BALANCE OF PAYMENTS STATISTICS YEARBOOK

Part 1: Country Tables

A Selection of Statistical Publications of the International Monetary Fund

International Financial Statistics (IFS)
Acknowledged as a standard source of statistics on all aspects of international and domestic finance, *IFS* publishes, for most countries of the world, current data on exchange rates, international liquidity, international banking, money and banking, interest rates, prices, production, international transactions (including balance of payments and international investment position), government finance, and national accounts. Information is presented in tables for specific countries and in tables for area and world aggregates. *IFS* is published monthly and annually. *Price:* Subscription price is US$289 a year (US$199 to university faculty and students) for twelve monthly issues and the yearbook. Single copy price is US$40 for a monthly issue and US$72 for a yearbook issue.

Balance of Payments Statistics Yearbook (BOPSY)
Issued in three parts, this annual publication contains balance of payments and international investment position data. Part 1 provides detailed tables on balance of payments statistics for approximately 165 countries and international investment position data for 81 countries. Part 2 presents tables of regional and world totals of major balance of payments components. Part 3 contains descriptions of methodologies, compilation practices, and data sources used by reporting countries *Price:* US$78.

Direction of Trade Statistics (DOTS)
Quarterly issues of this publication provide, for about 156 countries, tables with current data (or estimates) on the value of imports from and exports to their most important trading partners. In addition, similar summary tables for the world, industrial countries, and developing countries are included. The yearbook provides, for the most recent seven years, detailed trade data by country for approximately 186 countries, the world, and major areas. *Price:* Subscription price is US$128 a year (US$89 to university faculty and students) for the quarterly issues and the yearbook. Price for a quarterly issue only is US$25, the yearbook only is US$45, and a guide only is US$12.50.

Government Finance Statistics Yearbook (GFSY)
This annual publication provides detailed data on revenue, grants, expenditure, lending minus repayments, financing, and debt of central governments and indicates the amounts represented by social security funds and extrabudgetary operations. Also provided are data for state and local governments, and information on the institutional units of government. *Price:* US$65.

CD-ROM Subscriptions

International Financial Statistics (IFS), *Balance of Payments Statistics (BOPS)*, and *Direction of Trade Statistics (DOTS)* are available on CD-ROM by annual subscription. The CD-ROMs incorporate a Windows-based browser facility, as well as a flat file of the database in scientific notation. *Price of each subscription*: US$1,000 a year for single-user PC license (US$350 for university faculty and students). Network and redistribution licenses are negotiated on a case-by-case basis. Please contact Publication Services for information.

Subscription Packages

Combined Subscription Package
The combined subscription package includes all issues of *IFS, DOTS, BOPSY, GFSY,* and *Staff Papers,* the Fund's economic journal. *Combined subscription price:* US$446 a year. Airspeed delivery available at additional cost; please inquire.

Combined Statistical Yearbook Subscription
This subscription comprises *BOPSY*, *GFSY*, *IFSY,* and *DOTSY* at a combined rate of US$195. Because of different publication dates of the four yearbooks, it may take up to one year to service an order. Airspeed delivery available at additional cost; please inquire.

IFS on the Internet

The Statistics Department of the Fund is pleased to make available to subscribers the *International Financial Statistics (IFS)* database through an easy-to-use online service. The *IFS* database contains time series data beginning in 1948. The browser software provides a familiar and easy-to-use Windows interface for browsing the database, selecting series of interest, displaying the selected series in a spreadsheet format, and saving the selected series for transfer to other software systems, such as Microsoft Excel®. Single user license price for the *IFS Online Service* is $495, and $247 for academic users. Dependent on certain criteria, a range of scaled discounts is available. For full details of qualification for these discounts and online payment, please visit http://www.imfstatistics.org or email us directly at publications@imf.org.

Address orders to
Publication Services, IMF, Washington, DC 20431, USA
Telephone: (202) 623-7430 Telefax: (202) 623-7201 E-mail: publications@imf.org
Internet: http://www.imf.org

Note: Prices include the cost of delivery by surface mail. Enhanced delivery is available for an additional charge.

BALANCE OF PAYMENTS STATISTICS YEARBOOK

Part 1: Country Tables

2002

INTERNATIONAL MONETARY FUND

Balance of Payments Statistics Yearbook
Volume 53, Part 1: Country Tables, 2002
Prepared by Balance of Payments and
External Debt Divisions I and II, IMF Statistics Department
Carol S. Carson, Director, Statistics Department
Neil Patterson, Assistant Director,
Balance of Payments and External Debt Division I
Roger Pownall, Division Chief,
Balance of Payments and External Debt Division II

For information related to this publication, please:
fax the Statistics Department at (202) 623-6460,
or write Statistics Department
International Monetary Fund
Washington, D.C. 20431
or telephone (202) 623-6180.
For copyright inquiries, please fax the Editorial Division at (202) 623-6579.
For purchases only, please contact Publication Services (see information below).

Balance of Payments Statistics Yearbook (BOPSY): Issued in three parts, this annual publication contains balance of payments and international investment position data. Part 1 provides detailed tables on balance of payments statistics for approximately 165 countries and international investment position data for 81 countries. Part 2 presents tables of regional and world totals of major balance of payments components. Part 3 contains descriptions of methodologies, compilation practices, and data sources used by reporting countries.

Cutoff date: September 13, 2002

Address orders to:
International Monetary Fund
Attention: Publication Services
Washington, D.C. 20431
U.S.A.
Telephone (202) 623-7430
Telefax (202) 623-7201
E-mail: publications@imf.org
Internet: http://www.imf.org

ISSN 0252-3035
ISBN 1-58906-184-5
Recycled paper

Table of Contents

Country Tables

TABLE OF CONTENTS *(concluded)*

INTRODUCTION[1]

Volume 53 of the *Balance of Payments Statistics Yearbook*, published by the International Monetary Fund (the Fund), contains balance of payments data that member countries have reported to the Fund. The Fund is indebted to these countries for their cooperation in providing these data. For some of these countries, some data have been supplemented by details Fund economists have derived from other sources.

The yearbook consists of three parts. Part 1 presents balance of payments and international investment position (IIP) data of individual countries. Part 2 contains regional and world totals for major components of the balance of payments. Part 3 provides technical descriptions of selected reporting countries. Part 1 is separately bound, and Parts 2 and 3 are bound together.

This volume of the yearbook continues the features introduced in Volumes 46 through 52. As in Volume 46, balance of payments data are presented in accordance with the standard components of the fifth edition of the *Balance of Payments Manual (BPM5)*.[2] However, the standard components have changed with the publication of *Financial Derivatives, a Supplement to the Fifth Edition (1993) of the Balance of Payments Manual*, published in 2000 and amended in 2002. Thereafter, references to *BPM5* include the supplement and its addendum. In conformity with the recommendations in the addendum, this yearbook reflects the decision of the IMF Committee on Balance of Payments Statistics (BOPCOM) that the financial derivative transactions involving affiliated enterprises should be included in the financial derivatives component of the balance of payments statistics and the IIP. Similarly, as in Volume 47, IIP data also are presented in the *BPM5* format, and Part 3 of the yearbook publishes detailed reviews of the methodologies, compilation practices, and sources of data for most of the countries included in the volume.

The *BPM5*[3] introduced a number of methodological changes in the compilation of balance of payments data. Chapter I of the *BPM5* describes these changes in detail. Since Volume 46, a set of data codes has accompanied data presented in this yearbook under the standard components of the *BPM5*. These data codes were developed jointly by the Fund, the Organisation for Economic Cooperation and Development (OECD), and the Statistical Office of the European Union (Eurostat). An annex to this introduction explains the structure of the codes. In addition, beginning with Volume 46, the yearbook no longer presents quarterly balance of payments data for those countries that report quarterly balance of payments statistics to the Fund. Such quarterly data are published in the monthly Fund publication *International Financial Statistics (IFS)*.

Data conversion work undertaken by the Fund staff has made possible the presentation in the *BPM5* format of both historical data from the Fund's database and more recent statistics reported by those member countries who are still compiling their data in the format of the fourth edition of the *Balance of Payments Manual (BPM4)*. In 1995, the Fund staff developed formulas to transform reported balance of payments data for each country in the Fund's database to approximate the *BPM5* methodology and presentation. Converted data for each reporting country were sent to the respective authorities for review, and their comments were incorporated in the new *BPM5* database. In 1996, the Fund staff, in collaboration with country authorities, completed a similar conversion of the *BPM4* IIP data into the *BPM5* presentation. In principle, the IIP of a country is a balance sheet of its stock of external financial assets and liabilities.

The technical descriptions of reporting countries' methodologies, compiling practices, and data sources, shown in Part 3 of the yearbook, are largely based on information that the countries provide to the Fund. The descriptions are intended to enhance users' understanding of the coverage, as well as of the limitations, of individual country data published in this yearbook. They are also designed to inform compilers of data sources and practices used by their counterparts in other countries. In addition, detailed information on countries' practices in compiling direct investment (DI) statistics is available to compilers from the 2001 survey of DI methodologies, conducted jointly by the Fund and the Organisation for Economic Cooperation and Development (OECD). Compilers can consult the Internet database that contains the DI metadata at http://www.imf.org/external/np/sta/di/mdb97.htm.

The balance of this introduction is organized as follows:

- Section I describes essential features of the tables published in Part 1 of this volume of the yearbook. (Readers can find details on coverage for Parts 2 and 3 in the separately bound publication.)
- Section II offers information on the accessibility of the Fund's balance of payments data on CD-ROM.
- There are six annexes. Annex I shows an analytic presentation of balance of payments components (and related data codes) arranged in a summary form. Annex II presents the standard components of the *BPM5* (and related

[1]French and Spanish translations of this introduction appear after the annexes; data on individual countries follow immediately thereafter.

[2]Volume 1 of the yearbook, published in 1949, was based on the first edition of the Fund's *Balance of Payments Manual*, issued in 1948; Volumes 2-12 were compiled pursuant to the second edition of the manual, issued in 1950; Volumes 13-23 were based on the third edition of the manual, issued in 1961; and Volumes 24-29 were associated with that edition as well as the *Balance of Payments Manual: Supplement to Third Edition*, issued in 1973. Volumes 30-45 followed the guidance of the fourth edition of the manual, published in 1977.

[3]International Monetary Fund, *Balance of Payments Manual*, fifth edition, Washington, D.C., September 1993, and *Financial Derivatives, A Supplement to the Fifth Edition (1993) of the Balance of Payments Manual*, 2000.

data codes). Annex III explains the data coding scheme. Annex IV presents the standard components for IIP as shown in the *BPM5*. Annex V provides the conceptual framework of the balance of payments. Annex VI explains the coverage of major components of the balance of payments accounts, as set forth in the *BPM5*.

I. Part 1 of the Yearbook: Individual Country Data

Part 1 of the yearbook presents country pages alphabetically. "Country" in this publication does not always refer to a territorial entity that is a state as understood by international law and practice; the term also covers the euro area and some nonsovereign territorial entities for which statistical data are provided internationally on a separate basis.

For most countries, balance of payments data are presented in two tables. Table 1 is an analytical summary of the more detailed data of Table 2. This table provides an array of balance of payments components to highlight the financing items (the reserves and related items). (See also Annex I.) Table 2 displays data in the standard components described in the *BPM5*. (See also Annex II.)

For countries for which IIP statistics are available, Table 3 presents those data. Tables 1, 2, and 3 present data for the years 1994–2001 for each country. Unless otherwise indicated, the tables report figures for calendar years.

Analytic Presentation

In the analytic presentation, shown in Table 1, balance of payments components are classified into five major data categories (groups A through E), which the Fund regards as useful for analyzing balance of payments developments uniformly. The selected groups, however, should not be considered to reflect the Fund's recommendation about the analytic approach appropriate for every country. Other analytical presentations could be arrayed by regrouping the standard components of Table 2 in other ways to take account of the special circumstances of a specific country or to serve particular analytical requirements.

Note that the figures shown in Tables 1 and 2 differ for some countries for balances of the current account, the capital account, and the financial account. This is because in Table 1 certain transactions under these accounts are excluded and reclassified as "exceptional financing" under reserves and related items. "Exceptional financing" refers to transactions undertaken by the authorities to finance balance of payments needs, including such items as external borrowing, payment arrears, and debt forgiveness. Exceptional financing does not include reserves.

Standard Presentation

The standard components of *BPM5*, shown in Table 2, list a more detailed classification of goods and services than appears in *BPM4*. The designated "capital and financial account" has separate components for the "capital" and the "financial account." Under the "financial account," components are classified by types of investment (i.e., direct investment, portfolio investment, financial derivatives,[1] other investment, and reserve assets), assets/liabilities, domestic sectors (monetary authorities, general government, banks, and other sectors), and original maturity.

International Investment Position

IIP data, as shown in Table 3, are arrayed in accordance with the standard components for IIP, as set forth in the *BPM5*. (See also Annex IV.)

Although the classification of the IIP components in Table 3 is consistent with that of the financial account of the balance of payments as shown in Table 2, there are several differences between the two tables. As mentioned earlier, IIP data reflect a country's external financial assets and liabilities at a specific point in time. Table 3, therefore, provides the basic presentation of the IIP components under two general categories, namely, assets and liabilities, as opposed to the functional types of investment (direct investment, portfolio investment, financial derivatives, other investment, and reserve assets) shown in Table 2. Also, the data in Table 3 reflect a country's IIP at the end of the reporting period, as opposed to transactions during the period shown in Table 2. Furthermore, unlike Table 2, which shows the value of financial transactions over a period, the valuation of a country's IIP shown in Table 3 reflects the value of financial transactions, valuation changes, and other adjustments at the end of the reporting period. The net IIP shown in Table 3 is derived by taking the difference between the value of reported external financial assets and that of reported external financial liabilities.

Data Codes

Tables 1, 2, and 3 show codes for each data category and component. As mentioned earlier, these codes were developed jointly by the Fund, the OECD, and Eurostat and are intended to facilitate international data reporting. The codes are designed for the standard components of balance of payments and international investment position data as defined in the *BPM5*, as well as for the OECD/Eurostat components for trade in services.

There are six digits/characters for each code shown in the yearbook. The first digit designates credit/debit/net, with the number "2" assigned to credit, "3" to debit, and "4" to net (the difference between credit and debit). The next three digits are used to classify balance of payments components. For example the current account is coded 993, the capital

[1]Owing to the unique nature of financial derivatives, and the manner in which some institutions record transactions, some countries can provide only net transactions data. While such net data could be included under assets, in this yearbook it has been decided to include these net transactions, and net positions when reported, under liabilities. The reason is that one common source of demand for these instruments is from entities that are hedging cash flows associated with debt liabilities.

Box. International Investment Position

Countries in the early stages of IIP compilation are encouraged to submit partial IIP statements. In general, these partial statements include data on the monetary authorities (including international reserves) and at least one other sector. IIP statements for reporting countries are shown as Table 3 in the country pages. No totals are shown for partial IIP statements. Because of these data limitations, a country's IIP statement should be read in conjunction with the notes included in Part 3—Methodologies, Compilation Practices, and Data Sources—for that particular country. As countries collect more IIP data, the coverage of the IIP for these countries will be expanded in subsequent volumes of the yearbook.

Readers may refer to Chapter XXIII of the *BPM5* for a full discussion of the concept of international investment position.

External debt is not a separate component of the IIP but can be derived by summing up the non-equity liability components of the IIP (i.e., all recorded liabilities other than equity securities and direct investment equity capital [including reinvested earnings], and financial derivatives). Such a view is in general concordance with the core definition of gross external debt in the *External Debt Statistics: Guide for Compilers and Users*, prepared by the Inter-Agency Task Force on Finance Statistics. The Task Force was chaired by the IMF, and the work on the Guide involved representatives from the BIS, the Commonwealth Secretariat, the European Central Bank, Eurostat, the IMF, the OECD, the Paris Club Secretariat, the United Nations Conference on Trade and Development, and the World Bank.

Key Components [1]

A. Assets

1. Direct investment
- 1.1 Equity capital and reinvested earnings
- 1.2 Other capital[2]

2. Portfolio investment
- 2.1 Equity securities
- 2.2 Debt securities[4]

3. Financial derivatives
- 3.1 Monetary authorities
- 3.2 General government
- 3.3 Banks
- 3.4 Other sectors

4. Other investment
- 4.1 Trade credits
- 4.2 Loans
- 4.3 Currency and deposits
- 4.4 Other assets

5. Reserve assets
- 5.1 Monetary gold
- 5.2 Special drawing rights
- 5.3 Reserve position in the Fund
- 5.4 Foreign exchange
- 5.5 Other claims

B. Liabilities

1. Direct investment
- 1.1 Equity capital and reinvested earnings
- 1.2 Other capital[3]

2. Portfolio investment
- 2.1 Equity securities
- 2.2 Debt securities[3,4]

3. Financial derivatives
- 3.1 Monetary authorities
- 3.2 General government
- 3.3 Banks
- 3.4 Other sectors

4. Other investment
- 4.1 Trade credits[3]
- 4.2 Loans[3]
- 4.3 Currency and deposits[3]
- 4.4 Other liabilities[3]

[1] Not all components are shown, such as those broken down by sector (monetary authorities, general government, banks, and other) and, in some cases, by maturity.

[2] Liabilities to affiliated enterprises, which are netted under other capital in the functional classification, are a component of external debt.

[3] These components comprise gross external debt. (See also footnote 2.)

[4] Includes bonds, notes, and money market instruments.

account, 994, and the financial account, 995. Readers may refer to Annex III for details of the coding scheme.

The fifth and sixth digits/characters of the code shown in the yearbook denote special features about specific data components. For example, in Table 1, the fifth character Z indicates that the component excludes exceptional financing; W is used to show where exceptional financing and use of Fund credit and loans from the Fund are excluded. Letters A, B, C, and D in Table 1 differentiate the various domestic sectors. In Table 2, the letters A, B, and C indicate nonstandard subcomponents, such as those for transportation (viz., passenger, freight, and other).

Credits and Debits

In Tables 1 and 2, the transactions data are shown as gross credit or gross debit entries in the current and capital accounts. In the financial account, they are shown as net credit or net debit entries (to reflect net changes in liabilities and net changes in assets). Credit entries, gross or net, are positive (but without a plus sign), and debit entries, gross or net, are negative (with a minus sign). Thus, decreases in assets and increases in liabilities (credits) are shown as positive, and increases in assets and decreases in liabilities (debits) are shown as negative.

Nil or Unavailable Entries

It is often difficult to discern in data reported by countries whether missing numbers are not available or are zero or insignificant. In the yearbook tables, dots (...) indicate that data are either not available, zero, or insignificant.

A Note on the Components of Income and Other Investment

In Table 2, Standard Presentation, the data reported by certain countries under "income" and "other investment" are at a level of aggregation that does not allow all the individual components within this category to be separately identified. In these cases, therefore, the aggregate data for certain subcategories cannot be derived by summing the components for these subcategories. The same principle applies to "other investment" shown in Table 3, International Investment Position.

Previously, in Volumes 46 through 49, the tables showed data for "other investment" (assets and liabilities) under "long-term" and "short-term." Beginning with volume 50, tables now show the data for "other investment" (assets and liabilities) for monetary authorities, general government, banks, and other sectors as totals (of long- and short-term financing) and as "of which: short-term." (For "loans, monetary authorities," tables show the data as totals, as "of which: use of Fund credit and loans from the Fund," and as "of which: short-term.") However, in Annex II, the Standard Presentation has not been modified.

Rounding of Figures

Most data in the tables are expressed in units of one million; users should not assume that any table showing smaller units necessarily contains more accurate figures. The unit is chosen to present the figures conveniently. Because of the calculation routines used, there may be rounding differences between an aggregate and the sum of its components.

Currency Conversion

Most of the balance of payments data reported to the Fund are expressed in national currencies or in U.S. dollars, although some countries report certain data in SDRs. To ease comparisons among countries, all balance of payments statements published in the yearbook are expressed in U.S. dollars. In addition, all countries' reported data on transactions with the Fund and transactions in SDRs are replaced with data obtained from the Fund records, which are kept in SDRs. This information is, in turn, converted to U.S. dollars.

For countries that do not report in U.S. dollars, data are converted using the country conversion rates shown at the bottom of Table 1. These rates are normally the average exchange rates for a country for the relevant period taken from the *IFS*. For example, the *IFS* pages for the Netherlands contain line "rf," giving average rates for guilders per U.S. dollar. Conversions of transactions data from SDRs into U.S. dollars are made at the rates shown in line "sb" of the *IFS* pages for the United States. For countries reporting quarterly data in national currencies, annual U.S. dollar totals are obtained by aggregating the quarterly U.S. dollar figures.

Readers may find more information on the exchange rates that are used in the introduction to *IFS*, Section 1.

II. CD-ROM Subscription

Statistics published in the yearbook are also available on CD-ROM. The number of countries and time series covered in the CD-ROM version is slightly larger than that appearing in the printed version of the yearbook, as is the number of periods for which data observations of time series are given. Quarterly data reported by countries are also available on the CD-ROM. Moreover, the CD-ROM includes updates and revisions of the data as they become available. Inquiries about the CD-ROM should be addressed to:

Publication Services
International Monetary Fund
Washington, D.C. 20431, U.S.A.
Telephone (202) 623-7430
Telefax (202) 623-7201
E-mail publications@imf.org
Internet http://www.imf.org

ANNEX I. ANALYTIC PRESENTATION

	Data Codes
A. CURRENT ACCOUNT[1]	4 993 Z .
Goods: exports f.o.b.	2 100 . .
Goods: imports f.o.b.	3 100 . .
Balance on Goods	4 100 . .
Services: credit	2 200 . .
Services: debit	3 200 . .
Balance on Goods and Services	4 991 . .
Income: credit	2 300 . .
Income: debit	3 300 . .
Balance on Goods, Services, and Income	4 992 . .
Current transfers: credit	2 379 Z .
Current transfers: debit	3 379 . .
B. CAPITAL ACCOUNT[1]	4 994 Z .
Capital account: credit	2 994 Z .
Capital account: debit	3 994 . .
Total, Groups A plus B	4 981 . .
C. FINANCIAL ACCOUNT[1]	4 995 W .
Direct investment abroad	4 505 . .
Direct investment in reporting economy	4 555 Z .
Portfolio investment assets	4 602 . .
Equity securities	4 610 . .
Debt securities	4 619 . .
Portfolio investment liabilities	4 652 Z .
Equity securities	4 660 . .
Debt securities	4 669 Z .
Financial derivatives	4 910
Financial derivatives assets	4 900
Financial derivatives liabilities	4 905
Other investment assets	4 703 . .
Monetary authorities	4 701 . .
General government	4 704 . .
Banks	4 705 . .
Other sectors	4 728 . .
Other investment liabilities	4 753 W .
Monetary authorities	4 753 WA
General government	4 753 ZB
Banks	4 753 ZC
Other sectors	4 753 ZD
Total, Groups A through C	4 983 . .
D. NET ERRORS AND OMISSIONS	4 998 . .
Total, Groups A through D	4 984 . .
E. RESERVES AND RELATED ITEMS	4 802 A .
Reserve assets	4 802 . .
Use of Fund credit and loans	4 766 . .
Exceptional financing	4 920 . .
CONVERSION RATES: CURRENCY PER U.S. DOLLAR	0 101 . .

[1]Excludes components that have been classified in the categories of Group E.

Annex II. Standard Presentation

	Data Codes
CURRENT ACCOUNT	4 993 ..
A. GOODS	4 100 ..
Credit	2 100 ..
General merchandise: exports f.o.b.	2 110 ..
Goods for processing: exports f.o.b.	2 150 ..
Repairs on goods	2 160 ..
Goods procured in ports by carriers	2 170 ..
Nonmonetary gold	2 180 ..
Debit	3 100 ..
General merchandise: imports f.o.b.	3 110 ..
Goods for processing: imports f.o.b.	3 150 ..
Repairs on goods	3 160 ..
Goods procured in ports by carriers	3 170 ..
Nonmonetary gold	3 180 ..
B. SERVICES	4 200 ..
Total Credit	2 200 ..
Total Debit	3 200 ..
Transportation services, credit	2 205 ..
Passenger	2 850 ..
Freight	2 850 ..
Other	2 852 ..
Sea transport, passenger	2 207 ..
Sea transport, freight	2 208 ..
Sea transport, other	2 209 ..
Air transport, passenger	2 211 ..
Air transport, freight	2 212 ..
Air transport, other	2 213 ..
Other transport, passenger	2 215 ..
Other transport, freight	2 216 ..
Other transport, other	2 217 ..
Transportation services, debit	3 205 ..
Passenger	3 850 ..
Freight	3 851 ..
Other	3 852 ..
Sea transport, passenger	3 207 ..
Sea transport, freight	3 208 ..
Sea transport, other	3 209 ..
Air transport, passenger	3 211 ..
Air transport, freight	3 212 ..
Air transport, other	3 213 ..
Other transport, passenger	3 215 ..
Other transport, freight	3 216 ..
Other transport, other	3 217 ..
Travel, credit	2 236 ..
Business travel	2 237 ..
Personal travel	2 240 ..
Travel, debit	3 236 ..
Business travel	3 237 ..
Personal travel	3 240 ..

ANNEX II. STANDARD PRESENTATION *(continued)*

	Data Codes
Other services, credit	2 200 BA
Communications	2 245 . .
Construction	2 249 . .
Insurance	2 253 . .
Financial	2 260 . .
Computer and information	2 262 . .
Royalties and license fees	2 266 . .
Other business services	2 268 . .
Personal, cultural, and recreational	2 287 . .
Government, n.i.e.	2 291 . .
Other services, debit	3 200 BA
Communications	3 245 . .
Construction	3 249 . .
Insurance	3 253 . .
Financial	3 260 . .
Computer and information	3 262 . .
Royalties and license fees	3 266 . .
Other business services	3 268 . .
Personal, cultural, and recreational	3 287 . .
Government, n.i.e.	3 291 . .
C. INCOME	4 300 . .
Total Credit	2 300 . .
Total Debit	3 300 . .
Compensation of employees, credit	2 310 . .
Compensation of employees, debit	3 310 . .
Investment income, credit	2 320 . .
Direct investment income	2 330 . .
Dividends and distributed branch profits	2 332 . .
Reinvested earnings and undistributed branch profits	2 333 . .
Income on debt (interest)	2 334 . .
Portfolio investment income	2 339 . .
Income on equity	2 340 . .
Income on bonds and notes	2 350 . .
Income on money market instruments	2 360 . .
Other investment income	2 370 . .
Investment income, debit	3 320 . .
Direct investment income	3 330 . .
Dividends and distributed branch profits	3 332 . .
Reinvested earnings and undistributed branch profits	3 333 . .
Income on debt (interest)	3 334 . .
Portfolio investment income	3 339 . .
Income on equity	3 340 . .
Income on bonds and notes	3 350 . .
Income on money market instruments	3 360 . .
Other investment income	3 370 . .
D. CURRENT TRANSFERS	4 379 . .
Credit	2 379 . .
General government	2 380 . .
Other sectors	2 390 .
Workers' remittances	2 391 . .
Other current transfers	2 392 . .

	Data Codes	
Debit	3 379	..
General government	3 380	..
Other sectors	3 390	..
Workers' remittances	3 391	..
Other current transfers	3 392	..
CAPITAL AND FINANCIAL ACCOUNT	4 996	..
CAPITAL ACCOUNT	4 994	..
Total Credit	2 994	..
Total Debit	3 994	..
Capital transfers, credit	2 400	..
General government	2 401	..
Debt forgiveness	2 402	..
Other capital transfers	2 410	..
Other sectors	2 430	..
Migrants' transfers	2 431	..
Debt forgiveness	2 432	..
Other capital transfers	2 440	..
Capital transfers, debit	3 400	..
General government	3 401	..
Debt forgiveness	3 402	..
Other capital transfers	3 410	..
Other sectors	3 430	..
Migrants' transfers	3 431	..
Debt forgiveness	3 432	..
Other capital transfers	3 440	..
Nonproduced nonfinancial assets, credit	2 480	..
Nonproduced nonfinancial assets, debit	3 480	..
FINANCIAL ACCOUNT	4 995	..
A. DIRECT INVESTMENT	4 500	..
Direct investment abroad	4 505	..
Equity capital	4 510	..
Claims on affiliated enterprises	4 515	..
Liabilities to affiliated enterprises	4 520	..
Reinvested earnings	4 525	..
Other capital	4 530	..
Claims on affiliated enterprises	4 535	..
Liabilities to affiliated enterprises	4 540	..
Direct investment in reporting economy	4 555	..
Equity capital	4 560	..
Claims on direct investors	4 565	..
Liabilities to direct investors	4 570	..
Reinvested earnings	4 575	..
Other capital	4 580	..
Claims on direct investors	4 585	..
Liabilities to direct investors	4 590	..

	Data Codes	
B. PORTFOLIO INVESTMENT	4 600	..
Assets	4 602	..
Equity securities	4 610	..
Monetary authorities	4 611	..
General government	4 612	..
Banks	4 613	..
Other sectors	4 614	..
Debt securities	4 619	..
Bonds and notes	4 620	..
Monetary authorities	4 621	..
General government	4 622	..
Banks	4 623	..
Other sectors	4 624	..
Money market instruments	4 630	..
Monetary authorities	4 631	..
General government	4 632	..
Banks	4 633	..
Other sectors	4 634	..
Liabilities	4 652	..
Equity securities	4 660	..
Banks	4 663	..
Other sectors	4 664	..
Debt securities	4 669	..
Bonds and notes	4 670	..
Monetary authorities	4 671	..
General government	4 672	..
Banks	4 673	..
Other sectors	4 674	..
Money market instruments	4 680	..
Monetary authorities	4 681	..
General government	4 682	..
Banks	4 683	..
Other sectors	4 684	..
C. FINANCIAL DERIVATIVES	4 910	..
Monetary authorities	4 911	..
General government	4 912	..
Banks	4 913	..
Other sectors	4 914	..
Assets	4 900	..
Monetary authorities	4 901	..
General government	4 902	..
Banks	4 903	..
Other sectors	4 904	..
Liabilities	4 905	..
Monetary authorities	4 906	..
General government	4 907	..
Banks	4 908	..
Other sectors	4 909	..
D. OTHER INVESTMENT	4 700	..
Assets	4 703	..
Trade credits	4 706	..
General government	4 707	..
of which: short-term	4 709	..
Other sectors	4 710	..
of which: short-term	4 712	..

	Data Codes	
Loans	4 714	..
Monetary authorities	4 715	..
of which: short-term	4 718	..
General government	4 719	..
of which: short-term	4 721	..
Banks	4 722	..
of which: short-term	4 724	..
Other sectors	4 725	..
of which: short-term	4 727	..
Currency and deposits	4 730	..
Monetary authorities	4 731	..
General government	4 732	..
Banks	4 733	..
Other sectors	4 734	..
Other assets	4 736	..
Monetary authorities	4 737	..
of which: short-term	4 739	..
General government	4 740	..
of which: short-term	4 742	..
Banks	4 743	..
of which: short-term	4 745	..
Other sectors	4 746	..
of which: short-term	4 748	..
Liabilities	4 753	..
Trade credits	4 756	..
General government	4 757	..
of which: short-term	4 759	..
Other sectors	4 760	..
of which: short-term	4 762	..
Loans	4 764	..
Monetary authorities	4 765	..
of which: Use of Fund credit and loans from the Fund	4 766	..
of which: short-term	4 768	..
General government	4 769	..
of which: short-term	4 771	..
Banks	4 772	..
of which: short-term	4 774	..
Other sectors	4 775	..
of which: short-term	4 777	..
Currency and deposits	4 780	..
Monetary authorities	4 781	..
General government	4 782	..
Banks	4 783	..
Other sectors	4 784	..
Other liabilities	4 786	..
Monetary authorities	4 787	..
of which: short-term	4 789	..
General government	4 790	..
of which: short-term	4 792	..
Banks	4 793	..
of which: short-term	4 795	..
Other sectors	4 796	..
of which: short-term	4 798	..
E. RESERVE ASSETS	4 802	..
Monetary gold	4 812	..
Special drawing rights	4 811	..
Reserve position in the Fund	4 810	..
Foreign exchange	4 803	..
Other claims	4 813	..
NET ERRORS AND OMISSIONS	4 998	..

Annex III. IMF/OECD/Eurostat Coding System for Balance of Payments, International Investment Position, and Trade In Services[1]

This coding system incorporates all the standard components and supplementary information lines of the fifth edition of the *Balance of Payments Manual*, as well as the components and memorandum items of the OECD-Eurostat classification for international trade in services.

The code consists of three components or sections as follows:

<position>	one decimal digit (selected from the range of 1 to 8) that describes the position of the subject in the international investment position (IIP)/balance of payments (BOP) accounts;
<BOP topic>	three decimal digits (selected from the range of integers from 100 to 998) that identify all the BOP, trade-in-services, and selected supplementary information components; and
<tag>	a user defined component that may be of any length.

The complete code would take the form <position><topic><tag>. However, the tag component is optional. In contrast, the position and the topic components of the code are always required. Thus, a common implementation of the code will take the form <position><topic>.

The first section of the code describes the position in the IIP and BOP accounts and is defined as follows:

Code	Position in IIP/BOP Accounts
1	stock at the beginning of the period
2	credit flows
3	debit flows
4	net flows
5	price valuation adjustment
6	exchange rate valuation adjustment
7	other adjustments
8	stock at the end of the period
0	other

The first digit of the topic component identifies the section of the balance of payments as follows:

Code	Section of the accounts
1	goods
2	services
3	income and current transfers
4	capital account
5	direct investment
6	portfolio investment
7	other investment
8	reserves
9	aggregates and supplementary information

The second and third digits of the component are generally sequential counts of the components with some gaps to allow for the possibility of additional codes being included at a later time. In addition, with the exception of the direct investment accounts, the second digit of the topic component takes the numbers 0, 1, 2, 3, or 4 for assets and 5, 6, 7, 8, or 9 for liabilities in the financial accounts.

Examples of data codes for "Other Investment" of the financial account are shown below.

Topic	Single Field			Multiple Field		
	Credit	Debit	Net	Credit	Debit	Net
Other investment	2700	3700	4700	2700	3700	4700
Liabilities	2750	3750	4750	2750	3750	4750
Loans	2762	3762	4762	2762	3762	4762
General govt.	2767	3767	4767	2767	3767	4767
Long-term	2768	3768	4768	2768	3768	4768
Short-term	2769	3769	4769	2769	3769	4769
Banks	2770	3770	4770	2770	3770	4770
Long-term	2771	3771	4771	2771	3771	4771
Short-term	2772	3772	4772	2772	3772	4772
Other sectors	2773	3773	4773	2773	3773	4773
Long-term	2774	3774	4774	2774	3774	4774
Short-term	2775	3775	4775	2775	3775	4775

When considering credits and debits for loans, the language that is commonly used is drawings and repayments. The *BPM5* recommends reporting of all drawings and repayments for long-term loans as a supplementary classification. Most other financial account items are presently collected by the Fund on a net basis. Nevertheless, the coding system provides for the identification of all flows on a credit, debit, and net basis.

[1] This is adopted from International Monetary Fund, "Balance of Payments Codes for Standard Components and Additional Items," Washington, D.C., March 3, 1995.

Annex IV. Standard Components of International Investment Position

	Data Codes	
A. **ASSETS**	8 995	C .
Direct investment abroad	8 505	. .
Equity capital and reinvested earnings	8 506	. .
Claims on affiliated enterprises	8 507	. .
Liabilities to affiliated enterprises	8 508	. .
Other capital	8 530	. .
Claims on affiliated enterprises	8 535	. .
Liabilities to affiliated enterprises	8 540	. .
Portfolio investment	8 602	. .
Equity securities	8 610	. .
Monetary authorities	8 611	. .
General government	8 612	. .
Banks	8 613	. .
Other sectors	8 614	. .
Debt securities	8 619	. .
Bonds and notes	8 620	. .
Monetary authorities	8 621	. .
General government	8 622	. .
Banks	8 623	. .
Other sectors	8 624	. .
Money market instruments	8 630	. .
Monetary authorities	8 631	. .
General government	8 632	. .
Banks	8 633	. .
Other sectors	8 634	. .
Financial derivatives	8 900	. .
Monetary authorities	8 901	. .
General government	8 902	. .
Banks	8 903	. .
Other sectors	8 904	. .
Other investment	8 703	. .
Trade credits	8 706	. .
General government	8 707	. .
of which: short-term	8 709	. .
Other sectors	8 710	. .
of which: short-term	8 712	. .
Loans	8 714	. .
Monetary authorities	8 715	. .
of which: short-term	8 718	. .
General government	8 719	. .
of which: short-term	8 721	. .
Banks	8 722	. .
of which: short-term	8 724	. .
Other sectors	8 725	. .
of which: short-term	8 727	. .
Currency and deposits	8 730	. .
Monetary authorities	8 731	. .
General government	8 732	. .
Banks	8 733	. .
Other sectors	8 734	. .

Annex IV. Standard Components of International Investment Position
(continued)

	Data Codes
Other assets	8 736 . .
Monetary authorities	8 737 . .
of which: short-term	8 739 . .
General government	8 740 . .
of which: short-term	8 742 . .
Banks	8 743 . .
of which: short-term	8 745 . .
Other sectors	8 746 . .
of which: short-term	8 748 . .
Reserve assets	8 802 . .
Monetary gold	8 812 . .
Special drawing rights	8 811 . .
Reserve position in the Fund	8 810 . .
Foreign exchange	8 803 . .
Other claims	8 813 . .
B. LIABILITIES	8 995 D .
Direct investment in reporting economy	8 555 . .
Equity capital and reinvested earnings	8 556 . .
Claims on direct investors	8 557 . .
Liabilities to direct investors	8 558 . .
Other capital	8 580 . .
Claims on direct investors	8 585 . .
Liabilities to direct investors	8 590 . .
Portfolio investment	8 652 . .
Equity securities	8 660 . .
Banks	8 663 . .
Other sectors	8 664 . .
Debt securities	8 669 . .
Bonds and notes	8 670 . .
Monetary authorities	8 671 . .
General government	8 672 . .
Banks	8 673 . .
Other sectors	8 674 . .
Money market instruments	8 680 . .
Monetary authorities	8 681 . .
General government	8 682 . .
Banks	8 683 . .
Other sectors	8 684 . .
Financial derivatives	8 905 . .
Monetary authorities	8 906 . .
General government	8 907 . .
Banks	8 908 . .
Other sectors	8 909 . .
Other investment	8 753 . .
Trade credits	8 756 . .
General government	8 757 . .
of which: short-term	8 759 . .
Other sectors	8 760 . .
of which: short-term	8 762 . .

Annex IV. Standard Components of International Investment Position
(concluded)

	Data Codes	
Loans	8 764	..
Monetary authorities	8 765	..
of which: Use of Fund credit and loans from the Fund	8 766	..
of which: short-term	8 768	..
General government	8 769	..
of which: short-term	8 771	..
Banks	8 772	..
of which: short-term	8 774	..
Other sectors	8 775	..
of which: short-term	8 777	..
Currency and deposits	8 780	..
Monetary authorities	8 781	..
General government	8 782	..
Banks	8 783	..
Other sectors	8 784	..
Other liabilities	8 786	..
Monetary authorities	8 787	..
of which: short-term	8 789	..
General government	8 790	..
of which: short-term	8 792	..
Banks	8 793	..
of which: short-term	8 795	..
Other sectors	8 796	..
of which: short-term	8 798	..
NET INTERNATIONAL INVESTMENT POSITION	8 995	..
Conversion rates (end of period)	0 102	..

Annex V. Conceptual Framework of the Balance of Payments and International Investment Position

This annex is reproduced from Chapter II of the BPM5. *Please note that paragraph and page numbers cited in this annex refer to those that appear in the* BPM5.

Definitions

12. Part one of this *Manual* deals with the conceptual framework of balance of payments accounts and the international investment position. Part one covers their relationship to national accounts; to concepts of residence, valuation, and time of recording; and to the unit of account and conversion.

13. The balance of payments is a statistical statement that systematically summarizes, for a specific time period, the economic transactions of an economy with the rest of the world. Transactions, for the most part between residents and nonresidents,[1] consist of those involving goods, services, and income; those involving financial claims on, and liabilities to, the rest of the world; and those (such as gifts) classified as transfers, which involve offsetting entries to balance—in an accounting sense—one-sided transactions. (See paragraph 28.)[2] A transaction itself is defined as an economic flow that reflects the creation, transformation, exchange, transfer, or extinction of economic value and involves changes in ownership of goods and/or financial assets, the provision of services, or the provision of labor and capital.

14. Closely related to the flow-oriented balance of payments framework is the stock-oriented international investment position. Compiled at a specified date such as year end, this investment position is a statistical statement of: (i) the value and composition of the stock of an economy's financial assets or the economy's claims on the rest of the world, and (ii) the value and composition of the stock of an economy's liabilities to the rest of the world. In some instances, it may be of analytic interest to compute the difference between the two sides of the balance sheet. The calculation would provide a measure of the net position, and the measure would be equivalent to that portion of an economy's net worth attributable to, or derived from, its relationship with the rest of the world. A change in stocks during any defined period can be attributable to transactions (flows); to valuation changes reflecting changes in exchange rates, prices, etc.; or to other adjustments (e.g., uncompensated seizures). By contrast, balance of payments accounts reflect only transactions.

Principles and Concepts

15. The remainder of this chapter deals with the conceptual framework of international accounts, that is, the set of underlying principles and conventions that ensure the systematized and coherent recording of international transactions and stocks of foreign assets and liabilities. Relevant aspects of these principles, together with practical considerations and limitations, will be thoroughly discussed in subsequent chapters.

Double Entry System

16. The basic convention applied in constructing a balance of payments statement is that every recorded transaction is represented by two entries with equal values. One of these entries is designated a credit with a positive arithmetic sign; the other is designated a debit with a negative sign. In principle, the sum of all credit entries is identical to the sum of all the debit entries, and the net balance of all entries in the statement is zero.

17. In practice, however, the accounts frequently do not balance. Data for balance of payments estimates often are derived independently from different sources; as a result, there may be a summary net credit or net debit (i.e., net errors and omissions in the accounts). A separate entry, equal to that amount with the sign reversed, is then made to balance the accounts. Because inaccurate or missing estimates may be offsetting, the size of the net residual cannot be taken as an indicator of the relative accuracy of the balance of payments statement. Nonetheless, a large, persistent residual that is not reversed should cause concern. Such a residual impedes analysis or interpretation of estimates and diminishes the credibility of both. A large net residual may also have implications for interpretation of the investment position statement. (See the discussion in Chapter XXIII.)

18. Most entries in the balance of payments refer to transactions in which economic values are provided or received in exchange for other economic values; those values consist of real resources (goods, services, and income) and financial items. Therefore, the offsetting credit and debit entries called for by the recording system are often the result of equal amounts having been entered for the two items exchanged. When items are given away rather than exchanged, or when a recording is one-sided for other reasons, special types of entries—referred to as *transfers*—are made as the required offsets. (The various kinds of entries that may be made in the balance of payments are discussed in paragraphs 26 through 31.)

19. Under the conventions of the system, a compiling economy records credit entries (i) for real resources denoting exports and (ii) for financial items reflecting reductions in an economy's foreign assets or increases in an economy's foreign liabilities. Conversely, a compiling economy records debit entries (i) for real resources denoting imports and (ii) for financial items reflecting increases in assets or decreases in liabilities. In other words, for assets—whether real or financial—a positive figure (credit) represents a decrease in holdings, and a negative figure (debit) represents an increase. In contrast, for liabilities, a positive figure shows an increase, and a negative figure shows a decrease. Transfers are shown as credits when the entries to which they provide the offsets are debits and as debits when those entries are credits.

20. The content or coverage of a balance of payments statement depends somewhat on whether transactions are treated on a gross or on a net basis. The recommendations in this *Manual* specify which transactions should be recorded gross or net. The recommendations are appropriately reflected in the list of standard components and in suggested supplementary presentations.

[1] The exceptions to the resident/nonresident basis of the balance of payments are the exchange of transferable foreign financial assets between resident sectors and, to a lesser extent, the exchange of transferable foreign financial liabilities between nonresidents. (See paragraph 318.)

[2] The definitions and classifications of international accounts presented in this *Manual* are intended to facilitate reporting of data on international transactions to the Fund. These definitions and classifications do not purport to give effect to, or interpret, various provisions (which pertain to the legal characterization of official action or inaction in relation to such transactions) of the *Articles of Agreement of the International Monetary Fund.*

Concepts of Economic Territory, Residence, and Center of Economic Interest

21. Identical concepts of economic territory, residence, and center of economic interest are used in this *Manual* and in the *SNA*. (These concepts are discussed fully in Chapter IV.) Economic territory may not be identical with boundaries recognized for political purposes. A country's economic territory consists of a geographic territory administered by a government; within this geographic territory, persons, goods, and capital circulate freely. For maritime countries, geographic territory includes any islands subject to the same fiscal and monetary authorities as the mainland.

22. An institutional unit has a center of economic interest and is a resident unit of a country when, from some location (dwelling, place of production, or other premises) within the economic territory of the country, the unit engages and intends to continue engaging (indefinitely or for a finite period) in economic activities and transactions on a significant scale. (One year or more may be used as a guideline but not as an inflexible rule.)

Principles for Valuation and Time of Recording

23. A uniform basis of valuation for the international accounts (both real resources and financial claims and liabilities) is necessary for compiling, on a consistent basis, any aggregate of individual transactions and an asset/liability position consistent with such transactions. This *Manual* generally uses, as the basis of transaction valuations, actual market prices agreed upon by transactors. (This practice is consistent with that of the *SNA*.) Conceptually, all stocks of assets and liabilities are valued at market prices prevailing at the time to which the international investment position relates. A full exposition of valuation principles; recommended practices; limitations; and the valuation of transfers, financial items, and stocks of assets and liabilities appears in Chapter V. (The exposition includes cases in which conditions may not allow for the existence or assumption of market prices.)

24. In the *Manual* and the *SNA*, the principle of accrual accounting governs the *time of recording* for transactions. Therefore, transactions are recorded when economic value is created, transformed, exchanged, transferred, or extinguished. Claims and liabilities arise when there is a change in ownership. The change may be legal or physical (economic). In practice, when a change in ownership is not obvious, the change may be proxied by the time that parties to a transaction record it in their books or accounts. (The recommended timing and conventions for various balance of payments entries, together with exceptions to and departures from the change of ownership principle, are covered in Chapter VI.)

Concept and Types of Transactions

25. Broadly speaking, changes in economic relationships registered by the balance of payments stem primarily from dealings between two parties. These parties are, with one exception (see footnote 1), a resident and a nonresident, and all dealings of this kind are covered in the balance of payments. Recommendations for specific entries are embodied in the list of standard components (see Chapter VIII) and are spelled out in detail from Chapter IX onward.

26. Despite the connotation, the balance of payments is not concerned with *payments*, as that term is generally understood, but with *transactions*. A number of international transactions that are of interest in a balance of payments context may not involve the payment of money, and some are not paid for in any sense. The inclusion of these transactions, in addition to those matched by actual payments, constitutes a principal difference between a balance of payments statement and a record of foreign payments.

Exchanges

27. The most numerous and important transactions found in the balance of payments may be characterized as *exchanges*. A transactor (economic entity) provides an economic value to another transactor and receives in return an equal value. The economic values provided by one economy to another may be categorized broadly as real resources (goods, services, income) and financial items. The parties that engage in the exchange are residents of different economies, except in the case of an exchange of foreign financial items between resident sectors. The provision of a financial item may involve not only a change in the ownership of an existing claim or liability but also the creation of a new claim or liability or the cancellation of existing ones. Moreover, the terms of a contract pertaining to a financial item (e.g., contractual maturity) may be altered by agreement between the parties. Such a case is equivalent to fulfillment of the original contract and replacement by a contract with different terms. All exchanges of these kinds are covered in the balance of payments.

Transfers

28. Transactions involving *transfers* differ from exchanges in that one transactor provides an economic value to another transactor but does not receive a quid pro quo on which, according to the conventions and rules adopted for the system, economic value is placed. This absence of value on one side is represented by an entry referred to as a *transfer*. Such transfers (economic value provided and received without a quid pro quo) are shown in the balance of payments. ***Current transfers*** are included in the **current account** (see Chapter XV) and *capital transfers* appear in the ***capital account***. (See Chapter XVII.)

Migration

29. Because an economy is defined in terms of the economic entities associated with its territory, the scope of an economy is likely to be affected by changes in entities associated with the economy.

30. Migration occurs when the residence of an individual changes from one economy to another because the person moves his or her abode. Certain movable, tangible assets owned by the migrant are, in effect, imported into the new economy. The migrant's immovable assets and certain movable, tangible assets located in the old economy become claims of the new economy on the old economy. The migrant's claims on, or liabilities to, residents of an economy other than the new economy become foreign claims or liabilities of the new economy. The migrant's claims on, or liabilities to, residents of the new economy cease to be claims on, or liabilities to, the rest of the world for any economy. The net sum of all these shifts is equal to the net worth of the migrant, and his or her net worth must also be recorded as an offset if the other shifts are recorded. These entries are made in the balance of payments where the offset is conventionally included with transfers.

Other imputed transactions

31. In some instances, transactions may be imputed and entries may be made in balance of payments accounts when no actual flow occurs. Attribution of reinvested earnings to foreign direct investors is an example. The earnings of a foreign subsidiary or branch include earnings attributable to a direct investor. The earnings, whether distributed or reinvested in the enterprise, are proportionate to the direct investor's equity share in the enterprise. Reinvested earnings are recorded as part of direct investment income. An offsetting entry, with opposite sign, is made in the *financial account*, under direct investment, reinvested earnings, to reflect the direct investor's increased investment in the foreign subsidiary or branch. (Reinvested earnings are discussed in Chapters XIV and XVIII.)

Changes Other Than Transactions

Reclassification of claims and liabilities

32. The classification of financial items in the *Manual* reflects characteristics designed to reveal the motivation of creditor or debtor. Changes in motivation affect the characteristics, and financial items are subject to reclassification in accordance with such changes. A case in point is the distinction drawn between *direct investment* and other types of investment. For example, several independent holders of *portfolio investment* (in the form of corporate equities issued by a single enterprise abroad) may form an associated group to have a lasting, effective voice in the management of the enterprise. Their holdings will then meet the criteria for *direct investment*, and the change in the status of the investment could be recorded as a reclassification. Such a reclassification would be reflected, at the end of the period during which it occurred, in the international investment position but not in the balance of payments. Similarly, claims on nonresidents can come under, or be released from, the control of resident monetary authorities. In such cases, there are reclassifications between *reserve assets* and assets other than reserves.

Valuation changes

33. The values of real resources and financial items are constantly subject to change stemming from either or both of two causes: (i) The price at which transactions in a certain type of item customarily take place may undergo alteration in terms of the currency in which that price is quoted. (ii) The exchange rate for the currency in which the price is quoted may change in relation to the unit of account that is being used. Valuation changes are not included in the balance of payments but are included in the international investment position.

ANNEX VI. CLASSIFICATION AND STANDARD COMPONENTS OF THE BALANCE OF PAYMENTS

This annex is reproduced from Chapter VIII of the BPM5. *Please note that paragraph and page numbers cited in this annex refer to those that appear in the* BPM5.

Structure and Classification

139. Part two of this *Manual* deals with the structure and classification of balance of payments accounts and the international investment position. Part two encompasses the standard components of both sets of accounts and contains discussions and elaboration of the ***current account***, the ***capital and financial account***, selected supplementary information, and the international investment position.

140. Balance of payments statistics must be arranged within a coherent structure to facilitate their utilization and adaptation for multiple purposes—policy formulation, analytical studies, projections, bilateral comparisons of particular components or total transactions, regional and global aggregations, etc. (See paragraph 7.)

141. The standard classification and the list of components reflect conceptual and practical considerations, take into account views expressed by national balance of payments experts, and are in general concordance with the *SNA* and with harmonization of the expanded classification of international transactions in services with the Central Product Classification (CPC). (See Appendix III.)

142. The scheme also reflects efforts to link the structure of the ***capital account*** to income accounts and to the international investment position classification. The scheme is designed as a flexible framework to be used by many countries in the long-term development of external statistics. Some countries may not be able to provide data for many items; other countries may be able to provide additional data.

Standard Components

143. The determination of standard components (see list at end of this chapter) is based on a number of considerations. Those that have been given the greatest weight are:

> The item should exhibit distinctive behavior. The economic factor or factors that influence the item should be different from those that influence other items, or the item should respond differently to the same factor or combination. This response to economic influences is what the balance of payments purports to make evident.
>
> The item should be important for a number of countries. Importance may be defined as a function of behavior (unusual variability, for example) or as absolute size.
>
> It should be possible to collect statistics for the item without undue difficulty. However, the desirability of collection should be evaluated according to the two previous criteria.
>
> The item should be needed on a separate basis for other purposes, such as incorporation into, or reconciliation with, the national accounts. The list of standard components should not be unduly long. A large number of countries, including many that are statistically less advanced, are asked to report uniformly on the components.
>
> To the extent practicable, standard components should be in concordance with, and apply to, other IMF statistical systems, the *SNA*, and, for ***services*** in particular, the CPC.

144. The list of standard components carries no implication that recommendations made in this *Manual* are intended to inhibit countries from compiling and publishing additional data of national importance. IMF requests for information will not be limited to standard components when further details are needed to understand the circumstances of particular countries or to analyze new developments. Supplementary information can also be most useful for verifying and reconciling the statistics of partner countries and, for example, analyzing exceptional financing transactions. (See the table entitled *Selected Supplementary Information* at the end of this chapter.) IMF staff will, from time to time, consult with countries to decide on the reporting of additional details.

145. Few countries are likely to have significant information to report for every standard component. Furthermore, several components may be available only in combination, or a minor component may be grouped with one that is more significant. The standard components should nevertheless be reported to the IMF as completely and accurately as possible. National compilers are in better positions than IMF staff to make estimates and adjustments for those components that do not exactly correspond to the basic series of the compiling economy.

Net Errors and Omissions

146. Application of the principles recommended in this *Manual* should result in a consistent body of positive and negative entries with a net (conceptual) total of zero. In practice, however, when all actual entries are totaled, the resulting balance will almost inevitably show a net credit or a net debit. That balance is the result of errors and omissions in compilation of statements. Some of the errors and omissions may be related to recommendations for practical approximation to principles.

147. In balance of payments statements, the standard practice is to show separately an item for net errors and omissions. Labeled by some compilers as a balancing item or statistical discrepancy, that item is intended as an offset to the overstatement or understatement of the recorded components. Thus, if the balance of those components is a credit, the item for net errors and omissions will be shown as a debit of equal value, and vice versa.

148. Some of the errors and omissions that occur in the course of compilation usually offset one another. Therefore, the size of the residual item does not necessarily provide any indication of the overall accuracy of the statement. Nonetheless, interpretation of the statement is hampered by a large net residual.

Major Classifications

149. The standard components, which are listed at the end of this chapter, are comprised of two main groups of accounts:

> The **current account** refers to ***goods and services, income,*** and ***current transfers***.
>
> The **capital and financial account** refers to (i) *capital transfers* and *acquisition/disposal of nonproduced, nonfinancial assets* and (ii) financial assets and liabilities.

This arrangement is based on common historical usage in most countries and on a major change introduced in this *Manual*. The former capital account has been relabeled **capital and financial account**. Reflecting harmonization with the *SNA*, this change introduces that system's distinction between *capital transfers* and ***current transfers*** in balance of payments accounts and concordance of the account with *SNA* capital and financial accounts.

150. Current account entries for most items in the list of standard components should show gross debits and credits. Most **capital and financial account** entries should be made on a net basis; that is, each component is shown only as a credit or a debit. (The recommended treatments for specific items and exceptions are discussed in appropriate chapters.) Inflows of real resources, increases in financial assets, and decreases in liabilities should be shown as debits; outflows of real resources, decreases in financial assets, and increases in liabilities should be shown as credits. Transfers, both in sections 1.C and 2.A, should be numerically equal with opposite sign to the entries for which they provide offsets.

Detailed Classifications

151. The following classifications of standard components have been developed in accordance with the criteria set out in paragraph 143. The structure and characteristics of the **current account** and the **capital and financial account** and significant changes from the fourth to the fifth edition of the *Manual* are discussed in chapters IX and XVI, respectively. The standard components of the **current account** are described fully in chapters X through XV, and those of the **capital and financial account** are covered in chapters XVII through XXI, and in *Financial Derivatives, A Supplement to the Fifth Edition (1993) of the Balance of Payments Manual,* 2000.

Current Account (1.)

152. Covered in the **current account** are all transactions (other than those in financial items) that involve economic values and occur between resident and nonresident entities. Also covered are offsets to current economic values provided or acquired without a quid pro quo. Specifically, the major classifications are ***goods and services***, ***income***, and ***current transfers***.

Goods and services (1.A.)

Goods (1.A.a.)

153. *General merchandise* covers most movable goods that are exported to, or imported from, nonresidents by residents and that, with a few specified exceptions, undergo changes in ownership (actual or imputed).

154. *Goods for processing* cover exports (or imports, in the compiling economy) of goods crossing the frontier for processing abroad and subsequent reimport (or export, in the compiling economy) of the goods, which are valued on a gross basis before and after processing. This item is an exception to the change of ownership principle.

155. *Repairs on goods* cover repair activity on goods provided to or received from nonresidents on ships, aircraft, etc. Although the physical movement of these goods is similar to that described in paragraph 154, the repairs are valued at the prices (fees paid or received) of the repairs and not at the gross values of the goods before and after repairs are made.

156. *Goods procured in ports by carriers* cover all goods (such as fuels, provisions, stores, and supplies) that resident/nonresident carriers—air, shipping, etc.—procure abroad (in the compiling economy). The classification does not cover the provision of auxiliary services (towing, maintenance, etc.), which are covered under *transportation*.

157. *Nonmonetary gold* covers exports and imports of all gold that is not held as a reserve asset (monetary gold) by the authorities. *Nonmonetary gold* is treated the same as any other commodity and is subdivided, when feasible, into gold held as a store of value and other (industrial) gold.

Services (1.A.b.)

158. *Transportation* covers most of the services, performed by residents for nonresidents and vice versa, that were included in shipment and other transportation in the fourth edition of the *Manual*. However, freight insurance is now included with *insurance services* rather than with *transportation*. *Transportation* includes freight and passenger transportation by all modes of transportation and other distributive and auxiliary services, including rentals of transportation equipment with crew. Certain exceptions are noted in chapters X, XI, and XIII.

159. *Travel* covers goods and services—including those related to health and education—acquired from an economy by nonresident travelers (including excursionists) for business purposes and personal use during their visits (of less than one year) in that economy. *Travel* excludes international passenger services, which are included in *transportation*. Students and medical patients are treated as travelers, regardless of their length of stay. Certain others—military and embassy personnel and nonresident workers—are not regarded as travelers. However, expenditures by nonresident workers are included in *travel*, while those of military and embassy personnel are included in *government services, n.i.e.* These cases are noted in chapters XII and XIII.

160. *Communications services* cover communications transactions between residents and nonresidents. Such services comprise postal, courier, and telecommunications services (transmission of sound, images, and other information by various modes and associated maintenance provided by/for residents by/for nonresidents).

161. *Construction services* cover construction and installation project work that is, on a temporary basis, performed abroad/in the compiling economy or in extraterritorial enclaves by resident/nonresident enterprises and their personnel. Such work does not include that undertaken by a foreign affiliate of a resident enterprise or by an unincorporated site office that, if it meets certain criteria, is equivalent to a foreign affiliate. Such residency aspects are covered in chapters IV and XIII.

162. *Insurance services* cover the provision of insurance to nonresidents by resident insurance enterprises and vice versa. This item comprises services provided for freight insurance (on goods exported and imported), services provided for other types of direct insurance (including life and non-life), and services provided for reinsurance. (For the method of calculating the value of insurance services, see paragraphs 256 and 257.)

163. *Financial services* (other than those related to insurance enterprises and pension funds) cover financial intermediation services and auxiliary services conducted between residents and nonresidents. Included are commissions and fees for letters of credit, lines of credit, financial leasing services, foreign exchange transactions, consumer and business credit services, brokerage services, underwriting services, arrangements for various forms of hedging instruments, etc. Auxiliary services include financial market operational and regulatory services, security custody services, etc.

164. *Computer and information services* cover resident/nonresident transactions related to hardware consultancy, software implementation, information services (data processing, database, news agency), and maintenance and repair of computers and related equipment.

165. *Royalties and license fees* cover receipts (exports) and payments (imports) of residents and nonresidents for: (i) the authorized use of intangible nonproduced, nonfinancial assets and proprietary rights such as trademarks, copyrights, patents, processes, techniques, designs, manufacturing rights, franchises, etc. and (ii) the use, through licensing agreements, of produced originals or prototypes, such as manuscripts, films, etc.

166. *Other business services* provided by residents to nonresidents and vice versa cover merchanting and other trade-related services; operational leasing services; and miscellaneous business, professional, and technical services. (See the table on *Selected Supplementary Information* following this chapter and paragraphs 261 through 264 for details.)

167. *Personal, cultural, and recreational services* cover (i) audiovisual and related services and (ii) other cultural services provided by residents to nonresidents and vice versa. Included under (i) are services associated with the production of motion pictures on films or video tape, radio and television programs, and musical recordings. (Examples of these services are rentals and fees received by actors, producers, etc. for productions and for distribution rights sold to the media.) Included under (ii) are other personal, cultural, and recreational services, such as those associated with libraries, museums, and other cultural and sporting activities.

168. *Government services, n.i.e.* cover all services (such as expenditures of embassies and consulates) associated with government sectors or international and regional organizations and not classified under other items.

Income (1.B.)

169. *Compensation of employees* covers wages, salaries, and other benefits, in cash or in kind, and includes those of border, seasonal, and other nonresident workers (e.g., local staff of embassies).

170. *Investment income* covers receipts and payments of income associated, respectively, with holdings of external financial assets by residents and with liabilities to nonresidents. *Investment income* consists of direct investment income, portfolio investment income, and other investment income. The direct investment component is broken down into income on equity (dividends, branch profits, and reinvested earnings) and income on debt (interest); portfolio investment income is broken down into income on equity (dividends) and income on debt (interest); other investment income covers interest earned on other capital (loans, etc.) and, in principle, imputed income to households from net equity in life insurance reserves and in pension funds.

Current transfers (1.C.)

171. ***Current transfers*** are distinguished from *capital transfers*, which are included in the **capital and financial account** in accordance with the *SNA* treatment of transfers. Transfers are the offsets to changes, which take place between residents and nonresidents, in ownership of real resources or financial items and, whether the changes are voluntary or compulsory, do not involve a quid pro quo in economic value. ***Current transfers*** consist of all transfers that **do not involve**: (i) transfers of ownership of fixed assets; (ii) transfers of funds linked to, or conditioned upon, acquisition or disposal of fixed assets; (iii) forgiveness, without any counterparts being received in return, of liabilities by creditors. All of these are *capital transfers*. ***Current transfers*** include those of general government (e.g., current international cooperation between different governments, payments of current taxes on income and wealth, etc.) and other transfers (e.g., workers' remittances, premiums—less service charges, and claims on non-life insurance). A full discussion of the distinction between ***current transfers*** and *capital transfers* appears in Chapter XV; see also paragraphs 175 and 344.

Capital and Financial Account (2.)

172. The **capital and financial account** has two major components—the ***capital account*** and the ***financial account***—that are in concordance with those same accounts in the *SNA*. Assets represent claims on nonresidents, and liabilities represent indebtedness to nonresidents. The two parties to a transaction in assets or liabilities are usually a resident and a nonresident but, in some instances, both parties may both be residents or nonresidents. (See paragraph 318.)

173. All valuation and other changes in foreign assets and liabilities, which do not reflect transactions (see paragraph 310), are excluded from the **capital and financial account** but are reflected in the international investment position. Supplementary statements identify certain items that are of analytical interest and that affect various accounts. Examples of such items are liabilities constituting foreign authorities' reserves and exceptional financing transactions, which are discussed in Chapter XXII.

174. Classification of the ***financial account*** and the income components of the **current account** are interrelated and must be consistent to facilitate analysis, to form an effective link between the balance of payments and the international investment position, and to be compatible with the *SNA* and other IMF statistical systems.

Capital account (2.A.)

175. The major components of the ***capital account*** are *capital transfers* and *acquisition/disposal of nonproduced, nonfinancial assets*. *Capital transfers* consist of those involving transfers of ownership of fixed assets; transfers of funds linked to, or conditional upon, acquisition or disposal of fixed assets; or cancellation, without any counterparts being received in return, of liabilities by creditors. *Capital transfers* include two components: (i) general government, subdivided into debt forgiveness and other, and (ii) other, subdivided into migrants' transfers, debt forgiveness, and other transfers. (See Chapter XV for discussion of the distinction between *capital transfers* and ***current transfers***. *Acquisition/disposal of nonproduced, nonfinancial assets* largely covers intangibles, such as patented entities, leases or other transferable contracts, goodwill, etc. This item does not cover land in a specific economic territory but may include the purchase or sale of land by a foreign embassy. (See paragraph 312.)

Financial account (2.B.)

176. The classification of standard components in the ***financial account*** is based on these criteria:

> All components are classified according to type of investment or by functional breakdown (*direct investment, portfolio investment, financial derivatives, other investment, reserve assets*).
>
> For the category of *direct investment*, there are directional distinctions (abroad or in the reporting economy) and for the equity capital, other capital.

For the categories of *portfolio investment, financial derivatives,* and *other investment*, there are the customary asset/liability distinctions.

Particularly significant for *portfolio investment* and *other investment* is the distinction by type of instrument (equity or debt securities, trade credits, loans, currency and deposits, other assets or liabilities). In this *Manual*, traditional and new money market and other financial instruments are included in *portfolio investment.*

For *portfolio investment, financial derivatives,* and *other investment*, there are distinctions by sector of the domestic creditor for assets or by sector of the domestic debtor for liabilities. These distinctions serve to facilitate links with the income accounts, the international investment position, the *SNA*, and other statistical systems.

The traditional distinction, which is based on original contractual maturity of more than one year or one year or less, between long- and short-term assets and liabilities applies only to *other investment.* In recent years, the significance of this distinction has clearly diminished for many domestic and international transactions. Consequently, the long- and short-term distinction is accorded less importance in the *SNA* and in this *Manual* than in previous editions. However, because the maturity factor remains important for specific purposes—analysis of external debt, for example—it is retained in the *Manual* for *other investment.*

177. *Direct investment*—reflecting the lasting interest of a resident entity in one economy (direct investor) in an entity resident in another economy (direct investment enterprise)—covers all transactions between direct investors and direct investment enterprises. That is, *direct investment* covers the initial transaction between the two and all subsequent transactions between them and among affiliated enterprises, both incorporated and unincorporated. Direct investment transactions occurring abroad and in the reporting economy are subclassified into equity capital, reinvested earnings, other capital (intercompany transactions). For equity capital and other capital, claims on and liabilities to affiliated enterprises and to direct investors are distinguished. Transactions between affiliated banks and between other affiliated financial intermediaries are limited to equity and permanent debt capital. (See paragraph 372.)

178. *Portfolio investment* covers transactions in equity securities and debt securities; the latter are subclassified, into bonds and notes and money market instruments. Various new financial instruments, other than financial derivatives, are covered under appropriate instrument classifications. (Transactions covered under *direct investment* and *reserve assets* are excluded.)

179. The *financial derivatives* category covers financial instruments that are linked to other specific financial instruments, indicators, or commodities and through which specific financial risks (such as interest rate risk, foreign exchange risk, equity and commodity price risks, credit risk. etc.) can, in their own right, be traded in financial markets. Transactions in financial derivatives should be treated as separate transactions rather than as integral parts of the values of the underlying transactions to which they are linked.

180. *Other investment* covers short- and long-term trade credits; loans (including use of Fund credit, loans from the Fund, and loans associated with financial leases); currency and deposits (transferable and other—such as savings and term deposits, savings and loan shares, shares in credit unions, etc.); and other accounts receivable and payable. (Transactions covered under *direct investment* are excluded.)

181. *Reserve assets* cover transactions in those assets that are considered, by the monetary authorities of an economy, to be available for use in meeting balance of payments and, in some instances, other needs. Such availability is not closely linked in principle to formal criteria such as ownership or currency of denomination. The items covered are monetary gold, SDRs, reserve position in the Fund, foreign exchange assets (currency, deposits, and securities), and other claims.

182. Coverage and identification of *reserve asset* components are linked to an analytic concept, are in part judgmental, and are not always amenable to application of objective, formal criteria or clear rankings as to conditionality and other considerations. In contrast to the treatment in the fourth edition of the *Manual*, valuation changes in *reserve assets* are excluded, along with counterparts to such changes, in the fifth edition. Also excluded are the allocation/cancellation of SDRs, the monetization/demonetization of gold, and counterpart entries. These changes, which do not constitute transactions, are reflected in the international investment position.

Introduction

Le volume 53 du *Balance of Payments Statistics Yearbook* (Annuaire de statistiques de balance des paiements) (l'annuaire), publié par le Fonds monétaire international (FMI), présente les données de balance des paiements que lui ont communiqué ses pays membres. Le FMI est redevable à ces derniers d'avoir collaboré au présent ouvrage en lui fournissant ces informations. Pour certains pays, les données sont parfois complétées par des renseignements que les économistes ont tirées d'autres sources.

Le présent volume de l'annuaire se compose de trois parties. La première présente les données de la balance des paiements et de la position extérieure globale (PEG) pour les divers pays. La deuxième contient des totaux régionaux et mondiaux pour les principales composantes de la balance des paiements. La troisième partie fournit une description technique des méthodes de certains pays qui ont communiqué les données. La première partie constitue une publication distincte, et les deuxième et troisième parties sont reliées ensemble.

Les caractéristiques introduites dans les volumes 46 à 52 sont conservées dans le présent ouvrage. Comme dans le volume 46, les données de balance des paiements sont présentées conformément à la classification des composantes types adoptées dans la cinquième édition du *Manuel de la balance des paiements (MBP5)*[1]. . Il convient toutefois de noter que les composantes types ont été modifiées par suite de la publication, en 2000, puis de la modification en 2002, de l'ouvrage intitulé «*Dérivés financiers — Supplément à la cinquième édition (1993) du Manuel de la balance des paiements*» (le Supplément). À compter de cette date, toute référence au *MBP5* renvoie également au Supplément et à son addendum. Conformément aux recommandations formulées dans l'addendum, le présent annuaire rend compte de la décision prise par le Comité d'experts de la balance des paiements créé sous les auspices du FMI (Comité d'experts) qui préconise d'inclure les transactions sur dérivés financiers effectuées par les entreprises apparentées dans la composante dérivés financiers de la balance des paiements et de la position extérieure globale (PEG). Parallèlement, comme pour le volume 47, les données sur la PEG sont elles aussi présentées conformément au *MBP5*, et la troisième partie de l'annuaire présente une analyse détaillée des méthodologies, méthodes de calcul et sources de données utilisées par la plupart des pays compris dans l'annuaire. Le *MBP5*[2] apporte un certain nombre de changements à la méthodologie utilisée pour l'établissement des données de balance des paiements. Ces changements sont décrits en détail au chapitre I du *MBP5*. Depuis la publication du volume 46, une série de codes accompagne les données présentées dans le présent Annuaire conformément à la classification des composantes types du *MBP5*. Ces codes ont été mis au point conjointement par le FMI, l'Organisation de coopération et de développement économiques (OCDE) et l'Office statistique de l'Union européenne (Eurostat). La structure de ces codes est décrite en annexe. En outre, à partir du volume 46, l'annuaire ne présente plus de données trimestrielles de balance des paiements pour les pays qui communiquent ce type de statistiques au FMI. Ces données trimestrielles sont publiées dans l'édition mensuelle de *Statistiques financières internationales (SFI)*.

La conversion des données par les services du FMI a permis de présenter, selon la classification retenue dans le *MBP5*, les statistiques de la base de données du FMI qui se rapportent à des périodes antérieures, ainsi que les données communiquées pour des périodes plus récentes par les pays membres qui continuent à suivre les recommandations de la quatrième édition du *Manuel de la balance des paiements*. En 1995, les services du FMI ont mis au point des formules de conversion permettant de mettre sous une forme à peu près conforme à la méthodologie et à la présentation retenues dans la cinquième édition les données de balance des paiements reçues de chaque pays et figurant dans la base de données du FMI. Une fois converties, les données ont été soumises à l'examen des autorités des pays en question, et les observations formulées ont été incorporées dans la nouvelle base de données du *MBP5*. En 1996, avec la collaboration des autorités nationales, les services du FMI ont procédé d'une manière analogue pour présenter conformément au *MBP5* les données sur la PEG établies selon les recommandations de la quatrième édition. En principe, la PEG d'un pays est un relevé du stock de ses avoirs et engagements financiers extérieurs.

La troisième partie présente une description technique des méthodologies, méthodes de calcul et sources de données qui se fonde en grande partie sur les renseignements que les pays transmettent au FMI. Les descriptions ont pour but de mieux renseigner les utilisateurs sur la couverture et les limitations des données publiées pour les différents pays dans cet annuaire, de même que les statisticiens sur les sources de données et méthodes utilisées par leurs homologues étrangers. En outre, des renseignements détaillés sont mis à la disposition des statisticiens sur les pratiques d'établissement nationales des statistiques d'investissement direct suite à l'enquête sur l'application des normes méthodologiques concernant l'investissement direct menée conjointement en 2001 par le FMI et l'OCDE. Les statisticiens peuvent consulter la base de métadonnées sur l'investissement direct à l'adresse http://www.imf.org/external/np/sta/di/mdb97.htm.

[1]Le volume 1 de l'annuaire, paru en 1949, était fondé sur la première édition du *Manuel de la balance des paiements* du FMI, publiée en 1948; les volumes 2 à 12, sur la deuxième édition du *Manuel*, publiée en 1950; les volumes 13 à 23, sur la troisième édition du *Manuel*, publiée en 1961; et les volumes 24 à 29, sur la troisième édition, ainsi que sur le *Manuel de la balance des paiements : supplément à la troisième édition*, paru en 1973. Les volumes 30 à 45 ont été établis sur la base des directives de la quatrième édition du *Manuel*, publiée en 1977.

[2]Fonds monétaire international, *Manuel de la balance des paiements*, cinquième édition, Washington, Septembre 1993, et *Dérivés financiers — Supplément à la cinquième édition (1993) du Manuel de la balance des paiements*, Washington, 2000.

Le reste de la présente introduction s'articule comme suit :

- La section I décrit les caractéristiques fondamentales des tableaux publiés dans la première partie du présent volume de l'annuaire. (Les lecteurs trouveront dans les deuxième et troisième parties des précisions sur le champ d'application des données.)
- La section II donne des indications sur l'abonnement aux données de balance des paiements du FMI sur disques optiques compacts (CD-ROM).
- Il y a six annexes. L'annexe I contient une présentation analytique des composantes de la balance des paiements (accompagnées des codes correspondants) sous forme résumée. L'annexe II présente les composantes types définies dans le *MBP5* (et les codes correspondants). L'annexe III explique le système de codage des données. L'annexe IV présente les composantes types de la PEG, telles qu'elles ressortent du *MBP5*. L'annexe V est consacrée au cadre conceptuel de la balance des paiements. L'annexe VI décrit le champ couvert par les principales composantes de la balance des paiements, telles qu'elles sont définies dans le *MBP5*.

I. Première partie de l'annuaire : données relatives aux pays

La première partie de l'annuaire présente les pages consacrées aux divers pays suivant un ordre alphabétique. Il convient de noter toutefois que, dans la présente publication, le terme «pays» ne désigne pas toujours une entité territoriale constituant un État tel qu'il est défini selon l'usage et le droit internationaux; ce terme recouvre également la zone euro et certaines entités territoriales qui ne sont pas des États souverains mais sur lesquelles des données statistiques sont disponibles séparément au niveau international.

Pour la plupart des pays, les données de balance des paiements se présentent sous la forme de deux tableaux. Le tableau 1 constitue un résumé analytique des données plus détaillées contenues au tableau 2, et présente toute une série de composantes de la balance des paiements de manière à mettre en relief les postes de financement (réserves et postes apparentés). (Voir aussi l'annexe I). Le tableau 2 présente des données correspondant aux composantes types décrites dans le *MBP5*. (Voir aussi l'annexe II). Dans le cas des pays pour lesquels on dispose de statistiques sur la PEG, ces dernières figurent au tableau 3. Les tableaux 1, 2 et 3 présentent, pour chaque pays, des données pour les années 1994 à 2001. Sauf indication contraire, les chiffres portent sur l'année civile.

Présentation analytique

Dans la présentation analytique, qui fait l'objet du tableau 1, les composantes de la balance des paiements sont réparties entre cinq grandes catégories (groupes A à E), que le FMI juge utiles à une analyse homogène de l'évolution de la balance des paiements. Cependant, le choix des groupes ne saurait être considéré comme découlant de la recommandation du FMI quant à l'approche analytique à retenir pour chaque pays. Il existe d'autres types de présentation analytique, qui consisteraient à regrouper les composantes types du tableau 2 d'une manière différente, soit pour tenir compte de la situation particulière d'un pays donné, soit pour répondre à des besoins analytiques précis.

Il convient de noter que les données présentées au tableau 1 sur le solde du compte des transactions courantes, du compte de capital et du compte d'opérations financières de certains pays ne concordent pas avec les données correspondantes du tableau 2. Cela tient au fait que, dans le tableau 1, certaines transactions relevant de ces comptes en sont exclues et sont reclassées en tant que «financement exceptionnel» à la rubrique des réserves et postes apparentés. Le «financement exceptionnel» se rapporte aux transactions que les autorités effectuent pour répondre aux besoins de financement de la balance des paiements et prend notamment la forme d'emprunts extérieurs, d'arriérés de paiements et de remises de dette. Le financement exceptionnel ne comprend pas les réserves.

Présentation type

Comme le montre le tableau 2, la liste des composantes types du *MBP5* présentée au tableau 2 fait apparaître une classification plus détaillée des biens et services que celle qui figure dans la quatrième édition. Le compte dénommé «compte de capital et d'opérations financières» comporte deux volets distincts, qui sont le «compte de capital» et le «compte d'opérations financières». Les composantes du «compte d'opérations financières» sont classées selon plusieurs critères : type d'investissement (c'est-à-dire investissements directs, investissements de portefeuille, dérivés financiers[1], autres investissements et avoirs de réserve), avoirs et engagements, secteurs intérieurs (autorités monétaires, administrations publiques, banques et autres secteurs) et échéances initiales (long terme et court terme).

Position extérieure globale

Comme le montre le tableau 3, les données de la PEG sont disposées conformément à la classification des composantes types de la PEG retenue dans le *MBP5*. (Voir aussi l'annexe IV.)

La classification des composantes de la PEG présentée au tableau 3 correspond à celle des composantes du compte d'opérations financières de la balance des paiements figurant au tableau 2, mais plusieurs différences apparaissent toutefois entre les deux tableaux. Comme indiqué précédemment, la PEG est un relevé des avoirs et

[1]Compte tenu du caractère spécifique des dérivés financiers et de la manière dont certaines institutions comptabilisent les transactions, certains pays ne peuvent communiquer que des chiffres nets. Bien qu'il soit possible de classer ces transactions nettes parmi les actifs, il a été décidé dans le présent annuaire de les classer parmi les passifs, tout comme les positions nettes lorsqu'elles sont communiquées, parce que la demande de ces instruments émane habituellement d'entités qui couvrent des flux monétaires liés à des opérations d'endettement.

Encadré – Position extérieure globale

Les pays qui commencent seulement à établir des données sur la position extérieure globale PEG) sont encouragés à communiquer des relevés partiels. En général, ces relevés partiels comprennent des données sur les autorités monétaires (y compris les réserves internationales) et sur un autre secteur au moins. Les relevés de la PEG des pays déclarants font l'objet du tableau 3 aux pages par pays. Aucun total n'est présenté pour les relevés partiels de la PEG. En raison des limitations inhérentes à ces données, il convient, pour chaque pays donné, de lire le relevé de la PEG en consultant simultanément les notes de la troisième partie — Méthodologies, méthodes de calcul et sources de données — qui se rapportent au pays concerné. Au fur et à mesure que les pays recueilleront davantage de données pour la PEG, la couverture des données de la PEG de ces pays sera élargie dans les éditions ultérieures de l'Annuaire.

Voir le chapitre XXIII du *MBP5* pour une étude exhaustive du concept de position extérieure globale.

La **dette extérieure** ne constitue pas une composante distincte de la PEG, mais elle peut être calculée par addition des composantes de la PEG autres que le capital social (c'est-à-dire tous les engagements autres que les titres de participation et le capital social correspondant à des investissements directs [y compris les bénéfices réinvestis] et les dérivés financiers). Cette conception cadre dans l'ensemble avec la définition de référence de la dette extérieure brute qui est retenue dans l'ouvrage intitulé Statistiques de la dette extérieure : Guide du statisticien et de l'utilisateur (External Debt Statistics : Guide for Compilers and Users), mis au point par l'Équipe spéciale interinstitutions des statistiques financières. L'Équipe spéciale était présidée par le FMI et des représentants de la Banque centrale européenne, de la Banque mondiale, de la BRI, de la CNUCED, d'Eurostat, du FMI, de l'OCDE, du Secrétariat du Club de Paris et du Secrétariat du Commonwealth ont pris part aux travaux du Guide.

Position extérieure globale : composantes types[1]

A. Avoirs

1. Investissements directs
- 1.1 Capital social et bénéfices réinvestis
- 1.2 Autres capitaux[2]

2. Investissements de portefeuille
- 2.1 Titres de participation
- 2.2 Titres de créance[4]

3. Dérivés financiers
- 3.1 Autorités monétaires
- 3.2 Administrations publiques
- 3.3 Banques
- 3.4 Autres secteurs

4. Autres investissements
- 4.1 Crédits commerciaux
- 4.2 Prêts
- 4.3 Monnaie fiduciaire et dépôts
- 4.4 Autres avoirs

4. Avoirs de réserve
- 4.1 Or monétaire
- 4.2 Droits de tirage spéciaux
- 4.3 Position de réserve au FMI
- 4.4 Devises étrangères
- 4.5 Autres créances

B. Engagements

1. Investissements directs
- 1.1 Capital social et bénéfices réinvestis
- 1.2 Autres capitaux[3]

2. Investissements de portefeuille
- 2.1 Titres de participation
- 2.2 Titres d'engagement[3,4]

3. Dérivés financiers
- 3.1 Autorités monétaires
- 3.2 Administrations publiques
- 3.3 Banques
- 3.4 Autres secteurs

4. Autres investissements
- 4.1 Crédits commerciaux[3]
- 4.2 Prêts[3]
- 4.3 Monnaie fiduciaire et dépôts[3]
- 4.4 Autres engagements[3]

[1] Les composantes ne sont pas toutes présentées, comme par exemple celles qui sont ventilées par secteur (autorités monétaires, administrations publiques, banques, autres secteurs) ou, dans certains cas, par échéance.

[2] Les passifs à l'égard des entreprises apparentées, qui figurent en chiffres nets au poste des «Autres capitaux » dans la classification fonctionnelle, constituent une composante de la dette extérieure.

[3] Ces composantes comprennent la dette extérieure brute (voir aussi la note 2).

[4] Ce poste comprend les obligations, les effets et les instruments du marché monétaire.

engagements extérieurs d'un pays à un moment précis. Par conséquent, au tableau 3, la présentation de base des composantes de la PEG comporte deux catégories générales, celles des avoirs et des engagements, par opposition à la classification fonctionnelle des investissements retenue au tableau 2 (investissements directs, investissements de portefeuille, dérivés financiers, autres investissements et avoirs de réserve). En outre, le tableau 3 présente la PEG d'un pays à la fin de la période considérée, alors que le tableau 2 retrace les transactions effectuées pendant cette période. Par ailleurs, contrairement au tableau 2, qui indique la valeur des transactions financières pendant une période, le tableau 3 présente de la PEG d'un pays une évaluation qui reflète les transactions financières, réévaluations et autres ajustements opérés à la fin de la période considérée. La PEG nette indiquée au tableau 3 est égale à la différence entre la valeur des avoirs financiers extérieurs recensés et celle des engagements financiers extérieurs recensés.

Codage des données

Aux tableaux 1, 2 et 3, chaque catégorie de données et chaque composante s'accompagnent d'un code. Comme indiqué plus haut, ces codes ont été établis conjointement par le FMI, l'OCDE et Eurostat en vue de faciliter la communication des statistiques au niveau international. Les codes s'appliquent aux composantes types de la balance des paiements et de la position extérieure globale, telles qu'elles sont définies dans le *MBP5*, ainsi qu'aux composantes de la classification OCDE/Eurostat pour le commerce des services.

Chaque code figurant dans l'annuaire est un code alphanumérique à six composantes. Le chiffre placé en première position indique s'il s'agit d'un crédit, d'un débit ou d'un solde; le chiffre «2» désigne un crédit, «3» un débit et «4» un solde (différence entre crédit et débit). Les trois chiffres suivants correspondent au code attribué à la composante de la balance des paiements. Par exemple, le compte des transactions courantes a pour code 993, le compte de capital, 994, et le compte d'opérations financières, 995. Pour plus de précisions sur le système de codage, les lecteurs pourront se référer à l'annexe III.

Les cinquième et sixième chiffres ou lettres du code figurant dans l'annuaire signalent l'existence de caractéristiques particulières à certaines composantes. Par exemple, dans le tableau 1, la lettre Z, placée en cinquième position, indique que la composante exclut le financement exceptionnel; W signifie que, outre le financement exceptionnel, les données excluent l'utilisation des crédits et les prêts du FMI. Au tableau 1, les lettres A, B, C et D différencient les divers secteurs intérieurs. Au tableau 2, les lettres A, B et C servent à indiquer qu'il ne s'agit pas de sous-composantes types, comme c'est le cas, par exemple, pour les postes ayant trait aux transports (passagers, fret et autres).

Écritures passées au crédit et au débit

Aux tableaux 1 et 2, les données sur les transactions sont présentées sous forme de chiffres bruts inscrits au crédit ou au débit du compte des transactions courantes et du compte de capital. Au compte d'opérations financières, les données sont présentées en chiffres nets au crédit ou au débit (pour rendre compte des variations nettes des passifs et des actifs). Les montants inscrits au crédit, qu'ils soient bruts ou nets, sont positifs (mais ne sont pas accompagnés du signe plus) et les montants portés au débit, bruts ou nets, sont négatifs (ils sont affectés du signe moins). En conséquence, la diminution des avoirs et l'augmentation des engagements (crédit) sont indiquées par des chiffres positifs, et l'accroissement des avoirs et la diminution des engagements (débit), par des chiffres négatifs.

Montants nuls ou non disponibles

Lorsqu'il manque des chiffres dans les statistiques communiquées par les pays, il est souvent difficile de savoir si ces données font défaut parce qu'elles ne sont pas disponibles, ou parce qu'il s'agit de montants nuls ou négligeables. Dans les tableaux de l'annuaire, le symbole (...) indique que les données ne sont pas disponibles, ou que les montants sont nuls ou négligeables.

Note sur les composantes du *Revenu* et des *Autres investissements*

Au tableau 2, Standard Presentation (Présentation type), les chiffres que certains pays communiquent pour les postes "Income" (Revenu) et "Other Investment" (Autres investissements) présentent un niveau d'agrégation qui ne permet pas d'identifier séparément chaque composante de la catégorie intéressée. En pareil cas, il n'est donc pas possible de faire la somme des composantes de certaines sous-catégories pour calculer le total agrégé de ces mêmes sous-catégories. Il en va de même pour le poste "Other Investment" (Autres investissements) du tableau 3, International Investment Position (Position extérieure globale).

Auparavant, dans les volumes 46 à 49, les données concernant les «Autres investissements» (avoirs et engagements) étaient ventilées sous les rubriques «long terme» et «court terme». Depuis la publication du volume 50, les tableaux présentent dorénavant les chiffres des «autres investissements» (actifs et passifs) pour les autorités monétaires, les administrations publiques, les banques et les autres secteurs sous forme de totaux (du financement à long terme et du financement à court terme), avec une rubrique «dont : court terme». (Au poste «prêts, autorités monétaires», les chiffrent sont présentés sous forme de totaux, avec une rubrique «dont : utilisation des crédits et des prêts du FMI» et une rubrique «dont : court terme»). La présentation type n'a toutefois pas été modifiée à l'annexe II.

Présentation de chiffres arrondis

La plupart des chiffres des tableaux sont exprimés en millions; les utilisateurs ne doivent pas présumer qu'un tableau présentant des chiffres exprimés en unités plus petites fournit nécessairement des données plus exactes. L'unité est choisie pour des raisons de commodité. Compte tenu des pratiques couramment utilisées pour le calcul, il peut exister un écart, dû au fait que les chiffres ont été arrondis, entre le total indiqué et la somme de ses composantes.

Méthodes de conversion

La plupart des données de balance des paiements communiquées au FMI sont exprimées en monnaie nationale ou en dollars E.U., bien que quelques pays fournissent certaines données en DTS. Pour faciliter les comparaisons entre pays, tous les états de balance des paiements publiés dans l'annuaire sont exprimés en dollars E.U. En outre, dans tous les cas, les données que les pays communiquent sur leurs transactions avec le FMI et sur leurs transactions en DTS sont remplacées par des données tirées des registres du FMI, qui sont exprimées en DTS; celles-ci sont à leur tour converties en dollars E.U.

Pour les pays qui communiquent des données exprimées en unités autres que le dollar E.U., les chiffres sont convertis à l'aide des taux de conversion figurant au bas du tableau 1. Ces taux de conversion sont normalement les taux de change moyens de la monnaie du pays pour la période considérée publiés dans *SFI*. Par exemple, les pages consacrées aux Pays-Bas dans *SFI* comportent la ligne «rf», qui présente le taux moyen du dollar en florins. Les données de flux exprimées en DTS sont converties en dollars E.U. à l'aide des taux indiqués à la ligne «sb» de la page consacrée aux États-Unis dans *SFI*. Pour les pays qui transmettent des données trimestrielles exprimées en monnaie nationale, le total annuel en dollars E.U. est égal à la somme des données trimestrielles en dollars E.U.

Les lecteurs trouveront à la section 1 de l'introduction de *International Financial Statistics (IFS)* de plus amples renseignements sur les taux de change retenus.

II. Abonnement aux disques optiques compacts (CD-ROM)

Les statistiques publiées dans l'annuaire sont également disponibles sur CD-ROM. Le nombre de pays et de séries chronologiques figurant sur les CD-ROM est légèrement supérieur à celui de la version imprimée de l'annuaire, et il en est de même pour le nombre de périodes auxquelles se rapportent les séries chronologiques. Les CD-ROM contiennent également les données trimestrielles communiquées par les pays, et présentent en outre des révisions et des mises à jour dès que les données actualisées sont disponibles. Les demandes de renseignements concernant les CD-ROM doivent être adressées à :

Publication Services
International Monetary Fund
Washington, DC 20431, U.S.A.
Téléphone : (202) 623–7430
Télécopie : (202) 623–7201
Messagerie électronique : publications@imf.org
Internet : http://www.imf.org

Annexe I. Présentation analytique

	Codes
A. COMPTE DES TRANSACTIONS COURANTES[1]	4 993 Z .
Biens : exportations, f.à.b.	2 100 .
Biens : importations, f.à.b.	3 100 .
Solde au titre des biens	4 100 .
Services : crédit	2 200 ..
Services : débit	3 200 ..
Solde au titre des biens et services	4 991 ..
Revenus : crédit	2 300 ..
Revenus : débit	3 300 ..
Solde au titre des biens, services et revenus	4 992 ..
Transferts courants : crédit	2 379 Z .
Transferts courants : débit	3 379 ..
B. COMPTE DE CAPITAL[1]	4 994 Z .
Compte de capital : crédit	2 994 Z .
Compte de capital : débit	3 994 ..
Total, groupes A plus B	4 981 ..
C. COMPTE D'OPÉRATIONS FINANCIÈRES[1]	4 995 W .
Investissements directs à l'étranger	4 505 ..
Investissements directs dans l'économie	4 555 Z .
Investissements de portefeuille : avoirs	4 602 ..
Titres de participation	4 610 ..
Titres de créance	4 619 ..
Investissements de portefeuille : engagements	4 652 Z .
Titres de participation	4 660 ..
Titres d'engagement	4 669 Z .
Dérivés financiers	4 910 ..
Dérivés financiers (actifs)	4 900 ..
Dérivés financiers (passifs)	4 905 ..
Autres investissements : avoirs	4 703 ..
Autorités monétaires	4 701 ..
Administrations publiques	4 704 ..
Banques	4 705 ..
Autres secteurs	4 728 ..
Autres investissements : engagements	4 753 W .
Autorités monétaires	4 753 WA
Administrations publiques	4 753 ZB
Banques	4 753 ZC
Autres secteurs	4 753 ZD
Total, groupes A à C inclus	4 983 ..
D. ERREURS ET OMISSIONS NETTES	4 998 ..
Total, groupes A à D inclus	4 984 ..
E. RÉSERVES ET POSTES APPARENTÉS	4 802.A.
Avoirs de réserve	4 802 ..
Utilisation des crédits et prêts du FMI	4 766 ..
Engagements constituant des réserves pour les autorités étrangères	4 900 ..
Financements exceptionnels	4 920 ..
TAUX DE CONVERSION : MONTANT D'UNITÉS MONÉTAIRES POUR UN DOLLAR E.U.	0 101 ..

[1]Non compris les composantes qui font partie des catégories du groupe E.

ANNEXE II. COMPOSANTES TYPES

	Codes	
COMPTE DES TRANSACTIONS COURANTES	4 993	. .
A. BIENS	4 100	. .
Crédit	2 100	. .
Marchandises générales : exportations, f.à.b.	2 110	. .
Biens exportés pour transformation, f.à.b.	2 150	. .
Réparations de biens	2 160	. .
Achats de biens dans les ports par les transporteurs	2 170	. .
Or non monétaire	2 180	. .
Débit	3 100	. .
Marchandises générales : importations, f.à.b.	3 110	. .
Biens importés pour transformation, f.à.b.	3 150	. .
Réparations de biens	3 160	. .
Achats de biens dans les ports par les transporteurs	3 170	. .
Or non monétaire	3 180	. .
B. SERVICES	4 200	. .
Total, crédit	2 200	. .
Total, débit	3 200	. .
Services de transport, crédit	2 205	. .
Passagers	2 850	. .
Fret	2 851	. .
Autres	2 852	. .
Transports maritimes, passagers	2 207	. .
Transports maritimes, fret	2 208	. .
Transports maritimes, autres	2 209	. .
Transports aériens, passagers	2 211	. .
Transports aériens, fret	2 212	. .
Transports aériens, autres	2 213	. .
Autres transports, passagers	2 215	. .
Autres transports, fret	2 216	. .
Autres transports, autres	2 217	. .
Services de transport, débit	3 205	. .
Passagers	3 850	. .
Fret	3 851	. .
Autres	3 852	. .
Transports maritimes, passagers	3 207	. .
Transports maritimes, fret	3 208	. .
Transports maritimes, autres	3 209	. .
Transports aériens, passagers	3 211	. .
Transports aériens, fret	3 212	. .
Transports aériens, autres	3 213	. .
Autres transports, passagers	3 215	. .
Autres transports, fret	3 216	. .
Autres transports, autres	3 217	. .
Voyages, crédit	2 236	. .
Voyages à titre professionnel	2 237	. .
Voyages à titre personnel	2 240	. .
Voyages, débit	3 236	. .
Voyages à titre professionnel	3 237	. .
Voyages à titre personnel	3 240	. .

Annexe II. Composantes types *(suite)*

	Codes
Autres services, crédit	2 200 BA
Services de communication	2 245 . .
Services de bâtiment et travaux publics	2 249 . .
Services d'assurance	2 253 . .
Services financiers	2 260 . .
Services d'informatique et d'information	2 262 . .
Redevances et droits de licence	2 266 . .
Autres services aux entreprises	2 268 . .
Services personnels, culturels et relatifs aux loisirs	2 287 . .
Services fournis ou reçus par les administrations publiques, n.c.a.	2 291 . .
Autres services, débit	3 200 BA
Services de communication	3 245 . .
Services de bâtiment et travaux publics	3 249 . .
Services d'assurance	3 253 . .
Services financiers	3 260 . .
Services d'informatique et d'information	3 262 . .
Redevances et droits de licence	3 266 . .
Autres services aux entreprises	3 268 . .
Services personnels, culturels et relatifs aux loisirs	3 287 . .
Services fournis ou reçus par les administrations publiques, n.c.a.	3 291 . .
C. REVENUS	4 300 . .
Total, crédit	2 300 . .
Total, débit	3 300 . .
Rémunération des salariés, crédit	2 310 . .
Rémunération des salariés, débit	3 310 . .
Revenu des investissements, crédit	2 320 . .
Revenu des investissements directs	2 330 . .
Dividendes et bénéfices distribués des succursales	2 332 . .
Bénéfices réinvestis et bénéfices non distribués des succursales	2 333 . .
Revenu des titres de créance (intérêts)	2 334 . .
Revenu des investissements de portefeuille	2 339 . .
Revenu des titres de participation	2 340 . .
Revenu des obligations et autres titres d'emprunt	2 350 . .
Revenu des instruments du marché monétaire	2 360 . .
Revenu des autres investissements	2 370 . .
Revenu des investissements, débit	3 320 . .
Revenu des investissements directs	3 330 . .
Dividendes et bénéfices distribués des succursales	3 332 . .
Bénéfices réinvestis et bénéfices non distribués des succursales	3 333 . .
Revenu des titres de créance (intérêts)	3 334 . .
Revenu des investissements de portefeuille	3 339 . .
Revenu des titres de participation	3 340 . .
Revenu des obligations et autres titres d'emprunt	3 350 . .
Revenu des instruments du marché monétaire	3 360 . .
Revenu des autres investissements	3 370 . .
D.TRANSFERTS COURANTS	4 379 . .
Crédit	2 379 . .
Administrations publiques	2 380 . .
Autres secteurs	2 390 . .
Envois de fonds des travailleurs	2 391 . .
Autres transferts courants	2 392 . .

Annexe II. Composantes types (*suite*)

	Codes	
Débit	3 379	. .
Administrations publiques	3 380	. .
Autres secteurs	3 390	. .
Envois de fonds des travailleurs	3 391	. .
Autres transferts courants	3 392	. .
COMPTE DE CAPITAL ET D'OPÉRATIONS FINANCIÈRES	4 996	. .
COMPTE DE CAPITAL	4 994	. .
Total, crédit	2 994	. .
Total, débit	3 994	. .
Transferts de capital, crédit	2 400	. .
Administrations publiques	2 401	. .
Remise de dettes	2 402	. .
Autres transferts de capital	2 410	. .
Autres secteurs	2 430	. .
Transferts des migrants	2 431	. .
Remise de dettes	2 432	. .
Autres transferts de capital	2 440	. .
Transferts de capital, débit	3 400	. .
Administrations publiques	3 401	. .
Remise de dettes	3 402	. .
Autres transferts de capital	3 410	. .
Autres secteurs	3 430	. .
Transferts des migrants	3 431	. .
Remise de dettes	3 432	. .
Autres transferts de capital	3 440	. .
Acquisitions et cessions d'actifs non financiers non produits, crédit	2 480	. .
Acquisitions et cessions d'actifs non financiers non produits, débit	3 480	. .
COMPTE D'OPÉRATIONS FINANCIÈRES	4 995	. .
A. INVESTISSEMENTS DIRECTS	4 500	. .
De l'économie à l'étranger	4 505	. .
Capital social	4 510	. .
Créances sur les entreprises apparentées	4 515	. .
Engagements envers les entreprises apparentées	4 520	. .
Bénéfices réinvestis	4 525	. .
Autres transactions	4 530	. .
Créances sur les entreprises apparentées	4 535	. .
Engagements envers les entreprises apparentées	4 540	. .
De l'étranger dans l'économie	4 555	. .
Capital social	4 560	. .
Créances sur les investisseurs directs	4 565	. .
Engagements envers les investisseurs directs	4 570	. .
Bénéfices réinvestis	4 575	. .
Autres transactions	4 580	. .
Créances sur les investisseurs directs	4 585	. .
Engagements envers les investisseurs directs	4 590	. .

ANNEXE II. COMPOSANTES TYPES *(suite)*

	Codes	
B. INVESTISSEMENTS DE PORTEFEUILLE	4 600	. .
Avoirs	4 602	. .
Titres de participation	4 610	. .
Autorités monétaires	4 611	. .
Administrations publiques	4 612	. .
Banques	4 613	. .
Autres secteurs	4 614	. .
Titres de créance	4 619	. .
Obligations et autres titres d'emprunt	4 620	. .
Autorités monétaires	4 621	. .
Administrations publiques	4 622	. .
Banques	4 623	. .
Autres secteurs	4 624	. .
Instruments du marché monétaire	4 630	. .
Autorités monétaires	4 631	. .
Administrations publiques	4 632	. .
Banques	4 633	. .
Autres secteurs	4 634	. .
Engagements	4 652	. .
Titres de participation	4 660	. .
Banques	4 663	. .
Autres secteurs	4 664	. .
Titres d'engagement	4 669	. .
Obligations et autres titres d'emprunt	4 670	. .
Autorités monétaires	4 671	. .
Administrations publiques	4 672	. .
Banques	4 673	. .
Autres secteurs	4 674	. .
Instruments du marché monétaire	4 680	. .
Autorités monétaires	4 681	. .
Administrations publiques	4 682	. .
Banques	4 683	. .
Autres secteurs	4 684	. .
C. DÉRIVÉS FINANCIERS	4 910	. .
Autorités monétaires	4 911	. .
Administrations publiques	4 912	. .
Banques	4 913	. .
Autres secteurs	4 914	. .
Avoirs	4 900	. .
Autorités monétaires	4 901	. .
Administrations publiques	4 902	. .
Banques	4 903	. .
Autres secteurs	4 904	. .
Engagements	4 905	. .
Autorités monétaires	4 906	. .
Administrations publiques	4 907	. .
Banques	4 908	. .
Autres secteurs	4 909	. .
D.AUTRES INVESTISSEMENTS	4 700	. .
Avoirs	4 703	. .
Crédits commerciaux	4 706	. .
Administrations publiques	4 707	. .
dont : court terme	4 709	. .

Annexe II. Composantes types (*suite*)

	Codes	
Autres secteurs	4 710	. .
dont : court terme	4 712	. .
Prêts	4 714	. .
Autorités monétaires	4 715	. .
dont : court terme	4 718	. .
Administrations publiques	4 719	. .
dont : court terme	4 721	. .
Banques	4 722	. .
dont : court terme	4 724	. .
Autres secteurs	4 725	. .
dont : court terme	4 727	. .
Monnaie fiduciaire et dépôts	4 730	. .
Autorités monétaires	4 731	. .
Administrations publiques	4 732	. .
Banques	4 733	. .
Autres secteurs	4 734	. .
Autres avoirs	4 736	. .
Autorités monétaires	4 737	. .
dont : court terme	4 739	. .
Administrations publiques	4 740	. .
dont : court terme	4 742	. .
Banques	4 743	. .
dont : court terme	4 745	. .
Autres secteurs	4 746	. .
dont : court terme	4 748	. .
Engagements	4 753	. .
Crédits commerciaux	4 756	. .
Administrations publiques	4 757	. .
dont : court terme	4 759	. .
Autres secteurs	4 760	. .
dont : court terme	4 762	. .
Prêts	4 764	. .
Autorités monétaires	4 765	. .
dont : utilisation des crédits et prêts du FMI	4 766	. .
dont : court terme	4 768	. .
Administrations publiques : long terme	4 769	. .
dont : court terme	4 771	. .
Banques	4 772	. .
dont : court terme	4 774	. .
Autres secteurs	4 775	. .
dont : court terme	4 777	. .
Monnaie fiduciaire et dépôts	4 780	. .
Autorités monétaires	4 781	. .
Administrations publiques	4 782	. .
Banques	4 783	. .
Autres secteurs	4 784	. .
Autres engagements	4 786	. .
Autorités monétaires	4 787	. .
dont : court terme	4 789	. .
Administrations publiques	4 790	. .
dont : court terme	4 792	. .
Banques	4 793	. .
dont : court terme	4 795	. .
Autres secteurs	4 796	. .
dont : court terme	4 798	. .

ANNEXE II. COMPOSANTES TYPES (*fin*)

	Codes	
E. AVOIRS DE RÉSERVE	4 802	. .
Or monétaire	4 812	. .
Droits de tirage spéciaux	4 811	. .
Position de réserve au FMI	4 810	. .
Avoirs en devises	4 803	. .
Autres créances	4 813	. .
ERREURS ET OMISSIONS NETTES	4 998	. .

Annexe III. Système de codage FMI/OCDE/Eurostat applicable à la balance des paiements, à la position extérieure globale et au commerce international de services[1]

Le système de codage examiné ici s'applique à toutes les composantes types et aux postes complémentaires définis dans la cinquième édition du *Manuel de la balance des paiements*; il s'applique également aux composantes et postes pour mémoire de la classification OCDE-Eurostat des données sur le commerce international de services.

Le code a trois composantes ou sections, qui sont :

<position>	un nombre à un chiffre (compris entre 1 et 8) décrivant la position du poste dans les comptes de la position extérieure globale (PEG) ou de la balance des paiements (BP);
<sujet>	un nombre à trois chiffres (choisi parmi les nombres entiers compris entre 100 et 998) permettant d'identifier toutes les composantes de la balance des paiements et de la classification du commerce international des services et certains postes complémentaires;
<sous-code>	une composante définie par l'utilisateur et de longueur illimitée.

Le code complet comprendrait ces trois éléments dans l'ordre suivant : <position><sujet><sous-code>. Cependant, le sous-code est facultatif, contrairement au code de la position et au code du sujet. En conséquence, le code comportera, sous sa forme couramment utilisée, les composantes suivantes : <position><sujet>.

La première composante du code indique la position du poste dans les comptes de la position extérieure globale (PEG) et de la balance des paiements (BP); elle est définie comme suit :

Code	Position dans les comptes de la PEG et de la BP
1	Stock au début de la période
2	Flux, crédit
3	Flux, débit
4	Flux nets
5	Ajustement de la valeur en fonction des variations du prix
6	Ajustement de la valeur en fonction des variations du taux de change
7	Autres ajustements
8	Stock à la fin de la période
0	Autres

Le premier chiffre de la composante indicative du sujet correspond à la rubrique de la balance des paiements, c'est-à-dire :

Code	Rubrique de la BP
1	Biens
2	Services
3	Revenus et transferts courants
4	Compte de capital
5	Investissements directs
6	Investissements de portefeuille
7	Autres investissements
8	Avoirs de réserve
9	Principaux agrégats et détails complémentaires

Les deuxième et troisième chiffres de la composante sont généralement attribués dans un ordre consécutif et sont séparés par des espaces permettant l'inclusion ultérieure de codes additionnels, le cas échéant. En outre, dans le compte d'opérations financières, à l'exception des comptes des investissements directs, le deuxième chiffre de cette composante est 0, 1, 2, 3 ou 4 pour les avoirs et 5, 6, 7, 8 ou 9 pour les engagements.

Un exemple des codes appliqués aux «Autres investissements» dans le compte d'opérations financières est donné ci-après.

Sujet	Champ unique			Champ multiple		
	Crédit	Débit	Net	Crédit	Débit	Net
Autres investissements	2.700	3.700	4.700	2.700	3.700	4.700
Engagements	2.750	3.750	4.750	2.750	3.750	4.750
Prêts	2.762	3.762	4.762	2.762	3.762	4.762
Administrations publiques	2.767	3.767	4.767	2.767	3.767	4.767
Long terme	2.768	3.768	4.768	2.768	3.768	4.768
Court terme	2.769	3.769	4.769	2.769	3.769	4.769
Banques	2.770	3.770	4.770	2.770	3.770	4.770
Long terme	2.771	3.771	4.771	2.771	3.771	4.771
Court terme	2.772	3.772	4.772	2.772	3.772	4.772
Autres secteurs	2.773	3.773	4.773	2.773	3.773	4.773
Long terme	2.774	3.774	4.774	2.774	3.774	4.774
Court terme	2.775	3.775	4.775	2.775	3.775	4.775

Pour les prêts, les écritures passées au crédit et au débit servent à comptabiliser les transactions communément dénommées tirages et remboursements. La cinquième édition du *Manuel* recommande de classer tous les tirages sur prêts à long terme et tous les remboursements de ces prêts parmi les postes complémentaires. À l'heure actuelle, le FMI recueille des données nettes sur la plupart des autres postes du compte d'opérations financières. Néanmoins, le système de codage permet d'identifier tous les flux, qu'il s'agisse de transactions nettes ou de transactions inscrites au crédit ou au débit.

[1]Tiré de l'ouvrage du FMI intitulé «Balance des paiements : codes utilisés pour les composantes types et les postes complémentaires», Washington, DC, 3 mars 1995.

Annexe IV. Position extérieure globale : composantes types

	Codes	
A. AVOIRS	8 995	C .
Investissements directs à l'étranger	8 505	. .
Capital social et bénéfices réinvestis	8 506	. .
Créances sur les entreprises apparentées	8 507	. .
Engagements envers les entreprises apparentées	8 508	. .
Autres capitaux	8 530	. .
Créances sur les entreprises apparentées	8 535	. .
Engagements envers les entreprises apparentées	8 540	. .
Investissements de portefeuille	8 602	. .
Titres de participation	8 610	. .
Autorités monétaires	8 611	. .
Administrations publiques	8 612	. .
Banques	8 613	. .
Autres secteurs	8 614	. .
Titres de créances	8 619	. .
Obligations et autres titres d'emprunt	8 620	. .
Autorités monétaires	8 621	. .
Administrations publiques	8 622	. .
Banques	8 623	. .
Autres secteurs	8 624	. .
Instruments du marché monétaire	8 630	. .
Autorités monétaires	8 631	. .
Administrations publiques	8 632	. .
Banques	8 633	. .
Autres secteurs	8 634	. .
Dérivés financiers	8 900	. .
Autorités monétaires	8 901	. .
Administrations publiques	8 902	. .
Banques	8 903	. .
Autres secteurs	8 904	. .
Autres investissements	8 703	. .
Crédits commerciaux	8 706	. .
Administrations publiques	8 707	. .
dont : court terme	8 709	. .
Autres secteurs	8 710	. .
dont : court terme	8 712	. .
Prêts	8 714	. .
Autorités monétaires	8 715	. .
dont : court terme	8 718	. .
Administrations publiques	8 719	. .
dont : court terme	8 721	. .
Banques	8 722	. .
dont : court terme	8 724	. .
Autres secteurs	8 725	. .
dont : court terme	8 727	. .
Monnaie fiduciaire et dépôts	8 730	. .
Autorités monétaires	8 731	. .
Administrations publiques	8 732	. .
Banques	8 733	. .
Autres secteurs	8 734	. .

ANNEXE IV. POSITION EXTÉRIEURE GLOBALE : COMPOSANTES TYPES *(suite)*

	Codes	
Autres avoirs	8 736	..
Autorités monétaires	8 737	..
dont : court terme	8 739	..
Administrations publiques	8 740	..
dont : court terme	8 742	..
Banques	8 743	..
dont : court terme	8 745	..
Autres secteurs	8 746	..
dont : court terme	8 748	..
Avoirs de réserve	8 802	..
Or monétaire	8 812	..
Droits de tirage spéciaux	8 811	..
Position de réserve au FMI	8 810	..
Devises étrangères	8 803	..
Autres créances	8 813	..
B. ENGAGEMENTS	8 995	D .
Investissements directs de l'étranger dans l'économie	8 555	..
Capital social et bénéfices réinvestis	8 556	..
Créances sur les investisseurs directs	8 557	..
Engagements envers les investisseurs directs	8 558	..
Autres capitaux	8 580	..
Créances sur les investisseurs directs	8 585	..
Engagements envers les investisseurs directs	8 590	..
Investissements de portefeuille	8 652	..
Titres de participation	8 660	..
Banques	8 663	..
Autres secteurs	8 664	..
Titres d'engagement	8 669	..
Obligations et autres titres d'emprunt	8 670	..
Autorités monétaires	8 671	..
Administrations publiques	8 672	..
Banques	8 673	..
Autres secteurs	8 674	..
Instruments du marché monétaire	8 680	..
Autorités monétaires	8 681	..
Administrations publiques	8 682	..
Banques	8 683	..
Autres secteurs	8 684	..
Dérivés financiers	8 905	..
Autorités monétaires	8 906	..
Administrations publiques	8 907	..
Banques	8 908	..
Autres secteurs	8 909	..
Autres investissements	8 753	..
Crédits commerciaux	8 756	..
Administrations publiques	8 757	..
dont : court terme	8 759	..
Autres secteurs	8 760	..
dont : court terme	8 762	..

Annexe IV. Position extérieure globale : composantes types *(fin)*

	Codes	
Prêts	8 764	..
Autorités monétaires	8 765	..
dont : utilisation des crédits et des prêts du FMI	8 766	..
dont : court terme	8 768	..
Administrations publiques	8 769	..
dont : court terme	8 771	..
Banques	8 772	..
dont : court terme	8 774	..
Autres secteurs	8 775	..
dont : court terme	8 727	..
Monnaie fiduciaire et dépôts	8 780	..
Autorités monétaires	8 781	..
Administrations publiques	8 782	..
Banques	8 783	..
Autres secteurs	8 784	..
Autres engagements	8 786	..
Autorités monétaires	8 787	..
dont : court terme	8 789	..
Administrations publiques	8 790	..
dont : court terme	8 792	..
Banques	8 793	..
dont : court terme	8 795	..
Autres secteurs	8 796	..
dont : court terme	8 798	..
POSITION EXTÉRIEURE GLOBALE NETTE	8 995	..
Taux de conversion (fin de période)	0 102	..

Annexe V. Cadre conceptuel de la balance des paiements et de la position extérieure globale

La présente annexe reprend le texte du chapitre II de la cinquième édition du Manuel. *Il convient de noter que les numéros de paragraphe et page cités dans cette annexe sont ceux du* Manuel.

Définitions

12. La première partie du présent *Manuel* décrit le cadre conceptuel de la balance des paiements et de la position extérieure globale. Elle traite de leur relation avec la comptabilité nationale, du concept de résidence, des principes d'évaluation et de chronologie, enfin des notions d'unité de compte et de conversion.

13. La balance des paiements est un état statistique où sont systématiquement résumées, pour une période donnée, les transactions économiques d'une économie avec le reste du monde. Les transactions, pour la plupart entre résidents et non-résidents[1], sont celles qui portent sur les biens, services et revenus; celles qui font naître des créances financières sur le reste du monde ou des engagements financiers envers celui-ci; et celles qui, telles les donations, sont considérées comme des transferts, pour lesquels il y a lieu de passer des contre-écritures de manière à solder — au sens comptable du terme — les transactions à sens unique (voir paragraphe 28)[2]. Une transaction se définit comme un flux économique découlant de la création, de la transformation, de l'échange, du transfert ou de l'extinction d'une valeur économique et faisant intervenir le transfert de propriété de biens ou d'actifs financiers, la prestation de services ou la fourniture de travail et de capital.

14. De même que la balance des paiements retrace des flux, la position extérieure globale est un relevé de stocks. C'est un état statistique qui présente, à une date donnée, par exemple en fin d'année, i) la valeur et la composition du stock des actifs financiers d'une économie ou de ses créances sur le reste du monde, ainsi que ii) la valeur et la composition du stock de ses engagements envers le reste du monde. Dans certains cas, il peut être utile, pour les besoins de l'analyse, de calculer la différence entre avoirs et engagements extérieurs de ce bilan pour évaluer la position nette de l'économie, qui équivaut à la partie de la valeur nette de son patrimoine attribuable à ses relations avec le reste du monde ou en résultant. Une variation des stocks pendant une période définie peut être attribuable soit à des transactions (flux), soit à des réévaluations (qui rendent compte des variations des taux de change, des prix, etc.), soit à d'autres ajustements (des confiscations sans dédommagement, par exemple). Au contraire, la balance des paiements n'enregistre que des transactions.

Principes et concepts

15. Le reste du présent chapitre est consacré au cadre conceptuel des comptes internationaux — c'est-à-dire l'ensemble de conventions et principes sous-jacents qui assurent l'enregistrement systématisé et cohérent des transactions internationales et des stocks d'avoirs et engagements extérieurs. Les aspects pertinents de ces principes, ainsi que les considérations et contraintes pratiques qui s'y rapportent, seront examinés en détail dans les chapitres suivants.

Système d'enregistrement en partie double

16. La convention de base à respecter pour l'établissement d'un état de balance des paiements est que toute transaction enregistrée doit donner lieu à deux inscriptions de montants égaux. L'un de ces montants est inscrit en crédit et est affecté du signe plus, tandis que l'autre est inscrit en débit et affecté du signe moins. En théorie, donc, la somme des montants inscrits en crédit est censée être identique à celle des montants inscrits en débit et le solde de toutes les inscriptions est égal à zéro.

17. Dans la pratique, toutefois, il arrive fréquemment que les comptes ne s'équilibrent pas. Les données servant à établir les estimations pour la balance des paiements sont souvent obtenues séparément de sources différentes. C'est pourquoi le solde peut être un crédit net ou un débit net, qui correspond au montant net des erreurs et omissions. Une écriture distincte, de montant égal mais de signe contraire, doit alors être passée pour équilibrer les comptes. Comme les estimations erronées ou manquantes peuvent s'annuler, on ne peut juger du degré d'exactitude de l'état de balance des paiements d'après le montant de la différence entre la somme des crédits et celle des débits. Néanmoins, il y a lieu de s'inquiéter lorsqu'il subsiste une différence non négligeable qui n'est pas corrigée, car cela gêne l'analyse ou l'interprétation des estimations et en mine la crédibilité (il peut en aller de même pour l'interprétation de l'état de la position extérieure globale dont il sera question au chapitre XXIII).

18. La plupart des inscriptions à la balance des paiements se rapportent à des transactions dans lesquelles des valeurs économiques sont fournies ou reçues en échange d'autres valeurs économiques; ces valeurs sont soit des ressources réelles (biens, services et revenus), soit des actifs financiers. Les écritures compensatoires en crédit et en débit que requiert le système d'enregistrement résultent donc souvent de l'inscription de montants égaux pour les deux éléments échangés. Dans le cas où il y a don, et non échange, ou quand, pour d'autres raisons, la transaction donne lieu à un enregistrement unique, et non à deux enregistrements, une écriture — dénommée *transfert* — spécifiquement conçue pour assurer la compensation nécessaire doit être passée. (Les diverses sortes d'inscriptions qui peuvent être faites à la balance des paiements sont décrites aux paragraphes 26 à 31.)

19. Par convention de ce système, les inscriptions effectuées en crédit par l'économie qui établit sa balance des paiements reflètent i) des exportations lorsqu'il s'agit de ressources réelles et ii) soit une diminution des avoirs extérieurs de l'économie, soit une augmentation de ses engagements extérieurs, lorsqu'il s'agit d'actifs financiers. Parallèlement, les inscriptions faites en débit par l'économie qui établit les données reflètent i) des importations lorsqu'il s'agit de ressources réelles et ii) soit une augmentation des avoirs, soit une diminution des engagements lorsqu'il s'agit d'actifs financiers. En d'autres termes, pour les avoirs — qu'ils soient réels ou financiers —, un chiffre positif (crédit) dénote une baisse, tandis qu'un chiffre négatif (débit) correspond à une

[1]Sauf dans le cas d'échanges d'avoirs financiers extérieurs transférables entre secteurs résidents et, dans une moindre mesure, d'engagements financiers extérieurs entre non-résidents (voir paragraphe 318).

[2]Les définitions et classifications des comptes internationaux contenues dans le présent *Manuel* visent à faciliter la communication au FMI des données sur les transactions internationales, et non à donner effet ou à interpréter les diverses dispositions des statuts du Fonds monétaire international qui ont trait aux aspects juridiques de l'action (ou du manque d'action) officielle concernant ces transactions.

hausse. Par contre, pour les engagements, un chiffre positif indique une augmentation et un chiffre négatif une diminution. Les transferts sont portés au crédit lorsque les inscriptions qu'ils compensent sont faites en débit et ils sont portés au débit lorsque ces inscriptions sont effectuées en crédit.

20. La teneur ou la composition d'un état de balance des paiements varie quelque peu selon que les transactions sont enregistrées sur une base brute ou sur une base nette; les recommandations énoncées dans le présent *Manuel* indiquent quelles transactions sont à enregistrer sur une base brute et lesquelles sont à comptabiliser sur une base nette. Les inscriptions qu'il est recommandé d'effectuer sont énumérées dans la liste des composantes types de la balance des paiements et des renseignements complémentaires qui peuvent être présentés séparément.

Concepts de territoire économique, de résidence et de pôle d'intérêt économique

21. Les concepts de territoire économique, de résidence et de pôle d'intérêt économique utilisés dans le présent *Manuel* sont identiques à ceux qui ont été adoptés dans le *SCN* et seront examinés en détail au chapitre IV. Le territoire économique ne correspond pas forcément à la zone délimitée par les frontières reconnues sur le plan politique. Il recouvre un territoire géographique administré par un gouvernement. À l'intérieur de ce territoire géographique circulent librement des personnes, des biens et des capitaux. Dans le cas de pays maritimes, le territoire géographique comprend toutes les îles régies par les mêmes autorités fiscales et monétaires que le territoire principal.

22. Une unité institutionnelle a son pôle d'intérêt économique dans un pays et est résidente dudit pays lorsqu'il existe, sur le territoire économique de celui-ci, un endroit (domicile, lieu de production ou locaux à autre usage) auquel ou à partir duquel elle exerce et a l'intention de continuer à exercer des activités économiques et effectue ou a l'intention de continuer à effectuer des transactions sur une grande échelle, que ce soit pendant une période de temps indéfinie ou déterminée — en principe d'un an au moins, mais c'est là un critère indicatif et non une règle absolue.

Principes d'évaluation et de chronologie

23. Il est nécessaire d'utiliser une base d'évaluation uniforme pour l'ensemble des transactions internationales (qu'elles portent sur des ressources réelles ou sur des créances et engagements financiers) afin de pouvoir établir de façon systématique et cohérente la somme des transactions individuelles et une position des avoirs et des engagements qui corresponde bien à ces transactions. La base d'évaluation des transactions retenue dans le présent *Manuel* — comme dans le *SCN* — est généralement le prix de marché effectif convenu entre les agents. En théorie, tous les stocks d'avoirs et engagements doivent être évalués aux prix en vigueur sur le marché à la date à laquelle se rapporte la position extérieure globale. Les principes d'évaluation, les pratiques recommandées et leurs limites sont décrits au chapitre V, de même que la méthode d'évaluation des transferts, des actifs financiers et des stocks d'avoirs et engagements. (On y traitera aussi des cas où un prix de marché ne peut ni exister, ni être présumé.)

24. Dans le *Manuel* comme dans le *SCN*, c'est le principe de la comptabilité sur la base des faits générateurs (des droits constatés) qui régit le *moment de l'enregistrement* des transactions. Elles sont donc enregistrées au moment où une valeur économique est créée, transformée, échangée, transférée ou éteinte. Des créances et des engagements se créent lorsqu'il y a transfert de propriété. Le transfert peut être soit juridique, soit matériel (économique). Dans la pratique, lorsque le transfert de propriété n'est pas manifeste, on peut considérer comme une approximation raisonnable de cette date celle à laquelle les parties à une transaction l'enregistrent dans leurs livres ou dans leurs comptes. (Les principes de chronologie et les conventions qu'il est recommandé de respecter pour les diverses inscriptions à la balance des paiements, ainsi que les cas où il est possible de faire exception à la règle du transfert de propriété ou de s'en écarter, sont traités au chapitre VI.)

Le concept et les différents types de transactions

25. En général, les modifications des rapports économiques qu'enregistre la balance des paiements résultent principalement de la relation qui se noue entre deux parties, c'est-à-dire, à une exception près (voir la note 1), entre un résident et un non-résident, et toutes les transactions de cet ordre sont comptabilisées à la balance des paiements. Les inscriptions spécifiques qu'il est recommandé d'effectuer sont celles qui figurent dans la liste des composantes types (voir le chapitre VIII) et elles sont décrites en détail dans les chapitres IX et suivants.

26. En dépit de son appellation, la balance des paiements ne rend pas compte des *paiements*, au sens usuel du terme, mais des *transactions*. Un certain nombre de transactions internationales qui ont leur place à la balance des paiements peuvent ne pas donner lieu à un paiement monétaire et certaines ne comportent même aucun type de paiement. L'enregistrement de ces transactions, en plus de celles qui ont un paiement pour contrepartie, constitue la principale différence entre un état de balance des paiements et un relevé des paiements extérieurs.

Échanges

27. Parmi les transactions qui figurent à la balance des paiements, les plus nombreuses et les plus importantes sont celles qui peuvent être dénommées *échanges*. Un agent économique (entité économique) fournit une valeur économique à un autre et reçoit en échange une valeur égale. Les valeurs économiques fournies par une économie à une autre appartiennent à deux grandes catégories : les ressources réelles (biens, services, revenus), d'une part, et les instruments financiers, d'autre part. Les deux parties à l'échange sont des résidents d'économies différentes, sauf lorsqu'il s'agit d'échanges d'actifs financiers extérieurs entre secteurs résidents. Il se peut que la fourniture d'un instrument financier fasse intervenir non seulement le transfert de propriété d'une créance ou d'un engagement existant, mais aussi la création d'un nouvel avoir ou engagement ou l'annulation d'un avoir ou engagement existant. En outre, les modalités d'un contrat afférent à un instrument financier (par exemple son échéance) peuvent être modifiées par accord entre les parties; on considère dans ce cas que le contrat initial a été exécuté et est remplacé par un autre, assorti de modalités différentes. Tous les échanges de cet ordre doivent être enregistrés à la balance des paiements.

Transferts

28. Les transactions donnant lieu à un *transfert* diffèrent des échanges en ce qu'un agent économique fournit une valeur économique à un autre agent économique sans en recevoir une contrepartie qui, d'après les conventions et règles adoptées aux fins de ce système, a une valeur économique. La valeur qui fait défaut d'un côté de la transaction est représentée par une inscription dénommée *transfert*. Les transferts (valeurs économiques fournies et reçues sans réciprocité) doivent figurer à la balance des paiements. Les ***transferts courants*** figurent au **compte des transactions courantes** (voir le chapitre XV), tandis que les *transferts de capital* sont classés dans le ***compte de capital*** (voir le chapitre XVII).

Migration

29. Comme une économie se définit en fonction des entités économiques qui sont associées à son territoire, il est probable que toute modification touchant ces entités influera sur le champ que recouvre l'économie.

30. Il y a migration lorsqu'un particulier devient résident d'une nouvelle économie parce qu'il y transfère son lieu d'habitation principal. Certains avoirs mobiliers corporels appartenant au migrant sont effectivement importés dans la nouvelle économie; les avoirs immobiliers du migrant et certains de ses avoirs mobiliers corporels qui sont situés sur le territoire de l'ancienne économie deviennent des créances de la nouvelle économie sur l'ancienne; les créances du migrant sur les résidents d'une économie autre que la nouvelle ou ses engagements envers ceux-ci deviennent des créances ou engagements extérieurs de la nouvelle économie; et les créances du migrant sur les résidents de la nouvelle économie ou ses engagements envers ceux-ci cessent d'être des créances d'une économie, quelle qu'elle soit, sur le reste du monde, ou des engagements de cette économie envers celui-ci. La somme nette de tous ces changements est égale à la valeur nette du patrimoine du migrant, qui doit être inscrite en contrepartie si les autres changements sont enregistrés; ces inscriptions doivent être effectuées à la balance des paiements, où, par convention, la contre-écriture est passée sous la rubrique des transferts.

Autres transactions imputées

31. Dans quelques autres cas, des transactions peuvent être imputées et des inscriptions faites à la balance des paiements sans que des flux aient été effectivement engendrés. L'attribution des bénéfices réinvestis aux investisseurs directs étrangers en constitue un exemple. Les bénéfices d'une filiale ou succursale étrangère comprennent les bénéfices attribuables à l'investisseur direct. Ces bénéfices, qu'ils soient distribués ou réinvestis dans l'entreprise, sont proportionnels à sa participation au capital de l'entreprise. Les bénéfices réinvestis sont classés parmi les revenus des investissements directs. Un montant affecté du signe contraire est inscrit en contrepartie au poste investissement direct du *compte d'opérations financières* et représente l'augmentation de la participation des investisseurs directs étrangers au capital de la filiale ou succursale étrangère. (Les bénéfices réinvestis sont traités aux chapitres XIV et XVIII.)

Modifications non dues aux transactions

Reclassement des créances et engagements

32. Dans le *Manuel*, la classification des actifs financiers est établie en fonction de caractéristiques choisies de manière à révéler les intentions du créancier ou du débiteur. Les changements d'intentions influent sur les caractéristiques retenues, et il y a lieu de reclasser les actifs financiers en conséquence. L'un des cas typiques est celui de la distinction qui est faite entre les *investissements directs* et les autres catégories d'opérations financières. Par exemple, plusieurs détenteurs indépendants d'*investissements de portefeuille* (sous forme d'actions émises par une même entreprise à l'étranger) peuvent s'associer de manière à avoir, de façon durable, un pouvoir de décision effectif dans la gestion de l'entreprise. Leurs avoirs répondront alors à la définition de l'*investissement direct*, et la modification de la nature de l'investissement pourrait être assimilée à un reclassement. Ce reclassement se reflétera, à la fin de la période pendant laquelle il aura eu lieu, dans la position extérieure globale, mais non dans la balance des paiements. De même, les créances sur les non-résidents peuvent être soumises, ou cesser d'être assujetties, au contrôle des autorités monétaires résidentes. En pareil cas, il y aura reclassement entre les *actifs de réserve* et les actifs autres que les réserves.

Réévaluations

33. La valeur des ressources réelles et des actifs financiers est constamment sujette à variation. Cette variation peut être due à l'une ou à l'autre des causes suivantes, ou aux deux à la fois : i) le prix auquel les transactions sur une certaine sorte d'avoirs s'effectuent habituellement peut subir des variations qui sont liées à la monnaie dans laquelle le prix est exprimé; ii) le taux de change de la monnaie dans laquelle le prix est exprimé peut varier par rapport à l'unité de compte utilisée. Les réévaluations ne doivent pas être reportées à la balance des paiements, mais doivent figurer dans la position extérieure globale.

Annexe VI. Classification et composantes types de la balance des paiements

La présente annexe reprend le texte du chapitre VIII de la cinquième édition du Manuel. *Il convient de noter que les numéros de paragraphe et de page cités dans cette annexe sont ceux du* Manuel.

Structure et classification

139. La deuxième partie de ce *Manuel* a trait à la structure et à la classification des comptes de la balance des paiements et de la position extérieure globale. À l'examen des composantes types de ces deux séries de comptes succéderont l'analyse et la description détaillée du ***compte des transactions courantes***, du ***compte de capital et d'opérations financières***, des renseignements complémentaires qui peuvent être requis sur certains postes et de la position extérieure globale.

140. Il importe d'ordonner les statistiques de la balance des paiements selon une structure cohérente afin d'en faciliter l'utilisation et l'adaptation à des fins multiples : élaboration de politiques, études analytiques, projections, comparaisons bilatérales de telle ou telle composante ou de l'ensemble des transactions, agrégations régionales ou mondiales, etc. (Voir paragraphe 7.)

141. La classification et la liste des composantes types reposent sur des considérations théoriques et pratiques qui tiennent compte des opinions exprimées par les experts nationaux de la balance des paiements; elles concordent en général avec les définitions que donne le *SCN*. La classification élargie des transactions internationales au titre des services est conforme aux principes de la Classification centrale des produits (CCP). (Voir l'appendice III.)

142. Le système de classification est aussi le résultat d'efforts entrepris pour rattacher la structure du ***compte de capital*** aux comptes de revenu et à la classification de la position extérieure globale. Il a été conçu de manière à offrir un cadre flexible pouvant être utilisé par de nombreux pays pour développer au fil des années leurs statistiques extérieures. Certains pays ne sont peut-être pas en mesure de communiquer des chiffres pour de nombreux postes. D'autres sont peut-être en mesure de fournir des données supplémentaires.

Composantes types

143. Le choix des composantes types (dont la liste figure à la fin du présent chapitre) est fonction d'un certain nombre de considérations; celles qui suivent ont été jugées primordiales.

> Le poste doit manifester un comportement distinct. Il doit être influencé par un facteur économique ou un ensemble de facteurs différents de ceux qui influent sur les autres postes, ou réagir différemment au même facteur ou ensemble de facteurs. C'est cette réaction aux facteurs économiques que la balance des paiements cherche à mettre en évidence.
>
> Le poste doit revêtir de l'importance pour plusieurs pays; cette importance peut être fonction soit de son comportement (par exemple une variabilité exceptionnelle), soit de son ordre de grandeur.
>
> Les données relatives à ce poste ne doivent pas être excessivement difficiles à obtenir. L'utilité qu'il présente doit cependant être évaluée à la lumière des deux considérations qui précèdent.
>
> Le poste doit être utilisable séparément à d'autres fins, par exemple pouvoir être incorporé dans la comptabilité nationale ou servir au rapprochement avec cette dernière. La liste des composantes types ne doit pas être trop longue. En effet, un très grand nombre de pays, dont beaucoup ne disposent pas d'un système statistique très développé, sont censés utiliser les mêmes catégories lorsqu'ils communiquent leurs données.
>
> Dans la mesure du possible, les composantes types doivent être conformes et applicables aux autres systèmes statistiques du FMI et au *SCN* et concorder, pour les *services* en particulier, avec la CCP.

144. La liste type n'implique nullement que les recommandations formulées dans ce *Manuel* empêchent les pays d'établir et de publier d'autres données qu'ils jugent importantes. En fait, lorsque de plus amples détails sont nécessaires pour comprendre les circonstances particulières à tel ou tel pays ou pour analyser les situations nouvelles, les demandes de renseignements que le FMI adresse à ses pays membres ne se limitent pas aux composantes types. Des renseignements complémentaires peuvent être aussi très utiles pour vérifier et rapprocher les statistiques de pays partenaires, et, par exemple, pour analyser les financements exceptionnels. (Voir, à la fin du chapitre, le tableau intitulé *Renseignements complémentaires qui peuvent être requis sur certains postes*.) De temps en temps, les services du FMI tiennent des consultations avec les pays membres afin de déterminer avec eux quelles données complémentaires ils devraient lui communiquer.

145. Rares sont les pays qui ont des renseignements significatifs à communiquer pour chacune des composantes types. Il se peut aussi que certaines des composantes n'existent que regroupées ou qu'une composante mineure soit incluse dans une composante plus importante. Les composantes types doivent néanmoins être communiquées au FMI de manière aussi complète et exacte que possible. Les statisticiens nationaux sont incontestablement mieux placés que les services du FMI pour estimer et ajuster les composantes qui ne correspondent pas exactement aux séries de base de l'économie établissant ses statistiques.

Erreurs et omissions nettes

146. L'application des principes recommandés dans le présent *Manuel* devrait donner un ensemble cohérent d'inscriptions positives et négatives dont la somme est (en principe) égale à zéro. Or, en pratique, si l'on additionne toutes les inscriptions effectuées, on obtient presque inévitablement un crédit net ou un débit net. Ce solde est le résultat d'erreurs et d'omissions dont certaines peuvent être liées aux méthodes d'approximation recommandées pour la mise en pratique des principes.

147. La balance des paiements comprend normalement un poste distinct réservé aux erreurs et omissions nettes, appelé par certains statisticiens «solde» ou «écart statistique». Ce poste vise à compenser la surévaluation ou la sous-évaluation des composantes enregistrées. Ainsi donc, si ces composantes se soldent par un crédit, le poste des erreurs et omissions nettes constituera un débit de valeur égale et vice versa.

148. Certaines erreurs et omissions qui se produisent au cours de l'établissement des données se neutralisent habituellement. C'est pourquoi le montant du solde ne renseigne pas nécessairement sur la précision globale du relevé. Cependant, l'interprétation du relevé devient difficile si ce solde est considérable.

Classification générale

149. Les composantes types, dont la liste est donnée à la fin du présent chapitre, sont réparties en deux principales sections :

> Le compte des transactions courantes, qui se subdivise en : ***biens et services***, ***revenus*** et ***transferts courants***.
>
> Le **compte de capital et d'opérations financières**, qui enregistre i) les *transferts de capital* et les *acquisitions ou cessions d'actifs non financiers non produits*, et ii) les opérations portant sur des avoirs et engagements financiers.

Cette répartition correspond à la pratique suivie par la plupart des pays depuis de longues années et dénote un changement important apporté dans le présent *Manuel*. L'ancien compte des mouvements de capitaux a été rebaptisé **compte de capital et d'opérations financières**. Dicté par un souci d'harmonisation avec le *SCN*, ce changement consiste à adopter pour la balance des paiements la distinction que le *SCN* établit entre les *transferts de capital* et les ***transferts courants*** et à faire concorder le nouveau compte avec le compte de capital et le compte financier du *SCN*.

150. Les inscriptions à la plupart des rubriques du **compte des transactions courantes** doivent faire apparaître les crédits ou débits bruts. La plupart des inscriptions au **compte de capital et d'opérations financières** doivent être effectuées sur une base nette, c'est-à-dire que chaque composante ne doit y figurer que comme un crédit ou un débit (le mode de traitement recommandé pour certains postes spécifiques et les exceptions seront examinés dans les chapitres correspondants). Les entrées de ressources réelles et les augmentations d'avoirs financiers (ou diminutions d'engagements) seront enregistrées au débit; les sorties de ressources réelles et les diminutions d'avoirs financiers (ou augmentations d'engagements) seront enregistrées au crédit. Les transferts, dans les sections 1.C et 2.A, doivent avoir la même valeur numérique, mais affectée du signe opposé, que les inscriptions dont ils sont la contre-écriture.

Classification détaillée

151. La classification des composantes types qui suit a été mise au point conformément aux critères exposés au paragraphe 143. La structure et les caractéristiques du **compte des transactions courantes** et du **compte de capital et d'opérations financières**, sensiblement modifiées par rapport à la quatrième édition du *Manuel*, sont exposées aux chapitres IX et XVI, respectivement. Les composantes types du **compte des transactions courantes** sont décrites en détail aux chapitres X à XV, celles du **compte de capital et d'opérations financières** aux chapitres XVII à XXI et dans *Dérivés financiers — Supplément à la cinquième édition (1993) du Manuel de la balance des paiements*, Washington, 2000.

Transactions courantes (1.)

152. Sont incluses dans le **compte des transactions courantes** toutes les transactions portant sur des valeurs économiques (autres que des actifs financiers) entre entités résidentes et non résidentes. On y inscrit aussi les contreparties des valeurs économiques courantes qui sont fournies ou acquises sans réciprocité. Les grandes subdivisions (postes) sont les ***biens et services***, les ***revenus*** et les ***transferts courants***.

Biens et services (1.A)

Biens (1.A.a.)

153. La rubrique *marchandises générales* recouvre la plupart des biens meubles que les résidents exportent à destination de non-résidents ou qu'ils importent en provenance de non-résidents et qui, à quelques exceptions près, font l'objet d'un transfert de propriété (effectif ou présumé).

154. La rubrique *biens importés ou exportés pour transformation* recouvre les exportations (ou importations dans l'économie établissant sa balance des paiements) de biens franchissant une frontière pour faire l'objet à l'étranger d'une transformation, suivie d'une réimportation (ou exportation) des biens, dont la valeur est établie sur une base brute avant et après la transformation. Cette rubrique fait exception au principe du transfert de propriété.

155. La rubrique *réparations de biens* recouvre les travaux de réparation de biens — bateaux, avions, etc. — fournis à des non-résidents ou reçus de non-résidents. Bien que le mouvement physique de ces biens soit analogue à celui qui est décrit au paragraphe 154, la valeur de la réparation correspond à son prix (c'est-à-dire au montant payé ou reçu pour cette réparation) et non à la valeur brute des biens avant et après la réparation.

156. La rubrique *achats de biens dans les ports par les transporteurs* recouvre tous les biens, tels que carburants, vivres, approvisionnements et fournitures, que les transporteurs résidents ou non résidents — aériens ou maritimes, par exemple — ont achetés à l'étranger (ou dans l'économie établissant sa balance des paiements). Cette rubrique n'enregistre pas les services auxiliaires fournis (remorquage, entretien, etc.), qui sont inclus dans les services de *transports*.

157. La rubrique *or non monétaire* recouvre les exportations et importations de tout or non détenu sous la forme d'avoir de réserve (or monétaire) par les autorités. L'*or non monétaire* est traité comme n'importe quel autre produit et se décompose, lorsque cela est possible, en or détenu à titre de réserve de valeur et or détenu à d'autres fins (industrielles).

Services (1.A.b.)

158. La rubrique *transports* recouvre la plupart des services fournis par les résidents aux non-résidents et vice versa, qui étaient précédemment classés aux rubriques *expéditions* et *autres transports* dans la quatrième édition du *Manuel*. Cependant, l'assurance du fret ne figure pas ici, mais à la rubrique des *services d'assurance*. Sous la rubrique *transports*, on enregistre le transport de marchandises et de passagers, quel qu'en soit le mode, ainsi que les autres services de distribution et services auxiliaires, y compris l'affrètement de véhicules de transport avec leur équipage. Certaines exceptions sont signalées aux chapitres X, XI et XIII.

159. La rubrique *voyages* recouvre les biens et les services acquis dans une économie par les voyageurs non résidents (y compris les excursionnistes), à des fins professionnelles ou personnelles — notamment pour des raisons de santé ou à titre éducatif —, au cours de leur séjour (de moins d'un an) sur le territoire de cette économie. Cette rubrique exclut les services internationaux fournis aux passagers, qui sont inclus dans les *transports*. Les étudiants et les personnes en traitement médical sont considérés comme étant des voyageurs, quelle que soit la durée de leur séjour, contrairement à certaines autres catégories — militaires, personnel des ambassades et travailleurs non résidents. Les dépenses des travailleurs non résidents sont toutefois comprises dans les *voyages*, tandis que celles des militaires et du personnel des ambassades sont incluses dans les *services fournis ou reçus par les administrations publiques, n.c.a.* Ces cas sont signalés aux chapitres XII et XIII.

160. La rubrique *services de communication* recouvre les opérations de communication entre résidents et non-résidents. Ce sont les services postaux (y compris les messageries) et les services de télécommunication (transmission du son, des images et d'autres types d'information par divers moyens et entretien des installations correspondantes, assuré par des résidents pour le compte de non-résidents et vice versa).

161. La rubrique *services de bâtiment et travaux publics (BTP)* recouvre les travaux de construction et d'installation effectués à l'étranger (ou dans l'économie qui établit sa balance des paiements) ou dans les enclaves extraterritoriales, à titre temporaire, par les entreprises résidentes (ou non résidentes) et leur personnel mais qui ne sont effectués ni par une entreprise étrangère apparentée à une entreprise résidente, ni par un bureau sur place non constitué en société qui, dans certaines conditions, équivaut à une entreprise étrangère apparentée. Ces aspects de la résidence sont traités aux chapitres IV et XIII.

162. La rubrique *services d'assurance* recouvre les assurances fournies aux non-résidents par des compagnies d'assurances résidentes et vice versa. On entend par là l'assurance du fret (pour les biens exportés ou importés) et les autres types d'assurance directe (notamment l'assurance-vie et autres formes d'assurances), ainsi que la réassurance. (Pour la méthode de calcul de la valeur des services d'assurance, voir paragraphes 256 et 257.)

163. La rubrique *services financiers* (autres que ceux qui sont offerts par les compagnies d'assurances et les caisses de retraite) recouvre les services d'intermédiation financière et les services auxiliaires entre résidents et non-résidents. Sont inclus les commissions et les frais ayant trait aux services suivants : lettres de crédit, lignes de crédit, crédit-bail, opérations de change, services de crédit aux consommateurs et aux entreprises, opérations de courtage, souscriptions de titres, différentes formes de couverture des opérations à terme, etc. Les services auxiliaires se rapportent à l'administration et à la réglementation des marchés financiers, à la garde de titres, etc.

164. La rubrique *services d'informatique et d'information* recouvre les transactions entre résidents et non-résidents concernant le conseil en matériel, l'installation de logiciels, les services d'information (traitement de données, banques de données, agences de presse) et l'entretien et la réparation des ordinateurs et du matériel connexe.

165. La rubrique *redevances et droits de licence* recouvre les recettes (exportations) et paiements (importations) des résidents et non-résidents se rapportant à i) l'exploitation d'actifs incorporels non financiers non produits et de droits de propriété — marques, droits d'auteur, brevets, procédés, techniques, dessins, licences de fabrication, franchises, etc. — et à ii) l'utilisation, dans le cadre d'accords de licence, de brevets, d'oeuvres originales ou de prototypes, tels que les manuscrits, films, etc.

166. La rubrique *autres services aux entreprises* recouvre les services fournis par des résidents à des non-résidents et vice versa : le négoce international et les autres services liés au commerce, la location-exploitation et divers services aux entreprises, spécialisés et techniques. (Voir, à la fin du chapitre, le tableau des *Renseignements complémentaires qui peuvent être requis sur certains postes*, et les paragraphes 261 à 264 pour de plus amples détails.)

167. La rubrique *services personnels, culturels et relatifs aux loisirs* recouvre i) les services audio-visuels et connexes et ii) les autres services culturels fournis par des résidents à des non-résidents et vice versa. Sont compris dans la catégorie i) les services qui ont trait à la production de films cinématographiques (films ou bandes vidéo), d'émissions de radio ou de télévision et d'enregistrements musicaux, par exemple les droits de location, les redevances perçues par les acteurs, producteurs etc., pour les productions et pour les droits de distribution cédés aux médias. Dans la catégorie ii) figurent les autres services personnels, culturels et relatifs aux loisirs tels que ceux qui ont associés aux bibliothèques, musées et autres activités culturelles ou sportives.

168. La rubrique *services fournis ou reçus par les administrations publiques, n.c.a.* recouvre tous les services (auxquels correspondent par exemple les dépenses des ambassades et consulats) fournis ou reçus par le secteur public ou les organisations internationales ou régionales et non classés ailleurs.

Revenus (1.B.)

169. La rubrique *rémunération des salariés* recouvre les salaires, traitements et autres émoluments versés, en espèces ou en nature, aux travailleurs frontaliers, saisonniers et autres travailleurs non résidents, (par exemple le personnel local des ambassades).

170. La rubrique *revenus des investissements* recouvre les recettes et paiements se rapportant respectivement à la détention d'avoirs financiers extérieurs par les résidents et aux engagements envers les non-résidents. Cela comprend les revenus des investissements directs, les revenus des investissements de portefeuille et les autres revenus d'investissement. La composante investissements directs se subdivise en revenus des participations au capital (dividendes, bénéfices des succursales et bénéfices réinvestis) et en revenus des titres de créance (intérêts); les revenus des investissements de portefeuille se subdivisent en revenus des participations au capital (dividendes) et en revenus des titres de créance (intérêts); les autres revenus d'investissement recouvrent les intérêts provenant d'autres opérations financières (prêts, etc.) et, en principe, les droits nets des ménages sur les réserves techniques d'assurance-vie et les réserves des caisses de retraite.

Transferts courants (1.C.)

171. À l'instar du *SCN*, le *Manuel* distingue les ***transferts courants*** des *transferts de capital* (ces derniers sont enregistrés au **compte de capital et d'opérations financières**). Les transferts sont la contrepartie des transferts de propriété, volontaires ou forcés, de ressources réelles ou d'actifs financiers entre résidents et non-résidents, qui ne reçoivent pas en échange une valeur économique. Les ***transferts courants*** sont tous ceux qui **ne font pas intervenir** i) le transfert de propriété d'un actif fixe, ii) le transfert de fonds lié ou subordonné à l'acquisition ou à la cession d'un actif fixe, ni iii) la remise, sans contrepartie, d'une dette par un créancier (toutes ces opérations sont des *transferts de capital*). Les ***transferts courants*** comprennent ceux des administrations publiques — par exemple la coopération internationale courante (entre des administrations publiques appartenant à différentes économies), les paiements des impôts courants sur le revenu et sur la fortune, etc. — et les autres transferts, tels que les envois de fonds des travailleurs, les primes (moins les commissions de service) et les indemnités au titre des assurances autres que l'assurance-vie, etc. La distinction entre les ***transferts courants*** et les *transferts de capital* fait l'objet d'un examen approfondi au chapitre XV (voir également les paragraphes 175 et 344).

Le compte de capital et d'opérations financières (2.)

172. Le **compte de capital et d'opérations financières** a deux principales composantes — le ***compte de capital*** correspond au compte de capital du *SCN* et le ***compte d'opérations financières*** au compte financier du *SCN*. Les avoirs (ou actifs) sont des créances sur les non-résidents et les engagements (ou passifs) des dettes envers les non-résidents. Les deux parties à une transaction portant sur des avoirs ou des engagements sont en général un résident et un non-résident mais, dans certains cas, il peut s'agir de deux résidents ou de deux non-résidents. (Voir paragraphe 318.)

173. Toutes les réévaluations et toutes les autres variations d'actifs et de passifs extérieurs qui ne sont pas dues à des transactions (voir paragraphe 310) sont exclues du **compte de capital et d'opérations financières** mais apparaissent dans la position extérieure globale. Des relevés complémentaires identifient certains postes qui présentent un intérêt pour l'analyse et qui relèvent de plusieurs comptes. C'est le cas, par exemple, des engagements qui constituent des réserves pour les autorités étrangères et des financements exceptionnels, dont il est question au chapitre XXII.

174. La classification des ***opérations financières*** et celle des composantes des revenus dans les **transactions courantes** sont liées et doivent être cohérentes pour faciliter l'analyse, permettre le rapprochement effectif entre la balance des paiements et la position extérieure globale, et assurer la compatibilité avec le *SCN* et avec les autres systèmes statistiques du FMI.

Compte de capital (2.A.)

175. Les grandes subdivisions du ***compte de capital*** sont les *transferts de capital* et les *acquisitions et cessions d'actifs non financiers non produits*. Les *transferts de capital* sont ceux qui font intervenir le transfert de propriété d'un actif fixe; le transfert de fonds lié ou subordonné à l'acquisition ou à la cession d'un actif fixe; ou la remise, sans contrepartie, d'une dette par un créancier. Ils se subdivisent en deux catégories : i) les transferts des administrations publiques, qui se décomposent en remises de dettes et autres transferts et ii) les autres transferts, qui se subdivisent en transferts des migrants, remises de dettes et autres transferts. (Voir le chapitre XV, qui traite de la distinction entre les *transferts de capital* et les ***transferts courants***). Les *acquisitions et cessions d'actifs non financiers non produits* se rapportent généralement aux avoirs incorporels tels que les brevets, les contrats de location et autres contrats transférables, la marque, etc. Ce poste ne recouvre pas les propriétés non bâties situées sur le territoire d'une économie donnée mais peut inclure l'achat (ou la vente) de terrains par une ambassade étrangère. (Voir paragraphe 312.)

Compte d'opérations financières (2.B.)

176. La classification des composantes types comprises sous ce poste est fondée sur les critères suivants :

La nature des investissements ou leur ventilation fonctionnelle (*investissements directs*, *investissements de portefeuille*, *dérivés financiers*, *autres investissements* et *avoirs de réserve*).

Dans le cas des *investissements directs*, la distinction en fonction du sens des mouvements de capitaux — entre l'étranger et l'économie qui établit sa balance des paiements — étant entendu que, dans chaque sous-catégorie, les avoirs sont distingués des engagements.

Pour ce qui est des *investissements de portefeuille*, des *dérivés financiers* et des *autres investissements*, la distinction traditionnelle entre avoirs et engagements.

La nature de l'instrument est particulièrement importante pour les *investissements de portefeuille* et les *autres investissements* (titres de participation ou d'engagement, crédits commerciaux, prêts, monnaie et dépôts, autres avoirs ou engagements). Le présent *Manuel* regroupe dans les *investissements de portefeuille* les instruments du marché monétaire, ainsi que les autres instruments financiers, tant traditionnels que nouveaux.

Pour ce qui est des *investissements de portefeuille*, des *dérivés financiers*, et des *autres investissements*, on distingue le secteur dont relève le créancier intérieur en ce qui concerne les avoirs et le secteur dont relève le débiteur intérieur en ce qui concerne les engagements. Cette distinction facilite les rapprochements avec les comptes de revenu et la position extérieure globale ainsi qu'avec le *SCN* et les autres systèmes statistiques;

La distinction habituelle entre les avoirs et engagements à long et à court terme, le long terme étant défini par une échéance contractuelle initiale de plus d'un an et le court terme par une échéance ne dépassant pas un an, n'est faite que pour les *autres investissements*. Depuis quelques années, cette distinction a perdu à l'évidence beaucoup de son utilité pour de nombreuses transactions, intérieures ou internationales. C'est pourquoi la différenciation du long et du court terme a moins d'importance dans le présent *Manuel* — et dans le *SCN* — que dans les éditions précédentes. Cependant, parce qu'elle est importante à certains égards, par exemple pour l'analyse de la dette extérieure, elle est retenue dans le présent *Manuel* pour les *autres investissements*.

177. La rubrique *investissements directs* — lesquels témoignent d'un intérêt durable de la part d'une entité résidente d'une économie (l'investisseur direct) pour une entité résidente d'une autre économie (l'entreprise d'investissement direct) — recouvre toutes les transactions entre les investisseurs directs et les entreprises d'investissement direct. Les *investissements directs* recouvrent donc la transaction initiale entre les uns et les autres et toutes les transactions ultérieures entre eux, ainsi que les transactions entre les entreprises apparentées, constituées ou non en sociétés. Les opérations d'investissement direct effectuées à l'étranger et dans l'économie déclarante se décomposent en capital social, bénéfices réinvestis, autres opérations en capital (entre entreprises d'un même groupe). En ce qui concerne le capital social et les autres capitaux, les créances et les engagements à l'égard des entreprises affiliées et à l'égard des investisseurs directs sont ventilés séparément. Les transactions entre banques apparentées et entre autres intermédiaires financiers apparentés se limitent aux transactions portant sur des titres de participation (capital social) et des dettes/créances permanentes. (Voir paragraphe 372.)

178. Les investissements de portefeuille comprennent les titres de participation et les titres de créance; ces derniers se subdivisent en obligations et autres titres d'emprunt, et instruments du marché monétaire. Divers nouveaux instruments financiers, autres que les dérivés financiers, sont classés dans les catégories d'instruments appropriées. (Les opérations classées parmi les investissements directs et les avoirs de réserve sont exclues.)

179. La catégorie des *dérivés financiers* recouvre les instruments financiers qui sont liés à un autre instrument ou indicateur financier ou produit de base spécifique et par le biais desquels des risques financiers spécifiques (de taux d'intérêt, de taux de change, de participation ou de prix des produits de base, de crédit, etc.) peuvent être négociés en tant que tels sur les marchés financiers. Les opérations sur dérivés financiers doivent être traitées en tant qu'opérations distinctes et non comme faisant partie intégrante de la valeur des opérations sous-jacentes auxquelles elles sont liées.

180. La rubrique *autres investissements* recouvre les crédits commerciaux et les prêts à court et à long terme (y compris l'utilisation des crédits et des prêts du FMI, ainsi que les prêts/emprunts au titre de la location-vente; la monnaie fiduciaire et les dépôts (transférables et autres, tels que les dépôts d'épargne et les dépôts à terme, les parts des associations d'épargne et de prêt, des associations de crédit mutuel, etc.); et d'autres comptes à payer et à recevoir. (Les transactions classées parmi les *investissements directs* sont exclues de la présente rubrique.)

181. La rubrique *avoirs de réserve* recouvre les transactions portant sur les avoirs dont les autorités monétaires d'une économie considèrent qu'elles disposent pour répondre aux besoins de financement de la balance des paiements et, dans certains cas, à d'autres besoins; en principe, cette disponibilité n'est pas étroitement liée à des critères formels tels que la propriété des avoirs ou la monnaie dans laquelle ils sont libel-lés. Les rubriques incluses sous ce poste sont l'or monétaire, les DTS, la position de réserve au FMI, les avoirs en devises (monnaie fiduciaire et dépôts, et valeurs mobilières) et les autres créances.

182. Le champ couvert par les composantes des *avoirs de réserve* et leur définition répondent aux besoins de l'analyse, comportent un élément d'appréciation et ne se prêtent pas toujours à l'application de critères objectifs formels ou de systèmes de classement précis fondés sur la conditionnalité ou sur d'autres facteurs. Contrairement à la quatrième édition du *Manuel*, la cinquième édition prescrit d'exclure de ce poste les réévaluations des *avoirs de réserve*, ainsi que leurs contreparties. Sont aussi exclues les allocations ou annulations de DTS, la monétisation ou la démonétisation de l'or et les inscriptions de contrepartie. Ces variations, qui ne sont pas des transactions, apparaissent dans la position extérieure globale.

INTRODUCCIÓN

El volumen 53 de *Balance of Payments Statistics Yearbook* (anuario) que publica el Fondo Monetario Internacional (FMI) presenta las estadísticas de balanza de pagos declaradas por los países miembros al FMI. El FMI agradece a los países miembros su cooperación en la declaración de estos datos. En el caso de algunos países, esta información se complementa con detalles que los economistas de la institución obtienen de diferentes fuentes.

El anuario consta de tres partes. En la parte 1 se presentan datos de balanza de pagos y datos sobre la posición de inversión internacional de cada país. En la parte 2 figuran los totales regionales y mundiales de los componentes principales de la balanza de pagos. En la parte 3 se presentan descripciones técnicas sobre algunos países declarantes. La parte 1 se publica en un tomo separado y las partes 2 y 3 en un mismo tomo.

En este volumen del anuario se mantienen las características introducidas en los volúmenes 46 al 52 inclusive. Como en el volumen 46, los datos de balanza de pagos se desglosan conforme a los componentes normalizados de la quinta edición del *Manual de Balanza de Pagos (Manual)*[1]. No obstante, se han modificado los componentes normalizados tras la publicación de *Instrumentos financieros derivados: Suplemento a la quinta edición (1993) del* Manual de Balanza de Pagos, en 2000 y las modificaciones de dicha publicación en 2002. Por consiguiente, las referencias a la quinta edición del *Manual* incluyen el suplemento y el apéndice. De conformidad con las recomendaciones del suplemento y el apéndice, el presente anuario refleja la decisión del Comité del FMI de Estadísticas de Balanza de Pagos en el sentido de que las transacciones de instrumentos financieros derivados relacionadas con empresas afiliadas deben incluirse en el componente correspondiente a los instrumentos financieros derivados de las estadísticas de balanza de pagos y de la posición de inversión internacional. Además, como en el volumen 47, se incluyen los datos sobre la posición de inversión internacional en el formato de la quinta edición del *Manual*, y en la parte 3 del anuario, se publican descripciones detalladas de las metodologías, los procedimientos de compilación y las fuentes de datos que se utilizan en la mayoría de los países incluidos en el presente volumen. En el *Manual*[2], se introducen varios cambios metodológicos en la compilación de los datos de balanza de pagos, cambios que se describen con detalle en el capítulo I del *Manual*. A partir del volumen 46, en este anuario los datos presentados conforme a los componentes normalizados del *Manual* están acompañados de una lista de códigos, preparada conjuntamente por el FMI, la Organización de Cooperación y Desarrollo Económicos (OCDE) y la Oficina Estadística de las Comunidades Europeas (Eurostat). La estructura de estos códigos se explica en un anexo de esta introducción. Además, a partir del volumen 46, no se presentan datos trimestrales de balanza de pagos en el caso de los países que declaran estadísticas trimestrales de balanza de pagos al FMI. Estos datos trimestrales se publican en las ediciones mensuales de la publicación del FMI *International financial statistics (IFS)*.

La conversión de los datos realizada por el personal del FMI ha permitido presentar en el formato de la quinta edición los datos históricos extraídos de la base de datos del FMI, así como los datos más recientes declarados por los países miembros en el formato de la cuarta edición del *Manual de Balanza de Pagos*. En 1995, el personal del FMI elaboró fórmulas para transformar la información de balanza de pagos de cada país incluida en la base de datos del FMI a fin de adaptarla a la metodología y presentación que se establecen en la quinta edición. Seguidamente se enviaron los datos convertidos a las autoridades de los respectivos países para su revisión y se incorporaron los comentarios recibidos a la nueva base de datos. En 1996, el personal del FMI, en colaboración con las autoridades de los países, convirtió en forma similar los datos sobre la posición de inversión internacional declarados en el formato de la cuarta edición a la presentación de la quinta edición. En principio, la posición de inversión internacional de un país es un balance general de las tenencias de activos y pasivos financieros frente al exterior.

En la parte 3 del anuario se incluyen las descripciones técnicas de la metodología, los procedimientos de compilación y las fuentes de datos que utilizan los países que declaran datos. Las descripciones se basan en gran medida en la información que los países suministran al FMI. Se incluyen estas descripciones para que los usuarios comprendan mejor la cobertura de los datos de los distintos países publicados en el anuario, así como sus limitaciones, y para informar a los compiladores sobre las fuentes de datos y los métodos utilizados por los compiladores de otros países. Además, los compiladores tienen acceso a información detallada sobre las prácticas de los países en materia de compilación de las estadísticas sobre la inversión directa (ID) como resultado del estudio sobre las metodologías relativas a la ID realizado conjuntamente por el FMI y la Organización de Cooperación y Desarrollo Económicos (OCDE) en 2001. Los compiladores pueden consultar la base de

[1]El volumen 1 del anuario, publicado en 1949, se basó en la primera edición del *Manual de Balanza de Pagos* del FMI, publicado en 1948; los volúmenes 2–12 se basaron en la segunda edición del manual, publicada en 1950; los volúmenes 13–23 se basaron en la tercera edición, publicada en 1961, y los volúmenes 24–29 se basaron en esa edición así como en el *Manual de Balanza de Pagos: Suplemento a la tercera edición*, que apareció en 1973. Desde el volumen 30 al 45, las presentaciones siguieron las recomendaciones de la cuarta edición del manual, publicada en 1977.

[2]Fondo Monetario Internacional, *Manual de Balanza de Pagos*, quinta edición, Washington, septiembre de 1993, e *Instrumentos financieros derivados: Suplemento a la quinta edición (1993) del* Manual de Balanza de Pagos, 2000.

datos en Internet que contiene los metadatos sobre la ID en *http://www.imf.org/external/np/sta/di/mdb97.htm.*

El resto de esta introducción se ha organizado de la siguiente manera:

- En la sección I se describen las características básicas de los cuadros que se publican en la parte 1 del anuario. (Pueden consultarse los detalles sobre cobertura de los datos de las partes 2 y 3 en el segundo tomo.)
- La sección II contiene información sobre la manera de acceder a la información del FMI sobre balanza de pagos en CD-ROM.
- Se han incluido seis anexos. En el anexo I se incluye una presentación analítica sucinta de los componentes de la balanza de pagos (y los códigos correspondientes). En el anexo II se presentan los componentes normalizados (con sus respectivos códigos) de la quinta edición del *Manual*. En el anexo III se explica el sistema de codificación empleado. En el anexo IV se presentan los componentes normalizados de la posición de inversión internacional que figuran en la quinta edición del *Manual*. En el anexo V se describe el marco conceptual de la balanza de pagos y, en el anexo VI, se explica la cobertura de los componentes principales de las cuentas de la balanza de pagos conforme a las directrices establecidas en la quinta edición del *Manual*.

I. Parte 1 del anuario: Datos de cada país

En la parte 1 del anuario se presentan las páginas de países en orden alfabético. Debe hacerse la salvedad de que el término "país", según se emplea en esta publicación, no siempre se refiere a una entidad territorial que constituya un Estado conforme al derecho y la práctica internacionales; el término también abarca la zona del euro y ciertas entidades territoriales que no son Estados soberanos, sobre las cuales también se facilitan datos estadísticos a nivel internacional en forma separada.

Los datos de balanza de pagos de la mayoría de los países se presentan en dos cuadros. El cuadro 1 es un resumen analítico de los datos más detallados que se presentan en el cuadro 2. En el cuadro 1 se presentan los componentes de la balanza de pagos que están ordenados de tal manera que se destacan las partidas de financiamiento (reservas y partidas conexas). (Véase también el anexo I.) El cuadro 2 presenta los datos correspondientes a los componentes normalizados que se describen en la quinta edición del *Manual*. (Véase también el anexo II.) En el caso de los países sobre los que se dispone de información relativa a la posición de inversión internacional, los datos se presentan en el cuadro 3. En los cuadros 1, 2 y 3, los datos corresponden al período 1994–2001 para cada país. Los datos que figuran en los cuadros se declaran en base a los años calendario, salvo indicación contraria.

Presentación analítica

En la presentación analítica, que figura en el cuadro 1, los componentes de la balanza de pagos se clasifican en cinco categorías principales de datos (grupos A a E) que el FMI considera útiles para analizar de manera uniforme la evolución de la balanza de pagos. No obstante, no debe interpretarse que esta división en grupos refleja una recomendación del FMI sobre el enfoque analítico más apropiado para todos los países. Los componentes normalizados del cuadro 2 podrían agruparse conforme a una presentación analítica diferente en función de las circunstancias especiales de determinado país o de ciertos requisitos analíticos.

Obsérvese que las cifras que aparecen en los cuadros 1 y 2 en lo que respecta a los saldos de la cuenta corriente, la cuenta de capital y la cuenta financiera difieren en el caso de algunos países. Esto se debe a que en el cuadro 1 se excluyen ciertas transacciones que se clasifican en estas cuentas porque han sido reclasificadas como "financiamiento excepcional" en reservas y partidas conexas. El "financiamiento excepcional" se refiere a las transacciones efectuadas por las autoridades para financiar su balanza de pagos, e incluye la obtención de recursos en préstamo del exterior, los atrasos en los pagos y la condonación de deudas, pero no incluye las reservas.

Presentación normalizada

Los componentes normalizados conforme a la quinta edición del *Manual*, que figuran en el cuadro 2, ofrecen una clasificación más detallada de los bienes y servicios que en la cuarta edición. La llamada "cuenta de capital y financiera" agrupa diferentes componentes bajo la "cuenta de capital" y la "cuenta financiera". En esta última se clasifican los componentes según la clase de inversión (es decir, inversión directa, inversión de cartera, instrumentos financieros derivados1, otra inversión y activos de reserva), activos/pasivos, sectores internos (autoridades monetarias, gobierno general, bancos y otros sectores) y vencimiento original.

Posición de inversión internacional

Los datos sobre la posición de inversión internacional, que figuran en el cuadro 3, se agrupan conforme a los componentes normalizados de la posición de inversión

internacional que se establecen en la quinta edición del *Manual*. (Véase también el anexo IV.)

La clasificación de los componentes de la posición de inversión internacional en el cuadro 3 coincide con la de la cuenta financiera de la balanza de pagos que figura en el

[1]Debido a la naturaleza única de los instrumentos financieros derivados, y a la forma en que algunas instituciones registran las transacciones, algunos países sólo pueden declarar datos en cifras netas. Si bien estos datos en cifras netas podrían incluirse en la categoría de activos, en el presente anuario estas transacciones se incluyen en cifras netas, y las posiciones en cifras netas cuando se declaran, en la categoría de pasivos, porque las entidades que negocian con flujos de efectivo relacionados con obligaciones de deuda son las que generan mayor demanda de estos instrumentos.

Recuadro. Posición de inversión internacional

Se alienta a los países que se encuentran en las primeras etapas de compilación de la posición de inversión internacional a que presenten declaraciones parciales de la posición de inversión internacional. En general, estas declaraciones parciales contienen datos sobre las autoridades monetarias (incluidas las reservas internacionales) y por lo menos otro sector. Las declaraciones de la posición de inversión internacional de los países declarantes figuran como cuadro 3 en las páginas de países. No se presentan totales en el caso de las declaraciones parciales de la posición de inversión internacional. Debido a estas limitaciones de los datos, las declaraciones sobre la posición de inversión internacional de algunos países deben interpretarse teniendo en cuenta las notas que figuran en la parte 3 en la que se presentan las metodologías, los procedimientos de compilación y las fuentes de datos que utilizan estos países. A medida que los países sigan recopilando datos más completos, se publicará una presentación más extensa de los datos sobre la posición de inversión internacional de estos países en volúmenes subsiguientes del anuario.

Véase el capítulo XXIII de la quinta edición del *Manual* en el que se presenta un análisis detallado del concepto de posición de inversión internacional.

Deuda externa no es un componente aparte de la posición de inversión internacional sino que se deriva mediante la suma de los componentes del pasivo de la posición de inversión internacional que no corresponden a capital (es decir, todos los pasivos registrados que no sean títulos de participación en el capital ni acciones y otras participaciones de capital mediante inversión directa, incluidas las utilidades reinvertidas, y los instrumentos financieros derivados). Esta opinión concuerda, en general, con la definición básica de la deuda externa bruta adoptada en la publicación *Estadísticas de la deuda externa: Guía para compiladores y usuarios (Guía)* realizada por el Grupo de tareas interinstitucional sobre estadísticas financieras. Este grupo de tareas, que se reunió bajo la presidencia del FMI, se encargó de la elaboración de la *Guía* en la que participaron representantes del Banco de Pagos Internacionales, la Secretaría del Commonwealth, el Banco Central Europeo, Eurostat, el FMI, la OCDE, la Secretaría del Club de París, la Conferencia de las Naciones Unidas sobre Comercio y Desarrollo (UNCTAD) y el Banco Mundial.

Posición de inversión internacional: Componentes clave[1]

A. Activos

1. Inversión directa
- 1.1 Acciones y otras participaciones de capital y utilidades reinvertidas
- 1.2 Otro capital[2]

2. Inversión de cartera
- 2.1 Títulos de participación en el capital
- 2.2 Títulos de deuda[4]

3. Instrumentos financieros derivados
- 3.1 Autoridades monetarias
- 3.2 Gobierno general
- 3.3 Bancos
- 3.4 Otros sectores

4. Otra inversión
- 4.1 Créditos comerciales
- 4.2 Préstamos
- 4.3 Moneda y depósitos
- 4.4 Otros activos

5. Activos de reserva
- 5.1 Oro monetario
- 5.2 Derechos especiales de giro
- 5.3 Posición de reserva en el FMI
- 5.4 Divisas
- 5.5 AOtros activos

B. Pasivos

1. Inversión directa
- 1.1 Acciones y otras participaciones de capital y utilidades reinvertidas
- 1.2 Otro capital[3]

2. Inversión de cartera
- 2.1 Títulos de participación en el capital
- 2.2 Títulos de deuda[3,4]

3. Instrumentos financieros derivados
- 3.1 Autoridades monetarias
- 3.2 Gobierno general
- 3.3 Bancos
- 3.4 Otros sectores

4. Otra inversión
- 4.1 Créditos comerciales[3]
- 4.2 Préstamos [3]
- 4.3 Moneda y depósitos[3]
- 4.4 Otros pasivos[3]

[1] No se indican todos los componentes, por ejemplo, los que están desglosados por sectores (autoridades monetarias, gobierno general, bancos y otros) y, en algunos casos, por vencimientos.

[2] Los pasivos frente a empresas afiliadas, que se cancelan mutuamente con el otro capital en la clasificación funcional, son un componente de la deuda externa.

[3] Estos componentes comprenden la deuda externa bruta. (Véase también la nota de pie de página 2).

[4] Incluye bonos, pagarés e instrumentos del mercado de dinero.

cuadro 2. Sin embargo, hay varias diferencias entre los dos cuadros. Como se mencionó anteriormente, los datos sobre la posición de inversión internacional reflejan los activos y pasivos financieros de un país frente al exterior en un momento determinado. Por lo tanto, en el cuadro 3 los componentes de la posición de inversión internacional se agrupan en la presentación básica en dos categorías generales, a saber, activos y pasivos, a diferencia de la clasificación funcional de la inversión (es decir, inversión directa, inversión de cartera, instrumentos financieros derivados, otra inversión y activos de reserva) que figura en el cuadro 2. Además, los datos del cuadro 3 reflejan la posición de inversión internacional de un país al final del período de declaración de datos, a diferencia de las transacciones que tuvieron lugar durante el período, que se presentan en el cuadro 2. Asimismo, a diferencia del cuadro 2, en el que se indica el valor de las transacciones a lo largo de un período, la valoración de la posición de inversión internacional de un país, que se presenta en el cuadro 3, refleja el valor de las transacciones financieras, las variaciones por valoración y otros ajustes al final del período de declaración. La posición de inversión internacional neta, que figura en el cuadro 3, se calcula como diferencia entre el valor de los activos financieros externos declarados y el de los pasivos financieros externos declarados.

Códigos de datos

En los cuadros 1, 2 y 3 se indican los códigos de cada categoría y componente. Como se señaló anteriormente, los códigos fueron elaborados conjuntamente por el FMI, la OCDE y Eurostat, a efectos de facilitar la declaración de datos a nivel internacional. Los códigos corresponden a los componentes normalizados de la balanza de pagos y de la posición de inversión internacional según se definen en la quinta edición del *Manual*, así como a los componentes de la clasificación conjunta OCDE/Eurostat para el comercio de servicios.

Cada uno de los códigos que figuran en el anuario está formado por seis dígitos/caracteres. El primer dígito indica si se trata de un crédito, un débito o del valor neto (el número "2" corresponde a un crédito, el "3" a un débito y el "4" al valor neto, es decir, la diferencia entre créditos y débitos). Los tres dígitos siguientes se utilizan para clasificar los componentes de la balanza de pagos. Por ejemplo, para la cuenta corriente se utiliza el código 993, para la cuenta de capital 994 y para la cuenta financiera 995. Los detalles del sistema de codificación figuran en el anexo III.

Los dígitos/caracteres que ocupan los lugares quinto y sexto de los códigos que figuran en el anuario se reservan para indicar características especiales de ciertos componentes específicos. Por ejemplo, en el cuadro 1, la Z del quinto carácter señala que se excluye de ese componente el financiamiento excepcional; la W indica que se excluyen esta misma partida y el uso del crédito del FMI y préstamos del FMI. Las letras A, B, C y D del cuadro 1 indican los distintos sectores internos. En el cuadro 2, las letras A, B y C se refieren a subcomponentes no normalizados, como los de transportes (pasajeros, fletes y otros).

Créditos y débitos

En los cuadros 1 y 2, los datos sobre transacciones figuran como asientos de crédito bruto o débito bruto en la cuenta corriente y la cuenta de capital. En la cuenta financiera se presentan como asientos de crédito neto o débito neto (para reflejar variaciones netas de los pasivos y de los activos) en la cuenta financiera. Los asientos de crédito, bruto o neto, representan valores positivos (aunque no se indica el signo) y los asientos de débito, bruto o neto, son negativos (y sí se indica el signo). Por lo tanto, toda disminución de los activos y todo aumento de los pasivos (crédito) figuran como valores positivos y todo aumento de los activos y toda disminución de los pasivos (débito) aparecen con signo negativo.

Asientos nulos o carencia de datos

Con frecuencia es difícil discernir en la información declarada por los países si faltan cifras porque no se dispone de datos o porque el valor de esa partida es cero o insignificante. La inclusión de tres puntos (...) en los cuadros del anuario significa cualquiera de las dos posibilidades: bien que no se dispone de datos o bien que el valor es cero o insignificante.

Nota sobre los componentes de *renta* y *otra inversión*

En el cuadro 2 relativo a la presentación normalizada, los datos declarados por algunos países en las categorías de "renta" y "otra inversión" presentan un grado de agregación que no permite identificar por separado cada uno de los componentes que figuran en esta categoría. Por consiguiente, en estos casos, los datos agregados de ciertas subcategorías no pueden obtenerse sumando los componentes de estas subcategorías. Lo mismo ocurre en el caso de los datos relativos a "otra inversión" que figuran en el cuadro 3 relativo a la posición de inversión internacional.

Anteriormente, en los volúmenes 46 al 49, en los cuadros se presentaban los datos correspondientes a "otra inversión" (activos y pasivos) desglosados en "a largo plazo" y "a corto plazo". Desde el Volumen 50, en los cuadros se presentan los datos correspondientes a "otra inversión" (activos y pasivos) de las autoridades monetarias, el gobierno general, los bancos y otros sectores en cifras totales (del financiamiento a largo plazo y a corto plazo) y en partidas "de los cuales: a corto plazo". (En el caso de los préstamos, autoridades monetarias, los datos se indican en cifras totales, desglosados en "de los cuales: uso del crédito del FMI y préstamos del FMI" y "de los cuales: a corto plazo".) Sin embargo, en el Anexo II, no se ha modificado la presentación normalizada.

Redondeo de las cifras

La mayor parte de las cifras de los cuadros se expresan en unidades de un millón; no debe suponerse que los cuadros que incluyen unidades más pequeñas representan, necesariamente, cifras más exactas. La unidad se elige con el fin de presentar las cifras de una manera práctica. Debido al redondeo en el cálculo de las cifras, puede haber diferencias entre un total y la suma de sus componentes.

Conversión de monedas

La mayoría de los datos de balanza de pagos declarados al FMI se expresan en unidades de moneda nacional o en dólares de EE.UU., pero algunos países declaran ciertos datos en DEG. Para facilitar la comparación de datos entre los países, todos los estados de balanza de pagos publicados en el anuario se expresan en dólares de EE.UU. Además, los datos sobre transacciones con el FMI y sobre transacciones en DEG declarados por todos los países se remplazan por los datos que figuran en los registros del FMI, expresados en DEG. Esta información se convierte, a su vez, a dólares de EE.UU.

En el caso de los países que no declaran sus estadísticas en dólares de EE.UU., los datos se convierten utilizando el tipo de cambio que figura al pie del cuadro 1 para cada país, que normalmente es el tipo promedio vigente en el país en el período correspondiente y se obtiene de *IFS*. Por ejemplo, en las páginas de *IFS* correspondientes a los Países Bajos figura la línea "rf", en la que se indica el tipo de cambio promedio del florín frente al dólar de EE.UU. La conversión de los datos sobre transacciones de DEG a dólares de EE.UU. se efectúa a los tipos de cambio que se indican en la línea "sb" de las páginas de *IFS* correspondientes a Estados Unidos. En lo que respecta a los países que declaran datos trimestrales en unidades de moneda nacional, los totales anuales en dólares de EE.UU. se obtienen sumando los montos trimestrales en dólares de EE.UU.

En la introducción de *IFS*, sección 1, se presenta mayor información sobre los tipos de cambio empleados.

II. Suscripciones en CD-ROM

Las estadísticas publicadas en el anuario también se presentan en CD-ROM. El número de países y las series cronológicas que cubre la versión en CD-ROM son ligeramente mayores que en la versión impresa del anuario. También es mayor el número de períodos sobre los cuales se incluyen observaciones estadísticas en las series cronológicas. También se incluyen en la versión en CD-ROM los datos trimestrales declarados por los países. Además, la versión en CD-ROM incluye datos actualizados y corregidos a medida que se dispone de los mismos. Para mayor información, sírvase dirigirse a:

Publication Services
International Monetary Fund
Washington, D.C. 20431, EE.UU.
Teléfono: (202) 623–7430
Fax: (202) 623–7201
Correo electrónico: publications@imf.org
Internet: http://www.imf.org

Anexo I. Presentación Analítica

	Códigos
A. CUENTA CORRIENTE[1]	4 993 Z .
Bienes: exportaciones f.o.b.	2 100 . .
Bienes: importaciones f.o.b.	3 100 . .
Balanza de bienes	4 100 . .
Servicios: crédito	2 200 . .
Servicios: débito	3 200 . .
Balanza de bienes y servicios	4 991 . .
Renta: crédito	2 300 . .
Renta: débito	3 300 . .
Balanza de bienes, servicios y renta	4 992 . .
Transferencias corrientes: crédito	2 379 Z .
Transferencias corrientes: débito	3 379 . .
B. CUENTA DE CAPITAL[1]	4 994 Z .
Cuenta de capital: crédito	2 994 Z .
Cuenta de capital: débito	3 994 . .
Total, grupos A más B	4 981 . .
C. CUENTA FINANCIERA[1]	4 995 W .
Inversión directa en el extranjero	4 505 . .
Inversión directa en la economía declarante	4 555 Z .
Activos de inversión de cartera	4 602 . .
Títulos de participación en el capital	4 610 . .
Títulos de deuda	4 619 . .
Pasivos de inversión de cartera	4 652 Z .
Títulos de participación en el capital	4 660 . .
Títulos de deuda	4 669 Z .
Instrumentos financieros derivados	4 910 . .
Activos financieros derivados	4 900 . .
Pasivos financieros derivados	4 905 . .
Activos de otra inversión	4 703 . .
Autoridades monetarias	4 701 . .
Gobierno general	4 704 . .
Bancos	4 705 . .
Otros sectores	4 728 . .
Pasivos de otra inversión	4 753 W .
Autoridades monetarias	4 753 WA
Gobierno general	4 753 ZB
Bancos	4 753 ZC
Otros sectores	4 753 ZD
Total, grupos A a C	4 983 . .
D. ERRORES Y OMISIONES NETOS	4 998 . .
Total, grupos A a D	4 984 . .
E. RESERVAS Y PARTIDAS CONEXAS	4 802 A .
Activos de reserva	4 802 . .
Uso del crédito del FMI y préstamos del FMI	4 766 . .
Pasivos que constituyen reservas de autoridades extranjeras	4 900 . .
Financiamiento excepcional	4 920 . .
TIPOS DE CONVERSIÓN: MONEDA DEL PAÍS POR DÓLAR DE EE.UU.	0 101 . .

[1]Excluidos los componentes que se han clasificado en las categorías del Grupo E.

Anexo II. Presentación Normalizada

	Códigos	
CUENTA CORRIENTE	4 993	. .
A. **BIENES**	4 100	. .
Crédito	2 100	. .
Mercancías generales: exportaciones f.o.b.	2 110	. .
Bienes para transformación: exportaciones f.o.b.	2 150	. .
Reparaciones de bienes	2 160	. .
Bienes adquiridos en puerto por medios de transporte	2 170	. .
Oro no monetario	2 180	. .
Débito	3 100	. .
Mercancías generales: importaciones f.o.b.	3 110	. .
Bienes para transformación: importaciones f.o.b.	3 150	. .
Reparaciones de bienes	3 160	. .
Bienes adquiridos en puerto por medios de transporte	3 170	. .
Oro no monetario	3 180	. .
B. SERVICIOS	4 200	. .
Crédito total	2 200	. .
Débito total	3 200	. .
Servicios de transportes, crédito	2 205	. .
Pasajeros	2 850	. .
Fletes	2 851	. .
Otros	2 852	. .
Transporte marítimo, pasajeros	2 207	. .
Transporte marítimo, fletes	2 208	. .
Transporte marítimo, otros	2 209	. .
Transporte aéreo, pasajeros	2 211	. .
Transporte aéreo, fletes	2 212	. .
Transporte aéreo, otros	2 213	. .
Otros transportes, pasajeros	2 215	. .
Otros transportes, fletes	2 216	. .
Otros transportes, otros	2 217	. .
Servicios de transportes, débito	3 205	. .
Pasajeros	3 850	. .
Fletes	3 851	. .
Otros	3 852	. .
Transporte marítimo, pasajeros	3 207	. .
Transporte marítimo, fletes	3 208	. .
Transporte marítimo, otros	3 209	. .
Transporte aéreo, pasajeros	3 211	. .
Transporte aéreo, fletes	3 212	. .
Transporte aéreo, otros	3 213	. .
Otros transportes, pasajeros	3 215	. .
Otros transportes, fletes	3 216	. .
Otros transportes, otros	3 217	. .
Viajes, crédito	2 236	. .
De negocios	2 237	. .
Personales	2 240	. .
Viajes, débito	3 236	. .
De negocios	3 237	. .
Personales	3 240	. .
Otros servicios, crédito	2 200	BA
Comunicaciones	2 245	. .
Construcción	2 249	. .
Seguros	2 253	. .

ANEXO II. PRESENTACIÓN NORMALIZADA *(continuación)*

	Códigos	
Financieros	2 260	..
Informática e información	2 262	..
Regalías y derechos de licencia	2 266	..
Otros servicios empresariales	2 268	..
Personales, culturales y recreativos	2 287	..
Servicios del gobierno, n.i.o.p.	2 291	..
Otros servicios, débito	3 200	BA
Comunicaciones	3 245	..
Construcción	3 249	..
Seguros	3 253	..
Financieros	3 260	..
Informática e información	3 262	..
Regalías y derechos de licencia	3 266	..
Otros servicios empresariales	3 268	..
Personales, culturales y recreativos	3 287	..
Servicios del gobierno, n.i.o.p.	3 291	..
C. RENTA	4 300	..
Crédito total	2 300	..
Débito total	3 300	..
Remuneración de empleados, crédito	2 310	..
Remuneración de empleados, débito	3 310	..
Renta de la inversión, crédito	2 320	..
Renta de la inversión directa	2 330	..
Dividendos y utilidades distribuidas de sucursales	2 332	..
Utilidades reinvertidas y utilidades no distribuidas de sucursales	2 333	..
Renta procedente de la deuda (intereses)	2 334	..
Renta de la inversión de cartera	2 339	..
Renta procedente de acciones y otras participaciones de capital	2 340	..
Renta procedente de bonos y pagarés	2 350	..
Renta procedente de instrumentos del mercado monetario	2 360	..
Renta de otra inversión	2 370	..
Renta de la inversión, débito	3 320	..
Renta de la inversión directa	3 330	..
Dividendos y utilidades distribuidas de sucursales	3 332	..
Utilidades reinvertidas y utilidades no distribuidas de sucursales	3 333	..
Renta procedente de la deuda (intereses)	3 334	..
Renta de la inversión de cartera	3 339	..
Renta procedente de acciones y otras participaciones de capital	3 340	..
Renta procedente de bonos y pagarés	3 350	..
Renta procedente de instrumentos del mercado monetario	3 360	..
Renta de otra inversión	3 370	..
D.Transferencias corrientes	4 379	..
Crédito	2 379	..
Gobierno general	2 380	..
Otros sectores	2 390	..
Remesas de trabajadores	2 391	..
Otras transferencias corrientes	2 392	..
Débito	3 379	..
Gobierno general	3 380	..
Otros sectores	3 390	..
Remesas de trabajadores	3 391	..
Otras transferencias corrientes	3 392	..

Anexo II. Presentación Normalizada *(continuación)*

	Códigos	
CUENTA DE CAPITAL Y FINANCIERA	4 996	..
CUENTA DE CAPITAL	4 994	..
Crédito total	2 994	..
Débito total	3 994	..
Transferencias de capital, crédito	2 400	..
Gobierno general	2 401	..
Condonación de deudas	2 402	..
Otras transferencias de capital	2 410	..
Otros sectores	2 430	..
Transferencias de emigrantes	2 431	..
Condonación de deudas	2 432	..
Otras transferencias de capital	2 440	..
Transferencias de capital, débito	3 400	..
Gobierno general	3 401	..
Condonación de deudas	3 402	..
Otras transferencias de capital	3 410	..
Otros sectores	3 430	..
Transferencias de emigrantes	3 431	..
Condonación de deudas	3 432	..
Otras transferencias de capital	3 440	..
Activos no financieros no producidos, crédito	2 480	..
Activos no financieros no producidos, débito	3 480	..
CUENTA FINANCIERA	4 995	..
A. INVERSIÓN DIRECTA	4 500	..
Inversión directa en el extranjero	4 505	..
Acciones y otras participaciones de capital	4 510	..
Activos frente a empresas filiales	4 515	..
Pasivos frente a empresas filiales	4 520	..
Utilidades reinvertidas	4 525	..
Otro capital	4 530	..
Activos frente a empresas filiales	4 535	..
Pasivos frente a empresas filiales	4 540	..
Inversión directa en la economía declarante	4 555	..
Acciones y otras participaciones de capital	4 560	..
Activos frente a inversionistas directos	4 565	..
Pasivos frente a inversionistas directos	4 570	..
Utilidades reinvertidas	4 575	..
Otro capital	4 580	..
Activos frente a inversionistas directos	4 585	..
Pasivos frente a inversionistas directos	4 590	..
B. INVERSIÓN DE CARTERA	4 600	..
Activos	4 602	..
Títulos de participación en el capital	4 610	..
Autoridades monetarias	4 611	..
Gobierno general	4 612	..
Bancos	4 613	..
Otros sectores	4 614	..
Títulos de deuda	4 619	..
Bonos y pagarés	4 620	..
Autoridades monetarias	4 621	..

Anexo II. Presentación Normalizada *(continuación)*

	Códigos	
Gobierno general	4 622	..
Bancos	4 623	..
Otros sectores	4 624	..
Instrumentos del mercado monetario	4 630	..
Autoridades monetarias	4 631	..
Gobierno general	4 632	..
Bancos	4 633	..
Otros sectores	4 634	..
Pasivos	4 652	..
Títulos de participación en el capital	4 660	..
Bancos	4 663	..
Otros sectores	4 664	..
Títulos de deuda	4 669	..
Bonos y pagarés	4 670	..
Autoridades monetarias	4 671	..
Gobierno general	4 672	..
Bancos	4 673	..
Otros sectores	4 674	..
Instrumentos del mercado monetario	4 680	..
Autoridades monetarias	4 681	..
Gobierno general	4 682	..
Bancos	4 683	..
Otros sectores	4 684	..
C. INSTRUMENTOS FINANCIEROS DERIVADOS	4 910	..
Autoridades monetarias	4 911	..
Gobierno general	4 912	..
Bancos	4 913	..
Otros sectores	4 914	..
Activos	4 900	..
Autoridades monetarias	4 901	..
Gobierno general	4 902	..
Bancos	4 903	..
Otros sectores	4 904	..
Pasivos	4 905	..
Autoridades monetarias	4 906	..
Gobierno general	4 907	..
Bancos	4 908	..
Otros sectores	4 909	..
D.OTRA INVERSIÓN	4 700	..
Activos	4 703	..
Créditos comerciales	4 706	..
Gobierno general	4 707	..
de la cual: a corto plazo	4 709	..
Otros sectores	4 710	..
de la cual: a corto plazo	4 712	..
Préstamos	4 714	..
Autoridades monetarias	4 715	..
de la cual: a corto plazo	4 718	..
Gobierno general	4 719	..
de la cual: a corto plazo	4 721	..
Bancos	4 722	..
de la cual: a corto plazo	4 724	..

Anexo II. Presentación Normalizada *(conclusión)*

	Códigos	
Otros sectores	4 725	..
de la cual: a corto plazo	4 727	..
Moneda y depósitos	4 730	..
Autoridades monetarias	4 731	..
Gobierno general	4 732	..
Bancos	4 733	..
Otros sectores	4 734	..
Otros pasivos	4 736	..
Autoridades monetarias	4 737	..
de la cual: a corto plazo	4 739	..
Gobierno general	4 740	..
de la cual: a corto plazo	4 742	..
Bancos	4 743	..
de la cual: a corto plazo	4 745	..
Otros sectores	4 746	..
de la cual: a corto plazo	4 748	..
Pasivos	4 753	..
Créditos comerciales	4 756	..
Gobierno general	4 757	..
de la cual: a corto plazo	4 759	..
Otros sectores	4 760	..
de la cual: a corto plazo	4 762	..
Préstamos	4 764	..
Autoridades monetarias: otros	4 765	..
de la cual: uso del crédito del FMI y préstamos del FMI	4 766	..
de la cual: a corto plazo	4 768	..
Gobierno general	4 769	..
de la cual: a corto plazo	4 771	..
Bancos	4 772	..
de la cual: a corto plazo	4 774	..
Otros sectores	4 775	..
de la cual: a corto plazoo	4 777	..
Moneda y depósitos	4 780	..
Autoridades monetarias	4 781	..
Gobierno general	4 782	..
Bancos	4 783	..
Otros sectores	4 784	..
Otros pasivos	4 786	..
Autoridades monetarias	4 787	..
de la cual: a corto plazo	4 789	..
Gobierno general	4 790	..
de la cual: a corto plazo	4 792	..
Bancos	4 793	..
de la cual: a corto plazo	4 795	..
Otros sectores	4 796	..
de la cual: a corto plazo	4 798	..
D.ACTIVOS DE RESERVA	4 802	..
Oro monetario	4 812	..
Derechos especiales de giro	4 811	..
Posición de reserva en el FMI	4 810	..
Divisas	4 803	..
Otros activos	4 813	..
ERRORES Y OMISIONES NETOS	4 998	..

Anexo III. Sistema de codificación FMI/OCDE/Eurostat para la balanza de pagos, la posición de inversión internacional y el comercio de servicios[1]

Este sistema de codificación incorpora todos los componentes normalizados y las líneas de información suplementaria de la quinta edición del *Manual de Balanza de Pagos*, así como los componentes y partidas informativas de la clasificación OCDE/Eurostat para el comercio internacional de servicios.

El código consta de tres partes:

<posición>	Un dígito (del 1 al 8) que describe la posición de la partida en las cuentas de la posición de inversión internacional o de la balanza de pagos.
<tema>	Tres dígitos (del 100 al 998) que identifican todos los componentes de la balanza de pagos, del comercio de servicios y de información suplementaria seleccionada.
<sufijo>	Serie de caracteres definidos por el usuario; puede ser de cualquier longitud.

El código completo deberá tener la siguiente configuración: <posición><tema><sufijo>, aunque el sufijo es optativo. Los dígitos de posición y tema, en cambio, son obligatorios. Por esa razón, en la mayoría de los casos, la configuración del código es <posición><tema>.

El primer dígito del código describe la posición de la partida en las cuentas de la posición de inversión internacional y de la balanza de pagos, a saber:

Código	Posición en las cuentas de la posición de inversión internacional y la balanza de pagos
1	Posición al comienzo del período
2	Flujos de crédito
3	Flujos de débito
4	Flujos netos
5	Ajuste por variaciones de precios
6	Ajuste por variaciones de tipos de cambio
7	Otros ajustes
8	Posición al final del período
0	Otros

El primer dígito del tema identifica la sección de la balanza de pagos, a saber:

Código	Sección de las cuentas
1	Bienes
2	Servicios
3	Renta y transferencias corrientes
4	Cuenta de capital
5	Inversión directa
6	Inversión de cartera
7	Otra inversión
8	Activos de reserva
9	Agregados principales e información suplementaria

El segundo y tercer dígito del tema corresponden al orden consecutivo de los componentes con interrupciones para poder incluir códigos adicionales posteriormente. Además, en la cuenta financiera, salvo las cuentas de inversión directa, el segundo dígito del tema puede ser 0, 1, 2, 3 ó 4 en el caso de los activos y 5, 6, 7, 8 ó 9 en el caso de los pasivos.

A continuación se presentan ejemplos de códigos para "Otra inversión" en la cuenta financiera.

Tema	Campo único			Campo múltiple		
	Crédito	Débito	Neto	Crédito	Débito	Neto
Otra inversión	2700	3700	4700	2700	3700	4700
Pasivos	2750	3750	4750	2750	3750	4750
Préstamos	2762	3762	4762	2762	3762	4762
Gobierno general	2767	3767	4767	2767	3767	4767
A largo plazo	2768	3768	4768	2768	3768	4768
A corto plazo	2769	3769	4769	2769	3769	4769
Bancos	2770	3770	4770	2770	3770	4770
A largo plazo	2771	3771	4771	2771	3771	4771
A corto plazo	2772	3772	4772	2772	3772	4772
Otros sectores	2773	3773	4773	2773	3773	4773
A largo plazo	2774	3774	4774	2774	3774	4774
A corto plazo	2775	3775	4775	2775	3775	4775

Tratándose de créditos y débitos correspondientes a préstamos, los términos que se emplean comúnmente son giros y rembolsos. La quinta edición del *Manual* recomienda declarar todos los giros y rembolsos de los préstamos a largo plazo en una clasificación suplementaria. Actualmente, el FMI recopila la mayoría de las demás partidas de la cuenta financiera en cifras netas. No obstante, el sistema de codificación permite identificar todos los flujos como créditos, débitos o flujos netos.

[1]Adoptado de "Balance of Payments Codes for Standard Components and Additional Items", FMI, Washington, 3 de marzo de 1995.

ANEXO IV. POSICIÓN DE INVERSIÓN INTERNACIONAL COMPONENTES NORMALIZADOS

		Códigos
A. ACTIVOS	8 995	C .
Inversión directa en el extranjero	8 505	. .
Acciones y otras participaciones de capital y utilidades reinvertidas	8 506	. .
Activos frente a empresas filiales	8 507	. .
Pasivos frente a empresas filiales	8 508	. .
Otro capital	8 530	. .
Activos frente a empresas filiales	8 535	. .
Pasivos frente a empresas filiales	8 540	. .
Inversión de cartera	8 602	. .
Títulos de participación en el capital	8 610	. .
Autoridades monetarias	8 611	. .
Gobierno general	8 612	. .
Bancos	8 613	. .
Otros sectores	8 614	. .
Títulos de deuda	8 619	. .
Bonos y pagarés	8 620	. .
Autoridades monetarias	8 621	. .
Gobierno general	8 622	. .
Bancos	8 623	. .
Otros sectores	8 624	. .
Instrumentos del mercado monetario	8 630	. .
Autoridades monetarias	8 631	. .
Gobierno general	8 632	. .
Bancos	8 633	. .
Otros sectores	8 634	. .
Instrumentos financieros derivados	8 900	. .
Autoridades monetarias	8 901	. .
Gobierno general	8 902	. .
Bancos	8 903	. .
Otros sectores	8 904	. .
Otra inversión	8 703	. .
Créditos comerciales	8 706	. .
Gobierno general	8 707	. .
de la cual: a corto plazo	8 709	. .
Otros sectores	8 710	. .
de la cual: a corto plazo	8 712	. .
Préstamos	8 714	. .
Autoridades monetarias	8 715	. .
de la cual: a corto plazo	8 718	. .
Gobierno general	8 719	. .
de la cual: a corto plazo	8 721	. .
Bancos	8 722	. .
de la cual: a corto plazo	8 724	. .
Otros sectores	8 725	. .
de la cual: a corto plazo	8 727	. .
Moneda y depósitos	8 730	. .
Autoridades monetarias	8 731	. .
Gobierno general	8 732	. .
Bancos	8 733	. .
Otros sectores	8 734	. .

ANEXO IV. POSICIÓN DE INVERSIÓN INTERNACIONAL COMPONENTES NORMALIZADOS *(continuación)*

	Códigos
Otros activos	8 736 ..
Autoridades monetarias	8 737 ..
de la cual: a corto plazo	8 739 ..
Gobierno general	8 740 ..
de la cual: a corto plazo	8 742 ..
Bancos	8 743 ..
de la cual: a corto plazo	8 745 ..
Otros sectores	8 746 ..
de la cual: a corto plazo	8 748 ..
Activos de reserva	8 802 ..
Oro monetario	8 812 ..
Derechos especiales de giro	8 811 ..
Posición de reserva en el FMI	8 810 ..
Divisas	8 803 ..
Otros activos	8 813 ..
B. PASIVOS	8 995 D .
Inversión directa en la economía declarante	8 555 ..
Acciones y otras participaciones de capital y utilidades reinvertidas	8 556 ..
Activos frente a inversionistas directos	8 557 ..
Pasivos frente a inversionistas directos	8 558 ..
Otro capital	8 580 ..
Activos frente a inversionistas directos	8 585 ..
Pasivos frente a inversionistas directos	8 590 ..
Inversión de cartera	8 652 ..
Títulos de participación en el capital	8 660 ..
Bancos	8 663 ..
Otros sectores	8 664 ..
Títulos de deuda	8 669 ..
Bonos y pagarés	8 670 ..
Autoridades monetarias	8 671 ..
Gobierno general	8 672 ..
Bancos	8 673 ..
Otros sectores	8 674 ..
Instrumentos del mercado monetario	8 680 ..
Autoridades monetarias	8 681 ..
Gobierno general	8 682 ..
Bancos	8 683 ..
Otros sectores	8 684 ..
Instrumentos financieros derivados	8 905 ..
Autoridades monetarias	8 906 ..
Gobierno general	8 907 ..
Bancos	8 908 ..
Otros sectores	8 909 ..
Otra inversión	8 753 ..
Créditos comerciales	8 756 ..
Gobierno general	8 757 ..
de la cual: a corto plazo	8 759 ..
Otros sectores	8 760 ..
de la cual: a corto plazo	8 762 ..

ANEXO IV. POSICIÓN DE INVERSIÓN INTERNACIONAL COMPONENTES NORMALIZADOS
(conclusión)

	Códigos	
Préstamos	8 764	. .
Autoridades monetarias	8 765	. .
de la cual: uso del crédito del FMI y préstamos del FMI	8 766	. .
de la cual: a corto plazo	8 768	. .
Gobierno general	8 769	. .
de la cual: a corto plazo	8 771	. .
Bancos	8 772	. .
de la cual: a corto plazo	8 774	. .
Otros sectores	8 775	. .
de la cual: a corto plazo	8 777	. .
Moneda y depósitos	8 780	. .
Autoridades monetarias	8 781	. .
Gobierno general	8 782	. .
Bancos	8 783	. .
Otros sectores	8 784	. .
Otros pasivos	8 786	. .
Autoridades monetarias	8 787	. .
de la cual: a corto plazo	8 789	. .
Gobierno general	8 790	. .
de la cual: a corto plazo	8 792	. .
Bancos	8 793	. .
de la cual: a corto plazo	8 795	. .
Otros sectores	8 796	. .
de la cual: a corto plazo	8 798	. .
POSICIÓN DE INVERSIÓN INTERNACIONAL NETA	8 995	. .
Tipos de conversión (fin de período)	0 102	. .

Anexo V. Marco conceptual de la balanza de pagos y de la posición de inversión internacional

Este anexo es la reproducción del capítulo II del Manual de Balanza de Pagos, 5a. edición. *Los párrafos y los números de página citados en este anexo corresponden a los del* Manual.

Definiciones

12. La primera parte de este *Manual* abarca el marco conceptual de las cuentas de la balanza de pagos y de la posición de inversión internacional, examinándose su relación con las cuentas nacionales y con los conceptos de residencia, valoración, momento de registro, unidad de cuenta y conversión.

13. La balanza de pagos es un estado estadístico que resume sistemáticamente, para un período específico dado, las transacciones económicas entre una economía y el resto del mundo. Las transacciones, que en su mayoría tienen lugar entre residentes y no residentes[1], comprenden las que se refieren a bienes, servicios y renta, las que entrañan activos y pasivos financieros frente al resto del mundo y las que se clasifican como transferencias (como los regalos), en las que se efectúan asientos compensatorios para equilibrar —desde el punto de vista contable— las transacciones unilaterales (véase el párrafo 28)[2]. Una transacción en sí se define como un flujo económico que refleja la creación, transformación, intercambio, transferencia o extinción de un valor económico y entraña traspasos de propiedad de bienes y/o activos financieros, la prestación de servicios o el suministro de mano de obra y capital.

14. En estrecha relación con el marco de la balanza de pagos, basado en los flujos, se encuentra la posición de inversión internacional, definida por las tenencias de recursos financieros. Esta última, que corresponde a una fecha específica como el fin del año, es un estado estadístico que representa: i) el valor y la composición de las tenencias de activos financieros de una economía, o de los créditos adquiridos por una economía frente al resto del mundo, y ii) el valor y la composición de las tenencias de pasivos de una economía a favor del resto del mundo. En algunos casos, puede ser de interés analítico calcular la diferencia entre los dos lados del balance para tener una medida de la posición neta. Dicha medida sería equivalente a la porción del patrimonio de una economía atribuible a su relación con el resto del mundo, o derivado de ella. Toda variación de las tenencias en cualquier período definido puede atribuirse a transacciones (flujos), a variaciones de valoración debidas a fluctuaciones del tipo de cambio, precios, etc., o a otros ajustes (por ejemplo, confiscaciones sin indemnización). En cambio, las cuentas de la balanza de pagos sólo reflejan transacciones.

Criterios y conceptos

15. El resto de este capítulo se refiere al marco conceptual de las cuentas internacionales, vale decir, al conjunto de criterios y convenciones básicos que permite el registro sistematizado y coherente de las transacciones internacionales y de las tenencias de activos y pasivos sobre el exterior. En los capítulos subsiguientes se analizarán detenidamente los aspectos sobresalientes de estos criterios, así como sus consideraciones y limitaciones prácticas.

Método de contabilidad por partida doble

16. El criterio básico aplicado a la preparación del estado de balanza de pagos es que toda transacción registrada está representada por dos asientos de igual valor. Uno de ellos se denomina crédito y tiene signo aritmético positivo. El otro se llama débito y tiene signo negativo. En principio, la suma de todos los asientos de crédito es igual a la suma de todos los asientos de débito y el saldo neto de la totalidad de los asientos del estado es igual a cero.

17. En la práctica, sin embargo, las cuentas no suelen estar en equilibrio. A menudo, los datos empleados para estimar la balanza de pagos suelen derivarse en forma independiente de diferentes fuentes; en consecuencia, puede haber un crédito neto o débito neto agregado (es decir, errores y omisiones netos en las cuentas). Para equilibrar las cuentas, se deberá efectuar un asiento separado por un monto equivalente pero de signo contrario. Debe observarse que, como hay estimaciones imprecisas o faltantes de signo contrario que suelen compensarse mutuamente, la magnitud del residuo neto no es indicativa de la exactitud relativa del estado de balanza de pagos. No obstante, la existencia de un residuo significativo y persistente que no se corrige debe ser motivo de preocupación, porque esta situación impide el análisis o la interpretación de las estimaciones y les resta credibilidad. Por otra parte, un residuo neto elevado también puede afectar a la interpretación del estado de la posición de inversión internacional. (Véase la explicación en el capítulo XXIII.)

18. La mayoría de los asientos de la balanza de pagos se refieren a transacciones en las que se entregan o reciben valores económicos a cambio de otros. Dichos valores comprenden recursos reales (bienes, servicios y renta) y financieros. Así, los asientos compensatorios de crédito y débito que exige el método de registro suelen resultar del hecho de que se han anotado montos iguales para los dos recursos que se han intercambiado. Si en vez de ser intercambiados se ceden gratuitamente, o si el registro es unilateral por otras razones, se efectúan asientos especiales —llamados transferencias—para saldarlos. En los párrafos 26 a 31 se describen las distintas clases de asientos que pueden figurar en la balanza de pagos.

19. Conforme a las convenciones del método contable, una economía compiladora registra asientos de crédito i) para los recursos reales que denotan exportaciones y ii) para los recursos financieros que indican reducciones de sus activos sobre el exterior o aumentos de sus pasivos sobre el exterior. A su vez, registra asientos de débito i) para los recursos reales que denotan importaciones y ii) para los recursos financieros que indican aumentos de los activos o disminuciones de los pasivos. En otras palabras, en los activos —reales o financieros— una cifra con signo positivo

[1]En la balanza de pagos, las únicas transacciones que no se efectúan entre residentes y no residentes son el intercambio de activos financieros sobre el exterior transferibles entre sectores residentes y, en menor medida, el intercambio de pasivos financieros sobre el exterior transferibles entre no residentes. (Véase el párrafo 318.)

[2]Cabe destacar que las definiciones y clasificaciones de las cuentas internacionales que se presentan en este *Manual* tienen por objeto facilitar a los países miembros la tarea de declarar al FMI la información sobre transacciones internacionales y no pretenden hacer efectivas ni interpretar las disposiciones del *Convenio Constitutivo del Fondo Monetario Internacional* que se refieren al carácter jurídico de la acción (o falta de acción) oficial en relación con dichas transacciones.

(crédito) representa una disminución de las tenencias y una cifra con signo negativo (débito) indica un incremento. En cambio, en los pasivos, una cifra con signo positivo significa un aumento, y una cifra con signo negativo, una disminución. Las transferencias aparecen como créditos si compensan asientos de débito, y como débitos si saldan asientos de crédito.

20. El contenido o la cobertura del estado de balanza de pagos depende, en cierto modo, de que las transacciones sean tratadas en base a valores brutos o netos. Las recomendaciones de este *Manual* especifican cuáles deberán registrarse en valores brutos y cuáles en valores netos, como se refleja en la lista de componentes normalizados y en las presentaciones suplementarias sugeridas.

Conceptos de territorio económico, residencia y centro de interés económico

21. Los conceptos de territorio económico, residencia y centro de interés económico que se utilizan en este *Manual* son idénticos a los del *SCN* y se describen detalladamente en el capítulo IV. El territorio económico puede no coincidir con las fronteras políticas reconocidas. El territorio económico de un país comprende el territorio geográfico administrado por un gobierno dentro del cual circulan libremente personas, bienes y capital. En el caso de países marítimos, incluye también las islas que están sujetas a las mismas autoridades fiscales y monetarias que el territorio continental.

22. Una unidad institucional tiene un centro de interés económico y es residente de un país cuando desde algún lugar (vivienda, planta de producción u otro establecimiento), ubicado dentro del territorio económico del país, dicha unidad realiza e intenta seguir realizando (indefinidamente o durante un período finito) actividades económicas y transacciones en gran escala. (Se sugiere emplear un año o más como referencia, aunque no se trata de una regla inflexible.)

Criterios de valoración y momento de registro

23. Para compilar de manera uniforme cualquier agregado de transacciones individuales y registrar la posición de los activos y pasivos que les corresponden, es necesario contar con una base uniforme de valoración de las cuentas internacionales (tanto los recursos reales como los activos y pasivos financieros). En general, en este *Manual* se utiliza como base para la valoración de las transacciones el precio efectivo de mercado acordado por las partes que intervienen en la transacción. (Este criterio coincide con el adoptado en el *SCN*.) Desde el punto de vista conceptual, todas las tenencias de activos y pasivos deberán valorarse de acuerdo a los precios de mercado vigentes en el momento al cual se refiere la posición de inversión internacional. En el capítulo V se presenta una exposición completa de los criterios de valoración, las prácticas recomendadas, las limitaciones y la valoración de transferencias, recursos financieros y tenencias de activos y pasivos. (Se incluyen también casos en que no existe un precio de mercado o no es posible suponerlo.)

24. En el *Manual* y en el *SCN*, el criterio que se aplica con respecto al *momento de registro* de las transacciones es el de contabilidad en valores devengados. Por lo tanto, las transacciones deben registrarse con referencia al momento en que se crea, transforma, intercambia, transfiere o extingue un valor económico. Se crean activos y pasivos cuando tiene lugar un traspaso de propiedad, ya sea de índole legal o física (económica). En la práctica, cuando no sea evidente el traspaso de propiedad, el momento en que éste ocurre puede determinarse de una forma aproximada utilizando la fecha en que las partes de una transacción la registran en sus libros o en sus cuentas. (El capítulo VI trata sobre los momentos de registro y convenciones recomendados para diferentes asientos de la balanza de pagos, e incluye excepciones y desviaciones del criterio de traspaso de propiedad.)

Concepto y clase de transacción

25. En general, las variaciones de las relaciones económicas que se registran en la balanza de pagos provienen básicamente de las transacciones realizadas entre dos partes. Dichas partes son, con una excepción (véase la nota 1), un residente y un no residente, y todas las transacciones de esta clase aparecen en la balanza de pagos. Las recomendaciones sobre los asientos específicos necesarios se hallan incorporadas en la lista de componentes normalizados (véase el capítulo VIII) y se detallan a partir del capítulo IX.

26. A pesar de su nombre, la balanza de pagos no se refiere a *pagos* en su acepción común, sino a *transacciones*. Algunas transacciones internacionales que revisten interés a efectos de la balanza de pagos pueden no entrañar un pago en efectivo y algunas no se pagan en ningún sentido. La inclusión de estas transacciones, además de las que tienen como contrapartida un pago, constituye la diferencia principal entre un estado de balanza de pagos y un registro de pagos externos.

Intercambios

27. Las transacciones más comunes e importantes de la balanza de pagos pueden caracterizarse como *intercambios*. Una parte (entidad económica) suministra un valor económico a otra y recibe a cambio un valor igual. Los valores económicos suministrados por una economía a otra pueden clasificarse en términos generales como recursos reales (bienes, servicios, renta) y recursos financieros. Las partes que intervienen en la transacción son residentes de distintas economías, salvo en el caso de intercambio de recursos financieros externos entre sectores residentes. El suministro de un recurso financiero puede suponer no sólo un traspaso de propiedad de un activo o de un pasivo existente sino también la creación de uno nuevo o la cancelación de uno existente. Es más, las condiciones de un contrato relativo a un recurso financiero (por ejemplo, el plazo de vencimiento contractual) pueden modificarse por acuerdo entre las partes, en cuyo caso se da por cumplido el primer contrato y se considera que éste ha sido remplazado por otro con condiciones distintas. Todos estos intercambios se deberán incluir en la balanza de pagos.

Transferencias

28. Las transacciones que comprenden *transferencias* difieren de los intercambios porque una de las partes entrega un valor económico a la otra sin recibir un quid pro quo que, según las normas y reglas adoptadas en el sistema, tiene valor económico. Esta ausencia de valor por un lado de la transacción está representado por un asiento denominado *transferencia*. Las transferencias de esta clase (valores económicos suministrados y recibidos sin quid pro quo) se registran en la balanza de pagos. Las ***transferencias corrientes*** se incluyen en la **cuenta corriente** (véase el capítulo XV), en tanto que las *transferencias de capital* aparecen en la ***cuenta de capital*** (véase el capítulo XVII).

Migración

29. Como una economía se define en función de las entidades económicas vinculadas a su territorio, su ámbito posiblemente se vea afectado por los cambios que tengan lugar en las entidades vinculadas a ella.

30. Se produce una migración cuando la residencia de una persona se traslada de una economía a otra por haber cambiado su domicilio. Ciertos bienes muebles del emigrante se importan, de hecho, a la nueva economía. Sus bienes inmuebles y ciertos bienes muebles que se encuentran en la economía anterior se transforman en activos de la nueva economía frente a la anterior. Sus activos o pasivos frente a residentes de otra economía distinta de la nueva pasan a ser activos o pasivos sobre el exterior de la nueva economía. Sus activos o pasivos frente a residentes de la nueva economía dejan de ser activos o pasivos de una economía frente al resto del mundo. La suma neta de todas estas variaciones es igual al patrimonio del emigrante, que también debe registrarse como asiento compensatorio, si se registran los demás cambios. Estos asientos se efectúan en la balanza de pagos donde, por norma, se incluyen en las transferencias.

Otras transacciones imputadas

31. En algunos casos, las transacciones pueden ser imputadas y pueden efectuarse asientos en las cuentas de la balanza de pagos cuando no exista un flujo efectivo. Cabe citar como ejemplo la atribución de las utilidades reinvertidas a inversionistas directos extranjeros. Las utilidades de una filial o sucursal extranjera incluyen utilidades atribuibles a un inversionista directo residente. Dichas utilidades, independientemente de que se hayan distribuido o reinvertido en la empresa, son proporcionales a la participación del inversionista directo residente en el capital de la empresa. Las utilidades reinvertidas se registran como parte de la renta de la inversión directa. Se efectúa un asiento compensatorio, con signo contrario, en el rubro inversión directa de la *cuenta financiera* para reflejar el hecho de que aumentó la inversión del inversionista directo extranjero en la filial o sucursal extranjera. (En los capítulos XIV y XVIII se trata el tema de las utilidades reinvertidas.)

Otras variaciones que no entrañan transacciones

Reclasificación de activos y pasivos

32. En este *Manual*, la clasificación de los recursos financieros se basa en características que revelan los motivos del acreedor o del deudor. Si cambian los motivos, varían también dichas características, de modo que los recursos financieros quedan sujetos a reclasificación en función de dichos cambios. Cabe destacar la diferencia que se establece entre la *inversión directa* y otras clases de inversión. Por ejemplo, varios tenedores independientes de *inversiones de cartera* (en forma de acciones y otras participaciones de capital social emitidas por una sola empresa en el extranjero) pueden asociarse para adquirir una participación efectiva duradera en la dirección de la empresa. Sus tenencias reúnen así las condiciones de una *inversión directa* y el cambio de situación de la inversión puede registrarse como reclasificación. Dicha reclasificación se reflejará, al final del período en el que tuvo lugar, en la posición de inversión internacional, pero no en la balanza de pagos. Análogamente, ciertos activos frente a no residentes pueden pasar al control de las autoridades monetarias residentes o quedar fuera de su control, lo cual da lugar a una reclasificación entre *activos de reserva* y activos que no constituyen reservas.

Variaciones de valoración

33. El valor de los recursos reales y financieros está sujeto a constantes cambios, que pueden atribuirse a una de las dos, o a las dos, causas siguientes: i) el precio habitual al que se efectúan transacciones de ciertos tipos de recursos puede variar en relación con la moneda en que se cotiza dicho precio; ii) el tipo de cambio de la moneda en que se cotiza el precio puede variar en relación con la unidad de cuenta utilizada. Las variaciones de valoración no se registran en la balanza de pagos, pero sí en la posición de inversión internacional.

Anexo VI. Clasificación y componentes normalizados de la balanza de pagos

Este anexo es la reproducción del capítulo VIII del Manual de Balanza de Pagos, 5ª edición. *Los párrafos y los números de página citados en este anexo corresponden a los del* Manual.

Estructura y clasificación

139. En la segunda parte de este *Manual* se definen la estructura y la clasificación de las cuentas de la balanza de pagos y de la posición de inversión internacional. Abarca, asimismo, los componentes normalizados de ambos grupos de cuentas; se examina y explica la forma de preparar la **cuenta corriente**, la **cuenta de capital y financiera**, la información suplementaria seleccionada y la posición de inversión internacional.

140. Las estadísticas de balanza de pagos deben organizarse dentro de una estructura coherente para facilitar su utilización y adaptación para diferentes fines, tales como formulación de la política económica, estudios analíticos, proyecciones, comparaciones bilaterales de componentes específicos o transacciones totales, agregados regionales y mundiales, etc. (Véase el párrafo 7.)

141. La clasificación y la lista de componentes normalizados reflejan consideraciones de índole conceptual y práctica, toman en cuenta opiniones expresadas por expertos nacionales en balanza de pagos y, en general, concuerdan con el *SCN* y con la armonización entre la nueva clasificación de las transacciones internacionales de servicios y la Clasificación Central de Productos (CCP). (Véase el apéndice III.)

142. Se ha hecho todo lo posible para vincular la estructura de la ***cuenta de capital*** a las cuentas de renta y a la clasificación de la posición de inversión internacional. El objetivo es que muchos países puedan utilizarla como marco flexible para desarrollar a largo plazo sus estadísticas del sector externo. Si bien puede ocurrir que algunos países no puedan proporcionar datos para muchas partidas, este marco permitirá a otros países declarar datos adicionales.

Componentes normalizados

143. La determinación de los componentes normalizados (véase la lista al final de este capítulo) depende de una serie de factores, considerándose los más importantes los siguientes:

> La partida debe exhibir un comportamiento característico, que indique que influyen en ella un factor o una combinación de factores económicos distintos de los que influyen en las demás partidas o que responde de diferente manera ante el mismo factor o combinación de factores. En la balanza de pagos se trata precisamente de poner de manifiesto esta respuesta ante las influencias económicas.
>
> La partida debe ser importante para una serie de países, ya sea en función de su comportamiento (por ejemplo, variabilidad excepcional) o de su valor absoluto.
>
> Deberá ser posible obtener los datos estadísticos de la partida sin demasiada dificultad, aunque cabe tener en cuenta la conveniencia de recopilarlos en razón de las dos primeras consideraciones citadas.
>
> La partida deberá también ser necesaria para otros fines, por ejemplo, para incluirla en las cuentas nacionales o conciliarla con éstas. La lista de componentes normalizados no debe ser demasiado larga, dado el gran número de países, entre ellos muchos con sistemas estadísticos menos adelantados, a los cuales se solicita que presenten esos datos de manera uniforme.
>
> En la medida en que sea posible, los componentes normalizados deberán ser compatibles con otros sistemas estadísticos del FMI, el *SCN* y, en el caso específico de los ***servicios***, con la CCP.

144. La presentación de una lista de componentes normalizados no significa que las recomendaciones formuladas en este *Manual* tengan por objeto disuadir a los países de compilar y publicar otros datos de importancia nacional. Si se requieren mayores datos para comprender las circunstancias que rodean a determinados países o para analizar nuevas situaciones que puedan surgir, la información que solicite el FMI a los países miembros no se limitará a la lista de componentes normalizados. La información suplementaria también puede ser sumamente útil para verificar y conciliar las estadísticas de países que comercian entre sí y, por ejemplo, para analizar transacciones de financiamiento excepcional. (Véase el cuadro *Información suplementaria seleccionada* al final de este capítulo.) El personal del FMI consultará periódicamente con los países para decidir qué otros datos deberán presentar.

145. Es probable que sean pocos los países que cuentan con información significativa sobre todos los componentes normalizados. Tal vez los datos sobre varios de los componentes sólo puedan obtenerse en combinación con otros, o quizás un componente de menor importancia esté agrupado con otro más importante. No obstante, los componentes normalizados deberán declararse al FMI de la manera más completa y exacta que sea posible. En este sentido, los compiladores nacionales se encuentran en mejores condiciones que el personal del FMI para estimar y ajustar los componentes que no correspondan exactamente a los datos básicos de la economía declarante.

Errores y omisiones netos

146. Al aplicar los criterios recomendados en este *Manual*, se obtiene un conjunto coherente de asientos con signo positivo y negativo cuyo total neto es teóricamente igual a cero. En la práctica, sin embargo, una vez sumados todos los asientos, la balanza de pagos casi siempre arroja un crédito neto o un débito neto. Este saldo se debe a errores y omisiones en la compilación de las estadísticas, algunos de los cuales pueden tener relación con recomendaciones para una aproximación práctica a los criterios establecidos.

147. Por regla general, en el estado de balanza de pagos se presenta una partida separada de errores y omisiones netos, que algunos compiladores denominan partida equilibradora o discrepancia estadística, para compensar toda sobrestimación o subestimación de los componentes registrados. Así, si el saldo de estos componentes refleja un crédito, la partida de errores y omisiones netos aparece como un débito de igual valor, y viceversa.

148. Como algunos de los errores y omisiones que se producen al compilar los datos suelen compensarse entre sí, la magnitud de la partida residual no es necesariamente un indicio de la exactitud global del estado. Aun así, cuando el residuo neto es grande, es difícil interpretar un estado.

Clasificaciones principales

149. Los componentes normalizados, cuya lista figura al final de este capítulo, se clasifican en dos grupos principales de cuentas:

La **cuenta corriente**, que comprende ***bienes y servicios, renta*** y ***transferencias corrientes***.

La **cuenta de capital y financiera**, que se refiere a i) *transferencias de capital* y *adquisición/enajenación de activos no financieros no producidos* y ii) activos y pasivos financieros.

Esta presentación general refleja el uso común adoptado en la mayoría de los países en el transcurso de los años y un importante cambio que se introduce en este *Manual*. La cuenta de capital se denomina ahora **cuenta de capital y financiera**. A efectos de mantener la uniformidad con el *SCN*, se hace la distinción entre *transferencias de capital* y ***transferencias corrientes*** en las cuentas de la balanza de pagos, y se procura la concordancia con la cuenta de capital y la cuenta financiera del *SCN*.

150. Los asientos de la mayoría de las partidas de la lista de componentes normalizados de la **cuenta corriente** deberán mostrar créditos y débitos en cifras brutas. La mayoría de los asientos de la **cuenta de capital y financiera** deberán registrarse en cifras netas, es decir, cada componente se indicará únicamente como un crédito o como un débito. (Los tratamientos recomendados para determinadas partidas y las excepciones se describen en los capítulos correspondientes.) Las entradas de recursos reales, los aumentos de activos financieros y las disminuciones de pasivos deberán aparecer como débitos, en tanto que las salidas de recursos reales, las disminuciones de activos financieros y los aumentos de pasivos deberán figurar como créditos. Las transferencias de las secciones 1.C. y 2.A. deben ser numéricamente iguales, pero con signo contrario, a los asientos que saldan.

Clasificaciones detalladas

151. De acuerdo con los criterios establecidos en el párrafo 143, se han determinado las siguientes clasificaciones de los componentes normalizados. En los capítulos IX y XVI, respectivamente, se analizan la estructura y las características de la **cuenta corriente** y de la **cuenta de capital y financiera**, mencionándose los cambios significativos con respecto a la cuarta edición. En los capítulos X al XV se describen detalladamente los componentes normalizados de la **cuenta corriente**, y en los capítulos XVII al XXI, los de la **cuenta de capital y financiera** e *Instrumentos financieros derivados: Suplemento a la quinta edición (1993) del* Manual de Balanza de Pagos, 2000..

Cuenta corriente (1.)

152. En la **cuenta corriente** se registran todas las transacciones en valores económicos, salvo recursos financieros, que tienen lugar entre entidades residentes y no residentes; asimismo se registran los asientos compensatorios de los valores económicos corrientes que se suministren o adquieran sin un quid pro quo. Concretamente, las clasificaciones principales son ***bienes y servicios, renta*** y ***transferencias corrientes***.

Bienes y servicios (1.A.)
Bienes (1.A.a.)

153. *Mercancías generales* comprende la mayoría de los bienes muebles que los residentes exportan a no residentes, o importan de ellos, dando lugar, salvo algunas excepciones especificadas, a un traspaso de propiedad (efectivo o imputado).

154. *Bienes para transformación* comprende la exportación (o importación, en la economía compiladora) de bienes que cruzan la frontera para ser transformados en el extranjero y la reimportación (o exportación, en la economía compiladora) subsiguiente de dichos bienes, valorados en cifras brutas antes y después de su transformación. Esta partida constituye una excepción al criterio de traspaso de propiedad.

155. *Reparaciones de bienes* comprende las reparaciones de bienes efectuadas para no residentes o recibidas de ellos en embarcaciones, aeronaves, etc. Si bien el movimiento físico de estos bienes es similar al descrito en el párrafo 154, las reparaciones deben valorarse según el precio (derechos pagados o recibidos) de las mismas y no según el valor bruto de los bienes antes y después de las reparaciones.

156. *Bienes adquiridos en puerto por medios de transporte* comprende todos los bienes (como combustibles, víveres, pertrechos y suministros) que las empresas residentes/no residentes de transporte —aéreo, marítimo, etc.— adquieren en el extranjero/en la economía compiladora. Esta clasificación no cubre los servicios auxiliares prestados (remolque, mantenimiento, etc.), que se clasifican en la categoría *transportes*.

157. *Oro no monetario* comprende las exportaciones e importaciones de todo el oro que no esté en poder de las autoridades como activo de reserva (oro monetario). El *oro no monetario* se trata como cualquier otra mercancía y se subdivide, toda vez que sea posible, en oro que se mantiene como reserva de valor y oro para otros usos (industrial).

Servicios (1.A.b.)

158. *Transportes* abarca la mayoría de los servicios prestados por residentes a no residentes, y viceversa, que se incluían en las partidas embarques y otros transportes en la cuarta edición del *Manual*. En esta edición se excluye el seguro de fletes, que ahora forma parte de *servicios de seguros*. *Transportes* incluye el transporte de carga y de pasajeros por todos los medios, así como otros servicios de distribución y auxiliares, incluido el arrendamiento de equipo de transporte tripulado, con ciertas excepciones indicadas en los capítulos X, XI y XIII.

159. *Viajes* comprende bienes y servicios —incluidos los relacionados con salud y educación— adquiridos en una economía por viajeros no residentes (incluidos los excursionistas) para fines de negocios y para uso personal durante su estancia (inferior a un año) en esa economía. En *viajes* no se incluyen los servicios de transporte internacional de pasajeros, que forman parte de *transportes*. Los estudiantes y las personas que están bajo tratamiento médico se tratan como viajeros, independientemente de la duración de su estancia, en tanto que otros individuos —personal militar y de embajadas y trabajadores no residentes— no se consideran viajeros. No obstante, los gastos incurridos por los trabajadores no residentes se incluyen en *viajes*, mientras que los del personal militar y de embajadas se incluyen en *servicios del gobierno, n.i.o.p.* Estos casos se tratan en los capítulos XII y XIII.

160. *Servicios de comunicaciones* abarca las transacciones de comunicaciones entre residentes y no residentes, incluidos los servicios postales, de mensajería y de telecomunicaciones (transmisión de sonido, imagen y otra información por diferentes medios, así como el mantenimiento pertinente proporcionado por residentes a no residentes y viceversa).

161. *Servicios de construcción* incluye las obras de proyectos de construcción e instalación realizadas, con carácter temporal, en el extranjero/en la economía compiladora o en enclaves extraterritoriales por empresas residentes/no residentes y su personal. En este concepto no se incluyen las obras realizadas por una filial extranjera de una empresa residente o una oficina local no constituida en sociedad que sea equivalente siempre y cuando satisfaga ciertos criterios a una filial extranjera. En los capítulos IV y XIII se explica lo relativo a la residencia de esta clase de empresas.

162. *Servicios de seguros* comprende la contratación de seguros de no residentes con aseguradoras residentes y viceversa, incluidos los seguros de fletes (de bienes exportados e importados), los servicios correspondientes a otras clases de seguros directos (de vida y otros) y los servicios correspondientes a reaseguros. (En los párrafos 256 y 257 se describe el método que se emplea para calcular el valor de los servicios de seguros.)

163. *Servicios financieros* (salvo los relacionados con las empresas aseguradoras y las cajas de pensiones) abarca los servicios de intermediación financiera y los servicios auxiliares entre residentes y no residentes. Se incluyen las comisiones y derechos relacionados con cartas de crédito, líneas de crédito, arrendamiento financiero, transacciones en divisas, crédito al consumidor y a las empresas, corretaje, colocación y suscripción de valores, instrumentos de coberturas de riesgo de diferentes clases, etc. En los servicios auxiliares se incluyen los servicios de operación y reglamentación de los mercados financieros, servicios de custodia de valores, etc.

164. *Servicios de informática y de información* abarca las transacciones entre residentes y no residentes relacionadas con el asesoramiento en soporte técnico (*hardware*), aplicación de soporte lógico (*software*), servicios de información (procesamiento de datos, bases de datos, agencias noticiosas), y mantenimiento y reparación de computadores y equipo conexo.

165. *Regalías y derechos de licencia* comprende ingresos (exportación) y pagos (importación) de residentes y no residentes por: i) el uso autorizado de activos intangibles no financieros no producidos y derechos de propiedad como marcas registradas, derechos de autor, patentes, procesos, técnicas, diseños, derechos de fabricación, concesiones, etc., y ii) el uso, mediante convenios de licencia, de originales o prototipos producidos, como manuscritos, películas, etc.

166. *Otros servicios empresariales* prestados por residentes a no residentes y viceversa se refiere a servicios de compraventa y otros servicios relacionados con el comercio, servicios de arrendamiento de explotación y servicios empresariales, profesionales y técnicos varios. (Para información más detallada, véase el cuadro *Información suplementaria seleccionada* al final de este capítulo y los párrafos 261 a 264.)

167. *Servicios personales, culturales y recreativos* abarca i) servicios audiovisuales y conexos y ii) otros servicios culturales prestados por residentes a no residentes y viceversa. En el inciso i) se incluyen servicios relacionados con la producción de películas cinematográficas o videocintas, programas de radio y televisión y grabaciones musicales. (Ejemplos de estos servicios son los alquileres y honorarios percibidos por artistas, productores, etc. por sus producciones y por la venta de derechos de distribución a los medios de comunicación.) En el inciso ii) se incluyen otros servicios personales, culturales y recreativos, como los relacionados con bibliotecas, museos y otras actividades culturales y deportivas.

168. *Servicios del gobierno, n.i.o.p.* incluye todos los servicios (como los gastos incurridos por embajadas y consulados) relacionados con sectores gubernamentales u organismos internacionales y regionales y no clasificados en otras partidas.

Renta (1.B.)

169. *Remuneración de empleados* abarca los salarios, sueldos y otras prestaciones, en efectivo o en especie, incluidos los de los trabajadores fronterizos, de temporada y otros no residentes (por ejemplo, personal local de embajadas).

170. *Renta de la inversión* comprende los ingresos y pagos de la renta derivados, respectivamente, de las tenencias de activos financieros de residentes frente al exterior y de pasivos frente a no residentes, y se divide en renta de la inversión directa, renta de la inversión de cartera y renta de otra inversión. El componente inversión directa se desglosa en renta procedente de acciones y otras participaciones de capital (dividendos, utilidades de sucursales y utilidades reinvertidas) y en renta procedente de la deuda (intereses); la renta de la inversión de cartera se desglosa también en renta procedente de acciones y otras participaciones de capital (dividendos) y renta procedente de la deuda (intereses); en renta de otra inversión se registran los intereses devengados por otra inversión (préstamos, etc.) y, en principio, la renta imputada a las unidades familiares procedente de su participación neta de capital en las reservas de los seguros de vida y en las cajas de pensiones.

Transferencias corrientes (1.C.)

171. Las ***transferencias corrientes*** se distinguen de las *transferencias de capital*, que se incluyen en la **cuenta de capital y financiera** para guardar la uniformidad con el tratamiento de las transferencias que hace el *SCN*. Las transferencias son los asientos compensatorios de los traspasos de propiedad de recursos reales o financieros entre residentes y no residentes, ya sea en forma voluntaria u obligatoria, que no entrañan un quid pro quo en valor económico. Las ***transferencias corrientes*** comprenden todas aque-llas en las que **no tiene lugar**: i) un ***traspaso*** de propiedad de activos fijos; ii) un traspaso de fondos vinculados o condicionados a la adquisición o enajenación de activos fijos; iii) una condonación de un pasivo por parte de un acreedor, sin que se reciba a cambio una contrapartida. Todas éstas son *transferencias de capital*. En las ***transferencias corrientes*** se distinguen las del gobierno general (por ejemplo, cooperación internacional corriente entre diferentes go-biernos, pagos de impuestos corrientes sobre la renta y el patrimonio, etc.) y otras transferencias (por ejemplo, remesas de trabajadores, primas —menos cargos por servicio— e indemnizaciones de seguros excepto los de vida). En el capítulo XV se examina en forma detallada la distinción entre ***transferencias corrientes*** y *transferencias de capital*; véanse también los párrafos 175 y 344.

Cuenta de capital y financiera (2.)

172. Esta cuenta tiene dos componentes principales —la ***cuenta de capital*** y la ***cuenta financiera***— coincidiendo así con la clasificación adoptada en el *SCN*. Los activos representan créditos frente a no residentes y los pasivos representan deudas contraídas con no residentes. Las dos partes de una transacción de activos o pasivos son, generalmente, un residente y un no residente pero, en algunos casos, ambas partes pueden ser residentes o bien no residentes. (Véase el párrafo 318.)

173. Todas las variaciones de valoración y de otra índole de los activos y pasivos frente al exterior que no reflejen transacciones (véase el párrafo 310) se excluyen de la **cuenta de capital y financiera** pero figuran en la posición de inversión internacional. Los estados suplementarios identifican ciertas partidas que tienen interés analítico y que afectan a varias cuentas, como los pasivos que constituyen reservas de autoridades extranjeras y las transacciones de financiamiento excepcional, que se describen en el capítulo XXII.

174. La clasificación de la ***cuenta financiera*** y de los componentes de renta de la **cuenta corriente** están interrelacionadas y deben ser coherentes para facilitar el análisis, permitir una vinculación eficaz de la balanza de pagos con la posición de inversión internacional y mantener la compatibilidad con el *SCN* y con otros sistemas estadísticos del FMI.

Cuenta de capital (2.A.)

175. Los componentes principales de la ***cuenta de capital*** son las *transferencias de capital* y la *adquisición/enajenación de activos no financieros no producidos*. Las *transferencias de capital* son aquéllas en las que tiene lugar un traspaso de propiedad de un activo fijo, un traspaso de fondos vinculado o condicionado a la adquisición o enajenación de un activo fijo, o la cancelación de un pasivo por parte de un acreedor sin que se reciba a cambio una contrapartida. Las *transferencias de capital* se dividen en: i) las del gobierno general, que a su vez se subdividen en condonación de deudas y otras y ii) las de otros sectores, haciéndose el desglose en transferencias de emigrantes, condonación de deudas y otras. (Véase el capítulo XV, donde se explica la diferencia entre las *transferencias de capital* y las ***transferencias corrientes***.) La *adquisición/enajenación de activos no financieros no producidos* abarca, en general, los factores intangibles, como las patentes, arrendamientos u otros contratos transferibles, el buen nombre, etc. En esta partida no se incluyen las tierras situadas en un territorio económico específico, pero puede incluirse la compra o venta de tierras por una embajada. (Véase el párrafo 312.)

Cuenta financiera (2.B.)

176. La clasificación de los componentes normalizados de la cuenta financiera se basa en los siguientes criterios:

Todos los componentes se clasifican según la clase de inversión o haciéndose un desglose funcional (*inversión directa, inversión de cartera, instrumentos financieros derivados, otra inversión, activos de reserva*).

Para la categoría *inversión directa*, se hace la distinción según la dirección (en el extranjero o en la economía declarante); para los componentes acciones y otras participaciones de capital, otro capital.

En *inversión de cartera, instrumentos financieros derivados* y *otra inversión* se hace la distinción habitual entre activos y pasivos.

Cobra particular importancia en *inversión de cartera* y *otra inversión* la distinción por clases de instrumentos (títulos de participación en el capital, títulos de deuda, créditos comerciales, préstamos, moneda y depósitos, otros activos o pasivos). En este *Manual*, se incluyen en *inversión de cartera* los instrumentos tradicionales y nuevos del mercado monetario y otros instrumentos financieros básicos.

En *inversión de cartera, instrumentos financieros derivados* y *otra inversión*, se hace la distinción por sectores de acreedores internos en el caso de los activos o por sectores de deudores internos en el caso de los pasivos, a efectos de facilitar la vinculación con las cuentas de renta, la posición de inversión internacional, el *SCN* y otros sistemas estadísticos.

La distinción tradicional entre activos y pasivos a largo y a corto plazo, basada en un plazo contractual original de más de un año o de un año o menos, se efectúa solamente en *otra inversión*. En los últimos años, este desglose ha perdido importancia para muchas transacciones internas e internacionales. En consecuencia, tanto en el *SCN* como en este *Manual*, se da menos importancia a la diferencia entre largo y corto plazo que en ediciones previas. Sin embargo, debido a que el vencimiento sigue siendo importante para fines específicos —el análisis de la deuda externa, por ejemplo—, esta distinción se mantiene en el *Manual* para *otra inversión*.

177. *Inversión directa*, categoría que refleja el interés duradero de una entidad residente de una economía (inversionista directo) en una entidad residente de otra economía (empresa de inversión directa), abarca todas las transacciones entre inversionistas directos y empresas de inversión directa. Es decir, la *inversión directa* abarca la transacción inicial entre las dos partes y todas las transacciones subsiguientes que tienen lugar entre ellas y entre empresas filiales, constituidas o no en sociedad. Las transacciones de inversión directa (en el extranjero y en la economía declarante) se subclasifican en acciones y otras participaciones de capital, utilidades reinvertidas y otro capital (transacciones entre empresas afiliadas). En el caso de las acciones y otras participaciones de capital y otro capital, se hace la distinción entre activos y pasivos frente a empresas filiales y frente a inversionistas directos. Las transacciones entre bancos filiales y entre otros intermediarios financieros filiales se limitan al capital en acciones y al que está relacionado con la deuda permanente. (Véase el párrafo 372.)

178. *Inversión de cartera* comprende las transacciones en títulos de participación en el capital y títulos de deuda. Los títulos de deuda están subdivididos en bonos y pagarés e instrumentos del mercado monetario. Se incluyen, asimismo, varios instrumentos financieros nuevos, además de los derivados financieros, en las clasificaciones de instrumentos pertinentes.(Se excluyen las transacciones clasificadas como *inversión directa* y *activos de reserva*.)

179. La categoría de instrumentos financieros derivados abarca los instrumentos financieros vinculados a otros instrumentos financieros específicos o indicadores o productos primarios, a través de los cuales pueden negociarse en los mercados financieros, por derecho propio, riesgos financieros específicos (como riesgos de variaciones de tasas de interés, riesgo cambiario, riesgos de variaciones de las cotizaciones bursátiles y de los precios de los productos primarios, riesgo de crédito, etc.). Las transacciones de instrumentos financieros derivados deberán tratarse por separado y no como parte integral del valor de las transacciones a las que estén vinculadas.

180. *Otra inversión* incluye créditos comerciales a corto y largo plazo; préstamos (entre ellos, el uso de crédito del FMI, préstamos del FMI y préstamos relacionados con arrendamientos financieros); moneda y depósitos (transferibles y otros, como depósitos de ahorro y a plazo, acciones de asociaciones de ahorro y préstamo, acciones de cooperativas de crédito, etc.); otras cuentas por cobrar y por pagar. (Se excluyen las transacciones clasificadas como *inversión directa*.)

181. *Activos de reserva* comprende las transacciones de aquellos activos que las autoridades monetarias de una economía consideran disponibles para atender necesidades de financiamiento de la balanza de pagos y, en algunos casos, otras necesidades. Tal disponibilidad, en principio, no guarda estrecha relación con criterios formales tales como los de propiedad o moneda de denominación. Esta categoría se divide en oro monetario, DEG, posición de reserva en el FMI, activos en divisas (moneda, depósitos y valores) y otros activos.

182. La cobertura e identificación de los componentes de los *activos de reserva* están relacionadas con un concepto analítico, son en parte resultado de una decisión razonada y no siempre se prestan a la aplicación de criterios objetivos y formales ni a clasificaciones bien delimitadas respecto a la condicionalidad y otras consideraciones. A diferencia de la cuarta edición del *Manual*, en la quinta edición se excluyen las variaciones de valoración de los *activos de reserva* y sus contrapartidas. También se excluyen la asignación y cancelación de DEG, la monetización y desmonetización del oro y los asientos de contrapartida. Estas variaciones, que no constituyen transacciones, figuran en la posición de inversión internacional.

COUNTRY TABLES

Table 1. ANALYTIC PRESENTATION, 1994–2001
(Millions of U.S. dollars)

	Code		1994	1995	1996	1997	1998	1999	2000	2001
A. Current Account [1]	4 993	Z.	**−157.3**	**−11.5**	**−107.3**	**−272.2**	**−65.1**	**−155.4**	**−156.3**	**−220.3**
Goods: exports f.o.b.	2 100	. .	141.3	204.9	243.7	158.6	208.0	275.0	255.7	304.5
Goods: imports f.o.b.	3 100	. .	−601.0	−679.7	−922.0	−693.6	−811.7	−938.0	−1,070.0	−1,331.6
Balance on Goods	4 100	. .	*−459.7*	*−474.8*	*−678.3*	*−535.0*	*−603.6*	*−663.0*	*−814.3*	*−1,027.1*
Services: credit	2 200	. .	79.1	98.8	129.2	63.8	86.6	269.4	447.8	534.3
Services: debit	3 200	. .	−132.5	−156.5	−189.4	−115.2	−129.3	−163.1	−429.3	−444.1
Balance on Goods and Services	4 991	. .	*−513.1*	*−532.5*	*−738.5*	*−586.4*	*−646.3*	*−556.7*	*−795.8*	*−936.9*
Income: credit	2 300	. .	55.1	72.0	83.7	61.4	86.1	85.5	115.9	159.5
Income: debit	3 300	. .	−41.3	−28.4	−11.9	−11.8	−8.7	−10.2	−9.3	−13.5
Balance on Goods, Services, and Income	4 992	. .	*−499.3*	*−488.9*	*−666.7*	*−536.8*	*−569.0*	*−481.4*	*−689.2*	*−790.9*
Current transfers: credit	2 379	Z.	347.5	521.2	595.9	299.8	560.8	508.9	629.0	647.5
Current transfers: debit	3 379	. .	−5.5	−43.8	−36.5	−35.2	−56.9	−182.9	−96.1	−76.9
B. Capital Account [1]	4 994	Z.	**. . .**	**389.4**	**4.8**	**2.0**	**31.0**	**22.6**	**78.0**	**117.7**
Capital account: credit	2 994	Z.	. . .	389.4	4.8	2.0	31.0	22.6	78.0	117.7
Capital account: debit	3 994	. .	. . .	. . .	. . .	. . .	. . .	. . .	. . .	. . .
Total, Groups A Plus B	4 981	. .	*−157.3*	*377.9*	*−102.5*	*−270.2*	*−34.1*	*−132.8*	*−78.3*	*−102.6*
C. Financial Account [1]	4 995	W.	**40.2**	**−411.0**	**61.5**	**151.4**	**15.4**	**33.7**	**188.4**	**110.0**
Direct investment abroad	4 505	. .	. . .	. . .	. . .	. . .	. . .	. . .	. . .	. . .
Direct investment in Albania	4 555	Z.	53.0	70.0	90.1	47.5	45.0	41.2	143.0	207.3
Portfolio investment assets	4 602	. .	. . .	. . .	. . .	. . .	. . .	. . .	−25.0	−23.5
Equity securities	4 610	. .	. . .	. . .	. . .	. . .	. . .	. . .	. . .	. . .
Debt securities	4 619	. .	. . .	. . .	. . .	. . .	. . .	. . .	−25.0	−23.5
Portfolio investment liabilities	4 652	Z.	. . .	. . .	. . .	. . .	. . .	. . .	. . .	. . .
Equity securities	4 660	. .	. . .	. . .	. . .	. . .	. . .	. . .	. . .	. . .
Debt securities	4 669	Z.	. . .	. . .	. . .	. . .	. . .	. . .	. . .	. . .
Financial derivatives	4 910	. .	. . .	. . .	. . .	. . .	. . .	. . .	. . .	. . .
Financial derivatives assets	4 900	. .	. . .	. . .	. . .	. . .	. . .	. . .	. . .	. . .
Financial derivatives liabilities	4 905	. .	. . .	. . .	. . .	. . .	. . .	. . .	. . .	. . .
Other investment assets	4 703	. .	−97.3	−97.0	−138.6	59.8	−126.9	−130.1	−40.2	−197.2
Monetary authorities	4 701	. .	. . .	. . .	. . .	. . .	. . .	. . .	. . .	−1.8
General government	4 704	. .	. . .	. . .	. . .	. . .	. . .	. . .	. . .	. . .
Banks	4 705	. .	−22.9	−68.4	−110.5	81.5	−91.2	−96.8	−2.5	−132.3
Other sectors	4 728	. .	−74.4	−28.6	−28.1	−21.7	−35.7	−33.3	−37.7	−63.1
Other investment liabilities	4 753	W.	84.5	−384.0	110.0	44.1	97.3	122.6	110.6	123.4
Monetary authorities	4 753	WA	. . .	−9.1	10.4	16.0	10.4	8.9	−.2	−.3
General government	4 753	ZB	74.6	−404.5	61.3	40.3	81.3	97.9	90.8	86.1
Banks	4 753	ZC	2.6	−3.3	4.0	−.6	3.5	16.0	5.2	42.1
Other sectors	4 753	ZD	7.3	32.9	34.3	−11.6	2.0	−.2	14.8	−4.5
Total, Groups A Through C	4 983	. .	*−117.1*	*−33.1*	*−41.0*	*−118.8*	*−18.6*	*−99.1*	*110.1*	*7.4*
D. Net Errors and Omissions	4 998	. .	**123.9**	**53.7**	**96.9**	**158.4**	**71.1**	**206.2**	**9.8**	**139.3**
Total, Groups A Through D	4 984	. .	*6.8*	*20.6*	*55.9*	*39.5*	*52.4*	*107.1*	*119.9*	*146.7*
E. Reserves and Related Items	4 802	A.	**−6.8**	**−20.6**	**−55.9**	**−39.5**	**−52.4**	**−107.1**	**−119.9**	**−146.7**
Reserve assets	4 802	. .	−55.2	−30.5	−47.6	−43.7	−60.0	−124.7	−132.0	−145.1
Use of Fund credit and loans	4 766	. .	22.3	9.9	−8.3	4.2	6.8	17.5	12.1	−1.6
Exceptional financing	4 920	. .	26.1	. . .	. . .	. . .	.8	.1	. . .	. . .
Conversion rates: leks per U.S. dollar	0 101	. .	**94.62**	**92.70**	**104.50**	**148.93**	**150.63**	**137.69**	**143.71**	**143.48**

[1] Excludes components that have been classified in the categories of Group E.

Table 2. STANDARD PRESENTATION, 1994–2001
(Millions of U.S. dollars)

	Code		1994	1995	1996	1997	1998	1999	2000	2001
CURRENT ACCOUNT	4 993	. .	**–157.3**	**–11.5**	**–107.3**	**–272.2**	**–65.1**	**–155.4**	**–156.3**	**–220.3**
A. GOODS	4 100	. .	–459.7	–474.8	–678.3	–535.0	–603.6	–663.0	–814.3	–1,027.1
Credit	2 100	. .	**141.3**	**204.9**	**243.7**	**158.6**	**208.0**	**275.0**	**255.7**	**304.5**
General merchandise: exports f.o.b.	2 110	. .	141.3	204.9	243.7	90.9	100.7	91.7	95.2	109.5
Goods for processing: exports f.o.b.	2 150	. .	. . .	. . .	. . .	67.7	107.3	183.3	160.5	195.0
Repairs on goods	2 160	. .	. . .	. . .	. . .	. . .	. . .	. . .	. . .	. . .
Goods procured in ports by carriers	2 170	. .	. . .	. . .	. . .	. . .	. . .	. . .	. . .	. . .
Nonmonetary gold	2 180	. .	. . .	. . .	. . .	. . .	. . .	. . .	. . .	. . .
Debit	3 100	. .	**–601.0**	**–679.7**	**–922.0**	**–693.6**	**–811.7**	**–938.0**	**–1,070.0**	**–1,331.6**
General merchandise: imports f.o.b.	3 110	. .	–601.0	–679.7	–922.0	–570.6	–654.2	–783.1	–921.0	–1,151.0
Goods for processing: imports f.o.b.	3 150	. .	. . .	. . .	. . .	–123.0	–157.4	–154.9	–149.0	–180.6
Repairs on goods	3 160	. .	. . .	. . .	. . .	. . .	. . .	. . .	. . .	. . .
Goods procured in ports by carriers	3 170	. .	. . .	. . .	. . .	. . .	. . .	. . .	. . .	. . .
Nonmonetary gold	3 180	. .	. . .	. . .	. . .	. . .	. . .	. . .	. . .	. . .
B. SERVICES	4 200	. .	–53.4	–57.7	–60.2	–51.4	–42.7	106.3	18.5	90.2
Total credit	2 200	. .	*79.1*	*98.8*	*129.2*	*63.8*	*86.6*	*269.4*	*447.8*	*534.3*
Total debit	3 200	. .	*–132.5*	*–156.5*	*–189.4*	*–115.2*	*–129.3*	*–163.1*	*–429.3*	*–444.1*
Transportation services, credit	2 205	. .	**11.6**	**17.9**	**30.2**	**12.2**	**12.8**	**15.5**	**17.2**	**15.4**
Passenger	2 850	. .	*2.0*	*5.4*	*16.8*	*6.6*	*6.2*	*7.0*	*9.4*	*5.4*
Freight	2 851	. .	*6.5*	*10.2*	*9.2*	*4.7*	*6.2*	*8.4*	*7.7*	*9.2*
Other	2 852	. .	*3.1*	*2.3*	*4.2*	*.9*	*.3*	*.1*	*.1*	*.8*
Sea transport, passenger	2 207	. .	. . .	. . .	. . .	. . .	. . .	. . .	. . .	2.2
Sea transport, freight	2 208	. .	. . .	. . .	. . .	. . .	. . .	. . .	. . .	8.3
Sea transport, other	2 209	. .	. . .	. . .	. . .	. . .	. . .	. . .	. . .	. . .
Air transport, passenger	2 211	. .	. . .	. . .	. . .	. . .	. . .	. . .	. . .	3.2
Air transport, freight	2 212	. .	. . .	. . .	. . .	. . .	. . .	. . .	. . .	.9
Air transport, other	2 213	. .	. . .	. . .	. . .	. . .	. . .	. . .	. . .	. . .
Other transport, passenger	2 215	. .	. . .	. . .	. . .	. . .	. . .	. . .	. . .	. . .
Other transport, freight	2 216	. .	. . .	. . .	. . .	. . .	. . .	. . .	. . .	. . .
Other transport, other	2 217	. .	. . .	. . .	. . .	. . .	. . .	. . .	. . .	. . .
Transportation services, debit	3 205	. .	**–47.4**	**–60.3**	**–82.0**	**–55.3**	**–74.9**	**–90.1**	**–93.9**	**–107.0**
Passenger	3 850	. .	*–7.8*	*–11.6*	*–13.4*	*–7.9*	*–17.2*	*–23.4*	*–18.0*	*–12.1*
Freight	3 851	. .	*–38.9*	*–48.6*	*–65.4*	*–46.5*	*–57.7*	*–66.7*	*–75.9*	*–94.1*
Other	3 852	. .	*–.7*	*–.1*	*–3.2*	*–.9*	*–.1*	. . .	. . .	*–.8*
Sea transport, passenger	3 207	. .	. . .	. . .	. . .	. . .	. . .	. . .	. . .	–4.9
Sea transport, freight	3 208	. .	. . .	. . .	. . .	. . .	. . .	. . .	. . .	–84.8
Sea transport, other	3 209	. .	. . .	. . .	. . .	. . .	. . .	. . .	. . .	–.4
Air transport, passenger	3 211	. .	. . .	. . .	. . .	. . .	. . .	. . .	. . .	–7.2
Air transport, freight	3 212	. .	. . .	. . .	. . .	. . .	. . .	. . .	. . .	–9.3
Air transport, other	3 213	. .	. . .	. . .	. . .	. . .	. . .	. . .	. . .	–.4
Other transport, passenger	3 215	. .	. . .	. . .	. . .	. . .	. . .	. . .	. . .	. . .
Other transport, freight	3 216	. .	. . .	. . .	. . .	. . .	. . .	. . .	. . .	. . .
Other transport, other	3 217	. .	. . .	. . .	. . .	. . .	. . .	. . .	. . .	. . .
Travel, credit	2 236	. .	**58.4**	**65.1**	**76.8**	**27.1**	**53.9**	**211.0**	**389.4**	**446.4**
Business travel	2 237	. .	. . .	. . .	. . .	27.1	53.9	211.0	389.4	446.4
Personal travel	2 240	. .	. . .	. . .	. . .	. . .	. . .	. . .	. . .	. . .
Travel, debit	3 236	. .	**–5.6**	**–6.6**	**–11.8**	**–4.8**	**–5.3**	**–12.3**	**–272.2**	**–257.4**
Business travel	3 237	. .	. . .	. . .	. . .	–1.6	–1.7	–4.2	–90.7	–85.8
Personal travel	3 240	. .	. . .	. . .	. . .	–3.2	–3.6	–8.1	–181.5	171.6
Other services, credit	2 200	BA	**9.1**	**15.8**	**22.2**	**24.5**	**19.9**	**42.9**	**41.2**	**72.5**
Communications	2 245	. .	. . .	7.5	10.2	10.7	14.3	23.7	19.1	31.5
Construction	2 249	. .	. . .	. . .	. . .	. . .	. . .	. . .	. . .	. . .
Insurance	2 253	. .	.7	. . .	. . .	. . .	. . .	. . .	. . .	1.2
Financial	2 260	. .	. . .	1.3	4.7	1.3	.7	.9	.9	.5
Computer and information	2 262	. .	. . .	.8	.9	.8	1.0	2.1	2.2	. . .
Royalties and licence fees	2 266	. .	. . .	. . .	. . .	. . .	. . .	. . .	. . .	. . .
Other business services	2 268	. .	7.9	1.3	. . .	. . .	. . .	. . .	. . .	. . .
Personal, cultural, and recreational	2 287	. .	. . .	. . .	. . .	. . .	. . .	. . .	. . .	. . .
Government, n.i.e.	2 291	. .	.5	4.9	6.4	11.7	3.8	16.2	19.0	39.3
Other services, debit	3 200	BA	**–79.5**	**–89.6**	**–95.6**	**–55.1**	**–49.1**	**–60.7**	**–63.2**	**–79.7**
Communications	3 245	. .	. . .	–9.0	–10.1	–11.2	–12.9	–19.3	–12.1	–14.1
Construction	3 249	. .	. . .	. . .	. . .	. . .	. . .	. . .	. . .	. . .
Insurance	3 253	. .	–4.3	–21.1	–28.8	–20.7	–25.7	–29.5	–33.3	–43.2
Financial	3 260	. .	. . .	–.6	–1.4	–.6	–.5	–.9	–.8	. . .
Computer and information	3 262	. .	. . .	. . .	. . .	. . .	–.1	. . .	–.8	. . .
Royalties and licence fees	3 266	. .	. . .	. . .	. . .	. . .	. . .	. . .	. . .	. . .
Other business services	3 268	. .	–70.9	–.6	–.2	. . .	. . .	. . .	. . .	. . .
Personal, cultural, and recreational	3 287	. .	. . .	. . .	. . .	. . .	. . .	. . .	. . .	. . .
Government, n.i.e.	3 291	. .	–4.3	–58.3	–55.1	–22.6	–10.0	–11.0	–16.2	–22.4

Table 2 (Continued). STANDARD PRESENTATION, 1994–2001
(Millions of U.S. dollars)

	Code	1994	1995	1996	1997	1998	1999	2000	2001
C. INCOME	4 300 . .	13.8	43.6	71.8	49.6	77.4	75.3	106.6	146.0
Total credit	2 300 . .	*55.1*	*72.0*	*83.7*	*61.4*	*86.1*	*85.5*	*115.9*	*159.5*
Total debit	3 300 . .	*-41.3*	*-28.4*	*-11.9*	*-11.8*	*-8.7*	*-10.2*	*-9.3*	*-13.5*
Compensation of employees, credit	2 310 . .	**42.4**	**42.7**	**51.3**	**33.4**	**51.9**	**50.6**	**67.0**	**84.4**
Compensation of employees, debit	3 310 . .	...	...	...	...	...	...	...	...
Investment income, credit	2 320 . .	**12.7**	**29.3**	**32.4**	**28.0**	**34.2**	**34.9**	**48.9**	**75.1**
Direct investment income	2 330 . .	...	.2	...	...	...	...	...	...
Dividends and distributed branch profits	2 332 . .	...	...	...	...	...	...	...	...
Reinvested earnings and undistributed branch profits	2 333 . .	...	...	...	...	...	...	...	...
Income on debt (interest)	2 334 . .	...	...	...	...	...	...	...	...
Portfolio investment income	2 339 . .	...	...	...	...	...	...	...	...
Income on equity	2 340 . .	...	...	...	...	...	...	...	...
Income on bonds and notes	2 350 . .	...	...	...	...	...	...	...	...
Income on money market instruments	2 360 . .	...	...	...	...	...	...	...	...
Other investment income	2 370 . .	12.7	29.1	32.4	28.0	34.2	34.9	48.9	75.1
Investment income, debit	3 320 . .	**-41.3**	**-28.4**	**-11.9**	**-11.8**	**-8.7**	**-10.2**	**-9.3**	**-13.5**
Direct investment income	3 330 . .	...	-4.0	-2.0	-2.1	...	...	-.1	-.1
Dividends and distributed branch profits	3 332 . .	...	...	...	-2.1	...	...	-.1	-.1
Reinvested earnings and undistributed branch profits	3 333 . .	...	...	...	...	...	...	...	...
Income on debt (interest)	3 334 . .	...	...	...	...	...	...	...	...
Portfolio investment income	3 339 . .	...	...	...	...	...	...	...	...
Income on equity	3 340 . .	...	...	...	...	...	...	...	...
Income on bonds and notes	3 350 . .	...	...	...	...	...	...	...	...
Income on money market instruments	3 360 . .	...	...	...	...	...	...	...	...
Other investment income	3 370 . .	-41.3	-24.4	-9.9	-9.7	-8.7	-10.2	-9.2	-13.4
D. CURRENT TRANSFERS	4 379 . .	342.0	477.4	559.4	264.6	503.9	326.0	532.9	570.6
Credit	2 379 . .	**347.5**	**521.2**	**595.9**	**299.8**	**560.8**	**508.9**	**629.0**	**647.5**
General government	2 380 . .	82.8	136.6	96.3	32.7	87.7	151.8	97.2	32.4
Other sectors	2 390 . .	264.7	384.6	499.6	267.1	473.0	357.1	531.8	615.1
Workers' remittances	2 391 . .	264.7	384.6	499.6	266.9	452.3	356.6	530.8	614.9
Other current transfers	2 392 . .	...	...	...	.2	20.8	.5	1.0	.2
Debit	3 379 . .	**-5.5**	**-43.8**	**-36.5**	**-35.2**	**-56.9**	**-182.9**	**-96.1**	**-76.9**
General government	3 380 . .	-1.7	-8.1	-12.9	-3.8	-5.1	-2.8	-2.8	-4.4
Other sectors	3 390 . .	-3.8	-35.7	-23.6	-31.4	-51.7	-180.1	-93.3	-72.5
Workers' remittances	3 391 . .	...	...	...	...	...	...	...	...
Other current transfers	3 392 . .	-3.8	-35.7	-23.6	-31.4	-51.7	-180.1	-93.3	-72.5
CAPITAL AND FINANCIAL ACCOUNT	4 996 . .	**33.4**	**-42.2**	**10.4**	**113.9**	**-6.0**	**-50.8**	**146.5**	**81.0**
CAPITAL ACCOUNT	4 994 . .	...	**389.4**	**4.8**	**2.0**	**31.0**	**22.6**	**78.0**	**117.7**
Total credit	2 994 . .	...	*389.4*	*4.8*	*2.0*	*31.0*	*22.6*	*78.0*	*117.7*
Total debit	3 994 . .	...	...	...	...	...	...	...	...
Capital transfers, credit	2 400 . .	...	**389.4**	**4.8**	**2.0**	**31.0**	**22.6**	**78.0**	**117.7**
General government	2 401 . .	...	389.4	4.8	2.0	31.0	22.6	78.0	117.7
Debt forgiveness	2 402 . .	...	383.0	...	...	...	...	...	9.4
Other capital transfers	2 410 . .	...	6.4	4.8	2.0	31.0	22.6	78.0	108.3
Other sectors	2 430 . .	...	...	...	...	...	...	...	...
Migrants' transfers	2 431 . .	...	...	...	...	...	...	...	...
Debt forgiveness	2 432 . .	...	...	...	...	...	...	...	...
Other capital transfers	2 440 . .	...	...	...	...	...	...	...	...
Capital transfers, debit	3 400 . .	...	...	...	...	...	...	...	...
General government	3 401 . .	...	...	...	...	...	...	...	...
Debt forgiveness	3 402 . .	...	...	...	...	...	...	...	...
Other capital transfers	3 410 . .	...	...	...	...	...	...	...	...
Other sectors	3 430 . .	...	...	...	...	...	...	...	...
Migrants' transfers	3 431 . .	...	...	...	...	...	...	...	...
Debt forgiveness	3 432 . .	...	...	...	...	...	...	...	...
Other capital transfers	3 440 . .	...	...	...	...	...	...	...	...
Nonproduced nonfinancial assets, credit	2 480 . .	...	...	...	...	...	...	...	...
Nonproduced nonfinancial assets, debit	3 480 . .	...	...	...	...	...	...	...	...

Table 2 (Continued). STANDARD PRESENTATION, 1994–2001
(Millions of U.S. dollars)

	Code	1994	1995	1996	1997	1998	1999	2000	2001
FINANCIAL ACCOUNT	4 995 . .	**33.4**	**–431.6**	**5.6**	**111.9**	**–37.0**	**–73.4**	**68.5**	**–36.7**
A. DIRECT INVESTMENT	4 500 . .	53.0	70.0	90.1	47.5	45.0	41.2	143.0	207.3
Direct investment abroad	4 505 . .	**. . .**	**. . .**	**. . .**	**. . .**	**. . .**	**. . .**	**. . .**	**. . .**
Equity capital	4 510 . .	. . .	. . .	. . .	. . .	. . .	. . .	. . .	. . .
Claims on affiliated enterprises	4 515 . .	. . .	. . .	. . .	. . .	. . .	. . .	. . .	. . .
Liabilities to affiliated enterprises	4 520 . .	. . .	. . .	. . .	. . .	. . .	. . .	. . .	. . .
Reinvested earnings	4 525 . .	. . .	. . .	. . .	. . .	. . .	. . .	. . .	. . .
Other capital	4 530 . .	. . .	. . .	. . .	. . .	. . .	. . .	. . .	. . .
Claims on affiliated enterprises	4 535 . .	. . .	. . .	. . .	. . .	. . .	. . .	. . .	. . .
Liabilities to affiliated enterprises	4 540 . .	. . .	. . .	. . .	. . .	. . .	. . .	. . .	. . .
Direct investment in Albania	4 555 . .	**53.0**	**70.0**	**90.1**	**47.5**	**45.0**	**41.2**	**143.0**	**207.3**
Equity capital	4 560 . .	53.0	70.0	90.1	47.5	45.0	41.2	143.0	207.3
Claims on direct investors	4 565 . .	. . .	. . .	. . .	. . .	. . .	. . .	. . .	. . .
Liabilities to direct investors	4 570 . .	. . .	70.0	90.1	47.5	45.0	41.2	143.0	207.3
Reinvested earnings	4 575 . .	. . .	. . .	. . .	. . .	. . .	. . .	. . .	. . .
Other capital	4 580 . .	. . .	. . .	. . .	. . .	. . .	. . .	. . .	. . .
Claims on direct investors	4 585 . .	. . .	. . .	. . .	. . .	. . .	. . .	. . .	. . .
Liabilities to direct investors	4 590 . .	. . .	. . .	. . .	. . .	. . .	. . .	. . .	. . .
B. PORTFOLIO INVESTMENT	4 600 . .	. . .	. . .	. . .	. . .	. . .	. . .	–25.0	–23.5
Assets	4 602 . .	**. . .**	**. . .**	**. . .**	**. . .**	**. . .**	**. . .**	**–25.0**	**–23.5**
Equity securities	4 610 . .	. . .	. . .	. . .	. . .	. . .	. . .	. . .	. . .
Monetary authorities	4 611 . .	. . .	. . .	. . .	. . .	. . .	. . .	. . .	. . .
General government	4 612 . .	. . .	. . .	. . .	. . .	. . .	. . .	. . .	. . .
Banks	4 613 . .	. . .	. . .	. . .	. . .	. . .	. . .	. . .	. . .
Other sectors	4 614 . .	. . .	. . .	. . .	. . .	. . .	. . .	. . .	. . .
Debt securities	4 619 . .	. . .	. . .	. . .	. . .	. . .	. . .	–25.0	–23.5
Bonds and notes	4 620 . .	. . .	. . .	. . .	. . .	. . .	. . .	–25.0	–23.5
Monetary authorities	4 621 . .	. . .	. . .	. . .	. . .	. . .	. . .	. . .	. . .
General government	4 622 . .	. . .	. . .	. . .	. . .	. . .	. . .	. . .	. . .
Banks	4 623 . .	. . .	. . .	. . .	. . .	. . .	. . .	–25.0	–23.5
Other sectors	4 624 . .	. . .	. . .	. . .	. . .	. . .	. . .	. . .	. . .
Money market instruments	4 630 . .	. . .	. . .	. . .	. . .	. . .	. . .	. . .	. . .
Monetary authorities	4 631 . .	. . .	. . .	. . .	. . .	. . .	. . .	. . .	. . .
General government	4 632 . .	. . .	. . .	. . .	. . .	. . .	. . .	. . .	. . .
Banks	4 633 . .	. . .	. . .	. . .	. . .	. . .	. . .	. . .	. . .
Other sectors	4 634 . .	. . .	. . .	. . .	. . .	. . .	. . .	. . .	. . .
Liabilities	4 652 . .	**. . .**	**. . .**	**. . .**	**. . .**	**. . .**	**. . .**	**. . .**	**. . .**
Equity securities	4 660 . .	. . .	. . .	. . .	. . .	. . .	. . .	. . .	. . .
Banks	4 663 . .	. . .	. . .	. . .	. . .	. . .	. . .	. . .	. . .
Other sectors	4 664 . .	. . .	. . .	. . .	. . .	. . .	. . .	. . .	. . .
Debt securities	4 669 . .	. . .	. . .	. . .	. . .	. . .	. . .	. . .	. . .
Bonds and notes	4 670 . .	. . .	. . .	. . .	. . .	. . .	. . .	. . .	. . .
Monetary authorities	4 671 . .	. . .	. . .	. . .	. . .	. . .	. . .	. . .	. . .
General government	4 672 . .	. . .	. . .	. . .	. . .	. . .	. . .	. . .	. . .
Banks	4 673 . .	. . .	. . .	. . .	. . .	. . .	. . .	. . .	. . .
Other sectors	4 674 . .	. . .	. . .	. . .	. . .	. . .	. . .	. . .	. . .
Money market instruments	4 680 . .	. . .	. . .	. . .	. . .	. . .	. . .	. . .	. . .
Monetary authorities	4 681 . .	. . .	. . .	. . .	. . .	. . .	. . .	. . .	. . .
General government	4 682 . .	. . .	. . .	. . .	. . .	. . .	. . .	. . .	. . .
Banks	4 683 . .	. . .	. . .	. . .	. . .	. . .	. . .	. . .	. . .
Other sectors	4 684 . .	. . .	. . .	. . .	. . .	. . .	. . .	. . .	. . .
C. FINANCIAL DERIVATIVES	4 910 . .	. . .	. . .	. . .	. . .	. . .	. . .	. . .	. . .
Monetary authorities	4 911 . .	. . .	. . .	. . .	. . .	. . .	. . .	. . .	. . .
General government	4 912 . .	. . .	. . .	. . .	. . .	. . .	. . .	. . .	. . .
Banks	4 913 . .	. . .	. . .	. . .	. . .	. . .	. . .	. . .	. . .
Other sectors	4 914 . .	. . .	. . .	. . .	. . .	. . .	. . .	. . .	. . .
Assets	4 900 . .	**. . .**	**. . .**	**. . .**	**. . .**	**. . .**	**. . .**	**. . .**	**. . .**
Monetary authorities	4 901 . .	. . .	. . .	. . .	. . .	. . .	. . .	. . .	. . .
General government	4 902 . .	. . .	. . .	. . .	. . .	. . .	. . .	. . .	. . .
Banks	4 903 . .	. . .	. . .	. . .	. . .	. . .	. . .	. . .	. . .
Other sectors	4 904 . .	. . .	. . .	. . .	. . .	. . .	. . .	. . .	. . .
Liabilities	4 905 . .	**. . .**	**. . .**	**. . .**	**. . .**	**. . .**	**. . .**	**. . .**	**. . .**
Monetary authorities	4 906 . .	. . .	. . .	. . .	. . .	. . .	. . .	. . .	. . .
General government	4 907 . .	. . .	. . .	. . .	. . .	. . .	. . .	. . .	. . .
Banks	4 908 . .	. . .	. . .	. . .	. . .	. . .	. . .	. . .	. . .
Other sectors	4 909 . .	. . .	. . .	. . .	. . .	. . .	. . .	. . .	. . .

Table 2 (Concluded). STANDARD PRESENTATION, 1994–2001

(Millions of U.S. dollars)

	Code		1994	1995	1996	1997	1998	1999	2000	2001
D. OTHER INVESTMENT	4 700	. .	35.6	–471.1	–36.9	108.1	–22.0	10.1	82.5	–75.4
Assets	4 703	. .	**–97.3**	**–97.0**	**–138.6**	**59.8**	**–126.9**	**–130.1**	**–40.2**	**–197.2**
Trade credits	4 706	. .	. . .	. . .	. . .	. . .	. . .	. . .	. . .	. . .
General government	4 707	. .	. . .	. . .	. . .	. . .	. . .	. . .	. . .	. . .
of which: Short-term	4 709	. .	. . .	. . .	. . .	. . .	. . .	. . .	. . .	. . .
Other sectors	4 710	. .	. . .	. . .	. . .	. . .	. . .	. . .	. . .	. . .
of which: Short-term	4 712	. .	. . .	. . .	. . .	. . .	. . .	. . .	. . .	. . .
Loans	4 714	. .	. . .	. . .	. . .	. . .	. . .	. . .	. . .	–17.1
Monetary authorities	4 715	. .	. . .	. . .	. . .	. . .	. . .	. . .	. . .	. . .
of which: Short-term	4 718	. .	. . .	. . .	. . .	. . .	. . .	. . .	. . .	. . .
General government	4 719	. .	. . .	. . .	. . .	. . .	. . .	. . .	. . .	. . .
of which: Short-term	4 721	. .	. . .	. . .	. . .	. . .	. . .	. . .	. . .	. . .
Banks	4 722	. .	. . .	. . .	. . .	. . .	. . .	. . .	. . .	. . .
of which: Short-term	4 724	. .	. . .	. . .	. . .	. . .	. . .	. . .	. . .	. . .
Other sectors	4 725	. .	. . .	. . .	. . .	. . .	. . .	. . .	. . .	–17.1
of which: Short-term	4 727	. .	. . .	. . .	. . .	. . .	. . .	. . .	. . .	*–17.1*
Currency and deposits	4 730	. .	–102.3	–96.8	–137.3	60.6	–126.9	–130.1	–40.2	–180.1
Monetary authorities	4 731	. .	. . .	. . .	. . .	. . .	. . .	. . .	. . .	–1.8
General government	4 732	. .	. . .	. . .	. . .	. . .	. . .	. . .	. . .	. . .
Banks	4 733	. .	–22.9	–68.2	–110.5	81.5	–91.2	–96.8	–2.5	–132.3
Other sectors	4 734	. .	–79.4	–28.6	–26.8	–20.9	–35.7	–33.3	–37.7	–46.0
Other assets	4 736	. .	5.0	–.2	–1.3	–.8	. . .	. . .	. . .	. . .
Monetary authorities	4 737	. .	. . .	. . .	. . .	. . .	. . .	. . .	. . .	. . .
of which: Short-term	4 739	. .	. . .	. . .	. . .	. . .	. . .	. . .	. . .	. . .
General government	4 740	. .	. . .	. . .	. . .	. . .	. . .	. . .	. . .	. . .
of which: Short-term	4 742	. .	. . .	. . .	. . .	. . .	. . .	. . .	. . .	. . .
Banks	4 743	. .	. . .	–.2	. . .	. . .	. . .	. . .	. . .	. . .
of which: Short-term	4 745	. .	. . .	*–.2*	. . .	. . .	. . .	. . .	. . .	. . .
Other sectors	4 746	. .	5.0	. . .	–1.3	–.8	. . .	. . .	. . .	. . .
of which: Short-term	4 748	. .	. . .	. . .	*–1.3*	*–.8*	. . .	. . .	. . .	. . .
Liabilities	4 753	. .	**132.9**	**–374.1**	**101.7**	**48.3**	**104.8**	**140.2**	**122.7**	**121.8**
Trade credits	4 756	. .	. . .	7.8	25.7	–16.0	4.0	–2.8	22.6	–2.9
General government	4 757	. .	. . .	. . .	. . .	. . .	. . .	. . .	. . .	. . .
of which: Short-term	4 759	. .	. . .	. . .	. . .	. . .	. . .	. . .	. . .	. . .
Other sectors	4 760	. .	. . .	7.8	25.7	–16.0	4.0	–2.8	22.6	–2.9
of which: Short-term	4 762	. .	. . .	*7.8*	*25.7*	*–16.0*	*4.0*	*–2.8*	*22.6*	*–2.9*
Loans	4 764	. .	104.2	89.3	72.4	62.8	98.4	130.8	101.4	82.6
Monetary authorities	4 765	. .	22.3	9.9	1.6	18.8	17.7	26.3	11.9	–1.9
of which: Use of Fund credit and loans from the Fund	4 766	. .	*22.3*	*9.9*	*–8.3*	*4.2*	*6.8*	*17.5*	*12.1*	*–1.6*
of which: Short-term	4 768	. .	. . .	. . .	. . .	. . .	. . .	. . .	. . .	. . .
General government	4 769	. .	74.6	57.5	60.9	40.6	81.3	97.9	90.8	86.1
of which: Short-term	4 771	. .	. . .	. . .	. . .	. . .	. . .	. . .	. . .	. . .
Banks	4 772	. .	. . .	.1	1.7	.4	. . .	. . .	. . .	. . .
of which: Short-term	4 774	. .	. . .	. . .	. . .	. . .	. . .	. . .	. . .	. . .
Other sectors	4 775	. .	7.3	21.8	8.2	3.0	–.6	6.6	–1.3	–1.6
of which: Short-term	4 777	. .	*7.3*	. . .	. . .	. . .	. . .	. . .	. . .	. . .
Currency and deposits	4 780	. .	. . .	–3.4	2.8	.4	3.0	16.1	5.2	42.1
Monetary authorities	4 781	. .	. . .	. . .	.5	1.4	–.5	.1	. . .	. . .
General government	4 782	. .	. . .	. . .	. . .	. . .	. . .	. . .	. . .	. . .
Banks	4 783	. .	. . .	–3.4	2.3	–1.0	3.5	16.0	5.2	42.1
Other sectors	4 784	. .	. . .	. . .	. . .	. . .	. . .	. . .	. . .	. . .
Other liabilities	4 786	. .	28.7	–467.8	.8	1.1	–.6	–3.9	–6.5	. . .
Monetary authorities	4 787	. .	. . .	–9.1	. . .	. . .	.3	.1	. . .	. . .
of which: Short-term	4 789	. .	. . .	*–9.1*	. . .	. . .	*.3*	*.1*	. . .	. . .
General government	4 790	. .	26.1	–462.0	.4	–.3	.5	. . .	. . .	. . .
of which: Short-term	4 792	. .	*26.1*	*–462.0*	*.4*	*–.3*	*.5*	. . .	. . .	. . .
Banks	4 793	. .	2.6	. . .	. . .	. . .	. . .	. . .	. . .	. . .
of which: Short-term	4 795	. .	. . .	. . .	. . .	. . .	. . .	. . .	. . .	. . .
Other sectors	4 796	. .	. . .	3.3	.4	1.4	–1.4	–4.0	–6.5	. . .
of which: Short-term	4 798	. .	. . .	*3.3*	*.4*	*1.4*	*–1.4*	*–4.0*	*–6.5*	. . .
E. RESERVE ASSETS	4 802	. .	–55.2	–30.5	–47.6	–43.7	–60.0	–124.7	–132.0	–145.1
Monetary gold	4 812	. .	. . .	. . .	. . .	. . .	. . .	. . .	. . .	. . .
Special drawing rights	4 811	. .	–.3	.1	–.6	.1	–57.3	–16.9	–3.5	–8.4
Reserve position in the Fund	4 810	. .	. . .	. . .	. . .	. . .	. . .	–4.7	. . .	. . .
Foreign exchange	4 803	. .	–54.9	–30.6	–47.0	–43.8	–2.7	–103.0	–128.5	–136.7
Other claims	4 813	. .	. . .	. . .	. . .	. . .	. . .	. . .	. . .	. . .
NET ERRORS AND OMISSIONS	4 998	. .	**123.9**	**53.7**	**96.9**	**158.4**	**71.1**	**206.2**	**9.8**	**139.3**

Part 3 of the *Yearbook* contains descriptions of the methodologies, compilation practices, and sources used to compile these data.

Table 1. ANALYTIC PRESENTATION, 1994–2001
(Millions of U.S. dollars)

	Code	1994	1995	1996	1997	1998	1999	2000	2001
A. Current Account [1]	4 993 Z.	**–339.8**	**–295.0**	**3,266.4**	**–883.4**	**–1,867.2**	**–1,710.4**	**795.8**	**. . .**
Goods: exports f.o.b	2 100 . .	3,016.6	3,722.7	5,095.0	5,006.8	3,542.9	5,156.5	7,920.7	. . .
Goods: imports f.o.b	3 100 . .	–1,454.1	–1,467.7	–2,040.5	–2,597.0	–2,079.4	–3,109.1	–3,039.5	. . .
Balance on Goods	4 100 . .	*1,562.5*	*2,255.0*	*3,054.5*	*2,409.8*	*1,463.5*	*2,047.4*	*4,881.2*	. . .
Services: credit	2 200 . .	150.2	113.1	267.7	138.6	121.8	153.0	267.3	. . .
Services: debit	3 200 . .	–1,562.9	–2,051.4	–2,423.3	–2,605.4	–2,635.3	–2,594.6	–2,699.4	. . .
Balance on Goods and Services	4 991 . .	*149.8*	*316.7*	*898.9*	*–57.0*	*–1,050.0*	*–394.2*	*2,449.1*	. . .
Income: credit	2 300 . .	13.0	15.9	43.3	112.1	34.5	24.1	34.4	. . .
Income: debit	3 300 . .	–747.7	–783.2	–1,516.7	–1,033.1	–1,003.2	–1,396.1	–1,715.2	. . .
Balance on Goods, Services, and Income	4 992 . .	*–584.9*	*–450.6*	*–574.4*	*–978.0*	*–2,018.7*	*–1,766.2*	*768.3*	. . .
Current transfers: credit	2 379 Z.	333.2	312.2	3,949.4	176.4	238.2	154.5	123.5	. . .
Current transfers: debit	3 379 . .	–88.1	–156.7	–108.6	–81.8	–86.7	–98.7	–95.9	. . .
B. Capital Account [1]	4 994 Z.	**. . .**	**. . .**	**. . .**	**11.2**	**8.4**	**6.8**	**18.3**	**. . .**
Capital account: credit	2 994 Z.	. . .	. . .	. . .	11.2	8.4	6.8	18.3	. . .
Capital account: debit	3 994 . .	. . .	. . .	. . .	. . .	. . .	. . .	. . .	. . .
Total, Groups A Plus B	4 981 . .	*–339.8*	*–295.0*	*3,266.4*	*–872.2*	*–1,858.8*	*–1,703.7*	*814.1*	. . .
C. Financial Account [1]	4 995 W.	**–443.4**	**–924.8**	**–654.5**	**489.5**	**368.4**	**1,739.6**	**–494.1**	**. . .**
Direct investment abroad	4 505 . .	. . .	. . .	. . .	. . .	. . .	. . .	. . .	. . .
Direct investment in Angola	4 555 Z.	170.3	472.4	180.6	411.7	1,114.0	2,471.5	878.6	. . .
Portfolio investment assets	4 602 . .	. . .	. . .	. . .	. . .	. . .	. . .	. . .	. . .
Equity securities	4 610 . .	. . .	. . .	. . .	. . .	. . .	. . .	. . .	. . .
Debt securities	4 619 . .	. . .	. . .	. . .	. . .	. . .	. . .	. . .	. . .
Portfolio investment liabilities	4 652 Z.	. . .	. . .	. . .	. . .	. . .	. . .	. . .	. . .
Equity securities	4 660 . .	. . .	. . .	. . .	. . .	. . .	. . .	. . .	. . .
Debt securities	4 669 Z.	. . .	. . .	. . .	. . .	. . .	. . .	. . .	. . .
Financial derivatives	4 910 . .	. . .	. . .	. . .	. . .	. . .	. . .	. . .	. . .
Financial derivatives assets	4 900 . .	. . .	. . .	. . .	. . .	. . .	. . .	. . .	. . .
Financial derivatives liabilities	4 905 . .	. . .	. . .	. . .	. . .	. . .	. . .	. . .	. . .
Other investment assets	4 703 . .	214.1	–168.4	–327.6	–330.7	–40.8	–186.2	–702.1	. . .
Monetary authorities	4 701 . .	. . .	. . .	. . .	. . .	. . .	. . .	. . .	. . .
General government	4 704 . .	. . .	. . .	. . .	. . .	. . .	. . .	. . .	. . .
Banks	4 705 . .	. . .	–4.4	–48.8	. . .	. . .	. . .	. . .	. . .
Other sectors	4 728 . .	214.1	–164.1	–278.8	–330.7	–40.8	–186.2	–702.1	. . .
Other investment liabilities	4 753 W.	–827.8	–1,228.8	–507.4	408.5	–704.8	–545.7	–670.6	. . .
Monetary authorities	4 753 WA	–185.9	–114.3	–143.9	39.5	–303.0	–272.2	17.3	. . .
General government	4 753 ZB	–792.6	–778.1	–202.7	–69.0	–478.6	–180.5	–713.7	. . .
Banks	4 753 ZC	. . .	. . .	–1.6	4.8	2.4	3.5	. . .	. . .
Other sectors	4 753 ZD	150.7	–336.4	–159.2	433.2	74.4	–96.5	25.8	. . .
Total, Groups A Through C	4 983 . .	*–783.2*	*–1,219.9*	*2,611.9*	*–382.7*	*–1,490.4*	*35.9*	*320.0*	. . .
D. Net Errors and Omissions	4 998 . .	**–244.5**	**–19.4**	**149.2**	**–182.1**	**378.4**	**–78.8**	**–50.5**	**. . .**
Total, Groups A Through D	4 984 . .	*–1,027.7*	*–1,239.3*	*2,761.0*	*–564.8*	*–1,112.0*	*–42.9*	*269.5*	. . .
E. Reserves and Related Items	4 802 A.	**1,027.7**	**1,239.3**	**–2,761.0**	**564.8**	**1,112.0**	**42.9**	**–269.5**	**. . .**
Reserve assets	4 802 . .	14.2	–30.7	–330.3	162.6	318.0	–530.1	–631.3	. . .
Use of Fund credit and loans	4 766 . .	. . .	. . .	. . .	. . .	. . .	. . .	. . .	. . .
Exceptional financing	4 920 . .	1,013.5	1,270.0	–2,430.7	402.2	794.0	573.0	361.8	. . .
Conversion rates: kwanzas per U.S. dollar	0 101 . .	**. . .**	**.003**	**.128**	**.229**	**.393**	**2.791**	**10.041**	**22.058**

[1] Excludes components that have been classified in the categories of Group E.

Table 2. STANDARD PRESENTATION, 1994–2001

(Millions of U.S. dollars)

	Code	1994	1995	1996	1997	1998	1999	2000	2001
CURRENT ACCOUNT	4 993 . .	**–339.8**	**–295.0**	**3,266.4**	**–883.4**	**–1,867.2**	**–1,710.4**	**795.8**	. . .
A. GOODS	4 100 . .	1,562.5	2,255.0	3,054.5	2,409.8	1,463.5	2,047.4	4,881.2	. . .
Credit	2 100 . .	**3,016.6**	**3,722.7**	**5,095.0**	**5,006.8**	**3,542.9**	**5,156.5**	**7,920.7**	. . .
General merchandise: exports f.o.b.	2 110 . .	3,016.6	3,722.7	5,095.0	5,006.8	3,542.9	5,156.5	7,920.7	. . .
Goods for processing: exports f.o.b.	2 150 . .	. . .	. . .	. . .	. . .	. . .	. . .	. . .	. . .
Repairs on goods	2 160 . .	. . .	. . .	. . .	. . .	. . .	. . .	. . .	. . .
Goods procured in ports by carriers	2 170 . .	. . .	. . .	. . .	. . .	. . .	. . .	. . .	. . .
Nonmonetary gold	2 180 . .	. . .	. . .	. . .	. . .	. . .	. . .	. . .	. . .
Debit	3 100 . .	**–1,454.1**	**–1,467.7**	**–2,040.5**	**–2,597.0**	**–2,079.4**	**–3,109.1**	**–3,039.5**	. . .
General merchandise: imports f.o.b.	3 110 . .	–1,454.1	–1,467.7	–2,040.5	–2,597.0	–2,079.4	–3,109.1	–3,039.5	. . .
Goods for processing: imports f.o.b.	3 150 . .	. . .	. . .	. . .	. . .	. . .	. . .	. . .	. . .
Repairs on goods	3 160 . .	. . .	. . .	. . .	. . .	. . .	. . .	. . .	. . .
Goods procured in ports by carriers	3 170 . .	. . .	. . .	. . .	. . .	. . .	. . .	. . .	. . .
Nonmonetary gold	3 180 . .	. . .	. . .	. . .	. . .	. . .	. . .	. . .	. . .
B. SERVICES	4 200 . .	–1,412.7	–1,938.3	–2,155.6	–2,466.8	–2,513.5	–2,441.6	–2,432.1	. . .
Total credit	2 200 . .	*150.2*	*113.1*	*267.7*	*138.6*	*121.8*	*153.0*	*267.3*	. . .
Total debit	3 200 . .	*–1,562.9*	*–2,051.4*	*–2,423.3*	*–2,605.4*	*–2,635.3*	*–2,594.6*	*–2,699.4*	. . .
Transportation services, credit	2 205 . .	**32.2**	**35.9**	**81.5**	**44.8**	**55.3**	**47.0**	**16.1**	. . .
Passenger	2 850 . .	*10.6*	*17.0*	*28.9*	*15.3*	*30.9*	*17.6*	*16.1*	. . .
Freight	2 851 . .	*1.3*	. . .	*23.4*	*.1*	*1.4*	. . .	. . .	. . .
Other	2 852 . .	*20.3*	*19.0*	*29.1*	*29.5*	*23.0*	*29.4*	. . .	. . .
Sea transport, passenger	2 207 . .	. . .	. . .	. . .	. . .	. . .	. . .	. . .	. . .
Sea transport, freight	2 208 . .	. . .	. . .	. . .	. . .	. . .	. . .	. . .	. . .
Sea transport, other	2 209 . .	. . .	. . .	. . .	. . .	. . .	. . .	. . .	. . .
Air transport, passenger	2 211 . .	. . .	. . .	. . .	. . .	. . .	. . .	. . .	. . .
Air transport, freight	2 212 . .	. . .	. . .	. . .	. . .	. . .	. . .	. . .	. . .
Air transport, other	2 213 . .	. . .	. . .	. . .	. . .	. . .	. . .	. . .	. . .
Other transport, passenger	2 215 . .	. . .	. . .	. . .	. . .	. . .	. . .	. . .	. . .
Other transport, freight	2 216 . .	. . .	. . .	. . .	. . .	. . .	. . .	. . .	. . .
Other transport, other	2 217 . .	. . .	. . .	. . .	. . .	. . .	. . .	. . .	. . .
Transportation services, debit	3 205 . .	**–313.5**	**–303.3**	**–310.7**	**–381.3**	**–316.9**	**–395.1**	**–311.3**	. . .
Passenger	3 850 . .	*–35.2*	*–37.8*	*–37.4*	*–27.2*	*–20.5*	*–14.6*	*–10.0*	. . .
Freight	3 851 . .	*–137.1*	*–154.9*	*–198.6*	*–270.4*	*–188.0*	*–267.9*	*–211.2*	. . .
Other	3 852 . .	*–141.2*	*–110.6*	*–74.7*	*–83.7*	*–108.4*	*–112.6*	*–90.1*	. . .
Sea transport, passenger	3 207 . .	. . .	. . .	. . .	. . .	. . .	. . .	. . .	. . .
Sea transport, freight	3 208 . .	. . .	. . .	. . .	. . .	. . .	. . .	. . .	. . .
Sea transport, other	3 209 . .	. . .	. . .	. . .	. . .	. . .	. . .	. . .	. . .
Air transport, passenger	3 211 . .	. . .	. . .	. . .	. . .	. . .	. . .	. . .	. . .
Air transport, freight	3 212 . .	. . .	. . .	. . .	. . .	. . .	. . .	. . .	. . .
Air transport, other	3 213 . .	. . .	. . .	. . .	. . .	. . .	. . .	. . .	. . .
Other transport, passenger	3 215 . .	. . .	. . .	. . .	. . .	. . .	. . .	. . .	. . .
Other transport, freight	3 216 . .	. . .	. . .	. . .	. . .	. . .	. . .	. . .	. . .
Other transport, other	3 217 . .	. . .	. . .	. . .	. . .	. . .	. . .	. . .	. . .
Travel, credit	2 236 . .	**. . .**	**. . .**	**1.5**	**. . .**	**. . .**	**. . .**	**. . .**	**. . .**
Business travel	2 237 . .	. . .	. . .	. . .	. . .	. . .	. . .	. . .	. . .
Personal travel	2 240 . .	. . .	. . .	. . .	. . .	. . .	. . .	. . .	. . .
Travel, debit	3 236 . .	**–87.5**	**–75.3**	**–73.5**	**–97.5**	**–74.8**	**–126.8**	**–136.3**	**. . .**
Business travel	3 237 . .	. . .	. . .	. . .	. . .	. . .	. . .	. . .	. . .
Personal travel	3 240 . .	. . .	. . .	. . .	. . .	. . .	. . .	. . .	. . .
Other services, credit	2 200 BA	**118.0**	**77.1**	**184.7**	**93.8**	**66.5**	**106.0**	**251.2**	**. . .**
Communications	2 245 . .	. . .	. . .	. . .	. . .	. . .	. . .	. . .	. . .
Construction	2 249 . .	. . .	. . .	. . .	. . .	. . .	. . .	. . .	. . .
Insurance	2 253 . .	15.1	10.5	22.2	13.2	8.9	15.7	35.3	. . .
Financial	2 260 . .	. . .	. . .	. . .	. . .	. . .	. . .	. . .	. . .
Computer and information	2 262 . .	. . .	. . .	. . .	. . .	. . .	. . .	. . .	. . .
Royalties and licence fees	2 266 . .	18.3	7.4	16.6	6.0	9.5	2.8	15.8	. . .
Other business services	2 268 . .	84.6	59.2	104.1	74.6	48.1	87.5	200.1	. . .
Personal, cultural, and recreational	2 287 . .	. . .	. . .	. . .	. . .	. . .	. . .	. . .	. . .
Government, n.i.e.	2 291 . .	. . .	. . .	41.8	. . .	. . .	. . .	. . .	. . .
Other services, debit	3 200 BA	**–1,161.9**	**–1,672.8**	**–2,039.1**	**–2,126.6**	**–2,243.6**	**–2,072.7**	**–2,251.8**	**. . .**
Communications	3 245 . .	. . .	. . .	. . .	. . .	. . .	. . .	. . .	. . .
Construction	3 249 . .	. . .	. . .	. . .	. . .	. . .	. . .	. . .	. . .
Insurance	3 253 . .	–36.3	–44.9	–48.7	–57.9	–67.7	–60.9	–63.1	. . .
Financial	3 260 . .	. . .	. . .	. . .	. . .	. . .	. . .	. . .	. . .
Computer and information	3 262 . .	. . .	. . .	. . .	. . .	. . .	. . .	. . .	. . .
Royalties and licence fees	3 266 . .	. . .	. . .	. . .	–.3	–1.2	–1.7	–5.6	. . .
Other business services	3 268 . .	–988.1	–1,241.5	–1,305.5	–1,508.6	–1,934.6	–1,609.0	–1,754.3	. . .
Personal, cultural, and recreational	3 287 . .	. . .	. . .	. . .	. . .	. . .	. . .	. . .	. . .
Government, n.i.e.	3 291 . .	–137.5	–386.4	–685.0	–559.8	–240.1	–401.1	–428.8	. . .

Table 2 (Continued). STANDARD PRESENTATION, 1994–2001
(Millions of U.S. dollars)

	Code	1994	1995	1996	1997	1998	1999	2000	2001
C. INCOME	4 300 . .	–734.7	–767.3	–1,473.4	–921.0	–968.7	–1,372.0	–1,680.8	. . .
Total credit	2 300 . .	*13.0*	*15.9*	*43.3*	*112.1*	*34.5*	*24.1*	*34.4*	. . .
Total debit	3 300 . .	*–747.7*	*–783.2*	*–1,516.7*	*–1,033.1*	*–1,003.2*	*–1,396.1*	*–1,715.2*	. . .
Compensation of employees, credit	2 310 . .	. . .	. . .	**5.1**	. . .	. . .	. . .	. . .	. . .
Compensation of employees, debit	3 310 . .	**–64.7**	**–60.3**	**–71.1**	**–107.0**	**–121.5**	**–173.8**	**–189.9**	. . .
Investment income, credit	2 320 . .	**13.0**	**15.9**	**38.2**	**112.1**	**34.5**	**24.1**	**34.4**	. . .
Direct investment income	2 330 . .	. . .	. . .	. . .	. . .	. . .	. . .	. . .	. . .
Dividends and distributed branch profits	2 332 . .	. . .	. . .	. . .	. . .	. . .	. . .	. . .	. . .
Reinvested earnings and undistributed branch profits	2 333 . .	. . .	. . .	. . .	. . .	. . .	. . .	. . .	. . .
Income on debt (interest)	2 334 . .	. . .	. . .	. . .	. . .	. . .	. . .	. . .	. . .
Portfolio investment income	2 339 . .	. . .	. . .	. . .	. . .	. . .	. . .	. . .	. . .
Income on equity	2 340 . .	. . .	. . .	. . .	. . .	. . .	. . .	. . .	. . .
Income on bonds and notes	2 350 . .	. . .	. . .	. . .	. . .	. . .	. . .	. . .	. . .
Income on money market instruments	2 360 . .	. . .	. . .	. . .	. . .	. . .	. . .	. . .	. . .
Other investment income	2 370 . .	13.0	15.9	38.2	112.1	34.5	24.1	34.4	. . .
Investment income, debit	3 320 . .	**–683.0**	**–722.9**	**–1,445.6**	**–926.1**	**–881.7**	**–1,222.3**	**–1,525.3**	. . .
Direct investment income	3 330 . .	–357.5	–385.8	–536.3	–559.3	–377.8	–653.4	–928.6	. . .
Dividends and distributed branch profits	3 332 . .	–357.5	–385.8	–536.3	–559.3	–377.8	–653.4	–928.6	. . .
Reinvested earnings and undistributed branch profits	3 333 . .	. . .	. . .	. . .	. . .	. . .	. . .	. . .	. . .
Income on debt (interest)	3 334 . .	. . .	. . .	. . .	. . .	. . .	. . .	. . .	. . .
Portfolio investment income	3 339 . .	. . .	. . .	. . .	. . .	. . .	. . .	. . .	. . .
Income on equity	3 340 . .	. . .	. . .	. . .	. . .	. . .	. . .	. . .	. . .
Income on bonds and notes	3 350 . .	. . .	. . .	. . .	. . .	. . .	. . .	. . .	. . .
Income on money market instruments	3 360 . .	. . .	. . .	. . .	. . .	. . .	. . .	. . .	. . .
Other investment income	3 370 . .	–325.5	–337.1	–909.3	–366.8	–503.9	–568.9	–596.7	. . .
D. CURRENT TRANSFERS	4 379 . .	245.1	155.5	3,840.8	94.6	151.5	55.8	27.6	. . .
Credit	2 379 . .	**333.2**	**312.2**	**3,949.4**	**176.4**	**238.2**	**154.5**	**123.5**	. . .
General government	2 380 . .	160.9	165.9	3,728.1	50.4	77.9	33.2	9.0	. . .
Other sectors	2 390 . .	172.3	146.3	221.3	126.0	160.4	121.3	114.5	. . .
Workers' remittances	2 391 . .	. . .	. . .	. . .	. . .	. . .	. . .	. . .	. . .
Other current transfers	2 392 . .	172.3	146.3	221.3	126.0	160.4	121.3	114.5	. . .
Debit	3 379 . .	**–88.1**	**–156.7**	**–108.6**	**–81.8**	**–86.7**	**–98.7**	**–95.9**	. . .
General government	3 380 . .	–.3	–3.2	–1.3	–1.4	–1.7	–6.0	–4.7	. . .
Other sectors	3 390 . .	–87.8	–153.5	–107.3	–80.4	–85.0	–92.8	–91.2	. . .
Workers' remittances	3 391 . .	–84.2	–149.3	–102.7	–73.0	–80.1	–89.3	–76.4	. . .
Other current transfers	3 392 . .	–3.6	–4.2	–4.5	–7.4	–4.9	–3.5	–14.8	. . .
CAPITAL AND FINANCIAL ACCOUNT	4 996 . .	**584.3**	**314.4**	**–3,415.5**	**1,065.5**	**1,488.8**	**1,789.3**	**–745.3**	. . .
CAPITAL ACCOUNT	4 994 . .	. . .	. . .	. . .	**11.2**	**8.4**	**6.8**	**18.3**	. . .
Total credit	2 994 . .	. . .	. . .	. . .	*11.2*	*8.4*	*6.8*	*18.3*	. . .
Total debit	3 994 . .	. . .	. . .	. . .	. . .	. . .	. . .	. . .	. . .
Capital transfers, credit	2 400 . .	. . .	. . .	. . .	**11.2**	**8.4**	**6.8**	**18.3**	. . .
General government	2 401 . .	. . .	. . .	. . .	11.2	8.4	6.8	18.3	. . .
Debt forgiveness	2 402 . .	. . .	. . .	. . .	11.2	8.4	6.8	18.1	. . .
Other capital transfers	2 410 . .	. . .	. . .	. . .	. . .	. . .	. . .	.2	. . .
Other sectors	2 430 . .	. . .	. . .	. . .	. . .	. . .	. . .	. . .	. . .
Migrants' transfers	2 431 . .	. . .	. . .	. . .	. . .	. . .	. . .	. . .	. . .
Debt forgiveness	2 432 . .	. . .	. . .	. . .	. . .	. . .	. . .	. . .	. . .
Other capital transfers	2 440 . .	. . .	. . .	. . .	. . .	. . .	. . .	. . .	. . .
Capital transfers, debit	3 400 . .	. . .	. . .	. . .	. . .	. . .	. . .	. . .	. . .
General government	3 401 . .	. . .	. . .	. . .	. . .	. . .	. . .	. . .	. . .
Debt forgiveness	3 402 . .	. . .	. . .	. . .	. . .	. . .	. . .	. . .	. . .
Other capital transfers	3 410 . .	. . .	. . .	. . .	. . .	. . .	. . .	. . .	. . .
Other sectors	3 430 . .	. . .	. . .	. . .	. . .	. . .	. . .	. . .	. . .
Migrants' transfers	3 431 . .	. . .	. . .	. . .	. . .	. . .	. . .	. . .	. . .
Debt forgiveness	3 432 . .	. . .	. . .	. . .	. . .	. . .	. . .	. . .	. . .
Other capital transfers	3 440 . .	. . .	. . .	. . .	. . .	. . .	. . .	. . .	. . .
Nonproduced nonfinancial assets, credit	2 480 . .	. . .	. . .	. . .	. . .	. . .	. . .	. . .	. . .
Nonproduced nonfinancial assets, debit	3 480 . .	. . .	. . .	. . .	. . .	. . .	. . .	. . .	. . .

Table 2 (Continued). STANDARD PRESENTATION, 1994–2001
(Millions of U.S. dollars)

	Code	1994	1995	1996	1997	1998	1999	2000	2001
FINANCIAL ACCOUNT	4 995 . .	**584.3**	**314.4**	**–3,415.5**	**1,054.3**	**1,480.4**	**1,782.5**	**–763.6**	. . .
A. DIRECT INVESTMENT	4 500 . .	170.3	472.4	180.6	411.7	1,114.0	2,471.5	878.6	. . .
Direct investment abroad	4 505 . .	. . .	. . .	. . .	. . .	. . .	. . .	. . .	. . .
Equity capital	4 510 . .	. . .	. . .	. . .	. . .	. . .	. . .	. . .	. . .
Claims on affiliated enterprises	4 515 . .	. . .	. . .	. . .	. . .	. . .	. . .	. . .	. . .
Liabilities to affiliated enterprises	4 520 . .	. . .	. . .	. . .	. . .	. . .	. . .	. . .	. . .
Reinvested earnings	4 525 . .	. . .	. . .	. . .	. . .	. . .	. . .	. . .	. . .
Other capital	4 530 . .	. . .	. . .	. . .	. . .	. . .	. . .	. . .	. . .
Claims on affiliated enterprises	4 535 . .	. . .	. . .	. . .	. . .	. . .	. . .	. . .	. . .
Liabilities to affiliated enterprises	4 540 . .	. . .	. . .	. . .	. . .	. . .	. . .	. . .	. . .
Direct investment in Angola	4 555 . .	**170.3**	**472.4**	**180.6**	**411.7**	**1,114.0**	**2,471.5**	**878.6**	. . .
Equity capital	4 560 . .	. . .	. . .	. . .	. . .	. . .	. . .	. . .	. . .
Claims on direct investors	4 565 . .	. . .	. . .	. . .	. . .	. . .	. . .	. . .	. . .
Liabilities to direct investors	4 570 . .	. . .	. . .	. . .	. . .	. . .	. . .	. . .	. . .
Reinvested earnings	4 575 . .	. . .	. . .	. . .	. . .	. . .	. . .	. . .	. . .
Other capital	4 580 . .	170.3	472.4	180.6	411.7	1,114.0	2,471.5	878.6	. . .
Claims on direct investors	4 585 . .	. . .	. . .	. . .	. . .	. . .	. . .	. . .	. . .
Liabilities to direct investors	4 590 . .	. . .	. . .	. . .	. . .	. . .	. . .	. . .	. . .
B. PORTFOLIO INVESTMENT	4 600 . .	. . .	. . .	. . .	. . .	. . .	. . .	. . .	. . .
Assets	4 602 . .	. . .	. . .	. . .	. . .	. . .	. . .	. . .	. . .
Equity securities	4 610 . .	. . .	. . .	. . .	. . .	. . .	. . .	. . .	. . .
Monetary authorities	4 611 . .	. . .	. . .	. . .	. . .	. . .	. . .	. . .	. . .
General government	4 612 . .	. . .	. . .	. . .	. . .	. . .	. . .	. . .	. . .
Banks	4 613 . .	. . .	. . .	. . .	. . .	. . .	. . .	. . .	. . .
Other sectors	4 614 . .	. . .	. . .	. . .	. . .	. . .	. . .	. . .	. . .
Debt securities	4 619 . .	. . .	. . .	. . .	. . .	. . .	. . .	. . .	. . .
Bonds and notes	4 620 . .	. . .	. . .	. . .	. . .	. . .	. . .	. . .	. . .
Monetary authorities	4 621 . .	. . .	. . .	. . .	. . .	. . .	. . .	. . .	. . .
General government	4 622 . .	. . .	. . .	. . .	. . .	. . .	. . .	. . .	. . .
Banks	4 623 . .	. . .	. . .	. . .	. . .	. . .	. . .	. . .	. . .
Other sectors	4 624 . .	. . .	. . .	. . .	. . .	. . .	. . .	. . .	. . .
Money market instruments	4 630 . .	. . .	. . .	. . .	. . .	. . .	. . .	. . .	. . .
Monetary authorities	4 631 . .	. . .	. . .	. . .	. . .	. . .	. . .	. . .	. . .
General government	4 632 . .	. . .	. . .	. . .	. . .	. . .	. . .	. . .	. . .
Banks	4 633 . .	. . .	. . .	. . .	. . .	. . .	. . .	. . .	. . .
Other sectors	4 634 . .	. . .	. . .	. . .	. . .	. . .	. . .	. . .	. . .
Liabilities	4 652 . .	. . .	. . .	. . .	. . .	. . .	. . .	. . .	. . .
Equity securities	4 660 . .	. . .	. . .	. . .	. . .	. . .	. . .	. . .	. . .
Banks	4 663 . .	. . .	. . .	. . .	. . .	. . .	. . .	. . .	. . .
Other sectors	4 664 . .	. . .	. . .	. . .	. . .	. . .	. . .	. . .	. . .
Debt securities	4 669 . .	. . .	. . .	. . .	. . .	. . .	. . .	. . .	. . .
Bonds and notes	4 670 . .	. . .	. . .	. . .	. . .	. . .	. . .	. . .	. . .
Monetary authorities	4 671 . .	. . .	. . .	. . .	. . .	. . .	. . .	. . .	. . .
General government	4 672 . .	. . .	. . .	. . .	. . .	. . .	. . .	. . .	. . .
Banks	4 673 . .	. . .	. . .	. . .	. . .	. . .	. . .	. . .	. . .
Other sectors	4 674 . .	. . .	. . .	. . .	. . .	. . .	. . .	. . .	. . .
Money market instruments	4 680 . .	. . .	. . .	. . .	. . .	. . .	. . .	. . .	. . .
Monetary authorities	4 681 . .	. . .	. . .	. . .	. . .	. . .	. . .	. . .	. . .
General government	4 682 . .	. . .	. . .	. . .	. . .	. . .	. . .	. . .	. . .
Banks	4 683 . .	. . .	. . .	. . .	. . .	. . .	. . .	. . .	. . .
Other sectors	4 684 . .	. . .	. . .	. . .	. . .	. . .	. . .	. . .	. . .
C. FINANCIAL DERIVATIVES	4 910 . .	. . .	. . .	. . .	. . .	. . .	. . .	. . .	. . .
Monetary authorities	4 911 . .	. . .	. . .	. . .	. . .	. . .	. . .	. . .	. . .
General government	4 912 . .	. . .	. . .	. . .	. . .	. . .	. . .	. . .	. . .
Banks	4 913 . .	. . .	. . .	. . .	. . .	. . .	. . .	. . .	. . .
Other sectors	4 914 . .	. . .	. . .	. . .	. . .	. . .	. . .	. . .	. . .
Assets	4 900 . .	. . .	. . .	. . .	. . .	. . .	. . .	. . .	. . .
Monetary authorities	4 901 . .	. . .	. . .	. . .	. . .	. . .	. . .	. . .	. . .
General government	4 902 . .	. . .	. . .	. . .	. . .	. . .	. . .	. . .	. . .
Banks	4 903 . .	. . .	. . .	. . .	. . .	. . .	. . .	. . .	. . .
Other sectors	4 904 . .	. . .	. . .	. . .	. . .	. . .	. . .	. . .	. . .
Liabilities	4 905 . .	. . .	. . .	. . .	. . .	. . .	. . .	. . .	. . .
Monetary authorities	4 906 . .	. . .	. . .	. . .	. . .	. . .	. . .	. . .	. . .
General government	4 907 . .	. . .	. . .	. . .	. . .	. . .	. . .	. . .	. . .
Banks	4 908 . .	. . .	. . .	. . .	. . .	. . .	. . .	. . .	. . .
Other sectors	4 909 . .	. . .	. . .	. . .	. . .	. . .	. . .	. . .	. . .

Table 2 (Concluded). STANDARD PRESENTATION, 1994–2001
(Millions of U.S. dollars)

	Code	1994	1995	1996	1997	1998	1999	2000	2001
D. OTHER INVESTMENT	4 700	399.8	-127.3	-3,265.8	480.0	48.4	-158.9	-1,010.9	...
Assets	4 703	**214.1**	**-168.4**	**-327.6**	**-330.7**	**-40.8**	**-186.2**	**-702.1**	**...**
Trade credits	4 706	...	...	...	...	...	...	...	...
General government	4 707	...	...	...	...	...	...	...	...
of which: Short-term	4 709	...	...	...	...	...	...	...	...
Other sectors	4 710	...	...	...	...	...	...	...	...
of which: Short-term	4 712	...	...	...	...	...	...	...	...
Loans	4 714	211.8	-238.2	-285.3	-330.7	202.8	-181.8	-501.4	...
Monetary authorities	4 715	...	...	...	...	...	...	...	...
of which: Short-term	4 718	...	...	...	...	...	...	...	...
General government	4 719	...	...	...	...	...	...	...	...
of which: Short-term	4 721	...	...	...	...	...	...	...	...
Banks	4 722	...	...	...	...	...	...	...	...
of which: Short-term	4 724	...	...	...	...	...	...	...	...
Other sectors	4 725	211.8	-238.2	-285.3	-330.7	202.8	-181.8	-501.4	...
of which: Short-term	4 727	*211.8*	*-238.2*	*-285.3*	*-330.7*	*202.8*	*-181.8*	*-501.4*	...
Currency and deposits	4 730	2.3	69.8	-42.3	...	-243.6	-4.4	-200.7	...
Monetary authorities	4 731	...	...	...	...	...	...	...	...
General government	4 732	...	...	...	...	...	...	...	...
Banks	4 733	...	-4.4	-48.8	...	...	...	...	...
Other sectors	4 734	2.3	74.2	6.5	...	-243.6	-4.4	-200.7	...
Other assets	4 736	...	...	...	...	...	...	...	...
Monetary authorities	4 737	...	...	...	...	...	...	...	...
of which: Short-term	4 739	...	...	...	...	...	...	...	...
General government	4 740	...	...	...	...	...	...	...	...
of which: Short-term	4 742	...	...	...	...	...	...	...	...
Banks	4 743	...	...	...	...	...	...	...	...
of which: Short-term	4 745	...	...	...	...	...	...	...	...
Other sectors	4 746	...	...	...	...	...	...	...	...
of which: Short-term	4 748	...	...	...	...	...	...	...	...
Liabilities	4 753	**185.7**	**41.2**	**-2,938.1**	**810.7**	**89.2**	**27.3**	**-308.8**	**...**
Trade credits	4 756	...	...	...	...	...	...	...	...
General government	4 757	...	...	...	...	...	...	...	...
of which: Short-term	4 759	...	...	...	...	...	...	...	...
Other sectors	4 760	...	...	...	...	...	...	...	...
of which: Short-term	4 762	...	...	...	...	...	...	...	...
Loans	4 764	-514.5	-389.2	527.7	430.0	-661.6	-560.4	-490.1	...
Monetary authorities	4 765	-185.9	-114.6	-147.1	39.5	-303.0	-272.2	27.6	...
of which: Use of Fund credit and loans from the Fund	4 766	...	...	...	...	...	...	...	...
of which: Short-term	4 768	...	...	...	...	...	...	*17.3*	...
General government	4 769	-479.3	-304.9	709.9	-39.2	-411.9	-180.2	-473.7	...
of which: Short-term	4 771	*-1.8*	*1.9*	*-22.9*	*47.9*	*466.3*	*37.1*	*.4*	...
Banks	4 772	...	...	-2.4	...	...	...	...	...
of which: Short-term	4 774	...	...	...	...	...	...	...	...
Other sectors	4 775	150.7	30.3	-32.7	429.7	53.3	-108.0	-44.0	...
of which: Short-term	4 777	...	*6.8*	*9.9*	*144.9*	*82.5*	*-34.3*	*56.4*	...
Currency and deposits	4 780	...	...	.8	4.8	2.4	3.5	...	...
Monetary authorities	4 781	...	...	...	...	...	...	...	...
General government	4 782	...	...	...	...	...	...	...	...
Banks	4 783	...	...	.8	4.8	2.4	3.5	...	...
Other sectors	4 784	...	...	...	...	...	...	...	...
Other liabilities	4 786	700.2	430.4	-3,466.6	375.9	748.4	584.2	181.3	...
Monetary authorities	4 787	.2	.3	2.8	9.4	216.6	11.7	-141.6	...
of which: Short-term	4 789	*.2*	*.3*	*2.8*	*9.4*	*216.6*	*11.7*	*-141.6*	...
General government	4 790	939.2	833.7	-3,296.8	363.0	510.7	561.0	253.1	...
of which: Short-term	4 792	*939.2*	*833.7*	*-3,296.8*	*363.0*	*510.7*	*561.0*	*253.1*	...
Banks	4 793	...	...	...	...	...	...	...	...
of which: Short-term	4 795	...	...	...	...	...	...	...	...
Other sectors	4 796	-239.2	-403.6	-172.6	3.5	21.1	11.5	69.8	...
of which: Short-term	4 798	*-239.2*	*-403.6*	*-172.6*	*3.5*	*21.1*	*11.5*	*69.8*	...
E. RESERVE ASSETS	4 802	14.2	-30.7	-330.3	162.6	318.0	-530.1	-631.3	...
Monetary gold	4 812	...	.5	12.8	...	...	...	...	...
Special drawing rights	4 811	...	...	...	...	...	...	...	...
Reserve position in the Fund	4 810	...	...	...	...	...	...	...	...
Foreign exchange	4 803	14.2	-31.3	-343.2	162.6	318.0	-530.1	-631.3	...
Other claims	4 813	...	...	...	...	...	...	...	...
NET ERRORS AND OMISSIONS	4 998	**-244.5**	**-19.4**	**149.2**	**-182.1**	**378.4**	**-78.8**	**-50.5**	**...**

Part 3 of the *Yearbook* contains descriptions of the methodologies, compilation practices, and sources used to compile these data.

Table 1. ANALYTIC PRESENTATION, 1994–2001
(Millions of U.S. dollars)

	Code	1994	1995	1996	1997	1998	1999	2000	2001
A. Current Account [1]	4 993 Z.	**–11.46**	**–9.47**	**–20.26**	**–18.74**	**–19.92**	**–51.03**	**–55.76**	...
Goods: exports f.o.b.	2 100 ..	1.67	1.23	1.76	1.60	3.16	2.90	4.43	...
Goods: imports f.o.b.	3 100 ..	–39.09	–47.00	–52.86	–54.26	–63.00	–80.86	–83.29	...
Balance on Goods	4 100 ..	*–37.41*	*–45.78*	*–51.10*	*–52.66*	*–59.83*	*–77.96*	*–78.86*	...
Services: credit	2 200 ..	61.43	55.56	57.22	66.01	79.44	68.80	65.07	...
Services: debit	3 200 ..	–24.78	–27.81	–27.59	–28.96	–38.19	–38.31	–40.69	...
Balance on Goods and Services	4 991 ..	*–.76*	*–18.03*	*–21.47*	*–15.61*	*–18.58*	*–47.46*	*–54.47*	...
Income: credit	2 300 ..	1.47	2.06	2.27	3.28	1.56	3.67	3.97	...
Income: debit	3 300 ..	–10.78	–9.60	–8.48	–7.07	–5.29	–6.93	–6.80	...
Balance on Goods, Services, and Income	4 992 ..	*–10.06*	*–25.57*	*–27.67*	*–19.40*	*–22.31*	*–50.71*	*–57.31*	...
Current transfers: credit	2 379 Z.	5.28	21.51	12.63	7.20	8.77	6.84	8.87	...
Current transfers: debit	3 379 ..	–6.68	–5.42	–5.22	–6.54	–6.38	–7.16	–7.32	...
B. Capital Account [1]	4 994 Z.	**6.80**	**5.40**	**5.23**	**2.51**	**2.07**	**2.65**	**4.81**	...
Capital account: credit	2 994 Z.	8.11	6.71	6.54	3.87	3.42	4.00	6.16	...
Capital account: debit	3 994 ..	–1.31	–1.31	–1.31	–1.35	–1.35	–1.35	–1.35	...
Total, Groups A Plus B	4 981 ..	*–4.67*	*–4.08*	*–15.02*	*–16.22*	*–17.85*	*–48.38*	*–50.94*	...
C. Financial Account [1]	4 995 W.	**–1.50**	**–.95**	**36.01**	**20.22**	**10.84**	**58.97**	**41.01**	...
Direct investment abroad	4 505 ..	...	...	...	...	...	...	...	...
Direct investment in Anguilla	4 555 Z.	11.14	17.58	33.23	21.24	28.06	38.01	39.36	...
Portfolio investment assets	4 602 ..	...	–.18	...	...	...	...	...	...
Equity securities	4 610 ..	...	...	...	...	...	...	...	...
Debt securities	4 619 ..	...	...	...	...	...	...	...	...
Portfolio investment liabilities	4 652 Z.	...	...	...	...	–.23	...	...	...
Equity securities	4 660 ..	...	...	...	...	...	...	...	...
Debt securities	4 669 Z.	...	...	...	...	...	...	...	...
Financial derivatives	4 910 ..	...	...	...	...	...	...	...	...
Financial derivatives assets	4 900 ..	...	...	...	...	...	...	...	...
Financial derivatives liabilities	4 905 ..	...	...	...	...	...	...	...	...
Other investment assets	4 703 ..	–10.68	–18.40	–8.67	–2.84	–31.99	17.26	–.69	...
Monetary authorities	4 701 ..	...	...	...	...	...	...	...	...
General government	4 704 ..	...	...	...	...	...	...	...	...
Banks	4 705 ..	...	...	...	...	...	...	...	...
Other sectors	4 728 ..	...	...	...	...	...	...	...	...
Other investment liabilities	4 753 W.	–1.96	.05	11.45	1.81	14.99	3.70	2.34	...
Monetary authorities	4 753 WA	...	...	...	...	...	...	...	...
General government	4 753 ZB	...	...	...	...	...	...	...	...
Banks	4 753 ZC	...	...	...	...	...	...	...	...
Other sectors	4 753 ZD	...	...	...	...	...	...	...	...
Total, Groups A Through C	4 983 ..	*–6.16*	*–5.03*	*20.99*	*4.00*	*–7.01*	*10.59*	*–9.93*	...
D. Net Errors and Omissions	4 998 ..	**6.16**	**5.03**	**–19.54**	**–2.13**	**8.84**	**–8.82**	**10.32**	...
Total, Groups A Through D	4 984 ..	...	...	*1.44*	*1.87*	*1.83*	*1.77*	*.38*	...
E. Reserves and Related Items	4 802 A.	...	...	**–1.44**	**–1.86**	**–1.84**	**–1.76**	**–.39**	...
Reserve assets	4 802 ..	...	...	–1.44	–1.86	–1.84	–1.76	–.39	...
Use of Fund credit and loans	4 766 ..	...	...	...	...	...	...	...	...
Exceptional financing	4 920 ..	...	...	...	...	...	...	...	...
Conversion rates: Eastern Caribbean dollars per U.S. dollar	0 101 ..	**2.7000**	**2.7000**	**2.7000**	**2.7000**	**2.7000**	**2.7000**	**2.7000**	**2.7000**

[1] Excludes components that have been classified in the categories of Group E.

Table 2. STANDARD PRESENTATION, 1994–2001

(Millions of U.S. dollars)

	Code	1994	1995	1996	1997	1998	1999	2000	2001
CURRENT ACCOUNT	4 993 . .	**-11.46**	**-9.47**	**-20.26**	**-18.74**	**-19.92**	**-51.03**	**-55.76**	**. . .**
A. GOODS	4 100 . .	-37.41	-45.78	-51.10	-52.66	-59.83	-77.96	-78.86	. . .
Credit	2 100 . .	**1.67**	**1.23**	**1.76**	**1.60**	**3.16**	**2.90**	**4.43**	**. . .**
General merchandise: exports f.o.b.	2 110 . .	1.67	1.22	1.76	1.59	3.16	2.90	4.42	. . .
Goods for processing: exports f.o.b.	2 150 . .	. . .	. . .	. . .	. . .	. . .	. . .	. . .	. . .
Repairs on goods	2 160 . .	. . .	. . .	. . .	.01	.01	. . .	.01	. . .
Goods procured in ports by carriers	2 170 . .	. . .	. . .	. . .	. . .	. . .	. . .	. . .	. . .
Nonmonetary gold	2 180 . .	. . .	. . .	. . .	. . .	. . .	. . .	. . .	. . .
Debit	3 100 . .	**-39.09**	**-47.00**	**-52.86**	**-54.26**	**-63.00**	**-80.86**	**-83.29**	**. . .**
General merchandise: imports f.o.b.	3 110 . .	-38.94	-46.89	-52.75	-54.21	-62.80	-80.86	-83.17	. . .
Goods for processing: imports f.o.b.	3 150 . .	. . .	. . .	. . .	. . .	. . .	. . .	. . .	. . .
Repairs on goods	3 160 . .	. . .	. . .	. . .	. . .	. . .	. . .	. . .	. . .
Goods procured in ports by carriers	3 170 . .	-.15	-.11	-.11	-.05	-.20	. . .	-.11	. . .
Nonmonetary gold	3 180 . .	. . .	. . .	. . .	. . .	. . .	. . .	. . .	. . .
B. SERVICES	4 200 . .	36.65	27.75	29.63	37.05	41.25	30.49	24.39	. . .
Total credit	2 200 . .	*61.43*	*55.56*	*57.22*	*66.01*	*79.44*	*68.80*	*65.07*	. . .
Total debit	3 200 . .	*-24.78*	*-27.81*	*-27.59*	*-28.96*	*-38.19*	*-38.31*	*-40.69*	. . .
Transportation services, credit	2 205 . .	**1.33**	**1.27**	**1.24**	**1.23**	**1.38**	**.84**	**1.69**	**. . .**
Passenger	2 850 . .	. . .	. . .	. . .	. . .	. . .	. . .	. . .	. . .
Freight	2 851 . .	. . .	. . .	. . .	. . .	. . .	. . .	. . .	. . .
Other	2 852 . .	. . .	. . .	. . .	. . .	. . .	. . .	. . .	. . .
Sea transport, passenger	2 207 . .	. . .	. . .	. . .	. . .	. . .	. . .	. . .	. . .
Sea transport, freight	2 208 . .	. . .	. . .	. . .	. . .	. . .	. . .	. . .	. . .
Sea transport, other	2 209 . .	. . .	. . .	. . .	. . .	. . .	. . .	. . .	. . .
Air transport, passenger	2 211 . .	. . .	. . .	. . .	. . .	. . .	. . .	. . .	. . .
Air transport, freight	2 212 . .	. . .	. . .	. . .	. . .	. . .	. . .	. . .	. . .
Air transport, other	2 213 . .	. . .	. . .	. . .	. . .	. . .	. . .	. . .	. . .
Other transport, passenger	2 215 . .	. . .	. . .	. . .	. . .	. . .	. . .	. . .	. . .
Other transport, freight	2 216 . .	. . .	. . .	. . .	. . .	. . .	. . .	. . .	. . .
Other transport, other	2 217 . .	. . .	. . .	. . .	. . .	. . .	. . .	. . .	. . .
Transportation services, debit	3 205 . .	**-9.64**	**-9.75**	**-9.84**	**-9.82**	**-15.93**	**-14.13**	**-14.27**	**. . .**
Passenger	3 850 . .	. . .	. . .	. . .	. . .	. . .	. . .	. . .	. . .
Freight	3 851 . .	. . .	. . .	. . .	. . .	. . .	. . .	. . .	. . .
Other	3 852 . .	. . .	. . .	. . .	. . .	. . .	. . .	. . .	. . .
Sea transport, passenger	3 207 . .	. . .	. . .	. . .	. . .	. . .	. . .	. . .	. . .
Sea transport, freight	3 208 . .	. . .	. . .	. . .	. . .	. . .	. . .	. . .	. . .
Sea transport, other	3 209 . .	. . .	. . .	. . .	. . .	. . .	. . .	. . .	. . .
Air transport, passenger	3 211 . .	. . .	. . .	. . .	. . .	. . .	. . .	. . .	. . .
Air transport, freight	3 212 . .	. . .	. . .	. . .	. . .	. . .	. . .	. . .	. . .
Air transport, other	3 213 . .	. . .	. . .	. . .	. . .	. . .	. . .	. . .	. . .
Other transport, passenger	3 215 . .	. . .	. . .	. . .	. . .	. . .	. . .	. . .	. . .
Other transport, freight	3 216 . .	. . .	. . .	. . .	. . .	. . .	. . .	. . .	. . .
Other transport, other	3 217 . .	. . .	. . .	. . .	. . .	. . .	. . .	. . .	. . .
Travel, credit	2 236 . .	**56.30**	**50.26**	**50.81**	**60.37**	**61.68**	**57.68**	**56.89**	**. . .**
Business travel	2 237 . .	. . .	. . .	. . .	. . .	. . .	. . .	. . .	. . .
Personal travel	2 240 . .	. . .	. . .	. . .	. . .	. . .	. . .	. . .	. . .
Travel, debit	3 236 . .	**-5.70**	**-5.79**	**-5.99**	**-7.00**	**-8.24**	**-8.35**	**-8.64**	**. . .**
Business travel	3 237 . .	. . .	. . .	. . .	. . .	. . .	. . .	. . .	. . .
Personal travel	3 240 . .	. . .	. . .	. . .	. . .	. . .	. . .	. . .	. . .
Other services, credit	2 200 BA	**3.81**	**4.03**	**5.16**	**4.42**	**16.39**	**10.28**	**6.50**	**. . .**
Communications	2 245 . .	. . .	. . .	. . .	. . .	. . .	. . .	. . .	. . .
Construction	2 249 . .	. . .	. . .	. . .	. . .	. . .	. . .	. . .	. . .
Insurance	2 253 . .	.17	.22	.79	.47	.56	.79	.38	. . .
Financial	2 260 . .	. . .	. . .	. . .	. . .	. . .	1.07	1.31	. . .
Computer and information	2 262 . .	. . .	. . .	. . .	. . .	. . .	. . .	. . .	. . .
Royalties and licence fees	2 266 . .	.26	.29	.31	. . .	.31	. . .	. . .	. . .
Other business services	2 268 . .	3.34	3.46	3.93	3.76	3.76	2.84	3.24	. . .
Personal, cultural, and recreational	2 287 . .	. . .	. . .	. . .	. . .	. . .	. . .	. . .	. . .
Government, n.i.e.	2 291 . .	.04	.07	.13	.19	11.76	5.59	1.57	. . .
Other services, debit	3 200 BA	**-9.44**	**-12.27**	**-11.76**	**-12.15**	**-14.01**	**-15.83**	**-17.79**	**. . .**
Communications	3 245 . .	. . .	. . .	. . .	. . .	. . .	. . .	. . .	. . .
Construction	3 249 . .	. . .	-.29	. . .	. . .	. . .	. . .	. . .	. . .
Insurance	3 253 . .	-1.11	-1.83	-1.93	-1.55	-1.65	-2.43	-1.98	. . .
Financial	3 260 . .	-.06	. . .	. . .	. . .	. . .	. . .	. . .	. . .
Computer and information	3 262 . .	. . .	. . .	. . .	. . .	. . .	. . .	. . .	. . .
Royalties and licence fees	3 266 . .	-.07	-.10	-.02	-.04	-.02	. . .	. . .	. . .
Other business services	3 268 . .	-7.39	-7.84	-6.36	-8.25	-9.01	-10.53	-14.27	. . .
Personal, cultural, and recreational	3 287 . .	. . .	. . .	. . .	. . .	. . .	. . .	. . .	. . .
Government, n.i.e.	3 291 . .	-.81	-2.20	-3.44	-2.31	-3.33	-2.87	-1.53	. . .

Table 2 (Continued). STANDARD PRESENTATION, 1994–2001
(Millions of U.S. dollars)

	Code	1994	1995	1996	1997	1998	1999	2000	2001
C. INCOME	4 300	−9.30	−7.54	−6.20	−3.80	−3.73	−3.25	−2.84	. . .
Total credit	2 300	*1.47*	*2.06*	*2.27*	*3.28*	*1.56*	*3.67*	*3.97*	. . .
Total debit	3 300	*−10.78*	*−9.60*	*−8.48*	*−7.07*	*−5.29*	*−6.93*	*−6.80*	. . .
Compensation of employees, credit	2 310	. . .	. . .	. . .	. . .	. . .	. . .	. . .	. . .
Compensation of employees, debit	3 310	. . .	. . .	. . .	. . .	. . .	. . .	. . .	. . .
Investment income, credit	2 320	**1.47**	**2.06**	**2.27**	**3.28**	**1.56**	**3.67**	**3.97**	. . .
Direct investment income	2 330	. . .	. . .	. . .	. . .	. . .	. . .	.02	. . .
Dividends and distributed branch profits	2 332	. . .	. . .	. . .	. . .	. . .	. . .	. . .	. . .
Reinvested earnings and undistributed branch profits	2 333	. . .	. . .	. . .	. . .	. . .	. . .	. . .	. . .
Income on debt (interest)	2 334	. . .	. . .	. . .	. . .	. . .	. . .	.02	. . .
Portfolio investment income	2 339	.17	.15	.16	.16	.15	.08	.22	. . .
Income on equity	2 340	.17	.15	.16	.16	.15	.08	.22	. . .
Income on bonds and notes	2 350	. . .	. . .	. . .	. . .	. . .	. . .	. . .	. . .
Income on money market instruments	2 360	. . .	. . .	. . .	. . .	. . .	. . .	. . .	. . .
Other investment income	2 370	1.31	1.91	2.12	3.12	1.40	3.59	3.72	. . .
Investment income, debit	3 320	**−10.78**	**−9.60**	**−8.48**	**−7.07**	**−5.29**	**−6.93**	**−6.80**	. . .
Direct investment income	3 330	−9.20	−8.06	−6.74	−5.61	−4.91	−4.40	−3.55	. . .
Dividends and distributed branch profits	3 332	−4.77	−1.73	−.99	−.68	. . .	−1.14	−1.09	. . .
Reinvested earnings and undistributed branch profits	3 333	−3.18	−6.14	−5.40	−4.67	−4.62	−3.00	−2.25	. . .
Income on debt (interest)	3 334	−1.25	−.20	−.35	−.26	−.30	−.27	−.21	. . .
Portfolio investment income	3 339	. . .	. . .	. . .	. . .	. . .	. . .	. . .	. . .
Income on equity	3 340	. . .	. . .	. . .	. . .	. . .	. . .	. . .	. . .
Income on bonds and notes	3 350	. . .	. . .	. . .	. . .	. . .	. . .	. . .	. . .
Income on money market instruments	3 360	. . .	. . .	. . .	. . .	. . .	. . .	. . .	. . .
Other investment income	3 370	−1.57	−1.53	−1.74	−1.47	−.37	−2.52	−3.26	. . .
D. CURRENT TRANSFERS	4 379	−1.40	16.10	7.41	.67	2.39	−.31	1.55	. . .
Credit	2 379	**5.28**	**21.51**	**12.63**	**7.20**	**8.77**	**6.84**	**8.87**	. . .
General government	2 380	.73	2.02	3.17	1.93	2.95	2.53	1.46	. . .
Other sectors	2 390	4.55	19.49	9.46	5.27	5.82	4.31	7.41	. . .
Workers' remittances	2 391	. . .	. . .	. . .	. . .	. . .	. . .	. . .	. . .
Other current transfers	2 392	. . .	. . .	. . .	. . .	. . .	. . .	. . .	. . .
Debit	3 379	**−6.68**	**−5.42**	**−5.22**	**−6.54**	**−6.38**	**−7.16**	**−7.32**	. . .
General government	3 380	−.17	−.17	−.27	−.27	−.31	−.39	−.56	. . .
Other sectors	3 390	−6.50	−5.24	−4.95	−6.26	−6.07	−6.77	−6.76	. . .
Workers' remittances	3 391	. . .	. . .	. . .	. . .	. . .	. . .	. . .	. . .
Other current transfers	3 392	. . .	. . .	. . .	. . .	. . .	. . .	. . .	. . .
CAPITAL AND FINANCIAL ACCOUNT	4 996	**5.30**	**4.44**	**39.80**	**20.87**	**11.08**	**59.85**	**45.44**	. . .
CAPITAL ACCOUNT	4 994	**6.80**	**5.40**	**5.23**	**2.51**	**2.07**	**2.65**	**4.81**	. . .
Total credit	2 994	*8.11*	*6.71*	*6.54*	*3.87*	*3.42*	*4.00*	*6.16*	. . .
Total debit	3 994	*−1.31*	*−1.31*	*−1.31*	*−1.35*	*−1.35*	*−1.35*	*−1.35*	. . .
Capital transfers, credit	2 400	**8.11**	**6.71**	**6.54**	**3.87**	**3.42**	**4.00**	**6.16**	. . .
General government	2 401	3.57	1.26	1.41	1.93	1.43	1.89	3.63	. . .
Debt forgiveness	2 402	. . .	. . .	. . .	. . .	. . .	. . .	. . .	. . .
Other capital transfers	2 410	3.57	1.26	1.41	1.93	1.43	1.89	3.63	. . .
Other sectors	2 430	4.54	5.45	5.14	1.94	1.99	2.11	2.53	. . .
Migrants' transfers	2 431	4.54	5.45	5.14	1.94	1.99	2.11	2.53	. . .
Debt forgiveness	2 432	. . .	. . .	. . .	. . .	. . .	. . .	. . .	. . .
Other capital transfers	2 440	. . .	. . .	. . .	. . .	. . .	. . .	. . .	. . .
Capital transfers, debit	3 400	**−1.31**	**−1.31**	**−1.31**	**−1.35**	**−1.35**	**−1.35**	**−1.35**	. . .
General government	3 401	. . .	. . .	. . .	. . .	. . .	. . .	. . .	. . .
Debt forgiveness	3 402	. . .	. . .	. . .	. . .	. . .	. . .	. . .	. . .
Other capital transfers	3 410	. . .	. . .	. . .	. . .	. . .	. . .	. . .	. . .
Other sectors	3 430	−1.31	−1.31	−1.31	−1.35	−1.35	−1.35	−1.35	. . .
Migrants' transfers	3 431	−1.31	−1.31	−1.31	−1.35	−1.35	−1.35	−1.35	. . .
Debt forgiveness	3 432	. . .	. . .	. . .	. . .	. . .	. . .	. . .	. . .
Other capital transfers	3 440	. . .	. . .	. . .	. . .	. . .	. . .	. . .	. . .
Nonproduced nonfinancial assets, credit	2 480	. . .	. . .	. . .	. . .	. . .	. . .	. . .	. . .
Nonproduced nonfinancial assets, debit	3 480	. . .	. . .	. . .	. . .	. . .	. . .	. . .	. . .

Table 2 (Continued). STANDARD PRESENTATION, 1994–2001
(Millions of U.S. dollars)

	Code	1994	1995	1996	1997	1998	1999	2000	2001
FINANCIAL ACCOUNT	4 995 . .	**–1.50**	**–.95**	**34.57**	**18.35**	**9.00**	**57.20**	**40.62**	**. . .**
A. DIRECT INVESTMENT	4 500 . .	11.14	17.58	33.23	21.24	28.06	38.01	39.36	. . .
Direct investment abroad	4 505 . .	**. . .**	**. . .**	**. . .**	**. . .**	**. . .**	**. . .**	**. . .**	**. . .**
Equity capital	4 510 . .	. . .	. . .	. . .	. . .	. . .	. . .	. . .	. . .
Claims on affiliated enterprises	4 515 . .	. . .	. . .	. . .	. . .	. . .	. . .	. . .	. . .
Liabilities to affiliated enterprises	4 520 . .	. . .	. . .	. . .	. . .	. . .	. . .	. . .	. . .
Reinvested earnings	4 525 . .	. . .	. . .	. . .	. . .	. . .	. . .	. . .	. . .
Other capital	4 530 . .	. . .	. . .	. . .	. . .	. . .	. . .	. . .	. . .
Claims on affiliated enterprises	4 535 . .	. . .	. . .	. . .	. . .	. . .	. . .	. . .	. . .
Liabilities to affiliated enterprises	4 540 . .	. . .	. . .	. . .	. . .	. . .	. . .	. . .	. . .
Direct investment in Anguilla	4 555 . .	**11.14**	**17.58**	**33.23**	**21.24**	**28.06**	**38.01**	**39.36**	**. . .**
Equity capital	4 560 . .	7.50	11.25	27.13	16.52	.74	3.36	1.93	. . .
Claims on direct investors	4 565 . .	. . .	. . .	. . .	. . .	. . .	. . .	. . .	. . .
Liabilities to direct investors	4 570 . .	7.50	11.25	27.13	16.52	.74	3.36	1.93	. . .
Reinvested earnings	4 575 . .	3.18	6.14	5.40	4.67	4.62	3.00	2.25	. . .
Other capital	4 580 . .	.46	.20	.70	.06	22.70	31.65	35.17	. . .
Claims on direct investors	4 585 . .	. . .	. . .	. . .	. . .	. . .	. . .	. . .	. . .
Liabilities to direct investors	4 590 . .	.46	.20	.70	.06	22.70	31.65	35.17	. . .
B. PORTFOLIO INVESTMENT	4 600 . .	. . .	–.18	. . .	. . .	–.23	. . .	. . .	. . .
Assets	4 602 . .	**. . .**	**–.18**	**. . .**	**. . .**	**. . .**	**. . .**	**. . .**	**. . .**
Equity securities	4 610 . .	. . .	. . .	. . .	. . .	. . .	. . .	. . .	. . .
Monetary authorities	4 611 . .	. . .	. . .	. . .	. . .	. . .	. . .	. . .	. . .
General government	4 612 . .	. . .	. . .	. . .	. . .	. . .	. . .	. . .	. . .
Banks	4 613 . .	. . .	. . .	. . .	. . .	. . .	. . .	. . .	. . .
Other sectors	4 614 . .	. . .	. . .	. . .	. . .	. . .	. . .	. . .	. . .
Debt securities	4 619 . .	. . .	. . .	. . .	. . .	. . .	. . .	. . .	. . .
Bonds and notes	4 620 . .	. . .	. . .	. . .	. . .	. . .	. . .	. . .	. . .
Monetary authorities	4 621 . .	. . .	. . .	. . .	. . .	. . .	. . .	. . .	. . .
General government	4 622 . .	. . .	. . .	. . .	. . .	. . .	. . .	. . .	. . .
Banks	4 623 . .	. . .	. . .	. . .	. . .	. . .	. . .	. . .	. . .
Other sectors	4 624 . .	. . .	. . .	. . .	. . .	. . .	. . .	. . .	. . .
Money market instruments	4 630 . .	. . .	. . .	. . .	. . .	. . .	. . .	. . .	. . .
Monetary authorities	4 631 . .	. . .	. . .	. . .	. . .	. . .	. . .	. . .	. . .
General government	4 632 . .	. . .	. . .	. . .	. . .	. . .	. . .	. . .	. . .
Banks	4 633 . .	. . .	. . .	. . .	. . .	. . .	. . .	. . .	. . .
Other sectors	4 634 . .	. . .	. . .	. . .	. . .	. . .	. . .	. . .	. . .
Liabilities	4 652 . .	**. . .**	**. . .**	**. . .**	**. . .**	**–.23**	**. . .**	**. . .**	**. . .**
Equity securities	4 660 . .	. . .	. . .	. . .	. . .	. . .	. . .	. . .	. . .
Banks	4 663 . .	. . .	. . .	. . .	. . .	. . .	. . .	. . .	. . .
Other sectors	4 664 . .	. . .	. . .	. . .	. . .	. . .	. . .	. . .	. . .
Debt securities	4 669 . .	. . .	. . .	. . .	. . .	. . .	. . .	. . .	. . .
Bonds and notes	4 670 . .	. . .	. . .	. . .	. . .	. . .	. . .	. . .	. . .
Monetary authorities	4 671	. . .	. . .	. . .	. . .	. . .	. . .	. . .	. . .
General government	4 672 . .	. . .	. . .	. . .	. . .	. . .	. . .	. . .	. . .
Banks	4 673 . .	. . .	. . .	. . .	. . .	. . .	. . .	. . .	. . .
Other sectors	4 674 . .	. . .	. . .	. . .	. . .	. . .	. . .	. . .	. . .
Money market instruments	4 680 . .	. . .	. . .	. . .	. . .	. . .	. . .	. . .	. . .
Monetary authorities	4 681 . .	. . .	. . .	. . .	. . .	. . .	. . .	. . .	. . .
General government	4 682 . .	. . .	. . .	. . .	. . .	. . .	. . .	. . .	. . .
Banks	4 683 . .	. . .	. . .	. . .	. . .	. . .	. . .	. . .	. . .
Other sectors	4 684 . .	. . .	. . .	. . .	. . .	. . .	. . .	. . .	. . .
C. FINANCIAL DERIVATIVES	4 910 . .	. . .	. . .	. . .	. . .	. . .	. . .	. . .	. . .
Monetary authorities	4 911 . .	. . .	. . .	. . .	. . .	. . .	. . .	. . .	. . .
General government	4 912 . .	. . .	. . .	. . .	. . .	. . .	. . .	. . .	. . .
Banks	4 913 . .	. . .	. . .	. . .	. . .	. . .	. . .	. . .	. . .
Other sectors	4 914 . .	. . .	. . .	. . .	. . .	. . .	. . .	. . .	. . .
Assets	4 900 . .	**. . .**	**. . .**	**. . .**	**. . .**	**. . .**	**. . .**	**. . .**	**. . .**
Monetary authorities	4 901 . .	. . .	. . .	. . .	. . .	. . .	. . .	. . .	. . .
General government	4 902 . .	. . .	. . .	. . .	. . .	. . .	. . .	. . .	. . .
Banks	4 903 . .	. . .	. . .	. . .	. . .	. . .	. . .	. . .	. . .
Other sectors	4 904 . .	. . .	. . .	. . .	. . .	. . .	. . .	. . .	. . .
Liabilities	4 905 . .	**. . .**	**. . .**	**. . .**	**. . .**	**. . .**	**. . .**	**. . .**	**. . .**
Monetary authorities	4 906 . .	. . .	. . .	. . .	. . .	. . .	. . .	. . .	. . .
General government	4 907 . .	. . .	. . .	. . .	. . .	. . .	. . .	. . .	. . .
Banks	4 908 . .	. . .	. . .	. . .	. . .	. . .	. . .	. . .	. . .
Other sectors	4 909 . .	. . .	. . .	. . .	. . .	. . .	. . .	. . .	. . .

Table 2 (Concluded). STANDARD PRESENTATION, 1994–2001
(Millions of U.S. dollars)

	Code	1994	1995	1996	1997	1998	1999	2000	2001
D. OTHER INVESTMENT	4 700 . .	–12.64	–18.35	2.78	–1.03	–16.99	20.95	1.65	...
Assets	4 703 . .	**–10.68**	**–18.40**	**–8.67**	**–2.84**	**–31.99**	**17.26**	**–.69**	...
Trade credits	4 706 . .	...	...	...	...	...	...	...	...
General government	4 707 . .	...	...	...	...	...	...	...	...
of which: Short-term	4 709 . .	...	...	...	...	...	...	...	...
Other sectors	4 710 . .	...	...	...	...	...	...	...	...
of which: Short-term	4 712 . .	...	...	...	...	...	...	...	...
Loans	4 714 . .	...	...	...	...	...	...	...	...
Monetary authorities	4 715 . .	...	...	...	...	...	...	...	...
of which: Short-term	4 718 . .	...	...	...	...	...	...	...	...
General government	4 719 . .	...	...	...	...	...	...	...	...
of which: Short-term	4 721 . .	...	...	...	...	...	...	...	...
Banks	4 722 . .	...	...	...	...	...	...	...	...
of which: Short-term	4 724 . .	...	...	...	...	...	...	...	...
Other sectors	4 725 . .	...	...	...	...	...	...	...	...
of which: Short-term	4 727 . .	...	...	...	...	...	...	...	...
Currency and deposits	4 730 . .	...	...	...	...	...	...	...	...
Monetary authorities	4 731 . .	...	...	...	...	...	...	...	...
General government	4 732 . .	...	...	...	...	...	...	...	...
Banks	4 733 . .	...	...	...	...	...	...	...	...
Other sectors	4 734 . .	...	...	...	...	...	...	...	...
Other assets	4 736 . .	...	...	...	...	...	...	...	...
Monetary authorities	4 737 . .	...	...	...	...	...	...	...	...
of which: Short-term	4 739 . .	...	...	...	...	...	...	...	...
General government	4 740 . .	...	...	...	...	...	...	...	...
of which: Short-term	4 742 . .	...	...	...	...	...	...	...	...
Banks	4 743 . .	...	...	...	...	...	...	...	...
of which: Short-term	4 745 . .	...	...	...	...	...	...	...	...
Other sectors	4 746 . .	...	...	...	...	...	...	...	...
of which: Short-term	4 748 . .	...	...	...	...	...	...	...	...
Liabilities	4 753 . .	**–1.96**	**.05**	**11.45**	**1.81**	**14.99**	**3.70**	**2.34**	...
Trade credits	4 756 . .	...	...	...	...	...	...	...	...
General government	4 757 . .	...	...	...	...	...	...	...	...
of which: Short-term	4 759 . .	...	...	...	...	...	...	...	...
Other sectors	4 760 . .	...	...	...	...	...	...	...	...
of which: Short-term	4 762 . .	...	...	...	...	...	...	...	...
Loans	4 764 . .	...	...	...	...	...	...	...	...
Monetary authorities	4 765 . .	...	...	...	...	...	...	...	...
of which: Use of Fund credit and loans from the Fund	4 766 . .	...	...	...	...	...	...	...	...
of which: Short-term	4 768 . .	...	...	...	...	...	...	...	...
General government	4 769 . .	...	...	...	...	...	...	...	...
of which: Short-term	4 771 . .	...	...	...	...	...	...	...	...
Banks	4 772 . .	...	...	...	...	...	...	...	...
of which: Short-term	4 774 . .	...	...	...	...	...	...	...	...
Other sectors	4 775 . .	...	...	...	...	...	...	...	...
of which: Short-term	4 777 . .	...	...	...	...	...	...	...	...
Currency and deposits	4 780 . .	...	...	...	...	...	...	...	...
Monetary authorities	4 781 . .	...	...	...	...	...	...	...	...
General government	4 782 . .	...	...	...	...	...	...	...	...
Banks	4 783 . .	...	...	...	...	...	...	...	...
Other sectors	4 784 . .	...	...	...	...	...	...	...	...
Other liabilities	4 786 . .	...	...	...	...	...	...	...	...
Monetary authorities	4 787 . .	...	...	...	...	...	...	...	...
of which: Short-term	4 789 . .	...	...	...	...	...	...	...	...
General government	4 790 . .	...	...	...	...	...	...	...	...
of which: Short-term	4 792 . .	...	...	...	...	...	...	...	...
Banks	4 793 . .	...	...	...	...	...	...	...	...
of which: Short-term	4 795 . .	...	...	...	...	...	...	...	...
Other sectors	4 796 . .	...	...	...	...	...	...	...	...
of which: Short-term	4 798 . .	...	...	...	...	...	...	...	...
E. RESERVE ASSETS	4 802 . .	...	...	–1.44	–1.86	–1.84	–1.76	–.39	...
Monetary gold	4 812 . .	...	...	...	...	...	...	...	...
Special drawing rights	4 811 . .	...	...	...	...	...	...	...	...
Reserve position in the Fund	4 810 . .	...	...	...	...	...	...	...	...
Foreign exchange	4 803 . .	...	...	–1.66	–1.86	–1.84	–1.76	–.39	...
Other claims	4 813 . .	...	...	.22	...	...	...	...	...
NET ERRORS AND OMISSIONS	4 998 . .	**6.16**	**5.03**	**–19.54**	**–2.13**	**8.84**	**–8.82**	**10.32**	...

Part 3 of the *Yearbook* contains descriptions of the methodologies, compilation practices, and sources used to compile these data.

Table 1. ANALYTIC PRESENTATION, 1994–2001

(Millions of U.S. dollars)

	Code	1994	1995	1996	1997	1998	1999	2000	2001
A. Current Account[1]	4 993 Z.	**–6.34**	**–.52**	**–59.60**	**–47.24**	**–63.13**	**–77.48**	**–79.13**	**. . .**
Goods: exports f.o.b	2 100 . .	45.23	53.15	38.88	38.80	37.38	36.84	42.28	. . .
Goods: imports f.o.b	3 100 . .	–287.50	–291.04	–309.94	–313.86	–320.84	–352.70	–341.33	. . .
Balance on Goods	4 100 . .	*–242.27*	*–237.89*	*–271.06*	*–275.06*	*–283.46*	*–315.87*	*–299.05*	. . .
Services: credit	2 200 . .	391.23	348.46	363.64	404.49	425.86	438.86	414.81	. . .
Services: debit	3 200 . .	–134.42	–147.89	–157.43	–164.43	–173.74	–183.36	–164.34	. . .
Balance on Goods and Services	4 991 . .	*14.53*	*–37.32*	*–64.84*	*–35.00*	*–31.33*	*–60.37*	*–48.57*	. . .
Income: credit	2 300 . .	4.26	5.21	5.79	3.71	4.14	3.60	8.87	. . .
Income: debit	3 300 . .	–30.81	–32.07	–32.17	–25.73	–33.30	–39.50	–47.75	. . .
Balance on Goods, Services, and Income	4 992 . .	*–12.03*	*–64.18*	*–91.22*	*–57.03*	*–60.48*	*–96.27*	*–87.46*	. . .
Current transfers: credit	2 379 Z.	15.15	78.04	35.19	19.90	11.70	22.66	17.24	. . .
Current transfers: debit	3 379 . .	–9.47	–14.38	–3.56	–10.12	–14.34	–3.88	–8.91	. . .
B. Capital Account[1]	4 994 Z.	**5.91**	**6.99**	**4.36**	**9.17**	**13.52**	**8.44**	**17.79**	**. . .**
Capital account: credit	2 994 Z.	6.53	6.99	4.36	9.17	13.52	8.44	17.79	. . .
Capital account: debit	3 994 . .	–.62	. . .	. . .	. . .	. . .	. . .	. . .	. . .
Total, Groups A Plus B	4 981 . .	*–.44*	*6.47*	*–55.24*	*–38.07*	*–49.61*	*–69.04*	*–61.34*	. . .
C. Financial Account[1]	4 995 W.	**–19.88**	**–10.66**	**57.61**	**66.90**	**57.88**	**51.17**	**64.01**	**. . .**
Direct investment abroad	4 505 . .	. . .	. . .	. . .	. . .	. . .	. . .	. . .	. . .
Direct investment in Antigua & Barbuda	4 555 Z.	24.79	31.49	19.35	22.94	27.43	36.53	33.15	. . .
Portfolio investment assets	4 602 . .	–1.38	1.19	–.78	. . .	. . .	–.09	–.10	. . .
Equity securities	4 610 . .	. . .	. . .	. . .	. . .	. . .	. . .	. . .	. . .
Debt securities	4 619 . .	. . .	. . .	. . .	. . .	. . .	. . .	. . .	. . .
Portfolio investment liabilities	4 652 Z.	. . .	–1.28	–.81	. . .	–.29	2.78	2.35	. . .
Equity securities	4 660 . .	. . .	. . .	. . .	. . .	. . .	. . .	. . .	. . .
Debt securities	4 669 Z.	. . .	. . .	. . .	. . .	. . .	. . .	. . .	. . .
Financial derivatives	4 910 . .	. . .	. . .	. . .	. . .	. . .	. . .	. . .	. . .
Financial derivatives assets	4 900 . .	. . .	. . .	. . .	. . .	. . .	. . .	. . .	. . .
Financial derivatives liabilities	4 905 . .	. . .	. . .	. . .	. . .	. . .	. . .	. . .	. . .
Other investment assets	4 703 . .	–23.89	–31.34	–1.16	10.84	–32.97	–92.28	–.39	. . .
Monetary authorities	4 701 . .	. . .	. . .	. . .	. . .	. . .	. . .	. . .	. . .
General government	4 704 . .	. . .	. . .	. . .	. . .	. . .	. . .	. . .	. . .
Banks	4 705 . .	. . .	. . .	. . .	. . .	. . .	. . .	. . .	. . .
Other sectors	4 728 . .	. . .	. . .	. . .	. . .	. . .	. . .	. . .	. . .
Other investment liabilities	4 753 W.	–19.40	–10.71	41.01	33.12	63.71	104.23	29.00	. . .
Monetary authorities	4 753 WA	. . .	. . .	. . .	. . .	. . .	. . .	. . .	. . .
General government	4 753 ZB	. . .	. . .	. . .	. . .	. . .	. . .	. . .	. . .
Banks	4 753 ZC	. . .	. . .	. . .	. . .	. . .	. . .	. . .	. . .
Other sectors	4 753 ZD	. . .	. . .	. . .	. . .	. . .	. . .	. . .	. . .
Total, Groups A Through C	4 983 . .	*–20.31*	*–4.20*	*2.37*	*28.83*	*8.27*	*–17.88*	*2.67*	. . .
D. Net Errors and Omissions	4 998 . .	**28.39**	**17.78**	**–13.63**	**–25.87**	**.40**	**28.25**	**–8.85**	**. . .**
Total, Groups A Through D	4 984 . .	*8.08*	*13.59*	*–11.26*	*2.96*	*8.67*	*10.37*	*–6.18*	. . .
E. Reserves and Related Items	4 802 A.	**–8.08**	**–13.59**	**11.26**	**–2.96**	**–8.67**	**–10.37**	**6.18**	**. . .**
Reserve assets	4 802 . .	–8.08	–13.59	11.26	–2.96	–8.67	–10.37	6.18	. . .
Use of Fund credit and loans	4 766 . .	. . .	. . .	. . .	. . .	. . .	. . .	. . .	. . .
Exceptional financing	4 920 . .	. . .	. . .	. . .	. . .	. . .	. . .	. . .	. . .
Conversion rates: Eastern Caribbean dollars per U.S. dollar	0 101 . .	**2.7000**	**2.7000**	**2.7000**	**2.7000**	**2.7000**	**2.7000**	**2.7000**	**2.7000**

[1] Excludes components that have been classified in the categories of Group E.

Table 2. STANDARD PRESENTATION, 1994–2001

(Millions of U.S. dollars)

	Code		1994	1995	1996	1997	1998	1999	2000	2001
CURRENT ACCOUNT	4 993	. .	**–6.34**	**–.52**	**–59.60**	**–47.24**	**–63.13**	**–77.48**	**–79.13**	. . .
A. GOODS	4 100	. .	–242.27	–237.89	–271.06	–275.06	–283.46	–315.87	–299.05	. . .
Credit	2 100	. .	**45.23**	**53.15**	**38.88**	**38.80**	**37.38**	**36.84**	**42.28**	. . .
General merchandise: exports f.o.b.	2 110	. .	27.42	30.09	16.82	12.96	14.81	15.77	16.34	. . .
Goods for processing: exports f.o.b.	2 150	. .	. . .	. . .	. . .	. . .	. . .	. . .	. . .	. . .
Repairs on goods	2 160	. .	.79	. . .	.84	.92	.95	.01	.01	. . .
Goods procured in ports by carriers	2 170	. .	17.03	23.06	21.21	24.91	21.62	21.06	25.93	. . .
Nonmonetary gold	2 180	. .	. . .	. . .	. . .	. . .	. . .	. . .	. . .	. . .
Debit	3 100	. .	**–287.50**	**–291.04**	**–309.94**	**–313.86**	**–320.84**	**–352.70**	**–341.33**	. . .
General merchandise: imports f.o.b.	3 110	. .	–283.84	–288.16	–306.56	–309.65	–318.33	–350.41	–338.29	. . .
Goods for processing: imports f.o.b.	3 150	. .	. . .	. . .	. . .	. . .	. . .	. . .	. . .	. . .
Repairs on goods	3 160	. .	. . .	. . .	. . .	. . .	. . .	. . .	. . .	. . .
Goods procured in ports by carriers	3 170	. .	–3.66	–2.88	–3.39	–4.20	–2.51	–2.30	–3.04	. . .
Nonmonetary gold	3 180	. .	. . .	. . .	. . .	. . .	. . .	. . .	. . .	. . .
B. SERVICES	4 200	. .	256.80	200.57	206.22	240.06	252.13	255.50	250.48	. . .
Total credit	2 200	. .	*391.23*	*348.46*	*363.64*	*404.49*	*425.86*	*438.86*	*414.81*	. . .
Total debit	3 200	. .	*–134.42*	*–147.89*	*–157.43*	*–164.43*	*–173.74*	*–183.36*	*–164.34*	. . .
Transportation services, credit	2 205	. .	**66.23**	**66.95**	**66.78**	**73.02**	**66.15**	**60.00**	**64.00**	. . .
Passenger	2 850	. .	. . .	. . .	. . .	. . .	. . .	. . .	. . .	. . .
Freight	2 851	. .	. . .	. . .	. . .	. . .	. . .	. . .	. . .	. . .
Other	2 852	. .	. . .	. . .	. . .	. . .	. . .	. . .	. . .	. . .
Sea transport, passenger	2 207	. .	. . .	. . .	. . .	. . .	. . .	. . .	. . .	. . .
Sea transport, freight	2 208	. .	. . .	. . .	. . .	. . .	. . .	. . .	. . .	. . .
Sea transport, other	2 209	. .	. . .	. . .	. . .	. . .	. . .	. . .	. . .	. . .
Air transport, passenger	2 211	. .	. . .	. . .	. . .	. . .	. . .	. . .	. . .	. . .
Air transport, freight	2 212	. .	. . .	. . .	. . .	. . .	. . .	. . .	. . .	. . .
Air transport, other	2 213	. .	. . .	. . .	. . .	. . .	. . .	. . .	. . .	. . .
Other transport, passenger	2 215	. .	. . .	. . .	. . .	. . .	. . .	. . .	. . .	. . .
Other transport, freight	2 216	. .	. . .	. . .	. . .	. . .	. . .	. . .	. . .	. . .
Other transport, other	2 217	. .	. . .	. . .	. . .	. . .	. . .	. . .	. . .	. . .
Transportation services, debit	3 205	. .	**–55.53**	**–56.24**	**–56.24**	**–58.20**	**–60.44**	**–62.14**	**–58.85**	. . .
Passenger	3 850	. .	. . .	. . .	. . .	. . .	. . .	. . .	. . .	. . .
Freight	3 851	. .	. . .	. . .	. . .	. . .	. . .	. . .	. . .	. . .
Other	3 852	. .	. . .	. . .	. . .	. . .	. . .	. . .	. . .	. . .
Sea transport, passenger	3 207	. .	. . .	. . .	. . .	. . .	. . .	. . .	. . .	. . .
Sea transport, freight	3 208	. .	. . .	. . .	. . .	. . .	. . .	. . .	. . .	. . .
Sea transport, other	3 209	. .	. . .	. . .	. . .	. . .	. . .	. . .	. . .	. . .
Air transport, passenger	3 211	. .	. . .	. . .	. . .	. . .	. . .	. . .	. . .	. . .
Air transport, freight	3 212	. .	. . .	. . .	. . .	. . .	. . .	. . .	. . .	. . .
Air transport, other	3 213	. .	. . .	. . .	. . .	. . .	. . .	. . .	. . .	. . .
Other transport, passenger	3 215	. .	. . .	. . .	. . .	. . .	. . .	. . .	. . .	. . .
Other transport, freight	3 216	. .	. . .	. . .	. . .	. . .	. . .	. . .	. . .	. . .
Other transport, other	3 217	. .	. . .	. . .	. . .	. . .	. . .	. . .	. . .	. . .
Travel, credit	2 236	. .	**293.44**	**246.71**	**257.94**	**277.53**	**281.33**	**289.98**	**291.09**	. . .
Business travel	2 237	. .	. . .	. . .	. . .	. . .	. . .	. . .	. . .	. . .
Personal travel	2 240	. .	. . .	. . .	. . .	. . .	. . .	. . .	. . .	. . .
Travel, debit	3 236	. .	**–24.03**	**–23.15**	**–26.07**	**–26.75**	**–28.96**	**–30.24**	**–30.70**	. . .
Business travel	3 237	. .	. . .	. . .	. . .	. . .	. . .	. . .	. . .	. . .
Personal travel	3 240	. .	. . .	. . .	. . .	. . .	. . .	. . .	. . .	. . .
Other services, credit	2 200	BA	**31.56**	**34.80**	**38.92**	**53.94**	**78.39**	**88.88**	**59.72**	. . .
Communications	2 245	. .	. . .	. . .	. . .	. . .	. . .	. . .	. . .	. . .
Construction	2 249	. .	. . .	. . .	. . .	. . .	. . .	. . .	. . .	. . .
Insurance	2 253	. .	2.37	2.16	3.59	3.57	19.74	30.29	15.91	. . .
Financial	2 260	. .	. . .	. . .	. . .	. . .	6.76	6.26	5.14	. . .
Computer and information	2 262	. .	. . .	. . .	. . .	. . .	. . .	. . .	. . .	. . .
Royalties and licence fees	2 266	. .	. . .	. . .	. . .	. . .	. . .	. . .	. . .	. . .
Other business services	2 268	. .	28.61	32.23	34.94	47.39	49.79	43.69	30.23	. . .
Personal, cultural, and recreational	2 287	. .	. . .	. . .	. . .	. . .	. . .	. . .	. . .	. . .
Government, n.i.e.	2 291	. .	.57	.41	.39	2.99	2.10	8.66	8.44	. . .
Other services, debit	3 200	BA	**–54.86**	**–68.50**	**–75.11**	**–79.48**	**–84.33**	**–90.97**	**–74.79**	. . .
Communications	3 245	. .	. . .	. . .	. . .	. . .	. . .	. . .	. . .	. . .
Construction	3 249	. .	. . .	. . .	–1.51	–.56	–1.83	–2.55	–1.90	. . .
Insurance	3 253	. .	–10.50	–16.33	–19.24	–16.16	–15.92	–26.97	–15.69	. . .
Financial	3 260	. .	. . .	. . .	. . .	–.72	. . .	. . .	. . .	. . .
Computer and information	3 262	. .	. . .	. . .	. . .	. . .	. . .	. . .	. . .	. . .
Royalties and licence fees	3 266	. .	. . .	. . .	–.13	. . .	–.31	–.26	–.29	. . .
Other business services	3 268	. .	–37.42	–44.59	–49.44	–57.64	–62.80	–54.82	–50.01	. . .
Personal, cultural, and recreational	3 287	. .	. . .	. . .	. . .	. . .	. . .	. . .	. . .	. . .
Government, n.i.e.	3 291	. .	–6.94	–7.59	–4.79	–4.41	–3.47	–6.37	–6.91	. . .

Table 2 (Continued). STANDARD PRESENTATION, 1994–2001
(Millions of U.S. dollars)

	Code	1994	1995	1996	1997	1998	1999	2000	2001
C. INCOME	4 300 . .	–26.56	–26.86	–26.37	–22.03	–29.15	–35.90	–38.88	. . .
Total credit	2 300 . .	*4.26*	*5.21*	*5.79*	*3.71*	*4.14*	*3.60*	*8.87*	. . .
Total debit	3 300 . .	*–30.81*	*–32.07*	*–32.17*	*–25.73*	*–33.30*	*–39.50*	*–47.75*	. . .
Compensation of employees, credit	2 310 . .	. . .	. . .	. . .	. . .	. . .	. . .	. . .	. . .
Compensation of employees, debit	3 310 . .	. . .	**–.21**	. . .	. . .	. . .	. . .	. . .	. . .
Investment income, credit	2 320 . .	**4.26**	**5.21**	**5.79**	**3.71**	**4.14**	**3.60**	**8.87**	. . .
Direct investment income	2 330 . .	. . .	. . .	. . .	. . .	. . .	. . .	. . .	. . .
Dividends and distributed branch profits	2 332 . .	. . .	. . .	. . .	. . .	. . .	. . .	. . .	. . .
Reinvested earnings and undistributed branch profits	2 333 . .	. . .	. . .	. . .	. . .	. . .	. . .	. . .	. . .
Income on debt (interest)	2 334 . .	. . .	. . .	. . .	. . .	. . .	. . .	. . .	. . .
Portfolio investment income	2 339 . .	1.56	1.61	1.75	1.63	1.63	.78	1.19	. . .
Income on equity	2 340 . .	1.56	1.61	1.75	1.63	1.63	.78	1.19	. . .
Income on bonds and notes	2 350 . .	. . .	. . .	. . .	. . .	. . .	. . .	. . .	. . .
Income on money market instruments	2 360 . .	. . .	. . .	. . .	. . .	. . .	. . .	. . .	. . .
Other investment income	2 370 . .	2.69	3.59	4.04	2.07	2.52	2.82	7.68	. . .
Investment income, debit	3 320 . .	**–30.81**	**–31.86**	**–32.17**	**–25.73**	**–33.30**	**–39.50**	**–47.75**	. . .
Direct investment income	3 330 . .	–15.84	–13.17	–15.06	–15.08	–15.51	–21.75	–22.83	. . .
Dividends and distributed branch profits	3 332 . .	–10.76	–1.39	–5.05	–10.41	–8.17	–14.24	–14.48	. . .
Reinvested earnings and undistributed branch profits	3 333 . .	–4.68	–5.27	–5.31	–4.32	–6.99	–6.70	–7.48	. . .
Income on debt (interest)	3 334 . .	–.41	–6.52	–4.70	–.35	–.36	–.81	–.87	. . .
Portfolio investment income	3 339 . .	. . .	. . .	. . .	. . .	. . .	. . .	. . .	. . .
Income on equity	3 340 . .	. . .	. . .	. . .	. . .	. . .	. . .	. . .	. . .
Income on bonds and notes	3 350 . .	. . .	. . .	. . .	. . .	. . .	. . .	. . .	. . .
Income on money market instruments	3 360 . .	. . .	. . .	. . .	. . .	. . .	. . .	. . .	. . .
Other investment income	3 370 . .	–14.97	–18.69	–17.11	–10.65	–17.78	–17.75	–24.93	. . .
D. CURRENT TRANSFERS	4 379 . .	5.68	63.66	31.62	9.78	–2.64	18.79	8.33	. . .
Credit	2 379 . .	**15.15**	**78.04**	**35.19**	**19.90**	**11.70**	**22.66**	**17.24**	. . .
General government	2 380 . .	1.75	3.09	2.38	1.01	1.21	1.88	2.48	. . .
Other sectors	2 390 . .	13.40	74.95	32.81	18.89	10.49	20.78	14.76	. . .
Workers' remittances	2 391 . .	. . .	. . .	. . .	. . .	. . .	. . .	. . .	. . .
Other current transfers	2 392 . .	. . .	. . .	. . .	. . .	. . .	. . .	. . .	. . .
Debit	3 379 . .	**–9.47**	**–14.38**	**–3.56**	**–10.12**	**–14.34**	**–3.88**	**–8.91**	. . .
General government	3 380 . .	–1.07	–2.81	–1.51	–1.73	–1.67	–1.27	–1.27	. . .
Other sectors	3 390 . .	–8.40	–11.57	–2.05	–8.39	–12.68	–2.61	–7.64	. . .
Workers' remittances	3 391 . .	. . .	. . .	. . .	. . .	. . .	. . .	. . .	. . .
Other current transfers	3 392 . .	. . .	. . .	. . .	. . .	. . .	. . .	. . .	. . .
CAPITAL AND FINANCIAL ACCOUNT	4 996 . .	**–22.05**	**–17.27**	**73.23**	**73.12**	**62.73**	**49.23**	**87.98**	. . .
CAPITAL ACCOUNT	4 994 . .	**5.91**	**6.99**	**4.36**	**9.17**	**13.52**	**8.44**	**17.79**	. . .
Total credit	2 994 . .	*6.53*	*6.99*	*4.36*	*9.17*	*13.52*	*8.44*	*17.79*	. . .
Total debit	3 994 . .	*–.62*	. . .	. . .	. . .	. . .	. . .	. . .	. . .
Capital transfers, credit	2 400 . .	**6.53**	**6.99**	**4.36**	**9.17**	**13.52**	**8.44**	**16.82**	. . .
General government	2 401 . .	3.19	3.65	1.02	2.76	10.07	4.99	13.49	. . .
Debt forgiveness	2 402 . .	. . .	. . .	. . .	. . .	. . .	. . .	. . .	. . .
Other capital transfers	2 410 . .	3.19	3.65	1.02	2.76	10.07	4.99	13.49	. . .
Other sectors	2 430 . .	3.33	3.33	3.33	6.41	3.44	3.44	3.33	. . .
Migrants' transfers	2 431 . .	3.33	3.33	3.33	6.41	3.44	3.44	3.33	. . .
Debt forgiveness	2 432 . .	. . .	. . .	. . .	. . .	. . .	. . .	. . .	. . .
Other capital transfers	2 440 . .	. . .	. . .	. . .	. . .	. . .	. . .	. . .	. . .
Capital transfers, debit	3 400 . .	. . .	. . .	. . .	. . .	. . .	. . .	. . .	. . .
General government	3 401 . .	. . .	. . .	. . .	. . .	. . .	. . .	. . .	. . .
Debt forgiveness	3 402 . .	. . .	. . .	. . .	. . .	. . .	. . .	. . .	. . .
Other capital transfers	3 410 . .	. . .	. . .	. . .	. . .	. . .	. . .	. . .	. . .
Other sectors	3 430 . .	. . .	. . .	. . .	. . .	. . .	. . .	. . .	. . .
Migrants' transfers	3 431 . .	. . .	. . .	. . .	. . .	. . .	. . .	. . .	. . .
Debt forgiveness	3 432 . .	. . .	. . .	. . .	. . .	. . .	. . .	. . .	. . .
Other capital transfers	3 440 . .	. . .	. . .	. . .	. . .	. . .	. . .	. . .	. . .
Nonproduced nonfinancial assets, credit	2 480 . .	. . .	. . .	. . .	. . .	. . .	. . .	**.96**	. . .
Nonproduced nonfinancial assets, debit	3 480 . .	**–.62**	. . .	. . .	. . .	. . .	. . .	. . .	. . .

Table 2 (Continued). STANDARD PRESENTATION, 1994–2001

(Millions of U.S. dollars)

	Code	1994	1995	1996	1997	1998	1999	2000	2001
FINANCIAL ACCOUNT	4 995 . .	**–27.95**	**–24.25**	**68.87**	**63.95**	**49.21**	**40.80**	**70.19**	**...**
A. DIRECT INVESTMENT	4 500 . .	24.79	31.49	19.35	22.94	27.43	36.53	33.15	...
Direct investment abroad	4 505 . .	**...**	**...**	**...**	**...**	**...**	**...**	**...**	**...**
Equity capital	4 510 . .	...	...	...	...	...	...	...	...
Claims on affiliated enterprises	4 515 . .	...	...	...	...	...	...	...	...
Liabilities to affiliated enterprises	4 520 . .	...	...	...	...	...	...	...	...
Reinvested earnings	4 525 . .	...	...	...	...	...	...	...	...
Other capital	4 530 . .	...	...	...	...	...	...	...	...
Claims on affiliated enterprises	4 535 . .	...	...	...	...	...	...	...	...
Liabilities to affiliated enterprises	4 540 . .	...	...	...	...	...	...	...	...
Direct investment in Antigua & Barbuda	4 555 . .	**24.79**	**31.49**	**19.35**	**22.94**	**27.43**	**36.53**	**33.15**	**...**
Equity capital	4 560 . .	15.52	6.16	11.43	15.48	17.53	33.02	10.26	...
Claims on direct investors	4 565 . .	...	...	...	...	...	...	...	...
Liabilities to direct investors	4 570 . .	15.52	6.16	11.43	15.48	17.53	33.02	10.26	...
Reinvested earnings	4 575 . .	4.68	5.27	5.31	4.32	6.99	6.70	7.48	...
Other capital	4 580 . .	4.59	20.06	2.61	3.14	2.91	–3.19	15.41	...
Claims on direct investors	4 585 . .	...	...	...	...	...	...	...	...
Liabilities to direct investors	4 590 . .	4.59	20.06	2.61	3.14	2.91	–3.19	15.41	...
B. PORTFOLIO INVESTMENT	4 600 . .	–1.38	–.09	–1.59	...	–.29	2.69	2.25	...
Assets	4 602 . .	**–1.38**	**1.19**	**–.78**	**...**	**...**	**–.09**	**–.10**	**...**
Equity securities	4 610 . .	...	...	...	...	...	...	...	...
Monetary authorities	4 611 . .	...	...	...	...	...	...	...	...
General government	4 612 . .	...	...	...	...	...	...	...	...
Banks	4 613 . .	...	...	...	...	...	...	...	...
Other sectors	4 614 . .	...	...	...	...	...	...	...	...
Debt securities	4 619 . .	...	...	...	...	...	...	...	...
Bonds and notes	4 620 . .	...	...	...	...	...	...	...	...
Monetary authorities	4 621 . .	...	...	...	...	...	...	...	...
General government	4 622 . .	...	...	...	...	...	...	...	...
Banks	4 623 . .	...	...	...	...	...	...	...	...
Other sectors	4 624 . .	...	...	...	...	...	...	...	...
Money market instruments	4 630 . .	...	...	...	...	...	...	...	...
Monetary authorities	4 631 . .	...	...	...	...	...	...	...	...
General government	4 632 . .	...	...	...	...	...	...	...	...
Banks	4 633 . .	...	...	...	...	...	...	...	...
Other sectors	4 634 . .	...	...	...	...	...	...	...	...
Liabilities	4 652 . .	**...**	**–1.28**	**–.81**	**...**	**–.29**	**2.78**	**2.35**	**...**
Equity securities	4 660 . .	...	...	...	...	...	...	...	...
Banks	4 663 . .	...	...	...	...	...	...	...	...
Other sectors	4 664 . .	...	...	...	...	...	...	...	...
Debt securities	4 669 . .	...	...	...	...	...	...	...	...
Bonds and notes	4 670 . .	...	...	...	...	...	...	...	...
Monetary authorities	4 671 . .	...	...	...	...	...	...	...	...
General government	4 672 . .	...	...	...	...	...	...	...	...
Banks	4 673 . .	...	...	...	...	...	...	...	...
Other sectors	4 674 . .	...	...	...	...	...	...	...	...
Money market instruments	4 680 . .	...	...	...	...	...	...	...	...
Monetary authorities	4 681 . .	...	...	...	...	...	...	...	...
General government	4 682 . .	...	...	...	...	...	...	...	...
Banks	4 683 . .	...	...	...	...	...	...	...	...
Other sectors	4 684 . .	...	...	...	...	...	...	...	...
C. FINANCIAL DERIVATIVES	4 910 . .	...	...	...	...	...	...	...	...
Monetary authorities	4 911 . .	...	...	...	...	...	...	...	...
General government	4 912 . .	...	...	...	...	...	...	...	...
Banks	4 913 . .	...	...	...	...	...	...	...	...
Other sectors	4 914 . .	...	...	...	...	...	...	...	...
Assets	4 900 . .	**...**	**...**	**...**	**...**	**...**	**...**	**...**	**...**
Monetary authorities	4 901 . .	...	...	...	...	...	...	...	...
General government	4 902 . .	...	...	...	...	...	...	...	...
Banks	4 903 . .	...	...	...	...	...	...	...	...
Other sectors	4 904 . .	...	...	...	...	...	...	...	...
Liabilities	4 905 . .	**...**	**...**	**...**	**...**	**...**	**...**	**...**	**...**
Monetary authorities	4 906 . .	...	...	...	...	...	...	...	...
General government	4 907 . .	...	...	...	...	...	...	...	...
Banks	4 908 . .	...	...	...	...	...	...	...	...
Other sectors	4 909 . .	...	...	...	...	...	...	...	...

Table 2 (Concluded). STANDARD PRESENTATION, 1994–2001
(Millions of U.S. dollars)

	Code	1994	1995	1996	1997	1998	1999	2000	2001
D. OTHER INVESTMENT	4 700 . .	–43.29	–42.05	39.85	43.96	30.74	11.95	28.61	. . .
Assets	4 703 . .	**–23.89**	**–31.34**	**–1.16**	**10.84**	**–32.97**	**–92.28**	**–.39**	**. . .**
Trade credits	4 706 . .	. . .	. . .	. . .	. . .	. . .	. . .	. . .	. . .
General government	4 707 . .	. . .	. . .	. . .	. . .	. . .	. . .	. . .	. . .
of which: Short-term	4 709 . .	. . .	. . .	. . .	. . .	. . .	. . .	. . .	. . .
Other sectors	4 710 . .	. . .	. . .	. . .	. . .	. . .	. . .	. . .	. . .
of which: Short-term	4 712 . .	. . .	. . .	. . .	. . .	. . .	. . .	. . .	. . .
Loans	4 714 . .	. . .	. . .	. . .	. . .	. . .	. . .	. . .	. . .
Monetary authorities	4 715 . .	. . .	. . .	. . .	. . .	. . .	. . .	. . .	. . .
of which: Short-term	4 718 . .	. . .	. . .	. . .	. . .	. . .	. . .	. . .	. . .
General government	4 719 . .	. . .	. . .	. . .	. . .	. . .	. . .	. . .	. . .
of which: Short-term	4 721 . .	. . .	. . .	. . .	. . .	. . .	. . .	. . .	. . .
Banks	4 722 . .	. . .	. . .	. . .	. . .	. . .	. . .	. . .	. . .
of which: Short-term	4 724 . .	. . .	. . .	. . .	. . .	. . .	. . .	. . .	. . .
Other sectors	4 725 . .	. . .	. . .	. . .	. . .	. . .	. . .	. . .	. . .
of which: Short-term	4 727 . .	. . .	. . .	. . .	. . .	. . .	. . .	. . .	. . .
Currency and deposits	4 730 . .	. . .	. . .	. . .	. . .	. . .	. . .	. . .	. . .
Monetary authorities	4 731 . .	. . .	. . .	. . .	. . .	. . .	. . .	. . .	. . .
General government	4 732 . .	. . .	. . .	. . .	. . .	. . .	. . .	. . .	. . .
Banks	4 733 . .	. . .	. . .	. . .	. . .	. . .	. . .	. . .	. . .
Other sectors	4 734 . .	. . .	. . .	. . .	. . .	. . .	. . .	. . .	. . .
Other assets	4 736 . .	. . .	. . .	. . .	. . .	. . .	. . .	. . .	. . .
Monetary authorities	4 737 . .	. . .	. . .	. . .	. . .	. . .	. . .	. . .	. . .
of which: Short-term	4 739 . .	. . .	. . .	. . .	. . .	. . .	. . .	. . .	. . .
General government	4 740 . .	. . .	. . .	. . .	. . .	. . .	. . .	. . .	. . .
of which: Short-term	4 742 . .	. . .	. . .	. . .	. . .	. . .	. . .	. . .	. . .
Banks	4 743 . .	. . .	. . .	. . .	. . .	. . .	. . .	. . .	. . .
of which: Short-term	4 745 . .	. . .	. . .	. . .	. . .	. . .	. . .	. . .	. . .
Other sectors	4 746 . .	. . .	. . .	. . .	. . .	. . .	. . .	. . .	. . .
of which: Short-term	4 748 . .	. . .	. . .	. . .	. . .	. . .	. . .	. . .	. . .
Liabilities	4 753 . .	**–19.40**	**–10.71**	**41.01**	**33.12**	**63.71**	**104.23**	**29.00**	**. . .**
Trade credits	4 756 . .	. . .	. . .	. . .	. . .	. . .	. . .	. . .	. . .
General government	4 757 . .	. . .	. . .	. . .	. . .	. . .	. . .	. . .	. . .
of which: Short-term	4 759 . .	. . .	. . .	. . .	. . .	. . .	. . .	. . .	. . .
Other sectors	4 760 . .	. . .	. . .	. . .	. . .	. . .	. . .	. . .	. . .
of which: Short-term	4 762 . .	. . .	. . .	. . .	. . .	. . .	. . .	. . .	. . .
Loans	4 764 . .	. . .	. . .	. . .	. . .	. . .	. . .	. . .	. . .
Monetary authorities	4 765 . .	. . .	. . .	. . .	. . .	. . .	. . .	. . .	. . .
of which: Use of Fund credit and loans from the Fund	4 766 . .	. . .	. . .	. . .	. . .	. . .	. . .	. . .	. . .
of which: Short-term	4 768 . .	. . .	. . .	. . .	. . .	. . .	. . .	. . .	. . .
General government	4 769 . .	. . .	. . .	. . .	. . .	. . .	. . .	. . .	. . .
of which: Short-term	4 771 . .	. . .	. . .	. . .	. . .	. . .	. . .	. . .	. . .
Banks	4 772 . .	. . .	. . .	. . .	. . .	. . .	. . .	. . .	. . .
of which: Short-term	4 774 . .	. . .	. . .	. . .	. . .	. . .	. . .	. . .	. . .
Other sectors	4 775 . .	. . .	. . .	. . .	. . .	. . .	. . .	. . .	. . .
of which: Short-term	4 777 . .	. . .	. . .	. . .	. . .	. . .	. . .	. . .	. . .
Currency and deposits	4 780 . .	. . .	. . .	. . .	. . .	. . .	. . .	. . .	. . .
Monetary authorities	4 781 . .	. . .	. . .	. . .	. . .	. . .	. . .	. . .	. . .
General government	4 782 . .	. . .	. . .	. . .	. . .	. . .	. . .	. . .	. . .
Banks	4 783 . .	. . .	. . .	. . .	. . .	. . .	. . .	. . .	. . .
Other sectors	4 784 . .	. . .	. . .	. . .	. . .	. . .	. . .	. . .	. . .
Other liabilities	4 786 . .	. . .	. . .	. . .	. . .	. . .	. . .	. . .	. . .
Monetary authorities	4 787 . .	. . .	. . .	. . .	. . .	. . .	. . .	. . .	. . .
of which: Short-term	4 789 . .	. . .	. . .	. . .	. . .	. . .	. . .	. . .	. . .
General government	4 790 . .	. . .	. . .	. . .	. . .	. . .	. . .	. . .	. . .
of which: Short-term	4 792 . .	. . .	. . .	. . .	. . .	. . .	. . .	. . .	. . .
Banks	4 793 . .	. . .	. . .	. . .	. . .	. . .	. . .	. . .	. . .
of which: Short-term	4 795 . .	. . .	. . .	. . .	. . .	. . .	. . .	. . .	. . .
Other sectors	4 796 . .	. . .	. . .	. . .	. . .	. . .	. . .	. . .	. . .
of which: Short-term	4 798 . .	. . .	. . .	. . .	. . .	. . .	. . .	. . .	. . .
E. RESERVE ASSETS	4 802 . .	–8.08	–13.59	11.26	–2.96	–8.67	–10.37	6.18	. . .
Monetary gold	4 812 . .	. . .	. . .	. . .	. . .	. . .	. . .	. . .	. . .
Special drawing rights	4 811 . .	. . .	. . .	. . .	. . .	. . .	. . .	. . .	. . .
Reserve position in the Fund	4 810 . .	. . .	. . .	. . .	. . .	. . .	. . .	. . .	. . .
Foreign exchange	4 803 . .	–8.07	–13.59	11.70	–2.96	–8.67	–10.37	6.18	. . .
Other claims	4 813 . .	. . .	. . .	–.44	. . .	. . .	. . .	. . .	. . .
NET ERRORS AND OMISSIONS	4 998 . .	**28.39**	**17.78**	**–13.63**	**–25.87**	**.40**	**28.25**	**–8.85**	**. . .**

Part 3 of the *Yearbook* contains descriptions of the methodologies, compilation practices, and sources used to compile these data.

Table 1. ANALYTIC PRESENTATION, 1994–2001
(Millions of U.S. dollars)

	Code	1994	1995	1996	1997	1998	1999	2000	2001
A. Current Account [1]	4 993 Z.	**-11,171**	**-5,175**	**-6,825**	**-12,243**	**-14,532**	**-11,902**	**-8,879**	**-4,553**
Goods: exports f.o.b.	2 100 ..	16,043	21,162	24,043	26,431	26,434	23,309	26,410	26,610
Goods: imports f.o.b.	3 100 ..	-20,202	-18,804	-22,283	-28,554	-29,531	-24,103	-23,852	-19,159
Balance on Goods	4 100 ..	*-4,160*	*2,357*	*1,760*	*-2,123*	*-3,097*	*-795*	*2,558*	*7,451*
Services: credit	2 200 ..	3,364	3,819	4,341	4,500	4,706	4,556	4,704	4,310
Services: debit	3 200 ..	-7,141	-7,236	-7,869	-8,864	-9,140	-8,662	-9,011	-8,402
Balance on Goods and Services	4 991 ..	*-7,936*	*-1,060*	*-1,768*	*-6,487*	*-7,532*	*-4,901*	*-1,749*	*3,358*
Income: credit	2 300 ..	3,461	4,385	4,440	5,486	6,125	6,160	7,520	5,660
Income: debit	3 300 ..	-7,158	-9,055	-9,943	-11,705	-13,531	-13,558	-14,892	-13,755
Balance on Goods, Services, and Income	4 992 ..	*-11,633*	*-5,729*	*-7,271*	*-12,706*	*-14,938*	*-12,298*	*-9,121*	*-4,737*
Current transfers: credit	2 379 Z.	799	823	703	760	719	704	601	572
Current transfers: debit	3 379 ..	-336	-269	-257	-297	-314	-307	-360	-389
B. Capital Account [1]	4 994 Z.	**18**	**14**	**51**	**94**	**73**	**86**	**87**	**101**
Capital account: credit	2 994 Z.	27	25	72	112	92	98	102	109
Capital account: debit	3 994 ..	-10	-11	-21	-17	-19	-12	-15	-8
Total, Groups A Plus B	4 981 ..	*-11,153*	*-5,161*	*-6,774*	*-12,148*	*-14,459*	*-11,815*	*-8,793*	*-4,453*
C. Financial Account [1]	4 995 W.	**11,360**	**4,990**	**11,713**	**16,755**	**18,996**	**14,926**	**8,770**	**-13,590**
Direct investment abroad	4 505 ..	-1,013	-1,497	-1,601	-3,653	-2,326	-1,175	-1,018	123
Direct investment in Argentina	4 555 Z.	3,635	5,610	6,948	9,160	7,291	23,988	11,657	3,214
Portfolio investment assets	4 602 ..	-1,486	-2,882	-2,381	-1,570	-1,906	-2,128	-1,060	2,019
Equity securities	4 610 ..	-763	-401	-594	-838	-839	167	-1,454	-946
Debt securities	4 619 ..	-723	-2,481	-1,788	-733	-1,067	-2,296	394	2,965
Portfolio investment liabilities	4 652 Z.	9,843	4,734	12,098	11,666	10,693	-4,780	-1,331	-9,516
Equity securities	4 660 ..	3,116	1,091	990	1,391	-210	-10,773	-3,227	-81
Debt securities	4 669 Z.	6,727	3,643	11,108	10,276	10,903	5,993	1,896	-9,435
Financial derivatives	4 910 ..	...	...	...	...	...	...	...	...
Financial derivatives assets	4 900 ..	...	...	...	...	...	...	...	...
Financial derivatives liabilities	4 905 ..	...	...	...	...	...	...	...	...
Other investment assets	4 703 ..	-3,163	-8,123	-5,217	-7,107	-113	-2,817	-1,764	-3,940
Monetary authorities	4 701 ..	...	...	...	...	...	...	...	...
General government	4 704 ..	442	-686	62	-89	111	-1,594	921	55
Banks	4 705 ..	-297	-603	-3,039	-5,337	613	995	-2,348	8,937
Other sectors	4 728 ..	-3,308	-6,834	-2,240	-1,681	-837	-2,218	-337	-12,933
Other investment liabilities	4 753 W.	3,544	7,149	1,865	8,259	5,357	1,838	2,287	-5,490
Monetary authorities	4 753 WA	-16	-94	-214	-11	-10	-13	-16	1,130
General government	4 753 ZB	535	1,903	-151	311	1,924	1,203	440	1,495
Banks	4 753 ZC	1,098	3,251	443	3,843	621	1,134	898	-6,836
Other sectors	4 753 ZD	1,928	2,089	1,788	4,116	2,822	-486	964	-1,280
Total, Groups A Through C	4 983 ..	*206*	*-171*	*4,939*	*4,607*	*4,537*	*3,110*	*-22*	*-18,043*
D. Net Errors and Omissions	4 998 ..	**-881**	**-2,140**	**-1,682**	**-1,276**	**-447**	**-1,098**	**-1,154**	**-3,362**
Total, Groups A Through D	4 984 ..	*-675*	*-2,311*	*3,258*	*3,331*	*4,090*	*2,013*	*-1,176*	*-21,405*
E. Reserves and Related Items	4 802 A.	**675**	**2,311**	**-3,258**	**-3,331**	**-4,090**	**-2,013**	**1,176**	**21,405**
Reserve assets	4 802 ..	-685	82	-3,875	-3,293	-3,436	-1,186	403	12,070
Use of Fund credit and loans	4 766 ..	455	1,924	367	-38	-654	-826	773	9,335
Exceptional financing	4 920 ..	904	305	250	...	...	...	...	...
Conversion rates: Argentine peso per U.S. dollar	0 101 ..	**.99901**	**.99975**	**.99966**	**.99950**	**.99950**	**.99950**	**.99950**	**.99950**

[1] Excludes components that have been classified in the categories of Group E.

Table 2. STANDARD PRESENTATION, 1994–2001
(Millions of U.S. dollars)

	Code		1994	1995	1996	1997	1998	1999	2000	2001
CURRENT ACCOUNT	4 993	. .	**–11,171**	**–5,175**	**–6,825**	**–12,243**	**–14,532**	**–11,902**	**–8,879**	**–4,553**
A. GOODS	4 100	. .	–4,160	2,357	1,760	–2,123	–3,097	–795	2,558	7,451
Credit	2 100	. .	**16,043**	**21,162**	**24,043**	**26,431**	**26,434**	**23,309**	**26,410**	**26,610**
General merchandise: exports f.o.b.	2 110	. .	15,814	20,963	23,811	26,181	26,169	22,947	25,994	26,209
Goods for processing: exports f.o.b.	2 150	. .	. . .	. . .	. . .	. . .	. . .	. . .	. . .	. . .
Repairs on goods	2 160	. .	. . .	. . .	. . .	. . .	. . .	. . .	. . .	. . .
Goods procured in ports by carriers	2 170	. .	204	199	232	248	237	252	319	305
Nonmonetary gold	2 180	. .	25	. . .	. . .	1	27	110	96	96
Debit	3 100	. .	**–20,202**	**–18,804**	**–22,283**	**–28,554**	**–29,531**	**–24,103**	**–23,852**	**–19,159**
General merchandise: imports f.o.b.	3 110	. .	–20,077	–18,726	–22,190	–28,459	–29,457	–24,040	–23,735	–19,109
Goods for processing: imports f.o.b.	3 150	. .	. . .	. . .	. . .	. . .	. . .	. . .	. . .	. . .
Repairs on goods	3 160	. .	. . .	. . .	. . .	. . .	. . .	. . .	. . .	. . .
Goods procured in ports by carriers	3 170	. .	–125	–78	–93	–94	–74	–64	–116	–50
Nonmonetary gold	3 180	. .	. . .	. . .	. . .	. . .	. . .	. . .	. . .	. . .
B. SERVICES	4 200	. .	–3,777	–3,417	–3,528	–4,365	–4,435	–4,106	–4,307	–4,093
Total credit	2 200	. .	*3,364*	*3,819*	*4,341*	*4,500*	*4,706*	*4,556*	*4,704*	*4,310*
Total debit	3 200	. .	*–7,141*	*–7,236*	*–7,869*	*–8,864*	*–9,140*	*–8,662*	*–9,011*	*–8,402*
Transportation services, credit	2 205	. .	**892**	**1,010**	**1,073**	**1,125**	**1,112**	**1,055**	**1,106**	**853**
Passenger	2 850	. .	*312*	*328*	*354*	*375*	*328*	*277*	*291*	*114*
Freight	2 851	. .	*204*	*238*	*227*	*242*	*224*	*212*	*226*	*219*
Other	2 852	. .	*376*	*444*	*492*	*508*	*560*	*565*	*590*	*520*
Sea transport, passenger	2 207	. .	11	5	6	7	7	9	9	7
Sea transport, freight	2 208	. .	111	135	117	125	121	128	136	133
Sea transport, other	2 209	. .	165	226	254	258	274	253	244	237
Air transport, passenger	2 211	. .	289	311	335	355	306	255	268	93
Air transport, freight	2 212	. .	37	22	24	20	14	13	9	5
Air transport, other	2 213	. .	207	214	234	246	282	308	345	281
Other transport, passenger	2 215	. .	12	13	13	13	15	14	14	14
Other transport, freight	2 216	. .	56	81	86	98	89	71	81	81
Other transport, other	2 217	. .	4	4	4	4	4	4	2	2
Transportation services, debit	3 205	. .	**–2,120**	**–2,113**	**–2,388**	**–2,808**	**–2,791**	**–2,425**	**–2,424**	**–2,123**
Passenger	3 850	. .	*–743*	*–741*	*–872*	*–1,017*	*–1,058*	*–1,039*	*–1,044*	*–1,009*
Freight	3 851	. .	*–1,110*	*–1,053*	*–1,206*	*–1,456*	*–1,425*	*–1,092*	*–1,090*	*–917*
Other	3 852	. .	*–268*	*–318*	*–310*	*–335*	*–308*	*–294*	*–289*	*–198*
Sea transport, passenger	3 207	. .	–41	–39	–49	–55	–56	–55	–51	–51
Sea transport, freight	3 208	. .	–797	–762	–830	–996	–936	–718	–715	–613
Sea transport, other	3 209	. .	–47	–48	–43	–48	–47	–45	–47	–45
Air transport, passenger	3 211	. .	–681	–683	–805	–944	–983	–965	–974	–940
Air transport, freight	3 212	. .	–188	–173	–221	–268	–279	–235	–225	–169
Air transport, other	3 213	. .	–221	–270	–267	–286	–260	–249	–240	–152
Other transport, passenger	3 215	. .	–21	–19	–18	–19	–19	–19	–19	–19
Other transport, freight	3 216	. .	–124	–118	–156	–192	–210	–139	–150	–135
Other transport, other	3 217	. .	. . .	. . .	. . .	–1	–1	–1	–2	. . .
Travel, credit	2 236	. .	**1,933**	**2,222**	**2,621**	**2,778**	**3,025**	**2,898**	**2,904**	**2,615**
Business travel	2 237	. .	659	759	916	958	1,046	997	1,010	828
Personal travel	2 240	. .	1,274	1,463	1,705	1,819	1,979	1,901	1,893	1,787
Travel, debit	3 236	. .	**–3,398**	**–3,278**	**–3,584**	**–3,962**	**–4,230**	**–4,195**	**–4,425**	**–3,967**
Business travel	3 237	. .	811	–786	–847	–920	–983	–975	–1,046	–863
Personal travel	3 240	. .	–2,587	–2,492	–2,737	–3,043	–3,247	–3,220	–3,379	–3,104
Other services, credit	2 200	BA	**540**	**588**	**648**	**597**	**569**	**603**	**694**	**842**
Communications	2 245	. .	277	333	360	270	193	169	154	170
Construction	2 249	. .	. . .	1	8	8	22	28	7	. . .
Insurance	2 253	. .	7	2	1	2	. . .	. . .	13	. . .
Financial	2 260	. .	8	7	6	6	6	5	6	4
Computer and information	2 262	. .	11	13	21	44	63	68	125	168
Royalties and licence fees	2 266	. .	9	12	13	15	21	20	14	23
Other business services	2 268	. .	77	66	81	84	103	137	200	289
Personal, cultural, and recreational	2 287	. .	4	4	8	17	9	13	15	31
Government, n.i.e.	2 291	. .	148	150	151	152	153	161	160	158
Other services, debit	3 200	BA	**–1,623**	**–1,846**	**–1,897**	**–2,094**	**–2,119**	**–2,043**	**–2,163**	**–2,312**
Communications	3 245	. .	–187	–193	–182	–190	–173	–140	–168	–197
Construction	3 249	. .	–7	–2	–14	–10	–4	–6	. . .	. . .
Insurance	3 253	. .	–210	–371	–302	–317	–296	–271	–200	–297
Financial	3 260	. .	–79	–126	–164	–207	–203	–189	–168	–186
Computer and information	3 262	. .	–43	–41	–45	–62	–67	–76	–136	–183
Royalties and licence fees	3 266	. .	–369	–370	–433	–470	–492	–478	–475	–465
Other business services	3 268	. .	–389	–381	–362	–405	–509	–538	–585	–527
Personal, cultural, and recreational	3 287	. .	–85	–92	–91	–149	–155	–113	–171	–230
Government, n.i.e.	3 291	. .	–255	–270	–305	–283	–220	–231	–260	–228

Table 2 (Continued). STANDARD PRESENTATION, 1994–2001

(Millions of U.S. dollars)

	Code	1994	1995	1996	1997	1998	1999	2000	2001
C. INCOME	4 300	–3,697	–4,669	–5,502	–6,218	–7,406	–7,398	–7,372	–8,095
Total credit	2 300	*3,461*	*4,385*	*4,440*	*5,486*	*6,125*	*6,160*	*7,520*	*5,660*
Total debit	3 300	*–7,158*	*–9,055*	*–9,943*	*–11,705*	*–13,531*	*–13,558*	*–14,892*	*–13,755*
Compensation of employees, credit	2 310	**16**	**16**	**16**	**16**	**16**	**24**	**23**	**21**
Compensation of employees, debit	3 310	**–6**	**–6**	**–8**	**–21**	**–23**	**–16**	**–19**	**–20**
Investment income, credit	2 320	**3,445**	**4,369**	**4,424**	**5,470**	**6,109**	**6,137**	**7,497**	**5,639**
Direct investment income	2 330	457	522	457	853	866	663	1,010	817
Dividends and distributed branch profits	2 332	282	494	479	447	335	441	520	437
Reinvested earnings and undistributed branch profits	2 333	175	28	–22	405	530	222	490	381
Income on debt (interest)	2 334	. . .	. . .	. . .	. . .	. . .	. . .	. . .	. . .
Portfolio investment income	2 339	3	5	407	506	460	389	216	262
Income on equity	2 340	3	3	4	5	3	. . .	. . .	. . .
Income on bonds and notes	2 350	. . .	2	402	502	457	389	216	262
Income on money market instruments	2 360	. . .	. . .	. . .	. . .	. . .	. . .	. . .	. . .
Other investment income	2 370	2,985	3,843	3,561	4,111	4,784	5,085	6,271	4,559
Investment income, debit	3 320	**–7,152**	**–9,049**	**–9,935**	**–11,684**	**–13,508**	**–13,541**	**–14,873**	**–13,735**
Direct investment income	3 330	–2,023	–2,130	–2,083	–2,739	–2,765	–2,100	–3,020	–2,153
Dividends and distributed branch profits	3 332	–1,031	–1,308	–1,453	–1,644	–1,592	–1,803	–858	–2,372
Reinvested earnings and undistributed branch profits	3 333	–898	–659	–398	–726	–788	144	–1,548	844
Income on debt (interest)	3 334	–94	–163	–231	–370	–385	–441	–614	–626
Portfolio investment income	3 339	–2,773	–3,876	–4,572	–5,572	–6,889	–7,336	–7,344	–6,844
Income on equity	3 340	–450	–707	–731	–488	–782	–554	–115	–122
Income on bonds and notes	3 350	–2,323	–3,169	–3,841	–5,083	–6,107	–6,782	–7,228	–6,722
Income on money market instruments	3 360	. . .	. . .	. . .	. . .	. . .	. . .	. . .	. . .
Other investment income	3 370	–2,357	–3,043	–3,281	–3,373	–3,854	–4,106	–4,510	–4,738
D. CURRENT TRANSFERS	4 379	463	553	446	463	406	397	241	183
Credit	2 379	**799**	**823**	**703**	**760**	**719**	**704**	**601**	**572**
General government	2 380	166	163	162	185	215	228	271	261
Other sectors	2 390	633	660	541	575	504	476	330	311
Workers' remittances	2 391	46	40	41	41	43	29	. . .	. . .
Other current transfers	2 392	586	619	500	533	461	447	330	311
Debit	3 379	**–336**	**–269**	**–257**	**–297**	**–314**	**–307**	**–360**	**–389**
General government	3 380	–110	–43	–25	–71	–64	–39	–49	–55
Other sectors	3 390	–226	–226	–232	–226	–249	–267	–311	–334
Workers' remittances	3 391	–171	–185	–193	–204	–217	–226	–240	–227
Other current transfers	3 392	–55	–42	–38	–22	–33	–41	–72	–107
CAPITAL AND FINANCIAL ACCOUNT	4 996	**12,052**	**7,315**	**8,506**	**13,519**	**14,979**	**12,999**	**10,033**	**7,916**
CAPITAL ACCOUNT	4 994	**18**	**14**	**51**	**94**	**73**	**86**	**87**	**101**
Total credit	2 994	*27*	*25*	*72*	*112*	*92*	*98*	*102*	*109*
Total debit	3 994	*–10*	*–11*	*–21*	*–17*	*–19*	*–12*	*–15*	*–8*
Capital transfers, credit	2 400	**. . .**	**. . .**	**. . .**	**. . .**	**. . .**	**. . .**	**. . .**	**. . .**
General government	2 401	. . .	. . .	. . .	. . .	. . .	. . .	. . .	. . .
Debt forgiveness	2 402	. . .	. . .	. . .	. . .	. . .	. . .	. . .	. . .
Other capital transfers	2 410	. . .	. . .	. . .	. . .	. . .	. . .	. . .	. . .
Other sectors	2 430	. . .	. . .	. . .	. . .	. . .	. . .	. . .	. . .
Migrants' transfers	2 431	. . .	. . .	. . .	. . .	. . .	. . .	. . .	. . .
Debt forgiveness	2 432	. . .	. . .	. . .	. . .	. . .	. . .	. . .	. . .
Other capital transfers	2 440	. . .	. . .	. . .	. . .	. . .	. . .	. . .	. . .
Capital transfers, debit	3 400	**. . .**	**. . .**	**. . .**	**. . .**	**. . .**	**. . .**	**. . .**	**. . .**
General government	3 401	. . .	. . .	. . .	. . .	. . .	. . .	. . .	. . .
Debt forgiveness	3 402	. . .	. . .	. . .	. . .	. . .	. . .	. . .	. . .
Other capital transfers	3 410	. . .	. . .	. . .	. . .	. . .	. . .	. . .	. . .
Other sectors	3 430	. . .	. . .	. . .	. . .	. . .	. . .	. . .	. . .
Migrants' transfers	3 431	. . .	. . .	. . .	. . .	. . .	. . .	. . .	. . .
Debt forgiveness	3 432	. . .	. . .	. . .	. . .	. . .	. . .	. . .	. . .
Other capital transfers	3 440	. . .	. . .	. . .	. . .	. . .	. . .	. . .	. . .
Nonproduced nonfinancial assets, credit	2 480	**27**	**25**	**72**	**112**	**92**	**98**	**102**	**109**
Nonproduced nonfinancial assets, debit	3 480	**–10**	**–11**	**–21**	**–17**	**–19**	**–12**	**–15**	**–8**

Table 2 (Continued). STANDARD PRESENTATION, 1994–2001
(Millions of U.S. dollars)

	Code	1994	1995	1996	1997	1998	1999	2000	2001
FINANCIAL ACCOUNT	4 995 . .	**12,034**	**7,301**	**8,455**	**13,424**	**14,906**	**12,913**	**9,947**	**7,815**
A. DIRECT INVESTMENT	4 500 . .	2,622	4,112	5,348	5,507	4,965	22,812	10,639	3,337
Direct investment abroad	4 505 . .	**–1,013**	**–1,497**	**–1,601**	**–3,653**	**–2,326**	**–1,175**	**–1,018**	**123**
Equity capital	4 510 . .	–846	–1,438	–1,633	–3,259	–1,625	–940	–346	552
Claims on affiliated enterprises	4 515 . .	–846	–1,438	–1,633	–3,259	–1,625	–940	–346	552
Liabilities to affiliated enterprises	4 520 . .	. . .	. . .	. . .	. . .	. . .	. . .	. . .	. . .
Reinvested earnings	4 525 . .	–175	–28	22	–405	–530	–222	–490	–381
Other capital	4 530 . .	8	–31	10	11	–170	–13	–182	–49
Claims on affiliated enterprises	4 535 . .	8	–31	10	11	–170	–13	–182	–49
Liabilities to affiliated enterprises	4 540 . .	. . .	. . .	. . .	. . .	. . .	. . .	. . .	. . .
Direct investment in Argentina	4 555 . .	**3,635**	**5,610**	**6,948**	**9,160**	**7,291**	**23,988**	**11,657**	**3,214**
Equity capital	4 560 . .	2,350	4,251	5,025	7,276	5,701	22,504	9,422	3,558
Claims on direct investors	4 565 . .	. . .	. . .	. . .	. . .	. . .	. . .	. . .	. . .
Liabilities to direct investors	4 570 . .	2,350	4,251	5,025	7,276	5,701	22,504	9,422	3,558
Reinvested earnings	4 575 . .	898	659	398	726	788	–144	1,548	–844
Other capital	4 580 . .	387	700	1,525	1,159	802	1,628	688	500
Claims on direct investors	4 585 . .	. . .	. . .	. . .	. . .	. . .	. . .	. . .	. . .
Liabilities to direct investors	4 590 . .	387	700	1,525	1,159	802	1,628	688	500
B. PORTFOLIO INVESTMENT	4 600 . .	8,357	1,852	9,717	10,096	8,788	–6,908	–2,392	–7,496
Assets	4 602 . .	**–1,486**	**–2,882**	**–2,381**	**–1,570**	**–1,906**	**–2,128**	**–1,060**	**2,019**
Equity securities	4 610 . .	–763	–401	–594	–838	–839	167	–1,454	–946
Monetary authorities	4 611 . .	. . .	. . .	. . .	. . .	. . .	. . .	. . .	. . .
General government	4 612 . .	. . .	. . .	. . .	. . .	. . .	. . .	. . .	. . .
Banks	4 613 . .	–15	–40	6	–115	166	20	–12	7
Other sectors	4 614 . .	–748	–361	–600	–723	–1,004	147	–1,442	–952
Debt securities	4 619 . .	–723	–2,481	–1,788	–733	–1,067	–2,296	394	2,965
Bonds and notes	4 620 . .	–723	–2,481	–1,788	–733	–1,067	–2,296	394	2,965
Monetary authorities	4 621 . .	. . .	. . .	. . .	. . .	. . .	. . .	. . .	. . .
General government	4 622 . .	–240	179	–138	421	867	55	1,122	360
Banks	4 623 . .	1	–49	–455	–561	195	–446	–88	1,315
Other sectors	4 624 . .	–484	–2,611	–1,195	–593	–2,129	–1,905	–640	1,290
Money market instruments	4 630 . .	. . .	. . .	. . .	. . .	. . .	. . .	. . .	. . .
Monetary authorities	4 631 . .	. . .	. . .	. . .	. . .	. . .	. . .	. . .	. . .
General government	4 632 . .	. . .	. . .	. . .	. . .	. . .	. . .	. . .	. . .
Banks	4 633 . .	. . .	. . .	. . .	. . .	. . .	. . .	. . .	. . .
Other sectors	4 634 . .	. . .	. . .	. . .	. . .	. . .	. . .	. . .	. . .
Liabilities	4 652 . .	**9,843**	**4,734**	**12,098**	**11,666**	**10,693**	**–4,780**	**–1,331**	**–9,516**
Equity securities	4 660 . .	3,116	1,091	990	1,391	–210	–10,773	–3,227	–81
Banks	4 663 . .	182	248	322	52	13	–75	–274	–72
Other sectors	4 664 . .	2,935	843	669	1,339	–223	–10,698	–2,953	–9
Debt securities	4 669 . .	6,727	3,643	11,108	10,276	10,903	5,993	1,896	–9,435
Bonds and notes	4 670 . .	6,727	3,643	11,108	10,276	10,903	5,993	1,896	–9,435
Monetary authorities	4 671 . .	. . .	. . .	. . .	. . .	. . .	. . .	. . .	. . .
General government	4 672 . .	4,470	2,504	9,116	4,536	5,955	5,297	2,634	–7,185
Banks	4 673 . .	821	–298	1,465	1,086	1,096	188	250	–1,262
Other sectors	4 674 . .	1,436	1,437	527	4,654	3,851	508	–987	–988
Money market instruments	4 680 . .	. . .	. . .	. . .	. . .	. . .	. . .	. . .	. . .
Monetary authorities	4 681 . .	. . .	. . .	. . .	. . .	. . .	. . .	. . .	. . .
General government	4 682 . .	. . .	. . .	. . .	. . .	. . .	. . .	. . .	. . .
Banks	4 683 . .	. . .	. . .	. . .	. . .	. . .	. . .	. . .	. . .
Other sectors	4 684 . .	. . .	. . .	. . .	. . .	. . .	. . .	. . .	. . .
C. FINANCIAL DERIVATIVES	4 910 . .	. . .	. . .	. . .	. . .	. . .	. . .	. . .	. . .
Monetary authorities	4 911 . .	. . .	. . .	. . .	. . .	. . .	. . .	. . .	. . .
General government	4 912 . .	. . .	. . .	. . .	. . .	. . .	. . .	. . .	. . .
Banks	4 913 . .	. . .	. . .	. . .	. . .	. . .	. . .	. . .	. . .
Other sectors	4 914 . .	. . .	. . .	. . .	. . .	. . .	. . .	. . .	. . .
Assets	4 900 . .	**. . .**	**. . .**	**. . .**	**. . .**	**. . .**	**. . .**	**. . .**	**. . .**
Monetary authorities	4 901 . .	. . .	. . .	. . .	. . .	. . .	. . .	. . .	. . .
General government	4 902 . .	. . .	. . .	. . .	. . .	. . .	. . .	. . .	. . .
Banks	4 903 . .	. . .	. . .	. . .	. . .	. . .	. . .	. . .	. . .
Other sectors	4 904 . .	. . .	. . .	. . .	. . .	. . .	. . .	. . .	. . .
Liabilities	4 905 . .	**. . .**	**. . .**	**. . .**	**. . .**	**. . .**	**. . .**	**. . .**	**. . .**
Monetary authorities	4 906 . .	. . .	. . .	. . .	. . .	. . .	. . .	. . .	. . .
General government	4 907 . .	. . .	. . .	. . .	. . .	. . .	. . .	. . .	. . .
Banks	4 908 . .	. . .	. . .	. . .	. . .	. . .	. . .	. . .	. . .
Other sectors	4 909 . .	. . .	. . .	. . .	. . .	. . .	. . .	. . .	. . .

Table 2 (Concluded). STANDARD PRESENTATION, 1994–2001
(Millions of U.S. dollars)

	Code	1994	1995	1996	1997	1998	1999	2000	2001
D. OTHER INVESTMENT	4 700	1,740	1,255	–2,735	1,114	4,589	–1,805	1,296	–96
Assets	4 703	**–3,163**	**–8,123**	**–5,217**	**–7,107**	**–113**	**–2,817**	**–1,764**	**–3,940**
Trade credits	4 706	–352	–230	–193	–275	226	–221	–774	–330
General government	4 707	. . .	. . .	. . .	. . .	. . .	. . .	. . .	. . .
of which: Short-term	4 709	. . .	. . .	. . .	. . .	. . .	. . .	. . .	. . .
Other sectors	4 710	–352	–230	–193	–275	226	–221	–774	–330
of which: Short-term	4 712	*–352*	*–230*	*–193*	*–275*	*226*	*–221*	*–774*	*–330*
Loans	4 714	–211	–1,174	–1,024	–2,813	–1,243	168	–2,334	4,700
Monetary authorities	4 715	. . .	. . .	. . .	. . .	. . .	. . .	. . .	. . .
of which: Short-term	4 718	. . .	. . .	. . .	. . .	. . .	. . .	. . .	. . .
General government	4 719	135	–227	–122	17	–16	–131	–165	–170
of which: Short-term	4 721	. . .	. . .	. . .	. . .	. . .	. . .	. . .	. . .
Banks	4 722	–346	–947	–902	–2,830	–1,227	299	–2,169	4,870
of which: Short-term	4 724	*–346*	*–947*	*–902*	*–2,830*	*–1,227*	*299*	*–2,169*	*4,870*
Other sectors	4 725	. . .	. . .	. . .	. . .	. . .	. . .	. . .	. . .
of which: Short-term	4 727	. . .	. . .	. . .	. . .	. . .	. . .	. . .	. . .
Currency and deposits	4 730	–2,570	–6,695	–3,983	–4,006	912	–2,764	1,344	–8,309
Monetary authorities	4 731	. . .	. . .	. . .	. . .	. . .	. . .	. . .	. . .
General government	4 732	338	–435	201	–94	135	–1,463	1,086	226
Banks	4 733	48	345	–2,137	–2,506	1,840	696	–179	4,068
Other sectors	4 734	–2,956	–6,604	–2,047	–1,406	–1,063	–1,997	437	–12,603
Other assets	4 736	–31	–24	–17	–12	–8	. . .	. . .	–1
Monetary authorities	4 737	. . .	. . .	. . .	. . .	. . .	. . .	. . .	. . .
of which: Short-term	4 739	. . .	. . .	. . .	. . .	. . .	. . .	. . .	. . .
General government	4 740	–31	–24	–17	–12	–8	. . .	. . .	–1
of which: Short-term	4 742	. . .	. . .	. . .	. . .	. . .	. . .	. . .	. . .
Banks	4 743	. . .	. . .	. . .	. . .	. . .	. . .	. . .	. . .
of which: Short-term	4 745	. . .	. . .	. . .	. . .	. . .	. . .	. . .	. . .
Other sectors	4 746	. . .	. . .	. . .	. . .	. . .	. . .	. . .	. . .
of which: Short-term	4 748	. . .	. . .	. . .	. . .	. . .	. . .	. . .	. . .
Liabilities	4 753	**4,903**	**9,378**	**2,483**	**8,221**	**4,702**	**1,012**	**3,060**	**3,845**
Trade credits	4 756	198	2	55	247	630	360	–64	–139
General government	4 757	. . .	. . .	. . .	. . .	. . .	. . .	. . .	. . .
of which: Short-term	4 759	. . .	. . .	. . .	. . .	. . .	. . .	. . .	. . .
Other sectors	4 760	198	2	55	247	630	360	–64	–139
of which: Short-term	4 762	*198*	*2*	*55*	*247*	*630*	*360*	*–64*	*–139*
Loans	4 764	4,538	8,214	1,465	4,241	4,225	574	527	9,695
Monetary authorities	4 765	452	1,921	364	–42	–654	–833	767	10,327
of which: Use of Fund credit and loans from the Fund	4 766	*455*	*1,924*	*367*	*–38*	*–654*	*–826*	*773*	*9,335*
of which: Short-term	4 768	. . .	. . .	. . .	. . .	. . .	. . .	. . .	. . .
General government	4 769	1,431	2,088	–261	225	1,788	1,044	362	1,249
of which: Short-term	4 771	. . .	. . .	. . .	. . .	. . .	. . .	. . .	. . .
Banks	4 772	947	2,152	–255	415	1,088	1,326	–1,481	–1,013
of which: Short-term	4 774	*914*	*2,148*	*–425*	*458*	*1,116*	*1,259*	*–1,447*	*–1,051*
Other sectors	4 775	1,708	2,053	1,617	3,642	2,004	–964	879	–868
of which: Short-term	4 777	. . .	. . .	. . .	. . .	. . .	. . .	. . .	. . .
Currency and deposits	4 780	675	20	–124	1,219	–468	276	1,158	–2,557
Monetary authorities	4 781	. . .	. . .	. . .	. . .	. . .	. . .	. . .	. . .
General government	4 782	. . .	. . .	. . .	. . .	. . .	. . .	. . .	. . .
Banks	4 783	675	20	–124	1,219	–468	276	1,158	–2,557
Other sectors	4 784	. . .	. . .	. . .	. . .	. . .	. . .	. . .	. . .
Other liabilities	4 786	–508	1,141	1,086	2,514	315	–198	1,438	–3,154
Monetary authorities	4 787	–13	9	39	–7	–10	–6	–10	138
of which: Short-term	4 789	*16*	*26*	*54*	*1*	. . .	. . .	*–7*	*145*
General government	4 790	8	20	110	86	135	159	79	246
of which: Short-term	4 792	*8*	*20*	*110*	*86*	*135*	*159*	*79*	*246*
Banks	4 793	–524	1,078	821	2,208	2	–469	1,221	–3,265
of which: Short-term	4 795	*–524*	*1,078*	*821*	*2,208*	*2*	*–469*	*1,221*	*–3,265*
Other sectors	4 796	22	34	116	227	188	118	149	–273
of which: Short-term	4 798	*22*	*34*	*116*	*227*	*188*	*118*	*149*	*–273*
E. RESERVE ASSETS	4 802	–685	82	–3,875	–3,293	–3,436	–1,186	403	12,070
Monetary gold	4 812	. . .	. . .	53	1,490	–4	6	111	4
Special drawing rights	4 811	–82	23	122	212	–95	121	–603	705
Reserve position in the Fund	4 810	. . .	. . .	. . .	. . .	. . .	. . .	. . .	. . .
Foreign exchange	4 803	–603	59	–4,050	–4,995	–3,337	–1,313	895	11,361
Other claims	4 813	. . .	. . .	. . .	. . .	. . .	. . .	. . .	. . .
NET ERRORS AND OMISSIONS	4 998	**–881**	**–2,140**	**–1,682**	**–1,276**	**–447**	**–1,098**	**–1,154**	**–3,362**

Part 3 of the *Yearbook* contains descriptions of the methodologies, compilation practices, and sources used to compile these data.

Table 3. INTERNATIONAL INVESTMENT POSITION (End–period stocks), 1994–2001
(Millions of U.S. dollars)

	Code	1994	1995	1996	1997	1998	1999	2000	2001
ASSETS	8 995 C.	...	...	...	...	139,970	149,583	152,430	132,497
Direct investment abroad	8 505 ..	...	...	...	...	**18,334**	**19,564**	**20,681**	**20,473**
Equity capital and reinvested earnings	8 506 ..	...	...	...	...	18,334	19,564	20,681	20,473
Claims on affiliated enterprises	8 507 ..	...	...	...	...	...	...	...	...
Liabilities to affiliated enterprises	8 508 ..	...	...	...	...	...	...	...	...
Other capital	8 530 ..	...	...	...	...	...	...	...	...
Claims on affiliated enterprises	8 535 ..	...	...	...	...	...	...	...	...
Liabilities to affiliated enterprises	8 540 ..	...	...	...	...	...	...	...	...
Portfolio investment	8 602 ..	...	...	...	...	**29,955**	**34,504**	**34,998**	**23,143**
Equity securities	8 610 ..	...	...	...	...	51	31	43	36
Monetary authorities	8 611 ..	...	...	...	...	...	...	...	...
General government	8 612 ..	...	...	...	...	...	...	...	...
Banks	8 613 ..	...	...	...	...	51	31	43	36
Other sectors	8 614 ..	...	...	...	...	...	...	...	...
Debt securities	8 619 ..	...	...	...	...	29,904	34,473	34,955	23,107
Bonds and notes	8 620 ..	...	...	...	...	29,904	34,473	34,955	23,107
Monetary authorities	8 621 ..	...	...	...	...	...	...	...	...
General government	8 622 ..	...	...	...	...	2,566	2,547	1,782	1,082
Banks	8 623 ..	...	...	...	...	879	1,325	1,413	98
Other sectors	8 624 ..	...	...	...	...	26,459	30,601	31,760	21,927
Money market instruments	8 630 ..	...	...	...	...	...	...	...	...
Monetary authorities	8 631 ..	...	...	...	...	...	...	...	...
General government	8 632 ..	...	...	...	...	...	...	...	...
Banks	8 633 ..	...	...	...	...	...	...	...	...
Other sectors	8 634 ..	...	...	...	...	...	...	...	...
Financial derivatives	8 900 ..	...	...	...	...	...	...	...	...
Monetary authorities	8 901 ..	...	...	...	...	...	...	...	...
General government	8 902 ..	...	...	...	...	...	...	...	...
Banks	8 903 ..	...	...	...	...	...	...	...	...
Other sectors	8 904 ..	...	...	...	...	...	...	...	...
Other investment	8 703 ..	...	...	...	...	**65,432**	**68,194**	**69,826**	**73,963**
Trade credits	8 706 ..	...	...	...	...	2,522	2,743	3,516	3,847
General government	8 707 ..	...	...	...	...	...	...	...	...
of which: Short-term	8 709 ..	...	...	...	...	...	...	...	...
Other sectors	8 710 ..	...	...	...	...	2,522	2,743	3,516	3,847
of which: Short-term	8 712 ..	...	...	...	...	*2,522*	*2,743*	*3,516*	*3,847*
Loans	8 714 ..	...	...	...	...	...	...	...	...
Monetary authorities	8 715 ..	...	...	...	...	...	...	...	...
of which: Short-term	8 718 ..	...	...	...	...	...	...	...	...
General government	8 719 ..	...	...	...	...	...	...	...	...
of which: Short-term	8 721 ..	...	...	...	...	...	...	...	...
Banks	8 722 ..	...	...	...	...	...	...	...	...
of which: Short-term	8 724 ..	...	...	...	...	...	...	...	...
Other sectors	8 725 ..	...	...	...	...	...	...	...	...
of which: Short-term	8 727 ..	...	...	...	...	...	...	...	...
Currency and deposits	8 730 ..	...	...	...	...	49,660	50,961	50,703	59,238
Monetary authorities	8 731 ..	...	...	...	...	...	...	...	...
General government	8 732 ..	...	...	...	...	...	...	...	...
Banks	8 733 ..	...	...	...	...	6,443	5,747	5,926	1,858
Other sectors	8 734 ..	...	...	...	...	43,217	45,214	44,777	57,380
Other assets	8 736 ..	...	...	...	...	13,250	14,490	15,607	10,878
Monetary authorities	8 737 ..	...	...	...	...	...	...	...	...
of which: Short-term	8 739 ..	...	...	...	...	...	...	...	...
General government	8 740 ..	...	...	...	...	5,950	7,489	6,437	6,825
of which: Short-term	8 742 ..	...	...	...	...	...	...	...	...
Banks	8 743 ..	...	...	...	...	7,300	7,001	9,170	4,053
of which: Short-term	8 745 ..	...	...	...	...	...	...	...	...
Other sectors	8 746 ..	...	...	...	...	...	...	...	...
of which: Short-term	8 748 ..	...	...	...	...	...	...	...	...
Reserve assets	8 802 ..	...	...	...	...	**26,249**	**27,321**	**26,925**	**14,918**
Monetary gold	8 812 ..	...	...	...	...	124	121	7	3
Special drawing rights	8 811 ..	563	539	399	167	264	138	733	11
Reserve position in the Fund	8 810 ..	...	...	...	...	...	...	...	...
Foreign exchange	8 803 ..	...	...	...	...	25,832	27,049	26,182	14,909
Other claims	8 813 ..	...	...	...	...	29	13	3	-5

Table 3 (Concluded). INTERNATIONAL INVESTMENT POSITION (End–period stocks), 1994–2001
(Millions of U.S. dollars)

	Code		1994	1995	1996	1997	1998	1999	2000	2001
LIABILITIES	8 995	D.	...	...	...	...	206,758	218,957	227,127	222,117
Direct investment in Argentina	8 555	..	...	...	...	...	**47,898**	**62,088**	**73,104**	**76,167**
Equity capital and reinvested earnings	8 556	..	...	...	...	...	42,193	54,814	65,150	67,713
Claims on direct investors	8 557	..	...	...	...	...	...	...	...	...
Liabilities to direct investors	8 558	..	...	...	...	...	...	...	...	...
Other capital	8 580	..	...	...	...	...	5,705	7,274	7,954	8,454
Claims on direct investors	8 585	..	...	...	...	...	...	...	...	...
Liabilities to direct investors	8 590	..	...	...	...	...	5,705	7,274	7,954	8,454
Portfolio investment	8 652	..	...	...	...	...	**94,566**	**91,776**	**86,691**	**75,808**
Equity securities	8 660	..	...	...	...	...	14,297	8,389	3,636	2,103
Banks	8 663	..	...	...	...	...	1,672	1,612	994	263
Other sectors	8 664	..	...	...	...	...	12,625	6,777	2,642	1,840
Debt securities	8 669	..	...	...	...	...	80,269	83,387	83,055	73,705
Bonds and notes	8 670	..	...	...	...	...	80,269	83,387	83,055	73,705
Monetary authorities	8 671	..	...	...	...	...	...	...	...	...
General government	8 672	..	...	...	...	...	56,794	59,271	59,673	52,677
Banks	8 673	..	...	...	...	...	6,161	6,349	6,598	5,337
Other sectors	8 674	..	...	...	...	...	17,314	17,767	16,784	15,691
Money market instruments	8 680	..	...	...	...	...	...	...	...	...
Monetary authorities	8 681	..	...	...	...	...	...	...	...	...
General government	8 682	..	...	...	...	...	...	...	...	...
Banks	8 683	..	...	...	...	...	...	...	...	...
Other sectors	8 684	..	...	...	...	...	...	...	...	...
Financial derivatives	8 905	..	...	...	...	...	...	...	...	...
Monetary authorities	8 906	..	...	...	...	...	...	...	...	...
General government	8 907	..	...	...	...	...	...	...	...	...
Banks	8 908	..	...	...	...	...	...	...	...	...
Other sectors	8 909	..	...	...	...	...	...	...	...	...
Other investment	8 753	..	...	...	...	...	**64,294**	**65,093**	**67,332**	**70,142**
Trade credits	8 756	..	...	...	...	...	2,219	2,576	2,557	2,354
General government	8 757	..	...	...	...	...	158	163	245	208
of which: Short-term	8 759	..	...	...	...	...	...	...	...	...
Other sectors	8 760	..	...	...	...	...	2,061	2,413	2,312	2,146
of which: Short-term	8 762	..	...	...	...	...	*1,443*	*1,689*	*1,618*	*1,502*
Loans	8 764	..	...	...	...	...	59,721	59,887	60,987	66,557
Monetary authorities	8 765	..	...	...	...	...	5,462	4,493	5,067	14,980
of which: Use of Fund credit and loans from the Fund	8 766	..	*4,211*	*6,131*	*6,293*	*5,868*	*5,442*	*4,478*	*5,056*	*13,976*
of which: Short-term	8 768	..	...	...	...	...	...	...	...	...
General government	8 769	..	...	...	...	...	22,607	23,171	22,685	23,322
of which: Short-term	8 771	..	...	...	...	...	...	...	...	...
Banks	8 772	..	...	...	...	...	13,791	14,649	14,389	10,111
of which: Short-term	8 774	..	...	...	...	...	...	...	...	...
Other sectors	8 775	..	...	...	...	...	17,861	17,574	18,846	18,144
of which: Short-term	8 777	..	...	...	...	...	...	...	...	...
Currency and deposits	8 780	..	...	...	...	...	2,354	2,630	3,788	1,231
Monetary authorities	8 781	..	...	...	...	...	...	...	...	...
General government	8 782	..	...	...	...	...	...	...	...	...
Banks	8 783	..	...	...	...	...	2,354	2,630	3,788	1,231
Other sectors	8 784	..	...	...	...	...	...	...	...	...
Other liabilities	8 786	..	...	...	...	...	...	...	...	...
Monetary authorities	8 787	..	...	...	...	...	...	...	...	...
of which: Short-term	8 789	..	...	...	...	...	...	...	...	...
General government	8 790	..	...	...	...	...	...	...	...	...
of which: Short-term	8 792	..	...	...	...	...	...	...	...	...
Banks	8 793	..	...	...	...	...	...	...	...	...
of which: Short-term	8 795	..	...	...	...	...	...	...	...	...
Other sectors	8 796	..	...	...	...	...	...	...	...	...
of which: Short-term	8 798	..	...	...	...	...	...	...	...	...
NET INTERNATIONAL INVESTMENT POSITION	8 995	..	...	...	...	...	**–66,788**	**–69,374**	**–74,697**	**–89,621**
Conversion rates: Argentine peso per U.S. dollar (end of period)	0 102	..	**.99950**	**1.00000**	**.99950**	**.99950**	**.99950**	**.99950**	**.99950**	**.99950**

Table 1. ANALYTIC PRESENTATION, 1994–2001
(Millions of U.S. dollars)

	Code	1994	1995	1996	1997	1998	1999	2000	2001
A. Current Account[1]	4 993 Z.	**–103.78**	**–218.37**	**–290.68**	**–306.51**	**–417.96**	**–307.05**	**–278.34**	**–200.52**
Goods: exports f.o.b	2 100 ..	215.35	270.90	290.44	233.64	228.89	247.31	309.92	353.11
Goods: imports f.o.b	3 100 ..	–393.63	–673.87	–759.63	–793.10	–806.29	–721.35	–773.41	–773.34
Balance on Goods	4 100 ..	*–178.28*	*–402.97*	*–469.19*	*–559.46*	*–577.40*	*–474.04*	*–463.49*	*–420.23*
Services: credit	2 200 ..	13.67	28.60	77.71	96.60	130.34	135.81	136.94	186.54
Services: debit	3 200 ..	–40.70	–52.27	–128.52	–159.38	–208.71	–197.87	–192.75	–204.34
Balance on Goods and Services	4 991 ..	*–205.31*	*–426.64*	*–520.00*	*–622.24*	*–655.77*	*–536.10*	*–519.30*	*–438.03*
Income: credit	2 300 ..	...	54.63	78.04	138.95	103.91	93.57	103.74	103.08
Income: debit	3 300 ..	–4.02	–14.61	–33.31	–40.44	–43.51	–38.64	–50.84	–39.55
Balance on Goods, Services, and Income	4 992 ..	*–209.33*	*–386.62*	*–475.27*	*–523.73*	*–595.37*	*–481.17*	*–466.40*	*–374.50*
Current transfers: credit	2 379 Z.	106.33	169.95	198.99	252.41	203.02	200.57	208.52	200.79
Current transfers: debit	3 379 ..	–.78	–1.70	–14.40	–35.19	–25.61	–26.45	–20.46	–26.81
B. Capital Account[1]	4 994 Z.	**5.74**	**8.05**	**13.40**	**10.88**	**9.74**	**12.55**	**28.31**	**30.12**
Capital account: credit	2 994 Z.	5.74	8.05	13.40	10.88	9.74	16.85	29.49	32.57
Capital account: debit	3 994 ..	...	...	...	...	...	–4.30	–1.18	–2.45
Total, Groups A Plus B	4 981 ..	*–98.04*	*–210.32*	*–277.28*	*–295.63*	*–408.22*	*–294.50*	*–250.03*	*–170.40*
C. Financial Account[1]	4 995 W.	**89.94**	**227.48**	**216.76**	**334.82**	**390.43**	**286.18**	**249.88**	**176.86**
Direct investment abroad	4 505 ..	...	...	...	...	...	...	...	...
Direct investment in Armenia	4 555 Z.	8.00	25.32	17.57	51.94	220.83	122.04	104.19	69.87
Portfolio investment assets	4 602 ..	...	...	–.01	–.14	.63	.06	–19.10	–5.76
Equity securities	4 610 ..	...	...	–.01	–.03	.53	.01	–3.01	–.53
Debt securities	4 619 ..	...	...	...	–.11	.10	.05	–16.09	–5.23
Portfolio investment liabilities	4 652 Z.	...	...	7.23	15.90	–16.57	1.58	.25	–.09
Equity securities	4 660 ..	...	...	1.88	.46	.72	–.32	.40	.50
Debt securities	4 669 Z.	...	...	5.35	15.44	–17.29	1.90	–.15	–.59
Financial derivatives	4 910 ..	...	...	...	...	...	...	...	...
Financial derivatives assets	4 900 ..	...	...	...	...	...	...	...	...
Financial derivatives liabilities	4 905 ..	...	...	...	...	...	...	...	...
Other investment assets	4 703 ..	35.89	–8.60	35.34	40.76	19.97	2.97	–9.49	–18.23
Monetary authorities	4 701 ..	...	–8.58	–.08	1.36	.07	.06	–.10	.14
General government	4 704 ..	–6.24	...	...	...	–43.27	15.56	11.33	12.76
Banks	4 705 ..	.27	–.02	7.33	–17.57	6.17	–34.42	–14.11	–19.70
Other sectors	4 728 ..	41.86	...	28.09	56.97	57.00	21.77	–6.61	–11.43
Other investment liabilities	4 753 W.	46.05	210.76	156.63	226.36	165.57	159.53	174.03	131.07
Monetary authorities	4 753 WA	–9.18	.53	4.68	.04	–2.92	–.93	1.59	3.79
General government	4 753 ZB	55.26	151.20	44.21	122.86	35.01	80.16	44.28	64.25
Banks	4 753 ZC	–.03	.03	26.18	29.04	23.99	11.19	8.78	–3.70
Other sectors	4 753 ZD	...	59.00	81.56	74.50	109.49	69.11	119.38	66.73
Total, Groups A Through C	4 983 ..	*–8.10*	*17.16*	*–60.52*	*39.19*	*–17.79*	*–8.32*	*–.15*	*6.46*
D. Net Errors and Omissions	4 998 ..	**4.83**	**12.35**	**15.06**	**10.83**	**18.39**	**13.11**	**17.05**	**12.14**
Total, Groups A Through D	4 984 ..	*–3.27*	*29.51*	*–45.46*	*50.02*	*.60*	*4.79*	*16.90*	*18.60*
E. Reserves and Related Items	4 802 A.	**3.27**	**–29.51**	**45.46**	**–50.02**	**–.60**	**–4.79**	**–16.90**	**–18.60**
Reserve assets	4 802 ..	–21.24	–76.22	–60.35	–73.48	–52.13	–20.79	–19.75	–20.02
Use of Fund credit and loans	4 766 ..	24.50	46.71	49.04	23.46	51.53	16.00	–15.91	3.35
Exceptional financing	4 920 ..	...	...	56.77	...	...	...	18.77	–1.93
Conversion rates: drams per U.S. dollar	0 101 ..	**288.65**	**405.91**	**414.04**	**490.85**	**504.92**	**535.06**	**539.53**	**555.08**

[1] Excludes components that have been classified in the categories of Group E.

Table 2. STANDARD PRESENTATION, 1994–2001

(Millions of U.S. dollars)

	Code		1994	1995	1996	1997	1998	1999	2000	2001
CURRENT ACCOUNT	4 993	. .	**–103.78**	**–218.37**	**–290.68**	**–306.51**	**–417.96**	**–307.05**	**–278.34**	**–200.52**
A. GOODS	4 100	. .	–178.28	–402.97	–469.19	–559.46	–577.40	–474.04	–463.49	–420.23
Credit	2 100	. .	**215.35**	**270.90**	**290.44**	**233.64**	**228.89**	**247.31**	**309.92**	**353.11**
General merchandise: exports f.o.b.	2 110	. .	215.35	270.90	290.30	232.50	220.52	231.67	300.49	341.83
Goods for processing: exports f.o.b.	2 150	. .	. . .	. . .	. . .	. . .	. . .	12.23	5.45	3.01
Repairs on goods	2 160	. .	. . .	. . .	. . .	. . .	. . .	. . .	. . .	. . .
Goods procured in ports by carriers	2 170	. .	. . .	. . .	.14	1.14	8.37	3.41	3.98	8.27
Nonmonetary gold	2 180	. .	. . .	. . .	. . .	. . .	. . .	. . .	. . .	. . .
Debit	3 100	. .	**–393.63**	**–673.87**	**–759.63**	**–793.10**	**–806.29**	**–721.35**	**–773.41**	**–773.34**
General merchandise: imports f.o.b.	3 110	. .	–393.63	–673.87	–757.37	–779.43	–794.64	–697.38	–759.44	–753.90
Goods for processing: imports f.o.b.	3 150	. .	. . .	. . .	. . .	. . .	. . .	–13.96	–3.54	–1.80
Repairs on goods	3 160	. .	. . .	. . .	. . .	. . .	–.45	. . .	. . .	. . .
Goods procured in ports by carriers	3 170	. .	. . .	. . .	–2.26	–13.67	–11.20	–10.01	–10.43	–17.64
Nonmonetary gold	3 180	. .	. . .	. . .	. . .	. . .	. . .	. . .	. . .	. . .
B. SERVICES	4 200	. .	–27.03	–23.67	–50.81	–62.78	–78.37	–62.06	–55.81	–17.80
Total credit	2 200	. .	*13.67*	*28.60*	*77.71*	*96.60*	*130.34*	*135.81*	*136.94*	*186.54*
Total debit	3 200	. .	*–40.70*	*–52.27*	*–128.52*	*–159.38*	*–208.71*	*–197.87*	*–192.75*	*–204.34*
Transportation services, credit	2 205	. .	**3.56**	**14.27**	**36.17**	**50.63**	**52.63**	**53.12**	**63.95**	**71.16**
Passenger	2 850	. .	*3.56*	*12.82*	*5.80*	*12.69*	*16.56*	*15.62*	*13.57*	*16.14*
Freight	2 851	. .	. . .	*1.45*	*30.37*	*37.94*	*31.85*	*33.30*	*42.79*	*46.92*
Other	2 852	. .	. . .	. . .	. . .	. . .	*4.22*	*4.20*	*7.59*	*8.10*
Sea transport, passenger	2 207	. .	. . .	. . .	. . .	. . .	. . .	. . .	. . .	. . .
Sea transport, freight	2 208	. .	. . .	. . .	. . .	. . .	. . .	. . .	. . .	. . .
Sea transport, other	2 209	. .	. . .	. . .	. . .	. . .	. . .	. . .	. . .	. . .
Air transport, passenger	2 211	. .	3.56	12.31	5.34	8.19	12.42	12.34	10.85	13.53
Air transport, freight	2 212	. .	. . .	.95	1.77	10.58	2.61	1.78	1.73	1.60
Air transport, other	2 213	. .	. . .	. . .	. . .	. . .	4.22	4.20	7.59	8.10
Other transport, passenger	2 215	. .	. . .	.51	.46	4.50	4.14	3.28	2.72	2.61
Other transport, freight	2 216	. .	. . .	.50	28.60	27.36	29.24	31.52	41.06	45.32
Other transport, other	2 217	. .	. . .	. . .	. . .	. . .	. . .	. . .	. . .	. . .
Transportation services, debit	3 205	. .	**–32.23**	**–43.19**	**–92.11**	**–91.84**	**–124.94**	**–107.14**	**–115.95**	**–120.60**
Passenger	3 850	. .	. . .	*–8.86*	*–3.55*	*–3.86*	*–13.79*	*–14.17*	*–15.56*	*–19.30*
Freight	3 851	. .	. . .	*–34.33*	*–88.56*	*–87.98*	*–72.80*	*–75.30*	*–82.54*	*–82.64*
Other	3 852	. .	. . .	. . .	. . .	. . .	*–38.35*	*–17.67*	*–17.85*	*–18.66*
Sea transport, passenger	3 207	. .	. . .	. . .	. . .	. . .	. . .	. . .	. . .	. . .
Sea transport, freight	3 208	. .	. . .	. . .	. . .	. . .	. . .	–8.12	–11.10	–10.05
Sea transport, other	3 209	. .	. . .	. . .	. . .	. . .	. . .	. . .	. . .	. . .
Air transport, passenger	3 211	. .	. . .	–8.01	–3.14	–2.45	–10.11	–11.38	–12.04	–15.75
Air transport, freight	3 212	. .	. . .	–6.83	–1.64	–4.40	–1.03	–.36	–.65	–.62
Air transport, other	3 213	. .	. . .	. . .	. . .	. . .	–23.20	–17.63	–17.85	–18.66
Other transport, passenger	3 215	. .	. . .	–.85	–.41	–1.41	–3.68	–2.79	–3.52	–3.55
Other transport, freight	3 216	. .	. . .	–27.50	–86.92	–83.58	–71.77	–66.82	–70.79	–71.97
Other transport, other	3 217	. .	. . .	. . .	. . .	. . .	–15.15	–.04	. . .	. . .
Travel, credit	2 236	. .	**. . .**	**1.40**	**11.80**	**19.55**	**23.56**	**30.99**	**37.76**	**64.89**
Business travel	2 237	. .	. . .	1.00	3.86	13.78	8.02	23.42	14.35	33.42
Personal travel	2 240	. .	. . .	.40	7.94	5.77	15.54	7.57	23.41	31.47
Travel, debit	3 236	. .	**–.79**	**–3.26**	**–21.80**	**–41.43**	**–41.12**	**–36.72**	**–39.68**	**–39.74**
Business travel	3 237	. .	–.79	–1.71	–17.00	–30.63	–38.10	–29.35	–27.71	–25.17
Personal travel	3 240	. .	. . .	–1.55	–4.80	–10.80	–3.02	–7.37	–11.97	–14.57
Other services, credit	2 200	BA	**10.11**	**12.93**	**29.74**	**26.42**	**54.15**	**51.70**	**35.23**	**50.49**
Communications	2 245	. .	8.47	11.03	18.95	14.33	25.65	32.06	15.84	22.69
Construction	2 249	. .	.20	. . .	1.18	1.63	. . .	. . .	. . .	.67
Insurance	2 253	. .	. . .	. . .	2.91	2.32	2.21	2.32	3.01	3.52
Financial	2 260	. .	. . .	. . .	2.10	.64	.88	1.34	1.38	.88
Computer and information	2 262	. .	. . .	. . .	. . .	. . .	. . .	.28	1.97	8.36
Royalties and licence fees	2 266	. .	. . .	. . .	. . .	. . .	. . .	. . .	. . .	. . .
Other business services	2 268	. .	. . .	. . .	. . .	4.83	6.65	4.52	5.60	5.56
Personal, cultural, and recreational	2 287	. .	. . .	. . .	2.00	2.67	6.51	4.81	.78	1.70
Government, n.i.e.	2 291	. .	1.44	1.90	2.60	. . .	12.25	6.37	6.65	7.11
Other services, debit	3 200	BA	**–7.68**	**–5.82**	**–14.61**	**–26.11**	**–42.65**	**–54.01**	**–37.12**	**–44.00**
Communications	3 245	. .	. . .	–.45	–3.04	–3.08	–4.85	–20.47	–8.70	–13.95
Construction	3 249	. .	–.18	. . .	–1.05	–2.17	. . .	. . .	. . .	–.78
Insurance	3 253	. .	–3.57	–5.37	–9.84	–11.29	–10.76	–9.59	–10.19	–10.36
Financial	3 260	. .	. . .	. . .	–.15	–.59	–1.69	–3.52	–1.16	–.41
Computer and information	3 262	. .	. . .	. . .	. . .	. . .	. . .	–.06	. . .	. . .
Royalties and licence fees	3 266	. .	. . .	. . .	. . .	. . .	. . .	. . .	. . .	. . .
Other business services	3 268	. .	–3.93	. . .	–.47	–3.25	–2.78	–2.16	–.46	–1.53
Personal, cultural, and recreational	3 287	. .	. . .	. . .	–.06	–3.13	–4.03	–3.40	–.75	–4.55
Government, n.i.e.	3 291	. .	. . .	. . .	. . .	–2.60	–18.54	–14.81	–15.86	–12.42

Table 2 (Continued). STANDARD PRESENTATION, 1994–2001
(Millions of U.S. dollars)

	Code		1994	1995	1996	1997	1998	1999	2000	2001
C. INCOME	4 300	. .	–4.02	40.02	44.73	98.51	60.40	54.93	52.90	63.53
Total credit	2 300	. .	*. . .*	*54.63*	*78.04*	*138.95*	*103.91*	*93.57*	*103.74*	*103.08*
Total debit	3 300	. .	*–4.02*	*–14.61*	*–33.31*	*–40.44*	*–43.51*	*–38.64*	*–50.84*	*–39.55*
Compensation of employees, credit	2 310	. .	**. . .**	**53.00**	**72.74**	**127.40**	**82.31**	**79.73**	**78.16**	**84.23**
Compensation of employees, debit	3 310	. .	**. . .**	**. . .**	**–17.00**	**–3.40**	**. . .**	**–.92**	**–1.21**	**–11.70**
Investment income, credit	2 320	. .	**. . .**	**1.63**	**5.30**	**11.55**	**21.60**	**13.84**	**25.58**	**18.85**
Direct investment income	2 330	. .	. . .	. . .	. . .	. . .	.80	. . .	. . .	. . .
Dividends and distributed branch profits	2 332	. .	. . .	. . .	. . .	. . .	. . .	. . .	. . .	. . .
Reinvested earnings and undistributed branch profits	2 333	. .	. . .	. . .	. . .	. . .	. . .	. . .	. . .	. . .
Income on debt (interest)	2 334	. .	. . .	. . .	. . .	. . .	.80	. . .	. . .	. . .
Portfolio investment income	2 339	. .	. . .	1.00	.30	.20	2.57	1.33	1.99	1.44
Income on equity	2 340	. .	. . .	.50	.30	. . .	. . .	. . .	. . .	. . .
Income on bonds and notes	2 350	. .	. . .	.50	. . .	. . .	2.57	. . .	. . .	. . .
Income on money market instruments	2 360	. .	. . .	. . .	. . .	.20	. . .	1.33	1.99	1.44
Other investment income	2 370	. .	. . .	.63	5.00	11.35	18.23	12.51	23.59	17.41
Investment income, debit	3 320	. .	**–4.02**	**–14.61**	**–16.31**	**–37.04**	**–43.51**	**–37.72**	**–49.63**	**–27.85**
Direct investment income	3 330	. .	. . .	. . .	–3.28	–11.12	–19.84	–13.97	–22.02	–3.58
Dividends and distributed branch profits	3 332	. .	. . .	. . .	–3.28	–7.20	. . .	. . .	. . .	. . .
Reinvested earnings and undistributed branch profits	3 333	. .	. . .	. . .	. . .	–3.92	–19.84	–13.97	–22.02	–3.58
Income on debt (interest)	3 334	. .	. . .	. . .	. . .	. . .	. . .	. . .	. . .	. . .
Portfolio investment income	3 339	. .	. . .	. . .	–.70	–8.52	–1.17	–1.91	–1.21	–1.33
Income on equity	3 340	. .	. . .	. . .	–.70	. . .	. . .	. . .	. . .	. . .
Income on bonds and notes	3 350	. .	. . .	. . .	. . .	. . .	. . .	–.04	. . .	–.15
Income on money market instruments	3 360	. .	. . .	. . .	. . .	–8.52	–1.17	–1.87	–1.21	–1.18
Other investment income	3 370	. .	–4.02	–14.61	–12.33	–17.40	–22.50	–21.84	–26.40	–22.94
D. CURRENT TRANSFERS	4 379	. .	105.55	168.25	184.59	217.22	177.41	174.12	188.06	173.98
Credit	2 379	. .	**106.33**	**169.95**	**198.99**	**252.41**	**203.02**	**200.57**	**208.52**	**200.79**
General government	2 380	. .	95.21	151.60	118.00	150.82	118.67	97.64	104.52	75.77
Other sectors	2 390	. .	11.12	18.35	80.99	101.59	84.35	102.93	104.00	125.02
Workers' remittances	2 391	. .	. . .	12.35	11.12	8.74	10.10	14.92	9.31	10.16
Other current transfers	2 392	. .	11.12	6.00	69.87	92.85	74.25	88.01	94.69	114.86
Debit	3 379	. .	**–.78**	**–1.70**	**–14.40**	**–35.19**	**–25.61**	**–26.45**	**–20.46**	**–26.81**
General government	3 380	. .	–.78	–1.70	–.90	–1.40	–5.94	–3.87	–2.01	–3.88
Other sectors	3 390	. .	. . .	. . .	–13.50	–33.79	–19.67	–22.58	–18.45	–22.93
Workers' remittances	3 391	. .	. . .	. . .	. . .	–1.94	–3.21	–7.13	–2.31	–6.38
Other current transfers	3 392	. .	. . .	. . .	–13.50	–31.85	–16.46	–15.45	–16.14	–16.55
CAPITAL AND FINANCIAL ACCOUNT	4 996	. .	**98.95**	**206.02**	**275.62**	**295.68**	**399.57**	**293.94**	**261.29**	**188.38**
CAPITAL ACCOUNT	4 994	. .	**5.74**	**8.05**	**13.40**	**10.88**	**9.74**	**12.55**	**28.31**	**30.12**
Total credit	2 994	. .	*5.74*	*8.05*	*13.40*	*10.88*	*9.74*	*16.85*	*29.49*	*32.57*
Total debit	3 994	. .	*. . .*	*. . .*	*. . .*	*. . .*	*. . .*	*–4.30*	*–1.18*	*–2.45*
Capital transfers, credit	2 400	. .	**5.74**	**8.05**	**13.40**	**10.88**	**9.74**	**16.85**	**29.49**	**32.57**
General government	2 401	. .	5.74	8.05	13.40	10.88	9.74	16.85	29.49	32.57
Debt forgiveness	2 402	. .	. . .	. . .	. . .	. . .	. . .	. . .	. . .	. . .
Other capital transfers	2 410	. .	5.74	8.05	13.40	10.88	9.74	16.85	29.49	32.57
Other sectors	2 430	. .	. . .	. . .	. . .	. . .	. . .	. . .	. . .	. . .
Migrants' transfers	2 431	. .	. . .	. . .	. . .	. . .	. . .	. . .	. . .	. . .
Debt forgiveness	2 432	. .	. . .	. . .	. . .	. . .	. . .	. . .	. . .	. . .
Other capital transfers	2 440	. .	. . .	. . .	. . .	. . .	. . .	. . .	. . .	. . .
Capital transfers, debit	3 400	. .	**. . .**	**. . .**	**. . .**	**. . .**	**. . .**	**–4.30**	**–1.18**	**–2.45**
General government	3 401	. .	. . .	. . .	. . .	. . .	. . .	. . .	. . .	. . .
Debt forgiveness	3 402	. .	. . .	. . .	. . .	. . .	. . .	. . .	. . .	. . .
Other capital transfers	3 410	. .	. . .	. . .	. . .	. . .	. . .	. . .	. . .	. . .
Other sectors	3 430	. .	. . .	. . .	. . .	. . .	. . .	–4.30	–1.18	–2.45
Migrants' transfers	3 431	. .	. . .	. . .	. . .	. . .	. . .	–4.30	–1.18	–2.45
Debt forgiveness	3 432	. .	. . .	. . .	. . .	. . .	. . .	. . .	. . .	. . .
Other capital transfers	3 440	. .	. . .	. . .	. . .	. . .	. . .	. . .	. . .	. . .
Nonproduced nonfinancial assets, credit	2 480	. .	**. . .**	**. . .**	**. . .**	**. . .**	**. . .**	**. . .**	**. . .**	**. . .**
Nonproduced nonfinancial assets, debit	3 480	. .	**. . .**	**. . .**	**. . .**	**. . .**	**. . .**	**. . .**	**. . .**	**. . .**

Table 2 (Continued). STANDARD PRESENTATION, 1994–2001

(Millions of U.S. dollars)

	Code		1994	1995	1996	1997	1998	1999	2000	2001
FINANCIAL ACCOUNT	4 995	. .	**93.21**	**197.97**	**262.22**	**284.80**	**389.83**	**281.39**	**232.98**	**158.26**
A. DIRECT INVESTMENT	4 500	. .	8.00	25.32	17.57	51.94	220.83	122.04	104.19	69.87
Direct investment abroad	4 505	. .	**. . .**	**. . .**	**. . .**	**. . .**	**. . .**	**. . .**	**. . .**	**. . .**
Equity capital	4 510	. .	. . .	. . .	. . .	. . .	. . .	. . .	. . .	. . .
Claims on affiliated enterprises	4 515	. .	. . .	. . .	. . .	. . .	. . .	. . .	. . .	. . .
Liabilities to affiliated enterprises	4 520	. .	. . .	. . .	. . .	. . .	. . .	. . .	. . .	. . .
Reinvested earnings	4 525	. .	. . .	. . .	. . .	. . .	. . .	. . .	. . .	. . .
Other capital	4 530	. .	. . .	. . .	. . .	. . .	. . .	. . .	. . .	. . .
Claims on affiliated enterprises	4 535	. .	. . .	. . .	. . .	. . .	. . .	. . .	. . .	. . .
Liabilities to affiliated enterprise	4 540	. .	. . .	. . .	. . .	. . .	. . .	. . .	. . .	. . .
Direct investment in Armenia	4 555	. .	**8.00**	**25.32**	**17.57**	**51.94**	**220.83**	**122.04**	**104.19**	**69.87**
Equity capital	4 560	. .	8.00	5.32	17.57	48.02	118.40	61.14	68.47	60.80
Claims on direct investors	4 565	. .	. . .	. . .	. . .	. . .	. . .	. . .	. . .	. . .
Liabilities to direct investors	4 570	. .	8.00	5.32	17.57	48.02	118.40	61.14	68.47	60.80
Reinvested earnings	4 575	. .	. . .	. . .	. . .	3.92	19.84	13.97	22.02	3.58
Other capital	4 580	. .	. . .	20.00	. . .	. . .	82.59	46.93	13.70	5.49
Claims on direct investors	4 585	. .	. . .	. . .	. . .	. . .	. . .	. . .	. . .	. . .
Liabilities to direct investors	4 590	. .	. . .	20.00	. . .	. . .	82.59	46.93	13.70	5.49
B. PORTFOLIO INVESTMENT	4 600	. .	. . .	. . .	7.22	15.76	–15.94	1.64	–18.85	–5.85
Assets	4 602	. .	**. . .**	**. . .**	**–.01**	**–.14**	**.63**	**.06**	**–19.10**	**–5.76**
Equity securities	4 610	. .	. . .	. . .	–.01	–.03	.53	.01	–3.01	–.53
Monetary authorities	4 611	. .	. . .	. . .	. . .	. . .	. . .	. . .	. . .	. . .
General government	4 612	. .	. . .	. . .	. . .	. . .	. . .	. . .	. . .	. . .
Banks	4 613	. .	. . .	. . .	–.01	–.03	.39	.01	–.41	.20
Other sectors	4 614	. .	. . .	. . .	. . .	. . .	.14	. . .	–2.60	–.73
Debt securities	4 619	. .	. . .	. . .	. . .	–.11	.10	.05	–16.09	–5.23
Bonds and notes	4 620	. .	. . .	. . .	. . .	–.11	.03	. . .	–16.09	–5.23
Monetary authorities	4 621	. .	. . .	. . .	. . .	. . .	. . .	. . .	. . .	. . .
General government	4 622	. .	. . .	. . .	. . .	. . .	. . .	. . .	. . .	. . .
Banks	4 623	. .	. . .	. . .	. . .	. . .	. . .	. . .	. . .	. . .
Other sectors	4 624	. .	. . .	. . .	. . .	–.11	.03	. . .	–16.09	–5.23
Money market instruments	4 630	. .	. . .	. . .	. . .	. . .	.07	.05	. . .	. . .
Monetary authorities	4 631	. .	. . .	. . .	. . .	. . .	. . .	. . .	. . .	. . .
General government	4 632	. .	. . .	. . .	. . .	. . .	. . .	. . .	. . .	. . .
Banks	4 633	. .	. . .	. . .	. . .	. . .	.07	.05	. . .	. . .
Other sectors	4 634	. .	. . .	. . .	. . .	. . .	. . .	. . .	. . .	. . .
Liabilities	4 652	. .	**. . .**	**. . .**	**7.23**	**15.90**	**–16.57**	**1.58**	**.25**	**–.09**
Equity securities	4 660	. .	. . .	. . .	1.88	.46	.72	–.32	.40	.50
Banks	4 663	. .	. . .	. . .	1.88	.46	.72	–.32	.20	.50
Other sectors	4 664	. .	. . .	. . .	. . .	. . .	. . .	. . .	.20	. . .
Debt securities	4 669	. .	. . .	. . .	5.35	15.44	–17.29	1.90	–.15	–.59
Bonds and notes	4 670	. .	. . .	. . .	–.02	5.62	.14	. . .	. . .	. . .
Monetary authorities	4 671	. .	. . .	. . .	. . .	. . .	. . .	. . .	. . .	. . .
General government	4 672	. .	. . .	. . .	. . .	. . .	. . .	. . .	. . .	. . .
Banks	4 673	. .	. . .	. . .	–.02	.02	. . .	. . .	. . .	. . .
Other sectors	4 674	. .	. . .	. . .	. . .	5.60	.14	. . .	. . .	. . .
Money market instruments	4 680	. .	. . .	. . .	5.37	9.82	–17.43	1.90	–.15	–.59
Monetary authorities	4 681	. .	. . .	. . .	. . .	. . .	. . .	. . .	. . .	. . .
General government	4 682	. .	. . .	. . .	5.37	9.80	–21.17	1.90	–.15	–.59
Banks	4 683	. .	. . .	. . .	. . .	.02	3.74	. . .	. . .	. . .
Other sectors	4 684	. .	. . .	. . .	. . .	. . .	. . .	. . .	. . .	. . .
C. FINANCIAL DERIVATIVES	4 910	. .	. . .	. . .	. . .	. . .	. . .	. . .	. . .	. . .
Monetary authorities	4 911	. .	. . .	. . .	. . .	. . .	. . .	. . .	. . .	. . .
General government	4 912	. .	. . .	. . .	. . .	. . .	. . .	. . .	. . .	. . .
Banks	4 913	. .	. . .	. . .	. . .	. . .	. . .	. . .	. . .	. . .
Other sectors	4 914	. .	. . .	. . .	. . .	. . .	. . .	. . .	. . .	. . .
Assets	4 900	. .	**. . .**	**. . .**	**. . .**	**. . .**	**. . .**	**. . .**	**. . .**	**. . .**
Monetary authorities	4 901	. .	. . .	. . .	. . .	. . .	. . .	. . .	. . .	. . .
General government	4 902	. .	. . .	. . .	. . .	. . .	. . .	. . .	. . .	. . .
Banks	4 903	. .	. . .	. . .	. . .	. . .	. . .	. . .	. . .	. . .
Other sectors	4 904	. .	. . .	. . .	. . .	. . .	. . .	. . .	. . .	. . .
Liabilities	4 905	. .	**. . .**	**. . .**	**. . .**	**. . .**	**. . .**	**. . .**	**. . .**	**. . .**
Monetary authorities	4 906	. .	. . .	. . .	. . .	. . .	. . .	. . .	. . .	. . .
General government	4 907	. .	. . .	. . .	. . .	. . .	. . .	. . .	. . .	. . .
Banks	4 908	. .	. . .	. . .	. . .	. . .	. . .	. . .	. . .	. . .
Other sectors	4 909	. .	. . .	. . .	. . .	. . .	. . .	. . .	. . .	. . .

Table 2 (Concluded). STANDARD PRESENTATION, 1994–2001
(Millions of U.S. dollars)

	Code	1994	1995	1996	1997	1998	1999	2000	2001
D. OTHER INVESTMENT	4 700 . .	106.44	248.87	297.78	290.58	237.07	178.50	167.40	114.26
Assets	4 703 . .	**35.89**	**–8.60**	**35.34**	**40.76**	**19.97**	**2.97**	**–9.49**	**–18.23**
Trade credits	4 706 . .	42.12	. . .	. . .	. . .	. . .	–20.06	–21.82	–22.34
General government	4 707 . .	.26	. . .	. . .	. . .	. . .	. . .	. . .	. . .
of which: Short-term	4 709 . .	. . .	. . .	. . .	. . .	. . .	. . .	. . .	. . .
Other sectors	4 710 . .	41.86	. . .	. . .	. . .	. . .	–20.06	–21.82	–22.34
of which: Short-term	4 712 . .	*41.86*	. . .	. . .	. . .	. . .	*–20.06*	*–21.82*	*–22.34*
Loans	4 714 . .	.01	–.01	.41	–1.09	–.15	–.34	–4.55	5.21
Monetary authorities	4 715 . .	. . .	. . .	. . .	. . .	. . .	. . .	. . .	. . .
of which: Short-term	4 718 . .	. . .	. . .	. . .	. . .	. . .	. . .	. . .	. . .
General government	4 719 . .	. . .	. . .	. . .	. . .	. . .	. . .	. . .	. . .
of which: Short-term	4 721 . .	. . .	. . .	. . .	. . .	. . .	. . .	. . .	. . .
Banks	4 722 . .	.01	–.01	.41	–1.09	–.15	–.34	–4.55	5.21
of which: Short-term	4 724 . .	. . .	*–.01*	*.41*	*–1.09*	*–.11*	*–.34*	*–4.55*	*5.21*
Other sectors	4 725 . .	. . .	. . .	. . .	. . .	. . .	. . .	. . .	. . .
of which: Short-term	4 727 . .	. . .	. . .	. . .	. . .	. . .	. . .	. . .	. . .
Currency and deposits	4 730 . .	.19	–.15	34.00	41.66	20.41	23.26	17.89	–1.55
Monetary authorities	4 731 . .	. . .	–.15	–.08	1.36	.07	.09	–.08	.09
General government	4 732 . .	. . .	. . .	. . .	. . .	–43.27	15.57	11.33	12.76
Banks	4 733 . .	.19	. . .	5.99	–16.67	6.61	–34.23	–8.57	–25.31
Other sectors	4 734 . .	. . .	. . .	28.09	56.97	57.00	41.83	15.21	10.91
Other assets	4 736 . .	–6.43	–8.44	.93	.19	–.29	.11	–1.01	.45
Monetary authorities	4 737 . .	. . .	–8.43	. . .	. . .	. . .	–.03	–.02	.05
of which: Short-term	4 739 . .	. . .	*–8.43*	. . .	. . .	. . .	*–.03*	*–.02*	*.05*
General government	4 740 . .	–6.50	. . .	. . .	. . .	. . .	–.01	. . .	. . .
of which: Short-term	4 742 . .	*–6.50*	. . .	. . .	. . .	. . .	*–.01*	. . .	. . .
Banks	4 743 . .	.07	–.01	.93	.19	–.29	.15	–.99	.40
of which: Short-term	4 745 . .	*.07*	*–.01*	*.93*	*.19*	*–.29*	*.15*	*–.99*	*.40*
Other sectors	4 746 . .	. . .	. . .	. . .	. . .	. . .	. . .	. . .	. . .
of which: Short-term	4 748 . .	. . .	. . .	. . .	. . .	. . .	. . .	. . .	. . .
Liabilities	4 753 . .	**70.55**	**257.47**	**262.44**	**249.82**	**217.10**	**175.53**	**176.89**	**132.49**
Trade credits	4 756 . .	. . .	59.00	53.00	52.50	91.72	61.73	92.19	47.89
General government	4 757 . .	. . .	. . .	. . .	. . .	. . .	. . .	. . .	. . .
of which: Short-term	4 759 . .	. . .	. . .	. . .	. . .	. . .	. . .	. . .	. . .
Other sectors	4 760 . .	. . .	59.00	53.00	52.50	91.72	61.73	92.19	47.89
of which: Short-term	4 762 . .	. . .	*59.00*	*53.00*	*55.00*	*89.70*	*68.18*	*59.20*	*43.55*
Loans	4 764 . .	79.76	197.92	202.33	179.71	106.32	95.40	59.74	78.28
Monetary authorities	4 765 . .	24.50	46.71	54.04	23.46	49.03	15.07	–14.37	7.16
of which: Use of Fund credit and loans from the Fund	4 766 . .	*24.50*	*46.71*	*49.04*	*23.46*	*51.53*	*16.00*	*–15.91*	*3.35*
of which: Short-term	4 768 . .	. . .	. . .	. . .	. . .	. . .	. . .	. . .	. . .
General government	4 769 . .	55.26	151.20	102.23	122.86	35.01	80.16	44.28	64.25
of which: Short-term	4 771 . .	. . .	. . .	. . .	*–78.40*	. . .	. . .	. . .	. . .
Banks	4 772 . .	. . .	.01	17.50	11.39	20.19	–7.21	2.64	–11.28
of which: Short-term	4 774 . .	. . .	*.01*	*17.50*	*11.39*	*19.23*	*–7.21*	*2.64*	*–11.28*
Other sectors	4 775 . .	. . .	. . .	28.56	22.00	2.09	7.38	27.19	18.15
of which: Short-term	4 777 . .	. . .	. . .	. . .	*5.80*	*.06*	*5.80*	*.31*	. . .
Currency and deposits	4 780 . .	–8.38	.30	21.30	15.25	9.87	18.59	5.42	7.71
Monetary authorities	4 781 . .	–8.38	.29	4.89	–.04	. . .	. . .	. . .	. . .
General government	4 782 . .	. . .	. . .	. . .	. . .	. . .	. . .	. . .	. . .
Banks	4 783 . .	. . .	.01	16.41	15.29	9.72	18.59	5.42	7.71
Other sectors	4 784 . .	. . .	. . .	. . .	. . .	.15	. . .	. . .	. . .
Other liabilities	4 786 . .	–.83	.25	–14.19	2.36	9.19	–.19	19.54	–1.39
Monetary authorities	4 787 . .	–.80	.24	–.21	. . .	–.42	. . .	.05	–.02
of which: Short-term	4 789 . .	*–.80*	. . .	*–.21*	. . .	*–.42*	. . .	. . .	. . .
General government	4 790 . .	. . .	. . .	–6.25	. . .	. . .	. . .	18.77	–1.93
of which: Short-term	4 792 . .	. . .	. . .	*–6.25*	. . .	. . .	. . .	*18.77*	*–1.93*
Banks	4 793 . .	–.03	.01	–7.73	2.36	–5.92	–.19	.72	–.13
of which: Short-term	4 795 . .	*–.03*	*.01*	*–7.73*	*2.36*	*–5.92*	*–.19*	*.72*	*–.13*
Other sectors	4 796 . .	. . .	. . .	. . .	. . .	15.53	. . .	. . .	.69
of which: Short-term	4 798 . .	. . .	. . .	. . .	. . .	*3.93*	. . .	. . .	*.08*
E. RESERVE ASSETS	4 802 . .	–21.24	–76.22	–60.35	–73.48	–52.13	–20.79	–19.75	–20.02
Monetary gold	4 812 . .	–2.44	–7.98	–2.40	2.12	.02	. . .	.36	. . .
Special drawing rights	4 811 . .	–.28	–45.59	1.40	1.69	10.80	–13.77	17.42	10.64
Reserve position in the Fund	4 810 . .	. . .	. . .	. . .	. . .	. . .	–.02	. . .	. . .
Foreign exchange	4 803 . .	–14.30	–20.01	–63.67	–77.11	–54.54	–16.56	–37.72	–30.67
Other claims	4 813 . .	–4.22	–2.64	4.32	–.18	–8.41	9.56	.19	.01
NET ERRORS AND OMISSIONS	4 998 . .	**4.83**	**12.35**	**15.06**	**10.83**	**18.39**	**13.11**	**17.05**	**12.14**

Part 3 of the *Yearbook* contains descriptions of the methodologies, compilation practices, and sources used to compile these data.

Table 3. INTERNATIONAL INVESTMENT POSITION (End–period stocks), 1994–2001

(Millions of U.S. dollars)

	Code	1994	1995	1996	1997	1998	1999	2000	2001
ASSETS	8 995 C.	...	...	...	381.90	417.38	488.89	529.43	542.28
Direct investment abroad	8 505 ..	...	...	...	...	...	...	**.01**	**.02**
Equity capital and reinvested earnings	8 506 ..	...	...	...	...	...	...	.01	.02
Claims on affiliated enterprises	8 507 ..	...	...	...	...	...	...	.01	.02
Liabilities to affiliated enterprises	8 508 ..	...	...	...	...	...	...	...	...
Other capital	8 530 ..	...	...	...	...	...	...	...	...
Claims on affiliated enterprises	8 535 ..	...	...	...	...	...	...	...	...
Liabilities to affiliated enterprises	8 540 ..	...	...	...	...	...	...	...	...
Portfolio investment	8 602 ..	...	...	...	**.61**	**.18**	**.12**	**19.27**	**8.91**
Equity securities	8 610 ..	...	...	...	.50	.10	.09	3.09	3.61
Monetary authorities	8 611 ..	...	...	...	...	...	...	...	...
General government	8 612 ..	...	...	...	...	...	...	...	...
Banks	8 613 ..	...	...	...	.30	.03	.02	.42	.20
Other sectors	8 614 ..	...	...	...	.20	.07	.07	2.67	3.41
Debt securities	8 619 ..	...	...	...	.11	.08	.03	16.18	5.30
Bonds and notes	8 620 ..	...	...	...	.01	.01	.01	16.11	5.24
Monetary authorities	8 621 ..	...	...	...	.01	.01	.01	.01	...
General government	8 622 ..	...	...	...	...	...	...	...	...
Banks	8 623 ..	...	...	...	...	...	...	16.10	5.24
Other sectors	8 624 ..	...	...	...	...	...	...	...	...
Money market instruments	8 630 ..	...	...	...	.10	.07	.02	.07	.06
Monetary authorities	8 631 ..	...	...	...	...	...	...	...	...
General government	8 632 ..	...	...	...	...	...	...	...	...
Banks	8 633 ..	...	...	...	.10	.07	.02	.07	.06
Other sectors	8 634 ..	...	...	...	...	...	...	...	...
Financial derivatives	8 900 ..	...	...	...	...	...	...	...	...
Monetary authorities	8 901 ..	...	...	...	...	...	...	...	...
General government	8 902 ..	...	...	...	...	...	...	...	...
Banks	8 903 ..	...	...	...	...	...	...	...	...
Other sectors	8 904 ..	...	...	...	...	...	...	...	...
Other investment	8 703 ..	...	...	...	**141.82**	**124.09**	**185.77**	**196.02**	**203.89**
Trade credits	8 706 ..	...	...	...	...	...	20.61	40.61	61.03
General government	8 707 ..	...	...	...	...	...	...	...	...
of which: Short-term	8 709 ..	...	...	...	...	...	...	...	...
Other sectors	8 710 ..	...	...	...	...	...	20.61	40.61	61.03
of which: Short-term	8 712 ..	...	...	...	...	...	*20.61*	*40.61*	*61.03*
Loans	8 714 ..	...	...	...	19.08	19.72	20.09	26.14	20.89
Monetary authorities	8 715 ..	...	...	...	...	...	...	...	...
of which: Short-term	8 718 ..	...	...	...	...	...	...	...	...
General government	8 719 ..	...	...	...	18.00	18.00	18.00	19.59	19.59
of which: Short-term	8 721 ..	...	...	...	...	...	...	...	...
Banks	8 722 ..	...	...	...	1.08	1.72	2.09	6.55	1.30
of which: Short-term	8 724 ..	...	...	...	*1.08*	*1.72*	*2.09*	*6.55*	*1.30*
Other sectors	8 725 ..	...	...	...	...	...	...	...	...
of which: Short-term	8 727 ..	...	...	...	...	...	...	...	...
Currency and deposits	8 730 ..	...	...	...	122.42	104.10	144.90	128.10	121.88
Monetary authorities	8 731 ..	...	...	...	.18	.10	.01	.09	...
General government	8 732 ..	...	...	...	...	43.27	27.70	16.37	3.60
Banks	8 733 ..	...	...	...	36.37	31.86	67.90	75.70	97.13
Other sectors	8 734 ..	...	...	...	85.87	28.87	49.29	35.94	21.15
Other assets	8 736 ..	...	...	...	.32	.27	.17	1.17	.09
Monetary authorities	8 737 ..	...	...	...	...	...	.03	.05	...
of which: Short-term	8 739 ..	...	...	...	...	...	*.03*	*.03*	...
General government	8 740 ..	...	...	...	...	...	.01	...	...
of which: Short-term	8 742 ..	...	...	...	...	...	*.01*	...	...
Banks	8 743 ..	...	...	...	.32	.27	.13	1.12	.09
of which: Short-term	8 745 ..	...	...	...	*.32*	*.27*	*.13*	*1.12*	*.09*
Other sectors	8 746 ..	...	...	...	...	...	...	...	...
of which: Short-term	8 748 ..	...	...	...	...	...	...	...	...
Reserve assets	8 802 ..	...	...	...	**239.47**	**293.11**	**303.00**	**314.13**	**329.46**
Monetary gold	8 812 ..	...	...	...	.38	.36	.36	...	...
Special drawing rights	8 811 ..	.28	44.33	41.50	37.28	28.00	40.68	21.55	10.24
Reserve position in the Fund	8 810 ..	.01	.01	.01	.01	.01	...	...	...
Foreign exchange	8 803 ..	...	...	...	201.48	256.01	261.76	292.57	319.23
Other claims	8 813 ..	...	...	...	.32	8.73	.20	.01	–.01

Table 3 (Concluded). INTERNATIONAL INVESTMENT POSITION (End–period stocks), 1994–2001
(Millions of U.S. dollars)

	Code	1994	1995	1996	1997	1998	1999	2000	2001
LIABILITIES	8 995 D.	...	...	...	949.92	1,332.16	1,607.72	1,829.71	1,978.04
Direct investment in Armenia	8 555 ..	**...**	**...**	**...**	**103.44**	**312.67**	**421.36**	**513.09**	**579.85**
Equity capital and reinvested earnings	8 556 ..	...	...	...	72.25	202.95	268.90	350.21	416.91
Claims on direct investors	8 557 ..	...	...	...	...	...	...	...	...
Liabilities to direct investors	8 558 ..	...	...	...	72.25	202.95	268.90	350.21	416.91
Other capital	8 580 ..	...	...	...	31.19	109.72	152.46	162.88	162.94
Claims on direct investors	8 585 ..	...	...	...	...	...	...	...	...
Liabilities to direct investors	8 590 ..	...	...	...	31.19	109.72	152.46	162.88	162.94
Portfolio investment	8 652 ..	**...**	**...**	**...**	**21.18**	**3.44**	**4.47**	**4.79**	**5.92**
Equity securities	8 660 ..	...	...	...	.44	1.09	.75	1.09	1.55
Banks	8 663 ..	...	...	...	.44	1.09	.75	.89	1.35
Other sectors	8 664 ..	...	...	...	...	...	...	.20	.20
Debt securities	8 669 ..	...	...	...	20.74	2.35	3.72	3.70	4.37
Bonds and notes	8 670 ..	...	...	...	...	.14	–.14	–.14	.19
Monetary authorities	8 671 ..	...	...	...	...	...	...	...	...
General government	8 672 ..	...	...	...	...	...	...	...	.33
Banks	8 673 ..	...	...	...	...	...	...	...	...
Other sectors	8 674 ..	...	...	...	...	.14	–.14	–.14	–.14
Money market instruments	8 680 ..	...	...	...	20.74	2.21	3.86	3.84	4.18
Monetary authorities	8 681 ..	...	...	...	...	...	...	...	...
General government	8 682 ..	...	...	...	20.74	2.21	4.01	3.84	4.18
Banks	8 683 ..	...	...	...	...	...	–.15	...	...
Other sectors	8 684 ..	...	...	...	...	...	...	...	...
Financial derivatives	8 905 ..	**...**	**...**	**...**	**...**	**...**	**...**	**...**	**...**
Monetary authorities	8 906 ..	...	...	...	...	...	...	...	...
General government	8 907 ..	...	...	...	...	...	...	...	...
Banks	8 908 ..	...	...	...	...	...	...	...	...
Other sectors	8 909 ..	...	...	...	...	...	...	...	...
Other investment	8 753 ..	**...**	**...**	**...**	**825.30**	**1,016.05**	**1,181.89**	**1,311.83**	**1,392.27**
Trade credits	8 756 ..	...	...	...	78.50	170.22	230.44	268.52	269.55
General government	8 758 ..	...	...	...	...	...	...	...	...
of which: Short-term	8 759 ..	...	...	...	...	...	...	...	...
Other sectors	8 760 ..	...	...	...	78.50	170.22	230.44	268.52	269.55
of which: Short-term	8 762 ..	...	...	...	*30.00*	*119.70*	*186.60*	*192.22*	*195.00*
Loans	8 764 ..	...	...	...	698.00	778.82	863.91	932.32	1,005.17
Monetary authorities	8 765 ..	...	...	...	137.06	192.94	202.80	178.32	178.92
of which: Use of Fund credit and loans from the Fund	8 766 ..	*24.63*	*70.24*	*116.47*	*132.06*	*190.44*	*201.23*	*175.45*	*172.61*
of which: Short-term	8 768 ..	...	...	...	...	...	...	...	...
General government	8 769 ..	...	...	...	496.80	538.29	611.83	675.48	740.87
of which: Short-term	8 771 ..	...	...	...	...	...	...	...	...
Banks	8 772 ..	...	...	...	64.14	45.40	39.72	42.02	30.73
of which: Short-term	8 774 ..	...	...	...	*26.94*	*45.40*	*39.72*	*42.02*	*42.00*
Other sectors	8 775 ..	...	...	...	...	2.19	9.56	36.50	54.65
of which: Short-term	8 777 ..	...	...	...	...	*.06*	*5.86*	*6.17*	*6.17*
Currency and deposits	8 780 ..	...	...	...	42.07	51.09	71.72	76.41	83.58
Monetary authorities	8 781 ..	...	...	...	.01	...	...	...	...
General government	8 782 ..	...	...	...	...	...	...	...	...
Banks	8 783 ..	...	...	...	42.06	50.94	71.57	76.26	83.43
Other sectors	8 784 ..	...	...	...	...	.15	.15	.15	.15
Other liabilities	8 786 ..	...	...	...	6.73	15.92	15.82	34.58	33.97
Monetary authorities	8 787 ..	...	...	...	.42	...	...	.03	.01
of which: Short-term	8 789 ..	...	...	...	*.42*	...	...	...	...
General government	8 790 ..	...	...	...	...	...	...	18.75	16.84
of which: Short-term	8 792 ..	...	...	...	...	...	...	*18.75*	*16.84*
Banks	8 793 ..	...	...	...	6.31	.39	.22	.20	.81
of which: Short-term	8 795 ..	...	...	...	*6.31*	*.39*	*.22*	*.20*	*.81*
Other sectors	8 796 ..	...	...	...	...	15.53	15.60	15.60	16.31
of which: Short-term	8 798 ..	...	...	...	...	*3.93*	*3.93*	*3.93*	*4.02*
NET INTERNATIONAL INVESTMENT POSITION	8 995 ..	**...**	**...**	**...**	**–568.02**	**–914.78**	**–1,118.83**	**–1,300.29**	**–1,435.76**
Conversion rates: drams per U.S. dollar (end of period)	0 102 ..	**405.51**	**402.00**	**435.07**	**494.98**	**522.03**	**523.77**	**552.18**	**561.81**

Table 1. ANALYTIC PRESENTATION, 1994–2001
(Millions of U.S. dollars)

	Code	1994	1995	1996	1997	1998	1999	2000	2001
A. Current Account [1]	4 993 Z.	**81.1**	**-.3**	**-69.1**	**-195.8**	**-18.8**	**-333.2**	**282.3**	. . .
Goods: exports f.o.b	2 100 . .	1,296.8	1,347.2	1,735.7	1,728.7	1,164.8	1,413.5	2,582.1	. . .
Goods: imports f.o.b	3 100 . .	-1,607.3	-1,772.5	-2,043.4	-2,115.9	-1,518.2	-2,005.2	-2,610.4	. . .
Balance on Goods	4 100 . .	*-310.6*	*-425.3*	*-307.7*	*-387.2*	*-353.4*	*-591.7*	*-28.3*	. . .
Services: credit	2 200 . .	624.2	645.1	769.9	815.8	892.1	989.7	1,032.0	. . .
Services: debit	3 200 . .	-228.7	-245.5	-515.9	-596.1	-553.1	-712.9	-678.7	. . .
Balance on Goods and Services	4 991 . .	*85.0*	*-25.6*	*-53.6*	*-167.5*	*-14.4*	*-315.0*	*325.0*	. . .
Income: credit	2 300 . .	9.6	16.4	19.2	20.7	40.5	37.4	46.8	. . .
Income: debit	3 300 . .	-22.3	-24.6	-31.0	-37.9	-40.1	-69.0	-53.5	. . .
Balance on Goods, Services, and Income	4 992 . .	*72.3*	*-33.8*	*-65.5*	*-184.7*	*-14.0*	*-346.6*	*318.3*	. . .
Current transfers: credit	2 379 Z.	47.5	71.5	18.4	18.4	29.3	59.3	46.2	. . .
Current transfers: debit	3 379 . .	-38.7	-37.9	-22.0	-29.5	-34.1	-45.9	-82.2	. . .
B. Capital Account [1]	4 994 Z.	**-4.1**	**-.5**	**28.0**	**21.0**	**5.2**	**. . .**	**9.9**	. . .
Capital account: credit	2 994 Z.	.3	3.1	28.7	21.6	10.2	.9	10.5	. . .
Capital account: debit	3 994 . .	-4.4	-3.6	-.7	-.6	-5.0	-.9	-.6	. . .
Total, Groups A Plus B	4 981 . .	*76.9*	*-.8*	*-41.1*	*-174.8*	*-13.6*	*-333.2*	*292.2*	. . .
C. Financial Account [1]	4 995 W.	**-75.4**	**41.6**	**10.7**	**158.9**	**64.2**	**336.4**	**-314.6**	. . .
Direct investment abroad	4 505 . .	. . .	. . .	-.3	1.7	-1.4	8.9	-11.7	. . .
Direct investment in Aruba	4 555 Z.	-73.2	-5.5	84.5	195.9	83.6	392.1	-227.5	. . .
Portfolio investment assets	4 602 . .	16.5	-16.6	-7.8	-1.6	-44.1	-65.6	-42.9	. . .
Equity securities	4 610 . .	. . .	. . .	. . .	. . .	. . .	. . .	. . .	. . .
Debt securities	4 619 . .	16.5	-16.6	-7.8	-1.6	-44.1	-65.6	-42.9	. . .
Portfolio investment liabilities	4 652 Z.	-25.8	. . .	1.6	-17.4	-3.4	12.2	2.1	. . .
Equity securities	4 660 . .	. . .	. . .	. . .	. . .	. . .	. . .	. . .	. . .
Debt securities	4 669 Z.	-25.8	. . .	1.6	-17.4	-3.4	12.2	2.1	. . .
Financial derivatives	4 910 . .	. . .	. . .	. . .	. . .	. . .	. . .	. . .	. . .
Financial derivatives assets	4 900 . .	. . .	. . .	. . .	. . .	. . .	. . .	. . .	. . .
Financial derivatives liabilities	4 905 . .	. . .	. . .	. . .	. . .	. . .	. . .	. . .	. . .
Other investment assets	4 703 . .	5.8	12.5	-11.3	-49.7	29.2	-15.7	-97.7	. . .
Monetary authorities	4 701 . .	. . .	. . .	. . .	. . .	. . .	. . .	. . .	. . .
General government	4 704 . .	-.8	. . .	. . .	. . .	. . .	. . .	. . .	. . .
Banks	4 705 . .	-3.7	15.6	-17.0	-30.7	-11.5	-12.2	-21.1	. . .
Other sectors	4 728 . .	10.4	-3.1	5.7	-19.0	40.7	-3.5	-76.6	. . .
Other investment liabilities	4 753 W.	1.3	51.2	-55.9	30.0	.4	4.5	63.1	. . .
Monetary authorities	4 753 WA	. . .	. . .	. . .	. . .	. . .	. . .	. . .	. . .
General government	4 753 ZB	.4	.6	-10.6	-8.9	22.2	7.5	34.0	. . .
Banks	4 753 ZC	-8.7	10.7	17.0	37.3	-26.4	.5	29.2	. . .
Other sectors	4 753 ZD	9.6	39.9	-62.3	1.6	4.6	-3.5	. . .	. . .
Total, Groups A Through C	4 983 . .	*1.6*	*40.8*	*-30.4*	*-15.9*	*50.7*	*3.2*	*-22.3*	. . .
D. Net Errors and Omissions	4 998 . .	**-4.7**	**2.0**	**4.3**	**-2.5**	**.6**	**-.7**	**6.5**	. . .
Total, Groups A Through D	4 984 . .	*-3.2*	*42.7*	*-26.1*	*-18.4*	*51.3*	*2.5*	*-15.9*	. . .
E. Reserves and Related Items	4 802 A.	**3.2**	**-42.7**	**26.1**	**18.4**	**-51.3**	**-2.5**	**15.9**	. . .
Reserve assets	4 802 . .	3.2	-42.7	26.1	18.4	-51.3	-2.5	15.9	. . .
Use of Fund credit and loans	4 766 . .	. . .	. . .	. . .	. . .	. . .	. . .	. . .	. . .
Exceptional financing	4 920 . .	. . .	. . .	. . .	. . .	. . .	. . .	. . .	. . .
Conversion rates: florins per U.S. dollar	0 101 . .	**1.7900**	**1.7900**	**1.7900**	**1.7900**	**1.7900**	**1.7900**	**1.7900**	**1.7900**

[1] Excludes components that have been classified in the categories of Group E.

Table 2. STANDARD PRESENTATION, 1994–2001

(Millions of U.S. dollars)

	Code	1994	1995	1996	1997	1998	1999	2000	2001
CURRENT ACCOUNT	4 993 . .	**81.1**	**–.3**	**–69.1**	**–195.8**	**–18.8**	**–333.2**	**282.3**	**. . .**
A. GOODS	4 100 . .	–310.6	–425.3	–307.7	–387.2	–353.4	–591.7	–28.3	. . .
Credit	2 100 . .	**1,296.8**	**1,347.2**	**1,735.7**	**1,728.7**	**1,164.8**	**1,413.5**	**2,582.1**	**. . .**
General merchandise: exports f.o.b.	2 110 . .	1,296.8	1,289.8	1,644.9	1,631.1	1,091.7	1,317.4	2,430.6	. . .
Goods for processing: exports f.o.b.	2 150 . .	. . .	. . .	. . .	. . .	. . .	. . .	. . .	. . .
Repairs on goods	2 160 . .	. . .	1.1	.8	.3	.3	.2	.5	. . .
Goods procured in ports by carriers	2 170 . .	. . .	56.3	89.1	97.3	72.7	95.9	151.0	. . .
Nonmonetary gold	2 180 . .	. . .	. . .	.9	. . .	. . .	. . .	. . .	. . .
Debit	3 100 . .	**–1,607.3**	**–1,772.5**	**–2,043.4**	**–2,115.9**	**–1,518.2**	**–2,005.2**	**–2,610.4**	**. . .**
General merchandise: imports f.o.b.	3 110 . .	–1,607.3	–917.9	–749.5	–826.7	–956.1	–852.3	–763.9	. . .
Goods for processing: imports f.o.b.	3 150 . .	. . .	–838.9	–1,266.0	–1,271.7	–544.6	–1,137.0	–1,832.8	. . .
Repairs on goods	3 160 . .	. . .	–6.6	–8.5	–7.3	–6.9	–5.1	–2.6	. . .
Goods procured in ports by carriers	3 170 . .	. . .	–9.1	–13.2	–10.1	–10.6	–10.7	–11.1	. . .
Nonmonetary gold	3 180 . .	. . .	. . .	–6.1	. . .	. . .	. . .	. . .	. . .
B. SERVICES	4 200 . .	395.6	399.7	254.0	219.7	339.0	276.8	353.3	. . .
Total credit	2 200 . .	*624.2*	*645.1*	*769.9*	*815.8*	*892.1*	*989.7*	*1,032.0*	. . .
Total debit	3 200 . .	*–228.7*	*–245.5*	*–515.9*	*–596.1*	*–553.1*	*–712.9*	*–678.7*	. . .
Transportation services, credit	2 205 . .	**109.4**	**49.0**	**65.0**	**49.2**	**63.1**	**81.5**	**76.4**	**. . .**
Passenger	2 850 . .	*17.8*	*33.4*	*46.0*	*36.5*	*45.4*	*54.6*	*36.3*	. . .
Freight	2 851 . .	*11.4*	*15.6*	*15.1*	*1.6*	*1.0*	*1.9*	*.9*	. . .
Other	2 852 . .	*80.2*	. . .	*3.9*	*11.1*	*16.7*	*25.0*	*39.2*	. . .
Sea transport, passenger	2 207 . .	. . .	. . .	. . .	.1	.1	. . .	. . .	. . .
Sea transport, freight	2 208 . .	. . .	. . .	3.3	1.5	.9	1.6	.6	. . .
Sea transport, other	2 209 . .	. . .	. . .	1.4	3.2	8.8	12.6	24.5	. . .
Air transport, passenger	2 211 . .	. . .	. . .	46.0	36.5	45.3	54.6	36.3	. . .
Air transport, freight	2 212 . .	. . .	. . .	11.8	.2	.1	.3	.4	. . .
Air transport, other	2 213 . .	. . .	. . .	2.5	7.9	7.9	12.4	14.7	. . .
Other transport, passenger	2 215 . .	. . .	. . .	. . .	. . .	. . .	. . .	. . .	. . .
Other transport, freight	2 216 . .	. . .	. . .	. . .	. . .	. . .	. . .	. . .	. . .
Other transport, other	2 217 . .	. . .	. . .	. . .	. . .	. . .	. . .	. . .	. . .
Transportation services, debit	3 205 . .	**–19.2**	**–13.9**	**–221.5**	**–235.2**	**–164.4**	**–210.8**	**–270.8**	**. . .**
Passenger	3 850 . .	*–4.4*	*–6.4*	*–7.7*	*–4.6*	*–5.3*	*–7.9*	*–9.1*	. . .
Freight	3 851 . .	*–8.5*	*–7.5*	*–202.2*	*–218.1*	*–152.7*	*–194.3*	*–254.4*	. . .
Other	3 852 . .	*–6.3*	. . .	*–11.6*	*–12.5*	*–6.4*	*–8.6*	*–7.3*	. . .
Sea transport, passenger	3 207 . .	. . .	. . .	–.4	–.1	–.6	–.1	. . .	. . .
Sea transport, freight	3 208 . .	. . .	. . .	–198.7	–216.4	–149.7	–191.5	–252.5	. . .
Sea transport, other	3 209 . .	. . .	. . .	–2.6	–4.0	–2.0	–.9	–3.9	. . .
Air transport, passenger	3 211 . .	. . .	. . .	–7.3	–4.5	–4.7	–7.8	–9.1	. . .
Air transport, freight	3 212 . .	. . .	. . .	–3.5	–1.7	–3.0	–2.8	–1.9	. . .
Air transport, other	3 213 . .	. . .	. . .	–9.0	–8.5	–4.4	–7.7	–3.4	. . .
Other transport, passenger	3 215 . .	. . .	. . .	. . .	. . .	. . .	. . .	. . .	. . .
Other transport, freight	3 216 . .	. . .	. . .	. . .	. . .	. . .	. . .	. . .	. . .
Other transport, other	3 217 . .	. . .	. . .	. . .	. . .	. . .	. . .	. . .	. . .
Travel, credit	2 236 . .	**453.2**	**520.6**	**619.8**	**689.2**	**740.9**	**788.9**	**843.0**	. . .
Business travel	2 237 . .	. . .	. . .	. . .	. . .	. . .	. . .	. . .	. . .
Personal travel	2 240 . .	453.2	520.6	619.8	689.2	740.9	788.9	843.0	. . .
Travel, debit	3 236 . .	**–65.1**	**–72.7**	**–119.8**	**–156.5**	**–134.7**	**–148.2**	**–158.2**	**. . .**
Business travel	3 237 . .	. . .	. . .	. . .	. . .	. . .	. . .	. . .	. . .
Personal travel	3 240 . .	–65.1	–72.7	–119.8	–156.5	–134.7	–148.2	–158.2	. . .
Other services, credit	2 200 BA	**61.7**	**75.6**	**85.0**	**77.4**	**88.0**	**119.3**	**112.5**	**. . .**
Communications	2 245 . .	. . .	2.3	3.9	5.3	5.0	7.2	4.5	. . .
Construction	2 249 . .	. . .	11.4	5.9	5.9	8.4	10.2	1.2	. . .
Insurance	2 253 . .	1.7	2.2	16.3	4.0	8.9	7.3	6.6	. . .
Financial	2 260 . .	22.2	19.7	.4	1.1	1.7	.6	5.1	. . .
Computer and information	2 262 . .	. . .	. . .	.4	.2	.1	.2	.4	. . .
Royalties and licence fees	2 266 . .	. . .	. . .	. . .	. . .	. . .	. . .	. . .	. . .
Other business services	2 268 . .	18.3	20.8	39.4	43.8	49.0	76.0	77.8	. . .
Personal, cultural, and recreational	2 287 . .	. . .	. . .	. . .	. . .	. . .	. . .	. . .	. . .
Government, n.i.e.	2 291 . .	19.6	19.1	18.7	17.2	14.9	17.8	16.9	. . .
Other services, debit	3 200 BA	**–144.4**	**–158.9**	**–174.6**	**–204.4**	**–254.0**	**–353.9**	**–249.7**	**. . .**
Communications	3 245 . .	–1.1	–3.2	–15.9	–17.4	–17.5	–14.6	–12.0	. . .
Construction	3 249 . .	. . .	–47.6	–20.6	–23.7	–45.1	–111.9	–19.9	. . .
Insurance	3 253 . .	–4.5	–3.3	–6.1	–32.2	–27.4	–37.3	–39.0	. . .
Financial	3 260 . .	–35.7	–53.2	–2.3	–1.8	–5.8	–3.9	–7.5	. . .
Computer and information	3 262 . .	. . .	. . .	–3.0	–3.6	–3.3	–5.1	–5.0	. . .
Royalties and licence fees	3 266 . .	. . .	. . .	. . .	. . .	. . .	. . .	. . .	. . .
Other business services	3 268 . .	–72.1	–13.4	–93.7	–86.1	–129.9	–153.0	–142.1	. . .
Personal, cultural, and recreational	3 287 . .	. . .	. . .	. . .	. . .	. . .	. . .	. . .	. . .
Government, n.i.e.	3 291 . .	–30.9	–38.3	–33.0	–39.4	–25.0	–28.1	–24.3	. . .

Table 2 (Continued). STANDARD PRESENTATION, 1994–2001
(Millions of U.S. dollars)

	Code		1994	1995	1996	1997	1998	1999	2000	2001
C. INCOME	4 300	. .	–12.7	–8.2	–11.8	–17.2	.4	–31.6	–6.8	. . .
Total credit	2 300	. .	*9.6*	*16.4*	*19.2*	*20.7*	*40.5*	*37.4*	*46.8*	. . .
Total debit	3 300	. .	*–22.3*	*–24.6*	*–31.0*	*–37.9*	*–40.1*	*–69.0*	*–53.5*	. . .
Compensation of employees, credit	2 310	. .	**. . .**	**. . .**	**1.1**	**.9**	**.4**	**.7**	**.1**	**. . .**
Compensation of employees, debit	3 310	. .	**. . .**	**. . .**	**–2.4**	**–.2**	**–.3**	**–.6**	**–.3**	**. . .**
Investment income, credit	2 320	. .	**9.6**	**16.4**	**18.1**	**19.8**	**40.1**	**36.6**	**46.6**	**. . .**
Direct investment income	2 330	. .	. . .	. . .	2.2	1.0	1.0	.5	. . .	. . .
Dividends and distributed branch profits	2 332	. .	. . .	. . .	2.2	1.0	.2	.5	. . .	. . .
Reinvested earnings and undistributed branch profits	2 333	. .	. . .	. . .	. . .	. . .	. . .	. . .	. . .	. . .
Income on debt (interest)	2 334	. .	. . .	. . .	. . .	. . .	.8	. . .	. . .	. . .
Portfolio investment income	2 339	. .	. . .	. . .	. . .	3.5	7.3	16.0	15.3	. . .
Income on equity	2 340	. .	. . .	. . .	. . .	.8	.8	. . .	4.7	. . .
Income on bonds and notes	2 350	. .	. . .	. . .	. . .	2.7	6.5	16.0	10.6	. . .
Income on money market instruments	2 360	. .	. . .	. . .	. . .	. . .	. . .	. . .	. . .	. . .
Other investment income	2 370	. .	9.6	16.4	15.9	15.3	31.8	20.1	31.4	. . .
Investment income, debit	3 320	. .	**–22.3**	**–24.6**	**–28.6**	**–37.7**	**–39.8**	**–68.4**	**–53.2**	**. . .**
Direct investment income	3 330	. .	–.8	–6.0	–8.8	–13.0	–9.2	–37.0	. . .	. . .
Dividends and distributed branch profits	3 332	. .	–.8	–6.0	–8.8	–11.9	–8.8	–37.0	. . .	. . .
Reinvested earnings and undistributed branch profits	3 333	. .	. . .	. . .	. . .	. . .	. . .	. . .	. . .	. . .
Income on debt (interest)	3 334	. .	. . .	. . .	. . .	–1.1	–.3	. . .	. . .	. . .
Portfolio investment income	3 339	. .	. . .	. . .	. . .	. . .	–10.2	–10.7	–21.5	. . .
Income on equity	3 340	. .	. . .	. . .	. . .	. . .	. . .	. . .	–17.1	. . .
Income on bonds and notes	3 350	. .	. . .	. . .	. . .	. . .	–10.2	–10.7	–4.4	. . .
Income on money market instruments	3 360	. .	. . .	. . .	. . .	. . .	. . .	. . .	. . .	. . .
Other investment income	3 370	. .	–21.5	–18.5	–19.8	–24.7	–20.4	–20.7	–31.7	. . .
D. CURRENT TRANSFERS	4 379	. .	8.8	33.5	–3.6	–11.1	–4.8	13.4	–36.0	. . .
Credit	2 379	. .	**47.5**	**71.5**	**18.4**	**18.4**	**29.3**	**59.3**	**46.2**	**. . .**
General government	2 380	. .	11.2	15.1	5.1	7.4	12.3	14.7	14.6	. . .
Other sectors	2 390	. .	36.3	56.3	13.3	11.1	16.9	44.5	31.6	. . .
Workers' remittances	2 391	. .	3.6	1.3	.6	.9	1.2	3.7	1.3	. . .
Other current transfers	2 392	. .	32.6	55.0	12.7	10.2	15.7	40.8	30.3	. . .
Debit	3 379	. .	**–38.7**	**–37.9**	**–22.0**	**–29.5**	**–34.1**	**–45.9**	**–82.2**	**. . .**
General government	3 380	. .	–2.8	–2.8	–7.0	–10.7	–12.2	–15.6	–35.8	. . .
Other sectors	3 390	. .	–35.9	–35.1	–15.0	–18.8	–21.8	–30.2	–46.4	. . .
Workers' remittances	3 391	. .	–3.7	–5.0	–4.8	–9.8	–11.3	–18.9	–29.9	. . .
Other current transfers	3 392	. .	–32.2	–30.1	–10.2	–9.0	–10.6	–11.3	–16.5	. . .
CAPITAL AND FINANCIAL ACCOUNT	4 996	. .	**–76.3**	**–1.7**	**64.8**	**198.3**	**18.2**	**333.9**	**–288.8**	**. . .**
CAPITAL ACCOUNT	4 994	. .	**–4.1**	**–.5**	**28.0**	**21.0**	**5.2**	**. . .**	**9.9**	**. . .**
Total credit	2 994	. .	*.3*	*3.1*	*28.7*	*21.6*	*10.2*	*.9*	*10.5*	. . .
Total debit	3 994	. .	*–4.4*	*–3.6*	*–.7*	*–.6*	*–5.0*	*–.9*	*–.6*	. . .
Capital transfers, credit	2 400	. .	**.3**	**3.1**	**26.1**	**21.6**	**10.2**	**.9**	**10.5**	**. . .**
General government	2 401	. .	. . .	. . .	15.6	21.4	8.8	.8	9.4	. . .
Debt forgiveness	2 402	. .	. . .	. . .	. . .	. . .	. . .	. . .	. . .	. . .
Other capital transfers	2 410	. .	. . .	. . .	. . .	. . .	. . .	. . .	9.4	. . .
Other sectors	2 430	. .	.3	3.1	10.5	.2	1.4	.1	1.1	. . .
Migrants' transfers	2 431	. .	.3	3.1	10.5	.2	1.4	.1	1.1	. . .
Debt forgiveness	2 432	. .	. . .	. . .	. . .	. . .	. . .	. . .	. . .	. . .
Other capital transfers	2 440	. .	. . .	. . .	. . .	. . .	. . .	. . .	. . .	. . .
Capital transfers, debit	3 400	. .	**–4.4**	**–3.6**	**–.7**	**–.6**	**–5.0**	**–.9**	**–.6**	**. . .**
General government	3 401	. .	. . .	. . .	. . .	. . .	. . .	. . .	. . .	. . .
Debt forgiveness	3 402	. .	. . .	. . .	. . .	. . .	. . .	. . .	. . .	. . .
Other capital transfers	3 410	. .	. . .	. . .	. . .	. . .	. . .	. . .	. . .	. . .
Other sectors	3 430	. .	–4.4	–3.6	–.7	–.6	–5.0	–.9	–.6	. . .
Migrants' transfers	3 431	. .	–4.4	–3.6	–.7	–.6	–5.0	–.9	–.6	. . .
Debt forgiveness	3 432	. .	. . .	. . .	. . .	. . .	. . .	. . .	. . .	. . .
Other capital transfers	3 440	. .	. . .	. . .	. . .	. . .	. . .	. . .	. . .	. . .
Nonproduced nonfinancial assets, credit	2 480	. .	**. . .**	**. . .**	**2.6**	**. . .**	**. . .**	**. . .**	**. . .**	**. . .**
Nonproduced nonfinancial assets, debit	3 480	. .	**. . .**	**. . .**	**. . .**	**. . .**	**. . .**	**. . .**	**. . .**	**. . .**

Table 2 (Continued). STANDARD PRESENTATION, 1994–2001
(Millions of U.S. dollars)

	Code	1994	1995	1996	1997	1998	1999	2000	2001
FINANCIAL ACCOUNT	4 995 . .	**–72.2**	**–1.2**	**36.8**	**177.3**	**13.0**	**333.9**	**–298.7**	. . .
A. DIRECT INVESTMENT	4 500 . .	–73.2	–5.5	84.1	197.6	82.2	401.0	–239.2	. . .
Direct investment abroad	4 505 . .	. . .	. . .	**–.3**	**1.7**	**–1.4**	**8.9**	**–11.7**	. . .
Equity capital	4 510 . .	. . .	. . .	–.3	1.7	–1.4	8.9	–11.7	. . .
Claims on affiliated enterprises	4 515 . .	. . .	. . .	–.9	–.2	–1.4	8.9	–11.7	. . .
Liabilities to affiliated enterprises	4 520 . .	. . .	. . .	.6	1.9	. . .	. . .	. . .	. . .
Reinvested earnings	4 525 . .	. . .	. . .	. . .	. . .	. . .	. . .	. . .	. . .
Other capital	4 530 . .	. . .	. . .	. . .	. . .	. . .	. . .	. . .	. . .
Claims on affiliated enterprises	4 535 . .	. . .	. . .	. . .	. . .	. . .	. . .	. . .	. . .
Liabilities to affiliated enterprises	4 540 . .	. . .	. . .	. . .	. . .	. . .	. . .	. . .	. . .
Direct investment in Aruba	4 555 . .	**–73.2**	**–5.5**	**84.5**	**195.9**	**83.6**	**392.1**	**–227.5**	. . .
Equity capital	4 560 . .	. . .	. . .	. . .	. . .	. . .	. . .	. . .	. . .
Claims on direct investors	4 565 . .	. . .	. . .	. . .	. . .	. . .	. . .	. . .	. . .
Liabilities to direct investors	4 570 . .	. . .	. . .	. . .	. . .	. . .	. . .	. . .	. . .
Reinvested earnings	4 575 . .	. . .	. . .	. . .	. . .	. . .	. . .	. . .	. . .
Other capital	4 580 . .	–73.2	–5.5	84.5	195.9	83.6	392.1	–227.5	. . .
Claims on direct investors	4 585 . .	. . .	. . .	. . .	. . .	–29.9	–67.8	58.8	. . .
Liabilities to direct investors	4 590 . .	. . .	. . .	. . .	. . .	113.5	459.9	–286.3	. . .
B. PORTFOLIO INVESTMENT	4 600 . .	–9.3	–16.6	–6.3	–19.0	–47.5	–53.4	–40.8	. . .
Assets	4 602 . .	**16.5**	**–16.6**	**–7.8**	**–1.6**	**–44.1**	**–65.6**	**–42.9**	. . .
Equity securities	4 610 . .	. . .	. . .	. . .	. . .	. . .	. . .	. . .	. . .
Monetary authorities	4 611 . .	. . .	. . .	. . .	. . .	. . .	. . .	. . .	. . .
General government	4 612 . .	. . .	. . .	. . .	. . .	. . .	. . .	. . .	. . .
Banks	4 613 . .	. . .	. . .	. . .	. . .	. . .	. . .	. . .	. . .
Other sectors	4 614 . .	. . .	. . .	. . .	. . .	. . .	. . .	. . .	. . .
Debt securities	4 619 . .	16.5	–16.6	–7.8	–1.6	–44.1	–65.6	–42.9	. . .
Bonds and notes	4 620 . .	16.5	–16.6	–7.8	–1.6	–44.1	–65.6	–42.9	. . .
Monetary authorities	4 621 . .	. . .	. . .	. . .	. . .	. . .	. . .	. . .	. . .
General government	4 622 . .	. . .	. . .	. . .	. . .	. . .	. . .	. . .	. . .
Banks	4 623 . .	. . .	. . .	. . .	. . .	. . .	. . .	. . .	. . .
Other sectors	4 624 . .	. . .	–16.6	–7.8	–1.6	–44.1	–65.6	–42.9	. . .
Money market instruments	4 630 . .	. . .	. . .	. . .	. . .	. . .	. . .	. . .	. . .
Monetary authorities	4 631 . .	. . .	. . .	. . .	. . .	. . .	. . .	. . .	. . .
General government	4 632 . .	. . .	. . .	. . .	. . .	. . .	. . .	. . .	. . .
Banks	4 633 . .	. . .	. . .	. . .	. . .	. . .	. . .	. . .	. . .
Other sectors	4 634 . .	. . .	. . .	. . .	. . .	. . .	. . .	. . .	. . .
Liabilities	4 652 . .	**–25.8**	. . .	**1.6**	**–17.4**	**–3.4**	**12.2**	**2.1**	. . .
Equity securities	4 660 . .	. . .	. . .	. . .	. . .	. . .	. . .	. . .	. . .
Banks	4 663 . .	. . .	. . .	. . .	. . .	. . .	. . .	. . .	. . .
Other sectors	4 664 . .	. . .	. . .	. . .	. . .	. . .	. . .	. . .	. . .
Debt securities	4 669 . .	–25.8	. . .	1.6	–17.4	–3.4	12.2	2.1	. . .
Bonds and notes	4 670 . .	–25.8	. . .	1.6	–17.4	–3.4	12.2	2.1	. . .
Monetary authorities	4 671 . .	. . .	. . .	. . .	. . .	. . .	. . .	. . .	. . .
General government	4 672 . .	. . .	. . .	. . .	. . .	. . .	. . .	. . .	. . .
Banks	4 673 . .	. . .	. . .	. . .	. . .	. . .	. . .	. . .	. . .
Other sectors	4 674 . .	–25.8	. . .	1.6	–17.4	–3.4	12.2	2.1	. . .
Money market instruments	4 680 . .	. . .	. . .	. . .	. . .	. . .	. . .	. . .	. . .
Monetary authorities	4 681 . .	. . .	. . .	. . .	. . .	. . .	. . .	. . .	. . .
General government	4 682 . .	. . .	. . .	. . .	. . .	. . .	. . .	. . .	. . .
Banks	4 683 . .	. . .	. . .	. . .	. . .	. . .	. . .	. . .	. . .
Other sectors	4 684 . .	. . .	. . .	. . .	. . .	. . .	. . .	. . .	. . .
C. FINANCIAL DERIVATIVES	4 910 . .	. . .	. . .	. . .	. . .	. . .	. . .	. . .	. . .
Monetary authorities	4 911 . .	. . .	. . .	. . .	. . .	. . .	. . .	. . .	. . .
General government	4 912 . .	. . .	. . .	. . .	. . .	. . .	. . .	. . .	. . .
Banks	4 913 . .	. . .	. . .	. . .	. . .	. . .	. . .	. . .	. . .
Other sectors	4 914 . .	. . .	. . .	. . .	. . .	. . .	. . .	. . .	. . .
Assets	4 900 . .	. . .	. . .	. . .	. . .	. . .	. . .	. . .	. . .
Monetary authorities	4 901 . .	. . .	. . .	. . .	. . .	. . .	. . .	. . .	. . .
General government	4 902 . .	. . .	. . .	. . .	. . .	. . .	. . .	. . .	. . .
Banks	4 903 . .	. . .	. . .	. . .	. . .	. . .	. . .	. . .	. . .
Other sectors	4 904 . .	. . .	. . .	. . .	. . .	. . .	. . .	. . .	. . .
Liabilities	4 905 . .	. . .	. . .	. . .	. . .	. . .	. . .	. . .	. . .
Monetary authorities	4 906 . .	. . .	. . .	. . .	. . .	. . .	. . .	. . .	. . .
General government	4 907 . .	. . .	. . .	. . .	. . .	. . .	. . .	. . .	. . .
Banks	4 908 . .	. . .	. . .	. . .	. . .	. . .	. . .	. . .	. . .
Other sectors	4 909 . .	. . .	. . .	. . .	. . .	. . .	. . .	. . .	. . .

Table 2 (Concluded). STANDARD PRESENTATION, 1994–2001
(Millions of U.S. dollars)

	Code	1994	1995	1996	1997	1998	1999	2000	2001
D. OTHER INVESTMENT	4 700 . .	7.2	63.7	–67.2	–19.7	29.6	–11.2	–34.6	. . .
Assets	4 703 . .	**5.8**	**12.5**	**–11.3**	**–49.7**	**29.2**	**–15.7**	**–97.7**	**. . .**
Trade credits	4 706 . .	. . .	. . .	. . .	. . .	. . .	. . .	. . .	. . .
General government	4 707 . .	. . .	. . .	. . .	. . .	. . .	. . .	. . .	. . .
of which: Short-term	4 709 . .	. . .	. . .	. . .	. . .	. . .	. . .	. . .	. . .
Other sectors	4 710 . .	. . .	. . .	. . .	. . .	. . .	. . .	. . .	. . .
of which: Short-term	4 712 . .	. . .	. . .	. . .	. . .	. . .	. . .	. . .	. . .
Loans	4 714 . .	–19.7	–10.4	–36.5	7.0	–.9	–6.4	–5.6	. . .
Monetary authorities	4 715 . .	. . .	. . .	. . .	. . .	. . .	. . .	. . .	. . .
of which: Short-term	4 718 . .	. . .	. . .	. . .	. . .	. . .	. . .	. . .	. . .
General government	4 719 . .	. . .	. . .	. . .	. . .	. . .	. . .	. . .	. . .
of which: Short-term	4 721 . .	. . .	. . .	. . .	. . .	. . .	. . .	. . .	. . .
Banks	4 722 . .	. . .	. . .	–36.5	7.0	–.9	–6.4	–5.6	. . .
of which: Short-term	4 724 . .	. . .	. . .	. . .	. . .	. . .	. . .	. . .	. . .
Other sectors	4 725 . .	–19.7	–10.4	. . .	. . .	. . .	. . .	. . .	. . .
of which: Short-term	4 727 . .	*–21.5*	*–13.3*	. . .	. . .	. . .	. . .	. . .	. . .
Currency and deposits	4 730 . .	4.2	23.0	5.7	–59.3	31.4	–4.2	–91.0	. . .
Monetary authorities	4 731 . .	. . .	. . .	. . .	. . .	. . .	. . .	. . .	. . .
General government	4 732 . .	–.8	. . .	. . .	. . .	. . .	. . .	. . .	. . .
Banks	4 733 . .	–3.7	15.6	. . .	–40.3	–9.3	–.7	–14.4	. . .
Other sectors	4 734 . .	8.8	7.4	5.7	–19.0	40.7	–3.5	–76.6	. . .
Other assets	4 736 . .	21.2	. . .	19.5	2.6	–1.2	–5.1	–1.1	. . .
Monetary authorities	4 737 . .	. . .	. . .	. . .	. . .	. . .	. . .	. . .	. . .
of which: Short-term	4 739 . .	. . .	. . .	. . .	. . .	. . .	. . .	. . .	. . .
General government	4 740 . .	. . .	. . .	. . .	. . .	. . .	. . .	. . .	. . .
of which: Short-term	4 742 . .	. . .	. . .	. . .	. . .	. . .	. . .	. . .	. . .
Banks	4 743 . .	. . .	. . .	19.5	2.6	–1.2	–5.1	–1.1	. . .
of which: Short-term	4 745 . .	. . .	. . .	. . .	. . .	. . .	. . .	. . .	. . .
Other sectors	4 746 . .	21.2	. . .	. . .	. . .	. . .	. . .	. . .	. . .
of which: Short-term	4 748 . .	. . .	. . .	. . .	. . .	. . .	. . .	. . .	. . .
Liabilities	4 753 . .	**1.3**	**51.2**	**–55.9**	**30.0**	**.4**	**4.5**	**63.1**	**. . .**
Trade credits	4 756 . .	. . .	. . .	. . .	. . .	. . .	. . .	. . .	. . .
General government	4 757 . .	. . .	. . .	. . .	. . .	. . .	. . .	. . .	. . .
of which: Short-term	4 759 . .	. . .	. . .	. . .	. . .	. . .	. . .	. . .	. . .
Other sectors	4 760 . .	. . .	. . .	. . .	. . .	. . .	. . .	. . .	. . .
of which: Short-term	4 762 . .	. . .	. . .	. . .	. . .	. . .	. . .	. . .	. . .
Loans	4 764 . .	46.3	40.4	–72.9	–7.3	26.8	4.0	34.0	. . .
Monetary authorities	4 765 . .	. . .	. . .	. . .	. . .	. . .	. . .	. . .	. . .
of which: Use of Fund credit and loans from the Fund	4 766 . .	. . .	. . .	. . .	. . .	. . .	. . .	. . .	. . .
of which: Short-term	4 768 . .	. . .	. . .	. . .	. . .	. . .	. . .	. . .	. . .
General government	4 769 . .	.4	.6	–10.6	–8.9	22.2	7.5	34.0	. . .
of which: Short-term	4 771 . .	. . .	. . .	. . .	. . .	. . .	. . .	. . .	. . .
Banks	4 772 . .	. . .	. . .	. . .	. . .	. . .	. . .	. . .	. . .
of which: Short-term	4 774 . .	. . .	. . .	. . .	. . .	. . .	. . .	. . .	. . .
Other sectors	4 775 . .	45.9	39.9	–62.3	1.6	4.6	–3.5	. . .	. . .
of which: Short-term	4 777 . .	*11.1*	. . .	*–32.3*	*15.3*	*5.4*	*–26.6*	. . .	. . .
Currency and deposits	4 780 . .	–8.7	10.7	. . .	. . .	. . .	. . .	. . .	. . .
Monetary authorities	4 781 . .	. . .	. . .	. . .	. . .	. . .	. . .	. . .	. . .
General government	4 782 . .	. . .	. . .	. . .	. . .	. . .	. . .	. . .	. . .
Banks	4 783 . .	–8.7	10.7	. . .	. . .	. . .	. . .	. . .	. . .
Other sectors	4 784 . .	. . .	. . .	. . .	. . .	. . .	. . .	. . .	. . .
Other liabilities	4 786 . .	–36.3	. . .	17.0	37.3	–26.4	.5	29.2	. . .
Monetary authorities	4 787 . .	. . .	. . .	. . .	. . .	. . .	. . .	. . .	. . .
of which: Short-term	4 789 . .	. . .	. . .	. . .	. . .	. . .	. . .	. . .	. . .
General government	4 790 . .	. . .	. . .	. . .	. . .	. . .	. . .	. . .	. . .
of which: Short-term	4 792 . .	. . .	. . .	. . .	. . .	. . .	. . .	. . .	. . .
Banks	4 793 . .	. . .	. . .	17.0	37.3	–26.4	.5	29.2	. . .
of which: Short-term	4 795 . .	. . .	. . .	. . .	*37.3*	. . .	. . .	. . .	. . .
Other sectors	4 796 . .	–36.3	. . .	. . .	. . .	. . .	. . .	. . .	. . .
of which: Short-term	4 798 . .	*–7.8*	. . .	. . .	. . .	. . .	. . .	. . .	. . .
E. RESERVE ASSETS	4 802 . .	3.2	–42.7	26.1	18.4	–51.3	–2.5	15.9	. . .
Monetary gold	4 812 . .	. . .	–.7	. . .	. . .	5.1	. . .	. . .	. . .
Special drawing rights	4 811 . .	. . .	. . .	. . .	. . .	. . .	. . .	. . .	. . .
Reserve position in the Fund	4 810 . .	. . .	. . .	. . .	. . .	. . .	. . .	. . .	. . .
Foreign exchange	4 803 . .	3.2	–42.1	26.1	18.4	–56.4	–2.5	15.9	. . .
Other claims	4 813 . .	. . .	. . .	. . .	. . .	. . .	. . .	. . .	. . .
NET ERRORS AND OMISSIONS	4 998 . .	**–4.7**	**2.0**	**4.3**	**–2.5**	**.6**	**–.7**	**6.5**	**. . .**

Part 3 of the *Yearbook* contains descriptions of the methodologies, compilation practices, and sources used to compile these data.

Table 1. ANALYTIC PRESENTATION, 1994–2001
(Millions of U.S. dollars)

	Code	1994	1995	1996	1997	1998	1999	2000	2001
A. Current Account [1]	4 993 Z.	**–17,146**	**–19,323**	**–15,810**	**–12,384**	**–18,014**	**–23,012**	**–15,391**	**–8,876**
Goods: exports f.o.b	2 100 . .	47,371	53,220	60,397	64,893	55,884	56,096	64,041	63,673
Goods: imports f.o.b	3 100 . .	–50,648	–57,443	–61,032	–63,044	–61,215	–65,826	–68,752	–61,761
Balance on Goods	4 100 . .	*–3,277*	*–4,223*	*–635*	*1,849*	*–5,332*	*–9,730*	*–4,711*	*1,912*
Services: credit	2 200 . .	14,185	16,156	18,531	18,488	16,181	17,354	18,390	16,236
Services: debit	3 200 . .	–15,458	–17,110	–18,606	–18,844	–17,272	–18,304	–18,075	–16,751
Balance on Goods and Services	4 991 . .	*–4,550*	*–5,177*	*–710*	*1,493*	*–6,422*	*–10,680*	*–4,396*	*1,396*
Income: credit	2 300 . .	4,462	5,258	6,027	7,162	6,532	6,909	8,586	7,934
Income: debit	3 300 . .	–16,829	–19,294	–21,220	–21,000	–17,842	–19,211	–19,533	–18,228
Balance on Goods, Services, and Income	4 992 . .	*–16,917*	*–19,213*	*–15,903*	*–12,345*	*–17,732*	*–22,983*	*–15,344*	*–8,897*
Current transfers: credit	2 379 Z.	2,206	2,364	2,699	2,765	2,651	3,003	2,622	2,242
Current transfers: debit	3 379 . .	–2,434	–2,474	–2,606	–2,805	–2,933	–3,032	–2,669	–2,221
B. Capital Account [1]	4 994 Z.	**323**	**558**	**964**	**903**	**670**	**819**	**615**	**591**
Capital account: credit	2 994 Z.	908	1,250	1,674	1,606	1,315	1,535	1,406	1,320
Capital account: debit	3 994 . .	–586	–692	–710	–703	–646	–716	–791	–729
Total, Groups A Plus B	4 981 . .	*–16,823*	*–18,765*	*–14,846*	*–11,482*	*–17,344*	*–22,193*	*–14,776*	*–8,285*
C. Financial Account [1]	4 995 W.	**15,897**	**18,632**	**16,070**	**16,820**	**15,117**	**27,969**	**14,313**	**8,003**
Direct investment abroad	4 505 . .	–2,817	–3,267	–7,052	–6,368	–3,368	2,989	–5,133	–11,611
Direct investment in Australia	4 555 Z.	5,001	12,026	6,181	7,631	6,046	5,699	11,512	4,394
Portfolio investment assets	4 602 . .	1,503	–2,842	–3,307	–79	–3,127	–6,443	–4,714	–8,690
Equity securities	4 610 . .	–543	–1,175	–2,416	–567	–2,882	–3,718	–3,877	–7,761
Debt securities	4 619 . .	2,045	–1,668	–892	489	–245	–2,724	–838	–929
Portfolio investment liabilities	4 652 Z.	14,593	15,200	23,738	13,219	6,917	17,224	14,484	19,034
Equity securities	4 660 . .	8,120	2,585	2,068	8,775	10,776	5,973	–757	10,777
Debt securities	4 669 Z.	6,473	12,615	21,670	4,444	–3,859	11,251	15,240	8,256
Financial derivatives	4 910 . .	373	584	293	622	–1,017	1,301	–580	316
Financial derivatives assets	4 900 . .	1,004	2,801	974	–470	–382	247	–966	168
Financial derivatives liabilities	4 905 . .	–632	–2,217	–681	1,092	–636	1,054	387	148
Other investment assets	4 703 . .	–1,597	–3,223	–5,613	–6,735	–243	–2,907	–4,210	144
Monetary authorities	4 701 . .	. . .	. . .	–246	–414	–180	–327	133	275
General government	4 704 . .	137	–57	–94	–840	–412	–214	–22	–153
Banks	4 705 . .	–2,438	–2,824	–4,618	–4,233	–609	–2,386	–1,177	–3,323
Other sectors	4 728 . .	704	–342	–656	–1,248	956	20	–3,144	3,345
Other investment liabilities	4 753 W.	–1,158	154	1,829	8,530	9,909	10,105	2,954	4,416
Monetary authorities	4 753 WA	–4	27	–29	3	9	61	–70	3
General government	4 753 ZB	157	133	103	–91	129	–228	75	–125
Banks	4 753 ZC	–1,375	2,998	2,717	7,207	7,654	7,833	4,339	2,958
Other sectors	4 753 ZD	64	–3,004	–963	1,417	2,116	2,439	–1,390	1,579
Total, Groups A Through C	4 983 . .	*–926*	*–133*	*1,223*	*5,339*	*–2,228*	*5,776*	*–463*	*–282*
D. Net Errors and Omissions	4 998 . .	**–34**	**529**	**1,248**	**–2,466**	**188**	**929**	**–902**	**1,378**
Total, Groups A Through D	4 984 . .	*–960*	*396*	*2,471*	*2,873*	*–2,040*	*6,705*	*–1,365*	*1,096*
E. Reserves and Related Items	4 802 A.	**960**	**–396**	**–2,471**	**–2,873**	**2,040**	**–6,705**	**1,365**	**–1,096**
Reserve assets	4 802 . .	960	–396	–2,471	–2,873	2,040	–6,705	1,365	–1,096
Use of Fund credit and loans	4 766 . .	. . .	. . .	. . .	. . .	. . .	. . .	. . .	. . .
Exceptional financing	4 920 . .	. . .	. . .	. . .	. . .	. . .	. . .	. . .	. . .
Conversion rates: Australian dollars per U.S. dollar	0 101 . .	**1.3678**	**1.3490**	**1.2779**	**1.3474**	**1.5918**	**1.5500**	**1.7248**	**1.9334**

[1] Excludes components that have been classified in the categories of Group E.

Table 2. STANDARD PRESENTATION, 1994–2001
(Millions of U.S. dollars)

	Code		1994	1995	1996	1997	1998	1999	2000	2001
CURRENT ACCOUNT	4 993	. .	**–17,146**	**–19,323**	**–15,810**	**–12,384**	**–18,014**	**–23,012**	**–15,391**	**–8,876**
A. GOODS	4 100	. .	–3,277	–4,223	–635	1,849	–5,332	–9,730	–4,711	1,912
Credit	2 100	. .	**47,371**	**53,220**	**60,397**	**64,893**	**55,884**	**56,096**	**64,041**	**63,673**
General merchandise: exports f.o.b.	2 110	. .	43,339	48,684	55,433	58,635	50,381	51,793	59,881	59,661
Goods for processing: exports f.o.b.	2 150	. .	49	61	59	64	165	781	630	767
Repairs on goods	2 160	. .	17	13	17	19	36	41	33	31
Goods procured in ports by carriers	2 170	. .	374	412	457	456	321	365	528	477
Nonmonetary gold	2 180	. .	3,591	4,049	4,430	5,719	4,980	3,115	2,969	2,737
Debit	3 100	. .	**–50,648**	**–57,443**	**–61,032**	**–63,044**	**–61,215**	**–65,826**	**–68,752**	**–61,761**
General merchandise: imports f.o.b.	3 110	. .	–49,508	–56,126	–59,665	–60,572	–57,944	–63,522	–66,682	–59,042
Goods for processing: imports f.o.b.	3 150	. .	–220	–357	–377	–641	–1,037	–1,487	–1,242	–1,823
Repairs on goods	3 160	. .	–26	–21	–41	–45	–62	–72	–63	–116
Goods procured in ports by carriers	3 170	. .	–333	–397	–456	–476	–342	–361	–470	–536
Nonmonetary gold	3 180	. .	–562	–540	–493	–1,310	–1,830	–383	–294	–245
B. SERVICES	4 200	. .	–1,273	–954	–76	–356	–1,091	–950	315	–516
Total credit	2 200	. .	*14,185*	*16,156*	*18,531*	*18,488*	*16,181*	*17,354*	*18,390*	*16,236*
Total debit	3 200	. .	*–15,458*	*–17,110*	*–18,606*	*–18,844*	*–17,272*	*–18,304*	*–18,075*	*–16,751*
Transportation services, credit	2 205	. .	**4,316**	**4,711**	**5,103**	**4,942**	**4,297**	**4,296**	**4,324**	**4,124**
Passenger	2 850	. .	*2,622*	*3,785*	*4,260*	*4,242*	*3,533*	*3,610*	*3,727*	*3,580*
Freight	2 851	. .	*776*	*927*	*843*	*700*	*763*	*685*	*597*	*545*
Other	2 852	. .	*919*	. . .	. . .	. . .	. . .	. . .	. . .	. . .
Sea transport, passenger	2 207	. .	. . .	. . .	. . .	. . .	. . .	. . .	. . .	. . .
Sea transport, freight	2 208	. .	776	927	843	. . .	. . .	. . .	. . .	. . .
Sea transport, other	2 209	. .	419	. . .	. . .	. . .	. . .	. . .	. . .	. . .
Air transport, passenger	2 211	. .	2,622	3,785	4,260	. . .	. . .	. . .	. . .	. . .
Air transport, freight	2 212	. .	. . .	. . .	. . .	. . .	. . .	. . .	. . .	. . .
Air transport, other	2 213	. .	500	. . .	. . .	. . .	. . .	. . .	. . .	. . .
Other transport, passenger	2 215	. .	. . .	. . .	. . .	. . .	. . .	. . .	. . .	. . .
Other transport, freight	2 216	. .	. . .	. . .	. . .	. . .	. . .	. . .	. . .	. . .
Other transport, other	2 217	. .	. . .	. . .	. . .	. . .	. . .	. . .	. . .	. . .
Transportation services, debit	3 205	. .	**–5,479**	**–6,260**	**–6,647**	**–6,467**	**–5,937**	**–6,040**	**–6,292**	**–5,750**
Passenger	3 850	. .	*–1,887*	*–2,095*	*–2,303*	*–2,325*	*–2,127*	*–2,347*	*–2,393*	*–2,193*
Freight	3 851	. .	*–2,968*	*–3,256*	*–3,459*	*–3,426*	*–3,268*	*–3,136*	*–3,343*	*–3,031*
Other	3 852	. .	*–624*	*–909*	*–886*	*–716*	*–542*	*–558*	*–556*	*–526*
Sea transport, passenger	3 207	. .	. . .	. . .	. . .	. . .	. . .	. . .	. . .	. . .
Sea transport, freight	3 208	. .	–2,674	–2,906	–3,058	. . .	. . .	. . .	. . .	. . .
Sea transport, other	3 209	. .	–624	–909	–886	. . .	. . .	. . .	. . .	. . .
Air transport, passenger	3 211	. .	–1,887	–2,095	–2,303	. . .	. . .	. . .	. . .	. . .
Air transport, freight	3 212	. .	–294	–350	–400	. . .	. . .	. . .	. . .	. . .
Air transport, other	3 213	. .	. . .	. . .	. . .	. . .	. . .	. . .	. . .	. . .
Other transport, passenger	3 215	. .	. . .	. . .	. . .	. . .	. . .	. . .	. . .	. . .
Other transport, freight	3 216	. .	. . .	. . .	. . .	. . .	. . .	. . .	. . .	. . .
Other transport, other	3 217	. .	. . .	. . .	. . .	. . .	. . .	. . .	. . .	. . .
Travel, credit	2 236	. .	**6,564**	**7,873**	**9,072**	**8,782**	**7,336**	**8,014**	**8,463**	**7,693**
Business travel	2 237	. .	454	575	534	589	622	631	648	585
Personal travel	2 240	. .	6,110	7,298	8,537	8,193	6,714	7,383	7,815	7,108
Travel, debit	3 236	. .	**–4,325**	**–4,979**	**–5,786**	**–6,136**	**–5,417**	**–6,046**	**–6,107**	**–5,807**
Business travel	3 237	. .	–1,129	–1,405	–1,697	–1,838	–1,398	–1,538	–1,594	–1,419
Personal travel	3 240	. .	–3,196	–3,574	–4,089	–4,298	–4,018	–4,508	–4,513	–4,388
Other services, credit	2 200	BA	**3,305**	**3,571**	**4,356**	**4,764**	**4,549**	**5,044**	**5,604**	**4,418**
Communications	2 245	. .	545	645	752	823	806	897	887	579
Construction	2 249	. .	37	68	58	44	9	14	19	45
Insurance	2 253	. .	390	455	566	598	535	525	437	351
Financial	2 260	. .	415	408	483	503	447	472	435	396
Computer and information	2 262	. .	197	127	168	333	375	424	423	435
Royalties and licence fees	2 266	. .	235	234	265	325	275	343	343	298
Other business services	2 268	. .	933	1,058	1,433	1,463	1,502	1,755	1,737	1,668
Personal, cultural, and recreational	2 287	. .	136	161	207	245	248	266	841	248
Government, n.i.e.	2 291	. .	418	415	425	431	352	348	482	399
Other services, debit	3 200	BA	**–5,655**	**–5,871**	**–6,173**	**–6,242**	**–5,919**	**–6,217**	**–5,676**	**–5,194**
Communications	3 245	. .	–703	–788	–843	–866	–940	–967	–1,064	–840
Construction	3 249	. .	. . .	. . .	. . .	. . .	. . .	. . .	. . .	. . .
Insurance	3 253	. .	–768	–789	–812	–718	–578	–589	–525	–442
Financial	3 260	. .	–458	–427	–361	–333	–284	–321	–307	–280
Computer and information	3 262	. .	–144	–142	–173	–221	–244	–310	–248	–212
Royalties and licence fees	3 266	. .	–930	–947	–1,069	–1,100	–1,010	–1,132	–999	–868
Other business services	3 268	. .	–1,872	–1,961	–2,059	–2,126	–2,007	–2,025	–1,683	–1,825
Personal, cultural, and recreational	3 287	. .	–385	–400	–445	–461	–464	–482	–471	–396
Government, n.i.e.	3 291	. .	–394	–419	–409	–417	–392	–392	–379	–330

Table 2 (Continued). STANDARD PRESENTATION, 1994–2001

(Millions of U.S. dollars)

	Code	1994	1995	1996	1997	1998	1999	2000	2001
C. INCOME	4 300 . .	-12,367	-14,036	-15,193	-13,838	-11,310	-12,302	-10,948	-10,293
Total credit	2 300 . .	*4,462*	*5,258*	*6,027*	*7,162*	*6,532*	*6,909*	*8,586*	*7,934*
Total debit	3 300 . .	*-16,829*	*-19,294*	*-21,220*	*-21,000*	*-17,842*	*-19,211*	*-19,533*	*-18,228*
Compensation of employees, credit	2 310 . .	**387**	**431**	**507**	**527**	**490**	**518**	**504**	**466**
Compensation of employees, debit	3 310 . .	**-235**	**-309**	**-420**	**-463**	**-525**	**-577**	**-592**	**-549**
Investment income, credit	2 320 . .	**4,075**	**4,827**	**5,520**	**6,635**	**6,042**	**6,391**	**8,082**	**7,468**
Direct investment income	2 330 . .	2,419	2,759	3,501	4,147	3,608	4,027	5,407	4,584
Dividends and distributed branch profits	2 332 . .	660	427	1,535	950	1,667	2,069	2,278	1,247
Reinvested earnings and undistributed branch profits	2 333 . .	1,850	2,328	1,906	3,161	1,927	2,043	3,235	3,400
Income on debt (interest)	2 334 . .	-91	4	59	36	15	-85	-107	-63
Portfolio investment income	2 339 . .	1,156	1,499	1,215	1,465	1,427	1,498	1,506	1,907
Income on equity	2 340 . .	266	353	389	491	490	527	475	746
Income on bonds and notes	2 350 . .	890	1,146	826	975	936	972	1,031	1,161
Income on money market instruments	2 360 . .	. . .	. . .	. . .	. . .	. . .	. . .	. . .	. . .
Other investment income	2 370 . .	500	569	804	1,023	1,007	865	1,169	977
Investment income, debit	3 320 . .	**-16,595**	**-18,985**	**-20,799**	**-20,536**	**-17,317**	**-18,634**	**-18,942**	**-17,679**
Direct investment income	3 330 . .	-7,290	-8,235	-8,856	-8,822	-7,733	-7,718	-7,609	-6,844
Dividends and distributed branch profits	3 332 . .	-2,457	-3,161	-4,366	-3,780	-4,124	-3,624	-3,248	-3,654
Reinvested earnings and undistributed branch profits	3 333 . .	-4,298	-4,525	-3,865	-4,492	-3,097	-3,746	-3,910	-2,658
Income on debt (interest)	3 334 . .	-536	-549	-625	-550	-512	-348	-452	-531
Portfolio investment income	3 339 . .	-7,704	-9,075	-10,173	-10,139	-8,256	-9,080	-9,298	-8,844
Income on equity	3 340 . .	-1,101	-1,529	-1,632	-1,651	-1,618	-2,084	-1,739	-1,805
Income on bonds and notes	3 350 . .	-5,350	-5,802	-6,616	-6,833	-5,297	-5,691	-6,006	-5,721
Income on money market instruments	3 360 . .	-1,253	-1,744	-1,925	-1,655	-1,341	-1,305	-1,553	-1,318
Other investment income	3 370 . .	-1,601	-1,676	-1,771	-1,576	-1,328	-1,836	-2,034	-1,991
D. CURRENT TRANSFERS	4 379 . .	-228	-109	93	-40	-282	-29	-47	21
Credit	2 379 . .	**2,206**	**2,364**	**2,699**	**2,765**	**2,651**	**3,003**	**2,622**	**2,242**
General government	2 380 . .	559	660	772	728	687	838	686	640
Other sectors	2 390 . .	1,646	1,704	1,927	2,037	1,963	2,165	1,936	1,602
Workers' remittances	2 391 . .	. . .	. . .	. . .	. . .	. . .	. . .	. . .	. . .
Other current transfers	2 392 . .	1,646	1,704	1,927	2,037	1,963	2,165	1,936	1,602
Debit	3 379 . .	**-2,434**	**-2,474**	**-2,606**	**-2,805**	**-2,933**	**-3,032**	**-2,669**	**-2,221**
General government	3 380 . .	-952	-952	-881	-860	-825	-854	-991	-790
Other sectors	3 390 . .	-1,482	-1,522	-1,726	-1,944	-2,107	-2,178	-1,678	-1,431
Workers' remittances	3 391 . .	. . .	. . .	. . .	. . .	. . .	. . .	. . .	. . .
Other current transfers	3 392 . .	-1,482	-1,522	-1,726	-1,944	-2,107	-2,178	-1,678	-1,431
CAPITAL AND FINANCIAL ACCOUNT	4 996 . .	**17,180**	**18,794**	**14,562**	**14,850**	**17,826**	**22,082**	**16,293**	**7,498**
CAPITAL ACCOUNT	4 994 . .	**323**	**558**	**964**	**903**	**670**	**819**	**615**	**591**
Total credit	2 994 . .	*908*	*1,250*	*1,674*	*1,606*	*1,315*	*1,535*	*1,406*	*1,320*
Total debit	3 994 . .	*-586*	*-692*	*-710*	*-703*	*-646*	*-716*	*-791*	*-729*
Capital transfers, credit	2 400 . .	**890**	**1,220**	**1,652**	**1,591**	**1,291**	**1,511**	**1,399**	**1,311**
General government	2 401 . .	. . .	. . .	. . .	. . .	. . .	. . .	. . .	. . .
Debt forgiveness	2 402 . .	. . .	. . .	. . .	. . .	. . .	. . .	. . .	. . .
Other capital transfers	2 410 . .	. . .	. . .	. . .	. . .	. . .	. . .	. . .	. . .
Other sectors	2 430 . .	890	1,220	1,652	1,591	1,291	1,511	1,399	1,311
Migrants' transfers	2 431 . .	890	1,220	1,652	1,591	1,291	1,511	1,399	1,311
Debt forgiveness	2 432 . .	. . .	. . .	. . .	. . .	. . .	. . .	. . .	. . .
Other capital transfers	2 440 . .	. . .	. . .	. . .	. . .	. . .	. . .	. . .	. . .
Capital transfers, debit	3 400 . .	**-577**	**-684**	**-687**	**-693**	**-642**	**-669**	**-728**	**-685**
General government	3 401 . .	-225	-292	-236	-206	-201	-191	-253	-224
Debt forgiveness	3 402 . .	. . .	. . .	. . .	. . .	. . .	. . .	. . .	. . .
Other capital transfers	3 410 . .	-225	-292	-236	-206	-201	-191	-253	-224
Other sectors	3 430 . .	-352	-392	-451	-487	-441	-478	-475	-460
Migrants' transfers	3 431 . .	-352	-392	-451	-487	-441	-478	-475	-460
Debt forgiveness	3 432 . .	. . .	. . .	. . .	. . .	. . .	. . .	. . .	. . .
Other capital transfers	3 440 . .	. . .	. . .	. . .	. . .	. . .	. . .	. . .	. . .
Nonproduced nonfinancial assets, credit	2 480 . .	**18**	**30**	**22**	**15**	**24**	**24**	**6**	**9**
Nonproduced nonfinancial assets, debit	3 480 . .	**-9**	**-8**	**-23**	**-10**	**-4**	**-46**	**-63**	**-44**

Table 2 (Continued). STANDARD PRESENTATION, 1994–2001
(Millions of U.S. dollars)

	Code		1994	1995	1996	1997	1998	1999	2000	2001
FINANCIAL ACCOUNT	4 995	. .	**16,857**	**18,236**	**13,598**	**13,947**	**17,157**	**21,263**	**15,678**	**6,907**
A. DIRECT INVESTMENT	4 500	. .	2,184	8,760	–871	1,263	2,678	8,688	6,379	–7,217
Direct investment abroad	4 505	. .	**–2,817**	**–3,267**	**–7,052**	**–6,368**	**–3,368**	**2,989**	**–5,133**	**–11,611**
Equity capital	4 510	. .	399	–1,776	–3,582	–3,548	–1,613	3,283	–2,097	–5,547
Claims on affiliated enterprises	4 515	. .	. . .	. . .	. . .	. . .	. . .	. . .	. . .	. . .
Liabilities to affiliated enterprises	4 520	. .	. . .	. . .	. . .	. . .	. . .	. . .	. . .	. . .
Reinvested earnings	4 525	. .	–1,850	–2,328	–1,906	–3,161	–1,927	–2,043	–3,235	–3,400
Other capital	4 530	. .	–1,366	837	–1,563	342	172	1,748	200	–2,665
Claims on affiliated enterprises	4 535	. .	–200	135	–358	363	–442	–182	–998	–1,833
Liabilities to affiliated enterprises	4 540	. .	–1,166	702	–1,206	–21	615	1,930	1,198	–832
Direct investment in Australia	4 555	. .	**5,001**	**12,026**	**6,181**	**7,631**	**6,046**	**5,699**	**11,512**	**4,394**
Equity capital	4 560	. .	836	5,745	3,476	3,059	3,534	765	2,449	2,636
Claims on direct investors	4 565	. .	. . .	. . .	. . .	. . .	. . .	. . .	. . .	. . .
Liabilities to direct investors	4 570	. .	. . .	. . .	. . .	. . .	. . .	. . .	. . .	. . .
Reinvested earnings	4 575	. .	4,298	4,525	3,865	4,492	3,097	3,746	3,910	2,658
Other capital	4 580	. .	–133	1,757	–1,160	81	–585	1,188	5,153	–900
Claims on direct investors	4 585	. .	–739	–828	–75	–386	–1,529	337	–934	–306
Liabilities to direct investors	4 590	. .	605	2,585	–1,085	467	944	850	6,087	–594
B. PORTFOLIO INVESTMENT	4 600	. .	16,095	12,358	20,431	13,140	3,790	10,781	9,769	10,344
Assets	4 602	. .	**1,503**	**–2,842**	**–3,307**	**–79**	**–3,127**	**–6,443**	**–4,714**	**–8,690**
Equity securities	4 610	. .	–543	–1,175	–2,416	–567	–2,882	–3,718	–3,877	–7,761
Monetary authorities	4 611	. .	. . .	. . .	. . .	. . .	. . .	. . .	. . .	. . .
General government	4 612	. .	. . .	. . .	. . .	. . .	. . .	. . .	. . .	. . .
Banks	4 613	. .	–84	195	–23	47	5	91	–131	. . .
Other sectors	4 614	. .	–458	–1,369	–2,392	–614	–2,887	–3,809	–3,746	–7,761
Debt securities	4 619	. .	2,045	–1,668	–892	489	–245	–2,724	–838	–929
Bonds and notes	4 620	. .	1,434	–1,127	164	–1,086	–521	–2,501	–638	–1,325
Monetary authorities	4 621	. .	. . .	. . .	. . .	. . .	. . .	. . .	. . .	. . .
General government	4 622	. .	. . .	. . .	. . .	. . .	. . .	. . .	. . .	. . .
Banks	4 623	. .	46	–113	247	–92	88	–146	–111	–281
Other sectors	4 624	. .	1,388	–1,013	–83	–993	–609	–2,355	–527	–1,044
Money market instruments	4 630	. .	611	–541	–1,056	1,574	276	–223	–200	396
Monetary authorities	4 631	. .	. . .	. . .	. . .	. . .	. . .	. . .	. . .	. . .
General government	4 632	. .	. . .	. . .	. . .	. . .	. . .	. . .	. . .	. . .
Banks	4 633	. .	611	–541	–23	416	235	59	–208	109
Other sectors	4 634	. .	. . .	. . .	–1,032	1,158	40	–282	8	287
Liabilities	4 652	. .	**14,593**	**15,200**	**23,738**	**13,219**	**6,917**	**17,224**	**14,484**	**19,034**
Equity securities	4 660	. .	8,120	2,585	2,068	8,775	10,776	5,973	–757	10,777
Banks	4 663	. .	79	65	479	1,079	1,399	1,498	1,880	716
Other sectors	4 664	. .	8,041	2,520	1,590	7,696	9,378	4,476	–2,637	10,061
Debt securities	4 669	. .	6,473	12,615	21,670	4,444	–3,859	11,251	15,240	8,256
Bonds and notes	4 670	. .	12,446	5,857	18,360	6,069	–5,645	4,639	5,443	12,530
Monetary authorities	4 671	. .	. . .	. . .	. . .	. . .	. . .	. . .	. . .	. . .
General government	4 672	. .	6,454	–316	9,062	–2,783	–4,851	–1,567	–3,924	–592
Banks	4 673	. .	4,000	4,194	10,285	6,873	–2,373	4,237	5,450	7,309
Other sectors	4 674	. .	1,992	1,979	–986	1,979	1,579	1,969	3,917	5,812
Money market instruments	4 680	. .	–5,974	6,758	3,310	–1,625	1,786	6,612	9,797	–4,274
Monetary authorities	4 681	. .	. . .	. . .	. . .	. . .	. . .	. . .	. . .	. . .
General government	4 682	. .	–151	257	–92	189	–406	–10	–11	363
Banks	4 683	. .	–3,527	6,610	6,095	–1,363	3,061	7,012	5,261	–1,265
Other sectors	4 684	. .	–2,296	–110	–2,693	–451	–869	–390	4,548	–3,371
C. FINANCIAL DERIVATIVES	4 910	. .	373	584	293	622	–1,017	1,301	–580	316
Monetary authorities	4 911	. .	. . .	. . .	. . .	. . .	. . .	. . .	. . .	. . .
General government	4 912	. .	. . .	. . .	. . .	. . .	. . .	. . .	. . .	. . .
Banks	4 913	. .	113	703	–548	321	–873	121	–356	600
Other sectors	4 914	. .	260	–119	841	301	–144	1,180	–223	–284
Assets	4 900	. .	**1,004**	**2,801**	**974**	**–470**	**–382**	**247**	**–966**	**168**
Monetary authorities	4 901	. .	. . .	. . .	. . .	. . .	. . .	. . .	. . .	. . .
General government	4 902	. .	. . .	. . .	. . .	. . .	. . .	. . .	. . .	. . .
Banks	4 903	. .	632	2,757	581	–902	–319	–740	–898	452
Other sectors	4 904	. .	373	44	393	432	–62	986	–68	–284
Liabilities	4 905	. .	**–632**	**–2,217**	**–681**	**1,092**	**–636**	**1,054**	**387**	**148**
Monetary authorities	4 906	. .	. . .	. . .	. . .	. . .	. . .	. . .	. . .	. . .
General government	4 907	. .	. . .	. . .	. . .	. . .	. . .	. . .	. . .	. . .
Banks	4 908	. .	–519	–2,053	–1,129	1,223	–554	860	542	148
Other sectors	4 909	. .	–113	–163	447	–131	–82	193	–155	. . .

Table 2 (Concluded). STANDARD PRESENTATION, 1994–2001
(Millions of U.S. dollars)

	Code	1994	1995	1996	1997	1998	1999	2000	2001
D. OTHER INVESTMENT	4 700	–2,755	–3,070	–3,783	1,795	9,666	7,199	–1,255	4,560
Assets	4 703	**–1,597**	**–3,223**	**–5,613**	**–6,735**	**–243**	**–2,907**	**–4,210**	**144**
Trade credits	4 706	56	–526	–328	–1,535	–247	–453	622	–181
General government	4 707	137	–57	–74	–539	–238	–201	153	–153
of which: Short-term	4 709	*57*	. . .	. . .	. . .	. . .	. . .	. . .	. . .
Other sectors	4 710	–81	–468	–254	–995	–9	–252	469	–28
of which: Short-term	4 712	*–81*	*–468*	*–262*	*–978*	*–2*	*–253*	*436*	*–27*
Loans	4 714	–2,385	–1,850	–3,849	–3,139	–285	–2,775	117	–2,088
Monetary authorities	4 715	. . .	. . .	–246	–414	–180	–327	133	275
of which: Short-term	4 718	. . .	. . .	. . .	. . .	. . .	. . .	. . .	. . .
General government	4 719	. . .	. . .	. . .	. . .	. . .	. . .	. . .	. . .
of which: Short-term	4 721	. . .	. . .	. . .	. . .	. . .	. . .	. . .	. . .
Banks	4 722	–2,236	–2,427	–4,194	–2,953	–444	–2,645	–85	–2,562
of which: Short-term	4 724	*1,103*	*–1,327*	*–2,569*	*–977*	*–774*	*–2,548*	*472*	*–935*
Other sectors	4 725	–149	576	591	227	339	197	69	200
of which: Short-term	4 727	. . .	. . .	*13*	*63*	*8*	*28*	*–34*	*65*
Currency and deposits	4 730	698	–809	–1,410	–1,776	629	338	–4,616	2,830
Monetary authorities	4 731	. . .	. . .	. . .	. . .	. . .	. . .	. . .	. . .
General government	4 732	. . .	. . .	. . .	. . .	. . .	. . .	. . .	. . .
Banks	4 733	–202	–397	–407	–1,302	–21	124	–1,075	–786
Other sectors	4 734	900	–412	–1,003	–473	650	214	–3,540	3,617
Other assets	4 736	35	–39	–26	–285	–340	–17	–333	–418
Monetary authorities	4 737	. . .	. . .	. . .	. . .	. . .	. . .	. . .	. . .
of which: Short-term	4 739	. . .	. . .	. . .	. . .	. . .	. . .	. . .	. . .
General government	4 740	. . .	. . .	–20	–300	–173	–13	–175	. . .
of which: Short-term	4 742	. . .	. . .	. . .	. . .	. . .	. . .	. . .	. . .
Banks	4 743	. . .	. . .	–17	22	–144	135	–16	26
of which: Short-term	4 745	. . .	. . .	*–17*	*22*	*–130*	*102*	*–14*	*26*
Other sectors	4 746	35	–39	10	–7	–23	–140	–142	–444
of which: Short-term	4 748	*35*	*–39*	*21*	*–7*	*–31*	*–143*	*–139*	*–452*
Liabilities	4 753	**–1,158**	**154**	**1,829**	**8,530**	**9,909**	**10,105**	**2,954**	**4,416**
Trade credits	4 756	467	487	707	1	620	27	211	–110
General government	4 757	73	75	84	–337	40	–150	. . .	. . .
of which: Short-term	4 759	. . .	. . .	. . .	. . .	. . .	. . .	. . .	. . .
Other sectors	4 760	394	412	623	338	580	177	211	–110
of which: Short-term	4 762	*394*	*412*	*616*	*336*	*504*	*176*	*103*	*15*
Loans	4 764	–1,807	–1,484	–1,628	2,472	2,027	8,229	–1,111	711
Monetary authorities	4 765	. . .	. . .	. . .	. . .	. . .	. . .	. . .	1
of which: Use of Fund credit and loans from the Fund	4 766	. . .	. . .	. . .	. . .	. . .	. . .	. . .	. . .
of which: Short-term	4 768	. . .	. . .	. . .	. . .	. . .	. . .	. . .	. . .
General government	4 769	84	58	19	–3	. . .	. . .	. . .	. . .
of which: Short-term	4 771	. . .	. . .	. . .	. . .	. . .	. . .	. . .	. . .
Banks	4 772	–1,587	2,185	157	1,825	861	6,533	410	–510
of which: Short-term	4 774	*103*	*1,382*	*1,430*	*1,891*	*–2*	*2,539*	*1,710*	*548*
Other sectors	4 775	–304	–3,727	–1,804	649	1,166	1,695	–1,521	1,220
of which: Short-term	4 777	. . .	. . .	*372*	*270*	*181*	*2,268*	*–704*	*1,403*
Currency and deposits	4 780	204	842	2,576	5,365	6,767	1,342	3,565	3,504
Monetary authorities	4 781	–4	27	–29	–3	9	61	–70	3
General government	4 782	. . .	. . .	. . .	. . .	. . .	. . .	. . .	. . .
Banks	4 783	208	815	2,605	5,368	6,758	1,281	3,635	3,501
Other sectors	4 784	. . .	. . .	. . .	. . .	. . .	. . .	. . .	. . .
Other liabilities	4 786	–22	309	174	692	494	508	289	311
Monetary authorities	4 787	. . .	. . .	. . .	. . .	. . .	. . .	. . .	. . .
of which: Short-term	4 789	. . .	. . .	. . .	. . .	. . .	. . .	. . .	. . .
General government	4 790	. . .	. . .	. . .	248	89	–78	75	–125
of which: Short-term	4 792	. . .	. . .	. . .	. . .	. . .	. . .	. . .	. . .
Banks	4 793	4	–2	–44	14	35	18	294	–33
of which: Short-term	4 795	*4*	*–2*	*–44*	*14*	*35*	*19*	*296*	*–33*
Other sectors	4 796	–25	311	218	430	370	567	–80	469
of which: Short-term	4 798	*–25*	*311*	*219*	*425*	*337*	*602*	*–89*	*484*
E. RESERVE ASSETS	4 802	960	–396	–2,471	–2,873	2,040	–6,705	1,365	–1,096
Monetary gold	4 812	. . .	. . .	. . .	. . .	. . .	. . .	. . .	. . .
Special drawing rights	4 811	14	20	17	16	2	–55	–25	–19
Reserve position in the Fund	4 810	77	14	4	–277	–481	–408	315	–216
Foreign exchange	4 803	869	–430	–2,492	–2,613	2,519	–6,243	1,075	–861
Other claims	4 813	. . .	. . .	. . .	. . .	. . .	. . .	. . .	. . .
NET ERRORS AND OMISSIONS	4 998	**–34**	**529**	**1,248**	**–2,466**	**188**	**929**	**–902**	**1,378**

Part 3 of the *Yearbook* contains descriptions of the methodologies, compilation practices, and sources used to compile these data.

Australia
193

Table 3. INTERNATIONAL INVESTMENT POSITION (End-period stocks), 1994–2001
(Millions of U.S. dollars)

	Code	1994	1995	1996	1997	1998	1999	2000	2001
ASSETS	8 995 C.	119,962	133,885	161,821	173,545	185,349	232,482	229,939	239,881
Direct investment abroad	8 505 . .	**47,774**	**53,010**	**66,816**	**71,936**	**78,635**	**89,559**	**83,232**	**91,352**
Equity capital and reinvested earnings	8 506 . .	48,529	54,392	66,096	71,497	78,030	90,730	84,955	90,515
Claims on affiliated enterprises	8 507 . .	. . .	. . .	. . .	. . .	. . .	. . .	. . .	. . .
Liabilities to affiliated enterprises	8 508 . .	. . .	. . .	. . .	. . .	. . .	. . .	. . .	. . .
Other capital	8 530 . .	–755	–1,383	720	439	605	–1,171	–1,723	837
Claims on affiliated enterprises	8 535 . .	2,626	2,567	3,495	2,835	3,621	3,521	3,984	5,426
Liabilities to affiliated enterprises	8 540 . .	–3,381	–3,950	–2,775	–2,395	–3,016	–4,692	–5,707	–4,589
Portfolio investment	8 602 . .	**29,375**	**35,658**	**42,023**	**42,451**	**48,651**	**72,875**	**77,154**	**79,352**
Equity securities	8 610 . .	22,538	27,029	31,518	32,947	36,652	57,060	61,119	64,160
Monetary authorities	8 611 . .	. . .	. . .	. . .	. . .	. . .	. . .	. . .	. . .
General government	8 612 . .	. . .	. . .	. . .	. . .	. . .	. . .	. . .	. . .
Banks	8 613 . .	554	404	448	413	21	1	. . .	. . .
Other sectors	8 614 . .	21,984	26,625	31,069	32,534	36,631	57,059	61,119	64,160
Debt securities	8 619 . .	6,837	8,629	10,506	9,504	11,999	15,815	16,035	15,192
Bonds and notes	8 620 . .	5,970	7,260	7,640	8,382	10,673	14,094	14,511	14,396
Monetary authorities	8 621 . .	. . .	. . .	. . .	. . .	. . .	. . .	. . .	. . .
General government	8 622 . .	. . .	. . .	. . .	. . .	. . .	. . .	. . .	. . .
Banks	8 623 . .	629	694	730	662	596	718	721	903
Other sectors	8 624 . .	5,340	6,566	6,910	7,719	10,077	13,376	13,790	13,493
Money market instruments	8 630 . .	868	1,369	2,866	1,122	1,325	1,721	1,524	796
Monetary authorities	8 631 . .	. . .	. . .	. . .	. . .	. . .	. . .	. . .	. . .
General government	8 632 . .	. . .	. . .	. . .	. . .	. . .	. . .	. . .	. . .
Banks	8 633 . .	868	1,369	1,529	779	512	465	513	362
Other sectors	8 634 . .	. . .	. . .	1,337	343	813	1,256	1,011	433
Financial derivatives	8 900 . .	**8,924**	**7,679**	**6,733**	**8,058**	**9,282**	**10,716**	**12,592**	**14,774**
Monetary authorities	8 901 . .	. . .	. . .	. . .	. . .	. . .	. . .	. . .	. . .
General government	8 902 . .	. . .	. . .	. . .	. . .	. . .	. . .	. . .	. . .
Banks	8 903 . .	7,815	6,288	5,466	6,751	7,776	9,402	11,164	12,497
Other sectors	8 904 . .	1,109	1,391	1,266	1,307	1,506	1,313	1,429	2,277
Other investment	8 703 . .	**19,581**	**22,589**	**28,847**	**34,006**	**33,404**	**37,377**	**38,145**	**35,739**
Trade credits	8 706 . .	3,852	4,250	5,007	6,052	6,156	6,508	5,303	5,277
General government	8 707 . .	656	685	798	1,324	1,559	1,763	1,585	1,723
of which: Short-term	8 709 . .	*–32*	. . .	. . .	. . .	. . .	. . .	. . .	. . .
Other sectors	8 710 . .	3,197	3,566	4,209	4,729	4,597	4,745	3,718	3,554
of which: Short-term	8 712 . .	*3,197*	*3,566*	*4,178*	*4,683*	*4,552*	*4,707*	*3,716*	*3,551*
Loans	8 714 . .	13,384	15,153	19,073	19,975	19,418	22,860	21,048	21,694
Monetary authorities	8 715 . .	. . .	. . .	. . .	491	766	953	875	536
of which: Short-term	8 718 . .	. . .	. . .	. . .	. . .	. . .	. . .	. . .	. . .
General government	8 719 . .	. . .	. . .	. . .	. . .	. . .	. . .	. . .	. . .
of which: Short-term	8 721 . .	. . .	. . .	. . .	. . .	. . .	. . .	. . .	. . .
Banks	8 722 . .	8,643	10,958	15,567	16,529	16,009	19,201	17,591	18,780
of which: Short-term	8 724 . .	*4,134*	*5,298*	*8,292*	*7,988*	*8,420*	*11,404*	*9,866*	*9,859*
Other sectors	8 725 . .	4,741	4,194	3,506	2,954	2,642	2,705	2,583	2,378
of which: Short-term	8 727 . .	. . .	. . .	*147*	*75*	*48*	*37*	*141*	*82*
Currency and deposits	8 730 . .	1,355	2,201	3,592	4,764	4,415	4,197	8,235	5,030
Monetary authorities	8 731 . .	. . .	. . .	. . .	. . .	. . .	. . .	. . .	. . .
General government	8 732 . .	8	7	8	7	. . .	. . .	. . .	. . .
Banks	8 733 . .	589	947	1,352	2,310	2,268	2,208	2,849	3,415
Other sectors	8 734 . .	758	1,247	2,232	2,448	2,147	1,990	5,385	1,615
Other assets	8 736 . .	990	985	1,175	3,215	3,415	3,812	3,558	3,738
Monetary authorities	8 737 . .	. . .	. . .	. . .	. . .	. . .	. . .	. . .	. . .
of which: Short-term	8 739 . .	. . .	. . .	. . .	. . .	. . .	. . .	. . .	. . .
General government	8 740 . .	538	516	571	2,714	2,724	2,914	2,638	2,431
of which: Short-term	8 742 . .	. . .	. . .	. . .	*7*	. . .	. . .	. . .	. . .
Banks	8 743 . .	. . .	. . .	69	53	192	136	53	21
of which: Short-term	8 745 . .	. . .	. . .	*69*	*52*	*177*	*96*	*53*	*21*
Other sectors	8 746 . .	452	469	534	448	499	762	867	1,285
of which: Short-term	8 748 . .	*452*	*469*	*534*	*448*	*499*	*753*	*853*	*1,281*
Reserve assets	8 802 . .	**14,308**	**14,949**	**17,402**	**17,094**	**15,377**	**21,956**	**18,817**	**18,664**
Monetary gold	8 812 . .	3,023	3,055	2,918	740	737	743	699	709
Special drawing rights	8 811 . .	73	55	37	19	18	72	94	109
Reserve position in the Fund	8 810 . .	506	502	482	727	1,256	1,633	1,243	1,412
Foreign exchange	8 803 . .	10,706	11,337	13,967	15,608	13,366	19,507	16,782	16,434
Other claims	8 813 . .	. . .	. . .	. . .	. . .	. . .	. . .	. . .	. . .

Table 3 (Concluded). INTERNATIONAL INVESTMENT POSITION (End–period stocks), 1994–2001
(Millions of U.S. dollars)

	Code	1994	1995	1996	1997	1998	1999	2000	2001
LIABILITIES	8 995 D.	309,880	335,211	388,362	360,313	380,429	450,518	424,088	428,863
Direct investment in Australia	8 555 ..	**95,519**	**104,074**	**116,724**	**101,043**	**105,944**	**120,316**	**109,263**	**106,416**
Equity capital and reinvested earnings	8 556 ..	80,214	87,523	100,514	87,043	92,251	105,932	90,823	90,666
Claims on direct investors	8 557 ..	...	...	...	...	...	...	...	...
Liabilities to direct investors	8 558 ..	...	...	...	...	...	...	...	...
Other capital	8 580 ..	15,305	16,550	16,210	13,999	13,693	14,384	18,439	15,749
Claims on direct investors	8 585 ..	–2,389	–3,232	–3,453	–3,211	–4,503	–4,511	–4,636	–5,046
Liabilities to direct investors	8 590 ..	17,695	19,782	19,663	17,210	18,196	18,895	23,076	20,795
Portfolio investment	8 652 ..	**162,325**	**181,223**	**218,728**	**203,158**	**208,590**	**246,355**	**234,302**	**243,148**
Equity securities	8 660 ..	46,544	51,314	61,123	60,297	72,987	96,748	80,339	88,949
Banks	8 663 ..	6,325	7,193	10,234	11,967	14,164	15,358	18,151	19,895
Other sectors	8 664 ..	40,219	44,121	50,888	48,330	58,823	81,390	62,188	69,055
Debt securities	8 669 ..	115,780	129,909	157,605	142,861	135,603	149,607	153,963	154,199
Bonds and notes	8 670 ..	91,836	99,082	122,108	112,781	106,011	115,188	112,918	118,402
Monetary authorities	8 671 ..	...	...	...	...	...	...	...	...
General government	8 672 ..	22,929	23,770	34,390	26,711	20,690	18,386	13,066	11,265
Banks	8 673 ..	20,542	24,280	34,340	38,141	36,544	45,137	47,847	52,655
Other sectors	8 674 ..	48,365	51,033	53,378	47,929	48,776	51,666	52,005	54,482
Money market instruments	8 680 ..	23,945	30,827	35,497	30,080	29,592	34,419	41,045	35,798
Monetary authorities	8 681 ..	...	...	...	...	...	...	...	...
General government	8 682 ..	378	624	592	625	205	204	125	465
Banks	8 683 ..	14,094	20,844	27,959	23,579	24,911	29,953	31,750	29,277
Other sectors	8 684 ..	9,472	9,359	6,946	5,876	4,477	4,261	9,170	6,056
Financial derivatives	8 905 ..	**7,564**	**7,250**	**8,275**	**9,884**	**9,862**	**12,526**	**13,350**	**12,632**
Monetary authorities	8 906 ..	...	...	...	...	...	...	...	...
General government	8 907 ..	...	...	...	...	...	...	...	...
Banks	8 908 ..	7,166	6,218	6,354	8,610	8,590	10,705	11,312	11,131
Other sectors	8 909 ..	398	1,033	1,921	1,274	1,271	1,821	2,038	1,501
Other investment	8 753 ..	**44,472**	**42,665**	**44,636**	**46,227**	**56,034**	**71,320**	**67,173**	**66,667**
Trade credits	8 756 ..	4,001	4,191	4,922	4,057	4,437	4,412	4,005	3,298
General government	8 757 ..	308	370	481	110	174	34	...	...
of which: Short-term	8 759 ..	...	...	...	...	*31*	*34*	...	...
Other sectors	8 760 ..	3,693	3,821	4,440	3,946	4,264	4,378	4,005	3,298
of which: Short-term	8 762 ..	*3,693*	*3,821*	*4,437*	*3,942*	*4,178*	*4,300*	*3,819*	*3,236*
Loans	8 764 ..	29,732	27,093	24,738	23,331	24,791	33,633	28,998	27,826
Monetary authorities	8 765 ..	...	...	...	...	...	...	...	...
of which: Use of Fund credit and loans from the Fund	8 766 ..	...	...	...	...	...	...	...	...
of which: Short-term	8 768 ..	...	...	...	...	...	...	...	...
General government	8 769 ..	89	69	92	27	...	...	30	23
of which: Short-term	8 771 ..	...	...	...	...	...	...	...	...
Banks	8 772 ..	14,076	15,096	14,602	13,887	14,594	21,791	19,901	18,279
of which: Short-term	8 774 ..	*4,352*	*5,576*	*8,865*	*9,270*	*9,008*	*11,925*	*12,183*	*11,782*
Other sectors	8 775 ..	15,567	11,929	10,044	9,417	10,197	11,842	9,067	9,524
of which: Short-term	8 777 ..	...	...	*986*	*1,119*	*1,353*	*3,540*	*2,638*	*4,020*
Currency and deposits	8 780 ..	9,607	9,985	13,303	16,981	22,941	24,900	27,144	29,063
Monetary authorities	8 781 ..	46	71	45	33	36	100	18	19
General government	8 782 ..	...	...	...	...	...	...	...	...
Banks	8 783 ..	9,562	9,914	13,258	16,947	22,905	24,800	27,126	29,043
Other sectors	8 784 ..	...	...	...	...	...	...	...	...
Other liabilities	8 786 ..	1,132	1,395	1,673	1,860	3,865	8,376	7,026	6,480
Monetary authorities	8 787 ..	...	...	...	...	...	...	...	...
of which: Short-term	8 789 ..	...	...	...	...	...	...	...	...
General government	8 790 ..	...	...	...	99	186	119	179	41
of which: Short-term	8 792 ..	...	...	...	...	...	...	...	...
Banks	8 793 ..	...	...	23	17	23	41	307	318
of which: Short-term	8 795 ..	...	...	*23*	*16*	*21*	*41*	*307*	*318*
Other sectors	8 796 ..	1,132	1,395	1,650	1,743	3,656	8,216	6,539	6,121
of which: Short-term	8 798 ..	*1,132*	*1,395*	*1,649*	*1,720*	*3,603*	*8,201*	*6,522*	*6,121*
NET INTERNATIONAL INVESTMENT POSITION	8 995 ..	**–189,919**	**–201,327**	**–226,541**	**–186,768**	**–195,080**	**–218,035**	**–194,148**	**–188,982**
Conversion rates: Australian dollars per U.S. dollar (end of period)	0 102 ..	**1.2873**	**1.3423**	**1.2555**	**1.5321**	**1.6289**	**1.5295**	**1.8051**	**1.9585**

Table 1. ANALYTIC PRESENTATION, 1994–2001
(Millions of U.S. dollars)

	Code	1994	1995	1996	1997	1998	1999	2000	2001
A. Current Account [1]	4 993 Z.	**–2,992**	**–5,448**	**–4,890**	**–5,221**	**–5,258**	**–6,655**	**–4,864**	**–4,103**
Goods: exports f.o.b	2 100 . .	45,175	57,695	57,937	58,662	63,299	64,422	64,684	66,899
Goods: imports f.o.b	3 100 . .	–53,089	–64,352	–65,252	–62,936	–66,983	–68,051	–67,421	–68,227
Balance on Goods	4 100 . .	*–7,914*	*–6,656*	*–7,315*	*–4,274*	*–3,684*	*–3,629*	*–2,737*	*–1,328*
Services: credit	2 200 . .	28,019	32,211	33,977	29,605	29,759	31,306	31,342	32,896
Services: debit	3 200 . .	–20,743	–27,703	–29,331	–28,569	–27,398	–29,421	–29,653	–31,535
Balance on Goods and Services	4 991 . .	*–639*	*–2,149*	*–2,669*	*–3,239*	*–1,323*	*–1,745*	*–1,048*	*33*
Income: credit	2 300 . .	7,074	8,900	9,852	10,393	9,957	12,673	11,992	12,297
Income: debit	3 300 . .	–8,344	–10,498	–10,291	–10,682	–11,958	–15,552	–14,456	–15,292
Balance on Goods, Services, and Income	4 992 . .	*–1,909*	*–3,746*	*–3,107*	*–3,527*	*–3,325*	*–4,624*	*–3,512*	*–2,962*
Current transfers: credit	2 379 Z.	1,370	2,972	3,145	2,912	2,940	2,925	2,914	3,264
Current transfers: debit	3 379 . .	–2,453	–4,674	–4,928	–4,605	–4,874	–4,956	–4,267	–4,404
B. Capital Account [1]	4 994 Z.	**–68**	**–62**	**78**	**26**	**–347**	**–265**	**–432**	**–514**
Capital account: credit	2 994 Z.	676	540	591	590	483	555	530	485
Capital account: debit	3 994 . .	–744	–602	–513	–564	–831	–820	–962	–999
Total, Groups A Plus B	4 981 . .	*–3,060*	*–5,510*	*–4,812*	*–5,195*	*–5,606*	*–6,921*	*–5,296*	*–4,617*
C. Financial Account [1]	4 995 W.	**4,311**	**7,365**	**5,325**	**1,666**	**9,535**	**4,789**	**3,407**	**1,809**
Direct investment abroad	4 505 . .	–1,256	–1,134	–1,848	–1,984	–2,794	–3,306	–5,599	–3,046
Direct investment in Austria	4 555 Z.	2,117	1,901	4,485	2,624	4,661	3,008	8,523	5,898
Portfolio investment assets	4 602 . .	–4,475	–2,836	–8,296	–10,157	–11,210	–29,216	–27,145	–11,867
Equity securities	4 610 . .	–842	–545	–1,146	–2,405	–5,280	–5,281	–15,387	–996
Debt securities	4 619 . .	–3,633	–2,291	–7,150	–7,752	–5,930	–23,935	–11,757	–10,871
Portfolio investment liabilities	4 652 Z.	4,253	12,292	5,607	10,956	17,942	26,364	30,360	16,583
Equity securities	4 660 . .	1,304	1,262	2,652	2,610	1,005	2,131	3,436	–4,441
Debt securities	4 669 Z.	2,949	11,030	2,955	8,345	16,937	24,232	26,924	21,024
Financial derivatives	4 910 . .	–85	–133	215	32	204	–417	–187	–299
Financial derivatives assets	4 900 . .	–85	–133	215	–191	303	–517	–441	–394
Financial derivatives liabilities	4 905 . .	. . .	. . .	. . .	223	–99	100	254	96
Other investment assets	4 703 . .	–2,545	–9,923	719	–5,208	–690	–11,592	–16,334	–6,172
Monetary authorities	4 701 . .	–17	–131	131	. . .	–115	–3,561	1,760	539
General government	4 704 . .	–183	–231	324	–647	–512	331	–1,003	–284
Banks	4 705 . .	–1,307	–10,848	2,292	–3,873	924	–5,242	–13,593	–5,904
Other sectors	4 728 . .	–1,039	1,287	–2,027	–687	–988	–3,121	–3,498	–523
Other investment liabilities	4 753 W.	6,303	7,199	4,442	5,403	1,423	19,948	13,790	712
Monetary authorities	4 753 WA	. . .	. . .	. . .	. . .	–1	6,684	–647	–6,129
General government	4 753 ZB	1,558	467	–715	–319	526	101	157	491
Banks	4 753 ZC	4,584	6,077	5,142	5,695	1,695	10,740	11,721	6,207
Other sectors	4 753 ZD	160	655	15	27	–797	2,422	2,559	143
Total, Groups A Through C	4 983 . .	*1,251*	*1,855*	*513*	*–3,529*	*3,929*	*–2,132*	*–1,889*	*–2,807*
D. Net Errors and Omissions	4 998 . .	**–417**	**–464**	**562**	**476**	**–447**	**–40**	**1,143**	**919**
Total, Groups A Through D	4 984 . .	*834*	*1,391*	*1,075*	*–3,053*	*3,482*	*–2,172*	*–746*	*–1,888*
E. Reserves and Related Items	4 802 A.	**–834**	**–1,391**	**–1,075**	**3,053**	**–3,482**	**2,172**	**746**	**1,888**
Reserve assets	4 802 . .	–834	–1,391	–1,075	3,053	–3,482	2,172	746	1,888
Use of Fund credit and loans	4 766 . .	. . .	. . .	. . .	. . .	. . .	. . .	. . .	. . .
Exceptional financing	4 920 . .	. . .	. . .	. . .	. . .	. . .	. . .	. . .	. . .
Conversion rates: schillings per U.S. dollar	0 101 . .	**11.422**	**10.081**	**10.587**	**12.204**	**12.379**	. . .	. . .	. . .
Conversion rates: euros per U.S. dollar	0 103 . .	. . .	. . .	. . .	. . .	. . .	**.93863**	**1.08540**	**1.11751**

[1] Excludes components that have been classified in the categories of Group E.

Table 2. STANDARD PRESENTATION, 1994–2001
(Millions of U.S. dollars)

	Code		1994	1995	1996	1997	1998	1999	2000	2001
CURRENT ACCOUNT	4 993	. .	**–2,992**	**–5,448**	**–4,890**	**–5,221**	**–5,258**	**–6,655**	**–4,864**	**–4,103**
A. GOODS	4 100	. .	–7,914	–6,656	–7,315	–4,274	–3,684	–3,629	–2,737	–1,328
Credit	2 100	. .	**45,175**	**57,695**	**57,937**	**58,662**	**63,299**	**64,422**	**64,684**	**66,899**
General merchandise: exports f.o.b.	2 110	. .	45,175	57,695	57,937	58,662	60,214	61,223	61,199	63,811
Goods for processing: exports f.o.b.	2 150	. .	. . .	. . .	. . .	. . .	3,038	3,106	3,359	3,046
Repairs on goods	2 160	. .	. . .	. . .	. . .	. . .	. . .	. . .	. . .	. . .
Goods procured in ports by carriers	2 170	. .	. . .	. . .	. . .	. . .	. . .	. . .	. . .	. . .
Nonmonetary gold	2 180	. .	. . .	. . .	. . .	. . .	47	92	126	41
Debit	3 100	. .	**–53,089**	**–64,352**	**–65,252**	**–62,936**	**–66,983**	**–68,051**	**–67,421**	**–68,227**
General merchandise: imports f.o.b.	3 110	. .	–53,089	–64,352	–65,252	–62,936	–64,674	–65,407	–64,257	–65,016
Goods for processing: imports f.o.b.	3 150	. .	. . .	. . .	. . .	. . .	–2,274	–2,642	–3,162	–3,208
Repairs on goods	3 160	. .	. . .	. . .	. . .	. . .	. . .	. . .	. . .	. . .
Goods procured in ports by carriers	3 170	. .	. . .	. . .	. . .	. . .	. . .	. . .	. . .	. . .
Nonmonetary gold	3 180	. .	. . .	. . .	. . .	. . .	–35	–3	–2	–3
B. SERVICES	4 200	. .	7,275	4,508	4,646	1,035	2,361	1,884	1,689	1,361
Total credit	2 200	. .	*28,019*	*32,211*	*33,977*	*29,605*	*29,759*	*31,306*	*31,342*	*32,896*
Total debit	3 200	. .	*–20,743*	*–27,703*	*–29,331*	*–28,569*	*–27,398*	*–29,421*	*–29,653*	*–31,535*
Transportation services, credit	2 205	. .	**3,508**	**3,730**	**4,006**	**4,050**	**4,558**	**4,303**	**4,354**	**4,972**
Passenger	2 850	. .	*900*	*1,094*	*1,150*	*1,257*	*1,453*	*1,509*	*1,485*	*1,777*
Freight	2 851	. .	*2,608*	*2,636*	*2,856*	*2,792*	*2,268*	*2,084*	*2,147*	*2,422*
Other	2 852	. .	. . .	. . .	. . .	. . .	*837*	*710*	*722*	*773*
Sea transport, passenger	2 207	. .	. . .	. . .	. . .	. . .	. . .	. . .	. . .	. . .
Sea transport, freight	2 208	. .	. . .	. . .	. . .	. . .	. . .	. . .	. . .	. . .
Sea transport, other	2 209	. .	. . .	. . .	. . .	. . .	. . .	. . .	. . .	. . .
Air transport, passenger	2 211	. .	. . .	. . .	. . .	. . .	. . .	. . .	. . .	. . .
Air transport, freight	2 212	. .	. . .	. . .	. . .	. . .	. . .	. . .	. . .	. . .
Air transport, other	2 213	. .	. . .	. . .	. . .	. . .	. . .	. . .	. . .	. . .
Other transport, passenger	2 215	. .	. . .	. . .	. . .	. . .	. . .	. . .	. . .	. . .
Other transport, freight	2 216	. .	. . .	. . .	. . .	. . .	. . .	. . .	. . .	. . .
Other transport, other	2 217	. .	. . .	. . .	. . .	. . .	. . .	. . .	. . .	. . .
Transportation services, debit	3 205	. .	**–3,046**	**–3,274**	**–3,226**	**–2,919**	**–3,160**	**–2,918**	**–2,995**	**–3,342**
Passenger	3 850	. .	*–617*	*–799*	*–762*	*–610*	*–818*	*–790*	*–768*	*–818*
Freight	3 851	. .	*–2,429*	*–2,476*	*–2,463*	*–2,309*	*–1,982*	*–1,798*	*–1,888*	*–2,144*
Other	3 852	. .	. . .	. . .	. . .	. . .	*–361*	*–330*	*–339*	*–380*
Sea transport, passenger	3 207	. .	. . .	. . .	. . .	. . .	. . .	. . .	. . .	. . .
Sea transport, freight	3 208	. .	. . .	. . .	. . .	. . .	. . .	. . .	. . .	. . .
Sea transport, other	3 209	. .	. . .	. . .	. . .	. . .	. . .	. . .	. . .	. . .
Air transport, passenger	3 211	. .	. . .	. . .	. . .	. . .	. . .	. . .	. . .	. . .
Air transport, freight	3 212	. .	. . .	. . .	. . .	. . .	. . .	. . .	. . .	. . .
Air transport, other	3 213	. .	. . .	. . .	. . .	. . .	. . .	. . .	. . .	. . .
Other transport, passenger	3 215	. .	. . .	. . .	. . .	. . .	. . .	. . .	. . .	. . .
Other transport, freight	3 216	. .	. . .	. . .	. . .	. . .	. . .	. . .	. . .	. . .
Other transport, other	3 217	. .	. . .	. . .	. . .	. . .	. . .	. . .	. . .	. . .
Travel, credit	2 236	. .	**12,202**	**13,435**	**12,830**	**11,018**	**11,241**	**11,096**	**9,998**	**10,244**
Business travel	2 237	. .	. . .	. . .	. . .	. . .	. . .	. . .	. . .	. . .
Personal travel	2 240	. .	. . .	. . .	. . .	. . .	. . .	. . .	. . .	. . .
Travel, debit	3 236	. .	**–8,854**	**–10,887**	**–11,015**	**–10,062**	**–9,581**	**–9,151**	**–8,463**	**–8,885**
Business travel	3 237	. .	. . .	. . .	. . .	. . .	. . .	. . .	. . .	. . .
Personal travel	3 240	. .	. . .	. . .	. . .	. . .	. . .	. . .	. . .	. . .
Other services, credit	2 200	BA	**12,310**	**15,046**	**17,141**	**14,537**	**13,960**	**15,906**	**16,990**	**17,680**
Communications	2 245	. .	122	298	338	317	425	428	479	552
Construction	2 249	. .	830	766	741	755	746	704	585	661
Insurance	2 253	. .	541	637	756	652	805	838	765	1,026
Financial	2 260	. .	445	614	882	592	763	941	1,335	903
Computer and information	2 262	. .	57	82	83	80	88	113	135	131
Royalties and licence fees	2 266	. .	129	133	182	185	99	120	162	138
Other business services	2 268	. .	9,498	11,836	13,406	11,356	10,289	12,097	13,055	13,697
Personal, cultural, and recreational	2 287	. .	162	160	202	211	212	224	193	212
Government, n.i.e.	2 291	. .	525	520	552	390	534	441	282	361
Other services, debit	3 200	BA	**–8,844**	**–13,542**	**–15,090**	**–15,589**	**–14,657**	**–17,353**	**–18,195**	**–19,307**
Communications	3 245	. .	–141	–303	–360	–374	–495	–523	–430	–479
Construction	3 249	. .	–502	–595	–618	–492	–469	–545	–312	–466
Insurance	3 253	. .	–639	–822	–832	–788	–943	–950	–928	–987
Financial	3 260	. .	–514	–715	–873	–581	–716	–835	–1,185	–853
Computer and information	3 262	. .	–106	–150	–170	–157	–231	–237	–212	–221
Royalties and licence fees	3 266	. .	–456	–533	–696	–691	–817	–625	–566	–602
Other business services	3 268	. .	–6,190	–10,079	–11,177	–12,120	–10,630	–13,314	–14,308	–15,448
Personal, cultural, and recreational	3 287	. .	–146	–194	–228	–248	–229	–208	–174	–187
Government, n.i.e.	3 291	. .	–149	–152	–136	–138	–127	–116	–80	–64

Table 2 (Continued). STANDARD PRESENTATION, 1994–2001
(Millions of U.S. dollars)

	Code	1994	1995	1996	1997	1998	1999	2000	2001
C. INCOME	4 300	–1,270	–1,597	–439	–289	–2,001	–2,879	–2,464	–2,995
Total credit	2 300	*7,074*	*8,900*	*9,852*	*10,393*	*9,957*	*12,673*	*11,992*	*12,297*
Total debit	3 300	*–8,344*	*–10,498*	*–10,291*	*–10,682*	*–11,958*	*–15,552*	*–14,456*	*–15,292*
Compensation of employees, credit	2 310	**845**	**1,012**	**984**	**915**	**944**	**1,019**	**911**	**946**
Compensation of employees, debit	3 310	**–292**	**–346**	**–346**	**–343**	**–377**	**–424**	**–383**	**–421**
Investment income, credit	2 320	**6,229**	**7,888**	**8,868**	**9,478**	**9,013**	**11,654**	**11,081**	**11,351**
Direct investment income	2 330	236	12	616	831	763	1,251	1,279	1,469
Dividends and distributed branch profits	2 332	...	...	...	...	328	452	1,103	776
Reinvested earnings and undistributed branch profits	2 333	...	...	...	...	384	714	115	624
Income on debt (interest)	2 334	...	...	...	...	51	85	61	69
Portfolio investment income	2 339	1,433	2,194	2,155	3,116	2,564	3,432	4,399	4,361
Income on equity	2 340	...	...	...	...	198	281	393	151
Income on bonds and notes	2 350	...	...	...	...	2,345	3,040	3,916	4,124
Income on money market instruments	2 360	...	...	...	...	20	110	90	87
Other investment income	2 370	4,561	5,682	6,097	5,531	5,686	6,971	5,403	5,521
Investment income, debit	3 320	**–8,052**	**–10,152**	**–9,944**	**–10,339**	**–11,581**	**–15,129**	**–14,073**	**–14,871**
Direct investment income	3 330	–1,383	–2,113	–1,889	–1,965	–1,944	–2,522	–2,598	–2,936
Dividends and distributed branch profits	3 332	...	...	...	...	–959	–963	–1,693	–1,520
Reinvested earnings and undistributed branch profits	3 333	...	...	...	...	–981	–1,555	–900	–1,414
Income on debt (interest)	3 334	...	...	...	...	–4	–3	–5	–2
Portfolio investment income	3 339	–3,342	–3,754	–4,063	–4,079	–5,213	–6,210	–6,774	–7,446
Income on equity	3 340	...	...	...	...	–290	–271	–228	–258
Income on bonds and notes	3 350	...	...	...	...	–4,768	–5,761	–6,225	–6,921
Income on money market instruments	3 360	...	...	...	...	–155	–178	–321	–268
Other investment income	3 370	–3,327	–4,285	–3,992	–4,295	–4,425	–6,397	–4,701	–4,489
D. CURRENT TRANSFERS	4 379	–1,083	–1,702	–1,783	–1,694	–1,934	–2,031	–1,352	–1,141
Credit	2 379	**1,370**	**2,972**	**3,145**	**2,912**	**2,940**	**2,925**	**2,914**	**3,264**
General government	2 380	204	1,881	1,948	1,723	1,666	1,702	1,696	1,830
Other sectors	2 390	1,166	1,092	1,197	1,188	1,274	1,223	1,218	1,433
Workers' remittances	2 391	...	...	...	...	329	327	305	315
Other current transfers	2 392	...	...	...	...	945	896	914	1,119
Debit	3 379	**–2,453**	**–4,674**	**–4,928**	**–4,605**	**–4,874**	**–4,956**	**–4,267**	**–4,404**
General government	3 380	–928	–3,289	–3,421	–3,266	–3,168	–3,213	–2,771	–2,804
Other sectors	3 390	–1,526	–1,385	–1,507	–1,340	–1,706	–1,743	–1,496	–1,600
Workers' remittances	3 391	...	...	...	...	–370	–355	–280	–243
Other current transfers	3 392	...	...	...	...	–1,336	–1,388	–1,216	–1,358
CAPITAL AND FINANCIAL ACCOUNT	4 996	**3,409**	**5,912**	**4,328**	**4,745**	**5,706**	**6,695**	**3,721**	**3,184**
CAPITAL ACCOUNT	4 994	**–68**	**–62**	**78**	**26**	**–347**	**–265**	**–432**	**–514**
Total credit	2 994	*676*	*540*	*591*	*590*	*483*	*555*	*530*	*485*
Total debit	3 994	*–744*	*–602*	*–513*	*–564*	*–831*	*–820*	*–962*	*–999*
Capital transfers, credit	2 400	**676**	**528**	**586**	**540**	**461**	**498**	**490**	**438**
General government	2 401	...	42	220	209	187	213	152	57
Debt forgiveness	2 402	...	...	...	...	...	...	...	...
Other capital transfers	2 410	...	...	...	...	187	213	152	57
Other sectors	2 430	676	486	366	332	274	285	338	381
Migrants' transfers	2 431	...	...	...	...	143	180	225	252
Debt forgiveness	2 432	...	...	...	...	16	28	8	16
Other capital transfers	2 440	...	...	...	...	114	77	105	113
Capital transfers, debit	3 400	**–744**	**–599**	**–510**	**–531**	**–795**	**–790**	**–895**	**–910**
General government	3 401	...	...	...	–4	–64	–16	–8	–152
Debt forgiveness	3 402	...	...	...	...	–63	...	...	...
Other capital transfers	3 410	...	...	...	...	–1	–16	–8	–152
Other sectors	3 430	–744	–599	–510	–527	–732	–774	–887	–758
Migrants' transfers	3 431	...	...	...	...	–184	–166	–196	–261
Debt forgiveness	3 432	...	...	...	...	–457	–496	–481	–391
Other capital transfers	3 440	...	...	...	...	–90	–113	–210	–106
Nonproduced nonfinancial assets, credit	2 480	**...**	**12**	**6**	**50**	**23**	**56**	**40**	**47**
Nonproduced nonfinancial assets, debit	3 480	**...**	**–3**	**–3**	**–32**	**–35**	**–30**	**–67**	**–88**

Table 2 (Continued). STANDARD PRESENTATION, 1994–2001
(Millions of U.S. dollars)

	Code		1994	1995	1996	1997	1998	1999	2000	2001
FINANCIAL ACCOUNT	4 995	. .	**3,477**	**5,974**	**4,250**	**4,719**	**6,053**	**6,961**	**4,153**	**3,698**
A. DIRECT INVESTMENT	4 500	. .	860	767	2,637	641	1,866	–298	2,924	2,852
Direct investment abroad	4 505	. .	**–1,256**	**–1,134**	**–1,848**	**–1,984**	**–2,794**	**–3,306**	**–5,599**	**–3,046**
Equity capital	4 510	. .	–1,256	–1,134	–1,848	–1,984	–2,379	–2,756	–4,820	–2,340
Claims on affiliated enterprises	4 515	. .	. . .	. . .	. . .	. . .	–2,379	–2,756	–4,820	–2,340
Liabilities to affiliated enterprises	4 520	. .	. . .	. . .	. . .	. . .	. . .	. . .	. . .	. . .
Reinvested earnings	4 525	. .	. . .	. . .	. . .	. . .	–384	–714	–115	–624
Other capital	4 530	. .	. . .	. . .	. . .	. . .	–31	163	–664	–81
Claims on affiliated enterprises	4 535	. .	. . .	. . .	. . .	. . .	–2	219	–683	–86
Liabilities to affiliated enterprises	4 540	. .	. . .	. . .	. . .	. . .	–29	–55	19	5
Direct investment in Austria	4 555	. .	**2,117**	**1,901**	**4,485**	**2,624**	**4,661**	**3,008**	**8,523**	**5,898**
Equity capital	4 560	. .	2,117	1,901	4,485	2,624	3,687	1,395	7,475	3,655
Claims on direct investors	4 565	. .	. . .	. . .	. . .	. . .	. . .	. . .	. . .	. . .
Liabilities to direct investors	4 570	. .	. . .	. . .	. . .	. . .	3,687	1,395	7,475	3,655
Reinvested earnings	4 575	. .	. . .	. . .	. . .	. . .	981	1,555	900	1,414
Other capital	4 580	. .	. . .	. . .	. . .	. . .	–7	57	148	829
Claims on direct investors	4 585	. .	. . .	. . .	. . .	. . .	–40	75	90	–196
Liabilities to direct investors	4 590	. .	. . .	. . .	. . .	. . .	33	–18	58	1,025
B. PORTFOLIO INVESTMENT	4 600	. .	–222	9,456	–2,688	798	6,732	–2,852	3,215	4,716
Assets	4 602	. .	**–4,475**	**–2,836**	**–8,296**	**–10,157**	**–11,210**	**–29,216**	**–27,145**	**–11,867**
Equity securities	4 610	. .	–842	–545	–1,146	–2,405	–5,280	–5,281	–15,387	–996
Monetary authorities	4 611	. .	. . .	. . .	. . .	. . .	–1,174	–95	–75	173
General government	4 612	. .	. . .	. . .	. . .	. . .	–18	–58	–78	–82
Banks	4 613	. .	. . .	. . .	. . .	. . .	–533	–880	102	24
Other sectors	4 614	. .	. . .	. . .	. . .	. . .	–3,554	–4,247	–15,337	–1,111
Debt securities	4 619	. .	–3,633	–2,291	–7,150	–7,752	–5,930	–23,935	–11,757	–10,871
Bonds and notes	4 620	. .	–3,435	–2,430	–6,530	–8,134	–6,324	–23,744	–10,906	–11,222
Monetary authorities	4 621	. .	. . .	. . .	. . .	. . .	257	247	–395	–299
General government	4 622	. .	. . .	. . .	. . .	. . .	–165	–30	–387	–319
Banks	4 623	. .	. . .	. . .	. . .	. . .	–2,617	–10,342	–4,314	–5,277
Other sectors	4 624	. .	. . .	. . .	. . .	. . .	–3,798	–13,619	–5,810	–5,328
Money market instruments	4 630	. .	–198	139	–620	382	394	–191	–852	351
Monetary authorities	4 631	. .	. . .	. . .	. . .	. . .	216	835	345	209
General government	4 632	. .	. . .	. . .	. . .	. . .	–3	31	–1,553	75
Banks	4 633	. .	. . .	. . .	. . .	. . .	–536	–454	81	49
Other sectors	4 634	. .	. . .	. . .	. . .	. . .	717	–603	275	18
Liabilities	4 652	. .	**4,253**	**12,292**	**5,607**	**10,956**	**17,942**	**26,364**	**30,360**	**16,583**
Equity securities	4 660	. .	1,304	1,262	2,652	2,610	1,005	2,131	3,436	–4,441
Banks	4 663	. .	. . .	. . .	. . .	. . .	754	130	475	170
Other sectors	4 664	. .	. . .	. . .	. . .	. . .	250	2,002	2,960	–4,611
Debt securities	4 669	. .	2,949	11,030	2,955	8,345	16,937	24,232	26,924	21,024
Bonds and notes	4 670	. .	3,001	11,794	4,119	7,090	16,566	20,496	25,031	23,358
Monetary authorities	4 671	. .	. . .	. . .	. . .	. . .	. . .	. . .	. . .	. . .
General government	4 672	. .	. . .	. . .	. . .	. . .	10,761	14,655	11,125	9,199
Banks	4 673	. .	. . .	. . .	. . .	. . .	3,857	5,647	12,964	9,950
Other sectors	4 674	. .	. . .	. . .	. . .	. . .	1,948	193	943	4,209
Money market instruments	4 680	. .	–52	–764	–1,163	1,255	371	3,737	1,893	–2,334
Monetary authorities	4 681	. .	. . .	. . .	. . .	. . .	. . .	. . .	. . .	. . .
General government	4 682	. .	. . .	. . .	. . .	. . .	1,476	1,066	–202	–511
Banks	4 683	. .	. . .	. . .	. . .	. . .	–1,149	2,295	2,330	–1,623
Other sectors	4 684	. .	. . .	. . .	. . .	. . .	44	376	–236	–200
C. FINANCIAL DERIVATIVES	4 910	. .	–85	–133	215	32	204	–417	–187	–299
Monetary authorities	4 911	. .	. . .	. . .	. . .	. . .	1	12	2	–37
General government	4 912	. .	. . .	. . .	. . .	. . .	284	213	235	313
Banks	4 913	. .	. . .	. . .	. . .	. . .	–37	–680	–86	–1,355
Other sectors	4 914	. .	. . .	. . .	. . .	. . .	–44	39	–338	780
Assets	4 900	. .	**–85**	**–133**	**215**	**–191**	**303**	**–517**	**–441**	**–394**
Monetary authorities	4 901	. .	. . .	. . .	. . .	. . .	1	12	2	–37
General government	4 902	. .	. . .	. . .	. . .	. . .	284	213	235	313
Banks	4 903	. .	. . .	. . .	. . .	. . .	64	–779	–361	–1,506
Other sectors	4 904	. .	. . .	. . .	. . .	. . .	–46	38	–317	835
Liabilities	4 905	. .	**. . .**	**. . .**	**. . .**	**223**	**–99**	**100**	**254**	**96**
Monetary authorities	4 906	. .	. . .	. . .	. . .	. . .	. . .	. . .	. . .	. . .
General government	4 907	. .	. . .	. . .	. . .	. . .	. . .	. . .	. . .	. . .
Banks	4 908	. .	. . .	. . .	. . .	. . .	–101	99	275	150
Other sectors	4 909	. .	. . .	. . .	. . .	. . .	2	2	–21	–55

Table 2 (Concluded). STANDARD PRESENTATION, 1994–2001
(Millions of U.S. dollars)

	Code		1994	1995	1996	1997	1998	1999	2000	2001
D. OTHER INVESTMENT	4 700	. .	3,758	–2,724	5,161	195	732	8,355	–2,544	–5,460
Assets	4 703	. .	**–2,545**	**–9,923**	**719**	**–5,208**	**–690**	**–11,592**	**–16,334**	**–6,172**
Trade credits	4 706	. .	–391	347	1,034	237	716	–688	–2,046	264
General government	4 707	. .	. . .	. . .	. . .	. . .	. . .	. . .	. . .	. . .
of which: Short-term	4 709	. .	. . .	. . .	. . .	. . .	. . .	. . .	. . .	. . .
Other sectors	4 710	. .	–391	347	1,034	237	716	–688	–2,046	264
of which: Short-term	4 712	. .	*–391*	*347*	*1,034*	*237*	*716*	*–688*	*–2,046*	*264*
Loans	4 714	. .	–889	–2,189	–3,577	–4,158	–4,285	–12,074	–9,302	–6,084
Monetary authorities	4 715	. .	. . .	. . .	. . .	. . .	. . .	–1,046	821	93
of which: Short-term	4 718	. .	. . .	. . .	. . .	. . .	. . .	. . .	. . .	. . .
General government	4 719	. .	–124	184	11	10	61	82	16	11
of which: Short-term	4 721	. .	. . .	. . .	. . .	. . .	. . .	. . .	. . .	. . .
Banks	4 722	. .	265	–2,404	–2,287	–3,280	–2,724	–8,383	–8,520	–5,906
of which: Short-term	4 724	. .	*–260*	*–199*	*–673*	*–1,281*	*–497*	*–4,240*	*–4,007*	*–569*
Other sectors	4 725	. .	–1,030	32	–1,300	–888	–1,622	–2,728	–1,618	–282
of which: Short-term	4 727	. .	. . .	. . .	. . .	. . .	. . .	. . .	. . .	. . .
Currency and deposits	4 730	. .	–1,212	–7,814	2,636	989	2,908	1,238	–4,985	327
Monetary authorities	4 731	. .	–17	–131	131	. . .	17	–2,515	940	447
General government	4 732	. .	29	–126	588	–414	–447	324	–917	–199
Banks	4 733	. .	–1,488	–8,213	3,232	1,091	3,435	2,996	–5,373	581
Other sectors	4 734	. .	263	656	–1,315	311	–97	433	365	–502
Other assets	4 736	. .	–52	–268	626	–2,275	–29	–69	. . .	–678
Monetary authorities	4 737	. .	. . .	. . .	. . .	. . .	–132	. . .	. . .	. . .
of which: Short-term	4 739	. .	. . .	. . .	. . .	. . .	. . .	. . .	. . .	. . .
General government	4 740	. .	–88	–289	–274	–244	–125	–75	–101	–96
of which: Short-term	4 742	. .	. . .	. . .	. . .	. . .	. . .	. . .	. . .	. . .
Banks	4 743	. .	–83	–231	1,346	–1,684	213	144	300	–579
of which: Short-term	4 745	. .	. . .	. . .	. . .	. . .	*175*	*156*	*205*	*–565*
Other sectors	4 746	. .	119	252	–446	–346	15	–138	–199	–3
of which: Short-term	4 748	. .	. . .	. . .	. . .	. . .	. . .	. . .	. . .	. . .
Liabilities	4 753	. .	**6,303**	**7,199**	**4,442**	**5,403**	**1,423**	**19,948**	**13,790**	**712**
Trade credits	4 756	. .	614	–294	–104	392	–293	1,252	454	–505
General government	4 757	. .	. . .	. . .	. . .	. . .	. . .	. . .	. . .	. . .
of which: Short-term	4 759	. .	. . .	. . .	. . .	. . .	. . .	. . .	. . .	. . .
Other sectors	4 760	. .	614	–294	–104	392	–293	1,252	454	–505
of which: Short-term	4 762	. .	*614*	*–294*	*–104*	*392*	*–293*	*1,252*	*454*	*–505*
Loans	4 764	. .	1,230	1,590	168	–417	49	1,980	3,807	744
Monetary authorities	4 765	. .	. . .	. . .	. . .	. . .	–1	498	–643	–17
of which: Use of Fund credit and loans from the Fund	4 766	. .	. . .	. . .	. . .	. . .	. . .	. . .	. . .	. . .
of which: Short-term	4 768	. .	. . .	. . .	. . .	. . .	. . .	*498*	*–643*	*–17*
General government	4 769	. .	1,627	624	–205	–136	365	65	–114	406
of which: Short-term	4 771	. .	. . .	. . .	. . .	. . .	. . .	. . .	. . .	. . .
Banks	4 772	. .	179	147	284	96	176	581	2,160	–326
of which: Short-term	4 774	. .	. . .	. . .	. . .	. . .	*201*	*301*	*1,422*	*–690*
Other sectors	4 775	. .	–576	818	89	–377	–491	836	2,404	680
of which: Short-term	4 777	. .	. . .	. . .	. . .	. . .	. . .	. . .	. . .	. . .
Currency and deposits	4 780	. .	4,083	5,518	5,081	5,679	1,320	16,178	9,370	465
Monetary authorities	4 781	. .	. . .	. . .	. . .	. . .	. . .	6,186	–4	–6,112
General government	4 782	. .	. . .	. . .	. . .	. . .	. . .	. . .	. . .	. . .
Banks	4 783	. .	4,083	5,518	5,081	5,679	1,320	9,992	9,374	6,578
Other sectors	4 784	. .	. . .	. . .	. . .	. . .	. . .	. . .	. . .	. . .
Other liabilities	4 786	. .	376	387	–704	–251	347	538	159	7
Monetary authorities	4 787	. .	. . .	. . .	. . .	. . .	. . .	. . .	. . .	. . .
of which: Short-term	4 789	. .	. . .	. . .	. . .	. . .	. . .	. . .	. . .	. . .
General government	4 790	. .	–69	–157	–511	–183	162	36	271	85
of which: Short-term	4 792	. .	. . .	. . .	. . .	. . .	. . .	. . .	. . .	. . .
Banks	4 793	. .	323	413	–223	–79	198	168	188	–45
of which: Short-term	4 795	. .	. . .	. . .	. . .	. . .	*270*	*137*	*195*	*–107*
Other sectors	4 796	. .	122	131	30	12	–13	334	–300	–32
of which: Short-term	4 798	. .	. . .	. . .	. . .	. . .	. . .	. . .	. . .	. . .
E. RESERVE ASSETS	4 802	. .	–834	–1,391	–1,075	3,053	–3,482	2,172	746	1,888
Monetary gold	4 812	. .	43	1,152	319	403	–770	172	254	254
Special drawing rights	4 811	. .	–53	116	–20	15	27	1	4	–105
Reserve position in the Fund	4 810	. .	26	–147	–151	–204	–347	372	221	–166
Foreign exchange	4 803	. .	–850	–2,512	–1,222	2,839	–2,391	1,626	267	1,905
Other claims	4 813	. .	. . .	. . .	. . .	. . .	. . .	1	. . .	. . .
NET ERRORS AND OMISSIONS	4 998	. .	**–417**	**–464**	**562**	**476**	**–447**	**–40**	**1,143**	**919**

Part 3 of the *Yearbook* contains descriptions of the methodologies, compilation practices, and sources used to compile these data.

Table 3. INTERNATIONAL INVESTMENT POSITION (End–period stocks), 1994–2001

(Millions of U.S. dollars)

	Code	1994	1995	1996	1997	1998	1999	2000	2001
ASSETS	8 995 C.	137,955	160,211	161,785	166,135	194,856	225,924	261,554	267,497
Direct investment abroad	8 505 . .	**9,390**	**11,707**	**11,868**	**15,159**	**18,726**	**20,458**	**26,262**	**27,761**
Equity capital and reinvested earnings	8 506 . .	7,658	9,447	9,586	13,386	16,794	18,748	23,653	25,211
Claims on affiliated enterprises	8 507 . .	...	...	...	...	...	...	...	...
Liabilities to affiliated enterprises	8 508 . .	...	...	...	...	...	...	...	...
Other capital	8 530 . .	1,732	2,260	2,282	1,773	1,932	1,709	2,609	2,550
Claims on affiliated enterprises	8 535 . .	...	...	...	...	...	...	...	...
Liabilities to affiliated enterprises	8 540 . .	...	...	...	...	...	...	...	...
Portfolio investment	8 602 . .	**22,673**	**27,389**	**33,303**	**44,051**	**58,747**	**93,299**	**115,680**	**119,137**
Equity securities	8 610 . .	4,941	5,868	6,454	11,502	17,225	28,936	42,698	36,905
Monetary authorities	8 611 . .	...	...	...	...	1,014	1,455	1,347	998
General government	8 612 . .	...	...	...	25	12	55	56	78
Banks	8 613 . .	428	456	548	1,257	1,041	2,541	1,908	2,781
Other sectors	8 614 . .	4,513	5,412	5,907	10,219	15,158	24,885	39,388	33,049
Debt securities	8 619 . .	17,732	21,521	26,849	32,549	41,522	64,363	72,982	82,232
Bonds and notes	8 620 . .	17,148	20,718	25,826	32,162	40,873	62,573	71,377	81,275
Monetary authorities	8 621 . .	...	...	...	545	...	2,917	2,784	3,005
General government	8 622 . .	356	268	37	153	283	147	153	538
Banks	8 623 . .	5,771	6,483	9,138	11,946	14,996	22,880	26,851	30,757
Other sectors	8 624 . .	11,022	13,967	16,651	19,517	25,594	36,629	41,589	46,973
Money market instruments	8 630 . .	583	803	1,022	388	649	1,790	1,605	958
Monetary authorities	8 631 . .	...	...	...	128	...	662	629	232
General government	8 632 . .	...	...	...	...	1	1	222	66
Banks	8 633 . .	529	406	621	59	432	777	393	355
Other sectors	8 634 . .	55	397	402	200	216	350	361	304
Financial derivatives	8 900 . .	**109**	**169**	**219**	**201**	**...**	**...**	**...**	**...**
Monetary authorities	8 901 . .	...	...	...	...	...	...	...	...
General government	8 902 . .	...	...	...	–4	...	...	...	...
Banks	8 903 . .	64	119	219	239	...	...	...	...
Other sectors	8 904 . .	46	50	...	–33	...	...	...	...
Other investment	8 703 . .	**82,040**	**95,054**	**89,730**	**84,853**	**90,959**	**93,236**	**101,985**	**104,988**
Trade credits	8 706 . .	6,199	6,384	5,058	4,621	4,219	3,675	5,482	4,921
General government	8 707 . .	...	...	...	...	...	...	...	...
of which: Short-term	8 709 . .	...	...	...	...	...	...	...	...
Other sectors	8 710 . .	6,199	6,384	5,058	4,621	4,219	3,675	5,482	4,921
of which: Short-term	8 712 . .	...	...	...	...	*4,219*	*3,675*	*5,482*	*4,921*
Loans	8 714 . .	26,247	33,297	32,445	35,734	41,291	47,340	54,634	59,248
Monetary authorities	8 715 . .	...	...	...	6	...	995	93	...
of which: Short-term	8 718 . .	...	...	...	...	...	*995*	*93*	...
General government	8 719 . .	109	139	119	99	107	13	20	9
of which: Short-term	8 721 . .	...	...	...	...	...	...	...	...
Banks	8 722 . .	26,137	33,228	31,678	33,357	37,236	39,890	46,211	50,565
of which: Short-term	8 724 . .	...	...	...	*8,066*	*8,236*	*9,879*	*13,431*	*15,506*
Other sectors	8 725 . .	...	–69	648	2,272	3,949	6,442	8,310	8,674
of which: Short-term	8 727 . .	...	...	...	...	*1,881*	*3,401*	*4,698*	*4,281*
Currency and deposits	8 730 . .	46,577	50,922	48,046	38,203	38,418	35,976	35,965	34,663
Monetary authorities	8 731 . .	...	...	...	6	50	3,242	2,180	1,660
General government	8 732 . .	91	...	...	423	961	483	1,265	1,412
Banks	8 733 . .	44,042	49,623	45,874	37,085	36,553	31,520	32,009	30,717
Other sectors	8 734 . .	2,443	1,299	2,173	689	854	730	512	873
Other assets	8 736 . .	3,018	4,451	4,181	6,295	7,031	6,246	5,904	6,156
Monetary authorities	8 737 . .	...	...	...	...	138	119	110	104
of which: Short-term	8 739 . .	...	...	...	...	...	...	...	...
General government	8 740 . .	820	1,071	1,488	1,517	1,761	1,581	1,568	1,580
of which: Short-term	8 742 . .	*456*	*496*	*456*	...	...	...	...	...
Banks	8 743 . .	201	416	164	3,209	3,478	3,037	2,677	3,024
of which: Short-term	8 745 . .	...	...	...	...	...	...	...	...
Other sectors	8 746 . .	1,997	2,964	2,529	1,569	1,654	1,509	1,548	1,448
of which: Short-term	8 748 . .	*1,112*	*1,675*	*1,004*	...	...	...	...	...
Reserve assets	8 802 . .	**23,742**	**25,893**	**26,666**	**21,871**	**26,423**	**18,931**	**17,627**	**15,611**
Monetary gold	8 812 . .	7,047	4,609	3,971	2,311	3,989	3,811	3,308	3,102
Special drawing rights	8 811 . .	283	181	195	168	149	145	134	233
Reserve position in the Fund	8 810 . .	531	682	809	963	1,365	959	692	833
Foreign exchange	8 803 . .	15,872	20,410	21,682	18,428	20,920	14,016	13,492	11,444
Other claims	8 813 . .	9	10	9	...	...	...	...	...

Table 3 (Concluded). INTERNATIONAL INVESTMENT POSITION (End–period stocks), 1994–2001
(Millions of U.S. dollars)

	Code	1994	1995	1996	1997	1998	1999	2000	2001
LIABILITIES	8 995 D.	155,538	189,790	189,264	198,918	236,547	262,994	299,033	311,227
Direct investment in Austria	8 555 . .	**13,246**	**17,536**	**18,258**	**19,694**	**23,837**	**23,991**	**31,280**	**35,442**
Equity capital and reinvested earnings	8 556 . .	11,350	15,702	16,432	18,816	23,242	23,104	29,841	33,262
Claims on direct investors	8 557 . .	. . .	. . .	. . .	. . .	. . .	. . .	. . .	. . .
Liabilities to direct investors	8 558 . .	. . .	. . .	. . .	. . .	. . .	. . .	. . .	. . .
Other capital	8 580 . .	1,896	1,834	1,826	879	595	887	1,439	2,180
Claims on direct investors	8 585 . .	. . .	. . .	. . .	. . .	. . .	. . .	. . .	. . .
Liabilities to direct investors	8 590 . .	. . .	. . .	. . .	. . .	. . .	. . .	. . .	. . .
Portfolio investment	8 652 . .	**69,469**	**89,473**	**87,676**	**97,091**	**121,674**	**139,054**	**161,082**	**171,603**
Equity securities	8 660 . .	5,379	6,989	9,056	15,662	15,623	14,745	19,569	13,662
Banks	8 663 . .	328	367	593	2,564	3,039	3,057	2,793	2,878
Other sectors	8 664 . .	5,051	6,622	8,463	13,098	12,584	11,688	16,776	10,784
Debt securities	8 669 . .	64,090	82,484	78,620	81,430	106,052	124,309	141,512	157,941
Bonds and notes	8 670 . .	59,285	77,716	75,251	78,247	101,785	116,979	132,689	150,753
Monetary authorities	8 671 . .	. . .	. . .	. . .	. . .	. . .	. . .	. . .	. . .
General government	8 672 . .	28,909	39,750	36,270	38,132	53,800	61,578	66,531	72,732
Banks	8 673 . .	22,308	27,805	29,167	31,658	37,673	43,939	54,248	62,238
Other sectors	8 674 . .	8,068	10,161	9,814	8,457	10,313	11,463	11,910	15,782
Money market instruments	8 680 . .	4,804	4,768	3,369	3,182	4,266	7,329	8,823	7,188
Monetary authorities	8 681 . .	. . .	. . .	. . .	. . .	. . .	. . .	. . .	. . .
General government	8 682 . .	109	59	110	34	1,392	2,166	1,801	1,321
Banks	8 683 . .	4,668	4,580	3,232	2,719	2,470	4,557	6,781	5,840
Other sectors	8 684 . .	27	129	27	429	404	606	240	27
Financial derivatives	8 905 . .	**119**	**129**	**110**	**12**	. . .	. . .	. . .	. . .
Monetary authorities	8 906 . .	. . .	. . .	. . .	. . .	. . .	. . .	. . .	. . .
General government	8 907 . .	. . .	. . .	. . .	. . .	. . .	. . .	. . .	. . .
Banks	8 908 . .	119	129	110	. . .	. . .	. . .	. . .	. . .
Other sectors	8 909 . .	. . .	. . .	. . .	12	. . .	. . .	. . .	. . .
Other investment	8 753 . .	**72,705**	**82,653**	**83,221**	**82,121**	**91,036**	**99,949**	**106,672**	**104,183**
Trade credits	8 756 . .	4,285	4,362	3,834	3,693	3,661	3,527	3,734	3,041
General government	8 757 . .	. . .	. . .	. . .	. . .	. . .	. . .	. . .	. . .
of which: Short-term	8 759 . .	. . .	. . .	. . .	. . .	. . .	. . .	. . .	. . .
Other sectors	8 760 . .	4,285	4,362	3,834	3,693	3,661	3,527	3,734	3,041
of which: Short-term	8 762 . .	. . .	. . .	. . .	. . .	. . .	*3,527*	*3,734*	*3,041*
Loans	8 764 . .	7,895	11,410	10,727	8,723	10,010	12,064	16,031	16,835
Monetary authorities	8 765 . .	. . .	. . .	. . .	. . .	. . .	956	958	1,017
of which: Use of Fund credit and loans from the Fund	8 766 . .	. . .	. . .	. . .	. . .	. . .	. . .	. . .	. . .
of which: Short-term	8 768 . .	. . .	. . .	. . .	. . .	. . .	*956*	*90*	*209*
General government	8 769 . .	1,750	3,033	2,930	2,375	2,933	2,845	2,510	2,728
of which: Short-term	8 771 . .	. . .	. . .	. . .	. . .	. . .	. . .	. . .	. . .
Banks	8 772 . .	3,008	4,738	4,400	2,066	2,398	3,695	5,545	5,212
of which: Short-term	8 774 . .	. . .	. . .	. . .	*546*	*834*	*1,198*	*2,494*	*1,696*
Other sectors	8 775 . .	3,136	3,638	3,396	4,282	4,679	4,568	7,018	7,879
of which: Short-term	8 777 . .	. . .	. . .	. . .	. . .	*909*	*924*	*2,634*	*2,908*
Currency and deposits	8 780 . .	56,769	61,866	64,908	66,390	73,616	80,677	83,441	81,004
Monetary authorities	8 781 . .	. . .	. . .	. . .	. . .	. . .	5,185	4,681	–1,579
General government	8 782 . .	748	446	. . .	. . .	. . .	. . .	. . .	. . .
Banks	8 783 . .	54,581	60,061	63,630	66,390	73,616	75,493	78,760	82,583
Other sectors	8 784 . .	1,440	1,358	1,278	. . .	. . .	. . .	. . .	. . .
Other liabilities	8 786 . .	3,756	5,016	3,752	3,315	3,750	3,680	3,467	3,302
Monetary authorities	8 787 . .	18	20	9	. . .	. . .	. . .	. . .	. . .
of which: Short-term	8 789 . .	*18*	*20*	*9*	. . .	. . .	. . .	. . .	. . .
General government	8 790 . .	547	595	548	581	786	719	902	947
of which: Short-term	8 792 . .	*547*	*595*	*548*	*581*	. . .	. . .	. . .	. . .
Banks	8 793 . .	91	585	237	213	424	440	601	514
of which: Short-term	8 795 . .	. . .	*169*	. . .	. . .	. . .	. . .	. . .	. . .
Other sectors	8 796 . .	3,100	3,816	2,958	2,521	2,540	2,520	1,963	1,841
of which: Short-term	8 798 . .	*547*	*872*	*265*	. . .	. . .	. . .	. . .	. . .
NET INTERNATIONAL INVESTMENT POSITION	8 995 . .	**–17,583**	**–29,579**	**–27,479**	**–32,784**	**–41,691**	**–37,070**	**–37,480**	**–43,730**
Conversion rates: schillings per U.S. dollar (end of period)	0 102 . .	**10.969**	**10.088**	**10.954**	**12.633**	**11.747**	. . .	. . .	. . .
Conversion rates: euros per U.S. dollar (end of period)	0 104 . .	. . .	. . .	. . .	. . .	. . .	**.99542**	**1.07469**	**1.13469**

Table 1. ANALYTIC PRESENTATION, 1994–2001
(Millions of U.S. dollars)

	Code	1994	1995	1996	1997	1998	1999	2000	2001
A. Current Account[1]	4 993 Z.	...	**–400.7**	**–931.2**	**–915.8**	**–1,364.5**	**–599.7**	**–167.8**	**–51.8**
Goods: exports f.o.b	2 100 . .	...	612.3	643.7	808.3	677.8	1,025.2	1,858.3	2,078.9
Goods: imports f.o.b	3 100 . .	...	–985.4	–1,337.6	–1,375.2	–1,723.9	–1,433.4	–1,539.0	–1,465.1
Balance on Goods	4 100 . .	...	*–373.1*	*–693.9*	*–566.9*	*–1,046.2*	*–408.2*	*319.3*	*613.9*
Services: credit	2 200 . .	...	172.4	149.3	341.8	331.7	256.8	259.8	289.8
Services: debit	3 200 . .	...	–304.6	–440.9	–726.0	–700.8	–485.1	–484.5	–664.9
Balance on Goods and Services	4 991 . .	...	*–505.4*	*–985.6*	*–951.1*	*–1,415.2*	*–636.5*	*94.6*	*238.8*
Income: credit	2 300 . .	...	9.9	15.1	22.8	38.3	11.0	55.9	41.5
Income: debit	3 300 . .	...	–16.0	–27.2	–32.3	–51.6	–56.0	–391.4	–408.7
Balance on Goods, Services, and Income	4 992 . .	...	*–511.4*	*–997.7*	*–960.6*	*–1,428.5*	*–681.5*	*–240.9*	*–128.4*
Current transfers: credit	2 379 Z.	...	129.3	107.2	95.7	145.0	134.5	135.0	176.5
Current transfers: debit	3 379 . .	...	–18.5	–40.7	–50.9	–80.9	–52.8	–62.0	–99.9
B. Capital Account[1]	4 994 Z.	...	**–1.6**	...	**–10.2**	**–.7**	...	...	...
Capital account: credit	2 994 Z.	...	...	...	...	...	...	...	...
Capital account: debit	3 994 . .	...	–1.6	...	–10.2	–.7	...	...	...
Total, Groups A Plus B	4 981 . .	...	*–402.2*	*–931.2*	*–926.0*	*–1,365.2*	*–599.7*	*–167.8*	*–51.8*
C. Financial Account[1]	4 995 W.	...	**400.3**	**822.5**	**1,092.1**	**1,326.0**	**690.2**	**493.4**	**126.0**
Direct investment abroad	4 505 . .	...	...	...	...	...	...	–.8	...
Direct investment in Azerbaijan	4 555 Z.	...	330.1	627.3	1,114.8	1,023.0	510.3	129.9	226.5
Portfolio investment assets	4 602 . .	...	–1.7	...	1.1	...	...	...	...
Equity securities	4 610 . .	...	...	...	...	...	...	...	...
Debt securities	4 619 . .	...	–1.7	...	1.1	...	...	...	...
Portfolio investment liabilities	4 652 Z.	...	...	...	...	.4	...	...	...
Equity securities	4 660 . .	...	...	...	...	...	...	...	...
Debt securities	4 669 Z.	...	...	...	...	.4	...	...	...
Financial derivatives	4 910 . .	...	...	...	...	...	...	...	...
Financial derivatives assets	4 900 . .	...	...	...	...	...	...	...	...
Financial derivatives liabilities	4 905 . .	...	...	...	...	...	...	...	...
Other investment assets	4 703 . .	...	–22.1	–216.8	–102.6	22.3	–81.0	–114.2	–394.0
Monetary authorities	4 701 . .	...	...	...	...	...	...	...	...
General government	4 704 . .	...	...	...	...	...	...	...	–220.5
Banks	4 705 . .	...	–19.6	–136.9	5.3	62.4	–44.2	7.1	–77.7
Other sectors	4 728 . .	...	–2.5	–79.8	–107.9	–40.1	–36.8	–121.2	–95.8
Other investment liabilities	4 753 W.	...	94.1	412.0	78.8	280.4	260.9	478.4	293.5
Monetary authorities	4 753 WA	...	...	...	...	...	...	...	...
General government	4 753 ZB	...	30.0	...	70.8	75.6	161.6	246.2	138.6
Banks	4 753 ZC	...	–.3	26.5	–18.8	–1.7	–.1	–22.9	3.0
Other sectors	4 753 ZD	...	64.3	385.5	26.8	206.5	99.3	255.0	151.9
Total, Groups A Through C	4 983 . .	...	*–1.9*	*–108.7*	*166.1*	*–39.2*	*90.5*	*325.6*	*74.3*
D. Net Errors and Omissions	4 998 . .	...	**59.7**	**23.6**	**–27.0**	**–20.1**	**42.4**	...	**–.9**
Total, Groups A Through D	4 984 . .	...	*57.8*	*–85.0*	*139.2*	*–59.2*	*132.9*	*325.6*	*73.4*
E. Reserves and Related Items	4 802 A.	...	**–57.8**	**85.0**	**–139.2**	**59.2**	**–132.9**	**–325.6**	**–73.4**
Reserve assets	4 802 . .	...	–161.6	7.1	–244.2	18.7	–228.5	–274.2	–44.1
Use of Fund credit and loans	4 766 . .	...	103.8	77.9	105.0	40.5	95.6	–51.4	–29.3
Exceptional financing	4 920 . .	...	...	...	...	...	...	...	...
Conversion rates: manat per U.S. dollar	0 101 . .	**1,570.23**	**4,413.54**	**4,301.26**	**3,985.38**	**3,869.00**	**4,120.17**	**4,474.15**	**4,656.58**

[1] Excludes components that have been classified in the categories of Group E.

Table 2. STANDARD PRESENTATION, 1994–2001
(Millions of U.S. dollars)

	Code		1994	1995	1996	1997	1998	1999	2000	2001
CURRENT ACCOUNT	4 993	. .	**. . .**	**–400.7**	**–931.2**	**–915.8**	**–1,364.5**	**–599.7**	**–167.8**	**–51.8**
A. GOODS	4 100	. .	. . .	–373.1	–693.9	–566.9	–1,046.2	–408.2	319.3	613.9
Credit	2 100	. .	**. . .**	**612.3**	**643.7**	**808.3**	**677.8**	**1,025.2**	**1,858.3**	**2,078.9**
General merchandise: exports f.o.b.	2 110	. .	. . .	606.7	636.5	804.6	675.7	1,025.2	1,858.3	2,077.2
Goods for processing: exports f.o.b.	2 150	. .	. . .	. . .	. . .	. . .	. . .	. . .	. . .	. . .
Repairs on goods	2 160	. .	. . .	. . .	. . .	. . .	. . .	. . .	. . .	. . .
Goods procured in ports by carriers	2 170	. .	. . .	5.6	7.2	3.7	2.1	. . .	. . .	1.7
Nonmonetary gold	2 180	. .	. . .	. . .	. . .	. . .	. . .	. . .	. . .	. . .
Debit	3 100	. .	**. . .**	**–985.4**	**–1,337.6**	**–1,375.2**	**–1,723.9**	**–1,433.4**	**–1,539.0**	**–1,465.1**
General merchandise: imports f.o.b.	3 110	. .	. . .	–980.0	–1,327.1	–1,358.2	–1,711.0	–1,433.4	–1,539.0	–1,455.5
Goods for processing: imports f.o.b.	3 150	. .	. . .	. . .	. . .	. . .	. . .	. . .	. . .	. . .
Repairs on goods	3 160	. .	. . .	. . .	. . .	. . .	. . .	. . .	. . .	. . .
Goods procured in ports by carriers	3 170	. .	. . .	–5.5	–10.5	–16.9	–12.9	. . .	. . .	–9.6
Nonmonetary gold	3 180	. .	. . .	. . .	. . .	. . .	. . .	. . .	. . .	. . .
B. SERVICES	4 200	. .	. . .	–132.3	–291.6	–384.2	–369.1	–228.3	–224.7	–375.0
Total credit	2 200	. .	. . .	*172.4*	*149.3*	*341.8*	*331.7*	*256.8*	*259.8*	*289.8*
Total debit	3 200	. .	. . .	*–304.6*	*–440.9*	*–726.0*	*–700.8*	*–485.1*	*–484.5*	*–664.9*
Transportation services, credit	2 205	. .	**. . .**	**76.2**	**53.7**	**96.9**	**129.0**	**114.0**	**119.3**	**161.7**
Passenger	2 850	. .	. . .	*17.5*	*11.1*	*13.7*	*18.1*	*12.1*	*5.2*	*14.3*
Freight	2 851	. .	. . .	*47.8*	*34.5*	*67.2*	*90.4*	*90.5*	*88.5*	*125.8*
Other	2 852	. .	. . .	*10.9*	*8.1*	*16.0*	*20.6*	*11.5*	*25.6*	*21.6*
Sea transport, passenger	2 207	. .	. . .	. . .	. . .	. . .	. . .	. . .	. . .	. . .
Sea transport, freight	2 208	. .	. . .	. . .	. . .	. . .	. . .	. . .	. . .	. . .
Sea transport, other	2 209	. .	. . .	. . .	. . .	. . .	. . .	. . .	. . .	. . .
Air transport, passenger	2 211	. .	. . .	. . .	. . .	. . .	. . .	. . .	. . .	. . .
Air transport, freight	2 212	. .	. . .	. . .	. . .	. . .	. . .	. . .	. . .	. . .
Air transport, other	2 213	. .	. . .	. . .	. . .	. . .	. . .	. . .	. . .	. . .
Other transport, passenger	2 215	. .	. . .	. . .	. . .	. . .	. . .	. . .	. . .	. . .
Other transport, freight	2 216	. .	. . .	. . .	. . .	. . .	. . .	. . .	. . .	. . .
Other transport, other	2 217	. .	. . .	. . .	. . .	. . .	. . .	. . .	. . .	. . .
Transportation services, debit	3 205	. .	**. . .**	**–92.1**	**–116.1**	**–109.3**	**–194.3**	**–68.0**	**–144.1**	**–156.6**
Passenger	3 850	. .	. . .	*–18.9*	*–14.9*	*–6.7*	*–10.7*	*–9.9*	*–6.4*	*–9.9*
Freight	3 851	. .	. . .	*–63.5*	*–89.9*	*–77.3*	*–150.1*	*–38.7*	*–101.2*	*–118.4*
Other	3 852	. .	. . .	*–9.7*	*–11.3*	*–25.3*	*–33.5*	*–19.5*	*–36.5*	*–28.4*
Sea transport, passenger	3 207	. .	. . .	. . .	. . .	. . .	. . .	. . .	. . .	. . .
Sea transport, freight	3 208	. .	. . .	. . .	. . .	. . .	. . .	. . .	. . .	. . .
Sea transport, other	3 209	. .	. . .	. . .	. . .	. . .	. . .	. . .	. . .	. . .
Air transport, passenger	3 211	. .	. . .	. . .	. . .	. . .	. . .	. . .	. . .	. . .
Air transport, freight	3 212	. .	. . .	. . .	. . .	. . .	. . .	. . .	. . .	. . .
Air transport, other	3 213	. .	. . .	. . .	. . .	. . .	. . .	. . .	. . .	. . .
Other transport, passenger	3 215	. .	. . .	. . .	. . .	. . .	. . .	. . .	. . .	. . .
Other transport, freight	3 216	. .	. . .	. . .	. . .	. . .	. . .	. . .	. . .	. . .
Other transport, other	3 217	. .	. . .	. . .	. . .	. . .	. . .	. . .	. . .	. . .
Travel, credit	2 236	. .	**. . .**	**70.2**	**45.6**	**161.8**	**125.0**	**81.1**	**63.1**	**42.6**
Business travel	2 237	. .	. . .	10.1	21.2	125.9	102.3	52.1	32.7	20.8
Personal travel	2 240	. .	. . .	60.1	24.4	35.8	22.8	29.0	30.4	21.7
Travel, debit	3 236	. .	**. . .**	**–145.6**	**–99.7**	**–186.3**	**–169.6**	**–138.8**	**–131.6**	**–108.9**
Business travel	3 237	. .	. . .	–9.7	–14.2	–28.0	–20.9	–20.6	–17.5	–12.9
Personal travel	3 240	. .	. . .	–135.9	–85.5	–158.3	–148.7	–118.3	–114.2	–96.0
Other services, credit	2 200	BA	**. . .**	**26.0**	**50.0**	**83.1**	**77.6**	**61.6**	**77.4**	**85.6**
Communications	2 245	. .	. . .	8.3	7.5	12.7	15.7	15.8	16.1	14.0
Construction	2 249	. .	. . .	1.7	3.9	17.1	13.7	4.1	5.1	6.8
Insurance	2 253	. .	. . .	. . .	1.0	1.0	3.0	. . .	. . .	. . .
Financial	2 260	. .	. . .	.2	.3	.1	1.0	. . .	. . .	. . .
Computer and information	2 262	. .	. . .	. . .	. . .	. . .	. . .	. . .	. . .	. . .
Royalties and licence fees	2 266	. .	. . .	. . .	. . .	. . .	. . .	. . .	. . .	. . .
Other business services	2 268	. .	. . .	9.4	27.2	42.5	32.8	21.4	30.9	30.8
Personal, cultural, and recreational	2 287	. .	. . .	. . .	. . .	. . .	. . .	. . .	. . .	. . .
Government, n.i.e.	2 291	. .	. . .	6.4	10.1	9.7	11.4	20.3	25.3	34.0
Other services, debit	3 200	BA	**. . .**	**–67.0**	**–225.1**	**–430.4**	**–336.9**	**–278.2**	**–208.8**	**–399.3**
Communications	3 245	. .	. . .	–3.7	–2.3	–6.0	–6.1	–7.1	–6.8	–6.8
Construction	3 249	. .	. . .	–18.8	–60.9	–189.1	–137.9	–177.2	–90.8	–186.8
Insurance	3 253	. .	. . .	–2.4	–1.9	–5.4	–6.5	. . .	. . .	–11.7
Financial	3 260	. .	. . .	. . .	–1.3	–4.3	–.5	. . .	. . .	. . .
Computer and information	3 262	. .	. . .	. . .	. . .	. . .	. . .	. . .	. . .	. . .
Royalties and licence fees	3 266	. .	. . .	. . .	. . .	. . .	. . .	. . .	. . .	. . .
Other business services	3 268	. .	. . .	–33.8	–150.4	–213.8	–177.4	–84.5	–102.0	–179.5
Personal, cultural, and recreational	3 287	. .	. . .	. . .	. . .	. . .	. . .	. . .	. . .	. . .
Government, n.i.e.	3 291	. .	. . .	–8.1	–8.3	–11.8	–8.5	–9.3	–9.3	–14.6

Table 2 (Continued). STANDARD PRESENTATION, 1994–2001

(Millions of U.S. dollars)

	Code	1994	1995	1996	1997	1998	1999	2000	2001
C. INCOME	4 300 . .	. . .	–6.0	–12.1	–9.5	–13.3	–45.0	–335.5	–367.2
Total credit	2 300 . .	. . .	*9.9*	*15.1*	*22.8*	*38.3*	*11.0*	*55.9*	*41.5*
Total debit	3 300 . .	. . .	*–16.0*	*–27.2*	*–32.3*	*–51.6*	*–56.0*	*–391.4*	*–408.7*
Compensation of employees, credit	2 310 . .	**. . .**	**3.0**	**. . .**	**. . .**	**6.3**	**. . .**	**. . .**	**. . .**
Compensation of employees, debit	3 310 . .	**. . .**	**–9.3**	**–14.9**	**–19.0**	**–30.3**	**–31.8**	**–47.4**	**–47.3**
Investment income, credit	2 320 . .	**. . .**	**6.9**	**15.1**	**22.8**	**32.0**	**11.0**	**55.9**	**41.5**
Direct investment income	2 330 . .	. . .	.3	. . .	. . .	. . .	–22.8	. . .	. . .
Dividends and distributed branch profits	2 332 . .	. . .	. . .	. . .	. . .	. . .	. . .	. . .	. . .
Reinvested earnings and undistributed branch profits	2 333 . .	. . .	. . .	. . .	. . .	. . .	. . .	. . .	. . .
Income on debt (interest)	2 334 . .	. . .	. . .	. . .	. . .	. . .	. . .	. . .	. . .
Portfolio investment income	2 339 . .	. . .	. . .	. . .	. . .	. . .	. . .	. . .	. . .
Income on equity	2 340 . .	. . .	. . .	. . .	. . .	. . .	. . .	. . .	. . .
Income on bonds and notes	2 350 . .	. . .	. . .	. . .	. . .	. . .	. . .	. . .	. . .
Income on money market instruments	2 360 . .	. . .	. . .	. . .	. . .	. . .	. . .	. . .	. . .
Other investment income	2 370 . .	. . .	6.6	15.1	22.8	32.0	33.9	55.9	41.5
Investment income, debit	3 320 . .	**. . .**	**–6.7**	**–12.3**	**–13.2**	**–21.3**	**–24.2**	**–344.0**	**–361.4**
Direct investment income	3 330 . .	. . .	. . .	. . .	–7.3	–8.0	–2.0	–317.2	–329.2
Dividends and distributed branch profits	3 332 . .	. . .	. . .	. . .	. . .	. . .	. . .	. . .	. . .
Reinvested earnings and undistributed branch profits	3 333 . .	. . .	. . .	. . .	. . .	. . .	. . .	. . .	. . .
Income on debt (interest)	3 334 . .	. . .	. . .	. . .	. . .	. . .	. . .	. . .	. . .
Portfolio investment income	3 339 . .	. . .	. . .	. . .	. . .	. . .	. . .	. . .	. . .
Income on equity	3 340 . .	. . .	. . .	. . .	. . .	. . .	. . .	. . .	. . .
Income on bonds and notes	3 350 . .	. . .	. . .	. . .	. . .	. . .	. . .	. . .	. . .
Income on money market instruments	3 360 . .	. . .	. . .	. . .	. . .	. . .	. . .	. . .	. . .
Other investment income	3 370 . .	. . .	–6.6	–12.3	–6.0	–13.3	–22.2	–26.7	–32.2
D. CURRENT TRANSFERS	4 379 . .	. . .	110.8	66.5	44.8	64.0	81.8	73.1	76.6
Credit	2 379 . .	**. . .**	**129.3**	**107.2**	**95.7**	**145.0**	**134.5**	**135.0**	**176.5**
General government	2 380 . .	. . .	86.7	86.3	57.5	68.7	63.4	65.7	66.3
Other sectors	2 390 . .	. . .	42.6	21.0	38.2	76.3	71.2	69.3	110.2
Workers' remittances	2 391 . .	. . .	. . .	. . .	. . .	. . .	54.5	57.1	104.1
Other current transfers	2 392 . .	. . .	42.6	21.0	38.2	76.3	16.7	12.2	6.1
Debit	3 379 . .	**. . .**	**–18.5**	**–40.7**	**–50.9**	**–80.9**	**–52.8**	**–62.0**	**–99.9**
General government	3 380 . .	. . .	–5.3	–.2	–3.9	–4.6	–7.0	–3.3	–2.6
Other sectors	3 390 . .	. . .	–13.2	–40.5	–47.0	–76.4	–45.8	–58.6	–97.3
Workers' remittances	3 391 . .	. . .	. . .	. . .	. . .	. . .	–45.2	–53.6	–94.6
Other current transfers	3 392 . .	. . .	–13.2	–40.5	–47.0	–76.4	–.6	–5.0	–2.7
CAPITAL AND FINANCIAL ACCOUNT	4 996 . .	**. . .**	**340.9**	**907.6**	**942.7**	**1,384.6**	**557.3**	**167.8**	**52.6**
CAPITAL ACCOUNT	4 994 . .	**. . .**	**–1.6**	**. . .**	**–10.2**	**–.7**	**. . .**	**. . .**	**. . .**
Total credit	2 994 . .	. . .	. . .	. . .	. . .	. . .	. . .	. . .	. . .
Total debit	3 994 . .	. . .	*–1.6*	. . .	*–10.2*	*–.7*	. . .	. . .	. . .
Capital transfers, credit	2 400 . .	**. . .**	**. . .**	**. . .**	**. . .**	**. . .**	**. . .**	**. . .**	**. . .**
General government	2 401 . .	. . .	. . .	. . .	. . .	. . .	. . .	. . .	. . .
Debt forgiveness	2 402 . .	. . .	. . .	. . .	. . .	. . .	. . .	. . .	. . .
Other capital transfers	2 410 . .	. . .	. . .	. . .	. . .	. . .	. . .	. . .	. . .
Other sectors	2 430 . .	. . .	. . .	. . .	. . .	. . .	. . .	. . .	. . .
Migrants' transfers	2 431 . .	. . .	. . .	. . .	. . .	. . .	. . .	. . .	. . .
Debt forgiveness	2 432 . .	. . .	. . .	. . .	. . .	. . .	. . .	. . .	. . .
Other capital transfers	2 440 . .	. . .	. . .	. . .	. . .	. . .	. . .	. . .	. . .
Capital transfers, debit	3 400 . .	**. . .**	**. . .**	**. . .**	**. . .**	**. . .**	**. . .**	**. . .**	**. . .**
General government	3 401 . .	. . .	. . .	. . .	. . .	. . .	. . .	. . .	. . .
Debt forgiveness	3 402 . .	. . .	. . .	. . .	. . .	. . .	. . .	. . .	. . .
Other capital transfers	3 410 . .	. . .	. . .	. . .	. . .	. . .	. . .	. . .	. . .
Other sectors	3 430 . .	. . .	. . .	. . .	. . .	. . .	. . .	. . .	. . .
Migrants' transfers	3 431 . .	. . .	. . .	. . .	. . .	. . .	. . .	. . .	. . .
Debt forgiveness	3 432 . .	. . .	. . .	. . .	. . .	. . .	. . .	. . .	. . .
Other capital transfers	3 440 . .	. . .	. . .	. . .	. . .	. . .	. . .	. . .	. . .
Nonproduced nonfinancial assets, credit	2 480 . .	**. . .**	**. . .**	**. . .**	**. . .**	**. . .**	**. . .**	**. . .**	**. . .**
Nonproduced nonfinancial assets, debit	3 480 . .	**. . .**	**–1.6**	**. . .**	**–10.2**	**–.7**	**. . .**	**. . .**	**. . .**

Table 2 (Continued). STANDARD PRESENTATION, 1994–2001

(Millions of U.S. dollars)

	Code	1994	1995	1996	1997	1998	1999	2000	2001
FINANCIAL ACCOUNT	4 995 . .	**...**	**342.5**	**907.6**	**952.9**	**1,385.3**	**557.3**	**167.8**	**52.6**
A. DIRECT INVESTMENT	4 500 . .	...	330.1	627.3	1,114.8	1,022.9	510.3	129.2	226.5
Direct investment abroad	4 505 . .	**...**	**...**	**...**	**...**	**...**	**...**	**–.8**	**...**
Equity capital	4 510 . .	...	...	...	...	...	...	...	...
Claims on affiliated enterprises	4 515 . .	...	...	...	...	...	...	...	...
Liabilities to affiliated enterprises	4 520 . .	...	...	...	...	...	...	...	...
Reinvested earnings	4 525 . .	...	...	...	...	...	...	...	...
Other capital	4 530 . .	...	...	...	...	...	...	...	...
Claims on affiliated enterprises	4 535 . .	...	...	...	...	...	...	...	...
Liabilities to affiliated enterprises	4 540 . .	...	...	...	...	...	...	...	...
Direct investment in Azerbaijan	4 555 . .	**...**	**330.1**	**627.3**	**1,114.8**	**1,023.0**	**510.3**	**129.9**	**226.5**
Equity capital	4 560 . .	...	148.9	447.4	824.7	850.7	510.3	129.9	226.5
Claims on direct investors	4 565 . .	...	...	...	...	...	...	...	–593.1
Liabilities to direct investors	4 570 . .	...	...	...	...	...	...	...	819.6
Reinvested earnings	4 575 . .	...	...	...	...	...	...	...	...
Other capital	4 580 . .	...	181.2	179.9	290.2	172.2	...	...	...
Claims on direct investors	4 585 . .	...	...	...	...	...	...	...	...
Liabilities to direct investors	4 590 . .	...	...	...	...	...	...	...	...
B. PORTFOLIO INVESTMENT	4 600 . .	...	–1.7	...	1.1	.4	...	...	...
Assets	4 602 . .	**...**	**–1.7**	**...**	**1.1**	**...**	**...**	**...**	**...**
Equity securities	4 610 . .	...	...	...	...	...	...	...	...
Monetary authorities	4 611 . .	...	...	...	...	...	...	...	...
General government	4 612 . .	...	...	...	...	...	...	...	...
Banks	4 613 . .	...	...	...	...	...	...	...	...
Other sectors	4 614 . .	...	...	...	...	...	...	...	...
Debt securities	4 619 . .	...	–1.7	...	1.1	...	...	...	...
Bonds and notes	4 620 . .	...	–1.7	...	1.1	...	...	...	...
Monetary authorities	4 621 . .	...	...	...	...	...	...	...	...
General government	4 622 . .	...	...	...	...	...	...	...	...
Banks	4 623 . .	...	...	...	...	...	...	...	...
Other sectors	4 624 . .	...	–1.7	...	1.1	...	...	...	...
Money market instruments	4 630 . .	...	...	...	...	...	...	...	...
Monetary authorities	4 631 . .	...	...	...	...	...	...	...	...
General government	4 632 . .	...	...	...	...	...	...	...	...
Banks	4 633 . .	...	...	...	...	...	...	...	...
Other sectors	4 634 . .	...	...	...	...	...	...	...	...
Liabilities	4 652 . .	**...**	**...**	**...**	**...**	**.4**	**...**	**...**	**...**
Equity securities	4 660 . .	...	...	...	...	...	...	...	...
Banks	4 663 . .	...	...	...	...	...	...	...	...
Other sectors	4 664 . .	...	...	...	...	...	...	...	...
Debt securities	4 669 . .	...	...	...	...	.4	...	...	...
Bonds and notes	4 670 . .	...	...	...	...	.4	...	...	...
Monetary authorities	4 671 . .	...	...	...	...	...	...	...	...
General government	4 672 . .	...	...	...	...	...	...	...	...
Banks	4 673 . .	...	...	...	...	...	...	...	...
Other sectors	4 674 . .	...	...	...	...	.4	...	...	...
Money market instruments	4 680 . .	...	...	...	...	...	...	...	...
Monetary authorities	4 681 . .	...	...	...	...	...	...	...	...
General government	4 682 . .	...	...	...	...	...	...	...	...
Banks	4 683 . .	...	...	...	...	...	...	...	...
Other sectors	4 684 . .	...	...	...	...	...	...	...	...
C. FINANCIAL DERIVATIVES	4 910 . .	...	...	...	...	...	...	...	...
Monetary authorities	4 911 . .	...	...	...	...	...	...	...	...
General government	4 912 . .	...	...	...	...	...	...	...	...
Banks	4 913 . .	...	...	...	...	...	...	...	...
Other sectors	4 914 . .	...	...	...	...	...	...	...	...
Assets	4 900 . .	**...**	**...**	**...**	**...**	**...**	**...**	**...**	**...**
Monetary authorities	4 901 . .	...	...	...	...	...	...	...	...
General government	4 902 . .	...	...	...	...	...	...	...	...
Banks	4 903 . .	...	...	...	...	...	...	...	...
Other sectors	4 904 . .	...	...	...	...	...	...	...	...
Liabilities	4 905 . .	**...**	**...**	**...**	**...**	**...**	**...**	**...**	**...**
Monetary authorities	4 906 . .	...	...	...	...	...	...	...	...
General government	4 907 . .	...	...	...	...	...	...	...	...
Banks	4 908 . .	...	...	...	...	...	...	...	...
Other sectors	4 909 . .	...	...	...	...	...	...	...	...

Table 2 (Concluded). STANDARD PRESENTATION, 1994–2001
(Millions of U.S. dollars)

	Code	1994	1995	1996	1997	1998	1999	2000	2001
D. OTHER INVESTMENT	4 700 . .	...	175.7	273.1	81.2	343.3	275.5	312.8	–129.8
Assets	4 703 . .	**...**	**–22.1**	**–216.8**	**–102.6**	**22.3**	**–81.0**	**–114.2**	**–394.0**
Trade credits	4 706 . .	...	...	–77.5	–97.4	–28.8	–28.0	–119.9	–93.2
General government	4 707 . .	...	...	...	...	...	...	...	...
of which: Short-term	4 709 . .	...	...	...	...	...	...	...	...
Other sectors	4 710 . .	...	...	–77.5	–97.4	–28.8	–28.0	–119.9	–93.2
of which: Short-term	4 712 . .	...	...	...	...	...	...	...	*–93.2*
Loans	4 714 . .	...	.2	.8	.3	...	–.2	...	...
Monetary authorities	4 715 . .	...	...	...	...	...	...	...	...
of which: Short-term	4 718 . .	...	...	...	...	...	...	...	...
General government	4 719 . .	...	...	...	...	...	...	...	...
of which: Short-term	4 721 . .	...	...	...	...	...	...	...	...
Banks	4 722 . .	...	.2	.8	.3	....	–.2	...	...
of which: Short-term	4 724 . .	...	...	...	...	...	...	...	...
Other sectors	4 725 . .	...	...	...	...	...	...	...	...
of which: Short-term	4 727 . .	...	...	...	...	...	...	...	...
Currency and deposits	4 730 . .	...	–19.8	–137.8	5.0	62.4	–44.0	7.1	–298.2
Monetary authorities	4 731 . .	...	...	...	...	...	...	...	...
General government	4 732 . .	...	...	...	...	...	...	...	–220.5
Banks	4 733 . .	...	–19.8	–137.8	5.0	62.4	–44.0	7.1	–77.7
Other sectors	4 734 . .	...	...	...	...	...	...	...	...
Other assets	4 736 . .	...	–2.5	–2.4	–10.5	–11.3	–8.8	–1.4	–2.6
Monetary authorities	4 737 . .	...	...	...	...	...	...	...	...
of which: Short-term	4 739 . .	...	...	...	...	...	...	...	...
General government	4 740 . .	...	...	...	...	...	...	...	...
of which: Short-term	4 742 . .	...	...	...	...	...	...	...	...
Banks	4 743 . .	...	...	...	...	...	...	...	...
of which: Short-term	4 745 . .	...	...	...	...	...	...	...	...
Other sectors	4 746 . .	...	–2.5	–2.4	–10.5	–11.3	–8.8	–1.4	–2.6
of which: Short-term	4 748 . .	...	...	...	...	...	...	...	*–2.6*
Liabilities	4 753 . .	**...**	**197.9**	**489.9**	**183.9**	**321.0**	**356.5**	**427.0**	**264.3**
Trade credits	4 756 . .	...	69.3	301.4	–49.7	81.0	–67.0	33.5	74.5
General government	4 757 . .	...	...	...	...	...	...	...	...
of which: Short-term	4 759 . .	...	...	...	...	...	...	...	...
Other sectors	4 760 . .	...	69.3	301.4	–49.7	81.0	–67.0	33.5	74.5
of which: Short-term	4 762 . .	...	...	...	...	...	...	...	*74.5*
Loans	4 764 . .	...	133.3	114.9	186.9	121.2	259.7	203.4	104.1
Monetary authorities	4 765 . .	...	103.8	77.9	105.0	40.5	95.6	–51.4	–29.3
of which: Use of Fund credit and loans from the Fund	4 766 . .	...	*103.8*	*77.9*	*105.0*	*40.5*	*95.6*	*–51.4*	*–29.3*
of which: Short-term	4 768 . .	...	...	...	...	...	...	...	...
General government	4 769 . .	...	30.0	...	70.8	75.6	161.6	246.2	138.6
of which: Short-term	4 771 . .	...	...	...	...	...	...	...	*–46.7*
Banks	4 772 . .	...	...	...	...	.3	–.1	–.3	5.2
of which: Short-term	4 774 . .	...	...	...	...	...	...	...	*–1.7*
Other sectors	4 775 . .	...	–.5	37.0	11.0	4.7	2.6	8.9	–10.5
of which: Short-term	4 777 . .	...	...	...	...	...	...	...	*–20.8*
Currency and deposits	4 780 . .	...	–.3	26.5	–18.8	–2.0	...	–22.6	–2.2
Monetary authorities	4 781 . .	...	...	...	...	...	...	...	...
General government	4 782 . .	...	...	...	...	...	...	...	...
Banks	4 783 . .	...	–.3	26.5	–18.8	–2.0	...	–22.6	–2.2
Other sectors	4 784 . .	...	...	...	...	...	...	...	...
Other liabilities	4 786 . .	...	–4.4	47.1	65.5	120.8	163.7	212.6	87.8
Monetary authorities	4 787 . .	...	...	...	...	...	...	...	...
of which: Short-term	4 789 . .	...	...	...	...	...	...	...	...
General government	4 790 . .	...	...	...	...	...	...	...	...
of which: Short-term	4 792 . .	...	...	...	...	...	...	...	...
Banks	4 793 . .	...	...	...	...	...	...	...	...
of which: Short-term	4 795 . .	...	...	...	...	...	...	...	...
Other sectors	4 796 . .	...	–4.4	47.1	65.5	120.8	163.7	212.6	87.8
of which: Short-term	4 798 . .	...	...	...	...	...	...	...	*87.8*
E. RESERVE ASSETS	4 802 . .	...	–161.6	7.1	–244.2	18.7	–228.5	–274.2	–44.1
Monetary gold	4 812 . .	...	...	...	...	...	...	...	...
Special drawing rights	4 811 . .	...	–1.3	–19.7	14.4	5.5	–6.9	.1	4.1
Reserve position in the Fund	4 810 . .	...	...	...	...	...	...	...	...
Foreign exchange	4 803 . .	...	–160.3	26.9	–258.6	13.2	–221.6	–274.2	–48.2
Other claims	4 813 . .	...	...	...	...	...	...	...	...
NET ERRORS AND OMISSIONS	4 998 . .	**...**	**59.7**	**23.6**	**–27.0**	**–20.1**	**42.4**	**...**	**–.9**

Part 3 of the *Yearbook* contains descriptions of the methodologies, compilation practices, and sources used to compile these data.

Table 3. INTERNATIONAL INVESTMENT POSITION (End–period stocks), 1994–2001

(Millions of U.S. dollars)

	Code		1994	1995	1996	1997	1998	1999	2000	2001
ASSETS	8 995	C.	...	...	...	...	...	...	...	...
Direct investment abroad	8 505	. .	...	...	...	...	...	...	**.8**	**.8**
Equity capital and reinvested earnings	8 506	. .	...	...	...	...	...	...	...	.8
Claims on affiliated enterprises	8 507	. .	...	...	...	...	...	...	...	.8
Liabilities to affiliated enterprises	8 508	. .	...	...	...	...	...	...	...	...
Other capital	8 530	. .	...	...	...	...	...	...	...	...
Claims on affiliated enterprises	8 535	. .	...	...	...	...	...	...	...	...
Liabilities to affiliated enterprises	8 540	. .	...	...	...	...	...	...	...	...
Portfolio investment	8 602	. .	...	...	...	...	...	...	...	...
Equity securities	8 610	. .	...	...	...	...	...	...	...	...
Monetary authorities	8 611	. .	...	...	...	...	...	...	...	...
General government	8 612	. .	...	...	...	...	...	...	...	...
Banks	8 613	. .	...	...	...	...	...	...	...	...
Other sectors	8 614	. .	...	...	...	...	...	...	...	...
Debt securities	8 619	. .	...	...	...	...	...	...	...	...
Bonds and notes	8 620	. .	...	...	...	...	...	...	...	...
Monetary authorities	8 621	. .	...	...	...	...	...	...	...	...
General government	8 622	. .	...	...	...	...	...	...	...	...
Banks	8 623	. .	...	...	...	...	...	...	...	...
Other sectors	8 624	. .	...	...	...	...	...	...	...	...
Money market instruments	8 630	. .	...	...	...	...	...	...	...	...
Monetary authorities	8 631	. .	...	...	...	...	...	...	...	...
General government	8 632	. .	...	...	...	...	...	...	...	...
Banks	8 633	. .	...	...	...	...	...	...	...	...
Other sectors	8 634	. .	...	...	...	...	...	...	...	...
Financial derivatives	8 900	. .	...	...	...	...	...	...	...	...
Monetary authorities	8 901	. .	...	...	...	...	...	...	...	...
General government	8 902	. .	...	...	...	...	...	...	...	...
Banks	8 903	. .	...	...	...	...	...	...	...	...
Other sectors	8 904	. .	...	...	...	...	...	...	...	...
Other investment	8 703	. .	...	...	...	...	...	**385.1**	**282.4**	**827.5**
Trade credits	8 706	. .	...	...	...	...	...	231.7	119.9	93.2
General government	8 707	. .	...	...	...	...	...	...	...	...
of which: Short-term	8 709	. .	...	...	...	...	...	...	...	...
Other sectors	8 710	. .	...	...	...	...	...	...	...	93.2
of which: Short-term	8 712	. .	...	...	...	...	...	...	...	*93.2*
Loans	8 714	. .	...	...	...	...	...	...	...	...
Monetary authorities	8 715	. .	...	...	...	...	...	...	...	...
of which: Short-term	8 718	. .	...	...	...	...	...	...	...	...
General government	8 719	. .	...	...	...	...	...	...	...	...
of which: Short-term	8 721	. .	...	...	...	...	...	...	...	...
Banks	8 722	. .	...	...	...	...	...	...	...	...
of which: Short-term	8 724	. .	...	...	...	...	...	...	...	...
Other sectors	8 725	. .	...	...	...	...	...	...	...	...
of which: Short-term	8 727	. .	...	...	...	...	...	...	...	...
Currency and deposits	8 730	. .	...	...	...	...	...	120.1	113.0	682.2
Monetary authorities	8 731	. .	...	...	...	...	...	...	...	...
General government	8 732	. .	...	...	...	...	...	...	...	491.5
Banks	8 733	. .	...	...	...	...	...	...	...	190.7
Other sectors	8 734	. .	...	...	...	...	...	...	...	...
Other assets	8 736	. .	...	...	...	...	...	33.3	49.5	52.1
Monetary authorities	8 737	. .	...	...	...	...	...	...	...	...
of which: Short-term	8 739	. .	...	...	...	...	...	...	...	...
General government	8 740	. .	...	...	...	...	...	...	...	...
of which: Short-term	8 742	. .	...	...	...	...	...	...	...	...
Banks	8 743	. .	...	...	...	...	...	...	...	...
of which: Short-term	8 745	. .	...	...	...	...	...	...	...	...
Other sectors	8 746	. .	...	...	...	...	...	...	...	52.1
of which: Short-term	8 748	. .	...	...	...	...	...	...	...	*52.1*
Reserve assets	8 802	. .	...	...	...	...	...	**675.8**	**950.8**	**725.4**
Monetary gold	8 812	. .	...	...	...	...	...	...	...	...
Special drawing rights	8 811	. .	...	1.2	20.8	5.6	.1	7.1	6.6	2.5
Reserve position in the Fund	8 810	. .	...	...	...	...	...	...	...	...
Foreign exchange	8 803	. .	...	...	...	...	...	668.7	944.2	722.9
Other claims	8 813	. .	...	...	...	...	...	...	...	...

Table 3 (Concluded). INTERNATIONAL INVESTMENT POSITION (End–period stocks), 1994–2001
(Millions of U.S. dollars)

	Code		1994	1995	1996	1997	1998	1999	2000	2001
LIABILITIES	8 995	D	...	...	...	...	...	...	...	...
Direct investment in Azerbaijan	8 555	..	**...**	**...**	**...**	**...**	**...**	**3,099.5**	**3,735.2**	**3,961.7**
Equity capital and reinvested earnings	8 556	..	...	...	...	...	...	...	...	3,961.7
Claims on direct investors	8 557	..	...	...	...	...	...	...	...	–1,641.3
Liabilities to direct investors	8 558	..	...	...	...	...	...	...	...	5,603.0
Other capital	8 580	..	...	...	...	...	...	...	...	...
Claims on direct investors	8 585	..	...	...	...	...	...	...	...	...
Liabilities to direct investors	8 590	..	...	...	...	...	...	...	...	...
Portfolio investment	8 652	..	**...**	**...**	**...**	**...**	**...**	**...**	**...**	**...**
Equity securities	8 660	..	...	...	...	...	...	...	...	...
Banks	8 663	..	...	...	...	...	...	...	...	...
Other sectors	8 664	..	...	...	...	...	...	...	...	...
Debt securities	8 669	..	...	...	...	...	...	...	...	...
Bonds and notes	8 670	..	...	...	...	...	...	...	...	...
Monetary authorities	8 671	..	...	...	...	...	...	...	...	...
General government	8 672	..	...	...	...	...	...	...	...	...
Banks	8 673	..	...	...	...	...	...	...	...	...
Other sectors	8 674	..	...	...	...	...	...	...	...	...
Money market instruments	8 680	..	...	...	...	...	...	...	...	...
Monetary authorities	8 681	..	...	...	...	...	...	...	...	...
General government	8 682	..	...	...	...	...	...	...	...	...
Banks	8 683	..	...	...	...	...	...	...	...	...
Other sectors	8 684	..	...	...	...	...	...	...	...	...
Financial derivatives	8 905	..	**...**	**...**	**...**	**...**	**...**	**...**	**...**	**...**
Monetary authorities	8 906	..	...	...	...	...	...	...	...	...
General government	8 907	..	...	...	...	...	...	...	...	...
Banks	8 908	..	...	...	...	...	...	...	...	...
Other sectors	8 909	..	...	...	...	...	...	...	...	...
Other investment	8 753	..	**...**	**...**	**...**	**...**	**...**	**1,616.4**	**1,497.1**	**1,797.9**
Trade credits	8 756	..	...	...	...	...	...	334.9	33.5	74.5
General government	8 757	..	...	...	...	...	...	...	...	...
of which: Short-term	8 759	..	...	...	...	...	...	...	...	...
Other sectors	8 760	..	...	...	...	...	...	...	...	74.5
of which: Short-term	8 762	..	...	...	...	...	...	...	...	*74.5*
Loans	8 764	..	...	...	...	...	...	858.1	1,061.5	1,235.7
Monetary authorities	8 765	..	...	...	...	...	...	570.9	519.5	446.9
of which: Use of Fund credit and loans from the Fund	8 766	..	...	*100.9*	*175.0*	*266.8*	*321.2*	*407.3*	*335.8*	*295.2*
of which: Short-term	8 768	..	...	...	...	...	...	...	...	...
General government	8 769	..	...	...	...	...	...	279.7	525.9	56.8
of which: Short-term	8 771	..	...	...	...	...	...	...	...	...
Banks	8 772	..	...	...	...	...	...	...	.4	5.6
of which: Short-term	8 774	..	...	...	...	...	...	...	...	*5.6*
Other sectors	8 775	..	...	...	...	...	...	7.5	15.7	726.4
of which: Short-term	8 777	..	...	...	...	...	...	...	...	...
Currency and deposits	8 780	..	...	...	...	...	...	42.3	94.8	92.6
Monetary authorities	8 781	..	...	...	...	...	...	...	...	...
General government	8 782	..	...	...	...	...	...	...	...	...
Banks	8 783	..	...	...	...	...	...	...	...	92.6
Other sectors	8 784	..	...	...	...	...	...	...	...	...
Other liabilities	8 786	..	...	...	...	...	...	381.1	307.3	395.1
Monetary authorities	8 787	..	...	...	...	...	...	...	...	...
of which: Short-term	8 789	..	...	...	...	...	...	...	...	...
General government	8 790	..	...	...	...	...	...	...	...	...
of which: Short-term	8 792	..	...	...	...	...	...	...	...	...
Banks	8 793	..	...	...	...	...	...	...	...	...
of which: Short-term	8 795	..	...	...	...	...	...	...	...	...
Other sectors	8 796	..	...	...	...	...	...	...	...	395.1
of which: Short-term	8 798	..	...	...	...	...	...	...	...	*395.1*
NET INTERNATIONAL INVESTMENT POSITION	8 995	..	**...**	**...**	**...**	**...**	**...**	**...**	**...**	**...**
Conversion rates: manat per U.S. dollar (end of period)	0 102	..	**4,182.00**	**4,440.00**	**4,098.00**	**3,888.00**	**3,890.00**	**4,378.00**	**4,565.00**	**4,775.00**

Table 1. ANALYTIC PRESENTATION, 1994–2001
(Millions of U.S. dollars)

	Code	1994	1995	1996	1997	1998	1999	2000	2001
A. Current Account [1]	4 993 Z.	**–42.2**	**–145.9**	**–263.3**	**–472.1**	**–995.4**	**–671.9**	**–471.3**	**–348.0**
Goods: exports f.o.b.	2 100 . .	198.5	225.4	273.3	295.0	362.9	379.9	805.3	614.1
Goods: imports f.o.b.	3 100 . .	–1,013.8	–1,156.7	–1,287.4	–1,410.7	–1,737.1	–1,808.1	–2,176.4	–1,764.7
Balance on Goods	4 100 . .	*–815.3*	*–931.3*	*–1,014.1*	*–1,115.7*	*–1,374.2*	*–1,428.2*	*–1,371.1*	*–1,150.6*
Services: credit	2 200 . .	1,510.6	1,542.3	1,578.2	1,592.9	1,533.0	1,811.2	2,036.6	1,889.7
Services: debit	3 200 . .	–627.2	–639.1	–715.8	–836.0	–990.9	–953.8	–1,007.2	–939.1
Balance on Goods and Services	4 991 . .	*68.1*	*–28.1*	*–151.7*	*–358.8*	*–832.1*	*–570.8*	*–341.7*	*–200.0*
Income: credit	2 300 . .	61.2	75.1	84.6	105.7	147.9	229.6	212.0	94.0
Income: debit	3 300 . .	–198.8	–210.8	–233.4	–258.3	–345.4	–367.2	–385.0	–283.8
Balance on Goods, Services, and Income	4 992 . .	*–69.5*	*–163.8*	*–300.5*	*–511.4*	*–1,029.6*	*–708.4*	*–514.7*	*–389.8*
Current transfers: credit	2 379 Z.	33.1	25.1	45.9	50.0	45.0	49.0	53.8	52.7
Current transfers: debit	3 379 . .	–5.8	–7.2	–8.7	–10.7	–10.8	–12.5	–10.5	–10.9
B. Capital Account [1]	4 994 Z.	**–11.6**	**–12.5**	**–24.4**	**–12.9**	**–11.7**	**–14.5**	**–16.4**	**–20.3**
Capital account: credit	2 994 Z.	. . .	. . .	. . .	. . .	. . .	. . .	. . .	. . .
Capital account: debit	3 994 . .	–11.6	–12.5	–24.4	–12.9	–11.7	–14.5	–16.4	–20.3
Total, Groups A Plus B	4 981 . .	*–53.8*	*–158.4*	*–287.7*	*–485.0*	*–1,007.1*	*–686.4*	*–487.7*	*–368.3*
C. Financial Account [1]	4 995 W.	**66.8**	**104.6**	**181.1**	**412.0**	**817.7**	**611.4**	**429.3**	**279.8**
Direct investment abroad	4 505 . .	.1	–.1	.3	–.4	–1.0	–.2	. . .	. . .
Direct investment in The Bahamas	4 555 Z.	23.4	106.8	87.8	210.0	146.9	144.6	249.7	100.8
Portfolio investment assets	4 602 . .	. . .	. . .	. . .	. . .	. . .	. . .	. . .	. . .
Equity securities	4 610 . .	. . .	. . .	. . .	. . .	. . .	. . .	. . .	. . .
Debt securities	4 619 . .	. . .	. . .	. . .	. . .	. . .	. . .	. . .	. . .
Portfolio investment liabilities	4 652 Z.	. . .	. . .	. . .	. . .	. . .	. . .	. . .	. . .
Equity securities	4 660 . .	. . .	. . .	. . .	. . .	. . .	. . .	. . .	. . .
Debt securities	4 669 Z.	. . .	. . .	. . .	. . .	. . .	. . .	. . .	. . .
Financial derivatives	4 910 . .	. . .	. . .	. . .	. . .	. . .	. . .	. . .	. . .
Financial derivatives assets	4 900 . .	. . .	. . .	. . .	. . .	. . .	. . .	. . .	. . .
Financial derivatives liabilities	4 905 . .	. . .	. . .	. . .	. . .	. . .	. . .	. . .	. . .
Other investment assets	4 703 . .	–7,455.9	7,436.6	–6,428.8	–80.7	–4,872.0	–12,487.1	–19,067.2	–25,411.7
Monetary authorities	4 701 . .	. . .	. . .	. . .	. . .	. . .	. . .	. . .	. . .
General government	4 704 . .	. . .	. . .	. . .	. . .	. . .	. . .	. . .	. . .
Banks	4 705 . .	–7,455.9	7,436.6	–6,428.8	–80.7	–4,872.0	–12,487.1	–19,067.2	–25,411.7
Other sectors	4 728 . .	. . .	. . .	. . .	. . .	. . .	. . .	. . .	. . .
Other investment liabilities	4 753 W.	7,499.2	–7,438.7	6,521.8	283.1	5,543.8	12,954.1	19,246.9	25,590.7
Monetary authorities	4 753 WA	. . .	. . .	. . .	. . .	. . .	. . .	. . .	. . .
General government	4 753 ZB	–5.8	–26.9	–25.2	19.2	–5.9	11.7	–11.2	. . .
Banks	4 753 ZC	7,459.6	–7,417.9	6,451.8	141.9	4,901.8	12,578.9	19,039.1	25,533.1
Other sectors	4 753 ZD	45.4	6.1	95.2	122.0	647.9	363.5	218.9	57.6
Total, Groups A Through C	4 983 . .	*13.0*	*–53.8*	*–106.6*	*–73.0*	*–189.4*	*–75.0*	*–58.4*	*–88.5*
D. Net Errors and Omissions	4 998 . .	**–3.9**	**50.9**	**99.0**	**129.5**	**308.6**	**140.2**	**–2.6**	**58.6**
Total, Groups A Through D	4 984 . .	*9.1*	*–2.9*	*–7.6*	*56.5*	*119.2*	*65.2*	*–61.0*	*–29.9*
E. Reserves and Related Items	4 802 A.	**–9.1**	**2.9**	**7.6**	**–56.5**	**–119.2**	**–65.2**	**61.0**	**29.9**
Reserve assets	4 802 . .	–9.1	2.9	7.6	–56.5	–119.2	–65.2	61.0	29.9
Use of Fund credit and loans	4 766 . .	. . .	. . .	. . .	. . .	. . .	. . .	. . .	. . .
Exceptional financing	4 920 . .	. . .	. . .	. . .	. . .	. . .	. . .	. . .	. . .
Conversion rates: Bahamian dollar per U.S. dollar	0 101 . .	**1.0000**	**1.0000**	**1.0000**	**1.0000**	**1.0000**	**1.0000**	**1.0000**	**1.0000**

[1] Excludes components that have been classified in the categories of Group E.

Table 2. STANDARD PRESENTATION, 1994–2001
(Millions of U.S. dollars)

	Code		1994	1995	1996	1997	1998	1999	2000	2001
CURRENT ACCOUNT	4 993	. .	**–42.2**	**–145.9**	**–263.3**	**–472.1**	**–995.4**	**–671.9**	**–471.3**	**–348.0**
A. GOODS	4 100	. .	–815.3	–931.3	–1,014.1	–1,115.7	–1,374.2	–1,428.2	–1,371.1	–1,150.6
Credit	2 100	. .	**198.5**	**225.4**	**273.3**	**295.0**	**362.9**	**379.9**	**805.3**	**614.1**
General merchandise: exports f.o.b.	2 110	. .	163.7	175.9	201.7	230.4	300.3	309.9	683.1	497.5
Goods for processing: exports f.o.b.	2 150	. .	. . .	. . .	. . .	. . .	. . .	. . .	. . .	. . .
Repairs on goods	2 160	. .	. . .	. . .	. . .	. . .	. . .	. . .	. . .	. . .
Goods procured in ports by carriers	2 170	. .	34.8	49.5	71.6	64.6	62.6	70.0	122.3	116.6
Nonmonetary gold	2 180	. .	. . .	. . .	. . .	. . .	. . .	. . .	. . .	. . .
Debit	3 100	. .	**–1,013.8**	**–1,156.7**	**–1,287.4**	**–1,410.7**	**–1,737.1**	**–1,808.1**	**–2,176.4**	**–1,764.7**
General merchandise: imports f.o.b.	3 110	. .	–1,013.0	–1,155.6	–1,285.8	–1,409.1	–1,735.5	–1,806.1	–2,173.7	–1,760.9
Goods for processing: imports f.o.b.	3 150	. .	. . .	. . .	. . .	. . .	. . .	. . .	. . .	. . .
Repairs on goods	3 160	. .	. . .	. . .	. . .	. . .	. . .	. . .	. . .	. . .
Goods procured in ports by carriers	3 170	. .	–.8	–1.1	–1.6	–1.6	–1.6	–2.0	–2.7	–3.8
Nonmonetary gold	3 180	. .	. . .	. . .	. . .	. . .	. . .	. . .	. . .	. . .
B. SERVICES	4 200	. .	883.4	903.2	862.4	756.9	542.1	857.4	1,029.4	950.6
Total credit	2 200	. .	*1,510.6*	*1,542.3*	*1,578.2*	*1,592.9*	*1,533.0*	*1,811.2*	*2,036.6*	*1,889.7*
Total debit	3 200	. .	*–627.2*	*–639.1*	*–715.8*	*–836.0*	*–990.9*	*–953.8*	*–1,007.2*	*–939.1*
Transportation services, credit	2 205	. .	**45.6**	**52.6**	**41.2**	**52.7**	**57.8**	**60.0**	**54.6**	**50.5**
Passenger	2 850	. .	*10.4*	*9.6*	*10.5*	*10.8*	*10.8*	*14.8*	*15.3*	*16.9*
Freight	2 851	. .	. . .	. . .	. . .	. . .	. . .	. . .	. . .	. . .
Other	2 852	. .	*35.2*	*43.0*	*30.7*	*41.9*	*47.0*	*45.2*	*39.3*	*33.6*
Sea transport, passenger	2 207	. .	. . .	. . .	. . .	. . .	. . .	. . .	. . .	. . .
Sea transport, freight	2 208	. .	. . .	. . .	. . .	. . .	. . .	. . .	. . .	. . .
Sea transport, other	2 209	. .	23.7	33.8	19.6	27.8	32.5	35.9	30.9	24.1
Air transport, passenger	2 211	. .	10.4	9.6	10.5	10.8	10.8	14.8	15.3	16.9
Air transport, freight	2 212	. .	. . .	. . .	. . .	. . .	. . .	. . .	. . .	. . .
Air transport, other	2 213	. .	11.5	9.2	11.1	14.1	14.5	9.3	8.4	9.6
Other transport, passenger	2 215	. .	. . .	. . .	. . .	. . .	. . .	. . .	. . .	. . .
Other transport, freight	2 216	. .	. . .	. . .	. . .	. . .	. . .	. . .	. . .	. . .
Other transport, other	2 217	. .	. . .	. . .	. . .	. . .	. . .	. . .	. . .	. . .
Transportation services, debit	3 205	. .	**–110.6**	**–134.4**	**–156.6**	**–182.8**	**–205.1**	**–176.4**	**–188.1**	**–184.3**
Passenger	3 850	. .	*–19.1*	*–28.3*	*–44.2*	*–59.7*	*–54.2*	*–34.2*	*–28.7*	*–35.2*
Freight	3 851	. .	*–69.8*	*–79.3*	*–86.4*	*–96.5*	*–124.2*	*–130.2*	*–149.0*	*–117.8*
Other	3 852	. .	*–21.7*	*–26.8*	*–26.0*	*–26.6*	*–26.7*	*–12.0*	*–10.5*	*–31.4*
Sea transport, passenger	3 207	. .	–1.6	–1.2	–.9	–2.5	–1.3	–1.0	–4.1	–.4
Sea transport, freight	3 208	. .	–55.8	–63.4	–69.2	–77.2	–99.4	–104.1	–119.2	–94.3
Sea transport, other	3 209	. .	–1.6	–1.6	–1.6	–1.8	–1.9	–2.0	–1.4	–1.8
Air transport, passenger	3 211	. .	–17.5	–27.1	–43.3	–57.2	–52.9	–33.2	–24.6	–34.7
Air transport, freight	3 212	. .	–14.0	–15.9	–17.2	–19.3	–24.8	–26.1	–29.8	–23.6
Air transport, other	3 213	. .	–20.1	–25.2	–24.4	–24.8	–24.8	–10.0	–9.1	–29.6
Other transport, passenger	3 215	. .	. . .	. . .	. . .	. . .	. . .	. . .	. . .	. . .
Other transport, freight	3 216	. .	. . .	. . .	. . .	. . .	. . .	. . .	. . .	. . .
Other transport, other	3 217		. . .	. . .	. . .	. . .	. . .	. . .	. . .	. . .
Travel, credit	2 236	. .	**1,327.3**	**1,345.8**	**1,397.9**	**1,416.0**	**1,354.0**	**1,502.9**	**1,814.0**	**1,750.5**
Business travel	2 237	. .	. . .	. . .	. . .	. . .	. . .	. . .	. . .	. . .
Personal travel	2 240	. .	. . .	. . .	. . .	. . .	. . .	. . .	1,814.0	1,750.5
Travel, debit	3 236	. .	**–193.3**	**–212.8**	**–234.6**	**–249.8**	**–255.8**	**–308.5**	**–293.0**	**–297.0**
Business travel	3 237	. .	–32.3	–37.9	–36.8	–36.1	–36.9	–56.9	–40.9	–42.6
Personal travel	3 240	. .	–161.0	–174.9	–197.8	–213.7	–218.9	–251.6	252.0	–254.4
Other services, credit	2 200	BA	**137.7**	**143.9**	**139.1**	**124.2**	**121.2**	**248.3**	**168.0**	**88.7**
Communications	2 245	. .	. . .	. . .	. . .	. . .	. . .	. . .	. . .	. . .
Construction	2 249	. .	. . .	. . .	. . .	. . .	. . .	. . .	. . .	. . .
Insurance	2 253	. .	. . .	. . .	. . .	. . .	. . .	134.3	12.8	. . .
Financial	2 260	. .	. . .	. . .	. . .	. . .	. . .	. . .	. . .	. . .
Computer and information	2 262	. .	. . .	. . .	. . .	. . .	. . .	. . .	. . .	. . .
Royalties and licence fees	2 266	. .	. . .	. . .	. . .	. . .	. . .	. . .	. . .	. . .
Other business services	2 268	. .	117.0	124.2	119.2	104.4	104.9	91.3	127.9	59.9
Personal, cultural, and recreational	2 287	. .	. . .	. . .	. . .	. . .	. . .	. . .	. . .	. . .
Government, n.i.e.	2 291	. .	20.7	19.7	19.9	19.8	16.3	22.7	27.4	28.9
Other services, debit	3 200	BA	**–323.3**	**–291.9**	**–324.6**	**–403.4**	**–530.0**	**–468.9**	**–526.1**	**–457.8**
Communications	3 245	. .	–1.2	–1.2	–1.2	–1.2	–1.2	–1.2	–1.0	–1.0
Construction	3 249	. .	–64.8	–12.3	–20.4	–75.1	–145.8	–101.0	–102.9	–33.1
Insurance	3 253	. .	–71.9	–74.4	–72.2	–64.8	–59.7	–59.6	–73.7	–81.4
Financial	3 260	. .	. . .	. . .	. . .	. . .	. . .	. . .	. . .	. . .
Computer and information	3 262	. .	. . .	. . .	. . .	. . .	. . .	. . .	. . .	. . .
Royalties and licence fees	3 266	. .	–5.1	–4.6	–6.4	–9.6	–9.1	–12.2	–14.2	–13.3
Other business services	3 268	. .	–143.7	–163.7	–175.8	–205.1	–260.1	–243.4	–275.6	–250.2
Personal, cultural, and recreational	3 287	. .	–2.0	–2.0	–2.0	–2.0	–2.0	–2.0	–2.0	–2.0
Government, n.i.e.	3 291	. .	–34.6	–33.7	–46.6	–45.6	–52.1	–49.5	–56.8	–76.9

Table 2 (Continued). STANDARD PRESENTATION, 1994–2001

(Millions of U.S. dollars)

	Code	1994	1995	1996	1997	1998	1999	2000	2001
C. INCOME	4 300	–137.6	–135.7	–148.8	–152.6	–197.5	–137.6	–173.0	–189.8
Total credit	2 300	*61.2*	*75.1*	*84.6*	*105.7*	*147.9*	*229.6*	*212.0*	*94.0*
Total debit	3 300	*–198.8*	*–210.8*	*–233.4*	*–258.3*	*–345.4*	*–367.2*	*–385.0*	*–283.8*
Compensation of employees, credit	2 310	...	...	...	...	...	...	...	...
Compensation of employees, debit	3 310	**–25.0**	**–27.8**	**–29.1**	**–31.1**	**–34.4**	**–40.4**	**–51.1**	**–46.8**
Investment income, credit	2 320	**61.2**	**75.1**	**84.6**	**105.7**	**147.9**	**229.6**	**212.0**	**94.0**
Direct investment income	2 330	...	...	...	...	...	...	...	...
Dividends and distributed branch profits	2 332	...	...	...	...	...	...	...	...
Reinvested earnings and undistributed branch profits	2 333	...	...	...	...	...	...	...	...
Income on debt (interest)	2 334	...	...	...	...	...	...	...	...
Portfolio investment income	2 339	...	...	...	...	...	...	...	...
Income on equity	2 340	...	...	...	...	...	...	...	...
Income on bonds and notes	2 350	...	...	...	...	...	...	...	...
Income on money market instruments	2 360	...	...	...	...	...	...	...	...
Other investment income	2 370	61.2	75.1	84.6	105.7	147.9	229.6	212.0	94.0
Investment income, debit	3 320	**–173.8**	**–183.0**	**–204.3**	**–227.2**	**–311.0**	**–326.8**	**–333.9**	**–237.0**
Direct investment income	3 330	...	...	...	...	...	...	...	...
Dividends and distributed branch profits	3 332	...	...	...	...	...	...	...	...
Reinvested earnings and undistributed branch profits	3 333	...	...	...	...	...	...	...	...
Income on debt (interest)	3 334	...	...	...	...	...	...	...	...
Portfolio investment income	3 339	...	...	...	...	...	...	...	...
Income on equity	3 340	...	...	...	...	...	...	...	...
Income on bonds and notes	3 350	...	...	...	...	...	...	...	...
Income on money market instruments	3 360	...	...	...	...	...	...	...	...
Other investment income	3 370	–173.8	–183.0	–204.3	–227.2	–311.0	–326.8	–333.9	–237.0
D. CURRENT TRANSFERS	4 379	27.3	17.9	37.2	39.3	34.2	36.5	43.4	41.8
Credit	2 379	**33.1**	**25.1**	**45.9**	**50.0**	**45.0**	**49.0**	**53.8**	**52.7**
General government	2 380	31.9	23.9	44.7	48.8	43.8	47.8	52.6	51.5
Other sectors	2 390	1.2	1.2	1.2	1.2	1.2	1.2	1.2	1.2
Workers' remittances	2 391	...	...	...	...	...	...	...	...
Other current transfers	2 392	1.2	1.2	1.2	1.2	1.2	1.2	1.2	1.2
Debit	3 379	**–5.8**	**–7.2**	**–8.7**	**–10.7**	**–10.8**	**–12.5**	**–10.5**	**–10.9**
General government	3 380	–2.8	–3.3	–4.6	–5.0	–5.9	–6.3	–5.3	–5.8
Other sectors	3 390	–3.0	–3.9	–4.1	–5.7	–4.9	–6.2	–5.2	–5.1
Workers' remittances	3 391	–3.0	–3.9	–4.1	–5.7	–4.9	–6.2	–5.2	–5.1
Other current transfers	3 392	...	...	...	...	...	...	...	...
CAPITAL AND FINANCIAL ACCOUNT	4 996	**46.1**	**95.0**	**164.3**	**342.6**	**686.8**	**531.7**	**473.9**	**289.4**
CAPITAL ACCOUNT	4 994	**–11.6**	**–12.5**	**–24.4**	**–12.9**	**–11.7**	**–14.5**	**–16.4**	**–20.3**
Total credit	2 994	...	...	...	...	...	...	...	...
Total debit	3 994	*–11.6*	*–12.5*	*–24.4*	*–12.9*	*–11.7*	*–14.5*	*–16.4*	*–20.3*
Capital transfers, credit	2 400	...	...	...	...	...	...	...	...
General government	2 401	...	...	...	...	...	...	...	...
Debt forgiveness	2 402	...	...	...	...	...	...	...	...
Other capital transfers	2 410	...	...	...	...	...	...	...	...
Other sectors	2 430	...	...	...	...	...	...	...	...
Migrants' transfers	2 431	...	...	...	...	...	...	...	...
Debt forgiveness	2 432	...	...	...	...	...	...	...	...
Other capital transfers	2 440	...	...	...	...	...	...	...	...
Capital transfers, debit	3 400	**–11.6**	**–12.5**	**–24.4**	**–12.9**	**–11.7**	**–14.5**	**–16.4**	**–20.3**
General government	3 401	...	...	...	...	...	...	...	...
Debt forgiveness	3 402	...	...	...	...	...	...	...	...
Other capital transfers	3 410	...	...	...	...	...	...	...	...
Other sectors	3 430	–11.6	–12.5	–24.4	–12.9	–11.7	–14.5	–16.4	–20.3
Migrants' transfers	3 431	–11.6	–12.5	–24.4	–12.9	–11.7	–14.5	–16.4	–20.3
Debt forgiveness	3 432	...	...	...	...	...	...	...	...
Other capital transfers	3 440	...	...	...	...	...	...	...	...
Nonproduced nonfinancial assets, credit	2 480	...	...	...	...	...	...	...	...
Nonproduced nonfinancial assets, debit	3 480	...	...	...	...	...	...	...	...

Table 2 (Continued). STANDARD PRESENTATION, 1994–2001
(Millions of U.S. dollars)

	Code	1994	1995	1996	1997	1998	1999	2000	2001
FINANCIAL ACCOUNT	4 995 . .	**57.7**	**107.5**	**188.7**	**355.5**	**698.5**	**546.2**	**490.3**	**309.7**
A. DIRECT INVESTMENT	4 500 . .	23.5	106.7	88.1	209.6	145.9	144.4	249.7	100.8
Direct investment abroad	4 505 . .	**.1**	**–.1**	**.3**	**–.4**	**–1.0**	**–.2**	**...**	**...**
Equity capital	4 510 . .	–.1	–.1	–.1	–.1	–.6	–.6	...	...
Claims on affiliated enterprises	4 515 . .	–.1	–.1	–.1	–.1	–.6	–.6	...	...
Liabilities to affiliated enterprises	4 520 . .	...	...	...	...	...	...	...	...
Reinvested earnings	4 525 . .	...	...	...	...	...	...	...	...
Other capital	4 530 . .	.2	...	.4	–.3	–.4	.4	...	...
Claims on affiliated enterprises	4 535 . .	...	–.1	.4	–.3	–.4	.4	...	...
Liabilities to affiliated enterprises	4 540 . .	.2	.1	...	...	...	...	...	...
Direct investment in The Bahamas	4 555 . .	**23.4**	**106.8**	**87.8**	**210.0**	**146.9**	**144.6**	**249.7**	**100.8**
Equity capital	4 560 . .	–18.2	20.9	9.7	14.8	8.9	23.7	106.2	38.1
Claims on direct investors	4 565 . .	...	...	...	...	...	...	...	...
Liabilities to direct investors	4 570 . .	–18.2	20.9	9.7	14.8	8.9	23.7	106.2	38.1
Reinvested earnings	4 575 . .	...	...	...	...	...	...	...	...
Other capital	4 580 . .	41.6	85.9	78.1	195.2	138.0	120.9	143.4	62.7
Claims on direct investors	4 585 . .	...	...	...	...	...	...	...	...
Liabilities to direct investors	4 590 . .	41.6	85.9	78.1	195.2	138.0	120.9	143.4	62.7
B. PORTFOLIO INVESTMENT	4 600 . .	...	...	...	...	...	...	...	...
Assets	4 602 . .	**...**	**...**	**...**	**...**	**...**	**...**	**...**	**...**
Equity securities	4 610 . .	...	...	...	...	...	...	...	...
Monetary authorities	4 611 . .	...	...	...	...	...	...	...	...
General government	4 612 . .	...	...	...	...	...	...	...	...
Banks	4 613 . .	...	...	...	...	...	...	...	...
Other sectors	4 614 . .	...	...	...	...	...	...	...	...
Debt securities	4 619 . .	...	...	...	...	...	...	...	...
Bonds and notes	4 620 . .	...	...	...	...	...	...	...	...
Monetary authorities	4 621 . .	...	...	...	...	...	...	...	...
General government	4 622 . .	...	...	...	...	...	...	...	...
Banks	4 623 . .	...	...	...	...	...	...	...	...
Other sectors	4 624 . .	...	...	...	...	...	...	...	...
Money market instruments	4 630 . .	...	...	...	...	...	...	...	...
Monetary authorities	4 631 . .	...	...	...	...	...	...	...	...
General government	4 632 . .	...	...	...	...	...	...	...	...
Banks	4 633 . .	...	...	...	...	...	...	...	...
Other sectors	4 634 . .	...	...	...	...	...	...	...	...
Liabilities	4 652 . .	**...**	**...**	**...**	**...**	**...**	**...**	**...**	**...**
Equity securities	4 660 . .	...	...	...	...	...	...	...	...
Banks	4 663 . .	...	...	...	...	...	...	...	...
Other sectors	4 664 . .	...	...	...	...	...	...	...	...
Debt securities	4 669 . .	...	...	...	...	...	...	...	...
Bonds and notes	4 670 . .	...	...	...	...	...	...	...	...
Monetary authorities	4 671 . .	...	...	...	...	...	...	...	...
General government	4 672 . .	...	...	...	...	...	...	...	...
Banks	4 673 . .	...	...	...	...	...	...	...	...
Other sectors	4 674 . .	...	...	...	...	...	...	...	...
Money market instruments	4 680 . .	...	...	...	...	...	...	...	...
Monetary authorities	4 681 . .	...	...	...	...	...	...	...	...
General government	4 682 . .	...	...	...	...	...	...	...	...
Banks	4 683 . .	...	...	...	...	...	...	...	...
Other sectors	4 684 . .	...	...	...	...	...	...	...	...
C. FINANCIAL DERIVATIVES	4 910 . .	...	...	...	...	...	...	...	...
Monetary authorities	4 911 . .	...	...	...	...	...	...	...	...
General government	4 912 . .	...	...	...	...	...	...	...	...
Banks	4 913 . .	...	...	...	...	...	...	...	...
Other sectors	4 914 . .	...	...	...	...	...	...	...	...
Assets	4 900 . .	**...**	**...**	**...**	**...**	**...**	**...**	**...**	**...**
Monetary authorities	4 901 . .	...	...	...	...	...	...	...	...
General government	4 902 . .	...	...	...	...	...	...	...	...
Banks	4 903 . .	...	...	...	...	...	...	...	...
Other sectors	4 904 . .	...	...	...	...	...	...	...	...
Liabilities	4 905 . .	**...**	**...**	**...**	**...**	**...**	**...**	**...**	**...**
Monetary authorities	4 906 . .	...	...	...	...	...	...	...	...
General government	4 907 . .	...	...	...	...	...	...	...	...
Banks	4 908 . .	...	...	...	...	...	...	...	...
Other sectors	4 909 . .	...	...	...	...	...	...	...	...

Table 2 (Concluded). STANDARD PRESENTATION, 1994–2001
(Millions of U.S. dollars)

	Code		1994	1995	1996	1997	1998	1999	2000	2001
D. OTHER INVESTMENT	4 700	. .	43.3	-2.1	93.0	202.4	671.8	467.0	179.7	179.0
Assets	4 703	. .	**-7,455.9**	**7,436.6**	**-6,428.8**	**-80.7**	**-4,872.0**	**-12,487.1**	**-19,067.2**	**-25,411.7**
Trade credits	4 706	. .	...	...	...	...	...	...	...	...
General government	4 707	. .	...	...	...	...	...	...	...	...
of which: Short-term	4 709	. .	...	...	...	...	...	...	...	...
Other sectors	4 710	. .	...	...	...	...	...	...	...	...
of which: Short-term	4 712	. .	...	...	...	...	...	...	...	...
Loans	4 714	. .	...	...	...	...	...	...	...	...
Monetary authorities	4 715	. .	...	...	...	...	...	...	...	...
of which: Short-term	4 718	. .	...	...	...	...	...	...	...	...
General government	4 719	. .	...	...	...	...	...	...	...	...
of which: Short-term	4 721	. .	...	...	...	...	...	...	...	...
Banks	4 722	. .	...	...	...	...	...	...	...	...
of which: Short-term	4 724	. .	...	...	...	...	...	...	...	...
Other sectors	4 725	. .	...	...	...	...	...	...	...	...
of which: Short-term	4 727	. .	...	...	...	...	...	...	...	...
Currency and deposits	4 730	. .	-7,455.9	7,436.6	-6,428.8	-80.7	-4,872.0	-12,487.1	-19,067.2	-25,411.7
Monetary authorities	4 731	. .	...	...	...	...	...	...	...	...
General government	4 732	. .	...	...	...	...	...	...	...	...
Banks	4 733	. .	-7,455.9	7,436.6	-6,428.8	-80.7	-4,872.0	-12,487.1	-19,067.2	-25,411.7
Other sectors	4 734	. .	...	...	...	...	...	...	...	...
Other assets	4 736	. .	...	...	...	...	...	...	...	...
Monetary authorities	4 737	. .	...	...	...	...	...	...	...	...
of which: Short-term	4 739	. .	...	...	...	...	...	...	...	...
General government	4 740	. .	...	...	...	...	...	...	...	...
of which: Short-term	4 742	. .	...	...	...	...	...	...	...	...
Banks	4 743	. .	...	...	...	...	...	...	...	...
of which: Short-term	4 745	. .	...	...	...	...	...	...	...	...
Other sectors	4 746	. .	...	...	...	...	...	...	...	...
of which: Short-term	4 748	. .	...	...	...	...	...	...	...	...
Liabilities	4 753	. .	**7,499.2**	**-7,438.7**	**6,521.8**	**283.1**	**5,543.8**	**12,954.1**	**19,246.9**	**25,590.7**
Trade credits	4 756	. .	...	...	...	...	...	...	...	-4.0
General government	4 757	. .	...	...	...	...	...	...	...	...
of which: Short-term	4 759	. .	...	...	...	...	...	...	...	...
Other sectors	4 760	. .	...	...	...	...	...	...	...	-4.0
of which: Short-term	4 762	. .	...	...	...	...	...	...	...	...
Loans	4 764	. .	39.6	-20.8	70.0	141.2	642.0	375.2	207.7	62.6
Monetary authorities	4 765	. .	...	...	...	...	...	...	...	...
of which: Use of Fund credit and loans from the Fund	4 766	. .	...	...	...	...	...	...	...	...
of which: Short-term	4 768	. .	...	...	...	...	...	...	...	...
General government	4 769	. .	-5.8	-26.9	-25.2	19.2	-5.9	11.7	-11.2	...
of which: Short-term	4 771	. .	...	...	...	...	...	...	...	...
Banks	4 772	. .	...	...	...	...	...	...	...	1.0
of which: Short-term	4 774	. .	...	...	...	...	...	...	...	...
Other sectors	4 775	. .	45.4	6.1	95.2	122.0	647.9	363.5	218.9	61.6
of which: Short-term	4 777	. .	...	...	...	...	...	...	...	...
Currency and deposits	4 780	. .	7,459.6	-7,417.9	6,451.8	141.9	4,901.8	12,578.9	19,039.1	25,532.1
Monetary authorities	4 781	. .	...	...	...	...	...	...	...	...
General government	4 782	. .	...	...	...	...	...	...	...	...
Banks	4 783	. .	7,459.6	-7,417.9	6,451.8	141.9	4,901.8	12,578.9	19,039.1	25,532.1
Other sectors	4 784	. .	...	...	...	...	...	...	...	...
Other liabilities	4 786	. .	...	...	...	...	...	...	...	...
Monetary authorities	4 787	. .	...	...	...	...	...	...	...	...
of which: Short-term	4 789	. .	...	...	...	...	...	...	...	...
General government	4 790	. .	...	...	...	...	...	...	...	...
of which: Short-term	4 792	. .	...	...	...	...	...	...	...	...
Banks	4 793	. .	...	...	...	...	...	...	...	...
of which: Short-term	4 795	. .	...	...	...	...	...	...	...	...
Other sectors	4 796	. .	...	...	...	...	...	...	...	...
of which: Short-term	4 798	. .	...	...	...	...	...	...	...	...
E. RESERVE ASSETS	4 802	. .	-9.1	2.9	7.6	-56.5	-119.2	-65.2	61.0	29.9
Monetary gold	4 812	. .	...	...	...	...	...	...	...	...
Special drawing rights	4 811	. .	...	...	...	...	...	...	-.1	...
Reserve position in the Fund	4 810	. .	...	...	...	...	...	...	...	...
Foreign exchange	4 803	. .	-9.1	2.9	7.6	-56.5	-119.2	-65.2	61.1	29.9
Other claims	4 813	. .	...	...	...	...	...	...	...	...
NET ERRORS AND OMISSIONS	4 998	. .	**-3.9**	**50.9**	**99.0**	**129.5**	**308.6**	**140.2**	**-2.6**	**58.6**

Part 3 of the *Yearbook* contains descriptions of the methodologies, compilation practices, and sources used to compile these data.

Table 1. ANALYTIC PRESENTATION, 1994–2001
(Millions of U.S. dollars)

	Code	1994	1995	1996	1997	1998	1999	2000	2001
A. Current Account [1]	4 993 Z.	**–255.6**	**237.2**	**260.6**	**–31.1**	**–777.7**	**–36.7**	**782.4**	**157.2**
Goods: exports f.o.b.	2 100 ..	3,617.0	4,114.4	4,702.1	4,383.0	3,270.2	4,362.8	6,194.9	5,544.7
Goods: imports f.o.b.	3 100 ..	–3,497.3	–3,488.3	–4,037.0	–3,778.2	–3,298.7	–3,468.4	–4,393.6	–4,008.2
Balance on Goods	4 100 ..	*119.7*	*626.1*	*665.2*	*604.8*	*–28.5*	*894.4*	*1,801.3*	*1,536.4*
Services: credit	2 200 ..	818.6	683.2	666.2	637.2	724.7	858.8	933.5	950.3
Services: debit	3 200 ..	–621.8	–634.0	–612.8	–634.8	–651.9	–700.3	–738.6	–743.9
Balance on Goods and Services	4 991 ..	*316.5*	*675.3*	*718.6*	*607.2*	*44.4*	*1,052.9*	*1,996.3*	*1,742.8*
Income: credit	2 300 ..	3,112.5	4,087.0	3,815.2	4,270.7	4,763.8	5,118.6	6,327.9	3,794.4
Income: debit	3 300 ..	–3,355.1	–4,146.0	–3,840.2	–4,506.9	–4,926.1	–5,388.8	–6,551.3	–4,116.0
Balance on Goods, Services, and Income	4 992 ..	*73.9*	*616.2*	*693.6*	*371.0*	*–117.8*	*782.7*	*1,772.9*	*1,421.3*
Current transfers: credit	2 379 Z.	101.1	120.7	126.3	232.7	65.2	36.7	22.3	22.9
Current transfers: debit	3 379 ..	–430.6	–499.7	–559.3	–634.8	–725.0	–856.1	–1,012.8	–1,287.0
B. Capital Account [1]	4 994 Z.	**319.1**	**156.9**	**50.0**	**125.0**	**100.0**	**100.0**	**50.0**	**100.0**
Capital account: credit	2 994 Z.	319.1	156.9	50.0	125.0	100.0	100.0	50.0	100.0
Capital account: debit	3 994 ..	...	...	...	...	...	...	...	...
Total, Groups A Plus B	4 981 ..	*63.6*	*394.1*	*310.6*	*93.9*	*–677.7*	*63.3*	*832.4*	*257.2*
C. Financial Account [1]	4 995 W.	**1,301.1**	**–1,726.6**	**–510.4**	**15.4**	**22.3**	**230.1**	**–29.8**	**–417.0**
Direct investment abroad	4 505 ..	–198.7	16.0	–305.1	–47.6	–180.9	–163.3	–9.6	–216.0
Direct investment in Bahrain	4 555 Z.	208.2	430.6	2,048.1	329.3	179.5	453.7	363.6	80.3
Portfolio investment assets	4 602 ..	–454.0	–113.3	–779.8	–1,150.8	–1,206.6	–2,105.9	–88.3	–1,448.1
Equity securities	4 610 ..	...	...	...	...	...	–119.9	–161.2	–389.1
Debt securities	4 619 ..	–454.0	–113.3	–779.8	–1,150.8	–1,206.6	–1,985.9	72.9	–1,059.0
Portfolio investment liabilities	4 652 Z.	...	...	...	...	194.7	112.8	282.4	–30.6
Equity securities	4 660 ..	...	...	...	...	...	...	...	1.3
Debt securities	4 669 Z.	...	...	...	...	194.7	112.8	282.4	–31.9
Financial derivatives	4 910 ..	...	...	...	...	...	...	...	...
Financial derivatives assets	4 900 ..	...	...	...	...	...	...	...	...
Financial derivatives liabilities	4 905 ..	...	...	...	...	...	...	...	...
Other investment assets	4 703 ..	–4,527.1	1,124.5	–2,579.8	–4,342.0	–14,677.9	967.0	–3,833.8	5,623.4
Monetary authorities	4 701 ..	...	...	...	...	...	...	...	...
General government	4 704 ..	–8.0	–5.3	–8.0	–8.0	–5.1	–7.7	–5.9	–6.9
Banks	4 705 ..	–4,519.1	1,129.8	–2,571.8	–4,334.0	–14,672.9	974.7	–3,827.9	5,629.3
Other sectors	4 728 ..	...	...	...	...	...	...	...	1.1
Other investment liabilities	4 753 W.	6,272.6	–3,184.3	1,106.1	5,226.6	15,713.6	965.7	3,255.9	–4,426.1
Monetary authorities	4 753 WA	...	...	...	...	...	...	...	...
General government	4 753 ZB	4.0	11.2	1.3	52.4	44.1	54.8	59.0	34.6
Banks	4 753 ZC	6,268.4	–2,901.9	1,056.4	5,175.5	15,394.4	875.8	3,249.2	–4,289.6
Other sectors	4 753 ZD	.3	–293.6	48.4	–1.3	275.0	35.1	–52.4	–171.0
Total, Groups A Through C	4 983 ..	*1,364.6*	*–1,332.4*	*–199.7*	*109.3*	*–655.3*	*293.4*	*802.7*	*–159.8*
D. Net Errors and Omissions	4 998 ..	**–1,412.2**	**1,501.4**	**193.3**	**–6.5**	**638.7**	**–268.1**	**–602.6**	**283.3**
Total, Groups A Through D	4 984 ..	*–47.5*	*168.9*	*–6.4*	*102.8*	*–16.6*	*25.3*	*200.1*	*123.5*
E. Reserves and Related Items	4 802 A.	**47.5**	**–168.9**	**6.4**	**–102.8**	**16.6**	**–25.3**	**–200.1**	**–123.5**
Reserve assets	4 802 ..	47.5	–168.9	6.4	–102.8	16.6	–25.3	–200.1	–123.5
Use of Fund credit and loans	4 766 ..	...	...	...	...	...	...	...	...
Exceptional financing	4 920 ..	...	...	...	...	...	...	...	...
Conversion rates: Bahrain dinar per U.S. dollar	0 101 ..	**.3760**	**.3760**	**.3760**	**.3760**	**.3760**	**.3760**	**.3760**	**.3760**

[1] Excludes components that have been classified in the categories of Group E.

Table 2. STANDARD PRESENTATION, 1994–2001
(Millions of U.S. dollars)

	Code		1994	1995	1996	1997	1998	1999	2000	2001
CURRENT ACCOUNT	4 993	. .	**–255.6**	**237.2**	**260.6**	**–31.1**	**–777.7**	**–36.7**	**782.4**	**157.2**
A. GOODS	4 100	. .	119.7	626.1	665.2	604.8	–28.5	894.4	1,801.3	1,536.4
Credit	2 100	. .	**3,617.0**	**4,114.4**	**4,702.1**	**4,383.0**	**3,270.2**	**4,362.8**	**6,194.9**	**5,544.7**
General merchandise: exports f.o.b.	2 110	. .	3,617.0	4,114.4	4,702.1	4,383.0	3,270.2	4,362.8	6,194.9	5,544.7
Goods for processing: exports f.o.b.	2 150	. .	. . .	. . .	. . .	. . .	. . .	. . .	. . .	. . .
Repairs on goods	2 160	. .	. . .	. . .	. . .	. . .	. . .	. . .	. . .	. . .
Goods procured in ports by carriers	2 170	. .	. . .	. . .	. . .	. . .	. . .	. . .	. . .	. . .
Nonmonetary gold	2 180	. .	. . .	. . .	. . .	. . .	. . .	. . .	. . .	. . .
Debit	3 100	. .	**–3,497.3**	**–3,488.3**	**–4,037.0**	**–3,778.2**	**–3,298.7**	**–3,468.4**	**–4,393.6**	**–4,008.2**
General merchandise: imports f.o.b.	3 110	. .	–3,497.3	–3,488.3	–4,037.0	–3,778.2	–3,298.7	–3,468.4	–4,393.6	–4,008.2
Goods for processing: imports f.o.b.	3 150	. .	. . .	. . .	. . .	. . .	. . .	. . .	. . .	. . .
Repairs on goods	3 160	. .	. . .	. . .	. . .	. . .	. . .	. . .	. . .	. . .
Goods procured in ports by carriers	3 170	. .	. . .	. . .	. . .	. . .	. . .	. . .	. . .	. . .
Nonmonetary gold	3 180	. .	. . .	. . .	. . .	. . .	. . .	. . .	. . .	. . .
B. SERVICES	4 200	. .	196.8	49.2	53.5	2.4	72.9	158.5	194.9	206.4
Total credit	2 200	. .	*818.6*	*683.2*	*666.2*	*637.2*	*724.7*	*858.8*	*933.5*	*950.3*
Total debit	3 200	. .	*–621.8*	*–634.0*	*–612.8*	*–634.8*	*–651.9*	*–700.3*	*–738.6*	*–743.9*
Transportation services, credit	2 205	. .	**427.1**	**345.7**	**326.3**	**267.3**	**259.0**	**267.3**	**281.4**	**255.9**
Passenger	2 850	. .	*427.1*	*345.7*	*326.3*	*267.3*	*259.0*	*267.3*	*281.4*	*255.9*
Freight	2 851	. .	. . .	. . .	. . .	. . .	. . .	. . .	. . .	. . .
Other	2 852	. .	. . .	. . .	. . .	. . .	. . .	. . .	. . .	. . .
Sea transport, passenger	2 207	. .	. . .	. . .	. . .	. . .	. . .	. . .	. . .	. . .
Sea transport, freight	2 208	. .	. . .	. . .	. . .	. . .	. . .	. . .	. . .	. . .
Sea transport, other	2 209	. .	. . .	. . .	. . .	. . .	. . .	. . .	. . .	. . .
Air transport, passenger	2 211	. .	427.1	345.7	326.3	267.3	259.0	267.3	281.4	255.9
Air transport, freight	2 212	. .	. . .	. . .	. . .	. . .	. . .	. . .	. . .	. . .
Air transport, other	2 213	. .	. . .	. . .	. . .	. . .	. . .	. . .	. . .	. . .
Other transport, passenger	2 215	. .	. . .	. . .	. . .	. . .	. . .	. . .	. . .	. . .
Other transport, freight	2 216	. .	. . .	. . .	. . .	. . .	. . .	. . .	. . .	. . .
Other transport, other	2 217	. .	. . .	. . .	. . .	. . .	. . .	. . .	. . .	. . .
Transportation services, debit	3 205	. .	**–379.3**	**–402.7**	**–401.9**	**–419.1**	**–425.5**	**–389.6**	**–417.3**	**–401.9**
Passenger	3 850	. .	*–154.3*	*–198.1*	*–188.6*	*–195.5*	*–184.8*	*–183.2*	*–201.3*	*–172.6*
Freight	3 851	. .	*–225.0*	*–204.5*	*–213.3*	*–223.7*	*–240.7*	*–206.4*	*–216.0*	*–229.3*
Other	3 852	. .	. . .	. . .	. . .	. . .	. . .	. . .	. . .	. . .
Sea transport, passenger	3 207	. .	. . .	. . .	. . .	. . .	. . .	. . .	. . .	. . .
Sea transport, freight	3 208	. .	–225.0	–204.5	–213.3	–223.7	–240.7	–206.4	–216.0	–229.3
Sea transport, other	3 209	. .	. . .	. . .	. . .	. . .	. . .	. . .	. . .	. . .
Air transport, passenger	3 211	. .	–154.3	–198.1	–188.6	–195.5	–184.8	–183.2	–201.3	–172.6
Air transport, freight	3 212	. .	. . .	. . .	. . .	. . .	. . .	. . .	. . .	. . .
Air transport, other	3 213	. .	. . .	. . .	. . .	. . .	. . .	. . .	. . .	. . .
Other transport, passenger	3 215	. .	. . .	. . .	. . .	. . .	. . .	. . .	. . .	. . .
Other transport, freight	3 216	. .	. . .	. . .	. . .	. . .	. . .	. . .	. . .	. . .
Other transport, other	3 217	. .	. . .	. . .	. . .	. . .	. . .	. . .	. . .	. . .
Travel, credit	2 236	. .	**303.2**	**247.3**	**263.3**	**311.2**	**366.2**	**518.4**	**572.9**	**630.1**
Business travel	2 237	. .	. . .	. . .	. . .	. . .	. . .	. . .	. . .	. . .
Personal travel	2 240	. .	. . .	. . .	. . .	. . .	. . .	. . .	. . .	. . .
Travel, debit	3 236	. .	**–146.3**	**–122.3**	**–109.0**	**–122.3**	**–142.0**	**–212.2**	**–223.7**	**–250.0**
Business travel	3 237	. .	. . .	. . .	. . .	. . .	. . .	. . .	. . .	. . .
Personal travel	3 240	. .	. . .	. . .	. . .	. . .	. . .	. . .	. . .	. . .
Other services, credit	2 200	BA	**88.3**	**90.2**	**76.6**	**58.8**	**99.5**	**73.1**	**79.3**	**64.4**
Communications	2 245	. .	. . .	. . .	. . .	. . .	. . .	. . .	. . .	. . .
Construction	2 249	. .	. . .	. . .	. . .	. . .	. . .	. . .	. . .	. . .
Insurance	2 253	. .	. . .	. . .	. . .	. . .	. . .	. . .	. . .	. . .
Financial	2 260	. .	. . .	. . .	. . .	. . .	. . .	. . .	. . .	. . .
Computer and information	2 262	. .	. . .	. . .	. . .	. . .	. . .	. . .	. . .	. . .
Royalties and licence fees	2 266	. .	. . .	. . .	. . .	. . .	. . .	. . .	. . .	. . .
Other business services	2 268	. .	88.3	90.2	76.6	58.8	99.5	73.1	79.3	64.4
Personal, cultural, and recreational	2 287	. .	. . .	. . .	. . .	. . .	. . .	. . .	. . .	. . .
Government, n.i.e.	2 291	. .	. . .	. . .	. . .	. . .	. . .	. . .	. . .	. . .
Other services, debit	3 200	BA	**–96.3**	**–109.0**	**–101.9**	**–93.4**	**–84.3**	**–98.4**	**–97.6**	**–92.0**
Communications	3 245	. .	. . .	. . .	. . .	. . .	. . .	. . .	. . .	. . .
Construction	3 249	. .	. . .	. . .	. . .	. . .	. . .	. . .	. . .	. . .
Insurance	3 253	. .	–25.0	–22.6	–23.7	–24.7	–26.9	–22.9	–23.9	–25.5
Financial	3 260	. .	. . .	. . .	. . .	. . .	. . .	. . .	. . .	. . .
Computer and information	3 262	. .	. . .	. . .	. . .	. . .	. . .	. . .	. . .	. . .
Royalties and licence fees	3 266	. .	. . .	. . .	. . .	. . .	. . .	. . .	. . .	. . .
Other business services	3 268	. .	–71.3	–86.4	–78.2	–68.6	–57.4	–75.5	–73.7	–66.5
Personal, cultural, and recreational	3 287	. .	. . .	. . .	. . .	. . .	. . .	. . .	. . .	. . .
Government, n.i.e.	3 291	. .	. . .	. . .	. . .	. . .	. . .	. . .	. . .	. . .

Table 2 (Continued). STANDARD PRESENTATION, 1994–2001

(Millions of U.S. dollars)

	Code		1994	1995	1996	1997	1998	1999	2000	2001
C. INCOME	4 300	. .	-242.6	-59.0	-25.0	-236.2	-162.2	-270.2	-223.4	-321.5
Total credit	2 300	. .	*3,112.5*	*4,087.0*	*3,815.2*	*4,270.7*	*4,763.8*	*5,118.6*	*6,327.9*	*3,794.4*
Total debit	3 300	. .	*-3,355.1*	*-4,146.0*	*-3,840.2*	*-4,506.9*	*-4,926.1*	*-5,388.8*	*-6,551.3*	*-4,116.0*
Compensation of employees, credit	2 310	. .	**. . .**	**. . .**	**. . .**	**. . .**	**. . .**	**. . .**	**. . .**	**. . .**
Compensation of employees, debit	3 310	. .	**. . .**	**. . .**	**. . .**	**. . .**	**. . .**	**. . .**	**. . .**	**. . .**
Investment income, credit	2 320	. .	**3,112.5**	**4,087.0**	**3,815.2**	**4,270.7**	**4,763.8**	**5,118.6**	**6,327.9**	**3,794.4**
Direct investment income	2 330	. .	103.2	127.1	125.3	161.7	167.6	189.4	208.8	208.8
Dividends and distributed branch profits	2 332	. .	41.2	50.8	50.0	64.6	67.0	75.8	83.5	83.5
Reinvested earnings and undistributed branch profits	2 333	. .	62.0	76.3	75.3	97.1	100.5	113.6	125.3	125.3
Income on debt (interest)	2 334	. .	. . .	. . .	. . .	. . .	. . .	. . .	. . .	. . .
Portfolio investment income	2 339	. .	304.5	405.1	393.9	467.6	519.7	615.4	824.7	501.6
Income on equity	2 340	. .	. . .	. . .	. . .	. . .	. . .	77.9	114.1	75.0
Income on bonds and notes	2 350	. .	304.5	405.1	393.9	467.6	519.7	537.5	710.6	426.6
Income on money market instruments	2 360	. .	. . .	. . .	. . .	. . .	. . .	. . .	. . .	. . .
Other investment income	2 370	. .	2,704.8	3,554.8	3,296.0	3,641.5	4,076.6	4,313.8	5,294.4	3,084.0
Investment income, debit	3 320	. .	**-3,355.1**	**-4,146.0**	**-3,840.2**	**-4,506.9**	**-4,926.1**	**-5,388.8**	**-6,551.3**	**-4,116.0**
Direct investment income	3 330	. .	-275.0	-388.6	-409.8	-725.3	-770.2	-784.3	-880.9	-922.1
Dividends and distributed branch profits	3 332	. .	-110.6	-164.1	-168.6	-293.9	-311.4	-316.0	-357.2	-372.3
Reinvested earnings and undistributed branch profits	3 333	. .	-164.4	-224.5	-241.2	-431.4	-458.8	-468.4	-523.7	-549.7
Income on debt (interest)	3 334	. .	. . .	. . .	. . .	. . .	. . .	. . .	. . .	. . .
Portfolio investment income	3 339	. .	. . .	. . .	. . .	. . .	-5.3	-13.6	-29.3	-21.8
Income on equity	3 340	. .	. . .	. . .	. . .	. . .	. . .	. . .	. . .	. . .
Income on bonds and notes	3 350	. .	. . .	. . .	. . .	. . .	-5.3	-13.6	-29.3	-21.8
Income on money market instruments	3 360	. .	. . .	. . .	. . .	. . .	. . .	. . .	. . .	. . .
Other investment income	3 370	. .	-3,080.1	-3,757.4	-3,430.3	-3,781.6	-4,150.5	-4,591.0	-5,641.2	-3,172.1
D. CURRENT TRANSFERS	4 379	. .	-329.5	-379.0	-433.0	-402.1	-659.8	-819.4	-990.4	-1,264.1
Credit	2 379	. .	**101.1**	**120.7**	**126.3**	**232.7**	**65.2**	**36.7**	**22.3**	**22.9**
General government	2 380	. .	. . .	. . .	. . .	. . .	. . .	. . .	. . .	. . .
Other sectors	2 390	. .	101.1	120.7	126.3	232.7	65.2	36.7	22.3	22.9
Workers' remittances	2 391	. .	. . .	. . .	. . .	. . .	. . .	. . .	. . .	. . .
Other current transfers	2 392	. .	101.1	120.7	126.3	232.7	65.2	36.7	22.3	22.9
Debit	3 379	. .	**-430.6**	**-499.7**	**-559.3**	**-634.8**	**-725.0**	**-856.1**	**-1,012.8**	**-1,287.0**
General government	3 380	. .	. . .	. . .	. . .	. . .	. . .	. . .	. . .	. . .
Other sectors	3 390	. .	-430.6	-499.7	-559.3	-634.8	-725.0	-856.1	-1,012.8	-1,287.0
Workers' remittances	3 391	. .	-430.6	-499.7	-559.3	-634.8	-725.0	-856.1	-1,012.8	-1,287.0
Other current transfers	3 392	. .	. . .	. . .	. . .	. . .	. . .	. . .	. . .	. . .
CAPITAL AND FINANCIAL ACCOUNT	4 996	. .	**1,667.8**	**-1,738.6**	**-453.9**	**37.6**	**139.0**	**304.8**	**-179.9**	**-440.5**
CAPITAL ACCOUNT	4 994	. .	**319.1**	**156.9**	**50.0**	**125.0**	**100.0**	**100.0**	**50.0**	**100.0**
Total credit	2 994	. .	*319.1*	*156.9*	*50.0*	*125.0*	*100.0*	*100.0*	*50.0*	*100.0*
Total debit	3 994	. .	. . .	. . .	. . .	. . .	. . .	. . .	. . .	. . .
Capital transfers, credit	2 400	. .	**319.1**	**156.9**	**50.0**	**125.0**	**100.0**	**100.0**	**50.0**	**100.0**
General government	2 401	. .	319.1	156.9	50.0	125.0	100.0	100.0	50.0	100.0
Debt forgiveness	2 402	. .	. . .	. . .	. . .	. . .	. . .	. . .	. . .	. . .
Other capital transfers	2 410	. .	319.1	156.9	50.0	125.0	100.0	100.0	50.0	100.0
Other sectors	2 430	. .	. . .	. . .	. . .	. . .	. . .	. . .	. . .	. . .
Migrants' transfers	2 431	. .	. . .	. . .	. . .	. . .	. . .	. . .	. . .	. . .
Debt forgiveness	2 432	. .	. . .	. . .	. . .	. . .	. . .	. . .	. . .	. . .
Other capital transfers	2 440	. .	. . .	. . .	. . .	. . .	. . .	. . .	. . .	. . .
Capital transfers, debit	3 400	. .	**. . .**	**. . .**	**. . .**	**. . .**	**. . .**	**. . .**	**. . .**	**. . .**
General government	3 401	. .	. . .	. . .	. . .	. . .	. . .	. . .	. . .	. . .
Debt forgiveness	3 402	. .	. . .	. . .	. . .	. . .	. . .	. . .	. . .	. . .
Other capital transfers	3 410	. .	. . .	. . .	. . .	. . .	. . .	. . .	. . .	. . .
Other sectors	3 430	. .	. . .	. . .	. . .	. . .	. . .	. . .	. . .	. . .
Migrants' transfers	3 431	. .	. . .	. . .	. . .	. . .	. . .	. . .	. . .	. . .
Debt forgiveness	3 432	. .	. . .	. . .	. . .	. . .	. . .	. . .	. . .	. . .
Other capital transfers	3 440	. .	. . .	. . .	. . .	. . .	. . .	. . .	. . .	. . .
Nonproduced nonfinancial assets, credit	2 480	. .	**. . .**	**. . .**	**. . .**	**. . .**	**. . .**	**. . .**	**. . .**	**. . .**
Nonproduced nonfinancial assets, debit	3 480	. .	**. . .**	**. . .**	**. . .**	**. . .**	**. . .**	**. . .**	**. . .**	**. . .**

Table 2 (Continued). STANDARD PRESENTATION, 1994–2001

(Millions of U.S. dollars)

	Code	1994	1995	1996	1997	1998	1999	2000	2001
FINANCIAL ACCOUNT	4 995	**1,348.6**	**–1,895.5**	**–503.9**	**–87.4**	**39.0**	**204.8**	**–229.9**	**–540.5**
A. DIRECT INVESTMENT	4 500	9.6	446.5	1,743.1	281.6	–1.3	290.4	354.0	–135.6
Direct investment abroad	4 505	**–198.7**	**16.0**	**–305.1**	**–47.6**	**–180.9**	**–163.3**	**–9.6**	**–216.0**
Equity capital	4 510	–136.7	92.3	–229.8	49.5	–80.3	–49.7	115.7	–90.7
Claims on affiliated enterprises	4 515	–136.7	92.3	–229.8	49.5	–80.3	–49.7	115.7	–90.7
Liabilities to affiliated enterprises	4 520	. . .	. . .	. . .	. . .	. . .	. . .	. . .	. . .
Reinvested earnings	4 525	–62.0	–76.3	–75.3	–97.1	–100.5	–113.6	–125.3	–125.3
Other capital	4 530	. . .	. . .	. . .	. . .	. . .	. . .	. . .	. . .
Claims on affiliated enterprises	4 535	. . .	. . .	. . .	. . .	. . .	. . .	. . .	. . .
Liabilities to affiliated enterprises	4 540	. . .	. . .	. . .	. . .	. . .	. . .	. . .	. . .
Direct investment in Bahrain	4 555	**208.2**	**430.6**	**2,048.1**	**329.3**	**179.5**	**453.7**	**363.6**	**80.3**
Equity capital	4 560	43.9	206.1	1,806.9	–102.1	–279.3	–14.6	–160.1	–469.4
Claims on direct investors	4 565	. . .	. . .	. . .	. . .	. . .	. . .	. . .	. . .
Liabilities to direct investors	4 570	43.9	206.1	1,806.9	–102.1	–279.3	–14.6	–160.1	–469.4
Reinvested earnings	4 575	164.4	224.5	241.2	431.4	458.8	468.4	523.7	549.7
Other capital	4 580	. . .	. . .	. . .	. . .	. . .	. . .	. . .	. . .
Claims on direct investors	4 585	. . .	. . .	. . .	. . .	. . .	. . .	. . .	. . .
Liabilities to direct investors	4 590	. . .	. . .	. . .	. . .	. . .	. . .	. . .	. . .

	Code	1994	1995	1996	1997	1998	1999	2000	2001
B. PORTFOLIO INVESTMENT	4 600	–454.0	–113.3	–779.8	–1,150.8	–1,012.0	–1,993.1	194.1	–1,478.7
Assets	4 602	**–454.0**	**–113.3**	**–779.8**	**–1,150.8**	**–1,206.6**	**–2,105.9**	**–88.3**	**–1,448.1**
Equity securities	4 610	. . .	. . .	. . .	. . .	. . .	–119.9	–161.2	–389.1
Monetary authorities	4 611	. . .	. . .	. . .	. . .	. . .	. . .	. . .	. . .
General government	4 612	. . .	. . .	. . .	. . .	. . .	. . .	. . .	. . .
Banks	4 613	. . .	. . .	. . .	. . .	. . .	–75.5	–150.5	–300.0
Other sectors	4 614	. . .	. . .	. . .	. . .	. . .	–44.4	–10.6	–89.1
Debt securities	4 619	–454.0	–113.3	–779.8	–1,150.8	–1,206.6	–1,985.9	72.9	–1,059.0
Bonds and notes	4 620	–454.0	–113.3	–779.8	–1,150.8	–1,206.6	–1,985.9	72.9	–1,059.0
Monetary authorities	4 621	. . .	. . .	. . .	. . .	. . .	. . .	. . .	. . .
General government	4 622	. . .	. . .	. . .	. . .	. . .	. . .	. . .	. . .
Banks	4 623	–446.3	–113.0	–778.2	–1,158.0	–1,202.4	–1,972.9	66.8	–1,036.2
Other sectors	4 624	–7.7	–.3	–1.6	7.2	–4.3	–13.0	6.1	–22.9
Money market instruments	4 630	. . .	. . .	. . .	. . .	. . .	. . .	. . .	. . .
Monetary authorities	4 631	. . .	. . .	. . .	. . .	. . .	. . .	. . .	. . .
General government	4 632	. . .	. . .	. . .	. . .	. . .	. . .	. . .	. . .
Banks	4 633	. . .	. . .	. . .	. . .	. . .	. . .	. . .	. . .
Other sectors	4 634	. . .	. . .	. . .	. . .	. . .	. . .	. . .	. . .
Liabilities	4 652	**. . .**	**. . .**	**. . .**	**. . .**	**194.7**	**112.8**	**282.4**	**–30.6**
Equity securities	4 660	. . .	. . .	. . .	. . .	. . .	. . .	. . .	1.3
Banks	4 663	. . .	. . .	. . .	. . .	. . .	. . .	. . .	. . .
Other sectors	4 664	. . .	. . .	. . .	. . .	. . .	. . .	. . .	1.3
Debt securities	4 669	. . .	. . .	. . .	. . .	194.7	112.8	282.4	–31.9
Bonds and notes	4 670	. . .	. . .	. . .	. . .	194.7	112.8	282.4	–31.9
Monetary authorities	4 671	. . .	. . .	. . .	. . .	. . .	. . .	. . .	. . .
General government	4 672	. . .	. . .	. . .	. . .	. . .	. . .	. . .	. . .
Banks	4 673	. . .	. . .	. . .	. . .	194.7	112.8	282.4	–31.9
Other sectors	4 674	. . .	. . .	. . .	. . .	. . .	. . .	. . .	. . .
Money market instruments	4 680	. . .	. . .	. . .	. . .	. . .	. . .	. . .	. . .
Monetary authorities	4 681	. . .	. . .	. . .	. . .	. . .	. . .	. . .	. . .
General government	4 682	. . .	. . .	. . .	. . .	. . .	. . .	. . .	. . .
Banks	4 683	. . .	. . .	. . .	. . .	. . .	. . .	. . .	. . .
Other sectors	4 684	. . .	. . .	. . .	. . .	. . .	. . .	. . .	. . .
C. FINANCIAL DERIVATIVES	4 910	. . .	. . .	. . .	. . .	. . .	. . .	. . .	. . .
Monetary authorities	4 911	. . .	. . .	. . .	. . .	. . .	. . .	. . .	. . .
General government	4 912	. . .	. . .	. . .	. . .	. . .	. . .	. . .	. . .
Banks	4 913	. . .	. . .	. . .	. . .	. . .	. . .	. . .	. . .
Other sectors	4 914	. . .	. . .	. . .	. . .	. . .	. . .	. . .	. . .
Assets	4 900	**. . .**	**. . .**	**. . .**	**. . .**	**. . .**	**. . .**	**. . .**	**. . .**
Monetary authorities	4 901	. . .	. . .	. . .	. . .	. . .	. . .	. . .	. . .
General government	4 902	. . .	. . .	. . .	. . .	. . .	. . .	. . .	. . .
Banks	4 903	. . .	. . .	. . .	. . .	. . .	. . .	. . .	. . .
Other sectors	4 904	. . .	. . .	. . .	. . .	. . .	. . .	. . .	. . .
Liabilities	4 905	**. . .**	**. . .**	**. . .**	**. . .**	**. . .**	**. . .**	**. . .**	**. . .**
Monetary authorities	4 906	. . .	. . .	. . .	. . .	. . .	. . .	. . .	. . .
General government	4 907	. . .	. . .	. . .	. . .	. . .	. . .	. . .	. . .
Banks	4 908	. . .	. . .	. . .	. . .	. . .	. . .	. . .	. . .
Other sectors	4 909	. . .	. . .	. . .	. . .	. . .	. . .	. . .	. . .

Table 2 (Concluded). STANDARD PRESENTATION, 1994–2001
(Millions of U.S. dollars)

	Code	1994	1995	1996	1997	1998	1999	2000	2001
D. OTHER INVESTMENT	4 700 . .	1,745.5	–2,059.8	–1,473.7	884.6	1,035.6	1,932.7	–577.9	1,197.3
Assets	4 703 . .	**–4,527.1**	**1,124.5**	**–2,579.8**	**–4,342.0**	**–14,677.9**	**967.0**	**–3,833.8**	**5,623.4**
Trade credits	4 706 . .	...	...	...	...	...	...	...	...
General government	4 707 . .	...	...	...	...	...	...	...	...
of which: Short-term	4 709 . .	...	...	...	...	...	...	...	...
Other sectors	4 710 . .	...	...	...	...	...	...	...	...
of which: Short-term	4 712 . .	...	...	...	...	...	...	...	...
Loans	4 714 . .	–4,590.7	8,861.7	1,076.6	–2,650.5	–1,944.4	451.1	–1,258.0	1,954.3
Monetary authorities	4 715 . .	...	...	...	...	...	...	...	...
of which: Short-term	4 718 . .	...	...	...	...	...	...	...	...
General government	4 719 . .	...	...	...	...	...	...	...	...
of which: Short-term	4 721 . .	...	...	...	...	...	...	...	...
Banks	4 722 . .	–4,590.7	8,861.7	1,076.6	–2,650.5	–1,944.4	451.1	–1,258.0	1,954.3
of which: Short-term	4 724 . .	...	...	...	...	...	...	...	...
Other sectors	4 725 . .	...	...	...	...	...	...	...	...
of which: Short-term	4 727 . .	...	...	...	...	...	...	...	...
Currency and deposits	4 730 . .	71.5	–7,731.9	–3,648.4	–1,683.5	–12,728.5	523.7	–2,569.9	3,675.0
Monetary authorities	4 731 . .	...	...	...	...	...	...	...	...
General government	4 732 . .	...	...	...	...	...	...	...	...
Banks	4 733 . .	71.5	–7,731.9	–3,648.4	–1,683.5	–12,728.5	523.7	–2,569.9	3,675.0
Other sectors	4 734 . .	...	...	...	...	...	...	...	...
Other assets	4 736 . .	–8.0	–5.3	–8.0	–8.0	–5.1	–7.7	–5.9	–5.9
Monetary authorities	4 737 . .	...	...	...	...	...	...	...	...
of which: Short-term	4 739 . .	...	...	...	...	...	...	...	...
General government	4 740 . .	–8.0	–5.3	–8.0	–8.0	–5.1	–7.7	–5.9	–6.9
of which: Short-term	4 742 . .	...	...	...	...	...	...	...	...
Banks	4 743 . .	...	...	...	...	...	...	...	...
of which: Short-term	4 745 . .	...	...	...	...	...	...	...	...
Other sectors	4 746 . .	...	...	...	...	...	...	...	1.1
of which: Short-term	4 748 . .	...	...	...	...	...	...	...	...
Liabilities	4 753 . .	**6,272.6**	**–3,184.3**	**1,106.1**	**5,226.6**	**15,713.6**	**965.7**	**3,255.9**	**–4,426.1**
Trade credits	4 756 . .	...	...	...	...	...	...	...	...
General government	4 757 . .	...	...	...	...	...	...	...	...
of which: Short-term	4 759 . .	...	...	...	...	...	...	...	...
Other sectors	4 760 . .	...	...	...	...	...	...	...	...
of which: Short-term	4 762 . .	...	...	...	...	...	...	...	...
Loans	4 764 . .	4.3	–282.4	49.7	51.1	319.1	89.9	6.6	–136.7
Monetary authorities	4 765 . .	...	...	...	...	...	...	...	...
of which: Use of Fund credit and loans from the Fund	4 766 . .	...	...	...	...	...	...	...	...
of which: Short-term	4 768 . .	...	...	...	...	...	...	...	...
General government	4 769 . .	4.0	11.2	1.3	52.4	44.1	54.8	59.0	34.6
of which: Short-term	4 771 . .	...	...	...	...	...	...	...	...
Banks	4 772 . .	...	...	...	...	...	...	...	...
of which: Short-term	4 774 . .	...	...	...	...	...	...	...	...
Other sectors	4 775 . .	.3	–293.6	48.4	–1.3	275.0	35.1	–52.4	–171.3
of which: Short-term	4 777 . .	...	...	...	...	...	...	...	...
Currency and deposits	4 780 . .	6,268.4	–2,901.9	1,056.4	5,175.5	15,394.4	875.8	3,249.2	–4,289.6
Monetary authorities	4 781 . .	...	...	...	...	...	...	...	...
General government	4 782 . .	...	...	...	...	...	...	...	...
Banks	4 783 . .	6,268.4	–2,901.9	1,056.4	5,175.5	15,394.4	875.8	3,249.2	–4,289.6
Other sectors	4 784 . .	...	...	...	...	...	...	...	...
Other liabilities	4 786 . .	...	...	...	...	...	...	...	.3
Monetary authorities	4 787 . .	...	...	...	...	...	...	...	...
of which: Short-term	4 789 . .	...	...	...	...	...	...	...	...
General government	4 790 . .	...	...	...	...	...	...	...	...
of which: Short-term	4 792 . .	...	...	...	...	...	...	...	...
Banks	4 793 . .	...	...	...	...	...	...	...	...
of which: Short-term	4 795 . .	...	...	...	...	...	...	...	...
Other sectors	4 796 . .	...	...	...	...	...	...	...	.3
of which: Short-term	4 798 . .	...	...	...	...	...	...	...	...
E. RESERVE ASSETS	4 802 . .	47.5	–168.9	6.4	–102.8	16.6	–25.3	–200.1	–123.5
Monetary gold	4 812 . .	...	...	...	...	...	...	...	...
Special drawing rights	4 811 . .	–.3	–.4	–.6	–.3	–.3	16.7	–1.4	.2
Reserve position in the Fund	4 810 . .	–1.9	–2.3	–2.0	–2.2	–2.4	–19.1	–3.3	–3.0
Foreign exchange	4 803 . .	49.2	–166.0	9.3	–100.5	19.7	–23.4	–194.9	–121.5
Other claims	4 813 . .	.5	–.3	–.3	.3	–.3	.5	–.5	.8
NET ERRORS AND OMISSIONS	4 998 . .	**–1,412.2**	**1,501.4**	**193.3**	**–6.5**	**638.7**	**–268.1**	**–602.6**	**283.3**

Part 3 of the *Yearbook* contains descriptions of the methodologies, compilation practices, and sources used to compile these data.

Table 3. INTERNATIONAL INVESTMENT POSITION (End–period stocks), 1994–2001

(Millions of U.S. dollars)

	Code	1994	1995	1996	1997	1998	1999	2000	2001
ASSETS	8 995 C.	66,735.3	65,872.8	69,518.5	75,156.1	91,569.8	92,887.3	97,291.5	93,445.7
Direct investment abroad	8 505	**1,059.8**	**1,043.9**	**1,348.7**	**1,396.3**	**1,579.3**	**1,742.6**	**1,752.1**	**1,968.1**
Equity capital and reinvested earnings	8 506	1,059.8	1,043.9	1,348.7	1,396.3	1,579.3	1,742.6	1,752.1	1,968.1
Claims on affiliated enterprises	8 507	1,059.8	1,043.9	1,348.7	1,396.3	1,579.3	1,742.6	1,752.1	1,968.1
Liabilities to affiliated enterprises	8 508	...	...	...	...	...	...	...	...
Other capital	8 530	...	...	...	...	...	...	...	...
Claims on affiliated enterprises	8 535	...	...	...	...	...	...	...	...
Liabilities to affiliated enterprises	8 540	...	...	...	...	...	...	...	...
Portfolio investment	8 602	**6,647.6**	**6,760.6**	**7,538.8**	**8,696.8**	**10,268.1**	**12,373.9**	**12,719.1**	**14,166.7**
Equity securities	8 610	...	...	...	...	1,342.6	1,462.5	1,840.2	2,229.3
Monetary authorities	8 611	...	...	...	...	...	...	...	...
General government	8 612	...	...	...	...	...	...	...	...
Banks	8 613	...	...	...	...	1,064.1	1,139.6	1,289.9	1,589.9
Other sectors	8 614	...	...	...	...	278.5	322.9	550.3	639.4
Debt securities	8 619	6,647.6	6,760.6	7,538.8	8,696.8	8,925.5	10,911.4	10,879.0	11,937.5
Bonds and notes	8 620	6,647.6	6,760.6	7,538.8	8,696.8	8,925.5	10,911.4	10,879.0	11,937.5
Monetary authorities	8 621	...	...	...	...	...	...	...	...
General government	8 622	...	...	...	...	...	...	...	...
Banks	8 623	6,647.6	6,760.6	7,538.8	8,696.8	8,835.1	10,808.2	10,741.5	11,777.6
Other sectors	8 624	...	...	...	...	90.4	103.2	137.5	159.8
Money market instruments	8 630	...	...	...	...	...	...	...	...
Monetary authorities	8 631	...	...	...	...	...	...	...	...
General government	8 632	...	...	...	...	...	...	...	...
Banks	8 633	...	...	...	...	...	...	...	...
Other sectors	8 634	...	...	...	...	...	...	...	...
Financial derivatives	8 900	**...**	**...**	**...**	**...**	**...**	**...**	**...**	**...**
Monetary authorities	8 901	...	...	...	...	...	...	...	...
General government	8 902	...	...	...	...	...	...	...	...
Banks	8 903	...	...	...	...	...	...	...	...
Other sectors	8 904	...	...	...	...	...	...	...	...
Other investment	8 703	**57,917.7**	**56,787.9**	**59,359.7**	**63,693.8**	**78,366.6**	**77,391.9**	**81,245.6**	**75,615.8**
Trade credits	8 706	...	...	...	...	...	...	...	...
General government	8 707	...	...	...	...	...	...	...	...
of which: Short-term	8 709	...	...	...	...	...	...	...	...
Other sectors	8 710	...	...	...	...	...	...	...	...
of which: Short-term	8 712	...	...	...	...	...	...	...	...
Loans	8 714	21,670.4	12,808.8	11,732.2	14,382.7	16,327.1	15,876.0	17,134.3	15,180.0
Monetary authorities	8 715	...	...	...	...	...	...	...	...
of which: Short-term	8 718	...	...	...	...	...	...	...	...
General government	8 719	...	...	...	...	...	...	...	...
of which: Short-term	8 721	...	...	...	...	...	...	...	...
Banks	8 722	21,670.4	12,808.8	11,732.2	14,382.7	16,327.1	15,876.0	17,134.3	15,180.0
of which: Short-term	8 724	...	...	...	...	...	...	...	...
Other sectors	8 725	...	...	...	...	...	...	...	...
of which: Short-term	8 727	...	...	...	...	...	...	...	...
Currency and deposits	8 730	36,247.3	43,979.2	47,627.6	49,311.1	62,039.5	61,515.9	64,085.8	60,411.1
Monetary authorities	8 731	...	...	...	...	...	...	...	...
General government	8 732	...	...	...	...	...	...	...	...
Banks	8 733	36,247.3	43,979.2	47,627.6	49,311.1	62,039.5	61,515.9	64,085.8	60,411.1
Other sectors	8 734	...	...	...	...	...	...	...	...
Other assets	8 736	...	...	...	...	...	...	25.5	24.7
Monetary authorities	8 737	...	...	...	...	...	...	...	...
of which: Short-term	8 739	...	...	...	...	...	...	...	...
General government	8 740	...	...	...	...	...	...	...	...
of which: Short-term	8 742	...	...	...	...	...	...	...	...
Banks	8 743	...	...	...	...	...	...	...	...
of which: Short-term	8 745	...	...	...	...	...	...	...	...
Other sectors	8 746	...	...	...	...	...	...	25.5	24.7
of which: Short-term	8 748	...	...	...	...	...	...	...	...
Reserve assets	8 802	**1,110.1**	**1,280.4**	**1,271.3**	**1,369.0**	**1,355.9**	**1,379.0**	**1,574.7**	**1,695.1**
Monetary gold	8 812	6.6	6.6	6.6	6.6	6.6	6.6	6.6	6.6
Special drawing rights	8 811	16.1	16.8	16.8	16.1	17.1	...	1.3	1.1
Reserve position in the Fund	8 810	61.6	65.0	64.8	63.0	68.3	85.6	84.5	84.4
Foreign exchange	8 803	774.7	940.7	931.4	1,031.9	1,012.2	1,035.6	1,230.6	1,352.1
Other claims	8 813	251.1	251.3	251.6	251.3	251.6	251.1	251.6	250.8

Table 3 (Concluded). INTERNATIONAL INVESTMENT POSITION (End–period stocks), 1994–2001

(Millions of U.S. dollars)

	Code		1994	1995	1996	1997	1998	1999	2000	2001
LIABILITIES	8 995	D.	64,529.7	62,081.8	65,187.7	70,744.6	86,515.3	88,016.3	92,136.3	87,929.9
Direct investment in Bahrain	8 555	..	**1,972.9**	**2,403.5**	**4,451.6**	**4,780.8**	**4,960.4**	**5,414.1**	**5,905.8**	**5,986.2**
Equity capital and reinvested earnings	8 556	..	1,972.9	2,403.5	4,451.6	4,780.8	4,960.4	5,414.1	5,905.8	5,986.2
Claims on direct investors	8 557	..	...	...	...	...	...	...	...	...
Liabilities to direct investors	8 558	..	1,972.9	2,403.5	4,451.6	4,780.8	4,960.4	5,414.1	5,905.8	5,986.2
Other capital	8 580	..	...	...	...	...	...	...	...	...
Claims on direct investors	8 585	..	...	...	...	...	...	...	...	...
Liabilities to direct investors	8 590	..	...	...	...	...	...	...	...	...
Portfolio investment	8 652	..	**...**	**...**	**...**	**...**	**194.7**	**307.7**	**616.0**	**585.4**
Equity securities	8 660	..	...	...	...	...	...	...	25.8	27.1
Banks	8 663	..	...	...	...	...	...	...	...	...
Other sectors	8 664	..	...	...	...	...	...	...	25.8	27.1
Debt securities	8 669	..	...	...	...	...	194.7	307.7	590.2	558.2
Bonds and notes	8 670	..	...	...	...	...	194.7	307.7	590.2	558.2
Monetary authorities	8 671	..	...	...	...	...	...	...	...	...
General government	8 672	..	...	...	...	...	...	...	...	...
Banks	8 673	..	...	...	...	...	194.7	307.7	590.2	558.2
Other sectors	8 674	..	...	...	...	...	...	...	...	...
Money market instruments	8 680	..	...	...	...	...	...	...	...	...
Monetary authorities	8 681	..	...	...	...	...	...	...	...	...
General government	8 682	..	...	...	...	...	...	...	...	...
Banks	8 683	..	...	...	...	...	...	...	...	...
Other sectors	8 684	..	...	...	...	...	...	...	...	...
Financial derivatives	8 905	..	**...**	**...**	**...**	**...**	**...**	**...**	**...**	**...**
Monetary authorities	8 906	..	...	...	...	...	...	...	...	...
General government	8 907	..	...	...	...	...	...	...	...	...
Banks	8 908	..	...	...	...	...	...	...	...	...
Other sectors	8 909	..	...	...	...	...	...	...	...	...
Other investment	8 753	..	**62,556.8**	**59,678.4**	**60,736.1**	**65,963.7**	**81,360.2**	**82,294.5**	**85,614.5**	**81,358.4**
Trade credits	8 756	..	...	...	...	...	...	...	3.5	3.5
General government	8 757	..	...	...	...	...	...	...	...	...
of which: Short-term	8 759	..	...	...	...	...	...	...	...	...
Other sectors	8 760	..	...	...	...	...	...	...	3.5	3.5
of which: Short-term	8 762	..	...	...	...	...	...	...	...	...
Loans	8 764	..	150.3	173.7	175.0	227.1	229.3	287.8	345.7	378.7
Monetary authorities	8 765	..	...	...	...	...	...	...	...	...
of which: Use of Fund credit and loans from the Fund	8 766	..	...	...	...	...	...	...	...	...
of which: Short-term	8 768	..	...	...	...	...	...	...	...	...
General government	8 769	..	150.3	173.7	175.0	227.1	229.3	287.8	345.7	378.7
of which: Short-term	8 771	..	...	...	...	...	...	...	...	...
Banks	8 772	..	...	...	...	...	...	...	...	...
of which: Short-term	8 774	..	...	...	...	...	...	...	...	...
Other sectors	8 775	..	...	...	...	...	...	...	...	...
of which: Short-term	8 777	..	...	...	...	...	...	...	...	...
Currency and deposits	8 780	..	62,406.5	59,504.7	60,561.1	65,736.6	81,131.0	82,006.8	85,256.0	80,966.4
Monetary authorities	8 781	..	...	...	...	...	...	...	...	...
General government	8 782	..	...	...	...	...	...	...	...	...
Banks	8 783	..	62,406.5	59,504.7	60,561.1	65,736.6	81,131.0	82,006.8	85,256.0	80,966.4
Other sectors	8 784	..	...	...	...	...	...	...	...	...
Other liabilities	8 786	..	...	...	...	...	...	...	9.3	9.8
Monetary authorities	8 787	..	...	...	...	...	...	...	...	...
of which: Short-term	8 789	..	...	...	...	...	...	...	...	...
General government	8 790	..	...	...	...	...	...	...	...	...
of which: Short-term	8 792	..	...	...	...	...	...	...	...	...
Banks	8 793	..	...	...	...	...	...	...	...	...
of which: Short-term	8 795	..	...	...	...	...	...	...	...	...
Other sectors	8 796	..	...	...	...	...	...	...	9.3	9.8
of which: Short-term	8 798	..	...	...	...	...	...	...	...	...
NET INTERNATIONAL INVESTMENT POSITION	8 995	..	**2,205.6**	**3,791.0**	**4,330.8**	**4,411.5**	**5,054.5**	**4,871.0**	**5,155.2**	**5,515.8**
Conversion rates: Bahrain dinar per U.S. dollar (end of period)	0 102	..	**.3760**	**.3760**	**.3760**	**.3760**	**.3760**	**.3760**	**.3760**	**.3760**

Table 1. ANALYTIC PRESENTATION, 1994–2001
(Millions of U.S. dollars)

	Code	1994	1995	1996	1997	1998	1999	2000	2001
A. Current Account [1]	4 993 Z.	**199.6**	**–823.9**	**–991.4**	**–286.3**	**–35.2**	**–364.4**	**–305.8**	**–490.1**
Goods: exports f.o.b	2 100 ..	2,934.4	3,733.3	4,009.3	4,839.9	5,141.4	5,458.3	6,399.2	6,084.7
Goods: imports f.o.b	3 100 ..	–4,350.5	–6,057.4	–6,284.6	–6,550.7	–6,715.7	–7,535.5	–8,052.9	–8,133.4
Balance on Goods	4 100 ..	*–1,416.1*	*–2,324.1*	*–2,275.3*	*–1,710.8*	*–1,574.3*	*–2,077.2*	*–1,653.7*	*–2,048.7*
Services: credit	2 200 ..	589.8	698.2	604.8	687.3	723.9	777.7	815.1	751.4
Services: debit	3 200 ..	–1,025.0	–1,531.2	–1,166.0	–1,283.7	–1,237.1	–1,396.7	–1,620.2	–1,473.6
Balance on Goods and Services	4 991 ..	*–1,851.3*	*–3,157.1*	*–2,836.5*	*–2,307.2*	*–2,087.4*	*–2,696.3*	*–2,458.9*	*–2,770.9*
Income: credit	2 300 ..	150.5	270.1	129.4	86.6	91.5	94.3	78.4	74.8
Income: debit	3 300 ..	–188.7	–201.8	–193.1	–198.0	–206.1	–258.5	–344.8	–361.9
Balance on Goods, Services, and Income	4 992 ..	*–1,889.6*	*–3,088.8*	*–2,900.2*	*–2,418.6*	*–2,202.1*	*–2,860.4*	*–2,725.3*	*–3,058.0*
Current transfers: credit	2 379 Z.	2,091.4	2,266.7	1,912.8	2,136.5	2,172.9	2,501.4	2,426.5	2,572.8
Current transfers: debit	3 379 ..	–2.2	–1.8	–4.0	–4.3	–5.9	–5.3	–7.0	–4.9
B. Capital Account [1]	4 994 Z.	**...**	**...**	**371.2**	**366.8**	**238.7**	**364.1**	**248.7**	**235.4**
Capital account: credit	2 994 Z.	...	...	371.2	366.8	238.7	364.1	248.7	235.4
Capital account: debit	3 994 ..	...	...	...	...	...	...	...	...
Total, Groups A Plus B	4 981 ..	*199.6*	*–823.9*	*–620.2*	*80.5*	*203.5*	*–.2*	*–57.1*	*–254.7*
C. Financial Account [1]	4 995 W.	**748.8**	**178.8**	**92.4**	**–140.2**	**–116.0**	**–446.9**	**–256.0**	**261.5**
Direct investment abroad	4 505 ..	...	...	...	–3.1	–3.0	–.1	...	...
Direct investment in Bangladesh	4 555 Z.	11.1	1.9	13.5	139.4	190.1	179.7	280.4	77.5
Portfolio investment assets	4 602 ..	...	...	...	...	...	–.2	...	...
Equity securities	4 610 ..	...	...	...	...	...	–.2	...	...
Debt securities	4 619 ..	...	...	...	...	...	...	...	...
Portfolio investment liabilities	4 652 Z.	105.9	–15.2	–117.0	–9.9	–4.1	–1.1	1.3	–3.5
Equity securities	4 660 ..	105.9	–15.2	–117.0	–9.9	–4.2	–1.1	1.2	–3.5
Debt securities	4 669 Z.	...	...	...	...	.1	...	.1	...
Financial derivatives	4 910 ..	...	...	...	...	...	...	...	...
Financial derivatives assets	4 900 ..	...	...	...	...	...	...	...	...
Financial derivatives liabilities	4 905 ..	...	...	...	...	...	...	...	...
Other investment assets	4 703 ..	–1.6	–243.9	–426.7	–677.8	–859.7	–1,143.7	–1,246.8	–433.9
Monetary authorities	4 701 ..	...	...	...	...	...	...	...	...
General government	4 704 ..	–.1	...	...	...	...	...	...	...
Banks	4 705 ..	–1.5	–243.9	–41.1	–70.2	–38.1	–131.4	–315.7	151.7
Other sectors	4 728 ..	...	...	–385.6	–607.6	–821.6	–1,012.3	–931.0	–585.6
Other investment liabilities	4 753 W.	633.4	436.1	622.6	411.2	560.7	518.4	709.1	621.4
Monetary authorities	4 753 WA	15.0	58.3	–4.3	–25.5	126.6	–118.9	35.2	132.7
General government	4 753 ZB	718.5	374.2	511.3	294.1	404.6	524.7	537.9	413.7
Banks	4 753 ZC	–116.3	–34.2	83.0	118.4	2.6	30.7	105.7	29.6
Other sectors	4 753 ZD	16.2	37.9	32.7	24.2	26.9	82.0	30.4	45.3
Total, Groups A Through C	4 983 ..	*948.4*	*–645.1*	*–527.8*	*–59.7*	*87.5*	*–447.1*	*–313.1*	*6.8*
D. Net Errors and Omissions	4 998 ..	**–257.1**	**133.3**	**113.5**	**–75.5**	**201.0**	**258.0**	**282.4**	**–150.7**
Total, Groups A Through D	4 984 ..	*691.3*	*–511.7*	*–414.3*	*–135.1*	*288.5*	*–189.2*	*–30.7*	*–143.9*
E. Reserves and Related Items	4 802 A.	**–691.3**	**511.7**	**414.3**	**135.1**	**–288.5**	**189.2**	**30.7**	**143.9**
Reserve assets	4 802 ..	–636.2	572.8	499.9	253.8	–319.1	286.0	121.0	207.9
Use of Fund credit and loans	4 766 ..	–55.1	–61.0	–85.6	–118.7	30.6	–96.8	–90.3	–64.0
Exceptional financing	4 920 ..	...	...	...	...	...	...	...	...
Conversion rates: taka per U.S. dollar	0 101 ..	**40.212**	**40.278**	**41.794**	**43.892**	**46.906**	**49.085**	**52.142**	**55.807**

[1] Excludes components that have been classified in the categories of Group E.

Table 2. STANDARD PRESENTATION, 1994–2001

(Millions of U.S. dollars)

	Code		1994	1995	1996	1997	1998	1999	2000	2001
CURRENT ACCOUNT	4 993	. .	**199.6**	**–823.9**	**–991.4**	**–286.3**	**–35.2**	**–364.4**	**–305.8**	**–490.1**
A. GOODS	4 100	. .	–1,416.1	–2,324.1	–2,275.3	–1,710.8	–1,574.3	–2,077.2	–1,653.7	–2,048.7
Credit	2 100	. .	**2,934.4**	**3,733.3**	**4,009.3**	**4,839.9**	**5,141.4**	**5,458.3**	**6,399.2**	**6,084.7**
General merchandise: exports f.o.b.	2 110	. .	2,934.4	3,733.3	4,004.4	4,836.8	5,138.8	5,454.9	6,392.7	6,078.7
Goods for processing: exports f.o.b.	2 150	. .	. . .	. . .	. . .	. . .	. . .	. . .	. . .	. . .
Repairs on goods	2 160	. .	. . .	. . .	.6	.2	.6	.6	.7	1.1
Goods procured in ports by carriers	2 170	. .	. . .	. . .	4.3	3.0	2.1	2.8	5.7	5.0
Nonmonetary gold	2 180	. .	. . .	. . .	. . .	. . .	. . .	. . .	. . .	. . .
Debit	3 100	. .	**–4,350.5**	**–6,057.4**	**–6,284.6**	**–6,550.7**	**–6,715.7**	**–7,535.5**	**–8,052.9**	**–8,133.4**
General merchandise: imports f.o.b.	3 110	. .	–4,350.5	–6,057.4	–6,260.8	–6,544.6	–6,713.5	–7,517.6	–8,023.0	–8,109.3
Goods for processing: imports f.o.b.	3 150	. .	. . .	. . .	. . .	. . .	. . .	. . .	. . .	. . .
Repairs on goods	3 160	. .	. . .	. . .	–21.8	–3.5	–2.2	–16.8	–27.5	–16.7
Goods procured in ports by carriers	3 170	. .	. . .	. . .	–2.0	–2.6	. . .	–1.2	–2.4	–7.5
Nonmonetary gold	3 180	. .	. . .	. . .	. . .	. . .	. . .	. . .	. . .	. . .
B. SERVICES	4 200	. .	–435.2	–833.0	–561.2	–596.4	–513.2	–619.1	–805.1	–722.2
Total credit	2 200	. .	*589.8*	*698.2*	*604.8*	*687.3*	*723.9*	*777.7*	*815.1*	*751.4*
Total debit	3 200	. .	*–1,025.0*	*–1,531.2*	*–1,166.0*	*–1,283.7*	*–1,237.1*	*–1,396.7*	*–1,620.2*	*–1,473.6*
Transportation services, credit	2 205	. .	**55.1**	**70.2**	**80.1**	**90.8**	**92.3**	**94.5**	**91.4**	**71.6**
Passenger	2 850	. .	. . .	. . .	*.2*	. . .	. . .	. . .	. . .	. . .
Freight	2 851	. .	*4.8*	*3.7*	*10.6*	*15.7*	*15.4*	*13.5*	*10.0*	*1.5*
Other	2 852	. .	*50.3*	*66.5*	*69.3*	*75.1*	*76.9*	*81.0*	*81.4*	*70.1*
Sea transport, passenger	2 207	. .	. . .	. . .	. . .	. . .	. . .	. . .	. . .	. . .
Sea transport, freight	2 208	. .	. . .	. . .	3.0	7.1	5.4	5.4	5.5	1.5
Sea transport, other	2 209	. .	. . .	. . .	61.2	70.2	71.5	69.2	61.9	59.7
Air transport, passenger	2 211	. .	. . .	. . .	.1	. . .	. . .	. . .	. . .	. . .
Air transport, freight	2 212	. .	. . .	. . .	1.2	5.4	8.9	8.0	4.5	. . .
Air transport, other	2 213	. .	. . .	. . .	7.0	4.0	4.5	11.8	19.1	10.4
Other transport, passenger	2 215	. .	. . .	. . .	.1	. . .	. . .	. . .	. . .	. . .
Other transport, freight	2 216	. .	. . .	. . .	6.4	3.1	1.1	. . .	. . .	. . .
Other transport, other	2 217	. .	. . .	. . .	1.1	.9	.8	. . .	.3	. . .
Transportation services, debit	3 205	. .	**–549.6**	**–775.4**	**–767.6**	**–850.2**	**–845.8**	**–933.8**	**–1,012.8**	**–1,032.1**
Passenger	3 850	. .	. . .	. . .	*–116.4*	*–135.9*	*–143.4*	*–163.5*	*–181.3*	*–175.9*
Freight	3 851	. .	*–436.8*	*–603.9*	*–639.9*	*–700.6*	*–688.4*	*–760.4*	*–822.7*	*–833.7*
Other	3 852	. .	*–112.8*	*–171.5*	*–11.3*	*–13.8*	*–14.0*	*–9.8*	*–8.7*	*–22.5*
Sea transport, passenger	3 207	. .	. . .	. . .	. . .	. . .	. . .	. . .	. . .	. . .
Sea transport, freight	3 208	. .	. . .	. . .	–637.3	–698.4	–688.4	–760.4	–822.7	–833.7
Sea transport, other	3 209	. .	. . .	. . .	–1.5	–2.6	–1.7	–1.3	–3.3	–1.3
Air transport, passenger	3 211	. .	. . .	. . .	–116.4	–135.9	–143.4	–163.5	–181.3	–175.9
Air transport, freight	3 212	. .	. . .	. . .	–2.6	–2.2	. . .	. . .	–.1	. . .
Air transport, other	3 213	. .	. . .	. . .	–9.8	–11.2	–12.3	–8.5	–5.4	–21.2
Other transport, passenger	3 215	. .	. . .	. . .	. . .	. . .	. . .	. . .	. . .	. . .
Other transport, freight	3 216	. .	. . .	. . .	. . .	. . .	. . .	. . .	. . .	. . .
Other transport, other	3 217	. .	. . .	. . .	. . .	. . .	. . .	. . .	. . .	. . .
Travel, credit	2 236	. .	**21.3**	**25.1**	**33.4**	**62.2**	**52.4**	**50.0**	**50.4**	**47.6**
Business travel	2 237	. .	. . .	. . .	.4	.4	.7	3.4	2.6	1.5
Personal travel	2 240	. .	. . .	. . .	33.0	61.8	51.7	46.5	47.8	46.1
Travel, debit	3 236	. .	**–193.6**	**–233.5**	**–135.4**	**–178.2**	**–150.9**	**–210.9**	**–289.9**	**–165.4**
Business travel	3 237	. .	. . .	. . .	–17.3	–18.9	–19.8	–21.0	–33.0	–29.9
Personal travel	3 240	. .	. . .	. . .	–118.1	–159.3	–131.2	–189.9	–256.9	–135.5
Other services, credit	2 200	BA	**513.4**	**602.9**	**491.3**	**534.3**	**579.3**	**633.2**	**673.3**	**632.1**
Communications	2 245	. .	. . .	. . .	28.4	36.1	28.5	46.1	21.5	10.8
Construction	2 249	. .	. . .	. . .	. . .	2.6	.3	. . .	.2	. . .
Insurance	2 253	. .	.5	.4	.6	.5	2.9	1.7	3.5	1.7
Financial	2 260	. .	. . .	. . .	12.0	12.4	11.4	18.8	13.1	9.9
Computer and information	2 262	. .	. . .	. . .	.5	1.3	.9	1.6	3.2	2.5
Royalties and licence fees	2 266	. .	. . .	. . .	. . .	. . .	. . .	.1	.1	. . .
Other business services	2 268	. .	341.8	372.8	67.7	60.2	62.4	53.0	99.3	97.8
Personal, cultural, and recreational	2 287	. .	. . .	. . .	.1	.3	.8	.5	.5	.4
Government, n.i.e.	2 291	. .	171.0	229.7	382.0	420.8	472.2	511.5	531.9	509.0
Other services, debit	3 200	BA	**–281.8**	**–522.3**	**–263.1**	**–255.3**	**–240.3**	**–252.0**	**–317.5**	**–276.1**
Communications	3 245	. .	. . .	. . .	–4.6	–10.8	–12.7	–7.8	–7.4	–5.6
Construction	3 249	. .	. . .	. . .	–10.5	–1.3	–12.2	–5.6	–2.1	–3.2
Insurance	3 253	. .	–48.5	–67.1	–75.4	–81.0	–79.4	–88.7	–91.1	–97.6
Financial	3 260	. .	. . .	. . .	–25.9	–21.6	–21.1	–16.4	–30.8	–16.0
Computer and information	3 262	. .	. . .	. . .	–.3	–.7	–1.4	–1.4	–1.5	–1.2
Royalties and licence fees	3 266	. .	. . .	. . .	–4.6	–7.7	–5.1	–5.5	–4.4	–5.5
Other business services	3 268	. .	–64.9	–116.1	–33.7	–32.1	–35.5	–47.7	–83.3	–48.8
Personal, cultural, and recreational	3 287	. .	. . .	. . .	–.8	–.5	. . .	. . .	–.1	. . .
Government, n.i.e.	3 291	. .	–168.4	–339.0	–107.4	–99.5	–72.9	–78.9	–96.9	–98.2

Table 2 (Continued). STANDARD PRESENTATION, 1994–2001
(Millions of U.S. dollars)

	Code	1994	1995	1996	1997	1998	1999	2000	2001
C. INCOME	4 300 . .	−38.3	68.3	−63.7	−111.4	−114.7	−164.1	−266.5	−287.1
Total credit	2 300 . .	*150.5*	*270.1*	*129.4*	*86.6*	*91.5*	*94.3*	*78.4*	*74.8*
Total debit	3 300 . .	*−188.7*	*−201.8*	*−193.1*	*−198.0*	*−206.1*	*−258.5*	*−344.8*	*−361.9*
Compensation of employees, credit	2 310 . .	**. . .**	**. . .**	**. . .**	**.7**	**6.1**	**10.1**	**9.4**	**10.4**
Compensation of employees, debit	3 310 . .	**. . .**	**. . .**	**. . .**	**−.3**	**−1.0**	**−1.8**	**−1.8**	**−1.8**
Investment income, credit	2 320 . .	**150.5**	**270.1**	**129.4**	**85.9**	**85.3**	**84.2**	**68.9**	**64.4**
Direct investment income	2 330 . .	. . .	. . .	.2	.3	1.6	2.0	1.8	. . .
Dividends and distributed branch profits	2 332 . .	. . .	. . .	.2	.3	1.6	2.0	1.8	. . .
Reinvested earnings and undistributed branch profits	2 333 . .	. . .	. . .	. . .	. . .	. . .	. . .	. . .	. . .
Income on debt (interest)	2 334 . .	. . .	. . .	. . .	. . .	. . .	. . .	. . .	. . .
Portfolio investment income	2 339 . .	. . .	. . .	.6	.4	.3	.1	. . .	. . .
Income on equity	2 340 . .	. . .	. . .	.6	.3	.2	.1	. . .	. . .
Income on bonds and notes	2 350 . .	. . .	. . .	. . .	.1	.1	. . .	. . .	. . .
Income on money market instruments	2 360 . .	. . .	. . .	. . .	. . .	. . .	. . .	. . .	. . .
Other investment income	2 370 . .	150.5	270.1	128.6	85.2	83.4	82.1	67.1	64.4
Investment income, debit	3 320 . .	**−188.7**	**−201.8**	**−193.1**	**−197.7**	**−205.1**	**−256.7**	**−343.0**	**−360.1**
Direct investment income	3 330 . .	. . .	. . .	−18.6	−26.5	−40.1	−82.4	−149.0	−175.2
Dividends and distributed branch profits	3 332 . .	. . .	. . .	−17.9	−26.5	−40.1	−82.4	−149.0	−175.2
Reinvested earnings and undistributed branch profits	3 333 . .	. . .	. . .	. . .	. . .	. . .	. . .	. . .	. . .
Income on debt (interest)	3 334 . .	. . .	. . .	−.7	. . .	. . .	. . .	. . .	. . .
Portfolio investment income	3 339 . .	. . .	. . .	−2.9	−.6	−1.2	−.7	−.8	−.8
Income on equity	3 340 . .	. . .	. . .	−2.8	−.6	−1.2	−.7	−.8	−.8
Income on bonds and notes	3 350 . .	. . .	. . .	−.1	. . .	. . .	. . .	. . .	. . .
Income on money market instruments	3 360 . .	. . .	. . .	. . .	. . .	. . .	. . .	. . .	. . .
Other investment income	3 370 . .	−188.7	−201.8	−171.5	−170.5	−163.8	−173.6	−193.3	−184.0
D. CURRENT TRANSFERS	4 379 . .	2,089.2	2,264.9	1,908.8	2,132.3	2,167.0	2,496.1	2,419.5	2,567.9
Credit	2 379 . .	**2,091.4**	**2,266.7**	**1,912.8**	**2,136.5**	**2,172.9**	**2,501.4**	**2,426.5**	**2,572.8**
General government	2 380 . .	739.6	810.8	292.3	330.2	311.1	438.5	212.0	243.1
Other sectors	2 390 . .	1,351.7	1,456.0	1,620.4	1,806.3	1,861.8	2,062.9	2,214.5	2,329.6
Workers' remittances	2 391 . .	1,150.9	1,201.7	1,344.7	1,525.8	1,599.7	1,796.7	1,958.1	2,094.1
Other current transfers	2 392 . .	200.8	254.3	275.8	280.5	262.1	266.2	256.4	235.5
Debit	3 379 . .	**−2.2**	**−1.8**	**−4.0**	**−4.3**	**−5.9**	**−5.3**	**−7.0**	**−4.9**
General government	3 380 . .	. . .	. . .	−.7	−.5	−.9	−1.1	−.7	−.5
Other sectors	3 390 . .	−2.2	−1.8	−3.3	−3.7	−5.0	−4.3	−6.2	−4.4
Workers' remittances	3 391 . .	. . .	. . .	−.8	−1.4	−1.5	−1.9	−2.6	−1.9
Other current transfers	3 392 . .	−2.2	−1.8	−2.5	−2.3	−3.5	−2.3	−3.7	−2.5
CAPITAL AND FINANCIAL ACCOUNT	4 996 . .	**57.5**	**690.5**	**878.0**	**361.8**	**−165.8**	**106.4**	**23.5**	**640.8**
CAPITAL ACCOUNT	4 994 . .	**. . .**	**. . .**	**371.2**	**366.8**	**238.7**	**364.1**	**248.7**	**235.4**
Total credit	2 994 . .	. . .	. . .	*371.2*	*366.8*	*238.7*	*364.1*	*248.7*	*235.4*
Total debit	3 994 . .	. . .	. . .	. . .	. . .	. . .	. . .	. . .	. . .
Capital transfers, credit	2 400 . .	. . .	. . .	**371.2**	**366.8**	**238.7**	**364.1**	**248.7**	**235.4**
General government	2 401 . .	. . .	. . .	370.9	365.7	238.4	364.1	248.6	235.4
Debt forgiveness	2 402 . .	. . .	. . .	. . .	. . .	. . .	. . .	. . .	. . .
Other capital transfers	2 410 . .	. . .	. . .	370.9	365.7	238.4	364.1	248.6	235.4
Other sectors	2 430 . .	. . .	. . .	.4	1.2	.3	. . .	.1	. . .
Migrants' transfers	2 431 . .	. . .	. . .	. . .	. . .	.3	. . .	. . .	. . .
Debt forgiveness	2 432 . .	. . .	. . .	. . .	. . .	. . .	. . .	. . .	. . .
Other capital transfers	2 440 . .	. . .	. . .	.4	1.2	. . .	. . .	.1	. . .
Capital transfers, debit	3 400 . .	**. . .**	**. . .**	**. . .**	**. . .**	**. . .**	**. . .**	**. . .**	**. . .**
General government	3 401 . .	. . .	. . .	. . .	. . .	. . .	. . .	. . .	. . .
Debt forgiveness	3 402 . .	. . .	. . .	. . .	. . .	. . .	. . .	. . .	. . .
Other capital transfers	3 410 . .	. . .	. . .	. . .	. . .	. . .	. . .	. . .	. . .
Other sectors	3 430 . .	. . .	. . .	. . .	. . .	. . .	. . .	. . .	. . .
Migrants' transfers	3 431 . .	. . .	. . .	. . .	. . .	. . .	. . .	. . .	. . .
Debt forgiveness	3 432 . .	. . .	. . .	. . .	. . .	. . .	. . .	. . .	. . .
Other capital transfers	3 440 . .	. . .	. . .	. . .	. . .	. . .	. . .	. . .	. . .
Nonproduced nonfinancial assets, credit	2 480 . .	**. . .**	**. . .**	**. . .**	**. . .**	**. . .**	**. . .**	**. . .**	**. . .**
Nonproduced nonfinancial assets, debit	3 480 . .	**. . .**	**. . .**	**. . .**	**. . .**	**. . .**	**. . .**	**. . .**	**. . .**

Table 2 (Continued). STANDARD PRESENTATION, 1994–2001
(Millions of U.S. dollars)

	Code	1994	1995	1996	1997	1998	1999	2000	2001
FINANCIAL ACCOUNT	4 995	**57.5**	**690.5**	**506.7**	**–5.1**	**–404.5**	**–257.8**	**–225.2**	**405.4**
A. DIRECT INVESTMENT	4 500	11.1	1.9	13.5	136.3	187.1	179.6	280.4	77.5
Direct investment abroad	4 505	**. . .**	**. . .**	**. . .**	**–3.1**	**–3.0**	**–.1**	**. . .**	**. . .**
Equity capital	4 510	. . .	. . .	. . .	–3.0	–3.0	–.1	. . .	. . .
Claims on affiliated enterprises	4 515	. . .	. . .	. . .	–3.0	–3.0	. . .	. . .	. . .
Liabilities to affiliated enterprises	4 520	. . .	. . .	. . .	. . .	. . .	–.1	. . .	. . .
Reinvested earnings	4 525	. . .	. . .	. . .	. . .	. . .	. . .	. . .	. . .
Other capital	4 530	. . .	. . .	. . .	. . .	. . .	. . .	. . .	. . .
Claims on affiliated enterprises	4 535	. . .	. . .	. . .	. . .	. . .	. . .	. . .	. . .
Liabilities to affiliated enterprises	4 540	. . .	. . .	. . .	. . .	. . .	. . .	. . .	. . .
Direct investment in Bangladesh	4 555	**11.1**	**1.9**	**13.5**	**139.4**	**190.1**	**179.7**	**280.4**	**77.5**
Equity capital	4 560	5.8	1.8	11.7	139.4	188.2	179.4	278.9	77.5
Claims on direct investors	4 565	. . .	. . .	. . .	. . .	. . .	. . .	. . .	. . .
Liabilities to direct investors	4 570	. . .	. . .	11.7	139.4	188.2	179.4	278.9	77.5
Reinvested earnings	4 575	. . .	. . .	. . .	. . .	. . .	. . .	. . .	. . .
Other capital	4 580	5.4	.1	1.8	. . .	1.9	.2	1.5	. . .
Claims on direct investors	4 585	. . .	. . .	. . .	. . .	. . .	. . .	. . .	. . .
Liabilities to direct investors	4 590	. . .	. . .	1.8	. . .	1.9	.2	1.5	. . .
B. PORTFOLIO INVESTMENT	4 600	105.9	–15.2	–117.0	–9.9	–4.1	–1.3	1.3	–3.5
Assets	4 602	**. . .**	**. . .**	**. . .**	**. . .**	**. . .**	**–.2**	**. . .**	**. . .**
Equity securities	4 610	. . .	. . .	. . .	. . .	. . .	–.2	. . .	. . .
Monetary authorities	4 611	. . .	. . .	. . .	. . .	. . .	. . .	. . .	. . .
General government	4 612	. . .	. . .	. . .	. . .	. . .	. . .	. . .	. . .
Banks	4 613	. . .	. . .	. . .	. . .	. . .	–.2	. . .	. . .
Other sectors	4 614	. . .	. . .	. . .	. . .	. . .	. . .	. . .	. . .
Debt securities	4 619	. . .	. . .	. . .	. . .	. . .	. . .	. . .	. . .
Bonds and notes	4 620	. . .	. . .	. . .	. . .	. . .	. . .	. . .	. . .
Monetary authorities	4 621	. . .	. . .	. . .	. . .	. . .	. . .	. . .	. . .
General government	4 622	. . .	. . .	. . .	. . .	. . .	. . .	. . .	. . .
Banks	4 623	. . .	. . .	. . .	. . .	. . .	. . .	. . .	. . .
Other sectors	4 624	. . .	. . .	. . .	. . .	. . .	. . .	. . .	. . .
Money market instruments	4 630	. . .	. . .	. . .	. . .	. . .	. . .	. . .	. . .
Monetary authorities	4 631	. . .	. . .	. . .	. . .	. . .	. . .	. . .	. . .
General government	4 632	. . .	. . .	. . .	. . .	. . .	. . .	. . .	. . .
Banks	4 633	. . .	. . .	. . .	. . .	. . .	. . .	. . .	. . .
Other sectors	4 634	. . .	. . .	. . .	. . .	. . .	. . .	. . .	. . .
Liabilities	4 652	**105.9**	**–15.2**	**–117.0**	**–9.9**	**–4.1**	**–1.1**	**1.3**	**–3.5**
Equity securities	4 660	105.9	–15.2	–117.0	–9.9	–4.2	–1.1	1.2	–3.5
Banks	4 663	. . .	. . .	.2	. . .	. . .	. . .	. . .	. . .
Other sectors	4 664	. . .	. . .	–117.2	–9.9	–4.2	–1.1	1.2	–3.5
Debt securities	4 669	. . .	. . .	. . .	. . .	.1	. . .	.1	. . .
Bonds and notes	4 670	. . .	. . .	. . .	. . .	.1	. . .	.1	. . .
Monetary authorities	4 671	. . .	. . .	. . .	. . .	. . .	. . .	. . .	. . .
General government	4 672	. . .	. . .	. . .	. . .	.1	. . .	. . .	. . .
Banks	4 673	. . .	. . .	. . .	. . .	. . .	. . .	.1	. . .
Other sectors	4 674	. . .	. . .	. . .	. . .	. . .	. . .	. . .	. . .
Money market instruments	4 680	. . .	. . .	. . .	. . .	. . .	. . .	. . .	. . .
Monetary authorities	4 681	. . .	. . .	. . .	. . .	. . .	. . .	. . .	. . .
General government	4 682	. . .	. . .	. . .	. . .	. . .	. . .	. . .	. . .
Banks	4 683	. . .	. . .	. . .	. . .	. . .	. . .	. . .	. . .
Other sectors	4 684	. . .	. . .	. . .	. . .	. . .	. . .	. . .	. . .
C. FINANCIAL DERIVATIVES	4 910	. . .	. . .	. . .	. . .	. . .	. . .	. . .	. . .
Monetary authorities	4 911	. . .	. . .	. . .	. . .	. . .	. . .	. . .	. . .
General government	4 912	. . .	. . .	. . .	. . .	. . .	. . .	. . .	. . .
Banks	4 913	. . .	. . .	. . .	. . .	. . .	. . .	. . .	. . .
Other sectors	4 914	. . .	. . .	. . .	. . .	. . .	. . .	. . .	. . .
Assets	4 900	**. . .**	**. . .**	**. . .**	**. . .**	**. . .**	**. . .**	**. . .**	**. . .**
Monetary authorities	4 901	. . .	. . .	. . .	. . .	. . .	. . .	. . .	. . .
General government	4 902	. . .	. . .	. . .	. . .	. . .	. . .	. . .	. . .
Banks	4 903	. . .	. . .	. . .	. . .	. . .	. . .	. . .	. . .
Other sectors	4 904	. . .	. . .	. . .	. . .	. . .	. . .	. . .	. . .
Liabilities	4 905	**. . .**	**. . .**	**. . .**	**. . .**	**. . .**	**. . .**	**. . .**	**. . .**
Monetary authorities	4 906	. . .	. . .	. . .	. . .	. . .	. . .	. . .	. . .
General government	4 907	. . .	. . .	. . .	. . .	. . .	. . .	. . .	. . .
Banks	4 908	. . .	. . .	. . .	. . .	. . .	. . .	. . .	. . .
Other sectors	4 909	. . .	. . .	. . .	. . .	. . .	. . .	. . .	. . .

Table 2 (Concluded). STANDARD PRESENTATION, 1994–2001
(Millions of U.S. dollars)

	Code	1994	1995	1996	1997	1998	1999	2000	2001
D. OTHER INVESTMENT	4 700	576.7	131.1	110.3	–385.3	–268.3	–722.1	–627.9	123.6
Assets	4 703	**–1.6**	**–243.9**	**–426.7**	**–677.8**	**–859.7**	**–1,143.7**	**–1,246.8**	**–433.9**
Trade credits	4 706	...	...	–385.6	–607.6	–821.6	–1,012.7	–935.7	–585.9
General government	4 707	...	...	...	...	...	...	...	...
of which: Short-term	4 709	...	...	...	...	...	...	...	...
Other sectors	4 710	...	...	–385.6	–607.6	–821.6	–1,012.7	–935.7	–585.9
of which: Short-term	4 712	...	...	*–385.6*	*–607.6*	*–821.6*	*–1,012.7*	*–935.7*	*–585.9*
Loans	4 714	...	...	...	–13.6	–71.5	–10.0	–27.1	30.9
Monetary authorities	4 715	...	...	...	...	...	...	...	...
of which: Short-term	4 718	...	...	...	...	...	...	...	...
General government	4 719	...	...	...	...	...	...	...	...
of which: Short-term	4 721	...	...	...	...	...	...	...	...
Banks	4 722	...	...	...	–13.6	–71.5	–10.5	–31.8	30.6
of which: Short-term	4 724	...	...	...	*–13.6*	*–72.4*	*–10.7*	*–31.8*	*30.6*
Other sectors	4 725	...	...	...	...	...	.4	4.7	.3
of which: Short-term	4 727	...	...	...	...	...	*.3*	...	*.3*
Currency and deposits	4 730	–1.5	–243.9	–41.1	–56.6	33.4	–120.9	–284.0	121.2
Monetary authorities	4 731	...	...	...	...	...	...	...	...
General government	4 732	...	...	...	...	...	...	...	...
Banks	4 733	–1.5	–243.9	–41.1	–56.6	33.4	–120.9	–284.0	121.2
Other sectors	4 734	...	...	...	...	...	...	...	...
Other assets	4 736	–.1	...	...	...	...	...	...	...
Monetary authorities	4 737	...	...	...	...	...	...	...	...
of which: Short-term	4 739	...	...	...	...	...	...	...	...
General government	4 740	–.1	...	...	...	...	...	...	...
of which: Short-term	4 742	...	...	...	...	...	...	...	...
Banks	4 743	...	...	...	...	...	...	...	...
of which: Short-term	4 745	...	...	...	...	...	...	...	...
Other sectors	4 746	...	...	...	...	...	...	...	...
of which: Short-term	4 748	...	...	...	...	...	...	...	...
Liabilities	4 753	**578.3**	**375.0**	**537.0**	**292.6**	**591.3**	**421.6**	**618.9**	**557.4**
Trade credits	4 756	...	...	...	...	...	...	...	...
General government	4 757	...	...	...	...	...	...	...	...
of which: Short-term	4 759	...	...	...	...	...	...	...	...
Other sectors	4 760	...	...	...	...	...	...	...	...
of which: Short-term	4 762	...	...	...	...	...	...	...	...
Loans	4 764	678.2	351.8	465.1	204.8	535.1	515.3	477.4	321.4
Monetary authorities	4 765	–55.1	–61.0	–85.6	–118.7	30.6	–96.8	–90.3	–64.0
of which: Use of Fund credit and loans from the Fund	4 766	*–55.1*	*–61.0*	*–85.6*	*–118.7*	*30.6*	*–96.8*	*–90.3*	*–64.0*
of which: Short-term	4 768	...	...	...	...	...	...	...	...
General government	4 769	718.5	374.2	511.3	294.1	404.6	524.7	537.9	413.7
of which: Short-term	4 771	...	...	...	...	...	...	...	...
Banks	4 772	...	...	6.7	5.1	72.9	5.5	–.6	–73.6
of which: Short-term	4 774	...	...	*6.6*	*–5.2*	*73.3*	*5.9*	*–.2*	*–73.6*
Other sectors	4 775	14.8	38.7	32.7	24.2	26.9	82.0	30.4	45.3
of which: Short-term	4 777	...	...	*15.6*	*–5.2*	*32.0*	*56.9*	*15.9*	*46.9*
Currency and deposits	4 780	–116.3	–34.2	76.3	113.9	–70.8	27.9	104.4	103.2
Monetary authorities	4 781	...	...	...	.6	–.4	2.7	–2.0	...
General government	4 782	...	...	...	...	...	...	...	...
Banks	4 783	–116.3	–34.2	76.3	113.3	–70.4	25.2	106.3	103.2
Other sectors	4 784	...	...	...	...	...	...	...	...
Other liabilities	4 786	16.4	57.4	–4.4	–26.1	127.0	–121.6	37.1	132.7
Monetary authorities	4 787	15.0	58.3	–4.4	–26.1	127.0	–121.6	37.1	132.7
of which: Short-term	4 789	*15.0*	*58.3*	*–4.4*	*–26.1*	*127.0*	*–121.6*	*37.1*	*132.7*
General government	4 790	...	...	...	...	...	...	...	...
of which: Short-term	4 792	...	...	...	...	...	...	...	...
Banks	4 793	...	...	...	...	...	...	...	...
of which: Short-term	4 795	...	...	...	...	...	...	...	...
Other sectors	4 796	1.4	–.8	...	...	...	...	...	...
of which: Short-term	4 798	...	...	...	...	...	...	...	...
E. RESERVE ASSETS	4 802	–636.2	572.8	499.9	253.8	–319.1	286.0	121.0	207.9
Monetary gold	4 812	...	...	1.3	5.6	–.8	–1.1	1.8	–1.3
Special drawing rights	4 811	–12.1	–125.4	45.2	75.2	16.3	11.0	–.3	–1.1
Reserve position in the Fund	4 810	...	...	...	...	–.1	...	...	...
Foreign exchange	4 803	–617.2	746.1	453.4	172.9	–334.5	276.2	119.5	210.3
Other claims	4 813	–6.8	–47.9	...	...	...	...	...	...
NET ERRORS AND OMISSIONS	4 998	**–257.1**	**133.3**	**113.5**	**–75.5**	**201.0**	**258.0**	**282.4**	**–150.7**

Part 3 of the *Yearbook* contains descriptions of the methodologies, compilation practices, and sources used to compile these data.

Table 3. INTERNATIONAL INVESTMENT POSITION (End–period stocks), 1994–2001
(Millions of U.S. dollars)

	Code	1994	1995	1996	1997	1998	1999	2000	2001
ASSETS	8 995 C.	...	...	...	...	...	...	...	...
Direct investment abroad	8 505 . .	...	...	...	...	...	...	...	...
Equity capital and reinvested earnings	8 506 . .	...	...	...	...	...	...	...	...
Claims on affiliated enterprises	8 507 . .	...	...	...	...	...	...	...	...
Liabilities to affiliated enterprises	8 508 . .	...	...	...	...	...	...	...	...
Other capital	8 530 . .	...	...	...	...	...	...	...	...
Claims on affiliated enterprises	8 535 . .	...	...	...	...	...	...	...	...
Liabilities to affiliated enterprises	8 540 . .	...	...	...	...	...	...	...	...
Portfolio investment	8 602 . .	...	...	...	...	...	...	...	...
Equity securities	8 610 . .	...	...	...	...	...	...	...	...
Monetary authorities	8 611 . .	...	...	...	...	...	...	...	...
General government	8 612 . .	...	...	...	...	...	...	...	...
Banks	8 613 . .	...	...	...	...	...	...	...	...
Other sectors	8 614 . .	...	...	...	...	...	...	...	...
Debt securities	8 619 . .	...	...	...	...	...	...	...	...
Bonds and notes	8 620 . .	...	...	...	...	...	...	...	...
Monetary authorities	8 621 . .	...	...	...	...	...	...	...	...
General government	8 622 . .	...	...	...	...	...	...	...	...
Banks	8 623 . .	...	...	...	...	...	...	...	...
Other sectors	8 624 . .	...	...	...	...	...	...	...	...
Money market instruments	8 630 . .	...	...	...	...	...	...	...	...
Monetary authorities	8 631 . .	...	...	...	...	...	...	...	...
General government	8 632 . .	...	...	...	...	...	...	...	...
Banks	8 633 . .	...	...	...	...	...	...	...	...
Other sectors	8 634 . .	...	...	...	...	...	...	...	...
Financial derivatives	8 900 . .	...	...	...	...	...	...	...	...
Monetary authorities	8 901 . .	...	...	...	...	...	...	...	...
General government	8 902 . .	...	...	...	...	...	...	...	...
Banks	8 903 . .	...	...	...	...	...	...	...	...
Other sectors	8 904 . .	...	...	...	...	...	...	...	...
Other investment	8 703 . .	...	**730.6**	**771.6**	**827.9**	**794.9**	**917.0**	**1,203.4**	**1,081.0**
Trade credits	8 706 . .	...	...	...	...	...	...	...	...
General government	8 707 . .	...	...	...	...	...	...	...	...
of which: Short-term	8 709 . .	...	...	...	...	...	...	...	...
Other sectors	8 710 . .	...	...	...	...	...	...	...	...
of which: Short-term	8 712 . .	...	...	...	...	...	...	...	...
Loans	8 714 . .	...	...	...	...	...	...	...	...
Monetary authorities	8 715 . .	...	...	...	...	...	...	...	...
of which: Short-term	8 718 . .	...	...	...	...	...	...	...	...
General government	8 719 . .	...	...	...	...	...	...	...	...
of which: Short-term	8 721 . .	...	...	...	...	...	...	...	...
Banks	8 722 . .	...	...	...	...	...	...	...	...
of which: Short-term	8 724 . .	...	...	...	...	...	...	...	...
Other sectors	8 725 . .	...	...	...	...	...	...	...	...
of which: Short-term	8 727 . .	...	...	...	...	...	...	...	...
Currency and deposits	8 730 . .	...	730.6	771.6	827.9	794.9	917.0	1,203.4	1,081.0
Monetary authorities	8 731 . .	...	...	...	...	...	...	...	...
General government	8 732 . .	...	...	...	...	...	...	...	...
Banks	8 733 . .	...	730.6	771.6	827.9	794.9	917.0	1,203.4	1,081.0
Other sectors	8 734 . .	...	...	...	...	...	...	...	...
Other assets	8 736 . .	...	...	...	...	...	...	...	...
Monetary authorities	8 737 . .	...	...	...	...	...	...	...	...
of which: Short-term	8 739 . .	...	...	...	...	...	...	...	...
General government	8 740 . .	...	...	...	...	...	...	...	...
of which: Short-term	8 742 . .	...	...	...	...	...	...	...	...
Banks	8 743 . .	...	...	...	...	...	...	...	...
of which: Short-term	8 745 . .	...	...	...	...	...	...	...	...
Other sectors	8 746 . .	...	...	...	...	...	...	...	...
of which: Short-term	8 748 . .	...	...	...	...	...	...	...	...
Reserve assets	8 802 . .	...	**2,337.2**	**1,842.4**	**1,558.2**	**1,920.8**	**1,617.6**	**1,511.4**	**1,305.7**
Monetary gold	8 812 . .	...	26.9	28.0	25.3	22.3	19.6	29.6	30.6
Special drawing rights	8 811 . .	36.0	159.5	109.6	29.2	12.9	.9	.4	1.2
Reserve position in the Fund	8 810 . .	.1	.1	.2	.1	.2	.3	.2	.2
Foreign exchange	8 803 . .	...	2,150.7	1,704.7	1,503.6	1,885.4	1,596.8	1,481.1	1,273.6
Other claims	8 813 . .	...	...	...	...	...	...	...	...

Table 3 (Concluded). INTERNATIONAL INVESTMENT POSITION (End-period stocks), 1994–2001
(Millions of U.S. dollars)

	Code		1994	1995	1996	1997	1998	1999	2000	2001
LIABILITIES	8 995	D.	...	...	...	...	...	...	...	...
Direct investment in Bangladesh	8 555	..	**...**	**...**	**...**	**...**	**...**	**...**	**...**	**...**
Equity capital and reinvested earnings	8 556	..	...	...	...	...	...	...	...	...
Claims on direct investors	8 557	..	...	...	...	...	...	...	...	...
Liabilities to direct investors	8 558	..	...	...	...	...	...	...	...	...
Other capital	8 580	..	...	...	...	...	...	...	...	...
Claims on direct investors	8 585	..	...	...	...	...	...	...	...	...
Liabilities to direct investors	8 590	..	...	...	...	...	...	...	...	...
Portfolio investment	8 652	..	**...**	**...**	**...**	**...**	**...**	**...**	**...**	**...**
Equity securities	8 660	..	...	...	...	...	...	...	...	...
Banks	8 663	..	...	...	...	...	...	...	...	...
Other sectors	8 664	..	...	...	...	...	...	...	...	...
Debt securities	8 669	..	...	...	...	...	...	...	...	...
Bonds and notes	8 670	..	...	...	...	...	...	...	...	...
Monetary authorities	8 671	..	...	...	...	...	...	...	...	...
General government	8 672	..	...	...	...	...	...	...	...	...
Banks	8 673	..	...	...	...	...	...	...	...	...
Other sectors	8 674	..	...	...	...	...	...	...	...	...
Money market instruments	8 680	..	...	...	...	...	...	...	...	...
Monetary authorities	8 681	..	...	...	...	...	...	...	...	...
General government	8 682	..	...	...	...	...	...	...	...	...
Banks	8 683	..	...	...	...	...	...	...	...	...
Other sectors	8 684	..	...	...	...	...	...	...	...	...
Financial derivatives	8 905	..	**...**	**...**	**...**	**...**	**...**	**...**	**...**	**...**
Monetary authorities	8 906	..	...	...	...	...	...	...	...	...
General government	8 907	..	...	...	...	...	...	...	...	...
Banks	8 908	..	...	...	...	...	...	...	...	...
Other sectors	8 909	..	...	...	...	...	...	...	...	...
Other investment	8 753	..	**...**	**17,018.2**	**15,509.7**	**15,462.1**	**14,569.4**	**15,267.0**	**16,764.2**	**15,746.6**
Trade credits	8 756	..	...	...	...	...	...	...	...	...
General government	8 757	..	...	...	...	...	...	...	...	...
of which: Short-term	8 759	..	...	...	...	...	...	...	...	...
Other sectors	8 760	..	...	...	...	...	...	...	...	...
of which: Short-term	8 762	..	...	...	...	...	...	...	...	...
Loans	8 764	..	...	16,699.3	15,114.4	14,953.6	14,134.1	14,805.2	16,194.5	15,074.7
Monetary authorities	8 765	..	...	643.8	538.1	388.5	434.3	326.1	219.6	148.6
of which: Use of Fund credit and loans from the Fund	8 766	..	*691.0*	*643.8*	*538.1*	*388.5*	*434.3*	*326.1*	*219.6*	*148.6*
of which: Short-term	8 768	..	...	...	...	...	...	...	...	...
General government	8 769	..	...	16,055.5	14,576.3	14,565.1	13,699.8	14,479.1	15,974.9	14,926.1
of which: Short-term	8 771	..	...	...	...	...	...	...	...	...
Banks	8 772	..	...	...	...	...	...	...	...	...
of which: Short-term	8 774	..	...	...	...	...	...	...	...	...
Other sectors	8 775	..	...	...	...	...	...	...	...	...
of which: Short-term	8 777	..	...	...	...	...	...	...	...	...
Currency and deposits	8 780	..	...	318.8	395.3	508.5	435.4	461.8	569.7	671.9
Monetary authorities	8 781	..	...	...	...	...	...	...	...	...
General government	8 782	..	...	...	...	...	...	...	...	...
Banks	8 783	..	...	318.8	395.3	508.5	435.4	461.8	569.7	671.9
Other sectors	8 784	..	...	...	...	...	...	...	...	...
Other liabilities	8 786	..	...	...	...	...	...	...	...	...
Monetary authorities	8 787	..	...	...	...	...	...	...	...	...
of which: Short-term	8 789	..	...	...	...	...	...	...	...	...
General government	8 790	..	...	...	...	...	...	...	...	...
of which: Short-term	8 792	..	...	...	...	...	...	...	...	...
Banks	8 793	..	...	...	...	...	...	...	...	...
of which: Short-term	8 795	..	...	...	...	...	...	...	...	...
Other sectors	8 796	..	...	...	...	...	...	...	...	...
of which: Short-term	8 798	..	...	...	...	...	...	...	...	...
NET INTERNATIONAL INVESTMENT POSITION	8 995	..	**...**	**...**	**...**	**...**	**...**	**...**	**...**	**...**
Conversion rates: taka per U.S. dollar (end of period)	0 102	..	**40.250**	**40.750**	**42.450**	**45.450**	**48.500**	**51.000**	**54.000**	**57.000**

Table 1. ANALYTIC PRESENTATION, 1994–2001
(Millions of U.S. dollars)

	Code		1994	1995	1996	1997	1998	1999	2000	2001
A. Current Account [1]	4 993	Z.	**133.6**	**42.5**	**69.7**	**–50.0**	**–63.0**	**–148.2**	**–145.5**	**. . .**
Goods: exports f.o.b	2 100	. .	190.0	245.4	286.7	289.0	270.1	275.3	286.4	. . .
Goods: imports f.o.b	3 100	. .	–544.7	–691.2	–743.0	–887.7	–920.7	–989.4	–1,030.3	. . .
Balance on Goods	4 100	. .	*–354.7*	*–445.9*	*–456.3*	*–598.7*	*–650.6*	*–714.1*	*–743.9*	. . .
Services: credit	2 200	. .	813.6	866.6	926.9	959.3	1,023.6	1,029.4	1,090.2	. . .
Services: debit	3 200	. .	–319.0	–363.2	–387.1	–409.5	–432.3	–458.3	–487.4	. . .
Balance on Goods and Services	4 991	. .	*140.0*	*57.6*	*83.6*	*–48.9*	*–59.2*	*–143.0*	*–141.1*	. . .
Income: credit	2 300	. .	46.1	48.4	54.2	60.5	63.5	66.7	70.2	. . .
Income: debit	3 300	. .	–86.8	–96.1	–106.3	–108.2	–119.4	–138.1	–152.5	. . .
Balance on Goods, Services, and Income	4 992	. .	*99.3*	*9.9*	*31.4*	*–96.6*	*–115.2*	*–214.5*	*–223.4*	. . .
Current transfers: credit	2 379	Z.	54.5	56.2	64.8	71.7	78.4	94.0	108.9	. . .
Current transfers: debit	3 379	. .	–20.2	–23.6	–26.6	–25.1	–26.2	–27.7	–31.0	. . .
B. Capital Account [1]	4 994	Z.	**. . .**	**. . .**	**.4**	**. . .**	**.7**	**.7**	**–1.8**	**. . .**
Capital account: credit	2 994	Z.	. . .	. . .	.4	. . .	.7	.7	. . .	. . .
Capital account: debit	3 994	. .	. . .	. . .	. . .	. . .	. . .	. . .	–1.8	. . .
Total, Groups A Plus B	4 981	. .	*133.6*	*42.5*	*70.1*	*–50.0*	*–62.3*	*–147.6*	*–147.3*	. . .
C. Financial Account [1]	4 995	W.	**–6.4**	**–26.4**	**–22.2**	**20.0**	**55.5**	**118.4**	**302.9**	**. . .**
Direct investment abroad	4 505	. .	–1.1	–3.3	–3.6	–1.2	–1.0	–1.3	–1.1	. . .
Direct investment in Barbados	4 555	Z.	13.0	11.8	13.3	14.8	15.8	17.4	19.4	. . .
Portfolio investment assets	4 602	. .	–1.8	–3.1	–17.4	–17.3	–24.8	–18.6	–11.8	. . .
Equity securities	4 610	. .	–13.3	–7.6	–9.7	–11.3	–14.0	–16.3	–13.9	. . .
Debt securities	4 619	. .	11.5	4.6	–7.8	–6.0	–10.8	–2.3	2.1	. . .
Portfolio investment liabilities	4 652	Z.	48.7	40.4	–1.6	–25.5	–25.6	44.9	100.0	. . .
Equity securities	4 660	. .	. . .	. . .	. . .	–.1	–.1	–.1	. . .	. . .
Debt securities	4 669	Z.	48.7	40.4	–1.6	–25.4	–25.6	45.0	100.0	. . .
Financial derivatives	4 910	. .	. . .	. . .	. . .	. . .	. . .	. . .	. . .	. . .
Financial derivatives assets	4 900	. .	. . .	. . .	. . .	. . .	. . .	. . .	. . .	. . .
Financial derivatives liabilities	4 905	. .	. . .	. . .	. . .	. . .	. . .	. . .	. . .	. . .
Other investment assets	4 703	. .	–88.9	–167.0	–210.9	–12.1	–16.9	–93.9	52.6	. . .
Monetary authorities	4 701	. .	. . .	. . .	. . .	. . .	. . .	. . .	. . .	. . .
General government	4 704	. .	–7.8	–9.3	–7.1	–14.1	–11.0	–4.4	–4.6	. . .
Banks	4 705	. .	–32.6	–87.5	–154.1	24.5	21.5	–72.5	66.9	. . .
Other sectors	4 728	. .	–48.6	–70.3	–49.8	–22.5	–27.4	–17.1	–9.7	. . .
Other investment liabilities	4 753	W.	23.8	94.8	198.0	61.1	107.9	169.9	143.7	. . .
Monetary authorities	4 753	WA	–5.2	–8.5	–6.7	–6.7	. . .	. . .	. . .	. . .
General government	4 753	ZB	–41.1	–34.4	10.3	7.9	23.9	4.1	15.7	. . .
Banks	4 753	ZC	16.6	101.4	127.3	–19.8	19.0	49.1	–77.0	. . .
Other sectors	4 753	ZD	53.5	36.3	67.1	79.6	65.1	116.8	204.9	. . .
Total, Groups A Through C	4 983	. .	*127.3*	*16.1*	*47.9*	*–30.0*	*–6.9*	*–29.2*	*155.6*	. . .
D. Net Errors and Omissions	4 998	. .	**–89.4**	**26.0**	**38.5**	**47.4**	**.7**	**65.5**	**22.1**	**. . .**
Total, Groups A Through D	4 984	. .	*37.8*	*42.1*	*86.4*	*17.4*	*–6.1*	*36.3*	*177.6*	. . .
E. Reserves and Related Items	4 802	A.	**–37.8**	**–42.1**	**–86.4**	**–17.4**	**6.1**	**–36.3**	**–177.6**	**. . .**
Reserve assets	4 802	. .	–59.1	–25.0	–61.1	–9.1	5.6	–37.1	–178.1	. . .
Use of Fund credit and loans	4 766	. .	. . .	–18.1	–26.8	–9.0	. . .	. . .	. . .	. . .
Exceptional financing	4 920	. .	21.3	1.0	1.5	.7	.6	.8	.5	. . .
Conversion rates: Barbados dollars per U.S. dollar	0 101	. .	**2.0000**	**2.0000**	**2.0000**	**2.0000**	**2.0000**	**2.0000**	**2.0000**	**2.0000**

[1] Excludes components that have been classified in the categories of Group E.

Table 2. STANDARD PRESENTATION, 1994–2001
(Millions of U.S. dollars)

	Code	1994	1995	1996	1997	1998	1999	2000	2001
CURRENT ACCOUNT	4 993 . .	**134.6**	**43.5**	**71.2**	**–49.3**	**–62.4**	**–147.5**	**–145.0**	**. . .**
A. GOODS	4 100 . .	–354.7	–445.9	–456.3	–598.7	–650.6	–714.1	–743.9	. . .
Credit	2 100 . .	**190.0**	**245.4**	**286.7**	**289.0**	**270.1**	**275.3**	**286.4**	**. . .**
General merchandise: exports f.o.b.	2 110 . .	153.6	205.5	243.7	239.8	217.8	220.6	229.1	. . .
Goods for processing: exports f.o.b.	2 150 . .	7.6	5.6	5.4	5.0	7.5	10.3	11.5	. . .
Repairs on goods	2 160 . .	2.2	.1	.2	.2	.2	.2	.7	. . .
Goods procured in ports by carriers	2 170 . .	26.6	34.2	37.5	44.1	44.7	44.3	45.1	. . .
Nonmonetary gold	2 180 . .	. . .	. . .	. . .	. . .	. . .	. . .	. . .	. . .
Debit	3 100 . .	**–544.7**	**–691.2**	**–743.0**	**–887.7**	**–920.7**	**–989.4**	**–1,030.3**	**. . .**
General merchandise: imports f.o.b.	3 110 . .	–544.5	–688.8	–742.7	–887.6	–918.9	–988.1	–1,029.7	. . .
Goods for processing: imports f.o.b.	3 150 . .	. . .	–2.4	–.2	. . .	–.1	–1.2	. . .	. . .
Repairs on goods	3 160 . .	–.1	. . .	. . .	. . .	–.4	. . .	. . .	. . .
Goods procured in ports by carriers	3 170 . .	–.1	–.1	–.1	–.1	–1.4	–.2	–.6	. . .
Nonmonetary gold	3 180 . .	. . .	. . .	. . .	. . .	. . .	. . .	. . .	. . .
B. SERVICES	4 200 . .	494.7	503.5	539.8	549.8	591.4	571.1	602.9	. . .
Total credit	2 200 . .	*813.6*	*866.6*	*926.9*	*959.3*	*1,023.6*	*1,029.4*	*1,090.2*	. . .
Total debit	3 200 . .	*–319.0*	*–363.2*	*–387.1*	*–409.5*	*–432.3*	*–458.3*	*–487.4*	. . .
Transportation services, credit	2 205 . .	**14.5**	**16.4**	**17.6**	**20.6**	**21.1**	**23.2**	**24.8**	**. . .**
Passenger	2 850 . .	*7.5*	*8.0*	*8.1*	*9.2*	*9.1*	*9.5*	*10.5*	. . .
Freight	2 851 . .	*2.9*	*3.8*	*4.4*	*4.4*	*4.6*	*4.9*	*4.6*	. . .
Other	2 852 . .	*4.2*	*4.7*	*5.2*	*7.0*	*7.5*	*8.8*	*9.7*	. . .
Sea transport, passenger	2 207 . .	. . .	3.6	3.5	3.8	3.9	4.1	4.6	. . .
Sea transport, freight	2 208 . .	. . .	. . .	. . .	. . .	. . .	. . .	. . .	. . .
Sea transport, other	2 209 . .	. . .	. . .	. . .	. . .	. . .	. . .	. . .	. . .
Air transport, passenger	2 211 . .	.5	.7	.7	.5	.7	.7	.8	. . .
Air transport, freight	2 212 . .	. . .	. . .	. . .	. . .	. . .	. . .	. . .	. . .
Air transport, other	2 213 . .	2.4	2.1	2.1	2.3	2.7	3.5	3.5	. . .
Other transport, passenger	2 215 . .	7.0	3.8	3.9	5.0	4.5	4.8	5.2	. . .
Other transport, freight	2 216 . .	2.9	3.8	4.4	4.4	4.6	4.9	4.6	. . .
Other transport, other	2 217 . .	1.8	2.6	3.1	4.7	4.8	5.3	6.2	. . .
Transportation services, debit	3 205 . .	**–97.4**	**–116.9**	**–123.6**	**–140.9**	**–146.8**	**–156.8**	**–163.5**	**. . .**
Passenger	3 850 . .	*–32.0*	*–38.5*	*–40.2*	*–41.3*	*–44.1*	*–45.0*	*–46.7*	. . .
Freight	3 851 . .	*–61.5*	*–77.1*	*–83.4*	*–99.6*	*–101.0*	*–110.8*	*–115.6*	. . .
Other	3 852 . .	*–4.0*	*–1.3*	*–.1*	*–.1*	*–1.7*	*–1.0*	*–1.2*	. . .
Sea transport, passenger	3 207 . .	–.1	–.1	. . .	. . .	–.1	–.1	–.1	. . .
Sea transport, freight	3 208 . .	–49.2	–61.7	–66.7	–79.7	–80.8	–88.7	–92.5	. . .
Sea transport, other	3 209 . .	–.1	–.1	–.1	–.1	–1.4	–.2	–.1	. . .
Air transport, passenger	3 211 . .	–31.9	–38.5	–40.2	–41.3	–44.0	–45.0	–46.7	. . .
Air transport, freight	3 212 . .	–12.3	–15.4	–16.7	–19.9	–20.2	–22.2	–23.1	. . .
Air transport, other	3 213 . .	–2.7	–.3	. . .	. . .	–.4	–.9	–1.1	. . .
Other transport, passenger	3 215 . .	. . .	. . .	. . .	. . .	. . .	. . .	. . .	. . .
Other transport, freight	3 216 . .	. . .	. . .	. . .	. . .	. . .	. . .	. . .	. . .
Other transport, other	3 217 . .	–1.2	–1.0	. . .	. . .	. . .	. . .	. . .	. . .
Travel, credit	2 236 . .	**603.0**	**622.4**	**659.3**	**663.5**	**711.9**	**686.8**	**723.0**	**. . .**
Business travel	2 237 . .	2.7	2.8	2.5	2.9	3.1	3.5	3.8	. . .
Personal travel	2 240 . .	600.3	619.6	656.9	660.6	708.9	683.4	719.2	. . .
Travel, debit	3 236 . .	**–59.1**	**–71.1**	**–74.1**	**–78.8**	**–82.2**	**–86.7**	**–94.1**	**. . .**
Business travel	3 237 . .	–21.4	–25.9	–28.0	–29.4	–30.6	–31.5	–32.7	. . .
Personal travel	3 240 . .	–37.8	–45.2	–46.2	–49.4	–51.6	–55.3	–61.4	. . .
Other services, credit	2 200 BA	**196.2**	**227.9**	**250.0**	**275.3**	**290.7**	**319.5**	**342.5**	**. . .**
Communications	2 245 . .	22.6	25.1	25.8	26.0	26.9	27.3	27.8	. . .
Construction	2 249 . .	. . .	1.3	2.0	1.8	2.1	2.3	2.8	. . .
Insurance	2 253 . .	54.4	49.9	59.9	65.2	68.3	75.0	79.5	. . .
Financial	2 260 . .	. . .	50.3	55.2	59.2	64.3	68.3	75.2	. . .
Computer and information	2 262 . .	20.0	21.8	25.2	26.2	23.6	17.8	17.4	. . .
Royalties and licence fees	2 266 . .	.4	.1	. . .	. . .	.3	.2	.3	. . .
Other business services	2 268 . .	70.2	56.8	55.7	70.4	76.3	96.2	104.5	. . .
Personal, cultural, and recreational	2 287 . .	.1	.1	.5	.1	.1	.3	.3	. . .
Government, n.i.e.	2 291 . .	28.6	22.8	25.9	26.5	29.0	32.3	34.9	. . .
Other services, debit	3 200 BA	**–162.5**	**–175.3**	**–189.4**	**–189.8**	**–203.4**	**–214.8**	**–229.8**	**. . .**
Communications	3 245 . .	–1.9	–.3	–3.3	–4.7	–5.1	–6.8	–7.9	. . .
Construction	3 249 . .	. . .	. . .	–.5	–1.6	–1.6	–2.1	–2.1	. . .
Insurance	3 253 . .	–98.7	–95.3	–94.2	–90.8	–95.7	–101.6	–109.5	. . .
Financial	3 260 . .	. . .	–5.6	–4.4	–3.2	–4.4	–4.9	–5.1	. . .
Computer and information	3 262 . .	–2.2	–4.8	–3.7	–4.4	–4.9	–5.2	–5.2	. . .
Royalties and licence fees	3 266 . .	–13.0	–14.7	–17.8	–20.7	–22.2	–22.6	–23.7	. . .
Other business services	3 268 . .	–27.1	–38.3	–43.3	–44.2	–46.5	–46.3	–48.9	. . .
Personal, cultural, and recreational	3 287 . .	–.1	–.1	–.3	–.1	–.1	–.2	–.2	. . .
Government, n.i.e.	3 291 . .	–19.8	–16.4	–22.0	–20.4	–23.1	–25.3	–27.4	. . .

Table 2 (Continued). STANDARD PRESENTATION, 1994–2001

(Millions of U.S. dollars)

	Code	1994	1995	1996	1997	1998	1999	2000	2001
C. INCOME	4 300 . .	–40.7	–47.7	–52.2	–47.7	–56.0	–71.5	–82.3	. . .
Total credit	2 300 . .	*46.1*	*48.4*	*54.2*	*60.5*	*63.5*	*66.7*	*70.2*	. . .
Total debit	3 300 . .	*–86.8*	*–96.1*	*–106.3*	*–108.2*	*–119.4*	*–138.1*	*–152.5*	. . .
Compensation of employees, credit	2 310 . .	**8.7**	**10.3**	**12.0**	**14.3**	**14.6**	**14.9**	**15.8**	. . .
Compensation of employees, debit	3 310 . .	**–1.6**	**–2.3**	**–3.0**	**–2.3**	**–2.8**	**–2.9**	**–2.2**	. . .
Investment income, credit	2 320 . .	**37.4**	**38.1**	**42.2**	**46.2**	**48.9**	**51.8**	**54.4**	. . .
Direct investment income	2 330 . .	.8	1.2	4.5	3.7	4.3	4.7	5.8	. . .
Dividends and distributed branch profits	2 332 . .	.2	.6	3.6	2.0	3.5	4.0	5.1	. . .
Reinvested earnings and undistributed branch profits	2 333 . .	.6	.6	1.0	1.7	.8	.8	.7	. . .
Income on debt (interest)	2 334 . .	. . .	. . .	. . .	. . .	. . .	. . .	. . .	. . .
Portfolio investment income	2 339 . .	36.6	36.9	37.7	42.5	44.2	46.2	48.2	. . .
Income on equity	2 340 . .	12.6	12.2	12.9	12.2	13.3	14.3	15.7	. . .
Income on bonds and notes	2 350 . .	. . .	. . .	. . .	. . .	. . .	. . .	. . .	. . .
Income on money market instruments	2 360 . .	. . .	. . .	. . .	. . .	. . .	. . .	. . .	. . .
Other investment income	2 370 . .	. . .	. . .	. . .	. . .	.5	.9	.5	. . .
Investment income, debit	3 320 . .	**–85.2**	**–93.9**	**–103.4**	**–105.9**	**–116.6**	**–135.2**	**–150.3**	. . .
Direct investment income	3 330 . .	–7.8	–6.8	–9.7	–11.6	–12.8	–15.5	–17.0	. . .
Dividends and distributed branch profits	3 332 . .	–.8	–.5	–2.2	–1.3	–3.3	–5.4	–5.6	. . .
Reinvested earnings and undistributed branch profits	3 333 . .	–7.0	–6.3	–7.5	–9.3	–9.5	–10.1	–11.4	. . .
Income on debt (interest)	3 334 . .	. . .	. . .	. . .	–1.1	. . .	. . .	. . .	. . .
Portfolio investment income	3 339 . .	–77.5	–86.4	–93.1	–93.6	–102.7	–118.2	–131.2	. . .
Income on equity	3 340 . .	–20.6	–24.3	–26.4	–25.5	–29.4	–33.9	–39.3	. . .
Income on bonds and notes	3 350 . .	. . .	. . .	. . .	. . .	. . .	. . .	. . .	. . .
Income on money market instruments	3 360 . .	. . .	. . .	. . .	. . .	. . .	. . .	. . .	. . .
Other investment income	3 370 . .	. . .	–.8	–.6	–.8	–1.2	–1.6	–2.2	. . .
D. CURRENT TRANSFERS	4 379 . .	35.3	33.6	39.8	47.3	52.8	67.0	78.4	. . .
Credit	2 379 . .	**55.5**	**57.2**	**66.3**	**72.3**	**78.9**	**94.7**	**109.4**	. . .
General government	2 380 . .	1.4	1.5	1.8	1.2	1.2	2.4	3.4	. . .
Other sectors	2 390 . .	54.1	55.7	64.5	71.2	77.8	92.4	106.0	. . .
Workers' remittances	2 391 . .	37.4	42.4	48.3	55.0	61.2	71.1	84.2	. . .
Other current transfers	2 392 . .	16.8	13.4	16.3	16.2	16.6	21.3	21.9	. . .
Debit	3 379 . .	**–20.2**	**–23.6**	**–26.6**	**–25.1**	**–26.2**	**–27.7**	**–31.0**	. . .
General government	3 380 . .	–6.3	–2.8	–3.6	–4.1	–5.2	–4.6	–6.1	. . .
Other sectors	3 390 . .	–13.9	–20.8	–23.0	–21.0	–21.0	–23.1	–25.0	. . .
Workers' remittances	3 391 . .	–7.2	–11.6	–15.3	–12.0	–12.6	–13.8	–14.3	. . .
Other current transfers	3 392 . .	–6.7	–9.2	–7.8	–9.1	–8.4	–9.3	–10.7	. . .
CAPITAL AND FINANCIAL ACCOUNT	4 996 . .	**–45.1**	**–69.5**	**–109.6**	**1.9**	**61.7**	**81.9**	**122.9**	. . .
CAPITAL ACCOUNT	4 994 . .	**20.4**	. . .	**.4**	. . .	**.7**	**.7**	**–1.8**	. . .
Total credit	2 994 . .	*20.4*	. . .	*.4*	. . .	*.7*	*.7*	. . .	. . .
Total debit	3 994 . .	. . .	. . .	. . .	. . .	. . .	. . .	*–1.8*	. . .
Capital transfers, credit	2 400 . .	**20.4**	. . .	**.4**	. . .	**.7**	**.7**	. . .	. . .
General government	2 401 . .	20.4	. . .	. . .	. . .	. . .	. . .	. . .	. . .
Debt forgiveness	2 402 . .	20.4	. . .	. . .	. . .	. . .	. . .	. . .	. . .
Other capital transfers	2 410 . .	. . .	. . .	. . .	. . .	. . .	. . .	. . .	. . .
Other sectors	2 430 . .	. . .	. . .	.4	. . .	.7	.7	. . .	. . .
Migrants' transfers	2 431 . .	. . .	. . .	.2	. . .	.7	.7	. . .	. . .
Debt forgiveness	2 432 . .	. . .	. . .	. . .	. . .	. . .	. . .	. . .	. . .
Other capital transfers	2 440 . .	. . .	. . .	.2	. . .	. . .	. . .	. . .	. . .
Capital transfers, debit	3 400 . .	. . .	. . .	. . .	. . .	. . .	. . .	**–1.8**	. . .
General government	3 401 . .	. . .	. . .	. . .	. . .	. . .	. . .	. . .	. . .
Debt forgiveness	3 402 . .	. . .	. . .	. . .	. . .	. . .	. . .	. . .	. . .
Other capital transfers	3 410 . .	. . .	. . .	. . .	. . .	. . .	. . .	. . .	. . .
Other sectors	3 430 . .	. . .	. . .	. . .	. . .	. . .	. . .	–1.8	. . .
Migrants' transfers	3 431 . .	. . .	. . .	. . .	. . .	. . .	. . .	–1.8	. . .
Debt forgiveness	3 432 . .	. . .	. . .	. . .	. . .	. . .	. . .	. . .	. . .
Other capital transfers	3 440 . .	. . .	. . .	. . .	. . .	. . .	. . .	. . .	. . .
Nonproduced nonfinancial assets, credit	2 480 . .	. . .	. . .	. . .	. . .	. . .	. . .	. . .	. . .
Nonproduced nonfinancial assets, debit	3 480 . .	. . .	. . .	. . .	. . .	. . .	. . .	. . .	. . .

Table 2 (Continued). STANDARD PRESENTATION, 1994–2001
(Millions of U.S. dollars)

	Code	1994	1995	1996	1997	1998	1999	2000	2001
FINANCIAL ACCOUNT	4 995	**–65.5**	**–69.5**	**–110.0**	**1.9**	**61.0**	**81.3**	**124.7**	**. . .**
A. DIRECT INVESTMENT	4 500	11.9	8.5	9.8	13.6	14.8	16.1	18.4	. . .
Direct investment abroad	4 505	**–1.1**	**–3.3**	**–3.6**	**–1.2**	**–1.0**	**–1.3**	**–1.1**	**. . .**
Equity capital	4 510	. . .	–.4	–.5	–.3	–.1	–.2	–.1	. . .
Claims on affiliated enterprises	4 515	. . .	. . .	. . .	. . .	. . .	. . .	. . .	. . .
Liabilities to affiliated enterprises	4 520	. . .	. . .	. . .	. . .	. . .	. . .	. . .	. . .
Reinvested earnings	4 525	–.6	–.6	–1.0	–1.7	–.8	–.8	–.7	. . .
Other capital	4 530	–.5	–2.4	–2.1	.8	–.2	–.4	–.3	. . .
Claims on affiliated enterprises	4 535	. . .	. . .	. . .	. . .	. . .	. . .	. . .	. . .
Liabilities to affiliated enterprises	4 540	. . .	. . .	. . .	. . .	. . .	. . .	. . .	. . .
Direct investment in Barbados	4 555	**13.0**	**11.8**	**13.3**	**14.8**	**15.8**	**17.4**	**19.4**	**. . .**
Equity capital	4 560	6.0	4.7	3.1	3.8	4.1	4.2	4.6	. . .
Claims on direct investors	4 565	. . .	. . .	. . .	. . .	. . .	. . .	. . .	. . .
Liabilities to direct investors	4 570	. . .	. . .	. . .	. . .	. . .	. . .	. . .	. . .
Reinvested earnings	4 575	7.0	6.3	7.5	9.3	9.5	10.1	11.4	. . .
Other capital	4 580	.1	.9	2.8	1.8	2.3	3.2	3.5	. . .
Claims on direct investors	4 585	. . .	. . .	. . .	. . .	. . .	. . .	. . .	. . .
Liabilities to direct investors	4 590	. . .	. . .	. . .	. . .	. . .	. . .	. . .	. . .
B. PORTFOLIO INVESTMENT	4 600	46.9	37.4	–19.0	–42.7	–50.4	26.3	88.3	. . .
Assets	4 602	**–1.8**	**–3.1**	**–17.4**	**–17.3**	**–24.8**	**–18.6**	**–11.8**	**. . .**
Equity securities	4 610	–13.3	–7.6	–9.7	–11.3	–14.0	–16.3	–13.9	. . .
Monetary authorities	4 611	. . .	. . .	. . .	. . .	. . .	. . .	. . .	. . .
General government	4 612	. . .	. . .	–1.0	. . .	. . .	. . .	. . .	. . .
Banks	4 613	. . .	. . .	. . .	. . .	. . .	. . .	. . .	. . .
Other sectors	4 614	–13.3	–7.6	–8.7	–11.3	–14.0	–16.3	–13.9	. . .
Debt securities	4 619	11.5	4.6	–7.8	–6.0	–10.8	–2.3	2.1	. . .
Bonds and notes	4 620	7.6	9.4	–2.4	1.4	–3.2	3.0	6.4	. . .
Monetary authorities	4 621	. . .	. . .	. . .	. . .	. . .	. . .	. . .	. . .
General government	4 622	.2	1.6	.5	. . .	–1.7	5.6	8.7	. . .
Banks	4 623	. . .	. . .	. . .	. . .	. . .	. . .	. . .	. . .
Other sectors	4 624	7.5	7.9	–2.9	1.4	–1.6	–2.6	–2.4	. . .
Money market instruments	4 630	3.9	–4.9	–5.4	–7.4	–7.6	–5.3	–4.3	. . .
Monetary authorities	4 631	. . .	. . .	. . .	. . .	. . .	. . .	. . .	. . .
General government	4 632	. . .	. . .	. . .	. . .	. . .	. . .	. . .	. . .
Banks	4 633	. . .	. . .	. . .	. . .	. . .	. . .	. . .	. . .
Other sectors	4 634	3.9	–4.9	–5.4	–7.4	–7.6	–5.3	–4.3	. . .
Liabilities	4 652	**48.7**	**40.4**	**–1.6**	**–25.5**	**–25.6**	**44.9**	**100.0**	**. . .**
Equity securities	4 660	. . .	. . .	. . .	–.1	–.1	–.1	. . .	. . .
Banks	4 663	. . .	. . .	. . .	. . .	. . .	. . .	. . .	. . .
Other sectors	4 664	. . .	. . .	. . .	–.1	–.1	–.1	. . .	. . .
Debt securities	4 669	48.7	40.4	–1.6	–25.4	–25.6	45.0	100.0	. . .
Bonds and notes	4 670	48.6	40.4	–4.0	–24.0	–24.1	45.0	100.0	. . .
Monetary authorities	4 671	. . .	. . .	. . .	. . .	. . .	. . .	. . .	. . .
General government	4 672	45.5	40.4	–4.0	–24.0	–24.1	45.0	100.0	. . .
Banks	4 673	. . .	. . .	. . .	. . .	. . .	. . .	. . .	. . .
Other sectors	4 674	3.2	. . .	. . .	. . .	. . .	. . .	. . .	. . .
Money market instruments	4 680	.1	. . .	2.5	–1.4	–1.5	–.1	. . .	. . .
Monetary authorities	4 681	.1	. . .	. . .	. . .	. . .	. . .	. . .	. . .
General government	4 682	. . .	. . .	. . .	. . .	. . .	. . .	. . .	. . .
Banks	4 683	. . .	. . .	. . .	. . .	. . .	. . .	. . .	. . .
Other sectors	4 684	. . .	. . .	2.5	–1.4	–1.5	–.1	. . .	. . .
C. FINANCIAL DERIVATIVES	4 910	. . .	. . .	. . .	. . .	. . .	. . .	. . .	. . .
Monetary authorities	4 911	. . .	. . .	. . .	. . .	. . .	. . .	. . .	. . .
General government	4 912	. . .	. . .	. . .	. . .	. . .	. . .	. . .	. . .
Banks	4 913	. . .	. . .	. . .	. . .	. . .	. . .	. . .	. . .
Other sectors	4 914	. . .	. . .	. . .	. . .	. . .	. . .	. . .	. . .
Assets	4 900	**. . .**	**. . .**	**. . .**	**. . .**	**. . .**	**. . .**	**. . .**	**. . .**
Monetary authorities	4 901	. . .	. . .	. . .	. . .	. . .	. . .	. . .	. . .
General government	4 902	. . .	. . .	. . .	. . .	. . .	. . .	. . .	. . .
Banks	4 903	. . .	. . .	. . .	. . .	. . .	. . .	. . .	. . .
Other sectors	4 904	. . .	. . .	. . .	. . .	. . .	. . .	. . .	. . .
Liabilities	4 905	**. . .**	**. . .**	**. . .**	**. . .**	**. . .**	**. . .**	**. . .**	**. . .**
Monetary authorities	4 906	. . .	. . .	. . .	. . .	. . .	. . .	. . .	. . .
General government	4 907	. . .	. . .	. . .	. . .	. . .	. . .	. . .	. . .
Banks	4 908	. . .	. . .	. . .	. . .	. . .	. . .	. . .	. . .
Other sectors	4 909	. . .	. . .	. . .	. . .	. . .	. . .	. . .	. . .

Table 2 (Concluded). STANDARD PRESENTATION, 1994–2001
(Millions of U.S. dollars)

	Code	1994	1995	1996	1997	1998	1999	2000	2001
D. OTHER INVESTMENT	4 700 . .	-65.1	-90.3	-39.8	40.0	91.0	76.0	196.3	. . .
Assets	4 703 . .	**-88.9**	**-167.0**	**-210.9**	**-12.1**	**-16.9**	**-93.9**	**52.6**	**. . .**
Trade credits	4 706 . .	-32.1	-54.0	-28.8	-7.0	-9.0	-9.0	-7.1	. . .
General government	4 707 . .	. . .	. . .	. . .	. . .	. . .	. . .	. . .	. . .
of which: Short-term	4 709 . .	. . .	. . .	. . .	. . .	. . .	. . .	. . .	. . .
Other sectors	4 710 . .	-32.1	-54.0	-28.8	-7.0	-9.0	-9.0	-7.1	. . .
of which: Short-term	4 712 . .	*-32.1*	*-48.5*	*-23.7*	*-1.3*	*-2.4*	*-1.8*	*-1.9*	. . .
Loans	4 714 . .	-15.5	-17.2	-19.3	-9.8	-10.9	-8.3	-5.8	. . .
Monetary authorities	4 715 . .	. . .	. . .	. . .	. . .	. . .	. . .	. . .	. . .
of which: Short-term	4 718 . .	. . .	. . .	. . .	. . .	. . .	. . .	. . .	. . .
General government	4 719 . .	-.7	-.7	-.8	-.7	-.7	-.7	-.7	. . .
of which: Short-term	4 721 . .	*-.7*	*-.7*	*-.8*	*-.7*	*-.7*	*-.7*	*-.7*	. . .
Banks	4 722 . .	. . .	. . .	. . .	. . .	. . .	. . .	. . .	. . .
of which: Short-term	4 724 . .	. . .	. . .	. . .	. . .	. . .	. . .	. . .	. . .
Other sectors	4 725 . .	-14.9	-16.6	-18.5	-9.1	-10.3	-7.7	-5.2	. . .
of which: Short-term	4 727 . .	. . .	. . .	. . .	. . .	. . .	. . .	. . .	. . .
Currency and deposits	4 730 . .	-1.7	-10.0	-17.1	-7.2	-10.4	-10.7	-9.7	. . .
Monetary authorities	4 731 . .	. . .	. . .	. . .	. . .	. . .	. . .	. . .	. . .
General government	4 732 . .	. . .	. . .	. . .	. . .	. . .	. . .	. . .	. . .
Banks	4 733 . .	-1.7	-10.0	-17.1	-7.2	-10.4	-10.7	-9.7	. . .
Other sectors	4 734 . .	. . .	. . .	. . .	. . .	. . .	. . .	. . .	. . .
Other assets	4 736 . .	-39.6	-85.9	-145.8	11.9	13.4	-66.0	75.1	. . .
Monetary authorities	4 737 . .	. . .	. . .	. . .	. . .	. . .	. . .	. . .	. . .
of which: Short-term	4 739 . .	. . .	. . .	. . .	. . .	. . .	. . .	. . .	. . .
General government	4 740 . .	-7.1	-8.6	-6.3	-13.4	-10.3	-3.8	-3.9	. . .
of which: Short-term	4 742 . .	*-1.3*	*-1.7*	*-2.3*	*-2.4*	. . .	*-2.6*	*-3.5*	. . .
Banks	4 743 . .	-30.9	-77.5	-137.1	31.6	31.8	-61.8	76.5	. . .
of which: Short-term	4 745 . .	. . .	. . .	. . .	. . .	. . .	. . .	. . .	. . .
Other sectors	4 746 . .	-1.6	.2	-2.5	-6.4	-8.2	-.5	2.5	. . .
of which: Short-term	4 748 . .	*-7.5*	*-5.1*	*-1.8*	*-5.1*	*-5.6*	*1.3*	*1.4*	. . .
Liabilities	4 753 . .	**23.8**	**76.7**	**171.1**	**52.1**	**107.9**	**169.9**	**143.7**	**. . .**
Trade credits	4 756 . .	11.7	32.3	19.0	28.0	20.8	38.7	35.7	. . .
General government	4 757 . .	-2.6	-2.6	-1.1	-.7	-.1	. . .	. . .	. . .
of which: Short-term	4 759 . .	. . .	. . .	. . .	. . .	. . .	. . .	. . .	. . .
Other sectors	4 760 . .	14.3	34.9	20.1	28.7	20.8	38.7	35.7	. . .
of which: Short-term	4 762 . .	*14.3*	*26.1*	*11.7*	*21.1*	*15.3*	*28.4*	*26.3*	. . .
Loans	4 764 . .	-14.8	-66.2	10.8	23.8	44.3	43.4	147.3	. . .
Monetary authorities	4 765 . .	. . .	-18.1	-26.8	-9.0	. . .	. . .	. . .	. . .
of which: Use of Fund credit and loans from the Fund	4 766 . .	. . .	*-18.1*	*-26.8*	*-9.0*	. . .	. . .	. . .	. . .
of which: Short-term	4 768 . .	. . .	. . .	. . .	. . .	. . .	. . .	. . .	. . .
General government	4 769 . .	-38.6	-31.8	11.4	8.6	23.9	4.1	15.7	. . .
of which: Short-term	4 771 . .	. . .	. . .	. . .	. . .	. . .	. . .	. . .	. . .
Banks	4 772 . .	. . .	. . .	. . .	. . .	. . .	. . .	. . .	. . .
of which: Short-term	4 774 . .	. . .	. . .	. . .	. . .	. . .	. . .	. . .	. . .
Other sectors	4 775 . .	23.8	-16.3	26.2	24.3	20.4	39.4	131.6	. . .
of which: Short-term	4 777 . .	. . .	. . .	. . .	. . .	. . .	. . .	. . .	. . .
Currency and deposits	4 780 . .	. . .	. . .	. . .	. . .	. . .	. . .	. . .	. . .
Monetary authorities	4 781 . .	. . .	. . .	. . .	. . .	. . .	. . .	. . .	. . .
General government	4 782 . .	. . .	. . .	. . .	. . .	. . .	. . .	. . .	. . .
Banks	4 783 . .	. . .	. . .	. . .	. . .	. . .	. . .	. . .	. . .
Other sectors	4 784 . .	. . .	. . .	. . .	. . .	. . .	. . .	. . .	. . .
Other liabilities	4 786 . .	26.9	110.6	141.4	.3	42.9	87.9	-39.3	. . .
Monetary authorities	4 787 . .	-5.2	-8.5	-6.7	-6.7	. . .	. . .	. . .	. . .
of which: Short-term	4 789 . .	. . .	. . .	. . .	. . .	. . .	. . .	. . .	. . .
General government	4 790 . .	. . .	. . .	. . .	. . .	. . .	. . .	. . .	. . .
of which: Short-term	4 792 . .	. . .	. . .	. . .	. . .	. . .	. . .	. . .	. . .
Banks	4 793 . .	16.6	101.4	127.3	-19.8	19.0	49.1	-77.0	. . .
of which: Short-term	4 795 . .	. . .	. . .	. . .	. . .	. . .	. . .	. . .	. . .
Other sectors	4 796 . .	15.5	17.7	20.8	26.7	23.9	38.8	37.7	. . .
of which: Short-term	4 798 . .	*2.6*	*2.6*	*3.1*	*5.6*	*4.5*	*9.5*	*10.1*	. . .
E. RESERVE ASSETS	4 802 . .	-59.1	-25.0	-61.1	-9.1	5.6	-37.1	-178.1	. . .
Monetary gold	4 812 . .	. . .	. . .	. . .	. . .	. . .	. . .	. . .	. . .
Special drawing rights	4 811 . .	. . .	. . .	. . .	. . .	. . .	. . .	. . .	. . .
Reserve position in the Fund	4 810 . .	. . .	. . .	. . .	. . .	. . .	-6.4	. . .	. . .
Foreign exchange	4 803 . .	-58.7	-24.6	-57.3	25.1	22.3	-7.1	-155.4	. . .
Other claims	4 813 . .	-.5	-.4	-3.8	-34.2	-16.7	-23.7	-22.8	. . .
NET ERRORS AND OMISSIONS	4 998 . .	**-89.4**	**26.0**	**38.5**	**47.4**	**.7**	**65.5**	**22.1**	**. . .**

Part 3 of the *Yearbook* contains descriptions of the methodologies, compilation practices, and sources used to compile these data.

Belarus
913

Table 1. ANALYTIC PRESENTATION, 1994–2001

(Millions of U.S. dollars)

	Code	1994	1995	1996	1997	1998	1999	2000	2001
A. Current Account [1]	4 993 Z.	**–443.8**	**–458.3**	**–515.9**	**–859.2**	**–1,016.5**	**–193.7**	**–323.1**	**–285.2**
Goods: exports f.o.b.	2 100 . .	2,510.0	4,803.0	5,790.1	6,918.7	6,172.3	5,646.4	6,640.5	7,256.2
Goods: imports f.o.b.	3 100 . .	–2,999.8	–5,468.7	–6,938.6	–8,325.7	–7,673.4	–6,216.4	–7,524.6	–8,063.1
Balance on Goods	4 100 . .	*–489.8*	*–665.7*	*–1,148.5*	*–1,407.0*	*–1,501.1*	*–570.0*	*–884.1*	*–806.9*
Services: credit	2 200 . .	251.4	466.1	908.0	918.8	925.1	753.3	1,015.6	1,013.1
Services: debit	3 200 . .	–199.3	–283.7	–335.9	–364.8	–443.2	–438.8	–562.6	–602.7
Balance on Goods and Services	4 991 . .	*–437.7*	*–483.3*	*–576.4*	*–853.0*	*–1,019.2*	*–255.5*	*–431.1*	*–396.5*
Income: credit	2 300 . .	.5	1.9	74.1	31.2	26.8	20.8	25.7	27.0
Income: debit	3 300 . .	–29.3	–52.9	–104.9	–115.8	–119.7	–62.8	–72.4	–69.8
Balance on Goods, Services, and Income	4 992 . .	*–466.5*	*–534.3*	*–607.2*	*–937.6*	*–1,112.1*	*–297.5*	*–477.8*	*–439.3*
Current transfers: credit	2 379 Z.	50.9	107.2	135.5	106.1	120.9	137.0	177.1	202.6
Current transfers: debit	3 379 . .	–28.2	–31.2	–44.2	–27.7	–25.3	–33.2	–22.4	–48.5
B. Capital Account [1]	4 994 Z.	**23.8**	**7.3**	**101.1**	**133.2**	**170.1**	**60.4**	**69.4**	**56.3**
Capital account: credit	2 994 Z.	23.8	7.3	257.2	248.0	261.3	131.1	125.6	132.3
Capital account: debit	3 994 . .	. . .	. . .	–156.1	–114.8	–91.2	–70.7	–56.2	–76.0
Total, Groups A Plus B	4 981 . .	*–420.0*	*–451.0*	*–414.8*	*–726.0*	*–846.4*	*–133.3*	*–253.7*	*–228.9*
C. Financial Account [1]	4 995 W.	**144.6**	**204.0**	**378.7**	**738.1**	**354.8**	**399.5**	**140.1**	**247.1**
Direct investment abroad	4 505 . .	. . .	. . .	. . .	–2.1	–2.3	–.8	–.2	–.3
Direct investment in Belarus	4 555 Z.	10.5	14.7	104.5	351.6	203.2	444.0	118.8	95.8
Portfolio investment assets	4 602 . .	. . .	. . .	–17.7	–61.6	28.0	–15.4	–5.7	10.5
Equity securities	4 610 . .	. . .	. . .	. . .	–.6	.3	–7.3	.5	.7
Debt securities	4 619 . .	. . .	. . .	–17.7	–61.0	27.7	–8.1	–6.2	9.8
Portfolio investment liabilities	4 652 Z.	. . .	. . .	3.2	41.8	–13.4	–5.2	50.1	–45.4
Equity securities	4 660 . .	. . .	. . .	. . .	. . .	2.7	. . .	.5	2.5
Debt securities	4 669 Z.	. . .	. . .	3.2	41.8	–16.1	–5.2	49.6	–47.9
Financial derivatives	4 910 . .	. . .	. . .	. . .	. . .	. . .	. . .	. . .	. . .
Financial derivatives assets	4 900 . .	. . .	. . .	. . .	. . .	. . .	. . .	. . .	. . .
Financial derivatives liabilities	4 905 . .	. . .	. . .	. . .	. . .	. . .	. . .	. . .	. . .
Other investment assets	4 703 . .	–232.5	–155.4	–131.5	49.9	199.4	–36.7	41.7	–139.2
Monetary authorities	4 701 . .	. . .	. . .	. . .	1.5	–.9	1.1	–.2	–99.3
General government	4 704 . .	. . .	14.0	. . .	. . .	. . .	. . .	. . .	. . .
Banks	4 705 . .	–94.2	58.6	–40.2	–12.6	19.0	–16.4	8.4	17.5
Other sectors	4 728 . .	–138.3	–228.0	–91.3	61.0	181.3	–21.4	33.5	–57.4
Other investment liabilities	4 753 W.	366.6	344.7	420.2	358.5	–60.1	13.6	–64.6	325.7
Monetary authorities	4 753 WA	–.3	3.7	133.1	–86.8	6.8	.7	–21.2	17.3
General government	4 753 ZB	239.4	81.7	33.4	62.4	24.7	–28.5	–37.2	27.6
Banks	4 753 ZC	34.9	24.1	23.1	16.6	–20.3	–24.1	1.9	81.4
Other sectors	4 753 ZD	92.6	235.2	230.6	366.3	–71.3	65.5	–8.1	199.4
Total, Groups A Through C	4 983 . .	*–275.4*	*–247.0*	*–36.1*	*12.1*	*–491.6*	*266.2*	*–113.6*	*18.2*
D. Net Errors and Omissions	4 998 . .	**–41.6**	**168.6**	**–178.1**	**53.0**	**172.3**	**–246.3**	**238.9**	**–99.6**
Total, Groups A Through D	4 984 . .	*–317.0*	*–78.4*	*–214.2*	*65.1*	*–319.3*	*19.9*	*125.3*	*–81.4*
E. Reserves and Related Items	4 802 A.	**317.0**	**78.4**	**214.2**	**–65.1**	**319.3**	**–19.9**	**–125.3**	**81.4**
Reserve assets	4 802 . .	–58.6	–283.7	–78.6	75.3	54.6	34.6	–75.7	5.2
Use of Fund credit and loans	4 766 . .	. . .	177.8	. . .	. . .	–24.4	–58.1	–55.8	–29.8
Exceptional financing	4 920 . .	375.6	184.3	292.8	–140.4	289.1	3.6	6.2	106.0
Conversion rates: rubels per U.S. dollar	0 101 . .	**. . .**	**11.52**	**13.23**	**26.02**	**46.13**	**248.79**	**876.75**	**1,390.00**

[1] Excludes components that have been classified in the categories of Group E.

Table 2. STANDARD PRESENTATION, 1994–2001
(Millions of U.S. dollars)

	Code	1994	1995	1996	1997	1998	1999	2000	2001
CURRENT ACCOUNT	4 993 . .	**–443.8**	**–458.3**	**–515.9**	**–859.2**	**–1,016.5**	**–193.7**	**–323.1**	**–285.2**
A. GOODS	4 100 . .	–489.8	–665.7	–1,148.5	–1,407.0	–1,501.1	–570.0	–884.1	–806.9
Credit	2 100 . .	**2,510.0**	**4,803.0**	**5,790.1**	**6,918.7**	**6,172.3**	**5,646.4**	**6,640.5**	**7,256.2**
General merchandise: exports f.o.b.	2 110 . .	2,510.0	4,803.0	5,790.1	6,918.7	6,157.4	5,645.1	6,054.8	6,617.1
Goods for processing: exports f.o.b.	2 150 . .	. . .	. . .	. . .	. . .	. . .	. . .	572.6	628.4
Repairs on goods	2 160 . .	. . .	. . .	. . .	. . .	14.9	1.3	12.2	8.7
Goods procured in ports by carriers	2 170 . .	. . .	. . .	. . .	. . .	. . .	. . .	.9	2.0
Nonmonetary gold	2 180 . .	. . .	. . .	. . .	. . .	. . .	. . .	. . .	. . .
Debit	3 100 . .	**–2,999.8**	**–5,468.7**	**–6,938.6**	**–8,325.7**	**–7,673.4**	**–6,216.4**	**–7,524.6**	**–8,063.1**
General merchandise: imports f.o.b.	3 110 . .	–2,999.8	–5,468.7	–6,938.6	–8,325.7	–7,666.9	–6,213.1	–7,076.0	–7,573.2
Goods for processing: imports f.o.b.	3 150 . .	. . .	. . .	. . .	. . .	. . .	. . .	–422.8	–464.3
Repairs on goods	3 160 . .	. . .	. . .	. . .	. . .	–6.5	–3.3	–16.7	–8.2
Goods procured in ports by carriers	3 170 . .	. . .	. . .	. . .	. . .	. . .	. . .	–9.1	–17.4
Nonmonetary gold	3 180 . .	. . .	. . .	. . .	. . .	. . .	. . .	. . .	. . .
B. SERVICES	4 200 . .	52.1	182.4	572.1	554.0	481.9	314.5	453.0	410.4
Total credit	2 200 . .	*251.4*	*466.1*	*908.0*	*918.8*	*925.1*	*753.3*	*1,015.6*	*1,013.1*
Total debit	3 200 . .	*–199.3*	*–283.7*	*–335.9*	*–364.8*	*–443.2*	*–438.8*	*–562.6*	*–602.7*
Transportation services, credit	2 205 . .	**183.7**	**302.1**	**477.9**	**495.9**	**495.0**	**465.7**	**583.6**	**628.0**
Passenger	2 850 . .	*3.3*	*4.5*	*6.2*	*15.1*	*31.6*	*80.0*	*94.5*	*60.6*
Freight	2 851 . .	*163.5*	*297.6*	*417.9*	*451.0*	*453.6*	*376.5*	*457.5*	*516.9*
Other	2 852 . .	*16.9*	. . .	*53.8*	*29.8*	*9.8*	*9.2*	*31.6*	*50.5*
Sea transport, passenger	2 207 . .	. . .	. . .	. . .	. . .	. . .	. . .	. . .	. . .
Sea transport, freight	2 208 . .	. . .	. . .	. . .	. . .	. . .	. . .	. . .	. . .
Sea transport, other	2 209 . .	. . .	. . .	. . .	. . .	. . .	. . .	. . .	. . .
Air transport, passenger	2 211 . .	2.0	2.6	5.0	11.3	12.3	24.9	24.7	23.8
Air transport, freight	2 212 . .	.2	15.9	20.4	11.7	3.2	9.8	8.7	10.1
Air transport, other	2 213 . .	. . .	. . .	. . .	. . .	. . .	. . .	18.5	15.6
Other transport, passenger	2 215 . .	1.3	1.9	1.2	3.8	19.3	55.1	69.8	36.8
Other transport, freight	2 216 . .	163.3	281.7	397.5	439.3	450.4	366.7	448.8	506.8
Other transport, other	2 217 . .	16.9	. . .	53.8	29.8	9.8	9.2	13.1	34.9
Transportation services, debit	3 205 . .	**–74.9**	**–99.1**	**–153.7**	**–132.5**	**–133.2**	**–118.4**	**–109.5**	**–124.7**
Passenger	3 850 . .	*–5.1*	*–14.1*	*–22.5*	*–8.2*	*–13.8*	*–17.2*	*–31.1*	*–32.1*
Freight	3 851 . .	*–63.6*	*–85.0*	*–117.6*	*–81.8*	*–101.7*	*–74.5*	*–55.1*	*–57.4*
Other	3 852 . .	*–6.2*	. . .	*–13.6*	*–42.5*	*–17.7*	*–26.7*	*–23.3*	*–35.2*
Sea transport, passenger	3 207 . .	. . .	. . .	. . .	. . .	. . .	. . .	. . .	. . .
Sea transport, freight	3 208 . .	. . .	. . .	. . .	. . .	. . .	. . .	–3.1	–3.4
Sea transport, other	3 209 . .	. . .	. . .	. . .	. . .	. . .	. . .	. . .	. . .
Air transport, passenger	3 211 . .	–.1	–1.1	–22.3	–5.6	–13.0	–16.9	–12.2	–14.5
Air transport, freight	3 212 . .	–.4	–.4	–.7	–7.5	–2.6	–3.2	–2.4	–1.7
Air transport, other	3 213 . .	. . .	. . .	. . .	. . .	. . .	. . .	–16.3	–17.0
Other transport, passenger	3 215 . .	–5.0	–13.0	–.2	–2.6	–.8	–.3	–18.9	–17.6
Other transport, freight	3 216 . .	–63.2	–84.6	–116.9	–74.3	–99.1	–71.3	–49.6	–52.3
Other transport, other	3 217 . .	–6.2	. . .	–13.6	–42.5	–17.7	–26.7	–7.0	–18.2
Travel, credit	2 236 . .	**38.6**	**23.2**	**55.0**	**25.1**	**22.4**	**11.6**	**93.2**	**82.2**
Business travel	2 237 . .	. . .	. . .	. . .	.5	8.1	2.7	28.1	13.5
Personal travel	2 240 . .	. . .	. . .	. . .	24.6	14.3	8.9	65.1	68.7
Travel, debit	3 236 . .	**–74.1**	**–86.9**	**–118.6**	**–114.1**	**–124.0**	**–115.7**	**–243.2**	**–262.6**
Business travel	3 237 . .	. . .	. . .	. . .	–87.0	–89.7	–86.6	–103.7	–103.1
Personal travel	3 240 . .	. . .	. . .	. . .	–27.1	–34.3	–29.1	–139.5	–159.5
Other services, credit	2 200 BA	**29.1**	**140.8**	**375.1**	**397.8**	**407.7**	**276.0**	**338.8**	**302.9**
Communications	2 245 . .	8.1	8.6	16.7	29.4	42.7	43.8	50.0	54.0
Construction	2 249 . .	3.4	26.8	54.2	103.7	69.3	37.8	42.0	46.3
Insurance	2 253 . .	.4	2.1	3.1	1.5	2.1	1.5	3.6	3.2
Financial	2 260 . .	. . .	. . .	. . .	1.3	11.4	.8	2.1	3.7
Computer and information	2 262 . .	. . .	.2	1.1	2.1	5.9	3.9	4.5	6.7
Royalties and licence fees	2 266 . .	. . .	. . .	. . .	1.7	.9	.7	.9	.5
Other business services	2 268 . .	17.2	102.9	299.2	257.8	269.4	179.4	222.2	168.6
Personal, cultural, and recreational	2 287 . .	. . .	. . .	. . .	. . .	. . .	. . .	1.9	1.3
Government, n.i.e.	2 291 . .	. . .	.2	.8	.3	6.0	8.1	11.6	18.6
Other services, debit	3 200 BA	**–50.3**	**–97.7**	**–63.6**	**–118.2**	**–186.0**	**–204.7**	**–209.9**	**–215.4**
Communications	3 245 . .	–.9	–2.9	–3.5	–11.4	–32.1	–35.3	–40.4	–46.7
Construction	3 249 . .	–6.0	–6.1	–4.8	–22.5	–14.2	–9.9	–11.0	–15.8
Insurance	3 253 . .	–2.8	–9.9	–11.7	–7.0	–9.7	–9.3	–10.7	–12.2
Financial	3 260 . .	–8.3	. . .	. . .	–4.7	–6.7	–5.8	–3.2	–3.6
Computer and information	3 262 . .	–1.6	–.2	–.4	–3.9	–7.6	–3.0	–4.4	–5.8
Royalties and licence fees	3 266 . .	. . .	. . .	. . .	–1.8	–1.1	–.8	–2.7	–3.8
Other business services	3 268 . .	–28.0	–70.7	–37.4	–55.9	–109.3	–132.9	–123.3	–111.5
Personal, cultural, and recreational	3 287 . .	. . .	. . .	. . .	. . .	. . .	. . .	–3.0	–4.1
Government, n.i.e.	3 291 . .	–2.7	–7.9	–5.8	–11.0	–5.3	–7.7	–11.2	–11.9

Table 2 (Continued). STANDARD PRESENTATION, 1994–2001
(Millions of U.S. dollars)

	Code		1994	1995	1996	1997	1998	1999	2000	2001
C. INCOME	4 300	. .	−28.8	−51.0	−30.8	−84.6	−92.9	−42.0	−46.7	−42.8
Total credit	2 300	. .	*.5*	*1.9*	*74.1*	*31.2*	*26.8*	*20.8*	*25.7*	*27.0*
Total debit	3 300	. .	*−29.3*	*−52.9*	*−104.9*	*−115.8*	*−119.7*	*−62.8*	*−72.4*	*−69.8*
Compensation of employees, credit	2 310	. .	**. . .**	**. . .**	**70.7**	**17.4**	**22.2**	**8.4**	**13.6**	**16.9**
Compensation of employees, debit	3 310	. .	**. . .**	**. . .**	**−23.1**	**−22.0**	**−17.8**	**−3.4**	**−2.2**	**−.7**
Investment income, credit	2 320	. .	**.5**	**1.9**	**3.4**	**13.8**	**4.6**	**12.4**	**12.1**	**10.1**
Direct investment income	2 330	. .	. . .	. . .	. . .	. . .	. . .	.2	.1	.4
Dividends and distributed branch profits	2 332	. .	. . .	. . .	. . .	. . .	. . .	.2	.1	.4
Reinvested earnings and undistributed branch profits	2 333	. .	. . .	. . .	. . .	. . .	. . .	. . .	. . .	. . .
Income on debt (interest)	2 334	. .	. . .	. . .	. . .	. . .	. . .	. . .	. . .	. . .
Portfolio investment income	2 339	. .	. . .	. . .	3.2	13.5	4.5	.4	.5	.3
Income on equity	2 340	. .	. . .	. . .	3.2	. . .	.4	. . .	. . .	. . .
Income on bonds and notes	2 350	. .	. . .	. . .	. . .	13.5	4.1	.4	.5	.3
Income on money market instruments	2 360	. .	. . .	. . .	. . .	. . .	. . .	. . .	. . .	. . .
Other investment income	2 370	. .	.5	1.9	.2	.3	.1	11.8	11.5	9.4
Investment income, debit	3 320	. .	**−29.3**	**−52.9**	**−81.8**	**−93.8**	**−101.9**	**−59.4**	**−70.2**	**−69.1**
Direct investment income	3 330	. .	. . .	. . .	. . .	−7.5	−18.2	−.7	−4.6	−5.3
Dividends and distributed branch profits	3 332	. .	. . .	. . .	. . .	. . .	. . .	−.5	−4.2	−5.2
Reinvested earnings and undistributed branch profits	3 333	. .	. . .	. . .	. . .	−7.5	−18.2	−.2	−.4	−.1
Income on debt (interest)	3 334	. .	. . .	. . .	. . .	. . .	. . .	. . .	. . .	. . .
Portfolio investment income	3 339	. .	. . .	. . .	. . .	−.3	−1.3	−.3	−1.0	−.5
Income on equity	3 340	. .	. . .	. . .	. . .	−.3	−1.3	. . .	. . .	−.2
Income on bonds and notes	3 350	. .	. . .	. . .	. . .	. . .	. . .	−.3	−1.0	−.3
Income on money market instruments	3 360	. .	. . .	. . .	. . .	. . .	. . .	. . .	. . .	. . .
Other investment income	3 370	. .	−29.3	−52.9	−81.8	−86.0	−82.4	−58.4	−64.6	−63.3
D. CURRENT TRANSFERS	4 379	. .	22.7	76.0	91.3	78.4	95.6	103.8	154.7	154.1
Credit	2 379	. .	**50.9**	**107.2**	**135.5**	**106.1**	**120.9**	**137.0**	**177.1**	**202.6**
General government	2 380	. .	43.7	64.9	81.3	59.0	81.4	60.5	57.3	81.0
Other sectors	2 390	. .	7.2	42.3	54.2	47.1	39.5	76.5	119.8	121.6
Workers' remittances	2 391	. .	.4	28.5	22.6	29.1	31.7	53.6	. . .	. . .
Other current transfers	2 392	. .	6.8	13.8	31.6	18.0	7.8	22.9	119.8	121.6
Debit	3 379	. .	**−28.2**	**−31.2**	**−44.2**	**−27.7**	**−25.3**	**−33.2**	**−22.4**	**−48.5**
General government	3 380	. .	−3.7	−2.6	−10.5	−9.9	−22.3	−23.1	−10.4	−14.3
Other sectors	3 390	. .	−24.5	−28.6	−33.7	−17.8	−3.0	−10.1	−12.0	−34.2
Workers' remittances	3 391	. .	−17.0	−11.9	−12.5	−3.7	−2.1	−1.4	. . .	. . .
Other current transfers	3 392	. .	−7.5	−16.7	−21.2	−14.1	−.9	−8.7	−12.0	−34.2
CAPITAL AND FINANCIAL ACCOUNT	4 996	. .	**485.4**	**289.7**	**694.0**	**806.2**	**844.2**	**440.0**	**84.2**	**384.8**
CAPITAL ACCOUNT	4 994	. .	**23.8**	**7.3**	**1,006.0**	**133.2**	**170.1**	**60.4**	**69.4**	**56.3**
Total credit	2 994	. .	*23.8*	*7.3*	*1,162.1*	*248.0*	*261.3*	*131.1*	*125.6*	*132.3*
Total debit	3 994	. .	. . .	. . .	*−156.1*	*−114.8*	*−91.2*	*−70.7*	*−56.2*	*−76.0*
Capital transfers, credit	2 400	. .	**23.8**	**7.3**	**1,162.1**	**248.0**	**261.3**	**131.1**	**125.6**	**132.3**
General government	2 401	. .	23.8	7.3	904.9	. . .	. . .	. . .	. . .	. . .
Debt forgiveness	2 402	. .	. . .	. . .	904.9	. . .	. . .	. . .	. . .	. . .
Other capital transfers	2 410	. .	23.8	7.3	. . .	. . .	. . .	. . .	. . .	. . .
Other sectors	2 430	. .	. . .	. . .	257.2	248.0	261.3	131.1	125.6	132.3
Migrants' transfers	2 431	. .	. . .	. . .	257.2	248.0	261.3	131.1	125.6	132.3
Debt forgiveness	2 432	. .	. . .	. . .	. . .	. . .	. . .	. . .	. . .	. . .
Other capital transfers	2 440	. .	. . .	. . .	. . .	. . .	. . .	. . .	. . .	. . .
Capital transfers, debit	3 400	. .	**. . .**	**. . .**	**−156.1**	**−114.8**	**−91.2**	**−70.7**	**−56.2**	**−76.0**
General government	3 401	. .	. . .	. . .	. . .	. . .	. . .	. . .	. . .	. . .
Debt forgiveness	3 402	. .	. . .	. . .	. . .	. . .	. . .	. . .	. . .	. . .
Other capital transfers	3 410	. .	. . .	. . .	. . .	. . .	. . .	. . .	. . .	. . .
Other sectors	3 430	. .	. . .	. . .	−156.1	−114.8	−91.2	−70.7	−56.2	−76.0
Migrants' transfers	3 431	. .	. . .	. . .	−156.1	−114.8	−91.2	−70.7	−56.2	−76.0
Debt forgiveness	3 432	. .	. . .	. . .	. . .	. . .	. . .	. . .	. . .	. . .
Other capital transfers	3 440	. .	. . .	. . .	. . .	. . .	. . .	. . .	. . .	. . .
Nonproduced nonfinancial assets, credit	2 480	. .	**. . .**	**. . .**	**. . .**	**. . .**	**. . .**	**. . .**	**. . .**	**. . .**
Nonproduced nonfinancial assets, debit	3 480	. .	**. . .**	**. . .**	**. . .**	**. . .**	**. . .**	**. . .**	**. . .**	**. . .**

Table 2 (Continued). STANDARD PRESENTATION, 1994–2001
(Millions of U.S. dollars)

	Code	1994	1995	1996	1997	1998	1999	2000	2001
FINANCIAL ACCOUNT	4 995 . .	**461.6**	**282.4**	**–312.0**	**673.0**	**674.1**	**379.6**	**14.8**	**328.5**
A. DIRECT INVESTMENT	4 500 . .	10.5	14.7	104.5	349.5	200.9	443.2	118.6	95.5
Direct investment abroad	4 505 . .	**. . .**	**. . .**	**. . .**	**–2.1**	**–2.3**	**–.8**	**–.2**	**–.3**
Equity capital	4 510 . .	. . .	. . .	. . .	–2.1	–2.3	–.8	–.2	–.3
Claims on affiliated enterprises	4 515 . .	. . .	. . .	. . .	–2.1	–2.3	–.8	–.2	–.3
Liabilities to affiliated enterprises	4 520 . .	. . .	. . .	. . .	. . .	. . .	. . .	. . .	. . .
Reinvested earnings	4 525 . .	. . .	. . .	. . .	. . .	. . .	. . .	. . .	. . .
Other capital	4 530 . .	. . .	. . .	. . .	. . .	. . .	. . .	. . .	. . .
Claims on affiliated enterprises	4 535 . .	. . .	. . .	. . .	. . .	. . .	. . .	. . .	. . .
Liabilities to affiliated enterprises	4 540 . .	. . .	. . .	. . .	. . .	. . .	. . .	. . .	. . .
Direct investment in Belarus	4 555 . .	**10.5**	**14.7**	**104.5**	**351.6**	**203.2**	**444.0**	**118.8**	**95.8**
Equity capital	4 560 . .	10.5	14.7	104.5	344.1	185.0	443.8	115.2	89.8
Claims on direct investors	4 565 . .	. . .	. . .	. . .	. . .	. . .	. . .	. . .	. . .
Liabilities to direct investors	4 570 . .	10.5	14.7	104.5	344.1	185.0	443.8	115.2	89.8
Reinvested earnings	4 575 . .	. . .	. . .	. . .	7.5	18.2	.2	.4	.1
Other capital	4 580 . .	. . .	. . .	. . .	. . .	. . .	. . .	3.2	5.9
Claims on direct investors	4 585 . .	. . .	. . .	. . .	. . .	. . .	. . .	. . .	. . .
Liabilities to direct investors	4 590 . .	. . .	. . .	. . .	. . .	. . .	. . .	3.2	5.9
B. PORTFOLIO INVESTMENT	4 600 . .	. . .	. . .	–14.5	–19.8	14.6	–20.6	44.4	–34.9
Assets	4 602 . .	**. . .**	**. . .**	**–17.7**	**–61.6**	**28.0**	**–15.4**	**–5.7**	**10.5**
Equity securities	4 610 . .	. . .	. . .	. . .	–.6	.3	–7.3	.5	.7
Monetary authorities	4 611 . .	. . .	. . .	. . .	. . .	. . .	. . .	. . .	. . .
General government	4 612 . .	. . .	. . .	. . .	. . .	. . .	. . .	. . .	. . .
Banks	4 613 . .	. . .	. . .	. . .	–.6	.3	–7.3	–.1	.2
Other sectors	4 614 . .	. . .	. . .	. . .	. . .	. . .	. . .	.6	.5
Debt securities	4 619 . .	. . .	. . .	–17.7	–61.0	27.7	–8.1	–6.2	9.8
Bonds and notes	4 620 . .	. . .	. . .	–17.7	–61.0	27.7	–8.1	–6.2	9.8
Monetary authorities	4 621 . .	. . .	. . .	. . .	–14.8	. . .	. . .	. . .	. . .
General government	4 622 . .	. . .	. . .	. . .	. . .	. . .	. . .	. . .	. . .
Banks	4 623 . .	. . .	. . .	–17.7	–27.1	26.5	–10.2	–7.0	7.0
Other sectors	4 624 . .	. . .	. . .	. . .	–19.1	1.2	2.1	.8	2.8
Money market instruments	4 630 . .	. . .	. . .	. . .	. . .	. . .	. . .	. . .	. . .
Monetary authorities	4 631 . .	. . .	. . .	. . .	. . .	. . .	. . .	. . .	. . .
General government	4 632 . .	. . .	. . .	. . .	. . .	. . .	. . .	. . .	. . .
Banks	4 633 . .	. . .	. . .	. . .	. . .	. . .	. . .	. . .	. . .
Other sectors	4 634 . .	. . .	. . .	. . .	. . .	. . .	. . .	. . .	. . .
Liabilities	4 652 . .	**. . .**	**. . .**	**3.2**	**41.8**	**–13.4**	**–5.2**	**50.1**	**–45.4**
Equity securities	4 660 . .	. . .	. . .	. . .	. . .	2.7	. . .	.5	2.5
Banks	4 663 . .	. . .	. . .	. . .	. . .	2.7	. . .	.1	–.4
Other sectors	4 664 . .	. . .	. . .	. . .	. . .	. . .	. . .	.4	2.9
Debt securities	4 669 . .	. . .	. . .	3.2	41.8	–16.1	–5.2	49.6	–47.9
Bonds and notes	4 670 . .	. . .	. . .	3.2	41.8	–16.1	–5.2	49.6	–47.9
Monetary authorities	4 671 . .	. . .	. . .	. . .	21.2	. . .	. . .	50.0	–48.9
General government	4 672 . .	. . .	. . .	. . .	. . .	. . .	. . .	.6	–2.5
Banks	4 673 . .	. . .	. . .	–.2	4.2	–14.0	–4.4	1.4	4.0
Other sectors	4 674 . .	. . .	. . .	3.4	16.4	–2.1	–.8	–2.4	–.5
Money market instruments	4 680 . .	. . .	. . .	. . .	. . .	. . .	. . .	. . .	. . .
Monetary authorities	4 681 . .	. . .	. . .	. . .	. . .	. . .	. . .	. . .	. . .
General government	4 682 . .	. . .	. . .	. . .	. . .	. . .	. . .	. . .	. . .
Banks	4 683 . .	. . .	. . .	. . .	. . .	. . .	. . .	. . .	. . .
Other sectors	4 684 . .	. . .	. . .	. . .	. . .	. . .	. . .	. . .	. . .
C. FINANCIAL DERIVATIVES	4 910 . .	. . .	. . .	. . .	. . .	. . .	. . .	. . .	. . .
Monetary authorities	4 911 . .	. . .	. . .	. . .	. . .	. . .	. . .	. . .	. . .
General government	4 912 . .	. . .	. . .	. . .	. . .	. . .	. . .	. . .	. . .
Banks	4 913 . .	. . .	. . .	. . .	. . .	. . .	. . .	. . .	. . .
Other sectors	4 914 . .	. . .	. . .	. . .	. . .	. . .	. . .	. . .	. . .
Assets	4 900 . .	**. . .**	**. . .**	**. . .**	**. . .**	**. . .**	**. . .**	**. . .**	**. . .**
Monetary authorities	4 901 . .	. . .	. . .	. . .	. . .	. . .	. . .	. . .	. . .
General government	4 902 . .	. . .	. . .	. . .	. . .	. . .	. . .	. . .	. . .
Banks	4 903 . .	. . .	. . .	. . .	. . .	. . .	. . .	. . .	. . .
Other sectors	4 904 . .	. . .	. . .	. . .	. . .	. . .	. . .	. . .	. . .
Liabilities	4 905 . .	**. . .**	**. . .**	**. . .**	**. . .**	**. . .**	**. . .**	**. . .**	**. . .**
Monetary authorities	4 906 . .	. . .	. . .	. . .	. . .	. . .	. . .	. . .	. . .
General government	4 907 . .	. . .	. . .	. . .	. . .	. . .	. . .	. . .	. . .
Banks	4 908 . .	. . .	. . .	. . .	. . .	. . .	. . .	. . .	. . .
Other sectors	4 909 . .	. . .	. . .	. . .	. . .	. . .	. . .	. . .	. . .

Table 2 (Concluded). STANDARD PRESENTATION, 1994–2001

(Millions of U.S. dollars)

	Code	1994	1995	1996	1997	1998	1999	2000	2001
D. OTHER INVESTMENT	4 700	509.7	551.4	–323.4	268.0	404.0	–77.6	–72.5	262.7
Assets	4 703	**–232.5**	**–155.4**	**–131.5**	**49.9**	**199.4**	**–36.7**	**41.7**	**–139.2**
Trade credits	4 706	–144.6	–230.2	–93.9	59.6	187.9	–8.8	55.8	–36.5
General government	4 707	. . .	. . .	. . .	. . .	. . .	. . .	. . .	. . .
of which: Short-term	4 709	. . .	. . .	. . .	. . .	. . .	. . .	. . .	. . .
Other sectors	4 710	–144.6	–230.2	–93.9	59.6	187.9	–8.8	55.8	–36.5
of which: Short-term	4 712	*–144.6*	*–230.2*	*–93.9*	*59.6*	*187.9*	*–8.8*	*55.8*	*–36.5*
Loans	4 714	. . .	14.0	. . .	–4.2	7.1	–7.0	1.6	–21.2
Monetary authorities	4 715	. . .	. . .	. . .	. . .	. . .	. . .	. . .	–20.0
of which: Short-term	4 718	. . .	. . .	. . .	. . .	. . .	. . .	. . .	*–20.0*
General government	4 719	. . .	14.0	. . .	. . .	. . .	. . .	. . .	. . .
of which: Short-term	4 721	. . .	. . .	. . .	. . .	. . .	. . .	. . .	. . .
Banks	4 722	. . .	. . .	. . .	–5.9	8.1	–5.4	1.0	–1.7
of which: Short-term	4 724	. . .	. . .	. . .	*–5.9*	*8.1*	*–5.4*	*1.0*	*–1.8*
Other sectors	4 725	. . .	. . .	. . .	1.7	–1.0	–1.6	.6	.5
of which: Short-term	4 727	. . .	. . .	. . .	. . .	. . .	. . .	. . .	. . .
Currency and deposits	4 730	. . .	. . .	–40.2	–7.4	18.8	–6.1	9.8	–64.6
Monetary authorities	4 731	. . .	. . .	. . .	1.5	5.2	.2	.3	–79.7
General government	4 732	. . .	. . .	. . .	. . .	. . .	. . .	. . .	. . .
Banks	4 733	. . .	. . .	–40.2	–8.9	13.6	–8.1	9.1	19.2
Other sectors	4 734	. . .	. . .	. . .	. . .	. . .	1.8	.4	–4.1
Other assets	4 736	–87.9	60.8	2.6	1.9	–14.4	–14.8	–25.5	–16.9
Monetary authorities	4 737	. . .	. . .	. . .	. . .	–6.1	.9	–.5	.4
of which: Short-term	4 739	. . .	. . .	. . .	. . .	*–6.1*	*.9*	*–.5*	*.4*
General government	4 740	. . .	. . .	. . .	. . .	. . .	. . .	. . .	. . .
of which: Short-term	4 742	. . .	. . .	. . .	. . .	. . .	. . .	. . .	. . .
Banks	4 743	–94.2	58.6	. . .	2.2	–2.7	–2.9	–1.7	. . .
of which: Short-term	4 745	*–94.2*	*58.6*	. . .	*2.2*	*–2.7*	*–2.9*	*–1.7*	. . .
Other sectors	4 746	6.3	2.2	2.6	–.3	–5.6	–12.8	–23.3	–17.3
of which: Short-term	4 748	*6.3*	*2.2*	*2.6*	*–.3*	*–5.6*	*–12.8*	*–23.3*	*–17.3*
Liabilities	4 753	**742.2**	**706.8**	**–191.9**	**218.1**	**204.6**	**–40.9**	**–114.2**	**401.9**
Trade credits	4 756	92.6	227.2	187.1	359.0	–59.7	–5.0	–125.5	–19.1
General government	4 757	. . .	. . .	. . .	. . .	. . .	. . .	. . .	. . .
of which: Short-term	4 759	. . .	. . .	. . .	. . .	. . .	. . .	. . .	. . .
Other sectors	4 760	92.6	227.2	187.1	359.0	–59.7	–5.0	–125.5	–19.1
of which: Short-term	4 762	*92.6*	*227.2*	*187.1*	*359.0*	*–59.7*	*–5.0*	*–125.5*	*–19.1*
Loans	4 764	239.4	267.5	76.9	76.6	–19.0	–26.9	50.4	321.7
Monetary authorities	4 765	. . .	177.8	. . .	. . .	–24.4	–58.1	–55.8	38.6
of which: Use of Fund credit and loans from the Fund	4 766	. . .	*177.8*	. . .	. . .	*–24.4*	*–58.1*	*–55.8*	*–29.8*
of which: Short-term	4 768	. . .	. . .	. . .	. . .	. . .	. . .	. . .	. . .
General government	4 769	239.4	81.7	33.4	62.4	24.7	–28.5	–37.2	27.6
of which: Short-term	4 771	. . .	. . .	. . .	. . .	. . .	. . .	. . .	. . .
Banks	4 772	. . .	. . .	. . .	11.5	–6.5	–16.0	25.5	38.9
of which: Short-term	4 774	. . .	. . .	. . .	*11.5*	*–6.5*	*–16.0*	*25.5*	*38.9*
Other sectors	4 775	. . .	8.0	43.5	2.7	–12.8	75.7	117.9	216.6
of which: Short-term	4 777	. . .	*3.1*	*33.0*	*.4*	*–2.5*	*49.3*	*22.1*	*18.0*
Currency and deposits	4 780	. . .	. . .	156.2	–81.7	–7.4	–7.1	–44.7	61.5
Monetary authorities	4 781	. . .	. . .	133.1	–86.8	6.8	.7	–21.2	20.2
General government	4 782	. . .	. . .	. . .	. . .	. . .	. . .	. . .	. . .
Banks	4 783	. . .	. . .	23.1	5.1	–14.2	–7.8	–23.5	41.3
Other sectors	4 784	. . .	. . .	. . .	. . .	. . .	. . .	. . .	. . .
Other liabilities	4 786	410.2	212.1	–612.1	–135.8	290.7	–1.9	5.6	37.8
Monetary authorities	4 787	–.3	3.7	. . .	. . .	. . .	. . .	. . .	. . .
of which: Short-term	4 789	*–.3*	*3.7*	. . .	. . .	. . .	. . .	. . .	. . .
General government	4 790	4.3	–1.3	–843.1	–21.0	11.1	21.0	9.4	–38.0
of which: Short-term	4 792	*4.3*	*–1.3*	*–843.1*	*–21.0*	*11.1*	*21.0*	*9.4*	*–38.0*
Banks	4 793	34.9	24.1	. . .	. . .	.4	–.3	–.1	1.2
of which: Short-term	4 795	*34.9*	*24.1*	. . .	. . .	*.4*	*–.3*	*–.1*	*1.2*
Other sectors	4 796	371.3	185.6	231.0	–114.8	279.2	–22.6	–3.7	74.6
of which: Short-term	4 798	*371.3*	*185.6*	*231.0*	*–114.8*	*279.2*	*–22.6*	*–3.7*	*74.6*
E. RESERVE ASSETS	4 802	–58.6	–283.7	–78.6	75.3	54.6	34.6	–75.7	5.2
Monetary gold	4 812	. . .	. . .	. . .	. . .	–6.0	–4.4	. . .	. . .
Special drawing rights	4 811	4.6	–4.5	4.4	. . .	–.4	.1	–.2	–.2
Reserve position in the Fund	4 810	. . .	. . .	. . .	. . .	. . .	. . .	. . .	. . .
Foreign exchange	4 803	–63.1	–279.3	–27.3	75.3	61.0	38.9	–61.7	9.5
Other claims	4 813	–.1	.1	–55.7	. . .	. . .	. . .	–13.8	–4.1
NET ERRORS AND OMISSIONS	4 998	**–41.6**	**168.6**	**–178.1**	**53.0**	**172.3**	**–246.3**	**238.9**	**–99.6**

Part 3 of the *Yearbook* contains descriptions of the methodologies, compilation practices, and sources used to compile these data.

Table 3. INTERNATIONAL INVESTMENT POSITION (End–period stocks), 1994–2001

(Millions of U.S. dollars)

	Code	1994	1995	1996	1997	1998	1999	2000	2001
ASSETS	8 995 C.	...	...	1,335.4	1,273.7	991.3	1,004.2	996.9	1,107.8
Direct investment abroad	8 505 . .	**...**	**...**	**...**	**2.1**	**4.4**	**5.2**	**5.5**	**5.8**
Equity capital and reinvested earnings	8 506 . .	...	...	...	2.1	4.4	5.2	5.5	5.8
Claims on affiliated enterprises	8 507 . .	...	...	...	2.1	4.4	5.2	5.5	5.8
Liabilities to affiliated enterprises	8 508 . .	...	...	...	...	...	...	...	...
Other capital	8 530 . .	...	...	...	...	...	...	...	...
Claims on affiliated enterprises	8 535 . .	...	...	...	...	...	...	...	...
Liabilities to affiliated enterprises	8 540 . .	...	...	...	...	...	...	...	...
Portfolio investment	8 602 . .	**...**	**...**	**21.5**	**83.1**	**55.1**	**69.0**	**57.5**	**46.6**
Equity securities	8 610 . .	...	...	2.3	2.9	2.6	9.8	9.3	8.3
Monetary authorities	8 611 . .	...	...	...	...	...	...	.1	.1
General government	8 612 . .	...	...	...	...	...	...	...	...
Banks	8 613 . .	...	...	.2	.8	.5	7.7	7.8	7.3
Other sectors	8 614 . .	...	...	2.1	2.1	2.1	2.1	1.4	.9
Debt securities	8 619 . .	...	...	19.2	80.2	52.5	59.2	48.2	38.3
Bonds and notes	8 620 . .	...	...	19.2	80.2	52.5	59.2	48.2	38.3
Monetary authorities	8 621 . .	...	...	...	14.8	14.8	14.8	...	...
General government	8 622 . .	...	...	1.5	1.5	1.5	1.5	...	...
Banks	8 623 . .	...	...	17.7	44.8	18.3	27.1	34.0	26.9
Other sectors	8 624 . .	...	...	...	19.1	17.9	15.8	14.2	11.4
Money market instruments	8 630 . .	...	...	...	...	...	...	...	...
Monetary authorities	8 631 . .	...	...	...	...	...	...	...	...
General government	8 632 . .	...	...	...	...	...	...	...	...
Banks	8 633 . .	...	...	...	...	...	...	...	...
Other sectors	8 634 . .	...	...	...	...	...	...	...	...
Financial derivatives	8 900 . .	**...**	**...**	**...**	**...**	**...**	**...**	**...**	**...**
Monetary authorities	8 901 . .	...	...	...	...	...	...	...	...
General government	8 902 . .	...	...	...	...	...	...	...	...
Banks	8 903 . .	...	...	...	...	...	...	...	...
Other sectors	8 904 . .	...	...	...	...	...	...	...	...
Other investment	8 703 . .	**...**	**...**	**844.8**	**794.9**	**592.8**	**625.4**	**577.1**	**709.8**
Trade credits	8 706 . .	...	...	538.3	478.7	260.0	301.5	245.8	282.3
General government	8 707 . .	...	...	...	...	...	...	...	...
of which: Short-term	8 709 . .	...	...	...	...	...	...	...	...
Other sectors	8 710 . .	...	...	538.3	478.7	260.0	301.5	245.8	282.3
of which: Short-term	8 712 . .	...	...	*538.3*	*478.7*	*260.0*	*301.5*	*245.8*	*282.3*
Loans	8 714 . .	...	...	5.7	9.9	2.7	9.7	8.1	29.0
Monetary authorities	8 715 . .	...	...	...	...	...	...	...	20.0
of which: Short-term	8 718 . .	...	...	...	...	...	...	...	*20.0*
General government	8 719 . .	...	...	...	...	...	...	...	...
of which: Short-term	8 721 . .	...	...	...	...	...	...	...	...
Banks	8 722 . .	...	...	3.7	9.6	1.4	6.8	5.8	7.2
of which: Short-term	8 724 . .	...	...	*3.7*	*9.6*	*1.4*	*6.8*	*5.7*	*7.2*
Other sectors	8 725 . .	...	...	2.0	.3	1.3	2.9	2.3	1.8
of which: Short-term	8 727 . .	...	...	...	...	...	...	...	...
Currency and deposits	8 730 . .	...	...	291.1	298.5	279.7	288.8	276.7	335.4
Monetary authorities	8 731 . .	...	...	9.0	7.5	2.3	2.1	1.6	78.0
General government	8 732 . .	...	...	...	...	...	...	...	...
Banks	8 733 . .	...	...	282.1	291.0	277.4	282.0	271.5	250.0
Other sectors	8 734 . .	...	...	...	...	...	4.7	3.6	7.4
Other assets	8 736 . .	...	...	9.7	7.8	50.4	25.4	46.5	63.1
Monetary authorities	8 737 . .	...	...	...	...	6.1	5.3	.6	.1
of which: Short-term	8 739 . .	...	...	...	...	*6.1*	*5.3*	*.6*	*.1*
General government	8 740 . .	...	...	...	...	...	...	...	...
of which: Short-term	8 742 . .	...	...	...	...	...	...	...	...
Banks	8 743 . .	...	...	5.9	3.7	6.6	9.4	11.6	11.4
of which: Short-term	8 745 . .	...	...	*5.9*	*3.7*	*6.6*	*9.4*	*11.6*	*11.4*
Other sectors	8 746 . .	...	...	3.8	4.1	37.7	10.7	34.3	51.6
of which: Short-term	8 748 . .	...	...	*3.8*	*4.1*	*37.7*	*10.7*	*34.3*	*51.6*
Reserve assets	8 802 . .	**...**	**...**	**469.1**	**393.6**	**339.0**	**304.6**	**356.8**	**345.6**
Monetary gold	8 812 . .	...	...	...	...	...	...	...	...
Special drawing rights	8 811 . .	...	4.5	.1	...	.4	.4	.2	.4
Reserve position in the Fund	8 810 . .	...	...	...	...	...	...	...	...
Foreign exchange	8 803 . .	...	...	468.9	393.6	332.6	293.8	350.0	336.8
Other claims	8 813 . .	...	...	...	...	6.0	10.4	6.6	8.4

Table 3 (Concluded). INTERNATIONAL INVESTMENT POSITION (End–period stocks), 1994–2001
(Millions of U.S. dollars)

	Code	1994	1995	1996	1997	1998	1999	2000	2001
LIABILITIES	8 995 D.	...	...	2,064.7	2,656.7	3,086.9	3,419.6	3,436.8	3,868.9
Direct investment in Belarus	8 555 ..	**...**	**...**	**154.3**	**505.9**	**709.1**	**1,153.1**	**1,305.5**	**1,412.8**
Equity capital and reinvested earnings	8 556 ..	...	...	154.3	505.9	709.1	1,153.1	1,305.5	1,412.8
Claims on direct investors	8 557 ..	...	...	...	...	...	...	...	...
Liabilities to direct investors	8 558 ..	...	...	154.3	505.9	709.1	1,153.1	1,305.5	1,412.8
Other capital	8 580 ..	...	...	...	...	...	...	...	...
Claims on direct investors	8 585 ..	...	...	...	...	...	...	...	...
Liabilities to direct investors	8 590 ..	...	...	...	...	...	...	...	...
Portfolio investment	8 652 ..	**...**	**...**	**34.6**	**76.4**	**63.0**	**44.7**	**78.6**	**36.1**
Equity securities	8 660 ..	...	...	5.5	5.5	8.2	8.2	8.8	11.4
Banks	8 663 ..	...	...	4.5	4.5	7.2	7.2	7.3	6.9
Other sectors	8 664 ..	...	...	1.0	1.0	1.0	1.0	1.5	4.5
Debt securities	8 669 ..	...	...	29.1	70.9	54.8	36.5	69.8	24.7
Bonds and notes	8 670 ..	...	...	29.1	70.9	54.8	36.5	69.8	24.7
Monetary authorities	8 671 ..	...	...	...	21.2	21.2	21.2	50.0	1.1
General government	8 672 ..	...	...	...	...	...	...	...	.2
Banks	8 673 ..	...	...	25.7	29.9	15.9	.4	7.4	11.5
Other sectors	8 674 ..	...	...	3.4	19.8	17.7	14.9	12.4	11.9
Money market instruments	8 680 ..	...	...	...	...	...	...	...	...
Monetary authorities	8 681 ..	...	...	...	...	...	...	...	...
General government	8 682 ..	...	...	...	...	...	...	...	...
Banks	8 683 ..	...	...	...	...	...	...	...	...
Other sectors	8 684 ..	...	...	...	...	...	...	...	...
Financial derivatives	8 905 ..	**...**	**...**	**...**	**...**	**...**	**...**	**...**	**...**
Monetary authorities	8 906 ..	...	...	...	...	...	...	...	...
General government	8 907 ..	...	...	...	...	...	...	...	...
Banks	8 908 ..	...	...	...	...	...	...	...	...
Other sectors	8 909 ..	...	...	...	...	...	...	...	...
Other investment	8 753 ..	**...**	**...**	**1,875.8**	**2,074.4**	**2,314.8**	**2,221.8**	**2,052.7**	**2,420.0**
Trade credits	8 756 ..	...	...	338.1	697.1	510.4	622.3	494.6	475.5
General government	8 757 ..	...	...	...	...	...	...	...	...
of which: Short-term	8 759 ..	...	...	...	...	...	...	...	...
Other sectors	8 760 ..	...	...	338.1	697.1	510.4	622.3	494.6	475.5
of which: Short-term	8 762 ..	...	...	*338.1*	*697.1*	*510.4*	*622.3*	*494.6*	*475.5*
Loans	8 764 ..	...	...	1,045.2	1,102.4	1,114.9	1,039.6	1,051.0	1,341.9
Monetary authorities	8 765 ..	...	...	309.0	289.3	277.7	208.4	142.1	174.4
of which: Use of Fund credit and loans from the Fund	8 766 ..	*102.3*	*282.7*	*273.5*	*256.6*	*242.6*	*178.1*	*114.2*	*80.8*
of which: Short-term	8 768 ..	...	...	...	...	...	...	...	...
General government	8 769 ..	...	...	615.9	680.3	371.1	340.0	302.8	330.4
of which: Short-term	8 771 ..	...	...	...	...	...	...	...	...
Banks	8 772 ..	...	...	47.7	59.2	52.8	36.8	62.4	99.5
of which: Short-term	8 774 ..	...	...	*47.7*	*59.2*	*52.8*	*36.8*	*62.4*	*99.5*
Other sectors	8 775 ..	...	...	72.6	73.6	413.3	454.4	543.7	737.6
of which: Short-term	8 777 ..	...	...	*39.5*	*39.2*	*33.7*	*79.6*	*90.9*	*107.3*
Currency and deposits	8 780 ..	...	...	195.9	114.2	106.7	97.1	51.0	106.9
Monetary authorities	8 781 ..	...	...	100.9	14.1	20.9	21.7	.3	20.5
General government	8 782 ..	...	...	...	...	...	...	...	...
Banks	8 783 ..	...	...	95.0	100.1	85.8	75.4	50.7	86.4
Other sectors	8 784 ..	...	...	...	...	...	...	...	...
Other liabilities	8 786 ..	...	...	296.6	160.7	582.8	462.8	456.1	495.7
Monetary authorities	8 787 ..	...	...	...	...	...	...	...	...
of which: Short-term	8 789 ..	...	...	...	...	...	...	...	...
General government	8 790 ..	...	...	23.6	2.7	15.2	35.9	43.2	3.8
of which: Short-term	8 792 ..	...	...	*23.6*	*2.7*	*15.2*	*35.9*	*43.2*	*3.8*
Banks	8 793 ..	...	...	.1	.1	.5	.2	1.0	2.2
of which: Short-term	8 795 ..	...	...	*.1*	*.1*	*.5*	*.2*	*1.0*	*2.2*
Other sectors	8 796 ..	...	...	272.9	157.9	567.1	426.7	411.9	489.7
of which: Short-term	8 798 ..	...	...	*272.9*	*157.9*	*567.1*	*426.7*	*411.9*	*489.7*
NET INTERNATIONAL INVESTMENT POSITION	8 995 ..	**...**	**...**	**–729.3**	**–1,383.0**	**–2,095.5**	**–2,415.3**	**–2,439.9**	**–2,761.0**
Conversion rates: rubels per U.S. dollar (end of period)	0 102 ..	**10.60**	**11.50**	**15.50**	**30.74**	**220.00**	**320.00**	**1,180.00**	**1,580.00**

Table 1. ANALYTIC PRESENTATION, 1994–2001
(Millions of U.S. dollars)

	Code	1994	1995	1996	1997	1998	1999	2000	2001
A. Current Account[1]	4 993 Z.	**12,571**	**14,232**	**13,762**	**13,914**	**12,168**	**14,579**	**11,360**	**13,534**
Goods: exports f.o.b	2 100 . .	122,795	155,219	154,695	149,497	153,558	161,278	164,471	162,970
Goods: imports f.o.b	3 100 . .	–115,895	–145,664	–146,004	–141,794	–146,577	–154,782	–162,246	–159,302
Balance on Goods	4 100 . .	*6,901*	*9,555*	*8,690*	*7,703*	*6,981*	*6,496*	*2,225*	*3,668*
Services: credit	2 200 . .	40,440	35,466	34,702	35,503	38,081	41,749	44,008	44,480
Services: debit	3 200 . .	–36,500	–33,134	–32,069	–31,664	–34,411	–36,839	–38,866	–40,043
Balance on Goods and Services	4 991 . .	*10,841*	*11,887*	*11,322*	*11,542*	*10,651*	*11,406*	*7,368*	*8,106*
Income: credit	2 300 . .	89,403	74,798	62,884	58,237	65,251	71,487	75,740	79,912
Income: debit	3 300 . .	–84,166	–67,990	–55,838	–51,882	–59,315	–63,485	–67,569	–70,403
Balance on Goods, Services, and Income	4 992 . .	*16,078*	*18,695*	*18,368*	*17,896*	*16,588*	*19,409*	*15,538*	*17,614*
Current transfers: credit	2 379 Z.	4,501	7,822	7,474	7,142	7,006	7,041	7,010	7,303
Current transfers: debit	3 379 . .	–8,009	–12,285	–12,081	–11,124	–11,426	–11,871	–11,188	–11,384
B. Capital Account[1]	4 994 Z.	**. . .**	**378**	**179**	**403**	**–113**	**–78**	**–213**	**23**
Capital account: credit	2 994 Z.	. . .	734	673	783	323	420	222	482
Capital account: debit	3 994 . .	. . .	–356	–494	–379	–436	–497	–436	–460
Total, Groups A Plus B	4 981 . .	*12,571*	*14,610*	*13,941*	*14,318*	*12,055*	*14,501*	*11,147*	*13,557*
C. Financial Account[1]	4 995 W.	**–10,182**	**–12,912**	**–12,257**	**–12,091**	**–16,043**	**–15,139**	**–10,861**	**–11,109**
Direct investment abroad	4 505 . .	–1,371	–11,603	–8,026	–7,252	–28,845	–121,722	–229,355	–66,376
Direct investment in Belgium-Luxembourg	4 555 Z.	8,514	10,689	14,064	11,998	22,690	133,055	234,757	50,460
Portfolio investment assets	4 602 . .	–40,963	–29,472	–48,409	–62,657	–100,234	–161,579	–122,972	–126,612
Equity securities	4 610 . .	–10,649	–3,525	–3,582	–21,006	–29,087	–60,737	–103,445	–57,232
Debt securities	4 619 . .	–30,314	–25,946	–44,827	–41,651	–71,147	–100,842	–19,528	–69,380
Portfolio investment liabilities	4 652 Z.	17,445	4,649	36,666	54,047	59,253	135,259	132,130	147,117
Equity securities	4 660 . .	22,489	6,505	34,243	47,207	58,418	91,794	82,405	97,304
Debt securities	4 669 Z.	–5,043	–1,856	2,423	6,840	835	43,466	49,725	49,813
Financial derivatives	4 910 . .	. . .	1,843	–487	113	791	2,026	–2,401	–6,799
Financial derivatives assets	4 900 . .	. . .	1,213	–970	–330	489	884	–3,653	–7,740
Financial derivatives liabilities	4 905 . .	. . .	630	483	444	302	1,142	1,252	942
Other investment assets	4 703 . .	11,269	–23,445	–14,977	–48,692	7,467	–58,340	–37,983	–71,883
Monetary authorities	4 701 . .	. . .	. . .	. . .	. . .	–147	–991	–342	13
General government	4 704 . .	–294	–72	–372	–306	371	–1,848	–236	–137
Banks	4 705 . .	9,829	–16,926	9,164	–28,220	3,886	–12,806	–22,296	–58,022
Other sectors	4 728 . .	1,734	6,447	–23,769	–20,166	3,357	–42,694	–15,109	–13,737
Other investment liabilities	4 753 W.	–5,076	34,426	8,913	40,352	22,836	56,162	14,963	62,984
Monetary authorities	4 753 WA	. . .	223	–458	–50	193	23,578	–1,386	–3,903
General government	4 753 ZB	–5,233	322	40	–161	203	1,405	–1,231	493
Banks	4 753 ZC	64	42,121	6,469	31,211	18,087	6,702	7,139	67,223
Other sectors	4 753 ZD	93	–8,240	2,941	9,352	4,352	24,476	10,441	–829
Total, Groups A Through C	4 983 . .	*2,388*	*1,698*	*1,683*	*2,227*	*–3,988*	*–638*	*285*	*2,448*
D. Net Errors and Omissions	4 998 . .	**–2,169**	**–1,456**	**–1,091**	**–1,171**	**1,893**	**–1,230**	**–1,244**	**–1,006**
Total, Groups A Through D	4 984 . .	*219*	*243*	*593*	*1,056*	*–2,095*	*–1,867*	*–959*	*1,442*
E. Reserves and Related Items	4 802 A.	**–219**	**–243**	**–593**	**–1,056**	**2,095**	**1,867**	**959**	**–1,442**
Reserve assets	4 802 . .	–219	–243	–593	–1,056	2,095	1,867	959	–1,442
Use of Fund credit and loans	4 766 . .	. . .	. . .	. . .	. . .	. . .	. . .	. . .	. . .
Exceptional financing	4 920 . .	. . .	. . .	. . .	. . .	. . .	. . .	. . .	. . .
Conversion rates: Belgian francs (or Luxembourg francs) per U.S. dollar	0 101 . .	**33.456**	**29.480**	**30.962**	**35.774**	**36.299**	**. . .**	**. . .**	**. . .**
Conversion rates: euros per U.S. dollar	0 103 . .	**. . .**	**. . .**	**. . .**	**. . .**	**. . .**	**.93863**	**1.08540**	**1.11751**

[1] Excludes components that have been classified in the categories of Group E.

Table 2. STANDARD PRESENTATION, 1994–2001
(Millions of U.S. dollars)

	Code			1994	1995	1996	1997	1998	1999	2000	2001
CURRENT ACCOUNT	4	993	. .	**12,571**	**14,232**	**13,762**	**13,914**	**12,168**	**14,579**	**11,360**	**13,534**
A. GOODS	4	100	. .	6,901	9,555	8,690	7,703	6,981	6,496	2,225	3,668
Credit	2	100	. .	**122,795**	**155,219**	**154,695**	**149,497**	**153,558**	**161,278**	**164,471**	**162,970**
General merchandise: exports f.o.b.	2	110	. .	118,790	150,443	149,702	144,984	148,907	145,187	149,212	146,162
Goods for processing: exports f.o.b.	2	150	. .	2,878	3,377	3,668	3,216	3,202	14,177	12,984	14,625
Repairs on goods	2	160	. .	202	245	256	166	203	308	372	384
Goods procured in ports by carriers	2	170	. .	344	543	627	736	667	948	1,299	1,245
Nonmonetary gold	2	180	. .	581	611	441	396	579	657	605	554
Debit	3	100	. .	**-115,895**	**-145,664**	**-146,004**	**-141,794**	**-146,577**	**-154,782**	**-162,246**	**-159,302**
General merchandise: imports f.o.b.	3	110	. .	-114,517	-143,868	-143,903	-139,730	-144,467	-141,245	-149,093	-144,511
Goods for processing: imports f.o.b.	3	150	. .	-511	-797	-1,042	-1,066	-853	-12,388	-11,607	-13,496
Repairs on goods	3	160	. .	-153	-259	-331	-283	-342	-383	-396	-331
Goods procured in ports by carriers	3	170	. .	-245	-307	-352	-326	-361	-393	-642	-546
Nonmonetary gold	3	180	. .	-468	-433	-377	-389	-553	-373	-508	-417
B. SERVICES	4	200	. .	3,940	2,332	2,632	3,839	3,670	4,910	5,142	4,437
Total credit	2	200	. .	*40,440*	*35,466*	*34,702*	*35,503*	*38,081*	*41,749*	*44,008*	*44,480*
Total debit	3	200	. .	*-36,500*	*-33,134*	*-32,069*	*-31,664*	*-34,411*	*-36,839*	*-38,866*	*-40,043*
Transportation services, credit	2	205	. .	**9,666**	**9,869**	**9,557**	**9,647**	**9,909**	**10,071**	**10,640**	**10,006**
Passenger	2	850	. .	*1,422*	*1,208*	*1,152*	*1,167*	*1,437*	*1,586*	*1,692*	*1,325*
Freight	2	851	. .	*7,282*	*7,659*	*7,143*	*6,826*	*6,918*	*7,047*	*7,721*	*7,576*
Other	2	852	. .	*962*	*1,001*	*1,262*	*1,654*	*1,554*	*1,438*	*1,227*	*1,104*
Sea transport, passenger	2	207	. .	. . .	3	2	2	6	13	11	9
Sea transport, freight	2	208	. .	. . .	4,120	3,746	3,547	3,258	3,177	3,900	3,819
Sea transport, other	2	209	. .	. . .	657	635	681	713	733	704	622
Air transport, passenger	2	211	. .	. . .	1,050	1,044	1,082	1,329	1,501	1,602	1,228
Air transport, freight	2	212	. .	. . .	513	535	537	693	839	796	896
Air transport, other	2	213	. .	. . .	53	224	313	334	324	269	156
Other transport, passenger	2	215	. .	1,422	155	106	83	101	73	79	88
Other transport, freight	2	216	. .	7,282	3,026	2,861	2,742	2,966	3,031	3,025	2,862
Other transport, other	2	217	. .	962	291	404	659	507	381	254	327
Transportation services, debit	3	205	. .	**-7,699**	**-7,842**	**-7,547**	**-7,604**	**-7,455**	**-7,388**	**-8,345**	**-8,187**
Passenger	3	850	. .	*-1,239*	*-1,016*	*-1,061*	*-1,032*	*-1,131*	*-1,137*	*-1,225*	*-995*
Freight	3	851	. .	*-5,639*	*-6,281*	*-5,897*	*-5,893*	*-5,619*	*-5,603*	*-6,431*	*-6,538*
Other	3	852	. .	*-820*	*-545*	*-589*	*-679*	*-705*	*-648*	*-688*	*-653*
Sea transport, passenger	3	207	. .	. . .	-9	-6	-7	-7	-11	-7	-10
Sea transport, freight	3	208	. .	. . .	-3,572	-3,211	-3,283	-2,929	-2,784	-3,583	-3,604
Sea transport, other	3	209	. .	. . .	-317	-337	-287	-245	-232	-182	-175
Air transport, passenger	3	211	. .	. . .	-871	-955	-950	-1,024	-1,047	-1,151	-912
Air transport, freight	3	212	. .	. . .	-229	-292	-392	-496	-546	-563	-592
Air transport, other	3	213	. .	. . .	-134	-174	-303	-383	-347	-436	-375
Other transport, passenger	3	215	. .	-1,239	-136	-100	-76	-100	-80	-67	-73
Other transport, freight	3	216	. .	-5,639	-2,481	-2,394	-2,218	-2,195	-2,273	-2,285	-2,342
Other transport, other	3	217	. .	-820	-94	-77	-88	-78	-68	-70	-103
Travel, credit	2	236	. .	**5,182**	**5,859**	**4,893**	**5,267**	**5,443**	**7,316**	**7,442**	**7,622**
Business travel	2	237	. .	25	1,154	882	995	1,115	2,868	2,924	3,363
Personal travel	2	240	. .	5,157	4,705	4,011	4,271	4,328	4,448	4,518	4,259
Travel, debit	3	236	. .	**-7,773**	**-9,003**	**-8,562**	**-8,281**	**-8,794**	**-10,437**	**-10,178**	**-10,548**
Business travel	3	237	. .	. . .	-2,046	-2,185	-2,057	-2,328	-3,662	-3,513	-4,045
Personal travel	3	240	. .	-7,773	-6,957	-6,378	-6,224	-6,466	-6,775	-6,665	-6,504
Other services, credit	2	200	BA	**25,592**	**19,738**	**20,253**	**20,589**	**22,729**	**24,362**	**25,926**	**26,852**
Communications	2	245	. .	. . .	1,001	1,277	1,302	1,469	1,762	1,893	2,075
Construction	2	249	. .	736	616	691	986	895	968	921	884
Insurance	2	253	. .	4,016	881	903	913	898	1,012	1,068	1,031
Financial	2	260	. .	5,465	4,089	4,217	4,726	5,353	6,726	7,393	7,181
Computer and information	2	262	. .	. . .	1,197	1,322	1,290	1,407	1,709	1,777	1,887
Royalties and licence fees	2	266	. .	1,075	582	668	667	703	774	780	862
Other business services	2	268	. .	11,140	9,203	9,122	8,904	9,959	9,586	10,234	10,978
Personal, cultural, and recreational	2	287	. .	681	322	414	397	652	607	628	615
Government, n.i.e.	2	291	. .	2,480	1,847	1,638	1,405	1,394	1,219	1,232	1,339
Other services, debit	3	200	BA	**-21,028**	**-16,289**	**-15,960**	**-15,778**	**-18,162**	**-19,014**	**-20,343**	**-21,308**
Communications	3	245	. .	. . .	-399	-448	-505	-573	-699	-989	-1,187
Construction	3	249	. .	-553	-728	-701	-935	-860	-656	-607	-581
Insurance	3	253	. .	-3,410	-784	-814	-769	-769	-858	-868	-858
Financial	3	260	. .	-4,273	-2,534	-2,463	-2,835	-3,616	-4,576	-4,918	-4,251
Computer and information	3	262	. .	. . .	-623	-680	-809	-1,076	-1,265	-1,318	-1,462
Royalties and licence fees	3	266	. .	-1,533	-1,158	-1,194	-1,092	-1,150	-1,113	-913	-1,222
Other business services	3	268	. .	-9,966	-8,643	-8,255	-7,919	-9,013	-8,655	-9,479	-10,526
Personal, cultural, and recreational	3	287	. .	-528	-795	-754	-687	-789	-840	-827	-763
Government, n.i.e.	3	291	. .	-766	-623	-651	-227	-316	-352	-424	-458

Table 2 (Continued). STANDARD PRESENTATION, 1994–2001
(Millions of U.S. dollars)

	Code		1994	1995	1996	1997	1998	1999	2000	2001
C. INCOME	4 300	. .	5,237	6,808	7,046	6,354	5,936	8,003	8,170	9,509
Total credit	2 300	. .	*89,403*	*74,798*	*62,884*	*58,237*	*65,251*	*71,487*	*75,740*	*79,912*
Total debit	3 300	. .	*–84,166*	*–67,990*	*–55,838*	*–51,882*	*–59,315*	*–63,485*	*–67,569*	*–70,403*
Compensation of employees, credit	2 310	. .	**3,524**	**4,481**	**4,490**	**3,983**	**3,898**	**4,109**	**3,720**	**3,219**
Compensation of employees, debit	3 310	. .	**–1,712**	**–2,491**	**–2,578**	**–2,508**	**–2,712**	**–2,974**	**–2,932**	**–3,267**
Investment income, credit	2 320	. .	**85,879**	**70,316**	**58,394**	**54,254**	**61,353**	**67,379**	**72,020**	**76,693**
Direct investment income	2 330	. .	. . .	6,161	4,520	3,916	3,870	4,068	5,062	5,733
Dividends and distributed branch profits	2 332	. .	. . .	4,335	3,181	2,760	2,733	1,529	1,766	1,974
Reinvested earnings and undistributed branch profits	2 333	. .	. . .	. . .	. . .	. . .	. . .	666	860	. . .
Income on debt (interest)	2 334	. .	. . .	1,826	1,339	1,156	1,137	1,873	2,436	3,758
Portfolio investment income	2 339	. .	31,556	25,470	18,801	17,291	19,367	33,850	34,244	36,333
Income on equity	2 340	. .	. . .	1,361	998	892	958	3,757	4,972	5,090
Income on bonds and notes	2 350	. .	31,556	23,324	17,227	15,801	17,534	27,385	26,457	27,524
Income on money market instruments	2 360	. .	. . .	785	576	598	875	2,708	2,814	3,719
Other investment income	2 370	. .	54,324	38,685	35,073	33,046	38,117	29,461	32,715	34,627
Investment income, debit	3 320	. .	**–82,454**	**–65,498**	**–53,259**	**–49,374**	**–56,603**	**–60,510**	**–64,637**	**–67,137**
Direct investment income	3 330	. .	. . .	–10,772	–7,985	–6,936	–6,861	–8,635	–8,574	–7,579
Dividends and distributed branch profits	3 332	. .	. . .	–9,224	–6,905	–6,001	–5,942	–4,351	–4,589	–5,460
Reinvested earnings and undistributed branch profits	3 333	. .	. . .	. . .	. . .	. . .	. . .	–2,565	–2,350	. . .
Income on debt (interest)	3 334	. .	. . .	–1,547	–1,080	–935	–920	–1,719	–1,634	–2,119
Portfolio investment income	3 339	. .	–24,646	–19,122	–13,350	–12,399	–14,618	–22,894	–23,765	–25,401
Income on equity	3 340	. .	. . .	–14,554	–10,163	–9,639	–11,697	–18,140	–17,488	–18,221
Income on bonds and notes	3 350	. .	–24,646	–3,478	–2,427	–2,101	–2,243	–3,988	–5,034	–5,494
Income on money market instruments	3 360	. .	. . .	–1,089	–760	–659	–678	–767	–1,243	–1,687
Other investment income	3 370	. .	–57,808	–35,605	–31,925	–30,039	–35,123	–28,982	–32,298	–34,156
D. CURRENT TRANSFERS	4 379	. .	–3,507	–4,463	–4,607	–3,982	–4,420	–4,830	–4,178	–4,080
Credit	2 379	. .	**4,501**	**7,822**	**7,474**	**7,142**	**7,006**	**7,041**	**7,010**	**7,303**
General government	2 380	. .	2,206	3,350	2,669	2,589	2,531	2,211	1,987	2,090
Other sectors	2 390	. .	2,295	4,472	4,804	4,553	4,475	4,830	5,023	5,213
Workers' remittances	2 391	. .	1,089	82	95	96	120	101	101	92
Other current transfers	2 392	. .	1,206	4,390	4,710	4,457	4,355	4,729	4,922	5,121
Debit	3 379	. .	**–8,009**	**–12,285**	**–12,081**	**–11,124**	**–11,426**	**–11,871**	**–11,188**	**–11,384**
General government	3 380	. .	–4,695	–6,598	–5,826	–5,493	–5,765	–5,652	–5,080	–5,167
Other sectors	3 390	. .	–3,313	–5,686	–6,254	–5,631	–5,661	–6,219	–6,108	–6,216
Workers' remittances	3 391	. .	–1,948	–456	–443	–394	–389	–393	–431	–360
Other current transfers	3 392	. .	–1,365	–5,230	–5,811	–5,236	–5,272	–5,826	–5,677	–5,856
CAPITAL AND FINANCIAL ACCOUNT	4 996	. .	**–10,402**	**–12,777**	**–12,671**	**–12,743**	**–14,061**	**–13,349**	**–10,116**	**–12,528**
CAPITAL ACCOUNT	4 994	. .	**. . .**	**378**	**179**	**403**	**–113**	**–78**	**–213**	**23**
Total credit	2 994	. .	. . .	*734*	*673*	*783*	*323*	*420*	*222*	*482*
Total debit	3 994	. .	. . .	*–356*	*–494*	*–379*	*–436*	*–497*	*–436*	*–460*
Capital transfers, credit	2 400	. .	**. . .**	**531**	**636**	**760**	**246**	**280**	**214**	**221**
General government	2 401	. .	. . .	119	234	435	33	. . .	1	1
Debt forgiveness	2 402	. .	. . .	. . .	. . .	. . .	. . .	. . .	. . .	. . .
Other capital transfers	2 410	. .	. . .	119	234	435	33	. . .	1	1
Other sectors	2 430	. .	. . .	411	402	325	214	280	213	220
Migrants' transfers	2 431	. .	. . .	374	363	250	186	257	184	182
Debt forgiveness	2 432	. .	. . .	. . .	. . .	. . .	. . .	. . .	. . .	. . .
Other capital transfers	2 440	. .	. . .	37	40	75	27	23	29	38
Capital transfers, debit	3 400	. .	**. . .**	**–343**	**–449**	**–297**	**–290**	**–378**	**–344**	**–358**
General government	3 401	. .	. . .	–9	–10	–44	–12	–64	–84	–71
Debt forgiveness	3 402	. .	. . .	. . .	. . .	. . .	. . .	. . .	. . .	. . .
Other capital transfers	3 410	. .	. . .	–9	–10	–44	–12	–64	–84	–71
Other sectors	3 430	. .	. . .	–333	–439	–254	–278	–314	–260	–288
Migrants' transfers	3 431	. .	. . .	–304	–397	–223	–247	–286	–225	–271
Debt forgiveness	3 432	. .	. . .	. . .	. . .	. . .	. . .	. . .	. . .	. . .
Other capital transfers	3 440	. .	. . .	–29	–42	–31	–31	–29	–35	–17
Nonproduced nonfinancial assets, credit	2 480	. .	**. . .**	**204**	**37**	**23**	**77**	**140**	**8**	**262**
Nonproduced nonfinancial assets, debit	3 480	. .	**. . .**	**–14**	**–46**	**–82**	**–146**	**–119**	**–91**	**–101**

Table 2 (Continued). STANDARD PRESENTATION, 1994–2001
(Millions of U.S. dollars)

	Code	1994	1995	1996	1997	1998	1999	2000	2001
FINANCIAL ACCOUNT	4 995	**–10,402**	**–13,155**	**–12,850**	**–13,147**	**–13,948**	**–13,271**	**–9,902**	**–12,551**
A. DIRECT INVESTMENT	4 500	7,142	–914	6,038	4,746	–6,155	11,333	5,402	–15,917
Direct investment abroad	4 505	**–1,371**	**–11,603**	**–8,026**	**–7,252**	**–28,845**	**–121,722**	**–229,355**	**–66,376**
Equity capital	4 510	–2,403	–4,520	–5,161	–4,187	–14,934	–87,300	–163,331	–27,966
Claims on affiliated enterprises	4 515	...	...	...	...	...	...	...	...
Liabilities to affiliated enterprises	4 520	...	...	...	...	...	...	...	...
Reinvested earnings	4 525	...	...	...	...	...	–666	–860	...
Other capital	4 530	1,032	–7,083	–2,865	–3,065	–13,911	–33,756	–65,164	–38,410
Claims on affiliated enterprises	4 535	...	...	...	...	...	...	...	...
Liabilities to affiliated enterprises	4 540	...	...	...	...	...	...	...	...
Direct investment in Belgium-Luxembourg	4 555	**8,514**	**10,689**	**14,064**	**11,998**	**22,690**	**133,055**	**234,757**	**50,460**
Equity capital	4 560	7,483	6,332	8,401	5,972	11,237	121,060	165,069	44,429
Claims on direct investors	4 565	...	...	...	...	...	...	...	...
Liabilities to direct investors	4 570	...	...	...	...	...	...	...	...
Reinvested earnings	4 575	...	...	...	...	...	2,565	2,350	...
Other capital	4 580	1,031	4,356	5,663	6,026	11,453	9,430	67,338	6,031
Claims on direct investors	4 585	...	...	...	...	...	...	...	...
Liabilities to direct investors	4 590	...	...	...	...	...	...	...	...
B. PORTFOLIO INVESTMENT	4 600	–23,518	–24,822	–11,743	–8,610	–40,981	–26,320	9,158	20,505
Assets	4 602	**–40,963**	**–29,472**	**–48,409**	**–62,657**	**–100,234**	**–161,579**	**–122,972**	**–126,612**
Equity securities	4 610	–10,649	–3,525	–3,582	–21,006	–29,087	–60,737	–103,445	–57,232
Monetary authorities	4 611	...	...	...	...	...	...	...	...
General government	4 612	...	...	...	...	...	...	...	...
Banks	4 613	...	1,130	219	–772	–903	–838	–1,164	756
Other sectors	4 614	–10,649	–4,655	–3,801	–20,234	–28,185	–59,899	–102,280	–57,988
Debt securities	4 619	–30,314	–25,946	–44,827	–41,651	–71,147	–100,842	–19,528	–69,380
Bonds and notes	4 620	–30,314	–21,890	–45,813	–38,798	–79,997	–102,482	–48,024	–75,615
Monetary authorities	4 621	...	...	...	...	...	697	143	–413
General government	4 622	...	...	...	...	...	...	...	...
Banks	4 623	...	–28,131	–24,121	–12,473	–14,024	–38,356	–19,303	–61,541
Other sectors	4 624	–30,314	6,241	–21,691	–26,325	–65,973	–64,824	–28,864	–13,662
Money market instruments	4 630	...	–4,056	985	–2,852	8,850	1,640	28,496	6,236
Monetary authorities	4 631	...	...	...	...	...	...	...	...
General government	4 632	...	...	...	...	...	...	...	...
Banks	4 633	...	1,958	–174	–290	–5,809	–20,096	20,121	694
Other sectors	4 634	...	–6,015	1,159	–2,562	14,659	21,736	8,375	5,542
Liabilities	4 652	**17,445**	**4,649**	**36,666**	**54,047**	**59,253**	**135,259**	**132,130**	**147,117**
Equity securities	4 660	22,489	6,505	34,243	47,207	58,418	91,794	82,405	97,304
Banks	4 663	...	...	...	...	...	...	...	...
Other sectors	4 664	...	...	...	...	...	...	...	...
Debt securities	4 669	–5,043	–1,856	2,423	6,840	835	43,466	49,725	49,813
Bonds and notes	4 670	–5,595	5,477	–276	1,059	–6,915	46,489	55,659	20,408
Monetary authorities	4 671	...	...	...	...	...	...	...	...
General government	4 672	–4,416	4,938	–4,289	–128	–5,793	23,462	24,792	14,959
Banks	4 673	...	3,391	–1,336	2,196	–642	5,588	973	959
Other sectors	4 674	–1,179	–2,852	5,349	–1,009	–480	17,439	29,894	4,490
Money market instruments	4 680	552	–7,332	2,699	5,781	7,749	–3,023	–5,934	29,405
Monetary authorities	4 681	...	...	...	...	...	...	...	...
General government	4 682	552	–2,270	1,733	154	1,754	–4,484	–1,899	655
Banks	4 683	...	–212	2,410	450	1,020	3,655	–1,537	7,206
Other sectors	4 684	...	–4,850	–1,445	5,176	4,975	–2,194	–2,498	21,544
C. FINANCIAL DERIVATIVES	4 910	...	1,843	–487	113	791	2,026	–2,401	–6,799
Monetary authorities	4 911	...	...	...	...	...	...	...	...
General government	4 912	...	...	...	...	...	248	70	–642
Banks	4 913	...	1,616	–120	187	464	2,720	–692	–563
Other sectors	4 914	...	227	–367	–73	327	–943	–1,779	–5,594
Assets	4 900	**...**	**1,213**	**–970**	**–330**	**489**	**884**	**–3,653**	**–7,740**
Monetary authorities	4 901	...	...	...	...	...	...	...	...
General government	4 902	...	...	...	...	...	248	70	–642
Banks	4 903	...	1,616	–120	187	464	2,720	–692	–563
Other sectors	4 904	...	–403	–850	–517	25	–2,084	–3,031	–6,535
Liabilities	4 905	**...**	**630**	**483**	**444**	**302**	**1,142**	**1,252**	**942**
Monetary authorities	4 906	...	...	...	...	...	...	...	...
General government	4 907	...	...	...	...	...	...	...	...
Banks	4 908	...	...	...	...	...	...	...	...
Other sectors	4 909	...	630	483	444	302	1,142	1,252	942

Table 2 (Concluded). STANDARD PRESENTATION, 1994–2001

(Millions of U.S. dollars)

	Code		1994	1995	1996	1997	1998	1999	2000	2001
D. OTHER INVESTMENT	4 700	. .	6,193	10,981	–6,065	–8,340	30,303	–2,178	–23,020	–8,899
Assets	4 703	. .	**11,269**	**–23,445**	**–14,977**	**–48,692**	**7,467**	**–58,340**	**–37,983**	**–71,883**
Trade credits	4 706	. .	303	–100	–377	–1,796	–76	–1,362	–2,002	151
General government	4 707	. .	. . .	. . .	. . .	. . .	. . .	. . .	. . .	. . .
of which: Short-term	4 709	. .	. . .	. . .	. . .	. . .	. . .	. . .	. . .	. . .
Other sectors	4 710	. .	303	–100	–377	–1,796	–76	–1,362	–2,002	151
of which: Short-term	4 712	. .	. . .	. . .	. . .	. . .	. . .	. . .	. . .	. . .
Loans	4 714	. .	4,242	–3,372	–790	–11,093	–4,476	–12,092	–1,632	765
Monetary authorities	4 715	. .	. . .	. . .	. . .	. . .	. . .	. . .	. . .	. . .
of which: Short-term	4 718	. .	. . .	. . .	. . .	. . .	. . .	. . .	. . .	. . .
General government	4 719	. .	–114	28	3	. . .	–6	. . .	15	–2
of which: Short-term	4 721	. .	. . .	*24*	*7*	. . .	*3*	. . .	*–1*	*–6*
Banks	4 722	. .	4,356	–3,256	–867	–11,270	–4,434	–10,819	–1,505	661
of which: Short-term	4 724	. .	*4,356*	*24*	*179*	*–38*	*–95*	*9*	*61*	*–52*
Other sectors	4 725	. .	. . .	–144	74	178	–36	–1,273	–142	106
of which: Short-term	4 727	. .	. . .	. . .	. . .	. . .	. . .	. . .	. . .	. . .
Currency and deposits	4 730	. .	6,725	–21,453	–15,336	–37,203	10,584	–42,909	–35,305	–73,636
Monetary authorities	4 731	. .	. . .	. . .	. . .	. . .	. . .	701	–342	13
General government	4 732	. .	–180	21	–46	–33	447	–284	–237	25
Banks	4 733	. .	5,473	–13,669	10,031	–16,950	8,321	–1,987	–20,791	–58,683
Other sectors	4 734	. .	1,432	–7,805	–25,321	–20,220	1,816	–41,339	–13,936	–14,991
Other assets	4 736	. .	. . .	1,481	1,526	1,400	1,434	–1,977	956	837
Monetary authorities	4 737	. .	. . .	. . .	. . .	. . .	–147	–1,693	. . .	. . .
of which: Short-term	4 739	. .	. . .	. . .	. . .	. . .	. . .	. . .	. . .	. . .
General government	4 740	. .	. . .	–122	–329	–272	–70	–1,564	–15	–160
of which: Short-term	4 742	. .	. . .	. . .	. . .	. . .	. . .	. . .	. . .	. . .
Banks	4 743	. .	. . .	. . .	. . .	. . .	. . .	. . .	. . .	. . .
of which: Short-term	4 745	. .	. . .	. . .	. . .	. . .	. . .	. . .	. . .	. . .
Other sectors	4 746	. .	. . .	1,602	1,855	1,672	1,652	1,280	971	997
of which: Short-term	4 748	. .	. . .	. . .	. . .	. . .	. . .	. . .	. . .	. . .
Liabilities	4 753	. .	**–5,076**	**34,426**	**8,913**	**40,352**	**22,836**	**56,162**	**14,963**	**62,984**
Trade credits	4 756	. .	. . .	329	410	1,051	509	1,073	893	–313
General government	4 757	. .	. . .	. . .	. . .	. . .	. . .	. . .	. . .	. . .
of which: Short-term	4 759	. .	. . .	. . .	. . .	. . .	. . .	. . .	. . .	. . .
Other sectors	4 760	. .	. . .	329	410	1,051	509	1,073	893	–313
of which: Short-term	4 762	. .	. . .	. . .	. . .	. . .	. . .	. . .	. . .	. . .
Loans	4 764	. .	–5,471	–1,271	3,861	18,469	–3,534	25,865	10,857	3,840
Monetary authorities	4 765	. .	. . .	. . .	. . .	. . .	. . .	. . .	. . .	. . .
of which: Use of Fund credit and loans from the Fund	4 766	. .	. . .	. . .	. . .	. . .	. . .	. . .	. . .	. . .
of which: Short-term	4 768	. .	. . .	. . .	. . .	. . .	. . .	. . .	. . .	. . .
General government	4 769	. .	–5,233	322	–40	–161	203	1,405	–1,231	493
of which: Short-term	4 771	. .	*–5,233*	*136*	*–86*	*–337*	*204*	*1,403*	*–1,337*	*260*
Banks	4 772	. .	. . .	9,590	3,944	12,154	–3,321	2,211	4,044	6,468
of which: Short-term	4 774	. .	. . .	. . .	. . .	. . .	. . .	. . .	. . .	. . .
Other sectors	4 775	. .	–238	–11,182	–43	6,477	–417	22,249	8,044	–3,121
of which: Short-term	4 777	. .	*302*	*–11,281*	*–2,378*	*4,667*	*–1,957*	*22,140*	*5,587*	*–3,258*
Currency and deposits	4 780	. .	64	32,754	2,067	19,007	21,602	28,069	1,709	56,852
Monetary authorities	4 781	. .	. . .	223	–458	–50	193	23,578	–1,386	–3,903
General government	4 782	. .	. . .	. . .	. . .	. . .	. . .	. . .	. . .	. . .
Banks	4 783	. .	64	32,531	2,525	19,057	21,408	4,491	3,095	60,755
Other sectors	4 784	. .	. . .	. . .	. . .	. . .	. . .	. . .	. . .	. . .
Other liabilities	4 786	. .	331	2,614	2,574	1,824	4,260	1,154	1,504	2,605
Monetary authorities	4 787	. .	. . .	. . .	. . .	. . .	. . .	. . .	. . .	. . .
of which: Short-term	4 789	. .	. . .	. . .	. . .	. . .	. . .	. . .	. . .	. . .
General government	4 790	. .	. . .	. . .	. . .	. . .	. . .	. . .	. . .	. . .
of which: Short-term	4 792	. .	. . .	. . .	. . .	. . .	. . .	. . .	. . .	. . .
Banks	4 793	. .	. . .	. . .	. . .	. . .	. . .	. . .	. . .	. . .
of which: Short-term	4 795	. .	. . .	. . .	. . .	. . .	. . .	. . .	. . .	. . .
Other sectors	4 796	. .	331	2,614	2,574	1,824	4,260	1,154	1,504	2,605
of which: Short-term	4 798	. .	*331*	*159*	*645*	*–289*	*2,148*	*583*	*875*	*1,997*
E. RESERVE ASSETS	4 802	. .	–219	–243	–593	–1,056	2,095	1,867	959	–1,442
Monetary gold	4 812	. .	. . .	1,751	2,123	. . .	1,759	281	. . .	. . .
Special drawing rights	4 811	. .	. . .	–308	–23	–23	–96	325	–53	–183
Reserve position in the Fund	4 810	. .	6	–180	–105	–170	–692	–424	483	–451
Foreign exchange	4 803	. .	–225	–1,506	–2,587	–864	1,125	1,685	528	–808
Other claims	4 813	. .	. . .	. . .	. . .	. . .	. . .	. . .	. . .	. . .
NET ERRORS AND OMISSIONS	4 998	. .	**–2,169**	**–1,456**	**–1,091**	**–1,171**	**1,893**	**–1,230**	**–1,244**	**–1,006**

Part 3 of the *Yearbook* contains descriptions of the methodologies, compilation practices, and sources used to compile these data.

Table 3. INTERNATIONAL INVESTMENT POSITION (End–period stocks), 1994–2001, BELGIUM ONLY

(Millions of U.S. dollars)

	Code		1994	1995	1996	1997	1998	1999	2000	2001
ASSETS	8 995	C.	533,478	601,893	609,225	608,945	702,911	759,627	744,917	...
Direct investment abroad	8 505	..	**69,541**	**80,639**	**87,221**	**94,840**	**134,877**	**151,695**	**175,027**	**...**
Equity capital and reinvested earnings	8 506	..	...	52,113	61,005	69,054	95,790	107,794	107,752	...
Claims on affiliated enterprises	8 507	..	...	...	...	...	...	...	...	...
Liabilities to affiliated enterprises	8 508	..	...	...	...	...	...	...	...	...
Other capital	8 530	..	...	28,525	26,217	25,786	39,086	43,901	67,275	...
Claims on affiliated enterprises	8 535	..	...	...	...	...	...	...	...	...
Liabilities to affiliated enterprises	8 540	..	...	...	...	...	...	...	...	...
Portfolio investment	8 602	..	**161,256**	**190,488**	**194,863**	**200,054**	**250,265**	**311,627**	**301,575**	**...**
Equity securities	8 610	..	59,804	63,770	64,534	64,572	94,272	124,470	124,594	...
Monetary authorities	8 611	..	...	...	...	...	...	...	...	...
General government	8 612	..	534	687	503	328	466	...	...	...
Banks	8 613	..	565	959	756	764	1,750	1,507	1,954	...
Other sectors	8 614	..	58,704	62,125	63,274	63,480	92,056	122,963	122,640	...
Debt securities	8 619	..	101,453	126,718	130,330	135,482	155,994	187,157	176,981	...
Bonds and notes	8 620	..	100,353	124,250	127,808	132,752	152,144	171,586	170,375	...
Monetary authorities	8 621	..	...	...	...	...	...	2,612	2,233	...
General government	8 622	..	94	...	125	108	...	...	...	...
Banks	8 623	..	36,561	43,886	49,536	54,085	58,453	70,623	80,116	...
Other sectors	8 624	..	63,698	80,364	78,147	78,559	93,690	98,350	88,025	...
Money market instruments	8 630	..	1,099	2,468	2,521	2,730	3,850	15,571	6,607	...
Monetary authorities	8 631	..	...	...	...	...	...	...	...	...
General government	8 632	..	...	...	...	...	...	...	...	...
Banks	8 633	..	1,099	2,468	2,521	2,730	3,850	15,571	6,607	...
Other sectors	8 634	..	...	...	...	...	...	...	...	...
Financial derivatives	8 900	..	**...**	**687**	**1,387**	**1,855**	**2,218**	**3,516**	**4,932**	**...**
Monetary authorities	8 901	..	...	...	...	...	...	...	...	...
General government	8 902	..	...	...	...	...	...	...	...	...
Banks	8 903	..	...	275	253	108	–116	...	931	...
Other sectors	8 904	..	...	411	1,134	1,747	2,334	3,516	4,001	...
Other investment	8 703	..	**279,199**	**306,639**	**302,754**	**290,747**	**295,074**	**279,480**	**251,142**	**...**
Trade credits	8 706	..	2,513	2,880	3,025	4,261	4,667	5,224	6,607	...
General government	8 707	..	...	...	...	...	...	...	...	...
of which: Short-term	8 709	..	...	...	...	...	...	...	...	...
Other sectors	8 710	..	2,513	2,880	3,025	4,261	4,667	5,224	6,607	...
of which: Short-term	8 712	..	...	...	...	...	...	...	...	...
Loans	8 714	..	196,906	229,158	216,161	205,412	203,365	187,961	167,118	...
Monetary authorities	8 715	..	597	1,645	1,009	108	466	...	372	...
of which: Short-term	8 718	..	...	*1,645*	*1,009*	*108*	*466*	...	*372*	...
General government	8 719	..	1,947	7,952	7,183	6,335	6,299	5,425	5,025	...
of which: Short-term	8 721	..	...	*547*	*503*	*436*	*466*	*402*	*372*	...
Banks	8 722	..	193,388	218,463	207,086	198,313	196,133	182,134	161,349	...
of which: Short-term	8 724	..	...	*197,756*	*187,424*	*179,629*	*178,747*	*164,955*	*143,297*	...
Other sectors	8 725	..	974	1,097	882	656	467	402	372	...
of which: Short-term	8 727	..	*974*	...	...	...	...	...	...	...
Currency and deposits	8 730	..	55,029	51,973	59,872	55,507	64,640	67,107	68,671	...
Monetary authorities	8 731	..	...	...	...	...	...	...	...	...
General government	8 732	..	...	...	...	...	...	...	...	...
Banks	8 733	..	188	136	253	219	234	...	...	...
Other sectors	8 734	..	54,841	51,837	59,619	55,287	64,406	67,107	68,671	...
Other assets	8 736	..	24,751	22,628	23,696	25,568	22,402	19,188	8,747	...
Monetary authorities	8 737	..	...	...	...	...	...	1,607	1,489	...
of which: Short-term	8 739	..	...	...	...	...	...	...	...	...
General government	8 740	..	...	...	...	...	...	...	...	...
of which: Short-term	8 742	..	...	...	...	...	...	...	...	...
Banks	8 743	..	10,239	960	504	765	933	1,105	1,489	...
of which: Short-term	8 745	..	...	...	...	...	...	...	...	...
Other sectors	8 746	..	14,511	21,668	23,192	24,803	21,468	16,475	5,769	...
of which: Short-term	8 748	..	...	...	...	...	...	...	...	...
Reserve assets	8 802	..	**23,482**	**23,440**	**22,999**	**21,448**	**20,477**	**13,310**	**12,242**	**...**
Monetary gold	8 812	..	...	7,955	5,671	4,480	2,684	2,411	2,233	...
Special drawing rights	8 811	..	180	492	498	489	610	271	307	472
Reserve position in the Fund	8 810	..	812	1,005	1,075	1,182	1,899	2,290	1,699	2,051
Foreign exchange	8 803	..	22,489	13,988	15,755	15,297	15,284	8,338	8,002	...
Other claims	8 813	..	...	...	...	...	...	...	...	...

Table 3 (Concluded). INTERNATIONAL INVESTMENT POSITION (End–period stocks), 1994–2001, BELGIUM ONLY
(Millions of U.S. dollars)

	Code		1994	1995	1996	1997	1998	1999	2000	2001
LIABILITIES	8 995	D.	495,611	553,636	542,358	528,949	603,909	616,222	603,522	...
Direct investment in Belgium	8 555	. .	**105,881**	**112,867**	**123,900**	**128,712**	**180,497**	**179,924**	**187,961**	**...**
Equity capital and reinvested earnings	8 556	. .	...	87,907	95,414	97,572	142,461	145,366	149,345	...
Claims on direct investors	8 557	. .	...	...	...	...	...	...	...	...
Liabilities to direct investors	8 558	. .	...	...	...	...	...	...	...	...
Other capital	8 580	. .	...	24,960	28,486	31,140	38,036	34,558	38,616	...
Claims on direct investors	8 585	. .	...	...	...	...	...	...	...	...
Liabilities to direct investors	8 590	. .	...	...	...	...	...	...	...	...
Portfolio investment	8 652	. .	**103,808**	**106,694**	**97,432**	**90,146**	**91,241**	**112,214**	**124,687**	**...**
Equity securities	8 660	. .	9,737	10,012	11,217	12,129	17,851	15,571	12,283	...
Banks	8 663	. .	...	...	...	...	...	...	...	...
Other sectors	8 664	. .	...	10,012	11,217	12,129	17,851	15,571	12,283	...
Debt securities	8 669	. .	94,071	96,682	86,215	78,017	73,389	96,643	112,404	...
Bonds and notes	8 670	. .	54,841	70,076	60,125	55,726	49,354	69,217	83,559	...
Monetary authorities	8 671	. .	...	1,234	631	983	...	...	...	...
General government	8 672	. .	44,727	64,729	55,082	51,354	44,686	64,294	78,255	...
Banks	8 673	. .	8,418	4,114	4,159	3,388	3,968	3,817	4,187	...
Other sectors	8 674	. .	1,696	...	253	...	700	1,105	1,117	...
Money market instruments	8 680	. .	39,230	26,605	26,090	22,291	24,035	27,426	28,846	...
Monetary authorities	8 681	. .	...	...	...	...	...	...	...	...
General government	8 682	. .	36,843	23,451	23,949	21,089	22,985	16,576	12,003	...
Banks	8 683	. .	1,508	823	125	219	466	201	3,722	...
Other sectors	8 684	. .	879	2,332	2,015	983	584	10,649	13,120	...
Financial derivatives	8 905	. .	**...**	**547**	**881**	**1,311**	**1,866**	**3,516**	**3,722**	**...**
Monetary authorities	8 906	. .	...	...	...	...	...	...	...	...
General government	8 907	. .	...	...	...	...	...	...	...	...
Banks	8 908	. .	...	...	...	...	116	804	...	...
Other sectors	8 909	. .	...	547	881	1,311	1,750	2,712	3,722	...
Other investment	8 753	. .	**285,921**	**333,528**	**320,146**	**308,780**	**330,306**	**320,568**	**287,152**	**...**
Trade credits	8 756	. .	...	274	756	1,639	2,217	3,014	3,722	...
General government	8 757	. .	...	...	...	...	...	...	...	...
of which: Short-term	8 759	. .	...	...	...	...	...	...	...	...
Other sectors	8 760	. .	...	274	756	1,639	2,217	3,014	3,722	...
of which: Short-term	8 762	. .	...	...	...	...	...	...	...	...
Loans	8 764	. .	215,092	262,353	249,942	235,355	248,284	226,839	200,337	...
Monetary authorities	8 765	. .	...	...	...	...	...	...	...	...
of which: Use of Fund credit and loans from the Fund	8 766	. .	...	...	...	...	...	...	...	...
of which: Short-term	8 768	. .	...	...	...	...	...	...	...	...
General government	8 769	. .	534	823	756	328	350	301	372	...
of which: Short-term	8 771	. .	...	*687*	*631*	*219*	*234*	*201*	*372*	...
Banks	8 772	. .	201,995	245,208	232,045	217,324	222,965	202,929	174,097	...
of which: Short-term	8 774	. .	...	*227,928*	*215,910*	*201,809*	*208,382*	*189,166*	*160,046*	...
Other sectors	8 775	. .	12,564	16,322	17,141	17,703	24,969	23,608	25,868	...
of which: Short-term	8 777	. .	...	*3,155*	*2,900*	*3,716*	*9,333*	*9,544*	*10,515*	...
Currency and deposits	8 780	. .	52,517	59,793	57,347	54,959	64,987	73,537	60,110	...
Monetary authorities	8 781	. .	848	1,098	503	436	816	17,279	7,165	...
General government	8 782	. .	408	...	...	...	...	...	...	...
Banks	8 783	. .	49,596	58,695	56,844	54,523	64,172	56,258	52,945	...
Other sectors	8 784	. .	1,665	...	...	...	...	...	...	...
Other liabilities	8 786	. .	18,312	11,108	12,100	16,827	14,818	17,179	22,983	...
Monetary authorities	8 787	. .	...	...	...	...	...	...	...	...
of which: Short-term	8 789	. .	...	...	...	...	...	...	...	...
General government	8 790	. .	...	...	...	...	...	...	...	...
of which: Short-term	8 792	. .	...	...	...	...	...	...	...	...
Banks	8 793	. .	...	6,308	7,437	12,456	10,384	12,959	18,889	...
of which: Short-term	8 795	. .	...	...	...	...	...	...	...	...
Other sectors	8 796	. .	18,312	4,800	4,664	4,371	4,434	4,219	4,094	...
of which: Short-term	8 798	. .	...	...	...	...	...	...	...	...
NET INTERNATIONAL INVESTMENT POSITION	8 995	. .	**37,867**	**48,257**	**66,867**	**79,996**	**99,002**	**143,405**	**141,395**	**...**
Conversion rates: Belgian francs per U.S. dollar (end of period)	0 102	. .	**31.838**	**29.415**	**32.005**	**36.920**	**34.575**	**...**	**...**	**...**
Conversion rates: euros per U.S. dollar (end of period)	0 104	. .	**...**	**...**	**...**	**...**	**...**	**.99542**	**1.07469**	**1.13469**

Table 1. ANALYTIC PRESENTATION, 1994–2001
(Millions of U.S. dollars)

	Code	1994	1995	1996	1997	1998	1999	2000	2001
A. Current Account [1]	4 993 Z.	**-40.1**	**-17.2**	**-6.6**	**-31.9**	**-59.8**	**-77.5**	**-139.5**	**...**
Goods: exports f.o.b.	2 100 ..	156.5	164.6	171.3	193.4	186.2	213.2	212.3	...
Goods: imports f.o.b.	3 100 ..	-231.9	-230.6	-229.5	-282.9	-290.9	-337.5	-403.7	...
Balance on Goods	4 100 ..	*-75.4*	*-66.1*	*-58.2*	*-89.5*	*-104.7*	*-124.3*	*-191.4*	...
Services: credit	2 200 ..	121.1	132.8	137.9	137.8	140.5	161.6	172.4	...
Services: debit	3 200 ..	-88.0	-94.9	-91.3	-91.7	-99.0	-108.2	-119.8	...
Balance on Goods and Services	4 991 ..	*-42.2*	*-28.1*	*-11.7*	*-43.3*	*-63.3*	*-70.8*	*-138.8*	...
Income: credit	2 300 ..	2.9	2.8	6.3	7.5	7.2	2.7	4.8	...
Income: debit	3 300 ..	-28.2	-25.1	-32.4	-30.8	-39.3	-46.6	-58.9	...
Balance on Goods, Services, and Income	4 992 ..	*-67.5*	*-50.4*	*-37.8*	*-66.7*	*-95.4*	*-114.7*	*-192.9*	...
Current transfers: credit	2 379 Z.	34.4	38.3	34.2	38.2	38.4	40.6	56.6	...
Current transfers: debit	3 379 ..	-6.9	-5.2	-3.1	-3.4	-2.8	-3.5	-3.2	...
B. Capital Account [1]	4 994 Z.	**...**	**...**	**-2.2**	**-3.4**	**-1.9**	**-2.0**	**.5**	**...**
Capital account: credit	2 994 Z.	...	...	...	...	...	.5	.9	...
Capital account: debit	3 994 ..	...	...	-2.2	-3.4	-1.9	-2.4	-.5	...
Total, Groups A Plus B	4 981 ..	*-40.1*	*-17.2*	*-8.8*	*-35.3*	*-61.7*	*-79.5*	*-139.0*	...
C. Financial Account [1]	4 995 W.	**3.6**	**-1.0**	**11.0**	**27.6**	**23.5**	**91.5**	**88.4**	**...**
Direct investment abroad	4 505 ..	...	...	-5.7	-3.9	-4.5	...	...	...
Direct investment in Belize	4 555 Z.	15.4	21.1	16.6	12.0	17.7	47.4	17.7	...
Portfolio investment assets	4 602 ..	...	...	...	...	...	...	...	...
Equity securities	4 610 ..	...	...	...	...	...	...	...	...
Debt securities	4 619 ..	...	...	...	...	...	...	...	...
Portfolio investment liabilities	4 652 Z.	6.1	3.5	10.1	10.2	12.5	32.9	26.9	...
Equity securities	4 660 ..	...	...	...	...	...	...	...	...
Debt securities	4 669 Z.	6.1	3.5	10.1	10.2	12.5	32.9	26.9	...
Financial derivatives	4 910 ..	...	...	...	...	...	...	...	...
Financial derivatives assets	4 900 ..	...	...	...	...	...	...	...	...
Financial derivatives liabilities	4 905 ..	...	...	...	...	...	...	...	...
Other investment assets	4 703 ..	-17.1	-14.1	-12.2	2.8	...	-8.9	-39.4	...
Monetary authorities	4 701 ..	...	...	...	...	...	...	...	...
General government	4 704 ..	...	...	...	...	...	...	-11.1	...
Banks	4 705 ..	-3.3	-1.7	-12.2	2.8	...	-6.3	-26.3	...
Other sectors	4 728 ..	-13.8	-12.4	...	...	...	-2.7	-2.1	...
Other investment liabilities	4 753 W.	-.8	-11.5	2.2	6.5	-2.2	20.2	83.3	...
Monetary authorities	4 753 WA	...	...	...	...	...	-.6	41.8	...
General government	4 753 ZB	8.9	-2.6	19.7	11.5	8.8	14.9	46.1	...
Banks	4 753 ZC	-9.3	-12.1	-6.3	4.8	7.2	-8.9	15.5	...
Other sectors	4 753 ZD	-.3	3.2	-11.2	-9.8	-18.2	14.8	-20.2	...
Total, Groups A Through C	4 983 ..	*-36.4*	*-18.3*	*2.2*	*-7.7*	*-38.2*	*12.0*	*-50.6*	...
D. Net Errors and Omissions	4 998 ..	**32.8**	**22.4**	**18.4**	**9.1**	**24.5**	**.9**	**7.3**	**...**
Total, Groups A Through D	4 984 ..	*-3.6*	*4.1*	*20.6*	*1.4*	*-13.7*	*12.9*	*-43.3*	...
E. Reserves and Related Items	4 802 A.	**3.6**	**-4.1**	**-20.6**	**-1.4**	**13.7**	**-12.9**	**43.3**	**...**
Reserve assets	4 802 ..	3.6	-4.1	-20.6	-1.4	13.7	-27.5	-51.8	...
Use of Fund credit and loans	4 766 ..	...	...	...	...	...	...	...	...
Exceptional financing	4 920 ..	...	...	...	...	...	14.6	95.2	...
Conversion rates: Belize dollars per U.S. dollar	0 101 ..	**2.0000**	**2.0000**	**2.0000**	**2.0000**	**2.0000**	**2.0000**	**2.0000**	**2.0000**

[1] Excludes components that have been classified in the categories of Group E.

Table 2. STANDARD PRESENTATION, 1994–2001
(Millions of U.S. dollars)

	Code		1994	1995	1996	1997	1998	1999	2000	2001
CURRENT ACCOUNT	4 993	. .	**–40.1**	**–17.2**	**–6.6**	**–31.9**	**–59.8**	**–65.7**	**–131.0**	**. . .**
A. GOODS	4 100	. .	–75.4	–66.1	–58.2	–89.5	–104.7	–124.3	–191.4	. . .
Credit	2 100	. .	**156.5**	**164.6**	**171.3**	**193.4**	**186.2**	**213.2**	**212.3**	**. . .**
General merchandise: exports f.o.b.	2 110	. .	151.4	162.1	171.3	193.4	186.2	213.2	212.3	. . .
Goods for processing: exports f.o.b.	2 150	. .	. . .	. . .	. . .	. . .	. . .	. . .	. . .	. . .
Repairs on goods	2 160	. .	. . .	. . .	. . .	. . .	. . .	. . .	. . .	. . .
Goods procured in ports by carriers	2 170	. .	5.0	2.5	. . .	. . .	. . .	. . .	. . .	. . .
Nonmonetary gold	2 180	. .	. . .	. . .	. . .	. . .	. . .	. . .	. . .	. . .
Debit	3 100	. .	**–231.9**	**–230.6**	**–229.5**	**–282.9**	**–290.9**	**–337.5**	**–403.7**	**. . .**
General merchandise: imports f.o.b.	3 110	. .	–231.9	–230.6	–229.5	–282.9	–290.9	–337.5	–403.7	. . .
Goods for processing: imports f.o.b.	3 150	. .	. . .	. . .	. . .	. . .	. . .	. . .	. . .	. . .
Repairs on goods	3 160	. .	. . .	. . .	. . .	. . .	. . .	. . .	. . .	. . .
Goods procured in ports by carriers	3 170	. .	. . .	. . .	. . .	. . .	. . .	. . .	. . .	. . .
Nonmonetary gold	3 180	. .	. . .	. . .	. . .	. . .	. . .	. . .	. . .	. . .
B. SERVICES	4 200	. .	33.2	37.9	46.5	46.2	41.5	53.5	52.6	. . .
Total credit	2 200	. .	*121.1*	*132.8*	*137.9*	*137.8*	*140.5*	*161.6*	*172.4*	. . .
Total debit	3 200	. .	*–88.0*	*–94.9*	*–91.3*	*–91.7*	*–99.0*	*–108.2*	*–119.8*	. . .
Transportation services, credit	2 205	. .	**10.3**	**6.2**	**6.2**	**6.5**	**6.9**	**8.5**	**11.3**	**. . .**
Passenger	2 850	. .	. . .	. . .	*2.0*	*2.0*	*2.3*	. . .	. . .	. . .
Freight	2 851	. .	. . .	. . .	*3.5*	*3.6*	*3.8*	. . .	. . .	. . .
Other	2 852	. .	*10.3*	*6.2*	*.7*	*.9*	*.9*	*8.5*	*11.3*	. . .
Sea transport, passenger	2 207	. .	. . .	. . .	. . .	. . .	. . .	. . .	. . .	. . .
Sea transport, freight	2 208	. .	. . .	. . .	3.5	3.6	3.8	. . .	. . .	. . .
Sea transport, other	2 209	. .	. . .	. . .	. . .	. . .	. . .	6.2	8.2	. . .
Air transport, passenger	2 211	. .	. . .	. . .	2.0	2.0	2.3	. . .	. . .	. . .
Air transport, freight	2 212	. .	. . .	. . .	. . .	. . .	. . .	. . .	. . .	. . .
Air transport, other	2 213	. .	. . .	. . .	.7	. . .	. . .	2.4	3.2	. . .
Other transport, passenger	2 215	. .	. . .	. . .	. . .	. . .	. . .	. . .	. . .	. . .
Other transport, freight	2 216	. .	. . .	. . .	. . .	. . .	. . .	. . .	. . .	. . .
Other transport, other	2 217	. .	10.3	6.2	. . .	.9	.9	. . .	. . .	. . .
Transportation services, debit	3 205	. .	**–37.0**	**–40.7**	**–37.9**	**–43.1**	**–44.5**	**–40.5**	**–48.4**	**. . .**
Passenger	3 850	. .	*–11.0*	*–12.2*	*–12.3*	*–11.6*	*–12.0*	*–3.0*	*–3.9*	. . .
Freight	3 851	. .	*–26.0*	*–25.9*	*–25.6*	*–31.5*	*–32.5*	*–37.5*	*–44.6*	. . .
Other	3 852	. .	. . .	*–2.6*	. . .	. . .	. . .	. . .	. . .	. . .
Sea transport, passenger	3 207	. .	. . .	. . .	. . .	. . .	. . .	. . .	. . .	. . .
Sea transport, freight	3 208	. .	. . .	. . .	–25.6	–31.5	–32.5	–37.5	–44.6	. . .
Sea transport, other	3 209	. .	. . .	. . .	. . .	. . .	. . .	. . .	. . .	. . .
Air transport, passenger	3 211	. .	. . .	. . .	–12.3	–11.6	–12.0	–3.0	–3.9	. . .
Air transport, freight	3 212	. .	. . .	. . .	. . .	. . .	. . .	. . .	. . .	. . .
Air transport, other	3 213	. .	. . .	. . .	. . .	. . .	. . .	. . .	. . .	. . .
Other transport, passenger	3 215	. .	. . .	. . .	. . .	. . .	. . .	. . .	. . .	. . .
Other transport, freight	3 216	. .	. . .	. . .	. . .	. . .	. . .	. . .	. . .	. . .
Other transport, other	3 217	. .	. . .	–2.6	. . .	. . .	. . .	. . .	. . .	. . .
Travel, credit	2 236	. .	**71.4**	**77.6**	**93.1**	**95.0**	**99.0**	**111.4**	**122.0**	**. . .**
Business travel	2 237	. .	. . .	. . .	. . .	. . .	. . .	3.2	3.4	. . .
Personal travel	2 240	. .	71.4	77.6	93.1	95.0	99.0	108.2	118.6	. . .
Travel, debit	3 236	. .	**–18.6**	**–20.8**	**–26.2**	**–17.9**	**–21.2**	**–25.8**	**–30.0**	**. . .**
Business travel	3 237	. .	–4.1	–2.5	–2.4	–3.4	–2.9	–4.3	–5.1	. . .
Personal travel	3 240	. .	–14.5	–18.3	–23.7	–14.5	–18.3	–21.5	–25.0	. . .
Other services, credit	2 200	BA	**39.5**	**49.0**	**38.6**	**36.4**	**34.6**	**41.7**	**39.1**	**. . .**
Communications	2 245	. .	7.4	9.0	10.9	7.9	5.4	7.5	6.7	. . .
Construction	2 249	. .	. . .	. . .	. . .	. . .	. . .	. . .	. . .	. . .
Insurance	2 253	. .	1.6	1.3	1.6	2.0	1.1	. . .	. . .	. . .
Financial	2 260	. .	. . .	. . .	. . .	. . .	. . .	. . .	. . .	. . .
Computer and information	2 262	. .	. . .	. . .	. . .	. . .	. . .	. . .	. . .	. . .
Royalties and licence fees	2 266	. .	. . .	. . .	. . .	. . .	. . .	. . .	. . .	. . .
Other business services	2 268	. .	18.2	23.1	13.3	12.9	9.3	13.1	12.3	. . .
Personal, cultural, and recreational	2 287	. .	. . .	. . .	. . .	. . .	. . .	. . .	. . .	. . .
Government, n.i.e.	2 291	. .	12.3	15.7	12.9	13.7	18.8	21.1	20.2	. . .
Other services, debit	3 200	BA	**–32.3**	**–33.4**	**–27.3**	**–30.7**	**–33.4**	**–41.9**	**–41.4**	**. . .**
Communications	3 245	. .	–4.1	–4.0	–.1	–.2	–.2	–4.2	–4.1	. . .
Construction	3 249	. .	. . .	. . .	. . .	. . .	. . .	. . .	–1.1	. . .
Insurance	3 253	. .	–8.2	–8.3	–8.0	–7.9	–8.6	–8.7	–9.6	. . .
Financial	3 260	. .	. . .	. . .	. . .	. . .	. . .	. . .	. . .	. . .
Computer and information	3 262	. .	. . .	. . .	–.4	–.5	–.6	–.4	–.6	. . .
Royalties and licence fees	3 266	. .	–.1	–.1	–.4	–.5	–.1	–.2	–.2	. . .
Other business services	3 268	. .	–18.0	–14.5	–14.7	–17.5	–18.7	–20.5	–19.6	. . .
Personal, cultural, and recreational	3 287	. .	. . .	. . .	. . .	. . .	. . .	. . .	. . .	. . .
Government, n.i.e.	3 291	. .	–2.1	–6.5	–3.7	–4.3	–5.2	–8.1	–6.3	. . .

Table 2 (Continued). STANDARD PRESENTATION, 1994–2001
(Millions of U.S. dollars)

	Code		1994	1995	1996	1997	1998	1999	2000	2001
C. INCOME	4 300	. .	–25.3	–22.3	–26.1	–23.4	–32.1	–43.9	–54.1	. . .
Total credit	2 300	. .	*2.9*	*2.8*	*6.3*	*7.5*	*7.2*	*2.7*	*4.8*	. . .
Total debit	3 300	. .	*–28.2*	*–25.1*	*–32.4*	*–30.8*	*–39.3*	*–46.6*	*–58.9*	. . .
Compensation of employees, credit	2 310	. .	**. . .**	**. . .**	**4.1**	**4.9**	**4.5**	**. . .**	**. . .**	**. . .**
Compensation of employees, debit	3 310	. .	**–5.3**	**–5.7**	**–6.2**	**–6.8**	**–6.1**	**–6.5**	**–6.8**	**. . .**
Investment income, credit	2 320	. .	**2.9**	**2.8**	**2.3**	**2.6**	**2.8**	**2.7**	**4.8**	**. . .**
Direct investment income	2 330	. .	. . .	. . .	2.3	2.6	2.8	. . .	. . .	. . .
Dividends and distributed branch profits	2 332	. .	. . .	. . .	. . .	. . .	. . .	. . .	. . .	. . .
Reinvested earnings and undistributed branch profits	2 333	. .	. . .	. . .	. . .	. . .	. . .	. . .	. . .	. . .
Income on debt (interest)	2 334	. .	. . .	. . .	2.3	2.6	2.8	. . .	. . .	. . .
Portfolio investment income	2 339	. .	. . .	. . .	. . .	. . .	. . .	.1	. . .	. . .
Income on equity	2 340	. .	. . .	. . .	. . .	. . .	. . .	. . .	. . .	. . .
Income on bonds and notes	2 350	. .	. . .	. . .	. . .	. . .	. . .	.1	. . .	. . .
Income on money market instruments	2 360	. .	. . .	. . .	. . .	. . .	. . .	. . .	. . .	. . .
Other investment income	2 370	. .	2.9	2.8	. . .	. . .	. . .	2.6	4.8	. . .
Investment income, debit	3 320	. .	**–22.9**	**–19.3**	**–26.2**	**–24.1**	**–33.2**	**–40.1**	**–52.1**	**. . .**
Direct investment income	3 330	. .	–13.1	–8.0	–26.2	–24.1	–30.2	–23.2	–28.4	. . .
Dividends and distributed branch profits	3 332	. .	–10.1	–2.8	–11.2	–8.1	–11.4	–14.7	–17.3	. . .
Reinvested earnings and undistributed branch profits	3 333	. .	–3.0	–5.3	–3.4	–3.8	–3.5	–8.5	–11.1	. . .
Income on debt (interest)	3 334	. .	. . .	. . .	–11.5	–12.2	–15.3	. . .	. . .	. . .
Portfolio investment income	3 339	. .	. . .	. . .	. . .	. . .	–3.0	–3.7	–4.2	. . .
Income on equity	3 340	. .	. . .	. . .	. . .	. . .	. . .	. . .	. . .	. . .
Income on bonds and notes	3 350	. .	. . .	. . .	. . .	. . .	–3.0	–3.7	–4.2	. . .
Income on money market instruments	3 360	. .	. . .	. . .	. . .	. . .	. . .	. . .	. . .	. . .
Other investment income	3 370	. .	–9.8	–11.3	. . .	. . .	. . .	–13.3	–19.6	. . .
D. CURRENT TRANSFERS	4 379	. .	27.5	33.1	31.1	34.7	35.6	49.0	61.9	. . .
Credit	2 379	. .	**34.4**	**38.3**	**34.2**	**38.2**	**38.4**	**52.4**	**65.1**	**. . .**
General government	2 380	. .	15.5	17.8	12.6	12.0	10.7	11.8	8.5	. . .
Other sectors	2 390	. .	18.9	20.5	21.6	26.2	27.7	40.6	56.6	. . .
Workers' remittances	2 391	. .	13.0	13.9	13.2	17.8	19.0	21.3	21.8	. . .
Other current transfers	2 392	. .	5.9	6.6	8.4	8.4	8.8	19.3	34.8	. . .
Debit	3 379	. .	**–6.9**	**–5.2**	**–3.1**	**–3.4**	**–2.8**	**–3.5**	**–3.2**	**. . .**
General government	3 380	. .	–3.0	–1.5	–2.1	–2.3	–1.7	–1.6	–1.6	. . .
Other sectors	3 390	. .	–3.9	–3.7	–1.0	–1.2	–1.1	–1.9	–1.6	. . .
Workers' remittances	3 391	. .	–1.3	–1.2	–.7	–.8	–.8	–1.1	–.9	. . .
Other current transfers	3 392	. .	–2.6	–2.6	–.3	–.4	–.3	–.9	–.7	. . .
CAPITAL AND FINANCIAL ACCOUNT	4 996	. .	**7.2**	**–5.1**	**–11.7**	**22.9**	**35.3**	**64.8**	**123.7**	. . .
CAPITAL ACCOUNT	4 994	. .	. . .	. . .	**–2.2**	**–3.4**	**–1.9**	**.8**	**.8**	. . .
Total credit	2 994	. .	. . .	. . .	. . .	. . .	. . .	*3.2*	*1.2*	. . .
Total debit	3 994	. .	. . .	. . .	*–2.2*	*–3.4*	*–1.9*	*–2.4*	*–.5*	. . .
Capital transfers, credit	2 400	. .	**. . .**	**. . .**	**. . .**	**. . .**	**. . .**	**3.2**	**1.2**	**. . .**
General government	2 401	. .	. . .	. . .	. . .	. . .	. . .	2.8	.3	. . .
Debt forgiveness	2 402	. .	. . .	. . .	. . .	. . .	. . .	2.8	.3	. . .
Other capital transfers	2 410	. .	. . .	. . .	. . .	. . .	. . .	. . .	. . .	. . .
Other sectors	2 430	. .	. . .	. . .	. . .	. . .	. . .	.5	.9	. . .
Migrants' transfers	2 431	. .	. . .	. . .	. . .	. . .	. . .	. . .	. . .	. . .
Debt forgiveness	2 432	. .	. . .	. . .	. . .	. . .	. . .	. . .	. . .	. . .
Other capital transfers	2 440	. .	. . .	. . .	. . .	. . .	. . .	.5	.9	. . .
Capital transfers, debit	3 400	. .	**. . .**	**. . .**	**–2.2**	**–3.4**	**–2.5**	**–2.4**	**–.5**	**. . .**
General government	3 401	. .	. . .	. . .	–.6	–.9	–.5	–1.1	–.3	. . .
Debt forgiveness	3 402	. .	. . .	. . .	. . .	. . .	. . .	. . .	. . .	. . .
Other capital transfers	3 410	. .	. . .	. . .	–.6	–.9	–.5	–1.1	–.3	. . .
Other sectors	3 430	. .	. . .	. . .	–1.6	–2.5	–2.1	–1.3	–.2	. . .
Migrants' transfers	3 431	. .	. . .	. . .	–1.6	–2.5	–2.1	–1.3	–.2	. . .
Debt forgiveness	3 432	. .	. . .	. . .	. . .	. . .	. . .	. . .	. . .	. . .
Other capital transfers	3 440	. .	. . .	. . .	. . .	. . .	. . .	. . .	. . .	. . .
Nonproduced nonfinancial assets, credit	2 480	. .	**. . .**	**. . .**	**. . .**	**. . .**	**. . .**	**. . .**	**. . .**	**. . .**
Nonproduced nonfinancial assets, debit	3 480	. .	**. . .**	**. . .**	**. . .**	**. . .**	**.7**	**. . .**	**. . .**	**. . .**

Table 2 (Continued). STANDARD PRESENTATION, 1994–2001
(Millions of U.S. dollars)

	Code	1994	1995	1996	1997	1998	1999	2000	2001
FINANCIAL ACCOUNT	4 995 . .	**7.2**	**–5.1**	**–9.6**	**26.2**	**37.2**	**64.0**	**122.9**	**. . .**
A. DIRECT INVESTMENT	4 500 . .	15.4	21.1	10.9	8.1	13.2	47.4	17.7	. . .
Direct investment abroad	4 505 . .	**. . .**	**. . .**	**–5.7**	**–3.9**	**–4.5**	**. . .**	**. . .**	**. . .**
Equity capital	4 510 . .	. . .	. . .	–5.7	–3.9	–4.5	. . .	. . .	. . .
Claims on affiliated enterprises	4 515 . .	. . .	. . .	–5.7	–3.9	–4.5	. . .	. . .	. . .
Liabilities to affiliated enterprises	4 520 . .	. . .	. . .	. . .	. . .	. . .	. . .	. . .	. . .
Reinvested earnings	4 525 . .	. . .	. . .	. . .	. . .	. . .	. . .	. . .	. . .
Other capital	4 530 . .	. . .	. . .	. . .	. . .	. . .	. . .	. . .	. . .
Claims on affiliated enterprises	4 535 . .	. . .	. . .	. . .	. . .	. . .	. . .	. . .	. . .
Liabilities to affiliated enterprises	4 540 . .	. . .	. . .	. . .	. . .	. . .	. . .	. . .	. . .
Direct investment in Belize	4 555 . .	**15.4**	**21.1**	**16.6**	**12.0**	**17.7**	**47.4**	**17.7**	**. . .**
Equity capital	4 560 . .	5.6	5.8	13.1	8.2	14.2	37.6	.7	. . .
Claims on direct investors	4 565 . .	. . .	. . .	. . .	. . .	. . .	–10.0	–9.9	. . .
Liabilities to direct investors	4 570 . .	. . .	. . .	13.1	8.2	14.2	47.6	10.6	. . .
Reinvested earnings	4 575 . .	3.0	5.3	3.4	3.8	3.5	8.5	11.1	. . .
Other capital	4 580 . .	6.8	10.0	. . .	. . .	. . .	1.3	6.0	. . .
Claims on direct investors	4 585 . .	. . .	. . .	. . .	. . .	. . .	. . .	. . .	. . .
Liabilities to direct investors	4 590 . .	. . .	. . .	. . .	. . .	. . .	1.3	6.0	. . .
B. PORTFOLIO INVESTMENT	4 600 . .	6.1	3.5	10.1	10.2	12.5	32.9	113.2	. . .
Assets	4 602 . .	**. . .**	**. . .**	**. . .**	**. . .**	**. . .**	**. . .**	**. . .**	**. . .**
Equity securities	4 610 . .	. . .	. . .	. . .	. . .	. . .	. . .	. . .	. . .
Monetary authorities	4 611 . .	. . .	. . .	. . .	. . .	. . .	. . .	. . .	. . .
General government	4 612 . .	. . .	. . .	. . .	. . .	. . .	. . .	. . .	. . .
Banks	4 613 . .	. . .	. . .	. . .	. . .	. . .	. . .	. . .	. . .
Other sectors	4 614 . .	. . .	. . .	. . .	. . .	. . .	. . .	. . .	. . .
Debt securities	4 619 . .	. . .	. . .	. . .	. . .	. . .	. . .	. . .	. . .
Bonds and notes	4 620 . .	. . .	. . .	. . .	. . .	. . .	. . .	. . .	. . .
Monetary authorities	4 621 . .	. . .	. . .	. . .	. . .	. . .	. . .	. . .	. . .
General government	4 622 . .	. . .	. . .	. . .	. . .	. . .	. . .	. . .	. . .
Banks	4 623 . .	. . .	. . .	. . .	. . .	. . .	. . .	. . .	. . .
Other sectors	4 624 . .	. . .	. . .	. . .	. . .	. . .	. . .	. . .	. . .
Money market instruments	4 630 . .	. . .	. . .	. . .	. . .	. . .	. . .	. . .	. . .
Monetary authorities	4 631 . .	. . .	. . .	. . .	. . .	. . .	. . .	. . .	. . .
General government	4 632 . .	. . .	. . .	. . .	. . .	. . .	. . .	. . .	. . .
Banks	4 633 . .	. . .	. . .	. . .	. . .	. . .	. . .	. . .	. . .
Other sectors	4 634 . .	. . .	. . .	. . .	. . .	. . .	. . .	. . .	. . .
Liabilities	4 652 . .	**6.1**	**3.5**	**10.1**	**10.2**	**12.5**	**32.9**	**113.2**	**. . .**
Equity securities	4 660 . .	. . .	. . .	. . .	. . .	. . .	. . .	. . .	. . .
Banks	4 663 . .	. . .	. . .	. . .	. . .	. . .	. . .	. . .	. . .
Other sectors	4 664 . .	. . .	. . .	. . .	. . .	. . .	. . .	. . .	. . .
Debt securities	4 669 . .	6.1	3.5	10.1	10.2	12.5	32.9	113.2	. . .
Bonds and notes	4 670 . .	6.1	3.5	7.8	10.1	12.0	. . .	83.4	. . .
Monetary authorities	4 671 . .	. . .	. . .	12.0	. . .	. . .	. . .	–3.0	. . .
General government	4 672 . .	. . .	. . .	. . .	10.0	12.0	. . .	86.4	. . .
Banks	4 673 . .	. . .	. . .	–4.2	.1	. . .	. . .	. . .	. . .
Other sectors	4 674 . .	6.1	3.5	. . .	. . .	. . .	. . .	. . .	. . .
Money market instruments	4 680 . .	. . .	. . .	2.3	.1	.5	32.9	29.9	. . .
Monetary authorities	4 681 . .	. . .	. . .	. . .	. . .	. . .	. . .	. . .	. . .
General government	4 682 . .	. . .	. . .	.3	.1	.5	33.6	39.7	. . .
Banks	4 683 . .	. . .	. . .	. . .	. . .	. . .	. . .	. . .	. . .
Other sectors	4 684 . .	. . .	. . .	2.1	. . .	. . .	–.7	–9.8	. . .
C. FINANCIAL DERIVATIVES	4 910 . .	. . .	. . .	. . .	. . .	. . .	. . .	. . .	. . .
Monetary authorities	4 911 . .	. . .	. . .	. . .	. . .	. . .	. . .	. . .	. . .
General government	4 912 . .	. . .	. . .	. . .	. . .	. . .	. . .	. . .	. . .
Banks	4 913 . .	. . .	. . .	. . .	. . .	. . .	. . .	. . .	. . .
Other sectors	4 914 . .	. . .	. . .	. . .	. . .	. . .	. . .	. . .	. . .
Assets	4 900 . .	**. . .**	**. . .**	**. . .**	**. . .**	**. . .**	**. . .**	**. . .**	**. . .**
Monetary authorities	4 901 . .	. . .	. . .	. . .	. . .	. . .	. . .	. . .	. . .
General government	4 902 . .	. . .	. . .	. . .	. . .	. . .	. . .	. . .	. . .
Banks	4 903 . .	. . .	. . .	. . .	. . .	. . .	. . .	. . .	. . .
Other sectors	4 904 . .	. . .	. . .	. . .	. . .	. . .	. . .	. . .	. . .
Liabilities	4 905 . .	**. . .**	**. . .**	**. . .**	**. . .**	**. . .**	**. . .**	**. . .**	**. . .**
Monetary authorities	4 906 . .	. . .	. . .	. . .	. . .	. . .	. . .	. . .	. . .
General government	4 907 . .	. . .	. . .	. . .	. . .	. . .	. . .	. . .	. . .
Banks	4 908 . .	. . .	. . .	. . .	. . .	. . .	. . .	. . .	. . .
Other sectors	4 909 . .	. . .	. . .	. . .	. . .	. . .	. . .	. . .	. . .

Table 2 (Concluded). STANDARD PRESENTATION, 1994–2001
(Millions of U.S. dollars)

	Code	1994	1995	1996	1997	1998	1999	2000	2001
D. OTHER INVESTMENT	4 700	–17.9	–25.5	–10.0	9.3	–2.2	11.3	43.9	...
Assets	4 703	**–17.1**	**–14.1**	**–12.2**	**2.8**	**...**	**–8.9**	**–39.4**	**...**
Trade credits	4 706	...	...	...	...	...	–2.7	–2.1	...
General government	4 707	...	...	...	...	...	...	...	...
of which: Short-term	4 709	...	...	...	...	...	...	...	...
Other sectors	4 710	...	...	...	...	...	–2.7	–2.1	...
of which: Short-term	4 712	...	...	...	...	...	*–2.7*	*–2.1*	...
Loans	4 714	...	...	...	...	...	...	–.1	...
Monetary authorities	4 715	...	...	...	...	...	...	...	...
of which: Short-term	4 718	...	...	...	...	...	...	...	...
General government	4 719	...	...	...	...	...	...	...	...
of which: Short-term	4 721	...	...	...	...	...	...	...	...
Banks	4 722	...	...	...	...	...	...	...	...
of which: Short-term	4 724	...	...	...	...	...	...	...	...
Other sectors	4 725	...	...	...	...	...	...	–.1	...
of which: Short-term	4 727	...	...	...	...	...	...	...	...
Currency and deposits	4 730	–3.3	–1.7	...	...	...	–6.3	–37.3	...
Monetary authorities	4 731	...	...	...	...	...	...	...	...
General government	4 732	...	...	...	...	...	...	–11.1	...
Banks	4 733	–3.3	–1.7	...	...	...	–6.3	–26.3	...
Other sectors	4 734	...	...	...	...	...	...	...	...
Other assets	4 736	–13.8	–12.4	–12.2	2.8	...	...	...	...
Monetary authorities	4 737	...	...	...	...	...	...	...	...
of which: Short-term	4 739	...	...	...	...	...	...	...	...
General government	4 740	...	...	...	...	...	...	...	...
of which: Short-term	4 742	...	...	...	...	...	...	...	...
Banks	4 743	...	...	–12.2	2.8	...	...	...	...
of which: Short-term	4 745	...	...	*–12.2*	*2.8*	...	...	...	...
Other sectors	4 746	–13.8	–12.4	...	...	...	...	...	...
of which: Short-term	4 748	...	...	...	...	...	...	...	...
Liabilities	4 753	**–.8**	**–11.5**	**2.2**	**6.5**	**–2.2**	**20.2**	**83.3**	**...**
Trade credits	4 756	...	...	...	...	...	3.6	2.9	...
General government	4 757	...	...	...	...	...	...	...	...
of which: Short-term	4 759	...	...	...	...	...	...	...	...
Other sectors	4 760	...	...	...	...	...	3.6	2.9	...
of which: Short-term	4 762	...	...	...	...	...	*3.6*	*2.9*	...
Loans	4 764	8.5	.6	28.9	13.7	15.3	30.2	104.0	...
Monetary authorities	4 765	...	...	...	...	...	...	42.0	...
of which: Use of Fund credit and loans from the Fund	4 766	...	...	...	...	...	...	...	...
of which: Short-term	4 768	...	...	...	...	...	...	...	...
General government	4 769	8.9	–2.6	19.4	11.3	12.9	14.9	46.8	...
of which: Short-term	4 771	...	...	...	...	...	...	...	...
Banks	4 772	...	...	...	...	...	...	...	...
of which: Short-term	4 774	...	...	...	...	...	...	...	...
Other sectors	4 775	–.3	3.2	9.4	2.5	2.5	15.4	15.2	...
of which: Short-term	4 777	*.5*	*2.0*	*–.5*	*–1.2*	*–.3*	*.8*	*3.3*	...
Currency and deposits	4 780	–9.3	–12.1	...	...	7.2	–9.5	14.6	...
Monetary authorities	4 781	...	...	...	...	...	–.6	–.2	...
General government	4 782	...	...	...	...	...	...	–.7	...
Banks	4 783	–9.3	–12.1	...	...	7.2	–8.9	15.5	...
Other sectors	4 784	...	...	...	...	...	...	...	...
Other liabilities	4 786	...	...	–26.6	–7.2	–24.7	–4.2	–38.2	...
Monetary authorities	4 787	...	...	...	...	...	...	...	...
of which: Short-term	4 789	...	...	...	...	...	...	...	...
General government	4 790	...	...	.3	.2	–4.1	...	...	...
of which: Short-term	4 792	...	...	*.3*	*.2*	*–4.1*	...	...	...
Banks	4 793	...	...	–6.3	4.8	...	...	...	...
of which: Short-term	4 795	...	...	*–6.3*	*4.8*	...	...	...	...
Other sectors	4 796	...	...	–20.6	–12.3	–20.6	–4.2	–38.2	...
of which: Short-term	4 798	...	...	*–20.6*	*–9.4*	*–13.4*	*–4.2*	*–38.2*	...
E. RESERVE ASSETS	4 802	3.6	–4.1	–20.6	–1.4	13.7	–27.5	–51.8	...
Monetary gold	4 812	...	...	...	...	...	...	...	...
Special drawing rights	4 811	–.1	–.1	–.2	–.1	–.2	–.3	–.2	...
Reserve position in the Fund	4 810	...	...	...	...	...	–1.8	...	...
Foreign exchange	4 803	3.7	–4.0	–19.9	–1.2	13.8	–25.4	–51.6	...
Other claims	4 813	...	...	–.5	...	...	...	...	...
NET ERRORS AND OMISSIONS	4 998	**32.8**	**22.4**	**18.4**	**9.1**	**24.5**	**.9**	**7.3**	**...**

Part 3 of the *Yearbook* contains descriptions of the methodologies, compilation practices, and sources used to compile these data.

Table 1. ANALYTIC PRESENTATION, 1994–2001
(Millions of U.S. dollars)

	Code		1994	1995	1996	1997	1998	1999	2000	2001
A. Current Account[1]	4 993	Z.	**–23.2**	**–206.6**	**–57.4**	**–169.9**	**–151.5**	**–191.4**	**–111.0**	**. . .**
Goods: exports f.o.b	2 100	. .	397.9	419.9	527.7	424.0	414.3	421.5	392.4	. . .
Goods: imports f.o.b	3 100	. .	–451.5	–622.5	–559.7	–576.9	–572.6	–635.2	–516.1	. . .
Balance on Goods	4 100	. .	*–53.6*	*–202.5*	*–32.0*	*–152.9*	*–158.3*	*–213.7*	*–123.7*	. . .
Services: credit	2 200	. .	142.2	194.3	126.1	116.0	142.3	176.9	136.1	. . .
Services: debit	3 200	. .	–181.4	–272.2	–188.8	–172.3	–191.4	–215.3	–191.7	. . .
Balance on Goods and Services	4 991	. .	*–92.8*	*–280.4*	*–94.7*	*–209.2*	*–207.4*	*–252.2*	*–179.4*	. . .
Income: credit	2 300	. .	18.8	24.0	29.6	24.4	27.8	27.7	28.0	. . .
Income: debit	3 300	. .	–21.7	–25.1	–50.6	–44.4	–41.2	–39.1	–40.3	. . .
Balance on Goods, Services, and Income	4 992	. .	*–95.7*	*–281.5*	*–115.6*	*–229.2*	*–220.8*	*–263.6*	*–191.6*	. . .
Current transfers: credit	2 379	Z.	98.5	105.4	92.4	77.8	102.0	87.1	91.3	. . .
Current transfers: debit	3 379	. .	–25.9	–30.5	–34.2	–18.5	–32.7	–14.9	–10.7	. . .
B. Capital Account[1]	4 994	Z.	**75.2**	**85.6**	**6.4**	**84.5**	**66.6**	**69.9**	**73.3**	**. . .**
Capital account: credit	2 994	Z.	75.2	85.6	6.4	84.5	66.6	69.9	73.4	. . .
Capital account: debit	3 994	. .	. . .	. . .	. . .	. . .	. . .	. . .	–.1	. . .
Total, Groups A Plus B	4 981	. .	*52.0*	*–121.1*	*–51.0*	*–85.4*	*–84.9*	*–121.5*	*–37.7*	. . .
C. Financial Account[1]	4 995	W.	**–17.6**	**–132.9**	**–104.2**	**–21.3**	**–8.4**	**25.4**	**11.2**	**. . .**
Direct investment abroad	4 505	. .	. . .	–.6	–15.0	–12.1	–1.9	–1.4	–8.1	. . .
Direct investment in Benin	4 555	Z.	13.6	7.4	28.6	26.0	34.7	39.3	64.3	. . .
Portfolio investment assets	4 602	. .	–26.4	–64.2	–7.7	–7.8	1.2	–1.4	5.7	. . .
Equity securities	4 610	. .	. . .	. . .	1.4	. . .	.1	–.9	.9	. . .
Debt securities	4 619	. .	–26.4	–64.2	–9.1	–7.7	1.1	–.5	4.7	. . .
Portfolio investment liabilities	4 652	Z.	. . .	.3	2.5	2.0	1.7	2.0	.5	. . .
Equity securities	4 660	. .	. . .	.3	2.5	2.0	1.2	2.0	.1	. . .
Debt securities	4 669	Z.	. . .	. . .	. . .	. . .	.5	. . .	.4	. . .
Financial derivatives	4 910	. .	. . .	. . .	. . .	. . .	. . .	8.5	. . .	. . .
Financial derivatives assets	4 900	. .	. . .	. . .	. . .	. . .	. . .	–.1	. . .	. . .
Financial derivatives liabilities	4 905	. .	. . .	. . .	. . .	. . .	. . .	8.6	. . .	. . .
Other investment assets	4 703	. .	–52.2	–62.1	–4.0	–12.4	–9.6	–58.3	25.1	. . .
Monetary authorities	4 701	. .	. . .	. . .	. . .	. . .	. . .	. . .	. . .	. . .
General government	4 704	. .	11.9	–6.9	. . .	–.1	. . .	. . .	. . .	. . .
Banks	4 705	. .	–50.8	–44.2	11.8	–41.1	12.4	–26.7	1.8	. . .
Other sectors	4 728	. .	–13.3	–10.9	–15.8	28.8	22.0	–31.6	23.4	. . .
Other investment liabilities	4 753	W.	47.4	–13.7	–108.6	–17.0	–34.4	36.8	–76.2	. . .
Monetary authorities	4 753	WA	.6	–2.7	5.2	4.7	–5.4	.3	–1.4	. . .
General government	4 753	ZB	–28.1	–36.0	–129.4	–26.8	–29.7	33.6	–49.2	. . .
Banks	4 753	ZC	9.8	–.5	4.5	–11.6	21.1	33.3	–21.0	. . .
Other sectors	4 753	ZD	65.1	25.4	11.1	16.7	–20.4	36.8	–4.7	. . .
Total, Groups A Through C	4 983	. .	*34.4*	*–253.9*	*–155.2*	*–106.7*	*–93.3*	*–96.0*	*–26.5*	. . .
D. Net Errors and Omissions	4 998	. .	**–16.3**	**–1.0**	**6.3**	**6.7**	**7.1**	**7.3**	**6.7**	**. . .**
Total, Groups A Through D	4 984	. .	*18.1*	*–254.9*	*–149.0*	*–100.0*	*–86.2*	*–88.7*	*–19.8*	. . .
E. Reserves and Related Items	4 802	A.	**–18.1**	**254.9**	**149.0**	**100.0**	**86.2**	**88.7**	**19.8**	**. . .**
Reserve assets	4 802	. .	–117.7	81.9	–78.3	–24.5	7.0	–40.2	–87.3	. . .
Use of Fund credit and loans	4 766	. .	24.9	12.2	18.0	1.9	–5.3	1.1	–3.6	. . .
Exceptional financing	4 920	. .	74.6	160.7	209.3	122.6	84.5	127.8	110.8	. . .
Conversion rates: CFA francs per U.S. dollar	0 101	. .	**555.20**	**499.15**	**511.55**	**583.67**	**589.95**	**615.70**	**711.98**	**733.04**

[1] Excludes components that have been classified in the categories of Group E.

Table 2. STANDARD PRESENTATION, 1994–2001
(Millions of U.S. dollars)

	Code	1994	1995	1996	1997	1998	1999	2000	2001
CURRENT ACCOUNT	4 993 . .	**10.6**	**–160.5**	**–41.0**	**–154.0**	**–132.5**	**–155.6**	**–80.6**	. . .
A. GOODS	4 100 . .	–53.6	–202.5	–32.0	–152.9	–158.3	–213.7	–123.7	. . .
Credit	2 100 . .	**397.9**	**419.9**	**527.7**	**424.0**	**414.3**	**421.5**	**392.4**	. . .
General merchandise: exports f.o.b.	2 110 . .	391.2	413.8	519.5	417.1	407.5	415.7	384.4	. . .
Goods for processing: exports f.o.b.	2 150 . .	. . .	. . .	. . .	. . .	. . .	. . .	. . .	. . .
Repairs on goods	2 160 . .	. . .	. . .	. . .	. . .	. . .	. . .	. . .	. . .
Goods procured in ports by carriers	2 170 . .	6.7	6.2	8.2	7.0	6.8	5.7	8.0	. . .
Nonmonetary gold	2 180 . .	. . .	. . .	. . .	. . .	. . .	. . .	. . .	. . .
Debit	3 100 . .	**–451.5**	**–622.5**	**–559.7**	**–576.9**	**–572.6**	**–635.2**	**–516.1**	. . .
General merchandise: imports f.o.b.	3 110 . .	–451.5	–622.5	–557.8	–576.9	–572.4	–632.8	–514.8	. . .
Goods for processing: imports f.o.b.	3 150 . .	. . .	. . .	. . .	. . .	. . .	. . .	. . .	. . .
Repairs on goods	3 160 . .	. . .	. . .	–1.9	–.1	–.2	–2.4	–1.3	. . .
Goods procured in ports by carriers	3 170 . .	. . .	. . .	. . .	. . .	. . .	. . .	. . .	. . .
Nonmonetary gold	3 180 . .	. . .	. . .	. . .	. . .	. . .	. . .	. . .	. . .
B. SERVICES	4 200 . .	–39.2	–77.9	–62.6	–56.3	–49.1	–38.5	–55.6	. . .
Total credit	2 200 . .	*142.2*	*194.3*	*126.1*	*116.0*	*142.3*	*176.9*	*136.1*	. . .
Total debit	3 200 . .	*–181.4*	*–272.2*	*–188.8*	*–172.3*	*–191.4*	*–215.3*	*–191.7*	. . .
Transportation services, credit	2 205 . .	**36.4**	**41.1**	**15.5**	**25.5**	**26.4**	**19.9**	**18.1**	. . .
Passenger	2 850 . .	. . .	. . .	*.1*	*.2*	*.2*	*.4*	*.4*	. . .
Freight	2 851 . .	*15.1*	*13.9*	*4.5*	*13.7*	*15.2*	*12.3*	*11.9*	. . .
Other	2 852 . .	*21.2*	*27.1*	*10.9*	*11.6*	*11.1*	*7.2*	*5.8*	. . .
Sea transport, passenger	2 207 . .	. . .	. . .	. . .	. . .	. . .	. . .	. . .	. . .
Sea transport, freight	2 208 . .	2.9	5.3	. . .	. . .	. . .	. . .	1.3	. . .
Sea transport, other	2 209 . .	21.2	27.1	10.4	11.3	10.5	6.4	5.4	. . .
Air transport, passenger	2 211 . .	. . .	. . .	. . .	. . .	. . .	. . .	. . .	. . .
Air transport, freight	2 212 . .	. . .	. . .	. . .	. . .	. . .	. . .	. . .	. . .
Air transport, other	2 213 . .	. . .	. . .	.5	.3	.6	.8	.3	. . .
Other transport, passenger	2 215 . .	. . .	. . .	.1	.2	.2	.4	.4	. . .
Other transport, freight	2 216 . .	12.3	8.6	4.5	13.7	15.2	12.3	10.6	. . .
Other transport, other	2 217 . .	. . .	. . .	. . .	. . .	. . .	. . .	. . .	. . .
Transportation services, debit	3 205 . .	**–103.6**	**–139.2**	**–108.6**	**–112.4**	**–112.8**	**–143.7**	**–125.6**	. . .
Passenger	3 850 . .	*–11.7*	*–13.3*	*–21.7*	*–17.6*	*–11.9*	*–37.0*	*–38.3*	. . .
Freight	3 851 . .	*–89.5*	*–123.3*	*–85.2*	*–93.0*	*–99.8*	*–104.6*	*–83.2*	. . .
Other	3 852 . .	*–2.3*	*–2.6*	*–1.8*	*–1.9*	*–1.0*	*–2.1*	*–4.2*	. . .
Sea transport, passenger	3 207 . .	. . .	. . .	. . .	. . .	. . .	. . .	. . .	. . .
Sea transport, freight	3 208 . .	–89.5	–123.3	–65.8	–71.6	–76.6	–83.0	–64.0	. . .
Sea transport, other	3 209 . .	–2.3	–2.6	–.8	–.9	–1.0	–1.0	–3.1	. . .
Air transport, passenger	3 211 . .	–11.7	–13.3	–20.6	–16.6	–10.9	–32.8	–34.9	. . .
Air transport, freight	3 212 . .	. . .	. . .	–16.5	–17.9	–19.2	–20.8	–16.0	. . .
Air transport, other	3 213 . .	. . .	. . .	–.9	–1.0	. . .	–1.1	–1.1	. . .
Other transport, passenger	3 215 . .	. . .	. . .	–1.1	–1.0	–1.0	–4.2	–3.4	. . .
Other transport, freight	3 216 . .	. . .	. . .	–2.9	–3.5	–4.0	–.8	–3.2	. . .
Other transport, other	3 217 . .	. . .	. . .	. . .	. . .	. . .	. . .	. . .	. . .
Travel, credit	2 236 . .	**58.8**	**84.8**	**78.5**	**55.7**	**64.3**	**93.6**	**76.8**	. . .
Business travel	2 237 . .	. . .	. . .	7.3	7.5	22.0	27.3	25.1	. . .
Personal travel	2 240 . .	58.8	84.8	71.3	48.2	42.3	66.3	51.7	. . .
Travel, debit	3 236 . .	**–16.2**	**–34.5**	**–28.8**	**–15.5**	**–20.2**	**–25.6**	**–12.3**	. . .
Business travel	3 237 . .	–1.1	–1.1	–9.8	–2.7	–8.0	–11.1	–4.2	. . .
Personal travel	3 240 . .	–15.1	–33.4	–19.0	–12.8	–12.2	–14.5	–8.1	. . .
Other services, credit	2 200 BA	**47.1**	**68.5**	**32.1**	**34.8**	**51.6**	**63.4**	**41.1**	. . .
Communications	2 245 . .	.1	.1	4.6	4.4	5.6	3.8	4.2	. . .
Construction	2 249 . .	. . .	. . .	. . .	. . .	7.6	11.7	.1	. . .
Insurance	2 253 . .	.7	1.6	.8	1.1	.6	.4	.4	. . .
Financial	2 260 . .	6.5	9.4	2.5	2.7	6.1	5.9	2.6	. . .
Computer and information	2 262 . .	. . .	. . .	. . .	. . .	. . .	. . .	. . .	. . .
Royalties and licence fees	2 266 . .	. . .	. . .	. . .	. . .	. . .	. . .	. . .	. . .
Other business services	2 268 . .	11.8	22.4	20.6	13.0	16.3	19.4	24.2	. . .
Personal, cultural, and recreational	2 287 . .	. . .	. . .	.1	.1	.1	. . .	. . .	. . .
Government, n.i.e.	2 291 . .	28.1	34.9	3.4	13.6	15.3	22.1	9.8	. . .
Other services, debit	3 200 BA	**–61.6**	**–98.5**	**–51.3**	**–44.3**	**–58.5**	**–46.0**	**–53.8**	. . .
Communications	3 245 . .	. . .	. . .	–2.3	–.7	–3.7	–1.3	–4.0	. . .
Construction	3 249 . .	. . .	. . .	. . .	–.1	. . .	–.2	–13.1	. . .
Insurance	3 253 . .	–1.3	–2.4	–17.3	–18.7	–18.3	–18.8	–15.5	. . .
Financial	3 260 . .	–10.4	–22.0	–.8	–2.0	–.4	–1.2	–1.8	. . .
Computer and information	3 262 . .	. . .	. . .	–.6	–.6	–.6	–1.4	–.7	. . .
Royalties and licence fees	3 266 . .	. . .	. . .	–.4	–.4	–1.6	–.5	–.4	. . .
Other business services	3 268 . .	–23.5	–36.1	–29.8	–19.5	–33.9	–20.6	–13.0	. . .
Personal, cultural, and recreational	3 287 . .	–.6	–.9	–.1	. . .	–.1	–.2	–.1	. . .
Government, n.i.e.	3 291 . .	–25.9	–37.1	. . .	–2.3	. . .	–1.9	–5.3	. . .

Table 2 (Continued). STANDARD PRESENTATION, 1994–2001
(Millions of U.S. dollars)

	Code	1994	1995	1996	1997	1998	1999	2000	2001
C. INCOME	4 300 . .	–2.9	–1.1	–21.0	–20.0	–13.4	–11.4	–12.3	. . .
Total credit	2 300 . .	*18.8*	*24.0*	*29.6*	*24.4*	*27.8*	*27.7*	*28.0*	. . .
Total debit	3 300 . .	*–21.7*	*–25.1*	*–50.6*	*–44.4*	*–41.2*	*–39.1*	*–40.3*	. . .
Compensation of employees, credit	2 310 . .	**6.1**	**6.5**	**3.8**	**3.3**	**2.6**	**5.5**	**5.2**	**. . .**
Compensation of employees, debit	3 310 . .	**–.6**	**–.8**	**–1.8**	**–1.4**	**–.2**	**–1.4**	**–2.3**	**. . .**
Investment income, credit	2 320 . .	**12.7**	**17.6**	**25.9**	**21.1**	**25.2**	**22.2**	**22.8**	**. . .**
Direct investment income	2 330 . .	. . .	.6	3.4	.5	.3	.1	4.8	. . .
Dividends and distributed branch profits	2 332 . .	. . .	. . .	.1	.4	.2	. . .	. . .	. . .
Reinvested earnings and undistributed branch profits	2 333 . .	. . .	.6	3.2	. . .	. . .	. . .	4.8	. . .
Income on debt (interest)	2 334 . .	. . .	. . .	.1	.1	.1	.1	. . .	. . .
Portfolio investment income	2 339 . .	. . .	. . .	3.6	5.9	3.4	5.7	3.4	. . .
Income on equity	2 340 . .	. . .	. . .	.1	. . .	.1	.1	.1	. . .
Income on bonds and notes	2 350 . .	. . .	. . .	1.9	5.5	3.1	3.9	2.5	. . .
Income on money market instruments	2 360 . .	. . .	. . .	1.7	.4	.1	1.7	.9	. . .
Other investment income	2 370 . .	12.7	17.0	18.8	14.7	21.5	16.4	14.6	. . .
Investment income, debit	3 320 . .	**–21.1**	**–24.3**	**–48.8**	**–43.0**	**–41.0**	**–37.7**	**–38.0**	**. . .**
Direct investment income	3 330 . .	–.3	. . .	–2.1	–11.5	–11.7	–8.5	–3.8	. . .
Dividends and distributed branch profits	3 332 . .	. . .	. . .	–1.4	–2.3	–2.1	–2.1	–2.8	. . .
Reinvested earnings and undistributed branch profits	3 333 . .	–.3	. . .	. . .	–9.3	–9.2	–6.3	. . .	. . .
Income on debt (interest)	3 334 . .	. . .	. . .	–.7	. . .	–.3	. . .	–1.0	. . .
Portfolio investment income	3 339 . .	. . .	. . .	–9.6	–9.5	–3.5	–6.5	–5.4	. . .
Income on equity	3 340 . .	. . .	. . .	–1.2	–1.3	–1.6	–1.3	–1.6	. . .
Income on bonds and notes	3 350 . .	. . .	. . .	–8.4	–8.2	–1.9	–4.8	–3.7	. . .
Income on money market instruments	3 360 . .	. . .	. . .	. . .	. . .	. . .	–.4	. . .	. . .
Other investment income	3 370 . .	–20.8	–24.3	–37.1	–22.0	–25.8	–22.7	–28.8	. . .
D. CURRENT TRANSFERS	4 379 . .	106.3	121.1	74.7	75.2	88.3	108.0	111.0	. . .
Credit	2 379 . .	**132.2**	**151.6**	**108.9**	**93.7**	**121.0**	**122.9**	**121.7**	**. . .**
General government	2 380 . .	33.7	46.2	16.4	16.0	19.0	35.8	30.4	. . .
Other sectors	2 390 . .	98.5	105.4	92.4	77.8	102.0	87.1	91.3	. . .
Workers' remittances	2 391 . .	82.3	92.4	81.2	66.8	86.6	69.5	80.5	. . .
Other current transfers	2 392 . .	16.2	13.0	11.3	11.0	15.4	17.5	10.8	. . .
Debit	3 379 . .	**–25.9**	**–30.5**	**–34.2**	**–18.5**	**–32.7**	**–14.9**	**–10.7**	**. . .**
General government	3 380 . .	–1.5	–2.9	–1.6	–1.7	–2.2	–1.4	–2.9	. . .
Other sectors	3 390 . .	–24.4	–27.7	–32.6	–16.7	–30.5	–13.5	–7.7	. . .
Workers' remittances	3 391 . .	–22.6	–25.7	–31.8	–15.7	–29.7	–4.6	–6.6	. . .
Other current transfers	3 392 . .	–1.8	–2.0	–.8	–1.1	–.8	–8.9	–1.2	. . .
CAPITAL AND FINANCIAL ACCOUNT	4 996 . .	**5.7**	**161.4**	**34.7**	**147.2**	**125.4**	**148.3**	**73.9**	**. . .**
CAPITAL ACCOUNT	4 994 . .	**76.2**	**89.2**	**111.1**	**84.5**	**66.6**	**69.9**	**73.3**	**. . .**
Total credit	2 994 . .	*76.2*	*89.2*	*111.1*	*84.5*	*66.6*	*69.9*	*73.4*	. . .
Total debit	3 994 . .	. . .	. . .	. . .	. . .	. . .	. . .	*–.1*	. . .
Capital transfers, credit	2 400 . .	**76.2**	**89.2**	**111.1**	**84.5**	**66.6**	**69.9**	**73.4**	**. . .**
General government	2 401 . .	75.2	88.0	108.1	80.0	62.3	64.3	68.6	. . .
Debt forgiveness	2 402 . .	1.1	3.7	104.7	. . .	. . .	. . .	23.2	. . .
Other capital transfers	2 410 . .	74.1	84.4	3.4	80.0	62.3	64.3	45.4	. . .
Other sectors	2 430 . .	1.1	1.2	3.0	4.4	4.2	5.6	4.8	. . .
Migrants' transfers	2 431 . .	1.1	1.2	1.3	1.1	1.1	1.6	1.4	. . .
Debt forgiveness	2 432 . .	. . .	. . .	. . .	. . .	. . .	. . .	. . .	. . .
Other capital transfers	2 440 . .	. . .	. . .	1.7	3.3	3.1	4.0	3.4	. . .
Capital transfers, debit	3 400 . .	**. . .**	**. . .**	**. . .**	**. . .**	**. . .**	**. . .**	**. . .**	**. . .**
General government	3 401 . .	. . .	. . .	. . .	. . .	. . .	. . .	. . .	. . .
Debt forgiveness	3 402 . .	. . .	. . .	. . .	. . .	. . .	. . .	. . .	. . .
Other capital transfers	3 410 . .	. . .	. . .	. . .	. . .	. . .	. . .	. . .	. . .
Other sectors	3 430 . .	. . .	. . .	. . .	. . .	. . .	. . .	. . .	. . .
Migrants' transfers	3 431 . .	. . .	. . .	. . .	. . .	. . .	. . .	. . .	. . .
Debt forgiveness	3 432 . .	. . .	. . .	. . .	. . .	. . .	. . .	. . .	. . .
Other capital transfers	3 440 . .	. . .	. . .	. . .	. . .	. . .	. . .	. . .	. . .
Nonproduced nonfinancial assets, credit	2 480 . .	**. . .**	**. . .**	**. . .**	**. . .**	**. . .**	**. . .**	**. . .**	**. . .**
Nonproduced nonfinancial assets, debit	3 480 . .	**. . .**	**. . .**	**. . .**	**. . .**	**. . .**	**. . .**	**–.1**	**. . .**

Table 2 (Continued). STANDARD PRESENTATION, 1994–2001

(Millions of U.S. dollars)

	Code		1994	1995	1996	1997	1998	1999	2000	2001
FINANCIAL ACCOUNT	4 995	. .	**–70.5**	**72.2**	**–76.4**	**62.7**	**58.9**	**78.4**	**.6**	**. . .**
A. DIRECT INVESTMENT	4 500	. .	13.6	6.8	13.6	13.9	32.7	37.8	56.2	. . .
Direct investment abroad	4 505	. .	**. . .**	**–.6**	**–15.0**	**–12.1**	**–1.9**	**–1.4**	**–8.1**	**. . .**
Equity capital	4 510	. .	. . .	. . .	–12.0	–.1	–3.0	–.8	. . .	. . .
Claims on affiliated enterprises	4 515	. .	. . .	. . .	. . .	. . .	. . .	. . .	. . .	. . .
Liabilities to affiliated enterprises	4 520	. .	. . .	. . .	–12.0	–.1	–3.0	–.8	. . .	. . .
Reinvested earnings	4 525	. .	. . .	–.6	–3.2	. . .	. . .	. . .	–4.8	. . .
Other capital	4 530	. .	. . .	. . .	.2	–12.0	1.0	–.7	–3.4	. . .
Claims on affiliated enterprises	4 535	. .	. . .	. . .	. . .	–18.3	1.1	–.7	–4.0	. . .
Liabilities to affiliated enterprises	4 540	. .	. . .	. . .	.2	6.3	–.1	.1	.6	. . .
Direct investment in Benin	4 555	. .	**13.6**	**7.4**	**28.6**	**26.0**	**34.7**	**39.3**	**64.3**	**. . .**
Equity capital	4 560	. .	9.6	11.4	28.3	18.1	20.3	35.3	73.5	. . .
Claims on direct investors	4 565	. .	10.3	12.6	38.3	21.0	24.2	37.7	70.2	. . .
Liabilities to direct investors	4 570	. .	–.8	–1.2	–10.1	–3.0	–3.9	–2.4	3.3	. . .
Reinvested earnings	4 575	. .	.3	. . .	. . .	9.3	9.2	6.3	. . .	. . .
Other capital	4 580	. .	3.8	–4.0	.3	–1.4	5.2	–2.3	–9.2	. . .
Claims on direct investors	4 585	. .	10.4	8.5	. . .	–.1	–.6	–8.4	3.0	. . .
Liabilities to direct investors	4 590	. .	–6.6	–12.4	.3	–1.3	5.7	6.1	–12.2	. . .
B. PORTFOLIO INVESTMENT	4 600	. .	–26.4	–63.9	–11.6	–17.2	26.1	13.8	3.2	. . .
Assets	4 602	. .	**–26.4**	**–64.2**	**–7.7**	**–7.8**	**1.2**	**–1.4**	**5.7**	**. . .**
Equity securities	4 610	. .	. . .	. . .	1.4	. . .	.1	–.9	.9	. . .
Monetary authorities	4 611	. .	. . .	. . .	. . .	. . .	. . .	. . .	. . .	. . .
General government	4 612	. .	. . .	. . .	. . .	. . .	. . .	. . .	. . .	. . .
Banks	4 613	. .	. . .	. . .	1.5	. . .	.2	–.1	3.0	. . .
Other sectors	4 614	. .	. . .	. . .	–.2	. . .	–.1	–.8	–2.1	. . .
Debt securities	4 619	. .	–26.4	–64.2	–9.1	–7.7	1.1	–.5	4.7	. . .
Bonds and notes	4 620	. .	–26.4	–64.2	–.8	–11.7	–2.6	11.3	–9.4	. . .
Monetary authorities	4 621	. .	. . .	. . .	. . .	. . .	. . .	. . .	. . .	. . .
General government	4 622	. .	–1.6	–.7	. . .	. . .	. . .	. . .	. . .	. . .
Banks	4 623	. .	–24.8	–63.5	. . .	–13.4	–5.4	13.6	–8.1	. . .
Other sectors	4 624	. .	. . .	. . .	–.8	1.7	2.8	–2.2	–1.3	. . .
Money market instruments	4 630	. .	. . .	. . .	–8.3	3.9	3.7	–11.8	14.2	. . .
Monetary authorities	4 631	. .	. . .	. . .	. . .	. . .	. . .	. . .	. . .	. . .
General government	4 632	. .	. . .	. . .	. . .	. . .	. . .	. . .	. . .	. . .
Banks	4 633	. .	. . .	. . .	–8.3	3.9	3.7	–11.8	12.1	. . .
Other sectors	4 634	. .	. . .	. . .	. . .	. . .	. . .	. . .	2.1	. . .
Liabilities	4 652	. .	**. . .**	**.3**	**–3.9**	**–9.4**	**24.9**	**15.1**	**–2.4**	**. . .**
Equity securities	4 660	. .	. . .	.3	2.5	2.0	1.2	2.0	.1	. . .
Banks	4 663	. .	. . .	. . .	2.1	1.8	1.2	1.2	–1.0	. . .
Other sectors	4 664	. .	. . .	.3	.4	.2	. . .	.8	1.1	. . .
Debt securities	4 669	. .	. . .	. . .	–6.5	–11.4	23.7	13.1	–2.5	. . .
Bonds and notes	4 670	. .	. . .	. . .	–6.5	–11.4	23.2	13.1	–2.9	. . .
Monetary authorities	4 671	. .	. . .	. . .	. . .	. . .	. . .	. . .	. . .	. . .
General government	4 672	. .	. . .	. . .	–6.5	. . .	–.1	. . .	–.2	. . .
Banks	4 673	. .	. . .	. . .	. . .	–.3	–.1	1.6	–.6	. . .
Other sectors	4 674	. .	. . .	. . .	. . .	–11.1	23.4	11.5	–2.1	. . .
Money market instruments	4 680	. .	. . .	. . .	. . .	. . .	.5	. . .	.4	. . .
Monetary authorities	4 681	. .	. . .	. . .	. . .	. . .	. . .	. . .	. . .	. . .
General government	4 682	. .	. . .	. . .	. . .	. . .	. . .	. . .	. . .	. . .
Banks	4 683	. .	. . .	. . .	. . .	. . .	. . .	. . .	. . .	. . .
Other sectors	4 684	. .	. . .	. . .	. . .	. . .	. . .	. . .	. . .	. . .
C. FINANCIAL DERIVATIVES	4 910	. .	. . .	. . .	. . .	. . .	. . .	8.5	. . .	. . .
Monetary authorities	4 911	. .	. . .	. . .	. . .	. . .	. . .	. . .	. . .	. . .
General government	4 912	. .	. . .	. . .	. . .	. . .	. . .	. . .	. . .	. . .
Banks	4 913	. .	. . .	. . .	. . .	. . .	. . .	. . .	. . .	. . .
Other sectors	4 914	. .	. . .	. . .	. . .	. . .	. . .	8.5	. . .	. . .
Assets	4 900	. .	**. . .**	**. . .**	**. . .**	**. . .**	**. . .**	**–.1**	**. . .**	**. . .**
Monetary authorities	4 901	. .	. . .	. . .	. . .	. . .	. . .	. . .	. . .	. . .
General government	4 902	. .	. . .	. . .	. . .	. . .	. . .	. . .	. . .	. . .
Banks	4 903	. .	. . .	. . .	. . .	. . .	. . .	. . .	. . .	. . .
Other sectors	4 904	. .	. . .	. . .	. . .	. . .	. . .	–.1	. . .	. . .
Liabilities	4 905	. .	**. . .**	**. . .**	**. . .**	**. . .**	**. . .**	**8.6**	**. . .**	**. . .**
Monetary authorities	4 906	. .	. . .	. . .	. . .	. . .	. . .	. . .	. . .	. . .
General government	4 907	. .	. . .	. . .	. . .	. . .	. . .	. . .	. . .	. . .
Banks	4 908	. .	. . .	. . .	. . .	. . .	. . .	. . .	. . .	. . .
Other sectors	4 909	. .	. . .	. . .	. . .	. . .	. . .	8.6	. . .	. . .

Table 2 (Concluded). STANDARD PRESENTATION, 1994–2001
(Millions of U.S. dollars)

	Code	1994	1995	1996	1997	1998	1999	2000	2001
D. OTHER INVESTMENT	4 700 . .	59.9	47.3	. . .	90.5	–7.0	58.5	28.5	. . .
Assets	4 703 . .	**–52.2**	**–62.1**	**–4.0**	**–12.4**	**–9.6**	**–58.3**	**25.1**	**. . .**
Trade credits	4 706 . .	13.0	–2.8	. . .	9.7	–16.2	–34.8	13.6	. . .
General government	4 707 . .	. . .	. . .	. . .	. . .	. . .	. . .	. . .	. . .
of which: Short-term	4 709 . .	. . .	. . .	. . .	. . .	. . .	. . .	. . .	. . .
Other sectors	4 710 . .	13.0	–2.8	. . .	9.7	–16.2	–34.8	13.6	. . .
of which: Short-term	4 712 . .	*13.0*	*–2.8*	. . .	*8.1*	*–16.2*	*–34.8*	*13.6*	. . .
Loans	4 714 . .	–28.0	–2.5	–11.2	–17.3	8.5	–17.9	–6.7	. . .
Monetary authorities	4 715 . .	. . .	. . .	. . .	. . .	. . .	. . .	. . .	. . .
of which: Short-term	4 718 . .	. . .	. . .	. . .	. . .	. . .	. . .	. . .	. . .
General government	4 719 . .	. . .	. . .	. . .	. . .	. . .	. . .	. . .	. . .
of which: Short-term	4 721 . .	. . .	. . .	. . .	. . .	. . .	. . .	. . .	. . .
Banks	4 722 . .	–28.0	–2.5	–11.2	–15.3	8.8	–17.9	–6.7	. . .
of which: Short-term	4 724 . .	. . .	. . .	*–7.1*	*–11.6*	*12.2*	*–11.8*	*.8*	. . .
Other sectors	4 725 . .	. . .	. . .	. . .	–2.0	–.3	. . .	. . .	. . .
of which: Short-term	4 727 . .	. . .	. . .	. . .	*–2.0*	*–.3*	. . .	. . .	. . .
Currency and deposits	4 730 . .	–25.3	–26.4	13.0	–33.5	4.2	–16.5	15.6	. . .
Monetary authorities	4 731 . .	. . .	. . .	. . .	. . .	. . .	. . .	. . .	. . .
General government	4 732 . .	. . .	. . .	. . .	. . .	. . .	. . .	. . .	. . .
Banks	4 733 . .	–21.7	–26.4	21.0	–25.9	4.5	–8.1	12.7	. . .
Other sectors	4 734 . .	–3.6	. . .	–8.0	–7.6	–.3	–8.4	2.9	. . .
Other assets	4 736 . .	–12.0	–30.4	–5.9	28.6	–6.2	10.9	2.6	. . .
Monetary authorities	4 737 . .	. . .	. . .	. . .	. . .	. . .	. . .	. . .	. . .
of which: Short-term	4 739 . .	. . .	. . .	. . .	. . .	. . .	. . .	. . .	. . .
General government	4 740 . .	11.9	–6.9	. . .	–.1	. . .	. . .	. . .	. . .
of which: Short-term	4 742 . .	*–.1*	*–.1*	. . .	*–.1*	. . .	. . .	. . .	. . .
Banks	4 743 . .	–1.1	–15.4	1.9	. . .	–.8	–.8	–4.2	. . .
of which: Short-term	4 745 . .	*.2*	*–14.3*	*1.9*	. . .	*–.8*	*–.7*	*–4.2*	. . .
Other sectors	4 746 . .	–22.7	–8.0	–7.7	28.7	–5.3	11.6	6.8	. . .
of which: Short-term	4 748 . .	*–22.7*	*–8.0*	*–7.7*	*28.7*	*–5.3*	*12.1*	*9.0*	. . .
Liabilities	4 753 . .	**112.1**	**109.4**	**4.0**	**102.9**	**2.7**	**116.8**	**3.4**	**. . .**
Trade credits	4 756 . .	43.4	1.9	12.3	36.0	5.1	43.2	–15.9	. . .
General government	4 757 . .	. . .	. . .	. . .	. . .	. . .	. . .	. . .	. . .
of which: Short-term	4 759 . .	. . .	. . .	. . .	. . .	. . .	. . .	. . .	. . .
Other sectors	4 760 . .	43.4	1.9	12.3	36.0	5.1	43.2	–15.9	. . .
of which: Short-term	4 762 . .	*43.4*	*1.9*	. . .	*–5.8*	. . .	. . .	. . .	. . .
Loans	4 764 . .	35.0	85.4	–18.6	91.7	7.2	45.1	–9.1	. . .
Monetary authorities	4 765 . .	24.9	12.2	18.0	1.9	–5.3	1.1	–3.6	. . .
of which: Use of Fund credit and loans from the Fund	4 766 . .	*24.9*	*12.2*	*18.0*	*1.9*	*–5.3*	*1.1*	*–3.6*	. . .
of which: Short-term	4 768 . .	. . .	. . .	. . .	. . .	. . .	. . .	. . .	. . .
General government	4 769 . .	9.3	58.6	–41.2	18.5	1.5	10.8	24.4	. . .
of which: Short-term	4 771 . .	. . .	. . .	. . .	. . .	. . .	. . .	*–4.5*	. . .
Banks	4 772 . .	2.4	15.2	–.2	.4	1.4	.4	9.9	. . .
of which: Short-term	4 774 . .	. . .	. . .	*1.1*	*.1*	*1.8*	*2.2*	*5.8*	. . .
Other sectors	4 775 . .	–1.7	–.6	4.7	70.9	9.6	32.7	–39.7	. . .
of which: Short-term	4 777 . .	. . .	. . .	*6.4*	*72.3*	*11.2*	*34.2*	*–43.4*	. . .
Currency and deposits	4 780 . .	5.9	–3.7	9.0	9.4	16.1	31.8	–19.9	. . .
Monetary authorities	4 781 . .	.6	–2.7	4.2	3.9	–3.5	–1.1	1.1	. . .
General government	4 782 . .	. . .	. . .	. . .	. . .	. . .	. . .	. . .	. . .
Banks	4 783 . .	5.3	–1.0	4.8	–13.2	19.7	32.9	–21.0	. . .
Other sectors	4 784 . .	. . .	. . .	. . .	. . .	. . .	. . .	. . .	. . .
Other liabilities	4 786 . .	27.8	25.8	1.4	–15.5	–25.7	–3.3	48.3	. . .
Monetary authorities	4 787 . .	. . .	. . .	1.0	.8	–1.8	1.4	–2.4	. . .
of which: Short-term	4 789 . .	. . .	. . .	. . .	*–.1*	. . .	. . .	. . .	. . .
General government	4 790 . .	. . .	. . .	. . .	. . .	. . .	.2	. . .	. . .
of which: Short-term	4 792 . .	. . .	. . .	. . .	. . .	. . .	*.2*	. . .	. . .
Banks	4 793 . .	4.5	.6	. . .	1.6	. . .	. . .	–.2	. . .
of which: Short-term	4 795 . .	*5.8*	*–1.2*	. . .	*1.6*	. . .	. . .	*–.2*	. . .
Other sectors	4 796 . .	23.3	25.2	.4	–17.9	–23.9	–4.9	50.9	. . .
of which: Short-term	4 798 . .	*23.3*	*25.2*	. . .	*–49.3*	*–23.9*	*–4.9*	*50.9*	. . .
E. RESERVE ASSETS	4 802 . .	–117.7	81.9	–78.3	–24.5	7.0	–40.2	–87.3	. . .
Monetary gold	4 812 . .	. . .	. . .	. . .	. . .	. . .	. . .	. . .	. . .
Special drawing rights	4 811 . .	.1	–.1	–.2	.2	. . .	–.1	.1	. . .
Reserve position in the Fund	4 810 . .	. . .	. . .	. . .	. . .	. . .	. . .	. . .	. . .
Foreign exchange	4 803 . .	–117.8	82.4	–78.1	–24.7	7.0	–40.1	–87.4	. . .
Other claims	4 813 . .	.1	–.3	. . .	. . .	. . .	. . .	. . .	. . .
NET ERRORS AND OMISSIONS	4 998 . .	**–16.3**	**–1.0**	**6.3**	**6.7**	**7.1**	**7.3**	**6.7**	**. . .**

Part 3 of the *Yearbook* contains descriptions of the methodologies, compilation practices, and sources used to compile these data.

Table 3. INTERNATIONAL INVESTMENT POSITION (End–period stocks), 1994–2001
(Millions of U.S. dollars)

	Code	1994	1995	1996	1997	1998	1999	2000	2001
ASSETS	8 995 C.	...	...	613.1	664.5	598.7	726.4	737.4	...
Direct investment abroad	8 505	**...**	**...**	**13.7**	**–2.3**	**5.3**	**5.6**	**10.5**	**...**
Equity capital and reinvested earnings	8 506	...	...	11.8	1.7	4.9	4.9	6.5	...
Claims on affiliated enterprises	8 507	...	...	11.8	1.7	4.9	4.9	6.5	...
Liabilities to affiliated enterprises	8 508	...	...	...	...	...	...	...	...
Other capital	8 530	...	...	1.9	–4.0	.4	.7	4.0	...
Claims on affiliated enterprises	8 535	...	...	1.9	...	.4	.7	4.0	...
Liabilities to affiliated enterprises	8 540	...	...	...	–4.0	...	...	...	...
Portfolio investment	8 602	**...**	**...**	**76.0**	**75.2**	**94.4**	**81.4**	**67.6**	**...**
Equity securities	8 610	...	...	.2	...	2.5	1.7	3.2	...
Monetary authorities	8 611	...	...	...	...	...	...	...	...
General government	8 612	...	...	...	...	...	...	...	...
Banks	8 613	...	...	.2	...	1.9	.5	.5	...
Other sectors	8 614	...	...	...	...	.6	1.2	2.7	...
Debt securities	8 619	...	...	75.8	75.2	91.9	79.7	64.4	...
Bonds and notes	8 620	...	...	15.4	26.2	12.3	17.2	46.2	...
Monetary authorities	8 621	...	...	...	...	...	...	...	...
General government	8 622	...	...	...	...	...	...	...	...
Banks	8 623	...	...	5.2	17.6	5.7	9.4	43.3	...
Other sectors	8 624	...	...	10.1	8.5	6.6	7.8	2.8	...
Money market instruments	8 630	...	...	60.4	49.0	79.6	62.5	18.3	...
Monetary authorities	8 631	...	...	...	...	...	...	...	...
General government	8 632	...	...	...	...	...	...	...	...
Banks	8 633	...	...	60.4	49.0	79.5	62.5	16.2	...
Other sectors	8 634	...	...	...	...	...	...	2.1	...
Financial derivatives	8 900	**...**	**...**	**.1**	**...**	**...**	**.1**	**...**	**...**
Monetary authorities	8 901	...	...	...	...	...	...	...	...
General government	8 902	...	...	...	...	...	...	...	...
Banks	8 903	...	...	...	...	...	...	...	...
Other sectors	8 904	...	...	.1	...	...	.1	...	...
Other investment	8 703	**...**	**...**	**261.6**	**338.4**	**236.9**	**239.2**	**200.5**	**...**
Trade credits	8 706	...	...	16.7	118.3	36.4	51.2	30.5	...
General government	8 707	...	...	...	...	...	...	...	...
of which: Short-term	8 709	...	...	...	...	...	...	...	...
Other sectors	8 710	...	...	16.7	118.3	36.4	51.2	30.5	...
of which: Short-term	8 712	...	...	*16.7*	*118.3*	*36.4*	*51.2*	*30.5*	...
Loans	8 714	...	...	75.2	82.6	76.8	68.1	69.4	...
Monetary authorities	8 715	...	...	...	...	...	...	...	...
of which: Short-term	8 718	...	...	...	...	...	...	...	...
General government	8 719	...	...	.1	...	...	...	...	...
of which: Short-term	8 721	...	...	...	...	...	...	...	...
Banks	8 722	...	...	75.1	80.6	76.5	68.1	69.4	...
of which: Short-term	8 724	...	...	*64.8*	*67.6*	*59.1*	*62.1*	*56.4*	...
Other sectors	8 725	...	...	...	2.0	.3	...	...	...
of which: Short-term	8 727	...	...	...	*2.0*	*.3*	...	...	...
Currency and deposits	8 730	...	...	105.1	119.4	119.0	115.7	90.5	...
Monetary authorities	8 731	...	...	...	...	...	...	...	...
General government	8 732	...	...	...	...	...	...	...	...
Banks	8 733	...	...	90.7	104.5	106.6	99.5	79.3	...
Other sectors	8 734	...	...	14.4	14.9	12.4	16.2	11.2	...
Other assets	8 736	...	...	64.7	18.1	4.7	4.3	10.0	...
Monetary authorities	8 737	...	...	...	...	...	...	...	...
of which: Short-term	8 739	...	...	...	...	...	...	...	...
General government	8 740	...	...	...	.1	.1	.1	.1	...
of which: Short-term	8 742	...	...	...	*.1*	*.1*	*.1*	*.1*	...
Banks	8 743	...	...	1.2	1.0	2.0	2.4	6.5	...
of which: Short-term	8 745	...	...	*1.2*	*1.0*	*2.0*	*2.4*	*6.5*	...
Other sectors	8 746	...	...	63.5	17.1	2.7	1.8	3.4	...
of which: Short-term	8 748	...	...	*63.5*	*17.1*	*2.7*	*1.8*	*3.4*	...
Reserve assets	8 802	**...**	**...**	**261.8**	**253.1**	**262.2**	**400.1**	**458.8**	**...**
Monetary gold	8 812	...	...	...	...	...	...	...	...
Special drawing rights	8 811	...	.1	.3	.1	.1	.2	.1	.4
Reserve position in the Fund	8 810	3.1	3.2	3.1	2.9	3.1	3.0	2.9	2.7
Foreign exchange	8 803	...	...	258.4	250.1	259.0	396.9	455.8	...
Other claims	8 813	...	...	...	...	...	...	...	...

Table 3 (Concluded). INTERNATIONAL INVESTMENT POSITION (End-period stocks), 1994–2001
(Millions of U.S. dollars)

	Code	1994	1995	1996	1997	1998	1999	2000	2001
LIABILITIES	8 995 D.	...	...	1,802.5	1,628.9	1,776.1	1,748.1	1,842.2	...
Direct investment in Benin	8 555 . .	...	...	**62.3**	**46.9**	**67.0**	**73.5**	**213.2**	...
Equity capital and reinvested earnings	8 556 . .	...	...	52.3	42.2	56.1	68.5	136.5	...
Claims on direct investors	8 557 . .	...	...	...	...	...	...	...	...
Liabilities to direct investors	8 558 . .	...	...	52.3	42.2	56.1	68.5	136.5	...
Other capital	8 580 . .	...	...	10.0	4.7	10.8	4.9	76.7	...
Claims on direct investors	8 585 . .	...	...	...	...	...	...	...	...
Liabilities to direct investors	8 590 . .	...	...	10.0	4.7	10.8	4.9	76.7	...
Portfolio investment	8 652 . .	...	...	**81.7**	**62.2**	**91.2**	**95.1**	**16.3**	...
Equity securities	8 660 . .	...	...	2.5	3.5	6.3	6.5	6.1	...
Banks	8 663 . .	...	...	2.1	3.1	5.1	5.6	4.1	...
Other sectors	8 664 . .	...	...	.4	.4	1.2	.9	1.9	...
Debt securities	8 669 . .	...	...	79.2	58.7	84.9	88.6	10.2	...
Bonds and notes	8 670 . .	...	...	79.2	58.7	84.4	88.6	9.8	...
Monetary authorities	8 671 . .	...	...	...	...	...	...	...	...
General government	8 672 . .	...	...	...	...	...	...	...	...
Banks	8 673 . .	...	...	...	1.5	.5	2.6	1.8	...
Other sectors	8 674 . .	...	...	79.2	57.2	83.9	86.0	8.0	...
Money market instruments	8 680 . .	...	...	...	...	.5	...	.4	...
Monetary authorities	8 681 . .	...	...	...	...	...	...	...	...
General government	8 682 . .	...	...	...	...	...	...	...	...
Banks	8 683 . .	...	...	...	...	.5	...	.4	...
Other sectors	8 684 . .	...	...	...	...	...	...	...	...
Financial derivatives	8 905 . .	...	...	**.8**	...	...	**8.1**	...	...
Monetary authorities	8 906 . .	...	...	...	...	...	...	...	...
General government	8 907 . .	...	...	...	...	...	...	...	...
Banks	8 908 . .	...	...	.8	...	...	8.1	...	...
Other sectors	8 909 . .	...	...	...	...	...	...	...	...
Other investment	8 753 . .	...	...	**1,657.8**	**1,519.7**	**1,618.0**	**1,571.4**	**1,612.7**	...
Trade credits	8 756 . .	...	...	59.4	69.0	71.9	74.3	38.0	...
General government	8 757 . .	...	...	...	...	...	...	...	...
of which: Short-term	8 759 . .	...	...	...	...	...	...	...	...
Other sectors	8 760 . .	...	...	59.4	69.0	71.9	74.3	38.0	...
of which: Short-term	8 762 . .	...	...	*59.4*	*69.0*	*71.9*	*74.3*	*38.0*	...
Loans	8 764 . .	...	...	1,446.3	1,346.5	1,444.2	1,390.3	1,446.8	...
Monetary authorities	8 765 . .	...	...	99.1	94.9	93.5	92.1	83.9	...
of which: Use of Fund credit and loans from the Fund	8 766 . .	*71.2*	*84.1*	*99.1*	*94.9*	*93.5*	*92.1*	*83.9*	...
of which: Short-term	8 768 . .	...	...	...	...	...	...	...	...
General government	8 769 . .	...	...	1,318.3	1,165.8	1,288.4	1,204.2	1,291.5	...
of which: Short-term	8 771 . .	...	...	*12.0*	*10.5*	*11.2*	*9.6*	...	...
Banks	8 772 . .	...	...	3.2	1.6	3.1	3.1	12.8	...
of which: Short-term	8 774 . .	...	...	*2.1*	*.2*	*2.1*	*3.9*	*9.5*	...
Other sectors	8 775 . .	...	...	25.6	84.2	59.1	90.9	58.6	...
of which: Short-term	8 777 . .	...	...	*3.3*	*2.9*	*3.0*	*84.5*	*36.3*	...
Currency and deposits	8 780 . .	...	...	64.2	44.8	64.7	86.9	64.6	...
Monetary authorities	8 781 . .	...	...	14.0	11.7	8.8	6.3	6.7	...
General government	8 782 . .	...	...	50.2	...	...	...	...	...
Banks	8 783 . .	...	...	...	33.0	55.9	80.6	57.9	...
Other sectors	8 784 . .	...	...	...	...	...	...	...	...
Other liabilities	8 786 . .	...	...	87.9	59.5	37.3	19.9	63.3	...
Monetary authorities	8 787 . .	...	...	1.9	2.4	–.2	1.1	–1.4	...
of which: Short-term	8 789 . .	...	...	...	...	...	...	...	...
General government	8 790 . .	...	...	...	...	...	...	...	...
of which: Short-term	8 792 . .	...	...	...	...	...	...	...	...
Banks	8 793 . .	...	...	...	...	...	...	...	...
of which: Short-term	8 795 . .	...	...	...	...	...	...	...	...
Other sectors	8 796 . .	...	...	86.0	57.0	37.5	18.8	64.7	...
of which: Short-term	8 798 . .	...	...	...	...	...	...	...	...
NET INTERNATIONAL INVESTMENT POSITION	8 995 . .	...	...	**–1,189.4**	**–964.4**	**–1,177.5**	**–1,021.7**	**–1,104.8**	...
Conversion rates: CFA francs per U.S. dollar (end of period)	0 102 . .	**534.60**	**490.00**	**523.70**	**598.81**	**562.21**	**652.95**	**704.95**	**744.31**

Table 1. ANALYTIC PRESENTATION, 1994–2001
(Millions of U.S. dollars)

	Code	1994	1995	1996	1997	1998	1999	2000	2001
A. Current Account [1]	4 993 Z.	**–90.2**	**–302.5**	**–404.3**	**–553.5**	**–666.1**	**–488.0**	**–447.0**	**–292.5**
Goods: exports f.o.b.	2 100 . .	985.1	1,041.4	1,132.0	1,166.6	1,104.0	1,051.2	1,246.0	1,284.9
Goods: imports f.o.b.	3 100 . .	–1,015.3	–1,223.7	–1,368.0	–1,643.6	–1,759.5	–1,539.0	–1,610.1	–1,493.9
Balance on Goods	4 100 . .	*–30.2*	*–182.3*	*–236.0*	*–477.0*	*–655.5*	*–487.8*	*–364.1*	*–209.0*
Services: credit	2 200 . .	196.0	192.4	180.9	247.2	251.2	259.4	224.1	235.8
Services: debit	3 200 . .	–337.5	–350.2	–363.4	–418.7	–440.5	–449.7	–468.1	–501.9
Balance on Goods and Services	4 991 . .	*–171.7*	*–340.1*	*–418.5*	*–648.5*	*–844.8*	*–678.1*	*–608.1*	*–475.1*
Income: credit	2 300 . .	18.7	28.3	28.6	98.2	127.4	157.3	139.7	121.2
Income: debit	3 300 . .	–201.2	–234.9	–236.8	–294.7	–289.3	–353.3	–365.3	–331.6
Balance on Goods, Services, and Income	4 992 . .	*–354.2*	*–546.7*	*–626.7*	*–845.0*	*–1,006.7*	*–874.1*	*–833.7*	*–685.5*
Current transfers: credit	2 379 Z.	269.2	248.0	226.2	300.3	352.3	414.7	419.9	428.4
Current transfers: debit	3 379 . .	–5.2	–3.8	–3.8	–8.8	–11.7	–28.6	–33.2	–35.4
B. Capital Account [1]	4 994 Z.	**1.2**	**2.0**	**2.8**	**25.3**	**9.9**	**. . .**	**. . .**	**3.2**
Capital account: credit	2 994 Z.	1.2	2.0	2.8	25.3	9.9	. . .	. . .	3.2
Capital account: debit	3 994 . .	. . .	. . .	. . .	. . .	. . .	. . .	. . .	. . .
Total, Groups A Plus B	4 981 . .	*–89.0*	*–300.5*	*–401.5*	*–528.2*	*–656.2*	*–488.0*	*–447.0*	*–289.3*
C. Financial Account [1]	4 995 W.	**315.3**	**505.2**	**701.0**	**889.8**	**1,181.9**	**868.6**	**428.2**	**330.8**
Direct investment abroad	4 505 . .	–2.2	–2.0	–2.1	–2.5	–2.5	–2.4	–2.4	–2.4
Direct investment in Bolivia	4 555 Z.	130.2	392.7	474.1	730.6	949.3	1,010.5	725.1	662.3
Portfolio investment assets	4 602 . .	. . .	. . .	.3	–53.2	–74.5	–44.4	55.4	–23.0
Equity securities	4 610 . .	. . .	. . .	. . .	. . .	. . .	. . .	. . .	. . .
Debt securities	4 619 . .	. . .	. . .	.3	–53.2	–74.5	–44.4	55.4	–23.0
Portfolio investment liabilities	4 652 Z.	. . .	. . .	. . .	. . .	. . .	–16.9	. . .	. . .
Equity securities	4 660 . .	. . .	. . .	. . .	. . .	. . .	. . .	. . .	. . .
Debt securities	4 669 Z.	. . .	. . .	. . .	. . .	. . .	–16.9	. . .	. . .
Financial derivatives	4 910 . .	. . .	. . .	. . .	. . .	. . .	. . .	. . .	. . .
Financial derivatives assets	4 900 . .	. . .	. . .	. . .	. . .	. . .	. . .	. . .	. . .
Financial derivatives liabilities	4 905 . .	. . .	. . .	. . .	. . .	. . .	. . .	. . .	. . .
Other investment assets	4 703 . .	–104.0	–38.4	12.2	–19.9	–13.2	–47.7	–164.0	–202.0
Monetary authorities	4 701 . .	. . .	. . .	. . .	. . .	–8.4	–9.2	–9.1	–9.0
General government	4 704 . .	. . .	. . .	–.2	. . .	. . .	. . .	. . .	. . .
Banks	4 705 . .	–104.0	–38.4	12.4	–19.9	66.1	–24.2	–85.3	–155.6
Other sectors	4 728 . .	. . .	. . .	. . .	. . .	–70.9	–14.3	–69.6	–37.4
Other investment liabilities	4 753 W.	291.3	152.9	216.5	234.8	322.8	–30.5	–185.9	–104.1
Monetary authorities	4 753 WA	40.8	78.0	11.7	1.5	–46.0	–11.6	–20.9	–22.5
General government	4 753 ZB	–16.9	–41.0	206.9	199.7	149.4	123.1	131.4	232.9
Banks	4 753 ZC	206.3	78.8	2.8	169.7	137.9	–138.1	–282.9	–246.6
Other sectors	4 753 ZD	61.1	37.1	–4.9	–136.1	81.5	–3.9	–13.5	–67.9
Total, Groups A Through C	4 983 . .	*226.3*	*204.7*	*299.5*	*361.6*	*525.7*	*380.6*	*–18.8*	*41.5*
D. Net Errors and Omissions	4 998 . .	**–315.8**	**–112.3**	**–31.6**	**–260.6**	**–401.0**	**–353.6**	**–20.7**	**–78.8**
Total, Groups A Through D	4 984 . .	*–89.5*	*92.4*	*268.0*	*101.0*	*124.7*	*27.0*	*–39.5*	*–37.3*
E. Reserves and Related Items	4 802 A.	**89.5**	**–92.4**	**–268.0**	**–101.0**	**–124.7**	**–27.0**	**39.5**	**37.3**
Reserve assets	4 802 . .	–26.4	–147.4	–310.1	–89.6	–133.0	–31.9	38.8	33.9
Use of Fund credit and loans	4 766 . .	28.7	–1.1	17.1	–11.4	5.7	–10.9	–14.5	–5.3
Exceptional financing	4 920 . .	87.3	56.1	25.1	. . .	2.6	15.8	15.2	8.7
Conversion rates: bolivianos per U.S. dollar	0 101 . .	**4.6205**	**4.8003**	**5.0746**	**5.2543**	**5.5101**	**5.8124**	**6.1835**	**6.6069**

[1] Excludes components that have been classified in the categories of Group E.

Table 2. STANDARD PRESENTATION, 1994–2001

(Millions of U.S. dollars)

	Code		1994	1995	1996	1997	1998	1999	2000	2001
CURRENT ACCOUNT	4 993	. .	**–90.2**	**–302.5**	**–379.7**	**–553.5**	**–666.1**	**–488.0**	**–447.0**	**–292.5**
A. GOODS	4 100	. .	–30.2	–182.3	–236.0	–477.0	–655.5	–487.8	–364.1	–209.0
Credit	2 100	. .	**985.1**	**1,041.4**	**1,132.0**	**1,166.6**	**1,104.0**	**1,051.2**	**1,246.0**	**1,284.9**
General merchandise: exports f.o.b.	2 110	. .	985.1	1,041.4	1,132.0	971.1	909.4	909.5	1,039.2	1,092.8
Goods for processing: exports f.o.b.	2 150	. .	. . .	. . .	. . .	74.1	60.4	40.8	98.3	86.5
Repairs on goods	2 160	. .	. . .	. . .	. . .	2.5	11.6	4.9	8.6	9.6
Goods procured in ports by carriers	2 170	. .	. . .	. . .	. . .	8.6	10.8	6.9	12.0	9.8
Nonmonetary gold	2 180	. .	. . .	. . .	. . .	110.3	111.8	89.1	87.9	86.2
Debit	3 100	. .	**–1,015.3**	**–1,223.7**	**–1,368.0**	**–1,643.6**	**–1,759.5**	**–1,539.0**	**–1,610.1**	**–1,493.9**
General merchandise: imports f.o.b.	3 110	. .	–1,015.3	–1,223.7	–1,368.0	–1,643.6	–1,759.5	–1,539.0	–1,610.1	–1,493.9
Goods for processing: imports f.o.b.	3 150	. .	. . .	. . .	. . .	. . .	. . .	. . .	. . .	. . .
Repairs on goods	3 160	. .	. . .	. . .	. . .	. . .	. . .	. . .	. . .	. . .
Goods procured in ports by carriers	3 170	. .	. . .	. . .	. . .	. . .	. . .	. . .	. . .	. . .
Nonmonetary gold	3 180	. .	. . .	. . .	. . .	. . .	. . .	. . .	. . .	. . .
B. SERVICES	4 200	. .	–141.5	–157.8	–182.5	–171.5	–189.3	–190.3	–244.0	–266.1
Total credit	2 200	. .	*196.0*	*192.4*	*180.9*	*247.2*	*251.2*	*259.4*	*224.1*	*235.8*
Total debit	3 200	. .	*–337.5*	*–350.2*	*–363.4*	*–418.7*	*–440.5*	*–449.7*	*–468.1*	*–501.9*
Transportation services, credit	2 205	. .	**63.9**	**78.1**	**75.6**	**70.8**	**77.7**	**52.7**	**49.9**	**67.2**
Passenger	2 850	. .	*28.9*	*36.9*	*39.4*	*65.2*	*68.1*	*36.7*	*32.6*	*42.8*
Freight	2 851	. .	*18.9*	*22.0*	*23.6*	*4.5*	*4.5*	*4.5*	*4.1*	*9.7*
Other	2 852	. .	*16.1*	*19.2*	*12.6*	*1.1*	*5.1*	*11.5*	*13.2*	*14.7*
Sea transport, passenger	2 207	. .	. . .	. . .	. . .	. . .	. . .	. . .	. . .	. . .
Sea transport, freight	2 208	. .	. . .	. . .	. . .	. . .	. . .	. . .	. . .	. . .
Sea transport, other	2 209	. .	. . .	. . .	. . .	. . .	. . .	. . .	. . .	. . .
Air transport, passenger	2 211	. .	. . .	. . .	. . .	62.4	65.3	34.7	30.0	41.1
Air transport, freight	2 212	. .	. . .	. . .	. . .	2.9	2.9	2.8	1.9	1.8
Air transport, other	2 213	. .	. . .	. . .	. . .	.7	4.7	11.1	12.6	13.9
Other transport, passenger	2 215	. .	. . .	. . .	. . .	2.8	2.8	2.0	2.6	1.7
Other transport, freight	2 216	. .	. . .	. . .	. . .	1.6	1.6	1.7	2.2	7.9
Other transport, other	2 217	. .	. . .	. . .	. . .	.4	.4	.4	.6	.8
Transportation services, debit	3 205	. .	**–177.8**	**–211.2**	**–216.5**	**–259.0**	**–269.3**	**–263.8**	**–270.1**	**–282.1**
Passenger	3 850	. .	*–27.0*	*–24.0*	*–33.3*	*–39.0*	*–38.0*	*–41.5*	*–38.6*	*–30.6*
Freight	3 851	. .	*–127.7*	*–149.3*	*–169.9*	*–177.9*	*–180.2*	*–174.7*	*–176.3*	*–195.2*
Other	3 852	. .	*–23.1*	*–37.9*	*–13.3*	*–42.1*	*–51.1*	*–47.6*	*–55.2*	*–56.3*
Sea transport, passenger	3 207	. .	. . .	. . .	. . .	. . .	. . .	. . .	. . .	. . .
Sea transport, freight	3 208	. .	. . .	. . .	. . .	–176.3	–178.6	–172.7	–173.3	–191.3
Sea transport, other	3 209	. .	. . .	. . .	. . .	–28.5	–30.9	–28.5	–30.0	–23.3
Air transport, passenger	3 211	. .	. . .	. . .	. . .	–36.1	–35.1	–39.2	–35.7	–28.4
Air transport, freight	3 212	. .	. . .	. . .	. . .	. . .	. . .	. . .	–.6	–1.4
Air transport, other	3 213	. .	. . .	. . .	. . .	–13.4	–20.2	–18.3	–24.4	–32.2
Other transport, passenger	3 215	. .	. . .	. . .	. . .	–2.9	–2.9	–2.3	–2.9	–2.2
Other transport, freight	3 216	. .	. . .	. . .	. . .	–1.6	–1.6	–2.0	–2.4	–2.5
Other transport, other	3 217	. .	. . .	. . .	. . .	–.2	. . .	–.8	–.8	–.8
Travel, credit	2 236	. .	**72.2**	**55.0**	**60.7**	**64.2**	**69.2**	**86.8**	**68.4**	**75.7**
Business travel	2 237	. .	. . .	. . .	. . .	18.2	18.7	23.5	20.8	24.2
Personal travel	2 240	. .	. . .	. . .	. . .	46.0	50.5	63.3	47.6	51.5
Travel, debit	3 236	. .	**–68.1**	**–48.1**	**–53.7**	**–57.2**	**–59.8**	**–74.6**	**–77.2**	**–83.1**
Business travel	3 237	. .	. . .	. . .	. . .	–18.6	–22.0	–17.3	–17.8	20.1
Personal travel	3 240	. .	–68.1	–48.1	–53.7	–38.6	–37.8	–57.3	–59.4	–63.0
Other services, credit	2 200	BA	**59.9**	**59.3**	**44.6**	**112.2**	**104.3**	**119.9**	**105.8**	**92.9**
Communications	2 245	. .	. . .	. . .	. . .	64.2	52.6	40.0	35.4	31.8
Construction	2 249	. .	. . .	. . .	. . .	. . .	. . .	. . .	. . .	. . .
Insurance	2 253	. .	18.5	17.1	18.3	21.2	22.3	51.8	41.2	35.4
Financial	2 260	. .	. . .	. . .	. . .	3.2	3.5	4.3	4.5	3.6
Computer and information	2 262	. .	. . .	. . .	. . .	. . .	. . .	.5	.4	.4
Royalties and licence fees	2 266	. .	. . .	. . .	. . .	. . .	. . .	1.6	1.6	1.6
Other business services	2 268	. .	22.3	24.2	12.0	8.4	10.0	4.5	4.8	4.7
Personal, cultural, and recreational	2 287	. .	. . .	. . .	. . .	. . .	. . .	1.1	1.1	.9
Government, n.i.e.	2 291	. .	19.1	18.0	14.4	15.2	15.9	16.1	16.8	14.5
Other services, debit	3 200	BA	**–91.6**	**–90.9**	**–93.2**	**–102.5**	**–111.4**	**–111.3**	**–120.8**	**–136.7**
Communications	3 245	. .	. . .	. . .	. . .	–27.1	–19.4	–16.6	–13.9	–9.2
Construction	3 249	. .	. . .	. . .	. . .	. . .	. . .	. . .	. . .	. . .
Insurance	3 253	. .	–37.5	–29.8	–35.2	–25.4	–37.2	–53.7	–61.7	–81.6
Financial	3 260	. .	. . .	. . .	. . .	. . .	. . .	–3.0	–3.0	–2.6
Computer and information	3 262	. .	. . .	. . .	. . .	–4.0	–5.2	–4.0	–4.2	–4.5
Royalties and licence fees	3 266	. .	–4.1	–4.4	–4.0	–5.2	–5.2	–4.8	–5.1	–5.2
Other business services	3 268	. .	–26.8	–27.2	–27.3	–17.3	–20.7	–13.0	–13.7	–14.3
Personal, cultural, and recreational	3 287	. .	. . .	. . .	. . .	–5.4	–5.7	–2.0	–2.0	–2.2
Government, n.i.e.	3 291	. .	–23.2	–29.5	–26.7	–18.1	–18.0	–14.2	–17.2	–17.1

Table 2 (Continued). STANDARD PRESENTATION, 1994–2001
(Millions of U.S. dollars)

	Code	1994	1995	1996	1997	1998	1999	2000	2001
C. INCOME	4 300	−182.5	−206.6	−208.2	−196.5	−161.9	−196.0	−225.6	−210.4
Total credit	2 300	*18.7*	*28.3*	*28.6*	*98.2*	*127.4*	*157.3*	*139.7*	*121.2*
Total debit	3 300	*−201.2*	*−234.9*	*−236.8*	*−294.7*	*−289.3*	*−353.3*	*−365.3*	*−331.6*
Compensation of employees, credit	2 310	**2.1**	**3.6**	**8.6**	**16.8**	**24.5**	**23.5**	**25.8**	**28.1**
Compensation of employees, debit	3 310	**−7.8**	**−7.2**	**−10.2**	**−5.2**	**−5.4**	**−5.5**	**−5.9**	**−6.4**
Investment income, credit	2 320	**16.6**	**24.7**	**20.0**	**81.4**	**102.9**	**133.8**	**113.9**	**93.1**
Direct investment income	2 330	...	...	20.0	2.8	3.2	3.2	3.2	3.0
Dividends and distributed branch profits	2 332	...	...	20.0	.4	.4	.4	.4	.4
Reinvested earnings and undistributed branch profits	2 333	...	...	...	2.4	2.8	2.8	2.8	2.6
Income on debt (interest)	2 334	...	...	...	...	...	...	...	...
Portfolio investment income	2 339	...	...	...	78.6	99.7	130.6	110.7	90.1
Income on equity	2 340	...	...	...	...	...	...	...	...
Income on bonds and notes	2 350	...	...	...	4.2	24.8	12.4	14.3	25.0
Income on money market instruments	2 360	...	...	...	74.4	74.9	118.2	96.4	65.1
Other investment income	2 370	16.6	24.7	...	...	...	...	...	...
Investment income, debit	3 320	**−193.4**	**−227.7**	**−226.6**	**−289.5**	**−283.9**	**−347.8**	**−359.4**	**−325.2**
Direct investment income	3 330	−20.0	−24.4	−40.0	−80.4	−81.2	−142.4	−148.4	−167.7
Dividends and distributed branch profits	3 332	...	...	−19.2	−65.6	−66.2	−115.4	−86.0	−78.2
Reinvested earnings and undistributed branch profits	3 333	−20.0	−24.4	−20.8	−14.8	−15.0	−27.0	−62.4	−89.5
Income on debt (interest)	3 334	...	...	...	...	...	...	...	...
Portfolio investment income	3 339	...	...	...	...	...	...	...	...
Income on equity	3 340	...	...	...	...	...	...	...	...
Income on bonds and notes	3 350	...	...	...	...	...	...	...	...
Income on money market instruments	3 360	...	...	...	...	...	...	...	...
Other investment income	3 370	−173.4	−203.3	−186.6	−209.1	−202.7	−205.4	−211.0	−157.5
D. CURRENT TRANSFERS	4 379	264.0	244.2	247.0	291.5	340.6	386.1	386.7	393.0
Credit	2 379	**269.2**	**248.0**	**250.8**	**300.3**	**352.3**	**414.7**	**419.9**	**428.4**
General government	2 380	244.0	226.9	232.2	189.2	210.8	243.9	243.8	256.9
Other sectors	2 390	25.2	21.1	18.6	111.1	141.5	170.8	176.1	171.5
Workers' remittances	2 391	1.2	1.8	2.1	68.1	63.9	72.5	101.0	107.1
Other current transfers	2 392	24.0	19.3	16.5	43.0	77.6	98.3	75.1	64.4
Debit	3 379	**−5.2**	**−3.8**	**−3.8**	**−8.8**	**−11.7**	**−28.6**	**−33.2**	**−35.4**
General government	3 380	−3.2	−1.8	−1.0	−2.0	−2.0	−2.0	−2.0	−5.3
Other sectors	3 390	−2.0	−2.0	−2.8	−6.8	−9.7	−26.6	−31.2	−30.1
Workers' remittances	3 391	−2.0	−2.0	−2.8	−6.8	−9.7	−26.6	−31.2	−30.1
Other current transfers	3 392	...	...	...	...	...	...	...	...
CAPITAL AND FINANCIAL ACCOUNT	4 996	**406.0**	**414.8**	**411.2**	**814.1**	**1,067.1**	**841.6**	**467.7**	**371.3**
CAPITAL ACCOUNT	4 994	**1.2**	**2.0**	**2.8**	**25.3**	**9.9**	...	...	**3.2**
Total credit	2 994	*1.2*	*2.0*	*2.8*	*25.3*	*9.9*	...	...	*3.2*
Total debit	3 994	...	...	...	...	...	...	...	...
Capital transfers, credit	2 400	**1.2**	**2.0**	**2.8**	**25.3**	**9.9**	...	...	**3.2**
General government	2 401	...	...	...	25.3	9.9	...	...	3.2
Debt forgiveness	2 402	...	...	...	...	...	...	...	3.2
Other capital transfers	2 410	...	...	...	25.3	9.9	...	...	...
Other sectors	2 430	1.2	2.0	2.8	...	...	...	...	...
Migrants' transfers	2 431	1.2	2.0	2.8	...	...	...	...	...
Debt forgiveness	2 432	...	...	...	...	...	...	...	...
Other capital transfers	2 440	...	...	...	...	...	...	...	...
Capital transfers, debit	3 400	...	...	...	...	...	...	...	...
General government	3 401	...	...	...	...	...	...	...	...
Debt forgiveness	3 402	...	...	...	...	...	...	...	...
Other capital transfers	3 410	...	...	...	...	...	...	...	...
Other sectors	3 430	...	...	...	...	...	...	...	...
Migrants' transfers	3 431	...	...	...	...	...	...	...	...
Debt forgiveness	3 432	...	...	...	...	...	...	...	...
Other capital transfers	3 440	...	...	...	...	...	...	...	...
Nonproduced nonfinancial assets, credit	2 480	...	...	...	...	...	...	...	...
Nonproduced nonfinancial assets, debit	3 480	...	...	...	...	...	...	...	...

Table 2 (Continued). STANDARD PRESENTATION, 1994–2001
(Millions of U.S. dollars)

	Code	1994	1995	1996	1997	1998	1999	2000	2001
FINANCIAL ACCOUNT	4 995 . .	**404.8**	**412.8**	**408.4**	**788.8**	**1,057.2**	**841.6**	**467.7**	**368.1**
A. DIRECT INVESTMENT	4 500 . .	128.0	390.7	472.0	728.1	946.8	1,008.1	722.7	659.9
Direct investment abroad	4 505 . .	**–2.2**	**–2.0**	**–2.1**	**–2.5**	**–2.5**	**–2.4**	**–2.4**	**–2.4**
Equity capital	4 510 . .	–2.2	–2.0	–2.1	. . .	. . .	. . .	. . .	. . .
Claims on affiliated enterprises	4 515 . .	. . .	. . .	. . .	. . .	. . .	. . .	. . .	. . .
Liabilities to affiliated enterprises	4 520 . .	. . .	. . .	. . .	. . .	. . .	. . .	. . .	. . .
Reinvested earnings	4 525 . .	. . .	. . .	. . .	–2.5	–2.5	–2.4	–2.4	–2.4
Other capital	4 530 . .	. . .	. . .	. . .	. . .	. . .	. . .	. . .	. . .
Claims on affiliated enterprises	4 535 . .	. . .	. . .	. . .	. . .	. . .	. . .	. . .	. . .
Liabilities to affiliated enterprises	4 540 . .	. . .	. . .	. . .	. . .	. . .	. . .	. . .	. . .
Direct investment in Bolivia	4 555 . .	**130.2**	**392.7**	**474.1**	**730.6**	**949.3**	**1,010.5**	**725.1**	**662.3**
Equity capital	4 560 . .	110.2	368.3	453.3	715.8	725.4	597.7	273.9	196.5
Claims on direct investors	4 565 . .	. . .	. . .	. . .	. . .	. . .	. . .	. . .	. . .
Liabilities to direct investors	4 570 . .	110.2	368.3	453.3	715.8	725.4	597.7	273.9	196.5
Reinvested earnings	4 575 . .	20.0	24.4	20.8	14.8	15.0	27.0	62.4	89.5
Other capital	4 580 . .	. . .	. . .	. . .	. . .	208.9	385.8	388.8	376.3
Claims on direct investors	4 585 . .	. . .	. . .	. . .	. . .	. . .	. . .	. . .	. . .
Liabilities to direct investors	4 590 . .	. . .	. . .	. . .	. . .	208.9	385.8	388.8	376.3
B. PORTFOLIO INVESTMENT	4 600 . .	. . .	. . .	.3	–53.2	–74.5	–61.3	55.4	–23.0
Assets	4 602 . .	**. . .**	**. . .**	**.3**	**–53.2**	**–74.5**	**–44.4**	**55.4**	**–23.0**
Equity securities	4 610 . .	. . .	. . .	. . .	. . .	. . .	. . .	. . .	. . .
Monetary authorities	4 611 . .	. . .	. . .	. . .	. . .	. . .	. . .	. . .	. . .
General government	4 612 . .	. . .	. . .	. . .	. . .	. . .	. . .	. . .	. . .
Banks	4 613 . .	. . .	. . .	. . .	. . .	. . .	. . .	. . .	. . .
Other sectors	4 614 . .	. . .	. . .	. . .	. . .	. . .	. . .	. . .	. . .
Debt securities	4 619 . .	. . .	. . .	.3	–53.2	–74.5	–44.4	55.4	–23.0
Bonds and notes	4 620 . .	. . .	. . .	.3	. . .	. . .	. . .	. . .	. . .
Monetary authorities	4 621 . .	. . .	. . .	. . .	. . .	. . .	. . .	. . .	. . .
General government	4 622 . .	. . .	. . .	. . .	. . .	. . .	. . .	. . .	. . .
Banks	4 623 . .	. . .	. . .	. . .	. . .	. . .	. . .	. . .	. . .
Other sectors	4 624 . .	. . .	. . .	. . .	. . .	. . .	. . .	. . .	. . .
Money market instruments	4 630 . .	. . .	. . .	. . .	–53.2	–74.5	–44.4	55.4	–23.0
Monetary authorities	4 631 . .	. . .	. . .	. . .	. . .	. . .	. . .	. . .	. . .
General government	4 632 . .	. . .	. . .	. . .	. . .	. . .	. . .	. . .	. . .
Banks	4 633 . .	. . .	. . .	. . .	–53.2	. . .	. . .	. . .	. . .
Other sectors	4 634 . .	. . .	. . .	. . .	. . .	–74.5	–44.4	55.4	–23.0
Liabilities	4 652 . .	**. . .**	**. . .**	**. . .**	**. . .**	**. . .**	**–16.9**	**. . .**	**. . .**
Equity securities	4 660 . .	. . .	. . .	. . .	. . .	. . .	. . .	. . .	. . .
Banks	4 663 . .	. . .	. . .	. . .	. . .	. . .	. . .	. . .	. . .
Other sectors	4 664 . .	. . .	. . .	. . .	. . .	. . .	. . .	. . .	. . .
Debt securities	4 669 . .	. . .	. . .	. . .	. . .	. . .	–16.9	. . .	. . .
Bonds and notes	4 670 . .	. . .	. . .	. . .	. . .	. . .	–16.9	. . .	. . .
Monetary authorities	4 671 . .	. . .	. . .	. . .	. . .	. . .	. . .	. . .	. . .
General government	4 672 . .	. . .	. . .	. . .	. . .	. . .	–16.9	. . .	. . .
Banks	4 673 . .	. . .	. . .	. . .	. . .	. . .	. . .	. . .	. . .
Other sectors	4 674 . .	. . .	. . .	. . .	. . .	. . .	. . .	. . .	. . .
Money market instruments	4 680 . .	. . .	. . .	. . .	. . .	. . .	. . .	. . .	. . .
Monetary authorities	4 681 . .	. . .	. . .	. . .	. . .	. . .	. . .	. . .	. . .
General government	4 682 . .	. . .	. . .	. . .	. . .	. . .	. . .	. . .	. . .
Banks	4 683 . .	. . .	. . .	. . .	. . .	. . .	. . .	. . .	. . .
Other sectors	4 684 . .	. . .	. . .	. . .	. . .	. . .	. . .	. . .	. . .
C. FINANCIAL DERIVATIVES	4 910 . .	. . .	. . .	. . .	. . .	. . .	. . .	. . .	. . .
Monetary authorities	4 911 . .	. . .	. . .	. . .	. . .	. . .	. . .	. . .	. . .
General government	4 912 . .	. . .	. . .	. . .	. . .	. . .	. . .	. . .	. . .
Banks	4 913 . .	. . .	. . .	. . .	. . .	. . .	. . .	. . .	. . .
Other sectors	4 914 . .	. . .	. . .	. . .	. . .	. . .	. . .	. . .	. . .
Assets	4 900 . .	**. . .**	**. . .**	**. . .**	**. . .**	**. . .**	**. . .**	**. . .**	**. . .**
Monetary authorities	4 901 . .	. . .	. . .	. . .	. . .	. . .	. . .	. . .	. . .
General government	4 902 . .	. . .	. . .	. . .	. . .	. . .	. . .	. . .	. . .
Banks	4 903 . .	. . .	. . .	. . .	. . .	. . .	. . .	. . .	. . .
Other sectors	4 904 . .	. . .	. . .	. . .	. . .	. . .	. . .	. . .	. . .
Liabilities	4 905 . .	**. . .**	**. . .**	**. . .**	**. . .**	**. . .**	**. . .**	**. . .**	**. . .**
Monetary authorities	4 906 . .	. . .	. . .	. . .	. . .	. . .	. . .	. . .	. . .
General government	4 907 . .	. . .	. . .	. . .	. . .	. . .	. . .	. . .	. . .
Banks	4 908 . .	. . .	. . .	. . .	. . .	. . .	. . .	. . .	. . .
Other sectors	4 909 . .	. . .	. . .	. . .	. . .	. . .	. . .	. . .	. . .

Table 2 (Concluded). STANDARD PRESENTATION, 1994–2001
(Millions of U.S. dollars)

	Code	1994	1995	1996	1997	1998	1999	2000	2001
D. OTHER INVESTMENT	4 700	303.3	169.5	246.3	203.5	317.9	–73.3	–349.2	–302.7
Assets	4 703	**–104.0**	**–38.4**	**12.2**	**–19.9**	**–13.2**	**–47.7**	**–164.0**	**–202.0**
Trade credits	4 706	...	...	...	...	...	...	...	...
General government	4 707	...	...	...	...	...	...	...	...
of which: Short-term	4 709	...	...	...	...	...	...	...	...
Other sectors	4 710	...	...	...	...	...	...	...	...
of which: Short-term	4 712	...	...	...	...	...	...	...	...
Loans	4 714	16.0	...	...	...	...	...	...	...
Monetary authorities	4 715	...	...	...	...	...	...	...	...
of which: Short-term	4 718	...	...	...	...	...	...	...	...
General government	4 719	...	...	...	...	...	...	...	...
of which: Short-term	4 721	...	...	...	...	...	...	...	...
Banks	4 722	16.0	...	...	...	...	...	...	...
of which: Short-term	4 724	...	...	...	...	...	...	...	...
Other sectors	4 725	...	...	...	...	...	...	...	...
of which: Short-term	4 727	...	...	...	...	...	...	...	...
Currency and deposits	4 730	–120.0	–38.4	12.4	–19.9	66.1	–24.2	–85.3	–155.6
Monetary authorities	4 731	...	...	...	...	...	...	...	...
General government	4 732	...	...	...	...	...	...	...	...
Banks	4 733	–120.0	–38.4	12.4	–19.9	66.1	–24.2	–85.3	–155.6
Other sectors	4 734	...	...	...	...	...	...	...	...
Other assets	4 736	...	...	–.2	...	–79.3	–23.5	–78.7	–46.4
Monetary authorities	4 737	...	...	...	...	–8.4	–9.2	–9.1	–9.0
of which: Short-term	4 739	...	...	...	...	...	...	...	...
General government	4 740	...	...	–.2	...	...	...	...	...
of which: Short-term	4 742	...	...	...	...	...	...	...	...
Banks	4 743	...	...	...	...	...	...	...	...
of which: Short-term	4 745	...	...	...	...	...	...	...	...
Other sectors	4 746	...	...	...	...	–70.9	–14.3	–69.6	–37.4
of which: Short-term	4 748	...	...	...	...	...	...	...	...
Liabilities	4 753	**407.3**	**207.9**	**234.1**	**223.4**	**331.1**	**–25.6**	**–185.2**	**–100.7**
Trade credits	4 756	...	...	...	...	...	...	...	...
General government	4 757	...	...	...	...	...	...	...	...
of which: Short-term	4 759	...	...	...	...	...	...	...	...
Other sectors	4 760	...	...	...	...	...	...	...	...
of which: Short-term	4 762	...	...	...	...	...	...	...	...
Loans	4 764	202.6	95.7	235.6	140.8	237.4	88.7	–.5	111.9
Monetary authorities	4 765	78.0	79.1	30.3	–8.4	–44.4	–25.1	–37.3	–30.3
of which: Use of Fund credit and loans from the Fund	4 766	*28.7*	*–1.1*	*17.1*	*–11.4*	*5.7*	*–10.9*	*–14.5*	*–5.3*
of which: Short-term	4 768	...	...	...	...	...	...	...	...
General government	4 769	70.4	15.1	207.4	199.7	152.0	138.9	146.6	241.6
of which: Short-term	4 771	...	...	...	...	...	...	...	...
Banks	4 772	–6.9	–35.6	2.8	85.6	48.3	–21.2	–96.3	–31.5
of which: Short-term	4 774	...	...	...	...	...	...	...	...
Other sectors	4 775	61.1	37.1	–4.9	–136.1	81.5	–3.9	–13.5	–67.9
of which: Short-term	4 777	...	...	*14.7*	*–145.2*	...	...	...	...
Currency and deposits	4 780	204.7	112.2	–1.5	84.1	93.7	–114.3	–184.7	–212.6
Monetary authorities	4 781	–8.5	–2.2	–1.5	...	4.1	2.6	1.9	2.5
General government	4 782	...	...	...	...	...	...	...	...
Banks	4 783	213.2	114.4	...	84.1	89.6	–116.9	–186.6	–215.1
Other sectors	4 784	...	...	...	...	...	...	...	...
Other liabilities	4 786	...	...	...	–1.5	...	...	...	...
Monetary authorities	4 787	...	...	...	–1.5	...	...	...	...
of which: Short-term	4 789	...	...	...	*–1.5*	...	...	...	...
General government	4 790	...	...	...	...	...	...	...	...
of which: Short-term	4 792	...	...	...	...	...	...	...	...
Banks	4 793	...	...	...	...	...	...	...	...
of which: Short-term	4 795	...	...	...	...	...	...	...	...
Other sectors	4 796	...	...	...	...	...	...	...	...
of which: Short-term	4 798	...	...	...	...	...	...	...	...
E. RESERVE ASSETS	4 802	–26.4	–147.4	–310.1	–89.6	–133.0	–31.9	38.8	33.9
Monetary gold	4 812	...	...	...	...	–.1	–.8	1.0	...
Special drawing rights	4 811	–8.6	–14.9	.1	...	...	–.6	...	...
Reserve position in the Fund	4 810	...	...	...	...	...	...	...	...
Foreign exchange	4 803	–35.8	–137.3	–313.1	–84.4	–123.7	–27.1	46.0	43.8
Other claims	4 813	18.0	4.8	2.9	–5.2	–9.2	–3.4	–8.2	–9.9
NET ERRORS AND OMISSIONS	4 998	**–315.8**	**–112.3**	**–31.6**	**–260.6**	**–401.0**	**–353.6**	**–20.7**	**–78.8**

Part 3 of the *Yearbook* contains descriptions of the methodologies, compilation practices, and sources used to compile these data.

Table 3. INTERNATIONAL INVESTMENT POSITION (End–period stocks), 1994–2001

(Millions of U.S. dollars)

	Code	1994	1995	1996	1997	1998	1999	2000	2001
ASSETS	8 995 C.	...	...	...	2,058.0	2,520.5	2,606.6	2,640.6	2,838.0
Direct investment abroad	8 505 ..	...	...	...	**21.9**	**24.4**	**26.9**	**29.4**	**31.9**
Equity capital and reinvested earnings	8 506 ..	...	...	...	21.9	24.4	26.9	29.4	31.9
Claims on affiliated enterprises	8 507 ..	...	...	...	21.9	24.4	26.9	29.4	31.9
Liabilities to affiliated enterprises	8 508 ..	...	...	...	...	...	...	...	...
Other capital	8 530 ..	...	...	...	...	...	...	...	...
Claims on affiliated enterprises	8 535 ..	...	...	...	...	...	...	...	...
Liabilities to affiliated enterprises	8 540 ..	...	...	...	...	...	...	...	...
Portfolio investment	8 602 ..	...	...	...	**293.7**	**689.2**	**733.6**	**678.2**	**701.2**
Equity securities	8 610 ..	...	...	...	...	...	...	...	...
Monetary authorities	8 611 ..	...	...	...	...	...	...	...	...
General government	8 612 ..	...	...	...	...	...	...	...	...
Banks	8 613 ..	...	...	...	...	...	...	...	...
Other sectors	8 614 ..	...	...	...	...	...	...	...	...
Debt securities	8 619 ..	...	...	...	293.7	689.2	733.6	678.2	701.2
Bonds and notes	8 620 ..	...	...	...	...	...	...	...	...
Monetary authorities	8 621 ..	...	...	...	...	...	...	...	...
General government	8 622 ..	...	...	...	...	...	...	...	...
Banks	8 623 ..	...	...	...	...	...	...	...	...
Other sectors	8 624 ..	...	...	...	...	...	...	...	...
Money market instruments	8 630 ..	...	...	...	293.7	689.2	733.6	678.2	701.2
Monetary authorities	8 631 ..	...	...	...	...	...	...	...	...
General government	8 632 ..	...	...	...	...	...	...	...	...
Banks	8 633 ..	...	...	...	...	260.7	299.0	294.8	284.2
Other sectors	8 634 ..	...	...	...	293.7	428.5	434.6	383.4	417.0
Financial derivatives	8 900 ..	...	...	...	...	...	...	...	...
Monetary authorities	8 901 ..	...	...	...	...	...	...	...	...
General government	8 902 ..	...	...	...	...	...	...	...	...
Banks	8 903 ..	...	...	...	...	...	...	...	...
Other sectors	8 904 ..	...	...	...	...	...	...	...	...
Other investment	8 703 ..	...	...	...	**428.1**	**479.4**	**485.7**	**628.1**	**819.8**
Trade credits	8 706 ..	...	...	...	...	...	...	...	...
General government	8 707 ..	...	...	...	...	...	...	...	...
of which: Short-term	8 709 ..	...	...	...	...	...	...	...	...
Other sectors	8 710 ..	...	...	...	...	...	...	...	...
of which: Short-term	8 712 ..	...	...	...	...	...	...	...	...
Loans	8 714 ..	...	...	...	...	...	...	...	...
Monetary authorities	8 715 ..	...	...	...	...	...	...	...	...
of which: Short-term	8 718 ..	...	...	...	...	...	...	...	...
General government	8 719 ..	...	...	...	...	...	...	...	...
of which: Short-term	8 721 ..	...	...	...	...	...	...	...	...
Banks	8 722 ..	...	...	...	...	...	...	...	...
of which: Short-term	8 724 ..	...	...	...	...	...	...	...	...
Other sectors	8 725 ..	...	...	...	...	...	...	...	...
of which: Short-term	8 727 ..	...	...	...	...	...	...	...	...
Currency and deposits	8 730 ..	...	...	...	284.0	307.4	304.5	437.8	620.4
Monetary authorities	8 731 ..	...	...	...	...	...	...	...	...
General government	8 732 ..	...	...	...	...	...	...	...	...
Banks	8 733 ..	...	...	...	124.0	136.4	160.5	245.8	398.4
Other sectors	8 734 ..	...	...	...	160.0	171.0	144.0	192.0	222.0
Other assets	8 736 ..	...	...	...	144.1	172.0	181.2	190.3	199.4
Monetary authorities	8 737 ..	...	...	...	139.4	167.3	176.5	185.6	194.7
of which: Short-term	8 739 ..	...	...	...	...	...	...	...	...
General government	8 740 ..	...	...	...	...	...	...	...	...
of which: Short-term	8 742 ..	...	...	...	...	...	...	...	...
Banks	8 743 ..	...	...	...	4.7	4.7	4.7	4.7	4.7
of which: Short-term	8 745 ..	...	...	...	*.4*	*.4*	*.4*	*.4*	*.4*
Other sectors	8 746 ..	...	...	...	...	...	...	...	...
of which: Short-term	8 748 ..	...	...	...	...	...	...	...	...
Reserve assets	8 802 ..	...	...	...	**1,314.3**	**1,327.5**	**1,360.4**	**1,304.9**	**1,285.1**
Monetary gold	8 812 ..	...	...	...	39.6	256.9	260.0	244.8	259.6
Special drawing rights	8 811 ..	24.8	40.0	38.5	36.2	37.7	37.4	35.6	34.3
Reserve position in the Fund	8 810 ..	13.0	13.2	12.8	12.0	12.5	12.2	11.6	11.2
Foreign exchange	8 803 ..	...	...	...	1,103.7	888.3	915.2	869.2	826.3
Other claims	8 813 ..	...	...	...	122.9	132.1	135.6	143.8	153.7

Table 3 (Concluded). INTERNATIONAL INVESTMENT POSITION (End–period stocks), 1994–2001

(Millions of U.S. dollars)

	Code	1994	1995	1996	1997	1998	1999	2000	2001
LIABILITIES	8 995 D.	...	...	...	7,822.9	9,277.4	10,056.1	10,388.8	10,725.8
Direct investment in Bolivia	8 555 . .	**...**	**...**	**...**	**2,414.7**	**3,440.8**	**4,451.3**	**5,176.4**	**5,838.6**
Equity capital and reinvested earnings	8 556 . .	...	...	...	2,215.3	3,032.5	3,657.2	3,993.5	4,279.4
Claims on direct investors	8 557 . .	...	...	...	...	...	...	...	...
Liabilities to direct investors	8 558 . .	...	...	...	2,215.3	3,032.5	3,657.2	3,993.5	4,279.4
Other capital	8 580 . .	...	...	...	199.4	408.3	794.1	1,182.9	1,559.2
Claims on direct investors	8 585 . .	...	...	...	...	...	...	...	...
Liabilities to direct investors	8 590 . .	...	...	...	199.4	408.3	794.1	1,182.9	1,559.2
Portfolio investment	8 652 . .	**...**	**...**	**...**	**15.0**	**36.9**	**20.0**	**20.0**	**20.0**
Equity securities	8 660 . .	...	...	...	...	...	...	...	...
Banks	8 663 . .	...	...	...	...	...	...	...	...
Other sectors	8 664 . .	...	...	...	...	...	...	...	...
Debt securities	8 669 . .	...	...	...	15.0	36.9	20.0	20.0	20.0
Bonds and notes	8 670 . .	...	...	...	15.0	36.9	20.0	20.0	20.0
Monetary authorities	8 671 . .	...	...	...	...	...	...	...	...
General government	8 672 . .	...	...	...	15.0	36.9	20.0	20.0	20.0
Banks	8 673 . .	...	...	...	...	...	...	...	...
Other sectors	8 674 . .	...	...	...	...	...	...	...	...
Money market instruments	8 680 . .	...	...	...	...	...	...	...	...
Monetary authorities	8 681 . .	...	...	...	...	...	...	...	...
General government	8 682 . .	...	...	...	...	...	...	...	...
Banks	8 683 . .	...	...	...	...	...	...	...	...
Other sectors	8 684 . .	...	...	...	...	...	...	...	...
Financial derivatives	8 905 . .	**...**	**...**	**...**	**...**	**...**	**...**	**...**	**...**
Monetary authorities	8 906 . .	...	...	...	...	...	...	...	...
General government	8 907 . .	...	...	...	...	...	...	...	...
Banks	8 908 . .	...	...	...	...	...	...	...	...
Other sectors	8 909 . .	...	...	...	...	...	...	...	...
Other investment	8 753 . .	**...**	**...**	**...**	**5,393.2**	**5,799.7**	**5,584.8**	**5,192.4**	**4,867.2**
Trade credits	8 756 . .	...	...	...	...	...	...	...	...
General government	8 757 . .	...	...	...	...	...	...	...	...
of which: Short-term	8 759 . .	...	...	...	...	...	...	...	...
Other sectors	8 760 . .	...	...	...	...	...	...	...	...
of which: Short-term	8 762 . .	...	...	...	...	...	...	...	...
Loans	8 764 . .	...	...	...	5,376.4	5,778.8	5,561.3	5,167.1	4,839.4
Monetary authorities	8 765 . .	...	...	...	716.3	686.2	644.3	572.5	456.1
of which: Use of Fund credit and loans from the Fund	8 766 . .	*263.6*	*267.8*	*276.1*	*248.1*	*264.2*	*247.0*	*219.9*	*207.2*
of which: Short-term	8 768 . .	...	...	...	...	...	...	...	...
General government	8 769 . .	...	...	...	3,304.7	3,490.1	3,454.8	3,434.5	3,562.2
of which: Short-term	8 771 . .	...	...	...	...	...	...	...	...
Banks	8 772 . .	...	...	...	847.6	1,006.8	854.2	579.5	321.7
of which: Short-term	8 774 . .	...	...	...	*506.8*	*596.4*	*479.5*	*292.8*	*77.4*
Other sectors	8 775 . .	...	...	...	507.8	595.7	608.0	580.6	499.4
of which: Short-term	8 777 . .	...	...	...	*20.0*	*35.0*	*45.0*	*64.1*	*80.0*
Currency and deposits	8 780 . .	...	...	...	...	...	...	...	...
Monetary authorities	8 781 . .	...	...	...	...	...	...	...	...
General government	8 782 . .	...	...	...	...	...	...	...	...
Banks	8 783 . .	...	...	...	...	...	...	...	...
Other sectors	8 784 . .	...	...	...	...	...	...	...	...
Other liabilities	8 786 . .	...	...	...	16.8	20.9	23.5	25.3	27.8
Monetary authorities	8 787 . .	...	...	...	16.8	20.9	23.5	25.3	27.8
of which: Short-term	8 789 . .	...	...	...	...	...	...	...	...
General government	8 790 . .	...	...	...	...	...	...	...	...
of which: Short-term	8 792 . .	...	...	...	...	...	...	...	...
Banks	8 793 . .	...	...	...	...	...	...	...	...
of which: Short-term	8 795 . .	...	...	...	...	...	...	...	...
Other sectors	8 796 . .	...	...	...	...	...	...	...	...
of which: Short-term	8 798 . .	...	...	...	...	...	...	...	...
NET INTERNATIONAL INVESTMENT POSITION	8 995 . .	**...**	**...**	**...**	**–5,764.9**	**–6,756.8**	**–7,449.5**	**–7,748.2**	**–7,887.8**
Conversion rates: bolivianos per U.S. dollar (end of period)	0 102 . .	**4.6950**	**4.9350**	**5.1850**	**5.3650**	**5.6450**	**5.9900**	**6.3900**	**6.8200**

Table 1. ANALYTIC PRESENTATION, 1994–2001
(Millions of U.S. dollars)

	Code	1994	1995	1996	1997	1998	1999	2000	2001
A. Current Account [1]	4 993 Z.	**...**	**...**	**...**	**...**	**–1,249.4**	**–1,545.5**	**–1,281.1**	**–1,361.6**
Goods: exports f.o.b	2 100 . .	...	...	...	...	652.0	816.2	1,151.5	1,166.4
Goods: imports f.o.b	3 100 . .	...	...	...	...	–3,807.0	–4,149.2	–3,811.3	–3,917.9
Balance on Goods	4 100 . .	...	...	...	...	*–3,155.0*	*–3,333.1*	*–2,659.9*	*–2,751.5*
Services: credit	2 200 . .	...	...	...	...	304.8	285.0	261.3	288.0
Services: debit	3 200 . .	...	...	...	...	–230.7	–249.9	–224.1	–228.4
Balance on Goods and Services	4 991 . .	...	...	...	...	*–3,081.0*	*–3,298.0*	*–2,622.7*	*–2,691.9*
Income: credit	2 300 . .	...	...	...	...	481.2	454.7	391.8	401.3
Income: debit	3 300 . .	...	...	...	...	–52.1	–61.2	–68.4	–65.2
Balance on Goods, Services, and Income	4 992 . .	...	...	...	...	*–2,651.9*	*–2,904.6*	*–2,299.2*	*–2,355.7*
Current transfers: credit	2 379 Z.	...	...	...	...	1,404.9	1,361.5	1,020.9	997.6
Current transfers: debit	3 379 . .	...	...	...	...	–2.4	–2.5	–2.8	–3.5
B. Capital Account [1]	4 994 Z.	**...**	**...**	**...**	**...**	**435.2**	**531.5**	**406.0**	**390.6**
Capital account: credit	2 994 Z.	...	...	...	...	435.2	531.5	406.0	390.6
Capital account: debit	3 994 . .	...	...	...	...	...	...	...	...
Total, Groups A Plus B	4 981 . .	...	...	...	...	*–814.2*	*–1,014.1*	*–875.2*	*–971.0*
C. Financial Account [1]	4 995 W.	**...**	**...**	**...**	**...**	**58.0**	**433.8**	**677.6**	**1,550.9**
Direct investment abroad	4 505 . .	...	...	...	...	...	...	...	...
Direct investment in Bosnia & Herzegovina	4 555 Z.	...	...	...	...	66.7	176.6	146.0	221.9
Portfolio investment assets	4 602 . .	...	...	...	...	...	...	...	...
Equity securities	4 610 . .	...	...	...	...	...	...	...	...
Debt securities	4 619 . .	...	...	...	...	...	...	...	...
Portfolio investment liabilities	4 652 Z.	...	...	...	...	...	...	...	...
Equity securities	4 660 . .	...	...	...	...	...	...	...	...
Debt securities	4 669 Z.	...	...	...	...	...	...	...	...
Financial derivatives	4 910 . .	...	...	...	...	...	...	...	...
Financial derivatives assets	4 900 . .	...	...	...	...	...	...	...	...
Financial derivatives liabilities	4 905 . .	...	...	...	...	...	...	...	...
Other investment assets	4 703 . .	...	...	...	...	34.8	297.4	493.3	1,309.2
Monetary authorities	4 701 . .	...	...	...	...	...	...	...	...
General government	4 704 . .	...	...	...	...	...	...	...	...
Banks	4 705 . .	...	...	...	...	71.9	21.1	–52.9	–185.5
Other sectors	4 728 . .	...	...	...	...	–37.1	276.3	546.2	1,494.7
Other investment liabilities	4 753 W.	...	...	...	...	–43.5	–40.2	38.3	19.8
Monetary authorities	4 753 WA	...	...	...	...	...	...	.7	13.6
General government	4 753 ZB	...	...	...	...	–44.8	–31.3	–29.9	–22.2
Banks	4 753 ZC	...	...	...	...	–29.8	–47.1	27.2	–22.5
Other sectors	4 753 ZD	...	...	...	...	31.2	38.2	40.4	50.9
Total, Groups A Through C	4 983 . .	...	...	...	...	*–756.2*	*–580.2*	*–197.6*	*579.8*
D. Net Errors and Omissions	4 998 . .	**...**	**...**	**...**	**...**	**227.5**	**246.9**	**166.2**	**75.5**
Total, Groups A Through D	4 984 . .	...	...	...	...	*–528.7*	*–333.3*	*–31.4*	*655.3*
E. Reserves and Related Items	4 802 A.	**...**	**...**	**...**	**...**	**528.7**	**333.3**	**31.4**	**–655.3**
Reserve assets	4 802 . .	...	...	...	...	–84.0	–319.2	–76.4	–761.1
Use of Fund credit and loans	4 766 . .	...	...	...	...	32.3	18.2	15.5	9.9
Exceptional financing	4 920 . .	...	...	...	...	580.4	634.3	92.3	95.8
Conversion rates: convertible marka per U.S. dollar	0 101 . .	**...**	**.0143**	**.0150**	**1.7341**	**1.7597**	**1.8371**	**2.1243**	**2.1872**

[1] Excludes components that have been classified in the categories of Group E.

Table 2. STANDARD PRESENTATION, 1994–2001
(Millions of U.S. dollars)

	Code	1994	1995	1996	1997	1998	1999	2000	2001
CURRENT ACCOUNT	4 993 . .	**...**	**...**	**...**	**...**	**–1,249.4**	**–1,545.5**	**–1,281.1**	**–1,361.6**
A. GOODS	4 100 . .	...	...	...	...	–3,155.0	–3,333.1	–2,659.9	–2,751.5
Credit	2 100 . .	**...**	**...**	**...**	**...**	**652.0**	**816.2**	**1,151.5**	**1,166.4**
General merchandise: exports f.o.b.	2 110 . .	...	...	...	...	652.0	816.2	1,151.5	1,166.4
Goods for processing: exports f.o.b.	2 150 . .	...	...	...	...	...	...	...	...
Repairs on goods	2 160 . .	...	...	...	...	...	...	...	...
Goods procured in ports by carriers	2 170 . .	...	...	...	...	...	...	...	...
Nonmonetary gold	2 180 . .	...	...	...	...	...	...	...	...
Debit	3 100 . .	**...**	**...**	**...**	**...**	**–3,807.0**	**–4,149.2**	**–3,811.3**	**–3,917.9**
General merchandise: imports f.o.b.	3 110 . .	...	...	...	...	–3,807.0	–4,149.2	–3,811.3	–3,917.9
Goods for processing: imports f.o.b.	3 150 . .	...	...	...	...	...	...	...	...
Repairs on goods	3 160 . .	...	...	...	...	...	...	...	...
Goods procured in ports by carriers	3 170 . .	...	...	...	...	...	...	...	...
Nonmonetary gold	3 180 . .	...	...	...	...	...	...	...	...
B. SERVICES	4 200 . .	...	...	...	...	74.0	35.1	37.2	59.6
Total credit	2 200 . .	...	...	...	...	*304.8*	*285.0*	*261.3*	*288.0*
Total debit	3 200 . .	...	...	...	...	*–230.7*	*–249.9*	*–224.1*	*–228.4*
Transportation services, credit	2 205 . .	**...**	**...**	**...**	**...**	**16.1**	**21.3**	**24.7**	**26.0**
Passenger	2 850 . .	...	...	...	...	*9.5*	*13.1*	*13.1*	*14.3*
Freight	2 851 . .	...	...	...	...	*6.5*	*8.2*	*11.5*	*11.7*
Other	2 852 . .	...	...	...	...	...	...	...	...
Sea transport, passenger	2 207 . .	...	...	...	...	...	...	...	...
Sea transport, freight	2 208 . .	...	...	...	...	...	...	...	...
Sea transport, other	2 209 . .	...	...	...	...	...	...	...	...
Air transport, passenger	2 211 . .	...	...	...	...	7.9	10.0	9.8	10.5
Air transport, freight	2 212 . .	...	...	...	...	...	...	...	...
Air transport, other	2 213 . .	...	...	...	...	...	...	...	...
Other transport, passenger	2 215 . .	...	...	...	...	1.6	3.1	3.3	3.8
Other transport, freight	2 216 . .	...	...	...	...	6.5	8.2	11.5	11.7
Other transport, other	2 217 . .	...	...	...	...	...	...	...	...
Transportation services, debit	3 205 . .	**...**	**...**	**...**	**...**	**–134.9**	**–137.3**	**–120.8**	**–111.4**
Passenger	3 850 . .	...	...	...	...	*–15.9*	*–17.7*	*–18.7*	*–22.1*
Freight	3 851 . .	...	...	...	...	*–118.9*	*–119.5*	*–102.1*	*–89.4*
Other	3 852 . .	...	...	...	...	...	...	...	...
Sea transport, passenger	3 207 . .	...	...	...	...	...	...	...	...
Sea transport, freight	3 208 . .	...	...	...	...	...	...	...	...
Sea transport, other	3 209 . .	...	...	...	...	...	...	...	...
Air transport, passenger	3 211 . .	...	...	...	...	–14.9	–15.9	–16.8	–19.8
Air transport, freight	3 212 . .	...	...	...	...	...	...	...	...
Air transport, other	3 213 . .	...	...	...	...	...	...	...	...
Other transport, passenger	3 215 . .	...	...	...	...	–1.0	–1.9	–2.0	–2.3
Other transport, freight	3 216 . .	...	...	...	...	–118.9	–119.5	–102.1	–89.4
Other transport, other	3 217 . .	...	...	...	...	...	...	...	...
Travel, credit	2 236 . .	**...**	**...**	**...**	**...**	**97.7**	**81.6**	**68.6**	**72.5**
Business travel	2 237 . .	...	...	...	...	2.5	2.4	2.4	4.6
Personal travel	2 240 . .	...	...	...	...	95.2	79.1	66.2	67.9
Travel, debit	3 236 . .	**...**	**...**	**...**	**...**	**–56.8**	**–60.5**	**–67.7**	**–79.3**
Business travel	3 237 . .	...	...	...	...	–1.6	–1.9	–2.8	–4.6
Personal travel	3 240 . .	...	...	...	...	–55.2	–58.7	–64.9	–74.7
Other services, credit	2 200 BA	**...**	**...**	**...**	**...**	**191.0**	**182.1**	**168.0**	**189.4**
Communications	2 245 . .	...	...	...	...	3.8	3.3	2.5	2.4
Construction	2 249 . .	...	...	...	...	72.3	64.7	63.5	66.4
Insurance	2 253 . .	...	...	...	...	25.5	28.7	27.5	30.6
Financial	2 260 . .	...	...	...	...	9.1	8.9	11.5	29.5
Computer and information	2 262 . .	...	...	...	...	...	...	...	...
Royalties and licence fees	2 266 . .	...	...	...	...	...	...	...	...
Other business services	2 268 . .	...	...	...	...	80.3	76.5	62.9	60.6
Personal, cultural, and recreational	2 287 . .	...	...	...	...	...	...	...	...
Government, n.i.e.	2 291 . .	...	...	...	...	...	...	...	...
Other services, debit	3 200 BA	**...**	**...**	**...**	**...**	**–39.1**	**–52.1**	**–35.5**	**–37.6**
Communications	3 245 . .	...	...	...	...	–9.4	–21.0	–6.0	–6.7
Construction	3 249 . .	...	...	...	...	...	...	...	...
Insurance	3 253 . .	...	...	...	...	–6.3	–7.1	–6.8	–7.7
Financial	3 260 . .	...	...	...	...	–8.2	–8.4	–7.9	–8.4
Computer and information	3 262 . .	...	...	...	...	...	...	...	...
Royalties and licence fees	3 266 . .	...	...	...	...	...	...	...	...
Other business services	3 268 . .	...	...	...	...	...	...	...	...
Personal, cultural, and recreational	3 287 . .	...	...	...	...	...	...	...	...
Government, n.i.e.	3 291 . .	...	...	...	...	–15.2	–15.5	–14.8	–14.8

Table 2 (Continued). STANDARD PRESENTATION, 1994–2001
(Millions of U.S. dollars)

	Code	1994	1995	1996	1997	1998	1999	2000	2001
C. INCOME	4 300	...	...	...	...	429.1	393.5	323.4	336.2
Total credit	2 300	...	...	...	...	*481.2*	*454.7*	*391.8*	*401.3*
Total debit	3 300	...	...	...	...	*–52.1*	*–61.2*	*–68.4*	*–65.2*
Compensation of employees, credit	2 310	...	...	...	...	**448.2**	**411.1**	**339.8**	**328.8**
Compensation of employees, debit	3 310	...	...	...	...	...	...	...	...
Investment income, credit	2 320	...	...	...	...	**33.0**	**43.6**	**52.0**	**72.5**
Direct investment income	2 330	...	...	...	...	...	...	...	...
Dividends and distributed branch profits	2 332	...	...	...	...	...	...	...	...
Reinvested earnings and undistributed branch profits	2 333	...	...	...	...	...	...	...	...
Income on debt (interest)	2 334	...	...	...	...	...	...	...	...
Portfolio investment income	2 339	...	...	...	...	...	...	...	...
Income on equity	2 340	...	...	...	...	...	...	...	...
Income on bonds and notes	2 350	...	...	...	...	...	...	...	...
Income on money market instruments	2 360	...	...	...	...	...	...	...	...
Other investment income	2 370	...	...	...	...	33.0	43.6	52.0	72.5
Investment income, debit	3 320	...	...	...	...	**–52.1**	**–61.2**	**–68.4**	**–65.2**
Direct investment income	3 330	...	...	...	...	...	...	...	...
Dividends and distributed branch profits	3 332	...	...	...	...	...	...	...	...
Reinvested earnings and undistributed branch profits	3 333	...	...	...	...	...	...	...	...
Income on debt (interest)	3 334	...	...	...	...	...	...	...	...
Portfolio investment income	3 339	...	...	...	...	...	...	...	...
Income on equity	3 340	...	...	...	...	...	...	...	...
Income on bonds and notes	3 350	...	...	...	...	...	...	...	...
Income on money market instruments	3 360	...	...	...	...	...	...	...	...
Other investment income	3 370	...	...	...	...	–52.1	–61.2	–68.4	–65.2
D. CURRENT TRANSFERS	4 379	...	...	...	...	1,402.5	1,359.0	1,018.1	994.1
Credit	2 379	...	...	...	...	**1,404.9**	**1,361.5**	**1,020.9**	**997.6**
General government	2 380	...	...	...	...	524.8	557.0	337.1	328.2
Other sectors	2 390	...	...	...	...	880.2	804.5	683.7	669.4
Workers' remittances	2 391	...	...	...	...	714.5	661.0	549.4	526.0
Other current transfers	2 392	...	...	...	...	165.7	143.5	134.3	143.4
Debit	3 379	...	...	...	...	**–2.4**	**–2.5**	**–2.8**	**–3.5**
General government	3 380	...	...	...	...	...	...	...	...
Other sectors	3 390	...	...	...	...	–2.4	–2.5	–2.8	–3.5
Workers' remittances	3 391	...	...	...	...	...	...	...	...
Other current transfers	3 392	...	...	...	...	–2.4	–2.5	–2.8	–3.5
CAPITAL AND FINANCIAL ACCOUNT	4 996	...	...	...	...	**1,021.9**	**1,298.6**	**1,115.0**	**1,286.1**
CAPITAL ACCOUNT	4 994	...	...	...	...	**435.2**	**531.5**	**406.0**	**390.6**
Total credit	2 994	...	...	...	...	*435.2*	*531.5*	*406.0*	*390.6*
Total debit	3 994	...	...	...	...	...	...	...	...
Capital transfers, credit	2 400	...	...	...	...	**435.2**	**531.5**	**406.0**	**390.6**
General government	2 401	...	...	...	...	381.1	516.3	398.0	385.3
Debt forgiveness	2 402	...	...	...	...	...	...	...	...
Other capital transfers	2 410	...	...	...	...	381.1	516.3	398.0	385.3
Other sectors	2 430	...	...	...	...	54.1	15.2	8.0	5.3
Migrants' transfers	2 431	...	...	...	...	54.1	15.2	8.0	5.3
Debt forgiveness	2 432	...	...	...	...	...	...	...	...
Other capital transfers	2 440	...	...	...	...	...	...	...	...
Capital transfers, debit	3 400	...	...	...	...	...	...	...	...
General government	3 401	...	...	...	...	...	...	...	...
Debt forgiveness	3 402	...	...	...	...	...	...	...	...
Other capital transfers	3 410	...	...	...	...	...	...	...	...
Other sectors	3 430	...	...	...	...	...	...	...	...
Migrants' transfers	3 431	...	...	...	...	...	...	...	...
Debt forgiveness	3 432	...	...	...	...	...	...	...	...
Other capital transfers	3 440	...	...	...	...	...	...	...	...
Nonproduced nonfinancial assets, credit	2 480	...	...	...	...	...	...	...	...
Nonproduced nonfinancial assets, debit	3 480	...	...	...	...	...	...	...	...

Table 2 (Continued). STANDARD PRESENTATION, 1994–2001

(Millions of U.S. dollars)

	Code	1994	1995	1996	1997	1998	1999	2000	2001
FINANCIAL ACCOUNT	4 995	**...**	**...**	**...**	**...**	**586.7**	**767.1**	**709.0**	**895.5**
A. DIRECT INVESTMENT	4 500	...	...	...	...	66.7	176.6	146.0	221.9
Direct investment abroad	4 505	**...**	**...**	**...**	**...**	**...**	**...**	**...**	**...**
Equity capital	4 510	...	...	...	...	...	...	...	...
Claims on affiliated enterprises	4 515	...	...	...	...	...	...	...	...
Liabilities to affiliated enterprises	4 520	...	...	...	...	...	...	...	...
Reinvested earnings	4 525	...	...	...	...	...	...	...	...
Other capital	4 530	...	...	...	...	...	...	...	...
Claims on affiliated enterprises	4 535	...	...	...	...	...	...	...	...
Liabilities to affiliated enterprises	4 540	...	...	...	...	...	...	...	...
Direct investment in Bosnia & Herzegovina	4 555	**...**	**...**	**...**	**...**	**66.7**	**176.6**	**146.0**	**221.9**
Equity capital	4 560	...	...	...	...	66.7	176.6	146.0	221.9
Claims on direct investors	4 565	...	...	...	...	...	...	...	...
Liabilities to direct investors	4 570	...	...	...	...	66.7	176.6	146.0	221.9
Reinvested earnings	4 575	...	...	...	...	...	...	...	...
Other capital	4 580	...	...	...	...	...	...	...	...
Claims on direct investors	4 585	...	...	...	...	...	...	...	...
Liabilities to direct investors	4 590	...	...	...	...	...	...	...	...
B. PORTFOLIO INVESTMENT	4 600	...	...	...	...	...	...	...	...
Assets	4 602	**...**	**...**	**...**	**...**	**...**	**...**	**...**	**...**
Equity securities	4 610	...	...	...	...	...	...	...	...
Monetary authorities	4 611	...	...	...	...	...	...	...	...
General government	4 612	...	...	...	...	...	...	...	...
Banks	4 613	...	...	...	...	...	...	...	...
Other sectors	4 614	...	...	...	...	...	...	...	...
Debt securities	4 619	...	...	...	...	...	...	...	...
Bonds and notes	4 620	...	...	...	...	...	...	...	...
Monetary authorities	4 621	...	...	...	...	...	...	...	...
General government	4 622	...	...	...	...	...	...	...	...
Banks	4 623	...	...	...	...	...	...	...	...
Other sectors	4 624	...	...	...	...	...	...	...	...
Money market instruments	4 630	...	...	...	...	...	...	...	...
Monetary authorities	4 631	...	...	...	...	...	...	...	...
General government	4 632	...	...	...	...	...	...	...	...
Banks	4 633	...	...	...	...	...	...	...	...
Other sectors	4 634	...	...	...	...	...	...	...	...
Liabilities	4 652	**...**	**...**	**...**	**...**	**...**	**...**	**...**	**...**
Equity securities	4 660	...	...	...	...	...	...	...	...
Banks	4 663	...	...	...	...	...	...	...	...
Other sectors	4 664	...	...	...	...	...	...	...	...
Debt securities	4 669	...	...	...	...	...	...	...	...
Bonds and notes	4 670	...	...	...	...	...	...	...	...
Monetary authorities	4 671	...	...	...	...	...	...	...	...
General government	4 672	...	...	...	...	...	...	...	...
Banks	4 673	...	...	...	...	...	...	...	...
Other sectors	4 674	...	...	...	...	...	...	...	...
Money market instruments	4 680	...	...	...	...	...	...	...	...
Monetary authorities	4 681	...	...	...	...	...	...	...	...
General government	4 682	...	...	...	...	...	...	...	...
Banks	4 683	...	...	...	...	...	...	...	...
Other sectors	4 684	...	...	...	...	...	...	...	...
C. FINANCIAL DERIVATIVES	4 910	...	...	...	...	...	...	...	...
Monetary authorities	4 911	...	...	...	...	...	...	...	...
General government	4 912	...	...	...	...	...	...	...	...
Banks	4 913	...	...	...	...	...	...	...	...
Other sectors	4 914	...	...	...	...	...	...	...	...
Assets	4 900	**...**	**...**	**...**	**...**	**...**	**...**	**...**	**...**
Monetary authorities	4 901	...	...	...	...	...	...	...	...
General government	4 902	...	...	...	...	...	...	...	...
Banks	4 903	...	...	...	...	...	...	...	...
Other sectors	4 904	...	...	...	...	...	...	...	...
Liabilities	4 905	**...**	**...**	**...**	**...**	**...**	**...**	**...**	**...**
Monetary authorities	4 906	...	...	...	...	...	...	...	...
General government	4 907	...	...	...	...	...	...	...	...
Banks	4 908	...	...	...	...	...	...	...	...
Other sectors	4 909	...	...	...	...	...	...	...	...

Table 2 (Concluded). STANDARD PRESENTATION, 1994–2001
(Millions of U.S. dollars)

	Code	1994	1995	1996	1997	1998	1999	2000	2001
D. OTHER INVESTMENT	4 700	...	...	...	...	604.0	909.7	639.5	1,434.7
Assets	4 703	**...**	**...**	**...**	**...**	**34.8**	**297.4**	**493.3**	**1,309.2**
Trade credits	4 706	...	...	...	...	...	...	...	...
General government	4 707	...	...	...	...	...	...	...	...
of which: Short-term	4 709	...	...	...	...	...	...	...	...
Other sectors	4 710	...	...	...	...	...	...	...	...
of which: Short-term	4 712	...	...	...	...	...	...	...	...
Loans	4 714	...	...	...	...	...	...	...	...
Monetary authorities	4 715	...	...	...	...	...	...	...	...
of which: Short-term	4 718	...	...	...	...	...	...	...	...
General government	4 719	...	...	...	...	...	...	...	...
of which: Short-term	4 721	...	...	...	...	...	...	...	...
Banks	4 722	...	...	...	...	...	...	...	...
of which: Short-term	4 724	...	...	...	...	...	...	...	...
Other sectors	4 725	...	...	...	...	...	...	...	...
of which: Short-term	4 727	...	...	...	...	...	...	...	...
Currency and deposits	4 730	...	...	...	...	34.8	297.4	493.3	1,309.2
Monetary authorities	4 731	...	...	...	...	...	...	...	...
General government	4 732	...	...	...	...	...	...	...	...
Banks	4 733	...	...	...	...	71.9	21.1	–52.9	–185.5
Other sectors	4 734	...	...	...	...	–37.1	276.3	546.2	1,494.7
Other assets	4 736	...	...	...	...	...	...	...	...
Monetary authorities	4 737	...	...	...	...	...	...	...	...
of which: Short-term	4 739	...	...	...	...	...	...	...	...
General government	4 740	...	...	...	...	...	...	...	...
of which: Short-term	4 742	...	...	...	...	...	...	...	...
Banks	4 743	...	...	...	...	...	...	...	...
of which: Short-term	4 745	...	...	...	...	...	...	...	...
Other sectors	4 746	...	...	...	...	...	...	...	...
of which: Short-term	4 748	...	...	...	...	...	...	...	...
Liabilities	4 753	**...**	**...**	**...**	**...**	**569.2**	**612.3**	**146.2**	**125.5**
Trade credits	4 756	...	...	...	...	31.2	38.2	40.4	50.9
General government	4 757	...	...	...	...	...	...	...	...
of which: Short-term	4 759	...	...	...	...	...	...	...	...
Other sectors	4 760	...	...	...	...	31.2	38.2	40.4	50.9
of which: Short-term	4 762	...	...	...	...	*31.2*	*38.2*	*40.4*	*50.9*
Loans	4 764	...	...	...	...	567.9	621.2	77.9	83.5
Monetary authorities	4 765	...	...	...	...	32.3	18.2	15.5	9.9
of which: Use of Fund credit and loans from the Fund	4 766	...	...	...	...	*32.3*	*18.2*	*15.5*	*9.9*
of which: Short-term	4 768	...	...	...	...	...	...	...	...
General government	4 769	...	...	...	...	535.6	603.0	62.4	73.6
of which: Short-term	4 771	...	...	...	...	...	...	...	...
Banks	4 772	...	...	...	...	...	...	...	...
of which: Short-term	4 774	...	...	...	...	...	...	...	...
Other sectors	4 775	...	...	...	...	...	...	...	...
of which: Short-term	4 777	...	...	...	...	...	...	...	...
Currency and deposits	4 780	...	...	...	...	...	...	...	...
Monetary authorities	4 781	...	...	...	...	...	...	...	...
General government	4 782	...	...	...	...	...	...	...	...
Banks	4 783	...	...	...	...	...	...	...	...
Other sectors	4 784	...	...	...	...	...	...	...	...
Other liabilities	4 786	...	...	...	...	–29.8	–47.1	27.9	–8.8
Monetary authorities	4 787	...	...	...	...	...	...	.7	13.6
of which: Short-term	4 789	...	...	...	...	...	...	*.7*	*13.6*
General government	4 790	...	...	...	...	...	...	...	...
of which: Short-term	4 792	...	...	...	...	...	...	...	...
Banks	4 793	...	...	...	...	–29.8	–47.1	27.2	–22.5
of which: Short-term	4 795	...	...	...	...	*–29.8*	*–47.1*	*27.2*	*–22.5*
Other sectors	4 796	...	...	...	...	...	...	...	...
of which: Short-term	4 798	...	...	...	...	...	...	...	...
E. RESERVE ASSETS	4 802	...	...	...	...	–84.0	–319.2	–76.4	–761.1
Monetary gold	4 812	...	...	...	...	...	...	...	...
Special drawing rights	4 811	...	...	...	...	–4.9	–2.1	–3.2	4.3
Reserve position in the Fund	4 810	...	...	...	...	...	...	...	...
Foreign exchange	4 803	...	...	...	...	–79.1	–317.1	–73.2	–765.4
Other claims	4 813	...	...	...	...	...	...	...	...
NET ERRORS AND OMISSIONS	4 998	**...**	**...**	**...**	**...**	**227.5**	**246.9**	**166.2**	**75.5**

Part 3 of the *Yearbook* contains descriptions of the methodologies, compilation practices, and sources used to compile these data.

Table 1. ANALYTIC PRESENTATION, 1994–2001
(Millions of U.S. dollars)

	Code	1994	1995	1996	1997	1998	1999	2000	2001
A. Current Account [1]	4 993 Z.	**211.6**	**299.7**	**495.0**	**721.5**	**170.1**	**516.8**	**...**	**...**
Goods: exports f.o.b.	2 100 . .	1,874.3	2,160.2	2,217.5	2,819.8	2,060.6	2,671.0	...	...
Goods: imports f.o.b.	3 100 . .	-1,364.3	-1,605.4	-1,467.7	-1,924.4	-1,983.1	-1,996.5	...	...
Balance on Goods	4 100 . .	*510.0*	*554.8*	*749.8*	*895.4*	*77.5*	*674.5*	...	...
Services: credit	2 200 . .	186.1	260.4	163.0	210.2	255.3	372.6	...	...
Services: debit	3 200 . .	-322.0	-444.2	-343.6	-440.7	-522.4	-515.9	...	...
Balance on Goods and Services	4 991 . .	*374.2*	*370.9*	*569.2*	*664.9*	*-189.6*	*531.2*	...	...
Income: credit	2 300 . .	230.8	483.2	501.7	622.1	622.7	429.8	...	...
Income: debit	3 300 . .	-455.1	-515.6	-754.8	-766.9	-503.1	-696.0	...	...
Balance on Goods, Services, and Income	4 992 . .	*149.9*	*338.5*	*316.1*	*520.1*	*-70.0*	*265.1*	...	...
Current transfers: credit	2 379 Z.	356.8	330.7	355.4	456.8	460.9	474.4	...	...
Current transfers: debit	3 379 . .	-295.1	-369.5	-176.6	-255.5	-220.8	-222.6	...	...
B. Capital Account [1]	4 994 Z.	**19.2**	**14.4**	**6.2**	**16.9**	**31.8**	**20.6**	**...**	**...**
Capital account: credit	2 994 Z.	19.6	15.4	18.0	29.4	44.2	33.5	...	...
Capital account: debit	3 994 . .	-.4	-.9	-11.9	-12.5	-12.4	-12.9	...	...
Total, Groups A Plus B	4 981 . .	*230.8*	*314.1*	*501.2*	*738.4*	*202.0*	*537.5*	...	...
C. Financial Account [1]	4 995 W.	**41.1**	**-33.9**	**42.4**	**5.6**	**-202.4**	**-175.2**	**...**	**...**
Direct investment abroad	4 505 . .	-9.5	-40.9	1.1	-4.1	-3.5	-1.5	...	...
Direct investment in Botswana	4 555 Z.	-14.2	70.4	71.2	100.1	95.3	36.7	...	...
Portfolio investment assets	4 602 . .	...	-36.2	-35.5	-28.5	-42.8	-22.8	...	...
Equity securities	4 610 . .	...	-30.8	-26.7	-33.1	-16.9	6.5	...	...
Debt securities	4 619 . .	...	-5.4	-8.9	4.7	-25.9	-29.3	...	...
Portfolio investment liabilities	4 652 Z.	-.1	5.5	28.9	10.8	-14.1	-7.5	...	...
Equity securities	4 660 . .	...	5.5	28.7	10.8	-14.1	-7.5	...	...
Debt securities	4 669 Z.	-.1	...	.2	...	...	...	...	...
Financial derivatives	4 910 . .	...	.1	2.1	-15.4	5.2	-4.6	...	...
Financial derivatives assets	4 900 . .	...	-.2	...	-15.4	5.2	-4.6	...	...
Financial derivatives liabilities	4 905 . .	...	.3	2.1	...	...	...	...	...
Other investment assets	4 703 . .	15.8	-88.7	-95.6	-166.5	-310.8	-206.1	...	...
Monetary authorities	4 701 . .	...	...	...	...	...	...	...	...
General government	4 704 . .	19.7	-46.1	-28.7	-78.0	-101.1	-17.8	...	...
Banks	4 705 . .	.4	-8.7	-35.1	-76.9	-139.7	-154.7	...	...
Other sectors	4 728 . .	-4.3	-34.0	-31.8	-11.6	-70.0	-33.7	...	...
Other investment liabilities	4 753 W.	49.0	55.9	70.3	109.3	68.2	30.7	...	...
Monetary authorities	4 753 WA	...	...	...	...	...	...	...	...
General government	4 753 ZB	6.5	-12.3	-19.6	51.3	22.2	-16.1	...	...
Banks	4 753 ZC	-2.8	-2.5	17.8	-3.4	-3.5	1.4	...	...
Other sectors	4 753 ZD	45.3	70.7	72.1	61.4	49.5	45.4	...	...
Total, Groups A Through C	4 983 . .	*271.9*	*280.2*	*543.6*	*744.0*	*-.4*	*362.2*	...	...
D. Net Errors and Omissions	4 998 . .	**-136.7**	**-73.6**	**-32.9**	**-108.9**	**44.6**	**8.7**	**...**	**...**
Total, Groups A Through D	4 984 . .	*135.2*	*206.6*	*510.7*	*635.1*	*44.2*	*371.0*	...	...
E. Reserves and Related Items	4 802 A.	**-135.2**	**-206.6**	**-510.7**	**-635.1**	**-44.2**	**-371.0**	**...**	**...**
Reserve assets	4 802 . .	-135.2	-206.6	-510.7	-635.1	-44.2	-371.0	...	...
Use of Fund credit and loans	4 766 . .	...	...	...	...	...	...	...	...
Exceptional financing	4 920 . .	...	...	...	...	...	...	...	...
Conversion rates: pula per U.S. dollar	0 101 . .	**2.6846**	**2.7722**	**3.3242**	**3.6508**	**4.2259**	**4.6244**	**5.1018**	**5.8412**

[1] Excludes components that have been classified in the categories of Group E.

Table 2. STANDARD PRESENTATION, 1994–2001

(Millions of U.S. dollars)

	Code	1994	1995	1996	1997	1998	1999	2000	2001
CURRENT ACCOUNT	4 993 . .	**211.6**	**299.7**	**495.0**	**721.5**	**170.1**	**516.8**	**. . .**	**. . .**
A. GOODS	4 100 . .	510.0	554.8	749.8	895.4	77.5	674.5	. . .	. . .
Credit	2 100 . .	**1,874.3**	**2,160.2**	**2,217.5**	**2,819.8**	**2,060.6**	**2,671.0**	**. . .**	**. . .**
General merchandise: exports f.o.b.	2 110 . .	1,874.3	2,160.2	2,217.5	2,819.8	2,060.6	2,671.0	. . .	. . .
Goods for processing: exports f.o.b.	2 150 . .	. . .	. . .	. . .	. . .	. . .	. . .	. . .	. . .
Repairs on goods	2 160 . .	. . .	. . .	. . .	. . .	. . .	. . .	. . .	. . .
Goods procured in ports by carriers	2 170 . .	. . .	. . .	. . .	. . .	. . .	. . .	. . .	. . .
Nonmonetary gold	2 180 . .	. . .	. . .	. . .	. . .	. . .	. . .	. . .	. . .
Debit	3 100 . .	**–1,364.3**	**–1,605.4**	**–1,467.7**	**–1,924.4**	**–1,983.1**	**–1,996.5**	**. . .**	**. . .**
General merchandise: imports f.o.b.	3 110 . .	–1,364.3	–1,605.4	–1,463.3	–1,920.9	–1,980.1	–1,996.5	. . .	. . .
Goods for processing: imports f.o.b.	3 150 . .	. . .	. . .	. . .	. . .	. . .	. . .	. . .	. . .
Repairs on goods	3 160 . .	. . .	. . .	–4.5	–3.5	–3.0	. . .	. . .	. . .
Goods procured in ports by carriers	3 170 . .	. . .	. . .	. . .	–.1	. . .	. . .	. . .	. . .
Nonmonetary gold	3 180 . .	. . .	. . .	. . .	. . .	. . .	. . .	. . .	. . .
B. SERVICES	4 200 . .	–135.8	–183.9	–180.6	–230.5	–267.1	–143.3	. . .	. . .
Total credit	2 200 . .	*186.1*	*260.4*	*163.0*	*210.2*	*255.3*	*372.6*	. . .	. . .
Total debit	3 200 . .	*–322.0*	*–444.2*	*–343.6*	*–440.7*	*–522.4*	*–515.9*	. . .	. . .
Transportation services, credit	2 205 . .	**35.7**	**38.3**	**40.2**	**37.7**	**43.6**	**95.8**	**. . .**	**. . .**
Passenger	2 850 . .	*9.7*	*14.0*	*11.9*	*4.5*	*5.0*	*18.5*	. . .	. . .
Freight	2 851 . .	. . .	. . .	. . .	*9.3*	*9.6*	*29.1*	. . .	. . .
Other	2 852 . .	*26.0*	*24.3*	*28.2*	*23.9*	*29.1*	*48.1*	. . .	. . .
Sea transport, passenger	2 207 . .	. . .	. . .	. . .	. . .	. . .	. . .	. . .	. . .
Sea transport, freight	2 208 . .	. . .	. . .	. . .	. . .	. . .	. . .	. . .	. . .
Sea transport, other	2 209 . .	. . .	. . .	. . .	. . .	. . .	. . .	. . .	. . .
Air transport, passenger	2 211 . .	8.8	13.3	. . .	. . .	. . .	. . .	. . .	. . .
Air transport, freight	2 212 . .	. . .	. . .	. . .	. . .	. . .	. . .	. . .	. . .
Air transport, other	2 213 . .	2.7	2.1	. . .	. . .	. . .	. . .	. . .	. . .
Other transport, passenger	2 215 . .	.9	.7	. . .	. . .	. . .	. . .	. . .	. . .
Other transport, freight	2 216 . .	. . .	. . .	. . .	. . .	. . .	. . .	. . .	. . .
Other transport, other	2 217 . .	23.3	22.3	. . .	. . .	. . .	. . .	. . .	. . .
Transportation services, debit	3 205 . .	**–164.6**	**–187.4**	**–180.0**	**–212.5**	**–218.1**	**–216.5**	**. . .**	**. . .**
Passenger	3 850 . .	*–13.0*	*–8.3*	*–14.2*	*–12.5*	*–12.3*	*–8.5*	. . .	. . .
Freight	3 851 . .	*–139.1*	*–162.7*	*–146.5*	*–192.2*	*–197.3*	*–199.4*	. . .	. . .
Other	3 852 . .	*–12.6*	*–16.5*	*–19.4*	*–7.8*	*–8.4*	*–8.6*	. . .	. . .
Sea transport, passenger	3 207 . .	. . .	. . .	. . .	. . .	. . .	. . .	. . .	. . .
Sea transport, freight	3 208 . .	–8.3	–8.1	. . .	. . .	. . .	. . .	. . .	. . .
Sea transport, other	3 209 . .	–1.4	–2.5	. . .	. . .	. . .	. . .	. . .	. . .
Air transport, passenger	3 211 . .	–6.1	–7.1	. . .	. . .	. . .	. . .	. . .	. . .
Air transport, freight	3 212 . .	–48.7	–56.9	. . .	. . .	. . .	. . .	. . .	. . .
Air transport, other	3 213 . .	–2.6	–4.5	. . .	. . .	. . .	. . .	. . .	. . .
Other transport, passenger	3 215 . .	–6.9	–1.1	. . .	. . .	. . .	. . .	. . .	. . .
Other transport, freight	3 216 . .	–82.1	–97.6	. . .	. . .	. . .	. . .	. . .	. . .
Other transport, other	3 217 . .	–8.6	–9.6	. . .	. . .	. . .	. . .	. . .	. . .
Travel, credit	2 236 . .	**123.7**	**161.9**	**93.3**	**135.5**	**174.7**	**234.1**	**. . .**	**. . .**
Business travel	2 237 . .	4.5	14.6	4.3	26.2	33.9	42.8	. . .	. . .
Personal travel	2 240 . .	119.3	147.4	89.0	109.3	140.8	191.3	. . .	. . .
Travel, debit	3 236 . .	**–76.2**	**–145.2**	**–77.6**	**–92.4**	**–125.7**	**–142.9**	**. . .**	**. . .**
Business travel	3 237 . .	–16.0	–47.9	–18.6	–22.2	–30.2	–31.2	. . .	. . .
Personal travel	3 240 . .	–60.2	–97.3	–59.0	–70.2	–95.5	–111.6	. . .	. . .
Other services, credit	2 200 BA	**26.7**	**60.1**	**29.6**	**37.0**	**37.0**	**42.7**	**. . .**	**. . .**
Communications	2 245 . .	2.4	2.8	. . .	. . .	.5	.6	. . .	. . .
Construction	2 249 . .	.3	.7	. . .	.3	1.4	.1	. . .	. . .
Insurance	2 253 . .	3.1	8.8	1.3	1.7	3.3	3.6	. . .	. . .
Financial	2 260 . .	5.8	9.8	. . .	1.5	3.1	1.1	. . .	. . .
Computer and information	2 262 . .	. . .	. . .	. . .	. . .	. . .	. . .	. . .	. . .
Royalties and licence fees	2 266 . .	. . .	. . .	. . .	.1	.2	. . .	. . .	. . .
Other business services	2 268 . .	3.5	14.1	10.7	10.2	13.7	10.6	. . .	. . .
Personal, cultural, and recreational	2 287 . .	. . .	. . .	. . .	. . .	. . .	. . .	. . .	. . .
Government, n.i.e.	2 291 . .	11.5	24.0	17.6	23.2	14.8	26.6	. . .	. . .
Other services, debit	3 200 BA	**–81.2**	**–111.6**	**–86.0**	**–135.8**	**–178.7**	**–156.6**	**. . .**	**. . .**
Communications	3 245 . .	–.1	–.7	. . .	–1.6	–3.1	–2.6	. . .	. . .
Construction	3 249 . .	–1.2	–.7	. . .	–.7	–2.1	–12.5	. . .	. . .
Insurance	3 253 . .	–28.1	–28.1	–14.4	–17.1	–15.9	–17.4	. . .	. . .
Financial	3 260 . .	–10.7	–7.4	. . .	–2.4	–3.3	–3.8	. . .	. . .
Computer and information	3 262 . .	. . .	. . .	. . .	–.3	–.3	–2.0	. . .	. . .
Royalties and licence fees	3 266 . .	–2.1	–5.8	. . .	–3.3	–8.5	–6.4	. . .	. . .
Other business services	3 268 . .	–33.7	–64.5	–67.4	–104.9	–139.5	–107.1	. . .	. . .
Personal, cultural, and recreational	3 287 . .	. . .	–.1	. . .	. . .	. . .	. . .	. . .	. . .
Government, n.i.e.	3 291 . .	–5.2	–4.3	–4.2	–5.6	–5.8	–4.8	. . .	. . .

Table 2 (Continued). STANDARD PRESENTATION, 1994–2001
(Millions of U.S. dollars)

	Code	1994	1995	1996	1997	1998	1999	2000	2001
C. INCOME	4 300	-224.3	-32.4	-253.1	-144.8	119.6	-266.2	...	...
Total credit	2 300	*230.8*	*483.2*	*501.7*	*622.1*	*622.7*	*429.8*	...	...
Total debit	3 300	*-455.1*	*-515.6*	*-754.8*	*-766.9*	*-503.1*	*-696.0*	...	...
Compensation of employees, credit	2 310	**63.4**	**55.3**	**34.9**	**40.9**	**35.9**	**26.2**	...	...
Compensation of employees, debit	3 310	**-47.4**	**-42.2**	**-48.8**	**-51.4**	**-50.8**	**-52.5**	...	...
Investment income, credit	2 320	**167.4**	**427.9**	**466.8**	**581.2**	**586.8**	**403.6**	...	...
Direct investment income	2 330	25.6	58.3	20.1	23.9	31.8	21.9	...	...
Dividends and distributed branch profits	2 332	16.1	17.0	21.5	20.9	19.4	15.4	...	...
Reinvested earnings and undistributed branch profits	2 333	9.1	40.9	-1.4	-.2	6.3	5.3	...	...
Income on debt (interest)	2 334	.4	.4	...	3.2	6.1	1.3	...	...
Portfolio investment income	2 339	136.1	359.6	438.0	546.8	532.9	361.5	...	...
Income on equity	2 340	136.1	359.6	438.0	546.1	531.3	347.6	...	...
Income on bonds and notes	2 350	...	...	...	.7	1.7	13.9	...	...
Income on money market instruments	2 360	...	...	...	...	...	...	...	...
Other investment income	2 370	5.6	9.9	8.7	10.5	22.1	20.2	...	...
Investment income, debit	3 320	**-407.7**	**-473.4**	**-705.9**	**-715.5**	**-452.3**	**-643.4**	...	...
Direct investment income	3 330	-265.5	-415.7	-656.5	-669.3	-407.4	-607.0	...	...
Dividends and distributed branch profits	3 332	-314.5	-346.4	-591.2	-593.9	-333.5	-587.0	...	...
Reinvested earnings and undistributed branch profits	3 333	68.8	-48.0	-37.5	-45.8	-43.8	12.4	...	...
Income on debt (interest)	3 334	-19.8	-21.2	-27.9	-29.6	-30.1	-32.4	...	...
Portfolio investment income	3 339	...	...	-3.7	-.5	-.4	-3.4	...	...
Income on equity	3 340	...	...	-3.7	-.5	-.4	-3.4	...	...
Income on bonds and notes	3 350	...	...	...	...	...	...	...	...
Income on money market instruments	3 360	...	...	...	...	...	...	...	...
Other investment income	3 370	-142.3	-57.8	-45.7	-45.8	-44.5	-33.0	...	...
D. CURRENT TRANSFERS	4 379	61.8	-38.8	178.9	201.4	240.2	251.8	...	...
Credit	2 379	**356.8**	**330.7**	**355.4**	**456.8**	**460.9**	**474.4**	...	...
General government	2 380	345.2	321.8	340.5	445.6	446.9	459.0	...	...
Other sectors	2 390	11.6	8.9	14.9	11.3	14.1	15.4	...	...
Workers' remittances	2 391	...	...	8.3	.1	.4	.2	...	...
Other current transfers	2 392	11.6	8.9	6.6	11.2	13.7	15.3	...	...
Debit	3 379	**-295.1**	**-369.5**	**-176.6**	**-255.5**	**-220.8**	**-222.6**	...	...
General government	3 380	-192.2	-202.9	-138.6	-187.8	-153.8	-152.9	...	...
Other sectors	3 390	-102.9	-166.6	-38.0	-67.7	-66.9	-69.7	...	...
Workers' remittances	3 391	-97.9	-156.8	-37.5	-67.7	-66.9	-69.7	...	...
Other current transfers	3 392	-5.0	-9.8	-.4	...	...	...	...	...
CAPITAL AND FINANCIAL ACCOUNT	4 996	**-74.9**	**-226.0**	**-462.1**	**-612.6**	**-214.7**	**-525.6**	...	...
CAPITAL ACCOUNT	4 994	**19.2**	**14.4**	**6.2**	**16.9**	**31.8**	**20.6**	...	...
Total credit	2 994	*19.6*	*15.4*	*18.0*	*29.4*	*44.2*	*33.5*	...	...
Total debit	3 994	*-.4*	*-.9*	*-11.9*	*-12.5*	*-12.4*	*-12.9*	...	...
Capital transfers, credit	2 400	**19.6**	**15.4**	**18.0**	**29.4**	**44.2**	**33.5**	...	...
General government	2 401	13.1	11.5	11.2	22.2	37.1	26.1	...	...
Debt forgiveness	2 402	...	...	...	...	...	...	...	...
Other capital transfers	2 410	13.1	11.5	11.2	22.2	37.1	26.1	...	...
Other sectors	2 430	6.5	3.8	6.9	7.2	7.1	7.5	...	...
Migrants' transfers	2 431	6.5	3.8	6.9	7.2	7.1	7.5	...	...
Debt forgiveness	2 432	...	...	...	...	...	...	...	...
Other capital transfers	2 440	...	...	...	...	...	...	...	...
Capital transfers, debit	3 400	**-.4**	**-.9**	**-11.9**	**-12.5**	**-12.4**	**-12.9**	...	...
General government	3 401	...	...	...	...	...	...	...	...
Debt forgiveness	3 402	...	...	...	...	...	...	...	...
Other capital transfers	3 410	...	...	...	...	...	...	...	...
Other sectors	3 430	-.4	-.9	-11.9	-12.5	-12.4	-12.9	...	...
Migrants' transfers	3 431	-.4	-.9	-11.9	-12.5	-12.4	-12.9	...	...
Debt forgiveness	3 432	...	...	...	...	...	...	...	...
Other capital transfers	3 440	...	...	...	...	...	...	...	...
Nonproduced nonfinancial assets, credit	2 480	...	...	...	...	...	...	...	...
Nonproduced nonfinancial assets, debit	3 480	...	...	...	...	...	...	...	...

Table 2 (Continued). STANDARD PRESENTATION, 1994–2001
(Millions of U.S. dollars)

	Code	1994	1995	1996	1997	1998	1999	2000	2001
FINANCIAL ACCOUNT	4 995 . .	**–94.1**	**–240.4**	**–468.3**	**–629.5**	**–246.6**	**–546.2**	**. . .**	**. . .**
A. DIRECT INVESTMENT	4 500 . .	–23.6	29.5	72.2	96.0	91.8	35.2	. . .	. . .
Direct investment abroad	4 505 . .	**–9.5**	**–40.9**	**1.1**	**–4.1**	**–3.5**	**–1.5**	**. . .**	**. . .**
Equity capital	4 510 . .	–.4	. . .	. . .	. . .	. . .	. . .	. . .	. . .
Claims on affiliated enterprises	4 515 . .	. . .	. . .	. . .	. . .	. . .	. . .	. . .	. . .
Liabilities to affiliated enterprises	4 520 . .	. . .	. . .	. . .	. . .	. . .	. . .	. . .	. . .
Reinvested earnings	4 525 . .	–9.1	–40.9	1.4	.2	–6.3	–5.3	. . .	. . .
Other capital	4 530 . .	. . .	. . .	–.4	–4.3	2.8	3.7	. . .	. . .
Claims on affiliated enterprises	4 535 . .	. . .	. . .	–.4	–4.3	2.8	3.7	. . .	. . .
Liabilities to affiliated enterprises	4 540 . .	. . .	. . .	. . .	. . .	. . .	. . .	. . .	. . .
Direct investment in Botswana	4 555 . .	**–14.2**	**70.4**	**71.2**	**100.1**	**95.3**	**36.7**	**. . .**	**. . .**
Equity capital	4 560 . .	12.2	18.4	6.2	11.0	24.1	20.5	. . .	. . .
Claims on direct investors	4 565 . .	. . .	. . .	. . .	. . .	. . .	. . .	. . .	. . .
Liabilities to direct investors	4 570 . .	. . .	. . .	6.2	11.0	24.1	20.5	. . .	. . .
Reinvested earnings	4 575 . .	–68.8	48.0	37.5	45.8	43.8	–12.4	. . .	. . .
Other capital	4 580 . .	42.5	4.0	27.5	43.3	27.4	28.6	. . .	. . .
Claims on direct investors	4 585 . .	. . .	. . .	. . .	. . .	. . .	. . .	. . .	. . .
Liabilities to direct investors	4 590 . .	. . .	. . .	27.5	43.3	27.4	28.6	. . .	. . .
B. PORTFOLIO INVESTMENT	4 600 . .	–.1	–30.7	–6.6	–17.7	–56.9	–30.3	. . .	. . .
Assets	4 602 . .	**. . .**	**–36.2**	**–35.5**	**–28.5**	**–42.8**	**–22.8**	**. . .**	**. . .**
Equity securities	4 610 . .	. . .	–30.8	–26.7	–33.1	–16.9	6.5	. . .	. . .
Monetary authorities	4 611 . .	. . .	. . .	. . .	. . .	. . .	. . .	. . .	. . .
General government	4 612 . .	. . .	. . .	. . .	. . .	. . .	. . .	. . .	. . .
Banks	4 613 . .	. . .	. . .	. . .	. . .	. . .	. . .	. . .	. . .
Other sectors	4 614 . .	. . .	–30.8	–26.7	–33.1	–16.9	6.5	. . .	. . .
Debt securities	4 619 . .	. . .	–5.4	–8.9	4.7	–25.9	–29.3	. . .	. . .
Bonds and notes	4 620 . .	. . .	–5.4	–8.9	.2	–15.6	–22.9	. . .	. . .
Monetary authorities	4 621 . .	. . .	. . .	. . .	. . .	. . .	. . .	. . .	. . .
General government	4 622 . .	. . .	. . .	. . .	. . .	. . .	. . .	. . .	. . .
Banks	4 623 . .	. . .	. . .	. . .	. . .	. . .	. . .	. . .	. . .
Other sectors	4 624 . .	. . .	–5.4	–8.9	.2	–15.6	–22.9	. . .	. . .
Money market instruments	4 630 . .	. . .	. . .	. . .	4.4	–10.3	–6.5	. . .	. . .
Monetary authorities	4 631 . .	. . .	. . .	. . .	. . .	. . .	. . .	. . .	. . .
General government	4 632 . .	. . .	. . .	. . .	. . .	. . .	. . .	. . .	. . .
Banks	4 633 . .	. . .	. . .	. . .	4.4	. . .	. . .	. . .	. . .
Other sectors	4 634 . .	. . .	. . .	. . .	. . .	–10.3	–6.5	. . .	. . .
Liabilities	4 652 . .	**–.1**	**5.5**	**28.9**	**10.8**	**–14.1**	**–7.5**	**. . .**	**. . .**
Equity securities	4 660 . .	. . .	5.5	28.7	10.8	–14.1	–7.5	. . .	. . .
Banks	4 663 . .	. . .	. . .	. . .	.1	. . .	. . .	. . .	. . .
Other sectors	4 664 . .	. . .	5.5	28.7	10.7	–14.1	–7.5	. . .	. . .
Debt securities	4 669 . .	–.1	. . .	.2	. . .	. . .	. . .	. . .	. . .
Bonds and notes	4 670 . .	. . .	. . .	.2	. . .	. . .	. . .	. . .	. . .
Monetary authorities	4 671 . .	. . .	. . .	. . .	. . .	. . .	. . .	. . .	. . .
General government	4 672 . .	. . .	. . .	. . .	. . .	. . .	. . .	. . .	. . .
Banks	4 673 . .	. . .	. . .	. . .	. . .	. . .	. . .	. . .	. . .
Other sectors	4 674 . .	. . .	. . .	.2	. . .	. . .	. . .	. . .	. . .
Money market instruments	4 680 . .	–.1	. . .	. . .	. . .	. . .	. . .	. . .	. . .
Monetary authorities	4 681 . .	. . .	. . .	. . .	. . .	. . .	. . .	. . .	. . .
General government	4 682 . .	. . .	. . .	. . .	. . .	. . .	. . .	. . .	. . .
Banks	4 683 . .	. . .	. . .	. . .	. . .	. . .	. . .	. . .	. . .
Other sectors	4 684 . .	. . .	. . .	. . .	. . .	. . .	. . .	. . .	. . .
C. FINANCIAL DERIVATIVES	4 910 . .	. . .	.1	2.1	–15.4	5.2	–4.6	. . .	. . .
Monetary authorities	4 911 . .	. . .	. . .	. . .	. . .	. . .	. . .	. . .	. . .
General government	4 912 . .	. . .	. . .	. . .	. . .	. . .	. . .	. . .	. . .
Banks	4 913 . .	. . .	–.2	2.1	–15.4	5.2	–4.6	. . .	. . .
Other sectors	4 914 . .	. . .	.3	. . .	. . .	. . .	. . .	. . .	. . .
Assets	4 900 . .	**. . .**	**–.2**	**. . .**	**–15.4**	**5.2**	**–4.6**	**. . .**	**. . .**
Monetary authorities	4 901 . .	. . .	. . .	. . .	. . .	. . .	. . .	. . .	. . .
General government	4 902 . .	. . .	. . .	. . .	. . .	. . .	. . .	. . .	. . .
Banks	4 903 . .	. . .	–.2	. . .	–15.4	5.2	–4.6	. . .	. . .
Other sectors	4 904 . .	. . .	. . .	. . .	. . .	. . .	. . .	. . .	. . .
Liabilities	4 905 . .	**. . .**	**.3**	**2.1**	**. . .**	**. . .**	**. . .**	**. . .**	**. . .**
Monetary authorities	4 906 . .	. . .	. . .	. . .	. . .	. . .	. . .	. . .	. . .
General government	4 907 . .	. . .	. . .	. . .	. . .	. . .	. . .	. . .	. . .
Banks	4 908 . .	. . .	. . .	2.1	. . .	. . .	. . .	. . .	. . .
Other sectors	4 909 . .	. . .	.3	. . .	. . .	. . .	. . .	. . .	. . .

Table 2 (Concluded). STANDARD PRESENTATION, 1994–2001
(Millions of U.S. dollars)

	Code	1994	1995	1996	1997	1998	1999	2000	2001
D. OTHER INVESTMENT	4 700	64.8	–32.8	–25.3	–57.2	–242.6	–175.4	...	...
Assets	4 703	**15.8**	**–88.7**	**–95.6**	**–166.5**	**–310.8**	**–206.1**	...	...
Trade credits	4 706	–11.2	–40.0	–8.1	–8.7	–29.4	–2.3	...	...
General government	4 707	...	...	...	...	...	...	...	...
of which: Short-term	4 709	...	...	...	...	...	...	...	...
Other sectors	4 710	–11.2	–40.0	–8.1	–8.7	–29.4	–2.3	...	...
of which: Short-term	4 712	*–11.1*	*–39.8*	*–8.1*	*–8.7*	*–29.4*	*–2.3*	...	...
Loans	4 714	–1.2	–.1	.1	...	...	–2.2	...	...
Monetary authorities	4 715	...	...	...	...	...	...	...	...
of which: Short-term	4 718	...	...	...	...	...	...	...	...
General government	4 719	...	...	...	...	...	...	...	...
of which: Short-term	4 721	...	...	...	...	...	...	...	...
Banks	4 722	...	...	...	...	...	...	...	...
of which: Short-term	4 724	...	...	...	...	...	...	...	...
Other sectors	4 725	–1.2	–.1	.1	...	...	–2.2	...	...
of which: Short-term	4 727	...	...	*.1*	...	...	*–2.2*	...	...
Currency and deposits	4 730	.4	2.2	–61.4	–79.1	–179.2	–183.9	...	...
Monetary authorities	4 731	...	...	...	...	...	...	...	...
General government	4 732	...	...	...	...	...	...	...	...
Banks	4 733	.4	–8.7	–38.6	–76.9	–139.7	–154.7	...	...
Other sectors	4 734	...	10.9	–22.8	–2.2	–39.5	–29.1	...	...
Other assets	4 736	27.8	–50.9	–26.3	–78.8	–102.2	–17.8	...	...
Monetary authorities	4 737	...	...	...	...	...	...	...	...
of which: Short-term	4 739	...	...	...	...	...	...	...	...
General government	4 740	19.7	–46.1	–28.7	–78.0	–101.1	–17.8	...	...
of which: Short-term	4 742	...	...	...	...	...	...	...	...
Banks	4 743	...	...	3.4	...	...	...	...	...
of which: Short-term	4 745	...	...	*3.4*	...	...	...	...	...
Other sectors	4 746	8.1	–4.8	–1.0	–.7	–1.1	...	...	...
of which: Short-term	4 748	*6.9*	*–1.9*	*–.4*	*–.7*	*–1.1*	...	...	...
Liabilities	4 753	**49.0**	**55.9**	**70.3**	**109.3**	**68.2**	**30.7**	...	...
Trade credits	4 756	18.8	40.0	41.5	34.5	7.5	22.1	...	...
General government	4 757	...	...	...	...	...	...	...	...
of which: Short-term	4 759	...	...	...	...	...	...	...	...
Other sectors	4 760	18.8	40.0	41.5	34.5	7.5	22.1	...	...
of which: Short-term	4 762	*18.0*	*40.0*	*40.6*	*34.5*	*7.5*	*22.1*	...	...
Loans	4 764	71.2	–34.8	–7.3	49.6	40.6	–14.5	...	...
Monetary authorities	4 765	...	...	...	...	...	...	...	...
of which: Use of Fund credit and loans from the Fund	4 766	...	...	...	...	...	...	...	...
of which: Short-term	4 768	...	...	...	...	...	...	...	...
General government	4 769	6.5	–12.3	–19.6	51.3	22.2	–16.1	...	...
of which: Short-term	4 771	...	...	...	...	...	...	...	...
Banks	4 772	...	...	...	...	...	...	...	...
of which: Short-term	4 774	...	...	...	...	...	...	...	...
Other sectors	4 775	64.7	–22.5	12.3	–1.7	18.4	1.6	...	...
of which: Short-term	4 777	...	*–18.7*	*–.7*	*8.3*	*–9.0*	*–.2*	...	...
Currency and deposits	4 780	–2.8	–2.5	17.8	–3.4	–3.5	1.4	...	...
Monetary authorities	4 781	...	...	...	...	...	...	...	...
General government	4 782	...	...	...	...	...	...	...	...
Banks	4 783	–2.8	–2.5	17.8	–3.4	–3.5	1.4	...	...
Other sectors	4 784	...	...	...	...	...	...	...	...
Other liabilities	4 786	–38.2	53.2	18.3	28.7	23.6	21.7	...	...
Monetary authorities	4 787	...	...	...	...	...	...	...	...
of which: Short-term	4 789	...	...	...	...	...	...	...	...
General government	4 790	...	...	...	...	...	...	...	...
of which: Short-term	4 792	...	...	...	...	...	...	...	...
Banks	4 793	...	...	...	...	...	...	...	...
of which: Short-term	4 795	...	...	...	...	...	...	...	...
Other sectors	4 796	–38.2	53.2	18.3	28.7	23.6	21.7	...	...
of which: Short-term	4 798	*–37.4*	*15.1*	*18.3*	*28.7*	*21.6*	*19.9*	...	...
E. RESERVE ASSETS	4 802	–135.2	–206.6	–510.7	–635.1	–44.2	–371.0	...	...
Monetary gold	4 812	...	...	...	...	...	...	...	...
Special drawing rights	4 811	–2.0	–2.5	–2.4	–2.3	–2.8	6.0	...	...
Reserve position in the Fund	4 810	.4	–4.4	–.9	2.5	–12.7	6.7	...	...
Foreign exchange	4 803	–529.0	–451.3	–507.4	–635.3	–28.7	–383.7	...	...
Other claims	4 813	395.4	251.7	...	...	...	...	...	...
NET ERRORS AND OMISSIONS	4 998	**–136.7**	**–73.6**	**–32.9**	**–108.9**	**44.6**	**8.7**	...	...

Part 3 of the *Yearbook* contains descriptions of the methodologies, compilation practices, and sources used to compile these data.

Table 3. INTERNATIONAL INVESTMENT POSITION (End–period stocks), 1994–2001

(Millions of U.S. dollars)

	Code	1994	1995	1996	1997	1998	1999	2000	2001
ASSETS	8 995 C.	5,084.0	5,643.9	6,001.0	6,510.5	6,855.1	7,356.3	...	...
Direct investment abroad	8 505 . .	**484.5**	**650.1**	**576.7**	**404.5**	**257.5**	**596.9**	**...**	**...**
Equity capital and reinvested earnings	8 506 . .	481.5	647.1	576.7	398.8	256.6	583.6	...	...
Claims on affiliated enterprises	8 507 . .	481.5	647.1	576.7	398.8	256.6	583.6	...	...
Liabilities to affiliated enterprises	8 508 . .	...	...	...	...	...	...	...	...
Other capital	8 530 . .	3.1	3.0	...	5.6	.9	13.3	...	...
Claims on affiliated enterprises	8 535 . .	...	...	...	...	...	...	...	...
Liabilities to affiliated enterprises	8 540 . .	...	...	...	...	...	...	...	...
Portfolio investment	8 602 . .	**26.9**	**61.5**	**139.1**	**132.2**	**214.6**	**148.2**	**...**	**...**
Equity securities	8 610 . .	16.1	45.8	105.8	81.7	73.6	120.2	...	...
Monetary authorities	8 611 . .	...	...	...	...	...	...	...	...
General government	8 612 . .	...	...	...	...	...	...	...	...
Banks	8 613 . .	...	...	...	...	...	...	...	...
Other sectors	8 614 . .	16.1	45.8	105.8	81.7	73.6	120.2	...	...
Debt securities	8 619 . .	10.9	15.8	33.3	50.5	141.0	28.0	...	...
Bonds and notes	8 620 . .	10.9	15.8	33.3	50.5	125.1	28.0	...	...
Monetary authorities	8 621 . .	...	...	...	...	...	...	...	...
General government	8 622 . .	...	...	...	...	...	...	...	...
Banks	8 623 . .	...	...	...	...	...	...	...	...
Other sectors	8 624 . .	10.9	15.8	33.3	50.5	125.1	28.0	...	...
Money market instruments	8 630 . .	...	...	...	...	15.9	...	...	...
Monetary authorities	8 631 . .	...	...	...	...	...	...	...	...
General government	8 632 . .	...	...	...	...	...	...	...	...
Banks	8 633 . .	...	...	...	...	...	...	...	...
Other sectors	8 634 . .	...	...	...	...	15.9	...	...	...
Financial derivatives	8 900 . .	**...**	**.2**	**...**	**17.1**	**9.6**	**...**	**...**	**...**
Monetary authorities	8 901 . .	...	...	...	...	...	...	...	...
General government	8 902 . .	...	...	...	...	...	...	...	...
Banks	8 903 . .	...	...	...	17.1	9.6	...	...	...
Other sectors	8 904 . .	...	.2	...	...	...	...	...	...
Other investment	8 703 . .	**171.3**	**239.1**	**253.1**	**280.3**	**433.0**	**382.4**	**...**	**...**
Trade credits	8 706 . .	38.7	76.5	95.7	46.8	62.0	29.1	...	...
General government	8 707 . .	...	...	...	...	...	...	...	...
of which: Short-term	8 709 . .	...	...	...	...	...	...	...	...
Other sectors	8 710 . .	38.7	76.5	95.7	46.8	62.0	29.1	...	...
of which: Short-term	8 712 . .	*38.4*	*76.2*	*95.7*	*46.8*	*62.0*	*29.1*	...	...
Loans	8 714 . .	3.1	3.0	.1	.1	...	...	...	...
Monetary authorities	8 715 . .	...	...	...	...	...	...	...	...
of which: Short-term	8 718 . .	...	...	...	...	...	...	...	...
General government	8 719 . .	...	...	...	...	...	...	...	...
of which: Short-term	8 721 . .	...	...	...	...	...	...	...	...
Banks	8 722 . .	...	...	...	...	...	...	...	...
of which: Short-term	8 724 . .	...	...	...	...	...	...	...	...
Other sectors	8 725 . .	3.1	3.0	.1	.1	...	...	...	...
of which: Short-term	8 727 . .	*3.1*	*3.0*	*.1*	*.1*	...	...	...	...
Currency and deposits	8 730 . .	80.7	75.6	135.1	232.0	367.5	353.1	...	...
Monetary authorities	8 731 . .	...	...	...	...	...	...	...	...
General government	8 732 . .	...	...	...	...	...	...	...	...
Banks	8 733 . .	63.3	69.5	91.5	186.2	291.5	289.9	...	...
Other sectors	8 734 . .	17.4	6.1	43.7	45.8	76.0	63.2	...	...
Other assets	8 736 . .	48.8	84.0	22.3	1.5	3.5	.2	...	...
Monetary authorities	8 737 . .	...	...	...	...	...	...	...	...
of which: Short-term	8 739 . .	...	...	...	...	...	...	...	...
General government	8 740 . .	...	...	...	...	...	...	...	...
of which: Short-term	8 742 . .	...	...	...	...	...	...	...	...
Banks	8 743 . .	...	...	8.4	...	...	...	...	...
of which: Short-term	8 745 . .	...	...	*8.4*	...	...	...	...	...
Other sectors	8 746 . .	48.8	84.0	13.9	1.5	3.5	.2	...	...
of which: Short-term	8 748 . .	*39.5*	*31.6*	*7.2*	*1.5*	*3.5*	*.2*	...	...
Reserve assets	8 802 . .	**4,401.3**	**4,693.0**	**5,032.1**	**5,676.5**	**5,940.3**	**6,228.8**	**...**	**...**
Monetary gold	8 812 . .	...	...	...	...	...	...	...	...
Special drawing rights	8 811 . .	37.1	40.2	41.3	41.0	45.6	38.5	38.9	...
Reserve position in the Fund	8 810 . .	23.9	28.7	28.6	24.5	38.9	31.0	23.1	...
Foreign exchange	8 803 . .	4,340.4	4,624.1	4,962.2	5,611.0	5,855.8	6,159.3	...	...
Other claims	8 813 . .	...	...	...	...	...	...	...	...

Table 3 (Concluded). INTERNATIONAL INVESTMENT POSITION (End–period stocks), 1994–2001
(Millions of U.S. dollars)

	Code	1994	1995	1996	1997	1998	1999	2000	2001
LIABILITIES	8 995 D.	2,005.3	1,995.1	1,941.9	2,151.9	2,248.7	2,514.8	...	...
Direct investment in Botswana	8 555 . .	**998.5**	**1,126.4**	**1,058.1**	**1,172.9**	**1,294.8**	**1,387.3**	...	...
Equity capital and reinvested earnings	8 556 . .	277.4	441.7	389.3	421.5	531.5	644.9	...	...
Claims on direct investors	8 557 . .	...	...	...	...	...	...	...	...
Liabilities to direct investors	8 558 . .	277.4	441.7	389.3	421.5	531.5	644.9	...	...
Other capital	8 580 . .	721.0	684.7	668.8	751.5	763.3	742.3	...	...
Claims on direct investors	8 585 . .	...	...	...	...	...	...	...	...
Liabilities to direct investors	8 590 . .	721.0	684.7	668.8	751.5	763.3	742.3	...	...
Portfolio investment	8 652 . .	**10.9**	**15.9**	**50.4**	**60.5**	**34.2**	**24.0**	...	...
Equity securities	8 660 . .	10.9	15.9	50.4	60.0	33.4	22.7	...	...
Banks	8 663 . .	...	...	...	2.0	.1	...	...	...
Other sectors	8 664 . .	10.9	15.9	50.4	58.0	33.3	22.7	...	...
Debt securities	8 669 . .	...	...	...	.5	.8	1.3	...	...
Bonds and notes	8 670 . .	...	...	...	...	.8	1.3	...	...
Monetary authorities	8 671 . .	...	...	...	...	...	...	...	...
General government	8 672 . .	...	...	...	...	...	...	...	...
Banks	8 673 . .	...	...	...	...	...	...	...	...
Other sectors	8 674 . .	...	...	...	...	.8	1.3	...	...
Money market instruments	8 680 . .	...	...	...	.5	...	...	...	...
Monetary authorities	8 681 . .	...	...	...	...	...	...	...	...
General government	8 682 . .	...	...	...	...	...	...	...	...
Banks	8 683 . .	...	...	...	...	...	...	...	...
Other sectors	8 684 . .	...	...	...	.5	...	...	...	...
Financial derivatives	8 905 . .	**...**	**.2**	**1.9**	**...**	**...**	**...**	...	...
Monetary authorities	8 906 . .	...	...	...	...	...	...	...	...
General government	8 907 . .	...	...	...	...	...	...	...	...
Banks	8 908 . .	...	...	1.9	...	...	...	...	...
Other sectors	8 909 . .	...	.2	...	...	...	...	...	...
Other investment	8 753 . .	**996.0**	**852.6**	**831.5**	**918.5**	**919.7**	**1,103.5**	...	...
Trade credits	8 756 . .	49.8	87.2	182.4	132.7	122.2	62.5	...	...
General government	8 757 . .	...	...	...	...	...	...	...	...
of which: Short-term	8 759 . .	...	...	...	...	...	...	...	...
Other sectors	8 760 . .	49.8	87.2	182.4	132.7	122.2	62.5	...	...
of which: Short-term	8 762 . .	*49.5*	*86.9*	*179.5*	*132.7*	*122.2*	*62.5*	...	...
Loans	8 764 . .	729.0	564.3	496.4	610.2	624.8	851.2	...	...
Monetary authorities	8 765 . .	...	...	...	...	...	...	...	...
of which: Use of Fund credit and loans from the Fund	8 766 . .	...	...	...	...	...	...	...	...
of which: Short-term	8 768 . .	...	...	...	...	...	...	...	...
General government	8 769 . .	496.9	495.8	387.9	483.1	482.6	523.6	...	...
of which: Short-term	8 771 . .	...	...	...	...	...	...	...	...
Banks	8 772 . .	...	...	...	...	...	...	...	...
of which: Short-term	8 774 . .	...	...	...	...	...	...	...	...
Other sectors	8 775 . .	232.2	68.5	108.5	127.0	142.2	327.6	...	...
of which: Short-term	8 777 . .	*37.9*	*18.1*	*15.8*	*46.4*	*2.6*	*6.4*	...	...
Currency and deposits	8 780 . .	38.9	35.1	27.4	23.7	16.8	15.3	...	...
Monetary authorities	8 781 . .	...	...	...	...	...	...	...	...
General government	8 782 . .	...	...	...	...	...	...	...	...
Banks	8 783 . .	38.9	35.1	27.4	23.7	16.8	15.3	...	...
Other sectors	8 784 . .	...	...	...	...	...	...	...	...
Other liabilities	8 786 . .	178.2	166.0	125.3	152.0	156.0	174.6	...	...
Monetary authorities	8 787 . .	...	...	...	...	...	...	...	...
of which: Short-term	8 789 . .	...	...	...	...	...	...	...	...
General government	8 790 . .	...	...	...	...	...	...	...	...
of which: Short-term	8 792 . .	...	...	...	...	...	...	...	...
Banks	8 793 . .	...	...	...	...	...	...	...	...
of which: Short-term	8 795 . .	...	...	...	...	...	...	...	...
Other sectors	8 796 . .	178.2	166.0	125.3	152.0	156.0	174.6	...	...
of which: Short-term	8 798 . .	*84.6*	*125.2*	*105.9*	*123.3*	*143.4*	*165.6*	...	...
NET INTERNATIONAL INVESTMENT POSITION	8 995 . .	**3,078.7**	**3,648.8**	**4,059.1**	**4,358.6**	**4,606.4**	**4,841.5**	...	...
Conversion rates: pula per U.S. dollar (end of period)	0 102 . .	**2.7174**	**2.8217**	**3.6443**	**3.8095**	**4.4583**	**4.6318**	**5.3619**	**6.9832**

Table 1. ANALYTIC PRESENTATION, 1994–2001
(Millions of U.S. dollars)

	Code	1994	1995	1996	1997	1998	1999	2000	2001
A. Current Account[1]	4 993 Z.	**–1,153**	**–18,136**	**–23,248**	**–30,491**	**–33,829**	**–25,400**	**–24,632**	**–23,211**
Goods: exports f.o.b	2 100 . .	44,102	46,506	47,851	53,189	51,136	48,011	55,087	58,224
Goods: imports f.o.b	3 100 . .	–33,241	–49,663	–53,304	–59,841	–57,739	–49,272	–55,783	–55,579
Balance on Goods	4 100 . .	*10,861*	*–3,157*	*–5,453*	*–6,652*	*–6,603*	*–1,261*	*–696*	*2,645*
Services: credit	2 200 . .	4,908	6,135	4,655	5,989	7,631	7,189	9,382	9,323
Services: debit	3 200 . .	–10,254	–13,630	–12,714	–15,298	–16,676	–14,172	–16,956	–17,073
Balance on Goods and Services	4 991 . .	*5,515*	*–10,652*	*–13,512*	*–15,961*	*–15,648*	*–8,244*	*–8,270*	*–5,105*
Income: credit	2 300 . .	2,202	3,457	5,350	5,344	4,914	3,936	3,620	3,279
Income: debit	3 300 . .	–11,293	–14,562	–17,527	–21,688	–24,531	–22,780	–21,504	–23,024
Balance on Goods, Services, and Income	4 992 . .	*–3,576*	*–21,757*	*–25,689*	*–32,305*	*–35,265*	*–27,088*	*–26,154*	*–24,850*
Current transfers: credit	2 379 Z.	2,577	3,861	2,699	2,130	1,795	1,969	1,828	1,934
Current transfers: debit	3 379 . .	–154	–240	–258	–316	–359	–281	–306	–295
B. Capital Account[1]	4 994 Z.	**173**	**352**	**494**	**482**	**375**	**339**	**272**	**–36**
Capital account: credit	2 994 Z.	175	363	507	519	488	361	300	329
Capital account: debit	3 994 . .	–2	–11	–13	–37	–113	–22	–28	–365
Total, Groups A Plus B	4 981 . .	*–980*	*–17,784*	*–22,754*	*–30,009*	*–33,454*	*–25,061*	*–24,360*	*–23,247*
C. Financial Account[1]	4 995 W.	**8,020**	**29,306**	**33,428**	**24,918**	**20,063**	**8,056**	**29,369**	**20,079**
Direct investment abroad	4 505 . .	–1,037	–1,384	467	–1,042	–2,721	–1,690	–2,280	2,259
Direct investment in Brazil	4 555 Z.	3,072	4,859	11,200	19,650	31,913	28,576	32,779	22,636
Portfolio investment assets	4 602 . .	–3,052	–936	–257	–335	–594	258	–1,697	–796
Equity securities	4 610 . .	. . .	–168	–49	–306	–553	–865	–1,954	–1,122
Debt securities	4 619 . .	–3,052	–768	–208	–29	–41	1,123	257	326
Portfolio investment liabilities	4 652 Z.	47,784	10,171	21,089	10,393	19,013	3,542	8,646	873
Equity securities	4 660 . .	7,280	2,775	5,785	5,099	–1,768	2,572	3,075	2,482
Debt securities	4 669 Z.	40,504	7,396	15,304	5,294	20,781	970	5,571	–1,609
Financial derivatives	4 910 . .	. . .	. . .	. . .	. . .	. . .	–87	–197	–471
Financial derivatives assets	4 900 . .	. . .	. . .	. . .	. . .	. . .	642	386	567
Financial derivatives liabilities	4 905 . .	. . .	. . .	. . .	. . .	. . .	–729	–583	–1,038
Other investment assets	4 703 . .	–4,368	–1,783	–3,327	2,251	–5,992	–4,399	–2,992	–6,284
Monetary authorities	4 701 . .	. . .	. . .	–44	–67	–84	1,668	88	471
General government	4 704 . .	. . .	. . .	. . .	2,146	60	–880	192	–1,086
Banks	4 705 . .	–4,077	–228	–4,610	5,133	3,383	–121	1,444	–1,300
Other sectors	4 728 . .	–291	–1,555	1,327	–4,961	–9,351	–5,066	–4,716	–4,369
Other investment liabilities	4 753 W.	–34,379	18,379	4,256	–5,999	–21,556	–18,144	–4,890	1,862
Monetary authorities	4 753 WA	–545	–1,652	–3,773	1,698	–1,704	–6,671	–200	–138
General government	4 753 ZB	–35,609	. . .	. . .	. . .	. . .	934	1,539	–61
Banks	4 753 ZC	–1,439	7,071	6,450	–897	–8,570	–5,059	1,717	–1,569
Other sectors	4 753 ZD	3,214	12,960	1,579	–3,404	–11,282	–7,348	–7,946	3,630
Total, Groups A Through C	4 983 . .	*7,040*	*11,522*	*10,674*	*–5,091*	*–13,391*	*–17,005*	*5,009*	*–3,168*
D. Net Errors and Omissions	4 998 . .	**–442**	**1,447**	**–1,992**	**–3,160**	**–2,911**	**240**	**2,971**	**–250**
Total, Groups A Through D	4 984 . .	*6,598*	*12,969*	*8,682*	*–8,251*	*–16,302*	*–16,765*	*7,980*	*–3,418*
E. Reserves and Related Items	4 802 A.	**–6,598**	**–12,969**	**–8,682**	**8,251**	**16,302**	**16,765**	**–7,980**	**3,418**
Reserve assets	4 802 . .	–7,215	–12,920	–8,326	8,284	6,990	7,783	2,261	–3,311
Use of Fund credit and loans	4 766 . .	–133	–49	–70	–33	4,773	4,059	–6,795	6,729
Exceptional financing	4 920 . .	750	. . .	–286	. . .	4,539	4,924	–3,446	. . .
Conversion rates: reais per U.S. dollar	0 101 . .	**.63931**	**.91767**	**1.00510**	**1.07799**	**1.16052**	**1.81473**	**1.83014**	**2.35771**

[1] Excludes components that have been classified in the categories of Group E.

Table 2. STANDARD PRESENTATION, 1994–2001

(Millions of U.S. dollars)

	Code	1994	1995	1996	1997	1998	1999	2000	2001
CURRENT ACCOUNT	4 993 . .	**–1,153**	**–18,136**	**–23,248**	**–30,491**	**–33,829**	**–25,400**	**–24,632**	**–23,211**
A. GOODS	4 100 . .	10,861	–3,157	–5,453	–6,652	–6,603	–1,261	–696	2,645
Credit	2 100 . .	**44,102**	**46,506**	**47,851**	**53,189**	**51,136**	**48,011**	**55,087**	**58,224**
General merchandise: exports f.o.b.	2 110 . .	43,558	46,506	47,368	52,527	50,701	46,890	53,676	57,223
Goods for processing: exports f.o.b.	2 150 . .	...	...	...	...	...	...	...	...
Repairs on goods	2 160 . .	...	...	105	198	15	...	...	...
Goods procured in ports by carriers	2 170 . .	...	...	378	464	420	773	1,035	776
Nonmonetary gold	2 180 . .	544	...	...	...	...	348	376	225
Debit	3 100 . .	**–33,241**	**–49,663**	**–53,304**	**–59,841**	**–57,739**	**–49,272**	**–55,783**	**–55,579**
General merchandise: imports f.o.b.	3 110 . .	–33,168	–49,663	–53,285	–59,824	–57,687	–49,009	–55,121	–54,920
Goods for processing: imports f.o.b.	3 150 . .	...	...	...	...	...	–263	–472	–595
Repairs on goods	3 160 . .	...	...	–3	–3	–28	...	...	...
Goods procured in ports by carriers	3 170 . .	...	...	–16	–14	–24	...	...	...
Nonmonetary gold	3 180 . .	–73	...	...	...	...	...	–190	–64
B. SERVICES	4 200 . .	–5,346	–7,495	–8,059	–9,309	–9,045	–6,983	–7,574	–7,750
Total credit	2 200 . .	*4,908*	*6,135*	*4,655*	*5,989*	*7,631*	*7,189*	*9,382*	*9,323*
Total debit	3 200 . .	*–10,254*	*–13,630*	*–12,714*	*–15,298*	*–16,676*	*–14,172*	*–16,956*	*–17,073*
Transportation services, credit	2 205 . .	**2,200**	**2,600**	**1,428**	**1,405**	**1,862**	**1,141**	**1,294**	**1,423**
Passenger	2 850 . .	*229*	*113*	*26*	*48*	*81*	*92*	*159*	*114*
Freight	2 851 . .	*1,184*	*1,200*	*516*	*500*	*471*	*367*	*470*	*498*
Other	2 852 . .	*787*	*1,287*	*886*	*857*	*1,310*	*682*	*665*	*811*
Sea transport, passenger	2 207 . .	...	...	–3	–5	–10	...	...	...
Sea transport, freight	2 208 . .	...	...	342	335	309	256	366	328
Sea transport, other	2 209 . .	...	...	13	9	8	647	621	752
Air transport, passenger	2 211 . .	...	...	29	53	91	92	159	114
Air transport, freight	2 212 . .	...	...	–71	–71	–71	84	78	149
Air transport, other	2 213 . .	...	...	1	5	12	35	36	48
Other transport, passenger	2 215 . .	...	...	...	...	...	...	...	...
Other transport, freight	2 216 . .	...	...	245	236	233	27	26	21
Other transport, other	2 217 . .	...	...	872	843	1,290	...	8	11
Transportation services, debit	3 205 . .	**–4,300**	**–5,800**	**–4,151**	**–4,874**	**–5,090**	**–4,213**	**–4,602**	**–4,379**
Passenger	3 850 . .	*–437*	*–591*	*–601*	*–789*	*–634*	*–466*	*–654*	*–566*
Freight	3 851 . .	*–1,485*	*–2,200*	*–1,619*	*–1,895*	*–2,135*	*–1,484*	*–1,801*	*–1,789*
Other	3 852 . .	*–2,378*	*–3,009*	*–1,931*	*–2,190*	*–2,321*	*–2,263*	*–2,147*	*–2,024*
Sea transport, passenger	3 207 . .	...	...	–3	...	–1	...	–2	–6
Sea transport, freight	3 208 . .	...	...	–1,371	–1,603	–1,539	–1,334	–1,660	–1,636
Sea transport, other	3 209 . .	...	...	–698	–698	–741	–1,286	–1,290	–1,252
Air transport, passenger	3 211 . .	...	...	–598	–788	–633	–466	–652	–560
Air transport, freight	3 212 . .	...	...	66	76	72	–91	–71	–83
Air transport, other	3 213 . .	...	...	–14	–156	–180	–977	–857	–772
Other transport, passenger	3 215 . .	...	...	...	–1	...	...	...	...
Other transport, freight	3 216 . .	...	...	–314	–368	–668	–59	–70	–70
Other transport, other	3 217 . .	...	...	–1,219	–1,336	–1,400	...	...	...
Travel, credit	2 236 . .	**944**	**972**	**718**	**977**	**1,317**	**1,626**	**1,811**	**1,732**
Business travel	2 237 . .	...	20	20	22	25	26	31	25
Personal travel	2 240 . .	...	952	698	955	1,292	1,600	1,780	1,707
Travel, debit	3 236 . .	**–2,156**	**–3,391**	**–4,387**	**–5,419**	**–5,385**	**–3,085**	**–3,895**	**–3,198**
Business travel	3 237 . .	...	–154	–164	–185	–202	–164	–206	–194
Personal travel	3 240 . .	...	–3,237	–4,223	–5,234	–5,183	–2,921	–3,689	–3,004
Other services, credit	2 200 BA	**1,764**	**2,563**	**2,509**	**3,607**	**4,452**	**4,422**	**6,277**	**6,168**
Communications	2 245 . .	...	36	227	146	157	29	36	241
Construction	2 249 . .	...	14	...	...	...	16	96	17
Insurance	2 253 . .	152	186	2	–37	...	164	311	180
Financial	2 260 . .	...	827	353	316	323	305	376	316
Computer and information	2 262 . .	...	43	4	6	6	16	32	28
Royalties and licence fees	2 266 . .	19	32	78	97	142	133	126	112
Other business services	2 268 . .	1,502	1,249	1,582	2,449	3,160	3,402	4,701	4,612
Personal, cultural, and recreational	2 287 . .	...	46	61	129	116	41	63	58
Government, n.i.e.	2 291 . .	91	130	202	501	548	316	536	604
Other services, debit	3 200 BA	**–3,798**	**–4,439**	**–4,176**	**–5,005**	**–6,201**	**–6,874**	**–8,459**	**–9,496**
Communications	3 245 . .	...	–53	–91	–84	–230	–15	–30	–213
Construction	3 249 . .	...	–4	...	...	...	...	...	...
Insurance	3 253 . .	–262	–308	56	239	198	–294	–318	–453
Financial	3 260 . .	...	–950	–432	–289	–348	–574	–670	–624
Computer and information	3 262 . .	...	–251	–112	–205	–310	–1,025	–1,146	–1,135
Royalties and licence fees	3 266 . .	–239	–529	–797	–887	–1,075	–1,283	–1,415	–1,245
Other business services	3 268 . .	–2,879	–1,619	–2,005	–2,632	–3,169	–2,493	–3,430	–4,204
Personal, cultural, and recreational	3 287 . .	...	–256	–281	–296	–334	–375	–363	–365
Government, n.i.e.	3 291 . .	–418	–469	–514	–851	–933	–815	–1,087	–1,257

Table 2 (Continued). STANDARD PRESENTATION, 1994–2001

(Millions of U.S. dollars)

	Code		1994	1995	1996	1997	1998	1999	2000	2001
C. INCOME	4 300	. .	–9,091	–11,105	–12,177	–16,344	–19,617	–18,844	–17,884	–19,745
Total credit	2 300	. .	*2,202*	*3,457*	*5,350*	*5,344*	*4,914*	*3,936*	*3,620*	*3,279*
Total debit	3 300	. .	*–11,293*	*–14,562*	*–17,527*	*–21,688*	*–24,531*	*–22,780*	*–21,504*	*–23,024*
Compensation of employees, credit	2 310	. .	**59**	**61**	**193**	**248**	**273**	**311**	**237**	**271**
Compensation of employees, debit	3 310	. .	**–190**	**–218**	**–254**	**–203**	**–177**	**–169**	**–158**	**–176**
Investment income, credit	2 320	. .	**2,143**	**3,396**	**5,157**	**5,096**	**4,641**	**3,625**	**3,383**	**3,008**
Direct investment income	2 330	. .	365	770	1,409	864	421	1,487	998	368
Dividends and distributed branch profits	2 332	. .	365	770	1,409	864	421	1,389	932	265
Reinvested earnings and undistributed branch profits	2 333	. .	. . .	. . .	. . .	. . .	. . .	. . .	. . .	. . .
Income on debt (interest)	2 334	. .	. . .	. . .	. . .	. . .	. . .	98	66	103
Portfolio investment income	2 339	. .	35	153	158	211	325	772	859	1,464
Income on equity	2 340	. .	35	141	59	46	68	11	4	. . .
Income on bonds and notes	2 350	. .	. . .	12	. . .	. . .	. . .	680	820	1,463
Income on money market instruments	2 360	. .	. . .	. . .	99	165	257	81	35	1
Other investment income	2 370	. .	1,743	2,473	3,590	4,021	3,895	1,366	1,526	1,176
Investment income, debit	3 320	. .	**–11,103**	**–14,344**	**–17,273**	**–21,485**	**–24,354**	**–22,611**	**–21,346**	**–22,848**
Direct investment income	3 330	. .	–2,315	–2,814	–3,975	–6,070	–6,456	–5,150	–4,237	–5,007
Dividends and distributed branch profits	3 332	. .	–2,235	–2,614	–2,695	–4,718	–5,076	–4,221	–3,104	–3,703
Reinvested earnings and undistributed branch profits	3 333	. .	–80	–200	–532	–151	–124	. . .	. . .	. . .
Income on debt (interest)	3 334	. .	. . .	. . .	–748	–1,201	–1,256	–929	–1,133	–1,304
Portfolio investment income	3 339	. .	–648	–4,896	–5,522	–7,864	–9,641	–8,480	–9,387	–11,084
Income on equity	3 340	. .	–648	–887	–1,146	–1,790	–2,593	–1,292	–1,148	–1,524
Income on bonds and notes	3 350	. .	. . .	–4,009	–4,239	–5,657	–6,330	–7,188	–8,239	–9,560
Income on money market instruments	3 360	. .	. . .	. . .	–137	–417	–718	. . .	. . .	. . .
Other investment income	3 370	. .	–8,140	–6,634	–7,776	–7,551	–8,257	–8,981	–7,722	–6,757
D. CURRENT TRANSFERS	4 379	. .	2,423	3,621	2,441	1,814	1,436	1,688	1,522	1,639
Credit	2 379	. .	**2,577**	**3,861**	**2,699**	**2,130**	**1,795**	**1,969**	**1,828**	**1,934**
General government	2 380	. .	76	37	46	47	82	43	42	73
Other sectors	2 390	. .	2,501	3,824	2,653	2,083	1,713	1,926	1,786	1,861
Workers' remittances	2 391	. .	1,834	2,891	1,866	1,324	963	1,190	1,113	1,179
Other current transfers	2 392	. .	667	933	787	759	750	736	673	682
Debit	3 379	. .	**–154**	**–240**	**–258**	**–316**	**–359**	**–281**	**–306**	**–295**
General government	3 380	. .	–44	–79	–78	–74	–109	–81	–73	–64
Other sectors	3 390	. .	–110	–161	–180	–242	–250	–200	–233	–231
Workers' remittances	3 391	. .	–60	–118	–142	–158	–182	–139	–180	–169
Other current transfers	3 392	. .	–50	–43	–38	–84	–68	–61	–53	–62
CAPITAL AND FINANCIAL ACCOUNT	4 996	. .	**1,595**	**16,689**	**25,240**	**33,651**	**36,740**	**25,160**	**21,661**	**23,461**
CAPITAL ACCOUNT	4 994	. .	**173**	**352**	**494**	**482**	**375**	**339**	**272**	**–36**
Total credit	2 994	. .	*175*	*363*	*507*	*519*	*488*	*361*	*300*	*329*
Total debit	3 994	. .	*–2*	*–11*	*–13*	*–37*	*–113*	*–22*	*–28*	*–365*
Capital transfers, credit	2 400	. .	**175**	**363**	**468**	**410**	**406**	**361**	**300**	**327**
General government	2 401	. .	. . .	. . .	. . .	. . .	. . .	. . .	. . .	. . .
Debt forgiveness	2 402	. .	. . .	. . .	. . .	. . .	. . .	. . .	. . .	. . .
Other capital transfers	2 410	. .	. . .	. . .	. . .	. . .	. . .	. . .	. . .	. . .
Other sectors	2 430	. .	175	363	468	410	406	361	300	327
Migrants' transfers	2 431	. .	175	363	468	410	406	361	300	327
Debt forgiveness	2 432	. .	. . .	. . .	. . .	. . .	. . .	. . .	. . .	. . .
Other capital transfers	2 440	. .	. . .	. . .	. . .	. . .	. . .	. . .	. . .	. . .
Capital transfers, debit	3 400	. .	**–2**	**–11**	**–13**	**–14**	**–85**	**–22**	**–28**	**–365**
General government	3 401	. .	. . .	. . .	. . .	. . .	. . .	. . .	. . .	. . .
Debt forgiveness	3 402	. .	. . .	. . .	. . .	. . .	. . .	. . .	. . .	. . .
Other capital transfers	3 410	. .	. . .	. . .	. . .	. . .	. . .	. . .	. . .	. . .
Other sectors	3 430	. .	–2	–11	–13	–14	–85	–22	–28	–365
Migrants' transfers	3 431	. .	–2	–11	–13	–14	–85	–22	–28	–365
Debt forgiveness	3 432	. .	. . .	. . .	. . .	. . .	. . .	. . .	. . .	. . .
Other capital transfers	3 440	. .	. . .	. . .	. . .	. . .	. . .	. . .	. . .	. . .
Nonproduced nonfinancial assets, credit	2 480	. .	**. . .**	**. . .**	**39**	**109**	**82**	**. . .**	**. . .**	**2**
Nonproduced nonfinancial assets, debit	3 480	. .	**. . .**	**. . .**	**. . .**	**–23**	**–28**	**. . .**	**. . .**	**. . .**

Table 2 (Continued). STANDARD PRESENTATION, 1994–2001

(Millions of U.S. dollars)

	Code	1994	1995	1996	1997	1998	1999	2000	2001
FINANCIAL ACCOUNT	4 995	**1,422**	**16,337**	**24,746**	**33,169**	**36,365**	**24,821**	**21,389**	**23,497**
A. DIRECT INVESTMENT	4 500	2,035	3,475	11,667	18,608	29,192	26,886	30,499	24,895
Direct investment abroad	4 505	**–1,037**	**–1,384**	**467**	**–1,042**	**–2,721**	**–1,690**	**–2,280**	**2,259**
Equity capital	4 510	–1,037	–1,384	467	–1,042	–2,721	–1,110	–1,754	1,753
Claims on affiliated enterprises	4 515	–1,037	–1,384	–885	–1,042	–2,721	–1,110	–1,754	1,753
Liabilities to affiliated enterprises	4 520	. . .	. . .	1,352	. . .	. . .	. . .	. . .	. . .
Reinvested earnings	4 525	. . .	. . .	. . .	. . .	. . .	. . .	. . .	. . .
Other capital	4 530	. . .	. . .	. . .	. . .	. . .	–580	–526	506
Claims on affiliated enterprises	4 535	. . .	. . .	. . .	. . .	. . .	–385	–546	–267
Liabilities to affiliated enterprises	4 540	. . .	. . .	. . .	. . .	. . .	–195	20	773
Direct investment in Brazil	4 555	**3,072**	**4,859**	**11,200**	**19,650**	**31,913**	**28,576**	**32,779**	**22,636**
Equity capital	4 560	1,888	3,928	9,445	16,932	26,009	29,982	30,016	18,944
Claims on direct investors	4 565	. . .	. . .	. . .	. . .	. . .	. . .	. . .	. . .
Liabilities to direct investors	4 570	1,888	3,928	9,445	16,932	26,009	29,982	30,016	18,944
Reinvested earnings	4 575	80	200	532	151	124	. . .	. . .	. . .
Other capital	4 580	1,104	731	1,223	2,567	5,780	–1,406	2,763	3,692
Claims on direct investors	4 585	. . .	. . .	. . .	. . .	. . .	–3	–196	4
Liabilities to direct investors	4 590	1,104	731	1,223	2,567	5,780	–1,403	2,959	3,688
B. PORTFOLIO INVESTMENT	4 600	51,135	9,745	20,832	10,058	18,419	3,800	6,949	77
Assets	4 602	**–3,052**	**–936**	**–257**	**–335**	**–594**	**258**	**–1,697**	**–796**
Equity securities	4 610	. . .	–168	–49	–306	–553	–865	–1,954	–1,122
Monetary authorities	4 611	. . .	. . .	. . .	. . .	. . .	. . .	. . .	. . .
General government	4 612	. . .	. . .	. . .	. . .	. . .	. . .	. . .	. . .
Banks	4 613	. . .	. . .	. . .	. . .	. . .	–770	–2,892	–605
Other sectors	4 614	. . .	–168	–49	–306	–553	–95	938	–517
Debt securities	4 619	–3,052	–768	–208	–29	–41	1,123	257	326
Bonds and notes	4 620	–3,052	–768	–208	–29	–168	1,123	257	326
Monetary authorities	4 621	. . .	. . .	. . .	. . .	. . .	. . .	. . .	. . .
General government	4 622	–3,052	–768	. . .	. . .	. . .	431	245	353
Banks	4 623	. . .	. . .	. . .	. . .	. . .	602	27	75
Other sectors	4 624	. . .	. . .	–208	–29	–168	90	–15	–102
Money market instruments	4 630	. . .	. . .	. . .	. . .	127	. . .	. . .	. . .
Monetary authorities	4 631	. . .	. . .	. . .	. . .	. . .	. . .	. . .	. . .
General government	4 632	. . .	. . .	. . .	. . .	. . .	. . .	. . .	. . .
Banks	4 633	. . .	. . .	. . .	. . .	. . .	. . .	. . .	. . .
Other sectors	4 634	. . .	. . .	. . .	. . .	127	. . .	. . .	. . .
Liabilities	4 652	**54,187**	**10,681**	**21,089**	**10,393**	**19,013**	**3,542**	**8,646**	**873**
Equity securities	4 660	7,280	2,775	5,785	5,099	–1,768	2,572	3,075	2,482
Banks	4 663	. . .	. . .	. . .	. . .	. . .	1,066	517	1,410
Other sectors	4 664	. . .	2,775	5,785	5,099	–1,768	1,506	2,558	1,072
Debt securities	4 669	46,907	7,906	15,304	5,294	20,781	970	5,571	–1,609
Bonds and notes	4 670	46,907	8,227	14,856	5,735	20,541	689	5,334	–2,206
Monetary authorities	4 671	. . .	199	. . .	. . .	. . .	. . .	–16	–6
General government	4 672	42,612	311	. . .	. . .	. . .	3,172	3,809	3,397
Banks	4 673	. . .	. . .	. . .	. . .	. . .	–5,126	–104	–4,473
Other sectors	4 674	4,295	7,717	14,856	5,735	20,541	2,643	1,645	–1,124
Money market instruments	4 680	. . .	–321	448	–441	240	281	237	597
Monetary authorities	4 681	. . .	. . .	44	–110	7	. . .	–11	–4
General government	4 682	. . .	. . .	. . .	. . .	. . .	. . .	–54	–21
Banks	4 683	. . .	. . .	. . .	. . .	. . .	436	153	555
Other sectors	4 684	. . .	–321	404	–331	233	–155	149	67
C. FINANCIAL DERIVATIVES	4 910	. . .	. . .	. . .	. . .	. . .	–87	–197	–471
Monetary authorities	4 911	. . .	. . .	. . .	. . .	. . .	. . .	. . .	. . .
General government	4 912	. . .	. . .	. . .	. . .	. . .	. . .	. . .	. . .
Banks	4 913	. . .	. . .	. . .	. . .	. . .	–13	–194	–440
Other sectors	4 914	. . .	. . .	. . .	. . .	. . .	–74	–3	–31
Assets	4 900	**. . .**	**. . .**	**. . .**	**. . .**	**. . .**	**642**	**386**	**567**
Monetary authorities	4 901	. . .	. . .	. . .	. . .	. . .	. . .	. . .	. . .
General government	4 902	. . .	. . .	. . .	. . .	. . .	. . .	. . .	. . .
Banks	4 903	. . .	. . .	. . .	. . .	. . .	524	296	459
Other sectors	4 904	. . .	. . .	. . .	. . .	. . .	118	90	108
Liabilities	4 905	**. . .**	**. . .**	**. . .**	**. . .**	**. . .**	**–729**	**–583**	**–1,038**
Monetary authorities	4 906	. . .	. . .	. . .	. . .	. . .	. . .	. . .	. . .
General government	4 907	. . .	. . .	. . .	. . .	. . .	. . .	. . .	. . .
Banks	4 908	. . .	. . .	. . .	. . .	. . .	–537	–490	–899
Other sectors	4 909	. . .	. . .	. . .	. . .	. . .	–192	–93	–139

Table 2 (Concluded). STANDARD PRESENTATION, 1994–2001
(Millions of U.S. dollars)

	Code	1994	1995	1996	1997	1998	1999	2000	2001
D. OTHER INVESTMENT	4 700 . .	–44,533	16,037	573	–3,781	–18,236	–13,560	–18,123	2,307
Assets	4 703 . .	**–4,368**	**–1,783**	**–3,327**	**2,251**	**–5,992**	**–4,399**	**–2,992**	**–6,284**
Trade credits	4 706 . .	. . .	. . .	4,074	1,005	2,633	. . .	. . .	. . .
General government	4 707 . .	. . .	. . .	. . .	. . .	. . .	. . .	. . .	. . .
of which: Short-term	4 709 . .	. . .	. . .	. . .	. . .	. . .	. . .	. . .	. . .
Other sectors	4 710 . .	. . .	. . .	4,074	1,005	2,633	. . .	. . .	. . .
of which: Short-term	4 712 . .	. . .	. . .	*4,074*	*1,005*	*2,633*	. . .	. . .	. . .
Loans	4 714 . .	–291	–1,514	–2,336	3,518	–5,259	–1,279	–283	–1,063
Monetary authorities	4 715 . .	. . .	. . .	. . .	. . .	. . .	. . .	. . .	. . .
of which: Short-term	4 718 . .	. . .	. . .	. . .	. . .	. . .	. . .	. . .	. . .
General government	4 719 . .	. . .	. . .	. . .	2,146	60	498	365	–1,286
of which: Short-term	4 721 . .	. . .	. . .	. . .	. . .	. . .	*64*	*12*	*14*
Banks	4 722 . .	. . .	. . .	–1,866	2,748	1,091	–540	238	377
of which: Short-term	4 724 . .	. . .	. . .	*–2,031*	*2,310*	. . .	*–543*	*238*	*377*
Other sectors	4 725 . .	–291	–1,514	–470	–1,376	–6,410	–1,237	–886	–154
of which: Short-term	4 727 . .	. . .	*–651*	*–195*	*–381*	*–2,554*	*–76*	*–158*	*–96*
Currency and deposits	4 730 . .	–4,077	–228	–5,060	–2,208	–3,285	–2,303	–1,775	–7,685
Monetary authorities	4 731 . .	. . .	. . .	. . .	. . .	. . .	–113	106	–1,968
General government	4 732 . .	. . .	. . .	. . .	. . .	. . .	444	–127	200
Banks	4 733 . .	–4,077	–228	–2,744	2,385	2,292	458	1,214	–1,583
Other sectors	4 734 . .	. . .	. . .	–2,316	–4,593	–5,577	–3,092	–2,968	–4,334
Other assets	4 736 . .	. . .	–41	–5	–64	–81	–817	–934	2,464
Monetary authorities	4 737 . .	. . .	. . .	–44	–67	–84	1,781	–18	2,439
of which: Short-term	4 739 . .	. . .	. . .	. . .	. . .	. . .	. . .	. . .	. . .
General government	4 740 . .	. . .	. . .	. . .	. . .	. . .	–1,822	–46	. . .
of which: Short-term	4 742 . .	. . .	. . .	. . .	. . .	. . .	. . .	. . .	*–3*
Banks	4 743 . .	. . .	. . .	. . .	. . .	. . .	–39	–8	–94
of which: Short-term	4 745 . .	. . .	. . .	. . .	. . .	. . .	*–39*	*–8*	*–94*
Other sectors	4 746 . .	. . .	–41	39	3	3	–737	–862	119
of which: Short-term	4 748 . .	. . .	. . .	*39*	*3*	*3*	*–724*	*–820*	*138*
Liabilities	4 753 . .	**–40,165**	**17,820**	**3,900**	**–6,032**	**–12,244**	**–9,161**	**–15,131**	**8,591**
Trade credits	4 756 . .	5,099	8,659	9,122	6,904	210	–7,233	–6,408	3,672
General government	4 757 . .	. . .	. . .	. . .	. . .	. . .	. . .	. . .	. . .
of which: Short-term	4 759 . .	. . .	. . .	. . .	. . .	. . .	. . .	. . .	. . .
Other sectors	4 760 . .	5,099	8,659	9,122	6,904	210	–7,233	–6,408	3,672
of which: Short-term	4 762 . .	*5,099*	*8,659*	*10,198*	*–5,744*	*–1,775*	*–2,451*	*–3,421*	*3,849*
Loans	4 764 . .	–40,799	381	45	–1,074	3,797	1,354	–8,693	5,496
Monetary authorities	4 765 . .	–733	–1,697	–3,849	–1,703	7,623	2,803	–10,351	6,645
of which: Use of Fund credit and loans from the Fund	4 766 . .	*–133*	*–49*	*–70*	*–33*	*4,773*	*4,059*	*–6,795*	*6,729*
of which: Short-term	4 768 . .	*–600*	. . .	. . .	. . .	. . .	. . .	. . .	. . .
General government	4 769 . .	–35,609	. . .	. . .	. . .	. . .	553	1,539	–61
of which: Short-term	4 771 . .	. . .	. . .	. . .	. . .	. . .	. . .	. . .	. . .
Banks	4 772 . .	. . .	476	4,469	895	–5,665	–1,888	1,657	–1,047
of which: Short-term	4 774 . .	. . .	. . .	*4,684*	*–1,816*	*–5,952*	*–368*	*–254*	*–1,504*
Other sectors	4 775 . .	–4,457	1,602	–575	1,524	1,839	–114	–1,538	–41
of which: Short-term	4 777 . .	*–986*	*2,294*	*–513*	*–3*	*–202*	*916*	*–822*	*–1,219*
Currency and deposits	4 780 . .	–1,384	6,591	415	–944	–814	–3,250	–34	–579
Monetary authorities	4 781 . .	55	–4	. . .	. . .	. . .	–454	–90	–54
General government	4 782 . .	. . .	. . .	. . .	. . .	. . .	381	. . .	. . .
Banks	4 783 . .	–1,439	6,595	–20	33	36	–3,177	56	–525
Other sectors	4 784 . .	. . .	. . .	435	–977	–850	. . .	. . .	. . .
Other liabilities	4 786 . .	–3,081	2,189	–5,682	–10,918	–15,437	–32	4	2
Monetary authorities	4 787 . .	–5,653	–510	6	–28	–14	–37	. . .	. . .
of which: Short-term	4 789 . .	*–5,653*	*–510*	*6*	*–28*	*–14*	*–37*	. . .	. . .
General government	4 790 . .	. . .	. . .	–286	. . .	. . .	. . .	. . .	. . .
of which: Short-term	4 792 . .	. . .	. . .	*–286*	. . .	. . .	. . .	. . .	. . .
Banks	4 793 . .	. . .	. . .	2,001	–35	–2,942	6	4	3
of which: Short-term	4 795 . .	. . .	. . .	*2,001*	*–35*	*–2,942*	. . .	. . .	. . .
Other sectors	4 796 . .	2,572	2,699	–7,403	–10,855	–12,481	–1	. . .	–1
of which: Short-term	4 798 . .	*2,572*	*2,699*	*–7,403*	*–10,855*	*–12,481*	*–1*	. . .	*–1*
E. RESERVE ASSETS	4 802 . .	–7,215	–12,920	–8,326	8,284	6,990	7,783	2,261	–3,311
Monetary gold	4 812 . .	–297	–331	341	376	–978	380	330	394
Special drawing rights	4 811 . .	2	–1	. . .	. . .	–1	–8	6	–11
Reserve position in the Fund	4 810 . .	. . .	. . .	. . .	. . .	. . .	. . .	. . .	. . .
Foreign exchange	4 803 . .	–6,920	–12,588	–8,667	7,908	7,969	7,378	1,896	–3,720
Other claims	4 813 . .	. . .	. . .	. . .	. . .	. . .	33	29	26
NET ERRORS AND OMISSIONS	4 998 . .	**–442**	**1,447**	**–1,992**	**–3,160**	**–2,911**	**240**	**2,971**	**–250**

Part 3 of the *Yearbook* contains descriptions of the methodologies, compilation practices, and sources used to compile these data.

Table 3. INTERNATIONAL INVESTMENT POSITION (End–period stocks), 1994–2001
(Millions of U.S. dollars)

	Code	1994	1995	1996	1997	1998	1999	2000	2001
ASSETS	8 995 C.	...	...	...	...	...	...	...	108,145
Direct investment abroad	8 505	...	...	...	...	...	...	...	**50,745**
Equity capital and reinvested earnings	8 506	...	...	...	...	...	...	...	43,641
Claims on affiliated enterprises	8 507	...	...	...	...	...	...	...	43,641
Liabilities to affiliated enterprises	8 508	...	...	...	...	...	...	...	...
Other capital	8 530	...	...	...	...	...	...	...	7,104
Claims on affiliated enterprises	8 535	...	...	...	...	...	...	...	7,104
Liabilities to affiliated enterprises	8 540	...	...	...	...	...	...	...	...
Portfolio investment	8 602	...	...	...	...	...	...	...	**6,402**
Equity securities	8 610	...	...	...	...	...	...	...	3,001
Monetary authorities	8 611	...	...	...	...	...	...	...	...
General government	8 612	...	...	...	...	...	...	...	...
Banks	8 613	...	...	...	...	...	...	...	626
Other sectors	8 614	...	...	...	...	...	...	...	2,375
Debt securities	8 619	...	...	...	...	...	...	...	3,401
Bonds and notes	8 620	...	...	...	...	...	...	...	1,816
Monetary authorities	8 621	...	...	...	...	...	...	...	1,239
General government	8 622	...	...	...	...	...	...	...	...
Banks	8 623	...	...	...	...	...	...	...	84
Other sectors	8 624	...	...	...	...	...	...	...	493
Money market instruments	8 630	...	...	...	...	...	...	...	1,585
Monetary authorities	8 631	...	...	...	...	...	...	...	...
General government	8 632	...	...	...	...	...	...	...	...
Banks	8 633	...	...	...	...	...	...	...	230
Other sectors	8 634	...	...	...	...	...	...	...	1,355
Financial derivatives	8 900	...	...	...	...	...	...	...	**42**
Monetary authorities	8 901	...	...	...	...	...	...	...	...
General government	8 902	...	...	...	...	...	...	...	...
Banks	8 903	...	...	...	...	...	...	...	...
Other sectors	8 904	...	...	...	...	...	...	...	42
Other investment	8 703	...	...	...	...	...	...	...	**15,090**
Trade credits	8 706	...	...	...	...	...	...	...	155
General government	8 707	...	...	...	...	...	...	...	...
of which: Short-term	8 709	...	...	...	...	...	...	...	...
Other sectors	8 710	...	...	...	...	...	...	...	155
of which: Short-term	8 712	...	...	...	...	...	...	...	*99*
Loans	8 714	...	...	...	...	...	...	...	697
Monetary authorities	8 715	...	...	...	...	...	...	...	...
of which: Short-term	8 718	...	...	...	...	...	...	...	...
General government	8 719	...	...	...	...	...	...	...	...
of which: Short-term	8 721	...	...	...	...	...	...	...	...
Banks	8 722	...	...	...	...	...	...	...	5
of which: Short-term	8 724	...	...	...	...	...	...	...	...
Other sectors	8 725	...	...	...	...	...	...	...	692
of which: Short-term	8 727	...	...	...	...	...	...	...	*213*
Currency and deposits	8 730	...	...	...	...	...	...	...	9,442
Monetary authorities	8 731	...	...	...	...	...	...	...	...
General government	8 732	...	...	...	...	...	...	...	...
Banks	8 733	...	...	...	...	...	...	...	5,328
Other sectors	8 734	...	...	...	...	...	...	...	4,114
Other assets	8 736	...	...	...	...	...	...	...	4,796
Monetary authorities	8 737	...	...	...	...	...	...	...	1,383
of which: Short-term	8 739	...	...	...	...	...	...	...	...
General government	8 740	...	...	...	...	...	...	...	...
of which: Short-term	8 742	...	...	...	...	...	...	...	...
Banks	8 743	...	...	...	...	...	...	...	189
of which: Short-term	8 745	...	...	...	...	...	...	...	*188*
Other sectors	8 746	...	...	...	...	...	...	...	3,224
of which: Short-term	8 748	...	...	...	...	...	...	...	*429*
Reserve assets	8 802	...	...	...	...	...	...	...	**35,866**
Monetary gold	8 812	...	...	...	...	...	...	...	127
Special drawing rights	8 811	...	1	1	1	2	10	...	11
Reserve position in the Fund	8 810	...	...	...	...	...	...	...	...
Foreign exchange	8 803	...	...	...	...	...	...	...	35,699
Other claims	8 813	...	...	...	...	...	...	...	29

Table 3 (Concluded). INTERNATIONAL INVESTMENT POSITION (End-period stocks), 1994–2001

(Millions of U.S. dollars)

	Code		1994	1995	1996	1997	1998	1999	2000	2001
LIABILITIES	8 995	D.	...	...	...	...	...	...	...	372,617
Direct investment in Brazil	8 555	..	...	...	...	...	...	...	...	**121,948**
Equity capital and reinvested earnings	8 556	..	...	...	...	...	...	...	...	105,815
Claims on direct investors	8 557	..	...	...	...	...	...	...	...	...
Liabilities to direct investors	8 558	..	...	...	...	...	...	...	...	105,815
Other capital	8 580	..	...	...	...	...	...	...	...	16,133
Claims on direct investors	8 585	..	...	...	...	...	...	...	...	...
Liabilities to direct investors	8 590	..	...	...	...	...	...	...	...	16,133
Portfolio investment	8 652	..	...	...	...	...	...	...	...	**152,306**
Equity securities	8 660	..	...	...	...	...	...	...	...	37,407
Banks	8 663	..	...	...	...	...	...	...	...	...
Other sectors	8 664	..	...	...	...	...	...	...	...	37,407
Debt securities	8 669	..	...	...	...	...	...	...	...	114,899
Bonds and notes	8 670	..	...	...	...	...	...	...	...	113,699
Monetary authorities	8 671	..	...	...	...	...	...	...	...	...
General government	8 672	..	...	...	...	...	...	...	...	...
Banks	8 673	..	...	...	...	...	...	...	...	...
Other sectors	8 674	..	...	...	...	...	...	...	...	113,699
Money market instruments	8 680	..	...	...	...	...	...	...	...	1,200
Monetary authorities	8 681	..	...	...	...	...	...	...	...	...
General government	8 682	..	...	...	...	...	...	...	...	...
Banks	8 683	..	...	...	...	...	...	...	...	...
Other sectors	8 684	..	...	...	...	...	...	...	...	1,200
Financial derivatives	8 905	..	...	...	...	...	...	...	...	**45**
Monetary authorities	8 906	..	...	...	...	...	...	...	...	...
General government	8 907	..	...	...	...	...	...	...	...	...
Banks	8 908	..	...	...	...	...	...	...	...	...
Other sectors	8 909	..	...	...	...	...	...	...	...	45
Other investment	8 753	..	...	...	...	...	...	...	...	**98,318**
Trade credits	8 756	..	...	...	...	...	...	...	...	6,026
General government	8 757	..	...	...	...	...	...	...	...	...
of which: Short-term	8 759	..	...	...	...	...	...	...	...	...
Other sectors	8 760	..	...	...	...	...	...	...	...	6,026
of which: Short-term	8 762	..	...	...	...	...	...	...	...	*628*
Loans	8 764	..	...	...	...	...	...	...	...	90,710
Monetary authorities	8 765	..	...	...	...	...	...	...	...	9,121
of which: Use of Fund credit and loans from the Fund	8 766	..	*186*	*142*	*68*	*31*	*4,825*	*8,827*	*1,768*	*8,337*
of which: Short-term	8 768	..	...	...	...	...	...	...	...	...
General government	8 769	..	...	...	...	...	...	...	...	...
of which: Short-term	8 771	..	...	...	...	...	...	...	...	...
Banks	8 772	..	...	...	...	...	...	...	...	6,324
of which: Short-term	8 774	..	...	...	...	...	...	...	...	*6,324*
Other sectors	8 775	..	...	...	...	...	...	...	...	75,265
of which: Short-term	8 777	..	...	...	...	...	...	...	...	*19,506*
Currency and deposits	8 780	..	...	...	...	...	...	...	...	1,582
Monetary authorities	8 781	..	...	...	...	...	...	...	...	129
General government	8 782	..	...	...	...	...	...	...	...	...
Banks	8 783	..	...	...	...	...	...	...	...	1,453
Other sectors	8 784	..	...	...	...	...	...	...	...	...
Other liabilities	8 786	..	...	...	...	...	...	...	...	...
Monetary authorities	8 787	..	...	...	...	...	...	...	...	...
of which: Short-term	8 789	..	...	...	...	...	...	...	...	...
General government	8 790	..	...	...	...	...	...	...	...	...
of which: Short-term	8 792	..	...	...	...	...	...	...	...	...
Banks	8 793	..	...	...	...	...	...	...	...	...
of which: Short-term	8 795	..	...	...	...	...	...	...	...	...
Other sectors	8 796	..	...	...	...	...	...	...	...	...
of which: Short-term	8 798	..	...	...	...	...	...	...	...	...
NET INTERNATIONAL INVESTMENT POSITION	8 995	..	...	...	...	...	...	...	...	**–264,472**
Conversion rates: reais per U.S. dollar (end of period)	0 102	..	**.8460**	**.9730**	**1.0394**	**1.1164**	**1.2087**	**1.7890**	**1.9546**	**2.3204**

Table 1. ANALYTIC PRESENTATION, 1994–2001
(Millions of U.S. dollars)

	Code	1994	1995	1996	1997	1998	1999	2000	2001
A. Current Account [1]	4 993 Z.	**–31.8**	**–25.8**	**15.7**	**426.9**	**–61.8**	**–684.7**	**–701.2**	**–846.8**
Goods: exports f.o.b.	2 100 . .	3,935.1	5,345.0	4,890.2	4,939.6	4,193.5	4,006.4	4,824.6	5,106.8
Goods: imports f.o.b.	3 100 . .	–3,951.9	–5,224.0	–4,702.6	–4,559.3	–4,574.2	–5,087.4	–6,000.1	–6,682.4
Balance on Goods	4 100 . .	*–16.8*	*121.0*	*187.6*	*380.3*	*–380.7*	*–1,081.0*	*–1,175.5*	*–1,575.6*
Services: credit	2 200 . .	1,256.9	1,431.4	1,366.0	1,337.4	1,787.9	1,786.3	2,175.3	2,419.2
Services: debit	3 200 . .	–1,246.1	–1,277.9	–1,245.9	–1,171.0	–1,415.1	–1,471.1	–1,669.4	–1,879.2
Balance on Goods and Services	4 991 . .	*–6.0*	*274.5*	*307.7*	*546.7*	*–7.9*	*–765.8*	*–669.6*	*–1,035.6*
Income: credit	2 300 . .	84.6	149.7	181.0	210.8	306.6	265.5	322.9	351.6
Income: debit	3 300 . .	–277.1	–581.9	–577.2	–567.4	–590.3	–484.2	–644.2	–651.2
Balance on Goods, Services, and Income	4 992 . .	*–198.5*	*–157.7*	*–88.5*	*190.1*	*–291.6*	*–984.5*	*–990.9*	*–1,335.2*
Current transfers: credit	2 379 Z.	357.1	256.8	231.8	275.5	261.4	328.7	354.1	588.5
Current transfers: debit	3 379 . .	–190.4	–124.9	–127.6	–38.7	–31.6	–28.9	–64.4	–100.1
B. Capital Account [1]	4 994 Z.	**763.3**	**. . .**	**65.9**	**. . .**	**. . .**	**–2.4**	**25.0**	**. . .**
Capital account: credit	2 994 Z.	763.3	. . .	65.9	. . .	. . .	. . .	25.0	. . .
Capital account: debit	3 994 . .	. . .	. . .	. . .	. . .	. . .	–2.4	. . .	. . .
Total, Groups A Plus B	4 981 . .	*731.5*	*–25.8*	*81.6*	*426.9*	*–61.8*	*–687.1*	*–676.2*	*–846.8*
C. Financial Account [1]	4 995 W.	**–1,018.7**	**326.6**	**–715.0**	**462.0**	**266.7**	**777.4**	**881.5**	**1,002.1**
Direct investment abroad	4 505 . .	. . .	8.0	28.5	1.7	–.1	–16.8	1.9	–9.8
Direct investment in Bulgaria	4 555 Z.	105.4	90.4	109.0	504.8	537.2	806.1	1,001.5	691.9
Portfolio investment assets	4 602 . .	–222.0	9.7	–7.1	–13.7	–129.5	–207.5	–62.0	–120.3
Equity securities	4 610 . .	. . .	9.7	–7.1	–8.5	–10.7	. . .	–8.1	–33.5
Debt securities	4 619 . .	–222.0	. . .	. . .	–5.2	–118.8	–207.5	–53.9	–86.8
Portfolio investment liabilities	4 652 Z.	–9.8	–75.4	–122.2	146.5	–112.0	8.0	–114.9	105.1
Equity securities	4 660 . .	. . .	. . .	2.0	52.0	19.2	1.9	4.8	–8.7
Debt securities	4 669 Z.	–9.8	–75.4	–124.2	94.5	–131.2	6.1	–119.7	113.8
Financial derivatives	4 910 . .	. . .	. . .	. . .	. . .	. . .	. . .	–3.6	17.5
Financial derivatives assets	4 900 . .	. . .	. . .	. . .	. . .	. . .	. . .	–1.8	. . .
Financial derivatives liabilities	4 905 . .	. . .	. . .	. . .	. . .	. . .	. . .	–1.8	17.5
Other investment assets	4 703 . .	–209.2	404.2	–568.1	–53.9	222.2	16.6	–136.6	348.3
Monetary authorities	4 701 . .	. . .	. . .	. . .	. . .	. . .	. . .	.9	–2.2
General government	4 704 . .	90.1	292.6	293.7	106.5	–19.8	–17.5	–9.1	–20.7
Banks	4 705 . .	–299.3	111.6	113.7	–440.6	103.0	25.7	–495.7	–130.6
Other sectors	4 728 . .	. . .	. . .	–975.5	280.2	139.0	8.4	367.3	501.8
Other investment liabilities	4 753 W.	–683.1	–110.3	–155.1	–123.4	–251.1	171.0	195.2	–30.6
Monetary authorities	4 753 WA	. . .	. . .	. . .	. . .	. . .	. . .	. . .	. . .
General government	4 753 ZB	–951.0	–1.9	44.0	–82.1	–213.7	–105.0	–224.0	–307.9
Banks	4 753 ZC	–39.2	–94.8	–179.7	–52.3	–65.1	10.1	108.4	102.8
Other sectors	4 753 ZD	307.1	–13.6	–19.4	11.0	27.7	265.9	310.8	174.5
Total, Groups A Through C	4 983 . .	*–287.2*	*300.8*	*–633.4*	*888.9*	*204.9*	*90.3*	*205.3*	*155.3*
D. Net Errors and Omissions	4 998 . .	**71.6**	**143.8**	**–105.3**	**256.4**	**–299.2**	**6.1**	**–68.3**	**288.5**
Total, Groups A Through D	4 984 . .	*–215.6*	*444.6*	*–738.7*	*1,145.3*	*–94.3*	*96.4*	*137.0*	*443.8*
E. Reserves and Related Items	4 802 A.	**215.6**	**–444.6**	**738.7**	**–1,145.3**	**94.3**	**–96.4**	**–137.0**	**–443.8**
Reserve assets	4 802 . .	–341.6	–233.7	750.9	–1,641.3	–461.5	–527.6	–408.9	–275.3
Use of Fund credit and loans	4 766 . .	262.4	–245.9	–108.7	396.9	129.4	161.9	136.0	–168.5
Exceptional financing	4 920 . .	294.8	35.0	96.5	99.1	426.4	269.4	136.0	. . .
Conversion rates: leva per U.S. dollar	0 101 . .	**.0541**	**.0672**	**.1779**	**1.6819**	**1.7604**	**1.8364**	**2.1233**	**2.1847**

[1] Excludes components that have been classified in the categories of Group E.

Table 2. STANDARD PRESENTATION, 1994–2001

(Millions of U.S. dollars)

	Code			1994	1995	1996	1997	1998	1999	2000	2001
CURRENT ACCOUNT	4	993	..	**–31.8**	**–25.8**	**15.7**	**426.9**	**–61.8**	**–684.7**	**–701.2**	**–846.8**
A. GOODS	4	100	..	–16.8	121.0	187.6	380.3	–380.7	–1,081.0	–1,175.5	–1,575.6
Credit	2	100	..	**3,935.1**	**5,345.0**	**4,890.2**	**4,939.6**	**4,193.5**	**4,006.4**	**4,824.6**	**5,106.8**
General merchandise: exports f.o.b.	2	110	..	3,935.1	5,345.0	4,890.2	3,358.5	4,193.5	4,006.4	4,824.6	5,106.8
Goods for processing: exports f.o.b.	2	150	..	...	...	...	1,581.1	...	...	...	...
Repairs on goods	2	160	..	...	...	...	...	...	...	...	...
Goods procured in ports by carriers	2	170	..	...	...	...	...	...	...	...	...
Nonmonetary gold	2	180	..	...	...	...	...	...	...	...	...
Debit	3	100	..	**–3,951.9**	**–5,224.0**	**–4,702.6**	**–4,559.3**	**–4,574.2**	**–5,087.4**	**–6,000.1**	**–6,682.4**
General merchandise: imports f.o.b.	3	110	..	–3,951.9	–5,224.0	–4,702.6	–3,059.1	–3,421.4	–5,087.4	–6,000.1	–6,682.4
Goods for processing: imports f.o.b.	3	150	..	...	...	...	–1,500.2	–1,152.8	...	...	...
Repairs on goods	3	160	..	...	...	...	...	...	...	...	...
Goods procured in ports by carriers	3	170	..	...	...	...	...	...	...	...	...
Nonmonetary gold	3	180	..	...	...	...	...	...	...	...	...
B. SERVICES	4	200	..	10.8	153.5	120.1	166.4	372.8	315.2	505.9	540.0
Total credit	2	200	..	*1,256.9*	*1,431.4*	*1,366.0*	*1,337.4*	*1,787.9*	*1,786.3*	*2,175.3*	*2,419.2*
Total debit	3	200	..	*–1,246.1*	*–1,277.9*	*–1,245.9*	*–1,171.0*	*–1,415.1*	*–1,471.1*	*–1,669.4*	*–1,879.2*
Transportation services, credit	2	205	..	**375.7**	**494.0**	**439.2**	**448.8**	**452.3**	**521.3**	**631.9**	**696.4**
Passenger	2	850	..	*144.6*	*189.2*	*153.1*	*147.6*	*183.7*	...	*290.1*	...
Freight	2	851	..	*196.8*	*267.4*	*244.6*	*247.0*	*209.7*	...	*241.2*	...
Other	2	852	..	*34.3*	*37.4*	*41.5*	*54.2*	*58.9*	...	*100.6*	...
Sea transport, passenger	2	207	..	...	...	...	...	...	...	...	...
Sea transport, freight	2	208	..	...	...	...	...	...	...	...	...
Sea transport, other	2	209	..	...	...	...	...	...	...	...	...
Air transport, passenger	2	211	..	...	...	...	...	...	...	...	...
Air transport, freight	2	212	..	...	...	...	...	...	...	...	...
Air transport, other	2	213	..	...	...	...	...	...	...	...	...
Other transport, passenger	2	215	..	...	...	...	...	...	...	...	...
Other transport, freight	2	216	..	...	...	...	...	...	...	...	...
Other transport, other	2	217	..	...	...	...	...	...	...	...	...
Transportation services, debit	3	205	..	**–465.6**	**–530.9**	**–486.1**	**–505.6**	**–529.7**	**–647.8**	**–732.8**	**–805.3**
Passenger	3	850	..	*–146.2*	*–116.9*	*–114.6*	*–132.9*	*–135.1*	...	*–225.9*	...
Freight	3	851	..	*–319.4*	*–414.0*	*–371.5*	*–372.7*	*–394.6*	...	*–506.9*	...
Other	3	852	..	...	...	...	...	...	...	...	...
Sea transport, passenger	3	207	..	...	...	...	...	...	...	...	...
Sea transport, freight	3	208	..	...	...	...	...	...	...	...	...
Sea transport, other	3	209	..	...	...	...	...	...	...	...	...
Air transport, passenger	3	211	..	...	...	...	...	...	...	...	...
Air transport, freight	3	212	..	...	...	...	...	...	...	...	...
Air transport, other	3	213	..	...	...	...	...	...	...	...	...
Other transport, passenger	3	215	..	...	...	...	...	...	...	...	...
Other transport, freight	3	216	..	...	...	...	...	...	...	...	...
Other transport, other	3	217	..	...	...	...	...	...	...	...	...
Travel, credit	2	236	..	**361.6**	**472.6**	**388.4**	**369.1**	**966.2**	**930.0**	**1,074.1**	**1,197.5**
Business travel	2	237	..	...	19.2	13.8	13.6	47.2	122.8	136.5	141.2
Personal travel	2	240	..	...	453.4	374.6	355.5	919.0	807.2	937.6	1,056.3
Travel, debit	3	236	..	**–243.7**	**–195.1**	**–198.6**	**–221.6**	**–519.1**	**–524.3**	**–537.9**	**–568.5**
Business travel	3	237	..	...	–14.4	–2.8	–4.5	–19.3	–245.2	–230.5	–269.1
Personal travel	3	240	..	...	–180.7	–195.8	–217.1	–499.8	–279.1	–307.4	–299.4
Other services, credit	2	200	BA	**519.6**	**464.8**	**538.4**	**519.5**	**369.4**	**335.0**	**469.3**	**525.3**
Communications	2	245	..	...	...	...	25.1	27.8	29.4	45.3	47.0
Construction	2	249	..	...	...	...	106.0	74.3	35.2	50.2	67.7
Insurance	2	253	..	...	...	...	18.7	9.9	10.0	17.3	12.1
Financial	2	260	..	...	...	...	80.1	33.4	16.2	12.9	33.3
Computer and information	2	262	..	...	...	...	...	...	...	5.1	12.3
Royalties and licence fees	2	266	..	...	...	...	...	...	...	3.5	2.6
Other business services	2	268	..	519.6	464.8	538.4	258.8	202.5	215.4	266.3	279.7
Personal, cultural, and recreational	2	287	..	...	...	...	...	...	...	22.3	28.1
Government, n.i.e.	2	291	..	...	...	...	30.8	21.5	28.8	46.4	42.5
Other services, debit	3	200	BA	**–536.8**	**–551.9**	**–561.2**	**–443.8**	**–366.3**	**–299.0**	**–398.7**	**–505.4**
Communications	3	245	..	...	...	...	–34.0	–61.1	–24.5	–28.9	–19.6
Construction	3	249	..	...	...	...	–13.5	–22.3	–11.5	–21.7	–54.4
Insurance	3	253	..	...	...	...	–29.5	–24.1	–26.5	–42.6	–37.5
Financial	3	260	..	...	...	...	–75.5	–39.1	–39.1	–46.7	–23.0
Computer and information	3	262	..	...	...	...	...	...	...	–5.3	–13.7
Royalties and licence fees	3	266	..	...	...	...	...	...	...	–9.9	–11.5
Other business services	3	268	..	–536.8	–551.9	–561.2	–277.0	–202.4	–195.9	–230.2	–321.0
Personal, cultural, and recreational	3	287	..	...	...	...	...	...	...	–4.1	–8.5
Government, n.i.e.	3	291	..	...	...	...	–14.3	–17.3	–1.5	–9.3	–16.2

Table 2 (Continued). STANDARD PRESENTATION, 1994–2001
(Millions of U.S. dollars)

	Code		1994	1995	1996	1997	1998	1999	2000	2001
C. INCOME	4 300	. .	–192.5	–432.2	–396.2	–356.6	–283.7	–218.7	–321.3	–299.6
Total credit	2 300	. .	*84.6*	*149.7*	*181.0*	*210.8*	*306.6*	*265.5*	*322.9*	*351.6*
Total debit	3 300	. .	*–277.1*	*–581.9*	*–577.2*	*–567.4*	*–590.3*	*–484.2*	*–644.2*	*–651.2*
Compensation of employees, credit	2 310	. .	**. . .**	**. . .**	**41.5**	**50.6**	**50.6**	**42.5**	**58.2**	**70.5**
Compensation of employees, debit	3 310	. .	**. . .**	**. . .**	**–33.5**	**–15.5**	**–3.5**	**–3.8**	**–26.0**	**–27.0**
Investment income, credit	2 320	. .	**84.6**	**149.7**	**139.5**	**160.2**	**256.0**	**223.0**	**264.7**	**281.1**
Direct investment income	2 330	. .	. . .	. . .	. . .	. . .	1.0	–1.1	. . .	.6
Dividends and distributed branch profits	2 332	. .	. . .	. . .	. . .	. . .	1.0	.1	. . .	.6
Reinvested earnings and undistributed branch profits	2 333	. .	. . .	. . .	. . .	. . .	. . .	–1.2	. . .	. . .
Income on debt (interest)	2 334	. .	. . .	. . .	. . .	. . .	. . .	. . .	. . .	. . .
Portfolio investment income	2 339	. .	. . .	. . .	. . .	. . .	.5	.4	48.8	64.4
Income on equity	2 340	. .	. . .	. . .	. . .	. . .	. . .	. . .	. . .	. . .
Income on bonds and notes	2 350	. .	. . .	. . .	. . .	. . .	. . .	. . .	47.7	62.9
Income on money market instruments	2 360	. .	. . .	. . .	. . .	. . .	. . .	. . .	1.1	1.5
Other investment income	2 370	. .	84.6	149.7	139.5	160.2	254.5	223.7	215.9	216.1
Investment income, debit	3 320	. .	**–277.1**	**–581.9**	**–543.7**	**–551.9**	**–586.8**	**–480.4**	**–618.2**	**–624.2**
Direct investment income	3 330	. .	. . .	. . .	. . .	. . .	–55.8	–11.9	–107.0	–159.7
Dividends and distributed branch profits	3 332	. .	. . .	. . .	. . .	. . .	–6.1	–32.4	–19.8	–112.8
Reinvested earnings and undistributed branch profits	3 333	. .	. . .	. . .	. . .	. . .	–49.7	20.5	–58.3	–19.2
Income on debt (interest)	3 334	. .	. . .	. . .	. . .	. . .	. . .	. . .	–28.9	–27.7
Portfolio investment income	3 339	. .	. . .	. . .	. . .	–37.8	–282.7	–265.1	–293.8	–301.7
Income on equity	3 340	. .	. . .	. . .	. . .	. . .	. . .	. . .	–3.7	–2.4
Income on bonds and notes	3 350	. .	. . .	. . .	. . .	–37.8	. . .	. . .	–290.1	–299.3
Income on money market instruments	3 360	. .	. . .	. . .	. . .	. . .	. . .	. . .	. . .	. . .
Other investment income	3 370	. .	–277.1	–581.9	–543.7	–514.1	–248.3	–203.4	–217.4	–162.8
D. CURRENT TRANSFERS	4 379	. .	166.7	131.9	104.2	236.8	229.8	299.8	289.7	488.4
Credit	2 379	. .	**357.1**	**256.8**	**231.8**	**275.5**	**261.4**	**328.7**	**354.1**	**588.5**
General government	2 380	. .	9.6	14.9	37.0	129.3	70.5	80.5	74.3	177.2
Other sectors	2 390	. .	347.5	241.9	194.8	146.2	190.9	248.2	279.8	411.3
Workers' remittances	2 391	. .	. . .	. . .	. . .	. . .	. . .	. . .	. . .	. . .
Other current transfers	2 392	. .	347.5	241.9	194.8	146.2	190.9	248.2	279.8	411.3
Debit	3 379	. .	**–190.4**	**–124.9**	**–127.6**	**–38.7**	**–31.6**	**–28.9**	**–64.4**	**–100.1**
General government	3 380	. .	–7.0	. . .	–.2	–.6	–11.3	–12.8	–19.5	–40.8
Other sectors	3 390	. .	–183.4	–124.9	–127.4	–38.1	–20.3	–16.1	–44.9	–59.3
Workers' remittances	3 391	. .	. . .	. . .	. . .	. . .	. . .	. . .	. . .	. . .
Other current transfers	3 392	. .	–183.4	–124.9	–127.4	–38.1	–20.3	–16.1	–44.9	–59.3
CAPITAL AND FINANCIAL ACCOUNT	4 996	. .	**–39.8**	**–118.0**	**89.6**	**–683.3**	**361.0**	**678.6**	**769.5**	**558.3**
CAPITAL ACCOUNT	4 994	. .	**763.3**	**. . .**	**65.9**	**. . .**	**. . .**	**–2.4**	**25.0**	**. . .**
Total credit	2 994	. .	*763.3*	. . .	*65.9*	. . .	. . .	. . .	*25.0*	. . .
Total debit	3 994	. .	. . .	. . .	. . .	. . .	. . .	*–2.4*	. . .	. . .
Capital transfers, credit	2 400	. .	**763.3**	**. . .**	**65.9**	**. . .**	**. . .**	**. . .**	**25.0**	**. . .**
General government	2 401	. .	763.3	. . .	65.9	. . .	. . .	. . .	25.0	. . .
Debt forgiveness	2 402	. .	763.3	. . .	. . .	. . .	. . .	. . .	. . .	. . .
Other capital transfers	2 410	. .	. . .	. . .	65.9	. . .	. . .	. . .	25.0	. . .
Other sectors	2 430	. .	. . .	. . .	. . .	. . .	. . .	. . .	. . .	. . .
Migrants' transfers	2 431	. .	. . .	. . .	. . .	. . .	. . .	. . .	. . .	. . .
Debt forgiveness	2 432	. .	. . .	. . .	. . .	. . .	. . .	. . .	. . .	. . .
Other capital transfers	2 440	. .	. . .	. . .	. . .	. . .	. . .	. . .	. . .	. . .
Capital transfers, debit	3 400	. .	**. . .**	**. . .**	**. . .**	**. . .**	**. . .**	**–2.4**	**. . .**	**. . .**
General government	3 401	. .	. . .	. . .	. . .	. . .	. . .	–2.4	. . .	. . .
Debt forgiveness	3 402	. .	. . .	. . .	. . .	. . .	. . .	–2.4	. . .	. . .
Other capital transfers	3 410	. .	. . .	. . .	. . .	. . .	. . .	. . .	. . .	. . .
Other sectors	3 430	. .	. . .	. . .	. . .	. . .	. . .	. . .	. . .	. . .
Migrants' transfers	3 431	. .	. . .	. . .	. . .	. . .	. . .	. . .	. . .	. . .
Debt forgiveness	3 432	. .	. . .	. . .	. . .	. . .	. . .	. . .	. . .	. . .
Other capital transfers	3 440	. .	. . .	. . .	. . .	. . .	. . .	. . .	. . .	. . .
Nonproduced nonfinancial assets, credit	2 480	. .	**. . .**	**. . .**	**. . .**	**. . .**	**. . .**	**. . .**	**. . .**	**. . .**
Nonproduced nonfinancial assets, debit	3 480	. .	**. . .**	**. . .**	**. . .**	**. . .**	**. . .**	**. . .**	**. . .**	**. . .**

Table 2 (Continued). STANDARD PRESENTATION, 1994–2001
(Millions of U.S. dollars)

	Code	1994	1995	1996	1997	1998	1999	2000	2001
FINANCIAL ACCOUNT	4 995 . .	**–803.1**	**–118.0**	**23.7**	**–683.3**	**361.0**	**681.0**	**744.5**	**558.3**
A. DIRECT INVESTMENT	4 500 . .	105.4	98.4	137.5	506.5	537.1	789.3	1,003.4	682.1
Direct investment abroad	4 505 . .	**. . .**	**8.0**	**28.5**	**1.7**	**–.1**	**–16.8**	**1.9**	**–9.8**
Equity capital	4 510 . .	. . .	8.0	28.5	.7	. . .	–11.5	4.0	–6.3
Claims on affiliated enterprises	4 515 . .	. . .	. . .	. . .	.7	. . .	. . .	. . .	. . .
Liabilities to affiliated enterprises	4 520 . .	. . .	. . .	. . .	. . .	. . .	. . .	. . .	. . .
Reinvested earnings	4 525 . .	. . .	. . .	. . .	. . .	. . .	1.2	. . .	. . .
Other capital	4 530 . .	. . .	. . .	. . .	1.0	–.1	–6.5	–2.1	–3.5
Claims on affiliated enterprises	4 535 . .	. . .	. . .	. . .	1.0	–.1	–6.5	–2.1	–3.5
Liabilities to affiliated enterprises	4 540 . .	. . .	. . .	. . .	. . .	. . .	. . .	. . .	. . .
Direct investment in Bulgaria	4 555 . .	**105.4**	**90.4**	**109.0**	**504.8**	**537.2**	**806.1**	**1,001.5**	**691.9**
Equity capital	4 560 . .	105.4	90.4	109.0	491.8	504.6	475.6	750.5	470.7
Claims on direct investors	4 565 . .	. . .	. . .	. . .	. . .	. . .	. . .	. . .	. . .
Liabilities to direct investors	4 570 . .	. . .	. . .	. . .	. . .	. . .	. . .	. . .	. . .
Reinvested earnings	4 575 . .	. . .	. . .	. . .	. . .	49.7	–20.5	58.3	19.2
Other capital	4 580 . .	. . .	. . .	. . .	13.0	–17.1	351.0	192.7	202.0
Claims on direct investors	4 585 . .	. . .	. . .	. . .	. . .	. . .	. . .	. . .	. . .
Liabilities to direct investors	4 590 . .	. . .	. . .	. . .	. . .	. . .	. . .	192.7	202.0
B. PORTFOLIO INVESTMENT	4 600 . .	–231.8	–65.7	–129.3	132.8	–241.5	–199.5	–176.9	–15.2
Assets	4 602 . .	**–222.0**	**9.7**	**–7.1**	**–13.7**	**–129.5**	**–207.5**	**–62.0**	**–120.3**
Equity securities	4 610 . .	. . .	9.7	–7.1	–8.5	–10.7	. . .	–8.1	–33.5
Monetary authorities	4 611 . .	. . .	. . .	. . .	. . .	. . .	. . .	. . .	. . .
General government	4 612 . .	. . .	. . .	. . .	. . .	. . .	. . .	. . .	. . .
Banks	4 613 . .	. . .	9.7	–7.1	–8.5	–10.7	.5	–7.7	–31.2
Other sectors	4 614 . .	. . .	. . .	. . .	. . .	. . .	–.5	–.4	–2.3
Debt securities	4 619 . .	–222.0	. . .	. . .	–5.2	–118.8	–207.5	–53.9	–86.8
Bonds and notes	4 620 . .	–222.0	. . .	. . .	–5.2	–54.2	–165.3	–43.4	–133.3
Monetary authorities	4 621 . .	. . .	. . .	. . .	. . .	. . .	. . .	. . .	–2.7
General government	4 622 . .	–222.0	. . .	. . .	. . .	–21.9	–23.7	–25.6	–40.1
Banks	4 623 . .	. . .	. . .	. . .	–5.2	–32.3	–131.6	–2.1	–90.7
Other sectors	4 624 . .	. . .	. . .	. . .	. . .	. . .	–10.0	–15.7	.2
Money market instruments	4 630 . .	. . .	. . .	. . .	. . .	–64.6	–42.2	–10.5	46.5
Monetary authorities	4 631 . .	. . .	. . .	. . .	. . .	. . .	.2	.1	. . .
General government	4 632 . .	. . .	. . .	. . .	. . .	. . .	–.1	. . .	39.7
Banks	4 633 . .	. . .	. . .	. . .	. . .	–64.6	–37.2	–10.6	6.8
Other sectors	4 634 . .	. . .	. . .	. . .	. . .	. . .	–5.1	. . .	. . .
Liabilities	4 652 . .	**–9.8**	**–75.4**	**–122.2**	**146.5**	**–112.0**	**8.0**	**–114.9**	**105.1**
Equity securities	4 660 . .	. . .	. . .	2.0	52.0	19.2	1.9	4.8	–8.7
Banks	4 663 . .	. . .	. . .	2.0	2.3	7.8	4.7	6.8	2.9
Other sectors	4 664 . .	. . .	. . .	. . .	49.7	11.4	–2.8	–2.0	–11.6
Debt securities	4 669 . .	–9.8	–75.4	–124.2	94.5	–131.2	6.1	–119.7	113.8
Bonds and notes	4 670 . .	–9.8	–75.4	–124.2	94.5	–131.2	–8.5	–119.5	113.8
Monetary authorities	4 671 . .	. . .	. . .	. . .	. . .	. . .	. . .	. . .	. . .
General government	4 672 . .	–9.8	–75.4	–124.2	94.5	–161.1	–8.5	–120.8	123.3
Banks	4 673 . .	. . .	. . .	. . .	. . .	29.9	. . .	1.0	–9.5
Other sectors	4 674 . .	. . .	. . .	. . .	. . .	. . .	. . .	.3	. . .
Money market instruments	4 680 . .	. . .	. . .	. . .	. . .	. . .	14.6	–.2	. . .
Monetary authorities	4 681 . .	. . .	. . .	. . .	. . .	. . .	. . .	. . .	. . .
General government	4 682 . .	. . .	. . .	. . .	. . .	. . .	.4	–.6	. . .
Banks	4 683 . .	. . .	. . .	. . .	. . .	. . .	14.2	. . .	. . .
Other sectors	4 684 . .	. . .	. . .	. . .	. . .	. . .	. . .	.4	. . .
C. FINANCIAL DERIVATIVES	4 910 . .	. . .	. . .	. . .	. . .	. . .	. . .	–3.6	17.5
Monetary authorities	4 911 . .	. . .	. . .	. . .	. . .	. . .	. . .	. . .	. . .
General government	4 912 . .	. . .	. . .	. . .	. . .	. . .	. . .	. . .	. . .
Banks	4 913 . .	. . .	. . .	. . .	. . .	. . .	. . .	–3.6	17.5
Other sectors	4 914 . .	. . .	. . .	. . .	. . .	. . .	. . .	. . .	. . .
Assets	4 900 . .	**. . .**	**. . .**	**. . .**	**. . .**	**. . .**	**. . .**	**–1.8**	**. . .**
Monetary authorities	4 901 . .	. . .	. . .	. . .	. . .	. . .	. . .	. . .	. . .
General government	4 902 . .	. . .	. . .	. . .	. . .	. . .	. . .	. . .	. . .
Banks	4 903 . .	. . .	. . .	. . .	. . .	. . .	. . .	–1.8	. . .
Other sectors	4 904 . .	. . .	. . .	. . .	. . .	. . .	. . .	. . .	. . .
Liabilities	4 905 . .	**. . .**	**. . .**	**. . .**	**. . .**	**. . .**	**. . .**	**–1.8**	**17.5**
Monetary authorities	4 906 . .	. . .	. . .	. . .	. . .	. . .	. . .	. . .	. . .
General government	4 907 . .	. . .	. . .	. . .	. . .	. . .	. . .	. . .	. . .
Banks	4 908 . .	. . .	. . .	. . .	. . .	. . .	. . .	–1.8	17.5
Other sectors	4 909 . .	. . .	. . .	. . .	. . .	. . .	. . .	. . .	. . .

Table 2 (Concluded). STANDARD PRESENTATION, 1994–2001

(Millions of U.S. dollars)

	Code	1994	1995	1996	1997	1998	1999	2000	2001
D. OTHER INVESTMENT	4 700 . .	–335.1	83.0	–735.4	318.7	526.9	618.9	330.6	149.2
Assets	4 703 . .	**–209.2**	**404.2**	**–568.1**	**–53.9**	**222.2**	**16.6**	**–136.6**	**348.3**
Trade credits	4 706 . .	...	...	–1.0	–.2	...	–.6	120.9	...
General government	4 707 . .	...	...	...	...	...	...	...	...
of which: Short-term	4 709 . .	...	...	...	...	...	...	...	...
Other sectors	4 710 . .	...	...	–1.0	–.2	...	–.6	120.9	...
of which: Short-term	4 712 . .	...	...	*–1.0*	*–.2*	...	*–.6*	*120.9*	...
Loans	4 714 . .	263.1	292.6	339.2	139.3	17.1	11.1	–7.5	15.2
Monetary authorities	4 715 . .	...	...	...	...	...	...	...	...
of which: Short-term	4 718 . .	...	...	...	...	...	...	...	...
General government	4 719 . .	263.1	292.6	339.5	129.2	...	...	...	...
of which: Short-term	4 721 . .	...	...	...	...	...	...	...	...
Banks	4 722 . .	...	...	–.5	.4	6.3	...	–7.5	–.8
of which: Short-term	4 724 . .	...	...	*–.5*	*.4*	*.8*	...	*–3.3*	*–.8*
Other sectors	4 725 . .	...	...	.2	9.7	10.8	11.1	...	16.0
of which: Short-term	4 727 . .	...	...	*.2*	*6.6*	*10.5*	*.7*	...	*–.5*
Currency and deposits	4 730 . .	–472.3	171.4	109.4	–421.4	42.4	–53.4	–240.1	357.1
Monetary authorities	4 731 . .	...	...	...	...	...	...	...	...
General government	4 732 . .	–173.0	...	...	...	...	...	...	...
Banks	4 733 . .	–299.3	171.4	68.1	–436.0	69.4	22.7	–486.5	–128.7
Other sectors	4 734 . .	...	...	41.3	14.6	–27.0	–76.1	246.4	485.8
Other assets	4 736 . .	...	–59.8	–1,015.7	228.4	162.7	59.5	–9.9	–24.0
Monetary authorities	4 737 . .	...	...	...	...	...	...	.9	–2.2
of which: Short-term	4 739 . .	...	...	...	...	...	...	*.9*	*–2.2*
General government	4 740 . .	...	...	–45.8	–22.7	–19.8	–17.5	–9.1	–20.7
of which: Short-term	4 742 . .	...	...	*–45.8*	*–22.7*	*–19.8*	*–17.5*	*–9.1*	*–20.7*
Banks	4 743 . .	...	–59.8	46.1	–5.0	27.3	3.0	–1.7	–1.1
of which: Short-term	4 745 . .	...	*–59.8*	*46.1*	*–5.0*	*27.3*	*3.0*	*–1.7*	*–1.1*
Other sectors	4 746 . .	...	...	–1,016.0	256.1	155.2	74.0	...	...
of which: Short-term	4 748 . .	...	...	*–1,016.0*	*256.1*	*155.2*	*74.0*	...	...
Liabilities	4 753 . .	**–125.9**	**–321.2**	**–167.3**	**372.6**	**304.7**	**602.3**	**467.2**	**–199.1**
Trade credits	4 756 . .	...	...	.3	16.3	9.2	79.7	29.5	–27.4
General government	4 757 . .	...	...	...	...	...	...	...	...
of which: Short-term	4 759 . .	...	...	...	...	...	...	...	...
Other sectors	4 760 . .	...	...	.3	16.3	9.2	79.7	29.5	–27.4
of which: Short-term	4 762 . .	...	...	*.3*	*16.3*	*9.2*	*79.7*	*29.5*	*–27.4*
Loans	4 764 . .	–393.0	–310.8	–204.3	254.5	377.9	504.1	330.2	–358.1
Monetary authorities	4 765 . .	557.2	–245.9	–108.7	396.9	129.4	161.9	136.0	–168.5
of which: Use of Fund credit and loans from the Fund	4 766 . .	*262.4*	*–245.9*	*–108.7*	*396.9*	*129.4*	*161.9*	*136.0*	*–168.5*
of which: Short-term	4 768 . .	...	...	...	...	...	...	...	...
General government	4 769 . .	–894.0	–1.9	44.0	–82.1	220.6	164.4	–80.3	–307.9
of which: Short-term	4 771 . .	...	...	...	...	*–2.1*	...	...	...
Banks	4 772 . .	–56.2	–63.0	–119.9	–55.0	13.2	...	37.5	8.4
of which: Short-term	4 774 . .	...	*–12.4*	*–13.9*	*–7.8*	*–.2*	*–.1*	*5.5*	*1.7*
Other sectors	4 775 . .	...	...	–19.7	–5.3	14.7	177.8	237.0	109.9
of which: Short-term	4 777 . .	...	...	*–45.5*	*–8.7*	*7.9*	*17.7*	*79.7*	*–60.7*
Currency and deposits	4 780 . .	17.0	–29.8	–94.9	16.3	–79.5	44.5	73.1	44.7
Monetary authorities	4 781 . .	...	...	...	...	...	...	...	...
General government	4 782 . .	...	...	...	...	...	...	...	...
Banks	4 783 . .	17.0	–29.8	–94.9	16.3	–79.5	44.5	73.1	44.7
Other sectors	4 784 . .	...	...	...	...	...	...	...	...
Other liabilities	4 786 . .	250.1	19.4	131.6	85.5	–2.9	–26.0	34.4	141.7
Monetary authorities	4 787 . .	...	...	...	...	...	...	...	...
of which: Short-term	4 789 . .	...	...	...	...	...	...	...	...
General government	4 790 . .	–57.0	...	...	53.8	–7.9	...	–7.7	...
of which: Short-term	4 792 . .	*–57.0*	...	...	*53.8*	*–275.5*	...	*–7.7*	...
Banks	4 793 . .	...	33.0	131.6	31.7	1.2	–34.4	–2.2	49.7
of which: Short-term	4 795 . .	...	*33.0*	*131.6*	*31.7*	*1.2*	*–34.4*	*–2.2*	*49.7*
Other sectors	4 796 . .	307.1	–13.6	...	...	3.8	8.4	44.3	92.0
of which: Short-term	4 798 . .	*307.1*	*–13.6*	...	...	*3.8*	*8.4*	*44.3*	*92.0*
E. RESERVE ASSETS	4 802 . .	–341.6	–233.7	750.9	–1,641.3	–461.5	–527.6	–408.9	–275.3
Monetary gold	4 812 . .	...	...	...	...	...	...	...	...
Special drawing rights	4 811 . .	–11.9	–14.7	17.5	–.1	–17.9	–51.6	–6.0	81.4
Reserve position in the Fund	4 810 . .	...	...	...	...	...	–.1	–.1	...
Foreign exchange	4 803 . .	–329.7	–219.0	733.4	–1,641.2	–443.6	–476.0	–402.9	–356.7
Other claims	4 813 . .	...	...	...	...	...	...	...	...
NET ERRORS AND OMISSIONS	4 998 . .	**71.6**	**143.8**	**–105.3**	**256.4**	**–299.2**	**6.1**	**–68.3**	**288.5**

Part 3 of the *Yearbook* contains descriptions of the methodologies, compilation practices, and sources used to compile these data.

Table 3. INTERNATIONAL INVESTMENT POSITION (End-period stocks), 1994–2001
(Millions of U.S. dollars)

	Code	1994	1995	1996	1997	1998	1999	2000	2001
ASSETS	8 995 C.	...	...	...	...	8,708.0	9,022.6	9,956.1	10,799.2
Direct investment abroad	8 505 . .	...	...	...	...	**74.5**	**90.0**	**87.0**	**96.6**
Equity capital and reinvested earnings	8 506 . .	...	...	...	...	37.9	50.4	45.2	51.5
Claims on affiliated enterprises	8 507 . .	...	...	...	...	37.9	50.4	45.2	51.5
Liabilities to affiliated enterprises	8 508 . .	...	...	...	...	...	...	...	...
Other capital	8 530 . .	...	...	...	...	36.6	39.6	41.8	45.2
Claims on affiliated enterprises	8 535 . .	...	...	...	...	53.4	79.1	95.6	99.0
Liabilities to affiliated enterprises	8 540 . .	...	...	...	...	–16.8	–39.5	–53.8	–53.8
Portfolio investment	8 602 . .	...	...	...	...	**521.9**	**677.6**	**728.2**	**755.0**
Equity securities	8 610 . .	...	...	...	...	20.5	20.6	28.7	13.9
Monetary authorities	8 611 . .	...	...	...	...	...	...	...	...
General government	8 612 . .	...	...	...	...	...	...	...	...
Banks	8 613 . .	...	...	...	...	20.5	20.1	27.8	10.6
Other sectors	8 614 . .	...	...	...	...	...	.5	.9	3.3
Debt securities	8 619 . .	...	...	...	...	501.4	657.0	699.5	741.1
Bonds and notes	8 620 . .	...	...	...	...	335.1	485.9	517.9	628.8
Monetary authorities	8 621 . .	...	...	...	...	...	...	...	...
General government	8 622 . .	...	...	...	...	307.5	331.2	356.9	337.2
Banks	8 623 . .	...	...	...	...	27.6	144.7	135.3	265.8
Other sectors	8 624 . .	...	...	...	...	...	10.0	25.7	25.8
Money market instruments	8 630 . .	...	...	...	...	166.2	171.1	181.6	112.3
Monetary authorities	8 631 . .	...	...	...	...	80.0	79.9	79.8	...
General government	8 632 . .	...	...	...	...	85.5	85.6	85.5	102.4
Banks	8 633 . .	...	...	...	...	.8	.7	11.3	4.5
Other sectors	8 634 . .	...	...	...	...	...	5.1	5.1	5.4
Financial derivatives	8 900 . .	...	...	...	...	...	...	**1.8**	**19.2**
Monetary authorities	8 901 . .	...	...	...	...	...	...	...	...
General government	8 902 . .	...	...	...	...	...	...	...	...
Banks	8 903 . .	...	...	...	...	...	...	1.8	19.2
Other sectors	8 904 . .	...	...	...	...	...	...	...	...
Other investment	8 703 . .	...	...	...	...	**5,055.3**	**5,033.4**	**5,678.9**	**6,348.0**
Trade credits	8 706 . .	...	...	...	...	...	...	...	...
General government	8 707 . .	...	...	...	...	...	...	...	...
of which: Short-term	8 709 . .	...	...	...	...	...	...	...	...
Other sectors	8 710 . .	...	...	...	...	...	...	...	...
of which: Short-term	8 712 . .	...	...	...	...	...	...	...	...
Loans	8 714 . .	...	...	...	...	42.3	36.8	21.6	18.3
Monetary authorities	8 715 . .	...	...	...	...	...	...	...	...
of which: Short-term	8 718 . .	...	...	...	...	...	...	...	...
General government	8 719 . .	...	...	...	...	...	...	...	...
of which: Short-term	8 721 . .	...	...	...	...	...	...	...	...
Banks	8 722 . .	...	...	...	...	42.3	36.8	21.5	18.2
of which: Short-term	8 724 . .	...	...	...	...	*42.3*	*36.8*	*11.3*	*7.3*
Other sectors	8 725 . .	...	...	...	...	...	...	.1	.1
of which: Short-term	8 727 . .	...	...	...	...	...	...	...	...
Currency and deposits	8 730 . .	...	...	...	...	1,807.8	1,707.1	2,093.6	2,184.5
Monetary authorities	8 731 . .	...	...	...	...	...	...	...	...
General government	8 732 . .	...	...	...	...	...	...	...	...
Banks	8 733 . .	...	...	...	...	1,466.8	1,348.1	1,766.6	1,810.5
Other sectors	8 734 . .	...	...	...	...	341.0	359.0	327.0	374.0
Other assets	8 736 . .	...	...	...	...	3,205.2	3,289.5	3,563.7	4,145.2
Monetary authorities	8 737 . .	...	...	...	...	3.0	2.5	2.3	2.2
of which: Short-term	8 739 . .	...	...	...	...	*.5*	...	...	...
General government	8 740 . .	...	...	...	...	2,348.2	2,389.9	2,416.7	2,446.7
of which: Short-term	8 742 . .	...	...	...	...	*2,348.2*	*2,389.9*	*2,416.7*	*2,446.7*
Banks	8 743 . .	...	...	...	...	15.5	12.4	18.1	20.0
of which: Short-term	8 745 . .	...	...	...	...	*15.5*	*12.4*	*18.1*	*20.0*
Other sectors	8 746 . .	...	...	...	...	838.5	884.7	1,126.6	1,676.3
of which: Short-term	8 748 . .	...	...	...	...	*838.5*	*884.7*	*1,126.6*	*1,676.3*
Reserve assets	8 802 . .	...	...	...	...	**3,056.4**	**3,221.6**	**3,460.3**	**3,580.4**
Monetary gold	8 812 . .	...	...	...	...	296.3	264.8	245.3	232.3
Special drawing rights	8 811 . .	15.2	29.8	11.9	11.3	30.1	81.7	84.6	2.3
Reserve position in the Fund	8 810 . .	47.6	48.5	46.9	44.0	46.0	44.9	42.7	41.2
Foreign exchange	8 803 . .	...	...	...	...	2,674.5	2,791.6	3,058.2	3,278.3
Other claims	8 813 . .	...	...	...	...	9.5	38.6	29.5	26.3

Table 3 (Concluded). INTERNATIONAL INVESTMENT POSITION (End-period stocks), 1994–2001
(Millions of U.S. dollars)

	Code	1994	1995	1996	1997	1998	1999	2000	2001
LIABILITIES	8 995 D.	...	...	...	...	12,539.9	13,086.8	13,674.9	13,663.7
Direct investment in Bulgaria	8 555 ..	...	...	...	...	**1,596.6**	**2,402.7**	**2,716.0**	**3,410.2**
Equity capital and reinvested earnings	8 556 ..	...	...	...	...	1,382.3	1,837.4	2,124.0	2,608.6
Claims on direct investors	8 557 ..	...	...	...	...	...	...	...	...
Liabilities to direct investors	8 558 ..	...	...	...	...	1,382.3	1,837.4	2,124.0	2,608.6
Other capital	8 580 ..	...	...	...	...	214.3	565.3	592.0	801.6
Claims on direct investors	8 585 ..	...	...	...	...	...	...	–20.3	–39.8
Liabilities to direct investors	8 590 ..	...	...	...	...	214.3	565.3	612.3	841.4
Portfolio investment	8 652 ..	...	...	...	...	**5,173.1**	**5,195.4**	**5,193.6**	**5,083.3**
Equity securities	8 660 ..	...	...	...	...	113.4	97.9	99.9	95.3
Banks	8 663 ..	...	...	...	...	28.0	27.7	24.4	31.3
Other sectors	8 664 ..	...	...	...	...	85.4	70.2	75.5	64.0
Debt securities	8 669 ..	...	...	...	...	5,059.7	5,097.5	5,093.7	4,988.0
Bonds and notes	8 670 ..	...	...	...	...	5,059.5	5,082.6	5,093.7	4,988.0
Monetary authorities	8 671 ..	...	...	...	...	...	...	...	...
General government	8 672 ..	...	...	...	...	5,059.5	5,082.6	5,093.7	4,988.0
Banks	8 673 ..	...	...	...	...	...	...	...	...
Other sectors	8 674 ..	...	...	...	...	...	...	...	...
Money market instruments	8 680 ..	...	...	...	...	.2	14.9	...	...
Monetary authorities	8 681 ..	...	...	...	...	...	...	...	...
General government	8 682 ..	...	...	...	...	.2	.6	...	...
Banks	8 683 ..	...	...	...	...	...	14.3	...	...
Other sectors	8 684 ..	...	...	...	...	...	...	...	...
Financial derivatives	8 905 ..	...	...	...	...	...	...	...	...
Monetary authorities	8 906 ..	...	...	...	...	...	...	...	...
General government	8 907 ..	...	...	...	...	...	...	...	...
Banks	8 908 ..	...	...	...	...	...	...	...	...
Other sectors	8 909 ..	...	...	...	...	...	...	...	...
Other investment	8 753 ..	...	...	...	...	**5,770.2**	**5,488.7**	**5,765.3**	**5,170.2**
Trade credits	8 756 ..	...	...	...	...	617.6	709.6	837.4	712.4
General government	8 757 ..	...	...	...	...	...	...	...	...
of which: Short-term	8 759 ..	...	...	...	...	...	...	...	...
Other sectors	8 760 ..	...	...	...	...	617.6	709.6	837.4	712.4
of which: Short-term	8 762 ..	...	...	...	...	*585.4*	*672.3*	*803.7*	*654.5*
Loans	8 764 ..	...	...	...	...	4,201.4	4,442.7	4,568.2	4,130.2
Monetary authorities	8 765 ..	...	...	...	...	1,115.5	1,250.0	1,322.0	1,109.7
of which: Use of Fund credit and loans from the Fund	8 766 ..	*940.7*	*716.7*	*585.6*	*941.8*	*1,115.5*	*1,250.0*	*1,322.0*	*1,109.7*
of which: Short-term	8 768 ..	...	...	...	...	...	...	...	...
General government	8 769 ..	...	...	...	...	2,457.7	2,260.6	2,257.3	1,969.5
of which: Short-term	8 771 ..	...	...	...	...	...	...	...	...
Banks	8 772 ..	...	...	...	...	3.7	2.8	43.2	49.9
of which: Short-term	8 774 ..	...	...	...	...	*.5*	*.1*	*9.3*	*10.6*
Other sectors	8 775 ..	...	...	...	...	624.5	929.3	945.7	1,001.1
of which: Short-term	8 777 ..	...	...	...	...	*63.0*	*101.3*	*155.2*	*97.4*
Currency and deposits	8 780 ..	...	...	...	...	99.3	129.8	174.5	195.7
Monetary authorities	8 781 ..	...	...	...	...	...	...	...	...
General government	8 782 ..	...	...	...	...	...	...	...	...
Banks	8 783 ..	...	...	...	...	99.3	129.8	174.5	195.7
Other sectors	8 784 ..	...	...	...	...	...	...	...	...
Other liabilities	8 786 ..	...	...	...	...	851.9	206.6	185.2	131.9
Monetary authorities	8 787 ..	...	...	...	...	2.5	2.8	3.1	2.3
of which: Short-term	8 789 ..	...	...	...	...	*.8*	*.8*	*.9*	*.3*
General government	8 790 ..	...	...	...	...	511.1	11.1	3.5	1.4
of which: Short-term	8 792 ..	...	...	...	...	*511.1*	*11.1*	*3.5*	*1.4*
Banks	8 793 ..	...	...	...	...	337.9	192.7	178.6	128.2
of which: Short-term	8 795 ..	...	...	...	...	*337.9*	*192.7*	*178.6*	*128.2*
Other sectors	8 796 ..	...	...	...	...	.4	...	...	...
of which: Short-term	8 798 ..	...	...	...	...	*.4*	...	...	...
NET INTERNATIONAL INVESTMENT POSITION	8 995 ..	...	...	...	...	**–3,831.9**	**–4,064.2**	**–3,718.7**	**–2,864.5**
Conversion rates: leva per U.S. dollar (end of period)	0 102 ..	**.0660**	**.0707**	**.4874**	**1.7765**	**1.6751**	**1.9469**	**2.1019**	**2.2193**

Table 1. ANALYTIC PRESENTATION, 1994–2001
(Millions of U.S. dollars)

	Code		1994	1995	1996	1997	1998	1999	2000	2001
A. Current Account [1]	4 993	Z.	**–16.9**	**10.4**	**–40.0**	**–1.0**	**–53.6**	**–27.0**	**–48.8**	**. . .**
Goods: exports f.o.b	2 100	. .	80.7	112.9	40.4	87.5	64.0	55.0	49.1	. . .
Goods: imports f.o.b	3 100	. .	–172.6	–175.6	–100.0	–96.1	–123.5	–97.3	–107.9	. . .
Balance on Goods	4 100	. .	*–91.9*	*–62.7*	*–59.6*	*–8.6*	*–59.5*	*–42.3*	*–58.8*	. . .
Services: credit	2 200	. .	14.9	16.4	10.5	8.7	7.6	6.3	6.1	. . .
Services: debit	3 200	. .	–93.9	–83.3	–38.4	–45.4	–49.5	–32.6	–43.4	. . .
Balance on Goods and Services	4 991	. .	*–170.9*	*–129.6*	*–87.4*	*–45.3*	*–101.3*	*–68.7*	*–96.1*	. . .
Income: credit	2 300	. .	8.1	10.4	6.4	4.3	3.6	1.9	2.4	. . .
Income: debit	3 300	. .	–19.5	–22.9	–20.4	–16.8	–11.9	–11.3	–14.5	. . .
Balance on Goods, Services, and Income	4 992	. .	*–182.3*	*–142.1*	*–101.4*	*–57.8*	*–109.6*	*–78.1*	*–108.2*	. . .
Current transfers: credit	2 379	Z.	167.0	154.7	62.5	61.3	59.3	52.9	61.1	. . .
Current transfers: debit	3 379	. .	–1.6	–2.1	–1.1	–4.5	–3.3	–1.8	–1.8	. . .
B. Capital Account [1]	4 994	Z.	**–.2**	**–.8**	**–.3**	**–.1**	**. . .**	**. . .**	**. . .**	**. . .**
Capital account: credit	2 994	Z.	. . .	. . .	. . .	. . .	. . .	. . .	. . .	. . .
Capital account: debit	3 994	. .	–.2	–.8	–.3	–.1	. . .	. . .	. . .	. . .
Total, Groups A Plus B	4 981	. .	*–17.1*	*9.7*	*–40.3*	*–1.1*	*–53.6*	*–27.0*	*–48.8*	. . .
C. Financial Account [1]	4 995	W.	**31.1**	**21.1**	**14.1**	**13.7**	**28.8**	**17.0**	**58.9**	**. . .**
Direct investment abroad	4 505	. .	–.1	–.6	. . .	. . .	. . .	. . .	. . .	. . .
Direct investment in Burundi	4 555	Z.	. . .	2.0	. . .	. . .	. . .	.2	11.7	. . .
Portfolio investment assets	4 602	. .	. . .	. . .	. . .	. . .	. . .	. . .	. . .	. . .
Equity securities	4 610	. .	. . .	. . .	. . .	. . .	. . .	. . .	. . .	. . .
Debt securities	4 619	. .	. . .	. . .	. . .	. . .	. . .	. . .	. . .	. . .
Portfolio investment liabilities	4 652	Z.	. . .	. . .	. . .	. . .	. . .	. . .	. . .	. . .
Equity securities	4 660	. .	. . .	. . .	. . .	. . .	. . .	. . .	. . .	. . .
Debt securities	4 669	Z.	. . .	. . .	. . .	. . .	. . .	. . .	. . .	. . .
Financial derivatives	4 910	. .	. . .	. . .	. . .	. . .	. . .	. . .	. . .	. . .
Financial derivatives assets	4 900	. .	. . .	. . .	. . .	. . .	. . .	. . .	. . .	. . .
Financial derivatives liabilities	4 905	. .	. . .	. . .	. . .	. . .	. . .	. . .	. . .	. . .
Other investment assets	4 703	. .	–1.6	8.2	6.6	15.3	10.7	13.7	5.1	. . .
Monetary authorities	4 701	. .	. . .	. . .	. . .	. . .	. . .	. . .	. . .	. . .
General government	4 704	. .	–.8	–.4	–.3	–.4	–.3	–.3	. . .	. . .
Banks	4 705	. .	–8.8	.1	–10.4	8.5	5.0	–10.3	–8.2	. . .
Other sectors	4 728	. .	7.9	8.6	17.3	7.1	6.0	24.3	13.3	. . .
Other investment liabilities	4 753	W.	32.9	11.5	7.6	–1.6	18.1	3.1	42.2	. . .
Monetary authorities	4 753	WA	. . .	. . .	. . .	. . .	. . .	. . .	. . .	. . .
General government	4 753	ZB	25.2	4.9	7.3	–8.0	15.3	.2	32.2	. . .
Banks	4 753	ZC	4.7	–.4	–2.0	1.6	1.7	1.9	8.7	. . .
Other sectors	4 753	ZD	3.0	7.0	2.2	4.8	1.1	1.1	1.2	. . .
Total, Groups A Through C	4 983	. .	*14.1*	*30.8*	*–26.2*	*12.6*	*–24.9*	*–10.0*	*10.1*	. . .
D. Net Errors and Omissions	4 998	. .	**21.1**	**5.9**	**–9.2**	**–2.4**	**5.4**	**8.7**	**–6.2**	**. . .**
Total, Groups A Through D	4 984	. .	*35.2*	*36.7*	*–35.3*	*10.2*	*–19.5*	*–1.2*	*3.9*	. . .
E. Reserves and Related Items	4 802	A.	**–35.2**	**–36.7**	**35.3**	**–10.2**	**19.5**	**1.2**	**–3.9**	**. . .**
Reserve assets	4 802	. .	–29.0	–27.6	44.0	–2.0	28.7	8.8	1.2	. . .
Use of Fund credit and loans	4 766	. .	–6.1	–9.0	–8.7	–8.3	–9.3	–7.6	–5.0	. . .
Exceptional financing	4 920	. .	. . .	. . .	. . .	. . .	. . .	. . .	. . .	. . .
Conversion rates: Burundi francs per U.S. dollar	0 101	. .	**252.66**	**249.76**	**302.75**	**352.35**	**447.77**	**563.56**	**720.67**	**830.35**

[1] Excludes components that have been classified in the categories of Group E.

Table 2. STANDARD PRESENTATION, 1994–2001
(Millions of U.S. dollars)

	Code		1994	1995	1996	1997	1998	1999	2000	2001
CURRENT ACCOUNT	4 993	. .	**–16.9**	**10.4**	**–40.0**	**–1.0**	**–53.6**	**–27.0**	**–48.8**	**. . .**
A. GOODS	4 100	. .	–91.9	–62.7	–59.6	–8.6	–59.5	–42.3	–58.8	. . .
Credit	2 100	. .	**80.7**	**112.9**	**40.4**	**87.5**	**64.0**	**55.0**	**49.1**	**. . .**
General merchandise: exports f.o.b.	2 110	. .	80.7	112.9	40.4	87.5	64.0	55.0	49.1	. . .
Goods for processing: exports f.o.b.	2 150	. .	. . .	. . .	. . .	. . .	. . .	. . .	. . .	. . .
Repairs on goods	2 160	. .	. . .	. . .	. . .	. . .	. . .	. . .	. . .	. . .
Goods procured in ports by carriers	2 170	. .	. . .	. . .	. . .	. . .	. . .	. . .	. . .	. . .
Nonmonetary gold	2 180	. .	. . .	. . .	. . .	. . .	. . .	. . .	. . .	. . .
Debit	3 100	. .	**–172.6**	**–175.6**	**–100.0**	**–96.1**	**–123.5**	**–97.3**	**–107.9**	**. . .**
General merchandise: imports f.o.b.	3 110	. .	–172.6	–175.6	–100.0	–96.1	–123.5	–97.3	–107.9	. . .
Goods for processing: imports f.o.b.	3 150	. .	. . .	. . .	. . .	. . .	. . .	. . .	. . .	. . .
Repairs on goods	3 160	. .	. . .	. . .	. . .	. . .	. . .	. . .	. . .	. . .
Goods procured in ports by carriers	3 170	. .	. . .	. . .	. . .	. . .	. . .	. . .	. . .	. . .
Nonmonetary gold	3 180	. .	. . .	. . .	. . .	. . .	. . .	. . .	. . .	. . .
B. SERVICES	4 200	. .	–79.0	–66.9	–27.8	–36.7	–41.9	–26.4	–37.3	. . .
Total credit	2 200	. .	*14.9*	*16.4*	*10.5*	*8.7*	*7.6*	*6.3*	*6.1*	. . .
Total debit	3 200	. .	*–93.9*	*–83.3*	*–38.4*	*–45.4*	*–49.5*	*–32.6*	*–43.4*	. . .
Transportation services, credit	2 205	. .	**3.1**	**2.0**	**1.4**	**1.6**	**1.6**	**.9**	**.9**	**. . .**
Passenger	2 850	. .	*1.3*	*1.0*	*.9*	*.8*	*.9*	*.5*	*.6*	. . .
Freight	2 851	. .	*1.8*	*1.0*	*.5*	*.8*	*.8*	*.4*	*.2*	. . .
Other	2 852	. .	. . .	. . .	. . .	. . .	. . .	. . .	. . .	. . .
Sea transport, passenger	2 207	. .	. . .	. . .	. . .	. . .	. . .	. . .	. . .	. . .
Sea transport, freight	2 208	. .	. . .	. . .	. . .	. . .	. . .	. . .	. . .	. . .
Sea transport, other	2 209	. .	. . .	. . .	. . .	. . .	. . .	. . .	. . .	. . .
Air transport, passenger	2 211	. .	. . .	. . .	. . .	. . .	. . .	. . .	. . .	. . .
Air transport, freight	2 212	. .	. . .	. . .	. . .	. . .	. . .	. . .	. . .	. . .
Air transport, other	2 213	. .	. . .	. . .	. . .	. . .	. . .	. . .	. . .	. . .
Other transport, passenger	2 215	. .	. . .	. . .	. . .	. . .	. . .	. . .	. . .	. . .
Other transport, freight	2 216	. .	. . .	. . .	. . .	. . .	. . .	. . .	. . .	. . .
Other transport, other	2 217	. .	. . .	. . .	. . .	. . .	. . .	. . .	. . .	. . .
Transportation services, debit	3 205	. .	**–35.8**	**–30.6**	**–13.8**	**–21.9**	**–28.2**	**–13.6**	**–19.0**	**. . .**
Passenger	3 850	. .	. . .	. . .	. . .	. . .	. . .	. . .	. . .	. . .
Freight	3 851	. .	*–35.8*	*–30.6*	*–13.8*	*–21.9*	*–28.2*	*–13.6*	*–19.0*	. . .
Other	3 852	. .	. . .	. . .	. . .	. . .	. . .	. . .	. . .	. . .
Sea transport, passenger	3 207	. .	. . .	. . .	. . .	. . .	. . .	. . .	. . .	. . .
Sea transport, freight	3 208	. .	. . .	. . .	. . .	. . .	. . .	. . .	. . .	. . .
Sea transport, other	3 209	. .	. . .	. . .	. . .	. . .	. . .	. . .	. . .	. . .
Air transport, passenger	3 211	. .	. . .	. . .	. . .	. . .	. . .	. . .	. . .	. . .
Air transport, freight	3 212	. .	. . .	. . .	. . .	. . .	. . .	. . .	. . .	. . .
Air transport, other	3 213	. .	. . .	. . .	. . .	. . .	. . .	. . .	. . .	. . .
Other transport, passenger	3 215	. .	. . .	. . .	. . .	. . .	. . .	. . .	. . .	. . .
Other transport, freight	3 216	. .	. . .	. . .	. . .	. . .	. . .	. . .	. . .	. . .
Other transport, other	3 217	. .	. . .	. . .	. . .	. . .	. . .	. . .	. . .	. . .
Travel, credit	2 236	. .	**1.9**	**1.4**	**1.2**	**.6**	**.4**	**.7**	**.8**	**. . .**
Business travel	2 237	. .	. . .	. . .	. . .	. . .	. . .	. . .	. . .	. . .
Personal travel	2 240	. .	. . .	. . .	. . .	. . .	. . .	. . .	. . .	. . .
Travel, debit	3 236	. .	**–18.0**	**–25.4**	**–12.1**	**–12.1**	**–10.5**	**–8.2**	**–13.5**	**. . .**
Business travel	3 237	. .	. . .	. . .	. . .	. . .	. . .	. . .	. . .	. . .
Personal travel	3 240	. .	. . .	. . .	. . .	. . .	. . .	. . .	. . .	. . .
Other services, credit	2 200	BA	**9.9**	**13.0**	**7.9**	**6.4**	**5.6**	**4.7**	**4.5**	**. . .**
Communications	2 245	. .	. . .	. . .	. . .	. . .	. . .	. . .	. . .	. . .
Construction	2 249	. .	. . .	. . .	. . .	. . .	. . .	. . .	. . .	. . .
Insurance	2 253	. .	.5	. . .	.4	.3	.1	. . .	. . .	. . .
Financial	2 260	. .	. . .	. . .	. . .	. . .	. . .	. . .	. . .	. . .
Computer and information	2 262	. .	. . .	. . .	. . .	. . .	. . .	. . .	. . .	. . .
Royalties and licence fees	2 266	. .	. . .	. . .	. . .	. . .	. . .	. . .	. . .	. . .
Other business services	2 268	. .	.9	.9	1.5	.8	.4	.3	.4	. . .
Personal, cultural, and recreational	2 287	. .	. . .	. . .	. . .	. . .	. . .	. . .	. . .	. . .
Government, n.i.e.	2 291	. .	8.5	12.1	6.0	5.3	5.0	4.3	4.1	. . .
Other services, debit	3 200	BA	**–40.1**	**–27.4**	**–12.5**	**–11.3**	**–10.8**	**–10.8**	**–10.9**	**. . .**
Communications	3 245	. .	. . .	. . .	. . .	. . .	. . .	. . .	. . .	. . .
Construction	3 249	. .	. . .	. . .	. . .	. . .	. . .	. . .	. . .	. . .
Insurance	3 253	. .	–2.9	–3.7	–1.4	–1.0	–.6	–.9	–.6	. . .
Financial	3 260	. .	. . .	. . .	. . .	. . .	. . .	. . .	. . .	. . .
Computer and information	3 262	. .	. . .	. . .	. . .	. . .	. . .	. . .	. . .	. . .
Royalties and licence fees	3 266	. .	. . .	–.1	. . .	–.1	. . .	. . .	. . .	. . .
Other business services	3 268	. .	–1.8	–2.2	–1.6	–1.7	–.7	–1.0	–1.0	. . .
Personal, cultural, and recreational	3 287	. .	. . .	. . .	. . .	. . .	. . .	. . .	. . .	. . .
Government, n.i.e.	3 291	. .	–35.4	–21.4	–9.4	–8.6	–9.5	–8.9	–9.4	. . .

Table 2 (Continued). STANDARD PRESENTATION, 1994–2001
(Millions of U.S. dollars)

	Code	1994	1995	1996	1997	1998	1999	2000	2001
C. INCOME	4 300 . .	–11.4	–12.5	–13.9	–12.5	–8.3	–9.4	–12.1	. . .
Total credit	2 300 . .	*8.1*	*10.4*	*6.4*	*4.3*	*3.6*	*1.9*	*2.4*	. . .
Total debit	3 300 . .	*–19.5*	*–22.9*	*–20.4*	*–16.8*	*–11.9*	*–11.3*	*–14.5*	. . .
Compensation of employees, credit	2 310 . .	**. . .**	**. . .**	**. . .**	**. . .**	**. . .**	**. . .**	**. . .**	**. . .**
Compensation of employees, debit	3 310 . .	**–3.9**	**–4.5**	**–4.5**	**–2.3**	**–2.2**	**–2.1**	**–2.5**	**. . .**
Investment income, credit	2 320 . .	**8.1**	**10.4**	**6.4**	**4.3**	**3.6**	**1.9**	**2.4**	**. . .**
Direct investment income	2 330 . .	. . .	. . .	. . .	. . .	. . .	. . .	. . .	. . .
Dividends and distributed branch profits	2 332 . .	. . .	. . .	. . .	. . .	. . .	. . .	. . .	. . .
Reinvested earnings and undistributed branch profits	2 333 . .	. . .	. . .	. . .	. . .	. . .	. . .	. . .	. . .
Income on debt (interest)	2 334 . .	. . .	. . .	. . .	. . .	. . .	. . .	. . .	. . .
Portfolio investment income	2 339 . .	. . .	. . .	. . .	. . .	. . .	. . .	. . .	. . .
Income on equity	2 340 . .	. . .	. . .	. . .	. . .	. . .	. . .	. . .	. . .
Income on bonds and notes	2 350 . .	. . .	. . .	. . .	. . .	. . .	. . .	. . .	. . .
Income on money market instruments	2 360 . .	. . .	. . .	. . .	. . .	. . .	. . .	. . .	. . .
Other investment income	2 370 . .	8.1	10.4	6.4	4.3	3.6	1.9	2.4	. . .
Investment income, debit	3 320 . .	**–15.5**	**–18.4**	**–15.8**	**–14.5**	**–9.7**	**–9.2**	**–12.0**	**. . .**
Direct investment income	3 330 . .	–3.4	–3.1	–1.4	–.6	. . .	. . .	–.4	. . .
Dividends and distributed branch profits	3 332 . .	–3.4	–3.1	–1.4	–.6	. . .	. . .	–.4	. . .
Reinvested earnings and undistributed branch profits	3 333 . .	. . .	. . .	. . .	. . .	. . .	. . .	. . .	. . .
Income on debt (interest)	3 334 . .	. . .	. . .	. . .	. . .	. . .	. . .	. . .	. . .
Portfolio investment income	3 339 . .	. . .	. . .	. . .	. . .	. . .	. . .	. . .	. . .
Income on equity	3 340 . .	. . .	. . .	. . .	. . .	. . .	. . .	. . .	. . .
Income on bonds and notes	3 350 . .	. . .	. . .	. . .	. . .	. . .	. . .	. . .	. . .
Income on money market instruments	3 360 . .	. . .	. . .	. . .	. . .	. . .	. . .	. . .	. . .
Other investment income	3 370 . .	–12.1	–15.3	–14.5	–13.9	–9.7	–9.2	–11.6	. . .
D. CURRENT TRANSFERS	4 379 . .	165.4	152.5	61.4	56.8	56.0	51.1	59.4	. . .
Credit	2 379 . .	**167.0**	**154.7**	**62.5**	**61.3**	**59.3**	**52.9**	**61.1**	**. . .**
General government	2 380 . .	144.6	137.1	50.4	51.5	51.5	46.6	55.8	. . .
Other sectors	2 390 . .	22.3	17.5	12.1	9.8	7.8	6.2	5.4	. . .
Workers' remittances	2 391 . .	. . .	. . .	. . .	. . .	. . .	. . .	. . .	. . .
Other current transfers	2 392 . .	22.3	17.5	12.1	9.8	7.8	6.2	5.4	. . .
Debit	3 379 . .	**–1.6**	**–2.1**	**–1.1**	**–4.5**	**–3.3**	**–1.8**	**–1.8**	**. . .**
General government	3 380 . .	–.8	–1.0	–.6	–.5	–1.6	–1.1	–1.0	. . .
Other sectors	3 390 . .	–.7	–1.1	–.5	–4.0	–1.7	–.7	–.7	. . .
Workers' remittances	3 391 . .	. . .	. . .	. . .	. . .	. . .	. . .	. . .	. . .
Other current transfers	3 392 . .	–.7	–1.1	–.5	–4.0	–1.7	–.7	–.7	. . .
CAPITAL AND FINANCIAL ACCOUNT	4 996 . .	**–4.2**	**–16.4**	**49.2**	**3.4**	**48.2**	**18.3**	**55.0**	**. . .**
CAPITAL ACCOUNT	4 994 . .	**–.2**	**–.8**	**–.3**	**–.1**	**. . .**	**. . .**	**. . .**	**. . .**
Total credit	2 994 . .	. . .	. . .	. . .	. . .	. . .	. . .	. . .	. . .
Total debit	3 994 . .	*–.2*	*–.8*	*–.3*	*–.1*	. . .	. . .	. . .	. . .
Capital transfers, credit	2 400 . .	**. . .**	**. . .**	**. . .**	**. . .**	**. . .**	**. . .**	**. . .**	**. . .**
General government	2 401 . .	. . .	. . .	. . .	. . .	. . .	. . .	. . .	. . .
Debt forgiveness	2 402 . .	. . .	. . .	. . .	. . .	. . .	. . .	. . .	. . .
Other capital transfers	2 410 . .	. . .	. . .	. . .	. . .	. . .	. . .	. . .	. . .
Other sectors	2 430 . .	. . .	. . .	. . .	. . .	. . .	. . .	. . .	. . .
Migrants' transfers	2 431 . .	. . .	. . .	. . .	. . .	. . .	. . .	. . .	. . .
Debt forgiveness	2 432 . .	. . .	. . .	. . .	. . .	. . .	. . .	. . .	. . .
Other capital transfers	2 440 . .	. . .	. . .	. . .	. . .	. . .	. . .	. . .	. . .
Capital transfers, debit	3 400 . .	**–.2**	**–.8**	**–.3**	**–.1**	**. . .**	**. . .**	**. . .**	**. . .**
General government	3 401 . .	. . .	. . .	. . .	. . .	. . .	. . .	. . .	. . .
Debt forgiveness	3 402 . .	. . .	. . .	. . .	. . .	. . .	. . .	. . .	. . .
Other capital transfers	3 410 . .	. . .	. . .	. . .	. . .	. . .	. . .	. . .	. . .
Other sectors	3 430 . .	–.2	–.8	–.3	–.1	. . .	. . .	. . .	. . .
Migrants' transfers	3 431 . .	–.2	–.8	–.3	–.1	. . .	. . .	. . .	. . .
Debt forgiveness	3 432 . .	. . .	. . .	. . .	. . .	. . .	. . .	. . .	. . .
Other capital transfers	3 440 . .	. . .	. . .	. . .	. . .	. . .	. . .	. . .	. . .
Nonproduced nonfinancial assets, credit	2 480 . .	**. . .**	**. . .**	**. . .**	**. . .**	**. . .**	**. . .**	**. . .**	**. . .**
Nonproduced nonfinancial assets, debit	3 480 . .	**. . .**	**. . .**	**. . .**	**. . .**	**. . .**	**. . .**	**. . .**	**. . .**

Table 2 (Continued). STANDARD PRESENTATION, 1994–2001

(Millions of U.S. dollars)

	Code	1994	1995	1996	1997	1998	1999	2000	2001
FINANCIAL ACCOUNT	4 995 . .	**–4.0**	**–15.6**	**49.5**	**3.4**	**48.2**	**18.3**	**55.1**	**. . .**
A. DIRECT INVESTMENT	4 500 . .	–.1	1.4	. . .	. . .	. . .	.2	11.7	. . .
Direct investment abroad	4 505 . .	**–.1**	**–.6**	**. . .**	**. . .**	**. . .**	**. . .**	**. . .**	**. . .**
Equity capital	4 510 . .	–.1	–.6	. . .	. . .	. . .	. . .	. . .	. . .
Claims on affiliated enterprises	4 515 . .	. . .	. . .	. . .	. . .	. . .	. . .	. . .	. . .
Liabilities to affiliated enterprises	4 520 . .	. . .	. . .	. . .	. . .	. . .	. . .	. . .	. . .
Reinvested earnings	4 525 . .	. . .	. . .	. . .	. . .	. . .	. . .	. . .	. . .
Other capital	4 530 . .	. . .	. . .	. . .	. . .	. . .	. . .	. . .	. . .
Claims on affiliated enterprises	4 535 . .	. . .	. . .	. . .	. . .	. . .	. . .	. . .	. . .
Liabilities to affiliated enterprises	4 540 . .	. . .	. . .	. . .	. . .	. . .	. . .	. . .	. . .
Direct investment in Burundi	4 555 . .	**. . .**	**2.0**	**. . .**	**. . .**	**. . .**	**.2**	**11.7**	**. . .**
Equity capital	4 560 . .	. . .	2.0	. . .	. . .	. . .	.2	11.7	. . .
Claims on direct investors	4 565 . .	. . .	. . .	. . .	. . .	. . .	.2	11.7	. . .
Liabilities to direct investors	4 570 . .	. . .	. . .	. . .	. . .	. . .	. . .	. . .	. . .
Reinvested earnings	4 575 . .	. . .	. . .	. . .	. . .	. . .	. . .	. . .	. . .
Other capital	4 580 . .	. . .	. . .	. . .	. . .	. . .	. . .	. . .	. . .
Claims on direct investors	4 585 . .	. . .	. . .	. . .	. . .	. . .	. . .	. . .	. . .
Liabilities to direct investors	4 590 . .	. . .	. . .	. . .	. . .	. . .	. . .	. . .	. . .
B. PORTFOLIO INVESTMENT	4 600 . .	. . .	. . .	. . .	. . .	. . .	. . .	. . .	. . .
Assets	4 602 . .	**. . .**	**. . .**	**. . .**	**. . .**	**. . .**	**. . .**	**. . .**	**. . .**
Equity securities	4 610 . .	. . .	. . .	. . .	. . .	. . .	. . .	. . .	. . .
Monetary authorities	4 611 . .	. . .	. . .	. . .	. . .	. . .	. . .	. . .	. . .
General government	4 612 . .	. . .	. . .	. . .	. . .	. . .	. . .	. . .	. . .
Banks	4 613 . .	. . .	. . .	. . .	. . .	. . .	. . .	. . .	. . .
Other sectors	4 614 . .	. . .	. . .	. . .	. . .	. . .	. . .	. . .	. . .
Debt securities	4 619 . .	. . .	. . .	. . .	. . .	. . .	. . .	. . .	. . .
Bonds and notes	4 620 . .	. . .	. . .	. . .	. . .	. . .	. . .	. . .	. . .
Monetary authorities	4 621 . .	. . .	. . .	. . .	. . .	. . .	. . .	. . .	. . .
General government	4 622 . .	. . .	. . .	. . .	. . .	. . .	. . .	. . .	. . .
Banks	4 623 . .	. . .	. . .	. . .	. . .	. . .	. . .	. . .	. . .
Other sectors	4 624 . .	. . .	. . .	. . .	. . .	. . .	. . .	. . .	. . .
Money market instruments	4 630 . .	. . .	. . .	. . .	. . .	. . .	. . .	. . .	. . .
Monetary authorities	4 631 . .	. . .	. . .	. . .	. . .	. . .	. . .	. . .	. . .
General government	4 632 . .	. . .	. . .	. . .	. . .	. . .	. . .	. . .	. . .
Banks	4 633 . .	. . .	. . .	. . .	. . .	. . .	. . .	. . .	. . .
Other sectors	4 634 . .	. . .	. . .	. . .	. . .	. . .	. . .	. . .	. . .
Liabilities	4 652 . .	**. . .**	**. . .**	**. . .**	**. . .**	**. . .**	**. . .**	**. . .**	**. . .**
Equity securities	4 660 . .	. . .	. . .	. . .	. . .	. . .	. . .	. . .	. . .
Banks	4 663 . .	. . .	. . .	. . .	. . .	. . .	. . .	. . .	. . .
Other sectors	4 664 . .	. . .	. . .	. . .	. . .	. . .	. . .	. . .	. . .
Debt securities	4 669 . .	. . .	. . .	. . .	. . .	. . .	. . .	. . .	. . .
Bonds and notes	4 670 . .	. . .	. . .	. . .	. . .	. . .	. . .	. . .	. . .
Monetary authorities	4 671 . .	. . .	. . .	. . .	. . .	. . .	. . .	. . .	. . .
General government	4 672 . .	. . .	. . .	. . .	. . .	. . .	. . .	. . .	. . .
Banks	4 673 . .	. . .	. . .	. . .	. . .	. . .	. . .	. . .	. . .
Other sectors	4 674 . .	. . .	. . .	. . .	. . .	. . .	. . .	. . .	. . .
Money market instruments	4 680 . .	. . .	. . .	. . .	. . .	. . .	. . .	. . .	. . .
Monetary authorities	4 681 . .	. . .	. . .	. . .	. . .	. . .	. . .	. . .	. . .
General government	4 682 . .	. . .	. . .	. . .	. . .	. . .	. . .	. . .	. . .
Banks	4 683 . .	. . .	. . .	. . .	. . .	. . .	. . .	. . .	. . .
Other sectors	4 684 . .	. . .	. . .	. . .	. . .	. . .	. . .	. . .	. . .
C. FINANCIAL DERIVATIVES	4 910 . .	. . .	. . .	. . .	. . .	. . .	. . .	. . .	. . .
Monetary authorities	4 911 . .	. . .	. . .	. . .	. . .	. . .	. . .	. . .	. . .
General government	4 912 . .	. . .	. . .	. . .	. . .	. . .	. . .	. . .	. . .
Banks	4 913 . .	. . .	. . .	. . .	. . .	. . .	. . .	. . .	. . .
Other sectors	4 914 . .	. . .	. . .	. . .	. . .	. . .	. . .	. . .	. . .
Assets	4 900 . .	**. . .**	**. . .**	**. . .**	**. . .**	**. . .**	**. . .**	**. . .**	**. . .**
Monetary authorities	4 901 . .	. . .	. . .	. . .	. . .	. . .	. . .	. . .	. . .
General government	4 902 . .	. . .	. . .	. . .	. . .	. . .	. . .	. . .	. . .
Banks	4 903 . .	. . .	. . .	. . .	. . .	. . .	. . .	. . .	. . .
Other sectors	4 904 . .	. . .	. . .	. . .	. . .	. . .	. . .	. . .	. . .
Liabilities	4 905 . .	**. . .**	**. . .**	**. . .**	**. . .**	**. . .**	**. . .**	**. . .**	**. . .**
Monetary authorities	4 906 . .	. . .	. . .	. . .	. . .	. . .	. . .	. . .	. . .
General government	4 907 . .	. . .	. . .	. . .	. . .	. . .	. . .	. . .	. . .
Banks	4 908 . .	. . .	. . .	. . .	. . .	. . .	. . .	. . .	. . .
Other sectors	4 909 . .	. . .	. . .	. . .	. . .	. . .	. . .	. . .	. . .

Table 2 (Concluded). STANDARD PRESENTATION, 1994–2001
(Millions of U.S. dollars)

	Code	1994	1995	1996	1997	1998	1999	2000	2001
D. OTHER INVESTMENT	4 700 . .	25.1	10.7	5.4	5.4	19.5	9.2	42.2	. . .
Assets	4 703 . .	**–1.6**	**8.2**	**6.6**	**15.3**	**10.7**	**13.7**	**5.1**	**. . .**
Trade credits	4 706 . .	. . .	. . .	. . .	. . .	. . .	. . .	. . .	. . .
General government	4 707 . .	. . .	. . .	. . .	. . .	. . .	. . .	. . .	. . .
of which: Short-term	4 709 . .	. . .	. . .	. . .	. . .	. . .	. . .	. . .	. . .
Other sectors	4 710 . .	. . .	. . .	. . .	. . .	. . .	. . .	. . .	. . .
of which: Short-term	4 712 . .	. . .	. . .	. . .	. . .	. . .	. . .	. . .	. . .
Loans	4 714 . .	15.2	13.5	18.3	7.7	7.1	25.6	13.7	. . .
Monetary authorities	4 715 . .	. . .	. . .	. . .	. . .	. . .	. . .	. . .	. . .
of which: Short-term	4 718 . .	. . .	. . .	. . .	. . .	. . .	. . .	. . .	. . .
General government	4 719 . .	. . .	. . .	. . .	. . .	. . .	. . .	. . .	. . .
of which: Short-term	4 721 . .	. . .	. . .	. . .	. . .	. . .	. . .	. . .	. . .
Banks	4 722 . .	. . .	. . .	. . .	. . .	. . .	. . .	. . .	. . .
of which: Short-term	4 724 . .	. . .	. . .	. . .	. . .	. . .	. . .	. . .	. . .
Other sectors	4 725 . .	15.2	13.5	18.3	7.7	7.1	25.6	13.7	. . .
of which: Short-term	4 727 . .	*15.2*	*13.5*	*18.3*	*7.7*	*7.1*	*25.6*	*13.7*	. . .
Currency and deposits	4 730 . .	–16.1	–4.9	–11.4	8.0	3.9	–11.1	–8.6	. . .
Monetary authorities	4 731 . .	. . .	. . .	. . .	. . .	. . .	. . .	. . .	. . .
General government	4 732 . .	. . .	. . .	. . .	. . .	. . .	. . .	. . .	. . .
Banks	4 733 . .	–8.8	.1	–10.4	8.5	5.0	–10.3	–8.2	. . .
Other sectors	4 734 . .	–7.3	–4.9	–1.0	–.5	–1.1	–.8	–.4	. . .
Other assets	4 736 . .	–.8	–.4	–.3	–.4	–.3	–.8	. . .	. . .
Monetary authorities	4 737 . .	. . .	. . .	. . .	. . .	. . .	. . .	. . .	. . .
of which: Short-term	4 739 . .	. . .	. . .	. . .	. . .	. . .	. . .	. . .	. . .
General government	4 740 . .	–.8	–.4	–.3	–.4	–.3	–.3	. . .	. . .
of which: Short-term	4 742 . .	. . .	. . .	. . .	. . .	. . .	. . .	. . .	. . .
Banks	4 743 . .	. . .	. . .	. . .	. . .	. . .	. . .	. . .	. . .
of which: Short-term	4 745 . .	. . .	. . .	. . .	. . .	. . .	. . .	. . .	. . .
Other sectors	4 746 . .	. . .	. . .	. . .	. . .	. . .	–.5	. . .	. . .
of which: Short-term	4 748 . .	. . .	. . .	. . .	. . .	. . .	. . .	. . .	. . .
Liabilities	4 753 . .	**26.8**	**2.4**	**–1.1**	**–9.9**	**8.8**	**–4.4**	**37.1**	**. . .**
Trade credits	4 756 . .	. . .	. . .	. . .	. . .	. . .	. . .	. . .	. . .
General government	4 757 . .	. . .	. . .	. . .	. . .	. . .	. . .	. . .	. . .
of which: Short-term	4 759 . .	. . .	. . .	. . .	. . .	. . .	. . .	. . .	. . .
Other sectors	4 760 . .	. . .	. . .	. . .	. . .	. . .	. . .	. . .	. . .
of which: Short-term	4 762 . .	. . .	. . .	. . .	. . .	. . .	. . .	. . .	. . .
Loans	4 764 . .	19.1	–4.1	–1.4	–16.2	6.0	–7.4	27.2	. . .
Monetary authorities	4 765 . .	–6.1	–9.0	–8.7	–8.3	–9.3	–7.6	–5.0	. . .
of which: Use of Fund credit and loans from the Fund	4 766 . .	*–6.1*	*–9.0*	*–8.7*	*–8.3*	*–9.3*	*–7.6*	*–5.0*	. . .
of which: Short-term	4 768 . .	. . .	. . .	. . .	. . .	. . .	. . .	. . .	. . .
General government	4 769 . .	25.2	4.9	7.3	–8.0	15.3	.2	32.2	. . .
of which: Short-term	4 771 . .	. . .	. . .	. . .	. . .	. . .	. . .	. . .	. . .
Banks	4 772 . .	. . .	. . .	. . .	. . .	. . .	. . .	. . .	. . .
of which: Short-term	4 774 . .	. . .	. . .	. . .	. . .	. . .	. . .	. . .	. . .
Other sectors	4 775 . .	. . .	. . .	. . .	. . .	. . .	. . .	. . .	. . .
of which: Short-term	4 777 . .	. . .	. . .	. . .	. . .	. . .	. . .	. . .	. . .
Currency and deposits	4 780 . .	4.7	–.4	–2.0	1.6	1.7	1.9	8.7	. . .
Monetary authorities	4 781 . .	. . .	. . .	. . .	. . .	. . .	. . .	. . .	. . .
General government	4 782 . .	. . .	. . .	. . .	. . .	. . .	. . .	. . .	. . .
Banks	4 783 . .	4.7	–.4	–2.0	1.6	1.7	1.9	8.7	. . .
Other sectors	4 784 . .	. . .	. . .	. . .	. . .	. . .	. . .	. . .	. . .
Other liabilities	4 786 . .	3.0	7.0	2.2	4.8	1.1	1.1	1.2	. . .
Monetary authorities	4 787 . .	. . .	. . .	. . .	. . .	. . .	. . .	. . .	. . .
of which: Short-term	4 789 . .	. . .	. . .	. . .	. . .	. . .	. . .	. . .	. . .
General government	4 790 . .	. . .	. . .	. . .	. . .	. . .	. . .	. . .	. . .
of which: Short-term	4 792 . .	. . .	. . .	. . .	. . .	. . .	. . .	. . .	. . .
Banks	4 793 . .	. . .	. . .	. . .	. . .	. . .	. . .	. . .	. . .
of which: Short-term	4 795 . .	. . .	. . .	. . .	. . .	. . .	. . .	. . .	. . .
Other sectors	4 796 . .	3.0	7.0	2.2	4.8	1.1	1.1	1.2	. . .
of which: Short-term	4 798 . .	*3.0*	*7.0*	*2.2*	*4.8*	*1.1*	*1.1*	*1.2*	. . .
E. RESERVE ASSETS	4 802 . .	–29.0	–27.6	44.0	–2.0	28.7	8.8	1.2	. . .
Monetary gold	4 812 . .	.5	–.9	–.7	. . .	–1.0	–1.1	–.7	. . .
Special drawing rights	4 811 . .	.5	.1	. . .	. . .	. . .	. . .	. . .	. . .
Reserve position in the Fund	4 810 . .	. . .	. . .	. . .	. . .	. . .	. . .	. . .	. . .
Foreign exchange	4 803 . .	–30.1	–26.9	44.7	–2.1	29.8	10.0	1.9	. . .
Other claims	4 813 . .	. . .	. . .	. . .	. . .	. . .	. . .	. . .	. . .
NET ERRORS AND OMISSIONS	4 998 . .	**21.1**	**5.9**	**–9.2**	**–2.4**	**5.4**	**8.7**	**–6.2**	**. . .**

Part 3 of the *Yearbook* contains descriptions of the methodologies, compilation practices, and sources used to compile these data.

Table 1. ANALYTIC PRESENTATION, 1994–2001
(Millions of U.S. dollars)

	Code	1994	1995	1996	1997	1998	1999	2000	2001
A. Current Account [1]	4 993 Z.	**–156.6**	**–185.7**	**–184.9**	**–209.9**	**–109.3**	**–155.0**	**–105.8**	**–104.6**
Goods: exports f.o.b	2 100 . .	489.9	855.2	643.6	736.0	903.4	886.4	1,264.0	1,377.5
Goods: imports f.o.b	3 100 . .	–744.4	–1,186.8	–1,071.8	–1,064.0	–1,149.1	–1,239.0	–1,628.2	–1,725.0
Balance on Goods	4 100 . .	*–254.5*	*–331.6*	*–428.2*	*–328.0*	*–245.7*	*–352.6*	*–364.2*	*–347.5*
Services: credit	2 200 . .	54.5	114.0	162.8	160.4	109.8	198.7	244.2	256.9
Services: debit	3 200 . .	–139.6	–187.9	–214.8	–188.0	–163.2	–194.4	–240.4	–243.8
Balance on Goods and Services	4 991 . .	*–339.6*	*–405.5*	*–480.2*	*–355.6*	*–299.1*	*–348.3*	*–360.4*	*–334.4*
Income: credit	2 300 . .	2.1	9.7	12.6	16.0	17.8	20.6	32.0	21.0
Income: debit	3 300 . .	–49.1	–66.9	–98.3	–58.5	–51.4	–61.6	–82.3	–63.9
Balance on Goods, Services, and Income	4 992 . .	*–386.6*	*–462.7*	*–565.9*	*–398.1*	*–332.7*	*–389.3*	*–410.7*	*–377.3*
Current transfers: credit	2 379 Z.	230.0	277.9	383.4	188.5	224.0	235.9	305.3	273.1
Current transfers: debit	3 379 . .	. . .	–.9	–2.4	–.3	–.6	–1.6	–.4	–.4
B. Capital Account [1]	4 994 Z.	**73.2**	**78.0**	**75.8**	**65.2**	**42.0**	**44.0**	**38.1**	**63.3**
Capital account: credit	2 994 Z.	73.2	78.0	75.8	65.2	42.0	44.0	38.1	63.3
Capital account: debit	3 994 . .	. . .	. . .	. . .	. . .	. . .	. . .	. . .	. . .
Total, Groups A Plus B	4 981 . .	*–83.4*	*–107.7*	*–109.1*	*–144.7*	*–67.3*	*–111.0*	*–67.7*	*–41.3*
C. Financial Account [1]	4 995 W.	**54.0**	**122.4**	**259.1**	**219.8**	**154.1**	**126.2**	**99.3**	**74.8**
Direct investment abroad	4 505 . .	. . .	. . .	. . .	. . .	. . .	. . .	. . .	. . .
Direct investment in Cambodia	4 555 Z.	68.9	150.8	293.6	203.7	120.7	143.6	111.7	113.1
Portfolio investment assets	4 602 . .	. . .	. . .	. . .	. . .	. . .	. . .	. . .	. . .
Equity securities	4 610 . .	. . .	. . .	. . .	. . .	. . .	. . .	. . .	. . .
Debt securities	4 619 . .	. . .	. . .	. . .	. . .	. . .	. . .	. . .	. . .
Portfolio investment liabilities	4 652 Z.	. . .	. . .	. . .	. . .	. . .	. . .	. . .	. . .
Equity securities	4 660 . .	. . .	. . .	. . .	. . .	. . .	. . .	. . .	. . .
Debt securities	4 669 Z.	. . .	. . .	. . .	. . .	. . .	. . .	. . .	. . .
Financial derivatives	4 910 . .	. . .	. . .	. . .	. . .	. . .	. . .	. . .	. . .
Financial derivatives assets	4 900 . .	. . .	. . .	. . .	. . .	. . .	. . .	. . .	. . .
Financial derivatives liabilities	4 905 . .	. . .	. . .	. . .	. . .	. . .	. . .	. . .	. . .
Other investment assets	4 703 . .	–46.8	–103.4	–118.0	–23.6	–21.2	–61.1	–80.3	–103.0
Monetary authorities	4 701 . .	. . .	. . .	. . .	. . .	. . .	. . .	. . .	. . .
General government	4 704 . .	. . .	. . .	. . .	. . .	. . .	. . .	. . .	. . .
Banks	4 705 . .	. . .	–39.8	–23.6	23.6	23.2	–15.1	–13.5	–49.0
Other sectors	4 728 . .	–46.8	–63.6	–94.4	–47.2	–44.4	–46.0	–66.8	–54.0
Other investment liabilities	4 753 W.	31.9	75.0	83.5	39.7	54.6	43.7	67.9	64.7
Monetary authorities	4 753 WA	. . .	. . .	. . .	. . .	. . .	. . .	. . .	. . .
General government	4 753 ZB	51.4	73.1	89.7	41.2	53.3	46.4	74.6	64.6
Banks	4 753 ZC	–19.5	1.9	–6.2	–1.5	1.3	–2.7	–6.7	.1
Other sectors	4 753 ZD	. . .	. . .	. . .	. . .	. . .	. . .	. . .	. . .
Total, Groups A Through C	4 983 . .	*–29.4*	*14.7*	*150.0*	*75.1*	*86.8*	*15.2*	*31.6*	*33.5*
D. Net Errors and Omissions	4 998 . .	**65.6**	**11.5**	**–78.0**	**–41.2**	**–56.1**	**34.8**	**54.3**	**39.0**
Total, Groups A Through D	4 984 . .	*36.2*	*26.2*	*72.0*	*33.9*	*30.7*	*50.0*	*85.9*	*72.5*
E. Reserves and Related Items	4 802 A.	**–36.2**	**–26.2**	**–72.0**	**–33.9**	**–30.7**	**–50.0**	**–85.9**	**–72.5**
Reserve assets	4 802 . .	–71.2	–73.2	–68.9	–34.3	–29.3	–65.1	–101.4	–90.2
Use of Fund credit and loans	4 766 . .	19.8	42.3	. . .	. . .	–1.4	8.3	4.0	9.3
Exceptional financing	4 920 . .	15.2	4.7	–3.1	.4	. . .	6.8	11.5	8.4
Conversion rates: riel per U.S. dollar	0 101 . .	**2,545.3**	**2,450.8**	**2,624.1**	**2,946.3**	**3,744.4**	**3,807.8**	**3,840.8**	**3,916.3**

[1] Excludes components that have been classified in the categories of Group E.

Table 2. STANDARD PRESENTATION, 1994–2001
(Millions of U.S. dollars)

	Code	1994	1995	1996	1997	1998	1999	2000	2001
CURRENT ACCOUNT	4 993 . .	**–156.6**	**–185.7**	**–184.9**	**–209.9**	**–109.3**	**–155.0**	**–105.8**	**–104.6**
A. GOODS	4 100 . .	–254.5	–331.6	–428.2	–328.0	–245.7	–352.6	–364.2	–347.5
Credit	2 100 . .	**489.9**	**855.2**	**643.6**	**736.0**	**903.4**	**886.4**	**1,264.0**	**1,377.5**
General merchandise: exports f.o.b.	2 110 . .	486.5	852.4	641.4	732.3	897.5	881.0	1,256.7	1,369.8
Goods for processing: exports f.o.b.	2 150 . .	...	...	...	...	...	...	...	...
Repairs on goods	2 160 . .	...	...	...	...	...	...	...	...
Goods procured in ports by carriers	2 170 . .	3.4	2.8	2.2	3.7	5.9	5.4	7.3	7.7
Nonmonetary gold	2 180 . .	...	...	...	...	...	...	...	...
Debit	3 100 . .	**–744.4**	**–1,186.8**	**–1,071.8**	**–1,064.0**	**–1,149.1**	**–1,239.0**	**–1,628.2**	**–1,725.0**
General merchandise: imports f.o.b.	3 110 . .	–744.4	–1,186.1	–1,067.5	–1,057.0	–1,068.6	–1,153.9	–1,516.2	–1,605.0
Goods for processing: imports f.o.b.	3 150 . .	...	...	...	...	...	...	...	...
Repairs on goods	3 160 . .	...	...	...	...	...	...	...	...
Goods procured in ports by carriers	3 170 . .	...	–.7	–4.3	–7.0	–80.5	–85.1	–112.0	–120.0
Nonmonetary gold	3 180 . .	...	...	...	...	...	...	...	...
B. SERVICES	4 200 . .	–85.1	–73.9	–52.0	–27.6	–53.4	4.3	3.8	13.1
Total credit	2 200 . .	*54.5*	*114.0*	*162.8*	*160.4*	*109.8*	*198.7*	*244.2*	*256.9*
Total debit	3 200 . .	*–139.6*	*–187.9*	*–214.8*	*–188.0*	*–163.2*	*–194.4*	*–240.4*	*–243.8*
Transportation services, credit	2 205 . .	**11.2**	**31.5**	**49.6**	**50.4**	**37.7**	**47.4**	**71.4**	**87.0**
Passenger	2 850 . .	*3.7*	*17.7*	*35.2*	*31.4*	*22.3*	*27.8*	*41.2*	*48.6*
Freight	2 851 . .	*.3*	*.7*	*.8*	*1.0*	*1.7*	*3.2*	*5.6*	*2.9*
Other	2 852 . .	*7.2*	*13.1*	*13.6*	*18.0*	*13.7*	*16.4*	*24.6*	*35.5*
Sea transport, passenger	2 207 . .	...	...	...	...	...	...	...	...
Sea transport, freight	2 208 . .	.3	.5	.1	.1	.3	...	2.4	.1
Sea transport, other	2 209 . .	4.7	11.1	8.1	8.8	7.5	9.7	13.5	23.7
Air transport, passenger	2 211 . .	3.7	17.7	35.2	31.4	22.3	27.8	41.2	48.6
Air transport, freight	2 212 . .	...	.2	.7	.9	1.4	3.2	3.2	2.8
Air transport, other	2 213 . .	2.5	2.0	5.5	9.2	6.2	6.7	11.1	11.8
Other transport, passenger	2 215 . .	...	...	...	...	...	...	...	...
Other transport, freight	2 216 . .	...	...	...	...	...	...	...	...
Other transport, other	2 217 . .	...	...	...	...	...	...	...	...
Transportation services, debit	3 205 . .	**–71.7**	**–83.9**	**–99.6**	**–92.2**	**–97.7**	**–105.4**	**–142.7**	**–154.9**
Passenger	3 850 . .	*–13.5*	*–13.9*	*–16.1*	*–14.5*	*–10.3*	*–12.8*	*–19.0*	*–22.4*
Freight	3 851 . .	*–58.2*	*–69.6*	*–79.9*	*–71.8*	*–83.5*	*–88.3*	*–116.0*	*–124.8*
Other	3 852 . .	...	*–.4*	*–3.6*	*–5.9*	*–3.9*	*–4.3*	*–7.7*	*–7.7*
Sea transport, passenger	3 207 . .	...	...	...	...	...	...	...	...
Sea transport, freight	3 208 . .	–56.4	–67.6	–76.9	–69.2	–80.5	–85.1	–112.0	–120.0
Sea transport, other	3 209 . .	...	...	...	...	...	...	–.5	...
Air transport, passenger	3 211 . .	–13.5	–13.9	–16.1	–14.5	–10.3	–12.8	–19.0	–22.4
Air transport, freight	3 212 . .	–1.8	–2.0	–3.0	–2.6	–3.0	–3.2	–4.0	–4.8
Air transport, other	3 213 . .	...	–.4	–3.6	–5.9	–3.9	–4.3	–7.2	–7.7
Other transport, passenger	3 215 . .	...	...	...	...	...	...	...	...
Other transport, freight	3 216 . .	...	...	...	...	...	...	...	...
Other transport, other	3 217 . .	...	...	...	...	...	...	...	...
Travel, credit	2 236 . .	**33.8**	**53.4**	**81.7**	**68.1**	**43.9**	**129.9**	**139.2**	**148.5**
Business travel	2 237 . .	...	...	...	...	...	...	...	...
Personal travel	2 240 . .	...	...	...	...	...	...	...	...
Travel, debit	3 236 . .	**–7.5**	**–8.3**	**–14.5**	**–12.8**	**–6.7**	**–23.8**	**–29.0**	**–34.5**
Business travel	3 237 . .	...	...	...	...	...	...	...	...
Personal travel	3 240 . .	...	...	...	...	...	...	...	...
Other services, credit	2 200 BA	**9.5**	**29.1**	**31.5**	**41.9**	**28.2**	**21.4**	**33.6**	**21.4**
Communications	2 245 . .	...	18.3	20.7	21.5	17.0	17.4	29.6	17.4
Construction	2 249 . .	...	...	...	...	...	...	...	...
Insurance	2 253 . .	...	...	...	...	...	...	...	...
Financial	2 260 . .	...	...	...	...	...	...	...	...
Computer and information	2 262 . .	...	...	...	...	...	...	...	...
Royalties and licence fees	2 266 . .	...	...	...	...	...	...	...	...
Other business services	2 268 . .	...	...	...	9.6	...	...	...	...
Personal, cultural, and recreational	2 287 . .	...	...	...	...	...	...	...	...
Government, n.i.e.	2 291 . .	9.5	10.8	10.8	10.8	11.2	4.0	4.0	4.0
Other services, debit	3 200 BA	**–60.4**	**–95.7**	**–100.7**	**–83.0**	**–58.8**	**–65.2**	**–68.7**	**–54.4**
Communications	3 245 . .	–3.4	–17.5	–21.2	–12.1	–10.6	–19.9	–25.5	–9.3
Construction	3 249 . .	–44.4	–47.4	–46.1	–39.5	–25.6	–26.8	–23.2	–23.1
Insurance	3 253 . .	–4.4	–7.8	–8.8	–8.0	–9.2	–9.7	–12.8	–16.0
Financial	3 260 . .	–.2	...	...	...	...	...	...	...
Computer and information	3 262 . .	...	...	...	...	...	...	...	...
Royalties and licence fees	3 266 . .	...	...	...	...	...	...	...	...
Other business services	3 268 . .	...	–16.0	–18.5	–17.6	–10.8	–8.8	–7.2	–6.0
Personal, cultural, and recreational	3 287 . .	...	...	...	...	...	...	...	...
Government, n.i.e.	3 291 . .	–8.0	–7.0	–6.1	–5.8	–2.6	...	...	...

Table 2 (Continued). STANDARD PRESENTATION, 1994–2001
(Millions of U.S. dollars)

	Code	1994	1995	1996	1997	1998	1999	2000	2001
C. INCOME	4 300 . .	–47.0	–57.2	–85.7	–42.5	–33.6	–41.0	–50.3	–42.9
Total credit	2 300 . .	*2.1*	*9.7*	*12.6*	*16.0*	*17.8*	*20.6*	*32.0*	*21.0*
Total debit	3 300 . .	*–49.1*	*–66.9*	*–98.3*	*–58.5*	*–51.4*	*–61.6*	*–82.3*	*–63.9*
Compensation of employees, credit	2 310 . .	**1.3**	**1.6**	**1.6**	**1.7**	**2.0**	**2.4**	**2.4**	**2.4**
Compensation of employees, debit	3 310 . .	**–38.4**	**–52.0**	**–77.2**	**–38.8**	**–36.4**	**–37.6**	**–54.8**	**–44.4**
Investment income, credit	2 320 . .	**.8**	**8.1**	**11.0**	**14.3**	**15.8**	**18.2**	**29.6**	**18.6**
Direct investment income	2 330 . .	. . .	. . .	. . .	. . .	. . .	. . .	. . .	. . .
Dividends and distributed branch profits	2 332 . .	. . .	. . .	. . .	. . .	. . .	. . .	. . .	. . .
Reinvested earnings and undistributed branch profits	2 333 . .	. . .	. . .	. . .	. . .	. . .	. . .	. . .	. . .
Income on debt (interest)	2 334 . .	. . .	. . .	. . .	. . .	. . .	. . .	. . .	. . .
Portfolio investment income	2 339 . .	. . .	. . .	. . .	. . .	. . .	. . .	. . .	. . .
Income on equity	2 340 . .	. . .	. . .	. . .	. . .	. . .	. . .	. . .	. . .
Income on bonds and notes	2 350 . .	. . .	. . .	. . .	. . .	. . .	. . .	. . .	. . .
Income on money market instruments	2 360 . .	. . .	. . .	. . .	. . .	. . .	. . .	. . .	. . .
Other investment income	2 370 . .	.8	8.1	11.0	14.3	15.8	18.2	29.6	18.6
Investment income, debit	3 320 . .	**–10.7**	**–14.9**	**–21.1**	**–19.7**	**–15.0**	**–24.0**	**–27.5**	**–19.5**
Direct investment income	3 330 . .	4.0	3.8	–4.4	–4.4	–2.0	–12.6	–12.9	–6.4
Dividends and distributed branch profits	3 332 . .	. . .	. . .	. . .	. . .	. . .	. . .	. . .	. . .
Reinvested earnings and undistributed branch profits	3 333 . .	4.0	3.8	–1.6	–1.1	1.6	–8.6	–8.9	–2.4
Income on debt (interest)	3 334 . .	. . .	. . .	–2.8	–3.3	–3.6	–4.0	–4.0	–4.0
Portfolio investment income	3 339 . .	. . .	. . .	. . .	. . .	. . .	. . .	. . .	. . .
Income on equity	3 340 . .	. . .	. . .	. . .	. . .	. . .	. . .	. . .	. . .
Income on bonds and notes	3 350 . .	. . .	. . .	. . .	. . .	. . .	. . .	. . .	. . .
Income on money market instruments	3 360 . .	. . .	. . .	. . .	. . .	. . .	. . .	. . .	. . .
Other investment income	3 370 . .	–14.7	–18.7	–16.7	–15.3	–13.0	–11.4	–14.6	–13.1
D. CURRENT TRANSFERS	4 379 . .	230.0	277.0	381.0	188.2	223.4	234.3	304.9	272.7
Credit	2 379 . .	**230.0**	**277.9**	**383.4**	**188.5**	**224.0**	**235.9**	**305.3**	**273.1**
General government	2 380 . .	210.0	257.9	363.4	168.5	158.0	165.9	232.9	202.7
Other sectors	2 390 . .	20.0	20.0	20.0	20.0	66.0	70.0	72.4	70.4
Workers' remittances	2 391 . .	10.0	10.0	10.0	10.0	10.0	12.0	17.2	15.2
Other current transfers	2 392 . .	10.0	10.0	10.0	10.0	56.0	58.0	55.2	55.2
Debit	3 379 . .	**. . .**	**–.9**	**–2.4**	**–.3**	**–.6**	**–1.6**	**–.4**	**–.4**
General government	3 380 . .	. . .	–.9	–2.4	–.3	–.6	–1.6	–.4	–.4
Other sectors	3 390 . .	. . .	. . .	. . .	. . .	. . .	. . .	. . .	. . .
Workers' remittances	3 391 . .	. . .	. . .	. . .	. . .	. . .	. . .	. . .	. . .
Other current transfers	3 392 . .	. . .	. . .	. . .	. . .	. . .	. . .	. . .	. . .
CAPITAL AND FINANCIAL ACCOUNT	4 996 . .	**91.0**	**174.2**	**262.9**	**251.1**	**165.4**	**120.2**	**51.5**	**65.6**
CAPITAL ACCOUNT	4 994 . .	**73.2**	**91.9**	**75.8**	**65.2**	**42.0**	**44.0**	**38.1**	**63.3**
Total credit	2 994 . .	*73.2*	*91.9*	*75.8*	*65.2*	*42.0*	*44.0*	*38.1*	*63.3*
Total debit	3 994 . .	. . .	. . .	. . .	. . .	. . .	. . .	. . .	. . .
Capital transfers, credit	2 400 . .	**73.2**	**91.9**	**75.8**	**65.2**	**42.0**	**44.0**	**38.1**	**63.3**
General government	2 401 . .	73.2	91.9	75.8	65.2	42.0	44.0	38.1	63.3
Debt forgiveness	2 402 . .	. . .	13.9	. . .	. . .	. . .	. . .	. . .	. . .
Other capital transfers	2 410 . .	73.2	78.0	75.8	65.2	42.0	44.0	38.1	63.3
Other sectors	2 430 . .	. . .	. . .	. . .	. . .	. . .	. . .	. . .	. . .
Migrants' transfers	2 431 . .	. . .	. . .	. . .	. . .	. . .	. . .	. . .	. . .
Debt forgiveness	2 432 . .	. . .	. . .	. . .	. . .	. . .	. . .	. . .	. . .
Other capital transfers	2 440 . .	. . .	. . .	. . .	. . .	. . .	. . .	. . .	. . .
Capital transfers, debit	3 400 . .	**. . .**	**. . .**	**. . .**	**. . .**	**. . .**	**. . .**	**. . .**	**. . .**
General government	3 401 . .	. . .	. . .	. . .	. . .	. . .	. . .	. . .	. . .
Debt forgiveness	3 402 . .	. . .	. . .	. . .	. . .	. . .	. . .	. . .	. . .
Other capital transfers	3 410 . .	. . .	. . .	. . .	. . .	. . .	. . .	. . .	. . .
Other sectors	3 430 . .	. . .	. . .	. . .	. . .	. . .	. . .	. . .	. . .
Migrants' transfers	3 431 . .	. . .	. . .	. . .	. . .	. . .	. . .	. . .	. . .
Debt forgiveness	3 432 . .	. . .	. . .	. . .	. . .	. . .	. . .	. . .	. . .
Other capital transfers	3 440 . .	. . .	. . .	. . .	. . .	. . .	. . .	. . .	. . .
Nonproduced nonfinancial assets, credit	2 480 . .	**. . .**	**. . .**	**. . .**	**. . .**	**. . .**	**. . .**	**. . .**	**. . .**
Nonproduced nonfinancial assets, debit	3 480 . .	**. . .**	**. . .**	**. . .**	**. . .**	**. . .**	**. . .**	**. . .**	**. . .**

Table 2 (Continued). STANDARD PRESENTATION, 1994–2001
(Millions of U.S. dollars)

	Code		1994	1995	1996	1997	1998	1999	2000	2001
FINANCIAL ACCOUNT	4 995	. .	**17.8**	**82.3**	**187.1**	**185.9**	**123.4**	**76.2**	**13.4**	**2.3**
A. DIRECT INVESTMENT	4 500	. .	68.9	150.8	293.6	203.7	120.7	143.6	111.7	113.1
Direct investment abroad	4 505	. .	...	...	...	...	...	...	...	...
Equity capital	4 510	. .	...	...	...	...	...	...	...	...
Claims on affiliated enterprises	4 515	. .	...	...	...	...	...	...	...	...
Liabilities to affiliated enterprises	4 520	. .	...	...	...	...	...	...	...	...
Reinvested earnings	4 525	. .	...	...	...	...	...	...	...	...
Other capital	4 530	. .	...	...	...	...	...	...	...	...
Claims on affiliated enterprises	4 535	. .	...	...	...	...	...	...	...	...
Liabilities to affiliated enterprises	4 540	. .	...	...	...	...	...	...	...	...
Direct investment in Cambodia	4 555	. .	**68.9**	**150.8**	**293.6**	**203.7**	**120.7**	**143.6**	**111.7**	**113.1**
Equity capital	4 560	. .	72.9	154.6	131.8	51.6	34.3	51.0	26.8	50.7
Claims on direct investors	4 565	. .	...	...	...	...	...	...	...	...
Liabilities to direct investors	4 570	. .	72.9	154.6	131.8	51.6	34.3	51.0	26.8	50.7
Reinvested earnings	4 575	. .	-4.0	-3.8	1.6	1.1	-1.6	8.6	8.9	2.4
Other capital	4 580	. .	...	...	160.2	151.0	88.0	84.0	76.0	60.0
Claims on direct investors	4 585	. .	...	...	...	...	...	...	...	...
Liabilities to direct investors	4 590	. .	...	...	160.2	151.0	88.0	84.0	76.0	60.0
B. PORTFOLIO INVESTMENT	4 600	. .	...	...	...	...	...	...	...	...
Assets	4 602	. .	...	...	...	...	...	...	...	...
Equity securities	4 610	. .	...	...	...	...	...	...	...	...
Monetary authorities	4 611	. .	...	...	...	...	...	...	...	...
General government	4 612	. .	...	...	...	...	...	...	...	...
Banks	4 613	. .	...	...	...	...	...	...	...	...
Other sectors	4 614	. .	...	...	...	...	...	...	...	...
Debt securities	4 619	. .	...	...	...	...	...	...	...	...
Bonds and notes	4 620	. .	...	...	...	...	...	...	...	...
Monetary authorities	4 621	. .	...	...	...	...	...	...	...	...
General government	4 622	. .	...	...	...	...	...	...	...	...
Banks	4 623	. .	...	...	...	...	...	...	...	...
Other sectors	4 624	. .	...	...	...	...	...	...	...	...
Money market instruments	4 630	. .	...	...	...	...	...	...	...	...
Monetary authorities	4 631	. .	...	...	...	...	...	...	...	...
General government	4 632	. .	...	...	...	...	...	...	...	...
Banks	4 633	. .	...	...	...	...	...	...	...	...
Other sectors	4 634	. .	...	...	...	...	...	...	...	...
Liabilities	4 652	. .	...	...	...	...	...	...	...	...
Equity securities	4 660	. .	...	...	...	...	...	...	...	...
Banks	4 663	. .	...	...	...	...	...	...	...	...
Other sectors	4 664	. .	...	...	...	...	...	...	...	...
Debt securities	4 669	. .	...	...	...	...	...	...	...	...
Bonds and notes	4 670	. .	...	...	...	...	...	...	...	...
Monctary authorities	4 671	. .	...	...	...	...	...	...	...	...
General government	4 672	. .	...	...	...	...	...	...	...	...
Banks	4 673	. .	...	...	...	...	...	...	...	...
Other sectors	4 674	. .	...	...	...	...	...	...	...	...
Money market instruments	4 680	. .	...	...	...	...	...	...	...	...
Monetary authorities	4 681	. .	...	...	...	...	...	...	...	...
General government	4 682	. .	...	...	...	...	...	...	...	...
Banks	4 683	. .	...	...	...	...	...	...	...	...
Other sectors	4 684	. .	...	...	...	...	...	...	...	...
C. FINANCIAL DERIVATIVES	4 910	. .	...	...	...	...	...	...	...	...
Monetary authorities	4 911	. .	...	...	...	...	...	...	...	...
General government	4 912	. .	...	...	...	...	...	...	...	...
Banks	4 913	. .	...	...	...	...	...	...	...	...
Other sectors	4 914	. .	...	...	...	...	...	...	...	...
Assets	4 900	. .	...	...	...	...	...	...	...	...
Monetary authorities	4 901	. .	...	...	...	...	...	...	...	...
General government	4 902	. .	...	...	...	...	...	...	...	...
Banks	4 903	. .	...	...	...	...	...	...	...	...
Other sectors	4 904	. .	...	...	...	...	...	...	...	...
Liabilities	4 905	. .	...	...	...	...	...	...	...	...
Monetary authorities	4 906	. .	...	...	...	...	...	...	...	...
General government	4 907	. .	...	...	...	...	...	...	...	...
Banks	4 908	. .	...	...	...	...	...	...	...	...
Other sectors	4 909	. .	...	...	...	...	...	...	...	...

Table 2 (Concluded). STANDARD PRESENTATION, 1994–2001
(Millions of U.S. dollars)

	Code	1994	1995	1996	1997	1998	1999	2000	2001
D. OTHER INVESTMENT	4 700 . .	20.1	4.7	–37.6	16.5	32.0	–2.3	3.1	–20.6
Assets	4 703 . .	**–46.8**	**–103.4**	**–118.0**	**–23.6**	**–21.2**	**–61.1**	**–80.3**	**–103.0**
Trade credits	4 706 . .	. . .	. . .	. . .	. . .	. . .	. . .	. . .	. . .
General government	4 707 . .	. . .	. . .	. . .	. . .	. . .	. . .	. . .	. . .
of which: Short-term	4 709 . .	. . .	. . .	. . .	. . .	. . .	. . .	. . .	. . .
Other sectors	4 710 . .	. . .	. . .	. . .	. . .	. . .	. . .	. . .	. . .
of which: Short-term	4 712 . .	. . .	. . .	. . .	. . .	. . .	. . .	. . .	. . .
Loans	4 714 . .	. . .	. . .	. . .	. . .	. . .	. . .	. . .	. . .
Monetary authorities	4 715 . .	. . .	. . .	. . .	. . .	. . .	. . .	. . .	. . .
of which: Short-term	4 718 . .	. . .	. . .	. . .	. . .	. . .	. . .	. . .	. . .
General government	4 719 . .	. . .	. . .	. . .	. . .	. . .	. . .	. . .	. . .
of which: Short-term	4 721 . .	. . .	. . .	. . .	. . .	. . .	. . .	. . .	. . .
Banks	4 722 . .	. . .	. . .	. . .	. . .	. . .	. . .	. . .	. . .
of which: Short-term	4 724 . .	. . .	. . .	. . .	. . .	. . .	. . .	. . .	. . .
Other sectors	4 725 . .	. . .	. . .	. . .	. . .	. . .	. . .	. . .	. . .
of which: Short-term	4 727 . .	. . .	. . .	. . .	. . .	. . .	. . .	. . .	. . .
Currency and deposits	4 730 . .	–38.6	–107.6	–118.9	–19.3	–24.5	–63.9	–77.9	–99.1
Monetary authorities	4 731 . .	. . .	. . .	. . .	. . .	. . .	. . .	. . .	. . .
General government	4 732 . .	. . .	. . .	. . .	. . .	. . .	. . .	. . .	. . .
Banks	4 733 . .	8.2	–44.0	–24.5	27.9	19.9	–17.9	–11.1	–45.1
Other sectors	4 734 . .	–46.8	–63.6	–94.4	–47.2	–44.4	–46.0	–66.8	–54.0
Other assets	4 736 . .	–8.2	4.2	.9	–4.3	3.3	2.8	–2.4	–3.9
Monetary authorities	4 737 . .	. . .	. . .	. . .	. . .	. . .	. . .	. . .	. . .
of which: Short-term	4 739 . .	. . .	. . .	. . .	. . .	. . .	. . .	. . .	. . .
General government	4 740 . .	. . .	. . .	. . .	. . .	. . .	. . .	. . .	. . .
of which: Short-term	4 742 . .	. . .	. . .	. . .	. . .	. . .	. . .	. . .	. . .
Banks	4 743 . .	–8.2	4.2	.9	–4.3	3.3	2.8	–2.4	–3.9
of which: Short-term	4 745 . .	*–8.2*	*4.2*	*.9*	*–4.3*	. . .	. . .	. . .	. . .
Other sectors	4 746 . .	. . .	. . .	. . .	. . .	. . .	. . .	. . .	. . .
of which: Short-term	4 748 . .	. . .	. . .	. . .	. . .	. . .	. . .	. . .	. . .
Liabilities	4 753 . .	**66.9**	**108.1**	**80.4**	**40.1**	**53.2**	**58.8**	**83.4**	**82.4**
Trade credits	4 756 . .	. . .	. . .	. . .	. . .	. . .	. . .	. . .	. . .
General government	4 757 . .	. . .	. . .	. . .	. . .	. . .	. . .	. . .	. . .
of which: Short-term	4 759 . .	. . .	. . .	. . .	. . .	. . .	. . .	. . .	. . .
Other sectors	4 760 . .	. . .	. . .	. . .	. . .	. . .	. . .	. . .	. . .
of which: Short-term	4 762 . .	. . .	. . .	. . .	. . .	. . .	. . .	. . .	. . .
Loans	4 764 . .	50.3	334.2	90.0	42.2	39.3	50.9	81.3	71.5
Monetary authorities	4 765 . .	19.8	42.3	. . .	. . .	–1.4	8.3	4.0	9.3
of which: Use of Fund credit and loans from the Fund	4 766 . .	*19.8*	*42.3*	. . .	. . .	*–1.4*	*8.3*	*4.0*	*9.3*
of which: Short-term	4 768 . .	. . .	. . .	. . .	. . .	. . .	. . .	. . .	. . .
General government	4 769 . .	51.4	308.4	89.7	41.2	42.5	43.8	74.6	64.6
of which: Short-term	4 771 . .	. . .	. . .	. . .	. . .	. . .	. . .	. . .	. . .
Banks	4 772 . .	–20.9	–16.5	.3	1.0	–1.8	–1.2	2.7	–2.4
of which: Short-term	4 774 . .	*–20.9*	*–16.5*	*.3*	*1.0*	. . .	. . .	. . .	. . .
Other sectors	4 775 . .	. . .	. . .	. . .	. . .	. . .	. . .	. . .	. . .
of which: Short-term	4 777 . .	. . .	. . .	. . .	. . .	. . .	. . .	. . .	. . .
Currency and deposits	4 780 . .	1.7	16.8	–6.8	–.7	3.6	–3.0	–7.3	.1
Monetary authorities	4 781 . .	. . .	. . .	. . .	. . .	. . .	. . .	. . .	. . .
General government	4 782 . .	. . .	. . .	. . .	. . .	. . .	. . .	. . .	. . .
Banks	4 783 . .	1.7	16.8	–6.8	–.7	3.6	–3.0	–7.3	.1
Other sectors	4 784 . .	. . .	. . .	. . .	. . .	. . .	. . .	. . .	. . .
Other liabilities	4 786 . .	14.9	–242.9	–2.8	–1.4	10.3	10.9	9.4	10.8
Monetary authorities	4 787 . .	. . .	. . .	. . .	. . .	. . .	. . .	. . .	. . .
of which: Short-term	4 789 . .	. . .	. . .	. . .	. . .	. . .	. . .	. . .	. . .
General government	4 790 . .	15.2	–244.5	–3.1	.4	10.8	9.4	11.5	8.4
of which: Short-term	4 792 . .	*15.2*	*–244.5*	*–3.1*	*.4*	*10.8*	*9.4*	*11.5*	*8.4*
Banks	4 793 . .	–.3	1.6	.3	–1.8	–.5	1.5	–2.1	2.4
of which: Short-term	4 795 . .	*–.3*	*1.6*	*.3*	*–1.8*	. . .	. . .	. . .	. . .
Other sectors	4 796 . .	. . .	. . .	. . .	. . .	. . .	. . .	. . .	. . .
of which: Short-term	4 798 . .	. . .	. . .	. . .	. . .	. . .	. . .	. . .	. . .
E. RESERVE ASSETS	4 802 . .	–71.2	–73.2	–68.9	–34.3	–29.3	–65.1	–101.4	–90.2
Monetary gold	4 812 . .	. . .	. . .	. . .	. . .	. . .	. . .	7.3	. . .
Special drawing rights	4 811 . .	.8	1.0	1.0	1.0	2.5	4.3	4.8	–.4
Reserve position in the Fund	4 810 . .	. . .	. . .	. . .	. . .	. . .	. . .	. . .	. . .
Foreign exchange	4 803 . .	–72.0	–74.2	–69.9	–35.3	–31.8	–69.4	–113.5	–89.8
Other claims	4 813 . .	. . .	. . .	. . .	. . .	. . .	. . .	. . .	. . .
NET ERRORS AND OMISSIONS	4 998 . .	**65.6**	**11.5**	**–78.0**	**–41.2**	**–56.1**	**34.8**	**54.3**	**39.0**

Part 3 of the *Yearbook* contains descriptions of the methodologies, compilation practices, and sources used to compile these data.

Table 3. INTERNATIONAL INVESTMENT POSITION (End–period stocks), 1994–2001
(Millions of U.S. dollars)

	Code		1994	1995	1996	1997	1998	1999	2000	2001
ASSETS	8 995	C.	...	...	...	...	...	...	...	...
Direct investment abroad	8 505	. .	**...**	**...**	**...**	**...**	**...**	**...**	**...**	**...**
Equity capital and reinvested earnings	8 506	. .	...	...	...	...	...	...	...	...
Claims on affiliated enterprises	8 507	. .	...	...	...	...	...	...	...	...
Liabilities to affiliated enterprises	8 508	. .	...	...	...	...	...	...	...	...
Other capital	8 530	. .	...	...	...	...	...	...	...	...
Claims on affiliated enterprises	8 535	. .	...	...	...	...	...	...	...	...
Liabilities to affiliated enterprises	8 540	. .	...	...	...	...	...	...	...	...
Portfolio investment	8 602	. .	**...**	**...**	**...**	**...**	**...**	**...**	**...**	**...**
Equity securities	8 610	. .	...	...	...	...	...	...	...	...
Monetary authorities	8 611	. .	...	...	...	...	...	...	...	...
General government	8 612	. .	...	...	...	...	...	...	...	...
Banks	8 613	. .	...	...	...	...	...	...	...	...
Other sectors	8 614	. .	...	...	...	...	...	...	...	...
Debt securities	8 619	. .	...	...	...	...	...	...	...	...
Bonds and notes	8 620	. .	...	...	...	...	...	...	...	...
Monetary authorities	8 621	. .	...	...	...	...	...	...	...	...
General government	8 622	. .	...	...	...	...	...	...	...	...
Banks	8 623	. .	...	...	...	...	...	...	...	...
Other sectors	8 624	. .	...	...	...	...	...	...	...	...
Money market instruments	8 630	. .	...	...	...	...	...	...	...	...
Monetary authorities	8 631	. .	...	...	...	...	...	...	...	...
General government	8 632	. .	...	...	...	...	...	...	...	...
Banks	8 633	. .	...	...	...	...	...	...	...	...
Other sectors	8 634	. .	...	...	...	...	...	...	...	...
Financial derivatives	8 900	. .	**...**	**...**	**...**	**...**	**...**	**...**	**...**	**...**
Monetary authorities	8 901	. .	...	...	...	...	...	...	...	...
General government	8 902	. .	...	...	...	...	...	...	...	...
Banks	8 903	. .	...	...	...	...	...	...	...	...
Other sectors	8 904	. .	...	...	...	...	...	...	...	...
Other investment	8 703	. .	**...**	**182.3**	**206.9**	**223.2**	**206.1**	**225.0**	**240.6**	**287.5**
Trade credits	8 706	. .	...	...	...	...	...	...	...	...
General government	8 707	. .	...	...	...	...	...	...	...	...
of which: Short-term	8 709	. .	...	...	...	...	...	...	...	...
Other sectors	8 710	. .	...	...	...	...	...	...	...	...
of which: Short-term	8 712	. .	...	...	...	...	...	...	...	...
Loans	8 714	. .	...	...	...	...	...	...	...	...
Monetary authorities	8 715	. .	...	...	...	...	...	...	...	...
of which: Short-term	8 718	. .	...	...	...	...	...	...	...	...
General government	8 719	. .	...	...	...	...	...	...	...	...
of which: Short-term	8 721	. .	...	...	...	...	...	...	...	...
Banks	8 722	. .	...	...	...	...	...	...	...	...
of which: Short-term	8 724	. .	...	...	...	...	...	...	...	...
Other sectors	8 725	. .	...	...	...	...	...	...	...	...
of which: Short-term	8 727	. .	...	...	...	...	...	...	...	...
Currency and deposits	8 730	. .	...	174.3	199.7	211.8	197.9	219.7	232.8	275.8
Monetary authorities	8 731	. .	...	...	...	...	...	...	...	...
General government	8 732	. .	...	...	...	...	...	...	...	...
Banks	8 733	. .	...	155.3	179.7	151.8	131.9	149.7	160.8	205.8
Other sectors	8 734	. .	...	19.0	20.0	60.0	66.0	70.0	72.0	70.0
Other assets	8 736	. .	...	8.0	7.2	11.4	8.2	5.3	7.8	11.7
Monetary authorities	8 737	. .	...	...	...	...	...	...	...	...
of which: Short-term	8 739	. .	...	...	...	...	...	...	...	...
General government	8 740	. .	...	...	...	...	...	...	...	...
of which: Short-term	8 742	. .	...	...	...	...	...	...	...	...
Banks	8 743	. .	...	8.0	7.2	11.4	8.2	5.3	7.8	11.7
of which: Short-term	8 745	. .	...	*8.0*	*7.2*	*11.4*	*8.2*	*5.3*	*7.8*	*11.7*
Other sectors	8 746	. .	...	...	...	...	...	...	...	...
of which: Short-term	8 748	. .	...	...	...	...	...	...	...	...
Reserve assets	8 802	. .	**...**	**192.1**	**504.1**	**575.2**	**446.8**	**509.2**	**610.6**	**696.2**
Monetary gold	8 812	. .	...	...	...	...	118.5	116.2	109.0	110.8
Special drawing rights	8 811	. .	15.9	15.2	13.7	11.8	9.8	5.2	.2	.5
Reserve position in the Fund	8 810	. .	...	...	...	...	...	...	...	...
Foreign exchange	8 803	. .	...	176.9	490.4	563.4	318.5	387.8	501.4	584.9
Other claims	8 813	. .	...	...	...	...	...	...	...	...

Table 3 (Concluded). INTERNATIONAL INVESTMENT POSITION (End–period stocks), 1994–2001

(Millions of U.S. dollars)

	Code		1994	1995	1996	1997	1998	1999	2000	2001
LIABILITIES	8 995	D.	...	...	...	...	...	...	...	...
Direct investment in Cambodia	8 555	. .	**...**	**498.1**	**677.6**	**580.4**	**1,080.7**	**1,224.2**	**1,336.0**	**1,448.9**
Equity capital and reinvested earnings	8 556	. .	...	360.4	361.0	430.2	584.8	644.3	680.1	733.0
Claims on direct investors	8 557	. .	...	...	...	...	...	...	...	...
Liabilities to direct investors	8 558	. .	...	360.4	361.0	430.2	584.8	644.3	680.1	733.0
Other capital	8 580	. .	...	137.7	316.6	150.2	495.9	579.9	655.9	715.9
Claims on direct investors	8 585	. .	...	...	...	...	...	...	...	...
Liabilities to direct investors	8 590	. .	...	137.7	316.6	150.2	495.9	579.9	655.9	715.9
Portfolio investment	8 652	. .	**...**	**...**	**...**	**...**	**...**	**...**	**...**	**...**
Equity securities	8 660	. .	...	...	...	...	...	...	...	...
Banks	8 663	. .	...	...	...	...	...	...	...	...
Other sectors	8 664	. .	...	...	...	...	...	...	...	...
Debt securities	8 669	. .	...	...	...	...	...	...	...	...
Bonds and notes	8 670	. .	...	...	...	...	...	...	...	...
Monetary authorities	8 671	. .	...	...	...	...	...	...	...	...
General government	8 672	. .	...	...	...	...	...	...	...	...
Banks	8 673	. .	...	...	...	...	...	...	...	...
Other sectors	8 674	. .	...	...	...	...	...	...	...	...
Money market instruments	8 680	. .	...	...	...	...	...	...	...	...
Monetary authorities	8 681	. .	...	...	...	...	...	...	...	...
General government	8 682	. .	...	...	...	...	...	...	...	...
Banks	8 683	. .	...	...	...	...	...	...	...	...
Other sectors	8 684	. .	...	...	...	...	...	...	...	...
Financial derivatives	8 905	. .	**...**	**...**	**...**	**...**	**...**	**...**	**...**	**...**
Monetary authorities	8 906	. .	...	...	...	...	...	...	...	...
General government	8 907	. .	...	...	...	...	...	...	...	...
Banks	8 908	. .	...	...	...	...	...	...	...	...
Other sectors	8 909	. .	...	...	...	...	...	...	...	...
Other investment	8 753	. .	**...**	**609.9**	**673.6**	**630.1**	**753.9**	**841.3**	**1,132.2**	**1,131.4**
Trade credits	8 756	. .	...	...	...	...	...	...	...	...
General government	8 757	. .	...	...	...	...	...	...	...	...
of which: Short-term	8 759	. .	...	...	...	...	...	...	...	...
Other sectors	8 760	. .	...	...	...	...	...	...	...	...
of which: Short-term	8 762	. .	...	...	...	...	...	...	...	...
Loans	8 764	. .	...	328.6	418.0	359.4	490.4	540.2	856.1	852.9
Monetary authorities	8 765	. .	...	71.7	69.4	65.1	66.5	72.9	73.3	79.8
of which: Use of Fund credit and loans from the Fund	8 766	. .	*29.6*	*71.7*	*69.4*	*65.1*	*66.5*	*72.9*	*73.3*	*79.8*
of which: Short-term	8 768	. .	...	...	...	...	...	...	...	...
General government	8 769	. .	...	255.1	346.5	291.3	422.7	467.2	780.1	772.8
of which: Short-term	8 771	. .	...	...	...	...	...	...	...	...
Banks	8 772	. .	...	1.8	2.1	3.0	1.2	.1	2.7	.3
of which: Short-term	8 774	. .	...	*1.8*	*2.1*	*3.0*	*1.2*	*.1*	*2.7*	*.3*
Other sectors	8 775	. .	...	...	...	...	...	...	...	...
of which: Short-term	8 777	. .	...	...	...	...	...	...	...	...
Currency and deposits	8 780	. .	...	61.4	54.7	54.0	57.7	54.7	47.5	47.5
Monetary authorities	8 781	. .	...	...	...	...	...	...	...	...
General government	8 782	. .	...	...	...	...	...	...	...	...
Banks	8 783	. .	...	61.4	54.7	54.0	57.7	54.7	47.5	47.5
Other sectors	8 784	. .	...	...	...	...	...	...	...	...
Other liabilities	8 786	. .	...	219.9	201.0	216.7	205.8	246.4	228.6	231.0
Monetary authorities	8 787	. .	...	...	...	...	...	...	...	...
of which: Short-term	8 789	. .	...	...	...	...	...	...	...	...
General government	8 790	. .	...	217.4	198.2	215.6	205.2	244.3	228.6	228.6
of which: Short-term	8 792	. .	...	*217.4*	*198.2*	*215.6*	*205.2*	*244.3*	*228.6*	*228.6*
Banks	8 793	. .	...	2.5	2.8	1.1	.6	2.1	...	2.4
of which: Short-term	8 795	. .	...	*2.5*	*2.8*	*1.1*	*.6*	*2.1*	...	*2.4*
Other sectors	8 796	. .	...	...	...	...	...	...	...	...
of which: Short-term	8 798	. .	...	...	...	...	...	...	...	...
NET INTERNATIONAL INVESTMENT POSITION	8 995	. .	**...**	**...**	**...**	**...**	**...**	**...**	**...**	**...**
Conversion rates: riel per U.S. dollar (end of period)	0 102	. .	**2,575.0**	**2,526.0**	**2,713.0**	**3,452.0**	**3,770.0**	**3,770.0**	**3,905.0**	**3,895.0**

Table 1. ANALYTIC PRESENTATION, 1994–2001
(Millions of U.S. dollars)

	Code		1994	1995	1996	1997	1998	1999	2000	2001
A. Current Account [1]	4 993	Z.	**–56.1**	**89.9**	...	...	...	...	...	...
Goods: exports f.o.b	2 100	..	1,454.2	1,735.9	...	...	...	...	...	...
Goods: imports f.o.b	3 100	..	–1,052.3	–1,109.0	...	...	...	...	...	...
Balance on Goods	4 100	..	*401.9*	*626.9*	...	...	...	...	...	...
Services: credit	2 200	..	330.8	304.4	...	...	...	...	...	...
Services: debit	3 200	..	–493.2	–498.6	...	...	...	...	...	...
Balance on Goods and Services	4 991	..	*239.6*	*432.6*	...	...	...	...	...	...
Income: credit	2 300	..	19.9	12.4	...	...	...	...	...	...
Income: debit	3 300	..	–336.4	–424.6	...	...	...	...	...	...
Balance on Goods, Services, and Income	4 992	..	*–76.9*	*20.4*	...	...	...	...	...	...
Current transfers: credit	2 379	Z.	83.8	100.7	...	...	...	...	...	...
Current transfers: debit	3 379	..	–63.0	–31.2	...	...	...	...	...	...
B. Capital Account [1]	4 994	Z.	**14.1**	**20.4**	...	...	...	...	...	...
Capital account: credit	2 994	Z.	14.1	21.1	...	...	...	...	...	...
Capital account: debit	3 994	..	...	–.7	...	...	...	...	...	...
Total, Groups A Plus B	4 981	..	*–41.9*	*110.2*	...	...	...	...	...	...
C. Financial Account [1]	4 995	W.	**–626.4**	**43.3**	...	...	...	...	...	...
Direct investment abroad	4 505	..	–.4	–.6	...	...	...	...	...	...
Direct investment in Cameroon	4 555	Z.	–9.0	7.3	...	...	...	...	...	...
Portfolio investment assets	4 602	..	–74.6	–26.2	...	...	...	...	...	...
Equity securities	4 610	..	6.4	...	...	...	...	...	...	...
Debt securities	4 619	..	–81.1	–26.2	...	...	...	...	...	...
Portfolio investment liabilities	4 652	Z.	...	...	...	...	...	...	...	...
Equity securities	4 660	..	...	...	...	...	...	...	...	...
Debt securities	4 669	Z.	...	...	...	...	...	...	...	...
Financial derivatives	4 910	..	...	...	...	...	...	...	...	...
Financial derivatives assets	4 900	..	...	...	...	...	...	...	...	...
Financial derivatives liabilities	4 905	..	...	...	...	...	...	...	...	...
Other investment assets	4 703	..	138.4	–146.8	...	...	...	...	...	...
Monetary authorities	4 701	..	...	...	...	...	...	...	...	...
General government	4 704	..	...	...	...	...	...	...	...	...
Banks	4 705	..	–27.9	6.6	...	...	...	...	...	...
Other sectors	4 728	..	166.3	–153.4	...	...	...	...	...	...
Other investment liabilities	4 753	W.	–680.7	209.6	...	...	...	...	...	...
Monetary authorities	4 753	WA	–181.3	666.9	...	...	...	...	...	...
General government	4 753	ZB	–272.3	–457.0	...	...	...	...	...	...
Banks	4 753	ZC	–76.2	17.0	...	...	...	...	...	...
Other sectors	4 753	ZD	–150.9	–17.3	...	...	...	...	...	...
Total, Groups A Through C	4 983	..	*–668.3*	*153.5*	...	...	...	...	...	...
D. Net Errors and Omissions	4 998	..	**117.0**	**–138.1**	...	...	...	...	...	...
Total, Groups A Through D	4 984	..	*–551.3*	*15.4*	...	...	...	...	...	...
E. Reserves and Related Items	4 802	A.	**551.3**	**–15.4**	...	...	...	...	...	...
Reserve assets	4 802	..	.4	14.5	...	...	...	...	...	...
Use of Fund credit and loans	4 766	..	25.3	6.7	...	...	...	...	...	...
Exceptional financing	4 920	..	525.6	–36.6	...	...	...	...	...	...
Conversion rates: CFA francs per U.S. dollar	0 101	..	**555.20**	**499.15**	**511.55**	**583.67**	**589.95**	**615.70**	**711.98**	**733.04**

[1] Excludes components that have been classified in the categories of Group E.

Table 2. STANDARD PRESENTATION, 1994–2001

(Millions of U.S. dollars)

	Code	1994	1995	1996	1997	1998	1999	2000	2001
CURRENT ACCOUNT	4 993 . .	**–56.1**	**89.9**	**. . .**	**. . .**	**. . .**	**. . .**	**. . .**	**. . .**
A. GOODS	4 100 . .	401.9	626.9	. . .	. . .	. . .	. . .	. . .	. . .
Credit	2 100 . .	**1,454.2**	**1,735.9**	**. . .**	**. . .**	**. . .**	**. . .**	**. . .**	**. . .**
General merchandise: exports f.o.b.	2 110 . .	1,454.2	1,735.9	. . .	. . .	. . .	. . .	. . .	. . .
Goods for processing: exports f.o.b.	2 150 . .	. . .	. . .	. . .	. . .	. . .	. . .	. . .	. . .
Repairs on goods	2 160 . .	. . .	. . .	. . .	. . .	. . .	. . .	. . .	. . .
Goods procured in ports by carriers	2 170 . .	. . .	. . .	. . .	. . .	. . .	. . .	. . .	. . .
Nonmonetary gold	2 180 . .	. . .	. . .	. . .	. . .	. . .	. . .	. . .	. . .
Debit	3 100 . .	**–1,052.3**	**–1,109.0**	**. . .**	**. . .**	**. . .**	**. . .**	**. . .**	**. . .**
General merchandise: imports f.o.b.	3 110 . .	–1,052.3	–1,109.0	. . .	. . .	. . .	. . .	. . .	. . .
Goods for processing: imports f.o.b.	3 150 . .	. . .	. . .	. . .	. . .	. . .	. . .	. . .	. . .
Repairs on goods	3 160 . .	. . .	. . .	. . .	. . .	. . .	. . .	. . .	. . .
Goods procured in ports by carriers	3 170 . .	. . .	. . .	. . .	. . .	. . .	. . .	. . .	. . .
Nonmonetary gold	3 180 . .	. . .	. . .	. . .	. . .	. . .	. . .	. . .	. . .
B. SERVICES	4 200 . .	–162.3	–194.3	. . .	. . .	. . .	. . .	. . .	. . .
Total credit	2 200 . .	*330.8*	*304.4*	. . .	. . .	. . .	. . .	. . .	. . .
Total debit	3 200 . .	*–493.2*	*–498.6*	. . .	. . .	. . .	. . .	. . .	. . .
Transportation services, credit	2 205 . .	**119.6**	**117.1**	**. . .**	**. . .**	**. . .**	**. . .**	**. . .**	**. . .**
Passenger	2 850 . .	*36.1*	*39.1*	. . .	. . .	. . .	. . .	. . .	. . .
Freight	2 851 . .	*51.3*	*43.7*	. . .	. . .	. . .	. . .	. . .	. . .
Other	2 852 . .	*32.2*	*34.3*	. . .	. . .	. . .	. . .	. . .	. . .
Sea transport, passenger	2 207 . .	. . .	. . .	. . .	. . .	. . .	. . .	. . .	. . .
Sea transport, freight	2 208 . .	32.3	31.7	. . .	. . .	. . .	. . .	. . .	. . .
Sea transport, other	2 209 . .	32.2	34.3	. . .	. . .	. . .	. . .	. . .	. . .
Air transport, passenger	2 211 . .	36.1	39.1	. . .	. . .	. . .	. . .	. . .	. . .
Air transport, freight	2 212 . .	19.1	12.0	. . .	. . .	. . .	. . .	. . .	. . .
Air transport, other	2 213 . .	. . .	. . .	. . .	. . .	. . .	. . .	. . .	. . .
Other transport, passenger	2 215 . .	. . .	. . .	. . .	. . .	. . .	. . .	. . .	. . .
Other transport, freight	2 216 . .	. . .	. . .	. . .	. . .	. . .	. . .	. . .	. . .
Other transport, other	2 217 . .	. . .	. . .	. . .	. . .	. . .	. . .	. . .	. . .
Transportation services, debit	3 205 . .	**–215.8**	**–171.6**	**. . .**	**. . .**	**. . .**	**. . .**	**. . .**	**. . .**
Passenger	3 850 . .	*–44.1*	*–34.6*	. . .	. . .	. . .	. . .	. . .	. . .
Freight	3 851 . .	*–128.2*	*–94.9*	. . .	. . .	. . .	. . .	. . .	. . .
Other	3 852 . .	*–43.5*	*–42.1*	. . .	. . .	. . .	. . .	. . .	. . .
Sea transport, passenger	3 207 . .	. . .	. . .	. . .	. . .	. . .	. . .	. . .	. . .
Sea transport, freight	3 208 . .	–119.0	–89.3	. . .	. . .	. . .	. . .	. . .	. . .
Sea transport, other	3 209 . .	–43.5	–42.1	. . .	. . .	. . .	. . .	. . .	. . .
Air transport, passenger	3 211 . .	–44.1	–34.6	. . .	. . .	. . .	. . .	. . .	. . .
Air transport, freight	3 212 . .	–9.2	–5.6	. . .	. . .	. . .	. . .	. . .	. . .
Air transport, other	3 213 . .	. . .	. . .	. . .	. . .	. . .	. . .	. . .	. . .
Other transport, passenger	3 215 . .	. . .	. . .	. . .	. . .	. . .	. . .	. . .	. . .
Other transport, freight	3 216 . .	. . .	. . .	. . .	. . .	. . .	. . .	. . .	. . .
Other transport, other	3 217 . .	. . .	. . .	. . .	. . .	. . .	. . .	. . .	. . .
Travel, credit	2 236 . .	**27.8**	**35.8**	**. . .**	**. . .**	**. . .**	**. . .**	**. . .**	**. . .**
Business travel	2 237 . .	13.2	24.7	. . .	. . .	. . .	. . .	. . .	. . .
Personal travel	2 240 . .	14.6	11.2	. . .	. . .	. . .	. . .	. . .	. . .
Travel, debit	3 236 . .	**–58.4**	**–105.3**	**. . .**	**. . .**	**. . .**	**. . .**	**. . .**	**. . .**
Business travel	3 237 . .	–22.0	–79.4	. . .	. . .	. . .	. . .	. . .	. . .
Personal travel	3 240 . .	–36.5	–25.8	. . .	. . .	. . .	. . .	. . .	. . .
Other services, credit	2 200 BA	**183.4**	**151.4**	**. . .**	**. . .**	**. . .**	**. . .**	**. . .**	**. . .**
Communications	2 245 . .	2.5	2.4	. . .	. . .	. . .	. . .	. . .	. . .
Construction	2 249 . .	8.5	12.8	. . .	. . .	. . .	. . .	. . .	. . .
Insurance	2 253 . .	12.7	15.0	. . .	. . .	. . .	. . .	. . .	. . .
Financial	2 260 . .	4.3	2.4	. . .	. . .	. . .	. . .	. . .	. . .
Computer and information	2 262 . .	. . .	. . .	. . .	. . .	. . .	. . .	. . .	. . .
Royalties and licence fees	2 266 . .	.4	.2	. . .	. . .	. . .	. . .	. . .	. . .
Other business services	2 268 . .	132.8	56.6	. . .	. . .	. . .	. . .	. . .	. . .
Personal, cultural, and recreational	2 287 . .	. . .	. . .	. . .	. . .	. . .	. . .	. . .	. . .
Government, n.i.e.	2 291 . .	22.3	62.0	. . .	. . .	. . .	. . .	. . .	. . .
Other services, debit	3 200 BA	**–218.9**	**–221.8**	**. . .**	**. . .**	**. . .**	**. . .**	**. . .**	**. . .**
Communications	3 245 . .	–1.1	–3.9	. . .	. . .	. . .	. . .	. . .	. . .
Construction	3 249 . .	–81.8	–41.8	. . .	. . .	. . .	. . .	. . .	. . .
Insurance	3 253 . .	–26.5	–31.4	. . .	. . .	. . .	. . .	. . .	. . .
Financial	3 260 . .	–5.7	–3.7	. . .	. . .	. . .	. . .	. . .	. . .
Computer and information	3 262 . .	. . .	. . .	. . .	. . .	. . .	. . .	. . .	. . .
Royalties and licence fees	3 266 . .	–.3	–1.0	. . .	. . .	. . .	. . .	. . .	. . .
Other business services	3 268 . .	–87.3	–126.1	. . .	. . .	. . .	. . .	. . .	. . .
Personal, cultural, and recreational	3 287 . .	. . .	. . .	. . .	. . .	. . .	. . .	. . .	. . .
Government, n.i.e.	3 291 . .	–16.2	–13.9	. . .	. . .	. . .	. . .	. . .	. . .

Table 2 (Continued). STANDARD PRESENTATION, 1994–2001
(Millions of U.S. dollars)

	Code	1994	1995	1996	1997	1998	1999	2000	2001
C. INCOME	4 300 . .	–316.4	–412.2	. . .	. . .	. . .	. . .	. . .	. . .
Total credit	2 300 . .	*19.9*	*12.4*	. . .	. . .	. . .	. . .	. . .	. . .
Total debit	3 300 . .	*–336.4*	*–424.6*	. . .	. . .	. . .	. . .	. . .	. . .
Compensation of employees, credit	2 310 . .	**5.6**	**2.2**	. . .	. . .	. . .	. . .	. . .	. . .
Compensation of employees, debit	3 310 . .	**–10.9**	**–5.7**	. . .	. . .	. . .	. . .	. . .	. . .
Investment income, credit	2 320 . .	**14.4**	**10.2**	. . .	. . .	. . .	. . .	. . .	. . .
Direct investment income	2 330 . .	8.9	4.5	. . .	. . .	. . .	. . .	. . .	. . .
Dividends and distributed branch profits	2 332 . .	8.8	4.5	. . .	. . .	. . .	. . .	. . .	. . .
Reinvested earnings and undistributed branch profits	2 333 . .	. . .	. . .	. . .	. . .	. . .	. . .	. . .	. . .
Income on debt (interest)	2 334 . .	.1	. . .	. . .	. . .	. . .	. . .	. . .	. . .
Portfolio investment income	2 339 . .	. . .	. . .	. . .	. . .	. . .	. . .	. . .	. . .
Income on equity	2 340 . .	. . .	. . .	. . .	. . .	. . .	. . .	. . .	. . .
Income on bonds and notes	2 350 . .	. . .	. . .	. . .	. . .	. . .	. . .	. . .	. . .
Income on money market instruments	2 360 . .	. . .	. . .	. . .	. . .	. . .	. . .	. . .	. . .
Other investment income	2 370 . .	5.5	5.6	. . .	. . .	. . .	. . .	. . .	. . .
Investment income, debit	3 320 . .	**–325.5**	**–418.9**	. . .	. . .	. . .	. . .	. . .	. . .
Direct investment income	3 330 . .	–27.1	–20.7	. . .	. . .	. . .	. . .	. . .	. . .
Dividends and distributed branch profits	3 332 . .	–22.6	–17.4	. . .	. . .	. . .	. . .	. . .	. . .
Reinvested earnings and undistributed branch profits	3 333 . .	–3.7	–.4	. . .	. . .	. . .	. . .	. . .	. . .
Income on debt (interest)	3 334 . .	–.9	–2.8	. . .	. . .	. . .	. . .	. . .	. . .
Portfolio investment income	3 339 . .	. . .	. . .	. . .	. . .	. . .	. . .	. . .	. . .
Income on equity	3 340 . .	. . .	. . .	. . .	. . .	. . .	. . .	. . .	. . .
Income on bonds and notes	3 350 . .	. . .	. . .	. . .	. . .	. . .	. . .	. . .	. . .
Income on money market instruments	3 360 . .	. . .	. . .	. . .	. . .	. . .	. . .	. . .	. . .
Other investment income	3 370 . .	–298.3	–398.3	. . .	. . .	. . .	. . .	. . .	. . .
D. CURRENT TRANSFERS	4 379 . .	20.8	69.5	. . .	. . .	. . .	. . .	. . .	. . .
Credit	2 379 . .	**83.8**	**100.7**	. . .	. . .	. . .	. . .	. . .	. . .
General government	2 380 . .	55.9	66.8	. . .	. . .	. . .	. . .	. . .	. . .
Other sectors	2 390 . .	27.9	33.9	. . .	. . .	. . .	. . .	. . .	. . .
Workers' remittances	2 391 . .	5.8	9.1	. . .	. . .	. . .	. . .	. . .	. . .
Other current transfers	2 392 . .	22.1	24.8	. . .	. . .	. . .	. . .	. . .	. . .
Debit	3 379 . .	**–63.0**	**–31.2**	. . .	. . .	. . .	. . .	. . .	. . .
General government	3 380 . .	–1.0	–9.3	. . .	. . .	. . .	. . .	. . .	. . .
Other sectors	3 390 . .	–62.0	–21.9	. . .	. . .	. . .	. . .	. . .	. . .
Workers' remittances	3 391 . .	–51.3	–16.7	. . .	. . .	. . .	. . .	. . .	. . .
Other current transfers	3 392 . .	–10.7	–5.3	. . .	. . .	. . .	. . .	. . .	. . .
CAPITAL AND FINANCIAL ACCOUNT	4 996 . .	**–61.0**	**48.2**	. . .	. . .	. . .	. . .	. . .	. . .
CAPITAL ACCOUNT	4 994 . .	**14.1**	**20.4**	. . .	. . .	. . .	. . .	. . .	. . .
Total credit	2 994 . .	*14.1*	*21.1*	. . .	. . .	. . .	. . .	. . .	. . .
Total debit	3 994 . .	. . .	*–.7*	. . .	. . .	. . .	. . .	. . .	. . .
Capital transfers, credit	2 400 . .	**14.1**	**21.1**	. . .	. . .	. . .	. . .	. . .	. . .
General government	2 401 . .	14.1	21.1	. . .	. . .	. . .	. . .	. . .	. . .
Debt forgiveness	2 402 . .	. . .	. . .	. . .	. . .	. . .	. . .	. . .	. . .
Other capital transfers	2 410 . .	14.1	21.1	. . .	. . .	. . .	. . .	. . .	. . .
Other sectors	2 430 . .	. . .	. . .	. . .	. . .	. . .	. . .	. . .	. . .
Migrants' transfers	2 431 . .	. . .	. . .	. . .	. . .	. . .	. . .	. . .	. . .
Debt forgiveness	2 432 . .	. . .	. . .	. . .	. . .	. . .	. . .	. . .	. . .
Other capital transfers	2 440 . .	. . .	. . .	. . .	. . .	. . .	. . .	. . .	. . .
Capital transfers, debit	3 400 . .	. . .	**–.7**	. . .	. . .	. . .	. . .	. . .	. . .
General government	3 401 . .	. . .	–.7	. . .	. . .	. . .	. . .	. . .	. . .
Debt forgiveness	3 402 . .	. . .	. . .	. . .	. . .	. . .	. . .	. . .	. . .
Other capital transfers	3 410 . .	. . .	–.7	. . .	. . .	. . .	. . .	. . .	. . .
Other sectors	3 430 . .	. . .	. . .	. . .	. . .	. . .	. . .	. . .	. . .
Migrants' transfers	3 431 . .	. . .	. . .	. . .	. . .	. . .	. . .	. . .	. . .
Debt forgiveness	3 432 . .	. . .	. . .	. . .	. . .	. . .	. . .	. . .	. . .
Other capital transfers	3 440 . .	. . .	. . .	. . .	. . .	. . .	. . .	. . .	. . .
Nonproduced nonfinancial assets, credit	2 480 . .	. . .	. . .	. . .	. . .	. . .	. . .	. . .	. . .
Nonproduced nonfinancial assets, debit	3 480 . .	. . .	. . .	. . .	. . .	. . .	. . .	. . .	. . .

Table 2 (Continued). STANDARD PRESENTATION, 1994–2001
(Millions of U.S. dollars)

	Code	1994	1995	1996	1997	1998	1999	2000	2001
FINANCIAL ACCOUNT	4 995	**–75.1**	**27.8**	**...**	**...**	**...**	**...**	**...**	**...**
A. DIRECT INVESTMENT	4 500	–9.4	6.7	...	...	...	...	...	...
Direct investment abroad	4 505	**–.4**	**–.6**	**...**	**...**	**...**	**...**	**...**	**...**
Equity capital	4 510	–.4	–.6	...	...	...	...	...	...
Claims on affiliated enterprises	4 515	–.4	–.6	...	...	...	...	...	...
Liabilities to affiliated enterprises	4 520	...	...	...	...	...	...	...	...
Reinvested earnings	4 525	...	...	...	...	...	...	...	...
Other capital	4 530	...	...	...	...	...	...	...	...
Claims on affiliated enterprises	4 535	...	...	...	...	...	...	...	...
Liabilities to affiliated enterprises	4 540	...	...	...	...	...	...	...	...
Direct investment in Cameroon	4 555	**–9.0**	**7.3**	**...**	**...**	**...**	**...**	**...**	**...**
Equity capital	4 560	–5.2	14.7	...	...	...	...	...	...
Claims on direct investors	4 565	–5.2	...	...	...	...	...	...	...
Liabilities to direct investors	4 570	...	14.7	...	...	...	...	...	...
Reinvested earnings	4 575	3.7	.4	...	...	...	...	...	...
Other capital	4 580	–7.4	–7.8	...	...	...	...	...	...
Claims on direct investors	4 585	–7.4	–7.8	...	...	...	...	...	...
Liabilities to direct investors	4 590	...	...	...	...	...	...	...	...
B. PORTFOLIO INVESTMENT	4 600	–74.6	–26.2	...	...	...	...	...	...
Assets	4 602	**–74.6**	**–26.2**	**...**	**...**	**...**	**...**	**...**	**...**
Equity securities	4 610	6.4	...	...	...	...	...	...	...
Monetary authorities	4 611	...	...	...	...	...	...	...	...
General government	4 612	...	...	...	...	...	...	...	...
Banks	4 613	...	...	...	...	...	...	...	...
Other sectors	4 614	6.4	...	...	...	...	...	...	...
Debt securities	4 619	–81.1	–26.2	...	...	...	...	...	...
Bonds and notes	4 620	–81.1	–26.2	...	...	...	...	...	...
Monetary authorities	4 621	...	...	...	...	...	...	...	...
General government	4 622	...	...	...	...	...	...	...	...
Banks	4 623	...	...	...	...	...	...	...	...
Other sectors	4 624	–81.1	–26.2	...	...	...	...	...	...
Money market instruments	4 630	...	...	...	...	...	...	...	...
Monetary authorities	4 631	...	...	...	...	...	...	...	...
General government	4 632	...	...	...	...	...	...	...	...
Banks	4 633	...	...	...	...	...	...	...	...
Other sectors	4 634	...	...	...	...	...	...	...	...
Liabilities	4 652	**...**	**...**	**...**	**...**	**...**	**...**	**...**	**...**
Equity securities	4 660	...	...	...	...	...	...	...	...
Banks	4 663	...	...	...	...	...	...	...	...
Other sectors	4 664	...	...	...	...	...	...	...	...
Debt securities	4 669	...	...	...	...	...	...	...	...
Bonds and notes	4 670	...	...	...	...	...	...	...	...
Monetary authorities	4 671	...	...	...	...	...	...	...	...
General government	4 672	...	...	...	...	...	...	...	...
Banks	4 673	...	...	...	...	...	...	...	...
Other sectors	4 674	...	...	...	...	...	...	...	...
Money market instruments	4 680	...	...	...	...	...	...	...	...
Monetary authorities	4 681	...	...	...	...	...	...	...	...
General government	4 682	...	...	...	...	...	...	...	...
Banks	4 683	...	...	...	...	...	...	...	...
Other sectors	4 684	...	...	...	...	...	...	...	...
C. FINANCIAL DERIVATIVES	4 910	...	...	...	...	...	...	...	...
Monetary authorities	4 911	...	...	...	...	...	...	...	...
General government	4 912	...	...	...	...	...	...	...	...
Banks	4 913	...	...	...	...	...	...	...	...
Other sectors	4 914	...	...	...	...	...	...	...	...
Assets	4 900	**...**	**...**	**...**	**...**	**...**	**...**	**...**	**...**
Monetary authorities	4 901	...	...	...	...	...	...	...	...
General government	4 902	...	...	...	...	...	...	...	...
Banks	4 903	...	...	...	...	...	...	...	...
Other sectors	4 904	...	...	...	...	...	...	...	...
Liabilities	4 905	**...**	**...**	**...**	**...**	**...**	**...**	**...**	**...**
Monetary authorities	4 906	...	...	...	...	...	...	...	...
General government	4 907	...	...	...	...	...	...	...	...
Banks	4 908	...	...	...	...	...	...	...	...
Other sectors	4 909	...	...	...	...	...	...	...	...

Table 2 (Concluded). STANDARD PRESENTATION, 1994–2001
(Millions of U.S. dollars)

	Code	1994	1995	1996	1997	1998	1999	2000	2001
D. OTHER INVESTMENT	4 700	8.6	32.8	...	...	...	...	...	...
Assets	4 703	**138.4**	**–146.8**	...	...	...	...	...	...
Trade credits	4 706	252.4	183.0	...	...	...	...	...	...
General government	4 707	...	...	...	...	...	...	...	...
of which: Short-term	4 709	...	...	...	...	...	...	...	...
Other sectors	4 710	252.4	183.0	...	...	...	...	...	...
of which: Short-term	4 712	*252.4*	*183.0*	...	...	...	...	...	...
Loans	4 714	–2.5	–22.8	...	...	...	...	...	...
Monetary authorities	4 715	...	...	...	...	...	...	...	...
of which: Short-term	4 718	...	...	...	...	...	...	...	...
General government	4 719	...	...	...	...	...	...	...	...
of which: Short-term	4 721	...	...	...	...	...	...	...	...
Banks	4 722	...	...	...	...	...	...	...	...
of which: Short-term	4 724	...	...	...	...	...	...	...	...
Other sectors	4 725	–2.5	–22.8	...	...	...	...	...	...
of which: Short-term	4 727	...	...	...	...	...	...	...	...
Currency and deposits	4 730	–27.9	6.6	...	...	...	...	...	...
Monetary authorities	4 731	...	...	...	...	...	...	...	...
General government	4 732	...	...	...	...	...	...	...	...
Banks	4 733	–27.9	6.6	...	...	...	...	...	...
Other sectors	4 734	...	...	...	...	...	...	...	...
Other assets	4 736	–83.6	–313.6	...	...	...	...	...	...
Monetary authorities	4 737	...	...	...	...	...	...	...	...
of which: Short-term	4 739	...	...	...	...	...	...	...	...
General government	4 740	...	...	...	...	...	...	...	...
of which: Short-term	4 742	...	...	...	...	...	...	...	...
Banks	4 743	...	...	...	...	...	...	...	...
of which: Short-term	4 745	...	...	...	...	...	...	...	...
Other sectors	4 746	–83.6	–313.6	...	...	...	...	...	...
of which: Short-term	4 748	*–83.6*	*–313.6*	...	...	...	...	...	...
Liabilities	4 753	**–129.8**	**179.6**	...	...	...	...	...	...
Trade credits	4 756	–212.3	–273.8	...	...	...	...	...	...
General government	4 757	...	...	...	...	...	...	...	...
of which: Short-term	4 759	...	...	...	...	...	...	...	...
Other sectors	4 760	–212.3	–273.8	...	...	...	...	...	...
of which: Short-term	4 762	*–212.3*	*–273.8*	...	...	...	...	...	...
Loans	4 764	–15.4	254.5	...	...	...	...	...	...
Monetary authorities	4 765	–154.0	667.5	...	...	...	...	...	...
of which: Use of Fund credit and loans from the Fund	4 766	*25.3*	*6.7*	...	...	...	...	...	...
of which: Short-term	4 768	...	...	...	...	...	...	...	...
General government	4 769	168.5	–400.7	...	...	...	...	...	...
of which: Short-term	4 771	...	...	...	...	...	...	...	...
Banks	4 772	...	...	...	...	...	...	...	...
of which: Short-term	4 774	...	...	...	...	...	...	...	...
Other sectors	4 775	–29.8	–12.3	...	...	...	...	...	...
of which: Short-term	4 777	...	...	...	...	...	...	...	...
Currency and deposits	4 780	–78.2	23.1	...	...	...	...	...	...
Monetary authorities	4 781	–2.0	6.1	...	...	...	...	...	...
General government	4 782	...	...	...	...	...	...	...	...
Banks	4 783	–76.2	17.0	...	...	...	...	...	...
Other sectors	4 784	...	...	...	...	...	...	...	...
Other liabilities	4 786	176.0	175.8	...	...	...	...	...	...
Monetary authorities	4 787	62.7	–161.5	...	...	...	...	...	...
of which: Short-term	4 789	*62.7*	*–161.5*	...	...	...	...	...	...
General government	4 790	...	...	...	...	...	...	...	...
of which: Short-term	4 792	...	...	...	...	...	...	...	...
Banks	4 793	...	...	...	...	...	...	...	...
of which: Short-term	4 795	...	...	...	...	...	...	...	...
Other sectors	4 796	113.3	337.3	...	...	...	...	...	...
of which: Short-term	4 798	*113.3*	*337.3*	...	...	...	...	...	...
E. RESERVE ASSETS	4 802	.4	14.5	...	...	...	...	...	...
Monetary gold	4 812	...	11.4	...	...	...	...	...	...
Special drawing rights	4 811	.1	...	...	...	...	...	...	...
Reserve position in the Fund	4 810	...	...	...	...	...	...	...	...
Foreign exchange	4 803	.3	3.2	...	...	...	...	...	...
Other claims	4 813	...	...	...	...	...	...	...	...
NET ERRORS AND OMISSIONS	4 998	**117.0**	**–138.1**	...	...	...	...	...	...

Part 3 of the *Yearbook* contains descriptions of the methodologies, compilation practices, and sources used to compile these data.

Table 1. ANALYTIC PRESENTATION, 1994–2001
(Millions of U.S. dollars)

	Code	1994	1995	1996	1997	1998	1999	2000	2001
A. Current Account [1]	4 993 Z.	**–13,024**	**–4,328**	**3,378**	**–8,233**	**–7,839**	**1,367**	**18,596**	**19,479**
Goods: exports f.o.b.	2 100 ..	166,990	193,373	205,443	219,063	220,539	247,240	286,476	267,915
Goods: imports f.o.b.	3 100 ..	–152,155	–167,517	–174,352	–200,498	–204,617	–220,159	–244,714	–226,490
Balance on Goods	4 100 ..	*14,834*	*25,855*	*31,091*	*18,565*	*15,922*	*27,080*	*41,763*	*41,425*
Services: credit	2 200 ..	23,958	26,128	29,243	31,596	33,836	35,715	38,496	36,576
Services: debit	3 200 ..	–32,530	–33,473	–35,906	–38,013	–38,156	–40,517	–43,493	–42,000
Balance on Goods and Services	4 991 ..	*6,262*	*18,510*	*24,428*	*12,148*	*11,602*	*22,278*	*36,766*	*36,001*
Income: credit	2 300 ..	15,443	18,888	19,204	23,998	21,830	22,165	26,811	22,633
Income: debit	3 300 ..	–34,382	–41,609	–40,755	–44,878	–41,815	–43,759	–45,970	–40,411
Balance on Goods, Services, and Income	4 992 ..	*–12,676*	*–4,211*	*2,877*	*–8,732*	*–8,383*	*685*	*17,607*	*18,223*
Current transfers: credit	2 379 Z.	2,625	2,878	3,594	3,634	3,407	3,796	4,109	4,535
Current transfers: debit	3 379 ..	–2,973	–2,995	–3,092	–3,135	–2,863	–3,114	–3,120	–3,280
B. Capital Account [1]	4 994 Z.	**7,498**	**4,950**	**5,833**	**5,429**	**3,336**	**3,400**	**3,552**	**3,673**
Capital account: credit	2 994 Z.	7,876	5,416	6,262	5,862	3,794	3,858	4,044	4,163
Capital account: debit	3 994 ..	–378	–466	–429	–433	–457	–458	–492	–490
Total, Groups A Plus B	4 981 ..	*–5,526*	*622*	*9,212*	*–2,804*	*–4,503*	*4,767*	*22,148*	*23,151*
C. Financial Account [1]	4 995 W.	**5,159**	**–1,277**	**–9,277**	**3,394**	**4,944**	**–6,470**	**–14,295**	**–15,008**
Direct investment abroad	4 505 ..	–9,303	–11,490	–13,107	–23,069	–34,112	–15,623	–47,311	–35,567
Direct investment in Canada	4 555 Z.	8,224	9,319	9,635	11,523	22,742	24,488	66,017	27,438
Portfolio investment assets	4 602 ..	–6,587	–5,328	–14,183	–8,568	–15,106	–15,556	–41,866	–24,468
Equity securities	4 610 ..	–6,898	–4,570	–12,661	–3,777	–10,428	–13,888	–39,123	–23,239
Debt securities	4 619 ..	311	–759	–1,522	–4,792	–4,678	–1,669	–2,743	–1,230
Portfolio investment liabilities	4 652 Z.	17,155	18,402	13,718	11,692	16,590	2,315	9,875	19,750
Equity securities	4 660 ..	4,718	–3,077	5,900	5,461	9,645	9,534	24,064	3,020
Debt securities	4 669 Z.	12,437	21,479	7,818	6,230	6,945	–7,219	–14,189	16,730
Financial derivatives	4 910 ..	...	...	...	...	...	...	...	...
Financial derivatives assets	4 900 ..	...	...	...	...	...	...	...	...
Financial derivatives liabilities	4 905 ..	...	...	...	...	...	...	...	...
Other investment assets	4 703 ..	–20,378	–8,328	–21,064	–16,167	9,400	9,395	–2,759	–8,940
Monetary authorities	4 701 ..	...	...	...	...	...	...	...	...
General government	4 704 ..	–436	–336	–119	–515	–579	–305	–235	–127
Banks	4 705 ..	–12,575	–8,314	–13,847	–5,419	969	13,368	–7,301	–2,096
Other sectors	4 728 ..	–7,366	322	–7,098	–10,233	9,010	–3,668	4,776	–6,718
Other investment liabilities	4 753 W.	16,049	–3,852	15,724	27,983	5,430	–11,489	1,749	6,780
Monetary authorities	4 753 WA	...	...	...	...	...	...	...	...
General government	4 753 ZB	586	–484	–508	–321	–270	–318	–350	–237
Banks	4 753 ZC	15,233	–4,579	12,707	24,630	953	–16,200	–697	15,155
Other sectors	4 753 ZD	230	1,211	3,525	3,673	4,747	5,029	2,796	–8,137
Total, Groups A Through C	4 983 ..	*–366*	*–655*	*–65*	*590*	*441*	*–1,703*	*7,852*	*8,144*
D. Net Errors and Omissions	4 998 ..	**–26**	**3,366**	**5,563**	**–2,983**	**4,555**	**7,637**	**–4,133**	**–5,972**
Total, Groups A Through D	4 984 ..	*–392*	*2,711*	*5,498*	*–2,393*	*4,996*	*5,933*	*3,720*	*2,172*
E. Reserves and Related Items	4 802 A.	**392**	**–2,711**	**–5,498**	**2,393**	**–4,996**	**–5,933**	**–3,720**	**–2,172**
Reserve assets	4 802 ..	392	–2,711	–5,498	2,393	–4,996	–5,933	–3,720	–2,172
Use of Fund credit and loans	4 766 ..	...	...	...	...	...	...	...	...
Exceptional financing	4 920 ..	...	...	...	...	...	...	...	...
Conversion rates: Canadian dollars per U.S. dollar	0 101 ..	**1.3656**	**1.3724**	**1.3635**	**1.3846**	**1.4835**	**1.4857**	**1.4851**	**1.5488**

[1] Excludes components that have been classified in the categories of Group E.

Table 2. STANDARD PRESENTATION, 1994–2001
(Millions of U.S. dollars)

	Code	1994	1995	1996	1997	1998	1999	2000	2001
CURRENT ACCOUNT	4 993 . .	**–13,024**	**–4,328**	**3,378**	**–8,233**	**–7,839**	**1,367**	**18,596**	**19,479**
A. GOODS	4 100 . .	14,834	25,855	31,091	18,565	15,922	27,080	41,763	41,425
Credit	2 100 . .	**166,990**	**193,373**	**205,443**	**219,063**	**220,539**	**247,240**	**286,476**	**267,915**
General merchandise: exports f.o.b.	2 110 . .	164,302	191,226	202,933	216,566	218,281	245,414	284,724	266,442
Goods for processing: exports f.o.b.	2 150 . .	. . .	. . .	. . .	. . .	. . .	. . .	. . .	. . .
Repairs on goods	2 160 . .	. . .	. . .	. . .	. . .	. . .	. . .	. . .	. . .
Goods procured in ports by carriers	2 170 . .	. . .	. . .	. . .	. . .	. . .	. . .	. . .	. . .
Nonmonetary gold	2 180 . .	2,688	2,147	2,510	2,496	2,258	1,826	1,752	1,473
Debit	3 100 . .	**–152,155**	**–167,517**	**–174,352**	**–200,498**	**–204,617**	**–220,159**	**–244,714**	**–226,490**
General merchandise: imports f.o.b.	3 110 . .	–151,526	–166,971	–173,567	–199,468	–203,551	–219,454	–244,071	–225,982
Goods for processing: imports f.o.b.	3 150 . .	. . .	. . .	. . .	. . .	. . .	. . .	. . .	. . .
Repairs on goods	3 160 . .	. . .	. . .	. . .	. . .	. . .	. . .	. . .	. . .
Goods procured in ports by carriers	3 170 . .	. . .	. . .	. . .	. . .	. . .	. . .	. . .	. . .
Nonmonetary gold	3 180 . .	–629	–547	–785	–1,030	–1,066	–705	–643	–508
B. SERVICES	4 200 . .	–8,572	–7,345	–6,664	–6,417	–4,320	–4,802	–4,997	–5,424
Total credit	2 200 . .	*23,958*	*26,128*	*29,243*	*31,596*	*33,836*	*35,715*	*38,496*	*36,576*
Total debit	3 200 . .	*–32,530*	*–33,473*	*–35,906*	*–38,013*	*–38,156*	*–40,517*	*–43,493*	*–42,000*
Transportation services, credit	2 205 . .	**4,884**	**5,262**	**5,796**	**6,069**	**6,158**	**6,527**	**7,520**	**6,797**
Passenger	2 850 . .	*1,091*	*1,259*	*1,466*	*1,571*	*1,635*	*1,821*	*2,151*	*1,923*
Freight	2 851 . .	*2,096*	*2,339*	*2,546*	*2,712*	*2,556*	*2,668*	*3,143*	*2,768*
Other	2 852 . .	*1,697*	*1,664*	*1,784*	*1,785*	*1,967*	*2,038*	*2,226*	*2,107*
Sea transport, passenger	2 207 . .	3	3	4	4	9	8	10	15
Sea transport, freight	2 208 . .	526	666	564	621	538	429	681	618
Sea transport, other	2 209 . .	882	790	833	824	832	867	970	934
Air transport, passenger	2 211 . .	1,081	1,242	1,445	1,555	1,611	1,790	2,118	1,885
Air transport, freight	2 212 . .	. . .	. . .	. . .	. . .	. . .	. . .	. . .	. . .
Air transport, other	2 213 . .	815	874	950	961	1,135	1,171	1,256	1,173
Other transport, passenger	2 215 . .	7	14	17	13	15	23	23	22
Other transport, freight	2 216 . .	1,570	1,673	1,982	2,091	2,018	2,240	2,462	2,150
Other transport, other	2 217 . .	. . .	. . .	. . .	. . .	. . .	. . .	. . .	. . .
Transportation services, debit	3 205 . .	**–7,708**	**–7,949**	**–7,750**	**–8,249**	**–7,933**	**–8,273**	**–9,431**	**–9,183**
Passenger	3 850 . .	*–2,174*	*–2,398*	*–2,561*	*–2,671*	*–2,535*	*–2,500*	*–2,750*	*–2,704*
Freight	3 851 . .	*–5,122*	*–5,127*	*–4,797*	*–5,173*	*–5,054*	*–5,466*	*–6,339*	*–6,165*
Other	3 852 . .	*–412*	*–424*	*–392*	*–404*	*–344*	*–307*	*–343*	*–314*
Sea transport, passenger	3 207 . .	–15	–26	–27	–59	–59	–49	–64	–75
Sea transport, freight	3 208 . .	–2,674	–2,524	–2,062	–2,215	–2,281	–2,578	–3,086	–3,010
Sea transport, other	3 209 . .	–412	–424	–392	–404	–344	–307	–343	–314
Air transport, passenger	3 211 . .	–2,105	–2,320	–2,469	–2,547	–2,421	–2,395	–2,624	–2,569
Air transport, freight	3 212 . .	–1,090	–1,058	–1,153	–1,259	–1,177	–1,201	–1,467	–1,550
Air transport, other	3 213 . .	. . .	. . .	. . .	. . .	. . .	. . .	. . .	. . .
Other transport, passenger	3 215 . .	–54	–52	–65	–65	–54	–56	–62	–60
Other transport, freight	3 216 . .	–1,358	–1,546	–1,582	–1,700	–1,597	–1,687	–1,785	–1,605
Other transport, other	3 217 . .	. . .	. . .	. . .	. . .	. . .	. . .	. . .	. . .
Travel, credit	2 236 . .	**6,981**	**7,917**	**8,607**	**8,819**	**9,414**	**10,203**	**10,847**	**10,783**
Business travel	2 237 . .	1,323	1,451	1,632	1,777	1,868	2,027	2,149	1,794
Personal travel	2 240 . .	5,658	6,466	6,975	7,043	7,546	8,176	8,697	8,988
Travel, debit	3 236 . .	**–10,021**	**–10,260**	**–11,254**	**–11,480**	**–10,849**	**–11,469**	**–12,352**	**–11,646**
Business travel	3 237 . .	–2,030	–2,223	–2,501	–2,508	–2,665	–2,894	–3,045	–2,436
Personal travel	3 240 . .	–7,992	–8,037	–8,753	–8,972	–8,185	–8,576	–9,307	–9,210
Other services, credit	2 200 BA	**12,094**	**12,950**	**14,839**	**16,708**	**18,265**	**18,986**	**20,129**	**18,996**
Communications	2 245 . .	. . .	1,278	1,283	1,472	1,481	1,376	1,320	1,208
Construction	2 249 . .	. . .	95	103	135	184	196	216	193
Insurance	2 253 . .	. . .	2,256	2,192	2,122	2,376	2,230	1,938	1,980
Financial	2 260 . .	. . .	632	729	841	812	971	1,319	1,515
Computer and information	2 262 . .	. . .	1,011	788	1,083	1,385	1,628	1,622	1,441
Royalties and licence fees	2 266 . .	. . .	374	877	1,164	1,401	1,569	1,564	1,499
Other business services	2 268 . .	11,238	5,853	7,325	7,953	8,724	8,798	9,845	8,863
Personal, cultural, and recreational	2 287 . .	108	748	901	1,066	1,107	1,329	1,358	1,364
Government, n.i.e.	2 291 . .	748	703	642	872	796	889	946	933
Other services, debit	3 200 BA	**–14,801**	**–15,264**	**–16,902**	**–18,284**	**–19,374**	**–20,775**	**–21,709**	**–21,170**
Communications	3 245 . .	. . .	–1,271	–1,244	–1,614	–1,540	–1,359	–1,361	–1,276
Construction	3 249 . .	. . .	–194	–68	–109	–117	–192	–79	–93
Insurance	3 253 . .	. . .	–2,778	–2,885	–2,908	–2,901	–2,965	–2,833	–2,882
Financial	3 260 . .	. . .	–942	–1,229	–1,269	–1,386	–1,318	–1,641	–1,657
Computer and information	3 262 . .	. . .	–495	–529	–688	–748	–871	–871	–883
Royalties and licence fees	3 266 . .	. . .	–1,885	–1,951	–2,327	–2,708	–3,334	–3,603	–3,474
Other business services	3 268 . .	–14,276	–6,212	–7,301	–7,682	–8,231	–8,883	–9,277	–8,893
Personal, cultural, and recreational	3 287 . .	–82	–1,000	–1,211	–1,202	–1,256	–1,344	–1,523	–1,507
Government, n.i.e.	3 291 . .	–443	–488	–485	–484	–486	–508	–522	–507

Table 2 (Continued). STANDARD PRESENTATION, 1994–2001
(Millions of U.S. dollars)

	Code	1994	1995	1996	1997	1998	1999	2000	2001
C. INCOME	4 300	-18,938	-22,721	-21,551	-20,880	-19,985	-21,594	-19,159	-17,778
Total credit	2 300	*15,443*	*18,888*	*19,204*	*23,998*	*21,830*	*22,165*	*26,811*	*22,633*
Total debit	3 300	*-34,382*	*-41,609*	*-40,755*	*-44,878*	*-41,815*	*-43,759*	*-45,970*	*-40,411*
Compensation of employees, credit	2 310	...	...	...	...	...	...	...	...
Compensation of employees, debit	3 310	...	...	...	...	...	...	...	...
Investment income, credit	2 320	**15,443**	**18,888**	**19,204**	**23,998**	**21,830**	**22,165**	**26,811**	**22,633**
Direct investment income	2 330	6,721	7,321	8,038	10,940	8,752	9,531	12,400	10,222
Dividends and distributed branch profits	2 332	3,297	3,554	4,270	6,209	5,179	6,108	7,619	6,287
Reinvested earnings and undistributed branch profits	2 333	3,159	3,420	3,428	4,475	3,426	3,252	4,395	3,713
Income on debt (interest)	2 334	265	347	340	256	147	171	385	222
Portfolio investment income	2 339	2,298	2,335	2,202	3,541	3,819	4,031	4,600	4,897
Income on equity	2 340	1,549	1,611	1,529	2,649	2,837	2,909	3,202	3,660
Income on bonds and notes	2 350	750	724	674	891	982	1,122	1,398	1,237
Income on money market instruments	2 360	...	...	...	...	...	...	...	...
Other investment income	2 370	6,424	9,231	8,963	9,518	9,259	8,603	9,811	7,514
Investment income, debit	3 320	**-34,382**	**-41,609**	**-40,755**	**-44,878**	**-41,815**	**-43,759**	**-45,970**	**-40,411**
Direct investment income	3 330	-6,279	-10,283	-10,119	-13,646	-10,998	-13,871	-15,818	-13,534
Dividends and distributed branch profits	3 332	-3,270	-3,329	-4,480	-6,791	-6,396	-7,590	-5,832	-6,343
Reinvested earnings and undistributed branch profits	3 333	-1,959	-5,785	-4,483	-5,727	-3,525	-5,172	-8,924	-6,325
Income on debt (interest)	3 334	-1,050	-1,169	-1,157	-1,129	-1,077	-1,108	-1,063	-866
Portfolio investment income	3 339	-20,320	-21,909	-21,254	-21,317	-21,104	-20,498	-19,697	-19,146
Income on equity	3 340	-707	-821	-861	-1,257	-1,387	-1,138	-1,190	-1,566
Income on bonds and notes	3 350	-17,766	-18,688	-18,969	-19,076	-18,477	-18,358	-17,456	-16,720
Income on money market instruments	3 360	-1,847	-2,400	-1,424	-984	-1,241	-1,002	-1,051	-860
Other investment income	3 370	-7,782	-9,417	-9,382	-9,914	-9,713	-9,390	-10,455	-7,732
D. CURRENT TRANSFERS	4 379	-348	-117	502	499	544	682	989	1,255
Credit	2 379	**2,625**	**2,878**	**3,594**	**3,634**	**3,407**	**3,796**	**4,109**	**4,535**
General government	2 380	1,244	1,431	2,087	2,137	1,898	2,277	2,526	2,925
Other sectors	2 390	1,381	1,447	1,506	1,497	1,509	1,519	1,583	1,610
Workers' remittances	2 391	...	...	...	...	...	...	...	...
Other current transfers	2 392	1,381	1,447	1,506	1,497	1,509	1,519	1,583	1,610
Debit	3 379	**-2,973**	**-2,995**	**-3,092**	**-3,135**	**-2,863**	**-3,114**	**-3,120**	**-3,280**
General government	3 380	-1,796	-1,749	-1,701	-1,613	-1,440	-1,554	-1,495	-1,561
Other sectors	3 390	-1,177	-1,246	-1,391	-1,522	-1,423	-1,560	-1,625	-1,719
Workers' remittances	3 391	...	...	...	...	...	...	...	...
Other current transfers	3 392	-1,177	-1,246	-1,391	-1,522	-1,423	-1,560	-1,625	-1,719
CAPITAL AND FINANCIAL ACCOUNT	4 996	**13,050**	**962**	**-8,941**	**11,216**	**3,284**	**-9,003**	**-14,463**	**-13,507**
CAPITAL ACCOUNT	4 994	**7,498**	**4,950**	**5,833**	**5,429**	**3,336**	**3,400**	**3,552**	**3,673**
Total credit	2 994	*7,876*	*5,416*	*6,262*	*5,862*	*3,794*	*3,858*	*4,044*	*4,163*
Total debit	3 994	*-378*	*-466*	*-429*	*-433*	*-457*	*-458*	*-492*	*-490*
Capital transfers, credit	2 400	**7,876**	**5,666**	**6,262**	**5,862**	**3,794**	**3,862**	**4,045**	**4,163**
General government	2 401	...	...	...	...	...	...	...	...
Debt forgiveness	2 402	...	...	...	...	...	...	...	...
Other capital transfers	2 410	...	...	...	...	...	...	...	...
Other sectors	2 430	...	...	...	...	...	...	...	...
Migrants' transfers	2 431	...	...	...	...	...	...	...	...
Debt forgiveness	2 432	...	...	...	...	...	...	...	...
Other capital transfers	2 440	...	...	...	...	...	...	...	...
Capital transfers, debit	3 400	**-305**	**-466**	**-429**	**-433**	**-457**	**-458**	**-492**	**-519**
General government	3 401	...	...	...	...	...	...	...	...
Debt forgiveness	3 402	...	...	...	...	...	...	...	...
Other capital transfers	3 410	...	...	...	...	...	...	...	...
Other sectors	3 430	...	...	...	...	...	...	...	...
Migrants' transfers	3 431	...	...	...	...	...	...	...	...
Debt forgiveness	3 432	...	...	...	...	...	...	...	...
Other capital transfers	3 440	...	...	...	...	...	...	...	...
Nonproduced nonfinancial assets, credit	2 480	...	**-250**	...	...	...	**-4**	**-1**	...
Nonproduced nonfinancial assets, debit	3 480	**-72**	...	...	...	...	...	...	**28**

Table 2 (Continued). STANDARD PRESENTATION, 1994–2001
(Millions of U.S. dollars)

	Code	1994	1995	1996	1997	1998	1999	2000	2001
FINANCIAL ACCOUNT	4 995 . .	**5,552**	**–3,988**	**–14,774**	**5,787**	**–52**	**–12,404**	**–18,015**	**–17,180**
A. DIRECT INVESTMENT	4 500 . .	–1,080	–2,171	–3,472	–11,546	–11,370	8,865	18,706	–8,129
Direct investment abroad	4 505 . .	**–9,303**	**–11,490**	**–13,107**	**–23,069**	**–34,112**	**–15,623**	**–47,311**	**–35,567**
Equity capital	4 510 . .	. . .	. . .	. . .	. . .	. . .	. . .	. . .	. . .
Claims on affiliated enterprises	4 515 . .	. . .	. . .	. . .	. . .	. . .	. . .	. . .	. . .
Liabilities to affiliated enterprises	4 520 . .	. . .	. . .	. . .	. . .	. . .	. . .	. . .	. . .
Reinvested earnings	4 525 . .	–3,159	–3,420	–3,428	–4,475	–3,426	–3,252	–4,395	–3,713
Other capital	4 530 . .	–6,144	–8,070	–9,679	–18,594	–30,687	–12,371	–42,916	–31,854
Claims on affiliated enterprises	4 535 . .	–6,308	–9,305	–9,552	–19,709	–33,120	–13,437	–45,920	–33,648
Liabilities to affiliated enterprises	4 540 . .	164	1,235	–127	1,116	2,434	1,066	3,004	1,795
Direct investment in Canada	4 555 . .	**8,224**	**9,319**	**9,635**	**11,523**	**22,742**	**24,488**	**66,017**	**27,438**
Equity capital	4 560 . .	. . .	. . .	. . .	. . .	. . .	. . .	. . .	. . .
Claims on direct investors	4 565 . .	. . .	. . .	. . .	. . .	. . .	. . .	. . .	. . .
Liabilities to direct investors	4 570 . .	. . .	. . .	. . .	. . .	. . .	. . .	. . .	. . .
Reinvested earnings	4 575 . .	1,959	5,785	4,483	5,727	3,525	5,172	8,924	6,325
Other capital	4 580 . .	6,265	3,534	5,152	5,796	19,217	19,316	57,094	21,113
Claims on direct investors	4 585 . .	–1,154	–3,103	690	–2,544	196	–2,482	1,139	1,842
Liabilities to direct investors	4 590 . .	7,419	6,638	4,462	8,340	19,021	21,797	55,955	19,271
B. PORTFOLIO INVESTMENT	4 600 . .	10,568	13,074	–465	3,123	1,484	–13,241	–31,991	–4,718
Assets	4 602 . .	**–6,587**	**–5,328**	**–14,183**	**–8,568**	**–15,106**	**–15,556**	**–41,866**	**–24,468**
Equity securities	4 610 . .	–6,898	–4,570	–12,661	–3,777	–10,428	–13,888	–39,123	–23,239
Monetary authorities	4 611 . .	. . .	. . .	. . .	. . .	. . .	. . .	. . .	. . .
General government	4 612 . .	. . .	. . .	. . .	. . .	. . .	. . .	. . .	. . .
Banks	4 613 . .	. . .	. . .	. . .	. . .	. . .	. . .	. . .	. . .
Other sectors	4 614 . .	–6,898	–4,570	–12,661	–3,777	–10,428	–13,888	–39,123	–23,239
Debt securities	4 619 . .	311	–759	–1,522	–4,792	–4,678	–1,669	–2,743	–1,230
Bonds and notes	4 620 . .	311	–759	–1,522	–4,792	–4,678	–1,669	–2,743	–1,230
Monetary authorities	4 621 . .	. . .	. . .	. . .	. . .	. . .	. . .	. . .	. . .
General government	4 622 . .	. . .	. . .	. . .	. . .	. . .	. . .	. . .	. . .
Banks	4 623 . .	. . .	. . .	. . .	. . .	. . .	. . .	. . .	. . .
Other sectors	4 624 . .	311	–759	–1,522	–4,792	–4,678	–1,669	–2,743	–1,230
Money market instruments	4 630 . .	. . .	. . .	. . .	. . .	. . .	. . .	. . .	. . .
Monetary authorities	4 631 . .	. . .	. . .	. . .	. . .	. . .	. . .	. . .	. . .
General government	4 632 . .	. . .	. . .	. . .	. . .	. . .	. . .	. . .	. . .
Banks	4 633 . .	. . .	. . .	. . .	. . .	. . .	. . .	. . .	. . .
Other sectors	4 634 . .	. . .	. . .	. . .	. . .	. . .	. . .	. . .	. . .
Liabilities	4 652 . .	**17,155**	**18,402**	**13,718**	**11,692**	**16,590**	**2,315**	**9,875**	**19,750**
Equity securities	4 660 . .	4,718	–3,077	5,900	5,461	9,645	9,534	24,064	3,020
Banks	4 663 . .	. . .	. . .	. . .	. . .	. . .	. . .	. . .	. . .
Other sectors	4 664 . .	4,718	–3,077	5,900	5,461	9,645	9,534	24,064	3,020
Debt securities	4 669 . .	12,437	21,479	7,818	6,230	6,945	–7,219	–14,189	16,730
Bonds and notes	4 670 . .	11,799	22,483	13,240	4,523	7,001	1,593	–15,320	21,548
Monetary authorities	4 671 . .	. . .	. . .	. . .	. . .	. . .	. . .	. . .	. . .
General government	4 672 . .	8,746	14,308	8,847	–5,753	–4,870	–2,218	–12,828	–4,531
Banks	4 673 . .	–307	–182	–320	–122	–639	–470	–74	–397
Other sectors	4 674 . .	3,361	8,357	4,713	10,399	12,510	4,281	–2,417	26,476
Money market instruments	4 680 . .	638	–1,004	–5,422	1,707	–56	–8,811	1,131	–4,818
Monetary authorities	4 681 . .	. . .	. . .	. . .	. . .	. . .	. . .	. . .	. . .
General government	4 682 . .	1,199	–232	–6,556	–2,769	–751	–4,480	687	3,678
Banks	4 683 . .	. . .	. . .	. . .	. . .	. . .	. . .	. . .	. . .
Other sectors	4 684 . .	–561	–772	1,134	4,476	695	–4,331	444	–1,140
C. FINANCIAL DERIVATIVES	4 910 . .	. . .	. . .	. . .	. . .	. . .	. . .	. . .	. . .
Monetary authorities	4 911 . .	. . .	. . .	. . .	. . .	. . .	. . .	. . .	. . .
General government	4 912 . .	. . .	. . .	. . .	. . .	. . .	. . .	. . .	. . .
Banks	4 913 . .	. . .	. . .	. . .	. . .	. . .	. . .	. . .	. . .
Other sectors	4 914 . .	. . .	. . .	. . .	. . .	. . .	. . .	. . .	. . .
Assets	4 900 . .	**. . .**	**. . .**	**. . .**	**. . .**	**. . .**	**. . .**	**. . .**	**. . .**
Monetary authorities	4 901 . .	. . .	. . .	. . .	. . .	. . .	. . .	. . .	. . .
General government	4 902 . .	. . .	. . .	. . .	. . .	. . .	. . .	. . .	. . .
Banks	4 903 . .	. . .	. . .	. . .	. . .	. . .	. . .	. . .	. . .
Other sectors	4 904 . .	. . .	. . .	. . .	. . .	. . .	. . .	. . .	. . .
Liabilities	4 905 . .	**. . .**	**. . .**	**. . .**	**. . .**	**. . .**	**. . .**	**. . .**	**. . .**
Monetary authorities	4 906 . .	. . .	. . .	. . .	. . .	. . .	. . .	. . .	. . .
General government	4 907 . .	. . .	. . .	. . .	. . .	. . .	. . .	. . .	. . .
Banks	4 908 . .	. . .	. . .	. . .	. . .	. . .	. . .	. . .	. . .
Other sectors	4 909 . .	. . .	. . .	. . .	. . .	. . .	. . .	. . .	. . .

Table 2 (Concluded). STANDARD PRESENTATION, 1994–2001
(Millions of U.S. dollars)

	Code	1994	1995	1996	1997	1998	1999	2000	2001
D. OTHER INVESTMENT	4 700	-4,329	-12,180	-5,340	11,816	14,830	-2,094	-1,011	-2,161
Assets	4 703	**-20,378**	**-8,328**	**-21,064**	**-16,167**	**9,400**	**9,395**	**-2,759**	**-8,940**
Trade credits	4 706	-791	-406	-212	-280	-426	110	-1,340	-241
General government	4 707	...	...	...	...	...	...	...	...
of which: Short-term	4 709	...	...	...	...	...	...	...	...
Other sectors	4 710	-791	-406	-212	-280	-426	110	-1,340	-241
of which: Short-term	4 712	...	...	...	...	...	...	...	...
Loans	4 714	81	-2,468	-3,068	-13,828	8,351	1,727	-3,404	-4,982
Monetary authorities	4 715	...	...	...	...	...	...	...	...
of which: Short-term	4 718	...	...	...	...	...	...	...	...
General government	4 719	-99	36	53	-198	-435	-141	-80	-109
of which: Short-term	4 721	...	...	...	...	...	...	...	...
Banks	4 722	1,327	-1,780	-2,633	-2,259	-346	1,435	-863	-1,884
of which: Short-term	4 724	...	...	...	...	...	...	...	...
Other sectors	4 725	-1,146	-724	-487	-11,371	9,132	432	-2,462	-2,989
of which: Short-term	4 727	...	...	...	...	...	...	...	...
Currency and deposits	4 730	-14,518	-5,178	-13,306	-2,126	-4,015	6,962	2,609	-665
Monetary authorities	4 731	...	...	...	...	...	...	...	...
General government	4 732	...	...	...	...	...	...	...	...
Banks	4 733	-11,183	-6,025	-6,571	-3,017	-2,113	11,529	-5,293	1,423
Other sectors	4 734	-3,334	847	-6,736	891	-1,902	-4,567	7,903	-2,088
Other assets	4 736	-5,150	-275	-4,478	68	5,490	596	-625	-3,052
Monetary authorities	4 737	...	...	...	...	...	...	...	...
of which: Short-term	4 739	...	...	...	...	...	...	...	...
General government	4 740	-337	-372	-172	-317	-145	-164	-155	-18
of which: Short-term	4 742	...	...	...	...	...	...	...	...
Banks	4 743	-2,718	-508	-4,643	-143	3,429	404	-1,145	-1,634
of which: Short-term	4 745	...	...	...	...	...	...	...	...
Other sectors	4 746	-2,095	605	337	528	2,206	356	675	-1,400
of which: Short-term	4 748	...	...	...	...	...	...	...	...
Liabilities	4 753	**16,049**	**-3,852**	**15,724**	**27,983**	**5,430**	**-11,489**	**1,749**	**6,780**
Trade credits	4 756	664	437	-486	520	843	961	378	-1,512
General government	4 757	...	...	...	...	...	...	...	...
of which: Short-term	4 759	...	...	...	...	...	...	...	...
Other sectors	4 760	664	437	-486	520	843	961	378	-1,512
of which: Short-term	4 762	...	...	...	...	...	...	...	...
Loans	4 764	-111	860	4,354	1,450	2,330	4,329	1,910	-4,929
Monetary authorities	4 765	...	...	...	...	...	...	...	...
of which: Use of Fund credit and loans from the Fund	4 766	...	...	...	...	...	...	...	...
of which: Short-term	4 768	...	...	...	...	...	...	...	...
General government	4 769	604	-199	-253	-442	-150	-48	-83	-24
of which: Short-term	4 771	...	...	...	...	...	...	...	...
Banks	4 772	...	...	...	...	...	...	...	...
of which: Short-term	4 774	...	...	...	...	...	...	...	...
Other sectors	4 775	-715	1,059	4,607	1,892	2,480	4,377	1,993	-4,906
of which: Short-term	4 777	...	...	...	...	...	...	...	...
Currency and deposits	4 780	15,307	-4,607	12,499	24,597	2,019	-16,087	-818	15,159
Monetary authorities	4 781	...	...	...	...	...	...	...	...
General government	4 782	...	...	...	...	...	...	...	...
Banks	4 783	15,233	-4,579	12,707	24,630	953	-16,200	-697	15,155
Other sectors	4 784	73	-28	-208	-34	1,067	113	-120	4
Other liabilities	4 786	189	-543	-643	1,416	238	-693	278	-1,937
Monetary authorities	4 787	...	...	...	...	...	...	...	...
of which: Short-term	4 789	...	...	...	...	...	...	...	...
General government	4 790	-18	-285	-255	121	-120	-271	-266	-213
of which: Short-term	4 792	...	...	...	...	...	...	...	...
Banks	4 793	...	...	...	...	...	...	...	...
of which: Short-term	4 795	...	...	...	...	...	...	...	...
Other sectors	4 796	208	-258	-388	1,295	358	-422	544	-1,724
of which: Short-term	4 798	...	...	...	...	...	...	...	...
E. RESERVE ASSETS	4 802	392	-2,711	-5,498	2,393	-4,996	-5,933	-3,720	-2,172
Monetary gold	4 812	...	...	...	...	...	...	...	...
Special drawing rights	4 811	-19	1	-30	-30	73	548	-75	-62
Reserve position in the Fund	4 810	86	-309	-24	-424	-634	-932	514	-457
Foreign exchange	4 803	325	-2,403	-5,443	2,847	-4,436	-5,550	-4,160	-1,653
Other claims	4 813	...	...	...	...	...	...	...	...
NET ERRORS AND OMISSIONS	4 998	**-26**	**3,366**	**5,563**	**-2,983**	**4,555**	**7,637**	**-4,133**	**-5,972**

Part 3 of the *Yearbook* contains descriptions of the methodologies, compilation practices, and sources used to compile these data.

Table 3. INTERNATIONAL INVESTMENT POSITION (End–period stocks), 1994–2001
(Millions of U.S. dollars)

	Code		1994	1995	1996	1997	1998	1999	2000	2001
ASSETS	8 995	C.	282,944	324,692	371,736	419,480	448,443	496,988	546,006	567,947
Direct investment abroad	8 505	..	**104,302**	**118,105**	**132,329**	**152,969**	**171,780**	**196,236**	**226,880**	**244,522**
Equity capital and reinvested earnings	8 506	..	86,168	102,143	115,062	134,851	148,967	171,540	200,583	216,180
Claims on affiliated enterprises	8 507	..	...	...	...	...	...	...	...	...
Liabilities to affiliated enterprises	8 508	..	...	...	...	...	...	...	...	...
Other capital	8 530	..	18,134	15,961	17,268	18,118	22,813	24,697	26,298	28,342
Claims on affiliated enterprises	8 535	..	...	...	...	...	...	...	...	...
Liabilities to affiliated enterprises	8 540	..	...	...	...	...	...	...	...	...
Portfolio investment	8 602	..	**59,601**	**66,487**	**79,054**	**91,222**	**102,845**	**124,584**	**143,533**	**145,160**
Equity securities	8 610	..	46,543	52,700	63,529	72,619	81,118	103,291	120,219	123,105
Monetary authorities	8 611	..	...	...	...	...	...	...	...	...
General government	8 612	..	...	...	...	...	...	...	...	...
Banks	8 613	..	...	...	...	...	...	...	...	...
Other sectors	8 614	..	46,543	52,700	63,529	72,619	81,118	103,291	120,219	123,105
Debt securities	8 619	..	13,057	13,787	15,525	18,603	21,728	21,294	23,314	22,055
Bonds and notes	8 620	..	13,057	13,787	15,525	18,603	21,728	21,294	23,314	22,055
Monetary authorities	8 621	..	...	...	...	...	...	...	...	...
General government	8 622	..	...	...	...	...	...	...	...	...
Banks	8 623	..	...	...	...	...	...	...	...	...
Other sectors	8 624	..	13,057	13,787	15,525	18,603	21,728	21,294	23,314	22,055
Money market instruments	8 630	..	...	...	...	...	...	...	...	...
Monetary authorities	8 631	..	...	...	...	...	...	...	...	...
General government	8 632	..	...	...	...	...	...	...	...	...
Banks	8 633	..	...	...	...	...	...	...	...	...
Other sectors	8 634	..	...	...	...	...	...	...	...	...
Financial derivatives	8 900	..	**...**	**...**	**...**	**...**	**...**	**...**	**...**	**...**
Monetary authorities	8 901	..	...	...	...	...	...	...	...	...
General government	8 902	..	...	...	...	...	...	...	...	...
Banks	8 903	..	...	...	...	...	...	...	...	...
Other sectors	8 904	..	...	...	...	...	...	...	...	...
Other investment	8 703	..	**106,564**	**124,885**	**139,761**	**157,305**	**150,351**	**147,435**	**143,727**	**144,776**
Trade credits	8 706	..	3,563	4,021	4,020	4,294	4,325	4,421	5,552	5,243
General government	8 707	..	...	...	...	...	...	...	...	...
of which: Short-term	8 709	..	...	...	...	...	...	...	...	...
Other sectors	8 710	..	3,563	4,021	4,020	4,294	4,325	4,421	5,552	5,243
of which: Short-term	8 712	..	...	...	...	...	...	...	...	...
Loans	8 714	..	21,984	31,659	35,840	49,428	39,503	38,807	40,333	43,337
Monetary authorities	8 715	..	...	...	...	...	...	...	...	...
of which: Short-term	8 718	..	...	...	...	...	...	...	...	...
General government	8 719	..	15,419	15,656	15,868	16,759	18,716	20,835	21,983	22,717
of which: Short-term	8 721	..	...	...	...	...	...	...	...	...
Banks	8 722	..	6,107	7,962	10,553	12,478	12,191	11,024	11,704	13,200
of which: Short-term	8 724	..	...	...	...	...	...	...	...	...
Other sectors	8 725	..	459	8,041	9,419	20,192	8,595	6,948	6,646	7,419
of which: Short-term	8 727	..	...	...	...	...	...	...	...	...
Currency and deposits	8 730	..	52,134	59,008	72,317	71,446	77,392	75,401	72,384	68,262
Monetary authorities	8 731	..	...	...	...	...	...	...	...	...
General government	8 732	..	...	...	...	...	...	...	...	...
Banks	8 733	..	36,103	43,967	50,593	50,913	53,020	41,588	46,745	45,124
Other sectors	8 734	..	16,031	15,041	21,724	20,533	24,373	33,812	25,639	23,138
Other assets	8 736	..	28,883	30,196	27,583	32,137	29,131	28,806	25,458	27,935
Monetary authorities	8 737	..	...	...	...	...	...	...	...	...
of which: Short-term	8 739	..	...	...	...	...	...	...	...	...
General government	8 740	..	...	...	...	...	...	...	...	...
of which: Short-term	8 742	..	...	...	...	...	...	...	...	...
Banks	8 743	..	7,766	8,339	12,511	12,633	9,339	8,752	7,788	9,773
of which: Short-term	8 745	..	...	...	...	...	...	...	...	...
Other sectors	8 746	..	21,117	21,858	15,073	19,504	19,791	20,055	17,670	18,162
of which: Short-term	8 748	..	...	...	...	...	...	...	...	...
Reserve assets	8 802	..	**12,476**	**15,216**	**20,591**	**17,984**	**23,467**	**28,732**	**31,866**	**33,488**
Monetary gold	8 812	..	198	177	155	146	123	87	54	46
Special drawing rights	8 811	..	1,148	1,177	1,168	1,126	1,098	527	574	614
Reserve position in the Fund	8 810	..	919	1,243	1,226	1,575	2,299	3,168	2,509	2,863
Foreign exchange	8 803	..	10,211	12,618	18,041	15,138	19,948	24,951	28,728	29,964
Other claims	8 813	..	...	...	...	...	...	...	...	...

Table 3 (Concluded). INTERNATIONAL INVESTMENT POSITION (End-period stocks), 1994–2001
(Millions of U.S. dollars)

	Code	1994	1995	1996	1997	1998	1999	2000	2001
LIABILITIES	8 995 D.	520,374	562,156	599,081	622,564	644,239	668,106	680,971	695,675
Direct investment in Canada	8 555 . .	**110,204**	**123,181**	**132,978**	**135,944**	**143,344**	**172,256**	**201,506**	**201,514**
Equity capital and reinvested earnings	8 556 . .	87,363	102,371	114,051	117,359	121,832	149,532	169,144	171,755
Claims on direct investors	8 557 . .	...	...	...	...	...	...	...	...
Liabilities to direct investors	8 558 . .	...	...	...	...	...	...	...	...
Other capital	8 580 . .	22,841	20,810	18,927	18,585	21,512	22,725	32,362	29,758
Claims on direct investors	8 585 . .	...	...	...	...	...	...	...	...
Liabilities to direct investors	8 590 . .	...	...	...	...	...	...	...	...
Portfolio investment	8 652 . .	**281,767**	**309,774**	**323,661**	**321,742**	**334,129**	**336,914**	**323,433**	**330,957**
Equity securities	8 660 . .	22,001	27,170	34,537	35,968	42,041	47,881	56,993	55,117
Banks	8 663 . .	...	...	...	...	...	...	...	...
Other sectors	8 664 . .	22,001	27,170	34,537	35,968	42,041	47,881	56,993	55,117
Debt securities	8 669 . .	259,766	282,604	289,125	285,774	292,088	289,033	266,440	275,840
Bonds and notes	8 670 . .	225,884	250,292	261,282	257,434	265,124	270,001	247,354	261,919
Monetary authorities	8 671 . .	...	...	...	...	...	...	...	...
General government	8 672 . .	136,496	153,090	159,830	149,037	143,947	144,850	127,435	117,577
Banks	8 673 . .	4,705	4,612	4,088	3,829	3,327	2,900	2,906	2,580
Other sectors	8 674 . .	84,684	92,590	97,364	104,567	117,849	122,252	117,013	141,762
Money market instruments	8 680 . .	33,881	32,312	27,843	28,340	26,964	19,032	19,086	13,921
Monetary authorities	8 681 . .	...	...	...	...	...	...	...	...
General government	8 682 . .	28,348	25,731	20,296	16,547	14,848	11,094	11,201	7,367
Banks	8 683 . .	...	...	...	...	...	...	...	...
Other sectors	8 684 . .	5,533	6,582	7,547	11,793	12,116	7,939	7,885	6,554
Financial derivatives	8 905 . .	...	...	...	...	...	...	...	...
Monetary authorities	8 906 . .	...	...	...	...	...	...	...	...
General government	8 907 . .	...	...	...	...	...	...	...	...
Banks	8 908 . .	...	...	...	...	...	...	...	...
Other sectors	8 909 . .	...	...	...	...	...	...	...	...
Other investment	8 753 . .	**128,403**	**129,201**	**142,442**	**164,879**	**166,766**	**158,935**	**156,032**	**163,204**
Trade credits	8 756 . .	3,435	3,889	3,251	3,619	3,457	4,589	4,697	4,636
General government	8 757 . .	...	...	...	...	...	...	...	...
of which: Short-term	8 759 . .	...	...	...	...	...	...	...	...
Other sectors	8 760 . .	3,435	3,889	3,251	3,619	3,457	4,589	4,697	4,636
of which: Short-term	8 762 . .	...	...	...	...	...	...	...	...
Loans	8 764 . .	31,832	35,754	37,270	36,159	36,198	39,359	38,162	31,072
Monetary authorities	8 765 . .	...	...	...	...	...	...	...	...
of which: Use of Fund credit and loans from the Fund	8 766 . .	...	...	...	...	...	...	...	...
of which: Short-term	8 768 . .	...	...	...	...	...	...	...	...
General government	8 769 . .	2,912	2,587	2,098	1,444	1,475	1,551	1,306	1,126
of which: Short-term	8 771 . .	...	...	...	...	...	...	...	...
Banks	8 772 . .	...	...	...	...	...	...	...	...
of which: Short-term	8 774 . .	...	...	...	...	...	...	...	...
Other sectors	8 775 . .	28,920	33,167	35,172	34,715	34,724	37,808	36,856	29,947
of which: Short-term	8 777 . .	...	...	...	...	...	...	...	...
Currency and deposits	8 780 . .	84,031	80,067	92,608	115,707	118,056	105,322	103,436	118,502
Monetary authorities	8 781 . .	...	...	...	...	...	...	...	...
General government	8 782 . .	...	...	...	...	...	...	...	...
Banks	8 783 . .	83,691	79,735	92,486	115,623	118,008	105,157	103,391	118,456
Other sectors	8 784 . .	340	332	123	84	48	165	44	46
Other liabilities	8 786 . .	9,106	9,491	9,313	9,393	9,054	9,664	9,736	8,994
Monetary authorities	8 787 . .	...	...	...	...	...	...	...	...
of which: Short-term	8 789 . .	...	...	...	...	...	...	...	...
General government	8 790 . .	1,656	1,473	1,236	1,346	1,173	993	714	474
of which: Short-term	8 792 . .	...	...	...	...	...	...	...	...
Banks	8 793 . .	...	...	...	...	...	...	...	...
of which: Short-term	8 795 . .	...	...	...	...	...	...	...	...
Other sectors	8 796 . .	7,450	8,018	8,077	8,048	7,881	8,671	9,022	8,520
of which: Short-term	8 798 . .	...	...	...	...	...	...	...	...
NET INTERNATIONAL INVESTMENT POSITION	8 995 . .	**–237,430**	**–237,464**	**–227,345**	**–203,085**	**–195,796**	**–171,118**	**–134,965**	**–127,728**
Conversion rates: Canadian dollars per U.S. dollar (end of period)	0 102 . .	**1.4028**	**1.3652**	**1.3696**	**1.4291**	**1.5305**	**1.4433**	**1.5002**	**1.5926**

Table 1. ANALYTIC PRESENTATION, 1994–2001
(Millions of U.S. dollars)

	Code	1994	1995	1996	1997	1998	1999	2000	2001
A. Current Account[1]	4 993 Z.	**-45.73**	**-61.62**	**-35.04**	**-29.72**	**-58.51**	**-74.76**	**. . .**	**. . .**
Goods: exports f.o.b	2 100 . .	14.16	16.58	23.88	43.24	32.69	26.24	. . .	. . .
Goods: imports f.o.b	3 100 . .	-195.26	-233.63	-207.52	-215.10	-218.81	-240.94	. . .	. . .
Balance on Goods	4 100 . .	*-181.10*	*-217.05*	*-183.64*	*-171.87*	*-186.13*	*-214.71*	. . .	. . .
Services: credit	2 200 . .	47.01	66.90	77.52	91.31	86.45	105.90	. . .	. . .
Services: debit	3 200 . .	-34.52	-60.50	-70.03	-71.90	-90.59	-116.70	. . .	. . .
Balance on Goods and Services	4 991 . .	*-168.61*	*-210.65*	*-176.15*	*-152.46*	*-190.27*	*-225.51*	. . .	. . .
Income: credit	2 300 . .	4.22	4.00	2.98	4.87	2.51	1.91	. . .	. . .
Income: debit	3 300 . .	-4.56	-6.57	-7.38	-8.46	-8.07	-10.47	. . .	. . .
Balance on Goods, Services, and Income	4 992 . .	*-168.95*	*-213.22*	*-180.55*	*-156.05*	*-195.83*	*-234.08*	. . .	. . .
Current transfers: credit	2 379 Z.	125.55	155.96	148.38	129.91	142.46	168.42	. . .	. . .
Current transfers: debit	3 379 . .	-2.33	-4.36	-2.87	-3.58	-5.15	-9.11	. . .	. . .
B. Capital Account[1]	4 994 Z.	**20.07**	**20.88**	**12.83**	**6.30**	**19.01**	**4.49**	**. . .**	**. . .**
Capital account: credit	2 994 Z.	20.07	20.88	12.83	6.30	19.01	4.49	. . .	. . .
Capital account: debit	3 994 . .	. . .	. . .	. . .	. . .	. . .	. . .	. . .	. . .
Total, Groups A Plus B	4 981 . .	*-25.66*	*-40.74*	*-22.21*	*-23.42*	*-39.50*	*-70.27*	. . .	. . .
C. Financial Account[1]	4 995 W.	**39.60**	**44.51**	**46.00**	**44.06**	**36.99**	**128.91**	**. . .**	**. . .**
Direct investment abroad	4 505 . .	-.42	-.57	-.26	-.05	. . .	-.42	. . .	. . .
Direct investment in Cape Verde	4 555 Z.	2.13	26.18	28.53	11.58	9.04	53.94	. . .	. . .
Portfolio investment assets	4 602 . .	. . .	. . .	. . .	. . .	. . .	. . .	. . .	. . .
Equity securities	4 610 . .	. . .	. . .	. . .	. . .	. . .	. . .	. . .	. . .
Debt securities	4 619 . .	. . .	. . .	. . .	. . .	. . .	. . .	. . .	. . .
Portfolio investment liabilities	4 652 Z.	. . .	. . .	. . .	. . .	. . .	2.99	. . .	. . .
Equity securities	4 660 . .	. . .	. . .	. . .	. . .	. . .	2.99	. . .	. . .
Debt securities	4 669 Z.	. . .	. . .	. . .	. . .	. . .	. . .	. . .	. . .
Financial derivatives	4 910 . .	. . .	. . .	. . .	. . .	. . .	. . .	. . .	. . .
Financial derivatives assets	4 900 . .	. . .	. . .	. . .	. . .	. . .	. . .	. . .	. . .
Financial derivatives liabilities	4 905 . .	. . .	. . .	. . .	. . .	. . .	. . .	. . .	. . .
Other investment assets	4 703 . .	1.61	-1.67	-2.25	-1.79	-22.44	-14.05	. . .	. . .
Monetary authorities	4 701 . .	1.61	2.32	-2.34	-1.84	4.02	5.23	. . .	. . .
General government	4 704 . .	. . .	. . .	. . .	. . .	-28.39	-18.72	. . .	. . .
Banks	4 705 . .	. . .	-3.99	.09	.05	3.02	-.05	. . .	. . .
Other sectors	4 728 . .	. . .	. . .	. . .	. . .	-1.09	-.51	. . .	. . .
Other investment liabilities	4 753 W.	36.28	20.57	19.99	34.33	50.39	86.46	. . .	. . .
Monetary authorities	4 753 WA	-1.21	-.93	-.12	-.12	-.01	.17	. . .	. . .
General government	4 753 ZB	22.74	17.57	22.88	19.79	28.49	43.34	. . .	. . .
Banks	4 753 ZC	1.11	2.38	.02	4.94	8.00	27.33	. . .	. . .
Other sectors	4 753 ZD	13.64	1.55	-2.80	9.72	13.91	15.62	. . .	. . .
Total, Groups A Through C	4 983 . .	*13.93*	*3.77*	*23.79*	*20.64*	*-2.51*	*58.64*	. . .	. . .
D. Net Errors and Omissions	4 998 . .	**8.31**	**-35.64**	**-1.34**	**-20.40**	**13.28**	**-8.84**	**. . .**	**. . .**
Total, Groups A Through D	4 984 . .	*22.24*	*-31.87*	*22.46*	*.24*	*10.76*	*49.79*	. . .	. . .
E. Reserves and Related Items	4 802 A.	**-22.24**	**31.87**	**-22.46**	**-.24**	**-10.76**	**-49.79**	**. . .**	**. . .**
Reserve assets	4 802 . .	-20.78	30.93	-19.76	9.84	-8.50	-42.27	. . .	. . .
Use of Fund credit and loans	4 766 . .	. . .	. . .	. . .	. . .	. . .	. . .	. . .	. . .
Exceptional financing	4 920 . .	-1.46	.95	-2.70	-10.08	-2.26	-7.52	. . .	. . .
Conversion rates: Cape Verde escudos per U.S. dollar	0 101 . .	**81.891**	**76.853**	**82.591**	**93.177**	**98.158**	**102.700**	**115.877**	**123.213**

[1] Excludes components that have been classified in the categories of Group E.

Table 2. STANDARD PRESENTATION, 1994–2001
(Millions of U.S. dollars)

	Code	1994	1995	1996	1997	1998	1999	2000	2001
CURRENT ACCOUNT	4 993 . .	**–45.73**	**–61.62**	**–35.04**	**–29.72**	**–58.51**	**–74.76**	**. . .**	**. . .**
A. GOODS	4 100 . .	–181.10	–217.05	–183.64	–171.87	–186.13	–214.71	. . .	. . .
Credit	2 100 . .	**14.16**	**16.58**	**23.88**	**43.24**	**32.69**	**26.24**	**. . .**	**. . .**
General merchandise: exports f.o.b.	2 110 . .	4.86	8.41	12.57	13.88	4.03	3.17	. . .	. . .
Goods for processing: exports f.o.b.	2 150 . .	. . .	. . .	. . .	. . .	7.11	8.81	. . .	. . .
Repairs on goods	2 160 . .	1.99	2.10	4.94	3.06	4.48	2.69	. . .	. . .
Goods procured in ports by carriers	2 170 . .	7.32	6.07	6.36	26.29	17.06	11.57	. . .	. . .
Nonmonetary gold	2 180 . .	. . .	. . .	. . .	. . .	. . .	. . .	. . .	. . .
Debit	3 100 . .	**–195.26**	**–233.63**	**–207.52**	**–215.10**	**–218.81**	**–240.94**	**. . .**	**. . .**
General merchandise: imports f.o.b.	3 110 . .	–195.07	–233.55	–205.66	–211.13	–208.67	–222.60	. . .	. . .
Goods for processing: imports f.o.b.	3 150 . .	. . .	. . .	. . .	. . .	–6.60	–9.12	. . .	. . .
Repairs on goods	3 160 . .	–.11	–.02	–1.76	–1.49	–2.43	–3.58	. . .	. . .
Goods procured in ports by carriers	3 170 . .	–.08	–.06	–.09	–2.48	–1.12	–5.64	. . .	. . .
Nonmonetary gold	3 180 . .	. . .	. . .	. . .	. . .	. . .	. . .	. . .	. . .
B. SERVICES	4 200 . .	12.49	6.40	7.49	19.41	–4.14	–10.81	. . .	. . .
Total credit	2 200 . .	*47.01*	*66.90*	*77.52*	*91.31*	*86.45*	*105.90*	. . .	. . .
Total debit	3 200 . .	*–34.52*	*–60.50*	*–70.03*	*–71.90*	*–90.59*	*–116.70*	. . .	. . .
Transportation services, credit	2 205 . .	**22.27**	**34.17**	**44.58**	**53.48**	**45.03**	**43.99**	**. . .**	**. . .**
Passenger	2 850 . .	*11.42*	*18.73*	*26.03*	*35.42*	*24.76*	*27.13*	. . .	. . .
Freight	2 851 . .	*.02*	*.01*	. . .	*.31*	*.40*	*.86*	. . .	. . .
Other	2 852 . .	*10.83*	*15.43*	*18.54*	*17.75*	*19.87*	*16.00*	. . .	. . .
Sea transport, passenger	2 207 . .	. . .	. . .	. . .	. . .	. . .	. . .	. . .	. . .
Sea transport, freight	2 208 . .	.02	.01	. . .	.31	. . .	.45	. . .	. . .
Sea transport, other	2 209 . .	10.17	14.71	15.40	17.44	3.84	3.29	. . .	. . .
Air transport, passenger	2 211 . .	11.42	18.73	26.03	35.42	24.76	27.13	. . .	. . .
Air transport, freight	2 212 . .	. . .	. . .	. . .	. . .	.40	.41	. . .	. . .
Air transport, other	2 213 . .	.66	.72	3.15	.31	16.03	12.71	. . .	. . .
Other transport, passenger	2 215 . .	. . .	. . .	. . .	. . .	. . .	. . .	. . .	. . .
Other transport, freight	2 216 . .	. . .	. . .	. . .	. . .	. . .	. . .	. . .	. . .
Other transport, other	2 217 . .	. . .	. . .	. . .	. . .	. . .	. . .	. . .	. . .
Transportation services, debit	3 205 . .	**–12.00**	**–25.21**	**–37.18**	**–37.22**	**–39.86**	**–45.68**	**. . .**	**. . .**
Passenger	3 850 . .	*–2.82*	*–3.56*	*–6.24*	*–7.50*	*–7.66*	*–5.78*	. . .	. . .
Freight	3 851 . .	*–4.23*	*–10.12*	*–12.66*	*–15.52*	*–18.22*	*–23.15*	. . .	. . .
Other	3 852 . .	*–4.95*	*–11.53*	*–18.27*	*–14.21*	*–13.98*	*–16.75*	. . .	. . .
Sea transport, passenger	3 207 . .	. . .	. . .	. . .	. . .	. . .	. . .	. . .	. . .
Sea transport, freight	3 208 . .	–4.23	–10.12	–12.66	–15.52	–18.18	–23.14	. . .	. . .
Sea transport, other	3 209 . .	–4.90	–9.19	–15.78	–9.02	–4.47	–5.48	. . .	. . .
Air transport, passenger	3 211 . .	–2.82	–3.56	–6.24	–7.50	–7.66	–5.78	. . .	. . .
Air transport, freight	3 212 . .	. . .	. . .	. . .	. . .	–.04	. . .	. . .	. . .
Air transport, other	3 213 . .	–.05	–2.34	–2.49	–5.19	–9.51	–11.28	. . .	. . .
Other transport, passenger	3 215 . .	. . .	. . .	. . .	. . .	. . .	. . .	. . .	. . .
Other transport, freight	3 216 . .	. . .	. . .	. . .	. . .	. . .	. . .	. . .	. . .
Other transport, other	3 217 . .	. . .	. . .	. . .	. . .	. . .	. . .	. . .	. . .
Travel, credit	2 236 . .	**8.76**	**9.68**	**11.23**	**15.01**	**20.29**	**28.75**	**. . .**	**. . .**
Business travel	2 237 . .	8.76	9.68	11.23	15.01	.05	.59	. . .	. . .
Personal travel	2 240 . .	. . .	. . .	. . .	. . .	20.24	28.17	. . .	. . .
Travel, debit	3 236 . .	**–11.63**	**–16.19**	**–17.79**	**–17.25**	**–23.82**	**–40.89**	**. . .**	**. . .**
Business travel	3 237 . .	–9.08	–12.30	–13.35	–10.73	–2.99	–5.39	. . .	. . .
Personal travel	3 240 . .	–2.55	–3.89	–4.45	–6.52	–20.82	–35.50	. . .	. . .
Other services, credit	2 200 BA	**15.97**	**23.05**	**21.71**	**22.82**	**21.13**	**33.15**	**. . .**	**. . .**
Communications	2 245 . .	7.09	9.84	4.81	3.40	4.72	5.45	. . .	. . .
Construction	2 249 . .	.07	2.30	1.86	2.61	2.10	7.35	. . .	. . .
Insurance	2 253 . .	. . .	. . .	. . .	. . .	.18	2.51	. . .	. . .
Financial	2 260 . .	. . .	. . .	. . .	. . .	. . .	.53	. . .	. . .
Computer and information	2 262 . .	. . .	. . .	. . .	. . .	.01	.15	. . .	. . .
Royalties and licence fees	2 266 . .	.09	.03	.01	.42	. . .	.04	. . .	. . .
Other business services	2 268 . .	1.09	1.45	2.94	3.63	2.12	7.42	. . .	. . .
Personal, cultural, and recreational	2 287 . .	. . .	. . .	. . .	. . .	. . .	.01	. . .	. . .
Government, n.i.e.	2 291 . .	7.63	9.43	12.09	12.75	11.99	9.70	. . .	. . .
Other services, debit	3 200 BA	**–10.89**	**–19.10**	**–15.06**	**–17.43**	**–26.91**	**–30.13**	**. . .**	**. . .**
Communications	3 245 . .	–1.72	–3.91	–.49	–.40	–.65	–2.60	. . .	. . .
Construction	3 249 . .	–.14	–.23	–.23	–.70	–1.49	–.54	. . .	. . .
Insurance	3 253 . .	. . .	. . .	. . .	. . .	–2.02	–3.30	. . .	. . .
Financial	3 260 . .	. . .	. . .	. . .	. . .	–.41	–3.02	. . .	. . .
Computer and information	3 262 . .	. . .	. . .	. . .	. . .	–4.79	–4.74	. . .	. . .
Royalties and licence fees	3 266 . .	–.06	–.09	–.03	–.08	–.34	–.20	. . .	. . .
Other business services	3 268 . .	–4.21	–8.88	–6.48	–9.90	–11.92	–10.89	. . .	. . .
Personal, cultural, and recreational	3 287 . .	. . .	. . .	. . .	. . .	–.11	–.53	. . .	. . .
Government, n.i.e.	3 291 . .	–4.76	–5.98	–7.82	–6.36	–5.18	–4.33	. . .	. . .

Table 2 (Continued). STANDARD PRESENTATION, 1994–2001

(Millions of U.S. dollars)

	Code	1994	1995	1996	1997	1998	1999	2000	2001
C. INCOME	4 300	–.34	–2.57	–4.40	–3.59	–5.56	–8.56	. . .	. . .
Total credit	2 300	*4.22*	*4.00*	*2.98*	*4.87*	*2.51*	*1.91*	. . .	. . .
Total debit	3 300	*–4.56*	*–6.57*	*–7.38*	*–8.46*	*–8.07*	*–10.47*	. . .	. . .
Compensation of employees, credit	2 310	**2.35**	**1.92**	**1.61**	**2.18**	**1.81**	**1.18**	. . .	. . .
Compensation of employees, debit	3 310	**–.42**	**–.80**	**–.61**	**–1.65**	**–.41**	**–.47**	. . .	. . .
Investment income, credit	2 320	**1.87**	**2.08**	**1.36**	**2.70**	**.69**	**.73**	. . .	. . .
Direct investment income	2 330	.42	.57	.23	. . .	. . .	. . .	. . .	. . .
Dividends and distributed branch profits	2 332	. . .	. . .	. . .	. . .	. . .	. . .	. . .	. . .
Reinvested earnings and undistributed branch profits	2 333	.42	.57	.23	. . .	. . .	. . .	. . .	. . .
Income on debt (interest)	2 334	. . .	. . .	. . .	. . .	. . .	. . .	. . .	. . .
Portfolio investment income	2 339	. . .	. . .	. . .	. . .	. . .	. . .	. . .	. . .
Income on equity	2 340	. . .	. . .	. . .	. . .	. . .	. . .	. . .	. . .
Income on bonds and notes	2 350	. . .	. . .	. . .	. . .	. . .	. . .	. . .	. . .
Income on money market instruments	2 360	. . .	. . .	. . .	. . .	. . .	. . .	. . .	. . .
Other investment income	2 370	1.45	1.51	1.13	2.70	.69	.73	. . .	. . .
Investment income, debit	3 320	**–4.15**	**–5.76**	**–6.76**	**–6.81**	**–7.65**	**–10.00**	. . .	. . .
Direct investment income	3 330	–.15	–.51	–.33	. . .	–2.39	–2.01	. . .	. . .
Dividends and distributed branch profits	3 332	. . .	. . .	. . .	. . .	–2.30	–2.01	. . .	. . .
Reinvested earnings and undistributed branch profits	3 333	–.15	–.51	–.33	. . .	–.09	. . .	. . .	. . .
Income on debt (interest)	3 334	. . .	. . .	. . .	. . .	. . .	. . .	. . .	. . .
Portfolio investment income	3 339	. . .	. . .	. . .	. . .	. . .	. . .	. . .	. . .
Income on equity	3 340	. . .	. . .	. . .	. . .	. . .	. . .	. . .	. . .
Income on bonds and notes	3 350	. . .	. . .	. . .	. . .	. . .	. . .	. . .	. . .
Income on money market instruments	3 360	. . .	. . .	. . .	. . .	. . .	. . .	. . .	. . .
Other investment income	3 370	–3.99	–5.25	–6.43	–6.81	–5.27	–7.99	. . .	. . .
D. CURRENT TRANSFERS	4 379	123.22	151.60	145.51	126.33	137.32	159.31	. . .	. . .
Credit	2 379	**125.55**	**155.96**	**148.38**	**129.91**	**142.46**	**168.42**	. . .	. . .
General government	2 380	42.45	52.02	49.64	55.67	56.62	50.79	. . .	. . .
Other sectors	2 390	83.10	103.95	98.74	74.24	85.84	117.64	. . .	. . .
Workers' remittances	2 391	83.10	103.95	98.74	74.24	71.93	78.53	. . .	. . .
Other current transfers	2 392	. . .	. . .	. . .	. . .	13.91	39.10	. . .	. . .
Debit	3 379	**–2.33**	**–4.36**	**–2.87**	**–3.58**	**–5.15**	**–9.11**	. . .	. . .
General government	3 380	. . .	. . .	. . .	. . .	–1.86	–1.66	. . .	. . .
Other sectors	3 390	–2.33	–4.36	–2.87	–3.58	–3.29	–7.45	. . .	. . .
Workers' remittances	3 391	–2.33	–4.36	–2.87	–3.58	. . .	. . .	. . .	. . .
Other current transfers	3 392	. . .	. . .	. . .	. . .	–3.29	–7.45	. . .	. . .
CAPITAL AND FINANCIAL ACCOUNT	4 996	**37.42**	**97.26**	**36.38**	**50.12**	**45.23**	**83.61**	. . .	. . .
CAPITAL ACCOUNT	4 994	**20.07**	**20.88**	**12.83**	**6.30**	**19.01**	**8.91**	. . .	. . .
Total credit	2 994	*20.07*	*20.88*	*12.83*	*6.30*	*19.01*	*8.91*	. . .	. . .
Total debit	3 994	. . .	. . .	. . .	. . .	. . .	. . .	. . .	. . .
Capital transfers, credit	2 400	**20.07**	**20.88**	**12.83**	**6.30**	**19.01**	**8.91**	. . .	. . .
General government	2 401	20.07	20.88	12.83	6.30	19.01	8.91	. . .	. . .
Debt forgiveness	2 402	. . .	. . .	. . .	. . .	. . .	4.42	. . .	. . .
Other capital transfers	2 410	20.07	20.88	12.83	6.30	19.01	4.49	. . .	. . .
Other sectors	2 430	. . .	. . .	. . .	. . .	. . .	. . .	. . .	. . .
Migrants' transfers	2 431	. . .	. . .	. . .	. . .	. . .	. . .	. . .	. . .
Debt forgiveness	2 432	. . .	. . .	. . .	. . .	. . .	. . .	. . .	. . .
Other capital transfers	2 440	. . .	. . .	. . .	. . .	. . .	. . .	. . .	. . .
Capital transfers, debit	3 400	. . .	. . .	. . .	. . .	. . .	. . .	. . .	. . .
General government	3 401	. . .	. . .	. . .	. . .	. . .	. . .	. . .	. . .
Debt forgiveness	3 402	. . .	. . .	. . .	. . .	. . .	. . .	. . .	. . .
Other capital transfers	3 410	. . .	. . .	. . .	. . .	. . .	. . .	. . .	. . .
Other sectors	3 430	. . .	. . .	. . .	. . .	. . .	. . .	. . .	. . .
Migrants' transfers	3 431	. . .	. . .	. . .	. . .	. . .	. . .	. . .	. . .
Debt forgiveness	3 432	. . .	. . .	. . .	. . .	. . .	. . .	. . .	. . .
Other capital transfers	3 440	. . .	. . .	. . .	. . .	. . .	. . .	. . .	. . .
Nonproduced nonfinancial assets, credit	2 480	. . .	. . .	. . .	. . .	. . .	. . .	. . .	. . .
Nonproduced nonfinancial assets, debit	3 480	. . .	. . .	. . .	. . .	. . .	. . .	. . .	. . .

Table 2 (Continued). STANDARD PRESENTATION, 1994–2001

(Millions of U.S. dollars)

	Code	1994	1995	1996	1997	1998	1999	2000	2001
FINANCIAL ACCOUNT	4 995 . .	**17.36**	**76.38**	**23.55**	**43.82**	**26.22**	**74.70**	**. . .**	**. . .**
A. DIRECT INVESTMENT	4 500 . .	1.71	25.61	28.26	11.53	9.04	53.52	. . .	. . .
Direct investment abroad	4 505 . .	**–.42**	**–.57**	**–.26**	**–.05**	**. . .**	**–.42**	**. . .**	**. . .**
Equity capital	4 510 . .	. . .	. . .	–.03	–.05	. . .	. . .	. . .	. . .
Claims on affiliated enterprises	4 515 . .	. . .	. . .	–.03	–.05	. . .	. . .	. . .	. . .
Liabilities to affiliated enterprises	4 520 . .	. . .	. . .	. . .	. . .	. . .	. . .	. . .	. . .
Reinvested earnings	4 525 . .	–.42	–.57	–.23	. . .	. . .	. . .	. . .	. . .
Other capital	4 530 . .	. . .	. . .	. . .	. . .	. . .	–.42	. . .	. . .
Claims on affiliated enterprises	4 535 . .	. . .	. . .	. . .	. . .	. . .	–.42	. . .	. . .
Liabilities to affiliated enterprises	4 540 . .	. . .	. . .	. . .	. . .	. . .	. . .	. . .	. . .
Direct investment in Cape Verde	4 555 . .	**2.13**	**26.18**	**28.53**	**11.58**	**9.04**	**53.94**	**. . .**	**. . .**
Equity capital	4 560 . .	1.97	25.67	28.20	11.58	6.70	53.94	. . .	. . .
Claims on direct investors	4 565 . .	. . .	. . .	. . .	. . .	6.70	3.55	. . .	. . .
Liabilities to direct investors	4 570 . .	1.97	25.67	28.20	11.58	. . .	50.38	. . .	. . .
Reinvested earnings	4 575 . .	.15	.51	.33	. . .	.09	. . .	. . .	. . .
Other capital	4 580 . .	. . .	. . .	. . .	. . .	2.25	. . .	. . .	. . .
Claims on direct investors	4 585 . .	. . .	. . .	. . .	. . .	2.25	. . .	. . .	. . .
Liabilities to direct investors	4 590 . .	. . .	. . .	. . .	. . .	. . .	. . .	. . .	. . .
B. PORTFOLIO INVESTMENT	4 600 . .	. . .	. . .	. . .	. . .	. . .	2.99	. . .	. . .
Assets	4 602 . .	**. . .**	**. . .**	**. . .**	**. . .**	**. . .**	**. . .**	**. . .**	**. . .**
Equity securities	4 610 . .	. . .	. . .	. . .	. . .	. . .	. . .	. . .	. . .
Monetary authorities	4 611 . .	. . .	. . .	. . .	. . .	. . .	. . .	. . .	. . .
General government	4 612 . .	. . .	. . .	. . .	. . .	. . .	. . .	. . .	. . .
Banks	4 613 . .	. . .	. . .	. . .	. . .	. . .	. . .	. . .	. . .
Other sectors	4 614 . .	. . .	. . .	. . .	. . .	. . .	. . .	. . .	. . .
Debt securities	4 619 . .	. . .	. . .	. . .	. . .	. . .	. . .	. . .	. . .
Bonds and notes	4 620 . .	. . .	. . .	. . .	. . .	. . .	. . .	. . .	. . .
Monetary authorities	4 621 . .	. . .	. . .	. . .	. . .	. . .	. . .	. . .	. . .
General government	4 622 . .	. . .	. . .	. . .	. . .	. . .	. . .	. . .	. . .
Banks	4 623 . .	. . .	. . .	. . .	. . .	. . .	. . .	. . .	. . .
Other sectors	4 624 . .	. . .	. . .	. . .	. . .	. . .	. . .	. . .	. . .
Money market instruments	4 630 . .	. . .	. . .	. . .	. . .	. . .	. . .	. . .	. . .
Monetary authorities	4 631 . .	. . .	. . .	. . .	. . .	. . .	. . .	. . .	. . .
General government	4 632 . .	. . .	. . .	. . .	. . .	. . .	. . .	. . .	. . .
Banks	4 633 . .	. . .	. . .	. . .	. . .	. . .	. . .	. . .	. . .
Other sectors	4 634 . .	. . .	. . .	. . .	. . .	. . .	. . .	. . .	. . .
Liabilities	4 652 . .	**. . .**	**. . .**	**. . .**	**. . .**	**. . .**	**2.99**	**. . .**	**. . .**
Equity securities	4 660 . .	. . .	. . .	. . .	. . .	. . .	2.99	. . .	. . .
Banks	4 663 . .	. . .	. . .	. . .	. . .	. . .	. . .	. . .	. . .
Other sectors	4 664 . .	. . .	. . .	. . .	. . .	. . .	2.99	. . .	. . .
Debt securities	4 669 . .	. . .	. . .	. . .	. . .	. . .	. . .	. . .	. . .
Bonds and notes	4 670 . .	. . .	. . .	. . .	. . .	. . .	. . .	. . .	. . .
Monetary authorities	4 671 . .	. . .	. . .	. . .	. . .	. . .	. . .	. . .	. . .
General government	4 672 . .	. . .	. . .	. . .	. . .	. . .	. . .	. . .	. . .
Banks	4 673 . .	. . .	. . .	. . .	. . .	. . .	. . .	. . .	. . .
Other sectors	4 674 . .	. . .	. . .	. . .	. . .	. . .	. . .	. . .	. . .
Money market instruments	4 680 . .	. . .	. . .	. . .	. . .	. . .	. . .	. . .	. . .
Monetary authorities	4 681 . .	. . .	. . .	. . .	. . .	. . .	. . .	. . .	. . .
General government	4 682 . .	. . .	. . .	. . .	. . .	. . .	. . .	. . .	. . .
Banks	4 683 . .	. . .	. . .	. . .	. . .	. . .	. . .	. . .	. . .
Other sectors	4 684 . .	. . .	. . .	. . .	. . .	. . .	. . .	. . .	. . .
C. FINANCIAL DERIVATIVES	4 910 . .	. . .	. . .	. . .	. . .	. . .	. . .	. . .	. . .
Monetary authorities	4 911 . .	. . .	. . .	. . .	. . .	. . .	. . .	. . .	. . .
General government	4 912 . .	. . .	. . .	. . .	. . .	. . .	. . .	. . .	. . .
Banks	4 913 . .	. . .	. . .	. . .	. . .	. . .	. . .	. . .	. . .
Other sectors	4 914 . .	. . .	. . .	. . .	. . .	. . .	. . .	. . .	. . .
Assets	4 900 . .	**. . .**	**. . .**	**. . .**	**. . .**	**. . .**	**. . .**	**. . .**	**. . .**
Monetary authorities	4 901 . .	. . .	. . .	. . .	. . .	. . .	. . .	. . .	. . .
General government	4 902 . .	. . .	. . .	. . .	. . .	. . .	. . .	. . .	. . .
Banks	4 903 . .	. . .	. . .	. . .	. . .	. . .	. . .	. . .	. . .
Other sectors	4 904 . .	. . .	. . .	. . .	. . .	. . .	. . .	. . .	. . .
Liabilities	4 905 . .	**. . .**	**. . .**	**. . .**	**. . .**	**. . .**	**. . .**	**. . .**	**. . .**
Monetary authorities	4 906 . .	. . .	. . .	. . .	. . .	. . .	. . .	. . .	. . .
General government	4 907 . .	. . .	. . .	. . .	. . .	. . .	. . .	. . .	. . .
Banks	4 908 . .	. . .	. . .	. . .	. . .	. . .	. . .	. . .	. . .
Other sectors	4 909 . .	. . .	. . .	. . .	. . .	. . .	. . .	. . .	. . .

Table 2 (Concluded). STANDARD PRESENTATION, 1994–2001
(Millions of U.S. dollars)

	Code	1994	1995	1996	1997	1998	1999	2000	2001
D. OTHER INVESTMENT	4 700 . .	36.43	19.85	15.04	22.45	25.68	60.47	...	...
Assets	4 703 . .	**1.61**	**–1.67**	**–2.25**	**–1.79**	**–22.44**	**–14.05**	...	...
Trade credits	4 706 . .	...	...	...	...	...	...	...	...
General government	4 707 . .	...	...	...	...	...	...	...	...
of which: Short-term	4 709 . .	...	...	...	...	...	...	...	...
Other sectors	4 710 . .	...	...	...	...	...	...	...	...
of which: Short-term	4 712 . .	...	...	...	...	...	...	...	...
Loans	4 714 . .	...	...	...	...	...	.11	...	...
Monetary authorities	4 715 . .	...	...	...	...	...	...	...	...
of which: Short-term	4 718 . .	...	...	...	...	...	...	...	...
General government	4 719 . .	...	...	...	...	...	...	...	...
of which: Short-term	4 721 . .	...	...	...	...	...	...	...	...
Banks	4 722 . .	...	...	...	...	...	.02	...	...
of which: Short-term	4 724 . .	...	...	...	...	...	*.02*	...	...
Other sectors	4 725 . .	...	...	...	...	...	.09	...	...
of which: Short-term	4 727 . .	...	...	...	...	...	...	...	...
Currency and deposits	4 730 . .	...	...	...	...	–.69	–.44	...	...
Monetary authorities	4 731 . .	...	...	...	...	...	...	...	...
General government	4 732 . .	...	...	...	...	...	...	...	...
Banks	4 733 . .	...	...	...	...	...	...	...	...
Other sectors	4 734 . .	...	...	...	...	–.69	–.44	...	...
Other assets	4 736 . .	1.61	–1.67	–2.25	–1.79	–21.75	–13.73	...	...
Monetary authorities	4 737 . .	1.61	2.32	–2.34	–1.84	4.02	5.23	...	...
of which: Short-term	4 739 . .	...	...	...	...	*.90*	*–.41*	...	...
General government	4 740 . .	...	...	...	...	–28.39	–18.72	...	...
of which: Short-term	4 742 . .	...	...	...	...	*–28.39*	*–18.72*	...	...
Banks	4 743 . .	...	–3.99	.09	.05	3.02	–.08	...	...
of which: Short-term	4 745 . .	...	...	...	...	*2.43*	*–.09*	...	...
Other sectors	4 746 . .	...	...	...	...	–.41	–.16	...	...
of which: Short-term	4 748 . .	...	...	...	...	*–.41*	*–.16*	...	...
Liabilities	4 753 . .	**34.82**	**21.51**	**17.29**	**24.25**	**48.12**	**74.52**	...	...
Trade credits	4 756 . .	...	–2.99	.42	3.30	2.48	12.93	...	...
General government	4 757 . .	...	...	...	...	...	...	...	...
of which: Short-term	4 759 . .	...	...	...	...	...	...	...	...
Other sectors	4 760 . .	...	–2.99	.42	3.30	2.48	12.93	...	...
of which: Short-term	4 762 . .	...	*–2.99*	*.42*	*3.30*	*2.48*	*12.93*	...	...
Loans	4 764 . .	28.88	14.56	13.33	35.94	37.26	50.04	...	...
Monetary authorities	4 765 . .	...	...	...	...	...	.17	...	...
of which: Use of Fund credit and loans from the Fund	4 766 . .	...	...	...	...	...	...	...	...
of which: Short-term	4 768 . .	...	...	...	...	...	*.12*	...	...
General government	4 769 . .	15.24	10.02	16.55	29.52	28.67	43.48	...	...
of which: Short-term	4 771 . .	...	...	...	...	*8.58*	*11.76*	...	...
Banks	4 772 . .	...	...	...	...	...	9.93	...	...
of which: Short-term	4 774 . .	...	...	...	...	...	*10.35*	...	...
Other sectors	4 775 . .	13.64	4.55	–3.22	6.42	8.59	–3.53	...	...
of which: Short-term	4 777 . .	...	...	...	...	*.20*	*.82*	...	...
Currency and deposits	4 780 . .	...	...	...	...	7.89	18.61	...	...
Monetary authorities	4 781 . .	...	...	...	...	...	...	...	...
General government	4 782 . .	...	...	...	...	...	...	...	...
Banks	4 783 . .	...	...	...	...	7.89	18.61	...	...
Other sectors	4 784 . .	...	...	...	...	...	...	...	...
Other liabilities	4 786 . .	5.94	9.94	3.53	–14.99	.49	–7.07	...	...
Monetary authorities	4 787 . .	1.81	3.31	3.51	–19.93	–.01	...	...	...
of which: Short-term	4 789 . .	*2.77*	*4.22*	*3.69*	*–19.74*	*–.01*	...	...	...
General government	4 790 . .	3.02	4.25	...	...	.40	–2.42	...	...
of which: Short-term	4 792 . .	*3.02*	*4.25*	...	...	*.40*	*–2.42*	...	...
Banks	4 793 . .	1.11	2.38	.02	4.94	.11	–3.82	...	...
of which: Short-term	4 795 . .	*.75*	*.71*	*–.94*	*2.32*	*.87*	*1.96*	...	...
Other sectors	4 796 . .	...	...	...	...	...	–.83	...	...
of which: Short-term	4 798 . .	...	...	...	...	...	*–.83*	...	...
E. RESERVE ASSETS	4 802 . .	–20.78	30.93	–19.76	9.84	–8.50	–42.27	...	...
Monetary gold	4 812 . .	...	...	...	...	...	...	...	...
Special drawing rights	4 811 . .	–.04	.04	–.04	.03	–.03	.04	...	...
Reserve position in the Fund	4 810 . .	...	...	...	...	...	...	...	...
Foreign exchange	4 803 . .	–20.75	30.89	–19.72	9.81	–8.48	–42.31	...	...
Other claims	4 813 . .	...	...	...	...	...	...	...	...
NET ERRORS AND OMISSIONS	4 998 . .	**8.31**	**–35.64**	**–1.34**	**–20.40**	**13.28**	**–8.84**	...	...

Part 3 of the *Yearbook* contains descriptions of the methodologies, compilation practices, and sources used to compile these data.

Table 1. ANALYTIC PRESENTATION, 1994–2001
(Millions of U.S. dollars)

	Code	1994	1995	1996	1997	1998	1999	2000	2001
A. Current Account [1]	4 993 Z.	**–1,586**	**–1,350**	**–3,145**	**–3,668**	**–4,008**	**–301**	**–1,078**	**–1,243**
Goods: exports f.o.b	2 100 . .	11,604	16,025	16,653	17,900	16,355	17,192	19,246	18,508
Goods: imports f.o.b	3 100 . .	–10,872	–14,644	–17,699	–19,297	–18,364	–14,737	–17,093	–16,413
Balance on Goods	4 100 . .	*732*	*1,381*	*–1,046*	*–1,397*	*–2,009*	*2,455*	*2,153*	*2,095*
Services: credit	2 200 . .	2,840	3,333	3,532	3,850	3,809	3,595	3,725	3,809
Services: debit	3 200 . .	–2,990	–3,657	–3,619	–4,027	–4,383	–4,552	–4,609	–4,813
Balance on Goods and Services	4 991 . .	*582*	*1,057*	*–1,133*	*–1,574*	*–2,583*	*1,498*	*1,269*	*1,091*
Income: credit	2 300 . .	556	869	1,007	1,175	1,378	1,143	1,581	1,268
Income: debit	3 300 . .	–3,056	–3,582	–3,525	–3,793	–3,264	–3,372	–4,381	–4,025
Balance on Goods, Services, and Income	4 992 . .	*–1,917*	*–1,657*	*–3,651*	*–4,192*	*–4,469*	*–731*	*–1,531*	*–1,666*
Current transfers: credit	2 379 Z.	449	482	664	836	810	769	821	795
Current transfers: debit	3 379 . .	–118	–175	–158	–312	–349	–339	–368	–372
B. Capital Account [1]	4 994 Z.	**. . .**	**. . .**	**. . .**	**. . .**	**. . .**	**. . .**	**. . .**	**. . .**
Capital account: credit	2 994 Z.	. . .	. . .	. . .	. . .	. . .	. . .	. . .	. . .
Capital account: debit	3 994 . .	. . .	. . .	. . .	. . .	. . .	. . .	. . .	. . .
Total, Groups A Plus B	4 981 . .	*–1,586*	*–1,350*	*–3,145*	*–3,668*	*–4,008*	*–301*	*–1,078*	*–1,243*
C. Financial Account [1]	4 995 W.	**5,294**	**2,357**	**4,185**	**6,741**	**1,968**	**236**	**829**	**1,758**
Direct investment abroad	4 505 . .	–911	–752	–1,300	–1,466	–1,662	–2,785	–3,985	–1,432
Direct investment in Chile	4 555 Z.	2,583	2,957	4,979	5,277	4,808	8,988	3,639	4,476
Portfolio investment assets	4 602 . .	–351	–14	–135	–988	–3,311	–5,795	767	–1,385
Equity securities	4 610 . .	–351	–14	–43	–743	–2,518	–3,474	821	–2,094
Debt securities	4 619 . .	. . .	. . .	–92	–245	–793	–2,321	–54	709
Portfolio investment liabilities	4 652 Z.	1,259	48	1,269	2,614	843	2,579	–127	1,431
Equity securities	4 660 . .	1,259	–249	699	1,720	581	525	–427	–219
Debt securities	4 669 Z.	. . .	297	570	894	262	2,054	300	1,650
Financial derivatives	4 910 . .	. . .	. . .	–21	166	–60	–6	3	–87
Financial derivatives assets	4 900 . .	. . .	. . .	. . .	. . .	. . .	. . .	. . .	. . .
Financial derivatives liabilities	4 905 . .	. . .	. . .	–21	166	–60	–6	3	–87
Other investment assets	4 703 . .	–152	–309	–856	–459	–1,953	–3,371	–2,066	–737
Monetary authorities	4 701 . .	–57	10	. . .	. . .	. . .	. . .	. . .	. . .
General government	4 704 . .	. . .	. . .	. . .	. . .	. . .	. . .	. . .	. . .
Banks	4 705 . .	–26	57	–89	–549	–381	–1,643	651	145
Other sectors	4 728 . .	–70	–376	–767	90	–1,572	–1,728	–2,717	–882
Other investment liabilities	4 753 W.	2,865	427	249	1,597	3,303	626	2,598	–508
Monetary authorities	4 753 WA	–99	–402	–1,547	–25	–74	–65	36	–48
General government	4 753 ZB	–99	–1,323	–545	–387	–171	–101	–129	–132
Banks	4 753 ZC	407	–322	–444	–1,497	–35	–840	–241	456
Other sectors	4 753 ZD	2,656	2,474	2,785	3,507	3,583	1,632	2,932	–784
Total, Groups A Through C	4 983 . .	*3,708*	*1,007*	*1,040*	*3,073*	*–2,040*	*–65*	*–249*	*515*
D. Net Errors and Omissions	4 998 . .	**–557**	**132**	**78**	**245**	**–123**	**–588**	**566**	**–1,114**
Total, Groups A Through D	4 984 . .	*3,151*	*1,139*	*1,118*	*3,318*	*–2,163*	*–653*	*317*	*–599*
E. Reserves and Related Items	4 802 A.	**–3,151**	**–1,139**	**–1,118**	**–3,318**	**2,163**	**653**	**–317**	**599**
Reserve assets	4 802 . .	–2,918	–740	–1,118	–3,318	2,163	653	–317	599
Use of Fund credit and loans	4 766 . .	–210	–298	. . .	. . .	. . .	. . .	. . .	. . .
Exceptional financing	4 920 . .	–22	–101	. . .	. . .	. . .	. . .	. . .	. . .
Conversion rates: Chilean pesos per U.S. dollar	0 101 . .	**420.18**	**396.77**	**412.27**	**419.30**	**460.29**	**508.78**	**535.47**	**634.94**

[1] Excludes components that have been classified in the categories of Group E.

Table 2. STANDARD PRESENTATION, 1994–2001
(Millions of U.S. dollars)

	Code		1994	1995	1996	1997	1998	1999	2000	2001
CURRENT ACCOUNT	4 993	. .	**–1,586**	**–1,350**	**–3,145**	**–3,668**	**–4,008**	**–301**	**–1,078**	**–1,243**
A. GOODS	4 100	. .	732	1,381	–1,046	–1,397	–2,009	2,455	2,153	2,095
Credit	2 100	. .	**11,604**	**16,025**	**16,653**	**17,900**	**16,355**	**17,192**	**19,246**	**18,508**
General merchandise: exports f.o.b.	2 110	. .	11,604	16,025	16,049	17,325	15,913	16,733	18,679	17,991
Goods for processing: exports f.o.b.	2 150	. .	. . .	. . .	. . .	. . .	. . .	. . .	. . .	. . .
Repairs on goods	2 160	. .	. . .	. . .	30	31	31	31	35	40
Goods procured in ports by carriers	2 170	. .	. . .	. . .	93	127	132	124	189	208
Nonmonetary gold	2 180	. .	. . .	. . .	481	417	279	304	343	269
Debit	3 100	. .	**–10,872**	**–14,644**	**–17,699**	**–19,297**	**–18,364**	**–14,737**	**–17,093**	**–16,413**
General merchandise: imports f.o.b.	3 110	. .	–10,872	–14,644	–17,371	–18,965	–18,035	–14,489	–16,806	–16,117
Goods for processing: imports f.o.b.	3 150	. .	. . .	. . .	. . .	. . .	. . .	. . .	. . .	. . .
Repairs on goods	3 160	. .	. . .	. . .	–75	–76	–75	–54	–63	–72
Goods procured in ports by carriers	3 170	. .	. . .	. . .	–253	–256	–254	–194	–224	–224
Nonmonetary gold	3 180	. .	. . .	. . .	. . .	. . .	. . .	. . .	. . .	. . .
B. SERVICES	4 200	. .	–150	–324	–87	–177	–574	–957	–884	–1,004
Total credit	2 200	. .	*2,840*	*3,333*	*3,532*	*3,850*	*3,809*	*3,595*	*3,725*	*3,809*
Total debit	3 200	. .	*–2,990*	*–3,657*	*–3,619*	*–4,027*	*–4,383*	*–4,552*	*–4,609*	*–4,813*
Transportation services, credit	2 205	. .	**1,142**	**1,194**	**1,543**	**1,707**	**1,672**	**1,636**	**1,650**	**1,657**
Passenger	2 850	. .	*335*	*275*	*329*	*408*	*369*	*353*	*383*	*347*
Freight	2 851	. .	*555*	*656*	*932*	*1,005*	*991*	*994*	*999*	*985*
Other	2 852	. .	*252*	*263*	*282*	*294*	*312*	*289*	*268*	*325*
Sea transport, passenger	2 207	. .	. . .	. . .	4	5	4	4	4	4
Sea transport, freight	2 208	. .	. . .	. . .	725	870	857	861	862	853
Sea transport, other	2 209	. .	. . .	. . .	223	227	231	213	200	243
Air transport, passenger	2 211	. .	. . .	. . .	. . .	. . .	. . .	. . .	. . .	. . .
Air transport, freight	2 212	. .	. . .	. . .	. . .	. . .	. . .	. . .	. . .	. . .
Air transport, other	2 213	. .	. . .	. . .	. . .	. . .	. . .	. . .	. . .	. . .
Other transport, passenger	2 215	. .	. . .	. . .	325	403	365	349	379	343
Other transport, freight	2 216	. .	. . .	. . .	207	135	134	133	137	132
Other transport, other	2 217	. .	. . .	. . .	59	67	81	76	68	82
Transportation services, debit	3 205	. .	**–1,299**	**–1,904**	**–1,483**	**–1,566**	**–1,615**	**–1,598**	**–1,713**	**–1,731**
Passenger	3 850	. .	*–169*	*–231*	*–274*	*–297*	*–323*	*–282*	*–320*	*–277*
Freight	3 851	. .	*–431*	*–797*	*–804*	*–820*	*–752*	*–750*	*–784*	*–896*
Other	3 852	. .	*–699*	*–876*	*–405*	*–449*	*–540*	*–566*	*–609*	*–558*
Sea transport, passenger	3 207	. .	. . .	. . .	–33	–34	–37	–32	–37	–32
Sea transport, freight	3 208	. .	. . .	. . .	–482	–491	–451	–467	–482	–537
Sea transport, other	3 209	. .	. . .	. . .	–264	–291	–320	–352	–388	–427
Air transport, passenger	3 211	. .	. . .	. . .	. . .	. . .	. . .	. . .	. . .	. . .
Air transport, freight	3 212	. .	. . .	. . .	. . .	. . .	. . .	. . .	. . .	. . .
Air transport, other	3 213	. .	. . .	. . .	. . .	. . .	. . .	. . .	. . .	. . .
Other transport, passenger	3 215	. .	. . .	. . .	–241	–263	–286	–250	–283	–245
Other transport, freight	3 216	. .	. . .	. . .	–322	–329	–301	–283	–302	–359
Other transport, other	3 217	. .	. . .	. . .	–141	–158	–220	–214	–221	–131
Travel, credit	2 236	. .	**825**	**911**	**932**	**1,103**	**1,106**	**910**	**820**	**856**
Business travel	2 237	. .	. . .	. . .	120	102	68	85	79	73
Personal travel	2 240	. .	. . .	. . .	812	1,001	1,038	825	741	783
Travel, debit	3 236	. .	**–506**	**–703**	**–737**	**–838**	**–889**	**–753**	**–619**	**–581**
Business travel	3 237	. .	. . .	. . .	–158	–115	–54	–48	–40	–37
Personal travel	3 240	. .	. . .	. . .	–579	–723	–835	–705	–579	–544
Other services, credit	2 200	BA	**873**	**1,228**	**1,057**	**1,040**	**1,031**	**1,049**	**1,255**	**1,296**
Communications	2 245	. .	77	179	194	192	203	182	207	210
Construction	2 249	. .	. . .	. . .	. . .	. . .	. . .	. . .	. . .	. . .
Insurance	2 253	. .	40	240	92	91	68	77	75	78
Financial	2 260	. .	. . .	. . .	28	26	27	42	38	34
Computer and information	2 262	. .	. . .	. . .	26	26	25	30	34	34
Royalties and licence fees	2 266	. .	6	2	10	11	4	6	4	5
Other business services	2 268	. .	674	723	586	574	584	601	787	834
Personal, cultural, and recreational	2 287	. .	. . .	. . .	28	28	28	22	22	22
Government, n.i.e.	2 291	. .	76	84	93	92	92	89	88	79
Other services, debit	3 200	BA	**–1,185**	**–1,050**	**–1,399**	**–1,623**	**–1,879**	**–2,201**	**–2,277**	**–2,501**
Communications	3 245	. .	–22	–158	–150	–179	–162	–130	–110	–122
Construction	3 249	. .	. . .	. . .	. . .	. . .	. . .	. . .	. . .	. . .
Insurance	3 253	. .	–155	–144	–139	–167	–137	–153	–96	–125
Financial	3 260	. .	. . .	. . .	–95	–115	–162	–241	–221	–202
Computer and information	3 262	. .	. . .	. . .	–23	–27	–39	–50	–79	–81
Royalties and licence fees	3 266	. .	–47	–50	–117	–141	–222	–324	–350	–360
Other business services	3 268	. .	–840	–565	–746	–839	–970	–1,129	–1,241	–1,426
Personal, cultural, and recreational	3 287	. .	. . .	. . .	–25	–29	–45	–42	–43	–45
Government, n.i.e.	3 291	. .	–121	–133	–104	–126	–142	–132	–137	–140

Table 2 (Continued). STANDARD PRESENTATION, 1994–2001
(Millions of U.S. dollars)

	Code	1994	1995	1996	1997	1998	1999	2000	2001
C. INCOME	4 300 . .	–2,499	–2,714	–2,518	–2,618	–1,886	–2,229	–2,800	–2,757
Total credit	2 300 . .	*556*	*869*	*1,007*	*1,175*	*1,378*	*1,143*	*1,581*	*1,268*
Total debit	3 300 . .	*–3,056*	*–3,582*	*–3,525*	*–3,793*	*–3,264*	*–3,372*	*–4,381*	*–4,025*
Compensation of employees, credit	2 310 . .	**. . .**	**. . .**	**. . .**	**. . .**	**. . .**	**. . .**	**. . .**	**. . .**
Compensation of employees, debit	3 310 . .	**. . .**	**. . .**	**–14**	**–20**	**–17**	**–13**	**–15**	**–15**
Investment income, credit	2 320 . .	**556**	**869**	**1,007**	**1,175**	**1,378**	**1,143**	**1,581**	**1,268**
Direct investment income	2 330 . .	–4	68	298	247	446	283	566	467
Dividends and distributed branch profits	2 332 . .	11	13	16	106	90	140	165	255
Reinvested earnings and undistributed branch profits	2 333 . .	–15	55	282	138	346	136	384	153
Income on debt (interest)	2 334 . .	. . .	. . .	. . .	3	10	7	17	59
Portfolio investment income	2 339 . .	. . .	. . .	. . .	4	7	55	87	26
Income on equity	2 340 . .	. . .	. . .	. . .	4	7	55	87	26
Income on bonds and notes	2 350 . .	. . .	. . .	. . .	. . .	. . .	. . .	. . .	. . .
Income on money market instruments	2 360 . .	. . .	. . .	. . .	. . .	. . .	. . .	. . .	. . .
Other investment income	2 370 . .	560	800	709	924	925	805	928	775
Investment income, debit	3 320 . .	**–3,056**	**–3,582**	**–3,511**	**–3,773**	**–3,247**	**–3,359**	**–4,366**	**–4,010**
Direct investment income	3 330 . .	–1,870	–2,178	–2,058	–2,190	–1,580	–1,695	–2,462	–2,256
Dividends and distributed branch profits	3 332 . .	–1,049	–902	–1,320	–1,256	–899	–956	–1,093	–858
Reinvested earnings and undistributed branch profits	3 333 . .	–821	–1,276	–643	–786	–520	–510	–1,123	–1,148
Income on debt (interest)	3 334 . .	. . .	. . .	–95	–148	–161	–229	–246	–250
Portfolio investment income	3 339 . .	. . .	. . .	–280	–360	–370	–402	–490	–527
Income on equity	3 340 . .	. . .	. . .	–218	–256	–218	–169	–154	–143
Income on bonds and notes	3 350 . .	. . .	. . .	–62	–104	–152	–233	–336	–384
Income on money market instruments	3 360 . .	. . .	. . .	. . .	. . .	. . .	. . .	. . .	. . .
Other investment income	3 370 . .	–1,186	–1,404	–1,173	–1,223	–1,297	–1,262	–1,414	–1,227
D. CURRENT TRANSFERS	4 379 . .	331	307	506	524	461	430	453	423
Credit	2 379 . .	**449**	**482**	**664**	**836**	**810**	**769**	**821**	**795**
General government	2 380 . .	301	291	436	441	345	337	371	329
Other sectors	2 390 . .	148	191	228	395	465	432	450	466
Workers' remittances	2 391 . .	. . .	. . .	. . .	. . .	. . .	. . .	. . .	. . .
Other current transfers	2 392 . .	148	191	228	395	465	432	450	466
Debit	3 379 . .	**–118**	**–175**	**–158**	**–312**	**–349**	**–339**	**–368**	**–372**
General government	3 380 . .	–30	–39	–30	–44	–45	–44	–46	–46
Other sectors	3 390 . .	–88	–136	–128	–268	–304	–295	–322	–326
Workers' remittances	3 391 . .	. . .	. . .	. . .	. . .	. . .	. . .	. . .	. . .
Other current transfers	3 392 . .	–88	–136	–128	–268	–304	–295	–322	–326
CAPITAL AND FINANCIAL ACCOUNT	4 996 . .	**2,143**	**1,218**	**3,067**	**3,423**	**4,131**	**889**	**512**	**2,357**
CAPITAL ACCOUNT	4 994 . .	. . .	. . .	. . .	. . .	. . .	. . .	. . .	. . .
Total credit	2 994 . .	. . .	. . .	. . .	. . .	. . .	. . .	. . .	. . .
Total debit	3 994 . .	. . .	. . .	. . .	. . .	. . .	. . .	. . .	. . .
Capital transfers, credit	2 400 . .	**. . .**	**. . .**	**. . .**	**. . .**	**. . .**	**. . .**	**. . .**	**. . .**
General government	2 401 . .	. . .	. . .	. . .	. . .	. . .	. . .	. . .	. . .
Debt forgiveness	2 402 . .	. . .	. . .	. . .	. . .	. . .	. . .	. . .	. . .
Other capital transfers	2 410 . .	. . .	. . .	. . .	. . .	. . .	. . .	. . .	. . .
Other sectors	2 430 . .	. . .	. . .	. . .	. . .	. . .	. . .	. . .	. . .
Migrants' transfers	2 431 . .	. . .	. . .	. . .	. . .	. . .	. . .	. . .	. . .
Debt forgiveness	2 432 . .	. . .	. . .	. . .	. . .	. . .	. . .	. . .	. . .
Other capital transfers	2 440 . .	. . .	. . .	. . .	. . .	. . .	. . .	. . .	. . .
Capital transfers, debit	3 400 . .	**. . .**	**. . .**	**. . .**	**. . .**	**. . .**	**. . .**	**. . .**	**. . .**
General government	3 401 . .	. . .	. . .	. . .	. . .	. . .	. . .	. . .	. . .
Debt forgiveness	3 402 . .	. . .	. . .	. . .	. . .	. . .	. . .	. . .	. . .
Other capital transfers	3 410 . .	. . .	. . .	. . .	. . .	. . .	. . .	. . .	. . .
Other sectors	3 430 . .	. . .	. . .	. . .	. . .	. . .	. . .	. . .	. . .
Migrants' transfers	3 431 . .	. . .	. . .	. . .	. . .	. . .	. . .	. . .	. . .
Debt forgiveness	3 432 . .	. . .	. . .	. . .	. . .	. . .	. . .	. . .	. . .
Other capital transfers	3 440 . .	. . .	. . .	. . .	. . .	. . .	. . .	. . .	. . .
Nonproduced nonfinancial assets, credit	2 480 . .	**. . .**	**. . .**	**. . .**	**. . .**	**. . .**	**. . .**	**. . .**	**. . .**
Nonproduced nonfinancial assets, debit	3 480 . .	**. . .**	**. . .**	**. . .**	**. . .**	**. . .**	**. . .**	**. . .**	**. . .**

Table 2 (Continued). STANDARD PRESENTATION, 1994–2001
(Millions of U.S. dollars)

	Code	1994	1995	1996	1997	1998	1999	2000	2001
FINANCIAL ACCOUNT	4 995 . .	**2,143**	**1,218**	**3,067**	**3,423**	**4,131**	**889**	**512**	**2,357**
A. DIRECT INVESTMENT	4 500 . .	1,672	2,205	3,679	3,811	3,146	6,203	–346	3,044
Direct investment abroad	4 505 . .	**–911**	**–752**	**–1,300**	**–1,466**	**–1,662**	**–2,785**	**–3,985**	**–1,432**
Equity capital	4 510 . .	–926	–697	–1,018	–1,148	–1,263	–1,896	–3,574	–1,112
Claims on affiliated enterprises	4 515 . .	. . .	. . .	–1,018	–1,148	–1,263	–1,896	–3,574	–1,112
Liabilities to affiliated enterprises	4 520 . .	. . .	. . .	. . .	. . .	. . .	. . .	. . .	. . .
Reinvested earnings	4 525 . .	15	–55	–282	–138	–346	–136	–384	–153
Other capital	4 530 . .	. . .	. . .	. . .	–180	–53	–753	–27	–167
Claims on affiliated enterprises	4 535 . .	. . .	. . .	. . .	–180	–53	–753	–27	–167
Liabilities to affiliated enterprises	4 540 . .	. . .	. . .	. . .	. . .	. . .	. . .	. . .	. . .
Direct investment in Chile	4 555 . .	**2,583**	**2,957**	**4,979**	**5,277**	**4,808**	**8,988**	**3,639**	**4,476**
Equity capital	4 560 . .	1,762	1,681	4,039	4,211	4,156	8,862	2,822	3,424
Claims on direct investors	4 565 . .	. . .	. . .	. . .	. . .	. . .	. . .	. . .	. . .
Liabilities to direct investors	4 570 . .	. . .	. . .	4,039	4,211	4,156	8,862	2,822	3,424
Reinvested earnings	4 575 . .	821	1,276	643	786	520	510	1,123	1,148
Other capital	4 580 . .	. . .	. . .	297	280	132	–384	–306	–96
Claims on direct investors	4 585 . .	. . .	. . .	. . .	. . .	. . .	. . .	. . .	. . .
Liabilities to direct investors	4 590 . .	. . .	. . .	297	280	132	–384	–306	–96
B. PORTFOLIO INVESTMENT	4 600 . .	908	34	1,134	1,626	–2,468	–3,216	640	46
Assets	4 602 . .	**–351**	**–14**	**–135**	**–988**	**–3,311**	**–5,795**	**767**	**–1,385**
Equity securities	4 610 . .	–351	–14	–43	–743	–2,518	–3,474	821	–2,094
Monetary authorities	4 611 . .	. . .	. . .	. . .	. . .	. . .	. . .	. . .	. . .
General government	4 612 . .	. . .	. . .	. . .	. . .	. . .	. . .	. . .	. . .
Banks	4 613 . .	. . .	. . .	. . .	. . .	. . .	. . .	. . .	. . .
Other sectors	4 614 . .	. . .	. . .	–43	–743	–2,518	–3,474	821	–2,094
Debt securities	4 619 . .	. . .	. . .	–92	–245	–793	–2,321	–54	709
Bonds and notes	4 620 . .	. . .	. . .	–92	–245	–793	–1,873	–63	742
Monetary authorities	4 621 . .	. . .	. . .	. . .	. . .	. . .	. . .	. . .	. . .
General government	4 622 . .	. . .	. . .	. . .	. . .	. . .	. . .	. . .	. . .
Banks	4 623 . .	. . .	. . .	–28	–110	–589	–1,407	79	1,210
Other sectors	4 624 . .	. . .	. . .	–64	–135	–204	–466	–142	–468
Money market instruments	4 630 . .	. . .	. . .	. . .	. . .	. . .	–448	9	–33
Monetary authorities	4 631 . .	. . .	. . .	. . .	. . .	. . .	. . .	. . .	. . .
General government	4 632 . .	. . .	. . .	. . .	. . .	. . .	. . .	. . .	. . .
Banks	4 633 . .	. . .	. . .	. . .	. . .	. . .	. . .	. . .	. . .
Other sectors	4 634 . .	. . .	. . .	. . .	. . .	. . .	–448	9	–33
Liabilities	4 652 . .	**1,259**	**48**	**1,269**	**2,614**	**843**	**2,579**	**–127**	**1,431**
Equity securities	4 660 . .	1,259	–249	699	1,720	581	525	–427	–219
Banks	4 663 . .	. . .	. . .	54	183	71	55	6	–35
Other sectors	4 664 . .	. . .	. . .	645	1,537	510	470	–433	–184
Debt securities	4 669 . .	. . .	297	570	894	262	2,054	300	1,650
Bonds and notes	4 670 . .	. . .	297	570	894	262	2,054	300	1,650
Monetary authorities	4 671 . .	. . .	. . .	. . .	. . .	. . .	. . .	. . .	. . .
General government	4 672 . .	. . .	. . .	. . .	. . .	. . .	500	. . .	650
Banks	4 673 . .	. . .	. . .	. . .	398	200	. . .	. . .	. . .
Other sectors	4 674 . .	. . .	297	570	496	62	1,554	300	1,000
Money market instruments	4 680 . .	. . .	. . .	. . .	. . .	. . .	. . .	. . .	. . .
Monetary authorities	4 681 . .	. . .	. . .	. . .	. . .	. . .	. . .	. . .	. . .
General government	4 682 . .	. . .	. . .	. . .	. . .	. . .	. . .	. . .	. . .
Banks	4 683 . .	. . .	. . .	. . .	. . .	. . .	. . .	. . .	. . .
Other sectors	4 684 . .	. . .	. . .	. . .	. . .	. . .	. . .	. . .	. . .
C. FINANCIAL DERIVATIVES	4 910 . .	. . .	. . .	–21	166	–60	–6	3	–87
Monetary authorities	4 911 . .	. . .	. . .	. . .	. . .	. . .	. . .	. . .	. . .
General government	4 912 . .	. . .	. . .	. . .	. . .	. . .	. . .	. . .	. . .
Banks	4 913 . .	. . .	. . .	. . .	. . .	. . .	. . .	. . .	. . .
Other sectors	4 914 . .	. . .	. . .	. . .	. . .	. . .	. . .	. . .	. . .
Assets	4 900 . .	**. . .**	**. . .**	**. . .**	**. . .**	**. . .**	**. . .**	**. . .**	**. . .**
Monetary authorities	4 901 . .	. . .	. . .	. . .	. . .	. . .	. . .	. . .	. . .
General government	4 902 . .	. . .	. . .	. . .	. . .	. . .	. . .	. . .	. . .
Banks	4 903 . .	. . .	. . .	. . .	. . .	. . .	. . .	. . .	. . .
Other sectors	4 904 . .	. . .	. . .	. . .	. . .	. . .	. . .	. . .	. . .
Liabilities	4 905 . .	**. . .**	**. . .**	**–21**	**166**	**–60**	**–6**	**3**	**–87**
Monetary authorities	4 906 . .	. . .	. . .	. . .	. . .	. . .	. . .	. . .	. . .
General government	4 907 . .	. . .	. . .	. . .	. . .	. . .	. . .	. . .	. . .
Banks	4 908 . .	. . .	. . .	. . .	. . .	. . .	. . .	. . .	. . .
Other sectors	4 909 . .	. . .	. . .	. . .	. . .	. . .	. . .	. . .	. . .

Table 2 (Concluded). STANDARD PRESENTATION, 1994–2001
(Millions of U.S. dollars)

	Code	1994	1995	1996	1997	1998	1999	2000	2001
D. OTHER INVESTMENT	4 700 . .	2,481	–281	–607	1,138	1,350	–2,745	532	–1,245
Assets	4 703 . .	**–152**	**–309**	**–856**	**–459**	**–1,953**	**–3,371**	**–2,066**	**–737**
Trade credits	4 706 . .	. . .	. . .	–491	–70	–118	–999	–1,134	191
General government	4 707 . .	. . .	. . .	. . .	. . .	. . .	. . .	. . .	. . .
of which: Short-term	4 709 . .	. . .	. . .	. . .	. . .	. . .	. . .	. . .	. . .
Other sectors	4 710 . .	. . .	. . .	–491	–70	–118	–999	–1,134	191
of which: Short-term	4 712 . .	. . .	. . .	*–491*	*–70*	*–118*	*–999*	*–1,134*	*191*
Loans	4 714 . .	–786	–1,921	–70	–33	–215	–381	–83	–193
Monetary authorities	4 715 . .	. . .	. . .	. . .	. . .	. . .	. . .	. . .	. . .
of which: Short-term	4 718 . .	. . .	. . .	. . .	. . .	. . .	. . .	. . .	. . .
General government	4 719 . .	. . .	. . .	. . .	. . .	. . .	. . .	. . .	. . .
of which: Short-term	4 721 . .	. . .	. . .	. . .	. . .	. . .	. . .	. . .	. . .
Banks	4 722 . .	. . .	. . .	–70	–33	–215	–381	–83	–193
of which: Short-term	4 724 . .	. . .	. . .	*–70*	*9*	*–208*	*–385*	*61*	*–105*
Other sectors	4 725 . .	–786	–1,921	. . .	. . .	. . .	. . .	. . .	. . .
of which: Short-term	4 727 . .	*–786*	*–1,921*	. . .	. . .	. . .	. . .	. . .	. . .
Currency and deposits	4 730 . .	696	1,606	–295	–356	–1,620	–1,991	1,503	648
Monetary authorities	4 731 . .	. . .	. . .	. . .	. . .	. . .	. . .	. . .	. . .
General government	4 732 . .	. . .	. . .	. . .	. . .	. . .	. . .	. . .	. . .
Banks	4 733 . .	–21	61	–19	–516	–166	–1,262	734	338
Other sectors	4 734 . .	717	1,545	–276	160	–1,454	–729	769	310
Other assets	4 736 . .	–62	5	. . .	. . .	. . .	. . .	–2,352	–1,383
Monetary authorities	4 737 . .	–57	10	. . .	. . .	. . .	. . .	. . .	. . .
of which: Short-term	4 739 . .	*–57*	*10*	. . .	. . .	. . .	. . .	. . .	. . .
General government	4 740 . .	. . .	. . .	. . .	. . .	. . .	. . .	. . .	. . .
of which: Short-term	4 742 . .	. . .	. . .	. . .	. . .	. . .	. . .	. . .	. . .
Banks	4 743 . .	–5	–5	. . .	. . .	. . .	. . .	. . .	. . .
of which: Short-term	4 745 . .	. . .	. . .	. . .	. . .	. . .	. . .	. . .	. . .
Other sectors	4 746 . .	. . .	. . .	. . .	. . .	. . .	. . .	–2,352	–1,383
of which: Short-term	4 748 . .	. . .	. . .	. . .	. . .	. . .	. . .	*–2,352*	*–1,383*
Liabilities	4 753 . .	**2,633**	**28**	**249**	**1,597**	**3,303**	**626**	**2,598**	**–508**
Trade credits	4 756 . .	. . .	. . .	840	–114	–595	–233	322	–228
General government	4 757 . .	. . .	. . .	. . .	. . .	. . .	. . .	. . .	. . .
of which: Short-term	4 759 . .	. . .	. . .	. . .	. . .	. . .	. . .	. . .	. . .
Other sectors	4 760 . .	. . .	. . .	840	–114	–595	–233	322	–228
of which: Short-term	4 762 . .	. . .	. . .	*840*	*–114*	*–595*	*–233*	*322*	*–228*
Loans	4 764 . .	2,407	605	–360	1,774	4,033	1,019	2,096	–88
Monetary authorities	4 765 . .	–243	–758	–1,474	. . .	. . .	. . .	. . .	. . .
of which: Use of Fund credit and loans from the Fund	4 766 . .	*–210*	*–298*	. . .	. . .	. . .	. . .	. . .	. . .
of which: Short-term	4 768 . .	. . .	. . .	. . .	. . .	. . .	. . .	. . .	. . .
General government	4 769 . .	–99	–1,323	–545	–387	–171	–101	–129	–132
of which: Short-term	4 771 . .	. . .	. . .	. . .	. . .	. . .	. . .	. . .	. . .
Banks	4 772 . .	82	206	–325	–1,459	4	–745	–389	600
of which: Short-term	4 774 . .	. . .	. . .	*–313*	*–1,601*	*163*	*–516*	*21*	*645*
Other sectors	4 775 . .	2,667	2,480	1,984	3,621	4,200	1,865	2,614	–556
of which: Short-term	4 777 . .	*1,253*	*1,123*	*–309*	*284*	*208*	*227*	*1,663*	*–666*
Currency and deposits	4 780 . .	260	–550	–3	–2	2	–1	. . .	5
Monetary authorities	4 781 . .	–66	–22	. . .	. . .	. . .	. . .	. . .	. . .
General government	4 782 . .	. . .	. . .	. . .	. . .	. . .	. . .	. . .	. . .
Banks	4 783 . .	325	–528	–3	–2	2	–1	. . .	5
Other sectors	4 784 . .	. . .	. . .	. . .	. . .	. . .	. . .	. . .	. . .
Other liabilities	4 786 . .	–34	–27	–228	–61	–137	–159	180	–197
Monetary authorities	4 787 . .	–22	–8	–73	–25	–74	–65	36	–48
of which: Short-term	4 789 . .	*–22*	*–8*	*–73*	*–25*	*–74*	*–65*	*36*	*–48*
General government	4 790 . .	. . .	–2	. . .	. . .	. . .	. . .	. . .	. . .
of which: Short-term	4 792 . .	. . .	*–2*	. . .	. . .	. . .	. . .	. . .	. . .
Banks	4 793 . .	. . .	–4	–116	–36	–41	–94	148	–149
of which: Short-term	4 795 . .	. . .	*–4*	*–116*	*–36*	*–41*	*–94*	*148*	*–149*
Other sectors	4 796 . .	–12	–13	–39	. . .	–22	. . .	–4	. . .
of which: Short-term	4 798 . .	. . .	*–7*	*–38*	. . .	*–22*	. . .	*–4*	. . .
E. RESERVE ASSETS	4 802 . .	–2,918	–740	–1,118	–3,318	2,163	653	–317	599
Monetary gold	4 812 . .	. . .	. . .	. . .	3	198	. . .	328	. . .
Special drawing rights	4 811 . .	1	–3	1	1	–7	–10	–7	–5
Reserve position in the Fund	4 810 . .	. . .	. . .	–51	–267	–267	176	67	4
Foreign exchange	4 803 . .	–2,919	–737	–1,161	–3,080	2,174	407	–663	550
Other claims	4 813 . .	. . .	. . .	93	25	65	81	–42	51
NET ERRORS AND OMISSIONS	4 998 . .	**–557**	**132**	**78**	**245**	**–123**	**–588**	**566**	**–1,114**

Part 3 of the *Yearbook* contains descriptions of the methodologies, compilation practices, and sources used to compile these data.

Table 3. INTERNATIONAL INVESTMENT POSITION (End-period stocks), 1994–2001

(Millions of U.S. dollars)

	Code	1994	1995	1996	1997	1998	1999	2000	2001
ASSETS	8 995 C.	...	...	...	35,404	40,540	55,427	53,213	53,630
Direct investment abroad	8 505 . .	...	...	...	**4,890**	**6,348**	**12,919**	**11,793**	**12,976**
Equity capital and reinvested earnings	8 506 . .	...	...	...	4,709	6,114	11,932	10,778	11,793
Claims on affiliated enterprises	8 507 . .	...	...	...	4,709	6,114	11,932	10,778	11,793
Liabilities to affiliated enterprises	8 508 . .	...	...	...	...	...	...	...	...
Other capital	8 530 . .	...	...	...	181	234	987	1,015	1,183
Claims on affiliated enterprises	8 535 . .	...	...	...	181	234	987	1,015	1,183
Liabilities to affiliated enterprises	8 540 . .	...	...	...	...	...	...	...	...
Portfolio investment	8 602 . .	...	...	...	**1,176**	**4,717**	**11,402**	**9,876**	**10,663**
Equity securities	8 610 . .	...	...	...	902	3,411	7,670	6,911	7,870
Monetary authorities	8 611 . .	...	...	...	...	...	...	...	...
General government	8 612 . .	...	...	...	...	...	...	...	...
Banks	8 613 . .	...	...	...	...	...	...	...	...
Other sectors	8 614 . .	...	...	...	902	3,411	7,670	6,911	7,870
Debt securities	8 619 . .	...	...	...	274	1,306	3,732	2,965	2,793
Bonds and notes	8 620 . .	...	...	...	274	1,306	3,213	2,894	2,756
Monetary authorities	8 621 . .	...	...	...	...	...	...	...	...
General government	8 622 . .	...	...	...	...	...	...	...	...
Banks	8 623 . .	...	...	...	140	728	2,135	1,990	781
Other sectors	8 624 . .	...	...	...	134	578	1,078	904	1,975
Money market instruments	8 630 . .	...	...	...	...	...	519	71	37
Monetary authorities	8 631 . .	...	...	...	...	...	...	...	...
General government	8 632 . .	...	...	...	...	...	...	...	...
Banks	8 633 . .	...	...	...	...	...	...	...	...
Other sectors	8 634 . .	...	...	...	...	...	519	71	37
Financial derivatives	8 900 . .	...	...	...	...	...	...	...	...
Monetary authorities	8 901 . .	...	...	...	...	...	...	...	...
General government	8 902 . .	...	...	...	...	...	...	...	...
Banks	8 903 . .	...	...	...	...	...	...	...	...
Other sectors	8 904 . .	...	...	...	...	...	...	...	...
Other investment	8 703 . .	...	...	**597**	**11,066**	**13,183**	**16,154**	**16,430**	**15,581**
Trade credits	8 706 . .	...	...	...	6,290	6,408	7,407	8,542	8,350
General government	8 707 . .	...	...	...	...	...	...	...	...
of which: Short-term	8 709 . .	...	...	...	...	...	...	...	...
Other sectors	8 710 . .	...	...	...	6,290	6,408	7,407	8,542	8,350
of which: Short-term	8 712 . .	...	...	...	*6,290*	*6,408*	*7,407*	*8,542*	*8,350*
Loans	8 714 . .	...	...	245	217	280	475	954	1,147
Monetary authorities	8 715 . .	...	...	...	...	...	...	...	...
of which: Short-term	8 718 . .	...	...	...	...	...	...	...	...
General government	8 719 . .	...	...	...	...	...	...	...	...
of which: Short-term	8 721 . .	...	...	...	...	...	...	...	...
Banks	8 722 . .	...	...	245	217	280	475	954	1,147
of which: Short-term	8 724 . .	...	...	*235*	*207*	*228*	*419*	*757*	*861*
Other sectors	8 725 . .	...	...	...	...	...	...	...	...
of which: Short-term	8 727 . .	...	...	...	...	...	...	...	...
Currency and deposits	8 730 . .	...	...	323	4,559	6,495	8,272	6,934	6,084
Monetary authorities	8 731 . .	...	...	...	...	...	...	...	...
General government	8 732 . .	...	...	...	...	...	...	...	...
Banks	8 733 . .	...	...	323	838	1,005	2,267	1,532	1,194
Other sectors	8 734 . .	...	...	...	3,721	5,490	6,005	5,402	4,890
Other assets	8 736 . .	...	...	29	...	...	...	...	...
Monetary authorities	8 737 . .	...	...	...	...	...	...	...	...
of which: Short-term	8 739 . .	...	...	...	...	...	...	...	...
General government	8 740 . .	...	...	...	...	...	...	...	...
of which: Short-term	8 742 . .	...	...	...	...	...	...	...	...
Banks	8 743 . .	...	...	29	...	...	...	...	...
of which: Short-term	8 745 . .	...	...	*26*	...	...	...	...	...
Other sectors	8 746 . .	...	...	...	...	...	...	...	...
of which: Short-term	8 748 . .	...	...	...	...	...	...	...	...
Reserve assets	8 802 . .	...	...	**15,660**	**18,272**	**16,292**	**14,952**	**15,114**	**14,410**
Monetary gold	8 812 . .	...	...	637	533	322	317	18	19
Special drawing rights	8 811 . .	1	3	2	1	8	18	25	29
Reserve position in the Fund	8 810 . .	...	...	50	313	605	411	324	309
Foreign exchange	8 803 . .	...	...	14,971	17,259	15,256	14,187	14,686	14,041
Other claims	8 813 . .	...	...	...	166	101	19	61	12

Table 3 (Concluded). INTERNATIONAL INVESTMENT POSITION (End–period stocks), 1994–2001

(Millions of U.S. dollars)

	Code	1994	1995	1996	1997	1998	1999	2000	2001
LIABILITIES	8 995 D.	...	...	...	63,339	70,451	81,271	81,204	81,344
Direct investment in Chile	8 555 . .	**...**	**...**	**...**	**33,950**	**38,483**	**45,839**	**44,954**	**44,693**
Equity capital and reinvested earnings	8 556 . .	...	...	...	30,630	34,965	42,563	41,989	41,873
Claims on direct investors	8 557 . .	...	...	...	...	...	...	...	...
Liabilities to direct investors	8 558 . .	...	...	...	30,630	34,965	42,563	41,989	41,873
Other capital	8 580 . .	...	...	...	3,320	3,518	3,276	2,965	2,820
Claims on direct investors	8 585 . .	...	...	...	...	...	...	...	...
Liabilities to direct investors	8 590 . .	...	...	...	3,320	3,518	3,276	2,965	2,820
Portfolio investment	8 652 . .	**...**	**...**	**6,418**	**9,172**	**7,966**	**10,611**	**9,188**	**10,136**
Equity securities	8 660 . .	...	...	5,224	7,111	5,704	6,451	4,701	3,770
Banks	8 663 . .	...	...	291	456	422	627	537	605
Other sectors	8 664 . .	...	...	4,933	6,655	5,282	5,824	4,164	3,165
Debt securities	8 669 . .	...	...	1,194	2,061	2,262	4,160	4,487	6,366
Bonds and notes	8 670 . .	...	...	1,194	2,061	2,262	4,160	4,487	6,366
Monetary authorities	8 671 . .	...	...	...	...	...	...	...	...
General government	8 672 . .	...	...	...	...	...	464	481	1,167
Banks	8 673 . .	...	...	...	400	595	576	593	620
Other sectors	8 674 . .	...	...	1,194	1,661	1,667	3,120	3,413	4,579
Money market instruments	8 680 . .	...	...	...	...	...	...	...	...
Monetary authorities	8 681 . .	...	...	...	...	...	...	...	...
General government	8 682 . .	...	...	...	...	...	...	...	...
Banks	8 683 . .	...	...	...	...	...	...	...	...
Other sectors	8 684 . .	...	...	...	...	...	...	...	...
Financial derivatives	8 905 . .	**...**	**...**	**...**	**...**	**...**	**...**	**...**	**...**
Monetary authorities	8 906 . .	...	...	...	...	...	...	...	...
General government	8 907 . .	...	...	...	...	...	...	...	...
Banks	8 908 . .	...	...	...	...	...	...	...	...
Other sectors	8 909 . .	...	...	...	...	...	...	...	...
Other investment	8 753 . .	**...**	**...**	**21,367**	**20,217**	**24,002**	**24,821**	**27,062**	**26,515**
Trade credits	8 756 . .	...	...	...	264	265	351	335	245
General government	8 757 . .	...	...	...	...	...	...	...	...
of which: Short-term	8 759 . .	...	...	...	...	...	...	...	...
Other sectors	8 760 . .	...	...	...	264	265	351	335	245
of which: Short-term	8 762 . .	...	...	...	*264*	*265*	*351*	*335*	*245*
Loans	8 764 . .	...	...	20,985	19,633	23,529	24,423	26,496	26,230
Monetary authorities	8 765 . .	...	...	3	3	3	2	2	2
of which: Use of Fund credit and loans from the Fund	8 766 . .	*291*	...	...	...	...	...	...	...
of which: Short-term	8 768 . .	...	...	...	...	...	...	...	...
General government	8 769 . .	...	...	2,653	2,269	2,169	2,082	1,910	1,734
of which: Short-term	8 771 . .	...	...	...	...	...	...	...	...
Banks	8 772 . .	...	...	3,403	1,932	1,924	1,326	962	1,558
of which: Short-term	8 774 . .	...	...	*2,196*	*595*	*758*	*243*	*264*	*909*
Other sectors	8 775 . .	...	...	14,926	15,429	19,433	21,013	23,622	22,936
of which: Short-term	8 777 . .	...	...	*439*	*692*	*841*	*936*	*2,268*	*1,013*
Currency and deposits	8 780 . .	...	...	8	6	8	6	7	12
Monetary authorities	8 781 . .	...	...	...	...	...	...	...	...
General government	8 782 . .	...	...	...	...	...	...	...	...
Banks	8 783 . .	...	...	8	6	8	6	7	12
Other sectors	8 784 . .	...	...	...	...	...	...	...	...
Other liabilities	8 786 . .	...	...	374	314	200	41	224	28
Monetary authorities	8 787 . .	...	...	186	162	89	24	60	13
of which: Short-term	8 789 . .	...	...	*186*	*162*	*89*	*24*	*60*	*13*
General government	8 790 . .	...	...	...	...	...	...	...	...
of which: Short-term	8 792 . .	...	...	...	...	...	...	...	...
Banks	8 793 . .	...	303	188	152	111	17	164	15
of which: Short-term	8 795 . .	...	*303*	*188*	*152*	*111*	*17*	*164*	*15*
Other sectors	8 796 . .	...	...	...	...	...	...	...	...
of which: Short-term	8 798 . .	...	...	...	...	...	...	...	...
NET INTERNATIONAL INVESTMENT POSITION	8 995 . .	**...**	**...**	**...**	**–27,935**	**–29,911**	**–25,844**	**–27,991**	**–27,714**
Conversion rates: Chilean pesos per U.S. dollar (end of period)	0 102 . .	**404.09**	**407.13**	**424.97**	**439.81**	**473.77**	**530.07**	**572.68**	**656.20**

Table 1. ANALYTIC PRESENTATION, 1994–2001
(Millions of U.S. dollars)

	Code	1994	1995	1996	1997	1998	1999	2000	2001
A. Current Account [1]	4 993 Z.	**6,908**	**1,618**	**7,243**	**36,963**	**31,472**	**21,115**	**20,518**	**17,401**
Goods: exports f.o.b	2 100 . .	102,561	128,110	151,077	182,670	183,529	194,716	249,131	266,075
Goods: imports f.o.b	3 100 . .	−95,271	−110,060	−131,542	−136,448	−136,915	−158,734	−214,657	−232,058
Balance on Goods	4 100 . .	*7,290*	*18,050*	*19,535*	*46,222*	*46,614*	*35,982*	*34,474*	*34,017*
Services: credit	2 200 . .	16,620	19,130	20,601	24,569	23,895	26,248	30,430	33,334
Services: debit	3 200 . .	−16,299	−25,223	−22,585	−27,967	−26,672	−31,589	−36,031	−39,267
Balance on Goods and Services	4 991 . .	*7,611*	*11,958*	*17,551*	*42,824*	*43,837*	*30,641*	*28,874*	*28,084*
Income: credit	2 300 . .	5,737	5,191	7,318	5,710	5,584	8,330	12,550	9,388
Income: debit	3 300 . .	−6,775	−16,965	−19,755	−16,715	−22,228	−22,800	−27,216	−28,563
Balance on Goods, Services, and Income	4 992 . .	*6,573*	*184*	*5,114*	*31,819*	*27,193*	*16,171*	*14,207*	*8,909*
Current transfers: credit	2 379 Z.	1,269	1,827	2,368	5,477	4,661	5,368	6,861	9,125
Current transfers: debit	3 379 . .	−934	−392	−239	−333	−382	−424	−550	−633
B. Capital Account [1]	4 994 Z.	**. . .**	**. . .**	**. . .**	**−21**	**−47**	**−26**	**−35**	**−54**
Capital account: credit	2 994 Z.	. . .	. . .	. . .	. . .	. . .	. . .	. . .	. . .
Capital account: debit	3 994 . .	. . .	. . .	. . .	−21	−47	−26	−35	−54
Total, Groups A Plus B	4 981 . .	*6,908*	*1,618*	*7,243*	*36,942*	*31,425*	*21,089*	*20,483*	*17,347*
C. Financial Account [1]	4 995 W.	**32,645**	**38,674**	**39,966**	**21,037**	**−6,275**	**5,204**	**1,958**	**34,832**
Direct investment abroad	4 505 . .	−2,000	−2,000	−2,114	−2,563	−2,634	−1,775	−916	−6,884
Direct investment in China, P.R.: Mainland	4 555 Z.	33,787	35,849	40,180	44,237	43,751	38,753	38,399	44,241
Portfolio investment assets	4 602 . .	−380	79	−628	−899	−3,830	−10,535	−11,307	−20,654
Equity securities	4 610 . .	. . .	. . .	. . .	. . .	. . .	. . .	. . .	32
Debt securities	4 619 . .	−380	79	−628	−899	−3,830	−10,535	−11,307	−20,686
Portfolio investment liabilities	4 652 Z.	3,923	710	2,372	7,842	98	−699	7,317	1,249
Equity securities	4 660 . .	. . .	. . .	. . .	5,657	765	612	6,912	849
Debt securities	4 669 Z.	3,923	710	2,372	2,185	−667	−1,311	405	400
Financial derivatives	4 910 . .	. . .	. . .	. . .	. . .	. . .	. . .	. . .	. . .
Financial derivatives assets	4 900 . .	. . .	. . .	. . .	. . .	. . .	. . .	. . .	. . .
Financial derivatives liabilities	4 905 . .	. . .	. . .	. . .	. . .	. . .	. . .	. . .	. . .
Other investment assets	4 703 . .	−1,189	−1,081	−1,126	−39,608	−35,041	−24,394	−43,864	20,813
Monetary authorities	4 701 . .	. . .	. . .	. . .	−7,977	−2,417	−5,715	−7,261	−5,387
General government	4 704 . .	−1,136	−367	−1,102	. . .	. . .	. . .	. . .	. . .
Banks	4 705 . .	. . .	. . .	. . .	−12,572	2,841	6,075	−21,430	16,800
Other sectors	4 728 . .	−53	−714	−24	−19,059	−35,465	−24,754	−15,173	9,400
Other investment liabilities	4 753 W.	−1,496	5,116	1,282	12,028	−8,619	3,854	12,329	−3,933
Monetary authorities	4 753 WA	1,004	1,154	1,256	−2,037	−5,441	−3,936	. . .	. . .
General government	4 753 ZB	5,178	6,021	4,995	. . .	. . .	3,233	3,153	1,124
Banks	4 753 ZC	−5,222	−4,045	−5,959	6,968	−3,150	−5,021	−8,281	−1,305
Other sectors	4 753 ZD	−2,456	1,986	990	7,097	−28	9,578	17,457	−3,752
Total, Groups A Through C	4 983 . .	*39,553*	*40,292*	*47,209*	*57,979*	*25,150*	*26,293*	*22,441*	*52,179*
D. Net Errors and Omissions	4 998 . .	**−9,100**	**−17,823**	**−15,504**	**−22,122**	**−18,902**	**−17,641**	**−11,748**	**−4,732**
Total, Groups A Through D	4 984 . .	*30,453*	*22,469*	*31,705*	*35,857*	*6,248*	*8,652*	*10,693*	*47,447*
E. Reserves and Related Items	4 802 A.	**−30,453**	**−22,469**	**−31,705**	**−35,857**	**−6,248**	**−8,652**	**−10,693**	**−47,447**
Reserve assets	4 802 . .	−30,453	−22,469	−31,705	−35,857	−6,248	−8,652	−10,693	−47,447
Use of Fund credit and loans	4 766 . .	. . .	. . .	. . .	. . .	. . .	. . .	. . .	. . .
Exceptional financing	4 920 . .	. . .	. . .	. . .	. . .	. . .	. . .	. . .	. . .
Conversion rates: yuan per U.S. dollar	0 101 . .	**8.6187**	**8.3514**	**8.3142**	**8.2898**	**8.2790**	**8.2783**	**8.2785**	**8.2771**

[1] Excludes components that have been classified in the categories of Group E.

China,P.R.: Mainland
924

Table 2. STANDARD PRESENTATION, 1994–2001
(Millions of U.S. dollars)

	Code	1994	1995	1996	1997	1998	1999	2000	2001
CURRENT ACCOUNT	4 993 . .	**6,908**	**1,618**	**7,243**	**36,963**	**31,472**	**21,115**	**20,518**	**17,401**
A. GOODS	4 100 . .	7,290	18,050	19,535	46,222	46,614	35,982	34,474	34,017
Credit	2 100 . .	**102,561**	**128,110**	**151,077**	**182,670**	**183,529**	**194,716**	**249,131**	**266,075**
General merchandise: exports f.o.b.	2 110 . .	102,561	128,110	151,077	82,846	78,889	83,708	111,178	118,210
Goods for processing: exports f.o.b.	2 150 . .	. . .	. . .	. . .	99,610	104,486	110,883	137,674	147,477
Repairs on goods	2 160 . .	. . .	. . .	. . .	77	58	39	125	135
Goods procured in ports by carriers	2 170 . .	. . .	. . .	. . .	137	96	86	154	253
Nonmonetary gold	2 180 . .	. . .	. . .	. . .	. . .	. . .	. . .	. . .	. . .
Debit	3 100 . .	**–95,271**	**–110,060**	**–131,542**	**–136,448**	**–136,915**	**–158,734**	**–214,657**	**–232,058**
General merchandise: imports f.o.b.	3 110 . .	–95,271	–110,060	–131,542	–68,967	–69,850	–86,618	–124,075	–140,329
Goods for processing: imports f.o.b.	3 150 . .	. . .	. . .	. . .	–66,706	–66,060	–71,080	–89,522	–90,837
Repairs on goods	3 160 . .	. . .	. . .	. . .	–311	–532	–518	–238	–190
Goods procured in ports by carriers	3 170 . .	. . .	. . .	. . .	–464	–473	–518	–822	–702
Nonmonetary gold	3 180 . .	. . .	. . .	. . .	. . .	. . .	. . .	. . .	. . .
B. SERVICES	4 200 . .	321	–6,093	–1,984	–3,398	–2,777	–5,341	–5,600	–5,933
Total credit	2 200 . .	*16,620*	*19,130*	*20,601*	*24,569*	*23,895*	*26,248*	*30,430*	*33,334*
Total debit	3 200 . .	*–16,299*	*–25,223*	*–22,585*	*–27,967*	*–26,672*	*–31,589*	*–36,031*	*–39,267*
Transportation services, credit	2 205 . .	**3,079**	**3,352**	**3,070**	**2,955**	**2,300**	**2,420**	**3,671**	**4,635**
Passenger	2 850 . .	*254*	. . .	. . .	*552*	*627*	*908*	*1,087*	*1,214*
Freight	2 851 . .	*2,065*	*2,478*	*2,833*	*1,358*	*1,223*	*1,004*	*1,826*	*2,358*
Other	2 852 . .	*760*	*874*	*237*	*1,045*	*450*	*508*	*757*	*1,063*
Sea transport, passenger	2 207 . .	. . .	. . .	. . .	51	47	90	111	68
Sea transport, freight	2 208 . .	. . .	. . .	. . .	941	902	760	1,440	1,944
Sea transport, other	2 209 . .	. . .	. . .	. . .	. . .	. . .	. . .	. . .	. . .
Air transport, passenger	2 211 . .	. . .	. . .	. . .	328	315	621	775	969
Air transport, freight	2 212 . .	. . .	. . .	. . .	339	239	155	268	299
Air transport, other	2 213 . .	. . .	. . .	. . .	. . .	. . .	. . .	. . .	. . .
Other transport, passenger	2 215 . .	. . .	. . .	. . .	173	265	197	201	177
Other transport, freight	2 216 . .	. . .	. . .	. . .	78	82	89	119	115
Other transport, other	2 217 . .	. . .	. . .	. . .	1,045	450	508	757	1,063
Transportation services, debit	3 205 . .	**–7,621**	**–9,526**	**–10,312**	**–9,945**	**–6,763**	**–7,899**	**–10,396**	**–11,325**
Passenger	3 850 . .	. . .	. . .	. . .	*–1,090*	*–738*	*–757*	*–1,055*	*–1,083*
Freight	3 851 . .	*–6,926*	*–8,727*	*–10,084*	*–8,594*	*–5,522*	*–6,478*	*–8,705*	*–9,378*
Other	3 852 . .	*–695*	*–799*	*–228*	*–261*	*–503*	*–664*	*–636*	*–864*
Sea transport, passenger	3 207 . .	. . .	. . .	. . .	–101	–135	–177	–149	–51
Sea transport, freight	3 208 . .	. . .	. . .	. . .	–6,704	–3,915	–4,883	–5,969	–6,844
Sea transport, other	3 209 . .	. . .	. . .	. . .	. . .	. . .	. . .	. . .	. . .
Air transport, passenger	3 211 . .	. . .	. . .	. . .	–906	–506	–507	–836	–969
Air transport, freight	3 212 . .	. . .	. . .	. . .	–905	–506	–599	–750	–1,397
Air transport, other	3 213 . .	. . .	. . .	. . .	. . .	. . .	. . .	. . .	. . .
Other transport, passenger	3 215 . .	. . .	. . .	. . .	–83	–97	–73	–70	–63
Other transport, freight	3 216 . .	. . .	. . .	. . .	–985	–1,101	–996	–1,986	–1,137
Other transport, other	3 217 . .	. . .	. . .	. . .	–261	–503	–664	–636	–864
Travel, credit	2 236 . .	**7,323**	**8,730**	**10,200**	**12,074**	**12,602**	**14,098**	**16,231**	**17,792**
Business travel	2 237 . .	. . .	. . .	. . .	. . .	. . .	. . .	. . .	. . .
Personal travel	2 240 . .	. . .	. . .	. . .	. . .	. . .	. . .	. . .	. . .
Travel, debit	3 236 . .	**–3,036**	**–3,688**	**–4,474**	**–8,130**	**–9,205**	**–10,864**	**–13,114**	**–13,909**
Business travel	3 237 . .	. . .	. . .	. . .	. . .	. . .	. . .	. . .	. . .
Personal travel	3 240 . .	. . .	. . .	. . .	. . .	. . .	. . .	. . .	. . .
Other services, credit	2 200 BA	**6,218**	**7,048**	**7,331**	**9,540**	**8,993**	**9,730**	**10,529**	**10,907**
Communications	2 245 . .	706	756	315	272	819	590	1,345	271
Construction	2 249 . .	. . .	. . .	. . .	590	594	985	602	830
Insurance	2 253 . .	1,700	1,852	123	174	384	204	108	227
Financial	2 260 . .	. . .	. . .	. . .	27	27	111	78	99
Computer and information	2 262 . .	. . .	. . .	. . .	84	134	265	356	461
Royalties and licence fees	2 266 . .	. . .	. . .	. . .	55	63	75	80	110
Other business services	2 268 . .	3,546	3,740	6,859	8,263	6,941	7,410	7,663	8,448
Personal, cultural, and recreational	2 287 . .	. . .	. . .	. . .	10	15	7	11	28
Government, n.i.e.	2 291 . .	266	700	34	65	16	83	285	433
Other services, debit	3 200 BA	**–5,642**	**–12,009**	**–7,799**	**–9,892**	**–10,704**	**–12,826**	**–12,521**	**–14,033**
Communications	3 245 . .	–146	–217	–134	–290	–207	–193	–242	–326
Construction	3 249 . .	. . .	. . .	. . .	–1,209	–1,120	–1,540	–994	–847
Insurance	3 253 . .	–1,880	–4,273	–233	–1,045	–1,758	–1,921	–2,471	–2,711
Financial	3 260 . .	. . .	. . .	. . .	–325	–163	–167	–97	–77
Computer and information	3 262 . .	. . .	. . .	. . .	–231	–333	–224	–265	–345
Royalties and licence fees	3 266 . .	. . .	. . .	. . .	–543	–420	–792	–1,281	–1,938
Other business services	3 268 . .	–3,098	–6,930	–7,216	–5,962	–6,459	–7,333	–6,959	–7,504
Personal, cultural, and recreational	3 287 . .	. . .	. . .	. . .	–44	–39	–34	–37	–50
Government, n.i.e.	3 291 . .	–518	–588	–216	–243	–205	–622	–173	–235

Table 2 (Continued). STANDARD PRESENTATION, 1994–2001
(Millions of U.S. dollars)

	Code	1994	1995	1996	1997	1998	1999	2000	2001
C. INCOME	4 300 . .	–1,038	–11,774	–12,437	–11,005	–16,644	–14,470	–14,666	–19,175
Total credit	2 300 . .	*5,737*	*5,191*	*7,318*	*5,710*	*5,584*	*8,330*	*12,550*	*9,388*
Total debit	3 300 . .	*–6,775*	*–16,965*	*–19,755*	*–16,715*	*–22,228*	*–22,800*	*–27,216*	*–28,563*
Compensation of employees, credit	2 310 . .	**. . .**	**. . .**	**. . .**	**166**	**97**	**146**	**202**	**297**
Compensation of employees, debit	3 310 . .	**. . .**	**. . .**	**. . .**	**. . .**	**–204**	**–523**	**–679**	**–852**
Investment income, credit	2 320 . .	**5,737**	**5,191**	**7,318**	**5,544**	**5,487**	**8,184**	**12,348**	**9,091**
Direct investment income	2 330 . .	. . .	1	7	60	23	18	62	146
Dividends and distributed branch profits	2 332 . .	. . .	1	7	60	23	18	62	146
Reinvested earnings and undistributed branch profits	2 333 . .	. . .	. . .	. . .	. . .	. . .	. . .	. . .	. . .
Income on debt (interest)	2 334 . .	. . .	. . .	. . .	. . .	. . .	. . .	. . .	. . .
Portfolio investment income	2 339 . .	. . .	. . .	. . .	7	48	66	173	173
Income on equity	2 340 . .	. . .	. . .	. . .	. . .	43	57	169	168
Income on bonds and notes	2 350 . .	. . .	. . .	. . .	. . .	. . .	. . .	. . .	. . .
Income on money market instruments	2 360 . .	. . .	. . .	. . .	. . .	. . .	. . .	. . .	. . .
Other investment income	2 370 . .	5,737	5,190	7,311	5,477	5,416	8,100	12,113	8,772
Investment income, debit	3 320 . .	**–6,775**	**–16,965**	**–19,755**	**–16,715**	**–22,024**	**–22,277**	**–26,537**	**–27,711**
Direct investment income	3 330 . .	–400	–9,953	–11,679	–13,311	–16,039	–16,039	–20,198	–21,489
Dividends and distributed branch profits	3 332 . .	–400	–9,953	–11,679	–2,056	–2,573	–3,841	–4,176	–6,808
Reinvested earnings and undistributed branch profits	3 333 . .	. . .	. . .	. . .	–11,255	–13,466	–12,198	–16,022	–14,681
Income on debt (interest)	3 334 . .	. . .	. . .	. . .	. . .	. . .	. . .	. . .	. . .
Portfolio investment income	3 339 . .	. . .	. . .	. . .	–450	–902	–787	–712	–714
Income on equity	3 340 . .	. . .	. . .	. . .	–106	–295	–266	–365	. . .
Income on bonds and notes	3 350 . .	. . .	. . .	. . .	. . .	. . .	. . .	. . .	. . .
Income on money market instruments	3 360 . .	. . .	. . .	. . .	. . .	. . .	. . .	. . .	. . .
Other investment income	3 370 . .	–6,375	–7,012	–8,076	–2,954	–5,083	–5,451	–5,626	–5,508
D. CURRENT TRANSFERS	4 379 . .	335	1,435	2,129	5,144	4,279	4,944	6,311	8,492
Credit	2 379 . .	**1,269**	**1,827**	**2,368**	**5,477**	**4,661**	**5,368**	**6,861**	**9,125**
General government	2 380 . .	174	657	379	483	183	201	147	138
Other sectors	2 390 . .	1,095	1,170	1,989	4,994	4,478	5,167	6,713	8,987
Workers' remittances	2 391 . .	395	350	1,672	4,423	247	384	556	912
Other current transfers	2 392 . .	700	820	317	571	4,231	4,783	6,157	8,075
Debit	3 379 . .	**–934**	**–392**	**–239**	**–333**	**–382**	**–424**	**–550**	**–633**
General government	3 380 . .	–675	–32	–78	. . .	–92	–93	–94	–205
Other sectors	3 390 . .	–259	–360	–161	–333	–290	–331	–456	–428
Workers' remittances	3 391 . .	–19	. . .	. . .	–198	–68	–70	–75	–84
Other current transfers	3 392 . .	–240	–360	–161	–135	–222	–261	–381	–344
CAPITAL AND FINANCIAL ACCOUNT	4 996 . .	**2,192**	**16,205**	**8,261**	**–14,841**	**–12,570**	**–3,474**	**–8,770**	**–12,669**
CAPITAL ACCOUNT	4 994 . .	**. . .**	**. . .**	**. . .**	**–21**	**–47**	**–26**	**–35**	**–54**
Total credit	2 994 . .	. . .	. . .	. . .	. . .	. . .	. . .	. . .	. . .
Total debit	3 994 . .	. . .	. . .	. . .	*–21*	*–47*	*–26*	*–35*	*–54*
Capital transfers, credit	2 400 . .	**. . .**	**. . .**	**. . .**	**. . .**	**. . .**	**. . .**	**. . .**	**. . .**
General government	2 401 . .	. . .	. . .	. . .	. . .	. . .	. . .	. . .	. . .
Debt forgiveness	2 402 . .	. . .	. . .	. . .	. . .	. . .	. . .	. . .	. . .
Other capital transfers	2 410 . .	. . .	. . .	. . .	. . .	. . .	. . .	. . .	. . .
Other sectors	2 430 . .	. . .	. . .	. . .	. . .	. . .	. . .	. . .	. . .
Migrants' transfers	2 431 . .	. . .	. . .	. . .	. . .	. . .	. . .	. . .	. . .
Debt forgiveness	2 432 . .	. . .	. . .	. . .	. . .	. . .	. . .	. . .	. . .
Other capital transfers	2 440 . .	. . .	. . .	. . .	. . .	. . .	. . .	. . .	. . .
Capital transfers, debit	3 400 . .	**. . .**	**. . .**	**. . .**	**–21**	**–47**	**–26**	**–35**	**–54**
General government	3 401 . .	. . .	. . .	. . .	. . .	. . .	. . .	. . .	. . .
Debt forgiveness	3 402 . .	. . .	. . .	. . .	. . .	. . .	. . .	. . .	. . .
Other capital transfers	3 410 . .	. . .	. . .	. . .	. . .	. . .	. . .	. . .	. . .
Other sectors	3 430 . .	. . .	. . .	. . .	–21	–47	–26	–35	–54
Migrants' transfers	3 431 . .	. . .	. . .	. . .	–21	–47	–26	–35	–54
Debt forgiveness	3 432 . .	. . .	. . .	. . .	. . .	. . .	. . .	. . .	. . .
Other capital transfers	3 440 . .	. . .	. . .	. . .	. . .	. . .	. . .	. . .	. . .
Nonproduced nonfinancial assets, credit	2 480 . .	**. . .**	**. . .**	**. . .**	**. . .**	**. . .**	**. . .**	**. . .**	**. . .**
Nonproduced nonfinancial assets, debit	3 480 . .	**. . .**	**. . .**	**. . .**	**. . .**	**. . .**	**. . .**	**. . .**	**. . .**

Table 2 (Continued). STANDARD PRESENTATION, 1994–2001
(Millions of U.S. dollars)

	Code		1994	1995	1996	1997	1998	1999	2000	2001
FINANCIAL ACCOUNT	4 995	. .	**2,192**	**16,205**	**8,261**	**–14,820**	**–12,523**	**–3,448**	**–8,735**	**–12,615**
A. DIRECT INVESTMENT	4 500	. .	31,787	33,849	38,066	41,674	41,117	36,978	37,483	37,357
Direct investment abroad	4 505	. .	**–2,000**	**–2,000**	**–2,114**	**–2,563**	**–2,634**	**–1,775**	**–916**	**–6,884**
Equity capital	4 510	. .	–2,000	–2,000	–2,114	–2,553	–706	–275	–587	–6,868
Claims on affiliated enterprises	4 515	. .	. . .	. . .	. . .	–2,565	–712	–290	–640	–6,973
Liabilities to affiliated enterprises	4 520	. .	. . .	. . .	. . .	12	6	15	53	105
Reinvested earnings	4 525	. .	. . .	. . .	. . .	. . .	. . .	. . .	. . .	. . .
Other capital	4 530	. .	. . .	. . .	. . .	–10	–1,928	–1,500	–329	–16
Claims on affiliated enterprises	4 535	. .	. . .	. . .	. . .	–159	–2,104	–2,087	–1,599	–118
Liabilities to affiliated enterprises	4 540	. .	. . .	. . .	. . .	149	176	587	1,270	102
Direct investment in China, P.R.: Mainland	4 555	. .	**33,787**	**35,849**	**40,180**	**44,237**	**43,751**	**38,753**	**38,399**	**44,241**
Equity capital	4 560	. .	33,787	35,849	40,180	28,981	21,469	16,772	20,841	27,361
Claims on direct investors	4 565	. .	. . .	. . .	. . .	–159	–460	–479	–872	–1,180
Liabilities to direct investors	4 570	. .	. . .	. . .	. . .	29,140	21,929	17,251	21,713	28,541
Reinvested earnings	4 575	. .	. . .	. . .	. . .	11,255	13,466	12,198	16,022	14,681
Other capital	4 580	. .	. . .	. . .	. . .	4,001	8,816	9,783	1,536	2,199
Claims on direct investors	4 585	. .	. . .	. . .	. . .	–882	–1,251	–1,180	–1,501	–1,425
Liabilities to direct investors	4 590	. .	. . .	. . .	. . .	4,883	10,067	10,963	3,037	3,624
B. PORTFOLIO INVESTMENT	4 600	. .	3,543	789	1,744	6,943	–3,732	–11,234	–3,991	–19,405
Assets	4 602	. .	**–380**	**79**	**–628**	**–899**	**–3,830**	**–10,535**	**–11,307**	**–20,654**
Equity securities	4 610	. .	. . .	. . .	. . .	. . .	. . .	. . .	. . .	32
Monetary authorities	4 611	. .	. . .	. . .	. . .	. . .	. . .	. . .	. . .	. . .
General government	4 612	. .	. . .	. . .	. . .	. . .	. . .	. . .	. . .	. . .
Banks	4 613	. .	. . .	. . .	. . .	. . .	. . .	. . .	. . .	32
Other sectors	4 614	. .	. . .	. . .	. . .	. . .	. . .	. . .	. . .	. . .
Debt securities	4 619	. .	–380	79	–628	–899	–3,830	–10,535	–11,307	–20,686
Bonds and notes	4 620	. .	–380	79	–628	–899	–3,830	–10,535	–11,307	–5,588
Monetary authorities	4 621	. .	. . .	. . .	. . .	. . .	. . .	. . .	. . .	. . .
General government	4 622	. .	. . .	. . .	. . .	. . .	. . .	. . .	. . .	. . .
Banks	4 623	. .	. . .	. . .	. . .	–899	–3,837	–10,631	–11,360	–5,584
Other sectors	4 624	. .	. . .	. . .	. . .	. . .	7	96	53	–4
Money market instruments	4 630	. .	. . .	. . .	. . .	. . .	. . .	. . .	. . .	–15,098
Monetary authorities	4 631	. .	. . .	. . .	. . .	. . .	. . .	. . .	. . .	. . .
General government	4 632	. .	. . .	. . .	. . .	. . .	. . .	. . .	. . .	. . .
Banks	4 633	. .	. . .	. . .	. . .	. . .	. . .	. . .	. . .	–15,098
Other sectors	4 634	. .	. . .	. . .	. . .	. . .	. . .	. . .	. . .	. . .
Liabilities	4 652	. .	**3,923**	**710**	**2,372**	**7,842**	**98**	**–699**	**7,317**	**1,249**
Equity securities	4 660	. .	. . .	. . .	. . .	5,657	765	612	6,912	849
Banks	4 663	. .	. . .	. . .	. . .	. . .	. . .	. . .	. . .	. . .
Other sectors	4 664	. .	. . .	. . .	. . .	5,657	765	612	6,912	849
Debt securities	4 669	. .	3,923	710	2,372	2,185	–667	–1,311	405	400
Bonds and notes	4 670	. .	3,923	710	2,372	2,115	–604	–1,254	405	400
Monetary authorities	4 671	. .	. . .	. . .	. . .	. . .	. . .	. . .	. . .	. . .
General government	4 672	. .	. . .	. . .	. . .	. . .	. . .	–285	276	786
Banks	4 673	. .	. . .	. . .	. . .	. . .	. . .	–984	129	–226
Other sectors	4 674	. .	3,923	710	2,372	2,115	–604	15	. . .	–160
Money market instruments	4 680	. .	. . .	. . .	. . .	70	–63	–57	. . .	. . .
Monetary authorities	4 681	. .	. . .	. . .	. . .	. . .	. . .	. . .	. . .	. . .
General government	4 682	. .	. . .	. . .	. . .	. . .	. . .	. . .	. . .	. . .
Banks	4 683	. .	. . .	. . .	. . .	. . .	. . .	. . .	. . .	. . .
Other sectors	4 684	. .	. . .	. . .	. . .	70	–63	–57	. . .	. . .
C. FINANCIAL DERIVATIVES	4 910	. .	. . .	. . .	. . .	. . .	. . .	. . .	. . .	. . .
Monetary authorities	4 911	. .	. . .	. . .	. . .	. . .	. . .	. . .	. . .	. . .
General government	4 912	. .	. . .	. . .	. . .	. . .	. . .	. . .	. . .	. . .
Banks	4 913	. .	. . .	. . .	. . .	. . .	. . .	. . .	. . .	. . .
Other sectors	4 914	. .	. . .	. . .	. . .	. . .	. . .	. . .	. . .	. . .
Assets	4 900	. .	**. . .**	**. . .**	**. . .**	**. . .**	**. . .**	**. . .**	**. . .**	**. . .**
Monetary authorities	4 901	. .	. . .	. . .	. . .	. . .	. . .	. . .	. . .	. . .
General government	4 902	. .	. . .	. . .	. . .	. . .	. . .	. . .	. . .	. . .
Banks	4 903	. .	. . .	. . .	. . .	. . .	. . .	. . .	. . .	. . .
Other sectors	4 904	. .	. . .	. . .	. . .	. . .	. . .	. . .	. . .	. . .
Liabilities	4 905	. .	**. . .**	**. . .**	**. . .**	**. . .**	**. . .**	**. . .**	**. . .**	**. . .**
Monetary authorities	4 906	. .	. . .	. . .	. . .	. . .	. . .	. . .	. . .	. . .
General government	4 907	. .	. . .	. . .	. . .	. . .	. . .	. . .	. . .	. . .
Banks	4 908	. .	. . .	. . .	. . .	. . .	. . .	. . .	. . .	. . .
Other sectors	4 909	. .	. . .	. . .	. . .	. . .	. . .	. . .	. . .	. . .

Table 2 (Concluded). STANDARD PRESENTATION, 1994–2001
(Millions of U.S. dollars)

	Code	1994	1995	1996	1997	1998	1999	2000	2001
D. OTHER INVESTMENT	4 700 . .	–2,685	4,035	156	–27,580	–43,660	–20,540	–31,535	16,880
Assets	4 703 . .	**–1,189**	**–1,081**	**–1,126**	**–39,608**	**–35,041**	**–24,394**	**–43,864**	**20,813**
Trade credits	4 706 . .	–53	–714	–24	–15,018	–22,092	–22,898	–12,960	702
General government	4 707 . .	. . .	. . .	. . .	. . .	. . .	. . .	. . .	. . .
of which: Short-term	4 709 . .	. . .	. . .	. . .	. . .	. . .	. . .	. . .	. . .
Other sectors	4 710 . .	–53	–714	–24	–15,018	–22,092	–22,898	–12,960	702
of which: Short-term	4 712 . .	. . .	. . .	. . .	*–15,018*	*–22,092*	*–22,898*	*–12,960*	*702*
Loans	4 714 . .	–1,136	–367	–1,102	–2,155	–1,411	–3,436	–18,430	15,314
Monetary authorities	4 715 . .	. . .	. . .	. . .	. . .	. . .	. . .	. . .	. . .
of which: Short-term	4 718 . .	. . .	. . .	. . .	. . .	. . .	. . .	. . .	. . .
General government	4 719 . .	–1,136	–367	–1,102	. . .	. . .	. . .	. . .	. . .
of which: Short-term	4 721 . .	. . .	. . .	. . .	. . .	. . .	. . .	. . .	. . .
Banks	4 722 . .	. . .	. . .	. . .	–2,155	–1,089	–3,214	–18,293	15,535
of which: Short-term	4 724 . .	. . .	. . .	. . .	. . .	*–897*	*–3,322*	*–18,293*	*15,712*
Other sectors	4 725 . .	. . .	. . .	. . .	. . .	–322	–222	–137	–221
of which: Short-term	4 727 . .	. . .	. . .	. . .	. . .	*–322*	*–222*	*–137*	*–221*
Currency and deposits	4 730 . .	. . .	. . .	. . .	–15,051	638	11,271	–6,049	–3,214
Monetary authorities	4 731 . .	. . .	. . .	. . .	–4,634	. . .	. . .	. . .	. . .
General government	4 732 . .	. . .	. . .	. . .	. . .	. . .	. . .	. . .	. . .
Banks	4 733 . .	. . .	. . .	. . .	–10,417	1,538	11,729	–5,870	–2,395
Other sectors	4 734 . .	. . .	. . .	. . .	. . .	–900	–458	–179	–819
Other assets	4 736 . .	. . .	. . .	. . .	–7,384	–12,176	–9,331	–6,425	8,011
Monetary authorities	4 737 . .	. . .	. . .	. . .	–3,343	–2,417	–5,715	–7,261	–5,387
of which: Short-term	4 739 . .	. . .	. . .	. . .	*–3,343*	*2,652*	*–302*	. . .	. . .
General government	4 740 . .	. . .	. . .	. . .	. . .	. . .	. . .	. . .	. . .
of which: Short-term	4 742 . .	. . .	. . .	. . .	. . .	. . .	. . .	. . .	. . .
Banks	4 743 . .	. . .	. . .	. . .	. . .	2,392	–2,440	2,733	3,660
of which: Short-term	4 745 . .	. . .	. . .	. . .	. . .	*2,392*	*–2,440*	*2,733*	*3,660*
Other sectors	4 746 . .	. . .	. . .	. . .	–4,041	–12,151	–1,176	–1,897	9,738
of which: Short-term	4 748 . .	. . .	. . .	. . .	*–4,041*	*–12,151*	*–1,176*	*–1,897*	*9,738*
Liabilities	4 753 . .	**–1,496**	**5,116**	**1,282**	**12,028**	**–8,619**	**3,854**	**12,329**	**–3,933**
Trade credits	4 756 . .	447	712	934	. . .	. . .	13,267	18,232	–2,442
General government	4 757 . .	. . .	. . .	. . .	. . .	. . .	. . .	. . .	. . .
of which: Short-term	4 759 . .	. . .	. . .	. . .	. . .	. . .	. . .	. . .	. . .
Other sectors	4 760 . .	447	712	934	. . .	. . .	13,267	18,232	–2,442
of which: Short-term	4 762 . .	. . .	. . .	. . .	. . .	. . .	*13,267*	*18,232*	*–2,442*
Loans	4 764 . .	1,169	3,979	1,935	3,411	–3,267	–548	–2,391	–1,489
Monetary authorities	4 765 . .	. . .	. . .	. . .	. . .	. . .	. . .	. . .	. . .
of which: Use of Fund credit and loans from the Fund	4 766 . .	. . .	. . .	. . .	. . .	. . .	. . .	. . .	. . .
of which: Short-term	4 768 . .	. . .	. . .	. . .	. . .	. . .	. . .	. . .	. . .
General government	4 769 . .	5,178	6,021	4,995	. . .	. . .	3,233	3,153	1,124
of which: Short-term	4 771 . .	. . .	. . .	. . .	. . .	. . .	. . .	. . .	. . .
Banks	4 772 . .	–4,808	–2,826	–4,030	. . .	. . .	–398	–3,712	–1,543
of which: Short-term	4 774 . .	. . .	. . .	. . .	. . .	. . .	*–685*	*–363*	*–314*
Other sectors	4 775 . .	799	784	970	3,411	–3,267	–3,383	–1,832	–1,070
of which: Short-term	4 777 . .	. . .	. . .	. . .	*201*	*–951*	*–17*	*–172*	*23*
Currency and deposits	4 780 . .	–414	–1,219	–1,929	–2,039	–5,287	–3,932	–54	492
Monetary authorities	4 781 . .	. . .	. . .	. . .	–2,037	–5,441	–3,936	. . .	. . .
General government	4 782 . .	. . .	. . .	. . .	. . .	. . .	. . .	. . .	. . .
Banks	4 783 . .	–414	–1,219	–1,929	–2	154	4	–54	490
Other sectors	4 784 . .	. . .	. . .	. . .	. . .	. . .	. . .	. . .	2
Other liabilities	4 786 . .	–2,698	1,644	342	10,656	–65	–4,933	–3,459	–494
Monetary authorities	4 787 . .	1,004	1,154	1,256	. . .	. . .	. . .	. . .	. . .
of which: Short-term	4 789 . .	*1,004*	*1,154*	*1,256*	. . .	. . .	. . .	. . .	. . .
General government	4 790 . .	. . .	. . .	. . .	. . .	. . .	. . .	. . .	. . .
of which: Short-term	4 792 . .	. . .	. . .	. . .	. . .	. . .	. . .	. . .	. . .
Banks	4 793 . .	. . .	. . .	. . .	6,970	–3,304	–4,627	–4,516	–252
of which: Short-term	4 795 . .	. . .	. . .	. . .	*6,970*	*–3,304*	*–4,780*	*–4,366*	*–4*
Other sectors	4 796 . .	–3,702	490	–914	3,686	3,239	–306	1,057	–242
of which: Short-term	4 798 . .	*–3,702*	*490*	*–914*	*616*	*654*	*876*	*431*	*616*
E. RESERVE ASSETS	4 802 . .	–30,453	–22,469	–31,705	–35,857	–6,248	–8,652	–10,693	–47,447
Monetary gold	4 812 . .	. . .	. . .	. . .	. . .	. . .	. . .	. . .	. . .
Special drawing rights	4 811 . .	–24	–34	–52	–26	–46	–81	–96	–82
Reserve position in the Fund	4 810 . .	–7	–458	–222	–969	–1,133	1,144	301	–774
Foreign exchange	4 803 . .	–30,421	–21,977	–31,431	–34,862	–5,069	–9,716	–10,898	–46,591
Other claims	4 813 . .	. . .	. . .	. . .	. . .	. . .	. . .	. . .	. . .
NET ERRORS AND OMISSIONS	4 998 . .	**–9,100**	**–17,823**	**–15,504**	**–22,122**	**–18,902**	**–17,641**	**–11,748**	**–4,732**

Part 3 of the *Yearbook* contains descriptions of the methodologies, compilation practices, and sources used to compile these data.

Table 1. ANALYTIC PRESENTATION, 1994–2001
(Millions of U.S. dollars)

	Code	1994	1995	1996	1997	1998	1999	2000	2001
A. Current Account [1]	4 993 Z.	...	...	...	...	**4,426**	**12,041**	**9,107**	**11,736**
Goods: exports f.o.b	2 100 ..	...	...	...	...	175,833	174,719	202,698	190,926
Goods: imports f.o.b	3 100 ..	...	...	...	...	–183,666	–177,878	–210,891	–199,257
Balance on Goods	4 100 ..	...	...	...	...	*–7,833*	*–3,159*	*–8,193*	*–8,331*
Services: credit	2 200 ..	...	...	...	...	35,132	35,983	40,759	41,428
Services: debit	3 200 ..	...	...	...	...	–24,991	–23,725	–24,584	–24,314
Balance on Goods and Services	4 991 ..	...	...	...	...	*2,309*	*9,098*	*7,981*	*8,783*
Income: credit	2 300 ..	...	...	...	...	46,831	47,031	53,494	48,010
Income: debit	3 300 ..	...	...	...	...	–43,117	–42,548	–50,699	–43,377
Balance on Goods, Services, and Income	4 992 ..	...	...	...	...	*6,023*	*13,581*	*10,777*	*13,417*
Current transfers: credit	2 379 Z.	...	...	...	...	669	570	538	813
Current transfers: debit	3 379 ..	...	...	...	...	–2,265	–2,109	–2,208	–2,495
B. Capital Account [1]	4 994 Z.	...	...	...	...	**–2,382**	**–1,780**	**–1,546**	**–1,162**
Capital account: credit	2 994 Z.	...	...	...	...	377	103	57	36
Capital account: debit	3 994 ..	...	...	...	...	–2,759	–1,883	–1,602	–1,198
Total, Groups A Plus B	4 981 ..	...	...	...	...	*2,045*	*10,261*	*7,561*	*10,574*
C. Financial Account [1]	4 995 W.	...	...	...	...	**–8,476**	**1,061**	**4,165**	**–5,146**
Direct investment abroad	4 505 ..	...	...	...	...	–16,985	–19,369	–59,352	–8,977
Direct investment in China, P.R.: Hong Kong	4 555 Z.	...	...	...	...	14,765	24,578	61,924	22,834
Portfolio investment assets	4 602 ..	...	...	...	...	25,492	–25,440	–22,022	–39,131
Equity securities	4 610 ..	...	...	...	...	8,507	–30,337	–17,606	–22,654
Debt securities	4 619 ..	...	...	...	...	16,985	4,897	–4,416	–16,478
Portfolio investment liabilities	4 652 Z.	...	...	...	...	–3,407	58,525	46,508	–531
Equity securities	4 660 ..	...	...	...	...	–2,106	60,470	46,976	596
Debt securities	4 669 Z.	...	...	...	...	–1,301	–1,944	–468	–1,127
Financial derivatives	4 910 ..	...	...	...	...	3,299	10,214	205	5,015
Financial derivatives assets	4 900 ..	...	...	...	...	10,837	21,224	8,445	17,506
Financial derivatives liabilities	4 905 ..	...	...	...	...	–7,538	–11,011	–8,240	–12,492
Other investment assets	4 703 ..	...	...	...	...	119,830	42,963	18,279	58,243
Monetary authorities	4 701 ..	...	...	...	...	...	...	...	...
General government	4 704 ..	...	...	...	...	...	...	...	...
Banks	4 705 ..	...	...	...	...	101,774	34,181	23,857	56,847
Other sectors	4 728 ..	...	...	...	...	18,057	8,781	–5,578	1,396
Other investment liabilities	4 753 W.	...	...	...	...	–151,470	–90,410	–41,375	–42,599
Monetary authorities	4 753 WA	...	...	...	...	...	...	...	...
General government	4 753 ZB	...	...	...	...	...	...	...	...
Banks	4 753 ZC	...	...	...	...	–148,616	–85,768	–44,259	–42,780
Other sectors	4 753 ZD	...	...	...	...	–2,854	–4,642	2,884	181
Total, Groups A Through C	4 983 ..	...	...	...	...	*–6,431*	*11,322*	*11,726*	*5,428*
D. Net Errors and Omissions	4 998 ..	...	...	...	...	**–358**	**–1,295**	**–1,683**	**–744**
Total, Groups A Through D	4 984 ..	...	...	...	...	*–6,789*	*10,028*	*10,044*	*4,684*
E. Reserves and Related Items	4 802 A.	...	...	...	...	**6,789**	**–10,028**	**–10,044**	**–4,684**
Reserve assets	4 802 ..	...	...	...	...	6,789	–10,028	–10,044	–4,684
Use of Fund credit and loans	4 766 ..	...	...	...	...	...	...	...	...
Exceptional financing	4 920 ..	...	...	...	...	...	...	...	...
Conversion rates: Hong Kong dollars per U.S. dollar	0 101 ..	**7.7284**	**7.7358**	**7.7343**	**7.7421**	**7.7453**	**7.7575**	**7.7912**	**7.7988**

[1] Excludes components that have been classified in the categories of Group E.

Table 2. STANDARD PRESENTATION, 1994–2001
(Millions of U.S. dollars)

	Code	1994	1995	1996	1997	1998	1999	2000	2001
CURRENT ACCOUNT	4 993 . .	**. . .**	**. . .**	**. . .**	**. . .**	**4,426**	**12,041**	**9,107**	**11,736**
A. GOODS	4 100 . .	. . .	. . .	. . .	. . .	–7,833	–3,159	–8,193	–8,331
Credit	2 100 . .	**. . .**	**. . .**	**. . .**	**. . .**	**175,833**	**174,719**	**202,698**	**190,926**
General merchandise: exports f.o.b.	2 110 . .	. . .	. . .	. . .	. . .	. . .	. . .	. . .	. . .
Goods for processing: exports f.o.b.	2 150 . .	. . .	. . .	. . .	. . .	. . .	. . .	. . .	. . .
Repairs on goods	2 160 . .	. . .	. . .	. . .	. . .	. . .	. . .	. . .	. . .
Goods procured in ports by carriers	2 170 . .	. . .	. . .	. . .	. . .	. . .	. . .	. . .	. . .
Nonmonetary gold	2 180 . .	. . .	. . .	. . .	. . .	. . .	. . .	. . .	. . .
Debit	3 100 . .	**. . .**	**. . .**	**. . .**	**. . .**	**–183,666**	**–177,878**	**–210,891**	**–199,257**
General merchandise: imports f.o.b.	3 110 . .	. . .	. . .	. . .	. . .	. . .	. . .	. . .	. . .
Goods for processing: imports f.o.b.	3 150 . .	. . .	. . .	. . .	. . .	. . .	. . .	. . .	. . .
Repairs on goods	3 160 . .	. . .	. . .	. . .	. . .	. . .	. . .	. . .	. . .
Goods procured in ports by carriers	3 170 . .	. . .	. . .	. . .	. . .	. . .	. . .	. . .	. . .
Nonmonetary gold	3 180 . .	. . .	. . .	. . .	. . .	. . .	. . .	. . .	. . .
B. SERVICES	4 200 . .	. . .	. . .	. . .	. . .	10,142	12,257	16,175	17,114
Total credit	2 200 . .	. . .	. . .	. . .	. . .	*35,132*	*35,983*	*40,759*	*41,428*
Total debit	3 200 . .	. . .	. . .	. . .	. . .	*–24,991*	*–23,725*	*–24,584*	*–24,314*
Transportation services, credit	2 205 . .	**. . .**	**. . .**	**. . .**	**. . .**	**10,984**	**11,502**	**12,772**	**. . .**
Passenger	2 850 . .	. . .	. . .	. . .	. . .	. . .	. . .	. . .	. . .
Freight	2 851 . .	. . .	. . .	. . .	. . .	. . .	. . .	. . .	. . .
Other	2 852 . .	. . .	. . .	. . .	. . .	. . .	. . .	. . .	. . .
Sea transport, passenger	2 207 . .	. . .	. . .	. . .	. . .	. . .	. . .	. . .	. . .
Sea transport, freight	2 208 . .	. . .	. . .	. . .	. . .	. . .	. . .	. . .	. . .
Sea transport, other	2 209 . .	. . .	. . .	. . .	. . .	. . .	. . .	. . .	. . .
Air transport, passenger	2 211 . .	. . .	. . .	. . .	. . .	. . .	. . .	. . .	. . .
Air transport, freight	2 212 . .	. . .	. . .	. . .	. . .	. . .	. . .	. . .	. . .
Air transport, other	2 213 . .	. . .	. . .	. . .	. . .	. . .	. . .	. . .	. . .
Other transport, passenger	2 215 . .	. . .	. . .	. . .	. . .	. . .	. . .	. . .	. . .
Other transport, freight	2 216 . .	. . .	. . .	. . .	. . .	. . .	. . .	. . .	. . .
Other transport, other	2 217 . .	. . .	. . .	. . .	. . .	. . .	. . .	. . .	. . .
Transportation services, debit	3 205 . .	**. . .**	**. . .**	**. . .**	**. . .**	**–5,534**	**–5,058**	**–6,241**	**. . .**
Passenger	3 850 . .	. . .	. . .	. . .	. . .	. . .	. . .	. . .	. . .
Freight	3 851 . .	. . .	. . .	. . .	. . .	. . .	. . .	. . .	. . .
Other	3 852 . .	. . .	. . .	. . .	. . .	. . .	. . .	. . .	. . .
Sea transport, passenger	3 207 . .	. . .	. . .	. . .	. . .	. . .	. . .	. . .	. . .
Sea transport, freight	3 208 . .	. . .	. . .	. . .	. . .	. . .	. . .	. . .	. . .
Sea transport, other	3 209 . .	. . .	. . .	. . .	. . .	. . .	. . .	. . .	. . .
Air transport, passenger	3 211 . .	. . .	. . .	. . .	. . .	. . .	. . .	. . .	. . .
Air transport, freight	3 212 . .	. . .	. . .	. . .	. . .	. . .	. . .	. . .	. . .
Air transport, other	3 213 . .	. . .	. . .	. . .	. . .	. . .	. . .	. . .	. . .
Other transport, passenger	3 215 . .	. . .	. . .	. . .	. . .	. . .	. . .	. . .	. . .
Other transport, freight	3 216 . .	. . .	. . .	. . .	. . .	. . .	. . .	. . .	. . .
Other transport, other	3 217 . .	. . .	. . .	. . .	. . .	. . .	. . .	. . .	. . .
Travel, credit	2 236 . .	**. . .**	**. . .**	**. . .**	**. . .**	**7,574**	**7,279**	**7,930**	**. . .**
Business travel	2 237 . .	. . .	. . .	. . .	. . .	. . .	. . .	. . .	. . .
Personal travel	2 240 . .	. . .	. . .	. . .	. . .	. . .	. . .	. . .	. . .
Travel, debit	3 236 . .	**. . .**	**. . .**	**. . .**	**. . .**	**–13,474**	**–13,135**	**–12,502**	**. . .**
Business travel	3 237 . .	. . .	. . .	. . .	. . .	. . .	. . .	. . .	. . .
Personal travel	3 240 . .	. . .	. . .	. . .	. . .	. . .	. . .	. . .	. . .
Other services, credit	2 200 BA	**. . .**	**. . .**	**. . .**	**. . .**	**16,575**	**17,202**	**20,057**	**. . .**
Communications	2 245 . .	. . .	. . .	. . .	. . .	835	450	362	. . .
Construction	2 249 . .	. . .	. . .	. . .	. . .	372	343	338	. . .
Insurance	2 253 . .	. . .	. . .	. . .	. . .	400	395	443	. . .
Financial	2 260 . .	. . .	. . .	. . .	. . .	2,108	2,475	2,677	. . .
Computer and information	2 262 . .	. . .	. . .	. . .	. . .	139	126	60	. . .
Royalties and licence fees	2 266 . .	. . .	. . .	. . .	. . .	155	78	107	. . .
Other business services	2 268 . .	. . .	. . .	. . .	. . .	12,403	13,193	15,952	. . .
Personal, cultural, and recreational	2 287 . .	. . .	. . .	. . .	. . .	113	85	51	. . .
Government, n.i.e.	2 291 . .	. . .	. . .	. . .	. . .	49	57	67	. . .
Other services, debit	3 200 BA	**. . .**	**. . .**	**. . .**	**. . .**	**–5,982**	**–5,533**	**–5,841**	**. . .**
Communications	3 245 . .	. . .	. . .	. . .	. . .	–1,138	–751	–698	. . .
Construction	3 249 . .	. . .	. . .	. . .	. . .	–547	–439	–415	. . .
Insurance	3 253 . .	. . .	. . .	. . .	. . .	–594	–641	–528	. . .
Financial	3 260 . .	. . .	. . .	. . .	. . .	–870	–738	–711	. . .
Computer and information	3 262 . .	. . .	. . .	. . .	. . .	–113	–110	–128	. . .
Royalties and licence fees	3 266 . .	. . .	. . .	. . .	. . .	–537	–281	–461	. . .
Other business services	3 268 . .	. . .	. . .	. . .	. . .	–2,016	–2,415	–2,726	. . .
Personal, cultural, and recreational	3 287 . .	. . .	. . .	. . .	. . .	–51	–47	–65	. . .
Government, n.i.e.	3 291 . .	. . .	. . .	. . .	. . .	–117	–111	–110	. . .

Table 2 (Continued). STANDARD PRESENTATION, 1994–2001
(Millions of U.S. dollars)

	Code	1994	1995	1996	1997	1998	1999	2000	2001
C. INCOME	4 300 . .	...	...	...	...	3,714	4,483	2,795	4,634
Total credit	2 300 . .	...	...	...	...	*46,831*	*47,031*	*53,494*	*48,010*
Total debit	3 300 . .	...	...	...	...	*–43,117*	*–42,548*	*–50,699*	*–43,377*
Compensation of employees, credit	2 310 . .	...	...	...	...	**47**	**14**	**7**	**5**
Compensation of employees, debit	3 310 . .	...	...	...	...	**–47**	**–14**	**–7**	**–5**
Investment income, credit	2 320 . .	...	...	...	...	**46,784**	**47,016**	**53,487**	**48,006**
Direct investment income	2 330 . .	...	...	...	...	16,139	17,587	19,748	20,170
Dividends and distributed branch profits	2 332 . .	...	...	...	...	8,609	8,291	8,402	7,879
Reinvested earnings and undistributed branch profits	2 333 . .	...	...	...	...	6,703	8,018	10,450	11,710
Income on debt (interest)	2 334 . .	...	...	...	...	827	1,279	896	581
Portfolio investment income	2 339 . .	...	...	...	...	9,612	11,124	12,204	12,275
Income on equity	2 340 . .	...	...	...	...	1,982	2,707	2,822	2,476
Income on bonds and notes	2 350 . .	...	...	...	...	6,841	7,643	8,388	9,010
Income on money market instruments	2 360 . .	...	...	...	...	789	774	994	788
Other investment income	2 370 . .	...	...	...	...	21,034	18,305	21,535	15,561
Investment income, debit	3 320 . .	...	...	...	...	**–43,070**	**–42,534**	**–50,692**	**–43,372**
Direct investment income	3 330 . .	...	...	...	...	–17,604	–25,403	–34,183	–30,735
Dividends and distributed branch profits	3 332 . .	...	...	...	...	–10,987	–12,170	–13,933	–17,345
Reinvested earnings and undistributed branch profits	3 333 . .	...	...	...	...	–5,771	–12,140	–19,289	–12,616
Income on debt (interest)	3 334 . .	...	...	...	...	–845	–1,093	–961	–774
Portfolio investment income	3 339 . .	...	...	...	...	–3,189	–3,275	–3,452	–3,501
Income on equity	3 340 . .	...	...	...	...	–2,271	–2,405	–2,645	–2,677
Income on bonds and notes	3 350 . .	...	...	...	...	–639	–649	–597	–670
Income on money market instruments	3 360 . .	...	...	...	...	–278	–221	–210	–153
Other investment income	3 370 . .	...	...	...	...	–22,278	–13,856	–13,057	–9,137
D. CURRENT TRANSFERS	4 379 . .	...	...	...	...	–1,596	–1,540	–1,670	–1,681
Credit	2 379 . .	...	...	...	...	**669**	**570**	**538**	**813**
General government	2 380 . .	...	...	...	...	...	...	...	...
Other sectors	2 390 . .	...	...	...	...	669	570	538	813
Workers' remittances	2 391 . .	...	...	...	...	...	...	...	...
Other current transfers	2 392 . .	...	...	...	...	...	...	...	...
Debit	3 379 . .	...	...	...	...	**–2,265**	**–2,109**	**–2,208**	**–2,495**
General government	3 380 . .	...	...	...	...	–165	–165	–166	–167
Other sectors	3 390 . .	...	...	...	...	–2,100	–1,944	–2,042	–2,327
Workers' remittances	3 391 . .	...	...	...	...	...	...	...	...
Other current transfers	3 392 . .	...	...	...	...	...	...	...	...
CAPITAL AND FINANCIAL ACCOUNT	4 996 . .	...	...	...	...	**–4,068**	**–10,747**	**–7,424**	**–10,991**
CAPITAL ACCOUNT	4 994 . .	...	...	...	...	**–2,382**	**–1,780**	**–1,546**	**–1,162**
Total credit	2 994 . .	...	...	...	...	*377*	*103*	*57*	*36*
Total debit	3 994 . .	...	...	...	...	*–2,759*	*–1,883*	*–1,602*	*–1,198*
Capital transfers, credit	2 400 . .	...	...	...	...	**377**	**103**	**57**	**36**
General government	2 401 . .	...	...	...	...	...	...	...	...
Debt forgiveness	2 402 . .	...	...	...	...	...	...	...	...
Other capital transfers	2 410 . .	...	...	...	...	...	...	...	...
Other sectors	2 430 . .	...	...	...	...	377	103	57	36
Migrants' transfers	2 431 . .	...	...	...	...	...	...	...	...
Debt forgiveness	2 432 . .	...	...	...	...	...	...	...	...
Other capital transfers	2 440 . .	...	...	...	...	...	...	...	...
Capital transfers, debit	3 400 . .	...	...	...	...	**–2,759**	**–1,883**	**–1,602**	**–1,198**
General government	3 401 . .	...	...	...	...	...	...	...	...
Debt forgiveness	3 402 . .	...	...	...	...	...	...	...	...
Other capital transfers	3 410 . .	...	...	...	...	...	...	...	...
Other sectors	3 430 . .	...	...	...	...	–2,759	–1,883	–1,602	–1,198
Migrants' transfers	3 431 . .	...	...	...	...	...	...	...	...
Debt forgiveness	3 432 . .	...	...	...	...	...	...	...	...
Other capital transfers	3 440 . .	...	...	...	...	...	...	...	...
Nonproduced nonfinancial assets, credit	2 480 . .	...	...	...	...	...	...	...	...
Nonproduced nonfinancial assets, debit	3 480 . .	...	...	...	...	...	...	...	...

Table 2 (Continued). STANDARD PRESENTATION, 1994–2001
(Millions of U.S. dollars)

	Code	1994	1995	1996	1997	1998	1999	2000	2001
FINANCIAL ACCOUNT	4 995	...	...	...	...	**–1,687**	**–8,967**	**–5,878**	**–9,830**
A. DIRECT INVESTMENT	4 500	...	...	...	...	–2,220	5,209	2,572	13,857
Direct investment abroad	4 505	...	...	...	...	**–16,985**	**–19,369**	**–59,352**	**–8,977**
Equity capital	4 510	...	...	...	...	–3,108	1,461	–49,153	–2,254
Claims on affiliated enterprises	4 515	...	...	...	...	–3,108	1,445	–49,153	–2,254
Liabilities to affiliated enterprises	4 520	...	...	...	...	...	16	...	...
Reinvested earnings	4 525	...	...	...	...	–6,703	–8,018	–10,450	–11,710
Other capital	4 530	...	...	...	...	–7,173	–12,812	251	4,987
Claims on affiliated enterprises	4 535	...	...	...	...	–6,778	–12,275	–8,270	–1,755
Liabilities to affiliated enterprises	4 540	...	...	...	...	–396	–537	8,521	6,742
Direct investment in China, P.R.: Hong Kong	4 555	...	...	...	...	**14,765**	**24,578**	**61,924**	**22,834**
Equity capital	4 560	...	...	...	...	1,323	4,311	32,940	7,003
Claims on direct investors	4 565	...	...	...	...	...	...	...	...
Liabilities to direct investors	4 570	...	...	...	...	1,323	4,311	32,940	7,003
Reinvested earnings	4 575	...	...	...	...	5,771	12,140	19,289	12,616
Other capital	4 580	...	...	...	...	7,671	8,126	9,695	3,215
Claims on direct investors	4 585	...	...	...	...	430	–1,518	–231	–646
Liabilities to direct investors	4 590	...	...	...	...	7,241	9,644	9,925	3,861
B. PORTFOLIO INVESTMENT	4 600	...	...	...	...	22,085	33,086	24,485	–39,662
Assets	4 602	...	...	...	...	**25,492**	**–25,440**	**–22,022**	**–39,131**
Equity securities	4 610	...	...	...	...	8,507	–30,337	–17,606	–22,654
Monetary authorities	4 611	...	...	...	...	...	...	...	...
General government	4 612	...	...	...	...	...	...	...	...
Banks	4 613	...	...	...	...	51	–30	–24	14
Other sectors	4 614	...	...	...	...	8,455	–30,307	–17,582	–22,668
Debt securities	4 619	...	...	...	...	16,985	4,897	–4,416	–16,478
Bonds and notes	4 620	...	...	...	...	15,907	4,489	–4,487	–16,186
Monetary authorities	4 621	...	...	...	...	...	...	...	...
General government	4 622	...	...	...	...	...	...	...	...
Banks	4 623	...	...	...	...	8,031	–4,230	–15,022	–12,921
Other sectors	4 624	...	...	...	...	7,876	8,719	10,535	–3,265
Money market instruments	4 630	...	...	...	...	1,078	408	71	–292
Monetary authorities	4 631	...	...	...	...	...	...	...	...
General government	4 632	...	...	...	...	...	...	...	...
Banks	4 633	...	...	...	...	802	1,489	344	–489
Other sectors	4 634	...	...	...	...	276	–1,081	–273	197
Liabilities	4 652	...	...	...	...	**–3,407**	**58,525**	**46,508**	**–531**
Equity securities	4 660	...	...	...	...	–2,106	60,470	46,976	596
Banks	4 663	...	...	...	...	–260	2,207	1,658	589
Other sectors	4 664	...	...	...	...	–1,846	58,263	45,318	7
Debt securities	4 669	...	...	...	...	–1,301	–1,944	–468	–1,127
Bonds and notes	4 670	...	...	...	...	–1,025	–3,371	–5	–1,467
Monetary authorities	4 671	...	...	...	...	...	...	...	...
General government	4 672	...	...	...	...	...	...	...	...
Banks	4 673	...	...	...	...	–667	–874	–378	–861
Other sectors	4 674	...	...	...	...	–358	–2,497	373	–605
Money market instruments	4 680	...	...	...	...	–276	1,427	–463	340
Monetary authorities	4 681	...	...	...	...	...	...	...	...
General government	4 682	...	...	...	...	...	...	...	...
Banks	4 683	...	...	...	...	–187	700	–59	169
Other sectors	4 684	...	...	...	...	–89	727	–404	171
C. FINANCIAL DERIVATIVES	4 910	...	...	...	...	3,299	10,214	205	5,015
Monetary authorities	4 911	...	...	...	...	...	...	...	...
General government	4 912	...	...	...	...	...	...	...	...
Banks	4 913	...	...	...	...	3,719	9,371	–741	4,577
Other sectors	4 914	...	...	...	...	–420	842	947	437
Assets	4 900	...	...	...	...	**10,837**	**21,224**	**8,445**	**17,506**
Monetary authorities	4 901	...	...	...	...	...	...	...	...
General government	4 902	...	...	...	...	...	...	...	...
Banks	4 903	...	...	...	...	10,046	18,963	7,146	16,627
Other sectors	4 904	...	...	...	...	791	2,262	1,298	879
Liabilities	4 905	...	...	...	...	**–7,538**	**–11,011**	**–8,240**	**–12,492**
Monetary authorities	4 906	...	...	...	...	...	...	...	...
General government	4 907	...	...	...	...	...	...	...	...
Banks	4 908	...	...	...	...	–6,327	–9,592	–7,888	–12,050
Other sectors	4 909	...	...	...	...	–1,211	–1,419	–352	–442

Table 2 (Concluded). STANDARD PRESENTATION, 1994–2001
(Millions of U.S. dollars)

	Code	1994	1995	1996	1997	1998	1999	2000	2001
D. OTHER INVESTMENT	4 700	...	...	...	...	–31,639	–47,447	–23,097	15,645
Assets	4 703	**...**	**...**	**...**	**...**	**119,830**	**42,963**	**18,279**	**58,243**
Trade credits	4 706	...	...	...	...	–810	–2,962	–712	417
General government	4 707	...	...	...	...	...	...	...	...
of which: Short-term	4 709	...	...	...	...	...	...	...	...
Other sectors	4 710	...	...	...	...	–810	–2,962	–712	417
of which: Short-term	4 712	...	...	...	...	...	...	...	...
Loans	4 714	...	...	...	...	107,480	43,159	42,591	27,607
Monetary authorities	4 715	...	...	...	...	...	...	...	...
of which: Short-term	4 718	...	...	...	...	...	...	...	...
General government	4 719	...	...	...	...	...	...	...	...
of which: Short-term	4 721	...	...	...	...	...	...	...	...
Banks	4 722	...	...	...	...	106,901	39,103	42,141	27,980
of which: Short-term	4 724	...	...	...	...	...	...	...	...
Other sectors	4 725	...	...	...	...	578	4,056	450	–373
of which: Short-term	4 727	...	...	...	...	...	...	...	...
Currency and deposits	4 730	...	...	...	...	13,653	3,941	–22,504	28,451
Monetary authorities	4 731	...	...	...	...	...	...	...	...
General government	4 732	...	...	...	...	...	...	...	...
Banks	4 733	...	...	...	...	–5,455	–4,934	–18,208	28,712
Other sectors	4 734	...	...	...	...	19,108	8,875	–4,296	–261
Other assets	4 736	...	...	...	...	–493	–1,176	–1,096	1,768
Monetary authorities	4 737	...	...	...	...	...	...	...	...
of which: Short-term	4 739	...	...	...	...	...	...	...	...
General government	4 740	...	...	...	...	...	...	...	...
of which: Short-term	4 742	...	...	...	...	...	...	...	...
Banks	4 743	...	...	...	...	327	13	–76	155
of which: Short-term	4 745	...	...	...	...	...	...	...	...
Other sectors	4 746	...	...	...	...	–820	–1,189	–1,020	1,613
of which: Short-term	4 748	...	...	...	...	...	...	...	...
Liabilities	4 753	**...**	**...**	**...**	**...**	**–151,470**	**–90,410**	**–41,375**	**–42,599**
Trade credits	4 756	...	...	...	...	–124	398	602	–894
General government	4 757	...	...	...	...	...	...	...	...
of which: Short-term	4 759	...	...	...	...	...	...	...	...
Other sectors	4 760	...	...	...	...	–124	398	602	–894
of which: Short-term	4 762	...	...	...	...	...	...	...	...
Loans	4 764	...	...	...	...	–3,503	–6,813	654	–1,741
Monetary authorities	4 765	...	...	...	...	...	...	...	...
of which: Use of Fund credit and loans from the Fund	4 766	...	...	...	...	...	...	...	...
of which: Short-term	4 768	...	...	...	...	...	...	...	...
General government	4 769	...	...	...	...	...	...	...	...
of which: Short-term	4 771	...	...	...	...	...	...	...	...
Banks	4 772	...	...	...	...	–288	–1,695	–1,272	–3,348
of which: Short-term	4 774	...	...	...	...	...	...	...	...
Other sectors	4 775	...	...	...	...	–3,215	–5,118	1,926	1,607
of which: Short-term	4 777	...	...	...	...	...	...	...	...
Currency and deposits	4 780	...	...	...	...	–149,157	–84,278	–43,004	–39,527
Monetary authorities	4 781	...	...	...	...	...	...	...	...
General government	4 782	...	...	...	...	...	...	...	...
Banks	4 783	...	...	...	...	–148,399	–84,189	–43,015	–39,545
Other sectors	4 784	...	...	...	...	–758	–88	12	18
Other liabilities	4 786	...	...	...	...	1,315	284	372	–436
Monetary authorities	4 787	...	...	...	...	...	...	...	...
of which: Short-term	4 789	...	...	...	...	...	...	...	...
General government	4 790	...	...	...	...	...	...	...	...
of which: Short-term	4 792	...	...	...	...	...	...	...	...
Banks	4 793	...	...	...	...	72	116	28	114
of which: Short-term	4 795	...	...	...	...	...	...	...	...
Other sectors	4 796	...	...	...	...	1,243	168	344	–550
of which: Short-term	4 798	...	...	...	...	...	...	...	...
E. RESERVE ASSETS	4 802	...	...	...	...	6,789	–10,028	–10,044	–4,684
Monetary gold	4 812	...	...	...	...	...	...	...	...
Special drawing rights	4 811	...	...	...	...	...	...	...	...
Reserve position in the Fund	4 810	...	...	...	...	–44	43	...	...
Foreign exchange	4 803	...	...	...	...	6,833	–10,070	–10,044	–4,684
Other claims	4 813	...	...	...	...	...	...	...	...
NET ERRORS AND OMISSIONS	4 998	**...**	**...**	**...**	**...**	**–358**	**–1,295**	**–1,683**	**–744**

Part 3 of the *Yearbook* contains descriptions of the methodologies, compilation practices, and sources used to compile these data.

Table 3. INTERNATIONAL INVESTMENT POSITION (End–period stocks), 1994–2001

(Millions of U.S. dollars)

	Code	1994	1995	1996	1997	1998	1999	2000	2001
ASSETS	8 995 C.	...	...	...	...	...	...	1,141,521	1,088,595
Direct investment abroad	8 505 . .	...	...	...	**235,796**	**223,907**	**321,692**	**388,380**	**360,030**
Equity capital and reinvested earnings	8 506 . .	...	...	...	181,796	165,440	246,973	317,105	294,750
Claims on affiliated enterprises	8 507 . .	...	...	...	181,796	165,440	246,988	317,105	294,750
Liabilities to affiliated enterprises	8 508 . .	...	...	...	...	...	–15	...	...
Other capital	8 530 . .	...	...	...	54,000	58,467	74,719	71,274	65,280
Claims on affiliated enterprises	8 535 . .	...	...	...	69,124	73,098	90,212	94,384	94,991
Liabilities to affiliated enterprises	8 540 . .	...	...	...	–15,124	–14,631	–15,494	–23,110	–29,711
Portfolio investment	8 602 . .	...	...	...	...	...	...	**178,851**	**210,307**
Equity securities	8 610 . .	...	...	...	...	...	...	88,325	95,056
Monetary authorities	8 611 . .	...	...	...	...	...	...	...	...
General government	8 612 . .	...	...	...	...	...	...	...	...
Banks	8 613 . .	...	...	...	...	...	...	70	67
Other sectors	8 614 . .	...	...	...	...	...	...	88,255	94,989
Debt securities	8 619 . .	...	...	...	...	...	...	90,526	115,251
Bonds and notes	8 620 . .	...	...	...	...	...	...	67,217	90,229
Monetary authorities	8 621 . .	...	...	...	...	...	...	...	...
General government	8 622 . .	...	...	...	...	...	...	...	...
Banks	8 623 . .	...	...	...	...	...	...	41,959	59,307
Other sectors	8 624 . .	...	...	...	...	...	...	25,258	30,922
Money market instruments	8 630 . .	...	...	...	...	...	...	23,309	25,021
Monetary authorities	8 631 . .	...	...	...	...	...	...	...	...
General government	8 632 . .	...	...	...	...	...	...	...	...
Banks	8 633 . .	...	...	...	...	...	...	21,154	21,422
Other sectors	8 634 . .	...	...	...	...	...	...	2,155	3,599
Financial derivatives	8 900 . .	...	...	...	...	...	...	**16,812**	**18,019**
Monetary authorities	8 901 . .	...	...	...	...	...	...	...	...
General government	8 902 . .	...	...	...	...	...	...	...	...
Banks	8 903 . .	...	...	...	...	...	...	15,797	16,978
Other sectors	8 904 . .	...	...	...	...	...	...	1,015	1,041
Other investment	8 703 . .	...	...	...	...	...	...	**449,880**	**389,053**
Trade credits	8 706 . .	...	...	...	...	...	...	4,032	5,904
General government	8 707 . .	...	...	...	...	...	...	...	...
of which: Short-term	8 709 . .	...	...	...	...	...	...	...	...
Other sectors	8 710 . .	...	...	...	...	...	...	4,032	5,904
of which: Short-term	8 712 . .	...	...	...	...	...	...	...	...
Loans	8 714 . .	...	...	...	...	...	...	83,233	57,748
Monetary authorities	8 715 . .	...	...	...	...	...	...	...	...
of which: Short-term	8 718 . .	...	...	...	...	...	...	...	...
General government	8 719 . .	...	...	...	...	...	...	...	...
of which: Short-term	8 721 . .	...	...	...	...	...	...	...	...
Banks	8 722 . .	...	...	...	...	...	...	76,858	44,616
of which: Short-term	8 724 . .	...	...	...	...	...	...	...	...
Other sectors	8 725 . .	...	...	...	...	...	...	6,375	13,131
of which: Short-term	8 727 . .	...	...	...	...	...	...	...	...
Currency and deposits	8 730 . .	...	...	...	...	...	...	356,949	319,261
Monetary authorities	8 731 . .	...	...	...	...	...	...	...	...
General government	8 732 . .	...	...	...	...	...	...	...	...
Banks	8 733 . .	...	...	...	...	...	...	315,007	271,388
Other sectors	8 734 . .	...	...	...	...	...	...	41,942	47,873
Other assets	8 736 . .	...	...	...	...	...	...	5,666	6,139
Monetary authorities	8 737 . .	...	...	...	...	...	...	...	...
of which: Short-term	8 739 . .	...	...	...	...	...	...	...	...
General government	8 740 . .	...	...	...	...	...	...	...	...
of which: Short-term	8 742 . .	...	...	...	...	...	...	...	...
Banks	8 743 . .	...	...	...	...	...	...	1,291	1,181
of which: Short-term	8 745 . .	...	...	...	...	...	...	...	...
Other sectors	8 746 . .	...	...	...	...	...	...	4,374	4,959
of which: Short-term	8 748 . .	...	...	...	...	...	...	...	...
Reserve assets	8 802 . .	...	...	...	**92,855**	**89,639**	**96,287**	**107,599**	**111,187**
Monetary gold	8 812 . .	...	...	...	...	...	...	...	...
Special drawing rights	8 811 . .	...	...	...	...	...	...	...	...
Reserve position in the Fund	8 810 . .	...	...	...	...	44	...	...	...
Foreign exchange	8 803 . .	...	...	...	...	...	...	...	...
Other claims	8 813 . .	...	...	...	...	...	...	...	...

Table 3 (Concluded). INTERNATIONAL INVESTMENT POSITION (End–period stocks), 1994–2001

(Millions of U.S. dollars)

	Code	1994	1995	1996	1997	1998	1999	2000	2001
LIABILITIES	8 995 D.	...	...	...	...	...	...	919,670	816,294
Direct investment in China: P.R.: Hong Kong	8 555 . .	**...**	**...**	**...**	**249,393**	**225,142**	**405,325**	**455,469**	**429,579**
Equity capital and reinvested earnings	8 556 . .	...	...	...	212,261	181,439	355,613	402,077	362,559
Claims on direct investors	8 557 . .	...	...	...	...	...	–9	...	...
Liabilities to direct investors	8 558 . .	...	...	...	212,261	181,439	355,622	402,077	362,559
Other capital	8 580 . .	...	...	...	37,133	43,703	49,713	53,393	67,020
Claims on direct investors	8 585 . .	...	...	...	–7,937	–7,421	–8,522	–13,344	–11,203
Liabilities to direct investors	8 590 . .	...	...	...	45,069	51,124	58,235	66,736	78,223
Portfolio investment	8 652 . .	**...**	**...**	**...**	**...**	**...**	**...**	**153,217**	**119,323**
Equity securities	8 660 . .	...	...	...	...	...	...	138,078	103,138
Banks	8 663 . .	...	...	...	...	...	...	8,102	6,377
Other sectors	8 664 . .	...	...	...	...	...	...	129,976	96,761
Debt securities	8 669 . .	...	...	...	...	...	...	15,139	16,185
Bonds and notes	8 670 . .	...	...	...	...	...	...	9,614	10,164
Monetary authorities	8 671 . .	...	...	...	...	...	...	...	...
General government	8 672 . .	...	...	...	...	...	...	...	...
Banks	8 673 . .	...	...	...	...	...	...	3,556	3,347
Other sectors	8 674 . .	...	...	...	...	...	...	6,058	6,817
Money market instruments	8 680 . .	...	...	...	...	...	...	5,525	6,021
Monetary authorities	8 681 . .	...	...	...	...	...	...	...	...
General government	8 682 . .	...	...	...	...	...	...	...	...
Banks	8 683 . .	...	...	...	...	...	...	2,715	3,134
Other sectors	8 684 . .	...	...	...	...	...	...	2,810	2,887
Financial derivatives	8 905 . .	**...**	**...**	**...**	**...**	**...**	**...**	**12,517**	**10,574**
Monetary authorities	8 906 . .	...	...	...	...	...	...	...	...
General government	8 907 . .	...	...	...	...	...	...	...	...
Banks	8 908 . .	...	...	...	...	...	...	11,917	10,088
Other sectors	8 909 . .	...	...	...	...	...	...	600	485
Other investment	8 753 . .	**...**	**...**	**...**	**...**	**...**	**...**	**298,467**	**256,818**
Trade credits	8 756 . .	...	...	...	...	...	...	2,121	2,792
General government	8 757 . .	...	...	...	...	...	...	...	...
of which: Short-term	8 759 . .	...	...	...	...	...	...	...	...
Other sectors	8 760 . .	...	...	...	...	...	...	2,121	2,792
of which: Short-term	8 762 . .	...	...	...	...	...	...	...	...
Loans	8 764 . .	...	...	...	...	...	...	34,804	34,156
Monetary authorities	8 765 . .	...	...	...	...	...	...	...	...
of which: Use of Fund credit and loans from the Fund	8 766 . .	...	...	...	...	...	...	...	...
of which: Short-term	8 768 . .	...	...	...	...	...	...	...	...
General government	8 769 . .	...	...	...	...	...	...	...	...
of which: Short-term	8 771 . .	...	...	...	...	...	...	...	...
Banks	8 772 . .	...	...	...	...	...	...	19,532	13,152
of which: Short-term	8 774 . .	...	...	...	...	...	...	...	...
Other sectors	8 775 . .	...	...	...	...	...	...	15,272	21,004
of which: Short-term	8 777 . .	...	...	...	...	...	...	...	...
Currency and deposits	8 780 . .	...	...	...	...	...	...	259,346	217,183
Monetary authorities	8 781 . .	...	...	...	...	...	...	...	...
General government	8 782 . .	...	...	...	...	...	...	...	...
Banks	8 783 . .	...	...	...	...	...	...	259,097	217,140
Other sectors	8 784 . .	...	...	...	...	...	...	249	43
Other liabilities	8 786 . .	...	...	...	...	...	...	2,196	2,688
Monetary authorities	8 787 . .	...	...	...	...	...	...	...	...
of which: Short-term	8 789 . .	...	...	...	...	...	...	...	...
General government	8 790 . .	...	...	...	...	...	...	...	...
of which: Short-term	8 792 . .	...	...	...	...	...	...	...	...
Banks	8 793 . .	...	...	...	...	...	...	387	534
of which: Short-term	8 795 . .	...	...	...	...	...	...	...	...
Other sectors	8 796 . .	...	...	...	...	...	...	1,809	2,155
of which: Short-term	8 798 . .	...	...	...	...	...	...	...	...
NET INTERNATIONAL INVESTMENT POSITION	8 995 . .	**...**	**...**	**...**	**...**	**...**	**...**	**221,851**	**272,301**
Conversion rates: Hong Kong dollars per U.S. dollar (end of period)	0 102 . .	**7.74**	**7.73**	**7.74**	**7.75**	**7.75**	**7.77**	**7.80**	**7.80**

Table 1. ANALYTIC PRESENTATION, 1994–2001
(Millions of U.S. dollars)

	Code	1994	1995	1996	1997	1998	1999	2000	2001
A. Current Account [1]	4 993 Z.	**–3,673**	**–4,596**	**–4,755**	**–5,885**	**–5,225**	**353**	**356**	**–1,789**
Goods: exports f.o.b	2 100 . .	9,059	10,594	10,966	12,065	11,480	12,037	13,620	12,775
Goods: imports f.o.b	3 100 . .	–11,288	–13,139	–13,058	–14,703	–13,930	–10,262	–11,090	–12,267
Balance on Goods	4 100 . .	*–2,229*	*–2,545*	*–2,092*	*–2,638*	*–2,450*	*1,775*	*2,531*	*508*
Services: credit	2 200 . .	1,571	1,700	2,192	2,152	1,952	1,882	2,004	2,157
Services: debit	3 200 . .	–2,626	–2,880	–3,385	–3,655	–3,414	–3,143	–3,311	–3,573
Balance on Goods and Services	4 991 . .	*–3,283*	*–3,725*	*–3,284*	*–4,141*	*–3,913*	*514*	*1,224*	*–908*
Income: credit	2 300 . .	706	677	707	885	882	792	858	739
Income: debit	3 300 . .	–2,164	–2,277	–2,774	–3,243	–2,640	–2,388	–3,388	–3,714
Balance on Goods, Services, and Income	4 992 . .	*–4,741*	*–5,325*	*–5,351*	*–6,498*	*–5,671*	*–1,082*	*–1,306*	*–3,882*
Current transfers: credit	2 379 Z.	1,262	963	814	831	608	1,683	1,900	2,395
Current transfers: debit	3 379 . .	–193	–234	–217	–217	–162	–248	–238	–302
B. Capital Account [1]	4 994 Z.	**. . .**	**. . .**	**. . .**	**. . .**	**. . .**	**. . .**	**. . .**	**. . .**
Capital account: credit	2 994 Z.	. . .	. . .	. . .	. . .	. . .	. . .	. . .	. . .
Capital account: debit	3 994 . .	. . .	. . .	. . .	. . .	. . .	. . .	. . .	. . .
Total, Groups A Plus B	4 981 . .	*–3,673*	*–4,596*	*–4,755*	*–5,885*	*–5,225*	*353*	*356*	*–1,789*
C. Financial Account [1]	4 995 W.	**3,530**	**4,476**	**6,851**	**6,731**	**3,718**	**–593**	**490**	**2,477**
Direct investment abroad	4 505 . .	–149	–256	–328	–809	–796	–116	–250	–42
Direct investment in Colombia	4 555 Z.	1,447	968	3,112	5,562	2,829	1,468	2,281	2,328
Portfolio investment assets	4 602 . .	–1,381	394	–586	–770	606	–1,735	–1,014	–3,480
Equity securities	4 610 . .	. . .	. . .	. . .	. . .	. . .	. . .	. . .	. . .
Debt securities	4 619 . .	–1,381	394	–586	–770	606	–1,735	–1,014	–3,480
Portfolio investment liabilities	4 652 Z.	1,502	1,041	2,270	1,712	1,057	689	1,436	3,452
Equity securities	4 660 . .	478	165	292	278	47	–27	17	–42
Debt securities	4 669 Z.	1,024	876	1,978	1,435	1,010	716	1,419	3,494
Financial derivatives	4 910 . .	. . .	. . .	. . .	295	–39	101	–103	–112
Financial derivatives assets	4 900 . .	. . .	. . .	. . .	. . .	. . .	. . .	. . .	. . .
Financial derivatives liabilities	4 905 . .	. . .	. . .	. . .	295	–39	101	–103	–112
Other investment assets	4 703 . .	161	320	–855	–1,407	–535	–438	–551	129
Monetary authorities	4 701 . .	. . .	. . .	. . .	1	–7	5	–8	8
General government	4 704 . .	. . .	. . .	–20	–20	–15	–23	–40	–35
Banks	4 705 . .	–70	58	–41	–231	–177	118	145	102
Other sectors	4 728 . .	231	262	–794	–1,157	–337	–539	–648	55
Other investment liabilities	4 753 W.	1,950	2,009	3,238	2,147	597	–562	–1,310	202
Monetary authorities	4 753 WA	–191	52	20	–15	–20	–11	–15	–12
General government	4 753 ZB	–418	–80	–266	–54	347	910	341	225
Banks	4 753 ZC	726	579	417	487	–861	–1,208	–1,149	–403
Other sectors	4 753 ZD	1,832	1,458	3,068	1,730	1,131	–253	–486	392
Total, Groups A Through C	4 983 . .	*–143*	*–120*	*2,096*	*846*	*–1,507*	*–240*	*846*	*689*
D. Net Errors and Omissions	4 998 . .	**325**	**115**	**–367**	**–568**	**109**	**–72**	**17**	**537**
Total, Groups A Through D	4 984 . .	*182*	*–5*	*1,729*	*278*	*–1,398*	*–312*	*862*	*1,226*
E. Reserves and Related Items	4 802 A.	**–182**	**5**	**–1,729**	**–278**	**1,398**	**312**	**–862**	**–1,226**
Reserve assets	4 802 . .	–182	5	–1,729	–278	1,398	312	–862	–1,226
Use of Fund credit and loans	4 766 . .	. . .	. . .	. . .	. . .	. . .	. . .	. . .	. . .
Exceptional financing	4 920 . .	. . .	. . .	. . .	. . .	. . .	. . .	–1	. . .
Conversion rates: Colombian pesos per U.S. dollar	0 101 . .	**844.84**	**912.83**	**1,036.69**	**1,140.96**	**1,426.04**	**1,756.23**	**2,087.90**	**2,299.63**

[1] Excludes components that have been classified in the categories of Group E.

Table 2. STANDARD PRESENTATION, 1994–2001

(Millions of U.S. dollars)

	Code	1994	1995	1996	1997	1998	1999	2000	2001
CURRENT ACCOUNT	4 993 . .	**–3,673**	**–4,596**	**–4,755**	**–5,885**	**–5,225**	**353**	**356**	**–1,789**
A. GOODS	4 100 . .	–2,229	–2,545	–2,092	–2,638	–2,450	1,775	2,531	508
Credit	2 100 . .	**9,059**	**10,594**	**10,966**	**12,065**	**11,480**	**12,037**	**13,620**	**12,775**
General merchandise: exports f.o.b.	2 110 . .	8,687	10,248	10,643	11,797	11,243	11,861	13,443	12,646
Goods for processing: exports f.o.b.	2 150 . .	27	22	14	1	17	18	12	5
Repairs on goods	2 160 . .	. . .	. . .	. . .	. . .	. . .	. . .	. . .	7
Goods procured in ports by carriers	2 170 . .	65	73	75	76	70	63	74	62
Nonmonetary gold	2 180 . .	279	251	234	191	150	96	91	55
Debit	3 100 . .	**–11,288**	**–13,139**	**–13,058**	**–14,703**	**–13,930**	**–10,262**	**–11,090**	**–12,267**
General merchandise: imports f.o.b.	3 110 . .	–11,199	–13,041	–12,934	–14,524	–13,827	–10,151	–10,945	–12,154
Goods for processing: imports f.o.b.	3 150 . .	. . .	. . .	. . .	. . .	. . .	. . .	. . .	. . .
Repairs on goods	3 160 . .	–15	–11	–17	–40	–33	–35	–34	–39
Goods procured in ports by carriers	3 170 . .	–74	–87	–101	–93	–70	–76	–111	–74
Nonmonetary gold	3 180 . .	. . .	. . .	–6	–46	. . .	. . .	. . .	. . .
B. SERVICES	4 200 . .	–1,054	–1,180	–1,193	–1,503	–1,463	–1,261	–1,307	–1,416
Total credit	2 200 . .	*1,571*	*1,700*	*2,192*	*2,152*	*1,952*	*1,882*	*2,004*	*2,157*
Total debit	3 200 . .	*–2,626*	*–2,880*	*–3,385*	*–3,655*	*–3,414*	*–3,143*	*–3,311*	*–3,573*
Transportation services, credit	2 205 . .	**499**	**565**	**592**	**647**	**621**	**550**	**554**	**530**
Passenger	2 850 . .	*191*	*230*	*242*	*272*	*288*	*251*	*251*	*245*
Freight	2 851 . .	*198*	*209*	*220*	*226*	*175*	*159*	*143*	*115*
Other	2 852 . .	*111*	*126*	*130*	*149*	*159*	*140*	*159*	*171*
Sea transport, passenger	2 207 . .	. . .	. . .	. . .	. . .	. . .	. . .	. . .	. . .
Sea transport, freight	2 208 . .	126	131	139	96	71	51	19	9
Sea transport, other	2 209 . .	51	55	60	62	66	51	60	69
Air transport, passenger	2 211 . .	191	230	242	272	288	251	251	245
Air transport, freight	2 212 . .	55	51	49	91	66	71	88	66
Air transport, other	2 213 . .	58	68	68	85	92	88	98	100
Other transport, passenger	2 215 . .	. . .	. . .	. . .	. . .	. . .	. . .	. . .	. . .
Other transport, freight	2 216 . .	18	27	32	39	38	37	37	40
Other transport, other	2 217 . .	2	3	2	2	1	1	1	1
Transportation services, debit	3 205 . .	**–1,119**	**–1,191**	**–1,207**	**–1,312**	**–1,295**	**–1,168**	**–1,310**	**–1,400**
Passenger	3 850 . .	*–235*	*–284*	*–314*	*–351*	*–335*	*–327*	*–395*	*–386*
Freight	3 851 . .	*–579*	*–568*	*–564*	*–673*	*–699*	*–587*	*–672*	*–791*
Other	3 852 . .	*–305*	*–339*	*–329*	*–287*	*–261*	*–254*	*–242*	*–223*
Sea transport, passenger	3 207 . .	. . .	. . .	. . .	. . .	. . .	. . .	. . .	. . .
Sea transport, freight	3 208 . .	–501	–475	–472	–568	–517	–462	–545	–637
Sea transport, other	3 209 . .	–195	–206	–208	–153	–127	–83	–39	–14
Air transport, passenger	3 211 . .	–235	–284	–314	–351	–335	–327	–395	–386
Air transport, freight	3 212 . .	–49	–65	–62	–62	–145	–99	–96	–118
Air transport, other	3 213 . .	–110	–133	–121	–134	–134	–171	–203	–209
Other transport, passenger	3 215 . .	. . .	. . .	. . .	. . .	. . .	. . .	. . .	. . .
Other transport, freight	3 216 . .	–30	–28	–29	–44	–38	–27	–32	–36
Other transport, other	3 217 . .	. . .	. . .	. . .	. . .	. . .	. . .	. . .	. . .
Travel, credit	2 236 . .	**660**	**657**	**1,120**	**1,043**	**927**	**927**	**1,026**	**1,209**
Business travel	2 237 . .	. . .	. . .	. . .	. . .	. . .	. . .	. . .	. . .
Personal travel	2 240 . .	660	. . .	1,120	1,043	927	927	1,026	1,209
Travel, debit	3 236 . .	**–841**	**–878**	**–1,117**	**–1,209**	**–1,120**	**–1,013**	**–1,057**	**–1,160**
Business travel	3 237 . .	. . .	. . .	. . .	. . .	. . .	. . .	. . .	. . .
Personal travel	3 240 . .	–841	. . .	–1,117	–1,209	–1,120	–1,013	–1,057	–1,160
Other services, credit	2 200 BA	**412**	**478**	**480**	**461**	**403**	**405**	**424**	**418**
Communications	2 245 . .	263	269	258	247	175	165	182	205
Construction	2 249 . .	. . .	. . .	. . .	. . .	. . .	. . .	. . .	. . .
Insurance	2 253 . .	. . .	. . .	1	1	. . .	. . .	. . .	. . .
Financial	2 260 . .	64	107	110	103	95	100	74	51
Computer and information	2 262 . .	2	2	2	3	4	3	4	7
Royalties and licence fees	2 266 . .	. . .	. . .	1	1	4	6	5	2
Other business services	2 268 . .	33	38	42	41	56	52	72	61
Personal, cultural, and recreational	2 287 . .	1	3	7	6	6	15	23	24
Government, n.i.e.	2 291 . .	49	59	59	60	63	64	64	68
Other services, debit	3 200 BA	**–665**	**–811**	**–1,061**	**–1,134**	**–1,000**	**–963**	**–944**	**–1,013**
Communications	3 245 . .	–126	–117	–119	–123	–113	–109	–124	–123
Construction	3 249 . .	. . .	–1	–1	. . .	–1	–1	. . .	. . .
Insurance	3 253 . .	–214	–230	–308	–366	–238	–190	–202	–239
Financial	3 260 . .	–82	–102	–111	–159	–139	–124	–138	–155
Computer and information	3 262 . .	–8	–13	–20	–28	–30	–69	–46	–40
Royalties and licence fees	3 266 . .	–26	–39	–60	–59	–61	–68	–71	–71
Other business services	3 268 . .	–156	–235	–372	–334	–341	–319	–278	–298
Personal, cultural, and recreational	3 287 . .	–7	–14	–9	–5	–15	–21	–25	–26
Government, n.i.e.	3 291 . .	–46	–60	–61	–60	–63	–62	–61	–62

Table 2 (Continued). STANDARD PRESENTATION, 1994–2001
(Millions of U.S. dollars)

	Code	1994	1995	1996	1997	1998	1999	2000	2001
C. INCOME	4 300 . .	–1,458	–1,600	–2,067	–2,358	–1,758	–1,596	–2,529	–2,975
Total credit	2 300 . .	*706*	*677*	*707*	*885*	*882*	*792*	*858*	*739*
Total debit	3 300 . .	*–2,164*	*–2,277*	*–2,774*	*–3,243*	*–2,640*	*–2,388*	*–3,388*	*–3,714*
Compensation of employees, credit	2 310 . .	**3**	**6**	**12**	**18**	**26**	**26**	**30**	**28**
Compensation of employees, debit	3 310 . .	**–2**	**–2**	**–3**	**–11**	**–8**	**–7**	**–10**	**–16**
Investment income, credit	2 320 . .	**703**	**671**	**695**	**867**	**856**	**766**	**828**	**711**
Direct investment income	2 330 . .	189	34	32	45	47	59	31	29
Dividends and distributed branch profits	2 332 . .	189	34	32	45	47	59	31	29
Reinvested earnings and undistributed branch profits	2 333 . .	. . .	. . .	. . .	. . .	. . .	. . .	. . .	. . .
Income on debt (interest)	2 334 . .	. . .	. . .	. . .	. . .	. . .	. . .	. . .	. . .
Portfolio investment income	2 339 . .	441	562	569	755	658	558	665	600
Income on equity	2 340 . .	23	37	48	96	64	62	60	39
Income on bonds and notes	2 350 . .	. . .	. . .	. . .	. . .	. . .	. . .	. . .	. . .
Income on money market instruments	2 360 . .	418	525	521	660	594	496	606	561
Other investment income	2 370 . .	73	75	94	67	151	149	132	82
Investment income, debit	3 320 . .	**–2,163**	**–2,275**	**–2,771**	**–3,232**	**–2,632**	**–2,381**	**–3,377**	**–3,698**
Direct investment income	3 330 . .	–488	–359	–643	–569	29	204	–675	–1,082
Dividends and distributed branch profits	3 332 . .	–139	–509	–288	–301	–381	–200	–1,149	–766
Reinvested earnings and undistributed branch profits	3 333 . .	–349	150	–355	–268	410	405	474	–316
Income on debt (interest)	3 334 . .	. . .	. . .	. . .	. . .	. . .	. . .	. . .	. . .
Portfolio investment income	3 339 . .	–143	–205	–339	–558	–629	–676	–758	–960
Income on equity	3 340 . .	–83	–46	–55	–80	–90	–41	–18	–14
Income on bonds and notes	3 350 . .	–60	–159	–284	–479	–538	–635	–740	–946
Income on money market instruments	3 360 . .	. . .	. . .	. . .	. . .	. . .	. . .	. . .	. . .
Other investment income	3 370 . .	–1,531	–1,711	–1,789	–2,104	–2,033	–1,909	–1,945	–1,656
D. CURRENT TRANSFERS	4 379 . .	1,069	729	597	614	446	1,435	1,662	2,094
Credit	2 379 . .	**1,262**	**963**	**814**	**831**	**608**	**1,683**	**1,900**	**2,395**
General government	2 380 . .	234	172	143	96	67	168	239	601
Other sectors	2 390 . .	1,028	791	671	735	541	1,516	1,661	1,794
Workers' remittances	2 391 . .	966	739	635	658	483	1,297	1,578	1,756
Other current transfers	2 392 . .	63	52	36	77	57	218	83	39
Debit	3 379 . .	**–193**	**–234**	**–217**	**–217**	**–162**	**–248**	**–238**	**–302**
General government	3 380 . .	–49	–34	–37	–41	–15	–11	–10	–8
Other sectors	3 390 . .	–144	–200	–180	–176	–147	–237	–228	–293
Workers' remittances	3 391 . .	–144	–148	–132	–99	–137	–232	–207	–192
Other current transfers	3 392 . .	. . .	–52	–48	–77	–10	–5	–21	–101
CAPITAL AND FINANCIAL ACCOUNT	4 996 . .	**3,348**	**4,481**	**5,121**	**6,453**	**5,116**	**–281**	**–373**	**1,251**
CAPITAL ACCOUNT	4 994 . .	. . .	. . .	. . .	. . .	. . .	. . .	. . .	. . .
Total credit	2 994 . .	. . .	. . .	. . .	. . .	. . .	. . .	. . .	. . .
Total debit	3 994 . .	. . .	. . .	. . .	. . .	. . .	. . .	. . .	. . .
Capital transfers, credit	2 400 . .	. . .	. . .	. . .	. . .	. . .	. . .	. . .	. . .
General government	2 401 . .	. . .	. . .	. . .	. . .	. . .	. . .	. . .	. . .
Debt forgiveness	2 402 . .	. . .	. . .	. . .	. . .	. . .	. . .	. . .	. . .
Other capital transfers	2 410 . .	. . .	. . .	. . .	. . .	. . .	. . .	. . .	. . .
Other sectors	2 430 . .	. . .	. . .	. . .	. . .	. . .	. . .	. . .	. . .
Migrants' transfers	2 431 . .	. . .	. . .	. . .	. . .	. . .	. . .	. . .	. . .
Debt forgiveness	2 432 . .	. . .	. . .	. . .	. . .	. . .	. . .	. . .	. . .
Other capital transfers	2 440 . .	. . .	. . .	. . .	. . .	. . .	. . .	. . .	. . .
Capital transfers, debit	3 400 . .	. . .	. . .	. . .	. . .	. . .	. . .	. . .	. . .
General government	3 401 . .	. . .	. . .	. . .	. . .	. . .	. . .	. . .	. . .
Debt forgiveness	3 402 . .	. . .	. . .	. . .	. . .	. . .	. . .	. . .	. . .
Other capital transfers	3 410 . .	. . .	. . .	. . .	. . .	. . .	. . .	. . .	. . .
Other sectors	3 430 . .	. . .	. . .	. . .	. . .	. . .	. . .	. . .	. . .
Migrants' transfers	3 431 . .	. . .	. . .	. . .	. . .	. . .	. . .	. . .	. . .
Debt forgiveness	3 432 . .	. . .	. . .	. . .	. . .	. . .	. . .	. . .	. . .
Other capital transfers	3 440 . .	. . .	. . .	. . .	. . .	. . .	. . .	. . .	. . .
Nonproduced nonfinancial assets, credit	2 480 . .	. . .	. . .	. . .	. . .	. . .	. . .	. . .	. . .
Nonproduced nonfinancial assets, debit	3 480 . .	. . .	. . .	. . .	. . .	. . .	. . .	. . .	. . .

Table 2 (Continued). STANDARD PRESENTATION, 1994–2001
(Millions of U.S. dollars)

	Code	1994	1995	1996	1997	1998	1999	2000	2001
FINANCIAL ACCOUNT	4 995 . .	**3,348**	**4,481**	**5,121**	**6,453**	**5,116**	**–281**	**–373**	**1,251**
A. DIRECT INVESTMENT	4 500 . .	1,298	712	2,784	4,753	2,033	1,352	2,031	2,287
Direct investment abroad	4 505 . .	**–149**	**–256**	**–328**	**–809**	**–796**	**–116**	**–250**	**–42**
Equity capital	4 510 . .	–149	–256	–328	–809	–796	–116	–250	–42
Claims on affiliated enterprises	4 515 . .	–149	–256	–328	–809	–796	–116	–250	–42
Liabilities to affiliated enterprises	4 520 . .	. . .	. . .	. . .	. . .	. . .	. . .	. . .	. . .
Reinvested earnings	4 525 . .	. . .	. . .	. . .	. . .	. . .	. . .	. . .	. . .
Other capital	4 530 . .	. . .	. . .	. . .	. . .	. . .	. . .	. . .	. . .
Claims on affiliated enterprises	4 535 . .	. . .	. . .	. . .	. . .	. . .	. . .	. . .	. . .
Liabilities to affiliated enterprises	4 540 . .	. . .	. . .	. . .	. . .	. . .	. . .	. . .	. . .
Direct investment in Colombia	4 555 . .	**1,447**	**968**	**3,112**	**5,562**	**2,829**	**1,468**	**2,281**	**2,328**
Equity capital	4 560 . .	1,098	1,118	2,757	5,294	3,239	1,873	2,755	2,012
Claims on direct investors	4 565 . .	. . .	. . .	. . .	. . .	. . .	. . .	. . .	. . .
Liabilities to direct investors	4 570 . .	1,098	1,118	2,757	5,294	3,239	1,873	2,755	2,012
Reinvested earnings	4 575 . .	349	–150	355	268	–410	–405	–474	316
Other capital	4 580 . .	. . .	. . .	. . .	. . .	. . .	. . .	. . .	. . .
Claims on direct investors	4 585 . .	. . .	. . .	. . .	. . .	. . .	. . .	. . .	. . .
Liabilities to direct investors	4 590 . .	. . .	. . .	. . .	. . .	. . .	. . .	. . .	. . .
B. PORTFOLIO INVESTMENT	4 600 . .	121	1,435	1,684	942	1,662	–1,045	422	–29
Assets	4 602 . .	**–1,381**	**394**	**–586**	**–770**	**606**	**–1,735**	**–1,014**	**–3,480**
Equity securities	4 610 . .	. . .	. . .	. . .	. . .	. . .	. . .	. . .	. . .
Monetary authorities	4 611 . .	. . .	. . .	. . .	. . .	. . .	. . .	. . .	. . .
General government	4 612 . .	. . .	. . .	. . .	. . .	. . .	. . .	. . .	. . .
Banks	4 613 . .	. . .	. . .	. . .	. . .	. . .	. . .	. . .	. . .
Other sectors	4 614 . .	. . .	. . .	. . .	. . .	. . .	. . .	. . .	. . .
Debt securities	4 619 . .	–1,381	394	–586	–770	606	–1,735	–1,014	–3,480
Bonds and notes	4 620 . .	. . .	. . .	. . .	. . .	. . .	. . .	. . .	. . .
Monetary authorities	4 621 . .	. . .	. . .	. . .	. . .	. . .	. . .	. . .	. . .
General government	4 622 . .	. . .	. . .	. . .	. . .	. . .	. . .	. . .	. . .
Banks	4 623 . .	. . .	. . .	. . .	. . .	. . .	. . .	. . .	. . .
Other sectors	4 624 . .	. . .	. . .	. . .	. . .	. . .	. . .	. . .	. . .
Money market instruments	4 630 . .	–1,381	394	–586	–770	606	–1,735	–1,014	–3,480
Monetary authorities	4 631 . .	. . .	. . .	. . .	. . .	. . .	. . .	. . .	. . .
General government	4 632 . .	–948	582	–430	323	374	–395	106	–1,138
Banks	4 633 . .	14	–65	–110	167	124	–61	31	–77
Other sectors	4 634 . .	–446	–123	–46	–1,260	108	–1,278	–1,150	–2,266
Liabilities	4 652 . .	**1,502**	**1,041**	**2,270**	**1,712**	**1,057**	**689**	**1,436**	**3,452**
Equity securities	4 660 . .	478	165	292	278	47	–27	17	–42
Banks	4 663 . .	. . .	. . .	. . .	. . .	. . .	. . .	. . .	. . .
Other sectors	4 664 . .	478	165	292	278	47	–27	17	–42
Debt securities	4 669 . .	1,024	876	1,978	1,435	1,010	716	1,419	3,494
Bonds and notes	4 670 . .	1,024	876	1,978	1,435	1,010	716	1,419	3,494
Monetary authorities	4 671 . .	. . .	. . .	. . .	. . .	. . .	. . .	. . .	. . .
General government	4 672 . .	438	290	1,292	1,345	1,254	1,072	1,565	3,602
Banks	4 673 . .	301	105	323	–22	–95	–282	–124	–184
Other sectors	4 674 . .	285	481	363	111	–149	–73	–23	76
Money market instruments	4 680 . .	. . .	. . .	. . .	. . .	. . .	. . .	. . .	. . .
Monetary authorities	4 681 . .	. . .	. . .	. . .	. . .	. . .	. . .	. . .	. . .
General government	4 682 . .	. . .	. . .	. . .	. . .	. . .	. . .	. . .	. . .
Banks	4 683 . .	. . .	. . .	. . .	. . .	. . .	. . .	. . .	. . .
Other sectors	4 684 . .	. . .	. . .	. . .	. . .	. . .	. . .	. . .	. . .
C. FINANCIAL DERIVATIVES	4 910 . .	. . .	. . .	. . .	295	–39	101	–103	–112
Monetary authorities	4 911 . .	. . .	. . .	. . .	. . .	. . .	. . .	. . .	. . .
General government	4 912 . .	. . .	. . .	. . .	. . .	. . .	. . .	. . .	. . .
Banks	4 913 . .	. . .	. . .	. . .	. . .	. . .	. . .	. . .	. . .
Other sectors	4 914 . .	. . .	. . .	. . .	295	–39	101	–103	–112
Assets	4 900 . .	**. . .**	**. . .**	**. . .**	**. . .**	**. . .**	**. . .**	**. . .**	**. . .**
Monetary authorities	4 901 . .	. . .	. . .	. . .	. . .	. . .	. . .	. . .	. . .
General government	4 902 . .	. . .	. . .	. . .	. . .	. . .	. . .	. . .	. . .
Banks	4 903 . .	. . .	. . .	. . .	. . .	. . .	. . .	. . .	. . .
Other sectors	4 904 . .	. . .	. . .	. . .	. . .	. . .	. . .	. . .	. . .
Liabilities	4 905 . .	**. . .**	**. . .**	**. . .**	**295**	**–39**	**101**	**–103**	**–112**
Monetary authorities	4 906 . .	. . .	. . .	. . .	. . .	. . .	. . .	. . .	. . .
General government	4 907 . .	. . .	. . .	. . .	. . .	. . .	. . .	. . .	. . .
Banks	4 908 . .	. . .	. . .	. . .	. . .	. . .	. . .	. . .	. . .
Other sectors	4 909 . .	. . .	. . .	. . .	295	–39	101	–103	–112

Table 2 (Concluded). STANDARD PRESENTATION, 1994–2001
(Millions of U.S. dollars)

	Code	1994	1995	1996	1997	1998	1999	2000	2001
D. OTHER INVESTMENT	4 700 . .	2,111	2,329	2,383	741	62	–1,001	–1,861	331
Assets	4 703 . .	**161**	**320**	**–855**	**–1,407**	**–535**	**–438**	**–551**	**129**
Trade credits	4 706 . .	237	243	–221	–290	20	–421	–348	–20
General government	4 707 . .	. . .	. . .	. . .	. . .	. . .	. . .	. . .	. . .
of which: Short-term	4 709 . .	. . .	. . .	. . .	. . .	. . .	. . .	. . .	. . .
Other sectors	4 710 . .	237	243	–221	–290	20	–421	–348	–20
of which: Short-term	4 712 . .	*237*	*243*	*–221*	*–290*	*20*	*–421*	*–348*	*–20*
Loans	4 714 . .	–102	55	–88	–195	–190	36	103	135
Monetary authorities	4 715 . .	. . .	. . .	. . .	. . .	. . .	. . .	. . .	. . .
of which: Short-term	4 718 . .	. . .	. . .	. . .	. . .	. . .	. . .	. . .	. . .
General government	4 719 . .	. . .	. . .	. . .	. . .	. . .	. . .	. . .	. . .
of which: Short-term	4 721 . .	. . .	. . .	. . .	. . .	. . .	. . .	. . .	. . .
Banks	4 722 . .	–81	66	–33	–138	–138	5	113	94
of which: Short-term	4 724 . .	*–81*	*66*	*–33*	*–132*	*–123*	*5*	*112*	*92*
Other sectors	4 725 . .	–21	–11	–55	–57	–52	30	–10	42
of which: Short-term	4 727 . .	*–24*	*–10*	*–54*	*–58*	*–52*	*36*	*–10*	*42*
Currency and deposits	4 730 . .	26	22	–526	–903	–344	–35	–259	41
Monetary authorities	4 731 . .	. . .	. . .	. . .	. . .	. . .	. . .	. . .	. . .
General government	4 732 . .	. . .	. . .	. . .	. . .	. . .	. . .	. . .	. . .
Banks	4 733 . .	12	–8	–8	–93	–38	113	32	8
Other sectors	4 734 . .	14	30	–518	–810	–305	–148	–290	33
Other assets	4 736 . .	. . .	. . .	–20	–19	–21	–17	–48	–28
Monetary authorities	4 737 . .	. . .	. . .	. . .	1	–7	5	–8	8
of which: Short-term	4 739 . .	. . .	. . .	. . .	*1*	*–7*	*5*	*–8*	*8*
General government	4 740 . .	. . .	. . .	–20	–20	–15	–23	–40	–35
of which: Short-term	4 742 . .	. . .	. . .	. . .	. . .	. . .	. . .	. . .	. . .
Banks	4 743 . .	. . .	. . .	. . .	. . .	. . .	. . .	. . .	. . .
of which: Short-term	4 745 . .	. . .	. . .	. . .	. . .	. . .	. . .	. . .	. . .
Other sectors	4 746 . .	. . .	. . .	. . .	. . .	. . .	. . .	. . .	. . .
of which: Short-term	4 748 . .	. . .	. . .	. . .	. . .	. . .	. . .	. . .	. . .
Liabilities	4 753 . .	**1,950**	**2,009**	**3,238**	**2,147**	**597**	**–562**	**–1,310**	**202**
Trade credits	4 756 . .	10	100	112	–29	35	180	–63	141
General government	4 757 . .	–65	–36	–60	–46	–19	–17	–7	5
of which: Short-term	4 759 . .	. . .	. . .	. . .	. . .	. . .	. . .	*1*	. . .
Other sectors	4 760 . .	75	136	172	17	54	197	–56	137
of which: Short-term	4 762 . .	*47*	*46*	*147*	*13*	*–154*	*–69*	*–91*	*140*
Loans	4 764 . .	1,931	1,917	3,117	2,179	565	–744	–1,246	60
Monetary authorities	4 765 . .	–200	60	11	–12	–16	–14	–15	–13
of which: Use of Fund credit and loans from the Fund	4 766 . .	. . .	. . .	. . .	. . .	. . .	. . .	. . .	. . .
of which: Short-term	4 768 . .	. . .	. . .	. . .	*–2*	*–2*	. . .	. . .	. . .
General government	4 769 . .	–353	–44	–206	–8	366	927	348	221
of which: Short-term	4 771 . .	*–91*	. . .	. . .	. . .	. . .	*56*	*–56*	. . .
Banks	4 772 . .	726	579	417	487	–861	–1,208	–1,149	–403
of which: Short-term	4 774 . .	*608*	*562*	*79*	*140*	*–496*	*–778*	*–260*	*207*
Other sectors	4 775 . .	1,757	1,322	2,896	1,713	1,077	–450	–431	256
of which: Short-term	4 777 . .	*–79*	*256*	*102*	*–39*	*185*	*–160*	*340*	*493*
Currency and deposits	4 780 . .	. . .	. . .	. . .	. . .	. . .	. . .	. . .	. . .
Monetary authorities	4 781 . .	. . .	. . .	. . .	. . .	. . .	. . .	. . .	. . .
General government	4 782 . .	. . .	. . .	. . .	. . .	. . .	. . .	. . .	. . .
Banks	4 783 . .	. . .	. . .	. . .	. . .	. . .	. . .	. . .	. . .
Other sectors	4 784 . .	. . .	. . .	. . .	. . .	. . .	. . .	. . .	. . .
Other liabilities	4 786 . .	9	–8	9	–2	–4	2	–1	1
Monetary authorities	4 787 . .	9	–8	9	–2	–4	2	–1	1
of which: Short-term	4 789 . .	*9*	*–8*	*9*	*–2*	*–4*	*2*	*–1*	*1*
General government	4 790 . .	. . .	. . .	. . .	. . .	. . .	. . .	. . .	. . .
of which: Short-term	4 792 . .	. . .	. . .	. . .	. . .	. . .	. . .	. . .	. . .
Banks	4 793 . .	. . .	. . .	. . .	. . .	. . .	. . .	. . .	. . .
of which: Short-term	4 795 . .	. . .	. . .	. . .	. . .	. . .	. . .	. . .	. . .
Other sectors	4 796 . .	. . .	. . .	. . .	. . .	. . .	. . .	. . .	. . .
of which: Short-term	4 798 . .	. . .	. . .	. . .	. . .	. . .	. . .	. . .	. . .
E. RESERVE ASSETS	4 802 . .	–182	5	–1,729	–278	1,398	312	–862	–1,226
Monetary gold	4 812 . .	. . .	. . .	. . .	–1	–3	33	7	–1
Special drawing rights	4 811 . .	–2	–4	–6	–7	–16	61	–11	–6
Reserve position in the Fund	4 810 . .	–10	–74	–43	–133	–194	166	. . .	. . .
Foreign exchange	4 803 . .	–170	83	–1,680	–138	1,611	52	–858	–1,219
Other claims	4 813 . .	. . .	. . .	. . .	. . .	. . .	. . .	. . .	. . .
NET ERRORS AND OMISSIONS	4 998 . .	**325**	**115**	**–367**	**–568**	**109**	**–72**	**17**	**537**

Part 3 of the *Yearbook* contains descriptions of the methodologies, compilation practices, and sources used to compile these data.

Table 3. INTERNATIONAL INVESTMENT POSITION (End–period stocks), 1994–2001
(Millions of U.S. dollars)

	Code	1994	1995	1996	1997	1998	1999	2000	2001
ASSETS	8 995 C.	15,149	16,445	17,656	20,641	20,139	21,771	24,460	29,045
Direct investment abroad	8 505 . .	**744**	**1,028**	**1,096**	**1,893**	**2,648**	**2,703**	**2,914**	**2,903**
Equity capital and reinvested earnings	8 506 . .	744	1,028	1,096	1,893	2,648	2,703	2,914	2,903
Claims on affiliated enterprises	8 507 . .	744	1,028	1,096	1,893	2,648	2,703	2,914	2,903
Liabilities to affiliated enterprises	8 508 . .	...	...	...	...	...	...	...	...
Other capital	8 530 . .	...	...	...	...	...	...	...	...
Claims on affiliated enterprises	8 535 . .	...	...	...	...	...	...	...	...
Liabilities to affiliated enterprises	8 540 . .	...	...	...	...	...	...	...	...
Portfolio investment	8 602 . .	**447**	**1,171**	**2,453**	**3,268**	**2,662**	**4,427**	**5,440**	**8,921**
Equity securities	8 610 . .	447	1,171	...	...	...	...	...	...
Monetary authorities	8 611 . .	...	...	...	...	...	...	...	...
General government	8 612 . .	...	...	...	...	...	...	...	...
Banks	8 613 . .	...	...	...	...	...	...	...	...
Other sectors	8 614 . .	447	1,171	...	...	...	...	...	...
Debt securities	8 619 . .	...	...	2,453	3,268	2,662	4,427	5,440	8,921
Bonds and notes	8 620 . .	...	...	...	...	...	...	...	...
Monetary authorities	8 621 . .	...	...	...	...	...	...	...	...
General government	8 622 . .	...	...	...	...	...	...	...	...
Banks	8 623 . .	...	...	...	...	...	...	...	...
Other sectors	8 624 . .	...	...	...	...	...	...	...	...
Money market instruments	8 630 . .	...	...	2,453	3,268	2,662	4,427	5,440	8,921
Monetary authorities	8 631 . .	...	...	...	...	...	...	...	...
General government	8 632 . .	...	...	1,054	731	357	752	647	1,784
Banks	8 633 . .	...	...	458	291	167	228	198	274
Other sectors	8 634 . .	...	...	941	2,246	2,138	3,446	4,596	6,862
Financial derivatives	8 900 . .	...	...	...	...	...	...	...	...
Monetary authorities	8 901 . .	...	...	...	...	...	...	...	...
General government	8 902 . .	...	...	...	...	...	...	...	...
Banks	8 903 . .	...	...	...	...	...	...	...	...
Other sectors	8 904 . .	...	...	...	...	...	...	...	...
Other investment	8 703 . .	**5,845**	**5,786**	**4,169**	**5,572**	**6,096**	**6,540**	**7,111**	**6,980**
Trade credits	8 706 . .	1,805	1,970	1,420	1,710	1,690	2,111	2,459	2,479
General government	8 707 . .	...	...	...	...	...	...	...	...
of which: Short-term	8 709 . .	...	...	...	...	...	...	...	...
Other sectors	8 710 . .	1,805	1,970	1,420	1,710	1,690	2,111	2,459	2,479
of which: Short-term	8 712 . .	...	...	*1,420*	*1,710*	*1,690*	*2,111*	*2,459*	*2,479*
Loans	8 714 . .	...	...	189	387	577	543	438	302
Monetary authorities	8 715 . .	...	...	...	...	...	...	...	...
of which: Short-term	8 718 . .	...	...	...	...	...	...	...	...
General government	8 719 . .	...	...	...	...	...	...	...	...
of which: Short-term	8 721 . .	...	...	...	...	...	...	...	...
Banks	8 722 . .	...	...	77	214	353	349	234	140
of which: Short-term	8 724 . .	...	...	*77*	*208*	*332*	*328*	*214*	*122*
Other sectors	8 725 . .	...	...	113	172	224	194	204	162
of which: Short-term	8 727 . .	...	...	*113*	*171*	*223*	*187*	*197*	*155*
Currency and deposits	8 730 . .	2,775	1,840	1,969	2,871	3,214	3,248	3,509	3,468
Monetary authorities	8 731 . .	...	...	...	...	...	...	...	...
General government	8 732 . .	1,205	623	...	...	...	...	...	...
Banks	8 733 . .	1,150	1,051	186	279	316	202	172	164
Other sectors	8 734 . .	421	167	1,782	2,592	2,898	3,046	3,336	3,304
Other assets	8 736 . .	1,265	1,976	591	604	615	638	706	732
Monetary authorities	8 737 . .	40	40	482	476	473	473	501	502
of which: Short-term	8 739 . .	...	...	*5*	*4*	*7*	*2*	*10*	*2*
General government	8 740 . .	341	429	109	128	142	165	205	229
of which: Short-term	8 742 . .	...	...	...	...	...	...	...	...
Banks	8 743 . .	...	...	...	...	...	...	...	...
of which: Short-term	8 745 . .	...	...	...	...	...	...	...	...
Other sectors	8 746 . .	885	1,507	...	...	...	...	...	...
of which: Short-term	8 748 . .	*885*	*1,507*	...	...	...	...	...	...
Reserve assets	8 802 . .	**8,114**	**8,462**	**9,939**	**9,908**	**8,733**	**8,102**	**8,995**	**10,242**
Monetary gold	8 812 . .	112	104	94	104	103	95	89	91
Special drawing rights	8 811 . .	170	177	177	172	196	131	135	135
Reserve position in the Fund	8 810 . .	127	201	237	355	575	392	372	359
Foreign exchange	8 803 . .	7,485	7,742	9,432	9,276	7,859	7,483	8,399	9,657
Other claims	8 813 . .	220	238	...	...	...	...	...	...

Table 3 (Concluded). INTERNATIONAL INVESTMENT POSITION (End–period stocks), 1994–2001
(Millions of U.S. dollars)

	Code	1994	1995	1996	1997	1998	1999	2000	2001
LIABILITIES	8 995 D.	30,129	35,297	44,024	56,112	54,247	51,278	49,091	56,039
Direct investment in Colombia	8 555 ..	**6,916**	**8,563**	**11,773**	**19,694**	**16,644**	**13,929**	**12,204**	**15,859**
Equity capital and reinvested earnings	8 556 ..	6,916	8,563	11,773	19,694	16,644	13,929	12,204	15,859
Claims on direct investors	8 557 ..	...	...	...	...	...	...	...	...
Liabilities to direct investors	8 558 ..	...	...	11,773	19,694	16,644	13,929	12,204	15,859
Other capital	8 580 ..	...	...	...	...	...	...	...	...
Claims on direct investors	8 585 ..	...	...	...	...	...	...	...	...
Liabilities to direct investors	8 590 ..	...	...	...	...	...	...	...	...
Portfolio investment	8 652 ..	**2,026**	**2,591**	**5,945**	**7,936**	**8,261**	**8,534**	**9,724**	**13,109**
Equity securities	8 660 ..	693	858	942	1,553	880	586	397	325
Banks	8 663 ..	...	...	...	...	...	...	...	...
Other sectors	8 664 ..	693	858	942	1,553	880	586	397	325
Debt securities	8 669 ..	1,333	1,733	5,003	6,383	7,381	7,948	9,327	12,784
Bonds and notes	8 670 ..	1,333	1,733	5,003	6,383	7,381	7,948	9,327	12,784
Monetary authorities	8 671 ..	...	...	...	...	...	...	...	...
General government	8 672 ..	933	1,223	2,558	3,886	5,173	6,221	7,746	11,312
Banks	8 673 ..	250	360	1,165	1,106	966	558	434	250
Other sectors	8 674 ..	150	150	1,280	1,391	1,242	1,169	1,146	1,222
Money market instruments	8 680 ..	...	...	...	...	...	...	...	...
Monetary authorities	8 681 ..	...	...	...	...	...	...	...	...
General government	8 682 ..	...	...	...	...	...	...	...	...
Banks	8 683 ..	...	...	...	...	...	...	...	...
Other sectors	8 684 ..	...	...	...	...	...	...	...	...
Financial derivatives	8 905 ..	**...**	**...**	**...**	**295**	**256**	**356**	**253**	**141**
Monetary authorities	8 906 ..	...	...	...	...	...	...	...	...
General government	8 907 ..	...	...	...	...	...	...	...	...
Banks	8 908 ..	...	...	...	...	...	...	...	...
Other sectors	8 909 ..	...	...	...	295	256	356	253	141
Other investment	8 753 ..	**21,187**	**24,144**	**26,306**	**28,187**	**29,086**	**28,459**	**26,911**	**26,930**
Trade credits	8 756 ..	537	516	1,559	1,596	1,687	1,835	1,796	1,938
General government	8 757 ..	216	181	115	92	112	62	52	58
of which: Short-term	8 759 ..	...	...	...	...	...	...	...	...
Other sectors	8 760 ..	321	335	1,443	1,504	1,576	1,772	1,744	1,881
of which: Short-term	8 762 ..	...	...	*724*	*737*	*582*	*513*	*423*	*563*
Loans	8 764 ..	20,071	22,800	24,597	26,485	27,297	26,530	25,026	24,921
Monetary authorities	8 765 ..	231	301	164	143	134	117	96	79
of which: Use of Fund credit and loans from the Fund	8 766 ..	...	...	...	...	...	...	...	...
of which: Short-term	8 768 ..	*111*	*137*	...	*2*	...	...	...	...
General government	8 769 ..	4,887	4,963	4,608	4,424	4,888	5,802	6,529	6,821
of which: Short-term	8 771 ..	...	...	...	...	...	*56*	...	...
Banks	8 772 ..	4,518	5,169	5,460	6,003	5,059	3,885	2,714	2,262
of which: Short-term	8 774 ..	*2,858*	*3,430*	*2,483*	*2,498*	*2,001*	*1,226*	*917*	*1,124*
Other sectors	8 775 ..	10,436	12,368	14,365	15,915	17,215	16,727	15,688	15,760
of which: Short-term	8 777 ..	*1,513*	*1,977*	*1,232*	*1,193*	*1,377*	*1,218*	*1,557*	*2,050*
Currency and deposits	8 780 ..	...	...	...	...	...	...	...	...
Monetary authorities	8 781 ..	...	...	...	...	...	...	...	...
General government	8 782 ..	...	...	...	...	...	...	...	...
Banks	8 783 ..	...	...	...	...	...	...	...	...
Other sectors	8 784 ..	...	...	...	...	...	...	...	...
Other liabilities	8 786 ..	579	828	151	106	102	94	90	70
Monetary authorities	8 787 ..	...	...	151	106	102	94	90	70
of which: Short-term	8 789 ..	...	...	*5*	*3*	...	*2*	*2*	*3*
General government	8 790 ..	...	...	...	...	...	...	...	...
of which: Short-term	8 792 ..	...	...	...	...	...	...	...	...
Banks	8 793 ..	...	...	...	...	...	...	...	...
of which: Short-term	8 795 ..	...	...	...	...	...	...	...	...
Other sectors	8 796 ..	579	828	...	...	...	...	...	...
of which: Short-term	8 798 ..	...	...	...	...	...	...	...	...
NET INTERNATIONAL INVESTMENT POSITION	8 995 ..	**-14,980**	**-18,852**	**-26,368**	**-35,471**	**-34,108**	**-29,507**	**-24,631**	**-26,995**
Conversion rates: Colombian pesos per U.S. dollar (end of period)	0 102 ..	**831.27**	**987.65**	**1,005.33**	**1,293.58**	**1,507.52**	**1,873.77**	**2,187.02**	**2,301.33**

Table 1. ANALYTIC PRESENTATION, 1994–2001
(Millions of U.S. dollars)

	Code	1994	1995	1996	1997	1998	1999	2000	2001
A. Current Account [1]	4 993 Z.	**–7.22**	**–18.96**	**. . .**	**. . .**	**. . .**	**. . .**	**. . .**	**. . .**
Goods: exports f.o.b	2 100 . .	10.79	11.32	. . .	. . .	. . .	. . .	. . .	. . .
Goods: imports f.o.b	3 100 . .	–44.94	–53.50	. . .	. . .	. . .	. . .	. . .	. . .
Balance on Goods	4 100 . .	*–34.16*	*–42.18*	. . .	. . .	. . .	. . .	. . .	. . .
Services: credit	2 200 . .	28.84	34.51	. . .	. . .	. . .	. . .	. . .	. . .
Services: debit	3 200 . .	–45.59	–49.85	. . .	. . .	. . .	. . .	. . .	. . .
Balance on Goods and Services	4 991 . .	*–50.91*	*–57.53*	. . .	. . .	. . .	. . .	. . .	. . .
Income: credit	2 300 . .	2.62	3.40	. . .	. . .	. . .	. . .	. . .	. . .
Income: debit	3 300 . .	–2.69	–2.39	. . .	. . .	. . .	. . .	. . .	. . .
Balance on Goods, Services, and Income	4 992 . .	*–50.98*	*–56.52*	. . .	. . .	. . .	. . .	. . .	. . .
Current transfers: credit	2 379 Z.	49.95	41.06	. . .	. . .	. . .	. . .	. . .	. . .
Current transfers: debit	3 379 . .	–6.19	–3.50	. . .	. . .	. . .	. . .	. . .	. . .
B. Capital Account [1]	4 994 Z.	**. . .**	**. . .**	**. . .**	**. . .**	**. . .**	**. . .**	**. . .**	**. . .**
Capital account: credit	2 994 Z.	. . .	. . .	. . .	. . .	. . .	. . .	. . .	. . .
Capital account: debit	3 994 . .	. . .	. . .	. . .	. . .	. . .	. . .	. . .	. . .
Total, Groups A Plus B	4 981 . .	*–7.22*	*–18.96*	. . .	. . .	. . .	. . .	. . .	. . .
C. Financial Account [1]	4 995 W.	**18.54**	**10.87**	**. . .**	**. . .**	**. . .**	**. . .**	**. . .**	**. . .**
Direct investment abroad	4 505 . .	. . .	. . .	. . .	. . .	. . .	. . .	. . .	. . .
Direct investment in Comoros	4 555 Z.	.18	.89	. . .	. . .	. . .	. . .	. . .	. . .
Portfolio investment assets	4 602 . .	. . .	. . .	. . .	. . .	. . .	. . .	. . .	. . .
Equity securities	4 610 . .	. . .	. . .	. . .	. . .	. . .	. . .	. . .	. . .
Debt securities	4 619 . .	. . .	. . .	. . .	. . .	. . .	. . .	. . .	. . .
Portfolio investment liabilities	4 652 Z.	. . .	. . .	. . .	. . .	. . .	. . .	. . .	. . .
Equity securities	4 660 . .	. . .	. . .	. . .	. . .	. . .	. . .	. . .	. . .
Debt securities	4 669 Z.	. . .	. . .	. . .	. . .	. . .	. . .	. . .	. . .
Financial derivatives	4 910 . .	. . .	. . .	. . .	. . .	. . .	. . .	. . .	. . .
Financial derivatives assets	4 900 . .	. . .	. . .	. . .	. . .	. . .	. . .	. . .	. . .
Financial derivatives liabilities	4 905 . .	. . .	. . .	. . .	. . .	. . .	. . .	. . .	. . .
Other investment assets	4 703 . .	1.66	–1.83	. . .	. . .	. . .	. . .	. . .	. . .
Monetary authorities	4 701 . .	. . .	. . .	. . .	. . .	. . .	. . .	. . .	. . .
General government	4 704 . .	. . .	. . .	. . .	. . .	. . .	. . .	. . .	. . .
Banks	4 705 . .	1.66	–1.83	. . .	. . .	. . .	. . .	. . .	. . .
Other sectors	4 728 . .	. . .	. . .	. . .	. . .	. . .	. . .	. . .	. . .
Other investment liabilities	4 753 W.	16.70	11.81	. . .	. . .	. . .	. . .	. . .	. . .
Monetary authorities	4 753 WA	7.93	2.02	. . .	. . .	. . .	. . .	. . .	. . .
General government	4 753 ZB	10.63	8.72	. . .	. . .	. . .	. . .	. . .	. . .
Banks	4 753 ZC	. . .	. . .	. . .	. . .	. . .	. . .	. . .	. . .
Other sectors	4 753 ZD	–1.86	1.06	. . .	. . .	. . .	. . .	. . .	. . .
Total, Groups A Through C	4 983 . .	*11.32*	*–8.09*	. . .	. . .	. . .	. . .	. . .	. . .
D. Net Errors and Omissions	4 998 . .	**–6.33**	**–1.77**	**. . .**	**. . .**	**. . .**	**. . .**	**. . .**	**. . .**
Total, Groups A Through D	4 984 . .	*4.99*	*–9.86*	. . .	. . .	. . .	. . .	. . .	. . .
E. Reserves and Related Items	4 802 A.	**–4.99**	**9.86**	**. . .**	**. . .**	**. . .**	**. . .**	**. . .**	**. . .**
Reserve assets	4 802 . .	–14.97	3.37	. . .	. . .	. . .	. . .	. . .	. . .
Use of Fund credit and loans	4 766 . .	1.89	. . .	. . .	. . .	. . .	. . .	. . .	. . .
Exceptional financing	4 920 . .	8.09	6.49	. . .	. . .	. . .	. . .	. . .	. . .
Conversion rates: Comorian francs per U.S. dollar	0 101 . .	**416.40**	**374.36**	**383.66**	**437.75**	**442.46**	**461.77**	**533.98**	**549.78**

[1] Excludes components that have been classified in the categories of Group E.

Table 2. STANDARD PRESENTATION, 1994–2001
(Millions of U.S. dollars)

	Code		1994	1995	1996	1997	1998	1999	2000	2001
CURRENT ACCOUNT	4 993	. .	**–7.22**	**–18.96**	. . .	. . .	. . .	. . .	. . .	. . .
A. GOODS	4 100	. .	–34.16	–42.18	. . .	. . .	. . .	. . .	. . .	. . .
Credit	2 100	. .	**10.79**	**11.32**	. . .	. . .	. . .	. . .	. . .	. . .
General merchandise: exports f.o.b.	2 110	. .	10.79	11.32	. . .	. . .	. . .	. . .	. . .	. . .
Goods for processing: exports f.o.b.	2 150	. .	. . .	. . .	. . .	. . .	. . .	. . .	. . .	. . .
Repairs on goods	2 160	. .	. . .	. . .	. . .	. . .	. . .	. . .	. . .	. . .
Goods procured in ports by carriers	2 170	. .	. . .	. . .	. . .	. . .	. . .	. . .	. . .	. . .
Nonmonetary gold	2 180	. .	. . .	. . .	. . .	. . .	. . .	. . .	. . .	. . .
Debit	3 100	. .	**–44.94**	**–53.50**	. . .	. . .	. . .	. . .	. . .	. . .
General merchandise: imports f.o.b.	3 110	. .	–44.94	–53.50	. . .	. . .	. . .	. . .	. . .	. . .
Goods for processing: imports f.o.b.	3 150	. .	. . .	. . .	. . .	. . .	. . .	. . .	. . .	. . .
Repairs on goods	3 160	. .	. . .	. . .	. . .	. . .	. . .	. . .	. . .	. . .
Goods procured in ports by carriers	3 170	. .	. . .	. . .	. . .	. . .	. . .	. . .	. . .	. . .
Nonmonetary gold	3 180	. .	. . .	. . .	. . .	. . .	. . .	. . .	. . .	. . .
B. SERVICES	4 200	. .	–16.76	–15.34	. . .	. . .	. . .	. . .	. . .	. . .
Total credit	2 200	. .	*28.84*	*34.51*	. . .	. . .	. . .	. . .	. . .	. . .
Total debit	3 200	. .	*–45.59*	*–49.85*	. . .	. . .	. . .	. . .	. . .	. . .
Transportation services, credit	2 205	. .	**3.28**	**4.28**	. . .	. . .	. . .	. . .	. . .	. . .
Passenger	2 850	. .	*.75*	*.92*	. . .	. . .	. . .	. . .	. . .	. . .
Freight	2 851	. .	. . .	. . .	. . .	. . .	. . .	. . .	. . .	. . .
Other	2 852	. .	*2.52*	*3.36*	. . .	. . .	. . .	. . .	. . .	. . .
Sea transport, passenger	2 207	. .	. . .	. . .	. . .	. . .	. . .	. . .	. . .	. . .
Sea transport, freight	2 208	. .	. . .	. . .	. . .	. . .	. . .	. . .	. . .	. . .
Sea transport, other	2 209	. .	. . .	. . .	. . .	. . .	. . .	. . .	. . .	. . .
Air transport, passenger	2 211	. .	. . .	. . .	. . .	. . .	. . .	. . .	. . .	. . .
Air transport, freight	2 212	. .	. . .	. . .	. . .	. . .	. . .	. . .	. . .	. . .
Air transport, other	2 213	. .	. . .	. . .	. . .	. . .	. . .	. . .	. . .	. . .
Other transport, passenger	2 215	. .	. . .	. . .	. . .	. . .	. . .	. . .	. . .	. . .
Other transport, freight	2 216	. .	. . .	. . .	. . .	. . .	. . .	. . .	. . .	. . .
Other transport, other	2 217	. .	. . .	. . .	. . .	. . .	. . .	. . .	. . .	. . .
Transportation services, debit	3 205	. .	**–18.83**	**–23.61**	. . .	. . .	. . .	. . .	. . .	. . .
Passenger	3 850	. .	*–6.11*	*–8.17*	. . .	. . .	. . .	. . .	. . .	. . .
Freight	3 851	. .	*–12.11*	*–14.38*	. . .	. . .	. . .	. . .	. . .	. . .
Other	3 852	. .	*–.61*	*–1.06*	. . .	. . .	. . .	. . .	. . .	. . .
Sea transport, passenger	3 207	. .	. . .	. . .	. . .	. . .	. . .	. . .	. . .	. . .
Sea transport, freight	3 208	. .	. . .	. . .	. . .	. . .	. . .	. . .	. . .	. . .
Sea transport, other	3 209	. .	. . .	. . .	. . .	. . .	. . .	. . .	. . .	. . .
Air transport, passenger	3 211	. .	. . .	. . .	. . .	. . .	. . .	. . .	. . .	. . .
Air transport, freight	3 212	. .	. . .	. . .	. . .	. . .	. . .	. . .	. . .	. . .
Air transport, other	3 213	. .	. . .	. . .	. . .	. . .	. . .	. . .	. . .	. . .
Other transport, passenger	3 215	. .	. . .	. . .	. . .	. . .	. . .	. . .	. . .	. . .
Other transport, freight	3 216	. .	. . .	. . .	. . .	. . .	. . .	. . .	. . .	. . .
Other transport, other	3 217	. .	. . .	. . .	. . .	. . .	. . .	. . .	. . .	. . .
Travel, credit	2 236	. .	**15.70**	**20.92**	. . .	. . .	. . .	. . .	. . .	. . .
Business travel	2 237	. .	. . .	. . .	. . .	. . .	. . .	. . .	. . .	. . .
Personal travel	2 240	. .	. . .	. . .	. . .	. . .	. . .	. . .	. . .	. . .
Travel, debit	3 236	. .	**–5.88**	**–6.59**	. . .	. . .	. . .	. . .	. . .	. . .
Business travel	3 237	. .	. . .	. . .	. . .	. . .	. . .	. . .	. . .	. . .
Personal travel	3 240	. .	. . .	. . .	. . .	. . .	. . .	. . .	. . .	. . .
Other services, credit	2 200	BA	**9.86**	**9.32**	. . .	. . .	. . .	. . .	. . .	. . .
Communications	2 245	. .	. . .	. . .	. . .	. . .	. . .	. . .	. . .	. . .
Construction	2 249	. .	. . .	. . .	. . .	. . .	. . .	. . .	. . .	. . .
Insurance	2 253	. .	. . .	. . .	. . .	. . .	. . .	. . .	. . .	. . .
Financial	2 260	. .	. . .	. . .	. . .	. . .	. . .	. . .	. . .	. . .
Computer and information	2 262	. .	. . .	. . .	. . .	. . .	. . .	. . .	. . .	. . .
Royalties and licence fees	2 266	. .	. . .	. . .	. . .	. . .	. . .	. . .	. . .	. . .
Other business services	2 268	. .	1.62	1.85	. . .	. . .	. . .	. . .	. . .	. . .
Personal, cultural, and recreational	2 287	. .	. . .	. . .	. . .	. . .	. . .	. . .	. . .	. . .
Government, n.i.e.	2 291	. .	8.24	7.46	. . .	. . .	. . .	. . .	. . .	. . .
Other services, debit	3 200	BA	**–20.88**	**–19.65**	. . .	. . .	. . .	. . .	. . .	. . .
Communications	3 245	. .	. . .	. . .	. . .	. . .	. . .	. . .	. . .	. . .
Construction	3 249	. .	. . .	. . .	. . .	. . .	. . .	. . .	. . .	. . .
Insurance	3 253	. .	. . .	. . .	. . .	. . .	. . .	. . .	. . .	. . .
Financial	3 260	. .	. . .	. . .	. . .	. . .	. . .	. . .	. . .	. . .
Computer and information	3 262	. .	. . .	. . .	. . .	. . .	. . .	. . .	. . .	. . .
Royalties and licence fees	3 266	. .	. . .	. . .	. . .	. . .	. . .	. . .	. . .	. . .
Other business services	3 268	. .	–4.42	–2.30	. . .	. . .	. . .	. . .	. . .	. . .
Personal, cultural, and recreational	3 287	. .	. . .	. . .	. . .	. . .	. . .	. . .	. . .	. . .
Government, n.i.e.	3 291	. .	–16.46	–17.35	. . .	. . .	. . .	. . .	. . .	. . .

Table 2 (Continued). STANDARD PRESENTATION, 1994–2001

(Millions of U.S. dollars)

	Code	1994	1995	1996	1997	1998	1999	2000	2001
C. INCOME	4 300 . .	–.07	1.01	...	...	...	...	...	...
Total credit	2 300 . .	*2.62*	*3.40*	...	...	...	...	...	...
Total debit	3 300 . .	*–2.69*	*–2.39*	...	...	...	...	...	...
Compensation of employees, credit	2 310 . .	...	...	...	...	...	...	...	...
Compensation of employees, debit	3 310 . .	...	...	...	...	...	...	...	...
Investment income, credit	2 320 . .	**2.62**	**3.40**	...	...	...	...	...	...
Direct investment income	2 330 . .	...	...	...	...	...	...	...	...
Dividends and distributed branch profits	2 332 . .	...	...	...	...	...	...	...	...
Reinvested earnings and undistributed branch profits	2 333 . .	...	...	...	...	...	...	...	...
Income on debt (interest)	2 334 . .	...	...	...	...	...	...	...	...
Portfolio investment income	2 339 . .	...	...	...	...	...	...	...	...
Income on equity	2 340 . .	...	...	...	...	...	...	...	...
Income on bonds and notes	2 350 . .	...	...	...	...	...	...	...	...
Income on money market instruments	2 360 . .	...	...	...	...	...	...	...	...
Other investment income	2 370 . .	2.62	3.40	...	...	...	...	...	...
Investment income, debit	3 320 . .	**–2.69**	**–2.39**	...	...	...	...	...	...
Direct investment income	3 330 . .	–.49	–.21	...	...	...	...	...	...
Dividends and distributed branch profits	3 332 . .	...	...	...	...	...	...	...	...
Reinvested earnings and undistributed branch profits	3 333 . .	...	...	...	...	...	...	...	...
Income on debt (interest)	3 334 . .	...	...	...	...	...	...	...	...
Portfolio investment income	3 339 . .	...	...	...	...	...	...	...	...
Income on equity	3 340 . .	...	...	...	...	...	...	...	...
Income on bonds and notes	3 350 . .	...	...	...	...	...	...	...	...
Income on money market instruments	3 360 . .	...	...	...	...	...	...	...	...
Other investment income	3 370 . .	–2.20	–2.18	...	...	...	...	...	...
D. CURRENT TRANSFERS	4 379 . .	43.76	37.55	...	...	...	...	...	...
Credit	2 379 . .	**49.95**	**41.06**	...	...	...	...	...	...
General government	2 380 . .	34.72	28.84	...	...	...	...	...	...
Other sectors	2 390 . .	15.23	12.21	...	...	...	...	...	...
Workers' remittances	2 391 . .	15.23	12.21	...	...	...	...	...	...
Other current transfers	2 392 . .	...	...	...	...	...	...	...	...
Debit	3 379 . .	**–6.19**	**–3.50**	...	...	...	...	...	...
General government	3 380 . .	–.14	...	...	...	...	...	...	...
Other sectors	3 390 . .	–6.05	–3.50	...	...	...	...	...	...
Workers' remittances	3 391 . .	–6.05	–3.50	...	...	...	...	...	...
Other current transfers	3 392 . .	...	...	...	...	...	...	...	...
CAPITAL AND FINANCIAL ACCOUNT	4 996 . .	**13.55**	**20.73**	...	...	...	...	...	...
CAPITAL ACCOUNT	4 994 . .	...	...	...	...	...	...	...	...
Total credit	2 994 . .	...	...	...	...	...	...	...	...
Total debit	3 994 . .	...	...	...	...	...	...	...	...
Capital transfers, credit	2 400 . .	...	...	...	...	...	...	...	...
General government	2 401 . .	...	...	...	...	...	...	...	...
Debt forgiveness	2 402 . .	...	...	...	...	...	...	...	...
Other capital transfers	2 410 . .	...	...	...	...	...	...	...	...
Other sectors	2 430 . .	...	...	...	...	...	...	...	...
Migrants' transfers	2 431 . .	...	...	...	...	...	...	...	...
Debt forgiveness	2 432 . .	...	...	...	...	...	...	...	...
Other capital transfers	2 440 . .	...	...	...	...	...	...	...	...
Capital transfers, debit	3 400 . .	...	...	...	...	...	...	...	...
General government	3 401 . .	...	...	...	...	...	...	...	...
Debt forgiveness	3 402 . .	...	...	...	...	...	...	...	...
Other capital transfers	3 410 . .	...	...	...	...	...	...	...	...
Other sectors	3 430 . .	...	...	...	...	...	...	...	...
Migrants' transfers	3 431 . .	...	...	...	...	...	...	...	...
Debt forgiveness	3 432 . .	...	...	...	...	...	...	...	...
Other capital transfers	3 440 . .	...	...	...	...	...	...	...	...
Nonproduced nonfinancial assets, credit	2 480 . .	...	...	...	...	...	...	...	...
Nonproduced nonfinancial assets, debit	3 480 . .	...	...	...	...	...	...	...	...

Table 2 (Continued). STANDARD PRESENTATION, 1994–2001
(Millions of U.S. dollars)

	Code		1994	1995	1996	1997	1998	1999	2000	2001
FINANCIAL ACCOUNT	4 995	. .	**13.55**	**20.73**	. . .	. . .	. . .	. . .	. . .	. . .
A. DIRECT INVESTMENT	4 500	. .	.18	.89	. . .	. . .	. . .	. . .	. . .	. . .
Direct investment abroad	4 505	. .	. . .	. . .	. . .	. . .	. . .	. . .	. . .	. . .
Equity capital	4 510	. .	. . .	. . .	. . .	. . .	. . .	. . .	. . .	. . .
Claims on affiliated enterprises	4 515	. .	. . .	. . .	. . .	. . .	. . .	. . .	. . .	. . .
Liabilities to affiliated enterprises	4 520	. .	. . .	. . .	. . .	. . .	. . .	. . .	. . .	. . .
Reinvested earnings	4 525	. .	. . .	. . .	. . .	. . .	. . .	. . .	. . .	. . .
Other capital	4 530	. .	. . .	. . .	. . .	. . .	. . .	. . .	. . .	. . .
Claims on affiliated enterprises	4 535	. .	. . .	. . .	. . .	. . .	. . .	. . .	. . .	. . .
Liabilities to affiliated enterprises	4 540	. .	. . .	. . .	. . .	. . .	. . .	. . .	. . .	. . .
Direct investment in Comoros	4 555	. .	**.18**	**.89**	. . .	. . .	. . .	. . .	. . .	. . .
Equity capital	4 560	. .	. . .	. . .	. . .	. . .	. . .	. . .	. . .	. . .
Claims on direct investors	4 565	. .	. . .	. . .	. . .	. . .	. . .	. . .	. . .	. . .
Liabilities to direct investors	4 570	. .	. . .	. . .	. . .	. . .	. . .	. . .	. . .	. . .
Reinvested earnings	4 575	. .	. . .	. . .	. . .	. . .	. . .	. . .	. . .	. . .
Other capital	4 580	. .	. . .	. . .	. . .	. . .	. . .	. . .	. . .	. . .
Claims on direct investors	4 585	. .	. . .	. . .	. . .	. . .	. . .	. . .	. . .	. . .
Liabilities to direct investors	4 590	. .	. . .	. . .	. . .	. . .	. . .	. . .	. . .	. . .
B. PORTFOLIO INVESTMENT	4 600	. .	. . .	. . .	. . .	. . .	. . .	. . .	. . .	. . .
Assets	4 602	. .	. . .	. . .	. . .	. . .	. . .	. . .	. . .	. . .
Equity securities	4 610	. .	. . .	. . .	. . .	. . .	. . .	. . .	. . .	. . .
Monetary authorities	4 611	. .	. . .	. . .	. . .	. . .	. . .	. . .	. . .	. . .
General government	4 612	. .	. . .	. . .	. . .	. . .	. . .	. . .	. . .	. . .
Banks	4 613	. .	. . .	. . .	. . .	. . .	. . .	. . .	. . .	. . .
Other sectors	4 614	. .	. . .	. . .	. . .	. . .	. . .	. . .	. . .	. . .
Debt securities	4 619	. .	. . .	. . .	. . .	. . .	. . .	. . .	. . .	. . .
Bonds and notes	4 620	. .	. . .	. . .	. . .	. . .	. . .	. . .	. . .	. . .
Monetary authorities	4 621	. .	. . .	. . .	. . .	. . .	. . .	. . .	. . .	. . .
General government	4 622	. .	. . .	. . .	. . .	. . .	. . .	. . .	. . .	. . .
Banks	4 623	. .	. . .	. . .	. . .	. . .	. . .	. . .	. . .	. . .
Other sectors	4 624	. .	. . .	. . .	. . .	. . .	. . .	. . .	. . .	. . .
Money market instruments	4 630	. .	. . .	. . .	. . .	. . .	. . .	. . .	. . .	. . .
Monetary authorities	4 631	. .	. . .	. . .	. . .	. . .	. . .	. . .	. . .	. . .
General government	4 632	. .	. . .	. . .	. . .	. . .	. . .	. . .	. . .	. . .
Banks	4 633	. .	. . .	. . .	. . .	. . .	. . .	. . .	. . .	. . .
Other sectors	4 634	. .	. . .	. . .	. . .	. . .	. . .	. . .	. . .	. . .
Liabilities	4 652	. .	. . .	. . .	. . .	. . .	. . .	. . .	. . .	. . .
Equity securities	4 660	. .	. . .	. . .	. . .	. . .	. . .	. . .	. . .	. . .
Banks	4 663	. .	. . .	. . .	. . .	. . .	. . .	. . .	. . .	. . .
Other sectors	4 664	. .	. . .	. . .	. . .	. . .	. . .	. . .	. . .	. . .
Debt securities	4 669	. .	. . .	. . .	. . .	. . .	. . .	. . .	. . .	. . .
Bonds and notes	4 670	. .	. . .	. . .	. . .	. . .	. . .	. . .	. . .	. . .
Monetary authorities	4 671	. .	. . .	. . .	. . .	. . .	. . .	. . .	. . .	. . .
General government	4 672	. .	. . .	. . .	. . .	. . .	. . .	. . .	. . .	. . .
Banks	4 673	. .	. . .	. . .	. . .	. . .	. . .	. . .	. . .	. . .
Other sectors	4 674	. .	. . .	. . .	. . .	. . .	. . .	. . .	. . .	. . .
Money market instruments	4 680	. .	. . .	. . .	. . .	. . .	. . .	. . .	. . .	. . .
Monetary authorities	4 681	. .	. . .	. . .	. . .	. . .	. . .	. . .	. . .	. . .
General government	4 682	. .	. . .	. . .	. . .	. . .	. . .	. . .	. . .	. . .
Banks	4 683	. .	. . .	. . .	. . .	. . .	. . .	. . .	. . .	. . .
Other sectors	4 684	. .	. . .	. . .	. . .	. . .	. . .	. . .	. . .	. . .
C. FINANCIAL DERIVATIVES	4 910	. .	. . .	. . .	. . .	. . .	. . .	. . .	. . .	. . .
Monetary authorities	4 911	. .	. . .	. . .	. . .	. . .	. . .	. . .	. . .	. . .
General government	4 912	. .	. . .	. . .	. . .	. . .	. . .	. . .	. . .	. . .
Banks	4 913	. .	. . .	. . .	. . .	. . .	. . .	. . .	. . .	. . .
Other sectors	4 914	. .	. . .	. . .	. . .	. . .	. . .	. . .	. . .	. . .
Assets	4 900	. .	. . .	. . .	. . .	. . .	. . .	. . .	. . .	. . .
Monetary authorities	4 901	. .	. . .	. . .	. . .	. . .	. . .	. . .	. . .	. . .
General government	4 902	. .	. . .	. . .	. . .	. . .	. . .	. . .	. . .	. . .
Banks	4 903	. .	. . .	. . .	. . .	. . .	. . .	. . .	. . .	. . .
Other sectors	4 904	. .	. . .	. . .	. . .	. . .	. . .	. . .	. . .	. . .
Liabilities	4 905	. .	. . .	. . .	. . .	. . .	. . .	. . .	. . .	. . .
Monetary authorities	4 906	. .	. . .	. . .	. . .	. . .	. . .	. . .	. . .	. . .
General government	4 907	. .	. . .	. . .	. . .	. . .	. . .	. . .	. . .	. . .
Banks	4 908	. .	. . .	. . .	. . .	. . .	. . .	. . .	. . .	. . .
Other sectors	4 909	. .	. . .	. . .	. . .	. . .	. . .	. . .	. . .	. . .

Table 2 (Concluded). STANDARD PRESENTATION, 1994–2001

(Millions of U.S. dollars)

	Code	1994	1995	1996	1997	1998	1999	2000	2001
D. OTHER INVESTMENT	4 700	28.34	16.47	...	...	...	...	...	...
Assets	4 703	**1.66**	**–1.83**	**...**	**...**	**...**	**...**	**...**	**...**
Trade credits	4 706	...	...	...	...	...	...	...	...
General government	4 707	...	...	...	...	...	...	...	...
of which: Short-term	4 709	...	...	...	...	...	...	...	...
Other sectors	4 710	...	...	...	...	...	...	...	...
of which: Short-term	4 712	...	...	...	...	...	...	...	...
Loans	4 714	...	...	...	...	...	...	...	...
Monetary authorities	4 715	...	...	...	...	...	...	...	...
of which: Short-term	4 718	...	...	...	...	...	...	...	...
General government	4 719	...	...	...	...	...	...	...	...
of which: Short-term	4 721	...	...	...	...	...	...	...	...
Banks	4 722	...	...	...	...	...	...	...	...
of which: Short-term	4 724	...	...	...	...	...	...	...	...
Other sectors	4 725	...	...	...	...	...	...	...	...
of which: Short-term	4 727	...	...	...	...	...	...	...	...
Currency and deposits	4 730	1.66	–1.83	...	...	...	...	...	...
Monetary authorities	4 731	...	...	...	...	...	...	...	...
General government	4 732	...	...	...	...	...	...	...	...
Banks	4 733	1.66	–1.83	...	...	...	...	...	...
Other sectors	4 734	...	...	...	...	...	...	...	...
Other assets	4 736	...	...	...	...	...	...	...	...
Monetary authorities	4 737	...	...	...	...	...	...	...	...
of which: Short-term	4 739	...	...	...	...	...	...	...	...
General government	4 740	...	...	...	...	...	...	...	...
of which: Short-term	4 742	...	...	...	...	...	...	...	...
Banks	4 743	...	...	...	...	...	...	...	...
of which: Short-term	4 745	...	...	...	...	...	...	...	...
Other sectors	4 746	...	...	...	...	...	...	...	...
of which: Short-term	4 748	...	...	...	...	...	...	...	...
Liabilities	4 753	**26.68**	**18.30**	**...**	**...**	**...**	**...**	**...**	**...**
Trade credits	4 756	3.97	1.29	...	...	...	...	...	...
General government	4 757	3.97	1.29	...	...	...	...	...	...
of which: Short-term	4 759	*3.97*	*1.29*	...	...	...	...	...	...
Other sectors	4 760	...	...	...	...	...	...	...	...
of which: Short-term	4 762	...	...	...	...	...	...	...	...
Loans	4 764	17.11	14.05	...	...	...	...	...	...
Monetary authorities	4 765	1.89	...	...	...	...	...	...	...
of which: Use of Fund credit and loans from the Fund	4 766	*1.89*	...	...	...	...	...	...	...
of which: Short-term	4 768	...	...	...	...	...	...	...	...
General government	4 769	6.66	7.43	...	...	...	...	...	...
of which: Short-term	4 771	...	...	...	...	...	...	...	...
Banks	4 772	8.09	6.49	...	...	...	...	...	...
of which: Short-term	4 774	...	...	...	...	...	...	...	...
Other sectors	4 775	.47	.14	...	...	...	...	...	...
of which: Short-term	4 777	...	...	...	...	...	...	...	...
Currency and deposits	4 780	...	...	...	...	...	...	...	...
Monetary authorities	4 781	...	...	...	...	...	...	...	...
General government	4 782	...	...	...	...	...	...	...	...
Banks	4 783	...	...	...	...	...	...	...	...
Other sectors	4 784	...	...	...	...	...	...	...	...
Other liabilities	4 786	5.60	2.95	...	...	...	...	...	...
Monetary authorities	4 787	7.93	2.02	...	...	...	...	...	...
of which: Short-term	4 789	*7.93*	*2.02*	...	...	...	...	...	...
General government	4 790	...	...	...	...	...	...	...	...
of which: Short-term	4 792	...	...	...	...	...	...	...	...
Banks	4 793	...	...	...	...	...	...	...	...
of which: Short-term	4 795	...	...	...	...	...	...	...	...
Other sectors	4 796	–2.33	.92	...	...	...	...	...	...
of which: Short-term	4 798	*–2.33*	*.92*	...	...	...	...	...	...
E. RESERVE ASSETS	4 802	–14.97	3.37	...	...	...	...	...	...
Monetary gold	4 812	...	...	...	...	...	...	...	...
Special drawing rights	4 811	.05	–.06	...	...	...	...	...	...
Reserve position in the Fund	4 810	–.03	–.02	...	...	...	...	...	...
Foreign exchange	4 803	–15.00	3.46	...	...	...	...	...	...
Other claims	4 813	...	...	...	...	...	...	...	...
NET ERRORS AND OMISSIONS	4 998	**–6.33**	**–1.77**	**...**	**...**	**...**	**...**	**...**	**...**

Table 1. ANALYTIC PRESENTATION, 1994–2001

(Millions of U.S. dollars)

	Code		1994	1995	1996	1997	1998	1999	2000	2001
A. Current Account [1]	4 993	Z.	**–793.4**	**–649.7**	**–1,109.0**	**–251.9**	...	...	...	...
Goods: exports f.o.b	2 100	..	958.9	1,167.0	1,554.5	1,744.1	...	...	...	...
Goods: imports f.o.b	3 100	..	–612.7	–650.7	–1,361.0	–802.9	...	...	...	...
Balance on Goods	4 100	..	*346.2*	*516.3*	*193.5*	*941.3*	...	...	...	...
Services: credit	2 200	..	67.0	76.3	91.1	55.7	...	...	...	...
Services: debit	3 200	..	–995.8	–778.5	–721.1	–565.2	...	...	...	...
Balance on Goods and Services	4 991	..	*–582.7*	*–185.9*	*–436.5*	*431.8*	...	...	...	...
Income: credit	2 300	..	2.0	3.0	11.7	5.1	...	...	...	...
Income: debit	3 300	..	–291.1	–459.4	–670.1	–668.9	...	...	...	...
Balance on Goods, Services, and Income	4 992	..	*–871.8*	*–642.3*	*–1,094.9*	*–232.0*	...	...	...	...
Current transfers: credit	2 379	Z.	111.3	30.9	29.9	24.7	...	...	...	...
Current transfers: debit	3 379	..	–33.0	–38.3	–44.0	–44.5	...	...	...	...
B. Capital Account [1]	4 994	Z.	...	...	...	...	...	...	...	...
Capital account: credit	2 994	Z.	...	...	...	...	...	...	...	...
Capital account: debit	3 994	..	...	...	...	...	...	...	...	...
Total, Groups A Plus B	4 981	..	*–793.4*	*–649.7*	*–1,109.0*	*–251.9*	...	...	...	...
C. Financial Account [1]	4 995	W.	**605.4**	**–80.3**	**657.2**	**–173.7**	...	...	...	...
Direct investment abroad	4 505	..	...	...	...	...	...	...	...	...
Direct investment in the Republic of Congo	4 555	Z.	...	...	...	...	...	...	...	...
Portfolio investment assets	4 602	..	...	...	...	...	...	...	...	...
Equity securities	4 610	..	...	...	...	...	...	...	...	...
Debt securities	4 619	..	...	...	...	...	...	...	...	...
Portfolio investment liabilities	4 652	Z.	...	...	...	...	...	...	...	...
Equity securities	4 660	..	...	...	...	...	...	...	...	...
Debt securities	4 669	Z.	...	...	...	...	...	...	...	...
Financial derivatives	4 910	..	...	...	...	...	...	...	...	...
Financial derivatives assets	4 900	..	...	...	...	...	...	...	...	...
Financial derivatives liabilities	4 905	..	...	...	...	...	...	...	...	...
Other investment assets	4 703	..	35.5	–10.4	.4	–3.6	...	...	...	...
Monetary authorities	4 701	..	...	...	...	...	...	...	...	...
General government	4 704	..	...	...	...	...	...	...	...	...
Banks	4 705	..	33.9	–13.4	–3.5	–7.4	...	...	...	...
Other sectors	4 728	..	1.6	3.0	3.9	3.8	...	...	...	...
Other investment liabilities	4 753	W.	569.9	–69.9	656.8	–170.1	...	...	...	...
Monetary authorities	4 753	WA	...	...	...	...	...	...	...	...
General government	4 753	ZB	88.4	–432.5	–317.3	–386.7	...	...	...	...
Banks	4 753	ZC	...	...	...	...	...	...	...	...
Other sectors	4 753	ZD	481.4	362.6	974.1	216.6	...	...	...	...
Total, Groups A Through C	4 983	..	*–188.0*	*–730.0*	*–451.8*	*–425.6*	...	...	...	...
D. Net Errors and Omissions	4 998	..	**33.1**	**120.7**	**102.1**	**–122.1**	...	...	...	...
Total, Groups A Through D	4 984	..	*–154.9*	*–609.3*	*–349.7*	*–547.7*	...	...	...	...
E. Reserves and Related Items	4 802	A.	**154.9**	**609.3**	**349.7**	**547.7**	...	...	...	...
Reserve assets	4 802	..	–55.5	–6.4	–16.8	21.6	...	...	...	...
Use of Fund credit and loans	4 766	..	15.0	–2.3	20.1	–2.1	...	...	...	...
Exceptional financing	4 920	..	195.4	618.1	346.4	528.2	...	...	...	...
Conversion rates: CFA francs per U.S. dollar	0 101	..	**555.20**	**499.15**	**511.55**	**583.67**	**589.95**	**615.70**	**711.98**	**733.04**

[1] Excludes components that have been classified in the categories of Group E.

Table 2. STANDARD PRESENTATION, 1994–2001
(Millions of U.S. dollars)

	Code		1994	1995	1996	1997	1998	1999	2000	2001
CURRENT ACCOUNT	4 993	. .	**–793.4**	**–649.7**	**–1,109.0**	**–251.9**	. . .	. . .	. . .	. . .
A. GOODS	4 100	. .	346.2	516.3	193.5	941.3	. . .	. . .	. . .	. . .
Credit	2 100	. .	**958.9**	**1,167.0**	**1,554.5**	**1,744.1**	. . .	. . .	. . .	. . .
General merchandise: exports f.o.b.	2 110	. .	958.9	1,167.0	1,554.5	1,744.1	. . .	. . .	. . .	. . .
Goods for processing: exports f.o.b.	2 150	. .	. . .	. . .	. . .	. . .	. . .	. . .	. . .	. . .
Repairs on goods	2 160	. .	. . .	. . .	. . .	. . .	. . .	. . .	. . .	. . .
Goods procured in ports by carriers	2 170	. .	. . .	. . .	. . .	. . .	. . .	. . .	. . .	. . .
Nonmonetary gold	2 180	. .	. . .	. . .	. . .	. . .	. . .	. . .	. . .	. . .
Debit	3 100	. .	**–612.7**	**–650.7**	**–1,361.0**	**–802.9**	. . .	. . .	. . .	. . .
General merchandise: imports f.o.b.	3 110	. .	–612.7	–650.7	–1,361.0	–802.9	. . .	. . .	. . .	. . .
Goods for processing: imports f.o.b.	3 150	. .	. . .	. . .	. . .	. . .	. . .	. . .	. . .	. . .
Repairs on goods	3 160	. .	. . .	. . .	. . .	. . .	. . .	. . .	. . .	. . .
Goods procured in ports by carriers	3 170	. .	. . .	. . .	. . .	. . .	. . .	. . .	. . .	. . .
Nonmonetary gold	3 180	. .	. . .	. . .	. . .	. . .	. . .	. . .	. . .	. . .
B. SERVICES	4 200	. .	–928.8	–702.2	–630.0	–509.5	. . .	. . .	. . .	. . .
Total credit	2 200	. .	*67.0*	*76.3*	*91.1*	*55.7*	. . .	. . .	. . .	. . .
Total debit	3 200	. .	*–995.8*	*–778.5*	*–721.1*	*–565.2*	. . .	. . .	. . .	. . .
Transportation services, credit	2 205	. .	**28.5**	**32.3**	**35.2**	**25.7**	. . .	. . .	. . .	. . .
Passenger	2 850	. .	. . .	. . .	. . .	. . .	. . .	. . .	. . .	. . .
Freight	2 851	. .	. . .	. . .	. . .	. . .	. . .	. . .	. . .	. . .
Other	2 852	. .	*28.5*	*32.3*	*35.2*	*25.7*	. . .	. . .	. . .	. . .
Sea transport, passenger	2 207	. .	. . .	. . .	. . .	. . .	. . .	. . .	. . .	. . .
Sea transport, freight	2 208	. .	. . .	. . .	. . .	. . .	. . .	. . .	. . .	. . .
Sea transport, other	2 209	. .	. . .	. . .	. . .	. . .	. . .	. . .	. . .	. . .
Air transport, passenger	2 211	. .	. . .	. . .	. . .	. . .	. . .	. . .	. . .	. . .
Air transport, freight	2 212	. .	. . .	. . .	. . .	. . .	. . .	. . .	. . .	. . .
Air transport, other	2 213	. .	. . .	. . .	. . .	. . .	. . .	. . .	. . .	. . .
Other transport, passenger	2 215	. .	. . .	. . .	. . .	. . .	. . .	. . .	. . .	. . .
Other transport, freight	2 216	. .	. . .	. . .	. . .	. . .	. . .	. . .	. . .	. . .
Other transport, other	2 217	. .	. . .	. . .	. . .	. . .	. . .	. . .	. . .	. . .
Transportation services, debit	3 205	. .	**–189.7**	**–210.4**	**–207.8**	**–237.5**	. . .	. . .	. . .	. . .
Passenger	3 850	. .	*–63.4*	*–73.3*	*–72.3*	*–68.5*	. . .	. . .	. . .	. . .
Freight	3 851	. .	*–126.3*	*–137.0*	*–135.5*	*–169.0*	. . .	. . .	. . .	. . .
Other	3 852	. .	. . .	. . .	. . .	. . .	. . .	. . .	. . .	. . .
Sea transport, passenger	3 207	. .	. . .	. . .	. . .	. . .	. . .	. . .	. . .	. . .
Sea transport, freight	3 208	. .	. . .	. . .	. . .	. . .	. . .	. . .	. . .	. . .
Sea transport, other	3 209	. .	. . .	. . .	. . .	. . .	. . .	. . .	. . .	. . .
Air transport, passenger	3 211	. .	. . .	. . .	. . .	. . .	. . .	. . .	. . .	. . .
Air transport, freight	3 212	. .	. . .	. . .	. . .	. . .	. . .	. . .	. . .	. . .
Air transport, other	3 213	. .	. . .	. . .	. . .	. . .	. . .	. . .	. . .	. . .
Other transport, passenger	3 215	. .	. . .	. . .	. . .	. . .	. . .	. . .	. . .	. . .
Other transport, freight	3 216	. .	. . .	. . .	. . .	. . .	. . .	. . .	. . .	. . .
Other transport, other	3 217	. .	. . .	. . .	. . .	. . .	. . .	. . .	. . .	. . .
Travel, credit	2 236	. .	**3.6**	**5.0**	**7.8**	**2.6**	. . .	. . .	. . .	. . .
Business travel	2 237	. .	. . .	. . .	. . .	. . .	. . .	. . .	. . .	. . .
Personal travel	2 240	. .	. . .	. . .	. . .	. . .	. . .	. . .	. . .	. . .
Travel, debit	3 236	. .	**–33.5**	**–39.1**	**–43.0**	**–51.4**	. . .	. . .	. . .	. . .
Business travel	3 237	. .	. . .	. . .	. . .	. . .	. . .	. . .	. . .	. . .
Personal travel	3 240	. .	. . .	. . .	. . .	. . .	. . .	. . .	. . .	. . .
Other services, credit	2 200	BA	**34.9**	**39.1**	**48.1**	**27.4**	. . .	. . .	. . .	. . .
Communications	2 245	. .	. . .	. . .	. . .	. . .	. . .	. . .	. . .	. . .
Construction	2 249	. .	. . .	. . .	. . .	. . .	. . .	. . .	. . .	. . .
Insurance	2 253	. .	. . .	. . .	. . .	. . .	. . .	. . .	. . .	. . .
Financial	2 260	. .	. . .	. . .	. . .	. . .	. . .	. . .	. . .	. . .
Computer and information	2 262	. .	. . .	. . .	. . .	. . .	. . .	. . .	. . .	. . .
Royalties and licence fees	2 266	. .	. . .	. . .	. . .	. . .	. . .	. . .	. . .	. . .
Other business services	2 268	. .	16.6	18.0	24.6	17.1	. . .	. . .	. . .	. . .
Personal, cultural, and recreational	2 287	. .	. . .	. . .	. . .	. . .	. . .	. . .	. . .	. . .
Government, n.i.e.	2 291	. .	18.4	21.0	23.5	10.3	. . .	. . .	. . .	. . .
Other services, debit	3 200	BA	**–772.7**	**–529.1**	**–470.3**	**–276.3**	. . .	. . .	. . .	. . .
Communications	3 245	. .	. . .	. . .	. . .	. . .	. . .	. . .	. . .	. . .
Construction	3 249	. .	. . .	. . .	. . .	. . .	. . .	. . .	. . .	. . .
Insurance	3 253	. .	–14.0	–15.2	–15.1	–18.8	. . .	. . .	. . .	. . .
Financial	3 260	. .	. . .	. . .	. . .	. . .	. . .	. . .	. . .	. . .
Computer and information	3 262	. .	. . .	. . .	. . .	. . .	. . .	. . .	. . .	. . .
Royalties and licence fees	3 266	. .	. . .	. . .	. . .	. . .	. . .	. . .	. . .	. . .
Other business services	3 268	. .	–745.7	–500.9	–441.8	–245.5	. . .	. . .	. . .	. . .
Personal, cultural, and recreational	3 287	. .	. . .	. . .	. . .	. . .	. . .	. . .	. . .	. . .
Government, n.i.e.	3 291	. .	–13.0	–13.0	–13.5	–12.0	. . .	. . .	. . .	. . .

Table 2 (Continued). STANDARD PRESENTATION, 1994–2001
(Millions of U.S. dollars)

	Code		1994	1995	1996	1997	1998	1999	2000	2001
C. INCOME	4 300	. .	–289.1	–456.4	–658.4	–663.7	...	...	...	...
Total credit	2 300	. .	*2.0*	*3.0*	*11.7*	*5.1*	...	...	...	...
Total debit	3 300	. .	*–291.1*	*–459.4*	*–670.1*	*–668.9*	...	...	...	...
Compensation of employees, credit	2 310	. .	...	...	...	...	...	...	...	...
Compensation of employees, debit	3 310	. .	...	...	...	...	...	...	...	...
Investment income, credit	2 320	. .	**2.0**	**3.0**	**11.7**	**5.1**	...	...	...	...
Direct investment income	2 330	. .	...	...	...	...	...	...	...	...
Dividends and distributed branch profits	2 332	. .	...	...	...	...	...	...	...	...
Reinvested earnings and undistributed branch profits	2 333	. .	...	...	...	...	...	...	...	...
Income on debt (interest)	2 334	. .	...	...	...	...	...	...	...	...
Portfolio investment income	2 339	. .	...	...	...	...	...	...	...	...
Income on equity	2 340	. .	...	...	...	...	...	...	...	...
Income on bonds and notes	2 350	. .	...	...	...	...	...	...	...	...
Income on money market instruments	2 360	. .	...	...	...	...	...	...	...	...
Other investment income	2 370	. .	2.0	3.0	11.7	5.1	...	...	...	...
Investment income, debit	3 320	. .	**–291.1**	**–459.4**	**–670.1**	**–668.9**	...	...	...	...
Direct investment income	3 330	. .	...	...	...	...	...	...	...	...
Dividends and distributed branch profits	3 332	. .	...	...	...	...	...	...	...	...
Reinvested earnings and undistributed branch profits	3 333	. .	...	...	...	...	...	...	...	...
Income on debt (interest)	3 334	. .	...	...	...	...	...	...	...	...
Portfolio investment income	3 339	. .	...	...	...	...	...	...	...	...
Income on equity	3 340	. .	...	...	...	...	...	...	...	...
Income on bonds and notes	3 350	. .	...	...	...	...	...	...	...	...
Income on money market instruments	3 360	. .	...	...	...	...	...	...	...	...
Other investment income	3 370	. .	–291.1	–459.4	–670.1	–668.9	...	...	...	...
D. CURRENT TRANSFERS	4 379	. .	78.3	–7.4	–14.1	–19.9	...	...	...	...
Credit	2 379	. .	**111.3**	**30.9**	**29.9**	**24.7**	...	...	...	...
General government	2 380	. .	108.2	26.8	20.1	21.8	...	...	...	...
Other sectors	2 390	. .	3.1	4.0	9.8	2.9	...	...	...	...
Workers' remittances	2 391	. .	...	...	...	...	...	...	...	...
Other current transfers	2 392	. .	3.1	4.0	9.8	2.9	...	...	...	...
Debit	3 379	. .	**–33.0**	**–38.3**	**–44.0**	**–44.5**	...	...	...	...
General government	3 380	. .	–1.6	–2.0	–2.9	–1.7	...	...	...	...
Other sectors	3 390	. .	–31.3	–36.3	–41.1	–42.8	...	...	...	...
Workers' remittances	3 391	. .	–23.2	–26.8	–30.3	–31.7	...	...	...	...
Other current transfers	3 392	. .	–8.1	–9.4	–10.8	–11.1	...	...	...	...
CAPITAL AND FINANCIAL ACCOUNT	4 996	. .	**760.3**	**529.0**	**1,006.9**	**374.0**	...	...	...	...
CAPITAL ACCOUNT	4 994	. .	...	...	...	...	...	...	...	...
Total credit	2 994	. .	...	...	...	...	...	...	...	...
Total debit	3 994	. .	...	...	...	...	...	...	...	...
Capital transfers, credit	2 400	. .	...	...	...	...	...	...	...	...
General government	2 401	. .	...	...	...	...	...	...	...	...
Debt forgiveness	2 402	. .	...	...	...	...	...	...	...	...
Other capital transfers	2 410	. .	...	...	...	...	...	...	...	...
Other sectors	2 430	. .	...	...	...	...	...	...	...	...
Migrants' transfers	2 431	. .	...	...	...	...	...	...	...	...
Debt forgiveness	2 432	. .	...	...	...	...	...	...	...	...
Other capital transfers	2 440	. .	...	...	...	...	...	...	...	...
Capital transfers, debit	3 400	. .	...	...	...	...	...	...	...	...
General government	3 401	. .	...	...	...	...	...	...	...	...
Debt forgiveness	3 402	. .	...	...	...	...	...	...	...	...
Other capital transfers	3 410	. .	...	...	...	...	...	...	...	...
Other sectors	3 430	. .	...	...	...	...	...	...	...	...
Migrants' transfers	3 431	. .	...	...	...	...	...	...	...	...
Debt forgiveness	3 432	. .	...	...	...	...	...	...	...	...
Other capital transfers	3 440	. .	...	...	...	...	...	...	...	...
Nonproduced nonfinancial assets, credit	2 480	. .	...	...	...	...	...	...	...	...
Nonproduced nonfinancial assets, debit	3 480	. .	...	...	...	...	...	...	...	...

Table 2 (Continued). STANDARD PRESENTATION, 1994–2001
(Millions of U.S. dollars)

	Code	1994	1995	1996	1997	1998	1999	2000	2001
FINANCIAL ACCOUNT	4 995	**760.3**	**529.0**	**1,006.9**	**374.0**	**...**	**...**	**...**	**...**
A. DIRECT INVESTMENT	4 500	...	...	...	...	...	...	...	...
Direct investment abroad	4 505	**...**	**...**	**...**	**...**	**...**	**...**	**...**	**...**
Equity capital	4 510	...	...	...	...	...	...	...	...
Claims on affiliated enterprises	4 515	...	...	...	...	...	...	...	...
Liabilities to affiliated enterprises	4 520	...	...	...	...	...	...	...	...
Reinvested earnings	4 525	...	...	...	...	...	...	...	...
Other capital	4 530	...	...	...	...	...	...	...	...
Claims on affiliated enterprises	4 535	...	...	...	...	...	...	...	...
Liabilities to affiliated enterprises	4 540	...	...	...	...	...	...	...	...
Direct investment in the Republic of Congo	4 555	**...**	**...**	**...**	**...**	**...**	**...**	**...**	**...**
Equity capital	4 560	...	...	...	...	...	...	...	...
Claims on direct investors	4 565	...	...	...	...	...	...	...	...
Liabilities to direct investors	4 570	...	...	...	...	...	...	...	...
Reinvested earnings	4 575	...	...	...	...	...	...	...	...
Other capital	4 580	...	...	...	...	...	...	...	...
Claims on direct investors	4 585	...	...	...	...	...	...	...	...
Liabilities to direct investors	4 590	...	...	...	...	...	...	...	...
B. PORTFOLIO INVESTMENT	4 600	...	...	...	...	...	...	...	...
Assets	4 602	**...**	**...**	**...**	**...**	**...**	**...**	**...**	**...**
Equity securities	4 610	...	...	...	...	...	...	...	...
Monetary authorities	4 611	...	...	...	...	...	...	...	...
General government	4 612	...	...	...	...	...	...	...	...
Banks	4 613	...	...	...	...	...	...	...	...
Other sectors	4 614	...	...	...	...	...	...	...	...
Debt securities	4 619	...	...	...	...	...	...	...	...
Bonds and notes	4 620	...	...	...	...	...	...	...	...
Monetary authorities	4 621	...	...	...	...	...	...	...	...
General government	4 622	...	...	...	...	...	...	...	...
Banks	4 623	...	...	...	...	...	...	...	...
Other sectors	4 624	...	...	...	...	...	...	...	...
Money market instruments	4 630	...	...	...	...	...	...	...	...
Monetary authorities	4 631	...	...	...	...	...	...	...	...
General government	4 632	...	...	...	...	...	...	...	...
Banks	4 633	...	...	...	...	...	...	...	...
Other sectors	4 634	...	...	...	...	...	...	...	...
Liabilities	4 652	**...**	**...**	**...**	**...**	**...**	**...**	**...**	**...**
Equity securities	4 660	...	...	...	...	...	...	...	...
Banks	4 663	...	...	...	...	...	...	...	...
Other sectors	4 664	...	...	...	...	...	...	...	...
Debt securities	4 669	...	...	...	...	...	...	...	...
Bonds and notes	4 670	...	...	...	...	...	...	...	...
Monetary authorities	4 671	...	...	...	...	...	...	...	...
General government	4 672	...	...	...	...	...	...	...	...
Banks	4 673	...	...	...	...	...	...	...	...
Other sectors	4 674	...	...	...	...	...	...	...	...
Money market instruments	4 680	...	...	...	...	...	...	...	...
Monetary authorities	4 681	...	...	...	...	...	...	...	...
General government	4 682	...	...	...	...	...	...	...	...
Banks	4 683	...	...	...	...	...	...	...	...
Other sectors	4 684	...	...	...	...	...	...	...	...
C. FINANCIAL DERIVATIVES	4 910	...	...	...	...	...	...	...	...
Monetary authorities	4 911	...	...	...	...	...	...	...	...
General government	4 912	...	...	...	...	...	...	...	...
Banks	4 913	...	...	...	...	...	...	...	...
Other sectors	4 914	...	...	...	...	...	...	...	...
Assets	4 900	**...**	**...**	**...**	**...**	**...**	**...**	**...**	**...**
Monetary authorities	4 901	...	...	...	...	...	...	...	...
General government	4 902	...	...	...	...	...	...	...	...
Banks	4 903	...	...	...	...	...	...	...	...
Other sectors	4 904	...	...	...	...	...	...	...	...
Liabilities	4 905	**...**	**...**	**...**	**...**	**...**	**...**	**...**	**...**
Monetary authorities	4 906	...	...	...	...	...	...	...	...
General government	4 907	...	...	...	...	...	...	...	...
Banks	4 908	...	...	...	...	...	...	...	...
Other sectors	4 909	...	...	...	...	...	...	...	...

Table 2 (Concluded). STANDARD PRESENTATION, 1994–2001

(Millions of U.S. dollars)

	Code	1994	1995	1996	1997	1998	1999	2000	2001
D. OTHER INVESTMENT	4 700	815.8	535.4	1,023.8	352.4	...	...	...	...
Assets	4 703	**35.5**	**–10.4**	**.4**	**–3.6**	**...**	**...**	**...**	**...**
Trade credits	4 706	...	...	...	...	...	...	...	...
General government	4 707	...	...	...	...	...	...	...	...
of which: Short-term	4 709	...	...	...	...	...	...	...	...
Other sectors	4 710	...	...	...	...	...	...	...	...
of which: Short-term	4 712	...	...	...	...	...	...	...	...
Loans	4 714	1.6	3.0	3.9	3.8	...	...	...	...
Monetary authorities	4 715	...	...	...	...	...	...	...	...
of which: Short-term	4 718	...	...	...	...	...	...	...	...
General government	4 719	...	...	...	...	...	...	...	...
of which: Short-term	4 721	...	...	...	...	...	...	...	...
Banks	4 722	...	...	...	...	...	...	...	...
of which: Short-term	4 724	...	...	...	...	...	...	...	...
Other sectors	4 725	1.6	3.0	3.9	3.8	...	...	...	...
of which: Short-term	4 727	...	...	...	...	...	...	...	...
Currency and deposits	4 730	33.9	–13.4	–3.5	–7.4	...	...	...	...
Monetary authorities	4 731	...	...	...	...	...	...	...	...
General government	4 732	...	...	...	...	...	...	...	...
Banks	4 733	33.9	–13.4	–3.5	–7.4	...	...	...	...
Other sectors	4 734	...	...	...	...	...	...	...	...
Other assets	4 736	...	...	...	...	...	...	...	...
Monetary authorities	4 737	...	...	...	...	...	...	...	...
of which: Short-term	4 739	...	...	...	...	...	...	...	...
General government	4 740	...	...	...	...	...	...	...	...
of which: Short-term	4 742	...	...	...	...	...	...	...	...
Banks	4 743	...	...	...	...	...	...	...	...
of which: Short-term	4 745	...	...	...	...	...	...	...	...
Other sectors	4 746	...	...	...	...	...	...	...	...
of which: Short-term	4 748	...	...	...	...	...	...	...	...
Liabilities	4 753	**780.3**	**545.8**	**1,023.4**	**356.0**	**...**	**...**	**...**	**...**
Trade credits	4 756	...	...	...	...	...	...	...	...
General government	4 757	...	...	...	...	...	...	...	...
of which: Short-term	4 759	...	...	...	...	...	...	...	...
Other sectors	4 760	...	...	...	...	...	...	...	...
of which: Short-term	4 762	...	...	...	...	...	...	...	...
Loans	4 764	1,464.5	–141.1	1,310.9	83.0	...	...	...	...
Monetary authorities	4 765	15.0	–2.3	20.1	–2.1	...	...	...	...
of which: Use of Fund credit and loans from the Fund	4 766	*15.0*	*–2.3*	*20.1*	*–2.1*	...	...	...	...
of which: Short-term	4 768	...	...	...	...	...	...	...	...
General government	4 769	1,208.7	–301.1	609.9	–54.3	...	...	...	...
of which: Short-term	4 771	...	...	...	...	...	...	...	...
Banks	4 772	...	...	...	...	...	...	...	...
of which: Short-term	4 774	...	...	...	...	...	...	...	...
Other sectors	4 775	240.8	162.3	680.9	139.5	...	...	...	...
of which: Short-term	4 777	...	...	...	...	...	...	...	...
Currency and deposits	4 780	...	...	...	...	...	...	...	...
Monetary authorities	4 781	...	...	...	...	...	...	...	...
General government	4 782	...	...	...	...	...	...	...	...
Banks	4 783	...	...	...	...	...	...	...	...
Other sectors	4 784	...	...	...	...	...	...	...	...
Other liabilities	4 786	–684.3	687.0	–287.6	272.9	...	...	...	...
Monetary authorities	4 787	–924.9	486.6	–580.8	195.8	...	...	...	...
of which: Short-term	4 789	*–924.9*	*486.6*	*–580.8*	*195.8*	...	...	...	...
General government	4 790	...	...	...	...	...	...	...	...
of which: Short-term	4 792	...	...	...	...	...	...	...	...
Banks	4 793	...	...	...	...	...	...	...	...
of which: Short-term	4 795	...	...	...	...	...	...	...	...
Other sectors	4 796	240.6	200.3	293.2	77.1	...	...	...	...
of which: Short-term	4 798	*240.6*	*200.3*	*293.2*	*77.1*	...	...	...	...
E. RESERVE ASSETS	4 802	–55.5	–6.4	–16.8	21.6	...	...	...	...
Monetary gold	4 812	...	...	...	...	...	...	...	...
Special drawing rights	4 811	...	...	...	...	...	...	...	...
Reserve position in the Fund	4 810	...	...	–.1	...	...	...	...	...
Foreign exchange	4 803	–55.5	–6.4	–16.8	21.6	...	...	...	...
Other claims	4 813	...	...	...	...	...	...	...	...
NET ERRORS AND OMISSIONS	4 998	**33.1**	**120.7**	**102.1**	**–122.1**	**...**	**...**	**...**	**...**

Part 3 of the *Yearbook* contains descriptions of the methodologies, compilation practices, and sources used to compile these data.

Table 1. ANALYTIC PRESENTATION, 1994–2001
(Millions of U.S. dollars)

	Code	1994	1995	1996	1997	1998	1999	2000	2001
A. Current Account [1]	4 993 Z.	**-244.0**	**-358.1**	**-263.7**	**-480.9**	**-520.8**	**-680.1**	**-757.8**	**-701.5**
Goods: exports f.o.b.	2 100 . .	2,122.0	3,481.8	3,774.1	4,220.6	5,538.3	6,576.8	5,813.7	4,907.8
Goods: imports f.o.b.	3 100 . .	-2,727.8	-3,804.4	-4,023.3	-4,718.2	-5,937.4	-5,996.3	-6,024.8	-6,117.9
Balance on Goods	4 100 . .	*-605.8*	*-322.6*	*-249.2*	*-497.6*	*-399.0*	*580.5*	*-211.1*	*-1,210.1*
Services: credit	2 200 . .	1,195.0	969.1	1,053.5	1,128.6	1,343.4	1,660.4	1,900.0	2,051.0
Services: debit	3 200 . .	-860.1	-913.0	-1,033.3	-988.4	-1,109.8	-1,201.9	-1,286.7	-1,275.2
Balance on Goods and Services	4 991 . .	*-270.9*	*-266.5*	*-228.9*	*-357.4*	*-165.5*	*1,039.0*	*402.2*	*-434.3*
Income: credit	2 300 . .	154.6	146.4	142.5	185.4	182.7	198.4	243.0	560.6
Income: debit	3 300 . .	-283.0	-371.9	-326.7	-434.4	-651.2	-2,019.9	-1,495.0	-975.5
Balance on Goods, Services, and Income	4 992 . .	*-399.3*	*-492.0*	*-413.2*	*-606.4*	*-634.0*	*-782.5*	*-849.8*	*-849.2*
Current transfers: credit	2 379 Z.	164.5	165.2	192.7	191.2	190.5	190.8	192.0	248.9
Current transfers: debit	3 379 . .	-9.2	-31.3	-43.2	-65.7	-77.3	-88.4	-100.0	-101.2
B. Capital Account [1]	4 994 Z.	**. . .**	**. . .**	**28.2**	**. . .**	**. . .**	**. . .**	**8.8**	**12.4**
Capital account: credit	2 994 Z.	. . .	. . .	28.2	. . .	. . .	. . .	8.8	12.4
Capital account: debit	3 994 . .	. . .	. . .	. . .	. . .	. . .	. . .	. . .	. . .
Total, Groups A Plus B	4 981 . .	*-244.0*	*-358.1*	*-235.5*	*-480.9*	*-520.8*	*-680.1*	*-749.0*	*-689.1*
C. Financial Account [1]	4 995 W.	**-108.4**	**517.3**	**47.5**	**129.7**	**199.0**	**568.0**	**-84.1**	**383.1**
Direct investment abroad	4 505 . .	-4.7	-5.5	-5.7	-4.4	-4.8	-5.0	-5.2	-5.2
Direct investment in Costa Rica	4 555 Z.	297.6	336.9	427.0	408.2	613.1	619.6	408.5	453.6
Portfolio investment assets	4 602 . .	. . .	-.4	. . .	-22.5	-33.9	-10.8	-18.4	-81.3
Equity securities	4 610 . .	. . .	-.4	. . .	-22.5	-33.9	-28.0	-4.0	-22.0
Debt securities	4 619 . .	. . .	. . .	. . .	. . .	. . .	17.2	-14.4	-59.3
Portfolio investment liabilities	4 652 Z.	-1.2	-24.4	-21.5	-190.8	-296.0	-253.8	-350.4	-200.3
Equity securities	4 660 . .	. . .	. . .	. . .	. . .	. . .	. . .	. . .	. . .
Debt securities	4 669 Z.	-1.2	-24.4	-21.5	-190.8	-296.0	-253.8	-350.4	-200.3
Financial derivatives	4 910 . .	. . .	. . .	. . .	. . .	. . .	. . .	. . .	. . .
Financial derivatives assets	4 900 . .	. . .	. . .	. . .	. . .	. . .	. . .	. . .	. . .
Financial derivatives liabilities	4 905 . .	. . .	. . .	. . .	. . .	. . .	. . .	. . .	. . .
Other investment assets	4 703 . .	-76.2	16.8	-159.3	-267.4	-95.6	161.7	-343.9	106.5
Monetary authorities	4 701 . .	. . .	.1	-6.3	-.1	. . .	. . .	. . .	. . .
General government	4 704 . .	-4.4	. . .	. . .	. . .	. . .	. . .	. . .	. . .
Banks	4 705 . .	. . .	-9.8	-17.8	43.3	-29.8	47.5	-76.3	54.3
Other sectors	4 728 . .	-71.8	26.5	-135.2	-310.6	-65.8	114.2	-267.6	52.2
Other investment liabilities	4 753 W.	-323.9	193.9	-192.9	206.7	16.2	56.3	225.3	109.8
Monetary authorities	4 753 WA	-216.1	-94.4	-104.0	-118.6	-98.5	-93.7	-175.9	-134.0
General government	4 753 ZB	-106.2	12.9	-85.2	-64.1	-60.7	-77.9	-74.6	11.6
Banks	4 753 ZC	-18.8	23.0	48.7	73.7	37.3	50.6	137.2	97.5
Other sectors	4 753 ZD	17.2	252.4	-52.3	315.7	138.1	177.3	338.6	134.7
Total, Groups A Through C	4 983 . .	*-352.4*	*159.2*	*-188.0*	*-351.1*	*-321.7*	*-112.1*	*-833.1*	*-306.0*
D. Net Errors and Omissions	4 998 . .	**249.1**	**57.1**	**118.7**	**157.8**	**-182.6**	**213.4**	**218.2**	**19.2**
Total, Groups A Through D	4 984 . .	*-103.3*	*216.2*	*-69.3*	*-193.3*	*-504.3*	*101.3*	*-614.9*	*-286.8*
E. Reserves and Related Items	4 802 A.	**103.3**	**-216.2**	**69.3**	**193.3**	**504.3**	**-101.3**	**614.9**	**286.8**
Reserve assets	4 802 . .	65.5	-179.2	77.3	-215.7	149.6	-481.0	152.9	-13.2
Use of Fund credit and loans	4 766 . .	-20.3	-44.4	-23.1	-.7	. . .	. . .	. . .	. . .
Exceptional financing	4 920 . .	58.1	7.4	15.0	409.7	354.7	379.7	462.0	300.0
Conversion rates: Costa Rican colones per U.S. dollar	0 101 . .	**157.07**	**179.73**	**207.69**	**232.60**	**257.23**	**285.68**	**308.19**	**328.87**

[1] Excludes components that have been classified in the categories of Group E.

Table 2. STANDARD PRESENTATION, 1994–2001
(Millions of U.S. dollars)

	Code		1994	1995	1996	1997	1998	1999	2000	2001
CURRENT ACCOUNT	4 993	. .	**-233.6**	**-358.1**	**-263.7**	**-480.9**	**-520.8**	**-680.1**	**-757.8**	**-701.5**
A. GOODS	4 100	. .	-605.8	-322.6	-249.2	-497.6	-399.0	580.5	-211.1	-1,210.1
Credit	2 100	. .	**2,122.0**	**3,481.8**	**3,774.1**	**4,220.6**	**5,538.3**	**6,576.8**	**5,813.7**	**4,907.8**
General merchandise: exports f.o.b.	2 110	. .	2,122.0	2,561.2	2,736.6	2,887.0	3,142.6	2,572.3	2,440.5	2,197.8
Goods for processing: exports f.o.b.	2 150	. .	. . .	909.8	1,021.8	1,318.5	2,380.7	3,984.9	3,355.2	2,692.4
Repairs on goods	2 160	. .	. . .	2.6	2.7	. . .	. . .	1.2	1.2	. . .
Goods procured in ports by carriers	2 170	. .	. . .	8.2	13.0	15.1	15.0	18.4	16.8	17.6
Nonmonetary gold	2 180	. .	. . .	. . .	. . .	. . .	. . .	. . .	. . .	. . .
Debit	3 100	. .	**-2,727.8**	**-3,804.4**	**-4,023.3**	**-4,718.2**	**-5,937.4**	**-5,996.3**	**-6,024.8**	**-6,117.9**
General merchandise: imports f.o.b.	3 110	. .	-2,727.8	-3,006.3	-3,233.7	-3,651.9	-4,266.8	-3,988.8	-4,080.7	-4,027.0
Goods for processing: imports f.o.b.	3 150	. .	. . .	-756.9	-762.3	-1,035.7	-1,629.1	-1,970.6	-1,906.6	-2,056.9
Repairs on goods	3 160	. .	. . .	-1.4	-1.6	-7.8	-8.0	-12.0	-12.0	-14.0
Goods procured in ports by carriers	3 170	. .	. . .	-39.8	-25.7	-22.9	-33.6	-24.9	-25.5	-20.0
Nonmonetary gold	3 180	. .	. . .	. . .	. . .	. . .	. . .	. . .	. . .	. . .
B. SERVICES	4 200	. .	334.9	56.1	20.3	140.2	233.6	458.5	613.3	775.8
Total credit	2 200	. .	*1,195.0*	*969.1*	*1,053.5*	*1,128.6*	*1,343.4*	*1,660.4*	*1,900.0*	*2,051.0*
Total debit	3 200	. .	*-860.1*	*-913.0*	*-1,033.3*	*-988.4*	*-1,109.8*	*-1,201.9*	*-1,286.7*	*-1,275.2*
Transportation services, credit	2 205	. .	**172.5**	**134.1**	**149.2**	**184.5**	**202.2**	**247.2**	**207.6**	**212.2**
Passenger	2 850	. .	*81.1*	*81.9*	*87.5*	*118.3*	*124.1*	*157.6*	*125.1*	*134.6*
Freight	2 851	. .	*13.6*	*24.2*	*21.6*	*20.4*	*26.7*	*20.3*	*18.7*	*15.3*
Other	2 852	. .	*77.8*	*28.0*	*40.2*	*45.8*	*51.4*	*69.3*	*63.8*	*62.3*
Sea transport, passenger	2 207	. .	. . .	. . .	. . .	. . .	. . .	. . .	. . .	. . .
Sea transport, freight	2 208	. .	. . .	. . .	. . .	. . .	. . .	. . .	. . .	. . .
Sea transport, other	2 209	. .	. . .	8.0	12.2	14.2	15.5	17.0	15.9	17.8
Air transport, passenger	2 211	. .	. . .	80.9	86.4	117.7	123.4	156.8	124.5	133.9
Air transport, freight	2 212	. .	. . .	15.0	12.5	10.9	16.9	9.5	7.2	2.9
Air transport, other	2 213	. .	. . .	19.8	28.0	31.7	35.9	52.3	47.9	44.5
Other transport, passenger	2 215	. .	. . .	1.0	1.1	.7	.7	.8	.6	.7
Other transport, freight	2 216	. .	. . .	9.2	9.0	9.5	9.7	10.8	11.5	12.4
Other transport, other	2 217	. .	. . .	.2	. . .	. . .	. . .	. . .	. . .	. . .
Transportation services, debit	3 205	. .	**-352.7**	**-370.9**	**-400.0**	**-373.6**	**-415.8**	**-439.4**	**-416.5**	**-423.9**
Passenger	3 850	. .	*-12.5*	*-13.3*	*-20.9*	*-53.1*	*-57.2*	*-62.3*	*-65.8*	*-70.4*
Freight	3 851	. .	*-262.5*	*-289.1*	*-311.2*	*-235.2*	*-288.5*	*-291.8*	*-302.0*	*-305.4*
Other	3 852	. .	*-77.7*	*-68.5*	*-67.9*	*-85.3*	*-70.1*	*-85.3*	*-48.7*	*-48.1*
Sea transport, passenger	3 207	. .	. . .	. . .	. . .	. . .	. . .	. . .	. . .	. . .
Sea transport, freight	3 208	. .	. . .	-289.0	-311.2	-235.2	-288.5	-291.8	-302.0	-305.4
Sea transport, other	3 209	. .	. . .	. . .	. . .	. . .	. . .	. . .	. . .	. . .
Air transport, passenger	3 211	. .	. . .	-13.3	-20.9	-53.1	-57.2	-62.3	-65.8	-70.4
Air transport, freight	3 212	. .	. . .	. . .	. . .	. . .	. . .	. . .	. . .	. . .
Air transport, other	3 213	. .	. . .	-66.8	-62.9	-84.9	-70.0	-83.5	-47.5	-47.2
Other transport, passenger	3 215	. .	. . .	. . .	. . .	. . .	. . .	. . .	. . .	. . .
Other transport, freight	3 216	. .	. . .	-.1	. . .	. . .	. . .	. . .	. . .	. . .
Other transport, other	3 217	. .	. . .	-1.7	-5.0	-.4	-.1	1.8	-1.2	-.9
Travel, credit	2 236	. .	**633.8**	**681.1**	**710.0**	**742.3**	**913.5**	**1,098.7**	**1,302.7**	**1,358.6**
Business travel	2 237	. .	. . .	. . .	. . .	. . .	. . .	.4	3.2	3.2
Personal travel	2 240	. .	. . .	681.1	710.0	742.3	913.5	1,098.3	1,299.5	1,355.4
Travel, debit	3 236	. .	**-303.3**	**-322.8**	**-336.0**	**-348.0**	**-408.9**	**-447.3**	**-485.4**	**-470.7**
Business travel	3 237	. .	-2.1	-.9	-.7	. . .	. . .	-1.0	-3.1	3.2
Personal travel	3 240	. .	-301.2	-321.9	-335.4	-348.0	-408.9	-446.3	-482.3	-467.5
Other services, credit	2 200	BA	**388.7**	**153.9**	**194.3**	**201.8**	**227.7**	**314.5**	**389.7**	**480.2**
Communications	2 245	. .	. . .	57.3	76.5	79.9	85.2	84.4	93.2	85.5
Construction	2 249	. .	. . .	. . .	. . .	. . .	. . .	. . .	. . .	. . .
Insurance	2 253	. .	. . .	-1.7	-1.2	. . .	. . .	15.1	15.6	15.5
Financial	2 260	. .	. . .	.1	3.3	5.2	7.1	9.2	4.0	4.8
Computer and information	2 262	. .	. . .	. . .	. . .	. . .	2.5	57.6	59.5	124.6
Royalties and licence fees	2 266	. .	2.5	2.6	2.2	.2	.2	1.2	.4	.8
Other business services	2 268	. .	354.0	83.1	101.7	103.9	117.9	124.2	192.2	222.7
Personal, cultural, and recreational	2 287	. .	. . .	. . .	. . .	.1	.1	. . .	. . .	. . .
Government, n.i.e.	2 291	. .	32.2	12.5	11.9	12.5	14.7	22.8	24.8	26.3
Other services, debit	3 200	BA	**-204.1**	**-219.3**	**-297.3**	**-266.8**	**-285.1**	**-315.2**	**-384.8**	**-380.6**
Communications	3 245	. .	. . .	-38.1	-56.9	-55.7	-51.7	-47.6	-51.7	-27.4
Construction	3 249	. .	. . .	. . .	. . .	. . .	. . .	. . .	. . .	. . .
Insurance	3 253	. .	-54.0	-39.6	-40.6	-39.7	-35.1	-56.7	-61.3	-64.8
Financial	3 260	. .	. . .	-1.8	-.6	-1.3	-.9	-1.6	-2.8	-2.0
Computer and information	3 262	. .	. . .	. . .	. . .	-1.2	-1.9	-3.2	-9.4	-14.2
Royalties and licence fees	3 266	. .	-11.0	-13.4	-23.6	-27.2	-32.0	-30.8	-49.9	-49.2
Other business services	3 268	. .	-124.7	-106.0	-160.5	-127.9	-152.6	-165.3	-197.7	-210.2
Personal, cultural, and recreational	3 287	. .	. . .	-2.4	-1.2	-.1	. . .	. . .	. . .	. . .
Government, n.i.e.	3 291	. .	-14.4	-18.0	-13.9	-13.8	-10.9	-10.0	-12.0	-12.8

Table 2 (Continued). STANDARD PRESENTATION, 1994–2001
(Millions of U.S. dollars)

	Code	1994	1995	1996	1997	1998	1999	2000	2001
C. INCOME	4 300	–128.4	–225.5	–184.2	–249.0	–468.5	–1,821.5	–1,252.0	–414.9
Total credit	2 300	*154.6*	*146.4*	*142.5*	*185.4*	*182.7*	*198.4*	*243.0*	*560.6*
Total debit	3 300	*–283.0*	*–371.9*	*–326.7*	*–434.4*	*–651.2*	*–2,019.9*	*–1,495.0*	*–975.5*
Compensation of employees, credit	2 310	**17.1**	**7.4**	**9.1**	**14.3**	**15.7**	**14.7**	**15.6**	**14.4**
Compensation of employees, debit	3 310	**–7.1**	**–7.5**	**–7.2**	**–8.8**	**–22.8**	**–29.4**	**–34.3**	**–33.7**
Investment income, credit	2 320	**137.5**	**139.0**	**133.4**	**171.2**	**167.0**	**183.7**	**227.4**	**546.2**
Direct investment income	2 330	5.7	5.5	7.8	19.8	11.2	7.7	11.2	385.9
Dividends and distributed branch profits	2 332	...	...	.4	14.1	5.0	2.7	6.0	380.7
Reinvested earnings and undistributed branch profits	2 333	5.7	5.5	7.4	5.7	6.2	5.0	5.2	5.2
Income on debt (interest)	2 334	...	...	...	...	...	...	...	...
Portfolio investment income	2 339	...	...	...	...	...	.4	1.2	5.2
Income on equity	2 340	...	...	...	...	...	...	...	...
Income on bonds and notes	2 350	...	...	...	...	...	.4	1.2	5.2
Income on money market instruments	2 360	...	...	...	...	...	...	...	...
Other investment income	2 370	131.8	133.5	125.6	151.4	155.8	175.6	215.0	155.1
Investment income, debit	3 320	**–275.9**	**–364.4**	**–319.5**	**–425.6**	**–628.4**	**–1,990.5**	**–1,460.7**	**–941.8**
Direct investment income	3 330	–64.7	–108.9	–89.2	–179.3	–382.6	–1,724.4	–1,140.9	–595.7
Dividends and distributed branch profits	3 332	–15.1	–23.8	–77.9	–53.8	–266.6	–1,512.7	–946.8	–272.9
Reinvested earnings and undistributed branch profits	3 333	–49.6	–85.1	–11.4	–125.5	–116.0	–211.7	–194.1	–322.8
Income on debt (interest)	3 334	...	...	...	...	...	...	...	...
Portfolio investment income	3 339	...	–44.0	–35.7	–33.3	–40.3	–79.1	–96.8	–128.0
Income on equity	3 340	...	–2.6	...	...	...	...	...	...
Income on bonds and notes	3 350	...	–41.4	–35.7	–33.3	–40.3	–79.1	–96.8	–128.0
Income on money market instruments	3 360	...	...	...	...	...	...	...	...
Other investment income	3 370	–211.2	–211.5	–194.6	–213.1	–205.5	–187.0	–223.0	–218.1
D. CURRENT TRANSFERS	4 379	165.7	133.9	149.5	125.5	113.2	102.4	92.0	147.7
Credit	2 379	**174.9**	**165.2**	**192.7**	**191.2**	**190.5**	**190.8**	**192.0**	**248.9**
General government	2 380	50.0	38.1	49.2	44.6	46.8	57.6	50.8	44.5
Other sectors	2 390	124.9	127.1	143.5	146.6	143.7	133.2	141.2	204.4
Workers' remittances	2 391	...	115.9	121.7	115.8	112.4	101.2	108.8	166.4
Other current transfers	2 392	124.9	11.2	21.8	30.8	31.3	32.0	32.4	38.0
Debit	3 379	**–9.2**	**–31.3**	**–43.2**	**–65.7**	**–77.3**	**–88.4**	**–100.0**	**–101.2**
General government	3 380	–3.5	–3.3	–3.5	–7.0	–7.0	–3.6	–2.0	–3.2
Other sectors	3 390	–5.7	–28.0	–39.6	–58.6	–70.3	–84.8	–98.0	–98.0
Workers' remittances	3 391	...	–28.0	–38.8	–58.4	–70.1	–84.0	–97.6	–96.8
Other current transfers	3 392	–5.7	...	–.8	–.2	–.2	–.8	–.4	–1.2
CAPITAL AND FINANCIAL ACCOUNT	4 996	**–15.5**	**301.1**	**145.0**	**323.0**	**703.3**	**466.7**	**539.6**	**682.3**
CAPITAL ACCOUNT	4 994	...	...	**28.2**	...	...	...	**8.8**	**12.4**
Total credit	2 994	...	...	*28.2*	...	...	...	*8.8*	*12.4*
Total debit	3 994	...	...	...	...	...	...	...	...
Capital transfers, credit	2 400	...	...	**28.2**	...	...	...	**8.8**	**12.4**
General government	2 401	...	...	10.0	...	...	...	8.8	12.4
Debt forgiveness	2 402	...	...	...	...	...	...	...	...
Other capital transfers	2 410	...	...	10.0	...	...	...	8.8	12.4
Other sectors	2 430	...	...	18.2	...	...	...	...	...
Migrants' transfers	2 431	...	...	...	...	...	...	...	...
Debt forgiveness	2 432	...	...	...	...	...	...	...	...
Other capital transfers	2 440	...	...	18.2	...	...	...	...	...
Capital transfers, debit	3 400	...	...	...	...	...	...	...	...
General government	3 401	...	...	...	...	...	...	...	...
Debt forgiveness	3 402	...	...	...	...	...	...	...	...
Other capital transfers	3 410	...	...	...	...	...	...	...	...
Other sectors	3 430	...	...	...	...	...	...	...	...
Migrants' transfers	3 431	...	...	...	...	...	...	...	...
Debt forgiveness	3 432	...	...	...	...	...	...	...	...
Other capital transfers	3 440	...	...	...	...	...	...	...	...
Nonproduced nonfinancial assets, credit	2 480	...	...	...	...	...	...	...	...
Nonproduced nonfinancial assets, debit	3 480	...	...	...	...	...	...	...	...

Table 2 (Continued). STANDARD PRESENTATION, 1994–2001
(Millions of U.S. dollars)

	Code	1994	1995	1996	1997	1998	1999	2000	2001
FINANCIAL ACCOUNT	4 995 . .	**–15.5**	**301.1**	**116.8**	**323.0**	**703.3**	**466.7**	**530.8**	**669.9**
A. DIRECT INVESTMENT	4 500 . .	292.9	331.4	421.3	403.8	608.3	614.6	403.3	448.4
Direct investment abroad	4 505 . .	**–4.7**	**–5.5**	**–5.7**	**–4.4**	**–4.8**	**–5.0**	**–5.2**	**–5.2**
Equity capital	4 510 . .	1.0	. . .	1.8	1.3	1.4	. . .	. . .	. . .
Claims on affiliated enterprises	4 515 . .	. . .	. . .	1.8	. . .	. . .	. . .	. . .	. . .
Liabilities to affiliated enterprises	4 520 . .	. . .	. . .	. . .	1.3	1.4	. . .	. . .	. . .
Reinvested earnings	4 525 . .	–5.7	–5.5	–7.4	–5.7	–6.2	–5.0	–5.2	–5.2
Other capital	4 530 . .	. . .	. . .	. . .	. . .	. . .	. . .	. . .	. . .
Claims on affiliated enterprises	4 535 . .	. . .	. . .	. . .	. . .	. . .	. . .	. . .	. . .
Liabilities to affiliated enterprises	4 540 . .	. . .	. . .	. . .	. . .	. . .	. . .	. . .	. . .
Direct investment in Costa Rica	4 555 . .	**297.6**	**336.9**	**427.0**	**408.2**	**613.1**	**619.6**	**408.5**	**453.6**
Equity capital	4 560 . .	38.7	181.8	211.7	131.0	226.2	278.2	159.2	236.4
Claims on direct investors	4 565 . .	. . .	. . .	. . .	. . .	. . .	. . .	. . .	. . .
Liabilities to direct investors	4 570 . .	. . .	181.8	211.7	131.0	226.2	278.2	159.2	236.4
Reinvested earnings	4 575 . .	49.6	85.1	11.4	125.5	116.0	211.7	194.1	322.8
Other capital	4 580 . .	209.3	70.0	203.9	151.6	270.9	129.7	55.2	–105.6
Claims on direct investors	4 585 . .	. . .	. . .	. . .	. . .	. . .	. . .	. . .	. . .
Liabilities to direct investors	4 590 . .	. . .	70.0	203.9	151.6	270.9	129.7	55.2	–105.6
B. PORTFOLIO INVESTMENT	4 600 . .	–1.2	–24.8	–21.5	76.7	–79.8	85.4	–68.8	18.4
Assets	4 602 . .	**. . .**	**–.4**	**. . .**	**–22.5**	**–33.9**	**–10.8**	**–18.4**	**–81.3**
Equity securities	4 610 . .	. . .	–.4	. . .	–22.5	–33.9	–28.0	–4.0	–22.0
Monetary authorities	4 611 . .	. . .	. . .	. . .	. . .	. . .	. . .	. . .	. . .
General government	4 612 . .	. . .	. . .	. . .	. . .	. . .	. . .	. . .	. . .
Banks	4 613 . .	. . .	. . .	. . .	. . .	. . .	. . .	. . .	. . .
Other sectors	4 614 . .	. . .	–.4	. . .	–22.5	–33.9	–28.0	–4.0	–22.0
Debt securities	4 619 . .	. . .	. . .	. . .	. . .	. . .	17.2	–14.4	–59.3
Bonds and notes	4 620 . .	. . .	. . .	. . .	. . .	. . .	17.2	–14.4	–59.3
Monetary authorities	4 621 . .	. . .	. . .	. . .	. . .	. . .	. . .	. . .	. . .
General government	4 622 . .	. . .	. . .	. . .	. . .	. . .	. . .	. . .	. . .
Banks	4 623 . .	. . .	. . .	. . .	. . .	. . .	. . .	. . .	. . .
Other sectors	4 624 . .	. . .	. . .	. . .	. . .	. . .	17.2	–14.4	–59.3
Money market instruments	4 630 . .	. . .	. . .	. . .	. . .	. . .	. . .	. . .	. . .
Monetary authorities	4 631 . .	. . .	. . .	. . .	. . .	. . .	. . .	. . .	. . .
General government	4 632 . .	. . .	. . .	. . .	. . .	. . .	. . .	. . .	. . .
Banks	4 633 . .	. . .	. . .	. . .	. . .	. . .	. . .	. . .	. . .
Other sectors	4 634 . .	. . .	. . .	. . .	. . .	. . .	. . .	. . .	. . .
Liabilities	4 652 . .	**–1.2**	**–24.4**	**–21.5**	**99.2**	**–46.0**	**96.2**	**–50.4**	**99.7**
Equity securities	4 660 . .	. . .	. . .	. . .	. . .	. . .	. . .	. . .	. . .
Banks	4 663 . .	. . .	. . .	. . .	. . .	. . .	. . .	. . .	. . .
Other sectors	4 664 . .	. . .	. . .	. . .	. . .	. . .	. . .	. . .	. . .
Debt securities	4 669 . .	–1.2	–24.4	–21.5	99.2	–46.0	96.2	–50.4	99.7
Bonds and notes	4 670 . .	–1.2	–24.4	–21.5	99.2	–46.0	96.2	–50.4	99.7
Monetary authorities	4 671 . .	–1.2	–24.4	–21.5	–24.0	25.8	–86.4	–55.6	29.2
General government	4 672 . .	. . .	. . .	. . .	125.0	–64.6	189.8	12.4	77.7
Banks	4 673 . .	. . .	. . .	. . .	. . .	. . .	. . .	. . .	. . .
Other sectors	4 674 . .	. . .	. . .	. . .	–1.8	–7.1	–7.2	–7.2	–7.2
Money market instruments	4 680 . .	. . .	. . .	. . .	. . .	. . .	. . .	. . .	. . .
Monetary authorities	4 681 . .	. . .	. . .	. . .	. . .	. . .	. . .	. . .	. . .
General government	4 682 . .	. . .	. . .	. . .	. . .	. . .	. . .	. . .	. . .
Banks	4 683 . .	. . .	. . .	. . .	. . .	. . .	. . .	. . .	. . .
Other sectors	4 684 . .	. . .	. . .	. . .	. . .	. . .	. . .	. . .	. . .
C. FINANCIAL DERIVATIVES	4 910 . .	. . .	. . .	. . .	. . .	. . .	. . .	. . .	. . .
Monetary authorities	4 911 . .	. . .	. . .	. . .	. . .	. . .	. . .	. . .	. . .
General government	4 912 . .	. . .	. . .	. . .	. . .	. . .	. . .	. . .	. . .
Banks	4 913 . .	. . .	. . .	. . .	. . .	. . .	. . .	. . .	. . .
Other sectors	4 914 . .	. . .	. . .	. . .	. . .	. . .	. . .	. . .	. . .
Assets	4 900 . .	**. . .**	**. . .**	**. . .**	**. . .**	**. . .**	**. . .**	**. . .**	**. . .**
Monetary authorities	4 901 . .	. . .	. . .	. . .	. . .	. . .	. . .	. . .	. . .
General government	4 902 . .	. . .	. . .	. . .	. . .	. . .	. . .	. . .	. . .
Banks	4 903 . .	. . .	. . .	. . .	. . .	. . .	. . .	. . .	. . .
Other sectors	4 904 . .	. . .	. . .	. . .	. . .	. . .	. . .	. . .	. . .
Liabilities	4 905 . .	**. . .**	**. . .**	**. . .**	**. . .**	**. . .**	**. . .**	**. . .**	**. . .**
Monetary authorities	4 906 . .	. . .	. . .	. . .	. . .	. . .	. . .	. . .	. . .
General government	4 907 . .	. . .	. . .	. . .	. . .	. . .	. . .	. . .	. . .
Banks	4 908 . .	. . .	. . .	. . .	. . .	. . .	. . .	. . .	. . .
Other sectors	4 909 . .	. . .	. . .	. . .	. . .	. . .	. . .	. . .	. . .

Table 2 (Concluded). STANDARD PRESENTATION, 1994–2001
(Millions of U.S. dollars)

	Code	1994	1995	1996	1997	1998	1999	2000	2001
D. OTHER INVESTMENT	4 700 . .	–372.7	173.7	–360.2	58.3	25.3	247.7	43.4	216.3
Assets	4 703 . .	**–76.2**	**16.8**	**–159.3**	**–267.4**	**–95.6**	**161.7**	**–343.9**	**106.5**
Trade credits	4 706 . .	13.6	–27.9	–24.4	–194.0	–100.5	–129.6	–44.6	5.0
General government	4 707 . .	. . .	. . .	. . .	. . .	. . .	. . .	. . .	. . .
of which: Short-term	4 709 . .	. . .	. . .	. . .	. . .	. . .	. . .	. . .	. . .
Other sectors	4 710 . .	13.6	–27.9	–24.4	–194.0	–100.5	–129.6	–44.6	5.0
of which: Short-term	4 712 . .	*13.6*	*–27.9*	*–24.4*	*–194.0*	*–100.5*	*–129.6*	*–44.6*	*5.0*
Loans	4 714 . .	. . .	. . .	. . .	. . .	. . .	–8.4	–30.4	–46.3
Monetary authorities	4 715 . .	. . .	. . .	. . .	. . .	. . .	. . .	. . .	. . .
of which: Short-term	4 718 . .	. . .	. . .	. . .	. . .	. . .	. . .	. . .	. . .
General government	4 719 . .	. . .	. . .	. . .	. . .	. . .	. . .	. . .	. . .
of which: Short-term	4 721 . .	. . .	. . .	. . .	. . .	. . .	. . .	. . .	. . .
Banks	4 722 . .	. . .	. . .	. . .	. . .	. . .	. . .	. . .	. . .
of which: Short-term	4 724 . .	. . .	. . .	. . .	. . .	. . .	. . .	. . .	. . .
Other sectors	4 725 . .	. . .	. . .	. . .	. . .	. . .	–8.4	–30.4	–46.3
of which: Short-term	4 727 . .	. . .	. . .	. . .	. . .	. . .	*–1.2*	*–3.6*	*–19.9*
Currency and deposits	4 730 . .	–85.4	71.2	–83.8	–70.8	4.1	311.7	–282.8	146.6
Monetary authorities	4 731 . .	. . .	. . .	. . .	. . .	. . .	. . .	. . .	. . .
General government	4 732 . .	. . .	. . .	. . .	. . .	. . .	. . .	. . .	. . .
Banks	4 733 . .	. . .	–9.8	–17.8	43.3	–29.8	47.5	–76.3	54.3
Other sectors	4 734 . .	–85.4	81.0	–66.0	–114.0	33.9	264.2	–206.5	92.3
Other assets	4 736 . .	–4.4	–26.5	–51.1	–2.7	.8	–12.0	13.9	1.2
Monetary authorities	4 737 . .	. . .	.1	–6.3	–.1	. . .	. . .	. . .	. . .
of which: Short-term	4 739 . .	. . .	. . .	. . .	. . .	. . .	. . .	. . .	. . .
General government	4 740 . .	–4.4	. . .	. . .	. . .	. . .	. . .	. . .	. . .
of which: Short-term	4 742 . .	. . .	. . .	. . .	. . .	. . .	. . .	. . .	. . .
Banks	4 743 . .	. . .	. . .	. . .	. . .	. . .	. . .	. . .	. . .
of which: Short-term	4 745 . .	. . .	. . .	. . .	. . .	. . .	. . .	. . .	. . .
Other sectors	4 746 . .	. . .	–26.6	–44.8	–2.6	.8	–12.0	13.9	1.2
of which: Short-term	4 748 . .	. . .	*–26.6*	*–44.8*	*–2.6*	*.8*	*–14.8*	*14.3*	*6.4*
Liabilities	4 753 . .	**–296.5**	**156.9**	**–201.0**	**325.7**	**120.9**	**86.0**	**387.3**	**109.8**
Trade credits	4 756 . .	–21.7	187.6	–43.0	301.8	101.5	75.2	311.3	134.8
General government	4 757 . .	. . .	. . .	. . .	. . .	. . .	. . .	. . .	. . .
of which: Short-term	4 759 . .	. . .	. . .	. . .	. . .	. . .	. . .	. . .	. . .
Other sectors	4 760 . .	–21.7	187.6	–43.0	301.8	101.5	75.2	311.3	134.8
of which: Short-term	4 762 . .	*–21.7*	*187.6*	*–43.0*	*301.8*	*101.5*	*75.2*	*311.3*	*134.8*
Loans	4 764 . .	–282.4	–55.7	–136.5	18.6	9.2	25.4	66.0	–37.4
Monetary authorities	4 765 . .	–205.5	–83.9	–95.8	–88.6	8.3	–62.5	–69.7	–132.8
of which: Use of Fund credit and loans from the Fund	4 766 . .	*–20.3*	*–44.4*	*–23.1*	*–.7*	. . .	. . .	. . .	. . .
of which: Short-term	4 768 . .	*–9.0*	. . .	. . .	. . .	. . .	. . .	. . .	. . .
General government	4 769 . .	–106.2	–27.1	–85.2	–5.6	–60.7	–77.9	–17.6	11.6
of which: Short-term	4 771 . .	. . .	. . .	. . .	. . .	. . .	. . .	. . .	. . .
Banks	4 772 . .	–2.9	–3.1	9.6	73.7	20.1	66.9	136.7	91.7
of which: Short-term	4 774 . .	. . .	. . .	. . .	*65.0*	*18.6*	*17.3*	*128.6*	*96.3*
Other sectors	4 775 . .	32.2	58.4	34.9	39.1	41.6	98.9	16.6	–7.9
of which: Short-term	4 777 . .	. . .	. . .	. . .	*7.0*	*–95.3*	*40.4*	*1.5*	*17.9*
Currency and deposits	4 780 . .	–16.6	26.1	39.1	. . .	17.2	–16.3	.5	5.8
Monetary authorities	4 781 . .	–.7	. . .	. . .	. . .	. . .	. . .	. . .	. . .
General government	4 782 . .	. . .	. . .	. . .	. . .	. . .	. . .	. . .	. . .
Banks	4 783 . .	–15.9	26.1	39.1	. . .	17.2	–16.3	.5	5.8
Other sectors	4 784 . .	. . .	. . .	. . .	. . .	. . .	. . .	. . .	. . .
Other liabilities	4 786 . .	24.2	–1.1	–60.6	5.4	–7.1	1.7	9.5	6.6
Monetary authorities	4 787 . .	–27.2	–1.7	11.1	–.7	–1.7	–1.2	–1.2	–1.2
of which: Short-term	4 789 . .	*–27.2*	*–1.7*	*11.1*	. . .	. . .	. . .	. . .	. . .
General government	4 790 . .	46.1	–6.1	–48.3	.3	–.3	–.3	. . .	. . .
of which: Short-term	4 792 . .	*46.1*	*–6.1*	*–48.3*	*.3*	*–.3*	*–.3*	. . .	. . .
Banks	4 793 . .	.2	.3	. . .	. . .	. . .	. . .	. . .	. . .
of which: Short-term	4 795 . .	*.2*	*.3*	. . .	. . .	. . .	. . .	. . .	. . .
Other sectors	4 796 . .	5.1	6.4	–23.3	5.8	–5.0	3.2	10.7	7.8
of which: Short-term	4 798 . .	*5.1*	*6.4*	*–23.3*	*5.8*	*–5.0*	*1.6*	*12.7*	*7.8*
E. RESERVE ASSETS	4 802 . .	65.5	–179.2	77.3	–215.7	149.6	–481.0	152.9	–13.2
Monetary gold	4 812 . .	. . .	–.2	13.1	. . .	. . .	. . .	. . .	. . .
Special drawing rights	4 811 . .	. . .	.1	. . .	. . .	. . .	–.8	.3	.3
Reserve position in the Fund	4 810 . .	. . .	. . .	. . .	. . .	. . .	–15.6	. . .	. . .
Foreign exchange	4 803 . .	129.9	–178.3	66.3	–232.4	151.2	–466.4	190.1	–1.4
Other claims	4 813 . .	–64.4	–.8	–2.1	16.7	–1.6	1.7	–37.5	–12.1
NET ERRORS AND OMISSIONS	4 998 . .	**249.1**	**57.1**	**118.7**	**157.8**	**–182.6**	**213.4**	**218.2**	**19.2**

Part 3 of the *Yearbook* contains descriptions of the methodologies, compilation practices, and sources used to compile these data.

Table 3. INTERNATIONAL INVESTMENT POSITION (End–period stocks), 1994–2001

(Millions of U.S. dollars)

	Code	1994	1995	1996	1997	1998	1999	2000	2001
ASSETS	8 995 C.	...	...	...	...	...	...	...	...
Direct investment abroad	8 505 . .	...	...	...	...	...	...	...	...
Equity capital and reinvested earnings	8 506 . .	...	...	...	...	...	...	...	...
Claims on affiliated enterprises	8 507 . .	...	...	...	...	...	...	...	...
Liabilities to affiliated enterprises	8 508 . .	...	...	...	...	...	...	...	...
Other capital	8 530 . .	...	...	...	...	...	...	...	...
Claims on affiliated enterprises	8 535 . .	...	...	...	...	...	...	...	...
Liabilities to affiliated enterprises	8 540 . .	...	...	...	...	...	...	...	...
Portfolio investment	8 602 . .	...	...	...	...	...	...	...	...
Equity securities	8 610 . .	...	...	...	...	...	...	...	...
Monetary authorities	8 611 . .	...	...	...	...	...	...	...	...
General government	8 612 . .	...	...	...	...	...	...	...	...
Banks	8 613 . .	...	...	...	...	...	...	...	...
Other sectors	8 614 . .	...	...	...	...	...	...	...	...
Debt securities	8 619 . .	...	...	...	...	...	...	...	...
Bonds and notes	8 620 . .	...	...	...	...	...	...	...	...
Monetary authorities	8 621 . .	...	...	...	...	...	...	...	...
General government	8 622 . .	...	...	...	...	...	...	...	...
Banks	8 623 . .	...	...	...	...	...	...	...	...
Other sectors	8 624 . .	...	...	...	...	...	...	...	...
Money market instruments	8 630 . .	...	...	...	...	...	...	...	...
Monetary authorities	8 631 . .	...	...	...	...	...	...	...	...
General government	8 632 . .	...	...	...	...	...	...	...	...
Banks	8 633 . .	...	...	...	...	...	...	...	...
Other sectors	8 634 . .	...	...	...	...	...	...	...	...
Financial derivatives	8 900 . .	...	...	...	...	...	...	...	...
Monetary authorities	8 901 . .	...	...	...	...	...	...	...	...
General government	8 902 . .	...	...	...	...	...	...	...	...
Banks	8 903 . .	...	...	...	...	...	...	...	...
Other sectors	8 904 . .	...	...	...	...	...	...	...	...
Other investment	8 703 . .	...	...	**412.4**	**361.2**	**415.3**	**363.2**	...	...
Trade credits	8 706 . .	...	...	1.6	1.6	1.7	1.3	...	...
General government	8 707 . .	...	...	...	...	...	...	...	...
of which: Short-term	8 709 . .	...	...	...	...	...	...	...	...
Other sectors	8 710 . .	...	...	1.6	1.6	1.7	1.3	...	...
of which: Short-term	8 712 . .	...	...	*1.6*	*1.6*	*1.7*	*1.3*	...	...
Loans	8 714 . .	...	...	...	...	...	...	...	...
Monetary authorities	8 715 . .	...	...	...	...	...	...	...	...
of which: Short-term	8 718 . .	...	...	...	...	...	...	...	...
General government	8 719 . .	...	...	...	...	...	...	...	...
of which: Short-term	8 721 . .	...	...	...	...	...	...	...	...
Banks	8 722 . .	...	...	...	...	...	...	...	...
of which: Short-term	8 724 . .	...	...	...	...	...	...	...	...
Other sectors	8 725 . .	...	...	...	...	...	...	...	...
of which: Short-term	8 727 . .	...	...	...	...	...	...	...	...
Currency and deposits	8 730 . .	...	...	313.9	262.7	316.6	264.8	...	...
Monetary authorities	8 731 . .	...	...	35.7	35.7	35.7	35.7	...	...
General government	8 732 . .	...	...	...	...	...	...	...	...
Banks	8 733 . .	...	...	247.6	204.4	245.2	198.6	...	...
Other sectors	8 734 . .	...	...	30.6	22.6	35.7	30.5	...	...
Other assets	8 736 . .	...	...	96.9	97.0	97.0	97.1	...	...
Monetary authorities	8 737 . .	...	...	96.9	97.0	97.0	97.1	...	...
of which: Short-term	8 739 . .	...	...	...	...	...	...	...	...
General government	8 740 . .	...	...	...	...	...	...	...	...
of which: Short-term	8 742 . .	...	...	...	...	...	...	...	...
Banks	8 743 . .	...	...	...	...	...	...	...	...
of which: Short-term	8 745 . .	...	...	...	...	...	...	...	...
Other sectors	8 746 . .	...	...	...	...	...	...	...	...
of which: Short-term	8 748 . .	...	...	...	...	...	...	...	...
Reserve assets	8 802 . .	...	...	**1,008.9**	**1,223.7**	**1,074.9**	**1,555.6**	...	...
Monetary gold	8 812 . .	...	...	...	...	...	...	...	...
Special drawing rights	8 811 . .	.2	.1	...	...	.1	.8	.4	.1
Reserve position in the Fund	8 810 . .	12.7	13.0	12.5	11.8	12.3	27.5	26.1	25.1
Foreign exchange	8 803 . .	...	...	967.7	1,200.1	1,049.1	1,515.5	...	...
Other claims	8 813 . .	...	...	28.6	11.8	13.4	11.8	...	...

Table 3 (Concluded). INTERNATIONAL INVESTMENT POSITION (End–period stocks), 1994–2001
(Millions of U.S. dollars)

	Code	1994	1995	1996	1997	1998	1999	2000	2001
LIABILITIES	8 995 D.	...	...	...	...	...	...	...	...
Direct investment in Costa Rica	8 555 ..	...	...	...	...	...	...	...	...
Equity capital and reinvested earnings	8 556 ..	...	...	...	...	...	...	...	...
Claims on direct investors	8 557 ..	...	...	...	...	...	...	...	...
Liabilities to direct investors	8 558 ..	...	...	...	...	...	...	...	...
Other capital	8 580 ..	...	...	...	...	...	...	...	...
Claims on direct investors	8 585 ..	...	...	...	...	...	...	...	...
Liabilities to direct investors	8 590 ..	...	...	...	...	...	...	...	...
Portfolio investment	8 652 ..	...	...	**728.4**	**827.3**	**781.0**	**841.3**	...	...
Equity securities	8 660 ..	...	...	...	...	...	...	...	...
Banks	8 663 ..	...	...	...	...	...	...	...	...
Other sectors	8 664 ..	...	...	...	...	...	...	...	...
Debt securities	8 669 ..	...	...	728.4	827.3	781.0	841.3	...	...
Bonds and notes	8 670 ..	...	...	728.4	827.3	781.0	841.3	...	...
Monetary authorities	8 671 ..	...	...	536.5	512.2	538.0	471.9	...	...
General government	8 672 ..	...	...	141.9	266.9	201.9	335.4	...	...
Banks	8 673 ..	...	...	...	...	...	...	...	...
Other sectors	8 674 ..	...	...	50.0	48.2	41.1	33.9	...	...
Money market instruments	8 680 ..	...	...	...	...	...	...	...	...
Monetary authorities	8 681 ..	...	...	...	...	...	...	...	...
General government	8 682 ..	...	...	...	...	...	...	...	...
Banks	8 683 ..	...	...	...	...	...	...	...	...
Other sectors	8 684 ..	...	...	...	...	...	...	...	...
Financial derivatives	8 905 ..	...	...	...	...	...	...	...	...
Monetary authorities	8 906 ..	...	...	...	...	...	...	...	...
General government	8 907 ..	...	...	...	...	...	...	...	...
Banks	8 908 ..	...	...	...	...	...	...	...	...
Other sectors	8 909 ..	...	...	...	...	...	...	...	...
Other investment	8 753 ..	...	...	**2,539.9**	**2,438.8**	**2,543.2**	**2,499.4**	...	...
Trade credits	8 756 ..	...	...	16.2	16.2	32.2	32.2	...	...
General government	8 757 ..	...	...	...	...	...	...	...	...
of which: Short-term	8 759 ..	...	...	...	...	...	...	...	...
Other sectors	8 760 ..	...	...	16.2	16.2	32.2	32.2	...	...
of which: Short-term	8 762 ..	...	...	*16.2*	*16.2*	*32.2*	*32.2*	...	...
Loans	8 764 ..	...	...	2,491.1	2,392.0	2,465.3	2,439.7	...	...
Monetary authorities	8 765 ..	...	...	621.0	519.4	528.8	464.9	...	...
of which: Use of Fund credit and loans from the Fund	8 766 ..	*66.4*	*24.3*	*.7*	...	...	...	...	...
of which: Short-term	8 768 ..	...	...	...	...	...	...	...	...
General government	8 769 ..	...	...	1,025.0	967.2	932.9	864.5	...	...
of which: Short-term	8 771 ..	...	...	...	...	...	...	...	...
Banks	8 772 ..	...	...	189.8	264.4	285.0	362.3	...	...
of which: Short-term	8 774 ..	...	...	*96.7*	*161.7*	*180.3*	*211.8*	...	...
Other sectors	8 775 ..	...	...	655.3	641.0	718.6	748.0	...	...
of which: Short-term	8 777 ..	...	...	...	...	...	...	...	...
Currency and deposits	8 780 ..	...	...	...	...	17.2	.8	...	...
Monetary authorities	8 781 ..	...	...	...	...	...	...	...	...
General government	8 782 ..	...	...	...	...	...	...	...	...
Banks	8 783 ..	...	...	...	...	17.2	.8	...	...
Other sectors	8 784 ..	...	...	...	...	...	...	...	...
Other liabilities	8 786 ..	...	...	32.6	30.6	28.5	26.7	...	...
Monetary authorities	8 787 ..	...	...	30.8	30.0	28.1	26.7	...	...
of which: Short-term	8 789 ..	...	...	...	...	...	...	...	...
General government	8 790 ..	...	...	.3	.6	.3	...	...	...
of which: Short-term	8 792 ..	...	...	*.3*	*.6*	*.3*	...	...	...
Banks	8 793 ..	...	...	...	...	...	...	...	...
of which: Short-term	8 795 ..	...	...	...	...	...	...	...	...
Other sectors	8 796 ..	...	...	1.4	...	...	...	...	...
of which: Short-term	8 798 ..	...	...	*1.4*	...	...	...	...	...
NET INTERNATIONAL INVESTMENT POSITION	8 995 ..	...	...	...	...	...	...	...	...
Conversion rates: Costa Rican colones per U.S. dollar (end of period)	0 102 ..	**165.07**	**194.90**	**220.11**	**244.29**	**271.42**	**298.19**	**318.02**	**341.67**

Table 1. ANALYTIC PRESENTATION, 1994–2001
(Millions of U.S. dollars)

	Code	1994	1995	1996	1997	1998	1999	2000	2001
A. Current Account [1]	4 993 Z.	**–13.8**	**–492.4**	**–162.3**	**–154.7**	**–290.2**	**–120.4**	**–241.6**	**–57.7**
Goods: exports f.o.b	2 100 . .	2,895.9	3,805.9	4,446.1	4,451.2	4,606.5	4,661.4	3,888.1	3,947.4
Goods: imports f.o.b	3 100 . .	–1,606.8	–2,430.3	–2,622.4	–2,658.4	–2,886.5	–2,766.0	–2,401.8	–2,407.8
Balance on Goods	4 100 . .	*1,289.1*	*1,375.5*	*1,823.7*	*1,792.8*	*1,720.0*	*1,895.4*	*1,486.3*	*1,539.6*
Services: credit	2 200 . .	507.7	530.9	565.7	579.6	614.3	586.0	482.5	487.4
Services: debit	3 200 . .	–1,011.1	–1,375.7	–1,440.3	–1,478.6	–1,524.0	–1,459.0	–1,226.9	–1,232.7
Balance on Goods and Services	4 991 . .	*785.7*	*530.7*	*949.1*	*893.8*	*810.2*	*1,022.4*	*741.9*	*794.4*
Income: credit	2 300 . .	133.8	189.5	170.7	161.2	169.2	162.6	141.3	141.9
Income: debit	3 300 . .	–817.5	–976.1	–939.5	–829.2	–876.0	–919.4	–794.7	–719.2
Balance on Goods, Services, and Income	4 992 . .	*102.0*	*–255.8*	*180.2*	*225.8*	*103.4*	*265.6*	*88.5*	*217.0*
Current transfers: credit	2 379 Z.	246.8	277.7	204.1	137.7	148.1	136.8	79.4	85.0
Current transfers: debit	3 379 . .	–362.6	–514.3	–546.6	–518.3	–541.7	–522.7	–409.4	–359.7
B. Capital Account [1]	4 994 Z.	**527.6**	**291.3**	**47.1**	**40.6**	**25.6**	**13.8**	**8.4**	**10.0**
Capital account: credit	2 994 Z.	527.6	291.3	49.8	50.5	35.9	17.4	9.8	11.5
Capital account: debit	3 994 . .	. . .	. . .	–2.7	–9.9	–10.3	–3.6	–1.4	–1.5
Total, Groups A Plus B	4 981 . .	*513.8*	*–201.1*	*–115.1*	*–114.1*	*–264.6*	*–106.5*	*–233.2*	*–47.7*
C. Financial Account [1]	4 995 W.	**–523.1**	**–88.6**	**–717.8**	**–323.0**	**–417.0**	**–577.2**	**–362.5**	**–23.5**
Direct investment abroad	4 505 . .	. . .	. . .	–.4	. . .	. . .	. . .	. . .	. . .
Direct investment in Cote d'Ivoire	4 555 Z.	78.0	211.5	269.2	415.3	379.9	323.7	234.7	245.7
Portfolio investment assets	4 602 . .	–27.4	–8.4	–16.0	–26.9	–29.8	–28.7	–12.6	–12.7
Equity securities	4 610 . .	7.7	1.2	–1.6	.2	–1.7	–1.6	–1.4	–1.4
Debt securities	4 619 . .	–35.1	–9.6	–14.5	–27.1	–28.1	–27.1	–11.2	–11.3
Portfolio investment liabilities	4 652 Z.	–.7	10.0	25.0	19.2	19.5	13.5	4.5	4.8
Equity securities	4 660 . .	1.1	1.2	10.2	8.6	8.6	5.7	1.1	1.2
Debt securities	4 669 Z.	–1.8	8.8	14.9	10.6	10.8	7.8	3.4	3.5
Financial derivatives	4 910 . .	. . .	. . .	–3.3	–3.1	–3.2	–3.1	–2.5	–2.6
Financial derivatives assets	4 900 . .	. . .	. . .	. . .	. . .	. . .	. . .	. . .	. . .
Financial derivatives liabilities	4 905 . .	. . .	. . .	–3.3	–3.1	–3.2	–3.1	–2.5	–2.6
Other investment assets	4 703 . .	–39.6	–323.2	–256.5	–304.8	–317.5	–350.5	–182.2	–170.1
Monetary authorities	4 701 . .	. . .	. . .	. . .	. . .	. . .	. . .	. . .	. . .
General government	4 704 . .	–11.9	–14.2	–22.3	–9.9	–7.6	–5.2	–4.5	–5.0
Banks	4 705 . .	–95.3	–33.1	35.2	–25.7	–16.4	–49.0	2.8	3.0
Other sectors	4 728 . .	67.5	–275.9	–269.4	–269.2	–293.4	–296.2	–180.5	–168.1
Other investment liabilities	4 753 W.	–533.3	21.4	–735.8	–422.7	–465.8	–532.1	–404.4	–88.5
Monetary authorities	4 753 WA	–726.6	1.8	–1.2	4.3	3.2	–5.0	–.8	–5.3
General government	4 753 ZB	249.8	–105.8	–621.6	–473.6	–597.3	–583.6	–523.3	–469.7
Banks	4 753 ZC	75.1	77.1	–38.5	64.9	37.3	41.9	23.2	55.1
Other sectors	4 753 ZD	–131.7	48.3	–74.5	–18.3	91.0	14.6	96.6	331.4
Total, Groups A Through C	4 983 . .	*–9.3*	*–289.8*	*–833.0*	*–437.1*	*–681.6*	*–683.8*	*–595.7*	*–71.2*
D. Net Errors and Omissions	4 998 . .	**–11.1**	**35.6**	**–15.4**	**–39.6**	**32.0**	**–24.0**	**–10.2**	**–23.0**
Total, Groups A Through D	4 984 . .	*–20.3*	*–254.2*	*–848.4*	*–476.6*	*–649.6*	*–707.8*	*–605.9*	*–94.2*
E. Reserves and Related Items	4 802 A.	**20.3**	**254.2**	**848.4**	**476.6**	**649.6**	**707.8**	**605.9**	**94.2**
Reserve assets	4 802 . .	–194.5	–302.5	–113.4	–95.4	–179.8	109.7	–89.1	–384.7
Use of Fund credit and loans	4 766 . .	94.3	94.9	90.3	–22.3	168.8	–8.2	–38.8	–66.4
Exceptional financing	4 920 . .	120.5	461.8	871.5	594.3	660.6	606.3	733.7	545.3
Conversion rates: CFA francs per U.S. dollar	0 101 . .	**555.20**	**499.15**	**511.55**	**583.67**	**589.95**	**615.70**	**711.98**	**733.04**

[1] Excludes components that have been classified in the categories of Group E.

Table 2. STANDARD PRESENTATION, 1994–2001
(Millions of U.S. dollars)

	Code	1994	1995	1996	1997	1998	1999	2000	2001
CURRENT ACCOUNT	4 993 . .	**–13.8**	**–492.4**	**–162.3**	**–154.7**	**–290.2**	**–120.4**	**–241.6**	**–57.7**
A. GOODS	4 100 . .	1,289.1	1,375.5	1,823.7	1,792.8	1,720.0	1,895.4	1,486.3	1,539.6
Credit	2 100 . .	**2,895.9**	**3,805.9**	**4,446.1**	**4,451.2**	**4,606.5**	**4,661.4**	**3,888.1**	**3,947.4**
General merchandise: exports f.o.b.	2 110 . .	2,742.1	3,644.8	4,277.8	4,275.9	4,423.6	4,480.3	3,728.9	3,789.0
Goods for processing: exports f.o.b.	2 150 . .	84.5	85.1	88.9	84.5	87.5	87.5	72.5	72.2
Repairs on goods	2 160 . .	. . .	. . .	. . .	. . .	. . .	. . .	5.9	5.9
Goods procured in ports by carriers	2 170 . .	69.3	75.9	79.4	77.6	80.3	80.4	67.4	67.1
Nonmonetary gold	2 180 . .	. . .	. . .	. . .	13.2	15.1	13.2	13.3	13.2
Debit	3 100 . .	**–1,606.8**	**–2,430.3**	**–2,622.4**	**–2,658.4**	**–2,886.5**	**–2,766.0**	**–2,401.8**	**–2,407.8**
General merchandise: imports f.o.b.	3 110 . .	–1,518.4	–2,299.5	–2,510.0	–2,537.4	–2,755.0	–2,639.3	–2,293.6	–2,301.2
Goods for processing: imports f.o.b.	3 150 . .	–77.4	–123.4	–104.0	–111.2	–120.9	–116.5	–100.3	–98.8
Repairs on goods	3 160 . .	. . .	. . .	. . .	. . .	. . .	. . .	. . .	. . .
Goods procured in ports by carriers	3 170 . .	–11.0	–7.4	–8.4	–9.8	–10.7	–10.2	–7.9	–7.8
Nonmonetary gold	3 180 . .	. . .	. . .	. . .	. . .	. . .	. . .	. . .	. . .
B. SERVICES	4 200 . .	–503.3	–844.8	–874.6	–899.0	–909.7	–873.0	–744.4	–745.3
Total credit	2 200 . .	*507.7*	*530.9*	*565.7*	*579.6*	*614.3*	*586.0*	*482.5*	*487.4*
Total debit	3 200 . .	*–1,011.1*	*–1,375.7*	*–1,440.3*	*–1,478.6*	*–1,524.0*	*–1,459.0*	*–1,226.9*	*–1,232.7*
Transportation services, credit	2 205 . .	**161.0**	**123.0**	**125.3**	**116.5**	**120.7**	**113.2**	**84.4**	**85.9**
Passenger	2 850 . .	*11.7*	*13.6*	*13.7*	*12.8*	*13.4*	*6.5*	*3.9*	*4.0*
Freight	2 851 . .	*87.4*	*42.7*	*44.6*	*41.6*	*42.9*	*42.9*	*22.3*	*22.8*
Other	2 852 . .	*62.0*	*66.7*	*67.1*	*62.0*	*64.4*	*63.8*	*58.1*	*59.2*
Sea transport, passenger	2 207 . .	. . .	. . .	. . .	. . .	. . .	. . .	. . .	. . .
Sea transport, freight	2 208 . .	72.4	17.0	17.8	16.6	17.1	17.1	. . .	. . .
Sea transport, other	2 209 . .	42.0	47.3	47.7	43.9	45.4	45.5	42.6	43.4
Air transport, passenger	2 211 . .	8.8	10.2	10.2	9.6	10.0	3.2	1.0	1.0
Air transport, freight	2 212 . .	. . .	. . .	. . .	. . .	. . .	. . .	. . .	. . .
Air transport, other	2 213 . .	20.0	19.4	19.4	18.2	19.0	18.4	15.6	15.8
Other transport, passenger	2 215 . .	2.9	3.4	3.5	3.3	3.4	3.2	2.9	3.0
Other transport, freight	2 216 . .	14.9	25.6	26.8	25.0	25.8	25.8	22.3	22.8
Other transport, other	2 217 . .	. . .	. . .	. . .	. . .	. . .	. . .	. . .	. . .
Transportation services, debit	3 205 . .	**–454.3**	**–623.1**	**–571.6**	**–568.6**	**–604.3**	**–590.1**	**–516.3**	**–521.8**
Passenger	3 850 . .	*–108.6*	*–122.0*	*–125.7*	*–116.7*	*–117.8*	*–114.7*	*–102.0*	*–103.0*
Freight	3 851 . .	*–254.8*	*–452.4*	*–394.1*	*–398.3*	*–432.4*	*–422.6*	*–367.6*	*–374.5*
Other	3 852 . .	*–91.0*	*–48.7*	*–51.8*	*–53.6*	*–54.1*	*–52.8*	*–46.8*	*–44.3*
Sea transport, passenger	3 207 . .	. . .	. . .	. . .	. . .	. . .	. . .	. . .	. . .
Sea transport, freight	3 208 . .	–233.2	–414.3	–360.9	–364.9	–396.1	–387.0	–336.8	–343.1
Sea transport, other	3 209 . .	–73.3	–29.5	–32.5	–33.6	–33.9	–33.1	–29.4	–29.6
Air transport, passenger	3 211 . .	–108.6	–122.0	–125.7	–116.7	–117.8	–114.7	–102.0	–103.0
Air transport, freight	3 212 . .	–11.8	–20.8	–18.2	–18.3	–19.8	–19.5	–16.9	–17.2
Air transport, other	3 213 . .	–17.5	–19.0	–19.2	–19.7	–19.8	–19.3	–17.1	–14.5
Other transport, passenger	3 215 . .	. . .	. . .	. . .	. . .	. . .	. . .	. . .	. . .
Other transport, freight	3 216 . .	–9.7	–17.2	–15.1	–15.1	–16.4	–16.1	–13.9	–14.2
Other transport, other	3 217 . .	–.2	–.2	–.2	–.3	–.3	–.3	–.3	–.3
Travel, credit	2 236 . .	**53.5**	**88.8**	**93.4**	**90.5**	**97.8**	**99.9**	**49.3**	**48.4**
Business travel	2 237 . .	35.1	47.3	46.3	40.8	45.1	46.3	20.9	20.6
Personal travel	2 240 . .	18.4	41.5	47.1	49.7	52.7	53.6	28.4	27.8
Travel, debit	3 236 . .	**–157.4**	**–189.5**	**–220.7**	**–199.9**	**–212.9**	**–221.7**	**–189.1**	**–191.8**
Business travel	3 237 . .	–12.4	–11.2	–10.6	–10.6	–11.2	–13.3	–3.7	–4.1
Personal travel	3 240 . .	–145.0	–178.3	–210.1	–189.3	–201.7	–208.4	–185.4	–187.7
Other services, credit	2 200 BA	**293.2**	**319.1**	**347.0**	**372.6**	**395.8**	**372.9**	**348.7**	**353.1**
Communications	2 245 . .	4.5	5.0	5.1	49.3	56.8	44.3	39.3	40.0
Construction	2 249 . .	.2	.2	11.9	11.0	11.5	11.7	10.4	10.6
Insurance	2 253 . .	29.4	22.4	28.5	26.9	30.2	29.1	24.6	25.0
Financial	2 260 . .	24.0	30.1	31.1	23.1	24.2	23.4	28.2	28.8
Computer and information	2 262 . .	. . .	. . .	.4	.2	.2	.2	.1	.1
Royalties and licence fees	2 266 . .	.5	.2	.2	.2	.2	.2	.1	.1
Other business services	2 268 . .	138.5	155.9	176.7	183.8	191.5	185.2	178.0	181.3
Personal, cultural, and recreational	2 287 . .	7.6	. . .	. . .	. . .	. . .	. . .	.1	. . .
Government, n.i.e.	2 291 . .	88.6	105.4	93.1	78.1	81.2	78.9	67.8	67.1
Other services, debit	3 200 BA	**–399.3**	**–563.2**	**–648.0**	**–710.0**	**–706.8**	**–647.2**	**–521.5**	**–519.1**
Communications	3 245 . .	–4.1	–5.0	–4.9	–33.9	–51.0	–46.9	–33.8	–33.7
Construction	3 249 . .	. . .	. . .	–6.5	–6.5	–6.6	–6.3	–3.9	–4.0
Insurance	3 253 . .	–21.6	–30.7	–45.2	–41.8	–44.1	–42.4	–37.4	–37.2
Financial	3 260 . .	–60.5	–104.8	–115.5	–119.8	–106.6	–103.8	–87.6	–87.4
Computer and information	3 262 . .	–3.6	–3.8	–5.7	–8.1	–8.6	–8.4	–7.3	–7.2
Royalties and licence fees	3 266 . .	–4.7	–3.4	–15.8	–16.1	–25.8	–15.3	–8.6	–8.6
Other business services	3 268 . .	–192.4	–273.7	–309.6	–344.5	–347.7	–322.6	–257.6	–256.9
Personal, cultural, and recreational	3 287 . .	–.5	–.6	–.6	–.7	–.7	–.6	–.6	–.4
Government, n.i.e.	3 291 . .	–111.9	–141.2	–144.3	–138.6	–115.8	–100.9	–84.7	–83.6

Table 2 (Continued). STANDARD PRESENTATION, 1994–2001

(Millions of U.S. dollars)

	Code	1994	1995	1996	1997	1998	1999	2000	2001
C. INCOME	4 300 . .	–683.7	–786.5	–768.8	–668.0	–706.8	–756.9	–653.4	–577.3
Total credit	2 300 . .	*133.8*	*189.5*	*170.7*	*161.2*	*169.2*	*162.6*	*141.3*	*141.9*
Total debit	3 300 . .	*–817.5*	*–976.1*	*–939.5*	*–829.2*	*–876.0*	*–919.4*	*–794.7*	*–719.2*
Compensation of employees, credit	2 310 . .	**110.4**	**151.1**	**147.0**	**136.4**	**142.6**	**137.6**	**119.4**	**119.5**
Compensation of employees, debit	3 310 . .	**–14.4**	**. . .**	**–13.7**	**–12.7**	**–12.9**	**–12.5**	**–11.1**	**–11.3**
Investment income, credit	2 320 . .	**23.4**	**38.5**	**23.7**	**24.8**	**26.6**	**25.0**	**21.9**	**22.4**
Direct investment income	2 330 . .	1.8	2.0	3.1	2.7	2.7	2.6	2.4	2.6
Dividends and distributed branch profits	2 332 . .	1.8	2.0	2.2	2.1	2.0	1.9	1.7	1.8
Reinvested earnings and undistributed branch profits	2 333 . .	. . .	. . .	. . .	. . .	. . .	. . .	. . .	. . .
Income on debt (interest)	2 334 . .	. . .	. . .	1.0	.7	.7	.6	.7	.8
Portfolio investment income	2 339 . .	. . .	. . .	.8	1.7	3.6	4.7	2.9	3.1
Income on equity	2 340 . .	. . .	. . .	.2	. . .	. . .	. . .	. . .	. . .
Income on bonds and notes	2 350 . .	. . .	. . .	. . .	. . .	1.7	2.9	1.4	1.5
Income on money market instruments	2 360 . .	. . .	. . .	.6	1.7	1.9	1.8	1.5	1.6
Other investment income	2 370 . .	21.6	36.5	19.7	20.4	20.3	17.7	16.6	16.6
Investment income, debit	3 320 . .	**–803.1**	**–976.1**	**–925.8**	**–816.6**	**–863.1**	**–906.9**	**–783.6**	**–707.9**
Direct investment income	3 330 . .	–81.2	–203.7	–224.2	–227.2	–291.9	–333.8	–284.0	–256.6
Dividends and distributed branch profits	3 332 . .	–38.7	–51.7	–101.1	–106.4	–145.8	–171.8	–145.1	–131.1
Reinvested earnings and undistributed branch profits	3 333 . .	–11.2	–93.6	–60.2	–61.9	–84.6	–99.7	–84.3	–76.1
Income on debt (interest)	3 334 . .	–31.3	–58.5	–62.9	–58.9	–61.5	–62.2	–54.6	–49.4
Portfolio investment income	3 339 . .	–1.4	–7.2	–36.2	–34.3	–38.1	–38.5	–33.3	–30.0
Income on equity	3 340 . .	–1.4	–7.2	–33.4	–30.8	–32.4	–32.6	–28.7	–25.9
Income on bonds and notes	3 350 . .	. . .	. . .	–2.7	–3.4	–5.8	–5.8	–4.6	–4.1
Income on money market instruments	3 360 . .	. . .	. . .	. . .	. . .	. . .	. . .	. . .	. . .
Other investment income	3 370 . .	–720.5	–765.1	–665.4	–555.1	–533.1	–534.7	–466.3	–421.3
D. CURRENT TRANSFERS	4 379 . .	–115.8	–236.6	–342.5	–380.5	–393.6	–385.9	–330.1	–274.7
Credit	2 379 . .	**246.8**	**277.7**	**204.1**	**137.7**	**148.1**	**136.8**	**79.4**	**85.0**
General government	2 380 . .	211.8	225.0	148.6	88.1	98.7	88.4	37.2	43.5
Other sectors	2 390 . .	34.9	52.7	55.5	49.7	49.5	48.4	42.1	41.5
Workers' remittances	2 391 . .	. . .	. . .	. . .	. . .	. . .	. . .	. . .	. . .
Other current transfers	2 392 . .	34.9	52.7	55.5	49.7	49.5	48.4	42.1	41.5
Debit	3 379 . .	**–362.6**	**–514.3**	**–546.6**	**–518.3**	**–541.7**	**–522.7**	**–409.4**	**–359.7**
General government	3 380 . .	–19.1	–22.4	–17.0	–16.1	–17.8	–17.1	–14.6	–14.5
Other sectors	3 390 . .	–343.5	–491.8	–529.6	–502.2	–523.9	–505.6	–394.8	–345.3
Workers' remittances	3 391 . .	–340.6	–457.0	–510.2	–482.5	–504.1	–486.4	–378.7	–331.1
Other current transfers	3 392 . .	–2.9	–34.9	–19.4	–19.7	–19.8	–19.2	–16.2	–14.2
CAPITAL AND FINANCIAL ACCOUNT	4 996 . .	**24.8**	**456.9**	**177.7**	**194.3**	**258.2**	**144.4**	**251.8**	**80.7**
CAPITAL ACCOUNT	4 994 . .	**527.6**	**291.3**	**47.1**	**40.6**	**25.6**	**13.8**	**8.4**	**10.0**
Total credit	2 994 . .	*527.6*	*291.3*	*49.8*	*50.5*	*35.9*	*17.4*	*9.8*	*11.5*
Total debit	3 994 . .	*. . .*	*. . .*	*–2.7*	*–9.9*	*–10.3*	*–3.6*	*–1.4*	*–1.5*
Capital transfers, credit	2 400 . .	**527.6**	**291.3**	**49.8**	**50.5**	**35.9**	**17.4**	**9.8**	**11.5**
General government	2 401 . .	527.6	291.3	39.5	50.5	35.9	17.2	9.8	11.5
Debt forgiveness	2 402 . .	463.3	220.6	. . .	. . .	. . .	. . .	. . .	. . .
Other capital transfers	2 410 . .	64.3	70.7	39.5	50.5	35.9	17.2	9.8	11.5
Other sectors	2 430 . .	. . .	. . .	10.4	. . .	. . .	.2	. . .	. . .
Migrants' transfers	2 431 . .	. . .	. . .	. . .	. . .	. . .	. . .	. . .	. . .
Debt forgiveness	2 432 . .	. . .	. . .	. . .	. . .	. . .	. . .	. . .	. . .
Other capital transfers	2 440 . .	. . .	. . .	10.4	. . .	. . .	.2	. . .	. . .
Capital transfers, debit	3 400 . .	**. . .**	**. . .**	**. . .**	**. . .**	**. . .**	**. . .**	**. . .**	**. . .**
General government	3 401 . .	. . .	. . .	. . .	. . .	. . .	. . .	. . .	. . .
Debt forgiveness	3 402 . .	. . .	. . .	. . .	. . .	. . .	. . .	. . .	. . .
Other capital transfers	3 410 . .	. . .	. . .	. . .	. . .	. . .	. . .	. . .	. . .
Other sectors	3 430 . .	. . .	. . .	. . .	. . .	. . .	. . .	. . .	. . .
Migrants' transfers	3 431 . .	. . .	. . .	. . .	. . .	. . .	. . .	. . .	. . .
Debt forgiveness	3 432 . .	. . .	. . .	. . .	. . .	. . .	. . .	. . .	. . .
Other capital transfers	3 440 . .	. . .	. . .	. . .	. . .	. . .	. . .	. . .	. . .
Nonproduced nonfinancial assets, credit	2 480 . .	**. . .**	**. . .**	**. . .**	**. . .**	**. . .**	**. . .**	**. . .**	**. . .**
Nonproduced nonfinancial assets, debit	3 480 . .	**. . .**	**. . .**	**–2.7**	**–9.9**	**–10.3**	**–3.6**	**–1.4**	**–1.5**

Table 2 (Continued). STANDARD PRESENTATION, 1994–2001
(Millions of U.S. dollars)

	Code	1994	1995	1996	1997	1998	1999	2000	2001
FINANCIAL ACCOUNT	4 995	**–502.7**	**165.6**	**130.6**	**153.7**	**232.6**	**130.6**	**243.4**	**70.7**
A. DIRECT INVESTMENT	4 500	78.0	211.5	268.8	415.3	379.9	323.7	234.7	245.7
Direct investment abroad	4 505	**. . .**	**. . .**	**–.4**	**. . .**	**. . .**	**. . .**	**. . .**	**. . .**
Equity capital	4 510	. . .	. . .	. . .	. . .	. . .	. . .	. . .	. . .
Claims on affiliated enterprises	4 515	. . .	. . .	. . .	. . .	. . .	. . .	. . .	. . .
Liabilities to affiliated enterprises	4 520	. . .	. . .	. . .	. . .	. . .	. . .	. . .	. . .
Reinvested earnings	4 525	. . .	. . .	. . .	. . .	. . .	. . .	. . .	. . .
Other capital	4 530	. . .	. . .	. . .	. . .	. . .	. . .	. . .	. . .
Claims on affiliated enterprises	4 535	. . .	. . .	. . .	. . .	. . .	. . .	. . .	. . .
Liabilities to affiliated enterprises	4 540	. . .	. . .	. . .	. . .	. . .	. . .	. . .	. . .
Direct investment in Cote d'Ivoire	4 555	**78.0**	**211.5**	**269.2**	**415.3**	**379.9**	**323.7**	**234.7**	**245.7**
Equity capital	4 560	4.9	62.6	116.9	276.9	219.2	200.3	135.1	141.5
Claims on direct investors	4 565	–.5	. . .	. . .	. . .	. . .	. . .	. . .	. . .
Liabilities to direct investors	4 570	5.4	62.6	116.9	276.9	219.2	200.3	135.1	141.5
Reinvested earnings	4 575	11.2	93.6	60.2	61.9	84.6	99.7	84.3	76.1
Other capital	4 580	62.0	55.3	92.1	76.6	76.1	23.7	15.3	28.1
Claims on direct investors	4 585	–4.7	–14.2	–19.4	–21.6	–22.5	–29.4	–20.4	–9.3
Liabilities to direct investors	4 590	66.6	69.5	111.4	98.2	98.7	53.1	35.7	37.4
B. PORTFOLIO INVESTMENT	4 600	–28.1	1.6	9.0	–7.7	–10.3	–15.3	–8.1	–7.9
Assets	4 602	**–27.4**	**–8.4**	**–16.0**	**–26.9**	**–29.8**	**–28.7**	**–12.6**	**–12.7**
Equity securities	4 610	7.7	1.2	–1.6	.2	–1.7	–1.6	–1.4	–1.4
Monetary authorities	4 611	. . .	. . .	. . .	. . .	. . .	. . .	. . .	. . .
General government	4 612	. . .	. . .	. . .	. . .	. . .	. . .	. . .	. . .
Banks	4 613	. . .	. . .	. . .	. . .	. . .	. . .	. . .	. . .
Other sectors	4 614	7.7	1.2	–1.6	.2	–1.7	–1.6	–1.4	–1.4
Debt securities	4 619	–35.1	–9.6	–14.5	–27.1	–28.1	–27.1	–11.2	–11.3
Bonds and notes	4 620	–35.1	–9.6	–15.1	–19.7	–20.5	–19.8	–7.6	–7.6
Monetary authorities	4 621	. . .	. . .	. . .	. . .	. . .	. . .	. . .	. . .
General government	4 622	. . .	. . .	. . .	. . .	. . .	. . .	. . .	. . .
Banks	4 623	–40.7	–11.8	. . .	. . .	. . .	. . .	. . .	. . .
Other sectors	4 624	5.6	2.2	–15.1	–19.7	–20.5	–19.8	–7.6	–7.6
Money market instruments	4 630	. . .	. . .	.6	–7.4	–7.6	–7.3	–3.7	–3.7
Monetary authorities	4 631	. . .	. . .	. . .	. . .	. . .	. . .	. . .	. . .
General government	4 632	. . .	. . .	. . .	. . .	. . .	. . .	. . .	. . .
Banks	4 633	. . .	. . .	. . .	. . .	. . .	. . .	. . .	. . .
Other sectors	4 634	. . .	. . .	.6	–7.4	–7.6	–7.3	–3.7	–3.7
Liabilities	4 652	**–.7**	**10.0**	**25.0**	**19.2**	**19.5**	**13.5**	**4.5**	**4.8**
Equity securities	4 660	1.1	1.2	10.2	8.6	8.6	5.7	1.1	1.2
Banks	4 663	. . .	. . .	. . .	. . .	. . .	. . .	. . .	. . .
Other sectors	4 664	1.1	1.2	10.2	8.6	8.6	5.7	1.1	1.2
Debt securities	4 669	–1.8	8.8	14.9	10.6	10.8	7.8	3.4	3.5
Bonds and notes	4 670	–1.8	8.8	11.7	10.6	10.8	7.8	3.4	3.5
Monetary authorities	4 671	. . .	. . .	. . .	. . .	. . .	. . .	. . .	. . .
General government	4 672	. . .	. . .	. . .	. . .	. . .	. . .	. . .	. . .
Banks	4 673	. . .	. . .	. . .	. . .	. . .	. . .	. . .	. . .
Other sectors	4 674	–1.8	8.8	11.7	10.6	10.8	7.8	3.4	3.5
Money market instruments	4 680	. . .	. . .	3.1	. . .	. . .	. . .	. . .	. . .
Monetary authorities	4 681	. . .	. . .	. . .	. . .	. . .	. . .	. . .	. . .
General government	4 682	. . .	. . .	. . .	. . .	. . .	. . .	. . .	. . .
Banks	4 683	. . .	. . .	. . .	. . .	. . .	. . .	. . .	. . .
Other sectors	4 684	. . .	. . .	3.1	. . .	. . .	. . .	. . .	. . .
C. FINANCIAL DERIVATIVES	4 910	. . .	. . .	–3.3	–3.1	–3.2	–3.1	–2.5	–2.6
Monetary authorities	4 911	. . .	. . .	. . .	. . .	. . .	. . .	. . .	. . .
General government	4 912	. . .	. . .	. . .	. . .	. . .	. . .	. . .	. . .
Banks	4 913	. . .	. . .	. . .	. . .	. . .	. . .	. . .	. . .
Other sectors	4 914	. . .	. . .	–3.3	–3.1	–3.2	–3.1	–2.5	–2.6
Assets	4 900	**. . .**	**. . .**	**. . .**	**. . .**	**. . .**	**. . .**	**. . .**	**. . .**
Monetary authorities	4 901	. . .	. . .	. . .	. . .	. . .	. . .	. . .	. . .
General government	4 902	. . .	. . .	. . .	. . .	. . .	. . .	. . .	. . .
Banks	4 903	. . .	. . .	. . .	. . .	. . .	. . .	. . .	. . .
Other sectors	4 904	. . .	. . .	. . .	. . .	. . .	. . .	. . .	. . .
Liabilities	4 905	**. . .**	**. . .**	**–3.3**	**–3.1**	**–3.2**	**–3.1**	**–2.5**	**–2.6**
Monetary authorities	4 906	. . .	. . .	. . .	. . .	. . .	. . .	. . .	. . .
General government	4 907	. . .	. . .	. . .	. . .	. . .	. . .	. . .	. . .
Banks	4 908	. . .	. . .	. . .	. . .	. . .	. . .	. . .	. . .
Other sectors	4 909	. . .	. . .	–3.3	–3.1	–3.2	–3.1	–2.5	–2.6

Table 2 (Concluded). STANDARD PRESENTATION, 1994–2001
(Millions of U.S. dollars)

	Code		1994	1995	1996	1997	1998	1999	2000	2001
D. OTHER INVESTMENT	4 700	. .	–358.1	255.0	–30.5	–155.4	46.1	–284.5	108.4	220.2
Assets	4 703	. .	**–39.6**	**–323.2**	**–256.5**	**–304.8**	**–317.5**	**–350.5**	**–182.2**	**–170.1**
Trade credits	4 706	. .	–1.8	–99.6	–105.6	–109.3	–115.9	–117.9	–11.2	–11.3
General government	4 707	. .	. . .	. . .	. . .	. . .	. . .	. . .	. . .	. . .
of which: Short-term	4 709	. .	. . .	. . .	. . .	. . .	. . .	. . .	. . .	. . .
Other sectors	4 710	. .	–1.8	–99.6	–105.6	–109.3	–115.9	–117.9	–11.2	–11.3
of which: Short-term	4 712	. .	*–1.8*	*–99.6*	*–105.6*	*–109.3*	*–115.9*	*–117.9*	*–11.2*	*–11.3*
Loans	4 714	. .	67.5	–18.6	98.3	–15.4	–2.4	6.3	–18.4	–18.6
Monetary authorities	4 715	. .	. . .	. . .	. . .	. . .	. . .	. . .	. . .	. . .
of which: Short-term	4 718	. .	. . .	. . .	. . .	. . .	. . .	. . .	. . .	. . .
General government	4 719	. .	. . .	. . .	. . .	. . .	. . .	. . .	. . .	. . .
of which: Short-term	4 721	. .	. . .	. . .	. . .	. . .	. . .	. . .	. . .	. . .
Banks	4 722	. .	22.5	–17.4	106.0	–8.2	5.1	13.5	–12.4	–12.4
of which: Short-term	4 724	. .	*22.5*	*–17.4*	*106.1*	*–7.9*	*5.3*	*10.2*	*–11.9*	*–12.0*
Other sectors	4 725	. .	45.0	–1.2	–7.6	–7.2	–7.5	–7.1	–6.0	–6.1
of which: Short-term	4 727	. .	*17.3*	*–15.8*	. . .	. . .	. . .	. . .	. . .	. . .
Currency and deposits	4 730	. .	–93.5	–190.7	–219.3	–157.3	–185.3	–231.6	–75.6	–76.3
Monetary authorities	4 731	. .	. . .	. . .	. . .	. . .	. . .	. . .	. . .	. . .
General government	4 732	. .	. . .	. . .	–6.6	. . .	–2.2	. . .	. . .	. . .
Banks	4 733	. .	–117.8	–15.6	–59.6	–16.6	–17.5	–62.7	51.7	52.2
Other sectors	4 734	. .	24.3	–175.1	–153.1	–140.7	–165.6	–168.9	–127.3	–128.5
Other assets	4 736	. .	–11.9	–14.2	–29.9	–22.8	–13.9	–7.3	–77.0	–64.0
Monetary authorities	4 737	. .	. . .	. . .	. . .	. . .	. . .	. . .	. . .	. . .
of which: Short-term	4 739	. .	. . .	. . .	. . .	. . .	. . .	. . .	. . .	. . .
General government	4 740	. .	–11.9	–14.2	–15.6	–9.9	–5.4	–5.2	–4.5	–5.0
of which: Short-term	4 742	. .	*.2*	*.2*	*.2*	*.2*	*.2*	*.2*	*.1*	*.1*
Banks	4 743	. .	. . .	. . .	–11.1	–.9	–4.1	.2	–36.5	–36.8
of which: Short-term	4 745	. .	. . .	. . .	*–11.1*	*–.9*	*–4.1*	*.2*	*–36.5*	*–36.8*
Other sectors	4 746	. .	. . .	. . .	–3.1	–12.0	–4.4	–2.3	–36.0	–22.1
of which: Short-term	4 748	. .	. . .	. . .	*–3.1*	*–12.0*	*–4.4*	*–2.3*	*–36.0*	*–22.1*
Liabilities	4 753	. .	**–318.5**	**578.1**	**226.0**	**149.4**	**363.6**	**66.0**	**290.6**	**390.3**
Trade credits	4 756	. .	–49.5	66.3	14.7	36.3	56.6	32.3	63.2	99.3
General government	4 757	. .	. . .	. . .	. . .	. . .	. . .	. . .	. . .	. . .
of which: Short-term	4 759	. .	. . .	. . .	. . .	. . .	. . .	. . .	. . .	. . .
Other sectors	4 760	. .	–49.5	66.3	14.7	36.3	56.6	32.3	63.2	99.3
of which: Short-term	4 762	. .	*–49.5*	*66.3*	*14.7*	*36.3*	*56.6*	*32.3*	*63.2*	*99.3*
Loans	4 764	. .	1,372.2	409.1	183.2	–145.3	741.8	–84.0	–137.1	–143.3
Monetary authorities	4 765	. .	94.3	94.9	90.3	–22.3	168.8	–8.2	–38.8	–66.4
of which: Use of Fund credit and loans from the Fund	4 766	. .	*94.3*	*94.9*	*90.3*	*–22.3*	*168.8*	*–8.2*	*–38.8*	*–66.4*
of which: Short-term	4 768	. .	. . .	. . .	. . .	. . .	. . .	. . .	. . .	. . .
General government	4 769	. .	1,308.2	341.8	245.7	–86.4	512.9	–29.9	–53.8	–144.9
of which: Short-term	4 771	. .	. . .	. . .	. . .	. . .	. . .	. . .	. . .	. . .
Banks	4 772	. .	51.9	–9.6	–63.7	18.0	25.6	–9.7	–43.5	–5.7
of which: Short-term	4 774	. .	. . .	. . .	*58.1*	*–46.3*	*71.7*	*–30.2*	*–18.1*	. . .
Other sectors	4 775	. .	–82.1	–18.0	–89.1	–54.7	34.4	–36.2	–1.0	73.7
of which: Short-term	4 777	. .	*–30.8*	*16.6*	*–47.1*	*–35.6*	*30.2*	*–20.5*	*–8.8*	. . .
Currency and deposits	4 780	. .	–717.0	12.2	9.2	43.2	7.1	57.3	11.5	14.7
Monetary authorities	4 781	. .	–726.6	1.8	2.0	1.2	–.5	4.4	–7.0	. . .
General government	4 782	. .	. . .	. . .	. . .	. . .	. . .	. . .	. . .	. . .
Banks	4 783	. .	9.5	10.4	7.2	42.0	7.6	52.9	18.5	14.7
Other sectors	4 784	. .	. . .	. . .	. . .	. . .	. . .	. . .	. . .	. . .
Other liabilities	4 786	. .	–924.2	90.6	19.0	215.2	–441.9	60.4	353.0	419.6
Monetary authorities	4 787	. .	. . .	. . .	–3.1	3.1	3.7	–9.4	6.2	–5.3
of which: Short-term	4 789	. .	. . .	. . .	. . .	. . .	. . .	. . .	. . .	. . .
General government	4 790	. .	–937.9	14.2	4.1	207.1	–449.7	52.6	264.2	220.5
of which: Short-term	4 792	. .	*–937.9*	*14.2*	*4.1*	*207.1*	*–449.7*	*52.6*	*264.2*	*220.5*
Banks	4 793	. .	13.7	76.3	18.0	5.0	4.1	–1.3	48.2	46.1
of which: Short-term	4 795	. .	*13.7*	*76.3*	*18.0*	*5.0*	*4.1*	*–1.3*	*48.2*	*46.1*
Other sectors	4 796	. .	. . .	. . .	. . .	. . .	. . .	18.5	34.4	158.4
of which: Short-term	4 798	. .	. . .	. . .	. . .	. . .	. . .	*18.5*	*34.4*	*158.4*
E. RESERVE ASSETS	4 802	. .	–194.5	–302.5	–113.4	–95.4	–179.8	109.7	–89.1	–384.7
Monetary gold	4 812	. .	. . .	. . .	. . .	. . .	. . .	. . .	. . .	. . .
Special drawing rights	4 811	. .	1.0	–1.8	.6	1.1	–.1	–3.3	2.0	.5
Reserve position in the Fund	4 810	. .	. . .	. . .	. . .	–.1	. . .	–.1	–.1	. . .
Foreign exchange	4 803	. .	–195.4	–300.7	–114.0	–96.5	–179.7	113.0	–91.0	–385.1
Other claims	4 813	. .	. . .	. . .	. . .	. . .	. . .	. . .	. . .	. . .
NET ERRORS AND OMISSIONS	4 998	. .	**–11.1**	**35.6**	**–15.4**	**–39.6**	**32.0**	**–24.0**	**–10.2**	**–23.0**

Part 3 of the *Yearbook* contains descriptions of the methodologies, compilation practices, and sources used to compile these data.

Table 3. INTERNATIONAL INVESTMENT POSITION (End–period stocks), 1994–2001

(Millions of U.S. dollars)

	Code		1994	1995	1996	1997	1998	1999	2000	2001
ASSETS	8 995	C .	...	...	...	...	2,768.1	2,641.1	2,734.3	3,154.7
Direct investment abroad	8 505	. .	...	...	...	...	...	...	...	...
Equity capital and reinvested earnings	8 506	. .	...	...	...	...	...	...	...	...
Claims on affiliated enterprises	8 507	. .	...	...	...	...	...	...	...	...
Liabilities to affiliated enterprises	8 508	. .	...	...	...	...	...	...	...	...
Other capital	8 530	. .	...	...	...	...	...	...	...	...
Claims on affiliated enterprises	8 535	. .	...	...	...	...	...	...	...	...
Liabilities to affiliated enterprises	8 540	. .	...	...	...	...	...	...	...	...
Portfolio investment	8 602	. .	...	...	...	...	**158.8**	**166.9**	**169.8**	**176.0**
Equity securities	8 610	. .	...	...	...	...	10.5	10.6	11.1	12.0
Monetary authorities	8 611	. .	...	...	...	...	...	...	...	...
General government	8 612	. .	...	...	...	...	...	...	...	...
Banks	8 613	. .	...	...	...	...	...	...	...	...
Other sectors	8 614	. .	...	...	...	...	...	10.6	11.1	12.0
Debt securities	8 619	. .	...	...	...	...	148.3	156.4	158.7	164.0
Bonds and notes	8 620	. .	...	...	...	...	...	...	...	...
Monetary authorities	8 621	. .	...	...	...	...	...	...	...	...
General government	8 622	. .	...	...	...	...	...	...	...	...
Banks	8 623	. .	...	...	...	...	...	...	...	...
Other sectors	8 624	. .	...	...	...	...	...	...	...	...
Money market instruments	8 630	. .	...	...	...	3.3	148.3	156.4	158.7	164.0
Monetary authorities	8 631	. .	...	...	...	...	...	...	...	...
General government	8 632	. .	...	...	...	...	...	...	...	...
Banks	8 633	. .	...	...	...	...	...	...	...	...
Other sectors	8 634	. .	...	...	...	...	148.3	156.4	158.7	164.0
Financial derivatives	8 900	. .	...	...	...	...	...	...	...	...
Monetary authorities	8 901	. .	...	...	...	...	...	...	...	...
General government	8 902	. .	...	...	...	...	...	...	...	...
Banks	8 903	. .	...	...	...	...	...	...	...	...
Other sectors	8 904	. .	...	...	...	...	...	...	...	...
Other investment	8 703	. .	**337.4**	**378.6**	**268.3**	**266.9**	**1,757.2**	**1,843.8**	**1,891.9**	**1,959.7**
Trade credits	8 706	. .	...	...	...	...	644.1	665.9	628.1	606.1
General government	8 707	. .	...	...	...	...	...	...	...	...
of which: Short-term	8 709	. .	...	...	...	...	...	...	...	...
Other sectors	8 710	. .	...	...	...	...	644.1	665.9	628.1	606.1
of which: Short-term	8 712	. .	...	...	...	...	...	...	...	...
Loans	8 714	. .	14.6	33.7	...	...	68.7	53.1	67.8	82.6
Monetary authorities	8 715	. .	...	...	...	...	...	...	...	...
of which: Short-term	8 718	. .	...	...	...	...	...	...	...	...
General government	8 719	. .	...	...	...	...	...	...	...	...
of which: Short-term	8 721	. .	...	...	...	...	...	...	...	...
Banks	8 722	. .	14.6	33.7	...	...	...	...	...	...
of which: Short-term	8 724	. .	*14.6*	*33.7*	...	...	...	...	...	...
Other sectors	8 725	. .	...	...	...	...	68.7	53.1	67.8	82.6
of which: Short-term	8 727	. .	...	...	...	...	...	...	...	...
Currency and deposits	8 730	. .	107.0	128.8	187.3	166.2	905.4	998.1	1,000.8	1,023.1
Monetary authorities	8 731	. .	...	...	...	...	...	...	...	...
General government	8 732	. .	107.0	128.8	187.3	166.2	...	...	...	...
Banks	8 733	. .	...	...	...	...	...	...	...	...
Other sectors	8 734	. .	...	...	...	...	905.4	998.1	1,000.8	1,023.1
Other assets	8 736	. .	215.9	216.1	81.0	100.7	139.1	126.7	195.2	247.9
Monetary authorities	8 737	. .	...	...	...	...	...	...	...	...
of which: Short-term	8 739	. .	...	...	...	...	...	...	...	...
General government	8 740	. .	...	...	...	...	...	...	...	...
of which: Short-term	8 742	. .	...	...	...	...	...	...	...	...
Banks	8 743	. .	215.9	216.1	81.0	100.7	...	...	...	...
of which: Short-term	8 745	. .	*215.9*	*216.1*	*81.0*	*100.7*	...	...	...	...
Other sectors	8 746	. .	...	...	...	...	139.1	126.7	195.2	247.9
of which: Short-term	8 748	. .	...	...	...	...	...	...	...	...
Reserve assets	8 802	. .	**204.4**	**531.0**	**607.0**	**623.0**	**852.1**	**630.4**	**672.6**	**1,019.0**
Monetary gold	8 812	. .	...	...	...	...	...	...	...	...
Special drawing rights	8 811	. .	.2	1.8	1.2	...	.2	3.4	1.3	.7
Reserve position in the Fund	8 810	. .	.1	.1	.2	.2	.3	.3	.4	.4
Foreign exchange	8 803	. .	203.1	525.1	603.0	620.9	851.6	626.7	671.0	1,017.9
Other claims	8 813	. .	.9	3.9	2.7	1.8	...	...	...	...

Table 3 (Concluded). INTERNATIONAL INVESTMENT POSITION (End–period stocks), 1994–2001
(Millions of U.S. dollars)

	Code	1994	1995	1996	1997	1998	1999	2000	2001
LIABILITIES	8 995 D.	...	...	...	...	18,731.3	16,581.3	15,907.8	15,706.8
Direct investment in Cote d'Ivoire	8 555 . .	...	...	...	...	**1,858.2**	**1,905.2**	**2,001.7**	**2,137.7**
Equity capital and reinvested earnings	8 556 . .	...	...	...	...	...	...	...	...
Claims on direct investors	8 557 . .	...	...	...	...	...	...	...	...
Liabilities to direct investors	8 558 . .	...	...	...	...	...	...	...	...
Other capital	8 580 . .	...	...	...	...	1,858.2	1,905.2	2,001.7	2,137.7
Claims on direct investors	8 585 . .	...	...	...	...	...	...	...	...
Liabilities to direct investors	8 590 . .	...	...	...	...	...	...	...	...
Portfolio investment	8 652 . .	...	...	...	...	**244.4**	**223.1**	**211.2**	**204.8**
Equity securities	8 660 . .	...	...	...	...	...	...	...	...
Banks	8 663 . .	...	...	...	...	...	...	...	...
Other sectors	8 664 . .	...	...	...	...	...	...	...	...
Debt securities	8 669 . .	...	...	...	...	244.4	223.1	211.2	204.8
Bonds and notes	8 670 . .	...	...	...	...	...	...	...	...
Monetary authorities	8 671 . .	...	...	...	...	...	...	...	...
General government	8 672 . .	...	...	...	...	...	...	...	...
Banks	8 673 . .	...	...	...	...	...	...	...	...
Other sectors	8 674 . .	...	...	...	...	...	...	...	...
Money market instruments	8 680 . .	...	...	...	...	244.4	223.1	211.2	204.8
Monetary authorities	8 681 . .	...	...	...	...	...	...	...	...
General government	8 682 . .	...	...	...	...	...	...	...	...
Banks	8 683 . .	...	...	...	...	...	...	...	...
Other sectors	8 684 . .	...	...	...	...	244.4	223.1	211.2	204.8
Financial derivatives	8 905 . .	...	...	...	...	...	...	...	...
Monetary authorities	8 906 . .	...	...	...	...	...	...	...	...
General government	8 907 . .	...	...	...	...	...	...	...	...
Banks	8 908 . .	...	...	...	...	...	...	...	...
Other sectors	8 909 . .	...	...	...	...	...	...	...	...
Other investment	8 753 . .	**15,272.6**	**17,009.2**	**16,101.1**	**14,046.3**	**16,628.7**	**14,453.0**	**13,694.9**	**13,364.3**
Trade credits	8 756 . .	...	...	...	...	704.2	637.0	653.8	717.0
General government	8 757 . .	...	...	...	...	...	...	...	...
of which: Short-term	8 759 . .	...	...	...	...	...	...	...	...
Other sectors	8 760 . .	...	...	...	...	704.2	637.0	653.8	717.0
of which: Short-term	8 762 . .	...	...	...	...	...	...	...	...
Loans	8 764 . .	14,736.8	16,695.4	15,855.9	13,778.1	15,659.9	13,527.0	12,671.9	12,087.0
Monetary authorities	8 765 . .	328.1	426.8	502.7	449.9	644.0	619.5	549.3	464.0
of which: Use of Fund credit and loans from the Fund	8 766 . .	*328.1*	*426.8*	*502.7*	*449.9*	*644.0*	*619.5*	*549.3*	*464.0*
of which: Short-term	8 768 . .	...	...	...	...	...	...	...	...
General government	8 769 . .	14,199.2	16,049.6	15,324.2	13,289.5	14,790.0	12,756.0	12,027.5	11,466.0
of which: Short-term	8 771 . .	...	...	...	...	*6,363.1*	*5,528.4*	*5,389.9*	*5,322.0*
Banks	8 772 . .	209.5	219.0	29.0	38.6	173.2	140.1	85.7	75.5
of which: Short-term	8 774 . .	*209.5*	*219.0*	*29.0*	*38.6*	*173.2*	*140.1*	*85.7*	*75.5*
Other sectors	8 775 . .	...	...	...	...	52.6	11.3	9.4	81.6
of which: Short-term	8 777 . .	...	...	...	...	...	...	...	...
Currency and deposits	8 780 . .	377.5	63.3	125.8	155.5	172.9	202.8	199.6	203.4
Monetary authorities	8 781 . .	1.7	10.0	8.0	11.4	...	...	...	...
General government	8 782 . .	...	...	...	...	...	...	...	...
Banks	8 783 . .	375.8	53.3	117.8	144.1	172.9	202.8	199.6	203.4
Other sectors	8 784 . .	...	...	...	...	...	...	...	...
Other liabilities	8 786 . .	158.2	250.6	119.3	112.7	91.8	86.2	169.7	356.8
Monetary authorities	8 787 . .	...	...	...	...	...	...	...	...
of which: Short-term	8 789 . .	...	...	...	...	...	...	...	...
General government	8 790 . .	...	...	...	...	...	...	...	...
of which: Short-term	8 792 . .	...	...	...	...	...	...	...	...
Banks	8 793 . .	158.2	250.6	119.3	112.7	91.8	86.2	169.7	356.8
of which: Short-term	8 795 . .	*158.2*	*250.6*	*119.3*	*112.7*	*91.8*	*86.2*	*169.7*	*356.8*
Other sectors	8 796 . .	...	...	...	...	...	...	...	...
of which: Short-term	8 798 . .	...	...	...	...	...	...	...	...
NET INTERNATIONAL INVESTMENT POSITION	8 995 . .	...	...	...	...	**–15,963.3**	**–13,940.2**	**–13,173.5**	**–12,552.1**
Conversion rates: CFA francs per U.S. dollar (end of period)	0 102 . .	**534.60**	**490.00**	**523.70**	**598.81**	**562.21**	**652.95**	**704.95**	**744.31**

Croatia
960

Table 1. ANALYTIC PRESENTATION, 1994–2001
(Millions of U.S. dollars)

	Code	1994	1995	1996	1997	1998	1999	2000	2001
A. Current Account [1]	4 993 Z.	**554.1**	**–1,591.8**	**–1,049.1**	**–2,825.4**	**–1,468.0**	**–1,406.0**	**–447.5**	**–642.4**
Goods: exports f.o.b	2 100 . .	4,402.8	4,517.3	4,677.5	4,021.1	4,580.6	4,394.7	4,567.1	4,752.1
Goods: imports f.o.b	3 100 . .	–5,681.2	–7,744.8	–8,165.5	–9,404.1	–8,652.1	–7,693.4	–7,770.7	–8,763.8
Balance on Goods	4 100 . .	*–1,278.4*	*–3,227.5*	*–3,488.0*	*–5,383.0*	*–4,071.5*	*–3,298.7*	*–3,203.6*	*–4,011.7*
Services: credit	2 200 . .	2,660.6	2,223.4	3,193.2	3,984.6	3,949.1	3,707.7	4,081.0	4,872.7
Services: debit	3 200 . .	–1,190.3	–1,361.1	–1,707.0	–2,273.9	–1,887.1	–2,098.0	–1,828.0	–1,940.6
Balance on Goods and Services	4 991 . .	*191.9*	*–2,365.2*	*–2,001.8*	*–3,672.3*	*–2,009.5*	*–1,689.0*	*–950.6*	*–1,079.6*
Income: credit	2 300 . .	149.0	218.8	269.9	363.7	394.8	252.2	333.9	400.5
Income: debit	3 300 . .	–313.2	–247.7	–339.7	–386.1	–559.1	–601.6	–713.8	–929.0
Balance on Goods, Services, and Income	4 992 . .	*27.7*	*–2,394.1*	*–2,071.6*	*–3,694.7*	*–2,173.8*	*–2,038.4*	*–1,330.5*	*–1,608.1*
Current transfers: credit	2 379 Z.	669.2	971.2	1,173.3	963.8	919.1	967.3	1,101.0	1,174.6
Current transfers: debit	3 379 . .	–142.8	–168.9	–150.8	–94.5	–213.3	–334.9	–218.0	–208.9
B. Capital Account [1]	4 994 Z.	**. . .**	**. . .**	**16.2**	**21.3**	**19.1**	**25.0**	**20.9**	**133.0**
Capital account: credit	2 994 Z.	. . .	. . .	18.0	23.5	24.1	28.3	24.5	137.6
Capital account: debit	3 994 . .	. . .	. . .	–1.8	–2.2	–5.0	–3.3	–3.6	–4.6
Total, Groups A Plus B	4 981 . .	*554.1*	*–1,591.8*	*–1,032.9*	*–2,804.1*	*–1,448.9*	*–1,381.0*	*–426.6*	*–509.4*
C. Financial Account [1]	4 995 W.	**16.4**	**1,135.3**	**2,996.3**	**3,020.8**	**1,610.3**	**2,676.6**	**1,516.8**	**2,242.3**
Direct investment abroad	4 505 . .	–6.7	–5.5	–24.4	–186.1	–97.5	–34.5	–28.6	–121.3
Direct investment in Croatia	4 555 Z.	116.9	114.3	510.8	532.8	932.3	1,479.2	1,114.8	1,446.8
Portfolio investment assets	4 602 . .	1.0	.3	6.2	11.2	–.1	–.3	–.2	–6.2
Equity securities	4 610 . .	1.0	.3	6.2	.2	–.1	–.3	–.2	.3
Debt securities	4 619 . .	. . .	. . .	. . .	11.0	. . .	. . .	. . .	–6.5
Portfolio investment liabilities	4 652 Z.	9.9	4.5	622.0	565.7	15.1	574.5	722.2	722.3
Equity securities	4 660 . .	9.9	4.5	–6.8	15.9	1.3	–18.7	–8.3	5.8
Debt securities	4 669 Z.	. . .	. . .	628.8	549.8	13.8	593.2	730.5	716.5
Financial derivatives	4 910 . .	. . .	. . .	. . .	. . .	. . .	. . .	. . .	. . .
Financial derivatives assets	4 900 . .	. . .	. . .	. . .	. . .	. . .	. . .	. . .	. . .
Financial derivatives liabilities	4 905 . .	. . .	. . .	. . .	. . .	. . .	. . .	. . .	. . .
Other investment assets	4 703 . .	–15.9	419.5	794.5	171.2	348.8	–180.0	–848.4	312.4
Monetary authorities	4 701 . .	. . .	. . .	. . .	. . .	. . .	. . .	. . .	. . .
General government	4 704 . .	–.2	–15.5	–33.4	30.7	–22.3	13.3	–25.6	–18.4
Banks	4 705 . .	–189.3	–451.6	–589.2	–371.8	406.1	100.1	–915.2	–1,622.2
Other sectors	4 728 . .	173.6	886.6	1,417.1	512.3	–35.0	–293.4	92.4	1,953.0
Other investment liabilities	4 753 W.	–88.8	602.2	1,087.2	1,926.0	411.7	837.7	557.0	–111.7
Monetary authorities	4 753 WA	. . .	. . .	. . .	. . .	. . .	. . .	. . .	1.0
General government	4 753 ZB	–131.5	–47.2	268.8	95.7	–61.3	259.0	267.0	–342.4
Banks	4 753 ZC	52.6	492.5	226.2	670.3	135.7	–31.3	–270.2	281.6
Other sectors	4 753 ZD	–9.9	156.9	592.2	1,160.0	337.3	610.0	560.2	–51.9
Total, Groups A Through C	4 983 . .	*570.5*	*–456.5*	*1,963.4*	*216.7*	*161.4*	*1,295.6*	*1,090.2*	*1,732.9*
D. Net Errors and Omissions	4 998 . .	**–294.0**	**496.9**	**–946.1**	**173.7**	**–.9**	**–885.6**	**–479.4**	**–390.7**
Total, Groups A Through D	4 984 . .	*276.5*	*40.4*	*1,017.3*	*390.4*	*160.5*	*410.0*	*610.8*	*1,342.2*
E. Reserves and Related Items	4 802 A.	**–276.5**	**–40.4**	**–1,017.3**	**–390.4**	**–160.5**	**–410.0**	**–610.8**	**–1,342.2**
Reserve assets	4 802 . .	–742.8	–443.2	–533.4	–428.0	–151.7	–378.5	–582.1	–1,311.3
Use of Fund credit and loans	4 766 . .	107.0	97.1	–4.5	37.5	–8.9	–31.5	–28.6	–30.8
Exceptional financing	4 920 . .	359.3	305.7	–479.4	. . .	. . .	. . .	. . .	. . .
Conversion rates: kunas per U.S. dollar	0 101 . .	**5.9961**	**5.2300**	**5.4338**	**6.1007**	**6.3623**	**7.1124**	**8.2766**	**8.3400**

[1] Excludes components that have been classified in the categories of Group E.

Table 2. STANDARD PRESENTATION, 1994–2001
(Millions of U.S. dollars)

	Code	1994	1995	1996	1997	1998	1999	2000	2001
CURRENT ACCOUNT	4 993 . .	**554.1**	**–1,591.8**	**–1,049.1**	**–2,825.4**	**–1,468.0**	**–1,406.0**	**–447.5**	**–642.4**
A. GOODS	4 100 . .	–1,278.4	–3,227.5	–3,488.0	–5,383.0	–4,071.5	–3,298.7	–3,203.6	–4,011.7
Credit	2 100 . .	**4,402.8**	**4,517.3**	**4,677.5**	**4,021.1**	**4,580.6**	**4,394.7**	**4,567.1**	**4,752.1**
General merchandise: exports f.o.b.	2 110 . .	4,402.8	4,517.3	4,677.5	4,021.1	4,580.6	4,394.7	4,567.1	4,752.1
Goods for processing: exports f.o.b.	2 150 . .	. . .	. . .	. . .	. . .	. . .	. . .	. . .	. . .
Repairs on goods	2 160 . .	. . .	. . .	. . .	. . .	. . .	. . .	. . .	. . .
Goods procured in ports by carriers	2 170 . .	. . .	. . .	. . .	. . .	. . .	. . .	. . .	. . .
Nonmonetary gold	2 180 . .	. . .	. . .	. . .	. . .	. . .	. . .	. . .	. . .
Debit	3 100 . .	**–5,681.2**	**–7,744.8**	**–8,165.5**	**–9,404.1**	**–8,652.1**	**–7,693.4**	**–7,770.7**	**–8,763.8**
General merchandise: imports f.o.b.	3 110 . .	–5,681.2	–7,744.8	–8,165.5	–9,404.1	–8,652.1	–7,693.4	–7,770.7	–8,763.8
Goods for processing: imports f.o.b.	3 150 . .	. . .	. . .	. . .	. . .	. . .	. . .	. . .	. . .
Repairs on goods	3 160 . .	. . .	. . .	. . .	. . .	. . .	. . .	. . .	. . .
Goods procured in ports by carriers	3 170 . .	. . .	. . .	. . .	. . .	. . .	. . .	. . .	. . .
Nonmonetary gold	3 180 . .	. . .	. . .	. . .	. . .	. . .	. . .	. . .	. . .
B. SERVICES	4 200 . .	1,470.3	862.3	1,486.2	1,710.7	2,062.0	1,609.7	2,253.0	2,932.1
Total credit	2 200 . .	*2,660.6*	*2,223.4*	*3,193.2*	*3,984.6*	*3,949.1*	*3,707.7*	*4,081.0*	*4,872.7*
Total debit	3 200 . .	*–1,190.3*	*–1,361.1*	*–1,707.0*	*–2,273.9*	*–1,887.1*	*–2,098.0*	*–1,828.0*	*–1,940.6*
Transportation services, credit	2 205 . .	**665.1**	**707.3**	**710.5**	**681.5**	**565.7**	**483.9**	**557.3**	**588.6**
Passenger	2 850 . .	. . .	. . .	. . .	. . .	. . .	*101.6*	*112.8*	*127.7*
Freight	2 851 . .	. . .	. . .	. . .	. . .	. . .	*290.0*	*339.9*	*348.0*
Other	2 852 . .	. . .	. . .	. . .	. . .	. . .	*92.3*	*104.6*	*112.9*
Sea transport, passenger	2 207 . .	. . .	. . .	. . .	. . .	. . .	6.5	8.4	9.3
Sea transport, freight	2 208 . .	. . .	. . .	. . .	. . .	. . .	214.6	259.0	248.1
Sea transport, other	2 209 . .	. . .	. . .	. . .	. . .	. . .	32.1	27.2	28.5
Air transport, passenger	2 211 . .	. . .	. . .	. . .	. . .	. . .	85.3	93.2	106.4
Air transport, freight	2 212 . .	. . .	. . .	. . .	. . .	. . .	1.1	1.2	1.9
Air transport, other	2 213 . .	. . .	. . .	. . .	. . .	. . .	43.0	50.2	53.0
Other transport, passenger	2 215 . .	. . .	. . .	. . .	. . .	. . .	9.8	11.2	11.9
Other transport, freight	2 216 . .	. . .	. . .	. . .	. . .	. . .	74.3	79.8	98.1
Other transport, other	2 217 . .	. . .	. . .	. . .	. . .	. . .	17.3	27.2	31.4
Transportation services, debit	3 205 . .	**–349.3**	**–390.8**	**–400.5**	**–398.9**	**–336.2**	**–400.1**	**–378.7**	**–420.0**
Passenger	3 850 . .	. . .	. . .	. . .	. . .	. . .	*–54.8*	*–66.5*	*–70.7*
Freight	3 851 . .	. . .	. . .	. . .	. . .	. . .	*–182.5*	*–179.0*	*–204.9*
Other	3 852 . .	. . .	. . .	. . .	. . .	. . .	*–162.8*	*–133.3*	*–144.4*
Sea transport, passenger	3 207 . .	. . .	. . .	. . .	. . .	. . .	–.4	–.2	–.1
Sea transport, freight	3 208 . .	. . .	. . .	. . .	. . .	. . .	–17.2	–16.5	–19.1
Sea transport, other	3 209 . .	. . .	. . .	. . .	. . .	. . .	–103.1	–79.1	–84.6
Air transport, passenger	3 211 . .	. . .	. . .	. . .	. . .	. . .	–46.8	–59.0	–65.1
Air transport, freight	3 212 . .	. . .	. . .	. . .	. . .	. . .	–15.5	–15.4	–18.1
Air transport, other	3 213 . .	. . .	. . .	. . .	. . .	. . .	–44.0	–38.7	–42.7
Other transport, passenger	3 215 . .	. . .	. . .	. . .	. . .	. . .	–7.7	–7.2	–5.5
Other transport, freight	3 216 . .	. . .	. . .	. . .	. . .	. . .	–149.8	–147.1	–167.6
Other transport, other	3 217 . .	. . .	. . .	. . .	. . .	. . .	–15.8	–15.5	–17.1
Travel, credit	2 236 . .	**1,801.3**	**1,349.0**	**2,013.9**	**2,523.1**	**2,733.3**	**2,493.4**	**2,757.9**	**3,334.9**
Business travel	2 237 . .	. . .	. . .	4.3	6.7	10.5	233.5	263.6	274.0
Personal travel	2 240 . .	1,801.3	1,349.0	2,009.6	2,516.4	2,722.8	2,259.9	2,494.3	3,060.9
Travel, debit	3 236 . .	**–395.9**	**–421.6**	**–510.5**	**–529.9**	**–600.0**	**–751.4**	**–568.3**	**–606.5**
Business travel	3 237 . .	–86.0	–82.0	–95.1	–95.3	–86.7	–384.3	–260.5	–289.1
Personal travel	3 240 . .	–309.9	–339.6	–415.4	–434.6	–513.3	–367.1	–307.8	–317.4
Other services, credit	2 200 BA	**194.2**	**167.1**	**468.8**	**780.0**	**650.1**	**730.4**	**765.8**	**949.2**
Communications	2 245 . .	68.8	73.9	83.0	123.1	133.6	96.5	102.9	151.3
Construction	2 249 . .	12.9	26.0	74.9	106.2	149.0	212.3	199.3	231.2
Insurance	2 253 . .	21.6	22.0	38.7	33.2	27.8	36.5	35.0	38.6
Financial	2 260 . .	1.2	7.7	8.4	18.1	30.3	27.0	10.6	20.7
Computer and information	2 262 . .	. . .	. . .	1.6	5.6	14.6	20.1	33.6	43.3
Royalties and licence fees	2 266 . .	2.3	2.3	2.5	19.0	41.6	81.9	66.0	106.3
Other business services	2 268 . .	84.3	33.0	248.8	459.8	221.1	219.0	288.1	330.6
Personal, cultural, and recreational	2 287 . .	2.7	2.2	10.6	14.6	31.5	36.6	30.1	25.9
Government, n.i.e.	2 291 . .	.4	. . .	.3	.4	.6	.5	.2	1.3
Other services, debit	3 200 BA	**–445.1**	**–548.7**	**–796.0**	**–1,345.1**	**–950.9**	**–946.5**	**–881.0**	**–914.1**
Communications	3 245 . .	–7.3	–9.2	–12.3	–16.6	–43.1	–17.1	–25.1	–71.6
Construction	3 249 . .	–62.6	–60.4	–67.1	–109.0	–147.3	–108.9	–63.8	–70.9
Insurance	3 253 . .	–28.1	–32.6	–35.2	–39.6	–45.2	–40.9	–40.5	–44.8
Financial	3 260 . .	–16.3	–12.7	–35.6	–36.8	–63.2	–47.1	–48.8	–36.4
Computer and information	3 262 . .	. . .	. . .	–7.1	–21.6	–50.5	–40.2	–56.9	–70.2
Royalties and licence fees	3 266 . .	–27.2	–45.8	–33.3	–31.1	–47.2	–50.4	–60.8	–62.5
Other business services	3 268 . .	–279.9	–305.4	–509.1	–1,013.1	–475.7	–559.8	–515.8	–495.4
Personal, cultural, and recreational	3 287 . .	–23.6	–48.2	–50.4	–41.3	–41.5	–39.6	–30.0	–31.6
Government, n.i.e.	3 291 . .	–.1	–34.4	–45.9	–36.0	–37.2	–42.5	–39.3	–30.7

Table 2 (Continued). STANDARD PRESENTATION, 1994–2001

(Millions of U.S. dollars)

	Code		1994	1995	1996	1997	1998	1999	2000	2001
C. INCOME	4 300	. .	–164.2	–28.9	–69.8	–22.4	–164.3	–349.4	–379.9	–528.5
Total credit	2 300	. .	*149.0*	*218.8*	*269.9*	*363.7*	*394.8*	*252.2*	*333.9*	*400.5*
Total debit	3 300	. .	*–313.2*	*–247.7*	*–339.7*	*–386.1*	*–559.1*	*–601.6*	*–713.8*	*–929.0*
Compensation of employees, credit	2 310	. .	**35.4**	**38.6**	**46.8**	**70.1**	**81.1**	**75.1**	**82.7**	**137.2**
Compensation of employees, debit	3 310	. .	**. . .**	**. . .**	**–7.8**	**–14.6**	**–11.4**	**–14.9**	**–13.1**	**–12.7**
Investment income, credit	2 320	. .	**113.6**	**180.2**	**223.1**	**293.6**	**313.7**	**177.1**	**251.2**	**263.3**
Direct investment income	2 330	. .	13.3	7.0	17.5	17.0	5.2	4.2	7.4	18.1
Dividends and distributed branch profits	2 332	. .	13.3	7.0	17.5	4.1	1.3	.9	1.3	4.0
Reinvested earnings and undistributed branch profits	2 333	. .	. . .	. . .	. . .	9.7	1.8	.6	2.9	9.4
Income on debt (interest)	2 334	. .	. . .	. . .	. . .	3.2	2.1	2.7	3.2	4.7
Portfolio investment income	2 339	. .	.1	.2	.1	2.6	.2	.1	. . .	. . .
Income on equity	2 340	. .	.1	.2	.1	.2	.2	.1	. . .	. . .
Income on bonds and notes	2 350	. .	. . .	. . .	. . .	2.4	. . .	. . .	. . .	. . .
Income on money market instruments	2 360	. .	. . .	. . .	. . .	. . .	. . .	. . .	. . .	. . .
Other investment income	2 370	. .	100.2	173.0	205.5	274.0	308.3	172.8	243.8	245.2
Investment income, debit	3 320	. .	**–313.2**	**–247.7**	**–331.9**	**–371.5**	**–547.7**	**–586.7**	**–700.7**	**–916.3**
Direct investment income	3 330	. .	–1.0	–6.3	–7.6	–68.7	–106.0	–73.7	–148.0	–363.2
Dividends and distributed branch profits	3 332	. .	–1.0	–6.3	–7.6	–20.8	–27.4	–12.5	–55.7	–135.0
Reinvested earnings and undistributed branch profits	3 333	. .	. . .	. . .	. . .	–40.3	–68.3	–47.2	–70.9	–185.5
Income on debt (interest)	3 334	. .	. . .	. . .	. . .	–7.6	–10.3	–14.0	–21.4	–42.7
Portfolio investment income	3 339	. .	. . .	–.4	–2.1	–94.2	–102.8	–129.2	–178.7	–218.3
Income on equity	3 340	. .	. . .	–.4	–1.0	–.5	–.8	–.3	–11.5	–18.4
Income on bonds and notes	3 350	. .	. . .	. . .	–1.1	–93.7	–102.0	–128.3	–164.8	–199.3
Income on money market instruments	3 360	. .	. . .	. . .	. . .	. . .	. . .	–.6	–2.4	–.6
Other investment income	3 370	. .	–312.2	–241.0	–322.2	–208.6	–338.9	–383.8	–374.0	–334.8
D. CURRENT TRANSFERS	4 379	. .	526.4	802.3	1,022.5	869.3	705.8	632.4	883.0	965.7
Credit	2 379	. .	**669.2**	**971.2**	**1,173.3**	**963.8**	**919.1**	**967.3**	**1,101.0**	**1,174.6**
General government	2 380	. .	261.2	309.2	193.5	55.5	77.6	76.1	118.0	125.6
Other sectors	2 390	. .	408.0	662.0	979.8	908.3	841.5	891.2	983.0	1,049.0
Workers' remittances	2 391	. .	340.2	505.6	603.3	523.7	520.2	453.5	536.8	568.4
Other current transfers	2 392	. .	67.8	156.4	376.5	384.6	321.3	437.7	446.2	480.6
Debit	3 379	. .	**–142.8**	**–168.9**	**–150.8**	**–94.5**	**–213.3**	**–334.9**	**–218.0**	**–208.9**
General government	3 380	. .	–26.6	–29.3	–38.8	–22.7	–86.9	–206.5	–96.3	–68.9
Other sectors	3 390	. .	–116.2	–139.6	–112.0	–71.8	–126.4	–128.4	–121.7	–140.0
Workers' remittances	3 391	. .	. . .	. . .	–6.9	–22.8	–24.2	–28.4	–27.4	–29.6
Other current transfers	3 392	. .	–116.2	–139.6	–105.1	–49.0	–102.2	–100.0	–94.3	–110.4
CAPITAL AND FINANCIAL ACCOUNT	4 996	. .	**–260.1**	**1,094.9**	**1,995.2**	**2,651.7**	**1,468.9**	**2,291.6**	**926.9**	**1,033.1**
CAPITAL ACCOUNT	4 994	. .	**. . .**	**. . .**	**16.2**	**21.3**	**19.1**	**25.0**	**20.9**	**133.0**
Total credit	2 994	. .	. . .	. . .	*18.0*	*23.5*	*24.1*	*28.3*	*24.5*	*137.6*
Total debit	3 994	. .	. . .	. . .	*–1.8*	*–2.2*	*–5.0*	*–3.3*	*–3.6*	*–4.6*
Capital transfers, credit	2 400	. .	**. . .**	**. . .**	**18.0**	**23.5**	**24.1**	**28.3**	**24.5**	**137.6**
General government	2 401	. .	. . .	. . .	. . .	. . .	. . .	. . .	. . .	114.9
Debt forgiveness	2 402	. .	. . .	. . .	. . .	. . .	. . .	. . .	. . .	. . .
Other capital transfers	2 410	. .	. . .	. . .	. . .	. . .	. . .	. . .	. . .	114.9
Other sectors	2 430	. .	. . .	. . .	18.0	23.5	24.1	28.3	24.5	22.7
Migrants' transfers	2 431	. .	. . .	. . .	18.0	23.5	24.1	28.3	24.5	22.7
Debt forgiveness	2 432	. .	. . .	. . .	. . .	. . .	. . .	. . .	. . .	. . .
Other capital transfers	2 440	. .	. . .	. . .	. . .	. . .	. . .	. . .	. . .	. . .
Capital transfers, debit	3 400	. .	**. . .**	**. . .**	**–1.8**	**–2.2**	**–5.0**	**–3.3**	**–3.6**	**–4.6**
General government	3 401	. .	. . .	. . .	. . .	. . .	. . .	. . .	. . .	. . .
Debt forgiveness	3 402	. .	. . .	. . .	. . .	. . .	. . .	. . .	. . .	. . .
Other capital transfers	3 410	. .	. . .	. . .	. . .	. . .	. . .	. . .	. . .	. . .
Other sectors	3 430	. .	. . .	. . .	–1.8	–2.2	–5.0	–3.3	–3.6	–4.6
Migrants' transfers	3 431	. .	. . .	. . .	–1.8	–2.2	–5.0	–3.3	–3.6	–4.6
Debt forgiveness	3 432	. .	. . .	. . .	. . .	. . .	. . .	. . .	. . .	. . .
Other capital transfers	3 440	. .	. . .	. . .	. . .	. . .	. . .	. . .	. . .	. . .
Nonproduced nonfinancial assets, credit	2 480	. .	**. . .**	**. . .**	**. . .**	**. . .**	**. . .**	**. . .**	**. . .**	**. . .**
Nonproduced nonfinancial assets, debit	3 480	. .	**. . .**	**. . .**	**. . .**	**. . .**	**. . .**	**. . .**	**. . .**	**. . .**

Table 2 (Continued). STANDARD PRESENTATION, 1994–2001

(Millions of U.S. dollars)

	Code	1994	1995	1996	1997	1998	1999	2000	2001
FINANCIAL ACCOUNT	4 995	**–260.1**	**1,094.9**	**1,979.0**	**2,630.4**	**1,449.8**	**2,266.6**	**906.0**	**900.1**
A. DIRECT INVESTMENT	4 500	110.2	108.8	486.4	346.7	834.8	1,444.7	1,086.2	1,325.5
Direct investment abroad	4 505	**–6.7**	**–5.5**	**–24.4**	**–186.1**	**–97.5**	**–34.5**	**–28.6**	**–121.3**
Equity capital	4 510	–6.7	–5.5	–24.4	–171.3	–76.0	–42.9	–26.4	–103.8
Claims on affiliated enterprises	4 515	–6.7	–5.6	–24.4	–171.3	–76.0	–42.9	–26.4	–103.8
Liabilities to affiliated enterprises	4 520	...	.1	...	...	...	...	...	...
Reinvested earnings	4 525	...	...	...	–9.7	–1.8	–.6	–2.9	–9.4
Other capital	4 530	...	...	...	–5.1	–19.7	9.0	.7	–8.1
Claims on affiliated enterprises	4 535	...	...	...	–52.5	–68.3	–53.7	–45.9	–40.5
Liabilities to affiliated enterprises	4 540	...	...	...	47.4	48.6	62.7	46.6	32.4
Direct investment in Croatia	4 555	**116.9**	**114.3**	**510.8**	**532.8**	**932.3**	**1,479.2**	**1,114.8**	**1,446.8**
Equity capital	4 560	116.9	114.3	510.8	359.5	635.6	1,274.4	704.6	738.4
Claims on direct investors	4 565	...	...	...	...	...	...	...	...
Liabilities to direct investors	4 570	116.9	114.3	510.8	359.5	635.6	1,274.4	704.6	738.4
Reinvested earnings	4 575	...	...	...	40.3	68.3	47.2	70.9	185.5
Other capital	4 580	...	...	...	133.0	228.4	157.6	339.3	522.9
Claims on direct investors	4 585	...	...	...	–8.0	–14.8	3.7	–1.9	–33.2
Liabilities to direct investors	4 590	...	...	...	141.0	243.2	153.9	341.2	556.1
B. PORTFOLIO INVESTMENT	4 600	10.9	4.8	628.2	576.9	15.0	574.2	722.0	716.1
Assets	4 602	**1.0**	**.3**	**6.2**	**11.2**	**–.1**	**–.3**	**–.2**	**–6.2**
Equity securities	4 610	1.0	.3	6.2	.2	–.1	–.3	–.2	.3
Monetary authorities	4 611	...	...	...	...	...	...	...	...
General government	4 612	...	...	...	...	...	...	...	...
Banks	4 613	1.0	.3	...	.2	–.1	–.2	–.2	.3
Other sectors	4 614	...	...	6.2	...	...	–.1	...	...
Debt securities	4 619	...	...	...	11.0	...	...	...	–6.5
Bonds and notes	4 620	...	...	...	...	...	...	...	...
Monetary authorities	4 621	...	...	...	...	...	...	...	...
General government	4 622	...	...	...	...	...	...	...	...
Banks	4 623	...	...	...	...	...	...	...	...
Other sectors	4 624	...	...	...	...	...	...	...	...
Money market instruments	4 630	...	...	...	11.0	...	...	...	–6.5
Monetary authorities	4 631	...	...	...	...	...	...	...	...
General government	4 632	...	...	...	...	...	...	...	...
Banks	4 633	...	...	...	11.0	...	...	...	–6.5
Other sectors	4 634	...	...	...	...	...	...	...	...
Liabilities	4 652	**9.9**	**4.5**	**622.0**	**565.7**	**15.1**	**574.5**	**722.2**	**722.3**
Equity securities	4 660	9.9	4.5	–6.8	15.9	1.3	–18.7	–8.3	5.8
Banks	4 663	3.0	2.4	3.3	11.5	–.4	–4.5	–7.7	–5.0
Other sectors	4 664	6.9	2.1	–10.1	4.4	1.7	–14.2	–.6	10.8
Debt securities	4 669	...	...	628.8	549.8	13.8	593.2	730.5	716.5
Bonds and notes	4 670	...	...	628.8	549.8	13.8	582.6	736.2	698.6
Monetary authorities	4 671	...	...	...	...	...	...	...	...
General government	4 672	...	...	628.8	549.8	13.8	546.8	736.2	698.6
Banks	4 673	...	...	...	...	...	...	...	...
Other sectors	4 674	...	...	...	...	...	35.8	...	...
Money market instruments	4 680	...	...	...	...	...	10.6	–5.7	17.9
Monetary authorities	4 681	...	...	...	...	...	...	...	...
General government	4 682	...	...	...	...	...	...	...	...
Banks	4 683	...	...	...	...	...	...	...	...
Other sectors	4 684	...	...	...	...	...	10.6	–5.7	17.9
C. FINANCIAL DERIVATIVES	4 910	...	...	...	...	...	...	...	...
Monetary authorities	4 911	...	...	...	...	...	...	...	...
General government	4 912	...	...	...	...	...	...	...	...
Banks	4 913	...	...	...	...	...	...	...	...
Other sectors	4 914	...	...	...	...	...	...	...	...
Assets	4 900	**...**	**...**	**...**	**...**	**...**	**...**	**...**	**...**
Monetary authorities	4 901	...	...	...	...	...	...	...	...
General government	4 902	...	...	...	...	...	...	...	...
Banks	4 903	...	...	...	...	...	...	...	...
Other sectors	4 904	...	...	...	...	...	...	...	...
Liabilities	4 905	**...**	**...**	**...**	**...**	**...**	**...**	**...**	**...**
Monetary authorities	4 906	...	...	...	...	...	...	...	...
General government	4 907	...	...	...	...	...	...	...	...
Banks	4 908	...	...	...	...	...	...	...	...
Other sectors	4 909	...	...	...	...	...	...	...	...

Table 2 (Concluded). STANDARD PRESENTATION, 1994–2001

(Millions of U.S. dollars)

	Code	1994	1995	1996	1997	1998	1999	2000	2001
D. OTHER INVESTMENT	4 700 . .	361.6	1,424.5	1,397.8	2,134.7	751.6	626.2	–320.0	169.9
Assets	4 703 . .	**–15.9**	**419.5**	**794.5**	**171.2**	**348.8**	**–180.0**	**–848.4**	**312.4**
Trade credits	4 706 . .	. . .	. . .	36.4	18.1	–19.5	–293.4	92.4	60.0
General government	4 707 . .	. . .	. . .	. . .	. . .	. . .	. . .	. . .	. . .
of which: Short-term	4 709 . .	. . .	. . .	. . .	. . .	. . .	. . .	. . .	. . .
Other sectors	4 710 . .	. . .	. . .	36.4	18.1	–19.5	–293.4	92.4	60.0
of which: Short-term	4 712 . .	. . .	. . .	*36.4*	*18.1*	*–19.5*	*–279.6*	*94.9*	*51.7*
Loans	4 714 . .	. . .	. . .	. . .	. . .	. . .	–84.4	7.3	–11.7
Monetary authorities	4 715 . .	. . .	. . .	. . .	. . .	. . .	. . .	. . .	. . .
of which: Short-term	4 718 . .	. . .	. . .	. . .	. . .	. . .	. . .	. . .	. . .
General government	4 719 . .	. . .	. . .	. . .	. . .	. . .	1.1	1.1	–3.2
of which: Short-term	4 721 . .	. . .	. . .	. . .	. . .	. . .	. . .	. . .	. . .
Banks	4 722 . .	. . .	. . .	. . .	. . .	. . .	–85.5	6.2	–8.5
of which: Short-term	4 724 . .	. . .	. . .	. . .	. . .	. . .	*–9.4*	*–.3*	*–5.6*
Other sectors	4 725 . .	. . .	. . .	. . .	. . .	. . .	. . .	. . .	. . .
of which: Short-term	4 727 . .	. . .	. . .	. . .	. . .	. . .	. . .	. . .	. . .
Currency and deposits	4 730 . .	–15.9	419.5	758.1	153.1	368.3	197.8	–948.1	264.1
Monetary authorities	4 731 . .	. . .	. . .	. . .	. . .	. . .	. . .	. . .	. . .
General government	4 732 . .	–.2	–15.5	–33.4	30.7	–22.3	12.2	–26.7	–15.2
Banks	4 733 . .	–189.3	–451.6	–589.2	–371.8	406.1	185.6	–921.4	–1,613.7
Other sectors	4 734 . .	173.6	886.6	1,380.7	494.2	–15.5	. . .	. . .	1,893.0
Other assets	4 736 . .	. . .	. . .	. . .	. . .	. . .	. . .	. . .	. . .
Monetary authorities	4 737 . .	. . .	. . .	. . .	. . .	. . .	. . .	. . .	. . .
of which: Short-term	4 739 . .	. . .	. . .	. . .	. . .	. . .	. . .	. . .	. . .
General government	4 740 . .	. . .	. . .	. . .	. . .	. . .	. . .	. . .	. . .
of which: Short-term	4 742 . .	. . .	. . .	. . .	. . .	. . .	. . .	. . .	. . .
Banks	4 743 . .	. . .	. . .	. . .	. . .	. . .	. . .	. . .	. . .
of which: Short-term	4 745 . .	. . .	. . .	. . .	. . .	. . .	. . .	. . .	. . .
Other sectors	4 746 . .	. . .	. . .	. . .	. . .	. . .	. . .	. . .	. . .
of which: Short-term	4 748 . .	. . .	. . .	. . .	. . .	. . .	. . .	. . .	. . .
Liabilities	4 753 . .	**377.5**	**1,005.0**	**603.3**	**1,963.5**	**402.8**	**806.2**	**528.4**	**–142.5**
Trade credits	4 756 . .	. . .	. . .	390.2	218.0	–466.9	309.7	279.7	52.4
General government	4 757 . .	. . .	. . .	. . .	. . .	. . .	.7	–3.3	1.1
of which: Short-term	4 759 . .	. . .	. . .	. . .	. . .	. . .	*1.7*	*–2.7*	. . .
Other sectors	4 760 . .	. . .	. . .	390.2	218.0	–466.9	309.0	283.0	51.3
of which: Short-term	4 762 . .	. . .	. . .	*390.2*	*218.0*	*–466.9*	*345.7*	*292.8*	*81.1*
Loans	4 764 . .	–28.1	425.1	666.6	1,474.4	1,045.5	460.9	353.6	–396.7
Monetary authorities	4 765 . .	107.0	97.1	–4.5	37.5	–8.9	–31.5	–28.6	–30.8
of which: Use of Fund credit and loans from the Fund	4 766 . .	*107.0*	*97.1*	*–4.5*	*37.5*	*–8.9*	*–31.5*	*–28.6*	*–30.8*
of which: Short-term	4 768 . .	. . .	. . .	. . .	. . .	. . .	. . .	. . .	. . .
General government	4 769 . .	–131.5	–47.2	268.8	95.7	–61.3	258.3	270.3	–343.5
of which: Short-term	4 771 . .	. . .	*100.0*	*8.2*	*–8.6*	*–49.2*	*28.5*	*286.9*	*–360.0*
Banks	4 772 . .	6.3	218.3	200.3	399.2	311.5	–66.9	–165.3	80.8
of which: Short-term	4 774 . .	*15.0*	*270.4*	*135.9*	*61.8*	*–50.7*	*–13.0*	*–12.7*	*.1*
Other sectors	4 775 . .	–9.9	156.9	202.0	942.0	804.2	301.0	277.2	–103.2
of which: Short-term	4 777 . .	*–5.3*	*99.5*	*73.3*	*194.9*	*136.4*	*53.7*	*–59.5*	*–48.9*
Currency and deposits	4 780 . .	46.3	274.2	25.9	271.1	–175.8	35.6	–104.9	201.8
Monetary authorities	4 781 . .	. . .	. . .	. . .	. . .	. . .	. . .	. . .	1.0
General government	4 782 . .	. . .	. . .	. . .	. . .	. . .	. . .	. . .	. . .
Banks	4 783 . .	46.3	274.2	25.9	271.1	–175.8	35.6	–104.9	200.8
Other sectors	4 784 . .	. . .	. . .	. . .	. . .	. . .	. . .	. . .	. . .
Other liabilities	4 786 . .	359.3	305.7	–479.4	. . .	. . .	. . .	. . .	. . .
Monetary authorities	4 787 . .	. . .	. . .	. . .	. . .	. . .	. . .	. . .	. . .
of which: Short-term	4 789 . .	. . .	. . .	. . .	. . .	. . .	. . .	. . .	. . .
General government	4 790 . .	243.8	213.1	125.0	. . .	. . .	. . .	. . .	. . .
of which: Short-term	4 792 . .	*243.8*	*213.1*	*125.0*	. . .	. . .	. . .	. . .	. . .
Banks	4 793 . .	78.3	78.8	–604.4	. . .	. . .	. . .	. . .	. . .
of which: Short-term	4 795 . .	*78.3*	*78.8*	*–604.4*	. . .	. . .	. . .	. . .	. . .
Other sectors	4 796 . .	37.2	13.8	. . .	. . .	. . .	. . .	. . .	. . .
of which: Short-term	4 798 . .	*37.2*	*13.8*	. . .	. . .	. . .	. . .	. . .	. . .
E. RESERVE ASSETS	4 802 . .	–742.8	–443.2	–533.4	–428.0	–151.7	–378.5	–582.1	–1,311.3
Monetary gold	4 812 . .	. . .	. . .	. . .	. . .	. . .	. . .	. . .	. . .
Special drawing rights	4 811 . .	–3.4	–141.3	10.3	–29.9	–73.2	35.9	32.9	35.1
Reserve position in the Fund	4 810 . .	. . .	. . .	. . .	–.1	–.1	–.1	. . .	. . .
Foreign exchange	4 803 . .	–739.4	–301.9	–543.6	–398.0	–78.4	–414.4	–615.0	–1,346.4
Other claims	4 813 . .	. . .	. . .	. . .	. . .	. . .	. . .	. . .	. . .
NET ERRORS AND OMISSIONS	4 998 . .	**–294.0**	**496.9**	**–946.1**	**173.7**	**–.9**	**–885.6**	**–479.4**	**–390.7**

Part 3 of the *Yearbook* contains descriptions of the methodologies, compilation practices, and sources used to compile these data.

Table 3. INTERNATIONAL INVESTMENT POSITION (End–period stocks), 1994–2001

(Millions of U.S. dollars)

	Code	1994	1995	1996	1997	1998	1999	2000	2001
ASSETS	8 995 C.	...	...	...	...	6,186.8	5,871.8	7,152.3	9,976.9
Direct investment abroad	8 505 . .	...	...	...	...	**1,027.3**	**910.1**	**879.5**	**975.2**
Equity capital and reinvested earnings	8 506 . .	...	...	...	...	960.2	839.7	824.1	928.5
Claims on affiliated enterprises	8 507 . .	...	...	...	...	960.2	839.7	824.1	928.5
Liabilities to affiliated enterprises	8 508 . .	...	...	...	...	...	...	...	...
Other capital	8 530 . .	...	...	...	...	67.1	70.4	55.4	46.7
Claims on affiliated enterprises	8 535 . .	...	...	...	...	...	...	...	...
Liabilities to affiliated enterprises	8 540 . .	...	...	...	...	...	...	...	...
Portfolio investment	8 602 . .	...	...	...	...	**29.7**	**26.0**	**14.3**	**22.4**
Equity securities	8 610 . .	...	...	...	...	29.7	26.0	14.3	22.4
Monetary authorities	8 611 . .	...	...	...	...	...	...	...	...
General government	8 612 . .	...	...	...	...	...	...	...	...
Banks	8 613 . .	...	...	...	...	2.3	.7	7.2	7.1
Other sectors	8 614 . .	...	...	...	...	27.4	25.3	7.1	15.3
Debt securities	8 619 . .	...	...	...	...	...	...	...	...
Bonds and notes	8 620 . .	...	...	...	...	...	...	...	...
Monetary authorities	8 621 . .	...	...	...	...	...	...	...	...
General government	8 622 . .	...	...	...	...	...	...	...	...
Banks	8 623 . .	...	...	...	...	...	...	...	...
Other sectors	8 624 . .	...	...	...	...	...	...	...	...
Money market instruments	8 630 . .	...	...	...	...	...	...	...	...
Monetary authorities	8 631 . .	...	...	...	...	...	...	...	...
General government	8 632 . .	...	...	...	...	...	...	...	...
Banks	8 633 . .	...	...	...	...	...	...	...	...
Other sectors	8 634 . .	...	...	...	...	...	...	...	...
Financial derivatives	8 900 . .	...	...	...	...	...	...	...	...
Monetary authorities	8 901 . .	...	...	...	...	...	...	...	...
General government	8 902 . .	...	...	...	...	...	...	...	...
Banks	8 903 . .	...	...	...	...	...	...	...	...
Other sectors	8 904 . .	...	...	...	...	...	...	...	...
Other investment	8 703 . .	...	...	...	...	**2,314.1**	**1,910.7**	**2,734.0**	**4,276.1**
Trade credits	8 706 . .	...	...	...	...	219.6	198.7	184.1	175.8
General government	8 707 . .	...	...	...	...	...	...	...	...
of which: Short-term	8 709 . .	...	...	...	...	...	...	...	...
Other sectors	8 710 . .	...	...	...	...	219.6	198.7	184.1	175.8
of which: Short-term	8 712 . .	...	...	...	...	*37.3*	*16.9*	*14.9*	*18.7*
Loans	8 714 . .	...	...	...	...	145.1	103.1	91.7	101.8
Monetary authorities	8 715 . .	...	...	...	...	...	...	...	...
of which: Short-term	8 718 . .	...	...	...	...	...	...	...	...
General government	8 719 . .	...	...	...	...	5.8	3.7	2.3	5.4
of which: Short-term	8 721 . .	...	...	...	...	...	...	...	...
Banks	8 722 . .	...	...	...	...	109.8	69.7	60.2	66.9
of which: Short-term	8 724 . .	...	...	...	...	*40.8*	*26.7*	*26.0*	*30.2*
Other sectors	8 725 . .	...	...	...	...	29.5	29.7	29.2	29.5
of which: Short-term	8 727 . .	...	...	...	...	...	...	...	...
Currency and deposits	8 730 . .	...	...	...	...	1,949.4	1,608.9	2,458.2	3,998.5
Monetary authorities	8 731 . .	...	...	...	...	...	...	...	...
General government	8 732 . .	...	...	...	...	64.2	46.0	69.0	83.5
Banks	8 733 . .	...	...	...	...	1,885.2	1,562.9	2,389.2	3,915.0
Other sectors	8 734 . .	...	...	...	...	...	...	...	...
Other assets	8 736 . .	...	...	...	...	...	...	...	...
Monetary authorities	8 737 . .	...	...	...	...	...	...	...	...
of which: Short-term	8 739 . .	...	...	...	...	...	...	...	...
General government	8 740 . .	...	...	...	...	...	...	...	...
of which: Short-term	8 742 . .	...	...	...	...	...	...	...	...
Banks	8 743 . .	...	...	...	...	...	...	...	...
of which: Short-term	8 745 . .	...	...	...	...	...	...	...	...
Other sectors	8 746 . .	...	...	...	...	...	...	...	...
of which: Short-term	8 748 . .	...	...	...	...	...	...	...	...
Reserve assets	8 802 . .	...	...	...	...	**2,815.7**	**3,025.0**	**3,524.5**	**4,703.2**
Monetary gold	8 812 . .	...	...	...	...	...	...	...	...
Special drawing rights	8 811 . .	4.5	140.3	125.6	147.1	231.2	189.5	147.2	107.4
Reserve position in the Fund	8 810 . .	...	...	...	.1	.2	.2	.2	.2
Foreign exchange	8 803 . .	...	...	...	...	2,584.4	2,835.3	3,377.0	4,595.6
Other claims	8 813 . .	...	...	...	...	...	...	...	...

Table 3 (Concluded). INTERNATIONAL INVESTMENT POSITION (End–period stocks), 1994–2001
(Millions of U.S. dollars)

	Code	1994	1995	1996	1997	1998	1999	2000	2001
LIABILITIES	8 995 D.	...	...	...	...	11,332.5	12,206.2	14,014.6	15,273.9
Direct investment in Croatia	8 555 . .	**...**	**...**	**...**	**...**	**2,135.6**	**2,745.4**	**4,018.8**	**5,063.3**
Equity capital and reinvested earnings	8 556 . .	...	...	...	...	1,659.1	2,205.5	2,904.1	3,947.3
Claims on direct investors	8 557 . .	...	...	...	...	...	...	...	...
Liabilities to direct investors	8 558 . .	...	...	...	...	1,659.1	2,205.5	2,904.1	3,947.3
Other capital	8 580 . .	...	...	...	...	476.5	539.9	1,114.7	1,116.0
Claims on direct investors	8 585 . .	...	...	...	...	...	...	...	...
Liabilities to direct investors	8 590 . .	...	...	...	...	...	...	...	...
Portfolio investment	8 652 . .	**...**	**...**	**...**	**...**	**2,145.3**	**2,699.7**	**3,288.4**	**3,881.6**
Equity securities	8 660 . .	...	...	...	...	87.3	128.3	108.8	143.7
Banks	8 663 . .	...	...	...	...	36.5	61.5	36.5	36.4
Other sectors	8 664 . .	...	...	...	...	50.8	66.8	72.3	107.3
Debt securities	8 669 . .	...	...	...	...	2,058.0	2,571.4	3,179.6	3,737.9
Bonds and notes	8 670 . .	...	...	...	...	2,049.3	2,554.0	3,170.1	3,710.5
Monetary authorities	8 671 . .	...	...	...	...	...	...	...	...
General government	8 672 . .	...	...	...	...	2,049.3	2,522.9	3,141.2	3,683.1
Banks	8 673 . .	...	...	...	...	...	...	...	...
Other sectors	8 674 . .	...	...	...	...	...	31.1	28.9	27.4
Money market instruments	8 680 . .	...	...	...	...	8.7	17.4	9.5	27.4
Monetary authorities	8 681 . .	...	...	...	...	...	...	...	...
General government	8 682 . .	...	...	...	...	...	...	...	...
Banks	8 683 . .	...	...	...	...	...	...	...	...
Other sectors	8 684 . .	...	...	...	...	8.7	17.4	9.5	27.4
Financial derivatives	8 905 . .	**...**	**...**	**...**	**...**	**...**	**...**	**...**	**...**
Monetary authorities	8 906 . .	...	...	...	...	...	...	...	...
General government	8 907 . .	...	...	...	...	...	...	...	...
Banks	8 908 . .	...	...	...	...	...	...	...	...
Other sectors	8 909 . .	...	...	...	...	...	...	...	...
Other investment	8 753 . .	**...**	**...**	**...**	**...**	**7,051.6**	**6,761.1**	**6,707.4**	**6,329.0**
Trade credits	8 756 . .	...	...	...	...	443.7	377.2	341.8	300.2
General government	8 757 . .	...	...	...	...	2.6	3.4	.1	1.1
of which: Short-term	8 759 . .	...	...	...	...	*.8*	*2.7*	...	...
Other sectors	8 760 . .	...	...	...	...	441.1	373.8	341.7	299.1
of which: Short-term	8 762 . .	...	...	...	...	*117.7*	*99.5*	*64.4*	*56.8*
Loans	8 764 . .	...	...	...	...	5,993.3	5,846.2	5,932.8	5,395.3
Monetary authorities	8 765 . .	...	...	...	...	233.9	196.6	158.2	122.2
of which: Use of Fund credit and loans from the Fund	8 766 . .	*127.1*	*220.8*	*209.1*	*233.0*	*233.9*	*196.6*	*158.2*	*122.2*
of which: Short-term	8 768 . .	...	...	...	...	...	...	...	...
General government	8 769 . .	...	...	...	...	1,343.3	1,446.8	1,654.0	1,326.8
of which: Short-term	8 771 . .	...	...	...	...	*50.0*	*75.3*	*360.0*	...
Banks	8 772 . .	...	...	...	...	1,651.0	1,416.8	1,164.3	1,185.3
of which: Short-term	8 774 . .	...	...	...	...	*34.9*	*31.2*	*7.9*	*8.4*
Other sectors	8 775 . .	...	...	...	...	2,765.1	2,786.0	2,956.3	2,761.0
of which: Short-term	8 777 . .	...	...	...	...	*392.0*	*250.3*	*145.9*	*89.8*
Currency and deposits	8 780 . .	...	...	...	...	614.6	537.7	432.8	633.5
Monetary authorities	8 781 . .	...	...	...	...	...	...	...	...
General government	8 782 . .	...	...	...	...	...	...	...	...
Banks	8 783 . .	...	...	...	...	614.6	537.7	432.8	633.5
Other sectors	8 784 . .	...	...	...	...	...	...	...	...
Other liabilities	8 786 . .	...	...	...	...	...	...	...	...
Monetary authorities	8 787 . .	...	...	...	...	...	...	...	...
of which: Short-term	8 789 . .	...	...	...	...	...	...	...	...
General government	8 790 . .	...	...	...	...	...	...	...	...
of which: Short-term	8 792 . .	...	...	...	...	...	...	...	...
Banks	8 793 . .	...	...	...	...	...	...	...	...
of which: Short-term	8 795 . .	...	...	...	...	...	...	...	...
Other sectors	8 796 . .	...	...	...	...	...	...	...	...
of which: Short-term	8 798 . .	...	...	...	...	...	...	...	...
NET INTERNATIONAL INVESTMENT POSITION	8 995 . .	**...**	**...**	**...**	**...**	**–5,145.7**	**–6,334.4**	**–6,862.4**	**–5,297.0**
Conversion rates: kunas per U.S. dollar (end of period)	0 102 . .	**5.6287**	**5.3161**	**5.5396**	**6.3031**	**6.2475**	**7.6477**	**8.1553**	**8.3560**

Table 1. ANALYTIC PRESENTATION, 1994–2001
(Millions of U.S. dollars)

	Code	1994	1995	1996	1997	1998	1999	2000	2001
A. Current Account [1]	4 993 Z.	**74.4**	**-164.0**	**-465.6**	**-338.2**	**-602.9**	**-217.3**	**-455.6**	**-394.8**
Goods: exports f.o.b	2 100 . .	967.5	1,228.7	1,392.4	1,245.8	1,064.6	1,000.3	951.0	976.5
Goods: imports f.o.b	3 100 . .	-2,703.0	-3,314.2	-3,575.7	-3,317.2	-3,490.4	-3,309.5	-3,556.5	-3,526.9
Balance on Goods	4 100 . .	*-1,735.5*	*-2,085.5*	*-2,183.3*	*-2,071.4*	*-2,425.7*	*-2,309.2*	*-2,605.5*	*-2,550.4*
Services: credit	2 200 . .	2,646.7	2,991.2	2,872.3	2,827.6	2,954.7	3,190.0	3,206.4	3,352.9
Services: debit	3 200 . .	-862.1	-1,105.8	-1,160.6	-1,109.4	-1,132.6	-1,147.3	-1,160.0	-1,185.2
Balance on Goods and Services	4 991 . .	*49.2*	*-200.0*	*-471.6*	*-353.2*	*-603.7*	*-266.5*	*-559.1*	*-382.7*
Income: credit	2 300 . .	121.5	371.1	359.2	382.2	416.7	418.5	508.5	563.8
Income: debit	3 300 . .	-211.1	-363.8	-386.4	-393.1	-445.3	-456.6	-530.8	-597.6
Balance on Goods, Services, and Income	4 992 . .	*-40.4*	*-192.7*	*-498.8*	*-364.1*	*-632.3*	*-304.6*	*-581.5*	*-416.4*
Current transfers: credit	2 379 Z.	125.0	46.4	43.1	40.9	49.6	113.6	153.3	49.3
Current transfers: debit	3 379 . .	-10.2	-17.7	-9.9	-15.0	-20.3	-26.3	-27.5	-27.7
B. Capital Account [1]	4 994 Z.	**. . .**	**. . .**	**. . .**	**. . .**	**. . .**	**. . .**	**. . .**	**. . .**
Capital account: credit	2 994 Z.	. . .	. . .	. . .	. . .	. . .	. . .	. . .	. . .
Capital account: debit	3 994 . .	. . .	. . .	. . .	. . .	. . .	. . .	. . .	. . .
Total, Groups A Plus B	4 981 . .	*74.4*	*-164.0*	*-465.6*	*-338.2*	*-602.9*	*-217.3*	*-455.6*	*-394.8*
C. Financial Account [1]	4 995 W.	**185.7**	**-140.8**	**419.0**	**383.7**	**657.9**	**1,006.4**	**263.5**	**845.7**
Direct investment abroad	4 505 . .	-6.1	-27.6	-48.3	-32.7	-68.9	-146.2	-202.4	-217.7
Direct investment in Cyprus	4 555 Z.	75.2	85.8	54.3	75.9	68.7	121.4	162.6	163.3
Portfolio investment assets	4 602 . .	-244.6	-44.4	-117.5	-125.9	-106.2	-474.8	-292.7	-443.2
Equity securities	4 610 . .	. . .	. . .	. . .	. . .	. . .	. . .	. . .	. . .
Debt securities	4 619 . .	-244.6	-44.4	-117.5	-125.9	-106.2	-474.8	-292.7	-443.2
Portfolio investment liabilities	4 652 Z.	84.5	-27.4	69.7	268.3	303.0	476.5	89.3	524.0
Equity securities	4 660 . .	. . .	2.0	2.8	3.1	-12.0	139.2	177.1	15.5
Debt securities	4 669 Z.	84.5	-29.4	66.9	265.2	315.0	337.2	-87.7	508.5
Financial derivatives	4 910 . .	. . .	. . .	. . .	. . .	. . .	. . .	. . .	. . .
Financial derivatives assets	4 900 . .	. . .	. . .	. . .	. . .	. . .	. . .	. . .	. . .
Financial derivatives liabilities	4 905 . .	. . .	. . .	. . .	. . .	. . .	. . .	. . .	. . .
Other investment assets	4 703 . .	56.3	-1,075.5	-158.0	-700.5	659.1	-389.7	-1,388.6	-540.5
Monetary authorities	4 701 . .	. . .	. . .	. . .	. . .	. . .	. . .	. . .	. . .
General government	4 704 . .	1.0	-11.9	-7.7	-22.8	32.4	.6	-4.5	-9.2
Banks	4 705 . .	55.3	-1,063.6	-150.3	-677.8	626.7	-390.3	-1,384.1	531.3
Other sectors	4 728 . .	. . .	. . .	. . .	. . .	. . .	. . .	. . .	. . .
Other investment liabilities	4 753 W.	220.4	948.5	618.9	898.6	-197.7	1,419.3	1,895.4	1,359.8
Monetary authorities	4 753 WA	.4	29.2	-36.2	20.6	-24.3	5.7	-20.1	16.0
General government	4 753 ZB	-228.6	-147.2	-95.4	-112.9	-7.1	-39.6	31.8	-113.7
Banks	4 753 ZC	301.5	964.4	693.3	872.0	-125.7	1,411.0	1,742.6	1,489.3
Other sectors	4 753 ZD	147.1	102.1	57.3	118.9	-40.6	53.6	141.1	-31.9
Total, Groups A Through C	4 983 . .	*260.1*	*-304.8*	*-46.5*	*45.5*	*55.0*	*789.0*	*-192.2*	*450.9*
D. Net Errors and Omissions	4 998 . .	**-13.1**	**-58.2**	**-13.3**	**-92.5**	**-137.6**	**-150.0**	**184.0**	**161.4**
Total, Groups A Through D	4 984 . .	*246.9*	*-363.1*	*-59.8*	*-47.0*	*-82.5*	*639.0*	*-8.2*	*612.3*
E. Reserves and Related Items	4 802 A.	**-246.9**	**363.1**	**59.8**	**47.0**	**82.5**	**-639.0**	**8.2**	**-612.3**
Reserve assets	4 802 . .	-246.9	363.1	59.8	47.0	82.5	-639.0	8.2	-612.3
Use of Fund credit and loans	4 766 . .	. . .	. . .	. . .	. . .	. . .	. . .	. . .	. . .
Exceptional financing	4 920 . .	. . .	. . .	. . .	. . .	. . .	. . .	. . .	. . .
Conversion rates: Cyprus pound per U.S. dollar	0 101 . .	**.4922**	**.4524**	**.4663**	**.5139**	**.5178**	**.5429**	**.6224**	**.6431**

[1] Excludes components that have been classified in the categories of Group E.

Table 2. STANDARD PRESENTATION, 1994–2001

(Millions of U.S. dollars)

	Code		1994	1995	1996	1997	1998	1999	2000	2001
CURRENT ACCOUNT	4 993	. .	**74.4**	**–164.0**	**–465.6**	**–338.2**	**–602.9**	**–217.3**	**–455.6**	**–394.8**
A. GOODS	4 100	. .	–1,735.5	–2,085.5	–2,183.3	–2,071.4	–2,425.7	–2,309.2	–2,605.5	–2,550.4
Credit	2 100	. .	**967.5**	**1,228.7**	**1,392.4**	**1,245.8**	**1,064.6**	**1,000.3**	**951.0**	**976.5**
General merchandise: exports f.o.b.	2 110	. .	879.7	1,127.7	1,280.5	1,178.4	1,004.0	929.0	841.2	887.7
Goods for processing: exports f.o.b.	2 150	. .	...	...	...	...	...	...	...	...
Repairs on goods	2 160	. .	...	...	...	...	...	...	...	...
Goods procured in ports by carriers	2 170	. .	87.8	101.0	111.9	67.3	60.6	71.3	109.7	88.8
Nonmonetary gold	2 180	. .	...	...	...	...	...	...	...	...
Debit	3 100	. .	**–2,703.0**	**–3,314.2**	**–3,575.7**	**–3,317.2**	**–3,490.4**	**–3,309.5**	**–3,556.5**	**–3,526.9**
General merchandise: imports f.o.b.	3 110	. .	–2,703.0	–3,314.2	–3,575.7	–3,317.2	–3,490.4	–3,309.5	–3,556.5	–3,526.9
Goods for processing: imports f.o.b.	3 150	. .	...	...	...	...	...	...	...	...
Repairs on goods	3 160	. .	...	...	...	...	...	...	...	...
Goods procured in ports by carriers	3 170	. .	...	...	...	...	...	...	...	...
Nonmonetary gold	3 180	. .	...	...	...	...	...	...	...	...
B. SERVICES	4 200	. .	1,784.7	1,885.4	1,711.7	1,718.2	1,822.0	2,042.7	2,046.4	2,167.8
Total credit	2 200	. .	*2,646.7*	*2,991.2*	*2,872.3*	*2,827.6*	*2,954.7*	*3,190.0*	*3,206.4*	*3,352.9*
Total debit	3 200	. .	*–862.1*	*–1,105.8*	*–1,160.6*	*–1,109.4*	*–1,132.6*	*–1,147.3*	*–1,160.0*	*–1,185.2*
Transportation services, credit	2 205	. .	**343.6**	**384.8**	**393.3**	**368.0**	**368.9**	**374.8**	**402.8**	**431.5**
Passenger	2 850	. .	*246.2*	*219.9*	*223.7*	*191.3*	*199.9*	*204.3*	*195.9*	*209.8*
Freight	2 851	. .	*15.2*	*16.6*	*16.3*	*17.1*	*31.9*	*26.2*	*27.3*	*30.2*
Other	2 852	. .	*82.1*	*148.3*	*153.3*	*159.6*	*137.1*	*144.4*	*179.6*	*191.6*
Sea transport, passenger	2 207	. .	...	9.9	13.5	11.7	19.3	22.1	22.5	25.5
Sea transport, freight	2 208	. .	...	...	...	...	15.1	9.2	10.1	11.5
Sea transport, other	2 209	. .	...	58.8	68.4	65.6	52.9	53.4	50.0	53.5
Air transport, passenger	2 211	. .	...	210.0	210.2	179.6	180.6	182.2	173.4	184.3
Air transport, freight	2 212	. .	...	16.6	16.3	17.1	16.8	16.9	17.2	18.7
Air transport, other	2 213	. .	...	89.5	84.9	94.0	84.2	91.0	129.7	138.1
Other transport, passenger	2 215	. .	...	...	...	...	...	...	...	...
Other transport, freight	2 216	. .	...	...	...	...	...	...	...	...
Other transport, other	2 217	. .	...	...	...	...	...	...	...	...
Transportation services, debit	3 205	. .	**–465.9**	**–585.7**	**–598.3**	**–534.7**	**–560.8**	**–545.5**	**–576.1**	**–580.3**
Passenger	3 850	. .	*–101.6*	*–143.7*	*–135.1*	*–126.5*	*–128.4*	*–129.3*	*–129.7*	*–140.3*
Freight	3 851	. .	*–270.2*	*–331.3*	*–357.5*	*–331.8*	*–349.0*	*–331.0*	*–355.7*	*–352.7*
Other	3 852	. .	*–94.1*	*–110.7*	*–105.7*	*–76.5*	*–83.4*	*–85.3*	*–90.8*	*–87.4*
Sea transport, passenger	3 207	. .	...	...	...	...	...	...	...	...
Sea transport, freight	3 208	. .	...	–331.3	–357.5	–331.8	–349.0	–331.0	–355.7	–352.7
Sea transport, other	3 209	. .	...	–13.3	–12.9	–10.7	–10.6	–6.1	–7.9	–11.7
Air transport, passenger	3 211	. .	...	–143.7	–135.1	–126.5	–128.4	–129.3	–129.7	–140.3
Air transport, freight	3 212	. .	...	...	...	...	...	...	...	...
Air transport, other	3 213	. .	...	–97.5	–92.9	–65.8	–72.8	–79.2	–82.9	–75.7
Other transport, passenger	3 215	. .	...	...	...	...	...	...	...	...
Other transport, freight	3 216	. .	...	...	...	...	...	...	...	...
Other transport, other	3 217	. .	...	...	...	...	...	...	...	...
Travel, credit	2 236	. .	**1,650.8**	**1,796.8**	**1,679.4**	**1,656.9**	**1,715.4**	**1,908.1**	**1,937.6**	**2,005.9**
Business travel	2 237	. .	...	...	...	...	...	...	...	...
Personal travel	2 240	. .	...	1,796.8	1,679.4	1,656.9	1,715.4	1,908.1	1,937.6	2,005.9
Travel, debit	3 236	. .	**–246.2**	**–329.3**	**–365.2**	**–385.5**	**–407.9**	**–430.8**	**–413.4**	**–427.6**
Business travel	3 237	. .	...	–24.8	–21.7	–21.4	–24.9	–25.2	–20.4	–19.9
Personal travel	3 240	. .	...	–304.6	–343.5	–364.1	–382.9	–405.6	–393.0	–407.7
Other services, credit	2 200	BA	**652.4**	**809.6**	**799.7**	**802.7**	**870.4**	**907.1**	**866.0**	**915.6**
Communications	2 245	. .	14.6	16.1	15.9	19.3	37.1	37.8	27.2	30.3
Construction	2 249	. .	...	...	...	...	...	...	...	...
Insurance	2 253	. .	...	...	...	...	...	...	...	...
Financial	2 260	. .	...	...	...	...	...	...	...	...
Computer and information	2 262	. .	...	...	...	...	...	...	...	...
Royalties and licence fees	2 266	. .	...	...	...	...	...	...	...	...
Other business services	2 268	. .	388.9	517.4	520.7	499.9	535.7	576.9	568.6	612.0
Personal, cultural, and recreational	2 287	. .	...	...	...	...	.2	.4	.3	.3
Government, n.i.e.	2 291	. .	248.9	276.1	263.1	283.5	297.4	292.1	269.9	272.9
Other services, debit	3 200	BA	**–149.9**	**–190.8**	**–197.1**	**–189.1**	**–164.0**	**–170.9**	**–170.5**	**–177.3**
Communications	3 245	. .	–20.7	–22.1	–20.4	–20.2	–22.0	–18.0	–16.4	–19.9
Construction	3 249	. .	...	...	...	...	...	...	...	...
Insurance	3 253	. .	–48.4	–61.2	–66.9	–65.0	–65.9	–62.8	–66.0	–61.4
Financial	3 260	. .	...	...	...	...	...	...	...	...
Computer and information	3 262	. .	...	...	...	...	...	...	...	...
Royalties and licence fees	3 266	. .	–10.0	–12.2	–16.7	–14.8	–18.2	–21.4	–20.7	–20.2
Other business services	3 268	. .	–56.3	–71.6	–70.1	–54.9	–32.6	–41.4	–38.4	–48.7
Personal, cultural, and recreational	3 287	. .	...	–5.3	–5.1	–6.8	–3.7	–4.8	–6.6	–4.4
Government, n.i.e.	3 291	. .	–14.6	–18.3	–17.8	–27.4	–21.6	–22.5	–22.3	–22.7

Table 2 (Continued). STANDARD PRESENTATION, 1994–2001
(Millions of U.S. dollars)

	Code	1994	1995	1996	1997	1998	1999	2000	2001
C. INCOME	4 300	–89.6	7.3	–27.2	–10.9	–28.6	–38.1	–22.3	–33.7
Total credit	2 300	*121.5*	*371.1*	*359.2*	*382.2*	*416.7*	*418.5*	*508.5*	*563.8*
Total debit	3 300	*–211.1*	*–363.8*	*–386.4*	*–393.1*	*–445.3*	*–456.6*	*–530.8*	*–597.6*
Compensation of employees, credit	2 310	**...**	**88.4**	**84.7**	**77.8**	**83.0**	**82.9**	**75.5**	**77.7**
Compensation of employees, debit	3 310	**–33.7**	**–48.0**	**–67.3**	**–62.9**	**–80.7**	**–74.0**	**–72.1**	**–79.5**
Investment income, credit	2 320	**121.5**	**282.7**	**274.5**	**304.3**	**333.7**	**335.6**	**433.0**	**486.1**
Direct investment income	2 330	...	20.8	21.7	35.4	52.1	64.1	72.3	87.1
Dividends and distributed branch profits	2 332	...	...	...	22.2	23.8	17.3	22.5	28.0
Reinvested earnings and undistributed branch profits	2 333	...	20.8	21.7	13.2	28.4	46.8	49.8	59.1
Income on debt (interest)	2 334	...	...	...	...	...	...	...	...
Portfolio investment income	2 339	...	...	...	...	...	...	...	...
Income on equity	2 340	...	...	...	...	...	...	...	...
Income on bonds and notes	2 350	...	...	...	...	...	...	...	...
Income on money market instruments	2 360	...	...	...	...	...	...	...	...
Other investment income	2 370	121.5	261.9	252.8	268.9	281.6	271.5	360.7	399.0
Investment income, debit	3 320	**–177.4**	**–315.9**	**–319.1**	**–330.2**	**–364.6**	**–382.5**	**–458.7**	**–518.1**
Direct investment income	3 330	–17.9	–21.0	–26.2	–37.6	–35.9	–41.3	–44.0	–52.9
Dividends and distributed branch profits	3 332	–17.9	–17.7	–21.9	–32.9	–31.1	–26.7	–28.0	–34.2
Reinvested earnings and undistributed branch profits	3 333	...	–3.3	–4.3	–4.7	–4.8	–14.6	–16.1	–18.7
Income on debt (interest)	3 334	...	...	...	...	...	...	...	...
Portfolio investment income	3 339	–13.2	–18.3	–16.1	–15.2	–11.8	–7.0	–5.6	–7.3
Income on equity	3 340	...	...	...	...	...	...	...	...
Income on bonds and notes	3 350	...	...	...	...	...	...	...	...
Income on money market instruments	3 360	–13.2	–18.3	–16.1	–15.2	–11.8	–7.0	–5.6	–7.3
Other investment income	3 370	–146.3	–276.5	–276.9	–277.5	–316.9	–334.3	–409.1	–457.9
D. CURRENT TRANSFERS	4 379	114.8	28.7	33.2	25.9	29.4	87.3	125.8	21.6
Credit	2 379	**125.0**	**46.4**	**43.1**	**40.9**	**49.6**	**113.6**	**153.3**	**49.3**
General government	2 380	15.2	19.9	17.4	17.5	25.3	87.9	128.4	22.9
Other sectors	2 390	109.7	26.5	25.7	23.4	24.3	25.8	24.9	26.4
Workers' remittances	2 391	81.3	...	...	...	...	...	...	...
Other current transfers	2 392	28.4	26.5	25.7	23.4	24.3	25.8	24.9	26.4
Debit	3 379	**–10.2**	**–17.7**	**–9.9**	**–15.0**	**–20.3**	**–26.3**	**–27.5**	**–27.7**
General government	3 380	...	...	...	...	...	...	...	...
Other sectors	3 390	–10.2	–17.7	–9.9	–15.0	–20.3	–26.3	–27.5	–27.7
Workers' remittances	3 391	...	...	...	...	...	...	...	...
Other current transfers	3 392	–10.2	–17.7	–9.9	–15.0	–20.3	–26.3	–27.5	–27.7
CAPITAL AND FINANCIAL ACCOUNT	4 996	**–61.2**	**222.3**	**478.9**	**430.7**	**740.5**	**367.3**	**271.7**	**233.4**
CAPITAL ACCOUNT	4 994	...	...	...	...	...	...	...	...
Total credit	2 994	...	...	...	...	...	...	...	...
Total debit	3 994	...	...	...	...	...	...	...	...
Capital transfers, credit	2 400	**...**	**...**	**...**	**...**	**...**	**...**	**...**	**...**
General government	2 401	...	...	...	...	...	...	...	...
Debt forgiveness	2 402	...	...	...	...	...	...	...	...
Other capital transfers	2 410	...	...	...	...	...	...	...	...
Other sectors	2 430	...	...	...	...	...	...	...	...
Migrants' transfers	2 431	...	...	...	...	...	...	...	...
Debt forgiveness	2 432	...	...	...	...	...	...	...	...
Other capital transfers	2 440	...	...	...	...	...	...	...	...
Capital transfers, debit	3 400	**...**	**...**	**...**	**...**	**...**	**...**	**...**	**...**
General government	3 401	...	...	...	...	...	...	...	...
Debt forgiveness	3 402	...	...	...	...	...	...	...	...
Other capital transfers	3 410	...	...	...	...	...	...	...	...
Other sectors	3 430	...	...	...	...	...	...	...	...
Migrants' transfers	3 431	...	...	...	...	...	...	...	...
Debt forgiveness	3 432	...	...	...	...	...	...	...	...
Other capital transfers	3 440	...	...	...	...	...	...	...	...
Nonproduced nonfinancial assets, credit	2 480	**...**	**...**	**...**	**...**	**...**	**...**	**...**	**...**
Nonproduced nonfinancial assets, debit	3 480	**...**	**...**	**...**	**...**	**...**	**...**	**...**	**...**

Table 2 (Continued). STANDARD PRESENTATION, 1994–2001

(Millions of U.S. dollars)

	Code	1994	1995	1996	1997	1998	1999	2000	2001
FINANCIAL ACCOUNT	4 995	**–61.2**	**222.3**	**478.9**	**430.7**	**740.5**	**367.3**	**271.7**	**233.4**
A. DIRECT INVESTMENT	4 500	69.1	58.1	6.0	43.2	–.2	–24.9	–39.8	–54.4
Direct investment abroad	4 505	**–6.1**	**–27.6**	**–48.3**	**–32.7**	**–68.9**	**–146.2**	**–202.4**	**–217.7**
Equity capital	4 510	...	–6.9	–26.6	–19.5	–40.6	–99.5	–152.6	–158.6
Claims on affiliated enterprises	4 515	...	–6.9	–26.6	–19.5	–40.6	–99.5	–152.6	–158.6
Liabilities to affiliated enterprises	4 520	...	...	...	...	...	...	...	...
Reinvested earnings	4 525	...	–20.8	–21.7	–13.2	–28.4	–46.8	–49.8	–59.1
Other capital	4 530	–6.1	...	...	...	...	...	...	...
Claims on affiliated enterprises	4 535	...	...	...	...	...	...	...	...
Liabilities to affiliated enterprises	4 540	...	...	...	...	...	...	...	...
Direct investment in Cyprus	4 555	**75.2**	**85.8**	**54.3**	**75.9**	**68.7**	**121.4**	**162.6**	**163.3**
Equity capital	4 560	...	82.4	50.0	71.2	63.9	106.8	146.5	144.6
Claims on direct investors	4 565	...	...	...	...	...	...	...	...
Liabilities to direct investors	4 570	...	82.4	50.0	71.2	63.9	106.8	146.5	144.6
Reinvested earnings	4 575	...	3.3	4.3	4.7	4.8	14.6	16.1	18.7
Other capital	4 580	75.2	...	...	...	...	...	...	...
Claims on direct investors	4 585	...	...	...	...	...	...	...	...
Liabilities to direct investors	4 590	...	...	...	...	...	...	...	...
B. PORTFOLIO INVESTMENT	4 600	–160.1	–71.8	–47.8	142.4	196.8	1.7	–203.4	80.9
Assets	4 602	**–244.6**	**–44.4**	**–117.5**	**–125.9**	**–106.2**	**–474.8**	**–292.7**	**–443.2**
Equity securities	4 610	...	...	...	...	...	...	...	...
Monetary authorities	4 611	...	...	...	...	...	...	...	...
General government	4 612	...	...	...	...	...	...	...	...
Banks	4 613	...	...	...	...	...	...	...	...
Other sectors	4 614	...	...	...	...	...	...	...	...
Debt securities	4 619	–244.6	–44.4	–117.5	–125.9	–106.2	–474.8	–292.7	–443.2
Bonds and notes	4 620	–244.6	–44.4	–117.5	–125.9	–106.2	–474.8	–292.7	–443.2
Monetary authorities	4 621	...	...	...	...	...	...	...	...
General government	4 622	...	...	...	...	...	...	...	...
Banks	4 623	–244.6	–23.7	–111.1	–111.3	–81.9	–397.8	–258.2	–433.8
Other sectors	4 624	...	–20.8	–6.4	–14.6	–24.3	–77.0	–34.5	–9.3
Money market instruments	4 630	...	...	...	...	...	...	...	...
Monetary authorities	4 631	...	...	...	...	...	...	...	...
General government	4 632	...	...	...	...	...	...	...	...
Banks	4 633	...	...	...	...	...	...	...	...
Other sectors	4 634	...	...	...	...	...	...	...	...
Liabilities	4 652	**84.5**	**–27.4**	**69.7**	**268.3**	**303.0**	**476.5**	**89.3**	**524.0**
Equity securities	4 660	...	2.0	2.8	3.1	–12.0	139.2	177.1	15.5
Banks	4 663	...	...	...	...	...	...	...	...
Other sectors	4 664	...	...	...	...	...	...	...	...
Debt securities	4 669	84.5	–29.4	66.9	265.2	315.0	337.2	–87.7	508.5
Bonds and notes	4 670	...	...	83.2	299.3	389.7	294.3	...	496.0
Monetary authorities	4 671	...	...	...	...	...	...	...	...
General government	4 672	...	...	...	299.3	389.7	294.3	...	...
Banks	4 673	...	...	83.2	...	...	...	...	496.0
Other sectors	4 674	...	...	...	...	...	...	...	...
Money market instruments	4 680	84.5	–29.4	–16.3	–34.1	–74.7	42.9	–87.7	12.4
Monetary authorities	4 681	...	...	...	...	...	...	...	...
General government	4 682	84.5	–29.4	–16.3	–34.1	–74.7	42.9	–87.7	12.4
Banks	4 683	...	...	...	...	...	...	...	...
Other sectors	4 684	...	...	...	...	...	...	...	...
C. FINANCIAL DERIVATIVES	4 910	...	...	...	...	...	...	...	...
Monetary authorities	4 911	...	...	...	...	...	...	...	...
General government	4 912	...	...	...	...	...	...	...	...
Banks	4 913	...	...	...	...	...	...	...	...
Other sectors	4 914	...	...	...	...	...	...	...	...
Assets	4 900	**...**	**...**	**...**	**...**	**...**	**...**	**...**	**...**
Monetary authorities	4 901	...	...	...	...	...	...	...	...
General government	4 902	...	...	...	...	...	...	...	...
Banks	4 903	...	...	...	...	...	...	...	...
Other sectors	4 904	...	...	...	...	...	...	...	...
Liabilities	4 905	**...**	**...**	**...**	**...**	**...**	**...**	**...**	**...**
Monetary authorities	4 906	...	...	...	...	...	...	...	...
General government	4 907	...	...	...	...	...	...	...	...
Banks	4 908	...	...	...	...	...	...	...	...
Other sectors	4 909	...	...	...	...	...	...	...	...

Table 2 (Concluded). STANDARD PRESENTATION, 1994–2001
(Millions of U.S. dollars)

	Code	1994	1995	1996	1997	1998	1999	2000	2001
D. OTHER INVESTMENT	4 700 . .	276.7	–127.1	460.9	198.1	461.4	1,029.6	506.7	819.3
Assets	4 703 . .	**56.3**	**–1,075.5**	**–158.0**	**–700.5**	**659.1**	**–389.7**	**–1,388.6**	**–540.5**
Trade credits	4 706 . .	.8	–9.9	–5.6	–20.6	34.8	3.1	–2.1	–6.5
General government	4 707 . .	.8	–9.9	–5.6	–20.6	34.8	3.1	–2.1	–6.5
of which: Short-term	4 709 . .	. . .	. . .	. . .	. . .	. . .	. . .	. . .	. . .
Other sectors	4 710 . .	. . .	. . .	. . .	. . .	. . .	. . .	. . .	. . .
of which: Short-term	4 712 . .	. . .	. . .	. . .	. . .	. . .	. . .	. . .	. . .
Loans	4 714 . .	. . .	–17.0	–46.3	–85.6	72.8	–309.4	17.7	–23.3
Monetary authorities	4 715 . .	. . .	. . .	. . .	. . .	. . .	. . .	. . .	. . .
of which: Short-term	4 718 . .	. . .	. . .	. . .	. . .	. . .	. . .	. . .	. . .
General government	4 719 . .	. . .	. . .	. . .	. . .	. . .	. . .	. . .	. . .
of which: Short-term	4 721 . .	. . .	. . .	. . .	. . .	. . .	. . .	. . .	. . .
Banks	4 722 . .	. . .	–17.0	–46.3	–85.6	72.8	–309.4	17.7	–23.3
of which: Short-term	4 724 . .	. . .	. . .	. . .	. . .	. . .	. . .	. . .	. . .
Other sectors	4 725 . .	. . .	. . .	. . .	. . .	. . .	. . .	. . .	. . .
of which: Short-term	4 727 . .	. . .	. . .	. . .	. . .	. . .	. . .	. . .	. . .
Currency and deposits	4 730 . .	55.5	–1,045.9	–110.0	–590.2	550.6	–84.5	–1,400.5	–511.0
Monetary authorities	4 731 . .	. . .	. . .	. . .	. . .	. . .	. . .	. . .	. . .
General government	4 732 . .	.2	. . .	. . .	. . .	. . .	. . .	. . .	. . .
Banks	4 733 . .	55.3	–1,045.9	–110.0	–590.2	550.6	–84.5	–1,400.5	–511.0
Other sectors	4 734 . .	. . .	. . .	. . .	. . .	. . .	. . .	. . .	. . .
Other assets	4 736 . .	. . .	–2.7	3.9	–4.1	1.0	1.1	–3.7	.3
Monetary authorities	4 737 . .	. . .	. . .	. . .	. . .	. . .	. . .	. . .	. . .
of which: Short-term	4 739 . .	. . .	. . .	. . .	. . .	. . .	. . .	. . .	. . .
General government	4 740 . .	. . .	–2.0	–2.1	–2.1	–2.3	–2.6	–2.4	–2.6
of which: Short-term	4 742 . .	. . .	. . .	. . .	. . .	. . .	. . .	. . .	. . .
Banks	4 743 . .	. . .	–.7	6.0	–1.9	3.3	3.7	–1.3	3.0
of which: Short-term	4 745 . .	. . .	*–.7*	*6.0*	. . .	. . .	. . .	. . .	. . .
Other sectors	4 746 . .	. . .	. . .	. . .	. . .	. . .	. . .	. . .	. . .
of which: Short-term	4 748 . .	. . .	. . .	. . .	. . .	. . .	. . .	. . .	. . .
Liabilities	4 753 . .	**220.4**	**948.5**	**618.9**	**898.6**	**–197.7**	**1,419.3**	**1,895.4**	**1,359.8**
Trade credits	4 756 . .	50.8	13.9	–16.1	–23.9	29.7	35.9	91.6	–40.4
General government	4 757 . .	. . .	–33.8	–13.9	–1.9	21.0	. . .	. . .	. . .
of which: Short-term	4 759 . .	. . .	. . .	. . .	. . .	. . .	. . .	. . .	. . .
Other sectors	4 760 . .	50.8	47.7	–2.1	–22.0	8.7	35.9	91.6	–40.4
of which: Short-term	4 762 . .	*50.8*	*48.6*	*10.7*	*–19.5*	*9.7*	*36.8*	*93.2*	*–38.9*
Loans	4 764 . .	–130.6	–17.9	9.2	34.1	–38.0	–14.2	59.6	181.0
Monetary authorities	4 765 . .	. . .	. . .	. . .	. . .	. . .	. . .	. . .	. . .
of which: Use of Fund credit and loans from the Fund	4 766 . .	. . .	. . .	. . .	. . .	. . .	. . .	. . .	. . .
of which: Short-term	4 768 . .	. . .	. . .	. . .	. . .	. . .	. . .	. . .	. . .
General government	4 769 . .	–226.9	–113.4	–81.5	–110.9	–28.2	–39.6	31.8	–113.7
of which: Short-term	4 771 . .	. . .	. . .	. . .	. . .	. . .	. . .	. . .	. . .
Banks	4 772 . .	. . .	41.1	31.3	4.1	39.4	7.7	21.7	286.1
of which: Short-term	4 774 . .	. . .	. . .	. . .	. . .	. . .	. . .	. . .	. . .
Other sectors	4 775 . .	96.3	54.4	59.4	140.9	–49.2	17.7	49.5	8.6
of which: Short-term	4 777 . .	*–6.9*	*–4.4*	*15.0*	*9.7*	*–5.8*	*–3.3*	*3.7*	*–6.7*
Currency and deposits	4 780 . .	301.9	952.4	625.8	888.5	–189.4	1,397.6	1,744.2	1,219.2
Monetary authorities	4 781 . .	.4	29.2	–36.2	20.6	–24.3	–5.7	–20.1	16.0
General government	4 782 . .	. . .	. . .	. . .	. . .	. . .	. . .	. . .	. . .
Banks	4 783 . .	301.5	923.3	662.0	867.9	–165.1	1,403.3	1,764.3	1,203.2
Other sectors	4 784 . .	. . .	. . .	. . .	. . .	. . .	. . .	. . .	. . .
Other liabilities	4 786 . .	–1.6	. . .	. . .	. . .	. . .	. . .	. . .	. . .
Monetary authorities	4 787 . .	. . .	. . .	. . .	. . .	. . .	. . .	. . .	. . .
of which: Short-term	4 789 . .	. . .	. . .	. . .	. . .	. . .	. . .	. . .	. . .
General government	4 790 . .	–1.6	. . .	. . .	. . .	. . .	. . .	. . .	. . .
of which: Short-term	4 792 . .	. . .	. . .	. . .	. . .	. . .	. . .	. . .	. . .
Banks	4 793 . .	. . .	. . .	. . .	. . .	. . .	. . .	. . .	. . .
of which: Short-term	4 795 . .	. . .	. . .	. . .	. . .	. . .	. . .	. . .	. . .
Other sectors	4 796 . .	. . .	. . .	. . .	. . .	. . .	. . .	. . .	. . .
of which: Short-term	4 798 . .	. . .	. . .	. . .	. . .	. . .	. . .	. . .	. . .
E. RESERVE ASSETS	4 802 . .	–246.9	363.1	59.8	47.0	82.5	–639.0	8.2	–612.3
Monetary gold	4 812 . .	–.2	–.4	. . .	. . .	. . .	. . .	. . .	. . .
Special drawing rights	4 811 . .	–.1	.1	. . .	–.3	.1	–.3	–.5	–.5
Reserve position in the Fund	4 810 . .	. . .	. . .	. . .	. . .	. . .	–13.7	. . .	. . .
Foreign exchange	4 803 . .	–246.7	363.4	59.8	47.3	82.5	–625.1	8.7	–611.9
Other claims	4 813 . .	. . .	. . .	. . .	. . .	. . .	. . .	. . .	. . .
NET ERRORS AND OMISSIONS	4 998 . .	**–13.1**	**–58.2**	**–13.3**	**–92.5**	**–137.6**	**–150.0**	**184.0**	**161.4**

Part 3 of the *Yearbook* contains descriptions of the methodologies, compilation practices, and sources used to compile these data.

Table 1. ANALYTIC PRESENTATION, 1994–2001

(Millions of U.S. dollars)

	Code	1994	1995	1996	1997	1998	1999	2000	2001
A. Current Account[1]	4 993 Z.	**–820**	**–1,374**	**–4,128**	**–3,622**	**–1,308**	**–1,466**	**–2,690**	**–2,624**
Goods: exports f.o.b	2 100 . .	15,964	21,477	21,950	22,319	25,886	26,259	29,019	33,404
Goods: imports f.o.b	3 100 . .	–17,372	–25,162	–27,656	–27,257	–28,533	–28,161	–32,115	–36,482
Balance on Goods	4 100 . .	*–1,408*	*–3,685*	*–5,706*	*–4,938*	*–2,647*	*–1,902*	*–3,095*	*–3,078*
Services: credit	2 200 . .	5,167	6,725	8,181	7,132	7,665	7,049	6,840	7,092
Services: debit	3 200 . .	–4,685	–4,882	–6,264	–5,389	–5,750	–5,850	–5,436	–5,568
Balance on Goods and Services	4 991 . .	*–926*	*–1,842*	*–3,789*	*–3,196*	*–731*	*–704*	*–1,692*	*–1,554*
Income: credit	2 300 . .	791	1,197	1,170	1,405	1,713	1,859	1,952	2,170
Income: debit	3 300 . .	–812	–1,301	–1,892	–2,197	–2,807	–3,209	–3,323	–3,710
Balance on Goods, Services, and Income	4 992 . .	*–947*	*–1,945*	*–4,512*	*–3,987*	*–1,825*	*–2,053*	*–3,063*	*–3,094*
Current transfers: credit	2 379 Z.	298	664	617	866	1,067	1,310	948	959
Current transfers: debit	3 379 . .	–171	–92	–233	–501	–550	–722	–575	–489
B. Capital Account[1]	4 994 Z.	**. . .**	**7**	**1**	**11**	**2**	**–2**	**–5**	**–9**
Capital account: credit	2 994 Z.	. . .	12	1	17	14	18	6	2
Capital account: debit	3 994 . .	. . .	–5	. . .	–5	–12	–20	–11	–11
Total, Groups A Plus B	4 981 . .	*–820*	*–1,367*	*–4,127*	*–3,611*	*–1,306*	*–1,468*	*–2,695*	*–2,633*
C. Financial Account[1]	4 995 W.	**4,504**	**8,225**	**4,202**	**1,122**	**2,908**	**3,080**	**3,835**	**4,058**
Direct investment abroad	4 505 . .	–116	–37	–155	–28	–125	–90	–43	–95
Direct investment in Czech Republic	4 555 Z.	878	2,568	1,435	1,286	3,700	6,313	4,987	4,924
Portfolio investment assets	4 602 . .	–47	–325	–50	–159	–44	–1,882	–2,236	125
Equity securities	4 610 . .	–47	–325	–50	3	119	–1,409	–1,167	247
Debt securities	4 619 . .	. . .	. . .	. . .	–162	–163	–473	–1,069	–121
Portfolio investment liabilities	4 652 Z.	893	1,695	771	1,152	1,146	500	482	798
Equity securities	4 660 . .	497	1,236	601	378	1,096	120	619	616
Debt securities	4 669 Z.	396	460	170	774	49	380	–137	181
Financial derivatives	4 910 . .	. . .	. . .	. . .	. . .	. . .	. . .	–40	–87
Financial derivatives assets	4 900 . .	. . .	. . .	. . .	. . .	. . .	. . .	–129	–254
Financial derivatives liabilities	4 905 . .	. . .	. . .	. . .	. . .	. . .	. . .	89	168
Other investment assets	4 703 . .	–2,437	–2,492	–2,370	–4,427	–1,552	–2,688	984	–1,271
Monetary authorities	4 701 . .	. . .	. . .	. . .	. . .	. . .	. . .	. . .	. . .
General government	4 704 . .	–2,362	–2,138	48	16	20	28	76	180
Banks	4 705 . .	–163	–224	–2,317	–4,161	–1,652	–2,642	1,011	–1,299
Other sectors	4 728 . .	88	–130	–101	–281	80	–74	–102	–152
Other investment liabilities	4 753 W.	5,333	6,816	4,571	3,298	–217	928	–300	–337
Monetary authorities	4 753 WA	–47	40	–2	–11	–7	–57	. . .	1
General government	4 753 ZB	2,821	1,657	–295	–360	–364	–185	–49	–129
Banks	4 753 ZC	888	3,310	2,858	1,638	388	886	–974	–1,152
Other sectors	4 753 ZD	1,671	1,809	2,011	2,030	–234	283	723	943
Total, Groups A Through C	4 983 . .	*3,684*	*6,858*	*75*	*–2,488*	*1,602*	*1,612*	*1,140*	*1,425*
D. Net Errors and Omissions	4 998 . .	**–210**	**596**	**–901**	**730**	**288**	**27**	**–297**	**362**
Total, Groups A Through D	4 984 . .	*3,474*	*7,453*	*–825*	*–1,758*	*1,890*	*1,639*	*844*	*1,787*
E. Reserves and Related Items	4 802 A.	**–3,474**	**–7,453**	**825**	**1,758**	**–1,890**	**–1,639**	**–844**	**–1,787**
Reserve assets	4 802 . .	–2,357	–7,453	825	1,758	–1,890	–1,639	–844	–1,787
Use of Fund credit and loans	4 766 . .	–1,117	. . .	. . .	. . .	. . .	. . .	. . .	. . .
Exceptional financing	4 920 . .	. . .	. . .	. . .	. . .	. . .	. . .	. . .	. . .
Conversion rates: Czech koruny per U.S. dollar	0 101 . .	**28.785**	**26.541**	**27.145**	**31.698**	**32.281**	**34.569**	**38.598**	**38.035**

[1] Excludes components that have been classified in the categories of Group E.

Table 2. STANDARD PRESENTATION, 1994–2001
(Millions of U.S. dollars)

	Code	1994	1995	1996	1997	1998	1999	2000	2001
CURRENT ACCOUNT	4 993 . .	**–820**	**–1,374**	**–4,128**	**–3,622**	**–1,308**	**–1,466**	**–2,690**	**–2,624**
A. GOODS	4 100 . .	–1,408	–3,685	–5,706	–4,938	–2,647	–1,902	–3,095	–3,078
Credit	2 100 . .	**15,964**	**21,477**	**21,950**	**22,319**	**25,886**	**26,259**	**29,019**	**33,404**
General merchandise: exports f.o.b.	2 110 . .	12,290	15,799	16,534	16,460	18,783	18,023	19,660	22,926
Goods for processing: exports f.o.b.	2 150 . .	3,667	5,660	5,393	5,840	7,080	8,214	9,335	10,387
Repairs on goods	2 160 . .	. . .	. . .	. . .	. . .	. . .	. . .	. . .	59
Goods procured in ports by carriers	2 170 . .	. . .	. . .	. . .	. . .	. . .	. . .	. . .	. . .
Nonmonetary gold	2 180 . .	7	18	24	19	22	21	24	32
Debit	3 100 . .	**–17,372**	**–25,162**	**–27,656**	**–27,257**	**–28,533**	**–28,161**	**–32,115**	**–36,482**
General merchandise: imports f.o.b.	3 110 . .	–14,858	–20,823	–22,823	–22,244	–22,806	–22,480	–25,535	–28,788
Goods for processing: imports f.o.b.	3 150 . .	–2,506	–4,321	–4,824	–5,006	–5,714	–5,674	–6,570	–7,640
Repairs on goods	3 160 . .	. . .	. . .	. . .	. . .	. . .	. . .	. . .	–46
Goods procured in ports by carriers	3 170 . .	. . .	. . .	. . .	. . .	. . .	. . .	. . .	. . .
Nonmonetary gold	3 180 . .	–8	–18	–9	–7	–12	–7	–9	–7
B. SERVICES	4 200 . .	482	1,844	1,917	1,743	1,916	1,199	1,403	1,524
Total credit	2 200 . .	*5,167*	*6,725*	*8,181*	*7,132*	*7,665*	*7,049*	*6,840*	*7,092*
Total debit	3 200 . .	*–4,685*	*–4,882*	*–6,264*	*–5,389*	*–5,750*	*–5,850*	*–5,436*	*–5,568*
Transportation services, credit	2 205 . .	**1,244**	**1,463**	**1,334**	**1,317**	**1,390**	**1,546**	**1,390**	**1,512**
Passenger	2 850 . .	. . .	. . .	. . .	. . .	. . .	. . .	. . .	. . .
Freight	2 851 . .	. . .	. . .	. . .	. . .	. . .	. . .	. . .	. . .
Other	2 852 . .	*1,244*	*1,463*	*1,334*	*1,317*	. . .	. . .	. . .	. . .
Sea transport, passenger	2 207 . .	. . .	. . .	. . .	. . .	. . .	. . .	. . .	. . .
Sea transport, freight	2 208 . .	. . .	. . .	. . .	. . .	. . .	. . .	. . .	. . .
Sea transport, other	2 209 . .	56	29	28	23	. . .	. . .	. . .	. . .
Air transport, passenger	2 211 . .	. . .	. . .	. . .	. . .	. . .	. . .	. . .	. . .
Air transport, freight	2 212 . .	. . .	. . .	. . .	. . .	. . .	. . .	. . .	. . .
Air transport, other	2 213 . .	139	265	238	253	. . .	. . .	. . .	. . .
Other transport, passenger	2 215 . .	. . .	. . .	. . .	. . .	. . .	. . .	. . .	. . .
Other transport, freight	2 216 . .	. . .	. . .	. . .	. . .	. . .	. . .	. . .	. . .
Other transport, other	2 217 . .	1,049	1,169	1,068	1,041	. . .	. . .	. . .	. . .
Transportation services, debit	3 205 . .	**–855**	**–800**	**–700**	**–630**	**–700**	**–782**	**–715**	**–805**
Passenger	3 850 . .	. . .	. . .	. . .	. . .	. . .	. . .	. . .	. . .
Freight	3 851 . .	. . .	. . .	. . .	. . .	. . .	. . .	. . .	. . .
Other	3 852 . .	*–855*	*–800*	*–700*	*–630*	. . .	. . .	. . .	. . .
Sea transport, passenger	3 207 . .	. . .	. . .	. . .	. . .	. . .	. . .	. . .	. . .
Sea transport, freight	3 208 . .	. . .	. . .	. . .	. . .	. . .	. . .	. . .	. . .
Sea transport, other	3 209 . .	–63	–55	–42	–30	. . .	. . .	. . .	. . .
Air transport, passenger	3 211 . .	. . .	. . .	. . .	. . .	. . .	. . .	. . .	. . .
Air transport, freight	3 212 . .	. . .	. . .	. . .	. . .	. . .	. . .	. . .	. . .
Air transport, other	3 213 . .	–97	–219	–171	–198	. . .	. . .	. . .	. . .
Other transport, passenger	3 215 . .	. . .	. . .	. . .	. . .	. . .	. . .	. . .	. . .
Other transport, freight	3 216 . .	. . .	. . .	. . .	. . .	. . .	. . .	. . .	. . .
Other transport, other	3 217 . .	–695	–526	–487	–402	. . .	. . .	. . .	. . .
Travel, credit	2 236 . .	**2,237**	**2,880**	**4,079**	**3,620**	**3,894**	**3,153**	**2,973**	**3,104**
Business travel	2 237 . .	. . .	. . .	. . .	. . .	. . .	. . .	. . .	. . .
Personal travel	2 240 . .	2,237	2,880	4,079	3,620	. . .	. . .	. . .	. . .
Travel, debit	3 236 . .	**–1,593**	**–1,635**	**–2,960**	**–2,355**	**–1,908**	**–1,493**	**–1,276**	**–1,386**
Business travel	3 237 . .	. . .	. . .	. . .	. . .	. . .	. . .	. . .	. . .
Personal travel	3 240 . .	–1,593	–1,635	–2,960	–2,355	. . .	. . .	. . .	. . .
Other services, credit	2 200 BA	**1,686**	**2,383**	**2,767**	**2,195**	**2,381**	**2,350**	**2,476**	**2,477**
Communications	2 245 . .	331	292	77	61	71	100	122	211
Construction	2 249 . .	44	57	466	371	266	233	167	157
Insurance	2 253 . .	12	17	39	37	31	4	3	7
Financial	2 260 . .	88	53	145	186	224	227	376	196
Computer and information	2 262 . .	. . .	5	28	39	57	65	95	123
Royalties and licence fees	2 266 . .	4	13	43	34	57	43	44	36
Other business services	2 268 . .	1,162	1,783	1,764	1,250	1,243	1,315	1,393	1,526
Personal, cultural, and recreational	2 287 . .	. . .	74	97	118	284	244	189	161
Government, n.i.e.	2 291 . .	47	88	109	99	147	121	88	58
Other services, debit	3 200 BA	**–2,237**	**–2,446**	**–2,604**	**–2,404**	**–3,142**	**–3,574**	**–3,445**	**–3,377**
Communications	3 245 . .	–274	–256	–64	–55	–150	–99	–46	–69
Construction	3 249 . .	–124	–141	–231	–353	–295	–217	–146	–168
Insurance	3 253 . .	–72	–113	–93	–80	–117	. . .	–67	–78
Financial	3 260 . .	–114	–141	–190	–194	–280	–354	–408	–263
Computer and information	3 262 . .	. . .	–11	–22	–39	–68	–127	–83	–107
Royalties and licence fees	3 266 . .	–26	–53	–98	–78	–113	–137	–82	–93
Other business services	3 268 . .	–1,626	–1,583	–1,733	–1,310	–1,775	–2,408	–2,415	–2,382
Personal, cultural, and recreational	3 287 . .	. . .	–126	–108	–211	–286	–153	–127	–136
Government, n.i.e.	3 291 . .	–1	–22	–66	–84	–59	–77	–72	–81

Table 2 (Continued). STANDARD PRESENTATION, 1994–2001

(Millions of U.S. dollars)

	Code	1994	1995	1996	1997	1998	1999	2000	2001
C. INCOME	4 300	–21	–104	–722	–791	–1,094	–1,350	–1,371	–1,540
Total credit	2 300	*791*	*1,197*	*1,170*	*1,405*	*1,713*	*1,859*	*1,952*	*2,170*
Total debit	3 300	*–812*	*–1,301*	*–1,892*	*–2,197*	*–2,807*	*–3,209*	*–3,323*	*–3,710*
Compensation of employees, credit	2 310	**164**	**189**	**110**	**71**	**346**	**311**	**294**	**256**
Compensation of employees, debit	3 310	**–55**	**–100**	**–302**	**–340**	**–739**	**–634**	**–603**	**–711**
Investment income, credit	2 320	**627**	**1,008**	**1,060**	**1,334**	**1,367**	**1,549**	**1,658**	**1,913**
Direct investment income	2 330	3	19	32	53	–83	14	–11	7
Dividends and distributed branch profits	2 332	3	19	32	53	14	27	4	4
Reinvested earnings and undistributed branch profits	2 333	...	...	...	...	–97	–16	–19	...
Income on debt (interest)	2 334	...	...	...	...	...	3	4	3
Portfolio investment income	2 339	44	30	71	45	104	76	39	214
Income on equity	2 340	17	6	33	3	30	18	8	15
Income on bonds and notes	2 350	...	...	17	23	57	38	31	183
Income on money market instruments	2 360	27	24	21	19	17	21	...	16
Other investment income	2 370	580	958	957	1,236	1,346	1,458	1,630	1,692
Investment income, debit	3 320	**–757**	**–1,200**	**–1,590**	**–1,857**	**–2,068**	**–2,575**	**–2,720**	**–2,999**
Direct investment income	3 330	–9	–66	–75	–56	–354	–1,045	–1,379	–1,405
Dividends and distributed branch profits	3 332	–9	–66	–75	–56	–173	–247	–279	–431
Reinvested earnings and undistributed branch profits	3 333	...	...	...	...	–181	–691	–957	–842
Income on debt (interest)	3 334	...	...	...	...	...	–107	–144	–133
Portfolio investment income	3 339	–127	–248	–459	–480	–386	–408	–234	–446
Income on equity	3 340	–17	–20	–45	–38	–34	–28	–12	–76
Income on bonds and notes	3 350	–67	–196	–363	–399	–322	–359	–221	–370
Income on money market instruments	3 360	–43	–32	–51	–44	–31	–21	–1	...
Other investment income	3 370	–620	–886	–1,055	–1,320	–1,327	–1,122	–1,107	–1,148
D. CURRENT TRANSFERS	4 379	127	572	384	365	517	588	373	470
Credit	2 379	**298**	**664**	**617**	**866**	**1,067**	**1,310**	**948**	**959**
General government	2 380	...	128	165	90	400	383	331	373
Other sectors	2 390	...	536	452	776	666	927	617	586
Workers' remittances	2 391	...	...	...	...	...	...	...	...
Other current transfers	2 392	...	536	452	776	666	927	617	586
Debit	3 379	**–171**	**–92**	**–233**	**–501**	**–550**	**–722**	**–575**	**–489**
General government	3 380	...	–25	–35	–37	–43	–87	–92	–132
Other sectors	3 390	...	–67	–198	–464	–506	–635	–483	–357
Workers' remittances	3 391	...	...	...	...	...	...	...	...
Other current transfers	3 392	...	–67	–198	–464	–506	–635	–483	–357
CAPITAL AND FINANCIAL ACCOUNT	4 996	1,029	778	5,028	2,892	1,020	1,439	2,986	2,262
CAPITAL ACCOUNT	4 994	...	7	1	11	2	–2	–5	–9
Total credit	2 994	...	*12*	*1*	*17*	*14*	*18*	*6*	*2*
Total debit	3 994	...	*–5*	...	*–5*	*–12*	*–20*	*–11*	*–11*
Capital transfers, credit	2 400	...	**12**	**1**	**14**	**4**	**8**	**3**	...
General government	2 401	...	...	...	...	...	...	...	...
Debt forgiveness	2 402	...	...	...	...	...	...	...	...
Other capital transfers	2 410	...	...	...	...	...	...	...	...
Other sectors	2 430	...	12	1	14	4	8	3	...
Migrants' transfers	2 431	...	1	1	14	4	8	3	...
Debt forgiveness	2 432	...	...	...	...	...	...	...	...
Other capital transfers	2 440	...	10	...	...	...	...	...	...
Capital transfers, debit	3 400	...	**–5**	...	**–1**	**–6**	**–8**	**–2**	**–7**
General government	3 401	...	...	...	...	...	...	...	...
Debt forgiveness	3 402	...	...	...	...	...	...	...	...
Other capital transfers	3 410	...	...	...	...	...	...	...	...
Other sectors	3 430	...	–5	...	–1	–6	–8	–2	–7
Migrants' transfers	3 431	...	...	...	–1	–6	–8	–2	–7
Debt forgiveness	3 432	...	...	...	...	...	...	...	...
Other capital transfers	3 440	...	–5	...	...	...	...	...	...
Nonproduced nonfinancial assets, credit	2 480	...	...	...	**2**	**10**	**11**	**3**	**2**
Nonproduced nonfinancial assets, debit	3 480	...	...	...	**–4**	**–6**	**–13**	**–9**	**–4**

Table 2 (Continued). STANDARD PRESENTATION, 1994–2001
(Millions of U.S. dollars)

	Code	1994	1995	1996	1997	1998	1999	2000	2001
FINANCIAL ACCOUNT	4 995 . .	**1,029**	**771**	**5,028**	**2,881**	**1,018**	**1,441**	**2,991**	**2,271**
A. DIRECT INVESTMENT	4 500 . .	762	2,531	1,281	1,259	3,575	6,223	4,944	4,829
Direct investment abroad	4 505 . .	**–116**	**–37**	**–155**	**–28**	**–125**	**–90**	**–43**	**–95**
Equity capital	4 510 . .	–116	–37	–155	–28	–173	–91	–51	–91
Claims on affiliated enterprises	4 515 . .	–116	–37	–155	–28	–173	–91	–51	–91
Liabilities to affiliated enterprises	4 520 . .	. . .	. . .	. . .	. . .	. . .	. . .	. . .	. . .
Reinvested earnings	4 525 . .	. . .	. . .	. . .	. . .	97	16	19	. . .
Other capital	4 530 . .	. . .	. . .	. . .	. . .	–49	–15	–11	–4
Claims on affiliated enterprises	4 535 . .	. . .	. . .	. . .	. . .	–49	–15	–11	–4
Liabilities to affiliated enterprises	4 540 . .	. . .	. . .	. . .	. . .	. . .	. . .	. . .	. . .
Direct investment in Czech Republic	4 555 . .	**878**	**2,568**	**1,435**	**1,286**	**3,700**	**6,313**	**4,987**	**4,924**
Equity capital	4 560 . .	878	2,568	1,435	1,286	2,554	4,862	3,497	3,999
Claims on direct investors	4 565 . .	. . .	. . .	. . .	. . .	. . .	. . .	. . .	. . .
Liabilities to direct investors	4 570 . .	878	2,568	1,435	1,286	2,554	4,862	3,497	3,999
Reinvested earnings	4 575 . .	. . .	. . .	. . .	. . .	181	691	957	842
Other capital	4 580 . .	. . .	. . .	. . .	. . .	966	760	533	83
Claims on direct investors	4 585 . .	. . .	. . .	. . .	. . .	. . .	. . .	. . .	. . .
Liabilities to direct investors	4 590 . .	. . .	. . .	. . .	. . .	966	760	533	83
B. PORTFOLIO INVESTMENT	4 600 . .	847	1,370	720	993	1,102	–1,382	–1,754	923
Assets	4 602 . .	**–47**	**–325**	**–50**	**–159**	**–44**	**–1,882**	**–2,236**	**125**
Equity securities	4 610 . .	–47	–325	–50	3	119	–1,409	–1,167	247
Monetary authorities	4 611 . .	. . .	. . .	. . .	. . .	. . .	. . .	. . .	. . .
General government	4 612 . .	. . .	. . .	. . .	. . .	. . .	. . .	–1	. . .
Banks	4 613 . .	. . .	. . .	. . .	4	24	–934	–512	41
Other sectors	4 614 . .	–47	–325	–50	–1	95	–474	–654	206
Debt securities	4 619 . .	. . .	. . .	. . .	–162	–163	–473	–1,069	–121
Bonds and notes	4 620 . .	. . .	. . .	. . .	163	–321	44	–987	–147
Monetary authorities	4 621 . .	. . .	. . .	. . .	. . .	. . .	. . .	. . .	. . .
General government	4 622 . .	. . .	. . .	. . .	. . .	. . .	. . .	. . .	. . .
Banks	4 623 . .	. . .	. . .	. . .	41	–272	30	–873	167
Other sectors	4 624 . .	. . .	. . .	. . .	122	–49	14	–114	–314
Money market instruments	4 630 . .	. . .	. . .	. . .	–325	158	–518	–82	26
Monetary authorities	4 631 . .	. . .	. . .	. . .	. . .	. . .	. . .	. . .	. . .
General government	4 632 . .	. . .	. . .	. . .	. . .	. . .	. . .	6	50
Banks	4 633 . .	. . .	. . .	. . .	–12	62	28	–3	107
Other sectors	4 634 . .	. . .	. . .	. . .	–313	96	–546	–86	–132
Liabilities	4 652 . .	**893**	**1,695**	**771**	**1,152**	**1,146**	**500**	**482**	**798**
Equity securities	4 660 . .	497	1,236	601	378	1,096	120	619	616
Banks	4 663 . .	. . .	. . .	61	83	290	382	226	69
Other sectors	4 664 . .	497	1,236	540	295	806	–262	393	548
Debt securities	4 669 . .	396	460	170	774	49	380	–137	181
Bonds and notes	4 670 . .	60	153	343	685	302	441	–218	132
Monetary authorities	4 671 . .	–130	. . .	–368	–21	. . .	. . .	–319	. . .
General government	4 672 . .	246	. . .	125	–52	–84	–6	13	232
Banks	4 673 . .	. . .	. . .	135	379	112	240	28	79
Other sectors	4 674 . .	–56	153	450	379	273	208	61	–179
Money market instruments	4 680 . .	336	307	–173	89	–252	–61	81	49
Monetary authorities	4 681 . .	. . .	. . .	. . .	. . .	. . .	. . .	. . .	. . .
General government	4 682 . .	336	307	–452	96	–191	–61	76	–29
Banks	4 683 . .	. . .	. . .	106	24	–3	. . .	5	78
Other sectors	4 684 . .	. . .	. . .	173	–31	–58	. . .	. . .	. . .
C. FINANCIAL DERIVATIVES	4 910 . .	. . .	. . .	. . .	. . .	. . .	. . .	–40	–87
Monetary authorities	4 911 . .	. . .	. . .	. . .	. . .	. . .	. . .	. . .	. . .
General government	4 912 . .	. . .	. . .	. . .	. . .	. . .	. . .	. . .	. . .
Banks	4 913 . .	. . .	. . .	. . .	. . .	. . .	. . .	–40	–87
Other sectors	4 914 . .	. . .	. . .	. . .	. . .	. . .	. . .	. . .	. . .
Assets	4 900 . .	**. . .**	**. . .**	**. . .**	**. . .**	**. . .**	**. . .**	**–129**	**–254**
Monetary authorities	4 901 . .	. . .	. . .	. . .	. . .	. . .	. . .	. . .	. . .
General government	4 902 . .	. . .	. . .	. . .	. . .	. . .	. . .	. . .	. . .
Banks	4 903 . .	. . .	. . .	. . .	. . .	. . .	. . .	–129	–254
Other sectors	4 904 . .	. . .	. . .	. . .	. . .	. . .	. . .	. . .	. . .
Liabilities	4 905 . .	**. . .**	**. . .**	**. . .**	**. . .**	**. . .**	**. . .**	**89**	**168**
Monetary authorities	4 906 . .	. . .	. . .	. . .	. . .	. . .	. . .	. . .	. . .
General government	4 907 . .	. . .	. . .	. . .	. . .	. . .	. . .	. . .	. . .
Banks	4 908 . .	. . .	. . .	. . .	. . .	. . .	. . .	89	168
Other sectors	4 909 . .	. . .	. . .	. . .	. . .	. . .	. . .	. . .	. . .

Table 2 (Concluded). STANDARD PRESENTATION, 1994–2001
(Millions of U.S. dollars)

	Code	1994	1995	1996	1997	1998	1999	2000	2001
D. OTHER INVESTMENT	4 700 . .	1,778	4,324	2,202	–1,129	–1,768	–1,761	684	–1,608
Assets	4 703 . .	**–2,437**	**–2,492**	**–2,370**	**–4,427**	**–1,552**	**–2,688**	**984**	**–1,271**
Trade credits	4 706 . .	83	–94	44	–293	31	–114	–61	34
General government	4 707 . .	. . .	. . .	. . .	. . .	. . .	. . .	. . .	. . .
of which: Short-term	4 709 . .	. . .	. . .	. . .	. . .	. . .	. . .	. . .	. . .
Other sectors	4 710 . .	83	–94	44	–293	31	–114	–61	34
of which: Short-term	4 712 . .	*–52*	*–146*	*–35*	*–303*	*–15*	*–142*	*–166*	*–42*
Loans	4 714 . .	–97	–422	–898	–1,158	–1,151	74	315	368
Monetary authorities	4 715 . .	. . .	. . .	. . .	. . .	. . .	. . .	. . .	. . .
of which: Short-term	4 718 . .	. . .	. . .	. . .	. . .	. . .	. . .	. . .	. . .
General government	4 719 . .	. . .	. . .	. . .	. . .	. . .	. . .	. . .	–9
of which: Short-term	4 721 . .	. . .	. . .	. . .	. . .	. . .	. . .	. . .	. . .
Banks	4 722 . .	–97	–422	–865	–1,158	–1,210	41	332	406
of which: Short-term	4 724 . .	*–85*	*–312*	*–487*	*–916*	*–341*	*655*	*–218*	*235*
Other sectors	4 725 . .	. . .	. . .	–33	. . .	59	33	–18	–29
of which: Short-term	4 727 . .	. . .	. . .	*–33*	. . .	*42*	*33*	*–18*	*–29*
Currency and deposits	4 730 . .	–175	153	–1,356	–2,858	–420	–2,726	500	–1,762
Monetary authorities	4 731 . .	. . .	. . .	. . .	. . .	. . .	. . .	. . .	. . .
General government	4 732 . .	. . .	. . .	. . .	. . .	. . .	. . .	. . .	–2
Banks	4 733 . .	–180	189	–1,243	–2,870	–410	–2,733	524	–1,717
Other sectors	4 734 . .	5	–36	–112	12	–11	7	–24	–43
Other assets	4 736 . .	–2,249	–2,129	–160	–118	–12	78	230	89
Monetary authorities	4 737 . .	. . .	. . .	. . .	. . .	. . .	. . .	. . .	. . .
of which: Short-term	4 739 . .	. . .	. . .	. . .	. . .	. . .	. . .	. . .	. . .
General government	4 740 . .	–2,362	–2,138	48	16	20	28	76	191
of which: Short-term	4 742 . .	*–2,647*	*–2,264*	. . .	. . .	. . .	. . .	. . .	. . .
Banks	4 743 . .	114	9	–208	–134	–32	50	155	12
of which: Short-term	4 745 . .	*114*	*9*	*–191*	*–11*	*–69*	*27*	*154*	*11*
Other sectors	4 746 . .	. . .	. . .	. . .	. . .	. . .	. . .	. . .	–114
of which: Short-term	4 748 . .	. . .	. . .	. . .	. . .	. . .	. . .	. . .	. . .
Liabilities	4 753 . .	**4,215**	**6,816**	**4,571**	**3,298**	**–217**	**928**	**–300**	**–337**
Trade credits	4 756 . .	284	231	–283	308	315	97	171	–285
General government	4 757 . .	. . .	. . .	. . .	. . .	. . .	. . .	. . .	. . .
of which: Short-term	4 759 . .	. . .	. . .	. . .	. . .	. . .	. . .	. . .	. . .
Other sectors	4 760 . .	284	231	–283	308	315	97	171	–285
of which: Short-term	4 762 . .	*61*	*325*	*–167*	*268*	*8*	*60*	*385*	*–273*
Loans	4 764 . .	230	2,132	2,860	1,400	85	206	–400	530
Monetary authorities	4 765 . .	–1,165	37	. . .	–12	–7	–60	–1	–1
of which: Use of Fund credit and loans from the Fund	4 766 . .	*–1,117*	. . .	. . .	. . .	. . .	. . .	. . .	. . .
of which: Short-term	4 768 . .	*–55*	. . .	. . .	. . .	. . .	. . .	. . .	. . .
General government	4 769 . .	–185	–455	–262	–358	–356	–182	–49	–13
of which: Short-term	4 771 . .	. . .	. . .	. . .	. . .	. . .	. . .	. . .	. . .
Banks	4 772 . .	194	972	828	131	996	262	–902	–685
of which: Short-term	4 774 . .	*8*	*199*	*–68*	*153*	*549*	*430*	*–356*	*–388*
Other sectors	4 775 . .	1,387	1,578	2,294	1,638	–549	186	551	1,228
of which: Short-term	4 777 . .	*16*	*22*	*133*	*79*	*154*	*–202*	*140*	*844*
Currency and deposits	4 780 . .	663	2,307	1,940	1,311	–676	469	40	–452
Monetary authorities	4 781 . .	1	3	–2	1	. . .	2	1	1
General government	4 782 . .	. . .	. . .	. . .	. . .	. . .	. . .	. . .	. . .
Banks	4 783 . .	662	2,304	1,942	1,310	–676	467	39	–453
Other sectors	4 784 . .	. . .	. . .	. . .	. . .	. . .	. . .	. . .	. . .
Other liabilities	4 786 . .	3,038	2,145	54	278	60	155	–111	–129
Monetary authorities	4 787 . .	. . .	. . .	. . .	. . .	. . .	. . .	. . .	. . .
of which: Short-term	4 789 . .	. . .	. . .	. . .	. . .	. . .	. . .	. . .	. . .
General government	4 790 . .	3,006	2,112	–33	–2	–7	–3	. . .	–116
of which: Short-term	4 792 . .	*3,006*	*2,112*	*–33*	*–2*	*–7*	*–3*	. . .	. . .
Banks	4 793 . .	32	33	88	197	67	158	–111	–13
of which: Short-term	4 795 . .	*32*	*33*	*88*	*197*	*67*	*158*	*–111*	*–19*
Other sectors	4 796 . .	. . .	. . .	. . .	84	. . .	. . .	. . .	. . .
of which: Short-term	4 798 . .	. . .	. . .	. . .	*84*	. . .	. . .	. . .	. . .
E. RESERVE ASSETS	4 802 . .	–2,357	–7,453	825	1,758	–1,890	–1,639	–844	–1,787
Monetary gold	4 812 . .	. . .	. . .	. . .	. . .	. . .	. . .	. . .	. . .
Special drawing rights	4 811 . .	9	. . .	. . .	. . .	. . .	. . .	. . .	–1
Reserve position in the Fund	4 810 . .	. . .	. . .	. . .	. . .	. . .	. . .	–3	–150
Foreign exchange	4 803 . .	–2,366	–7,453	825	1,758	–1,890	–1,639	–840	–1,640
Other claims	4 813 . .	. . .	. . .	. . .	. . .	. . .	. . .	. . .	3
NET ERRORS AND OMISSIONS	4 998 . .	**–210**	**596**	**–901**	**730**	**288**	**27**	**–297**	**362**

Part 3 of the *Yearbook* contains descriptions of the methodologies, compilation practices, and sources used to compile these data.

Table 3. INTERNATIONAL INVESTMENT POSITION (End–period stocks), 1994–2001
(Millions of U.S. dollars)

	Code	1994	1995	1996	1997	1998	1999	2000	2001
ASSETS	8 995 C.	20,471	29,396	30,629	29,779	36,426	37,465	38,304	42,381
Direct investment abroad	8 505 . .	**300**	**345**	**498**	**548**	**804**	**698**	**738**	**832**
Equity capital and reinvested earnings	8 506 . .	300	345	498	531	734	623	656	747
Claims on affiliated enterprises	8 507 . .	300	345	498	531	734	623	656	747
Liabilities to affiliated enterprises	8 508 . .	...	...	...	...	...	...	...	...
Other capital	8 530 . .	...	...	...	17	70	75	82	85
Claims on affiliated enterprises	8 535 . .	...	...	...	17	70	75	82	85
Liabilities to affiliated enterprises	8 540 . .	...	...	...	...	...	...	...	...
Portfolio investment	8 602 . .	**433**	**755**	**1,372**	**1,032**	**1,202**	**2,900**	**4,772**	**5,106**
Equity securities	8 610 . .	334	693	748	417	449	1,843	2,439	1,894
Monetary authorities	8 611 . .	...	...	...	...	...	...	...	...
General government	8 612 . .	...	...	...	...	...	...	...	...
Banks	8 613 . .	11	34	43	33	54	950	1,191	1,245
Other sectors	8 614 . .	323	659	705	384	395	893	1,248	649
Debt securities	8 619 . .	99	62	624	615	752	1,057	2,333	3,212
Bonds and notes	8 620 . .	99	62	624	605	724	941	2,200	2,981
Monetary authorities	8 621 . .	...	...	...	...	...	...	...	...
General government	8 622 . .	...	...	...	...	...	...	...	...
Banks	8 623 . .	99	62	624	484	665	506	1,603	1,693
Other sectors	8 624 . .	...	...	...	121	60	435	596	1,287
Money market instruments	8 630 . .	...	...	...	10	28	115	133	231
Monetary authorities	8 631 . .	...	...	...	...	...	...	...	...
General government	8 632 . .	...	...	...	...	...	106	123	111
Banks	8 633 . .	...	...	...	10	28	10	10	120
Other sectors	8 634 . .	...	...	...	...	...	...	...	...
Financial derivatives	8 900 . .	**...**	**...**	**...**	**...**	**...**	**...**	**168**	**435**
Monetary authorities	8 901 . .	...	...	...	...	...	...	...	...
General government	8 902 . .	...	...	...	...	...	...	...	...
Banks	8 903 . .	...	...	...	...	...	...	168	435
Other sectors	8 904 . .	...	...	...	...	...	...	...	...
Other investment	8 703 . .	**13,494**	**14,273**	**16,323**	**18,425**	**21,804**	**21,042**	**19,488**	**21,544**
Trade credits	8 706 . .	3,396	3,833	3,674	3,332	3,763	3,358	3,335	3,461
General government	8 707 . .	...	...	...	...	...	...	...	...
of which: Short-term	8 709 . .	...	...	...	...	...	...	...	...
Other sectors	8 710 . .	3,396	3,833	3,674	3,332	3,763	3,358	3,335	3,461
of which: Short-term	8 712 . .	*2,401*	*2,886*	*2,847*	*2,585*	*3,061*	*2,719*	*2,833*	*3,068*
Loans	8 714 . .	419	859	1,858	2,544	4,182	3,437	2,916	2,630
Monetary authorities	8 715 . .	...	...	...	...	...	...	7	7
of which: Short-term	8 718 . .	...	...	...	...	...	...	...	...
General government	8 719 . .	...	...	...	...	...	...	...	9
of which: Short-term	8 721 . .	...	...	...	...	...	...	...	...
Banks	8 722 . .	419	859	1,825	2,512	4,182	3,437	2,909	2,614
of which: Short-term	8 724 . .	*369*	*697*	*1,043*	*1,662*	*2,308*	*1,304*	*1,420*	*1,244*
Other sectors	8 725 . .	...	...	33	32	...	...	...	...
of which: Short-term	8 727 . .	...	...	*33*	*32*	...	...	...	...
Currency and deposits	8 730 . .	2,180	2,577	3,662	5,558	6,684	8,127	7,285	9,389
Monetary authorities	8 731 . .	...	...	...	...	...	...	...	...
General government	8 732 . .	...	...	...	...	...	...	...	2
Banks	8 733 . .	2,180	2,577	3,555	5,483	6,684	8,127	7,285	9,387
Other sectors	8 734 . .	...	...	107	75	...	...	...	...
Other assets	8 736 . .	7,499	7,004	7,129	6,990	7,174	6,120	5,952	6,064
Monetary authorities	8 737 . .	876	984	956	754	875	...	3	3
of which: Short-term	8 739 . .	...	...	...	...	...	...	*1*	*1*
General government	8 740 . .	6,278	5,987	5,931	5,923	5,902	5,843	5,839	5,802
of which: Short-term	8 742 . .	...	...	...	...	...	...	...	...
Banks	8 743 . .	345	33	243	313	397	277	110	115
of which: Short-term	8 745 . .	*345*	*33*	*226*	*204*	*311*	*228*	*65*	*69*
Other sectors	8 746 . .	...	...	...	...	...	...	...	143
of which: Short-term	8 748 . .	...	...	...	...	...	...	...	...
Reserve assets	8 802 . .	**6,243**	**14,023**	**12,435**	**9,774**	**12,617**	**12,825**	**13,139**	**14,465**
Monetary gold	8 812 . .	82	84	84	44	12	19	123	123
Special drawing rights	8 811 . .	...	...	...	...	...	...	...	1
Reserve position in the Fund	8 810 . .	...	...	...	...	...	...	3	151
Foreign exchange	8 803 . .	6,161	13,938	12,351	9,730	12,604	12,806	12,985	14,181
Other claims	8 813 . .	...	...	...	...	...	...	28	8

Table 3 (Concluded). INTERNATIONAL INVESTMENT POSITION (End–period stocks), 1994–2001

(Millions of U.S. dollars)

	Code	1994	1995	1996	1997	1998	1999	2000	2001
LIABILITIES	8 995 D.	18,088	27,182	33,151	32,863	40,361	40,548	43,378	49,216
Direct investment in Czech Republic	8 555 . .	**4,547**	**7,350**	**8,572**	**9,234**	**14,375**	**17,552**	**21,644**	**26,764**
Equity capital and reinvested earnings	8 556 . .	4,547	7,350	8,572	8,219	12,220	14,964	18,571	23,652
Claims on direct investors	8 557 . .	. . .	. . .	. . .	. . .	. . .	. . .	. . .	. . .
Liabilities to direct investors	8 558 . .	4,547	7,350	8,572	8,219	12,220	14,964	18,571	23,652
Other capital	8 580 . .	. . .	. . .	. . .	1,015	2,155	2,588	3,073	3,112
Claims on direct investors	8 585 . .	. . .	. . .	. . .	. . .	. . .	. . .	. . .	. . .
Liabilities to direct investors	8 590 . .	. . .	. . .	. . .	1,015	2,155	2,588	3,073	3,112
Portfolio investment	8 652 . .	**2,910**	**4,696**	**5,298**	**4,880**	**5,564**	**4,602**	**4,353**	**4,974**
Equity securities	8 660 . .	1,331	2,642	3,398	3,028	3,793	2,724	3,059	3,551
Banks	8 663 . .	28	190	358	555	861	784	1,279	1,435
Other sectors	8 664 . .	1,303	2,452	3,040	2,473	2,932	1,940	1,780	2,115
Debt securities	8 669 . .	1,579	2,055	1,900	1,853	1,771	1,878	1,294	1,423
Bonds and notes	8 670 . .	1,239	1,486	1,434	1,470	1,733	1,845	1,233	1,357
Monetary authorities	8 671 . .	754	743	326	270	304	343	. . .	. . .
General government	8 672 . .	277	303	424	397	604	566	503	589
Banks	8 673 . .	56	284	268	444	304	287	294	406
Other sectors	8 674 . .	152	156	416	359	521	649	436	362
Money market instruments	8 680 . .	340	568	466	383	38	33	61	67
Monetary authorities	8 681 . .	. . .	. . .	. . .	. . .	. . .	. . .	. . .	. . .
General government	8 682 . .	340	568	102	236	1	. . .	56	13
Banks	8 683 . .	. . .	. . .	194	35	. . .	. . .	2	54
Other sectors	8 684 . .	. . .	. . .	170	112	37	32	3	. . .
Financial derivatives	8 905 . .	. . .	. . .	. . .	. . .	. . .	. . .	**140**	**317**
Monetary authorities	8 906 . .	. . .	. . .	. . .	. . .	. . .	. . .	. . .	. . .
General government	8 907 . .	. . .	. . .	. . .	. . .	. . .	. . .	. . .	. . .
Banks	8 908 . .	. . .	. . .	. . .	. . .	. . .	. . .	140	317
Other sectors	8 909 . .	. . .	. . .	. . .	. . .	. . .	. . .	. . .	. . .
Other investment	8 753 . .	**10,631**	**15,136**	**19,280**	**18,749**	**20,422**	**18,394**	**17,242**	**17,160**
Trade credits	8 756 . .	2,601	2,757	2,113	1,997	2,536	2,293	2,390	2,094
General government	8 757 . .	. . .	. . .	. . .	. . .	. . .	. . .	. . .	. . .
of which: Short-term	8 759 . .	. . .	. . .	. . .	. . .	. . .	. . .	. . .	. . .
Other sectors	8 760 . .	2,601	2,757	2,113	1,997	2,536	2,293	2,390	2,094
of which: Short-term	8 762 . .	*1,419*	*1,784*	*1,515*	*1,427*	*1,615*	*1,387*	*1,723*	*1,470*
Loans	8 764 . .	5,409	7,907	10,601	10,188	10,996	9,803	8,836	9,498
Monetary authorities	8 765 . .	60	94	83	63	63	5	4	4
of which: Use of Fund credit and loans from the Fund	8 766 . .	. . .	. . .	. . .	. . .	. . .	. . .	. . .	. . .
of which: Short-term	8 768 . .	. . .	. . .	. . .	. . .	. . .	. . .	. . .	. . .
General government	8 769 . .	1,928	1,645	1,283	834	500	331	284	261
of which: Short-term	8 771 . .	. . .	. . .	. . .	. . .	. . .	. . .	. . .	. . .
Banks	8 772 . .	765	1,926	2,736	2,710	4,053	3,633	2,440	1,719
of which: Short-term	8 774 . .	*75*	*276*	*105*	*232*	*844*	*1,103*	*668*	*295*
Other sectors	8 775 . .	2,656	4,242	6,499	6,580	6,380	5,833	6,107	7,513
of which: Short-term	8 777 . .	*168*	*191*	*323*	*129*	*317*	*76*	*220*	*1,086*
Currency and deposits	8 780 . .	1,512	4,042	6,102	6,019	6,183	5,564	5,429	5,215
Monetary authorities	8 781 . .	1	4	2	1	1	1	. . .	2
General government	8 782 . .	. . .	. . .	. . .	. . .	. . .	. . .	. . .	. . .
Banks	8 783 . .	1,511	4,038	6,100	6,017	6,182	5,563	5,429	5,213
Other sectors	8 784 . .	. . .	. . .	. . .	. . .	. . .	. . .	. . .	. . .
Other liabilities	8 786 . .	1,108	429	464	546	706	734	587	354
Monetary authorities	8 787 . .	. . .	. . .	. . .	. . .	. . .	. . .	. . .	. . .
of which: Short-term	8 789 . .	. . .	. . .	. . .	. . .	. . .	. . .	. . .	. . .
General government	8 790 . .	982	386	336	264	301	248	237	. . .
of which: Short-term	8 792 . .	*179*	*42*	*12*	*8*	*3*	. . .	. . .	. . .
Banks	8 793 . .	126	43	128	282	405	486	350	354
of which: Short-term	8 795 . .	*126*	*43*	*128*	*282*	*405*	*486*	*350*	*347*
Other sectors	8 796 . .	. . .	. . .	. . .	. . .	. . .	. . .	. . .	. . .
of which: Short-term	8 798 . .	. . .	. . .	. . .	. . .	. . .	. . .	. . .	. . .
NET INTERNATIONAL INVESTMENT POSITION	8 995 . .	**2,383**	**2,214**	**–2,522**	**–3,085**	**–3,935**	**–3,083**	**–5,074**	**–6,835**
Conversion rates: Czech koruny per U.S. dollar (end of period)	0 102 . .	**28.049**	**26.602**	**27.332**	**34.636**	**29.855**	**35.979**	**37.813**	**36.259**

Table 1. ANALYTIC PRESENTATION, 1994–2001
(Millions of U.S. dollars)

	Code	1994	1995	1996	1997	1998	1999	2000	2001
A. Current Account [1]	4 993 Z.	**3,189**	**1,855**	**3,090**	**921**	**–2,008**	**2,915**	**2,507**	**4,142**
Goods: exports f.o.b.	2 100 . .	41,741	50,348	50,735	48,103	47,908	49,932	50,754	50,943
Goods: imports f.o.b.	3 100 . .	–34,300	–43,821	–43,203	–42,734	–44,021	–43,533	–44,001	–43,983
Balance on Goods	4 100 . .	*7,441*	*6,528*	*7,532*	*5,369*	*3,886*	*6,399*	*6,754*	*6,960*
Services: credit	2 200 . .	13,661	15,307	16,502	14,044	15,212	20,090	24,385	26,913
Services: debit	3 200 . .	–12,067	–14,040	–14,771	–13,727	–15,779	–18,517	–22,082	–23,506
Balance on Goods and Services	4 991 . .	*9,035*	*7,795*	*9,263*	*5,685*	*3,319*	*7,972*	*9,056*	*10,367*
Income: credit	2 300 . .	22,743	28,433	37,626	18,774	10,401	9,100	11,838	10,997
Income: debit	3 300 . .	–27,385	–32,982	–42,235	–22,203	–14,247	–11,426	–15,395	–14,595
Balance on Goods, Services, and Income	4 992 . .	*4,394*	*3,246*	*4,655*	*2,256*	*–527*	*5,646*	*5,499*	*6,769*
Current transfers: credit	2 379 Z.	2,261	2,580	2,398	3,633	3,443	4,156	3,303	3,629
Current transfers: debit	3 379 . .	–3,466	–3,970	–3,963	–4,968	–4,924	–6,888	–6,296	–6,256
B. Capital Account [1]	4 994 Z.	**. . .**	**. . .**	**. . .**	**128**	**50**	**1,083**	**–14**	**–25**
Capital account: credit	2 994 Z.	. . .	. . .	. . .	128	81	1,331	320	253
Capital account: debit	3 994 . .	. . .	. . .	. . .	. . .	–31	–248	–334	–278
Total, Groups A Plus B	4 981 . .	*3,189*	*1,855*	*3,090*	*1,049*	*–1,958*	*3,998*	*2,493*	*4,117*
C. Financial Account [1]	4 995 W.	**–5,647**	**–432**	**1,882**	**8,496**	**–1,489**	**6,247**	**–3,689**	**–3,837**
Direct investment abroad	4 505 . .	–4,162	–2,969	–2,510	–4,355	–4,215	–17,039	–27,672	–9,631
Direct investment in Denmark	4 555 Z.	5,006	4,139	773	2,792	6,675	16,076	35,532	7,238
Portfolio investment assets	4 602 . .	–1,175	–1,171	–2,349	–6,239	–7,563	–9,719	–23,623	–14,355
Equity securities	4 610 . .	. . .	. . .	. . .	. . .	. . .	. . .	. . .	. . .
Debt securities	4 619 . .	–1,175	–1,171	–2,349	. . .	. . .	. . .	. . .	. . .
Portfolio investment liabilities	4 652 Z.	–10,596	7,487	7,865	11,186	–2,598	7,014	5,783	11,033
Equity securities	4 660 . .	. . .	. . .	. . .	. . .	. . .	. . .	. . .	. . .
Debt securities	4 669 Z.	–10,596	7,487	7,865	. . .	. . .	. . .	. . .	. . .
Financial derivatives	4 910 . .	. . .	. . .	. . .	. . .	. . .	325	328	522
Financial derivatives assets	4 900 . .	. . .	. . .	. . .	. . .	. . .	. . .	. . .	. . .
Financial derivatives liabilities	4 905 . .	. . .	. . .	. . .	. . .	. . .	325	328	522
Other investment assets	4 703 . .	12,136	–1,330	–9,339	–8,033	–1,797	–1,188	–1,677	10,045
Monetary authorities	4 701 . .	. . .	. . .	. . .	. . .	. . .	. . .	. . .	. . .
General government	4 704 . .	. . .	. . .	. . .	. . .	. . .	. . .	. . .	. . .
Banks	4 705 . .	12,136	–1,330	–9,339	. . .	. . .	. . .	. . .	. . .
Other sectors	4 728 . .	. . .	. . .	. . .	–8,033	–1,797	. . .	. . .	. . .
Other investment liabilities	4 753 W.	–6,856	–6,589	7,442	13,145	8,009	10,778	7,641	–8,690
Monetary authorities	4 753 WA	122	133	–108	. . .	. . .	. . .	. . .	. . .
General government	4 753 ZB	–4,058	–3,380	–1,563	. . .	. . .	. . .	. . .	. . .
Banks	4 753 ZC	414	15	9,343	. . .	. . .	. . .	. . .	. . .
Other sectors	4 753 ZD	–3,333	–3,357	–231	13,145	8,009	. . .	. . .	. . .
Total, Groups A Through C	4 983 . .	*–2,458*	*1,423*	*4,972*	*9,545*	*–3,447*	*10,245*	*–1,196*	*279*
D. Net Errors and Omissions	4 998 . .	**606**	**1,075**	**–1,408**	**–3,012**	**–792**	**–808**	**–4,453**	**2,990**
Total, Groups A Through D	4 984 . .	*–1,851*	*2,498*	*3,563*	*6,532*	*–4,239*	*9,437*	*–5,649*	*3,270*
E. Reserves and Related Items	4 802 A.	**1,851**	**–2,498**	**–3,563**	**–6,532**	**4,239**	**–9,437**	**5,649**	**–3,270**
Reserve assets	4 802 . .	1,851	–2,498	–3,563	–6,532	4,239	–9,437	5,649	–3,270
Use of Fund credit and loans	4 766 . .	. . .	. . .	. . .	. . .	. . .	. . .	. . .	. . .
Exceptional financing	4 920 . .	. . .	. . .	. . .	. . .	. . .	. . .	. . .	. . .
Conversion rates: Danish kroner per U.S. dollar	0 101 . .	**6.3606**	**5.6024**	**5.7987**	**6.6045**	**6.7008**	**6.9762**	**8.0831**	**8.3228**

[1] Excludes components that have been classified in the categories of Group E.

Table 2. STANDARD PRESENTATION, 1994–2001

(Millions of U.S. dollars)

	Code	1994	1995	1996	1997	1998	1999	2000	2001
CURRENT ACCOUNT	4 993 ..	**3,189**	**1,855**	**3,090**	**921**	**–2,008**	**2,915**	**2,507**	**4,142**
A. GOODS	4 100 ..	7,441	6,528	7,532	5,369	3,886	6,399	6,754	6,960
Credit	2 100 ..	**41,741**	**50,348**	**50,735**	**48,103**	**47,908**	**49,932**	**50,754**	**50,943**
General merchandise: exports f.o.b.	2 110 ..	41,741	50,348	50,735	48,103	47,908	49,932	50,754	50,943
Goods for processing: exports f.o.b.	2 150 ..	...	...	...	...	...	...	...	...
Repairs on goods	2 160 ..	...	...	...	...	...	...	...	...
Goods procured in ports by carriers	2 170 ..	...	...	...	...	...	...	...	...
Nonmonetary gold	2 180 ..	...	...	...	...	...	...	...	...
Debit	3 100 ..	**–34,300**	**–43,821**	**–43,203**	**–42,734**	**–44,021**	**–43,533**	**–44,001**	**–43,983**
General merchandise: imports f.o.b.	3 110 ..	–34,300	–43,821	–43,203	–42,734	–44,021	–43,533	–44,001	–43,983
Goods for processing: imports f.o.b.	3 150 ..	...	...	...	...	...	...	...	...
Repairs on goods	3 160 ..	...	...	...	...	...	...	...	...
Goods procured in ports by carriers	3 170 ..	...	...	...	...	...	...	...	...
Nonmonetary gold	3 180 ..	...	...	...	...	...	...	...	...
B. SERVICES	4 200 ..	1,594	1,267	1,731	317	–567	1,573	2,303	3,407
Total credit	2 200 ..	*13,661*	*15,307*	*16,502*	*14,044*	*15,212*	*20,090*	*24,385*	*26,913*
Total debit	3 200 ..	*–12,067*	*–14,040*	*–14,771*	*–13,727*	*–15,779*	*–18,517*	*–22,082*	*–23,506*
Transportation services, credit	2 205 ..	**6,136**	**6,772**	**7,187**	**7,018**	**7,300**	**11,004**	**14,236**	**16,144**
Passenger	2 850 ..	...	...	...	...	...	...	...	...
Freight	2 851 ..	...	...	...	...	...	...	...	...
Other	2 852 ..	...	...	...	...	...	...	...	...
Sea transport, passenger	2 207 ..	...	...	...	...	...	...	...	...
Sea transport, freight	2 208 ..	...	...	...	...	...	...	...	...
Sea transport, other	2 209 ..	...	...	...	...	...	...	...	...
Air transport, passenger	2 211 ..	...	...	...	...	...	...	...	...
Air transport, freight	2 212 ..	...	...	...	...	...	...	...	...
Air transport, other	2 213 ..	...	...	...	...	...	...	...	...
Other transport, passenger	2 215 ..	...	...	...	...	...	...	...	...
Other transport, freight	2 216 ..	...	...	...	...	...	...	...	...
Other transport, other	2 217 ..	...	...	...	...	...	...	...	...
Transportation services, debit	3 205 ..	**–5,553**	**–6,293**	**–6,582**	**–6,876**	**–7,024**	**–8,636**	**–11,162**	**–12,270**
Passenger	3 850 ..	...	...	...	...	...	...	...	...
Freight	3 851 ..	...	...	...	...	...	...	...	...
Other	3 852 ..	...	...	...	...	...	...	...	...
Sea transport, passenger	3 207 ..	...	...	...	...	...	...	...	...
Sea transport, freight	3 208 ..	...	...	...	...	...	...	...	...
Sea transport, other	3 209 ..	...	...	...	...	...	...	...	...
Air transport, passenger	3 211 ..	...	...	...	...	...	...	...	...
Air transport, freight	3 212 ..	...	...	...	...	...	...	...	...
Air transport, other	3 213 ..	...	...	...	...	...	...	...	...
Other transport, passenger	3 215 ..	...	...	...	...	...	...	...	...
Other transport, freight	3 216 ..	...	...	...	...	...	...	...	...
Other transport, other	3 217 ..	...	...	...	...	...	...	...	...
Travel, credit	2 236 ..	**3,302**	**3,691**	**3,420**	**3,156**	**3,236**	**3,698**	**4,056**	**4,624**
Business travel	2 237 ..	...	...	...	...	...	...	...	...
Personal travel	2 240 ..	...	...	...	...	...	...	...	...
Travel, debit	3 236 ..	**–3,597**	**–4,288**	**–4,140**	**–4,194**	**–4,577**	**–4,899**	**–5,099**	**–5,534**
Business travel	3 237 ..	...	...	...	...	...	...	...	...
Personal travel	3 240 ..	...	...	...	...	...	...	...	...
Other services, credit	2 200 BA	**4,223**	**4,843**	**5,895**	**3,869**	**4,676**	**5,388**	**6,093**	**6,146**
Communications	2 245 ..	...	...	...	...	...	...	...	...
Construction	2 249 ..	...	...	...	...	...	...	...	...
Insurance	2 253 ..	...	...	...	...	...	...	...	...
Financial	2 260 ..	...	...	...	...	...	...	...	...
Computer and information	2 262 ..	...	...	...	...	...	...	...	...
Royalties and licence fees	2 266 ..	...	...	...	...	...	...	...	...
Other business services	2 268 ..	4,140	4,707	5,734	3,869	4,676	5,388	6,093	6,146
Personal, cultural, and recreational	2 287 ..	...	...	...	...	...	...	...	...
Government, n.i.e.	2 291 ..	83	136	161	...	...	...	...	...
Other services, debit	3 200 BA	**–2,917**	**–3,459**	**–4,049**	**–2,657**	**–4,178**	**–4,981**	**–5,820**	**–5,702**
Communications	3 245 ..	...	...	...	...	...	...	...	...
Construction	3 249 ..	...	...	...	...	...	...	...	...
Insurance	3 253 ..	...	...	...	...	...	...	...	...
Financial	3 260 ..	...	...	...	...	...	...	...	...
Computer and information	3 262 ..	...	...	...	...	...	...	...	...
Royalties and licence fees	3 266 ..	...	...	...	...	...	...	...	...
Other business services	3 268 ..	–2,847	–3,364	–3,920	–2,657	–4,178	–4,981	–5,820	–5,702
Personal, cultural, and recreational	3 287 ..	...	...	...	...	...	...	...	...
Government, n.i.e.	3 291 ..	–70	–95	–129	...	...	...	...	...

Table 2 (Continued). STANDARD PRESENTATION, 1994–2001
(Millions of U.S. dollars)

	Code	1994	1995	1996	1997	1998	1999	2000	2001
C. INCOME	4 300 . .	–4,642	–4,549	–4,609	–3,429	–3,846	–2,326	–3,557	–3,598
Total credit	2 300 . .	*22,743*	*28,433*	*37,626*	*18,774*	*10,401*	*9,100*	*11,838*	*10,997*
Total debit	3 300 . .	*–27,385*	*–32,982*	*–42,235*	*–22,203*	*–14,247*	*–11,426*	*–15,395*	*–14,595*
Compensation of employees, credit	2 310 . .	**439**	**523**	**. . .**	**852**	**765**	**803**	**682**	**742**
Compensation of employees, debit	3 310 . .	**–200**	**–209**	**. . .**	**–370**	**–346**	**–694**	**–662**	**–744**
Investment income, credit	2 320 . .	**22,304**	**27,910**	**37,626**	**17,922**	**9,636**	**8,297**	**11,156**	**10,255**
Direct investment income	2 330 . .	. . .	. . .	. . .	. . .	. . .	. . .	. . .	. . .
Dividends and distributed branch profits	2 332 . .	. . .	. . .	. . .	. . .	. . .	. . .	. . .	. . .
Reinvested earnings and undistributed branch profits	2 333 . .	. . .	. . .	. . .	. . .	. . .	. . .	. . .	. . .
Income on debt (interest)	2 334 . .	. . .	. . .	. . .	. . .	. . .	. . .	. . .	. . .
Portfolio investment income	2 339 . .	. . .	. . .	. . .	. . .	. . .	. . .	. . .	. . .
Income on equity	2 340 . .	. . .	. . .	. . .	. . .	. . .	. . .	. . .	. . .
Income on bonds and notes	2 350 . .	. . .	. . .	. . .	. . .	. . .	. . .	. . .	. . .
Income on money market instruments	2 360 . .	. . .	. . .	. . .	. . .	. . .	. . .	. . .	. . .
Other investment income	2 370 . .	22,304	27,910	37,626	17,922	9,636	. . .	. . .	. . .
Investment income, debit	3 320 . .	**–27,185**	**–32,773**	**–42,235**	**–21,833**	**–13,901**	**–10,732**	**–14,733**	**–13,851**
Direct investment income	3 330 . .	. . .	. . .	. . .	. . .	. . .	. . .	. . .	. . .
Dividends and distributed branch profits	3 332 . .	. . .	. . .	. . .	. . .	. . .	. . .	. . .	. . .
Reinvested earnings and undistributed branch profits	3 333 . .	. . .	. . .	. . .	. . .	. . .	. . .	. . .	. . .
Income on debt (interest)	3 334 . .	. . .	. . .	. . .	. . .	. . .	. . .	. . .	. . .
Portfolio investment income	3 339 . .	. . .	. . .	. . .	. . .	. . .	. . .	. . .	. . .
Income on equity	3 340 . .	. . .	. . .	. . .	. . .	. . .	. . .	. . .	. . .
Income on bonds and notes	3 350 . .	. . .	. . .	. . .	. . .	. . .	. . .	. . .	. . .
Income on money market instruments	3 360 . .	. . .	. . .	. . .	. . .	. . .	. . .	. . .	. . .
Other investment income	3 370 . .	–27,185	–32,773	–42,235	–21,833	–13,901	. . .	. . .	. . .
D. CURRENT TRANSFERS	4 379 . .	–1,204	–1,391	–1,565	–1,335	–1,481	–2,731	–2,992	–2,627
Credit	2 379 . .	**2,261**	**2,580**	**2,398**	**3,633**	**3,443**	**4,156**	**3,303**	**3,629**
General government	2 380 . .	1,914	2,180	1,981	. . .	. . .	469	392	572
Other sectors	2 390 . .	348	399	417	. . .	. . .	3,687	2,911	3,057
Workers' remittances	2 391 . .	. . .	. . .	. . .	. . .	. . .	. . .	. . .	. . .
Other current transfers	2 392 . .	348	399	417	. . .	. . .	. . .	. . .	. . .
Debit	3 379 . .	**–3,466**	**–3,970**	**–3,963**	**–4,968**	**–4,924**	**–6,888**	**–6,296**	**–6,256**
General government	3 380 . .	–3,025	–3,479	–3,434	. . .	. . .	–3,950	–3,544	–3,623
Other sectors	3 390 . .	–441	–491	–530	. . .	. . .	–2,938	–2,752	–2,633
Workers' remittances	3 391 . .	. . .	. . .	. . .	. . .	. . .	. . .	. . .	. . .
Other current transfers	3 392 . .	–441	–491	–530	. . .	. . .	. . .	. . .	. . .
CAPITAL AND FINANCIAL ACCOUNT	4 996 . .	**–3,796**	**–2,929**	**–1,681**	**2,091**	**2,800**	**–2,107**	**1,947**	**–7,132**
CAPITAL ACCOUNT	4 994 . .	**. . .**	**. . .**	**. . .**	**128**	**50**	**1,083**	**–14**	**–25**
Total credit	2 994 . .	. . .	. . .	. . .	*128*	*81*	*1,331*	*320*	*253*
Total debit	3 994 . .	. . .	. . .	. . .	. . .	*–31*	*–248*	*–334*	*–278*
Capital transfers, credit	2 400 . .	**. . .**	**. . .**	**. . .**	**128**	**81**	**1,331**	**320**	**253**
General government	2 401 . .	. . .	. . .	. . .	. . .	. . .	. . .	. . .	. . .
Debt forgiveness	2 402 . .	. . .	. . .	. . .	. . .	. . .	. . .	. . .	. . .
Other capital transfers	2 410 . .	. . .	. . .	. . .	. . .	. . .	. . .	. . .	. . .
Other sectors	2 430 . .	. . .	. . .	. . .	. . .	. . .	. . .	. . .	. . .
Migrants' transfers	2 431 . .	. . .	. . .	. . .	. . .	. . .	. . .	. . .	. . .
Debt forgiveness	2 432 . .	. . .	. . .	. . .	. . .	. . .	. . .	. . .	. . .
Other capital transfers	2 440 . .	. . .	. . .	. . .	. . .	. . .	. . .	. . .	. . .
Capital transfers, debit	3 400 . .	**. . .**	**. . .**	**. . .**	**. . .**	**–31**	**–248**	**–334**	**–278**
General government	3 401 . .	. . .	. . .	. . .	. . .	. . .	. . .	. . .	. . .
Debt forgiveness	3 402 . .	. . .	. . .	. . .	. . .	. . .	. . .	. . .	. . .
Other capital transfers	3 410 . .	. . .	. . .	. . .	. . .	. . .	. . .	. . .	. . .
Other sectors	3 430 . .	. . .	. . .	. . .	. . .	. . .	. . .	. . .	. . .
Migrants' transfers	3 431 . .	. . .	. . .	. . .	. . .	. . .	. . .	. . .	. . .
Debt forgiveness	3 432 . .	. . .	. . .	. . .	. . .	. . .	. . .	. . .	. . .
Other capital transfers	3 440 . .	. . .	. . .	. . .	. . .	. . .	. . .	. . .	. . .
Nonproduced nonfinancial assets, credit	2 480 . .	**. . .**	**. . .**	**. . .**	**. . .**	**. . .**	**. . .**	**. . .**	**. . .**
Nonproduced nonfinancial assets, debit	3 480 . .	**. . .**	**. . .**	**. . .**	**. . .**	**. . .**	**. . .**	**. . .**	**. . .**

Table 2 (Continued). STANDARD PRESENTATION, 1994–2001

(Millions of U.S. dollars)

	Code	1994	1995	1996	1997	1998	1999	2000	2001
FINANCIAL ACCOUNT	4 995 . .	**–3,796**	**–2,929**	**–1,681**	**1,963**	**2,750**	**–3,190**	**1,961**	**–7,107**
A. DIRECT INVESTMENT	4 500 . .	844	1,171	–1,737	–1,563	2,460	–962	7,860	–2,393
Direct investment abroad	4 505 . .	**–4,162**	**–2,969**	**–2,510**	**–4,355**	**–4,215**	**–17,039**	**–27,672**	**–9,631**
Equity capital	4 510 . .	–4,162	–2,969	–2,510	–4,355	–4,215	–17,039	–27,672	–9,631
Claims on affiliated enterprises	4 515 . .	...	...	...	...	...	...	...	...
Liabilities to affiliated enterprises	4 520 . .	...	...	...	...	...	...	...	...
Reinvested earnings	4 525 . .	...	...	...	...	...	...	...	...
Other capital	4 530 . .	...	...	...	...	...	...	...	...
Claims on affiliated enterprises	4 535 . .	...	...	...	...	...	...	...	...
Liabilities to affiliated enterprises	4 540 . .	...	...	...	...	...	...	...	...
Direct investment in Denmark	4 555 . .	**5,006**	**4,139**	**773**	**2,792**	**6,675**	**16,076**	**35,532**	**7,238**
Equity capital	4 560 . .	5,006	4,139	773	2,792	6,675	16,076	35,532	7,238
Claims on direct investors	4 565 . .	...	...	...	...	...	...	...	...
Liabilities to direct investors	4 570 . .	...	...	...	...	...	...	...	...
Reinvested earnings	4 575 . .	...	...	...	...	...	...	...	...
Other capital	4 580 . .	...	...	...	...	...	...	...	...
Claims on direct investors	4 585 . .	...	...	...	...	...	...	...	...
Liabilities to direct investors	4 590 . .	...	...	...	...	...	...	...	...
B. PORTFOLIO INVESTMENT	4 600 . .	–11,771	6,316	5,516	4,946	–10,161	–2,706	–17,840	–3,322
Assets	4 602 . .	**–1,175**	**–1,171**	**–2,349**	**–6,239**	**–7,563**	**–9,719**	**–23,623**	**–14,355**
Equity securities	4 610 . .	...	...	...	...	...	...	...	...
Monetary authorities	4 611 . .	...	...	...	...	...	...	...	...
General government	4 612 . .	...	...	...	...	...	...	...	...
Banks	4 613 . .	...	...	...	...	...	...	...	...
Other sectors	4 614 . .	...	...	...	...	...	...	...	...
Debt securities	4 619 . .	–1,175	–1,171	–2,349	...	...	...	...	...
Bonds and notes	4 620 . .	–1,175	–1,171	–2,349	...	...	...	...	...
Monetary authorities	4 621 . .	...	...	...	...	...	...	...	...
General government	4 622 . .	...	...	...	...	...	...	...	...
Banks	4 623 . .	...	...	...	...	...	...	...	...
Other sectors	4 624 . .	...	...	...	...	...	...	...	...
Money market instruments	4 630 . .	...	...	...	...	...	...	...	...
Monetary authorities	4 631 . .	...	...	...	...	...	...	...	...
General government	4 632 . .	...	...	...	...	...	...	...	...
Banks	4 633 . .	...	...	...	...	...	...	...	...
Other sectors	4 634 . .	...	...	...	...	...	...	...	...
Liabilities	4 652 . .	**–10,596**	**7,487**	**7,865**	**11,186**	**–2,598**	**7,014**	**5,783**	**11,033**
Equity securities	4 660 . .	...	...	...	...	...	...	...	...
Banks	4 663 . .	...	...	...	...	...	...	...	...
Other sectors	4 664 . .	...	...	...	...	...	...	...	...
Debt securities	4 669 . .	–10,596	7,487	7,865	...	...	...	...	...
Bonds and notes	4 670 . .	–10,596	7,487	7,865	...	...	...	...	...
Monetary authorities	4 671 . .	...	...	...	...	...	...	...	...
General government	4 672 . .	–10,596	7,487	7,865	...	...	...	...	...
Banks	4 673 . .	...	...	...	...	...	...	...	...
Other sectors	4 674 . .	...	...	...	...	...	...	...	...
Money market instruments	4 680 . .	...	...	...	...	...	...	...	...
Monetary authorities	4 681 . .	...	...	...	...	...	...	...	...
General government	4 682 . .	...	...	...	...	...	...	...	...
Banks	4 683 . .	...	...	...	...	...	...	...	...
Other sectors	4 684 . .	...	...	...	...	...	...	...	...
C. FINANCIAL DERIVATIVES	4 910 . .	...	...	...	...	...	325	328	522
Monetary authorities	4 911 . .	...	...	...	...	...	...	...	...
General government	4 912 . .	...	...	...	...	...	...	...	...
Banks	4 913 . .	...	...	...	...	...	...	...	...
Other sectors	4 914 . .	...	...	...	...	...	...	...	...
Assets	4 900 . .	**...**	**...**	**...**	**...**	**...**	**...**	**...**	**...**
Monetary authorities	4 901 . .	...	...	...	...	...	...	...	...
General government	4 902 . .	...	...	...	...	...	...	...	...
Banks	4 903 . .	...	...	...	...	...	...	...	...
Other sectors	4 904 . .	...	...	...	...	...	...	...	...
Liabilities	4 905 . .	**...**	**...**	**...**	**...**	**...**	**325**	**328**	**522**
Monetary authorities	4 906 . .	...	...	...	...	...	...	...	...
General government	4 907 . .	...	...	...	...	...	...	...	...
Banks	4 908 . .	...	...	...	...	...	...	...	...
Other sectors	4 909 . .	...	...	...	...	...	...	...	...

Table 2 (Concluded). STANDARD PRESENTATION, 1994–2001
(Millions of U.S. dollars)

	Code	1994	1995	1996	1997	1998	1999	2000	2001
D. OTHER INVESTMENT	4 700 . .	5,280	−7,918	−1,897	5,112	6,212	9,590	5,964	1,355
Assets	4 703 . .	**12,136**	**−1,330**	**−9,339**	**−8,033**	**−1,797**	**−1,188**	**−1,677**	**10,045**
Trade credits	4 706 . .	. . .	. . .	. . .	. . .	. . .	. . .	. . .	. . .
General government	4 707 . .	. . .	. . .	. . .	. . .	. . .	. . .	. . .	. . .
of which: Short-term	4 709 . .	. . .	. . .	. . .	. . .	. . .	. . .	. . .	. . .
Other sectors	4 710 . .	. . .	. . .	. . .	. . .	. . .	. . .	. . .	. . .
of which: Short-term	4 712 . .	. . .	. . .	. . .	. . .	. . .	. . .	. . .	. . .
Loans	4 714 . .	. . .	. . .	. . .	. . .	. . .	. . .	. . .	. . .
Monetary authorities	4 715 . .	. . .	. . .	. . .	. . .	. . .	. . .	. . .	. . .
of which: Short-term	4 718 . .	. . .	. . .	. . .	. . .	. . .	. . .	. . .	. . .
General government	4 719 . .	. . .	. . .	. . .	. . .	. . .	. . .	. . .	. . .
of which: Short-term	4 721 . .	. . .	. . .	. . .	. . .	. . .	. . .	. . .	. . .
Banks	4 722 . .	. . .	. . .	. . .	. . .	. . .	. . .	. . .	. . .
of which: Short-term	4 724 . .	. . .	. . .	. . .	. . .	. . .	. . .	. . .	. . .
Other sectors	4 725 . .	. . .	. . .	. . .	. . .	. . .	. . .	. . .	. . .
of which: Short-term	4 727 . .	. . .	. . .	. . .	. . .	. . .	. . .	. . .	. . .
Currency and deposits	4 730 . .	12,136	−1,330	−9,339	. . .	. . .	. . .	. . .	. . .
Monetary authorities	4 731 . .	. . .	. . .	. . .	. . .	. . .	. . .	. . .	. . .
General government	4 732 . .	. . .	. . .	. . .	. . .	. . .	. . .	. . .	. . .
Banks	4 733 . .	12,136	−1,330	−9,339	. . .	. . .	. . .	. . .	. . .
Other sectors	4 734 . .	. . .	. . .	. . .	. . .	. . .	. . .	. . .	. . .
Other assets	4 736 . .	. . .	. . .	. . .	−8,033	−1,797	. . .	. . .	. . .
Monetary authorities	4 737 . .	. . .	. . .	. . .	. . .	. . .	. . .	. . .	. . .
of which: Short-term	4 739 . .	. . .	. . .	. . .	. . .	. . .	. . .	. . .	. . .
General government	4 740 . .	. . .	. . .	. . .	. . .	. . .	. . .	. . .	. . .
of which: Short-term	4 742 . .	. . .	. . .	. . .	. . .	. . .	. . .	. . .	. . .
Banks	4 743 . .	. . .	. . .	. . .	. . .	. . .	. . .	. . .	. . .
of which: Short-term	4 745 . .	. . .	. . .	. . .	. . .	. . .	. . .	. . .	. . .
Other sectors	4 746 . .	. . .	. . .	. . .	−8,033	−1,797	. . .	. . .	. . .
of which: Short-term	4 748 . .	. . .	. . .	. . .	. . .	. . .	. . .	. . .	. . .
Liabilities	4 753 . .	**−6,856**	**−6,589**	**7,442**	**13,145**	**8,009**	**10,778**	**7,641**	**−8,690**
Trade credits	4 756 . .	. . .	. . .	. . .	. . .	. . .	. . .	. . .	. . .
General government	4 757 . .	. . .	. . .	. . .	. . .	. . .	. . .	. . .	. . .
of which: Short-term	4 759 . .	. . .	. . .	. . .	. . .	. . .	. . .	. . .	. . .
Other sectors	4 760 . .	. . .	. . .	. . .	. . .	. . .	. . .	. . .	. . .
of which: Short-term	4 762 . .	. . .	. . .	. . .	. . .	. . .	. . .	. . .	. . .
Loans	4 764 . .	−7,590	−6,667	−1,230	. . .	. . .	. . .	. . .	. . .
Monetary authorities	4 765 . .	. . .	. . .	. . .	. . .	. . .	. . .	. . .	. . .
of which: Use of Fund credit and loans from the Fund	4 766 . .	. . .	. . .	. . .	. . .	. . .	. . .	. . .	. . .
of which: Short-term	4 768 . .	. . .	. . .	. . .	. . .	. . .	. . .	. . .	. . .
General government	4 769 . .	−4,257	−3,310	−999	. . .	. . .	. . .	. . .	. . .
of which: Short-term	4 771 . .	. . .	. . .	. . .	. . .	. . .	. . .	. . .	. . .
Banks	4 772 . .	. . .	. . .	. . .	. . .	. . .	. . .	. . .	. . .
of which: Short-term	4 774 . .	. . .	. . .	. . .	. . .	. . .	. . .	. . .	. . .
Other sectors	4 775 . .	−3,333	−3,357	−231	. . .	. . .	. . .	. . .	. . .
of which: Short-term	4 777 . .	. . .	. . .	. . .	. . .	. . .	. . .	. . .	. . .
Currency and deposits	4 780 . .	536	148	9,235	. . .	. . .	. . .	. . .	. . .
Monetary authorities	4 781 . .	122	133	−108	. . .	. . .	. . .	. . .	. . .
General government	4 782 . .	. . .	. . .	. . .	. . .	. . .	. . .	. . .	. . .
Banks	4 783 . .	414	15	9,343	. . .	. . .	. . .	. . .	. . .
Other sectors	4 784 . .	. . .	. . .	. . .	. . .	. . .	. . .	. . .	. . .
Other liabilities	4 786 . .	198	−70	−564	13,145	8,009	. . .	. . .	. . .
Monetary authorities	4 787 . .	. . .	. . .	. . .	. . .	. . .	. . .	. . .	. . .
of which: Short-term	4 789 . .	. . .	. . .	. . .	. . .	. . .	. . .	. . .	. . .
General government	4 790 . .	198	−70	−564	. . .	. . .	. . .	. . .	. . .
of which: Short-term	4 792 . .	. . .	. . .	. . .	. . .	. . .	. . .	. . .	. . .
Banks	4 793 . .	. . .	. . .	. . .	. . .	. . .	. . .	. . .	. . .
of which: Short-term	4 795 . .	. . .	. . .	. . .	. . .	. . .	. . .	. . .	. . .
Other sectors	4 796 . .	. . .	. . .	. . .	13,145	8,009	. . .	. . .	. . .
of which: Short-term	4 798 . .	. . .	. . .	. . .	. . .	. . .	. . .	. . .	. . .
E. RESERVE ASSETS	4 802 . .	1,851	−2,498	−3,563	−6,532	4,239	−9,437	5,649	−3,270
Monetary gold	4 812 . .	9	−30	4	−10	−155	. . .	. . .	. . .
Special drawing rights	4 811 . .	−90	30	−15	−181	1	−7	262	−221
Reserve position in the Fund	4 810 . .	21	−157	−32	−61	−482	334	187	−160
Foreign exchange	4 803 . .	1,911	−2,341	−3,522	−6,280	4,875	−9,765	5,200	−2,889
Other claims	4 813 . .	. . .	. . .	. . .	. . .	. . .	. . .	. . .	. . .
NET ERRORS AND OMISSIONS	4 998 . .	**606**	**1,075**	**−1,408**	**−3,012**	**−792**	**−808**	**−4,453**	**2,990**

Part 3 of the *Yearbook* contains descriptions of the methodologies, compilation practices, and sources used to compile these data.

Table 3. INTERNATIONAL INVESTMENT POSITION (End–period stocks), 1994–2001
(Millions of U.S. dollars)

	Code	1994	1995	1996	1997	1998	1999	2000	2001
ASSETS	8 995 C.	109,111	123,004	145,614	156,402	187,516	213,446	224,140	. . .
Direct investment abroad	8 505 . .	**19,892**	**24,702**	**27,589**	**28,128**	**34,664**	**38,374**	**43,011**	**. . .**
Equity capital and reinvested earnings	8 506 . .	16,110	20,195	21,869	21,682	28,728	31,749	32,810	. . .
Claims on affiliated enterprises	8 507 . .	16,110	20,195	21,869	21,682	. . .	. . .	. . .	. . .
Liabilities to affiliated enterprises	8 508 . .	. . .	. . .	. . .	. . .	. . .	. . .	. . .	. . .
Other capital	8 530 . .	3,781	4,508	5,720	6,446	5,936	6,625	10,201	. . .
Claims on affiliated enterprises	8 535 . .	5,918	7,212	7,906	8,936	8,036	9,081	12,466	. . .
Liabilities to affiliated enterprises	8 540 . .	–2,137	–2,705	–2,187	–2,490	–2,099	–2,456	–2,265	. . .
Portfolio investment	8 602 . .	**17,261**	**22,899**	**29,944**	**37,064**	**51,792**	**70,982**	**84,322**	**. . .**
Equity securities	8 610 . .	8,877	10,819	16,149	22,414	32,623	50,353	55,187	. . .
Monetary authorities	8 611 . .	. . .	. . .	. . .	. . .	. . .	. . .	. . .	. . .
General government	8 612 . .	658	1,082	2,019	2,783	3,755	4,913	5,394	. . .
Banks	8 613 . .	822	902	1,346	1,758	2,175	3,071	2,879	. . .
Other sectors	8 614 . .	7,398	8,835	12,785	17,873	26,693	42,368	46,914	. . .
Debt securities	8 619 . .	8,384	12,081	13,794	14,650	19,169	20,629	29,135	. . .
Bonds and notes	8 620 . .	7,562	10,097	12,617	13,917	17,811	19,423	28,811	. . .
Monetary authorities	8 621 . .	. . .	. . .	. . .	. . .	. . .	. . .	. . .	. . .
General government	8 622 . .	329	541	505	439	802	1,241	3,295	. . .
Banks	8 623 . .	2,466	4,147	5,720	7,471	8,791	8,805	11,316	. . .
Other sectors	8 624 . .	4,767	5,409	6,392	6,006	8,218	9,376	14,200	. . .
Money market instruments	8 630 . .	822	1,983	1,178	732	1,358	1,206	324	. . .
Monetary authorities	8 631 . .	. . .	. . .	. . .	. . .	. . .	. . .	. . .	. . .
General government	8 632 . .	. . .	. . .	. . .	. . .	. . .	. . .	. . .	. . .
Banks	8 633 . .	493	1,623	673	293	813	904	236	. . .
Other sectors	8 634 . .	329	361	505	439	545	302	88	. . .
Financial derivatives	8 900 . .	**. . .**	**. . .**	**. . .**	**. . .**	**2,502**	**9,231**	**12,716**	**. . .**
Monetary authorities	8 901 . .	. . .	. . .	. . .	. . .	. . .	. . .	. . .	. . .
General government	8 902 . .	. . .	. . .	. . .	. . .	110	112	104	. . .
Banks	8 903 . .	. . .	. . .	. . .	. . .	925	7,932	11,518	. . .
Other sectors	8 904 . .	. . .	. . .	. . .	. . .	1,467	1,186	1,094	. . .
Other investment	8 703 . .	**62,798**	**63,469**	**73,513**	**71,931**	**82,423**	**72,189**	**69,047**	**. . .**
Trade credits	8 706 . .	6,247	5,409	7,906	6,885	6,924	6,578	6,068	. . .
General government	8 707 . .	493	361	168	146	14	522	481	. . .
of which: Short-term	8 709 . .	. . .	. . .	. . .	. . .	. . .	. . .	. . .	. . .
Other sectors	8 710 . .	5,754	5,049	7,738	6,739	6,910	6,056	5,586	. . .
of which: Short-term	8 712 . .	. . .	. . .	. . .	. . .	. . .	. . .	. . .	. . .
Loans	8 714 . .	12,329	12,081	14,635	16,701	14,000	16,458	17,153	. . .
Monetary authorities	8 715 . .	. . .	. . .	. . .	. . .	. . .	. . .	. . .	. . .
of which: Short-term	8 718 . .	. . .	. . .	. . .	. . .	. . .	. . .	. . .	. . .
General government	8 719 . .	. . .	. . .	. . .	. . .	162	93	60	. . .
of which: Short-term	8 721 . .	. . .	. . .	. . .	. . .	. . .	. . .	. . .	. . .
Banks	8 722 . .	12,329	12,081	14,635	16,701	11,499	12,673	13,050	. . .
of which: Short-term	8 724 . .	. . .	. . .	. . .	. . .	. . .	. . .	. . .	. . .
Other sectors	8 725 . .	. . .	. . .	. . .	. . .	2,339	3,692	4,042	. . .
of which: Short-term	8 727 . .	. . .	. . .	. . .	. . .	. . .	. . .	. . .	. . .
Currency and deposits	8 730 . .	36,166	39,308	43,065	41,313	53,028	42,453	38,529	. . .
Monetary authorities	8 731 . .	. . .	. . .	. . .	. . .	. . .	. . .	. . .	. . .
General government	8 732 . .	. . .	. . .	. . .	. . .	. . .	. . .	. . .	. . .
Banks	8 733 . .	33,700	37,324	40,373	39,262	53,028	42,453	38,529	. . .
Other sectors	8 734 . .	2,466	1,983	2,692	2,051	. . .	. . .	. . .	. . .
Other assets	8 736 . .	8,055	6,671	7,906	7,032	8,471	6,700	7,297	. . .
Monetary authorities	8 737 . .	. . .	. . .	. . .	. . .	. . .	. . .	. . .	. . .
of which: Short-term	8 739 . .	. . .	. . .	. . .	. . .	. . .	. . .	. . .	. . .
General government	8 740 . .	2,301	2,164	2,019	1,904	2,348	2,007	2,406	. . .
of which: Short-term	8 742 . .	. . .	. . .	. . .	. . .	. . .	. . .	. . .	. . .
Banks	8 743 . .	329	361	168	293	7	5	. . .	. . .
of which: Short-term	8 745 . .	. . .	. . .	. . .	. . .	. . .	. . .	. . .	. . .
Other sectors	8 746 . .	5,425	4,147	5,720	4,834	6,116	4,688	4,891	. . .
of which: Short-term	8 748 . .	. . .	. . .	. . .	. . .	. . .	. . .	. . .	. . .
Reserve assets	8 802 . .	**9,160**	**11,933**	**14,569**	**19,279**	**16,136**	**22,670**	**15,044**	**. . .**
Monetary gold	8 812 . .	658	721	673	439	611	617	584	. . .
Special drawing rights	8 811 . .	182	159	168	336	346	343	66	281
Reserve position in the Fund	8 810 . .	430	595	607	631	1,165	799	573	712
Foreign exchange	8 803 . .	7,891	10,458	13,121	17,873	12,448	20,911	13,821	. . .
Other claims	8 813 . .	. . .	. . .	. . .	. . .	1,566	. . .	. . .	. . .

Table 3 (Continued). INTERNATIONAL INVESTMENT POSITION (End–period stocks), 1994–2001

(Millions of U.S. dollars)

	Code	1994	1995	1996	1997	1998	1999	2000	2001
LIABILITIES	8 995 D.	151,734	170,934	187,737	197,480	235,320	237,097	251,462	...
Direct investment in Denmark	8 555 . .	**18,083**	**23,801**	**22,205**	**22,268**	**31,055**	**36,595**	**47,137**	**...**
Equity capital and reinvested earnings	8 556 . .	13,480	17,670	15,308	14,503	23,244	29,059	37,554	...
Claims on direct investors	8 557 . .	...	...	...	...	...	...	...	...
Liabilities to direct investors	8 558 . .	13,480	17,670	15,308	14,503	...	...	...	...
Other capital	8 580 . .	4,603	6,131	6,897	7,764	7,811	7,536	9,583	...
Claims on direct investors	8 585 . .	–3,452	–3,606	–2,187	–1,318	–2,509	–3,008	–2,774	...
Liabilities to direct investors	8 590 . .	8,055	9,737	9,084	9,083	10,320	10,544	12,357	...
Portfolio investment	8 652 . .	**72,826**	**88,713**	**101,607**	**106,505**	**117,215**	**104,705**	**103,580**	**...**
Equity securities	8 660 . .	6,740	8,294	12,448	20,363	20,556	20,702	26,170	...
Banks	8 663 . .	1,480	1,623	3,196	8,350	9,147	3,708	3,865	...
Other sectors	8 664 . .	5,261	6,671	9,252	12,013	11,409	16,994	22,305	...
Debt securities	8 669 . .	66,086	80,418	89,158	86,141	96,658	84,002	77,409	...
Bonds and notes	8 670 . .	63,949	77,894	86,130	84,237	91,824	79,546	72,221	...
Monetary authorities	8 671 . .	...	...	...	...	...	...	...	...
General government	8 672 . .	47,674	59,863	61,065	59,039	57,708	45,345	37,829	...
Banks	8 673 . .	2,466	2,705	4,878	6,592	5,110	6,405	6,526	...
Other sectors	8 674 . .	13,809	15,326	20,187	18,605	29,006	27,795	27,866	...
Money market instruments	8 680 . .	2,137	2,524	3,028	1,904	4,835	4,456	5,189	...
Monetary authorities	8 681 . .	...	...	...	...	...	...	...	...
General government	8 682 . .	1,480	721	2,187	586	962	733	1,135	...
Banks	8 683 . .	493	1,623	505	1,025	2,530	3,294	3,711	...
Other sectors	8 684 . .	164	180	336	293	1,342	429	343	...
Financial derivatives	8 905 . .	**...**	**...**	**...**	**...**	**2,159**	**8,871**	**12,393**	**...**
Monetary authorities	8 906 . .	...	...	...	...	...	...	...	...
General government	8 907 . .	...	...	...	...	26	41	38	...
Banks	8 908 . .	...	...	...	...	1,022	8,144	11,723	...
Other sectors	8 909 . .	...	...	...	...	1,111	686	633	...
Other investment	8 753 . .	**60,825**	**58,420**	**63,925**	**68,708**	**84,891**	**86,926**	**88,352**	**...**
Trade credits	8 756 . .	2,959	3,787	5,383	4,541	3,293	3,229	2,979	...
General government	8 758 . .	...	...	...	...	...	...	...	...
of which: Short-term	8 759 . .	...	...	...	...	...	...	...	...
Other sectors	8 760 . .	2,959	3,787	5,383	4,541	3,293	3,229	2,979	...
of which: Short-term	8 762 . .	...	...	...	...	...	...	...	...
Loans	8 764 . .	32,714	30,653	28,934	29,446	67,133	72,038	76,506	...
Monetary authorities	8 765 . .	...	...	...	...	204	328	392	...
of which: Use of Fund credit and loans from the Fund	8 766 . .	...	...	...	...	...	...	...	...
of which: Short-term	8 768 . .	...	...	...	...	...	...	...	...
General government	8 769 . .	2,630	1,623	841	586	548	871	479	...
of which: Short-term	8 771 . .	...	...	...	...	...	...	...	...
Banks	8 772 . .	7,069	8,294	8,075	9,229	44,189	43,568	55,067	...
of which: Short-term	8 774 . .	...	...	...	...	...	...	...	...
Other sectors	8 775 . .	23,015	20,736	20,019	19,631	22,192	27,271	20,567	...
of which: Short-term	8 777 . .	...	...	...	...	...	...	...	...
Currency and deposits	8 780 . .	20,056	20,375	25,906	31,497	9,286	9,476	5,267	...
Monetary authorities	8 781 . .	329	361	336	146	...	...	...	...
General government	8 782 . .	...	...	...	...	...	...	...	...
Banks	8 783 . .	19,727	20,014	25,570	31,351	9,286	9,476	5,267	...
Other sectors	8 784 . .	...	...	...	...	...	...	...	...
Other liabilities	8 786 . .	5,096	3,606	3,701	3,223	5,180	2,183	3,601	...
Monetary authorities	8 787 . .	...	...	...	...	...	...	...	...
of which: Short-term	8 789 . .	...	...	...	...	...	...	...	...
General government	8 790 . .	493	361	336	146	717	78	...	...
of which: Short-term	8 792 . .	...	...	...	...	...	...	...	...
Banks	8 793 . .	493	902	1,514	2,051	...	5	...	...
of which: Short-term	8 795 . .	...	...	...	...	...	...	...	...
Other sectors	8 796 . .	4,110	2,344	1,850	1,025	4,463	2,101	3,601	...
of which: Short-term	8 798 . .	...	...	...	...	...	...	...	...
NET INTERNATIONAL INVESTMENT POSITION	8 995 . .	**–42,623**	**–47,930**	**–42,122**	**–41,078**	**–47,804**	**–23,651**	**–27,322**	**...**
Conversion rates: Danish kroner per U.S. dollar (end of period)	0 102 . .	**6.0830**	**5.5460**	**5.9445**	**6.8260**	**6.3865**	**7.3988**	**8.0205**	**8.4095**

Djibouti
611

Table 1. ANALYTIC PRESENTATION, 1994–2001

(Millions of U.S. dollars)

	Code	1994	1995	1996	1997	1998	1999	2000	2001
A. Current Account [1]	4 993 Z.	**–46.1**	**–23.0**	**. . .**	**. . .**	**. . .**	**. . .**	**. . .**	**. . .**
Goods: exports f.o.b	2 100 . .	56.4	33.5	. . .	. . .	. . .	. . .	. . .	. . .
Goods: imports f.o.b	3 100 . .	–237.1	–205.0	. . .	. . .	. . .	. . .	. . .	. . .
Balance on Goods	4 100 . .	*–180.7*	*–171.5*	. . .	. . .	. . .	. . .	. . .	. . .
Services: credit	2 200 . .	152.3	151.4	. . .	. . .	. . .	. . .	. . .	. . .
Services: debit	3 200 . .	–89.7	–87.2	. . .	. . .	. . .	. . .	. . .	. . .
Balance on Goods and Services	4 991 . .	*–118.1*	*–107.3*	. . .	. . .	. . .	. . .	. . .	. . .
Income: credit	2 300 . .	23.7	25.9	. . .	. . .	. . .	. . .	. . .	. . .
Income: debit	3 300 . .	–7.0	–8.7	. . .	. . .	. . .	. . .	. . .	. . .
Balance on Goods, Services, and Income	4 992 . .	*–101.4*	*–90.0*	. . .	. . .	. . .	. . .	. . .	. . .
Current transfers: credit	2 379 Z.	73.7	85.4	. . .	. . .	. . .	. . .	. . .	. . .
Current transfers: debit	3 379 . .	–18.3	–18.4	. . .	. . .	. . .	. . .	. . .	. . .
B. Capital Account [1]	4 994 Z.	**. . .**	**. . .**	**. . .**	**. . .**	**. . .**	**. . .**	**. . .**	**. . .**
Capital account: credit	2 994 Z.	. . .	. . .	. . .	. . .	. . .	. . .	. . .	. . .
Capital account: debit	3 994 . .	. . .	. . .	. . .	. . .	. . .	. . .	. . .	. . .
Total, Groups A Plus B	4 981 . .	*–46.1*	*–23.0*	. . .	. . .	. . .	. . .	. . .	. . .
C. Financial Account [1]	4 995 W.	**39.0**	**–2.1**	**. . .**	**. . .**	**. . .**	**. . .**	**. . .**	**. . .**
Direct investment abroad	4 505 . .	. . .	. . .	. . .	. . .	. . .	. . .	. . .	. . .
Direct investment in Djibouti	4 555 Z.	1.4	3.2	. . .	. . .	. . .	. . .	. . .	. . .
Portfolio investment assets	4 602 . .	. . .	. . .	. . .	. . .	. . .	. . .	. . .	. . .
Equity securities	4 610 . .	. . .	. . .	. . .	. . .	. . .	. . .	. . .	. . .
Debt securities	4 619 . .	. . .	. . .	. . .	. . .	. . .	. . .	. . .	. . .
Portfolio investment liabilities	4 652 Z.	. . .	. . .	. . .	. . .	. . .	. . .	. . .	. . .
Equity securities	4 660 . .	. . .	. . .	. . .	. . .	. . .	. . .	. . .	. . .
Debt securities	4 669 Z.	. . .	. . .	. . .	. . .	. . .	. . .	. . .	. . .
Financial derivatives	4 910 . .	. . .	. . .	. . .	. . .	. . .	. . .	. . .	. . .
Financial derivatives assets	4 900 . .	. . .	. . .	. . .	. . .	. . .	. . .	. . .	. . .
Financial derivatives liabilities	4 905 . .	. . .	. . .	. . .	. . .	. . .	. . .	. . .	. . .
Other investment assets	4 703 . .	. . .	. . .	. . .	. . .	. . .	. . .	. . .	. . .
Monetary authorities	4 701 . .	. . .	. . .	. . .	. . .	. . .	. . .	. . .	. . .
General government	4 704 . .	. . .	. . .	. . .	. . .	. . .	. . .	. . .	. . .
Banks	4 705 . .	. . .	. . .	. . .	. . .	. . .	. . .	. . .	. . .
Other sectors	4 728 . .	. . .	. . .	. . .	. . .	. . .	. . .	. . .	. . .
Other investment liabilities	4 753 W.	37.6	–5.4	. . .	. . .	. . .	. . .	. . .	. . .
Monetary authorities	4 753 WA	. . .	. . .	. . .	. . .	. . .	. . .	. . .	. . .
General government	4 753 ZB	12.0	–9.4	. . .	. . .	. . .	. . .	. . .	. . .
Banks	4 753 ZC	11.6	4.0	. . .	. . .	. . .	. . .	. . .	. . .
Other sectors	4 753 ZD	14.1	.1	. . .	. . .	. . .	. . .	. . .	. . .
Total, Groups A Through C	4 983 . .	*–7.0*	*–25.1*	. . .	. . .	. . .	. . .	. . .	. . .
D. Net Errors and Omissions	4 998 . .	**7.9**	**.7**	**. . .**	**. . .**	**. . .**	**. . .**	**. . .**	**. . .**
Total, Groups A Through D	4 984 . .	*.8*	*–24.5*	. . .	. . .	. . .	. . .	. . .	. . .
E. Reserves and Related Items	4 802 A.	**–.8**	**24.5**	**. . .**	**. . .**	**. . .**	**. . .**	**. . .**	**. . .**
Reserve assets	4 802 . .	–3.4	7.3	. . .	. . .	. . .	. . .	. . .	. . .
Use of Fund credit and loans	4 766 . .	. . .	. . .	. . .	. . .	. . .	. . .	. . .	. . .
Exceptional financing	4 920 . .	2.6	17.2	. . .	. . .	. . .	. . .	. . .	. . .
Conversion rates: Djibouti francs per U.S. dollar	0 101 . .	**177.72**	**177.72**	**177.72**	**177.72**	**177.72**	**177.72**	**177.72**	**177.72**

[1] Excludes components that have been classified in the categories of Group E.

Table 2. STANDARD PRESENTATION, 1994–2001

(Millions of U.S. dollars)

	Code	1994	1995	1996	1997	1998	1999	2000	2001
CURRENT ACCOUNT	4 993 . .	**–46.1**	**–23.0**	**. . .**	**. . .**	**. . .**	**. . .**	**. . .**	**. . .**
A. GOODS	4 100 . .	–180.7	–171.5	. . .	. . .	. . .	. . .	. . .	. . .
Credit	2 100 . .	**56.4**	**33.5**	**. . .**	**. . .**	**. . .**	**. . .**	**. . .**	**. . .**
General merchandise: exports f.o.b.	2 110 . .	56.4	33.5	. . .	. . .	. . .	. . .	. . .	. . .
Goods for processing: exports f.o.b.	2 150 . .	. . .	. . .	. . .	. . .	. . .	. . .	. . .	. . .
Repairs on goods	2 160 . .	. . .	. . .	. . .	. . .	. . .	. . .	. . .	. . .
Goods procured in ports by carriers	2 170 . .	. . .	. . .	. . .	. . .	. . .	. . .	. . .	. . .
Nonmonetary gold	2 180 . .	. . .	. . .	. . .	. . .	. . .	. . .	. . .	. . .
Debit	3 100 . .	**–237.1**	**–205.0**	**. . .**	**. . .**	**. . .**	**. . .**	**. . .**	**. . .**
General merchandise: imports f.o.b.	3 110 . .	–237.1	–205.0	. . .	. . .	. . .	. . .	. . .	. . .
Goods for processing: imports f.o.b.	3 150 . .	. . .	. . .	. . .	. . .	. . .	. . .	. . .	. . .
Repairs on goods	3 160 . .	. . .	. . .	. . .	. . .	. . .	. . .	. . .	. . .
Goods procured in ports by carriers	3 170 . .	. . .	. . .	. . .	. . .	. . .	. . .	. . .	. . .
Nonmonetary gold	3 180 . .	. . .	. . .	. . .	. . .	. . .	. . .	. . .	. . .
B. SERVICES	4 200 . .	62.7	64.2	. . .	. . .	. . .	. . .	. . .	. . .
Total credit	2 200 . .	*152.3*	*151.4*	. . .	. . .	. . .	. . .	. . .	. . .
Total debit	3 200 . .	*–89.7*	*–87.2*	. . .	. . .	. . .	. . .	. . .	. . .
Transportation services, credit	2 205 . .	**23.2**	**16.3**	**. . .**	**. . .**	**. . .**	**. . .**	**. . .**	**. . .**
Passenger	2 850 . .	*3.1*	*2.3*	. . .	. . .	. . .	. . .	. . .	. . .
Freight	2 851 . .	*4.2*	*3.5*	. . .	. . .	. . .	. . .	. . .	. . .
Other	2 852 . .	*15.9*	*10.5*	. . .	. . .	. . .	. . .	. . .	. . .
Sea transport, passenger	2 207 . .	. . .	. . .	. . .	. . .	. . .	. . .	. . .	. . .
Sea transport, freight	2 208 . .	. . .	. . .	. . .	. . .	. . .	. . .	. . .	. . .
Sea transport, other	2 209 . .	6.5	6.2	. . .	. . .	. . .	. . .	. . .	. . .
Air transport, passenger	2 211 . .	. . .	. . .	. . .	. . .	. . .	. . .	. . .	. . .
Air transport, freight	2 212 . .	. . .	. . .	. . .	. . .	. . .	. . .	. . .	. . .
Air transport, other	2 213 . .	9.3	4.3	. . .	. . .	. . .	. . .	. . .	. . .
Other transport, passenger	2 215 . .	3.1	2.3	. . .	. . .	. . .	. . .	. . .	. . .
Other transport, freight	2 216 . .	4.2	3.5	. . .	. . .	. . .	. . .	. . .	. . .
Other transport, other	2 217 . .	. . .	. . .	. . .	. . .	. . .	. . .	. . .	. . .
Transportation services, debit	3 205 . .	**–49.9**	**–43.7**	**. . .**	**. . .**	**. . .**	**. . .**	**. . .**	**. . .**
Passenger	3 850 . .	*–14.2*	*–12.5*	. . .	. . .	. . .	. . .	. . .	. . .
Freight	3 851 . .	*–35.7*	*–31.2*	. . .	. . .	. . .	. . .	. . .	. . .
Other	3 852 . .	. . .	. . .	. . .	. . .	. . .	. . .	. . .	. . .
Sea transport, passenger	3 207 . .	. . .	. . .	. . .	. . .	. . .	. . .	. . .	. . .
Sea transport, freight	3 208 . .	–35.7	–31.2	. . .	. . .	. . .	. . .	. . .	. . .
Sea transport, other	3 209 . .	. . .	. . .	. . .	. . .	. . .	. . .	. . .	. . .
Air transport, passenger	3 211 . .	–14.2	–12.5	. . .	. . .	. . .	. . .	. . .	. . .
Air transport, freight	3 212 . .	. . .	. . .	. . .	. . .	. . .	. . .	. . .	. . .
Air transport, other	3 213 . .	. . .	. . .	. . .	. . .	. . .	. . .	. . .	. . .
Other transport, passenger	3 215 . .	. . .	. . .	. . .	. . .	. . .	. . .	. . .	. . .
Other transport, freight	3 216 . .	. . .	. . .	. . .	. . .	. . .	. . .	. . .	. . .
Other transport, other	3 217 . .	. . .	. . .	. . .	. . .	. . .	. . .	. . .	. . .
Travel, credit	2 236 . .	**3.3**	**4.4**	**. . .**	**. . .**	**. . .**	**. . .**	**. . .**	**. . .**
Business travel	2 237 . .	. . .	. . .	. . .	. . .	. . .	. . .	. . .	. . .
Personal travel	2 240 . .	. . .	. . .	. . .	. . .	. . .	. . .	. . .	. . .
Travel, debit	3 236 . .	**–2.6**	**–3.8**	**. . .**	**. . .**	**. . .**	**. . .**	**. . .**	**. . .**
Business travel	3 237 . .	. . .	. . .	. . .	. . .	. . .	. . .	. . .	. . .
Personal travel	3 240 . .	. . .	. . .	. . .	. . .	. . .	. . .	. . .	. . .
Other services, credit	2 200 BA	**125.9**	**130.7**	**. . .**	**. . .**	**. . .**	**. . .**	**. . .**	**. . .**
Communications	2 245 . .	1.5	1.1	. . .	. . .	. . .	. . .	. . .	. . .
Construction	2 249 . .	. . .	. . .	. . .	. . .	. . .	. . .	. . .	. . .
Insurance	2 253 . .	. . .	. . .	. . .	. . .	. . .	. . .	. . .	. . .
Financial	2 260 . .	. . .	. . .	. . .	. . .	. . .	. . .	. . .	. . .
Computer and information	2 262 . .	. . .	. . .	. . .	. . .	. . .	. . .	. . .	. . .
Royalties and licence fees	2 266 . .	. . .	. . .	. . .	. . .	. . .	. . .	. . .	. . .
Other business services	2 268 . .	5.4	6.1	. . .	. . .	. . .	. . .	. . .	. . .
Personal, cultural, and recreational	2 287 . .	. . .	. . .	. . .	. . .	. . .	. . .	. . .	. . .
Government, n.i.e.	2 291 . .	119.0	123.5	. . .	. . .	. . .	. . .	. . .	. . .
Other services, debit	3 200 BA	**–37.1**	**–39.7**	**. . .**	**. . .**	**. . .**	**. . .**	**. . .**	**. . .**
Communications	3 245 . .	. . .	. . .	. . .	. . .	. . .	. . .	. . .	. . .
Construction	3 249 . .	. . .	. . .	. . .	. . .	. . .	. . .	. . .	. . .
Insurance	3 253 . .	–7.6	–6.8	. . .	. . .	. . .	. . .	. . .	. . .
Financial	3 260 . .	. . .	. . .	. . .	. . .	. . .	. . .	. . .	. . .
Computer and information	3 262 . .	. . .	. . .	. . .	. . .	. . .	. . .	. . .	. . .
Royalties and licence fees	3 266 . .	. . .	. . .	. . .	. . .	. . .	. . .	. . .	. . .
Other business services	3 268 . .	–23.5	–22.3	. . .	. . .	. . .	. . .	. . .	. . .
Personal, cultural, and recreational	3 287 . .	. . .	. . .	. . .	. . .	. . .	. . .	. . .	. . .
Government, n.i.e.	3 291 . .	–6.0	–10.6	. . .	. . .	. . .	. . .	. . .	. . .

Table 2 (Continued). STANDARD PRESENTATION, 1994–2001
(Millions of U.S. dollars)

	Code		1994	1995	1996	1997	1998	1999	2000	2001
C. INCOME	4 300	. .	16.6	17.2	...	...	...	...	...	...
Total credit	2 300	. .	*23.7*	*25.9*	...	...	...	...	...	...
Total debit	3 300	. .	*–7.0*	*–8.7*	...	...	...	...	...	...
Compensation of employees, credit	2 310	. .	**12.0**	**10.9**	...	...	...	...	...	...
Compensation of employees, debit	3 310	. .	...	...	...	...	...	...	...	...
Investment income, credit	2 320	. .	**11.6**	**15.0**	...	...	...	...	...	...
Direct investment income	2 330	. .	...	...	...	...	...	...	...	...
Dividends and distributed branch profits	2 332	. .	...	...	...	...	...	...	...	...
Reinvested earnings and undistributed branch profits	2 333	. .	...	...	...	...	...	...	...	...
Income on debt (interest)	2 334	. .	...	...	...	...	...	...	...	...
Portfolio investment income	2 339	. .	11.6	15.0	...	...	...	...	...	...
Income on equity	2 340	. .	11.6	15.0	...	...	...	...	...	...
Income on bonds and notes	2 350	. .	...	...	...	...	...	...	...	...
Income on money market instruments	2 360	. .	...	...	...	...	...	...	...	...
Other investment income	2 370	. .	...	...	...	...	...	...	...	...
Investment income, debit	3 320	. .	**–7.0**	**–8.7**	...	...	...	...	...	...
Direct investment income	3 330	. .	–2.9	–4.6	...	...	...	...	...	...
Dividends and distributed branch profits	3 332	. .	–1.4	–1.4	...	...	...	...	...	...
Reinvested earnings and undistributed branch profits	3 333	. .	–1.4	–3.2	...	...	...	...	...	...
Income on debt (interest)	3 334	. .	...	...	...	...	...	...	...	...
Portfolio investment income	3 339	. .	...	...	...	...	...	...	...	...
Income on equity	3 340	. .	...	...	...	...	...	...	...	...
Income on bonds and notes	3 350	. .	...	...	...	...	...	...	...	...
Income on money market instruments	3 360	. .	...	...	...	...	...	...	...	...
Other investment income	3 370	. .	–4.2	–4.0	...	...	...	...	...	...
D. CURRENT TRANSFERS	4 379	. .	55.3	67.0	...	...	...	...	...	...
Credit	2 379	. .	**73.7**	**85.4**	...	...	...	...	...	...
General government	2 380	. .	67.2	80.7	...	...	...	...	...	...
Other sectors	2 390	. .	6.5	4.7	...	...	...	...	...	...
Workers' remittances	2 391	. .	1.5	1.0	...	...	...	...	...	...
Other current transfers	2 392	. .	5.0	3.7	...	...	...	...	...	...
Debit	3 379	. .	**–18.3**	**–18.4**	...	...	...	...	...	...
General government	3 380	. .	–1.0	–.8	...	...	...	...	...	...
Other sectors	3 390	. .	–17.3	–17.5	...	...	...	...	...	...
Workers' remittances	3 391	. .	–17.3	–17.5	...	...	...	...	...	...
Other current transfers	3 392	. .	...	...	...	...	...	...	...	...
CAPITAL AND FINANCIAL ACCOUNT	4 996	. .	**38.2**	**22.4**	...	...	...	...	...	...
CAPITAL ACCOUNT	4 994	. .	...	**18.4**	...	...	...	...	...	...
Total credit	2 994	. .	...	*18.4*	...	...	...	...	...	...
Total debit	3 994	. .	...	...	...	...	...	...	...	...
Capital transfers, credit	2 400	. .	...	**18.4**	...	...	...	...	...	...
General government	2 401	. .	...	18.4	...	...	...	...	...	...
Debt forgiveness	2 402	. .	...	18.4	...	...	...	...	...	...
Other capital transfers	2 410	. .	...	...	...	...	...	...	...	...
Other sectors	2 430	. .	...	...	...	...	...	...	...	...
Migrants' transfers	2 431	. .	...	...	...	...	...	...	...	...
Debt forgiveness	2 432	. .	...	...	...	...	...	...	...	...
Other capital transfers	2 440	. .	...	...	...	...	...	...	...	...
Capital transfers, debit	3 400	. .	...	...	...	...	...	...	...	...
General government	3 401	. .	...	...	...	...	...	...	...	...
Debt forgiveness	3 402	. .	...	...	...	...	...	...	...	...
Other capital transfers	3 410	. .	...	...	...	...	...	...	...	...
Other sectors	3 430	. .	...	...	...	...	...	...	...	...
Migrants' transfers	3 431	. .	...	...	...	...	...	...	...	...
Debt forgiveness	3 432	. .	...	...	...	...	...	...	...	...
Other capital transfers	3 440	. .	...	...	...	...	...	...	...	...
Nonproduced nonfinancial assets, credit	2 480	. .	...	...	...	...	...	...	...	...
Nonproduced nonfinancial assets, debit	3 480	. .	...	...	...	...	...	...	...	...

Table 2 (Continued). STANDARD PRESENTATION, 1994–2001
(Millions of U.S. dollars)

	Code	1994	1995	1996	1997	1998	1999	2000	2001
FINANCIAL ACCOUNT	4 995 . .	**38.2**	**4.0**	...	...	...	...	...	...
A. DIRECT INVESTMENT	4 500 . .	1.4	3.2	...	...	...	...	...	...
Direct investment abroad	4 505 . .	...	...	...	...	...	...	...	...
Equity capital	4 510 . .	...	...	...	...	...	...	...	...
Claims on affiliated enterprises	4 515 . .	...	...	...	...	...	...	...	...
Liabilities to affiliated enterprises	4 520 . .	...	...	...	...	...	...	...	...
Reinvested earnings	4 525 . .	...	...	...	...	...	...	...	...
Other capital	4 530 . .	...	...	...	...	...	...	...	...
Claims on affiliated enterprises	4 535 . .	...	...	...	...	...	...	...	...
Liabilities to affiliated enterprises	4 540 . .	...	...	...	...	...	...	...	...
Direct investment in Djibouti	4 555 . .	**1.4**	**3.2**	...	...	...	...	...	...
Equity capital	4 560 . .	...	...	...	...	...	...	...	...
Claims on direct investors	4 565 . .	...	...	...	...	...	...	...	...
Liabilities to direct investors	4 570 . .	...	...	...	...	...	...	...	...
Reinvested earnings	4 575 . .	1.4	3.2	...	...	...	...	...	...
Other capital	4 580 . .	...	...	...	...	...	...	...	...
Claims on direct investors	4 585 . .	...	...	...	...	...	...	...	...
Liabilities to direct investors	4 590 . .	...	...	...	...	...	...	...	...
B. PORTFOLIO INVESTMENT	4 600 . .	...	...	...	...	...	...	...	...
Assets	4 602 . .	...	...	...	...	...	...	...	...
Equity securities	4 610 . .	...	...	...	...	...	...	...	...
Monetary authorities	4 611 . .	...	...	...	...	...	...	...	...
General government	4 612 . .	...	...	...	...	...	...	...	...
Banks	4 613 . .	...	...	...	...	...	...	...	...
Other sectors	4 614 . .	...	...	...	...	...	...	...	...
Debt securities	4 619 . .	...	...	...	...	...	...	...	...
Bonds and notes	4 620 . .	...	...	...	...	...	...	...	...
Monetary authorities	4 621 . .	...	...	...	...	...	...	...	...
General government	4 622 . .	...	...	...	...	...	...	...	...
Banks	4 623 . .	...	...	...	...	...	...	...	...
Other sectors	4 624 . .	...	...	...	...	...	...	...	...
Money market instruments	4 630 . .	...	...	...	...	...	...	...	...
Monetary authorities	4 631 . .	...	...	...	...	...	...	...	...
General government	4 632 . .	...	...	...	...	...	...	...	...
Banks	4 633 . .	...	...	...	...	...	...	...	...
Other sectors	4 634 . .	...	...	...	...	...	...	...	...
Liabilities	4 652 . .	...	...	...	...	...	...	...	...
Equity securities	4 660 . .	...	...	...	...	...	...	...	...
Banks	4 663 . .	...	...	...	...	...	...	...	...
Other sectors	4 664 . .	...	...	...	...	...	...	...	...
Debt securities	4 669 . .	...	...	...	...	...	...	...	...
Bonds and notes	4 670 . .	...	...	...	...	...	...	...	...
Monetary authorities	4 671 . .	...	...	...	...	...	...	...	...
General government	4 672 . .	...	...	...	...	...	...	...	...
Banks	4 673 . .	...	...	...	...	...	...	...	...
Other sectors	4 674 . .	...	...	...	...	...	...	...	...
Money market instruments	4 680 . .	...	...	...	...	...	...	...	...
Monetary authorities	4 681 . .	...	...	...	...	...	...	...	...
General government	4 682 . .	...	...	...	...	...	...	...	...
Banks	4 683 . .	...	...	...	...	...	...	...	...
Other sectors	4 684 . .	...	...	...	...	...	...	...	...
C. FINANCIAL DERIVATIVES	4 910 . .	...	...	...	...	...	...	...	...
Monetary authorities	4 911 . .	...	...	...	...	...	...	...	...
General government	4 912 . .	...	...	...	...	...	...	...	...
Banks	4 913 . .	...	...	...	...	...	...	...	...
Other sectors	4 914 . .	...	...	...	...	...	...	...	...
Assets	4 900 . .	...	...	...	...	...	...	...	...
Monetary authorities	4 901 . .	...	...	...	...	...	...	...	...
General government	4 902 . .	...	...	...	...	...	...	...	...
Banks	4 903 . .	...	...	...	...	...	...	...	...
Other sectors	4 904 . .	...	...	...	...	...	...	...	...
Liabilities	4 905 . .	...	...	...	...	...	...	...	...
Monetary authorities	4 906 . .	...	...	...	...	...	...	...	...
General government	4 907 . .	...	...	...	...	...	...	...	...
Banks	4 908 . .	...	...	...	...	...	...	...	...
Other sectors	4 909 . .	...	...	...	...	...	...	...	...

Table 2 (Concluded). STANDARD PRESENTATION, 1994–2001
(Millions of U.S. dollars)

	Code	1994	1995	1996	1997	1998	1999	2000	2001
D. OTHER INVESTMENT	4 700	40.2	–6.5	...	...	...	...	...	...
Assets	4 703	...	...	...	...	...	...	...	...
Trade credits	4 706	...	...	...	...	...	...	...	...
General government	4 707	...	...	...	...	...	...	...	...
of which: Short-term	4 709	...	...	...	...	...	...	...	...
Other sectors	4 710	...	...	...	...	...	...	...	...
of which: Short-term	4 712	...	...	...	...	...	...	...	...
Loans	4 714	...	...	...	...	...	...	...	...
Monetary authorities	4 715	...	...	...	...	...	...	...	...
of which: Short-term	4 718	...	...	...	...	...	...	...	...
General government	4 719	...	...	...	...	...	...	...	...
of which: Short-term	4 721	...	...	...	...	...	...	...	...
Banks	4 722	...	...	...	...	...	...	...	...
of which: Short-term	4 724	...	...	...	...	...	...	...	...
Other sectors	4 725	...	...	...	...	...	...	...	...
of which: Short-term	4 727	...	...	...	...	...	...	...	...
Currency and deposits	4 730	...	...	...	...	...	...	...	...
Monetary authorities	4 731	...	...	...	...	...	...	...	...
General government	4 732	...	...	...	...	...	...	...	...
Banks	4 733	...	...	...	...	...	...	...	...
Other sectors	4 734	...	...	...	...	...	...	...	...
Other assets	4 736	...	...	...	...	...	...	...	...
Monetary authorities	4 737	...	...	...	...	...	...	...	...
of which: Short-term	4 739	...	...	...	...	...	...	...	...
General government	4 740	...	...	...	...	...	...	...	...
of which: Short-term	4 742	...	...	...	...	...	...	...	...
Banks	4 743	...	...	...	...	...	...	...	...
of which: Short-term	4 745	...	...	...	...	...	...	...	...
Other sectors	4 746	...	...	...	...	...	...	...	...
of which: Short-term	4 748	...	...	...	...	...	...	...	...
Liabilities	4 753	**40.2**	**–6.5**	...	...	...	...	...	...
Trade credits	4 756	...	...	...	...	...	...	...	...
General government	4 757	...	...	...	...	...	...	...	...
of which: Short-term	4 759	...	...	...	...	...	...	...	...
Other sectors	4 760	...	...	...	...	...	...	...	...
of which: Short-term	4 762	...	...	...	...	...	...	...	...
Loans	4 764	26.1	–9.4	...	...	...	...	...	...
Monetary authorities	4 765	...	...	...	...	...	...	...	...
of which: Use of Fund credit and loans from the Fund	4 766	...	...	...	...	...	...	...	...
of which: Short-term	4 768	...	...	...	...	...	...	...	...
General government	4 769	12.0	–9.4	...	...	...	...	...	...
of which: Short-term	4 771	...	...	...	...	...	...	...	...
Banks	4 772	...	...	...	...	...	...	...	...
of which: Short-term	4 774	...	...	...	...	...	...	...	...
Other sectors	4 775	14.1	.1	...	...	...	...	...	...
of which: Short-term	4 777	...	...	...	...	...	...	...	...
Currency and deposits	4 780	11.6	4.0	...	...	...	...	...	...
Monetary authorities	4 781	...	...	...	...	...	...	...	...
General government	4 782	...	...	...	...	...	...	...	...
Banks	4 783	11.6	4.0	...	...	...	...	...	...
Other sectors	4 784	...	...	...	...	...	...	...	...
Other liabilities	4 786	2.6	–1.2	...	...	...	...	...	...
Monetary authorities	4 787	...	...	...	...	...	...	...	...
of which: Short-term	4 789	...	...	...	...	...	...	...	...
General government	4 790	2.6	–1.2	...	...	...	...	...	...
of which: Short-term	4 792	*2.6*	*–1.2*	...	...	...	...	...	...
Banks	4 793	...	...	...	...	...	...	...	...
of which: Short-term	4 795	...	...	...	...	...	...	...	...
Other sectors	4 796	...	...	...	...	...	...	...	...
of which: Short-term	4 798	...	...	...	...	...	...	...	...
E. RESERVE ASSETS	4 802	–3.4	7.3	...	...	...	...	...	...
Monetary gold	4 812	...	...	...	...	...	...	...	...
Special drawing rights	4 811	.1	.1	...	...	...	...	...	...
Reserve position in the Fund	4 810	...	...	...	...	...	...	...	...
Foreign exchange	4 803	–3.5	7.2	...	...	...	...	...	...
Other claims	4 813	...	...	...	...	...	...	...	...
NET ERRORS AND OMISSIONS	4 998	**7.9**	**.7**	...	...	...	...	...	...

Part 3 of the *Yearbook* contains descriptions of the methodologies, compilation practices, and sources used to compile these data.

Table 1. ANALYTIC PRESENTATION, 1994–2001
(Millions of U.S. dollars)

	Code	1994	1995	1996	1997	1998	1999	2000	2001
A. Current Account [1]	4 993 Z.	**-37.55**	**-40.73**	**-33.27**	**-26.20**	**-12.20**	**-41.17**	**-68.93**	**. . .**
Goods: exports f.o.b	2 100 . .	48.33	50.27	52.75	53.77	63.10	54.61	50.29	. . .
Goods: imports f.o.b	3 100 . .	-95.76	-103.21	-100.50	-104.31	-106.93	-123.35	-129.60	. . .
Balance on Goods	4 100 . .	*-47.43*	*-52.94*	*-47.75*	*-50.54*	*-43.84*	*-68.74*	*-79.31*	. . .
Services: credit	2 200 . .	51.59	61.36	68.94	83.39	88.41	98.93	88.03	. . .
Services: debit	3 200 . .	-37.76	-43.72	-44.89	-52.17	-54.03	-59.27	-50.56	. . .
Balance on Goods and Services	4 991 . .	*-33.60*	*-35.30*	*-23.70*	*-19.33*	*-9.45*	*-29.08*	*-41.84*	. . .
Income: credit	2 300 . .	3.08	3.29	2.84	3.60	4.65	4.63	4.67	. . .
Income: debit	3 300 . .	-14.10	-16.59	-22.58	-20.83	-20.14	-30.27	-41.86	. . .
Balance on Goods, Services, and Income	4 992 . .	*-44.62*	*-48.59*	*-43.44*	*-36.55*	*-24.94*	*-54.73*	*-79.03*	. . .
Current transfers: credit	2 379 Z.	14.86	16.26	17.83	17.44	19.92	20.46	17.12	. . .
Current transfers: debit	3 379 . .	-7.79	-8.39	-7.66	-7.09	-7.18	-6.90	-7.02	. . .
B. Capital Account [1]	4 994 Z.	**6.90**	**24.54**	**25.30**	**22.52**	**14.75**	**11.76**	**14.16**	**. . .**
Capital account: credit	2 994 Z.	9.37	24.65	25.42	22.64	14.87	12.06	15.67	. . .
Capital account: debit	3 994 . .	-2.47	-.11	-.12	-.12	-.13	-.30	-1.52	. . .
Total, Groups A Plus B	4 981 . .	*-30.64*	*-16.19*	*-7.97*	*-3.68*	*2.54*	*-29.41*	*-54.77*	. . .
C. Financial Account [1]	4 995 W.	**30.00**	**42.15**	**5.18**	**15.48**	**-3.65**	**36.23**	**53.23**	**. . .**
Direct investment abroad	4 505 . .	. . .	. . .	. . .	. . .	. . .	. . .	. . .	. . .
Direct investment in Dominica	4 555 Z.	22.60	54.09	17.80	21.11	6.53	17.96	10.62	. . .
Portfolio investment assets	4 602 . .	.01	-7.96	. . .	. . .	. . .	-1.70	-.40	. . .
Equity securities	4 610 . .	. . .	. . .	. . .	. . .	. . .	. . .	. . .	. . .
Debt securities	4 619 . .	. . .	. . .	. . .	. . .	. . .	. . .	. . .	. . .
Portfolio investment liabilities	4 652 Z.	. . .	. . .	.46	-.18	1.30	30.44	14.03	. . .
Equity securities	4 660 . .	. . .	. . .	. . .	. . .	. . .	. . .	. . .	. . .
Debt securities	4 669 Z.	. . .	. . .	. . .	. . .	. . .	. . .	. . .	. . .
Financial derivatives	4 910 . .	. . .	. . .	. . .	. . .	. . .	. . .	. . .	. . .
Financial derivatives assets	4 900 . .	. . .	. . .	. . .	. . .	. . .	. . .	. . .	. . .
Financial derivatives liabilities	4 905 . .	. . .	. . .	. . .	. . .	. . .	. . .	. . .	. . .
Other investment assets	4 703 . .	-4.31	-3.60	-16.45	-7.28	-14.13	-12.37	-10.42	. . .
Monetary authorities	4 701 . .	. . .	. . .	. . .	. . .	. . .	. . .	. . .	. . .
General government	4 704 . .	. . .	. . .	. . .	. . .	. . .	. . .	. . .	. . .
Banks	4 705 . .	. . .	. . .	. . .	. . .	. . .	. . .	. . .	. . .
Other sectors	4 728 . .	. . .	. . .	. . .	. . .	. . .	. . .	. . .	. . .
Other investment liabilities	4 753 W.	11.71	-.38	3.37	1.82	2.65	1.90	39.40	. . .
Monetary authorities	4 753 WA	. . .	. . .	. . .	. . .	. . .	. . .	. . .	. . .
General government	4 753 ZB	. . .	. . .	. . .	. . .	. . .	. . .	. . .	. . .
Banks	4 753 ZC	. . .	. . .	. . .	. . .	. . .	. . .	. . .	. . .
Other sectors	4 753 ZD	. . .	. . .	. . .	. . .	. . .	. . .	. . .	. . .
Total, Groups A Through C	4 983 . .	*-.64*	*25.96*	*-2.79*	*11.80*	*-1.11*	*6.83*	*-1.55*	. . .
D. Net Errors and Omissions	4 998 . .	**-2.71**	**-17.62**	**4.66**	**-10.20**	**5.55**	**4.22**	**2.01**	**. . .**
Total, Groups A Through D	4 984 . .	*-3.35*	*8.34*	*1.87*	*1.60*	*4.44*	*11.04*	*.47*	. . .
E. Reserves and Related Items	4 802 A.	**3.35**	**-8.34**	**-1.87**	**-1.60**	**-4.44**	**-11.04**	**-.47**	**. . .**
Reserve assets	4 802 . .	4.15	-7.48	-1.06	-1.05	-4.22	-11.00	-.47	. . .
Use of Fund credit and loans	4 766 . .	-.80	-.86	-.81	-.55	-.22	-.04	. . .	. . .
Exceptional financing	4 920 . .	. . .	. . .	. . .	. . .	. . .	. . .	. . .	. . .
Conversion rates: Eastern Caribbean dollars per U.S. dollar	0 101 . .	**2.7000**	**2.7000**	**2.7000**	**2.7000**	**2.7000**	**2.7000**	**2.7000**	**2.7000**

[1] Excludes components that have been classified in the categories of Group E.

Table 2. STANDARD PRESENTATION, 1994–2001
(Millions of U.S. dollars)

	Code		1994	1995	1996	1997	1998	1999	2000	2001
CURRENT ACCOUNT	4 993	. .	**–37.55**	**–40.73**	**–33.27**	**–26.20**	**–12.20**	**–41.17**	**–68.93**	**. . .**
A. GOODS	4 100	. .	–47.43	–52.94	–47.75	–50.54	–43.84	–68.74	–79.31	. . .
Credit	2 100	. .	**48.33**	**50.27**	**52.75**	**53.77**	**63.10**	**54.61**	**50.29**	**. . .**
General merchandise: exports f.o.b.	2 110	. .	47.15	49.26	51.15	52.32	61.92	54.32	49.13	. . .
Goods for processing: exports f.o.b.	2 150	. .	. . .	. . .	. . .	. . .	. . .	. . .	. . .	. . .
Repairs on goods	2 160	. .	.49	.01	. . .	.01	.01	.01	. . .	. . .
Goods procured in ports by carriers	2 170	. .	.69	1.00	1.59	1.44	1.17	.28	1.16	. . .
Nonmonetary gold	2 180	. .	. . .	. . .	. . .	. . .	. . .	. . .	. . .	. . .
Debit	3 100	. .	**–95.76**	**–103.21**	**–100.50**	**–104.31**	**–106.93**	**–123.35**	**–129.60**	**. . .**
General merchandise: imports f.o.b.	3 110	. .	–95.76	–103.21	–100.20	–104.01	–106.93	–123.35	–129.60	. . .
Goods for processing: imports f.o.b.	3 150	. .	. . .	. . .	. . .	. . .	. . .	. . .	. . .	. . .
Repairs on goods	3 160	. .	. . .	. . .	. . .	. . .	. . .	. . .	. . .	. . .
Goods procured in ports by carriers	3 170	. .	. . .	. . .	–.30	–.30	. . .	. . .	. . .	. . .
Nonmonetary gold	3 180	. .	. . .	. . .	. . .	. . .	. . .	. . .	. . .	. . .
B. SERVICES	4 200	. .	13.83	17.64	24.04	31.21	34.39	39.66	37.47	. . .
Total credit	2 200	. .	*51.59*	*61.36*	*68.94*	*83.39*	*88.41*	*98.93*	*88.03*	. . .
Total debit	3 200	. .	*–37.76*	*–43.72*	*–44.89*	*–52.17*	*–54.03*	*–59.27*	*–50.56*	. . .
Transportation services, credit	2 205	. .	**5.39**	**5.64**	**6.53**	**7.03**	**7.05**	**7.39**	**6.45**	**. . .**
Passenger	2 850	. .	. . .	. . .	. . .	. . .	. . .	. . .	. . .	. . .
Freight	2 851	. .	. . .	. . .	. . .	. . .	. . .	. . .	. . .	. . .
Other	2 852	. .	. . .	. . .	. . .	. . .	. . .	. . .	. . .	. . .
Sea transport, passenger	2 207	. .	. . .	. . .	. . .	. . .	. . .	. . .	. . .	. . .
Sea transport, freight	2 208	. .	. . .	. . .	. . .	. . .	. . .	. . .	. . .	. . .
Sea transport, other	2 209	. .	. . .	. . .	. . .	. . .	. . .	. . .	. . .	. . .
Air transport, passenger	2 211	. .	. . .	. . .	. . .	. . .	. . .	. . .	. . .	. . .
Air transport, freight	2 212	. .	. . .	. . .	. . .	. . .	. . .	. . .	. . .	. . .
Air transport, other	2 213	. .	. . .	. . .	. . .	. . .	. . .	. . .	. . .	. . .
Other transport, passenger	2 215	. .	. . .	. . .	. . .	. . .	. . .	. . .	. . .	. . .
Other transport, freight	2 216	. .	. . .	. . .	. . .	. . .	. . .	. . .	. . .	. . .
Other transport, other	2 217	. .	. . .	. . .	. . .	. . .	. . .	. . .	. . .	. . .
Transportation services, debit	3 205	. .	**–16.73**	**–16.60**	**–18.24**	**–21.20**	**–18.89**	**–20.91**	**–21.69**	**. . .**
Passenger	3 850	. .	. . .	. . .	. . .	. . .	. . .	. . .	. . .	. . .
Freight	3 851	. .	. . .	. . .	. . .	. . .	. . .	. . .	. . .	. . .
Other	3 852	. .	. . .	. . .	. . .	. . .	. . .	. . .	. . .	. . .
Sea transport, passenger	3 207	. .	. . .	. . .	. . .	. . .	. . .	. . .	. . .	. . .
Sea transport, freight	3 208	. .	. . .	. . .	. . .	. . .	. . .	. . .	. . .	. . .
Sea transport, other	3 209	. .	. . .	. . .	. . .	. . .	. . .	. . .	. . .	. . .
Air transport, passenger	3 211	. .	. . .	. . .	. . .	. . .	. . .	. . .	. . .	. . .
Air transport, freight	3 212	. .	. . .	. . .	. . .	. . .	. . .	. . .	. . .	. . .
Air transport, other	3 213	. .	. . .	. . .	. . .	. . .	. . .	. . .	. . .	. . .
Other transport, passenger	3 215	. .	. . .	. . .	. . .	. . .	. . .	. . .	. . .	. . .
Other transport, freight	3 216	. .	. . .	. . .	. . .	. . .	. . .	. . .	. . .	. . .
Other transport, other	3 217	. .	. . .	. . .	. . .	. . .	. . .	. . .	. . .	. . .
Travel, credit	2 236	. .	**32.44**	**41.52**	**44.12**	**48.26**	**46.53**	**48.88**	**47.20**	**. . .**
Business travel	2 237	. .	. . .	. . .	. . .	. . .	. . .	. . .	. . .	. . .
Personal travel	2 240	. .	. . .	. . .	. . .	. . .	. . .	. . .	. . .	. . .
Travel, debit	3 236	. .	**–5.52**	**–5.94**	**–6.93**	**–7.34**	**–8.23**	**–9.43**	**–8.93**	**. . .**
Business travel	3 237	. .	. . .	. . .	. . .	. . .	. . .	. . .	. . .	. . .
Personal travel	3 240	. .	. . .	. . .	. . .	. . .	. . .	. . .	. . .	. . .
Other services, credit	2 200	BA	**13.76**	**14.20**	**18.29**	**28.10**	**34.83**	**42.66**	**34.38**	**. . .**
Communications	2 245	. .	. . .	. . .	. . .	. . .	. . .	. . .	. . .	. . .
Construction	2 249	. .	. . .	. . .	. . .	. . .	.18	. . .	. . .	. . .
Insurance	2 253	. .	1.83	2.04	2.70	2.63	2.64	2.71	3.41	. . .
Financial	2 260	. .	. . .	. . .	. . .	. . .	3.02	1.70	.91	. . .
Computer and information	2 262	. .	. . .	. . .	. . .	. . .	. . .	. . .	. . .	. . .
Royalties and licence fees	2 266	. .	. . .	. . .	. . .	. . .	.20	.10	.03	. . .
Other business services	2 268	. .	11.54	11.89	13.79	21.59	24.80	34.36	27.67	. . .
Personal, cultural, and recreational	2 287	. .	. . .	. . .	. . .	. . .	. . .	. . .	. . .	. . .
Government, n.i.e.	2 291	. .	.39	.28	1.79	3.87	3.98	3.80	2.36	. . .
Other services, debit	3 200	BA	**–15.51**	**–21.18**	**–19.73**	**–23.63**	**–26.90**	**–28.93**	**–19.95**	**. . .**
Communications	3 245	. .	. . .	. . .	. . .	. . .	. . .	. . .	. . .	. . .
Construction	3 249	. .	–.82	–3.81	–.61	–1.14	–.13	–.84	–.51	. . .
Insurance	3 253	. .	–3.49	–3.90	–3.87	–4.12	–4.63	–4.30	–4.69	. . .
Financial	3 260	. .	–2.03	–1.39	–.74	. . .	. . .	–.01	–.01	. . .
Computer and information	3 262	. .	. . .	. . .	. . .	. . .	. . .	. . .	. . .	. . .
Royalties and licence fees	3 266	. .	–.09	–.21	–.10	–.21	–.40	–.14	–.12	. . .
Other business services	3 268	. .	–4.24	–7.61	–10.12	–13.13	–13.54	–17.82	–10.64	. . .
Personal, cultural, and recreational	3 287	. .	. . .	. . .	. . .	. . .	. . .	. . .	. . .	. . .
Government, n.i.e.	3 291	. .	–4.84	–4.27	–4.28	–5.03	–8.20	–5.83	–3.99	. . .

Table 2 (Continued). STANDARD PRESENTATION, 1994–2001
(Millions of U.S. dollars)

	Code	1994	1995	1996	1997	1998	1999	2000	2001
C. INCOME	4 300	–11.02	–13.30	–19.74	–17.22	–15.49	–25.65	–37.19	...
Total credit	2 300	*3.08*	*3.29*	*2.84*	*3.60*	*4.65*	*4.63*	*4.67*	...
Total debit	3 300	*–14.10*	*–16.59*	*–22.58*	*–20.83*	*–20.14*	*–30.27*	*–41.86*	...
Compensation of employees, credit	2 310	**.03**	**.03**	**.03**	**.03**	**.24**	**.70**	**.65**	...
Compensation of employees, debit	3 310	**–.37**	**–.10**	...	**–.06**	...	...	...	...
Investment income, credit	2 320	**3.05**	**3.26**	**2.82**	**3.58**	**4.40**	**3.93**	**4.03**	...
Direct investment income	2 330	...	.11	.11	.07	.91	.05	.41	...
Dividends and distributed branch profits	2 332	...	...	...	...	.75	.05	.41	...
Reinvested earnings and undistributed branch profits	2 333	...	...	...	...	...	...	...	...
Income on debt (interest)	2 334	...	.11	.11	.07	.16	...	...	...
Portfolio investment income	2 339	1.21	1.06	.79	.77	.72	.71	.55	...
Income on equity	2 340	1.21	1.06	.79	.77	.72	.71	.55	...
Income on bonds and notes	2 350	...	...	...	...	...	...	...	...
Income on money market instruments	2 360	...	...	...	...	...	...	...	...
Other investment income	2 370	1.84	2.09	1.91	2.74	2.77	3.17	3.06	...
Investment income, debit	3 320	**–13.73**	**–16.49**	**–22.58**	**–20.76**	**–20.14**	**–30.27**	**–41.86**	...
Direct investment income	3 330	–9.62	–12.17	–16.97	–15.65	–15.19	–22.81	–26.07	...
Dividends and distributed branch profits	3 332	–4.52	–5.84	–6.04	–6.63	–7.36	–12.41	–17.96	...
Reinvested earnings and undistributed branch profits	3 333	–5.10	–5.70	–10.36	–8.57	–6.50	–9.61	–7.56	...
Income on debt (interest)	3 334	...	–.63	–.57	–.45	–1.33	–.79	–.55	...
Portfolio investment income	3 339	...	...	...	...	...	–1.20	–9.21	...
Income on equity	3 340	...	...	...	...	...	–1.20	–9.21	...
Income on bonds and notes	3 350	...	...	...	...	...	...	...	...
Income on money market instruments	3 360	...	...	...	...	...	...	...	...
Other investment income	3 370	–4.10	–4.32	–5.61	–5.11	–4.95	–6.26	–6.58	...
D. CURRENT TRANSFERS	4 379	7.07	7.87	10.17	10.35	12.74	13.56	10.10	...
Credit	2 379	**14.86**	**16.26**	**17.83**	**17.44**	**19.92**	**20.46**	**17.12**	...
General government	2 380	3.34	3.70	4.26	4.15	6.28	6.17	2.43	...
Other sectors	2 390	11.52	12.56	13.57	13.29	13.64	14.29	14.69	...
Workers' remittances	2 391	...	...	...	...	...	...	...	...
Other current transfers	2 392	...	...	...	...	...	...	...	...
Debit	3 379	**–7.79**	**–8.39**	**–7.66**	**–7.09**	**–7.18**	**–6.90**	**–7.02**	...
General government	3 380	–3.06	–5.04	–4.51	–3.21	–3.00	–2.96	–2.96	...
Other sectors	3 390	–4.73	–3.35	–3.15	–3.88	–4.17	–3.94	–4.06	...
Workers' remittances	3 391	...	...	...	...	...	...	...	...
Other current transfers	3 392	...	...	...	...	...	...	...	...
CAPITAL AND FINANCIAL ACCOUNT	4 996	**40.25**	**58.35**	**28.61**	**36.40**	**6.66**	**36.95**	**66.92**	...
CAPITAL ACCOUNT	4 994	**6.90**	**24.54**	**25.30**	**22.52**	**14.75**	**11.76**	**14.16**	...
Total credit	2 994	*9.37*	*24.65*	*25.42*	*22.64*	*14.87*	*12.06*	*15.67*	...
Total debit	3 994	*–2.47*	*–.11*	*–.12*	*–.12*	*–.13*	*–.30*	*–1.52*	...
Capital transfers, credit	2 400	**8.79**	**19.49**	**21.37**	**22.64**	**14.87**	**12.06**	**15.67**	...
General government	2 401	5.83	16.89	18.73	20.19	12.32	9.40	12.89	...
Debt forgiveness	2 402	...	...	...	...	...	...	...	...
Other capital transfers	2 410	5.83	16.89	18.73	20.19	12.32	9.40	12.89	...
Other sectors	2 430	2.96	2.59	2.64	2.46	2.55	2.66	2.79	...
Migrants' transfers	2 431	2.96	2.59	2.64	2.46	2.55	2.66	2.79	...
Debt forgiveness	2 432	...	...	...	...	...	...	...	...
Other capital transfers	2 440	...	...	...	...	...	...	...	...
Capital transfers, debit	3 400	**–1.85**	**–.11**	**–.12**	**–.12**	**–.13**	**–.13**	**–.13**	...
General government	3 401	...	...	...	...	...	...	...	...
Debt forgiveness	3 402	...	...	...	...	...	...	...	...
Other capital transfers	3 410	...	...	...	...	...	...	...	...
Other sectors	3 430	–1.85	–.11	–.12	–.12	–.13	–.13	–.13	...
Migrants' transfers	3 431	–1.85	–.11	–.12	–.12	–.13	–.13	–.13	...
Debt forgiveness	3 432	...	...	...	...	...	...	...	...
Other capital transfers	3 440	...	...	...	...	...	...	...	...
Nonproduced nonfinancial assets, credit	2 480	**.59**	**5.17**	**4.05**	...	...	...	...	...
Nonproduced nonfinancial assets, debit	3 480	**–.62**	...	...	...	...	**–.17**	**–1.39**	...

Table 2 (Continued). STANDARD PRESENTATION, 1994–2001

(Millions of U.S. dollars)

	Code	1994	1995	1996	1997	1998	1999	2000	2001
FINANCIAL ACCOUNT	4 995	**33.35**	**33.80**	**3.31**	**13.88**	**–8.09**	**25.19**	**52.76**	...
A. DIRECT INVESTMENT	4 500	22.60	54.09	17.80	21.11	6.53	17.96	10.62	...
Direct investment abroad	4 505	...	...	...	...	...	...	...	...
Equity capital	4 510	...	...	...	...	...	...	...	...
Claims on affiliated enterprises	4 515	...	...	...	...	...	...	...	...
Liabilities to affiliated enterprises	4 520	...	...	...	...	...	...	...	...
Reinvested earnings	4 525	...	...	...	...	...	...	...	...
Other capital	4 530	...	...	...	...	...	...	...	...
Claims on affiliated enterprises	4 535	...	...	...	...	...	...	...	...
Liabilities to affiliated enterprises	4 540	...	...	...	...	...	...	...	...
Direct investment in Dominica	4 555	**22.60**	**54.09**	**17.80**	**21.11**	**6.53**	**17.96**	**10.62**	...
Equity capital	4 560	15.16	39.12	6.99	11.87	2.19	8.44	5.45	...
Claims on direct investors	4 565	...	...	...	...	...	...	...	...
Liabilities to direct investors	4 570	15.16	39.12	6.99	11.87	2.19	8.44	5.45	...
Reinvested earnings	4 575	5.10	5.70	10.36	8.57	6.50	9.61	7.56	...
Other capital	4 580	2.34	9.27	.46	.67	–2.16	–.10	–2.39	...
Claims on direct investors	4 585	...	...	...	...	...	...	...	...
Liabilities to direct investors	4 590	2.34	9.27	.46	.67	–2.16	–.10	–2.39	...
B. PORTFOLIO INVESTMENT	4 600	.01	–7.96	.46	–.18	1.30	28.74	13.63	...
Assets	4 602	**.01**	**–7.96**	...	...	...	**–1.70**	**–.40**	...
Equity securities	4 610	...	...	...	...	...	...	...	...
Monetary authorities	4 611	...	...	...	...	...	...	...	...
General government	4 612	...	...	...	...	...	...	...	...
Banks	4 613	...	...	...	...	...	...	...	...
Other sectors	4 614	...	...	...	...	...	...	...	...
Debt securities	4 619	...	...	...	...	...	...	...	...
Bonds and notes	4 620	...	...	...	...	...	...	...	...
Monetary authorities	4 621	...	...	...	...	...	...	...	...
General government	4 622	...	...	...	...	...	...	...	...
Banks	4 623	...	...	...	...	...	...	...	...
Other sectors	4 624	...	...	...	...	...	...	...	...
Money market instruments	4 630	...	...	...	...	...	...	...	...
Monetary authorities	4 631	...	...	...	...	...	...	...	...
General government	4 632	...	...	...	...	...	...	...	...
Banks	4 633	...	...	...	...	...	...	...	...
Other sectors	4 634	...	...	...	...	...	...	...	...
Liabilities	4 652	...	...	**.46**	**–.18**	**1.30**	**30.44**	**14.03**	...
Equity securities	4 660	...	...	...	...	...	...	...	...
Banks	4 663	...	...	...	...	...	...	...	...
Other sectors	4 664	...	...	...	...	...	...	...	...
Debt securities	4 669	...	...	...	...	...	...	...	...
Bonds and notes	4 670	...	...	...	...	...	...	...	...
Monetary authorities	4 671	...	...	...	...	...	...	...	...
General government	4 672	...	...	...	...	...	...	...	...
Banks	4 673	...	...	...	...	...	...	...	...
Other sectors	4 674	...	...	...	...	...	...	...	...
Money market instruments	4 680	...	...	...	...	...	...	...	...
Monetary authorities	4 681	...	...	...	...	...	...	...	...
General government	4 682	...	...	...	...	...	...	...	...
Banks	4 683	...	...	...	...	...	...	...	...
Other sectors	4 684	...	...	...	...	...	...	...	...
C. FINANCIAL DERIVATIVES	4 910	...	...	...	...	...	...	...	...
Monetary authorities	4 911	...	...	...	...	...	...	...	...
General government	4 912	...	...	...	...	...	...	...	...
Banks	4 913	...	...	...	...	...	...	...	...
Other sectors	4 914	...	...	...	...	...	...	...	...
Assets	4 900	...	...	...	...	...	...	...	...
Monetary authorities	4 901	...	...	...	...	...	...	...	...
General government	4 902	...	...	...	...	...	...	...	...
Banks	4 903	...	...	...	...	...	...	...	...
Other sectors	4 904	...	...	...	...	...	...	...	...
Liabilities	4 905	...	...	...	...	...	...	...	...
Monetary authorities	4 906	...	...	...	...	...	...	...	...
General government	4 907	...	...	...	...	...	...	...	...
Banks	4 908	...	...	...	...	...	...	...	...
Other sectors	4 909	...	...	...	...	...	...	...	...

Table 2 (Concluded). STANDARD PRESENTATION, 1994–2001
(Millions of U.S. dollars)

	Code	1994	1995	1996	1997	1998	1999	2000	2001
D. OTHER INVESTMENT	4 700 . .	6.60	–4.84	–13.89	–6.01	–11.70	–10.51	28.98	. . .
Assets	4 703 . .	**–4.31**	**–3.60**	**–16.45**	**–7.28**	**–14.13**	**–12.37**	**–10.42**	**. . .**
Trade credits	4 706 . .	. . .	. . .	. . .	. . .	. . .	. . .	. . .	. . .
General government	4 707 . .	. . .	. . .	. . .	. . .	. . .	. . .	. . .	. . .
of which: Short-term	4 709 . .	. . .	. . .	. . .	. . .	. . .	. . .	. . .	. . .
Other sectors	4 710 . .	. . .	. . .	. . .	. . .	. . .	. . .	. . .	. . .
of which: Short-term	4 712 . .	. . .	. . .	. . .	. . .	. . .	. . .	. . .	. . .
Loans	4 714 . .	. . .	. . .	. . .	. . .	. . .	. . .	. . .	. . .
Monetary authorities	4 715 . .	. . .	. . .	. . .	. . .	. . .	. . .	. . .	. . .
of which: Short-term	4 718 . .	. . .	. . .	. . .	. . .	. . .	. . .	. . .	. . .
General government	4 719 . .	. . .	. . .	. . .	. . .	. . .	. . .	. . .	. . .
of which: Short-term	4 721 . .	. . .	. . .	. . .	. . .	. . .	. . .	. . .	. . .
Banks	4 722 . .	. . .	. . .	. . .	. . .	. . .	. . .	. . .	. . .
of which: Short-term	4 724 . .	. . .	. . .	. . .	. . .	. . .	. . .	. . .	. . .
Other sectors	4 725 . .	. . .	. . .	. . .	. . .	. . .	. . .	. . .	. . .
of which: Short-term	4 727 . .	. . .	. . .	. . .	. . .	. . .	. . .	. . .	. . .
Currency and deposits	4 730 . .	. . .	. . .	. . .	. . .	. . .	. . .	. . .	. . .
Monetary authorities	4 731 . .	. . .	. . .	. . .	. . .	. . .	. . .	. . .	. . .
General government	4 732 . .	. . .	. . .	. . .	. . .	. . .	. . .	. . .	. . .
Banks	4 733 . .	. . .	. . .	. . .	. . .	. . .	. . .	. . .	. . .
Other sectors	4 734 . .	. . .	. . .	. . .	. . .	. . .	. . .	. . .	. . .
Other assets	4 736 . .	. . .	. . .	. . .	. . .	. . .	. . .	. . .	. . .
Monetary authorities	4 737 . .	. . .	. . .	. . .	. . .	. . .	. . .	. . .	. . .
of which: Short-term	4 739 . .	. . .	. . .	. . .	. . .	. . .	. . .	. . .	. . .
General government	4 740 . .	. . .	. . .	. . .	. . .	. . .	. . .	. . .	. . .
of which: Short-term	4 742 . .	. . .	. . .	. . .	. . .	. . .	. . .	. . .	. . .
Banks	4 743 . .	. . .	. . .	. . .	. . .	. . .	. . .	. . .	. . .
of which: Short-term	4 745 . .	. . .	. . .	. . .	. . .	. . .	. . .	. . .	. . .
Other sectors	4 746 . .	. . .	. . .	. . .	. . .	. . .	. . .	. . .	. . .
of which: Short-term	4 748 . .	. . .	. . .	. . .	. . .	. . .	. . .	. . .	. . .
Liabilities	4 753 . .	**10.91**	**–1.24**	**2.56**	**1.27**	**2.43**	**1.86**	**39.40**	**. . .**
Trade credits	4 756 . .	. . .	. . .	. . .	. . .	. . .	. . .	. . .	. . .
General government	4 757 . .	. . .	. . .	. . .	. . .	. . .	. . .	. . .	. . .
of which: Short-term	4 759 . .	. . .	. . .	. . .	. . .	. . .	. . .	. . .	. . .
Other sectors	4 760 . .	. . .	. . .	. . .	. . .	. . .	. . .	. . .	. . .
of which: Short-term	4 762 . .	. . .	. . .	. . .	. . .	. . .	. . .	. . .	. . .
Loans	4 764 . .	–.80	–.86	–.81	–.55	–.22	–.04	. . .	. . .
Monetary authorities	4 765 . .	–.80	–.86	–.81	–.55	–.22	–.04	. . .	. . .
of which: Use of Fund credit and loans from the Fund	4 766 . .	*–.80*	*–.86*	*–.81*	*–.55*	*–.22*	*–.04*	. . .	. . .
of which: Short-term	4 768 . .	. . .	. . .	. . .	. . .	. . .	. . .	. . .	. . .
General government	4 769 . .	. . .	. . .	. . .	. . .	. . .	. . .	. . .	. . .
of which: Short-term	4 771 . .	. . .	. . .	. . .	. . .	. . .	. . .	. . .	. . .
Banks	4 772 . .	. . .	. . .	. . .	. . .	. . .	. . .	. . .	. . .
of which: Short-term	4 774 . .	. . .	. . .	. . .	. . .	. . .	. . .	. . .	. . .
Other sectors	4 775 . .	. . .	. . .	. . .	. . .	. . .	. . .	. . .	. . .
of which: Short-term	4 777 . .	. . .	. . .	. . .	. . .	. . .	. . .	. . .	. . .
Currency and deposits	4 780 . .	. . .	. . .	. . .	. . .	. . .	. . .	. . .	. . .
Monetary authorities	4 781 . .	. . .	. . .	. . .	. . .	. . .	. . .	. . .	. . .
General government	4 782 . .	. . .	. . .	. . .	. . .	. . .	. . .	. . .	. . .
Banks	4 783 . .	. . .	. . .	. . .	. . .	. . .	. . .	. . .	. . .
Other sectors	4 784 . .	. . .	. . .	. . .	. . .	. . .	. . .	. . .	. . .
Other liabilities	4 786 . .	. . .	. . .	. . .	. . .	. . .	. . .	. . .	. . .
Monetary authorities	4 787 . .	. . .	. . .	. . .	. . .	. . .	. . .	. . .	. . .
of which: Short-term	4 789 . .	. . .	. . .	. . .	. . .	. . .	. . .	. . .	. . .
General government	4 790 . .	. . .	. . .	. . .	. . .	. . .	. . .	. . .	. . .
of which: Short-term	4 792 . .	. . .	. . .	. . .	. . .	. . .	. . .	. . .	. . .
Banks	4 793 . .	. . .	. . .	. . .	. . .	. . .	. . .	. . .	. . .
of which: Short-term	4 795 . .	. . .	. . .	. . .	. . .	. . .	. . .	. . .	. . .
Other sectors	4 796 . .	. . .	. . .	. . .	. . .	. . .	. . .	. . .	. . .
of which: Short-term	4 798 . .	. . .	. . .	. . .	. . .	. . .	. . .	. . .	. . .
E. RESERVE ASSETS	4 802 . .	4.15	–7.48	–1.06	–1.05	–4.22	–11.00	–.47	. . .
Monetary gold	4 812 . .	. . .	. . .	. . .	. . .	. . .	. . .	. . .	. . .
Special drawing rights	4 811 . .	. . .	. . .	. . .	. . .	. . .	–.01	.01	. . .
Reserve position in the Fund	4 810 . .	. . .	. . .	. . .	. . .	. . .	. . .	. . .	. . .
Foreign exchange	4 803 . .	4.44	–6.98	–.79	–.69	–3.77	–3.91	2.20	. . .
Other claims	4 813 . .	–.30	–.50	–.27	–.36	–.45	–7.09	–2.67	. . .
NET ERRORS AND OMISSIONS	4 998 . .	**–2.71**	**–17.62**	**4.66**	**–10.20**	**5.55**	**4.22**	**2.01**	**. . .**

Part 3 of the *Yearbook* contains descriptions of the methodologies, compilation practices, and sources used to compile these data.

Table 1. ANALYTIC PRESENTATION, 1994–2001
(Millions of U.S. dollars)

	Code	1994	1995	1996	1997	1998	1999	2000	2001
A. Current Account [1]	4 993 Z.	**–283.0**	**–182.8**	**–212.7**	**–163.0**	**–338.4**	**–429.2**	**–1,026.5**	**–838.9**
Goods: exports f.o.b.	2 100 ..	3,452.5	3,779.5	4,052.8	4,613.7	4,980.5	5,136.7	5,736.7	5,332.9
Goods: imports f.o.b.	3 100 ..	–4,903.2	–5,170.4	–5,727.0	–6,608.7	–7,597.3	–8,041.1	–9,478.5	–8,784.2
Balance on Goods	4 100 ..	*–1,450.7*	*–1,390.9*	*–1,674.2*	*–1,995.0*	*–2,616.8*	*–2,904.4*	*–3,741.8*	*–3,451.3*
Services: credit	2 200 ..	1,787.9	1,951.3	2,140.0	2,446.6	2,501.5	2,850.3	3,227.6	2,998.8
Services: debit	3 200 ..	–921.1	–966.4	–1,121.4	–1,171.3	–1,319.5	–1,248.0	–1,373.3	–1,295.0
Balance on Goods and Services	4 991 ..	*–583.9*	*–406.0*	*–655.6*	*–719.7*	*–1,434.8*	*–1,302.1*	*–1,887.5*	*–1,747.5*
Income: credit	2 300 ..	101.4	128.1	130.3	140.4	168.2	218.3	299.7	271.2
Income: debit	3 300 ..	–783.3	–897.1	–855.1	–935.8	–1,058.3	–1,193.2	–1,341.0	–1,390.1
Balance on Goods, Services, and Income	4 992 ..	*–1,265.8*	*–1,175.0*	*–1,380.4*	*–1,515.1*	*–2,324.9*	*–2,277.0*	*–2,928.8*	*–2,866.4*
Current transfers: credit	2 379 Z.	996.8	1,007.7	1,187.6	1,373.1	2,016.9	1,997.1	2,095.6	2,232.0
Current transfers: debit	3 379 ..	–14.0	–15.5	–19.9	–21.0	–30.4	–149.3	–193.3	–204.5
B. Capital Account [1]	4 994 Z.	**...**	**...**	**...**	**...**	**...**	**...**	**...**	**...**
Capital account: credit	2 994 Z.	...	...	...	...	...	...	...	...
Capital account: debit	3 994 ..	...	...	...	...	...	...	...	...
Total, Groups A Plus B	4 981 ..	*–283.0*	*–182.8*	*–212.7*	*–163.0*	*–338.4*	*–429.2*	*–1,026.5*	*–838.9*
C. Financial Account [1]	4 995 W.	**368.0**	**253.6**	**64.1**	**447.6**	**688.1**	**1,061.0**	**1,596.6**	**1,722.9**
Direct investment abroad	4 505 ..	...	...	...	...	...	...	...	...
Direct investment in Dominican Republic	4 555 Z.	206.8	414.3	96.5	420.6	699.8	1,337.8	952.9	1,198.4
Portfolio investment assets	4 602 ..	–38.9	–2.9	–7.3	–5.6	–17.5	–433.0	268.4	123.5
Equity securities	4 610 ..	...	...	–4.0	–2.1	–13.7	–428.9	270.6	128.2
Debt securities	4 619 ..	–38.9	–2.9	–3.3	–3.5	–3.8	–4.1	–2.2	–4.7
Portfolio investment liabilities	4 652 Z.	...	...	...	–1.9	–3.8	–3.8	–3.9	480.2
Equity securities	4 660 ..	...	...	...	...	...	...	...	...
Debt securities	4 669 Z.	...	...	...	–1.9	–3.8	–3.8	–3.9	480.2
Financial derivatives	4 910 ..	...	...	...	...	...	...	...	...
Financial derivatives assets	4 900 ..	...	...	...	...	...	...	...	...
Financial derivatives liabilities	4 905 ..	...	...	...	...	...	...	...	...
Other investment assets	4 703 ..	176.8	–263.1	42.3	–220.1	–66.4	–53.4	–165.0	–155.5
Monetary authorities	4 701 ..	–15.2	–.6	–.9	–.9	–1.0	–1.0	–1.2	–.8
General government	4 704 ..	...	...	...	...	...	...	...	...
Banks	4 705 ..	18.0	–39.0	17.0	–40.7	–53.2	–18.8	–64.4	–94.9
Other sectors	4 728 ..	174.0	–223.5	26.2	–178.5	–12.2	–33.6	–99.4	–59.8
Other investment liabilities	4 753 W.	23.3	105.3	–67.4	254.6	76.0	213.4	544.2	76.3
Monetary authorities	4 753 WA	31.1	27.1	–22.8	–17.3	–88.7	–24.7	72.0	–25.1
General government	4 753 ZB	–59.5	–18.8	–35.3	–64.2	–38.5	124.2	119.1	71.4
Banks	4 753 ZC	45.4	32.1	89.7	172.3	218.5	106.9	234.2	–48.5
Other sectors	4 753 ZD	6.3	64.9	–99.0	163.8	–15.3	7.0	118.9	78.5
Total, Groups A Through C	4 983 ..	*85.0*	*70.8*	*–148.6*	*284.6*	*349.7*	*631.8*	*570.1*	*884.0*
D. Net Errors and Omissions	4 998 ..	**–596.0**	**75.3**	**108.8**	**–193.7**	**–338.6**	**–480.4**	**–618.5**	**–371.1**
Total, Groups A Through D	4 984 ..	*–511.0*	*146.1*	*–39.8*	*90.9*	*11.1*	*151.4*	*–48.4*	*512.9*
E. Reserves and Related Items	4 802 A.	**511.0**	**–146.1**	**39.8**	**–90.9**	**–11.1**	**–151.4**	**48.4**	**–512.9**
Reserve assets	4 802 ..	384.7	–131.2	15.2	–39.5	–98.2	–193.6	69.9	–518.2
Use of Fund credit and loans	4 766 ..	–8.1	–34.0	–59.4	–62.4	26.8	...	...	...
Exceptional financing	4 920 ..	134.4	19.1	84.1	11.0	60.3	42.2	–21.5	5.3
Conversion rates: Dominican pesos per U.S. dollar	0 101 ..	**13.160**	**13.597**	**13.775**	**14.265**	**15.267**	**16.033**	**16.415**	**16.952**

[1] Excludes components that have been classified in the categories of Group E.

Table 2. STANDARD PRESENTATION, 1994–2001
(Millions of U.S. dollars)

	Code	1994	1995	1996	1997	1998	1999	2000	2001
CURRENT ACCOUNT	4 993 . .	**–283.0**	**–182.8**	**–212.7**	**–163.0**	**–338.4**	**–429.2**	**–1,026.5**	**–838.9**
A. GOODS	4 100 . .	–1,450.7	–1,390.9	–1,674.2	–1,995.0	–2,616.8	–2,904.4	–3,741.8	–3,451.3
Credit	2 100 . .	**3,452.5**	**3,779.5**	**4,052.8**	**4,613.7**	**4,980.5**	**5,136.7**	**5,736.7**	**5,332.9**
General merchandise: exports f.o.b.	2 110 . .	625.2	727.5	783.5	859.1	725.7	621.5	783.0	652.4
Goods for processing: exports f.o.b.	2 150 . .	2,716.1	2,907.4	3,107.3	3,596.4	4,100.2	4,331.5	4,770.6	4,538.2
Repairs on goods	2 160 . .	. . .	. . .	. . .	. . .	. . .	. . .	. . .	. . .
Goods procured in ports by carriers	2 170 . .	93.8	103.3	116.3	132.8	140.6	177.6	183.1	142.3
Nonmonetary gold	2 180 . .	17.4	41.3	45.7	25.4	14.0	6.1	. . .	. . .
Debit	3 100 . .	**–4,903.2**	**–5,170.4**	**–5,727.0**	**–6,608.7**	**–7,597.3**	**–8,041.1**	**–9,478.5**	**–8,784.2**
General merchandise: imports f.o.b.	3 110 . .	–2,991.7	–3,164.2	–3,580.7	–4,192.0	–4,896.6	–5,206.8	–6,416.0	–5,937.1
Goods for processing: imports f.o.b.	3 150 . .	–1,911.5	–2,006.2	–2,146.3	–2,416.7	–2,700.7	–2,834.3	–3,062.5	–2,847.1
Repairs on goods	3 160 . .	. . .	. . .	. . .	. . .	. . .	. . .	. . .	. . .
Goods procured in ports by carriers	3 170 . .	. . .	. . .	. . .	. . .	. . .	. . .	. . .	. . .
Nonmonetary gold	3 180 . .	. . .	. . .	. . .	. . .	. . .	. . .	. . .	. . .
B. SERVICES	4 200 . .	866.8	984.9	1,018.6	1,275.3	1,182.0	1,602.3	1,854.3	1,703.8
Total credit	2 200 . .	*1,787.9*	*1,951.3*	*2,140.0*	*2,446.6*	*2,501.5*	*2,850.3*	*3,227.6*	*2,998.8*
Total debit	3 200 . .	*–921.1*	*–966.4*	*–1,121.4*	*–1,171.3*	*–1,319.5*	*–1,248.0*	*–1,373.3*	*–1,295.0*
Transportation services, credit	2 205 . .	**38.0**	**41.6**	**57.6**	**61.0**	**61.7**	**67.3**	**71.3**	**67.1**
Passenger	2 850 . .	. . .	. . .	. . .	. . .	. . .	. . .	. . .	. . .
Freight	2 851 . .	*2.8*	*2.6*	*2.8*	*3.0*	*2.8*	*4.9*	*5.2*	*4.7*
Other	2 852 . .	*35.2*	*39.0*	*54.8*	*58.0*	*58.9*	*62.4*	*66.1*	*62.4*
Sea transport, passenger	2 207 . .	. . .	. . .	. . .	. . .	. . .	. . .	. . .	. . .
Sea transport, freight	2 208 . .	. . .	. . .	. . .	. . .	. . .	. . .	. . .	. . .
Sea transport, other	2 209 . .	25.5	28.3	38.5	40.3	42.7	46.6	51.1	50.6
Air transport, passenger	2 211 . .	. . .	. . .	. . .	. . .	. . .	. . .	. . .	. . .
Air transport, freight	2 212 . .	2.8	2.6	2.8	3.0	2.8	4.9	5.2	4.7
Air transport, other	2 213 . .	1.1	1.5	4.5	4.6	3.0	3.3	4.0	3.8
Other transport, passenger	2 215 . .	. . .	. . .	. . .	. . .	. . .	. . .	. . .	. . .
Other transport, freight	2 216 . .	. . .	. . .	. . .	. . .	. . .	. . .	. . .	. . .
Other transport, other	2 217 . .	8.6	9.2	11.8	13.1	13.2	12.5	11.0	8.0
Transportation services, debit	3 205 . .	**–575.0**	**–584.2**	**–648.8**	**–678.9**	**–781.0**	**–772.3**	**–828.0**	**–763.7**
Passenger	3 850 . .	*–86.8*	*–93.5*	*–114.5*	*–118.1*	*–126.0*	*–127.0*	*–130.8*	*–133.5*
Freight	3 851 . .	*–485.5*	*–488.2*	*–531.5*	*–557.9*	*–652.3*	*–642.4*	*–694.6*	*–627.6*
Other	3 852 . .	*–2.7*	*–2.5*	*–2.8*	*–2.9*	*–2.7*	*–2.9*	*–2.6*	*–2.6*
Sea transport, passenger	3 207 . .	. . .	. . .	. . .	. . .	. . .	. . .	. . .	. . .
Sea transport, freight	3 208 . .	–451.8	–455.7	–490.1	–520.2	–609.0	–598.6	–647.2	–585.6
Sea transport, other	3 209 . .	. . .	. . .	. . .	. . .	. . .	. . .	. . .	. . .
Air transport, passenger	3 211 . .	–86.8	–93.5	–114.5	–118.1	–126.0	–127.0	–130.8	–133.5
Air transport, freight	3 212 . .	–33.7	–32.5	–41.4	–37.7	–43.3	–43.8	–47.4	–42.0
Air transport, other	3 213 . .	–2.7	–2.5	–2.8	–2.9	–2.7	–2.9	–2.6	–2.6
Other transport, passenger	3 215 . .	. . .	. . .	. . .	. . .	. . .	. . .	. . .	. . .
Other transport, freight	3 216 . .	. . .	. . .	. . .	. . .	. . .	. . .	. . .	. . .
Other transport, other	3 217 . .	. . .	. . .	. . .	. . .	. . .	. . .	. . .	. . .
Travel, credit	2 236 . .	**1,428.8**	**1,570.8**	**1,780.5**	**2,099.4**	**2,153.1**	**2,483.3**	**2,860.2**	**2,689.8**
Business travel	2 237 . .	. . .	. . .	. . .	. . .	. . .	. . .	17.4	19.5
Personal travel	2 240 . .	1,428.8	1,570.8	1,780.5	2,099.4	2,153.1	2,483.3	2,842.8	2,670.3
Travel, debit	3 236 . .	**–144.5**	**–173.0**	**–198.2**	**–220.7**	**–254.2**	**–264.1**	**–309.0**	**–286.6**
Business travel	3 237 . .	. . .	. . .	. . .	. . .	. . .	. . .	. . .	. . .
Personal travel	3 240 . .	–144.5	–173.0	–198.2	–220.7	–254.2	–264.1	–309.0	–286.6
Other services, credit	2 200 BA	**321.1**	**338.9**	**301.9**	**286.2**	**286.7**	**299.7**	**296.1**	**241.9**
Communications	2 245 . .	237.5	246.5	191.4	158.6	144.8	141.6	139.2	98.7
Construction	2 249 . .	. . .	. . .	. . .	. . .	. . .	. . .	. . .	. . .
Insurance	2 253 . .	. . .	. . .	. . .	. . .	. . .	. . .	. . .	. . .
Financial	2 260 . .	. . .	. . .	. . .	. . .	. . .	. . .	. . .	. . .
Computer and information	2 262 . .	. . .	. . .	. . .	. . .	. . .	. . .	. . .	. . .
Royalties and licence fees	2 266 . .	. . .	. . .	. . .	. . .	. . .	. . .	. . .	. . .
Other business services	2 268 . .	32.4	35.0	48.8	53.7	60.9	74.8	71.8	56.4
Personal, cultural, and recreational	2 287 . .	. . .	. . .	. . .	. . .	. . .	. . .	. . .	. . .
Government, n.i.e.	2 291 . .	51.2	57.4	61.7	73.9	81.0	83.3	85.1	86.8
Other services, debit	3 200 BA	**–201.6**	**–209.2**	**–274.4**	**–271.7**	**–284.3**	**–211.6**	**–236.3**	**–244.7**
Communications	3 245 . .	–55.7	–75.9	–70.2	–63.2	–45.3	–46.5	–50.2	–37.8
Construction	3 249 . .	. . .	. . .	. . .	. . .	. . .	. . .	. . .	. . .
Insurance	3 253 . .	–113.6	–96.8	–139.4	–151.4	–166.0	–77.7	–86.9	–93.9
Financial	3 260 . .	–3.5	–1.2	–2.7	–11.6	–5.9	–8.4	–8.8	–13.1
Computer and information	3 262 . .	. . .	. . .	. . .	. . .	. . .	. . .	. . .	. . .
Royalties and licence fees	3 266 . .	–5.6	–10.2	–28.5	–16.1	–25.3	–29.8	–29.7	–22.0
Other business services	3 268 . .	–13.5	–15.5	–12.4	–17.9	–21.9	–25.6	–27.1	–42.5
Personal, cultural, and recreational	3 287 . .	. . .	. . .	. . .	. . .	. . .	. . .	. . .	. . .
Government, n.i.e.	3 291 . .	–9.7	–9.6	–21.2	–11.5	–19.9	–23.6	–33.6	–35.4

Table 2 (Continued). STANDARD PRESENTATION, 1994–2001

(Millions of U.S. dollars)

	Code	1994	1995	1996	1997	1998	1999	2000	2001
C. INCOME	4 300	–681.9	–769.0	–724.8	–795.4	–890.1	–974.9	–1,041.3	–1,118.9
Total credit	2 300	*101.4*	*128.1*	*130.3*	*140.4*	*168.2*	*218.3*	*299.7*	*271.2*
Total debit	3 300	*–783.3*	*–897.1*	*–855.1*	*–935.8*	*–1,058.3*	*–1,193.2*	*–1,341.0*	*–1,390.1*
Compensation of employees, credit	2 310	**40.8**	**44.7**	**48.7**	**53.3**	**79.8**	**112.4**	**149.8**	**173.9**
Compensation of employees, debit	3 310	**–7.4**	**–7.0**	**–8.9**	**–7.6**	**–18.5**	**–17.8**	**–19.3**	**–21.7**
Investment income, credit	2 320	**60.6**	**83.4**	**81.6**	**87.1**	**88.4**	**105.9**	**149.9**	**97.3**
Direct investment income	2 330	. . .	. . .	. . .	. . .	. . .	. . .	. . .	. . .
Dividends and distributed branch profits	2 332	. . .	. . .	. . .	. . .	. . .	. . .	. . .	. . .
Reinvested earnings and undistributed branch profits	2 333	. . .	. . .	. . .	. . .	. . .	. . .	. . .	. . .
Income on debt (interest)	2 334	. . .	. . .	. . .	. . .	. . .	. . .	. . .	. . .
Portfolio investment income	2 339	.1	4.3	4.4	4.0	5.0	12.3	20.4	17.0
Income on equity	2 340	. . .	. . .	. . .	. . .	. . .	. . .	. . .	. . .
Income on bonds and notes	2 350	.1	4.3	4.4	4.0	5.0	12.3	20.4	17.0
Income on money market instruments	2 360	. . .	. . .	. . .	. . .	. . .	. . .	. . .	. . .
Other investment income	2 370	60.5	79.1	77.2	83.1	83.4	93.6	129.5	80.3
Investment income, debit	3 320	**–775.9**	**–890.1**	**–846.2**	**–928.2**	**–1,039.8**	**–1,175.4**	**–1,321.7**	**–1,368.4**
Direct investment income	3 330	–559.2	–624.0	–604.0	–711.6	–830.7	–963.2	–1,068.3	–1,107.9
Dividends and distributed branch profits	3 332	–372.0	–339.2	–513.8	–437.8	–443.1	–560.4	–793.6	–723.3
Reinvested earnings and undistributed branch profits	3 333	–187.2	–284.8	–69.7	–245.1	–343.7	–343.4	–210.7	–301.3
Income on debt (interest)	3 334	. . .	. . .	–20.5	–28.7	–43.9	–59.4	–64.0	–83.3
Portfolio investment income	3 339	–6.2	–39.2	–35.5	–37.0	–35.7	–32.9	–47.6	–43.1
Income on equity	3 340	–1.4	–2.9	–1.4	–2.4	–.4	–.8	–10.0	–10.4
Income on bonds and notes	3 350	–4.8	–36.3	–34.1	–34.6	–35.3	–32.1	–37.6	–32.7
Income on money market instruments	3 360	. . .	. . .	. . .	. . .	. . .	. . .	. . .	. . .
Other investment income	3 370	–210.5	–226.9	–206.7	–179.6	–173.4	–179.3	–205.8	–217.4
D. CURRENT TRANSFERS	4 379	982.8	992.2	1,167.7	1,352.1	1,986.5	1,847.8	1,902.3	2,027.5
Credit	2 379	**996.8**	**1,007.7**	**1,187.6**	**1,373.1**	**2,016.9**	**1,997.1**	**2,095.6**	**2,232.0**
General government	2 380	71.3	63.7	72.0	65.9	143.5	128.1	115.5	116.2
Other sectors	2 390	925.5	944.0	1,115.6	1,307.2	1,873.4	1,869.0	1,980.1	2,115.8
Workers' remittances	2 391	756.7	794.5	914.0	1,088.9	1,326.0	1,518.7	1,689.0	1,807.9
Other current transfers	2 392	168.8	149.5	201.6	218.3	547.4	350.3	291.1	307.9
Debit	3 379	**–14.0**	**–15.5**	**–19.9**	**–21.0**	**–30.4**	**–149.3**	**–193.3**	**–204.5**
General government	3 380	. . .	–.2	–3.2	–2.8	–3.0	–3.1	–2.8	–2.5
Other sectors	3 390	–14.0	–15.3	–16.7	–18.2	–27.4	–146.2	–190.5	–202.0
Workers' remittances	3 391	. . .	. . .	. . .	. . .	. . .	. . .	. . .	. . .
Other current transfers	3 392	–14.0	–15.3	–16.7	–18.2	–27.4	–146.2	–190.5	–202.0
CAPITAL AND FINANCIAL ACCOUNT	4 996	**879.0**	**107.5**	**103.9**	**356.7**	**677.0**	**909.6**	**1,645.0**	**1,210.0**
CAPITAL ACCOUNT	4 994	**13.2**	**1.0**	**7.8**	**1.0**	**2.3**	**1.5**	**1.7**	**4.2**
Total credit	2 994	*13.2*	*1.0*	*7.8*	*1.0*	*2.3*	*1.5*	*1.7*	*4.2*
Total debit	3 994	. . .	. . .	. . .	. . .	. . .	. . .	. . .	. . .
Capital transfers, credit	2 400	**13.2**	**1.0**	**7.8**	**1.0**	**2.3**	**1.5**	**1.7**	**4.2**
General government	2 401	13.2	1.0	7.8	1.0	2.3	1.5	1.7	4.2
Debt forgiveness	2 402	13.2	1.0	7.8	1.0	2.3	1.5	1.7	4.2
Other capital transfers	2 410	. . .	. . .	. . .	. . .	. . .	. . .	. . .	. . .
Other sectors	2 430	. . .	. . .	. . .	. . .	. . .	. . .	. . .	. . .
Migrants' transfers	2 431	. . .	. . .	. . .	. . .	. . .	. . .	. . .	. . .
Debt forgiveness	2 432	. . .	. . .	. . .	. . .	. . .	. . .	. . .	. . .
Other capital transfers	2 440	. . .	. . .	. . .	. . .	. . .	. . .	. . .	. . .
Capital transfers, debit	3 400	**. . .**	**. . .**	**. . .**	**. . .**	**. . .**	**. . .**	**. . .**	**. . .**
General government	3 401	. . .	. . .	. . .	. . .	. . .	. . .	. . .	. . .
Debt forgiveness	3 402	. . .	. . .	. . .	. . .	. . .	. . .	. . .	. . .
Other capital transfers	3 410	. . .	. . .	. . .	. . .	. . .	. . .	. . .	. . .
Other sectors	3 430	. . .	. . .	. . .	. . .	. . .	. . .	. . .	. . .
Migrants' transfers	3 431	. . .	. . .	. . .	. . .	. . .	. . .	. . .	. . .
Debt forgiveness	3 432	. . .	. . .	. . .	. . .	. . .	. . .	. . .	. . .
Other capital transfers	3 440	. . .	. . .	. . .	. . .	. . .	. . .	. . .	. . .
Nonproduced nonfinancial assets, credit	2 480	**. . .**	**. . .**	**. . .**	**. . .**	**. . .**	**. . .**	**. . .**	**. . .**
Nonproduced nonfinancial assets, debit	3 480	**. . .**	**. . .**	**. . .**	**. . .**	**. . .**	**. . .**	**. . .**	**. . .**

Table 2 (Continued). STANDARD PRESENTATION, 1994–2001

(Millions of U.S. dollars)

	Code	1994	1995	1996	1997	1998	1999	2000	2001
FINANCIAL ACCOUNT	4 995 . .	**865.8**	**106.5**	**96.1**	**355.7**	**674.7**	**908.1**	**1,643.3**	**1,205.8**
A. DIRECT INVESTMENT	4 500 . .	206.8	414.3	96.5	420.6	699.8	1,337.8	952.9	1,198.4
Direct investment abroad	4 505 . .	**. . .**	**. . .**	**. . .**	**. . .**	**. . .**	**. . .**	**. . .**	**. . .**
Equity capital	4 510 . .	. . .	. . .	. . .	. . .	. . .	. . .	. . .	. . .
Claims on affiliated enterprises	4 515 . .	. . .	. . .	. . .	. . .	. . .	. . .	. . .	. . .
Liabilities to affiliated enterprises	4 520 . .	. . .	. . .	. . .	. . .	. . .	. . .	. . .	. . .
Reinvested earnings	4 525 . .	. . .	. . .	. . .	. . .	. . .	. . .	. . .	. . .
Other capital	4 530 . .	. . .	. . .	. . .	. . .	. . .	. . .	. . .	. . .
Claims on affiliated enterprises	4 535 . .	. . .	. . .	. . .	. . .	. . .	. . .	. . .	. . .
Liabilities to affiliated enterprises	4 540 . .	. . .	. . .	. . .	. . .	. . .	. . .	. . .	. . .
Direct investment in Dominican Republic	4 555 . .	**206.8**	**414.3**	**96.5**	**420.6**	**699.8**	**1,337.8**	**952.9**	**1,198.4**
Equity capital	4 560 . .	37.8	111.1	65.8	190.2	295.2	946.6	632.9	752.2
Claims on direct investors	4 565 . .	. . .	. . .	–9.8	. . .	. . .	–.2	–25.5	. . .
Liabilities to direct investors	4 570 . .	37.8	111.1	75.6	190.2	295.2	946.8	658.4	752.2
Reinvested earnings	4 575 . .	187.2	284.8	69.7	245.1	343.7	343.4	210.7	301.3
Other capital	4 580 . .	–18.2	18.4	–39.0	–14.7	60.9	47.8	109.3	144.9
Claims on direct investors	4 585 . .	–1.3	–3.1	–27.9	11.9	30.9	–6.9	–10.6	–8.8
Liabilities to direct investors	4 590 . .	–16.9	21.5	–11.1	–26.6	30.0	54.7	119.9	153.7
B. PORTFOLIO INVESTMENT	4 600 . .	481.0	–2.9	–7.3	–7.5	–21.3	–436.8	264.5	603.7
Assets	4 602 . .	**–38.9**	**–2.9**	**–7.3**	**–5.6**	**–17.5**	**–433.0**	**268.4**	**123.5**
Equity securities	4 610 . .	. . .	. . .	–4.0	–2.1	–13.7	–428.9	270.6	128.2
Monetary authorities	4 611 . .	. . .	. . .	. . .	. . .	. . .	. . .	. . .	. . .
General government	4 612 . .	. . .	. . .	. . .	. . .	. . .	. . .	. . .	. . .
Banks	4 613 . .	. . .	. . .	–4.0	–2.1	–13.7	–1.9	7.3	–2.7
Other sectors	4 614 . .	. . .	. . .	. . .	. . .	. . .	–427.0	263.3	130.9
Debt securities	4 619 . .	–38.9	–2.9	–3.3	–3.5	–3.8	–4.1	–2.2	–4.7
Bonds and notes	4 620 . .	–38.9	–2.9	–3.3	–3.5	–3.8	–4.1	–2.2	–4.7
Monetary authorities	4 621 . .	–38.9	–2.9	–3.3	–3.5	–3.8	–4.1	–2.2	–4.7
General government	4 622 . .	. . .	. . .	. . .	. . .	. . .	. . .	. . .	. . .
Banks	4 623 . .	. . .	. . .	. . .	. . .	. . .	. . .	. . .	. . .
Other sectors	4 624 . .	. . .	. . .	. . .	. . .	. . .	. . .	. . .	. . .
Money market instruments	4 630 . .	. . .	. . .	. . .	. . .	. . .	. . .	. . .	. . .
Monetary authorities	4 631 . .	. . .	. . .	. . .	. . .	. . .	. . .	. . .	. . .
General government	4 632 . .	. . .	. . .	. . .	. . .	. . .	. . .	. . .	. . .
Banks	4 633 . .	. . .	. . .	. . .	. . .	. . .	. . .	. . .	. . .
Other sectors	4 634 . .	. . .	. . .	. . .	. . .	. . .	. . .	. . .	. . .
Liabilities	4 652 . .	**519.9**	**. . .**	**. . .**	**–1.9**	**–3.8**	**–3.8**	**–3.9**	**480.2**
Equity securities	4 660 . .	. . .	. . .	. . .	. . .	. . .	. . .	. . .	. . .
Banks	4 663 . .	. . .	. . .	. . .	. . .	. . .	. . .	. . .	. . .
Other sectors	4 664 . .	. . .	. . .	. . .	. . .	. . .	. . .	. . .	. . .
Debt securities	4 669 . .	519.9	. . .	. . .	–1.9	–3.8	–3.8	–3.9	480.2
Bonds and notes	4 670 . .	519.9	. . .	. . .	–1.9	–3.8	–3.8	–3.9	480.2
Monetary authorities	4 671 . .	367.1	. . .	. . .	–1.8	–3.7	–3.7	–3.7	–19.0
General government	4 672 . .	73.9	. . .	. . .	. . .	. . .	. . .	. . .	500.0
Banks	4 673 . .	1.3	. . .	. . .	. . .	. . .	. . .	–.1	–.1
Other sectors	4 674 . .	77.6	. . .	. . .	–.1	–.1	–.1	–.1	–.7
Money market instruments	4 680 . .	. . .	. . .	. . .	. . .	. . .	. . .	. . .	. . .
Monetary authorities	4 681 . .	. . .	. . .	. . .	. . .	. . .	. . .	. . .	. . .
General government	4 682 . .	. . .	. . .	. . .	. . .	. . .	. . .	. . .	. . .
Banks	4 683 . .	. . .	. . .	. . .	. . .	. . .	. . .	. . .	. . .
Other sectors	4 684 . .	. . .	. . .	. . .	. . .	. . .	. . .	. . .	. . .
C. FINANCIAL DERIVATIVES	4 910 . .	. . .	. . .	. . .	. . .	. . .	. . .	. . .	. . .
Monetary authorities	4 911 . .	. . .	. . .	. . .	. . .	. . .	. . .	. . .	. . .
General government	4 912 . .	. . .	. . .	. . .	. . .	. . .	. . .	. . .	. . .
Banks	4 913 . .	. . .	. . .	. . .	. . .	. . .	. . .	. . .	. . .
Other sectors	4 914 . .	. . .	. . .	. . .	. . .	. . .	. . .	. . .	. . .
Assets	4 900 . .	**. . .**	**. . .**	**. . .**	**. . .**	**. . .**	**. . .**	**. . .**	**. . .**
Monetary authorities	4 901 . .	. . .	. . .	. . .	. . .	. . .	. . .	. . .	. . .
General government	4 902 . .	. . .	. . .	. . .	. . .	. . .	. . .	. . .	. . .
Banks	4 903 . .	. . .	. . .	. . .	. . .	. . .	. . .	. . .	. . .
Other sectors	4 904 . .	. . .	. . .	. . .	. . .	. . .	. . .	. . .	. . .
Liabilities	4 905 . .	**. . .**	**. . .**	**. . .**	**. . .**	**. . .**	**. . .**	**. . .**	**. . .**
Monetary authorities	4 906 . .	. . .	. . .	. . .	. . .	. . .	. . .	. . .	. . .
General government	4 907 . .	. . .	. . .	. . .	. . .	. . .	. . .	. . .	. . .
Banks	4 908 . .	. . .	. . .	. . .	. . .	. . .	. . .	. . .	. . .
Other sectors	4 909 . .	. . .	. . .	. . .	. . .	. . .	. . .	. . .	. . .

Table 2 (Concluded). STANDARD PRESENTATION, 1994–2001

(Millions of U.S. dollars)

	Code	1994	1995	1996	1997	1998	1999	2000	2001
D. OTHER INVESTMENT	4 700	–206.7	–173.7	–8.2	–17.9	94.4	200.7	356.0	–78.1
Assets	4 703	**176.8**	**–263.1**	**42.3**	**–220.1**	**–66.4**	**–53.4**	**–165.0**	**–155.5**
Trade credits	4 706	. . .	. . .	–.1	–32.3	–6.3	10.1	–10.7	–17.4
General government	4 707	. . .	. . .	. . .	. . .	. . .	. . .	. . .	. . .
of which: Short-term	4 709	. . .	. . .	. . .	. . .	. . .	. . .	. . .	. . .
Other sectors	4 710	. . .	. . .	–.1	–32.3	–6.3	10.1	–10.7	–17.4
of which: Short-term	4 712	. . .	. . .	*–.1*	*–32.3*	*–6.3*	*10.1*	*–10.7*	*–17.4*
Loans	4 714	. . .	. . .	. . .	. . .	. . .	. . .	. . .	. . .
Monetary authorities	4 715	. . .	. . .	. . .	. . .	. . .	. . .	. . .	. . .
of which: Short-term	4 718	. . .	. . .	. . .	. . .	. . .	. . .	. . .	. . .
General government	4 719	. . .	. . .	. . .	. . .	. . .	. . .	. . .	. . .
of which: Short-term	4 721	. . .	. . .	. . .	. . .	. . .	. . .	. . .	. . .
Banks	4 722	. . .	. . .	. . .	. . .	. . .	. . .	. . .	. . .
of which: Short-term	4 724	. . .	. . .	. . .	. . .	. . .	. . .	. . .	. . .
Other sectors	4 725	. . .	. . .	. . .	. . .	. . .	. . .	. . .	. . .
of which: Short-term	4 727	. . .	. . .	. . .	. . .	. . .	. . .	. . .	. . .
Currency and deposits	4 730	192.0	–262.5	44.0	–183.1	–57.7	–66.4	–154.6	–136.6
Monetary authorities	4 731	. . .	. . .	. . .	. . .	. . .	. . .	. . .	. . .
General government	4 732	. . .	. . .	. . .	. . .	. . .	. . .	. . .	. . .
Banks	4 733	18.0	–39.0	17.7	–36.9	–51.8	–22.7	–65.9	–94.2
Other sectors	4 734	174.0	–223.5	26.3	–146.2	–5.9	–43.7	–88.7	–42.4
Other assets	4 736	–15.2	–.6	–1.6	–4.7	–2.4	2.9	.3	–1.5
Monetary authorities	4 737	–15.2	–.6	–.9	–.9	–1.0	–1.0	–1.2	–.8
of which: Short-term	4 739	. . .	. . .	. . .	. . .	. . .	. . .	. . .	. . .
General government	4 740	. . .	. . .	. . .	. . .	. . .	. . .	. . .	. . .
of which: Short-term	4 742	. . .	. . .	. . .	. . .	. . .	. . .	. . .	. . .
Banks	4 743	. . .	. . .	–.7	–3.8	–1.4	3.9	1.5	–.7
of which: Short-term	4 745	. . .	. . .	*–.7*	*–3.8*	*–1.4*	*3.9*	*1.5*	*–.7*
Other sectors	4 746	. . .	. . .	. . .	. . .	. . .	. . .	. . .	. . .
of which: Short-term	4 748	. . .	. . .	. . .	. . .	. . .	. . .	. . .	. . .
Liabilities	4 753	**–383.5**	**89.4**	**–50.5**	**202.2**	**160.8**	**254.1**	**521.0**	**77.4**
Trade credits	4 756	–22.9	–8.1	–137.3	158.0	–12.7	21.7	26.6	–10.8
General government	4 757	. . .	. . .	. . .	. . .	. . .	. . .	. . .	. . .
of which: Short-term	4 759	. . .	. . .	. . .	. . .	. . .	. . .	. . .	. . .
Other sectors	4 760	–22.9	–8.1	–137.3	158.0	–12.7	21.7	26.6	–10.8
of which: Short-term	4 762	*–22.9*	*–8.1*	*–137.3*	*158.0*	*–12.7*	*21.7*	*26.6*	*–10.8*
Loans	4 764	43.5	47.0	51.9	166.2	103.5	272.1	465.4	90.6
Monetary authorities	4 765	–37.8	20.2	–70.5	–80.0	–28.6	–26.7	33.7	–25.2
of which: Use of Fund credit and loans from the Fund	4 766	*–8.1*	*–34.0*	*–59.4*	*–62.4*	*26.8*	. . .	. . .	. . .
of which: Short-term	4 768	*25.7*	*32.0*	*–17.3*	*–.2*	*–38.3*	*–9.7*	*54.3*	*–3.3*
General government	4 769	–59.5	–8.8	–13.5	66.0	–17.3	138.9	119.1	71.4
of which: Short-term	4 771	. . .	. . .	. . .	. . .	. . .	. . .	. . .	*1.0*
Banks	4 772	24.2	40.2	87.9	170.2	149.9	162.9	220.3	–44.9
of which: Short-term	4 774	*23.7*	*38.4*	*83.9*	*126.6*	*97.4*	*166.5*	*191.3*	*–46.8*
Other sectors	4 775	116.6	–4.6	48.0	10.0	–.5	–3.0	92.3	89.3
of which: Short-term	4 777	*61.4*	*–77.7*	*9.6*	*4.1*	*–3.6*	*–8.9*	*35.6*	*–23.6*
Currency and deposits	4 780	100.8	15.8	10.8	2.4	34.7	–56.3	49.2	–2.8
Monetary authorities	4 781	79.6	23.9	9.5	.6	–33.1	2.0	38.3	.1
General government	4 782	. . .	. . .	. . .	. . .	. . .	. . .	. . .	. . .
Banks	4 783	21.2	–8.1	1.3	1.8	67.8	–58.3	10.9	–2.9
Other sectors	4 784	. . .	. . .	. . .	. . .	. . .	. . .	. . .	. . .
Other liabilities	4 786	–504.9	34.7	24.1	–124.4	35.3	16.6	–20.2	.4
Monetary authorities	4 787	–413.9	–2.1	.6	–.2	.7	.5	–1.6	. . .
of which: Short-term	4 789	*–413.9*	*–2.1*	*.6*	*–.2*	*.7*	*.5*	*–1.6*	. . .
General government	4 790	–26.7	49.8	21.4	–125.6	31.0	14.1	–17.3	–.5
of which: Short-term	4 792	*–26.7*	*49.8*	*21.4*	*–125.6*	*31.0*	*14.1*	*–17.3*	*–.5*
Banks	4 793	–1.3	.4	.9	.4	.9	2.4	3.1	–.7
of which: Short-term	4 795	*–1.3*	*.4*	*.9*	*.4*	*.9*	*2.4*	*3.1*	*–.7*
Other sectors	4 796	–63.0	–13.4	1.2	1.0	2.7	–.4	–4.4	1.6
of which: Short-term	4 798	*–63.0*	*–13.4*	*1.2*	*1.0*	*2.7*	*–.4*	*–4.4*	*1.6*
E. RESERVE ASSETS	4 802	384.7	–131.2	15.2	–39.5	–98.2	–193.6	69.9	–518.2
Monetary gold	4 812	.1	–.2	.3	1.2	.3	.2	.2	–.1
Special drawing rights	4 811	11.1	3.0	.1	.1	.1	. . .	–.1	–.1
Reserve position in the Fund	4 810	. . .	. . .	. . .	. . .	. . .	. . .	. . .	. . .
Foreign exchange	4 803	373.5	–134.0	14.8	–40.8	–98.6	–193.8	69.8	–518.0
Other claims	4 813	. . .	. . .	. . .	. . .	. . .	. . .	. . .	. . .
NET ERRORS AND OMISSIONS	4 998	**–596.0**	**75.3**	**108.8**	**–193.7**	**–338.6**	**–480.4**	**–618.5**	**–371.1**

Part 3 of the *Yearbook* contains descriptions of the methodologies, compilation practices, and sources used to compile these data.

Table 1. ANALYTIC PRESENTATION, 1994–2001

(Millions of U.S. dollars)

	Code	1994	1995	1996	1997	1998	1999	2000	2001
A. Current Account [1]	4 993 Z.	**–898**	**–1,000**	**–55**	**–457**	**–2,099**	**918**	**921**	**–800**
Goods: exports f.o.b.	2 100 . .	3,936	4,468	4,929	5,360	4,326	4,615	5,137	4,862
Goods: imports f.o.b.	3 100 . .	–3,787	–4,535	–4,008	–4,869	–5,458	–3,028	–3,743	–5,325
Balance on Goods	4 100 . .	*149*	*–66*	*921*	*491*	*–1,132*	*1,588*	*1,395*	*–462*
Services: credit	2 200 . .	676	728	683	686	678	730	849	911
Services: debit	3 200 . .	–1,107	–1,173	–1,110	–1,230	–1,241	–1,181	–1,269	–1,430
Balance on Goods and Services	4 991 . .	*–283*	*–512*	*494*	*–52*	*–1,695*	*1,136*	*975*	*–981*
Income: credit	2 300 . .	61	98	80	128	119	75	70	48
Income: debit	3 300 . .	–999	–1,029	–1,121	–1,154	–1,290	–1,383	–1,476	–1,411
Balance on Goods, Services, and Income	4 992 . .	*–1,221*	*–1,442*	*–547*	*–1,078*	*–2,865*	*–171*	*–431*	*–2,344*
Current transfers: credit	2 379 Z.	391	506	616	738	933	1,188	1,437	1,550
Current transfers: debit	3 379 . .	–69	–64	–124	–117	–166	–99	–85	–6
B. Capital Account [1]	4 994 Z.	**18**	**17**	**14**	**11**	**14**	**2**	**–1**	**–67**
Capital account: credit	2 994 Z.	21	21	18	17	23	11	8	17
Capital account: debit	3 994 . .	–3	–4	–4	–6	–9	–9	–10	–84
Total, Groups A Plus B	4 981 . .	*–880*	*–983*	*–40*	*–446*	*–2,084*	*920*	*920*	*–867*
C. Financial Account [1]	4 995 W.	**332**	**–43**	**103**	**–14**	**1,448**	**–1,344**	**–6,602**	**1,007**
Direct investment abroad	4 505 . .	. . .	. . .	. . .	. . .	. . .	. . .	. . .	. . .
Direct investment in Ecuador	4 555 Z.	576	452	500	724	870	648	720	1,330
Portfolio investment assets	4 602 . .	. . .	. . .	. . .	. . .	. . .	. . .	. . .	. . .
Equity securities	4 610 . .	. . .	. . .	. . .	. . .	. . .	. . .	. . .	. . .
Debt securities	4 619 . .	. . .	. . .	. . .	. . .	. . .	. . .	. . .	. . .
Portfolio investment liabilities	4 652 Z.	6	3	–4	–242	–34	–46	–5,583	117
Equity securities	4 660 . .	6	13	6	22	5	1	. . .	1
Debt securities	4 669 Z.	. . .	–10	–10	–264	–40	–47	–5,583	116
Financial derivatives	4 910 . .	. . .	. . .	. . .	. . .	. . .	. . .	. . .	. . .
Financial derivatives assets	4 900 . .	. . .	. . .	. . .	. . .	. . .	. . .	. . .	. . .
Financial derivatives liabilities	4 905 . .	. . .	. . .	. . .	. . .	. . .	. . .	. . .	. . .
Other investment assets	4 703 . .	–177	–668	–302	–560	–54	–725	–1,274	–1,308
Monetary authorities	4 701 . .	. . .	. . .	. . .	. . .	. . .	. . .	. . .	. . .
General government	4 704 . .	. . .	. . .	. . .	. . .	. . .	. . .	. . .	. . .
Banks	4 705 . .	. . .	. . .	. . .	. . .	. . .	. . .	. . .	. . .
Other sectors	4 728 . .	–177	–668	–302	–560	–54	–725	–1,274	–1,308
Other investment liabilities	4 753 W.	–75	170	–91	64	666	–1,221	–465	868
Monetary authorities	4 753 WA	83	–54	–48	–18	230	–76	–135	–144
General government	4 753 ZB	–727	–692	127	–190	–37	117	206	188
Banks	4 753 ZC	26	31	95	26	–24	–72	–37	–108
Other sectors	4 753 ZD	544	885	–265	245	497	–1,190	–499	932
Total, Groups A Through C	4 983 . .	*–549*	*–1,026*	*63*	*–460*	*–637*	*–423*	*–5,683*	*140*
D. Net Errors and Omissions	4 998 . .	**–226**	**–433**	**–189**	**–62**	**–147**	**–521**	**–15**	**–399**
Total, Groups A Through D	4 984 . .	*–775*	*–1,459*	*–126*	*–521*	*–784*	*–944*	*–5,697*	*–259*
E. Reserves and Related Items	4 802 A.	**775**	**1,459**	**126**	**521**	**784**	**944**	**5,697**	**259**
Reserve assets	4 802 . .	–578	174	–247	–253	461	489	–307	105
Use of Fund credit and loans	4 766 . .	122	–29	–23	–3	–67	–68	151	48
Exceptional financing	4 920 . .	1,231	1,314	396	777	391	523	5,853	106

[1] Excludes components that have been classified in the categories of Group E.

Table 2. STANDARD PRESENTATION, 1994–2001
(Millions of U.S. dollars)

	Code		1994	1995	1996	1997	1998	1999	2000	2001
CURRENT ACCOUNT	4 993	. .	**–898**	**–1,000**	**–55**	**–457**	**–2,099**	**918**	**921**	**–800**
A. GOODS	4 100	. .	149	–66	921	491	–1,132	1,588	1,395	–462
Credit	2 100	. .	**3,936**	**4,468**	**4,929**	**5,360**	**4,326**	**4,615**	**5,137**	**4,862**
General merchandise: exports f.o.b.	2 110	. .	3,932	4,453	4,913	5,300	4,273	4,550	5,022	4,771
Goods for processing: exports f.o.b.	2 150	. .	. . .	. . .	. . .	. . .	. . .	. . .	. . .	. . .
Repairs on goods	2 160	. .	. . .	8	10	4	4	4	5	8
Goods procured in ports by carriers	2 170	. .	4	7	6	57	49	61	111	84
Nonmonetary gold	2 180	. .	. . .	. . .	. . .	. . .	. . .	. . .	. . .	. . .
Debit	3 100	. .	**–3,787**	**–4,535**	**–4,008**	**–4,869**	**–5,458**	**–3,028**	**–3,743**	**–5,325**
General merchandise: imports f.o.b.	3 110	. .	–3,747	–4,509	–3,986	–4,842	–5,444	–3,014	–3,723	–5,295
Goods for processing: imports f.o.b.	3 150	. .	. . .	. . .	. . .	. . .	. . .	. . .	. . .	. . .
Repairs on goods	3 160	. .	–10	–12	–15	–13	–5	–3	–4	–8
Goods procured in ports by carriers	3 170	. .	–30	–14	–7	–14	–9	–11	–16	–22
Nonmonetary gold	3 180	. .	. . .	. . .	. . .	. . .	. . .	. . .	. . .	. . .
B. SERVICES	4 200	. .	–432	–445	–427	–543	–563	–451	–420	–518
Total credit	2 200	. .	*676*	*728*	*683*	*686*	*678*	*730*	*849*	*911*
Total debit	3 200	. .	*–1,107*	*–1,173*	*–1,110*	*–1,230*	*–1,241*	*–1,181*	*–1,269*	*–1,430*
Transportation services, credit	2 205	. .	**308**	**322**	**262**	**239**	**228**	**261**	**290**	**298**
Passenger	2 850	. .	*57*	*60*	*49*	*45*	*39*	*34*	*49*	*57*
Freight	2 851	. .	*214*	*219*	*168*	*164*	*154*	*203*	*218*	*215*
Other	2 852	. .	*37*	*43*	*45*	*30*	*35*	*24*	*23*	*26*
Sea transport, passenger	2 207	. .	. . .	. . .	. . .	. . .	. . .	. . .	. . .	. . .
Sea transport, freight	2 208	. .	213	217	165	160	148	190	204	202
Sea transport, other	2 209	. .	28	29	29	18	20	14	18	12
Air transport, passenger	2 211	. .	57	60	49	45	39	34	49	57
Air transport, freight	2 212	. .	1	2	3	4	6	13	14	13
Air transport, other	2 213	. .	9	14	16	12	15	10	5	14
Other transport, passenger	2 215	. .	. . .	. . .	. . .	. . .	. . .	. . .	. . .	. . .
Other transport, freight	2 216	. .	. . .	. . .	. . .	. . .	. . .	. . .	. . .	. . .
Other transport, other	2 217	. .	. . .	. . .	. . .	. . .	. . .	. . .	. . .	. . .
Transportation services, debit	3 205	. .	**–509**	**–484**	**–443**	**–512**	**–504**	**–368**	**–439**	**–553**
Passenger	3 850	. .	*–91*	*–96*	*–94*	*–104*	*–84*	*–114*	*–117*	*–125*
Freight	3 851	. .	*–318*	*–314*	*–280*	*–347*	*–381*	*–227*	*–270*	*–369*
Other	3 852	. .	*–100*	*–74*	*–69*	*–61*	*–39*	*–27*	*–52*	*–59*
Sea transport, passenger	3 207	. .	. . .	. . .	. . .	. . .	. . .	. . .	. . .	. . .
Sea transport, freight	3 208	. .	–297	–294	–257	–321	–339	–203	–239	–304
Sea transport, other	3 209	. .	–74	–57	–47	–39	–25	–20	–44	–46
Air transport, passenger	3 211	. .	–91	–96	–94	–104	–84	–114	–117	–125
Air transport, freight	3 212	. .	–10	–9	–8	–10	–26	–8	–15	–50
Air transport, other	3 213	. .	–26	–17	–22	–22	–14	–7	–8	–13
Other transport, passenger	3 215	. .	. . .	. . .	. . .	. . .	. . .	. . .	. . .	. . .
Other transport, freight	3 216	. .	–11	–11	–15	–16	–16	–16	–16	–16
Other transport, other	3 217	. .	. . .	. . .	. . .	. . .	. . .	. . .	. . .	. . .
Travel, credit	2 236	. .	**252**	**255**	**281**	**290**	**291**	**343**	**402**	**430**
Business travel	2 237	. .	47	48	50	60	74	88	98	101
Personal travel	2 240	. .	205	207	231	230	217	255	304	329
Travel, debit	3 236	. .	**–203**	**–235**	**–219**	**–227**	**–241**	**–271**	**–299**	**–340**
Business travel	3 237	. .	–44	–54	–49	–52	–49	–68	–82	–99
Personal travel	3 240	. .	–159	–181	–170	–175	–192	–203	–217	–241
Other services, credit	2 200	BA	**116**	**151**	**140**	**157**	**160**	**126**	**157**	**184**
Communications	2 245	. .	64	87	77	96	85	64	61	96
Construction	2 249	. .	. . .	. . .	. . .	. . .	. . .	. . .	. . .	. . .
Insurance	2 253	. .	. . .	. . .	1	. . .	11	. . .	1	1
Financial	2 260	. .	. . .	. . .	. . .	. . .	. . .	. . .	. . .	. . .
Computer and information	2 262	. .	. . .	. . .	. . .	. . .	. . .	. . .	. . .	. . .
Royalties and licence fees	2 266	. .	. . .	. . .	. . .	. . .	. . .	. . .	. . .	. . .
Other business services	2 268	. .	1	. . .	2	. . .	. . .	. . .	. . .	. . .
Personal, cultural, and recreational	2 287	. .	15	23	17	14	17	12	39	24
Government, n.i.e.	2 291	. .	36	41	43	47	47	49	56	63
Other services, debit	3 200	BA	**–395**	**–454**	**–449**	**–491**	**–497**	**–542**	**–532**	**–536**
Communications	3 245	. .	–4	–7	–9	–62	–52	–40	–38	–19
Construction	3 249	. .	. . .	. . .	. . .	. . .	. . .	. . .	. . .	. . .
Insurance	3 253	. .	–55	–57	–39	–24	–3	–36	–33	–65
Financial	3 260	. .	–9	–10	–10	–12	–9	–6	–8	–12
Computer and information	3 262	. .	. . .	. . .	. . .	. . .	. . .	. . .	. . .	. . .
Royalties and licence fees	3 266	. .	–50	–53	–68	–64	–68	–70	–62	–52
Other business services	3 268	. .	–218	–263	–249	–268	–304	–316	–294	–277
Personal, cultural, and recreational	3 287	. .	–24	–32	–34	–29	–28	–34	–52	–71
Government, n.i.e.	3 291	. .	–36	–32	–40	–32	–33	–40	–44	–39

Table 2 (Continued). STANDARD PRESENTATION, 1994–2001
(Millions of U.S. dollars)

	Code	1994	1995	1996	1997	1998	1999	2000	2001
C. INCOME	4 300 . .	–938	–930	–1,040	–1,026	–1,171	–1,308	–1,405	–1,364
Total credit	2 300 . .	*61*	*98*	*80*	*128*	*119*	*75*	*70*	*48*
Total debit	3 300 . .	*–999*	*–1,029*	*–1,121*	*–1,154*	*–1,290*	*–1,383*	*–1,476*	*–1,411*
Compensation of employees, credit	2 310 . .	**3**	**4**	**4**	**4**	**5**	**5**	**6**	**6**
Compensation of employees, debit	3 310 . .	**–5**	**–4**	**–9**	**–4**	**–5**	**–5**	**–6**	**–6**
Investment income, credit	2 320 . .	**58**	**94**	**76**	**124**	**114**	**70**	**65**	**42**
Direct investment income	2 330 . .	. . .	. . .	. . .	. . .	. . .	. . .	. . .	. . .
Dividends and distributed branch profits	2 332 . .	. . .	. . .	. . .	. . .	. . .	. . .	. . .	. . .
Reinvested earnings and undistributed branch profits	2 333 . .	. . .	. . .	. . .	. . .	. . .	. . .	. . .	. . .
Income on debt (interest)	2 334 . .	. . .	. . .	. . .	. . .	. . .	. . .	. . .	. . .
Portfolio investment income	2 339 . .	. . .	. . .	. . .	. . .	. . .	. . .	. . .	. . .
Income on equity	2 340 . .	. . .	. . .	. . .	. . .	. . .	. . .	. . .	. . .
Income on bonds and notes	2 350 . .	. . .	. . .	. . .	. . .	. . .	. . .	. . .	. . .
Income on money market instruments	2 360 . .	. . .	. . .	. . .	. . .	. . .	. . .	. . .	. . .
Other investment income	2 370 . .	58	94	76	124	114	70	65	42
Investment income, debit	3 320 . .	**–994**	**–1,025**	**–1,112**	**–1,150**	**–1,285**	**–1,378**	**–1,470**	**–1,405**
Direct investment income	3 330 . .	–141	–144	–189	–194	–230	–249	–280	–333
Dividends and distributed branch profits	3 332 . .	–130	–126	–164	–185	–202	–236	–239	–286
Reinvested earnings and undistributed branch profits	3 333 . .	–11	–18	–25	–10	–29	–13	–41	–47
Income on debt (interest)	3 334 . .	. . .	. . .	. . .	. . .	. . .	. . .	. . .	. . .
Portfolio investment income	3 339 . .	–1	–200	–325	–368	–396	–390	–464	–301
Income on equity	3 340 . .	–1	–1	. . .	. . .	. . .	. . .	. . .	. . .
Income on bonds and notes	3 350 . .	. . .	–199	–324	–368	–396	–390	–464	–301
Income on money market instruments	3 360 . .	. . .	. . .	. . .	. . .	. . .	. . .	. . .	. . .
Other investment income	3 370 . .	–853	–681	–598	–588	–659	–739	–727	–771
D. CURRENT TRANSFERS	4 379 . .	322	442	492	621	767	1,090	1,352	1,544
Credit	2 379 . .	**391**	**506**	**616**	**738**	**933**	**1,188**	**1,437**	**1,550**
General government	2 380 . .	45	56	63	19	31	46	73	120
Other sectors	2 390 . .	346	450	553	719	902	1,142	1,364	1,430
Workers' remittances	2 391 . .	273	382	485	644	794	1,084	1,317	1,414
Other current transfers	2 392 . .	73	68	68	75	109	58	47	15
Debit	3 379 . .	**–69**	**–64**	**–124**	**–117**	**–166**	**–99**	**–85**	**–6**
General government	3 380 . .	–19	–19	–34	–3	–11	–16	–15	–5
Other sectors	3 390 . .	–49	–45	–90	–114	–155	–82	–70	–1
Workers' remittances	3 391 . .	. . .	. . .	. . .	. . .	. . .	. . .	. . .	. . .
Other current transfers	3 392 . .	–49	–45	–90	–114	–155	–82	–70	–1
CAPITAL AND FINANCIAL ACCOUNT	4 996 . .	**1,124**	**1,433**	**244**	**518**	**2,246**	**–397**	**–906**	**1,199**
CAPITAL ACCOUNT	4 994 . .	**72**	**2,078**	**30**	**151**	**33**	**19**	**1,977**	**–64**
Total credit	2 994 . .	*75*	*2,082*	*34*	*157*	*42*	*29*	*1,987*	*20*
Total debit	3 994 . .	*–3*	*–4*	*–4*	*–6*	*–9*	*–9*	*–10*	*–84*
Capital transfers, credit	2 400 . .	**75**	**2,082**	**34**	**157**	**42**	**29**	**1,987**	**20**
General government	2 401 . .	75	2,082	34	157	42	29	1,987	20
Debt forgiveness	2 402 . .	54	2,060	16	140	19	17	1,978	3
Other capital transfers	2 410 . .	21	21	18	17	23	11	8	17
Other sectors	2 430 . .	. . .	. . .	. . .	. . .	. . .	. . .	. . .	. . .
Migrants' transfers	2 431 . .	. . .	. . .	. . .	. . .	. . .	. . .	. . .	. . .
Debt forgiveness	2 432 . .	. . .	. . .	. . .	. . .	. . .	. . .	. . .	. . .
Other capital transfers	2 440 . .	. . .	. . .	. . .	. . .	. . .	. . .	. . .	. . .
Capital transfers, debit	3 400 . .	**. . .**	**. . .**	**. . .**	**. . .**	**. . .**	**. . .**	**. . .**	**–78**
General government	3 401 . .	. . .	. . .	. . .	. . .	. . .	. . .	. . .	–78
Debt forgiveness	3 402 . .	. . .	. . .	. . .	. . .	. . .	. . .	. . .	–78
Other capital transfers	3 410 . .	. . .	. . .	. . .	. . .	. . .	. . .	. . .	. . .
Other sectors	3 430 . .	. . .	. . .	. . .	. . .	. . .	. . .	. . .	. . .
Migrants' transfers	3 431 . .	. . .	. . .	. . .	. . .	. . .	. . .	. . .	. . .
Debt forgiveness	3 432 . .	. . .	. . .	. . .	. . .	. . .	. . .	. . .	. . .
Other capital transfers	3 440 . .	. . .	. . .	. . .	. . .	. . .	. . .	. . .	. . .
Nonproduced nonfinancial assets, credit	2 480 . .	**. . .**	**. . .**	**. . .**	**. . .**	**. . .**	**. . .**	**. . .**	**. . .**
Nonproduced nonfinancial assets, debit	3 480 . .	**–3**	**–4**	**–4**	**–6**	**–9**	**–9**	**–10**	**–7**

Table 2 (Continued). STANDARD PRESENTATION, 1994–2001
(Millions of U.S. dollars)

	Code		1994	1995	1996	1997	1998	1999	2000	2001
FINANCIAL ACCOUNT	4 995	. .	**1,052**	**–645**	**213**	**367**	**2,213**	**–417**	**–2,883**	**1,263**
A. DIRECT INVESTMENT	4 500	. .	576	452	500	724	870	648	720	1,330
Direct investment abroad	4 505	. .	**. . .**	**. . .**	**. . .**	**. . .**	**. . .**	**. . .**	**. . .**	**. . .**
Equity capital	4 510	. .	. . .	. . .	. . .	. . .	. . .	. . .	. . .	. . .
Claims on affiliated enterprises	4 515	. .	. . .	. . .	. . .	. . .	. . .	. . .	. . .	. . .
Liabilities to affiliated enterprises	4 520	. .	. . .	. . .	. . .	. . .	. . .	. . .	. . .	. . .
Reinvested earnings	4 525	. .	. . .	. . .	. . .	. . .	. . .	. . .	. . .	. . .
Other capital	4 530	. .	. . .	. . .	. . .	. . .	. . .	. . .	. . .	. . .
Claims on affiliated enterprises	4 535	. .	. . .	. . .	. . .	. . .	. . .	. . .	. . .	. . .
Liabilities to affiliated enterprises	4 540	. .	. . .	. . .	. . .	. . .	. . .	. . .	. . .	. . .
Direct investment in Ecuador	4 555	. .	**576**	**452**	**500**	**724**	**870**	**648**	**720**	**1,330**
Equity capital	4 560	. .	161	182	220	161	88	33	34	196
Claims on direct investors	4 565	. .	. . .	. . .	. . .	. . .	. . .	. . .	. . .	. . .
Liabilities to direct investors	4 570	. .	161	182	220	161	88	33	34	196
Reinvested earnings	4 575	. .	11	18	25	10	29	13	41	47
Other capital	4 580	. .	404	253	255	554	753	602	646	1,087
Claims on direct investors	4 585	. .	. . .	. . .	. . .	. . .	. . .	. . .	. . .	. . .
Liabilities to direct investors	4 590	. .	404	253	255	554	753	602	646	1,087
B. PORTFOLIO INVESTMENT	4 600	. .	197	5,821	80	343	54	29	–1,725	117
Assets	4 602	. .	**. . .**	**. . .**	**. . .**	**. . .**	**. . .**	**. . .**	**. . .**	**. . .**
Equity securities	4 610	. .	. . .	. . .	. . .	. . .	. . .	. . .	. . .	. . .
Monetary authorities	4 611	. .	. . .	. . .	. . .	. . .	. . .	. . .	. . .	. . .
General government	4 612	. .	. . .	. . .	. . .	. . .	. . .	. . .	. . .	. . .
Banks	4 613	. .	. . .	. . .	. . .	. . .	. . .	. . .	. . .	. . .
Other sectors	4 614	. .	. . .	. . .	. . .	. . .	. . .	. . .	. . .	. . .
Debt securities	4 619	. .	. . .	. . .	. . .	. . .	. . .	. . .	. . .	. . .
Bonds and notes	4 620	. .	. . .	. . .	. . .	. . .	. . .	. . .	. . .	. . .
Monetary authorities	4 621	. .	. . .	. . .	. . .	. . .	. . .	. . .	. . .	. . .
General government	4 622	. .	. . .	. . .	. . .	. . .	. . .	. . .	. . .	. . .
Banks	4 623	. .	. . .	. . .	. . .	. . .	. . .	. . .	. . .	. . .
Other sectors	4 624	. .	. . .	. . .	. . .	. . .	. . .	. . .	. . .	. . .
Money market instruments	4 630	. .	. . .	. . .	. . .	. . .	. . .	. . .	. . .	. . .
Monetary authorities	4 631	. .	. . .	. . .	. . .	. . .	. . .	. . .	. . .	. . .
General government	4 632	. .	. . .	. . .	. . .	. . .	. . .	. . .	. . .	. . .
Banks	4 633	. .	. . .	. . .	. . .	. . .	. . .	. . .	. . .	. . .
Other sectors	4 634	. .	. . .	. . .	. . .	. . .	. . .	. . .	. . .	. . .
Liabilities	4 652	. .	**197**	**5,821**	**80**	**343**	**54**	**29**	**–1,725**	**117**
Equity securities	4 660	. .	6	13	6	22	5	1	. . .	1
Banks	4 663	. .	. . .	. . .	. . .	. . .	. . .	. . .	. . .	. . .
Other sectors	4 664	. .	6	13	6	22	5	1	. . .	1
Debt securities	4 669	. .	191	5,808	74	321	49	28	–1,725	116
Bonds and notes	4 670	. .	191	5,808	74	321	49	28	–1,725	116
Monetary authorities	4 671	. .	. . .	. . .	. . .	. . .	. . .	. . .	. . .	. . .
General government	4 672	. .	190	5,794	74	321	49	28	–1,725	116
Banks	4 673	. .	. . .	. . .	. . .	. . .	. . .	. . .	. . .	. . .
Other sectors	4 674	. .	1	14	. . .	. . .	. . .	. . .	. . .	. . .
Money market instruments	4 680	. .	. . .	. . .	. . .	. . .	. . .	. . .	. . .	. . .
Monetary authorities	4 681	. .	. . .	. . .	. . .	. . .	. . .	. . .	. . .	. . .
General government	4 682	. .	. . .	. . .	. . .	. . .	. . .	. . .	. . .	. . .
Banks	4 683	. .	. . .	. . .	. . .	. . .	. . .	. . .	. . .	. . .
Other sectors	4 684	. .	. . .	. . .	. . .	. . .	. . .	. . .	. . .	. . .
C. FINANCIAL DERIVATIVES	4 910	. .	. . .	. . .	. . .	. . .	. . .	. . .	. . .	. . .
Monetary authorities	4 911	. .	. . .	. . .	. . .	. . .	. . .	. . .	. . .	. . .
General government	4 912	. .	. . .	. . .	. . .	. . .	. . .	. . .	. . .	. . .
Banks	4 913	. .	. . .	. . .	. . .	. . .	. . .	. . .	. . .	. . .
Other sectors	4 914	. .	. . .	. . .	. . .	. . .	. . .	. . .	. . .	. . .
Assets	4 900	. .	**. . .**	**. . .**	**. . .**	**. . .**	**. . .**	**. . .**	**. . .**	**. . .**
Monetary authorities	4 901	. .	. . .	. . .	. . .	. . .	. . .	. . .	. . .	. . .
General government	4 902	. .	. . .	. . .	. . .	. . .	. . .	. . .	. . .	. . .
Banks	4 903	. .	. . .	. . .	. . .	. . .	. . .	. . .	. . .	. . .
Other sectors	4 904	. .	. . .	. . .	. . .	. . .	. . .	. . .	. . .	. . .
Liabilities	4 905	. .	**. . .**	**. . .**	**. . .**	**. . .**	**. . .**	**. . .**	**. . .**	**. . .**
Monetary authorities	4 906	. .	. . .	. . .	. . .	. . .	. . .	. . .	. . .	. . .
General government	4 907	. .	. . .	. . .	. . .	. . .	. . .	. . .	. . .	. . .
Banks	4 908	. .	. . .	. . .	. . .	. . .	. . .	. . .	. . .	. . .
Other sectors	4 909	. .	. . .	. . .	. . .	. . .	. . .	. . .	. . .	. . .

Table 2 (Concluded). STANDARD PRESENTATION, 1994–2001
(Millions of U.S. dollars)

	Code	1994	1995	1996	1997	1998	1999	2000	2001
D. OTHER INVESTMENT	4 700 . .	857	–7,092	–119	–447	828	–1,583	–1,572	–289
Assets	4 703 . .	**–177**	**–668**	**–302**	**–560**	**–54**	**–725**	**–1,274**	**–1,308**
Trade credits	4 706 . .	. . .	. . .	–203	–145	–149	–169	–187	–217
General government	4 707 . .	. . .	. . .	. . .	. . .	. . .	. . .	. . .	. . .
of which: Short-term	4 709 . .	. . .	. . .	. . .	. . .	. . .	. . .	. . .	. . .
Other sectors	4 710 . .	. . .	. . .	–203	–145	–149	–169	–187	–217
of which: Short-term	4 712 . .	. . .	. . .	*–203*	*–145*	*–149*	*–169*	*–187*	*–217*
Loans	4 714 . .	. . .	. . .	. . .	. . .	. . .	. . .	. . .	. . .
Monetary authorities	4 715 . .	. . .	. . .	. . .	. . .	. . .	. . .	. . .	. . .
of which: Short-term	4 718 . .	. . .	. . .	. . .	. . .	. . .	. . .	. . .	. . .
General government	4 719 . .	. . .	. . .	. . .	. . .	. . .	. . .	. . .	. . .
of which: Short-term	4 721 . .	. . .	. . .	. . .	. . .	. . .	. . .	. . .	. . .
Banks	4 722 . .	. . .	. . .	. . .	. . .	. . .	. . .	. . .	. . .
of which: Short-term	4 724 . .	. . .	. . .	. . .	. . .	. . .	. . .	. . .	. . .
Other sectors	4 725 . .	. . .	. . .	. . .	. . .	. . .	. . .	. . .	. . .
of which: Short-term	4 727 . .	. . .	. . .	. . .	. . .	. . .	. . .	. . .	. . .
Currency and deposits	4 730 . .	–177	–668	–99	–416	95	–556	–1,088	–1,090
Monetary authorities	4 731 . .	. . .	. . .	. . .	. . .	. . .	. . .	. . .	. . .
General government	4 732 . .	. . .	. . .	. . .	. . .	. . .	. . .	. . .	. . .
Banks	4 733 . .	. . .	. . .	. . .	. . .	. . .	. . .	. . .	. . .
Other sectors	4 734 . .	–177	–668	–99	–416	95	–556	–1,088	–1,090
Other assets	4 736 . .	. . .	. . .	. . .	. . .	. . .	. . .	. . .	. . .
Monetary authorities	4 737 . .	. . .	. . .	. . .	. . .	. . .	. . .	. . .	. . .
of which: Short-term	4 739 . .	. . .	. . .	. . .	. . .	. . .	. . .	. . .	. . .
General government	4 740 . .	. . .	. . .	. . .	. . .	. . .	. . .	. . .	. . .
of which: Short-term	4 742 . .	. . .	. . .	. . .	. . .	. . .	. . .	. . .	. . .
Banks	4 743 . .	. . .	. . .	. . .	. . .	. . .	. . .	. . .	. . .
of which: Short-term	4 745 . .	. . .	. . .	. . .	. . .	. . .	. . .	. . .	. . .
Other sectors	4 746 . .	. . .	. . .	. . .	. . .	. . .	. . .	. . .	. . .
of which: Short-term	4 748 . .	. . .	. . .	. . .	. . .	. . .	. . .	. . .	. . .
Liabilities	4 753 . .	**1,034**	**–6,424**	**183**	**113**	**881**	**–858**	**–297**	**1,019**
Trade credits	4 756 . .	–48	–57	–691	–608	–382	–277	–8	–183
General government	4 757 . .	–24	–19	–12	–18	13	4	98	–113
of which: Short-term	4 759 . .	. . .	. . .	. . .	. . .	. . .	. . .	. . .	. . .
Other sectors	4 760 . .	–24	–38	–679	–590	–395	–280	–106	–69
of which: Short-term	4 762 . .	. . .	. . .	. . .	. . .	. . .	. . .	. . .	. . .
Loans	4 764 . .	–31	358	656	448	861	–610	–215	1,774
Monetary authorities	4 765 . .	205	–83	–71	–21	163	–44	16	–96
of which: Use of Fund credit and loans from the Fund	4 766 . .	*122*	*–29*	*–23*	*–3*	*–67*	*–68*	*151*	*48*
of which: Short-term	4 768 . .	*–58*	*–54*	*–48*	*–18*	*–82*	*–76*	*–135*	*–144*
General government	4 769 . .	–547	–315	139	–170	59	114	108	1,167
of which: Short-term	4 771 . .	. . .	. . .	. . .	. . .	. . .	. . .	. . .	. . .
Banks	4 772 . .	26	35	95	27	–23	–72	–33	–108
of which: Short-term	4 774 . .	. . .	. . .	. . .	. . .	. . .	. . .	. . .	. . .
Other sectors	4 775 . .	285	721	493	612	662	–609	–306	810
of which: Short-term	4 777 . .	. . .	. . .	. . .	. . .	. . .	. . .	. . .	. . .
Currency and deposits	4 780 . .	288	240	–79	223	230	–301	–87	191
Monetary authorities	4 781 . .	. . .	. . .	. . .	. . .	. . .	. . .	. . .	. . .
General government	4 782 . .	. . .	. . .	. . .	. . .	. . .	. . .	. . .	. . .
Banks	4 783 . .	. . .	. . .	. . .	. . .	. . .	. . .	. . .	. . .
Other sectors	4 784 . .	288	240	–79	223	230	–301	–87	191
Other liabilities	4 786 . .	824	–6,965	297	50	172	330	12	–763
Monetary authorities	4 787 . .	. . .	2	16	–1	–1	–9	. . .	. . .
of which: Short-term	4 789 . .	. . .	*2*	*16*	*–1*	*–1*	*–9*	. . .	. . .
General government	4 790 . .	815	–6,911	257	66	170	338	39	–772
of which: Short-term	4 792 . .	*815*	*–6,911*	*257*	*66*	*170*	*338*	*39*	*–772*
Banks	4 793 . .	4	–4	5	–3	. . .	1	–22	9
of which: Short-term	4 795 . .	*4*	*–4*	*5*	*–3*	. . .	*1*	*–22*	*9*
Other sectors	4 796 . .	5	–52	19	–12	2	. . .	–5	. . .
of which: Short-term	4 798 . .	*5*	*–52*	*19*	*–12*	*2*	. . .	*–5*	. . .
E. RESERVE ASSETS	4 802 . .	–578	174	–247	–253	461	489	–307	105
Monetary gold	4 812 . .	. . .	–1	. . .	. . .	. . .	. . .	13	–1
Special drawing rights	4 811 . .	. . .	1	. . .	2	. . .	–2	2	–2
Reserve position in the Fund	4 810 . .	. . .	. . .	. . .	. . .	. . .	. . .	. . .	. . .
Foreign exchange	4 803 . .	–453	231	–245	–237	469	387	–331	123
Other claims	4 813 . .	–126	–57	–3	–18	–9	104	10	–15
NET ERRORS AND OMISSIONS	4 998 . .	**–226**	**–433**	**–189**	**–62**	**–147**	**–521**	**–15**	**–399**

Part 3 of the *Yearbook* contains descriptions of the methodologies, compilation practices, and sources used to compile these data.

Table 3. INTERNATIONAL INVESTMENT POSITION (End–period stocks), 1994–2001

(Millions of U.S. dollars)

	Code	1994	1995	1996	1997	1998	1999	2000	2001
ASSETS	8 995 C .	2,442	2,388	2,650	2,942	2,387	1,319	1,904	2,173
Direct investment abroad	8 505 . .	...	...	...	...	...	...	...	...
Equity capital and reinvested earnings	8 506 . .	...	...	...	...	...	...	...	...
Claims on affiliated enterprises	8 507 . .	...	...	...	...	...	...	...	...
Liabilities to affiliated enterprises	8 508 . .	...	...	...	...	...	...	...	...
Other capital	8 530 . .	...	...	...	...	...	...	...	...
Claims on affiliated enterprises	8 535 . .	...	...	...	...	...	...	...	...
Liabilities to affiliated enterprises	8 540 . .	...	...	...	...	...	...	...	...
Portfolio investment	8 602 . .	...	...	...	...	...	...	...	...
Equity securities	8 610 . .	...	...	...	...	...	...	...	...
Monetary authorities	8 611 . .	...	...	...	...	...	...	...	...
General government	8 612 . .	...	...	...	...	...	...	...	...
Banks	8 613 . .	...	...	...	...	...	...	...	...
Other sectors	8 614 . .	...	...	...	...	...	...	...	...
Debt securities	8 619 . .	...	...	...	...	...	...	...	...
Bonds and notes	8 620 . .	...	...	...	...	...	...	...	...
Monetary authorities	8 621 . .	...	...	...	...	...	...	...	...
General government	8 622 . .	...	...	...	...	...	...	...	...
Banks	8 623 . .	...	...	...	...	...	...	...	...
Other sectors	8 624 . .	...	...	...	...	...	...	...	...
Money market instruments	8 630 . .	...	...	...	...	...	...	...	...
Monetary authorities	8 631 . .	...	...	...	...	...	...	...	...
General government	8 632 . .	...	...	...	...	...	...	...	...
Banks	8 633 . .	...	...	...	...	...	...	...	...
Other sectors	8 634 . .	...	...	...	...	...	...	...	...
Financial derivatives	8 900 . .	...	...	...	...	...	...	...	...
Monetary authorities	8 901 . .	...	...	...	...	...	...	...	...
General government	8 902 . .	...	...	...	...	...	...	...	...
Banks	8 903 . .	...	...	...	...	...	...	...	...
Other sectors	8 904 . .	...	...	...	...	...	...	...	...
Other investment	8 703 . .	**538**	**658**	**674**	**715**	**619**	**445**	**724**	**1,099**
Trade credits	8 706 . .	...	...	...	...	...	...	...	...
General government	8 707 . .	...	...	...	...	...	...	...	...
of which: Short-term	8 709 . .	...	...	...	...	...	...	...	...
Other sectors	8 710 . .	...	...	...	...	...	...	...	...
of which: Short-term	8 712 . .	...	...	...	...	...	...	...	...
Loans	8 714 . .	...	...	...	...	...	...	...	...
Monetary authorities	8 715 . .	...	...	...	...	...	...	...	...
of which: Short-term	8 718 . .	...	...	...	...	...	...	...	...
General government	8 719 . .	...	...	...	...	...	...	...	...
of which: Short-term	8 721 . .	...	...	...	...	...	...	...	...
Banks	8 722 . .	...	...	...	...	...	...	...	...
of which: Short-term	8 724 . .	...	...	...	...	...	...	...	...
Other sectors	8 725 . .	...	...	...	...	...	...	...	...
of which: Short-term	8 727 . .	...	...	...	...	...	...	...	...
Currency and deposits	8 730 . .	538	658	674	715	619	445	724	1,099
Monetary authorities	8 731 . .	...	...	...	...	...	...	...	...
General government	8 732 . .	...	...	...	...	...	...	...	...
Banks	8 733 . .	538	658	674	715	619	445	724	1,099
Other sectors	8 734 . .	...	...	...	...	...	...	...	...
Other assets	8 736 . .	...	...	...	...	...	...	...	...
Monetary authorities	8 737 . .	...	...	...	...	...	...	...	...
of which: Short-term	8 739 . .	...	...	...	...	...	...	...	...
General government	8 740 . .	...	...	...	...	...	...	...	...
of which: Short-term	8 742 . .	...	...	...	...	...	...	...	...
Banks	8 743 . .	...	...	...	...	...	...	...	...
of which: Short-term	8 745 . .	...	...	...	...	...	...	...	...
Other sectors	8 746 . .	...	...	...	...	...	...	...	...
of which: Short-term	8 748 . .	...	...	...	...	...	...	...	...
Reserve assets	8 802 . .	**1,904**	**1,730**	**1,976**	**2,227**	**1,768**	**874**	**1,180**	**1,074**
Monetary gold	8 812 . .	166	167	167	167	167	166	233	234
Special drawing rights	8 811 . .	4	3	3	1	...	2	...	2
Reserve position in the Fund	8 810 . .	25	25	25	23	24	24	22	22
Foreign exchange	8 803 . .	1,596	1,364	1,609	1,846	1,377	586	944	821
Other claims	8 813 . .	114	170	173	191	200	96	–20	–5

Table 3 (Concluded). INTERNATIONAL INVESTMENT POSITION (End–period stocks), 1994–2001

(Millions of U.S. dollars)

	Code	1994	1995	1996	1997	1998	1999	2000	2001
LIABILITIES	8 995 D.	18,366	18,391	19,442	20,912	23,255	23,416	21,486	23,902
Direct investment in Ecuador	8 555 . .	**3,166**	**3,619**	**4,118**	**4,842**	**5,712**	**6,361**	**7,081**	**8,410**
Equity capital and reinvested earnings	8 556 . .	3,166	3,619	4,118	4,842	5,712	6,361	7,081	8,410
Claims on direct investors	8 557 . .	...	...	...	...	...	...	...	...
Liabilities to direct investors	8 558 . .	3,166	3,619	4,118	4,842	5,712	6,361	7,081	8,410
Other capital	8 580 . .	...	...	...	...	...	...	...	...
Claims on direct investors	8 585 . .	...	...	...	...	...	...	...	...
Liabilities to direct investors	8 590 . .	...	...	...	...	...	...	...	...
Portfolio investment	8 652 . .	**199**	**6,019**	**6,039**	**6,382**	**6,437**	**6,465**	**4,017**	**4,134**
Equity securities	8 660 . .	8	20	26	48	53	54	54	55
Banks	8 663 . .	...	...	...	...	...	...	...	...
Other sectors	8 664 . .	8	20	26	48	53	54	54	55
Debt securities	8 669 . .	191	5,999	6,013	6,334	6,383	6,411	3,963	4,079
Bonds and notes	8 670 . .	191	5,999	6,013	6,334	6,383	6,411	3,963	4,079
Monetary authorities	8 671 . .	...	...	...	...	...	...	...	...
General government	8 672 . .	191	5,999	6,013	6,334	6,383	6,411	3,963	4,079
Banks	8 673 . .	...	...	...	...	...	...	...	...
Other sectors	8 674 . .	...	...	...	...	...	...	...	...
Money market instruments	8 680 . .	...	...	...	...	...	...	...	...
Monetary authorities	8 681 . .	...	...	...	...	...	...	...	...
General government	8 682 . .	...	...	...	...	...	...	...	...
Banks	8 683 . .	...	...	...	...	...	...	...	...
Other sectors	8 684 . .	...	...	...	...	...	...	...	...
Financial derivatives	8 905 . .	...	...	...	...	...	...	...	...
Monetary authorities	8 906 . .	...	...	...	...	...	...	...	...
General government	8 907 . .	...	...	...	...	...	...	...	...
Banks	8 908 . .	...	...	...	...	...	...	...	...
Other sectors	8 909 . .	...	...	...	...	...	...	...	...
Other investment	8 753 . .	**15,001**	**8,753**	**9,284**	**9,688**	**11,106**	**10,590**	**10,389**	**11,357**
Trade credits	8 756 . .	188	132	103	65	68	165	246	118
General government	8 757 . .	60	42	40	21	34	38	136	22
of which: Short-term	8 759 . .	...	...	...	...	...	...	...	...
Other sectors	8 760 . .	128	90	63	44	34	127	110	96
of which: Short-term	8 762 . .	...	...	...	...	...	...	...	...
Loans	8 764 . .	7,450	7,927	8,314	8,490	9,475	8,845	8,646	10,328
Monetary authorities	8 765 . .	729	669	589	549	721	665	832	777
of which: Use of Fund credit and loans from the Fund	8 766 . .	*198*	*173*	*145*	*133*	*70*	...	*148*	*190*
of which: Short-term	8 768 . .	...	...	...	...	...	...	...	...
General government	8 769 . .	4,569	4,322	4,254	3,911	4,093	4,213	4,205	5,249
of which: Short-term	8 771 . .	...	...	...	...	...	...	...	...
Banks	8 772 . .	444	494	567	574	654	578	524	409
of which: Short-term	8 774 . .	...	...	...	...	...	...	...	...
Other sectors	8 775 . .	1,708	2,442	2,905	3,456	4,007	3,390	3,084	3,892
of which: Short-term	8 777 . .	*818*	*1,555*	*1,958*	*2,520*	*3,160*	*2,530*	*2,229*	*3,038*
Currency and deposits	8 780 . .	405	645	566	789	1,019	719	632	822
Monetary authorities	8 781 . .	...	...	...	...	...	...	...	...
General government	8 782 . .	...	...	...	...	...	...	...	...
Banks	8 783 . .	405	645	566	789	1,019	719	632	822
Other sectors	8 784 . .	...	...	...	...	...	...	...	...
Other liabilities	8 786 . .	6,959	50	301	344	544	861	866	89
Monetary authorities	8 787 . .	...	...	2	...	...	...	...	...
of which: Short-term	8 789 . .	...	...	...	...	...	...	...	...
General government	8 790 . .	6,897	45	284	342	543	859	863	80
of which: Short-term	8 792 . .	...	...	...	...	...	...	...	...
Banks	8 793 . .	7	3	4	1	1	2	2	9
of which: Short-term	8 795 . .	...	...	...	...	...	...	...	...
Other sectors	8 796 . .	55	2	11	1	...	...	...	...
of which: Short-term	8 798 . .	*14*	...	...	...	...	...	...	...
NET INTERNATIONAL INVESTMENT POSITION	8 995 . .	**–15,924**	**–16,003**	**–16,792**	**–17,970**	**–20,868**	**–22,097**	**–19,583**	**–21,729**

Table 1. ANALYTIC PRESENTATION, 1994–2001
(Millions of U.S. dollars)

	Code	1994	1995	1996	1997	1998	1999	2000	2001
A. Current Account [1]	4 993 Z.	**31**	**–254**	**–192**	**–711**	**–2,566**	**–1,635**	**–971**	**–388**
Goods: exports f.o.b	2 100 . .	4,044	4,670	4,779	5,525	4,403	5,237	7,061	7,025
Goods: imports f.o.b	3 100 . .	–9,997	–12,267	–13,169	–14,157	–14,617	–15,165	–15,382	–13,960
Balance on Goods	4 100 . .	*–5,953*	*–7,597*	*–8,390*	*–8,632*	*–10,214*	*–9,928*	*–8,321*	*–6,935*
Services: credit	2 200 . .	8,070	8,590	9,271	9,380	8,141	9,494	9,803	9,042
Services: debit	3 200 . .	–5,645	–4,873	–5,084	–6,770	–6,492	–6,452	–7,513	–7,037
Balance on Goods and Services	4 991 . .	*–3,528*	*–3,880*	*–4,203*	*–6,021*	*–8,565*	*–6,886*	*–6,031*	*–4,929*
Income: credit	2 300 . .	1,330	1,578	1,901	2,122	2,030	1,788	1,871	1,468
Income: debit	3 300 . .	–2,114	–1,983	–1,556	–1,185	–1,075	–1,045	–983	–885
Balance on Goods, Services, and Income	4 992 . .	*–4,312*	*–4,285*	*–3,858*	*–5,085*	*–7,610*	*–6,143*	*–5,143*	*–4,346*
Current transfers: credit	2 379 Z.	4,622	4,284	3,888	4,738	5,166	4,564	4,224	4,056
Current transfers: debit	3 379 . .	–279	–253	–222	–363	–122	–55	–52	–98
B. Capital Account [1]	4 994 Z.	**. . .**	**. . .**	**. . .**	**. . .**	**. . .**	**. . .**	**. . .**	**. . .**
Capital account: credit	2 994 Z.	. . .	. . .	. . .	. . .	. . .	. . .	. . .	. . .
Capital account: debit	3 994 . .	. . .	. . .	. . .	. . .	. . .	. . .	. . .	. . .
Total, Groups A Plus B	4 981 . .	*31*	*–254*	*–192*	*–711*	*–2,566*	*–1,635*	*–971*	*–388*
C. Financial Account [1]	4 995 W.	**–1,450**	**–1,845**	**–1,459**	**1,958**	**1,901**	**–1,421**	**–1,646**	**190**
Direct investment abroad	4 505 . .	–43	–93	–5	–129	–45	–38	–51	–12
Direct investment in Egypt	4 555 Z.	1,256	598	636	891	1,076	1,065	1,235	510
Portfolio investment assets	4 602 . .	. . .	. . .	. . .	. . .	–63	–22	–3	–2
Equity securities	4 610 . .	. . .	. . .	. . .	. . .	–63	–22	–3	–2
Debt securities	4 619 . .	. . .	. . .	. . .	. . .	. . .	. . .	. . .	. . .
Portfolio investment liabilities	4 652 Z.	3	20	545	816	–537	617	269	1,463
Equity securities	4 660 . .	. . .	. . .	. . .	515	–160	658	269	39
Debt securities	4 669 Z.	3	20	545	301	–377	–41	. . .	1,424
Financial derivatives	4 910 . .	. . .	. . .	. . .	. . .	. . .	. . .	. . .	. . .
Financial derivatives assets	4 900 . .	. . .	. . .	. . .	. . .	. . .	. . .	. . .	. . .
Financial derivatives liabilities	4 905 . .	. . .	. . .	. . .	. . .	. . .	. . .	. . .	. . .
Other investment assets	4 703 . .	–905	–396	–565	–170	39	–1,805	–2,991	–1,261
Monetary authorities	4 701 . .	–25	65	65	37	24	–14	–21	–73
General government	4 704 . .	. . .	. . .	. . .	. . .	. . .	. . .	. . .	. . .
Banks	4 705 . .	–634	371	338	1,599	1,357	372	257	1,369
Other sectors	4 728 . .	–246	–832	–968	–1,806	–1,342	–2,163	–3,227	–2,556
Other investment liabilities	4 753 W.	–1,761	–1,974	–2,070	551	1,431	–1,240	–105	–509
Monetary authorities	4 753 WA	–5	–21	–4	–19	–204	–3	–5	104
General government	4 753 ZB	–1,536	–1,783	–2,578	–1,506	–946	–989	–1,109	–1,157
Banks	4 753 ZC	–256	–148	324	1,715	1,393	–692	–129	–56
Other sectors	4 753 ZD	36	–22	188	361	1,188	444	1,138	601
Total, Groups A Through C	4 983 . .	*–1,419*	*–2,099*	*–1,651*	*1,247*	*–665*	*–3,056*	*–2,617*	*–199*
D. Net Errors and Omissions	4 998 . .	**255**	**272**	**–74**	**–1,882**	**–722**	**–1,558**	**587**	**–1,146**
Total, Groups A Through D	4 984 . .	*–1,164*	*–1,827*	*–1,725*	*–635*	*–1,387*	*–4,614*	*–2,030*	*–1,345*
E. Reserves and Related Items	4 802 A.	**1,164**	**1,827**	**1,725**	**635**	**1,387**	**4,614**	**2,030**	**1,345**
Reserve assets	4 802 . .	–1,193	–409	–1,010	–1,185	535	4,027	1,306	507
Use of Fund credit and loans	4 766 . .	–22	–95	–85	–15	. . .	. . .	. . .	. . .
Exceptional financing	4 920 . .	2,379	2,331	2,820	1,836	852	587	724	838
Conversion rates: Egyptian pounds per U.S. dollar	0 101 . .	**3.3851**	**3.3922**	**3.3915**	**3.3888**	**3.3880**	**3.3953**	**3.4721**	**3.9730**

[1] Excludes components that have been classified in the categories of Group E.

Table 2. STANDARD PRESENTATION, 1994–2001

(Millions of U.S. dollars)

	Code	1994	1995	1996	1997	1998	1999	2000	2001
CURRENT ACCOUNT	4 993 . .	**31**	**–254**	**–192**	**–711**	**–2,566**	**–1,635**	**–971**	**–388**
A. GOODS	4 100 . .	–5,953	–7,597	–8,390	–8,632	–10,214	–9,928	–8,321	–6,935
Credit	2 100 . .	**4,044**	**4,670**	**4,779**	**5,525**	**4,403**	**5,237**	**7,061**	**7,025**
General merchandise: exports f.o.b.	2 110 . .	3,759	4,256	4,261	4,992	4,099	4,863	6,465	6,468
Goods for processing: exports f.o.b.	2 150 . .	. . .	. . .	. . .	. . .	. . .	. . .	. . .	. . .
Repairs on goods	2 160 . .	. . .	. . .	. . .	. . .	. . .	. . .	. . .	. . .
Goods procured in ports by carriers	2 170 . .	285	414	518	534	304	373	596	557
Nonmonetary gold	2 180 . .	. . .	. . .	. . .	. . .	. . .	. . .	. . .	. . .
Debit	3 100 . .	**–9,997**	**–12,267**	**–13,169**	**–14,157**	**–14,617**	**–15,165**	**–15,382**	**–13,960**
General merchandise: imports f.o.b.	3 110 . .	–9,942	–12,102	–13,039	–14,087	–14,572	–15,144	–15,346	–13,884
Goods for processing: imports f.o.b.	3 150 . .	. . .	. . .	. . .	. . .	. . .	. . .	. . .	. . .
Repairs on goods	3 160 . .	. . .	. . .	. . .	. . .	. . .	. . .	. . .	. . .
Goods procured in ports by carriers	3 170 . .	–55	–165	–130	–70	–45	–21	–36	–76
Nonmonetary gold	3 180 . .	. . .	. . .	. . .	. . .	. . .	. . .	. . .	. . .
B. SERVICES	4 200 . .	2,425	3,717	4,187	2,610	1,649	3,042	2,290	2,006
Total credit	2 200 . .	*8,070*	*8,590*	*9,271*	*9,380*	*8,141*	*9,494*	*9,803*	*9,042*
Total debit	3 200 . .	*–5,645*	*–4,873*	*–5,084*	*–6,770*	*–6,492*	*–6,452*	*–7,513*	*–7,037*
Transportation services, credit	2 205 . .	**3,165**	**3,202**	**2,689**	**2,524**	**2,494**	**2,658**	**2,645**	**2,738**
Passenger	2 850 . .	*213*	*270*	*379*	*319*	*377*	*458*	*312*	*319*
Freight	2 851 . .	*811*	*752*	*145*	*203*	*130*	*220*	*321*	*347*
Other	2 852 . .	*2,141*	*2,180*	*2,165*	*2,003*	*1,987*	*1,979*	*2,012*	*2,072*
Sea transport, passenger	2 207 . .	. . .	3	6	13	1	. . .	. . .	. . .
Sea transport, freight	2 208 . .	811	743	145	199	127	220	320	339
Sea transport, other	2 209 . .	. . .	. . .	. . .	. . .	. . .	. . .	. . .	. . .
Air transport, passenger	2 211 . .	213	267	373	306	376	458	312	319
Air transport, freight	2 212 . .	. . .	9	. . .	4	3	. . .	1	8
Air transport, other	2 213 . .	. . .	. . .	. . .	. . .	. . .	. . .	. . .	. . .
Other transport, passenger	2 215 . .	. . .	. . .	. . .	. . .	. . .	. . .	. . .	. . .
Other transport, freight	2 216 . .	. . .	. . .	. . .	. . .	. . .	. . .	. . .	. . .
Other transport, other	2 217 . .	2,141	2,180	2,165	2,003	1,987	1,979	2,012	2,072
Transportation services, debit	3 205 . .	**–1,413**	**–1,582**	**–1,655**	**–1,912**	**–2,033**	**–2,128**	**–2,212**	**–2,037**
Passenger	3 850 . .	*–222*	*–93*	*–65*	*–84*	*–118*	*–140*	*–134*	*–116*
Freight	3 851 . .	*–1,191*	*–1,477*	*–1,544*	*–1,725*	*–1,845*	*–1,926*	*–2,013*	*–1,857*
Other	3 852 . .	*. . .*	*–12*	*–46*	*–103*	*–70*	*–63*	*–65*	*–64*
Sea transport, passenger	3 207 . .	–190	–43	–4	–2	–1	–2	. . .	–11
Sea transport, freight	3 208 . .	–1,191	–1,476	–1,544	–1,713	–1,826	–1,911	–2,002	–1,849
Sea transport, other	3 209 . .	. . .	–3	. . .	–3	–1	–2	. . .	–11
Air transport, passenger	3 211 . .	–32	–50	–61	–81	–117	–137	–134	–105
Air transport, freight	3 212 . .	. . .	–1	. . .	–1	–1	–2	–2	–1
Air transport, other	3 213 . .	. . .	–9	–46	–101	–69	–60	–65	–53
Other transport, passenger	3 215 . .	. . .	. . .	. . .	. . .	. . .	. . .	. . .	. . .
Other transport, freight	3 216 . .	. . .	. . .	. . .	–12	–18	–12	–9	–7
Other transport, other	3 217 . .	. . .	. . .	. . .	. . .	. . .	. . .	. . .	. . .
Travel, credit	2 236 . .	**2,006**	**2,684**	**3,204**	**3,727**	**2,565**	**3,903**	**4,345**	**3,800**
Business travel	2 237 . .	. . .	. . .	. . .	. . .	. . .	. . .	. . .	. . .
Personal travel	2 240 . .	. . .	. . .	. . .	. . .	. . .	. . .	. . .	. . .
Travel, debit	3 236 . .	**–1,067**	**–1,278**	**–1,317**	**–1,347**	**–1,153**	**–1,078**	**–1,072**	**–1,132**
Business travel	3 237 . .	–77	–78	–82	–100	–110	–86	–88	–94
Personal travel	3 240 . .	–990	–1,200	–1,235	–1,248	–1,043	–991	–984	–1,038
Other services, credit	2 200 BA	**2,899**	**2,704**	**3,378**	**3,128**	**3,082**	**2,933**	**2,813**	**2,504**
Communications	2 245 . .	105	215	210	181	216	235	306	232
Construction	2 249 . .	. . .	1	12	78	49	116	93	141
Insurance	2 253 . .	34	12	33	38	38	90	30	9
Financial	2 260 . .	84	71	60	43	55	81	52	70
Computer and information	2 262 . .	. . .	1	1	5	10	9	23	22
Royalties and licence fees	2 266 . .	40	47	55	54	56	47	59	46
Other business services	2 268 . .	2,258	2,027	2,808	2,436	2,337	2,118	2,119	1,737
Personal, cultural, and recreational	2 287 . .	1	2	7	11	12	19	15	19
Government, n.i.e.	2 291 . .	377	328	192	284	309	218	116	227
Other services, debit	3 200 BA	**–3,165**	**–2,013**	**–2,112**	**–3,510**	**–3,306**	**–3,246**	**–4,229**	**–3,868**
Communications	3 245 . .	–6	–11	–12	–20	–29	–32	–102	–128
Construction	3 249 . .	. . .	. . .	. . .	. . .	. . .	. . .	. . .	. . .
Insurance	3 253 . .	–130	–167	–167	–170	–430	–457	–450	–411
Financial	3 260 . .	–62	–41	–27	–26	–24	–30	–21	–27
Computer and information	3 262 . .	. . .	–1	–2	–6	–11	–22	–20	–13
Royalties and licence fees	3 266 . .	–508	–97	–40	–365	–392	–329	–401	–361
Other business services	3 268 . .	–2,196	–1,333	–1,482	–1,946	–1,792	–1,863	–2,862	–2,225
Personal, cultural, and recreational	3 287 . .	. . .	–1	–7	–21	–22	–20	–21	–22
Government, n.i.e.	3 291 . .	–263	–362	–375	–957	–606	–493	–352	–680

Table 2 (Continued). STANDARD PRESENTATION, 1994–2001

(Millions of U.S. dollars)

	Code	1994	1995	1996	1997	1998	1999	2000	2001
C. INCOME	4 300 . .	–784	–405	345	936	955	743	888	583
Total credit	2 300 . .	*1,330*	*1,578*	*1,901*	*2,122*	*2,030*	*1,788*	*1,871*	*1,468*
Total debit	3 300 . .	*–2,114*	*–1,983*	*–1,556*	*–1,185*	*–1,075*	*–1,045*	*–983*	*–885*
Compensation of employees, credit	2 310 . .	...	...	...	...	...	...	...	...
Compensation of employees, debit	3 310 . .	...	...	...	...	...	...	...	...
Investment income, credit	2 320 . .	**1,330**	**1,578**	**1,901**	**2,122**	**2,030**	**1,788**	**1,871**	**1,468**
Direct investment income	2 330 . .	48	79	52	94	65	66	71	85
Dividends and distributed branch profits	2 332 . .	48	79	52	94	65	66	71	85
Reinvested earnings and undistributed branch profits	2 333 . .	...	...	...	...	...	...	...	...
Income on debt (interest)	2 334 . .	...	...	...	...	...	...	...	...
Portfolio investment income	2 339 . .	17	1	204	237	305	256	176	151
Income on equity	2 340 . .	...	...	...	...	...	...	...	...
Income on bonds and notes	2 350 . .	17	1	204	237	305	256	176	151
Income on money market instruments	2 360 . .	...	...	...	...	...	...	...	...
Other investment income	2 370 . .	1,265	1,498	1,645	1,791	1,660	1,466	1,624	1,232
Investment income, debit	3 320 . .	**–2,114**	**–1,983**	**–1,556**	**–1,185**	**–1,075**	**–1,045**	**–983**	**–885**
Direct investment income	3 330 . .	–329	–228	–34	–113	–134	–100	–92	–28
Dividends and distributed branch profits	3 332 . .	–329	–228	–34	–113	–134	–100	–92	–28
Reinvested earnings and undistributed branch profits	3 333 . .	...	...	...	...	...	...	...	...
Income on debt (interest)	3 334 . .	...	...	...	...	...	...	...	...
Portfolio investment income	3 339 . .	...	–10	–38	–57	–28	–4	...	...
Income on equity	3 340 . .	...	...	...	–36	–25	–3	...	...
Income on bonds and notes	3 350 . .	...	–10	–38	–21	–3	–1	...	...
Income on money market instruments	3 360 . .	...	...	...	...	...	...	...	...
Other investment income	3 370 . .	–1,785	–1,745	–1,484	–1,015	–913	–941	–891	–857
D. CURRENT TRANSFERS	4 379 . .	4,343	4,031	3,666	4,375	5,044	4,508	4,172	3,957
Credit	2 379 . .	**4,622**	**4,284**	**3,888**	**4,738**	**5,166**	**4,564**	**4,224**	**4,056**
General government	2 380 . .	939	1,033	766	780	1,301	885	857	849
Other sectors	2 390 . .	3,683	3,251	3,122	3,958	3,865	3,679	3,367	3,207
Workers' remittances	2 391 . .	3,672	3,226	3,107	3,697	3,370	3,235	2,852	2,911
Other current transfers	2 392 . .	11	25	15	261	495	443	515	295
Debit	3 379 . .	**–279**	**–253**	**–222**	**–363**	**–122**	**–55**	**–52**	**–98**
General government	3 380 . .	–22	–30	–17	–19	–14	–16	–17	–64
Other sectors	3 390 . .	–257	–223	–205	–344	–108	–40	–35	–35
Workers' remittances	3 391 . .	–255	–223	–142	–344	–108	–39	–32	–35
Other current transfers	3 392 . .	–2	...	–63	...	...	–1	–3	...
CAPITAL AND FINANCIAL ACCOUNT	4 996 . .	**–286**	**–18**	**266**	**2,593**	**3,288**	**3,192**	**384**	**1,534**
CAPITAL ACCOUNT	4 994 . .	...	...	**608**	...	...	...	...	...
Total credit	2 994 . .	...	...	*608*	...	...	...	...	...
Total debit	3 994 . .	...	...	...	...	...	...	...	...
Capital transfers, credit	2 400 . .	...	...	**608**	...	...	...	...	...
General government	2 401 . .	...	...	608	...	...	...	...	...
Debt forgiveness	2 402 . .	...	...	608	...	...	...	...	...
Other capital transfers	2 410 . .	...	...	...	...	...	...	...	...
Other sectors	2 430 . .	...	...	...	...	...	...	...	...
Migrants' transfers	2 431 . .	...	...	...	...	...	...	...	...
Debt forgiveness	2 432 . .	...	...	...	...	...	...	...	...
Other capital transfers	2 440 . .	...	...	...	...	...	...	...	...
Capital transfers, debit	3 400 . .	...	...	...	...	...	...	...	...
General government	3 401 . .	...	...	...	...	...	...	...	...
Debt forgiveness	3 402 . .	...	...	...	...	...	...	...	...
Other capital transfers	3 410 . .	...	...	...	...	...	...	...	...
Other sectors	3 430 . .	...	...	...	...	...	...	...	...
Migrants' transfers	3 431 . .	...	...	...	...	...	...	...	...
Debt forgiveness	3 432 . .	...	...	...	...	...	...	...	...
Other capital transfers	3 440 . .	...	...	...	...	...	...	...	...
Nonproduced nonfinancial assets, credit	2 480 . .	...	...	...	...	...	...	...	...
Nonproduced nonfinancial assets, debit	3 480 . .	...	...	...	...	...	...	...	...

Table 2 (Continued). STANDARD PRESENTATION, 1994–2001
(Millions of U.S. dollars)

	Code		1994	1995	1996	1997	1998	1999	2000	2001
FINANCIAL ACCOUNT	4 995	. .	**–286**	**–18**	**–342**	**2,593**	**3,288**	**3,192**	**384**	**1,534**
A. DIRECT INVESTMENT	4 500	. .	1,213	505	631	761	1,031	1,028	1,184	498
Direct investment abroad	4 505	. .	**–43**	**–93**	**–5**	**–129**	**–45**	**–38**	**–51**	**–12**
Equity capital	4 510	. .	...	...	...	...	...	...	...	...
Claims on affiliated enterprises	4 515	. .	...	...	...	...	...	...	...	...
Liabilities to affiliated enterprises	4 520	. .	...	...	...	...	...	...	...	...
Reinvested earnings	4 525	. .	...	...	...	...	...	...	...	...
Other capital	4 530	. .	–43	–93	–5	–129	–45	–38	–51	–12
Claims on affiliated enterprises	4 535	. .	–43	–93	–5	–129	–45	–38	–51	–12
Liabilities to affiliated enterprises	4 540	. .	...	...	...	...	...	...	...	...
Direct investment in Egypt	4 555	. .	**1,256**	**598**	**636**	**891**	**1,076**	**1,065**	**1,235**	**510**
Equity capital	4 560	. .	...	...	...	...	...	...	...	...
Claims on direct investors	4 565	. .	...	...	...	...	...	...	...	...
Liabilities to direct investors	4 570	. .	...	...	...	...	...	...	...	...
Reinvested earnings	4 575	. .	...	...	...	...	...	...	...	...
Other capital	4 580	. .	1,256	598	636	891	1,076	1,065	1,235	510
Claims on direct investors	4 585	. .	...	...	...	...	...	...	...	...
Liabilities to direct investors	4 590	. .	1,256	598	636	891	1,076	1,065	1,235	510
B. PORTFOLIO INVESTMENT	4 600	. .	3	20	545	816	–600	595	266	1,461
Assets	4 602	. .	**...**	**...**	**...**	**...**	**–63**	**–22**	**–3**	**–2**
Equity securities	4 610	. .	...	...	...	...	–63	–22	–3	–2
Monetary authorities	4 611	. .	...	...	...	...	...	...	...	...
General government	4 612	. .	...	...	...	...	...	...	...	...
Banks	4 613	. .	...	...	...	...	...	...	...	...
Other sectors	4 614	. .	...	...	...	...	–63	–22	–3	–2
Debt securities	4 619	. .	...	...	...	...	...	...	...	...
Bonds and notes	4 620	. .	...	...	...	...	...	...	...	...
Monetary authorities	4 621	. .	...	...	...	...	...	...	...	...
General government	4 622	. .	...	...	...	...	...	...	...	...
Banks	4 623	. .	...	...	...	...	...	...	...	...
Other sectors	4 624	. .	...	...	...	...	...	...	...	...
Money market instruments	4 630	. .	...	...	...	...	...	...	...	...
Monetary authorities	4 631	. .	...	...	...	...	...	...	...	...
General government	4 632	. .	...	...	...	...	...	...	...	...
Banks	4 633	. .	...	...	...	...	...	...	...	...
Other sectors	4 634	. .	...	...	...	...	...	...	...	...
Liabilities	4 652	. .	**3**	**20**	**545**	**816**	**–537**	**617**	**269**	**1,463**
Equity securities	4 660	. .	...	...	...	515	–160	658	269	39
Banks	4 663	. .	...	...	...	...	...	...	...	...
Other sectors	4 664	. .	...	...	...	515	–160	658	269	39
Debt securities	4 669	. .	3	20	545	301	–377	–41	...	1,424
Bonds and notes	4 670	. .	3	20	545	301	–377	–41	...	1,424
Monetary authorities	4 671	. .	...	...	...	...	...	...	...	...
General government	4 672	. .	3	20	545	301	377	–41	...	1,424
Banks	4 673	. .	...	...	...	...	...	...	...	...
Other sectors	4 674	. .	...	...	...	...	...	...	...	...
Money market instruments	4 680	. .	...	...	...	...	...	...	...	...
Monetary authorities	4 681	. .	...	...	...	...	...	...	...	...
General government	4 682	. .	...	...	...	...	...	...	...	...
Banks	4 683	. .	...	...	...	...	...	...	...	...
Other sectors	4 684	. .	...	...	...	...	...	...	...	...
C. FINANCIAL DERIVATIVES	4 910	. .	...	...	...	...	...	...	...	...
Monetary authorities	4 911	. .	...	...	...	...	...	...	...	...
General government	4 912	. .	...	...	...	...	...	...	...	...
Banks	4 913	. .	...	...	...	...	...	...	...	...
Other sectors	4 914	. .	...	...	...	...	...	...	...	...
Assets	4 900	. .	**...**	**...**	**...**	**...**	**...**	**...**	**...**	**...**
Monetary authorities	4 901	. .	...	...	...	...	...	...	...	...
General government	4 902	. .	...	...	...	...	...	...	...	...
Banks	4 903	. .	...	...	...	...	...	...	...	...
Other sectors	4 904	. .	...	...	...	...	...	...	...	...
Liabilities	4 905	. .	**...**	**...**	**...**	**...**	**...**	**...**	**...**	**...**
Monetary authorities	4 906	. .	...	...	...	...	...	...	...	...
General government	4 907	. .	...	...	...	...	...	...	...	...
Banks	4 908	. .	...	...	...	...	...	...	...	...
Other sectors	4 909	. .	...	...	...	...	...	...	...	...

Table 2 (Concluded). STANDARD PRESENTATION, 1994–2001
(Millions of U.S. dollars)

	Code	1994	1995	1996	1997	1998	1999	2000	2001
D. OTHER INVESTMENT	4 700 . .	–309	–134	–508	2,201	2,322	–2,458	–2,372	–932
Assets	4 703 . .	**–905**	**–396**	**–565**	**–170**	**39**	**–1,805**	**–2,991**	**–1,261**
Trade credits	4 706 . .	. . .	. . .	. . .	. . .	. . .	. . .	. . .	. . .
General government	4 707 . .	. . .	. . .	. . .	. . .	. . .	. . .	. . .	. . .
of which: Short-term	4 709 . .	. . .	. . .	. . .	. . .	. . .	. . .	. . .	. . .
Other sectors	4 710 . .	. . .	. . .	. . .	. . .	. . .	. . .	. . .	. . .
of which: Short-term	4 712 . .	. . .	. . .	. . .	. . .	. . .	. . .	. . .	. . .
Loans	4 714 . .	. . .	. . .	. . .	. . .	. . .	. . .	. . .	. . .
Monetary authorities	4 715 . .	. . .	. . .	. . .	. . .	. . .	. . .	. . .	. . .
of which: Short-term	4 718 . .	. . .	. . .	. . .	. . .	. . .	. . .	. . .	. . .
General government	4 719 . .	. . .	. . .	. . .	. . .	. . .	. . .	. . .	. . .
of which: Short-term	4 721 . .	. . .	. . .	. . .	. . .	. . .	. . .	. . .	. . .
Banks	4 722 . .	. . .	. . .	. . .	. . .	. . .	. . .	. . .	. . .
of which: Short-term	4 724 . .	. . .	. . .	. . .	. . .	. . .	. . .	. . .	. . .
Other sectors	4 725 . .	. . .	. . .	. . .	. . .	. . .	. . .	. . .	. . .
of which: Short-term	4 727 . .	. . .	. . .	. . .	. . .	. . .	. . .	. . .	. . .
Currency and deposits	4 730 . .	–634	371	338	1,599	1,357	372	257	1,369
Monetary authorities	4 731 . .	. . .	. . .	. . .	. . .	. . .	. . .	. . .	. . .
General government	4 732 . .	. . .	. . .	. . .	. . .	. . .	. . .	. . .	. . .
Banks	4 733 . .	–634	371	338	1,599	1,357	372	257	1,369
Other sectors	4 734 . .	. . .	. . .	. . .	. . .	. . .	. . .	. . .	. . .
Other assets	4 736 . .	–271	–767	–903	–1,769	–1,318	–2,177	–3,248	–2,629
Monetary authorities	4 737 . .	–25	65	65	37	24	–14	–21	–73
of which: Short-term	4 739 . .	*–25*	. . .	. . .	. . .	. . .	. . .	. . .	. . .
General government	4 740 . .	. . .	. . .	. . .	. . .	. . .	. . .	. . .	. . .
of which: Short-term	4 742 . .	. . .	. . .	. . .	. . .	. . .	. . .	. . .	. . .
Banks	4 743 . .	. . .	. . .	. . .	. . .	. . .	. . .	. . .	. . .
of which: Short-term	4 745 . .	. . .	. . .	. . .	. . .	. . .	. . .	. . .	. . .
Other sectors	4 746 . .	–246	–832	–968	–1,806	–1,342	–2,163	–3,227	–2,556
of which: Short-term	4 748 . .	*–246*	*–832*	*–968*	*–1,806*	*–1,342*	*–2,163*	*–3,227*	*–2,556*
Liabilities	4 753 . .	**596**	**262**	**57**	**2,371**	**2,283**	**–653**	**619**	**329**
Trade credits	4 756 . .	36	–22	188	361	1,188	444	1,138	601
General government	4 757 . .	. . .	. . .	. . .	. . .	. . .	. . .	. . .	. . .
of which: Short-term	4 759 . .	. . .	. . .	. . .	. . .	. . .	. . .	. . .	. . .
Other sectors	4 760 . .	36	–22	188	361	1,188	444	1,138	601
of which: Short-term	4 762 . .	*199*	*243*	*503*	*446*	*878*	*614*	*1,275*	*569*
Loans	4 764 . .	821	453	–451	315	–94	–402	–385	–320
Monetary authorities	4 765 . .	–22	–95	–85	–15	. . .	. . .	. . .	. . .
of which: Use of Fund credit and loans from the Fund	4 766 . .	*–22*	*–95*	*–85*	*–15*	. . .	. . .	. . .	. . .
of which: Short-term	4 768 . .	. . .	. . .	. . .	. . .	. . .	. . .	. . .	. . .
General government	4 769 . .	843	548	–366	330	–94	–402	–385	–320
of which: Short-term	4 771 . .	. . .	. . .	. . .	. . .	. . .	. . .	. . .	. . .
Banks	4 772 . .	. . .	. . .	. . .	. . .	. . .	. . .	. . .	. . .
of which: Short-term	4 774 . .	. . .	. . .	. . .	. . .	. . .	. . .	. . .	. . .
Other sectors	4 775 . .	. . .	. . .	. . .	. . .	. . .	. . .	. . .	. . .
of which: Short-term	4 777 . .	. . .	. . .	. . .	. . .	. . .	. . .	. . .	. . .
Currency and deposits	4 780 . .	–256	–148	324	1,715	1,393	–692	–129	–56
Monetary authorities	4 781 . .	. . .	. . .	. . .	. . .	. . .	. . .	. . .	. . .
General government	4 782 . .	. . .	. . .	. . .	. . .	. . .	. . .	. . .	. . .
Banks	4 783 . .	–256	–148	324	1,715	1,393	–692	–129	–56
Other sectors	4 784 . .	. . .	. . .	. . .	. . .	. . .	. . .	. . .	. . .
Other liabilities	4 786 . .	–5	–21	–4	–19	–204	–3	–5	104
Monetary authorities	4 787 . .	–5	–21	–4	–19	–204	–3	–5	104
of which: Short-term	4 789 . .	*–5*	*–19*	*–4*	*–18*	*–205*	*–4*	*–7*	*94*
General government	4 790 . .	. . .	. . .	. . .	. . .	. . .	. . .	. . .	. . .
of which: Short-term	4 792 . .	. . .	. . .	. . .	. . .	. . .	. . .	. . .	. . .
Banks	4 793 . .	. . .	. . .	. . .	. . .	. . .	. . .	. . .	. . .
of which: Short-term	4 795 . .	. . .	. . .	. . .	. . .	. . .	. . .	. . .	. . .
Other sectors	4 796 . .	. . .	. . .	. . .	. . .	. . .	. . .	. . .	. . .
of which: Short-term	4 798 . .	. . .	. . .	. . .	. . .	. . .	. . .	. . .	. . .
E. RESERVE ASSETS	4 802 . .	–1,193	–409	–1,010	–1,185	535	4,027	1,306	507
Monetary gold	4 812 . .	. . .	. . .	. . .	. . .	. . .	. . .	. . .	. . .
Special drawing rights	4 811 . .	–12	–16	–23	2	–40	115	–9	13
Reserve position in the Fund	4 810 . .	. . .	. . .	. . .	. . .	. . .	–92	. . .	152
Foreign exchange	4 803 . .	–1,181	–393	–987	–1,187	575	4,003	1,315	342
Other claims	4 813 . .	. . .	. . .	. . .	. . .	. . .	. . .	. . .	. . .
NET ERRORS AND OMISSIONS	4 998 . .	**255**	**272**	**–74**	**–1,882**	**–722**	**–1,558**	**587**	**–1,146**

Part 3 of the *Yearbook* contains descriptions of the methodologies, compilation practices, and sources used to compile these data.

Table 1. ANALYTIC PRESENTATION, 1994–2001
(Millions of U.S. dollars)

	Code	1994	1995	1996	1997	1998	1999	2000	2001
A. Current Account [1]	4 993 Z.	**–18.0**	**–261.6**	**–169.0**	**–97.8**	**–90.7**	**–239.2**	**–430.6**	**–176.9**
Goods: exports f.o.b.	2 100 . .	1,252.3	1,651.1	1,787.4	2,437.1	2,459.5	2,534.3	2,963.2	2,901.0
Goods: imports f.o.b.	3 100 . .	–2,422.3	–3,113.5	–3,029.7	–3,580.3	–3,765.2	–3,890.4	–4,702.9	–4,813.9
Balance on Goods	4 100 . .	*–1,170.0*	*–1,462.3*	*–1,242.3*	*–1,143.2*	*–1,305.7*	*–1,356.1*	*–1,739.7*	*–1,912.9*
Services: credit	2 200 . .	387.2	388.6	414.4	475.8	588.5	640.5	698.4	1,075.8
Services: debit	3 200 . .	–428.9	–509.8	–504.6	–628.0	–737.3	–823.0	–933.3	–1,077.8
Balance on Goods and Services	4 991 . .	*–1,211.7*	*–1,583.5*	*–1,332.5*	*–1,295.4*	*–1,454.5*	*–1,538.6*	*–1,974.7*	*–1,915.0*
Income: credit	2 300 . .	35.5	54.0	44.1	75.1	111.4	112.9	141.3	168.9
Income: debit	3 300 . .	–130.1	–120.7	–134.4	–238.3	–274.4	–395.1	–394.4	–434.7
Balance on Goods, Services, and Income	4 992 . .	*–1,306.4*	*–1,650.2*	*–1,422.8*	*–1,458.6*	*–1,617.5*	*–1,820.7*	*–2,227.7*	*–2,180.7*
Current transfers: credit	2 379 Z.	1,290.9	1,393.2	1,258.6	1,363.6	1,534.1	1,590.5	1,830.3	2,022.4
Current transfers: debit	3 379 . .	–2.5	–4.6	–4.8	–2.7	–7.3	–9.0	–33.2	–18.6
B. Capital Account [1]	4 994 Z.	**. . .**	**. . .**	**. . .**	**11.6**	**28.6**	**78.6**	**109.0**	**197.7**
Capital account: credit	2 994 Z.	. . .	. . .	. . .	11.6	28.9	78.8	109.4	197.8
Capital account: debit	3 994 . .	. . .	. . .	. . .	. . .	–.3	–.2	–.4	–.1
Total, Groups A Plus B	4 981 . .	*–18.0*	*–261.6*	*–169.0*	*–86.1*	*–62.1*	*–160.6*	*–321.6*	*20.8*
C. Financial Account [1]	4 995 W.	**115.8**	**438.3**	**358.1**	**653.2**	**1,034.3**	**574.3**	**287.4**	**145.7**
Direct investment abroad	4 505 . .	. . .	. . .	–2.4	. . .	–1.0	–53.8	5.0	9.7
Direct investment in El Salvador	4 555 Z.	. . .	38.0	–4.8	59.0	1,103.7	215.8	173.4	267.8
Portfolio investment assets	4 602 . .	. . .	. . .	.5	. . .	. . .	–1.7	–8.9	–126.5
Equity securities	4 610 . .	. . .	. . .	.5	. . .	. . .	. . .	. . .	. . .
Debt securities	4 619 . .	. . .	. . .	. . .	. . .	. . .	–1.7	–8.9	–126.5
Portfolio investment liabilities	4 652 Z.	. . .	68.5	150.0	115.9	–226.4	75.2	–16.8	160.6
Equity securities	4 660 . .	. . .	. . .	. . .	. . .	. . .	. . .	. . .	2.4
Debt securities	4 669 Z.	. . .	68.5	150.0	115.9	–226.4	75.2	–16.8	158.2
Financial derivatives	4 910 . .	. . .	. . .	. . .	. . .	. . .	. . .	. . .	. . .
Financial derivatives assets	4 900 . .	. . .	. . .	. . .	. . .	. . .	. . .	. . .	. . .
Financial derivatives liabilities	4 905 . .	. . .	. . .	. . .	. . .	. . .	. . .	. . .	. . .
Other investment assets	4 703 . .	–8.7	24.2	4.7	–19.9	12.2	–126.9	–245.4	–630.1
Monetary authorities	4 701 . .	. . .	35.0	. . .	. . .	. . .	. . .	. . .	. . .
General government	4 704 . .	. . .	. . .	. . .	. . .	. . .	. . .	. . .	. . .
Banks	4 705 . .	–8.7	–10.2	. . .	2.1	–8.0	–4.6	146.5	–390.9
Other sectors	4 728 . .	. . .	–.6	4.7	–21.9	20.2	–122.3	–98.8	–239.2
Other investment liabilities	4 753 W.	124.5	307.5	210.2	498.2	145.7	465.8	380.0	464.2
Monetary authorities	4 753 WA	–147.2	38.2	51.2	27.9	–72.2	2.1	–19.5	–30.8
General government	4 753 ZB	177.0	46.4	162.8	154.6	162.9	51.4	83.3	201.0
Banks	4 753 ZC	94.7	219.9	3.2	130.8	–20.4	35.0	120.0	278.4
Other sectors	4 753 ZD	. . .	3.1	–.6	184.9	75.5	381.5	196.2	15.6
Total, Groups A Through C	4 983 . .	*97.8*	*176.7*	*189.0*	*567.1*	*972.1*	*413.7*	*–34.2*	*166.5*
D. Net Errors and Omissions	4 998 . .	**15.4**	**–28.4**	**–24.2**	**–204.4**	**–668.9**	**–205.9**	**–11.3**	**–344.2**
Total, Groups A Through D	4 984 . .	*113.3*	*148.3*	*164.8*	*362.7*	*303.3*	*207.8*	*–45.5*	*–177.7*
E. Reserves and Related Items	4 802 A.	**–113.3**	**–148.3**	**–164.8**	**–362.7**	**–303.3**	**–207.8**	**45.5**	**177.7**
Reserve assets	4 802 . .	–113.3	–148.3	–164.8	–362.7	–303.3	–207.8	45.5	177.7
Use of Fund credit and loans	4 766 . .	. . .	. . .	. . .	. . .	. . .	. . .	. . .	. . .
Exceptional financing	4 920 . .	. . .	. . .	. . .	. . .	. . .	. . .	. . .	. . .
Conversion rates: Salvadoran colones per U.S. dollar	0 101 . .	**8.7288**	**8.7546**	**8.7550**	**8.7563**	**8.7550**	**8.7550**	**8.7550**	**8.7500**

[1] Excludes components that have been classified in the categories of Group E.

Table 2. STANDARD PRESENTATION, 1994–2001

(Millions of U.S. dollars)

	Code		1994	1995	1996	1997	1998	1999	2000	2001
CURRENT ACCOUNT	4 993	. .	**–18.0**	**–261.6**	**–169.0**	**–97.8**	**–90.7**	**–239.2**	**–430.6**	**–176.9**
A. GOODS	4 100	. .	–1,170.0	–1,462.3	–1,242.3	–1,143.2	–1,305.7	–1,356.1	–1,739.7	–1,912.9
Credit	2 100	. .	**1,252.3**	**1,651.1**	**1,787.4**	**2,437.1**	**2,459.5**	**2,534.3**	**2,963.2**	**2,901.0**
General merchandise: exports f.o.b.	2 110	. .	820.9	1,104.8	1,023.0	1,362.5	1,244.9	1,165.0	1,319.9	1,211.3
Goods for processing: exports f.o.b.	2 150	. .	431.4	546.3	764.5	1,055.0	1,184.7	1,333.4	1,609.0	1,651.6
Repairs on goods	2 160	. .	. . .	. . .	. . .	9.1	15.5	21.9	19.3	24.6
Goods procured in ports by carriers	2 170	. .	. . .	. . .	. . .	9.1	13.6	13.3	14.9	13.5
Nonmonetary gold	2 180	. .	. . .	. . .	. . .	1.4	.8	.7	.1	. . .
Debit	3 100	. .	**–2,422.3**	**–3,113.5**	**–3,029.7**	**–3,580.3**	**–3,765.2**	**–3,890.4**	**–4,702.9**	**–4,813.9**
General merchandise: imports f.o.b.	3 110	. .	–2,099.5	–2,640.7	–2,478.7	–2,764.4	–2,854.6	–2,876.3	–3,459.3	–3,555.2
Goods for processing: imports f.o.b.	3 150	. .	–322.8	–472.8	–551.0	–763.9	–846.8	–954.7	–1,152.7	–1,161.6
Repairs on goods	3 160	. .	. . .	. . .	. . .	–19.8	–25.7	–22.6	–35.6	–37.3
Goods procured in ports by carriers	3 170	. .	. . .	. . .	. . .	–32.0	–37.8	–36.5	–54.9	–59.4
Nonmonetary gold	3 180	. .	. . .	. . .	. . .	–.2	–.2	–.3	–.4	–.4
B. SERVICES	4 200	. .	–41.7	–121.2	–90.2	–152.2	–148.8	–182.5	–234.9	–2.1
Total credit	2 200	. .	*387.2*	*388.6*	*414.4*	*475.8*	*588.5*	*640.5*	*698.4*	*1,075.8*
Total debit	3 200	. .	*–428.9*	*–509.8*	*–504.6*	*–628.0*	*–737.3*	*–823.0*	*–933.3*	*–1,077.8*
Transportation services, credit	2 205	. .	**94.5**	**96.7**	**99.4**	**180.4**	**187.4**	**213.8**	**248.6**	**281.8**
Passenger	2 850	. .	*64.8*	*66.7*	*68.5*	. . .	. . .	*185.6*	*219.6*	*243.7*
Freight	2 851	. .	. . .	. . .	. . .	*10.2*	*10.3*	*15.0*	*11.4*	*19.3*
Other	2 852	. .	*29.7*	*30.0*	*30.8*	*170.3*	*177.2*	*13.2*	*17.6*	*18.8*
Sea transport, passenger	2 207	. .	. . .	. . .	. . .	. . .	. . .	. . .	. . .	. . .
Sea transport, freight	2 208	. .	. . .	. . .	. . .	. . .	. . .	. . .	. . .	. . .
Sea transport, other	2 209	. .	. . .	. . .	. . .	. . .	. . .	.5	1.1	7.1
Air transport, passenger	2 211	. .	. . .	. . .	. . .	. . .	. . .	185.0	218.6	242.6
Air transport, freight	2 212	. .	. . .	. . .	. . .	10.2	10.3	13.1	10.8	19.3
Air transport, other	2 213	. .	. . .	. . .	. . .	. . .	. . .	9.4	11.6	11.1
Other transport, passenger	2 215	. .	. . .	. . .	. . .	. . .	. . .	.6	1.0	1.1
Other transport, freight	2 216	. .	. . .	. . .	. . .	. . .	. . .	1.9	.6	. . .
Other transport, other	2 217	. .	. . .	. . .	. . .	170.3	177.2	3.3	4.9	.6
Transportation services, debit	3 205	. .	**–215.6**	**–268.5**	**–285.6**	**–261.4**	**–324.7**	**–330.9**	**–405.0**	**–386.8**
Passenger	3 850	. .	*–15.1*	*–27.3*	*–29.1*	. . .	. . .	*–36.0*	*–53.6*	*–51.9*
Freight	3 851	. .	*–135.2*	*–183.2*	*–190.3*	*–181.9*	*–237.1*	*–234.6*	*–300.5*	*–279.8*
Other	3 852	. .	*–65.3*	*–58.0*	*–66.1*	*–79.5*	*–87.6*	*–60.3*	*–50.9*	*–55.1*
Sea transport, passenger	3 207	. .	. . .	. . .	. . .	. . .	. . .	. . .	. . .	. . .
Sea transport, freight	3 208	. .	. . .	. . .	. . .	. . .	. . .	–73.9	–104.4	–91.1
Sea transport, other	3 209	. .	. . .	. . .	. . .	. . .	. . .	–.5	. . .	. . .
Air transport, passenger	3 211	. .	. . .	. . .	. . .	. . .	. . .	–35.9	–53.2	–51.8
Air transport, freight	3 212	. .	. . .	. . .	. . .	–181.9	–237.1	–2.9	–2.3	–9.7
Air transport, other	3 213	. .	. . .	. . .	. . .	. . .	. . .	–59.7	–50.6	–55.1
Other transport, passenger	3 215	. .	. . .	. . .	. . .	. . .	. . .	–.1	–.4	–.1
Other transport, freight	3 216	. .	. . .	. . .	. . .	. . .	. . .	–157.8	–193.8	–179.0
Other transport, other	3 217	. .	. . .	. . .	. . .	–79.5	–87.6	–.1	–.3	. . .
Travel, credit	2 236	. .	**85.5**	**85.4**	**86.5**	**149.4**	**206.2**	**222.3**	**216.9**	**201.1**
Business travel	2 237	. .	. . .	. . .	. . .	. . .	. . .	94.0	83.3	63.1
Personal travel	2 240	. .	. . .	. . .	. . .	149.4	206.2	128.3	133.6	138.0
Travel, debit	3 236	. .	**–70.3**	**–72.4**	**–72.8**	**–153.1**	**–179.4**	**–168.9**	**–165.2**	**–195.3**
Business travel	3 237	. .	. . .	. . .	. . .	. . .	. . .	–83.9	–33.1	–27.5
Personal travel	3 240	. .	. . .	. . .	. . .	–153.1	–179.4	–85.0	–132.1	–167.8
Other services, credit	2 200	BA	**207.2**	**206.4**	**228.6**	**146.0**	**194.9**	**204.3**	**232.9**	**592.8**
Communications	2 245	. .	. . .	70.7	89.5	78.3	98.3	81.2	86.3	108.8
Construction	2 249	. .	. . .	. . .	. . .	1.6	5.7	6.8	14.0	15.6
Insurance	2 253	. .	26.6	26.6	26.8	31.7	54.3	66.7	63.1	406.2
Financial	2 260	. .	. . .	. . .	6.2	7.7	10.1	12.3	6.7	2.0
Computer and information	2 262	. .	. . .	. . .	. . .	. . .	. . .	. . .	3.9	.2
Royalties and licence fees	2 266	. .	. . .	. . .	. . .	. . .	. . .	1.1	2.4	1.2
Other business services	2 268	. .	131.4	62.8	9.6	11.1	13.6	15.9	30.6	34.8
Personal, cultural, and recreational	2 287	. .	. . .	. . .	. . .	. . .	. . .	. . .	.6	.4
Government, n.i.e.	2 291	. .	49.3	46.3	96.4	15.5	12.9	20.3	25.3	23.5
Other services, debit	3 200	BA	**–143.0**	**–168.8**	**–146.3**	**–213.4**	**–233.1**	**–323.1**	**–363.1**	**–495.7**
Communications	3 245	. .	. . .	. . .	. . .	–7.4	–18.3	–20.8	–27.2	–40.4
Construction	3 249	. .	. . .	. . .	. . .	–1.7	–4.1	–8.9	–8.2	–8.6
Insurance	3 253	. .	–47.4	–53.8	–34.0	–87.5	–89.3	–113.5	–113.2	–173.4
Financial	3 260	. .	. . .	. . .	. . .	–17.5	–16.9	–31.4	–38.1	–40.1
Computer and information	3 262	. .	. . .	. . .	. . .	. . .	. . .	–11.8	–14.1	–9.6
Royalties and licence fees	3 266	. .	–.1	–2.9	–.2	. . .	. . .	–20.3	–20.5	–22.1
Other business services	3 268	. .	–75.0	–90.0	–88.7	–86.1	–90.5	–93.9	–119.2	–184.3
Personal, cultural, and recreational	3 287	. .	. . .	. . .	. . .	. . .	. . .	. . .	–1.0	–1.3
Government, n.i.e.	3 291	. .	–20.4	–22.2	–23.3	–13.2	–14.0	–22.5	–21.6	–15.8

Table 2 (Continued). STANDARD PRESENTATION, 1994–2001
(Millions of U.S. dollars)

	Code	1994	1995	1996	1997	1998	1999	2000	2001
C. INCOME	4 300 . .	–94.6	–66.7	–90.3	–163.2	–163.0	–282.2	–253.1	–265.8
Total credit	2 300 . .	*35.5*	*54.0*	*44.1*	*75.1*	*111.4*	*112.9*	*141.3*	*168.9*
Total debit	3 300 . .	*–130.1*	*–120.7*	*–134.4*	*–238.3*	*–274.4*	*–395.1*	*–394.4*	*–434.7*
Compensation of employees, credit	2 310 . .	**5.0**	**3.2**	**. . .**	**. . .**	**. . .**	**12.2**	**13.5**	**13.8**
Compensation of employees, debit	3 310 . .	**–.1**	**. . .**	**. . .**	**. . .**	**. . .**	**–7.0**	**–19.2**	**–25.7**
Investment income, credit	2 320 . .	**30.5**	**50.8**	**44.1**	**75.1**	**111.4**	**100.7**	**127.8**	**155.1**
Direct investment income	2 330 . .	. . .	. . .	. . .	. . .	. . .	. . .	. . .	3.4
Dividends and distributed branch profits	2 332 . .	. . .	. . .	. . .	. . .	. . .	. . .	. . .	3.4
Reinvested earnings and undistributed branch profits	2 333 . .	. . .	. . .	. . .	. . .	. . .	. . .	. . .	. . .
Income on debt (interest)	2 334 . .	. . .	. . .	. . .	. . .	. . .	. . .	. . .	. . .
Portfolio investment income	2 339 . .	. . .	. . .	. . .	. . .	. . .	. . .	. . .	.3
Income on equity	2 340 . .	. . .	. . .	. . .	. . .	. . .	. . .	. . .	. . .
Income on bonds and notes	2 350 . .	. . .	. . .	. . .	. . .	. . .	. . .	. . .	. . .
Income on money market instruments	2 360 . .	. . .	. . .	. . .	. . .	. . .	. . .	. . .	.3
Other investment income	2 370 . .	30.5	50.8	44.1	75.1	111.4	100.7	127.8	151.4
Investment income, debit	3 320 . .	**–130.0**	**–120.7**	**–134.4**	**–238.3**	**–274.4**	**–388.1**	**–375.2**	**–409.0**
Direct investment income	3 330 . .	–26.9	. . .	. . .	. . .	–29.4	–110.8	–59.5	–73.4
Dividends and distributed branch profits	3 332 . .	–26.9	. . .	. . .	. . .	–29.4	–84.8	–41.4	–39.8
Reinvested earnings and undistributed branch profits	3 333 . .	. . .	. . .	. . .	. . .	. . .	–26.0	–18.1	–33.6
Income on debt (interest)	3 334 . .	. . .	. . .	. . .	. . .	. . .	. . .	. . .	. . .
Portfolio investment income	3 339 . .	. . .	. . .	. . .	–14.4	–15.9	–10.0	–21.2	–10.4
Income on equity	3 340 . .	. . .	. . .	. . .	–14.4	–15.9	. . .	. . .	. . .
Income on bonds and notes	3 350 . .	. . .	. . .	. . .	. . .	. . .	. . .	. . .	. . .
Income on money market instruments	3 360 . .	. . .	. . .	. . .	. . .	. . .	–10.0	–21.2	–10.4
Other investment income	3 370 . .	–103.1	–120.7	–134.4	–224.0	–229.1	–267.3	–294.5	–325.1
D. CURRENT TRANSFERS	4 379 . .	1,288.4	1,388.6	1,253.8	1,360.9	1,526.8	1,581.5	1,797.1	2,003.8
Credit	2 379 . .	**1,290.9**	**1,393.2**	**1,258.6**	**1,363.6**	**1,534.1**	**1,590.5**	**1,830.3**	**2,022.4**
General government	2 380 . .	286.6	197.0	64.4	55.4	45.0	28.1	29.4	34.4
Other sectors	2 390 . .	1,004.3	1,196.2	1,194.2	1,308.2	1,489.1	1,562.4	1,800.9	1,988.0
Workers' remittances	2 391 . .	966.7	1,060.7	1,083.8	1,199.5	1,338.3	1,373.8	1,750.7	1,910.5
Other current transfers	2 392 . .	37.6	135.5	110.3	108.7	150.8	188.6	50.2	77.5
Debit	3 379 . .	**–2.5**	**–4.6**	**–4.8**	**–2.7**	**–7.3**	**–9.0**	**–33.2**	**–18.6**
General government	3 380 . .	–1.8	–2.9	–2.9	. . .	. . .	. . .	–1.3	. . .
Other sectors	3 390 . .	–.7	–1.7	–1.9	–2.7	–7.3	–9.0	–31.9	–18.6
Workers' remittances	3 391 . .	. . .	. . .	–1.5	. . .	. . .	. . .	. . .	. . .
Other current transfers	3 392 . .	–.7	–1.7	–.5	–2.7	–7.3	–9.0	–31.9	–18.6
CAPITAL AND FINANCIAL ACCOUNT	4 996 . .	**2.6**	**290.0**	**193.3**	**302.2**	**759.6**	**445.1**	**441.9**	**521.1**
CAPITAL ACCOUNT	4 994 . .	**. . .**	**. . .**	**. . .**	**11.6**	**28.6**	**78.6**	**109.0**	**197.7**
Total credit	2 994 . .	. . .	. . .	. . .	*11.6*	*28.9*	*78.8*	*109.4*	*197.8*
Total debit	3 994 . .	. . .	. . .	. . .	. . .	*–.3*	*–.2*	*–.4*	*–.1*
Capital transfers, credit	2 400 . .	**. . .**	**. . .**	**. . .**	**11.6**	**28.9**	**78.8**	**109.4**	**197.8**
General government	2 401 . .	. . .	. . .	. . .	11.6	25.0	48.5	22.7	59.4
Debt forgiveness	2 402 . .	. . .	. . .	. . .	11.6	25.0	. . .	. . .	. . .
Other capital transfers	2 410 . .	. . .	. . .	. . .	. . .	. . .	48.5	22.7	59.4
Other sectors	2 430 . .	. . .	. . .	. . .	. . .	3.9	30.3	86.7	138.4
Migrants' transfers	2 431 . .	. . .	. . .	. . .	. . .	1.5	1.3	1.2	.2
Debt forgiveness	2 432 . .	. . .	. . .	. . .	. . .	. . .	. . .	. . .	. . .
Other capital transfers	2 440 . .	. . .	. . .	. . .	. . .	2.4	29.0	85.5	138.2
Capital transfers, debit	3 400 . .	**. . .**	**. . .**	**. . .**	**. . .**	**–.3**	**–.2**	**–.4**	**–.1**
General government	3 401 . .	. . .	. . .	. . .	. . .	. . .	. . .	. . .	. . .
Debt forgiveness	3 402 . .	. . .	. . .	. . .	. . .	. . .	. . .	. . .	. . .
Other capital transfers	3 410 . .	. . .	. . .	. . .	. . .	. . .	. . .	. . .	. . .
Other sectors	3 430 . .	. . .	. . .	. . .	. . .	–.3	–.2	–.4	–.1
Migrants' transfers	3 431 . .	. . .	. . .	. . .	. . .	–.3	–.2	–.4	–.1
Debt forgiveness	3 432 . .	. . .	. . .	. . .	. . .	. . .	. . .	. . .	. . .
Other capital transfers	3 440 . .	. . .	. . .	. . .	. . .	. . .	. . .	. . .	. . .
Nonproduced nonfinancial assets, credit	2 480 . .	**. . .**	**. . .**	**. . .**	**. . .**	**. . .**	**. . .**	**. . .**	**. . .**
Nonproduced nonfinancial assets, debit	3 480 . .	**. . .**	**. . .**	**. . .**	**. . .**	**. . .**	**. . .**	**. . .**	**. . .**

Table 2 (Continued). STANDARD PRESENTATION, 1994–2001
(Millions of U.S. dollars)

	Code	1994	1995	1996	1997	1998	1999	2000	2001
FINANCIAL ACCOUNT	4 995	**2.6**	**290.0**	**193.3**	**290.5**	**731.0**	**366.5**	**332.9**	**323.4**
A. DIRECT INVESTMENT	4 500	...	38.0	–7.2	59.0	1,102.7	162.0	178.4	277.5
Direct investment abroad	4 505	**...**	**...**	**–2.4**	**...**	**–1.0**	**–53.8**	**5.0**	**9.7**
Equity capital	4 510	...	...	–2.4	...	–1.0	–53.8	5.0	9.7
Claims on affiliated enterprises	4 515	...	...	–2.4	...	...	–53.8	5.0	9.7
Liabilities to affiliated enterprises	4 520	...	...	...	...	–1.0	...	...	...
Reinvested earnings	4 525	...	...	...	...	...	...	...	...
Other capital	4 530	...	...	...	...	...	...	...	...
Claims on affiliated enterprises	4 535	...	...	...	...	...	...	...	...
Liabilities to affiliated enterprises	4 540	...	...	...	...	...	...	...	...
Direct investment in El Salvador	4 555	**...**	**38.0**	**–4.8**	**59.0**	**1,103.7**	**215.8**	**173.4**	**267.8**
Equity capital	4 560	...	14.8	...	59.0	1,103.7	189.9	155.3	234.1
Claims on direct investors	4 565	...	...	...	...	...	...	...	...
Liabilities to direct investors	4 570	...	...	...	59.0	1,103.7	189.9	155.3	234.1
Reinvested earnings	4 575	...	...	...	...	...	25.9	18.1	33.7
Other capital	4 580	...	23.2	–4.8	...	...	...	...	...
Claims on direct investors	4 585	...	...	–4.8	...	...	...	...	...
Liabilities to direct investors	4 590	...	...	...	...	...	...	...	...
B. PORTFOLIO INVESTMENT	4 600	...	68.5	150.4	115.9	–226.4	73.5	–25.7	34.1
Assets	4 602	**...**	**...**	**.5**	**...**	**...**	**–1.7**	**–8.9**	**–126.5**
Equity securities	4 610	...	...	.5	...	...	...	...	...
Monetary authorities	4 611	...	...	...	...	...	...	...	...
General government	4 612	...	...	...	...	...	...	...	...
Banks	4 613	...	...	...	...	...	...	...	...
Other sectors	4 614	...	...	.5	...	...	...	...	...
Debt securities	4 619	...	...	...	...	...	–1.7	–8.9	–126.5
Bonds and notes	4 620	...	...	...	...	...	...	...	...
Monetary authorities	4 621	...	...	...	...	...	...	...	...
General government	4 622	...	...	...	...	...	...	...	...
Banks	4 623	...	...	...	...	...	...	...	...
Other sectors	4 624	...	...	...	...	...	...	...	...
Money market instruments	4 630	...	...	...	...	...	–1.7	–8.9	–126.5
Monetary authorities	4 631	...	...	...	...	...	...	...	...
General government	4 632	...	...	...	...	...	...	...	...
Banks	4 633	...	...	...	...	...	.4	–8.1	–122.1
Other sectors	4 634	...	...	...	...	...	–2.1	–.8	–4.4
Liabilities	4 652	**...**	**68.5**	**150.0**	**115.9**	**–226.4**	**75.2**	**–16.8**	**160.6**
Equity securities	4 660	...	...	...	...	...	...	...	2.4
Banks	4 663	...	...	...	...	...	...	...	...
Other sectors	4 664	...	...	...	...	...	...	...	2.4
Debt securities	4 669	...	68.5	150.0	115.9	–226.4	75.2	–16.8	158.2
Bonds and notes	4 670	...	...	...	...	...	115.3	–95.2	106.2
Monetary authorities	4 671	...	...	...	...	...	...	...	...
General government	4 672	...	...	...	...	...	115.3	–95.2	106.2
Banks	4 673	...	...	...	...	...	...	...	...
Other sectors	4 674	...	...	...	...	...	...	...	...
Money market instruments	4 680	...	68.5	150.0	115.9	–226.4	–40.1	78.4	52.0
Monetary authorities	4 681	...	...	...	...	–85.7	–12.9	8.7	–9.7
General government	4 682	...	...	150.0	115.9	–140.7	–27.2	68.5	65.8
Banks	4 683	...	68.5	...	...	...	...	...	...
Other sectors	4 684	...	...	...	...	...	...	1.2	–4.1
C. FINANCIAL DERIVATIVES	4 910	...	...	...	...	...	...	...	...
Monetary authorities	4 911	...	...	...	...	...	...	...	...
General government	4 912	...	...	...	...	...	...	...	...
Banks	4 913	...	...	...	...	...	...	...	...
Other sectors	4 914	...	...	...	...	...	...	...	...
Assets	4 900	**...**	**...**	**...**	**...**	**...**	**...**	**...**	**...**
Monetary authorities	4 901	...	...	...	...	...	...	...	...
General government	4 902	...	...	...	...	...	...	...	...
Banks	4 903	...	...	...	...	...	...	...	...
Other sectors	4 904	...	...	...	...	...	...	...	...
Liabilities	4 905	**...**	**...**	**...**	**...**	**...**	**...**	**...**	**...**
Monetary authorities	4 906	...	...	...	...	...	...	...	...
General government	4 907	...	...	...	...	...	...	...	...
Banks	4 908	...	...	...	...	...	...	...	...
Other sectors	4 909	...	...	...	...	...	...	...	...

Table 2 (Concluded). STANDARD PRESENTATION, 1994–2001
(Millions of U.S. dollars)

	Code	1994	1995	1996	1997	1998	1999	2000	2001
D. OTHER INVESTMENT	4 700	115.8	331.7	214.8	478.3	158.0	338.9	134.7	–165.9
Assets	4 703	**–8.7**	**24.2**	**4.7**	**–19.9**	**12.2**	**–126.9**	**–245.4**	**–630.1**
Trade credits	4 706	. . .	–.6	4.0	–21.9	20.2	–81.2	–92.7	2.3
General government	4 707	. . .	. . .	. . .	. . .	. . .	. . .	. . .	. . .
of which: Short-term	4 709	. . .	. . .	. . .	. . .	. . .	. . .	. . .	. . .
Other sectors	4 710	. . .	–.6	4.0	–21.9	20.2	–81.2	–92.7	2.3
of which: Short-term	4 712	. . .	*–.6*	*4.0*	. . .	. . .	*–81.2*	*–92.7*	*2.3*
Loans	4 714	. . .	. . .	. . .	. . .	. . .	–3.5	–72.7	–186.7
Monetary authorities	4 715	. . .	. . .	. . .	. . .	. . .	. . .	. . .	. . .
of which: Short-term	4 718	. . .	. . .	. . .	. . .	. . .	. . .	. . .	. . .
General government	4 719	. . .	. . .	. . .	. . .	. . .	. . .	. . .	. . .
of which: Short-term	4 721	. . .	. . .	. . .	. . .	. . .	. . .	. . .	. . .
Banks	4 722	. . .	. . .	. . .	. . .	. . .	. . .	–65.9	–182.9
of which: Short-term	4 724	. . .	. . .	. . .	. . .	. . .	. . .	*–65.9*	*–182.9*
Other sectors	4 725	. . .	. . .	. . .	. . .	. . .	–3.5	–6.8	–3.8
of which: Short-term	4 727	. . .	. . .	. . .	. . .	. . .	. . .	. . .	. . .
Currency and deposits	4 730	–8.7	24.8	.6	2.1	–8.0	–42.2	–75.3	–448.6
Monetary authorities	4 731	. . .	35.0	. . .	. . .	. . .	. . .	. . .	. . .
General government	4 732	. . .	. . .	. . .	. . .	. . .	. . .	. . .	. . .
Banks	4 733	–8.7	–10.2	. . .	2.1	–8.0	–6.4	–77.8	–207.9
Other sectors	4 734	. . .	. . .	.6	. . .	. . .	–35.8	2.5	–240.7
Other assets	4 736	. . .	. . .	.1	. . .	. . .	. . .	–4.6	2.9
Monetary authorities	4 737	. . .	. . .	. . .	. . .	. . .	. . .	. . .	. . .
of which: Short-term	4 739	. . .	. . .	. . .	. . .	. . .	. . .	. . .	. . .
General government	4 740	. . .	. . .	. . .	. . .	. . .	. . .	. . .	. . .
of which: Short-term	4 742	. . .	. . .	. . .	. . .	. . .	. . .	. . .	. . .
Banks	4 743	. . .	. . .	. . .	. . .	. . .	1.8	–2.8	–.1
of which: Short-term	4 745	. . .	. . .	. . .	. . .	. . .	*1.8*	*–2.8*	*–.1*
Other sectors	4 746	. . .	. . .	.1	. . .	. . .	–1.8	–1.8	3.0
of which: Short-term	4 748	. . .	. . .	*.1*	. . .	. . .	*–1.8*	*–1.8*	*3.0*
Liabilities	4 753	**124.5**	**307.5**	**210.2**	**498.2**	**145.7**	**465.8**	**380.0**	**464.2**
Trade credits	4 756	. . .	–5.9	–.5	33.9	13.9	83.6	62.9	–87.7
General government	4 757	. . .	–9.0	. . .	33.9	13.9	. . .	. . .	. . .
of which: Short-term	4 759	. . .	. . .	. . .	. . .	. . .	. . .	. . .	. . .
Other sectors	4 760	. . .	3.1	–.5	. . .	. . .	83.6	62.9	–87.7
of which: Short-term	4 762	. . .	*3.1*	*–.8*	. . .	. . .	*83.6*	*62.9*	*–87.7*
Loans	4 764	154.8	313.6	210.7	464.2	131.8	378.6	317.4	556.1
Monetary authorities	4 765	–117.0	38.3	51.2	27.9	–72.2	–5.7	–15.0	–24.3
of which: Use of Fund credit and loans from the Fund	4 766	. . .	. . .	. . .	. . .	. . .	. . .	. . .	. . .
of which: Short-term	4 768	. . .	. . .	. . .	. . .	. . .	. . .	. . .	. . .
General government	4 769	177.0	55.4	162.8	120.7	148.9	51.4	83.3	201.0
of which: Short-term	4 771	*–.2*	*23.6*	*–.6*	*120.7*	*148.9*	*–15.0*	. . .	. . .
Banks	4 772	94.7	219.9	–3.2	130.8	–20.4	35.0	120.0	278.4
of which: Short-term	4 774	*86.2*	*198.8*	*–49.5*	. . .	. . .	*–14.1*	*77.4*	*317.2*
Other sectors	4 775	. . .	. . .	. . .	184.9	75.5	297.9	129.1	101.0
of which: Short-term	4 777	. . .	. . .	. . .	. . .	. . .	. . .	*–320.9*	*219.5*
Currency and deposits	4 780	. . .	. . .	. . .	. . .	. . .	. . .	–.3	–3.4
Monetary authorities	4 781	. . .	. . .	. . .	. . .	. . .	. . .	–4.5	–5.7
General government	4 782	. . .	. . .	. . .	. . .	. . .	. . .	. . .	. . .
Banks	4 783	. . .	. . .	. . .	. . .	. . .	. . .	. . .	. . .
Other sectors	4 784	. . .	. . .	. . .	. . .	. . .	. . .	4.2	2.3
Other liabilities	4 786	–30.2	–.1	–.1	. . .	. . .	3.6	. . .	–.8
Monetary authorities	4 787	–30.2	–.1	. . .	. . .	. . .	3.6	. . .	–.8
of which: Short-term	4 789	*–30.2*	*–.1*	. . .	. . .	. . .	. . .	. . .	. . .
General government	4 790	. . .	. . .	. . .	. . .	. . .	. . .	. . .	. . .
of which: Short-term	4 792	. . .	. . .	. . .	. . .	. . .	. . .	. . .	. . .
Banks	4 793	. . .	. . .	. . .	. . .	. . .	. . .	. . .	. . .
of which: Short-term	4 795	. . .	. . .	. . .	. . .	. . .	. . .	. . .	. . .
Other sectors	4 796	. . .	. . .	–.1	. . .	. . .	. . .	. . .	. . .
of which: Short-term	4 798	. . .	. . .	*–.1*	. . .	. . .	. . .	. . .	. . .
E. RESERVE ASSETS	4 802	–113.3	–148.3	–164.8	–362.7	–303.3	–207.8	45.5	177.7
Monetary gold	4 812	. . .	. . .	. . .	. . .	. . .	. . .	. . .	. . .
Special drawing rights	4 811	–.1	–38.2	. . .	. . .	. . .	. . .	. . .	. . .
Reserve position in the Fund	4 810	. . .	. . .	. . .	. . .	. . .	. . .	. . .	. . .
Foreign exchange	4 803	–113.2	–110.1	–161.5	–361.5	–303.3	–207.8	45.5	177.7
Other claims	4 813	. . .	. . .	–3.3	–1.3	. . .	. . .	. . .	. . .
NET ERRORS AND OMISSIONS	4 998	**15.4**	**–28.4**	**–24.2**	**–204.4**	**–668.9**	**–205.9**	**–11.3**	**–344.2**

Part 3 of the *Yearbook* contains descriptions of the methodologies, compilation practices, and sources used to compile these data.

Table 3. INTERNATIONAL INVESTMENT POSITION (End–period stocks), 1994–2001
(Millions of U.S. dollars)

	Code	1994	1995	1996	1997	1998	1999	2000	2001
ASSETS	8 995 C.	...	...	1,771.3	2,153.8	2,445.6	2,832.4	3,004.0	3,309.9
Direct investment abroad	8 505	...	...	**55.7**	**55.7**	**56.7**	**110.5**	**103.9**	**64.3**
Equity capital and reinvested earnings	8 506	...	...	55.7	55.7	56.7	110.5	103.9	64.3
Claims on affiliated enterprises	8 507	...	...	55.7	55.7	56.7	110.5	103.9	64.3
Liabilities to affiliated enterprises	8 508	...	...	...	...	...	...	...	...
Other capital	8 530	...	...	...	...	...	...	...	...
Claims on affiliated enterprises	8 535	...	...	...	...	...	...	...	...
Liabilities to affiliated enterprises	8 540	...	...	...	...	...	...	...	...
Portfolio investment	8 602	...	...	...	...	...	**2.1**	**11.0**	**152.5**
Equity securities	8 610	...	...	...	...	...	...	...	17.8
Monetary authorities	8 611	...	...	...	...	...	...	...	...
General government	8 612	...	...	...	...	...	...	...	...
Banks	8 613	...	...	...	...	...	...	...	...
Other sectors	8 614	...	...	...	...	...	...	...	17.8
Debt securities	8 619	...	...	...	...	...	2.1	11.0	134.7
Bonds and notes	8 620	...	...	...	...	...	...	...	134.7
Monetary authorities	8 621	...	...	...	...	...	...	...	...
General government	8 622	...	...	...	...	...	...	...	...
Banks	8 623	...	...	...	...	...	...	...	134.7
Other sectors	8 624	...	...	...	...	...	...	...	...
Money market instruments	8 630	...	...	...	...	...	2.1	11.0	...
Monetary authorities	8 631	...	...	...	...	...	...	...	...
General government	8 632	...	...	...	...	...	...	...	...
Banks	8 633	...	...	...	...	...	...	8.1	...
Other sectors	8 634	...	...	...	...	...	2.1	2.9	...
Financial derivatives	8 900	...	...	...	...	...	...	...	...
Monetary authorities	8 901	...	...	...	...	...	...	...	...
General government	8 902	...	...	...	...	...	...	...	...
Banks	8 903	...	...	...	...	...	...	...	...
Other sectors	8 904	...	...	...	...	...	...	...	...
Other investment	8 703	**59.9**	**70.1**	**615.9**	**635.8**	**623.5**	**747.5**	**995.8**	**1,381.5**
Trade credits	8 706	...	...	225.0	246.9	226.7	307.9	400.6	405.3
General government	8 707	...	...	...	...	...	...	...	...
of which: Short-term	8 709	...	...	...	...	...	...	...	...
Other sectors	8 710	...	...	225.0	246.9	226.7	307.9	400.6	405.3
of which: Short-term	8 712	...	...	*225.0*	*246.9*	*226.7*	*307.9*	*400.6*	*405.3*
Loans	8 714	...	...	...	−2.0	−2.0	1.5	74.2	274.0
Monetary authorities	8 715	...	...	...	...	...	...	...	...
of which: Short-term	8 718	...	...	...	...	...	...	...	...
General government	8 719	...	...	...	...	...	...	...	...
of which: Short-term	8 721	...	...	...	...	...	...	...	...
Banks	8 722	...	...	...	−2.0	−2.0	−2.0	63.9	248.8
of which: Short-term	8 724	...	...	...	*−2.0*	*−2.0*	*−2.0*	*63.9*	*248.8*
Other sectors	8 725	...	...	...	...	...	3.5	10.3	25.2
of which: Short-term	8 727	...	...	...	...	...	*3.5*	*10.3*	*25.2*
Currency and deposits	8 730	59.9	70.1	390.9	390.9	398.8	445.9	534.1	692.5
Monetary authorities	8 731	...	...	...	...	...	...	...	...
General government	8 732	...	...	22.0	22.0	22.0	22.0	22.0	...
Banks	8 733	59.9	70.1	115.8	115.8	123.8	135.1	225.8	400.0
Other sectors	8 734	...	...	253.0	253.0	253.0	288.8	286.3	292.5
Other assets	8 736	...	...	...	...	...	−7.8	−13.1	9.7
Monetary authorities	8 737	...	...	...	...	...	...	...	...
of which: Short-term	8 739	...	...	...	...	...	...	...	...
General government	8 740	...	...	...	...	...	...	...	...
of which: Short-term	8 742	...	...	...	...	...	...	...	...
Banks	8 743	...	...	...	...	...	−9.6	−16.6	9.7
of which: Short-term	8 745	...	...	...	...	...	*−9.6*	*−16.6*	*9.7*
Other sectors	8 746	...	...	...	...	...	1.8	3.5	...
of which: Short-term	8 748	...	...	...	...	...	*1.8*	*3.5*	...
Reserve assets	8 802	**812.9**	**959.6**	**1,099.7**	**1,462.3**	**1,765.4**	**1,972.3**	**1,893.2**	**1,711.6**
Monetary gold	8 812	152.5	152.4	152.5	152.5	152.5	152.5	120.7	117.8
Special drawing rights	8 811	.1	37.1	35.9	33.7	35.2	34.3	32.6	31.4
Reserve position in the Fund	8 810	...	...	...	...	...	...	...	...
Foreign exchange	8 803	634.5	744.3	904.4	1,268.0	1,577.7	1,757.2	1,706.7	1,535.3
Other claims	8 813	25.8	25.8	6.9	8.1	...	28.3	33.3	27.1

Table 3 (Concluded). INTERNATIONAL INVESTMENT POSITION (End–period stocks), 1994–2001

(Millions of U.S. dollars)

	Code	1994	1995	1996	1997	1998	1999	2000	2001
LIABILITIES	8 995 D.	...	...	4,335.6	4,990.5	6,025.5	6,854.7	7,358.3	8,340.2
Direct investment in El Salvador	8 555 . .	**...**	**...**	**421.2**	**480.3**	**1,583.9**	**1,815.2**	**2,000.6**	**2,240.9**
Equity capital and reinvested earnings	8 556 . .	...	...	421.2	480.3	1,583.9	1,815.2	2,000.6	2,240.9
Claims on direct investors	8 557 . .	...	...	...	...	...	...	...	...
Liabilities to direct investors	8 558 . .	...	...	421.2	480.3	1,583.9	1,815.2	2,000.6	2,240.9
Other capital	8 580 . .	...	...	...	...	...	...	...	...
Claims on direct investors	8 585 . .	...	...	...	...	...	...	...	...
Liabilities to direct investors	8 590 . .	...	...	...	...	...	...	...	...
Portfolio investment	8 652 . .	**...**	**...**	**241.0**	**357.0**	**130.5**	**205.0**	**202.8**	**352.6**
Equity securities	8 660 . .	...	...	...	...	...	...	...	2.4
Banks	8 663 . .	...	...	...	...	...	...	...	...
Other sectors	8 664 . .	...	...	...	...	...	...	...	2.4
Debt securities	8 669 . .	...	...	241.0	357.0	130.5	205.0	202.8	350.2
Bonds and notes	8 670 . .	...	...	...	...	...	115.7	34.0	126.3
Monetary authorities	8 671 . .	...	...	...	...	...	...	...	...
General government	8 672 . .	...	...	...	...	...	115.7	34.0	126.3
Banks	8 673 . .	...	...	...	...	...	...	...	...
Other sectors	8 674 . .	...	...	...	...	...	...	...	...
Money market instruments	8 680 . .	...	...	241.0	357.0	130.5	89.3	168.8	223.9
Monetary authorities	8 681 . .	...	...	99.6	99.6	13.9	...	9.7	...
General government	8 682 . .	...	...	141.4	257.3	116.6	89.3	157.9	223.2
Banks	8 683 . .	...	...	...	...	...	...	...	...
Other sectors	8 684 . .	...	...	...	...	...	...	1.2	.7
Financial derivatives	8 905 . .	**...**	**...**	**...**	**...**	**...**	**...**	**...**	**...**
Monetary authorities	8 906 . .	...	...	...	...	...	...	...	...
General government	8 907 . .	...	...	...	...	...	...	...	...
Banks	8 908 . .	...	...	...	...	...	...	...	...
Other sectors	8 909 . .	...	...	...	...	...	...	...	...
Other investment	8 753 . .	**2,198.1**	**2,530.1**	**3,673.3**	**4,153.3**	**4,311.1**	**4,834.5**	**5,154.9**	**5,746.7**
Trade credits	8 756 . .	...	...	206.5	240.4	254.3	337.9	400.8	397.0
General government	8 757 . .	...	...	...	...	...	...	...	...
of which: Short-term	8 759 . .	...	...	...	...	...	...	...	...
Other sectors	8 760 . .	...	...	206.5	240.4	254.3	337.9	400.8	397.0
of which: Short-term	8 762 . .	...	...	*206.5*	*240.4*	*254.3*	*337.9*	*400.8*	*397.0*
Loans	8 764 . .	2,198.1	2,530.1	3,466.8	3,912.9	4,056.8	4,454.9	4,712.6	5,309.6
Monetary authorities	8 765 . .	176.0	191.3	220.4	237.5	165.4	160.7	144.6	120.0
of which: Use of Fund credit and loans from the Fund	8 766 . .	...	...	...	...	...	...	...	...
of which: Short-term	8 768 . .	*25.7*	*25.6*	...	...	...	...	...	...
General government	8 769 . .	1,879.7	1,975.9	2,075.8	2,194.9	2,350.1	2,423.2	2,448.3	2,678.0
of which: Short-term	8 771 . .	...	...	*15.0*	*15.0*	*15.0*	...	...	...
Banks	8 772 . .	142.4	362.9	406.2	531.0	516.5	548.3	673.8	950.0
of which: Short-term	8 774 . .	*134.4*	*333.1*	*329.4*	*400.3*	*297.2*	*280.5*	*360.8*	*676.7*
Other sectors	8 775 . .	...	...	764.4	949.4	1,024.8	1,322.7	1,445.9	1,561.6
of which: Short-term	8 777 . .	...	...	*602.9*	*603.0*	*602.9*	*911.2*	*720.4*	*603.1*
Currency and deposits	8 780 . .	...	...	...	...	...	41.7	41.5	38.1
Monetary authorities	8 781 . .	...	...	...	...	...	41.7	37.3	31.6
General government	8 782 . .	...	...	...	...	...	...	...	...
Banks	8 783 . .	...	...	...	...	...	...	...	...
Other sectors	8 784 . .	...	...	...	...	...	...	4.2	6.5
Other liabilities	8 786 . .	...	...	...	...	...	...	...	2.0
Monetary authorities	8 787 . .	...	...	...	...	...	...	...	2.0
of which: Short-term	8 789 . .	...	...	...	...	...	...	...	*2.0*
General government	8 790 . .	...	...	...	...	...	...	...	...
of which: Short-term	8 792 . .	...	...	...	...	...	...	...	...
Banks	8 793 . .	...	...	...	...	...	...	...	...
of which: Short-term	8 795 . .	...	...	...	...	...	...	...	...
Other sectors	8 796 . .	...	...	...	...	...	...	...	...
of which: Short-term	8 798 . .	...	...	...	...	...	...	...	...
NET INTERNATIONAL INVESTMENT POSITION	8 995 . .	**...**	**...**	**–2,564.3**	**–2,836.7**	**–3,579.9**	**–4,022.3**	**–4,354.4**	**–5,030.3**
Conversion rates: Salvadoran colones per U.S. dollar (end of period)	0 102 . .	**8.7500**	**8.7550**	**8.7550**	**8.7550**	**8.7550**	**8.7550**	**8.7550**	**8.7500**

Table 1. ANALYTIC PRESENTATION, 1994–2001
(Millions of U.S. dollars)

	Code			1994	1995	1996	1997	1998	1999	2000	2001
A. Current Account [1]	4	993	Z.	**–.38**	**–123.40**	**–344.04**	**...**	**...**	**...**	**...**	**...**
Goods: exports f.o.b	2	100	..	62.00	89.93	175.31	...	...	...	...	...
Goods: imports f.o.b	3	100	..	–36.95	–120.57	–292.04	...	...	...	...	...
Balance on Goods	4	100	..	*25.05*	*–30.64*	*–116.73*	...	...	...	...	...
Services: credit	2	200	..	3.36	4.18	4.88	...	...	...	...	...
Services: debit	3	200	..	–23.82	–75.54	–184.58	...	...	...	...	...
Balance on Goods and Services	4	991	..	*4.59*	*–102.00*	*–296.43*	...	...	...	...	...
Income: credit	2	300	..	...	.10	.16	...	...	...	...	...
Income: debit	3	300	..	–8.75	–25.03	–45.18	...	...	...	...	...
Balance on Goods, Services, and Income	4	992	..	*–4.16*	*–126.93*	*–341.44*	...	...	...	...	...
Current transfers: credit	2	379	Z.	5.67	6.83	4.03	...	...	...	...	...
Current transfers: debit	3	379	..	–1.89	–3.30	–6.62	...	...	...	...	...
B. Capital Account [1]	4	994	Z.	**...**	**...**	**...**	**...**	**...**	**...**	**...**	**...**
Capital account: credit	2	994	Z.	...	...	...	...	...	...	...	...
Capital account: debit	3	994	..	...	...	...	...	...	...	...	...
Total, Groups A Plus B	4	981	..	*–.38*	*–123.40*	*–344.04*	...	...	...	...	...
C. Financial Account [1]	4	995	W.	**–15.04**	**101.56**	**313.75**	**...**	**...**	**...**	**...**	**...**
Direct investment abroad	4	505	..	...	...	...	...	...	...	...	...
Direct investment in Equatorial Guinea	4	555	Z.	17.00	126.92	376.18	...	...	...	...	...
Portfolio investment assets	4	602	..	...	...	...	...	...	...	...	...
Equity securities	4	610	..	...	...	...	...	...	...	...	...
Debt securities	4	619	..	...	...	...	...	...	...	...	...
Portfolio investment liabilities	4	652	Z.	...	...	...	...	...	...	...	...
Equity securities	4	660	..	...	...	...	...	...	...	...	...
Debt securities	4	669	Z.	...	...	...	...	...	...	...	...
Financial derivatives	4	910	..	...	...	...	...	...	...	...	...
Financial derivatives assets	4	900	..	...	...	...	...	...	...	...	...
Financial derivatives liabilities	4	905	..	...	...	...	...	...	...	...	...
Other investment assets	4	703	..	...	...	...	...	...	...	...	...
Monetary authorities	4	701	..	...	...	...	...	...	...	...	...
General government	4	704	..	...	...	...	...	...	...	...	...
Banks	4	705	..	...	...	...	...	...	...	...	...
Other sectors	4	728	..	...	...	...	...	...	...	...	...
Other investment liabilities	4	753	W.	–32.04	–25.36	–62.43	...	...	...	...	...
Monetary authorities	4	753	WA	...	...	...	...	...	...	...	...
General government	4	753	ZB	–7.32	–13.95	–3.84	...	...	...	...	...
Banks	4	753	ZC	–1.98	1.84	–1.57	...	...	...	...	...
Other sectors	4	753	ZD	–22.73	–13.25	–57.02	...	...	...	...	...
Total, Groups A Through C	4	983	..	*–15.42*	*–21.84*	*–30.29*	...	...	...	...	...
D. Net Errors and Omissions	4	998	..	**–2.93**	**10.33**	**24.82**	**...**	**...**	**...**	**...**	**...**
Total, Groups A Through D	4	984	..	*–18.36*	*–11.52*	*–5.46*	...	...	...	...	...
E. Reserves and Related Items	4	802	A.	**18.36**	**11.52**	**5.46**	**...**	**...**	**...**	**...**	**...**
Reserve assets	4	802	..	–.92	–8.98	–3.59	...	...	...	...	...
Use of Fund credit and loans	4	766	..	2.08	–1.11	–1.11	...	...	...	...	...
Exceptional financing	4	920	..	17.20	21.61	10.17	...	...	...	...	...
Conversion rates: CFA francs per U.S. dollar	0	101	..	**555.20**	**499.15**	**511.55**	**583.67**	**589.95**	**615.70**	**711.98**	**733.04**

[1] Excludes components that have been classified in the categories of Group E.

Table 2. STANDARD PRESENTATION, 1994–2001
(Millions of U.S. dollars)

	Code	1994	1995	1996	1997	1998	1999	2000	2001
CURRENT ACCOUNT	4 993 . .	**–.38**	**–123.40**	**–344.04**	**. . .**	**. . .**	**. . .**	**. . .**	**. . .**
A. GOODS	4 100 . .	25.05	–30.64	–116.73	. . .	. . .	. . .	. . .	. . .
Credit	2 100 . .	**62.00**	**89.93**	**175.31**	**. . .**	**. . .**	**. . .**	**. . .**	**. . .**
General merchandise: exports f.o.b.	2 110 . .	62.00	89.93	175.31	. . .	. . .	. . .	. . .	. . .
Goods for processing: exports f.o.b.	2 150 . .	. . .	. . .	. . .	. . .	. . .	. . .	. . .	. . .
Repairs on goods	2 160 . .	. . .	. . .	. . .	. . .	. . .	. . .	. . .	. . .
Goods procured in ports by carriers	2 170 . .	. . .	. . .	. . .	. . .	. . .	. . .	. . .	. . .
Nonmonetary gold	2 180 . .	. . .	. . .	. . .	. . .	. . .	. . .	. . .	. . .
Debit	3 100 . .	**–36.95**	**–120.57**	**–292.04**	**. . .**	**. . .**	**. . .**	**. . .**	**. . .**
General merchandise: imports f.o.b.	3 110 . .	–36.95	–120.57	–292.04	. . .	. . .	. . .	. . .	. . .
Goods for processing: imports f.o.b.	3 150 . .	. . .	. . .	. . .	. . .	. . .	. . .	. . .	. . .
Repairs on goods	3 160 . .	. . .	. . .	. . .	. . .	. . .	. . .	. . .	. . .
Goods procured in ports by carriers	3 170 . .	. . .	. . .	. . .	. . .	. . .	. . .	. . .	. . .
Nonmonetary gold	3 180 . .	. . .	. . .	. . .	. . .	. . .	. . .	. . .	. . .
B. SERVICES	4 200 . .	–20.45	–71.36	–179.70	. . .	. . .	. . .	. . .	. . .
Total credit	2 200 . .	*3.36*	*4.18*	*4.88*	. . .	. . .	. . .	. . .	. . .
Total debit	3 200 . .	*–23.82*	*–75.54*	*–184.58*	. . .	. . .	. . .	. . .	. . .
Transportation services, credit	2 205 . .	**. . .**	**. . .**	**. . .**	**. . .**	**. . .**	**. . .**	**. . .**	**. . .**
Passenger	2 850 . .	. . .	. . .	. . .	. . .	. . .	. . .	. . .	. . .
Freight	2 851 . .	. . .	. . .	. . .	. . .	. . .	. . .	. . .	. . .
Other	2 852 . .	. . .	. . .	. . .	. . .	. . .	. . .	. . .	. . .
Sea transport, passenger	2 207 . .	. . .	. . .	. . .	. . .	. . .	. . .	. . .	. . .
Sea transport, freight	2 208 . .	. . .	. . .	. . .	. . .	. . .	. . .	. . .	. . .
Sea transport, other	2 209 . .	. . .	. . .	. . .	. . .	. . .	. . .	. . .	. . .
Air transport, passenger	2 211 . .	. . .	. . .	. . .	. . .	. . .	. . .	. . .	. . .
Air transport, freight	2 212 . .	. . .	. . .	. . .	. . .	. . .	. . .	. . .	. . .
Air transport, other	2 213 . .	. . .	. . .	. . .	. . .	. . .	. . .	. . .	. . .
Other transport, passenger	2 215 . .	. . .	. . .	. . .	. . .	. . .	. . .	. . .	. . .
Other transport, freight	2 216 . .	. . .	. . .	. . .	. . .	. . .	. . .	. . .	. . .
Other transport, other	2 217 . .	. . .	. . .	. . .	. . .	. . .	. . .	. . .	. . .
Transportation services, debit	3 205 . .	**. . .**	**. . .**	**. . .**	**. . .**	**. . .**	**. . .**	**. . .**	**. . .**
Passenger	3 850 . .	. . .	. . .	. . .	. . .	. . .	. . .	. . .	. . .
Freight	3 851 . .	. . .	. . .	. . .	. . .	. . .	. . .	. . .	. . .
Other	3 852 . .	. . .	. . .	. . .	. . .	. . .	. . .	. . .	. . .
Sea transport, passenger	3 207 . .	. . .	. . .	. . .	. . .	. . .	. . .	. . .	. . .
Sea transport, freight	3 208 . .	. . .	. . .	. . .	. . .	. . .	. . .	. . .	. . .
Sea transport, other	3 209 . .	. . .	. . .	. . .	. . .	. . .	. . .	. . .	. . .
Air transport, passenger	3 211 . .	. . .	. . .	. . .	. . .	. . .	. . .	. . .	. . .
Air transport, freight	3 212 . .	. . .	. . .	. . .	. . .	. . .	. . .	. . .	. . .
Air transport, other	3 213 . .	. . .	. . .	. . .	. . .	. . .	. . .	. . .	. . .
Other transport, passenger	3 215 . .	. . .	. . .	. . .	. . .	. . .	. . .	. . .	. . .
Other transport, freight	3 216 . .	. . .	. . .	. . .	. . .	. . .	. . .	. . .	. . .
Other transport, other	3 217 . .	. . .	. . .	. . .	. . .	. . .	. . .	. . .	. . .
Travel, credit	2 236 . .	**. . .**	**. . .**	**. . .**	**. . .**	**. . .**	**. . .**	**. . .**	**. . .**
Business travel	2 237 . .	. . .	. . .	. . .	. . .	. . .	. . .	. . .	. . .
Personal travel	2 240 . .	. . .	. . .	. . .	. . .	. . .	. . .	. . .	. . .
Travel, debit	3 236 . .	**. . .**	**. . .**	**. . .**	**. . .**	**. . .**	**. . .**	**. . .**	**. . .**
Business travel	3 237 . .	. . .	. . .	. . .	. . .	. . .	. . .	. . .	. . .
Personal travel	3 240 . .	. . .	. . .	. . .	. . .	. . .	. . .	. . .	. . .
Other services, credit	2 200 BA	**. . .**	**. . .**	**. . .**	**. . .**	**. . .**	**. . .**	**. . .**	**. . .**
Communications	2 245 . .	. . .	. . .	. . .	. . .	. . .	. . .	. . .	. . .
Construction	2 249 . .	. . .	. . .	. . .	. . .	. . .	. . .	. . .	. . .
Insurance	2 253 . .	. . .	. . .	. . .	. . .	. . .	. . .	. . .	. . .
Financial	2 260 . .	. . .	. . .	. . .	. . .	. . .	. . .	. . .	. . .
Computer and information	2 262 . .	. . .	. . .	. . .	. . .	. . .	. . .	. . .	. . .
Royalties and licence fees	2 266 . .	. . .	. . .	. . .	. . .	. . .	. . .	. . .	. . .
Other business services	2 268 . .	. . .	. . .	. . .	. . .	. . .	. . .	. . .	. . .
Personal, cultural, and recreational	2 287 . .	. . .	. . .	. . .	. . .	. . .	. . .	. . .	. . .
Government, n.i.e.	2 291 . .	. . .	. . .	. . .	. . .	. . .	. . .	. . .	. . .
Other services, debit	3 200 BA	**. . .**	**. . .**	**. . .**	**. . .**	**. . .**	**. . .**	**. . .**	**. . .**
Communications	3 245 . .	. . .	. . .	. . .	. . .	. . .	. . .	. . .	. . .
Construction	3 249 . .	. . .	. . .	. . .	. . .	. . .	. . .	. . .	. . .
Insurance	3 253 . .	. . .	. . .	. . .	. . .	. . .	. . .	. . .	. . .
Financial	3 260 . .	. . .	. . .	. . .	. . .	. . .	. . .	. . .	. . .
Computer and information	3 262 . .	. . .	. . .	. . .	. . .	. . .	. . .	. . .	. . .
Royalties and licence fees	3 266 . .	. . .	. . .	. . .	. . .	. . .	. . .	. . .	. . .
Other business services	3 268 . .	. . .	. . .	. . .	. . .	. . .	. . .	. . .	. . .
Personal, cultural, and recreational	3 287 . .	. . .	. . .	. . .	. . .	. . .	. . .	. . .	. . .
Government, n.i.e.	3 291 . .	. . .	. . .	. . .	. . .	. . .	. . .	. . .	. . .

Table 2 (Continued). STANDARD PRESENTATION, 1994–2001
(Millions of U.S. dollars)

	Code	1994	1995	1996	1997	1998	1999	2000	2001
C. INCOME	4 300	-8.75	-24.93	-45.02	...	...	...	...	...
Total credit	2 300	...	*.10*	*.16*	...	...	...	...	...
Total debit	3 300	*-8.75*	*-25.03*	*-45.18*	...	...	...	...	...
Compensation of employees, credit	2 310	...	**.10**	**.16**	...	...	...	...	...
Compensation of employees, debit	3 310	**-.33**	...	...	...	...	...	...	...
Investment income, credit	2 320	...	...	...	...	...	...	...	...
Direct investment income	2 330	...	...	...	...	...	...	...	...
Dividends and distributed branch profits	2 332	...	...	...	...	...	...	...	...
Reinvested earnings and undistributed branch profits	2 333	...	...	...	...	...	...	...	...
Income on debt (interest)	2 334	...	...	...	...	...	...	...	...
Portfolio investment income	2 339	...	...	...	...	...	...	...	...
Income on equity	2 340	...	...	...	...	...	...	...	...
Income on bonds and notes	2 350	...	...	...	...	...	...	...	...
Income on money market instruments	2 360	...	...	...	...	...	...	...	...
Other investment income	2 370	...	...	...	...	...	...	...	...
Investment income, debit	3 320	**-8.42**	**-25.03**	**-45.18**	...	...	...	...	...
Direct investment income	3 330	...	...	...	...	...	...	...	...
Dividends and distributed branch profits	3 332	...	...	...	...	...	...	...	...
Reinvested earnings and undistributed branch profits	3 333	...	...	...	...	...	...	...	...
Income on debt (interest)	3 334	...	...	...	...	...	...	...	...
Portfolio investment income	3 339	...	...	...	...	...	...	...	...
Income on equity	3 340	...	...	...	...	...	...	...	...
Income on bonds and notes	3 350	...	...	...	...	...	...	...	...
Income on money market instruments	3 360	...	...	...	...	...	...	...	...
Other investment income	3 370	-8.42	-25.03	-45.18	...	...	...	...	...
D. CURRENT TRANSFERS	4 379	3.78	3.53	-2.59	...	...	...	...	...
Credit	2 379	**5.67**	**6.83**	**4.03**	...	...	...	...	...
General government	2 380	5.67	6.83	4.03	...	...	...	...	...
Other sectors	2 390	...	...	...	...	...	...	...	...
Workers' remittances	2 391	...	...	...	...	...	...	...	...
Other current transfers	2 392	...	...	...	...	...	...	...	...
Debit	3 379	**-1.89**	**-3.30**	**-6.62**	...	...	...	...	...
General government	3 380	...	...	...	...	...	...	...	...
Other sectors	3 390	-1.89	-3.30	-6.62	...	...	...	...	...
Workers' remittances	3 391	...	...	...	...	...	...	...	...
Other current transfers	3 392	-1.89	-3.30	-6.62	...	...	...	...	...
CAPITAL AND FINANCIAL ACCOUNT	4 996	**3.31**	**113.08**	**319.21**	...	...	...	...	...
CAPITAL ACCOUNT	4 994	**1.48**	**53.46**	...	...	...	...	...	...
Total credit	2 994	*1.48*	*53.46*	...	...	...	...	...	...
Total debit	3 994	...	...	...	...	...	...	...	...
Capital transfers, credit	2 400	**1.48**	**53.46**	...	...	...	...	...	...
General government	2 401	1.48	53.46	...	...	...	...	...	...
Debt forgiveness	2 402	1.48	53.46	...	...	...	...	...	...
Other capital transfers	2 410	...	...	...	...	...	...	...	...
Other sectors	2 430	...	...	...	...	...	...	...	...
Migrants' transfers	2 431	...	...	...	...	...	...	...	...
Debt forgiveness	2 432	...	...	...	...	...	...	...	...
Other capital transfers	2 440	...	...	...	...	...	...	...	...
Capital transfers, debit	3 400	...	...	...	...	...	...	...	...
General government	3 401	...	...	...	...	...	...	...	...
Debt forgiveness	3 402	...	...	...	...	...	...	...	...
Other capital transfers	3 410	...	...	...	...	...	...	...	...
Other sectors	3 430	...	...	...	...	...	...	...	...
Migrants' transfers	3 431	...	...	...	...	...	...	...	...
Debt forgiveness	3 432	...	...	...	...	...	...	...	...
Other capital transfers	3 440	...	...	...	...	...	...	...	...
Nonproduced nonfinancial assets, credit	2 480	...	...	...	...	...	...	...	...
Nonproduced nonfinancial assets, debit	3 480	...	...	...	...	...	...	...	...

Table 2 (Continued). STANDARD PRESENTATION, 1994–2001

(Millions of U.S. dollars)

	Code	1994	1995	1996	1997	1998	1999	2000	2001
FINANCIAL ACCOUNT	4 995 . .	**1.84**	**59.62**	**319.21**	**. . .**	**. . .**	**. . .**	**. . .**	**. . .**
A. DIRECT INVESTMENT	4 500 . .	17.00	126.92	376.18	. . .	. . .	. . .	. . .	. . .
Direct investment abroad	4 505 . .	**. . .**	**. . .**	**. . .**	**. . .**	**. . .**	**. . .**	**. . .**	**. . .**
Equity capital	4 510 . .	. . .	. . .	. . .	. . .	. . .	. . .	. . .	. . .
Claims on affiliated enterprises	4 515 . .	. . .	. . .	. . .	. . .	. . .	. . .	. . .	. . .
Liabilities to affiliated enterprises	4 520 . .	. . .	. . .	. . .	. . .	. . .	. . .	. . .	. . .
Reinvested earnings	4 525 . .	. . .	. . .	. . .	. . .	. . .	. . .	. . .	. . .
Other capital	4 530 . .	. . .	. . .	. . .	. . .	. . .	. . .	. . .	. . .
Claims on affiliated enterprises	4 535 . .	. . .	. . .	. . .	. . .	. . .	. . .	. . .	. . .
Liabilities to affiliated enterprises	4 540 . .	. . .	. . .	. . .	. . .	. . .	. . .	. . .	. . .
Direct investment in Equatorial Guinea	4 555 . .	**17.00**	**126.92**	**376.18**	**. . .**	**. . .**	**. . .**	**. . .**	**. . .**
Equity capital	4 560 . .	17.00	126.92	376.18	. . .	. . .	. . .	. . .	. . .
Claims on direct investors	4 565 . .	. . .	. . .	. . .	. . .	. . .	. . .	. . .	. . .
Liabilities to direct investors	4 570 . .	17.00	126.92	376.18	. . .	. . .	. . .	. . .	. . .
Reinvested earnings	4 575 . .	. . .	. . .	. . .	. . .	. . .	. . .	. . .	. . .
Other capital	4 580 . .	. . .	. . .	. . .	. . .	. . .	. . .	. . .	. . .
Claims on direct investors	4 585 . .	. . .	. . .	. . .	. . .	. . .	. . .	. . .	. . .
Liabilities to direct investors	4 590 . .	. . .	. . .	. . .	. . .	. . .	. . .	. . .	. . .
B. PORTFOLIO INVESTMENT	4 600 . .	. . .	. . .	. . .	. . .	. . .	. . .	. . .	. . .
Assets	4 602 . .	**. . .**	**. . .**	**. . .**	**. . .**	**. . .**	**. . .**	**. . .**	**. . .**
Equity securities	4 610 . .	. . .	. . .	. . .	. . .	. . .	. . .	. . .	. . .
Monetary authorities	4 611 . .	. . .	. . .	. . .	. . .	. . .	. . .	. . .	. . .
General government	4 612 . .	. . .	. . .	. . .	. . .	. . .	. . .	. . .	. . .
Banks	4 613 . .	. . .	. . .	. . .	. . .	. . .	. . .	. . .	. . .
Other sectors	4 614 . .	. . .	. . .	. . .	. . .	. . .	. . .	. . .	. . .
Debt securities	4 619 . .	. . .	. . .	. . .	. . .	. . .	. . .	. . .	. . .
Bonds and notes	4 620 . .	. . .	. . .	. . .	. . .	. . .	. . .	. . .	. . .
Monetary authorities	4 621 . .	. . .	. . .	. . .	. . .	. . .	. . .	. . .	. . .
General government	4 622 . .	. . .	. . .	. . .	. . .	. . .	. . .	. . .	. . .
Banks	4 623 . .	. . .	. . .	. . .	. . .	. . .	. . .	. . .	. . .
Other sectors	4 624 . .	. . .	. . .	. . .	. . .	. . .	. . .	. . .	. . .
Money market instruments	4 630 . .	. . .	. . .	. . .	. . .	. . .	. . .	. . .	. . .
Monetary authorities	4 631 . .	. . .	. . .	. . .	. . .	. . .	. . .	. . .	. . .
General government	4 632 . .	. . .	. . .	. . .	. . .	. . .	. . .	. . .	. . .
Banks	4 633 . .	. . .	. . .	. . .	. . .	. . .	. . .	. . .	. . .
Other sectors	4 634 . .	. . .	. . .	. . .	. . .	. . .	. . .	. . .	. . .
Liabilities	4 652 . .	**. . .**	**. . .**	**. . .**	**. . .**	**. . .**	**. . .**	**. . .**	**. . .**
Equity securities	4 660 . .	. . .	. . .	. . .	. . .	. . .	. . .	. . .	. . .
Banks	4 663 . .	. . .	. . .	. . .	. . .	. . .	. . .	. . .	. . .
Other sectors	4 664 . .	. . .	. . .	. . .	. . .	. . .	. . .	. . .	. . .
Debt securities	4 669 . .	. . .	. . .	. . .	. . .	. . .	. . .	. . .	. . .
Bonds and notes	4 670 . .	. . .	. . .	. . .	. . .	. . .	. . .	. . .	. . .
Monetary authorities	4 671 . .	. . .	. . .	. . .	. . .	. . .	. . .	. . .	. . .
General government	4 672 . .	. . .	. . .	. . .	. . .	. . .	. . .	. . .	. . .
Banks	4 673 . .	. . .	. . .	. . .	. . .	. . .	. . .	. . .	. . .
Other sectors	4 674 . .	. . .	. . .	. . .	. . .	. . .	. . .	. . .	. . .
Money market instruments	4 680 . .	. . .	. . .	. . .	. . .	. . .	. . .	. . .	. . .
Monetary authorities	4 681 . .	. . .	. . .	. . .	. . .	. . .	. . .	. . .	. . .
General government	4 682 . .	. . .	. . .	. . .	. . .	. . .	. . .	. . .	. . .
Banks	4 683 . .	. . .	. . .	. . .	. . .	. . .	. . .	. . .	. . .
Other sectors	4 684 . .	. . .	. . .	. . .	. . .	. . .	. . .	. . .	. . .
C. FINANCIAL DERIVATIVES	4 910 . .	. . .	. . .	. . .	. . .	. . .	. . .	. . .	. . .
Monetary authorities	4 911 . .	. . .	. . .	. . .	. . .	. . .	. . .	. . .	. . .
General government	4 912 . .	. . .	. . .	. . .	. . .	. . .	. . .	. . .	. . .
Banks	4 913 . .	. . .	. . .	. . .	. . .	. . .	. . .	. . .	. . .
Other sectors	4 914 . .	. . .	. . .	. . .	. . .	. . .	. . .	. . .	. . .
Assets	4 900 . .	**. . .**	**. . .**	**. . .**	**. . .**	**. . .**	**. . .**	**. . .**	**. . .**
Monetary authorities	4 901 . .	. . .	. . .	. . .	. . .	. . .	. . .	. . .	. . .
General government	4 902 . .	. . .	. . .	. . .	. . .	. . .	. . .	. . .	. . .
Banks	4 903 . .	. . .	. . .	. . .	. . .	. . .	. . .	. . .	. . .
Other sectors	4 904 . .	. . .	. . .	. . .	. . .	. . .	. . .	. . .	. . .
Liabilities	4 905 . .	**. . .**	**. . .**	**. . .**	**. . .**	**. . .**	**. . .**	**. . .**	**. . .**
Monetary authorities	4 906 . .	. . .	. . .	. . .	. . .	. . .	. . .	. . .	. . .
General government	4 907 . .	. . .	. . .	. . .	. . .	. . .	. . .	. . .	. . .
Banks	4 908 . .	. . .	. . .	. . .	. . .	. . .	. . .	. . .	. . .
Other sectors	4 909 . .	. . .	. . .	. . .	. . .	. . .	. . .	. . .	. . .

Table 2 (Concluded). STANDARD PRESENTATION, 1994–2001
(Millions of U.S. dollars)

	Code	1994	1995	1996	1997	1998	1999	2000	2001
D. OTHER INVESTMENT	4 700 . .	–14.23	–58.32	–53.37	. . .	. . .	. . .	. . .	. . .
Assets	4 703 . .	**. . .**	**. . .**	**. . .**	**. . .**	**. . .**	**. . .**	**. . .**	**. . .**
Trade credits	4 706 . .	. . .	. . .	. . .	. . .	. . .	. . .	. . .	. . .
General government	4 707 . .	. . .	. . .	. . .	. . .	. . .	. . .	. . .	. . .
of which: Short-term	4 709 . .	. . .	. . .	. . .	. . .	. . .	. . .	. . .	. . .
Other sectors	4 710 . .	. . .	. . .	. . .	. . .	. . .	. . .	. . .	. . .
of which: Short-term	4 712 . .	. . .	. . .	. . .	. . .	. . .	. . .	. . .	. . .
Loans	4 714 . .	. . .	. . .	. . .	. . .	. . .	. . .	. . .	. . .
Monetary authorities	4 715 . .	. . .	. . .	. . .	. . .	. . .	. . .	. . .	. . .
of which: Short-term	4 718 . .	. . .	. . .	. . .	. . .	. . .	. . .	. . .	. . .
General government	4 719 . .	. . .	. . .	. . .	. . .	. . .	. . .	. . .	. . .
of which: Short-term	4 721 . .	. . .	. . .	. . .	. . .	. . .	. . .	. . .	. . .
Banks	4 722 . .	. . .	. . .	. . .	. . .	. . .	. . .	. . .	. . .
of which: Short-term	4 724 . .	. . .	. . .	. . .	. . .	. . .	. . .	. . .	. . .
Other sectors	4 725 . .	. . .	. . .	. . .	. . .	. . .	. . .	. . .	. . .
of which: Short-term	4 727 . .	. . .	. . .	. . .	. . .	. . .	. . .	. . .	. . .
Currency and deposits	4 730 . .	. . .	. . .	. . .	. . .	. . .	. . .	. . .	. . .
Monetary authorities	4 731 . .	. . .	. . .	. . .	. . .	. . .	. . .	. . .	. . .
General government	4 732 . .	. . .	. . .	. . .	. . .	. . .	. . .	. . .	. . .
Banks	4 733 . .	. . .	. . .	. . .	. . .	. . .	. . .	. . .	. . .
Other sectors	4 734 . .	. . .	. . .	. . .	. . .	. . .	. . .	. . .	. . .
Other assets	4 736 . .	. . .	. . .	. . .	. . .	. . .	. . .	. . .	. . .
Monetary authorities	4 737 . .	. . .	. . .	. . .	. . .	. . .	. . .	. . .	. . .
of which: Short-term	4 739 . .	. . .	. . .	. . .	. . .	. . .	. . .	. . .	. . .
General government	4 740 . .	. . .	. . .	. . .	. . .	. . .	. . .	. . .	. . .
of which: Short-term	4 742 . .	. . .	. . .	. . .	. . .	. . .	. . .	. . .	. . .
Banks	4 743 . .	. . .	. . .	. . .	. . .	. . .	. . .	. . .	. . .
of which: Short-term	4 745 . .	. . .	. . .	. . .	. . .	. . .	. . .	. . .	. . .
Other sectors	4 746 . .	. . .	. . .	. . .	. . .	. . .	. . .	. . .	. . .
of which: Short-term	4 748 . .	. . .	. . .	. . .	. . .	. . .	. . .	. . .	. . .
Liabilities	4 753 . .	**–14.23**	**–58.32**	**–53.37**	**. . .**	**. . .**	**. . .**	**. . .**	**. . .**
Trade credits	4 756 . .	. . .	. . .	. . .	. . .	. . .	. . .	. . .	. . .
General government	4 757 . .	. . .	. . .	. . .	. . .	. . .	. . .	. . .	. . .
of which: Short-term	4 759 . .	. . .	. . .	. . .	. . .	. . .	. . .	. . .	. . .
Other sectors	4 760 . .	. . .	. . .	. . .	. . .	. . .	. . .	. . .	. . .
of which: Short-term	4 762 . .	. . .	. . .	. . .	. . .	. . .	. . .	. . .	. . .
Loans	4 764 . .	–29.95	–26.46	–63.50	. . .	. . .	. . .	. . .	. . .
Monetary authorities	4 765 . .	2.08	–1.11	–1.11	. . .	. . .	. . .	. . .	. . .
of which: Use of Fund credit and loans from the Fund	4 766 . .	*2.08*	*–1.11*	*–1.11*	. . .	. . .	. . .	. . .	. . .
of which: Short-term	4 768 . .	. . .	. . .	. . .	. . .	. . .	. . .	. . .	. . .
General government	4 769 . .	–7.32	–13.95	–3.84	. . .	. . .	. . .	. . .	. . .
of which: Short-term	4 771 . .	. . .	. . .	. . .	. . .	. . .	. . .	. . .	. . .
Banks	4 772 . .	–1.98	1.84	–1.57	. . .	. . .	. . .	. . .	. . .
of which: Short-term	4 774 . .	*–1.98*	*1.84*	*–1.57*	. . .	. . .	. . .	. . .	. . .
Other sectors	4 775 . .	–22.72	–13.23	–56.98	. . .	. . .	. . .	. . .	. . .
of which: Short-term	4 777 . .	*–7.42*	*8.01*	*20.53*	. . .	. . .	. . .	. . .	. . .
Currency and deposits	4 780 . .	. . .	. . .	. . .	. . .	. . .	. . .	. . .	. . .
Monetary authorities	4 781 . .	. . .	. . .	. . .	. . .	. . .	. . .	. . .	. . .
General government	4 782 . .	. . .	. . .	. . .	. . .	. . .	. . .	. . .	. . .
Banks	4 783 . .	. . .	. . .	. . .	. . .	. . .	. . .	. . .	. . .
Other sectors	4 784 . .	. . .	. . .	. . .	. . .	. . .	. . .	. . .	. . .
Other liabilities	4 786 . .	15.72	–31.86	10.13	. . .	. . .	. . .	. . .	. . .
Monetary authorities	4 787 . .	. . .	. . .	. . .	. . .	. . .	. . .	. . .	. . .
of which: Short-term	4 789 . .	. . .	. . .	. . .	. . .	. . .	. . .	. . .	. . .
General government	4 790 . .	15.73	–31.84	10.17	. . .	. . .	. . .	. . .	. . .
of which: Short-term	4 792 . .	*15.73*	*–31.84*	*10.17*	. . .	. . .	. . .	. . .	. . .
Banks	4 793 . .	. . .	. . .	. . .	. . .	. . .	. . .	. . .	. . .
of which: Short-term	4 795 . .	. . .	. . .	. . .	. . .	. . .	. . .	. . .	. . .
Other sectors	4 796 . .	–.01	–.02	–.04	. . .	. . .	. . .	. . .	. . .
of which: Short-term	4 798 . .	*–.01*	*–.02*	*–.04*	. . .	. . .	. . .	. . .	. . .
E. RESERVE ASSETS	4 802 . .	–.92	–8.98	–3.59	. . .	. . .	. . .	. . .	. . .
Monetary gold	4 812 . .	. . .	. . .	. . .	. . .	. . .	. . .	. . .	. . .
Special drawing rights	4 811 . .	.38	.01	. . .	. . .	. . .	. . .	. . .	. . .
Reserve position in the Fund	4 810 . .	. . .	. . .	. . .	. . .	. . .	. . .	. . .	. . .
Foreign exchange	4 803 . .	–1.30	–8.99	–3.59	. . .	. . .	. . .	. . .	. . .
Other claims	4 813 . .	. . .	. . .	. . .	. . .	. . .	. . .	. . .	. . .
NET ERRORS AND OMISSIONS	4 998 . .	**–2.93**	**10.33**	**24.82**	**. . .**	**. . .**	**. . .**	**. . .**	**. . .**

Table 1. ANALYTIC PRESENTATION, 1994–2001
(Millions of U.S. dollars)

	Code			1994	1995	1996	1997	1998	1999	2000	2001
A. Current Account [1]	4	993	Z.	**–166.3**	**–157.8**	**–398.3**	**–561.7**	**–478.4**	**–294.6**	**–294.0**	**–339.0**
Goods: exports f.o.b	2	100	. .	1,225.0	1,696.3	1,812.3	2,289.6	2,690.1	2,453.1	3,311.4	3,338.1
Goods: imports f.o.b	3	100	. .	–1,581.4	–2,362.3	–2,831.5	–3,413.7	–3,805.4	–3,330.6	–4,079.5	–4,125.0
Balance on Goods	4	100	. .	*–356.5*	*–666.0*	*–1,019.2*	*–1,124.1*	*–1,115.2*	*–877.5*	*–768.1*	*–786.9*
Services: credit	2	200	. .	515.3	876.8	1,108.3	1,318.0	1,479.6	1,489.7	1,499.0	1,642.8
Services: debit	3	200	. .	–410.2	–497.7	–589.8	–726.6	–910.1	–917.6	–936.3	–1,064.9
Balance on Goods and Services	4	991	. .	*–251.3*	*–286.9*	*–500.7*	*–532.7*	*–545.7*	*–305.4*	*–205.4*	*–209.0*
Income: credit	2	300	. .	37.3	63.6	112.2	115.1	133.5	133.8	117.6	170.6
Income: debit	3	300	. .	–66.9	–60.8	–110.3	–260.8	–214.5	–235.5	–321.7	–451.8
Balance on Goods, Services, and Income	4	992	. .	*–280.9*	*–284.1*	*–498.8*	*–678.4*	*–626.7*	*–407.1*	*–409.6*	*–490.1*
Current transfers: credit	2	379	Z.	120.3	134.5	116.8	135.3	172.9	153.7	144.7	180.4
Current transfers: debit	3	379	. .	–5.7	–8.2	–16.3	–18.6	–24.6	–41.3	–29.1	–29.3
B. Capital Account [1]	4	994	Z.	**–.6**	**–.8**	**–.7**	**–.2**	**1.8**	**1.2**	**16.5**	**5.1**
Capital account: credit	2	994	Z.	.5	1.4	.2	.7	2.1	1.4	16.8	5.5
Capital account: debit	3	994	. .	–1.1	–2.2	–.8	–.9	–.3	–.2	–.2	–.4
Total, Groups A Plus B	4	981	. .	*–166.9*	*–158.6*	*–399.0*	*–561.9*	*–476.7*	*–293.4*	*–277.5*	*–333.9*
C. Financial Account [1]	4	995	W.	**167.2**	**233.4**	**540.9**	**802.8**	**508.1**	**418.2**	**406.7**	**306.4**
Direct investment abroad	4	505	. .	–2.4	–2.5	–40.1	–136.6	–6.3	–82.9	–63.4	–199.6
Direct investment in Estonia	4	555	Z.	214.4	201.5	150.2	266.2	580.5	305.2	387.3	539.4
Portfolio investment assets	4	602	. .	–22.5	–33.2	–52.7	–165.0	–10.9	–132.3	39.8	13.0
Equity securities	4	610	. .	–14.5	5.1	–15.0	–87.8	35.1	12.9	3.5	13.9
Debt securities	4	619	. .	–8.0	–38.2	–37.6	–77.2	–46.0	–145.2	36.4	–.9
Portfolio investment liabilities	4	652	Z.	8.4	11.1	198.1	427.5	1.1	153.3	75.6	83.0
Equity securities	4	660	. .	8.4	9.9	172.3	127.8	25.7	235.4	–28.5	31.5
Debt securities	4	669	Z.	. . .	1.2	25.8	299.7	–24.6	–82.1	104.1	51.5
Financial derivatives	4	910	. .	. . .	. . .	. . .	. . .	. . .	. . .	.7	–2.1
Financial derivatives assets	4	900	. .	. . .	. . .	. . .	. . .	. . .	. . .	–4.7	–.1
Financial derivatives liabilities	4	905	. .	. . .	. . .	. . .	. . .	. . .	. . .	5.4	–2.0
Other investment assets	4	703	. .	–146.7	–98.9	–7.3	–334.2	–168.5	–110.3	–177.1	–297.7
Monetary authorities	4	701	. .	.1	.1	.1	. . .	. . .	–18.3	–9.6	–11.1
General government	4	704	. .	.4	–.4	–3.3	–24.7	–61.9	–60.8	32.7	–17.3
Banks	4	705	. .	–102.8	–41.1	20.8	–195.9	61.3	–53.8	–77.0	–214.4
Other sectors	4	728	. .	–44.4	57.5	–24.9	–113.5	–167.9	22.5	–123.3	–54.9
Other investment liabilities	4	753	W.	115.9	155.4	292.6	744.8	112.1	285.2	143.8	170.5
Monetary authorities	4	753	WA	6.2	–13.5	–6.7	–2.5	–1.1	7.3	1.7	–5.3
General government	4	753	ZB	19.8	61.0	31.3	–3.3	4.4	9.8	–17.2	–7.2
Banks	4	753	ZC	37.5	82.2	173.7	492.4	–17.3	188.3	76.8	58.2
Other sectors	4	753	ZD	52.3	25.7	94.4	258.2	126.0	79.8	82.5	124.7
Total, Groups A Through C	4	983	. .	*.2*	*74.8*	*141.9*	*240.9*	*31.4*	*124.7*	*129.2*	*–27.5*
D. Net Errors and Omissions	4	998	. .	**17.2**	**8.7**	**–35.6**	**–25.1**	**5.9**	**–5.5**	**–1.6**	**–12.8**
Total, Groups A Through D	4	984	. .	*17.5*	*83.5*	*106.3*	*215.9*	*37.3*	*119.3*	*127.6*	*–40.3*
E. Reserves and Related Items	4	802	A.	**–17.5**	**–83.5**	**–106.3**	**–215.9**	**–37.3**	**–119.3**	**–127.6**	**40.3**
Reserve assets	4	802	. .	–17.5	–112.9	–95.3	–196.4	–11.7	–115.3	–122.4	45.2
Use of Fund credit and loans	4	766	. .	. . .	29.4	–11.1	–19.4	–25.6	–4.0	–5.2	–4.9
Exceptional financing	4	920	. .	. . .	. . .	. . .	. . .	. . .	. . .	. . .	. . .
Conversion rates: krooni per U.S. dollar	0	101	. .	**12.991**	**11.465**	**12.034**	**13.882**	**14.075**	**14.678**	**16.969**	**17.564**

[1] Excludes components that have been classified in the categories of Group E.

Table 2. STANDARD PRESENTATION, 1994–2001
(Millions of U.S. dollars)

	Code	1994	1995	1996	1997	1998	1999	2000	2001
CURRENT ACCOUNT	4 993 . .	**–166.3**	**–157.8**	**–398.3**	**–561.7**	**–478.4**	**–294.6**	**–294.0**	**–339.0**
A. GOODS	4 100 . .	–356.5	–666.0	–1,019.2	–1,124.1	–1,115.2	–877.5	–768.1	–786.9
Credit	2 100 . .	**1,225.0**	**1,696.3**	**1,812.3**	**2,289.6**	**2,690.1**	**2,453.1**	**3,311.4**	**3,338.1**
General merchandise: exports f.o.b.	2 110 . .	995.0	1,278.3	1,370.0	1,695.3	1,859.3	1,652.9	1,896.9	2,045.6
Goods for processing: exports f.o.b.	2 150 . .	214.4	386.1	409.1	569.4	806.1	779.3	1,396.3	1,266.4
Repairs on goods	2 160 . .	15.4	14.1	21.6	17.1	17.1	12.8	9.3	12.5
Goods procured in ports by carriers	2 170 . .	. . .	17.7	11.6	7.7	7.6	8.0	9.0	13.5
Nonmonetary gold	2 180 . .	.1	.1	. . .	.1	. . .	. . .	. . .	. . .
Debit	3 100 . .	**–1,581.4**	**–2,362.3**	**–2,831.5**	**–3,413.7**	**–3,805.4**	**–3,330.6**	**–4,079.5**	**–4,125.0**
General merchandise: imports f.o.b.	3 110 . .	–1,359.6	–1,970.9	–2,428.6	–2,874.1	–3,056.1	–2,574.9	–2,780.5	–3,070.8
Goods for processing: imports f.o.b.	3 150 . .	–187.2	–359.8	–372.9	–510.1	–704.9	–719.6	–1,260.9	–1,017.6
Repairs on goods	3 160 . .	–2.6	–6.7	–5.2	–2.4	–7.0	–5.7	–2.7	–4.0
Goods procured in ports by carriers	3 170 . .	–31.5	–23.5	–23.8	–26.5	–36.7	–29.8	–34.7	–31.8
Nonmonetary gold	3 180 . .	–.5	–1.4	–1.1	–.6	–.7	–.5	–.8	–.7
B. SERVICES	4 200 . .	105.1	379.1	518.5	591.4	569.5	572.1	562.7	577.9
Total credit	2 200 . .	*515.3*	*876.8*	*1,108.3*	*1,318.0*	*1,479.6*	*1,489.7*	*1,499.0*	*1,642.8*
Total debit	3 200 . .	*–410.2*	*–497.7*	*–589.8*	*–726.6*	*–910.1*	*–917.6*	*–936.3*	*–1,064.9*
Transportation services, credit	2 205 . .	**337.2**	**373.7**	**441.2**	**658.0**	**708.3**	**699.5**	**724.2**	**790.0**
Passenger	2 850 . .	*76.5*	*95.4*	*81.1*	*124.4*	*129.3*	*153.0*	*148.5*	*153.4*
Freight	2 851 . .	*174.2*	*173.3*	*210.4*	*374.9*	*353.9*	*287.7*	*312.7*	*388.9*
Other	2 852 . .	*86.6*	*105.1*	*149.7*	*158.7*	*225.1*	*258.8*	*263.1*	*247.6*
Sea transport, passenger	2 207 . .	60.8	71.0	60.7	88.5	96.4	114.7	109.6	112.7
Sea transport, freight	2 208 . .	128.2	98.1	123.5	159.7	150.5	109.2	118.9	119.6
Sea transport, other	2 209 . .	54.4	58.9	70.3	65.8	78.8	134.1	144.7	155.0
Air transport, passenger	2 211 . .	11.1	16.7	17.3	30.2	27.8	34.6	35.3	35.7
Air transport, freight	2 212 . .	1.0	1.7	1.2	2.5	3.1	3.3	2.9	3.4
Air transport, other	2 213 . .	7.0	10.2	13.9	13.1	11.8	14.1	11.2	10.4
Other transport, passenger	2 215 . .	4.6	7.6	3.2	5.7	5.1	3.6	3.6	5.0
Other transport, freight	2 216 . .	45.0	73.5	85.7	212.7	200.3	175.2	190.8	265.9
Other transport, other	2 217 . .	25.1	36.0	65.4	79.8	134.5	110.7	107.2	82.2
Transportation services, debit	3 205 . .	**–184.5**	**–222.1**	**–267.4**	**–340.2**	**–409.1**	**–370.1**	**–419.7**	**–486.5**
Passenger	3 850 . .	*–18.5*	*–29.9*	*–39.9*	*–42.2*	*–41.5*	*–40.0*	*–48.7*	*–61.1*
Freight	3 851 . .	*–100.9*	*–122.1*	*–167.3*	*–251.9*	*–302.7*	*–254.3*	*–301.5*	*–362.3*
Other	3 852 . .	*–65.2*	*–70.1*	*–60.2*	*–46.1*	*–64.8*	*–75.8*	*–69.5*	*–63.1*
Sea transport, passenger	3 207 . .	–15.5	–19.0	–24.7	–25.0	–29.8	–30.7	–37.8	–48.0
Sea transport, freight	3 208 . .	–77.3	–69.9	–78.5	–80.3	–102.2	–89.5	–112.7	–96.5
Sea transport, other	3 209 . .	–52.1	–50.4	–42.2	–29.9	–41.7	–42.6	–38.2	–39.5
Air transport, passenger	3 211 . .	–2.1	–9.6	–13.5	–12.9	–9.3	–7.8	–8.7	–9.1
Air transport, freight	3 212 . .	–1.9	–.7	–.7	–1.4	–3.5	–2.9	–3.4	–4.2
Air transport, other	3 213 . .	–5.6	–10.3	–14.1	–6.4	–8.9	–14.5	–11.3	–11.4
Other transport, passenger	3 215 . .	–.9	–1.4	–1.7	–4.3	–2.4	–1.4	–2.2	–3.9
Other transport, freight	3 216 . .	–21.7	–51.5	–88.1	–170.2	–197.0	–161.9	–185.4	–261.6
Other transport, other	3 217 . .	–7.4	–9.4	–3.9	–9.8	–14.2	–18.7	–19.9	–12.2
Travel, credit	2 236 . .	**91.4**	**356.7**	**484.4**	**473.5**	**538.5**	**548.8**	**504.5**	**505.5**
Business travel	2 237 . .	22.9	67.5	183.7	178.4	210.6	175.3	146.1	128.4
Personal travel	2 240 . .	68.5	289.1	300.6	295.1	327.9	373.6	358.4	377.1
Travel, debit	3 236 . .	**–48.0**	**–90.5**	**–100.8**	**–120.0**	**–155.2**	**–214.6**	**–203.7**	**–191.0**
Business travel	3 237 . .	–12.0	–22.6	–54.4	–53.1	–68.0	–80.5	–73.7	–63.8
Personal travel	3 240 . .	–36.0	–67.9	–46.3	–66.9	–87.2	–134.1	–130.0	–127.1
Other services, credit	2 200 BA	**86.7**	**146.4**	**182.7**	**186.5**	**232.8**	**241.4**	**270.3**	**347.3**
Communications	2 245 . .	11.8	16.7	13.2	11.9	14.0	25.7	20.8	18.6
Construction	2 249 . .	31.7	63.4	64.2	58.7	57.5	30.4	38.0	78.5
Insurance	2 253 . .	.6	1.3	2.0	1.5	2.5	5.1	6.1	4.1
Financial	2 260 . .	1.0	1.9	9.8	11.8	12.5	7.0	10.4	16.6
Computer and information	2 262 . .	2.7	2.4	3.9	7.2	8.0	14.8	21.2	23.1
Royalties and licence fees	2 266 . .	.9	.9	1.3	1.0	1.2	1.7	1.6	2.1
Other business services	2 268 . .	30.6	51.1	79.4	89.6	132.8	152.1	167.1	193.0
Personal, cultural, and recreational	2 287 . .	.3	.3	.2	.5	.9	.6	.9	2.5
Government, n.i.e.	2 291 . .	7.2	8.5	8.6	4.4	3.3	3.9	4.3	8.9
Other services, debit	3 200 BA	**–177.7**	**–185.1**	**–221.7**	**–266.4**	**–345.8**	**–332.9**	**–313.0**	**–387.4**
Communications	3 245 . .	–12.4	–5.5	–7.9	–14.7	–17.6	–36.2	–19.0	–21.3
Construction	3 249 . .	–30.5	–28.9	–24.2	–20.6	–31.0	–19.5	–17.6	–31.2
Insurance	3 253 . .	–11.7	–14.6	–14.5	–14.2	–15.9	–8.6	–2.5	–1.1
Financial	3 260 . .	–1.9	–5.3	–11.7	–10.2	–15.4	–9.9	–8.2	–13.4
Computer and information	3 262 . .	–2.6	–6.4	–6.9	–8.7	–10.3	–13.5	–11.6	–13.1
Royalties and licence fees	3 266 . .	–.8	–1.1	–2.9	–4.6	–7.0	–5.6	–7.9	–11.2
Other business services	3 268 . .	–36.7	–45.0	–88.6	–112.7	–150.2	–149.5	–176.1	–200.3
Personal, cultural, and recreational	3 287 . .	–1.5	–.8	–.6	–2.9	–2.2	–1.4	–1.6	–3.4
Government, n.i.e.	3 291 . .	–79.6	–77.6	–64.4	–77.7	–96.4	–88.7	–68.5	–92.4

Table 2 (Continued). STANDARD PRESENTATION, 1994–2001
(Millions of U.S. dollars)

	Code	1994	1995	1996	1997	1998	1999	2000	2001
C. INCOME	4 300 . .	–29.6	2.8	1.9	–145.7	–81.0	–101.7	–204.2	–281.2
Total credit	2 300 . .	*37.3*	*63.6*	*112.2*	*115.1*	*133.5*	*133.8*	*117.6*	*170.6*
Total debit	3 300 . .	*–66.9*	*–60.8*	*–110.3*	*–260.8*	*–214.5*	*–235.5*	*–321.7*	*–451.8*
Compensation of employees, credit	2 310 . .	**2.8**	**1.3**	**1.6**	**1.7**	**2.6**	**2.2**	**2.3**	**6.2**
Compensation of employees, debit	3 310 . .	**–.5**	**–2.9**	**–.8**	**–.9**	**–1.4**	**–1.3**	**–1.6**	**–.9**
Investment income, credit	2 320 . .	**34.5**	**62.4**	**110.6**	**113.4**	**131.0**	**131.7**	**115.3**	**164.5**
Direct investment income	2 330 . .	.2	.8	13.3	10.7	7.4	24.2	13.0	26.2
Dividends and distributed branch profits	2 332 . .	. . .	.4	.4	1.2	1.0	2.0	1.6	2.5
Reinvested earnings and undistributed branch profits	2 333 . .	. . .	. . .	12.1	6.3	.4	7.8	3.6	17.6
Income on debt (interest)	2 334 . .	.2	.3	.7	3.2	6.0	14.4	7.8	6.1
Portfolio investment income	2 339 . .	20.4	44.8	74.0	72.1	86.5	69.7	60.3	92.2
Income on equity	2 340 . .	. . .	. . .	. . .	. . .	. . .	. . .	.5	4.0
Income on bonds and notes	2 350 . .	. . .	. . .	. . .	. . .	. . .	. . .	59.8	88.3
Income on money market instruments	2 360 . .	. . .	. . .	. . .	. . .	. . .	. . .	. . .	. . .
Other investment income	2 370 . .	13.9	16.8	23.3	30.6	37.2	37.7	42.0	46.1
Investment income, debit	3 320 . .	**–66.4**	**–57.9**	**–109.6**	**–259.8**	**–213.1**	**–234.2**	**–320.2**	**–450.9**
Direct investment income	3 330 . .	–48.3	–26.1	–38.2	–127.3	–79.5	–119.4	–204.6	–309.8
Dividends and distributed branch profits	3 332 . .	–2.0	–3.1	–9.3	–22.0	–28.5	–56.7	–83.2	–67.9
Reinvested earnings and undistributed branch profits	3 333 . .	–42.8	–15.4	–18.0	–94.9	–25.8	–47.4	–105.9	–223.6
Income on debt (interest)	3 334 . .	–3.5	–7.6	–11.0	–10.4	–25.2	–15.3	–15.5	–18.2
Portfolio investment income	3 339 . .	–4.3	–3.7	–30.2	–80.8	–51.6	–44.6	–41.8	–65.8
Income on equity	3 340 . .	. . .	. . .	. . .	. . .	. . .	. . .	–6.9	–19.0
Income on bonds and notes	3 350 . .	. . .	. . .	. . .	. . .	. . .	. . .	–34.9	–46.8
Income on money market instruments	3 360 . .	. . .	. . .	. . .	. . .	. . .	. . .	. . .	. . .
Other investment income	3 370 . .	–13.8	–28.1	–41.1	–51.7	–82.1	–70.3	–73.8	–75.3
D. CURRENT TRANSFERS	4 379 . .	114.7	126.3	100.5	116.7	148.3	112.5	115.6	151.2
Credit	2 379 . .	**120.3**	**134.5**	**116.8**	**135.3**	**172.9**	**153.7**	**144.7**	**180.4**
General government	2 380 . .	110.1	105.3	89.2	98.8	115.8	102.1	93.6	126.7
Other sectors	2 390 . .	10.2	29.2	27.6	36.5	57.1	51.6	51.1	53.7
Workers' remittances	2 391 . .	.1	. . .	. . .	.1	.1	.1	.3	3.2
Other current transfers	2 392 . .	10.1	29.2	27.5	36.4	57.0	51.4	50.7	50.5
Debit	3 379 . .	**–5.7**	**–8.2**	**–16.3**	**–18.6**	**–24.6**	**–41.3**	**–29.1**	**–29.3**
General government	3 380 . .	–1.3	–4.5	–5.7	–2.7	–5.3	–5.6	–4.2	–2.7
Other sectors	3 390 . .	–4.4	–3.7	–10.6	–15.8	–19.4	–35.6	–25.0	–26.6
Workers' remittances	3 391 . .	–.3	–.6	–1.4	–3.6	–1.7	–2.0	–1.5	–1.3
Other current transfers	3 392 . .	–4.1	–3.1	–9.2	–12.2	–17.6	–33.6	–23.5	–25.3
CAPITAL AND FINANCIAL ACCOUNT	4 996 . .	**149.0**	**149.1**	**433.9**	**586.8**	**472.5**	**300.1**	**295.6**	**351.8**
CAPITAL ACCOUNT	4 994 . .	**–.6**	**–.8**	**–.7**	**–.2**	**1.8**	**1.2**	**16.5**	**5.1**
Total credit	2 994 . .	*.5*	*1.4*	*.2*	*.7*	*2.1*	*1.4*	*16.8*	*5.5*
Total debit	3 994 . .	*1.1*	*–2.2*	*–.8*	*–.9*	*–.3*	*–.2*	*–.2*	*–.4*
Capital transfers, credit	2 400 . .	**.5**	**1.4**	**.2**	**.7**	**2.1**	**1.4**	**16.8**	**5.5**
General government	2 401 . .	. . .	1.1	. . .	. . .	. . .	. . .	15.0	1.7
Debt forgiveness	2 402 . .	. . .	. . .	. . .	. . .	. . .	. . .	. . .	. . .
Other capital transfers	2 410 . .	. . .	. . .	. . .	. . .	. . .	. . .	. . .	. . .
Other sectors	2 430 . .	.5	.3	.2	.7	2.1	1.4	1.8	3.8
Migrants' transfers	2 431 . .	. . .	. . .	. . .	. . .	. . .	. . .	. . .	. . .
Debt forgiveness	2 432 . .	. . .	. . .	. . .	. . .	. . .	. . .	. . .	. . .
Other capital transfers	2 440 . .	. . .	. . .	. . .	. . .	. . .	. . .	. . .	. . .
Capital transfers, debit	3 400 . .	**–1.1**	**–2.2**	**–.8**	**–.9**	**–.3**	**–.2**	**–.2**	**–.4**
General government	3 401 . .	–1.1	–1.9	–.7	–.9	–.3	–.2	–.2	–.3
Debt forgiveness	3 402 . .	. . .	. . .	. . .	. . .	. . .	. . .	. . .	. . .
Other capital transfers	3 410 . .	. . .	. . .	. . .	. . .	. . .	. . .	. . .	. . .
Other sectors	3 430 . .	. . .	–.3	–.1	. . .	. . .	. . .	. . .	–.1
Migrants' transfers	3 431 . .	. . .	. . .	. . .	. . .	. . .	. . .	. . .	. . .
Debt forgiveness	3 432 . .	. . .	. . .	. . .	. . .	. . .	. . .	. . .	. . .
Other capital transfers	3 440 . .	. . .	. . .	. . .	. . .	. . .	. . .	. . .	. . .
Nonproduced nonfinancial assets, credit	2 480 . .	. . .	. . .	. . .	. . .	. . .	. . .	. . .	. . .
Nonproduced nonfinancial assets, debit	3 480 . .	. . .	. . .	. . .	. . .	. . .	. . .	. . .	. . .

Table 2 (Continued). STANDARD PRESENTATION, 1994–2001

(Millions of U.S. dollars)

	Code		1994	1995	1996	1997	1998	1999	2000	2001
FINANCIAL ACCOUNT	4 995	. .	**149.7**	**149.9**	**434.6**	**587.0**	**470.8**	**298.9**	**279.1**	**346.7**
A. DIRECT INVESTMENT	4 500	. .	212.1	199.0	110.2	129.6	574.2	222.3	323.9	339.7
Direct investment abroad	4 505	. .	**–2.4**	**–2.5**	**–40.1**	**–136.6**	**–6.3**	**–82.9**	**–63.4**	**–199.6**
Equity capital	4 510	. .	–1.8	–.3	–8.9	–38.7	–33.0	–35.3	–36.0	–106.6
Claims on affiliated enterprises	4 515	. .	–1.8	–.3	–8.9	–38.7	–33.0	–35.3	–36.0	–106.6
Liabilities to affiliated enterprises	4 520	. .	...	...	...	...	...	...	...	...
Reinvested earnings	4 525	. .	...	...	–12.1	–6.3	–.4	–7.8	–3.6	–17.6
Other capital	4 530	. .	–.5	–2.2	–19.1	–91.5	27.2	–39.8	–23.8	–75.4
Claims on affiliated enterprises	4 535	. .	–.5	–2.3	–21.6	–93.0	26.2	–43.0	–28.7	–70.6
Liabilities to affiliated enterprises	4 540	. .	...	.1	2.6	1.5	.9	3.2	4.9	–4.9
Direct investment in Estonia	4 555	. .	**214.4**	**201.5**	**150.2**	**266.2**	**580.5**	**305.2**	**387.3**	**539.4**
Equity capital	4 560	. .	143.3	101.2	18.0	97.0	412.1	174.2	227.4	208.9
Claims on direct investors	4 565	. .	1.1	...	...	...	...	...	...	...
Liabilities to direct investors	4 570	. .	142.2	101.2	18.0	97.0	412.1	174.2	227.4	208.9
Reinvested earnings	4 575	. .	42.8	15.4	18.0	94.9	25.8	47.4	105.9	223.6
Other capital	4 580	. .	28.4	84.9	114.3	74.4	142.7	83.7	53.9	106.8
Claims on direct investors	4 585	. .	–5.1	–5.2	–13.1	–6.4	–14.1	–17.5	–24.0	–54.6
Liabilities to direct investors	4 590	. .	33.5	90.1	127.4	80.7	156.8	101.2	77.9	161.5
B. PORTFOLIO INVESTMENT	4 600	. .	–14.1	–22.1	145.4	262.5	–9.8	21.0	115.4	95.9
Assets	4 602	. .	**–22.5**	**–33.2**	**–52.7**	**–165.0**	**–10.9**	**–132.3**	**39.8**	**13.0**
Equity securities	4 610	. .	–14.5	5.1	–15.0	–87.8	35.1	12.9	3.5	13.9
Monetary authorities	4 611	. .	...	...	...	...	...	...	...	...
General government	4 612	. .	...	–1.2	...	–3.2	.4	...	...	...
Banks	4 613	. .	–2.9	1.5	–12.3	–33.5	37.9	3.2	–3.9	23.1
Other sectors	4 614	. .	–11.5	4.7	–2.6	–51.0	–3.2	9.7	7.4	–9.3
Debt securities	4 619	. .	–8.0	–38.2	–37.6	–77.2	–46.0	–145.2	36.4	–.9
Bonds and notes	4 620	. .	–8.0	–38.2	–37.6	–77.2	–46.0	–145.2	–14.2	–19.6
Monetary authorities	4 621	. .	...	...	...	...	...	...	...	4.5
General government	4 622	. .	...	...	–6.7	–.4	...	...	...	...
Banks	4 623	. .	–6.8	–24.3	–32.9	–70.3	–20.3	–101.5	3.5	–2.0
Other sectors	4 624	. .	–1.2	–13.9	2.0	–6.5	–25.7	–43.7	–17.7	–22.1
Money market instruments	4 630	. .	...	...	...	...	...	...	50.6	18.7
Monetary authorities	4 631	. .	...	...	...	...	...	...	...	...
General government	4 632	. .	...	...	...	...	...	...	...	–.2
Banks	4 633	. .	...	...	...	...	...	...	31.2	27.1
Other sectors	4 634	. .	...	...	...	...	...	...	19.3	–8.2
Liabilities	4 652	. .	**8.4**	**11.1**	**198.1**	**427.5**	**1.1**	**153.3**	**75.6**	**83.0**
Equity securities	4 660	. .	8.4	9.9	172.3	127.8	25.7	235.4	–28.5	31.5
Banks	4 663	. .	8.2	9.6	83.5	65.4	–16.2	1.4	–36.2	23.6
Other sectors	4 664	. .	.2	.2	88.8	62.4	41.9	233.9	7.7	7.9
Debt securities	4 669	. .	...	1.2	25.8	299.7	–24.6	–82.1	104.1	51.5
Bonds and notes	4 670	. .	...	1.2	25.8	299.7	–24.6	–82.1	107.0	64.1
Monetary authorities	4 671	. .	...	...	...	...	...	...	...	...
General government	4 672	. .	...	–6.0	4.8	–16.2	–.8	11.4	–4.0	–6.5
Banks	4 673	. .	...	7.0	13.4	226.4	.3	–40.9	99.5	47.7
Other sectors	4 674	. .	...	.2	7.6	89.5	–24.1	–52.6	11.5	22.9
Money market instruments	4 680	. .	...	...	...	...	...	...	–2.9	–12.6
Monetary authorities	4 681	. .	...	...	...	...	...	...	...	...
General government	4 682	. .	...	...	...	...	...	...	...	...
Banks	4 683	. .	...	...	...	...	...	...	–2.9	–12.6
Other sectors	4 684	. .	...	...	...	...	...	...	...	...
C. FINANCIAL DERIVATIVES	4 910	. .	...	...	...	...	...	...	.7	–2.1
Monetary authorities	4 911	. .	...	...	...	...	...	...	...	...
General government	4 912	. .	...	...	...	...	...	...	...	...
Banks	4 913	. .	...	...	...	...	...	...	1.2	–2.1
Other sectors	4 914	. .	...	...	...	...	...	...	–.5	...
Assets	4 900	. .	**...**	**...**	**...**	**...**	**...**	**...**	**–4.7**	**–.1**
Monetary authorities	4 901	. .	...	...	...	...	...	...	...	...
General government	4 902	. .	...	...	...	...	...	...	...	...
Banks	4 903	. .	...	...	...	...	...	...	–4.1	...
Other sectors	4 904	. .	...	...	...	...	...	...	–.6	...
Liabilities	4 905	. .	**...**	**...**	**...**	**...**	**...**	**...**	**5.4**	**–2.0**
Monetary authorities	4 906	. .	...	...	...	...	...	...	...	...
General government	4 907	. .	...	...	...	...	...	...	...	...
Banks	4 908	. .	...	...	...	...	...	...	5.3	–2.0
Other sectors	4 909	. .	...	...	...	...	...	...	.1	...

Table 2 (Concluded). STANDARD PRESENTATION, 1994–2001
(Millions of U.S. dollars)

	Code	1994	1995	1996	1997	1998	1999	2000	2001
D. OTHER INVESTMENT	4 700 . .	–30.8	85.9	274.2	391.2	–82.0	170.9	–38.5	–132.1
Assets	4 703 . .	**–146.7**	**–98.9**	**–7.3**	**–334.2**	**–168.5**	**–110.3**	**–177.1**	**–297.7**
Trade credits	4 706 . .	–46.0	–5.6	–46.8	–61.0	–68.5	–3.7	–5.7	–46.3
General government	4 707 . .	. . .	. . .	. . .	. . .	. . .	. . .	. . .	. . .
of which: Short-term	4 709 . .	. . .	. . .	. . .	. . .	. . .	. . .	. . .	. . .
Other sectors	4 710 . .	–46.0	–5.6	–46.8	–61.0	–68.5	–3.7	–5.7	–46.3
of which: Short-term	4 712 . .	*–46.0*	*–5.6*	*–46.8*	*–61.0*	*–68.5*	*–3.7*	*–5.7*	*–46.3*
Loans	4 714 . .	–2.9	–18.4	–1.4	–116.9	–37.5	–4.0	–165.6	–130.5
Monetary authorities	4 715 . .	. . .	. . .	. . .	. . .	. . .	. . .	. . .	. . .
of which: Short-term	4 718 . .	. . .	. . .	. . .	. . .	. . .	. . .	. . .	. . .
General government	4 719 . .	. . .	. . .	. . .	. . .	. . .	. . .	. . .	. . .
of which: Short-term	4 721 . .	. . .	. . .	. . .	. . .	. . .	. . .	. . .	. . .
Banks	4 722 . .	. . .	. . .	. . .	–82.5	27.9	–15.3	–58.6	–160.3
of which: Short-term	4 724 . .	. . .	. . .	. . .	*–35.3*	*44.3*	*–37.6*	*–45.5*	*–152.6*
Other sectors	4 725 . .	–2.9	–18.4	–1.4	–34.5	–65.3	11.3	–107.0	29.7
of which: Short-term	4 727 . .	. . .	. . .	*.1*	*–5.6*	*–25.6*	*4.6*	*–54.6*	*39.9*
Currency and deposits	4 730 . .	–97.9	–74.6	50.5	–133.4	–69.8	–80.8	–27.8	–114.3
Monetary authorities	4 731 . .	.1	.1	.1	. . .	. . .	. . .	. . .	. . .
General government	4 732 . .	.4	–.4	–3.3	–24.7	–61.9	–60.8	32.7	–17.3
Banks	4 733 . .	–102.8	–41.1	20.8	–101.7	34.7	–33.6	–47.2	–57.3
Other sectors	4 734 . .	4.3	–33.1	32.9	–7.0	–42.6	13.6	–13.2	–39.8
Other assets	4 736 . .	.1	–.3	–9.6	–22.9	7.2	–21.9	22.0	–6.4
Monetary authorities	4 737 . .	. . .	. . .	. . .	. . .	. . .	–18.3	–9.6	–11.1
of which: Short-term	4 739 . .	. . .	. . .	. . .	. . .	. . .	*–18.3*	*–9.6*	*–11.2*
General government	4 740 . .	. . .	. . .	. . .	. . .	. . .	. . .	. . .	. . .
of which: Short-term	4 742 . .	. . .	. . .	. . .	. . .	. . .	. . .	. . .	. . .
Banks	4 743 . .	. . .	. . .	. . .	–11.8	–1.3	–4.8	28.9	3.1
of which: Short-term	4 745 . .	. . .	. . .	. . .	*–11.8*	*–1.3*	*–4.8*	*28.9*	*3.1*
Other sectors	4 746 . .	.1	–.3	–9.6	–11.1	8.6	1.2	2.6	1.5
of which: Short-term	4 748 . .	*–.1*	. . .	*–9.6*	*–10.9*	*8.6*	*1.5*	*3.1*	*1.6*
Liabilities	4 753 . .	**115.9**	**184.8**	**281.5**	**725.4**	**86.5**	**281.2**	**138.7**	**165.6**
Trade credits	4 756 . .	77.9	20.5	35.3	27.3	–17.3	7.3	62.3	–7.7
General government	4 757 . .	. . .	. . .	. . .	. . .	. . .	. . .	. . .	. . .
of which: Short-term	4 759 . .	. . .	. . .	. . .	. . .	. . .	. . .	. . .	. . .
Other sectors	4 760 . .	77.9	20.5	35.3	27.3	–17.3	7.3	62.3	–7.7
of which: Short-term	4 762 . .	*77.9*	*20.5*	*35.3*	*27.3*	*–17.3*	*7.3*	*62.3*	*–7.7*
Loans	4 764 . .	.7	108.0	142.8	457.3	12.6	162.7	–59.2	142.0
Monetary authorities	4 765 . .	.2	28.6	–14.7	–21.0	–26.4	3.3	–2.9	–9.1
of which: Use of Fund credit and loans from the Fund	4 766 . .	. . .	*29.4*	*–11.1*	*–19.4*	*–25.6*	*–4.0*	*–5.2*	*–4.9*
of which: Short-term	4 768 . .	. . .	. . .	. . .	. . .	. . .	*7.4*	*2.5*	*–4.0*
General government	4 769 . .	19.8	61.0	31.3	–3.3	4.4	9.8	–17.2	–7.2
of which: Short-term	4 771 . .	. . .	. . .	. . .	. . .	. . .	. . .	. . .	. . .
Banks	4 772 . .	7.2	14.0	68.4	250.7	–110.2	65.1	59.3	24.1
of which: Short-term	4 774 . .	. . .	. . .	*1.8*	*146.1*	*–106.8*	*26.7*	*–14.2*	*34.5*
Other sectors	4 775 . .	–26.5	4.4	57.8	231.0	144.8	84.6	20.3	134.1
of which: Short-term	4 777 . .	*–7.1*	*1.9*	*–6.7*	*41.9*	*46.5*	*15.0*	*–7.0*	*33.8*
Currency and deposits	4 780 . .	36.4	55.6	102.2	172.2	27.6	95.9	116.8	2.0
Monetary authorities	4 781 . .	6.1	–12.7	–3.1	–.9	–.2	.1	–.5	.1
General government	4 782 . .	. . .	. . .	. . .	. . .	. . .	. . .	. . .	. . .
Banks	4 783 . .	30.3	68.3	105.2	173.1	27.8	95.8	117.3	1.9
Other sectors	4 784 . .	. . .	. . .	. . .	. . .	. . .	. . .	. . .	. . .
Other liabilities	4 786 . .	.9	.7	1.3	68.6	63.6	15.4	18.7	29.3
Monetary authorities	4 787 . .	. . .	. . .	. . .	. . .	. . .	. . .	. . .	–1.2
of which: Short-term	4 789 . .	. . .	. . .	. . .	. . .	. . .	. . .	. . .	*–1.2*
General government	4 790 . .	. . .	. . .	. . .	. . .	. . .	. . .	. . .	. . .
of which: Short-term	4 792 . .	. . .	. . .	. . .	. . .	. . .	. . .	. . .	. . .
Banks	4 793 . .	. . .	. . .	. . .	68.7	65.0	27.4	18.8	32.3
of which: Short-term	4 795 . .	. . .	. . .	. . .	*6.1*	*52.6*	*27.6*	*21.0*	*12.1*
Other sectors	4 796 . .	.9	.7	1.3	–.1	–1.4	–12.1	. . .	–1.7
of which: Short-term	4 798 . .	. . .	. . .	*1.3*	*–.1*	*–1.4*	*–12.1*	. . .	*–1.7*
E. RESERVE ASSETS	4 802 . .	–17.5	–112.9	–95.3	–196.4	–11.7	–115.3	–122.4	45.2
Monetary gold	4 812 . .	. . .	. . .	. . .	. . .	. . .	.1	. . .	. . .
Special drawing rights	4 811 . .	59.3	2.6	.1	.1	. . .	–1.3	1.3	. . .
Reserve position in the Fund	4 810 . .	. . .	. . .	. . .	. . .	. . .	. . .	. . .	. . .
Foreign exchange	4 803 . .	–76.8	–115.5	–95.4	–196.6	–11.7	–114.1	–123.8	45.2
Other claims	4 813 . .	. . .	. . .	. . .	. . .	. . .	. . .	. . .	. . .
NET ERRORS AND OMISSIONS	4 998 . .	**17.2**	**8.7**	**–35.6**	**–25.1**	**5.9**	**–5.5**	**–1.6**	**–12.8**

Part 3 of the *Yearbook* contains descriptions of the methodologies, compilation practices, and sources used to compile these data.

Table 3. INTERNATIONAL INVESTMENT POSITION (End–period stocks), 1994–2001
(Millions of U.S. dollars)

	Code	1994	1995	1996	1997	1998	1999	2000	2001
ASSETS	8 995 C.	...	...	1,344.1	2,045.5	2,300.4	2,415.1	2,614.0	2,920.5
Direct investment abroad	8 505 . .	**...**	**...**	**107.7**	**215.3**	**198.4**	**281.2**	**259.1**	**441.8**
Equity capital and reinvested earnings	8 506 . .	...	...	26.2	58.0	89.3	120.7	173.5	285.9
Claims on affiliated enterprises	8 507 . .	...	...	26.2	58.0	89.3	120.7	173.5	285.9
Liabilities to affiliated enterprises	8 508 . .	...	...	...	...	...	...	...	...
Other capital	8 530 . .	...	...	81.5	157.3	109.1	160.5	85.6	155.8
Claims on affiliated enterprises	8 535 . .	...	...	89.3	165.2	119.7	173.0	103.0	167.8
Liabilities to affiliated enterprises	8 540 . .	...	...	–7.8	–7.9	–10.6	–12.5	–17.4	–12.0
Portfolio investment	8 602 . .	**...**	**...**	**121.0**	**249.3**	**211.2**	**305.2**	**271.8**	**262.1**
Equity securities	8 610 . .	...	...	26.1	98.5	31.5	12.4	26.4	22.5
Monetary authorities	8 611 . .	...	...	...	...	...	...	...	...
General government	8 612 . .	...	...	...	.1	...	...	...	...
Banks	8 613 . .	...	...	18.8	45.6	5.7	2.1	15.1	2.5
Other sectors	8 614 . .	...	...	7.3	52.8	25.8	10.2	11.3	19.9
Debt securities	8 619 . .	...	...	94.9	150.9	179.7	292.9	245.4	239.6
Bonds and notes	8 620 . .	...	...	94.9	150.9	179.7	292.9	75.8	91.4
Monetary authorities	8 621 . .	...	...	...	...	...	...	...	...
General government	8 622 . .	...	...	...	...	...	...	...	...
Banks	8 623 . .	...	...	68.8	129.4	128.7	207.9	15.6	13.5
Other sectors	8 624 . .	...	...	26.1	21.5	51.0	85.0	60.1	77.8
Money market instruments	8 630 . .	...	...	...	...	...	...	169.6	148.3
Monetary authorities	8 631 . .	...	...	...	...	...	...	...	...
General government	8 632 . .	...	...	...	...	...	...	...	...
Banks	8 633 . .	...	...	...	...	...	...	151.0	124.5
Other sectors	8 634 . .	...	...	...	...	...	...	18.6	23.8
Financial derivatives	8 900 . .	**...**	**...**	**...**	**...**	**...**	**...**	**9.1**	**8.7**
Monetary authorities	8 901 . .	...	...	...	...	...	...	...	...
General government	8 902 . .	...	...	...	...	...	...	...	...
Banks	8 903 . .	...	...	...	...	...	...	9.1	8.7
Other sectors	8 904 . .	...	...	...	...	...	...	...	...
Other investment	8 703 . .	**...**	**...**	**475.9**	**820.4**	**1,077.4**	**972.4**	**1,151.0**	**1,385.3**
Trade credits	8 706 . .	...	...	153.1	196.1	285.5	237.5	229.5	282.1
General government	8 707 . .	...	...	...	...	...	...	...	...
of which: Short-term	8 709 . .	...	...	...	...	...	...	...	...
Other sectors	8 710 . .	...	...	153.1	196.1	285.5	237.5	229.5	282.1
of which: Short-term	8 712 . .	...	...	*153.1*	*196.1*	*285.5*	*237.5*	*229.5*	*282.1*
Loans	8 714 . .	...	...	61.4	178.3	229.1	174.2	416.2	523.1
Monetary authorities	8 715 . .	...	...	...	...	...	...	...	...
of which: Short-term	8 718 . .	...	...	...	...	...	...	...	...
General government	8 719 . .	...	...	...	...	...	...	...	...
of which: Short-term	8 721 . .	...	...	...	...	...	...	...	...
Banks	8 722 . .	...	...	55.8	121.6	102.3	103.2	155.6	305.7
of which: Short-term	8 724 . .	...	...	*14.3*	*65.6*	*25.2*	*57.6*	*100.8*	*246.3*
Other sectors	8 725 . .	...	...	5.7	56.7	126.7	70.9	260.7	217.4
of which: Short-term	8 727 . .	...	...	*2.6*	*17.4*	*43.2*	*7.4*	*100.3*	*53.3*
Currency and deposits	8 730 . .	...	...	241.6	402.1	519.5	498.1	474.2	551.7
Monetary authorities	8 731 . .	...	...	...	...	...	...	...	...
General government	8 732 . .	...	...	4.6	26.7	97.7	129.6	87.5	98.0
Banks	8 733 . .	...	...	174.2	243.7	228.0	218.4	235.3	278.9
Other sectors	8 734 . .	...	...	62.7	131.6	193.8	150.1	151.4	174.8
Other assets	8 736 . .	...	...	19.7	43.9	43.3	62.6	31.1	28.4
Monetary authorities	8 737 . .	...	...	...	...	...	...	1.0	6.9
of which: Short-term	8 739 . .	...	...	...	...	...	...	*1.0*	*5.9*
General government	8 740 . .	...	...	...	...	...	...	...	...
of which: Short-term	8 742 . .	...	...	...	...	...	...	...	...
Banks	8 743 . .	...	...	17.0	27.5	30.6	52.8	20.9	16.6
of which: Short-term	8 745 . .	...	...	*17.0*	*27.5*	*30.6*	*52.8*	*20.9*	*16.6*
Other sectors	8 746 . .	...	...	2.8	16.4	12.7	9.9	9.2	4.9
of which: Short-term	8 748 . .	...	...	*2.8*	*14.1*	*10.5*	*7.6*	*6.7*	*4.9*
Reserve assets	8 802 . .	**...**	**...**	**639.6**	**760.5**	**813.5**	**856.2**	**922.9**	**822.5**
Monetary gold	8 812 . .	...	...	3.0	2.4	2.4	2.4	2.3	2.3
Special drawing rights	8 811 . .	1.6	.3	.2	...	.1	1.4	...	...
Reserve position in the Fund	8 810 . .	...	...	...	...	...	...	...	...
Foreign exchange	8 803 . .	...	...	636.4	758.1	811.0	852.5	920.6	820.2
Other claims	8 813 . .	...	...	...	...	...	...	...	...

Table 3 (Concluded). INTERNATIONAL INVESTMENT POSITION (End–period stocks), 1994–2001

(Millions of U.S. dollars)

	Code	1994	1995	1996	1997	1998	1999	2000	2001
LIABILITIES	8 995 D.	...	...	1,974.9	3,757.8	4,451.9	5,199.6	5,389.5	6,017.7
Direct investment in Estonia	8 555 . .	**...**	**...**	**824.6**	**1,147.9**	**1,821.7**	**2,467.3**	**2,644.7**	**3,159.9**
Equity capital and reinvested earnings	8 556 . .	...	...	441.3	683.2	1,316.2	1,917.6	2,064.6	2,486.5
Claims on direct investors	8 557 . .	...	...	...	...	...	...	...	...
Liabilities to direct investors	8 558 . .	...	...	441.3	683.2	1,316.2	1,917.6	2,064.6	2,486.5
Other capital	8 580 . .	...	...	383.2	464.7	505.5	549.8	580.2	673.4
Claims on direct investors	8 585 . .	...	...	–44.3	–52.6	–79.1	–85.2	–106.6	–158.2
Liabilities to direct investors	8 590 . .	...	...	427.6	517.2	584.6	635.0	686.7	831.6
Portfolio investment	8 652 . .	**...**	**...**	**117.4**	**954.2**	**702.9**	**771.8**	**761.4**	**764.3**
Equity securities	8 660 . .	...	...	76.3	572.9	301.2	500.7	431.6	403.0
Banks	8 663 . .	...	...	43.3	417.2	139.8	174.6	187.5	230.7
Other sectors	8 664 . .	...	...	33.0	155.7	161.4	326.1	244.1	172.2
Debt securities	8 669 . .	...	...	41.1	381.3	401.7	271.2	329.8	361.3
Bonds and notes	8 670 . .	...	...	41.1	381.3	401.7	271.2	312.8	358.1
Monetary authorities	8 671 . .	...	...	...	...	...	...	...	...
General government	8 672 . .	...	...	9.5	...	29.8	34.6	20.8	13.2
Banks	8 673 . .	...	...	19.3	259.1	277.6	197.6	266.0	298.5
Other sectors	8 674 . .	...	...	12.3	122.1	94.3	38.9	26.0	46.3
Money market instruments	8 680 . .	...	...	...	...	...	...	17.1	3.2
Monetary authorities	8 681 . .	...	...	...	...	...	...	...	...
General government	8 682 . .	...	...	...	...	...	...	...	...
Banks	8 683 . .	...	...	...	...	...	...	17.1	3.2
Other sectors	8 684 . .	...	...	...	...	...	...	...	...
Financial derivatives	8 905 . .	**...**	**...**	**...**	**...**	**...**	**...**	**10.2**	**6.3**
Monetary authorities	8 906 . .	...	...	...	...	...	...	...	...
General government	8 907 . .	...	...	...	...	...	...	...	...
Banks	8 908 . .	...	...	...	...	...	...	10.1	6.3
Other sectors	8 909 . .	...	...	...	...	...	...	.1	...
Other investment	8 753 . .	**...**	**...**	**1,033.0**	**1,655.6**	**1,927.4**	**1,960.4**	**1,973.1**	**2,087.2**
Trade credits	8 756 . .	...	...	215.0	250.6	323.3	318.1	366.9	346.6
General government	8 757 . .	...	...	...	...	...	...	...	...
of which: Short-term	8 759 . .	...	...	...	...	...	...	...	...
Other sectors	8 760 . .	...	...	215.0	250.6	323.3	318.1	366.9	346.6
of which: Short-term	8 762 . .	...	...	*215.0*	*250.6*	*323.3*	*318.1*	*366.9*	*346.6*
Loans	8 764 . .	...	...	432.3	941.2	1,154.5	1,145.6	1,009.2	1,135.6
Monetary authorities	8 765 . .	...	...	81.1	55.4	30.8	25.7	22.0	13.4
of which: Use of Fund credit and loans from the Fund	8 766 . .	*61.1*	*91.9*	*77.9*	*54.0*	*30.0*	*25.3*	*18.9*	*13.4*
of which: Short-term	8 768 . .	...	...	...	...	...	...	*2.9*	...
General government	8 769 . .	...	...	175.3	161.4	173.6	178.6	153.6	155.6
of which: Short-term	8 771 . .	...	...	...	...	...	...	...	...
Banks	8 772 . .	...	...	27.9	332.8	269.3	292.5	216.9	230.3
of which: Short-term	8 774 . .	...	...	...	*175.4*	*72.6*	*88.7*	*69.8*	*100.7*
Other sectors	8 775 . .	...	...	148.0	391.7	681.0	648.9	616.7	736.4
of which: Short-term	8 777 . .	...	...	*16.7*	*70.3*	*130.8*	*128.2*	*108.7*	*144.6*
Currency and deposits	8 780 . .	...	...	341.6	321.5	342.5	389.1	476.7	457.8
Monetary authorities	8 781 . .	...	...	70.3	.3	...	.1	.1	.1
General government	8 782 . .	...	...	...	...	...	...	...	...
Banks	8 783 . .	...	...	271.2	321.2	342.5	389.0	476.7	457.7
Other sectors	8 784 . .	...	...	...	...	...	...	...	...
Other liabilities	8 786 . .	...	...	44.1	142.4	107.0	107.6	120.4	147.2
Monetary authorities	8 787 . .	...	...	...	...	...	.1	...	.9
of which: Short-term	8 789 . .	...	...	...	...	...	*.1*	...	*.9*
General government	8 790 . .	...	...	...	...	...	...	...	...
of which: Short-term	8 792 . .	...	...	...	...	...	...	...	...
Banks	8 793 . .	...	...	...	93.1	81.0	96.7	115.4	139.8
of which: Short-term	8 795 . .	...	...	...	*21.6*	*11.0*	*35.5*	*61.0*	*69.2*
Other sectors	8 796 . .	...	...	44.1	49.2	26.0	10.8	5.0	6.5
of which: Short-term	8 798 . .	...	...	*44.1*	*49.2*	*26.0*	*10.7*	*4.9*	*6.5*
NET INTERNATIONAL INVESTMENT POSITION	8 995 . .	**...**	**...**	**–630.8**	**–1,712.2**	**–2,151.5**	**–2,784.6**	**–2,775.5**	**–3,097.3**
Conversion rates: krooni per U.S. dollar (end of period)	0 102 . .	**12.390**	**11.462**	**12.440**	**14.336**	**13.410**	**15.562**	**16.820**	**17.692**

Ethiopia
644

Table 1. ANALYTIC PRESENTATION, 1994–2001
(Millions of U.S. dollars)

	Code	1994	1995	1996	1997	1998	1999	2000	2001
A. Current Account[1]	4 993 Z.	**125.4**	**39.4**	**79.6**	**–40.3**	**–332.6**	**–465.2**	**14.6**	**–476.9**
Goods: exports f.o.b.	2 100 ..	372.0	423.0	417.5	588.3	560.3	467.4	486.0	433.3
Goods: imports f.o.b.	3 100 ..	–925.7	–1,092.8	–1,002.8	–1,001.6	–1,359.8	–1,387.2	–1,131.4	–1,626.1
Balance on Goods	4 100 ..	*–553.7*	*–669.8*	*–585.3*	*–413.4*	*–799.4*	*–919.8*	*–645.4*	*–1,192.8*
Services: credit	2 200 ..	294.6	344.5	377.2	390.7	391.5	473.6	506.2	522.9
Services: debit	3 200 ..	–310.4	–352.8	–349.8	–394.2	–455.6	–466.3	–490.7	–525.6
Balance on Goods and Services	4 991 ..	*–569.5*	*–678.1*	*–557.9*	*–416.9*	*–863.5*	*–912.5*	*–629.8*	*–1,195.5*
Income: credit	2 300 ..	42.9	68.4	41.2	24.2	21.0	16.6	16.2	16.3
Income: debit	3 300 ..	–74.6	–87.1	–75.2	–65.5	–64.2	–50.4	–52.0	–48.3
Balance on Goods, Services, and Income	4 992 ..	*–601.1*	*–696.9*	*–591.8*	*–458.2*	*–906.7*	*–946.3*	*–665.7*	*–1,227.5*
Current transfers: credit	2 379 Z.	728.5	737.3	679.0	425.5	589.8	500.7	697.9	774.6
Current transfers: debit	3 379 ..	–2.0	–1.1	–7.5	–7.6	–15.7	–19.7	–17.6	–24.0
B. Capital Account[1]	4 994 Z.	**3.7**	**2.6**	**.9**	**. . .**	**1.4**	**1.8**	**. . .**	**. . .**
Capital account: credit	2 994 Z.	3.7	2.6	.9	. . .	1.4	1.8	. . .	. . .
Capital account: debit	3 994 ..	. . .	. . .	. . .	. . .	. . .	. . .	. . .	. . .
Total, Groups A Plus B	4 981 ..	*129.1*	*42.0*	*80.5*	*–40.3*	*–331.2*	*–463.4*	*14.6*	*–476.9*
C. Financial Account[1]	4 995 W.	**–199.0**	**–24.9**	**–499.6**	**241.2**	**–21.3**	**–180.1**	**22.8**	**–139.6**
Direct investment abroad	4 505 ..	. . .	. . .	. . .	. . .	. . .	. . .	. . .	. . .
Direct investment in Ethiopia	4 555 Z.	. . .	. . .	. . .	. . .	. . .	. . .	. . .	. . .
Portfolio investment assets	4 602 ..	. . .	. . .	. . .	. . .	. . .	. . .	. . .	. . .
Equity securities	4 610 ..	. . .	. . .	. . .	. . .	. . .	. . .	. . .	. . .
Debt securities	4 619 ..	. . .	. . .	. . .	. . .	. . .	. . .	. . .	. . .
Portfolio investment liabilities	4 652 Z.	. . .	. . .	. . .	. . .	. . .	. . .	. . .	. . .
Equity securities	4 660 ..	. . .	. . .	. . .	. . .	. . .	. . .	. . .	. . .
Debt securities	4 669 Z.	. . .	. . .	. . .	. . .	. . .	. . .	. . .	. . .
Financial derivatives	4 910 ..	. . .	. . .	. . .	. . .	. . .	. . .	. . .	. . .
Financial derivatives assets	4 900 ..	. . .	. . .	. . .	. . .	. . .	. . .	. . .	. . .
Financial derivatives liabilities	4 905 ..	. . .	. . .	. . .	. . .	. . .	. . .	. . .	. . .
Other investment assets	4 703 ..	–318.5	57.7	–306.8	318.5	59.8	–85.3	116.1	60.5
Monetary authorities	4 701 ..	. . .	. . .	. . .	. . .	. . .	. . .	. . .	. . .
General government	4 704 ..	. . .	. . .	. . .	. . .	. . .	. . .	. . .	. . .
Banks	4 705 ..	–358.5	44.7	–283.0	350.7	26.3	–69.6	23.2	29.7
Other sectors	4 728 ..	40.0	13.1	–23.8	–32.2	33.5	–15.8	92.8	30.7
Other investment liabilities	4 753 W.	119.5	–82.6	–192.8	–77.3	–81.0	–94.7	–93.2	–200.1
Monetary authorities	4 753 WA	25.4	.4	–7.8	–.1	–.4	.4	47.0	–54.6
General government	4 753 ZB	82.4	–145.1	–131.5	–91.0	–79.9	–125.7	–178.3	–107.9
Banks	4 753 ZC	55.3	91.2	205.6	15.0	2.4	62.2	4.1	–70.5
Other sectors	4 753 ZD	–43.6	–29.1	–259.0	–1.2	–3.1	–31.6	34.0	33.0
Total, Groups A Through C	4 983 ..	*–69.9*	*17.2*	*–419.1*	*201.0*	*–352.5*	*–643.5*	*37.4*	*–616.5*
D. Net Errors and Omissions	4 998 ..	**69.5**	**–122.4**	**–45.8**	**–629.5**	**–7.9**	**407.2**	**–233.0**	**51.6**
Total, Groups A Through D	4 984 ..	*–.4*	*–105.2*	*–464.8*	*–428.6*	*–360.4*	*–236.3*	*–195.6*	*–564.9*
E. Reserves and Related Items	4 802 A.	**.4**	**105.2**	**464.8**	**428.6**	**360.4**	**236.3**	**195.6**	**564.9**
Reserve assets	4 802 ..	–124.7	–204.8	20.0	192.1	179.0	–49.7	–84.5	–32.0
Use of Fund credit and loans	4 766 ..	20.8	. . .	21.2	. . .	16.9	–9.7	–13.0	31.8
Exceptional financing	4 920 ..	104.3	310.0	423.6	236.5	164.5	295.7	293.0	565.1
Conversion rates: birr per U.S. dollar	0 101 ..	**5.465**	**6.158**	**6.352**	**6.709**	**7.116**	**7.942**	**8.217**	**8.457**

[1] Excludes components that have been classified in the categories of Group E.

Table 2. STANDARD PRESENTATION, 1994–2001

(Millions of U.S. dollars)

	Code	1994	1995	1996	1997	1998	1999	2000	2001
CURRENT ACCOUNT	4 993 . .	**125.4**	**39.4**	**79.6**	**–40.3**	**–332.6**	**–465.2**	**14.6**	**–476.9**
A. GOODS	4 100 . .	–553.7	–669.8	–585.3	–413.4	–799.4	–919.8	–645.4	–1,192.8
Credit	2 100 . .	**372.0**	**423.0**	**417.5**	**588.3**	**560.3**	**467.4**	**486.0**	**433.3**
General merchandise: exports f.o.b.	2 110 . .	372.0	423.0	417.5	588.3	560.3	467.4	486.0	433.3
Goods for processing: exports f.o.b.	2 150 . .	. . .	. . .	. . .	. . .	. . .	. . .	. . .	. . .
Repairs on goods	2 160 . .	. . .	. . .	. . .	. . .	. . .	. . .	. . .	. . .
Goods procured in ports by carriers	2 170 . .	. . .	. . .	. . .	. . .	. . .	. . .	. . .	. . .
Nonmonetary gold	2 180 . .	. . .	. . .	. . .	. . .	. . .	. . .	. . .	. . .
Debit	3 100 . .	**–925.7**	**–1,092.8**	**–1,002.8**	**–1,001.6**	**–1,359.8**	**–1,387.2**	**–1,131.4**	**–1,626.1**
General merchandise: imports f.o.b.	3 110 . .	–925.7	–1,092.8	–1,002.8	–1,001.6	–1,359.8	–1,387.2	–1,131.4	–1,626.1
Goods for processing: imports f.o.b.	3 150 . .	. . .	. . .	. . .	. . .	. . .	. . .	. . .	. . .
Repairs on goods	3 160 . .	. . .	. . .	. . .	. . .	. . .	. . .	. . .	. . .
Goods procured in ports by carriers	3 170 . .	. . .	. . .	. . .	. . .	. . .	. . .	. . .	. . .
Nonmonetary gold	3 180 . .	. . .	. . .	. . .	. . .	. . .	. . .	. . .	. . .
B. SERVICES	4 200 . .	–15.8	–8.3	27.4	–3.5	–64.0	7.3	15.5	–2.7
Total credit	2 200 . .	*294.6*	*344.5*	*377.2*	*390.7*	*391.5*	*473.6*	*506.2*	*522.9*
Total debit	3 200 . .	*–310.4*	*–352.8*	*–349.8*	*–394.2*	*–455.6*	*–466.3*	*–490.7*	*–525.6*
Transportation services, credit	2 205 . .	**218.0**	**238.0**	**217.2**	**211.2**	**142.3**	**189.4**	**215.4**	**234.3**
Passenger	2 850 . .	*142.4*	*160.6*	*146.9*	*135.3*	*115.1*	*128.6*	*148.4*	*166.7*
Freight	2 851 . .	*57.2*	*57.0*	*52.4*	*58.6*	*6.9*	*40.6*	*37.8*	*35.4*
Other	2 852 . .	*18.4*	*20.4*	*17.9*	*17.3*	*20.3*	*20.2*	*29.2*	*32.2*
Sea transport, passenger	2 207 . .	. . .	. . .	. . .	. . .	. . .	. . .	. . .	. . .
Sea transport, freight	2 208 . .	18.3	17.6	16.9	15.9	14.4	15.5	11.8	8.0
Sea transport, other	2 209 . .	. . .	. . .	. . .	. . .	. . .	. . .	. . .	. . .
Air transport, passenger	2 211 . .	142.4	160.6	146.9	135.3	115.1	128.6	148.4	166.7
Air transport, freight	2 212 . .	38.9	39.4	35.5	42.8	–7.5	25.2	26.0	27.4
Air transport, other	2 213 . .	13.8	14.8	12.4	11.7	14.4	15.8	22.7	27.5
Other transport, passenger	2 215 . .	. . .	. . .	. . .	. . .	. . .	. . .	. . .	. . .
Other transport, freight	2 216 . .	. . .	. . .	. . .	. . .	. . .	. . .	. . .	. . .
Other transport, other	2 217 . .	4.6	5.6	5.5	5.6	5.9	4.3	6.4	4.8
Transportation services, debit	3 205 . .	**–189.8**	**–213.8**	**–209.2**	**–219.2**	**–260.0**	**–292.0**	**–285.9**	**–326.8**
Passenger	3 850 . .	*–5.3*	*–4.6*	*–4.9*	*–7.5*	*–4.8*	*–5.6*	*–5.8*	*–6.0*
Freight	3 851 . .	*–92.4*	*–109.1*	*–100.1*	*–100.0*	*–135.7*	*–138.5*	*–112.9*	*–162.3*
Other	3 852 . .	*–92.1*	*–100.1*	*–104.3*	*–111.8*	*–119.5*	*–147.9*	*–167.2*	*–158.6*
Sea transport, passenger	3 207 . .	. . .	. . .	. . .	. . .	. . .	. . .	. . .	. . .
Sea transport, freight	3 208 . .	. . .	. . .	. . .	. . .	. . .	. . .	. . .	. . .
Sea transport, other	3 209 . .	–14.6	–10.9	–10.8	–10.0	–11.0	–20.2	–18.7	–13.2
Air transport, passenger	3 211 . .	–5.3	–4.6	–4.9	–7.5	–4.8	–5.6	–5.8	–6.0
Air transport, freight	3 212 . .	. . .	. . .	. . .	. . .	. . .	. . .	. . .	. . .
Air transport, other	3 213 . .	–74.5	–85.7	–90.3	–98.5	–104.1	–123.2	–144.8	–140.1
Other transport, passenger	3 215 . .	. . .	. . .	. . .	. . .	. . .	. . .	. . .	. . .
Other transport, freight	3 216 . .	. . .	. . .	. . .	. . .	. . .	. . .	. . .	. . .
Other transport, other	3 217 . .	–3.0	–3.5	–3.2	–3.2	–4.4	–4.5	–3.7	–5.3
Travel, credit	2 236 . .	**14.5**	**16.3**	**22.9**	**22.4**	**37.0**	**47.1**	**56.7**	**50.8**
Business travel	2 237 . .	. . .	. . .	4.7	1.4	9.6	10.5	1.0	.9
Personal travel	2 240 . .	. . .	. . .	18.2	21.1	27.5	36.5	55.7	49.8
Travel, debit	3 236 . .	**–15.2**	**–25.3**	**–24.8**	**–39.7**	**–45.7**	**–51.4**	**–73.8**	**–43.8**
Business travel	3 237 . .	. . .	. . .	–16.1	–28.9	–24.5	–28.5	–27.6	–27.5
Personal travel	3 240 . .	. . .	. . .	–8.8	–10.8	–21.3	–22.8	–46.2	–16.3
Other services, credit	2 200 BA	**62.1**	**90.2**	**137.1**	**157.0**	**212.2**	**237.1**	**234.1**	**237.8**
Communications	2 245 . .	18.5	25.6	25.6	24.7	37.3	32.0	17.7	15.7
Construction	2 249 . .	2.1	18.6	10.1	8.5	8.0	6.0	10.4	1.5
Insurance	2 253 . .	2.5	2.1	2.9	1.1	5.8	3.4	1.1	1.9
Financial	2 260 . .	2.5	2.6	3.6	3.6	2.6	9.6	3.6	4.1
Computer and information	2 262 . .	. . .	.1	. . .	.1	.3	.3	.4	2.0
Royalties and licence fees	2 266 . .	. . .	. . .	. . .	. . .	. . .	. . .	. . .	. . .
Other business services	2 268 . .	7.7	6.4	38.7	46.3	72.7	101.9	80.1	79.0
Personal, cultural, and recreational	2 287 . .	. . .	. . .	.1	. . .	2.0	2.2	1.5	1.3
Government, n.i.e.	2 291 . .	28.8	34.9	56.0	72.7	83.5	81.8	119.3	132.1
Other services, debit	3 200 BA	**–105.4**	**–113.8**	**–115.7**	**–135.3**	**–149.9**	**–122.9**	**–131.0**	**–154.9**
Communications	3 245 . .	–6.5	–6.9	–6.8	–5.8	–5.2	–5.2	–7.0	–7.2
Construction	3 249 . .	–3.4	–2.8	–1.3	–11.5	–33.2	–8.7	–10.3	–29.6
Insurance	3 253 . .	–22.9	–24.0	–18.9	–20.3	–23.5	–23.4	–16.3	–29.4
Financial	3 260 . .	–.4	–.9	–.3	–.4	–.5	–1.1	–.8	–.3
Computer and information	3 262 . .	–1.0	–.6	–1.4	–2.4	–2.8	–1.7	–1.6	–1.2
Royalties and licence fees	3 266 . .	. . .	. . .	. . .	. . .	. . .	–.1	–.3	–.1
Other business services	3 268 . .	–60.2	–62.9	–67.8	–77.6	–71.2	–79.2	–83.6	–77.6
Personal, cultural, and recreational	3 287 . .	. . .	. . .	–.2	–.2	–.1	–.1	–.2	–.6
Government, n.i.e.	3 291 . .	–11.0	–15.7	–18.9	–17.0	–13.4	–3.7	–10.7	–9.0

Table 2 (Continued). STANDARD PRESENTATION, 1994–2001

(Millions of U.S. dollars)

	Code	1994	1995	1996	1997	1998	1999	2000	2001
C. INCOME	4 300 . .	–31.6	–18.8	–33.9	–41.3	–43.2	–33.8	–35.8	–32.0
Total credit	2 300 . .	*42.9*	*68.4*	*41.2*	*24.2*	*21.0*	*16.6*	*16.2*	*16.3*
Total debit	3 300 . .	*–74.6*	*–87.1*	*–75.2*	*–65.5*	*–64.2*	*–50.4*	*–52.0*	*–48.3*
Compensation of employees, credit	2 310 . .	**24.6**	**27.4**	**6.0**	**. . .**	**. . .**	**. . .**	**. . .**	**. . .**
Compensation of employees, debit	3 310 . .	**–.3**	**–.2**	**–.2**	**. . .**	**–.1**	**. . .**	**. . .**	**. . .**
Investment income, credit	2 320 . .	**18.3**	**41.0**	**35.3**	**24.2**	**21.0**	**16.6**	**16.2**	**16.3**
Direct investment income	2 330 . .	. . .	. . .	. . .	. . .	. . .	1.1	. . .	. . .
Dividends and distributed branch profits	2 332 . .	. . .	. . .	. . .	. . .	. . .	1.1	. . .	. . .
Reinvested earnings and undistributed branch profits	2 333 . .	. . .	. . .	. . .	. . .	. . .	. . .	. . .	. . .
Income on debt (interest)	2 334 . .	. . .	. . .	. . .	. . .	. . .	. . .	. . .	. . .
Portfolio investment income	2 339 . .	. . .	. . .	. . .	. . .	. . .	. . .	. . .	. . .
Income on equity	2 340 . .	. . .	. . .	. . .	. . .	. . .	. . .	. . .	. . .
Income on bonds and notes	2 350 . .	. . .	. . .	. . .	. . .	. . .	. . .	. . .	. . .
Income on money market instruments	2 360 . .	. . .	. . .	. . .	. . .	. . .	. . .	. . .	. . .
Other investment income	2 370 . .	18.3	41.0	35.3	24.2	21.0	15.6	16.2	16.2
Investment income, debit	3 320 . .	**–74.2**	**–86.9**	**–75.0**	**–65.5**	**–64.1**	**–50.4**	**–52.0**	**–48.3**
Direct investment income	3 330 . .	. . .	. . .	–1.9	–7.2	–6.6	–2.0	–9.3	–11.7
Dividends and distributed branch profits	3 332 . .	. . .	. . .	–1.9	–7.2	–6.6	–2.0	–9.3	–11.7
Reinvested earnings and undistributed branch profits	3 333 . .	. . .	. . .	. . .	. . .	. . .	. . .	. . .	. . .
Income on debt (interest)	3 334 . .	. . .	. . .	. . .	. . .	. . .	. . .	. . .	. . .
Portfolio investment income	3 339 . .	. . .	. . .	. . .	. . .	. . .	. . .	. . .	. . .
Income on equity	3 340 . .	. . .	. . .	. . .	. . .	. . .	. . .	. . .	. . .
Income on bonds and notes	3 350 . .	. . .	. . .	. . .	. . .	. . .	. . .	. . .	. . .
Income on money market instruments	3 360 . .	. . .	. . .	. . .	. . .	. . .	. . .	. . .	. . .
Other investment income	3 370 . .	–74.2	–86.9	–73.1	–58.4	–57.5	–48.5	–42.7	–36.6
D. CURRENT TRANSFERS	4 379 . .	726.6	736.2	671.4	417.9	574.1	481.1	680.3	750.6
Credit	2 379 . .	**728.5**	**737.3**	**679.0**	**425.5**	**589.8**	**500.7**	**697.9**	**774.6**
General government	2 380 . .	422.8	379.9	373.4	161.7	264.9	188.5	257.8	456.2
Other sectors	2 390 . .	305.7	357.4	305.6	263.8	324.9	312.2	440.1	318.4
Workers' remittances	2 391 . .	. . .	. . .	10.1	9.2	27.3	33.7	53.2	18.3
Other current transfers	2 392 . .	305.7	357.4	295.5	254.6	297.5	278.5	387.0	300.1
Debit	3 379 . .	**–2.0**	**–1.1**	**–7.5**	**–7.6**	**–15.7**	**–19.7**	**–17.6**	**–24.0**
General government	3 380 . .	–1.8	–.8	–4.4	–5.4	–9.9	–13.5	–3.6	–8.6
Other sectors	3 390 . .	–.2	–.2	–3.1	–2.2	–5.8	–6.1	–14.1	–15.5
Workers' remittances	3 391 . .	. . .	. . .	–.9	–5.2	–4.1	–3.4	–12.6	–14.0
Other current transfers	3 392 . .	–.2	–.2	–2.3	3.0	–1.7	–2.7	–1.5	–1.4
CAPITAL AND FINANCIAL ACCOUNT	4 996 . .	**–194.9**	**83.0**	**–33.8**	**669.8**	**340.5**	**58.1**	**218.4**	**425.3**
CAPITAL ACCOUNT	4 994 . .	**16.2**	**11.4**	**2.6**	**.8**	**5.1**	**7.3**	**. . .**	**. . .**
Total credit	2 994 . .	*16.2*	*11.4*	*2.6*	*.8*	*5.1*	*7.3*	. . .	. . .
Total debit	3 994 . .	. . .	. . .	. . .	. . .	. . .	. . .	. . .	. . .
Capital transfers, credit	2 400 . .	**16.2**	**11.4**	**2.6**	**.8**	**5.1**	**7.3**	**. . .**	**. . .**
General government	2 401 . .	12.5	8.8	1.7	.8	3.7	5.4	. . .	. . .
Debt forgiveness	2 402 . .	12.5	8.8	1.7	.8	3.7	5.4	. . .	. . .
Other capital transfers	2 410 . .	. . .	. . .	. . .	. . .	. . .	. . .	. . .	. . .
Other sectors	2 430 . .	3.7	2.6	.9	. . .	1.4	1.8	. . .	. . .
Migrants' transfers	2 431 . .	. . .	. . .	. . .	. . .	. . .	. . .	. . .	. . .
Debt forgiveness	2 432 . .	3.7	2.6	.9	. . .	. . .	. . .	. . .	. . .
Other capital transfers	2 440 . .	. . .	. . .	. . .	. . .	. . .	. . .	. . .	. . .
Capital transfers, debit	3 400 . .	**. . .**	**. . .**	**. . .**	**. . .**	**. . .**	**. . .**	**. . .**	**. . .**
General government	3 401 . .	. . .	. . .	. . .	. . .	. . .	. . .	. . .	. . .
Debt forgiveness	3 402 . .	. . .	. . .	. . .	. . .	. . .	. . .	. . .	. . .
Other capital transfers	3 410 . .	. . .	. . .	. . .	. . .	. . .	. . .	. . .	. . .
Other sectors	3 430 . .	. . .	. . .	. . .	. . .	. . .	. . .	. . .	. . .
Migrants' transfers	3 431 . .	. . .	. . .	. . .	. . .	. . .	. . .	. . .	. . .
Debt forgiveness	3 432 . .	. . .	. . .	. . .	. . .	. . .	. . .	. . .	. . .
Other capital transfers	3 440 . .	. . .	. . .	. . .	. . .	. . .	. . .	. . .	. . .
Nonproduced nonfinancial assets, credit	2 480 . .	**. . .**	**. . .**	**. . .**	**. . .**	**. . .**	**. . .**	**. . .**	**. . .**
Nonproduced nonfinancial assets, debit	3 480 . .	**. . .**	**. . .**	**. . .**	**. . .**	**. . .**	**. . .**	**. . .**	**. . .**

Table 2 (Continued). STANDARD PRESENTATION, 1994–2001
(Millions of U.S. dollars)

	Code		1994	1995	1996	1997	1998	1999	2000	2001
FINANCIAL ACCOUNT	4 995	. .	**–211.0**	**71.6**	**–36.4**	**669.0**	**335.5**	**50.8**	**218.4**	**425.3**
A. DIRECT INVESTMENT	4 500	. .	. . .	. . .	. . .	. . .	. . .	. . .	. . .	. . .
Direct investment abroad	4 505	. .	. . .	. . .	. . .	. . .	. . .	. . .	. . .	. . .
Equity capital	4 510	. .	. . .	. . .	. . .	. . .	. . .	. . .	. . .	. . .
Claims on affiliated enterprises	4 515	. .	. . .	. . .	. . .	. . .	. . .	. . .	. . .	. . .
Liabilities to affiliated enterprises	4 520	. .	. . .	. . .	. . .	. . .	. . .	. . .	. . .	. . .
Reinvested earnings	4 525	. .	. . .	. . .	. . .	. . .	. . .	. . .	. . .	. . .
Other capital	4 530	. .	. . .	. . .	. . .	. . .	. . .	. . .	. . .	. . .
Claims on affiliated enterprises	4 535	. .	. . .	. . .	. . .	. . .	. . .	. . .	. . .	. . .
Liabilities to affiliated enterprises	4 540	. .	. . .	. . .	. . .	. . .	. . .	. . .	. . .	. . .
Direct investment in Ethiopia	4 555	. .	. . .	. . .	. . .	. . .	. . .	. . .	. . .	. . .
Equity capital	4 560	. .	. . .	. . .	. . .	. . .	. . .	. . .	. . .	. . .
Claims on direct investors	4 565	. .	. . .	. . .	. . .	. . .	. . .	. . .	. . .	. . .
Liabilities to direct investors	4 570	. .	. . .	. . .	. . .	. . .	. . .	. . .	. . .	. . .
Reinvested earnings	4 575	. .	. . .	. . .	. . .	. . .	. . .	. . .	. . .	. . .
Other capital	4 580	. .	. . .	. . .	. . .	. . .	. . .	. . .	. . .	. . .
Claims on direct investors	4 585	. .	. . .	. . .	. . .	. . .	. . .	. . .	. . .	. . .
Liabilities to direct investors	4 590	. .	. . .	. . .	. . .	. . .	. . .	. . .	. . .	. . .
B. PORTFOLIO INVESTMENT	4 600	. .	. . .	. . .	. . .	. . .	. . .	. . .	. . .	. . .
Assets	4 602	. .	. . .	. . .	. . .	. . .	. . .	. . .	. . .	. . .
Equity securities	4 610	. .	. . .	. . .	. . .	. . .	. . .	. . .	. . .	. . .
Monetary authorities	4 611	. .	. . .	. . .	. . .	. . .	. . .	. . .	. . .	. . .
General government	4 612	. .	. . .	. . .	. . .	. . .	. . .	. . .	. . .	. . .
Banks	4 613	. .	. . .	. . .	. . .	. . .	. . .	. . .	. . .	. . .
Other sectors	4 614	. .	. . .	. . .	. . .	. . .	. . .	. . .	. . .	. . .
Debt securities	4 619	. .	. . .	. . .	. . .	. . .	. . .	. . .	. . .	. . .
Bonds and notes	4 620	. .	. . .	. . .	. . .	. . .	. . .	. . .	. . .	. . .
Monetary authorities	4 621	. .	. . .	. . .	. . .	. . .	. . .	. . .	. . .	. . .
General government	4 622	. .	. . .	. . .	. . .	. . .	. . .	. . .	. . .	. . .
Banks	4 623	. .	. . .	. . .	. . .	. . .	. . .	. . .	. . .	. . .
Other sectors	4 624	. .	. . .	. . .	. . .	. . .	. . .	. . .	. . .	. . .
Money market instruments	4 630	. .	. . .	. . .	. . .	. . .	. . .	. . .	. . .	. . .
Monetary authorities	4 631	. .	. . .	. . .	. . .	. . .	. . .	. . .	. . .	. . .
General government	4 632	. .	. . .	. . .	. . .	. . .	. . .	. . .	. . .	. . .
Banks	4 633	. .	. . .	. . .	. . .	. . .	. . .	. . .	. . .	. . .
Other sectors	4 634	. .	. . .	. . .	. . .	. . .	. . .	. . .	. . .	. . .
Liabilities	4 652	. .	. . .	. . .	. . .	. . .	. . .	. . .	. . .	. . .
Equity securities	4 660	. .	. . .	. . .	. . .	. . .	. . .	. . .	. . .	. . .
Banks	4 663	. .	. . .	. . .	. . .	. . .	. . .	. . .	. . .	. . .
Other sectors	4 664	. .	. . .	. . .	. . .	. . .	. . .	. . .	. . .	. . .
Debt securities	4 669	. .	. . .	. . .	. . .	. . .	. . .	. . .	. . .	. . .
Bonds and notes	4 670	. .	. . .	. . .	. . .	. . .	. . .	. . .	. . .	. . .
Monetary authorities	4 671	. .	. . .	. . .	. . .	. . .	. . .	. . .	. . .	. . .
General government	4 672	. .	. . .	. . .	. . .	. . .	. . .	. . .	. . .	. . .
Banks	4 673	. .	. . .	. . .	. . .	. . .	. . .	. . .	. . .	. . .
Other sectors	4 674	. .	. . .	. . .	. . .	. . .	. . .	. . .	. . .	. . .
Money market instruments	4 680	. .	. . .	. . .	. . .	. . .	. . .	. . .	. . .	. . .
Monetary authorities	4 681	. .	. . .	. . .	. . .	. . .	. . .	. . .	. . .	. . .
General government	4 682	. .	. . .	. . .	. . .	. . .	. . .	. . .	. . .	. . .
Banks	4 683	. .	. . .	. . .	. . .	. . .	. . .	. . .	. . .	. . .
Other sectors	4 684	. .	. . .	. . .	. . .	. . .	. . .	. . .	. . .	. . .
C. FINANCIAL DERIVATIVES	4 910	. .	. . .	. . .	. . .	. . .	. . .	. . .	. . .	. . .
Monetary authorities	4 911	. .	. . .	. . .	. . .	. . .	. . .	. . .	. . .	. . .
General government	4 912	. .	. . .	. . .	. . .	. . .	. . .	. . .	. . .	. . .
Banks	4 913	. .	. . .	. . .	. . .	. . .	. . .	. . .	. . .	. . .
Other sectors	4 914	. .	. . .	. . .	. . .	. . .	. . .	. . .	. . .	. . .
Assets	4 900	. .	. . .	. . .	. . .	. . .	. . .	. . .	. . .	. . .
Monetary authorities	4 901	. .	. . .	. . .	. . .	. . .	. . .	. . .	. . .	. . .
General government	4 902	. .	. . .	. . .	. . .	. . .	. . .	. . .	. . .	. . .
Banks	4 903	. .	. . .	. . .	. . .	. . .	. . .	. . .	. . .	. . .
Other sectors	4 904	. .	. . .	. . .	. . .	. . .	. . .	. . .	. . .	. . .
Liabilities	4 905	. .	. . .	. . .	. . .	. . .	. . .	. . .	. . .	. . .
Monetary authorities	4 906	. .	. . .	. . .	. . .	. . .	. . .	. . .	. . .	. . .
General government	4 907	. .	. . .	. . .	. . .	. . .	. . .	. . .	. . .	. . .
Banks	4 908	. .	. . .	. . .	. . .	. . .	. . .	. . .	. . .	. . .
Other sectors	4 909	. .	. . .	. . .	. . .	. . .	. . .	. . .	. . .	. . .

Table 2 (Concluded). STANDARD PRESENTATION, 1994–2001
(Millions of U.S. dollars)

	Code	1994	1995	1996	1997	1998	1999	2000	2001
D. OTHER INVESTMENT	4 700 . .	–86.4	276.4	–56.5	476.9	156.5	100.5	302.9	457.3
Assets	4 703 . .	**–318.5**	**57.7**	**–306.8**	**318.5**	**59.8**	**–85.3**	**116.1**	**60.5**
Trade credits	4 706 . .	105.2	–16.3	–36.3	–27.0	33.9	–20.5	90.6	39.5
General government	4 707 . .	. . .	. . .	. . .	. . .	. . .	. . .	. . .	. . .
of which: Short-term	4 709 . .	. . .	. . .	. . .	. . .	. . .	. . .	. . .	. . .
Other sectors	4 710 . .	105.2	–16.3	–36.3	–27.0	33.9	–20.5	90.6	39.5
of which: Short-term	4 712 . .	*105.2*	*–16.3*	*–36.3*	*–27.0*	*33.9*	*–20.5*	*90.6*	*39.5*
Loans	4 714 . .	. . .	. . .	. . .	. . .	. . .	. . .	. . .	. . .
Monetary authorities	4 715 . .	. . .	. . .	. . .	. . .	. . .	. . .	. . .	. . .
of which: Short-term	4 718 . .	. . .	. . .	. . .	. . .	. . .	. . .	. . .	. . .
General government	4 719 . .	. . .	. . .	. . .	. . .	. . .	. . .	. . .	. . .
of which: Short-term	4 721 . .	. . .	. . .	. . .	. . .	. . .	. . .	. . .	. . .
Banks	4 722 . .	. . .	. . .	. . .	. . .	. . .	. . .	. . .	. . .
of which: Short-term	4 724 . .	. . .	. . .	. . .	. . .	. . .	. . .	. . .	. . .
Other sectors	4 725 . .	. . .	. . .	. . .	. . .	. . .	. . .	. . .	. . .
of which: Short-term	4 727 . .	. . .	. . .	. . .	. . .	. . .	. . .	. . .	. . .
Currency and deposits	4 730 . .	–423.7	74.0	–270.4	345.5	25.9	–64.9	25.4	20.9
Monetary authorities	4 731 . .	. . .	. . .	. . .	. . .	. . .	. . .	. . .	. . .
General government	4 732 . .	. . .	. . .	. . .	. . .	. . .	. . .	. . .	. . .
Banks	4 733 . .	–358.5	44.7	–283.0	350.7	26.3	–69.6	23.2	29.7
Other sectors	4 734 . .	–65.2	29.4	12.6	–5.2	–.4	4.7	2.2	–8.8
Other assets	4 736 . .	. . .	. . .	. . .	. . .	. . .	. . .	. . .	. . .
Monetary authorities	4 737 . .	. . .	. . .	. . .	. . .	. . .	. . .	. . .	. . .
of which: Short-term	4 739 . .	. . .	. . .	. . .	. . .	. . .	. . .	. . .	. . .
General government	4 740 . .	. . .	. . .	. . .	. . .	. . .	. . .	. . .	. . .
of which: Short-term	4 742 . .	. . .	. . .	. . .	. . .	. . .	. . .	. . .	. . .
Banks	4 743 . .	. . .	. . .	. . .	. . .	. . .	. . .	. . .	. . .
of which: Short-term	4 745 . .	. . .	. . .	. . .	. . .	. . .	. . .	. . .	. . .
Other sectors	4 746 . .	. . .	. . .	. . .	. . .	. . .	. . .	. . .	. . .
of which: Short-term	4 748 . .	. . .	. . .	. . .	. . .	. . .	. . .	. . .	. . .
Liabilities	4 753 . .	**232.1**	**218.6**	**250.3**	**158.4**	**96.7**	**185.9**	**186.8**	**396.8**
Trade credits	4 756 . .	.9	2.1	–10.9	.8	3.2	–1.4	29.4	6.5
General government	4 757 . .	. . .	. . .	. . .	. . .	. . .	. . .	. . .	. . .
of which: Short-term	4 759 . .	. . .	. . .	. . .	. . .	. . .	. . .	. . .	. . .
Other sectors	4 760 . .	.9	2.1	–10.9	.8	3.2	–1.4	29.4	6.5
of which: Short-term	4 762 . .	*.9*	*2.1*	*–10.9*	*.8*	*3.2*	*–1.4*	*29.4*	*6.5*
Loans	4 764 . .	99.9	43.1	–61.8	50.7	63.3	94.4	12.1	560.5
Monetary authorities	4 765 . .	20.8	. . .	21.2	. . .	16.9	–9.7	–13.0	31.8
of which: Use of Fund credit and loans from the Fund	4 766 . .	*20.8*	. . .	*21.2*	. . .	*16.9*	*–9.7*	*–13.0*	*31.8*
of which: Short-term	4 768 . .	. . .	. . .	. . .	. . .	. . .	. . .	. . .	. . .
General government	4 769 . .	107.5	74.0	124.3	52.2	42.8	126.4	16.8	497.0
of which: Short-term	4 771 . .	. . .	. . .	. . .	. . .	. . .	. . .	. . .	. . .
Banks	4 772 . .	. . .	. . .	. . .	. . .	. . .	. . .	. . .	. . .
of which: Short-term	4 774 . .	. . .	. . .	. . .	. . .	. . .	. . .	. . .	. . .
Other sectors	4 775 . .	–28.4	–30.9	–207.4	–1.5	3.7	–22.3	8.3	31.7
of which: Short-term	4 777 . .	*27.9*	*19.2*	*–1.4*	*10.3*	*6.1*	*–14.1*	*16.8*	*36.1*
Currency and deposits	4 780 . .	80.7	91.6	197.7	14.9	2.0	62.6	51.1	–125.1
Monetary authorities	4 781 . .	25.4	.4	–7.8	–.1	–.4	.4	47.0	–54.6
General government	4 782 . .	. . .	. . .	. . .	. . .	. . .	. . .	. . .	. . .
Banks	4 783 . .	55.3	91.2	205.6	15.0	2.4	62.2	4.1	–70.5
Other sectors	4 784 . .	. . .	. . .	. . .	. . .	. . .	. . .	. . .	. . .
Other liabilities	4 786 . .	50.6	81.8	125.3	92.0	28.1	30.2	94.2	–45.1
Monetary authorities	4 787 . .	. . .	. . .	. . .	. . .	. . .	. . .	. . .	. . .
of which: Short-term	4 789 . .	. . .	. . .	. . .	. . .	. . .	. . .	. . .	. . .
General government	4 790 . .	41.6	67.6	103.3	80.6	29.7	30.9	92.4	–40.5
of which: Short-term	4 792 . .	*41.6*	*67.6*	*103.3*	*80.6*	*29.7*	*30.9*	*92.4*	*–40.5*
Banks	4 793 . .	. . .	. . .	. . .	. . .	. . .	. . .	. . .	. . .
of which: Short-term	4 795 . .	. . .	. . .	. . .	. . .	. . .	. . .	. . .	. . .
Other sectors	4 796 . .	9.0	14.2	22.1	11.4	–1.6	–.7	1.8	–4.7
of which: Short-term	4 798 . .	*9.0*	*14.2*	*22.1*	*11.4*	*–1.6*	*–.7*	*1.8*	*–4.7*
E. RESERVE ASSETS	4 802 . .	–124.7	–204.8	20.0	192.1	179.0	–49.7	–84.5	–32.0
Monetary gold	4 812 . .	. . .	. . .	. . .	. . .	. . .	. . .	. . .	. . .
Special drawing rights	4 811 . .	–.1	.2	.2	–.1	. . .	. . .	.1	–.2
Reserve position in the Fund	4 810 . .	. . .	. . .	. . .	. . .	. . .	. . .	. . .	. . .
Foreign exchange	4 803 . .	–124.6	–204.9	19.8	192.3	178.9	–49.7	–84.5	–31.8
Other claims	4 813 . .	. . .	. . .	. . .	. . .	. . .	. . .	. . .	. . .
NET ERRORS AND OMISSIONS	4 998 . .	**69.5**	**–122.4**	**–45.8**	**–629.5**	**–7.9**	**407.2**	**–233.0**	**51.6**

Part 3 of the *Yearbook* contains descriptions of the methodologies, compilation practices, and sources used to compile these data.

Table 1. ANALYTIC PRESENTATION, 1994–2001
(Billions of U.S. dollars)

	Code		1994	1995	1996	1997	1998	1999	2000	2001
A. Current Account [1]	4 993	Z.	...	...	...	...	...	**–19.31**	**–54.91**	**–2.15**
Goods: exports f.o.b	2 100	..	...	...	...	...	...	870.74	908.17	929.28
Goods: imports f.o.b	3 100	..	...	...	...	...	...	–790.31	–875.64	–858.74
Balance on Goods	4 100	..	...	...	...	...	...	*80.43*	*32.53*	*70.53*
Services: credit	2 200	..	...	...	...	...	...	260.11	257.10	284.86
Services: debit	3 200	..	...	...	...	...	...	–272.90	–272.00	–282.03
Balance on Goods and Services	4 991	..	...	...	...	...	...	*67.65*	*17.63*	*73.36*
Income: credit	2 300	..	...	...	...	...	...	220.56	242.91	255.49
Income: debit	3 300	..	...	...	...	...	...	–258.54	–267.52	–288.28
Balance on Goods, Services, and Income	4 992	..	...	...	...	...	...	*29.67*	*–6.99*	*40.56*
Current transfers: credit	2 379	Z.	...	...	...	...	...	69.67	62.77	67.32
Current transfers: debit	3 379	..	...	...	...	...	...	–118.64	–110.69	–110.03
B. Capital Account [1]	4 994	Z.	...	...	...	...	...	**13.65**	**8.90**	**7.64**
Capital account: credit	2 994	Z.	...	...	...	...	...	20.32	16.82	14.71
Capital account: debit	3 994	..	...	...	...	...	...	–6.67	–7.92	–7.07
Total, Groups A Plus B	4 981	..	...	...	...	...	...	*–5.66*	*–46.01*	*5.49*
C. Financial Account [1]	4 995	W.	...	...	...	...	...	**.49**	**73.00**	**–79.51**
Direct investment abroad	4 505	..	...	...	...	...	...	–333.07	–351.28	–201.65
Direct investment in the Euro Area	4 555	Z.	...	...	...	...	...	208.14	378.55	109.36
Portfolio investment assets	4 602	..	...	...	...	...	...	–331.22	–385.31	–242.25
Equity securities	4 610	..	...	...	...	...	...	–165.35	–269.88	–86.68
Debt securities	4 619	..	...	...	...	...	...	–165.86	–115.43	–155.57
Portfolio investment liabilities	4 652	Z.	...	...	...	...	...	279.18	270.00	272.97
Equity securities	4 660	..	...	...	...	...	...	96.36	32.99	213.83
Debt securities	4 669	Z.	...	...	...	...	...	182.83	237.00	59.14
Financial derivatives	4 910	..	...	...	...	...	...	4.72	–.83	–18.49
Financial derivatives assets	4 900	..	...	...	...	...	...	...	...	...
Financial derivatives liabilities	4 905	..	...	...	...	...	...	4.72	–.83	–18.49
Other investment assets	4 703	..	...	...	...	...	...	–35.51	–166.71	–219.20
Monetary authorities	4 701	..	...	...	...	...	...	–2.20	–.98	.56
General government	4 704	..	...	...	...	...	...	3.56	–2.77	2.98
Banks	4 705	..	...	...	...	...	...	19.67	–119.34	–202.19
Other sectors	4 728	..	...	...	...	...	...	–56.53	–43.62	–20.55
Other investment liabilities	4 753	W.	...	...	...	...	...	208.24	328.59	219.75
Monetary authorities	4 753	WA	...	...	...	...	...	7.26	.54	3.82
General government	4 753	ZB	...	...	...	...	...	–14.03	.36	–1.38
Banks	4 753	ZC	...	...	...	...	...	174.14	273.44	213.82
Other sectors	4 753	ZD	...	...	...	...	...	40.87	54.24	3.50
Total, Groups A Through C	4 983	..	...	...	...	...	...	*–5.17*	*27.00*	*–74.02*
D. Net Errors and Omissions	4 998	..	...	...	...	...	...	**–6.41**	**–43.14**	**57.13**
Total, Groups A Through D	4 984	..	...	...	...	...	...	*–11.58*	*–16.14*	*–16.89*
E. Reserves and Related Items	4 802	A.	...	...	...	...	...	**11.58**	**16.14**	**16.89**
Reserve assets	4 802	..	...	...	...	...	...	11.58	16.14	16.89
Use of Fund credit and loans	4 766	..	...	...	...	...	...	...	...	...
Exceptional financing	4 920	..	...	...	...	...	...	...	...	...
Conversion rates: euros per U.S. dollar	0 103	..	...	...	...	...	...	**.9386**	**1.0854**	**1.1175**

[1] Excludes components that have been classified in the categories of Group E.

Table 2. STANDARD PRESENTATION, 1994–2001

(Billions of U.S. dollars)

	Code	1994	1995	1996	1997	1998	1999	2000	2001
CURRENT ACCOUNT	4 993 . .	...	...	...	...	...	**–19.31**	**–54.91**	**–2.15**
A. GOODS	4 100 . .	...	...	...	...	...	80.43	32.53	70.53
Credit	2 100 . .	...	...	...	...	...	**870.74**	**908.17**	**929.28**
General merchandise: exports f.o.b.	2 110 . .	...	...	...	...	...	...	...	...
Goods for processing: exports f.o.b.	2 150 . .	...	...	...	...	...	...	...	...
Repairs on goods	2 160 . .	...	...	...	...	...	...	...	...
Goods procured in ports by carriers	2 170 . .	...	...	...	...	...	...	...	...
Nonmonetary gold	2 180 . .	...	...	...	...	...	...	...	...
Debit	3 100 . .	...	...	...	...	...	**–790.31**	**–875.64**	**–858.74**
General merchandise: imports f.o.b.	3 110 . .	...	...	...	...	...	...	...	...
Goods for processing: imports f.o.b.	3 150 . .	...	...	...	...	...	...	...	...
Repairs on goods	3 160 . .	...	...	...	...	...	...	...	...
Goods procured in ports by carriers	3 170 . .	...	...	...	...	...	...	...	...
Nonmonetary gold	3 180 . .	...	...	...	...	...	...	...	...
B. SERVICES	4 200 . .	...	...	...	...	...	–12.79	–14.90	2.83
Total credit	2 200 . .	...	...	...	...	...	*260.11*	*257.10*	*284.86*
Total debit	3 200 . .	...	...	...	...	...	*–272.90*	*–272.00*	*–282.03*
Transportation services, credit	2 205 . .	...	...	...	...	...	...	...	...
Passenger	2 850 . .	...	...	...	...	...	...	...	...
Freight	2 851 . .	...	...	...	...	...	...	...	...
Other	2 852 . .	...	...	...	...	...	...	...	...
Sea transport, passenger	2 207 . .	...	...	...	...	...	...	...	...
Sea transport, freight	2 208 . .	...	...	...	...	...	...	...	...
Sea transport, other	2 209 . .	...	...	...	...	...	...	...	...
Air transport, passenger	2 211 . .	...	...	...	...	...	...	...	...
Air transport, freight	2 212 . .	...	...	...	...	...	...	...	...
Air transport, other	2 213 . .	...	...	...	...	...	...	...	...
Other transport, passenger	2 215 . .	...	...	...	...	...	...	...	...
Other transport, freight	2 216 . .	...	...	...	...	...	...	...	...
Other transport, other	2 217 . .	...	...	...	...	...	...	...	...
Transportation services, debit	3 205 . .	...	...	...	...	...	...	...	...
Passenger	3 850 . .	...	...	...	...	...	...	...	...
Freight	3 851 . .	...	...	...	...	...	...	...	...
Other	3 852 . .	...	...	...	...	...	...	...	...
Sea transport, passenger	3 207 . .	...	...	...	...	...	...	...	...
Sea transport, freight	3 208 . .	...	...	...	...	...	...	...	...
Sea transport, other	3 209 . .	...	...	...	...	...	...	...	...
Air transport, passenger	3 211 . .	...	...	...	...	...	...	...	...
Air transport, freight	3 212 . .	...	...	...	...	...	...	...	...
Air transport, other	3 213 . .	...	...	...	...	...	...	...	...
Other transport, passenger	3 215 . .	...	...	...	...	...	...	...	...
Other transport, freight	3 216 . .	...	...	...	...	...	...	...	...
Other transport, other	3 217 . .	...	...	...	...	...	...	...	...
Travel, credit	2 236 . .	...	...	...	...	...	...	...	...
Business travel	2 237 . .	...	...	...	...	...	...	...	...
Personal travel	2 240 . .	...	...	...	...	...	...	...	...
Travel, debit	3 236 . .	...	...	...	...	...	...	...	...
Business travel	3 237 . .	...	...	...	...	...	...	...	...
Personal travel	3 240 . .	...	...	...	...	...	...	...	...
Other services, credit	2 200 BA	...	...	...	...	...	...	...	...
Communications	2 245 . .	...	...	...	...	...	...	...	...
Construction	2 249 . .	...	...	...	...	...	...	...	...
Insurance	2 253 . .	...	...	...	...	...	...	...	...
Financial	2 260 . .	...	...	...	...	...	...	...	...
Computer and information	2 262 . .	...	...	...	...	...	...	...	...
Royalties and licence fees	2 266 . .	...	...	...	...	...	...	...	...
Other business services	2 268 . .	...	...	...	...	...	...	...	...
Personal, cultural, and recreational	2 287 . .	...	...	...	...	...	...	...	...
Government, n.i.e.	2 291 . .	...	...	...	...	...	...	...	...
Other services, debit	3 200 BA	...	...	...	...	...	...	...	...
Communications	3 245 . .	...	...	...	...	...	...	...	...
Construction	3 249 . .	...	...	...	...	...	...	...	...
Insurance	3 253 . .	...	...	...	...	...	...	...	...
Financial	3 260 . .	...	...	...	...	...	...	...	...
Computer and information	3 262 . .	...	...	...	...	...	...	...	...
Royalties and licence fees	3 266 . .	...	...	...	...	...	...	...	...
Other business services	3 268 . .	...	...	...	...	...	...	...	...
Personal, cultural, and recreational	3 287 . .	...	...	...	...	...	...	...	...
Government, n.i.e.	3 291 . .	...	...	...	...	...	...	...	...

Table 2 (Continued). STANDARD PRESENTATION, 1994–2001
(Billions of U.S. dollars)

	Code	1994	1995	1996	1997	1998	1999	2000	2001
C. INCOME	4 300 . .	...	...	...	...	...	–37.98	–24.62	–32.80
Total credit	2 300 . .	...	...	...	...	...	*220.56*	*242.91*	*255.49*
Total debit	3 300 . .	...	...	...	...	...	*–258.54*	*–267.52*	*–288.28*
Compensation of employees, credit	2 310 . .	**...**	**...**	**...**	**...**	**...**	**13.38**	**12.16**	**12.10**
Compensation of employees, debit	3 310 . .	**...**	**...**	**...**	**...**	**...**	**–5.28**	**–5.01**	**–5.20**
Investment income, credit	2 320 . .	**...**	**...**	**...**	**...**	**...**	**207.17**	**230.75**	**243.39**
Direct investment income	2 330 . .	...	...	...	...	...	45.36	52.64	61.35
Dividends and distributed branch profits	2 332 . .	...	...	...	...	...	...	...	...
Reinvested earnings and undistributed branch profits	2 333 . .	...	...	...	...	...	...	...	...
Income on debt (interest)	2 334 . .	...	...	...	...	...	6.86	9.12	9.11
Portfolio investment income	2 339 . .	...	...	...	...	...	68.26	68.81	75.20
Income on equity	2 340 . .	...	...	...	...	...	10.03	13.06	14.66
Income on bonds and notes	2 350 . .	...	...	...	...	...	...	...	...
Income on money market instruments	2 360 . .	...	...	...	...	...	...	...	...
Other investment income	2 370 . .	...	...	...	...	...	93.56	109.29	106.84
Investment income, debit	3 320 . .	**...**	**...**	**...**	**...**	**...**	**–253.25**	**–262.52**	**–283.09**
Direct investment income	3 330 . .	...	...	...	...	...	–53.56	–54.47	–60.14
Dividends and distributed branch profits	3 332 . .	...	...	...	...	...	...	...	...
Reinvested earnings and undistributed branch profits	3 333 . .	...	...	...	...	...	...	...	...
Income on debt (interest)	3 334 . .	...	...	...	...	...	–4.48	–6.49	–7.43
Portfolio investment income	3 339 . .	...	...	...	...	...	–108.11	–98.58	–105.01
Income on equity	3 340 . .	...	...	...	...	...	–36.09	–28.23	–34.50
Income on bonds and notes	3 350 . .	...	...	...	...	...	...	...	...
Income on money market instruments	3 360 . .	...	...	...	...	...	...	...	...
Other investment income	3 370 . .	...	...	...	...	...	–91.58	–109.46	–117.93
D. CURRENT TRANSFERS	4 379 . .	...	...	...	...	...	–48.97	–47.92	–42.71
Credit	2 379 . .	**...**	**...**	**...**	**...**	**...**	**69.67**	**62.77**	**67.32**
General government	2 380 . .	...	...	...	...	...	...	...	...
Other sectors	2 390 . .	...	...	...	...	...	...	...	...
Workers' remittances	2 391 . .	...	...	...	...	...	...	...	...
Other current transfers	2 392 . .	...	...	...	...	...	...	...	...
Debit	3 379 . .	**...**	**...**	**...**	**...**	**...**	**–118.64**	**–110.69**	**–110.03**
General government	3 380 . .	...	...	...	...	...	...	...	...
Other sectors	3 390 . .	...	...	...	...	...	...	...	...
Workers' remittances	3 391 . .	...	...	...	...	...	...	...	...
Other current transfers	3 392 . .	...	...	...	...	...	...	...	...
CAPITAL AND FINANCIAL ACCOUNT	4 996 . .	**...**	**...**	**...**	**...**	**...**	**25.72**	**98.05**	**–54.99**
CAPITAL ACCOUNT	4 994 . .	**...**	**...**	**...**	**...**	**...**	**13.65**	**8.90**	**7.64**
Total credit	2 994 . .	...	...	...	...	...	*20.32*	*16.82*	*14.71*
Total debit	3 994 . .	...	...	...	...	...	*–6.67*	*–7.92*	*–7.07*
Capital transfers, credit	2 400 . .	**...**	**...**	**...**	**...**	**...**	**...**	**...**	**...**
General government	2 401 . .	...	...	...	...	...	...	...	...
Debt forgiveness	2 402 . .	...	...	...	...	...	...	...	...
Other capital transfers	2 410 . .	...	...	...	...	...	...	...	...
Other sectors	2 430 . .	...	...	...	...	...	...	...	...
Migrants' transfers	2 431 . .	...	...	...	...	...	...	...	...
Debt forgiveness	2 432 . .	...	...	...	...	...	...	...	...
Other capital transfers	2 440 . .	...	...	...	...	...	...	...	...
Capital transfers, debit	3 400 . .	**...**	**...**	**...**	**...**	**...**	**...**	**...**	**...**
General government	3 401 . .	...	...	...	...	...	...	...	...
Debt forgiveness	3 402 . .	...	...	...	...	...	...	...	...
Other capital transfers	3 410 . .	...	...	...	...	...	...	...	...
Other sectors	3 430 . .	...	...	...	...	...	...	...	...
Migrants' transfers	3 431 . .	...	...	...	...	...	...	...	...
Debt forgiveness	3 432 . .	...	...	...	...	...	...	...	...
Other capital transfers	3 440 . .	...	...	...	...	...	...	...	...
Nonproduced nonfinancial assets, credit	2 480 . .	**...**	**...**	**...**	**...**	**...**	**...**	**...**	**...**
Nonproduced nonfinancial assets, debit	3 480 . .	**...**	**...**	**...**	**...**	**...**	**...**	**...**	**...**

Table 2 (Continued). STANDARD PRESENTATION, 1994–2001

(Billions of U.S. dollars)

	Code	1994	1995	1996	1997	1998	1999	2000	2001
FINANCIAL ACCOUNT	4 995 . .	**...**	**...**	**...**	**...**	**...**	**12.06**	**89.15**	**–62.62**
A. DIRECT INVESTMENT	4 500 . .	...	...	...	...	...	–124.93	27.27	–92.29
Direct investment abroad	4 505 . .	**...**	**...**	**...**	**...**	**...**	**–333.07**	**–351.28**	**–201.65**
Equity capital	4 510 . .	...	...	...	...	...	...	...	...
Claims on affiliated enterprises	4 515 . .	...	...	...	...	...	...	...	...
Liabilities to affiliated enterprises	4 520 . .	...	...	...	...	...	...	...	...
Reinvested earnings	4 525 . .	...	...	...	...	...	...	...	...
Other capital	4 530 . .	...	...	...	...	...	...	...	...
Claims on affiliated enterprises	4 535 . .	...	...	...	...	...	...	...	...
Liabilities to affiliated enterprises	4 540 . .	...	...	...	...	...	...	...	...
Direct investment in the Euro Area	4 555 . .	**...**	**...**	**...**	**...**	**...**	**208.14**	**378.55**	**109.36**
Equity capital	4 560 . .	...	...	...	...	...	...	...	...
Claims on direct investors	4 565 . .	...	...	...	...	...	...	...	...
Liabilities to direct investors	4 570 . .	...	...	...	...	...	...	...	...
Reinvested earnings	4 575 . .	...	...	...	...	...	...	...	...
Other capital	4 580 . .	...	...	...	...	...	...	...	...
Claims on direct investors	4 585 . .	...	...	...	...	...	...	...	...
Liabilities to direct investors	4 590 . .	...	...	...	...	...	...	...	...
B. PORTFOLIO INVESTMENT	4 600 . .	...	...	...	...	...	–52.03	–115.31	30.72
Assets	4 602 . .	**...**	**...**	**...**	**...**	**...**	**–331.22**	**–385.31**	**–242.25**
Equity securities	4 610 . .	...	...	...	...	...	–165.35	–269.88	–86.68
Monetary authorities	4 611 . .	...	...	...	...	...	.12	–.02	–.32
General government	4 612 . .	...	...	...	...	...	–2.24	–2.34	–1.83
Banks	4 613 . .	...	...	...	...	...	–1.41	–3.59	2.51
Other sectors	4 614 . .	...	...	...	...	...	–161.83	–263.93	–87.04
Debt securities	4 619 . .	...	...	...	...	...	–165.86	–115.43	–155.57
Bonds and notes	4 620 . .	...	...	...	...	...	–165.76	–95.34	–137.50
Monetary authorities	4 621 . .	...	...	...	...	...	.18	–1.59	1.69
General government	4 622 . .	...	...	...	...	...	–1.86	–1.12	–.85
Banks	4 623 . .	...	...	...	...	...	–16.05	–70.19	–63.07
Other sectors	4 624 . .	...	...	...	...	...	–148.04	–22.44	–75.26
Money market instruments	4 630 . .	...	...	...	...	...	–.10	–20.08	–18.07
Monetary authorities	4 631 . .	...	...	...	...	...	1.09	2.02	–2.14
General government	4 632 . .	...	...	...	...	...	–.14	–.71	.06
Banks	4 633 . .	...	...	...	...	...	–8.69	–10.56	–30.07
Other sectors	4 634 . .	...	...	...	...	...	7.64	–10.84	14.08
Liabilities	4 652 . .	**...**	**...**	**...**	**...**	**...**	**279.18**	**270.00**	**272.97**
Equity securities	4 660 . .	...	...	...	...	...	96.36	32.99	213.83
Banks	4 663 . .	...	...	...	...	...	...	...	...
Other sectors	4 664 . .	...	...	...	...	...	...	...	...
Debt securities	4 669 . .	...	...	...	...	...	182.83	237.00	59.14
Bonds and notes	4 670 . .	...	...	...	...	...	123.53	210.48	68.74
Monetary authorities	4 671 . .	...	...	...	...	...	...	...	...
General government	4 672 . .	...	...	...	...	...	...	...	...
Banks	4 673 . .	...	...	...	...	...	...	...	...
Other sectors	4 674 . .	...	...	...	...	...	...	...	...
Money market instruments	4 680 . .	...	...	...	...	...	59.29	26.53	–9.61
Monetary authorities	4 681 . .	...	...	...	...	...	...	...	...
General government	4 682 . .	...	...	...	...	...	...	...	...
Banks	4 683 . .	...	...	...	...	...	...	...	...
Other sectors	4 684 . .	...	...	...	...	...	...	...	...
C. FINANCIAL DERIVATIVES	4 910 . .	...	...	...	...	...	4.72	–.83	–18.49
Monetary authorities	4 911 . .	...	...	...	...	...	...	...	...
General government	4 912 . .	...	...	...	...	...	...	...	...
Banks	4 913 . .	...	...	...	...	...	...	...	...
Other sectors	4 914 . .	...	...	...	...	...	...	...	...
Assets	4 900 . .	**...**	**...**	**...**	**...**	**...**	**...**	**...**	**...**
Monetary authorities	4 901 . .	...	...	...	...	...	...	...	...
General government	4 902 . .	...	...	...	...	...	...	...	...
Banks	4 903 . .	...	...	...	...	...	...	...	...
Other sectors	4 904 . .	...	...	...	...	...	...	...	...
Liabilities	4 905 . .	**...**	**...**	**...**	**...**	**...**	**4.72**	**–.83**	**–18.49**
Monetary authorities	4 906 . .	...	...	...	...	...	...	...	...
General government	4 907 . .	...	...	...	...	...	...	...	...
Banks	4 908 . .	...	...	...	...	...	...	...	...
Other sectors	4 909 . .	...	...	...	...	...	...	...	...

Table 2 (Concluded). STANDARD PRESENTATION, 1994–2001
(Billions of U.S. dollars)

	Code	1994	1995	1996	1997	1998	1999	2000	2001
D. OTHER INVESTMENT	4 700 . .	. . .	. . .	. . .	. . .	. . .	172.74	161.88	.55
Assets	4 703 . .	**. . .**	**. . .**	**. . .**	**. . .**	**. . .**	**–35.51**	**–166.71**	**–219.20**
Trade credits	4 706 . .	. . .	. . .	. . .	. . .	. . .	–7.97	–13.60	–6.88
General government	4 707 . .	. . .	. . .	. . .	. . .	. . .	.04	.05	–.09
of which: Short-term	4 709 . .	. . .	. . .	. . .	. . .	. . .	. . .	. . .	. . .
Other sectors	4 710 . .	. . .	. . .	. . .	. . .	. . .	–8.00	–13.65	–6.79
of which: Short-term	4 712 . .	. . .	. . .	. . .	. . .	. . .	. . .	. . .	. . .
Loans	4 714 . .	. . .	. . .	. . .	. . .	. . .	–1.90	–143.78	–193.27
Monetary authorities	4 715 . .	. . .	. . .	. . .	. . .	. . .	–1.32	–.98	.56
of which: Short-term	4 718 . .	. . .	. . .	. . .	. . .	. . .	. . .	. . .	. . .
General government	4 719 . .	. . .	. . .	. . .	. . .	. . .	4.79	–2.01	4.23
of which: Short-term	4 721 . .	. . .	. . .	. . .	. . .	. . .	. . .	. . .	. . .
Banks	4 722 . .	. . .	. . .	. . .	. . .	. . .	18.56	–115.58	–189.86
of which: Short-term	4 724 . .	. . .	. . .	. . .	. . .	. . .	. . .	. . .	. . .
Other sectors	4 725 . .	. . .	. . .	. . .	. . .	. . .	–23.93	–25.20	–8.20
of which: Short-term	4 727 . .	. . .	. . .	. . .	. . .	. . .	. . .	. . .	. . .
Currency and deposits	4 730 . .	. . .	. . .	. . .	. . .	. . .	. . .	. . .	. . .
Monetary authorities	4 731 . .	. . .	. . .	. . .	. . .	. . .	. . .	. . .	. . .
General government	4 732 . .	. . .	. . .	. . .	. . .	. . .	. . .	. . .	. . .
Banks	4 733 . .	. . .	. . .	. . .	. . .	. . .	. . .	. . .	. . .
Other sectors	4 734 . .	. . .	. . .	. . .	. . .	. . .	. . .	. . .	. . .
Other assets	4 736 . .	. . .	. . .	. . .	. . .	. . .	–25.64	–9.33	–19.06
Monetary authorities	4 737 . .	. . .	. . .	. . .	. . .	. . .	–.88	. . .	. . .
of which: Short-term	4 739 . .	. . .	. . .	. . .	. . .	. . .	. . .	. . .	. . .
General government	4 740 . .	. . .	. . .	. . .	. . .	. . .	–1.27	–.81	–1.16
of which: Short-term	4 742 . .	. . .	. . .	. . .	. . .	. . .	. . .	. . .	. . .
Banks	4 743 . .	. . .	. . .	. . .	. . .	. . .	1.11	–3.76	–12.33
of which: Short-term	4 745 . .	. . .	. . .	. . .	. . .	. . .	. . .	. . .	. . .
Other sectors	4 746 . .	. . .	. . .	. . .	. . .	. . .	–24.60	–4.77	–5.56
of which: Short-term	4 748 . .	. . .	. . .	. . .	. . .	. . .	. . .	. . .	. . .
Liabilities	4 753 . .	**. . .**	**. . .**	**. . .**	**. . .**	**. . .**	**208.24**	**328.59**	**219.75**
Trade credits	4 756 . .	. . .	. . .	. . .	. . .	. . .	5.23	9.72	2.77
General government	4 757 . .	. . .	. . .	. . .	. . .	. . .	–.01	.01	.01
of which: Short-term	4 759 . .	. . .	. . .	. . .	. . .	. . .	. . .	. . .	. . .
Other sectors	4 760 . .	. . .	. . .	. . .	. . .	. . .	5.24	9.71	2.76
of which: Short-term	4 762 . .	. . .	. . .	. . .	. . .	. . .	. . .	. . .	. . .
Loans	4 764 . .	. . .	. . .	. . .	. . .	. . .	188.65	319.30	207.90
Monetary authorities	4 765 . .	. . .	. . .	. . .	. . .	. . .	7.40	.54	3.83
of which: Use of Fund credit and loans from the Fund	4 766 . .	. . .	. . .	. . .	. . .	. . .	. . .	. . .	. . .
of which: Short-term	4 768 . .	. . .	. . .	. . .	. . .	. . .	. . .	. . .	. . .
General government	4 769 . .	. . .	. . .	. . .	. . .	. . .	–14.21	.34	–1.37
of which: Short-term	4 771 . .	. . .	. . .	. . .	. . .	. . .	. . .	. . .	. . .
Banks	4 772 . .	. . .	. . .	. . .	. . .	. . .	173.62	268.75	205.01
of which: Short-term	4 774 . .	. . .	. . .	. . .	. . .	. . .	. . .	. . .	. . .
Other sectors	4 775 . .	. . .	. . .	. . .	. . .	. . .	21.85	49.67	.42
of which: Short-term	4 777 . .	. . .	. . .	. . .	. . .	. . .	. . .	. . .	. . .
Currency and deposits	4 780 . .	. . .	. . .	. . .	. . .	. . .	. . .	. . .	. . .
Monetary authorities	4 781 . .	. . .	. . .	. . .	. . .	. . .	. . .	. . .	. . .
General government	4 782 . .	. . .	. . .	. . .	. . .	. . .	. . .	. . .	. . .
Banks	4 783 . .	. . .	. . .	. . .	. . .	. . .	. . .	. . .	. . .
Other sectors	4 784 . .	. . .	. . .	. . .	. . .	. . .	. . .	. . .	. . .
Other liabilities	4 786 . .	. . .	. . .	. . .	. . .	. . .	14.36	–.43	9.08
Monetary authorities	4 787 . .	. . .	. . .	. . .	. . .	. . .	–.13	.01	–.01
of which: Short-term	4 789 . .	. . .	. . .	. . .	. . .	. . .	. . .	. . .	. . .
General government	4 790 . .	. . .	. . .	. . .	. . .	. . .	.19	.02	–.02
of which: Short-term	4 792 . .	. . .	. . .	. . .	. . .	. . .	. . .	. . .	. . .
Banks	4 793 . .	. . .	. . .	. . .	. . .	. . .	.52	4.69	8.80
of which: Short-term	4 795 . .	. . .	. . .	. . .	. . .	. . .	. . .	. . .	. . .
Other sectors	4 796 . .	. . .	. . .	. . .	. . .	. . .	13.78	–5.14	.31
of which: Short-term	4 798 . .	. . .	. . .	. . .	. . .	. . .	. . .	. . .	. . .
E. RESERVE ASSETS	4 802 . .	. . .	. . .	. . .	. . .	. . .	11.58	16.14	16.89
Monetary gold	4 812 . .	. . .	. . .	. . .	. . .	. . .	.28	.92	.50
Special drawing rights	4 811 . .	. . .	. . .	. . .	. . .	. . .	1.35	.30	–.87
Reserve position in the Fund	4 810 . .	. . .	. . .	. . .	. . .	. . .	2.41	3.45	–3.02
Foreign exchange	4 803 . .	. . .	. . .	. . .	. . .	. . .	7.35	9.86	22.03
Other claims	4 813 . .	. . .	. . .	. . .	. . .	. . .	.18	1.62	–1.74
NET ERRORS AND OMISSIONS	4 998 . .	**. . .**	**. . .**	**. . .**	**. . .**	**. . .**	**–6.41**	**–43.14**	**57.13**

Part 3 of the *Yearbook* contains descriptions of the methodologies, compilation practices, and sources used to compile these data.

Table 1. ANALYTIC PRESENTATION, 1994–2001
(Millions of U.S. dollars)

	Code	1994	1995	1996	1997	1998	1999	2000	2001
A. Current Account [1]	4 993 Z.	**–112.8**	**–112.7**	**13.5**	**–34.1**	**–59.9**	**12.7**	**. . .**	**. . .**
Goods: exports f.o.b	2 100 . .	490.2	519.6	672.2	535.6	428.9	537.7	. . .	. . .
Goods: imports f.o.b	3 100 . .	–719.7	–761.4	–839.9	–818.9	–614.6	–653.3	. . .	. . .
Balance on Goods	4 100 . .	*–229.5*	*–241.8*	*–167.7*	*–283.2*	*–185.6*	*–115.6*	. . .	. . .
Services: credit	2 200 . .	534.7	564.1	612.6	667.9	503.2	525.1	. . .	. . .
Services: debit	3 200 . .	–366.0	–398.6	–412.9	–405.6	–352.0	–389.8	. . .	. . .
Balance on Goods and Services	4 991 . .	*–60.8*	*–76.3*	*31.9*	*–20.9*	*–34.4*	*19.7*	. . .	. . .
Income: credit	2 300 . .	49.2	55.4	63.6	61.7	54.6	47.3	. . .	. . .
Income: debit	3 300 . .	–105.7	–94.6	–91.6	–99.2	–110.6	–82.8	. . .	. . .
Balance on Goods, Services, and Income	4 992 . .	*–117.3*	*–115.5*	*4.0*	*–58.4*	*–90.4*	*–15.8*	. . .	. . .
Current transfers: credit	2 379 Z.	38.1	36.0	44.1	54.6	45.3	42.7	. . .	. . .
Current transfers: debit	3 379 . .	–33.5	–33.1	–34.6	–30.3	–14.7	–14.2	. . .	. . .
B. Capital Account [1]	4 994 Z.	**43.4**	**87.0**	**70.8**	**48.5**	**60.6**	**14.0**	**. . .**	**. . .**
Capital account: credit	2 994 Z.	76.0	120.1	114.5	88.9	100.6	59.3	. . .	. . .
Capital account: debit	3 994 . .	–32.6	–33.1	–43.8	–40.5	–40.0	–45.3	. . .	. . .
Total, Groups A Plus B	4 981 . .	*–69.4*	*–25.7*	*84.3*	*14.3*	*.7*	*26.7*	. . .	. . .
C. Financial Account [1]	4 995 W.	**61.0**	**88.3**	**3.6**	**–15.1**	**28.7**	**–104.0**	**. . .**	**. . .**
Direct investment abroad	4 505 . .	.3	2.8	–9.8	–30.0	–62.6	–53.0	. . .	. . .
Direct investment in Fiji	4 555 Z.	67.5	69.5	2.4	15.6	107.0	–33.2	. . .	. . .
Portfolio investment assets	4 602 . .	. . .	. . .	. . .	. . .	. . .	. . .	. . .	. . .
Equity securities	4 610 . .	. . .	. . .	. . .	. . .	. . .	. . .	. . .	. . .
Debt securities	4 619 . .	. . .	. . .	. . .	. . .	. . .	. . .	. . .	. . .
Portfolio investment liabilities	4 652 Z.	. . .	. . .	. . .	. . .	. . .	. . .	. . .	. . .
Equity securities	4 660 . .	. . .	. . .	. . .	. . .	. . .	. . .	. . .	. . .
Debt securities	4 669 Z.	. . .	. . .	. . .	. . .	. . .	. . .	. . .	. . .
Financial derivatives	4 910 . .	. . .	. . .	. . .	. . .	. . .	. . .	. . .	. . .
Financial derivatives assets	4 900 . .	. . .	. . .	. . .	. . .	. . .	. . .	. . .	. . .
Financial derivatives liabilities	4 905 . .	. . .	. . .	. . .	. . .	. . .	. . .	. . .	. . .
Other investment assets	4 703 . .	1.2	12.0	–25.9	–21.1	–66.6	–62.2	. . .	. . .
Monetary authorities	4 701 . .	. . .	. . .	. . .	. . .	. . .	. . .	. . .	. . .
General government	4 704 . .	. . .	. . .	. . .	. . .	. . .	. . .	. . .	. . .
Banks	4 705 . .	1.2	12.0	–25.9	–21.1	–66.6	–62.2	. . .	. . .
Other sectors	4 728 . .	. . .	. . .	. . .	. . .	. . .	. . .	. . .	. . .
Other investment liabilities	4 753 W.	–8.1	3.9	36.8	20.4	51.0	44.4	. . .	. . .
Monetary authorities	4 753 WA	. . .	. . .	. . .	. . .	. . .	. . .	. . .	. . .
General government	4 753 ZB	. . .	. . .	. . .	. . .	. . .	. . .	. . .	. . .
Banks	4 753 ZC	–8.1	3.9	36.8	20.4	51.0	44.4	. . .	. . .
Other sectors	4 753 ZD	. . .	. . .	. . .	. . .	. . .	. . .	. . .	. . .
Total, Groups A Through C	4 983 . .	*–8.4*	*62.6*	*87.9*	*–.8*	*29.4*	*–77.4*	. . .	. . .
D. Net Errors and Omissions	4 998 . .	**30.9**	**30.4**	**–9.7**	**–24.3**	**–24.6**	**32.5**	**. . .**	**. . .**
Total, Groups A Through D	4 984 . .	*22.5*	*93.0*	*78.1*	*–25.1*	*4.9*	*–44.9*	. . .	. . .
E. Reserves and Related Items	4 802 A.	**–22.5**	**–93.0**	**–78.1**	**25.1**	**–4.9**	**44.9**	**. . .**	**. . .**
Reserve assets	4 802 . .	10.7	–76.6	–71.1	29.7	–27.4	–30.5	. . .	. . .
Use of Fund credit and loans	4 766 . .	. . .	. . .	. . .	. . .	. . .	. . .	. . .	. . .
Exceptional financing	4 920 . .	–33.2	–16.4	–7.0	–4.6	22.5	75.3	. . .	. . .
Conversion rates: Fiji dollars per U.S. dollar	0 101 . .	**1.4641**	**1.4063**	**1.4033**	**1.4437**	**1.9868**	**1.9696**	**2.1286**	**2.2766**

[1] Excludes components that have been classified in the categories of Group E.

Table 2. STANDARD PRESENTATION, 1994–2001

(Millions of U.S. dollars)

	Code		1994	1995	1996	1997	1998	1999	2000	2001
CURRENT ACCOUNT	4 993	. .	**–112.8**	**–112.7**	**13.5**	**–34.1**	**–59.9**	**12.7**	**. . .**	**. . .**
A. GOODS	4 100	. .	–229.5	–241.8	–167.7	–283.2	–185.6	–115.6	. . .	. . .
Credit	2 100	. .	**490.2**	**519.6**	**672.2**	**535.6**	**428.9**	**537.7**	**. . .**	**. . .**
General merchandise: exports f.o.b.	2 110	. .	475.4	502.3	649.4	527.0	422.5	533.9	. . .	. . .
Goods for processing: exports f.o.b.	2 150	. .	. . .	. . .	. . .	. . .	. . .	. . .	. . .	. . .
Repairs on goods	2 160	. .	. . .	. . .	. . .	. . .	. . .	. . .	. . .	. . .
Goods procured in ports by carriers	2 170	. .	14.8	17.4	22.8	8.7	6.4	3.8	. . .	. . .
Nonmonetary gold	2 180	. .	. . .	. . .	. . .	. . .	. . .	. . .	. . .	. . .
Debit	3 100	. .	**–719.7**	**–761.4**	**–839.9**	**–818.9**	**–614.6**	**–653.3**	**. . .**	**. . .**
General merchandise: imports f.o.b.	3 110	. .	–719.7	–761.4	–839.9	–818.9	–614.6	–653.3	. . .	. . .
Goods for processing: imports f.o.b.	3 150	. .	. . .	. . .	. . .	. . .	. . .	. . .	. . .	. . .
Repairs on goods	3 160	. .	. . .	. . .	. . .	. . .	. . .	. . .	. . .	. . .
Goods procured in ports by carriers	3 170	. .	. . .	. . .	. . .	. . .	. . .	. . .	. . .	. . .
Nonmonetary gold	3 180	. .	. . .	. . .	. . .	. . .	. . .	. . .	. . .	. . .
B. SERVICES	4 200	. .	168.7	165.5	199.7	262.3	151.2	135.3	. . .	. . .
Total credit	2 200	. .	*534.7*	*564.1*	*612.6*	*667.9*	*503.2*	*525.1*	. . .	. . .
Total debit	3 200	. .	*–366.0*	*–398.6*	*–412.9*	*–405.6*	*–352.0*	*–389.8*	. . .	. . .
Transportation services, credit	2 205	. .	**149.1**	**170.4**	**169.5**	**164.6**	**134.3**	**155.2**	**. . .**	**. . .**
Passenger	2 850	. .	*73.4*	*78.4*	*76.1*	*69.5*	*61.3*	*84.9*	. . .	. . .
Freight	2 851	. .	*23.7*	*24.9*	*24.9*	*28.7*	*22.3*	*28.0*	. . .	. . .
Other	2 852	. .	*52.0*	*67.2*	*68.4*	*66.4*	*50.7*	*42.2*	. . .	. . .
Sea transport, passenger	2 207	. .	. . .	. . .	. . .	. . .	. . .	. . .	. . .	. . .
Sea transport, freight	2 208	. .	. . .	. . .	. . .	. . .	. . .	. . .	. . .	. . .
Sea transport, other	2 209	. .	. . .	. . .	. . .	. . .	. . .	. . .	. . .	. . .
Air transport, passenger	2 211	. .	. . .	. . .	. . .	. . .	. . .	. . .	. . .	. . .
Air transport, freight	2 212	. .	. . .	. . .	. . .	. . .	. . .	. . .	. . .	. . .
Air transport, other	2 213	. .	. . .	. . .	. . .	. . .	. . .	. . .	. . .	. . .
Other transport, passenger	2 215	. .	. . .	. . .	. . .	. . .	. . .	. . .	. . .	. . .
Other transport, freight	2 216	. .	. . .	. . .	. . .	. . .	. . .	. . .	. . .	. . .
Other transport, other	2 217	. .	. . .	. . .	. . .	. . .	. . .	. . .	. . .	. . .
Transportation services, debit	3 205	. .	**–143.4**	**–156.4**	**–172.3**	**–161.3**	**–130.8**	**–148.4**	**. . .**	**. . .**
Passenger	3 850	. .	*–14.3*	*–18.1*	*–18.0*	*–17.7*	*–15.2*	*–16.2*	. . .	. . .
Freight	3 851	. .	*–92.3*	*–98.1*	*–108.5*	*–106.1*	*–79.4*	*–84.1*	. . .	. . .
Other	3 852	. .	*–36.7*	*–40.3*	*–45.9*	*–37.5*	*–36.2*	*–48.1*	. . .	. . .
Sea transport, passenger	3 207	. .	. . .	. . .	. . .	. . .	. . .	. . .	. . .	. . .
Sea transport, freight	3 208	. .	. . .	. . .	. . .	. . .	. . .	. . .	. . .	. . .
Sea transport, other	3 209	. .	. . .	. . .	. . .	. . .	. . .	. . .	. . .	. . .
Air transport, passenger	3 211	. .	. . .	. . .	. . .	. . .	. . .	. . .	. . .	. . .
Air transport, freight	3 212	. .	. . .	. . .	. . .	. . .	. . .	. . .	. . .	. . .
Air transport, other	3 213	. .	. . .	. . .	. . .	. . .	. . .	. . .	. . .	. . .
Other transport, passenger	3 215	. .	. . .	. . .	. . .	. . .	. . .	. . .	. . .	. . .
Other transport, freight	3 216	. .	. . .	. . .	. . .	. . .	. . .	. . .	. . .	. . .
Other transport, other	3 217	. .	. . .	. . .	. . .	. . .	. . .	. . .	. . .	. . .
Travel, credit	2 236	. .	**270.5**	**290.8**	**297.6**	**317.0**	**247.8**	**279.7**	**. . .**	**. . .**
Business travel	2 237	. .	. . .	. . .	. . .	. . .	. . .	. . .	. . .	. . .
Personal travel	2 240	. .	270.5	290.8	297.6	317.0	247.8	279.7	. . .	. . .
Travel, debit	3 236	. .	**–62.4**	**–64.5**	**–69.7**	**–69.1**	**–51.5**	**–65.9**	**. . .**	**. . .**
Business travel	3 237	. .	. . .	. . .	. . .	. . .	. . .	. . .	. . .	. . .
Personal travel	3 240	. .	–62.4	–64.5	–69.7	–69.1	–51.5	–65.9	. . .	. . .
Other services, credit	2 200	BA	**115.0**	**102.8**	**145.5**	**186.4**	**121.1**	**90.3**	**. . .**	**. . .**
Communications	2 245	. .	4.4	4.6	1.1	4.5	2.5	5.1	. . .	. . .
Construction	2 249	. .	. . .	. . .	. . .	. . .	. . .	. . .	. . .	. . .
Insurance	2 253	. .	15.6	6.8	5.4	12.1	16.6	4.8	. . .	. . .
Financial	2 260	. .	. . .	. . .	. . .	. . .	. . .	. . .	. . .	. . .
Computer and information	2 262	. .	. . .	. . .	. . .	. . .	. . .	. . .	. . .	. . .
Royalties and licence fees	2 266	. .	. . .	. . .	. . .	. . .	. . .	. . .	. . .	. . .
Other business services	2 268	. .	48.8	51.6	92.6	117.9	70.7	59.9	. . .	. . .
Personal, cultural, and recreational	2 287	. .	. . .	. . .	. . .	. . .	. . .	. . .	. . .	. . .
Government, n.i.e.	2 291	. .	46.1	39.8	46.3	52.0	31.4	20.5	. . .	. . .
Other services, debit	3 200	BA	**–160.2**	**–177.7**	**–170.9**	**–175.2**	**–169.6**	**–175.5**	**. . .**	**. . .**
Communications	3 245	. .	–.3	–.8	–.6	–.8	–10.5	–1.3	. . .	. . .
Construction	3 249	. .	. . .	. . .	. . .	. . .	. . .	. . .	. . .	. . .
Insurance	3 253	. .	–35.2	–32.6	–35.8	–31.0	–24.6	–27.3	. . .	. . .
Financial	3 260	. .	. . .	. . .	. . .	. . .	. . .	. . .	. . .	. . .
Computer and information	3 262	. .	. . .	. . .	. . .	. . .	. . .	. . .	. . .	. . .
Royalties and licence fees	3 266	. .	. . .	. . .	. . .	. . .	. . .	. . .	. . .	. . .
Other business services	3 268	. .	–102.6	–116.6	–108.9	–119.3	–113.3	–121.5	. . .	. . .
Personal, cultural, and recreational	3 287	. .	. . .	. . .	. . .	. . .	. . .	. . .	. . .	. . .
Government, n.i.e.	3 291	. .	–22.1	–27.7	–25.6	–24.2	–21.2	–25.4	. . .	. . .

Table 2 (Continued). STANDARD PRESENTATION, 1994–2001
(Millions of U.S. dollars)

	Code	1994	1995	1996	1997	1998	1999	2000	2001
C. INCOME	4 300 . .	–56.6	–39.3	–27.9	–37.5	–56.1	–35.5	...	...
Total credit	2 300 . .	*49.2*	*55.4*	*63.6*	*61.7*	*54.6*	*47.3*	...	...
Total debit	3 300 . .	*–105.7*	*–94.6*	*–91.6*	*–99.2*	*–110.6*	*–82.8*	...	...
Compensation of employees, credit	2 310 . .	**29.6**	**32.7**	**33.3**	**34.6**	**25.9**	**23.2**	...	...
Compensation of employees, debit	3 310 . .	...	...	...	...	...	...	...	...
Investment income, credit	2 320 . .	**19.6**	**22.7**	**30.3**	**27.1**	**28.7**	**24.1**	...	...
Direct investment income	2 330 . .	1.1	4.8	5.6	5.1	5.4	6.7	...	...
Dividends and distributed branch profits	2 332 . .	.8	.8	1.0	.8	1.7	1.6	...	...
Reinvested earnings and undistributed branch profits	2 333 . .	.3	4.1	4.6	4.2	3.7	5.1	...	...
Income on debt (interest)	2 334 . .	...	...	...	...	...	...	...	...
Portfolio investment income	2 339 . .	...	...	...	...	...	...	...	...
Income on equity	2 340 . .	...	...	...	...	...	...	...	...
Income on bonds and notes	2 350 . .	...	...	...	...	...	...	...	...
Income on money market instruments	2 360 . .	...	...	...	...	...	...	...	...
Other investment income	2 370 . .	18.5	17.8	24.7	22.0	23.3	17.4	...	...
Investment income, debit	3 320 . .	**–105.7**	**–94.6**	**–91.6**	**–99.2**	**–110.6**	**–82.8**	...	...
Direct investment income	3 330 . .	–91.0	–83.7	–81.9	–90.9	–103.0	–71.9	...	...
Dividends and distributed branch profits	3 332 . .	–44.9	–48.9	–40.9	–46.9	–48.8	–41.5	...	...
Reinvested earnings and undistributed branch profits	3 333 . .	–46.0	–34.8	–41.0	–44.0	–54.3	–30.5	...	...
Income on debt (interest)	3 334 . .	...	...	...	...	...	...	...	...
Portfolio investment income	3 339 . .	...	...	...	...	...	...	...	...
Income on equity	3 340 . .	...	...	...	...	...	...	...	...
Income on bonds and notes	3 350 . .	...	...	...	...	...	...	...	...
Income on money market instruments	3 360 . .	...	...	...	...	...	...	...	...
Other investment income	3 370 . .	–14.8	–11.0	–9.6	–8.3	–7.6	–10.9	...	...
D. CURRENT TRANSFERS	4 379 . .	4.6	2.8	9.5	24.2	30.6	28.5	...	...
Credit	2 379 . .	**38.1**	**36.0**	**44.1**	**54.6**	**45.3**	**42.7**	...	...
General government	2 380 . .	...	...	...	...	...	...	...	...
Other sectors	2 390 . .	38.1	36.0	44.1	54.6	45.3	42.7	...	...
Workers' remittances	2 391 . .	...	...	...	...	...	...	...	...
Other current transfers	2 392 . .	38.1	36.0	44.1	54.6	45.3	42.7	...	...
Debit	3 379 . .	**–33.5**	**–33.1**	**–34.6**	**–30.3**	**–14.7**	**–14.2**	...	...
General government	3 380 . .	...	...	...	...	...	...	...	...
Other sectors	3 390 . .	–33.5	–33.1	–34.6	–30.3	–14.7	–14.2	...	...
Workers' remittances	3 391 . .	...	...	...	...	...	...	...	...
Other current transfers	3 392 . .	–33.5	–33.1	–34.6	–30.3	–14.7	–14.2	...	...
CAPITAL AND FINANCIAL ACCOUNT	4 996 . .	**81.8**	**82.3**	**–3.8**	**58.5**	**84.5**	**–45.2**	...	...
CAPITAL ACCOUNT	4 994 . .	**43.4**	**87.0**	**70.8**	**48.5**	**60.6**	**14.0**	...	...
Total credit	2 994 . .	*76.0*	*120.1*	*114.5*	*88.9*	*100.6*	*59.3*	...	...
Total debit	3 994 . .	*–32.6*	*–33.1*	*–43.8*	*–40.5*	*–40.0*	*–45.3*	...	...
Capital transfers, credit	2 400 . .	**76.0**	**120.1**	**114.5**	**88.9**	**100.6**	**59.3**	...	...
General government	2 401 . .	75.9	119.9	114.4	88.2	100.6	58.1	...	...
Debt forgiveness	2 402 . .	...	...	...	...	...	...	...	...
Other capital transfers	2 410 . .	75.9	119.9	114.4	88.2	100.6	58.1	...	...
Other sectors	2 430 . .	.1	.2	.1	.7	.1	1.2	...	...
Migrants' transfers	2 431 . .	.1	.2	.1	.7	.1	1.2	...	...
Debt forgiveness	2 432 . .	...	...	...	...	...	...	...	...
Other capital transfers	2 440 . .	...	...	...	...	...	...	...	...
Capital transfers, debit	3 400 . .	**–32.6**	**–33.1**	**–43.8**	**–40.5**	**–40.0**	**–45.3**	...	...
General government	3 401 . .	–4.2	–3.6	–3.7	–4.1	–2.4	–4.9	...	...
Debt forgiveness	3 402 . .	...	...	...	...	...	...	...	...
Other capital transfers	3 410 . .	–4.2	–3.6	–3.7	–4.1	–2.4	–4.9	...	...
Other sectors	3 430 . .	–28.4	–29.5	–40.0	–36.4	–37.6	–40.4	...	...
Migrants' transfers	3 431 . .	–28.4	–29.5	–40.0	–36.4	–37.6	–40.4	...	...
Debt forgiveness	3 432 . .	...	...	...	...	...	...	...	...
Other capital transfers	3 440 . .	...	...	...	...	...	...	...	...
Nonproduced nonfinancial assets, credit	2 480 . .	...	...	...	...	...	...	...	...
Nonproduced nonfinancial assets, debit	3 480 . .	...	...	...	...	...	...	...	...

Table 2 (Continued). STANDARD PRESENTATION, 1994–2001
(Millions of U.S. dollars)

	Code	1994	1995	1996	1997	1998	1999	2000	2001
FINANCIAL ACCOUNT	4 995 . .	**38.5**	**–4.7**	**–74.6**	**10.0**	**23.9**	**–59.2**	**. . .**	**. . .**
A. DIRECT INVESTMENT	4 500 . .	67.8	72.4	–7.4	–14.4	44.4	–86.2	. . .	. . .
Direct investment abroad	4 505 . .	**.3**	**2.8**	**–9.8**	**–30.0**	**–62.6**	**–53.0**	**. . .**	**. . .**
Equity capital	4 510 . .	4.0	–7.8	–21.7	–23.1	–24.5	–24.9	. . .	. . .
Claims on affiliated enterprises	4 515 . .	. . .	–8.0	–23.3	–24.1	–28.0	–25.0	. . .	. . .
Liabilities to affiliated enterprises	4 520 . .	4.0	.2	1.6	1.0	3.5	.2	. . .	. . .
Reinvested earnings	4 525 . .	–.3	–4.1	–4.6	–4.2	–3.7	–5.1	. . .	. . .
Other capital	4 530 . .	–3.4	14.6	16.4	–2.6	–34.4	–23.1	. . .	. . .
Claims on affiliated enterprises	4 535 . .	99.4	107.1	92.6	74.1	55.8	91.0	. . .	. . .
Liabilities to affiliated enterprises	4 540 . .	–102.9	–92.4	–76.2	–76.7	–90.2	–114.0	. . .	. . .
Direct investment in Fiji	4 555 . .	**67.5**	**69.5**	**2.4**	**15.6**	**107.0**	**–33.2**	**. . .**	**. . .**
Equity capital	4 560 . .	25.5	22.3	–24.5	–17.5	48.6	–62.7	. . .	. . .
Claims on direct investors	4 565 . .	. . .	. . .	. . .	. . .	. . .	. . .	. . .	. . .
Liabilities to direct investors	4 570 . .	. . .	. . .	. . .	. . .	. . .	. . .	. . .	. . .
Reinvested earnings	4 575 . .	46.0	34.8	41.0	44.0	54.3	30.5	. . .	. . .
Other capital	4 580 . .	–4.0	12.4	–14.1	–10.9	4.2	–1.0	. . .	. . .
Claims on direct investors	4 585 . .	. . .	. . .	. . .	. . .	. . .	. . .	. . .	. . .
Liabilities to direct investors	4 590 . .	. . .	. . .	. . .	. . .	. . .	. . .	. . .	. . .
B. PORTFOLIO INVESTMENT	4 600 . .	. . .	. . .	. . .	. . .	. . .	. . .	. . .	. . .
Assets	4 602 . .	**. . .**	**. . .**	**. . .**	**. . .**	**. . .**	**. . .**	**. . .**	**. . .**
Equity securities	4 610 . .	. . .	. . .	. . .	. . .	. . .	. . .	. . .	. . .
Monetary authorities	4 611 . .	. . .	. . .	. . .	. . .	. . .	. . .	. . .	. . .
General government	4 612 . .	. . .	. . .	. . .	. . .	. . .	. . .	. . .	. . .
Banks	4 613 . .	. . .	. . .	. . .	. . .	. . .	. . .	. . .	. . .
Other sectors	4 614 . .	. . .	. . .	. . .	. . .	. . .	. . .	. . .	. . .
Debt securities	4 619 . .	. . .	. . .	. . .	. . .	. . .	. . .	. . .	. . .
Bonds and notes	4 620 . .	. . .	. . .	. . .	. . .	. . .	. . .	. . .	. . .
Monetary authorities	4 621 . .	. . .	. . .	. . .	. . .	. . .	. . .	. . .	. . .
General government	4 622 . .	. . .	. . .	. . .	. . .	. . .	. . .	. . .	. . .
Banks	4 623 . .	. . .	. . .	. . .	. . .	. . .	. . .	. . .	. . .
Other sectors	4 624 . .	. . .	. . .	. . .	. . .	. . .	. . .	. . .	. . .
Money market instruments	4 630 . .	. . .	. . .	. . .	. . .	. . .	. . .	. . .	. . .
Monetary authorities	4 631 . .	. . .	. . .	. . .	. . .	. . .	. . .	. . .	. . .
General government	4 632 . .	. . .	. . .	. . .	. . .	. . .	. . .	. . .	. . .
Banks	4 633 . .	. . .	. . .	. . .	. . .	. . .	. . .	. . .	. . .
Other sectors	4 634 . .	. . .	. . .	. . .	. . .	. . .	. . .	. . .	. . .
Liabilities	4 652 . .	**. . .**	**. . .**	**. . .**	**. . .**	**. . .**	**. . .**	**. . .**	**. . .**
Equity securities	4 660 . .	. . .	. . .	. . .	. . .	. . .	. . .	. . .	. . .
Banks	4 663 . .	. . .	. . .	. . .	. . .	. . .	. . .	. . .	. . .
Other sectors	4 664 . .	. . .	. . .	. . .	. . .	. . .	. . .	. . .	. . .
Debt securities	4 669 . .	. . .	. . .	. . .	. . .	. . .	. . .	. . .	. . .
Bonds and notes	4 670 . .	. . .	. . .	. . .	. . .	. . .	. . .	. . .	. . .
Monetary authorities	4 671 . .	. . .	. . .	. . .	. . .	. . .	. . .	. . .	. . .
General government	4 672 . .	. . .	. . .	. . .	. . .	. . .	. . .	. . .	. . .
Banks	4 673 . .	. . .	. . .	. . .	. . .	. . .	. . .	. . .	. . .
Other sectors	4 674 . .	. . .	. . .	. . .	. . .	. . .	. . .	. . .	. . .
Money market instruments	4 680 . .	. . .	. . .	. . .	. . .	. . .	. . .	. . .	. . .
Monetary authorities	4 681 . .	. . .	. . .	. . .	. . .	. . .	. . .	. . .	. . .
General government	4 682 . .	. . .	. . .	. . .	. . .	. . .	. . .	. . .	. . .
Banks	4 683 . .	. . .	. . .	. . .	. . .	. . .	. . .	. . .	. . .
Other sectors	4 684 . .	. . .	. . .	. . .	. . .	. . .	. . .	. . .	. . .
C. FINANCIAL DERIVATIVES	4 910 . .	. . .	. . .	. . .	. . .	. . .	. . .	. . .	. . .
Monetary authorities	4 911 . .	. . .	. . .	. . .	. . .	. . .	. . .	. . .	. . .
General government	4 912 . .	. . .	. . .	. . .	. . .	. . .	. . .	. . .	. . .
Banks	4 913 . .	. . .	. . .	. . .	. . .	. . .	. . .	. . .	. . .
Other sectors	4 914 . .	. . .	. . .	. . .	. . .	. . .	. . .	. . .	. . .
Assets	4 900 . .	**. . .**	**. . .**	**. . .**	**. . .**	**. . .**	**. . .**	**. . .**	**. . .**
Monetary authorities	4 901 . .	. . .	. . .	. . .	. . .	. . .	. . .	. . .	. . .
General government	4 902 . .	. . .	. . .	. . .	. . .	. . .	. . .	. . .	. . .
Banks	4 903 . .	. . .	. . .	. . .	. . .	. . .	. . .	. . .	. . .
Other sectors	4 904 . .	. . .	. . .	. . .	. . .	. . .	. . .	. . .	. . .
Liabilities	4 905 . .	**. . .**	**. . .**	**. . .**	**. . .**	**. . .**	**. . .**	**. . .**	**. . .**
Monetary authorities	4 906 . .	. . .	. . .	. . .	. . .	. . .	. . .	. . .	. . .
General government	4 907 . .	. . .	. . .	. . .	. . .	. . .	. . .	. . .	. . .
Banks	4 908 . .	. . .	. . .	. . .	. . .	. . .	. . .	. . .	. . .
Other sectors	4 909 . .	. . .	. . .	. . .	. . .	. . .	. . .	. . .	. . .

Table 2 (Concluded). STANDARD PRESENTATION, 1994–2001
(Millions of U.S. dollars)

	Code	1994	1995	1996	1997	1998	1999	2000	2001
D. OTHER INVESTMENT	4 700	-40.0	-.4	4.0	-5.3	6.8	57.5	...	...
Assets	4 703	**1.2**	**12.0**	**-25.9**	**-21.1**	**-66.6**	**-62.2**	**...**	**...**
Trade credits	4 706	...	...	...	...	...	...	...	...
General government	4 707	...	...	...	...	...	...	...	...
of which: Short-term	4 709	...	...	...	...	...	...	...	...
Other sectors	4 710	...	...	...	...	...	...	...	...
of which: Short-term	4 712	...	...	...	...	...	...	...	...
Loans	4 714	...	...	...	...	...	...	...	...
Monetary authorities	4 715	...	...	...	...	...	...	...	...
of which: Short-term	4 718	...	...	...	...	...	...	...	...
General government	4 719	...	...	...	...	...	...	...	...
of which: Short-term	4 721	...	...	...	...	...	...	...	...
Banks	4 722	...	...	...	...	...	...	...	...
of which: Short-term	4 724	...	...	...	...	...	...	...	...
Other sectors	4 725	...	...	...	...	...	...	...	...
of which: Short-term	4 727	...	...	...	...	...	...	...	...
Currency and deposits	4 730	1.2	12.0	-25.9	-21.1	-66.6	-62.2	...	...
Monetary authorities	4 731	...	...	...	...	...	...	...	...
General government	4 732	...	...	...	...	...	...	...	...
Banks	4 733	1.2	12.0	-25.9	-21.1	-66.6	-62.2	...	...
Other sectors	4 734	...	...	...	...	...	...	...	...
Other assets	4 736	...	...	...	...	...	...	...	...
Monetary authorities	4 737	...	...	...	...	...	...	...	...
of which: Short-term	4 739	...	...	...	...	...	...	...	...
General government	4 740	...	...	...	...	...	...	...	...
of which: Short-term	4 742	...	...	...	...	...	...	...	...
Banks	4 743	...	...	...	...	...	...	...	...
of which: Short-term	4 745	...	...	...	...	...	...	...	...
Other sectors	4 746	...	...	...	...	...	...	...	...
of which: Short-term	4 748	...	...	...	...	...	...	...	...
Liabilities	4 753	**-41.3**	**-12.4**	**29.9**	**15.7**	**73.5**	**119.7**	**...**	**...**
Trade credits	4 756	...	...	...	...	...	...	...	...
General government	4 757	...	...	...	...	...	...	...	...
of which: Short-term	4 759	...	...	...	...	...	...	...	...
Other sectors	4 760	...	...	...	...	...	...	...	...
of which: Short-term	4 762	...	...	...	...	...	...	...	...
Loans	4 764	-33.2	-16.4	-7.0	-4.6	22.5	75.3	...	...
Monetary authorities	4 765	...	...	...	...	...	...	...	...
of which: Use of Fund credit and loans from the Fund	4 766	...	...	...	...	...	...	...	...
of which: Short-term	4 768	...	...	...	...	...	...	...	...
General government	4 769	3.6	-3.6	-1.8	-2.8	-6.7	5.5	...	...
of which: Short-term	4 771	...	...	...	...	...	...	...	...
Banks	4 772	...	...	...	...	...	...	...	...
of which: Short-term	4 774	...	...	...	...	...	...	...	...
Other sectors	4 775	-36.8	-12.7	-5.2	-1.8	29.2	69.9	...	...
of which: Short-term	4 777	...	...	...	...	...	...	...	...
Currency and deposits	4 780	-8.1	3.9	36.8	20.4	51.0	44.4	...	...
Monetary authorities	4 781	...	...	...	...	...	...	...	...
General government	4 782	...	...	...	...	...	...	...	...
Banks	4 783	-8.1	3.9	36.8	20.4	51.0	44.4	...	...
Other sectors	4 784	...	...	...	...	...	...	...	...
Other liabilities	4 786	...	...	...	...	...	...	...	...
Monetary authorities	4 787	...	...	...	...	...	...	...	...
of which: Short-term	4 789	...	...	...	...	...	...	...	...
General government	4 790	...	...	...	...	...	...	...	...
of which: Short-term	4 792	...	...	...	...	...	...	...	...
Banks	4 793	...	...	...	...	...	...	...	...
of which: Short-term	4 795	...	...	...	...	...	...	...	...
Other sectors	4 796	...	...	...	...	...	...	...	...
of which: Short-term	4 798	...	...	...	...	...	...	...	...
E. RESERVE ASSETS	4 802	10.7	-76.6	-71.1	29.7	-27.4	-30.5	...	...
Monetary gold	4 812	.1	-.1	.1	-.1	...	...	...	...
Special drawing rights	4 811	-1.6	-.4	-.5	-.4	-.5	6.2	...	...
Reserve position in the Fund	4 810	...	...	-.1	...	...	-6.7	...	...
Foreign exchange	4 803	12.2	-76.1	-70.7	30.3	-26.9	-30.1	...	...
Other claims	4 813	...	...	...	...	...	...	...	...
NET ERRORS AND OMISSIONS	4 998	**30.9**	**30.4**	**-9.7**	**-24.3**	**-24.6**	**32.5**	**...**	**...**

Part 3 of the *Yearbook* contains descriptions of the methodologies, compilation practices, and sources used to compile these data.

Table 1. ANALYTIC PRESENTATION, 1994–2001
(Millions of U.S. dollars)

	Code	1994	1995	1996	1997	1998	1999	2000	2001
A. Current Account [1]	4 993 Z.	**1,110**	**5,231**	**5,003**	**6,633**	**7,340**	**7,657**	**9,038**	**8,357**
Goods: exports f.o.b	2 100 . .	29,881	40,558	40,725	41,148	43,393	41,983	45,703	42,980
Goods: imports f.o.b	3 100 . .	–22,158	–28,121	–29,411	–29,604	–30,903	–29,815	–32,019	–30,323
Balance on Goods	4 100 . .	*7,723*	*12,437*	*11,314*	*11,544*	*12,490*	*12,168*	*13,684*	*12,657*
Services: credit	2 200 . .	5,490	7,415	7,129	6,640	6,698	6,522	6,169	5,796
Services: debit	3 200 . .	–7,335	–9,584	–8,817	–8,235	–7,767	–7,952	–8,473	–8,221
Balance on Goods and Services	4 991 . .	*5,878*	*10,268*	*9,627*	*9,949*	*11,421*	*10,738*	*11,381*	*10,232*
Income: credit	2 300 . .	1,789	2,879	2,868	4,136	4,237	5,664	7,265	8,445
Income: debit	3 300 . .	–6,103	–7,318	–6,503	–6,600	–7,320	–7,712	–8,989	–9,637
Balance on Goods, Services, and Income	4 992 . .	*1,564*	*5,828*	*5,992*	*7,485*	*8,338*	*8,690*	*9,657*	*9,041*
Current transfers: credit	2 379 Z.	410	1,536	1,253	1,210	1,523	1,608	1,715	1,549
Current transfers: debit	3 379 . .	–863	–2,133	–2,242	–2,062	–2,521	–2,641	–2,334	–2,233
B. Capital Account [1]	4 994 Z.	**. . .**	**66**	**56**	**247**	**91**	**84**	**92**	**65**
Capital account: credit	2 994 Z.	. . .	114	130	247	91	149	100	75
Capital account: debit	3 994 . .	. . .	–48	–74	. . .	. . .	–65	–7	–10
Total, Groups A Plus B	4 981 . .	*1,110*	*5,297*	*5,058*	*6,880*	*7,430*	*7,741*	*9,130*	*8,422*
C. Financial Account [1]	4 995 W.	**4,093**	**–4,284**	**–7,718**	**–2,976**	**–1,722**	**–6,379**	**–8,841**	**–10,973**
Direct investment abroad	4 505 . .	–4,354	–1,494	–3,583	–5,260	–18,698	–6,739	–23,898	–8,363
Direct investment in Finland	4 555 Z.	1,496	1,044	1,118	2,129	12,029	4,649	9,125	3,427
Portfolio investment assets	4 602 . .	775	204	–4,186	–4,600	–3,906	–15,699	–18,920	–11,594
Equity securities	4 610 . .	–78	–209	–736	–1,694	–2,099	–5,527	–7,164	–5,153
Debt securities	4 619 . .	853	414	–3,450	–2,906	–1,807	–10,173	–11,756	–6,441
Portfolio investment liabilities	4 652 Z.	6,180	–1,779	1,153	3,843	3,866	13,550	17,116	5,985
Equity securities	4 660 . .	2,541	2,027	1,915	4,023	7,931	10,279	10,114	3,960
Debt securities	4 669 Z.	3,640	–3,807	–761	–181	–4,065	3,271	7,002	2,025
Financial derivatives	4 910 . .	56	639	363	42	–636	–419	–630	38
Financial derivatives assets	4 900 . .	51	38	38	–72	89	. . .	. . .	. . .
Financial derivatives liabilities	4 905 . .	5	600	325	114	–725	–419	–630	38
Other investment assets	4 703 . .	–668	–2,863	–4,683	–2,201	331	–3,288	–5,636	–10,118
Monetary authorities	4 701 . .	99	146	27	94	145	–307	–129	77
General government	4 704 . .	–445	–366	–719	–609	–126	–224	–171	–967
Banks	4 705 . .	–511	–1,926	–3,815	–1,725	41	–1,566	–4,107	–8,197
Other sectors	4 728 . .	189	–717	175	39	270	–1,191	–1,229	–1,032
Other investment liabilities	4 753 W.	607	–35	2,099	3,072	5,292	1,567	14,001	9,652
Monetary authorities	4 753 WA	–107	92	–96	–173	–180	–872	1,433	282
General government	4 753 ZB	965	–331	764	1,478	394	–420	–1,272	467
Banks	4 753 ZC	–1,088	869	–626	1,876	3,607	–154	4,098	8,703
Other sectors	4 753 ZD	837	–666	2,056	–110	1,471	3,014	9,742	200
Total, Groups A Through C	4 983 . .	*5,203*	*1,013*	*–2,660*	*3,904*	*5,708*	*1,362*	*289*	*–2,551*
D. Net Errors and Omissions	4 998 . .	**–489**	**–1,384**	**–375**	**–1,600**	**–5,412**	**–1,349**	**70**	**2,956**
Total, Groups A Through D	4 984 . .	*4,714*	*–372*	*–3,036*	*2,304*	*296*	*13*	*359*	*405*
E. Reserves and Related Items	4 802 A.	**–4,714**	**372**	**3,036**	**–2,304**	**–296**	**–13**	**–359**	**–405**
Reserve assets	4 802 . .	–4,714	372	3,036	–2,304	–296	–13	–359	–405
Use of Fund credit and loans	4 766 . .	. . .	. . .	. . .	. . .	. . .	. . .	. . .	. . .
Exceptional financing	4 920 . .	. . .	. . .	. . .	. . .	. . .	. . .	. . .	. . .
Conversion rates: markkaa per U.S. dollar	0 101 . .	**5.2235**	**4.3667**	**4.5936**	**5.1914**	**5.3441**	**. . .**	**. . .**	**. . .**
Conversion rates: euros per U.S. dollar	0 103 . .	**. . .**	**. . .**	**. . .**	**. . .**	**. . .**	**.9386**	**1.0854**	**1.1175**

[1] Excludes components that have been classified in the categories of Group E.

Table 2. STANDARD PRESENTATION, 1994–2001
(Millions of U.S. dollars)

	Code		1994	1995	1996	1997	1998	1999	2000	2001
CURRENT ACCOUNT	4 993	. .	**1,110**	**5,231**	**5,003**	**6,633**	**7,340**	**7,657**	**9,038**	**8,357**
A. GOODS	4 100	. .	7,723	12,437	11,314	11,544	12,490	12,168	13,684	12,657
Credit	2 100	. .	**29,881**	**40,558**	**40,725**	**41,148**	**43,393**	**41,983**	**45,703**	**42,980**
General merchandise: exports f.o.b.	2 110	. .	29,489	39,727	39,861	40,334	41,927	41,112	44,957	42,253
Goods for processing: exports f.o.b.	2 150	. .	337	773	766	722	1,353	751	650	630
Repairs on goods	2 160	. .	. . .	. . .	. . .	. . .	. . .	. . .	. . .	. . .
Goods procured in ports by carriers	2 170	. .	44	58	59	57	61	60	52	50
Nonmonetary gold	2 180	. .	11	. . .	39	35	53	61	45	46
Debit	3 100	. .	**–22,158**	**–28,121**	**–29,411**	**–29,604**	**–30,903**	**–29,815**	**–32,019**	**–30,323**
General merchandise: imports f.o.b.	3 110	. .	–21,627	–27,225	–28,455	–28,724	–28,994	–28,899	–31,161	–29,520
Goods for processing: imports f.o.b.	3 150	. .	–441	–783	–836	–775	–1,795	–793	–687	–666
Repairs on goods	3 160	. .	. . .	. . .	. . .	. . .	. . .	. . .	. . .	. . .
Goods procured in ports by carriers	3 170	. .	–80	–112	–114	–100	–101	–111	–160	–123
Nonmonetary gold	3 180	. .	–10	. . .	–6	–5	–12	–12	–10	–13
B. SERVICES	4 200	. .	–1,845	–2,169	–1,688	–1,595	–1,069	–1,430	–2,303	–2,425
Total credit	2 200	. .	*5,490*	*7,415*	*7,129*	*6,640*	*6,698*	*6,522*	*6,169*	*5,796*
Total debit	3 200	. .	*–7,335*	*–9,584*	*–8,817*	*–8,235*	*–7,767*	*–7,952*	*–8,473*	*–8,221*
Transportation services, credit	2 205	. .	**1,610**	**2,063**	**1,897**	**1,726**	**2,055**	**1,784**	**1,677**	**1,551**
Passenger	2 850	. .	*638*	*743*	*772*	*719*	*741*	*715*	*629*	*628*
Freight	2 851	. .	*681*	*810*	*792*	*688*	*933*	*699*	*657*	*568*
Other	2 852	. .	*291*	*511*	*334*	*319*	*381*	*369*	*391*	*355*
Sea transport, passenger	2 207	. .	300	313	331	301	330	322	270	273
Sea transport, freight	2 208	. .	523	611	591	486	725	499	479	392
Sea transport, other	2 209	. .	211	347	186	189	248	236	258	254
Air transport, passenger	2 211	. .	338	430	441	418	411	393	359	355
Air transport, freight	2 212	. .	57	59	68	73	71	68	67	64
Air transport, other	2 213	. .	77	160	145	128	131	129	129	97
Other transport, passenger	2 215	. .	. . .	. . .	. . .	. . .	. . .	. . .	. . .	. . .
Other transport, freight	2 216	. .	101	139	132	130	137	132	111	111
Other transport, other	2 217	. .	2	4	3	2	2	4	4	4
Transportation services, debit	3 205	. .	**–1,840**	**–2,149**	**–2,045**	**–1,929**	**–2,072**	**–2,510**	**–2,566**	**–2,573**
Passenger	3 850	. .	*–464*	*–575*	*–475*	*–461*	*–503*	*–490*	*–441*	*–590*
Freight	3 851	. .	*–1,022*	*–1,162*	*–1,182*	*–1,092*	*–1,174*	*–1,680*	*–1,818*	*–1,717*
Other	3 852	. .	*–355*	*–413*	*–387*	*–376*	*–396*	*–341*	*–307*	*–266*
Sea transport, passenger	3 207	. .	–223	–242	–185	–256	–224	–221	–185	–178
Sea transport, freight	3 208	. .	–913	–1,015	–1,035	–949	–1,025	–1,534	–1,688	–1,588
Sea transport, other	3 209	. .	–260	–297	–266	–266	–284	–233	–228	–189
Air transport, passenger	3 211	. .	–240	–333	–291	–205	–279	–269	–256	–412
Air transport, freight	3 212	. .	–56	–73	–77	–76	–80	–77	–70	–71
Air transport, other	3 213	. .	–85	–93	–110	–95	–86	–82	–79	–70
Other transport, passenger	3 215	. .	. . .	. . .	. . .	. . .	. . .	. . .	. . .	. . .
Other transport, freight	3 216	. .	–52	–73	–70	–66	–69	–69	–60	–59
Other transport, other	3 217	. .	–10	–23	–10	–15	–25	–26	. . .	–7
Travel, credit	2 236	. .	**1,365**	**1,640**	**1,636**	**1,639**	**1,630**	**1,521**	**1,406**	**1,437**
Business travel	2 237	. .	751	730	728	729	726	608	619	632
Personal travel	2 240	. .	614	910	908	909	905	913	787	805
Travel, debit	3 236	. .	**–1,619**	**–2,278**	**–2,285**	**–2,080**	**–2,062**	**–2,035**	**–1,852**	**–1,852**
Business travel	3 237	. .	–503	–707	–710	–646	–640	–733	–704	–704
Personal travel	3 240	. .	–1,116	–1,570	–1,576	–1,434	–1,421	–1,302	–1,148	–1,148
Other services, credit	2 200	BA	**2,516**	**3,711**	**3,596**	**3,275**	**3,013**	**3,217**	**3,087**	**2,808**
Communications	2 245	. .	122	173	155	147	163	162	259	229
Construction	2 249	. .	144	285	225	275	123	243	391	412
Insurance	2 253	. .	–118	–131	–120	–123	–49	–9	–33	–39
Financial	2 260	. .	247	275	84	27	32	. . .	. . .	. . .
Computer and information	2 262	. .	608	743	888	958	1,051	1,331	203	347
Royalties and licence fees	2 266	. .	75	58	66	93	106	648	912	573
Other business services	2 268	. .	1,363	2,227	2,229	1,826	1,519	772	1,289	1,222
Personal, cultural, and recreational	2 287	. .	. . .	. . .	. . .	. . .	. . .	4	7	7
Government, n.i.e.	2 291	. .	75	80	69	72	67	65	59	57
Other services, debit	3 200	BA	**–3,876**	**–5,157**	**–4,487**	**–4,226**	**–3,633**	**–3,406**	**–4,055**	**–3,796**
Communications	3 245	. .	–121	–197	–194	–193	–203	–183	–321	–365
Construction	3 249	. .	–51	–64	–66	–70	–7	–21	–52	–129
Insurance	3 253	. .	–65	–166	–64	–94	–71	–75	–37	–61
Financial	3 260	. .	–277	–303	–105	–20	–38	. . .	. . .	. . .
Computer and information	3 262	. .	–497	–757	–615	–679	–649	–614	–310	–390
Royalties and licence fees	3 266	. .	–325	–389	–465	–504	–411	–375	–572	–526
Other business services	3 268	. .	–2,299	–3,115	–2,772	–2,470	–2,113	–1,971	–2,587	–2,181
Personal, cultural, and recreational	3 287	. .	. . .	. . .	. . .	. . .	–16	–43	–59	–32
Government, n.i.e.	3 291	. .	–242	–166	–204	–196	–124	–124	–116	–111

Table 2 (Continued). STANDARD PRESENTATION, 1994–2001
(Millions of U.S. dollars)

	Code	1994	1995	1996	1997	1998	1999	2000	2001
C. INCOME	4 300 . .	–4,314	–4,440	–3,635	–2,464	–3,083	–2,048	–1,724	–1,192
Total credit	2 300 . .	*1,789*	*2,879*	*2,868*	*4,136*	*4,237*	*5,664*	*7,265*	*8,445*
Total debit	3 300 . .	*–6,103*	*–7,318*	*–6,503*	*–6,600*	*–7,320*	*–7,712*	*–8,989*	*–9,637*
Compensation of employees, credit	2 310 . .	**67**	**74**	**145**	**235**	**375**	**444**	**473**	**426**
Compensation of employees, debit	3 310 . .	**–42**	**–54**	**–55**	**–89**	**–104**	**–111**	**–100**	**–97**
Investment income, credit	2 320 . .	**1,722**	**2,805**	**2,722**	**3,901**	**3,861**	**5,221**	**6,793**	**8,019**
Direct investment income	2 330 . .	374	876	1,071	1,989	1,971	3,221	3,825	4,607
Dividends and distributed branch profits	2 332 . .	495	625	677	748	4,941	1,164	1,956	5,986
Reinvested earnings and undistributed branch profits	2 333 . .	–52	113	233	1,067	–3,202	1,718	1,288	–2,051
Income on debt (interest)	2 334 . .	–69	139	160	174	232	338	581	672
Portfolio investment income	2 339 . .	460	970	709	1,035	1,034	809	1,376	1,759
Income on equity	2 340 . .	3	7	10	24	31	74	203	214
Income on bonds and notes	2 350 . .	63	97	195	380	486	711	1,151	1,489
Income on money market instruments	2 360 . .	394	867	504	631	518	24	23	56
Other investment income	2 370 . .	888	958	943	876	856	1,191	1,592	1,653
Investment income, debit	3 320 . .	**–6,062**	**–7,264**	**–6,448**	**–6,511**	**–7,216**	**–7,602**	**–8,889**	**–9,540**
Direct investment income	3 330 . .	–656	–1,023	–1,151	–1,324	–2,029	–2,405	–2,837	–2,907
Dividends and distributed branch profits	3 332 . .	–252	–346	–604	–565	–696	–1,107	–1,213	–1,861
Reinvested earnings and undistributed branch profits	3 333 . .	–311	–596	–461	–692	–1,248	–1,167	–1,381	–806
Income on debt (interest)	3 334 . .	–93	–80	–85	–68	–86	–130	–243	–240
Portfolio investment income	3 339 . .	–3,867	–4,604	–4,046	–3,719	–3,808	–3,675	–4,047	–4,161
Income on equity	3 340 . .	–61	–213	–297	–293	–539	–946	–1,467	–1,662
Income on bonds and notes	3 350 . .	–3,699	–4,264	–3,582	–3,317	–2,978	–2,657	–2,530	–2,386
Income on money market instruments	3 360 . .	–107	–128	–168	–109	–292	–73	–50	–113
Other investment income	3 370 . .	–1,539	–1,638	–1,251	–1,467	–1,379	–1,522	–2,006	–2,472
D. CURRENT TRANSFERS	4 379 . .	–453	–597	–989	–852	–998	–1,033	–619	–684
Credit	2 379 . .	**410**	**1,536**	**1,253**	**1,210**	**1,523**	**1,608**	**1,715**	**1,549**
General government	2 380 . .	50	1,249	1,093	974	211	220	307	194
Other sectors	2 390 . .	360	287	160	236	1,311	1,387	1,408	1,355
Workers' remittances	2 391 . .	. . .	. . .	. . .	. . .	. . .	. . .	. . .	. . .
Other current transfers	2 392 . .	360	287	160	236	1,311	1,387	1,408	1,355
Debit	3 379 . .	**–863**	**–2,133**	**–2,242**	**–2,062**	**–2,521**	**–2,641**	**–2,334**	**–2,233**
General government	3 380 . .	–408	–1,653	–1,681	–1,606	–1,714	–1,980	–1,713	–1,668
Other sectors	3 390 . .	–456	–481	–561	–456	–807	–661	–620	–566
Workers' remittances	3 391 . .	. . .	. . .	. . .	. . .	. . .	. . .	. . .	. . .
Other current transfers	3 392 . .	–456	–481	–561	–456	–807	–661	–620	–566
CAPITAL AND FINANCIAL ACCOUNT	4 996 . .	**–621**	**–3,847**	**–4,627**	**–5,033**	**–1,927**	**–6,307**	**–9,108**	**–11,312**
CAPITAL ACCOUNT	4 994 . .	**. . .**	**66**	**56**	**247**	**91**	**84**	**92**	**65**
Total credit	2 994 . .	. . .	*114*	*130*	*247*	*91*	*149*	*100*	*75*
Total debit	3 994 . .	. . .	*48*	*–74*	. . .	. . .	*–65*	*–7*	*–10*
Capital transfers, credit	2 400 . .	**. . .**	**114**	**130**	**247**	**91**	**149**	**100**	**75**
General government	2 401 . .	. . .	114	130	247	52	107	63	32
Debt forgiveness	2 402 . .	. . .	. . .	. . .	. . .	. . .	. . .	. . .	. . .
Other capital transfers	2 410 . .	. . .	114	130	247	52	107	63	32
Other sectors	2 430 . .	. . .	. . .	. . .	. . .	39	43	37	43
Migrants' transfers	2 431 . .	. . .	. . .	. . .	. . .	. . .	. . .	. . .	. . .
Debt forgiveness	2 432 . .	. . .	. . .	. . .	. . .	. . .	. . .	. . .	. . .
Other capital transfers	2 440 . .	. . .	. . .	. . .	. . .	39	43	37	43
Capital transfers, debit	3 400 . .	**. . .**	**–48**	**–13**	**. . .**	**. . .**	**–65**	**–7**	**–10**
General government	3 401 . .	. . .	–48	–13	. . .	. . .	–65	–7	–10
Debt forgiveness	3 402 . .	. . .	–48	–13	. . .	. . .	–65	. . .	–3
Other capital transfers	3 410 . .	. . .	. . .	. . .	. . .	. . .	. . .	–7	–7
Other sectors	3 430 . .	. . .	. . .	. . .	. . .	. . .	. . .	. . .	. . .
Migrants' transfers	3 431 . .	. . .	. . .	. . .	. . .	. . .	. . .	. . .	. . .
Debt forgiveness	3 432 . .	. . .	. . .	. . .	. . .	. . .	. . .	. . .	. . .
Other capital transfers	3 440 . .	. . .	. . .	. . .	. . .	. . .	. . .	. . .	. . .
Nonproduced nonfinancial assets, credit	2 480 . .	**. . .**	**. . .**	**. . .**	**. . .**	**. . .**	**. . .**	**. . .**	**. . .**
Nonproduced nonfinancial assets, debit	3 480 . .	**. . .**	**. . .**	**–61**	**. . .**	**. . .**	**. . .**	**. . .**	**. . .**

Table 2 (Continued). STANDARD PRESENTATION, 1994–2001
(Millions of U.S. dollars)

	Code	1994	1995	1996	1997	1998	1999	2000	2001
FINANCIAL ACCOUNT	4 995	**–621**	**–3,913**	**–4,683**	**–5,280**	**–2,018**	**–6,391**	**–9,200**	**–11,378**
A. DIRECT INVESTMENT	4 500	–2,858	–450	–2,465	–3,132	–6,669	–2,090	–14,773	–4,936
Direct investment abroad	4 505	**–4,354**	**–1,494**	**–3,583**	**–5,260**	**–18,698**	**–6,739**	**–23,898**	**–8,363**
Equity capital	4 510	–2,268	–1,194	–1,385	–3,388	–19,882	–3,662	–15,725	–5,259
Claims on affiliated enterprises	4 515	. . .	. . .	. . .	–3,388	–19,882	–3,556	–15,725	–5,401
Liabilities to affiliated enterprises	4 520	. . .	. . .	. . .	. . .	. . .	–106	. . .	142
Reinvested earnings	4 525	52	–113	–233	–1,067	3,202	–1,718	–1,288	2,051
Other capital	4 530	–2,137	–187	–1,965	–805	–2,017	–1,360	–6,885	–5,155
Claims on affiliated enterprises	4 535	–804	–596	–1,525	–1,342	–2,018	–4,271	–11,215	–4,342
Liabilities to affiliated enterprises	4 540	–1,334	408	–440	537	1	2,911	4,329	–813
Direct investment in Finland	4 555	**1,496**	**1,044**	**1,118**	**2,129**	**12,029**	**4,649**	**9,125**	**3,427**
Equity capital	4 560	790	535	833	1,082	10,612	1,290	4,871	3,144
Claims on direct investors	4 565	. . .	. . .	. . .	. . .	. . .	. . .	. . .	. . .
Liabilities to direct investors	4 570	790	535	833	1,082	10,612	1,290	4,871	3,144
Reinvested earnings	4 575	311	596	461	692	1,248	1,167	1,381	806
Other capital	4 580	395	–87	–176	355	169	2,192	2,874	–523
Claims on direct investors	4 585	–116	2	–74	212	–485	–344	–45	–147
Liabilities to direct investors	4 590	511	–89	–102	143	655	2,536	2,918	–376
B. PORTFOLIO INVESTMENT	4 600	6,955	–1,575	–3,032	–758	–40	–2,149	–1,804	–5,609
Assets	4 602	**775**	**204**	**–4,186**	**–4,600**	**–3,906**	**–15,699**	**–18,920**	**–11,594**
Equity securities	4 610	–78	–209	–736	–1,694	–2,099	–5,527	–7,164	–5,153
Monetary authorities	4 611	. . .	. . .	. . .	. . .	. . .	. . .	. . .	. . .
General government	4 612	. . .	. . .	–503	–515	–611	–2,074	–2,743	–3,436
Banks	4 613	–2	–6	–11	–7	–41	–15	–21	–22
Other sectors	4 614	–76	–204	–221	–1,173	–1,447	–3,438	–4,400	–1,695
Debt securities	4 619	853	414	–3,450	–2,906	–1,807	–10,173	–11,756	–6,441
Bonds and notes	4 620	779	–834	–3,372	–2,972	–1,828	–9,238	–11,948	–6,678
Monetary authorities	4 621	. . .	. . .	. . .	. . .	. . .	–367	–130	–59
General government	4 622	. . .	–10	–830	–356	–1,754	–4,808	–9,239	–4,611
Banks	4 623	922	–145	–528	–277	–759	–2,102	–513	927
Other sectors	4 624	–142	–678	–2,013	–2,338	685	–1,961	–2,067	–2,935
Money market instruments	4 630	73	1,247	–79	66	21	–934	192	237
Monetary authorities	4 631	. . .	. . .	. . .	. . .	. . .	–164	102	69
General government	4 632	. . .	. . .	1	. . .	1	–253	106	–49
Banks	4 633	85	49	. . .	–13	–6	–41	–131	–134
Other sectors	4 634	–12	1,198	–79	79	26	–477	115	351
Liabilities	4 652	**6,180**	**–1,779**	**1,153**	**3,843**	**3,866**	**13,550**	**17,116**	**5,985**
Equity securities	4 660	2,541	2,027	1,915	4,023	7,931	10,279	10,114	3,960
Banks	4 663	15	46	100	248	321	124	–1,884	38
Other sectors	4 664	2,526	1,981	1,815	3,776	7,609	10,155	11,998	3,922
Debt securities	4 669	3,640	–3,807	–761	–181	–4,065	3,271	7,002	2,025
Bonds and notes	4 670	4,092	–4,166	–981	–734	–3,703	1,142	2,437	444
Monetary authorities	4 671	. . .	. . .	. . .	. . .	. . .	. . .	. . .	. . .
General government	4 672	5,070	–166	898	–1,755	–1,696	1,645	–72	–816
Banks	4 673	–473	–1,980	–2,343	–80	–846	–153	303	–1,190
Other sectors	4 674	–504	–2,020	463	1,100	–1,162	–350	2,206	2,449
Money market instruments	4 680	–453	359	220	553	–362	2,129	4,565	1,581
Monetary authorities	4 681	–7	1	3	2	. . .	. . .	. . .	. . .
General government	4 682	150	389	377	–406	230	312	3,102	461
Banks	4 683	–603	–302	133	–107	222	1,921	1,782	1,743
Other sectors	4 684	7	272	–293	1,064	–814	–105	–319	–623
C. FINANCIAL DERIVATIVES	4 910	56	639	363	42	–636	–419	–630	38
Monetary authorities	4 911	. . .	. . .	. . .	. . .	. . .	. . .	. . .	. . .
General government	4 912	52	221	51	229	–527	6	91	–7
Banks	4 913	133	68	89	–28	–8	–86	–164	–16
Other sectors	4 914	–129	351	223	–159	–102	–339	–557	62
Assets	4 900	**51**	**38**	**38**	**–72**	**89**	**. . .**	**. . .**	**. . .**
Monetary authorities	4 901	. . .	. . .	. . .	. . .	. . .	. . .	. . .	. . .
General government	4 902	. . .	. . .	. . .	. . .	. . .	. . .	. . .	. . .
Banks	4 903	68	10	26	–34	13	. . .	. . .	. . .
Other sectors	4 904	–17	29	12	–37	75	. . .	. . .	. . .
Liabilities	4 905	**5**	**600**	**325**	**114**	**–725**	**–419**	**–630**	**38**
Monetary authorities	4 906	. . .	. . .	. . .	. . .	. . .	. . .	. . .	. . .
General government	4 907	52	221	51	229	–527	6	91	–7
Banks	4 908	64	58	63	7	–21	–86	–164	–16
Other sectors	4 909	–111	322	211	–122	–177	–339	–557	62

Table 2 (Concluded). STANDARD PRESENTATION, 1994–2001
(Millions of U.S. dollars)

	Code	1994	1995	1996	1997	1998	1999	2000	2001
D. OTHER INVESTMENT	4 700	–61	–2,898	–2,585	871	5,623	–1,721	8,366	–466
Assets	4 703	**–668**	**–2,863**	**–4,683**	**–2,201**	**331**	**–3,288**	**–5,636**	**–10,118**
Trade credits	4 706	–278	–885	–206	–405	–59	31	–897	–332
General government	4 707	–132	–326	–332	–793	–40	31	–156	–190
of which: Short-term	4 709	*3*	*1*	*–1*	*–1*	...	...	*–1*	*1*
Other sectors	4 710	–145	–559	126	388	–19	...	–741	–142
of which: Short-term	4 712	*–233*	*–592*	*100*	*398*	*–12*	*–31*	*–767*	*–75*
Loans	4 714	1,438	616	–1,009	–1,261	–5	830	–1,189	809
Monetary authorities	4 715	...	...	...	...	...	...	...	...
of which: Short-term	4 718	...	...	...	...	...	...	...	...
General government	4 719	81	47	–2	5	3	41	2	4
of which: Short-term	4 721	...	...	...	...	...	...	...	...
Banks	4 722	765	650	–653	–1,407	–213	1,542	–1,096	2,002
of which: Short-term	4 724	*452*	*229*	*–974*	*–1,359*	*146*	*1,449*	*–953*	*1,288*
Other sectors	4 725	592	–81	–355	141	204	–752	–94	–1,196
of which: Short-term	4 727	*73*	*–48*	*–108*	*4*	*120*	*–391*	*–115*	*–16*
Currency and deposits	4 730	–565	289	401	–294	283	68	–85	–1,138
Monetary authorities	4 731	...	...	...	...	...	520	–129	77
General government	4 732	–238	168	–106	201	–66	–233	–23	–786
Banks	4 733	–23	228	371	8	–13	–66	71	–76
Other sectors	4 734	–304	–106	136	–503	362	–153	–4	–353
Other assets	4 736	–1,263	–2,883	–3,869	–241	112	–4,218	–3,465	–9,458
Monetary authorities	4 737	99	146	27	94	145	–827	...	...
of which: Short-term	4 739	*99*	*146*	*27*	*94*	*145*	...	...	...
General government	4 740	–156	–255	–279	–22	–24	–63	5	6
of which: Short-term	4 742	...	...	*–15*	*–1*	*–26*	*–54*	*51*	...
Banks	4 743	–1,253	–2,804	–3,534	–326	267	–3,041	–3,081	–10,122
of which: Short-term	4 745	*–1,226*	*–2,998*	*–3,512*	*131*	*686*	*–2,627*	*–3,727*	*–10,136*
Other sectors	4 746	46	29	–83	14	–277	–286	–390	658
of which: Short-term	4 748	*27*	*36*	*–70*	*27*	*–299*	*–301*	*–408*	*661*
Liabilities	4 753	**607**	**–35**	**2,099**	**3,072**	**5,292**	**1,567**	**14,001**	**9,652**
Trade credits	4 756	694	–242	–743	–394	126	345	622	–108
General government	4 757	...	...	...	...	...	...	...	...
of which: Short-term	4 759	...	...	...	...	...	...	...	...
Other sectors	4 760	694	–242	–743	–394	126	345	622	–108
of which: Short-term	4 762	*656*	*–437*	*–562*	*–201*	*115*	*339*	*663*	*–196*
Loans	4 764	249	–1,619	2,766	2,103	1,190	2,021	4,065	–1,836
Monetary authorities	4 765	...	...	...	...	...	24	49	–185
of which: Use of Fund credit and loans from the Fund	4 766	...	...	...	...	...	...	...	...
of which: Short-term	4 768	...	...	...	...	...	*24*	*49*	*–185*
General government	4 769	997	–295	802	1,524	377	–471	–1,189	483
of which: Short-term	4 771	...	...	...	...	*157*	*139*	*–244*	*54*
Banks	4 772	–842	–713	–744	201	–156	92	–91	–1,995
of which: Short-term	4 774	*65*	*189*	*–74*	*543*	*–408*	*156*	*756*	*–1,057*
Other sectors	4 775	94	–612	2,708	378	969	2,377	5,294	–138
of which: Short-term	4 777	*774*	*–123*	*472*	*142*	*–375*	*1,053*	*2,655*	*–2,168*
Currency and deposits	4 780	–41	–179	–184	188	350	–656	1,910	1,041
Monetary authorities	4 781	...	...	...	...	...	–939	1,383	467
General government	4 782	...	...	...	...	...	...	...	...
Banks	4 783	–41	–179	–184	188	350	230	19	574
Other sectors	4 784	...	...	...	...	...	53	508	...
Other liabilities	4 786	–296	2,006	259	1,175	3,626	–143	7,405	10,555
Monetary authorities	4 787	–107	92	–96	–173	–180	43	...	...
of which: Short-term	4 789	*–107*	*92*	*–96*	*–173*	*–180*	...	...	...
General government	4 790	–32	–36	–38	–45	16	51	–83	–15
of which: Short-term	4 792	*–5*	*1*	*5*	*–9*	*35*	*70*	*–79*	...
Banks	4 793	–205	1,761	302	1,487	3,413	–476	4,170	10,124
of which: Short-term	4 795	*–87*	*1,215*	*208*	*1,299*	*3,895*	*–1,773*	*5,087*	*9,296*
Other sectors	4 796	49	189	90	–94	377	239	3,318	446
of which: Short-term	4 798	*–15*	*130*	*157*	*–36*	*347*	*30*	*2,826*	*98*
E. RESERVE ASSETS	4 802	–4,714	372	3,036	–2,304	–296	–13	–359	–405
Monetary gold	4 812	...	96	...	...	–87	118	...	...
Special drawing rights	4 811	–204	–24	59	–54	–8	52	137	–101
Reserve position in the Fund	4 810	34	–97	–48	–164	–247	179	109	–71
Foreign exchange	4 803	–4,544	1,145	2,835	–1,808	–740	–626	–1,093	–233
Other claims	4 813	...	–748	190	–278	785	264	487	...
NET ERRORS AND OMISSIONS	4 998	**–489**	**–1,384**	**–375**	**–1,600**	**–5,412**	**–1,349**	**70**	**2,956**

Part 3 of the *Yearbook* contains descriptions of the methodologies, compilation practices, and sources used to compile these data.

Table 3. INTERNATIONAL INVESTMENT POSITION (End–period stocks), 1994–2001
(Millions of U.S. dollars)

	Code	1994	1995	1996	1997	1998	1999	2000	2001
ASSETS	8 995 C.	51,570	57,970	65,385	71,091	85,854	109,967	148,101	166,438
Direct investment abroad	8 505 . .	**12,534**	**14,993**	**17,666**	**20,297**	**29,407**	**33,850**	**52,109**	**57,632**
Equity capital and reinvested earnings	8 506 . .	10,389	12,333	13,461	15,543	22,594	24,724	36,445	37,889
Claims on affiliated enterprises	8 507 . .	10,389	12,333	13,461	15,543	22,594	24,750	36,474	38,056
Liabilities to affiliated enterprises	8 508 . .	. . .	. . .	. . .	. . .	. . .	–26	–29	–167
Other capital	8 530 . .	2,145	2,660	4,205	4,754	6,814	9,126	15,664	19,743
Claims on affiliated enterprises	8 535 . .	4,734	5,914	6,912	7,741	9,978	15,237	25,701	28,315
Liabilities to affiliated enterprises	8 540 . .	–2,589	–3,254	–2,707	–2,986	–3,164	–6,111	–10,037	–8,572
Portfolio investment	8 602 . .	**3,417**	**3,572**	**7,713**	**11,659**	**16,825**	**33,621**	**51,125**	**55,905**
Equity securities	8 610 . .	418	738	1,564	3,245	5,271	13,670	20,263	20,157
Monetary authorities	8 611 . .	. . .	. . .	. . .	. . .	. . .	. . .	. . .	. . .
General government	8 612 . .	. . .	. . .	719	1,195	1,874	4,899	7,057	8,471
Banks	8 613 . .	37	44	53	57	89	75	87	100
Other sectors	8 614 . .	382	694	792	1,993	3,308	8,695	13,119	11,586
Debt securities	8 619 . .	2,999	2,835	6,149	8,414	11,554	19,951	30,862	35,748
Bonds and notes	8 620 . .	1,077	2,207	5,400	7,819	10,985	18,683	29,817	34,897
Monetary authorities	8 621 . .	. . .	. . .	. . .	. . .	105	443	543	568
General government	8 622 . .	. . .	10	1,356	1,599	3,630	7,353	16,376	20,264
Banks	8 623 . .	605	801	1,221	1,377	2,664	4,483	4,679	4,394
Other sectors	8 624 . .	472	1,396	2,824	4,844	4,586	6,404	8,219	9,671
Money market instruments	8 630 . .	1,922	628	749	594	569	1,269	1,045	851
Monetary authorities	8 631 . .	. . .	. . .	. . .	. . .	29	184	70	. . .
General government	8 632 . .	. . .	. . .	. . .	. . .	. . .	263	118	160
Banks	8 633 . .	47	. . .	. . .	13	5	43	220	419
Other sectors	8 634 . .	1,875	628	749	582	535	779	637	272
Financial derivatives	8 900 . .	**103**	**41**	**–5**	**259**	**151**	**3,469**	**2,816**	**2,073**
Monetary authorities	8 901 . .	. . .	. . .	. . .	. . .	. . .	. . .	. . .	. . .
General government	8 902 . .	. . .	. . .	. . .	. . .	. . .	827	477	430
Banks	8 903 . .	96	29	–16	1	22	1,320	1,462	1,354
Other sectors	8 904 . .	6	12	12	258	130	1,322	877	289
Other investment	8 703 . .	**24,395**	**28,153**	**32,173**	**29,385**	**29,684**	**30,348**	**33,636**	**42,407**
Trade credits	8 706 . .	5,376	6,506	6,445	3,733	4,316	4,125	4,557	4,448
General government	8 707 . .	283	618	951	1,227	1,211	1,195	1,341	1,499
of which: Short-term	8 709 . .	*1*	. . .	*1*	*1*	. . .	. . .	*1*	. . .
Other sectors	8 710 . .	5,093	5,888	5,494	2,506	3,105	2,929	3,216	2,949
of which: Short-term	8 712 . .	*4,841*	*5,769*	*5,412*	*2,423*	*2,914*	*2,772*	*3,085*	*2,432*
Loans	8 714 . .	5,238	4,676	5,478	6,407	6,709	5,502	6,313	5,324
Monetary authorities	8 715 . .	. . .	. . .	. . .	. . .	. . .	. . .	. . .	. . .
of which: Short-term	8 718 . .	. . .	. . .	. . .	. . .	. . .	. . .	. . .	. . .
General government	8 719 . .	156	123	118	97	99	46	41	35
of which: Short-term	8 721 . .	. . .	. . .	. . .	. . .	. . .	. . .	. . .	. . .
Banks	8 722 . .	2,308	1,570	2,128	3,275	3,735	2,008	2,843	3,378
of which: Short-term	8 724 . .	*598*	*434*	*1,351*	*2,497*	*2,575*	*1,190*	*1,974*	*1,056*
Other sectors	8 725 . .	2,774	2,983	3,232	3,035	2,875	3,448	3,429	1,911
of which: Short-term	8 727 . .	*7*	*82*	*189*	*210*	*126*	*521*	*606*	*184*
Currency and deposits	8 730 . .	1,741	1,673	1,270	1,282	1,774	1,476	1,453	2,378
Monetary authorities	8 731 . .	. . .	. . .	. . .	. . .	622	49	171	90
General government	8 732 . .	259	102	242	27	103	304	315	1,097
Banks	8 733 . .	593	530	159	133	191	222	112	182
Other sectors	8 734 . .	889	1,040	869	1,122	858	900	856	1,009
Other assets	8 736 . .	12,039	15,298	18,981	17,964	16,885	19,245	21,313	30,258
Monetary authorities	8 737 . .	969	911	830	617	456	772	715	677
of which: Short-term	8 739 . .	*969*	*911*	*830*	*617*	. . .	. . .	. . .	. . .
General government	8 740 . .	1,782	2,122	2,325	2,147	2,197	2,124	1,763	1,720
of which: Short-term	8 742 . .	. . .	. . .	*24*	*21*	. . .	*48*	. . .	. . .
Banks	8 743 . .	9,120	12,103	15,585	15,023	14,078	15,939	18,002	27,743
of which: Short-term	8 745 . .	*8,624*	*11,803*	*15,269*	*14,232*	*12,872*	*14,372*	*17,092*	*26,859*
Other sectors	8 746 . .	168	162	241	178	154	411	833	117
of which: Short-term	8 748 . .	*122*	*71*	*132*	*70*	*65*	*350*	*786*	*71*
Reserve assets	8 802 . .	**11,122**	**11,210**	**7,839**	**9,490**	**9,787**	**8,679**	**8,415**	**8,420**
Monetary gold	8 812 . .	460	400	375	321	576	459	430	438
Special drawing rights	8 811 . .	325	359	290	326	349	290	139	234
Reserve position in the Fund	8 810 . .	286	386	421	559	838	637	498	552
Foreign exchange	8 803 . .	10,051	9,293	6,206	7,532	7,088	6,759	7,342	7,191
Other claims	8 813 . .	. . .	772	547	752	937	533	7	5

Table 3 (Concluded). INTERNATIONAL INVESTMENT POSITION (End-period stocks), 1994–2001

(Millions of U.S. dollars)

	Code	1994	1995	1996	1997	1998	1999	2000	2001
LIABILITIES	8 995 D.	107,281	111,245	118,245	119,705	186,126	327,251	330,167	261,225
Direct investment in Finland	8 555 ..	**6,714**	**8,465**	**8,797**	**9,530**	**16,455**	**18,320**	**24,272**	**25,411**
Equity capital and reinvested earnings	8 556 ..	5,002	6,659	7,209	7,559	14,203	14,251	17,636	19,675
Claims on direct investors	8 557 ..	...	...	...	...	...	–2	...	...
Liabilities to direct investors	8 558 ..	5,002	6,659	7,209	7,559	14,203	14,253	17,636	19,675
Other capital	8 580 ..	1,712	1,805	1,589	1,971	2,252	4,069	6,636	5,736
Claims on direct investors	8 585 ..	–614	–824	–842	–658	–1,225	–1,884	–1,807	–1,857
Liabilities to direct investors	8 590 ..	2,326	2,629	2,431	2,629	3,477	5,952	8,443	7,592
Portfolio investment	8 652 ..	**69,508**	**69,408**	**75,311**	**76,436**	**131,124**	**267,648**	**253,376**	**176,145**
Equity securities	8 660 ..	12,767	14,625	23,457	28,870	79,722	219,531	204,361	128,284
Banks	8 663 ..	270	326	617	1,446	2,097	2,213	291	395
Other sectors	8 664 ..	12,497	14,299	22,840	27,424	77,625	217,318	204,070	127,889
Debt securities	8 669 ..	56,741	54,782	51,855	47,566	51,403	48,116	49,015	47,861
Bonds and notes	8 670 ..	54,567	52,465	49,510	44,963	49,133	45,291	42,956	40,247
Monetary authorities	8 671 ..	...	...	...	...	...	...	...	...
General government	8 672 ..	36,845	38,271	37,832	32,918	38,070	34,694	30,016	27,797
Banks	8 673 ..	7,473	5,786	3,270	3,231	2,540	2,252	2,718	5,691
Other sectors	8 674 ..	10,249	8,409	8,408	8,813	8,524	8,345	10,222	6,759
Money market instruments	8 680 ..	2,173	2,317	2,345	2,603	2,269	2,825	6,059	7,614
Monetary authorities	8 681 ..	1	...	...	...	...	...	...	...
General government	8 682 ..	218	566	728	227	348	582	3,308	3,665
Banks	8 683 ..	683	217	365	260	632	1,183	2,122	3,712
Other sectors	8 684 ..	1,271	1,535	1,252	2,116	1,290	1,060	630	236
Financial derivatives	8 905 ..	**–1,092**	**354**	**723**	**1,153**	**229**	**2,965**	**1,925**	**1,633**
Monetary authorities	8 906 ..	...	...	...	...	...	...	...	...
General government	8 907 ..	–184	994	751	604	106	495	239	288
Banks	8 908 ..	–402	–424	–162	15	–124	1,200	1,037	1,153
Other sectors	8 909 ..	–506	–216	134	534	247	1,269	649	192
Other investment	8 753 ..	**32,151**	**33,018**	**33,414**	**32,586**	**38,317**	**38,319**	**50,594**	**58,037**
Trade credits	8 756 ..	4,185	4,254	3,200	2,119	2,400	2,411	2,908	2,644
General government	8 757 ..	...	...	...	...	...	...	...	...
of which: Short-term	8 759 ..	...	...	...	...	...	...	...	...
Other sectors	8 760 ..	4,185	4,254	3,200	2,119	2,400	2,411	2,908	2,644
of which: Short-term	8 762 ..	*3,717*	*3,548*	*2,717*	*1,898*	*2,123*	*2,161*	*2,723*	*2,387*
Loans	8 764 ..	17,425	15,888	17,936	18,104	21,104	21,618	24,719	23,317
Monetary authorities	8 765 ..	...	...	...	...	246	240	278	93
of which: Use of Fund credit and loans from the Fund	8 766 ..	...	...	...	...	...	...	...	...
of which: Short-term	8 768 ..	...	...	...	...	*246*	*240*	*278*	*93*
General government	8 769 ..	3,762	3,646	4,110	5,221	5,992	5,421	3,980	4,230
of which: Short-term	8 771 ..	...	...	...	...	*114*	*248*	...	*56*
Banks	8 772 ..	3,804	3,115	2,163	1,998	2,335	1,875	1,613	1,976
of which: Short-term	8 774 ..	*178*	*310*	*199*	*665*	*300*	*409*	*1,089*	*206*
Other sectors	8 775 ..	9,859	9,127	11,663	10,885	12,530	14,082	18,847	17,017
of which: Short-term	8 777 ..	*1,086*	*917*	*1,375*	*1,354*	*1,085*	*1,981*	*4,585*	*2,193*
Currency and deposits	8 780 ..	723	589	373	509	982	–85	1,634	2,089
Monetary authorities	8 781 ..	...	...	...	...	114	–930	336	794
General government	8 782 ..	...	...	...	...	...	...	...	...
Banks	8 783 ..	723	589	373	509	868	794	769	1,295
Other sectors	8 784 ..	...	...	...	...	...	51	529	...
Other liabilities	8 786 ..	9,817	12,287	11,904	11,854	13,832	14,376	21,334	29,988
Monetary authorities	8 787 ..	996	1,176	1,018	713	374	...	...	...
of which: Short-term	8 789 ..	*996*	*1,176*	*1,018*	*713*	...	...	...	...
General government	8 790 ..	254	240	188	120	140	154	60	42
of which: Short-term	8 792 ..	*8*	*9*	*14*	*5*	*39*	*84*	...	...
Banks	8 793 ..	8,092	10,120	9,990	10,496	12,932	11,816	15,443	28,090
of which: Short-term	8 795 ..	*7,275*	*8,720*	*8,538*	*8,901*	*11,820*	*9,275*	*13,874*	*25,756*
Other sectors	8 796 ..	475	751	707	526	386	2,406	5,831	1,856
of which: Short-term	8 798 ..	*378*	*472*	*516*	*412*	*152*	*158*	*3,162*	*147*
NET INTERNATIONAL INVESTMENT POSITION	8 995 ..	**–55,711**	**–53,276**	**–52,860**	**–48,614**	**–100,272**	**–217,285**	**–182,067**	**–94,788**
Conversion rates: markaa per U.S. dollar (end of period)	0 102 ..	**4.7432**	**4.3586**	**4.6439**	**5.4207**	**5.0960**	...	...	...
Conversion rates: euros per U.S. dollar (end of period)	0 104 ..	...	...	...	...	...	**.9954**	**1.0747**	**1.1347**

France
132

Table 1. ANALYTIC PRESENTATION, 1994–2001
(Billions of U.S. dollars)

	Code	1994	1995	1996	1997	1998	1999	2000	2001
A. Current Account [1]	4 993 Z.	**7.42**	**10.84**	**20.56**	**37.80**	**37.70**	**35.04**	**20.43**	**21.36**
Goods: exports f.o.b	2 100 . .	230.81	278.63	281.85	286.07	303.02	300.05	295.53	291.41
Goods: imports f.o.b	3 100 . .	–223.56	–267.63	–266.91	–259.17	–278.08	–282.06	–294.40	–288.56
Balance on Goods	4 100 . .	*7.25*	*11.00*	*14.94*	*26.90*	*24.94*	*17.99*	*1.13*	*2.85*
Services: credit	2 200 . .	75.52	84.09	83.53	80.79	84.96	82.39	81.74	80.39
Services: debit	3 200 . .	–57.67	–66.12	–67.28	–64.16	–67.73	–64.45	–62.63	–62.48
Balance on Goods and Services	4 991 . .	*25.10*	*28.97*	*31.19*	*43.52*	*42.17*	*35.93*	*20.24*	*20.76*
Income: credit	2 300 . .	41.56	45.18	47.55	57.13	66.67	64.96	71.36	79.57
Income: debit	3 300 . .	–48.32	–54.15	–50.25	–50.04	–58.00	–53.03	–57.65	–64.19
Balance on Goods, Services, and Income	4 992 . .	*18.34*	*20.01*	*28.48*	*50.62*	*50.83*	*47.86*	*33.95*	*36.15*
Current transfers: credit	2 379 Z.	18.22	22.01	22.76	19.61	19.65	18.88	17.35	17.16
Current transfers: debit	3 379 . .	–29.15	–31.17	–30.68	–32.43	–32.79	–31.70	–30.87	–31.95
B. Capital Account [1]	4 994 Z.	**–4.18**	**.51**	**1.23**	**1.48**	**1.47**	**1.57**	**1.39**	**–.12**
Capital account: credit	2 994 Z.	.99	1.16	1.88	2.41	2.10	1.89	1.92	1.15
Capital account: debit	3 994 . .	–5.16	–.66	–.65	–.93	–.63	–.31	–.53	–1.28
Total, Groups A Plus B	4 981 . .	*3.24*	*11.35*	*21.80*	*39.28*	*39.17*	*36.61*	*21.82*	*21.24*
C. Financial Account [1]	4 995 W.	**–4.78**	**–7.33**	**–22.34**	**–37.60**	**–29.29**	**–36.13**	**–30.28**	**–31.57**
Direct investment abroad	4 505 . .	–24.44	–15.82	–30.36	–35.49	–45.70	–119.49	–169.48	–83.19
Direct investment in France	4 555 Z.	15.80	23.73	21.97	23.05	29.52	46.63	43.17	52.50
Portfolio investment assets	4 602 . .	–21.96	–7.42	–46.63	–60.79	–105.22	–126.81	–96.80	–83.67
Equity securities	4 610 . .	. . .	1.78	–1.08	–9.67	–24.46	–20.73	–31.91	–17.30
Debt securities	4 619 . .	. . .	–9.20	–45.55	–51.12	–80.76	–106.08	–64.89	–66.37
Portfolio investment liabilities	4 652 Z.	–27.90	13.08	–15.35	35.32	59.75	117.52	132.96	102.24
Equity securities	4 660 . .	. . .	6.82	12.20	11.97	17.21	49.35	49.36	10.97
Debt securities	4 669 Z.	. . .	6.26	–27.56	23.36	42.54	68.17	83.60	91.28
Financial derivatives	4 910 . .	. . .	1.00	1.34	4.10	–.44	–2.23	4.14	.95
Financial derivatives assets	4 900 . .	. . .	. . .	–6.47	. . .	. . .	. . .	. . .	. . .
Financial derivatives liabilities	4 905 . .	. . .	1.00	7.81	4.10	–.44	–2.23	4.14	.95
Other investment assets	4 703 . .	23.06	–40.16	26.31	–53.64	26.11	–26.62	.96	–55.90
Monetary authorities	4 701 . .	–.24	.50	.13	–.43	–.05	–10.31	–6.00	–12.50
General government	4 704 . .	3.08	–.65	1.11	1.18	.86	.74	.68	–.09
Banks	4 705 . .	22.72	–43.19	28.59	–46.82	41.70	–11.66	6.64	–42.28
Other sectors	4 728 . .	–2.50	3.18	–3.52	–7.57	–16.40	–5.39	–.37	–1.03
Other investment liabilities	4 753 W.	30.67	18.26	20.38	49.85	6.70	74.88	54.77	35.50
Monetary authorities	4 753 WA	–14.41	.45	–.47	.13	.31	28.86	–23.39	1.15
General government	4 753 ZB	3.16	1.10	–.01	4.67	.15	2.14	2.18	1.32
Banks	4 753 ZC	32.11	13.12	15.83	39.05	2.26	43.89	56.41	39.11
Other sectors	4 753 ZD	9.81	3.59	5.04	6.00	3.98	–.01	19.56	–6.08
Total, Groups A Through C	4 983 . .	*–1.54*	*4.02*	*–.55*	*1.68*	*9.88*	*.48*	*–8.46*	*–10.33*
D. Net Errors and Omissions	4 998 . .	**3.99**	**–3.31**	**.79**	**4.26**	**9.94**	**–1.87**	**6.03**	**4.86**
Total, Groups A Through D	4 984 . .	*2.45*	*.71*	*.24*	*5.94*	*19.82*	*–1.39*	*–2.43*	*–5.47*
E. Reserves and Related Items	4 802 A.	**–2.45**	**–.71**	**–.24**	**–5.94**	**–19.82**	**1.39**	**2.43**	**5.47**
Reserve assets	4 802 . .	–2.45	–.71	–.24	–5.94	–19.82	1.39	2.43	5.47
Use of Fund credit and loans	4 766 . .	. . .	. . .	. . .	. . .	. . .	. . .	. . .	. . .
Exceptional financing	4 920 . .	. . .	. . .	. . .	. . .	. . .	. . .	. . .	. . .
Conversion rates: French francs per U.S. dollar	0 101 . .	**5.5520**	**4.9915**	**5.1155**	**5.8367**	**5.8995**	**. . .**	**. . .**	**. . .**
Conversion rates: euros per U.S. dollar	0 103 . .	**. . .**	**. . .**	**. . .**	**. . .**	**. . .**	**.9386**	**1.0854**	**1.1175**

[1] Excludes components that have been classified in the categories of Group E.

Table 2. STANDARD PRESENTATION, 1994–2001

(Billions of U.S. dollars)

	Code		1994	1995	1996	1997	1998	1999	2000	2001
CURRENT ACCOUNT	4 993	. .	**7.42**	**10.84**	**20.56**	**37.80**	**37.70**	**35.04**	**20.43**	**21.36**
A. GOODS	4 100	. .	7.25	11.00	14.94	26.90	24.94	17.99	1.13	2.85
Credit	2 100	. .	**230.81**	**278.63**	**281.85**	**286.07**	**303.02**	**300.05**	**295.53**	**291.41**
General merchandise: exports f.o.b.	2 110	. .	223.07	268.24	271.48	277.70	294.11	291.01	286.85	281.82
Goods for processing: exports f.o.b.	2 150	. .	. . .	. . .	. . .	. . .	. . .	. . .	. . .	. . .
Repairs on goods	2 160	. .	7.20	9.75	9.63	7.65	8.34	8.31	7.51	8.78
Goods procured in ports by carriers	2 170	. .	.54	.63	.74	.71	.57	.74	1.17	.81
Nonmonetary gold	2 180	. .	. . .	. . .	. . .	. . .	. . .	. . .	. . .	. . .
Debit	3 100	. .	**–223.56**	**–267.63**	**–266.91**	**–259.17**	**–278.08**	**–282.06**	**–294.40**	**–288.56**
General merchandise: imports f.o.b.	3 110	. .	–217.35	–258.92	–258.63	–252.43	–270.60	–274.50	–286.40	–279.33
Goods for processing: imports f.o.b.	3 150	. .	. . .	. . .	. . .	. . .	. . .	. . .	. . .	. . .
Repairs on goods	3 160	. .	–5.91	–8.44	–7.86	–6.38	–7.20	–6.93	–6.78	–8.06
Goods procured in ports by carriers	3 170	. .	–.30	–.27	–.42	–.36	–.29	–.64	–1.22	–1.17
Nonmonetary gold	3 180	. .	. . .	. . .	. . .	. . .	. . .	. . .	. . .	. . .
B. SERVICES	4 200	. .	17.85	17.97	16.25	16.63	17.23	17.94	19.11	17.91
Total credit	2 200	. .	*75.52*	*84.09*	*83.53*	*80.79*	*84.96*	*82.39*	*81.74*	*80.39*
Total debit	3 200	. .	*–57.67*	*–66.12*	*–67.28*	*–64.16*	*–67.73*	*–64.45*	*–62.63*	*–62.48*
Transportation services, credit	2 205	. .	**17.23**	**20.47**	**20.16**	**19.41**	**20.40**	**19.60**	**19.43**	**18.07**
Passenger	2 850	. .	*3.27*	*3.71*	*3.74*	. . .	. . .	. . .	. . .	. . .
Freight	2 851	. .	*4.27*	*4.88*	*4.87*	. . .	. . .	. . .	. . .	. . .
Other	2 852	. .	*9.70*	*11.88*	*11.56*	. . .	. . .	. . .	. . .	. . .
Sea transport, passenger	2 207	. .	.19	.19	.14	. . .	. . .	. . .	. . .	. . .
Sea transport, freight	2 208	. .	1.60	1.82	1.67	. . .	. . .	. . .	. . .	. . .
Sea transport, other	2 209	. .	1.46	1.70	1.50	. . .	. . .	. . .	. . .	. . .
Air transport, passenger	2 211	. .	2.75	3.08	3.23	. . .	. . .	. . .	. . .	. . .
Air transport, freight	2 212	. .	1.10	1.27	1.26	. . .	. . .	. . .	. . .	. . .
Air transport, other	2 213	. .	3.70	4.53	4.40	. . .	. . .	. . .	. . .	. . .
Other transport, passenger	2 215	. .	.33	.44	.36	. . .	. . .	. . .	. . .	. . .
Other transport, freight	2 216	. .	1.56	1.79	1.94	. . .	. . .	. . .	. . .	. . .
Other transport, other	2 217	. .	4.54	5.65	5.66	. . .	. . .	. . .	. . .	. . .
Transportation services, debit	3 205	. .	**–18.03**	**–21.25**	**–20.62**	**–19.19**	**–19.91**	**–19.18**	**–19.54**	**–17.36**
Passenger	3 850	. .	*–3.75*	*–4.34*	*–4.30*	. . .	. . .	. . .	. . .	. . .
Freight	3 851	. .	*–4.38*	*–5.08*	*–4.88*	. . .	. . .	. . .	. . .	. . .
Other	3 852	. .	*–9.91*	*–11.82*	*–11.44*	. . .	. . .	. . .	. . .	. . .
Sea transport, passenger	3 207	. .	–.06	–.04	–.06	. . .	. . .	. . .	. . .	. . .
Sea transport, freight	3 208	. .	–2.89	–3.19	–2.97	. . .	. . .	. . .	. . .	. . .
Sea transport, other	3 209	. .	–1.49	–1.57	–1.47	. . .	. . .	. . .	. . .	. . .
Air transport, passenger	3 211	. .	–3.53	–4.09	–4.07	. . .	. . .	. . .	. . .	. . .
Air transport, freight	3 212	. .	–1.18	–1.47	–1.52	. . .	. . .	. . .	. . .	. . .
Air transport, other	3 213	. .	–3.37	–3.82	–3.66	. . .	. . .	. . .	. . .	. . .
Other transport, passenger	3 215	. .	–.16	–.21	–.18	. . .	. . .	. . .	. . .	. . .
Other transport, freight	3 216	. .	–.31	–.42	–.38	. . .	. . .	. . .	. . .	. . .
Other transport, other	3 217	. .	–5.05	–6.43	–6.31	. . .	. . .	. . .	. . .	. . .
Travel, credit	2 236	. .	**24.80**	**27.59**	**28.35**	**27.40**	**29.49**	**31.56**	**30.92**	**30.45**
Business travel	2 237	. .	. . .	. . .	. . .	. . .	. . .	. . .	. . .	. . .
Personal travel	2 240	. .	. . .	. . .	. . .	. . .	. . .	. . .	. . .	. . .
Travel, debit	3 236	. .	**–13.85**	**–16.36**	**–17.75**	**–17.49**	**–18.82**	**–18.71**	**–17.92**	**–18.06**
Business travel	3 237	. .	. . .	. . .	. . .	. . .	. . .	. . .	. . .	. . .
Personal travel	3 240	. .	. . .	. . .	. . .	. . .	. . .	. . .	. . .	. . .
Other services, credit	2 200	BA	**33.49**	**36.04**	**35.02**	**33.98**	**35.07**	**31.23**	**31.39**	**31.86**
Communications	2 245	. .	.37	.47	.58	.64	.89	1.06	1.32	1.61
Construction	2 249	. .	2.28	3.10	3.79	3.95	4.93	3.96	2.87	2.69
Insurance	2 253	. .	1.46	1.85	1.49	1.41	.96	.96	1.32	.89
Financial	2 260	. .	2.55	2.54	1.88	1.69	1.50	1.39	1.26	1.07
Computer and information	2 262	. .	.25	.36	.51	.55	.77	.85	.81	1.17
Royalties and licence fees	2 266	. .	1.53	1.85	1.88	2.05	2.34	1.92	2.31	2.50
Other business services	2 268	. .	23.28	23.71	22.52	21.41	21.46	19.05	19.32	19.96
Personal, cultural, and recreational	2 287	. .	.94	1.18	1.42	1.41	1.43	1.38	1.59	1.43
Government, n.i.e.	2 291	. .	.83	.98	.94	.88	.79	.64	.59	.54
Other services, debit	3 200	BA	**–25.79**	**–28.51**	**–28.91**	**–27.48**	**–29.00**	**–26.56**	**–25.16**	**–27.05**
Communications	3 245	. .	–.41	–.41	–.42	–.67	–.90	–.96	–1.14	–1.52
Construction	3 249	. .	–.85	–1.02	–1.36	–1.84	–2.67	–2.03	–1.53	–1.61
Insurance	3 253	. .	–1.07	–1.57	–1.57	–1.18	–1.37	–1.17	.32	–.63
Financial	3 260	. .	–2.38	–2.35	–1.72	–1.61	–1.61	–1.38	–1.46	–1.44
Computer and information	3 262	. .	–.47	–.52	–.48	–.52	–.63	–.75	–.74	–.99
Royalties and licence fees	3 266	. .	–1.91	–2.32	–2.65	–2.48	–2.72	–2.35	–2.05	–1.88
Other business services	3 268	. .	–15.92	–17.39	–17.21	–15.81	–16.01	–15.15	–15.49	–16.12
Personal, cultural, and recreational	3 287	. .	–1.28	–1.34	–1.84	–1.82	–1.80	–1.81	–1.97	–1.97
Government, n.i.e.	3 291	. .	–1.50	–1.59	–1.66	–1.57	–1.30	–.96	–1.11	–.90

Table 2 (Continued). STANDARD PRESENTATION, 1994–2001

(Billions of U.S. dollars)

	Code	1994	1995	1996	1997	1998	1999	2000	2001
C. INCOME	4 300	-6.75	-8.96	-2.71	7.09	8.66	11.94	13.71	15.38
Total credit	2 300	*41.56*	*45.18*	*47.55*	*57.13*	*66.67*	*64.96*	*71.36*	*79.57*
Total debit	3 300	*-48.32*	*-54.15*	*-50.25*	*-50.04*	*-58.00*	*-53.03*	*-57.65*	*-64.19*
Compensation of employees, credit	2 310	**2.34**	**2.65**	**2.61**	**9.05**	**9.32**	**8.64**	**7.93**	**8.50**
Compensation of employees, debit	3 310	**-1.44**	**-1.65**	**-1.25**	**-1.12**	**-1.16**	**-1.28**	**-1.09**	**-1.07**
Investment income, credit	2 320	**39.23**	**42.53**	**44.94**	**48.08**	**57.35**	**56.33**	**63.43**	**71.07**
Direct investment income	2 330	6.30	2.23	7.68	9.99	10.22	14.83	13.75	19.45
Dividends and distributed branch profits	2 332	4.83	5.29	6.31	...	...	...	...	...
Reinvested earnings and undistributed branch profits	2 333	1.47	-3.06	1.37	1.87	2.16	6.40	6.48	5.73
Income on debt (interest)	2 334	...	...	...	8.12	8.06	8.43	7.26	13.72
Portfolio investment income	2 339	9.17	10.36	11.86	14.94	22.12	22.81	25.86	27.62
Income on equity	2 340	1.97	1.87	1.96	...	...	...	...	...
Income on bonds and notes	2 350	6.53	7.73	9.14	...	...	...	...	...
Income on money market instruments	2 360	.68	.76	.77	...	...	...	...	...
Other investment income	2 370	23.75	29.94	25.41	23.15	25.01	18.68	23.83	24.00
Investment income, debit	3 320	**-46.87**	**-52.50**	**-49.00**	**-48.92**	**-56.84**	**-51.75**	**-56.55**	**-63.12**
Direct investment income	3 330	-2.81	-2.91	-2.88	-4.23	-5.81	-5.77	-6.24	-6.79
Dividends and distributed branch profits	3 332	-3.64	-3.62	-3.94	...	...	...	...	...
Reinvested earnings and undistributed branch profits	3 333	.83	.72	1.06	-.54	-.53	-2.56	-3.22	-2.86
Income on debt (interest)	3 334	...	...	...	-3.69	-5.29	-3.21	-3.01	-3.92
Portfolio investment income	3 339	-22.94	-25.41	-24.81	-23.40	-27.29	-26.55	-25.89	-30.97
Income on equity	3 340	-2.47	-3.31	-3.74	...	...	...	...	...
Income on bonds and notes	3 350	-16.55	-20.29	-19.19	...	...	...	...	...
Income on money market instruments	3 360	-3.92	-1.81	-1.88	...	...	...	...	...
Other investment income	3 370	-21.12	-24.18	-21.31	-21.29	-23.74	-19.42	-24.43	-25.35
D. CURRENT TRANSFERS	4 379	-10.93	-9.17	-7.92	-12.82	-13.13	-12.82	-13.53	-14.79
Credit	2 379	**18.22**	**22.01**	**22.76**	**19.61**	**19.65**	**18.88**	**17.35**	**17.16**
General government	2 380	11.76	13.92	15.61	13.77	13.33	12.92	11.35	10.81
Other sectors	2 390	6.47	8.09	7.15	5.84	6.33	5.96	5.99	6.35
Workers' remittances	2 391	1.41	1.78	1.73	.69	.70	.85	.68	.72
Other current transfers	2 392	5.05	6.30	5.42	5.15	5.62	5.11	5.31	5.63
Debit	3 379	**-29.15**	**-31.17**	**-30.68**	**-32.43**	**-32.79**	**-31.70**	**-30.87**	**-31.95**
General government	3 380	-21.96	-23.24	-22.66	-21.64	-21.60	-20.42	-19.55	-19.43
Other sectors	3 390	-7.19	-7.93	-8.02	-10.79	-11.18	-11.29	-11.32	-12.52
Workers' remittances	3 391	-2.70	-3.15	-3.07	-2.87	-3.07	-2.87	-2.69	-2.86
Other current transfers	3 392	-4.49	-4.79	-4.96	-7.92	-8.11	-8.41	-8.63	-9.66
CAPITAL AND FINANCIAL ACCOUNT	4 996	**-11.40**	**-7.53**	**-21.35**	**-42.06**	**-47.64**	**-33.17**	**-26.45**	**-26.22**
CAPITAL ACCOUNT	4 994	**-4.18**	**.51**	**1.23**	**1.48**	**1.47**	**1.57**	**1.39**	**-.12**
Total credit	2 994	*.99*	*1.16*	*1.88*	*2.41*	*2.10*	*1.89*	*1.92*	*1.15*
Total debit	3 994	*-5.16*	*-.66*	*-.65*	*-.93*	*-.63*	*-.31*	*-.53*	*-1.28*
Capital transfers, credit	2 400	**.92**	**1.07**	**1.80**	**2.35**	**1.96**	**1.89**	**1.89**	**1.15**
General government	2 401	.72	.86	1.54	2.02	1.74	1.57	1.65	.80
Debt forgiveness	2 402	...	...	...	...	...	...	...	...
Other capital transfers	2 410	.72	.86	1.54	2.02	1.74	1.57	1.65	.80
Other sectors	2 430	.21	.21	.27	.33	.22	.31	.24	.36
Migrants' transfers	2 431	.21	.21	.20	...	...	...	...	...
Debt forgiveness	2 432	...	...	.07	.13	...	...	.01	...
Other capital transfers	2 440	...	...	...	.20	.22	.31	.23	.36
Capital transfers, debit	3 400	**-5.08**	**-.47**	**-.55**	**-.85**	**-.54**	**-.31**	**-.42**	**-1.09**
General government	3 401	-4.50	-.33	-.37	-.52	-.34	-.10	-.21	-.29
Debt forgiveness	3 402	-4.25	-.09	-.13	-.31	-.14	-.10	-.04	-.13
Other capital transfers	3 410	-.25	-.24	-.23	-.21	-.20	...	-.17	-.16
Other sectors	3 430	-.57	-.14	-.18	-.33	-.20	-.21	-.22	-.81
Migrants' transfers	3 431	-.13	-.14	-.14	...	...	...	...	...
Debt forgiveness	3 432	-.44	...	-.04	-.19	-.04	...	-.04	-.81
Other capital transfers	3 440	...	...	...	-.14	-.16	-.21	-.18	...
Nonproduced nonfinancial assets, credit	2 480	**.06**	**.09**	**.08**	**.06**	**.14**	**...**	**.03**	**...**
Nonproduced nonfinancial assets, debit	3 480	**-.09**	**-.18**	**-.10**	**-.08**	**-.09**	**...**	**-.10**	**-.18**

Table 2 (Continued). STANDARD PRESENTATION, 1994–2001
(Billions of U.S. dollars)

	Code	1994	1995	1996	1997	1998	1999	2000	2001
FINANCIAL ACCOUNT	4 995	**–7.22**	**–8.04**	**–22.58**	**–43.54**	**–49.10**	**–34.74**	**–27.85**	**–26.10**
A. DIRECT INVESTMENT	4 500	–8.64	7.91	–8.39	–12.44	–16.18	–72.87	–126.31	–30.69
Direct investment abroad	4 505	**–24.44**	**–15.82**	**–30.36**	**–35.49**	**–45.70**	**–119.49**	**–169.48**	**–83.19**
Equity capital	4 510	–10.15	–8.02	–15.21	–18.03	–24.19	–86.40	–131.19	–46.80
Claims on affiliated enterprises	4 515	...	...	...	–18.03	–24.19	–86.40	–131.19	–46.80
Liabilities to affiliated enterprises	4 520	...	...	...	...	...	...	...	...
Reinvested earnings	4 525	–1.47	3.06	–1.37	–1.87	–2.16	–6.40	–6.48	–5.73
Other capital	4 530	–12.82	–10.87	–13.79	–15.59	–19.35	–26.69	–31.81	–30.67
Claims on affiliated enterprises	4 535	...	...	...	–15.59	–19.35	–26.69	–31.81	–30.67
Liabilities to affiliated enterprises	4 540	...	...	...	...	...	...	...	...
Direct investment in France	4 555	**15.80**	**23.73**	**21.97**	**23.05**	**29.52**	**46.63**	**43.17**	**52.50**
Equity capital	4 560	9.35	11.86	9.97	12.88	17.09	19.07	26.65	18.00
Claims on direct investors	4 565	...	...	...	...	...	...	...	...
Liabilities to direct investors	4 570	...	...	...	12.88	17.09	19.07	26.65	18.00
Reinvested earnings	4 575	–.83	–.72	–1.06	.54	.53	2.56	3.22	2.86
Other capital	4 580	7.28	12.59	13.05	9.63	11.90	25.00	13.30	31.64
Claims on direct investors	4 585	...	...	...	...	...	...	...	...
Liabilities to direct investors	4 590	...	...	...	9.63	11.90	25.00	13.30	31.64
B. PORTFOLIO INVESTMENT	4 600	–49.86	5.66	–61.99	–25.47	–45.47	–9.29	36.16	18.58
Assets	4 602	**–21.96**	**–7.42**	**–46.63**	**–60.79**	**–105.22**	**–126.81**	**–96.80**	**–83.67**
Equity securities	4 610	...	1.78	–1.08	–9.67	–24.46	–20.73	–31.91	–17.30
Monetary authorities	4 611	...	...	...	...	...	...	...	...
General government	4 612	...	...	...	...	...	...	...	...
Banks	4 613	...	...	–.79	–3.48	–15.53	–8.92	–1.14	1.93
Other sectors	4 614	...	1.78	–.29	–6.19	–8.93	–11.81	–30.78	–19.23
Debt securities	4 619	...	–9.20	–45.55	–51.12	–80.76	–106.08	–64.89	–66.37
Bonds and notes	4 620	...	–15.48	–45.02	–44.23	–61.91	–73.61	–56.59	–56.34
Monetary authorities	4 621	...	...	...	...	...	...	...	...
General government	4 622	...	...	...	...	...	...	...	...
Banks	4 623	...	...	–23.72	–24.87	–31.00	–27.69	–41.00	–14.77
Other sectors	4 624	...	–15.48	–21.30	–19.36	–30.91	–45.92	–15.59	–41.57
Money market instruments	4 630	...	6.28	–.53	–6.89	–18.85	–32.47	–8.30	–10.03
Monetary authorities	4 631	...	...	...	...	...	...	...	...
General government	4 632	...	...	...	...	...	...	...	...
Banks	4 633	...	8.04	–.04	.06	–4.35	–9.48	8.36	–1.72
Other sectors	4 634	...	–1.76	–.50	–6.96	–14.50	–22.99	–16.66	–8.31
Liabilities	4 652	**–27.90**	**13.08**	**–15.35**	**35.32**	**59.75**	**117.52**	**132.96**	**102.24**
Equity securities	4 660	...	6.82	12.20	11.97	17.21	49.35	49.36	10.97
Banks	4 663	...	...	.65	1.18	.07	2.91	–2.18	3.91
Other sectors	4 664	...	6.82	11.56	10.78	17.14	46.44	51.55	7.06
Debt securities	4 669	...	6.26	–27.56	23.36	42.54	68.17	83.60	91.28
Bonds and notes	4 670	...	2.88	–25.27	16.16	46.66	58.07	66.87	84.10
Monetary authorities	4 671	...	...	...	...	...	...	...	...
General government	4 672	...	...	–25.68	5.49	43.01	36.17	33.17	27.84
Banks	4 673	...	...	–1.00	4.46	–.82	9.03	15.30	18.84
Other sectors	4 674	...	2.88	1.42	6.21	4.47	12.87	18.40	37.42
Money market instruments	4 680	...	3.38	–2.29	7.19	–4.12	10.10	16.73	7.18
Monetary authorities	4 681	...	...	...	...	...	...	...	...
General government	4 682	...	1.88	1.59	6.50	–2.74	–.95	7.97	2.85
Banks	4 683	...	1.50	–1.50	–.71	.33	7.29	3.62	12.57
Other sectors	4 684	...	...	–2.37	1.40	–1.72	3.76	5.14	–8.24
C. FINANCIAL DERIVATIVES	4 910	...	1.00	1.34	4.10	–.44	–2.23	4.14	.95
Monetary authorities	4 911	...	...	...	...	...	...	...	...
General government	4 912	...	...	...	...	...	...	...	...
Banks	4 913	...	...	...	4.10	–.44	–2.23	4.14	.95
Other sectors	4 914	...	1.00	1.34	...	...	...	...	...
Assets	4 900	**...**	**...**	**–6.47**	**...**	**...**	**...**	**...**	**...**
Monetary authorities	4 901	...	...	...	...	...	...	...	...
General government	4 902	...	...	...	...	...	...	...	...
Banks	4 903	...	...	...	...	...	...	...	...
Other sectors	4 904	...	...	–6.47	...	...	...	...	...
Liabilities	4 905	**...**	**1.00**	**7.81**	**4.10**	**–.44**	**–2.23**	**4.14**	**.95**
Monetary authorities	4 906	...	...	...	...	...	...	...	...
General government	4 907	...	...	...	...	...	...	...	...
Banks	4 908	...	...	...	4.10	–.44	–2.23	4.14	.95
Other sectors	4 909	...	1.00	7.81	...	...	...	...	...

Table 2 (Concluded). STANDARD PRESENTATION, 1994–2001
(Billions of U.S. dollars)

	Code	1994	1995	1996	1997	1998	1999	2000	2001
D. OTHER INVESTMENT	4 700	53.72	-21.89	46.69	-3.80	32.81	48.25	55.73	-20.40
Assets	4 703	**23.06**	**-40.16**	**26.31**	**-53.64**	**26.11**	**-26.62**	**.96**	**-55.90**
Trade credits	4 706	-4.24	-6.57	-5.13	-10.00	-8.02	-4.40	1.21	.65
General government	4 707	...	...	...	...	...	...	...	...
of which: Short-term	4 709	...	...	...	...	...	...	...	...
Other sectors	4 710	-4.24	-6.57	-5.13	-10.00	-8.02	-4.40	1.21	.65
of which: Short-term	4 712	...	...	...	...	...	...	...	...
Loans	4 714	27.63	-33.12	30.84	-43.32	35.23	-22.01	.10	-56.28
Monetary authorities	4 715	-.24	.50	.13	-.43	-.05	-10.31	-6.00	-12.50
of which: Short-term	4 718	...	...	...	...	...	...	...	...
General government	4 719	3.57	-.07	1.62	1.50	1.96	.95	1.03	.19
of which: Short-term	4 721	...	...	...	...	...	...	...	...
Banks	4 722	22.72	-43.19	28.59	-46.82	41.70	-11.66	6.64	-42.28
of which: Short-term	4 724	...	...	...	...	...	...	...	...
Other sectors	4 725	1.58	9.64	.50	2.43	-8.38	-.99	-1.57	-1.68
of which: Short-term	4 727	*-.38*	*-.33*	*-.47*	...	...	...	...	...
Currency and deposits	4 730	...	...	...	...	...	...	...	...
Monetary authorities	4 731	...	...	...	...	...	...	...	...
General government	4 732	...	...	...	...	...	...	...	...
Banks	4 733	...	...	...	...	...	...	...	...
Other sectors	4 734	...	...	...	...	...	...	...	...
Other assets	4 736	-.34	-.47	.60	-.32	-1.10	-.21	-.35	-.28
Monetary authorities	4 737	...	...	...	...	...	...	...	...
of which: Short-term	4 739	...	...	...	...	...	...	...	...
General government	4 740	-.49	-.57	-.51	-.32	-1.10	-.21	-.35	-.28
of which: Short-term	4 742	...	...	...	...	...	...	...	...
Banks	4 743	...	...	...	...	...	...	...	...
of which: Short-term	4 745	...	...	...	...	...	...	...	...
Other sectors	4 746	.16	.11	1.11	...	...	...	...	...
of which: Short-term	4 748	...	...	...	...	...	...	...	...
Liabilities	4 753	**30.67**	**18.26**	**20.38**	**49.85**	**6.70**	**74.88**	**54.77**	**35.50**
Trade credits	4 756	5.76	2.76	2.26	2.14	1.79	-1.24	3.08	-.61
General government	4 757	...	...	...	...	...	...	...	...
of which: Short-term	4 759	...	...	...	...	...	...	...	...
Other sectors	4 760	5.76	2.76	2.26	2.14	1.79	-1.24	3.08	-.61
of which: Short-term	4 762	*5.76*	*2.76*	*2.26*	*2.14*	*1.79*	*-1.24*	*3.08*	*-.61*
Loans	4 764	21.50	14.65	19.39	47.70	4.91	76.12	51.69	36.11
Monetary authorities	4 765	-14.96	.20	.30	.13	.31	28.86	-23.39	1.15
of which: Use of Fund credit and loans from the Fund	4 766	...	...	...	...	...	...	...	...
of which: Short-term	4 768	...	...	...	*.13*	*.31*	*28.86*	*-23.39*	*1.15*
General government	4 769	.30	.49	.48	4.67	.15	2.14	2.18	1.32
of which: Short-term	4 771	...	...	...	...	...	...	...	...
Banks	4 772	32.11	13.12	15.83	39.05	2.26	43.89	56.41	39.11
of which: Short-term	4 774	...	...	...	...	...	...	...	...
Other sectors	4 775	4.05	.83	2.78	3.85	2.19	1.22	16.48	-5.47
of which: Short-term	4 777	*.91*	*.76*	*.64*	...	...	...	...	...
Currency and deposits	4 780	3.10	.64	-.49	...	...	...	...	...
Monetary authorities	4 781	.24	.04	...	...	...	...	...	...
General government	4 782	2.86	.61	-.49	...	...	...	...	...
Banks	4 783	...	...	...	...	...	...	...	...
Other sectors	4 784	...	...	...	...	...	...	...	...
Other liabilities	4 786	.31	.21	-.77	...	...	...	...	...
Monetary authorities	4 787	.31	.21	-.77	...	...	...	...	...
of which: Short-term	4 789	...	...	...	...	...	...	...	...
General government	4 790	...	...	...	...	...	...	...	...
of which: Short-term	4 792	...	...	...	...	...	...	...	...
Banks	4 793	...	...	...	...	...	...	...	...
of which: Short-term	4 795	...	...	...	...	...	...	...	...
Other sectors	4 796	...	...	...	...	...	...	...	...
of which: Short-term	4 798	...	...	...	...	...	...	...	...
E. RESERVE ASSETS	4 802	-2.45	-.71	-.24	-5.94	-19.82	1.39	2.43	5.47
Monetary gold	4 812	...	...	...	...	-6.00	1.46	...	...
Special drawing rights	4 811	-.01	-.59	-.06	-.05	-.09	.74	-.07	-.11
Reserve position in the Fund	4 810	.08	-.34	-.03	-.33	-1.42	-1.09	.65	-.54
Foreign exchange	4 803	-2.51	.22	-.15	-5.56	-12.31	.28	1.86	6.11
Other claims	4 813	...	...	...	...	...	...	...	...
NET ERRORS AND OMISSIONS	4 998	**3.99**	**-3.31**	**.79**	**4.26**	**9.94**	**-1.87**	**6.03**	**4.86**

Part 3 of the *Yearbook* contains descriptions of the methodologies, compilation practices, and sources used to compile these data.

Table 3. INTERNATIONAL INVESTMENT POSITION (End–period stocks), 1994–2001
(Billions of U.S. dollars)

	Code		1994	1995	1996	1997	1998	1999	2000	2001
ASSETS	8 995	C.	1,194.77	1,349.18	1,495.49	1,709.96	2,049.12	2,321.27	2,429.34	2,397.59
Direct investment abroad	8 505	. .	**301.60**	**368.47**	**482.90**	**603.58**	**747.30**	**912.98**	**1,014.71**	**907.03**
Equity capital and reinvested earnings	8 506	. .	268.02	330.05	429.15	543.72	665.51	825.08	898.21	766.64
Claims on affiliated enterprises	8 507	. .	. . .	. . .	. . .	. . .	. . .	. . .	. . .	. . .
Liabilities to affiliated enterprises	8 508	. .	. . .	. . .	. . .	. . .	. . .	. . .	. . .	. . .
Other capital	8 530	. .	33.58	38.41	53.75	59.86	81.79	87.90	116.50	140.39
Claims on affiliated enterprises	8 535	. .	. . .	. . .	. . .	. . .	. . .	. . .	. . .	. . .
Liabilities to affiliated enterprises	8 540	. .	. . .	. . .	. . .	. . .	. . .	. . .	. . .	. . .
Portfolio investment	8 602	. .	**185.37**	**200.08**	**260.75**	**343.15**	**488.98**	**590.20**	**651.72**	**674.99**
Equity securities	8 610	. .	53.88	57.35	73.55	99.95	143.04	190.67	208.25	185.25
Monetary authorities	8 611	. .	.12	.13	.13	.22	.23	. . .	. . .	. . .
General government	8 612	. .	.12	.13	.13	.11	. . .	. . .	. . .	. . .
Banks	8 613	. .	10.95	11.97	18.42	26.73	44.10	27.63	30.15	29.08
Other sectors	8 614	. .	42.68	45.12	54.88	72.89	98.71	163.05	178.10	156.17
Debt securities	8 619	. .	131.49	142.73	187.20	243.20	345.94	399.53	443.48	489.74
Bonds and notes	8 620	. .	90.16	113.66	161.01	209.62	289.12	317.75	356.29	399.49
Monetary authorities	8 621	. .	. . .	. . .	. . .	. . .	. . .	. . .	. . .	. . .
General government	8 622	. .	.12	.13	.13	.11	.35	. . .	. . .	. . .
Banks	8 623	. .	59.29	73.53	100.99	128.11	140.83	147.48	165.91	183.05
Other sectors	8 624	. .	30.75	39.99	59.89	81.40	147.94	170.28	190.38	216.45
Money market instruments	8 630	. .	41.33	29.07	26.19	33.57	56.82	81.77	87.19	90.25
Monetary authorities	8 631	. .	. . .	. . .	. . .	. . .	. . .	. . .	. . .	. . .
General government	8 632	. .	. . .	. . .	. . .	. . .	. . .	. . .	. . .	. . .
Banks	8 633	. .	11.93	13.42	11.90	16.57	38.27	67.01	59.46	53.41
Other sectors	8 634	. .	29.40	15.66	14.28	17.01	18.55	14.77	27.73	36.84
Financial derivatives	8 900	. .	**24.85**	**30.78**	**34.71**	**42.96**	**76.07**	**110.00**	**95.00**	**109.81**
Monetary authorities	8 901	. .	. . .	. . .	. . .	. . .	. . .	. . .	. . .	. . .
General government	8 902	. .	. . .	. . .	. . .	. . .	. . .	. . .	. . .	. . .
Banks	8 903	. .	. . .	. . .	. . .	. . .	. . .	. . .	. . .	. . .
Other sectors	8 904	. .	24.85	30.78	34.71	42.96	76.07	110.00	95.00	109.81
Other investment	8 703	. .	**624.86**	**692.08**	**659.70**	**664.21**	**666.80**	**640.03**	**604.36**	**647.05**
Trade credits	8 706	. .	73.92	81.17	79.06	76.32	89.84	82.68	78.16	69.89
General government	8 707	. .	. . .	. . .	. . .	. . .	. . .	. . .	. . .	. . .
of which: Short-term	8 709	. .	. . .	. . .	. . .	. . .	. . .	. . .	. . .	. . .
Other sectors	8 710	. .	73.92	81.17	79.06	76.32	89.84	82.68	78.16	69.89
of which: Short-term	8 712	. .	. . .	. . .	. . .	. . .	. . .	. . .	. . .	. . .
Loans	8 714	. .	541.22	599.86	569.23	576.85	564.24	545.00	513.36	564.30
Monetary authorities	8 715	. .	1.23	.92	.75	1.88	1.17	10.75	15.35	27.23
of which: Short-term	8 718	. .	*1.23*	*.79*	*.63*	*1.10*	*1.17*	*10.75*	*15.35*	*27.23*
General government	8 719	. .	21.65	23.15	21.93	19.00	19.84	15.47	13.86	12.96
of which: Short-term	8 721	. .	*3.08*	*3.16*	*2.88*	*2.54*	*2.68*	*.60*	*.84*	*.97*
Banks	8 722	. .	470.49	521.06	484.78	502.52	487.70	457.70	429.61	450.08
of which: Short-term	8 724	. .	*379.71*	*426.87*	*398.70*	*417.04*	*391.91*	*356.63*	*321.77*	*337.27*
Other sectors	8 725	. .	47.85	54.72	61.77	53.45	55.54	61.08	54.53	74.03
of which: Short-term	8 727	. .	*47.85*	*54.72*	*61.77*	*52.35*	*54.37*	*59.87*	*53.50*	*72.71*
Currency and deposits	8 730	. .	. . .	. . .	. . .	. . .	. . .	. . .	. . .	. . .
Monetary authorities	8 731	. .	. . .	. . .	. . .	. . .	. . .	. . .	. . .	. . .
General government	8 732	. .	. . .	. . .	. . .	. . .	. . .	. . .	. . .	. . .
Banks	8 733	. .	. . .	. . .	. . .	. . .	. . .	. . .	. . .	. . .
Other sectors	8 734	. .	. . .	. . .	. . .	. . .	. . .	. . .	. . .	. . .
Other assets	8 736	. .	9.72	11.05	11.40	11.04	12.72	12.36	12.84	12.87
Monetary authorities	8 737	. .	. . .	. . .	. . .	. . .	.93	.80	.74	.71
of which: Short-term	8 739	. .	. . .	. . .	. . .	. . .	. . .	. . .	. . .	. . .
General government	8 740	. .	9.72	11.05	11.40	11.04	11.78	11.55	12.10	12.16
of which: Short-term	8 742	. .	. . .	. . .	. . .	. . .	. . .	. . .	. . .	. . .
Banks	8 743	. .	. . .	. . .	. . .	. . .	. . .	. . .	. . .	. . .
of which: Short-term	8 745	. .	. . .	. . .	. . .	. . .	. . .	. . .	. . .	. . .
Other sectors	8 746	. .	. . .	. . .	. . .	. . .	. . .	. . .	. . .	. . .
of which: Short-term	8 748	. .	. . .	. . .	. . .	. . .	. . .	. . .	. . .	. . .
Reserve assets	8 802	. .	**58.09**	**57.78**	**57.43**	**56.07**	**69.96**	**68.05**	**63.55**	**58.70**
Monetary gold	8 812	. .	31.37	31.18	30.45	25.07	29.87	28.33	26.52	26.97
Special drawing rights	8 811	. .	.36	.96	.98	.97	1.11	.35	.40	.49
Reserve position in the Fund	8 810	. .	2.37	2.76	2.70	2.86	4.45	5.42	4.52	4.89
Foreign exchange	8 803	. .	23.99	22.89	23.31	27.17	34.54	33.96	32.10	26.35
Other claims	8 813	. .	. . .	. . .	. . .	. . .	. . .	. . .	. . .	. . .

Table 3 (Concluded). INTERNATIONAL INVESTMENT POSITION (End–period stocks), 1994–2001

(Billions of U.S. dollars)

	Code	1994	1995	1996	1997	1998	1999	2000	2001
LIABILITIES	8 995 D.	1,162.26	1,276.41	1,331.18	1,452.23	1,816.51	2,243.37	2,353.79	2,247.58
Direct investment in France	8 555 . .	**302.59**	**335.18**	**359.36**	**403.01**	**548.60**	**648.87**	**646.14**	**561.21**
Equity capital and reinvested earnings	8 556 . .	277.25	303.88	320.39	361.59	491.90	581.66	568.07	455.98
Claims on direct investors	8 557 . .	. . .	. . .	. . .	. . .	. . .	. . .	. . .	. . .
Liabilities to direct investors	8 558 . .	. . .	. . .	. . .	. . .	. . .	. . .	. . .	. . .
Other capital	8 580 . .	25.34	31.31	38.97	41.42	56.70	67.21	78.07	105.23
Claims on direct investors	8 585 . .	. . .	. . .	. . .	. . .	. . .	. . .	. . .	. . .
Liabilities to direct investors	8 590 . .	. . .	. . .	. . .	. . .	. . .	. . .	. . .	. . .
Portfolio investment	8 652 . .	**367.54**	**410.43**	**424.39**	**481.86**	**638.09**	**854.51**	**944.74**	**913.20**
Equity securities	8 660 . .	102.46	118.66	155.37	201.67	300.55	499.59	522.57	416.33
Banks	8 663 . .	10.95	12.37	11.40	20.87	30.69	54.95	45.97	38.95
Other sectors	8 664 . .	91.52	106.29	143.97	180.80	269.87	444.64	476.60	377.37
Debt securities	8 669 . .	265.07	291.77	269.02	280.19	337.54	354.93	422.17	496.88
Bonds and notes	8 670 . .	244.04	266.25	240.20	247.28	307.67	319.56	377.69	447.52
Monetary authorities	8 671 . .	. . .	. . .	. . .	. . .	. . .	. . .	. . .	. . .
General government	8 672 . .	94.71	109.05	83.95	92.88	139.08	150.69	182.94	203.84
Banks	8 673 . .	104.31	108.79	106.63	103.49	107.34	102.77	112.96	128.05
Other sectors	8 674 . .	45.02	48.41	49.62	50.91	61.25	66.10	81.79	115.63
Money market instruments	8 680 . .	21.03	25.52	28.82	32.91	29.87	35.36	44.48	49.35
Monetary authorities	8 681 . .	. . .	. . .	. . .	. . .	. . .	. . .	. . .	. . .
General government	8 682 . .	4.67	6.84	12.78	18.56	16.33	11.25	14.05	16.13
Banks	8 683 . .	11.93	14.34	12.15	10.05	10.85	16.48	18.80	30.40
Other sectors	8 684 . .	4.43	4.34	3.88	4.31	2.68	7.63	11.63	2.82
Financial derivatives	8 905 . .	**20.30**	**32.36**	**38.34**	**45.61**	**81.09**	**105.08**	**98.26**	**104.79**
Monetary authorities	8 906 . .	. . .	. . .	. . .	. . .	. . .	. . .	. . .	. . .
General government	8 907 . .	. . .	. . .	. . .	. . .	. . .	. . .	. . .	. . .
Banks	8 908 . .	. . .	. . .	. . .	. . .	. . .	. . .	. . .	. . .
Other sectors	8 909 . .	20.30	32.36	38.34	45.61	81.09	105.08	98.26	104.79
Other investment	8 753 . .	**471.84**	**498.43**	**509.09**	**521.74**	**548.72**	**634.91**	**664.66**	**668.38**
Trade credits	8 756 . .	. . .	. . .	. . .	. . .	. . .	62.18	66.16	63.19
General government	8 757 . .	. . .	. . .	. . .	. . .	. . .	. . .	. . .	. . .
of which: Short-term	8 759 . .	. . .	. . .	. . .	. . .	. . .	. . .	. . .	. . .
Other sectors	8 760 . .	. . .	. . .	. . .	. . .	. . .	62.18	66.16	63.19
of which: Short-term	8 762 . .	. . .	. . .	. . .	. . .	. . .	. . .	. . .	. . .
Loans	8 764 . .	471.84	498.43	509.09	521.74	548.72	572.72	598.50	605.19
Monetary authorities	8 765 . .	1.72	1.97	2.26	2.32	2.68	28.03	2.33	3.35
of which: Use of Fund credit and loans from the Fund	8 766 . .	. . .	. . .	. . .	. . .	. . .	. . .	. . .	. . .
of which: Short-term	8 768 . .	*1.72*	*1.97*	*2.26*	*2.32*	*2.68*	*28.03*	*2.33*	*3.35*
General government	8 769 . .	9.47	11.05	10.65	16.46	15.05	14.47	15.82	15.95
of which: Short-term	8 771 . .	*8.49*	*9.60*	*8.77*	*8.62*	*6.65*	*7.13*	*8.84*	*9.17*
Banks	8 772 . .	436.17	458.31	469.12	476.79	501.82	500.79	530.29	543.32
of which: Short-term	8 774 . .	*400.25*	*416.48*	*430.28*	*441.66*	*462.15*	*446.04*	*476.70*	*488.15*
Other sectors	8 775 . .	24.48	27.10	27.07	26.18	29.17	29.43	50.06	42.57
of which: Short-term	8 777 . .	*13.04*	*15.66*	*11.78*	*16.68*	*18.20*	*19.19*	*39.83*	*33.84*
Currency and deposits	8 780 . .	. . .	. . .	. . .	. . .	. . .	. . .	. . .	. . .
Monetary authorities	8 781 . .	. . .	. . .	. . .	. . .	. . .	. . .	. . .	. . .
General government	8 782 . .	. . .	. . .	. . .	. . .	. . .	. . .	. . .	. . .
Banks	8 783 . .	. . .	. . .	. . .	. . .	. . .	. . .	. . .	. . .
Other sectors	8 784 . .	. . .	. . .	. . .	. . .	. . .	. . .	. . .	. . .
Other liabilities	8 786 . .	. . .	. . .	. . .	. . .	. . .	. . .	. . .	. . .
Monetary authorities	8 787 . .	. . .	. . .	. . .	. . .	. . .	. . .	. . .	. . .
of which: Short-term	8 789 . .	. . .	. . .	. . .	. . .	. . .	. . .	. . .	. . .
General government	8 790 . .	. . .	. . .	. . .	. . .	. . .	. . .	. . .	. . .
of which: Short-term	8 792 . .	. . .	. . .	. . .	. . .	. . .	. . .	. . .	. . .
Banks	8 793 . .	. . .	. . .	. . .	. . .	. . .	. . .	. . .	. . .
of which: Short-term	8 795 . .	. . .	. . .	. . .	. . .	. . .	. . .	. . .	. . .
Other sectors	8 796 . .	. . .	. . .	. . .	. . .	. . .	. . .	. . .	. . .
of which: Short-term	8 798 . .	. . .	. . .	. . .	. . .	. . .	. . .	. . .	. . .
NET INTERNATIONAL INVESTMENT POSITION	8 995 . .	**32.51**	**72.77**	**164.31**	**257.73**	**232.61**	**77.90**	**75.55**	**150.01**
Conversion rates: French francs per U.S. dollar (end of period)	0 102 . .	**5.3460**	**4.9000**	**5.2370**	**5.9881**	**5.6221**	. . .	. . .	. . .
Conversion rates: euros per U.S. dollar (end of period)	0 104 . .	. . .	. . .	. . .	. . .	. . .	**.9954**	**1.0747**	**1.1347**

Table 1. ANALYTIC PRESENTATION, 1994–2001
(Millions of U.S. dollars)

	Code	1994	1995	1996	1997	1998	1999	2000	2001
A. Current Account [1]	4 993 Z.	**317.4**	**464.7**	**888.6**	**531.4**	**–595.5**	**390.4**	**. . .**	**. . .**
Goods: exports f.o.b	2 100 . .	2,365.3	2,727.8	3,334.2	3,032.7	1,907.6	2,498.8	. . .	. . .
Goods: imports f.o.b	3 100 . .	–776.7	–880.9	–961.6	–1,030.6	–1,163.2	–910.5	. . .	. . .
Balance on Goods	4 100 . .	*1,588.6*	*1,846.9*	*2,372.5*	*2,002.1*	*744.4*	*1,588.3*	. . .	. . .
Services: credit	2 200 . .	219.6	217.1	233.9	232.9	219.6	280.9	. . .	. . .
Services: debit	3 200 . .	–826.7	–891.6	–917.8	–952.7	–991.0	–867.0	. . .	. . .
Balance on Goods and Services	4 991 . .	*981.4*	*1,172.4*	*1,688.6*	*1,282.3*	*–27.0*	*1,002.2*	. . .	. . .
Income: credit	2 300 . .	11.9	35.0	42.8	39.0	57.5	84.2	. . .	. . .
Income: debit	3 300 . .	–509.9	–700.5	–805.8	–755.5	–572.5	–653.1	. . .	. . .
Balance on Goods, Services, and Income	4 992 . .	*483.4*	*507.0*	*925.6*	*565.8*	*–542.1*	*433.3*	. . .	. . .
Current transfers: credit	2 379 Z.	18.7	58.0	65.2	62.7	36.6	42.6	. . .	. . .
Current transfers: debit	3 379 . .	–184.8	–100.3	–102.1	–97.1	–90.0	–85.6	. . .	. . .
B. Capital Account [1]	4 994 Z.	**. . .**	**4.8**	**5.1**	**5.8**	**1.8**	**5.4**	**. . .**	**. . .**
Capital account: credit	2 994 Z.	. . .	5.6	9.6	7.5	3.6	5.7	. . .	. . .
Capital account: debit	3 994 . .	. . .	–.8	–4.5	–1.7	–1.8	–.3	. . .	. . .
Total, Groups A Plus B	4 981 . .	*317.4*	*469.5*	*893.8*	*537.2*	*–593.7*	*395.7*	. . .	. . .
C. Financial Account [1]	4 995 W.	**–745.0**	**–724.7**	**–1,047.6**	**–626.2**	**–165.8**	**–686.8**	**. . .**	**. . .**
Direct investment abroad	4 505 . .	. . .	–35.0	–2.3	–21.0	–33.2	–73.9	. . .	. . .
Direct investment in Gabon	4 555 Z.	–99.6	–314.5	–489.1	–311.3	146.6	–156.6	. . .	. . .
Portfolio investment assets	4 602 . .	. . .	–29.8	–21.1	260.1	19.2	22.4	. . .	. . .
Equity securities	4 610 . .	. . .	–45.0	–16.7	311.3	19.2	44.0	. . .	. . .
Debt securities	4 619 . .	. . .	15.2	–4.4	–51.2	. . .	–21.6	. . .	. . .
Portfolio investment liabilities	4 652 Z.	. . .	80.3	4.6	–20.7	–.2	–.7	. . .	. . .
Equity securities	4 660 . .	. . .	. . .	–7.5	. . .	–.2	. . .	. . .	. . .
Debt securities	4 669 Z.	. . .	80.3	12.1	–20.7	. . .	–.7	. . .	. . .
Financial derivatives	4 910 . .	. . .	. . .	. . .	. . .	. . .	. . .	. . .	. . .
Financial derivatives assets	4 900 . .	. . .	. . .	. . .	. . .	. . .	. . .	. . .	. . .
Financial derivatives liabilities	4 905 . .	. . .	. . .	. . .	. . .	. . .	. . .	. . .	. . .
Other investment assets	4 703 . .	–258.6	–39.9	–215.1	18.3	–220.7	–109.0	. . .	. . .
Monetary authorities	4 701 . .	. . .	–2.1	1.2	25.0	–21.5	17.5	. . .	. . .
General government	4 704 . .	. . .	. . .	. . .	. . .	. . .	. . .	. . .	. . .
Banks	4 705 . .	–22.9	13.8	–90.3	76.5	–2.7	–14.0	. . .	. . .
Other sectors	4 728 . .	–235.8	–51.5	–126.0	–83.2	–196.4	–112.5	. . .	. . .
Other investment liabilities	4 753 W.	–386.7	–385.7	–324.7	–551.6	–77.5	–369.1	. . .	. . .
Monetary authorities	4 753 WA	–203.9	. . .	. . .	. . .	. . .	. . .	. . .	. . .
General government	4 753 ZB	–133.1	–280.3	–208.4	251.7	–276.0	–268.5	. . .	. . .
Banks	4 753 ZC	–54.9	34.3	19.8	–32.6	2.7	30.7	. . .	. . .
Other sectors	4 753 ZD	5.2	–139.7	–136.1	–267.3	195.8	–131.3	. . .	. . .
Total, Groups A Through C	4 983 . .	*–427.6*	*–255.2*	*–153.9*	*–89.0*	*–759.5*	*–291.1*	. . .	. . .
D. Net Errors and Omissions	4 998 . .	**254.6**	**–181.1**	**–97.4**	**–108.4**	**92.5**	**–106.7**	**. . .**	**. . .**
Total, Groups A Through D	4 984 . .	*–173.0*	*–436.3*	*–251.2*	*–197.4*	*–667.0*	*–397.8*	. . .	. . .
E. Reserves and Related Items	4 802 A.	**173.0**	**436.3**	**251.2**	**197.4**	**667.0**	**397.8**	**. . .**	**. . .**
Reserve assets	4 802 . .	–173.8	42.2	–112.8	–66.8	272.2	–4.9	. . .	. . .
Use of Fund credit and loans	4 766 . .	40.9	5.0	26.4	19.4	–22.7	–24.5	. . .	. . .
Exceptional financing	4 920 . .	306.0	389.1	337.6	244.8	417.5	427.3	. . .	. . .
Conversion rates: CFA francs per U.S. dollar	0 101 . .	**555.20**	**499.15**	**511.55**	**583.67**	**589.95**	**615.70**	**711.98**	**733.04**

[1] Excludes components that have been classified in the categories of Group E.

Table 2. STANDARD PRESENTATION, 1994–2001

(Millions of U.S. dollars)

	Code		1994	1995	1996	1997	1998	1999	2000	2001
CURRENT ACCOUNT	4 993	. .	**317.4**	**464.7**	**888.6**	**531.4**	**–595.5**	**390.4**	**. . .**	**. . .**
A. GOODS	4 100	. .	1,588.6	1,846.9	2,372.5	2,002.1	744.4	1,588.3	. . .	. . .
Credit	2 100	. .	**2,365.3**	**2,727.8**	**3,334.2**	**3,032.7**	**1,907.6**	**2,498.8**	**. . .**	**. . .**
General merchandise: exports f.o.b.	2 110	. .	2,365.3	2,713.9	3,319.6	3,021.2	1,894.9	2,481.5	. . .	. . .
Goods for processing: exports f.o.b.	2 150	. .	. . .	. . .	. . .	. . .	. . .	. . .	. . .	. . .
Repairs on goods	2 160	. .	. . .	2.9	5.1	2.5	5.9	2.1	. . .	. . .
Goods procured in ports by carriers	2 170	. .	. . .	11.0	9.5	9.1	6.8	15.2	. . .	. . .
Nonmonetary gold	2 180	. .	. . .	. . .	. . .	. . .	. . .	. . .	. . .	. . .
Debit	3 100	. .	**–776.7**	**–880.9**	**–961.6**	**–1,030.6**	**–1,163.2**	**–910.5**	**. . .**	**. . .**
General merchandise: imports f.o.b.	3 110	. .	–776.7	–822.5	–897.3	–967.1	–1,102.9	–852.0	. . .	. . .
Goods for processing: imports f.o.b.	3 150	. .	. . .	. . .	. . .	. . .	. . .	. . .	. . .	. . .
Repairs on goods	3 160	. .	. . .	–38.8	–42.0	–39.0	–39.8	–38.9	. . .	. . .
Goods procured in ports by carriers	3 170	. .	. . .	–19.6	–22.3	–24.5	–20.5	–19.7	. . .	. . .
Nonmonetary gold	3 180	. .	. . .	. . .	. . .	. . .	. . .	. . .	. . .	. . .
B. SERVICES	4 200	. .	–607.2	–674.5	–683.9	–719.8	–771.4	–586.0	. . .	. . .
Total credit	2 200	. .	*219.6*	*217.1*	*233.9*	*232.9*	*219.6*	*280.9*	. . .	. . .
Total debit	3 200	. .	*–826.7*	*–891.6*	*–917.8*	*–952.7*	*–991.0*	*–867.0*	. . .	. . .
Transportation services, credit	2 205	. .	**70.2**	**88.6**	**98.5**	**101.6**	**105.1**	**151.3**	**. . .**	**. . .**
Passenger	2 850	. .	. . .	*76.9*	*80.7*	*83.8*	*87.5*	*128.0*	. . .	. . .
Freight	2 851	. .	. . .	*7.0*	*12.4*	*11.4*	*12.0*	*16.5*	. . .	. . .
Other	2 852	. .	*70.2*	*4.7*	*5.4*	*6.4*	*5.6*	*6.8*	. . .	. . .
Sea transport, passenger	2 207	. .	. . .	. . .	. . .	. . .	. . .	. . .	. . .	. . .
Sea transport, freight	2 208	. .	. . .	. . .	. . .	. . .	. . .	. . .	. . .	. . .
Sea transport, other	2 209	. .	. . .	. . .	. . .	. . .	. . .	. . .	. . .	. . .
Air transport, passenger	2 211	. .	. . .	76.9	80.7	83.8	87.5	128.0	. . .	. . .
Air transport, freight	2 212	. .	. . .	7.0	12.4	11.4	12.0	16.5	. . .	. . .
Air transport, other	2 213	. .	. . .	. . .	. . .	. . .	. . .	. . .	. . .	. . .
Other transport, passenger	2 215	. .	. . .	. . .	. . .	. . .	. . .	. . .	. . .	. . .
Other transport, freight	2 216	. .	. . .	. . .	. . .	. . .	. . .	. . .	. . .	. . .
Other transport, other	2 217	. .	. . .	4.7	5.4	6.4	5.6	6.8	. . .	. . .
Transportation services, debit	3 205	. .	**–238.8**	**–197.0**	**–234.8**	**–251.6**	**–280.0**	**–287.8**	**. . .**	**. . .**
Passenger	3 850	. .	. . .	*–44.8*	*–67.9*	*–70.3*	*–74.2*	*–104.2*	. . .	. . .
Freight	3 851	. .	*–170.9*	*–149.9*	*–161.6*	*–176.9*	*–201.8*	*–155.9*	. . .	. . .
Other	3 852	. .	*–67.9*	*–2.3*	*–5.3*	*–4.4*	*–4.1*	*–27.8*	. . .	. . .
Sea transport, passenger	3 207	. .	. . .	. . .	. . .	. . .	. . .	. . .	. . .	. . .
Sea transport, freight	3 208	. .	. . .	. . .	. . .	. . .	. . .	. . .	. . .	. . .
Sea transport, other	3 209	. .	. . .	. . .	. . .	. . .	. . .	. . .	. . .	. . .
Air transport, passenger	3 211	. .	. . .	–44.8	–67.9	–70.3	–74.2	–104.2	. . .	. . .
Air transport, freight	3 212	. .	. . .	–149.9	–161.6	–176.9	–201.8	–155.9	. . .	. . .
Air transport, other	3 213	. .	. . .	. . .	. . .	. . .	. . .	. . .	. . .	. . .
Other transport, passenger	3 215	. .	. . .	. . .	. . .	. . .	. . .	. . .	. . .	. . .
Other transport, freight	3 216	. .	. . .	. . .	. . .	. . .	. . .	. . .	. . .	. . .
Other transport, other	3 217	. .	. . .	–2.3	–5.3	–4.4	–4.1	–27.8	. . .	. . .
Travel, credit	2 236	. .	**5.2**	**17.3**	**9.8**	**18.6**	**23.4**	**14.9**	**. . .**	**. . .**
Business travel	2 237	. .	. . .	1.4	.2	4.5	3.9	3.4	. . .	. . .
Personal travel	2 240	. .	. . .	15.9	9.6	14.0	19.5	11.5	. . .	. . .
Travel, debit	3 236	. .	**–143.4**	**–137.5**	**–99.6**	**–86.4**	**–84.4**	**–91.1**	**. . .**	**. . .**
Business travel	3 237	. .	. . .	–29.6	–52.0	–28.3	–27.4	–31.0	. . .	. . .
Personal travel	3 240	. .	. . .	–107.9	–47.6	–58.2	–57.0	–60.1	. . .	. . .
Other services, credit	2 200	BA	**144.1**	**111.2**	**125.6**	**112.7**	**91.1**	**114.7**	**. . .**	**. . .**
Communications	2 245	. .	. . .	1.2	1.5	1.4	.2	1.6	. . .	. . .
Construction	2 249	. .	. . .	. . .	. . .	. . .	. . .	. . .	. . .	. . .
Insurance	2 253	. .	11.9	6.3	10.0	12.8	5.7	12.5	. . .	. . .
Financial	2 260	. .	. . .	. . .	. . .	. . .	. . .	. . .	. . .	. . .
Computer and information	2 262	. .	. . .	. . .	. . .	. . .	. . .	. . .	. . .	. . .
Royalties and licence fees	2 266	. .	. . .	. . .	. . .	. . .	. . .	. . .	. . .	. . .
Other business services	2 268	. .	112.2	71.2	77.0	59.3	50.3	56.8	. . .	. . .
Personal, cultural, and recreational	2 287	. .	. . .	6.3	8.4	10.8	8.9	11.6	. . .	. . .
Government, n.i.e.	2 291	. .	20.0	26.1	28.7	28.3	26.1	32.3	. . .	. . .
Other services, debit	3 200	BA	**–444.5**	**–557.1**	**–583.5**	**–614.6**	**–626.6**	**–488.1**	**. . .**	**. . .**
Communications	3 245	. .	. . .	–35.6	–36.5	–32.1	–30.2	–32.1	. . .	. . .
Construction	3 249	. .	. . .	. . .	. . .	. . .	. . .	. . .	. . .	. . .
Insurance	3 253	. .	–30.1	–71.4	–79.7	–81.7	–81.9	–79.1	. . .	. . .
Financial	3 260	. .	. . .	. . .	. . .	. . .	. . .	. . .	. . .	. . .
Computer and information	3 262	. .	. . .	. . .	. . .	. . .	. . .	. . .	. . .	. . .
Royalties and licence fees	3 266	. .	. . .	. . .	. . .	. . .	. . .	. . .	. . .	. . .
Other business services	3 268	. .	–397.2	–400.9	–382.1	–353.3	–387.0	–275.2	. . .	. . .
Personal, cultural, and recreational	3 287	. .	. . .	–39.2	–75.5	–138.2	–116.8	–88.2	. . .	. . .
Government, n.i.e.	3 291	. .	–17.3	–9.9	–9.7	–9.4	–10.7	–13.4	. . .	. . .

Table 2 (Continued). STANDARD PRESENTATION, 1994–2001
(Millions of U.S. dollars)

	Code	1994	1995	1996	1997	1998	1999	2000	2001
C. INCOME	4 300 . .	–498.0	–665.4	–763.0	–716.5	–515.1	–568.9	. . .	. . .
Total credit	2 300 . .	*11.9*	*35.0*	*42.8*	*39.0*	*57.5*	*84.2*	. . .	. . .
Total debit	3 300 . .	*–509.9*	*–700.5*	*–805.8*	*–755.5*	*–572.5*	*–653.1*	. . .	. . .
Compensation of employees, credit	2 310 . .	**. . .**	**.8**	**3.4**	**2.3**	**2.3**	**2.0**	**. . .**	**. . .**
Compensation of employees, debit	3 310 . .	**–2.2**	**–37.1**	**–49.5**	**–48.2**	**–36.9**	**–40.0**	**. . .**	**. . .**
Investment income, credit	2 320 . .	**11.9**	**34.2**	**39.4**	**36.7**	**55.1**	**82.1**	**. . .**	**. . .**
Direct investment income	2 330 . .	1.8	3.4	10.0	7.3	47.5	61.2	. . .	. . .
Dividends and distributed branch profits	2 332 . .	1.8	2.2	.4	.2	. . .	.1	. . .	. . .
Reinvested earnings and undistributed branch profits	2 333 . .	. . .	1.2	9.5	7.1	47.5	61.1	. . .	. . .
Income on debt (interest)	2 334 . .	. . .	. . .	. . .	. . .	. . .	. . .	. . .	. . .
Portfolio investment income	2 339 . .	. . .	16.1	12.0	18.5	2.5	.5	. . .	. . .
Income on equity	2 340 . .	. . .	14.0	12.0	13.0	1.8	.3	. . .	. . .
Income on bonds and notes	2 350 . .	. . .	2.0	. . .	5.4	.7	.2	. . .	. . .
Income on money market instruments	2 360 . .	. . .	. . .	. . .	. . .	. . .	. . .	. . .	. . .
Other investment income	2 370 . .	10.1	14.7	17.4	11.0	5.1	20.5	. . .	. . .
Investment income, debit	3 320 . .	**–507.7**	**–663.3**	**–756.3**	**–707.3**	**–535.7**	**–613.1**	**. . .**	**. . .**
Direct investment income	3 330 . .	–130.9	–236.4	–386.0	–330.4	–176.6	–226.6	. . .	. . .
Dividends and distributed branch profits	3 332 . .	–46.8	–120.9	–221.8	–232.8	–157.3	–57.5	. . .	. . .
Reinvested earnings and undistributed branch profits	3 333 . .	–84.1	–115.5	–164.2	–97.6	–19.3	–169.1	. . .	. . .
Income on debt (interest)	3 334 . .	. . .	. . .	. . .	. . .	. . .	. . .	. . .	. . .
Portfolio investment income	3 339 . .	. . .	–17.5	–23.5	–25.5	–51.0	–.8	. . .	. . .
Income on equity	3 340 . .	. . .	–12.5	–14.8	–14.6	–50.7	–.5	. . .	. . .
Income on bonds and notes	3 350 . .	. . .	–5.0	–8.6	–10.9	–.3	–.4	. . .	. . .
Income on money market instruments	3 360 . .	. . .	. . .	. . .	. . .	. . .	. . .	. . .	. . .
Other investment income	3 370 . .	–376.8	–409.4	–346.8	–351.5	–308.0	–385.7	. . .	. . .
D. CURRENT TRANSFERS	4 379 . .	–166.1	–42.3	–36.9	–34.4	–53.4	–42.9	. . .	. . .
Credit	2 379 . .	**18.7**	**58.0**	**65.2**	**62.7**	**36.6**	**42.6**	**. . .**	**. . .**
General government	2 380 . .	15.1	49.9	51.1	41.7	32.8	35.0	. . .	. . .
Other sectors	2 390 . .	3.6	8.2	14.0	21.0	3.8	7.7	. . .	. . .
Workers' remittances	2 391 . .	. . .	3.6	2.3	3.8	3.2	2.2	. . .	. . .
Other current transfers	2 392 . .	3.6	4.5	11.7	17.2	.5	5.5	. . .	. . .
Debit	3 379 . .	**–184.8**	**–100.3**	**–102.1**	**–97.1**	**–90.0**	**–85.6**	**. . .**	**. . .**
General government	3 380 . .	–18.0	–10.3	–7.0	–4.2	–4.5	–12.2	. . .	. . .
Other sectors	3 390 . .	–166.8	–90.1	–95.1	–92.9	–85.5	–73.3	. . .	. . .
Workers' remittances	3 391 . .	–154.2	–62.1	–63.8	–56.0	–52.3	–44.7	. . .	. . .
Other current transfers	3 392 . .	–12.6	–28.0	–31.3	–36.9	–33.2	–28.6	. . .	. . .
CAPITAL AND FINANCIAL ACCOUNT	4 996 . .	**–571.9**	**–283.6**	**–791.3**	**–423.0**	**503.0**	**–283.6**	**. . .**	**. . .**
CAPITAL ACCOUNT	4 994 . .	**130.9**	**4.8**	**5.1**	**5.8**	**1.8**	**5.4**	**. . .**	**. . .**
Total credit	2 994 . .	*130.9*	*5.6*	*9.6*	*7.5*	*3.6*	*5.7*	. . .	. . .
Total debit	3 994 . .	. . .	*–.8*	*–4.5*	*–1.7*	*–1.8*	*–.3*	. . .	. . .
Capital transfers, credit	2 400 . .	**130.9**	**5.6**	**9.6**	**7.5**	**3.6**	**5.7**	**. . .**	. . .
General government	2 401 . .	130.9	5.3	9.6	7.5	3.6	5.3	. . .	. . .
Debt forgiveness	2 402 . .	130.9	. . .	. . .	. . .	. . .	. . .	. . .	. . .
Other capital transfers	2 410 . .	. . .	5.3	9.6	7.5	3.6	5.3	. . .	. . .
Other sectors	2 430 . .	. . .	.2	. . .	. . .	. . .	.4	. . .	. . .
Migrants' transfers	2 431 . .	. . .	. . .	. . .	. . .	. . .	. . .	. . .	. . .
Debt forgiveness	2 432 . .	. . .	. . .	. . .	. . .	. . .	. . .	. . .	. . .
Other capital transfers	2 440 . .	. . .	.2	. . .	. . .	. . .	.4	. . .	. . .
Capital transfers, debit	3 400 . .	**. . .**	**. . .**	**–2.8**	**. . .**	**. . .**	**. . .**	**. . .**	**. . .**
General government	3 401 . .	. . .	. . .	. . .	. . .	. . .	. . .	. . .	. . .
Debt forgiveness	3 402 . .	. . .	. . .	. . .	. . .	. . .	. . .	. . .	. . .
Other capital transfers	3 410 . .	. . .	. . .	. . .	. . .	. . .	. . .	. . .	. . .
Other sectors	3 430 . .	. . .	. . .	–2.8	. . .	. . .	. . .	. . .	. . .
Migrants' transfers	3 431 . .	. . .	. . .	. . .	. . .	. . .	. . .	. . .	. . .
Debt forgiveness	3 432 . .	. . .	. . .	. . .	. . .	. . .	. . .	. . .	. . .
Other capital transfers	3 440 . .	. . .	. . .	–2.8	. . .	. . .	. . .	. . .	. . .
Nonproduced nonfinancial assets, credit	2 480 . .	**. . .**	**. . .**	**. . .**	**. . .**	**. . .**	**. . .**	**. . .**	**. . .**
Nonproduced nonfinancial assets, debit	3 480 . .	**. . .**	**–.8**	**–1.7**	**–1.7**	**–1.8**	**–.3**	**. . .**	**. . .**

Table 2 (Continued). STANDARD PRESENTATION, 1994–2001

(Millions of U.S. dollars)

	Code	1994	1995	1996	1997	1998	1999	2000	2001
FINANCIAL ACCOUNT	4 995 . .	**–702.9**	**–288.4**	**–796.4**	**–428.8**	**501.2**	**–289.0**	**. . .**	**. . .**
A. DIRECT INVESTMENT	4 500 . .	–99.6	–349.6	–491.4	–332.2	113.4	–230.5	. . .	. . .
Direct investment abroad	4 505 . .	**. . .**	**–35.0**	**–2.3**	**–21.0**	**–33.2**	**–73.9**	**. . .**	**. . .**
Equity capital	4 510 . .	. . .	–33.9	.3	. . .	1.1	.8	. . .	. . .
Claims on affiliated enterprises	4 515 . .	. . .	. . .	.3	. . .	1.1	.8	. . .	. . .
Liabilities to affiliated enterprises	4 520 . .	. . .	–33.9	. . .	. . .	. . .	. . .	. . .	. . .
Reinvested earnings	4 525 . .	. . .	–1.2	–9.5	–7.1	–47.5	–61.1	. . .	. . .
Other capital	4 530 . .	. . .	.1	6.9	–13.8	13.1	–13.6	. . .	. . .
Claims on affiliated enterprises	4 535 . .	. . .	1.6	8.0	. . .	13.9	. . .	. . .	. . .
Liabilities to affiliated enterprises	4 540 . .	. . .	–1.5	–1.1	–13.8	–.8	–13.6	. . .	. . .
Direct investment in Gabon	4 555 . .	**–99.6**	**–314.5**	**–489.1**	**–311.3**	**146.6**	**–156.6**	**. . .**	**. . .**
Equity capital	4 560 . .	. . .	14.6	15.0	20.9	–12.7	30.4	. . .	. . .
Claims on direct investors	4 565 . .	. . .	14.6	15.0	20.9	–12.7	30.4	. . .	. . .
Liabilities to direct investors	4 570 . .	. . .	. . .	. . .	. . .	. . .	. . .	. . .	. . .
Reinvested earnings	4 575 . .	84.1	115.5	164.2	97.6	19.3	169.1	. . .	. . .
Other capital	4 580 . .	–183.7	–444.7	–668.3	–429.8	140.0	–356.1	. . .	. . .
Claims on direct investors	4 585 . .	. . .	14.1	15.4	17.1	176.8	. . .	. . .	. . .
Liabilities to direct investors	4 590 . .	. . .	–458.8	–683.7	–446.9	–36.9	–356.1	. . .	. . .
B. PORTFOLIO INVESTMENT	4 600 . .	. . .	50.4	–16.4	239.3	19.0	21.8	. . .	. . .
Assets	4 602 . .	**. . .**	**–29.8**	**–21.1**	**260.1**	**19.2**	**22.4**	**. . .**	**. . .**
Equity securities	4 610 . .	. . .	–45.0	–16.7	311.3	19.2	44.0	. . .	. . .
Monetary authorities	4 611 . .	. . .	. . .	. . .	. . .	. . .	. . .	. . .	. . .
General government	4 612 . .	. . .	. . .	. . .	. . .	. . .	. . .	. . .	. . .
Banks	4 613 . .	. . .	. . .	. . .	. . .	. . .	. . .	. . .	. . .
Other sectors	4 614 . .	. . .	–45.0	–16.7	311.2	19.2	44.0	. . .	. . .
Debt securities	4 619 . .	. . .	15.2	–4.4	–51.2	. . .	–21.6	. . .	. . .
Bonds and notes	4 620 . .	. . .	15.2	–4.4	–51.2	. . .	–21.6	. . .	. . .
Monetary authorities	4 621 . .	. . .	. . .	. . .	. . .	. . .	. . .	. . .	. . .
General government	4 622 . .	. . .	. . .	. . .	. . .	. . .	. . .	. . .	. . .
Banks	4 623 . .	. . .	. . .	. . .	. . .	. . .	. . .	. . .	. . .
Other sectors	4 624 . .	. . .	15.2	–4.4	–51.2	. . .	–21.6	. . .	. . .
Money market instruments	4 630 . .	. . .	. . .	. . .	. . .	. . .	. . .	. . .	. . .
Monetary authorities	4 631 . .	. . .	. . .	. . .	. . .	. . .	. . .	. . .	. . .
General government	4 632 . .	. . .	. . .	. . .	. . .	. . .	. . .	. . .	. . .
Banks	4 633 . .	. . .	. . .	. . .	. . .	. . .	. . .	. . .	. . .
Other sectors	4 634 . .	. . .	. . .	. . .	. . .	. . .	. . .	. . .	. . .
Liabilities	4 652 . .	**. . .**	**80.3**	**4.6**	**–20.7**	**–.2**	**–.7**	**. . .**	**. . .**
Equity securities	4 660 . .	. . .	. . .	–7.5	. . .	–.2	. . .	. . .	. . .
Banks	4 663 . .	. . .	. . .	. . .	. . .	. . .	. . .	. . .	. . .
Other sectors	4 664 . .	. . .	. . .	–7.5	. . .	–.2	. . .	. . .	. . .
Debt securities	4 669 . .	. . .	80.3	12.1	–20.7	. . .	–.7	. . .	. . .
Bonds and notes	4 670 . .	. . .	80.3	12.1	–20.7	. . .	–.7	. . .	. . .
Monetary authorities	4 671 . .	. . .	. . .	. . .	. . .	. . .	. . .	. . .	. . .
General government	4 672 . .	. . .	. . .	. . .	. . .	. . .	. . .	. . .	. . .
Banks	4 673 . .	. . .	. . .	. . .	–2.1	. . .	. . .	. . .	. . .
Other sectors	4 674 . .	. . .	80.3	12.1	–18.7	. . .	–.7	. . .	. . .
Money market instruments	4 680 . .	. . .	. . .	. . .	. . .	. . .	. . .	. . .	. . .
Monetary authorities	4 681 . .	. . .	. . .	. . .	. . .	. . .	. . .	. . .	. . .
General government	4 682 . .	. . .	. . .	. . .	. . .	. . .	. . .	. . .	. . .
Banks	4 683 . .	. . .	. . .	. . .	. . .	. . .	. . .	. . .	. . .
Other sectors	4 684 . .	. . .	. . .	. . .	. . .	. . .	. . .	. . .	. . .
C. FINANCIAL DERIVATIVES	4 910 . .	. . .	. . .	. . .	. . .	. . .	. . .	. . .	. . .
Monetary authorities	4 911 . .	. . .	. . .	. . .	. . .	. . .	. . .	. . .	. . .
General government	4 912 . .	. . .	. . .	. . .	. . .	. . .	. . .	. . .	. . .
Banks	4 913 . .	. . .	. . .	. . .	. . .	. . .	. . .	. . .	. . .
Other sectors	4 914 . .	. . .	. . .	. . .	. . .	. . .	. . .	. . .	. . .
Assets	4 900 . .	**. . .**	**. . .**	**. . .**	**. . .**	**. . .**	**. . .**	**. . .**	**. . .**
Monetary authorities	4 901 . .	. . .	. . .	. . .	. . .	. . .	. . .	. . .	. . .
General government	4 902 . .	. . .	. . .	. . .	. . .	. . .	. . .	. . .	. . .
Banks	4 903 . .	. . .	. . .	. . .	. . .	. . .	. . .	. . .	. . .
Other sectors	4 904 . .	. . .	. . .	. . .	. . .	. . .	. . .	. . .	. . .
Liabilities	4 905 . .	**. . .**	**. . .**	**. . .**	**. . .**	**. . .**	**. . .**	**. . .**	**. . .**
Monetary authorities	4 906 . .	. . .	. . .	. . .	. . .	. . .	. . .	. . .	. . .
General government	4 907 . .	. . .	. . .	. . .	. . .	. . .	. . .	. . .	. . .
Banks	4 908 . .	. . .	. . .	. . .	. . .	. . .	. . .	. . .	. . .
Other sectors	4 909 . .	. . .	. . .	. . .	. . .	. . .	. . .	. . .	. . .

Table 2 (Concluded). STANDARD PRESENTATION, 1994–2001
(Millions of U.S. dollars)

	Code	1994	1995	1996	1997	1998	1999	2000	2001
D. OTHER INVESTMENT	4 700 . .	–429.4	–31.5	–175.8	–269.1	96.6	–75.3	. . .	. . .
Assets	4 703 . .	**–258.6**	**–39.9**	**–215.1**	**18.3**	**–220.7**	**–109.0**	**. . .**	**. . .**
Trade credits	4 706 . .	–258.8	17.6	5.3	. . .	16.2	–25.3	. . .	. . .
General government	4 707 . .	. . .	. . .	. . .	. . .	. . .	. . .	. . .	. . .
of which: Short-term	4 709 . .	. . .	. . .	. . .	. . .	. . .	. . .	. . .	. . .
Other sectors	4 710 . .	–258.8	17.6	5.3	. . .	16.2	–25.3	. . .	. . .
of which: Short-term	4 712 . .	*–258.8*	*16.4*	*5.1*	. . .	*17.1*	*–25.3*	. . .	. . .
Loans	4 714 . .	21.1	–6.2	5.2	15.6	–116.4	29.4	. . .	. . .
Monetary authorities	4 715 . .	. . .	. . .	. . .	. . .	. . .	. . .	. . .	. . .
of which: Short-term	4 718 . .	. . .	. . .	. . .	. . .	. . .	. . .	. . .	. . .
General government	4 719 . .	. . .	. . .	. . .	. . .	. . .	. . .	. . .	. . .
of which: Short-term	4 721 . .	. . .	. . .	. . .	. . .	. . .	. . .	. . .	. . .
Banks	4 722 . .	. . .	–7.4	5.2	–13.1	11.3	–1.9	. . .	. . .
of which: Short-term	4 724 . .	. . .	*–7.5*	*5.1*	*–8.3*	*13.6*	*–2.7*	. . .	. . .
Other sectors	4 725 . .	21.1	1.2	. . .	28.7	–127.7	31.3	. . .	. . .
of which: Short-term	4 727 . .	. . .	*1.3*	*–.2*	*–.7*	*–120.0*	. . .	. . .	. . .
Currency and deposits	4 730 . .	–22.9	–53.8	–225.9	–29.1	–119.6	–118.3	. . .	. . .
Monetary authorities	4 731 . .	. . .	–2.1	1.2	25.0	–21.5	17.5	. . .	. . .
General government	4 732 . .	. . .	. . .	. . .	. . .	. . .	. . .	. . .	. . .
Banks	4 733 . .	–22.9	21.2	–92.8	88.8	–13.8	–14.1	. . .	. . .
Other sectors	4 734 . .	. . .	–72.8	–134.3	–143.0	–84.2	–121.7	. . .	. . .
Other assets	4 736 . .	2.0	2.5	.3	31.7	–.8	5.2	. . .	. . .
Monetary authorities	4 737 . .	. . .	. . .	. . .	. . .	. . .	. . .	. . .	. . .
of which: Short-term	4 739 . .	. . .	. . .	. . .	. . .	. . .	. . .	. . .	. . .
General government	4 740 . .	. . .	. . .	. . .	. . .	. . .	. . .	. . .	. . .
of which: Short-term	4 742 . .	. . .	. . .	. . .	. . .	. . .	. . .	. . .	. . .
Banks	4 743 . .	. . .	. . .	–2.7	.7	–.1	2.0	. . .	. . .
of which: Short-term	4 745 . .	. . .	. . .	*–2.7*	*.7*	*–.1*	*2.0*	. . .	. . .
Other sectors	4 746 . .	2.0	2.5	3.0	31.0	–.7	3.2	. . .	. . .
of which: Short-term	4 748 . .	. . .	*2.5*	*3.0*	*31.0*	*–.7*	*3.2*	. . .	. . .
Liabilities	4 753 . .	**–170.8**	**8.4**	**39.3**	**–287.4**	**317.3**	**33.7**	**. . .**	**. . .**
Trade credits	4 756 . .	65.4	–23.1	–16.2	–7.9	27.7	–37.2	. . .	. . .
General government	4 757 . .	. . .	. . .	. . .	. . .	. . .	. . .	. . .	. . .
of which: Short-term	4 759 . .	. . .	. . .	. . .	. . .	. . .	. . .	. . .	. . .
Other sectors	4 760 . .	65.4	–23.1	–16.2	–7.9	27.7	–37.2	. . .	. . .
of which: Short-term	4 762 . .	*65.4*	*–22.6*	*–14.9*	*–7.9*	*18.8*	*–37.2*	. . .	. . .
Loans	4 764 . .	1,299.0	46.7	52.0	8.5	163.5	74.4	. . .	. . .
Monetary authorities	4 765 . .	40.9	394.1	364.0	264.2	394.8	402.8	. . .	. . .
of which: Use of Fund credit and loans from the Fund	4 766 . .	*40.9*	*5.0*	*26.4*	*19.4*	*–22.7*	*–24.5*	. . .	. . .
of which: Short-term	4 768 . .	. . .	. . .	. . .	. . .	. . .	. . .	. . .	. . .
General government	4 769 . .	1,308.2	–280.3	–208.4	–251.7	–276.0	–268.5	. . .	. . .
of which: Short-term	4 771 . .	. . .	. . .	. . .	. . .	. . .	. . .	. . .	. . .
Banks	4 772 . .	. . .	12.8	–15.5	–.2	–.2	2.6	. . .	. . .
of which: Short-term	4 774 . .	. . .	*13.3*	*–15.4*	*2.9*	*–.2*	*2.6*	. . .	. . .
Other sectors	4 775 . .	–50.1	–80.0	–88.1	–3.8	44.9	–62.5	. . .	. . .
of which: Short-term	4 777 . .	. . .	*–35.3*	*–38.1*	*–20.9*	*10.3*	*–64.3*	. . .	. . .
Currency and deposits	4 780 . .	–81.2	20.5	37.6	–32.6	2.9	28.5	. . .	. . .
Monetary authorities	4 781 . .	–26.3	. . .	. . .	. . .	. . .	. . .	. . .	. . .
General government	4 782 . .	. . .	. . .	. . .	. . .	. . .	. . .	. . .	. . .
Banks	4 783 . .	–54.9	20.5	37.6	–32.6	2.9	28.5	. . .	. . .
Other sectors	4 784 . .	. . .	. . .	. . .	. . .	. . .	. . .	. . .	. . .
Other liabilities	4 786 . .	–1,453.9	–35.7	–34.1	–255.4	123.2	–32.1	. . .	. . .
Monetary authorities	4 787 . .	–1,443.8	. . .	. . .	. . .	. . .	. . .	. . .	. . .
of which: Short-term	4 789 . .	*–1,443.8*	. . .	. . .	. . .	. . .	. . .	. . .	. . .
General government	4 790 . .	. . .	. . .	. . .	. . .	. . .	. . .	. . .	. . .
of which: Short-term	4 792 . .	. . .	. . .	. . .	. . .	. . .	. . .	. . .	. . .
Banks	4 793 . .	. . .	.9	–2.2	.2	. . .	–.4	. . .	. . .
of which: Short-term	4 795 . .	. . .	*.9*	*–2.2*	*.2*	. . .	*–.4*	. . .	. . .
Other sectors	4 796 . .	–10.1	–36.6	–31.9	–255.6	123.2	–31.6	. . .	. . .
of which: Short-term	4 798 . .	*–10.1*	*–36.6*	*–31.9*	*–255.6*	*123.2*	*–31.6*	. . .	. . .
E. RESERVE ASSETS	4 802 . .	–173.8	42.2	–112.8	–66.8	272.2	–4.9	. . .	. . .
Monetary gold	4 812 . .	.5	. . .	. . .	. . .	. . .	. . .	. . .	. . .
Special drawing rights	4 811 . .	–.2	.3	. . .	. . .	. . .	. . .	. . .	. . .
Reserve position in the Fund	4 810 . .	. . .	. . .	. . .	. . .	. . .	–.1	. . .	. . .
Foreign exchange	4 803 . .	–174.2	42.0	–112.7	–66.8	272.2	–4.9	. . .	. . .
Other claims	4 813 . .	. . .	. . .	. . .	. . .	. . .	. . .	. . .	. . .
NET ERRORS AND OMISSIONS	4 998 . .	**254.6**	**–181.1**	**–97.4**	**–108.4**	**92.5**	**–106.7**	**. . .**	**. . .**

Part 3 of the *Yearbook* contains descriptions of the methodologies, compilation practices, and sources used to compile these data.

Table 1. ANALYTIC PRESENTATION, FISCAL YEARS 1994–2001 ENDING JUNE 30
(Millions of U.S. dollars)

	Code	1994	1995	1996	1997	1998	1999	2000	2001
A. Current Account [1]	4 993 Z.	**8.17**	**–8.19**	**–47.70**	**–23.56**	**. . .**	**. . .**	**. . .**	**. . .**
Goods: exports f.o.b	2 100 . .	124.97	122.96	118.75	119.61	. . .	. . .	. . .	. . .
Goods: imports f.o.b	3 100 . .	–181.62	–162.53	–217.10	–207.09	. . .	. . .	. . .	. . .
Balance on Goods	4 100 . .	*–56.65*	*–39.57*	*–98.35*	*–87.48*	. . .	. . .	. . .	. . .
Services: credit	2 200 . .	90.47	53.71	101.21	109.35	. . .	. . .	. . .	. . .
Services: debit	3 200 . .	–67.04	–69.25	–77.03	–74.67	. . .	. . .	. . .	. . .
Balance on Goods and Services	4 991 . .	*–33.22*	*–55.11*	*–74.17*	*–52.81*	. . .	. . .	. . .	. . .
Income: credit	2 300 . .	4.87	4.37	6.01	3.73	. . .	. . .	. . .	. . .
Income: debit	3 300 . .	–5.14	–9.58	–9.28	–11.30	. . .	. . .	. . .	. . .
Balance on Goods, Services, and Income	4 992 . .	*–33.50*	*–60.32*	*–77.44*	*–60.38*	. . .	. . .	. . .	. . .
Current transfers: credit	2 379 Z.	45.85	55.81	35.10	45.04	. . .	. . .	. . .	. . .
Current transfers: debit	3 379 . .	–4.18	–3.68	–5.35	–8.22	. . .	. . .	. . .	. . .
B. Capital Account [1]	4 994 Z.	**. . .**	**. . .**	**8.52**	**5.74**	**. . .**	**. . .**	**. . .**	**. . .**
Capital account: credit	2 994 Z.	. . .	. . .	8.52	5.74	. . .	. . .	. . .	. . .
Capital account: debit	3 994 . .	. . .	. . .	. . .	. . .	. . .	. . .	. . .	. . .
Total, Groups A Plus B	4 981 . .	*8.17*	*–8.19*	*–39.18*	*–17.83*	. . .	. . .	. . .	. . .
C. Financial Account [1]	4 995 W.	**33.13**	**24.77**	**58.59**	**39.44**	**. . .**	**. . .**	**. . .**	**. . .**
Direct investment abroad	4 505 . .	. . .	. . .	. . .	. . .	. . .	. . .	. . .	. . .
Direct investment in The Gambia	4 555 Z.	9.81	7.78	10.80	11.98	. . .	. . .	. . .	. . .
Portfolio investment assets	4 602 . .	. . .	. . .	. . .	. . .	. . .	. . .	. . .	. . .
Equity securities	4 610 . .	. . .	. . .	. . .	. . .	. . .	. . .	. . .	. . .
Debt securities	4 619 . .	. . .	. . .	. . .	. . .	. . .	. . .	. . .	. . .
Portfolio investment liabilities	4 652 Z.	. . .	. . .	. . .	. . .	. . .	. . .	. . .	. . .
Equity securities	4 660 . .	. . .	. . .	. . .	. . .	. . .	. . .	. . .	. . .
Debt securities	4 669 Z.	. . .	. . .	. . .	. . .	. . .	. . .	. . .	. . .
Financial derivatives	4 910 . .	. . .	. . .	. . .	. . .	. . .	. . .	. . .	. . .
Financial derivatives assets	4 900 . .	. . .	. . .	. . .	. . .	. . .	. . .	. . .	. . .
Financial derivatives liabilities	4 905 . .	. . .	. . .	. . .	. . .	. . .	. . .	. . .	. . .
Other investment assets	4 703 . .	3.79	–3.66	5.62	10.28	. . .	. . .	. . .	. . .
Monetary authorities	4 701 . .	. . .	. . .	. . .	. . .	. . .	. . .	. . .	. . .
General government	4 704 . .	. . .	. . .	. . .	. . .	. . .	. . .	. . .	. . .
Banks	4 705 . .	3.79	–3.66	4.71	7.14	. . .	. . .	. . .	. . .
Other sectors	4 728 . .	. . .	. . .	.91	3.14	. . .	. . .	. . .	. . .
Other investment liabilities	4 753 W.	19.54	20.65	42.18	17.19	. . .	. . .	. . .	. . .
Monetary authorities	4 753 WA	. . .	. . .	34.01	3.00	. . .	. . .	. . .	. . .
General government	4 753 ZB	17.79	22.60	3.11	10.49	. . .	. . .	. . .	. . .
Banks	4 753 ZC	1.75	–1.95	–.26	.13	. . .	. . .	. . .	. . .
Other sectors	4 753 ZD	. . .	. . .	5.32	3.57	. . .	. . .	. . .	. . .
Total, Groups A Through C	4 983 . .	*41.31*	*16.58*	*19.41*	*21.61*	. . .	. . .	. . .	. . .
D. Net Errors and Omissions	4 998 . .	**–35.12**	**–15.63**	**–4.94**	**–14.22**	**. . .**	**. . .**	**. . .**	**. . .**
Total, Groups A Through D	4 984 . .	*6.19*	*.94*	*14.47*	*7.40*	. . .	. . .	. . .	. . .
E. Reserves and Related Items	4 802 A.	**–6.19**	**–.94**	**–14.47**	**–7.40**	**. . .**	**. . .**	**. . .**	**. . .**
Reserve assets	4 802 . .	–3.30	4.23	–7.45	–.12	. . .	. . .	. . .	. . .
Use of Fund credit and loans	4 766 . .	–2.89	–5.17	–7.02	–7.27	. . .	. . .	. . .	. . .
Exceptional financing	4 920 . .	. . .	. . .	. . .	. . .	. . .	. . .	. . .	. . .
Conversion rates: dalasis per U.S. dollar	0 101 . .	**9.494**	**9.479**	**9.670**	**9.937**	**10.461**	**10.962**	**11.858**	**14.316**

[1] Excludes components that have been classified in the categories of Group E.

Table 2. STANDARD PRESENTATION, FISCAL YEARS 1994–2001 ENDING JUNE 30
(Millions of U.S. dollars)

	Code	1994	1995	1996	1997	1998	1999	2000	2001
CURRENT ACCOUNT	4 993 . .	**8.17**	**–8.19**	**–47.70**	**–23.56**	**. . .**	**. . .**	**. . .**	**. . .**
A. GOODS	4 100 . .	–56.65	–39.57	–98.35	–87.48	. . .	. . .	. . .	. . .
Credit	2 100 . .	**124.97**	**122.96**	**118.75**	**119.61**	**. . .**	**. . .**	**. . .**	**. . .**
General merchandise: exports f.o.b.	2 110 . .	124.97	122.96	118.75	119.61	. . .	. . .	. . .	. . .
Goods for processing: exports f.o.b.	2 150 . .	. . .	. . .	. . .	. . .	. . .	. . .	. . .	. . .
Repairs on goods	2 160 . .	. . .	. . .	. . .	. . .	. . .	. . .	. . .	. . .
Goods procured in ports by carriers	2 170 . .	. . .	. . .	. . .	. . .	. . .	. . .	. . .	. . .
Nonmonetary gold	2 180 . .	. . .	. . .	. . .	. . .	. . .	. . .	. . .	. . .
Debit	3 100 . .	**–181.62**	**–162.53**	**–217.10**	**–207.09**	**. . .**	**. . .**	**. . .**	**. . .**
General merchandise: imports f.o.b.	3 110 . .	–181.62	–162.53	–217.10	–207.09	. . .	. . .	. . .	. . .
Goods for processing: imports f.o.b.	3 150 . .	. . .	. . .	. . .	. . .	. . .	. . .	. . .	. . .
Repairs on goods	3 160 . .	. . .	. . .	. . .	. . .	. . .	. . .	. . .	. . .
Goods procured in ports by carriers	3 170 . .	. . .	. . .	. . .	. . .	. . .	. . .	. . .	. . .
Nonmonetary gold	3 180 . .	. . .	. . .	. . .	. . .	. . .	. . .	. . .	. . .
B. SERVICES	4 200 . .	23.43	–15.54	24.18	34.68	. . .	. . .	. . .	. . .
Total credit	2 200 . .	*90.47*	*53.71*	*101.21*	*109.35*	. . .	. . .	. . .	. . .
Total debit	3 200 . .	*–67.04*	*–69.25*	*–77.03*	*–74.67*	. . .	. . .	. . .	. . .
Transportation services, credit	2 205 . .	**7.87**	**8.31**	**9.59**	**8.90**	**. . .**	**. . .**	**. . .**	**. . .**
Passenger	2 850 . .	. . .	. . .	*1.05*	*1.12*	. . .	. . .	. . .	. . .
Freight	2 851 . .	*.88*	*.96*	*.99*	*1.01*	. . .	. . .	. . .	. . .
Other	2 852 . .	*6.99*	*7.36*	*7.55*	*6.77*	. . .	. . .	. . .	. . .
Sea transport, passenger	2 207 . .	. . .	. . .	1.05	1.12	. . .	. . .	. . .	. . .
Sea transport, freight	2 208 . .	. . .	. . .	. . .	. . .	. . .	. . .	. . .	. . .
Sea transport, other	2 209 . .	. . .	7.36	6.90	6.10	. . .	. . .	. . .	. . .
Air transport, passenger	2 211 . .	. . .	. . .	. . .	. . .	. . .	. . .	. . .	. . .
Air transport, freight	2 212 . .	. . .	. . .	. . .	. . .	. . .	. . .	. . .	. . .
Air transport, other	2 213 . .	. . .	. . .	.66	.67	. . .	. . .	. . .	. . .
Other transport, passenger	2 215 . .	. . .	. . .	. . .	. . .	. . .	. . .	. . .	. . .
Other transport, freight	2 216 . .	. . .	. . .	. . .	. . .	. . .	. . .	. . .	. . .
Other transport, other	2 217 . .	. . .	. . .	. . .	. . .	. . .	. . .	. . .	. . .
Transportation services, debit	3 205 . .	**–30.71**	**–27.93**	**–34.89**	**–33.34**	**. . .**	**. . .**	**. . .**	**. . .**
Passenger	3 850 . .	*–1.79*	*–1.85*	*–.48*	*–.51*	. . .	. . .	. . .	. . .
Freight	3 851 . .	*–27.33*	*–24.40*	*–32.60*	*–31.10*	. . .	. . .	. . .	. . .
Other	3 852 . .	*–1.58*	*–1.68*	*–1.81*	*–1.73*	. . .	. . .	. . .	. . .
Sea transport, passenger	3 207 . .	. . .	. . .	–.48	–.51	. . .	. . .	. . .	. . .
Sea transport, freight	3 208 . .	. . .	. . .	. . .	. . .	. . .	. . .	. . .	. . .
Sea transport, other	3 209 . .	. . .	–1.68	–1.72	–1.63	. . .	. . .	. . .	. . .
Air transport, passenger	3 211 . .	. . .	. . .	. . .	. . .	. . .	. . .	. . .	. . .
Air transport, freight	3 212 . .	. . .	. . .	. . .	. . .	. . .	. . .	. . .	. . .
Air transport, other	3 213 . .	. . .	. . .	–.09	–.10	. . .	. . .	. . .	. . .
Other transport, passenger	3 215 . .	. . .	. . .	. . .	. . .	. . .	. . .	. . .	. . .
Other transport, freight	3 216 . .	. . .	. . .	. . .	. . .	. . .	. . .	. . .	. . .
Other transport, other	3 217 . .	. . .	. . .	. . .	. . .	. . .	. . .	. . .	. . .
Travel, credit	2 236 . .	**66.29**	**28.14**	**65.70**	**75.26**	**. . .**	**. . .**	**. . .**	**. . .**
Business travel	2 237 . .	. . .	. . .	. . .	. . .	. . .	. . .	. . .	. . .
Personal travel	2 240 . .	. . .	. . .	. . .	. . .	. . .	. . .	. . .	. . .
Travel, debit	3 236 . .	**–13.55**	**–14.25**	**–15.36**	**–16.44**	**. . .**	**. . .**	**. . .**	**. . .**
Business travel	3 237 . .	. . .	. . .	. . .	. . .	. . .	. . .	. . .	. . .
Personal travel	3 240 . .	. . .	. . .	. . .	. . .	. . .	. . .	. . .	. . .
Other services, credit	2 200 BA	**16.31**	**17.26**	**25.92**	**25.19**	**. . .**	**. . .**	**. . .**	**. . .**
Communications	2 245 . .	. . .	. . .	10.45	10.68	. . .	. . .	. . .	. . .
Construction	2 249 . .	. . .	. . .	. . .	. . .	. . .	. . .	. . .	. . .
Insurance	2 253 . .	.10	.11	.11	.11	. . .	. . .	. . .	. . .
Financial	2 260 . .	. . .	. . .	. . .	. . .	. . .	. . .	. . .	. . .
Computer and information	2 262 . .	. . .	. . .	. . .	. . .	. . .	. . .	. . .	. . .
Royalties and licence fees	2 266 . .	. . .	. . .	. . .	. . .	. . .	. . .	. . .	. . .
Other business services	2 268 . .	1.69	1.79	1.81	1.86	. . .	. . .	. . .	. . .
Personal, cultural, and recreational	2 287 . .	. . .	. . .	. . .	. . .	. . .	. . .	. . .	. . .
Government, n.i.e.	2 291 . .	14.52	15.36	13.55	12.53	. . .	. . .	. . .	. . .
Other services, debit	3 200 BA	**–22.78**	**–27.07**	**–26.77**	**–24.88**	**. . .**	**. . .**	**. . .**	**. . .**
Communications	3 245 . .	. . .	. . .	–3.99	–4.55	. . .	. . .	. . .	. . .
Construction	3 249 . .	. . .	. . .	. . .	. . .	. . .	. . .	. . .	. . .
Insurance	3 253 . .	–2.97	–2.71	–3.62	–3.46	. . .	. . .	. . .	. . .
Financial	3 260 . .	. . .	. . .	. . .	. . .	. . .	. . .	. . .	. . .
Computer and information	3 262 . .	. . .	. . .	. . .	. . .	. . .	. . .	. . .	. . .
Royalties and licence fees	3 266 . .	. . .	. . .	. . .	. . .	. . .	. . .	. . .	. . .
Other business services	3 268 . .	–1.70	–1.97	–2.07	–1.97	. . .	. . .	. . .	. . .
Personal, cultural, and recreational	3 287 . .	. . .	. . .	. . .	. . .	. . .	. . .	. . .	. . .
Government, n.i.e.	3 291 . .	–18.12	–22.39	–17.09	–14.90	. . .	. . .	. . .	. . .

Table 2 (Continued). STANDARD PRESENTATION, FISCAL YEARS 1994–2001 ENDING JUNE 30

(Millions of U.S. dollars)

	Code	1994	1995	1996	1997	1998	1999	2000	2001
C. INCOME	4 300 . .	–.27	–5.21	–3.27	–7.58	...	...	...	...
Total credit	2 300 . .	*4.87*	*4.37*	*6.01*	*3.73*	...	...	...	...
Total debit	3 300 . .	*–5.14*	*–9.58*	*–9.28*	*–11.30*	...	...	...	...
Compensation of employees, credit	2 310 . .	...	...	...	...	...	...	...	...
Compensation of employees, debit	3 310 . .	...	...	...	...	...	...	...	...
Investment income, credit	2 320 . .	**4.87**	**4.37**	**6.01**	**3.73**	...	...	...	...
Direct investment income	2 330 . .	...	...	...	...	...	...	...	...
Dividends and distributed branch profits	2 332 . .	...	...	...	...	...	...	...	...
Reinvested earnings and undistributed branch profits	2 333 . .	...	...	...	...	...	...	...	...
Income on debt (interest)	2 334 . .	...	...	...	...	...	...	...	...
Portfolio investment income	2 339 . .	...	...	...	...	...	...	...	...
Income on equity	2 340 . .	...	...	...	...	...	...	...	...
Income on bonds and notes	2 350 . .	...	...	...	...	...	...	...	...
Income on money market instruments	2 360 . .	...	...	...	...	...	...	...	...
Other investment income	2 370 . .	4.87	4.37	6.01	3.73	...	...	...	...
Investment income, debit	3 320 . .	**–5.14**	**–9.58**	**–9.28**	**–11.30**	...	...	...	...
Direct investment income	3 330 . .	...	...	...	...	...	...	...	...
Dividends and distributed branch profits	3 332 . .	...	...	...	...	...	...	...	...
Reinvested earnings and undistributed branch profits	3 333 . .	...	...	...	...	...	...	...	...
Income on debt (interest)	3 334 . .	...	...	...	...	...	...	...	...
Portfolio investment income	3 339 . .	...	...	...	...	...	...	...	...
Income on equity	3 340 . .	...	...	...	...	...	...	...	...
Income on bonds and notes	3 350 . .	...	...	...	...	...	...	...	...
Income on money market instruments	3 360 . .	...	...	...	...	...	...	...	...
Other investment income	3 370 . .	–5.14	–9.58	–9.28	–11.30	...	...	...	...
D. CURRENT TRANSFERS	4 379 . .	41.67	52.12	29.74	36.82	...	...	...	...
Credit	2 379 . .	**45.85**	**55.81**	**35.10**	**45.04**	...	...	...	...
General government	2 380 . .	30.00	30.53	17.62	21.29	...	...	...	...
Other sectors	2 390 . .	15.85	25.28	17.47	23.74	...	...	...	...
Workers' remittances	2 391 . .	...	...	...	...	...	...	...	...
Other current transfers	2 392 . .	15.85	25.28	17.47	23.74	...	...	...	...
Debit	3 379 . .	**–4.18**	**–3.68**	**–5.35**	**–8.22**	...	...	...	...
General government	3 380 . .	–1.81	–1.26	–2.92	–5.80	...	...	...	...
Other sectors	3 390 . .	–2.37	–2.43	–2.43	–2.42	...	...	...	...
Workers' remittances	3 391 . .	...	...	...	...	...	...	...	...
Other current transfers	3 392 . .	–2.37	–2.43	–2.43	–2.42	...	...	...	...
CAPITAL AND FINANCIAL ACCOUNT	4 996 . .	**26.94**	**23.83**	**52.64**	**37.78**	...	...	...	...
CAPITAL ACCOUNT	4 994 . .	...	...	**8.52**	**5.74**	...	...	...	...
Total credit	2 994 . .	...	...	*8.52*	*5.74*	...	...	...	...
Total debit	3 994 . .	...	...	...	...	...	...	...	...
Capital transfers, credit	2 400 . .	...	...	**8.52**	**5.74**	...	...	...	...
General government	2 401 . .	...	...	8.52	5.74	...	...	...	...
Debt forgiveness	2 402 . .	...	...	...	...	...	...	...	...
Other capital transfers	2 410 . .	...	...	...	...	...	...	...	...
Other sectors	2 430 . .	...	...	...	...	...	...	...	...
Migrants' transfers	2 431 . .	...	...	...	...	...	...	...	...
Debt forgiveness	2 432 . .	...	...	...	...	...	...	...	...
Other capital transfers	2 440 . .	...	...	...	...	...	...	...	...
Capital transfers, debit	3 400 . .	...	...	...	...	...	...	...	...
General government	3 401 . .	...	...	...	...	...	...	...	...
Debt forgiveness	3 402 . .	...	...	...	...	...	...	...	...
Other capital transfers	3 410 . .	...	...	...	...	...	...	...	...
Other sectors	3 430 . .	...	...	...	...	...	...	...	...
Migrants' transfers	3 431 . .	...	...	...	...	...	...	...	...
Debt forgiveness	3 432 . .	...	...	...	...	...	...	...	...
Other capital transfers	3 440 . .	...	...	...	...	...	...	...	...
Nonproduced nonfinancial assets, credit	2 480 . .	...	...	...	...	...	...	...	...
Nonproduced nonfinancial assets, debit	3 480 . .	...	...	...	...	...	...	...	...

Table 2 (Continued). STANDARD PRESENTATION, FISCAL YEARS 1994–2001 ENDING JUNE 30
(Millions of U.S. dollars)

	Code	1994	1995	1996	1997	1998	1999	2000	2001
FINANCIAL ACCOUNT	4 995 . .	**26.94**	**23.83**	**44.12**	**32.05**	...	...	...	...
A. DIRECT INVESTMENT	4 500 . .	9.81	7.78	10.80	11.98	...	...	...	...
Direct investment abroad	4 505 . .	...	...	...	...	...	...	...	...
Equity capital	4 510 . .	...	...	...	...	...	...	...	...
Claims on affiliated enterprises	4 515 . .	...	...	...	...	...	...	...	...
Liabilities to affiliated enterprises	4 520 . .	...	...	...	...	...	...	...	...
Reinvested earnings	4 525 . .	...	...	...	...	...	...	...	...
Other capital	4 530 . .	...	...	...	...	...	...	...	...
Claims on affiliated enterprises	4 535 . .	...	...	...	...	...	...	...	...
Liabilities to affiliated enterprises	4 540 . .	...	...	...	...	...	...	...	...
Direct investment in The Gambia	4 555 . .	**9.81**	**7.78**	**10.80**	**11.98**	...	...	...	...
Equity capital	4 560 . .	9.81	7.78	10.80	11.98	...	...	...	...
Claims on direct investors	4 565 . .	...	...	...	...	...	...	...	...
Liabilities to direct investors	4 570 . .	...	...	...	...	...	...	...	...
Reinvested earnings	4 575 . .	...	...	...	...	...	...	...	...
Other capital	4 580 . .	...	...	...	...	...	...	...	...
Claims on direct investors	4 585 . .	...	...	...	...	...	...	...	...
Liabilities to direct investors	4 590 . .	...	...	...	...	...	...	...	...
B. PORTFOLIO INVESTMENT	4 600 . .	...	...	...	...	...	...	...	...
Assets	4 602 . .	...	...	...	...	...	...	...	...
Equity securities	4 610 . .	...	...	...	...	...	...	...	...
Monetary authorities	4 611 . .	...	...	...	...	...	...	...	...
General government	4 612 . .	...	...	...	...	...	...	...	...
Banks	4 613 . .	...	...	...	...	...	...	...	...
Other sectors	4 614 . .	...	...	...	...	...	...	...	...
Debt securities	4 619 . .	...	...	...	...	...	...	...	...
Bonds and notes	4 620 . .	...	...	...	...	...	...	...	...
Monetary authorities	4 621 . .	...	...	...	...	...	...	...	...
General government	4 622 . .	...	...	...	...	...	...	...	...
Banks	4 623 . .	...	...	...	...	...	...	...	...
Other sectors	4 624 . .	...	...	...	...	...	...	...	...
Money market instruments	4 630 . .	...	...	...	...	...	...	...	...
Monetary authorities	4 631 . .	...	...	...	...	...	...	...	...
General government	4 632 . .	...	...	...	...	...	...	...	...
Banks	4 633 . .	...	...	...	...	...	...	...	...
Other sectors	4 634 . .	...	...	...	...	...	...	...	...
Liabilities	4 652 . .	...	...	...	...	...	...	...	...
Equity securities	4 660 . .	...	...	...	...	...	...	...	...
Banks	4 663 . .	...	...	...	...	...	...	...	...
Other sectors	4 664 . .	...	...	...	...	...	...	...	...
Debt securities	4 669 . .	...	...	...	...	...	...	...	...
Bonds and notes	4 670 . .	...	...	...	...	...	...	...	...
Monetary authorities	4 671 . .	...	...	...	...	...	...	...	...
General government	4 672 . .	...	...	...	...	...	...	...	...
Banks	4 673 . .	...	...	...	...	...	...	...	...
Other sectors	4 674 . .	...	...	...	...	...	...	...	...
Money market instruments	4 680 . .	...	...	...	...	...	...	...	...
Monetary authorities	4 681 . .	...	...	...	...	...	...	...	...
General government	4 682 . .	...	...	...	...	...	...	...	...
Banks	4 683 . .	...	...	...	...	...	...	...	...
Other sectors	4 684 . .	...	...	...	...	...	...	...	...
C. FINANCIAL DERIVATIVES	4 910 . .	...	...	...	...	...	...	...	...
Monetary authorities	4 911 . .	...	...	...	...	...	...	...	...
General government	4 912 . .	...	...	...	...	...	...	...	...
Banks	4 913 . .	...	...	...	...	...	...	...	...
Other sectors	4 914 . .	...	...	...	...	...	...	...	...
Assets	4 900 . .	...	...	...	...	...	...	...	...
Monetary authorities	4 901 . .	...	...	...	...	...	...	...	...
General government	4 902 . .	...	...	...	...	...	...	...	...
Banks	4 903 . .	...	...	...	...	...	...	...	...
Other sectors	4 904 . .	...	...	...	...	...	...	...	...
Liabilities	4 905 . .	...	...	...	...	...	...	...	...
Monetary authorities	4 906 . .	...	...	...	...	...	...	...	...
General government	4 907 . .	...	...	...	...	...	...	...	...
Banks	4 908 . .	...	...	...	...	...	...	...	...
Other sectors	4 909 . .	...	...	...	...	...	...	...	...

Table 2 (Concluded). STANDARD PRESENTATION, FISCAL YEARS 1994–2001 ENDING JUNE 30

(Millions of U.S. dollars)

	Code	1994	1995	1996	1997	1998	1999	2000	2001
D. OTHER INVESTMENT	4 700 . .	20.43	11.82	40.78	20.19	...	...	...	...
Assets	4 703 . .	**3.79**	**–3.66**	**5.62**	**10.28**	**...**	**...**	**...**	**...**
Trade credits	4 706 . .	...	...	...	...	...	...	...	...
General government	4 707 . .	...	...	...	...	...	...	...	...
of which: Short-term	4 709 . .	...	...	...	...	...	...	...	...
Other sectors	4 710 . .	...	...	...	...	...	...	...	...
of which: Short-term	4 712 . .	...	...	...	...	...	...	...	...
Loans	4 714 . .	...	...	...	...	...	...	...	...
Monetary authorities	4 715 . .	...	...	...	...	...	...	...	...
of which: Short-term	4 718 . .	...	...	...	...	...	...	...	...
General government	4 719 . .	...	...	...	...	...	...	...	...
of which: Short-term	4 721 . .	...	...	...	...	...	...	...	...
Banks	4 722 . .	...	...	...	...	...	...	...	...
of which: Short-term	4 724 . .	...	...	...	...	...	...	...	...
Other sectors	4 725 . .	...	...	...	...	...	...	...	...
of which: Short-term	4 727 . .	...	...	...	...	...	...	...	...
Currency and deposits	4 730 . .	3.79	–3.66	5.62	10.28	...	...	...	...
Monetary authorities	4 731 . .	...	...	...	...	...	...	...	...
General government	4 732 . .	...	...	...	...	...	...	...	...
Banks	4 733 . .	3.79	–3.66	4.71	7.14	...	...	...	...
Other sectors	4 734 . .	...	...	.91	3.14	...	...	...	...
Other assets	4 736 . .	...	...	...	...	...	...	...	...
Monetary authorities	4 737 . .	...	...	...	...	...	...	...	...
of which: Short-term	4 739 . .	...	...	...	...	...	...	...	...
General government	4 740 . .	...	...	...	...	...	...	...	...
of which: Short-term	4 742 . .	...	...	...	...	...	...	...	...
Banks	4 743 . .	...	...	...	...	...	...	...	...
of which: Short-term	4 745 . .	...	...	...	...	...	...	...	...
Other sectors	4 746 . .	...	...	...	...	...	...	...	...
of which: Short-term	4 748 . .	...	...	...	...	...	...	...	...
Liabilities	4 753 . .	**16.64**	**15.47**	**35.16**	**9.91**	**...**	**...**	**...**	**...**
Trade credits	4 756 . .	...	...	5.32	3.57	...	...	...	...
General government	4 757 . .	...	...	...	...	...	...	...	...
of which: Short-term	4 759 . .	...	...	...	...	...	...	...	...
Other sectors	4 760 . .	...	...	5.32	3.57	...	...	...	...
of which: Short-term	4 762 . .	...	...	*5.32*	*3.57*	...	...	...	...
Loans	4 764 . .	14.90	17.43	30.10	6.22	...	...	...	...
Monetary authorities	4 765 . .	–2.89	–5.17	27.00	–4.27	...	...	...	...
of which: Use of Fund credit and loans from the Fund	4 766 . .	*–2.89*	*–5.17*	*–7.02*	*–7.27*	...	...	...	...
of which: Short-term	4 768 . .	...	...	...	...	...	...	...	...
General government	4 769 . .	17.79	22.60	3.11	10.49	...	...	...	...
of which: Short-term	4 771 . .	...	...	...	...	...	...	...	...
Banks	4 772 . .	...	...	...	...	...	...	...	...
of which: Short-term	4 774 . .	...	...	...	...	...	...	...	...
Other sectors	4 775 . .	...	...	...	...	...	...	...	...
of which: Short-term	4 777 . .	...	...	...	...	...	...	...	...
Currency and deposits	4 780 . .	1.75	–1.95	–.26	.13	...	...	...	...
Monetary authorities	4 781 . .	...	...	...	...	...	...	...	...
General government	4 782 . .	...	...	...	...	...	...	...	...
Banks	4 783 . .	1.75	–1.95	–.26	.13	...	...	...	...
Other sectors	4 784 . .	...	...	...	...	...	...	...	...
Other liabilities	4 786 . .	...	...	...	...	...	...	...	...
Monetary authorities	4 787 . .	...	...	...	...	...	...	...	...
of which: Short-term	4 789 . .	...	...	...	...	...	...	...	...
General government	4 790 . .	...	...	...	...	...	...	...	...
of which: Short-term	4 792 . .	...	...	...	...	...	...	...	...
Banks	4 793 . .	...	...	...	...	...	...	...	...
of which: Short-term	4 795 . .	...	...	...	...	...	...	...	...
Other sectors	4 796 . .	...	...	...	...	...	...	...	...
of which: Short-term	4 798 . .	...	...	...	...	...	...	...	...
E. RESERVE ASSETS	4 802 . .	–3.30	4.23	–7.45	–.12	...	...	...	...
Monetary gold	4 812 . .	...	...	...	...	...	...	...	...
Special drawing rights	4 811 . .	.18	.26	–.33	–.05	...	...	...	...
Reserve position in the Fund	4 810 . .	–.01	...	...	...	...	...	...	...
Foreign exchange	4 803 . .	–3.47	3.97	–7.12	–.07	...	...	...	...
Other claims	4 813 . .	...	...	...	...	...	...	...	...
NET ERRORS AND OMISSIONS	4 998 . .	**–35.12**	**–15.63**	**–4.94**	**–14.22**	**...**	**...**	**...**	**...**

Part 3 of the *Yearbook* contains descriptions of the methodologies, compilation practices, and sources used to compile these data.

Table 1. ANALYTIC PRESENTATION, 1994–2001
(Millions of U.S. dollars)

	Code	1994	1995	1996	1997	1998	1999	2000	2001
A. Current Account [1]	4 993 Z.	**...**	**...**	**...**	**–514.2**	**–275.7**	**–198.4**	**–269.0**	**...**
Goods: exports f.o.b	2 100 ..	...	...	...	376.5	299.9	329.5	459.0	...
Goods: imports f.o.b	3 100 ..	...	...	...	–1,162.9	–994.5	–863.4	–970.5	...
Balance on Goods	4 100 ..	...	...	...	*–786.4*	*–694.6*	*–533.9*	*–511.5*	...
Services: credit	2 200 ..	...	...	...	198.0	365.3	216.9	206.4	...
Services: debit	3 200 ..	...	...	...	–249.7	–345.2	–224.0	–216.3	...
Balance on Goods and Services	4 991 ..	...	...	...	*–838.1*	*–674.5*	*–541.0*	*–521.4*	...
Income: credit	2 300 ..	...	...	...	186.6	243.4	211.4	178.6	...
Income: debit	3 300 ..	...	...	...	–59.2	–52.7	–64.5	–61.1	...
Balance on Goods, Services, and Income	4 992 ..	...	...	...	*–710.7*	*–483.8*	*–394.1*	*–403.9*	...
Current transfers: credit	2 379 Z.	...	...	...	205.5	219.9	228.7	163.2	...
Current transfers: debit	3 379 ..	...	...	...	–9.0	–11.8	–33.0	–28.3	...
B. Capital Account [1]	4 994 Z.	**...**	**...**	**...**	**–6.5**	**–6.1**	**–7.1**	**–4.8**	**...**
Capital account: credit	2 994 Z.	...	...	...	...	...	...	...	...
Capital account: debit	3 994 ..	...	...	...	–6.5	–6.1	–7.1	–4.8	...
Total, Groups A Plus B	4 981 ..	...	...	...	*–520.7*	*–281.8*	*–205.5*	*–273.8*	...
C. Financial Account [1]	4 995 W.	**...**	**...**	**...**	**322.7**	**348.8**	**135.5**	**92.8**	**...**
Direct investment abroad	4 505 ..	...	...	...	...	...	–1.0	.5	...
Direct investment in Georgia	4 555 Z.	...	...	...	242.5	265.3	82.3	131.1	...
Portfolio investment assets	4 602 ..	...	...	...	...	...	...	2.7	...
Equity securities	4 610 ..	...	...	...	...	...	...	2.7	...
Debt securities	4 619 ..	...	...	...	...	...	...	...	...
Portfolio investment liabilities	4 652 Z.	...	...	...	2.4	...	6.2	...	...
Equity securities	4 660 ..	...	...	...	2.4	...	6.2	...	...
Debt securities	4 669 Z.	...	...	...	...	...	...	...	...
Financial derivatives	4 910 ..	...	...	...	...	...	...	...	...
Financial derivatives assets	4 900 ..	...	...	...	...	...	...	...	...
Financial derivatives liabilities	4 905 ..	...	...	...	...	...	...	...	...
Other investment assets	4 703 ..	...	...	...	–24.8	–86.9	9.3	–7.7	...
Monetary authorities	4 701 ..	...	...	...	...	...	...	...	...
General government	4 704 ..	...	...	...	...	–45.0	...	...	...
Banks	4 705 ..	...	...	...	–15.0	–23.2	9.3	–7.7	...
Other sectors	4 728 ..	...	...	...	–9.8	–18.7	...	...	...
Other investment liabilities	4 753 W.	...	...	...	102.6	170.4	38.7	–33.8	...
Monetary authorities	4 753 WA	...	...	...	...	...	...	...	...
General government	4 753 ZB	...	...	...	90.0	141.5	17.6	–41.1	...
Banks	4 753 ZC	...	...	...	7.4	37.4	26.3	7.3	...
Other sectors	4 753 ZD	...	...	...	5.2	–8.5	–5.2	...	...
Total, Groups A Through C	4 983 ..	...	...	...	*–198.0*	*67.0*	*–70.0*	*–181.0*	...
D. Net Errors and Omissions	4 998 ..	**...**	**...**	**...**	**136.0**	**–170.5**	**55.7**	**187.4**	**...**
Total, Groups A Through D	4 984 ..	...	...	...	*–62.0*	*–103.5*	*–14.3*	*6.4*	...
E. Reserves and Related Items	4 802 A.	**...**	**...**	**...**	**62.0**	**103.5**	**14.3**	**–6.4**	**...**
Reserve assets	4 802 ..	...	...	...	–14.1	67.6	–9.6	19.8	...
Use of Fund credit and loans	4 766 ..	...	...	...	76.1	35.8	23.9	–26.2	...
Exceptional financing	4 920 ..	...	...	...	...	...	...	...	...
Conversion rates: lari per U.S. dollar	0 101 ..	**...**	**...**	**1.2628**	**1.2975**	**1.3898**	**2.0245**	**1.9762**	**2.0730**

[1] Excludes components that have been classified in the categories of Group E.

Table 2. STANDARD PRESENTATION, 1994–2001

(Millions of U.S. dollars)

	Code	1994	1995	1996	1997	1998	1999	2000	2001
CURRENT ACCOUNT	4 993 . .	**. . .**	**. . .**	**. . .**	**–514.2**	**–275.7**	**–198.4**	**–269.0**	**. . .**
A. GOODS	4 100 . .	. . .	. . .	. . .	–786.4	–694.6	–533.9	–511.5	. . .
Credit	2 100 . .	**. . .**	**. . .**	**. . .**	**376.5**	**299.9**	**329.5**	**459.0**	**. . .**
General merchandise: exports f.o.b.	2 110 . .	. . .	. . .	. . .	376.5	299.9	329.5	459.0	. . .
Goods for processing: exports f.o.b.	2 150 . .	. . .	. . .	. . .	. . .	. . .	. . .	. . .	. . .
Repairs on goods	2 160 . .	. . .	. . .	. . .	. . .	. . .	. . .	. . .	. . .
Goods procured in ports by carriers	2 170 . .	. . .	. . .	. . .	. . .	. . .	. . .	. . .	. . .
Nonmonetary gold	2 180 . .	. . .	. . .	. . .	. . .	. . .	. . .	. . .	. . .
Debit	3 100 . .	**. . .**	**. . .**	**. . .**	**–1,162.9**	**–994.5**	**–863.4**	**–970.5**	**. . .**
General merchandise: imports f.o.b.	3 110 . .	. . .	. . .	. . .	–1,162.9	–994.5	–863.4	–970.5	. . .
Goods for processing: imports f.o.b.	3 150 . .	. . .	. . .	. . .	. . .	. . .	. . .	. . .	. . .
Repairs on goods	3 160 . .	. . .	. . .	. . .	. . .	. . .	. . .	. . .	. . .
Goods procured in ports by carriers	3 170 . .	. . .	. . .	. . .	. . .	. . .	. . .	. . .	. . .
Nonmonetary gold	3 180 . .	. . .	. . .	. . .	. . .	. . .	. . .	. . .	. . .
B. SERVICES	4 200 . .	. . .	. . .	. . .	–51.7	20.1	–7.1	–9.9	. . .
Total credit	2 200 . .	. . .	. . .	. . .	*198.0*	*365.3*	*216.9*	*206.4*	. . .
Total debit	3 200 . .	. . .	. . .	. . .	*–249.7*	*–345.2*	*–224.0*	*–216.3*	. . .
Transportation services, credit	2 205 . .	**. . .**	**. . .**	**. . .**	**90.5**	**150.1**	**97.1**	**102.5**	**. . .**
Passenger	2 850 . .	. . .	. . .	. . .	*27.5*	*41.1*	*12.9*	*9.5*	. . .
Freight	2 851 . .	. . .	. . .	. . .	*24.3*	*82.0*	*74.2*	*76.6*	. . .
Other	2 852 . .	. . .	. . .	. . .	*38.7*	*27.0*	*10.0*	*16.4*	. . .
Sea transport, passenger	2 207 . .	. . .	. . .	. . .	.2	.4	. . .	. . .	. . .
Sea transport, freight	2 208 . .	. . .	. . .	. . .	9.3	. . .	10.3	14.8	. . .
Sea transport, other	2 209 . .	. . .	. . .	. . .	16.9	15.0	7.1	12.9	. . .
Air transport, passenger	2 211 . .	. . .	. . .	. . .	24.7	38.0	12.8	9.5	. . .
Air transport, freight	2 212 . .	. . .	. . .	. . .	1.9	1.2	2.9	4.1	. . .
Air transport, other	2 213 . .	. . .	. . .	. . .	6.3	12.0	2.9	3.5	. . .
Other transport, passenger	2 215 . .	. . .	. . .	. . .	2.6	2.7	.1	. . .	. . .
Other transport, freight	2 216 . .	. . .	. . .	. . .	13.1	80.8	61.0	57.7	. . .
Other transport, other	2 217 . .	. . .	. . .	. . .	15.5	. . .	. . .	. . .	. . .
Transportation services, debit	3 205 . .	**. . .**	**. . .**	**. . .**	**–67.2**	**–80.1**	**–84.3**	**–89.2**	**. . .**
Passenger	3 850 . .	. . .	. . .	. . .	*–14.6*	*–13.1*	*–4.9*	*–19.0*	. . .
Freight	3 851 . .	. . .	. . .	. . .	*–35.5*	*–33.0*	*–35.2*	*–44.7*	. . .
Other	3 852 . .	. . .	. . .	. . .	*–17.1*	*–34.0*	*–44.2*	*–25.5*	. . .
Sea transport, passenger	3 207 . .	. . .	. . .	. . .	. . .	. . .	. . .	–9.3	. . .
Sea transport, freight	3 208 . .	. . .	. . .	. . .	–7.9	–2.4	–13.6	–16.4	. . .
Sea transport, other	3 209 . .	. . .	. . .	. . .	–7.7	–6.5	–20.9	–11.2	. . .
Air transport, passenger	3 211 . .	. . .	. . .	. . .	–9.3	–11.5	–4.9	–9.7	. . .
Air transport, freight	3 212 . .	. . .	. . .	. . .	–2.1	–2.7	–5.6	–6.8	. . .
Air transport, other	3 213 . .	. . .	. . .	. . .	–8.6	–25.5	–23.1	–14.3	. . .
Other transport, passenger	3 215 . .	. . .	. . .	. . .	–5.3	–1.6	. . .	. . .	. . .
Other transport, freight	3 216 . .	. . .	. . .	. . .	–25.5	–27.9	–16.0	–21.5	. . .
Other transport, other	3 217 . .	. . .	. . .	. . .	–.8	–2.0	–.2	. . .	. . .
Travel, credit	2 236 . .	**. . .**	**. . .**	**. . .**	**46.9**	**187.8**	**118.3**	**96.7**	**. . .**
Business travel	2 237 . .	. . .	. . .	. . .	33.8	116.8	82.8	67.7	. . .
Personal travel	2 240 . .	. . .	. . .	. . .	13.1	71.0	35.5	29.0	. . .
Travel, debit	3 236 . .	**. . .**	**. . .**	**. . .**	**–156.2**	**–226.2**	**–130.3**	**–110.3**	**. . .**
Business travel	3 237 . .	. . .	. . .	. . .	–147.0	–188.5	–91.2	–77.3	. . .
Personal travel	3 240 . .	. . .	. . .	. . .	–9.2	–37.7	–39.1	–33.0	. . .
Other services, credit	2 200 BA	**. . .**	**. . .**	**. . .**	**60.6**	**27.4**	**1.5**	**7.2**	**. . .**
Communications	2 245 . .	. . .	. . .	. . .	30.2	15.7	1.5	7.2	. . .
Construction	2 249 . .	. . .	. . .	. . .	8.3	. . .	. . .	. . .	. . .
Insurance	2 253 . .	. . .	. . .	. . .	. . .	. . .	. . .	. . .	. . .
Financial	2 260 . .	. . .	. . .	. . .	. . .	. . .	. . .	. . .	. . .
Computer and information	2 262 . .	. . .	. . .	. . .	. . .	. . .	. . .	. . .	. . .
Royalties and licence fees	2 266 . .	. . .	. . .	. . .	. . .	. . .	. . .	. . .	. . .
Other business services	2 268 . .	. . .	. . .	. . .	12.0	. . .	. . .	. . .	. . .
Personal, cultural, and recreational	2 287 . .	. . .	. . .	. . .	. . .	. . .	. . .	. . .	. . .
Government, n.i.e.	2 291 . .	. . .	. . .	. . .	10.1	11.7	. . .	. . .	. . .
Other services, debit	3 200 BA	**. . .**	**. . .**	**. . .**	**–26.3**	**–38.9**	**–9.4**	**–16.8**	**. . .**
Communications	3 245 . .	. . .	. . .	. . .	–.3	–5.7	–.4	–4.1	. . .
Construction	3 249 . .	. . .	. . .	. . .	. . .	. . .	. . .	. . .	. . .
Insurance	3 253 . .	. . .	. . .	. . .	–21.0	–18.0	–9.0	–12.7	. . .
Financial	3 260 . .	. . .	. . .	. . .	. . .	. . .	. . .	. . .	. . .
Computer and information	3 262 . .	. . .	. . .	. . .	. . .	. . .	. . .	. . .	. . .
Royalties and licence fees	3 266 . .	. . .	. . .	. . .	. . .	. . .	. . .	. . .	. . .
Other business services	3 268 . .	. . .	. . .	. . .	–4.2	–5.4	. . .	. . .	. . .
Personal, cultural, and recreational	3 287 . .	. . .	. . .	. . .	. . .	. . .	. . .	. . .	. . .
Government, n.i.e.	3 291 . .	. . .	. . .	. . .	–.8	–9.8	. . .	. . .	. . .

Table 2 (Continued). STANDARD PRESENTATION, 1994–2001
(Millions of U.S. dollars)

	Code	1994	1995	1996	1997	1998	1999	2000	2001
C. INCOME	4 300 . .	...	...	...	127.4	190.7	146.9	117.5	...
Total credit	2 300 . .	...	...	...	*186.6*	*243.4*	*211.4*	*178.6*	...
Total debit	3 300 . .	...	...	...	*–59.2*	*–52.7*	*–64.5*	*–61.1*	...
Compensation of employees, credit	2 310 . .	**...**	**...**	**...**	**180.8**	**235.7**	**211.4**	**178.6**	**...**
Compensation of employees, debit	3 310 . .	**...**	**...**	**...**	**–5.8**	**–4.5**	**–16.9**	**–14.6**	**...**
Investment income, credit	2 320 . .	**...**	**...**	**...**	**5.8**	**7.7**	**...**	**...**	**...**
Direct investment income	2 330 . .	...	...	...	...	...	...	...	...
Dividends and distributed branch profits	2 332 . .	...	...	...	...	...	...	...	...
Reinvested earnings and undistributed branch profits	2 333 . .	...	...	...	...	...	...	...	...
Income on debt (interest)	2 334 . .	...	...	...	...	...	...	...	...
Portfolio investment income	2 339 . .	...	...	...	...	...	...	...	...
Income on equity	2 340 . .	...	...	...	...	...	...	...	...
Income on bonds and notes	2 350 . .	...	...	...	...	...	...	...	...
Income on money market instruments	2 360 . .	...	...	...	...	...	...	...	...
Other investment income	2 370 . .	...	...	...	5.8	7.7	...	...	...
Investment income, debit	3 320 . .	**...**	**...**	**...**	**–53.4**	**–48.2**	**–47.6**	**–46.5**	**...**
Direct investment income	3 330 . .	...	...	...	–2.8	...	–.3	–.3	...
Dividends and distributed branch profits	3 332 . .	...	...	...	...	...	...	...	...
Reinvested earnings and undistributed branch profits	3 333 . .	...	...	...	...	...	...	...	...
Income on debt (interest)	3 334 . .	...	...	...	...	...	...	...	...
Portfolio investment income	3 339 . .	...	...	...	...	–.8	...	...	...
Income on equity	3 340 . .	...	...	...	...	...	...	...	...
Income on bonds and notes	3 350 . .	...	...	...	...	...	...	...	...
Income on money market instruments	3 360 . .	...	...	...	...	...	...	...	...
Other investment income	3 370 . .	...	...	...	–50.6	–47.4	–47.3	–46.2	...
D. CURRENT TRANSFERS	4 379 . .	...	...	...	196.5	208.1	195.7	134.9	...
Credit	2 379 . .	**...**	**...**	**...**	**205.5**	**219.9**	**228.7**	**163.2**	**...**
General government	2 380 . .	...	...	...	25.8	9.0	31.7	7.1	...
Other sectors	2 390 . .	...	...	...	179.7	210.9	197.0	156.1	...
Workers' remittances	2 391 . .	...	...	...	103.2	137.2	149.4	94.9	...
Other current transfers	2 392 . .	...	...	...	76.5	73.7	47.6	61.2	...
Debit	3 379 . .	**...**	**...**	**...**	**–9.0**	**–11.8**	**–33.0**	**–28.3**	**...**
General government	3 380 . .	...	...	...	–9.0	–11.8	–10.5	–8.9	...
Other sectors	3 390 . .	...	...	...	...	...	–22.5	–19.4	...
Workers' remittances	3 391 . .	...	...	...	...	...	–22.5	–19.4	...
Other current transfers	3 392 . .	...	...	...	...	...	...	...	...
CAPITAL AND FINANCIAL ACCOUNT	4 996 . .	**...**	**...**	**...**	**378.2**	**446.2**	**142.7**	**81.6**	**...**
CAPITAL ACCOUNT	4 994 . .	**...**	**...**	**...**	**–6.5**	**–6.1**	**–7.1**	**–4.8**	**...**
Total credit	2 994 . .	...	...	...	...	...	...	...	...
Total debit	3 994 . .	...	...	...	*–6.5*	*–6.1*	*–7.1*	*–4.8*	...
Capital transfers, credit	2 400 . .	**...**	**...**	**...**	**...**	**...**	**...**	**...**	**...**
General government	2 401 . .	...	...	...	...	...	...	...	...
Debt forgiveness	2 402 . .	...	...	...	...	...	...	...	...
Other capital transfers	2 410 . .	...	...	...	...	...	...	...	...
Other sectors	2 430 . .	...	...	...	...	...	...	...	...
Migrants' transfers	2 431 . .	...	...	...	...	...	...	...	...
Debt forgiveness	2 432 . .	...	...	...	...	...	...	...	...
Other capital transfers	2 440 . .	...	...	...	...	...	...	...	...
Capital transfers, debit	3 400 . .	**...**	**...**	**...**	**–6.5**	**–6.1**	**–7.1**	**–4.8**	**...**
General government	3 401 . .	...	...	...	...	...	...	...	...
Debt forgiveness	3 402 . .	...	...	...	...	...	...	...	...
Other capital transfers	3 410 . .	...	...	...	...	...	...	...	...
Other sectors	3 430 . .	...	...	...	–6.5	–6.1	–7.1	–4.8	...
Migrants' transfers	3 431 . .	...	...	...	–6.5	–6.1	–7.1	–4.8	...
Debt forgiveness	3 432 . .	...	...	...	...	...	...	...	...
Other capital transfers	3 440 . .	...	...	...	...	...	...	...	...
Nonproduced nonfinancial assets, credit	2 480 . .	**...**	**...**	**...**	**...**	**...**	**...**	**...**	**...**
Nonproduced nonfinancial assets, debit	3 480 . .	**...**	**...**	**...**	**...**	**...**	**...**	**...**	**...**

Table 2 (Continued). STANDARD PRESENTATION, 1994–2001

(Millions of U.S. dollars)

	Code	1994	1995	1996	1997	1998	1999	2000	2001
FINANCIAL ACCOUNT	4 995	**...**	**...**	**...**	**384.7**	**452.3**	**149.8**	**86.4**	**...**
A. DIRECT INVESTMENT	4 500	...	...	...	242.5	265.3	81.3	131.6	...
Direct investment abroad	4 505	**...**	**...**	**...**	**...**	**...**	**–1.0**	**.5**	**...**
Equity capital	4 510	...	...	...	...	...	–1.0	.5	...
Claims on affiliated enterprises	4 515	...	...	...	...	...	...	...	...
Liabilities to affiliated enterprises	4 520	...	...	...	...	...	...	...	...
Reinvested earnings	4 525	...	...	...	...	...	...	...	...
Other capital	4 530	...	...	...	...	...	...	...	...
Claims on affiliated enterprises	4 535	...	...	...	...	...	...	...	...
Liabilities to affiliated enterprises	4 540	...	...	...	...	...	...	...	...
Direct investment in Georgia	4 555	**...**	**...**	**...**	**242.5**	**265.3**	**82.3**	**131.1**	**...**
Equity capital	4 560	...	...	...	242.5	265.3	82.3	131.1	...
Claims on direct investors	4 565	...	...	...	...	...	...	...	...
Liabilities to direct investors	4 570	...	...	...	...	...	...	...	...
Reinvested earnings	4 575	...	...	...	...	...	...	...	...
Other capital	4 580	...	...	...	...	...	...	...	...
Claims on direct investors	4 585	...	...	...	...	...	...	...	...
Liabilities to direct investors	4 590	...	...	...	...	...	...	...	...
B. PORTFOLIO INVESTMENT	4 600	...	...	...	2.4	...	6.2	2.7	...
Assets	4 602	**...**	**...**	**...**	**...**	**...**	**...**	**2.7**	**...**
Equity securities	4 610	...	...	...	...	...	...	2.7	...
Monetary authorities	4 611	...	...	...	...	...	...	...	...
General government	4 612	...	...	...	...	...	...	...	...
Banks	4 613	...	...	...	...	...	...	...	...
Other sectors	4 614	...	...	...	...	...	...	...	...
Debt securities	4 619	...	...	...	...	...	...	...	...
Bonds and notes	4 620	...	...	...	...	...	...	...	...
Monetary authorities	4 621	...	...	...	...	...	...	...	...
General government	4 622	...	...	...	...	...	...	...	...
Banks	4 623	...	...	...	...	...	...	...	...
Other sectors	4 624	...	...	...	...	...	...	...	...
Money market instruments	4 630	...	...	...	...	...	...	...	...
Monetary authorities	4 631	...	...	...	...	...	...	...	...
General government	4 632	...	...	...	...	...	...	...	...
Banks	4 633	...	...	...	...	...	...	...	...
Other sectors	4 634	...	...	...	...	...	...	...	...
Liabilities	4 652	**...**	**...**	**...**	**2.4**	**...**	**6.2**	**...**	**...**
Equity securities	4 660	...	...	...	2.4	...	6.2	...	...
Banks	4 663	...	...	...	...	...	...	...	...
Other sectors	4 664	...	...	...	...	...	...	...	...
Debt securities	4 669	...	...	...	...	...	...	...	...
Bonds and notes	4 670	...	...	...	...	...	...	...	...
Monetary authorities	4 671	...	...	...	...	...	...	...	...
General government	4 672	...	...	...	...	...	...	...	...
Banks	4 673	...	...	...	...	...	...	...	...
Other sectors	4 674	...	...	...	...	...	...	...	...
Money market instruments	4 680	...	...	...	...	...	...	...	...
Monetary authorities	4 681	...	...	...	...	...	...	...	...
General government	4 682	...	...	...	...	...	...	...	...
Banks	4 683	...	...	...	...	...	...	...	...
Other sectors	4 684	...	...	...	...	...	...	...	...
C. FINANCIAL DERIVATIVES	4 910	...	...	...	...	...	...	...	...
Monetary authorities	4 911	...	...	...	...	...	...	...	...
General government	4 912	...	...	...	...	...	...	...	...
Banks	4 913	...	...	...	...	...	...	...	...
Other sectors	4 914	...	...	...	...	...	...	...	...
Assets	4 900	**...**	**...**	**...**	**...**	**...**	**...**	**...**	**...**
Monetary authorities	4 901	...	...	...	...	...	...	...	...
General government	4 902	...	...	...	...	...	...	...	...
Banks	4 903	...	...	...	...	...	...	...	...
Other sectors	4 904	...	...	...	...	...	...	...	...
Liabilities	4 905	**...**	**...**	**...**	**...**	**...**	**...**	**...**	**...**
Monetary authorities	4 906	...	...	...	...	...	...	...	...
General government	4 907	...	...	...	...	...	...	...	...
Banks	4 908	...	...	...	...	...	...	...	...
Other sectors	4 909	...	...	...	...	...	...	...	...

Table 2 (Concluded). STANDARD PRESENTATION, 1994–2001
(Millions of U.S. dollars)

	Code	1994	1995	1996	1997	1998	1999	2000	2001
D. OTHER INVESTMENT	4 700 . .	...	...	...	153.9	119.4	71.9	–67.7	...
Assets	4 703 . .	**...**	**...**	**...**	**–24.8**	**–86.9**	**9.3**	**–7.7**	**...**
Trade credits	4 706 . .	...	...	...	...	...	...	...	...
General government	4 707 . .	...	...	...	...	...	...	...	...
of which: Short-term	4 709 . .	...	...	...	...	...	...	...	...
Other sectors	4 710 . .	...	...	...	...	...	...	...	...
of which: Short-term	4 712 . .	...	...	...	...	...	...	...	...
Loans	4 714 . .	...	...	...	...	–45.0	7.2	–2.7	...
Monetary authorities	4 715 . .	...	...	...	...	...	...	...	...
of which: Short-term	4 718 . .	...	...	...	...	...	...	...	...
General government	4 719 . .	...	...	...	...	–45.0	...	...	...
of which: Short-term	4 721 . .	...	...	...	...	*–45.0*	...	...	...
Banks	4 722 . .	...	...	...	...	...	7.2	–2.7	...
of which: Short-term	4 724 . .	...	...	...	...	...	*5.4*	*–1.2*	...
Other sectors	4 725 . .	...	...	...	...	...	...	...	...
of which: Short-term	4 727 . .	...	...	...	...	...	...	...	...
Currency and deposits	4 730 . .	...	...	...	–24.8	–41.9	–2.1	–2.7	...
Monetary authorities	4 731 . .	...	...	...	...	...	...	...	...
General government	4 732 . .	...	...	...	...	...	...	...	...
Banks	4 733 . .	...	...	...	–15.0	–23.2	–2.1	–2.7	...
Other sectors	4 734 . .	...	...	...	–9.8	–18.7	...	...	...
Other assets	4 736 . .	...	...	...	...	...	4.2	–2.3	...
Monetary authorities	4 737 . .	...	...	...	...	...	...	...	...
of which: Short-term	4 739 . .	...	...	...	...	...	...	...	...
General government	4 740 . .	...	...	...	...	...	...	...	...
of which: Short-term	4 742 . .	...	...	...	...	...	...	...	...
Banks	4 743 . .	...	...	...	...	...	4.2	–2.3	...
of which: Short-term	4 745 . .	...	...	...	...	...	...	...	...
Other sectors	4 746 . .	...	...	...	...	...	...	...	...
of which: Short-term	4 748 . .	...	...	...	...	...	...	...	...
Liabilities	4 753 . .	**...**	**...**	**...**	**178.7**	**206.2**	**62.6**	**–60.0**	**...**
Trade credits	4 756 . .	...	...	...	6.6	6.5	–5.2	...	...
General government	4 757 . .	...	...	...	1.4	15.0	...	...	...
of which: Short-term	4 759 . .	...	...	...	*1.4*	...	...	...	...
Other sectors	4 760 . .	...	...	...	5.2	–8.5	–5.2	...	...
of which: Short-term	4 762 . .	...	...	...	...	...	...	...	...
Loans	4 764 . .	...	...	...	431.9	348.8	130.6	–127.7	...
Monetary authorities	4 765 . .	...	...	...	76.1	35.8	23.9	–26.2	...
of which: Use of Fund credit and loans from the Fund	4 766 . .	...	...	...	*76.1*	*35.8*	*23.9*	*–26.2*	...
of which: Short-term	4 768 . .	...	...	...	...	...	...	...	...
General government	4 769 . .	...	...	...	355.8	313.0	68.5	–108.2	...
of which: Short-term	4 771 . .	...	...	...	...	*45.0*	...	...	...
Banks	4 772 . .	...	...	...	...	...	38.2	6.7	...
of which: Short-term	4 774 . .	...	...	...	...	...	*30.3*	*2.3*	...
Other sectors	4 775 . .	...	...	...	...	...	...	...	...
of which: Short-term	4 777 . .	...	...	...	...	...	...	...	...
Currency and deposits	4 780 . .	...	...	...	7.4	37.4	2.4	.5	...
Monetary authorities	4 781 . .	...	...	...	...	...	...	...	...
General government	4 782 . .	...	...	...	...	...	...	...	...
Banks	4 783 . .	...	...	...	7.4	37.4	2.4	.5	...
Other sectors	4 784 . .	...	...	...	...	...	...	...	...
Other liabilities	4 786 . .	...	...	...	–267.2	–186.5	–65.2	67.2	...
Monetary authorities	4 787 . .	...	...	...	...	...	...	...	...
of which: Short-term	4 789 . .	...	...	...	...	...	...	...	...
General government	4 790 . .	...	...	...	–267.2	–186.5	–50.9	67.1	...
of which: Short-term	4 792 . .	...	...	...	*–257.8*	*–83.1*	*–50.9*	*67.1*	...
Banks	4 793 . .	...	...	...	...	...	–14.3	.1	...
of which: Short-term	4 795 . .	...	...	...	...	...	...	...	...
Other sectors	4 796 . .	...	...	...	...	...	...	...	...
of which: Short-term	4 798 . .	...	...	...	...	...	...	...	...
E. RESERVE ASSETS	4 802 . .	...	...	...	–14.1	67.6	–9.6	19.8	...
Monetary gold	4 812 . .	...	...	...	.7	...	–.1	...	...
Special drawing rights	4 811 . .	...	...	...	–.1	–5.0	–3.2	5.0	...
Reserve position in the Fund	4 810 . .	...	...	...	...	...	...	...	...
Foreign exchange	4 803 . .	...	...	...	–14.7	72.6	–6.3	14.8	...
Other claims	4 813 . .	...	...	...	...	...	...	...	...
NET ERRORS AND OMISSIONS	4 998 . .	**...**	**...**	**...**	**136.0**	**–170.5**	**55.7**	**187.4**	**...**

Part 3 of the *Yearbook* contains descriptions of the methodologies, compilation practices, and sources used to compile these data.

Table 1. ANALYTIC PRESENTATION, 1994–2001
(Billions of U.S. dollars)

	Code	1994	1995	1996	1997	1998	1999	2000	2001
A. Current Account [1]	4 993 Z.	**–20.94**	**–18.93**	**–7.97**	**–2.84**	**–6.11**	**–19.07**	**–20.39**	**2.44**
Goods: exports f.o.b	2 100 . .	430.54	523.58	522.58	510.02	542.62	542.73	549.84	569.95
Goods: imports f.o.b	3 100 . .	–379.63	–458.48	–453.20	–439.90	–465.71	–472.69	–492.33	–481.44
Balance on Goods	4 100 . .	*50.92*	*65.11*	*69.38*	*70.12*	*76.91*	*70.03*	*57.51*	*88.51*
Services: credit	2 200 . .	66.25	81.84	85.56	84.42	85.92	86.93	85.57	87.50
Services: debit	3 200 . .	–105.94	–127.20	–129.82	–125.63	–131.01	–139.15	–135.48	–138.48
Balance on Goods and Services	4 991 . .	*11.22*	*19.75*	*25.12*	*28.91*	*31.83*	*17.81*	*7.60*	*37.53*
Income: credit	2 300 . .	68.51	84.89	81.36	80.40	83.43	86.13	99.90	105.34
Income: debit	3 300 . .	–61.68	–84.59	–80.42	–81.77	–91.03	–95.71	–102.99	–116.61
Balance on Goods, Services, and Income	4 992 . .	*18.05*	*20.04*	*26.06*	*27.54*	*24.22*	*8.23*	*4.51*	*26.27*
Current transfers: credit	2 379 Z.	13.89	16.87	17.89	16.47	15.96	16.96	15.77	15.15
Current transfers: debit	3 379 . .	–52.88	–55.84	–51.92	–46.85	–46.30	–44.26	–40.67	–38.98
B. Capital Account [1]	4 994 Z.	**.15**	**–2.73**	**–2.18**	**. . .**	**.72**	**–.16**	**6.19**	**–.83**
Capital account: credit	2 994 Z.	1.56	1.68	2.76	2.83	3.31	3.00	9.41	1.87
Capital account: debit	3 994 . .	–1.42	–4.41	–4.94	–2.82	–2.59	–3.16	–3.22	–2.70
Total, Groups A Plus B	4 981 . .	*–20.79*	*–21.67*	*–10.15*	*–2.84*	*–5.39*	*–19.23*	*–14.20*	*1.61*
C. Financial Account [1]	4 995 W.	**30.43**	**43.98**	**16.13**	**1.13**	**8.36**	**–30.25**	**35.71**	**–26.28**
Direct investment abroad	4 505 . .	–17.26	–39.10	–50.75	–42.73	–89.93	–109.42	–53.00	–42.75
Direct investment in Germany	4 555 Z.	1.94	11.99	6.43	12.80	23.64	54.58	207.72	31.53
Portfolio investment assets	4 602 . .	–41.48	–18.05	–30.89	–90.08	–145.49	–190.32	–195.96	–115.26
Equity securities	4 610 . .	–20.97	.28	–17.52	–42.62	–78.33	–87.56	–129.44	–31.18
Debt securities	4 619 . .	–20.51	–18.33	–13.37	–47.46	–67.17	–102.77	–66.51	–84.07
Portfolio investment liabilities	4 652 Z.	10.64	53.15	93.90	91.04	150.91	176.31	39.34	114.19
Equity securities	4 660 . .	3.92	–1.51	12.98	12.87	56.77	27.98	–27.73	78.91
Debt securities	4 669 Z.	6.72	54.66	80.92	78.17	94.14	148.32	67.07	35.28
Financial derivatives	4 910 . .	.54	–.66	–5.73	–8.70	–7.99	–1.67	–3.91	5.92
Financial derivatives assets	4 900 . .	–10.71	. . .	. . .	. . .	. . .	. . .	. . .	. . .
Financial derivatives liabilities	4 905 . .	11.25	–.66	–5.73	–8.70	–7.99	–1.67	–3.91	5.92
Other investment assets	4 703 . .	–.62	–61.28	–39.77	–83.53	–95.50	–70.85	–79.68	–87.06
Monetary authorities	4 701 . .	.17	.28	.35	.29	–.11	–51.70	39.37	20.70
General government	4 704 . .	2.46	–6.72	–.34	–2.33	–.63	8.46	–17.98	14.84
Banks	4 705 . .	14.98	–55.18	–39.13	–80.40	–79.22	–46.32	–92.58	–118.47
Other sectors	4 728 . .	–18.23	.35	–.64	–1.09	–15.54	18.72	–8.49	–4.13
Other investment liabilities	4 753 W.	76.66	97.94	42.93	122.34	172.73	111.12	121.21	67.14
Monetary authorities	4 753 WA	–2.04	–2.65	–1.17	–.39	2.16	–2.21	.37	2.35
General government	4 753 ZB	2.12	3.84	3.45	–7.75	.10	–12.29	.52	.29
Banks	4 753 ZC	69.19	83.71	36.62	120.20	159.94	103.54	109.95	52.83
Other sectors	4 753 ZD	7.39	13.04	4.03	10.29	10.53	22.09	10.37	11.68
Total, Groups A Through C	4 983 . .	*9.64*	*22.31*	*5.98*	*–1.70*	*2.97*	*–49.47*	*21.51*	*–24.67*
D. Net Errors and Omissions	4 998 . .	**–11.68**	**–15.09**	**–7.17**	**–2.05**	**1.05**	**35.36**	**–26.73**	**19.21**
Total, Groups A Through D	4 984 . .	*–2.04*	*7.22*	*–1.20*	*–3.75*	*4.02*	*–14.11*	*–5.22*	*–5.47*
E. Reserves and Related Items	4 802 A.	**2.04**	**–7.22**	**1.20**	**3.75**	**–4.02**	**14.11**	**5.22**	**5.47**
Reserve assets	4 802 . .	2.04	–7.22	1.20	3.75	–4.02	14.11	5.22	5.47
Use of Fund credit and loans	4 766 . .	. . .	. . .	. . .	. . .	. . .	. . .	. . .	. . .
Exceptional financing	4 920 . .	. . .	. . .	. . .	. . .	. . .	. . .	. . .	. . .
Conversion rates: deutsche mark per U.S. dollar	0 101 . .	**1.6228**	**1.4331**	**1.5048**	**1.7341**	**1.7597**	**. . .**	**. . .**	**. . .**
Conversion rates: euros per U.S. dollar	0 103 . .	**. . .**	**. . .**	**. . .**	**. . .**	**. . .**	**.9386**	**1.0854**	**1.1175**

[1] Excludes components that have been classified in the categories of Group E.

Table 2. STANDARD PRESENTATION, 1994–2001
(Billions of U.S. dollars)

	Code	1994	1995	1996	1997	1998	1999	2000	2001
CURRENT ACCOUNT	4 993 . .	**–20.94**	**–18.93**	**–7.97**	**–2.84**	**–6.11**	**–19.07**	**–20.39**	**2.44**
A. GOODS	4 100 . .	50.92	65.11	69.38	70.12	76.91	70.03	57.51	88.51
Credit	2 100 . .	**430.54**	**523.58**	**522.58**	**510.02**	**542.62**	**542.73**	**549.84**	**569.95**
General merchandise: exports f.o.b.	2 110 . .	405.56	494.65	491.34	479.79	507.20	507.19	513.51	544.35
Goods for processing: exports f.o.b.	2 150 . .	19.16	23.05	25.27	24.34	28.58	29.06	28.53	19.31
Repairs on goods	2 160 . .	4.49	4.57	4.68	4.88	5.94	5.61	6.84	5.50
Goods procured in ports by carriers	2 170 . .	.52	.52	.42	.46	.43	.39	.40	.41
Nonmonetary gold	2 180 . .	.81	.80	.86	.55	.47	.48	.56	.38
Debit	3 100 . .	**–379.63**	**–458.48**	**–453.20**	**–439.90**	**–465.71**	**–472.69**	**–492.33**	**–481.44**
General merchandise: imports f.o.b.	3 110 . .	–351.05	–423.82	–417.64	–407.76	–430.40	–438.30	–458.81	–456.76
Goods for processing: imports f.o.b.	3 150 . .	–22.29	–27.51	–28.79	–26.03	–28.47	–28.27	–27.02	–19.35
Repairs on goods	3 160 . .	–3.81	–4.19	–4.17	–3.65	–4.02	–3.85	–4.22	–3.20
Goods procured in ports by carriers	3 170 . .	–1.09	–1.57	–1.23	–1.33	–1.35	–1.39	–1.59	–1.50
Nonmonetary gold	3 180 . .	–1.40	–1.38	–1.38	–1.14	–1.47	–.88	–.68	–.62
B. SERVICES	4 200 . .	–39.69	–45.36	–44.26	–41.21	–45.09	–52.22	–49.91	–50.98
Total credit	2 200 . .	*66.25*	*81.84*	*85.56*	*84.42*	*85.92*	*86.93*	*85.57*	*87.50*
Total debit	3 200 . .	*–105.94*	*–127.20*	*–129.82*	*–125.63*	*–131.01*	*–139.15*	*–135.48*	*–138.48*
Transportation services, credit	2 205 . .	**16.67**	**19.57**	**20.09**	**19.56**	**20.54**	**20.03**	**19.95**	**20.52**
Passenger	2 850 . .	*5.39*	*6.02*	*6.37*	*6.80*	*7.44*	*7.10*	*6.33*	*6.13*
Freight	2 851 . .	*8.01*	*9.79*	*10.13*	*9.31*	*9.61*	*9.59*	*10.43*	*11.27*
Other	2 852 . .	*3.27*	*3.76*	*3.60*	*3.45*	*3.49*	*3.34*	*3.18*	*3.12*
Sea transport, passenger	2 207 . .	.02	.03	.02	.01	.06	.05	.19	.21
Sea transport, freight	2 208 . .	4.49	5.10	5.78	5.64	5.62	5.73	6.77	7.51
Sea transport, other	2 209 . .	.97	1.04	.96	.94	.95	.88	.90	.91
Air transport, passenger	2 211 . .	4.82	5.61	5.95	6.43	7.00	6.66	5.78	5.57
Air transport, freight	2 212 . .	1.23	1.77	1.55	1.08	1.25	1.18	1.02	1.00
Air transport, other	2 213 . .	1.75	2.09	1.96	1.71	1.68	1.70	1.54	1.50
Other transport, passenger	2 215 . .	.55	.38	.40	.35	.38	.38	.37	.35
Other transport, freight	2 216 . .	2.30	2.92	2.80	2.60	2.74	2.68	2.65	2.77
Other transport, other	2 217 . .	.55	.63	.67	.80	.85	.76	.75	.71
Transportation services, debit	3 205 . .	**–20.77**	**–24.60**	**–24.13**	**–23.49**	**–25.18**	**–24.83**	**–25.54**	**–25.17**
Passenger	3 850 . .	*–5.86*	*–6.72*	*–6.01*	*–5.62*	*–6.12*	*–5.62*	*–5.06*	*–4.78*
Freight	3 851 . .	*–9.95*	*–12.09*	*–11.33*	*–11.22*	*–12.10*	*–12.12*	*–12.98*	*–12.86*
Other	3 852 . .	*–4.95*	*–5.78*	*–6.79*	*–6.66*	*–6.96*	*–7.08*	*–7.49*	*–7.53*
Sea transport, passenger	3 207 . .	–.56	. . .	. . .	. . .	. . .	. . .	. . .	. . .
Sea transport, freight	3 208 . .	–4.33	–4.97	–4.26	–4.20	–4.44	–4.46	–5.05	–4.80
Sea transport, other	3 209 . .	–2.28	–2.63	–3.09	–2.85	–3.08	–3.09	–3.42	–3.44
Air transport, passenger	3 211 . .	–4.80	–5.96	–5.38	–5.06	–5.56	–5.07	–4.52	–4.24
Air transport, freight	3 212 . .	–.26	–.49	–.41	–.43	–.48	–.47	–.45	–.41
Air transport, other	3 213 . .	–1.50	–1.72	–2.13	–2.05	–1.94	–1.88	–1.71	–1.72
Other transport, passenger	3 215 . .	–.50	–.76	–.62	–.55	–.56	–.55	–.54	–.54
Other transport, freight	3 216 . .	–5.36	–6.63	–6.65	–6.58	–7.18	–7.19	–7.48	–7.65
Other transport, other	3 217 . .	–1.17	–1.44	–1.58	–1.76	–1.93	–2.11	–2.36	–2.37
Travel, credit	2 236 . .	**14.91**	**17.90**	**17.70**	**17.83**	**18.38**	**18.07**	**18.40**	**17.20**
Business travel	2 237 . .	. . .	. . .	. . .	. . .	. . .	. . .	. . .	. . .
Personal travel	2 240 . .	. . .	. . .	. . .	. . .	. . .	. . .	. . .	. . .
Travel, debit	3 236 . .	**–45.46**	**–52.17**	**–52.95**	**–48.09**	**–48.91**	**–50.63**	**–47.50**	**–46.12**
Business travel	3 237 . .	. . .	. . .	. . .	. . .	. . .	. . .	. . .	. . .
Personal travel	3 240 . .	. . .	. . .	. . .	. . .	. . .	. . .	. . .	. . .
Other services, credit	2 200 BA	**34.67**	**44.37**	**47.77**	**47.03**	**47.01**	**48.82**	**47.22**	**49.79**
Communications	2 245 . .	.68	2.04	2.02	1.92	1.79	1.82	1.45	1.61
Construction	2 249 . .	3.77	5.24	5.00	5.19	4.72	4.67	4.09	3.56
Insurance	2 253 . .	1.52	1.25	2.74	1.82	.77	2.63	.52	1.61
Financial	2 260 . .	1.45	2.43	2.79	2.73	3.35	3.85	4.20	4.08
Computer and information	2 262 . .	.91	1.40	1.60	2.17	2.88	2.93	3.78	4.65
Royalties and licence fees	2 266 . .	2.40	3.13	3.37	3.22	3.35	3.11	2.88	3.15
Other business services	2 268 . .	16.55	22.04	23.89	24.61	25.38	25.90	26.46	26.51
Personal, cultural, and recreational	2 287 . .	.15	.19	.14	.15	.24	.21	.39	.34
Government, n.i.e.	2 291 . .	7.24	6.66	6.21	5.21	4.54	3.72	3.43	4.28
Other services, debit	3 200 BA	**–39.72**	**–50.43**	**–52.73**	**–54.04**	**–56.92**	**–63.69**	**–62.44**	**–67.20**
Communications	3 245 . .	–1.48	–2.95	–2.69	–2.93	–2.91	–3.24	–3.15	–3.13
Construction	3 249 . .	–4.56	–5.90	–5.82	–6.17	–6.13	–5.12	–4.92	–4.73
Insurance	3 253 . .	–1.68	–1.48	–2.33	–1.85	–1.85	–2.13	–1.01	–1.15
Financial	3 260 . .	–.44	–.56	–1.02	–1.40	–1.64	–2.76	–3.32	–3.70
Computer and information	3 262 . .	–1.24	–1.96	–2.38	–3.08	–3.64	–4.51	–4.94	–6.37
Royalties and licence fees	3 266 . .	–4.51	–5.92	–5.88	–5.73	–5.65	–5.14	–5.57	–5.24
Other business services	3 268 . .	–22.18	–27.79	–28.30	–28.92	–31.17	–35.63	–34.55	–38.22
Personal, cultural, and recreational	3 287 . .	–1.77	–1.97	–2.56	–2.58	–2.48	–3.55	–3.56	–3.34
Government, n.i.e.	3 291 . .	–1.85	–1.89	–1.75	–1.39	–1.45	–1.62	–1.42	–1.32

Table 2 (Continued). STANDARD PRESENTATION, 1994–2001
(Billions of U.S. dollars)

	Code	1994	1995	1996	1997	1998	1999	2000	2001
C. INCOME	4 300	6.83	.30	.93	-1.37	-7.60	-9.58	-3.09	-11.27
Total credit	2 300	*68.51*	*84.89*	*81.36*	*80.40*	*83.43*	*86.13*	*99.90*	*105.34*
Total debit	3 300	*-61.68*	*-84.59*	*-80.42*	*-81.77*	*-91.03*	*-95.71*	*-102.99*	*-116.61*
Compensation of employees, credit	2 310	**4.39**	**4.51**	**4.33**	**3.83**	**3.91**	**3.80**	**3.44**	**3.75**
Compensation of employees, debit	3 310	**-4.20**	**-5.51**	**-5.50**	**-4.79**	**-4.82**	**-4.67**	**-4.23**	**-5.06**
Investment income, credit	2 320	**64.11**	**80.38**	**77.03**	**76.57**	**79.52**	**82.32**	**96.46**	**101.59**
Direct investment income	2 330	5.35	9.22	14.51	15.23	15.64	14.73	18.28	14.82
Dividends and distributed branch profits	2 332	5.06	6.52	7.19	9.65	7.70	8.29	11.80	10.69
Reinvested earnings and undistributed branch profits	2 333	...	2.16	6.09	3.58	5.75	4.69	2.12	...
Income on debt (interest)	2 334	.28	.55	1.24	2.00	2.20	1.75	4.36	4.13
Portfolio investment income	2 339	20.27	23.39	22.31	22.28	25.24	28.67	33.90	39.58
Income on equity	2 340	6.42	7.22	7.13	6.84	8.20	9.80	13.24	13.94
Income on bonds and notes	2 350	...	...	...	...	...	...	...	...
Income on money market instruments	2 360	...	...	...	...	...	...	...	...
Other investment income	2 370	38.50	47.77	40.21	39.06	38.64	38.92	44.28	47.19
Investment income, debit	3 320	**-57.48**	**-79.08**	**-74.92**	**-76.98**	**-86.21**	**-91.03**	**-98.75**	**-111.55**
Direct investment income	3 330	-1.66	-6.35	-4.64	-9.20	-12.97	-8.11	-12.10	-15.98
Dividends and distributed branch profits	3 332	-6.26	-6.88	-6.89	-6.66	-9.95	-10.74	-8.28	-7.79
Reinvested earnings and undistributed branch profits	3 333	6.17	2.46	4.53	.46	.57	5.76	3.32	3.22
Income on debt (interest)	3 334	-1.58	-1.92	-2.28	-3.00	-3.58	-3.13	-7.15	-11.40
Portfolio investment income	3 339	-29.58	-35.80	-37.49	-35.57	-38.17	-42.95	-42.67	-47.90
Income on equity	3 340	-4.05	-5.03	-4.59	-5.12	-7.69	-8.30	-7.16	-7.33
Income on bonds and notes	3 350	...	...	...	...	...	...	...	...
Income on money market instruments	3 360	...	...	...	...	...	...	...	...
Other investment income	3 370	-26.23	-36.94	-32.79	-32.21	-35.08	-39.98	-43.99	-47.67
D. CURRENT TRANSFERS	4 379	-38.99	-38.97	-34.03	-30.38	-30.34	-27.30	-24.90	-23.82
Credit	2 379	**13.89**	**16.87**	**17.89**	**16.47**	**15.96**	**16.96**	**15.77**	**15.15**
General government	2 380	10.67	13.03	14.53	12.84	12.61	13.18	11.71	11.35
Other sectors	2 390	3.22	3.84	3.36	3.63	3.35	3.78	4.06	3.80
Workers' remittances	2 391	...	...	...	...	...	...	...	...
Other current transfers	2 392	3.22	3.84	3.36	3.63	3.35	3.78	4.06	3.80
Debit	3 379	**-52.88**	**-55.84**	**-51.92**	**-46.85**	**-46.30**	**-44.26**	**-40.67**	**-38.98**
General government	3 380	-39.46	-41.21	-37.92	-34.02	-33.86	-31.65	-29.13	-26.54
Other sectors	3 390	-13.43	-14.63	-14.00	-12.83	-12.45	-12.61	-11.54	-12.44
Workers' remittances	3 391	-4.63	-5.31	-4.92	-4.34	-3.95	-3.66	-3.19	-3.15
Other current transfers	3 392	-8.80	-9.32	-9.08	-8.49	-8.50	-8.95	-8.35	-9.29
CAPITAL AND FINANCIAL ACCOUNT	4 996	**32.61**	**34.02**	**15.14**	**4.89**	**5.06**	**-16.29**	**47.13**	**-21.65**
CAPITAL ACCOUNT	4 994	**.15**	**-2.73**	**-2.18**	...	**.72**	**-.16**	**6.19**	**-.83**
Total credit	2 994	*1.56*	*1.68*	*2.76*	*2.83*	*3.31*	*3.00*	*9.41*	*1.87*
Total debit	3 994	*-1.42*	*-4.41*	*-4.94*	*-2.82*	*-2.59*	*-3.16*	*-3.22*	*-2.70*
Capital transfers, credit	2 400	**1.56**	**1.68**	**2.76**	**2.83**	**3.31**	**3.00**	**1.79**	**1.87**
General government	2 401	...	...	...	...	...	...	...	...
Debt forgiveness	2 402	...	...	...	...	...	...	...	...
Other capital transfers	2 410	...	...	...	...	...	...	...	...
Other sectors	2 430	1.56	1.68	2.76	2.83	3.31	3.00	1.79	1.87
Migrants' transfers	2 431	.02	.02	.02	.03	.36	.57	.04	.05
Debt forgiveness	2 432	...	...	...	...	...	...	...	...
Other capital transfers	2 440	1.55	1.66	2.75	2.80	2.96	2.44	1.75	1.82
Capital transfers, debit	3 400	**-1.42**	**-4.41**	**-4.94**	**-2.82**	**-2.59**	**-3.16**	**-3.22**	**-2.70**
General government	3 401	-.39	-3.11	-1.74	-1.64	-1.40	-1.43	-1.09	-1.21
Debt forgiveness	3 402	-.19	-1.65	-.32	-.31	-.08	-.11	-.06	...
Other capital transfers	3 410	-.19	-1.46	-1.42	-1.32	-1.32	-1.32	-1.02	-1.21
Other sectors	3 430	-1.03	-1.30	-3.20	-1.19	-1.19	-1.73	-2.13	-1.49
Migrants' transfers	3 431	-.41	-.46	-.51	-.41	-.39	-.43	-.38	-.26
Debt forgiveness	3 432	-.62	-.01	-.36	-.01	-.01	...	-1.07	-.55
Other capital transfers	3 440	...	-.83	-2.33	-.76	-.79	-1.30	-.68	-.68
Nonproduced nonfinancial assets, credit	2 480	...	...	...	...	...	...	**7.62**	...
Nonproduced nonfinancial assets, debit	3 480	...	...	...	...	...	...	...	...

Table 2 (Continued). STANDARD PRESENTATION, 1994–2001

(Billions of U.S. dollars)

	Code	1994	1995	1996	1997	1998	1999	2000	2001
FINANCIAL ACCOUNT	4 995 . .	**32.47**	**36.76**	**17.32**	**4.88**	**4.34**	**–16.13**	**40.93**	**–20.82**
A. DIRECT INVESTMENT	4 500 . .	–15.32	–27.11	–44.32	–29.93	–66.29	–54.83	154.71	–11.22
Direct investment abroad	4 505 . .	**–17.26**	**–39.10**	**–50.75**	**–42.73**	**–89.93**	**–109.42**	**–53.00**	**–42.75**
Equity capital	4 510 . .	–15.13	–32.23	–24.19	–25.54	–61.05	–89.23	–46.91	–52.19
Claims on affiliated enterprises	4 515 . .	. . .	. . .	. . .	. . .	. . .	. . .	. . .	. . .
Liabilities to affiliated enterprises	4 520 . .	. . .	. . .	. . .	. . .	. . .	. . .	. . .	. . .
Reinvested earnings	4 525 . .	. . .	–2.16	–6.09	–3.58	–5.75	–4.69	–2.12	. . .
Other capital	4 530 . .	–2.12	–4.71	–20.47	–13.61	–23.14	–15.50	–3.97	9.45
Claims on affiliated enterprises	4 535 . .	. . .	. . .	. . .	. . .	. . .	. . .	. . .	. . .
Liabilities to affiliated enterprises	4 540 . .	. . .	. . .	. . .	. . .	. . .	. . .	. . .	. . .
Direct investment in Germany	4 555 . .	**1.94**	**11.99**	**6.43**	**12.80**	**23.64**	**54.58**	**207.72**	**31.53**
Equity capital	4 560 . .	4.22	8.73	3.23	5.70	6.50	26.00	119.35	28.96
Claims on direct investors	4 565 . .	. . .	. . .	. . .	. . .	. . .	. . .	. . .	. . .
Liabilities to direct investors	4 570 . .	. . .	. . .	. . .	. . .	. . .	. . .	. . .	. . .
Reinvested earnings	4 575 . .	–6.17	–2.46	–4.53	–.46	–.57	–5.76	–3.32	–3.22
Other capital	4 580 . .	3.89	5.72	7.73	7.56	17.70	34.34	91.69	5.79
Claims on direct investors	4 585 . .	. . .	. . .	. . .	. . .	. . .	. . .	. . .	. . .
Liabilities to direct investors	4 590 . .	. . .	. . .	. . .	. . .	. . .	. . .	. . .	. . .
B. PORTFOLIO INVESTMENT	4 600 . .	–30.83	35.10	63.02	.96	5.41	–14.01	–156.61	–1.07
Assets	4 602 . .	**–41.48**	**–18.05**	**–30.89**	**–90.08**	**–145.49**	**–190.32**	**–195.96**	**–115.26**
Equity securities	4 610 . .	–20.97	.28	–17.52	–42.62	–78.33	–87.56	–129.44	–31.18
Monetary authorities	4 611 . .	. . .	. . .	. . .	. . .	. . .	. . .	. . .	. . .
General government	4 612 . .	. . .	. . .	. . .	. . .	. . .	. . .	. . .	. . .
Banks	4 613 . .	. . .	. . .	. . .	. . .	. . .	. . .	. . .	. . .
Other sectors	4 614 . .	. . .	. . .	. . .	. . .	. . .	. . .	. . .	. . .
Debt securities	4 619 . .	–20.51	–18.33	–13.37	–47.46	–67.17	–102.77	–66.51	–84.07
Bonds and notes	4 620 . .	–16.94	–16.86	–13.92	–46.99	–63.24	–102.03	–68.24	–84.97
Monetary authorities	4 621 . .	. . .	. . .	. . .	. . .	. . .	. . .	. . .	. . .
General government	4 622 . .	. . .	. . .	. . .	. . .	. . .	. . .	. . .	. . .
Banks	4 623 . .	. . .	. . .	. . .	. . .	. . .	. . .	. . .	. . .
Other sectors	4 624 . .	. . .	. . .	. . .	. . .	. . .	. . .	. . .	. . .
Money market instruments	4 630 . .	–3.57	–1.47	.55	–.46	–3.92	–.73	1.73	.90
Monetary authorities	4 631 . .	. . .	. . .	. . .	. . .	. . .	. . .	. . .	. . .
General government	4 632 . .	. . .	. . .	. . .	. . .	. . .	. . .	. . .	. . .
Banks	4 633 . .	. . .	. . .	. . .	. . .	. . .	. . .	. . .	. . .
Other sectors	4 634 . .	. . .	. . .	. . .	. . .	. . .	. . .	. . .	. . .
Liabilities	4 652 . .	**10.64**	**53.15**	**93.90**	**91.04**	**150.91**	**176.31**	**39.34**	**114.19**
Equity securities	4 660 . .	3.92	–1.51	12.98	12.87	56.77	27.98	–27.73	78.91
Banks	4 663 . .	. . .	. . .	. . .	. . .	. . .	. . .	. . .	. . .
Other sectors	4 664 . .	. . .	. . .	. . .	. . .	. . .	. . .	. . .	. . .
Debt securities	4 669 . .	6.72	54.66	80.92	78.17	94.14	148.32	67.07	35.28
Bonds and notes	4 670 . .	8.13	60.29	67.95	70.94	87.07	105.07	63.55	49.03
Monetary authorities	4 671 . .	–7.75	. . .	. . .	. . .	. . .	. . .	. . .	. . .
General government	4 672 . .	3.66	34.81	29.19	45.15	44.47	34.53	20.42	–5.14
Banks	4 673 . .	. . .	. . .	. . .	. . .	. . .	. . .	. . .	. . .
Other sectors	4 674 . .	12.22	25.48	38.76	25.79	42.60	70.54	43.13	54.17
Money market instruments	4 680 . .	–1.41	–5.63	12.97	7.23	7.07	43.25	3.52	–13.75
Monetary authorities	4 681 . .	. . .	. . .	. . .	. . .	. . .	. . .	. . .	. . .
General government	4 682 . .	–.33	–2.66	9.86	3.98	–4.32	.09	.12	5.93
Banks	4 683 . .	.47	–.14	2.70	3.25	11.13	41.22	1.55	–20.37
Other sectors	4 684 . .	–1.54	–2.84	.41	. . .	.26	1.94	1.86	.69
C. FINANCIAL DERIVATIVES	4 910 . .	.54	–.66	–5.73	–8.70	–7.99	–1.67	–3.91	5.92
Monetary authorities	4 911 . .	. . .	. . .	. . .	. . .	. . .	. . .	. . .	. . .
General government	4 912 . .	. . .	. . .	. . .	. . .	. . .	. . .	. . .	. . .
Banks	4 913 . .	. . .	. . .	. . .	. . .	. . .	. . .	. . .	. . .
Other sectors	4 914 . .	. . .	. . .	. . .	. . .	. . .	. . .	. . .	. . .
Assets	4 900 . .	**–10.71**	**. . .**	**. . .**	**. . .**	**. . .**	**. . .**	**. . .**	**. . .**
Monetary authorities	4 901 . .	. . .	. . .	. . .	. . .	. . .	. . .	. . .	. . .
General government	4 902 . .	. . .	. . .	. . .	. . .	. . .	. . .	. . .	. . .
Banks	4 903 . .	. . .	. . .	. . .	. . .	. . .	. . .	. . .	. . .
Other sectors	4 904 . .	. . .	. . .	. . .	. . .	. . .	. . .	. . .	. . .
Liabilities	4 905 . .	**11.25**	**–.66**	**–5.73**	**–8.70**	**–7.99**	**–1.67**	**–3.91**	**5.92**
Monetary authorities	4 906 . .	. . .	. . .	. . .	. . .	. . .	. . .	. . .	. . .
General government	4 907 . .	. . .	. . .	. . .	. . .	. . .	. . .	. . .	. . .
Banks	4 908 . .	. . .	. . .	. . .	. . .	. . .	. . .	. . .	. . .
Other sectors	4 909 . .	. . .	. . .	. . .	. . .	. . .	. . .	. . .	. . .

Table 2 (Concluded). STANDARD PRESENTATION, 1994–2001

(Billions of U.S. dollars)

	Code	1994	1995	1996	1997	1998	1999	2000	2001
D. OTHER INVESTMENT	4 700 . .	76.05	36.66	3.16	38.81	77.23	40.27	41.53	–19.92
Assets	4 703 . .	**–.62**	**–61.28**	**–39.77**	**–83.53**	**–95.50**	**–70.85**	**–79.68**	**–87.06**
Trade credits	4 706 . .	–7.99	–5.46	–1.34	–4.94	2.91	–1.74	–7.98	1.62
General government	4 707 . .	. . .	. . .	. . .	. . .	. . .	. . .	. . .	. . .
of which: Short-term	4 709 . .	. . .	. . .	. . .	. . .	. . .	. . .	. . .	. . .
Other sectors	4 710 . .	–7.99	–5.46	–1.34	–4.94	2.91	–1.74	–7.98	1.62
of which: Short-term	4 712 . .	. . .	. . .	. . .	. . .	. . .	. . .	. . .	. . .
Loans	4 714 . .	8.80	–52.82	–35.78	–76.10	–93.81	–66.67	–69.65	–87.44
Monetary authorities	4 715 . .	.17	.28	.35	.29	–.11	–51.70	39.37	20.70
of which: Short-term	4 718 . .	. . .	. . .	. . .	. . .	. . .	. . .	. . .	. . .
General government	4 719 . .	2.46	–6.72	–.34	–2.33	–.63	8.46	–17.98	14.84
of which: Short-term	4 721 . .	*5.54*	*–5.13*	*.60*	*–.52*	*.35*	*8.85*	*–16.99*	*14.61*
Banks	4 722 . .	14.98	–55.18	–39.13	–80.40	–79.22	–46.32	–92.58	–118.47
of which: Short-term	4 724 . .	*28.36*	*–39.95*	*–28.75*	*–50.40*	*–44.42*	*–.87*	*–56.00*	*–75.95*
Other sectors	4 725 . .	–8.81	8.81	3.35	6.34	–13.85	22.90	1.54	–4.51
of which: Short-term	4 727 . .	*–9.05*	*10.96*	*4.83*	*7.53*	*–13.43*	*25.10*	*1.11*	*–2.99*
Currency and deposits	4 730 . .	. . .	. . .	. . .	. . .	. . .	. . .	. . .	. . .
Monetary authorities	4 731 . .	. . .	. . .	. . .	. . .	. . .	. . .	. . .	. . .
General government	4 732 . .	. . .	. . .	. . .	. . .	. . .	. . .	. . .	. . .
Banks	4 733 . .	. . .	. . .	. . .	. . .	. . .	. . .	. . .	. . .
Other sectors	4 734 . .	. . .	. . .	. . .	. . .	. . .	. . .	. . .	. . .
Other assets	4 736 . .	–1.43	–3.00	–2.66	–2.49	–4.60	–2.44	–2.05	–1.24
Monetary authorities	4 737 . .	. . .	. . .	. . .	. . .	. . .	. . .	. . .	. . .
of which: Short-term	4 739 . .	. . .	. . .	. . .	. . .	. . .	. . .	. . .	. . .
General government	4 740 . .	. . .	. . .	. . .	. . .	. . .	. . .	. . .	. . .
of which: Short-term	4 742 . .	. . .	. . .	. . .	. . .	. . .	. . .	. . .	. . .
Banks	4 743 . .	. . .	. . .	. . .	. . .	. . .	. . .	. . .	. . .
of which: Short-term	4 745 . .	. . .	. . .	. . .	. . .	. . .	. . .	. . .	. . .
Other sectors	4 746 . .	–1.43	–3.00	–2.66	–2.49	–4.60	–2.44	–2.05	–1.24
of which: Short-term	4 748 . .	*–1.43*	*–3.00*	*–2.66*	*–2.49*	*–4.60*	*–2.44*	*–2.05*	*–1.24*
Liabilities	4 753 . .	**76.66**	**97.94**	**42.93**	**122.34**	**172.73**	**111.12**	**121.21**	**67.14**
Trade credits	4 756 . .	7.38	4.40	2.01	4.67	–1.43	1.35	5.85	3.37
General government	4 757 . .	. . .	. . .	. . .	. . .	. . .	. . .	. . .	. . .
of which: Short-term	4 759 . .	. . .	. . .	. . .	. . .	. . .	. . .	. . .	. . .
Other sectors	4 760 . .	7.38	4.40	2.01	4.67	–1.43	1.35	5.85	3.37
of which: Short-term	4 762 . .	. . .	. . .	. . .	. . .	. . .	. . .	. . .	. . .
Loans	4 764 . .	70.78	94.15	40.91	118.10	174.29	109.88	115.31	63.74
Monetary authorities	4 765 . .	. . .	–2.65	–1.17	–.39	2.16	–2.21	.37	2.35
of which: Use of Fund credit and loans from the Fund	4 766 . .	. . .	. . .	. . .	. . .	. . .	. . .	. . .	. . .
of which: Short-term	4 768 . .	. . .	*–2.65*	*–1.17*	*–.39*	*2.16*	*–2.21*	*.37*	*2.35*
General government	4 769 . .	2.12	3.84	3.45	–7.75	.10	–12.29	.52	.29
of which: Short-term	4 771 . .	*3.06*	*2.26*	*2.07*	*–3.47*	*4.96*	*–3.42*	*.66*	*.83*
Banks	4 772 . .	69.19	83.71	36.62	120.20	159.94	103.54	109.95	52.83
of which: Short-term	4 774 . .	*46.04*	*41.46*	*10.60*	*91.34*	*125.24*	*65.54*	*94.90*	*49.27*
Other sectors	4 775 . .	–.53	9.25	2.00	6.05	12.09	20.86	4.47	8.28
of which: Short-term	4 777 . .	*.51*	*8.50*	*1.45*	*5.65*	*3.07*	*16.66*	*.38*	*.12*
Currency and deposits	4 780 . .	. . .	. . .	. . .	. . .	. . .	. . .	. . .	. . .
Monetary authorities	4 781 . .	. . .	. . .	. . .	. . .	. . .	. . .	. . .	. . .
General government	4 782 . .	. . .	. . .	. . .	. . .	. . .	. . .	. . .	. . .
Banks	4 783 . .	. . .	. . .	. . .	. . .	. . .	. . .	. . .	. . .
Other sectors	4 784 . .	. . .	. . .	. . .	. . .	. . .	. . .	. . .	. . .
Other liabilities	4 786 . .	–1.50	–.62	.02	–.44	–.13	–.11	.06	.03
Monetary authorities	4 787 . .	–2.04	. . .	. . .	. . .	. . .	. . .	. . .	. . .
of which: Short-term	4 789 . .	. . .	. . .	. . .	. . .	. . .	. . .	. . .	. . .
General government	4 790 . .	. . .	. . .	. . .	. . .	. . .	. . .	. . .	. . .
of which: Short-term	4 792 . .	. . .	. . .	. . .	. . .	. . .	. . .	. . .	. . .
Banks	4 793 . .	. . .	. . .	. . .	. . .	. . .	. . .	. . .	. . .
of which: Short-term	4 795 . .	. . .	. . .	. . .	. . .	. . .	. . .	. . .	. . .
Other sectors	4 796 . .	.54	–.62	.02	–.44	–.13	–.11	.06	.03
of which: Short-term	4 798 . .	. . .	. . .	. . .	. . .	. . .	. . .	. . .	. . .
E. RESERVE ASSETS	4 802 . .	2.04	–7.22	1.20	3.75	–4.02	14.11	5.22	5.47
Monetary gold	4 812 . .	. . .	. . .	. . .	. . .	–2.06	2.06	. . .	. . .
Special drawing rights	4 811 . .	–.09	–.86	.03	. . .	. . .	–.11	.10	–.09
Reserve position in the Fund	4 810 . .	.16	–1.13	–.44	–.81	–1.72	1.39	.66	–.65
Foreign exchange	4 803 . .	1.96	–5.23	1.60	4.56	–.24	10.78	4.46	6.21
Other claims	4 813 . .	. . .	. . .	. . .	. . .	. . .	. . .	. . .	. . .
NET ERRORS AND OMISSIONS	4 998 . .	**–11.68**	**–15.09**	**–7.17**	**–2.05**	**1.05**	**35.36**	**–26.73**	**19.21**

Part 3 of the *Yearbook* contains descriptions of the methodologies, compilation practices, and sources used to compile these data.

Table 3. INTERNATIONAL INVESTMENT POSITION (End–period stocks), 1994–2001

(Billions of U.S. dollars)

	Code	1994	1995	1996	1997	1998	1999	2000	2001
ASSETS	8 995 C.	1,431.95	1,663.83	1,699.68	1,749.47	2,220.08	2,389.36	2,595.89	2,668.77
Direct investment abroad	8 505 . .	**188.32**	**234.13**	**250.14**	**296.28**	**365.22**	**411.94**	**478.32**	**505.31**
Equity capital and reinvested earnings	8 506 . .	188.32	234.13	250.14	257.33	315.41	360.52	425.55	469.42
Claims on affiliated enterprises	8 507 . .	. . .	. . .	. . .	. . .	. . .	. . .	. . .	. . .
Liabilities to affiliated enterprises	8 508 . .	. . .	. . .	. . .	. . .	. . .	. . .	. . .	. . .
Other capital	8 530 . .	. . .	. . .	. . .	38.95	49.81	51.42	52.77	35.89
Claims on affiliated enterprises	8 535 . .	. . .	. . .	. . .	. . .	. . .	. . .	. . .	. . .
Liabilities to affiliated enterprises	8 540 . .	. . .	. . .	. . .	. . .	. . .	. . .	. . .	. . .
Portfolio investment	8 602 . .	**320.00**	**385.42**	**413.69**	**502.74**	**723.96**	**893.18**	**1,006.65**	**1,004.55**
Equity securities	8 610 . .	145.79	165.97	187.49	241.39	370.57	507.07	575.11	509.57
Monetary authorities	8 611 . .	. . .	. . .	. . .	. . .	. . .	. . .	. . .	. . .
General government	8 612 . .	. . .	. . .	. . .	. . .	. . .	. . .	. . .	. . .
Banks	8 613 . .	4.57	4.77	6.46	8.17	12.90	16.01	22.64	26.37
Other sectors	8 614 . .	141.22	161.21	181.03	233.22	357.68	491.06	552.46	483.20
Debt securities	8 619 . .	174.22	219.45	226.20	261.35	353.39	386.11	431.54	494.98
Bonds and notes	8 620 . .	167.79	211.28	219.01	253.70	341.44	374.46	422.02	486.81
Monetary authorities	8 621 . .	. . .	. . .	. . .	. . .	. . .	. . .	. . .	. . .
General government	8 622 . .	. . .	. . .	. . .	. . .	. . .	. . .	. . .	. . .
Banks	8 623 . .	53.24	68.73	80.63	97.00	152.85	186.86	214.16	240.35
Other sectors	8 624 . .	114.55	142.55	138.38	156.70	188.58	187.61	207.86	246.47
Money market instruments	8 630 . .	6.43	8.17	7.19	7.66	11.95	11.65	9.52	8.17
Monetary authorities	8 631 . .	. . .	. . .	. . .	. . .	. . .	. . .	. . .	. . .
General government	8 632 . .	. . .	. . .	. . .	. . .	. . .	. . .	. . .	. . .
Banks	8 633 . .	.43	1.24	3.31	4.08	7.90	9.57	8.17	6.79
Other sectors	8 634 . .	6.00	6.93	3.88	3.58	4.06	2.09	1.35	1.38
Financial derivatives	8 900 . .	**. . .**	**. . .**	**. . .**	**. . .**	**. . .**	**. . .**	**. . .**	**. . .**
Monetary authorities	8 901 . .	. . .	. . .	. . .	. . .	. . .	. . .	. . .	. . .
General government	8 902 . .	. . .	. . .	. . .	. . .	. . .	. . .	. . .	. . .
Banks	8 903 . .	. . .	. . .	. . .	. . .	. . .	. . .	. . .	. . .
Other sectors	8 904 . .	. . .	. . .	. . .	. . .	. . .	. . .	. . .	. . .
Other investment	8 703 . .	**850.27**	**959.66**	**958.95**	**879.65**	**1,050.79**	**990.77**	**1,023.63**	**1,076.75**
Trade credits	8 706 . .	111.02	120.00	116.65	81.93	87.64	79.41	85.40	80.40
General government	8 707 . .	. . .	. . .	. . .	. . .	. . .	. . .	. . .	. . .
of which: Short-term	8 709 . .	. . .	. . .	. . .	. . .	. . .	. . .	. . .	. . .
Other sectors	8 710 . .	111.02	120.00	116.65	81.93	87.64	79.41	85.40	80.40
of which: Short-term	8 712 . .	*111.02*	*120.00*	*116.65*	*81.93*	*87.64*	*79.41*	*85.40*	*80.40*
Loans	8 714 . .	707.82	802.95	805.48	762.44	920.79	871.20	898.45	956.50
Monetary authorities	8 715 . .	1.52	1.36	.93	.54	.64	47.90	5.31	–16.13
of which: Short-term	8 718 . .	. . .	. . .	. . .	. . .	. . .	. . .	. . .	. . .
General government	8 719 . .	39.81	48.13	44.73	40.89	44.47	28.89	46.03	29.76
of which: Short-term	8 721 . .	*15.53*	*21.90*	*19.72*	*17.61*	*18.71*	*6.46*	*24.34*	*9.20*
Banks	8 722 . .	426.43	504.41	515.95	545.01	661.75	624.48	678.49	767.58
of which: Short-term	8 724 . .	*223.04*	*275.05*	*288.24*	*309.19*	*376.61*	*336.13*	*369.95*	*427.93*
Other sectors	8 725 . .	240.05	249.05	243.88	176.00	213.93	169.92	168.61	175.29
of which: Short-term	8 727 . .	*223.53*	*229.03*	*224.86*	*163.88*	*198.26*	*153.82*	*151.38*	*154.58*
Currency and deposits	8 730 . .	. . .	. . .	. . .	. . .	. . .	. . .	. . .	. . .
Monetary authorities	8 731 . .	. . .	. . .	. . .	. . .	. . .	. . .	. . .	. . .
General government	8 732 . .	. . .	. . .	. . .	. . .	. . .	. . .	. . .	. . .
Banks	8 733 . .	. . .	. . .	. . .	. . .	. . .	. . .	. . .	. . .
Other sectors	8 734 . .	. . .	. . .	. . .	. . .	. . .	. . .	. . .	. . .
Other assets	8 736 . .	31.43	36.71	36.81	35.28	42.36	40.15	39.78	39.86
Monetary authorities	8 737 . .	. . .	. . .	. . .	. . .	. . .	1.24	1.15	1.09
of which: Short-term	8 739 . .	. . .	. . .	. . .	. . .	. . .	. . .	. . .	. . .
General government	8 740 . .	12.52	14.49	14.79	14.43	17.16	15.48	15.10	15.08
of which: Short-term	8 742 . .	. . .	. . .	. . .	. . .	. . .	. . .	. . .	. . .
Banks	8 743 . .	.53	.54	.54	.59	1.07	.62	.54	.55
of which: Short-term	8 745 . .	. . .	. . .	. . .	. . .	. . .	. . .	. . .	. . .
Other sectors	8 746 . .	18.38	21.67	21.48	20.26	24.12	22.81	22.98	23.14
of which: Short-term	8 748 . .	*.49*	*.47*	*.44*	*.41*	*.41*	*.35*	*.31*	*.30*
Reserve assets	8 802 . .	**73.35**	**84.62**	**76.90**	**70.79**	**80.11**	**93.48**	**87.30**	**82.16**
Monetary gold	8 812 . .	8.84	9.55	8.80	7.64	10.23	32.44	30.41	30.85
Special drawing rights	8 811 . .	1.11	2.00	1.91	1.79	1.87	1.96	1.76	1.79
Reserve position in the Fund	8 810 . .	4.03	5.21	5.47	5.95	8.02	6.42	5.46	5.90
Foreign exchange	8 803 . .	59.37	67.86	60.72	55.42	59.99	52.66	49.67	43.61
Other claims	8 813 . .	. . .	. . .	. . .	. . .	. . .	. . .	. . .	. . .

Table 3 (Concluded). INTERNATIONAL INVESTMENT POSITION (End-period stocks), 1994–2001

(Billions of U.S. dollars)

	Code		1994	1995	1996	1997	1998	1999	2000	2001
LIABILITIES	8 995	D.	1,236.60	1,534.68	1,610.14	1,675.87	2,215.51	2,307.87	2,534.41	2,566.72
Direct investment in Germany	8 555	. .	**85.72**	**101.48**	**101.73**	**188.88**	**250.34**	**288.56**	**439.51**	**447.62**
Equity capital and reinvested earnings	8 556	. .	...	101.48	101.73	100.04	130.30	136.78	230.69	243.31
Claims on direct investors	8 557	. .	...	...	...	...	...	...	...	...
Liabilities to direct investors	8 558	. .	...	...	...	...	...	...	...	...
Other capital	8 580	. .	...	...	...	88.84	120.04	151.78	208.83	204.31
Claims on direct investors	8 585	. .	...	...	...	...	...	...	...	...
Liabilities to direct investors	8 590	. .	...	...	...	...	...	...	...	...
Portfolio investment	8 652	. .	**493.72**	**636.90**	**705.19**	**756.01**	**1,023.21**	**1,081.96**	**1,039.80**	**1,036.56**
Equity securities	8 660	. .	99.51	110.78	140.29	186.98	289.98	374.53	300.14	295.99
Banks	8 663	. .	15.88	17.15	17.78	32.21	32.95	44.91	49.84	32.18
Other sectors	8 664	. .	83.62	93.63	122.51	154.77	257.02	329.62	250.29	263.81
Debt securities	8 669	. .	394.21	526.13	564.90	569.04	733.23	707.43	739.66	740.57
Bonds and notes	8 670	. .	386.14	522.37	548.92	547.16	704.65	641.37	675.24	692.90
Monetary authorities	8 671	. .	...	...	...	...	...	...	...	...
General government	8 672	. .	277.74	370.09	369.73	365.55	461.37	381.73	383.21	357.52
Banks	8 673	. .	100.54	141.88	169.44	174.57	235.91	252.11	282.93	322.77
Other sectors	8 674	. .	7.85	10.40	9.75	7.04	7.37	7.52	9.10	12.61
Money market instruments	8 680	. .	8.08	3.76	15.98	21.88	28.59	66.06	64.42	47.67
Monetary authorities	8 681	. .	2.98	1.10	1.65	2.53	...	...	...	...
General government	8 682	. .	.35	.44	9.35	11.89	8.47	7.44	7.03	12.57
Banks	8 683	. .	.82	.74	3.24	6.03	18.16	55.09	52.43	29.61
Other sectors	8 684	. .	3.93	1.48	1.75	1.43	1.95	3.52	4.96	5.49
Financial derivatives	8 905	. .	...	...	...	...	...	...	...	...
Monetary authorities	8 906	. .	...	...	...	...	...	...	...	...
General government	8 907	. .	...	...	...	...	...	...	...	...
Banks	8 908	. .	...	...	...	...	...	...	...	...
Other sectors	8 909	. .	...	...	...	...	...	...	...	...
Other investment	8 753	. .	**657.16**	**796.29**	**803.22**	**730.97**	**941.97**	**937.36**	**1,055.10**	**1,082.54**
Trade credits	8 756	. .	71.03	77.92	74.48	41.72	41.84	35.81	46.70	48.16
General government	8 757	. .	...	...	...	...	...	...	...	...
of which: Short-term	8 759	. .	...	...	...	...	...	...	...	...
Other sectors	8 760	. .	71.03	77.92	74.48	41.72	41.84	35.81	46.70	48.16
of which: Short-term	8 762	. .	*71.03*	*77.92*	*74.48*	*41.72*	*41.84*	*35.81*	*46.70*	*48.16*
Loans	8 764	. .	574.32	716.31	726.54	686.70	897.12	899.04	1,005.94	1,031.98
Monetary authorities	8 765	. .	12.64	20.88	18.88	16.02	19.31	14.59	13.90	15.07
of which: Use of Fund credit and loans from the Fund	8 766	. .	...	...	...	...	...	...	...	...
of which: Short-term	8 768	. .	*12.64*	*20.88*	*18.88*	*16.02*	*19.31*	*14.59*	*13.90*	*15.07*
General government	8 769	. .	33.29	45.87	45.07	31.83	34.12	18.02	17.39	16.87
of which: Short-term	8 771	. .	*5.49*	*6.61*	*7.45*	*3.29*	*8.50*	*4.34*	*4.86*	*5.53*
Banks	8 772	. .	379.70	484.40	492.57	563.89	759.37	779.38	844.09	862.47
of which: Short-term	8 774	. .	*213.41*	*266.62*	*262.84*	*330.71*	*476.63*	*491.96*	*556.69*	*582.97*
Other sectors	8 775	. .	148.69	165.16	170.01	74.95	84.32	87.05	130.56	137.57
of which: Short-term	8 777	. .	*82.65*	*94.37*	*103.19*	*50.34*	*51.61*	*56.32*	*74.69*	*75.72*
Currency and deposits	8 780	. .	...	...	...	...	...	...	...	...
Monetary authorities	8 781	. .	...	...	...	...	...	...	...	...
General government	8 782	. .	...	...	...	...	...	...	...	...
Banks	8 783	. .	...	...	...	...	...	...	...	...
Other sectors	8 784	. .	...	...	...	...	...	...	...	...
Other liabilities	8 786	. .	11.81	2.07	2.21	2.56	3.01	2.51	2.46	2.40
Monetary authorities	8 787	. .	9.48	...	...	...	...	...	...	...
of which: Short-term	8 789	. .	*9.48*	...	...	...	...	...	...	...
General government	8 790	. .	.22	.37	.47	.43	.43	.40	.46	.48
of which: Short-term	8 792	. .	...	...	...	...	...	...	...	...
Banks	8 793	. .	.54	.60	.64	.58	.96	.77	.56	.52
of which: Short-term	8 795	. .	...	...	...	...	...	...	...	...
Other sectors	8 796	. .	1.57	1.10	1.11	1.54	1.62	1.34	1.44	1.39
of which: Short-term	8 798	. .	...	...	...	...	...	...	...	...
NET INTERNATIONAL INVESTMENT POSITION	8 995	. .	**195.35**	**129.16**	**89.54**	**73.60**	**4.56**	**81.49**	**61.48**	**102.05**
Conversion rates: deutsche mark per U.S. dollar (end of period)	0 102	. .	**1.5488**	**1.4335**	**1.5548**	**1.7921**	**1.6730**	...	...	...
Conversion rates: euros per U.S. dollar (end of period)	0 104	. .	...	...	...	...	...	**.9954**	**1.0747**	**1.1347**

Table 1. ANALYTIC PRESENTATION, 1994–2001
(Millions of U.S. dollars)

	Code			1994	1995	1996	1997	1998	1999	2000	2001
A. Current Account [1]	4	993	Z.	**–254.6**	**–144.7**	**–324.7**	**–549.7**	**–443.1**	**–932.5**	**–412.6**	**. . .**
Goods: exports f.o.b	2	100	. .	1,237.7	1,431.2	1,570.1	1,489.9	2,090.8	2,005.5	1,898.4	. . .
Goods: imports f.o.b	3	100	. .	–1,579.9	–1,687.8	–1,937.0	–2,128.2	–2,896.5	–3,228.1	–2,741.3	. . .
Balance on Goods	4	100	. .	*–342.2*	*–256.6*	*–366.9*	*–638.3*	*–805.7*	*–1,222.6*	*–842.9*	. . .
Services: credit	2	200	. .	147.5	150.6	156.8	164.9	438.6	467.8	504.3	. . .
Services: debit	3	200	. .	–420.8	–432.7	–456.4	–505.0	–673.6	–665.9	–597.3	. . .
Balance on Goods and Services	4	991	. .	*–615.5*	*–538.7*	*–666.5*	*–978.4*	*–1,040.7*	*–1,420.7*	*–935.9*	. . .
Income: credit	2	300	. .	11.8	13.7	23.5	26.7	26.7	15.0	15.6	. . .
Income: debit	3	300	. .	–122.7	–142.9	–163.4	–158.1	–163.0	–146.8	–123.2	. . .
Balance on Goods, Services, and Income	4	992	. .	*–726.4*	*–667.9*	*–806.4*	*–1,109.8*	*–1,177.0*	*–1,552.5*	*–1,043.5*	. . .
Current transfers: credit	2	379	Z.	487.3	538.9	497.9	576.5	751.0	637.8	649.3	. . .
Current transfers: debit	3	379	. .	–15.5	–15.7	–16.2	–16.4	–17.1	–17.8	–18.4	. . .
B. Capital Account [1]	4	994	Z.	**–1.0**	**–1.0**	**–1.0**	**–1.0**	**–1.0**	**–1.0**	**. . .**	**. . .**
Capital account: credit	2	994	Z.	. . .	. . .	. . .	. . .	. . .	. . .	. . .	. . .
Capital account: debit	3	994	. .	–1.0	–1.0	–1.0	–1.0	–1.0	–1.0	. . .	. . .
Total, Groups A Plus B	4	981	. .	*–255.6*	*–145.7*	*–325.7*	*–550.7*	*–444.1*	*–933.5*	*–412.6*	. . .
C. Financial Account [1]	4	995	W.	**481.7**	**462.1**	**285.1**	**493.8**	**449.9**	**554.5**	**265.8**	**. . .**
Direct investment abroad	4	505	. .	. . .	. . .	. . .	. . .	. . .	. . .	. . .	. . .
Direct investment in Ghana	4	555	Z.	233.0	106.5	120.0	82.6	55.7	62.6	110.3	. . .
Portfolio investment assets	4	602	. .	. . .	. . .	. . .	. . .	. . .	. . .	. . .	. . .
Equity securities	4	610	. .	. . .	. . .	. . .	. . .	. . .	. . .	. . .	. . .
Debt securities	4	619	. .	. . .	. . .	. . .	. . .	. . .	. . .	. . .	. . .
Portfolio investment liabilities	4	652	Z.	. . .	. . .	. . .	. . .	. . .	. . .	. . .	. . .
Equity securities	4	660	. .	. . .	. . .	. . .	. . .	. . .	. . .	. . .	. . .
Debt securities	4	669	Z.	. . .	. . .	. . .	. . .	. . .	. . .	. . .	. . .
Financial derivatives	4	910	. .	. . .	. . .	. . .	. . .	. . .	. . .	. . .	. . .
Financial derivatives assets	4	900	. .	. . .	. . .	. . .	. . .	. . .	. . .	. . .	. . .
Financial derivatives liabilities	4	905	. .	. . .	. . .	. . .	. . .	. . .	. . .	. . .	. . .
Other investment assets	4	703	. .	–119.6	–20.0	–179.4	33.1	88.1	183.1	41.0	. . .
Monetary authorities	4	701	. .	3.2	3.0	–.4	.2	.1	–3.3	.2	. . .
General government	4	704	. .	. . .	. . .	. . .	. . .	. . .	. . .	. . .	. . .
Banks	4	705	. .	–93.3	77.6	–72.0	34.4	83.7	200.3	26.7	. . .
Other sectors	4	728	. .	–29.5	–100.6	–107.0	–1.5	4.3	–13.9	14.1	. . .
Other investment liabilities	4	753	W.	368.3	375.6	344.5	378.1	306.1	308.8	114.5	. . .
Monetary authorities	4	753	WA	–19.4	–39.1	. . .	. . .	. . .	. . .	. . .	. . .
General government	4	753	ZB	295.3	215.5	341.2	499.4	348.9	144.8	139.7	. . .
Banks	4	753	ZC	64.8	–31.2	30.6	. . .	. . .	. . .	. . .	. . .
Other sectors	4	753	ZD	27.6	230.4	–27.3	–121.3	–42.8	164.0	–25.2	. . .
Total, Groups A Through C	4	983	. .	*226.1*	*316.4*	*–40.6*	*–56.9*	*5.8*	*–379.0*	*–146.8*	. . .
D. Net Errors and Omissions	4	998	. .	**–54.0**	**–65.6**	**20.2**	**83.6**	**102.1**	**289.4**	**–111.7**	**. . .**
Total, Groups A Through D	4	984	. .	*172.1*	*250.8*	*–20.4*	*26.7*	*107.9*	*–89.6*	*–258.5*	. . .
E. Reserves and Related Items	4	802	A.	**–172.1**	**–250.8**	**20.4**	**–26.7**	**–107.9**	**89.6**	**258.5**	**. . .**
Reserve assets	4	802	. .	–89.2	–185.6	105.7	139.0	–81.8	104.6	260.8	. . .
Use of Fund credit and loans	4	766	. .	–82.9	–65.2	–85.3	–165.8	–26.1	–15.0	–2.3	. . .
Exceptional financing	4	920	. .	. . .	. . .	. . .	. . .	. . .	. . .	. . .	. . .
Conversion rates: cedis per U.S. dollar	0	101	. .	**956.7**	**1,200.4**	**1,637.2**	**2,050.2**	**2,314.1**	**2,669.3**	**5,455.1**	**7,170.8**

[1] Excludes components that have been classified in the categories of Group E.

Table 2. STANDARD PRESENTATION, 1994–2001
(Millions of U.S. dollars)

	Code	1994	1995	1996	1997	1998	1999	2000	2001
CURRENT ACCOUNT	4 993 . .	**–254.6**	**–144.7**	**–324.7**	**–549.7**	**–443.1**	**–932.5**	**–412.6**	**. . .**
A. GOODS	4 100 . .	–342.2	–256.6	–366.9	–638.3	–805.7	–1,222.6	–842.9	. . .
Credit	2 100 . .	**1,237.7**	**1,431.2**	**1,570.1**	**1,489.9**	**2,090.8**	**2,005.5**	**1,898.4**	**. . .**
General merchandise: exports f.o.b.	2 110 . .	689.1	783.9	957.7	910.7	1,403.0	1,294.7	1,196.4	. . .
Goods for processing: exports f.o.b.	2 150 . .	. . .	. . .	. . .	. . .	. . .	. . .	. . .	. . .
Repairs on goods	2 160 . .	. . .	. . .	. . .	. . .	. . .	. . .	. . .	. . .
Goods procured in ports by carriers	2 170 . .	. . .	. . .	. . .	. . .	. . .	. . .	. . .	. . .
Nonmonetary gold	2 180 . .	548.6	647.3	612.4	579.2	687.8	710.8	702.0	. . .
Debit	3 100 . .	**–1,579.9**	**–1,687.8**	**–1,937.0**	**–2,128.2**	**–2,896.5**	**–3,228.1**	**–2,741.3**	**. . .**
General merchandise: imports f.o.b.	3 110 . .	–1,579.9	–1,687.8	–1,937.0	–2,128.2	–2,896.5	–3,228.1	–2,741.3	. . .
Goods for processing: imports f.o.b.	3 150 . .	. . .	. . .	. . .	. . .	. . .	. . .	. . .	. . .
Repairs on goods	3 160 . .	. . .	. . .	. . .	. . .	. . .	. . .	. . .	. . .
Goods procured in ports by carriers	3 170 . .	. . .	. . .	. . .	. . .	. . .	. . .	. . .	. . .
Nonmonetary gold	3 180 . .	. . .	. . .	. . .	. . .	. . .	. . .	. . .	. . .
B. SERVICES	4 200 . .	–273.3	–282.1	–299.6	–340.1	–235.0	–198.1	–93.0	. . .
Total credit	2 200 . .	*147.5*	*150.6*	*156.8*	*164.9*	*438.6*	*467.8*	*504.3*	. . .
Total debit	3 200 . .	*–420.8*	*–432.7*	*–456.4*	*–505.0*	*–673.6*	*–665.9*	*–597.3*	. . .
Transportation services, credit	2 205 . .	**80.2**	**81.5**	**83.2**	**87.0**	**90.8**	**94.8**	**98.4**	**. . .**
Passenger	2 850 . .	*18.4*	*18.6*	*18.9*	*19.6*	*20.4*	*21.3*	*22.2*	. . .
Freight	2 851 . .	*33.4*	*33.7*	*35.1*	*36.8*	*38.4*	*40.1*	*41.6*	. . .
Other	2 852 . .	*28.4*	*29.2*	*29.2*	*30.6*	*32.0*	*33.4*	*34.6*	. . .
Sea transport, passenger	2 207 . .	. . .	. . .	. . .	. . .	. . .	. . .	. . .	. . .
Sea transport, freight	2 208 . .	. . .	. . .	. . .	. . .	. . .	. . .	. . .	. . .
Sea transport, other	2 209 . .	. . .	. . .	. . .	. . .	. . .	. . .	. . .	. . .
Air transport, passenger	2 211 . .	. . .	. . .	. . .	. . .	. . .	. . .	. . .	. . .
Air transport, freight	2 212 . .	. . .	. . .	. . .	. . .	. . .	. . .	. . .	. . .
Air transport, other	2 213 . .	. . .	. . .	. . .	. . .	. . .	. . .	. . .	. . .
Other transport, passenger	2 215 . .	. . .	. . .	. . .	. . .	. . .	. . .	. . .	. . .
Other transport, freight	2 216 . .	. . .	. . .	. . .	. . .	. . .	. . .	. . .	. . .
Other transport, other	2 217 . .	. . .	. . .	. . .	. . .	. . .	. . .	. . .	. . .
Transportation services, debit	3 205 . .	**–186.5**	**–202.9**	**–214.5**	**–245.0**	**–314.7**	**–336.0**	**–282.9**	**. . .**
Passenger	3 850 . .	*–50.5*	*–52.6*	*–54.4*	*–57.4*	*–59.9*	*–59.9*	*–62.1*	. . .
Freight	3 851 . .	*–116.8*	*–131.8*	*–140.3*	*–167.4*	*–233.8*	*–255.1*	*–199.0*	. . .
Other	3 852 . .	*–19.2*	*–18.5*	*–19.8*	*–20.2*	*–21.0*	*–21.0*	*–21.8*	. . .
Sea transport, passenger	3 207 . .	. . .	. . .	. . .	. . .	. . .	. . .	. . .	. . .
Sea transport, freight	3 208 . .	. . .	. . .	. . .	. . .	. . .	. . .	. . .	. . .
Sea transport, other	3 209 . .	. . .	. . .	. . .	. . .	. . .	. . .	. . .	. . .
Air transport, passenger	3 211 . .	. . .	. . .	. . .	. . .	. . .	. . .	. . .	. . .
Air transport, freight	3 212 . .	. . .	. . .	. . .	. . .	. . .	. . .	. . .	. . .
Air transport, other	3 213 . .	. . .	. . .	. . .	. . .	. . .	. . .	. . .	. . .
Other transport, passenger	3 215 . .	. . .	. . .	. . .	. . .	. . .	. . .	. . .	. . .
Other transport, freight	3 216 . .	. . .	. . .	. . .	. . .	. . .	. . .	. . .	. . .
Other transport, other	3 217 . .	. . .	. . .	. . .	. . .	. . .	. . .	. . .	. . .
Travel, credit	2 236 . .	**10.8**	**11.0**	**12.7**	**14.6**	**284.0**	**304.1**	**334.6**	**. . .**
Business travel	2 237 . .	7.6	7.7	8.4	10.2	198.8	212.9	234.2	. . .
Personal travel	2 240 . .	3.2	3.3	4.3	4.4	85.2	91.2	100.4	. . .
Travel, debit	3 236 . .	**–20.1**	**–20.6**	**–22.4**	**–23.4**	**–85.2**	**–91.2**	**–100.4**	**. . .**
Business travel	3 237 . .	–13.1	–14.4	–14.6	–16.4	–59.6	–27.4	–70.3	. . .
Personal travel	3 240 . .	–7.0	–6.2	–7.8	–7.0	–25.6	–63.8	–30.1	. . .
Other services, credit	2 200 BA	**56.5**	**58.1**	**60.9**	**63.3**	**63.8**	**68.9**	**71.3**	**. . .**
Communications	2 245 . .	. . .	. . .	. . .	. . .	. . .	. . .	. . .	. . .
Construction	2 249 . .	. . .	. . .	. . .	. . .	. . .	. . .	. . .	. . .
Insurance	2 253 . .	3.7	4.2	4.5	4.5	4.8	5.0	5.1	. . .
Financial	2 260 . .	. . .	. . .	. . .	. . .	. . .	. . .	. . .	. . .
Computer and information	2 262 . .	. . .	. . .	. . .	. . .	. . .	. . .	. . .	. . .
Royalties and licence fees	2 266 . .	. . .	. . .	. . .	. . .	. . .	. . .	. . .	. . .
Other business services	2 268 . .	41.3	42.1	44.0	45.8	47.8	49.9	51.7	. . .
Personal, cultural, and recreational	2 287 . .	. . .	. . .	. . .	. . .	. . .	. . .	. . .	. . .
Government, n.i.e.	2 291 . .	11.5	11.8	12.4	13.0	11.2	14.0	14.5	. . .
Other services, debit	3 200 BA	**–214.2**	**–209.2**	**–219.5**	**–236.6**	**–273.7**	**–238.7**	**–214.0**	**. . .**
Communications	3 245 . .	. . .	. . .	. . .	. . .	. . .	. . .	. . .	. . .
Construction	3 249 . .	. . .	. . .	. . .	. . .	. . .	. . .	. . .	. . .
Insurance	3 253 . .	–27.2	–21.5	–31.8	–27.2	–38.1	–41.5	–32.4	. . .
Financial	3 260 . .	. . .	. . .	. . .	. . .	. . .	. . .	. . .	. . .
Computer and information	3 262 . .	. . .	. . .	. . .	. . .	. . .	. . .	. . .	. . .
Royalties and licence fees	3 266 . .	–.7	–.9	–1.0	. . .	. . .	. . .	. . .	. . .
Other business services	3 268 . .	–84.5	–86.1	–93.9	–99.1	–110.3	–107.6	–111.6	. . .
Personal, cultural, and recreational	3 287 . .	. . .	. . .	. . .	. . .	. . .	. . .	. . .	. . .
Government, n.i.e.	3 291 . .	–101.8	–100.7	–92.8	–110.3	–125.3	–89.6	–70.0	. . .

Table 2 (Continued). STANDARD PRESENTATION, 1994–2001
(Millions of U.S. dollars)

	Code	1994	1995	1996	1997	1998	1999	2000	2001
C. INCOME	4 300 . .	–110.9	–129.2	–139.9	–131.4	–136.3	–131.8	–107.6	. . .
Total credit	2 300 . .	*11.8*	*13.7*	*23.5*	*26.7*	*26.7*	*15.0*	*15.6*	. . .
Total debit	3 300 . .	*–122.7*	*–142.9*	*–163.4*	*–158.1*	*–163.0*	*–146.8*	*–123.2*	. . .
Compensation of employees, credit	2 310 . .	**. . .**	**. . .**	**. . .**	**. . .**	**. . .**	**. . .**	**. . .**	**. . .**
Compensation of employees, debit	3 310 . .	**. . .**	**. . .**	**. . .**	**. . .**	**. . .**	**. . .**	**. . .**	**. . .**
Investment income, credit	2 320 . .	**11.8**	**13.7**	**23.5**	**26.7**	**26.7**	**15.0**	**15.6**	**. . .**
Direct investment income	2 330 . .	. . .	. . .	. . .	. . .	. . .	. . .	. . .	. . .
Dividends and distributed branch profits	2 332 . .	. . .	. . .	. . .	. . .	. . .	. . .	. . .	. . .
Reinvested earnings and undistributed branch profits	2 333 . .	. . .	. . .	. . .	. . .	. . .	. . .	. . .	. . .
Income on debt (interest)	2 334 . .	. . .	. . .	. . .	. . .	. . .	. . .	. . .	. . .
Portfolio investment income	2 339 . .	11.8	13.7	23.5	26.7	26.7	15.0	15.6	. . .
Income on equity	2 340 . .	11.8	13.7	23.5	26.7	26.7	15.0	15.6	. . .
Income on bonds and notes	2 350 . .	. . .	. . .	. . .	. . .	. . .	. . .	. . .	. . .
Income on money market instruments	2 360 . .	. . .	. . .	. . .	. . .	. . .	. . .	. . .	. . .
Other investment income	2 370 . .	. . .	. . .	. . .	. . .	. . .	. . .	. . .	. . .
Investment income, debit	3 320 . .	**–122.7**	**–142.9**	**–163.4**	**–158.1**	**–163.0**	**–146.8**	**–123.2**	**. . .**
Direct investment income	3 330 . .	–10.6	–10.6	–11.6	–12.7	–14.2	–15.6	–16.2	. . .
Dividends and distributed branch profits	3 332 . .	. . .	. . .	. . .	. . .	. . .	. . .	. . .	. . .
Reinvested earnings and undistributed branch profits	3 333 . .	. . .	. . .	. . .	. . .	. . .	. . .	. . .	. . .
Income on debt (interest)	3 334 . .	. . .	. . .	. . .	. . .	. . .	. . .	. . .	. . .
Portfolio investment income	3 339 . .	–112.1	–132.3	–151.8	–145.4	–148.8	–131.2	–107.0	. . .
Income on equity	3 340 . .	. . .	. . .	. . .	. . .	. . .	. . .	. . .	. . .
Income on bonds and notes	3 350 . .	–112.1	–132.3	–151.8	–145.4	–148.8	–131.2	–107.0	. . .
Income on money market instruments	3 360 . .	. . .	. . .	. . .	. . .	. . .	. . .	. . .	. . .
Other investment income	3 370 . .	. . .	. . .	. . .	. . .	. . .	. . .	. . .	. . .
D. CURRENT TRANSFERS	4 379 . .	471.8	523.2	481.7	560.1	733.9	620.0	630.9	. . .
Credit	2 379 . .	**487.3**	**538.9**	**497.9**	**576.5**	**751.0**	**637.8**	**649.3**	**. . .**
General government	2 380 . .	210.8	270.0	215.6	169.7	290.5	158.8	143.1	. . .
Other sectors	2 390 . .	276.5	268.9	282.3	406.8	460.5	479.0	506.2	. . .
Workers' remittances	2 391 . .	15.7	17.2	27.5	26.0	29.5	30.7	32.4	. . .
Other current transfers	2 392 . .	260.8	251.7	254.8	380.8	431.0	448.3	473.8	. . .
Debit	3 379 . .	**–15.5**	**–15.7**	**–16.2**	**–16.4**	**–17.1**	**–17.8**	**–18.4**	**. . .**
General government	3 380 . .	–10.0	–10.0	–10.0	–10.0	–10.4	–10.8	–11.2	. . .
Other sectors	3 390 . .	–5.5	–5.7	–6.2	–6.4	–6.7	–7.0	–7.2	. . .
Workers' remittances	3 391 . .	–4.6	–4.8	–5.0	–5.4	–5.6	–5.9	–6.1	. . .
Other current transfers	3 392 . .	–.9	–.9	–1.2	–1.0	–1.1	–1.1	–1.1	. . .
CAPITAL AND FINANCIAL ACCOUNT	4 996 . .	**308.6**	**210.3**	**304.5**	**466.1**	**341.0**	**643.1**	**524.3**	**. . .**
CAPITAL ACCOUNT	4 994 . .	**–1.0**	**–1.0**	**–1.0**	**–1.0**	**–1.0**	**–1.0**	**. . .**	**. . .**
Total credit	2 994 . .	. . .	. . .	. . .	. . .	. . .	. . .	. . .	. . .
Total debit	3 994 . .	*–1.0*	*–1.0*	*–1.0*	*–1.0*	*–1.0*	*–1.0*	. . .	. . .
Capital transfers, credit	2 400 . .	**. . .**	**. . .**	**. . .**	**. . .**	**. . .**	**. . .**	**. . .**	**. . .**
General government	2 401 . .	. . .	. . .	. . .	. . .	. . .	. . .	. . .	. . .
Debt forgiveness	2 402 . .	. . .	. . .	. . .	. . .	. . .	. . .	. . .	. . .
Other capital transfers	2 410 . .	. . .	. . .	. . .	. . .	. . .	. . .	. . .	. . .
Other sectors	2 430 . .	. . .	. . .	. . .	. . .	. . .	. . .	. . .	. . .
Migrants' transfers	2 431 . .	. . .	. . .	. . .	. . .	. . .	. . .	. . .	. . .
Debt forgiveness	2 432 . .	. . .	. . .	. . .	. . .	. . .	. . .	. . .	. . .
Other capital transfers	2 440 . .	. . .	. . .	. . .	. . .	. . .	. . .	. . .	. . .
Capital transfers, debit	3 400 . .	**–1.0**	**–1.0**	**–1.0**	**–1.0**	**–1.0**	**–1.0**	**. . .**	**. . .**
General government	3 401 . .	. . .	. . .	. . .	. . .	. . .	. . .	. . .	. . .
Debt forgiveness	3 402 . .	. . .	. . .	. . .	. . .	. . .	. . .	. . .	. . .
Other capital transfers	3 410 . .	. . .	. . .	. . .	. . .	. . .	. . .	. . .	. . .
Other sectors	3 430 . .	–1.0	–1.0	–1.0	–1.0	–1.0	–1.0	. . .	. . .
Migrants' transfers	3 431 . .	–1.0	–1.0	–1.0	–1.0	–1.0	–1.0	. . .	. . .
Debt forgiveness	3 432 . .	. . .	. . .	. . .	. . .	. . .	. . .	. . .	. . .
Other capital transfers	3 440 . .	. . .	. . .	. . .	. . .	. . .	. . .	. . .	. . .
Nonproduced nonfinancial assets, credit	2 480 . .	**. . .**	**. . .**	**. . .**	**. . .**	**. . .**	**. . .**	**. . .**	**. . .**
Nonproduced nonfinancial assets, debit	3 480 . .	**. . .**	**. . .**	**. . .**	**. . .**	**. . .**	**. . .**	**. . .**	**. . .**

Table 2 (Continued). STANDARD PRESENTATION, 1994–2001

(Millions of U.S. dollars)

	Code	1994	1995	1996	1997	1998	1999	2000	2001
FINANCIAL ACCOUNT	4 995 . .	**309.6**	**211.3**	**305.5**	**467.1**	**342.0**	**644.1**	**524.3**	**...**
A. DIRECT INVESTMENT	4 500 . .	233.0	106.5	120.0	82.6	55.7	62.6	110.3	...
Direct investment abroad	4 505 . .	**...**	**...**	**...**	**...**	**...**	**...**	**...**	**...**
Equity capital	4 510 . .	...	...	...	...	...	...	...	...
Claims on affiliated enterprises	4 515 . .	...	...	...	...	...	...	...	...
Liabilities to affiliated enterprises	4 520 . .	...	...	...	...	...	...	...	...
Reinvested earnings	4 525 . .	...	...	...	...	...	...	...	...
Other capital	4 530 . .	...	...	...	...	...	...	...	...
Claims on affiliated enterprises	4 535 . .	...	...	...	...	...	...	...	...
Liabilities to affiliated enterprises	4 540 . .	...	...	...	...	...	...	...	...
Direct investment in Ghana	4 555 . .	**233.0**	**106.5**	**120.0**	**82.6**	**55.7**	**62.6**	**110.3**	**...**
Equity capital	4 560 . .	233.0	106.5	120.0	82.6	55.7	62.6	110.3	...
Claims on direct investors	4 565 . .	...	...	...	...	...	...	...	...
Liabilities to direct investors	4 570 . .	...	...	...	...	...	...	...	...
Reinvested earnings	4 575 . .	...	...	...	...	...	...	...	...
Other capital	4 580 . .	...	...	...	...	...	...	...	...
Claims on direct investors	4 585 . .	...	...	...	...	...	...	...	...
Liabilities to direct investors	4 590 . .	...	...	...	...	...	...	...	...
B. PORTFOLIO INVESTMENT	4 600 . .	...	...	...	...	...	...	...	...
Assets	4 602 . .	**...**	**...**	**...**	**...**	**...**	**...**	**...**	**...**
Equity securities	4 610 . .	...	...	...	...	...	...	...	...
Monetary authorities	4 611 . .	...	...	...	...	...	...	...	...
General government	4 612 . .	...	...	...	...	...	...	...	...
Banks	4 613 . .	...	...	...	...	...	...	...	...
Other sectors	4 614 . .	...	...	...	...	...	...	...	...
Debt securities	4 619 . .	...	...	...	...	...	...	...	...
Bonds and notes	4 620 . .	...	...	...	...	...	...	...	...
Monetary authorities	4 621 . .	...	...	...	...	...	...	...	...
General government	4 622 . .	...	...	...	...	...	...	...	...
Banks	4 623 . .	...	...	...	...	...	...	...	...
Other sectors	4 624 . .	...	...	...	...	...	...	...	...
Money market instruments	4 630 . .	...	...	...	...	...	...	...	...
Monetary authorities	4 631 . .	...	...	...	...	...	...	...	...
General government	4 632 . .	...	...	...	...	...	...	...	...
Banks	4 633 . .	...	...	...	...	...	...	...	...
Other sectors	4 634 . .	...	...	...	...	...	...	...	...
Liabilities	4 652 . .	**...**	**...**	**...**	**...**	**...**	**...**	**...**	**...**
Equity securities	4 660 . .	...	...	...	...	...	...	...	...
Banks	4 663 . .	...	...	...	...	...	...	...	...
Other sectors	4 664 . .	...	...	...	...	...	...	...	...
Debt securities	4 669 . .	...	...	...	...	...	...	...	...
Bonds and notes	4 670 . .	...	...	...	...	...	...	...	...
Monetary authorities	4 671 . .	...	...	...	...	...	...	...	...
General government	4 672 . .	...	...	...	...	...	...	...	...
Banks	4 673 . .	...	...	...	...	...	...	...	...
Other sectors	4 674 . .	...	...	...	...	...	...	...	...
Money market instruments	4 680 . .	...	...	...	...	...	...	...	...
Monetary authorities	4 681 . .	...	...	...	...	...	...	...	...
General government	4 682 . .	...	...	...	...	...	...	...	...
Banks	4 683 . .	...	...	...	...	...	...	...	...
Other sectors	4 684 . .	...	...	...	...	...	...	...	...
C. FINANCIAL DERIVATIVES	4 910 . .	...	...	...	...	...	...	...	...
Monetary authorities	4 911 . .	...	...	...	...	...	...	...	...
General government	4 912 . .	...	...	...	...	...	...	...	...
Banks	4 913 . .	...	...	...	...	...	...	...	...
Other sectors	4 914 . .	...	...	...	...	...	...	...	...
Assets	4 900 . .	**...**	**...**	**...**	**...**	**...**	**...**	**...**	**...**
Monetary authorities	4 901 . .	...	...	...	...	...	...	...	...
General government	4 902 . .	...	...	...	...	...	...	...	...
Banks	4 903 . .	...	...	...	...	...	...	...	...
Other sectors	4 904 . .	...	...	...	...	...	...	...	...
Liabilities	4 905 . .	**...**	**...**	**...**	**...**	**...**	**...**	**...**	**...**
Monetary authorities	4 906 . .	...	...	...	...	...	...	...	...
General government	4 907 . .	...	...	...	...	...	...	...	...
Banks	4 908 . .	...	...	...	...	...	...	...	...
Other sectors	4 909 . .	...	...	...	...	...	...	...	...

Table 2 (Concluded). STANDARD PRESENTATION, 1994–2001
(Millions of U.S. dollars)

	Code	1994	1995	1996	1997	1998	1999	2000	2001
D. OTHER INVESTMENT	4 700 . .	165.8	290.4	79.8	245.4	368.1	476.9	153.2	. . .
Assets	4 703 . .	**–119.6**	**–20.0**	**–179.4**	**33.1**	**88.1**	**183.1**	**41.0**	**. . .**
Trade credits	4 706 . .	. . .	. . .	. . .	. . .	. . .	. . .	. . .	. . .
General government	4 707 . .	. . .	. . .	. . .	. . .	. . .	. . .	. . .	. . .
of which: Short-term	4 709 . .	. . .	. . .	. . .	. . .	. . .	. . .	. . .	. . .
Other sectors	4 710 . .	. . .	. . .	. . .	. . .	. . .	. . .	. . .	. . .
of which: Short-term	4 712 . .	. . .	. . .	. . .	. . .	. . .	. . .	. . .	. . .
Loans	4 714 . .	. . .	. . .	. . .	. . .	. . .	. . .	. . .	. . .
Monetary authorities	4 715 . .	. . .	. . .	. . .	. . .	. . .	. . .	. . .	. . .
of which: Short-term	4 718 . .	. . .	. . .	. . .	. . .	. . .	. . .	. . .	. . .
General government	4 719 . .	. . .	. . .	. . .	. . .	. . .	. . .	. . .	. . .
of which: Short-term	4 721 . .	. . .	. . .	. . .	. . .	. . .	. . .	. . .	. . .
Banks	4 722 . .	. . .	. . .	. . .	. . .	. . .	. . .	. . .	. . .
of which: Short-term	4 724 . .	. . .	. . .	. . .	. . .	. . .	. . .	. . .	. . .
Other sectors	4 725 . .	. . .	. . .	. . .	. . .	. . .	. . .	. . .	. . .
of which: Short-term	4 727 . .	. . .	. . .	. . .	. . .	. . .	. . .	. . .	. . .
Currency and deposits	4 730 . .	–122.8	–23.0	–179.0	32.9	88.0	186.4	40.8	. . .
Monetary authorities	4 731 . .	. . .	. . .	. . .	. . .	. . .	. . .	. . .	. . .
General government	4 732 . .	. . .	. . .	. . .	. . .	. . .	. . .	. . .	. . .
Banks	4 733 . .	–93.3	77.6	–72.0	34.4	83.7	200.3	26.7	. . .
Other sectors	4 734 . .	–29.5	–100.6	–107.0	–1.5	4.3	–13.9	14.1	. . .
Other assets	4 736 . .	3.2	3.0	–.4	.2	.1	–3.3	.2	. . .
Monetary authorities	4 737 . .	3.2	3.0	–.4	.2	.1	–3.3	.2	. . .
of which: Short-term	4 739 . .	*3.2*	*3.0*	*–.4*	*.2*	*.1*	*–3.3*	*.2*	. . .
General government	4 740 . .	. . .	. . .	. . .	. . .	. . .	. . .	. . .	. . .
of which: Short-term	4 742 . .	. . .	. . .	. . .	. . .	. . .	. . .	. . .	. . .
Banks	4 743 . .	. . .	. . .	. . .	. . .	. . .	. . .	. . .	. . .
of which: Short-term	4 745 . .	. . .	. . .	. . .	. . .	. . .	. . .	. . .	. . .
Other sectors	4 746 . .	. . .	. . .	. . .	. . .	. . .	. . .	. . .	. . .
of which: Short-term	4 748 . .	. . .	. . .	. . .	. . .	. . .	. . .	. . .	. . .
Liabilities	4 753 . .	**285.4**	**310.4**	**259.2**	**212.3**	**280.0**	**293.8**	**112.2**	**. . .**
Trade credits	4 756 . .	15.1	.7	–27.3	–94.9	–21.7	47.5	28.6	. . .
General government	4 757 . .	. . .	. . .	. . .	. . .	. . .	. . .	. . .	. . .
of which: Short-term	4 759 . .	. . .	. . .	. . .	. . .	. . .	. . .	. . .	. . .
Other sectors	4 760 . .	15.1	.7	–27.3	–94.9	–21.7	47.5	28.6	. . .
of which: Short-term	4 762 . .	*15.1*	*.7*	*–27.3*	*–94.9*	*–21.7*	*47.5*	*28.6*	. . .
Loans	4 764 . .	205.5	340.9	255.9	307.2	301.7	246.3	83.6	. . .
Monetary authorities	4 765 . .	–102.3	–104.3	–85.3	–165.8	–26.1	–15.0	–2.3	. . .
of which: Use of Fund credit and loans from the Fund	4 766 . .	*–82.9*	*–65.2*	*–85.3*	*–165.8*	*–26.1*	*–15.0*	*–2.3*	. . .
of which: Short-term	4 768 . .	*–19.4*	*–39.1*	. . .	. . .	. . .	. . .	. . .	. . .
General government	4 769 . .	295.3	215.5	341.2	499.4	348.9	144.8	139.7	. . .
of which: Short-term	4 771 . .	. . .	. . .	. . .	. . .	. . .	. . .	. . .	. . .
Banks	4 772 . .	. . .	. . .	. . .	. . .	. . .	. . .	. . .	. . .
of which: Short-term	4 774 . .	. . .	. . .	. . .	. . .	. . .	. . .	. . .	. . .
Other sectors	4 775 . .	12.5	229.7	. . .	–26.4	–21.1	116.5	–53.8	. . .
of which: Short-term	4 777 . .	. . .	. . .	. . .	. . .	. . .	. . .	. . .	. . .
Currency and deposits	4 780 . .	64.8	–31.2	30.6	. . .	. . .	. . .	. . .	. . .
Monetary authorities	4 781 . .	. . .	. . .	. . .	. . .	. . .	. . .	. . .	. . .
General government	4 782 . .	. . .	. . .	. . .	. . .	. . .	. . .	. . .	. . .
Banks	4 783 . .	64.8	–31.2	30.6	. . .	. . .	. . .	. . .	. . .
Other sectors	4 784 . .	. . .	. . .	. . .	. . .	. . .	. . .	. . .	. . .
Other liabilities	4 786 . .	. . .	. . .	. . .	. . .	. . .	. . .	. . .	. . .
Monetary authorities	4 787 . .	. . .	. . .	. . .	. . .	. . .	. . .	. . .	. . .
of which: Short-term	4 789 . .	. . .	. . .	. . .	. . .	. . .	. . .	. . .	. . .
General government	4 790 . .	. . .	. . .	. . .	. . .	. . .	. . .	. . .	. . .
of which: Short-term	4 792 . .	. . .	. . .	. . .	. . .	. . .	. . .	. . .	. . .
Banks	4 793 . .	. . .	. . .	. . .	. . .	. . .	. . .	. . .	. . .
of which: Short-term	4 795 . .	. . .	. . .	. . .	. . .	. . .	. . .	. . .	. . .
Other sectors	4 796 . .	. . .	. . .	. . .	. . .	. . .	. . .	. . .	. . .
of which: Short-term	4 798 . .	. . .	. . .	. . .	. . .	. . .	. . .	. . .	. . .
E. RESERVE ASSETS	4 802 . .	–89.2	–185.6	105.7	139.0	–81.8	104.6	260.8	. . .
Monetary gold	4 812 . .	. . .	. . .	. . .	. . .	–1.3	–.2	–.3	. . .
Special drawing rights	4 811 . .	–3.3	.7	.3	–1.4	–55.3	39.8	16.4	. . .
Reserve position in the Fund	4 810 . .	. . .	. . .	. . .	. . .	. . .	–32.8	54.7	. . .
Foreign exchange	4 803 . .	–178.2	–129.7	116.6	89.9	55.2	74.6	132.2	. . .
Other claims	4 813 . .	92.3	–56.6	–11.2	50.5	–80.4	23.2	57.8	. . .
NET ERRORS AND OMISSIONS	4 998 . .	**–54.0**	**–65.6**	**20.2**	**83.6**	**102.1**	**289.4**	**–111.7**	**. . .**

Part 3 of the *Yearbook* contains descriptions of the methodologies, compilation practices, and sources used to compile these data.

Table 1. ANALYTIC PRESENTATION, 1994–2001
(Millions of U.S. dollars)

	Code	1994	1995	1996	1997	1998	1999	2000	2001
A. Current Account [1]	4 993 Z.	**–146**	**–2,864**	**–4,554**	**–4,860**	**. . .**	**–7,295**	**–9,820**	**–9,400**
Goods: exports f.o.b.	2 100 . .	5,338	5,918	5,890	5,576	. . .	8,545	10,202	10,615
Goods: imports f.o.b.	3 100 . .	–16,611	–20,343	–21,395	–20,951	. . .	–26,496	–30,440	–29,702
Balance on Goods	4 100 . .	*–11,273*	*–14,425*	*–15,505*	*–15,375*	. . .	*–17,951*	*–20,239*	*–19,087*
Services: credit	2 200 . .	9,213	9,605	9,348	9,287	. . .	16,506	19,239	19,456
Services: debit	3 200 . .	–3,774	–4,368	–4,238	–4,650	. . .	–9,251	–11,286	–11,589
Balance on Goods and Services	4 991 . .	*–5,834*	*–9,188*	*–10,395*	*–10,738*	. . .	*–10,696*	*–12,286*	*–11,220*
Income: credit	2 300 . .	1,099	1,312	1,156	1,208	. . .	2,577	2,807	1,885
Income: debit	3 300 . .	–2,347	–2,996	–3,337	–2,840	. . .	–3,248	–3,692	–3,652
Balance on Goods, Services, and Income	4 992 . .	*–7,082*	*–10,872*	*–12,576*	*–12,370*	. . .	*–11,367*	*–13,171*	*–12,987*
Current transfers: credit	2 379 Z.	6,964	8,039	8,053	7,538	. . .	4,957	4,116	4,592
Current transfers: debit	3 379 . .	–28	–31	–31	–28	. . .	–884	–764	–1,005
B. Capital Account [1]	4 994 Z.	**. . .**	**. . .**	**. . .**	**. . .**	**. . .**	**2,211**	**2,112**	**2,153**
Capital account: credit	2 994 Z.	. . .	. . .	. . .	. . .	. . .	2,318	2,244	2,320
Capital account: debit	3 994 . .	. . .	. . .	. . .	. . .	. . .	–107	–131	–167
Total, Groups A Plus B	4 981 . .	*–146*	*–2,864*	*–4,554*	*–4,860*	. . .	*–5,084*	*–7,707*	*–7,247*
C. Financial Account [1]	4 995 W.	**6,903**	**3,162**	**8,658**	**119**	**. . .**	**7,478**	**10,830**	**537**
Direct investment abroad	4 505 . .	. . .	. . .	. . .	. . .	. . .	–542	–2,099	–611
Direct investment in Greece	4 555 Z.	981	1,053	1,058	984	. . .	567	1,083	1,585
Portfolio investment assets	4 602 . .	. . .	. . .	. . .	. . .	. . .	–858	–1,184	–474
Equity securities	4 610 . .	. . .	. . .	. . .	. . .	. . .	–166	–846	–1,020
Debt securities	4 619 . .	. . .	. . .	. . .	. . .	. . .	–692	–338	546
Portfolio investment liabilities	4 652 Z.	. . .	. . .	. . .	. . .	. . .	6,754	9,262	9,012
Equity securities	4 660 . .	. . .	. . .	. . .	. . .	. . .	–2,589	1,637	1,829
Debt securities	4 669 Z.	. . .	. . .	. . .	. . .	. . .	9,343	7,625	7,183
Financial derivatives	4 910 . .	. . .	. . .	. . .	. . .	. . .	419	348	74
Financial derivatives assets	4 900 . .	. . .	. . .	. . .	. . .	. . .	. . .	. . .	. . .
Financial derivatives liabilities	4 905 . .	. . .	. . .	. . .	. . .	. . .	419	348	74
Other investment assets	4 703 . .	. . .	. . .	. . .	980	. . .	–2,913	6,970	–1,539
Monetary authorities	4 701 . .	. . .	. . .	. . .	. . .	. . .	. . .	. . .	. . .
General government	4 704 . .	. . .	. . .	. . .	980	. . .	–2,913	6,970	–1,539
Banks	4 705 . .	. . .	. . .	. . .	. . .	. . .	. . .	. . .	. . .
Other sectors	4 728 . .	. . .	. . .	. . .	. . .	. . .	. . .	. . .	. . .
Other investment liabilities	4 753 W.	5,922	2,109	7,600	–1,845	. . .	4,050	–3,551	–7,511
Monetary authorities	4 753 WA	–1,791	–2,385	–2,194	–2,570	. . .	. . .	. . .	. . .
General government	4 753 ZB	4,703	3,441	3,530	7,101	. . .	. . .	. . .	. . .
Banks	4 753 ZC	89	–2,110	–598	–3,348	. . .	1,644	–3,425	–6,989
Other sectors	4 753 ZD	2,921	3,163	6,862	–3,028	. . .	2,406	–126	–522
Total, Groups A Through C	4 983 . .	*6,757*	*298*	*4,104*	*–4,741*	. . .	*2,394*	*3,123*	*–6,710*
D. Net Errors and Omissions	4 998 . .	**–448**	**–321**	**111**	**226**	**. . .**	**42**	**–550**	**1,011**
Total, Groups A Through D	4 984 . .	*6,309*	*–23*	*4,215*	*–4,515*	. . .	*2,435*	*2,573*	*–5,699*
E. Reserves and Related Items	4 802 A.	**–6,309**	**23**	**–4,215**	**4,515**	**. . .**	**–2,435**	**–2,573**	**5,699**
Reserve assets	4 802 . .	–6,309	23	–4,215	4,515	. . .	–2,435	–2,573	5,699
Use of Fund credit and loans	4 766 . .	. . .	. . .	. . .	. . .	. . .	. . .	. . .	. . .
Exceptional financing	4 920 . .	. . .	. . .	. . .	. . .	. . .	. . .	. . .	. . .
Conversion rates: drachmas per U.S. dollar	0 101 . .	**242.60**	**231.66**	**240.71**	**273.06**	**295.53**	**305.65**	**365.40**	**. . .**
Conversion rates: euros per U.S. dollar	0 103 . .	**. . .**	**. . .**	**. . .**	**. . .**	**. . .**	**.938627**	**1.085401**	**1.117510**

[1] Excludes components that have been classified in the categories of Group E.

Table 2. STANDARD PRESENTATION, 1994–2001
(Millions of U.S. dollars)

	Code	1994	1995	1996	1997	1998	1999	2000	2001
CURRENT ACCOUNT	4 993 . .	**–146**	**–2,864**	**–4,554**	**–4,860**	**. . .**	**–7,295**	**–9,820**	**–9,400**
A. GOODS	4 100 . .	–11,273	–14,425	–15,505	–15,375	. . .	–17,951	–20,239	–19,087
Credit	2 100 . .	**5,338**	**5,918**	**5,890**	**5,576**	**. . .**	**8,545**	**10,202**	**10,615**
General merchandise: exports f.o.b.	2 110 . .	5,219	5,783	5,770	5,373	. . .	7,889	9,460	9,549
Goods for processing: exports f.o.b.	2 150 . .	. . .	. . .	. . .	. . .	. . .	109	37	76
Repairs on goods	2 160 . .	. . .	. . .	. . .	. . .	. . .	40	55	54
Goods procured in ports by carriers	2 170 . .	119	135	120	203	. . .	506	651	936
Nonmonetary gold	2 180 . .	. . .	. . .	. . .	. . .	. . .	. . .	. . .	. . .
Debit	3 100 . .	**–16,611**	**–20,343**	**–21,395**	**–20,951**	**. . .**	**–26,496**	**–30,440**	**–29,702**
General merchandise: imports f.o.b.	3 110 . .	–16,588	–20,292	–21,359	–20,923	. . .	–25,822	–29,713	–29,218
Goods for processing: imports f.o.b.	3 150 . .	. . .	. . .	. . .	. . .	. . .	–31	–23	–26
Repairs on goods	3 160 . .	. . .	. . .	. . .	. . .	. . .	–89	–96	–64
Goods procured in ports by carriers	3 170 . .	–23	–51	–36	–28	. . .	–553	–609	–394
Nonmonetary gold	3 180 . .	. . .	. . .	. . .	. . .	. . .	. . .	. . .	. . .
B. SERVICES	4 200 . .	5,439	5,237	5,110	4,637	. . .	7,255	7,953	7,867
Total credit	2 200 . .	*9,213*	*9,605*	*9,348*	*9,287*	. . .	*16,506*	*19,239*	*19,456*
Total debit	3 200 . .	*–3,774*	*–4,368*	*–4,238*	*–4,650*	. . .	*–9,251*	*–11,286*	*–11,589*
Transportation services, credit	2 205 . .	**466**	**376**	**376**	**176**	**. . .**	**5,154**	**7,923**	**8,167**
Passenger	2 850 . .	*48*	*47*	*36*	*21*	. . .	*53*	*43*	*61*
Freight	2 851 . .	*100*	*48*	*92*	*54*	. . .	*251*	*92*	*107*
Other	2 852 . .	*318*	*281*	*248*	*101*	. . .	*4,849*	*7,788*	*7,999*
Sea transport, passenger	2 207 . .	. . .	. . .	. . .	. . .	. . .	53	43	61
Sea transport, freight	2 208 . .	. . .	. . .	. . .	. . .	. . .	251	91	106
Sea transport, other	2 209 . .	. . .	. . .	. . .	. . .	. . .	4,418	7,376	7,407
Air transport, passenger	2 211 . .	. . .	. . .	. . .	. . .	. . .	. . .	. . .	. . .
Air transport, freight	2 212 . .	. . .	. . .	. . .	. . .	. . .	. . .	. . .	. . .
Air transport, other	2 213 . .	. . .	. . .	. . .	. . .	. . .	. . .	. . .	404
Other transport, passenger	2 215 . .	. . .	. . .	. . .	. . .	. . .	. . .	. . .	. . .
Other transport, freight	2 216 . .	. . .	. . .	. . .	. . .	. . .	. . .	1	1
Other transport, other	2 217 . .	. . .	. . .	. . .	. . .	. . .	431	412	188
Transportation services, debit	3 205 . .	**–966**	**–1,197**	**–1,265**	**–1,219**	**. . .**	**–2,390**	**–4,088**	**–4,794**
Passenger	3 850 . .	*–130*	*–172*	*–186*	*–210*	. . .	*–23*	*–6*	*–12*
Freight	3 851 . .	*–675*	*–826*	*–870*	*–853*	. . .	*–284*	*–186*	*–247*
Other	3 852 . .	*–161*	*–199*	*–209*	*–156*	. . .	*–2,083*	*–3,896*	*–4,535*
Sea transport, passenger	3 207 . .	. . .	. . .	. . .	. . .	. . .	–23	–6	–12
Sea transport, freight	3 208 . .	. . .	. . .	. . .	. . .	. . .	–284	–185	–246
Sea transport, other	3 209 . .	. . .	. . .	. . .	. . .	. . .	–1,455	–3,100	–3,622
Air transport, passenger	3 211 . .	. . .	. . .	. . .	. . .	. . .	. . .	. . .	. . .
Air transport, freight	3 212 . .	. . .	. . .	. . .	. . .	. . .	. . .	. . .	. . .
Air transport, other	3 213 . .	. . .	. . .	. . .	. . .	. . .	. . .	. . .	–371
Other transport, passenger	3 215 . .	. . .	. . .	. . .	. . .	. . .	. . .	. . .	. . .
Other transport, freight	3 216 . .	. . .	. . .	. . .	. . .	. . .	1	–1	–1
Other transport, other	3 217 . .	. . .	. . .	. . .	. . .	. . .	–628	–796	–542
Travel, credit	2 236 . .	**3,905**	**4,135**	**3,723**	**3,773**	**. . .**	**8,786**	**9,219**	**9,155**
Business travel	2 237 . .	. . .	. . .	. . .	. . .	. . .	2,161	2,820	2,611
Personal travel	2 240 . .	. . .	. . .	. . .	. . .	. . .	6,625	6,399	6,544
Travel, debit	3 236 . .	**–1,125**	**–1,323**	**–1,210**	**–1,327**	**. . .**	**–3,991**	**–4,558**	**–4,177**
Business travel	3 237 . .	. . .	. . .	. . .	. . .	. . .	–1,199	–1,176	–991
Personal travel	3 240 . .	. . .	. . .	. . .	. . .	. . .	–2,792	–3,382	–3,186
Other services, credit	2 200 BA	**4,842**	**5,094**	**5,249**	**5,338**	**. . .**	**2,566**	**2,097**	**2,134**
Communications	2 245 . .	. . .	. . .	. . .	. . .	. . .	212	257	228
Construction	2 249 . .	. . .	. . .	. . .	. . .	. . .	339	233	211
Insurance	2 253 . .	17	24	28	26	. . .	146	169	120
Financial	2 260 . .	. . .	. . .	. . .	. . .	. . .	213	112	71
Computer and information	2 262 . .	. . .	. . .	. . .	. . .	. . .	145	89	82
Royalties and licence fees	2 266 . .	. . .	. . .	. . .	. . .	. . .	13	5	14
Other business services	2 268 . .	4,754	4,993	5,135	5,249	. . .	1,255	927	1,147
Personal, cultural, and recreational	2 287 . .	. . .	. . .	. . .	. . .	. . .	202	246	189
Government, n.i.e.	2 291 . .	71	77	86	63	. . .	42	58	72
Other services, debit	3 200 BA	**–1,683**	**–1,848**	**–1,763**	**–2,104**	**. . .**	**–2,870**	**–2,641**	**–2,618**
Communications	3 245 . .	. . .	. . .	. . .	. . .	. . .	–131	–288	–383
Construction	3 249 . .	. . .	. . .	. . .	. . .	. . .	–638	–417	–145
Insurance	3 253 . .	–151	–182	–201	–211	. . .	–167	–210	–240
Financial	3 260 . .	. . .	. . .	. . .	. . .	. . .	–130	–85	–54
Computer and information	3 262 . .	. . .	. . .	. . .	. . .	. . .	–197	–157	–125
Royalties and licence fees	3 266 . .	–46	–58	–57	–58	. . .	–205	–203	–225
Other business services	3 268 . .	–1,132	–1,243	–1,097	–1,381	. . .	–829	–754	–850
Personal, cultural, and recreational	3 287 . .	. . .	. . .	. . .	. . .	. . .	–154	–160	–196
Government, n.i.e.	3 291 . .	–354	–365	–408	–454	. . .	–420	–368	–400

Table 2 (Continued). STANDARD PRESENTATION, 1994–2001
(Millions of U.S. dollars)

	Code	1994	1995	1996	1997	1998	1999	2000	2001
C. INCOME	4 300 . .	–1,248	–1,684	–2,181	–1,632	. . .	–672	–885	–1,767
Total credit	2 300 . .	*1,099*	*1,312*	*1,156*	*1,208*	. . .	*2,577*	*2,807*	*1,885*
Total debit	3 300 . .	*–2,347*	*–2,996*	*–3,337*	*–2,840*	. . .	*–3,248*	*–3,692*	*–3,652*
Compensation of employees, credit	2 310 . .	**310**	**304**	**185**	**246**	**. . .**	**617**	**581**	**543**
Compensation of employees, debit	3 310 . .	**–222**	**–300**	**–319**	**–342**	**. . .**	**–246**	**–251**	**–251**
Investment income, credit	2 320 . .	**789**	**1,008**	**971**	**962**	**. . .**	**1,960**	**2,227**	**1,342**
Direct investment income	2 330 . .	45	22	62	33	. . .	108	48	44
Dividends and distributed branch profits	2 332 . .	45	22	62	33	. . .	98	42	42
Reinvested earnings and undistributed branch profits	2 333 . .	. . .	. . .	. . .	. . .	. . .	. . .	. . .	. . .
Income on debt (interest)	2 334 . .	. . .	. . .	. . .	. . .	. . .	10	6	2
Portfolio investment income	2 339 . .	. . .	. . .	. . .	. . .	. . .	291	356	170
Income on equity	2 340 . .	. . .	. . .	. . .	. . .	. . .	14	10	14
Income on bonds and notes	2 350 . .	. . .	. . .	. . .	. . .	. . .	236	325	155
Income on money market instruments	2 360 . .	. . .	. . .	. . .	. . .	. . .	41	21	1
Other investment income	2 370 . .	744	986	909	929	. . .	1,561	1,823	1,128
Investment income, debit	3 320 . .	**–2,125**	**–2,696**	**–3,018**	**–2,498**	**. . .**	**–3,002**	**–3,442**	**–3,401**
Direct investment income	3 330 . .	–141	–206	–199	–129	. . .	–156	–319	–241
Dividends and distributed branch profits	3 332 . .	–116	–193	–185	–112	. . .	–146	–294	–207
Reinvested earnings and undistributed branch profits	3 333 . .	–25	–13	–14	–17	. . .	. . .	. . .	. . .
Income on debt (interest)	3 334 . .	. . .	. . .	. . .	. . .	. . .	–10	–25	–34
Portfolio investment income	3 339 . .	. . .	. . .	. . .	. . .	. . .	–110	–212	–183
Income on equity	3 340 . .	. . .	. . .	. . .	. . .	. . .	–43	–96	–67
Income on bonds and notes	3 350 . .	. . .	. . .	. . .	. . .	. . .	–54	–104	–115
Income on money market instruments	3 360 . .	. . .	. . .	. . .	. . .	. . .	–12	–12	–1
Other investment income	3 370 . .	–1,984	–2,490	–2,819	–2,369	. . .	–2,736	–2,911	–2,977
D. CURRENT TRANSFERS	4 379 . .	6,936	8,008	8,022	7,510	. . .	4,073	3,352	3,587
Credit	2 379 . .	**6,964**	**8,039**	**8,053**	**7,538**	**. . .**	**4,957**	**4,116**	**4,592**
General government	2 380 . .	4,307	4,968	5,057	4,622	. . .	2,338	1,710	2,315
Other sectors	2 390 . .	2,657	3,071	2,996	2,916	. . .	2,619	2,406	2,277
Workers' remittances	2 391 . .	2,576	2,982	2,894	2,816	. . .	1,667	1,613	1,471
Other current transfers	2 392 . .	81	89	102	100	. . .	952	793	806
Debit	3 379 . .	**–28**	**–31**	**–31**	**–28**	**. . .**	**–884**	**–764**	**–1,005**
General government	3 380 . .	. . .	. . .	. . .	. . .	. . .	–185	–194	–451
Other sectors	3 390 . .	–28	–31	–31	–28	. . .	–699	–570	–554
Workers' remittances	3 391 . .	. . .	. . .	. . .	. . .	. . .	–385	–295	–285
Other current transfers	3 392 . .	–28	–31	–31	–28	. . .	–314	–275	–269
CAPITAL AND FINANCIAL ACCOUNT	4 996 . .	**594**	**3,185**	**4,443**	**4,634**	**. . .**	**7,253**	**10,369**	**8,389**
CAPITAL ACCOUNT	4 994 . .	**. . .**	**. . .**	**. . .**	**. . .**	**. . .**	**2,211**	**2,112**	**2,153**
Total credit	2 994 . .	. . .	. . .	. . .	. . .	. . .	*2,318*	*2,244*	*2,320*
Total debit	3 994 . .	. . .	. . .	. . .	. . .	. . .	*–107*	*–131*	*–167*
Capital transfers, credit	2 400 . .	**. . .**	**. . .**	**. . .**	**. . .**	**. . .**	**2,316**	**2,239**	**2,093**
General government	2 401 . .	. . .	. . .	. . .	. . .	. . .	2,233	2,116	1,940
Debt forgiveness	2 402 . .	. . .	. . .	. . .	. . .	. . .	6	9	18
Other capital transfers	2 410 . .	. . .	. . .	. . .	. . .	. . .	2,227	2,107	1,922
Other sectors	2 430 . .	. . .	. . .	. . .	. . .	. . .	83	123	153
Migrants' transfers	2 431 . .	. . .	. . .	. . .	. . .	. . .	. . .	. . .	. . .
Debt forgiveness	2 432 . .	. . .	. . .	. . .	. . .	. . .	12	9	6
Other capital transfers	2 440 . .	. . .	. . .	. . .	. . .	. . .	72	114	147
Capital transfers, debit	3 400 . .	**. . .**	**. . .**	**. . .**	**. . .**	**. . .**	**–105**	**–129**	**–145**
General government	3 401 . .	. . .	. . .	. . .	. . .	. . .	–46	–49	–32
Debt forgiveness	3 402 . .	. . .	. . .	. . .	. . .	. . .	–3	–5	–3
Other capital transfers	3 410 . .	. . .	. . .	. . .	. . .	. . .	–43	–45	–29
Other sectors	3 430 . .	. . .	. . .	. . .	. . .	. . .	–60	–80	–113
Migrants' transfers	3 431 . .	. . .	. . .	. . .	. . .	. . .	. . .	. . .	. . .
Debt forgiveness	3 432 . .	. . .	. . .	. . .	. . .	. . .	–9	–7	–8
Other capital transfers	3 440 . .	. . .	. . .	. . .	. . .	. . .	–51	–72	–105
Nonproduced nonfinancial assets, credit	2 480 . .	**. . .**	**. . .**	**. . .**	**. . .**	**. . .**	**2**	**4**	**227**
Nonproduced nonfinancial assets, debit	3 480 . .	**. . .**	**. . .**	**. . .**	**. . .**	**. . .**	**–2**	**–3**	**–22**

Table 2 (Continued). STANDARD PRESENTATION, 1994–2001
(Millions of U.S. dollars)

	Code	1994	1995	1996	1997	1998	1999	2000	2001
FINANCIAL ACCOUNT	4 995	**594**	**3,185**	**4,443**	**4,634**	...	**5,042**	**8,257**	**6,236**
A. DIRECT INVESTMENT	4 500	981	1,053	1,058	984	...	25	–1,015	974
Direct investment abroad	4 505	...	...	...	...	...	**–542**	**–2,099**	**–611**
Equity capital	4 510	...	...	...	...	...	–527	–2,071	–546
Claims on affiliated enterprises	4 515	...	...	...	...	...	–524	–2,092	–544
Liabilities to affiliated enterprises	4 520	...	...	...	...	...	–3	21	–2
Reinvested earnings	4 525	...	...	...	...	...	...	...	...
Other capital	4 530	...	...	...	...	...	–15	–27	–65
Claims on affiliated enterprises	4 535	...	...	...	...	...	–18	–19	–71
Liabilities to affiliated enterprises	4 540	...	...	...	...	...	3	–8	6
Direct investment in Greece	4 555	**981**	**1,053**	**1,058**	**984**	...	**567**	**1,083**	**1,585**
Equity capital	4 560	956	1,040	1,044	967	...	681	953	1,504
Claims on direct investors	4 565	...	...	...	...	...	595	958	1,501
Liabilities to direct investors	4 570	...	...	...	...	...	87	–5	3
Reinvested earnings	4 575	25	13	14	17	...	...	...	...
Other capital	4 580	...	...	...	...	...	–114	130	81
Claims on direct investors	4 585	...	...	...	...	...	–110	146	86
Liabilities to direct investors	4 590	...	...	...	...	...	–5	–16	–5
B. PORTFOLIO INVESTMENT	4 600	...	...	...	...	...	5,897	8,078	8,538
Assets	4 602	...	...	...	...	...	**–858**	**–1,184**	**–474**
Equity securities	4 610	...	...	...	...	...	–166	–846	–1,020
Monetary authorities	4 611	...	...	...	...	...	...	...	...
General government	4 612	...	...	...	...	...	...	...	...
Banks	4 613	...	...	...	...	...	–25	–79	–151
Other sectors	4 614	...	...	...	...	...	–140	–767	–869
Debt securities	4 619	...	...	...	...	...	–692	–338	546
Bonds and notes	4 620	...	...	...	...	...	–677	–308	546
Monetary authorities	4 621	...	...	...	...	...	...	...	–148
General government	4 622	...	...	...	...	...	...	...	...
Banks	4 623	...	...	...	...	...	–317	–133	304
Other sectors	4 624	...	...	...	...	...	–360	–175	390
Money market instruments	4 630	...	...	...	...	...	–15	–30	...
Monetary authorities	4 631	...	...	...	...	...	...	...	...
General government	4 632	...	...	...	...	...	...	...	...
Banks	4 633	...	...	...	...	...	–10	–35	...
Other sectors	4 634	...	...	...	...	...	–6	5	...
Liabilities	4 652	...	...	...	...	...	**6,754**	**9,262**	**9,012**
Equity securities	4 660	...	...	...	...	...	–2,589	1,637	1,829
Banks	4 663	...	...	...	...	...	–727	469	587
Other sectors	4 664	...	...	...	...	...	–1,861	1,168	1,242
Debt securities	4 669	...	...	...	...	...	9,343	7,625	7,183
Bonds and notes	4 670	...	...	...	...	...	9,190	7,734	7,298
Monetary authorities	4 671	...	...	...	...	...	...	...	...
General government	4 672	...	...	...	...	...	9,190	7,734	7,298
Banks	4 673	...	...	...	...	...	...	...	...
Other sectors	4 674	...	...	...	...	...	...	...	...
Money market instruments	4 680	...	...	...	...	...	153	–109	–115
Monetary authorities	4 681	...	...	...	...	...	...	...	...
General government	4 682	...	...	...	...	...	153	–243	–115
Banks	4 683	...	...	...	...	...	...	135	...
Other sectors	4 684	...	...	...	...	...	...	...	...
C. FINANCIAL DERIVATIVES	4 910	...	...	...	...	...	419	348	74
Monetary authorities	4 911	...	...	...	...	...	...	...	...
General government	4 912	...	...	...	...	...	...	...	...
Banks	4 913	...	...	...	...	...	419	348	74
Other sectors	4 914	...	...	...	...	...	...	...	...
Assets	4 900	...	...	...	...	...	...	...	...
Monetary authorities	4 901	...	...	...	...	...	...	...	...
General government	4 902	...	...	...	...	...	...	...	...
Banks	4 903	...	...	...	...	...	...	...	...
Other sectors	4 904	...	...	...	...	...	...	...	...
Liabilities	4 905	...	...	...	...	...	**419**	**348**	**74**
Monetary authorities	4 906	...	...	...	...	...	...	...	...
General government	4 907	...	...	...	...	...	...	...	...
Banks	4 908	...	...	...	...	...	419	348	74
Other sectors	4 909	...	...	...	...	...	...	...	...

Table 2 (Concluded). STANDARD PRESENTATION, 1994–2001
(Millions of U.S. dollars)

	Code	1994	1995	1996	1997	1998	1999	2000	2001
D. OTHER INVESTMENT	4 700	5,922	2,109	7,600	–865	...	1,137	3,419	–9,049
Assets	4 703	**...**	**...**	**...**	**980**	**...**	**–2,913**	**6,970**	**–1,539**
Trade credits	4 706	...	...	...	...	...	...	...	...
General government	4 707	...	...	...	...	...	...	...	...
of which: Short-term	4 709	...	...	...	...	...	...	...	...
Other sectors	4 710	...	...	...	...	...	...	...	...
of which: Short-term	4 712	...	...	...	...	...	...	...	...
Loans	4 714	...	...	...	980	...	–117	323	–311
Monetary authorities	4 715	...	...	...	...	...	...	...	...
of which: Short-term	4 718	...	...	...	...	...	...	...	...
General government	4 719	...	...	...	980	...	–117	323	–311
of which: Short-term	4 721	...	...	...	*980*	...	...	...	...
Banks	4 722	...	...	...	...	...	...	...	...
of which: Short-term	4 724	...	...	...	...	...	...	...	...
Other sectors	4 725	...	...	...	...	...	...	...	...
of which: Short-term	4 727	...	...	...	...	...	...	...	...
Currency and deposits	4 730	...	...	...	...	...	–2,513	6,520	–23
Monetary authorities	4 731	...	...	...	...	...	...	...	...
General government	4 732	...	...	...	...	...	–2,513	6,520	–23
Banks	4 733	...	...	...	...	...	...	...	...
Other sectors	4 734	...	...	...	...	...	...	...	...
Other assets	4 736	...	...	...	...	...	–283	127	–1,205
Monetary authorities	4 737	...	...	...	...	...	...	...	...
of which: Short-term	4 739	...	...	...	...	...	...	...	...
General government	4 740	...	...	...	...	...	–283	127	–1,205
of which: Short-term	4 742	...	...	...	...	...	...	...	...
Banks	4 743	...	...	...	...	...	...	...	...
of which: Short-term	4 745	...	...	...	...	...	...	...	...
Other sectors	4 746	...	...	...	...	...	...	...	...
of which: Short-term	4 748	...	...	...	...	...	...	...	...
Liabilities	4 753	**5,922**	**2,109**	**7,600**	**–1,845**	**...**	**4,050**	**–3,551**	**–7,511**
Trade credits	4 756	269	527	259	470	...	...	...	...
General government	4 757	...	...	...	...	...	...	...	...
of which: Short-term	4 759	...	...	...	...	...	...	...	...
Other sectors	4 760	269	527	259	470	...	...	...	...
of which: Short-term	4 762	*269*	*527*	*259*	*470*	...	...	...	...
Loans	4 764	5,216	4,539	6,273	6,111	...	2,771	–440	–2,277
Monetary authorities	4 765	–1,791	–2,385	–2,194	–2,570	...	...	...	...
of which: Use of Fund credit and loans from the Fund	4 766	...	...	...	...	...	...	...	...
of which: Short-term	4 768	...	...	...	...	...	...	...	...
General government	4 769	4,703	3,441	3,530	7,101	...	...	...	...
of which: Short-term	4 771	...	...	...	...	...	...	...	...
Banks	4 772	...	...	...	...	...	...	...	...
of which: Short-term	4 774	...	...	...	...	...	...	...	...
Other sectors	4 775	2,304	3,483	4,937	1,580	...	2,771	–440	–2,277
of which: Short-term	4 777	*–94*	...	...	...	...	...	...	...
Currency and deposits	4 780	60	–2,115	–603	–3,343	...	1,644	–3,425	–6,989
Monetary authorities	4 781	...	...	...	...	...	...	...	...
General government	4 782	...	...	...	...	...	...	...	...
Banks	4 783	60	–2,115	–603	–3,343	...	1,644	–3,425	–6,989
Other sectors	4 784	...	...	...	...	...	...	...	...
Other liabilities	4 786	377	–842	1,671	–5,083	...	–365	314	1,756
Monetary authorities	4 787	...	...	...	...	...	...	...	...
of which: Short-term	4 789	...	...	...	...	...	...	...	...
General government	4 790	...	...	...	...	...	...	...	...
of which: Short-term	4 792	...	...	...	...	...	...	...	...
Banks	4 793	29	5	5	–5	...	...	...	...
of which: Short-term	4 795	...	...	...	...	...	...	...	...
Other sectors	4 796	348	–847	1,666	–5,078	...	–365	314	1,756
of which: Short-term	4 798	...	...	...	...	...	...	...	...
E. RESERVE ASSETS	4 802	–6,309	23	–4,215	4,515	...	–2,435	–2,573	5,699
Monetary gold	4 812	51	–13	–9	2,438	...	–50	–24	180
Special drawing rights	4 811	...	...	–1	...	...	–5	–7	2
Reserve position in the Fund	4 810	...	...	...	...	...	–128	75	–72
Foreign exchange	4 803	–6,360	36	–4,205	2,077	...	–2,254	–2,616	5,589
Other claims	4 813	...	...	...	...	...	...	...	...
NET ERRORS AND OMISSIONS	4 998	**–448**	**–321**	**111**	**226**	**...**	**42**	**–550**	**1,011**

Table 3. INTERNATIONAL INVESTMENT POSITION (End–period stocks), 1994–2001

(Millions of U.S. dollars)

	Code	1994	1995	1996	1997	1998	1999	2000	2001
ASSETS	8 995 C.	...	...	...	...	55,491	59,106	57,195	61,344
Direct investment abroad	8 505 . .	**...**	**...**	**...**	**...**	**2,792**	**3,809**	**5,852**	**6,371**
Equity capital and reinvested earnings	8 506 . .	...	...	...	...	2,745	3,709	5,625	6,597
Claims on affiliated enterprises	8 507 . .	...	...	...	...	2,745	3,709	5,625	6,597
Liabilities to affiliated enterprises	8 508 . .	...	...	...	...	...	...	...	...
Other capital	8 530 . .	...	...	...	...	47	100	227	–226
Claims on affiliated enterprises	8 535 . .	...	...	...	...	47	100	227	–226
Liabilities to affiliated enterprises	8 540 . .	...	...	...	...	...	...	...	...
Portfolio investment	8 602 . .	**...**	**...**	**...**	**...**	**4,503**	**4,777**	**3,847**	**8,029**
Equity securities	8 610 . .	...	...	...	...	1,177	1,147	1,345	1,406
Monetary authorities	8 611 . .	...	...	...	...	...	...	...	...
General government	8 612 . .	...	...	...	...	...	...	...	...
Banks	8 613 . .	...	...	...	...	181	190	106	16
Other sectors	8 614 . .	...	...	...	...	996	957	1,239	1,390
Debt securities	8 619 . .	...	...	...	...	3,326	3,630	2,502	6,623
Bonds and notes	8 620 . .	...	...	...	...	3,314	3,627	2,479	6,514
Monetary authorities	8 621 . .	...	...	...	...	2,032	2,719	1,028	1,064
General government	8 622 . .	...	...	...	...	...	...	...	...
Banks	8 623 . .	...	...	...	...	422	428	913	2,806
Other sectors	8 624 . .	...	...	...	...	860	480	538	2,644
Money market instruments	8 630 . .	...	...	...	...	12	3	23	109
Monetary authorities	8 631 . .	...	...	...	...	...	...	...	...
General government	8 632 . .	...	...	...	...	...	...	...	...
Banks	8 633 . .	...	...	...	...	7	3	8	12
Other sectors	8 634 . .	...	...	...	...	5	...	15	97
Financial derivatives	8 900 . .	**...**	**...**	**...**	**...**	**12**	**13**	**12**	**15**
Monetary authorities	8 901 . .	...	...	...	...	...	...	...	...
General government	8 902 . .	...	...	...	...	...	...	...	...
Banks	8 903 . .	...	...	...	...	...	...	...	...
Other sectors	8 904 . .	...	...	...	...	12	13	12	15
Other investment	8 703 . .	**...**	**...**	**...**	**...**	**38,726**	**40,362**	**35,227**	**40,760**
Trade credits	8 706 . .	...	...	...	...	177	177	246	264
General government	8 707 . .	...	...	...	...	...	...	...	...
of which: Short-term	8 709 . .	...	...	...	...	...	...	...	...
Other sectors	8 710 . .	...	...	...	...	177	177	246	264
of which: Short-term	8 712 . .	...	...	...	...	...	...	...	...
Loans	8 714 . .	...	...	...	...	25,951	26,897	21,319	27,614
Monetary authorities	8 715 . .	...	...	...	...	7,239	6,016	411	5,505
of which: Short-term	8 718 . .	...	...	...	...	...	...	...	...
General government	8 719 . .	...	...	...	...	...	...	...	...
of which: Short-term	8 721 . .	...	...	...	...	...	...	...	...
Banks	8 722 . .	...	...	...	...	18,712	20,881	20,908	22,109
of which: Short-term	8 724 . .	...	...	...	...	...	...	...	...
Other sectors	8 725 . .	...	...	...	...	...	...	...	...
of which: Short-term	8 727 . .	...	...	...	...	...	...	...	...
Currency and deposits	8 730 . .	...	...	...	...	12,598	13,169	13,596	12,882
Monetary authorities	8 731 . .	...	...	...	...	...	...	...	...
General government	8 732 . .	...	...	...	...	...	...	...	...
Banks	8 733 . .	...	...	...	...	...	...	...	...
Other sectors	8 734 . .	...	...	...	...	12,598	13,169	13,596	12,882
Other assets	8 736 . .	...	...	...	...	...	119	66	...
Monetary authorities	8 737 . .	...	...	...	...	...	119	66	...
of which: Short-term	8 739 . .	...	...	...	...	...	...	...	...
General government	8 740 . .	...	...	...	...	...	...	...	...
of which: Short-term	8 742 . .	...	...	...	...	...	...	...	...
Banks	8 743 . .	...	...	...	...	...	...	...	...
of which: Short-term	8 745 . .	...	...	...	...	...	...	...	...
Other sectors	8 746 . .	...	...	...	...	...	...	...	...
of which: Short-term	8 748 . .	...	...	...	...	...	...	...	...
Reserve assets	8 802 . .	**...**	**...**	**...**	**...**	**9,458**	**10,145**	**12,257**	**6,169**
Monetary gold	8 812 . .	...	...	...	...	1,546	1,330	1,250	1,015
Special drawing rights	8 811 . .	...	...	1	...	...	5	12	10
Reserve position in the Fund	8 810 . .	166	169	163	153	270	391	297	357
Foreign exchange	8 803 . .	...	...	...	...	7,642	8,419	10,698	4,787
Other claims	8 813 . .	...	...	...	...	...	...	...	...

Table 3 (Concluded). INTERNATIONAL INVESTMENT POSITION (End–period stocks), 1994–2001
(Millions of U.S. dollars)

	Code	1994	1995	1996	1997	1998	1999	2000	2001
LIABILITIES	8 995 D.	...	...	...	...	91,539	100,463	105,246	108,844
Direct investment in Greece	8 555 ..	...	...	...	...	**13,084**	**15,387**	**12,480**	**12,006**
Equity capital and reinvested earnings	8 556 ..	...	...	...	...	11,954	14,548	11,551	10,536
Claims on direct investors	8 557 ..	...	...	...	...	...	...	...	...
Liabilities to direct investors	8 558 ..	...	...	...	...	11,954	14,548	11,551	10,536
Other capital	8 580 ..	...	...	...	...	1,130	839	929	1,470
Claims on direct investors	8 585 ..	...	...	...	...	...	...	...	...
Liabilities to direct investors	8 590 ..	...	...	...	...	1,130	839	929	1,470
Portfolio investment	8 652 ..	...	...	...	...	**45,330**	**51,152**	**55,665**	**54,640**
Equity securities	8 660 ..	...	...	...	...	12,001	15,211	9,584	8,575
Banks	8 663 ..	...	...	...	...	4,151	4,351	3,700	2,150
Other sectors	8 664 ..	...	...	...	...	7,850	10,860	5,884	6,425
Debt securities	8 669 ..	...	...	...	...	33,329	35,941	46,081	46,065
Bonds and notes	8 670 ..	...	...	...	...	31,898	35,218	45,734	45,913
Monetary authorities	8 671 ..	...	...	...	...	...	...	...	...
General government	8 672 ..	...	...	...	...	30,913	34,800	42,071	42,904
Banks	8 673 ..	...	...	...	...	...	...	...	...
Other sectors	8 674 ..	...	...	...	...	985	418	3,663	3,009
Money market instruments	8 680 ..	...	...	...	...	1,431	723	347	152
Monetary authorities	8 681 ..	...	...	...	...	...	...	...	...
General government	8 682 ..	...	...	...	...	1,431	723	347	152
Banks	8 683 ..	...	...	...	...	...	...	...	...
Other sectors	8 684 ..	...	...	...	...	...	...	...	...
Financial derivatives	8 905 ..	...	...	...	...	...	...	...	...
Monetary authorities	8 906 ..	...	...	...	...	...	...	...	...
General government	8 907 ..	...	...	...	...	...	...	...	...
Banks	8 908 ..	...	...	...	...	...	...	...	...
Other sectors	8 909 ..	...	...	...	...	...	...	...	...
Other investment	8 753 ..	...	...	...	...	**33,125**	**33,924**	**37,101**	**42,198**
Trade credits	8 756 ..	...	...	...	...	1,659	649	1,071	868
General government	8 757 ..	...	...	...	...	159	155	160	159
of which: Short-term	8 759 ..	...	...	...	...	...	...	...	...
Other sectors	8 760 ..	...	...	...	...	1,500	494	911	709
of which: Short-term	8 762 ..	...	...	...	...	...	...	...	...
Loans	8 764 ..	...	...	...	...	31,466	33,275	36,030	41,330
Monetary authorities	8 765 ..	...	...	...	...	...	...	...	7,132
of which: Use of Fund credit and loans from the Fund	8 766 ..	...	...	...	...	...	...	...	...
of which: Short-term	8 768 ..	...	...	...	...	...	...	...	*7,132*
General government	8 769 ..	...	...	...	...	7,912	7,490	8,863	10,946
of which: Short-term	8 771 ..	...	...	...	...	...	...	...	...
Banks	8 772 ..	...	...	...	...	15,384	16,551	18,846	14,935
of which: Short-term	8 774 ..	...	...	...	...	...	...	...	...
Other sectors	8 775 ..	...	...	...	...	8,170	9,234	8,321	8,317
of which: Short-term	8 777 ..	...	...	...	...	...	...	...	...
Currency and deposits	8 780 ..	...	...	...	...	...	...	...	...
Monetary authorities	8 781 ..	...	...	...	...	...	...	...	...
General government	8 782 ..	...	...	...	...	...	...	...	...
Banks	8 783 ..	...	...	...	...	...	...	...	...
Other sectors	8 784 ..	...	...	...	...	...	...	...	...
Other liabilities	8 786 ..	...	...	...	...	...	...	...	...
Monetary authorities	8 787 ..	...	...	...	...	...	...	...	...
of which: Short-term	8 789 ..	...	...	...	...	...	...	...	...
General government	8 790 ..	...	...	...	...	...	...	...	...
of which: Short-term	8 792 ..	...	...	...	...	...	...	...	...
Banks	8 793 ..	...	...	...	...	...	...	...	...
of which: Short-term	8 795 ..	...	...	...	...	...	...	...	...
Other sectors	8 796 ..	...	...	...	...	...	...	...	...
of which: Short-term	8 798 ..	...	...	...	...	...	...	...	...
NET INTERNATIONAL INVESTMENT POSITION	8 995 ..	...	...	...	...	**–36,048**	**–41,357**	**–48,051**	**–47,500**
Conversion rates: drachmas per U.S. dollar (end of period)	0 102 ..	**240.10**	**237.04**	**247.02**	**282.61**	**282.57**	**328.44**	**365.62**	...
Conversion rates: euros per U.S. dollar (end of period)	0 104 ..	...	...	...	...	...	**.995421**	**1.074691**	**1.134687**

Table 1. ANALYTIC PRESENTATION, 1994–2001
(Millions of U.S. dollars)

	Code	1994	1995	1996	1997	1998	1999	2000	2001
A. Current Account [1]	4 993 Z.	**–26.93**	**–40.84**	**–55.60**	**–67.15**	**–80.43**	**–46.60**	**–79.10**	**. . .**
Goods: exports f.o.b	2 100 . .	25.24	24.57	24.93	32.80	45.95	74.30	84.54	. . .
Goods: imports f.o.b	3 100 . .	–119.45	–129.78	–147.41	–154.90	–183.01	–184.57	–220.94	. . .
Balance on Goods	4 100 . .	*–94.21*	*–105.21*	*–122.49*	*–122.10*	*–137.06*	*–110.28*	*–136.40*	. . .
Services: credit	2 200 . .	101.53	99.19	106.69	106.14	119.77	148.49	151.30	. . .
Services: debit	3 200 . .	–41.26	–38.46	–45.77	–56.48	–69.27	–78.46	–83.31	. . .
Balance on Goods and Services	4 991 . .	*–33.94*	*–44.48*	*–61.57*	*–72.44*	*–86.56*	*–40.25*	*–68.41*	. . .
Income: credit	2 300 . .	3.61	4.91	4.68	4.70	4.13	4.33	5.08	. . .
Income: debit	3 300 . .	–12.43	–18.36	–20.08	–20.92	–27.19	–29.87	–35.88	. . .
Balance on Goods, Services, and Income	4 992 . .	*–42.76*	*–57.92*	*–76.97*	*–88.66*	*–109.62*	*–65.79*	*–99.21*	. . .
Current transfers: credit	2 379 Z.	19.75	21.58	25.46	25.53	34.19	26.76	30.35	. . .
Current transfers: debit	3 379 . .	–3.92	–4.50	–4.09	–4.01	–5.00	–7.57	–10.25	. . .
B. Capital Account [1]	4 994 Z.	**21.67**	**25.84**	**31.41**	**31.78**	**28.58**	**31.18**	**29.63**	**. . .**
Capital account: credit	2 994 Z.	23.04	27.28	31.41	33.42	30.36	33.10	31.71	. . .
Capital account: debit	3 994 . .	–1.38	–1.44	. . .	–1.64	–1.78	–1.92	–2.08	. . .
Total, Groups A Plus B	4 981 . .	*–5.26*	*–15.00*	*–24.19*	*–35.37*	*–51.86*	*–15.42*	*–49.47*	. . .
C. Financial Account [1]	4 995 W.	**4.06**	**3.10**	**26.19**	**55.08**	**57.14**	**33.63**	**68.69**	**. . .**
Direct investment abroad	4 505 . .	. . .	. . .	. . .	. . .	. . .	. . .	. . .	. . .
Direct investment in Grenada	4 555 Z.	19.31	19.98	16.96	33.50	48.69	41.55	37.41	. . .
Portfolio investment assets	4 602 . .	–.38	–.87	. . .	–.02	.04	–.36	–.07	. . .
Equity securities	4 610 . .	. . .	. . .	. . .	. . .	. . .	. . .	. . .	. . .
Debt securities	4 619 . .	. . .	. . .	. . .	. . .	. . .	. . .	. . .	. . .
Portfolio investment liabilities	4 652 Z.	. . .	. . .	. . .	. . .	–.11	.75	19.77	. . .
Equity securities	4 660 . .	. . .	. . .	. . .	. . .	. . .	. . .	. . .	. . .
Debt securities	4 669 Z.	. . .	. . .	. . .	. . .	. . .	. . .	. . .	. . .
Financial derivatives	4 910 . .	. . .	. . .	. . .	. . .	. . .	. . .	. . .	. . .
Financial derivatives assets	4 900 . .	. . .	. . .	. . .	. . .	. . .	. . .	. . .	. . .
Financial derivatives liabilities	4 905 . .	. . .	. . .	. . .	. . .	. . .	. . .	. . .	. . .
Other investment assets	4 703 . .	–23.59	–11.02	–6.51	–1.09	–1.71	–30.13	–11.07	. . .
Monetary authorities	4 701 . .	. . .	. . .	. . .	. . .	. . .	. . .	. . .	. . .
General government	4 704 . .	. . .	. . .	. . .	. . .	. . .	. . .	. . .	. . .
Banks	4 705 . .	. . .	. . .	. . .	. . .	. . .	. . .	. . .	. . .
Other sectors	4 728 . .	. . .	. . .	. . .	. . .	. . .	. . .	. . .	. . .
Other investment liabilities	4 753 W.	8.72	–4.99	15.74	22.69	10.23	21.82	22.66	. . .
Monetary authorities	4 753 WA	. . .	. . .	. . .	. . .	. . .	. . .	. . .	. . .
General government	4 753 ZB	. . .	. . .	. . .	. . .	. . .	. . .	. . .	. . .
Banks	4 753 ZC	. . .	. . .	. . .	. . .	. . .	. . .	. . .	. . .
Other sectors	4 753 ZD	. . .	. . .	. . .	. . .	. . .	. . .	. . .	. . .
Total, Groups A Through C	4 983 . .	*–1.20*	*–11.91*	*2.00*	*19.72*	*5.29*	*18.21*	*19.22*	. . .
D. Net Errors and Omissions	4 998 . .	**5.88**	**17.94**	**–1.55**	**–12.78**	**–1.10**	**–13.56**	**–12.61**	**. . .**
Total, Groups A Through D	4 984 . .	*4.68*	*6.03*	*.45*	*6.93*	*4.18*	*4.65*	*6.61*	. . .
E. Reserves and Related Items	4 802 A.	**–4.68**	**–6.03**	**–.45**	**–6.93**	**–4.18**	**–4.65**	**–6.61**	**. . .**
Reserve assets	4 802 . .	–4.68	–6.03	–.45	–6.93	–4.18	–4.65	–6.61	. . .
Use of Fund credit and loans	4 766 . .	. . .	. . .	. . .	. . .	. . .	. . .	. . .	. . .
Exceptional financing	4 920 . .	. . .	. . .	. . .	. . .	. . .	. . .	. . .	. . .
Conversion rates: Eastern Caribbean dollars per U.S. dollar	0 101 . .	**2.7000**	**2.7000**	**2.7000**	**2.7000**	**2.7000**	**2.7000**	**2.7000**	**2.7000**

[1] Excludes components that have been classified in the categories of Group E.

Table 2. STANDARD PRESENTATION, 1994–2001

(Millions of U.S. dollars)

	Code	1994	1995	1996	1997	1998	1999	2000	2001
CURRENT ACCOUNT	4 993 . .	**–26.93**	**–40.84**	**–55.60**	**–67.15**	**–80.43**	**–46.60**	**–79.10**	**. . .**
A. GOODS	4 100 . .	–94.21	–105.21	–122.49	–122.10	–137.06	–110.28	–136.40	. . .
Credit	2 100 . .	**25.24**	**24.57**	**24.93**	**32.80**	**45.95**	**74.30**	**84.54**	**. . .**
General merchandise: exports f.o.b.	2 110 . .	23.34	21.90	20.98	29.77	41.58	69.47	78.14	. . .
Goods for processing: exports f.o.b.	2 150 . .	. . .	. . .	. . .	. . .	. . .	. . .	. . .	. . .
Repairs on goods	2 160 . .	. . .	. . .	. . .	. . .	. . .	. . .	. . .	. . .
Goods procured in ports by carriers	2 170 . .	1.90	2.67	3.94	3.03	4.37	4.82	6.40	. . .
Nonmonetary gold	2 180 . .	. . .	. . .	. . .	. . .	. . .	. . .	. . .	. . .
Debit	3 100 . .	**–119.45**	**–129.78**	**–147.41**	**–154.90**	**–183.01**	**–184.57**	**–220.94**	**. . .**
General merchandise: imports f.o.b.	3 110 . .	–119.45	–129.78	–147.39	–154.90	–182.96	–184.52	–220.89	. . .
Goods for processing: imports f.o.b.	3 150 . .	. . .	. . .	. . .	. . .	. . .	. . .	. . .	. . .
Repairs on goods	3 160 . .	. . .	. . .	. . .	. . .	. . .	. . .	. . .	. . .
Goods procured in ports by carriers	3 170 . .	. . .	. . .	–.03	. . .	–.06	–.06	–.06	. . .
Nonmonetary gold	3 180 . .	. . .	. . .	. . .	. . .	. . .	. . .	. . .	. . .
B. SERVICES	4 200 . .	60.26	60.73	60.92	49.66	50.50	70.03	68.00	. . .
Total credit	2 200 . .	*101.53*	*99.19*	*106.69*	*106.14*	*119.77*	*148.49*	*151.30*	. . .
Total debit	3 200 . .	*–41.26*	*–38.46*	*–45.77*	*–56.48*	*–69.27*	*–78.46*	*–83.31*	. . .
Transportation services, credit	2 205 . .	**4.64**	**3.90**	**4.84**	**4.53**	**3.79**	**5.52**	**5.80**	**. . .**
Passenger	2 850 . .	. . .	. . .	. . .	. . .	. . .	. . .	. . .	. . .
Freight	2 851 . .	. . .	. . .	. . .	. . .	. . .	. . .	. . .	. . .
Other	2 852 . .	. . .	. . .	. . .	. . .	. . .	. . .	. . .	. . .
Sea transport, passenger	2 207 . .	. . .	. . .	. . .	. . .	. . .	. . .	. . .	. . .
Sea transport, freight	2 208 . .	. . .	. . .	. . .	. . .	. . .	. . .	. . .	. . .
Sea transport, other	2 209 . .	. . .	. . .	. . .	. . .	. . .	. . .	. . .	. . .
Air transport, passenger	2 211 . .	. . .	. . .	. . .	. . .	. . .	. . .	. . .	. . .
Air transport, freight	2 212 . .	. . .	. . .	. . .	. . .	. . .	. . .	. . .	. . .
Air transport, other	2 213 . .	. . .	. . .	. . .	. . .	. . .	. . .	. . .	. . .
Other transport, passenger	2 215 . .	. . .	. . .	. . .	. . .	. . .	. . .	. . .	. . .
Other transport, freight	2 216 . .	. . .	. . .	. . .	. . .	. . .	. . .	. . .	. . .
Other transport, other	2 217 . .	. . .	. . .	. . .	. . .	. . .	. . .	. . .	. . .
Transportation services, debit	3 205 . .	**–21.74**	**–20.71**	**–25.53**	**–27.63**	**–32.40**	**–30.25**	**–34.27**	**. . .**
Passenger	3 850 . .	. . .	. . .	. . .	. . .	. . .	. . .	. . .	. . .
Freight	3 851 . .	. . .	. . .	. . .	. . .	. . .	. . .	. . .	. . .
Other	3 852 . .	. . .	. . .	. . .	. . .	. . .	. . .	. . .	. . .
Sea transport, passenger	3 207 . .	. . .	. . .	. . .	. . .	. . .	. . .	. . .	. . .
Sea transport, freight	3 208 . .	. . .	. . .	. . .	. . .	. . .	. . .	. . .	. . .
Sea transport, other	3 209 . .	. . .	. . .	. . .	. . .	. . .	. . .	. . .	. . .
Air transport, passenger	3 211 . .	. . .	. . .	. . .	. . .	. . .	. . .	. . .	. . .
Air transport, freight	3 212 . .	. . .	. . .	. . .	. . .	. . .	. . .	. . .	. . .
Air transport, other	3 213 . .	. . .	. . .	. . .	. . .	. . .	. . .	. . .	. . .
Other transport, passenger	3 215 . .	. . .	. . .	. . .	. . .	. . .	. . .	. . .	. . .
Other transport, freight	3 216 . .	. . .	. . .	. . .	. . .	. . .	. . .	. . .	. . .
Other transport, other	3 217 . .	. . .	. . .	. . .	. . .	. . .	. . .	. . .	. . .
Travel, credit	2 236 . .	**77.61**	**76.23**	**78.74**	**78.43**	**83.11**	**88.18**	**92.50**	**. . .**
Business travel	2 237 . .	. . .	. . .	. . .	. . .	. . .	. . .	. . .	. . .
Personal travel	2 240 . .	. . .	. . .	. . .	. . .	. . .	. . .	. . .	. . .
Travel, debit	3 236 . .	**–4.24**	**–4.55**	**–4.91**	**–5.46**	**–5.71**	**–7.07**	**–7.67**	**. . .**
Business travel	3 237 . .	. . .	. . .	. . .	. . .	. . .	. . .	. . .	. . .
Personal travel	3 240 . .	. . .	. . .	. . .	. . .	. . .	. . .	. . .	. . .
Other services, credit	2 200 BA	**19.27**	**19.06**	**23.11**	**23.19**	**32.88**	**54.79**	**53.00**	**. . .**
Communications	2 245 . .	. . .	. . .	. . .	. . .	. . .	. . .	. . .	. . .
Construction	2 249 . .	. . .	. . .	. . .	. . .	. . .	. . .	. . .	. . .
Insurance	2 253 . .	1.18	1.13	.92	.70	1.47	2.04	3.20	. . .
Financial	2 260 . .	. . .	. . .	. . .	2.87	4.12	6.88	7.07	. . .
Computer and information	2 262 . .	. . .	. . .	. . .	. . .	. . .	. . .	. . .	. . .
Royalties and licence fees	2 266 . .	. . .	. . .	. . .	. . .	. . .	. . .	. . .	. . .
Other business services	2 268 . .	16.64	16.94	20.70	18.01	23.71	41.38	36.44	. . .
Personal, cultural, and recreational	2 287 . .	. . .	. . .	. . .	. . .	. . .	. . .	. . .	. . .
Government, n.i.e.	2 291 . .	1.45	.99	1.49	1.60	3.58	4.49	6.29	. . .
Other services, debit	3 200 BA	**–15.29**	**–13.20**	**–15.33**	**–23.39**	**–31.16**	**–41.13**	**–41.37**	**. . .**
Communications	3 245 . .	. . .	. . .	. . .	. . .	. . .	. . .	. . .	. . .
Construction	3 249 . .	. . .	. . .	. . .	. . .	. . .	. . .	. . .	. . .
Insurance	3 253 . .	–3.94	–3.09	–3.51	–5.43	–6.30	–6.58	–8.22	. . .
Financial	3 260 . .	. . .	. . .	. . .	. . .	. . .	. . .	. . .	. . .
Computer and information	3 262 . .	. . .	. . .	. . .	. . .	. . .	. . .	. . .	. . .
Royalties and licence fees	3 266 . .	–.27	–.23	–.51	–.51	–.60	–.61	–.61	. . .
Other business services	3 268 . .	–8.77	–7.94	–9.20	–14.60	–18.43	–30.06	–28.49	. . .
Personal, cultural, and recreational	3 287 . .	. . .	. . .	. . .	. . .	. . .	. . .	. . .	. . .
Government, n.i.e.	3 291 . .	–2.32	–1.94	–2.12	–2.84	–5.83	–3.88	–4.05	. . .

Table 2 (Continued). STANDARD PRESENTATION, 1994–2001

(Millions of U.S. dollars)

	Code	1994	1995	1996	1997	1998	1999	2000	2001
C. INCOME	4 300 . .	-8.81	-13.44	-15.40	-16.22	-23.06	-25.54	-30.80	. . .
Total credit	2 300 . .	*3.61*	*4.91*	*4.68*	*4.70*	*4.13*	*4.33*	*5.08*	. . .
Total debit	3 300 . .	*-12.43*	*-18.36*	*-20.08*	*-20.92*	*-27.19*	*-29.87*	*-35.88*	. . .
Compensation of employees, credit	2 310 . .	**.08**	**.09**	**.01**	**.04**	**.05**	**.04**	**.01**	**. . .**
Compensation of employees, debit	3 310 . .	**-.02**	**-.03**	**. . .**	**-.02**	**-.02**	**. . .**	**. . .**	**. . .**
Investment income, credit	2 320 . .	**3.54**	**4.83**	**4.67**	**4.66**	**4.09**	**4.29**	**5.07**	**. . .**
Direct investment income	2 330 . .	.05	.05	.10	.06	.08	.24	.19	. . .
Dividends and distributed branch profits	2 332 . .	. . .	. . .	. . .	. . .	. . .	. . .	. . .	. . .
Reinvested earnings and undistributed branch profits	2 333 . .	. . .	. . .	. . .	. . .	. . .	. . .	. . .	. . .
Income on debt (interest)	2 334 . .	.05	.05	.10	.06	.08	.24	.19	. . .
Portfolio investment income	2 339 . .	.74	1.81	1.70	1.24	1.37	.64	1.02	. . .
Income on equity	2 340 . .	.74	1.81	1.70	1.24	1.37	.64	1.02	. . .
Income on bonds and notes	2 350 . .	. . .	. . .	. . .	. . .	. . .	. . .	. . .	. . .
Income on money market instruments	2 360 . .	. . .	. . .	. . .	. . .	. . .	. . .	. . .	. . .
Other investment income	2 370 . .	2.74	2.97	2.87	3.35	2.64	3.41	3.86	. . .
Investment income, debit	3 320 . .	**-12.41**	**-18.33**	**-20.08**	**-20.90**	**-27.17**	**-29.87**	**-35.88**	**. . .**
Direct investment income	3 330 . .	-7.60	-12.59	-14.13	-15.59	-19.83	-20.93	-27.79	. . .
Dividends and distributed branch profits	3 332 . .	-4.59	-6.64	-5.11	-6.71	-10.04	-8.19	-12.85	. . .
Reinvested earnings and undistributed branch profits	3 333 . .	-1.75	-4.10	-7.51	-8.22	-9.28	-12.31	-14.53	. . .
Income on debt (interest)	3 334 . .	-1.26	-1.84	-1.51	-.66	-.50	-.43	-.41	. . .
Portfolio investment income	3 339 . .	. . .	. . .	. . .	. . .	. . .	. . .	. . .	. . .
Income on equity	3 340 . .	. . .	. . .	. . .	. . .	. . .	. . .	. . .	. . .
Income on bonds and notes	3 350 . .	. . .	. . .	. . .	. . .	. . .	. . .	. . .	. . .
Income on money market instruments	3 360 . .	. . .	. . .	. . .	. . .	. . .	. . .	. . .	. . .
Other investment income	3 370 . .	-4.81	-5.74	-5.95	-5.31	-7.34	-8.94	-8.09	. . .
D. CURRENT TRANSFERS	4 379 . .	15.83	17.08	21.37	21.51	29.19	19.19	20.10	. . .
Credit	2 379 . .	**19.75**	**21.58**	**25.46**	**25.53**	**34.19**	**26.76**	**30.35**	**. . .**
General government	2 380 . .	5.41	1.26	3.77	3.55	12.03	2.94	5.94	. . .
Other sectors	2 390 . .	14.34	20.32	21.69	21.98	22.16	23.82	24.41	. . .
Workers' remittances	2 391 . .	. . .	. . .	. . .	. . .	. . .	. . .	. . .	. . .
Other current transfers	2 392 . .	. . .	. . .	. . .	. . .	. . .	. . .	. . .	. . .
Debit	3 379 . .	**-3.92**	**-4.50**	**-4.09**	**-4.01**	**-5.00**	**-7.57**	**-10.25**	**. . .**
General government	3 380 . .	-1.88	-1.88	-1.71	-2.16	-2.69	-3.37	-3.65	. . .
Other sectors	3 390 . .	-2.04	-2.61	-2.38	-1.86	-2.31	-4.20	-6.60	. . .
Workers' remittances	3 391 . .	. . .	. . .	. . .	. . .	. . .	. . .	. . .	. . .
Other current transfers	3 392 . .	. . .	. . .	. . .	. . .	. . .	. . .	. . .	. . .
CAPITAL AND FINANCIAL ACCOUNT	4 996 . .	**21.05**	**22.90**	**57.15**	**79.93**	**81.54**	**60.17**	**91.72**	**. . .**
CAPITAL ACCOUNT	4 994 . .	**21.67**	**25.84**	**31.41**	**31.78**	**28.58**	**31.18**	**29.63**	**. . .**
Total credit	2 994 . .	*23.04*	*27.28*	*31.41*	*33.42*	*30.36*	*33.10*	*31.71*	. . .
Total debit	3 994 . .	*-1.38*	*-1.44*	. . .	*-1.64*	*-1.78*	*-1.92*	*-2.08*	. . .
Capital transfers, credit	2 400 . .	**23.04**	**27.28**	**31.41**	**33.42**	**30.36**	**33.10**	**31.71**	**. . .**
General government	2 401 . .	10.48	9.38	11.09	13.60	10.04	11.52	9.57	. . .
Debt forgiveness	2 402 . .	. . .	. . .	. . .	. . .	. . .	. . .	. . .	. . .
Other capital transfers	2 410 . .	10.48	9.38	11.09	13.60	10.04	11.52	9.57	. . .
Other sectors	2 430 . .	12.56	17.90	20.32	19.82	20.32	21.58	22.14	. . .
Migrants' transfers	2 431 . .	12.56	17.90	20.32	19.82	20.32	21.33	22.14	. . .
Debt forgiveness	2 432 . .	. . .	. . .	. . .	. . .	. . .	. . .	. . .	. . .
Other capital transfers	2 440 . .	. . .	. . .	. . .	. . .	. . .	.25	. . .	. . .
Capital transfers, debit	3 400 . .	**-1.38**	**-1.44**	**. . .**	**-1.64**	**-1.78**	**-1.92**	**-2.08**	**. . .**
General government	3 401 . .	. . .	. . .	. . .	. . .	. . .	. . .	. . .	. . .
Debt forgiveness	3 402 . .	. . .	. . .	. . .	. . .	. . .	. . .	. . .	. . .
Other capital transfers	3 410 . .	. . .	. . .	. . .	. . .	. . .	. . .	. . .	. . .
Other sectors	3 430 . .	-1.38	-1.44	. . .	-1.64	-1.78	-1.92	-2.08	. . .
Migrants' transfers	3 431 . .	-1.38	-1.44	. . .	-1.64	-1.78	-1.92	-2.08	. . .
Debt forgiveness	3 432 . .	. . .	. . .	. . .	. . .	. . .	. . .	. . .	. . .
Other capital transfers	3 440 . .	. . .	. . .	. . .	. . .	. . .	. . .	. . .	. . .
Nonproduced nonfinancial assets, credit	2 480 . .	**. . .**	**. . .**	**. . .**	**. . .**	**. . .**	**. . .**	**. . .**	**. . .**
Nonproduced nonfinancial assets, debit	3 480 . .	**. . .**	**. . .**	**. . .**	**. . .**	**. . .**	**. . .**	**. . .**	**. . .**

Table 2 (Continued). STANDARD PRESENTATION, 1994–2001
(Millions of U.S. dollars)

	Code		1994	1995	1996	1997	1998	1999	2000	2001
FINANCIAL ACCOUNT	4 995	. .	**–.62**	**–2.93**	**25.75**	**48.15**	**52.96**	**28.99**	**62.08**	**. . .**
A. DIRECT INVESTMENT	4 500	. .	19.31	19.98	16.96	33.50	48.69	41.55	37.41	. . .
Direct investment abroad	4 505	. .	**. . .**	**. . .**	**. . .**	**. . .**	**. . .**	**. . .**	**. . .**	**. . .**
Equity capital	4 510	. .	. . .	. . .	. . .	. . .	. . .	. . .	. . .	. . .
Claims on affiliated enterprises	4 515	. .	. . .	. . .	. . .	. . .	. . .	. . .	. . .	. . .
Liabilities to affiliated enterprises	4 520	. .	. . .	. . .	. . .	. . .	. . .	. . .	. . .	. . .
Reinvested earnings	4 525	. .	. . .	. . .	. . .	. . .	. . .	. . .	. . .	. . .
Other capital	4 530	. .	. . .	. . .	. . .	. . .	. . .	. . .	. . .	. . .
Claims on affiliated enterprises	4 535	. .	. . .	. . .	. . .	. . .	. . .	. . .	. . .	. . .
Liabilities to affiliated enterprises	4 540	. .	. . .	. . .	. . .	. . .	. . .	. . .	. . .	. . .
Direct investment in Grenada	4 555	. .	**19.31**	**19.98**	**16.96**	**33.50**	**48.69**	**41.55**	**37.41**	**. . .**
Equity capital	4 560	. .	15.38	16.94	10.89	8.51	8.16	8.47	6.56	. . .
Claims on direct investors	4 565	. .	. . .	. . .	. . .	. . .	. . .	. . .	. . .	. . .
Liabilities to direct investors	4 570	. .	15.38	16.94	10.89	8.51	8.16	8.47	6.56	. . .
Reinvested earnings	4 575	. .	1.75	4.10	7.51	8.22	9.28	12.31	14.53	. . .
Other capital	4 580	. .	2.18	–1.07	–1.44	16.77	31.25	20.77	16.32	. . .
Claims on direct investors	4 585	. .	. . .	. . .	. . .	. . .	. . .	. . .	. . .	. . .
Liabilities to direct investors	4 590	. .	2.18	–1.07	–1.44	16.77	31.25	20.77	16.32	. . .
B. PORTFOLIO INVESTMENT	4 600	. .	–.38	–.87	. . .	–.02	–.07	.40	19.70	. . .
Assets	4 602	. .	**–.38**	**–.87**	**. . .**	**–.02**	**.04**	**–.36**	**–.07**	**. . .**
Equity securities	4 610	. .	. . .	. . .	. . .	. . .	. . .	. . .	. . .	. . .
Monetary authorities	4 611	. .	. . .	. . .	. . .	. . .	. . .	. . .	. . .	. . .
General government	4 612	. .	. . .	. . .	. . .	. . .	. . .	. . .	. . .	. . .
Banks	4 613	. .	. . .	. . .	. . .	. . .	. . .	. . .	. . .	. . .
Other sectors	4 614	. .	. . .	. . .	. . .	. . .	. . .	. . .	. . .	. . .
Debt securities	4 619	. .	. . .	. . .	. . .	. . .	. . .	. . .	. . .	. . .
Bonds and notes	4 620	. .	. . .	. . .	. . .	. . .	. . .	. . .	. . .	. . .
Monetary authorities	4 621	. .	. . .	. . .	. . .	. . .	. . .	. . .	. . .	. . .
General government	4 622	. .	. . .	. . .	. . .	. . .	. . .	. . .	. . .	. . .
Banks	4 623	. .	. . .	. . .	. . .	. . .	. . .	. . .	. . .	. . .
Other sectors	4 624	. .	. . .	. . .	. . .	. . .	. . .	. . .	. . .	. . .
Money market instruments	4 630	. .	. . .	. . .	. . .	. . .	. . .	. . .	. . .	. . .
Monetary authorities	4 631	. .	. . .	. . .	. . .	. . .	. . .	. . .	. . .	. . .
General government	4 632	. .	. . .	. . .	. . .	. . .	. . .	. . .	. . .	. . .
Banks	4 633	. .	. . .	. . .	. . .	. . .	. . .	. . .	. . .	. . .
Other sectors	4 634	. .	. . .	. . .	. . .	. . .	. . .	. . .	. . .	. . .
Liabilities	4 652	. .	**. . .**	**. . .**	**. . .**	**. . .**	**–.11**	**.75**	**19.77**	**. . .**
Equity securities	4 660	. .	. . .	. . .	. . .	. . .	. . .	. . .	. . .	. . .
Banks	4 663	. .	. . .	. . .	. . .	. . .	. . .	. . .	. . .	. . .
Other sectors	4 664	. .	. . .	. . .	. . .	. . .	. . .	. . .	. . .	. . .
Debt securities	4 669	. .	. . .	. . .	. . .	. . .	. . .	. . .	. . .	. . .
Bonds and notes	4 670	. .	. . .	. . .	. . .	. . .	. . .	. . .	. . .	. . .
Monetary authorities	4 671	. .	. . .	. . .	. . .	. . .	. . .	. . .	. . .	. . .
General government	4 672	. .	. . .	. . .	. . .	. . .	. . .	. . .	. . .	. . .
Banks	4 673	. .	. . .	. . .	. . .	. . .	. . .	. . .	. . .	. . .
Other sectors	4 674	. .	. . .	. . .	. . .	. . .	. . .	. . .	. . .	. . .
Money market instruments	4 680	. .	. . .	. . .	. . .	. . .	. . .	. . .	. . .	. . .
Monetary authorities	4 681	. .	. . .	. . .	. . .	. . .	. . .	. . .	. . .	. . .
General government	4 682	. .	. . .	. . .	. . .	. . .	. . .	. . .	. . .	. . .
Banks	4 683	. .	. . .	. . .	. . .	. . .	. . .	. . .	. . .	. . .
Other sectors	4 684	. .	. . .	. . .	. . .	. . .	. . .	. . .	. . .	. . .
C. FINANCIAL DERIVATIVES	4 910	. .	. . .	. . .	. . .	. . .	. . .	. . .	. . .	. . .
Monetary authorities	4 911	. .	. . .	. . .	. . .	. . .	. . .	. . .	. . .	. . .
General government	4 912	. .	. . .	. . .	. . .	. . .	. . .	. . .	. . .	. . .
Banks	4 913	. .	. . .	. . .	. . .	. . .	. . .	. . .	. . .	. . .
Other sectors	4 914	. .	. . .	. . .	. . .	. . .	. . .	. . .	. . .	. . .
Assets	4 900	. .	**. . .**	**. . .**	**. . .**	**. . .**	**. . .**	**. . .**	**. . .**	**. . .**
Monetary authorities	4 901	. .	. . .	. . .	. . .	. . .	. . .	. . .	. . .	. . .
General government	4 902	. .	. . .	. . .	. . .	. . .	. . .	. . .	. . .	. . .
Banks	4 903	. .	. . .	. . .	. . .	. . .	. . .	. . .	. . .	. . .
Other sectors	4 904	. .	. . .	. . .	. . .	. . .	. . .	. . .	. . .	. . .
Liabilities	4 905	. .	**. . .**	**. . .**	**. . .**	**. . .**	**. . .**	**. . .**	**. . .**	**. . .**
Monetary authorities	4 906	. .	. . .	. . .	. . .	. . .	. . .	. . .	. . .	. . .
General government	4 907	. .	. . .	. . .	. . .	. . .	. . .	. . .	. . .	. . .
Banks	4 908	. .	. . .	. . .	. . .	. . .	. . .	. . .	. . .	. . .
Other sectors	4 909	. .	. . .	. . .	. . .	. . .	. . .	. . .	. . .	. . .

Table 2 (Concluded). STANDARD PRESENTATION, 1994–2001

(Millions of U.S. dollars)

	Code	1994	1995	1996	1997	1998	1999	2000	2001
D. OTHER INVESTMENT	4 700 . .	–14.87	–16.01	9.23	21.60	8.52	–8.31	11.59	...
Assets	4 703 . .	**–23.59**	**–11.02**	**–6.51**	**–1.09**	**–1.71**	**–30.13**	**–11.07**	**...**
Trade credits	4 706 . .	...	...	...	...	...	...	...	...
General government	4 707 . .	...	...	...	...	...	...	...	...
of which: Short-term	4 709 . .	...	...	...	...	...	...	...	...
Other sectors	4 710 . .	...	...	...	...	...	...	...	...
of which: Short-term	4 712 . .	...	...	...	...	...	...	...	...
Loans	4 714 . .	...	...	...	...	...	...	...	...
Monetary authorities	4 715 . .	...	...	...	...	...	...	...	...
of which: Short-term	4 718 . .	...	...	...	...	...	...	...	...
General government	4 719 . .	...	...	...	...	...	...	...	...
of which: Short-term	4 721 . .	...	...	...	...	...	...	...	...
Banks	4 722 . .	...	...	...	...	...	...	...	...
of which: Short-term	4 724 . .	...	...	...	...	...	...	...	...
Other sectors	4 725 . .	...	...	...	...	...	...	...	...
of which: Short-term	4 727 . .	...	...	...	...	...	...	...	...
Currency and deposits	4 730 . .	...	...	...	...	...	...	...	...
Monetary authorities	4 731 . .	...	...	...	...	...	...	...	...
General government	4 732 . .	...	...	...	...	...	...	...	...
Banks	4 733 . .	...	...	...	...	...	...	...	...
Other sectors	4 734 . .	...	...	...	...	...	...	...	...
Other assets	4 736 . .	...	...	...	...	...	...	...	...
Monetary authorities	4 737 . .	...	...	...	...	...	...	...	...
of which: Short-term	4 739 . .	...	...	...	...	...	...	...	...
General government	4 740 . .	...	...	...	...	...	...	...	...
of which: Short-term	4 742 . .	...	...	...	...	...	...	...	...
Banks	4 743 . .	...	...	...	...	...	...	...	...
of which: Short-term	4 745 . .	...	...	...	...	...	...	...	...
Other sectors	4 746 . .	...	...	...	...	...	...	...	...
of which: Short-term	4 748 . .	...	...	...	...	...	...	...	...
Liabilities	4 753 . .	**8.72**	**–4.99**	**15.74**	**22.69**	**10.23**	**21.82**	**22.66**	**...**
Trade credits	4 756 . .	...	...	...	...	...	...	...	...
General government	4 757 . .	...	...	...	...	...	...	...	...
of which: Short-term	4 759 . .	...	...	...	...	...	...	...	...
Other sectors	4 760 . .	...	...	...	...	...	...	...	...
of which: Short-term	4 762 . .	...	...	...	...	...	...	...	...
Loans	4 764 . .	...	...	...	...	...	...	...	...
Monetary authorities	4 765 . .	...	...	...	...	...	...	...	...
of which: Use of Fund credit and loans from the Fund	4 766 . .	...	...	...	...	...	...	...	...
of which: Short-term	4 768 . .	...	...	...	...	...	...	...	...
General government	4 769 . .	...	...	...	...	...	...	...	...
of which: Short-term	4 771 . .	...	...	...	...	...	...	...	...
Banks	4 772 . .	...	...	...	...	...	...	...	...
of which: Short-term	4 774 . .	...	...	...	...	...	...	...	...
Other sectors	4 775 . .	...	...	...	...	...	...	...	...
of which: Short-term	4 777 . .	...	...	...	...	...	...	...	...
Currency and deposits	4 780 . .	...	...	...	...	...	...	...	...
Monetary authorities	4 781 . .	...	...	...	...	...	...	...	...
General government	4 782 . .	...	...	...	...	...	...	...	...
Banks	4 783 . .	...	...	...	...	...	...	...	...
Other sectors	4 784 . .	...	...	...	...	...	...	...	...
Other liabilities	4 786 . .	...	...	...	...	...	...	...	...
Monetary authorities	4 787 . .	...	...	...	...	...	...	...	...
of which: Short-term	4 789 . .	...	...	...	...	...	...	...	...
General government	4 790 . .	...	...	...	...	...	...	...	...
of which: Short-term	4 792 . .	...	...	...	...	...	...	...	...
Banks	4 793 . .	...	...	...	...	...	...	...	...
of which: Short-term	4 795 . .	...	...	...	...	...	...	...	...
Other sectors	4 796 . .	...	...	...	...	...	...	...	...
of which: Short-term	4 798 . .	...	...	...	...	...	...	...	...
E. RESERVE ASSETS	4 802 . .	–4.68	–6.03	–.45	–6.93	–4.18	–4.65	–6.61	...
Monetary gold	4 812 . .	...	...	...	...	...	...	...	...
Special drawing rights	4 811 . .	–.03	.01	–.04	.05	–.03	.04	...	...
Reserve position in the Fund	4 810 . .	...	...	...	...	...	...	...	...
Foreign exchange	4 803 . .	–4.24	–5.55	1.04	–6.98	–4.15	–4.03	–6.83	...
Other claims	4 813 . .	–.41	–.48	–1.45	...	...	–.66	.22	...
NET ERRORS AND OMISSIONS	4 998 . .	**5.88**	**17.94**	**–1.55**	**–12.78**	**–1.10**	**–13.56**	**–12.61**	**...**

Part 3 of the *Yearbook* contains descriptions of the methodologies, compilation practices, and sources used to compile these data.

Table 1. ANALYTIC PRESENTATION, 1994–2001
(Millions of U.S. dollars)

	Code	1994	1995	1996	1997	1998	1999	2000	2001
A. Current Account [1]	4 993 Z.	**–625.3**	**–572.0**	**–451.5**	**–633.5**	**–1,039.1**	**–1,025.9**	**–1,049.6**	**–1,237.9**
Goods: exports f.o.b	2 100 . .	1,550.1	2,157.5	2,236.9	2,602.9	2,846.9	2,780.6	3,085.1	2,864.6
Goods: imports f.o.b	3 100 . .	–2,546.6	–3,032.6	–2,880.3	–3,542.7	–4,255.7	–4,225.7	–4,742.0	–5,142.1
Balance on Goods	4 100 . .	*–996.5*	*–875.1*	*–643.4*	*–939.8*	*–1,408.8*	*–1,445.1*	*–1,656.9*	*–2,277.5*
Services: credit	2 200 . .	697.5	665.9	559.0	588.8	639.9	699.5	777.0	1,031.0
Services: debit	3 200 . .	–644.9	–694.9	–659.7	–650.5	–791.8	–790.7	–825.4	–898.0
Balance on Goods and Services	4 991 . .	*–943.9*	*–904.1*	*–744.1*	*–1,001.5*	*–1,560.7*	*–1,536.3*	*–1,705.3*	*–2,144.5*
Income: credit	2 300 . .	63.6	46.6	40.2	72.4	91.4	76.2	214.4	317.5
Income: debit	3 300 . .	–193.6	–205.7	–270.1	–311.1	–275.1	–280.7	–424.0	–407.6
Balance on Goods, Services, and Income	4 992 . .	*–1,073.9*	*–1,063.2*	*–974.0*	*–1,240.2*	*–1,744.4*	*–1,740.8*	*–1,914.9*	*–2,234.6*
Current transfers: credit	2 379 Z.	456.4	508.2	537.1	628.8	742.9	754.4	908.2	1,031.8
Current transfers: debit	3 379 . .	–7.8	–17.0	–14.6	–22.1	–37.6	–39.5	–42.9	–35.1
B. Capital Account [1]	4 994 Z.	**. . .**	**61.6**	**65.0**	**85.0**	**71.0**	**68.4**	**85.5**	**93.3**
Capital account: credit	2 994 Z.	. . .	61.6	65.0	85.0	71.0	68.4	85.5	93.3
Capital account: debit	3 994 . .	. . .	. . .	. . .	. . .	. . .	. . .	. . .	. . .
Total, Groups A Plus B	4 981 . .	*–625.3*	*–510.4*	*–386.5*	*–548.5*	*–968.1*	*–957.5*	*–964.1*	*–1,144.6*
C. Financial Account [1]	4 995 W.	**655.2**	**494.8**	**672.3**	**737.4**	**1,136.7**	**637.5**	**1,520.7**	**1,520.8**
Direct investment abroad	4 505 . .	. . .	. . .	. . .	. . .	. . .	. . .	. . .	. . .
Direct investment in Guatemala	4 555 Z.	65.2	75.2	76.9	84.4	672.8	154.6	229.9	455.5
Portfolio investment assets	4 602 . .	–9.8	–22.2	–11.5	–18.1	–11.6	–26.0	–36.3	–44.9
Equity securities	4 610 . .	. . .	. . .	. . .	. . .	. . .	. . .	. . .	. . .
Debt securities	4 619 . .	–9.8	–22.2	–11.5	–18.1	–11.6	–26.0	–36.3	–44.9
Portfolio investment liabilities	4 652 Z.	7.1	5.9	–4.5	249.7	65.8	136.5	78.9	175.4
Equity securities	4 660 . .	. . .	. . .	. . .	. . .	. . .	. . .	. . .	. . .
Debt securities	4 669 Z.	7.1	5.9	–4.5	249.7	65.8	136.5	78.9	175.4
Financial derivatives	4 910 . .	. . .	. . .	. . .	. . .	. . .	. . .	. . .	. . .
Financial derivatives assets	4 900 . .	. . .	. . .	. . .	. . .	. . .	. . .	. . .	. . .
Financial derivatives liabilities	4 905 . .	. . .	. . .	. . .	. . .	. . .	. . .	. . .	. . .
Other investment assets	4 703 . .	116.8	125.1	199.2	221.2	241.7	199.9	213.2	156.7
Monetary authorities	4 701 . .	. . .	. . .	. . .	. . .	. . .	. . .	. . .	. . .
General government	4 704 . .	–49.2	. . .	. . .	. . .	. . .	. . .	. . .	. . .
Banks	4 705 . .	. . .	. . .	. . .	. . .	. . .	. . .	. . .	. . .
Other sectors	4 728 . .	166.0	125.1	199.2	221.2	241.7	199.9	213.2	156.7
Other investment liabilities	4 753 W.	475.9	310.8	412.2	200.2	168.0	172.5	1,035.0	778.1
Monetary authorities	4 753 WA	–63.9	–78.3	–56.3	–108.6	–54.2	–25.6	–24.0	–11.3
General government	4 753 ZB	132.7	11.8	91.1	89.5	252.4	295.9	92.7	44.8
Banks	4 753 ZC	. . .	7.3	19.4	–4.6	3.2	23.0	–17.4	21.9
Other sectors	4 753 ZD	407.1	370.0	358.0	223.9	–33.4	–120.8	983.7	722.7
Total, Groups A Through C	4 983 . .	*29.9*	*–15.6*	*285.8*	*188.9*	*168.6*	*–320.0*	*556.6*	*376.2*
D. Net Errors and Omissions	4 998 . .	**–23.6**	**–136.2**	**–71.7**	**40.7**	**66.8**	**195.0**	**86.1**	**98.1**
Total, Groups A Through D	4 984 . .	*6.3*	*–151.8*	*214.1*	*229.6*	*235.4*	*–125.0*	*642.7*	*474.3*
E. Reserves and Related Items	4 802 A.	**–6.3**	**151.8**	**–214.1**	**–229.6**	**–235.4**	**125.0**	**–642.7**	**–474.3**
Reserve assets	4 802 . .	–47.3	157.3	–199.0	–257.7	–263.0	125.0	–642.7	–474.3
Use of Fund credit and loans	4 766 . .	. . .	. . .	. . .	. . .	. . .	. . .	. . .	. . .
Exceptional financing	4 920 . .	41.0	–5.5	–15.1	28.1	27.6	. . .	. . .	. . .
Conversion rates: quetzales per U.S. dollar	0 101 . .	**5.7512**	**5.8103**	**6.0495**	**6.0653**	**6.3947**	**7.3856**	**7.7632**	**7.8586**

[1] Excludes components that have been classified in the categories of Group E.

Table 2. STANDARD PRESENTATION, 1994–2001

(Millions of U.S. dollars)

	Code		1994	1995	1996	1997	1998	1999	2000	2001
CURRENT ACCOUNT	4 993	. .	**–625.3**	**–572.0**	**–451.5**	**–633.5**	**–1,039.1**	**–1,025.9**	**–1,049.6**	**–1,237.9**
A. GOODS	4 100	. .	–996.5	–875.1	–643.4	–939.8	–1,408.8	–1,445.1	–1,656.9	–2,277.5
Credit	2 100	. .	**1,550.1**	**2,157.5**	**2,236.9**	**2,602.9**	**2,846.9**	**2,780.6**	**3,085.1**	**2,864.6**
General merchandise: exports f.o.b.	2 110	. .	1,550.1	1,991.0	2,061.3	2,390.7	2,561.9	2,492.9	2,711.2	2,468.3
Goods for processing: exports f.o.b.	2 150	. .	. . .	166.5	175.6	212.2	285.0	287.7	373.9	396.3
Repairs on goods	2 160	. .	. . .	. . .	. . .	. . .	. . .	. . .	. . .	. . .
Goods procured in ports by carriers	2 170	. .	. . .	. . .	. . .	. . .	. . .	. . .	. . .	. . .
Nonmonetary gold	2 180	. .	. . .	. . .	. . .	. . .	. . .	. . .	. . .	. . .
Debit	3 100	. .	**–2,546.6**	**–3,032.6**	**–2,880.3**	**–3,542.7**	**–4,255.7**	**–4,225.7**	**–4,742.0**	**–5,142.1**
General merchandise: imports f.o.b.	3 110	. .	–2,546.6	–3,032.6	–2,880.3	–3,542.7	–4,255.7	–4,225.7	–4,742.0	–5,142.1
Goods for processing: imports f.o.b.	3 150	. .	. . .	. . .	. . .	. . .	. . .	. . .	. . .	. . .
Repairs on goods	3 160	. .	. . .	. . .	. . .	. . .	. . .	. . .	. . .	. . .
Goods procured in ports by carriers	3 170	. .	. . .	. . .	. . .	. . .	. . .	. . .	. . .	. . .
Nonmonetary gold	3 180	. .	. . .	. . .	. . .	. . .	. . .	. . .	. . .	. . .
B. SERVICES	4 200	. .	52.6	–29.0	–100.7	–61.7	–151.9	–91.2	–48.4	133.0
Total credit	2 200	. .	*697.5*	*665.9*	*559.0*	*588.8*	*639.9*	*699.5*	*777.0*	*1,031.0*
Total debit	3 200	. .	*–644.9*	*–694.9*	*–659.7*	*–650.5*	*–791.8*	*–790.7*	*–825.4*	*–898.0*
Transportation services, credit	2 205	. .	**39.8**	**53.7**	**62.4**	**76.8**	**89.2**	**83.0**	**82.4**	**99.8**
Passenger	2 850	. .	. . .	*3.3*	*5.2*	*3.7*	*14.9*	*18.4*	*16.4*	*25.6*
Freight	2 851	. .	*6.6*	*13.8*	*11.3*	*17.6*	*28.7*	*21.4*	*23.2*	*21.4*
Other	2 852	. .	*33.2*	*36.6*	*45.9*	*55.5*	*45.6*	*43.2*	*42.8*	*52.8*
Sea transport, passenger	2 207	. .	. . .	. . .	. . .	. . .	. . .	. . .	. . .	2.9
Sea transport, freight	2 208	. .	. . .	8.6	7.1	11.1	18.2	13.5	14.6	10.7
Sea transport, other	2 209	. .	. . .	2.7	4.4	5.8	2.6	1.7	1.5	4.7
Air transport, passenger	2 211	. .	. . .	2.7	4.2	3.1	12.2	15.1	13.5	9.2
Air transport, freight	2 212	. .	. . .	.8	.5	.9	1.3	1.1	1.2	.8
Air transport, other	2 213	. .	. . .	31.8	38.0	45.0	40.9	40.1	40.0	43.4
Other transport, passenger	2 215	. .	. . .	.6	1.0	.6	2.7	3.3	2.9	13.5
Other transport, freight	2 216	. .	. . .	4.4	3.7	5.6	9.2	6.8	7.4	9.9
Other transport, other	2 217	. .	. . .	2.1	3.5	4.7	2.1	1.4	1.3	4.7
Transportation services, debit	3 205	. .	**–255.9**	**–278.6**	**–286.9**	**–327.9**	**–418.8**	**–363.8**	**–421.6**	**–465.8**
Passenger	3 850	. .	*–18.3*	*–25.7*	*–28.0*	*–27.0*	*–33.0*	*–33.0*	*–34.3*	*–40.5*
Freight	3 851	. .	*–222.2*	*–251.7*	*–257.7*	*–299.6*	*–381.9*	*–327.3*	*–386.8*	*–423.9*
Other	3 852	. .	*–15.4*	*–1.2*	*–1.2*	*–1.3*	*–3.9*	*–3.5*	*–.5*	*–1.4*
Sea transport, passenger	3 207	. .	. . .	. . .	. . .	. . .	. . .	. . .	. . .	. . .
Sea transport, freight	3 208	. .	. . .	–159.1	–162.8	–189.3	–241.4	–206.8	–244.4	–294.7
Sea transport, other	3 209	. .	. . .	. . .	. . .	. . .	–.4	–.4	. . .	–.2
Air transport, passenger	3 211	. .	. . .	–24.6	–26.7	–26.4	–31.8	–32.0	–33.2	–35.7
Air transport, freight	3 212	. .	. . .	–12.0	–12.4	–14.4	–18.4	–15.7	–18.6	–36.2
Air transport, other	3 213	. .	. . .	. . .	. . .	. . .	. . .	. . .	. . .	. . .
Other transport, passenger	3 215	. .	. . .	–1.1	–1.3	–.6	–1.2	–1.0	–1.1	–4.8
Other transport, freight	3 216	. .	. . .	–80.6	–82.5	–95.9	–122.1	–104.8	–123.8	–93.0
Other transport, other	3 217	. .	. . .	–1.2	–1.2	–1.3	–3.5	–3.1	–.5	–1.2
Travel, credit	2 236	. .	**205.0**	**212.5**	**216.3**	**266.1**	**314.4**	**356.1**	**482.2**	**561.5**
Business travel	2 237	. .	53.6	1.8	1.3	1.6	1.1	1.6	3.3	76.8
Personal travel	2 240	. .	151.4	210.7	215.0	264.5	313.3	354.5	478.9	484.7
Travel, debit	3 236	. .	**–150.7**	**–141.1**	**–135.4**	**–118.7**	**–157.0**	**–183.2**	**–181.7**	**–195.7**
Business travel	3 237	. .	–33.3	–1.9	–3.3	–3.1	–2.2	–2.2	–2.2	–1.8
Personal travel	3 240	. .	–117.4	–139.2	–132.1	–115.6	–154.8	–181.0	–179.5	–193.9
Other services, credit	2 200	BA	**452.7**	**399.7**	**280.3**	**245.9**	**236.3**	**260.4**	**212.4**	**369.7**
Communications	2 245	. .	. . .	66.1	68.5	49.2	.5	.2	.3	25.6
Construction	2 249	. .	. . .	. . .	. . .	1.4	. . .	. . .	. . .	2.8
Insurance	2 253	. .	5.3	8.2	7.3	6.1	23.3	31.7	18.8	30.3
Financial	2 260	. .	. . .	17.0	26.7	6.5	7.6	4.4	5.1	8.7
Computer and information	2 262	. .	. . .	1.7	3.9	1.4	4.1	4.3	3.7	4.7
Royalties and licence fees	2 266	. .	. . .	. . .	. . .	. . .	. . .	. . .	. . .	. . .
Other business services	2 268	. .	408.4	268.5	148.3	134.8	141.5	173.6	109.2	200.4
Personal, cultural, and recreational	2 287	. .	. . .	. . .	. . .	. . .	. . .	. . .	. . .	.3
Government, n.i.e.	2 291	. .	39.0	38.2	25.6	46.5	59.3	46.2	75.3	96.9
Other services, debit	3 200	BA	**–238.3**	**–275.2**	**–237.4**	**–203.9**	**–216.0**	**–243.7**	**–222.1**	**–236.5**
Communications	3 245	. .	. . .	–6.5	–7.4	–4.5	–3.4	–1.3	–.8	–10.9
Construction	3 249	. .	. . .	–23.6	–11.3	–10.2	–1.3	–14.3	–4.9	–1.0
Insurance	3 253	. .	–31.2	–31.7	–24.9	–26.7	–27.4	–26.5	–59.9	–77.5
Financial	3 260	. .	. . .	–26.5	–25.0	–15.9	–12.8	–5.6	–4.5	–13.0
Computer and information	3 262	. .	. . .	–2.1	–2.1	–1.5	–4.5	–5.0	–4.3	–1.8
Royalties and licence fees	3 266	. .	. . .	. . .	. . .	. . .	. . .	. . .	. . .	. . .
Other business services	3 268	. .	–163.9	–162.3	–145.1	–121.2	–133.7	–160.0	–107.9	–95.2
Personal, cultural, and recreational	3 287	. .	. . .	. . .	. . .	. . .	–.2	. . .	. . .	–.3
Government, n.i.e.	3 291	. .	–43.2	–22.5	–21.6	–23.9	–32.7	–31.0	–39.8	–36.8

Table 2 (Continued). STANDARD PRESENTATION, 1994–2001

(Millions of U.S. dollars)

	Code	1994	1995	1996	1997	1998	1999	2000	2001
C. INCOME	4 300 . .	−130.0	−159.1	−229.9	−238.7	−183.7	−204.5	−209.6	−90.1
Total credit	2 300 . .	*63.6*	*46.6*	*40.2*	*72.4*	*91.4*	*76.2*	*214.4*	*317.5*
Total debit	3 300 . .	*−193.6*	*−205.7*	*−270.1*	*−311.1*	*−275.1*	*−280.7*	*−424.0*	*−407.6*
Compensation of employees, credit	2 310 . .	**21.9**	**. . .**	**. . .**	**. . .**	**. . .**	**. . .**	**32.8**	**41.4**
Compensation of employees, debit	3 310 . .	**−3.2**	**. . .**	**. . .**	**. . .**	**. . .**	**. . .**	**−16.5**	**−11.4**
Investment income, credit	2 320 . .	**41.7**	**46.6**	**40.2**	**72.4**	**91.4**	**76.2**	**181.6**	**276.1**
Direct investment income	2 330 . .	6.8	11.9	14.5	22.4	43.4	18.5	77.7	80.4
Dividends and distributed branch profits	2 332 . .	6.8	7.0	3.8	11.3	2.2	1.9	49.8	53.6
Reinvested earnings and undistributed branch profits	2 333 . .	. . .	. . .	. . .	. . .	. . .	. . .	. . .	. . .
Income on debt (interest)	2 334 . .	. . .	4.9	10.7	11.1	41.2	16.6	27.9	26.8
Portfolio investment income	2 339 . .	. . .	. . .	. . .	. . .	. . .	. . .	. . .	. . .
Income on equity	2 340 . .	. . .	. . .	. . .	. . .	. . .	. . .	. . .	. . .
Income on bonds and notes	2 350 . .	. . .	. . .	. . .	. . .	. . .	. . .	. . .	. . .
Income on money market instruments	2 360 . .	. . .	. . .	. . .	. . .	. . .	. . .	. . .	. . .
Other investment income	2 370 . .	34.9	34.7	25.7	50.0	48.0	57.7	103.9	195.7
Investment income, debit	3 320 . .	**−190.4**	**−205.7**	**−270.1**	**−311.1**	**−275.1**	**−280.7**	**−407.5**	**−396.2**
Direct investment income	3 330 . .	−58.6	−95.3	−129.5	−163.7	−129.8	−150.2	−248.4	−205.1
Dividends and distributed branch profits	3 332 . .	−25.3	−35.2	−63.3	−99.5	−60.2	−88.8	−175.2	−118.0
Reinvested earnings and undistributed branch profits	3 333 . .	−33.3	−37.1	−37.4	−40.8	−45.9	−43.4	−48.9	−54.6
Income on debt (interest)	3 334 . .	. . .	−23.0	−28.8	−23.4	−23.7	−18.0	−24.3	−32.5
Portfolio investment income	3 339 . .	. . .	. . .	. . .	−14.4	−12.5	−23.6	−36.9	−54.5
Income on equity	3 340 . .	. . .	. . .	. . .	. . .	. . .	. . .	. . .	. . .
Income on bonds and notes	3 350 . .	. . .	. . .	. . .	−14.4	−12.5	−23.6	−36.9	−54.5
Income on money market instruments	3 360 . .	. . .	. . .	. . .	. . .	. . .	. . .	. . .	. . .
Other investment income	3 370 . .	−131.8	−110.4	−140.6	−133.0	−132.8	−106.9	−122.2	−136.6
D. CURRENT TRANSFERS	4 379 . .	448.6	491.2	522.5	606.7	705.3	714.9	865.3	996.7
Credit	2 379 . .	**456.4**	**508.2**	**537.1**	**628.8**	**742.9**	**754.4**	**908.2**	**1,031.8**
General government	2 380 . .	12.4	. . .	. . .	. . .	. . .	. . .	. . .	8.7
Other sectors	2 390 . .	444.0	508.2	537.1	628.8	742.9	754.4	908.2	1,023.1
Workers' remittances	2 391 . .	262.6	357.5	375.4	408.0	456.5	465.6	563.4	599.9
Other current transfers	2 392 . .	181.4	150.7	161.7	220.8	286.4	288.8	344.8	423.2
Debit	3 379 . .	**−7.8**	**−17.0**	**−14.6**	**−22.1**	**−37.6**	**−39.5**	**−42.9**	**−35.1**
General government	3 380 . .	. . .	. . .	. . .	. . .	. . .	. . .	. . .	.1
Other sectors	3 390 . .	−7.8	−17.0	−14.6	−22.1	−37.6	−39.5	−42.9	−35.2
Workers' remittances	3 391 . .	−7.4	−7.8	−12.7	−20.5	−33.3	−26.9	−39.1	−28.6
Other current transfers	3 392 . .	−.4	−9.2	−1.9	−1.6	−4.3	−12.6	−3.8	−6.6
CAPITAL AND FINANCIAL ACCOUNT	4 996 . .	**648.9**	**708.2**	**523.2**	**592.8**	**972.3**	**830.9**	**963.5**	**1,139.8**
CAPITAL ACCOUNT	4 994 . .	**. . .**	**61.6**	**65.0**	**85.0**	**71.0**	**68.4**	**85.5**	**93.3**
Total credit	2 994 . .	. . .	*61.6*	*65.0*	*85.0*	*71.0*	*68.4*	*85.5*	*93.3*
Total debit	3 994 . .	. . .	. . .	. . .	. . .	. . .	. . .	. . .	. . .
Capital transfers, credit	2 400 . .	**. . .**	**61.6**	**65.0**	**85.0**	**71.0**	**68.4**	**85.5**	**93.3**
General government	2 401 . .	. . .	61.6	65.0	85.0	71.0	68.4	85.5	93.3
Debt forgiveness	2 402 . .	. . .	. . .	. . .	20.0	. . .	. . .	. . .	. . .
Other capital transfers	2 410 . .	. . .	61.6	65.0	65.0	71.0	68.4	85.5	93.3
Other sectors	2 430 . .	. . .	. . .	. . .	. . .	. . .	. . .	. . .	. . .
Migrants' transfers	2 431 . .	. . .	. . .	. . .	. . .	. . .	. . .	. . .	. . .
Debt forgiveness	2 432 . .	. . .	. . .	. . .	. . .	. . .	. . .	. . .	. . .
Other capital transfers	2 440 . .	. . .	. . .	. . .	. . .	. . .	. . .	. . .	. . .
Capital transfers, debit	3 400 . .	**. . .**	**. . .**	**. . .**	**. . .**	**. . .**	**. . .**	**. . .**	**. . .**
General government	3 401 . .	. . .	. . .	. . .	. . .	. . .	. . .	. . .	. . .
Debt forgiveness	3 402 . .	. . .	. . .	. . .	. . .	. . .	. . .	. . .	. . .
Other capital transfers	3 410 . .	. . .	. . .	. . .	. . .	. . .	. . .	. . .	. . .
Other sectors	3 430 . .	. . .	. . .	. . .	. . .	. . .	. . .	. . .	. . .
Migrants' transfers	3 431 . .	. . .	. . .	. . .	. . .	. . .	. . .	. . .	. . .
Debt forgiveness	3 432 . .	. . .	. . .	. . .	. . .	. . .	. . .	. . .	. . .
Other capital transfers	3 440 . .	. . .	. . .	. . .	. . .	. . .	. . .	. . .	. . .
Nonproduced nonfinancial assets, credit	2 480 . .	**. . .**	**. . .**	**. . .**	**. . .**	**. . .**	**. . .**	**. . .**	**. . .**
Nonproduced nonfinancial assets, debit	3 480 . .	**. . .**	**. . .**	**. . .**	**. . .**	**. . .**	**. . .**	**. . .**	**. . .**

Table 2 (Continued). STANDARD PRESENTATION, 1994–2001
(Millions of U.S. dollars)

	Code	1994	1995	1996	1997	1998	1999	2000	2001
FINANCIAL ACCOUNT	4 995	**648.9**	**646.6**	**458.2**	**507.8**	**901.3**	**762.5**	**878.0**	**1,046.5**
A. DIRECT INVESTMENT	4 500	65.2	75.2	76.9	84.4	672.8	154.6	229.9	455.5
Direct investment abroad	4 505	**. . .**	**. . .**	**. . .**	**. . .**	**. . .**	**. . .**	**. . .**	**. . .**
Equity capital	4 510	. . .	. . .	. . .	. . .	. . .	. . .	. . .	. . .
Claims on affiliated enterprises	4 515	. . .	. . .	. . .	. . .	. . .	. . .	. . .	. . .
Liabilities to affiliated enterprises	4 520	. . .	. . .	. . .	. . .	. . .	. . .	. . .	. . .
Reinvested earnings	4 525	. . .	. . .	. . .	. . .	. . .	. . .	. . .	. . .
Other capital	4 530	. . .	. . .	. . .	. . .	. . .	. . .	. . .	. . .
Claims on affiliated enterprises	4 535	. . .	. . .	. . .	. . .	. . .	. . .	. . .	. . .
Liabilities to affiliated enterprises	4 540	. . .	. . .	. . .	. . .	. . .	. . .	. . .	. . .
Direct investment in Guatemala	4 555	**65.2**	**75.2**	**76.9**	**84.4**	**672.8**	**154.6**	**229.9**	**455.5**
Equity capital	4 560	27.2	32.5	34.1	37.1	619.0	103.4	170.6	389.5
Claims on direct investors	4 565	. . .	. . .	. . .	–547.0	–673.5	–770.0	1,018.5	1,392.0
Liabilities to direct investors	4 570	. . .	. . .	. . .	584.1	1,292.5	873.4	–847.9	–1,002.5
Reinvested earnings	4 575	33.3	37.1	37.4	40.8	45.9	43.4	48.9	54.6
Other capital	4 580	4.7	5.6	5.4	6.5	7.9	7.8	10.4	11.4
Claims on direct investors	4 585	. . .	. . .	. . .	. . .	. . .	. . .	. . .	. . .
Liabilities to direct investors	4 590	. . .	5.6	5.4	6.5	7.9	7.8	10.4	11.4
B. PORTFOLIO INVESTMENT	4 600	–4.0	–16.3	–16.0	231.6	54.2	110.5	42.6	130.5
Assets	4 602	**–9.8**	**–22.2**	**–11.5**	**–18.1**	**–11.6**	**–26.0**	**–36.3**	**–44.9**
Equity securities	4 610	. . .	. . .	. . .	. . .	. . .	. . .	. . .	. . .
Monetary authorities	4 611	. . .	. . .	. . .	. . .	. . .	. . .	. . .	. . .
General government	4 612	. . .	. . .	. . .	. . .	. . .	. . .	. . .	. . .
Banks	4 613	. . .	. . .	. . .	. . .	. . .	. . .	. . .	. . .
Other sectors	4 614	. . .	. . .	. . .	. . .	. . .	. . .	. . .	. . .
Debt securities	4 619	–9.8	–22.2	–11.5	–18.1	–11.6	–26.0	–36.3	–44.9
Bonds and notes	4 620	–9.8	–22.2	–11.5	–18.1	–11.6	–26.0	–36.3	–44.9
Monetary authorities	4 621	. . .	. . .	. . .	. . .	. . .	. . .	. . .	. . .
General government	4 622	. . .	. . .	. . .	. . .	. . .	. . .	. . .	. . .
Banks	4 623	. . .	. . .	. . .	. . .	. . .	. . .	. . .	. . .
Other sectors	4 624	. . .	–22.2	–11.5	–18.1	–11.6	–26.0	–36.3	–44.9
Money market instruments	4 630	. . .	. . .	. . .	. . .	. . .	. . .	. . .	. . .
Monetary authorities	4 631	. . .	. . .	. . .	. . .	. . .	. . .	. . .	. . .
General government	4 632	. . .	. . .	. . .	. . .	. . .	. . .	. . .	. . .
Banks	4 633	. . .	. . .	. . .	. . .	. . .	. . .	. . .	. . .
Other sectors	4 634	. . .	. . .	. . .	. . .	. . .	. . .	. . .	. . .
Liabilities	4 652	**5.8**	**5.9**	**–4.5**	**249.7**	**65.8**	**136.5**	**78.9**	**175.4**
Equity securities	4 660	. . .	. . .	. . .	. . .	. . .	. . .	. . .	. . .
Banks	4 663	. . .	. . .	. . .	. . .	. . .	. . .	. . .	. . .
Other sectors	4 664	. . .	. . .	. . .	. . .	. . .	. . .	. . .	. . .
Debt securities	4 669	5.8	5.9	–4.5	249.7	65.8	136.5	78.9	175.4
Bonds and notes	4 670	5.8	5.9	–4.5	249.7	65.8	136.5	78.9	175.4
Monetary authorities	4 671	–26.7	. . .	. . .	. . .	. . .	. . .	. . .	. . .
General government	4 672	32.5	5.9	–4.5	249.7	65.8	136.5	78.9	175.4
Banks	4 673	. . .	. . .	. . .	. . .	. . .	. . .	. . .	. . .
Other sectors	4 674	. . .	. . .	. . .	. . .	. . .	. . .	. . .	. . .
Money market instruments	4 680	. . .	. . .	. . .	. . .	. . .	. . .	. . .	. . .
Monetary authorities	4 681	. . .	. . .	. . .	. . .	. . .	. . .	. . .	. . .
General government	4 682	. . .	. . .	. . .	. . .	. . .	. . .	. . .	. . .
Banks	4 683	. . .	. . .	. . .	. . .	. . .	. . .	. . .	. . .
Other sectors	4 684	. . .	. . .	. . .	. . .	. . .	. . .	. . .	. . .
C. FINANCIAL DERIVATIVES	4 910	. . .	. . .	. . .	. . .	. . .	. . .	. . .	. . .
Monetary authorities	4 911	. . .	. . .	. . .	. . .	. . .	. . .	. . .	. . .
General government	4 912	. . .	. . .	. . .	. . .	. . .	. . .	. . .	. . .
Banks	4 913	. . .	. . .	. . .	. . .	. . .	. . .	. . .	. . .
Other sectors	4 914	. . .	. . .	. . .	. . .	. . .	. . .	. . .	. . .
Assets	4 900	**. . .**	**. . .**	**. . .**	**. . .**	**. . .**	**. . .**	**. . .**	**. . .**
Monetary authorities	4 901	. . .	. . .	. . .	. . .	. . .	. . .	. . .	. . .
General government	4 902	. . .	. . .	. . .	. . .	. . .	. . .	. . .	. . .
Banks	4 903	. . .	. . .	. . .	. . .	. . .	. . .	. . .	. . .
Other sectors	4 904	. . .	. . .	. . .	. . .	. . .	. . .	. . .	. . .
Liabilities	4 905	**. . .**	**. . .**	**. . .**	**. . .**	**. . .**	**. . .**	**. . .**	**. . .**
Monetary authorities	4 906	. . .	. . .	. . .	. . .	. . .	. . .	. . .	. . .
General government	4 907	. . .	. . .	. . .	. . .	. . .	. . .	. . .	. . .
Banks	4 908	. . .	. . .	. . .	. . .	. . .	. . .	. . .	. . .
Other sectors	4 909	. . .	. . .	. . .	. . .	. . .	. . .	. . .	. . .

Table 2 (Concluded). STANDARD PRESENTATION, 1994–2001
(Millions of U.S. dollars)

	Code	1994	1995	1996	1997	1998	1999	2000	2001
D. OTHER INVESTMENT	4 700 . .	635.0	430.4	596.3	449.5	437.3	372.4	1,248.2	934.8
Assets	4 703 . .	**116.8**	**125.1**	**199.2**	**221.2**	**241.7**	**199.9**	**213.2**	**156.7**
Trade credits	4 706 . .	. . .	. . .	. . .	. . .	. . .	. . .	. . .	. . .
General government	4 707 . .	. . .	. . .	. . .	. . .	. . .	. . .	. . .	. . .
of which: Short-term	4 709 . .	. . .	. . .	. . .	. . .	. . .	. . .	. . .	. . .
Other sectors	4 710 . .	. . .	. . .	. . .	. . .	. . .	. . .	. . .	. . .
of which: Short-term	4 712 . .	. . .	. . .	. . .	. . .	. . .	. . .	. . .	. . .
Loans	4 714 . .	–49.2	. . .	. . .	. . .	. . .	. . .	. . .	. . .
Monetary authorities	4 715 . .	. . .	. . .	. . .	. . .	. . .	. . .	. . .	. . .
of which: Short-term	4 718 . .	. . .	. . .	. . .	. . .	. . .	. . .	. . .	. . .
General government	4 719 . .	–49.2	. . .	. . .	. . .	. . .	. . .	. . .	. . .
of which: Short-term	4 721 . .	*–49.2*	. . .	. . .	. . .	. . .	. . .	. . .	. . .
Banks	4 722 . .	. . .	. . .	. . .	. . .	. . .	. . .	. . .	. . .
of which: Short-term	4 724 . .	. . .	. . .	. . .	. . .	. . .	. . .	. . .	. . .
Other sectors	4 725 . .	. . .	. . .	. . .	. . .	. . .	. . .	. . .	. . .
of which: Short-term	4 727 . .	. . .	. . .	. . .	. . .	. . .	. . .	. . .	. . .
Currency and deposits	4 730 . .	. . .	. . .	. . .	. . .	. . .	. . .	. . .	. . .
Monetary authorities	4 731 . .	. . .	. . .	. . .	. . .	. . .	. . .	. . .	. . .
General government	4 732 . .	. . .	. . .	. . .	. . .	. . .	. . .	. . .	. . .
Banks	4 733 . .	. . .	. . .	. . .	. . .	. . .	. . .	. . .	. . .
Other sectors	4 734 . .	. . .	. . .	. . .	. . .	. . .	. . .	. . .	. . .
Other assets	4 736 . .	166.0	125.1	199.2	221.2	241.7	199.9	213.2	156.7
Monetary authorities	4 737 . .	. . .	. . .	. . .	. . .	. . .	. . .	. . .	. . .
of which: Short-term	4 739 . .	. . .	. . .	. . .	. . .	. . .	. . .	. . .	. . .
General government	4 740 . .	. . .	. . .	. . .	. . .	. . .	. . .	. . .	. . .
of which: Short-term	4 742 . .	. . .	. . .	. . .	. . .	. . .	. . .	. . .	. . .
Banks	4 743 . .	. . .	. . .	. . .	. . .	. . .	. . .	. . .	. . .
of which: Short-term	4 745 . .	. . .	. . .	. . .	. . .	. . .	. . .	. . .	. . .
Other sectors	4 746 . .	166.0	125.1	199.2	221.2	241.7	199.9	213.2	156.7
of which: Short-term	4 748 . .	. . .	. . .	. . .	. . .	. . .	. . .	. . .	. . .
Liabilities	4 753 . .	**518.2**	**305.3**	**397.1**	**228.3**	**195.6**	**172.5**	**1,035.0**	**778.1**
Trade credits	4 756 . .	267.8	477.7	635.1	667.5	551.4	736.0	1,233.8	1,273.1
General government	4 757 . .	. . .	. . .	. . .	. . .	. . .	. . .	. . .	. . .
of which: Short-term	4 759 . .	. . .	. . .	. . .	. . .	. . .	. . .	. . .	. . .
Other sectors	4 760 . .	267.8	477.7	635.1	667.5	551.4	736.0	1,233.8	1,273.1
of which: Short-term	4 762 . .	*267.8*	*477.7*	*635.1*	*667.5*	*551.4*	*736.0*	*1,233.8*	*1,273.1*
Loans	4 764 . .	251.3	16.3	180.8	194.6	386.3	594.8	566.8	735.6
Monetary authorities	4 765 . .	–54.9	–77.7	–56.5	–82.0	–54.2	–25.8	–24.3	–11.2
of which: Use of Fund credit and loans from the Fund	4 766 . .	. . .	. . .	. . .	. . .	. . .	. . .	. . .	. . .
of which: Short-term	4 768 . .	. . .	. . .	. . .	. . .	. . .	. . .	. . .	. . .
General government	4 769 . .	132.7	11.8	91.1	85.6	252.4	295.9	92.7	44.8
of which: Short-term	4 771 . .	. . .	. . .	. . .	. . .	. . .	. . .	. . .	. . .
Banks	4 772 . .	. . .	. . .	. . .	. . .	. . .	. . .	. . .	. . .
of which: Short-term	4 774 . .	. . .	. . .	. . .	. . .	. . .	. . .	. . .	. . .
Other sectors	4 775 . .	173.5	82.2	146.2	191.0	188.1	324.7	498.4	702.0
of which: Short-term	4 777 . .	*37.8*	*19.2*	*–32.8*	*–41.7*	*–30.5*	*–65.3*	*–1.8*	*215.2*
Currency and deposits	4 780 . .	. . .	–.4	. . .	–1.0	–.2	–20.0	. . .	. . .
Monetary authorities	4 781 . .	. . .	. . .	. . .	. . .	. . .	. . .	. . .	. . .
General government	4 782 . .	. . .	. . .	. . .	. . .	. . .	. . .	. . .	. . .
Banks	4 783 . .	. . .	. . .	. . .	. . .	. . .	. . .	. . .	. . .
Other sectors	4 784 . .	. . .	–.4	. . .	–1.0	–.2	–20.0	. . .	. . .
Other liabilities	4 786 . .	–.9	–188.3	–418.8	–632.8	–741.9	–1,138.3	–765.6	–1,230.6
Monetary authorities	4 787 . .	33.3	–.6	.2	–26.6	. . .	.2	.3	–.1
of which: Short-term	4 789 . .	*33.3*	*–.6*	*.2*	*–26.6*	. . .	*.2*	*.3*	*–.1*
General government	4 790 . .	. . .	–5.5	–15.1	32.0	27.6	. . .	. . .	. . .
of which: Short-term	4 792 . .	. . .	*–5.5*	*–15.1*	*32.0*	*27.6*	. . .	. . .	. . .
Banks	4 793 . .	. . .	7.3	19.4	–4.6	3.2	23.0	–17.4	21.9
of which: Short-term	4 795 . .	. . .	*7.3*	*19.4*	*–4.6*	*3.2*	*23.0*	*–17.4*	*21.9*
Other sectors	4 796 . .	–34.2	–189.5	–423.3	–633.6	–772.7	–1,161.5	–748.5	–1,252.4
of which: Short-term	4 798 . .	*–34.2*	*–189.5*	*–423.3*	*–633.6*	*–772.7*	*–1,161.5*	*–748.5*	*–1,252.4*
E. RESERVE ASSETS	4 802 . .	–47.3	157.3	–199.0	–257.7	–263.0	125.0	–642.7	–474.3
Monetary gold	4 812 . .	. . .	. . .	. . .	. . .	–.1	. . .	–50.2	–.8
Special drawing rights	4 811 . .	.1	1.2	.7	1.0	1.1	.4	1.1	1.0
Reserve position in the Fund	4 810 . .	. . .	. . .	. . .	. . .	. . .	. . .	. . .	. . .
Foreign exchange	4 803 . .	5.6	156.1	–199.7	–258.7	–264.0	124.6	–593.6	–474.5
Other claims	4 813 . .	–53.0	. . .	. . .	. . .	. . .	. . .	. . .	. . .
NET ERRORS AND OMISSIONS	4 998 . .	**–23.6**	**–136.2**	**–71.7**	**40.7**	**66.8**	**195.0**	**86.1**	**98.1**

Part 3 of the *Yearbook* contains descriptions of the methodologies, compilation practices, and sources used to compile these data.

Table 1. ANALYTIC PRESENTATION, 1994–2001
(Millions of U.S. dollars)

	Code		1994	1995	1996	1997	1998	1999	2000	2001
A. Current Account [1]	4 993	Z.	**–248.0**	**–216.5**	**–177.3**	**–91.1**	**–183.6**	**–214.9**	**–155.1**	**–102.4**
Goods: exports f.o.b	2 100	. .	515.7	582.8	636.5	630.1	693.0	635.7	666.4	731.0
Goods: imports f.o.b	3 100	. .	–685.4	–621.7	–525.3	–512.5	–572.0	–581.8	–587.1	–561.8
Balance on Goods	4 100	. .	*–169.7*	*–39.0*	*111.2*	*117.6*	*121.0*	*53.9*	*79.3*	*169.2*
Services: credit	2 200	. .	152.9	117.5	124.1	110.7	110.8	113.1	68.0	102.8
Services: debit	3 200	. .	–366.0	–389.3	–422.2	–321.6	–382.7	–364.6	–284.9	–319.1
Balance on Goods and Services	4 991	. .	*–382.9*	*–310.8*	*–186.8*	*–93.3*	*–150.9*	*–197.6*	*–137.6*	*–47.1*
Income: credit	2 300	. .	6.5	12.9	12.8	7.8	9.0	24.7	23.5	11.4
Income: debit	3 300	. .	–79.8	–97.5	–105.7	–121.3	–133.5	–106.9	–101.1	–113.7
Balance on Goods, Services, and Income	4 992	. .	*–456.1*	*–395.5*	*–279.8*	*–206.9*	*–275.5*	*–279.8*	*–215.2*	*–149.4*
Current transfers: credit	2 379	Z.	280.6	258.3	137.8	131.4	116.2	80.0	88.6	91.5
Current transfers: debit	3 379	. .	–72.5	–79.3	–35.3	–15.6	–24.3	–15.1	–28.5	–44.5
B. Capital Account [1]	4 994	Z.	**. . .**	**. . .**	**. . .**	**. . .**	**. . .**	**. . .**	**. . .**	**. . .**
Capital account: credit	2 994	Z.	. . .	. . .	. . .	. . .	. . .	. . .	. . .	. . .
Capital account: debit	3 994	. .	. . .	. . .	. . .	. . .	. . .	. . .	. . .	. . .
Total, Groups A Plus B	4 981	. .	*–248.0*	*–216.5*	*–177.3*	*–91.1*	*–183.6*	*–214.9*	*–155.1*	*–102.4*
C. Financial Account [1]	4 995	W.	**84.2**	**109.2**	**47.5**	**–89.3**	**8.0**	**116.5**	**8.3**	**–12.2**
Direct investment abroad	4 505	. .	. . .	. . .	–.5	. . .	. . .	. . .	. . .	. . .
Direct investment in Guinea	4 555	Z.	.2	.8	23.8	17.3	17.8	63.4	9.9	1.6
Portfolio investment assets	4 602	. .	. . .	. . .	. . .	. . .	–82.7	–20.0	8.7	4.6
Equity securities	4 610	. .	. . .	. . .	. . .	. . .	. . .	. . .	. . .	. . .
Debt securities	4 619	. .	. . .	. . .	. . .	. . .	–82.7	–20.0	8.7	4.6
Portfolio investment liabilities	4 652	Z.	. . .	. . .	. . .	. . .	. . .	. . .	. . .	. . .
Equity securities	4 660	. .	. . .	. . .	. . .	. . .	. . .	. . .	. . .	. . .
Debt securities	4 669	Z.	. . .	. . .	. . .	. . .	. . .	. . .	. . .	. . .
Financial derivatives	4 910	. .	. . .	. . .	. . .	. . .	. . .	. . .	. . .	. . .
Financial derivatives assets	4 900	. .	. . .	. . .	. . .	. . .	. . .	. . .	. . .	. . .
Financial derivatives liabilities	4 905	. .	. . .	. . .	. . .	. . .	. . .	. . .	. . .	. . .
Other investment assets	4 703	. .	–14.5	–73.7	–19.8	–99.1	–14.6	.1	–17.0	11.6
Monetary authorities	4 701	. .	–6.5	9.0	6.0	2.4	1.2	–1.5	–13.7	1.5
General government	4 704	. .	. . .	. . .	. . .	. . .	. . .	. . .	. . .	. . .
Banks	4 705	. .	–2.2	–4.6	9.0	9.3	–12.5	7.6	–1.3	9.5
Other sectors	4 728	. .	–5.8	–78.2	–34.7	–110.8	–3.3	–6.0	–2.0	.6
Other investment liabilities	4 753	W.	98.5	182.2	44.0	–7.5	87.5	73.0	6.7	–30.0
Monetary authorities	4 753	WA	.1	–.5	39.1	35.3	–3.0	.2	–.8	13.4
General government	4 753	ZB	79.6	106.5	–14.4	48.2	37.6	84.1	61.5	26.5
Banks	4 753	ZC	8.3	26.0	–9.8	–18.1	6.7	3.8	–23.1	–12.4
Other sectors	4 753	ZD	10.5	50.2	29.0	–2.3	46.2	–15.1	–30.9	–57.5
Total, Groups A Through C	4 983	. .	*–163.8*	*–107.3*	*–129.8*	*–180.4*	*–175.6*	*–98.4*	*–146.8*	*–114.6*
D. Net Errors and Omissions	4 998	. .	**39.7**	**34.8**	**69.9**	**49.8**	**17.8**	**22.4**	**82.1**	**–1.9**
Total, Groups A Through D	4 984	. .	*–124.1*	*–72.5*	*–59.9*	*–130.6*	*–157.8*	*–76.0*	*–64.7*	*–116.5*
E. Reserves and Related Items	4 802	A.	**124.1**	**72.5**	**59.9**	**130.6**	**157.8**	**76.0**	**64.7**	**116.5**
Reserve assets	4 802	. .	32.4	–43.8	–6.5	–20.3	60.7	60.7	52.2	–3.9
Use of Fund credit and loans	4 766	. .	7.0	22.1	–8.4	22.4	22.8	3.7	–7.9	14.8
Exceptional financing	4 920	. .	84.7	94.2	74.9	128.5	74.3	11.6	20.4	105.7
Conversion rates: Guinean francs per U.S. dollar	0 101	. .	**976.6**	**991.4**	**1,004.0**	**1,095.3**	**1,236.8**	**1,387.4**	**1,746.9**	**1,950.6**

[1] Excludes components that have been classified in the categories of Group E.

Table 2. STANDARD PRESENTATION, 1994–2001

(Millions of U.S. dollars)

	Code			1994	1995	1996	1997	1998	1999	2000	2001
CURRENT ACCOUNT	4	993	. .	**–248.0**	**–216.5**	**–177.3**	**–91.1**	**–154.5**	**–201.5**	**–139.9**	**–59.6**
A. GOODS	4	100	. .	–169.7	–39.0	111.2	117.6	121.0	53.9	79.3	169.2
Credit	2	100	. .	**515.7**	**582.8**	**636.5**	**630.1**	**693.0**	**635.7**	**666.4**	**731.0**
General merchandise: exports f.o.b.	2	110	. .	452.5	521.2	554.7	592.1	575.7	541.2	547.5	534.0
Goods for processing: exports f.o.b.	2	150	. .	. . .	. . .	. . .	. . .	. . .	. . .	. . .	1.0
Repairs on goods	2	160	. .	. . .	. . .	. . .	4.0	. . .	. . .	. . .	3.4
Goods procured in ports by carriers	2	170	. .	.3	.9	1.4	8.0	8.3	. . .	8.2	27.5
Nonmonetary gold	2	180	. .	62.9	60.7	80.5	26.0	109.0	94.5	110.7	165.1
Debit	3	100	. .	**–685.4**	**–621.7**	**–525.3**	**–512.5**	**–572.0**	**–581.8**	**–587.1**	**–561.8**
General merchandise: imports f.o.b.	3	110	. .	–685.4	–621.5	–523.1	–511.1	–570.5	–580.0	–582.9	–531.8
Goods for processing: imports f.o.b.	3	150	. .	. . .	. . .	. . .	. . .	. . .	. . .	. . .	–22.5
Repairs on goods	3	160	. .	. . .	. . .	–1.0	. . .	. . .	–.8	–1.2	–.9
Goods procured in ports by carriers	3	170	. .	. . .	–.3	–1.3	–1.4	–1.5	–1.0	–3.0	–6.6
Nonmonetary gold	3	180	. .	. . .	. . .	. . .	. . .	. . .	. . .	. . .	. . .
B. SERVICES	4	200	. .	–213.2	–271.9	–298.0	–210.9	–272.0	–251.5	–216.9	–216.3
Total credit	2	200	. .	*152.9*	*117.5*	*124.1*	*110.7*	*110.8*	*113.1*	*68.0*	*102.8*
Total debit	3	200	. .	*–366.0*	*–389.3*	*–422.2*	*–321.6*	*–382.7*	*–364.6*	*–284.9*	*–319.1*
Transportation services, credit	2	205	. .	**11.5**	**12.8**	**15.2**	**47.5**	**48.7**	**19.3**	**15.6**	**31.7**
Passenger	2	850	. .	*.4*	. . .	*2.9*	*4.7*	*3.4*	*4.1*	*5.8*	*8.1*
Freight	2	851	. .	. . .	. . .	*.7*	*26.3*	*30.3*	*8.6*	*4.8*	*16.2*
Other	2	852	. .	*11.2*	*12.7*	*11.6*	*16.5*	*15.1*	*6.6*	*5.0*	*7.4*
Sea transport, passenger	2	207	. .	. . .	. . .	. . .	. . .	. . .	. . .	. . .	. . .
Sea transport, freight	2	208	. .	. . .	. . .	. . .	23.5	24.1	8.6	4.8	16.2
Sea transport, other	2	209	. .	3.4	12.1	7.9	15.6	13.5	5.8	3.3	5.7
Air transport, passenger	2	211	. .	. . .	. . .	2.9	4.7	3.4	4.1	5.8	8.1
Air transport, freight	2	212	. .	. . .	. . .	.7	. . .	2.0	. . .	. . .	. . .
Air transport, other	2	213	. .	7.8	.7	3.7	.9	1.6	.8	1.7	1.7
Other transport, passenger	2	215	. .	.4	. . .	. . .	. . .	. . .	. . .	. . .	. . .
Other transport, freight	2	216	. .	. . .	. . .	. . .	2.8	4.2	. . .	. . .	. . .
Other transport, other	2	217	. .	. . .	. . .	. . .	. . .	. . .	. . .	. . .	. . .
Transportation services, debit	3	205	. .	**–131.5**	**–147.1**	**–146.4**	**–124.3**	**–149.6**	**–123.2**	**–111.4**	**–112.5**
Passenger	3	850	. .	*–6.8*	*–7.9*	*–9.6*	*–16.2*	*–7.0*	*–4.9*	*–3.8*	*–7.8*
Freight	3	851	. .	*–124.7*	*–129.9*	*–130.7*	*–106.7*	*–134.5*	*–99.9*	*–104.2*	*–100.3*
Other	3	852	. .	*–.1*	*–9.3*	*–6.1*	*–1.5*	*–8.1*	*–18.4*	*–3.4*	*–4.4*
Sea transport, passenger	3	207	. .	. . .	. . .	. . .	. . .	. . .	. . .	. . .	. . .
Sea transport, freight	3	208	. .	–124.7	–119.7	–121.1	–100.4	–128.0	–94.9	–99.0	–95.3
Sea transport, other	3	209	. .	–.1	–7.5	–5.3	–.7	–7.2	–14.0	–1.0	–3.7
Air transport, passenger	3	211	. .	–6.5	–7.9	–9.6	–16.2	–7.0	–4.9	–3.8	–7.8
Air transport, freight	3	212	. .	. . .	–10.2	–9.6	–6.3	–5.3	–5.0	–5.2	–5.0
Air transport, other	3	213	. .	. . .	–1.9	–.8	–.8	–.9	–4.4	–2.4	–.7
Other transport, passenger	3	215	. .	–.3	. . .	. . .	. . .	. . .	. . .	. . .	. . .
Other transport, freight	3	216	. .	. . .	. . .	. . .	. . .	–1.3	. . .	. . .	. . .
Other transport, other	3	217	. .	. . .	. . .	. . .	. . .	. . .	. . .	. . .	. . .
Travel, credit	2	236	. .	**.5**	**.9**	**6.4**	**.1**	**.9**	**1.7**	**2.0**	**.1**
Business travel	2	237	. .	.5	.3	3.8	. . .	. . .	1.5	. . .	.1
Personal travel	2	240	. .	. . .	.6	2.6	.1	.9	.2	2.0	. . .
Travel, debit	3	236	. .	**–23.5**	**–21.2**	**–26.7**	**–23.3**	**–27.5**	**–23.7**	**–9.2**	**–17.9**
Business travel	3	237	. .	–7.7	–8.8	–10.2	–9.1	–13.1	–9.7	–1.0	–2.9
Personal travel	3	240	. .	–15.8	–12.4	–16.4	–14.3	–14.4	–14.0	–8.2	–15.0
Other services, credit	2	200	BA	**140.8**	**103.9**	**102.6**	**63.1**	**61.2**	**92.1**	**50.4**	**71.0**
Communications	2	245	. .	. . .	. . .	1.4	9.9	10.4	.9	1.1	2.2
Construction	2	249	. .	. . .	. . .	. . .	4.5	4.1	7.4	4.1	12.9
Insurance	2	253	. .	.9	.2	2.8	1.3	. . .	.1	. . .	3.7
Financial	2	260	. .	. . .	. . .	.2	. . .	.1	.3	.1	.3
Computer and information	2	262	. .	. . .	. . .	. . .	. . .	. . .	. . .	. . .	.1
Royalties and licence fees	2	266	. .	. . .	. . .	. . .	. . .	. . .	. . .	. . .	. . .
Other business services	2	268	. .	1.0	3.1	37.0	6.5	1.8	6.4	3.9	21.2
Personal, cultural, and recreational	2	287	. .	. . .	. . .	. . .	.1	. . .	. . .	. . .	. . .
Government, n.i.e.	2	291	. .	138.9	100.5	61.1	40.8	44.8	77.0	41.2	30.6
Other services, debit	3	200	BA	**–211.0**	**–221.0**	**–249.1**	**–174.0**	**–205.7**	**–217.7**	**–164.3**	**–188.7**
Communications	3	245	. .	–1.0	–.6	–2.4	–7.0	–8.7	–2.3	–9.9	–5.5
Construction	3	249	. .	. . .	. . .	. . .	–.8	–4.6	–3.7	–5.5	–2.1
Insurance	3	253	. .	–26.2	–18.1	–26.8	–6.9	–8.5	–6.7	–7.0	–6.7
Financial	3	260	. .	. . .	. . .	–.1	. . .	. . .	. . .	–.1	–.3
Computer and information	3	262	. .	. . .	. . .	. . .	–.7	–2.8	–1.2	–3.2	–1.3
Royalties and licence fees	3	266	. .	. . .	. . .	. . .	. . .	. . .	–.1	. . .	–1.0
Other business services	3	268	. .	–46.7	–64.6	–118.4	–41.3	–71.5	–97.5	–37.0	–72.9
Personal, cultural, and recreational	3	287	. .	–4.1	–.3	. . .	. . .	–1.0	. . .	–.1	–.2
Government, n.i.e.	3	291	. .	–133.0	–137.4	–101.4	–117.3	–108.5	–106.2	–101.5	–98.7

Table 2 (Continued). STANDARD PRESENTATION, 1994–2001

(Millions of U.S. dollars)

	Code	1994	1995	1996	1997	1998	1999	2000	2001
C. INCOME	4 300 . .	–73.2	–84.6	–92.9	–113.6	–124.6	–82.2	–77.6	–102.3
Total credit	2 300 . .	*6.5*	*12.9*	*12.8*	*7.8*	*9.0*	*24.7*	*23.5*	*11.4*
Total debit	3 300 . .	*–79.8*	*–97.5*	*–105.7*	*–121.3*	*–133.5*	*–106.9*	*–101.1*	*–113.7*
Compensation of employees, credit	2 310 . .	**. . .**	**.2**	**. . .**	**.5**	**.6**	**. . .**	**. . .**	**. . .**
Compensation of employees, debit	3 310 . .	**–.3**	**. . .**	**. . .**	**–1.5**	**–.8**	**–4.6**	**–1.4**	**–3.6**
Investment income, credit	2 320 . .	**6.5**	**12.6**	**12.8**	**7.2**	**8.3**	**24.7**	**23.5**	**11.4**
Direct investment income	2 330 . .	. . .	. . .	3.5	3.4	. . .	.2	. . .	.1
Dividends and distributed branch profits	2 332 . .	. . .	. . .	3.5	1.1	. . .	. . .	. . .	. . .
Reinvested earnings and undistributed branch profits	2 333 . .	. . .	. . .	. . .	. . .	. . .	. . .	. . .	. . .
Income on debt (interest)	2 334 . .	. . .	. . .	. . .	2.4	. . .	.2	. . .	.1
Portfolio investment income	2 339 . .	. . .	. . .	. . .	. . .	. . .	. . .	. . .	. . .
Income on equity	2 340 . .	. . .	. . .	. . .	. . .	. . .	. . .	. . .	. . .
Income on bonds and notes	2 350 . .	. . .	. . .	. . .	. . .	. . .	. . .	. . .	. . .
Income on money market instruments	2 360 . .	. . .	. . .	. . .	. . .	. . .	. . .	. . .	. . .
Other investment income	2 370 . .	6.5	12.6	9.3	3.8	8.3	24.5	23.5	11.3
Investment income, debit	3 320 . .	**–79.5**	**–97.5**	**–105.7**	**–119.8**	**–132.8**	**–102.3**	**–99.7**	**–110.1**
Direct investment income	3 330 . .	–15.9	–23.3	–35.8	–46.2	–60.1	–32.5	–8.4	–45.6
Dividends and distributed branch profits	3 332 . .	–15.7	–23.2	–35.7	–45.9	–60.1	–32.1	–8.3	–45.5
Reinvested earnings and undistributed branch profits	3 333 . .	–.2	–.1	–.1	. . .	. . .	–.2	. . .	–.1
Income on debt (interest)	3 334 . .	. . .	. . .	. . .	–.2	. . .	–.2	–.1	. . .
Portfolio investment income	3 339 . .	. . .	. . .	. . .	. . .	. . .	. . .	. . .	. . .
Income on equity	3 340 . .	. . .	. . .	. . .	. . .	. . .	. . .	. . .	. . .
Income on bonds and notes	3 350 . .	. . .	. . .	. . .	. . .	. . .	. . .	. . .	. . .
Income on money market instruments	3 360 . .	. . .	. . .	. . .	. . .	. . .	. . .	. . .	. . .
Other investment income	3 370 . .	–63.6	–74.3	–70.0	–73.7	–72.7	–69.8	–91.3	–64.5
D. CURRENT TRANSFERS	4 379 . .	208.1	179.0	102.5	115.8	121.0	78.3	75.3	89.8
Credit	2 379 . .	**280.6**	**258.3**	**137.8**	**131.4**	**145.3**	**93.4**	**103.8**	**134.3**
General government	2 380 . .	208.1	148.4	127.4	117.5	137.2	86.3	84.1	124.6
Other sectors	2 390 . .	72.6	109.9	10.3	14.0	8.1	7.1	19.7	9.7
Workers' remittances	2 391 . .	.5	.5	1.1	1.0	4.4	6.0	1.2	8.7
Other current transfers	2 392 . .	72.1	109.4	9.3	13.0	3.8	1.1	18.5	1.0
Debit	3 379 . .	**–72.5**	**–79.3**	**–35.3**	**–15.6**	**–24.3**	**–15.1**	**–28.5**	**–44.5**
General government	3 380 . .	–.9	–1.3	. . .	–.1	. . .	. . .	–.1	–6.7
Other sectors	3 390 . .	–71.6	–78.0	–35.2	–15.6	–24.3	–15.1	–28.4	–37.8
Workers' remittances	3 391 . .	–21.9	–10.4	–11.3	–12.9	–22.2	–13.3	–25.5	–33.2
Other current transfers	3 392 . .	–49.7	–67.6	–24.0	–2.6	–2.1	–1.8	–2.9	–4.6
CAPITAL AND FINANCIAL ACCOUNT	4 996 . .	**208.2**	**181.7**	**107.4**	**41.3**	**136.6**	**179.1**	**57.8**	**61.5**
CAPITAL ACCOUNT	4 994 . .	**.7**	**44.8**	**.8**	**108.6**	. . .	. . .	. . .	. . .
Total credit	2 994 . .	*.7*	*44.8*	*.8*	*108.6*	. . .	. . .	. . .	. . .
Total debit	3 994 . .	. . .	. . .	. . .	. . .	. . .	. . .	. . .	. . .
Capital transfers, credit	2 400 . .	**.7**	**44.8**	**.8**	**108.6**	**. . .**	**. . .**	**. . .**	**. . .**
General government	2 401 . .	.7	44.8	.8	108.6	. . .	. . .	. . .	. . .
Debt forgiveness	2 402 . .	.7	44.8	.8	108.6	. . .	. . .	. . .	. . .
Other capital transfers	2 410 . .	. . .	. . .	. . .	. . .	. . .	. . .	. . .	. . .
Other sectors	2 430 . .	. . .	. . .	. . .	. . .	. . .	. . .	. . .	. . .
Migrants' transfers	2 431 . .	. . .	. . .	. . .	. . .	. . .	. . .	. . .	. . .
Debt forgiveness	2 432 . .	. . .	. . .	. . .	. . .	. . .	. . .	. . .	. . .
Other capital transfers	2 440 . .	. . .	. . .	. . .	. . .	. . .	. . .	. . .	. . .
Capital transfers, debit	3 400 . .	**. . .**	**. . .**	**. . .**	**. . .**	**. . .**	**. . .**	**. . .**	**. . .**
General government	3 401 . .	. . .	. . .	. . .	. . .	. . .	. . .	. . .	. . .
Debt forgiveness	3 402 . .	. . .	. . .	. . .	. . .	. . .	. . .	. . .	. . .
Other capital transfers	3 410 . .	. . .	. . .	. . .	. . .	. . .	. . .	. . .	. . .
Other sectors	3 430 . .	. . .	. . .	. . .	. . .	. . .	. . .	. . .	. . .
Migrants' transfers	3 431 . .	. . .	. . .	. . .	. . .	. . .	. . .	. . .	. . .
Debt forgiveness	3 432 . .	. . .	. . .	. . .	. . .	. . .	. . .	. . .	. . .
Other capital transfers	3 440 . .	. . .	. . .	. . .	. . .	. . .	. . .	. . .	. . .
Nonproduced nonfinancial assets, credit	2 480 . .	**. . .**	**. . .**	**. . .**	**. . .**	**. . .**	**. . .**	**. . .**	**. . .**
Nonproduced nonfinancial assets, debit	3 480 . .	**. . .**	**. . .**	**. . .**	**. . .**	**. . .**	**. . .**	**. . .**	**. . .**

Table 2 (Continued). STANDARD PRESENTATION, 1994–2001

(Millions of U.S. dollars)

	Code		1994	1995	1996	1997	1998	1999	2000	2001
FINANCIAL ACCOUNT	4 995	. .	**207.6**	**136.9**	**106.6**	**–67.3**	**136.6**	**179.1**	**57.8**	**61.5**
A. DIRECT INVESTMENT	4 500	. .	.2	.8	23.3	17.3	17.8	63.4	9.9	1.6
Direct investment abroad	4 505	. .	**. . .**	**. . .**	**–.5**	**. . .**	**. . .**	**. . .**	**. . .**	**. . .**
Equity capital	4 510	. .	. . .	. . .	–.5	. . .	. . .	. . .	. . .	. . .
Claims on affiliated enterprises	4 515	. .	. . .	. . .	–.5	. . .	. . .	. . .	. . .	. . .
Liabilities to affiliated enterprises	4 520	. .	. . .	. . .	. . .	. . .	. . .	. . .	. . .	. . .
Reinvested earnings	4 525	. .	. . .	. . .	. . .	. . .	. . .	. . .	. . .	. . .
Other capital	4 530	. .	. . .	. . .	. . .	. . .	. . .	. . .	. . .	. . .
Claims on affiliated enterprises	4 535	. .	. . .	. . .	. . .	. . .	. . .	. . .	. . .	. . .
Liabilities to affiliated enterprises	4 540	. .	. . .	. . .	. . .	. . .	. . .	. . .	. . .	. . .
Direct investment in Guinea	4 555	. .	**.2**	**.8**	**23.8**	**17.3**	**17.8**	**63.4**	**9.9**	**1.6**
Equity capital	4 560	. .	. . .	.7	23.7	17.3	17.8	9.1	9.9	1.5
Claims on direct investors	4 565	. .	. . .	. . .	. . .	. . .	. . .	. . .	. . .	. . .
Liabilities to direct investors	4 570	. .	. . .	.7	23.7	17.3	17.8	9.1	9.9	1.5
Reinvested earnings	4 575	. .	.2	.1	.1	. . .	. . .	.2	. . .	.1
Other capital	4 580	. .	. . .	. . .	. . .	. . .	. . .	54.1	. . .	. . .
Claims on direct investors	4 585	. .	. . .	. . .	. . .	. . .	. . .	. . .	. . .	. . .
Liabilities to direct investors	4 590	. .	. . .	. . .	. . .	. . .	. . .	54.1	. . .	. . .
B. PORTFOLIO INVESTMENT	4 600	. .	. . .	. . .	. . .	. . .	–82.7	–20.0	8.7	4.6
Assets	4 602	. .	**. . .**	**. . .**	**. . .**	**. . .**	**–82.7**	**–20.0**	**8.7**	**4.6**
Equity securities	4 610	. .	. . .	. . .	. . .	. . .	. . .	. . .	. . .	. . .
Monetary authorities	4 611	. .	. . .	. . .	. . .	. . .	. . .	. . .	. . .	. . .
General government	4 612	. .	. . .	. . .	. . .	. . .	. . .	. . .	. . .	. . .
Banks	4 613	. .	. . .	. . .	. . .	. . .	. . .	. . .	. . .	. . .
Other sectors	4 614	. .	. . .	. . .	. . .	. . .	. . .	. . .	. . .	. . .
Debt securities	4 619	. .	. . .	. . .	. . .	. . .	–82.7	–20.0	8.7	4.6
Bonds and notes	4 620	. .	. . .	. . .	. . .	. . .	–82.7	–20.0	8.7	4.6
Monetary authorities	4 621	. .	. . .	. . .	. . .	. . .	–82.7	–20.0	8.7	4.6
General government	4 622	. .	. . .	. . .	. . .	. . .	. . .	. . .	. . .	. . .
Banks	4 623	. .	. . .	. . .	. . .	. . .	. . .	. . .	. . .	. . .
Other sectors	4 624	. .	. . .	. . .	. . .	. . .	. . .	. . .	. . .	. . .
Money market instruments	4 630	. .	. . .	. . .	. . .	. . .	. . .	. . .	. . .	. . .
Monetary authorities	4 631	. .	. . .	. . .	. . .	. . .	. . .	. . .	. . .	. . .
General government	4 632	. .	. . .	. . .	. . .	. . .	. . .	. . .	. . .	. . .
Banks	4 633	. .	. . .	. . .	. . .	. . .	. . .	. . .	. . .	. . .
Other sectors	4 634	. .	. . .	. . .	. . .	. . .	. . .	. . .	. . .	. . .
Liabilities	4 652	. .	**. . .**	**. . .**	**. . .**	**. . .**	**. . .**	**. . .**	**. . .**	**. . .**
Equity securities	4 660	. .	. . .	. . .	. . .	. . .	. . .	. . .	. . .	. . .
Banks	4 663	. .	. . .	. . .	. . .	. . .	. . .	. . .	. . .	. . .
Other sectors	4 664	. .	. . .	. . .	. . .	. . .	. . .	. . .	. . .	. . .
Debt securities	4 669	. .	. . .	. . .	. . .	. . .	. . .	. . .	. . .	. . .
Bonds and notes	4 670	. .	. . .	. . .	. . .	. . .	. . .	. . .	. . .	. . .
Monetary authorities	4 671	. .	. . .	. . .	. . .	. . .	. . .	. . .	. . .	. . .
General government	4 672	. .	. . .	. . .	. . .	. . .	. . .	. . .	. . .	. . .
Banks	4 673	. .	. . .	. . .	. . .	. . .	. . .	. . .	. . .	. . .
Other sectors	4 674	. .	. . .	. . .	. . .	. . .	. . .	. . .	. . .	. . .
Money market instruments	4 680	. .	. . .	. . .	. . .	. . .	. . .	. . .	. . .	. . .
Monetary authorities	4 681	. .	. . .	. . .	. . .	. . .	. . .	. . .	. . .	. . .
General government	4 682	. .	. . .	. . .	. . .	. . .	. . .	. . .	. . .	. . .
Banks	4 683	. .	. . .	. . .	. . .	. . .	. . .	. . .	. . .	. . .
Other sectors	4 684	. .	. . .	. . .	. . .	. . .	. . .	. . .	. . .	. . .
C. FINANCIAL DERIVATIVES	4 910	. .	. . .	. . .	. . .	. . .	. . .	. . .	. . .	. . .
Monetary authorities	4 911	. .	. . .	. . .	. . .	. . .	. . .	. . .	. . .	. . .
General government	4 912	. .	. . .	. . .	. . .	. . .	. . .	. . .	. . .	. . .
Banks	4 913	. .	. . .	. . .	. . .	. . .	. . .	. . .	. . .	. . .
Other sectors	4 914	. .	. . .	. . .	. . .	. . .	. . .	. . .	. . .	. . .
Assets	4 900	. .	**. . .**	**. . .**	**. . .**	**. . .**	**. . .**	**. . .**	**. . .**	**. . .**
Monetary authorities	4 901	. .	. . .	. . .	. . .	. . .	. . .	. . .	. . .	. . .
General government	4 902	. .	. . .	. . .	. . .	. . .	. . .	. . .	. . .	. . .
Banks	4 903	. .	. . .	. . .	. . .	. . .	. . .	. . .	. . .	. . .
Other sectors	4 904	. .	. . .	. . .	. . .	. . .	. . .	. . .	. . .	. . .
Liabilities	4 905	. .	**. . .**	**. . .**	**. . .**	**. . .**	**. . .**	**. . .**	**. . .**	**. . .**
Monetary authorities	4 906	. .	. . .	. . .	. . .	. . .	. . .	. . .	. . .	. . .
General government	4 907	. .	. . .	. . .	. . .	. . .	. . .	. . .	. . .	. . .
Banks	4 908	. .	. . .	. . .	. . .	. . .	. . .	. . .	. . .	. . .
Other sectors	4 909	. .	. . .	. . .	. . .	. . .	. . .	. . .	. . .	. . .

Table 2 (Concluded). STANDARD PRESENTATION, 1994–2001
(Millions of U.S. dollars)

	Code	1994	1995	1996	1997	1998	1999	2000	2001
D. OTHER INVESTMENT	4 700 . .	175.0	179.9	89.9	-64.3	140.8	75.0	-13.0	59.3
Assets	4 703 . .	**-14.5**	**-73.7**	**-19.8**	**-99.1**	**-14.6**	**.1**	**-17.0**	**11.6**
Trade credits	4 706 . .	-.2	11.1	-8.6	11.9	-2.7	. . .	. . .	. . .
General government	4 707 . .	. . .	. . .	. . .	. . .	. . .	. . .	. . .	. . .
of which: Short-term	4 709 . .	. . .	. . .	. . .	. . .	. . .	. . .	. . .	. . .
Other sectors	4 710 . .	-.2	11.1	-8.6	11.9	-2.7	. . .	. . .	. . .
of which: Short-term	4 712 . .	*-.2*	*11.1*	*-8.6*	*11.9*	*-2.7*	. . .	. . .	. . .
Loans	4 714 . .	. . .	. . .	. . .	. . .	. . .	. . .	. . .	. . .
Monetary authorities	4 715 . .	. . .	. . .	. . .	. . .	. . .	. . .	. . .	. . .
of which: Short-term	4 718 . .	. . .	. . .	. . .	. . .	. . .	. . .	. . .	. . .
General government	4 719 . .	. . .	. . .	. . .	. . .	. . .	. . .	. . .	. . .
of which: Short-term	4 721 . .	. . .	. . .	. . .	. . .	. . .	. . .	. . .	. . .
Banks	4 722 . .	. . .	. . .	. . .	. . .	. . .	. . .	. . .	. . .
of which: Short-term	4 724 . .	. . .	. . .	. . .	. . .	. . .	. . .	. . .	. . .
Other sectors	4 725 . .	. . .	. . .	. . .	. . .	. . .	. . .	. . .	. . .
of which: Short-term	4 727 . .	. . .	. . .	. . .	. . .	. . .	. . .	. . .	. . .
Currency and deposits	4 730 . .	-6.0	-29.7	12.1	8.3	-13.2	1.6	-3.3	10.1
Monetary authorities	4 731 . .	. . .	. . .	. . .	. . .	. . .	. . .	. . .	. . .
General government	4 732 . .	. . .	. . .	. . .	. . .	. . .	. . .	. . .	. . .
Banks	4 733 . .	-.4	-4.6	9.0	9.3	-12.5	7.6	-1.3	9.5
Other sectors	4 734 . .	-5.6	-25.1	3.0	-1.0	-.7	-6.0	-2.0	.6
Other assets	4 736 . .	-8.3	-55.1	-23.2	-119.2	1.2	-1.5	-13.7	1.5
Monetary authorities	4 737 . .	-6.5	9.0	6.0	2.4	1.2	-1.5	-13.7	1.5
of which: Short-term	4 739 . .	*-6.5*	*9.0*	*6.0*	*2.4*	*1.2*	*-1.5*	*-13.7*	*1.5*
General government	4 740 . .	. . .	. . .	. . .	. . .	. . .	. . .	. . .	. . .
of which: Short-term	4 742 . .	. . .	. . .	. . .	. . .	. . .	. . .	. . .	. . .
Banks	4 743 . .	-1.8	. . .	. . .	. . .	. . .	. . .	. . .	. . .
of which: Short-term	4 745 . .	*-1.8*	. . .	. . .	. . .	. . .	. . .	. . .	. . .
Other sectors	4 746 . .	. . .	-64.1	-29.2	-121.6	. . .	. . .	. . .	. . .
of which: Short-term	4 748 . .	. . .	*-64.1*	*-29.2*	*-121.6*	. . .	. . .	. . .	. . .
Liabilities	4 753 . .	**189.5**	**253.6**	**109.6**	**34.8**	**155.4**	**74.9**	**4.0**	**47.7**
Trade credits	4 756 . .	-3.5	-1.7	-3.7	. . .	.1	. . .	. . .	. . .
General government	4 757 . .	. . .	. . .	. . .	. . .	. . .	. . .	. . .	. . .
of which: Short-term	4 759 . .	. . .	. . .	. . .	. . .	. . .	. . .	. . .	. . .
Other sectors	4 760 . .	-3.5	-1.7	-3.7	. . .	.1	. . .	. . .	. . .
of which: Short-term	4 762 . .	. . .	*-1.7*	*-3.7*	. . .	*.1*	. . .	. . .	. . .
Loans	4 764 . .	128.8	344.6	59.3	194.0	140.5	74.3	23.9	45.3
Monetary authorities	4 765 . .	19.1	22.1	26.9	-13.0	22.8	3.7	-7.9	14.8
of which: Use of Fund credit and loans from the Fund	4 766 . .	*7.0*	*22.1*	*-8.4*	*22.4*	*22.8*	*3.7*	*-7.9*	*14.8*
of which: Short-term	4 768 . .	. . .	. . .	*35.4*	*-35.4*	. . .	. . .	. . .	. . .
General government	4 769 . .	94.8	272.6	-.3	217.5	69.6	86.0	63.2	88.0
of which: Short-term	4 771 . .	. . .	. . .	. . .	. . .	. . .	. . .	. . .	. . .
Banks	4 772 . .	1.0	-1.9	. . .	-1.8	2.0	-.3	-.5	. . .
of which: Short-term	4 774 . .	. . .	. . .	. . .	. . .	. . .	. . .	. . .	. . .
Other sectors	4 775 . .	14.0	51.9	32.7	-8.6	46.1	-15.1	-30.9	-57.5
of which: Short-term	4 777 . .	*16.5*	*16.6*	*26.1*	*-3.5*	*-13.0*	*10.9*	*10.9*	*4.9*
Currency and deposits	4 780 . .	7.4	27.9	-7.8	-18.1	5.0	4.4	-21.2	-13.0
Monetary authorities	4 781 . .	.1	. . .	2.0	-1.7	.2	.3	1.4	-.6
General government	4 782 . .	. . .	. . .	. . .	. . .	. . .	. . .	. . .	. . .
Banks	4 783 . .	7.3	27.9	-9.8	-16.3	4.8	4.1	-22.6	-12.4
Other sectors	4 784 . .	. . .	. . .	. . .	. . .	. . .	. . .	. . .	. . .
Other liabilities	4 786 . .	56.8	-117.1	61.8	-141.2	9.9	-3.8	1.3	15.4
Monetary authorities	4 787 . .	. . .	-.4	1.7	1.8	-3.2	-.1	-2.2	14.0
of which: Short-term	4 789 . .	. . .	*-.4*	*1.7*	*1.8*	*-3.2*	*-.1*	*-2.2*	*14.0*
General government	4 790 . .	56.8	-116.7	60.0	-149.4	13.1	-3.7	3.5	1.4
of which: Short-term	4 792 . .	*56.8*	*-116.7*	*60.0*	*-149.4*	*13.1*	*-3.7*	*3.5*	*1.4*
Banks	4 793 . .	. . .	. . .	. . .	. . .	. . .	. . .	. . .	. . .
of which: Short-term	4 795 . .	. . .	. . .	. . .	. . .	. . .	. . .	. . .	. . .
Other sectors	4 796 . .	. . .	. . .	. . .	6.4	. . .	. . .	. . .	. . .
of which: Short-term	4 798 . .	. . .	. . .	. . .	. . .	. . .	. . .	. . .	. . .
E. RESERVE ASSETS	4 802 . .	32.4	-43.8	-6.5	-20.3	60.7	60.7	52.2	-3.9
Monetary gold	4 812 . .	-11.5	-28.6	-7.4	6.0	88.3	3.6	-1.6	3.8
Special drawing rights	4 811 . .	6.8	-1.9	6.5	-2.0	1.4	.1	.9	-.5
Reserve position in the Fund	4 810 . .	. . .	. . .	. . .	. . .	. . .	. . .	. . .	. . .
Foreign exchange	4 803 . .	37.1	-13.3	-5.6	-24.3	-29.0	57.0	52.9	-7.2
Other claims	4 813 . .	. . .	. . .	. . .	. . .	. . .	. . .	. . .	. . .
NET ERRORS AND OMISSIONS	4 998 . .	**39.7**	**34.8**	**69.9**	**49.8**	**17.8**	**22.4**	**82.1**	**-1.9**

Part 3 of the *Yearbook* contains descriptions of the methodologies, compilation practices, and sources used to compile these data.

Table 1. ANALYTIC PRESENTATION, 1994–2001

(Millions of U.S. dollars)

	Code	1994	1995	1996	1997	1998	1999	2000	2001
A. Current Account [1]	4 993 Z.	**–47.63**	**–50.65**	**–60.43**	**–30.28**	...	...	...	...
Goods: exports f.o.b	2 100 ..	33.21	23.90	21.61	48.86	...	...	...	...
Goods: imports f.o.b	3 100 ..	–53.80	–59.34	–56.80	–62.49	...	...	...	...
Balance on Goods	4 100 ..	*–20.59*	*–35.44*	*–35.19*	*–13.63*	...	...	...	...
Services: credit	2 200 ..	5.61	5.69	6.96	8.00	...	...	...	...
Services: debit	3 200 ..	–27.11	–29.91	–29.25	–26.15	...	...	...	...
Balance on Goods and Services	4 991 ..	*–42.09*	*–59.66*	*–57.48*	*–31.78*	...	...	...	...
Income: credit	2 300 ..	...	...	...	...	...	...	...	...
Income: debit	3 300 ..	–26.27	–21.09	–18.65	–14.30	...	...	...	...
Balance on Goods, Services, and Income	4 992 ..	*–68.36*	*–80.75*	*–76.13*	*–46.08*	...	...	...	...
Current transfers: credit	2 379 Z.	21.79	31.42	15.70	15.80	...	...	...	...
Current transfers: debit	3 379 ..	–1.06	–1.32	...	...	...	...	...	...
B. Capital Account [1]	4 994 Z.	**44.42**	**49.20**	**40.70**	**32.20**	...	...	...	...
Capital account: credit	2 994 Z.	44.42	49.20	40.70	32.20	...	...	...	...
Capital account: debit	3 994 ..	...	...	...	...	...	...	...	...
Total, Groups A Plus B	4 981 ..	*–3.21*	*–1.45*	*–19.73*	*1.92*	...	...	...	...
C. Financial Account [1]	4 995 W.	**–26.98**	**–28.25**	**–12.30**	**2.03**	...	...	...	...
Direct investment abroad	4 505 ..	...	...	...	...	...	...	...	...
Direct investment in Guinea-Bissau	4 555 Z.	...	...	...	...	...	...	...	...
Portfolio investment assets	4 602 ..	...	...	...	...	...	...	...	...
Equity securities	4 610 ..	...	...	...	...	...	...	...	...
Debt securities	4 619 ..	...	...	...	...	...	...	...	...
Portfolio investment liabilities	4 652 Z.	...	...	...	...	...	...	...	...
Equity securities	4 660 ..	...	...	...	...	...	...	...	...
Debt securities	4 669 Z.	...	...	...	...	...	...	...	...
Financial derivatives	4 910 ..	...	...	...	...	...	...	...	...
Financial derivatives assets	4 900 ..	...	...	...	...	...	...	...	...
Financial derivatives liabilities	4 905 ..	...	...	...	...	...	...	...	...
Other investment assets	4 703 ..	...	...	...	–5.80	...	...	...	...
Monetary authorities	4 701 ..	...	...	...	...	...	...	...	...
General government	4 704 ..	...	...	...	...	...	...	...	...
Banks	4 705 ..	...	...	...	–5.80	...	...	...	...
Other sectors	4 728 ..	...	...	...	...	...	...	...	...
Other investment liabilities	4 753 W.	–26.98	–28.25	–12.30	7.83	...	...	...	...
Monetary authorities	4 753 WA	...	–6.88	...	.43	...	...	...	...
General government	4 753 ZB	–26.98	–21.37	–12.30	7.40	...	...	...	...
Banks	4 753 ZC	...	...	...	...	...	...	...	...
Other sectors	4 753 ZD	...	...	...	...	...	...	...	...
Total, Groups A Through C	4 983 ..	*–30.19*	*–29.70*	*–32.03*	*3.95*	...	...	...	...
D. Net Errors and Omissions	4 998 ..	**–24.34**	**–10.90**	**–11.47**	**–19.19**	...	...	...	...
Total, Groups A Through D	4 984 ..	*–54.53*	*–40.60*	*–43.50*	*–15.24*	...	...	...	...
E. Reserves and Related Items	4 802 A.	**54.53**	**40.60**	**43.50**	**15.24**	...	...	...	...
Reserve assets	4 802 ..	6.24	–3.64	–8.90	–35.15	...	...	...	...
Use of Fund credit and loans	4 766 ..	–.43	1.19	1.94	5.11	...	...	...	...
Exceptional financing	4 920 ..	48.72	43.05	50.46	45.28	...	...	...	...
Conversion rates: CFA francs per U.S. dollar	0 101 ..	**198.34**	**278.04**	**405.75**	**582.78**	**589.95**	**615.70**	**711.98**	**733.04**

[1] Excludes components that have been classified in the categories of Group E.

Table 2. STANDARD PRESENTATION, 1994–2001
(Millions of U.S. dollars)

	Code	1994	1995	1996	1997	1998	1999	2000	2001
CURRENT ACCOUNT	4 993 . .	**–45.94**	**–35.18**	**–44.47**	**–6.38**	...	...	...	...
A. GOODS	4 100 . .	–20.59	–35.44	–35.19	–13.63	...	...	...	...
Credit	2 100 . .	**33.21**	**23.90**	**21.61**	**48.86**	...	...	...	...
General merchandise: exports f.o.b.	2 110 . .	33.21	23.90	21.61	48.86	...	...	...	...
Goods for processing: exports f.o.b.	2 150 . .	...	...	...	...	...	...	...	...
Repairs on goods	2 160 . .	...	...	...	...	...	...	...	...
Goods procured in ports by carriers	2 170 . .	...	...	...	...	...	...	...	...
Nonmonetary gold	2 180 . .	...	...	...	...	...	...	...	...
Debit	3 100 . .	**–53.80**	**–59.34**	**–56.80**	**–62.49**	...	...	...	...
General merchandise: imports f.o.b.	3 110 . .	–53.80	–59.34	–56.80	–62.49	...	...	...	...
Goods for processing: imports f.o.b.	3 150 . .	...	...	...	...	...	...	...	...
Repairs on goods	3 160 . .	...	...	...	...	...	...	...	...
Goods procured in ports by carriers	3 170 . .	...	...	...	...	...	...	...	...
Nonmonetary gold	3 180 . .	...	...	...	...	...	...	...	...
B. SERVICES	4 200 . .	–21.50	–24.22	–22.29	–18.15	...	...	...	...
Total credit	2 200 . .	*5.61*	*5.69*	*6.96*	*8.00*	...	...	...	...
Total debit	3 200 . .	*–27.11*	*–29.91*	*–29.25*	*–26.15*	...	...	...	...
Transportation services, credit	2 205 . .	**.55**	**.44**	**.40**	**.45**	...	...	...	...
Passenger	2 850 . .	*.30*	*.31*	*.40*	*.32*	...	...	...	...
Freight	2 851 . .	...	...	...	*–.15*	...	...	...	...
Other	2 852 . .	*.25*	*.13*	...	*.28*	...	...	...	...
Sea transport, passenger	2 207 . .	...	...	...	...	...	...	...	...
Sea transport, freight	2 208 . .	...	...	...	...	...	...	...	...
Sea transport, other	2 209 . .	...	...	...	...	...	...	...	...
Air transport, passenger	2 211 . .	.30	.31	.40	.32	...	...	...	...
Air transport, freight	2 212 . .	...	...	...	...	...	...	...	...
Air transport, other	2 213 . .	...	...	...	...	...	...	...	...
Other transport, passenger	2 215 . .	...	...	...	...	...	...	...	...
Other transport, freight	2 216 . .	...	...	...	...	...	...	...	...
Other transport, other	2 217 . .	.25	.13	...	.28	...	...	...	...
Transportation services, debit	3 205 . .	**–12.69**	**–14.14**	**–12.61**	**–15.56**	...	...	...	...
Passenger	3 850 . .	*–1.79*	*–1.96*	*–1.80*	*–2.00*	...	...	...	...
Freight	3 851 . .	*–10.26*	*–11.33*	*–10.81*	*–13.56*	...	...	...	...
Other	3 852 . .	*–.64*	*–.85*	...	...	...	...	...	...
Sea transport, passenger	3 207 . .	...	...	...	...	...	...	...	...
Sea transport, freight	3 208 . .	–10.26	–11.33	–10.81	–13.41	...	...	...	...
Sea transport, other	3 209 . .	...	...	...	...	...	...	...	...
Air transport, passenger	3 211 . .	–1.79	–1.96	–1.80	–2.00	...	...	...	...
Air transport, freight	3 212 . .	...	...	...	–.15	...	...	...	...
Air transport, other	3 213 . .	...	...	...	...	...	...	...	...
Other transport, passenger	3 215 . .	...	...	...	...	...	...	...	...
Other transport, freight	3 216 . .	...	...	...	...	...	...	...	...
Other transport, other	3 217 . .	–.64	–.85	...	...	...	...	...	...
Travel, credit	2 236 . .	**...**	**...**	**.40**	**3.13**	...	...	...	...
Business travel	2 237 . .	...	...	...	...	...	...	...	...
Personal travel	2 240 . .	...	...	.40	3.13	...	...	...	...
Travel, debit	3 236 . .	**–3.80**	**–3.75**	**–2.88**	**–1.45**	...	...	...	...
Business travel	3 237 . .	–.60	–.45	–1.52	–.75	...	...	...	...
Personal travel	3 240 . .	–3.20	–3.30	–1.36	–.70	...	...	...	...
Other services, credit	2 200 BA	**5.06**	**5.25**	**6.16**	**4.42**	...	...	...	...
Communications	2 245 . .	...	...	.69	.32	...	...	...	...
Construction	2 249 . .	...	...	...	...	...	...	...	...
Insurance	2 253 . .	...	...	...	...	...	...	...	...
Financial	2 260 . .	...	...	...	...	...	...	...	...
Computer and information	2 262 . .	.41	...	...	...	...	...	...	...
Royalties and licence fees	2 266 . .	...	...	...	...	...	...	...	...
Other business services	2 268 . .	1.50	1.98	1.37	2.00	...	...	...	...
Personal, cultural, and recreational	2 287 . .	...	...	...	...	...	...	...	...
Government, n.i.e.	2 291 . .	3.15	3.27	4.10	2.10	...	...	...	...
Other services, debit	3 200 BA	**–10.62**	**–12.02**	**–13.76**	**–9.14**	...	...	...	...
Communications	3 245 . .	...	–.50	–.40	...	...	...	...	...
Construction	3 249 . .	...	...	...	...	...	...	...	...
Insurance	3 253 . .	–1.14	–1.26	–1.20	–1.34	...	...	...	...
Financial	3 260 . .	...	...	...	...	...	...	...	...
Computer and information	3 262 . .	...	...	...	...	...	...	...	...
Royalties and licence fees	3 266 . .	...	...	...	...	...	...	...	...
Other business services	3 268 . .	–6.52	–7.00	–9.36	–6.00	...	...	...	...
Personal, cultural, and recreational	3 287 . .	...	...	...	...	...	...	...	...
Government, n.i.e.	3 291 . .	–2.96	–3.26	–2.80	–1.80	...	...	...	...

Table 2 (Continued). STANDARD PRESENTATION, 1994–2001

(Millions of U.S. dollars)

	Code	1994	1995	1996	1997	1998	1999	2000	2001
C. INCOME	4 300	–26.27	–21.09	–18.65	–14.30	...	...	...	...
Total credit	2 300	...	...	...	...	...	...	...	...
Total debit	3 300	*–26.27*	*–21.09*	*–18.65*	*–14.30*	...	...	...	...
Compensation of employees, credit	2 310	**...**	**...**	**...**	**...**	**...**	**...**	**...**	**...**
Compensation of employees, debit	3 310	**–12.18**	**–2.09**	**...**	**...**	**...**	**...**	**...**	**...**
Investment income, credit	2 320	**...**	**...**	**...**	**...**	**...**	**...**	**...**	**...**
Direct investment income	2 330	...	...	...	...	...	...	...	...
Dividends and distributed branch profits	2 332	...	...	...	...	...	...	...	...
Reinvested earnings and undistributed branch profits	2 333	...	...	...	...	...	...	...	...
Income on debt (interest)	2 334	...	...	...	...	...	...	...	...
Portfolio investment income	2 339	...	...	...	...	...	...	...	...
Income on equity	2 340	...	...	...	...	...	...	...	...
Income on bonds and notes	2 350	...	...	...	...	...	...	...	...
Income on money market instruments	2 360	...	...	...	...	...	...	...	...
Other investment income	2 370	...	...	...	...	...	...	...	...
Investment income, debit	3 320	**–14.09**	**–19.00**	**–18.65**	**–14.30**	**...**	**...**	**...**	**...**
Direct investment income	3 330	...	...	...	...	...	...	...	...
Dividends and distributed branch profits	3 332	...	...	...	...	...	...	...	...
Reinvested earnings and undistributed branch profits	3 333	...	...	...	...	...	...	...	...
Income on debt (interest)	3 334	...	...	...	...	...	...	...	...
Portfolio investment income	3 339	...	...	...	...	...	...	...	...
Income on equity	3 340	...	...	...	...	...	...	...	...
Income on bonds and notes	3 350	...	...	...	...	...	...	...	...
Income on money market instruments	3 360	...	...	...	...	...	...	...	...
Other investment income	3 370	–14.09	–19.00	–18.65	–14.30	...	...	...	...
D. CURRENT TRANSFERS	4 379	22.42	45.57	31.66	39.70	...	...	...	...
Credit	2 379	**23.48**	**46.89**	**31.66**	**39.70**	**...**	**...**	**...**	**...**
General government	2 380	23.48	46.89	29.66	37.70	...	...	...	...
Other sectors	2 390	...	...	2.00	2.00	...	...	...	...
Workers' remittances	2 391	...	...	2.00	2.00	...	...	...	...
Other current transfers	2 392	...	...	...	...	...	...	...	...
Debit	3 379	**–1.06**	**–1.32**	**...**	**...**	**...**	**...**	**...**	**...**
General government	3 380	...	...	...	...	...	...	...	...
Other sectors	3 390	–1.06	–1.32	...	...	...	...	...	...
Workers' remittances	3 391	–1.06	–1.32	...	...	...	...	...	...
Other current transfers	3 392	...	...	...	...	...	...	...	...
CAPITAL AND FINANCIAL ACCOUNT	4 996	**70.28**	**46.08**	**55.94**	**25.57**	**...**	**...**	**...**	**...**
CAPITAL ACCOUNT	4 994	**44.42**	**49.20**	**40.70**	**32.20**	**...**	**...**	**...**	**...**
Total credit	2 994	*44.42*	*49.20*	*40.70*	*32.20*	...	...	...	...
Total debit	3 994	...	...	...	...	...	...	...	...
Capital transfers, credit	2 400	**44.42**	**49.20**	**40.70**	**32.20**	**...**	**...**	**...**	**...**
General government	2 401	44.42	49.20	38.68	32.20	...	...	...	...
Debt forgiveness	2 402	.15	9.90	11.80	...	...	...	...	...
Other capital transfers	2 410	44.27	39.30	26.88	32.20	...	...	...	...
Other sectors	2 430	...	...	2.02	...	...	...	...	...
Migrants' transfers	2 431	...	...	...	...	...	...	...	...
Debt forgiveness	2 432	...	...	...	...	...	...	...	...
Other capital transfers	2 440	...	...	2.02	...	...	...	...	...
Capital transfers, debit	3 400	**...**	**...**	**...**	**...**	**...**	**...**	**...**	**...**
General government	3 401	...	...	...	...	...	...	...	...
Debt forgiveness	3 402	...	...	...	...	...	...	...	...
Other capital transfers	3 410	...	...	...	...	...	...	...	...
Other sectors	3 430	...	...	...	...	...	...	...	...
Migrants' transfers	3 431	...	...	...	...	...	...	...	...
Debt forgiveness	3 432	...	...	...	...	...	...	...	...
Other capital transfers	3 440	...	...	...	...	...	...	...	...
Nonproduced nonfinancial assets, credit	2 480	**...**	**...**	**...**	**...**	**...**	**...**	**...**	**...**
Nonproduced nonfinancial assets, debit	3 480	**...**	**...**	**...**	**...**	**...**	**...**	**...**	**...**

Table 2 (Continued). STANDARD PRESENTATION, 1994–2001

(Millions of U.S. dollars)

	Code		1994	1995	1996	1997	1998	1999	2000	2001
FINANCIAL ACCOUNT	4 995	. .	**25.86**	**–3.12**	**15.24**	**–6.63**	...	...	...	...
A. DIRECT INVESTMENT	4 500	. .	...	...	...	...	...	...	...	...
Direct investment abroad	4 505	. .	...	...	...	...	...	...	...	...
Equity capital	4 510	. .	...	...	...	...	...	...	...	...
Claims on affiliated enterprises	4 515	. .	...	...	...	...	...	...	...	...
Liabilities to affiliated enterprises	4 520	. .	...	...	...	...	...	...	...	...
Reinvested earnings	4 525	. .	...	...	...	...	...	...	...	...
Other capital	4 530	. .	...	...	...	...	...	...	...	...
Claims on affiliated enterprises	4 535	. .	...	...	...	...	...	...	...	...
Liabilities to affiliated enterprises	4 540	. .	...	...	...	...	...	...	...	...
Direct investment in Guinea-Bissau	4 555	. .	...	...	...	...	...	...	...	...
Equity capital	4 560	. .	...	...	...	...	...	...	...	...
Claims on direct investors	4 565	. .	...	...	...	...	...	...	...	...
Liabilities to direct investors	4 570	. .	...	...	...	...	...	...	...	...
Reinvested earnings	4 575	. .	...	...	...	...	...	...	...	...
Other capital	4 580	. .	...	...	...	...	...	...	...	...
Claims on direct investors	4 585	. .	...	...	...	...	...	...	...	...
Liabilities to direct investors	4 590	. .	...	...	...	...	...	...	...	...
B. PORTFOLIO INVESTMENT	4 600	. .	...	...	...	...	...	...	...	...
Assets	4 602	. .	...	...	...	...	...	...	...	...
Equity securities	4 610	. .	...	...	...	...	...	...	...	...
Monetary authorities	4 611	. .	...	...	...	...	...	...	...	...
General government	4 612	. .	...	...	...	...	...	...	...	...
Banks	4 613	. .	...	...	...	...	...	...	...	...
Other sectors	4 614	. .	...	...	...	...	...	...	...	...
Debt securities	4 619	. .	...	...	...	...	...	...	...	...
Bonds and notes	4 620	. .	...	...	...	...	...	...	...	...
Monetary authorities	4 621	. .	...	...	...	...	...	...	...	...
General government	4 622	. .	...	...	...	...	...	...	...	...
Banks	4 623	. .	...	...	...	...	...	...	...	...
Other sectors	4 624	. .	...	...	...	...	...	...	...	...
Money market instruments	4 630	. .	...	...	...	...	...	...	...	...
Monetary authorities	4 631	. .	...	...	...	...	...	...	...	...
General government	4 632	. .	...	...	...	...	...	...	...	...
Banks	4 633	. .	...	...	...	...	...	...	...	...
Other sectors	4 634	. .	...	...	...	...	...	...	...	...
Liabilities	4 652	. .	...	...	...	...	...	...	...	...
Equity securities	4 660	. .	...	...	...	...	...	...	...	...
Banks	4 663	. .	...	...	...	...	...	...	...	...
Other sectors	4 664	. .	...	...	...	...	...	...	...	...
Debt securities	4 669	. .	...	...	...	...	...	...	...	...
Bonds and notes	4 670	. .	...	...	...	...	...	...	...	...
Monetary authorities	4 671	. .	...	...	...	...	...	...	...	...
General government	4 672	. .	...	...	...	...	...	...	...	...
Banks	4 673	. .	...	...	...	...	...	...	...	...
Other sectors	4 674	. .	...	...	...	...	...	...	...	...
Money market instruments	4 680	. .	...	...	...	...	...	...	...	...
Monetary authorities	4 681	. .	...	...	...	...	...	...	...	...
General government	4 682	. .	...	...	...	...	...	...	...	...
Banks	4 683	. .	...	...	...	...	...	...	...	...
Other sectors	4 684	. .	...	...	...	...	...	...	...	...
C. FINANCIAL DERIVATIVES	4 910	. .	...	...	...	...	...	...	...	...
Monetary authorities	4 911	. .	...	...	...	...	...	...	...	...
General government	4 912	. .	...	...	...	...	...	...	...	...
Banks	4 913	. .	...	...	...	...	...	...	...	...
Other sectors	4 914	. .	...	...	...	...	...	...	...	...
Assets	4 900	. .	...	...	...	...	...	...	...	...
Monetary authorities	4 901	. .	...	...	...	...	...	...	...	...
General government	4 902	. .	...	...	...	...	...	...	...	...
Banks	4 903	. .	...	...	...	...	...	...	...	...
Other sectors	4 904	. .	...	...	...	...	...	...	...	...
Liabilities	4 905	. .	...	...	...	...	...	...	...	...
Monetary authorities	4 906	. .	...	...	...	...	...	...	...	...
General government	4 907	. .	...	...	...	...	...	...	...	...
Banks	4 908	. .	...	...	...	...	...	...	...	...
Other sectors	4 909	. .	...	...	...	...	...	...	...	...

Table 2 (Concluded). STANDARD PRESENTATION, 1994–2001
(Millions of U.S. dollars)

	Code	1994	1995	1996	1997	1998	1999	2000	2001
D. OTHER INVESTMENT	4 700 . .	19.62	.52	24.14	28.52	...	...	...	...
Assets	4 703 . .	**...**	**...**	**...**	**–5.80**	**...**	**...**	**...**	**...**
Trade credits	4 706 . .	...	...	...	...	...	...	...	...
General government	4 707 . .	...	...	...	...	...	...	...	...
of which: Short-term	4 709 . .	...	...	...	...	...	...	...	...
Other sectors	4 710 . .	...	...	...	...	...	...	...	...
of which: Short-term	4 712 . .	...	...	...	...	...	...	...	...
Loans	4 714 . .	...	...	...	...	...	...	...	...
Monetary authorities	4 715 . .	...	...	...	...	...	...	...	...
of which: Short-term	4 718 . .	...	...	...	...	...	...	...	...
General government	4 719 . .	...	...	...	...	...	...	...	...
of which: Short-term	4 721 . .	...	...	...	...	...	...	...	...
Banks	4 722 . .	...	...	...	...	...	...	...	...
of which: Short-term	4 724 . .	...	...	...	...	...	...	...	...
Other sectors	4 725 . .	...	...	...	...	...	...	...	...
of which: Short-term	4 727 . .	...	...	...	...	...	...	...	...
Currency and deposits	4 730 . .	...	...	...	–5.80	...	...	...	...
Monetary authorities	4 731 . .	...	...	...	...	...	...	...	...
General government	4 732 . .	...	...	...	...	...	...	...	...
Banks	4 733 . .	...	...	...	–5.80	...	...	...	...
Other sectors	4 734 . .	...	...	...	...	...	...	...	...
Other assets	4 736 . .	...	...	...	...	...	...	...	...
Monetary authorities	4 737 . .	...	...	...	...	...	...	...	...
of which: Short-term	4 739 . .	...	...	...	...	...	...	...	...
General government	4 740 . .	...	...	...	...	...	...	...	...
of which: Short-term	4 742 . .	...	...	...	...	...	...	...	...
Banks	4 743 . .	...	...	...	...	...	...	...	...
of which: Short-term	4 745 . .	...	...	...	...	...	...	...	...
Other sectors	4 746 . .	...	...	...	...	...	...	...	...
of which: Short-term	4 748 . .	...	...	...	...	...	...	...	...
Liabilities	4 753 . .	**19.62**	**.52**	**24.14**	**34.32**	**...**	**...**	**...**	**...**
Trade credits	4 756 . .	...	...	...	...	...	...	...	...
General government	4 757 . .	...	...	...	...	...	...	...	...
of which: Short-term	4 759 . .	...	...	...	...	...	...	...	...
Other sectors	4 760 . .	...	...	...	...	...	...	...	...
of which: Short-term	4 762 . .	...	...	...	...	...	...	...	...
Loans	4 764 . .	–24.18	162.02	42.34	12.51	...	...	...	...
Monetary authorities	4 765 . .	–.43	1.19	1.94	5.11	...	...	...	...
of which: Use of Fund credit and loans from the Fund	4 766 . .	*–.43*	*1.19*	*1.94*	*5.11*	...	...	...	...
of which: Short-term	4 768 . .	...	...	...	...	...	...	...	...
General government	4 769 . .	–23.75	160.83	40.40	7.40	...	...	...	...
of which: Short-term	4 771 . .	...	...	...	...	...	...	...	...
Banks	4 772 . .	...	...	...	...	...	...	...	...
of which: Short-term	4 774 . .	...	...	...	...	...	...	...	...
Other sectors	4 775 . .	...	...	...	...	...	...	...	...
of which: Short-term	4 777 . .	...	...	...	...	...	...	...	...
Currency and deposits	4 780 . .	...	...	...	...	...	...	...	...
Monetary authorities	4 781 . .	...	...	...	...	...	...	...	...
General government	4 782 . .	...	...	...	...	...	...	...	...
Banks	4 783 . .	...	...	...	...	...	...	...	...
Other sectors	4 784 . .	...	...	...	...	...	...	...	...
Other liabilities	4 786 . .	43.80	–161.50	–18.20	21.81	...	...	...	...
Monetary authorities	4 787 . .	43.80	–161.50	–18.20	21.81	...	...	...	...
of which: Short-term	4 789 . .	*43.80*	*–161.50*	*–18.20*	*21.81*	...	...	...	...
General government	4 790 . .	...	...	...	...	...	...	...	...
of which: Short-term	4 792 . .	...	...	...	...	...	...	...	...
Banks	4 793 . .	...	...	...	...	...	...	...	...
of which: Short-term	4 795 . .	...	...	...	...	...	...	...	...
Other sectors	4 796 . .	...	...	...	...	...	...	...	...
of which: Short-term	4 798 . .	...	...	...	...	...	...	...	...
E. RESERVE ASSETS	4 802 . .	6.24	–3.64	–8.90	–35.15	...	...	...	...
Monetary gold	4 812 . .	...	...	...	...	...	...	...	...
Special drawing rights	4 811 . .	.01	–.01	...	–.05	...	...	...	...
Reserve position in the Fund	4 810 . .	...	...	...	...	...	...	...	...
Foreign exchange	4 803 . .	6.23	–3.63	–8.90	–35.10	...	...	...	...
Other claims	4 813 . .	...	...	...	...	...	...	...	...
NET ERRORS AND OMISSIONS	4 998 . .	**–24.34**	**–10.90**	**–11.47**	**–19.19**	**...**	**...**	**...**	**...**

Part 3 of the *Yearbook* contains descriptions of the methodologies, compilation practices, and sources used to compile these data.

Table 1. ANALYTIC PRESENTATION, 1994–2001
(Millions of U.S. dollars)

	Code		1994	1995	1996	1997	1998	1999	2000	2001
A. Current Account [1]	4 993	Z.	**–124.9**	**–134.8**	...	...	...	...	...	...
Goods: exports f.o.b	2 100	. .	463.4	495.7	...	...	...	...	...	...
Goods: imports f.o.b	3 100	. .	–504.0	–536.5	...	...	...	...	...	...
Balance on Goods	4 100	. .	*–40.6*	*–40.8*	...	...	...	...	...	...
Services: credit	2 200	. .	120.7	133.5	...	...	...	...	...	...
Services: debit	3 200	. .	–160.9	–171.8	...	...	...	...	...	...
Balance on Goods and Services	4 991	. .	*–80.8*	*–79.2*	...	...	...	...	...	...
Income: credit	2 300	. .	8.7	12.2	...	...	...	...	...	...
Income: debit	3 300	. .	–114.8	–129.9	...	...	...	...	...	...
Balance on Goods, Services, and Income	4 992	. .	*–186.9*	*–196.8*	...	...	...	...	...	...
Current transfers: credit	2 379	Z.	68.1	67.4	...	...	...	...	...	...
Current transfers: debit	3 379	. .	–6.2	–5.3	...	...	...	...	...	...
B. Capital Account [1]	4 994	Z.	**8.3**	**9.5**	...	...	...	...	...	...
Capital account: credit	2 994	Z.	11.0	12.5	...	...	...	...	...	...
Capital account: debit	3 994	. .	–2.7	–3.0	...	...	...	...	...	...
Total, Groups A Plus B	4 981	. .	*–116.6*	*–125.3*	...	...	...	...	...	...
C. Financial Account [1]	4 995	W.	**126.9**	**71.1**	...	...	...	...	...	...
Direct investment abroad	4 505	. .	...	...	...	...	...	...	...	...
Direct investment in Guyana	4 555	Z.	106.7	74.4	...	...	...	...	...	...
Portfolio investment assets	4 602	. .	...	...	...	...	...	...	...	...
Equity securities	4 610	. .	...	...	...	...	...	...	...	...
Debt securities	4 619	. .	...	...	...	...	...	...	...	...
Portfolio investment liabilities	4 652	Z.	15.8	3.2	...	...	...	...	...	...
Equity securities	4 660	. .	...	...	...	...	...	...	...	...
Debt securities	4 669	Z.	15.8	3.2	...	...	...	...	...	...
Financial derivatives	4 910	. .	...	...	...	...	...	...	...	...
Financial derivatives assets	4 900	. .	...	...	...	...	...	...	...	...
Financial derivatives liabilities	4 905	. .	...	...	...	...	...	...	...	...
Other investment assets	4 703	. .	–5.8	–8.9	...	...	...	...	...	...
Monetary authorities	4 701	. .	...	...	...	...	...	...	...	...
General government	4 704	. .	1.3	–2.2	...	...	...	...	...	...
Banks	4 705	. .	4.2	–2.8	...	...	...	...	...	...
Other sectors	4 728	. .	–11.2	–3.9	...	...	...	...	...	...
Other investment liabilities	4 753	W.	10.2	2.3	...	...	...	...	...	...
Monetary authorities	4 753	WA	1.3	18.6	...	...	...	...	...	...
General government	4 753	ZB	–1.0	–5.4	...	...	...	...	...	...
Banks	4 753	ZC	–2.9	–.4	...	...	...	...	...	...
Other sectors	4 753	ZD	12.9	–10.5	...	...	...	...	...	...
Total, Groups A Through C	4 983	. .	*10.3*	*–54.2*	...	...	...	...	...	...
D. Net Errors and Omissions	4 998	. .	**–16.3**	**11.2**	...	...	...	...	...	...
Total, Groups A Through D	4 984	. .	*–6.0*	*–43.0*	...	...	...	...	...	...
E. Reserves and Related Items	4 802	A.	**6.0**	**43.0**	...	...	...	...	...	...
Reserve assets	4 802	. .	–21.8	.8	...	...	...	...	...	...
Use of Fund credit and loans	4 766	. .	–8.8	–9.7	...	...	...	...	...	...
Exceptional financing	4 920	. .	36.6	52.0	...	...	...	...	...	...
Conversion rates: Guyana dollars per U.S. dollar	0 101	. .	**138.29**	**141.99**	**140.38**	**142.40**	**150.52**	**178.00**	**182.43**	**187.32**

[1] Excludes components that have been classified in the categories of Group E.

Table 2. STANDARD PRESENTATION, 1994–2001
(Millions of U.S. dollars)

	Code		1994	1995	1996	1997	1998	1999	2000	2001
CURRENT ACCOUNT	4 993	. .	**–124.9**	**–134.8**	**. . .**	**. . .**	**. . .**	**. . .**	**. . .**	**. . .**
A. GOODS	4 100	. .	–40.6	–40.8	. . .	. . .	. . .	. . .	. . .	. . .
Credit	2 100	. .	**463.4**	**495.7**	**. . .**	**. . .**	**. . .**	**. . .**	**. . .**	**. . .**
General merchandise: exports f.o.b.	2 110	. .	463.4	495.7	. . .	. . .	. . .	. . .	. . .	. . .
Goods for processing: exports f.o.b.	2 150	. .	. . .	. . .	. . .	. . .	. . .	. . .	. . .	. . .
Repairs on goods	2 160	. .	. . .	. . .	. . .	. . .	. . .	. . .	. . .	. . .
Goods procured in ports by carriers	2 170	. .	. . .	. . .	. . .	. . .	. . .	. . .	. . .	. . .
Nonmonetary gold	2 180	. .	. . .	. . .	. . .	. . .	. . .	. . .	. . .	. . .
Debit	3 100	. .	**–504.0**	**–536.5**	**. . .**	**. . .**	**. . .**	**. . .**	**. . .**	**. . .**
General merchandise: imports f.o.b.	3 110	. .	–504.0	–536.5	. . .	. . .	. . .	. . .	. . .	. . .
Goods for processing: imports f.o.b.	3 150	. .	. . .	. . .	. . .	. . .	. . .	. . .	. . .	. . .
Repairs on goods	3 160	. .	. . .	. . .	. . .	. . .	. . .	. . .	. . .	. . .
Goods procured in ports by carriers	3 170	. .	. . .	. . .	. . .	. . .	. . .	. . .	. . .	. . .
Nonmonetary gold	3 180	. .	. . .	. . .	. . .	. . .	. . .	. . .	. . .	. . .
B. SERVICES	4 200	. .	–40.2	–38.4	. . .	. . .	. . .	. . .	. . .	. . .
Total credit	2 200	. .	*120.7*	*133.5*	. . .	. . .	. . .	. . .	. . .	. . .
Total debit	3 200	. .	*–160.9*	*–171.8*	. . .	. . .	. . .	. . .	. . .	. . .
Transportation services, credit	2 205	. .	**26.7**	**33.1**	**. . .**	**. . .**	**. . .**	**. . .**	**. . .**	**. . .**
Passenger	2 850	. .	. . .	. . .	. . .	. . .	. . .	. . .	. . .	. . .
Freight	2 851	. .	. . .	. . .	. . .	. . .	. . .	. . .	. . .	. . .
Other	2 852	. .	. . .	. . .	. . .	. . .	. . .	. . .	. . .	. . .
Sea transport, passenger	2 207	. .	. . .	. . .	. . .	. . .	. . .	. . .	. . .	. . .
Sea transport, freight	2 208	. .	. . .	. . .	. . .	. . .	. . .	. . .	. . .	. . .
Sea transport, other	2 209	. .	. . .	. . .	. . .	. . .	. . .	. . .	. . .	. . .
Air transport, passenger	2 211	. .	. . .	. . .	. . .	. . .	. . .	. . .	. . .	. . .
Air transport, freight	2 212	. .	. . .	. . .	. . .	. . .	. . .	. . .	. . .	. . .
Air transport, other	2 213	. .	. . .	. . .	. . .	. . .	. . .	. . .	. . .	. . .
Other transport, passenger	2 215	. .	. . .	. . .	. . .	. . .	. . .	. . .	. . .	. . .
Other transport, freight	2 216	. .	. . .	. . .	. . .	. . .	. . .	. . .	. . .	. . .
Other transport, other	2 217	. .	. . .	. . .	. . .	. . .	. . .	. . .	. . .	. . .
Transportation services, debit	3 205	. .	**–63.1**	**–68.7**	**. . .**	**. . .**	**. . .**	**. . .**	**. . .**	**. . .**
Passenger	3 850	. .	. . .	. . .	. . .	. . .	. . .	. . .	. . .	. . .
Freight	3 851	. .	. . .	. . .	. . .	. . .	. . .	. . .	. . .	. . .
Other	3 852	. .	. . .	. . .	. . .	. . .	. . .	. . .	. . .	. . .
Sea transport, passenger	3 207	. .	. . .	. . .	. . .	. . .	. . .	. . .	. . .	. . .
Sea transport, freight	3 208	. .	. . .	. . .	. . .	. . .	. . .	. . .	. . .	. . .
Sea transport, other	3 209	. .	. . .	. . .	. . .	. . .	. . .	. . .	. . .	. . .
Air transport, passenger	3 211	. .	. . .	. . .	. . .	. . .	. . .	. . .	. . .	. . .
Air transport, freight	3 212	. .	. . .	. . .	. . .	. . .	. . .	. . .	. . .	. . .
Air transport, other	3 213	. .	. . .	. . .	. . .	. . .	. . .	. . .	. . .	. . .
Other transport, passenger	3 215	. .	. . .	. . .	. . .	. . .	. . .	. . .	. . .	. . .
Other transport, freight	3 216	. .	. . .	. . .	. . .	. . .	. . .	. . .	. . .	. . .
Other transport, other	3 217	. .	. . .	. . .	. . .	. . .	. . .	. . .	. . .	. . .
Travel, credit	2 236	. .	**34.0**	**32.6**	**. . .**	**. . .**	**. . .**	**. . .**	**. . .**	**. . .**
Business travel	2 237	. .	. . .	. . .	. . .	. . .	. . .	. . .	. . .	. . .
Personal travel	2 240	. .	. . .	. . .	. . .	. . .	. . .	. . .	. . .	. . .
Travel, debit	3 236	. .	**–23.0**	**–21.1**	**. . .**	**. . .**	**. . .**	**. . .**	**. . .**	**. . .**
Business travel	3 237	. .	. . .	. . .	. . .	. . .	. . .	. . .	. . .	. . .
Personal travel	3 240	. .	. . .	. . .	. . .	. . .	. . .	. . .	. . .	. . .
Other services, credit	2 200	BA	**60.0**	**67.8**	**. . .**	**. . .**	**. . .**	**. . .**	**. . .**	**. . .**
Communications	2 245	. .	53.2	60.5	. . .	. . .	. . .	. . .	. . .	. . .
Construction	2 249	. .	. . .	. . .	. . .	. . .	. . .	. . .	. . .	. . .
Insurance	2 253	. .	. . .	. . .	. . .	. . .	. . .	. . .	. . .	. . .
Financial	2 260	. .	. . .	. . .	. . .	. . .	. . .	. . .	. . .	. . .
Computer and information	2 262	. .	. . .	. . .	. . .	. . .	. . .	. . .	. . .	. . .
Royalties and licence fees	2 266	. .	. . .	. . .	. . .	. . .	. . .	. . .	. . .	. . .
Other business services	2 268	. .	3.2	3.4	. . .	. . .	. . .	. . .	. . .	. . .
Personal, cultural, and recreational	2 287	. .	. . .	. . .	. . .	. . .	. . .	. . .	. . .	. . .
Government, n.i.e.	2 291	. .	3.6	3.9	. . .	. . .	. . .	. . .	. . .	. . .
Other services, debit	3 200	BA	**–74.8**	**–82.0**	**. . .**	**. . .**	**. . .**	**. . .**	**. . .**	**. . .**
Communications	3 245	. .	–36.1	–50.5	. . .	. . .	. . .	. . .	. . .	. . .
Construction	3 249	. .	–9.0	–5.7	. . .	. . .	. . .	. . .	. . .	. . .
Insurance	3 253	. .	–5.0	–5.4	. . .	. . .	. . .	. . .	. . .	. . .
Financial	3 260	. .	. . .	. . .	. . .	. . .	. . .	. . .	. . .	. . .
Computer and information	3 262	. .	. . .	. . .	. . .	. . .	. . .	. . .	. . .	. . .
Royalties and licence fees	3 266	. .	. . .	. . .	. . .	. . .	. . .	. . .	. . .	. . .
Other business services	3 268	. .	–20.4	–16.1	. . .	. . .	. . .	. . .	. . .	. . .
Personal, cultural, and recreational	3 287	. .	. . .	. . .	. . .	. . .	. . .	. . .	. . .	. . .
Government, n.i.e.	3 291	. .	–4.3	–4.3	. . .	. . .	. . .	. . .	. . .	. . .

Table 2 (Continued). STANDARD PRESENTATION, 1994–2001
(Millions of U.S. dollars)

	Code		1994	1995	1996	1997	1998	1999	2000	2001
C. INCOME	4 300	. .	–106.1	–117.7	. . .	. . .	. . .	. . .	. . .	. . .
Total credit	2 300	. .	*8.7*	*12.2*	. . .	. . .	. . .	. . .	. . .	. . .
Total debit	3 300	. .	*–114.8*	*–129.9*	. . .	. . .	. . .	. . .	. . .	. . .
Compensation of employees, credit	2 310	. .	. . .	. . .	. . .	. . .	. . .	. . .	. . .	. . .
Compensation of employees, debit	3 310	. .	**–8.6**	**–9.0**	. . .	. . .	. . .	. . .	. . .	. . .
Investment income, credit	2 320	. .	**8.7**	**12.2**	. . .	. . .	. . .	. . .	. . .	. . .
Direct investment income	2 330	. .	. . .	. . .	. . .	. . .	. . .	. . .	. . .	. . .
Dividends and distributed branch profits	2 332	. .	. . .	. . .	. . .	. . .	. . .	. . .	. . .	. . .
Reinvested earnings and undistributed branch profits	2 333	. .	. . .	. . .	. . .	. . .	. . .	. . .	. . .	. . .
Income on debt (interest)	2 334	. .	. . .	. . .	. . .	. . .	. . .	. . .	. . .	. . .
Portfolio investment income	2 339	. .	. . .	. . .	. . .	. . .	. . .	. . .	. . .	. . .
Income on equity	2 340	. .	. . .	. . .	. . .	. . .	. . .	. . .	. . .	. . .
Income on bonds and notes	2 350	. .	. . .	. . .	. . .	. . .	. . .	. . .	. . .	. . .
Income on money market instruments	2 360	. .	. . .	. . .	. . .	. . .	. . .	. . .	. . .	. . .
Other investment income	2 370	. .	8.7	12.2	. . .	. . .	. . .	. . .	. . .	. . .
Investment income, debit	3 320	. .	**–106.3**	**–120.9**	. . .	. . .	. . .	. . .	. . .	. . .
Direct investment income	3 330	. .	. . .	. . .	. . .	. . .	. . .	. . .	. . .	. . .
Dividends and distributed branch profits	3 332	. .	. . .	. . .	. . .	. . .	. . .	. . .	. . .	. . .
Reinvested earnings and undistributed branch profits	3 333	. .	. . .	. . .	. . .	. . .	. . .	. . .	. . .	. . .
Income on debt (interest)	3 334	. .	. . .	. . .	. . .	. . .	. . .	. . .	. . .	. . .
Portfolio investment income	3 339	. .	–66.9	–70.3	. . .	. . .	. . .	. . .	. . .	. . .
Income on equity	3 340	. .	. . .	. . .	. . .	. . .	. . .	. . .	. . .	. . .
Income on bonds and notes	3 350	. .	–66.9	–70.3	. . .	. . .	. . .	. . .	. . .	. . .
Income on money market instruments	3 360	. .	. . .	. . .	. . .	. . .	. . .	. . .	. . .	. . .
Other investment income	3 370	. .	–39.4	–50.6	. . .	. . .	. . .	. . .	. . .	. . .
D. CURRENT TRANSFERS	4 379	. .	61.9	62.1	. . .	. . .	. . .	. . .	. . .	. . .
Credit	2 379	. .	**68.1**	**67.4**	. . .	. . .	. . .	. . .	. . .	. . .
General government	2 380	. .	15.0	6.1	. . .	. . .	. . .	. . .	. . .	. . .
Other sectors	2 390	. .	53.1	61.3	. . .	. . .	. . .	. . .	. . .	. . .
Workers' remittances	2 391	. .	. . .	. . .	. . .	. . .	. . .	. . .	. . .	. . .
Other current transfers	2 392	. .	. . .	. . .	. . .	. . .	. . .	. . .	. . .	. . .
Debit	3 379	. .	**–6.2**	**–5.3**	. . .	. . .	. . .	. . .	. . .	. . .
General government	3 380	. .	–4.2	–3.2	. . .	. . .	. . .	. . .	. . .	. . .
Other sectors	3 390	. .	–2.0	–2.1	. . .	. . .	. . .	. . .	. . .	. . .
Workers' remittances	3 391	. .	. . .	. . .	. . .	. . .	. . .	. . .	. . .	. . .
Other current transfers	3 392	. .	. . .	. . .	. . .	. . .	. . .	. . .	. . .	. . .
CAPITAL AND FINANCIAL ACCOUNT	4 996	. .	**141.2**	**123.6**	. . .	. . .	. . .	. . .	. . .	. . .
CAPITAL ACCOUNT	4 994	. .	**16.4**	**10.2**	. . .	. . .	. . .	. . .	. . .	. . .
Total credit	2 994	. .	*19.1*	*13.2*	. . .	. . .	. . .	. . .	. . .	. . .
Total debit	3 994	. .	*–2.7*	*–3.0*	. . .	. . .	. . .	. . .	. . .	. . .
Capital transfers, credit	2 400	. .	**19.1**	**13.2**	. . .	. . .	. . .	. . .	. . .	. . .
General government	2 401	. .	17.7	11.5	. . .	. . .	. . .	. . .	. . .	. . .
Debt forgiveness	2 402	. .	8.1	.7	. . .	. . .	. . .	. . .	. . .	. . .
Other capital transfers	2 410	. .	9.7	10.8	. . .	. . .	. . .	. . .	. . .	. . .
Other sectors	2 430	. .	1.3	1.7	. . .	. . .	. . .	. . .	. . .	. . .
Migrants' transfers	2 431	. .	1.3	1.7	. . .	. . .	. . .	. . .	. . .	. . .
Debt forgiveness	2 432	. .	. . .	. . .	. . .	. . .	. . .	. . .	. . .	. . .
Other capital transfers	2 440	. .	. . .	. . .	. . .	. . .	. . .	. . .	. . .	. . .
Capital transfers, debit	3 400	. .	**–2.7**	**–3.0**	. . .	. . .	. . .	. . .	. . .	. . .
General government	3 401	. .	. . .	. . .	. . .	. . .	. . .	. . .	. . .	. . .
Debt forgiveness	3 402	. .	. . .	. . .	. . .	. . .	. . .	. . .	. . .	. . .
Other capital transfers	3 410	. .	. . .	. . .	. . .	. . .	. . .	. . .	. . .	. . .
Other sectors	3 430	. .	–2.7	–3.0	. . .	. . .	. . .	. . .	. . .	. . .
Migrants' transfers	3 431	. .	–2.7	–3.0	. . .	. . .	. . .	. . .	. . .	. . .
Debt forgiveness	3 432	. .	. . .	. . .	. . .	. . .	. . .	. . .	. . .	. . .
Other capital transfers	3 440	. .	. . .	. . .	. . .	. . .	. . .	. . .	. . .	. . .
Nonproduced nonfinancial assets, credit	2 480	. .	. . .	. . .	. . .	. . .	. . .	. . .	. . .	. . .
Nonproduced nonfinancial assets, debit	3 480	. .	. . .	. . .	. . .	. . .	. . .	. . .	. . .	. . .

Table 2 (Continued). STANDARD PRESENTATION, 1994–2001
(Millions of U.S. dollars)

	Code	1994	1995	1996	1997	1998	1999	2000	2001
FINANCIAL ACCOUNT	4 995 . .	**124.8**	**113.4**	...	...	...	...	...	...
A. DIRECT INVESTMENT	4 500 . .	106.7	74.4	...	...	...	...	...	...
Direct investment abroad	4 505 . .	...	...	...	...	...	...	...	...
Equity capital	4 510 . .	...	...	...	...	...	...	...	...
Claims on affiliated enterprises	4 515 . .	...	...	...	...	...	...	...	...
Liabilities to affiliated enterprises	4 520 . .	...	...	...	...	...	...	...	...
Reinvested earnings	4 525 . .	...	...	...	...	...	...	...	...
Other capital	4 530 . .	...	...	...	...	...	...	...	...
Claims on affiliated enterprises	4 535 . .	...	...	...	...	...	...	...	...
Liabilities to affiliated enterprises	4 540 . .	...	...	...	...	...	...	...	...
Direct investment in Guyana	4 555 . .	**106.7**	**74.4**	...	...	...	...	...	...
Equity capital	4 560 . .	...	...	...	...	...	...	...	...
Claims on direct investors	4 565 . .	...	...	...	...	...	...	...	...
Liabilities to direct investors	4 570 . .	...	...	...	...	...	...	...	...
Reinvested earnings	4 575 . .	...	...	...	...	...	...	...	...
Other capital	4 580 . .	106.7	74.4	...	...	...	...	...	...
Claims on direct investors	4 585 . .	...	...	...	...	...	...	...	...
Liabilities to direct investors	4 590 . .	...	...	...	...	...	...	...	...
B. PORTFOLIO INVESTMENT	4 600 . .	15.8	3.2	...	...	...	...	...	...
Assets	4 602 . .	...	...	...	...	...	...	...	...
Equity securities	4 610 . .	...	...	...	...	...	...	...	...
Monetary authorities	4 611 . .	...	...	...	...	...	...	...	...
General government	4 612 . .	...	...	...	...	...	...	...	...
Banks	4 613 . .	...	...	...	...	...	...	...	...
Other sectors	4 614 . .	...	...	...	...	...	...	...	...
Debt securities	4 619 . .	...	...	...	...	...	...	...	...
Bonds and notes	4 620 . .	...	...	...	...	...	...	...	...
Monetary authorities	4 621 . .	...	...	...	...	...	...	...	...
General government	4 622 . .	...	...	...	...	...	...	...	...
Banks	4 623 . .	...	...	...	...	...	...	...	...
Other sectors	4 624 . .	...	...	...	...	...	...	...	...
Money market instruments	4 630 . .	...	...	...	...	...	...	...	...
Monetary authorities	4 631 . .	...	...	...	...	...	...	...	...
General government	4 632 . .	...	...	...	...	...	...	...	...
Banks	4 633 . .	...	...	...	...	...	...	...	...
Other sectors	4 634 . .	...	...	...	...	...	...	...	...
Liabilities	4 652 . .	**15.8**	**3.2**	...	...	...	...	...	...
Equity securities	4 660 . .	...	...	...	...	...	...	...	...
Banks	4 663 . .	...	...	...	...	...	...	...	...
Other sectors	4 664 . .	...	...	...	...	...	...	...	...
Debt securities	4 669 . .	15.8	3.2	...	...	...	...	...	...
Bonds and notes	4 670 . .	15.8	3.2	...	...	...	...	...	...
Monetary authorities	4 671 . .	...	...	...	...	...	...	...	...
General government	4 672 . .	...	...	...	...	...	...	...	...
Banks	4 673 . .	...	...	...	...	...	...	...	...
Other sectors	4 674 . .	...	...	...	...	...	...	...	...
Money market instruments	4 680 . .	...	...	...	...	...	...	...	...
Monetary authorities	4 681 . .	...	...	...	...	...	...	...	...
General government	4 682 . .	...	...	...	...	...	...	...	...
Banks	4 683 . .	...	...	...	...	...	...	...	...
Other sectors	4 684 . .	...	...	...	...	...	...	...	...
C. FINANCIAL DERIVATIVES	4 910 . .	...	...	...	...	...	...	...	...
Monetary authorities	4 911 . .	...	...	...	...	...	...	...	...
General government	4 912 . .	...	...	...	...	...	...	...	...
Banks	4 913 . .	...	...	...	...	...	...	...	...
Other sectors	4 914 . .	...	...	...	...	...	...	...	...
Assets	4 900 . .	...	...	...	...	...	...	...	...
Monetary authorities	4 901 . .	...	...	...	...	...	...	...	...
General government	4 902 . .	...	...	...	...	...	...	...	...
Banks	4 903 . .	...	...	...	...	...	...	...	...
Other sectors	4 904 . .	...	...	...	...	...	...	...	...
Liabilities	4 905 . .	...	...	...	...	...	...	...	...
Monetary authorities	4 906 . .	...	...	...	...	...	...	...	...
General government	4 907 . .	...	...	...	...	...	...	...	...
Banks	4 908 . .	...	...	...	...	...	...	...	...
Other sectors	4 909 . .	...	...	...	...	...	...	...	...

Table 2 (Concluded). STANDARD PRESENTATION, 1994–2001
(Millions of U.S. dollars)

	Code	1994	1995	1996	1997	1998	1999	2000	2001
D. OTHER INVESTMENT	4 700 . .	24.1	35.1	...	...	...	...	...	...
Assets	4 703 . .	**–5.8**	**–8.9**	**...**	**...**	**...**	**...**	**...**	**...**
Trade credits	4 706 . .	...	...	...	...	...	...	...	...
General government	4 707 . .	...	...	...	...	...	...	...	...
of which: Short-term	4 709 . .	...	...	...	...	...	...	...	...
Other sectors	4 710 . .	...	...	...	...	...	...	...	...
of which: Short-term	4 712 . .	...	...	...	...	...	...	...	...
Loans	4 714 . .	...	...	...	...	...	...	...	...
Monetary authorities	4 715 . .	...	...	...	...	...	...	...	...
of which: Short-term	4 718 . .	...	...	...	...	...	...	...	...
General government	4 719 . .	...	...	...	...	...	...	...	...
of which: Short-term	4 721 . .	...	...	...	...	...	...	...	...
Banks	4 722 . .	...	...	...	...	...	...	...	...
of which: Short-term	4 724 . .	...	...	...	...	...	...	...	...
Other sectors	4 725 . .	...	...	...	...	...	...	...	...
of which: Short-term	4 727 . .	...	...	...	...	...	...	...	...
Currency and deposits	4 730 . .	...	...	...	...	...	...	...	...
Monetary authorities	4 731 . .	...	...	...	...	...	...	...	...
General government	4 732 . .	...	...	...	...	...	...	...	...
Banks	4 733 . .	...	...	...	...	...	...	...	...
Other sectors	4 734 . .	...	...	...	...	...	...	...	...
Other assets	4 736 . .	–5.8	–8.9	...	...	...	...	...	...
Monetary authorities	4 737 . .	...	...	...	...	...	...	...	...
of which: Short-term	4 739 . .	...	...	...	...	...	...	...	...
General government	4 740 . .	1.3	–2.2	...	...	...	...	...	...
of which: Short-term	4 742 . .	*1.3*	*–2.2*	...	...	...	...	...	...
Banks	4 743 . .	4.2	–2.8	...	...	...	...	...	...
of which: Short-term	4 745 . .	*4.2*	*–2.8*	...	...	...	...	...	...
Other sectors	4 746 . .	–11.2	–3.9	...	...	...	...	...	...
of which: Short-term	4 748 . .	*–11.2*	*–3.9*	...	...	...	...	...	...
Liabilities	4 753 . .	**29.9**	**43.9**	**...**	**...**	**...**	**...**	**...**	**...**
Trade credits	4 756 . .	...	...	...	...	...	...	...	...
General government	4 757 . .	...	...	...	...	...	...	...	...
of which: Short-term	4 759 . .	...	...	...	...	...	...	...	...
Other sectors	4 760 . .	...	...	...	...	...	...	...	...
of which: Short-term	4 762 . .	...	...	...	...	...	...	...	...
Loans	4 764 . .	4.4	–25.2	...	...	...	...	...	...
Monetary authorities	4 765 . .	–7.6	–9.3	...	...	...	...	...	...
of which: Use of Fund credit and loans from the Fund	4 766 . .	*–8.8*	*–9.7*	...	...	...	...	...	...
of which: Short-term	4 768 . .	...	...	...	...	...	...	...	...
General government	4 769 . .	–1.0	–5.4	...	...	...	...	...	...
of which: Short-term	4 771 . .	...	...	...	...	...	...	...	...
Banks	4 772 . .	1.0	.6	...	...	...	...	...	...
of which: Short-term	4 774 . .	...	...	...	...	...	...	...	...
Other sectors	4 775 . .	12.0	–11.1	...	...	...	...	...	...
of which: Short-term	4 777 . .	...	...	...	...	...	...	...	...
Currency and deposits	4 780 . .	...	...	...	...	...	...	...	...
Monetary authorities	4 781 . .	...	...	...	...	...	...	...	...
General government	4 782 . .	...	...	...	...	...	...	...	...
Banks	4 783 . .	...	...	...	...	...	...	...	...
Other sectors	4 784 . .	...	...	...	...	...	...	...	...
Other liabilities	4 786 . .	25.5	69.1	...	...	...	...	...	...
Monetary authorities	4 787 . .	.1	18.2	...	...	...	...	...	...
of which: Short-term	4 789 . .	*–5.4*	*.6*	...	...	...	...	...	...
General government	4 790 . .	28.5	51.3	...	...	...	...	...	...
of which: Short-term	4 792 . .	*28.5*	*51.3*	...	...	...	...	...	...
Banks	4 793 . .	–3.9	–1.0	...	...	...	...	...	...
of which: Short-term	4 795 . .	*–3.9*	*–1.0*	...	...	...	...	...	...
Other sectors	4 796 . .	.8	.6	...	...	...	...	...	...
of which: Short-term	4 798 . .	*.8*	*.6*	...	...	...	...	...	...
E. RESERVE ASSETS	4 802 . .	–21.8	.8	...	...	...	...	...	...
Monetary gold	4 812 . .	–1.5	.4	...	...	...	...	...	...
Special drawing rights	4 811 . .	–.1	–.2	...	...	...	...	...	...
Reserve position in the Fund	4 810 . .	...	...	...	...	...	...	...	...
Foreign exchange	4 803 . .	–20.2	.6	...	...	...	...	...	...
Other claims	4 813 . .	...	...	...	...	...	...	...	...
NET ERRORS AND OMISSIONS	4 998 . .	**–16.3**	**11.2**	**...**	**...**	**...**	**...**	**...**	**...**

Table 1. ANALYTIC PRESENTATION, FISCAL YEARS 1994–2001 ENDING SEPTEMBER 30
(Millions of U.S. dollars)

	Code	1994	1995	1996	1997	1998	1999	2000	2001
A. Current Account [1]	4 993 Z.	**–23.4**	**–87.1**	**–137.7**	**–47.7**	**–38.1**	...	...	...
Goods: exports f.o.b	2 100 . .	60.3	88.3	82.5	205.4	299.3	...	...	...
Goods: imports f.o.b	3 100 . .	–171.5	–517.2	–498.6	–559.6	–640.7	...	...	...
Balance on Goods	4 100 . .	*–111.2*	*–428.9*	*–416.1*	*–354.2*	*–341.4*	...	...	...
Services: credit	2 200 . .	6.7	104.1	109.1	173.7	180.0	...	...	...
Services: debit	3 200 . .	–63.9	–284.5	–283.3	–331.5	–380.6	...	...	...
Balance on Goods and Services	4 991 . .	*–168.4*	*–609.3*	*–590.3*	*–512.0*	*–542.0*	...	...	...
Income: credit	2 300 . .	...	...	...	...	...	...	...	...
Income: debit	3 300 . .	–11.2	–30.6	–9.9	–13.6	–11.7	...	...	...
Balance on Goods, Services, and Income	4 992 . .	*–179.6*	*–639.9*	*–600.2*	*–525.6*	*–553.7*	...	...	...
Current transfers: credit	2 379 Z.	156.2	552.9	462.5	477.9	515.6	...	...	...
Current transfers: debit	3 379 . .	...	...	...	...	...	...	...	...
B. Capital Account [1]	4 994 Z.	...	...	...	...	...	...	...	...
Capital account: credit	2 994 Z.	...	...	...	...	...	...	...	...
Capital account: debit	3 994 . .	...	...	...	...	...	...	...	...
Total, Groups A Plus B	4 981 . .	*–23.4*	*–87.1*	*–137.7*	*–47.7*	*–38.1*	...	...	...
C. Financial Account [1]	4 995 W.	**–15.8**	**99.2**	**67.9**	**61.5**	**193.1**	...	...	...
Direct investment abroad	4 505 . .	...	...	...	...	...	...	...	...
Direct investment in Haiti	4 555 Z.	...	7.4	4.1	4.0	10.8	...	...	...
Portfolio investment assets	4 602 . .	...	...	...	...	...	...	...	...
Equity securities	4 610 . .	...	...	...	...	...	...	...	...
Debt securities	4 619 . .	...	...	...	...	...	...	...	...
Portfolio investment liabilities	4 652 Z.	...	...	...	...	...	...	...	...
Equity securities	4 660 . .	...	...	...	...	...	...	...	...
Debt securities	4 669 Z.	...	...	...	...	...	...	...	...
Financial derivatives	4 910 . .	...	...	...	...	...	...	...	...
Financial derivatives assets	4 900 . .	...	...	...	...	...	...	...	...
Financial derivatives liabilities	4 905 . .	...	...	...	...	...	...	...	...
Other investment assets	4 703 . .	–5.5	–11.2	–4.6	21.6	86.8	...	...	...
Monetary authorities	4 701 . .	...	...	...	...	...	...	...	...
General government	4 704 . .	...	...	...	...	...	...	...	...
Banks	4 705 . .	–5.5	–11.2	–4.6	3.6	2.8	...	...	...
Other sectors	4 728 . .	...	...	...	18.0	84.0	...	...	...
Other investment liabilities	4 753 W.	–10.3	103.1	68.4	35.9	95.5	...	...	...
Monetary authorities	4 753 WA	2.1	...	...	...	...	...	...	...
General government	4 753 ZB	–12.4	112.5	68.8	37.7	43.0	...	...	...
Banks	4 753 ZC	...	.4	–.4	12.3	–4.5	...	...	...
Other sectors	4 753 ZD	...	–9.8	.1	–14.1	57.0	...	...	...
Total, Groups A Through C	4 983 . .	*–39.2*	*12.2*	*–69.8*	*13.8*	*155.0*	...	...	...
D. Net Errors and Omissions	4 998 . .	**–10.5**	**124.9**	**19.4**	**16.0**	**–120.5**	...	...	...
Total, Groups A Through D	4 984 . .	*–49.7*	*137.1*	*–50.4*	*29.8*	*34.5*	...	...	...
E. Reserves and Related Items	4 802 A.	**49.7**	**–137.1**	**50.4**	**–29.8**	**–34.5**	...	...	...
Reserve assets	4 802 . .	12.8	–175.6	48.5	–50.6	–29.1	...	...	...
Use of Fund credit and loans	4 766 . .	...	–5.6	–2.6	20.8	–5.3	...	...	...
Exceptional financing	4 920 . .	36.9	44.1	4.4	...	...	...	...	...
Conversion rates: gourdes per U.S. dollar	0 101 . .	**14.744**	**14.477**	**16.044**	**16.175**	**16.917**	**16.673**	**19.621**	**23.829**

[1] Excludes components that have been classified in the categories of Group E.

Table 2. STANDARD PRESENTATION, FISCAL YEARS 1994–2001 ENDING SEPTEMBER 30
(Millions of U.S. dollars)

	Code		1994	1995	1996	1997	1998	1999	2000	2001
CURRENT ACCOUNT	4 993	. .	**–23.4**	**–87.1**	**–137.7**	**–47.7**	**–38.1**	**. . .**	**. . .**	**. . .**
A. GOODS	4 100	. .	–111.2	–428.9	–416.1	–354.2	–341.4	. . .	. . .	. . .
Credit	2 100	. .	**60.3**	**88.3**	**82.5**	**205.4**	**299.3**	**. . .**	**. . .**	**. . .**
General merchandise: exports f.o.b.	2 110	. .	60.3	88.3	82.5	205.4	299.3	. . .	. . .	. . .
Goods for processing: exports f.o.b.	2 150	. .	. . .	. . .	. . .	. . .	. . .	. . .	. . .	. . .
Repairs on goods	2 160	. .	. . .	. . .	. . .	. . .	. . .	. . .	. . .	. . .
Goods procured in ports by carriers	2 170	. .	. . .	. . .	. . .	. . .	. . .	. . .	. . .	. . .
Nonmonetary gold	2 180	. .	. . .	. . .	. . .	. . .	. . .	. . .	. . .	. . .
Debit	3 100	. .	**–171.5**	**–517.2**	**–498.6**	**–559.6**	**–640.7**	**. . .**	**. . .**	**. . .**
General merchandise: imports f.o.b.	3 110	. .	–171.5	–517.2	–498.6	–559.6	–640.7	. . .	. . .	. . .
Goods for processing: imports f.o.b.	3 150	. .	. . .	. . .	. . .	. . .	. . .	. . .	. . .	. . .
Repairs on goods	3 160	. .	. . .	. . .	. . .	. . .	. . .	. . .	. . .	. . .
Goods procured in ports by carriers	3 170	. .	. . .	. . .	. . .	. . .	. . .	. . .	. . .	. . .
Nonmonetary gold	3 180	. .	. . .	. . .	. . .	. . .	. . .	. . .	. . .	. . .
B. SERVICES	4 200	. .	–57.2	–180.5	–174.2	–157.8	–200.6	. . .	. . .	. . .
Total credit	2 200	. .	*6.7*	*104.1*	*109.1*	*173.7*	*180.0*	. . .	. . .	. . .
Total debit	3 200	. .	*–63.9*	*–284.5*	*–283.3*	*–331.5*	*–380.6*	. . .	. . .	. . .
Transportation services, credit	2 205	. .	**2.1**	**5.0**	**6.0**	**3.7**	**3.6**	**. . .**	**. . .**	**. . .**
Passenger	2 850	. .	*1.1*	. . .	. . .	. . .	. . .	. . .	. . .	. . .
Freight	2 851	. .	*1.0*	. . .	. . .	. . .	. . .	. . .	. . .	. . .
Other	2 852	. .	. . .	. . .	. . .	. . .	. . .	. . .	. . .	. . .
Sea transport, passenger	2 207	. .	. . .	. . .	. . .	. . .	. . .	. . .	. . .	. . .
Sea transport, freight	2 208	. .	. . .	. . .	. . .	. . .	. . .	. . .	. . .	. . .
Sea transport, other	2 209	. .	. . .	. . .	. . .	. . .	. . .	. . .	. . .	. . .
Air transport, passenger	2 211	. .	. . .	. . .	. . .	. . .	. . .	. . .	. . .	. . .
Air transport, freight	2 212	. .	. . .	. . .	. . .	. . .	. . .	. . .	. . .	. . .
Air transport, other	2 213	. .	. . .	. . .	. . .	. . .	. . .	. . .	. . .	. . .
Other transport, passenger	2 215	. .	. . .	. . .	. . .	. . .	. . .	. . .	. . .	. . .
Other transport, freight	2 216	. .	. . .	. . .	. . .	. . .	. . .	. . .	. . .	. . .
Other transport, other	2 217	. .	. . .	. . .	. . .	. . .	. . .	. . .	. . .	. . .
Transportation services, debit	3 205	. .	**–47.0**	**–183.0**	**–189.3**	**–279.6**	**–326.0**	**. . .**	**. . .**	**. . .**
Passenger	3 850	. .	*–17.7*	. . .	. . .	. . .	. . .	. . .	. . .	. . .
Freight	3 851	. .	*–29.3*	. . .	. . .	. . .	. . .	. . .	. . .	. . .
Other	3 852	. .	. . .	. . .	. . .	. . .	. . .	. . .	. . .	. . .
Sea transport, passenger	3 207	. .	. . .	. . .	. . .	. . .	. . .	. . .	. . .	. . .
Sea transport, freight	3 208	. .	. . .	. . .	. . .	. . .	. . .	. . .	. . .	. . .
Sea transport, other	3 209	. .	. . .	. . .	. . .	. . .	. . .	. . .	. . .	. . .
Air transport, passenger	3 211	. .	. . .	. . .	. . .	. . .	. . .	. . .	. . .	. . .
Air transport, freight	3 212	. .	. . .	. . .	. . .	. . .	. . .	. . .	. . .	. . .
Air transport, other	3 213	. .	. . .	. . .	. . .	. . .	. . .	. . .	. . .	. . .
Other transport, passenger	3 215	. .	. . .	. . .	. . .	. . .	. . .	. . .	. . .	. . .
Other transport, freight	3 216	. .	. . .	. . .	. . .	. . .	. . .	. . .	. . .	. . .
Other transport, other	3 217	. .	. . .	. . .	. . .	. . .	. . .	. . .	. . .	. . .
Travel, credit	2 236	. .	**4.5**	**90.2**	**95.6**	**107.1**	**113.2**	**. . .**	**. . .**	**. . .**
Business travel	2 237	. .	. . .	. . .	. . .	. . .	. . .	. . .	. . .	. . .
Personal travel	2 240	. .	. . .	. . .	. . .	. . .	. . .	. . .	. . .	. . .
Travel, debit	3 236	. .	**–13.7**	**–34.7**	**–37.0**	**–34.8**	**–36.5**	**. . .**	**. . .**	**. . .**
Business travel	3 237	. .	. . .	. . .	. . .	. . .	. . .	. . .	. . .	. . .
Personal travel	3 240	. .	. . .	. . .	. . .	. . .	. . .	. . .	. . .	. . .
Other services, credit	2 200	BA	**.1**	**8.9**	**7.5**	**62.9**	**63.2**	**. . .**	**. . .**	**. . .**
Communications	2 245	. .	. . .	. . .	. . .	61.6	61.0	. . .	. . .	. . .
Construction	2 249	. .	. . .	. . .	. . .	. . .	. . .	. . .	. . .	. . .
Insurance	2 253	. .	.1	.6	. . .	. . .	. . .	. . .	. . .	. . .
Financial	2 260	. .	. . .	. . .	. . .	. . .	. . .	. . .	. . .	. . .
Computer and information	2 262	. .	. . .	. . .	. . .	. . .	. . .	. . .	. . .	. . .
Royalties and licence fees	2 266	. .	. . .	. . .	. . .	. . .	. . .	. . .	. . .	. . .
Other business services	2 268	. .	. . .	2.4	2.5	. . .	. . .	. . .	. . .	. . .
Personal, cultural, and recreational	2 287	. .	. . .	. . .	. . .	. . .	. . .	. . .	. . .	. . .
Government, n.i.e.	2 291	. .	. . .	6.0	5.0	1.3	2.2	. . .	. . .	. . .
Other services, debit	3 200	BA	**–3.2**	**–66.8**	**–57.0**	**–17.1**	**–18.1**	**. . .**	**. . .**	**. . .**
Communications	3 245	. .	. . .	. . .	. . .	–6.3	–7.7	. . .	. . .	. . .
Construction	3 249	. .	. . .	. . .	. . .	. . .	. . .	. . .	. . .	. . .
Insurance	3 253	. .	–3.2	–4.0	. . .	. . .	. . .	. . .	. . .	. . .
Financial	3 260	. .	. . .	. . .	. . .	. . .	. . .	. . .	. . .	. . .
Computer and information	3 262	. .	. . .	. . .	. . .	. . .	. . .	. . .	. . .	. . .
Royalties and licence fees	3 266	. .	. . .	. . .	. . .	. . .	. . .	. . .	. . .	. . .
Other business services	3 268	. .	. . .	–14.0	–15.0	. . .	. . .	. . .	. . .	. . .
Personal, cultural, and recreational	3 287	. .	. . .	. . .	. . .	. . .	. . .	. . .	. . .	. . .
Government, n.i.e.	3 291	. .	. . .	–48.8	–42.0	–10.8	–10.4	. . .	. . .	. . .

Table 2 (Continued). STANDARD PRESENTATION, FISCAL YEARS 1994–2001 ENDING SEPTEMBER 30
(Millions of U.S. dollars)

	Code		1994	1995	1996	1997	1998	1999	2000	2001
C. INCOME	4 300	. .	–11.2	–30.6	–9.9	–13.6	–11.7	...	...	...
Total credit	2 300	. .	...	...	...	...	...	...	...	...
Total debit	3 300	. .	*–11.2*	*–30.6*	*–9.9*	*–13.6*	*–11.7*	...	...	...
Compensation of employees, credit	2 310	. .	...	...	...	...	...	...	...	...
Compensation of employees, debit	3 310	. .	...	...	...	...	...	...	...	...
Investment income, credit	2 320	. .	...	...	...	...	...	...	...	...
Direct investment income	2 330	. .	...	...	...	...	...	...	...	...
Dividends and distributed branch profits	2 332	. .	...	...	...	...	...	...	...	...
Reinvested earnings and undistributed branch profits	2 333	. .	...	...	...	...	...	...	...	...
Income on debt (interest)	2 334	. .	...	...	...	...	...	...	...	...
Portfolio investment income	2 339	. .	...	...	...	...	...	...	...	...
Income on equity	2 340	. .	...	...	...	...	...	...	...	...
Income on bonds and notes	2 350	. .	...	...	...	...	...	...	...	...
Income on money market instruments	2 360	. .	...	...	...	...	...	...	...	...
Other investment income	2 370	. .	...	...	...	...	...	...	...	...
Investment income, debit	3 320	. .	**–11.2**	**–30.6**	**–9.9**	**–13.6**	**–11.7**	...	...	...
Direct investment income	3 330	. .	...	–3.8	.4	...	...	...	...	...
Dividends and distributed branch profits	3 332	. .	...	...	...	...	...	...	...	...
Reinvested earnings and undistributed branch profits	3 333	. .	...	...	...	...	...	...	...	...
Income on debt (interest)	3 334	. .	...	...	...	...	...	...	...	...
Portfolio investment income	3 339	. .	...	...	...	...	...	...	...	...
Income on equity	3 340	. .	...	...	...	...	...	...	...	...
Income on bonds and notes	3 350	. .	...	...	...	...	...	...	...	...
Income on money market instruments	3 360	. .	...	...	...	...	...	...	...	...
Other investment income	3 370	. .	–11.2	–26.9	–10.3	–13.6	–11.7	...	...	...
D. CURRENT TRANSFERS	4 379	. .	156.2	552.9	462.5	477.9	515.6	...	...	...
Credit	2 379	. .	**156.2**	**552.9**	**462.5**	**477.9**	**515.6**	...	...	...
General government	2 380	. .	113.3	444.4	310.5	221.9	222.6	...	...	...
Other sectors	2 390	. .	42.9	108.5	152.0	256.0	293.0	...	...	...
Workers' remittances	2 391	. .	...	...	...	...	...	...	...	...
Other current transfers	2 392	. .	42.9	108.5	152.0	256.0	293.0	...	...	...
Debit	3 379	. .	...	...	...	...	...	...	...	...
General government	3 380	. .	...	...	...	...	...	...	...	...
Other sectors	3 390	. .	...	...	...	...	...	...	...	...
Workers' remittances	3 391	. .	...	...	...	...	...	...	...	...
Other current transfers	3 392	. .	...	...	...	...	...	...	...	...
CAPITAL AND FINANCIAL ACCOUNT	4 996	. .	**33.9**	**–37.9**	**118.3**	**31.7**	**158.6**	...	...	...
CAPITAL ACCOUNT	4 994	. .	...	**50.0**	...	...	...	...	...	...
Total credit	2 994	. .	...	*50.0*	...	...	...	...	...	...
Total debit	3 994	. .	...	...	...	...	...	...	...	...
Capital transfers, credit	2 400	. .	...	**50.0**	...	...	...	...	...	...
General government	2 401	. .	...	50.0	...	...	...	...	...	...
Debt forgiveness	2 402	. .	...	50.0	...	...	...	...	...	...
Other capital transfers	2 410	. .	...	...	...	...	...	...	...	...
Other sectors	2 430	. .	...	...	...	...	...	...	...	...
Migrants' transfers	2 431	. .	...	...	...	...	...	...	...	...
Debt forgiveness	2 432	. .	...	...	...	...	...	...	...	...
Other capital transfers	2 440	. .	...	...	...	...	...	...	...	...
Capital transfers, debit	3 400	. .	...	...	...	...	...	...	...	...
General government	3 401	. .	...	...	...	...	...	...	...	...
Debt forgiveness	3 402	. .	...	...	...	...	...	...	...	...
Other capital transfers	3 410	. .	...	...	...	...	...	...	...	...
Other sectors	3 430	. .	...	...	...	...	...	...	...	...
Migrants' transfers	3 431	. .	...	...	...	...	...	...	...	...
Debt forgiveness	3 432	. .	...	...	...	...	...	...	...	...
Other capital transfers	3 440	. .	...	...	...	...	...	...	...	...
Nonproduced nonfinancial assets, credit	2 480	. .	...	...	...	...	...	...	...	...
Nonproduced nonfinancial assets, debit	3 480	. .	...	...	...	...	...	...	...	...

Table 2 (Continued). STANDARD PRESENTATION, FISCAL YEARS 1994–2001 ENDING SEPTEMBER 30

(Millions of U.S. dollars)

	Code	1994	1995	1996	1997	1998	1999	2000	2001
FINANCIAL ACCOUNT	4 995 . .	**33.9**	**–87.9**	**118.3**	**31.7**	**158.6**	...	...	...
A. DIRECT INVESTMENT	4 500 . .	...	7.4	4.1	4.0	10.8	...	...	...
Direct investment abroad	4 505 . .	...	...	...	...	...	...	...	...
Equity capital	4 510 . .	...	...	...	...	...	...	...	...
Claims on affiliated enterprises	4 515 . .	...	...	...	...	...	...	...	...
Liabilities to affiliated enterprises	4 520 . .	...	...	...	...	...	...	...	...
Reinvested earnings	4 525 . .	...	...	...	...	...	...	...	...
Other capital	4 530 . .	...	...	...	...	...	...	...	...
Claims on affiliated enterprises	4 535 . .	...	...	...	...	...	...	...	...
Liabilities to affiliated enterprises	4 540 . .	...	...	...	...	...	...	...	...
Direct investment in Haiti	4 555 . .	...	**7.4**	**4.1**	**4.0**	**10.8**	...	...	...
Equity capital	4 560 . .	...	7.4	4.1	4.0	10.8	...	...	...
Claims on direct investors	4 565 . .	...	...	...	...	...	...	...	...
Liabilities to direct investors	4 570 . .	...	...	...	...	...	...	...	...
Reinvested earnings	4 575 . .	...	...	...	...	...	...	...	...
Other capital	4 580 . .	...	...	...	...	...	...	...	...
Claims on direct investors	4 585 . .	...	...	...	...	...	...	...	...
Liabilities to direct investors	4 590 . .	...	...	...	...	...	...	...	...
B. PORTFOLIO INVESTMENT	4 600 . .	...	...	...	...	...	...	...	...
Assets	4 602 . .	...	...	...	...	...	...	...	...
Equity securities	4 610 . .	...	...	...	...	...	...	...	...
Monetary authorities	4 611 . .	...	...	...	...	...	...	...	...
General government	4 612 . .	...	...	...	...	...	...	...	...
Banks	4 613 . .	...	...	...	...	...	...	...	...
Other sectors	4 614 . .	...	...	...	...	...	...	...	...
Debt securities	4 619 . .	...	...	...	...	...	...	...	...
Bonds and notes	4 620 . .	...	...	...	...	...	...	...	...
Monetary authorities	4 621 . .	...	...	...	...	...	...	...	...
General government	4 622 . .	...	...	...	...	...	...	...	...
Banks	4 623 . .	...	...	...	...	...	...	...	...
Other sectors	4 624 . .	...	...	...	...	...	...	...	...
Money market instruments	4 630 . .	...	...	...	...	...	...	...	...
Monetary authorities	4 631 . .	...	...	...	...	...	...	...	...
General government	4 632 . .	...	...	...	...	...	...	...	...
Banks	4 633 . .	...	...	...	...	...	...	...	...
Other sectors	4 634 . .	...	...	...	...	...	...	...	...
Liabilities	4 652 . .	...	...	...	...	...	...	...	...
Equity securities	4 660 . .	...	...	...	...	...	...	...	...
Banks	4 663 . .	...	...	...	...	...	...	...	...
Other sectors	4 664 . .	...	...	...	...	...	...	...	...
Debt securities	4 669 . .	...	...	...	...	...	...	...	...
Bonds and notes	4 670 . .	...	...	...	...	...	...	...	...
Monetary authorities	4 671 . .	...	...	...	...	...	...	...	...
General government	4 672 . .	...	...	...	...	...	...	...	...
Banks	4 673 . .	...	...	...	...	...	...	...	...
Other sectors	4 674 . .	...	...	...	...	...	...	...	...
Money market instruments	4 680 . .	...	...	...	...	...	...	...	...
Monetary authorities	4 681 . .	...	...	...	...	...	...	...	...
General government	4 682 . .	...	...	...	...	...	...	...	...
Banks	4 683 . .	...	...	...	...	...	...	...	...
Other sectors	4 684 . .	...	...	...	...	...	...	...	...
C. FINANCIAL DERIVATIVES	4 910 . .	...	...	...	...	...	...	...	...
Monetary authorities	4 911 . .	...	...	...	...	...	...	...	...
General government	4 912 . .	...	...	...	...	...	...	...	...
Banks	4 913 . .	...	...	...	...	...	...	...	...
Other sectors	4 914 . .	...	...	...	...	...	...	...	...
Assets	4 900 . .	...	...	...	...	...	...	...	...
Monetary authorities	4 901 . .	...	...	...	...	...	...	...	...
General government	4 902 . .	...	...	...	...	...	...	...	...
Banks	4 903 . .	...	...	...	...	...	...	...	...
Other sectors	4 904 . .	...	...	...	...	...	...	...	...
Liabilities	4 905 . .	...	...	...	...	...	...	...	...
Monetary authorities	4 906 . .	...	...	...	...	...	...	...	...
General government	4 907 . .	...	...	...	...	...	...	...	...
Banks	4 908 . .	...	...	...	...	...	...	...	...
Other sectors	4 909 . .	...	...	...	...	...	...	...	...

Table 2 (Concluded). STANDARD PRESENTATION, FISCAL YEARS 1994–2001 ENDING SEPTEMBER 30
(Millions of U.S. dollars)

	Code	1994	1995	1996	1997	1998	1999	2000	2001
D. OTHER INVESTMENT	4 700	21.1	80.3	65.6	78.3	177.0	...	...	...
Assets	4 703	**–5.5**	**–11.2**	**–4.6**	**21.6**	**86.8**	**...**	**...**	**...**
Trade credits	4 706	...	...	...	...	...	...	...	...
General government	4 707	...	...	...	...	...	...	...	...
of which: Short-term	4 709	...	...	...	...	...	...	...	...
Other sectors	4 710	...	...	...	...	...	...	...	...
of which: Short-term	4 712	...	...	...	...	...	...	...	...
Loans	4 714	...	...	...	...	...	...	...	...
Monetary authorities	4 715	...	...	...	...	...	...	...	...
of which: Short-term	4 718	...	...	...	...	...	...	...	...
General government	4 719	...	...	...	...	...	...	...	...
of which: Short-term	4 721	...	...	...	...	...	...	...	...
Banks	4 722	...	...	...	...	...	...	...	...
of which: Short-term	4 724	...	...	...	...	...	...	...	...
Other sectors	4 725	...	...	...	...	...	...	...	...
of which: Short-term	4 727	...	...	...	...	...	...	...	...
Currency and deposits	4 730	–5.5	–11.2	–4.6	21.6	86.8	...	...	...
Monetary authorities	4 731	...	...	...	...	...	...	...	...
General government	4 732	...	...	...	...	...	...	...	...
Banks	4 733	–5.5	–11.2	–4.6	3.6	2.8	...	...	...
Other sectors	4 734	...	...	...	18.0	84.0	...	...	...
Other assets	4 736	...	...	...	...	...	...	...	...
Monetary authorities	4 737	...	...	...	...	...	...	...	...
of which: Short-term	4 739	...	...	...	...	...	...	...	...
General government	4 740	...	...	...	...	...	...	...	...
of which: Short-term	4 742	...	...	...	...	...	...	...	...
Banks	4 743	...	...	...	...	...	...	...	...
of which: Short-term	4 745	...	...	...	...	...	...	...	...
Other sectors	4 746	...	...	...	...	...	...	...	...
of which: Short-term	4 748	...	...	...	...	...	...	...	...
Liabilities	4 753	**26.6**	**91.5**	**70.2**	**56.7**	**90.2**	**...**	**...**	**...**
Trade credits	4 756	...	...	...	–16.3	.5	...	...	...
General government	4 757	...	...	...	...	...	...	...	...
of which: Short-term	4 759	...	...	...	...	...	...	...	...
Other sectors	4 760	...	...	...	–16.3	.5	...	...	...
of which: Short-term	4 762	...	...	...	...	...	...	...	...
Loans	4 764	–12.4	100.1	65.3	58.5	37.7	...	...	...
Monetary authorities	4 765	...	–5.6	–2.6	20.8	–5.3	...	...	...
of which: Use of Fund credit and loans from the Fund	4 766	...	*–5.6*	*–2.6*	*20.8*	*–5.3*	...	...	...
of which: Short-term	4 768	...	...	...	...	...	...	...	...
General government	4 769	–12.4	112.5	68.8	37.7	43.0	...	...	...
of which: Short-term	4 771	...	...	...	...	...	...	...	...
Banks	4 772	...	...	...	...	...	...	...	...
of which: Short-term	4 774	...	...	...	...	...	...	...	...
Other sectors	4 775	...	–6.8	–.9	...	...	...	...	...
of which: Short-term	4 777	...	...	...	...	...	...	...	...
Currency and deposits	4 780	...	–2.6	.6	14.3	51.5	...	...	...
Monetary authorities	4 781	...	...	...	...	...	...	...	...
General government	4 782	...	...	...	...	...	...	...	...
Banks	4 783	...	.4	–.4	12.3	–4.5	...	...	...
Other sectors	4 784	...	–3.0	1.0	2.0	56.0	...	...	...
Other liabilities	4 786	39.0	–5.9	4.4	.2	.5	...	...	...
Monetary authorities	4 787	2.1	–34.4	...	...	...	...	...	...
of which: Short-term	4 789	*2.1*	*–34.4*	...	...	...	...	...	...
General government	4 790	36.9	28.5	4.4	...	...	...	...	...
of which: Short-term	4 792	*36.9*	*–84.4*	*4.4*	...	...	...	...	...
Banks	4 793	...	...	...	...	...	...	...	...
of which: Short-term	4 795	...	...	...	...	...	...	...	...
Other sectors	4 796	...	...	...	.2	.5	...	...	...
of which: Short-term	4 798	...	...	...	...	...	...	...	...
E. RESERVE ASSETS	4 802	12.8	–175.6	48.5	–50.6	–29.1	...	...	...
Monetary gold	4 812	...	–.6	...	.7	.6	...	...	...
Special drawing rights	4 811	...	–.6	.4	.1	–.3	...	...	...
Reserve position in the Fund	4 810	...	...	...	...	...	...	...	...
Foreign exchange	4 803	12.8	–167.9	44.6	–50.3	–30.8	...	...	...
Other claims	4 813	...	–6.5	3.6	–1.1	1.4	...	...	...
NET ERRORS AND OMISSIONS	4 998	**–10.5**	**124.9**	**19.4**	**16.0**	**–120.5**	**...**	**...**	**...**

Part 3 of the *Yearbook* contains descriptions of the methodologies, compilation practices, and sources used to compile these data.

Table 1. ANALYTIC PRESENTATION, 1994–2001

(Millions of U.S. dollars)

	Code	1994	1995	1996	1997	1998	1999	2000	2001
A. Current Account [1]	4 993 Z.	**–343.3**	**–200.9**	**–335.4**	**–272.2**	**–394.8**	**–624.6**	**–556.7**	**–669.8**
Goods: exports f.o.b	2 100 . .	1,101.5	1,377.2	1,638.4	1,856.5	2,047.9	1,756.3	2,001.2	1,930.9
Goods: imports f.o.b	3 100 . .	–1,351.1	–1,518.6	–1,925.8	–2,150.4	–2,370.5	–2,509.6	–2,669.6	–2,807.4
Balance on Goods	4 100 . .	*–249.6*	*–141.4*	*–287.4*	*–293.9*	*–322.6*	*–753.3*	*–668.4*	*–876.5*
Services: credit	2 200 . .	242.4	257.6	283.3	334.9	377.1	474.1	478.8	480.8
Services: debit	3 200 . .	–311.0	–333.7	–327.8	–360.9	–446.8	–502.4	–622.9	–653.4
Balance on Goods and Services	4 991 . .	*–318.2*	*–217.5*	*–331.9*	*–319.9*	*–392.3*	*–781.6*	*–812.5*	*–1,049.1*
Income: credit	2 300 . .	24.0	32.3	61.2	70.0	59.5	80.5	110.1	88.0
Income: debit	3 300 . .	–238.1	–258.2	–292.0	–281.8	–263.6	–235.7	–256.8	–235.2
Balance on Goods, Services, and Income	4 992 . .	*–532.3*	*–443.4*	*–562.7*	*–531.7*	*–596.4*	*–936.8*	*–959.2*	*–1,196.3*
Current transfers: credit	2 379 Z.	190.2	243.7	271.7	306.8	241.7	354.6	447.4	573.7
Current transfers: debit	3 379 . .	–1.2	–1.2	–44.4	–47.3	–40.1	–42.4	–44.9	–47.2
B. Capital Account [1]	4 994 Z.	**. . .**	**. . .**	**28.5**	**14.6**	**29.4**	**110.9**	**98.9**	**95.0**
Capital account: credit	2 994 Z.	. . .	. . .	29.2	15.3	29.4	110.9	98.9	95.0
Capital account: debit	3 994 . .	. . .	. . .	–.7	–.7	. . .	. . .	. . .	. . .
Total, Groups A Plus B	4 981 . .	*–343.3*	*–200.9*	*–306.9*	*–257.6*	*–365.4*	*–513.7*	*–457.8*	*–574.8*
C. Financial Account [1]	4 995 W.	**157.5**	**114.6**	**70.2**	**243.3**	**113.9**	**203.4**	**–29.5**	**154.9**
Direct investment abroad	4 505 . .	. . .	. . .	. . .	. . .	. . .	. . .	. . .	. . .
Direct investment in Honduras	4 555 Z.	34.8	50.0	90.9	121.5	99.0	237.3	282.0	195.0
Portfolio investment assets	4 602 . .	. . .	. . .	16.0	. . .	. . .	–72.4	–115.4	–46.7
Equity securities	4 610 . .	. . .	. . .	16.0	. . .	. . .	. . .	. . .	. . .
Debt securities	4 619 . .	. . .	. . .	. . .	. . .	. . .	–72.4	–115.4	–46.7
Portfolio investment liabilities	4 652 Z.	. . .	. . .	. . .	. . .	. . .	. . .	. . .	. . .
Equity securities	4 660 . .	. . .	. . .	. . .	. . .	. . .	. . .	. . .	. . .
Debt securities	4 669 Z.	. . .	. . .	. . .	. . .	. . .	. . .	. . .	. . .
Financial derivatives	4 910 . .	. . .	. . .	. . .	. . .	–25.8	–16.1	–1.2	. . .
Financial derivatives assets	4 900 . .	. . .	. . .	. . .	. . .	. . .	. . .	. . .	. . .
Financial derivatives liabilities	4 905 . .	. . .	. . .	. . .	. . .	–25.8	–16.1	–1.2	. . .
Other investment assets	4 703 . .	8.9	–12.8	–89.4	–53.4	–61.7	–132.2	–157.3	–68.8
Monetary authorities	4 701 . .	3.3	11.7	. . .	. . .	. . .	. . .	. . .	. . .
General government	4 704 . .	14.4	14.4	. . .	. . .	. . .	. . .	–59.4	–3.6
Banks	4 705 . .	–8.8	–38.9	–89.4	–53.4	–61.7	–132.2	–97.9	–65.2
Other sectors	4 728 . .	. . .	. . .	. . .	. . .	. . .	. . .	. . .	. . .
Other investment liabilities	4 753 W.	113.8	77.4	52.7	175.2	102.4	186.8	–37.6	75.4
Monetary authorities	4 753 WA	–60.7	–73.1	–180.1	–24.1	–27.2	–22.2	–32.4	–25.2
General government	4 753 ZB	96.2	101.7	141.9	–48.4	–30.3	168.8	10.5	121.4
Banks	4 753 ZC	–2.2	6.3	34.5	113.8	51.1	–11.5	–40.5	–45.9
Other sectors	4 753 ZD	80.5	42.5	56.4	133.9	108.8	51.7	24.8	25.1
Total, Groups A Through C	4 983 . .	*–185.8*	*–86.3*	*–236.7*	*–14.3*	*–251.5*	*–310.3*	*–487.3*	*–419.9*
D. Net Errors and Omissions	4 998 . .	**115.5**	**45.0**	**157.9**	**196.5**	**96.1**	**122.0**	**129.9**	**82.8**
Total, Groups A Through D	4 984 . .	*–70.3*	*–41.3*	*–78.8*	*182.2*	*–155.4*	*–188.3*	*–357.4*	*–337.1*
E. Reserves and Related Items	4 802 A.	**70.3**	**41.3**	**78.8**	**–182.2**	**155.4**	**188.3**	**357.4**	**337.1**
Reserve assets	4 802 . .	–74.1	–90.3	12.7	–307.9	–229.8	–441.9	–32.3	–85.6
Use of Fund credit and loans	4 766 . .	–16.1	–13.7	–38.0	–8.8	64.8	99.5	15.5	16.9
Exceptional financing	4 920 . .	160.4	145.3	104.1	134.5	320.4	530.6	374.3	405.8
Conversion rates: lempiras per U.S. dollar	0 101 . .	**8.4088**	**9.4710**	**11.7053**	**13.0035**	**13.3850**	**14.2132**	**14.8392**	**15.4737**

[1] Excludes components that have been classified in the categories of Group E.

Table 2. STANDARD PRESENTATION, 1994–2001

(Millions of U.S. dollars)

	Code		1994	1995	1996	1997	1998	1999	2000	2001
CURRENT ACCOUNT	4 993	. .	**–343.3**	**–200.9**	**–335.4**	**–272.2**	**–147.7**	**–240.9**	**–256.1**	**–325.0**
A. GOODS	4 100	. .	–249.6	–141.4	–287.4	–293.9	–322.6	–753.3	–668.4	–876.5
Credit	2 100	. .	**1,101.5**	**1,377.2**	**1,638.4**	**1,856.5**	**2,047.9**	**1,756.3**	**2,001.2**	**1,930.9**
General merchandise: exports f.o.b.	2 110	. .	939.5	1,189.7	1,422.5	1,535.6	1,611.9	1,217.8	1,425.8	1,379.4
Goods for processing: exports f.o.b.	2 150	. .	162.0	187.5	203.7	307.6	436.0	538.5	575.4	551.5
Repairs on goods	2 160	. .	. . .	. . .	.2	.3	. . .	. . .	. . .	. . .
Goods procured in ports by carriers	2 170	. .	. . .	. . .	12.0	13.0	. . .	. . .	. . .	. . .
Nonmonetary gold	2 180	. .	. . .	. . .	. . .	. . .	. . .	. . .	. . .	. . .
Debit	3 100	. .	**–1,351.1**	**–1,518.6**	**–1,925.8**	**–2,150.4**	**–2,370.5**	**–2,509.6**	**–2,669.6**	**–2,807.4**
General merchandise: imports f.o.b.	3 110	. .	–1,351.1	–1,518.6	–1,924.1	–2,148.5	–2,370.5	–2,509.6	–2,669.6	–2,807.4
Goods for processing: imports f.o.b.	3 150	. .	. . .	. . .	. . .	. . .	. . .	. . .	. . .	. . .
Repairs on goods	3 160	. .	. . .	. . .	–1.7	–1.9	. . .	. . .	. . .	. . .
Goods procured in ports by carriers	3 170	. .	. . .	. . .	. . .	. . .	. . .	. . .	. . .	. . .
Nonmonetary gold	3 180	. .	. . .	. . .	. . .	. . .	. . .	. . .	. . .	. . .
B. SERVICES	4 200	. .	–68.6	–76.1	–44.5	–26.0	–69.7	–28.3	–144.1	–172.6
Total credit	2 200	. .	*242.4*	*257.6*	*283.3*	*334.9*	*377.1*	*474.1*	*478.8*	*480.8*
Total debit	3 200	. .	*–311.0*	*–333.7*	*–327.8*	*–360.9*	*–446.8*	*–502.4*	*–622.9*	*–653.4*
Transportation services, credit	2 205	. .	**59.3**	**56.4**	**52.5**	**65.9**	**52.0**	**46.3**	**47.4**	**50.5**
Passenger	2 850	. .	*11.0*	*5.0*	*4.3*	*5.5*	*6.8*	*6.0*	*3.0*	*3.5*
Freight	2 851	. .	*12.0*	*13.3*	*16.7*	*17.9*	*19.3*	*14.6*	*17.1*	*16.6*
Other	2 852	. .	*36.3*	*38.1*	*31.5*	*42.5*	*25.9*	*25.7*	*27.3*	*30.4*
Sea transport, passenger	2 207	. .	. . .	. . .	. . .	. . .	. . .	. . .	. . .	. . .
Sea transport, freight	2 208	. .	. . .	. . .	. . .	. . .	19.3	14.6	17.1	16.6
Sea transport, other	2 209	. .	. . .	. . .	. . .	. . .	25.9	25.7	27.3	30.4
Air transport, passenger	2 211	. .	. . .	. . .	. . .	. . .	6.8	6.0	3.0	3.5
Air transport, freight	2 212	. .	. . .	. . .	. . .	. . .	. . .	. . .	. . .	. . .
Air transport, other	2 213	. .	. . .	. . .	. . .	. . .	. . .	. . .	. . .	. . .
Other transport, passenger	2 215	. .	. . .	. . .	. . .	. . .	. . .	. . .	. . .	. . .
Other transport, freight	2 216	. .	. . .	. . .	. . .	. . .	. . .	. . .	. . .	. . .
Other transport, other	2 217	. .	. . .	. . .	. . .	. . .	. . .	. . .	. . .	. . .
Transportation services, debit	3 205	. .	**–177.3**	**–196.7**	**–196.2**	**–215.6**	**–261.6**	**–283.7**	**–299.2**	**–310.8**
Passenger	3 850	. .	*–39.0*	*–42.0*	*–49.7*	*–52.5*	*–61.0*	*–71.9*	*–73.5*	*–74.5*
Freight	3 851	. .	*–130.3*	*–146.7*	*–145.7*	*–162.2*	*–192.1*	*–202.8*	*–216.3*	*–226.2*
Other	3 852	. .	*–8.0*	*–8.0*	*–.8*	*–.9*	*–8.5*	*–9.0*	*–9.4*	*–10.1*
Sea transport, passenger	3 207	. .	. . .	. . .	. . .	. . .	. . .	. . .	. . .	. . .
Sea transport, freight	3 208	. .	. . .	. . .	. . .	. . .	–192.1	–202.8	–216.3	–226.2
Sea transport, other	3 209	. .	. . .	. . .	. . .	. . .	–8.5	–9.0	–9.4	–10.1
Air transport, passenger	3 211	. .	. . .	. . .	. . .	. . .	–61.0	–71.9	–73.5	–74.5
Air transport, freight	3 212	. .	. . .	. . .	. . .	. . .	. . .	. . .	. . .	. . .
Air transport, other	3 213	. .	. . .	. . .	. . .	. . .	. . .	. . .	. . .	. . .
Other transport, passenger	3 215	. .	. . .	. . .	. . .	. . .	. . .	. . .	. . .	. . .
Other transport, freight	3 216	. .	. . .	. . .	. . .	. . .	. . .	. . .	. . .	. . .
Other transport, other	3 217	. .	. . .	. . .	. . .	. . .	. . .	. . .	. . .	. . .
Travel, credit	2 236	. .	**72.0**	**80.0**	**115.0**	**145.6**	**167.6**	**208.0**	**259.8**	**256.3**
Business travel	2 237	. .	. . .	. . .	. . .	. . .	. . .	. . .	. . .	. . .
Personal travel	2 240	. .	. . .	. . .	. . .	. . .	167.6	208.0	259.8	256.3
Travel, debit	3 236	. .	**–57.0**	**–57.0**	**–60.0**	**–62.1**	**–81.0**	**–94.0**	**–119.6**	**–127.6**
Business travel	3 237	. .	. . .	. . .	. . .	. . .	. . .	. . .	. . .	. . .
Personal travel	3 240	. .	. . .	. . .	. . .	. . .	–81.0	–94.0	–119.6	–127.6
Other services, credit	2 200	BA	**111.1**	**121.2**	**115.8**	**123.4**	**157.5**	**219.8**	**171.6**	**174.0**
Communications	2 245	. .	60.5	67.5	76.0	82.2	59.4	87.9	90.5	82.7
Construction	2 249	. .	. . .	. . .	. . .	. . .	. . .	. . .	. . .	. . .
Insurance	2 253	. .	3.9	4.5	6.2	6.5	47.1	78.6	24.5	26.3
Financial	2 260	. .	. . .	. . .	.9	1.0	. . .	. . .	. . .	. . .
Computer and information	2 262	. .	. . .	. . .	.2	.3	. . .	. . .	. . .	. . .
Royalties and licence fees	2 266	. .	. . .	. . .	. . .	. . .	. . .	. . .	. . .	. . .
Other business services	2 268	. .	11.7	12.2	26.3	26.2	6.0	6.3	6.6	10.0
Personal, cultural, and recreational	2 287	. .	. . .	. . .	. . .	. . .	. . .	. . .	. . .	. . .
Government, n.i.e.	2 291	. .	35.0	37.0	6.2	7.2	45.0	47.0	50.0	55.0
Other services, debit	3 200	BA	**–76.7**	**–80.0**	**–71.6**	**–83.2**	**–104.2**	**–124.7**	**–204.1**	**–215.0**
Communications	3 245	. .	–14.9	–16.0	–21.7	–22.1	–12.8	–13.9	–11.3	–8.4
Construction	3 249	. .	. . .	. . .	–9.0	–9.5	–9.0	–15.0	–40.0	–35.0
Insurance	3 253	. .	–7.5	–8.0	–2.7	–2.9	–3.3	–3.5	–25.5	–25.9
Financial	3 260	. .	. . .	. . .	–3.5	–4.0	. . .	. . .	. . .	. . .
Computer and information	3 262	. .	. . .	. . .	. . .	. . .	. . .	. . .	. . .	. . .
Royalties and licence fees	3 266	. .	–5.4	–8.9	–4.0	–4.5	–9.2	–9.5	–10.0	–10.5
Other business services	3 268	. .	–41.7	–39.1	–25.4	–34.5	–53.1	–64.8	–95.5	–113.0
Personal, cultural, and recreational	3 287	. .	. . .	. . .	–3.2	–3.5	–6.5	–7.0	–8.0	–8.2
Government, n.i.e.	3 291	. .	–7.2	–8.0	–2.1	–2.2	–10.3	–11.0	–13.8	–14.0

Table 2 (Continued). STANDARD PRESENTATION, 1994–2001

(Millions of U.S. dollars)

	Code	1994	1995	1996	1997	1998	1999	2000	2001
C. INCOME	4 300	−214.1	−225.9	−230.8	−211.8	−204.1	−155.2	−146.7	−147.2
Total credit	2 300	*24.0*	*32.3*	*61.2*	*70.0*	*59.5*	*80.5*	*110.1*	*88.0*
Total debit	3 300	*−238.1*	*−258.2*	*−292.0*	*−281.8*	*−263.6*	*−235.7*	*−256.8*	*−235.2*
Compensation of employees, credit	2 310	**4.0**	**4.0**	**28.9**	**30.0**	**5.0**	**8.3**	**6.0**	**6.5**
Compensation of employees, debit	3 310	**. . .**	**. . .**	**−8.1**	**−9.5**	**. . .**	**. . .**	**. . .**	**. . .**
Investment income, credit	2 320	**20.0**	**28.3**	**32.3**	**40.0**	**54.5**	**72.2**	**104.1**	**81.5**
Direct investment income	2 330	. . .	. . .	. . .	. . .	. . .	. . .	. . .	. . .
Dividends and distributed branch profits	2 332	. . .	. . .	. . .	. . .	. . .	. . .	. . .	. . .
Reinvested earnings and undistributed branch profits	2 333	. . .	. . .	. . .	. . .	. . .	. . .	. . .	. . .
Income on debt (interest)	2 334	. . .	. . .	. . .	. . .	. . .	. . .	. . .	. . .
Portfolio investment income	2 339	20.0	28.3	29.0	36.0	54.5	72.2	104.1	81.5
Income on equity	2 340	. . .	. . .	. . .	. . .	54.5	72.2	104.1	81.5
Income on bonds and notes	2 350	. . .	. . .	. . .	. . .	. . .	. . .	. . .	. . .
Income on money market instruments	2 360	20.0	28.3	29.0	36.0	. . .	. . .	. . .	. . .
Other investment income	2 370	. . .	. . .	3.3	4.0	. . .	. . .	. . .	. . .
Investment income, debit	3 320	**−238.1**	**−258.2**	**−283.9**	**−272.3**	**−263.6**	**−235.7**	**−256.8**	**−235.2**
Direct investment income	3 330	−30.0	−40.0	−66.5	−70.0	−70.0	−43.6	−70.0	−75.2
Dividends and distributed branch profits	3 332	−18.0	−30.0	−51.8	−50.0	−70.0	−43.6	−70.0	−75.2
Reinvested earnings and undistributed branch profits	3 333	−12.0	−10.0	−14.7	−20.0	. . .	. . .	. . .	. . .
Income on debt (interest)	3 334	. . .	. . .	. . .	. . .	. . .	. . .	. . .	. . .
Portfolio investment income	3 339	−208.1	−218.2	−217.4	−202.3	−193.6	−192.1	−186.8	−160.0
Income on equity	3 340	. . .	. . .	. . .	−8.0	. . .	. . .	. . .	. . .
Income on bonds and notes	3 350	−208.1	−218.2	−217.4	−194.3	−193.6	−192.1	−186.8	−160.0
Income on money market instruments	3 360	. . .	. . .	. . .	. . .	. . .	. . .	. . .	. . .
Other investment income	3 370	. . .	. . .	. . .	. . .	. . .	. . .	. . .	. . .
D. CURRENT TRANSFERS	4 379	189.0	242.5	227.3	259.5	448.7	695.9	703.1	871.3
Credit	2 379	**190.2**	**243.7**	**271.7**	**306.8**	**488.8**	**738.3**	**748.0**	**918.5**
General government	2 380	96.7	115.7	123.8	124.6	247.1	383.7	300.6	344.8
Other sectors	2 390	93.5	128.0	147.9	182.2	241.7	354.6	447.4	573.7
Workers' remittances	2 391	85.0	120.0	128.4	160.0	220.0	320.0	409.6	533.7
Other current transfers	2 392	8.5	8.0	19.5	22.2	21.7	34.6	37.8	40.0
Debit	3 379	**−1.2**	**−1.2**	**−44.4**	**−47.3**	**−40.1**	**−42.4**	**−44.9**	**−47.2**
General government	3 380	−.7	−.7	−.7	−.7	−.7	−.8	−.6	−.8
Other sectors	3 390	−.5	−.5	−43.7	−46.6	−39.4	−41.6	−44.3	−46.4
Workers' remittances	3 391	. . .	. . .	. . .	. . .	−.5	−.6	−.5	−.7
Other current transfers	3 392	−.5	−.5	−43.7	−46.6	−38.9	−41.0	−43.8	−45.7
CAPITAL AND FINANCIAL ACCOUNT	4 996	**227.8**	**155.9**	**177.5**	**75.7**	**51.6**	**118.9**	**126.2**	**242.2**
CAPITAL ACCOUNT	4 994	**31.9**	**17.4**	**31.0**	**18.7**	**29.4**	**110.9**	**98.9**	**95.0**
Total credit	2 994	*31.9*	*17.4*	*31.7*	*19.4*	*29.4*	*110.9*	*98.9*	*95.0*
Total debit	3 994	. . .	. . .	*−.7*	*−.7*	. . .	. . .	. . .	. . .
Capital transfers, credit	2 400	**31.9**	**17.4**	**31.7**	**19.4**	**29.4**	**110.9**	**98.9**	**95.0**
General government	2 401	31.9	17.4	30.5	18.0	11.9	110.9	98.9	87.2
Debt forgiveness	2 402	31.9	17.4	2.5	4.1	11.9	39.1	48.3	52.6
Other capital transfers	2 410	. . .	. . .	28.0	13.9	. . .	71.8	50.6	34.6
Other sectors	2 430	. . .	. . .	1.2	1.4	17.5	. . .	. . .	7.8
Migrants' transfers	2 431	. . .	. . .	. . .	. . .	. . .	. . .	. . .	. . .
Debt forgiveness	2 432	. . .	. . .	. . .	. . .	17.5	. . .	. . .	7.8
Other capital transfers	2 440	. . .	. . .	1.2	1.4	. . .	. . .	. . .	. . .
Capital transfers, debit	3 400	**. . .**	**. . .**	**−.7**	**−.7**	**. . .**	**. . .**	**. . .**	**. . .**
General government	3 401	. . .	. . .	. . .	. . .	. . .	. . .	. . .	. . .
Debt forgiveness	3 402	. . .	. . .	. . .	. . .	. . .	. . .	. . .	. . .
Other capital transfers	3 410	. . .	. . .	. . .	. . .	. . .	. . .	. . .	. . .
Other sectors	3 430	. . .	. . .	−.7	−.7	. . .	. . .	. . .	. . .
Migrants' transfers	3 431	. . .	. . .	. . .	. . .	. . .	. . .	. . .	. . .
Debt forgiveness	3 432	. . .	. . .	. . .	. . .	. . .	. . .	. . .	. . .
Other capital transfers	3 440	. . .	. . .	−.7	−.7	. . .	. . .	. . .	. . .
Nonproduced nonfinancial assets, credit	2 480	**. . .**	**. . .**	**. . .**	**. . .**	**. . .**	**. . .**	**. . .**	**. . .**
Nonproduced nonfinancial assets, debit	3 480	**. . .**	**. . .**	**. . .**	**. . .**	**. . .**	**. . .**	**. . .**	**. . .**

Table 2 (Continued). STANDARD PRESENTATION, 1994–2001
(Millions of U.S. dollars)

	Code	1994	1995	1996	1997	1998	1999	2000	2001
FINANCIAL ACCOUNT	4 995	**195.9**	**138.5**	**146.5**	**57.0**	**22.2**	**8.0**	**27.3**	**147.2**
A. DIRECT INVESTMENT	4 500	34.8	50.0	90.9	121.5	99.0	237.3	282.0	195.0
Direct investment abroad	4 505	**...**	**...**	**...**	**...**	**...**	**...**	**...**	**...**
Equity capital	4 510	...	...	...	...	...	...	...	...
Claims on affiliated enterprises	4 515	...	...	...	...	...	...	...	...
Liabilities to affiliated enterprises	4 520	...	...	...	...	...	...	...	...
Reinvested earnings	4 525	...	...	...	...	...	...	...	...
Other capital	4 530	...	...	...	...	...	...	...	...
Claims on affiliated enterprises	4 535	...	...	...	...	...	...	...	...
Liabilities to affiliated enterprises	4 540	...	...	...	...	...	...	...	...
Direct investment in Honduras	4 555	**34.8**	**50.0**	**90.9**	**121.5**	**99.0**	**237.3**	**282.0**	**195.0**
Equity capital	4 560	11.9	13.2	45.4	60.0	99.0	237.3	282.0	195.0
Claims on direct investors	4 565	...	...	...	...	...	...	...	...
Liabilities to direct investors	4 570	...	...	...	...	99.0	237.3	282.0	195.0
Reinvested earnings	4 575	12.0	10.0	14.7	20.0	...	...	...	...
Other capital	4 580	10.9	26.8	30.8	41.5	...	...	...	...
Claims on direct investors	4 585	...	...	...	...	...	...	...	...
Liabilities to direct investors	4 590	...	...	...	...	...	...	...	...
B. PORTFOLIO INVESTMENT	4 600	...	...	16.0	...	...	−72.4	−115.4	−46.7
Assets	4 602	**...**	**...**	**16.0**	**...**	**...**	**−72.4**	**−115.4**	**−46.7**
Equity securities	4 610	...	...	16.0	...	...	...	...	...
Monetary authorities	4 611	...	...	...	...	...	...	...	...
General government	4 612	...	...	...	...	...	...	...	...
Banks	4 613	...	...	...	...	...	...	...	...
Other sectors	4 614	...	...	16.0	...	...	...	...	...
Debt securities	4 619	...	...	...	...	...	−72.4	−115.4	−46.7
Bonds and notes	4 620	...	...	...	...	...	−72.4	−115.4	−46.7
Monetary authorities	4 621	...	...	...	...	...	...	...	...
General government	4 622	...	...	...	...	...	−72.4	−80.4	−46.7
Banks	4 623	...	...	...	...	...	...	...	...
Other sectors	4 624	...	...	...	...	...	...	−35.0	...
Money market instruments	4 630	...	...	...	...	...	...	...	...
Monetary authorities	4 631	...	...	...	...	...	...	...	...
General government	4 632	...	...	...	...	...	...	...	...
Banks	4 633	...	...	...	...	...	...	...	...
Other sectors	4 634	...	...	...	...	...	...	...	...
Liabilities	4 652	**...**	**...**	**...**	**...**	**...**	**...**	**...**	**...**
Equity securities	4 660	...	...	...	...	...	...	...	...
Banks	4 663	...	...	...	...	...	...	...	...
Other sectors	4 664	...	...	...	...	...	...	...	...
Debt securities	4 669	...	...	...	...	...	...	...	...
Bonds and notes	4 670	...	...	...	...	...	...	...	...
Monetary authorities	4 671	...	...	...	...	...	...	...	...
General government	4 672	...	...	...	...	...	...	...	...
Banks	4 673	...	...	...	...	...	...	...	...
Other sectors	4 674	...	...	...	...	...	...	...	...
Money market instruments	4 680	...	...	...	...	...	...	...	...
Monetary authorities	4 681	...	...	...	...	...	...	...	...
General government	4 682	...	...	...	...	...	...	...	...
Banks	4 683	...	...	...	...	...	...	...	...
Other sectors	4 684	...	...	...	...	...	...	...	...
C. FINANCIAL DERIVATIVES	4 910	...	...	...	...	−25.8	−16.1	−1.2	...
Monetary authorities	4 911	...	...	...	...	...	...	...	...
General government	4 912	...	...	...	...	...	...	...	...
Banks	4 913	...	...	...	...	...	...	...	...
Other sectors	4 914	...	...	...	...	−25.8	−16.1	−1.2	...
Assets	4 900	**...**	**...**	**...**	**...**	**...**	**...**	**...**	**...**
Monetary authorities	4 901	...	...	...	...	...	...	...	...
General government	4 902	...	...	...	...	...	...	...	...
Banks	4 903	...	...	...	...	...	...	...	...
Other sectors	4 904	...	...	...	...	...	...	...	...
Liabilities	4 905	**...**	**...**	**...**	**...**	**−25.8**	**−16.1**	**−1.2**	**...**
Monetary authorities	4 906	...	...	...	...	...	...	...	...
General government	4 907	...	...	...	...	...	...	...	...
Banks	4 908	...	...	...	...	...	...	...	...
Other sectors	4 909	...	...	...	...	−25.8	−16.1	−1.2	...

Table 2 (Concluded). STANDARD PRESENTATION, 1994–2001
(Millions of U.S. dollars)

	Code	1994	1995	1996	1997	1998	1999	2000	2001
D. OTHER INVESTMENT	4 700 . .	235.1	178.8	26.9	243.4	178.8	301.0	–105.7	84.5
Assets	4 703 . .	**8.9**	**–12.8**	**–89.4**	**–53.4**	**–61.7**	**–132.2**	**–157.3**	**–68.8**
Trade credits	4 706 . .	. . .	. . .	. . .	. . .	. . .	. . .	–59.4	–3.6
General government	4 707 . .	. . .	. . .	. . .	. . .	. . .	. . .	–59.4	–3.6
of which: Short-term	4 709 . .	. . .	. . .	. . .	. . .	. . .	. . .	. . .	. . .
Other sectors	4 710 . .	. . .	. . .	. . .	. . .	. . .	. . .	. . .	. . .
of which: Short-term	4 712 . .	. . .	. . .	. . .	. . .	. . .	. . .	. . .	. . .
Loans	4 714 . .	. . .	. . .	. . .	. . .	. . .	. . .	. . .	. . .
Monetary authorities	4 715 . .	. . .	. . .	. . .	. . .	. . .	. . .	. . .	. . .
of which: Short-term	4 718 . .	. . .	. . .	. . .	. . .	. . .	. . .	. . .	. . .
General government	4 719 . .	. . .	. . .	. . .	. . .	. . .	. . .	. . .	. . .
of which: Short-term	4 721 . .	. . .	. . .	. . .	. . .	. . .	. . .	. . .	. . .
Banks	4 722 . .	. . .	. . .	. . .	. . .	. . .	. . .	. . .	. . .
of which: Short-term	4 724 . .	. . .	. . .	. . .	. . .	. . .	. . .	. . .	. . .
Other sectors	4 725 . .	. . .	. . .	. . .	. . .	. . .	. . .	. . .	. . .
of which: Short-term	4 727 . .	. . .	. . .	. . .	. . .	. . .	. . .	. . .	. . .
Currency and deposits	4 730 . .	6.6	6.8	–89.4	–53.4	–61.7	–132.2	–97.9	–65.2
Monetary authorities	4 731 . .	. . .	. . .	. . .	. . .	. . .	. . .	. . .	. . .
General government	4 732 . .	15.4	45.7	. . .	. . .	. . .	. . .	. . .	. . .
Banks	4 733 . .	–8.8	–38.9	–89.4	–53.4	–61.7	–132.2	–97.9	–65.2
Other sectors	4 734 . .	. . .	. . .	. . .	. . .	. . .	. . .	. . .	. . .
Other assets	4 736 . .	2.3	–19.6	. . .	. . .	. . .	. . .	. . .	. . .
Monetary authorities	4 737 . .	3.3	11.7	. . .	. . .	. . .	. . .	. . .	. . .
of which: Short-term	4 739 . .	. . .	. . .	. . .	. . .	. . .	. . .	. . .	. . .
General government	4 740 . .	–1.0	–31.3	. . .	. . .	. . .	. . .	. . .	. . .
of which: Short-term	4 742 . .	. . .	. . .	. . .	. . .	. . .	. . .	. . .	. . .
Banks	4 743 . .	. . .	. . .	. . .	. . .	. . .	. . .	. . .	. . .
of which: Short-term	4 745 . .	. . .	. . .	. . .	. . .	. . .	. . .	. . .	. . .
Other sectors	4 746 . .	. . .	. . .	. . .	. . .	. . .	. . .	. . .	. . .
of which: Short-term	4 748 . .	. . .	. . .	. . .	. . .	. . .	. . .	. . .	. . .
Liabilities	4 753 . .	**226.2**	**191.6**	**116.3**	**296.8**	**240.5**	**433.2**	**51.6**	**153.3**
Trade credits	4 756 . .	83.5	40.1	22.7	4.0	. . .	. . .	. . .	. . .
General government	4 757 . .	. . .	. . .	. . .	. . .	. . .	. . .	. . .	. . .
of which: Short-term	4 759 . .	. . .	. . .	. . .	. . .	. . .	. . .	. . .	. . .
Other sectors	4 760 . .	83.5	40.1	22.7	4.0	. . .	. . .	. . .	. . .
of which: Short-term	4 762 . .	*83.5*	*40.1*	*22.7*	*4.0*	. . .	. . .	. . .	. . .
Loans	4 764 . .	95.3	194.8	145.3	216.0	263.0	341.8	218.4	166.6
Monetary authorities	4 765 . .	–107.5	–3.3	–70.2	–25.2	104.8	83.2	–6.3	–4.1
of which: Use of Fund credit and loans from the Fund	4 766 . .	*–16.1*	*–13.7*	*–38.0*	*–8.8*	*64.8*	*99.5*	*15.5*	*16.9*
of which: Short-term	4 768 . .	*–68.7*	*2.8*	*–1.1*	*1.3*	. . .	. . .	. . .	*–4.7*
General government	4 769 . .	190.4	169.4	160.3	34.8	–1.7	218.4	240.4	191.5
of which: Short-term	4 771 . .	*–16.5*	*39.0*	*150.7*	*–32.8*	*–3.9*	*–2.5*	*–31.9*	*–25.2*
Banks	4 772 . .	15.4	26.3	21.5	76.5	51.1	–11.5	–40.5	–45.9
of which: Short-term	4 774 . .	. . .	. . .	. . .	. . .	*–15.5*	. . .	. . .	. . .
Other sectors	4 775 . .	–3.0	2.4	33.7	129.9	108.8	51.7	24.8	25.1
of which: Short-term	4 777 . .	*–3.1*	*–2.6*	*20.4*	*134.0*	*37.4*	*–2.2*	*8.0*	*22.7*
Currency and deposits	4 780 . .	–1.2	–.8	. . .	. . .	. . .	. . .	. . .	. . .
Monetary authorities	4 781 . .	. . .	. . .	. . .	. . .	. . .	. . .	. . .	. . .
General government	4 782 . .	. . .	. . .	. . .	. . .	. . .	. . .	. . .	. . .
Banks	4 783 . .	–1.2	–.8	. . .	. . .	. . .	. . .	. . .	. . .
Other sectors	4 784 . .	. . .	. . .	. . .	. . .	. . .	. . .	. . .	. . .
Other liabilities	4 786 . .	48.6	–42.5	–51.7	76.8	–22.5	91.4	–166.8	–13.3
Monetary authorities	4 787 . .	65.0	–23.3	–64.7	39.5	–31.4	2.4	. . .	–4.0
of which: Short-term	4 789 . .	*65.0*	*–23.3*	*–64.7*	*39.5*	*–31.4*	*2.4*	. . .	*–4.0*
General government	4 790 . .	. . .	. . .	. . .	. . .	40.4	89.0	–166.8	–9.3
of which: Short-term	4 792 . .	. . .	. . .	. . .	. . .	*40.4*	*89.0*	*–166.8*	*–9.3*
Banks	4 793 . .	–16.4	–19.2	13.0	37.3	–31.5	. . .	. . .	. . .
of which: Short-term	4 795 . .	*–16.4*	*–19.2*	*13.0*	*37.3*	*–31.5*	. . .	. . .	. . .
Other sectors	4 796 . .	. . .	. . .	. . .	. . .	. . .	. . .	. . .	. . .
of which: Short-term	4 798 . .	. . .	. . .	. . .	. . .	. . .	. . .	. . .	. . .
E. RESERVE ASSETS	4 802 . .	–74.1	–90.3	12.7	–307.9	–229.8	–441.9	–32.3	–85.6
Monetary gold	4 812 . .	. . .	. . .	.4	1.6	.2	–.1	.3	–.1
Special drawing rights	4 811 . .	–.1	. . .	.1	. . .	. . .	–.9	.8	–.2
Reserve position in the Fund	4 810 . .	. . .	. . .	. . .	. . .	. . .	–11.9	. . .	. . .
Foreign exchange	4 803 . .	–74.0	–90.3	4.5	–331.3	–230.0	–429.0	–33.4	–85.3
Other claims	4 813 . .	. . .	. . .	7.7	21.8	. . .	. . .	. . .	. . .
NET ERRORS AND OMISSIONS	4 998 . .	**115.5**	**45.0**	**157.9**	**196.5**	**96.1**	**122.0**	**129.9**	**82.8**

Part 3 of the *Yearbook* contains descriptions of the methodologies, compilation practices, and sources used to compile these data.

Table 1. ANALYTIC PRESENTATION, 1994–2001
(Millions of U.S. dollars)

	Code	1994	1995	1996	1997	1998	1999	2000	2001
A. Current Account [1]	4 993 Z.	**-4,054**	**-2,530**	**-1,689**	**-982**	**-2,304**	**-2,106**	**-1,328**	**-1,097**
Goods: exports f.o.b.	2 100 . .	7,648	12,864	14,184	19,640	20,747	21,848	25,747	28,071
Goods: imports f.o.b.	3 100 . .	-11,364	-15,297	-16,836	-21,602	-23,101	-24,037	-27,506	-30,089
Balance on Goods	4 100 . .	*-3,716*	*-2,433*	*-2,652*	*-1,962*	*-2,354*	*-2,189*	*-1,760*	*-2,018*
Services: credit	2 200 . .	3,117	5,182	5,980	5,733	5,921	5,649	6,251	7,707
Services: debit	3 200 . .	-2,958	-3,616	-3,506	-3,465	-4,141	-4,263	-4,476	-5,544
Balance on Goods and Services	4 991 . .	*-3,557*	*-867*	*-178*	*306*	*-574*	*-803*	*15*	*146*
Income: credit	2 300 . .	676	798	1,202	1,382	1,111	775	942	1,111
Income: debit	3 300 . .	-2,082	-2,602	-2,658	-2,808	-2,990	-2,417	-2,516	-2,599
Balance on Goods, Services, and Income	4 992 . .	*-4,963*	*-2,671*	*-1,634*	*-1,120*	*-2,453*	*-2,446*	*-1,559*	*-1,342*
Current transfers: credit	2 379 Z.	2,871	364	160	335	379	582	520	589
Current transfers: debit	3 379 . .	-1,961	-222	-214	-197	-231	-243	-289	-344
B. Capital Account [1]	4 994 Z.	**. . .**	**59**	**156**	**117**	**189**	**29**	**270**	**317**
Capital account: credit	2 994 Z.	. . .	80	266	266	408	509	458	417
Capital account: debit	3 994 . .	. . .	-20	-110	-149	-219	-480	-188	-101
Total, Groups A Plus B	4 981 . .	*-4,054*	*-2,470*	*-1,533*	*-865*	*-2,115*	*-2,077*	*-1,058*	*-780*
C. Financial Account [1]	4 995 W.	**3,370**	**7,080**	**-687**	**658**	**3,017**	**4,693**	**2,219**	**617**
Direct investment abroad	4 505 . .	-49	-43	4	-433	-478	-252	-532	-337
Direct investment in Hungary	4 555 Z.	1,144	4,519	2,274	2,167	2,037	1,977	1,646	2,440
Portfolio investment assets	4 602 . .	6	-1	-35	-134	-93	-75	-309	-149
Equity securities	4 610 . .	-10	. . .	-15	-32	-45	16	-151	-55
Debt securities	4 619 . .	16	-1	-20	-102	-48	-91	-158	-95
Portfolio investment liabilities	4 652 Z.	2,458	2,213	-396	-914	1,925	2,065	-187	1,526
Equity securities	4 660 . .	224	. . .	359	1,004	556	1,191	-416	134
Debt securities	4 669 Z.	2,234	2,213	-754	-1,918	1,369	874	229	1,392
Financial derivatives	4 910 . .	. . .	. . .	16	8	147	-47	60	122
Financial derivatives assets	4 900 . .	. . .	. . .	17	12	185	852	753	579
Financial derivatives liabilities	4 905 . .	. . .	. . .	-1	-4	-38	-899	-692	-457
Other investment assets	4 703 . .	362	592	-1,256	-584	-507	-1,170	-1,014	-3,430
Monetary authorities	4 701 . .	. . .	-15	14	1	4	. . .	-8	4
General government	4 704 . .	156	27	45	189	75	30	64	30
Banks	4 705 . .	191	125	-1,129	-789	-333	-430	755	-1,490
Other sectors	4 728 . .	15	456	-185	15	-253	-770	-1,825	-1,975
Other investment liabilities	4 753 W.	-551	-199	-1,294	549	-13	2,197	2,555	446
Monetary authorities	4 753 WA	17	-904	-1,875	-659	-15	286	613	-644
General government	4 753 ZB	-1,761	-438	-331	-106	-288	235	-225	-33
Banks	4 753 ZC	365	321	394	1,123	619	522	401	294
Other sectors	4 753 ZD	828	823	518	190	-329	1,154	1,765	829
Total, Groups A Through C	4 983 . .	*-684*	*4,610*	*-2,220*	*-207*	*902*	*2,617*	*1,161*	*-162*
D. Net Errors and Omissions	4 998 . .	**209**	**789**	**976**	**32**	**49**	**-282**	**-109**	**79**
Total, Groups A Through D	4 984 . .	*-475*	*5,399*	*-1,244*	*-175*	*951*	*2,335*	*1,052*	*-84*
E. Reserves and Related Items	4 802 A.	**475**	**-5,399**	**1,244**	**175**	**-951**	**-2,335**	**-1,052**	**84**
Reserve assets	4 802 . .	640	-4,614	1,447	175	-790	-2,335	-1,052	84
Use of Fund credit and loans	4 766 . .	-165	-785	-203	. . .	-160	. . .	. . .	. . .
Exceptional financing	4 920 . .	. . .	. . .	. . .	. . .	. . .	. . .	. . .	. . .
Conversion rates: forint per U.S. dollar	0 101 . .	**105.16**	**125.68**	**152.65**	**186.79**	**214.40**	**237.15**	**282.18**	**286.49**

[1] Excludes components that have been classified in the categories of Group E.

Table 2. STANDARD PRESENTATION, 1994–2001
(Millions of U.S. dollars)

	Code	1994	1995	1996	1997	1998	1999	2000	2001
CURRENT ACCOUNT	4 993 . .	**–4,054**	**–2,530**	**–1,689**	**–982**	**–2,304**	**–2,106**	**–1,328**	**–1,097**
A. GOODS	4 100 . .	–3,716	–2,433	–2,652	–1,962	–2,354	–2,189	–1,760	–2,018
Credit	2 100 . .	**7,648**	**12,864**	**14,184**	**19,640**	**20,747**	**21,848**	**25,747**	**28,071**
General merchandise: exports f.o.b.	2 110 . .	7,648	12,864	14,184	19,640	20,747	21,848	25,747	28,071
Goods for processing: exports f.o.b.	2 150 . .	. . .	. . .	. . .	. . .	. . .	. . .	. . .	. . .
Repairs on goods	2 160 . .	. . .	. . .	. . .	. . .	. . .	. . .	. . .	. . .
Goods procured in ports by carriers	2 170 . .	. . .	. . .	. . .	. . .	. . .	. . .	. . .	. . .
Nonmonetary gold	2 180 . .	. . .	. . .	. . .	. . .	. . .	. . .	. . .	. . .
Debit	3 100 . .	**–11,364**	**–15,297**	**–16,836**	**–21,602**	**–23,101**	**–24,037**	**–27,506**	**–30,089**
General merchandise: imports f.o.b.	3 110 . .	–11,364	–15,297	–16,836	–21,602	–23,101	–24,037	–27,506	–30,089
Goods for processing: imports f.o.b.	3 150 . .	. . .	. . .	. . .	. . .	. . .	. . .	. . .	. . .
Repairs on goods	3 160 . .	. . .	. . .	. . .	. . .	. . .	. . .	. . .	. . .
Goods procured in ports by carriers	3 170 . .	. . .	. . .	. . .	. . .	. . .	. . .	. . .	. . .
Nonmonetary gold	3 180 . .	. . .	. . .	. . .	. . .	. . .	. . .	. . .	. . .
B. SERVICES	4 200 . .	159	1,566	2,473	2,267	1,780	1,386	1,775	2,163
Total credit	2 200 . .	*3,117*	*5,182*	*5,980*	*5,733*	*5,921*	*5,649*	*6,251*	*7,707*
Total debit	3 200 . .	*–2,958*	*–3,616*	*–3,506*	*–3,465*	*–4,141*	*–4,263*	*–4,476*	*–5,544*
Transportation services, credit	2 205 . .	**51**	**446**	**418**	**502**	**648**	**570**	**647**	**649**
Passenger	2 850 . .	. . .	*10*	*27*	*27*	*42*	*57*	*76*	*37*
Freight	2 851 . .	*51*	*348*	*240*	*272*	*411*	*403*	*452*	*509*
Other	2 852 . .	. . .	*88*	*150*	*203*	*195*	*110*	*119*	*103*
Sea transport, passenger	2 207 . .	. . .	. . .	. . .	. . .	. . .	. . .	. . .	. . .
Sea transport, freight	2 208 . .	. . .	. . .	. . .	. . .	. . .	. . .	. . .	. . .
Sea transport, other	2 209 . .	. . .	. . .	. . .	. . .	. . .	. . .	. . .	. . .
Air transport, passenger	2 211 . .	. . .	. . .	. . .	. . .	. . .	. . .	. . .	. . .
Air transport, freight	2 212 . .	. . .	. . .	. . .	. . .	. . .	. . .	. . .	. . .
Air transport, other	2 213 . .	. . .	. . .	. . .	. . .	. . .	. . .	. . .	. . .
Other transport, passenger	2 215 . .	. . .	. . .	. . .	. . .	. . .	. . .	. . .	. . .
Other transport, freight	2 216 . .	. . .	. . .	. . .	. . .	. . .	. . .	. . .	. . .
Other transport, other	2 217 . .	. . .	. . .	. . .	. . .	. . .	. . .	. . .	. . .
Transportation services, debit	3 205 . .	**–210**	**–370**	**–316**	**–426**	**–452**	**–450**	**–515**	**–564**
Passenger	3 850 . .	. . .	*–3*	*–9*	*–16*	*–20*	*–47*	*–71*	*–79*
Freight	3 851 . .	*–210*	*–84*	*–167*	*–270*	*–337*	*–287*	*–322*	*–341*
Other	3 852 . .	. . .	*–283*	*–140*	*–139*	*–96*	*–117*	*–122*	*–144*
Sea transport, passenger	3 207 . .	. . .	. . .	. . .	. . .	. . .	. . .	. . .	. . .
Sea transport, freight	3 208 . .	. . .	. . .	. . .	. . .	. . .	. . .	. . .	. . .
Sea transport, other	3 209 . .	. . .	. . .	. . .	. . .	. . .	. . .	. . .	. . .
Air transport, passenger	3 211 . .	. . .	. . .	. . .	. . .	. . .	. . .	. . .	. . .
Air transport, freight	3 212 . .	. . .	. . .	. . .	. . .	. . .	. . .	. . .	. . .
Air transport, other	3 213 . .	. . .	. . .	. . .	. . .	. . .	. . .	. . .	. . .
Other transport, passenger	3 215 . .	. . .	. . .	. . .	. . .	. . .	. . .	. . .	. . .
Other transport, freight	3 216 . .	. . .	. . .	. . .	. . .	. . .	. . .	. . .	. . .
Other transport, other	3 217 . .	. . .	. . .	. . .	. . .	. . .	. . .	. . .	. . .
Travel, credit	2 236 . .	**1,435**	**2,649**	**3,221**	**3,446**	**3,516**	**3,397**	**3,416**	**3,920**
Business travel	2 237 . .	. . .	. . .	68	118	122	148	174	179
Personal travel	2 240 . .	. . .	2,648	3,152	3,328	3,394	3,249	3,242	3,740
Travel, debit	3 236 . .	**–935**	**–1,071**	**–957**	**–925**	**–1,115**	**–1,193**	**–1,094**	**–1,306**
Business travel	3 237 . .	. . .	–164	–239	–264	–295	–277	–255	–264
Personal travel	3 240 . .	. . .	–907	–718	–660	–820	–916	–838	–1,041
Other services, credit	2 200 BA	**1,631**	**2,087**	**2,342**	**1,784**	**1,757**	**1,682**	**2,188**	**3,139**
Communications	2 245 . .	. . .	38	42	51	49	78	69	95
Construction	2 249 . .	. . .	21	32	60	108	72	107	108
Insurance	2 253 . .	6	62	20	27	28	37	16	16
Financial	2 260 . .	. . .	100	208	294	159	113	147	164
Computer and information	2 262 . .	. . .	. . .	93	79	59	86	121	176
Royalties and licence fees	2 266 . .	31	32	45	100	46	62	112	96
Other business services	2 268 . .	1,523	1,775	1,795	1,064	1,179	1,100	1,345	1,804
Personal, cultural, and recreational	2 287 . .	. . .	. . .	46	61	89	91	207	600
Government, n.i.e.	2 291 . .	71	60	60	48	40	43	65	80
Other services, debit	3 200 BA	**–1,813**	**–2,174**	**–2,233**	**–2,114**	**–2,574**	**–2,620**	**–2,868**	**–3,674**
Communications	3 245 . .	. . .	–22	–24	–41	–38	–53	–75	–78
Construction	3 249 . .	. . .	–36	–72	–67	–123	–186	–100	–114
Insurance	3 253 . .	–23	–31	–45	–87	–87	–101	–84	–113
Financial	3 260 . .	. . .	–152	–191	–257	–264	–205	–217	–214
Computer and information	3 262 . .	. . .	. . .	–59	–80	–96	–142	–127	–159
Royalties and licence fees	3 266 . .	–75	–70	–132	–192	–215	–307	–257	–263
Other business services	3 268 . .	–1,632	–1,789	–1,620	–1,292	–1,644	–1,506	–1,790	–2,090
Personal, cultural, and recreational	3 287 . .	. . .	. . .	–31	–38	–48	–43	–151	–563
Government, n.i.e.	3 291 . .	–83	–73	–60	–61	–59	–78	–67	–81

Table 2 (Continued). STANDARD PRESENTATION, 1994–2001
(Millions of U.S. dollars)

	Code	1994	1995	1996	1997	1998	1999	2000	2001
C. INCOME	4 300 . .	-1,406	-1,804	-1,456	-1,426	-1,878	-1,643	-1,574	-1,488
Total credit	2 300 . .	*676*	*798*	*1,202*	*1,382*	*1,111*	*775*	*942*	*1,111*
Total debit	3 300 . .	*-2,082*	*-2,602*	*-2,658*	*-2,808*	*-2,990*	*-2,417*	*-2,516*	*-2,599*
Compensation of employees, credit	2 310 . .	**. . .**	**21**	**36**	**38**	**45**	**33**	**39**	**50**
Compensation of employees, debit	3 310 . .	**. . .**	**-34**	**-56**	**-39**	**-21**	**-29**	**-37**	**-45**
Investment income, credit	2 320 . .	**676**	**778**	**1,166**	**1,344**	**1,067**	**741**	**903**	**1,061**
Direct investment income	2 330 . .	15	12	23	23	24	14	32	41
Dividends and distributed branch profits	2 332 . .	15	12	21	15	19	13	28	19
Reinvested earnings and undistributed branch profits	2 333 . .	. . .	. . .	. . .	. . .	. . .	. . .	. . .	. . .
Income on debt (interest)	2 334 . .	. . .	. . .	2	8	5	2	4	22
Portfolio investment income	2 339 . .	. . .	349	598	719	714	417	511	603
Income on equity	2 340 . .	. . .	. . .	. . .	15	6	5	10	15
Income on bonds and notes	2 350 . .	. . .	9	594	28	12	189	405	461
Income on money market instruments	2 360 . .	. . .	340	3	676	695	224	96	128
Other investment income	2 370 . .	660	417	545	602	329	310	360	417
Investment income, debit	3 320 . .	**-2,082**	**-2,568**	**-2,602**	**-2,769**	**-2,969**	**-2,388**	**-2,479**	**-2,554**
Direct investment income	3 330 . .	-132	-206	-281	-457	-963	-857	-832	-823
Dividends and distributed branch profits	3 332 . .	-132	-206	-259	-440	-925	-832	-786	-781
Reinvested earnings and undistributed branch profits	3 333 . .	. . .	. . .	. . .	. . .	. . .	. . .	. . .	. . .
Income on debt (interest)	3 334 . .	. . .	. . .	-21	-17	-38	-25	-46	-42
Portfolio investment income	3 339 . .	. . .	-1,136	-1,215	-1,306	-1,398	-985	-997	-1,000
Income on equity	3 340 . .	. . .	. . .	. . .	-61	-67	-78	-65	-58
Income on bonds and notes	3 350 . .	. . .	-1,135	-1,188	-954	-828	-893	-923	-938
Income on money market instruments	3 360 . .	. . .	-1	-27	-291	-504	-14	-9	-4
Other investment income	3 370 . .	-1,950	-1,226	-1,106	-1,005	-607	-546	-650	-732
D. CURRENT TRANSFERS	4 379 . .	910	141	-55	138	149	339	231	246
Credit	2 379 . .	**2,871**	**364**	**160**	**335**	**379**	**582**	**520**	**589**
General government	2 380 . .	82	62	22	46	52	68	88	100
Other sectors	2 390 . .	2,789	302	138	289	327	514	432	490
Workers' remittances	2 391 . .	. . .	6	11	18	26	26	53	51
Other current transfers	2 392 . .	2,789	296	127	271	302	488	379	439
Debit	3 379 . .	**-1,961**	**-222**	**-214**	**-197**	**-231**	**-243**	**-289**	**-344**
General government	3 380 . .	-68	-49	-37	-50	-98	-78	-99	-114
Other sectors	3 390 . .	-1,893	-173	-177	-146	-133	-165	-190	-230
Workers' remittances	3 391 . .	. . .	-20	-14	-12	-14	-17	-14	-16
Other current transfers	3 392 . .	-1,893	-154	-163	-134	-119	-148	-176	-215
CAPITAL AND FINANCIAL ACCOUNT	4 996 . .	**3,845**	**1,740**	**713**	**950**	**2,255**	**2,388**	**1,437**	**1,018**
CAPITAL ACCOUNT	4 994 . .	**. . .**	**59**	**156**	**117**	**189**	**29**	**270**	**317**
Total credit	2 994 . .	. . .	*80*	*266*	*266*	*408*	*509*	*458*	*417*
Total debit	3 994 . .	. . .	*-20*	*-110*	*-149*	*-219*	*-480*	*-188*	*-101*
Capital transfers, credit	2 400 . .	**. . .**	**80**	**266**	**222**	**335**	**373**	**317**	**395**
General government	2 401 . .	. . .	24	37	23	76	116	82	96
Debt forgiveness	2 402 . .	. . .	. . .	. . .	. . .	. . .	. . .	. . .	. . .
Other capital transfers	2 410 . .	. . .	24	37	23	76	116	82	96
Other sectors	2 430 . .	. . .	56	229	198	259	257	235	299
Migrants' transfers	2 431 . .	. . .	5	2	. . .	3	5	7	3
Debt forgiveness	2 432 . .	. . .	. . .	. . .	. . .	. . .	. . .	. . .	. . .
Other capital transfers	2 440 . .	. . .	50	227	198	256	253	229	296
Capital transfers, debit	3 400 . .	**. . .**	**-20**	**-109**	**-81**	**-127**	**-338**	**-50**	**-94**
General government	3 401 . .	. . .	-15	-14	-12	-24	-18	-2	-20
Debt forgiveness	3 402 . .	. . .	. . .	. . .	. . .	. . .	. . .	. . .	. . .
Other capital transfers	3 410 . .	. . .	-15	-14	-12	-24	-18	-2	-20
Other sectors	3 430 . .	. . .	-5	-95	-69	-103	-320	-47	-74
Migrants' transfers	3 431 . .	. . .	. . .	-1	-1	-1	-1	-3	-1
Debt forgiveness	3 432 . .	. . .	. . .	. . .	. . .	. . .	. . .	. . .	. . .
Other capital transfers	3 440 . .	. . .	-5	-95	-69	-102	-319	-45	-73
Nonproduced nonfinancial assets, credit	2 480 . .	**. . .**	**. . .**	**. . .**	**45**	**73**	**136**	**141**	**23**
Nonproduced nonfinancial assets, debit	3 480 . .	**. . .**	**. . .**	**-1**	**-68**	**-92**	**-141**	**-139**	**-6**

Table 2 (Continued). STANDARD PRESENTATION, 1994–2001
(Millions of U.S. dollars)

	Code	1994	1995	1996	1997	1998	1999	2000	2001
FINANCIAL ACCOUNT	4 995 . .	**3,845**	**1,681**	**557**	**833**	**2,067**	**2,358**	**1,167**	**701**
A. DIRECT INVESTMENT	4 500 . .	1,095	4,476	2,278	1,734	1,559	1,725	1,114	2,103
Direct investment abroad	4 505 . .	**–49**	**–43**	**4**	**–433**	**–478**	**–252**	**–532**	**–337**
Equity capital	4 510 . .	–49	–43	4	–289	–460	–249	–550	–328
Claims on affiliated enterprises	4 515 . .	. . .	–43	4	–289	–460	–249	–550	–328
Liabilities to affiliated enterprises	4 520 . .	. . .	. . .	. . .	. . .	. . .	. . .	. . .	. . .
Reinvested earnings	4 525 . .	. . .	. . .	. . .	. . .	. . .	. . .	. . .	. . .
Other capital	4 530 . .	. . .	. . .	. . .	–145	–18	–3	18	–9
Claims on affiliated enterprises	4 535 . .	. . .	. . .	. . .	–146	–18	–3	–1	–16
Liabilities to affiliated enterprises	4 540 . .	. . .	. . .	. . .	1	. . .	. . .	19	7
Direct investment in Hungary	4 555 . .	**1,144**	**4,519**	**2,274**	**2,167**	**2,037**	**1,977**	**1,646**	**2,440**
Equity capital	4 560 . .	1,144	4,519	1,787	1,807	1,409	1,656	1,353	986
Claims on direct investors	4 565 . .	. . .	. . .	. . .	. . .	. . .	. . .	. . .	. . .
Liabilities to direct investors	4 570 . .	. . .	4,519	1,787	1,807	1,409	1,656	1,353	986
Reinvested earnings	4 575 . .	. . .	. . .	. . .	. . .	. . .	. . .	. . .	. . .
Other capital	4 580 . .	. . .	. . .	487	360	628	320	293	1,454
Claims on direct investors	4 585 . .	. . .	. . .	. . .	–8	81	–37	–3	–98
Liabilities to direct investors	4 590 . .	. . .	. . .	487	368	547	357	296	1,552
B. PORTFOLIO INVESTMENT	4 600 . .	2,464	2,212	–431	–1,048	1,831	1,989	–496	1,377
Assets	4 602 . .	**6**	**–1**	**–35**	**–134**	**–93**	**–75**	**–309**	**–149**
Equity securities	4 610 . .	–10	. . .	–15	–32	–45	16	–151	–55
Monetary authorities	4 611 . .	. . .	. . .	. . .	. . .	. . .	. . .	. . .	. . .
General government	4 612 . .	. . .	. . .	. . .	. . .	. . .	. . .	. . .	. . .
Banks	4 613 . .	. . .	. . .	. . .	. . .	. . .	1	. . .	–20
Other sectors	4 614 . .	. . .	. . .	–15	–32	–45	14	–151	–34
Debt securities	4 619 . .	16	–1	–20	–102	–48	–91	–158	–95
Bonds and notes	4 620 . .	16	. . .	. . .	–53	–82	–75	–163	–102
Monetary authorities	4 621 . .	. . .	. . .	. . .	. . .	. . .	1	. . .	. . .
General government	4 622 . .	. . .	. . .	. . .	. . .	. . .	. . .	. . .	. . .
Banks	4 623 . .	. . .	. . .	. . .	–33	–55	–26	–46	–127
Other sectors	4 624 . .	. . .	. . .	. . .	–19	–27	–50	–117	25
Money market instruments	4 630 . .	. . .	. . .	–20	–49	34	–16	4	7
Monetary authorities	4 631 . .	. . .	. . .	. . .	. . .	1	. . .	. . .	. . .
General government	4 632 . .	. . .	. . .	. . .	. . .	. . .	. . .	. . .	. . .
Banks	4 633 . .	. . .	. . .	–9	–48	37	8	. . .	4
Other sectors	4 634 . .	. . .	. . .	–12	–1	–4	–24	4	2
Liabilities	4 652 . .	**2,458**	**2,213**	**–396**	**–914**	**1,925**	**2,065**	**–187**	**1,526**
Equity securities	4 660 . .	224	. . .	359	1,004	556	1,191	–416	134
Banks	4 663 . .	. . .	. . .	5	147	–8	188	66	142
Other sectors	4 664 . .	. . .	. . .	354	857	563	1,003	–481	–7
Debt securities	4 669 . .	2,234	2,213	–754	–1,918	1,369	874	229	1,392
Bonds and notes	4 670 . .	2,234	2,021	–694	–1,866	1,424	875	229	1,117
Monetary authorities	4 671 . .	. . .	2,056	–915	–2,024	323	–1,912	–1,313	–937
General government	4 672 . .	2,136	28	221	162	943	2,789	1,564	1,736
Banks	4 673 . .	. . .	. . .	. . .	–1	122	–1	–1	322
Other sectors	4 674 . .	98	–62	. . .	–2	36	–1	–21	–4
Money market instruments	4 680 . .	. . .	192	–60	–52	–56	–1	–1	275
Monetary authorities	4 681 . .	. . .	. . .	. . .	. . .	. . .	. . .	. . .	. . .
General government	4 682 . .	. . .	88	–113	–15	. . .	. . .	. . .	275
Banks	4 683 . .	. . .	. . .	. . .	51	–49	1	. . .	. . .
Other sectors	4 684 . .	. . .	103	52	–88	–6	–1	–1	. . .
C. FINANCIAL DERIVATIVES	4 910 . .	. . .	. . .	16	8	147	–47	60	122
Monetary authorities	4 911 . .	. . .	. . .	17	2	184	–83	23	–45
General government	4 912 . .	. . .	. . .	. . .	. . .	. . .	. . .	. . .	. . .
Banks	4 913 . .	. . .	. . .	–1	–4	–37	41	69	156
Other sectors	4 914 . .	. . .	. . .	. . .	10	. . .	–5	–31	11
Assets	4 900 . .	**. . .**	**. . .**	**17**	**12**	**185**	**852**	**753**	**579**
Monetary authorities	4 901 . .	. . .	. . .	17	2	184	520	366	185
General government	4 902 . .	. . .	. . .	. . .	. . .	. . .	. . .	. . .	. . .
Banks	4 903 . .	. . .	. . .	. . .	. . .	. . .	335	383	363
Other sectors	4 904 . .	. . .	. . .	. . .	10	. . .	–3	3	31
Liabilities	4 905 . .	**. . .**	**. . .**	**–1**	**–4**	**–38**	**–899**	**–692**	**–457**
Monetary authorities	4 906 . .	. . .	. . .	. . .	. . .	. . .	–604	–343	–230
General government	4 907 . .	. . .	. . .	. . .	. . .	. . .	. . .	. . .	. . .
Banks	4 908 . .	. . .	. . .	–1	–4	–38	–294	–314	–207
Other sectors	4 909 . .	. . .	. . .	. . .	. . .	. . .	–2	–35	–20

Table 2 (Concluded). STANDARD PRESENTATION, 1994–2001
(Millions of U.S. dollars)

	Code	1994	1995	1996	1997	1998	1999	2000	2001
D. OTHER INVESTMENT	4 700	–355	–393	–2,753	–35	–680	1,027	1,541	–2,984
Assets	4 703	**362**	**592**	**–1,256**	**–584**	**–507**	**–1,170**	**–1,014**	**–3,430**
Trade credits	4 706	...	56	–18	160	3	–271	–276	–143
General government	4 707	...	9	28	181	90	24	65	22
of which: Short-term	4 709	...	...	...	...	...	...	...	...
Other sectors	4 710	...	48	–46	–21	–88	–295	–341	–165
of which: Short-term	4 712	...	*45*	*–48*	*–10*	*–94*	*–20*	*–38*	*–23*
Loans	4 714	152	98	–170	–775	–906	–1,063	–855	–3,271
Monetary authorities	4 715	...	–17	14	1	4	...	–8	4
of which: Short-term	4 718	...	...	*4*	...	*4*	...	*–8*	*4*
General government	4 719	137	18	17	8	–15	6	–1	9
of which: Short-term	4 721	*32*	...	...	*2*	*–15*	*7*	*–1*	*9*
Banks	4 722	...	97	–63	–823	–731	–603	613	–1,329
of which: Short-term	4 724	...	*11*	*–320*	*–573*	*–577*	*–209*	*712*	*–1,079*
Other sectors	4 725	15	...	–137	39	–163	–466	–1,459	–1,955
of which: Short-term	4 727	*3*	...	*–137*	*77*	*–163*	*–492*	*–1,288*	*–1,448*
Currency and deposits	4 730	192	437	–1,068	31	397	163	117	–15
Monetary authorities	4 731	...	1	...	...	...	...	...	...
General government	4 732	...	...	...	...	...	...	...	...
Banks	4 733	192	28	–1,066	34	399	172	142	–161
Other sectors	4 734	...	408	–2	–4	–2	–9	–25	146
Other assets	4 736	18	...	...	...	...	...	...	...
Monetary authorities	4 737	...	...	...	...	...	...	...	...
of which: Short-term	4 739	...	...	...	...	...	...	...	...
General government	4 740	19	...	...	...	...	...	...	...
of which: Short-term	4 742	...	...	...	...	...	...	...	...
Banks	4 743	–1	...	...	...	...	...	...	...
of which: Short-term	4 745	...	...	...	...	...	...	...	...
Other sectors	4 746	...	...	...	...	...	...	...	...
of which: Short-term	4 748	...	...	...	...	...	...	...	...
Liabilities	4 753	**–716**	**–985**	**–1,497**	**549**	**–174**	**2,197**	**2,555**	**446**
Trade credits	4 756	...	–51	–476	–296	–1,046	–151	–141	–60
General government	4 757	...	53	18	–71	–293	–97	–114	–58
of which: Short-term	4 759	...	...	...	...	...	...	...	...
Other sectors	4 760	...	–103	–494	–224	–753	–53	–28	–2
of which: Short-term	4 762	...	*122*	*–107*	*–59*	*13*	*33*	*–12*	*6*
Loans	4 764	204	–526	–1,164	752	760	2,328	2,598	440
Monetary authorities	4 765	–165	–1,407	–1,956	–627	–247	284	616	–645
of which: Use of Fund credit and loans from the Fund	4 766	*–165*	*–785*	*–203*	...	*–160*	...	...	...
of which: Short-term	4 768	...	*3*	*–123*	...	*38*	*383*	*647*	*–209*
General government	4 769	–201	–491	–349	–35	5	332	–111	24
of which: Short-term	4 771	...	...	...	...	...	...	...	...
Banks	4 772	–11	447	129	999	578	504	301	229
of which: Short-term	4 774	...	*175*	*323*	*809*	*68*	*–40*	*–269*	*–206*
Other sectors	4 775	581	926	1,012	414	424	1,207	1,792	831
of which: Short-term	4 777	*20*	*125*	*198*	*91*	*13*	*152*	*784*	*657*
Currency and deposits	4 780	211	–408	143	92	112	19	98	66
Monetary authorities	4 781	...	–282	–123	–32	71	2	–3	1
General government	4 782	...	...	...	...	...	...	...	...
Banks	4 783	211	–126	266	124	41	18	101	64
Other sectors	4 784	...	...	...	...	...	...	...	...
Other liabilities	4 786	–1,131	...	...	...	...	...	...	...
Monetary authorities	4 787	17	...	...	...	...	...	...	...
of which: Short-term	4 789	*17*	...	...	...	...	...	...	...
General government	4 790	–1,560	...	...	...	...	...	...	...
of which: Short-term	4 792	...	...	...	...	...	...	...	...
Banks	4 793	165	...	...	...	...	...	...	...
of which: Short-term	4 795	...	...	...	...	...	...	...	...
Other sectors	4 796	247	...	...	...	...	...	...	...
of which: Short-term	4 798	*247*	...	...	...	...	...	...	...
E. RESERVE ASSETS	4 802	640	–4,614	1,447	175	–790	–2,335	–1,052	84
Monetary gold	4 812	1	...	4	...	...	...	...	...
Special drawing rights	4 811	2	...	...	...	–1	–4	–8	–9
Reserve position in the Fund	4 810	...	...	...	...	...	–165	–32	–152
Foreign exchange	4 803	637	–4,614	1,443	175	–790	–2,166	–2,037	495
Other claims	4 813	...	...	...	...	...	...	1,024	–250
NET ERRORS AND OMISSIONS	4 998	**209**	**789**	**976**	**32**	**49**	**–282**	**–109**	**79**

Part 3 of the *Yearbook* contains descriptions of the methodologies, compilation practices, and sources used to compile these data.

Table 3. INTERNATIONAL INVESTMENT POSITION (End–period stocks), 1994–2001
(Millions of U.S. dollars)

	Code	1994	1995	1996	1997	1998	1999	2000	2001
ASSETS	8 995 C.	...	...	...	13,335	15,651	19,353	21,344	25,066
Direct investment abroad	8 505 . .	**...**	**...**	**...**	**887**	**1,273**	**1,484**	**1,925**	**2,205**
Equity capital and reinvested earnings	8 506 . .	...	...	...	719	1,169	1,378	1,838	2,113
Claims on affiliated enterprises	8 507 . .	...	...	...	719	1,169	1,378	1,838	2,113
Liabilities to affiliated enterprises	8 508 . .	...	...	...	...	...	...	...	...
Other capital	8 530 . .	...	...	...	168	104	106	88	91
Claims on affiliated enterprises	8 535 . .	...	...	...	170	106	108	108	118
Liabilities to affiliated enterprises	8 540 . .	...	...	...	–2	–2	–2	–20	–27
Portfolio investment	8 602 . .	**...**	**...**	**...**	**171**	**293**	**367**	**667**	**814**
Equity securities	8 610 . .	...	...	...	32	87	73	221	271
Monetary authorities	8 611 . .	...	...	...	...	...	...	...	...
General government	8 612 . .	...	...	...	...	...	...	...	...
Banks	8 613 . .	...	...	...	1	3	1	...	21
Other sectors	8 614 . .	...	...	...	31	83	72	221	251
Debt securities	8 619 . .	...	...	...	139	206	294	447	543
Bonds and notes	8 620 . .	...	...	...	80	178	246	391	495
Monetary authorities	8 621 . .	...	...	...	...	...	...	...	...
General government	8 622 . .	...	...	...	...	...	...	...	...
Banks	8 623 . .	...	...	...	44	103	115	151	274
Other sectors	8 624 . .	...	...	...	36	75	131	240	221
Money market instruments	8 630 . .	...	...	...	58	29	48	55	48
Monetary authorities	8 631 . .	...	...	...	...	...	...	...	...
General government	8 632 . .	...	...	...	...	...	...	...	...
Banks	8 633 . .	...	...	...	48	13	7	7	3
Other sectors	8 634 . .	...	...	...	11	16	41	48	45
Financial derivatives	8 900 . .	**...**	**...**	**...**	**...**	**9**	**880**	**859**	**1,165**
Monetary authorities	8 901 . .	...	...	...	...	9	847	831	1,127
General government	8 902 . .	...	...	...	...	...	...	...	...
Banks	8 903 . .	...	...	...	...	...	33	28	38
Other sectors	8 904 . .	...	...	...	...	...	...	...	...
Other investment	8 703 . .	**...**	**...**	**...**	**3,841**	**4,730**	**5,639**	**6,675**	**10,127**
Trade credits	8 706 . .	...	...	...	1,015	937	1,099	1,308	1,432
General government	8 707 . .	...	...	...	569	468	438	354	334
of which: Short-term	8 709 . .	...	...	...	...	...	...	...	...
Other sectors	8 710 . .	...	...	...	446	469	661	954	1,098
of which: Short-term	8 712 . .	...	...	...	*102*	*146*	*94*	*117*	*132*
Loans	8 714 . .	...	...	...	2,423	3,405	4,225	5,116	8,208
Monetary authorities	8 715 . .	...	...	...	32	23	20	75	55
of which: Short-term	8 718 . .	...	...	...	*23*	*15*	*12*	*68*	*52*
General government	8 719 . .	...	...	...	24	37	30	27	19
of which: Short-term	8 721 . .	...	...	...	*15*	*28*	*21*	*20*	*11*
Banks	8 722 . .	...	...	...	1,928	2,704	3,082	2,330	3,594
of which: Short-term	8 724 . .	...	...	...	*1,607*	*2,213*	*2,203*	*1,374*	*2,424*
Other sectors	8 725 . .	...	...	...	440	640	1,093	2,684	4,541
of which: Short-term	8 727 . .	...	...	...	*401*	*601*	*1,017*	*2,384*	*3,733*
Currency and deposits	8 730 . .	...	...	...	403	388	315	252	487
Monetary authorities	8 731 . .	...	...	...	...	...	...	...	...
General government	8 732 . .	...	...	...	...	...	...	...	...
Banks	8 733 . .	...	...	...	395	379	305	230	473
Other sectors	8 734 . .	...	...	...	8	9	10	22	14
Other assets	8 736 . .	...	...	...	...	...	...	...	...
Monetary authorities	8 737 . .	...	...	...	...	...	...	...	...
of which: Short-term	8 739 . .	...	...	...	...	...	...	...	...
General government	8 740 . .	...	...	...	...	...	...	...	...
of which: Short-term	8 742 . .	...	...	...	...	...	...	...	...
Banks	8 743 . .	...	...	...	...	...	...	...	...
of which: Short-term	8 745 . .	...	...	...	...	...	...	...	...
Other sectors	8 746 . .	...	...	...	...	...	...	...	...
of which: Short-term	8 748 . .	...	...	...	...	...	...	...	...
Reserve assets	8 802 . .	**...**	**...**	**...**	**8,437**	**9,348**	**10,983**	**11,217**	**10,755**
Monetary gold	8 812 . .	...	...	...	29	29	29	28	28
Special drawing rights	8 811 . .	2	1	...	...	1	4	12	21
Reserve position in the Fund	8 810 . .	82	83	81	76	79	243	263	405
Foreign exchange	8 803 . .	...	...	...	8,332	9,239	10,707	10,822	9,967
Other claims	8 813 . .	...	...	...	...	...	...	93	335

Table 3 (Concluded). INTERNATIONAL INVESTMENT POSITION (End–period stocks), 1994–2001
(Millions of U.S. dollars)

	Code	1994	1995	1996	1997	1998	1999	2000	2001
LIABILITIES	8 995 D.	...	...	...	41,180	45,574	49,955	50,318	54,297
Direct investment in Hungary	8 555 ..	**...**	**...**	**...**	**16,073**	**18,505**	**19,217**	**19,662**	**22,584**
Equity capital and reinvested earnings	8 556 ..	...	...	...	14,200	15,989	16,365	16,704	18,255
Claims on direct investors	8 557 ..	...	...	...	...	...	...	...	...
Liabilities to direct investors	8 558 ..	...	...	...	14,200	15,989	16,365	16,704	18,255
Other capital	8 580 ..	...	...	...	1,872	2,515	2,852	2,957	4,329
Claims on direct investors	8 585 ..	...	...	...	–11	–11	–80	–122	–252
Liabilities to direct investors	8 590 ..	...	...	...	1,884	2,526	2,932	3,079	4,581
Portfolio investment	8 652 ..	**...**	**...**	**...**	**12,496**	**14,534**	**16,934**	**14,839**	**15,721**
Equity securities	8 660 ..	...	...	...	2,582	2,317	4,335	3,014	2,935
Banks	8 663 ..	...	...	...	161	110	354	342	464
Other sectors	8 664 ..	...	...	...	2,421	2,207	3,981	2,672	2,471
Debt securities	8 669 ..	...	...	...	9,914	12,217	12,599	11,825	12,786
Bonds and notes	8 670 ..	...	...	...	9,784	12,141	12,530	11,763	12,442
Monetary authorities	8 671 ..	...	...	...	9,289	10,471	8,360	6,404	4,973
General government	8 672 ..	...	...	...	363	1,358	3,900	5,130	6,904
Banks	8 673 ..	...	...	...	131	267	230	211	544
Other sectors	8 674 ..	...	...	...	1	45	40	17	22
Money market instruments	8 680 ..	...	...	...	130	76	69	63	344
Monetary authorities	8 681 ..	...	...	...	...	...	...	...	...
General government	8 682 ..	...	...	...	...	...	...	...	279
Banks	8 683 ..	...	...	...	50	...	1	1	1
Other sectors	8 684 ..	...	...	...	80	75	68	62	64
Financial derivatives	8 905 ..	**...**	**...**	**...**	**450**	**11**	**164**	**276**	**483**
Monetary authorities	8 906 ..	...	...	...	441	...	115	236	448
General government	8 907 ..	...	...	...	...	...	...	...	...
Banks	8 908 ..	...	...	...	9	11	49	40	35
Other sectors	8 909 ..	...	...	...	...	...	...	...	...
Other investment	8 753 ..	**...**	**...**	**...**	**12,161**	**12,524**	**13,640**	**15,541**	**15,509**
Trade credits	8 756 ..	...	...	...	1,816	743	533	382	307
General government	8 757 ..	...	...	...	737	467	328	193	129
of which: Short-term	8 759 ..	...	...	...	...	...	...	...	...
Other sectors	8 760 ..	...	...	...	1,079	276	205	188	178
of which: Short-term	8 762 ..	...	...	...	*42*	*76*	*98*	*86*	*84*
Loans	8 764 ..	...	...	...	9,569	10,889	12,359	14,342	14,332
Monetary authorities	8 765 ..	...	...	...	1,164	968	1,311	1,856	1,157
of which: Use of Fund credit and loans from the Fund	8 766 ..	*1,141*	*385*	*171*	*160*	...	...	...	...
of which: Short-term	8 768 ..	...	...	...	*26*	*69*	*532*	*1,168*	*941*
General government	8 769 ..	...	...	...	898	912	1,204	1,053	1,051
of which: Short-term	8 771 ..	...	...	...	...	...	...	...	...
Banks	8 772 ..	...	...	...	3,565	4,419	4,561	4,666	4,720
of which: Short-term	8 774 ..	...	...	...	*2,190*	*2,369*	*2,170*	*1,786*	*1,420*
Other sectors	8 775 ..	...	...	...	3,941	4,590	5,283	6,767	7,404
of which: Short-term	8 777 ..	...	...	...	*267*	*286*	*516*	*1,258*	*1,882*
Currency and deposits	8 780 ..	...	...	...	776	892	747	817	870
Monetary authorities	8 781 ..	...	...	...	51	126	10	7	8
General government	8 782 ..	...	...	...	...	...	...	...	...
Banks	8 783 ..	...	...	...	725	766	737	810	862
Other sectors	8 784 ..	...	...	...	...	...	...	...	...
Other liabilities	8 786 ..	...	...	...	...	...	...	...	...
Monetary authorities	8 787 ..	...	...	...	...	...	...	...	...
of which: Short-term	8 789 ..	...	...	...	...	...	...	...	...
General government	8 790 ..	...	...	...	...	...	...	...	...
of which: Short-term	8 792 ..	...	...	...	...	...	...	...	...
Banks	8 793 ..	...	...	...	...	...	...	...	...
of which: Short-term	8 795 ..	...	...	...	...	...	...	...	...
Other sectors	8 796 ..	...	...	...	...	...	...	...	...
of which: Short-term	8 798 ..	...	...	...	...	...	...	...	...
NET INTERNATIONAL INVESTMENT POSITION	8 995 ..	**...**	**...**	**...**	**–27,845**	**–29,923**	**–30,602**	**–28,974**	**–29,230**
Conversion rates: forint per U.S. dollar (end of period)	0 102 ..	**110.69**	**139.47**	**164.93**	**203.50**	**219.03**	**252.52**	**284.73**	**279.03**

Table 1. ANALYTIC PRESENTATION, 1994–2001

(Millions of U.S. dollars)

	Code		1994	1995	1996	1997	1998	1999	2000	2001
A. Current Account[1]	4 993	Z.	**109**	**54**	**–117**	**–125**	**–560**	**–591**	**–848**	**. . .**
Goods: exports f.o.b	2 100	. .	1,561	1,804	1,890	1,855	1,927	2,009	1,902	. . .
Goods: imports f.o.b	3 100	. .	–1,288	–1,598	–1,871	–1,850	–2,279	–2,317	–2,376	. . .
Balance on Goods	4 100	. .	*273*	*206*	*19*	*5*	*–352*	*–308*	*–474*	. . .
Services: credit	2 200	. .	615	689	768	844	947	941	1,049	. . .
Services: debit	3 200	. .	–577	–641	–739	–800	–964	–1,026	–1,164	. . .
Balance on Goods and Services	4 991	. .	*311*	*254*	*48*	*49*	*–369*	*–393*	*–589*	. . .
Income: credit	2 300	. .	73	91	113	104	123	119	154	. . .
Income: debit	3 300	. .	–267	–286	–272	–273	–298	–307	–403	. . .
Balance on Goods, Services, and Income	4 992	. .	*117*	*59*	*–111*	*–120*	*–544*	*–580*	*–839*	. . .
Current transfers: credit	2 379	Z.	12	15	10	17	4	5	6	. . .
Current transfers: debit	3 379	. .	–20	–20	–16	–22	–20	–15	–16	. . .
B. Capital Account[1]	4 994	Z.	**–6**	**–3**	**–1**	**1**	**–5**	**–1**	**–3**	**. . .**
Capital account: credit	2 994	Z.	6	13	10	11	9	17	18	. . .
Capital account: debit	3 994	. .	–12	–16	–11	–10	–14	–18	–21	. . .
Total, Groups A Plus B	4 981	. .	*103*	*51*	*–118*	*–124*	*–565*	*–591*	*–851*	. . .
C. Financial Account[1]	4 995	W.	**–293**	**–17**	**303**	**195**	**679**	**908**	**853**	**. . .**
Direct investment abroad	4 505	. .	–23	–25	–62	–50	–74	–107	–368	. . .
Direct investment in Iceland	4 555	Z.	1	–10	80	144	150	64	145	. . .
Portfolio investment assets	4 602	. .	–73	–76	–64	–201	–302	–448	–668	. . .
Equity securities	4 610	. .	–25	–55	–81	–180	–253	–369	–651	. . .
Debt securities	4 619	. .	–48	–21	17	–21	–49	–79	–17	. . .
Portfolio investment liabilities	4 652	Z.	242	214	176	–38	66	1,029	1,142	. . .
Equity securities	4 660	. .	. . .	. . .	1	–1	14	56	–44	. . .
Debt securities	4 669	Z.	242	214	175	–37	52	973	1,186	. . .
Financial derivatives	4 910	. .	5	–1	–1	–1	–1	3	–1	. . .
Financial derivatives assets	4 900	. .	–49	–17	–1	–1	–1	59	15	. . .
Financial derivatives liabilities	4 905	. .	54	16	. . .	. . .	. . .	–57	–16	. . .
Other investment assets	4 703	. .	–31	22	–30	–162	3	–174	–80	. . .
Monetary authorities	4 701	. .	. . .	. . .	. . .	. . .	. . .	. . .	. . .	. . .
General government	4 704	. .	. . .	. . .	. . .	. . .	. . .	. . .	. . .	. . .
Banks	4 705	. .	–16	47	–37	–86	28	–92	–71	. . .
Other sectors	4 728	. .	–15	–25	7	–76	–25	–82	–9	. . .
Other investment liabilities	4 753	W.	–414	–141	204	503	837	541	684	. . .
Monetary authorities	4 753	WA	39	21	–100	–1	55	–3	142	. . .
General government	4 753	ZB	–76	58	–17	34	81	43	25	. . .
Banks	4 753	ZC	–158	–54	288	306	422	441	332	. . .
Other sectors	4 753	ZD	–219	–166	33	164	279	61	184	. . .
Total, Groups A Through C	4 983	. .	*–190*	*34*	*185*	*71*	*114*	*316*	*2*	. . .
D. Net Errors and Omissions	4 998	. .	**40**	**–30**	**–32**	**–115**	**–82**	**–231**	**–71**	**. . .**
Total, Groups A Through D	4 984	. .	*–150*	*4*	*153*	*–44*	*32*	*86*	*–69*	. . .
E. Reserves and Related Items	4 802	A.	**150**	**–4**	**–153**	**44**	**–32**	**–86**	**69**	**. . .**
Reserve assets	4 802	. .	150	–4	–153	44	–32	–86	69	. . .
Use of Fund credit and loans	4 766	. .	. . .	. . .	. . .	. . .	. . .	. . .	. . .	. . .
Exceptional financing	4 920	. .	. . .	. . .	. . .	. . .	. . .	. . .	. . .	. . .
Conversion rates: krónur per U.S. dollar	0 101	. .	**69.944**	**64.692**	**66.500**	**70.904**	**70.958**	**72.335**	**78.616**	**97.425**

[1] Excludes components that have been classified in the categories of Group E.

Table 2. STANDARD PRESENTATION, 1994–2001

(Millions of U.S. dollars)

	Code	1994	1995	1996	1997	1998	1999	2000	2001
CURRENT ACCOUNT	4 993 . .	**109**	**54**	**–117**	**–125**	**–560**	**–591**	**–848**	**. . .**
A. GOODS	4 100 . .	273	206	19	5	–352	–308	–474	. . .
Credit	2 100 . .	**1,561**	**1,804**	**1,890**	**1,855**	**1,927**	**2,009**	**1,902**	**. . .**
General merchandise: exports f.o.b.	2 110 . .	1,561	1,804	1,890	1,855	1,927	2,009	1,902	. . .
Goods for processing: exports f.o.b.	2 150 . .	. . .	. . .	. . .	. . .	. . .	. . .	. . .	. . .
Repairs on goods	2 160 . .	. . .	. . .	. . .	. . .	. . .	. . .	. . .	. . .
Goods procured in ports by carriers	2 170 . .	. . .	. . .	. . .	. . .	. . .	. . .	. . .	. . .
Nonmonetary gold	2 180 . .	. . .	. . .	. . .	. . .	. . .	. . .	. . .	. . .
Debit	3 100 . .	**–1,288**	**–1,598**	**–1,871**	**–1,850**	**–2,279**	**–2,317**	**–2,376**	**. . .**
General merchandise: imports f.o.b.	3 110 . .	–1,288	–1,598	–1,871	–1,850	–2,279	–2,317	–2,376	. . .
Goods for processing: imports f.o.b.	3 150 . .	. . .	. . .	. . .	. . .	. . .	. . .	. . .	. . .
Repairs on goods	3 160 . .	. . .	. . .	. . .	. . .	. . .	. . .	. . .	. . .
Goods procured in ports by carriers	3 170 . .	. . .	. . .	. . .	. . .	. . .	. . .	. . .	. . .
Nonmonetary gold	3 180 . .	. . .	. . .	. . .	. . .	. . .	. . .	. . .	. . .
B. SERVICES	4 200 . .	38	48	29	44	–17	–85	–115	. . .
Total credit	2 200 . .	*615*	*689*	*768*	*844*	*947*	*941*	*1,049*	. . .
Total debit	3 200 . .	*–577*	*–641*	*–739*	*–800*	*–964*	*–1,026*	*–1,164*	. . .
Transportation services, credit	2 205 . .	**250**	**268**	**338**	**364**	**441**	**426**	**518**	**. . .**
Passenger	2 850 . .	*99*	*123*	*136*	*141*	*166*	*158*	*159*	. . .
Freight	2 851 . .	*91*	*82*	*95*	*102*	*108*	*107*	*126*	. . .
Other	2 852 . .	*60*	*63*	*107*	*121*	*167*	*161*	*233*	. . .
Sea transport, passenger	2 207 . .	. . .	. . .	. . .	. . .	. . .	. . .	. . .	. . .
Sea transport, freight	2 208 . .	86	77	84	88	93	86	90	. . .
Sea transport, other	2 209 . .	17	23	29	30	27	21	45	. . .
Air transport, passenger	2 211 . .	99	123	136	141	166	158	159	. . .
Air transport, freight	2 212 . .	5	5	11	14	15	22	36	. . .
Air transport, other	2 213 . .	43	40	78	91	140	140	188	. . .
Other transport, passenger	2 215 . .	. . .	. . .	. . .	. . .	. . .	. . .	. . .	. . .
Other transport, freight	2 216 . .	. . .	. . .	. . .	. . .	. . .	. . .	. . .	. . .
Other transport, other	2 217 . .	. . .	. . .	. . .	. . .	. . .	. . .	. . .	. . .
Transportation services, debit	3 205 . .	**–167**	**–206**	**–249**	**–252**	**–321**	**–355**	**–413**	**. . .**
Passenger	3 850 . .	. . .	. . .	*–4*	*–4*	*–3*	*–4*	. . .	. . .
Freight	3 851 . .	*–15*	*–17*	*–19*	*–18*	*–18*	*–12*	*–17*	. . .
Other	3 852 . .	*–152*	*–189*	*–226*	*–230*	*–300*	*–338*	*–396*	. . .
Sea transport, passenger	3 207 . .	. . .	. . .	. . .	. . .	. . .	. . .	. . .	. . .
Sea transport, freight	3 208 . .	–15	–17	–19	–18	–16	–11	–16	. . .
Sea transport, other	3 209 . .	–73	–87	–94	–85	–87	–130	–128	. . .
Air transport, passenger	3 211 . .	. . .	. . .	–4	–4	–3	–4	. . .	. . .
Air transport, freight	3 212 . .	. . .	. . .	. . .	. . .	–2	–1	–2	. . .
Air transport, other	3 213 . .	–79	–102	–132	–145	–213	–209	–268	. . .
Other transport, passenger	3 215 . .	. . .	. . .	. . .	. . .	. . .	. . .	. . .	. . .
Other transport, freight	3 216 . .	. . .	. . .	. . .	. . .	. . .	. . .	. . .	. . .
Other transport, other	3 217 . .	. . .	. . .	. . .	. . .	. . .	. . .	. . .	. . .
Travel, credit	2 236 . .	**145**	**185**	**176**	**173**	**205**	**222**	**227**	**. . .**
Business travel	2 237 . .	. . .	. . .	. . .	. . .	. . .	. . .	. . .	. . .
Personal travel	2 240 . .	145	185	176	173	205	222	227	. . .
Travel, debit	3 236 . .	**–247**	**–282**	**–308**	**–324**	**–396**	**–436**	**–470**	**. . .**
Business travel	3 237 . .	. . .	. . .	. . .	. . .	. . .	. . .	. . .	. . .
Personal travel	3 240 . .	–247	–282	–308	–324	–396	–436	–470	. . .
Other services, credit	2 200 BA	**220**	**236**	**254**	**307**	**301**	**294**	**304**	**. . .**
Communications	2 245 . .	20	23	24	24	19	10	10	. . .
Construction	2 249 . .	2	5	3	8	6	4	2	. . .
Insurance	2 253 . .	5	4	4	4	5	6	6	. . .
Financial	2 260 . .	. . .	. . .	. . .	. . .	. . .	1	. . .	. . .
Computer and information	2 262 . .	. . .	. . .	17	21	17	39	30	. . .
Royalties and licence fees	2 266 . .	. . .	. . .	. . .	. . .	. . .	. . .	. . .	. . .
Other business services	2 268 . .	105	99	87	126	141	121	138	. . .
Personal, cultural, and recreational	2 287 . .	. . .	2	4	4	6	10	11	. . .
Government, n.i.e.	2 291 . .	88	103	115	120	107	104	107	. . .
Other services, debit	3 200 BA	**–163**	**–153**	**–182**	**–224**	**–247**	**–236**	**–281**	**. . .**
Communications	3 245 . .	–17	–19	–24	–25	–21	–7	–2	. . .
Construction	3 249 . .	–21	–16	–8	–24	–22	–38	–19	. . .
Insurance	3 253 . .	–25	–21	–19	–13	–13	–10	–6	. . .
Financial	3 260 . .	–5	. . .	–2	–2	–2	–4	–11	. . .
Computer and information	3 262 . .	. . .	. . .	–2	. . .	–1	–2	–2	. . .
Royalties and licence fees	3 266 . .	. . .	. . .	–1	. . .	. . .	–1	–1	. . .
Other business services	3 268 . .	–85	–81	–104	–139	–159	–145	–211	. . .
Personal, cultural, and recreational	3 287 . .	. . .	–5	–11	–9	–12	–13	–15	. . .
Government, n.i.e.	3 291 . .	–10	–11	–11	–12	–17	–15	–16	. . .

Table 2 (Continued). STANDARD PRESENTATION, 1994–2001
(Millions of U.S. dollars)

	Code	1994	1995	1996	1997	1998	1999	2000	2001
C. INCOME	4 300 . .	–194	–195	–159	–169	–175	–188	–250	. . .
Total credit	2 300 . .	*73*	*91*	*113*	*104*	*123*	*119*	*154*	. . .
Total debit	3 300 . .	*–267*	*–286*	*–272*	*–273*	*–298*	*–307*	*–403*	. . .
Compensation of employees, credit	2 310 . .	**42**	**51**	**63**	**58**	**67**	**68**	**70**	**. . .**
Compensation of employees, debit	3 310 . .	**–8**	**–6**	**–5**	**–6**	**–4**	**–5**	**–10**	**. . .**
Investment income, credit	2 320 . .	**31**	**40**	**50**	**46**	**56**	**51**	**84**	**. . .**
Direct investment income	2 330 . .	–3	–4	5	7	8	10	19	. . .
Dividends and distributed branch profits	2 332 . .	1	. . .	1	1	2	1	2	. . .
Reinvested earnings and undistributed branch profits	2 333 . .	–4	–4	4	2	4	7	12	. . .
Income on debt (interest)	2 334 . .	. . .	. . .	. . .	4	2	1	6	. . .
Portfolio investment income	2 339 . .	4	15	16	4	8	24	30	. . .
Income on equity	2 340 . .	1	11	12	. . .	4	10	20	. . .
Income on bonds and notes	2 350 . .	3	4	4	4	4	8	8	. . .
Income on money market instruments	2 360 . .	. . .	. . .	. . .	. . .	. . .	6	3	. . .
Other investment income	2 370 . .	30	29	29	35	40	18	34	. . .
Investment income, debit	3 320 . .	**–259**	**–280**	**–267**	**–267**	**–294**	**–302**	**–393**	**. . .**
Direct investment income	3 330 . .	–18	–18	–19	–29	–34	–14	–28	. . .
Dividends and distributed branch profits	3 332 . .	–2	–10	–3	–5	–13	–56	–27	. . .
Reinvested earnings and undistributed branch profits	3 333 . .	–12	–4	–12	–20	–13	49	6	. . .
Income on debt (interest)	3 334 . .	–4	–4	–4	–4	–8	–7	–7	. . .
Portfolio investment income	3 339 . .	–111	–134	–139	–136	–128	–147	–182	. . .
Income on equity	3 340 . .	. . .	. . .	. . .	. . .	. . .	. . .	–2	. . .
Income on bonds and notes	3 350 . .	–101	–115	–122	–123	–119	–128	–162	. . .
Income on money market instruments	3 360 . .	–10	–19	–17	–13	–9	–19	–19	. . .
Other investment income	3 370 . .	–130	–128	–109	–102	–132	–142	–182	. . .
D. CURRENT TRANSFERS	4 379 . .	–8	–5	–6	–5	–16	–10	–10	. . .
Credit	2 379 . .	**12**	**15**	**10**	**17**	**4**	**5**	**6**	**. . .**
General government	2 380 . .	. . .	. . .	. . .	. . .	. . .	. . .	. . .	. . .
Other sectors	2 390 . .	12	15	10	17	4	5	6	. . .
Workers' remittances	2 391 . .	. . .	. . .	. . .	. . .	. . .	. . .	. . .	. . .
Other current transfers	2 392 . .	12	15	10	17	4	5	6	. . .
Debit	3 379 . .	**–20**	**–20**	**–16**	**–22**	**–20**	**–15**	**–16**	**. . .**
General government	3 380 . .	–7	–10	–9	–11	–10	–9	–10	. . .
Other sectors	3 390 . .	–13	–10	–7	–11	–10	–6	–5	. . .
Workers' remittances	3 391 . .	. . .	. . .	. . .	. . .	. . .	. . .	. . .	. . .
Other current transfers	3 392 . .	–13	–10	–7	–11	–10	–6	–5	. . .
CAPITAL AND FINANCIAL ACCOUNT	4 996 . .	**–149**	**–24**	**149**	**240**	**642**	**821**	**919**	**. . .**
CAPITAL ACCOUNT	4 994 . .	**–6**	**–3**	**–1**	**1**	**–5**	**–1**	**–3**	**. . .**
Total credit	2 994 . .	*6*	*13*	*10*	*11*	*9*	*17*	*18*	. . .
Total debit	3 994 . .	*–12*	*–16*	*–11*	*–10*	*–14*	*–18*	*–21*	. . .
Capital transfers, credit	2 400 . .	**6**	**13**	**10**	**11**	**9**	**17**	**18**	**. . .**
General government	2 401 . .	. . .	. . .	. . .	. . .	. . .	. . .	. . .	. . .
Debt forgiveness	2 402 . .	. . .	. . .	. . .	. . .	. . .	. . .	. . .	. . .
Other capital transfers	2 410 . .	. . .	. . .	. . .	. . .	. . .	. . .	. . .	. . .
Other sectors	2 430 . .	6	13	10	11	9	17	18	. . .
Migrants' transfers	2 431 . .	6	13	10	11	9	17	18	. . .
Debt forgiveness	2 432 . .	. . .	. . .	. . .	. . .	. . .	. . .	. . .	. . .
Other capital transfers	2 440 . .	. . .	. . .	. . .	. . .	. . .	. . .	. . .	. . .
Capital transfers, debit	3 400 . .	**–12**	**–16**	**–11**	**–10**	**–14**	**–18**	**–21**	**. . .**
General government	3 401 . .	. . .	. . .	. . .	. . .	. . .	. . .	. . .	. . .
Debt forgiveness	3 402 . .	. . .	. . .	. . .	. . .	. . .	. . .	. . .	. . .
Other capital transfers	3 410 . .	. . .	. . .	. . .	. . .	. . .	. . .	. . .	. . .
Other sectors	3 430 . .	–12	–16	–11	–10	–14	–18	–21	. . .
Migrants' transfers	3 431 . .	–10	–14	–11	–10	–14	–18	–21	. . .
Debt forgiveness	3 432 . .	–2	–2	. . .	. . .	. . .	. . .	. . .	. . .
Other capital transfers	3 440 . .	. . .	. . .	. . .	. . .	. . .	. . .	. . .	. . .
Nonproduced nonfinancial assets, credit	2 480 . .	**. . .**	**. . .**	**. . .**	**. . .**	**. . .**	**. . .**	**. . .**	**. . .**
Nonproduced nonfinancial assets, debit	3 480 . .	**. . .**	**. . .**	**. . .**	**. . .**	**. . .**	**. . .**	**. . .**	**. . .**

Table 2 (Continued). STANDARD PRESENTATION, 1994–2001
(Millions of U.S. dollars)

	Code	1994	1995	1996	1997	1998	1999	2000	2001
FINANCIAL ACCOUNT	4 995 . .	**–143**	**–21**	**150**	**239**	**647**	**822**	**922**	**. . .**
A. DIRECT INVESTMENT	4 500 . .	–22	–35	18	94	76	–43	–223	. . .
Direct investment abroad	4 505 . .	**–23**	**–25**	**–62**	**–50**	**–74**	**–107**	**–368**	**. . .**
Equity capital	4 510 . .	–11	–6	–10	–36	–26	–64	–380	. . .
Claims on affiliated enterprises	4 515 . .	. . .	. . .	. . .	. . .	. . .	. . .	. . .	. . .
Liabilities to affiliated enterprises	4 520 . .	. . .	. . .	. . .	. . .	. . .	. . .	. . .	. . .
Reinvested earnings	4 525 . .	4	4	–4	–2	–4	–7	–12	. . .
Other capital	4 530 . .	–16	–23	–48	–12	–44	–36	24	. . .
Claims on affiliated enterprises	4 535 . .	. . .	. . .	. . .	. . .	. . .	. . .	. . .	. . .
Liabilities to affiliated enterprises	4 540 . .	. . .	. . .	. . .	. . .	. . .	. . .	. . .	. . .
Direct investment in Iceland	4 555 . .	**1**	**–10**	**80**	**144**	**150**	**64**	**145**	**. . .**
Equity capital	4 560 . .	–2	6	–8	66	162	55	198	. . .
Claims on direct investors	4 565 . .	. . .	. . .	. . .	. . .	. . .	. . .	. . .	. . .
Liabilities to direct investors	4 570 . .	. . .	. . .	. . .	. . .	. . .	. . .	. . .	. . .
Reinvested earnings	4 575 . .	12	4	12	20	13	–49	–6	. . .
Other capital	4 580 . .	–9	–20	76	58	–25	58	–47	. . .
Claims on direct investors	4 585 . .	. . .	. . .	. . .	. . .	. . .	. . .	. . .	. . .
Liabilities to direct investors	4 590 . .	. . .	. . .	. . .	. . .	. . .	. . .	. . .	. . .
B. PORTFOLIO INVESTMENT	4 600 . .	169	138	112	–239	–236	581	474	. . .
Assets	4 602 . .	**–73**	**–76**	**–64**	**–201**	**–302**	**–448**	**–668**	**. . .**
Equity securities	4 610 . .	–25	–55	–81	–180	–253	–369	–651	. . .
Monetary authorities	4 611 . .	. . .	. . .	. . .	. . .	. . .	. . .	. . .	. . .
General government	4 612 . .	. . .	. . .	. . .	. . .	. . .	. . .	. . .	. . .
Banks	4 613 . .	. . .	. . .	. . .	. . .	. . .	. . .	. . .	. . .
Other sectors	4 614 . .	. . .	. . .	. . .	. . .	. . .	. . .	. . .	. . .
Debt securities	4 619 . .	–48	–21	17	–21	–49	–79	–17	. . .
Bonds and notes	4 620 . .	–48	–18	20	–23	–48	–71	–2	. . .
Monetary authorities	4 621 . .	. . .	. . .	. . .	. . .	. . .	. . .	. . .	. . .
General government	4 622 . .	. . .	. . .	. . .	. . .	. . .	. . .	–1	. . .
Banks	4 623 . .	. . .	. . .	. . .	. . .	–26	–29	45	. . .
Other sectors	4 624 . .	–48	–18	20	–23	–22	–42	–46	. . .
Money market instruments	4 630 . .	. . .	–3	–3	2	–1	–8	–15	. . .
Monetary authorities	4 631 . .	. . .	. . .	. . .	. . .	. . .	. . .	. . .	. . .
General government	4 632 . .	. . .	. . .	. . .	. . .	. . .	. . .	. . .	. . .
Banks	4 633 . .	. . .	. . .	. . .	. . .	. . .	–8	–15	. . .
Other sectors	4 634 . .	. . .	. . .	. . .	. . .	. . .	. . .	. . .	. . .
Liabilities	4 652 . .	**242**	**214**	**176**	**–38**	**66**	**1,029**	**1,142**	**. . .**
Equity securities	4 660 . .	. . .	. . .	1	–1	14	56	–44	. . .
Banks	4 663 . .	. . .	. . .	. . .	. . .	. . .	. . .	. . .	. . .
Other sectors	4 664 . .	. . .	. . .	. . .	. . .	. . .	. . .	. . .	. . .
Debt securities	4 669 . .	242	214	175	–37	52	973	1,186	. . .
Bonds and notes	4 670 . .	198	183	204	37	57	602	1,133	. . .
Monetary authorities	4 671 . .	. . .	. . .	. . .	29	. . .	–1	. . .	. . .
General government	4 672 . .	153	132	173	35	–125	–128	38	. . .
Banks	4 673 . .	. . .	. . .	. . .	1	75	323	762	. . .
Other sectors	4 674 . .	45	51	31	–28	107	408	334	. . .
Money market instruments	4 680 . .	44	31	–29	–74	–5	371	52	. . .
Monetary authorities	4 681 . .	. . .	. . .	. . .	. . .	. . .	. . .	. . .	. . .
General government	4 682 . .	. . .	. . .	. . .	. . .	. . .	161	134	. . .
Banks	4 683 . .	. . .	. . .	. . .	. . .	. . .	18	–129	. . .
Other sectors	4 684 . .	. . .	. . .	. . .	. . .	. . .	192	48	. . .
C. FINANCIAL DERIVATIVES	4 910 . .	5	–1	–1	–1	–1	3	–1	. . .
Monetary authorities	4 911 . .	. . .	. . .	. . .	. . .	. . .	. . .	. . .	. . .
General government	4 912 . .	. . .	. . .	. . .	. . .	. . .	. . .	. . .	. . .
Banks	4 913 . .	. . .	. . .	. . .	. . .	. . .	. . .	. . .	. . .
Other sectors	4 914 . .	. . .	. . .	. . .	. . .	. . .	. . .	. . .	. . .
Assets	4 900 . .	**–49**	**–17**	**–1**	**–1**	**–1**	**59**	**15**	**. . .**
Monetary authorities	4 901 . .	. . .	. . .	. . .	. . .	. . .	. . .	. . .	. . .
General government	4 902 . .	. . .	. . .	. . .	. . .	. . .	. . .	. . .	. . .
Banks	4 903 . .	. . .	. . .	. . .	. . .	. . .	. . .	. . .	. . .
Other sectors	4 904 . .	. . .	. . .	. . .	. . .	. . .	. . .	. . .	. . .
Liabilities	4 905 . .	**54**	**16**	**. . .**	**. . .**	**. . .**	**–57**	**–16**	**. . .**
Monetary authorities	4 906 . .	. . .	. . .	. . .	. . .	. . .	. . .	. . .	. . .
General government	4 907 . .	. . .	. . .	. . .	. . .	. . .	. . .	. . .	. . .
Banks	4 908 . .	. . .	. . .	. . .	. . .	. . .	. . .	. . .	. . .
Other sectors	4 909 . .	. . .	. . .	. . .	. . .	. . .	. . .	. . .	. . .

Table 2 (Concluded). STANDARD PRESENTATION, 1994–2001
(Millions of U.S. dollars)

	Code	1994	1995	1996	1997	1998	1999	2000	2001
D. OTHER INVESTMENT	4 700	–445	–119	174	341	840	367	603	. . .
Assets	4 703	**–31**	**22**	**–30**	**–162**	**3**	**–174**	**–80**	**. . .**
Trade credits	4 706	–2	–10	–15	–20	–19	–5	–19	. . .
General government	4 707	. . .	. . .	. . .	. . .	. . .	. . .	. . .	. . .
of which: Short-term	4 709	. . .	. . .	. . .	. . .	. . .	. . .	. . .	. . .
Other sectors	4 710	–2	–10	–15	–20	–19	–5	–19	. . .
of which: Short-term	4 712	. . .	. . .	. . .	. . .	. . .	. . .	. . .	. . .
Loans	4 714	. . .	. . .	–6	–30	–50	–48	–32	. . .
Monetary authorities	4 715	. . .	. . .	. . .	. . .	. . .	. . .	. . .	. . .
of which: Short-term	4 718	. . .	. . .	. . .	. . .	. . .	. . .	. . .	. . .
General government	4 719	. . .	. . .	. . .	. . .	. . .	. . .	. . .	. . .
of which: Short-term	4 721	. . .	. . .	. . .	. . .	. . .	. . .	. . .	. . .
Banks	4 722	. . .	. . .	–6	–30	9	3	–31	. . .
of which: Short-term	4 724	. . .	. . .	. . .	. . .	. . .	. . .	. . .	. . .
Other sectors	4 725	. . .	. . .	. . .	. . .	–59	–51	–1	. . .
of which: Short-term	4 727	. . .	. . .	. . .	. . .	. . .	. . .	. . .	. . .
Currency and deposits	4 730	–29	34	–11	–58	18	–121	–29	. . .
Monetary authorities	4 731	. . .	. . .	. . .	. . .	. . .	. . .	. . .	. . .
General government	4 732	. . .	. . .	. . .	. . .	. . .	. . .	. . .	. . .
Banks	4 733	–16	47	–31	–56	19	–95	–41	. . .
Other sectors	4 734	–13	–13	20	–2	–1	–25	11	. . .
Other assets	4 736	. . .	–2	2	–54	54	–1	–1	. . .
Monetary authorities	4 737	. . .	. . .	. . .	. . .	. . .	. . .	. . .	. . .
of which: Short-term	4 739	. . .	. . .	. . .	. . .	. . .	. . .	. . .	. . .
General government	4 740	. . .	. . .	. . .	. . .	. . .	. . .	. . .	. . .
of which: Short-term	4 742	. . .	. . .	. . .	. . .	. . .	. . .	. . .	. . .
Banks	4 743	. . .	. . .	. . .	. . .	. . .	. . .	. . .	. . .
of which: Short-term	4 745	. . .	. . .	. . .	. . .	. . .	. . .	. . .	. . .
Other sectors	4 746	. . .	–2	2	–54	54	–1	–1	. . .
of which: Short-term	4 748	. . .	. . .	. . .	. . .	. . .	. . .	. . .	. . .
Liabilities	4 753	**–414**	**–141**	**204**	**503**	**837**	**541**	**684**	**. . .**
Trade credits	4 756	2	2	22	31	–5	28	1	. . .
General government	4 757	. . .	. . .	. . .	. . .	. . .	. . .	. . .	. . .
of which: Short-term	4 759	. . .	. . .	. . .	. . .	. . .	. . .	. . .	. . .
Other sectors	4 760	2	2	22	31	–5	28	1	. . .
of which: Short-term	4 762	. . .	. . .	. . .	. . .	. . .	. . .	. . .	. . .
Loans	4 764	–403	–152	184	476	846	504	686	. . .
Monetary authorities	4 765	50	19	–100	. . .	54	–3	140	. . .
of which: Use of Fund credit and loans from the Fund	4 766	. . .	. . .	. . .	. . .	. . .	. . .	. . .	. . .
of which: Short-term	4 768	*50*	*19*	*–100*	. . .	*54*	*–3*	*140*	. . .
General government	4 769	–76	58	–17	34	81	43	25	. . .
of which: Short-term	4 771	. . .	. . .	. . .	. . .	. . .	. . .	. . .	. . .
Banks	4 772	–158	–54	288	306	422	440	347	. . .
of which: Short-term	4 774	*–81*	*74*	*257*	*178*	*–181*	*–83*	*160*	. . .
Other sectors	4 775	–219	–175	13	136	289	24	173	. . .
of which: Short-term	4 777	*–8*	*–3*	. . .	*11*	*78*	*58*	*35*	. . .
Currency and deposits	4 780	–11	2	. . .	–1	1	. . .	–13	. . .
Monetary authorities	4 781	–11	2	. . .	–1	1	–1	2	. . .
General government	4 782	. . .	. . .	. . .	. . .	. . .	. . .	. . .	. . .
Banks	4 783	. . .	. . .	. . .	. . .	. . .	1	–15	. . .
Other sectors	4 784	. . .	. . .	. . .	. . .	. . .	. . .	. . .	. . .
Other liabilities	4 786	–2	7	–2	–3	–5	9	10	. . .
Monetary authorities	4 787	. . .	. . .	. . .	. . .	. . .	. . .	. . .	. . .
of which: Short-term	4 789	. . .	. . .	. . .	. . .	. . .	. . .	. . .	. . .
General government	4 790	. . .	. . .	. . .	. . .	. . .	. . .	. . .	. . .
of which: Short-term	4 792	. . .	. . .	. . .	. . .	. . .	. . .	. . .	. . .
Banks	4 793	. . .	. . .	. . .	. . .	. . .	. . .	. . .	. . .
of which: Short-term	4 795	. . .	. . .	. . .	. . .	. . .	. . .	. . .	. . .
Other sectors	4 796	–2	7	–2	–3	–5	9	10	. . .
of which: Short-term	4 798	. . .	. . .	. . .	. . .	. . .	. . .	. . .	. . .
E. RESERVE ASSETS	4 802	150	–4	–153	44	–32	–86	69	. . .
Monetary gold	4 812	. . .	. . .	. . .	. . .	. . .	. . .	. . .	. . .
Special drawing rights	4 811	. . .	. . .	. . .	. . .	. . .	. . .	. . .	. . .
Reserve position in the Fund	4 810	. . .	. . .	. . .	. . .	. . .	–11	. . .	. . .
Foreign exchange	4 803	150	–4	–153	44	–32	–74	69	. . .
Other claims	4 813	. . .	. . .	. . .	. . .	. . .	. . .	. . .	. . .
NET ERRORS AND OMISSIONS	4 998	**40**	**–30**	**–32**	**–115**	**–82**	**–231**	**–71**	. . .

Part 3 of the *Yearbook* contains descriptions of the methodologies, compilation practices, and sources used to compile these data.

Table 3. INTERNATIONAL INVESTMENT POSITION (End–period stocks), 1994–2001

(Millions of U.S. dollars)

	Code	1994	1995	1996	1997	1998	1999	2000	2001
ASSETS	8 995 C.	872	1,008	1,319	1,601	2,196	3,370	3,741	...
Direct investment abroad	8 505 . .	**149**	**180**	**242**	**275**	**339**	**452**	**667**	**...**
Equity capital and reinvested earnings	8 506 . .	81	90	100	129	140	228	475	...
Claims on affiliated enterprises	8 507 . .	...	...	...	...	...	...	...	...
Liabilities to affiliated enterprises	8 508 . .	...	...	...	...	...	...	...	...
Other capital	8 530 . .	68	90	142	146	199	224	192	...
Claims on affiliated enterprises	8 535 . .	73	98	148	151	205	246	278	...
Liabilities to affiliated enterprises	8 540 . .	–5	–8	–6	–5	–6	–22	–86	...
Portfolio investment	8 602 . .	**118**	**198**	**264**	**488**	**967**	**1,902**	**2,205**	**...**
Equity securities	8 610 . .	48	103	183	398	830	1,718	2,128	...
Monetary authorities	8 611 . .	...	...	...	...	...	1	1	...
General government	8 612 . .	...	...	...	...	...	...	...	...
Banks	8 613 . .	...	...	...	...	...	28	73	...
Other sectors	8 614 . .	...	...	183	398	830	1,689	2,054	...
Debt securities	8 619 . .	71	95	81	90	137	184	78	...
Bonds and notes	8 620 . .	71	92	71	82	130	172	42	...
Monetary authorities	8 621 . .	...	...	...	...	2	1	1	...
General government	8 622 . .	...	...	...	...	...	...	...	...
Banks	8 623 . .	...	...	...	...	26	46	1	...
Other sectors	8 624 . .	71	92	71	82	102	125	40	...
Money market instruments	8 630 . .	...	3	10	8	8	12	36	...
Monetary authorities	8 631 . .	...	...	...	...	...	...	...	...
General government	8 632 . .	...	...	...	...	...	...	...	...
Banks	8 633 . .	...	3	10	8	8	12	36	...
Other sectors	8 634 . .	...	...	...	...	...	...	...	...
Financial derivatives	8 900 . .	**59**	**81**	**81**	**76**	**78**	**16**	**...**	**...**
Monetary authorities	8 901 . .	59	81	81	76	78	16	...	...
General government	8 902 . .	...	...	...	...	...	...	...	...
Banks	8 903 . .	...	...	...	...	...	...	...	...
Other sectors	8 904 . .	...	...	...	...	...	...	...	...
Other investment	8 703 . .	**248**	**235**	**259**	**376**	**384**	**505**	**463**	**...**
Trade credits	8 706 . .	103	115	126	139	165	163	160	...
General government	8 707 . .	...	...	...	...	...	...	...	...
of which: Short-term	8 709 . .	...	...	...	...	...	...	...	...
Other sectors	8 710 . .	103	115	126	139	165	163	160	...
of which: Short-term	8 712 . .	...	...	...	...	...	...	...	...
Loans	8 714 . .	...	...	6	34	86	136	106	...
Monetary authorities	8 715 . .	...	...	...	...	...	...	...	...
of which: Short-term	8 718 . .	...	...	...	...	...	...	...	...
General government	8 719 . .	...	...	...	...	...	...	...	...
of which: Short-term	8 721 . .	...	...	...	...	...	...	...	...
Banks	8 722 . .	...	...	6	34	27	24	57	...
of which: Short-term	8 724 . .	...	...	...	...	...	...	...	...
Other sectors	8 725 . .	...	...	...	...	59	112	48	...
of which: Short-term	8 727 . .	...	...	...	...	...	...	...	...
Currency and deposits	8 730 . .	145	118	126	150	133	206	197	...
Monetary authorities	8 731 . .	...	...	...	...	...	...	...	...
General government	8 732 . .	...	...	...	...	...	...	...	...
Banks	8 733 . .	119	80	109	131	115	160	172	...
Other sectors	8 734 . .	26	38	17	19	19	46	25	...
Other assets	8 736 . .	...	2	...	54	...	...	...	...
Monetary authorities	8 737 . .	...	...	...	...	...	...	...	...
of which: Short-term	8 739 . .	...	...	...	...	...	...	...	...
General government	8 740 . .	...	...	...	...	...	...	...	...
of which: Short-term	8 742 . .	...	...	...	...	...	...	...	...
Banks	8 743 . .	...	...	...	...	...	...	...	...
of which: Short-term	8 745 . .	...	...	...	...	...	...	...	...
Other sectors	8 746 . .	...	2	...	54	...	...	...	...
of which: Short-term	8 748 . .	...	...	...	...	...	...	...	...
Reserve assets	8 802 . .	**298**	**315**	**474**	**386**	**427**	**495**	**405**	**...**
Monetary gold	8 812 . .	3	3	1	3	3	17	16	...
Special drawing rights	8 811 . .	...	...	...	...	...	...	...	...
Reserve position in the Fund	8 810 . .	15	16	15	14	15	26	24	23
Foreign exchange	8 803 . .	280	297	458	369	410	452	365	...
Other claims	8 813 . .	...	...	...	...	...	...	...	...

Table 3 (Concluded). INTERNATIONAL INVESTMENT POSITION (End–period stocks), 1994–2001
(Millions of U.S. dollars)

	Code	1994	1995	1996	1997	1998	1999	2000	2001
LIABILITIES	8 995 D.	4,245	4,478	4,719	5,020	6,363	7,597	9,027	...
Direct investment in Iceland	8 555 . .	**127**	**129**	**199**	**332**	**458**	**477**	**483**	...
Equity capital and reinvested earnings	8 556 . .	97	114	115	198	343	350	405	...
Claims on direct investors	8 557 . .	...	...	...	...	...	...	...	...
Liabilities to direct investors	8 558 . .	...	...	...	...	...	...	...	...
Other capital	8 580 . .	30	15	84	134	115	127	78	...
Claims on direct investors	8 585 . .	–28	–26	98	160	147	170	112	...
Liabilities to direct investors	8 590 . .	58	41	–14	–26	–32	–43	–34	...
Portfolio investment	8 652 . .	**1,882**	**2,129**	**2,213**	**2,039**	**2,200**	**3,127**	**4,107**	...
Equity securities	8 660 . .	...	...	1	...	14	66	17	...
Banks	8 663 . .	...	...	...	...	...	...	10	...
Other sectors	8 664 . .	...	...	1	...	14	66	8	...
Debt securities	8 669 . .	1,882	2,128	2,212	2,039	2,186	3,061	4,090	...
Bonds and notes	8 670 . .	1,617	1,830	1,945	1,846	1,999	2,511	3,542	...
Monetary authorities	8 671 . .	...	...	...	...	...	...	...	...
General government	8 672 . .	1,178	1,337	1,448	1,371	1,318	1,128	1,103	...
Banks	8 673 . .	...	...	30	31	106	418	1,770	...
Other sectors	8 674 . .	439	494	467	445	575	965	670	...
Money market instruments	8 680 . .	265	298	267	193	187	550	548	...
Monetary authorities	8 681 . .	...	...	...	...	...	...	...	...
General government	8 682 . .	265	298	267	193	187	338	423	...
Banks	8 683 . .	...	...	...	...	...	18	124	...
Other sectors	8 684 . .	...	...	...	...	...	194	1	...
Financial derivatives	8 905 . .	**56**	**74**	**74**	**74**	**74**	**16**	...	...
Monetary authorities	8 906 . .	56	74	74	74	74	16	...	...
General government	8 907 . .	...	...	...	...	...	...	...	...
Banks	8 908 . .	...	...	...	...	...	...	...	...
Other sectors	8 909 . .	...	...	...	...	...	...	...	...
Other investment	8 753 . .	**2,180**	**2,146**	**2,233**	**2,575**	**3,631**	**3,976**	**4,436**	...
Trade credits	8 756 . .	82	86	104	129	130	153	146	...
General government	8 757 . .	...	...	...	...	...	...	...	...
of which: Short-term	8 759 . .	...	...	...	...	...	...	...	...
Other sectors	8 760 . .	82	86	104	129	130	153	146	...
of which: Short-term	8 762 . .	...	...	...	...	...	...	...	...
Loans	8 764 . .	2,076	2,026	2,078	2,390	3,473	3,780	4,228	...
Monetary authorities	8 765 . .	80	100	...	...	55	50	184	...
of which: Use of Fund credit and loans from the Fund	8 766 . .	...	...	...	...	...	...	...	...
of which: Short-term	8 768 . .	*80*	*100*	...	...	*55*	*50*	*184*	...
General government	8 769 . .	287	377	334	345	446	442	446	...
of which: Short-term	8 771 . .	...	...	...	...	...	...	*1*	...
Banks	8 772 . .	459	418	636	869	1,421	1,797	2,253	...
of which: Short-term	8 774 . .	*135*	*211*	*409*	*533*	*457*	*361*	*475*	...
Other sectors	8 775 . .	1,250	1,132	1,108	1,176	1,552	1,491	1,345	...
of which: Short-term	8 777 . .	*7*	*3*	*3*	*14*	*96*	*152*	*166*	...
Currency and deposits	8 780 . .	1	6	26	35	8	18	19	...
Monetary authorities	8 781 . .	1	3	2	1	2	1	3	...
General government	8 782 . .	...	...	...	...	...	...	...	...
Banks	8 783 . .	...	3	24	33	6	17	16	...
Other sectors	8 784 . .	...	...	...	...	...	...	...	...
Other liabilities	8 786 . .	21	28	25	21	19	25	43	...
Monetary authorities	8 787 . .	...	...	...	...	...	...	...	...
of which: Short-term	8 789 . .	...	...	...	...	...	...	...	...
General government	8 790 . .	...	...	...	...	...	...	...	...
of which: Short-term	8 792 . .	...	...	...	...	...	...	...	...
Banks	8 793 . .	...	...	...	...	...	...	...	...
of which: Short-term	8 795 . .	...	...	...	...	...	...	...	...
Other sectors	8 796 . .	21	28	25	21	19	25	43	...
of which: Short-term	8 798 . .	...	...	...	...	...	...	...	...
NET INTERNATIONAL INVESTMENT POSITION	8 995 . .	**–3,373**	**–3,470**	**–3,400**	**–3,419**	**–4,167**	**–4,227**	**–5,286**	...
Conversion rates: krónur per U.S. dollar (end of period)	0 102 . .	**68.300**	**65.230**	**66.890**	**72.180**	**69.320**	**72.550**	**84.700**	**102.950**

Table 1. ANALYTIC PRESENTATION, 1994–2001
(Millions of U.S. dollars)

	Code	1994	1995	1996	1997	1998	1999	2000	2001
A. Current Account [1]	4 993 Z.	**-1,676**	**-5,563**	**-5,956**	**-2,965**	**-6,903**	**-3,228**	**-4,198**	**. . .**
Goods: exports f.o.b.	2 100 . .	25,523	31,239	33,737	35,702	34,076	36,877	43,132	. . .
Goods: imports f.o.b.	3 100 . .	-29,673	-37,957	-43,789	-45,730	-44,828	-45,556	-55,325	. . .
Balance on Goods	4 100 . .	*-4,150*	*-6,719*	*-10,052*	*-10,028*	*-10,752*	*-8,679*	*-12,193*	. . .
Services: credit	2 200 . .	6,038	6,775	7,238	9,111	11,691	14,509	18,331	. . .
Services: debit	3 200 . .	-8,200	-10,268	-11,171	-12,443	-14,540	-17,271	-19,913	. . .
Balance on Goods and Services	4 991 . .	*-6,312*	*-10,212*	*-13,984*	*-13,360*	*-13,601*	*-11,441*	*-13,775*	. . .
Income: credit	2 300 . .	821	1,486	1,411	1,484	1,806	1,919	2,280	. . .
Income: debit	3 300 . .	-4,370	-5,219	-4,667	-5,002	-5,443	-5,629	-6,156	. . .
Balance on Goods, Services, and Income	4 992 . .	*-9,861*	*-13,945*	*-17,240*	*-16,878*	*-17,238*	*-15,151*	*-17,651*	. . .
Current transfers: credit	2 379 Z.	8,208	8,410	11,350	13,975	10,402	11,958	13,504	. . .
Current transfers: debit	3 379 . .	-23	-27	-66	-62	-67	-35	-51	. . .
B. Capital Account [1]	4 994 Z.	**. . .**	**. . .**	**. . .**	**. . .**	**. . .**	**. . .**	**. . .**	**. . .**
Capital account: credit	2 994 Z.	. . .	. . .	. . .	. . .	. . .	. . .	. . .	. . .
Capital account: debit	3 994 . .	. . .	. . .	. . .	. . .	. . .	. . .	. . .	. . .
Total, Groups A Plus B	4 981 . .	*-1,676*	*-5,563*	*-5,956*	*-2,965*	*-6,903*	*-3,228*	*-4,198*	. . .
C. Financial Account [1]	4 995 W.	**10,576**	**3,861**	**11,848**	**9,635**	**8,584**	**9,579**	**9,616**	**. . .**
Direct investment abroad	4 505 . .	-83	-117	-239	-113	-48	-79	-335	. . .
Direct investment in India	4 555 Z.	973	2,144	2,426	3,577	2,635	2,169	2,315	. . .
Portfolio investment assets	4 602 . .	. . .	. . .	. . .	. . .	. . .	. . .	. . .	. . .
Equity securities	4 610 . .	. . .	. . .	. . .	. . .	. . .	. . .	. . .	. . .
Debt securities	4 619 . .	. . .	. . .	. . .	. . .	. . .	. . .	. . .	. . .
Portfolio investment liabilities	4 652 Z.	5,491	1,590	3,958	2,556	-601	2,317	1,619	. . .
Equity securities	4 660 . .	5,491	1,590	3,958	2,556	-601	2,317	1,619	. . .
Debt securities	4 669 Z.	. . .	. . .	. . .	. . .	. . .	. . .	. . .	. . .
Financial derivatives	4 910 . .	. . .	. . .	. . .	. . .	. . .	. . .	. . .	. . .
Financial derivatives assets	4 900 . .	. . .	. . .	. . .	. . .	. . .	. . .	. . .	. . .
Financial derivatives liabilities	4 905 . .	. . .	. . .	. . .	. . .	. . .	. . .	. . .	. . .
Other investment assets	4 703 . .	1,170	-1,179	-4,710	-4,743	-3,239	-450	-1,136	. . .
Monetary authorities	4 701 . .	1	. . .	. . .	. . .	. . .	-498	-473	. . .
General government	4 704 . .	9	-29	-5	67	11	33	-15	. . .
Banks	4 705 . .	-1,029	-92	-1,642	-2,156	-1,355	1,140	-1,688	. . .
Other sectors	4 728 . .	2,189	-1,058	-3,063	-2,653	-1,896	-1,126	1,041	. . .
Other investment liabilities	4 753 W.	3,024	1,423	10,413	8,357	9,837	5,623	7,152	. . .
Monetary authorities	4 753 WA	142	-65	45	233	122	1,344	272	. . .
General government	4 753 ZB	92	1,483	1,698	397	-72	237	-416	. . .
Banks	4 753 ZC	1,307	266	2,989	1,098	1,739	2,458	1,396	. . .
Other sectors	4 753 ZD	1,483	-261	5,680	6,629	8,047	1,584	5,900	. . .
Total, Groups A Through C	4 983 . .	*8,899*	*-1,702*	*5,892*	*6,669*	*1,681*	*6,351*	*5,417*	. . .
D. Net Errors and Omissions	4 998 . .	**1,492**	**970**	**-1,934**	**-1,348**	**1,390**	**313**	**670**	**. . .**
Total, Groups A Through D	4 984 . .	*10,391*	*-733*	*3,958*	*5,321*	*3,071*	*6,664*	*6,087*	. . .
E. Reserves and Related Items	4 802 A.	**-10,391**	**733**	**-3,958**	**-5,321**	**-3,071**	**-6,664**	**-6,087**	**. . .**
Reserve assets	4 802 . .	-9,238	1,956	-2,676	-4,637	-2,659	-6,327	-6,035	. . .
Use of Fund credit and loans	4 766 . .	-1,153	-1,223	-1,282	-684	-412	-337	-52	. . .
Exceptional financing	4 920 . .	. . .	. . .	. . .	. . .	. . .	. . .	. . .	. . .
Conversion rates: Indian rupees per U.S. dollar	0 101 . .	**31.374**	**32.427**	**35.433**	**36.313**	**41.259**	**43.055**	**44.942**	**47.186**

[1] Excludes components that have been classified in the categories of Group E.

Table 2. STANDARD PRESENTATION, 1994–2001
(Millions of U.S. dollars)

	Code	1994	1995	1996	1997	1998	1999	2000	2001
CURRENT ACCOUNT	4 993 . .	**–1,676**	**–5,563**	**–5,956**	**–2,965**	**–6,903**	**–3,228**	**–4,198**	**. . .**
A. GOODS	4 100 . .	–4,150	–6,719	–10,052	–10,028	–10,752	–8,679	–12,193	. . .
Credit	2 100 . .	**25,523**	**31,239**	**33,737**	**35,702**	**34,076**	**36,877**	**43,132**	**. . .**
General merchandise: exports f.o.b.	2 110 . .	25,523	31,239	33,737	35,702	34,076	36,877	43,132	. . .
Goods for processing: exports f.o.b.	2 150 . .	. . .	. . .	. . .	. . .	. . .	. . .	. . .	. . .
Repairs on goods	2 160 . .	. . .	. . .	. . .	. . .	. . .	. . .	. . .	. . .
Goods procured in ports by carriers	2 170 . .	. . .	. . .	. . .	. . .	. . .	. . .	. . .	. . .
Nonmonetary gold	2 180 . .	. . .	. . .	. . .	. . .	. . .	. . .	. . .	. . .
Debit	3 100 . .	**–29,673**	**–37,957**	**–43,789**	**–45,730**	**–44,828**	**–45,556**	**–55,325**	**. . .**
General merchandise: imports f.o.b.	3 110 . .	–29,673	–37,957	–43,789	–45,730	–44,828	–45,556	–55,325	. . .
Goods for processing: imports f.o.b.	3 150 . .	. . .	. . .	. . .	. . .	. . .	. . .	. . .	. . .
Repairs on goods	3 160 . .	. . .	. . .	. . .	. . .	. . .	. . .	. . .	. . .
Goods procured in ports by carriers	3 170 . .	. . .	. . .	. . .	. . .	. . .	. . .	. . .	. . .
Nonmonetary gold	3 180 . .	. . .	. . .	. . .	. . .	. . .	. . .	. . .	. . .
B. SERVICES	4 200 . .	–2,162	–3,493	–3,933	–3,332	–2,849	–2,762	–1,582	. . .
Total credit	2 200 . .	*6,038*	*6,775*	*7,238*	*9,111*	*11,691*	*14,509*	*18,331*	. . .
Total debit	3 200 . .	*–8,200*	*–10,268*	*–11,171*	*–12,443*	*–14,540*	*–17,271*	*–19,913*	. . .
Transportation services, credit	2 205 . .	**1,714**	**1,890**	**1,989**	**1,942**	**1,773**	**1,844**	**1,882**	**. . .**
Passenger	2 850 . .	. . .	. . .	. . .	. . .	. . .	. . .	. . .	. . .
Freight	2 851 . .	*983*	*1,191*	*1,315*	*1,377*	*1,320*	*1,227*	*1,283*	. . .
Other	2 852 . .	*731*	*699*	*674*	*565*	*453*	*617*	*599*	. . .
Sea transport, passenger	2 207 . .	. . .	. . .	. . .	. . .	. . .	. . .	. . .	. . .
Sea transport, freight	2 208 . .	. . .	. . .	. . .	. . .	. . .	. . .	. . .	. . .
Sea transport, other	2 209 . .	. . .	. . .	. . .	. . .	. . .	. . .	. . .	. . .
Air transport, passenger	2 211 . .	. . .	. . .	. . .	. . .	. . .	. . .	. . .	. . .
Air transport, freight	2 212 . .	. . .	. . .	. . .	. . .	. . .	. . .	. . .	. . .
Air transport, other	2 213 . .	. . .	. . .	. . .	. . .	. . .	. . .	. . .	. . .
Other transport, passenger	2 215 . .	. . .	. . .	. . .	. . .	. . .	. . .	. . .	. . .
Other transport, freight	2 216 . .	. . .	. . .	. . .	. . .	. . .	. . .	. . .	. . .
Other transport, other	2 217 . .	. . .	. . .	. . .	. . .	. . .	. . .	. . .	. . .
Transportation services, debit	3 205 . .	**–4,564**	**–5,703**	**–6,447**	**–6,813**	**–7,093**	**–6,979**	**–8,047**	**. . .**
Passenger	3 850 . .	. . .	. . .	. . .	. . .	. . .	. . .	. . .	. . .
Freight	3 851 . .	*–3,009*	*–3,832*	*–4,314*	*–4,761*	*–4,908*	*–4,789*	*–5,629*	. . .
Other	3 852 . .	*–1,555*	*–1,871*	*–2,134*	*–2,052*	*–2,185*	*–2,190*	*–2,419*	. . .
Sea transport, passenger	3 207 . .	. . .	. . .	. . .	. . .	. . .	. . .	. . .	. . .
Sea transport, freight	3 208 . .	. . .	. . .	. . .	. . .	. . .	. . .	. . .	. . .
Sea transport, other	3 209 . .	. . .	. . .	. . .	. . .	. . .	. . .	. . .	. . .
Air transport, passenger	3 211 . .	. . .	. . .	. . .	. . .	. . .	. . .	. . .	. . .
Air transport, freight	3 212 . .	. . .	. . .	. . .	. . .	. . .	. . .	. . .	. . .
Air transport, other	3 213 . .	. . .	. . .	. . .	. . .	. . .	. . .	. . .	. . .
Other transport, passenger	3 215 . .	. . .	. . .	. . .	. . .	. . .	. . .	. . .	. . .
Other transport, freight	3 216 . .	. . .	. . .	. . .	. . .	. . .	. . .	. . .	. . .
Other transport, other	3 217 . .	. . .	. . .	. . .	. . .	. . .	. . .	. . .	. . .
Travel, credit	2 236 . .	**2,272**	**2,582**	**2,831**	**2,890**	**2,949**	**3,010**	**3,168**	**. . .**
Business travel	2 237 . .	. . .	. . .	. . .	. . .	. . .	. . .	. . .	. . .
Personal travel	2 240 . .	. . .	. . .	. . .	. . .	. . .	. . .	. . .	. . .
Travel, debit	3 236 . .	**–769**	**–996**	**–913**	**–1,342**	**–1,713**	**–2,010**	**–2,567**	**. . .**
Business travel	3 237 . .	. . .	. . .	. . .	. . .	. . .	. . .	. . .	. . .
Personal travel	3 240 . .	. . .	. . .	. . .	. . .	. . .	. . .	. . .	. . .
Other services, credit	2 200 BA	**2,052**	**2,303**	**2,418**	**4,279**	**6,970**	**9,656**	**13,281**	**. . .**
Communications	2 245 . .	. . .	. . .	. . .	. . .	. . .	. . .	. . .	. . .
Construction	2 249 . .	. . .	. . .	. . .	. . .	. . .	. . .	. . .	. . .
Insurance	2 253 . .	145	170	210	229	230	238	249	. . .
Financial	2 260 . .	. . .	. . .	. . .	. . .	. . .	. . .	. . .	. . .
Computer and information	2 262 . .	. . .	. . .	. . .	. . .	. . .	. . .	. . .	. . .
Royalties and licence fees	2 266 . .	. . .	1	7	12	19	23	83	. . .
Other business services	2 268 . .	1,899	2,120	2,142	3,852	6,096	8,892	12,289	. . .
Personal, cultural, and recreational	2 287 . .	. . .	. . .	. . .	. . .	. . .	. . .	. . .	. . .
Government, n.i.e.	2 291 . .	7	11	59	185	624	503	660	. . .
Other services, debit	3 200 BA	**–2,867**	**–3,569**	**–3,811**	**–4,288**	**–5,734**	**–8,282**	**–9,299**	**. . .**
Communications	3 245 . .	. . .	. . .	. . .	. . .	. . .	. . .	. . .	. . .
Construction	3 249 . .	. . .	. . .	. . .	. . .	. . .	. . .	. . .	. . .
Insurance	3 253 . .	–492	–559	–587	–650	–628	–614	–688	. . .
Financial	3 260 . .	. . .	. . .	. . .	. . .	. . .	. . .	. . .	. . .
Computer and information	3 262 . .	. . .	. . .	. . .	. . .	. . .	. . .	. . .	. . .
Royalties and licence fees	3 266 . .	–94	–90	–118	–150	–201	–315	–306	. . .
Other business services	3 268 . .	–2,112	–2,714	–2,935	–3,321	–4,557	–7,126	–7,992	. . .
Personal, cultural, and recreational	3 287 . .	. . .	. . .	. . .	. . .	. . .	. . .	. . .	. . .
Government, n.i.e.	3 291 . .	–169	–206	–171	–166	–348	–227	–312	. . .

Table 2 (Continued). STANDARD PRESENTATION, 1994–2001

(Millions of U.S. dollars)

	Code	1994	1995	1996	1997	1998	1999	2000	2001
C. INCOME	4 300	–3,549	–3,734	–3,256	–3,518	–3,636	–3,710	–3,875	...
Total credit	2 300	*821*	*1,486*	*1,411*	*1,484*	*1,806*	*1,919*	*2,280*	...
Total debit	3 300	*–4,370*	*–5,219*	*–4,667*	*–5,002*	*–5,443*	*–5,629*	*–6,156*	...
Compensation of employees, credit	2 310	**75**	**84**	**313**	**34**	**27**	**122**	**126**	...
Compensation of employees, debit	3 310	**–351**	**–419**	**–538**	**–162**	**–44**	**–15**	**–9**	...
Investment income, credit	2 320	**746**	**1,402**	**1,098**	**1,449**	**1,779**	**1,797**	**2,154**	...
Direct investment income	2 330	...	...	...	...	...	...	...	...
Dividends and distributed branch profits	2 332	...	...	...	...	...	...	...	...
Reinvested earnings and undistributed branch profits	2 333	...	...	...	...	...	...	...	...
Income on debt (interest)	2 334	...	...	...	...	...	...	...	...
Portfolio investment income	2 339	...	...	...	...	...	...	...	...
Income on equity	2 340	...	...	...	...	...	...	...	...
Income on bonds and notes	2 350	...	...	...	...	...	...	...	...
Income on money market instruments	2 360	...	...	...	...	...	...	...	...
Other investment income	2 370	746	1,402	1,098	1,449	1,779	1,797	2,154	...
Investment income, debit	3 320	**–4,019**	**–4,800**	**–4,129**	**–4,840**	**–5,398**	**–5,615**	**–6,146**	...
Direct investment income	3 330	...	...	...	...	...	...	...	...
Dividends and distributed branch profits	3 332	...	...	...	...	...	...	...	...
Reinvested earnings and undistributed branch profits	3 333	...	...	...	...	...	...	...	...
Income on debt (interest)	3 334	...	...	...	...	...	...	...	...
Portfolio investment income	3 339	...	...	...	...	...	...	...	...
Income on equity	3 340	...	...	...	...	...	...	...	...
Income on bonds and notes	3 350	...	...	...	...	...	...	...	...
Income on money market instruments	3 360	...	...	...	...	...	...	...	...
Other investment income	3 370	–4,019	–4,800	–4,129	–4,840	–5,398	–5,615	–6,146	...
D. CURRENT TRANSFERS	4 379	8,185	8,382	11,284	13,913	10,334	11,923	13,452	...
Credit	2 379	**8,208**	**8,410**	**11,350**	**13,975**	**10,402**	**11,958**	**13,504**	...
General government	2 380	429	339	421	445	323	341	352	...
Other sectors	2 390	7,779	8,070	10,928	13,531	10,079	11,617	13,152	...
Workers' remittances	2 391	5,782	6,139	8,453	10,297	9,453	11,002	9,034	...
Other current transfers	2 392	1,997	1,931	2,475	3,234	626	615	4,118	...
Debit	3 379	**–23**	**–27**	**–66**	**–62**	**–67**	**–35**	**–51**	...
General government	3 380	–7	–5	–11	–4	...	–1	–2	...
Other sectors	3 390	–16	–22	–55	–58	–67	–34	–50	...
Workers' remittances	3 391	...	...	...	...	...	–22	–33	...
Other current transfers	3 392	–16	–22	–55	–58	–67	–12	–17	...
CAPITAL AND FINANCIAL ACCOUNT	4 996	**185**	**4,594**	**7,890**	**4,314**	**5,513**	**2,915**	**3,529**	...
CAPITAL ACCOUNT	4 994	...	...	...	...	...	...	...	...
Total credit	2 994	...	...	...	...	...	...	...	...
Total debit	3 994	...	...	...	...	...	...	...	...
Capital transfers, credit	2 400	...	...	...	...	...	...	...	...
General government	2 401	...	...	...	...	...	...	...	...
Debt forgiveness	2 402	...	...	...	...	...	...	...	...
Other capital transfers	2 410	...	...	...	...	...	...	...	...
Other sectors	2 430	...	...	...	...	...	...	...	...
Migrants' transfers	2 431	...	...	...	...	...	...	...	...
Debt forgiveness	2 432	...	...	...	...	...	...	...	...
Other capital transfers	2 440	...	...	...	...	...	...	...	...
Capital transfers, debit	3 400	...	...	...	...	...	...	...	...
General government	3 401	...	...	...	...	...	...	...	...
Debt forgiveness	3 402	...	...	...	...	...	...	...	...
Other capital transfers	3 410	...	...	...	...	...	...	...	...
Other sectors	3 430	...	...	...	...	...	...	...	...
Migrants' transfers	3 431	...	...	...	...	...	...	...	...
Debt forgiveness	3 432	...	...	...	...	...	...	...	...
Other capital transfers	3 440	...	...	...	...	...	...	...	...
Nonproduced nonfinancial assets, credit	2 480	...	...	...	...	...	...	...	...
Nonproduced nonfinancial assets, debit	3 480	...	...	...	...	...	...	...	...

Table 2 (Continued). STANDARD PRESENTATION, 1994–2001
(Millions of U.S. dollars)

	Code	1994	1995	1996	1997	1998	1999	2000	2001
FINANCIAL ACCOUNT	4 995	**185**	**4,594**	**7,890**	**4,314**	**5,513**	**2,915**	**3,529**	**...**
A. DIRECT INVESTMENT	4 500	891	2,026	2,187	3,464	2,587	2,089	1,980	...
Direct investment abroad	4 505	**–83**	**–117**	**–239**	**–113**	**–48**	**–79**	**–335**	**...**
Equity capital	4 510	–83	–117	–239	–113	–48	–79	–335	...
Claims on affiliated enterprises	4 515	...	...	...	...	...	...	...	...
Liabilities to affiliated enterprises	4 520	...	...	...	...	...	...	...	...
Reinvested earnings	4 525	...	...	...	...	...	...	...	...
Other capital	4 530	...	...	...	...	...	...	...	...
Claims on affiliated enterprises	4 535	...	...	...	...	...	...	...	...
Liabilities to affiliated enterprises	4 540	...	...	...	...	...	...	...	...
Direct investment in India	4 555	**973**	**2,144**	**2,426**	**3,577**	**2,635**	**2,169**	**2,315**	**...**
Equity capital	4 560	973	2,144	2,426	3,577	2,635	2,169	2,315	...
Claims on direct investors	4 565	...	...	...	...	...	...	...	...
Liabilities to direct investors	4 570	973	2,144	2,426	3,577	2,635	2,169	2,315	...
Reinvested earnings	4 575	...	...	...	...	...	...	...	...
Other capital	4 580	...	...	...	...	...	...	...	...
Claims on direct investors	4 585	...	...	...	...	...	...	...	...
Liabilities to direct investors	4 590	...	...	...	...	...	...	...	...
B. PORTFOLIO INVESTMENT	4 600	5,491	1,590	3,958	2,556	–601	2,317	1,619	...
Assets	4 602	**...**	**...**	**...**	**...**	**...**	**...**	**...**	**...**
Equity securities	4 610	...	...	...	...	...	...	...	...
Monetary authorities	4 611	...	...	...	...	...	...	...	...
General government	4 612	...	...	...	...	...	...	...	...
Banks	4 613	...	...	...	...	...	...	...	...
Other sectors	4 614	...	...	...	...	...	...	...	...
Debt securities	4 619	...	...	...	...	...	...	...	...
Bonds and notes	4 620	...	...	...	...	...	...	...	...
Monetary authorities	4 621	...	...	...	...	...	...	...	...
General government	4 622	...	...	...	...	...	...	...	...
Banks	4 623	...	...	...	...	...	...	...	...
Other sectors	4 624	...	...	...	...	...	...	...	...
Money market instruments	4 630	...	...	...	...	...	...	...	...
Monetary authorities	4 631	...	...	...	...	...	...	...	...
General government	4 632	...	...	...	...	...	...	...	...
Banks	4 633	...	...	...	...	...	...	...	...
Other sectors	4 634	...	...	...	...	...	...	...	...
Liabilities	4 652	**5,491**	**1,590**	**3,958**	**2,556**	**–601**	**2,317**	**1,619**	**...**
Equity securities	4 660	5,491	1,590	3,958	2,556	–601	2,317	1,619	...
Banks	4 663	...	...	369	...	...	...	...	...
Other sectors	4 664	5,491	1,590	3,589	2,556	–601	2,317	1,619	...
Debt securities	4 669	...	...	...	...	...	...	...	...
Bonds and notes	4 670	...	...	...	...	...	...	...	...
Monetary authorities	4 671	...	...	...	...	...	...	...	...
General government	4 672	...	...	...	...	...	...	...	...
Banks	4 673	...	...	...	...	...	...	...	...
Other sectors	4 674	...	...	...	...	...	...	...	...
Money market instruments	4 680	...	...	...	...	...	...	...	...
Monetary authorities	4 681	...	...	...	...	...	...	...	...
General government	4 682	...	...	...	...	...	...	...	...
Banks	4 683	...	...	...	...	...	...	...	...
Other sectors	4 684	...	...	...	...	...	...	...	...
C. FINANCIAL DERIVATIVES	4 910	...	...	...	...	...	...	...	...
Monetary authorities	4 911	...	...	...	...	...	...	...	...
General government	4 912	...	...	...	...	...	...	...	...
Banks	4 913	...	...	...	...	...	...	...	...
Other sectors	4 914	...	...	...	...	...	...	...	...
Assets	4 900	**...**	**...**	**...**	**...**	**...**	**...**	**...**	**...**
Monetary authorities	4 901	...	...	...	...	...	...	...	...
General government	4 902	...	...	...	...	...	...	...	...
Banks	4 903	...	...	...	...	...	...	...	...
Other sectors	4 904	...	...	...	...	...	...	...	...
Liabilities	4 905	**...**	**...**	**...**	**...**	**...**	**...**	**...**	**...**
Monetary authorities	4 906	...	...	...	...	...	...	...	...
General government	4 907	...	...	...	...	...	...	...	...
Banks	4 908	...	...	...	...	...	...	...	...
Other sectors	4 909	...	...	...	...	...	...	...	...

Table 2 (Concluded). STANDARD PRESENTATION, 1994–2001
(Millions of U.S. dollars)

	Code	1994	1995	1996	1997	1998	1999	2000	2001
D. OTHER INVESTMENT	4 700	3,040	–979	4,421	2,931	6,186	4,835	5,965	...
Assets	4 703	**1,170**	**–1,179**	**–4,710**	**–4,743**	**–3,239**	**–450**	**–1,136**	**...**
Trade credits	4 706	...	...	...	...	...	...	...	...
General government	4 707	...	...	...	...	...	...	...	...
of which: Short-term	4 709	...	...	...	...	...	...	...	...
Other sectors	4 710	...	...	...	...	...	...	...	...
of which: Short-term	4 712	...	...	...	...	...	...	...	...
Loans	4 714	199	–15	8	–10	–15	10	–13	...
Monetary authorities	4 715	...	...	...	...	...	...	...	...
of which: Short-term	4 718	...	...	...	...	...	...	...	...
General government	4 719	20	–22	–3	–25	–20	–10	–18	...
of which: Short-term	4 721	*24*	...	...	...	...	...	...	...
Banks	4 722	...	...	...	...	...	...	...	...
of which: Short-term	4 724	...	...	...	...	...	...	...	...
Other sectors	4 725	179	7	11	14	5	20	5	...
of which: Short-term	4 727	...	...	...	...	...	...	...	...
Currency and deposits	4 730	–1,062	–92	–1,645	–2,065	–1,323	1,183	–1,685	...
Monetary authorities	4 731	...	...	...	...	...	...	...	...
General government	4 732	–4	...	–2	91	31	43	3	...
Banks	4 733	–1,029	–92	–1,642	–2,156	–1,355	1,140	–1,688	...
Other sectors	4 734	–30	...	...	...	...	...	...	...
Other assets	4 736	2,034	–1,073	–3,074	–2,668	–1,901	–1,643	563	...
Monetary authorities	4 737	1	...	...	...	...	–498	–473	...
of which: Short-term	4 739	...	...	...	...	...	...	...	...
General government	4 740	–7	–7	...	...	...	...	...	...
of which: Short-term	4 742	*–7*	*–7*	...	...	...	...	...	...
Banks	4 743	...	...	...	...	...	...	...	...
of which: Short-term	4 745	...	...	...	...	...	...	...	...
Other sectors	4 746	2,040	–1,065	–3,074	–2,668	–1,901	–1,146	1,036	...
of which: Short-term	4 748	...	...	...	...	...	...	...	...
Liabilities	4 753	**1,870**	**200**	**9,132**	**7,674**	**9,426**	**5,286**	**7,101**	**...**
Trade credits	4 756	...	...	...	...	...	...	...	...
General government	4 757	...	...	...	...	...	...	...	...
of which: Short-term	4 759	...	...	...	...	...	...	...	...
Other sectors	4 760	...	...	...	...	...	...	...	...
of which: Short-term	4 762	...	...	...	...	...	...	...	...
Loans	4 764	524	–29	4,119	3,450	2,686	525	5,230	...
Monetary authorities	4 765	–1,153	–1,223	–1,282	–684	–412	–337	–52	...
of which: Use of Fund credit and loans from the Fund	4 766	*–1,153*	*–1,223*	*–1,282*	*–684*	*–412*	*–337*	*–52*	...
of which: Short-term	4 768	...	...	...	...	...	...	...	...
General government	4 769	92	1,483	1,698	397	–72	237	–416	...
of which: Short-term	4 771	*–1,114*	*328*	*103*	...	...	...	...	...
Banks	4 772	...	...	...	...	...	...	...	...
of which: Short-term	4 774	...	...	...	...	...	...	...	...
Other sectors	4 775	1,585	–289	3,702	3,736	3,170	625	5,697	...
of which: Short-term	4 777	*459*	*345*	*–24*	*788*	*–1,303*	*431*	*616*	...
Currency and deposits	4 780	1,735	295	3,049	1,335	1,869	2,758	1,668	...
Monetary authorities	4 781	428	30	60	237	130	300	272	...
General government	4 782	...	...	...	...	...	...	...	...
Banks	4 783	1,307	266	2,989	1,098	1,739	2,458	1,396	...
Other sectors	4 784	...	...	...	...	...	...	...	...
Other liabilities	4 786	–388	–66	1,963	2,889	4,870	2,003	203	...
Monetary authorities	4 787	–286	–95	–15	–4	–7	1,044	...	...
of which: Short-term	4 789	*–24*	...	...	...	...	...	...	...
General government	4 790	...	...	...	...	...	...	...	...
of which: Short-term	4 792	...	...	...	...	...	...	...	...
Banks	4 793	...	...	...	...	...	...	...	...
of which: Short-term	4 795	...	...	...	...	...	...	...	...
Other sectors	4 796	–102	29	1,978	2,893	4,878	959	203	...
of which: Short-term	4 798	*–11*	...	...	...	...	...	...	...
E. RESERVE ASSETS	4 802	–9,238	1,956	–2,676	–4,637	–2,659	–6,327	–6,035	...
Monetary gold	4 812	...	...	...	...	...	...	...	...
Special drawing rights	4 811	103	–138	15	42	–6	78	2	...
Reserve position in the Fund	4 810	...	...	...	...	...	–381	...	...
Foreign exchange	4 803	–9,340	2,093	–2,691	–4,680	–2,653	–6,024	–6,037	...
Other claims	4 813	...	...	...	...	...	...	...	...
NET ERRORS AND OMISSIONS	4 998	**1,492**	**970**	**–1,934**	**–1,348**	**1,390**	**313**	**670**	**...**

Part 3 of the *Yearbook* contains descriptions of the methodologies, compilation practices, and sources used to compile these data.

Table 1. ANALYTIC PRESENTATION, 1994–2001
(Millions of U.S. dollars)

	Code	1994	1995	1996	1997	1998	1999	2000	2001
A. Current Account [1]	4 993 Z.	**–2,792**	**–6,431**	**–7,663**	**–4,889**	**4,096**	**5,785**	**7,985**	**6,899**
Goods: exports f.o.b.	2 100 . .	40,223	47,454	50,188	56,298	50,371	51,242	65,406	57,364
Goods: imports f.o.b.	3 100 . .	–32,322	–40,921	–44,240	–46,223	–31,942	–30,598	–40,366	–34,669
Balance on Goods	4 100 . .	*7,901*	*6,533*	*5,948*	*10,075*	*18,429*	*20,644*	*25,040*	*22,695*
Services: credit	2 200 . .	4,797	5,469	6,599	6,941	4,479	4,599	5,213	5,500
Services: debit	3 200 . .	–11,416	–13,540	–15,139	–16,607	–11,961	–11,573	–15,011	–15,880
Balance on Goods and Services	4 991 . .	*1,282*	*–1,538*	*–2,592*	*409*	*10,947*	*13,670*	*15,242*	*12,315*
Income: credit	2 300 . .	1,048	1,306	1,210	1,855	1,910	1,891	2,456	2,004
Income: debit	3 300 . .	–5,741	–7,180	–7,218	–8,187	–10,099	–11,690	–11,529	–8,940
Balance on Goods, Services, and Income	4 992 . .	*–3,411*	*–7,412*	*–8,600*	*–5,923*	*2,758*	*3,871*	*6,169*	*5,379*
Current transfers: credit	2 379 Z.	619	981	937	1,034	1,338	1,914	1,816	1,520
Current transfers: debit	3 379 . .	. . .	. . .	. . .	. . .	. . .	. . .	. . .	. . .
B. Capital Account [1]	4 994 Z.	**. . .**	**. . .**	**. . .**	**. . .**	**. . .**	**. . .**	**. . .**	**. . .**
Capital account: credit	2 994 Z.	. . .	. . .	. . .	. . .	. . .	. . .	. . .	. . .
Capital account: debit	3 994 . .	. . .	. . .	. . .	. . .	. . .	. . .	. . .	. . .
Total, Groups A Plus B	4 981 . .	*–2,792*	*–6,431*	*–7,663*	*–4,889*	*4,096*	*5,785*	*7,985*	*6,899*
C. Financial Account [1]	4 995 W.	**3,839**	**10,259**	**10,847**	**–603**	**–9,638**	**–5,941**	**–7,896**	**–7,616**
Direct investment abroad	4 505 . .	–609	–603	–600	–178	. . .	. . .	. . .	. . .
Direct investment in Indonesia	4 555 Z.	2,109	4,346	6,194	4,677	–356	–2,745	–4,550	–3,278
Portfolio investment assets	4 602 . .	. . .	. . .	. . .	. . .	. . .	. . .	. . .	. . .
Equity securities	4 610 . .	. . .	. . .	. . .	. . .	. . .	. . .	. . .	. . .
Debt securities	4 619 . .	. . .	. . .	. . .	. . .	. . .	. . .	. . .	. . .
Portfolio investment liabilities	4 652 Z.	3,877	4,100	5,005	–2,632	–1,878	–1,792	–1,909	–245
Equity securities	4 660 . .	1,900	1,493	1,819	–4,987	–4,371	–782	–1,020	. . .
Debt securities	4 669 Z.	1,977	2,607	3,186	2,355	2,493	–1,010	–889	. . .
Financial derivatives	4 910 . .	. . .	. . .	. . .	. . .	. . .	. . .	. . .	. . .
Financial derivatives assets	4 900 . .	. . .	. . .	. . .	. . .	. . .	. . .	. . .	. . .
Financial derivatives liabilities	4 905 . .	. . .	. . .	. . .	. . .	. . .	. . .	. . .	. . .
Other investment assets	4 703 . .	. . .	. . .	. . .	. . .	–44	–72	–150	–125
Monetary authorities	4 701 . .	. . .	. . .	. . .	. . .	. . .	. . .	. . .	. . .
General government	4 704 . .	. . .	. . .	. . .	. . .	. . .	. . .	. . .	. . .
Banks	4 705 . .	. . .	. . .	. . .	. . .	. . .	. . .	. . .	. . .
Other sectors	4 728 . .	. . .	. . .	. . .	. . .	–44	–72	–150	–125
Other investment liabilities	4 753 W.	–1,538	2,416	248	–2,470	–7,360	–1,332	–1,287	–3,968
Monetary authorities	4 753 WA	. . .	. . .	. . .	. . .	. . .	. . .	. . .	. . .
General government	4 753 ZB	137	6	–663	–265	4,209	3,979	2,093	636
Banks	4 753 ZC	527	1,953	–758	–276	–2,270	126	–1,420	–1,867
Other sectors	4 753 ZD	–2,202	457	1,669	–1,929	–9,299	–5,437	–1,960	–2,737
Total, Groups A Through C	4 983 . .	*1,047*	*3,828*	*3,184*	*–5,492*	*–5,542*	*–156*	*89*	*–717*
D. Net Errors and Omissions	4 998 . .	**–263**	**–2,255**	**1,319**	**–2,645**	**1,849**	**2,128**	**3,637**	**702**
Total, Groups A Through D	4 984 . .	*784*	*1,573*	*4,503*	*–8,137*	*–3,693*	*1,972*	*3,726*	*–15*
E. Reserves and Related Items	4 802 A.	**–784**	**–1,573**	**–4,503**	**8,137**	**3,693**	**–1,972**	**–3,726**	**15**
Reserve assets	4 802 . .	–784	–1,573	–4,503	5,113	–2,090	–3,342	–4,851	1,370
Use of Fund credit and loans	4 766 . .	. . .	. . .	. . .	3,025	5,782	1,371	1,125	–1,356
Exceptional financing	4 920 . .	. . .	. . .	. . .	. . .	. . .	. . .	. . .	. . .
Conversion rates: rupiah per U.S. dollar	0 101 . .	**2,160.8**	**2,248.6**	**2,342.3**	**2,909.4**	**10,013.6**	**7,855.2**	**8,421.8**	**10,260.9**

[1] Excludes components that have been classified in the categories of Group E.

Table 2. STANDARD PRESENTATION, 1994–2001

(Millions of U.S. dollars)

	Code		1994	1995	1996	1997	1998	1999	2000	2001
CURRENT ACCOUNT	4 993	. .	**–2,792**	**–6,431**	**–7,663**	**–4,889**	**4,096**	**5,785**	**7,985**	**6,899**
A. GOODS	4 100	. .	7,901	6,533	5,948	10,075	18,429	20,644	25,040	22,695
Credit	2 100	. .	**40,223**	**47,454**	**50,188**	**56,298**	**50,371**	**51,242**	**65,406**	**57,364**
General merchandise: exports f.o.b.	2 110	. .	40,223	47,454	50,188	56,298	50,371	51,242	65,406	57,364
Goods for processing: exports f.o.b.	2 150	. .	. . .	. . .	. . .	. . .	. . .	. . .	. . .	. . .
Repairs on goods	2 160	. .	. . .	. . .	. . .	. . .	. . .	. . .	. . .	. . .
Goods procured in ports by carriers	2 170	. .	. . .	. . .	. . .	. . .	. . .	. . .	. . .	. . .
Nonmonetary gold	2 180	. .	. . .	. . .	. . .	. . .	. . .	. . .	. . .	. . .
Debit	3 100	. .	**–32,322**	**–40,921**	**–44,240**	**–46,223**	**–31,942**	**–30,598**	**–40,366**	**–34,669**
General merchandise: imports f.o.b.	3 110	. .	–32,322	–40,921	–44,240	–46,223	–31,942	–30,598	–40,366	–34,669
Goods for processing: imports f.o.b.	3 150	. .	. . .	. . .	. . .	. . .	. . .	. . .	. . .	. . .
Repairs on goods	3 160	. .	. . .	. . .	. . .	. . .	. . .	. . .	. . .	. . .
Goods procured in ports by carriers	3 170	. .	. . .	. . .	. . .	. . .	. . .	. . .	. . .	. . .
Nonmonetary gold	3 180	. .	. . .	. . .	. . .	. . .	. . .	. . .	. . .	. . .
B. SERVICES	4 200	. .	–6,619	–8,071	–8,540	–9,666	–7,482	–6,974	–9,798	–10,380
Total credit	2 200	. .	*4,797*	*5,469*	*6,599*	*6,941*	*4,479*	*4,599*	*5,213*	*5,500*
Total debit	3 200	. .	*–11,416*	*–13,540*	*–15,139*	*–16,607*	*–11,961*	*–11,573*	*–15,011*	*–15,880*
Transportation services, credit	2 205	. .	**. . .**	**. . .**	**. . .**	**. . .**	**. . .**	**. . .**	**. . .**	**. . .**
Passenger	2 850	. .	. . .	. . .	. . .	. . .	. . .	. . .	. . .	. . .
Freight	2 851	. .	. . .	. . .	. . .	. . .	. . .	. . .	. . .	. . .
Other	2 852	. .	. . .	. . .	. . .	. . .	. . .	. . .	. . .	. . .
Sea transport, passenger	2 207	. .	. . .	. . .	. . .	. . .	. . .	. . .	. . .	. . .
Sea transport, freight	2 208	. .	. . .	. . .	. . .	. . .	. . .	. . .	. . .	. . .
Sea transport, other	2 209	. .	. . .	. . .	. . .	. . .	. . .	. . .	. . .	. . .
Air transport, passenger	2 211	. .	. . .	. . .	. . .	. . .	. . .	. . .	. . .	. . .
Air transport, freight	2 212	. .	. . .	. . .	. . .	. . .	. . .	. . .	. . .	. . .
Air transport, other	2 213	. .	. . .	. . .	. . .	. . .	. . .	. . .	. . .	. . .
Other transport, passenger	2 215	. .	. . .	. . .	. . .	. . .	. . .	. . .	. . .	. . .
Other transport, freight	2 216	. .	. . .	. . .	. . .	. . .	. . .	. . .	. . .	. . .
Other transport, other	2 217	. .	. . .	. . .	. . .	. . .	. . .	. . .	. . .	. . .
Transportation services, debit	3 205	. .	**–3,913**	**–4,861**	**–5,244**	**–5,400**	**–3,731**	**–3,275**	**–4,016**	**–3,876**
Passenger	3 850	. .	. . .	. . .	. . .	. . .	. . .	. . .	. . .	. . .
Freight	3 851	. .	*–3,196*	*–4,053*	*–4,381*	*–4,576*	*–3,003*	*–2,448*	*–2,906*	*–2,576*
Other	3 852	. .	*–717*	*–808*	*–863*	*–824*	*–728*	*–827*	*–1,110*	*–1,300*
Sea transport, passenger	3 207	. .	. . .	. . .	. . .	. . .	. . .	. . .	. . .	. . .
Sea transport, freight	3 208	. .	. . .	. . .	. . .	. . .	. . .	. . .	. . .	. . .
Sea transport, other	3 209	. .	. . .	. . .	. . .	. . .	. . .	. . .	. . .	. . .
Air transport, passenger	3 211	. .	. . .	. . .	. . .	. . .	. . .	. . .	. . .	. . .
Air transport, freight	3 212	. .	. . .	. . .	. . .	. . .	. . .	. . .	. . .	. . .
Air transport, other	3 213	. .	. . .	. . .	. . .	. . .	. . .	. . .	. . .	. . .
Other transport, passenger	3 215	. .	. . .	. . .	. . .	. . .	. . .	. . .	. . .	. . .
Other transport, freight	3 216	. .	. . .	. . .	. . .	. . .	. . .	. . .	. . .	. . .
Other transport, other	3 217	. .	. . .	. . .	. . .	. . .	. . .	. . .	. . .	. . .
Travel, credit	2 236	. .	**4,575**	**5,229**	**6,184**	**6,648**	**4,255**	**4,353**	**4,974**	**5,276**
Business travel	2 237	. .	1,190	1,360	1,607	1,728	1,106	1,132	1,294	1,372
Personal travel	2 240	. .	3,385	3,869	4,577	4,920	3,149	3,221	3,680	3,904
Travel, debit	3 236	. .	**–1,900**	**–2,172**	**–2,399**	**–2,411**	**–2,102**	**–2,353**	**–3,197**	**–3,406**
Business travel	3 237	. .	. . .	. . .	. . .	. . .	. . .	. . .	. . .	. . .
Personal travel	3 240	. .	–1,900	–2,172	–2,399	–2,411	–2,102	–2,353	–3,197	–3,406
Other services, credit	2 200	BA	**222**	**240**	**415**	**293**	**224**	**246**	**239**	**224**
Communications	2 245	. .	105	113	278	144	85	100	86	85
Construction	2 249	. .	. . .	. . .	. . .	. . .	. . .	. . .	. . .	. . .
Insurance	2 253	. .	. . .	. . .	. . .	. . .	. . .	. . .	. . .	. . .
Financial	2 260	. .	. . .	. . .	. . .	. . .	. . .	. . .	. . .	. . .
Computer and information	2 262	. .	. . .	. . .	. . .	. . .	. . .	. . .	. . .	. . .
Royalties and licence fees	2 266	. .	. . .	. . .	. . .	. . .	. . .	. . .	. . .	. . .
Other business services	2 268	. .	. . .	. . .	. . .	. . .	. . .	. . .	. . .	. . .
Personal, cultural, and recreational	2 287	. .	. . .	. . .	. . .	. . .	. . .	. . .	. . .	. . .
Government, n.i.e.	2 291	. .	117	127	137	149	139	146	153	139
Other services, debit	3 200	BA	**–5,603**	**–6,507**	**–7,496**	**–8,796**	**–6,128**	**–5,945**	**–7,798**	**–8,598**
Communications	3 245	. .	–57	–98	–187	–40	–40	–50	–49	–51
Construction	3 249	. .	. . .	. . .	. . .	. . .	. . .	. . .	. . .	. . .
Insurance	3 253	. .	–355	–451	–486	–509	–334	–272	–323	–286
Financial	3 260	. .	. . .	. . .	. . .	. . .	. . .	. . .	. . .	. . .
Computer and information	3 262	. .	. . .	. . .	. . .	. . .	. . .	. . .	. . .	. . .
Royalties and licence fees	3 266	. .	. . .	. . .	. . .	. . .	. . .	. . .	. . .	. . .
Other business services	3 268	. .	–4,911	–5,648	–6,461	–7,854	–5,537	–5,386	–7,170	–7,976
Personal, cultural, and recreational	3 287	. .	. . .	. . .	. . .	. . .	. . .	. . .	. . .	. . .
Government, n.i.e.	3 291	. .	–280	–310	–362	–393	–217	–237	–256	–285

Table 2 (Continued). STANDARD PRESENTATION, 1994–2001
(Millions of U.S. dollars)

	Code		1994	1995	1996	1997	1998	1999	2000	2001
C. INCOME	4 300	. .	–4,693	–5,874	–6,008	–6,332	–8,189	–9,799	–9,073	–6,936
Total credit	2 300	. .	*1,048*	*1,306*	*1,210*	*1,855*	*1,910*	*1,891*	*2,456*	*2,004*
Total debit	3 300	. .	*–5,741*	*–7,180*	*–7,218*	*–8,187*	*–10,099*	*–11,690*	*–11,529*	*–8,940*
Compensation of employees, credit	2 310	. .	...	...	...	...	...	...	...	...
Compensation of employees, debit	3 310	. .	...	...	...	...	...	...	...	...
Investment income, credit	2 320	. .	**1,048**	**1,306**	**1,210**	**1,855**	**1,910**	**1,891**	**2,456**	**2,004**
Direct investment income	2 330	. .	...	...	...	...	...	...	...	...
Dividends and distributed branch profits	2 332	. .	...	...	...	...	...	...	...	...
Reinvested earnings and undistributed branch profits	2 333	. .	...	...	...	...	...	...	...	...
Income on debt (interest)	2 334	. .	...	...	...	...	...	...	...	...
Portfolio investment income	2 339	. .	...	...	...	...	...	...	...	...
Income on equity	2 340	. .	...	...	...	...	...	...	...	...
Income on bonds and notes	2 350	. .	...	...	...	...	...	...	...	...
Income on money market instruments	2 360	. .	...	...	...	...	...	...	...	...
Other investment income	2 370	. .	1,048	1,306	1,210	1,855	1,910	1,891	2,456	2,004
Investment income, debit	3 320	. .	**–5,741**	**–7,180**	**–7,218**	**–8,187**	**–10,099**	**–11,690**	**–11,529**	**–8,940**
Direct investment income	3 330	. .	–597	–718	–964	–1,341	–3,541	–3,702	–3,574	–3,158
Dividends and distributed branch profits	3 332	. .	–597	–718	–964	–1,341	–1,145	–1,400	–1,475	–1,676
Reinvested earnings and undistributed branch profits	3 333	. .	...	...	...	...	...	...	...	...
Income on debt (interest)	3 334	. .	...	...	...	...	–2,396	–2,302	–2,099	–1,482
Portfolio investment income	3 339	. .	...	...	...	...	...	...	...	...
Income on equity	3 340	. .	...	...	...	...	...	...	...	...
Income on bonds and notes	3 350	. .	...	...	...	...	...	...	...	...
Income on money market instruments	3 360	. .	...	...	...	...	...	...	...	...
Other investment income	3 370	. .	–5,144	–6,462	–6,254	–6,846	–6,558	–7,988	–7,955	–5,782
D. CURRENT TRANSFERS	4 379	. .	619	981	937	1,034	1,338	1,914	1,816	1,520
Credit	2 379	. .	**619**	**981**	**937**	**1,034**	**1,338**	**1,914**	**1,816**	**1,520**
General government	2 380	. .	170	330	141	309	379	805	626	474
Other sectors	2 390	. .	449	651	796	725	959	1,109	1,190	1,046
Workers' remittances	2 391	. .	449	651	796	725	959	1,109	1,190	1,046
Other current transfers	2 392	. .	...	...	...	...	...	...	...	...
Debit	3 379	. .	...	...	...	...	...	...	...	...
General government	3 380	. .	...	...	...	...	...	...	...	...
Other sectors	3 390	. .	...	...	...	...	...	...	...	...
Workers' remittances	3 391	. .	...	...	...	...	...	...	...	...
Other current transfers	3 392	. .	...	...	...	...	...	...	...	...
CAPITAL AND FINANCIAL ACCOUNT	4 996	. .	**3,055**	**8,686**	**6,344**	**7,534**	**–5,945**	**–7,913**	**–11,622**	**–7,601**
CAPITAL ACCOUNT	4 994	. .	...	...	...	...	...	...	...	...
Total credit	2 994	. .	...	...	...	...	...	...	...	...
Total debit	3 994	. .	...	...	...	...	...	...	...	...
Capital transfers, credit	2 400	. .	...	...	...	...	...	...	...	...
General government	2 401	. .	...	...	...	...	...	...	...	...
Debt forgiveness	2 402	. .	...	...	...	...	...	...	...	...
Other capital transfers	2 410	. .	...	...	...	...	...	...	...	...
Other sectors	2 430	. .	...	...	...	...	...	...	...	...
Migrants' transfers	2 431	. .	...	...	...	...	...	...	...	...
Debt forgiveness	2 432	. .	...	...	...	...	...	...	...	...
Other capital transfers	2 440	. .	...	...	...	...	...	...	...	...
Capital transfers, debit	3 400	. .	...	...	...	...	...	...	...	...
General government	3 401	. .	...	...	...	...	...	...	...	...
Debt forgiveness	3 402	. .	...	...	...	...	...	...	...	...
Other capital transfers	3 410	. .	...	...	...	...	...	...	...	...
Other sectors	3 430	. .	...	...	...	...	...	...	...	...
Migrants' transfers	3 431	. .	...	...	...	...	...	...	...	...
Debt forgiveness	3 432	. .	...	...	...	...	...	...	...	...
Other capital transfers	3 440	. .	...	...	...	...	...	...	...	...
Nonproduced nonfinancial assets, credit	2 480	. .	...	...	...	...	...	...	...	...
Nonproduced nonfinancial assets, debit	3 480	. .	...	...	...	...	...	...	...	...

Table 2 (Continued). STANDARD PRESENTATION, 1994–2001

(Millions of U.S. dollars)

	Code	1994	1995	1996	1997	1998	1999	2000	2001
FINANCIAL ACCOUNT	4 995	**3,055**	**8,686**	**6,344**	**7,534**	**–5,945**	**–7,913**	**–11,622**	**–7,601**
A. DIRECT INVESTMENT	4 500	1,500	3,743	5,594	4,499	–356	–2,745	–4,550	–3,278
Direct investment abroad	4 505	**–609**	**–603**	**–600**	**–178**	**. . .**	**. . .**	**. . .**	**. . .**
Equity capital	4 510	. . .	. . .	. . .	. . .	. . .	. . .	. . .	. . .
Claims on affiliated enterprises	4 515	. . .	. . .	. . .	. . .	. . .	. . .	. . .	. . .
Liabilities to affiliated enterprises	4 520	. . .	. . .	. . .	. . .	. . .	. . .	. . .	. . .
Reinvested earnings	4 525	. . .	. . .	. . .	. . .	. . .	. . .	. . .	. . .
Other capital	4 530	. . .	. . .	. . .	. . .	. . .	. . .	. . .	. . .
Claims on affiliated enterprises	4 535	. . .	. . .	. . .	. . .	. . .	. . .	. . .	. . .
Liabilities to affiliated enterprises	4 540	. . .	. . .	. . .	. . .	. . .	. . .	. . .	. . .
Direct investment in Indonesia	4 555	**2,109**	**4,346**	**6,194**	**4,677**	**–356**	**–2,745**	**–4,550**	**–3,278**
Equity capital	4 560	1,024	1,793	2,447	3,001	2,097	1,111	892	687
Claims on direct investors	4 565	. . .	. . .	. . .	. . .	. . .	. . .	. . .	. . .
Liabilities to direct investors	4 570	. . .	. . .	. . .	. . .	. . .	. . .	. . .	. . .
Reinvested earnings	4 575	. . .	. . .	. . .	. . .	. . .	. . .	. . .	. . .
Other capital	4 580	1,085	2,553	3,747	1,676	–2,453	–3,856	–5,442	–3,965
Claims on direct investors	4 585	. . .	. . .	. . .	. . .	. . .	. . .	. . .	. . .
Liabilities to direct investors	4 590	. . .	. . .	. . .	. . .	. . .	. . .	. . .	. . .
B. PORTFOLIO INVESTMENT	4 600	3,877	4,100	5,005	–2,632	–1,878	–1,792	–1,909	–245
Assets	4 602	**. . .**	**. . .**	**. . .**	**. . .**	**. . .**	**. . .**	**. . .**	**. . .**
Equity securities	4 610	. . .	. . .	. . .	. . .	. . .	. . .	. . .	. . .
Monetary authorities	4 611	. . .	. . .	. . .	. . .	. . .	. . .	. . .	. . .
General government	4 612	. . .	. . .	. . .	. . .	. . .	. . .	. . .	. . .
Banks	4 613	. . .	. . .	. . .	. . .	. . .	. . .	. . .	. . .
Other sectors	4 614	. . .	. . .	. . .	. . .	. . .	. . .	. . .	. . .
Debt securities	4 619	. . .	. . .	. . .	. . .	. . .	. . .	. . .	. . .
Bonds and notes	4 620	. . .	. . .	. . .	. . .	. . .	. . .	. . .	. . .
Monetary authorities	4 621	. . .	. . .	. . .	. . .	. . .	. . .	. . .	. . .
General government	4 622	. . .	. . .	. . .	. . .	. . .	. . .	. . .	. . .
Banks	4 623	. . .	. . .	. . .	. . .	. . .	. . .	. . .	. . .
Other sectors	4 624	. . .	. . .	. . .	. . .	. . .	. . .	. . .	. . .
Money market instruments	4 630	. . .	. . .	. . .	. . .	. . .	. . .	. . .	. . .
Monetary authorities	4 631	. . .	. . .	. . .	. . .	. . .	. . .	. . .	. . .
General government	4 632	. . .	. . .	. . .	. . .	. . .	. . .	. . .	. . .
Banks	4 633	. . .	. . .	. . .	. . .	. . .	. . .	. . .	. . .
Other sectors	4 634	. . .	. . .	. . .	. . .	. . .	. . .	. . .	. . .
Liabilities	4 652	**3,877**	**4,100**	**5,005**	**–2,632**	**–1,878**	**–1,792**	**–1,909**	**–245**
Equity securities	4 660	1,900	1,493	1,819	–4,987	–4,371	–782	–1,020	. . .
Banks	4 663	. . .	. . .	. . .	. . .	. . .	. . .	. . .	. . .
Other sectors	4 664	1,900	1,493	1,819	–4,987	–4,371	–782	–1,020	. . .
Debt securities	4 669	1,977	2,607	3,186	2,355	2,493	–1,010	–889	. . .
Bonds and notes	4 670	1,977	2,607	3,186	2,355	2,493	–1,010	–889	. . .
Monetary authorities	4 671	. . .	. . .	. . .	. . .	. . .	. . .	. . .	. . .
General government	4 672	. . .	. . .	. . .	. . .	. . .	. . .	. . .	. . .
Banks	4 673	. . .	. . .	. . .	. . .	. . .	. . .	. . .	. . .
Other sectors	4 674	1,977	2,607	3,186	2,355	2,493	–1,010	–889	. . .
Money market instruments	4 680	. . .	. . .	. . .	. . .	. . .	. . .	. . .	. . .
Monetary authorities	4 681	. . .	. . .	. . .	. . .	. . .	. . .	. . .	. . .
General government	4 682	. . .	. . .	. . .	. . .	. . .	. . .	. . .	. . .
Banks	4 683	. . .	. . .	. . .	. . .	. . .	. . .	. . .	. . .
Other sectors	4 684	. . .	. . .	. . .	. . .	. . .	. . .	. . .	. . .
C. FINANCIAL DERIVATIVES	4 910	. . .	. . .	. . .	. . .	. . .	. . .	. . .	. . .
Monetary authorities	4 911	. . .	. . .	. . .	. . .	. . .	. . .	. . .	. . .
General government	4 912	. . .	. . .	. . .	. . .	. . .	. . .	. . .	. . .
Banks	4 913	. . .	. . .	. . .	. . .	. . .	. . .	. . .	. . .
Other sectors	4 914	. . .	. . .	. . .	. . .	. . .	. . .	. . .	. . .
Assets	4 900	**. . .**	**. . .**	**. . .**	**. . .**	**. . .**	**. . .**	**. . .**	**. . .**
Monetary authorities	4 901	. . .	. . .	. . .	. . .	. . .	. . .	. . .	. . .
General government	4 902	. . .	. . .	. . .	. . .	. . .	. . .	. . .	. . .
Banks	4 903	. . .	. . .	. . .	. . .	. . .	. . .	. . .	. . .
Other sectors	4 904	. . .	. . .	. . .	. . .	. . .	. . .	. . .	. . .
Liabilities	4 905	**. . .**	**. . .**	**. . .**	**. . .**	**. . .**	**. . .**	**. . .**	**. . .**
Monetary authorities	4 906	. . .	. . .	. . .	. . .	. . .	. . .	. . .	. . .
General government	4 907	. . .	. . .	. . .	. . .	. . .	. . .	. . .	. . .
Banks	4 908	. . .	. . .	. . .	. . .	. . .	. . .	. . .	. . .
Other sectors	4 909	. . .	. . .	. . .	. . .	. . .	. . .	. . .	. . .

Table 2 (Concluded). STANDARD PRESENTATION, 1994–2001
(Millions of U.S. dollars)

	Code	1994	1995	1996	1997	1998	1999	2000	2001
D. OTHER INVESTMENT	4 700	–1,538	2,416	248	555	–1,622	–33	–312	–5,449
Assets	4 703	**...**	**...**	**...**	**...**	**–44**	**–72**	**–150**	**–125**
Trade credits	4 706	...	...	...	...	...	...	...	...
General government	4 707	...	...	...	...	...	...	...	...
of which: Short-term	4 709	...	...	...	...	...	...	...	...
Other sectors	4 710	...	...	...	...	...	...	...	...
of which: Short-term	4 712	...	...	...	...	...	...	...	...
Loans	4 714	...	...	...	...	...	...	...	...
Monetary authorities	4 715	...	...	...	...	...	...	...	...
of which: Short-term	4 718	...	...	...	...	...	...	...	...
General government	4 719	...	...	...	...	...	...	...	...
of which: Short-term	4 721	...	...	...	...	...	...	...	...
Banks	4 722	...	...	...	...	...	...	...	...
of which: Short-term	4 724	...	...	...	...	...	...	...	...
Other sectors	4 725	...	...	...	...	...	...	...	...
of which: Short-term	4 727	...	...	...	...	...	...	...	...
Currency and deposits	4 730	...	...	...	...	...	...	...	...
Monetary authorities	4 731	...	...	...	...	...	...	...	...
General government	4 732	...	...	...	...	...	...	...	...
Banks	4 733	...	...	...	...	...	...	...	...
Other sectors	4 734	...	...	...	...	...	...	...	...
Other assets	4 736	...	...	...	...	–44	–72	–150	–125
Monetary authorities	4 737	...	...	...	...	...	...	...	...
of which: Short-term	4 739	...	...	...	...	...	...	...	...
General government	4 740	...	...	...	...	...	...	...	...
of which: Short-term	4 742	...	...	...	...	...	...	...	...
Banks	4 743	...	...	...	...	...	...	...	...
of which: Short-term	4 745	...	...	...	...	...	...	...	...
Other sectors	4 746	...	...	...	...	–44	–72	–150	–125
of which: Short-term	4 748	...	...	...	...	...	...	...	...
Liabilities	4 753	**–1,538**	**2,416**	**248**	**555**	**–1,578**	**39**	**–162**	**–5,324**
Trade credits	4 756	280	117	57	76	22	...	...	...
General government	4 757	...	...	...	...	...	...	...	...
of which: Short-term	4 759	...	...	...	...	...	...	...	...
Other sectors	4 760	280	117	57	76	22	...	...	...
of which: Short-term	4 762	*280*	*117*	*57*	*76*	*22*	...	...	...
Loans	4 764	–1,818	2,299	191	479	–1,600	39	–162	–5,324
Monetary authorities	4 765	...	...	...	3,025	5,782	1,371	1,125	–1,356
of which: Use of Fund credit and loans from the Fund	4 766	...	...	...	*3,025*	*5,782*	*1,371*	*1,125*	*–1,356*
of which: Short-term	4 768	...	...	...	...	...	...	...	...
General government	4 769	137	6	–663	–265	4,209	3,979	2,093	636
of which: Short-term	4 771	...	...	...	...	...	...	...	...
Banks	4 772	527	1,953	–758	–276	–2,270	126	–1,420	1,867
of which: Short term	4 774	...	...	...	...	...	*1,113*	*–401*	*–555*
Other sectors	4 775	–2,482	340	1,612	–2,005	–9,321	–5,437	–1,960	–2,737
of which: Short-term	4 777	*–2,674*	*–716*	...	...	...	*–2,496*	*–2,605*	*–2,247*
Currency and deposits	4 780	...	...	...	...	...	...	...	...
Monetary authorities	4 781	...	...	...	...	...	...	...	...
General government	4 782	...	...	...	...	...	...	...	...
Banks	4 783	...	...	...	...	...	...	...	...
Other sectors	4 784	...	...	...	...	...	...	...	...
Other liabilities	4 786	...	...	...	...	...	...	...	...
Monetary authorities	4 787	...	...	...	...	...	...	...	...
of which: Short-term	4 789	...	...	...	...	...	...	...	...
General government	4 790	...	...	...	...	...	...	...	...
of which: Short-term	4 792	...	...	...	...	...	...	...	...
Banks	4 793	...	...	...	...	...	...	...	...
of which: Short-term	4 795	...	...	...	...	...	...	...	...
Other sectors	4 796	...	...	...	...	...	...	...	...
of which: Short-term	4 798	...	...	...	...	...	...	...	...
E. RESERVE ASSETS	4 802	–784	–1,573	–4,503	5,113	–2,090	–3,342	–4,851	1,370
Monetary gold	4 812	–89	–2	50	219	7	–9	52	–7
Special drawing rights	4 811	...	–1	–1	–506	201	307	–40	14
Reserve position in the Fund	4 810	–21	–86	–41	410	...	–201	...	...
Foreign exchange	4 803	–674	–1,484	–4,511	4,990	–2,298	–3,439	–4,863	1,363
Other claims	4 813	...	...	...	...	...	...	...	...
NET ERRORS AND OMISSIONS	4 998	**–263**	**–2,255**	**1,319**	**–2,645**	**1,849**	**2,128**	**3,637**	**702**

Part 3 of the *Yearbook* contains descriptions of the methodologies, compilation practices, and sources used to compile these data.

Iran, Islamic Republic of
429

Table 1. ANALYTIC PRESENTATION, 1994–2001 YEARS BEGINNING MARCH 21

(Millions of U.S. dollars)

	Code		1994	1995	1996	1997	1998	1999	2000	2001
A. Current Account[1]	4 993	Z.	**4,956**	**3,358**	**5,232**	**2,213**	**–2,139**	**6,589**	**12,645**	**. . .**
Goods: exports f.o.b.	2 100	. .	19,434	18,360	22,391	18,381	13,118	21,030	28,345	. . .
Goods: imports f.o.b.	3 100	. .	–12,617	–12,774	–14,989	–14,123	–14,286	–13,433	–15,207	. . .
Balance on Goods	4 100	. .	*6,817*	*5,586*	*7,402*	*4,258*	*–1,168*	*7,597*	*13,138*	. . .
Services: credit	2 200	. .	438	593	860	1,192	1,793	1,216	1,382	. . .
Services: debit	3 200	. .	–3,226	–2,339	–3,083	–3,371	–2,760	–2,457	–2,296	. . .
Balance on Goods and Services	4 991	. .	*4,029*	*3,840*	*5,179*	*2,079*	*–2,135*	*6,356*	*12,224*	. . .
Income: credit	2 300	. .	142	316	488	466	230	181	404	. . .
Income: debit	3 300	. .	–413	–794	–898	–725	–731	–473	–604	. . .
Balance on Goods, Services, and Income	4 992	. .	*3,758*	*3,362*	*4,769*	*1,820*	*–2,636*	*6,064*	*12,024*	. . .
Current transfers: credit	2 379	Z.	1,200	. . .	471	400	500	508	539	. . .
Current transfers: debit	3 379	. .	–2	–4	–8	–7	–3	17	82	. . .
B. Capital Account[1]	4 994	Z.	**. . .**	**. . .**	**. . .**	**. . .**	**. . .**	**. . .**	**. . .**	**. . .**
Capital account: credit	2 994	Z.	. . .	. . .	. . .	. . .	. . .	. . .	. . .	. . .
Capital account: debit	3 994	. .	. . .	. . .	. . .	. . .	. . .	. . .	. . .	. . .
Total, Groups A Plus B	4 981	. .	*4,956*	*3,358*	*5,232*	*2,213*	*–2,139*	*6,589*	*12,645*	. . .
C. Financial Account[1]	4 995	W.	**–346**	**–774**	**–5,508**	**–4,822**	**2,270**	**–5,894**	**–10,189**	**. . .**
Direct investment abroad	4 505	. .	. . .	. . .	. . .	. . .	. . .	. . .	. . .	. . .
Direct investment in Iran	4 555	Z.	2	17	26	53	24	35	39	. . .
Portfolio investment assets	4 602	. .	. . .	. . .	. . .	. . .	. . .	. . .	. . .	. . .
Equity securities	4 610	. .	. . .	. . .	. . .	. . .	. . .	. . .	. . .	. . .
Debt securities	4 619	. .	. . .	. . .	. . .	. . .	. . .	. . .	. . .	. . .
Portfolio investment liabilities	4 652	Z.	. . .	. . .	. . .	. . .	. . .	. . .	. . .	. . .
Equity securities	4 660	. .	. . .	. . .	. . .	. . .	. . .	. . .	. . .	. . .
Debt securities	4 669	Z.	. . .	. . .	. . .	. . .	. . .	. . .	. . .	. . .
Financial derivatives	4 910	. .	. . .	. . .	. . .	. . .	. . .	. . .	. . .	. . .
Financial derivatives assets	4 900	. .	. . .	. . .	. . .	. . .	. . .	. . .	. . .	. . .
Financial derivatives liabilities	4 905	. .	. . .	. . .	. . .	. . .	. . .	. . .	. . .	. . .
Other investment assets	4 703	. .	–1,258	–419	–1,305	2,293	963	–1,650	–8,257	. . .
Monetary authorities	4 701	. .	. . .	. . .	. . .	. . .	. . .	. . .	. . .	. . .
General government	4 704	. .	–42	235	–48	–99	–21	–6	–5,932	. . .
Banks	4 705	. .	–1,216	–654	–1,257	2,392	984	–1,638	–1,783	. . .
Other sectors	4 728	. .	. . .	. . .	. . .	. . .	. . .	–6	–542	. . .
Other investment liabilities	4 753	W.	910	–372	–4,229	–7,168	1,283	–4,279	–1,971	. . .
Monetary authorities	4 753	WA	–252	–64	–283	179	93	–5,517	–1,410	. . .
General government	4 753	ZB	10,447	1,684	–4,523	–4,035	–489	104	–621	. . .
Banks	4 753	ZC	. . .	. . .	. . .	. . .	. . .	. . .	. . .	. . .
Other sectors	4 753	ZD	–9,285	–1,992	577	–3,312	1,679	1,134	60	. . .
Total, Groups A Through C	4 983	. .	*4,610*	*2,584*	*–276*	*–2,609*	*131*	*695*	*2,456*	. . .
D. Net Errors and Omissions	4 998	. .	**–3,702**	**202**	**2,717**	**–1,088**	**–1,122**	**–244**	**–1,373**	**. . .**
Total, Groups A Through D	4 984	. .	*908*	*2,786*	*2,441*	*–3,697*	*–991*	*451*	*1,083*	. . .
E. Reserves and Related Items	4 802	A.	**–908**	**–2,786**	**–2,441**	**3,697**	**991**	**–451**	**–1,083**	**. . .**
Reserve assets	4 802	. .	–908	–2,786	–2,441	3,697	991	–451	–1,083	. . .
Use of Fund credit and loans	4 766	. .	. . .	. . .	. . .	. . .	. . .	. . .	. . .	. . .
Exceptional financing	4 920	. .	. . .	. . .	. . .	. . .	. . .	. . .	. . .	. . .
Conversion rates: Iranian rials per U.S. dollar	0 101	. .	**1,748.3**	**1,748.2**	**1,752.2**	**1,752.7**	**1,752.3**	**1,752.6**	**1,764.9**	**2,266.9**

[1] Excludes components that have been classified in the categories of Group E.

Table 2. STANDARD PRESENTATION, 1994–2001 YEARS BEGINNING MARCH 21

(Millions of U.S. dollars)

	Code	1994	1995	1996	1997	1998	1999	2000	2001
CURRENT ACCOUNT	4 993 . .	**4,956**	**3,358**	**5,232**	**2,213**	**–2,139**	**6,589**	**12,645**	**. . .**
A. GOODS	4 100 . .	6,817	5,586	7,402	4,258	–1,168	7,597	13,138	. . .
Credit	2 100 . .	**19,434**	**18,360**	**22,391**	**18,381**	**13,118**	**21,030**	**28,345**	**. . .**
General merchandise: exports f.o.b.	2 110 . .	19,434	18,360	22,391	18,381	13,118	21,030	28,345	. . .
Goods for processing: exports f.o.b.	2 150 . .	. . .	. . .	. . .	. . .	. . .	. . .	. . .	. . .
Repairs on goods	2 160 . .	. . .	. . .	. . .	. . .	. . .	. . .	. . .	. . .
Goods procured in ports by carriers	2 170 . .	. . .	. . .	. . .	. . .	. . .	. . .	. . .	. . .
Nonmonetary gold	2 180 . .	. . .	. . .	. . .	. . .	. . .	. . .	. . .	. . .
Debit	3 100 . .	**–12,617**	**–12,774**	**–14,989**	**–14,123**	**–14,286**	**–13,433**	**–15,207**	**. . .**
General merchandise: imports f.o.b.	3 110 . .	–12,617	–12,774	–14,989	–14,123	–14,286	–13,433	–15,207	. . .
Goods for processing: imports f.o.b.	3 150 . .	. . .	. . .	. . .	. . .	. . .	. . .	. . .	. . .
Repairs on goods	3 160 . .	. . .	. . .	. . .	. . .	. . .	. . .	. . .	. . .
Goods procured in ports by carriers	3 170 . .	. . .	. . .	. . .	. . .	. . .	. . .	. . .	. . .
Nonmonetary gold	3 180 . .	. . .	. . .	. . .	. . .	. . .	. . .	. . .	. . .
B. SERVICES	4 200 . .	–2,788	–1,746	–2,223	–2,179	–967	–1,241	–914	. . .
Total credit	2 200 . .	*438*	*593*	*860*	*1,192*	*1,793*	*1,216*	*1,382*	. . .
Total debit	3 200 . .	*–3,226*	*–2,339*	*–3,083*	*–3,371*	*–2,760*	*–2,457*	*–2,296*	. . .
Transportation services, credit	2 205 . .	**91**	**138**	**434**	**449**	**419**	**420**	**671**	**. . .**
Passenger	2 850 . .	*91*	*138*	*123*	*174*	*166*	*156*	*500*	. . .
Freight	2 851 . .	. . .	. . .	*311*	*275*	*253*	*264*	*171*	. . .
Other	2 852 . .	. . .	. . .	. . .	. . .	. . .	. . .	. . .	. . .
Sea transport, passenger	2 207 . .	. . .	. . .	. . .	. . .	. . .	2	5	. . .
Sea transport, freight	2 208 . .	. . .	. . .	. . .	. . .	. . .	111	72	. . .
Sea transport, other	2 209 . .	. . .	. . .	. . .	. . .	. . .	. . .	. . .	. . .
Air transport, passenger	2 211 . .	. . .	. . .	. . .	. . .	. . .	30	95	. . .
Air transport, freight	2 212 . .	. . .	. . .	. . .	. . .	. . .	32	21	. . .
Air transport, other	2 213 . .	. . .	. . .	. . .	. . .	. . .	. . .	. . .	. . .
Other transport, passenger	2 215 . .	. . .	. . .	. . .	. . .	. . .	124	400	. . .
Other transport, freight	2 216 . .	. . .	. . .	. . .	. . .	. . .	121	78	. . .
Other transport, other	2 217 . .	. . .	. . .	. . .	. . .	. . .	. . .	. . .	. . .
Transportation services, debit	3 205 . .	**–990**	**–942**	**–1,434**	**–1,332**	**–1,456**	**–1,061**	**–1,142**	**. . .**
Passenger	3 850 . .	*–12*	*–6*	*–16*	*–14*	*–2*	*–6*	*–2*	. . .
Freight	3 851 . .	*–978*	*–936*	*–1,418*	*–1,318*	*–1,454*	*–1,055*	*–1,140*	. . .
Other	3 852 . .	. . .	. . .	. . .	. . .	. . .	. . .	. . .	. . .
Sea transport, passenger	3 207 . .	. . .	. . .	. . .	. . .	. . .	. . .	. . .	. . .
Sea transport, freight	3 208 . .	. . .	. . .	. . .	. . .	. . .	–444	–480	. . .
Sea transport, other	3 209 . .	. . .	. . .	. . .	. . .	. . .	. . .	. . .	. . .
Air transport, passenger	3 211 . .	. . .	. . .	. . .	. . .	. . .	–1	. . .	. . .
Air transport, freight	3 212 . .	. . .	. . .	. . .	. . .	. . .	–128	–138	. . .
Air transport, other	3 213 . .	. . .	. . .	. . .	. . .	. . .	. . .	. . .	. . .
Other transport, passenger	3 215 . .	. . .	. . .	. . .	. . .	. . .	–5	–2	. . .
Other transport, freight	3 216 . .	. . .	. . .	. . .	. . .	. . .	–483	–522	. . .
Other transport, other	3 217 . .	. . .	. . .	. . .	. . .	. . .	. . .	. . .	. . .
Travel, credit	2 236 . .	**11**	**67**	**19**	**16**	**490**	**403**	**501**	**. . .**
Business travel	2 237 . .	. . .	. . .	. . .	. . .	. . .	40	50	. . .
Personal travel	2 240 . .	11	67	19	16	490	363	451	. . .
Travel, debit	3 236 . .	**–149**	**–241**	**–258**	**–382**	**–153**	**–632**	**–205**	**. . .**
Business travel	3 237 . .	. . .	. . .	. . .	. . .	. . .	–63	–21	. . .
Personal travel	3 240 . .	–149	–241	–258	–382	–153	–569	–184	. . .
Other services, credit	2 200 BA	**336**	**388**	**407**	**727**	**884**	**393**	**210**	**. . .**
Communications	2 245 . .	. . .	. . .	. . .	. . .	. . .	. . .	. . .	. . .
Construction	2 249 . .	. . .	. . .	. . .	. . .	. . .	. . .	. . .	. . .
Insurance	2 253 . .	. . .	. . .	55	48	45	74	118	. . .
Financial	2 260 . .	49	47	44	24	22	32	27	. . .
Computer and information	2 262 . .	. . .	. . .	. . .	. . .	. . .	. . .	. . .	. . .
Royalties and licence fees	2 266 . .	. . .	. . .	. . .	. . .	. . .	. . .	. . .	. . .
Other business services	2 268 . .	259	281	191	481	404	48	40	. . .
Personal, cultural, and recreational	2 287 . .	. . .	. . .	. . .	. . .	. . .	. . .	. . .	. . .
Government, n.i.e.	2 291 . .	28	60	117	174	413	239	25	. . .
Other services, debit	3 200 BA	**–2,087**	**–1,156**	**–1,391**	**–1,657**	**–1,151**	**–764**	**–949**	**. . .**
Communications	3 245 . .	. . .	. . .	. . .	. . .	. . .	. . .	. . .	. . .
Construction	3 249 . .	. . .	. . .	. . .	. . .	. . .	. . .	. . .	. . .
Insurance	3 253 . .	–179	–172	–250	–232	–257	–187	–202	. . .
Financial	3 260 . .	–73	–45	–51	–30	–24	–10	–11	. . .
Computer and information	3 262 . .	. . .	. . .	. . .	. . .	. . .	. . .	. . .	. . .
Royalties and licence fees	3 266 . .	. . .	. . .	. . .	. . .	. . .	. . .	. . .	. . .
Other business services	3 268 . .	–1,671	–792	–906	–1,206	–681	–15	–17	. . .
Personal, cultural, and recreational	3 287 . .	. . .	. . .	. . .	. . .	. . .	. . .	. . .	. . .
Government, n.i.e.	3 291 . .	–164	–147	–184	–189	–189	–552	–719	. . .

Table 2 (Continued). STANDARD PRESENTATION, 1994–2001 YEARS BEGINNING MARCH 21

(Millions of U.S. dollars)

	Code	1994	1995	1996	1997	1998	1999	2000	2001
C. INCOME	4 300 . .	–271	–478	–410	–259	–501	–292	–200	. . .
Total credit	2 300 . .	*142*	*316*	*488*	*466*	*230*	*181*	*404*	. . .
Total debit	3 300 . .	*–413*	*–794*	*–898*	*–725*	*–731*	*–473*	*–604*	. . .
Compensation of employees, credit	2 310 . .	**. . .**	**. . .**	**. . .**	**. . .**	**. . .**	**. . .**	**. . .**	**. . .**
Compensation of employees, debit	3 310 . .	**. . .**	**. . .**	**. . .**	**. . .**	**. . .**	**. . .**	**. . .**	**. . .**
Investment income, credit	2 320 . .	**142**	**316**	**488**	**466**	**230**	**181**	**404**	**. . .**
Direct investment income	2 330 . .	. . .	. . .	. . .	. . .	. . .	. . .	. . .	. . .
Dividends and distributed branch profits	2 332 . .	. . .	. . .	. . .	. . .	. . .	. . .	. . .	. . .
Reinvested earnings and undistributed branch profits	2 333 . .	. . .	. . .	. . .	. . .	. . .	. . .	. . .	. . .
Income on debt (interest)	2 334 . .	. . .	. . .	. . .	. . .	. . .	. . .	. . .	. . .
Portfolio investment income	2 339 . .	. . .	. . .	. . .	. . .	. . .	181	404	. . .
Income on equity	2 340 . .	. . .	. . .	. . .	. . .	. . .	181	404	. . .
Income on bonds and notes	2 350 . .	. . .	. . .	. . .	. . .	. . .	. . .	. . .	. . .
Income on money market instruments	2 360 . .	. . .	. . .	. . .	. . .	. . .	. . .	. . .	. . .
Other investment income	2 370 . .	142	316	488	466	230	. . .	. . .	. . .
Investment income, debit	3 320 . .	**–413**	**–794**	**–898**	**–725**	**–731**	**–473**	**–604**	**. . .**
Direct investment income	3 330 . .	. . .	. . .	. . .	. . .	. . .	. . .	. . .	. . .
Dividends and distributed branch profits	3 332 . .	. . .	. . .	. . .	. . .	. . .	. . .	. . .	. . .
Reinvested earnings and undistributed branch profits	3 333 . .	. . .	. . .	. . .	. . .	. . .	. . .	. . .	. . .
Income on debt (interest)	3 334 . .	. . .	. . .	. . .	. . .	. . .	. . .	. . .	. . .
Portfolio investment income	3 339 . .	. . .	. . .	. . .	. . .	. . .	–473	–604	. . .
Income on equity	3 340 . .	. . .	. . .	. . .	. . .	. . .	–473	–604	. . .
Income on bonds and notes	3 350 . .	. . .	. . .	. . .	. . .	. . .	. . .	. . .	. . .
Income on money market instruments	3 360 . .	. . .	. . .	. . .	. . .	. . .	. . .	. . .	. . .
Other investment income	3 370 . .	–413	–794	–898	–725	–731	. . .	. . .	. . .
D. CURRENT TRANSFERS	4 379 . .	1,198	–4	463	393	497	525	621	. . .
Credit	2 379 . .	**1,200**	**. . .**	**471**	**400**	**500**	**508**	**539**	**. . .**
General government	2 380 . .	. . .	. . .	. . .	. . .	. . .	. . .	. . .	. . .
Other sectors	2 390 . .	1,200	. . .	471	400	500	508	539	. . .
Workers' remittances	2 391 . .	. . .	. . .	. . .	. . .	. . .	. . .	. . .	. . .
Other current transfers	2 392 . .	1,200	. . .	471	400	500	508	539	. . .
Debit	3 379 . .	**–2**	**–4**	**–8**	**–7**	**–3**	**17**	**82**	**. . .**
General government	3 380 . .	–2	–4	–8	–7	–3	. . .	. . .	. . .
Other sectors	3 390 . .	. . .	. . .	. . .	. . .	. . .	17	82	. . .
Workers' remittances	3 391 . .	. . .	. . .	. . .	. . .	. . .	. . .	. . .	. . .
Other current transfers	3 392 . .	. . .	. . .	. . .	. . .	. . .	17	82	. . .
CAPITAL AND FINANCIAL ACCOUNT	4 996 . .	**–1,254**	**–3,560**	**–7,949**	**–1,125**	**3,261**	**–6,345**	**–11,272**	**. . .**
CAPITAL ACCOUNT	4 994 . .	**. . .**	**. . .**	**. . .**	**. . .**	**. . .**	**. . .**	**. . .**	**. . .**
Total credit	2 994 . .	. . .	. . .	. . .	. . .	. . .	. . .	. . .	. . .
Total debit	3 994 . .	. . .	. . .	. . .	. . .	. . .	. . .	. . .	. . .
Capital transfers, credit	2 400 . .	**. . .**	**. . .**	**. . .**	**. . .**	**. . .**	**. . .**	**. . .**	**. . .**
General government	2 401 . .	. . .	. . .	. . .	. . .	. . .	. . .	. . .	. . .
Debt forgiveness	2 402 . .	. . .	. . .	. . .	. . .	. . .	. . .	. . .	. . .
Other capital transfers	2 410 . .	. . .	. . .	. . .	. . .	. . .	. . .	. . .	. . .
Other sectors	2 430 . .	. . .	. . .	. . .	. . .	. . .	. . .	. . .	. . .
Migrants' transfers	2 431 . .	. . .	. . .	. . .	. . .	. . .	. . .	. . .	. . .
Debt forgiveness	2 432 . .	. . .	. . .	. . .	. . .	. . .	. . .	. . .	. . .
Other capital transfers	2 440 . .	. . .	. . .	. . .	. . .	. . .	. . .	. . .	. . .
Capital transfers, debit	3 400 . .	**. . .**	**. . .**	**. . .**	**. . .**	**. . .**	**. . .**	**. . .**	**. . .**
General government	3 401 . .	. . .	. . .	. . .	. . .	. . .	. . .	. . .	. . .
Debt forgiveness	3 402 . .	. . .	. . .	. . .	. . .	. . .	. . .	. . .	. . .
Other capital transfers	3 410 . .	. . .	. . .	. . .	. . .	. . .	. . .	. . .	. . .
Other sectors	3 430 . .	. . .	. . .	. . .	. . .	. . .	. . .	. . .	. . .
Migrants' transfers	3 431 . .	. . .	. . .	. . .	. . .	. . .	. . .	. . .	. . .
Debt forgiveness	3 432 . .	. . .	. . .	. . .	. . .	. . .	. . .	. . .	. . .
Other capital transfers	3 440 . .	. . .	. . .	. . .	. . .	. . .	. . .	. . .	. . .
Nonproduced nonfinancial assets, credit	2 480 . .	**. . .**	**. . .**	**. . .**	**. . .**	**. . .**	**. . .**	**. . .**	**. . .**
Nonproduced nonfinancial assets, debit	3 480 . .	**. . .**	**. . .**	**. . .**	**. . .**	**. . .**	**. . .**	**. . .**	**. . .**

Table 2 (Continued). STANDARD PRESENTATION, 1994–2001 YEARS BEGINNING MARCH 21
(Millions of U.S. dollars)

	Code		1994	1995	1996	1997	1998	1999	2000	2001
FINANCIAL ACCOUNT	4 995	. .	**–1,254**	**–3,560**	**–7,949**	**–1,125**	**3,261**	**–6,345**	**–11,272**	**. . .**
A. DIRECT INVESTMENT	4 500	. .	2	17	26	53	24	35	39	. . .
Direct investment abroad	4 505	. .	**. . .**	**. . .**	**. . .**	**. . .**	**. . .**	**. . .**	**. . .**	**. . .**
Equity capital	4 510	. .	. . .	. . .	. . .	. . .	. . .	. . .	. . .	. . .
Claims on affiliated enterprises	4 515	. .	. . .	. . .	. . .	. . .	. . .	. . .	. . .	. . .
Liabilities to affiliated enterprises	4 520	. .	. . .	. . .	. . .	. . .	. . .	. . .	. . .	. . .
Reinvested earnings	4 525	. .	. . .	. . .	. . .	. . .	. . .	. . .	. . .	. . .
Other capital	4 530	. .	. . .	. . .	. . .	. . .	. . .	. . .	. . .	. . .
Claims on affiliated enterprises	4 535	. .	. . .	. . .	. . .	. . .	. . .	. . .	. . .	. . .
Liabilities to affiliated enterprises	4 540	. .	. . .	. . .	. . .	. . .	. . .	. . .	. . .	. . .
Direct investment in Iran	4 555	. .	**2**	**17**	**26**	**53**	**24**	**35**	**39**	**. . .**
Equity capital	4 560	. .	2	17	26	53	24	35	39	. . .
Claims on direct investors	4 565	. .	. . .	. . .	. . .	. . .	. . .	. . .	. . .	. . .
Liabilities to direct investors	4 570	. .	2	17	26	53	24	35	39	. . .
Reinvested earnings	4 575	. .	. . .	. . .	. . .	. . .	. . .	. . .	. . .	. . .
Other capital	4 580	. .	. . .	. . .	. . .	. . .	. . .	. . .	. . .	. . .
Claims on direct investors	4 585	. .	. . .	. . .	. . .	. . .	. . .	. . .	. . .	. . .
Liabilities to direct investors	4 590	. .	. . .	. . .	. . .	. . .	. . .	. . .	. . .	. . .
B. PORTFOLIO INVESTMENT	4 600	. .	. . .	. . .	. . .	. . .	. . .	. . .	. . .	. . .
Assets	4 602	. .	**. . .**	**. . .**	**. . .**	**. . .**	**. . .**	**. . .**	**. . .**	**. . .**
Equity securities	4 610	. .	. . .	. . .	. . .	. . .	. . .	. . .	. . .	. . .
Monetary authorities	4 611	. .	. . .	. . .	. . .	. . .	. . .	. . .	. . .	. . .
General government	4 612	. .	. . .	. . .	. . .	. . .	. . .	. . .	. . .	. . .
Banks	4 613	. .	. . .	. . .	. . .	. . .	. . .	. . .	. . .	. . .
Other sectors	4 614	. .	. . .	. . .	. . .	. . .	. . .	. . .	. . .	. . .
Debt securities	4 619	. .	. . .	. . .	. . .	. . .	. . .	. . .	. . .	. . .
Bonds and notes	4 620	. .	. . .	. . .	. . .	. . .	. . .	. . .	. . .	. . .
Monetary authorities	4 621	. .	. . .	. . .	. . .	. . .	. . .	. . .	. . .	. . .
General government	4 622	. .	. . .	. . .	. . .	. . .	. . .	. . .	. . .	. . .
Banks	4 623	. .	. . .	. . .	. . .	. . .	. . .	. . .	. . .	. . .
Other sectors	4 624	. .	. . .	. . .	. . .	. . .	. . .	. . .	. . .	. . .
Money market instruments	4 630	. .	. . .	. . .	. . .	. . .	. . .	. . .	. . .	. . .
Monetary authorities	4 631	. .	. . .	. . .	. . .	. . .	. . .	. . .	. . .	. . .
General government	4 632	. .	. . .	. . .	. . .	. . .	. . .	. . .	. . .	. . .
Banks	4 633	. .	. . .	. . .	. . .	. . .	. . .	. . .	. . .	. . .
Other sectors	4 634	. .	. . .	. . .	. . .	. . .	. . .	. . .	. . .	. . .
Liabilities	4 652	. .	**. . .**	**. . .**	**. . .**	**. . .**	**. . .**	**. . .**	**. . .**	**. . .**
Equity securities	4 660	. .	. . .	. . .	. . .	. . .	. . .	. . .	. . .	. . .
Banks	4 663	. .	. . .	. . .	. . .	. . .	. . .	. . .	. . .	. . .
Other sectors	4 664	. .	. . .	. . .	. . .	. . .	. . .	. . .	. . .	. . .
Debt securities	4 669	. .	. . .	. . .	. . .	. . .	. . .	. . .	. . .	. . .
Bonds and notes	4 670	. .	. . .	. . .	. . .	. . .	. . .	. . .	. . .	. . .
Monetary authorities	4 671	. .	. . .	. . .	. . .	. . .	. . .	. . .	. . .	. . .
General government	4 672	. .	. . .	. . .	. . .	. . .	. . .	. . .	. . .	. . .
Banks	4 673	. .	. . .	. . .	. . .	. . .	. . .	. . .	. . .	. . .
Other sectors	4 674	. .	. . .	. . .	. . .	. . .	. . .	. . .	. . .	. . .
Money market instruments	4 680	. .	. . .	. . .	. . .	. . .	. . .	. . .	. . .	. . .
Monetary authorities	4 681	. .	. . .	. . .	. . .	. . .	. . .	. . .	. . .	. . .
General government	4 682	. .	. . .	. . .	. . .	. . .	. . .	. . .	. . .	. . .
Banks	4 683	. .	. . .	. . .	. . .	. . .	. . .	. . .	. . .	. . .
Other sectors	4 684	. .	. . .	. . .	. . .	. . .	. . .	. . .	. . .	. . .
C. FINANCIAL DERIVATIVES	4 910	. .	. . .	. . .	. . .	. . .	. . .	. . .	. . .	. . .
Monetary authorities	4 911	. .	. . .	. . .	. . .	. . .	. . .	. . .	. . .	. . .
General government	4 912	. .	. . .	. . .	. . .	. . .	. . .	. . .	. . .	. . .
Banks	4 913	. .	. . .	. . .	. . .	. . .	. . .	. . .	. . .	. . .
Other sectors	4 914	. .	. . .	. . .	. . .	. . .	. . .	. . .	. . .	. . .
Assets	4 900	. .	**. . .**	**. . .**	**. . .**	**. . .**	**. . .**	**. . .**	**. . .**	**. . .**
Monetary authorities	4 901	. .	. . .	. . .	. . .	. . .	. . .	. . .	. . .	. . .
General government	4 902	. .	. . .	. . .	. . .	. . .	. . .	. . .	. . .	. . .
Banks	4 903	. .	. . .	. . .	. . .	. . .	. . .	. . .	. . .	. . .
Other sectors	4 904	. .	. . .	. . .	. . .	. . .	. . .	. . .	. . .	. . .
Liabilities	4 905	. .	**. . .**	**. . .**	**. . .**	**. . .**	**. . .**	**. . .**	**. . .**	**. . .**
Monetary authorities	4 906	. .	. . .	. . .	. . .	. . .	. . .	. . .	. . .	. . .
General government	4 907	. .	. . .	. . .	. . .	. . .	. . .	. . .	. . .	. . .
Banks	4 908	. .	. . .	. . .	. . .	. . .	. . .	. . .	. . .	. . .
Other sectors	4 909	. .	. . .	. . .	. . .	. . .	. . .	. . .	. . .	. . .

Table 2 (Concluded). STANDARD PRESENTATION, 1994–2001 YEARS BEGINNING MARCH 21

(Millions of U.S. dollars)

	Code	1994	1995	1996	1997	1998	1999	2000	2001
D. OTHER INVESTMENT	4 700	–348	–791	–5,534	–4,875	2,246	–5,929	–10,228	. . .
Assets	4 703	**–1,258**	**–419**	**–1,305**	**2,293**	**963**	**–1,650**	**–8,257**	**. . .**
Trade credits	4 706	. . .	. . .	. . .	. . .	. . .	. . .	. . .	. . .
General government	4 707	. . .	. . .	. . .	. . .	. . .	. . .	. . .	. . .
of which: Short-term	4 709	. . .	. . .	. . .	. . .	. . .	. . .	. . .	. . .
Other sectors	4 710	. . .	. . .	. . .	. . .	. . .	. . .	. . .	. . .
of which: Short-term	4 712	. . .	. . .	. . .	. . .	. . .	. . .	. . .	. . .
Loans	4 714	–42	235	–48	–99	–21	–12	12	. . .
Monetary authorities	4 715	. . .	. . .	. . .	. . .	. . .	. . .	. . .	. . .
of which: Short-term	4 718	. . .	. . .	. . .	. . .	. . .	. . .	. . .	. . .
General government	4 719	–42	235	–48	–99	–21	–6	12	. . .
of which: Short-term	4 721	. . .	. . .	. . .	. . .	. . .	. . .	. . .	. . .
Banks	4 722	. . .	. . .	. . .	. . .	. . .	. . .	. . .	. . .
of which: Short-term	4 724	. . .	. . .	. . .	. . .	. . .	. . .	. . .	. . .
Other sectors	4 725	. . .	. . .	. . .	. . .	. . .	–6	. . .	. . .
of which: Short-term	4 727	. . .	. . .	. . .	. . .	. . .	. . .	. . .	. . .
Currency and deposits	4 730	–1,216	–654	–1,257	2,392	984	–1,638	–7,727	. . .
Monetary authorities	4 731	. . .	. . .	. . .	. . .	. . .	. . .	. . .	. . .
General government	4 732	. . .	. . .	. . .	. . .	. . .	. . .	–5,944	. . .
Banks	4 733	–1,216	–654	–1,257	2,392	984	–1,638	–1,783	. . .
Other sectors	4 734	. . .	. . .	. . .	. . .	. . .	. . .	. . .	. . .
Other assets	4 736	. . .	. . .	. . .	. . .	. . .	. . .	–542	. . .
Monetary authorities	4 737	. . .	. . .	. . .	. . .	. . .	. . .	. . .	. . .
of which: Short-term	4 739	. . .	. . .	. . .	. . .	. . .	. . .	. . .	. . .
General government	4 740	. . .	. . .	. . .	. . .	. . .	. . .	. . .	. . .
of which: Short-term	4 742	. . .	. . .	. . .	. . .	. . .	. . .	. . .	. . .
Banks	4 743	. . .	. . .	. . .	. . .	. . .	. . .	. . .	. . .
of which: Short-term	4 745	. . .	. . .	. . .	. . .	. . .	. . .	. . .	. . .
Other sectors	4 746	. . .	. . .	. . .	. . .	. . .	. . .	–542	. . .
of which: Short-term	4 748	. . .	. . .	. . .	. . .	. . .	. . .	. . .	. . .
Liabilities	4 753	**910**	**–372**	**–4,229**	**–7,168**	**1,283**	**–4,279**	**–1,971**	**. . .**
Trade credits	4 756	1,203	–637	–4,525	–6,751	1,484	565	637	. . .
General government	4 757	10,488	1,362	–5,114	–3,450	–206	–569	577	. . .
of which: Short-term	4 759	. . .	. . .	. . .	. . .	. . .	*–130*	*232*	. . .
Other sectors	4 760	–9,285	–1,999	589	–3,301	1,690	1,134	60	. . .
of which: Short-term	4 762	*–9,285*	*–1,999*	*589*	*–3,301*	*1,690*	*1,134*	*60*	. . .
Loans	4 764	–31	–157	–110	–209	–294	–5,350	–2,608	. . .
Monetary authorities	4 765	. . .	. . .	. . .	. . .	. . .	–5,517	–1,410	. . .
of which: Use of Fund credit and loans from the Fund	4 766	. . .	. . .	. . .	. . .	. . .	. . .	. . .	. . .
of which: Short-term	4 768	. . .	. . .	. . .	. . .	. . .	*–2,424*	*–144*	. . .
General government	4 769	–31	–164	–98	–198	–283	167	–1,198	. . .
of which: Short-term	4 771	. . .	. . .	. . .	. . .	. . .	. . .	. . .	. . .
Banks	4 772	. . .	. . .	. . .	. . .	. . .	. . .	. . .	. . .
of which: Short-term	4 774	. . .	. . .	. . .	. . .	. . .	. . .	. . .	. . .
Other sectors	4 775	. . .	7	–12	–11	–11	. . .	. . .	. . .
of which: Short-term	4 777	. . .	. . .	. . .	. . .	. . .	. . .	. . .	. . .
Currency and deposits	4 780	. . .	. . .	. . .	. . .	. . .	. . .	. . .	. . .
Monetary authorities	4 781	. . .	. . .	. . .	. . .	. . .	. . .	. . .	. . .
General government	4 782	. . .	. . .	. . .	. . .	. . .	. . .	. . .	. . .
Banks	4 783	. . .	. . .	. . .	. . .	. . .	. . .	. . .	. . .
Other sectors	4 784	. . .	. . .	. . .	. . .	. . .	. . .	. . .	. . .
Other liabilities	4 786	–262	422	406	–208	93	506	. . .	. . .
Monetary authorities	4 787	–252	–64	–283	179	93	. . .	. . .	. . .
of which: Short-term	4 789	*–252*	*–64*	*–283*	*179*	*93*	. . .	. . .	. . .
General government	4 790	–10	486	689	–387	. . .	506	. . .	. . .
of which: Short-term	4 792	*–10*	*486*	*689*	*–387*	. . .	*506*	. . .	. . .
Banks	4 793	. . .	. . .	. . .	. . .	. . .	. . .	. . .	. . .
of which: Short-term	4 795	. . .	. . .	. . .	. . .	. . .	. . .	. . .	. . .
Other sectors	4 796	. . .	. . .	. . .	. . .	. . .	. . .	. . .	. . .
of which: Short-term	4 798	. . .	. . .	. . .	. . .	. . .	. . .	. . .	. . .
E. RESERVE ASSETS	4 802	–908	–2,786	–2,441	3,697	991	–451	–1,083	. . .
Monetary gold	4 812	–74	–593	–181	531	310	. . .	–10	. . .
Special drawing rights	4 811	10	12	–217	–7	325	–137	–221	. . .
Reserve position in the Fund	4 810	. . .	. . .	. . .	. . .	. . .	. . .	. . .	. . .
Foreign exchange	4 803	–680	–2,111	–2,342	3,688	189	–182	–871	. . .
Other claims	4 813	–164	–94	299	–515	167	–132	19	. . .
NET ERRORS AND OMISSIONS	4 998	**–3,702**	**202**	**2,717**	**–1,088**	**–1,122**	**–244**	**–1,373**	**. . .**

Part 3 of the *Yearbook* contains descriptions of the methodologies, compilation practices, and sources used to compile these data.

Table 1. ANALYTIC PRESENTATION, 1994–2001

(Millions of U.S. dollars)

	Code			1994	1995	1996	1997	1998	1999	2000	2001
A. Current Account [1]	4	993	Z.	**1,577**	**1,721**	**2,049**	**1,866**	**1,016**	**354**	**–593**	**–1,043**
Goods: exports f.o.b.	2	100	. .	33,642	44,423	49,184	55,293	78,562	68,540	73,433	78,371
Goods: imports f.o.b.	3	100	. .	–24,275	–30,866	–33,430	–36,668	–53,172	–44,284	–48,017	–48,369
Balance on Goods	4	100	. .	*9,366*	*13,557*	*15,754*	*18,625*	*25,390*	*24,256*	*25,416*	*30,003*
Services: credit	2	200	. .	4,319	5,017	5,749	6,186	16,735	15,522	16,788	20,194
Services: debit	3	200	. .	–8,452	–11,303	–13,448	–15,195	–29,626	–26,637	–28,745	–34,853
Balance on Goods and Services	4	991	. .	*5,233*	*7,270*	*8,055*	*9,616*	*12,499*	*13,142*	*13,459*	*15,344*
Income: credit	2	300	. .	3,513	5,110	5,576	7,353	25,430	24,442	29,973	28,697
Income: debit	3	300	. .	–8,919	–12,435	–13,772	–17,059	–38,800	–38,484	–44,974	–45,562
Balance on Goods, Services, and Income	4	992	. .	*–173*	*–55*	*–141*	*–90*	*–870*	*–899*	*–1,542*	*–1,520*
Current transfers: credit	2	379	Z.	2,850	3,009	3,538	3,083	7,428	5,308	4,304	4,295
Current transfers: debit	3	379	. .	–1,100	–1,233	–1,349	–1,128	–5,543	–4,055	–3,355	–3,818
B. Capital Account [1]	4	994	Z.	**387**	**817**	**785**	**871**	**1,218**	**593**	**1,097**	**598**
Capital account: credit	2	994	Z.	477	914	881	962	1,327	674	1,167	667
Capital account: debit	3	994	. .	–90	–96	–96	–91	–108	–81	–70	–69
Total, Groups A Plus B	4	981	. .	*1,964*	*2,538*	*2,833*	*2,736*	*2,234*	*947*	*504*	*–445*
C. Financial Account [1]	4	995	W.	**–3,963**	**–33**	**–2,780**	**–7,484**	**4,686**	**–3,893**	**8,901**	**37**
Direct investment abroad	4	505	. .	–438	–820	–727	–1,008	–4,955	–6,102	–3,983	–5,405
Direct investment in Ireland	4	555	Z.	838	1,447	2,618	2,743	11,035	18,615	22,778	9,865
Portfolio investment assets	4	602	. .	–1,019	–1,056	–183	–716	–66,738	–82,813	–78,817	–108,535
Equity securities	4	610	. .	. . .	. . .	. . .	. . .	–27,624	–36,357	–28,163	–23,886
Debt securities	4	619	. .	–1,019	–1,056	–183	–716	–39,114	–46,457	–50,654	–84,650
Portfolio investment liabilities	4	652	Z.	–379	771	982	–2,505	54,735	67,377	80,255	91,128
Equity securities	4	660	. .	. . .	. . .	. . .	. . .	47,948	52,061	67,533	78,250
Debt securities	4	669	Z.	–379	771	982	–2,505	6,787	15,316	12,721	12,878
Financial derivatives	4	910	. .	. . .	. . .	. . .	. . .	. . .	. . .	374	52
Financial derivatives assets	4	900	. .	. . .	. . .	. . .	. . .	. . .	. . .	416	–867
Financial derivatives liabilities	4	905	. .	. . .	. . .	. . .	. . .	. . .	. . .	–42	919
Other investment assets	4	703	. .	–4,483	–16,572	–22,162	–48,337	–25,211	–38,545	–41,048	–12,101
Monetary authorities	4	701	. .	. . .	. . .	. . .	. . .	. . .	. . .	3,311	–310
General government	4	704	. .	–76	76	. . .	. . .	. . .	. . .	–2,057	725
Banks	4	705	. .	–2,919	–14,083	–19,623	–43,421	. . .	. . .	–15,526	–6,779
Other sectors	4	728	. .	–1,489	–2,565	–2,539	–4,916	. . .	. . .	–26,776	–5,735
Other investment liabilities	4	753	W.	1,519	16,197	16,691	42,340	35,820	37,576	29,343	25,033
Monetary authorities	4	753	WA	. . .	. . .	. . .	. . .	. . .	. . .	165	1,111
General government	4	753	ZB	–1,585	–808	–947	–812	. . .	. . .	–135	–1
Banks	4	753	ZC	3,103	17,005	17,639	43,152	. . .	. . .	14,540	17,735
Other sectors	4	753	ZD	. . .	. . .	. . .	. . .	. . .	. . .	14,772	6,187
Total, Groups A Through C	4	983	. .	*–1,999*	*2,505*	*54*	*–4,748*	*6,920*	*–2,945*	*9,405*	*–408*
D. Net Errors and Omissions	4	998	. .	**1,823**	**–167**	**–106**	**3,639**	**–3,708**	**972**	**–9,284**	**803**
Total, Groups A Through D	4	984	. .	*–176*	*2,339*	*–52*	*–1,109*	*3,212*	*–1,973*	*121*	*395*
E. Reserves and Related Items	4	802	A.	**176**	**–2,339**	**52**	**1,109**	**–3,212**	**1,973**	**–121**	**–395**
Reserve assets	4	802	. .	176	–2,339	52	1,109	–3,212	1,973	–121	–395
Use of Fund credit and loans	4	766	. .	. . .	. . .	. . .	. . .	. . .	. . .	. . .	. . .
Exceptional financing	4	920	. .	. . .	. . .	. . .	. . .	. . .	. . .	. . .	. . .
Conversion rates: Irish pound per U.S. dollar	0	101	. .	**.66863**	**.62373**	**.62503**	**.65964**	**.70227**	**. . .**	**. . .**	**. . .**
Conversion rates: euros per U.S. dollar	0	103	. .	**. . .**	**. . .**	**. . .**	**. . .**	**. . .**	**.9386**	**1.0854**	**1.1175**

[1] Excludes components that have been classified in the categories of Group E.

Table 2. STANDARD PRESENTATION, 1994–2001

(Millions of U.S. dollars)

	Code	1994	1995	1996	1997	1998	1999	2000	2001
CURRENT ACCOUNT	4 993 . .	**1,577**	**1,721**	**2,049**	**1,866**	**1,016**	**354**	**–593**	**–1,043**
A. GOODS	4 100 . .	9,366	13,557	15,754	18,625	25,390	24,256	25,416	30,003
Credit	2 100 . .	**33,642**	**44,423**	**49,184**	**55,293**	**78,562**	**68,540**	**73,433**	**78,371**
General merchandise: exports f.o.b.	2 110 . .	33,642	44,423	49,184	55,293	78,562	68,540	73,433	78,371
Goods for processing: exports f.o.b.	2 150 . .	. . .	. . .	. . .	. . .	. . .	. . .	. . .	. . .
Repairs on goods	2 160 . .	. . .	. . .	. . .	. . .	. . .	. . .	. . .	. . .
Goods procured in ports by carriers	2 170 . .	. . .	. . .	. . .	. . .	. . .	. . .	. . .	. . .
Nonmonetary gold	2 180 . .	. . .	. . .	. . .	. . .	. . .	. . .	. . .	. . .
Debit	3 100 . .	**–24,275**	**–30,866**	**–33,430**	**–36,668**	**–53,172**	**–44,284**	**–48,017**	**–48,369**
General merchandise: imports f.o.b.	3 110 . .	–24,263	–30,850	–33,415	–36,654	–53,172	–44,284	–48,017	–48,369
Goods for processing: imports f.o.b.	3 150 . .	. . .	. . .	. . .	. . .	. . .	. . .	. . .	. . .
Repairs on goods	3 160 . .	. . .	. . .	. . .	. . .	. . .	. . .	. . .	. . .
Goods procured in ports by carriers	3 170 . .	. . .	. . .	. . .	. . .	. . .	. . .	. . .	. . .
Nonmonetary gold	3 180 . .	–12	–16	–14	–14	. . .	. . .	. . .	. . .
B. SERVICES	4 200 . .	–4,133	–6,287	–7,699	–9,009	–12,890	–11,114	–11,957	–14,658
Total credit	2 200 . .	*4,319*	*5,017*	*5,749*	*6,186*	*16,735*	*15,522*	*16,788*	*20,194*
Total debit	3 200 . .	*–8,452*	*–11,303*	*–13,448*	*–15,195*	*–29,626*	*–26,637*	*–28,745*	*–34,853*
Transportation services, credit	2 205 . .	**975**	**1,067**	**1,130**	**1,148**	**1,651**	**1,329**	**1,355**	**1,487**
Passenger	2 850 . .	*444*	*487*	*552*	*603*	. . .	*782*	*883*	*997*
Freight	2 851 . .	*26*	*34*	*35*	*33*	. . .	*142*	*122*	*149*
Other	2 852 . .	*506*	*547*	*543*	*511*	. . .	*405*	*351*	*340*
Sea transport, passenger	2 207 . .	. . .	. . .	. . .	. . .	. . .	. . .	. . .	. . .
Sea transport, freight	2 208 . .	. . .	. . .	. . .	. . .	. . .	. . .	. . .	. . .
Sea transport, other	2 209 . .	. . .	. . .	. . .	. . .	. . .	. . .	. . .	. . .
Air transport, passenger	2 211 . .	. . .	. . .	. . .	. . .	. . .	. . .	. . .	. . .
Air transport, freight	2 212 . .	. . .	. . .	. . .	. . .	. . .	. . .	. . .	. . .
Air transport, other	2 213 . .	. . .	. . .	. . .	. . .	. . .	. . .	. . .	. . .
Other transport, passenger	2 215 . .	. . .	. . .	. . .	. . .	. . .	. . .	. . .	. . .
Other transport, freight	2 216 . .	. . .	. . .	. . .	. . .	. . .	. . .	. . .	. . .
Other transport, other	2 217 . .	. . .	. . .	. . .	. . .	. . .	. . .	. . .	. . .
Transportation services, debit	3 205 . .	**–1,461**	**–1,791**	**–1,891**	**–2,016**	**–2,967**	**–2,438**	**–2,578**	**–2,567**
Passenger	3 850 . .	. . .	. . .	. . .	. . .	. . .	*–81*	*–81*	*–78*
Freight	3 851 . .	*–1,021*	*–1,315*	*–1,421*	*–1,567*	. . .	*–2,013*	*–2,178*	*–2,180*
Other	3 852 . .	*–440*	*–476*	*–470*	*–449*	. . .	*–344*	*–319*	*–309*
Sea transport, passenger	3 207 . .	. . .	. . .	. . .	. . .	. . .	. . .	. . .	. . .
Sea transport, freight	3 208 . .	. . .	. . .	. . .	. . .	. . .	. . .	. . .	. . .
Sea transport, other	3 209 . .	. . .	. . .	. . .	. . .	. . .	. . .	. . .	. . .
Air transport, passenger	3 211 . .	. . .	. . .	. . .	. . .	. . .	. . .	. . .	. . .
Air transport, freight	3 212 . .	. . .	. . .	. . .	. . .	. . .	. . .	. . .	. . .
Air transport, other	3 213 . .	. . .	. . .	. . .	. . .	. . .	. . .	. . .	. . .
Other transport, passenger	3 215 . .	. . .	. . .	. . .	. . .	. . .	. . .	. . .	. . .
Other transport, freight	3 216 . .	. . .	. . .	. . .	. . .	. . .	. . .	. . .	. . .
Other transport, other	3 217 . .	. . .	. . .	. . .	. . .	. . .	. . .	. . .	. . .
Travel, credit	2 236 . .	**1,811**	**2,211**	**2,470**	**2,578**	**3,297**	**2,621**	**2,647**	**2,753**
Business travel	2 237 . .	. . .	. . .	. . .	. . .	. . .	. . .	. . .	. . .
Personal travel	2 240 . .	. . .	. . .	. . .	. . .	. . .	. . .	. . .	. . .
Travel, debit	3 236 . .	**–1,615**	**–2,034**	**–2,198**	**–2,210**	**–3,015**	**–2,631**	**–2,623**	**–2,869**
Business travel	3 237 . .	. . .	. . .	. . .	. . .	. . .	. . .	. . .	. . .
Personal travel	3 240 . .	. . .	. . .	. . .	. . .	. . .	. . .	. . .	. . .
Other services, credit	2 200 BA	**1,532**	**1,738**	**2,149**	**2,460**	**11,787**	**11,572**	**12,785**	**15,954**
Communications	2 245 . .	. . .	. . .	. . .	. . .	332	284	328	726
Construction	2 249 . .	. . .	. . .	. . .	. . .	. . .	. . .	. . .	. . .
Insurance	2 253 . .	. . .	. . .	. . .	. . .	1,668	990	1,119	1,353
Financial	2 260 . .	. . .	. . .	. . .	. . .	1,288	1,660	2,073	2,620
Computer and information	2 262 . .	. . .	. . .	. . .	. . .	5,313	5,622	5,479	6,535
Royalties and licence fees	2 266 . .	91	132	101	117	249	417	504	346
Other business services	2 268 . .	1,267	1,389	1,862	2,203	2,706	2,271	2,971	4,053
Personal, cultural, and recreational	2 287 . .	. . .	. . .	. . .	. . .	. . .	166	163	158
Government, n.i.e.	2 291 . .	174	218	187	140	231	162	149	162
Other services, debit	3 200 BA	**–5,376**	**–7,478**	**–9,359**	**–10,970**	**–23,643**	**–21,568**	**–23,544**	**–29,417**
Communications	3 245 . .	. . .	. . .	. . .	. . .	–243	–331	–342	–297
Construction	3 249 . .	. . .	. . .	. . .	. . .	. . .	–21	–18	–18
Insurance	3 253 . .	–123	–159	–171	–189	–1,537	–1,421	–1,460	–1,574
Financial	3 260 . .	. . .	. . .	. . .	. . .	–1,363	–1,258	–1,446	–1,645
Computer and information	3 262 . .	. . .	. . .	. . .	. . .	–360	–282	–275	–335
Royalties and licence fees	3 266 . .	–1,917	–2,724	–3,418	–4,090	–7,935	–7,346	–7,899	–8,770
Other business services	3 268 . .	–3,288	–4,544	–5,738	–6,653	–12,039	–10,816	–12,039	–16,678
Personal, cultural, and recreational	3 287 . .	. . .	. . .	. . .	. . .	. . .	–32	–11	–11
Government, n.i.e.	3 291 . .	–48	–51	–32	–36	–167	–60	–53	–89

Table 2 (Continued). STANDARD PRESENTATION, 1994–2001
(Millions of U.S. dollars)

	Code	1994	1995	1996	1997	1998	1999	2000	2001
C. INCOME	4 300 . .	–5,406	–7,325	–8,196	–9,706	–13,369	–14,041	–15,002	–16,864
Total credit	2 300 . .	*3,513*	*5,110*	*5,576*	*7,353*	*25,430*	*24,442*	*29,973*	*28,697*
Total debit	3 300 . .	*–8,919*	*–12,435*	*–13,772*	*–17,059*	*–38,800*	*–38,484*	*–44,974*	*–45,562*
Compensation of employees, credit	2 310 . .	**324**	**347**	**362**	**314**	**274**	**295**	**255**	**238**
Compensation of employees, debit	3 310 . .	**–72**	**–77**	**–83**	**–79**	**–166**	**–120**	**–105**	**–228**
Investment income, credit	2 320 . .	**3,189**	**4,763**	**5,214**	**7,039**	**25,157**	**24,147**	**29,718**	**28,460**
Direct investment income	2 330 . .	444	891	764	1,014	3,621	2,984	3,036	3,504
Dividends and distributed branch profits	2 332 . .	6	71	37	6	165	59	466	291
Reinvested earnings and undistributed branch profits	2 333 . .	438	820	727	1,008	2,173	1,865	1,300	1,978
Income on debt (interest)	2 334 . .	. . .	. . .	. . .	. . .	1,284	1,060	1,269	1,236
Portfolio investment income	2 339 . .	. . .	. . .	. . .	. . .	5,143	5,943	6,762	9,584
Income on equity	2 340 . .	. . .	. . .	. . .	. . .	1,431	1,193	1,075	1,714
Income on bonds and notes	2 350 . .	. . .	. . .	. . .	. . .	. . .	. . .	3,893	4,878
Income on money market instruments	2 360 . .	. . .	. . .	. . .	. . .	. . .	. . .	1,793	2,993
Other investment income	2 370 . .	2,746	3,872	4,450	6,024	16,393	15,220	19,920	15,371
Investment income, debit	3 320 . .	**–8,847**	**–12,358**	**–13,689**	**–16,980**	**–38,633**	**–38,363**	**–44,869**	**–45,333**
Direct investment income	3 330 . .	–5,645	–8,334	–9,324	–11,219	–22,054	–22,834	–24,251	–25,260
Dividends and distributed branch profits	3 332 . .	–4,801	–6,328	–7,128	–9,090	–15,026	–12,427	–12,239	–13,788
Reinvested earnings and undistributed branch profits	3 333 . .	–844	–2,006	–2,196	–2,129	–6,113	–9,583	–10,818	–10,428
Income on debt (interest)	3 334 . .	. . .	. . .	. . .	. . .	–915	–823	–1,194	–1,044
Portfolio investment income	3 339 . .	. . .	. . .	. . .	. . .	–6,389	–6,240	–9,588	–10,215
Income on equity	3 340 . .	. . .	. . .	. . .	. . .	–3,216	–3,373	–4,231	–5,456
Income on bonds and notes	3 350 . .	. . .	. . .	. . .	. . .	. . .	. . .	–4,954	–2,260
Income on money market instruments	3 360 . .	. . .	. . .	. . .	. . .	. . .	. . .	–403	–2,499
Other investment income	3 370 . .	–3,203	–4,024	–4,365	–5,761	–10,191	–9,289	–11,030	–9,858
D. CURRENT TRANSFERS	4 379 . .	1,750	1,776	2,189	1,956	1,886	1,253	949	477
Credit	2 379 . .	**2,850**	**3,009**	**3,538**	**3,083**	**7,428**	**5,308**	**4,304**	**4,295**
General government	2 380 . .	587	584	588	608	792	421	305	204
Other sectors	2 390 . .	2,263	2,425	2,951	2,475	6,636	4,887	3,999	4,091
Workers' remittances	2 391 . .	. . .	. . .	. . .	. . .	. . .	. . .	55	54
Other current transfers	2 392 . .	2,263	2,425	2,951	2,475	. . .	. . .	3,943	4,037
Debit	3 379 . .	**–1,100**	**–1,233**	**–1,349**	**–1,128**	**–5,543**	**–4,055**	**–3,355**	**–3,818**
General government	3 380 . .	–311	–335	–545	–415	–781	–594	–548	–660
Other sectors	3 390 . .	–789	–898	–804	–712	–4,761	–3,460	–2,806	–3,158
Workers' remittances	3 391 . .	. . .	. . .	. . .	. . .	. . .	. . .	–4	–4
Other current transfers	3 392 . .	–789	–898	–804	–712	. . .	. . .	–2,802	–3,154
CAPITAL AND FINANCIAL ACCOUNT	4 996 . .	**–3,400**	**–1,554**	**–1,943**	**–5,505**	**2,692**	**–1,326**	**9,877**	**240**
CAPITAL ACCOUNT	4 994 . .	**387**	**817**	**785**	**871**	**1,218**	**593**	**1,097**	**598**
Total credit	2 994 . .	*477*	*914*	*881*	*962*	*1,327*	*674*	*1,167*	*667*
Total debit	3 994 . .	*–90*	*–96*	*–96*	*–91*	*–108*	*–81*	*–70*	*–69*
Capital transfers, credit	2 400 . .	**477**	**914**	**881**	**962**	**. . .**	**. . .**	**654**	**611**
General government	2 401 . .	471	907	874	956	. . .	. . .	651	607
Debt forgiveness	2 402 . .	. . .	. . .	. . .	. . .	. . .	. . .	. . .	. . .
Other capital transfers	2 410 . .	471	907	874	956	. . .	. . .	651	607
Other sectors	2 430 . .	6	6	6	6	. . .	. . .	4	4
Migrants' transfers	2 431 . .	. . .	. . .	. . .	. . .	. . .	. . .	. . .	. . .
Debt forgiveness	2 432 . .	. . .	. . .	. . .	. . .	. . .	. . .	. . .	. . .
Other capital transfers	2 440 . .	6	6	6	6	. . .	. . .	4	4
Capital transfers, debit	3 400 . .	**–90**	**–96**	**–96**	**–91**	**. . .**	**. . .**	**–70**	**–68**
General government	3 401 . .	. . .	. . .	. . .	. . .	. . .	. . .	. . .	. . .
Debt forgiveness	3 402 . .	. . .	. . .	. . .	. . .	. . .	. . .	. . .	. . .
Other capital transfers	3 410 . .	. . .	. . .	. . .	. . .	. . .	. . .	. . .	. . .
Other sectors	3 430 . .	–90	–96	–96	–91	. . .	. . .	–70	–68
Migrants' transfers	3 431 . .	–90	–96	–96	–91	. . .	. . .	–70	–68
Debt forgiveness	3 432 . .	. . .	. . .	. . .	. . .	. . .	. . .	. . .	. . .
Other capital transfers	3 440 . .	. . .	. . .	. . .	. . .	. . .	. . .	. . .	. . .
Nonproduced nonfinancial assets, credit	2 480 . .	**. . .**	**. . .**	**. . .**	**. . .**	**. . .**	**. . .**	**513**	**56**
Nonproduced nonfinancial assets, debit	3 480 . .	**. . .**	**. . .**	**. . .**	**. . .**	**. . .**	**. . .**	**. . .**	**–1**

Table 2 (Continued). STANDARD PRESENTATION, 1994–2001

(Millions of U.S. dollars)

	Code	1994	1995	1996	1997	1998	1999	2000	2001
FINANCIAL ACCOUNT	4 995 . .	**–3,787**	**–2,372**	**–2,727**	**–6,376**	**1,474**	**–1,919**	**8,780**	**–359**
A. DIRECT INVESTMENT	4 500 . .	401	627	1,891	1,735	6,080	12,514	18,795	4,460
Direct investment abroad	4 505 . .	**–438**	**–820**	**–727**	**–1,008**	**–4,955**	**–6,102**	**–3,983**	**–5,405**
Equity capital	4 510 . .	...	...	...	...	–1,290	–4,778	–3,254	–3,761
Claims on affiliated enterprises	4 515 . .	...	...	...	...	...	...	–3,304	–3,799
Liabilities to affiliated enterprises	4 520 . .	...	...	...	...	...	...	50	38
Reinvested earnings	4 525 . .	–438	–820	–727	–1,008	–2,173	–1,865	–1,300	–1,978
Other capital	4 530 . .	...	...	...	...	–1,492	542	571	334
Claims on affiliated enterprises	4 535 . .	...	...	...	...	...	...	534	–27
Liabilities to affiliated enterprises	4 540 . .	...	...	...	...	...	...	37	361
Direct investment in Ireland	4 555 . .	**838**	**1,447**	**2,618**	**2,743**	**11,035**	**18,615**	**22,778**	**9,865**
Equity capital	4 560 . .	...	...	...	...	8,293	7,699	12,127	5,343
Claims on direct investors	4 565 . .	...	...	...	...	...	...	–7,854	–2
Liabilities to direct investors	4 570 . .	...	...	...	...	...	...	19,981	5,345
Reinvested earnings	4 575 . .	844	2,006	2,196	2,129	6,113	9,583	10,818	10,428
Other capital	4 580 . .	–6	–560	422	614	–3,372	1,332	–168	–5,905
Claims on direct investors	4 585 . .	...	...	...	...	...	...	–1,350	–1,149
Liabilities to direct investors	4 590 . .	...	...	...	...	...	...	1,182	–4,756
B. PORTFOLIO INVESTMENT	4 600 . .	–1,399	–285	799	–3,221	–12,003	–15,437	1,437	–17,408
Assets	4 602 . .	**–1,019**	**–1,056**	**–183**	**–716**	**–66,738**	**–82,813**	**–78,817**	**–108,535**
Equity securities	4 610 . .	...	...	...	...	–27,624	–36,357	–28,163	–23,886
Monetary authorities	4 611 . .	...	...	...	...	...	...	...	...
General government	4 612 . .	...	...	...	...	...	...	...	...
Banks	4 613 . .	...	...	...	...	...	...	–23	–798
Other sectors	4 614 . .	...	...	...	...	...	...	–28,141	–23,088
Debt securities	4 619 . .	–1,019	–1,056	–183	–716	–39,114	–46,457	–50,654	–84,650
Bonds and notes	4 620 . .	–1,019	–1,056	–183	–716	–25,434	–31,861	–34,933	–45,262
Monetary authorities	4 621 . .	...	...	...	...	...	...	–119	–217
General government	4 622 . .	...	...	...	...	...	...	...	...
Banks	4 623 . .	...	...	...	...	...	...	–12,370	–17,219
Other sectors	4 624 . .	–1,019	–1,056	–183	–716	...	...	–22,444	–27,826
Money market instruments	4 630 . .	...	...	...	...	–13,680	–14,595	–15,721	–39,387
Monetary authorities	4 631 . .	...	...	...	...	...	...	–18	...
General government	4 632 . .	...	...	...	...	...	...	...	...
Banks	4 633 . .	...	...	...	...	...	...	–713	–17,585
Other sectors	4 634 . .	...	...	...	...	...	...	–14,989	–21,803
Liabilities	4 652 . .	**–379**	**771**	**982**	**–2,505**	**54,735**	**67,377**	**80,255**	**91,128**
Equity securities	4 660 . .	...	...	...	...	47,948	52,061	67,533	78,250
Banks	4 663 . .	...	...	...	...	...	...	1,003	15,826
Other sectors	4 664 . .	...	...	...	...	...	...	66,531	62,424
Debt securities	4 669 . .	–379	771	982	–2,505	6,787	15,316	12,721	12,878
Bonds and notes	4 670 . .	–379	771	982	–2,505	2,525	7,861	4,241	1,159
Monetary authorities	4 671 . .	...	...	...	...	...	...	...	...
General government	4 672 . .	–379	771	982	–2,505	...	...	1,959	309
Banks	4 673 . .	...	...	...	...	...	...	802	2,889
Other sectors	4 674 . .	...	...	...	...	...	...	1,480	–2,039
Money market instruments	4 680 . .	...	...	...	...	4,263	7,455	8,480	11,719
Monetary authorities	4 681 . .	...	...	...	...	...	...	...	...
General government	4 682 . .	...	...	...	...	...	...	–345	4,536
Banks	4 683 . .	...	...	...	...	...	...	7,377	9,483
Other sectors	4 684 . .	...	...	...	...	...	...	1,447	–2,299
C. FINANCIAL DERIVATIVES	4 910 . .	...	...	...	...	...	...	374	52
Monetary authorities	4 911 . .	...	...	...	...	...	...	...	...
General government	4 912 . .	...	...	...	...	...	...	–91	–32
Banks	4 913 . .	...	...	...	...	...	...	294	424
Other sectors	4 914 . .	...	...	...	...	...	...	171	–340
Assets	4 900 . .	**...**	**...**	**...**	**...**	**...**	**...**	**416**	**–867**
Monetary authorities	4 901 . .	...	...	...	...	...	...	...	...
General government	4 902 . .	...	...	...	...	...	...	–91	–32
Banks	4 903 . .	...	...	...	...	...	...	294	–440
Other sectors	4 904 . .	...	...	...	...	...	...	213	–395
Liabilities	4 905 . .	**...**	**...**	**...**	**...**	**...**	**...**	**–42**	**919**
Monetary authorities	4 906 . .	...	...	...	...	...	...	...	...
General government	4 907 . .	...	...	...	...	...	...	...	...
Banks	4 908 . .	...	...	...	...	...	...	...	864
Other sectors	4 909 . .	...	...	...	...	...	...	–42	54

Table 2 (Concluded). STANDARD PRESENTATION, 1994–2001
(Millions of U.S. dollars)

	Code	1994	1995	1996	1997	1998	1999	2000	2001
D. OTHER INVESTMENT	4 700	–2,964	–375	–5,470	–5,998	10,609	–969	–11,705	12,932
Assets	4 703	**–4,483**	**–16,572**	**–22,162**	**–48,337**	**–25,211**	**–38,545**	**–41,048**	**–12,101**
Trade credits	4 706	...	...	...	...	...	...	–2,437	–3,657
General government	4 707	...	...	...	...	...	...	170	...
of which: Short-term	4 709	...	...	...	...	...	...	*170*	...
Other sectors	4 710	...	...	...	...	...	...	–2,606	–3,657
of which: Short-term	4 712	...	...	...	...	...	...	*–1,777*	*–3,711*
Loans	4 714	...	...	...	...	...	...	–36,803	–12,340
Monetary authorities	4 715	...	...	...	...	...	...	...	...
of which: Short-term	4 718	...	...	...	...	...	...	...	...
General government	4 719	...	...	...	...	...	...	–2,250	–1,773
of which: Short-term	4 721	...	...	...	...	...	...	*–2,250*	*–1,773*
Banks	4 722	...	...	...	...	...	...	–13,761	–6,082
of which: Short-term	4 724	...	...	...	...	...	...	...	*–2,897*
Other sectors	4 725	...	...	...	...	...	...	–20,793	–4,484
of which: Short-term	4 727	...	...	...	...	...	...	*–6,933*	*–873*
Currency and deposits	4 730	–2,994	–14,008	–19,623	–43,421	...	...	1,400	5,306
Monetary authorities	4 731	...	...	...	...	...	...	3,308	–310
General government	4 732	–76	76	...	...	...	...	22	2,498
Banks	4 733	–2,919	–14,083	–19,623	–43,421	...	...	6	–30
Other sectors	4 734	...	...	...	...	...	...	–1,937	3,148
Other assets	4 736	–1,489	–2,565	–2,539	–4,916	...	...	–3,209	–1,410
Monetary authorities	4 737	...	...	...	...	...	...	3	...
of which: Short-term	4 739	...	...	...	...	...	...	*3*	...
General government	4 740	...	...	...	...	...	...	...	...
of which: Short-term	4 742	...	...	...	...	...	...	...	...
Banks	4 743	...	...	...	...	...	...	–1,771	–667
of which: Short-term	4 745	...	...	...	...	...	...	*–945*	*–279*
Other sectors	4 746	–1,489	–2,565	–2,539	–4,916	...	...	–1,440	–743
of which: Short-term	4 748	...	...	...	...	...	...	*–1,431*	*–1,200*
Liabilities	4 753	**1,519**	**16,197**	**16,691**	**42,340**	**35,820**	**37,576**	**29,343**	**25,033**
Trade credits	4 756	...	...	...	...	...	...	3,066	1,665
General government	4 757	...	...	...	...	...	...	–8	...
of which: Short-term	4 759	...	...	...	...	...	...	*–8*	...
Other sectors	4 760	...	...	...	...	...	...	3,075	1,665
of which: Short-term	4 762	...	...	...	...	...	...	*1,721*	*1,669*
Loans	4 764	–1,579	–795	–932	–801	...	...	28,106	20,508
Monetary authorities	4 765	...	...	...	...	...	...	...	...
of which: Use of Fund credit and loans from the Fund	4 766	...	...	...	...	...	...	...	...
of which: Short-term	4 768	...	...	...	...	...	...	...	...
General government	4 769	–1,579	–795	–932	–801	...	...	–126	–1
of which: Short-term	4 771	...	...	...	...	...	...	*–18*	*90*
Banks	4 772	...	...	...	...	...	...	14,915	17,669
of which: Short-term	4 774	...	...	...	...	...	...	...	*9,667*
Other sectors	4 775	...	...	...	...	...	...	13,317	2,839
of which: Short-term	4 777	...	...	...	...	...	...	*–627*	*2,849*
Currency and deposits	4 780	3,103	17,005	17,639	43,152	...	...	–50	2,269
Monetary authorities	4 781	...	...	...	...	...	...	...	1,117
General government	4 782	...	...	...	...	...	...	...	...
Banks	4 783	3,103	17,005	17,639	43,152	...	...	...	820
Other sectors	4 784	...	...	...	...	...	...	–50	332
Other liabilities	4 786	–6	–13	–16	–11	...	...	–1,779	591
Monetary authorities	4 787	...	...	...	...	...	...	165	–6
of which: Short-term	4 789	...	...	...	...	...	...	*165*	*–6*
General government	4 790	–6	–13	–16	–11	...	...	...	...
of which: Short-term	4 792	*–6*	*–13*	*–16*	*–11*	...	...	...	...
Banks	4 793	...	...	...	...	...	...	–375	–755
of which: Short-term	4 795	...	...	...	...	...	...	*–165*	*–273*
Other sectors	4 796	...	...	...	...	...	...	–1,569	1,351
of which: Short-term	4 798	...	...	...	...	...	...	*–1,569*	*1,346*
E. RESERVE ASSETS	4 802	176	–2,339	52	1,109	–3,212	1,973	–121	–395
Monetary gold	4 812	19	2	18	8	–40	72	–1	...
Special drawing rights	4 811	–7	–9	–11	–11	–19	149	–10	–8
Reserve position in the Fund	4 810	5	–69	–42	–35	–217	152	67	–20
Foreign exchange	4 803	159	–2,262	87	1,146	–2,925	1,613	–215	–367
Other claims	4 813	...	...	...	...	–11	–12	37	...
NET ERRORS AND OMISSIONS	4 998	**1,823**	**–167**	**–106**	**3,639**	**–3,708**	**972**	**–9,284**	**803**

Part 3 of the *Yearbook* contains descriptions of the methodologies, compilation practices, and sources used to compile these data.

Table 1. ANALYTIC PRESENTATION, 1994–2001
(Millions of U.S. dollars)

	Code	1994	1995	1996	1997	1998	1999	2000	2001
A. Current Account[1]	4 993 Z.	**–3,447**	**–4,972**	**–5,498**	**–3,845**	**–1,325**	**–3,277**	**–1,974**	**–1,852**
Goods: exports f.o.b	2 100 . .	17,242	19,663	21,333	22,698	22,974	25,577	30,947	27,678
Goods: imports f.o.b	3 100 . .	–22,728	–26,890	–28,469	–27,875	–26,241	–30,041	–34,036	–30,942
Balance on Goods	4 100 . .	*–5,486*	*–7,227*	*–7,136*	*–5,177*	*–3,267*	*–4,464*	*–3,089*	*–3,264*
Services: credit	2 200 . .	6,579	7,786	8,071	8,531	9,445	11,447	15,181	11,991
Services: debit	3 200 . .	–7,590	–8,401	–9,107	–9,288	–9,636	–10,708	–12,529	–12,563
Balance on Goods and Services	4 991 . .	*–6,497*	*–7,842*	*–8,173*	*–5,934*	*–3,457*	*–3,726*	*–437*	*–3,836*
Income: credit	2 300 . .	1,160	1,730	1,806	2,093	2,756	2,553	3,353	3,545
Income: debit	3 300 . .	–3,711	–4,533	–5,268	–6,053	–6,704	–8,420	–11,360	–7,959
Balance on Goods, Services, and Income	4 992 . .	*–9,048*	*–10,645*	*–11,635*	*–9,894*	*–7,405*	*–9,592*	*–8,443*	*–8,251*
Current transfers: credit	2 379 Z.	5,850	5,941	6,441	6,374	6,686	7,125	7,483	7,531
Current transfers: debit	3 379 . .	–250	–268	–304	–325	–606	–809	–1,015	–1,132
B. Capital Account[1]	4 994 Z.	**786**	**809**	**774**	**723**	**577**	**569**	**455**	**681**
Capital account: credit	2 994 Z.	786	809	774	723	577	569	455	681
Capital account: debit	3 994 . .	. . .	. . .	. . .	. . .	. . .	. . .	. . .	. . .
Total, Groups A Plus B	4 981 . .	*–2,662*	*–4,163*	*–4,724*	*–3,122*	*–748*	*–2,708*	*–1,519*	*–1,171*
C. Financial Account[1]	4 995 W.	**–959**	**4,217**	**4,535**	**7,238**	**–650**	**2,040**	**2,982**	**–110**
Direct investment abroad	4 505 . .	–742	–820	–815	–923	–1,125	–933	–2,859	–1,135
Direct investment in Israel	4 555 Z.	442	1,351	1,398	1,635	1,737	2,873	4,524	3,224
Portfolio investment assets	4 602 . .	–1,772	98	368	215	107	–830	–2,139	–1,199
Equity securities	4 610 . .	303	16	160	166	154	383	–1,538	–493
Debt securities	4 619 . .	–2,075	82	208	49	–47	–1,213	–601	–707
Portfolio investment liabilities	4 652 Z.	481	989	1,436	1,743	425	1,499	4,361	656
Equity securities	4 660 . .	469	991	1,440	1,719	476	1,500	4,397	664
Debt securities	4 669 Z.	13	–2	–4	25	–51	–1	–37	–8
Financial derivatives	4 910 . .	. . .	. . .	. . .	. . .	. . .	. . .	. . .	. . .
Financial derivatives assets	4 900 . .	. . .	. . .	. . .	. . .	. . .	. . .	. . .	. . .
Financial derivatives liabilities	4 905 . .	. . .	. . .	. . .	. . .	. . .	. . .	. . .	. . .
Other investment assets	4 703 . .	–1,063	–586	845	1,600	–2,152	–3,948	–2,854	–2,850
Monetary authorities	4 701 . .	. . .	. . .	. . .	. . .	. . .	. . .	. . .	. . .
General government	4 704 . .	–28	–1,230	864	–19	–13	–188	–142	–667
Banks	4 705 . .	–1,736	–216	–1,165	1,686	–1,808	–753	–1,198	–361
Other sectors	4 728 . .	701	860	1,146	–66	–332	–3,007	–1,513	–1,821
Other investment liabilities	4 753 W.	1,695	3,185	1,303	2,969	359	3,379	1,950	1,194
Monetary authorities	4 753 WA	. . .	. . .	. . .	. . .	. . .	. . .	. . .	. . .
General government	4 753 ZB	–64	215	77	–272	–307	–168	560	314
Banks	4 753 ZC	1,000	1,219	612	2,352	1,525	2,385	1,657	1,643
Other sectors	4 753 ZD	760	1,751	615	889	–859	1,162	–267	–763
Total, Groups A Through C	4 983 . .	*–3,620*	*54*	*–190*	*4,116*	*–1,398*	*–668*	*1,463*	*–1,281*
D. Net Errors and Omissions	4 998 . .	**1,510**	**426**	**1,396**	**2,960**	**1,305**	**677**	**–1,591**	**1,477**
Total, Groups A Through D	4 984 . .	*–2,111*	*480*	*1,206*	*7,077*	*–93*	*9*	*–128*	*196*
E. Reserves and Related Items	4 802 A.	**2,111**	**–480**	**–1,206**	**–7,077**	**93**	**–9**	**128**	**–196**
Reserve assets	4 802 . .	–124	–1,123	–3,413	–9,378	–1,880	–1,109	–597	170
Use of Fund credit and loans	4 766 . .	. . .	–101	–129	–31	. . .	. . .	. . .	. . .
Exceptional financing	4 920 . .	2,235	745	2,336	2,332	1,973	1,099	725	–366
Conversion rates: new sheqalim per U.S. dollar	0 101 . .	**3.0111**	**3.0113**	**3.1917**	**3.4494**	**3.8001**	**4.1397**	**4.0773**	**4.2057**

[1] Excludes components that have been classified in the categories of Group E.

Table 2. STANDARD PRESENTATION, 1994–2001

(Millions of U.S. dollars)

	Code	1994	1995	1996	1997	1998	1999	2000	2001
CURRENT ACCOUNT	4 993 . .	**–3,447**	**–4,972**	**–5,498**	**–3,845**	**–1,325**	**–3,277**	**–1,974**	**–1,852**
A. GOODS	4 100 . .	–5,486	–7,227	–7,136	–5,177	–3,267	–4,464	–3,089	–3,264
Credit	2 100 . .	**17,242**	**19,663**	**21,333**	**22,698**	**22,974**	**25,577**	**30,947**	**27,678**
General merchandise: exports f.o.b.	2 110 . .	17,150	19,562	21,226	22,583	22,863	25,449	30,726	27,602
Goods for processing: exports f.o.b.	2 150 . .	. . .	. . .	. . .	. . .	. . .	. . .	. . .	. . .
Repairs on goods	2 160 . .	. . .	. . .	. . .	. . .	. . .	. . .	. . .	. . .
Goods procured in ports by carriers	2 170 . .	91	101	107	115	111	127	221	77
Nonmonetary gold	2 180 . .	. . .	. . .	. . .	. . .	. . .	. . .	. . .	. . .
Debit	3 100 . .	**–22,728**	**–26,890**	**–28,469**	**–27,875**	**–26,241**	**–30,041**	**–34,036**	**–30,942**
General merchandise: imports f.o.b.	3 110 . .	–22,595	–26,721	–28,270	–27,690	–26,094	–29,874	–33,752	–30,690
Goods for processing: imports f.o.b.	3 150 . .	. . .	. . .	. . .	. . .	. . .	. . .	. . .	. . .
Repairs on goods	3 160 . .	. . .	. . .	. . .	. . .	. . .	. . .	. . .	. . .
Goods procured in ports by carriers	3 170 . .	–132	–169	–199	–186	–147	–167	–284	–252
Nonmonetary gold	3 180 . .	. . .	. . .	. . .	. . .	. . .	. . .	. . .	. . .
B. SERVICES	4 200 . .	–1,011	–615	–1,036	–757	–191	739	2,652	–573
Total credit	2 200 . .	*6,579*	*7,786*	*8,071*	*8,531*	*9,445*	*11,447*	*15,181*	*11,991*
Total debit	3 200 . .	*–7,590*	*–8,401*	*–9,107*	*–9,288*	*–9,636*	*–10,708*	*–12,529*	*–12,563*
Transportation services, credit	2 205 . .	**1,684**	**2,014**	**1,902**	**2,001**	**2,097**	**2,263**	**2,482**	**2,122**
Passenger	2 850 . .	*412*	*498*	*453*	*445*	*441*	*496*	*497*	*294*
Freight	2 851 . .	*1,045*	*1,210*	*1,182*	*1,205*	*1,298*	*1,407*	*1,633*	*1,519*
Other	2 852 . .	*227*	*306*	*267*	*351*	*357*	*360*	*351*	*310*
Sea transport, passenger	2 207 . .	. . .	. . .	. . .	. . .	. . .	. . .	. . .	. . .
Sea transport, freight	2 208 . .	921	1,058	1,023	1,042	1,134	1,252	1,478	1,398
Sea transport, other	2 209 . .	133	203	168	197	208	213	201	173
Air transport, passenger	2 211 . .	412	498	453	445	441	496	497	294
Air transport, freight	2 212 . .	125	152	159	164	164	155	156	120
Air transport, other	2 213 . .	64	73	79	120	122	116	116	113
Other transport, passenger	2 215 . .	. . .	. . .	. . .	. . .	. . .	. . .	. . .	. . .
Other transport, freight	2 216 . .	. . .	. . .	. . .	. . .	. . .	. . .	. . .	. . .
Other transport, other	2 217 . .	30	30	20	33	28	32	35	24
Transportation services, debit	3 205 . .	**–3,110**	**–3,730**	**–3,841**	**–3,913**	**–4,028**	**–4,291**	**–4,887**	**–4,475**
Passenger	3 850 . .	*–446*	*–506*	*–571*	*–669*	*–760*	*–845*	*–929*	*–1,022*
Freight	3 851 . .	*–1,239*	*–1,600*	*–1,663*	*–1,609*	*–1,634*	*–1,773*	*–2,032*	*–1,836*
Other	3 852 . .	*–1,425*	*–1,624*	*–1,606*	*–1,635*	*–1,635*	*–1,673*	*–1,925*	*–1,617*
Sea transport, passenger	3 207 . .	–5	–6	–6	–2	–6	–7	–7	–8
Sea transport, freight	3 208 . .	–1,169	–1,514	–1,580	–1,529	–1,554	–1,688	–1,938	–1,749
Sea transport, other	3 209 . .	–944	–1,102	–1,092	–1,114	–1,151	–1,202	–1,489	–1,262
Air transport, passenger	3 211 . .	–441	–500	–565	–667	–754	–838	–922	–1,014
Air transport, freight	3 212 . .	–70	–86	–83	–79	–80	–85	–94	–87
Air transport, other	3 213 . .	–472	–513	–508	–509	–470	–459	–422	–346
Other transport, passenger	3 215 . .	. . .	. . .	. . .	. . .	. . .	. . .	. . .	. . .
Other transport, freight	3 216 . .	. . .	. . .	. . .	. . .	. . .	. . .	. . .	. . .
Other transport, other	3 217 . .	–9	–9	–6	–12	–14	–12	–14	–9
Travel, credit	2 236 . .	**2,440**	**2,991**	**3,052**	**3,056**	**3,015**	**3,971**	**3,859**	**2,460**
Business travel	2 237 . .	. . .	. . .	. . .	. . .	. . .	. . .	. . .	. . .
Personal travel	2 240 . .	. . .	. . .	. . .	. . .	. . .	. . .	. . .	. . .
Travel, debit	3 236 . .	**–2,135**	**–2,120**	**–2,278**	**–2,283**	**–2,473**	**–2,566**	**–2,804**	**–2,945**
Business travel	3 237 . .	. . .	. . .	. . .	. . .	. . .	. . .	. . .	. . .
Personal travel	3 240 . .	. . .	. . .	. . .	. . .	. . .	. . .	. . .	. . .
Other services, credit	2 200 BA	**2,455**	**2,781**	**3,117**	**3,473**	**4,334**	**5,213**	**8,840**	**7,409**
Communications	2 245 . .	393	428	405	236	193	171	176	132
Construction	2 249 . .	36	41	67	114	138	163	182	233
Insurance	2 253 . .	12	18	13	15	17	18	17	13
Financial	2 260 . .	. . .	. . .	. . .	. . .	. . .	. . .	. . .	. . .
Computer and information	2 262 . .	. . .	. . .	. . .	. . .	. . .	. . .	. . .	. . .
Royalties and licence fees	2 266 . .	116	135	162	180	223	263	511	432
Other business services	2 268 . .	1,868	2,113	2,406	2,853	3,687	4,499	7,871	6,557
Personal, cultural, and recreational	2 287 . .	. . .	. . .	. . .	. . .	. . .	. . .	. . .	. . .
Government, n.i.e.	2 291 . .	30	47	64	75	76	99	83	41
Other services, debit	3 200 BA	**–2,345**	**–2,551**	**–2,989**	**–3,092**	**–3,135**	**–3,852**	**–4,838**	**–5,144**
Communications	3 245 . .	–273	–316	–296	–327	–209	–170	–232	–141
Construction	3 249 . .	–19	–25	–20	–13	. . .	. . .	. . .	. . .
Insurance	3 253 . .	–206	–241	–266	–292	–276	–340	–330	–313
Financial	3 260 . .	. . .	. . .	. . .	. . .	. . .	. . .	. . .	. . .
Computer and information	3 262 . .	. . .	. . .	. . .	. . .	. . .	. . .	. . .	. . .
Royalties and licence fees	3 266 . .	–148	–156	–184	–195	–213	–263	–357	–457
Other business services	3 268 . .	–1,521	–1,622	–2,032	–2,090	–2,238	–2,866	–3,721	–4,031
Personal, cultural, and recreational	3 287 . .	. . .	. . .	. . .	. . .	. . .	. . .	. . .	. . .
Government, n.i.e.	3 291 . .	–178	–192	–192	–175	–199	–213	–198	–202

Table 2 (Continued). STANDARD PRESENTATION, 1994–2001

(Millions of U.S. dollars)

	Code	1994	1995	1996	1997	1998	1999	2000	2001
C. INCOME	4 300	–2,551	–2,803	–3,462	–3,960	–3,948	–5,867	–8,006	–4,415
Total credit	2 300	*1,160*	*1,730*	*1,806*	*2,093*	*2,756*	*2,553*	*3,353*	*3,545*
Total debit	3 300	*–3,711*	*–4,533*	*–5,268*	*–6,053*	*–6,704*	*–8,420*	*–11,360*	*–7,959*
Compensation of employees, credit	2 310	**135**	**178**	**159**	**174**	**127**	**154**	**165**	**154**
Compensation of employees, debit	3 310	**–919**	**–1,408**	**–2,025**	**–2,400**	**–2,874**	**–3,092**	**–3,324**	**–2,983**
Investment income, credit	2 320	**1,025**	**1,552**	**1,647**	**1,919**	**2,630**	**2,399**	**3,188**	**3,391**
Direct investment income	2 330	28	91	87	120	25	92	92	115
Dividends and distributed branch profits	2 332	...	...	...	...	...	...	...	...
Reinvested earnings and undistributed branch profits	2 333	28	91	87	120	25	92	92	115
Income on debt (interest)	2 334	...	...	...	...	...	...	...	...
Portfolio investment income	2 339	...	...	...	...	...	...	...	...
Income on equity	2 340	...	...	...	...	...	...	...	...
Income on bonds and notes	2 350	...	...	...	...	...	...	...	...
Income on money market instruments	2 360	...	...	...	...	...	...	...	...
Other investment income	2 370	997	1,461	1,560	1,799	2,604	2,307	3,096	3,277
Investment income, debit	3 320	**–2,792**	**–3,126**	**–3,243**	**–3,654**	**–3,830**	**–5,328**	**–8,036**	**–4,977**
Direct investment income	3 330	–277	–161	–292	–456	–400	–1,528	–3,528	–986
Dividends and distributed branch profits	3 332	–240	–134	–265	–219	–348	–933	–1,850	–386
Reinvested earnings and undistributed branch profits	3 333	–37	–27	–27	–237	–52	–596	–1,678	–601
Income on debt (interest)	3 334	...	...	...	...	...	...	...	...
Portfolio investment income	3 339	...	...	...	...	...	...	...	...
Income on equity	3 340	...	...	...	...	...	...	...	...
Income on bonds and notes	3 350	...	...	...	...	...	...	...	...
Income on money market instruments	3 360	...	...	...	...	...	...	...	...
Other investment income	3 370	–2,515	–2,965	–2,951	–3,198	–3,430	–3,800	–4,508	–3,990
D. CURRENT TRANSFERS	4 379	5,600	5,673	6,137	6,049	6,080	6,316	6,469	6,399
Credit	2 379	**5,850**	**5,941**	**6,441**	**6,374**	**6,686**	**7,125**	**7,483**	**7,531**
General government	2 380	3,643	3,385	3,883	3,942	3,975	4,077	4,212	4,135
Other sectors	2 390	2,207	2,556	2,559	2,431	2,711	3,048	3,272	3,396
Workers' remittances	2 391	...	...	...	...	...	...	...	...
Other current transfers	2 392	2,207	2,556	2,559	2,431	2,711	3,048	3,272	3,396
Debit	3 379	**–250**	**–268**	**–304**	**–325**	**–606**	**–809**	**–1,015**	**–1,132**
General government	3 380	–38	–30	–32	–59	–59	–52	–86	–74
Other sectors	3 390	–211	–238	–272	–265	–547	–758	–928	–1,058
Workers' remittances	3 391	...	...	...	...	...	...	...	...
Other current transfers	3 392	–211	–238	–272	–265	–547	–758	–928	–1,058
CAPITAL AND FINANCIAL ACCOUNT	4 996	**1,938**	**4,546**	**4,102**	**885**	**20**	**2,600**	**3,565**	**376**
CAPITAL ACCOUNT	4 994	**786**	**809**	**774**	**723**	**577**	**569**	**455**	**681**
Total credit	2 994	*786*	*809*	*774*	*723*	*577*	*569*	*455*	*681*
Total debit	3 994	...	...	...	...	...	...	...	...
Capital transfers, credit	2 400	**786**	**809**	**774**	**723**	**577**	**569**	**455**	**681**
General government	2 401	186	200	198	176	180	163	161	162
Debt forgiveness	2 402	...	...	...	...	...	...	...	...
Other capital transfers	2 410	186	200	198	176	180	163	161	162
Other sectors	2 430	600	609	576	548	397	406	295	519
Migrants' transfers	2 431	1,467	1,590	1,619	1,757	1,336	1,386	895	233
Debt forgiveness	2 432	...	...	...	...	...	...	...	...
Other capital transfers	2 440	–867	–981	–1,043	–1,209	–939	–980	–600	286
Capital transfers, debit	3 400	...	...	...	...	...	...	...	...
General government	3 401	...	...	...	...	...	...	...	...
Debt forgiveness	3 402	...	...	...	...	...	...	...	...
Other capital transfers	3 410	...	...	...	...	...	...	...	...
Other sectors	3 430	...	...	...	...	...	...	...	...
Migrants' transfers	3 431	...	...	...	...	...	...	...	...
Debt forgiveness	3 432	...	...	...	...	...	...	...	...
Other capital transfers	3 440	...	...	...	...	...	...	...	...
Nonproduced nonfinancial assets, credit	2 480	...	...	...	...	...	...	...	...
Nonproduced nonfinancial assets, debit	3 480	...	...	...	...	...	...	...	...

Table 2 (Continued). STANDARD PRESENTATION, 1994–2001
(Millions of U.S. dollars)

	Code	1994	1995	1996	1997	1998	1999	2000	2001
FINANCIAL ACCOUNT	4 995 . .	**1,152**	**3,737**	**3,328**	**162**	**–557**	**2,031**	**3,110**	**–306**
A. DIRECT INVESTMENT	4 500 . .	–300	531	582	712	612	1,940	1,664	2,089
Direct investment abroad	4 505 . .	**–742**	**–820**	**–815**	**–923**	**–1,125**	**–933**	**–2,859**	**–1,135**
Equity capital	4 510 . .	–713	–376	–503	–241	–439	–387	–2,004	–317
Claims on affiliated enterprises	4 515 . .	. . .	. . .	. . .	. . .	. . .	. . .	. . .	. . .
Liabilities to affiliated enterprises	4 520 . .	. . .	. . .	. . .	. . .	. . .	. . .	. . .	. . .
Reinvested earnings	4 525 . .	–28	–91	–87	–120	–25	–92	–92	–115
Other capital	4 530 . .	. . .	–353	–225	–562	–661	–454	–763	–704
Claims on affiliated enterprises	4 535 . .	. . .	. . .	. . .	. . .	. . .	. . .	. . .	. . .
Liabilities to affiliated enterprises	4 540 . .	. . .	. . .	. . .	. . .	. . .	. . .	. . .	. . .
Direct investment in Israel	4 555 . .	**442**	**1,351**	**1,398**	**1,635**	**1,737**	**2,873**	**4,524**	**3,224**
Equity capital	4 560 . .	335	1,193	1,232	1,463	1,516	2,204	2,859	2,586
Claims on direct investors	4 565 . .	. . .	. . .	. . .	. . .	. . .	. . .	. . .	. . .
Liabilities to direct investors	4 570 . .	. . .	. . .	. . .	. . .	. . .	. . .	. . .	. . .
Reinvested earnings	4 575 . .	37	27	27	237	52	596	1,678	601
Other capital	4 580 . .	70	131	138	–65	169	74	–14	38
Claims on direct investors	4 585 . .	. . .	. . .	. . .	. . .	. . .	. . .	. . .	. . .
Liabilities to direct investors	4 590 . .	70	131	138	–65	169	74	–14	38
B. PORTFOLIO INVESTMENT	4 600 . .	944	1,831	4,140	4,290	2,505	1,768	2,947	–910
Assets	4 602 . .	**–1,772**	**98**	**368**	**215**	**107**	**–830**	**–2,139**	**–1,199**
Equity securities	4 610 . .	303	16	160	166	154	383	–1,538	–493
Monetary authorities	4 611 . .	. . .	. . .	. . .	. . .	. . .	. . .	. . .	. . .
General government	4 612 . .	. . .	. . .	. . .	. . .	. . .	. . .	. . .	. . .
Banks	4 613 . .	. . .	. . .	. . .	. . .	. . .	. . .	. . .	. . .
Other sectors	4 614 . .	303	16	160	166	154	383	–1,538	–493
Debt securities	4 619 . .	–2,075	82	208	49	–47	–1,213	–601	–707
Bonds and notes	4 620 . .	–512	138	116	–40	–255	–1,064	–1,265	–1,217
Monetary authorities	4 621 . .	. . .	. . .	. . .	. . .	. . .	. . .	. . .	. . .
General government	4 622 . .	43	41	34	29	26	22	19	17
Banks	4 623 . .	–555	97	83	80	–218	–568	–399	349
Other sectors	4 624 . .	. . .	. . .	. . .	–149	–63	–519	–885	–1,582
Money market instruments	4 630 . .	–1,563	–56	92	89	208	–149	663	510
Monetary authorities	4 631 . .	. . .	. . .	. . .	. . .	. . .	. . .	. . .	. . .
General government	4 632 . .	. . .	. . .	. . .	. . .	. . .	. . .	. . .	. . .
Banks	4 633 . .	. . .	. . .	. . .	. . .	. . .	. . .	. . .	. . .
Other sectors	4 634 . .	–1,563	–56	92	89	208	–149	663	510
Liabilities	4 652 . .	**2,716**	**1,734**	**3,772**	**4,075**	**2,399**	**2,598**	**5,086**	**290**
Equity securities	4 660 . .	469	991	1,440	1,719	476	1,500	4,397	664
Banks	4 663 . .	. . .	. . .	. . .	. . .	. . .	. . .	. . .	. . .
Other sectors	4 664 . .	469	991	1,440	1,719	476	1,500	4,397	664
Debt securities	4 669 . .	2,248	743	2,332	2,357	1,923	1,098	688	–374
Bonds and notes	4 670 . .	2,248	743	2,332	2,357	1,923	1,098	688	–374
Monetary authorities	4 671 . .	19	11	–2	32	2	–40	15	–4
General government	4 672 . .	2,235	745	1,737	1,461	1,453	17	–43	–537
Banks	4 673	6	–8	–6	. . .	–9	–41	. . .	. . .
Other sectors	4 674 . .	. . .	–5	603	864	477	1,163	716	167
Money market instruments	4 680 . .	. . .	. . .	. . .	. . .	. . .	. . .	. . .	. . .
Monetary authorities	4 681 . .	. . .	. . .	. . .	. . .	. . .	. . .	. . .	. . .
General government	4 682 . .	. . .	. . .	. . .	. . .	. . .	. . .	. . .	. . .
Banks	4 683 . .	. . .	. . .	. . .	. . .	. . .	. . .	. . .	. . .
Other sectors	4 684 . .	. . .	. . .	. . .	. . .	. . .	. . .	. . .	. . .
C. FINANCIAL DERIVATIVES	4 910 . .	. . .	. . .	. . .	. . .	. . .	. . .	. . .	. . .
Monetary authorities	4 911 . .	. . .	. . .	. . .	. . .	. . .	. . .	. . .	. . .
General government	4 912 . .	. . .	. . .	. . .	. . .	. . .	. . .	. . .	. . .
Banks	4 913 . .	. . .	. . .	. . .	. . .	. . .	. . .	. . .	. . .
Other sectors	4 914 . .	. . .	. . .	. . .	. . .	. . .	. . .	. . .	. . .
Assets	4 900 . .	**. . .**	**. . .**	**. . .**	**. . .**	**. . .**	**. . .**	**. . .**	**. . .**
Monetary authorities	4 901 . .	. . .	. . .	. . .	. . .	. . .	. . .	. . .	. . .
General government	4 902 . .	. . .	. . .	. . .	. . .	. . .	. . .	. . .	. . .
Banks	4 903 . .	. . .	. . .	. . .	. . .	. . .	. . .	. . .	. . .
Other sectors	4 904 . .	. . .	. . .	. . .	. . .	. . .	. . .	. . .	. . .
Liabilities	4 905 . .	**. . .**	**. . .**	**. . .**	**. . .**	**. . .**	**. . .**	**. . .**	**. . .**
Monetary authorities	4 906 . .	. . .	. . .	. . .	. . .	. . .	. . .	. . .	. . .
General government	4 907 . .	. . .	. . .	. . .	. . .	. . .	. . .	. . .	. . .
Banks	4 908 . .	. . .	. . .	. . .	. . .	. . .	. . .	. . .	. . .
Other sectors	4 909 . .	. . .	. . .	. . .	. . .	. . .	. . .	. . .	. . .

Table 2 (Concluded). STANDARD PRESENTATION, 1994–2001
(Millions of U.S. dollars)

	Code	1994	1995	1996	1997	1998	1999	2000	2001
D. OTHER INVESTMENT	4 700 . .	632	2,498	2,019	4,538	–1,794	–569	–904	–1,655
Assets	4 703 . .	**–1,063**	**–586**	**845**	**1,600**	**–2,152**	**–3,948**	**–2,854**	**–2,850**
Trade credits	4 706 . .	–206	–136	90	–1,010	–1,035	–2,167	–358	1,104
General government	4 707 . .	. . .	. . .	. . .	. . .	. . .	. . .	. . .	. . .
of which: *Short-term*	4 709 . .	. . .	. . .	. . .	. . .	. . .	. . .	. . .	. . .
Other sectors	4 710 . .	–206	–136	90	–1,010	–1,035	–2,167	–358	1,104
of which: *Short-term*	4 712 . .	*–206*	*–136*	*90*	*–1,010*	*–1,035*	*–2,167*	*–358*	*1,104*
Loans	4 714 . .	–162	–294	–376	–266	–798	–463	–797	–1,235
Monetary authorities	4 715 . .	. . .	. . .	. . .	. . .	. . .	. . .	. . .	. . .
of which: *Short-term*	4 718 . .	. . .	. . .	. . .	. . .	. . .	. . .	. . .	. . .
General government	4 719 . .	. . .	. . .	. . .	. . .	. . .	. . .	. . .	. . .
of which: *Short-term*	4 721 . .	. . .	. . .	. . .	. . .	. . .	. . .	. . .	. . .
Banks	4 722 . .	–162	–294	–376	–266	–798	–463	–797	–1,235
of which: *Short-term*	4 724 . .	*–162*	*–294*	*–376*	*–266*	*–798*	*–463*	*–797*	*–1,235*
Other sectors	4 725 . .	. . .	. . .	. . .	. . .	. . .	. . .	. . .	. . .
of which: *Short-term*	4 727 . .	. . .	. . .	. . .	. . .	. . .	. . .	. . .	. . .
Currency and deposits	4 730 . .	–593	1,199	261	3,032	–234	–1,070	–1,602	–1,988
Monetary authorities	4 731 . .	. . .	. . .	. . .	. . .	. . .	. . .	. . .	. . .
General government	4 732 . .	. . .	. . .	. . .	. . .	. . .	. . .	. . .	. . .
Banks	4 733 . .	–1,574	78	–789	1,952	–1,010	–290	–401	874
Other sectors	4 734 . .	982	1,121	1,050	1,080	776	–780	–1,201	–2,862
Other assets	4 736 . .	–102	–1,355	871	–156	–85	–248	–96	–730
Monetary authorities	4 737 . .	. . .	. . .	. . .	. . .	. . .	. . .	. . .	. . .
of which: *Short-term*	4 739 . .	. . .	. . .	. . .	. . .	. . .	. . .	. . .	. . .
General government	4 740 . .	–28	–1,230	864	–19	–13	–188	–142	–667
of which: *Short-term*	4 742 . .	*–28*	*–1,230*	*864*	*–19*	*–13*	*–188*	*–142*	*–667*
Banks	4 743 . .	. . .	. . .	. . .	. . .	. . .	. . .	. . .	. . .
of which: *Short-term*	4 745 . .	. . .	. . .	. . .	. . .	. . .	. . .	. . .	. . .
Other sectors	4 746 . .	–75	–125	6	–137	–73	–60	46	–63
of which: *Short-term*	4 748 . .	*–75*	*–125*	*6*	*–137*	*–73*	*–60*	*46*	*–63*
Liabilities	4 753 . .	**1,695**	**3,084**	**1,173**	**2,938**	**359**	**3,379**	**1,950**	**1,194**
Trade credits	4 756 . .	–368	735	–444	–207	–1,134	931	–238	–732
General government	4 757 . .	. . .	. . .	. . .	. . .	. . .	. . .	. . .	. . .
of which: *Short-term*	4 759 . .	. . .	. . .	. . .	. . .	. . .	. . .	. . .	. . .
Other sectors	4 760 . .	–368	735	–444	–207	–1,134	931	–238	–732
of which: *Short-term*	4 762 . .	*–368*	*735*	*–444*	*–207*	*–1,134*	*931*	*–238*	*–732*
Loans	4 764 . .	1,063	1,130	1,006	793	–32	63	531	284
Monetary authorities	4 765 . .	. . .	–101	–129	–31	. . .	. . .	. . .	. . .
of which: *Use of Fund credit and loans from the Fund*	4 766 . .	. . .	*–101*	*–129*	*–31*	. . .	. . .	. . .	. . .
of which: *Short-term*	4 768 . .	. . .	. . .	. . .	. . .	. . .	. . .	. . .	. . .
General government	4 769 . .	–64	215	77	–272	–307	–168	560	314
of which: *Short-term*	4 771 . .	*42*	*19*	*–8*	*–49*	*–12*	*23*	. . .	. . .
Banks	4 772 . .	. . .	. . .	. . .	. . .	. . .	. . .	. . .	. . .
of which: *Short-term*	4 774 . .	. . .	. . .	. . .	. . .	. . .	. . .	. . .	. . .
Other sectors	4 775 . .	1,128	1,016	1,059	1,096	275	231	–29	–31
of which: *Short-term*	4 777 . .	*529*	*655*	*370*	*310*	*329*	*304*	*25*	*–140*
Currency and deposits	4 780 . .	1,000	1,219	612	2,352	1,525	2,385	1,657	1,643
Monetary authorities	4 781 . .	. . .	. . .	. . .	. . .	. . .	. . .	. . .	. . .
General government	4 782 . .	. . .	. . .	. . .	. . .	. . .	. . .	. . .	. . .
Banks	4 783 . .	1,000	1,219	612	2,352	1,525	2,385	1,657	1,643
Other sectors	4 784 . .	. . .	. . .	. . .	. . .	. . .	. . .	. . .	. . .
Other liabilities	4 786 . .	. . .	. . .	. . .	. . .	. . .	. . .	. . .	. . .
Monetary authorities	4 787 . .	. . .	. . .	. . .	. . .	. . .	. . .	. . .	. . .
of which: *Short-term*	4 789 . .	. . .	. . .	. . .	. . .	. . .	. . .	. . .	. . .
General government	4 790 . .	. . .	. . .	. . .	. . .	. . .	. . .	. . .	. . .
of which: *Short-term*	4 792 . .	. . .	. . .	. . .	. . .	. . .	. . .	. . .	. . .
Banks	4 793 . .	. . .	. . .	. . .	. . .	. . .	. . .	. . .	. . .
of which: *Short-term*	4 795 . .	. . .	. . .	. . .	. . .	. . .	. . .	. . .	. . .
Other sectors	4 796 . .	. . .	. . .	. . .	. . .	. . .	. . .	. . .	. . .
of which: *Short-term*	4 798 . .	. . .	. . .	. . .	. . .	. . .	. . .	. . .	. . .
E. RESERVE ASSETS	4 802 . .	–124	–1,123	–3,413	–9,378	–1,880	–1,109	–597	170
Monetary gold	4 812 . .	. . .	. . .	. . .	. . .	. . .	. . .	. . .	. . .
Special drawing rights	4 811 . .	. . .	. . .	–1	1	. . .	. . .	–1	–1
Reserve position in the Fund	4 810 . .	. . .	. . .	. . .	. . .	. . .	–90	–32	–85
Foreign exchange	4 803 . .	–125	–1,022	–3,283	–9,340	–1,872	–1,014	–564	257
Other claims	4 813 . .	. . .	–101	–129	–39	–9	–4	. . .	–1
NET ERRORS AND OMISSIONS	4 998 . .	**1,510**	**426**	**1,396**	**2,960**	**1,305**	**677**	**–1,591**	**1,477**

Part 3 of the *Yearbook* contains descriptions of the methodologies, compilation practices, and sources used to compile these data.

Table 3. INTERNATIONAL INVESTMENT POSITION (End–period stocks), 1994–2001

(Millions of U.S. dollars)

	Code	1994	1995	1996	1997	1998	1999	2000	2001
ASSETS	8 995 C.	26,345	30,754	34,751	44,556	50,468	56,967	65,271	68,990
Direct investment abroad	8 505 . .	**. . .**	**2,867**	**3,283**	**5,223**	**5,376**	**6,180**	**8,735**	**9,727**
Equity capital and reinvested earnings	8 506 . .	. . .	2,109	2,300	3,678	3,170	3,520	5,312	5,600
Claims on affiliated enterprises	8 507 . .	. . .	2,109	2,300	3,678	3,170	3,520	5,312	5,600
Liabilities to affiliated enterprises	8 508 . .	. . .	. . .	. . .	. . .	. . .	. . .	. . .	. . .
Other capital	8 530 . .	. . .	758	983	1,545	2,206	2,660	3,423	4,127
Claims on affiliated enterprises	8 535 . .	. . .	758	983	1,545	2,206	2,660	3,423	4,127
Liabilities to affiliated enterprises	8 540 . .	. . .	. . .	. . .	. . .	. . .	. . .	. . .	. . .
Portfolio investment	8 602 . .	**2,866**	**2,801**	**2,609**	**2,711**	**3,027**	**5,001**	**7,294**	**8,033**
Equity securities	8 610 . .	374	430	356	447	499	1,449	2,518	2,067
Monetary authorities	8 611 . .	. . .	. . .	. . .	. . .	. . .	. . .	. . .	. . .
General government	8 612 . .	. . .	. . .	. . .	. . .	. . .	. . .	. . .	. . .
Banks	8 613 . .	. . .	. . .	. . .	. . .	. . .	. . .	. . .	. . .
Other sectors	8 614 . .	374	430	356	447	499	1,449	2,518	2,067
Debt securities	8 619 . .	2,492	2,371	2,253	2,264	2,528	3,552	4,776	5,966
Bonds and notes	8 620 . .	2,492	2,371	2,253	2,264	2,528	3,552	4,776	5,966
Monetary authorities	8 621 . .	. . .	. . .	. . .	. . .	. . .	. . .	. . .	. . .
General government	8 622 . .	270	229	195	166	140	118	99	82
Banks	8 623 . .	2,222	2,143	2,058	1,949	2,176	2,703	3,062	2,686
Other sectors	8 624 . .	. . .	. . .	. . .	149	212	731	1,616	3,198
Money market instruments	8 630 . .	. . .	. . .	. . .	. . .	. . .	. . .	. . .	. . .
Monetary authorities	8 631 . .	. . .	. . .	. . .	. . .	. . .	. . .	. . .	. . .
General government	8 632 . .	. . .	. . .	. . .	. . .	. . .	. . .	. . .	. . .
Banks	8 633 . .	. . .	. . .	. . .	. . .	. . .	. . .	. . .	. . .
Other sectors	8 634 . .	. . .	. . .	. . .	. . .	. . .	. . .	. . .	. . .
Financial derivatives	8 900 . .	**. . .**	**. . .**	**. . .**	**. . .**	**. . .**	**. . .**	**. . .**	**. . .**
Monetary authorities	8 901 . .	. . .	. . .	. . .	. . .	. . .	. . .	. . .	. . .
General government	8 902 . .	. . .	. . .	. . .	. . .	. . .	. . .	. . .	. . .
Banks	8 903 . .	. . .	. . .	. . .	. . .	. . .	. . .	. . .	. . .
Other sectors	8 904 . .	. . .	. . .	. . .	. . .	. . .	. . .	. . .	. . .
Other investment	8 703 . .	**16,315**	**16,476**	**17,107**	**16,022**	**19,022**	**22,515**	**25,370**	**27,358**
Trade credits	8 706 . .	4,969	4,678	4,229	4,965	5,747	6,827	6,722	5,574
General government	8 707 . .	. . .	. . .	. . .	. . .	. . .	. . .	. . .	. . .
of which: Short-term	8 709 . .	. . .	. . .	. . .	. . .	. . .	. . .	. . .	. . .
Other sectors	8 710 . .	4,969	4,678	4,229	4,965	5,747	6,827	6,722	5,574
of which: Short-term	8 712 . .	. . .	. . .	. . .	. . .	. . .	. . .	. . .	. . .
Loans	8 714 . .	1,554	1,862	2,221	2,456	3,290	3,751	4,901	6,471
Monetary authorities	8 715 . .	. . .	. . .	. . .	. . .	. . .	. . .	. . .	. . .
of which: Short-term	8 718 . .	. . .	. . .	. . .	. . .	. . .	. . .	. . .	. . .
General government	8 719 . .	. . .	. . .	. . .	. . .	. . .	. . .	. . .	. . .
of which: Short-term	8 721 . .	. . .	. . .	. . .	. . .	. . .	. . .	. . .	. . .
Banks	8 722 . .	1,554	1,862	2,221	2,456	3,266	3,698	4,472	5,694
of which: Short-term	8 724 . .	. . .	. . .	. . .	. . .	. . .	. . .	. . .	. . .
Other sectors	8 725 . .	. . .	. . .	. . .	. . .	24	54	429	778
of which: Short-term	8 727 . .	. . .	. . .	. . .	. . .	. . .	. . .	. . .	. . .
Currency and deposits	8 730 . .	9,792	9,936	10,658	8,602	9,984	11,936	13,747	15,313
Monetary authorities	8 731 . .	. . .	. . .	. . .	. . .	. . .	. . .	. . .	. . .
General government	8 732 . .	. . .	. . .	. . .	. . .	. . .	. . .	. . .	. . .
Banks	8 733 . .	8,235	8,400	9,003	6,700	7,804	7,873	8,142	7,194
Other sectors	8 734 . .	1,557	1,536	1,655	1,902	2,180	4,063	5,605	8,119
Other assets	8 736 . .	. . .	. . .	. . .	. . .	. . .	. . .	. . .	. . .
Monetary authorities	8 737 . .	. . .	. . .	. . .	. . .	. . .	. . .	. . .	. . .
of which: Short-term	8 739 . .	. . .	. . .	. . .	. . .	. . .	. . .	. . .	. . .
General government	8 740 . .	. . .	. . .	. . .	. . .	. . .	. . .	. . .	. . .
of which: Short-term	8 742 . .	. . .	. . .	. . .	. . .	. . .	. . .	. . .	. . .
Banks	8 743 . .	. . .	. . .	. . .	. . .	. . .	. . .	. . .	. . .
of which: Short-term	8 745 . .	. . .	. . .	. . .	. . .	. . .	. . .	. . .	. . .
Other sectors	8 746 . .	. . .	. . .	. . .	. . .	. . .	. . .	. . .	. . .
of which: Short-term	8 748 . .	. . .	. . .	. . .	. . .	. . .	. . .	. . .	. . .
Reserve assets	8 802 . .	**7,164**	**8,609**	**11,752**	**20,599**	**23,043**	**23,271**	**23,872**	**23,872**
Monetary gold	8 812 . .	. . .	1	. . .	. . .	. . .	. . .	. . .	. . .
Special drawing rights	8 811 . .	. . .	1	1	. . .	. . .	. . .	1	2
Reserve position in the Fund	8 810 . .	. . .	. . .	. . .	. . .	. . .	90	117	198
Foreign exchange	8 803 . .	6,895	8,308	11,576	20,333	22,675	22,507	23,158	23,181
Other claims	8 813 . .	268	300	175	267	368	674	596	492

Table 3 (Concluded). INTERNATIONAL INVESTMENT POSITION (End–period stocks), 1994–2001

(Millions of U.S. dollars)

	Code	1994	1995	1996	1997	1998	1999	2000	2001
LIABILITIES	8 995 D.	47,586	52,953	57,819	74,593	77,568	104,809	115,288	105,628
Direct investment in Israel	8 555 . .	**474**	**636**	**774**	**9,315**	**10,507**	**18,442**	**21,559**	**23,206**
Equity capital and reinvested earnings	8 556 . .	. . .	. . .	. . .	8,610	9,680	17,539	20,668	22,373
Claims on direct investors	8 557 . .	. . .	. . .	. . .	8,610	9,680	17,539	20,668	22,373
Liabilities to direct investors	8 558 . .	. . .	. . .	. . .	. . .	. . .	. . .	. . .	. . .
Other capital	8 580 . .	474	636	774	705	827	903	891	833
Claims on direct investors	8 585 . .	. . .	. . .	. . .	. . .	. . .	. . .	. . .	. . .
Liabilities to direct investors	8 590 . .	474	636	774	705	827	903	891	833
Portfolio investment	8 652 . .	**12,437**	**14,968**	**19,399**	**25,694**	**26,863**	**43,729**	**49,759**	**37,011**
Equity securities	8 660 . .	2,893	4,706	6,806	10,789	9,912	25,655	31,119	18,882
Banks	8 663 . .	. . .	. . .	. . .	. . .	. . .	. . .	. . .	. . .
Other sectors	8 664 . .	2,893	4,706	6,806	10,789	9,912	25,655	31,119	18,882
Debt securities	8 669 . .	9,544	10,262	12,593	14,905	16,951	18,074	18,640	18,129
Bonds and notes	8 670 . .	9,544	10,262	12,593	14,905	16,951	18,074	18,640	18,129
Monetary authorities	8 671 . .	. . .	. . .	. . .	. . .	. . .	. . .	. . .	. . .
General government	8 672 . .	9,480	10,206	11,943	13,404	14,807	14,858	14,705	14,109
Banks	8 673 . .	64	56	50	50	41	. . .	. . .	. . .
Other sectors	8 674 . .	. . .	. . .	600	1,451	2,104	3,217	3,935	4,020
Money market instruments	8 680 . .	. . .	. . .	. . .	. . .	. . .	. . .	. . .	. . .
Monetary authorities	8 681 . .	. . .	. . .	. . .	. . .	. . .	. . .	. . .	. . .
General government	8 682 . .	. . .	. . .	. . .	. . .	. . .	. . .	. . .	. . .
Banks	8 683 . .	. . .	. . .	. . .	. . .	. . .	. . .	. . .	. . .
Other sectors	8 684 . .	. . .	. . .	. . .	. . .	. . .	. . .	. . .	. . .
Financial derivatives	8 905 . .	**. . .**	**. . .**	**. . .**	**. . .**	**. . .**	**. . .**	**. . .**	**. . .**
Monetary authorities	8 906 . .	. . .	. . .	. . .	. . .	. . .	. . .	. . .	. . .
General government	8 907 . .	. . .	. . .	. . .	. . .	. . .	. . .	. . .	. . .
Banks	8 908 . .	. . .	. . .	. . .	. . .	. . .	. . .	. . .	. . .
Other sectors	8 909 . .	. . .	. . .	. . .	. . .	. . .	. . .	. . .	. . .
Other investment	8 753 . .	**34,676**	**37,350**	**37,647**	**39,584**	**40,198**	**42,637**	**43,970**	**45,411**
Trade credits	8 756 . .	4,834	5,313	4,691	4,400	3,502	4,036	3,741	3,377
General government	8 757 . .	. . .	. . .	. . .	. . .	. . .	. . .	. . .	. . .
of which: Short-term	8 759 . .	. . .	. . .	. . .	. . .	. . .	. . .	. . .	. . .
Other sectors	8 760 . .	4,834	5,313	4,691	4,400	3,502	4,036	3,741	3,377
of which: Short-term	8 762 . .	*4,834*	*5,313*	*4,691*	*4,400*	*3,502*	*4,036*	*3,741*	*3,377*
Loans	8 764 . .	16,342	17,079	17,528	17,714	17,566	17,383	17,561	17,872
Monetary authorities	8 765 . .	317	235	98	89	83	39	54	50
of which: Use of Fund credit and loans from the Fund	8 766 . .	*261*	*166*	*32*	. . .	. . .	. . .	. . .	. . .
of which: Short-term	8 768 . .	. . .	. . .	. . .	. . .	. . .	. . .	. . .	. . .
General government	8 769 . .	12,944	13,335	13,289	12,724	12,549	12,554	12,718	12,940
of which: Short-term	8 771 . .	. . .	*9*	*54*	. . .	*1*	. . .	. . .	. . .
Banks	8 772 . .	. . .	. . .	. . .	. . .	. . .	. . .	. . .	. . .
of which: Short-term	8 774 . .	. . .	. . .	. . .	. . .	. . .	. . .	. . .	. . .
Other sectors	8 775 . .	3,081	3,509	4,141	4,900	4,934	4,791	4,789	4,883
of which: Short-term	8 777 . .	*313*	*413*	*419*	*376*	*424*	*597*	*622*	*618*
Currency and deposits	8 780 . .	13,500	14,958	15,428	17,470	19,129	21,218	22,668	24,162
Monetary authorities	8 781 . .	. . .	. . .	. . .	. . .	. . .	. . .	. . .	. . .
General government	8 782 . .	. . .	. . .	. . .	. . .	. . .	. . .	. . .	. . .
Banks	8 783 . .	13,500	14,958	15,428	17,470	19,129	21,218	22,668	24,162
Other sectors	8 784 . .	. . .	. . .	. . .	. . .	. . .	. . .	. . .	. . .
Other liabilities	8 786 . .	. . .	. . .	. . .	. . .	. . .	. . .	. . .	. . .
Monetary authorities	8 787 . .	. . .	. . .	. . .	. . .	. . .	. . .	. . .	. . .
of which: Short-term	8 789 . .	. . .	. . .	. . .	. . .	. . .	. . .	. . .	. . .
General government	8 790 . .	. . .	. . .	. . .	. . .	. . .	. . .	. . .	. . .
of which: Short-term	8 792 . .	. . .	. . .	. . .	. . .	. . .	. . .	. . .	. . .
Banks	8 793 . .	. . .	. . .	. . .	. . .	. . .	. . .	. . .	. . .
of which: Short-term	8 795 . .	. . .	. . .	. . .	. . .	. . .	. . .	. . .	. . .
Other sectors	8 796 . .	. . .	. . .	. . .	. . .	. . .	. . .	. . .	. . .
of which: Short-term	8 798 . .	. . .	. . .	. . .	. . .	. . .	. . .	. . .	. . .
NET INTERNATIONAL INVESTMENT POSITION	8 995 . .	**–21,241**	**–22,200**	**–23,068**	**–30,037**	**–27,100**	**–47,842**	**–50,016**	**–36,637**
Conversion rates: new sheqalim per U.S. dollar (end of period)	0 102 . .	**3.0180**	**3.1350**	**3.2510**	**3.5360**	**4.1610**	**4.1530**	**4.0410**	**4.4160**

Table 1. ANALYTIC PRESENTATION, 1994–2001
(Millions of U.S. dollars)

	Code	1994	1995	1996	1997	1998	1999	2000	2001
A. Current Account [1]	4 993 Z.	**13,209**	**25,076**	**39,999**	**32,403**	**19,998**	**8,111**	**–5,781**	**–163**
Goods: exports f.o.b.	2 100 . .	191,421	233,998	252,039	240,404	242,572	235,856	240,473	242,430
Goods: imports f.o.b.	3 100 . .	–159,854	–195,269	–197,921	–200,527	–206,941	–212,420	–230,925	–226,568
Balance on Goods	4 100 . .	*31,568*	*38,729*	*54,118*	*39,878*	*35,631*	*23,437*	*9,549*	*15,862*
Services: credit	2 200 . .	53,681	61,619	65,660	66,991	67,549	58,788	56,556	57,548
Services: debit	3 200 . .	–48,238	–55,050	–57,605	–59,227	–63,379	–57,707	–55,601	–57,345
Balance on Goods and Services	4 991 . .	*37,011*	*45,299*	*62,173*	*47,642*	*39,801*	*24,517*	*10,504*	*16,065*
Income: credit	2 300 . .	28,599	34,168	40,142	45,734	51,319	46,361	38,671	38,649
Income: debit	3 300 . .	–45,289	–49,812	–55,101	–56,936	–63,636	–57,411	–50,680	–48,929
Balance on Goods, Services, and Income	4 992 . .	*20,321*	*29,655*	*47,213*	*36,440*	*27,483*	*13,467*	*–1,506*	*5,785*
Current transfers: credit	2 379 Z.	12,254	14,287	14,320	15,552	14,402	16,776	15,797	16,176
Current transfers: debit	3 379 . .	–19,366	–18,866	–21,535	–19,588	–21,887	–22,132	–20,073	–22,125
B. Capital Account [1]	4 994 Z.	**1,026**	**1,671**	**66**	**3,434**	**2,358**	**2,964**	**2,879**	**846**
Capital account: credit	2 994 Z.	2,213	2,797	1,414	4,582	3,359	4,572	4,172	2,098
Capital account: debit	3 994 . .	–1,187	–1,125	–1,348	–1,148	–1,001	–1,608	–1,293	–1,252
Total, Groups A Plus B	4 981 . .	*14,235*	*26,747*	*40,065*	*35,838*	*22,356*	*11,074*	*–2,902*	*683*
C. Financial Account [1]	4 995 W.	**–14,207**	**–2,889**	**–7,982**	**–6,878**	**–18,074**	**–17,415**	**7,504**	**–3,211**
Direct investment abroad	4 505 . .	–5,239	–7,024	–8,697	–10,414	–12,407	–6,723	–12,077	–21,758
Direct investment in Italy	4 555 Z.	2,199	4,842	3,546	3,700	2,635	6,943	13,176	14,874
Portfolio investment assets	4 602 . .	–37,718	–4,938	–25,598	–61,857	–109,064	–129,624	–80,263	–36,167
Equity securities	4 610 . .	–3,360	1,014	–1,036	–15,116	–26,570	–63,277	–77,036	–9,988
Debt securities	4 619 . .	–34,358	–5,952	–24,562	–46,741	–82,493	–66,347	–3,227	–26,179
Portfolio investment liabilities	4 652 Z.	29,895	45,583	74,655	73,375	111,987	104,607	57,020	29,329
Equity securities	4 660 . .	–1,395	5,358	9,331	9,414	14,423	–4,537	–2,426	–245
Debt securities	4 669 Z.	31,290	40,225	65,324	63,962	97,563	109,144	59,446	29,573
Financial derivatives	4 910 . .	715	227	264	156	191	1,869	2,332	–438
Financial derivatives assets	4 900 . .	87	–852	–1,009	–1,118	–850	161	744	–2,277
Financial derivatives liabilities	4 905 . .	628	1,079	1,272	1,273	1,041	1,709	1,588	1,839
Other investment assets	4 703 . .	2,092	–28,947	–68,358	–25,541	–21,232	–33,573	242	717
Monetary authorities	4 701 . .	. . .	. . .	. . .	. . .	. . .	5,396	3,034	–27,626
General government	4 704 . .	–2,023	–2,148	–1,112	–62	–1,101	–163	–649	–359
Banks	4 705 . .	22,599	–18,689	–45,046	–1,602	–7,052	–9,643	2,388	12,091
Other sectors	4 728 . .	–18,483	–8,110	–22,199	–23,877	–13,078	–29,163	–4,532	16,611
Other investment liabilities	4 753 W.	–6,152	–12,632	16,206	13,703	9,816	39,085	27,074	10,233
Monetary authorities	4 753 WA	–95	1,062	–1,269	–48	–128	916	–690	1,928
General government	4 753 ZB	–1,812	4,893	–2,583	–1,798	–5,739	–3,255	–3,549	–766
Banks	4 753 ZC	–1,527	–22,716	26,613	6,861	12,780	1,109	24,875	12,783
Other sectors	4 753 ZD	–2,719	4,129	–6,555	8,688	2,903	40,315	6,438	–3,712
Total, Groups A Through C	4 983 . .	*28*	*23,858*	*32,083*	*28,960*	*4,282*	*–6,340*	*4,602*	*–2,528*
D. Net Errors and Omissions	4 998 . .	**1,547**	**–21,054**	**–20,176**	**–15,810**	**–25,754**	**–1,711**	**–1,355**	**1,940**
Total, Groups A Through D	4 984 . .	*1,575*	*2,804*	*11,907*	*13,150*	*–21,472*	*–8,051*	*3,247*	*–588*
E. Reserves and Related Items	4 802 A.	**–1,575**	**–2,804**	**–11,907**	**–13,150**	**21,472**	**8,051**	**–3,247**	**588**
Reserve assets	4 802 . .	–1,575	–2,804	–11,907	–13,150	21,472	8,051	–3,247	588
Use of Fund credit and loans	4 766 . .	. . .	. . .	. . .	. . .	. . .	. . .	. . .	. . .
Exceptional financing	4 920 . .	. . .	. . .	. . .	. . .	. . .	. . .	. . .	. . .
Conversion rates: lire per U.S. dollar	0 101 . .	**1,612.4**	**1,628.9**	**1,542.9**	**1,703.1**	**1,736.2**	**. . .**	**. . .**	**. . .**
Conversion rates: euros per U.S. dollar	0 103 . .	**. . .**	**. . .**	**. . .**	**. . .**	**. . .**	**.9386**	**1.0854**	**1.1175**

[1] Excludes components that have been classified in the categories of Group E.

Table 2. STANDARD PRESENTATION, 1994–2001

(Millions of U.S. dollars)

	Code	1994	1995	1996	1997	1998	1999	2000	2001
CURRENT ACCOUNT	4 993 . .	**13,209**	**25,076**	**39,999**	**32,403**	**19,998**	**8,111**	**–5,781**	**–163**
A. GOODS	4 100 . .	31,568	38,729	54,118	39,878	35,631	23,437	9,549	15,862
Credit	2 100 . .	**191,421**	**233,998**	**252,039**	**240,404**	**242,572**	**235,856**	**240,473**	**242,430**
General merchandise: exports f.o.b.	2 110 . .	190,600	233,068	250,951	239,313	241,434	233,655	238,279	240,412
Goods for processing: exports f.o.b.	2 150 . .	. . .	. . .	. . .	. . .	. . .	635	680	761
Repairs on goods	2 160 . .	. . .	. . .	. . .	. . .	. . .	680	748	666
Goods procured in ports by carriers	2 170 . .	742	870	1,012	1,018	1,040	689	545	332
Nonmonetary gold	2 180 . .	79	59	75	73	98	197	221	259
Debit	3 100 . .	**–159,854**	**–195,269**	**–197,921**	**–200,527**	**–206,941**	**–212,420**	**–230,925**	**–226,568**
General merchandise: imports f.o.b.	3 110 . .	–155,249	–190,584	–193,564	–195,878	–202,416	–208,091	–226,168	–221,576
Goods for processing: imports f.o.b.	3 150 . .	. . .	. . .	. . .	. . .	. . .	–941	–1,071	–1,429
Repairs on goods	3 160 . .	. . .	. . .	. . .	. . .	. . .	–387	–464	–347
Goods procured in ports by carriers	3 170 . .	–455	–477	–465	–537	–416	–439	–634	–777
Nonmonetary gold	3 180 . .	–4,150	–4,208	–3,892	–4,111	–4,109	–2,562	–2,587	–2,438
B. SERVICES	4 200 . .	5,443	6,570	8,055	7,764	4,170	1,080	955	203
Total credit	2 200 . .	*53,681*	*61,619*	*65,660*	*66,991*	*67,549*	*58,788*	*56,556*	*57,548*
Total debit	3 200 . .	*–48,238*	*–55,050*	*–57,605*	*–59,227*	*–63,379*	*–57,707*	*–55,601*	*–57,345*
Transportation services, credit	2 205 . .	**9,657**	**10,823**	**10,883**	**10,669**	**10,641**	**9,514**	**9,291**	**8,215**
Passenger	2 850 . .	*1,715*	*1,695*	*1,869*	*1,702*	*1,526*	*1,220*	*1,213*	*1,019*
Freight	2 851 . .	*2,867*	*3,425*	*3,079*	*3,234*	*3,357*	*3,032*	*3,033*	*2,608*
Other	2 852 . .	*5,075*	*5,704*	*5,935*	*5,732*	*5,759*	*5,262*	*5,045*	*4,588*
Sea transport, passenger	2 207 . .	25	25	29	36	41	28	17	9
Sea transport, freight	2 208 . .	1,670	1,873	1,804	1,835	1,906	1,882	2,039	1,755
Sea transport, other	2 209 . .	2,342	2,670	2,782	2,620	2,735	2,399	2,207	2,096
Air transport, passenger	2 211 . .	1,563	1,534	1,694	1,542	1,361	1,035	1,032	824
Air transport, freight	2 212 . .	182	346	261	260	278	179	135	116
Air transport, other	2 213 . .	1,750	1,880	2,061	2,031	1,924	1,832	1,751	1,506
Other transport, passenger	2 215 . .	127	136	146	124	123	158	164	186
Other transport, freight	2 216 . .	1,015	1,205	1,014	1,139	1,173	970	859	736
Other transport, other	2 217 . .	983	1,154	1,093	1,081	1,100	1,031	1,087	986
Transportation services, debit	3 205 . .	**–11,479**	**–13,370**	**–13,784**	**–13,607**	**–13,627**	**–13,671**	**–13,140**	**–11,933**
Passenger	3 850 . .	*–2,099*	*–2,390*	*–2,813*	*–3,035*	*–2,942*	*–2,699*	*–2,484*	*–2,121*
Freight	3 851 . .	*–4,047*	*–4,779*	*–4,735*	*–4,435*	*–4,511*	*–5,163*	*–5,334*	*–5,068*
Other	3 852 . .	*–5,332*	*–6,201*	*–6,236*	*–6,137*	*–6,174*	*–5,809*	*–5,322*	*–4,744*
Sea transport, passenger	3 207 . .	–47	–46	–75	–66	–73	–55	–54	–61
Sea transport, freight	3 208 . .	–2,451	–3,109	–2,919	–2,762	–2,825	–3,405	–3,163	–2,976
Sea transport, other	3 209 . .	–2,793	–3,317	–3,176	–2,996	–3,100	–2,957	–2,442	–2,269
Air transport, passenger	3 211 . .	–1,953	–2,238	–2,624	–2,880	–2,770	–2,478	–2,272	–1,907
Air transport, freight	3 212 . .	–81	–86	–119	–132	–139	–314	–424	–390
Air transport, other	3 213 . .	–1,471	–1,628	–1,875	–1,968	–1,882	–1,700	–1,652	–1,360
Other transport, passenger	3 215 . .	–100	–106	–114	–88	–99	–167	–158	–153
Other transport, freight	3 216 . .	–1,516	–1,584	–1,697	–1,541	–1,548	–1,445	–1,747	–1,701
Other transport, other	3 217 . .	–1,068	–1,257	–1,185	–1,173	–1,192	–1,152	–1,228	–1,115
Travel, credit	2 236 . .	**24,741**	**28,731**	**30,017**	**29,714**	**29,809**	**28,350**	**27,493**	**25,815**
Business travel	2 237 . .	25	31	6,668	8,063	7,568	7,324	7,066	6,455
Personal travel	2 240 . .	24,716	28,700	23,349	21,651	22,241	21,026	20,427	19,360
Travel, debit	3 236 . .	**–13,942**	**–14,829**	**–15,805**	**–16,631**	**–17,579**	**–16,891**	**–15,685**	**–14,210**
Business travel	3 237 . .	–90	–149	–5,196	–6,560	–6,769	–6,846	–6,500	–5,858
Personal travel	3 240 . .	–13,852	–14,679	–10,609	–10,071	–10,810	–10,046	–9,185	–8,352
Other services, credit	2 200 BA	**19,282**	**22,066**	**24,759**	**26,608**	**27,099**	**20,923**	**19,772**	**23,517**
Communications	2 245 . .	310	293	538	684	674	1,169	1,274	1,430
Construction	2 249 . .	2,568	3,166	3,160	3,348	4,492	1,785	1,346	1,643
Insurance	2 253 . .	1,511	1,396	1,902	1,989	1,299	859	821	1,096
Financial	2 260 . .	2,353	2,620	3,222	3,769	2,261	514	428	409
Computer and information	2 262 . .	139	160	207	235	288	369	448	351
Royalties and licence fees	2 266 . .	323	462	381	490	477	563	563	443
Other business services	2 268 . .	11,194	13,154	14,207	15,066	16,247	14,412	13,789	17,024
Personal, cultural, and recreational	2 287 . .	375	368	395	444	433	482	544	543
Government, n.i.e.	2 291 . .	511	447	746	582	928	770	558	578
Other services, debit	3 200 BA	**–22,817**	**–26,851**	**–28,016**	**–28,989**	**–32,173**	**–27,145**	**–26,776**	**–31,202**
Communications	3 245 . .	–631	–627	–945	–1,055	–1,429	–1,778	–1,935	–2,609
Construction	3 249 . .	–1,102	–1,511	–1,208	–1,249	–1,405	–1,145	–1,143	–1,630
Insurance	3 253 . .	–1,402	–864	–906	–1,790	–1,818	–1,047	–1,104	–1,427
Financial	3 260 . .	–3,634	–4,454	–4,803	–4,984	–3,099	–830	–545	–563
Computer and information	3 262 . .	–401	–455	–589	–592	–783	–873	–926	–943
Royalties and licence fees	3 266 . .	–1,179	–1,166	–1,027	–1,004	–1,155	–1,382	–1,198	–1,312
Other business services	3 268 . .	–13,478	–16,225	–16,950	–16,943	–20,727	–17,509	–17,799	–19,962
Personal, cultural, and recreational	3 287 . .	–828	–1,113	–1,012	–1,089	–1,265	–1,114	–1,157	–1,090
Government, n.i.e.	3 291 . .	–163	–436	–575	–283	–492	–1,468	–969	–1,666

Table 2 (Continued). STANDARD PRESENTATION, 1994–2001
(Millions of U.S. dollars)

	Code		1994	1995	1996	1997	1998	1999	2000	2001
C. INCOME	4 300	. .	-16,689	-15,644	-14,959	-11,202	-12,318	-11,050	-12,010	-10,281
Total credit	2 300	. .	*28,599*	*34,168*	*40,142*	*45,734*	*51,319*	*46,361*	*38,671*	*38,649*
Total debit	3 300	. .	*-45,289*	*-49,812*	*-55,101*	*-56,936*	*-63,636*	*-57,411*	*-50,680*	*-48,929*
Compensation of employees, credit	2 310	. .	**1,901**	**1,934**	**2,189**	**1,844**	**1,745**	**1,581**	**1,511**	**1,845**
Compensation of employees, debit	3 310	. .	**-1,905**	**-1,441**	**-1,667**	**-1,698**	**-1,822**	**-1,927**	**-1,960**	**-1,905**
Investment income, credit	2 320	. .	**26,699**	**32,234**	**37,953**	**43,890**	**49,574**	**44,780**	**37,160**	**36,804**
Direct investment income	2 330	. .	1,124	1,494	1,023	1,311	1,716	3,896	1,936	3,005
Dividends and distributed branch profits	2 332	. .	1,124	1,494	1,023	1,311	1,716	514	1,694	4,081
Reinvested earnings and undistributed branch profits	2 333	. .	. . .	. . .	. . .	. . .	. . .	3,382	242	-1,076
Income on debt (interest)	2 334	. .	. . .	. . .	. . .	. . .	. . .	. . .	. . .	. . .
Portfolio investment income	2 339	. .	6,376	7,396	8,345	10,809	12,340	28,550	24,161	20,592
Income on equity	2 340	. .	. . .	. . .	. . .	. . .	. . .	3,518	4,008	4,553
Income on bonds and notes	2 350	. .	. . .	. . .	. . .	. . .	. . .	24,801	19,628	15,963
Income on money market instruments	2 360	. .	. . .	. . .	. . .	. . .	. . .	231	524	76
Other investment income	2 370	. .	19,198	23,344	28,584	31,770	35,519	12,333	11,063	13,207
Investment income, debit	3 320	. .	**-43,384**	**-48,370**	**-53,434**	**-55,239**	**-61,814**	**-55,483**	**-48,720**	**-47,024**
Direct investment income	3 330	. .	-412	-738	-862	-641	-1,424	-3,549	-3,535	-4,085
Dividends and distributed branch profits	3 332	. .	-412	-738	-862	-641	-1,424	-433	-630	-368
Reinvested earnings and undistributed branch profits	3 333	. .	. . .	. . .	. . .	. . .	. . .	-3,116	-2,906	-3,717
Income on debt (interest)	3 334	. .	. . .	. . .	. . .	. . .	. . .	. . .	. . .	. . .
Portfolio investment income	3 339	. .	-13,841	-15,415	-19,168	-21,814	-25,965	-38,137	-30,869	-26,196
Income on equity	3 340	. .	. . .	. . .	. . .	. . .	. . .	-6,092	-5,771	-6,066
Income on bonds and notes	3 350	. .	. . .	. . .	. . .	. . .	. . .	-31,902	-22,064	-18,081
Income on money market instruments	3 360	. .	. . .	. . .	. . .	. . .	. . .	-142	-3,033	-2,048
Other investment income	3 370	. .	-29,131	-32,217	-33,404	-32,783	-34,425	-13,798	-14,316	-16,744
D. CURRENT TRANSFERS	4 379	. .	-7,112	-4,579	-7,214	-4,036	-7,485	-5,356	-4,276	-5,948
Credit	2 379	. .	**12,254**	**14,287**	**14,320**	**15,552**	**14,402**	**16,776**	**15,797**	**16,176**
General government	2 380	. .	5,777	6,318	7,200	9,405	8,555	9,381	9,226	9,631
Other sectors	2 390	. .	6,478	7,969	7,120	6,147	5,847	7,395	6,571	6,546
Workers' remittances	2 391	. .	461	346	337	364	309	340	359	322
Other current transfers	2 392	. .	6,017	7,623	6,783	5,783	5,538	7,055	6,213	6,224
Debit	3 379	. .	**-19,366**	**-18,866**	**-21,535**	**-19,588**	**-21,887**	**-22,132**	**-20,073**	**-22,125**
General government	3 380	. .	-12,955	-11,675	-14,766	-12,803	-14,940	-13,787	-12,861	-13,107
Other sectors	3 390	. .	-6,411	-7,191	-6,769	-6,784	-6,947	-8,345	-7,212	-9,018
Workers' remittances	3 391	. .	-209	-248	-309	-332	-441	-544	-541	-670
Other current transfers	3 392	. .	-6,202	-6,944	-6,460	-6,452	-6,506	-7,801	-6,671	-8,347
CAPITAL AND FINANCIAL ACCOUNT	4 996	. .	**-14,757**	**-4,022**	**-19,823**	**-16,594**	**5,756**	**-6,400**	**7,136**	**-1,777**
CAPITAL ACCOUNT	4 994	. .	**1,026**	**1,671**	**66**	**3,434**	**2,358**	**2,964**	**2,879**	**846**
Total credit	2 994	. .	*2,213*	*2,797*	*1,414*	*4,582*	*3,359*	*4,572*	*4,172*	*2,098*
Total debit	3 994	. .	*-1,187*	*-1,125*	*-1,348*	*-1,148*	*-1,001*	*-1,608*	*-1,293*	*-1,252*
Capital transfers, credit	2 400	. .	**1,901**	**2,380**	**1,112**	**3,918**	**3,100**	**4,293**	**3,914**	**1,948**
General government	2 401	. .	1,844	2,295	1,054	3,841	3,038	3,405	3,273	1,571
Debt forgiveness	2 402	. .	. . .	. . .	. . .	. . .	. . .	. . .	. . .	. . .
Other capital transfers	2 410	. .	1,844	2,295	1,054	3,841	3,038	. . .	. . .	. . .
Other sectors	2 430	. .	57	84	58	76	62	888	641	377
Migrants' transfers	2 431	. .	57	84	58	76	62	77	67	99
Debt forgiveness	2 432	. .	. . .	. . .	. . .	. . .	. . .	. . .	. . .	. . .
Other capital transfers	2 440	. .	. . .	. . .	. . .	. . .	. . .	811	574	278
Capital transfers, debit	3 400	. .	**-640**	**-682**	**-628**	**-570**	**-567**	**-1,324**	**-963**	**-822**
General government	3 401	. .	-526	-547	-524	-434	-453	-426	-470	-507
Debt forgiveness	3 402	. .	. . .	. . .	. . .	. . .	. . .	. . .	. . .	. . .
Other capital transfers	3 410	. .	-526	-547	-524	-434	-453	. . .	. . .	. . .
Other sectors	3 430	. .	-115	-135	-104	-136	-114	-898	-493	-315
Migrants' transfers	3 431	. .	-115	-135	-104	-136	-114	-79	-81	-135
Debt forgiveness	3 432	. .	. . .	. . .	. . .	. . .	. . .	. . .	-1	-12
Other capital transfers	3 440	. .	. . .	. . .	. . .	. . .	. . .	-819	-411	-169
Nonproduced nonfinancial assets, credit	2 480	. .	**312**	**417**	**302**	**665**	**260**	**279**	**258**	**150**
Nonproduced nonfinancial assets, debit	3 480	. .	**-547**	**-444**	**-720**	**-578**	**-434**	**-284**	**-330**	**-429**

Table 2 (Continued). STANDARD PRESENTATION, 1994–2001
(Millions of U.S. dollars)

	Code	1994	1995	1996	1997	1998	1999	2000	2001
FINANCIAL ACCOUNT	4 995	**–15,782**	**–5,693**	**–19,889**	**–20,028**	**3,398**	**–9,364**	**4,257**	**–2,623**
A. DIRECT INVESTMENT	4 500	–3,039	–2,182	–5,151	–6,714	–9,772	220	1,099	–6,884
Direct investment abroad	4 505	**–5,239**	**–7,024**	**–8,697**	**–10,414**	**–12,407**	**–6,723**	**–12,077**	**–21,758**
Equity capital	4 510	–5,239	–7,024	–8,697	–10,414	–12,407	–282	–9,350	–13,372
Claims on affiliated enterprises	4 515	...	...	...	...	...	...	...	...
Liabilities to affiliated enterprises	4 520	...	...	...	...	...	...	...	...
Reinvested earnings	4 525	...	...	...	...	...	–3,382	–242	1,076
Other capital	4 530	...	...	...	...	...	–3,059	–2,485	–9,462
Claims on affiliated enterprises	4 535	...	...	...	...	...	...	...	...
Liabilities to affiliated enterprises	4 540	...	...	...	...	...	...	...	...
Direct investment in Italy	4 555	**2,199**	**4,842**	**3,546**	**3,700**	**2,635**	**6,943**	**13,176**	**14,874**
Equity capital	4 560	2,199	4,842	3,546	3,700	2,635	4,591	7,358	6,869
Claims on direct investors	4 565	...	...	...	...	...	...	...	...
Liabilities to direct investors	4 570	...	...	...	...	...	...	...	...
Reinvested earnings	4 575	...	...	...	...	...	3,116	2,906	3,717
Other capital	4 580	...	...	...	...	...	–763	2,912	4,288
Claims on direct investors	4 585	...	...	...	...	...	...	...	...
Liabilities to direct investors	4 590	...	...	...	...	...	...	...	...
B. PORTFOLIO INVESTMENT	4 600	–7,823	40,645	49,057	11,519	2,923	–25,016	–23,243	–6,838
Assets	4 602	**–37,718**	**–4,938**	**–25,598**	**–61,857**	**–109,064**	**–129,624**	**–80,263**	**–36,167**
Equity securities	4 610	–3,360	1,014	–1,036	–15,116	–26,570	–63,277	–77,036	–9,988
Monetary authorities	4 611	...	...	...	...	...	–1	...	...
General government	4 612	...	...	...	...	...	–1,147	–3,126	–2,696
Banks	4 613	...	...	...	...	...	5,391	–137	–910
Other sectors	4 614	–3,360	1,014	–1,036	–15,116	–26,570	–67,519	–73,773	–6,382
Debt securities	4 619	–34,358	–5,952	–24,562	–46,741	–82,493	–66,347	–3,227	–26,179
Bonds and notes	4 620	–34,358	–5,952	–24,562	–46,741	–82,493	–65,886	–1,584	–24,475
Monetary authorities	4 621	...	...	...	...	...	1	–31	10
General government	4 622	...	...	...	...	...	–1,838	–496	294
Banks	4 623	–11,673	–1,669	–4,402	–2,536	–6,487	3,628	1,644	4,987
Other sectors	4 624	–22,685	–4,283	–20,159	–44,205	–76,006	–67,678	–2,702	–29,766
Money market instruments	4 630	...	...	...	...	...	–461	–1,642	–1,704
Monetary authorities	4 631	...	...	...	...	...	–329	430	9
General government	4 632	...	...	...	...	...	...	–60	–5
Banks	4 633	...	...	...	...	...	29	–704	–1,196
Other sectors	4 634	...	...	...	...	...	–160	–1,309	–511
Liabilities	4 652	**29,895**	**45,583**	**74,655**	**73,375**	**111,987**	**104,607**	**57,020**	**29,329**
Equity securities	4 660	–1,395	5,358	9,331	9,414	14,423	–4,537	–2,426	–245
Banks	4 663	...	...	...	...	...	3,990	1,899	1,045
Other sectors	4 664	–1,395	5,358	9,331	9,414	14,423	–8,527	–4,325	–1,289
Debt securities	4 669	31,290	40,225	65,324	63,962	97,563	109,144	59,446	29,573
Bonds and notes	4 670	30,664	37,140	56,405	59,231	67,371	69,102	71,578	39,070
Monetary authorities	4 671	...	...	...	...	...	...	...	...
General government	4 672	23,771	27,984	56,477	55,805	56,128	59,652	63,075	20,228
Banks	4 673	4,993	8,510	–5,636	4,850	5,980	5,055	1,721	595
Other sectors	4 674	1,901	646	5,564	–1,424	5,263	4,395	6,782	18,247
Money market instruments	4 680	625	3,085	8,919	4,731	30,192	40,042	–12,131	–9,497
Monetary authorities	4 681	...	...	...	...	...	...	...	...
General government	4 682	625	3,085	8,919	4,731	30,192	39,878	–11,570	–7,540
Banks	4 683	...	...	...	...	...	–68	–579	–2,426
Other sectors	4 684	...	...	...	...	...	233	17	469
C. FINANCIAL DERIVATIVES	4 910	715	227	264	156	191	1,869	2,332	–438
Monetary authorities	4 911	...	...	...	...	...	...	...	...
General government	4 912	...	...	...	...	...	...	3	14
Banks	4 913	...	...	...	...	...	1,144	2,975	–1,081
Other sectors	4 914	715	227	264	156	191	726	–646	628
Assets	4 900	**87**	**–852**	**–1,009**	**–1,118**	**–850**	**161**	**744**	**–2,277**
Monetary authorities	4 901	...	...	...	...	...	...	...	...
General government	4 902	...	...	...	...	...	...	3	7
Banks	4 903	...	...	...	...	...	–220	1,597	–1,417
Other sectors	4 904	87	–852	–1,009	–1,118	–850	380	–856	–867
Liabilities	4 905	**628**	**1,079**	**1,272**	**1,273**	**1,041**	**1,709**	**1,588**	**1,839**
Monetary authorities	4 906	...	...	...	...	...	...	...	...
General government	4 907	...	...	...	...	...	...	...	7
Banks	4 908	...	...	...	...	...	1,363	1,378	337
Other sectors	4 909	628	1,079	1,272	1,273	1,041	345	210	1,495

Table 2 (Concluded). STANDARD PRESENTATION, 1994–2001
(Millions of U.S. dollars)

	Code	1994	1995	1996	1997	1998	1999	2000	2001
D. OTHER INVESTMENT	4 700	-4,060	-41,579	-52,151	-11,839	-11,415	5,512	27,316	10,950
Assets	4 703	**2,092**	**-28,947**	**-68,358**	**-25,541**	**-21,232**	**-33,573**	**242**	**717**
Trade credits	4 706	-6,350	-4,161	-878	-2,725	766	-4,774	-6,634	-830
General government	4 707	...	...	...	...	...	-6	-3	-4
of which: Short-term	4 709	...	...	...	...	...	...	...	...
Other sectors	4 710	-6,350	-4,161	-878	-2,725	766	-4,768	-6,631	-825
of which: Short-term	4 712	*-4,793*	*-2,818*	*-145*	*-2,066*	*2,263*	...	...	...
Loans	4 714	-12,941	-13,588	-29,852	-20,433	-13,101	-1,462	-19,226	-4,595
Monetary authorities	4 715	...	...	...	...	...	-41	45	...
of which: Short-term	4 718	...	...	...	...	...	...	...	...
General government	4 719	-1,702	-1,889	-548	258	36	104	66	38
of which: Short-term	4 721	...	...	...	...	...	...	...	...
Banks	4 722	-4,547	-10,897	-19,505	-5,400	-4,073	6,489	-17,183	-4,794
of which: Short-term	4 724	*-4,547*	*-10,897*	*-19,505*	*-5,400*	*-4,073*	...	...	...
Other sectors	4 725	-6,692	-802	-9,799	-15,291	-9,063	-8,014	-2,154	160
of which: Short-term	4 727	...	...	...	...	...	...	...	...
Currency and deposits	4 730	21,704	-10,939	-37,064	-2,063	-7,760	4,857	32,246	9,146
Monetary authorities	4 731	...	...	...	...	...	13,797	2,988	-27,624
General government	4 732	...	...	...	...	...	30	-403	-57
Banks	4 733	27,146	-7,791	-25,542	3,798	-2,979	-19,079	20,094	17,018
Other sectors	4 734	-5,441	-3,147	-11,523	-5,861	-4,781	10,108	9,567	19,809
Other assets	4 736	-322	-259	-564	-320	-1,137	-32,195	-6,144	-3,004
Monetary authorities	4 737	...	...	...	...	...	-8,360	1	-2
of which: Short-term	4 739	...	...	...	...	...	...	...	...
General government	4 740	-322	-259	-564	-320	-1,137	-291	-309	-336
of which: Short-term	4 742	...	...	...	...	...	...	...	...
Banks	4 743	...	...	...	...	...	2,946	-523	-133
of which: Short-term	4 745	...	...	...	...	...	...	...	...
Other sectors	4 746	...	...	...	...	...	-26,490	-5,312	-2,533
of which: Short-term	4 748	...	...	...	...	...	...	...	...
Liabilities	4 753	**-6,152**	**-12,632**	**16,206**	**13,703**	**9,816**	**39,085**	**27,074**	**10,233**
Trade credits	4 756	4,348	3,218	-3,137	3,363	-2,415	5,785	2,806	-47
General government	4 757	...	...	...	...	...	-6	7	3
of which: Short-term	4 759	...	...	...	...	...	...	...	...
Other sectors	4 760	4,348	3,218	-3,137	3,363	-2,415	5,791	2,800	-50
of which: Short-term	4 762	*4,274*	*2,946*	*-2,844*	*3,627*	*-2,339*	...	...	...
Loans	4 764	-4,249	8,630	126	11,183	-6,874	52,825	8,333	6,142
Monetary authorities	4 765	...	...	...	...	...	913	-680	1,911
of which: Use of Fund credit and loans from the Fund	4 766	...	...	...	...	...	...	...	...
of which: Short-term	4 768	...	...	...	...	...	*913*	*-680*	*1,911*
General government	4 769	-1,812	4,893	-2,583	-1,798	-5,739	-2,403	-2,022	-816
of which: Short-term	4 771	...	...	...	...	...	...	...	...
Banks	4 772	4,629	2,827	6,127	7,656	-6,453	33,392	812	3,091
of which: Short-term	4 774	*4,629*	*2,827*	*6,127*	*7,656*	*-6,453*	...	...	...
Other sectors	4 775	-7,066	910	-3,418	5,326	5,318	20,923	10,223	1,955
of which: Short-term	4 777	...	...	...	...	...	...	...	...
Currency and deposits	4 780	-6,156	-25,543	20,486	-795	19,234	-31,900	23,091	9,323
Monetary authorities	4 781	...	...	...	...	...	15	-12	17
General government	4 782	...	...	...	...	...	-892	-1,556	...
Banks	4 783	-6,156	-25,543	20,486	-795	19,234	-32,420	23,530	9,199
Other sectors	4 784	...	...	...	...	...	1,397	1,129	107
Other liabilities	4 786	-95	1,062	-1,269	-48	-128	12,374	-7,156	-5,185
Monetary authorities	4 787	-95	1,062	-1,269	-48	-128	-12	2	...
of which: Short-term	4 789	*-95*	*1,062*	*-1,269*	*-48*	*-128*	...	...	...
General government	4 790	...	...	...	...	...	46	23	46
of which: Short-term	4 792	...	...	...	...	...	...	...	...
Banks	4 793	...	...	...	...	...	137	533	493
of which: Short-term	4 795	...	...	...	...	...	...	...	...
Other sectors	4 796	...	...	...	...	...	12,204	-7,713	-5,724
of which: Short-term	4 798	...	...	...	...	...	...	...	...
E. RESERVE ASSETS	4 802	-1,575	-2,804	-11,907	-13,150	21,472	8,051	-3,247	588
Monetary gold	4 812	...	...	...	...	-4,952	1,254	...	...
Special drawing rights	4 811	126	130	-30	-40	-39	-61	-79	-68
Reserve position in the Fund	4 810	262	109	44	-502	-1,907	681	478	-424
Foreign exchange	4 803	-1,963	-3,042	-11,921	-12,607	28,370	6,252	-3,646	1,080
Other claims	4 813	...	...	...	...	...	-74	...	...
NET ERRORS AND OMISSIONS	4 998	**1,547**	**-21,054**	**-20,176**	**-15,810**	**-25,754**	**-1,711**	**-1,355**	**1,940**

Part 3 of the *Yearbook* contains descriptions of the methodologies, compilation practices, and sources used to compile these data.

Table 3. INTERNATIONAL INVESTMENT POSITION (End-period stocks), 1994–2001

(Millions of U.S. dollars)

	Code	1994	1995	1996	1997	1998	1999	2000	2001
ASSETS	8 995 C.	516,329	597,810	727,498	809,597	1,002,865	1,081,092	1,119,394	1,059,807
Direct investment abroad	8 505 . .	**91,097**	**109,176**	**113,251**	**130,668**	**165,412**	**181,852**	**180,275**	**182,375**
Equity capital and reinvested earnings	8 506 . .	91,097	109,176	113,251	130,668	165,412	179,010	172,295	166,021
Claims on affiliated enterprises	8 507 . .	...	...	...	...	...	...	...	...
Liabilities to affiliated enterprises	8 508 . .	...	...	...	...	...	...	...	...
Other capital	8 530 . .	...	...	...	...	...	2,842	7,980	16,354
Claims on affiliated enterprises	8 535 . .	...	...	...	...	...	...	...	...
Liabilities to affiliated enterprises	8 540 . .	...	...	...	...	...	...	...	...
Portfolio investment	8 602 . .	**150,426**	**171,793**	**192,351**	**257,494**	**394,501**	**546,903**	**590,753**	**545,708**
Equity securities	8 610 . .	14,015	13,982	16,915	26,600	37,690	210,929	285,553	225,162
Monetary authorities	8 611 . .	...	...	...	...	...	20	519	522
General government	8 612 . .	...	...	...	...	...	1,255	267	2,585
Banks	8 613 . .	...	...	...	...	...	4,800	7,008	7,422
Other sectors	8 614 . .	14,015	13,982	16,915	26,600	37,690	204,854	277,759	214,633
Debt securities	8 619 . .	136,411	157,811	175,436	230,894	356,811	335,974	305,200	320,546
Bonds and notes	8 620 . .	136,411	157,811	175,436	230,894	356,811	327,075	304,297	318,875
Monetary authorities	8 621 . .	...	...	...	...	...	...	36	182
General government	8 622 . .	...	...	...	...	...	4,962	1,545	1,163
Banks	8 623 . .	10,270	9,178	...	...	...	29,943	26,581	24,332
Other sectors	8 624 . .	126,141	148,633	175,436	230,894	356,811	292,170	276,135	293,197
Money market instruments	8 630 . .	...	...	...	...	...	8,900	904	1,672
Monetary authorities	8 631 . .	...	...	...	...	...	560	110	100
General government	8 632 . .	...	...	...	...	...	42	...	4
Banks	8 633 . .	...	...	...	...	...	364	183	457
Other sectors	8 634 . .	...	...	...	...	...	7,934	610	1,111
Financial derivatives	8 900 . .	**...**	**...**	**...**	**...**	**...**	**2,951**	**3,533**	**4,325**
Monetary authorities	8 901 . .	...	...	...	...	...	...	...	...
General government	8 902 . .	...	...	...	...	...	...	...	8
Banks	8 903 . .	...	...	...	...	...	1,569	1,296	1,351
Other sectors	8 904 . .	...	...	...	...	...	1,381	2,237	2,966
Other investment	8 703 . .	**217,192**	**256,520**	**350,907**	**344,344**	**388,310**	**304,085**	**297,775**	**281,183**
Trade credits	8 706 . .	43,625	49,914	52,594	48,252	50,581	46,972	45,012	43,691
General government	8 707 . .	...	...	...	...	...	16	28	19
of which: Short-term	8 709 . .	...	...	...	...	...	...	...	...
Other sectors	8 710 . .	43,625	49,914	52,594	48,252	50,581	46,956	44,984	43,673
of which: Short-term	8 712 . .	*25,008*	*28,670*	*29,863*	*27,834*	*27,280*	...	...	...
Loans	8 714 . .	50,287	65,513	98,584	107,938	128,278	214,375	199,189	187,362
Monetary authorities	8 715 . .	...	...	...	...	...	–4,190	–6,715	20,629
of which: Short-term	8 718 . .	...	...	...	...	...	...	...	...
General government	8 719 . .	13,340	16,073	17,687	16,284	17,233	15,680	18,608	18,280
of which: Short-term	8 721 . .	...	...	...	...	...	...	...	...
Banks	8 722 . .	18,905	30,314	50,980	49,717	58,421	125,674	119,943	103,077
of which: Short-term	8 724 . .	*18,905*	*30,314*	*50,980*	*49,717*	*58,421*	...	...	...
Other sectors	8 725 . .	18,042	19,126	29,916	41,938	52,625	77,211	67,353	45,376
of which: Short-term	8 727 . .	...	...	...	...	...	...	...	...
Currency and deposits	8 730 . .	120,160	137,624	195,640	184,258	204,116	...	...	...
Monetary authorities	8 731 . .	...	...	...	...	...	...	...	...
General government	8 732 . .	...	...	...	...	...	...	...	...
Banks	8 733 . .	102,821	116,631	163,544	148,804	166,669	...	...	...
Other sectors	8 734 . .	17,339	20,993	32,096	35,454	37,447	...	...	...
Other assets	8 736 . .	3,120	3,469	4,090	3,896	5,334	42,739	53,574	50,130
Monetary authorities	8 737 . .	...	...	...	...	...	...	...	...
of which: Short-term	8 739 . .	...	...	...	...	...	...	...	...
General government	8 740 . .	3,120	3,469	4,090	3,896	5,334	4,722	4,680	4,763
of which: Short-term	8 742 . .	...	...	...	...	...	...	...	...
Banks	8 743 . .	...	...	...	...	...	13,043	20,504	15,989
of which: Short-term	8 745 . .	...	...	...	...	...	...	...	...
Other sectors	8 746 . .	...	...	...	...	...	24,974	28,390	29,378
of which: Short-term	8 748 . .	...	...	...	...	...	...	...	...
Reserve assets	8 802 . .	**57,615**	**60,321**	**70,989**	**77,091**	**54,642**	**45,302**	**47,058**	**46,215**
Monetary gold	8 812 . .	25,365	25,403	25,066	21,361	24,759	22,880	21,493	21,796
Special drawing rights	8 811 . .	125	...	29	67	111	168	238	297
Reserve position in the Fund	8 810 . .	2,033	1,963	1,855	2,241	4,330	3,546	2,906	3,217
Foreign exchange	8 803 . .	30,091	32,955	44,038	53,423	25,443	18,708	22,422	20,904
Other claims	8 813 . .	...	...	...	...	...	...	...	...

Table 3 (Continued). INTERNATIONAL INVESTMENT POSITION (End–period stocks), 1994–2001

(Millions of U.S. dollars)

	Code	1994	1995	1996	1997	1998	1999	2000	2001
LIABILITIES	8 995 D.	587,612	650,102	761,656	807,436	1,022,771	1,027,672	1,072,544	1,047,630
Direct investment in Italy	8 555 . .	**60,955**	**65,980**	**74,640**	**83,158**	**105,397**	**108,638**	**113,047**	**107,921**
Equity capital and reinvested earnings	8 556 . .	60,955	65,980	74,640	83,158	105,397	104,772	106,438	97,734
Claims on direct investors	8 557 . .	. . .	. . .	. . .	. . .	. . .	. . .	. . .	. . .
Liabilities to direct investors	8 558 . .	. . .	. . .	. . .	. . .	. . .	. . .	. . .	. . .
Other capital	8 580 . .	. . .	. . .	. . .	. . .	. . .	3,867	6,609	10,187
Claims on direct investors	8 585 . .	. . .	. . .	. . .	. . .	. . .	. . .	. . .	. . .
Liabilities to direct investors	8 590 . .	. . .	. . .	. . .	. . .	. . .	. . .	. . .	. . .
Portfolio investment	8 652 . .	**188,595**	**237,861**	**333,422**	**385,388**	**544,602**	**549,251**	**570,236**	**560,957**
Equity securities	8 660 . .	11,118	16,434	27,245	35,500	65,833	53,380	53,182	35,743
Banks	8 663 . .	. . .	. . .	. . .	. . .	. . .	. . .	. . .	. . .
Other sectors	8 664 . .	11,118	16,434	27,245	35,500	65,833	53,380	53,182	35,743
Debt securities	8 669 . .	177,477	221,427	306,177	349,888	478,769	495,871	517,054	525,214
Bonds and notes	8 670 . .	174,171	214,893	290,387	331,553	426,994	409,572	450,004	470,842
Monetary authorities	8 671 . .	. . .	. . .	. . .	. . .	. . .	. . .	. . .	. . .
General government	8 672 . .	140,049	177,401	244,201	274,932	356,983	341,762	371,883	376,134
Banks	8 673 . .	919	1,444	. . .	. . .	. . .	5,456	12,219	13,595
Other sectors	8 674 . .	33,204	36,047	46,185	56,620	70,010	62,355	65,902	81,114
Money market instruments	8 680 . .	3,305	6,534	15,791	18,335	51,775	86,298	67,050	54,372
Monetary authorities	8 681 . .	. . .	. . .	. . .	. . .	. . .	. . .	. . .	. . .
General government	8 682 . .	3,305	6,534	15,791	18,335	51,775	86,298	67,050	53,677
Banks	8 683 . .	. . .	. . .	. . .	. . .	. . .	. . .	. . .	. . .
Other sectors	8 684 . .	. . .	. . .	. . .	. . .	. . .	. . .	. . .	694
Financial derivatives	8 905 . .	**. . .**	**. . .**	**. . .**	**. . .**	**. . .**	**3,244**	**2,641**	**4,550**
Monetary authorities	8 906 . .	. . .	. . .	. . .	. . .	. . .	. . .	. . .	. . .
General government	8 907 . .	. . .	. . .	. . .	. . .	. . .	. . .	. . .	6
Banks	8 908 . .	. . .	. . .	. . .	. . .	. . .	1,586	875	1,385
Other sectors	8 909 . .	. . .	. . .	. . .	. . .	. . .	1,658	1,766	3,159
Other investment	8 753 . .	**338,063**	**346,261**	**353,593**	**338,891**	**372,772**	**366,538**	**386,620**	**374,202**
Trade credits	8 756 . .	25,595	29,948	27,865	27,257	26,492	26,477	26,181	24,821
General government	8 758 . .	. . .	. . .	. . .	. . .	. . .	. . .	. . .	. . .
of which: Short-term	8 759 . .	. . .	. . .	. . .	. . .	. . .	. . .	. . .	. . .
Other sectors	8 760 . .	25,595	29,948	27,865	27,257	26,492	26,461	26,142	24,803
of which: Short-term	8 762 . .	*22,812*	*26,523*	*24,612*	*24,684*	*23,833*	. . .	. . .	. . .
Loans	8 764 . .	88,402	94,428	92,794	92,797	92,348	328,751	344,361	340,954
Monetary authorities	8 765 . .	. . .	. . .	. . .	. . .	. . .	950	235	2,197
of which: Use of Fund credit and loans from the Fund	8 766 . .	. . .	. . .	. . .	. . .	. . .	. . .	. . .	. . .
of which: Short-term	8 768 . .	. . .	. . .	. . .	. . .	. . .	*950*	*235*	*2,197*
General government	8 769 . .	21,551	26,328	22,187	21,470	15,595	8,865	7,170	5,934
of which: Short-term	8 771 . .	. . .	. . .	. . .	. . .	. . .	. . .	. . .	. . .
Banks	8 772 . .	5,540	8,528	15,038	20,510	15,059	241,669	254,405	252,492
of which: Short-term	8 774 . .	*5,540*	*8,528*	*15,038*	*20,510*	*15,059*	. . .	. . .	. . .
Other sectors	8 775 . .	61,312	59,573	55,570	50,817	61,694	77,268	82,550	80,331
of which: Short-term	8 777 . .	. . .	. . .	. . .	. . .	. . .	. . .	. . .	. . .
Currency and deposits	8 780 . .	223,580	220,331	232,694	218,661	253,876	. . .	. . .	. . .
Monetary authorities	8 781 . .	. . .	. . .	. . .	. . .	. . .	. . .	. . .	. . .
General government	8 782 . .	. . .	. . .	. . .	. . .	. . .	. . .	. . .	. . .
Banks	8 783 . .	223,580	220,331	232,694	218,661	253,876	. . .	. . .	. . .
Other sectors	8 784 . .	. . .	. . .	. . .	. . .	. . .	. . .	. . .	. . .
Other liabilities	8 786 . .	485	1,554	239	175	56	11,310	16,078	8,427
Monetary authorities	8 787 . .	485	1,554	239	175	56	. . .	. . .	. . .
of which: Short-term	8 789 . .	*485*	*1,554*	*239*	*175*	*56*	. . .	. . .	. . .
General government	8 790 . .	. . .	. . .	. . .	. . .	. . .	. . .	63	106
of which: Short-term	8 792 . .	. . .	. . .	. . .	. . .	. . .	. . .	. . .	. . .
Banks	8 793 . .	. . .	. . .	. . .	. . .	. . .	. . .	10,635	8,321
of which: Short-term	8 795 . .	. . .	. . .	. . .	. . .	. . .	. . .	. . .	. . .
Other sectors	8 796 . .	. . .	. . .	. . .	. . .	. . .	11,310	5,380	. . .
of which: Short-term	8 798 . .	. . .	. . .	. . .	. . .	. . .	. . .	. . .	. . .
NET INTERNATIONAL INVESTMENT POSITION	8 995 . .	**–71,283**	**–52,291**	**–34,158**	**2,160**	**–19,906**	**53,421**	**46,851**	**12,176**
Conversion rates: lire per U.S. dollar (end of period)	0 102 . .	**1,629.7**	**1,584.7**	**1,530.6**	**1,759.2**	**1,653.1**	**. . .**	**. . .**	**. . .**
Conversion rates: euros per U.S. dollar (end of period)	0 104 . .	**. . .**	**. . .**	**. . .**	**. . .**	**. . .**	**.9954**	**1.0747**	**1.1347**

Table 1. ANALYTIC PRESENTATION, 1994–2001
(Millions of U.S. dollars)

	Code	1994	1995	1996	1997	1998	1999	2000	2001
A. Current Account [1]	4 993 Z.	**81.6**	**–98.9**	**–142.6**	**–332.2**	**–327.9**	**–216.3**	**–387.0**	**–788.4**
Goods: exports f.o.b.	2 100 . .	1,548.0	1,796.0	1,721.0	1,700.3	1,613.4	1,499.1	1,562.8	1,454.4
Goods: imports f.o.b.	3 100 . .	–2,099.2	–2,625.3	–2,715.2	–2,832.6	–2,743.9	–2,685.6	–3,004.3	–3,072.6
Balance on Goods	4 100 . .	*–551.2*	*–829.3*	*–994.2*	*–1,132.3*	*–1,130.5*	*–1,186.5*	*–1,441.5*	*–1,618.2*
Services: credit	2 200 . .	1,480.2	1,597.9	1,601.9	1,698.9	1,770.4	1,978.4	2,025.7	1,900.7
Services: debit	3 200 . .	–955.3	–1,103.8	–1,149.2	–1,231.7	–1,293.6	–1,323.0	–1,442.1	–1,519.2
Balance on Goods and Services	4 991 . .	*–26.3*	*–335.2*	*–541.5*	*–665.1*	*–653.7*	*–531.1*	*–857.9*	*–1,236.7*
Income: credit	2 300 . .	104.6	146.6	141.8	147.3	156.3	165.8	193.1	218.2
Income: debit	3 300 . .	–456.6	–517.3	–366.5	–439.2	–464.4	–498.3	–543.0	–656.0
Balance on Goods, Services, and Income	4 992 . .	*–378.3*	*–705.9*	*–766.2*	*–957.0*	*–961.8*	*–863.6*	*–1,207.8*	*–1,674.5*
Current transfers: credit	2 379 Z.	504.2	669.6	709.3	705.7	733.5	757.9	969.4	1,062.7
Current transfers: debit	3 379 . .	–44.3	–62.6	–85.7	–80.9	–99.6	–110.6	–148.6	–176.6
B. Capital Account [1]	4 994 Z.	**10.4**	**10.5**	**16.6**	**–11.6**	**–8.7**	**–10.9**	**2.2**	**–22.3**
Capital account: credit	2 994 Z.	33.2	34.5	42.5	21.7	20.3	19.1	29.6	15.2
Capital account: debit	3 994 . .	–22.8	–24.0	–25.9	–33.3	–29.0	–30.0	–27.4	–37.5
Total, Groups A Plus B	4 981 . .	*92.0*	*–88.4*	*–126.0*	*–343.8*	*–336.6*	*–227.2*	*–384.8*	*–810.7*
C. Financial Account [1]	4 995 W.	**256.1**	**108.3**	**388.6**	**163.5**	**337.3**	**94.8**	**854.0**	**1,660.5**
Direct investment abroad	4 505 . .	–52.7	–66.3	–93.3	–56.6	–82.0	–94.9	–74.3	–89.0
Direct investment in Jamaica	4 555 Z.	129.7	147.4	183.7	203.3	369.1	523.7	468.4	613.9
Portfolio investment assets	4 602 . .	. . .	. . .	. . .	. . .	–3.9	–3.7	–70.0	–39.3
Equity securities	4 610 . .	. . .	. . .	. . .	. . .	. . .	. . .	. . .	. . .
Debt securities	4 619 . .	. . .	. . .	. . .	. . .	–3.9	–3.7	–70.0	–39.3
Portfolio investment liabilities	4 652 Z.	. . .	. . .	. . .	5.7	10.9	8.6	5.9	69.7
Equity securities	4 660 . .	. . .	. . .	. . .	. . .	. . .	. . .	. . .	. . .
Debt securities	4 669 Z.	. . .	. . .	. . .	5.7	10.9	8.6	5.9	69.7
Financial derivatives	4 910 . .	. . .	. . .	. . .	. . .	. . .	. . .	. . .	. . .
Financial derivatives assets	4 900 . .	. . .	. . .	. . .	. . .	. . .	. . .	. . .	. . .
Financial derivatives liabilities	4 905 . .	. . .	. . .	. . .	. . .	. . .	. . .	. . .	. . .
Other investment assets	4 703 . .	–141.3	–148.8	–13.8	–113.2	–59.1	–122.7	–95.5	–215.5
Monetary authorities	4 701 . .	. . .	. . .	. . .	. . .	. . .	. . .	. . .	. . .
General government	4 704 . .	. . .	. . .	. . .	. . .	. . .	. . .	. . .	. . .
Banks	4 705 . .	–177.9	–199.2	–88.1	–186.9	–142.3	–215.1	–181.5	–282.9
Other sectors	4 728 . .	36.6	50.4	74.3	73.7	83.2	92.4	86.0	67.4
Other investment liabilities	4 753 W.	320.4	176.0	312.0	124.3	102.3	–216.2	619.5	1,320.7
Monetary authorities	4 753 WA	. . .	. . .	. . .	. . .	. . .	. . .	. . .	. . .
General government	4 753 ZB	–127.4	–97.0	–144.7	43.1	–41.3	–331.4	383.6	653.4
Banks	4 753 ZC	142.2	74.7	130.7	156.7	205.5	122.2	167.9	250.5
Other sectors	4 753 ZD	305.6	198.3	326.0	–75.5	–61.9	–7.0	68.0	416.8
Total, Groups A Through C	4 983 . .	*348.1*	*19.9*	*262.6*	*–180.3*	*.7*	*–132.4*	*469.2*	*849.8*
D. Net Errors and Omissions	4 998 . .	**9.6**	**7.1**	**8.8**	**9.9**	**43.2**	**–4.0**	**49.2**	**15.2**
Total, Groups A Through D	4 984 . .	*357.7*	*27.0*	*271.4*	*–170.4*	*43.9*	*–136.4*	*518.4*	*865.0*
E. Reserves and Related Items	4 802 A.	**–357.7**	**–27.0**	**–271.4**	**170.4**	**–43.9**	**136.4**	**–518.4**	**–865.0**
Reserve assets	4 802 . .	–321.0	55.8	–201.7	205.0	–26.9	155.3	–499.4	–846.6
Use of Fund credit and loans	4 766 . .	–38.2	–84.6	–71.9	–34.6	–17.0	–18.9	–19.0	–18.3
Exceptional financing	4 920 . .	1.5	1.9	2.2	. . .	. . .	. . .	. . .	. . .
Conversion rates: Jamaica dollars per U.S. dollar	0 101 . .	**33.086**	**35.142**	**37.120**	**35.404**	**36.550**	**39.044**	**42.701**	**45.996**

[1] Excludes components that have been classified in the categories of Group E.

Table 2. STANDARD PRESENTATION, 1994–2001

(Millions of U.S. dollars)

	Code	1994	1995	1996	1997	1998	1999	2000	2001
CURRENT ACCOUNT	4 993 . .	**81.6**	**–98.9**	**–142.6**	**–332.2**	**–327.9**	**–216.3**	**–387.0**	**–788.4**
A. GOODS	4 100 . .	–551.2	–829.3	–994.2	–1,132.3	–1,130.5	–1,186.5	–1,441.5	–1,618.2
Credit	2 100 . .	**1,548.0**	**1,796.0**	**1,721.0**	**1,700.3**	**1,613.4**	**1,499.1**	**1,562.8**	**1,454.4**
General merchandise: exports f.o.b.	2 110 . .	1,519.0	1,767.7	1,688.4	1,671.0	1,586.4	1,469.6	1,524.9	1,419.0
Goods for processing: exports f.o.b.	2 150 . .	. . .	. . .	. . .	. . .	. . .	. . .	. . .	. . .
Repairs on goods	2 160 . .	. . .	. . .	. . .	. . .	. . .	. . .	. . .	. . .
Goods procured in ports by carriers	2 170 . .	29.0	28.3	32.6	29.3	27.0	29.5	37.9	35.4
Nonmonetary gold	2 180 . .	. . .	. . .	. . .	. . .	. . .	. . .	. . .	. . .
Debit	3 100 . .	**–2,099.2**	**–2,625.3**	**–2,715.2**	**–2,832.6**	**–2,743.9**	**–2,685.6**	**–3,004.3**	**–3,072.6**
General merchandise: imports f.o.b.	3 110 . .	–2,072.6	–2,594.3	–2,694.1	–2,811.5	–2,725.3	–2,663.2	–2,966.0	–3,033.9
Goods for processing: imports f.o.b.	3 150 . .	. . .	. . .	. . .	. . .	. . .	. . .	. . .	. . .
Repairs on goods	3 160 . .	. . .	. . .	. . .	. . .	. . .	. . .	. . .	. . .
Goods procured in ports by carriers	3 170 . .	–26.6	–31.0	–21.1	–21.1	–18.6	–22.4	–38.3	–38.7
Nonmonetary gold	3 180 . .	. . .	. . .	. . .	. . .	. . .	. . .	. . .	. . .
B. SERVICES	4 200 . .	524.9	494.1	452.7	467.2	476.8	655.4	583.6	381.5
Total credit	2 200 . .	*1,480.2*	*1,597.9*	*1,601.9*	*1,698.9*	*1,770.4*	*1,978.4*	*2,025.7*	*1,900.7*
Total debit	3 200 . .	*–955.3*	*–1,103.8*	*–1,149.2*	*–1,231.7*	*–1,293.6*	*–1,323.0*	*–1,442.1*	*–1,519.2*
Transportation services, credit	2 205 . .	**215.8**	**250.9**	**223.3**	**254.1**	**276.0**	**300.3**	**328.6**	**350.5**
Passenger	2 850 . .	*127.0*	*130.0*	*125.9*	*158.6*	*182.7*	*206.3*	*243.7*	*261.6*
Freight	2 851 . .	*13.4*	*3.6*	*1.1*	*6.3*	*7.2*	*7.7*	*6.5*	*6.9*
Other	2 852 . .	*75.4*	*117.3*	*96.3*	*89.2*	*86.1*	*86.3*	*78.4*	*82.0*
Sea transport, passenger	2 207 . .	. . .	. . .	. . .	. . .	. . .	. . .	. . .	. . .
Sea transport, freight	2 208 . .	. . .	. . .	. . .	. . .	. . .	. . .	. . .	. . .
Sea transport, other	2 209 . .	. . .	. . .	. . .	. . .	. . .	. . .	. . .	. . .
Air transport, passenger	2 211 . .	. . .	. . .	. . .	. . .	. . .	. . .	. . .	. . .
Air transport, freight	2 212 . .	. . .	. . .	. . .	. . .	. . .	. . .	. . .	. . .
Air transport, other	2 213 . .	. . .	. . .	. . .	. . .	. . .	. . .	. . .	. . .
Other transport, passenger	2 215 . .	. . .	. . .	. . .	. . .	. . .	. . .	. . .	. . .
Other transport, freight	2 216 . .	. . .	. . .	. . .	. . .	. . .	. . .	. . .	. . .
Other transport, other	2 217 . .	. . .	. . .	. . .	. . .	. . .	. . .	. . .	. . .
Transportation services, debit	3 205 . .	**–412.0**	**–496.9**	**–493.5**	**–527.5**	**–554.4**	**–533.9**	**–585.2**	**–606.7**
Passenger	3 850 . .	*–24.2*	*–24.5*	*–24.0*	*–24.0*	*–25.0*	*–28.6*	*–28.5*	*–20.9*
Freight	3 851 . .	*–315.3*	*–397.4*	*–408.4*	*–439.3*	*–437.7*	*–408.4*	*–431.4*	*–448.2*
Other	3 852 . .	*–72.5*	*–75.0*	*–61.1*	*–64.2*	*–91.7*	*–96.9*	*–125.3*	*–137.6*
Sea transport, passenger	3 207 . .	. . .	. . .	. . .	. . .	. . .	. . .	. . .	. . .
Sea transport, freight	3 208 . .	. . .	. . .	. . .	. . .	. . .	. . .	. . .	. . .
Sea transport, other	3 209 . .	. . .	. . .	. . .	. . .	. . .	. . .	. . .	. . .
Air transport, passenger	3 211 . .	. . .	. . .	. . .	. . .	. . .	. . .	. . .	. . .
Air transport, freight	3 212 . .	. . .	. . .	. . .	. . .	. . .	. . .	. . .	. . .
Air transport, other	3 213 . .	. . .	. . .	. . .	. . .	. . .	. . .	. . .	. . .
Other transport, passenger	3 215 . .	. . .	. . .	. . .	. . .	. . .	. . .	. . .	. . .
Other transport, freight	3 216 . .	. . .	. . .	. . .	. . .	. . .	. . .	. . .	. . .
Other transport, other	3 217 . .	. . .	. . .	. . .	. . .	. . .	. . .	. . .	. . .
Travel, credit	2 236 . .	**970.4**	**1,068.8**	**1,092.3**	**1,130.8**	**1,196.9**	**1,279.6**	**1,332.6**	**1,232.2**
Business travel	2 237 . .	. . .	. . .	. . .	. . .	. . .	. . .	. . .	. . .
Personal travel	2 240 . .	. . .	. . .	. . .	. . .	. . .	. . .	. . .	. . .
Travel, debit	3 236 . .	**–80.9**	**–147.6**	**–157.1**	**–181.3**	**–198.0**	**–227.2**	**–208.7**	**–206.0**
Business travel	3 237 . .	. . .	. . .	. . .	. . .	. . .	. . .	. . .	. . .
Personal travel	3 240 . .	. . .	. . .	. . .	. . .	. . .	. . .	. . .	. . .
Other services, credit	2 200 BA	**294.0**	**278.2**	**286.3**	**314.0**	**297.5**	**398.5**	**364.5**	**318.0**
Communications	2 245 . .	166.9	172.8	190.4	212.3	184.5	275.0	209.4	168.4
Construction	2 249 . .	. . .	. . .	. . .	. . .	1.0	. . .	. . .	. . .
Insurance	2 253 . .	21.6	11.3	6.4	6.0	5.9	6.4	12.1	11.9
Financial	2 260 . .	4.3	5.6	6.5	8.6	9.2	11.3	12.6	15.8
Computer and information	2 262 . .	30.0	31.3	32.0	33.0	37.0	40.0	40.4	36.6
Royalties and licence fees	2 266 . .	5.1	3.9	4.3	7.0	6.6	6.2	6.4	5.9
Other business services	2 268 . .	31.4	16.0	11.4	11.4	16.2	20.7	36.4	40.7
Personal, cultural, and recreational	2 287 . .	6.5	7.0	7.6	8.6	9.6	9.7	9.6	9.0
Government, n.i.e.	2 291 . .	28.2	30.3	27.7	27.1	27.5	29.2	37.6	29.7
Other services, debit	3 200 BA	**–462.4**	**–459.3**	**–498.6**	**–522.9**	**–541.2**	**–561.9**	**–648.2**	**–706.5**
Communications	3 245 . .	–38.0	–39.7	–41.8	–42.5	–40.0	–42.4	–51.4	–55.4
Construction	3 249 . .	. . .	. . .	. . .	–5.0	–6.0	–7.5	–10.2	–10.0
Insurance	3 253 . .	–80.1	–96.4	–85.0	–76.5	–71.7	–56.2	–87.2	–94.1
Financial	3 260 . .	–1.1	–1.9	–2.0	–2.9	–3.2	–3.5	–18.4	–29.7
Computer and information	3 262 . .	–.3	–.6	–1.4	–4.0	–5.0	–5.9	–7.1	–13.8
Royalties and licence fees	3 266 . .	–10.5	–19.4	–27.9	–27.6	–30.0	–40.5	–41.0	–38.3
Other business services	3 268 . .	–297.6	–267.3	–306.0	–325.8	–346.3	–365.6	–396.8	–427.2
Personal, cultural, and recreational	3 287 . .	–2.2	–3.5	–3.4	–3.0	–3.6	–3.7	–4.1	–4.0
Government, n.i.e.	3 291 . .	–32.6	–30.5	–31.1	–35.6	–35.4	–36.6	–32.0	–34.0

Table 2 (Continued). STANDARD PRESENTATION, 1994–2001

(Millions of U.S. dollars)

	Code	1994	1995	1996	1997	1998	1999	2000	2001
C. INCOME	4 300	–352.0	–370.7	–224.7	–291.9	–308.1	–332.5	–349.9	–437.8
Total credit	2 300	*104.6*	*146.6*	*141.8*	*147.3*	*156.3*	*165.8*	*193.1*	*218.2*
Total debit	3 300	*–456.6*	*–517.3*	*–366.5*	*–439.2*	*–464.4*	*–498.3*	*–543.0*	*–656.0*
Compensation of employees, credit	2 310	**49.2**	**56.8**	**54.8**	**72.8**	**86.8**	**94.0**	**88.2**	**106.7**
Compensation of employees, debit	3 310	**–7.8**	**–10.3**	**–7.5**	**–15.1**	**–20.7**	**–23.7**	**–20.8**	**–32.1**
Investment income, credit	2 320	**55.4**	**89.8**	**87.0**	**74.5**	**69.5**	**71.8**	**104.9**	**111.5**
Direct investment income	2 330	8.6	14.9	7.9	5.4	7.0	8.1	8.5	5.7
Dividends and distributed branch profits	2 332	8.6	14.9	7.9	5.4	7.0	8.1	6.3	5.7
Reinvested earnings and undistributed branch profits	2 333	...	...	...	...	...	...	...	...
Income on debt (interest)	2 334	...	...	...	...	...	...	2.2	...
Portfolio investment income	2 339	.5	.9	.6	.7	3.2	2.6	2.7	5.3
Income on equity	2 340	...	...	...	...	...	...	...	...
Income on bonds and notes	2 350	...	...	...	...	...	...	...	...
Income on money market instruments	2 360	...	...	...	...	...	...	...	...
Other investment income	2 370	46.3	74.0	78.5	68.4	59.3	61.1	93.7	100.5
Investment income, debit	3 320	**–448.8**	**–507.0**	**–359.0**	**–424.1**	**–443.7**	**–474.6**	**–522.2**	**–623.9**
Direct investment income	3 330	–181.9	–229.8	–107.5	–178.8	–184.2	–228.0	–289.9	–300.8
Dividends and distributed branch profits	3 332	–127.1	–155.3	–35.0	–86.5	–79.8	–137.4	–159.0	–171.6
Reinvested earnings and undistributed branch profits	3 333	–49.3	–69.4	–68.1	–88.6	–101.1	–87.3	–116.0	–115.9
Income on debt (interest)	3 334	–5.5	–5.1	–4.4	–3.7	–3.3	–3.3	–14.9	–13.3
Portfolio investment income	3 339	–11.9	–9.8	–10.2	–8.2	–8.9	–8.4	–7.6	–6.7
Income on equity	3 340	...	...	...	...	...	...	...	...
Income on bonds and notes	3 350	...	...	...	...	...	...	...	...
Income on money market instruments	3 360	...	...	...	...	...	...	...	...
Other investment income	3 370	–255.0	–267.4	–241.3	–237.1	–250.6	–238.2	–224.7	–316.4
D. CURRENT TRANSFERS	4 379	459.9	607.0	623.6	624.8	633.9	647.3	820.8	886.1
Credit	2 379	**504.2**	**669.6**	**709.3**	**705.7**	**733.5**	**757.9**	**969.4**	**1,062.7**
General government	2 380	24.2	57.0	57.1	44.5	50.5	53.5	155.1	97.0
Other sectors	2 390	480.0	612.6	652.2	661.2	683.0	704.4	814.3	965.7
Workers' remittances	2 391	457.9	582.3	635.5	642.3	660.6	681.0	789.5	939.9
Other current transfers	2 392	22.1	30.3	16.7	18.9	22.4	23.4	24.8	25.8
Debit	3 379	**–44.3**	**–62.6**	**–85.7**	**–80.9**	**–99.6**	**–110.6**	**–148.6**	**–176.6**
General government	3 380	–5.0	–4.8	–7.4	–4.7	–7.3	–7.7	–7.2	–6.6
Other sectors	3 390	–39.3	–57.8	–78.3	–76.2	–92.3	–102.9	–141.4	–170.0
Workers' remittances	3 391	–24.3	–39.8	–62.6	–68.5	–84.4	–95.8	–131.2	–147.3
Other current transfers	3 392	–15.0	–18.0	–15.7	–7.7	–7.9	–7.1	–10.2	–22.7
CAPITAL AND FINANCIAL ACCOUNT	4 996	**–91.2**	**91.8**	**133.8**	**322.3**	**284.7**	**220.3**	**337.8**	**773.2**
CAPITAL ACCOUNT	4 994	**10.4**	**10.5**	**16.6**	**–11.6**	**–8.7**	**–10.9**	**2.2**	**–22.3**
Total credit	2 994	*33.2*	*34.5*	*42.5*	*21.7*	*20.3*	*19.1*	*29.6*	*15.2*
Total debit	3 994	*–22.8*	*–24.0*	*–25.9*	*–33.3*	*–29.0*	*–30.0*	*–27.4*	*–37.5*
Capital transfers, credit	2 400	**33.2**	**34.5**	**42.5**	**21.7**	**20.3**	**19.1**	**29.6**	**15.2**
General government	2 401	18.2	20.5	18.7	7.0	4.2	4.1	15.6	3.5
Debt forgiveness	2 402	...	...	...	...	...	...	...	...
Other capital transfers	2 410	18.2	20.5	18.7	7.0	4.2	4.1	15.6	3.5
Other sectors	2 430	15.0	14.0	23.8	14.7	16.1	15.0	14.0	11.7
Migrants' transfers	2 431	15.0	14.0	23.8	14.7	16.1	15.0	14.0	11.7
Debt forgiveness	2 432	...	...	...	...	...	...	...	...
Other capital transfers	2 440	...	...	...	...	...	...	...	...
Capital transfers, debit	3 400	**–22.8**	**–24.0**	**–25.9**	**–33.3**	**–29.0**	**–30.0**	**–27.4**	**–37.5**
General government	3 401	...	...	...	...	...	...	...	...
Debt forgiveness	3 402	...	...	...	...	...	...	...	...
Other capital transfers	3 410	...	...	...	...	...	...	...	...
Other sectors	3 430	–22.8	–24.0	–25.9	–33.3	–29.0	–30.0	–27.4	–37.5
Migrants' transfers	3 431	–22.8	–24.0	–25.9	–33.3	–29.0	–30.0	–27.4	–37.5
Debt forgiveness	3 432	...	...	...	...	...	...	...	...
Other capital transfers	3 440	...	...	...	...	...	...	...	...
Nonproduced nonfinancial assets, credit	2 480	...	...	...	...	...	...	...	...
Nonproduced nonfinancial assets, debit	3 480	...	...	...	...	...	...	...	...

Table 2 (Continued). STANDARD PRESENTATION, 1994–2001

(Millions of U.S. dollars)

	Code	1994	1995	1996	1997	1998	1999	2000	2001
FINANCIAL ACCOUNT	4 995	**–101.6**	**81.3**	**117.2**	**333.9**	**293.4**	**231.2**	**335.6**	**795.5**
A. DIRECT INVESTMENT	4 500	77.0	81.1	90.4	146.7	287.1	428.8	394.1	524.9
Direct investment abroad	4 505	**–52.7**	**–66.3**	**–93.3**	**–56.6**	**–82.0**	**–94.9**	**–74.3**	**–89.0**
Equity capital	4 510	–2.0	–20.7	–45.3	–9.0	–35.0	–45.9	–25.6	–51.6
Claims on affiliated enterprises	4 515	–2.0	–20.7	–45.3	–9.0	–35.0	–45.9	–25.6	–51.6
Liabilities to affiliated enterprises	4 520	...	...	...	...	...	...	...	...
Reinvested earnings	4 525	...	...	...	...	...	...	...	...
Other capital	4 530	–50.7	–45.6	–48.0	–47.6	–47.0	–49.0	–48.7	–37.4
Claims on affiliated enterprises	4 535	...	...	...	...	...	...	...	...
Liabilities to affiliated enterprises	4 540	–50.7	–45.6	–48.0	–47.6	–47.0	–49.0	–48.7	–37.4
Direct investment in Jamaica	4 555	**129.7**	**147.4**	**183.7**	**203.3**	**369.1**	**523.7**	**468.4**	**613.9**
Equity capital	4 560	62.7	75.5	97.6	103.1	151.1	352.8	273.8	427.4
Claims on direct investors	4 565	...	...	...	...	...	...	...	...
Liabilities to direct investors	4 570	62.7	75.5	97.6	103.1	151.1	352.8	273.8	427.4
Reinvested earnings	4 575	49.3	69.4	68.1	88.6	101.1	87.3	116.1	115.9
Other capital	4 580	17.7	2.5	18.0	11.6	116.9	83.6	78.5	70.6
Claims on direct investors	4 585	...	...	...	...	...	...	...	...
Liabilities to direct investors	4 590	17.7	2.5	18.0	11.6	116.9	83.6	78.5	70.6
B. PORTFOLIO INVESTMENT	4 600	...	...	...	5.7	7.0	4.9	–64.1	30.4
Assets	4 602	**...**	**...**	**...**	**...**	**–3.9**	**–3.7**	**–70.0**	**–39.3**
Equity securities	4 610	...	...	...	...	...	...	...	...
Monetary authorities	4 611	...	...	...	...	...	...	...	...
General government	4 612	...	...	...	...	...	...	...	...
Banks	4 613	...	...	...	...	...	...	...	...
Other sectors	4 614	...	...	...	...	...	...	...	...
Debt securities	4 619	...	...	...	...	–3.9	–3.7	–70.0	–39.3
Bonds and notes	4 620	...	...	...	...	–3.9	–3.7	–70.0	–39.3
Monetary authorities	4 621	...	...	...	...	...	...	...	...
General government	4 622	...	...	...	...	...	...	...	...
Banks	4 623	...	...	...	...	...	...	...	...
Other sectors	4 624	...	...	...	...	–3.9	–3.7	–70.0	–39.3
Money market instruments	4 630	...	...	...	...	...	...	...	...
Monetary authorities	4 631	...	...	...	...	...	...	...	...
General government	4 632	...	...	...	...	...	...	...	...
Banks	4 633	...	...	...	...	...	...	...	...
Other sectors	4 634	...	...	...	...	...	...	...	...
Liabilities	4 652	**...**	**...**	**...**	**5.7**	**10.9**	**8.6**	**5.9**	**69.7**
Equity securities	4 660	...	...	...	...	...	...	...	...
Banks	4 663	...	...	...	...	...	...	...	...
Other sectors	4 664	...	...	...	...	...	...	...	...
Debt securities	4 669	...	...	...	5.7	10.9	8.6	5.9	69.7
Bonds and notes	4 670	...	...	...	5.7	10.9	8.6	5.9	69.7
Monetary authorities	4 671	...	...	...	...	...	...	...	...
General government	4 672	...	...	...	...	...	...	...	...
Banks	4 673	...	...	...	...	...	...	...	...
Other sectors	4 674	...	...	...	5.7	10.9	8.6	5.9	69.7
Money market instruments	4 680	...	...	...	...	...	...	...	...
Monetary authorities	4 681	...	...	...	...	...	...	...	...
General government	4 682	...	...	...	...	...	...	...	...
Banks	4 683	...	...	...	...	...	...	...	...
Other sectors	4 684	...	...	...	...	...	...	...	...
C. FINANCIAL DERIVATIVES	4 910	...	...	...	...	...	...	...	...
Monetary authorities	4 911	...	...	...	...	...	...	...	...
General government	4 912	...	...	...	...	...	...	...	...
Banks	4 913	...	...	...	...	...	...	...	...
Other sectors	4 914	...	...	...	...	...	...	...	...
Assets	4 900	**...**	**...**	**...**	**...**	**...**	**...**	**...**	**...**
Monetary authorities	4 901	...	...	...	...	...	...	...	...
General government	4 902	...	...	...	...	...	...	...	...
Banks	4 903	...	...	...	...	...	...	...	...
Other sectors	4 904	...	...	...	...	...	...	...	...
Liabilities	4 905	**...**	**...**	**...**	**...**	**...**	**...**	**...**	**...**
Monetary authorities	4 906	...	...	...	...	...	...	...	...
General government	4 907	...	...	...	...	...	...	...	...
Banks	4 908	...	...	...	...	...	...	...	...
Other sectors	4 909	...	...	...	...	...	...	...	...

Table 2 (Concluded). STANDARD PRESENTATION, 1994–2001
(Millions of U.S. dollars)

	Code	1994	1995	1996	1997	1998	1999	2000	2001
D. OTHER INVESTMENT	4 700 . .	142.4	–55.5	228.5	–23.5	26.2	–357.8	505.0	1,086.9
Assets	4 703 . .	**–141.3**	**–148.8**	**–13.8**	**–113.2**	**–59.1**	**–122.7**	**–95.5**	**–215.5**
Trade credits	4 706 . .	. . .	. . .	. . .	. . .	. . .	. . .	. . .	. . .
General government	4 707 . .	. . .	. . .	. . .	. . .	. . .	. . .	. . .	. . .
of which: Short-term	4 709 . .	. . .	. . .	. . .	. . .	. . .	. . .	. . .	. . .
Other sectors	4 710 . .	. . .	. . .	. . .	. . .	. . .	. . .	. . .	. . .
of which: Short-term	4 712 . .	. . .	. . .	. . .	. . .	. . .	. . .	. . .	. . .
Loans	4 714 . .	. . .	. . .	. . .	. . .	. . .	. . .	. . .	. . .
Monetary authorities	4 715 . .	. . .	. . .	. . .	. . .	. . .	. . .	. . .	. . .
of which: Short-term	4 718 . .	. . .	. . .	. . .	. . .	. . .	. . .	. . .	. . .
General government	4 719 . .	. . .	. . .	. . .	. . .	. . .	. . .	. . .	. . .
of which: Short-term	4 721 . .	. . .	. . .	. . .	. . .	. . .	. . .	. . .	. . .
Banks	4 722 . .	. . .	. . .	. . .	. . .	. . .	. . .	. . .	. . .
of which: Short-term	4 724 . .	. . .	. . .	. . .	. . .	. . .	. . .	. . .	. . .
Other sectors	4 725 . .	. . .	. . .	. . .	. . .	. . .	. . .	. . .	. . .
of which: Short-term	4 727 . .	. . .	. . .	. . .	. . .	. . .	. . .	. . .	. . .
Currency and deposits	4 730 . .	–177.9	–199.2	–88.1	–186.9	–142.3	–215.1	–181.5	–282.9
Monetary authorities	4 731 . .	. . .	. . .	. . .	. . .	. . .	. . .	. . .	. . .
General government	4 732 . .	. . .	. . .	. . .	. . .	. . .	. . .	. . .	. . .
Banks	4 733 . .	–177.9	–199.2	–88.1	–186.9	–142.3	–215.1	–181.5	–282.9
Other sectors	4 734 . .	. . .	. . .	. . .	. . .	. . .	. . .	. . .	. . .
Other assets	4 736 . .	36.6	50.4	74.3	73.7	83.2	92.4	86.0	67.4
Monetary authorities	4 737 . .	. . .	. . .	. . .	. . .	. . .	. . .	. . .	. . .
of which: Short-term	4 739 . .	. . .	. . .	. . .	. . .	. . .	. . .	. . .	. . .
General government	4 740 . .	. . .	. . .	. . .	. . .	. . .	. . .	. . .	. . .
of which: Short-term	4 742 . .	. . .	. . .	. . .	. . .	. . .	. . .	. . .	. . .
Banks	4 743 . .	. . .	. . .	. . .	. . .	. . .	. . .	. . .	. . .
of which: Short-term	4 745 . .	. . .	. . .	. . .	. . .	. . .	. . .	. . .	. . .
Other sectors	4 746 . .	36.6	50.4	74.3	73.7	83.2	92.4	86.0	67.4
of which: Short-term	4 748 . .	*46.5*	*61.0*	*79.8*	*79.4*	*83.9*	*93.3*	*87.6*	*88.5*
Liabilities	4 753 . .	**283.7**	**93.3**	**242.3**	**89.7**	**85.3**	**–235.1**	**600.5**	**1,302.4**
Trade credits	4 756 . .	95.4	3.1	40.6	1.7	–7.1	29.3	10.1	–42.9
General government	4 757 . .	. . .	. . .	. . .	. . .	. . .	. . .	. . .	. . .
of which: Short-term	4 759 . .	. . .	. . .	. . .	. . .	. . .	. . .	. . .	. . .
Other sectors	4 760 . .	95.4	3.1	40.6	1.7	–7.1	29.3	10.1	–42.9
of which: Short-term	4 762 . .	*95.4*	*3.1*	*40.6*	*1.7*	*–7.1*	*29.3*	*10.1*	*–42.9*
Loans	4 764 . .	–146.8	–114.9	–147.3	41.8	–223.1	–397.4	446.2	730.2
Monetary authorities	4 765 . .	–36.7	–82.7	–69.7	–34.6	–17.0	–18.9	–19.0	–18.3
of which: Use of Fund credit and loans from the Fund	4 766 . .	*–38.2*	*–84.6*	*–71.9*	*–34.6*	*–17.0*	*–18.9*	*–19.0*	*–18.3*
of which: Short-term	4 768 . .	. . .	. . .	. . .	. . .	. . .	. . .	. . .	. . .
General government	4 769 . .	–127.4	–97.0	–144.7	43.1	–41.3	–331.4	383.6	653.4
of which: Short-term	4 771 . .	. . .	. . .	. . .	. . .	. . .	. . .	. . .	. . .
Banks	4 772 . .	. . .	. . .	. . .	. . .	. . .	. . .	. . .	. . .
of which: Short-term	4 774 . .	. . .	. . .	. . .	. . .	. . .	. . .	. . .	. . .
Other sectors	4 775 . .	17.3	64.8	67.1	33.3	–164.8	–47.1	81.6	95.1
of which: Short-term	4 777 . .	. . .	. . .	. . .	. . .	. . .	. . .	. . .	. . .
Currency and deposits	4 780 . .	326.6	192.2	334.9	34.3	312.8	131.6	143.1	614.0
Monetary authorities	4 781 . .	. . .	. . .	. . .	. . .	. . .	. . .	. . .	. . .
General government	4 782 . .	. . .	. . .	. . .	. . .	. . .	. . .	. . .	. . .
Banks	4 783 . .	142.2	74.7	130.7	156.7	205.5	122.2	167.9	250.5
Other sectors	4 784 . .	184.4	117.5	204.2	–122.4	107.3	9.4	–24.8	363.5
Other liabilities	4 786 . .	8.5	12.9	14.1	11.9	2.7	1.4	1.1	1.1
Monetary authorities	4 787 . .	. . .	. . .	. . .	. . .	. . .	. . .	. . .	. . .
of which: Short-term	4 789 . .	. . .	. . .	. . .	. . .	. . .	. . .	. . .	. . .
General government	4 790 . .	. . .	. . .	. . .	. . .	. . .	. . .	. . .	. . .
of which: Short-term	4 792 . .	. . .	. . .	. . .	. . .	. . .	. . .	. . .	. . .
Banks	4 793 . .	. . .	. . .	. . .	. . .	. . .	. . .	. . .	. . .
of which: Short-term	4 795 . .	. . .	. . .	. . .	. . .	. . .	. . .	. . .	. . .
Other sectors	4 796 . .	8.5	12.9	14.1	11.9	2.7	1.4	1.1	1.1
of which: Short-term	4 798 . .	. . .	. . .	. . .	. . .	. . .	. . .	. . .	. . .
E. RESERVE ASSETS	4 802 . .	–321.0	55.8	–201.7	205.0	–26.9	155.3	–499.4	–846.6
Monetary gold	4 812 . .	. . .	. . .	. . .	. . .	. . .	. . .	. . .	. . .
Special drawing rights	4 811 . .	12.7	–.4	.4	–.2	–.4	–.1	.5	–1.4
Reserve position in the Fund	4 810 . .	. . .	. . .	. . .	. . .	. . .	. . .	. . .	. . .
Foreign exchange	4 803 . .	–343.7	55.9	–199.8	198.8	–26.6	154.9	–500.6	–845.4
Other claims	4 813 . .	10.0	.3	–2.3	6.4	.1	.5	.7	.2
NET ERRORS AND OMISSIONS	4 998 . .	**9.6**	**7.1**	**8.8**	**9.9**	**43.2**	**–4.0**	**49.2**	**15.2**

Part 3 of the *Yearbook* contains descriptions of the methodologies, compilation practices, and sources used to compile these data.

Table 1. ANALYTIC PRESENTATION, 1994–2001
(Billions of U.S. dollars)

	Code			1994	1995	1996	1997	1998	1999	2000	2001
A. Current Account [1]	4	993	Z.	**130.26**	**111.04**	**65.79**	**96.81**	**118.75**	**114.60**	**119.66**	**87.80**
Goods: exports f.o.b	2	100	..	385.70	428.72	400.29	409.24	374.04	403.69	459.51	383.59
Goods: imports f.o.b	3	100	..	–241.51	–296.93	–316.70	–307.64	–251.66	–280.37	–342.80	–313.38
Balance on Goods	4	100	..	*144.19*	*131.79*	*83.58*	*101.60*	*122.39*	*123.32*	*116.72*	*70.21*
Services: credit	2	200	..	58.30	65.27	67.71	69.30	62.41	61.00	69.24	64.52
Services: debit	3	200	..	–106.36	–122.63	–129.99	–123.45	–111.83	–115.16	–116.86	–108.25
Balance on Goods and Services	4	991	..	*96.13*	*74.43*	*21.31*	*47.45*	*72.97*	*69.16*	*69.09*	*26.48*
Income: credit	2	300	..	155.19	192.45	112.44	111.83	100.33	92.05	97.20	103.09
Income: debit	3	300	..	–114.96	–148.16	–58.95	–53.63	–45.71	–34.47	–36.80	–33.87
Balance on Goods, Services, and Income	4	992	..	*136.36*	*118.72*	*74.80*	*105.65*	*127.59*	*126.74*	*129.49*	*95.70*
Current transfers: credit	2	379	Z.	1.83	1.98	6.02	6.01	5.53	6.21	7.38	6.15
Current transfers: debit	3	379	..	–7.94	–9.66	–15.03	–14.84	–14.37	–18.35	–17.21	–14.06
B. Capital Account [1]	4	994	Z.	**–1.85**	**–2.23**	**–3.29**	**–4.05**	**–14.45**	**–16.47**	**–9.26**	**–2.87**
Capital account: credit	2	994	Z.	...	.01	1.22	1.52	1.57	.75	.78	.99
Capital account: debit	3	994	..	–1.85	–2.24	–4.51	–5.57	–16.02	–17.21	–10.04	–3.86
Total, Groups A Plus B	4	981	..	*128.41*	*108.82*	*62.50*	*92.76*	*104.29*	*98.14*	*110.40*	*84.93*
C. Financial Account [1]	4	995	W.	**–85.11**	**–63.98**	**–28.02**	**–120.51**	**–114.82**	**–38.85**	**–78.31**	**–48.16**
Direct investment abroad	4	505	..	–18.09	–22.51	–23.45	–26.06	–24.62	–22.27	–31.53	–38.50
Direct investment in Japan	4	555	Z.	.91	.04	.21	3.20	3.27	12.31	8.23	6.19
Portfolio investment assets	4	602	..	–91.97	–86.05	–100.61	–47.06	–95.24	–154.41	–83.36	–106.79
Equity securities	4	610	..	–14.00	.07	–8.17	–13.73	–14.00	–32.40	–19.72	–11.28
Debt securities	4	619	..	–77.97	–86.11	–92.43	–33.34	–81.24	–122.01	–63.64	–95.51
Portfolio investment liabilities	4	652	Z.	64.53	59.79	66.79	79.19	56.06	126.93	47.39	60.50
Equity securities	4	660	..	48.95	50.60	49.45	27.00	16.11	103.89	–1.29	39.10
Debt securities	4	669	Z.	15.58	9.19	17.34	52.19	39.95	23.04	48.67	21.40
Financial derivatives	4	910	..	.23	–10.31	–7.25	–5.85	1.10	–2.63	–4.67	1.39
Financial derivatives assets	4	900	..	.43	–1.20	98.70	86.17	90.75	83.80	106.74	102.79
Financial derivatives liabilities	4	905	..	–.20	–9.12	–105.95	–92.02	–89.65	–86.43	–111.41	–101.40
Other investment assets	4	703	..	–35.12	–102.24	5.21	–191.96	37.94	266.34	–4.15	46.59
Monetary authorities	4	701	..	...	...	...	...	...	...	...	...
General government	4	704	..	–8.76	–8.66	–5.28	–9.12	–15.50	–11.56	–1.89	–3.95
Banks	4	705	..	–10.67	–85.62	75.57	–140.18	54.14	239.40	36.51	15.59
Other sectors	4	728	..	–15.69	–7.96	–65.08	–42.66	–.70	38.50	–38.77	34.95
Other investment liabilities	4	753	W.	–5.60	97.30	31.08	68.03	–93.33	–265.12	–10.21	–17.55
Monetary authorities	4	753	WA	...	...	...	...	...	...	...	...
General government	4	753	ZB	–2.00	1.18	–2.12	–.11	–1.30	.55	–.93	7.01
Banks	4	753	ZC	4.87	17.27	–9.06	43.34	–23.75	–189.16	28.22	4.99
Other sectors	4	753	ZD	–8.47	78.86	42.27	24.80	–68.28	–76.50	–37.49	–29.54
Total, Groups A Through C	4	983	..	*43.30*	*44.84*	*34.49*	*–27.74*	*–10.52*	*59.29*	*32.09*	*36.77*
D. Net Errors and Omissions	4	998	..	**–18.03**	**13.78**	**.65**	**34.31**	**4.36**	**16.97**	**16.87**	**3.72**
Total, Groups A Through D	4	984	..	*25.27*	*58.61*	*35.14*	*6.57*	*–6.16*	*76.26*	*48.95*	*40.49*
E. Reserves and Related Items	4	802	A.	**–25.27**	**–58.61**	**–35.14**	**–6.57**	**6.16**	**–76.26**	**–48.95**	**–40.49**
Reserve assets	4	802	..	–25.27	–58.61	–35.14	–6.57	6.16	–76.26	–48.95	–40.49
Use of Fund credit and loans	4	766	..	...	...	...	...	...	...	...	...
Exceptional financing	4	920	..	...	...	...	...	...	...	...	...
Conversion rates: yen per U.S. dollar	0	101	..	**102.21**	**94.06**	**108.78**	**120.99**	**130.91**	**113.91**	**107.77**	**121.53**

[1] Excludes components that have been classified in the categories of Group E.

Table 2. STANDARD PRESENTATION, 1994–2001
(Billions of U.S. dollars)

	Code	1994	1995	1996	1997	1998	1999	2000	2001
CURRENT ACCOUNT	4 993 . .	**130.26**	**111.04**	**65.79**	**96.81**	**118.75**	**114.60**	**119.66**	**87.80**
A. GOODS	4 100 . .	144.19	131.79	83.58	101.60	122.39	123.32	116.72	70.21
Credit	2 100 . .	**385.70**	**428.72**	**400.29**	**409.24**	**374.04**	**403.69**	**459.51**	**383.59**
General merchandise: exports f.o.b.	2 110 . .	385.70	428.72	392.06	400.98	367.71	397.13	452.33	377.44
Goods for processing: exports f.o.b.	2 150 . .	. . .	. . .	4.68	4.90	4.18	4.61	5.07	4.30
Repairs on goods	2 160 . .	. . .	. . .	.36	.38	.24	.16	.14	.20
Goods procured in ports by carriers	2 170 . .	. . .	. . .	2.88	2.76	1.73	1.43	1.54	1.32
Nonmonetary gold	2 180 . .	. . .	. . .	.30	.22	.19	.37	.43	.33
Debit	3 100 . .	**–241.51**	**–296.93**	**–316.70**	**–307.64**	**–251.66**	**–280.37**	**–342.80**	**–313.38**
General merchandise: imports f.o.b.	3 110 . .	–241.51	–296.93	–306.07	–296.20	–241.67	–268.72	–328.86	–300.61
Goods for processing: imports f.o.b.	3 150 . .	. . .	. . .	–6.54	–7.32	–6.61	–7.64	–7.97	–7.80
Repairs on goods	3 160 . .	. . .	. . .	–.16	–.18	–.23	–.24	–.23	–.34
Goods procured in ports by carriers	3 170 . .	. . .	. . .	–3.08	–3.18	–2.42	–2.84	–5.17	–4.27
Nonmonetary gold	3 180 . .	. . .	. . .	–.85	–.76	–.72	–.93	–.57	–.36
B. SERVICES	4 200 . .	–48.06	–57.35	–62.28	–54.15	–49.42	–54.16	–47.63	–43.73
Total credit	2 200 . .	*58.30*	*65.27*	*67.71*	*69.30*	*62.41*	*61.00*	*69.24*	*64.52*
Total debit	3 200 . .	*–106.36*	*–122.63*	*–129.99*	*–123.45*	*–111.83*	*–115.16*	*–116.86*	*–108.25*
Transportation services, credit	2 205 . .	**20.31**	**22.51**	**21.60**	**21.83**	**21.27**	**22.93**	**25.60**	**24.01**
Passenger	2 850 . .	*1.52*	*1.67*	*1.69*	*1.85*	*1.92*	*2.28*	*2.60*	*2.44*
Freight	2 851 . .	*10.26*	*11.43*	*13.02*	*13.54*	*13.61*	*14.81*	*16.72*	*15.67*
Other	2 852 . .	*8.53*	*9.41*	*6.88*	*6.44*	*5.74*	*5.83*	*6.28*	*5.89*
Sea transport, passenger	2 207 . .	. . .	. . .	. . .	. . .	.01	.01	. . .	.01
Sea transport, freight	2 208 . .	8.53	9.45	11.11	11.54	11.82	12.48	14.05	13.70
Sea transport, other	2 209 . .	4.78	5.33	3.32	2.96	2.39	2.47	2.75	2.71
Air transport, passenger	2 211 . .	1.52	1.67	1.69	1.84	1.91	2.28	2.59	2.43
Air transport, freight	2 212 . .	1.73	1.98	1.89	1.98	1.78	2.32	2.66	1.96
Air transport, other	2 213 . .	3.76	4.08	3.56	3.48	3.34	3.35	3.52	3.18
Other transport, passenger	2 215 . .	. . .	. . .	. . .	. . .	. . .	. . .	. . .	. . .
Other transport, freight	2 216 . .	. . .	. . .	.02	.01	.01	.01	.01	.01
Other transport, other	2 217 . .	. . .	. . .	. . .	. . .	. . .	.01	.02	.01
Transportation services, debit	3 205 . .	**–31.70**	**–35.92**	**–33.62**	**–31.11**	**–28.38**	**–30.64**	**–35.10**	**–32.38**
Passenger	3 850 . .	*–9.55*	*–10.20*	*–9.74*	*–8.37*	*–6.53*	*–8.44*	*–10.76*	*–9.00*
Freight	3 851 . .	*–9.50*	*–11.87*	*–17.43*	*–16.50*	*–15.70*	*–16.14*	*–18.05*	*–17.31*
Other	3 852 . .	*–12.66*	*–13.85*	*–6.45*	*–6.23*	*–6.15*	*–6.06*	*–6.29*	*–6.07*
Sea transport, passenger	3 207 . .	. . .	. . .	–.01	–.01	–.02	–.02	. . .	. . .
Sea transport, freight	3 208 . .	–8.21	–10.19	–15.75	–15.06	–14.52	–14.43	–15.86	–15.29
Sea transport, other	3 209 . .	–11.78	–12.86	–5.64	–5.38	–5.19	–5.05	–5.21	–5.12
Air transport, passenger	3 211 . .	–9.55	–10.20	–9.73	–8.36	–6.50	–8.42	–10.75	–8.99
Air transport, freight	3 212 . .	–1.29	–1.68	–1.63	–1.38	–1.15	–1.66	–2.15	–1.96
Air transport, other	3 213 . .	–.88	–.99	–.81	–.85	–.93	–.99	–1.05	–.93
Other transport, passenger	3 215 . .	. . .	. . .	. . .	. . .	–.01	. . .	–.01	–.01
Other transport, freight	3 216 . .	. . .	. . .	–.05	–.06	–.03	–.04	–.05	–.07
Other transport, other	3 217 . .	. . .	. . .	. . .	–.01	–.04	–.02	–.03	–.01
Travel, credit	2 236 . .	**3.48**	**3.22**	**4.08**	**4.33**	**3.74**	**3.43**	**3.37**	**3.31**
Business travel	2 237 . .	1.08	1.03	1.22	1.25	1.03	.93	.93	. . .
Personal travel	2 240 . .	2.40	2.19	2.86	3.08	2.72	2.50	2.44	. . .
Travel, debit	3 236 . .	**–30.70**	**–36.76**	**–37.06**	**–33.01**	**–28.81**	**–32.77**	**–31.88**	**–26.53**
Business travel	3 237 . .	–5.67	–7.36	–7.36	–6.37	–5.75	–5.66	–5.73	. . .
Personal travel	3 240 . .	–25.03	–29.40	–29.70	–26.63	–23.06	–27.12	–26.16	. . .
Other services, credit	2 200 BA	**34.51**	**39.54**	**42.03**	**43.15**	**37.40**	**34.64**	**40.27**	**37.20**
Communications	2 245 . .	.47	.50	1.38	1.36	1.16	.76	.82	.72
Construction	2 249 . .	4.96	6.56	5.94	7.86	7.74	5.73	5.85	4.79
Insurance	2 253 . .	.37	.30	.49	.35	.04	–.08	.17	–.10
Financial	2 260 . .	.19	.31	2.84	1.85	1.61	2.04	2.86	2.71
Computer and information	2 262 . .	. . .	. . .	1.22	1.41	1.34	1.26	1.57	1.41
Royalties and licence fees	2 266 . .	5.18	6.01	6.68	7.30	7.39	8.19	10.23	10.46
Other business services	2 268 . .	21.71	24.44	21.98	21.61	17.08	15.81	17.71	16.24
Personal, cultural, and recreational	2 287 . .	.11	.13	.18	.23	.43	.24	.12	.12
Government, n.i.e.	2 291 . .	1.52	1.31	1.34	1.17	.62	.69	.94	.85
Other services, debit	3 200 BA	**–43.95**	**–49.94**	**–59.31**	**–59.33**	**–54.64**	**–51.74**	**–49.88**	**–49.34**
Communications	3 245 . .	–.79	–.84	–1.87	–1.71	–1.59	–1.41	–1.15	–1.07
Construction	3 249 . .	–2.34	–3.21	–4.80	–5.46	–5.53	–4.31	–4.00	–3.81
Insurance	3 253 . .	–2.58	–2.51	–1.91	–2.03	–2.37	–2.33	–2.03	–2.64
Financial	3 260 . .	–.56	–.46	–2.98	–2.68	–2.15	–2.72	–1.88	–1.65
Computer and information	3 262 . .	. . .	. . .	–2.44	–3.48	–3.53	–2.96	–3.07	–2.64
Royalties and licence fees	3 266 . .	–8.31	–9.42	–9.83	–9.62	–8.95	–9.85	–11.01	–11.10
Other business services	3 268 . .	–28.00	–31.87	–32.98	–31.89	–28.13	–26.03	–24.30	–23.81
Personal, cultural, and recreational	3 287 . .	–.48	–.56	–1.21	–1.09	–1.26	–1.14	–1.28	–1.39
Government, n.i.e.	3 291 . .	–.91	–1.08	–1.29	–1.37	–1.13	–.98	–1.18	–1.22

Table 2 (Continued). STANDARD PRESENTATION, 1994–2001

(Billions of U.S. dollars)

	Code	1994	1995	1996	1997	1998	1999	2000	2001
C. INCOME	4 300	40.23	44.29	53.49	58.20	54.62	57.58	60.40	69.22
Total credit	2 300	*155.19*	*192.45*	*112.44*	*111.83*	*100.33*	*92.05*	*97.20*	*103.09*
Total debit	3 300	*–114.96*	*–148.16*	*–58.95*	*–53.63*	*–45.71*	*–34.47*	*–36.80*	*–33.87*
Compensation of employees, credit	2 310	**.87**	**1.15**	**.25**	**.35**	**.33**	**.35**	**.27**	**.21**
Compensation of employees, debit	3 310	**–1.58**	**–1.82**	**–.26**	**–.34**	**–.31**	**–.31**	**–.27**	**–.25**
Investment income, credit	2 320	**154.32**	**191.29**	**112.18**	**111.47**	**100.00**	**91.70**	**96.93**	**102.88**
Direct investment income	2 330	9.71	9.40	14.64	16.12	12.36	6.11	8.24	16.81
Dividends and distributed branch profits	2 332	8.16	8.02	10.55	8.92	8.07	4.43	8.89	8.66
Reinvested earnings and undistributed branch profits	2 333	. . .	. . .	2.25	5.24	2.87	.52	–1.82	6.92
Income on debt (interest)	2 334	1.55	1.39	1.84	1.95	1.42	1.16	1.16	1.23
Portfolio investment income	2 339	48.60	56.75	57.08	59.05	53.09	54.77	61.35	63.15
Income on equity	2 340	. . .	. . .	4.94	5.56	5.73	6.71	7.39	7.26
Income on bonds and notes	2 350	. . .	. . .	48.85	49.15	43.71	44.73	47.87	50.12
Income on money market instruments	2 360	. . .	. . .	3.29	4.33	3.64	3.33	6.09	5.78
Other investment income	2 370	96.01	125.15	40.46	36.31	34.56	30.82	27.34	22.92
Investment income, debit	3 320	**–113.37**	**–146.34**	**–58.69**	**–53.29**	**–45.40**	**–34.16**	**–36.53**	**–33.62**
Direct investment income	3 330	–1.93	–2.54	–3.61	–4.00	–2.45	–2.32	–2.61	–4.12
Dividends and distributed branch profits	3 332	–1.80	–2.47	–2.51	–3.17	–2.10	–3.12	–2.40	–2.27
Reinvested earnings and undistributed branch profits	3 333	. . .	. . .	–.72	–.35	.20	1.08	.10	–1.55
Income on debt (interest)	3 334	–.14	–.07	–.39	–.47	–.54	–.28	–.32	–.31
Portfolio investment income	3 339	–18.24	–19.94	–16.98	–14.84	–12.82	–11.57	–13.87	–11.79
Income on equity	3 340	. . .	. . .	–1.67	–1.89	–1.70	–1.56	–2.79	–2.65
Income on bonds and notes	3 350	. . .	. . .	–15.30	–12.92	–11.12	–10.01	–11.08	–9.14
Income on money market instruments	3 360	. . .	. . .	–.01	–.03	–.01	. . .	. . .	. . .
Other investment income	3 370	–93.20	–123.86	–38.10	–34.45	–30.13	–20.27	–20.04	–17.71
D. CURRENT TRANSFERS	4 379	–6.11	–7.68	–9.01	–8.83	–8.84	–12.14	–9.83	–7.90
Credit	2 379	**1.83**	**1.98**	**6.02**	**6.01**	**5.53**	**6.21**	**7.38**	**6.15**
General government	2 380	.28	.33	.16	.18	.15	.13	.19	.16
Other sectors	2 390	1.55	1.66	5.86	5.83	5.38	6.09	7.19	5.99
Workers' remittances	2 391	. . .	. . .	.25	.26	.22	.22	.50	1.04
Other current transfers	2 392	. . .	. . .	5.61	5.57	5.16	5.87	6.69	4.95
Debit	3 379	**–7.94**	**–9.66**	**–15.03**	**–14.84**	**–14.37**	**–18.35**	**–17.21**	**–14.06**
General government	3 380	–3.11	–3.61	–2.13	–2.50	–2.34	–5.50	–3.09	–2.33
Other sectors	3 390	–4.83	–6.05	–12.90	–12.35	–12.03	–12.85	–14.12	–11.73
Workers' remittances	3 391	. . .	. . .	–2.78	–2.78	–2.60	–2.72	–2.26	–2.09
Other current transfers	3 392	. . .	. . .	–10.12	–9.57	–9.43	–10.13	–11.86	–9.64
CAPITAL AND FINANCIAL ACCOUNT	4 996	**–112.23**	**–124.82**	**–66.44**	**–131.13**	**–123.11**	**–131.57**	**–136.53**	**–91.52**
CAPITAL ACCOUNT	4 994	**–1.85**	**–2.23**	**–3.29**	**–4.05**	**–14.45**	**–16.47**	**–9.26**	**–2.87**
Total credit	2 994	. . .	*.01*	*1.22*	*1.52*	*1.57*	*.75*	*.78*	*.99*
Total debit	3 994	*–1.85*	*–2.24*	*4.51*	*–5.57*	*–16.02*	*–17.21*	*–10.04*	*–3.86*
Capital transfers, credit	2 400	**. . .**	**.01**	**.75**	**.75**	**1.24**	**.57**	**.65**	**.76**
General government	2 401	. . .	.01	. . .	. . .	. . .	. . .	.01	. . .
Debt forgiveness	2 402	. . .	. . .	. . .	. . .	. . .	. . .	. . .	. . .
Other capital transfers	2 410	. . .	. . .	. . .	. . .	. . .	. . .	.01	. . .
Other sectors	2 430	. . .	. . .	.75	.75	1.24	.57	.64	.75
Migrants' transfers	2 431	. . .	. . .	.73	.73	.69	.54	.60	.73
Debt forgiveness	2 432	. . .	. . .	. . .	. . .	. . .	. . .	. . .	. . .
Other capital transfers	2 440	. . .	. . .	.02	.02	.55	.03	.04	.02
Capital transfers, debit	3 400	**–1.85**	**–2.24**	**–4.35**	**–5.21**	**–14.40**	**–14.19**	**–9.18**	**–3.19**
General government	3 401	–1.85	–2.24	–1.79	–1.64	–1.75	–1.88	–1.65	–1.52
Debt forgiveness	3 402	. . .	. . .	. . .	. . .	. . .	. . .	. . .	. . .
Other capital transfers	3 410	. . .	. . .	–1.79	–1.64	–1.75	–1.88	–1.65	–1.52
Other sectors	3 430	. . .	. . .	–2.56	–3.57	–12.65	–12.31	–7.53	–1.67
Migrants' transfers	3 431	. . .	. . .	–.52	–.50	–.49	–.51	–.64	–.60
Debt forgiveness	3 432	. . .	. . .	–1.12	–1.11	–.88	–1.84	–1.91	–1.01
Other capital transfers	3 440	. . .	. . .	–.92	–1.96	–11.28	–9.97	–4.98	–.06
Nonproduced nonfinancial assets, credit	2 480	**. . .**	**. . .**	**.47**	**.76**	**.33**	**.17**	**.13**	**.24**
Nonproduced nonfinancial assets, debit	3 480	**. . .**	**. . .**	**–.17**	**–.36**	**–1.62**	**–3.03**	**–.86**	**–.67**

Table 2 (Continued). STANDARD PRESENTATION, 1994–2001
(Billions of U.S. dollars)

	Code	1994	1995	1996	1997	1998	1999	2000	2001
FINANCIAL ACCOUNT	4 995 . .	**–110.38**	**–122.59**	**–63.16**	**–127.08**	**–108.65**	**–115.10**	**–127.27**	**–88.65**
A. DIRECT INVESTMENT	4 500 . .	–17.18	–22.47	–23.24	–22.86	–21.36	–9.96	–23.31	–32.31
Direct investment abroad	4 505 . .	**–18.09**	**–22.51**	**–23.45**	**–26.06**	**–24.62**	**–22.27**	**–31.53**	**–38.50**
Equity capital	4 510 . .	–16.54	–23.26	–18.68	–21.64	–15.57	–19.65	–30.79	–27.50
Claims on affiliated enterprises	4 515 . .	. . .	. . .	–18.68	–21.64	–15.57	–19.65	–30.80	–26.28
Liabilities to affiliated enterprises	4 520 . .	. . .	. . .	. . .	. . .	. . .	.01	.01	–1.22
Reinvested earnings	4 525 . .	. . .	. . .	–2.25	–5.24	–2.87	–.52	1.82	–6.92
Other capital	4 530 . .	–1.55	.75	–2.52	.82	–6.19	–2.10	–2.56	–4.08
Claims on affiliated enterprises	4 535 . .	. . .	. . .	–2.47	.71	–6.06	–1.48	–2.32	–3.28
Liabilities to affiliated enterprises	4 540 . .	. . .	. . .	–.04	.11	–.12	–.62	–.24	–.80
Direct investment in Japan	4 555 . .	**.91**	**.04**	**.21**	**3.20**	**3.27**	**12.31**	**8.23**	**6.19**
Equity capital	4 560 . .	.69	.31	–.72	1.98	2.62	11.34	7.59	4.86
Claims on direct investors	4 565 . .	. . .	. . .	–.01	–.01	.10	–.06	–.07	. . .
Liabilities to direct investors	4 570 . .	. . .	. . .	–.70	1.99	2.53	11.40	7.66	4.86
Reinvested earnings	4 575 . .	. . .	. . .	.72	.35	–.20	–1.08	–.10	1.55
Other capital	4 580 . .	.22	–.28	.21	.87	.84	2.05	.74	–.22
Claims on direct investors	4 585 . .	. . .	. . .	–.66	–.04	–.56	–.74	–.64	–.92
Liabilities to direct investors	4 590 . .	. . .	. . .	.86	.91	1.40	2.79	1.38	.71
B. PORTFOLIO INVESTMENT	4 600 . .	–27.45	–26.26	–33.82	32.13	–39.17	–27.48	–35.98	–46.29
Assets	4 602 . .	**–91.97**	**–86.05**	**–100.61**	**–47.06**	**–95.24**	**–154.41**	**–83.36**	**–106.79**
Equity securities	4 610 . .	–14.00	.07	–8.17	–13.73	–14.00	–32.40	–19.72	–11.28
Monetary authorities	4 611 . .	. . .	. . .	. . .	. . .	. . .	. . .	. . .	. . .
General government	4 612 . .	. . .	. . .	. . .	. . .	. . .	. . .	. . .	. . .
Banks	4 613 . .	.27	–1.73	.03	.27	–.06	.82	–1.13	.29
Other sectors	4 614 . .	–14.27	1.80	–8.20	–13.99	–13.94	–33.23	–18.59	–11.57
Debt securities	4 619 . .	–77.97	–86.11	–92.43	–33.34	–81.24	–122.01	–63.64	–95.51
Bonds and notes	4 620 . .	–70.06	–92.28	–80.46	–24.82	–60.14	–84.73	–47.85	–96.71
Monetary authorities	4 621 . .	. . .	. . .	. . .	. . .	. . .	. . .	. . .	. . .
General government	4 622 . .	–9.11	1.15	2.73	2.24	3.34	4.76	3.88	12.35
Banks	4 623 . .	–3.51	–.98	.09	10.23	9.62	–15.78	–47.93	–18.31
Other sectors	4 624 . .	–57.44	–92.45	–83.28	–37.28	–73.10	–73.71	–3.80	–90.74
Money market instruments	4 630 . .	–7.91	6.17	–11.97	–8.52	–21.09	–37.28	–15.79	1.20
Monetary authorities	4 631 . .	. . .	. . .	. . .	. . .	. . .	. . .	. . .	. . .
General government	4 632 . .	. . .	. . .	. . .	3.15	.57	.19	.05	.22
Banks	4 633 . .	.38	–2.73	–2.52	–6.16	–19.21	–22.60	–8.66	–13.09
Other sectors	4 634 . .	–8.29	8.90	–9.45	–5.51	–2.45	–14.86	–7.18	14.08
Liabilities	4 652 . .	**64.53**	**59.79**	**66.79**	**79.19**	**56.06**	**126.93**	**47.39**	**60.50**
Equity securities	4 660 . .	48.95	50.60	49.45	27.00	16.11	103.89	–1.29	39.10
Banks	4 663 . .	5.38	9.00	8.64	2.54	3.59	15.48	2.72	–1.18
Other sectors	4 664 . .	43.56	41.60	40.81	24.47	12.52	88.40	–4.01	40.28
Debt securities	4 669 . .	15.58	9.19	17.34	52.19	39.95	23.04	48.67	21.40
Bonds and notes	4 670 . .	–14.43	–10.83	17.09	30.95	–19.37	18.09	56.53	28.35
Monetary authorities	4 671 . .	. . .	. . .	. . .	. . .	. . .	. . .	. . .	. . .
General government	4 672 . .	–.38	3.53	9.00	24.91	–11.29	12.80	54.19	27.87
Banks	4 673 . .	–.03	–.02	7.80	10.40	1.94	1.28	7.92	2.35
Other sectors	4 674 . .	–14.02	–14.35	.29	–4.36	–10.02	4.02	–5.57	–1.87
Money market instruments	4 680 . .	30.01	20.02	.24	21.24	59.32	4.95	–7.86	–6.95
Monetary authorities	4 681 . .	. . .	. . .	. . .	. . .	. . .	. . .	. . .	. . .
General government	4 682 . .	29.74	20.02	.07	21.20	59.08	4.92	–7.93	–7.33
Banks	4 683 . .	.02	–.01	–.02	–.03	–.08	–.04	.17	–.02
Other sectors	4 684 . .	.25	.01	.19	.07	.32	.06	–.10	.41
C. FINANCIAL DERIVATIVES	4 910 . .	.23	–10.31	–7.25	–5.85	1.10	–2.63	–4.67	1.39
Monetary authorities	4 911 . .	. . .	. . .	. . .	. . .	. . .	. . .	. . .	. . .
General government	4 912 . .	. . .	. . .	. . .	. . .	. . .	–.01	. . .	.06
Banks	4 913 . .	.41	–1.30	–3.39	–4.00	3.02	–1.00	–.87	.84
Other sectors	4 914 . .	–.18	–9.02	–3.86	–1.85	–1.93	–1.62	–3.80	.49
Assets	4 900 . .	**.43**	**–1.20**	**98.70**	**86.17**	**90.75**	**83.80**	**106.74**	**102.79**
Monetary authorities	4 901 . .	. . .	. . .	. . .	. . .	. . .	. . .	. . .	. . .
General government	4 902 . .	. . .	. . .	. . .	. . .	. . .	. . .	. . .	.07
Banks	4 903 . .	.43	–.75	107.93	106.12	106.13	98.31	110.07	105.03
Other sectors	4 904 . .	. . .	–.45	–9.23	–19.95	–15.38	–14.51	–3.33	–2.32
Liabilities	4 905 . .	**–.20**	**–9.12**	**–105.95**	**–92.02**	**–89.65**	**–86.43**	**–111.41**	**–101.40**
Monetary authorities	4 906 . .	. . .	. . .	. . .	. . .	. . .	. . .	. . .	. . .
General government	4 907 . .	. . .	. . .	. . .	. . .	. . .	–.01	. . .	–.01
Banks	4 908 . .	–.03	–.55	–111.33	–110.12	–103.11	–99.31	–110.95	–104.19
Other sectors	4 909 . .	–.17	–8.57	5.37	18.10	13.45	12.89	–.46	2.80

Table 2 (Concluded). STANDARD PRESENTATION, 1994–2001
(Billions of U.S. dollars)

	Code	1994	1995	1996	1997	1998	1999	2000	2001
D. OTHER INVESTMENT	4 700 . .	–40.71	–4.94	36.29	–123.93	–55.39	1.22	–14.36	29.04
Assets	4 703 . .	**–35.12**	**–102.24**	**5.21**	**–191.96**	**37.94**	**266.34**	**–4.15**	**46.59**
Trade credits	4 706 . .	2.53	2.37	1.00	1.49	–.58	2.82	–1.78	7.66
General government	4 707 . .	.32	–.22	.90	.20	–.07	.44	.30	.18
of which: Short-term	4 709 . .	. . .	. . .	*.03*	. . .	*.01*	*.04*	. . .	. . .
Other sectors	4 710 . .	2.20	2.59	.10	1.29	–.51	2.38	–2.08	7.48
of which: Short-term	4 712 . .	*–1.40*	*–2.26*	*–3.55*	*–1.75*	*–3.37*	*–.30*	*–4.86*	*5.89*
Loans	4 714 . .	–10.82	–165.52	–5.64	–159.08	–12.19	256.60	55.97	–25.32
Monetary authorities	4 715 . .	. . .	. . .	. . .	. . .	. . .	. . .	. . .	. . .
of which: Short-term	4 718 . .	. . .	. . .	. . .	. . .	. . .	. . .	. . .	. . .
General government	4 719 . .	–6.70	–8.97	–5.78	–7.24	–13.66	–12.46	–.82	–3.11
of which: Short-term	4 721 . .	. . .	. . .	. . .	. . .	. . .	. . .	. . .	. . .
Banks	4 722 . .	12.37	–148.29	28.59	–122.41	–.63	221.01	71.54	–31.40
of which: Short-term	4 724 . .	*–1.33*	*–153.46*	*14.13*	*–126.56*	*–29.82*	*210.45*	*47.21*	*–44.71*
Other sectors	4 725 . .	–16.48	–8.26	–28.45	–29.43	2.10	48.06	–14.76	9.20
of which: Short-term	4 727 . .	*–.86*	*–1.38*	*–22.47*	*–33.13*	*–6.45*	*36.55*	*–23.81*	*6.04*
Currency and deposits	4 730 . .	–25.35	40.87	46.53	–8.14	58.97	2.12	–46.56	61.84
Monetary authorities	4 731 . .	. . .	. . .	. . .	. . .	. . .	. . .	. . .	. . .
General government	4 732 . .	. . .	. . .	. . .	. . .	. . .	. . .	. . .	. . .
Banks	4 733 . .	–25.42	41.74	46.41	–7.95	53.62	–7.44	–29.90	43.70
Other sectors	4 734 . .	.06	–.87	.12	–.19	5.35	9.56	–16.66	18.14
Other assets	4 736 . .	–1.48	20.04	–36.68	–26.23	–8.25	4.80	–11.77	2.41
Monetary authorities	4 737 . .	. . .	. . .	. . .	. . .	. . .	. . .	. . .	. . .
of which: Short-term	4 739 . .	. . .	. . .	. . .	. . .	. . .	. . .	. . .	. . .
General government	4 740 . .	–2.38	.53	–.40	–2.07	–1.77	.46	–1.37	–1.02
of which: Short-term	4 742 . .	*.09*	*2.71*	*–.01*	*–.01*	*–.01*	*–.02*	*–.02*	*–.02*
Banks	4 743 . .	2.38	20.94	.57	–9.82	1.16	25.83	–5.13	3.29
of which: Short-term	4 745 . .	*1.39*	*20.70*	*.56*	*–9.39*	*2.46*	*27.61*	*–.94*	*4.52*
Other sectors	4 746 . .	–1.47	–1.42	–36.85	–14.34	–7.63	–21.49	–5.27	.14
of which: Short-term	4 748 . .	*.49*	*1.44*	*–.24*	*–.07*	*.34*	*.10*	*–.29*	*–14.93*
Liabilities	4 753 . .	**–5.60**	**97.30**	**31.08**	**68.03**	**–93.33**	**–265.12**	**–10.21**	**–17.55**
Trade credits	4 756 . .	–1.57	–.34	.49	–.73	–2.52	–1.67	–.25	–1.11
General government	4 757 . .	. . .	. . .	. . .	. . .	. . .	. . .	. . .	. . .
of which: Short-term	4 759 . .	. . .	. . .	. . .	. . .	. . .	. . .	. . .	. . .
Other sectors	4 760 . .	–1.57	–.34	.49	–.73	–2.52	–1.67	–.25	–1.11
of which: Short-term	4 762 . .	*–1.57*	*–.31*	*.71*	*–.51*	*–1.71*	*–1.37*	*.20*	*–.81*
Loans	4 764 . .	–.74	103.21	18.42	82.58	–45.07	–198.79	–18.18	–31.78
Monetary authorities	4 765 . .	. . .	. . .	. . .	. . .	. . .	. . .	. . .	. . .
of which: Use of Fund credit and loans from the Fund	4 766 . .	. . .	. . .	. . .	. . .	. . .	. . .	. . .	. . .
of which: Short-term	4 768 . .	. . .	. . .	. . .	. . .	. . .	. . .	. . .	. . .
General government	4 769 . .	. . .	. . .	.02	. . .	. . .	. . .	. . .	. . .
of which: Short-term	4 771 . .	. . .	. . .	*.02*	. . .	. . .	. . .	. . .	. . .
Banks	4 772 . .	.93	19.58	–16.87	65.44	25.22	127.10	25.74	–4.33
of which: Short-term	4 774 . .	*–.44*	*16.95*	*–21.91*	*55.48*	*22.89*	*–144.52*	*34.99*	*–7.29*
Other sectors	4 775 . .	–1.67	83.63	35.27	17.14	–70.29	–71.69	–43.92	–27.45
of which: Short-term	4 777 . .	*7.95*	*85.87*	*38.28*	*19.05*	*–55.73*	*–59.21*	*–25.10*	*–13.67*
Currency and deposits	4 780 . .	–.67	3.46	7.10	–29.05	–58.31	–59.12	6.62	15.83
Monetary authorities	4 781 . .	. . .	. . .	. . .	. . .	. . .	. . .	. . .	. . .
General government	4 782 . .	–2.17	.04	–.05	. . .	.06	–.19	–.16	7.41
Banks	4 783 . .	1.50	3.42	7.14	–29.05	–58.37	–58.93	6.78	8.42
Other sectors	4 784 . .	. . .	. . .	. . .	. . .	. . .	. . .	. . .	. . .
Other liabilities	4 786 . .	–2.61	–9.03	5.08	15.23	12.57	–5.53	1.60	–.49
Monetary authorities	4 787 . .	. . .	. . .	. . .	. . .	. . .	. . .	. . .	. . .
of which: Short-term	4 789 . .	. . .	. . .	. . .	. . .	. . .	. . .	. . .	. . .
General government	4 790 . .	.18	1.14	–2.10	–.11	–1.36	.74	–.77	–.40
of which: Short-term	4 792 . .	*.18*	*1.14*	*–2.10*	*–.11*	*–1.36*	*.74*	*–.77*	*–.40*
Banks	4 793 . .	2.44	–5.74	.67	6.95	9.40	–3.13	–4.30	.90
of which: Short-term	4 795 . .	*2.59*	*–6.64*	*.63*	*6.52*	*9.57*	*–3.18*	*–4.56*	*.65*
Other sectors	4 796 . .	–5.23	–4.43	6.51	8.39	4.53	–3.14	6.68	–.99
of which: Short-term	4 798 . .	*–5.39*	*–4.40*	*5.97*	*7.74*	*4.14*	*–3.85*	*9.13*	*–1.15*
E. RESERVE ASSETS	4 802 . .	–25.27	–58.61	–35.14	–6.57	6.16	–76.26	–48.95	–40.49
Monetary gold	4 812 . .	. . .	. . .	. . .	. . .	. . .	. . .	–.11	–.01
Special drawing rights	4 811 . .	–.44	–.54	–.02	–.16	.09	–.04	.09	–.03
Reserve position in the Fund	4 810 . .	.14	.69	1.19	–2.90	–.02	2.79	1.00	. . .
Foreign exchange	4 803 . .	–24.97	–58.76	–36.30	–3.51	6.10	–79.01	–49.93	–40.45
Other claims	4 813 . .	. . .	. . .	. . .	. . .	. . .	. . .	. . .	. . .
NET ERRORS AND OMISSIONS	4 998 . .	**–18.03**	**13.78**	**.65**	**34.31**	**4.36**	**16.97**	**16.87**	**3.72**

Part 3 of the *Yearbook* contains descriptions of the methodologies, compilation practices, and sources used to compile these data.

Table 3. INTERNATIONAL INVESTMENT POSITION (End–period stocks), 1994–2001
(Billions of U.S. dollars)

	Code		1994	1995	1996	1997	1998	1999	2000	2001
ASSETS	8 995	C.	2,424.24	2,632.86	2,652.61	2,737.45	2,986.33	3,013.60	2,969.59	2,881.51
Direct investment abroad	8 505	. .	**275.57**	**238.45**	**258.61**	**271.90**	**270.04**	**248.78**	**278.44**	**300.11**
Equity capital and reinvested earnings	8 506	. .	199.43	194.86	215.46	243.38	244.52	221.35	254.52	278.53
Claims on affiliated enterprises	8 507	. .	. . .	197.16	217.55	243.64	245.25	221.43	254.60	278.56
Liabilities to affiliated enterprises	8 508	. .	. . .	–2.30	–2.09	–.27	–.74	–.08	–.08	–.02
Other capital	8 530	. .	76.14	43.60	43.16	28.53	25.52	27.43	23.93	21.58
Claims on affiliated enterprises	8 535	. .	. . .	44.49	43.99	28.75	25.95	28.37	24.99	22.04
Liabilities to affiliated enterprises	8 540	. .	. . .	–.89	–.84	–.22	–.43	–.94	–1.06	–.46
Portfolio investment	8 602	. .	**858.69**	**855.07**	**933.20**	**902.26**	**1,056.49**	**1,242.37**	**1,306.48**	**1,289.75**
Equity securities	8 610	. .	. . .	146.26	154.90	158.77	209.38	285.34	262.25	227.35
Monetary authorities	8 611	. .	. . .	. . .	. . .	. . .	. . .	. . .	. . .	. . .
General government	8 612	. .	. . .	. . .	. . .	. . .	. . .	. . .	. . .	. . .
Banks	8 613	. .	. . .	17.74	17.85	27.24	17.44	19.83	6.40	4.82
Other sectors	8 614	. .	. . .	128.52	137.04	131.53	191.94	265.50	255.85	222.53
Debt securities	8 619	. .	. . .	708.81	778.30	743.49	847.11	957.04	1,044.23	1,062.40
Bonds and notes	8 620	. .	. . .	687.60	745.32	712.16	815.56	897.68	975.51	1,004.88
Monetary authorities	8 621	. .	. . .	. . .	. . .	. . .	. . .	. . .	. . .	. . .
General government	8 622	. .	. . .	71.12	64.79	64.52	74.08	73.00	67.17	52.72
Banks	8 623	. .	. . .	181.01	175.78	182.95	186.97	198.99	290.90	304.24
Other sectors	8 624	. .	. . .	435.48	504.74	464.69	554.50	625.70	617.43	647.92
Money market instruments	8 630	. .	. . .	21.21	32.98	31.32	31.55	59.35	68.72	57.52
Monetary authorities	8 631	. .	. . .	. . .	. . .	. . .	. . .	. . .	. . .	. . .
General government	8 632	. .	. . .	.61	.60	.30	.10	.16	.03	.06
Banks	8 633	. .	. . .	9.31	11.72	8.35	8.03	9.69	8.89	8.30
Other sectors	8 634	. .	. . .	11.29	20.66	22.68	23.43	49.50	59.80	49.16
Financial derivatives	8 900	. .	**. . .**	**3.21**	**3.97**	**4.41**	**5.09**	**4.46**	**3.31**	**3.00**
Monetary authorities	8 901	. .	. . .	. . .	. . .	. . .	. . .	. . .	. . .	. . .
General government	8 902	. .	. . .	. . .	. . .	. . .	. . .	. . .	. . .	. . .
Banks	8 903	. .	. . .	2.64	2.97	3.31	3.67	2.90	2.45	1.89
Other sectors	8 904	. .	. . .	.57	.99	1.10	1.42	1.55	.86	1.11
Other investment	8 703	. .	**1,162.87**	**1,351.31**	**1,239.23**	**1,338.08**	**1,438.88**	**1,230.34**	**1,020.36**	**888.23**
Trade credits	8 706	. .	. . .	60.10	54.98	51.48	55.11	54.68	41.40	32.75
General government	8 707	. .	. . .	12.66	10.44	8.29	9.50	10.54	7.76	6.96
of which: Short-term	8 709	. .	. . .	*.86*	*.74*	*.56*	*.59*	*.59*	*.44*	*.37*
Other sectors	8 710	. .	. . .	47.44	44.54	43.20	45.61	44.14	33.64	25.79
of which: Short-term	8 712	. .	. . .	*12.08*	*15.29*	*16.05*	*18.88*	*19.44*	*18.56*	*17.25*
Loans	8 714	. .	348.33	948.06	879.21	968.77	1,059.38	868.92	649.09	617.97
Monetary authorities	8 715	. .	. . .	. . .	. . .	. . .	. . .	. . .	. . .	. . .
of which: Short-term	8 718	. .	. . .	. . .	. . .	. . .	. . .	. . .	. . .	. . .
General government	8 719	. .	122.50	134.58	126.25	121.07	148.51	178.57	163.09	148.83
of which: Short-term	8 721	. .	. . .	. . .	. . .	. . .	. . .	. . .	. . .	. . .
Banks	8 722	. .	74.19	670.01	594.53	673.30	706.16	520.18	382.33	375.78
of which: Short-term	8 724	. .	. . .	*461.32*	*415.93*	*510.74*	*566.03*	*382.01*	*277.08*	*289.96*
Other sectors	8 725	. .	151.64	143.47	158.43	174.40	204.71	170.17	103.67	93.36
of which: Short-term	8 727	. .	*25.45*	*45.57*	*63.96*	*87.84*	*96.39*	*65.41*	*12.59*	*16.11*
Currency and deposits	8 730	. .	670.51	197.15	136.17	134.16	85.33	100.68	189.13	113.85
Monetary authorities	8 731	. .	. . .	. . .	. . .	. . .	. . .	. . .	. . .	. . .
General government	8 732	. .	. . .	. . .	. . .	. . .	. . .	. . .	. . .	. . .
Banks	8 733	. .	670.51	189.58	129.26	127.74	78.70	93.08	117.22	67.17
Other sectors	8 734	. .	. . .	7.57	6.91	6.42	6.63	7.60	71.91	46.67
Other assets	8 736	. .	144.03	146.00	168.87	183.66	239.07	206.06	140.74	123.66
Monetary authorities	8 737	. .	. . .	. . .	. . .	. . .	. . .	. . .	. . .	. . .
of which: Short-term	8 739	. .	. . .	. . .	. . .	. . .	. . .	. . .	. . .	. . .
General government	8 740	. .	42.51	36.81	33.78	32.96	38.14	41.81	39.31	36.14
of which: Short-term	8 742	. .	. . .	*.01*	*.02*	*.02*	*.04*	*.07*	*.08*	*.09*
Banks	8 743	. .	7.42	51.64	49.35	60.40	91.21	16.75	29.69	24.51
of which: Short-term	8 745	. .	. . .	*49.49*	*47.26*	*57.88*	*87.36*	*12.19*	*20.98*	*12.76*
Other sectors	8 746	. .	94.10	57.55	85.74	90.31	109.71	147.50	71.74	63.02
of which: Short-term	8 748	. .	*52.60*	*2.66*	*2.60*	*2.45*	*2.38*	*2.53*	*4.57*	*17.82*
Reserve assets	8 802	. .	**127.10**	**184.82**	**217.61**	**220.81**	**215.83**	**287.66**	**360.99**	**400.41**
Monetary gold	8 812	. .	1.24	1.26	1.22	1.14	1.19	1.16	6.74	6.79
Special drawing rights	8 811	. .	2.08	2.71	2.64	2.64	2.66	2.66	2.44	2.38
Reserve position in the Fund	8 810	. .	8.63	8.10	6.67	9.14	9.59	6.55	5.25	5.05
Foreign exchange	8 803	. .	115.15	172.75	207.08	207.88	202.38	277.29	346.56	386.20
Other claims	8 813	. .	. . .	. . .	. . .	. . .	. . .	. . .	. . .	. . .

Table 3 (Concluded). INTERNATIONAL INVESTMENT POSITION (End-period stocks), 1994–2001

(Billions of U.S. dollars)

	Code		1994	1995	1996	1997	1998	1999	2000	2001
LIABILITIES	8 995	D.	1,733.92	1,815.26	1,761.59	1,778.72	1,832.69	2,184.48	1,811.65	1,521.42
Direct investment in Japan	8 555	..	**19.17**	**33.51**	**29.94**	**27.08**	**26.07**	**46.12**	**50.32**	**50.32**
Equity capital and reinvested earnings	8 556	..	11.40	27.04	24.01	22.28	21.51	36.15	41.60	43.16
Claims on direct investors	8 557	..	...	–.80	–.70	–.34	–.11	–.15	–.28	–.05
Liabilities to direct investors	8 558	..	...	27.84	24.71	22.62	21.62	36.30	41.88	43.21
Other capital	8 580	..	7.77	6.46	5.93	4.80	4.55	9.97	8.73	7.16
Claims on direct investors	8 585	..	...	–.79	–1.31	–1.17	–1.36	–1.39	–1.31	–1.63
Liabilities to direct investors	8 590	..	...	7.25	7.24	5.97	5.91	11.36	10.03	8.79
Portfolio investment	8 652	..	**630.67**	**545.42**	**556.25**	**582.48**	**632.76**	**1,165.44**	**884.32**	**665.79**
Equity securities	8 660	..	250.88	306.28	315.65	279.53	304.33	833.43	550.23	376.05
Banks	8 663	..	...	25.95	31.05	19.94	19.62	41.97	32.30	11.32
Other sectors	8 664	..	...	280.34	284.59	259.60	284.71	791.46	517.93	364.73
Debt securities	8 669	..	379.79	239.14	240.60	302.95	328.43	332.01	334.09	289.75
Bonds and notes	8 670	..	379.79	183.36	190.57	244.87	240.45	270.75	287.04	254.52
Monetary authorities	8 671	..	...	...	...	...	...	...	...	...
General government	8 672	..	...	92.86	97.64	145.64	158.47	170.99	207.76	179.45
Banks	8 673	..	...	5.37	6.95	5.88	6.56	8.06	9.29	11.53
Other sectors	8 674	..	...	85.13	85.98	93.36	75.42	91.70	69.98	63.54
Money market instruments	8 680	..	...	55.78	50.03	58.07	87.97	61.26	47.05	35.23
Monetary authorities	8 681	..	...	...	...	...	...	...	...	...
General government	8 682	..	...	54.42	48.65	56.01	87.96	61.19	47.05	35.23
Banks	8 683	..	...	.02	...	1.28	.02	.01	...	...
Other sectors	8 684	..	...	1.34	1.39	.79	...	.06	...	...
Financial derivatives	8 905	..	**...**	**2.85**	**2.72**	**4.10**	**4.54**	**3.10**	**3.19**	**3.54**
Monetary authorities	8 906	..	...	...	...	...	...	...	...	...
General government	8 907	..	...	...	...	...	...	...	...	...
Banks	8 908	..	...	2.32	2.39	2.82	3.15	2.50	2.23	2.46
Other sectors	8 909	..	...	.53	.33	1.28	1.39	.60	.96	1.08
Other investment	8 753	..	**1,084.08**	**1,233.48**	**1,172.69**	**1,165.06**	**1,169.32**	**969.83**	**873.82**	**801.77**
Trade credits	8 756	..	...	12.70	12.16	11.40	10.81	10.15	9.49	8.71
General government	8 757	..	...	...	...	...	...	...	...	...
of which: Short-term	8 759	..	...	...	...	...	...	...	...	...
Other sectors	8 760	..	...	12.70	12.16	11.40	10.81	10.15	9.49	8.71
of which: Short-term	8 762	..	...	*11.00*	*10.86*	*10.46*	*9.74*	*8.95*	*8.43*	*7.78*
Loans	8 764	..	284.76	950.70	890.97	903.06	912.57	790.14	663.29	603.48
Monetary authorities	8 765	..	...	...	...	...	...	...	...	...
of which: Use of Fund credit and loans from the Fund	8 766	..	...	...	...	...	...	...	...	...
of which: Short-term	8 768	..	...	...	...	...	...	...	...	...
General government	8 769	..	...	...	...	...	...	...	...	...
of which: Short-term	8 771	..	...	...	...	...	...	...	...	...
Banks	8 772	..	...	504.52	462.22	501.12	545.07	442.16	441.88	411.98
of which: Short-term	8 774	..	...	*437.87*	*395.67*	*430.02*	*465.78*	*336.17*	*353.70*	*329.92*
Other sectors	8 775	..	284.76	446.17	428.75	401.94	367.50	347.98	221.41	191.50
of which: Short-term	8 777	..	*145.41*	*300.27*	*301.97*	*290.46*	*261.45*	*242.18*	*143.16*	*133.89*
Currency and deposits	8 780	..	678.96	220.22	219.15	179.70	128.09	74.07	85.30	95.95
Monetary authorities	8 781	..	...	...	...	...	...	...	...	...
General government	8 782	..	...	...	...	...	...	...	...	...
Banks	8 783	..	678.96	220.22	219.15	179.70	128.09	74.07	85.30	95.95
Other sectors	8 784	..	...	...	...	...	...	...	...	...
Other liabilities	8 786	..	120.36	49.87	50.42	70.90	117.85	95.47	115.74	93.62
Monetary authorities	8 787	..	99.85	...	...	...	...	...	...	...
of which: Short-term	8 789	..	*99.85*	...	...	...	...	...	...	...
General government	8 790	..	...	14.96	11.35	10.12	9.65	11.62	9.68	8.15
of which: Short-term	8 792	..	...	*14.96*	*11.35*	*10.12*	*9.65*	*11.62*	*9.68*	*8.15*
Banks	8 793	..	15.98	20.68	20.20	33.47	78.32	54.48	76.82	60.47
of which: Short-term	8 795	..	...	*20.31*	*19.78*	*32.62*	*77.66*	*53.77*	*75.87*	*58.17*
Other sectors	8 796	..	4.53	14.23	18.87	27.31	29.88	29.38	29.25	25.00
of which: Short-term	8 798	..	*4.16*	*13.64*	*17.84*	*25.78*	*27.73*	*26.15*	*28.67*	*24.35*
NET INTERNATIONAL INVESTMENT POSITION	8 995	..	**690.32**	**817.60**	**891.02**	**958.73**	**1,153.64**	**829.12**	**1,157.94**	**1,360.09**
Conversion rates: yen per U.S. dollar (end of period)	0 102	..	**99.74**	**102.83**	**116.00**	**129.95**	**115.60**	**102.20**	**114.90**	**131.80**

Table 1. ANALYTIC PRESENTATION, 1994–2001
(Millions of U.S. dollars)

	Code	1994	1995	1996	1997	1998	1999	2000	2001
A. Current Account [1]	4 993 Z.	**–398.0**	**–258.6**	**–221.9**	**29.3**	**14.1**	**404.9**	**58.5**	**–4.1**
Goods: exports f.o.b	2 100 . .	1,424.5	1,769.6	1,816.9	1,835.5	1,802.4	1,831.9	1,899.3	2,294.4
Goods: imports f.o.b	3 100 . .	–3,003.8	–3,287.8	–3,818.1	–3,648.5	–3,403.9	–3,292.0	–4,073.6	–4,301.4
Balance on Goods	4 100 . .	*–1,579.4*	*–1,518.2*	*–2,001.1*	*–1,813.0*	*–1,601.6*	*–1,460.1*	*–2,174.3*	*–2,007.0*
Services: credit	2 200 . .	1,562.0	1,709.2	1,846.3	1,736.8	1,825.1	1,701.7	1,636.7	1,481.7
Services: debit	3 200 . .	–1,392.7	–1,614.9	–1,597.7	–1,537.2	–1,783.8	–1,698.0	–1,722.6	–1,725.0
Balance on Goods and Services	4 991 . .	*–1,410.1*	*–1,424.0*	*–1,752.6*	*–1,613.4*	*–1,560.2*	*–1,456.4*	*–2,260.2*	*–2,250.3*
Income: credit	2 300 . .	72.7	115.7	111.7	248.2	306.9	467.6	670.1	648.5
Income: debit	3 300 . .	–387.5	–394.5	–412.7	–457.0	–445.0	–479.7	–535.4	–461.4
Balance on Goods, Services, and Income	4 992 . .	*–1,724.9*	*–1,702.8*	*–2,053.6*	*–1,822.1*	*–1,698.3*	*–1,468.5*	*–2,125.5*	*–2,063.1*
Current transfers: credit	2 379 Z.	1,447.4	1,591.8	1,970.2	2,096.1	1,984.3	2,154.9	2,461.5	2,361.8
Current transfers: debit	3 379 . .	–120.5	–147.6	–138.5	–244.6	–271.9	–281.4	–277.4	–302.8
B. Capital Account [1]	4 994 Z.	**. . .**	**197.2**	**157.7**	**163.8**	**81.1**	**90.3**	**64.9**	**21.6**
Capital account: credit	2 994 Z.	. . .	197.2	157.7	163.8	81.1	90.3	64.9	21.6
Capital account: debit	3 994 . .	. . .	. . .	. . .	. . .	. . .	. . .	. . .	. . .
Total, Groups A Plus B	4 981 . .	*–398.0*	*–61.4*	*–64.2*	*193.1*	*95.2*	*495.2*	*123.4*	*17.5*
C. Financial Account [1]	4 995 W.	**188.9**	**230.0**	**233.9**	**242.3**	**–177.3**	**725.1**	**1,387.6**	**527.8**
Direct investment abroad	4 505 . .	23.1	27.3	43.3	. . .	. . .	–4.5	–4.7	–7.9
Direct investment in Jordan	4 555 Z.	2.9	13.3	15.5	360.9	310.0	158.0	786.6	100.3
Portfolio investment assets	4 602 . .	. . .	. . .	. . .	. . .	. . .	32.2	. . .	. . .
Equity securities	4 610 . .	. . .	. . .	. . .	. . .	. . .	32.2	. . .	. . .
Debt securities	4 619 . .	. . .	. . .	. . .	. . .	. . .	. . .	. . .	. . .
Portfolio investment liabilities	4 652 Z.	. . .	. . .	. . .	. . .	. . .	–28.1	–140.9	–171.7
Equity securities	4 660 . .	. . .	. . .	. . .	. . .	. . .	21.9	–16.8	–145.1
Debt securities	4 669 Z.	. . .	. . .	. . .	. . .	. . .	–49.9	–124.1	–26.5
Financial derivatives	4 910 . .	. . .	. . .	. . .	. . .	. . .	. . .	. . .	. . .
Financial derivatives assets	4 900 . .	. . .	. . .	. . .	. . .	. . .	. . .	. . .	. . .
Financial derivatives liabilities	4 905 . .	. . .	. . .	. . .	. . .	. . .	. . .	. . .	. . .
Other investment assets	4 703 . .	62.5	–313.4	–5.9	16.4	–80.3	–41.9	146.4	26.8
Monetary authorities	4 701 . .	–163.5	–313.4	–5.9	16.4	–80.3	–40.5	148.4	30.6
General government	4 704 . .	. . .	. . .	. . .	. . .	. . .	–1.4	–2.0	–3.8
Banks	4 705 . .	. . .	. . .	. . .	. . .	. . .	. . .	. . .	. . .
Other sectors	4 728 . .	225.9	. . .	. . .	. . .	. . .	. . .	. . .	. . .
Other investment liabilities	4 753 W.	100.4	502.8	181.0	–135.0	–407.1	609.4	600.1	580.3
Monetary authorities	4 753 WA	–8.7	–34.4	–11.0	–27.6	–11.0	183.5	–69.8	4.7
General government	4 753 ZB	–235.4	96.8	17.8	–91.4	–391.0	277.3	15.7	146.7
Banks	4 753 ZC	344.5	440.5	174.2	–15.9	–5.1	205.5	533.9	394.5
Other sectors	4 753 ZD	. . .	. . .	. . .	. . .	. . .	–56.8	120.5	34.4
Total, Groups A Through C	4 983 . .	*–209.1*	*168.6*	*169.7*	*435.4*	*–82.1*	*1,220.3*	*1,511.0*	*545.3*
D. Net Errors and Omissions	4 998 . .	**–55.8**	**–339.9**	**–357.9**	**–160.8**	**–454.0**	**28.7**	**315.6**	**80.0**
Total, Groups A Through D	4 984 . .	*–264.9*	*–171.3*	*–188.2*	*274.6*	*–536.1*	*1,249.0*	*1,826.6*	*625.3*
E. Reserves and Related Items	4 802 A.	**264.9**	**171.3**	**188.2**	**–274.6**	**536.1**	**–1,249.0**	**–1,826.6**	**–625.3**
Reserve assets	4 802 . .	–216.8	–371.5	–280.7	–677.1	–83.4	–1,288.7	–1,815.4	–613.1
Use of Fund credit and loans	4 766 . .	57.6	106.5	97.6	110.3	22.4	39.7	–11.2	–12.1
Exceptional financing	4 920 . .	424.1	436.3	371.4	292.2	597.0	. . .	. . .	. . .
Conversion rates: Jordanian dinar per U.S. dollar	0 101 . .	**.6988**	**.7004**	**.7090**	**.7090**	**.7090**	**.7090**	**.7090**	**.7090**

[1] Excludes components that have been classified in the categories of Group E.

Table 2. STANDARD PRESENTATION, 1994–2001

(Millions of U.S. dollars)

	Code	1994	1995	1996	1997	1998	1999	2000	2001
CURRENT ACCOUNT	4 993 . .	**–398.0**	**–258.6**	**–221.9**	**29.3**	**14.1**	**404.9**	**58.5**	**–4.1**
A. GOODS	4 100 . .	–1,579.4	–1,518.2	–2,001.1	–1,813.0	–1,601.6	–1,460.1	–2,174.3	–2,007.0
Credit	2 100 . .	**1,424.5**	**1,769.6**	**1,816.9**	**1,835.5**	**1,802.4**	**1,831.9**	**1,899.3**	**2,294.4**
General merchandise: exports f.o.b.	2 110 . .	1,424.5	1,769.6	1,816.9	1,835.5	1,802.4	1,831.9	1,899.3	2,294.4
Goods for processing: exports f.o.b.	2 150 . .	...	...	...	...	...	...	...	...
Repairs on goods	2 160 . .	...	...	...	...	...	...	...	...
Goods procured in ports by carriers	2 170 . .	...	...	...	...	...	...	...	...
Nonmonetary gold	2 180 . .	...	...	...	...	...	...	...	...
Debit	3 100 . .	**–3,003.8**	**–3,287.8**	**–3,818.1**	**–3,648.5**	**–3,403.9**	**–3,292.0**	**–4,073.6**	**–4,301.4**
General merchandise: imports f.o.b.	3 110 . .	–3,003.8	–3,287.8	–3,818.1	–3,648.5	–3,403.9	–3,292.0	–4,073.6	–4,301.4
Goods for processing: imports f.o.b.	3 150 . .	...	...	...	...	...	...	...	...
Repairs on goods	3 160 . .	...	...	...	...	...	...	...	...
Goods procured in ports by carriers	3 170 . .	...	...	...	...	...	...	...	...
Nonmonetary gold	3 180 . .	...	...	...	...	...	...	...	...
B. SERVICES	4 200 . .	169.3	94.2	248.5	199.6	41.3	3.7	–85.9	–243.3
Total credit	2 200 . .	*1,562.0*	*1,709.2*	*1,846.3*	*1,736.8*	*1,825.1*	*1,701.7*	*1,636.7*	*1,481.7*
Total debit	3 200 . .	*–1,392.7*	*–1,614.9*	*–1,597.7*	*–1,537.2*	*–1,783.8*	*–1,698.0*	*–1,722.6*	*–1,725.0*
Transportation services, credit	2 205 . .	**352.8**	**418.8**	**376.9**	**390.4**	**310.4**	**298.2**	**297.7**	**257.3**
Passenger	2 850 . .	*262.7*	*313.0*	*282.2*	*288.9*	*230.5*	*221.2*	*212.0*	*181.5*
Freight	2 851 . .	*2.4*	*1.4*	*.6*	*5.4*	*3.2*	*3.4*	*15.2*	*12.1*
Other	2 852 . .	*87.6*	*104.3*	*94.1*	*96.2*	*76.7*	*73.6*	*70.5*	*63.6*
Sea transport, passenger	2 207 . .	...	...	...	...	...	...	...	...
Sea transport, freight	2 208 . .	...	...	...	...	...	...	...	...
Sea transport, other	2 209 . .	...	...	...	...	...	...	...	...
Air transport, passenger	2 211 . .	...	...	...	...	...	...	...	...
Air transport, freight	2 212 . .	...	...	...	...	...	...	...	...
Air transport, other	2 213 . .	...	...	...	...	...	...	...	...
Other transport, passenger	2 215 . .	...	...	...	...	...	...	...	...
Other transport, freight	2 216 . .	...	...	...	...	...	...	...	...
Other transport, other	2 217 . .	...	...	...	...	...	...	...	...
Transportation services, debit	3 205 . .	**–607.4**	**–724.1**	**–718.3**	**–684.9**	**–599.6**	**–573.3**	**–656.4**	**–696.6**
Passenger	3 850 . .	*–227.9*	*–293.7*	*–249.2*	*–237.0*	*–191.0*	*–180.5*	*–183.5*	*–196.3*
Freight	3 851 . .	*–303.6*	*–332.4*	*–386.0*	*–369.0*	*–345.0*	*–332.9*	*–411.8*	*–434.8*
Other	3 852 . .	*–75.9*	*–97.9*	*–83.1*	*–79.0*	*–63.6*	*–59.9*	*–61.1*	*–65.4*
Sea transport, passenger	3 207 . .	...	...	...	...	...	...	...	...
Sea transport, freight	3 208 . .	...	...	...	...	...	...	...	...
Sea transport, other	3 209 . .	...	...	...	...	...	...	...	...
Air transport, passenger	3 211 . .	...	...	...	...	...	...	...	...
Air transport, freight	3 212 . .	...	...	...	...	...	...	...	...
Air transport, other	3 213 . .	...	...	...	...	...	...	...	...
Other transport, passenger	3 215 . .	...	...	...	...	...	...	...	...
Other transport, freight	3 216 . .	...	...	...	...	...	...	...	...
Other transport, other	3 217 . .	...	...	...	...	...	...	...	...
Travel, credit	2 236 . .	**582.0**	**660.2**	**743.6**	**774.0**	**852.9**	**795.5**	**722.7**	**699.7**
Business travel	2 237 . .	...	...	...	...	...	...	...	...
Personal travel	2 240 . .	...	...	...	774.0	852.9	...	...	...
Travel, debit	3 236 . .	**–394.1**	**–424.6**	**–381.4**	**–398.0**	**–451.1**	**–355.3**	**–386.9**	**–420.0**
Business travel	3 237 . .	...	...	...	...	...	...	...	...
Personal travel	3 240 . .	–394.1	–424.6	–381.4	–398.0	–451.1	–355.3	–386.9	–420.0
Other services, credit	2 200 BA	**627.2**	**630.2**	**725.8**	**572.4**	**661.8**	**608.0**	**616.2**	**524.7**
Communications	2 245 . .	...	...	...	...	...	...	...	...
Construction	2 249 . .	...	...	...	...	...	...	...	...
Insurance	2 253 . .	...	...	...	3.9	2.0	1.7	...	...
Financial	2 260 . .	...	...	...	...	...	...	...	...
Computer and information	2 262 . .	...	...	...	...	...	...	...	...
Royalties and licence fees	2 266 . .	...	...	...	...	...	...	...	...
Other business services	2 268 . .	608.5	610.3	709.7	548.1	644.6	593.2	578.3	433.6
Personal, cultural, and recreational	2 287 . .	...	...	...	...	...	...	...	...
Government, n.i.e.	2 291 . .	18.8	19.9	16.1	20.3	15.2	13.1	37.9	91.1
Other services, debit	3 200 BA	**–391.2**	**–466.2**	**–498.0**	**–454.3**	**–733.1**	**–769.4**	**–679.3**	**–608.3**
Communications	3 245 . .	...	...	...	...	...	...	...	...
Construction	3 249 . .	...	...	...	...	...	...	...	...
Insurance	3 253 . .	–73.3	–84.8	–96.1	–81.9	–80.5	–79.7	–91.5	–96.6
Financial	3 260 . .	...	...	...	...	...	...	...	...
Computer and information	3 262 . .	...	...	...	...	...	...	...	...
Royalties and licence fees	3 266 . .	...	...	...	...	...	...	...	...
Other business services	3 268 . .	–121.8	–151.2	–152.3	–76.4	–457.1	–477.0	–328.5	–306.1
Personal, cultural, and recreational	3 287 . .	...	...	...	...	...	...	...	...
Government, n.i.e.	3 291 . .	–196.1	–230.3	–249.6	–295.9	–195.5	–212.7	–259.2	–205.6

Table 2 (Continued). STANDARD PRESENTATION, 1994–2001
(Millions of U.S. dollars)

	Code	1994	1995	1996	1997	1998	1999	2000	2001
C. INCOME	4 300	–314.7	–278.8	–301.0	–208.7	–138.1	–12.1	134.7	187.2
Total credit	2 300	*72.7*	*115.7*	*111.7*	*248.2*	*306.9*	*467.6*	*670.1*	*648.5*
Total debit	3 300	*–387.5*	*–394.5*	*–412.7*	*–457.0*	*–445.0*	*–479.7*	*–535.4*	*–461.4*
Compensation of employees, credit	2 310	**. . .**	**. . .**	**. . .**	**. . .**	**. . .**	**166.4**	**184.5**	**201.1**
Compensation of employees, debit	3 310	**. . .**	**. . .**	**. . .**	**. . .**	**. . .**	**–24.1**	**–23.1**	**–22.8**
Investment income, credit	2 320	**72.7**	**115.7**	**111.7**	**248.2**	**306.9**	**301.1**	**485.6**	**447.4**
Direct investment income	2 330	. . .	. . .	. . .	. . .	. . .	. . .	. . .	. . .
Dividends and distributed branch profits	2 332	. . .	. . .	. . .	. . .	. . .	. . .	. . .	. . .
Reinvested earnings and undistributed branch profits	2 333	. . .	. . .	. . .	. . .	. . .	. . .	. . .	. . .
Income on debt (interest)	2 334	. . .	. . .	. . .	. . .	. . .	. . .	. . .	. . .
Portfolio investment income	2 339	. . .	. . .	. . .	. . .	. . .	. . .	. . .	. . .
Income on equity	2 340	. . .	. . .	. . .	. . .	. . .	. . .	. . .	. . .
Income on bonds and notes	2 350	. . .	. . .	. . .	. . .	. . .	. . .	. . .	. . .
Income on money market instruments	2 360	. . .	. . .	. . .	. . .	. . .	. . .	. . .	. . .
Other investment income	2 370	72.7	115.7	111.7	248.2	306.9	301.1	485.6	447.4
Investment income, debit	3 320	**–387.5**	**–394.5**	**–412.7**	**–457.0**	**–445.0**	**–455.6**	**–512.3**	**–438.5**
Direct investment income	3 330	. . .	. . .	. . .	. . .	. . .	. . .	–1.1	–2.0
Dividends and distributed branch profits	3 332	. . .	. . .	. . .	. . .	. . .	. . .	. . .	. . .
Reinvested earnings and undistributed branch profits	3 333	. . .	. . .	. . .	. . .	. . .	. . .	. . .	. . .
Income on debt (interest)	3 334	. . .	. . .	. . .	. . .	. . .	. . .	. . .	. . .
Portfolio investment income	3 339	. . .	. . .	. . .	. . .	. . .	. . .	–8.0	–5.5
Income on equity	3 340	. . .	. . .	. . .	. . .	. . .	. . .	. . .	. . .
Income on bonds and notes	3 350	. . .	. . .	. . .	. . .	. . .	. . .	–8.0	–5.5
Income on money market instruments	3 360	. . .	. . .	. . .	. . .	. . .	. . .	. . .	. . .
Other investment income	3 370	–387.5	–394.5	–412.7	–457.0	–445.0	–455.6	–503.1	–431.0
D. CURRENT TRANSFERS	4 379	1,326.9	1,444.2	1,831.7	1,851.5	1,712.4	1,873.5	2,184.1	2,059.0
Credit	2 379	**1,447.4**	**1,591.8**	**1,970.2**	**2,096.1**	**1,984.3**	**2,154.9**	**2,461.5**	**2,361.8**
General government	2 380	324.1	325.8	407.8	414.4	358.1	396.2	410.9	465.5
Other sectors	2 390	1,123.2	1,266.0	1,562.5	1,681.7	1,626.2	1,758.7	2,050.6	1,896.4
Workers' remittances	2 391	1,093.9	1,244.0	1,544.1	1,655.1	1,542.7	1,497.6	1,660.6	1,810.2
Other current transfers	2 392	29.3	22.0	18.3	26.5	83.5	261.1	390.0	86.2
Debit	3 379	**–120.5**	**–147.6**	**–138.5**	**–244.6**	**–271.9**	**–281.4**	**–277.4**	**–302.8**
General government	3 380	. . .	. . .	. . .	. . .	. . .	–6.3	–6.2	–4.2
Other sectors	3 390	–120.5	–147.6	–138.5	–244.6	–271.9	–275.0	–271.2	–298.6
Workers' remittances	3 391	–93.0	–107.1	–99.9	–200.0	–207.1	–179.8	–174.3	–170.4
Other current transfers	3 392	–27.5	–40.5	–38.6	–44.6	–64.9	–95.2	–96.9	–128.2
CAPITAL AND FINANCIAL ACCOUNT	4 996	**453.7**	**598.5**	**579.8**	**131.5**	**439.9**	**–433.7**	**–374.1**	**–75.9**
CAPITAL ACCOUNT	4 994	**. . .**	**197.2**	**157.7**	**163.8**	**81.1**	**90.3**	**64.9**	**21.6**
Total credit	2 994	. . .	*197.2*	*157.7*	*163.8*	*81.1*	*90.3*	*64.9*	*21.6*
Total debit	3 994	. . .	. . .	. . .	. . .	. . .	. . .	. . .	. . .
Capital transfers, credit	2 400	**. . .**	**197.2**	**157.7**	**163.8**	**81.1**	**90.3**	**64.9**	**21.6**
General government	2 401	. . .	. . .	. . .	. . .	. . .	2.7	. . .	. . .
Debt forgiveness	2 402	. . .	. . .	. . .	. . .	. . .	. . .	. . .	. . .
Other capital transfers	2 410	. . .	. . .	. . .	. . .	. . .	. . .	. . .	. . .
Other sectors	2 430	. . .	197.2	157.7	163.8	81.1	87.6	64.9	21.6
Migrants' transfers	2 431	. . .	197.2	157.7	163.8	81.1	87.6	. . .	. . .
Debt forgiveness	2 432	. . .	. . .	. . .	. . .	. . .	. . .	. . .	. . .
Other capital transfers	2 440	. . .	. . .	. . .	. . .	. . .	. . .	64.9	21.6
Capital transfers, debit	3 400	**. . .**	**. . .**	**. . .**	**. . .**	**. . .**	**. . .**	**. . .**	**. . .**
General government	3 401	. . .	. . .	. . .	. . .	. . .	. . .	. . .	. . .
Debt forgiveness	3 402	. . .	. . .	. . .	. . .	. . .	. . .	. . .	. . .
Other capital transfers	3 410	. . .	. . .	. . .	. . .	. . .	. . .	. . .	. . .
Other sectors	3 430	. . .	. . .	. . .	. . .	. . .	. . .	. . .	. . .
Migrants' transfers	3 431	. . .	. . .	. . .	. . .	. . .	. . .	. . .	. . .
Debt forgiveness	3 432	. . .	. . .	. . .	. . .	. . .	. . .	. . .	. . .
Other capital transfers	3 440	. . .	. . .	. . .	. . .	. . .	. . .	. . .	. . .
Nonproduced nonfinancial assets, credit	2 480	**. . .**	**. . .**	**. . .**	**. . .**	**. . .**	**. . .**	**. . .**	**. . .**
Nonproduced nonfinancial assets, debit	3 480	**. . .**	**. . .**	**. . .**	**. . .**	**. . .**	**. . .**	**. . .**	**. . .**

Table 2 (Continued). STANDARD PRESENTATION, 1994–2001
(Millions of U.S. dollars)

	Code		1994	1995	1996	1997	1998	1999	2000	2001
FINANCIAL ACCOUNT	4 995	. .	**453.7**	**401.3**	**422.1**	**–32.3**	**358.8**	**–523.9**	**–439.0**	**–97.5**
A. DIRECT INVESTMENT	4 500	. .	26.0	40.6	58.8	360.9	310.0	153.5	781.9	92.4
Direct investment abroad	4 505	. .	**23.1**	**27.3**	**43.3**	**. . .**	**. . .**	**–4.5**	**–4.7**	**–7.9**
Equity capital	4 510	. .	. . .	. . .	. . .	. . .	. . .	. . .	. . .	. . .
Claims on affiliated enterprises	4 515	. .	. . .	. . .	. . .	. . .	. . .	. . .	. . .	. . .
Liabilities to affiliated enterprises	4 520	. .	. . .	. . .	. . .	. . .	. . .	. . .	. . .	. . .
Reinvested earnings	4 525	. .	. . .	. . .	. . .	. . .	. . .	. . .	. . .	. . .
Other capital	4 530	. .	23.1	27.3	43.3	. . .	. . .	. . .	. . .	. . .
Claims on affiliated enterprises	4 535	. .	. . .	. . .	. . .	. . .	. . .	. . .	. . .	. . .
Liabilities to affiliated enterprises	4 540	. .	. . .	. . .	. . .	. . .	. . .	. . .	. . .	. . .
Direct investment in Jordan	4 555	. .	**2.9**	**13.3**	**15.5**	**360.9**	**310.0**	**158.0**	**786.6**	**100.3**
Equity capital	4 560	. .	. . .	. . .	. . .	280.8	141.7	. . .	. . .	. . .
Claims on direct investors	4 565	. .	. . .	. . .	. . .	. . .	. . .	. . .	. . .	. . .
Liabilities to direct investors	4 570	. .	. . .	. . .	. . .	. . .	. . .	. . .	. . .	. . .
Reinvested earnings	4 575	. .	. . .	. . .	. . .	. . .	. . .	. . .	. . .	. . .
Other capital	4 580	. .	2.9	13.3	15.5	80.1	168.3	. . .	. . .	. . .
Claims on direct investors	4 585	. .	. . .	. . .	. . .	. . .	. . .	. . .	. . .	. . .
Liabilities to direct investors	4 590	. .	. . .	. . .	. . .	. . .	. . .	. . .	. . .	. . .
B. PORTFOLIO INVESTMENT	4 600	. .	. . .	. . .	. . .	. . .	. . .	4.1	–140.9	–171.7
Assets	4 602	. .	**. . .**	**. . .**	**. . .**	**. . .**	**. . .**	**32.2**	**. . .**	**. . .**
Equity securities	4 610	. .	. . .	. . .	. . .	. . .	. . .	32.2	. . .	. . .
Monetary authorities	4 611	. .	. . .	. . .	. . .	. . .	. . .	. . .	. . .	. . .
General government	4 612	. .	. . .	. . .	. . .	. . .	. . .	. . .	. . .	. . .
Banks	4 613	. .	. . .	. . .	. . .	. . .	. . .	. . .	. . .	. . .
Other sectors	4 614	. .	. . .	. . .	. . .	. . .	. . .	32.2	. . .	. . .
Debt securities	4 619	. .	. . .	. . .	. . .	. . .	. . .	. . .	. . .	. . .
Bonds and notes	4 620	. .	. . .	. . .	. . .	. . .	. . .	. . .	. . .	. . .
Monetary authorities	4 621	. .	. . .	. . .	. . .	. . .	. . .	. . .	. . .	. . .
General government	4 622	. .	. . .	. . .	. . .	. . .	. . .	. . .	. . .	. . .
Banks	4 623	. .	. . .	. . .	. . .	. . .	. . .	. . .	. . .	. . .
Other sectors	4 624	. .	. . .	. . .	. . .	. . .	. . .	. . .	. . .	. . .
Money market instruments	4 630	. .	. . .	. . .	. . .	. . .	. . .	. . .	. . .	. . .
Monetary authorities	4 631	. .	. . .	. . .	. . .	. . .	. . .	. . .	. . .	. . .
General government	4 632	. .	. . .	. . .	. . .	. . .	. . .	. . .	. . .	. . .
Banks	4 633	. .	. . .	. . .	. . .	. . .	. . .	. . .	. . .	. . .
Other sectors	4 634	. .	. . .	. . .	. . .	. . .	. . .	. . .	. . .	. . .
Liabilities	4 652	. .	**. . .**	**. . .**	**. . .**	**. . .**	**. . .**	**–28.1**	**–140.9**	**–171.7**
Equity securities	4 660	. .	. . .	. . .	. . .	. . .	. . .	21.9	–16.8	–145.1
Banks	4 663	. .	. . .	. . .	. . .	. . .	. . .	. . .	. . .	. . .
Other sectors	4 664	. .	. . .	. . .	. . .	. . .	. . .	21.9	–16.8	–145.1
Debt securities	4 669	. .	. . .	. . .	. . .	. . .	. . .	–49.9	–124.1	–26.5
Bonds and notes	4 670	. .	. . .	. . .	. . .	. . .	. . .	. . .	–124.1	–26.5
Monetary authorities	4 671	. .	. . .	. . .	. . .	. . .	. . .	. . .	. . .	. . .
General government	4 672	. .	. . .	. . .	. . .	. . .	. . .	. . .	–124.1	–26.5
Banks	4 673	. .	. . .	. . .	. . .	. . .	. . .	. . .	. . .	. . .
Other sectors	4 674	. .	. . .	. . .	. . .	. . .	. . .	. . .	. . .	. . .
Money market instruments	4 680	. .	. . .	. . .	. . .	. . .	. . .	–49.9	. . .	. . .
Monetary authorities	4 681	. .	. . .	. . .	. . .	. . .	. . .	–49.9	. . .	. . .
General government	4 682	. .	. . .	. . .	. . .	. . .	. . .	. . .	. . .	. . .
Banks	4 683	. .	. . .	. . .	. . .	. . .	. . .	. . .	. . .	. . .
Other sectors	4 684	. .	. . .	. . .	. . .	. . .	. . .	. . .	. . .	. . .
C. FINANCIAL DERIVATIVES	4 910	. .	. . .	. . .	. . .	. . .	. . .	. . .	. . .	. . .
Monetary authorities	4 911	. .	. . .	. . .	. . .	. . .	. . .	. . .	. . .	. . .
General government	4 912	. .	. . .	. . .	. . .	. . .	. . .	. . .	. . .	. . .
Banks	4 913	. .	. . .	. . .	. . .	. . .	. . .	. . .	. . .	. . .
Other sectors	4 914	. .	. . .	. . .	. . .	. . .	. . .	. . .	. . .	. . .
Assets	4 900	. .	**. . .**	**. . .**	**. . .**	**. . .**	**. . .**	**. . .**	**. . .**	**. . .**
Monetary authorities	4 901	. .	. . .	. . .	. . .	. . .	. . .	. . .	. . .	. . .
General government	4 902	. .	. . .	. . .	. . .	. . .	. . .	. . .	. . .	. . .
Banks	4 903	. .	. . .	. . .	. . .	. . .	. . .	. . .	. . .	. . .
Other sectors	4 904	. .	. . .	. . .	. . .	. . .	. . .	. . .	. . .	. . .
Liabilities	4 905	. .	**. . .**	**. . .**	**. . .**	**. . .**	**. . .**	**. . .**	**. . .**	**. . .**
Monetary authorities	4 906	. .	. . .	. . .	. . .	. . .	. . .	. . .	. . .	. . .
General government	4 907	. .	. . .	. . .	. . .	. . .	. . .	. . .	. . .	. . .
Banks	4 908	. .	. . .	. . .	. . .	. . .	. . .	. . .	. . .	. . .
Other sectors	4 909	. .	. . .	. . .	. . .	. . .	. . .	. . .	. . .	. . .

Table 2 (Concluded). STANDARD PRESENTATION, 1994–2001
(Millions of U.S. dollars)

	Code	1994	1995	1996	1997	1998	1999	2000	2001
D. OTHER INVESTMENT	4 700 . .	644.6	732.2	644.0	283.9	132.1	607.3	735.4	594.9
Assets	4 703 . .	**62.5**	**–313.4**	**–5.9**	**16.4**	**–80.3**	**–41.9**	**146.4**	**26.8**
Trade credits	4 706 . .	. . .	. . .	. . .	. . .	. . .	. . .	. . .	. . .
General government	4 707 . .	. . .	. . .	. . .	. . .	. . .	. . .	. . .	. . .
of which: Short-term	4 709 . .	. . .	. . .	. . .	. . .	. . .	. . .	. . .	. . .
Other sectors	4 710 . .	. . .	. . .	. . .	. . .	. . .	. . .	. . .	. . .
of which: Short-term	4 712 . .	. . .	. . .	. . .	. . .	. . .	. . .	. . .	. . .
Loans	4 714 . .	–163.5	–313.4	–5.9	16.4	–80.3	–40.5	148.4	30.6
Monetary authorities	4 715 . .	–163.5	–313.4	–5.9	16.4	–80.3	–40.5	148.4	30.6
of which: Short-term	4 718 . .	*–163.5*	*–313.4*	*–5.9*	*16.4*	*–80.3*	*–40.5*	*148.4*	*30.6*
General government	4 719 . .	. . .	. . .	. . .	. . .	. . .	. . .	. . .	. . .
of which: Short-term	4 721 . .	. . .	. . .	. . .	. . .	. . .	. . .	. . .	. . .
Banks	4 722 . .	. . .	. . .	. . .	. . .	. . .	. . .	. . .	. . .
of which: Short-term	4 724 . .	. . .	. . .	. . .	. . .	. . .	. . .	. . .	. . .
Other sectors	4 725 . .	. . .	. . .	. . .	. . .	. . .	. . .	. . .	. . .
of which: Short-term	4 727 . .	. . .	. . .	. . .	. . .	. . .	. . .	. . .	. . .
Currency and deposits	4 730 . .	225.9	. . .	. . .	. . .	. . .	. . .	. . .	. . .
Monetary authorities	4 731 . .	. . .	. . .	. . .	. . .	. . .	. . .	. . .	. . .
General government	4 732 . .	. . .	. . .	. . .	. . .	. . .	. . .	. . .	. . .
Banks	4 733 . .	. . .	. . .	. . .	. . .	. . .	. . .	. . .	. . .
Other sectors	4 734 . .	225.9	. . .	. . .	. . .	. . .	. . .	. . .	. . .
Other assets	4 736 . .	. . .	. . .	. . .	. . .	. . .	–1.4	–2.0	–3.8
Monetary authorities	4 737 . .	. . .	. . .	. . .	. . .	. . .	. . .	. . .	. . .
of which: Short-term	4 739 . .	. . .	. . .	. . .	. . .	. . .	. . .	. . .	. . .
General government	4 740 . .	. . .	. . .	. . .	. . .	. . .	–1.4	–2.0	–3.8
of which: Short-term	4 742 . .	. . .	. . .	. . .	. . .	. . .	. . .	. . .	. . .
Banks	4 743 . .	. . .	. . .	. . .	. . .	. . .	. . .	. . .	. . .
of which: Short-term	4 745 . .	. . .	. . .	. . .	. . .	. . .	. . .	. . .	. . .
Other sectors	4 746 . .	. . .	. . .	. . .	. . .	. . .	. . .	. . .	. . .
of which: Short-term	4 748 . .	. . .	. . .	. . .	. . .	. . .	. . .	. . .	. . .
Liabilities	4 753 . .	**582.1**	**1,045.6**	**649.9**	**267.5**	**212.4**	**649.2**	**589.0**	**568.1**
Trade credits	4 756 . .	. . .	. . .	. . .	. . .	. . .	–33.0	35.8	18.5
General government	4 757 . .	. . .	. . .	. . .	. . .	. . .	. . .	. . .	. . .
of which: Short-term	4 759 . .	. . .	. . .	. . .	. . .	. . .	. . .	. . .	. . .
Other sectors	4 760 . .	. . .	. . .	. . .	. . .	. . .	–33.0	35.8	18.5
of which: Short-term	4 762 . .	. . .	. . .	. . .	. . .	. . .	*–33.0*	*35.8*	*18.5*
Loans	4 764 . .	246.3	588.6	419.2	314.9	228.5	278.8	72.3	151.5
Monetary authorities	4 765 . .	57.6	106.5	97.6	110.3	22.4	25.3	–27.9	–11.1
of which: Use of Fund credit and loans from the Fund	4 766 . .	*57.6*	*106.5*	*97.6*	*110.3*	*22.4*	*39.7*	*–11.2*	*–12.1*
of which: Short-term	4 768 . .	. . .	. . .	. . .	. . .	. . .	. . .	. . .	. . .
General government	4 769 . .	188.7	482.1	321.6	204.7	206.1	277.3	15.7	146.7
of which: Short-term	4 771 . .	. . .	. . .	. . .	. . .	. . .	. . .	. . .	. . .
Banks	4 772 . .	. . .	. . .	. . .	. . .	. . .	. . .	. . .	. . .
of which: Short-term	4 774 . .	. . .	. . .	. . .	. . .	. . .	. . .	. . .	. . .
Other sectors	4 775 . .	. . .	. . .	. . .	. . .	. . .	–23.8	84.6	15.9
of which: Short-term	4 777 . .	. . .	. . .	. . .	. . .	. . .	. . .	. . .	. . .
Currency and deposits	4 780 . .	344.5	440.5	174.2	–15.9	–5.1	205.5	533.9	394.5
Monetary authorities	4 781 . .	. . .	. . .	. . .	. . .	. . .	. . .	. . .	. . .
General government	4 782 . .	. . .	. . .	. . .	. . .	. . .	. . .	. . .	. . .
Banks	4 783 . .	344.5	440.5	174.2	–15.9	–5.1	205.5	533.9	394.5
Other sectors	4 784 . .	. . .	. . .	. . .	. . .	. . .	. . .	. . .	. . .
Other liabilities	4 786 . .	–8.7	16.6	56.6	–31.5	–11.0	197.9	–53.0	3.7
Monetary authorities	4 787 . .	–8.7	–34.4	–11.0	–27.6	–11.0	197.9	–53.0	3.7
of which: Short-term	4 789 . .	*–8.7*	*–34.4*	*–11.0*	*–27.6*	*–11.0*	*197.9*	*–53.0*	*3.7*
General government	4 790 . .	. . .	51.0	67.6	–3.8	. . .	. . .	. . .	. . .
of which: Short-term	4 792 . .	. . .	*51.0*	*67.6*	*–3.8*	. . .	. . .	. . .	. . .
Banks	4 793 . .	. . .	. . .	. . .	. . .	. . .	. . .	. . .	. . .
of which: Short-term	4 795 . .	. . .	. . .	. . .	. . .	. . .	. . .	. . .	. . .
Other sectors	4 796 . .	. . .	. . .	. . .	. . .	. . .	. . .	. . .	. . .
of which: Short-term	4 798 . .	. . .	. . .	. . .	. . .	. . .	. . .	. . .	. . .
E. RESERVE ASSETS	4 802 . .	–216.8	–371.5	–280.7	–677.1	–83.4	–1,288.7	–1,815.4	–613.1
Monetary gold	4 812 . .	. . .	.3	–1.8	–3.0	–3.5	84.2	20.9	–13.0
Special drawing rights	4 811 . .	5.8	–.5	.4	.3	–.6	.4	–.7	–.6
Reserve position in the Fund	4 810 . .	. . .	. . .	. . .	. . .	. . .	. . .	–.1	. . .
Foreign exchange	4 803 . .	–47.9	–86.0	–89.6	–442.0	450.5	–879.1	–701.8	269.7
Other claims	4 813 . .	–174.7	–285.3	–189.7	–232.4	–529.8	–494.2	–1,133.7	–869.3
NET ERRORS AND OMISSIONS	4 998 . .	**–55.8**	**–339.9**	**–357.9**	**–160.8**	**–454.0**	**28.7**	**315.6**	**80.0**

Part 3 of the *Yearbook* contains descriptions of the methodologies, compilation practices, and sources used to compile these data.

Table 3. INTERNATIONAL INVESTMENT POSITION (End–period stocks), 1994–2001

(Millions of U.S. dollars)

	Code	1994	1995	1996	1997	1998	1999	2000	2001
ASSETS	8 995 C.	...	...	...	...	...	...	...	...
Direct investment abroad	8 505 . .	...	...	...	...	...	...	...	...
Equity capital and reinvested earnings	8 506 . .	...	...	...	...	...	...	...	...
Claims on affiliated enterprises	8 507 . .	...	...	...	...	...	...	...	...
Liabilities to affiliated enterprises	8 508 . .	...	...	...	...	...	...	...	...
Other capital	8 530 . .	...	...	...	...	...	...	...	...
Claims on affiliated enterprises	8 535 . .	...	...	...	...	...	...	...	...
Liabilities to affiliated enterprises	8 540 . .	...	...	...	...	...	...	...	...
Portfolio investment	8 602 . .	...	...	**118.9**	**188.6**	**190.0**	**184.6**	**229.9**	**457.8**
Equity securities	8 610 . .	...	...	89.1	110.6	109.7	93.1	102.0	136.0
Monetary authorities	8 611 . .	...	...	44.6	44.7	44.9	45.1	45.3	46.1
General government	8 612 . .	...	...	...	...	...	...	...	...
Banks	8 613 . .	...	...	44.6	65.9	64.9	48.0	56.7	89.8
Other sectors	8 614 . .	...	...	...	...	...	...	...	...
Debt securities	8 619 . .	...	...	29.8	78.0	80.3	91.5	127.9	321.9
Bonds and notes	8 620 . .	...	...	29.8	78.0	80.3	91.5	127.9	321.9
Monetary authorities	8 621 . .	...	...	...	...	...	...	...	...
General government	8 622 . .	...	...	...	...	...	...	...	...
Banks	8 623 . .	...	...	29.8	78.0	80.3	91.5	127.9	321.9
Other sectors	8 624 . .	...	...	...	...	...	...	...	...
Money market instruments	8 630 . .	...	...	...	...	...	...	...	...
Monetary authorities	8 631 . .	...	...	...	...	...	...	...	...
General government	8 632 . .	...	...	...	...	...	...	...	...
Banks	8 633 . .	...	...	...	...	...	...	...	...
Other sectors	8 634 . .	...	...	...	...	...	...	...	...
Financial derivatives	8 900 . .	...	...	...	...	...	...	...	...
Monetary authorities	8 901 . .	...	...	...	...	...	...	...	...
General government	8 902 . .	...	...	...	...	...	...	...	...
Banks	8 903 . .	...	...	...	...	...	...	...	...
Other sectors	8 904 . .	...	...	...	...	...	...	...	...
Other investment	8 703 . .	...	...	**3,992.5**	**4,139.2**	**4,748.0**	**5,288.4**	**6,228.6**	**6,840.2**
Trade credits	8 706 . .	...	...	...	...	...	...	...	...
General government	8 707 . .	...	...	...	...	...	...	...	...
of which: Short-term	8 709 . .	...	...	...	...	...	...	...	...
Other sectors	8 710 . .	...	...	...	...	...	...	...	...
of which: Short-term	8 712 . .	...	...	...	...	...	...	...	...
Loans	8 714 . .	...	...	1,440.2	1,417.6	1,568.3	1,633.7	1,488.9	1,478.4
Monetary authorities	8 715 . .	...	...	1,221.9	1,205.6	1,286.0	1,326.5	1,178.1	1,147.5
of which: Short-term	8 718 . .	...	...	...	...	...	...	...	...
General government	8 719 . .	...	...	...	...	...	...	...	...
of which: Short-term	8 721 . .	...	...	...	...	...	...	...	...
Banks	8 722 . .	...	...	218.3	212.0	282.2	307.2	310.7	330.9
of which: Short-term	8 724 . .	...	...	...	...	...	...	...	...
Other sectors	8 725 . .	...	...	...	...	...	...	...	...
of which: Short-term	8 727 . .	...	...	...	...	...	...	...	...
Currency and deposits	8 730 . .	...	...	2,494.1	2,574.8	2,982.1	3,379.7	4,322.0	4,853.0
Monetary authorities	8 731 . .	...	...	...	...	...	...	...	...
General government	8 732 . .	...	...	...	...	...	...	...	...
Banks	8 733 . .	...	...	2,494.1	2,574.8	2,982.1	3,379.7	4,322.0	4,853.0
Other sectors	8 734 . .	...	...	...	...	...	...	...	...
Other assets	8 736 . .	...	...	58.3	146.8	197.6	275.0	417.8	508.7
Monetary authorities	8 737 . .	...	...	...	...	...	...	...	...
of which: Short-term	8 739 . .	...	...	...	...	...	...	...	...
General government	8 740 . .	...	...	...	...	...	...	...	...
of which: Short-term	8 742 . .	...	...	...	...	...	...	...	...
Banks	8 743 . .	...	...	58.3	146.8	197.6	275.0	417.8	508.7
of which: Short-term	8 745 . .	...	...	...	...	...	...	...	...
Other sectors	8 746 . .	...	...	...	...	...	...	...	...
of which: Short-term	8 748 . .	...	...	...	...	...	...	...	...
Reserve assets	8 802 . .	...	...	**1,957.0**	**2,401.0**	**1,954.8**	**2,749.1**	**3,430.5**	**3,174.3**
Monetary gold	8 812 . .	...	...	197.7	200.7	204.4	120.0	99.2	112.1
Special drawing rights	8 811 . .	.7	1.2	.8	.2	.8	.3	.6	1.2
Reserve position in the Fund	8 810 . .	...	...	...	...	...	...	.1	.1
Foreign exchange	8 803 . .	...	...	1,758.4	2,200.1	1,749.7	2,628.8	3,330.6	3,060.9
Other claims	8 813 . .	...	...	...	...	...	...	...	...

Table 3 (Concluded). INTERNATIONAL INVESTMENT POSITION (End–period stocks), 1994–2001
(Millions of U.S. dollars)

	Code	1994	1995	1996	1997	1998	1999	2000	2001
LIABILITIES	8 995 D.	...	...	...	...	...	...	...	...
Direct investment in Jordan	8 555 . .	...	...	...	...	...	...	...	...
Equity capital and reinvested earnings	8 556 . .	...	...	...	...	...	...	...	...
Claims on direct investors	8 557 . .	...	...	...	...	...	...	...	...
Liabilities to direct investors	8 558 . .	...	...	...	...	...	...	...	...
Other capital	8 580 . .	...	...	...	...	...	...	...	...
Claims on direct investors	8 585 . .	...	...	...	...	...	...	...	...
Liabilities to direct investors	8 590 . .	...	...	...	...	...	...	...	...
Portfolio investment	8 652 . .	...	...	**622.6**	**588.9**	**456.8**	**456.8**	**354.0**	**318.8**
Equity securities	8 660 . .	...	...	...	...	...	...	...	...
Banks	8 663 . .	...	...	...	...	...	...	...	...
Other sectors	8 664 . .	...	...	...	...	...	...	...	...
Debt securities	8 669 . .	...	...	622.6	588.9	456.8	456.8	354.0	318.8
Bonds and notes	8 670 . .	...	...	622.6	588.9	456.8	456.8	354.0	318.8
Monetary authorities	8 671 . .	...	...	...	...	...	...	...	...
General government	8 672 . .	...	...	622.6	588.9	456.8	456.8	354.0	318.8
Banks	8 673 . .	...	...	...	...	...	...	...	...
Other sectors	8 674 . .	...	...	...	...	...	...	...	...
Money market instruments	8 680 . .	...	...	...	...	...	...	...	...
Monetary authorities	8 681 . .	...	...	...	...	...	...	...	...
General government	8 682 . .	...	...	...	...	...	...	...	...
Banks	8 683 . .	...	...	...	...	...	...	...	...
Other sectors	8 684 . .	...	...	...	...	...	...	...	...
Financial derivatives	8 905 . .	...	...	...	...	...	...	...	...
Monetary authorities	8 906 . .	...	...	...	...	...	...	...	...
General government	8 907 . .	...	...	...	...	...	...	...	...
Banks	8 908 . .	...	...	...	...	...	...	...	...
Other sectors	8 909 . .	...	...	...	...	...	...	...	...
Other investment	8 753 . .	...	...	**9,833.2**	**9,611.8**	**10,169.3**	**10,830.1**	**10,757.9**	**11,084.0**
Trade credits	8 756 . .	...	...	...	...	...	...	...	...
General government	8 757 . .	...	...	...	...	...	...	...	...
of which: *Short-term*	8 759 . .	...	...	...	...	...	...	...	...
Other sectors	8 760 . .	...	...	...	...	...	...	...	...
of which: *Short-term*	8 762 . .	...	...	...	...	...	...	...	...
Loans	8 764 . .	...	...	6,661.1	6,483.3	7,057.0	7,314.4	6,761.5	6,689.2
Monetary authorities	8 765 . .	...	...	339.5	427.1	469.4	498.0	461.6	432.9
of which: Use of Fund credit and loans from the Fund	8 766 . .	*144.4*	*251.5*	*339.5*	*427.1*	*469.4*	*498.0*	*461.6*	*432.9*
of which: *Short-term*	8 768 . .	...	...	...	...	...	...	...	...
General government	8 769 . .	...	...	6,321.6	6,056.1	6,587.6	6,816.4	6,299.9	6,256.3
of which: *Short-term*	8 771 . .	...	...	...	...	...	...	...	...
Banks	8 772 . .	...	...	...	...	...	...	...	...
of which: *Short-term*	8 774 . .	...	...	...	...	...	...	...	...
Other sectors	8 775 . .	...	...	...	...	...	...	...	...
of which: *Short-term*	8 777 . .	...	...	...	...	...	...	...	...
Currency and deposits	8 780 . .	...	...	3,094.2	3,045.4	2,956.3	3,366.0	3,709.6	4,022.4
Monetary authorities	8 781 . .	...	...	71.4	43.7	32.7	230.6	177.6	181.2
General government	8 782 . .	...	...	...	...	...	...	...	...
Banks	8 783 . .	...	...	3,022.9	3,001.7	2,923.6	3,135.4	3,532.0	3,841.2
Other sectors	8 784 . .	...	...	...	...	...	...	...	...
Other liabilities	8 786 . .	...	...	77.9	83.1	156.0	149.6	286.9	372.4
Monetary authorities	8 787 . .	...	...	...	...	...	...	...	...
of which: *Short-term*	8 789 . .	...	...	...	...	...	...	...	...
General government	8 790 . .	...	...	...	...	...	...	...	...
of which: *Short-term*	8 792 . .	...	...	...	...	...	...	...	...
Banks	8 793 . .	...	...	77.9	83.1	156.0	149.6	286.9	372.4
of which: *Short-term*	8 795 . .	...	...	...	...	...	...	...	...
Other sectors	8 796 . .	...	...	...	...	...	...	...	...
of which: *Short-term*	8 798 . .	...	...	...	...	...	...	...	...
NET INTERNATIONAL INVESTMENT POSITION	8 995 . .	...	...	...	...	...	...	...	...
Conversion rates: Jordanian dinar per U.S. dollar (end of period)	0 102 . .	**.7010**	**.7090**	**.7090**	**.7090**	**.7090**	**.7090**	**.7090**	**.7090**

Table 1. ANALYTIC PRESENTATION, 1994–2001
(Millions of U.S. dollars)

	Code	1994	1995	1996	1997	1998	1999	2000	2001
A. Current Account [1]	4 993 Z.	**. . .**	**–213.1**	**–751.0**	**–799.3**	**–1,224.9**	**–171.0**	**675.5**	**–1,415.5**
Goods: exports f.o.b	2 100 . .	. . .	5,440.0	6,291.6	6,899.3	5,870.5	5,988.7	9,288.1	9,104.3
Goods: imports f.o.b	3 100 . .	. . .	–5,325.9	–6,626.7	–7,175.7	–6,671.7	–5,645.0	–6,848.2	–8,295.5
Balance on Goods	4 100 . .	. . .	*114.1*	*–335.1*	*–276.4*	*–801.2*	*343.7*	*2,439.9*	*808.8*
Services: credit	2 200 . .	. . .	535.1	674.4	841.9	904.3	932.5	1,133.3	1,273.8
Services: debit	3 200 . .	. . .	–775.8	–928.3	–1,124.4	–1,154.1	–1,104.2	–2,004.3	–2,613.2
Balance on Goods and Services	4 991 . .	. . .	*–126.6*	*–589.0*	*–558.9*	*–1,051.0*	*172.0*	*1,568.9*	*–530.6*
Income: credit	2 300 . .	. . .	44.6	56.7	73.8	95.5	108.6	138.8	233.2
Income: debit	3 300 . .	. . .	–190.1	–277.1	–388.8	–391.8	–608.3	–1,281.2	–1,347.8
Balance on Goods, Services, and Income	4 992 . .	. . .	*–272.1*	*–809.4*	*–873.9*	*–1,347.3*	*–327.7*	*426.5*	*–1,645.2*
Current transfers: credit	2 379 Z.	. . .	79.9	83.4	104.7	141.4	174.7	352.2	392.7
Current transfers: debit	3 379 . .	. . .	–20.9	–25.0	–30.1	–19.0	–18.0	–103.2	–163.0
B. Capital Account [1]	4 994 Z.	**. . .**	**–380.6**	**–315.5**	**–439.8**	**–369.1**	**–234.0**	**–290.6**	**–197.3**
Capital account: credit	2 994 Z.	. . .	116.1	87.9	58.3	65.9	61.1	66.3	89.2
Capital account: debit	3 994 . .	. . .	–496.7	–403.4	–498.1	–435.0	–295.1	–356.9	–286.5
Total, Groups A Plus B	4 981 . .	. . .	*–593.7*	*–1,066.5*	*–1,239.1*	*–1,594.0*	*–405.0*	*384.9*	*–1,612.8*
C. Financial Account [1]	4 995 W.	**. . .**	**1,162.5**	**2,005.1**	**2,901.6**	**2,229.1**	**1,299.2**	**1,308.1**	**2,717.4**
Direct investment abroad	4 505 . .	. . .	–.3	. . .	–1.4	–8.1	–3.6	–4.4	–15.5
Direct investment in Kazakhstan	4 555 Z.	. . .	964.2	1,137.0	1,321.4	1,151.4	1,587.0	1,282.5	2,763.0
Portfolio investment assets	4 602 . .	. . .	. . .	. . .	–1.2	–5.3	–5.6	–85.5	–1,354.0
Equity securities	4 610 . .	. . .	. . .	. . .	–1.2	–.4	–1.8	.7	–10.4
Debt securities	4 619 . .	. . .	. . .	. . .	. . .	–4.9	–3.8	–86.2	–1,343.6
Portfolio investment liabilities	4 652 Z.	. . .	7.2	223.5	405.4	66.2	–39.9	30.7	31.7
Equity securities	4 660 . .	. . .	. . .	. . .	. . .	. . .	. . .	19.4	55.4
Debt securities	4 669 Z.	. . .	7.2	223.5	405.4	66.2	–39.9	11.3	–23.7
Financial derivatives	4 910 . .	. . .	. . .	. . .	. . .	. . .	. . .	. . .	. . .
Financial derivatives assets	4 900 . .	. . .	. . .	. . .	. . .	. . .	. . .	. . .	. . .
Financial derivatives liabilities	4 905 . .	. . .	. . .	. . .	. . .	. . .	. . .	. . .	. . .
Other investment assets	4 703 . .	. . .	–657.4	243.8	–139.5	–220.5	–778.4	43.6	514.5
Monetary authorities	4 701 . .	. . .	21.3	2.1	. . .	. . .	–.3	–.4	.3
General government	4 704 . .	. . .	. . .	27.8	.3	–41.1	16.3	–.3	209.6
Banks	4 705 . .	. . .	–152.3	174.4	–66.0	–67.9	–205.8	154.4	–63.6
Other sectors	4 728 . .	. . .	–526.4	39.5	–73.8	–111.5	–588.6	–110.1	368.2
Other investment liabilities	4 753 W.	. . .	848.8	400.8	1,316.9	1,245.4	539.7	41.2	777.7
Monetary authorities	4 753 WA	. . .	–4.9	12.1	–5.0	–37.7	. . .	–2.6	.3
General government	4 753 ZB	. . .	331.3	323.4	317.2	673.3	291.5	88.2	51.5
Banks	4 753 ZC	. . .	–251.5	–125.7	161.4	60.2	–20.2	165.1	457.6
Other sectors	4 753 ZD	. . .	773.9	191.0	843.3	549.6	268.4	–209.5	268.3
Total, Groups A Through C	4 983 . .	. . .	*568.8*	*938.6*	*1,662.5*	*635.1*	*894.2*	*1,693.0*	*1,104.6*
D. Net Errors and Omissions	4 998 . .	**. . .**	**–270.1**	**–780.0**	**–1,114.1**	**–1,078.4**	**–641.6**	**–1,122.7**	**–719.7**
Total, Groups A Through D	4 984 . .	. . .	*298.7*	*158.6*	*548.4*	*–443.3*	*252.6*	*570.3*	*384.9*
E. Reserves and Related Items	4 802 A.	**. . .**	**–298.7**	**–158.6**	**–548.4**	**443.3**	**–252.6**	**–570.3**	**–384.9**
Reserve assets	4 802 . .	. . .	–440.1	–293.7	–542.0	321.7	–77.1	–129.2	–384.9
Use of Fund credit and loans	4 766 . .	. . .	141.4	135.1	–6.4	121.6	–175.5	–441.0	. . .
Exceptional financing	4 920 . .	. . .	. . .	. . .	. . .	. . .	. . .	. . .	. . .
Conversion rates: tenge per U.S. dollar	0 101 . .	**35.54**	**60.95**	**67.30**	**75.44**	**78.30**	**119.52**	**142.13**	**146.74**

[1] Excludes components that have been classified in the categories of Group E.

Table 2. STANDARD PRESENTATION, 1994–2001

(Millions of U.S. dollars)

	Code		1994	1995	1996	1997	1998	1999	2000	2001
CURRENT ACCOUNT	4 993	. .	...	**–213.1**	**–751.0**	**–799.3**	**–1,224.9**	**–171.0**	**675.5**	**–1,415.5**
A. GOODS	4 100	. .	...	114.1	–335.1	–276.4	–801.2	343.7	2,439.9	808.8
Credit	2 100	. .	...	**5,440.0**	**6,291.6**	**6,899.3**	**5,870.5**	**5,988.7**	**9,288.1**	**9,104.3**
General merchandise: exports f.o.b.	2 110	. .	...	5,440.0	6,291.6	6,899.3	5,870.5	5,988.7	9,276.7	9,085.6
Goods for processing: exports f.o.b.	2 150	. .	...	...	...	...	...	...	...	...
Repairs on goods	2 160	. .	...	...	...	...	...	...	1.1	5.0
Goods procured in ports by carriers	2 170	. .	...	...	...	...	...	...	10.3	13.7
Nonmonetary gold	2 180	. .	...	...	...	...	...	...	...	...
Debit	3 100	. .	...	**–5,325.9**	**–6,626.7**	**–7,175.7**	**–6,671.7**	**–5,645.0**	**–6,848.2**	**–8,295.5**
General merchandise: imports f.o.b.	3 110	. .	...	–5,325.9	–6,626.7	–7,175.7	–6,671.7	–5,645.0	–6,777.3	–8,113.5
Goods for processing: imports f.o.b.	3 150	. .	...	...	...	...	...	...	...	...
Repairs on goods	3 160	. .	...	...	...	...	...	...	–59.4	–168.8
Goods procured in ports by carriers	3 170	. .	...	...	...	...	...	...	–11.5	–13.2
Nonmonetary gold	3 180	. .	...	...	...	...	...	...	...	...
B. SERVICES	4 200	. .	...	–240.7	–253.9	–282.5	–249.8	–171.7	–871.0	–1,339.4
Total credit	2 200	. .	...	*535.1*	*674.4*	*841.9*	*904.3*	*932.5*	*1,133.3*	*1,273.8*
Total debit	3 200	. .	...	*–775.8*	*–928.3*	*–1,124.4*	*–1,154.1*	*–1,104.2*	*–2,004.3*	*–2,613.2*
Transportation services, credit	2 205	. .	...	**351.5**	**431.8**	**494.9**	**387.8**	**420.5**	**540.2**	**624.0**
Passenger	2 850	. .	...	*32.9*	*59.0*	*60.7*	*46.7*	*30.6*	*47.2*	*50.5*
Freight	2 851	. .	...	*291.5*	*342.9*	*375.9*	*261.4*	*323.5*	*429.3*	*501.6*
Other	2 852	. .	...	*27.1*	*29.9*	*58.3*	*79.7*	*66.4*	*63.7*	*71.9*
Sea transport, passenger	2 207	. .	...	...	...	...	...	...	...	...
Sea transport, freight	2 208	. .	...	...	...	...	...	...	...	.1
Sea transport, other	2 209	. .	...	...	...	...	...	...	5.6	11.5
Air transport, passenger	2 211	. .	...	...	...	...	...	...	29.1	30.3
Air transport, freight	2 212	. .	...	...	...	...	...	...	32.5	28.2
Air transport, other	2 213	. .	...	...	...	...	...	...	55.1	56.1
Other transport, passenger	2 215	. .	...	...	...	...	...	...	18.1	20.2
Other transport, freight	2 216	. .	...	...	...	...	...	...	396.8	473.3
Other transport, other	2 217	. .	...	...	...	...	...	...	3.0	4.3
Transportation services, debit	3 205	. .	...	**–297.6**	**–357.2**	**–391.9**	**–418.2**	**–399.6**	**–483.7**	**–627.4**
Passenger	3 850	. .	...	*–12.9*	*–44.8*	*–48.8*	*–51.3*	*–60.6*	*–75.1*	*–87.8*
Freight	3 851	. .	...	*–259.6*	*–287.1*	*–333.2*	*–354.9*	*–309.4*	*–394.6*	*–513.8*
Other	3 852	. .	...	*–25.1*	*–25.3*	*–9.9*	*–12.0*	*–29.6*	*–14.0*	*–25.8*
Sea transport, passenger	3 207	. .	...	...	...	...	...	...	–.1	–.1
Sea transport, freight	3 208	. .	...	...	...	...	...	...	–3.2	–4.0
Sea transport, other	3 209	. .	...	...	...	...	...	...	...	–2.2
Air transport, passenger	3 211	. .	...	...	...	...	...	...	–63.1	–75.1
Air transport, freight	3 212	. .	...	...	...	...	...	...	–54.8	–68.9
Air transport, other	3 213	. .	...	...	...	...	...	...	–12.0	–22.2
Other transport, passenger	3 215	. .	...	...	...	...	...	...	–11.9	–12.6
Other transport, freight	3 216	. .	...	...	...	...	...	...	–336.6	–440.9
Other transport, other	3 217	. .	...	...	...	...	...	...	–2.0	–1.4
Travel, credit	2 236	. .	...	**121.7**	**199.2**	**289.2**	**407.1**	**362.8**	**356.3**	**396.2**
Business travel	2 237	. .	...	...	...	...	...	...	124.2	102.2
Personal travel	2 240	. .	...	...	...	...	...	...	232.1	294.0
Travel, debit	3 236	. .	...	**–282.6**	**–319.3**	**–445.4**	**–497.5**	**–394.0**	**–407.8**	**–473.7**
Business travel	3 237	. .	...	...	...	...	...	...	–59.3	–40.6
Personal travel	3 240	. .	...	...	...	...	...	...	–348.5	–433.1
Other services, credit	2 200	BA	...	**61.9**	**43.4**	**57.8**	**109.4**	**149.2**	**236.8**	**253.6**
Communications	2 245	. .	...	35.2	17.7	38.2	44.9	51.9	34.4	35.5
Construction	2 249	. .	...	...	...	1.6	8.6	6.9	.2	1.8
Insurance	2 253	. .	...	...	...	...	...	...	3.8	5.2
Financial	2 260	. .	...	...	...	.1	1.4	1.8	10.9	5.2
Computer and information	2 262	. .	...	...	...	...	...	...	1.2	.6
Royalties and licence fees	2 266	. .	...	...	...	...	...	...	...	...
Other business services	2 268	. .	...	20.5	18.5	9.3	27.4	16.1	38.3	44.9
Personal, cultural, and recreational	2 287	. .	...	6.2	7.2	8.6	27.1	72.5	.2	.1
Government, n.i.e.	2 291	. .	...	...	...	...	...	...	147.8	160.3
Other services, debit	3 200	BA	...	**–195.6**	**–251.8**	**–287.1**	**–238.4**	**–310.6**	**–1,112.8**	**–1,512.1**
Communications	3 245	. .	...	–53.6	–10.6	–12.5	–17.2	–30.6	–30.2	–39.1
Construction	3 249	. .	...	...	...	–10.9	–44.3	–48.4	–538.8	–763.1
Insurance	3 253	. .	...	...	...	...	...	...	–39.7	–43.4
Financial	3 260	. .	...	...	...	...	–20.6	–31.7	–12.7	–9.9
Computer and information	3 262	. .	...	...	...	...	...	...	–11.7	–17.6
Royalties and licence fees	3 266	. .	...	...	...	...	...	...	–11.8	–13.8
Other business services	3 268	. .	...	–108.7	–108.0	–225.3	–126.7	–176.0	–447.7	–597.8
Personal, cultural, and recreational	3 287	. .	...	–33.3	–133.2	–38.4	–29.6	–23.9	–1.6	–2.1
Government, n.i.e.	3 291	. .	...	...	...	...	...	...	–18.6	–25.3

Table 2 (Continued). STANDARD PRESENTATION, 1994–2001
(Millions of U.S. dollars)

	Code	1994	1995	1996	1997	1998	1999	2000	2001
C. INCOME	4 300 . .	. . .	–145.5	–220.4	–315.0	–296.3	–499.7	–1,142.4	–1,114.6
Total credit	2 300 . .	. . .	*44.6*	*56.7*	*73.8*	*95.5*	*108.6*	*138.8*	*233.2*
Total debit	3 300 . .	. . .	*–190.1*	*–277.1*	*–388.8*	*–391.8*	*–608.3*	*–1,281.2*	*–1,347.8*
Compensation of employees, credit	2 310 . .	**. . .**	**. . .**	**1.2**	**1.2**	**6.4**	**3.6**	**3.6**	**3.6**
Compensation of employees, debit	3 310 . .	**. . .**	**–6.6**	**–19.2**	**–24.1**	**–35.9**	**–60.5**	**–47.2**	**–57.2**
Investment income, credit	2 320 . .	**. . .**	**44.6**	**55.5**	**72.6**	**89.1**	**105.0**	**135.2**	**229.6**
Direct investment income	2 330 . .	. . .	. . .	. . .	. . .	. . .	. . .	. . .	.4
Dividends and distributed branch profits	2 332 . .	. . .	. . .	. . .	. . .	. . .	. . .	. . .	.4
Reinvested earnings and undistributed branch profits	2 333 . .	. . .	. . .	. . .	. . .	. . .	. . .	. . .	. . .
Income on debt (interest)	2 334 . .	. . .	. . .	. . .	. . .	. . .	. . .	. . .	. . .
Portfolio investment income	2 339 . .	. . .	. . .	. . .	1.4	.2	.1	73.7	150.8
Income on equity	2 340 . .	. . .	. . .	. . .	. . .	. . .	. . .	.8	1.9
Income on bonds and notes	2 350 . .	. . .	. . .	. . .	. . .	. . .	. . .	28.8	96.6
Income on money market instruments	2 360 . .	. . .	. . .	. . .	. . .	. . .	. . .	44.1	52.3
Other investment income	2 370 . .	. . .	44.6	55.5	71.2	88.9	104.9	61.5	78.4
Investment income, debit	3 320 . .	**. . .**	**–183.5**	**–257.9**	**–364.7**	**–355.9**	**–547.8**	**–1,234.0**	**–1,290.6**
Direct investment income	3 330 . .	. . .	–73.7	–118.6	–155.3	–97.4	–273.7	–934.4	–1,013.8
Dividends and distributed branch profits	3 332 . .	. . .	. . .	. . .	–.2	–.5	–.8	–62.1	–204.2
Reinvested earnings and undistributed branch profits	3 333 . .	. . .	. . .	–11.0	–17.5	–2.6	–178.2	–474.2	–448.5
Income on debt (interest)	3 334 . .	. . .	–73.7	–107.6	–137.6	–94.3	–94.7	–398.1	–361.1
Portfolio investment income	3 339 . .	. . .	. . .	. . .	–19.3	–47.9	–56.5	–64.1	–56.5
Income on equity	3 340 . .	. . .	. . .	. . .	. . .	. . .	. . .	–.4	–5.7
Income on bonds and notes	3 350 . .	. . .	. . .	. . .	. . .	. . .	. . .	–63.7	–50.8
Income on money market instruments	3 360 . .	. . .	. . .	. . .	. . .	. . .	. . .	. . .	. . .
Other investment income	3 370 . .	. . .	–109.8	–139.3	–190.1	–210.6	–217.6	–235.5	–220.3
D. CURRENT TRANSFERS	4 379 . .	. . .	59.0	58.4	74.6	122.4	156.7	249.0	229.7
Credit	2 379 . .	**. . .**	**79.9**	**83.4**	**104.7**	**141.4**	**174.7**	**352.2**	**392.7**
General government	2 380 . .	. . .	73.1	73.7	86.6	131.9	162.2	287.6	305.0
Other sectors	2 390 . .	. . .	6.8	9.7	18.1	9.5	12.5	64.6	87.7
Workers' remittances	2 391 . .	. . .	. . .	. . .	. . .	. . .	. . .	63.8	81.5
Other current transfers	2 392 . .	. . .	6.8	9.7	18.1	9.5	12.5	.8	6.2
Debit	3 379 . .	**. . .**	**–20.9**	**–25.0**	**–30.1**	**–19.0**	**–18.0**	**–103.2**	**–163.0**
General government	3 380 . .	. . .	. . .	–13.0	–13.5	–4.0	–4.8	–5.8	–7.3
Other sectors	3 390 . .	. . .	–20.9	–12.0	–16.6	–15.0	–13.2	–97.4	–155.7
Workers' remittances	3 391 . .	. . .	. . .	. . .	. . .	. . .	. . .	–74.3	–143.3
Other current transfers	3 392 . .	. . .	–20.9	–12.0	–16.6	–15.0	–13.2	–23.1	–12.4
CAPITAL AND FINANCIAL ACCOUNT	4 996 . .	**. . .**	**483.2**	**1,531.0**	**1,913.4**	**2,303.3**	**812.6**	**447.2**	**2,135.2**
CAPITAL ACCOUNT	4 994 . .	**. . .**	**–380.6**	**–315.5**	**–439.8**	**–369.1**	**–234.0**	**–290.6**	**–197.3**
Total credit	2 994 . .	. . .	*116.1*	*87.9*	*58.3*	*65.9*	*61.1*	*66.3*	*89.2*
Total debit	3 994 . .	. . .	*–496.7*	*–403.4*	*–498.1*	*–435.0*	*–295.1*	*–356.9*	*–286.5*
Capital transfers, credit	2 400 . .	**. . .**	**116.1**	**87.9**	**58.3**	**65.9**	**61.1**	**66.3**	**89.2**
General government	2 401 . .	. . .	. . .	. . .	. . .	. . .	.7	11.9	.4
Debt forgiveness	2 402 . .	. . .	. . .	. . .	. . .	. . .	. . .	. . .	. . .
Other capital transfers	2 410 . .	. . .	. . .	. . .	. . .	. . .	.7	11.9	.4
Other sectors	2 430 . .	. . .	116.1	87.9	58.3	65.9	60.4	54.4	88.8
Migrants' transfers	2 431 . .	. . .	116.1	87.9	58.3	65.9	60.4	54.3	79.5
Debt forgiveness	2 432 . .	. . .	. . .	. . .	. . .	. . .	. . .	. . .	. . .
Other capital transfers	2 440 . .	. . .	. . .	. . .	. . .	. . .	. . .	.1	9.3
Capital transfers, debit	3 400 . .	**. . .**	**–496.7**	**–403.4**	**–498.1**	**–435.0**	**–295.1**	**–356.9**	**–286.5**
General government	3 401 . .	. . .	. . .	. . .	. . .	. . .	. . .	–.2	. . .
Debt forgiveness	3 402 . .	. . .	. . .	. . .	. . .	. . .	. . .	. . .	. . .
Other capital transfers	3 410 . .	. . .	. . .	. . .	. . .	. . .	. . .	–.2	. . .
Other sectors	3 430 . .	. . .	–496.7	–403.4	–498.1	–435.0	–295.1	–356.7	–286.5
Migrants' transfers	3 431 . .	. . .	–496.7	–403.4	–498.1	–435.0	–295.1	–318.5	–286.5
Debt forgiveness	3 432 . .	. . .	. . .	. . .	. . .	. . .	. . .	–38.2	. . .
Other capital transfers	3 440 . .	. . .	. . .	. . .	. . .	. . .	. . .	. . .	. . .
Nonproduced nonfinancial assets, credit	2 480 . .	**. . .**	**. . .**	**. . .**	**. . .**	**. . .**	**. . .**	**. . .**	**. . .**
Nonproduced nonfinancial assets, debit	3 480 . .	**. . .**	**. . .**	**. . .**	**. . .**	**. . .**	**. . .**	**. . .**	**. . .**

Table 2 (Continued). STANDARD PRESENTATION, 1994–2001

(Millions of U.S. dollars)

	Code	1994	1995	1996	1997	1998	1999	2000	2001
FINANCIAL ACCOUNT	4 995 . .	**...**	**863.8**	**1,846.5**	**2,353.2**	**2,672.4**	**1,046.6**	**737.8**	**2,332.5**
A. DIRECT INVESTMENT	4 500 . .	...	963.9	1,137.0	1,320.0	1,143.3	1,583.4	1,278.1	2,747.5
Direct investment abroad	4 505 . .	**...**	**–.3**	**...**	**–1.4**	**–8.1**	**–3.6**	**–4.4**	**–15.5**
Equity capital	4 510 . .	...	–.3	...	–1.4	–8.1	–3.6	–4.4	–1.1
Claims on affiliated enterprises	4 515 . .	...	...	...	...	...	...	–4.4	–1.1
Liabilities to affiliated enterprises	4 520 . .	...	...	...	...	...	...	...	...
Reinvested earnings	4 525 . .	...	...	...	...	...	...	...	...
Other capital	4 530 . .	...	...	...	...	...	...	...	–14.4
Claims on affiliated enterprises	4 535 . .	...	...	...	...	...	...	...	–14.4
Liabilities to affiliated enterprises	4 540 . .	...	...	...	...	...	...	...	...
Direct investment in Kazakhstan	4 555 . .	**...**	**964.2**	**1,137.0**	**1,321.4**	**1,151.4**	**1,587.0**	**1,282.5**	**2,763.0**
Equity capital	4 560 . .	...	220.4	299.5	707.6	493.5	316.1	272.2	539.3
Claims on direct investors	4 565 . .	...	...	...	...	...	...	...	–.3
Liabilities to direct investors	4 570 . .	...	...	...	...	...	...	272.2	539.6
Reinvested earnings	4 575 . .	...	...	11.0	17.5	2.6	178.2	474.2	448.5
Other capital	4 580 . .	...	743.8	826.5	596.3	655.3	1,092.7	536.1	1,775.2
Claims on direct investors	4 585 . .	...	...	...	...	...	...	–88.0	70.5
Liabilities to direct investors	4 590 . .	...	...	...	...	...	...	624.1	1,704.7
B. PORTFOLIO INVESTMENT	4 600 . .	...	7.2	223.5	404.2	60.9	–45.5	–54.8	–1,322.3
Assets	4 602 . .	**...**	**...**	**...**	**–1.2**	**–5.3**	**–5.6**	**–85.5**	**–1,354.0**
Equity securities	4 610 . .	...	...	...	–1.2	–.4	–1.8	.7	–10.4
Monetary authorities	4 611 . .	...	...	...	...	...	...	...	...
General government	4 612 . .	...	...	...	...	...	...	...	...
Banks	4 613 . .	...	...	...	...	...	...	...	...
Other sectors	4 614 . .	...	...	...	–1.2	–.4	–1.8	.7	–10.4
Debt securities	4 619 . .	...	...	...	...	–4.9	–3.8	–86.2	–1,343.6
Bonds and notes	4 620 . .	...	...	...	...	–.8	.3	–86.2	–402.8
Monetary authorities	4 621 . .	...	...	...	...	...	...	...	–288.7
General government	4 622 . .	...	...	...	...	...	...	...	...
Banks	4 623 . .	...	...	...	...	–.8	.4	–39.5	–65.7
Other sectors	4 624 . .	...	...	...	...	...	–.1	–46.7	–48.4
Money market instruments	4 630 . .	...	...	...	...	–4.1	–4.1	...	–940.8
Monetary authorities	4 631 . .	...	...	...	...	...	...	...	–940.8
General government	4 632 . .	...	...	...	...	...	...	...	...
Banks	4 633 . .	...	...	...	...	–4.1	–4.1	...	...
Other sectors	4 634 . .	...	...	...	...	...	...	...	...
Liabilities	4 652 . .	**...**	**7.2**	**223.5**	**405.4**	**66.2**	**–39.9**	**30.7**	**31.7**
Equity securities	4 660 . .	...	...	...	...	...	...	19.4	55.4
Banks	4 663 . .	...	...	...	...	...	...	.6	31.7
Other sectors	4 664 . .	...	...	...	...	...	...	18.8	23.7
Debt securities	4 669 . .	...	7.2	223.5	405.4	66.2	–39.9	11.3	–23.7
Bonds and notes	4 670 . .	...	7.2	223.5	405.4	66.2	–39.9	11.6	–23.7
Monetary authorities	4 671 . .	...	...	...	...	...	...	...	...
General government	4 672 . .	...	.2	223.5	336.8	–60.7	31.0	10.7	–102.6
Banks	4 673 . .	...	...	...	...	...	...	–10.2	–31.1
Other sectors	4 674 . .	...	7.0	...	68.6	126.9	–70.9	11.1	110.0
Money market instruments	4 680 . .	...	...	...	...	...	...	–.3	...
Monetary authorities	4 681 . .	...	...	...	...	...	...	...	...
General government	4 682 . .	...	...	...	...	...	...	–.3	...
Banks	4 683 . .	...	...	...	...	...	...	...	...
Other sectors	4 684 . .	...	...	...	...	...	...	...	...
C. FINANCIAL DERIVATIVES	4 910 . .	...	...	...	...	...	...	...	...
Monetary authorities	4 911 . .	...	...	...	...	...	...	...	...
General government	4 912 . .	...	...	...	...	...	...	...	...
Banks	4 913 . .	...	...	...	...	...	...	...	...
Other sectors	4 914 . .	...	...	...	...	...	...	...	...
Assets	4 900 . .	**...**	**...**	**...**	**...**	**...**	**...**	**...**	**...**
Monetary authorities	4 901 . .	...	...	...	...	...	...	...	...
General government	4 902 . .	...	...	...	...	...	...	...	...
Banks	4 903 . .	...	...	...	...	...	...	...	...
Other sectors	4 904 . .	...	...	...	...	...	...	...	...
Liabilities	4 905 . .	**...**	**...**	**...**	**...**	**...**	**...**	**...**	**...**
Monetary authorities	4 906 . .	...	...	...	...	...	...	...	...
General government	4 907 . .	...	...	...	...	...	...	...	...
Banks	4 908 . .	...	...	...	...	...	...	...	...
Other sectors	4 909 . .	...	...	...	...	...	...	...	...

Table 2 (Concluded). STANDARD PRESENTATION, 1994–2001
(Millions of U.S. dollars)

	Code	1994	1995	1996	1997	1998	1999	2000	2001
D. OTHER INVESTMENT	4 700	...	332.8	779.7	1,171.0	1,146.5	–414.2	–356.2	1,292.2
Assets	4 703	**...**	**–657.4**	**243.8**	**–139.5**	**–220.5**	**–778.4**	**43.6**	**514.5**
Trade credits	4 706	...	...	...	...	–41.1	16.3	–115.3	79.1
General government	4 707	...	...	...	...	–41.1	16.3	...	...
of which: Short-term	4 709	...	...	...	...	*–1.0*	*.1*	...	...
Other sectors	4 710	...	...	...	...	...	...	–115.3	79.1
of which: Short-term	4 712	...	...	...	...	...	...	*–48.2*	*51.2*
Loans	4 714	...	18.6	22.8	–90.4	–22.5	13.6	43.3	–10.4
Monetary authorities	4 715	...	...	...	...	...	...	...	...
of which: Short-term	4 718	...	...	...	...	...	...	...	...
General government	4 719	...	18.6	21.3	...	...	...	...	...
of which: Short-term	4 721	...	*.2*	...	...	...	...	...	...
Banks	4 722	...	...	1.5	–90.4	–22.5	13.6	42.9	–10.2
of which: Short-term	4 724	...	...	*1.5*	*–90.4*	*–20.7*	*13.3*	*42.4*	*–10.5*
Other sectors	4 725	...	...	...	...	...	...	.4	–.2
of which: Short-term	4 727	...	...	...	...	...	...	...	*.2*
Currency and deposits	4 730	...	–140.4	136.7	26.1	–33.3	–350.4	63.2	245.1
Monetary authorities	4 731	...	1.0	2.1	...	...	–.3	–.4	.3
General government	4 732	...	...	...	...	...	...	...	...
Banks	4 733	...	–133.1	128.4	24.8	–40.9	–224.5	109.2	–45.6
Other sectors	4 734	...	–8.3	6.2	1.3	7.6	–125.6	–45.6	290.4
Other assets	4 736	...	–535.6	84.3	–75.2	–123.6	–457.9	52.4	200.7
Monetary authorities	4 737	...	20.3	...	...	...	...	...	...
of which: Short-term	4 739	...	*20.3*	...	...	...	...	...	...
General government	4 740	...	–18.6	6.5	.3	...	...	–.3	209.6
of which: Short-term	4 742	...	*–18.6*	*6.5*	*.3*	...	...	*–.3*	*–.4*
Banks	4 743	...	–19.2	44.5	–.4	–4.5	5.1	2.3	–7.8
of which: Short-term	4 745	...	*–19.2*	*44.5*	*–.4*	*–4.5*	*5.1*	*2.3*	*–7.8*
Other sectors	4 746	...	–518.1	33.3	–75.1	–119.1	–463.0	50.4	–1.1
of which: Short-term	4 748	...	*–518.1*	*33.3*	*–75.1*	*–119.1*	*–463.0*	*50.4*	*–1.1*
Liabilities	4 753	**...**	**990.2**	**535.9**	**1,310.5**	**1,367.0**	**364.2**	**–399.8**	**777.7**
Trade credits	4 756	...	129.1	–91.7	150.2	–161.3	–132.1	19.9	–60.9
General government	4 757	...	...	...	...	...	...	...	...
of which: Short-term	4 759	...	...	...	...	...	...	...	...
Other sectors	4 760	...	129.1	–91.7	150.2	–161.3	–132.1	19.9	–60.9
of which: Short-term	4 762	...	*16.1*	*–16.1*	...	...	...	*42.5*	*–1.9*
Loans	4 764	...	605.2	683.8	625.5	1,103.9	109.9	–502.0	719.6
Monetary authorities	4 765	...	162.9	148.7	–11.4	92.7	–175.5	–443.6	...
of which: Use of Fund credit and loans from the Fund	4 766	...	*141.4*	*135.1*	*–6.4*	*121.6*	*–175.5*	*–441.0*	...
of which: Short-term	4 768	...	...	...	...	...	...	...	...
General government	4 769	...	330.9	338.4	317.2	673.3	291.5	88.2	54.8
of which: Short-term	4 771	...	...	...	...	...	...	...	...
Banks	4 772	...	–1.5	3.9	120.6	46.7	–37.8	79.1	311.6
of which: Short-term	4 774	...	*–1.5*	*–.5*	*83.9*	*.1*	*–50.8*	*52.1*	*212.2*
Other sectors	4 775	...	112.9	192.8	199.1	291.2	31.7	–225.7	353.2
of which: Short-term	4 777	...	*90.3*	*89.8*	*–119.6*	*111.7*	*13.7*	*–144.1*	*127.7*
Currency and deposits	4 780	...	24.9	–32.2	.4	15.4	16.6	84.2	144.3
Monetary authorities	4 781	...	–1.1	–1.3	–.1	...	...	...	.1
General government	4 782	...	...	...	...	...	...	...	...
Banks	4 783	...	26.0	–30.9	.5	15.4	16.6	84.2	144.2
Other sectors	4 784	...	...	...	...	...	...	...	...
Other liabilities	4 786	...	231.0	–24.0	534.4	409.0	369.8	–1.9	–25.3
Monetary authorities	4 787	...	–25.3	–.2	.1	–8.8	...	...	.2
of which: Short-term	4 789	...	*–25.3*	*–.2*	*.1*	*–8.8*	...	...	*.2*
General government	4 790	...	.4	–15.0	...	...	...	...	–3.3
of which: Short-term	4 792	...	*.4*	*–15.0*	...	...	...	...	...
Banks	4 793	...	–276.0	–98.7	40.3	–1.9	1.0	1.8	1.8
of which: Short-term	4 795	...	*–276.0*	*–98.7*	*40.3*	*–1.9*	*1.0*	*1.8*	*1.8*
Other sectors	4 796	...	531.9	89.9	494.0	419.7	368.8	–3.7	–24.0
of which: Short-term	4 798	...	*531.9*	*89.9*	*494.0*	*419.7*	*368.8*	*–3.7*	*–24.0*
E. RESERVE ASSETS	4 802	...	–440.1	–293.7	–542.0	321.7	–77.1	–129.2	–384.9
Monetary gold	4 812	...	...	...	...	...	...	...	...
Special drawing rights	4 811	...	–130.1	–124.2	–118.6	71.5	151.7	217.1	...
Reserve position in the Fund	4 810	...	...	...	...	...	...	...	...
Foreign exchange	4 803	...	–310.0	–169.5	–423.4	250.2	–228.8	–346.3	–377.7
Other claims	4 813	...	...	...	...	...	...	...	–7.2
NET ERRORS AND OMISSIONS	4 998	**...**	**–270.1**	**–780.0**	**–1,114.1**	**–1,078.4**	**–641.6**	**–1,122.7**	**–719.7**

Part 3 of the *Yearbook* contains descriptions of the methodologies, compilation practices, and sources used to compile these data.

Table 3. INTERNATIONAL INVESTMENT POSITION (End–period stocks), 1994–2001

(Millions of U.S. dollars)

	Code	1994	1995	1996	1997	1998	1999	2000	2001
ASSETS	8 995 C.	...	...	...	2,629.1	2,391.8	2,598.4	4,541.8	6,041.0
Direct investment abroad	8 505 . .	**...**	**...**	**...**	**2.6**	**3.1**	**3.1**	**13.4**	**29.3**
Equity capital and reinvested earnings	8 506 . .	...	...	...	2.6	3.1	3.1	13.3	14.6
Claims on affiliated enterprises	8 507 . .	...	...	...	2.6	3.1	3.1	13.3	14.6
Liabilities to affiliated enterprises	8 508 . .	...	...	...	...	...	...	...	...
Other capital	8 530 . .	...	...	...	...	...	...	.1	14.7
Claims on affiliated enterprises	8 535 . .	...	...	...	...	...	...	.1	14.7
Liabilities to affiliated enterprises	8 540 . .	...	...	...	...	...	...	...	...
Portfolio investment	8 602 . .	**...**	**...**	**...**	**2.0**	**4.2**	**1.0**	**69.5**	**1,435.9**
Equity securities	8 610 . .	...	...	...	...	...	...	3.2	15.1
Monetary authorities	8 611 . .	...	...	...	...	...	...	...	...
General government	8 612 . .	...	...	...	...	...	...	...	...
Banks	8 613 . .	...	...	...	...	...	...	...	...
Other sectors	8 614 . .	...	...	...	...	...	...	3.2	15.1
Debt securities	8 619 . .	...	...	...	2.0	4.2	1.0	66.3	1,420.8
Bonds and notes	8 620 . .	...	...	...	.3	1.0	1.0	66.3	464.1
Monetary authorities	8 621 . .	...	...	...	...	...	...	...	283.5
General government	8 622 . .	...	...	...	...	...	...	...	...
Banks	8 623 . .	...	...	...	.3	1.0	1.0	41.3	110.7
Other sectors	8 624 . .	...	...	...	...	...	...	25.0	69.9
Money market instruments	8 630 . .	...	...	...	1.7	3.2	...	...	956.7
Monetary authorities	8 631 . .	...	...	...	...	...	...	...	956.7
General government	8 632 . .	...	...	...	...	...	...	...	...
Banks	8 633 . .	...	...	...	1.7	3.2	...	...	...
Other sectors	8 634 . .	...	...	...	...	...	...	...	...
Financial derivatives	8 900 . .	**...**	**...**	**...**	**...**	**2.0**	**...**	**...**	**...**
Monetary authorities	8 901 . .	...	...	...	...	...	...	...	...
General government	8 902 . .	...	...	...	...	...	...	...	...
Banks	8 903 . .	...	...	...	...	2.0	...	...	...
Other sectors	8 904 . .	...	...	...	...	...	...	...	...
Other investment	8 703 . .	**...**	**...**	**...**	**335.3**	**417.7**	**592.2**	**2,363.3**	**2,067.6**
Trade credits	8 706 . .	...	...	...	...	...	...	825.0	782.8
General government	8 707 . .	...	...	...	...	...	...	...	...
of which: Short-term	8 709 . .	...	...	...	...	...	...	...	...
Other sectors	8 710 . .	...	...	...	...	...	...	825.0	782.8
of which: Short-term	8 712 . .	...	...	...	...	...	...	*704.0*	*689.4*
Loans	8 714 . .	...	...	...	146.9	167.7	150.2	70.5	75.4
Monetary authorities	8 715 . .	...	...	...	...	...	...	...	...
of which: Short-term	8 718 . .	...	...	...	...	...	...	...	...
General government	8 719 . .	...	...	...	46.8	46.8	46.8	46.1	39.9
of which: Short-term	8 721 . .	...	...	...	...	...	...	...	...
Banks	8 722 . .	...	...	...	100.1	120.9	103.4	24.1	34.9
of which: Short-term	8 724 . .	...	...	...	*94.3*	*113.8*	*97.1*	*12.8*	*23.7*
Other sectors	8 725 . .	...	...	...	...	...	...	.3	.6
of which: Short-term	8 727 . .	...	...	...	...	...	...	*.2*	...
Currency and deposits	8 730 . .	...	...	...	179.3	236.0	433.3	952.5	895.8
Monetary authorities	8 731 . .	...	...	...	.3	.1	.3	.7	.3
General government	8 732 . .	...	...	...	...	...	...	321.2	321.2
Banks	8 733 . .	...	...	...	179.0	235.9	433.0	329.7	374.1
Other sectors	8 734 . .	...	...	...	...	...	...	300.9	200.2
Other assets	8 736 . .	...	...	...	9.1	14.0	8.7	515.3	313.6
Monetary authorities	8 737 . .	...	...	...	...	...	...	...	...
of which: Short-term	8 739 . .	...	...	...	...	...	...	...	...
General government	8 740 . .	...	...	...	...	...	...	420.0	210.0
of which: Short-term	8 742 . .	...	...	...	...	...	...	...	...
Banks	8 743 . .	...	...	...	9.1	14.0	8.7	6.1	14.0
of which: Short-term	8 745 . .	...	...	...	*9.1*	*14.0*	*8.7*	*6.1*	*14.0*
Other sectors	8 746 . .	...	...	...	...	...	...	89.2	89.6
of which: Short-term	8 748 . .	...	...	...	...	...	...	*89.2*	*89.6*
Reserve assets	8 802 . .	**...**	**...**	**...**	**2,289.2**	**1,964.8**	**2,002.1**	**2,095.6**	**2,508.2**
Monetary gold	8 812 . .	...	...	...	523.9	503.6	522.8	501.5	510.7
Special drawing rights	8 811 . .	101.5	230.2	345.4	441.4	387.3	225.4	...	...
Reserve position in the Fund	8 810 . .	...	...	...	...	...	...	...	...
Foreign exchange	8 803 . .	...	...	...	1,323.9	1,073.9	1,253.9	1,594.1	1,990.3
Other claims	8 813 . .	...	...	...	...	...	...	...	7.2

Table 3 (Concluded). INTERNATIONAL INVESTMENT POSITION (End–period stocks), 1994–2001

(Millions of U.S. dollars)

	Code	1994	1995	1996	1997	1998	1999	2000	2001
LIABILITIES	8 995 D.	...	...	...	2,595.3	3,594.3	3,678.4	15,687.9	19,198.7
Direct investment in Kazakhstan	8 555 . .	**...**	**...**	**...**	**50.1**	**122.3**	**115.9**	**9,982.2**	**12,716.1**
Equity capital and reinvested earnings	8 556 . .	...	...	...	50.1	122.3	115.9	3,144.4	4,141.9
Claims on direct investors	8 557 . .	...	...	...	...	...	...	...	...
Liabilities to direct investors	8 558 . .	...	...	...	50.1	122.3	115.9	3,144.4	4,141.9
Other capital	8 580 . .	...	...	...	...	...	...	6,837.8	8,574.2
Claims on direct investors	8 585 . .	...	...	...	...	...	...	–101.9	–34.2
Liabilities to direct investors	8 590 . .	...	...	...	...	...	...	6,939.7	8,608.4
Portfolio investment	8 652 . .	**...**	**...**	**...**	**623.9**	**663.4**	**617.2**	**695.9**	**725.1**
Equity securities	8 660 . .	...	...	...	53.9	49.9	37.7	101.6	146.9
Banks	8 663 . .	...	...	...	53.9	49.9	37.7	32.9	64.6
Other sectors	8 664 . .	...	...	...	...	...	...	68.7	82.3
Debt securities	8 669 . .	...	...	...	570.0	613.5	579.5	594.3	578.2
Bonds and notes	8 670 . .	...	...	...	550.0	603.0	578.7	593.8	578.1
Monetary authorities	8 671 . .	...	...	...	...	...	...	...	...
General government	8 672 . .	...	...	...	550.0	503.0	537.1	547.7	445.0
Banks	8 673 . .	...	...	...	...	100.0	41.6	31.3	.2
Other sectors	8 674 . .	...	...	...	...	...	...	14.8	132.9
Money market instruments	8 680 . .	...	...	...	20.0	10.5	.8	.5	.1
Monetary authorities	8 681 . .	...	...	...	4.4	...	...	...	.1
General government	8 682 . .	...	...	...	15.6	6.0	.8	.5	...
Banks	8 683 . .	...	...	...	...	4.5	...	...	...
Other sectors	8 684 . .	...	...	...	...	...	...	...	...
Financial derivatives	8 905 . .	**...**	**...**	**...**	**...**	**...**	**...**	**...**	**...**
Monetary authorities	8 906 . .	...	...	...	...	...	...	...	...
General government	8 907 . .	...	...	...	...	...	...	...	...
Banks	8 908 . .	...	...	...	...	...	...	...	...
Other sectors	8 909 . .	...	...	...	...	...	...	...	...
Other investment	8 753 . .	**...**	**...**	**...**	**1,921.3**	**2,808.6**	**2,945.3**	**5,009.8**	**5,757.5**
Trade credits	8 756 . .	...	...	...	...	...	...	1,441.3	1,429.1
General government	8 757 . .	...	...	...	...	...	...	...	...
of which: Short-term	8 759 . .	...	...	...	...	...	...	...	...
Other sectors	8 760 . .	...	...	...	...	...	...	1,441.3	1,429.1
of which: Short-term	8 762 . .	...	...	...	...	...	...	*534.7*	*552.9*
Loans	8 764 . .	...	...	...	1,843.9	2,725.0	2,839.6	3,167.9	3,836.0
Monetary authorities	8 765 . .	...	...	...	542.8	655.4	462.6	...	...
of which: Use of Fund credit and loans from the Fund	8 766 . .	*289.1*	*432.3*	*551.6*	*511.3*	*652.8*	*460.0*	...	...
of which: Short-term	8 768 . .	...	...	...	...	...	...	...	...
General government	8 769 . .	...	...	...	1,175.3	1,896.4	2,231.3	2,272.0	2,247.3
of which: Short-term	8 771 . .	...	...	...	...	...	...	...	...
Banks	8 772 . .	...	...	...	125.8	173.2	145.7	222.5	563.0
of which: Short-term	8 774 . .	...	...	...	*83.3*	*82.6*	*30.7*	*98.2*	*310.4*
Other sectors	8 775 . .	...	...	...	...	...	...	673.4	1,025.7
of which: Short-term	8 777 . .	...	...	...	...	...	...	*38.5*	*167.3*
Currency and deposits	8 780 . .	...	...	...	67.2	82.1	103.8	175.6	325.7
Monetary authorities	8 781 . .	...	...	...	.4	...	...	...	.2
General government	8 782 . .	...	...	...	...	...	...	...	...
Banks	8 783 . .	...	...	...	66.8	82.1	103.8	175.6	325.5
Other sectors	8 784 . .	...	...	...	...	...	...	...	...
Other liabilities	8 786 . .	...	...	...	10.2	1.5	1.9	225.0	166.7
Monetary authorities	8 787 . .	...	...	...	9.8	...	...	1.9	2.1
of which: Short-term	8 789 . .	...	...	...	*9.8*	...	...	...	*.2*
General government	8 790 . .	...	...	...	...	...	...	5.0	1.7
of which: Short-term	8 792 . .	...	...	...	...	...	...	...	...
Banks	8 793 . .	...	...	...	.4	1.5	1.9	4.4	6.2
of which: Short-term	8 795 . .	...	...	...	*.4*	*1.5*	*1.9*	*4.4*	*6.2*
Other sectors	8 796 . .	...	...	...	...	...	...	213.7	156.7
of which: Short-term	8 798 . .	...	...	...	...	...	...	*213.7*	*156.7*
NET INTERNATIONAL INVESTMENT POSITION	8 995 . .	**...**	**...**	**...**	**33.8**	**–1,202.5**	**–1,080.0**	**–11,146.1**	**–13,157.7**
Conversion rates: tenge per U.S. dollar (end of period)	0 102 . .	**54.26**	**63.95**	**73.30**	**75.55**	**83.80**	**138.20**	**144.50**	**150.20**

Table 1. ANALYTIC PRESENTATION, 1994–2001

(Millions of U.S. dollars)

	Code	1994	1995	1996	1997	1998	1999	2000	2001
A. Current Account [1]	4 993 Z.	**97.9**	**–400.4**	**–73.5**	**–456.8**	**–475.3**	**–89.6**	**–203.7**	**–317.8**
Goods: exports f.o.b.	2 100 ..	1,537.0	1,923.7	2,083.3	2,062.6	2,017.0	1,756.7	1,782.2	1,894.0
Goods: imports f.o.b.	3 100 ..	–1,775.3	–2,673.9	–2,598.2	–2,948.4	–3,028.7	–2,731.8	–3,044.0	–3,176.1
Balance on Goods	4 100 ..	*–238.4*	*–750.1*	*–514.8*	*–885.9*	*–1,011.7*	*–975.1*	*–1,261.7*	*–1,282.1*
Services: credit	2 200 ..	1,117.3	1,024.5	936.2	914.5	830.4	934.5	993.4	1,087.2
Services: debit	3 200 ..	–686.8	–868.1	–854.0	–826.0	–694.7	–570.4	–724.5	–825.5
Balance on Goods and Services	4 991 ..	*192.2*	*–593.7*	*–432.6*	*–797.4*	*–876.0*	*–611.0*	*–992.9*	*–1,020.4*
Income: credit	2 300 ..	20.9	25.6	21.4	23.0	41.2	31.7	45.0	42.8
Income: debit	3 300 ..	–385.7	–350.5	–242.2	–254.9	–214.7	–190.9	–178.1	–190.3
Balance on Goods, Services, and Income	4 992 ..	*–172.6*	*–918.6*	*–653.4*	*–1,029.4*	*–1,049.4*	*–770.2*	*–1,126.0*	*–1,167.8*
Current transfers: credit	2 379 Z.	333.7	563.6	585.4	572.5	578.6	685.3	926.6	850.0
Current transfers: debit	3 379 ..	–63.2	–45.5	–5.4	...	–4.5	–4.7	–4.2	...
B. Capital Account [1]	4 994 Z.	**–.4**	**–.4**	**–.4**	**76.8**	**84.3**	**55.4**	**49.6**	**69.0**
Capital account: credit	2 994 Z.	...	...	...	76.8	84.3	55.4	49.6	69.0
Capital account: debit	3 994 ..	–.4	–.4	–.4	...	...	...	...	...
Total, Groups A Plus B	4 981 ..	*97.5*	*–400.9*	*–73.9*	*–380.0*	*–391.0*	*–34.3*	*–154.1*	*–248.8*
C. Financial Account [1]	4 995 W.	**–41.7**	**247.9**	**589.1**	**362.6**	**562.1**	**165.7**	**157.4**	**84.3**
Direct investment abroad	4 505 ..	...	...	.5	–2.1	...	...	...	...
Direct investment in Kenya	4 555 Z.	3.7	32.5	12.7	19.7	11.4	13.8	110.9	5.3
Portfolio investment assets	4 602 ..	...	...	...	...	...	...	–10.9	–7.3
Equity securities	4 610 ..	...	...	...	...	...	...	–.5	–.9
Debt securities	4 619 ..	...	...	...	...	...	...	–10.4	–6.4
Portfolio investment liabilities	4 652 Z.	...	6.0	7.5	34.2	1.3	–8.0	–3.5	5.5
Equity securities	4 660 ..	...	6.0	7.5	26.9	1.3	–8.0	–6.0	2.4
Debt securities	4 669 Z.	...	...	...	7.3	...	...	2.5	3.1
Financial derivatives	4 910 ..	...	...	...	...	...	...	...	...
Financial derivatives assets	4 900 ..	...	...	...	...	...	...	...	...
Financial derivatives liabilities	4 905 ..	...	...	...	...	...	...	...	...
Other investment assets	4 703 ..	171.1	277.1	628.2	–53.6	–58.6	–89.8	–55.7	–86.4
Monetary authorities	4 701 ..	...	...	...	...	...	...	...	...
General government	4 704 ..	...	...	...	–4.7	...	...	...	...
Banks	4 705 ..	–61.2	...	...	–44.2	–44.4	–74.3	–5.3	–6.6
Other sectors	4 728 ..	232.3	277.1	628.2	–4.7	–14.3	–15.5	–50.4	–79.8
Other investment liabilities	4 753 W.	–216.5	–67.7	–59.9	364.6	608.0	249.7	116.5	167.2
Monetary authorities	4 753 WA	...	...	...	...	...	...	...	...
General government	4 753 ZB	–113.3	–5.7	5.0	–110.9	–109.4	–257.4	–100.6	–221.8
Banks	4 753 ZC	32.1	...	...	...	22.6	31.0	...	92.0
Other sectors	4 753 ZD	–135.3	–61.9	–64.9	475.5	694.8	476.1	217.1	297.0
Total, Groups A Through C	4 983 ..	*55.8*	*–153.0*	*515.2*	*–17.4*	*171.2*	*131.5*	*3.3*	*–164.5*
D. Net Errors and Omissions	4 998 ..	**5.8**	**11.4**	**–128.2**	**32.8**	**–88.6**	**–165.5**	**–10.0**	**117.0**
Total, Groups A Through D	4 984 ..	*61.6*	*–141.6*	*387.0*	*15.5*	*82.6*	*–34.0*	*–6.8*	*–47.5*
E. Reserves and Related Items	4 802 A.	**–61.6**	**141.6**	**–387.0**	**–15.5**	**–82.6**	**34.0**	**6.8**	**47.5**
Reserve assets	4 802 ..	–95.3	174.2	–378.1	70.8	5.4	–9.2	–107.1	–167.8
Use of Fund credit and loans	4 766 ..	19.3	–39.1	–24.6	–67.3	–62.8	–59.5	1.3	–23.6
Exceptional financing	4 920 ..	14.4	6.5	15.8	–19.0	–25.2	102.7	112.6	238.8
Conversion rates: Kenya shillings per U.S. dollar	0 101 ..	**56.051**	**51.430**	**57.115**	**58.732**	**60.367**	**70.326**	**76.176**	**78.563**

[1] Excludes components that have been classified in the categories of Group E.

Table 2. STANDARD PRESENTATION, 1994–2001
(Millions of U.S. dollars)

	Code		1994	1995	1996	1997	1998	1999	2000	2001
CURRENT ACCOUNT	4 993	. .	**97.9**	**–400.4**	**–73.5**	**–456.8**	**–475.3**	**–89.6**	**–203.7**	**–317.8**
A. GOODS	4 100	. .	–238.4	–750.1	–514.8	–885.9	–1,011.7	–975.1	–1,261.7	–1,282.1
Credit	2 100	. .	**1,537.0**	**1,923.7**	**2,083.3**	**2,062.6**	**2,017.0**	**1,756.7**	**1,782.2**	**1,894.0**
General merchandise: exports f.o.b.	2 110	. .	1,481.1	1,875.4	2,039.0	2,008.7	1,977.9	1,726.6	1,735.7	1,840.5
Goods for processing: exports f.o.b.	2 150	. .	. . .	. . .	. . .	. . .	. . .	. . .	. . .	. . .
Repairs on goods	2 160	. .	9.8	21.7	2.2	. . .	3.9	3.2	3.8	2.9
Goods procured in ports by carriers	2 170	. .	46.0	26.7	42.1	53.9	35.2	20.1	35.6	38.3
Nonmonetary gold	2 180	. .	. . .	. . .	. . .	. . .	. . .	6.8	7.1	12.4
Debit	3 100	. .	**–1,775.3**	**–2,673.9**	**–2,598.2**	**–2,948.4**	**–3,028.7**	**–2,731.8**	**–3,044.0**	**–3,176.1**
General merchandise: imports f.o.b.	3 110	. .	–1,761.3	–2,639.4	–2,571.6	–2,921.5	–2,998.8	–2,693.4	–2,985.6	–3,121.7
Goods for processing: imports f.o.b.	3 150	. .	. . .	. . .	. . .	. . .	. . .	. . .	. . .	. . .
Repairs on goods	3 160	. .	–14.0	–13.0	–12.7	–12.6	–13.7	–15.8	–22.4	–23.0
Goods procured in ports by carriers	3 170	. .	. . .	–21.4	–13.9	–14.4	–16.2	–22.6	–36.0	–31.4
Nonmonetary gold	3 180	. .	. . .	. . .	. . .	. . .	. . .	. . .	. . .	. . .
B. SERVICES	4 200	. .	430.6	156.4	82.2	88.4	135.7	364.1	268.8	261.8
Total credit	2 200	. .	*1,117.3*	*1,024.5*	*936.2*	*914.5*	*830.4*	*934.5*	*993.4*	*1,087.2*
Total debit	3 200	. .	*–686.8*	*–868.1*	*–854.0*	*–826.0*	*–694.7*	*–570.4*	*–724.5*	*–825.5*
Transportation services, credit	2 205	. .	**242.2**	**282.9**	**289.2**	**285.6**	**305.7**	**375.9**	**411.1**	**427.9**
Passenger	2 850	. .	*113.5*	*104.4*	*101.6*	*114.0*	*128.3*	*181.1*	*217.3*	*227.2*
Freight	2 851	. .	*49.0*	*115.0*	*91.9*	*99.3*	*110.9*	*104.2*	*64.6*	*71.6*
Other	2 852	. .	*79.8*	*63.6*	*95.6*	*72.2*	*66.5*	*90.6*	*129.3*	*129.1*
Sea transport, passenger	2 207	. .	. . .	. . .	. . .	. . .	. . .	. . .	. . .	. . .
Sea transport, freight	2 208	. .	. . .	. . .	. . .	. . .	. . .	. . .	. . .	. . .
Sea transport, other	2 209	. .	. . .	54.8	86.5	72.2	57.4	79.5	75.4	80.2
Air transport, passenger	2 211	. .	. . .	104.4	101.6	114.0	127.2	180.1	210.0	226.7
Air transport, freight	2 212	. .	. . .	8.2	6.7	9.1	7.7	9.6	12.7	14.0
Air transport, other	2 213	. .	. . .	8.8	9.2	. . .	. . .	11.1	11.5	12.1
Other transport, passenger	2 215	. .	. . .	. . .	. . .	. . .	1.1	1.0	7.3	.5
Other transport, freight	2 216	. .	. . .	106.7	85.3	90.3	103.2	94.5	51.8	57.6
Other transport, other	2 217	. .	. . .	. . .	. . .	. . .	9.1	. . .	42.3	36.8
Transportation services, debit	3 205	. .	**–353.6**	**–431.0**	**–415.8**	**–339.5**	**–309.0**	**–236.0**	**–341.5**	**–372.8**
Passenger	3 850	. .	*–34.0*	*–37.7*	*–35.7*	*–6.9*	. . .	. . .	*–24.4*	*–40.1*
Freight	3 851	. .	*–253.8*	*–380.3*	*–370.1*	*–291.4*	*–261.9*	*–221.6*	*–279.1*	*–309.1*
Other	3 852	. .	*–65.8*	*–12.9*	*–10.0*	*–41.2*	*–47.1*	*–14.3*	*–38.0*	*–23.5*
Sea transport, passenger	3 207	. .	. . .	. . .	. . .	. . .	. . .	. . .	. . .	. . .
Sea transport, freight	3 208	. .	. . .	–380.3	–370.1	–291.4	–261.9	–221.6	–252.8	–282.9
Sea transport, other	3 209	. .	. . .	–4.7	. . .	–41.2	–46.7	–.3	–2.5	–1.1
Air transport, passenger	3 211	. .	. . .	–37.7	–35.7	–6.9	. . .	. . .	–24.1	–38.3
Air transport, freight	3 212	. .	. . .	. . .	. . .	. . .	. . .	. . .	–20.2	–18.6
Air transport, other	3 213	. .	. . .	–8.3	–10.0	. . .	. . .	–13.6	–16.9	–5.9
Other transport, passenger	3 215	. .	. . .	. . .	. . .	. . .	. . .	. . .	–.2	–1.8
Other transport, freight	3 216	. .	. . .	. . .	. . .	. . .	. . .	. . .	–6.2	–7.6
Other transport, other	3 217	. .	. . .	. . .	. . .	. . .	–.4	–.4	–18.6	–16.5
Travel, credit	2 236	. .	**501.3**	**486.0**	**448.1**	**385.4**	**290.0**	**303.8**	**282.9**	**308.5**
Business travel	2 237	. .	. . .	486.0	. . .	. . .	. . .	. . .	62.7	72.0
Personal travel	2 240	. .	. . .	. . .	448.1	385.4	290.0	303.8	220.2	236.6
Travel, debit	3 236	. .	**–113.8**	**–144.8**	**–167.1**	**–194.4**	**–189.9**	**–114.6**	**–131.5**	**–143.1**
Business travel	3 237	. .	. . .	–144.8	–123.8	–95.5	–87.7	–72.3	–45.4	–61.2
Personal travel	3 240	. .	. . .	. . .	–43.3	–98.9	–102.2	–42.3	–86.1	–81.8
Other services, credit	2 200	BA	**373.8**	**255.6**	**198.9**	**243.5**	**234.7**	**254.8**	**299.3**	**350.8**
Communications	2 245	. .	54.6	57.2	33.1	24.1	26.9	34.5	22.0	45.5
Construction	2 249	. .	. . .	. . .	. . .	. . .	. . .	. . .	. . .	. . .
Insurance	2 253	. .	5.4	18.3	11.3	14.9	5.4	4.1	3.7	3.6
Financial	2 260	. .	. . .	1.2	1.3	1.7	. . .	. . .	. . .	. . .
Computer and information	2 262	. .	. . .	. . .	.6	. . .	.5	1.3	.4	.3
Royalties and licence fees	2 266	. .	6.9	5.5	5.2	4.3	1.9	.9	7.1	5.0
Other business services	2 268	. .	4.3	. . .	. . .	. . .	. . .	. . .	. . .	. . .
Personal, cultural, and recreational	2 287	. .	. . .	. . .	. . .	. . .	. . .	. . .	. . .	.1
Government, n.i.e.	2 291	. .	302.6	173.5	147.4	198.4	199.9	214.0	266.2	296.3
Other services, debit	3 200	BA	**–219.4**	**–292.3**	**–271.1**	**–292.1**	**–195.9**	**–219.8**	**–251.5**	**–309.6**
Communications	3 245	. .	–21.4	–33.5	–8.6	–6.0	–6.8	–19.5	–7.1	–31.5
Construction	3 249	. .	. . .	. . .	. . .	. . .	. . .	. . .	. . .	. . .
Insurance	3 253	. .	–46.5	–66.3	–61.5	–88.7	–52.2	–42.8	–47.7	–52.3
Financial	3 260	. .	. . .	–5.2	–8.1	–10.3	–10.7	–12.8	–16.2	–24.3
Computer and information	3 262	. .	. . .	–2.3	–2.7	–1.7	–1.9	–1.6	–1.3	–1.1
Royalties and licence fees	3 266	. .	–3.5	. . .	. . .	–38.9	–39.9	–44.2	–77.3	–62.1
Other business services	3 268	. .	–61.9	–49.6	–47.8	–28.7	–21.9	–33.1	–41.0	–74.9
Personal, cultural, and recreational	3 287	. .	. . .	. . .	. . .	. . .	. . .	–.5	–1.6	–1.5
Government, n.i.e.	3 291	. .	–86.1	–135.4	–142.4	–117.7	–62.4	–65.4	–59.3	–61.8

Table 2 (Continued). STANDARD PRESENTATION, 1994–2001
(Millions of U.S. dollars)

	Code	1994	1995	1996	1997	1998	1999	2000	2001
C. INCOME	4 300 . .	–364.8	–324.9	–220.8	–231.9	–173.4	–159.2	–133.1	–147.5
Total credit	2 300 . .	*20.9*	*25.6*	*21.4*	*23.0*	*41.2*	*31.7*	*45.0*	*42.8*
Total debit	3 300 . .	*–385.7*	*–350.5*	*–242.2*	*–254.9*	*–214.7*	*–190.9*	*–178.1*	*–190.3*
Compensation of employees, credit	2 310 . .	**. . .**	**. . .**	**. . .**	**. . .**	**. . .**	**. . .**	**. . .**	**. . .**
Compensation of employees, debit	3 310 . .	**. . .**	**. . .**	**. . .**	**–31.0**	**–34.8**	**–34.5**	**. . .**	**. . .**
Investment income, credit	2 320 . .	**20.9**	**25.6**	**21.4**	**23.0**	**41.2**	**31.7**	**45.0**	**42.8**
Direct investment income	2 330 . .	. . .	. . .	. . .	. . .	. . .	. . .	. . .	. . .
Dividends and distributed branch profits	2 332 . .	. . .	. . .	. . .	. . .	. . .	. . .	. . .	. . .
Reinvested earnings and undistributed branch profits	2 333 . .	. . .	. . .	. . .	. . .	. . .	. . .	. . .	. . .
Income on debt (interest)	2 334 . .	. . .	. . .	. . .	. . .	. . .	. . .	. . .	. . .
Portfolio investment income	2 339 . .	. . .	. . .	. . .	. . .	. . .	. . .	. . .	. . .
Income on equity	2 340 . .	. . .	. . .	. . .	. . .	. . .	. . .	. . .	. . .
Income on bonds and notes	2 350 . .	. . .	. . .	. . .	. . .	. . .	. . .	. . .	. . .
Income on money market instruments	2 360 . .	. . .	. . .	. . .	. . .	. . .	. . .	. . .	. . .
Other investment income	2 370 . .	20.9	25.6	21.4	23.0	41.2	31.7	45.0	42.8
Investment income, debit	3 320 . .	**–385.7**	**–350.5**	**–242.2**	**–223.9**	**–179.8**	**–156.5**	**–178.1**	**–190.3**
Direct investment income	3 330 . .	–86.9	–90.7	–23.6	–37.6	–8.1	–15.5	–28.7	–50.1
Dividends and distributed branch profits	3 332 . .	–83.2	–86.4	–19.3	–37.6	–8.1	–15.5	–21.9	–44.3
Reinvested earnings and undistributed branch profits	3 333 . .	–3.7	–4.3	–4.3	. . .	. . .	. . .	. . .	. . .
Income on debt (interest)	3 334 . .	. . .	. . .	. . .	. . .	. . .	. . .	–6.8	–5.8
Portfolio investment income	3 339 . .	. . .	. . .	. . .	. . .	. . .	. . .	–1.4	–2.7
Income on equity	3 340 . .	. . .	. . .	. . .	. . .	. . .	. . .	–1.2	–.6
Income on bonds and notes	3 350 . .	. . .	. . .	. . .	. . .	. . .	. . .	–.2	–2.1
Income on money market instruments	3 360 . .	. . .	. . .	. . .	. . .	. . .	. . .	. . .	. . .
Other investment income	3 370 . .	–298.8	–259.8	–218.6	–186.3	–171.8	–141.0	–148.0	–137.4
D. CURRENT TRANSFERS	4 379 . .	270.5	518.1	580.0	572.5	574.1	680.5	922.4	850.0
Credit	2 379 . .	**333.7**	**563.6**	**585.4**	**572.5**	**578.6**	**685.3**	**926.6**	**850.0**
General government	2 380 . .	125.4	111.7	148.4	39.2	51.4	31.5	111.2	151.2
Other sectors	2 390 . .	208.3	451.9	436.9	533.3	527.2	653.8	815.3	698.8
Workers' remittances	2 391 . .	. . .	. . .	. . .	. . .	. . .	. . .	. . .	. . .
Other current transfers	2 392 . .	208.3	451.9	436.9	533.3	527.2	653.8	815.3	698.8
Debit	3 379 . .	**–63.2**	**–45.5**	**–5.4**	**. . .**	**–4.5**	**–4.7**	**–4.2**	**. . .**
General government	3 380 . .	–2.5	–2.3	–1.6	. . .	. . .	. . .	. . .	. . .
Other sectors	3 390 . .	–60.6	–43.2	–3.8	. . .	–4.5	–4.7	–4.2	. . .
Workers' remittances	3 391 . .	–3.5	–3.6	–3.6	. . .	. . .	. . .	. . .	. . .
Other current transfers	3 392 . .	–57.2	–39.6	–.2	. . .	–4.5	–4.7	–4.2	. . .
CAPITAL AND FINANCIAL ACCOUNT	4 996 . .	**–103.8**	**389.1**	**201.6**	**424.0**	**563.9**	**255.2**	**213.7**	**200.8**
CAPITAL ACCOUNT	4 994 . .	**–.4**	**–.4**	**–.4**	**76.8**	**84.3**	**55.4**	**49.6**	**73.0**
Total credit	2 994 . .	. . .	. . .	. . .	*76.8*	*84.3*	*55.4*	*49.6*	*73.0*
Total debit	3 994 . .	*–.4*	*–.4*	*–.4*	. . .	. . .	. . .	. . .	. . .
Capital transfers, credit	2 400 . .	**. . .**	**. . .**	**. . .**	**76.8**	**84.3**	**55.4**	**49.6**	**73.0**
General government	2 401 . .	. . .	. . .	. . .	76.8	84.3	55.4	49.6	73.0
Debt forgiveness	2 402 . .	. . .	. . .	. . .	. . .	. . .	. . .	. . .	4.0
Other capital transfers	2 410 . .	. . .	. . .	. . .	76.8	84.3	55.4	49.6	69.0
Other sectors	2 430 . .	. . .	. . .	. . .	. . .	. . .	. . .	. . .	. . .
Migrants' transfers	2 431 . .	. . .	. . .	. . .	. . .	. . .	. . .	. . .	. . .
Debt forgiveness	2 432 . .	. . .	. . .	. . .	. . .	. . .	. . .	. . .	. . .
Other capital transfers	2 440 . .	. . .	. . .	. . .	. . .	. . .	. . .	. . .	. . .
Capital transfers, debit	3 400 . .	**–.4**	**–.4**	**–.4**	**. . .**	**. . .**	**. . .**	**. . .**	**. . .**
General government	3 401 . .	. . .	. . .	. . .	. . .	. . .	. . .	. . .	. . .
Debt forgiveness	3 402 . .	. . .	. . .	. . .	. . .	. . .	. . .	. . .	. . .
Other capital transfers	3 410 . .	. . .	. . .	. . .	. . .	. . .	. . .	. . .	. . .
Other sectors	3 430 . .	–.4	–.4	–.4	. . .	. . .	. . .	. . .	. . .
Migrants' transfers	3 431 . .	–.4	–.4	–.4	. . .	. . .	. . .	. . .	. . .
Debt forgiveness	3 432 . .	. . .	. . .	. . .	. . .	. . .	. . .	. . .	. . .
Other capital transfers	3 440 . .	. . .	. . .	. . .	. . .	. . .	. . .	. . .	. . .
Nonproduced nonfinancial assets, credit	2 480 . .	**. . .**	**. . .**	**. . .**	**. . .**	**. . .**	**. . .**	**. . .**	**. . .**
Nonproduced nonfinancial assets, debit	3 480 . .	**. . .**	**. . .**	**. . .**	**. . .**	**. . .**	**. . .**	**. . .**	**. . .**

Table 2 (Continued). STANDARD PRESENTATION, 1994–2001

(Millions of U.S. dollars)

	Code	1994	1995	1996	1997	1998	1999	2000	2001
FINANCIAL ACCOUNT	4 995	**–103.4**	**389.5**	**202.1**	**347.2**	**479.6**	**199.8**	**164.1**	**127.8**
A. DIRECT INVESTMENT	4 500	3.7	32.5	13.2	17.5	11.4	13.8	110.9	5.3
Direct investment abroad	4 505	**. . .**	**. . .**	**.5**	**–2.1**	**. . .**	**. . .**	**. . .**	**. . .**
Equity capital	4 510	. . .	. . .	. . .	. . .	. . .	. . .	. . .	. . .
Claims on affiliated enterprises	4 515	. . .	. . .	. . .	. . .	. . .	. . .	. . .	. . .
Liabilities to affiliated enterprises	4 520	. . .	. . .	. . .	. . .	. . .	. . .	. . .	. . .
Reinvested earnings	4 525	. . .	. . .	. . .	. . .	. . .	. . .	. . .	. . .
Other capital	4 530	. . .	. . .	.5	–2.1	. . .	. . .	. . .	. . .
Claims on affiliated enterprises	4 535	. . .	. . .	. . .	. . .	. . .	. . .	. . .	. . .
Liabilities to affiliated enterprises	4 540	. . .	. . .	. . .	. . .	. . .	. . .	. . .	. . .
Direct investment in Kenya	4 555	**3.7**	**32.5**	**12.7**	**19.7**	**11.4**	**13.8**	**110.9**	**5.3**
Equity capital	4 560	. . .	28.2	8.4	19.7	11.4	13.8	83.3	.8
Claims on direct investors	4 565	. . .	28.2	8.4	19.7	. . .	. . .	. . .	. . .
Liabilities to direct investors	4 570	. . .	. . .	. . .	. . .	11.4	13.8	83.3	.8
Reinvested earnings	4 575	3.7	4.3	4.3	. . .	. . .	. . .	. . .	. . .
Other capital	4 580	. . .	. . .	. . .	. . .	. . .	. . .	27.6	4.5
Claims on direct investors	4 585	. . .	. . .	. . .	. . .	. . .	. . .	. . .	. . .
Liabilities to direct investors	4 590	. . .	. . .	. . .	. . .	. . .	. . .	27.6	4.5
B. PORTFOLIO INVESTMENT	4 600	. . .	6.0	7.5	34.2	1.3	–8.0	–14.4	–1.8
Assets	4 602	**. . .**	**. . .**	**. . .**	**. . .**	**. . .**	**. . .**	**–10.9**	**–7.3**
Equity securities	4 610	. . .	. . .	. . .	. . .	. . .	. . .	–.5	–.9
Monetary authorities	4 611	. . .	. . .	. . .	. . .	. . .	. . .	. . .	. . .
General government	4 612	. . .	. . .	. . .	. . .	. . .	. . .	. . .	. . .
Banks	4 613	. . .	. . .	. . .	. . .	. . .	. . .	–.5	–.9
Other sectors	4 614	. . .	. . .	. . .	. . .	. . .	. . .	. . .	. . .
Debt securities	4 619	. . .	. . .	. . .	. . .	. . .	. . .	–10.4	–6.4
Bonds and notes	4 620	. . .	. . .	. . .	. . .	. . .	. . .	–10.4	–6.4
Monetary authorities	4 621	. . .	. . .	. . .	. . .	. . .	. . .	–.4	–1.3
General government	4 622	. . .	. . .	. . .	. . .	. . .	. . .	. . .	. . .
Banks	4 623	. . .	. . .	. . .	. . .	. . .	. . .	. . .	. . .
Other sectors	4 624	. . .	. . .	. . .	. . .	. . .	. . .	–10.0	–5.1
Money market instruments	4 630	. . .	. . .	. . .	. . .	. . .	. . .	. . .	. . .
Monetary authorities	4 631	. . .	. . .	. . .	. . .	. . .	. . .	. . .	. . .
General government	4 632	. . .	. . .	. . .	. . .	. . .	. . .	. . .	. . .
Banks	4 633	. . .	. . .	. . .	. . .	. . .	. . .	. . .	. . .
Other sectors	4 634	. . .	. . .	. . .	. . .	. . .	. . .	. . .	. . .
Liabilities	4 652	**. . .**	**6.0**	**7.5**	**34.2**	**1.3**	**–8.0**	**–3.5**	**5.5**
Equity securities	4 660	. . .	6.0	7.5	26.9	1.3	–8.0	–6.0	2.4
Banks	4 663	. . .	. . .	. . .	. . .	. . .	. . .	.4	1.0
Other sectors	4 664	. . .	6.0	7.5	26.9	1.3	–8.0	–6.4	1.4
Debt securities	4 669	. . .	. . .	. . .	7.3	. . .	. . .	2.5	3.1
Bonds and notes	4 670	. . .	. . .	. . .	7.3	. . .	. . .	2.5	3.1
Monetary authorities	4 671	. . .	. . .	. . .	. . .	. . .	. . .	2.5	3.1
General government	4 672	. . .	. . .	. . .	4.1	. . .	. . .	. . .	. . .
Banks	4 673	. . .	. . .	. . .	3.2	. . .	. . .	. . .	. . .
Other sectors	4 674	. . .	. . .	. . .	. . .	. . .	. . .	. . .	. . .
Money market instruments	4 680	. . .	. . .	. . .	. . .	. . .	. . .	. . .	. . .
Monetary authorities	4 681	. . .	. . .	. . .	. . .	. . .	. . .	. . .	. . .
General government	4 682	. . .	. . .	. . .	. . .	. . .	. . .	. . .	. . .
Banks	4 683	. . .	. . .	. . .	. . .	. . .	. . .	. . .	. . .
Other sectors	4 684	. . .	. . .	. . .	. . .	. . .	. . .	. . .	. . .
C. FINANCIAL DERIVATIVES	4 910	. . .	. . .	. . .	. . .	. . .	. . .	. . .	. . .
Monetary authorities	4 911	. . .	. . .	. . .	. . .	. . .	. . .	. . .	. . .
General government	4 912	. . .	. . .	. . .	. . .	. . .	. . .	. . .	. . .
Banks	4 913	. . .	. . .	. . .	. . .	. . .	. . .	. . .	. . .
Other sectors	4 914	. . .	. . .	. . .	. . .	. . .	. . .	. . .	. . .
Assets	4 900	**. . .**	**. . .**	**. . .**	**. . .**	**. . .**	**. . .**	**. . .**	**. . .**
Monetary authorities	4 901	. . .	. . .	. . .	. . .	. . .	. . .	. . .	. . .
General government	4 902	. . .	. . .	. . .	. . .	. . .	. . .	. . .	. . .
Banks	4 903	. . .	. . .	. . .	. . .	. . .	. . .	. . .	. . .
Other sectors	4 904	. . .	. . .	. . .	. . .	. . .	. . .	. . .	. . .
Liabilities	4 905	**. . .**	**. . .**	**. . .**	**. . .**	**. . .**	**. . .**	**. . .**	**. . .**
Monetary authorities	4 906	. . .	. . .	. . .	. . .	. . .	. . .	. . .	. . .
General government	4 907	. . .	. . .	. . .	. . .	. . .	. . .	. . .	. . .
Banks	4 908	. . .	. . .	. . .	. . .	. . .	. . .	. . .	. . .
Other sectors	4 909	. . .	. . .	. . .	. . .	. . .	. . .	. . .	. . .

Table 2 (Concluded). STANDARD PRESENTATION, 1994–2001
(Millions of U.S. dollars)

	Code	1994	1995	1996	1997	1998	1999	2000	2001
D. OTHER INVESTMENT	4 700	–11.8	176.9	559.4	224.7	461.4	203.1	174.7	292.1
Assets	4 703	**171.1**	**277.1**	**628.2**	**–53.6**	**–58.6**	**–89.8**	**–55.7**	**–86.4**
Trade credits	4 706	...	...	...	...	...	...	...	...
General government	4 707	...	...	...	...	...	...	...	...
of which: Short-term	4 709	...	...	...	...	...	...	...	...
Other sectors	4 710	...	...	...	...	...	...	...	...
of which: Short-term	4 712	...	...	...	...	...	...	...	...
Loans	4 714	...	...	...	...	...	...	...	...
Monetary authorities	4 715	...	...	...	...	...	...	...	...
of which: Short-term	4 718	...	...	...	...	...	...	...	...
General government	4 719	...	...	...	...	...	...	...	...
of which: Short-term	4 721	...	...	...	...	...	...	...	...
Banks	4 722	...	...	...	...	...	...	...	...
of which: Short-term	4 724	...	...	...	...	...	...	...	...
Other sectors	4 725	...	...	...	...	...	...	...	...
of which: Short-term	4 727	...	...	...	...	...	...	...	...
Currency and deposits	4 730	171.1	289.7	653.4	–35.8	–43.1	–69.0	...	...
Monetary authorities	4 731	...	...	...	...	...	...	...	...
General government	4 732	...	...	...	...	...	...	...	...
Banks	4 733	–61.2	...	...	–35.8	–43.1	–69.0	...	...
Other sectors	4 734	232.3	289.7	653.4	...	...	...	...	...
Other assets	4 736	–.1	–12.6	–25.1	–17.8	–15.5	–20.8	–55.7	–86.4
Monetary authorities	4 737	...	...	...	...	...	...	...	...
of which: Short-term	4 739	...	...	...	...	...	...	...	...
General government	4 740	...	...	...	–4.7	...	...	...	...
of which: Short-term	4 742	...	...	...	*–4.7*	...	...	...	...
Banks	4 743	...	...	...	–8.4	–1.3	–5.3	–5.3	–6.6
of which: Short-term	4 745	...	...	...	*–8.4*	*–1.3*	*–5.3*	*–5.3*	*–6.6*
Other sectors	4 746	–.1	–12.6	–25.1	–4.7	–14.3	–15.5	–50.4	–79.8
of which: Short-term	4 748	...	...	...	...	...	*14.6*	*13.0*	*12.1*
Liabilities	4 753	**–182.8**	**–100.2**	**–68.8**	**278.3**	**520.1**	**292.9**	**230.4**	**378.4**
Trade credits	4 756	...	29.0	187.6	...	...	...	...	...
General government	4 757	...	...	187.6	...	...	...	...	...
of which: Short-term	4 759	...	...	...	...	...	...	...	...
Other sectors	4 760	...	29.0	...	...	...	...	...	...
of which: Short-term	4 762	...	*29.0*	...	...	...	...	...	...
Loans	4 764	–242.7	–135.8	–272.2	–305.6	–191.7	–339.3	–52.8	–55.4
Monetary authorities	4 765	19.3	–39.1	–24.6	–67.3	–62.8	–59.5	1.3	–23.6
of which: Use of Fund credit and loans from the Fund	4 766	*19.3*	*–39.1*	*–24.6*	*–67.3*	*–62.8*	*–59.5*	*1.3*	*–23.6*
of which: Short-term	4 768	...	...	...	...	...	...	...	...
General government	4 769	–113.3	–5.7	–182.6	–110.9	–109.4	–257.4	65.4	–93.8
of which: Short-term	4 771	...	...	...	...	...	...	...	...
Banks	4 772	...	...	...	...	22.6	31.0	...	92.0
of which: Short-term	4 774	...	...	...	...	...	...	...	...
Other sectors	4 775	–148.7	–91.0	–64.9	–127.4	–42.2	–53.4	–119.5	–30.0
of which: Short-term	4 777	...	...	...	...	*35.2*	*22.1*	*20.9*	*17.0*
Currency and deposits	4 780	32.1	...	...	...	...	...	...	...
Monetary authorities	4 781	...	...	...	...	...	...	...	...
General government	4 782	...	...	...	...	...	...	...	...
Banks	4 783	32.1	...	...	...	...	...	...	...
Other sectors	4 784	...	...	...	...	...	...	...	...
Other liabilities	4 786	27.8	6.5	15.8	583.9	711.8	632.2	283.2	433.8
Monetary authorities	4 787	14.4	...	...	...	...	...	...	...
of which: Short-term	4 789	*14.4*	...	...	...	...	...	...	...
General government	4 790	...	6.5	15.8	–19.0	–25.2	102.7	–53.4	106.8
of which: Short-term	4 792	...	*6.5*	*15.8*	*–19.0*	*–25.2*	*102.7*	*–53.4*	*106.8*
Banks	4 793	...	...	...	...	...	...	...	...
of which: Short-term	4 795	...	...	...	...	...	...	...	...
Other sectors	4 796	13.4	...	...	602.9	737.0	529.5	336.6	327.0
of which: Short-term	4 798	*13.4*	...	...	*602.9*	*737.0*	*529.5*	*336.6*	*327.0*
E. RESERVE ASSETS	4 802	–95.3	174.2	–378.1	70.8	5.4	–9.2	–107.1	–167.8
Monetary gold	4 812	...	...	...	...	...	...	...	...
Special drawing rights	4 811	.5	.3	–.5	–.3	–.1	–1.9	2.0	–.7
Reserve position in the Fund	4 810	–.1	...	...	–.1	–.1	...	...	–.1
Foreign exchange	4 803	–97.8	174.6	–378.0	70.3	5.8	–7.3	–108.8	–167.2
Other claims	4 813	2.1	–.8	.4	.9	–.2	.1	–.2	.2
NET ERRORS AND OMISSIONS	4 998	**5.8**	**11.4**	**–128.2**	**32.8**	**–88.6**	**–165.5**	**–10.0**	**117.0**

Part 3 of the *Yearbook* contains descriptions of the methodologies, compilation practices, and sources used to compile these data.

Table 1. ANALYTIC PRESENTATION, 1994–2001
(Millions of U.S. dollars)

	Code			1994	1995	1996	1997	1998	1999	2000	2001
A. Current Account [1]	4	993	Z.	**–3,867**	**–8,507**	**–23,006**	**–8,167**	**40,365**	**24,477**	**12,241**	**8,617**
Goods: exports f.o.b	2	100	. .	94,964	124,632	129,968	138,619	132,122	145,164	175,948	151,371
Goods: imports f.o.b	3	100	. .	–97,824	–129,076	–144,933	–141,798	–90,495	–116,793	–159,076	–137,979
Balance on Goods	4	100	. .	*–2,860*	*–4,444*	*–14,965*	*–3,179*	*41,627*	*28,371*	*16,872*	*13,392*
Services: credit	2	200	. .	16,805	22,827	23,412	26,301	25,565	26,529	30,534	29,602
Services: debit	3	200	. .	–18,606	–25,806	–29,592	–29,502	–24,541	–27,180	–33,423	–33,129
Balance on Goods and Services	4	991	. .	*–4,661*	*–7,423*	*–21,144*	*–6,379*	*42,651*	*27,720*	*13,982*	*9,866*
Income: credit	2	300	. .	2,836	3,486	3,666	3,878	2,675	3,245	6,375	7,040
Income: debit	3	300	. .	–3,322	–4,787	–5,482	–6,333	–8,313	–8,404	–8,797	–7,926
Balance on Goods, Services, and Income	4	992	. .	*–5,147*	*–8,725*	*–22,960*	*–8,834*	*37,013*	*22,561*	*11,561*	*8,980*
Current transfers: credit	2	379	Z.	3,672	4,104	4,279	5,288	6,737	6,421	6,500	6,548
Current transfers: debit	3	379	. .	–2,392	–3,886	–4,325	–4,621	–3,384	–4,506	–5,820	–6,911
B. Capital Account [1]	4	994	Z.	**–437**	**–488**	**–598**	**–608**	**171**	**–389**	**–615**	**–443**
Capital account: credit	2	994	Z.	8	15	19	17	464	95	98	29
Capital account: debit	3	994	. .	–445	–502	–617	–624	–293	–484	–713	–471
Total, Groups A Plus B	4	981	. .	*–4,304*	*–8,994*	*–23,603*	*–8,775*	*40,536*	*24,087*	*11,626*	*8,174*
C. Financial Account [1]	4	995	W.	**10,733**	**17,273**	**23,924**	**–9,195**	**–8,381**	**12,709**	**12,725**	**2,543**
Direct investment abroad	4	505	. .	–2,461	–3,552	–4,671	–4,449	–4,740	–4,198	–4,999	–2,600
Direct investment in Korea	4	555	Z.	810	1,776	2,326	2,844	5,412	9,333	9,283	3,198
Portfolio investment assets	4	602	. .	–2,481	–2,907	–6,413	1,076	–1,999	1,282	–520	–5,499
Equity securities	4	610	. .	–382	–238	–653	–320	42	–271	–480	–273
Debt securities	4	619	. .	–2,098	–2,669	–5,760	1,395	–2,041	1,553	–40	–5,226
Portfolio investment liabilities	4	652	Z.	8,713	14,619	21,514	13,308	775	7,908	12,697	11,856
Equity securities	4	660	. .	3,614	4,219	5,954	2,525	3,856	12,072	13,094	10,165
Debt securities	4	669	Z.	5,099	10,400	15,561	10,783	–3,081	–4,164	–397	1,691
Financial derivatives	4	910	. .	–112	–121	83	–89	–654	–514	–179	–106
Financial derivatives assets	4	900	. .	452	623	414	932	412	401	532	272
Financial derivatives liabilities	4	905	. .	–565	–744	–331	–1,021	–1,066	–915	–711	–378
Other investment assets	4	703	. .	–7,369	–13,991	–13,487	–13,568	6,693	–2,606	–2,289	7,458
Monetary authorities	4	701	. .	–72	–36	. . .	–86	–36	–164	–44	–56
General government	4	704	. .	–296	–156	–543	–149	–46	–169	–155	–485
Banks	4	705	. .	–5,061	–9,199	–8,173	–8,336	6,970	–203	–1,219	9,048
Other sectors	4	728	. .	–1,940	–4,600	–4,770	–4,996	–194	–2,071	–871	–1,048
Other investment liabilities	4	753	W.	13,632	21,450	24,571	–8,317	–13,868	1,502	–1,268	–11,764
Monetary authorities	4	753	WA	–2	–10	–29	23	25	148	28	63
General government	4	753	ZB	–335	–593	–493	4,671	4,628	3,309	110	–400
Banks	4	753	ZC	7,368	11,389	9,952	–9,785	–6,233	1,418	–4,538	–5,315
Other sectors	4	753	ZD	6,600	10,664	15,142	–3,226	–12,288	–3,372	3,132	–6,112
Total, Groups A Through C	4	983	. .	*6,429*	*8,279*	*321*	*–17,970*	*32,155*	*36,796*	*24,351*	*10,718*
D. Net Errors and Omissions	4	998	. .	**–1,816**	**–1,240**	**1,095**	**–5,010**	**–6,225**	**–3,536**	**–561**	**2,698**
Total, Groups A Through D	4	984	. .	*4,614*	*7,039*	*1,416*	*–22,979*	*25,930*	*33,260*	*23,790*	*13,416*
E. Reserves and Related Items	4	802	A.	**–4,614**	**–7,039**	**–1,416**	**22,979**	**–25,930**	**–33,260**	**–23,790**	**–13,416**
Reserve assets	4	802	. .	–4,614	–7,039	–1,416	11,875	–30,968	–22,989	–23,790	–7,724
Use of Fund credit and loans	4	766	. .	. . .	. . .	. . .	11,104	5,038	–10,271	. . .	–5,692
Exceptional financing	4	920	. .	. . .	. . .	. . .	. . .	. . .	. . .	. . .	. . .
Conversion rates: won per U.S. dollar	0	101	. .	**803.4**	**771.3**	**804.5**	**951.3**	**1,401.4**	**1,188.8**	**1,131.0**	**1,291.0**

[1] Excludes components that have been classified in the categories of Group E.

Table 2. STANDARD PRESENTATION, 1994–2001
(Millions of U.S. dollars)

	Code		1994	1995	1996	1997	1998	1999	2000	2001
CURRENT ACCOUNT	4 993	. .	**–3,867**	**–8,507**	**–23,006**	**–8,167**	**40,365**	**24,477**	**12,241**	**8,617**
A. GOODS	4 100	. .	–2,860	–4,444	–14,965	–3,179	41,627	28,371	16,872	13,392
Credit	2 100	. .	**94,964**	**124,632**	**129,968**	**138,619**	**132,122**	**145,164**	**175,948**	**151,371**
General merchandise: exports f.o.b.	2 110	. .	89,248	114,941	116,096	121,953	114,660	129,231	159,137	139,538
Goods for processing: exports f.o.b.	2 150	. .	4,327	6,297	7,392	9,290	9,932	11,995	13,907	9,642
Repairs on goods	2 160	. .	225	229	237	240	235	127	103	37
Goods procured in ports by carriers	2 170	. .	597	735	933	978	603	860	1,278	1,097
Nonmonetary gold	2 180	. .	567	2,431	5,310	6,158	6,692	2,951	1,523	1,056
Debit	3 100	. .	**–97,824**	**–129,076**	**–144,933**	**–141,798**	**–90,495**	**–116,793**	**–159,076**	**–137,979**
General merchandise: imports f.o.b.	3 110	. .	–93,635	–121,512	–133,640	–127,633	–79,037	–104,503	–146,824	–128,926
Goods for processing: imports f.o.b.	3 150	. .	–2,618	–3,785	–4,491	–6,011	–6,005	–7,860	–8,508	–6,091
Repairs on goods	3 160	. .	. . .	–19	–82	–16	–3	–29	–24	–32
Goods procured in ports by carriers	3 170	. .	–888	–1,140	–1,339	–1,884	–1,143	–1,199	–1,567	–1,365
Nonmonetary gold	3 180	. .	–683	–2,621	–5,382	–6,255	–4,307	–3,201	–2,153	–1,565
B. SERVICES	4 200	. .	–1,801	–2,979	–6,179	–3,200	1,024	–651	–2,889	–3,526
Total credit	2 200	. .	*16,805*	*22,827*	*23,412*	*26,301*	*25,565*	*26,529*	*30,534*	*29,602*
Total debit	3 200	. .	*–18,606*	*–25,806*	*–29,592*	*–29,502*	*–24,541*	*–27,180*	*–33,423*	*–33,129*
Transportation services, credit	2 205	. .	**7,362**	**9,272**	**8,765**	**11,005**	**10,204**	**11,466**	**13,687**	**13,498**
Passenger	2 850	. .	*1,317*	*1,520*	*1,470*	*1,586*	*1,355*	*1,496*	*1,693*	. . .
Freight	2 851	. .	*5,187*	*6,684*	*7,019*	*8,759*	*8,076*	*9,010*	*9,995*	. . .
Other	2 852	. .	*857*	*1,068*	*277*	*660*	*774*	*961*	*2,000*	. . .
Sea transport, passenger	2 207	. .	. . .	. . .	. . .	. . .	. . .	. . .	. . .	. . .
Sea transport, freight	2 208	. .	. . .	. . .	. . .	. . .	. . .	. . .	. . .	. . .
Sea transport, other	2 209	. .	. . .	. . .	. . .	. . .	. . .	. . .	. . .	. . .
Air transport, passenger	2 211	. .	. . .	. . .	. . .	. . .	. . .	. . .	. . .	. . .
Air transport, freight	2 212	. .	. . .	. . .	. . .	. . .	. . .	. . .	. . .	. . .
Air transport, other	2 213	. .	. . .	. . .	. . .	. . .	. . .	. . .	. . .	. . .
Other transport, passenger	2 215	. .	. . .	. . .	. . .	. . .	. . .	. . .	. . .	. . .
Other transport, freight	2 216	. .	. . .	. . .	. . .	. . .	. . .	. . .	. . .	. . .
Other transport, other	2 217	. .	. . .	. . .	. . .	. . .	. . .	. . .	. . .	. . .
Transportation services, debit	3 205	. .	**–7,114**	**–9,645**	**–10,230**	**–10,310**	**–8,983**	**–9,980**	**–10,879**	**–10,741**
Passenger	3 850	. .	*–452*	*–606*	*–809*	*–1,051*	*–557*	*–674*	*–813*	. . .
Freight	3 851	. .	*–3,028*	*–3,875*	*–3,421*	*–2,737*	*–1,985*	*–2,825*	*–3,203*	. . .
Other	3 852	. .	*–3,634*	*–5,163*	*–6,001*	*–6,522*	*–6,441*	*–6,481*	*–6,863*	. . .
Sea transport, passenger	3 207	. .	. . .	. . .	. . .	. . .	. . .	. . .	. . .	. . .
Sea transport, freight	3 208	. .	. . .	. . .	. . .	. . .	. . .	. . .	. . .	. . .
Sea transport, other	3 209	. .	. . .	. . .	. . .	. . .	. . .	. . .	. . .	. . .
Air transport, passenger	3 211	. .	. . .	. . .	. . .	. . .	. . .	. . .	. . .	. . .
Air transport, freight	3 212	. .	. . .	. . .	. . .	. . .	. . .	. . .	. . .	. . .
Air transport, other	3 213	. .	. . .	. . .	. . .	. . .	. . .	. . .	. . .	. . .
Other transport, passenger	3 215	. .	. . .	. . .	. . .	. . .	. . .	. . .	. . .	. . .
Other transport, freight	3 216	. .	. . .	. . .	. . .	. . .	. . .	. . .	. . .	. . .
Other transport, other	3 217	. .	. . .	. . .	. . .	. . .	. . .	. . .	. . .	. . .
Travel, credit	2 236	. .	**3,340**	**5,150**	**4,880**	**4,731**	**6,908**	**6,841**	**6,834**	**6,292**
Business travel	2 237	. .	. . .	. . .	. . .	. . .	. . .	. . .	. . .	. . .
Personal travel	2 240	. .	. . .	. . .	. . .	. . .	. . .	. . .	. . .	. . .
Travel, debit	3 236	. .	**–4,513**	**–6,341**	**–7,482**	**–6,988**	**–3,470**	**–4,881**	**–7,132**	**–7,585**
Business travel	3 237	. .	. . .	. . .	. . .	. . .	. . .	. . .	. . .	. . .
Personal travel	3 240	. .	. . .	. . .	. . .	. . .	. . .	. . .	. . .	. . .
Other services, credit	2 200	BA	**6,104**	**8,405**	**9,768**	**10,565**	**8,452**	**8,222**	**10,012**	**8,951**
Communications	2 245	. .	490	561	643	652	656	400	387	. . .
Construction	2 249	. .	. . .	. . .	. . .	. . .	5	10	29	. . .
Insurance	2 253	. .	50	–20	95	–2	52	48	68	. . .
Financial	2 260	. .	92	105	123	159	145	478	705	. . .
Computer and information	2 262	. .	7	5	6	3	5	4	11	. . .
Royalties and licence fees	2 266	. .	155	299	185	252	260	455	688	. . .
Other business services	2 268	. .	4,738	6,761	7,952	8,633	6,580	6,035	7,200	. . .
Personal, cultural, and recreational	2 287	. .	. . .	. . .	. . .	5	14	29	137	. . .
Government, n.i.e.	2 291	. .	573	694	764	862	737	763	787	. . .
Other services, debit	3 200	BA	**–6,979**	**–9,820**	**–11,880**	**–12,204**	**–12,088**	**–12,319**	**–15,412**	**–13,656**
Communications	3 245	. .	–445	–642	–706	–865	–1,133	–677	–623	. . .
Construction	3 249	. .	. . .	. . .	. . .	. . .	–6	–5	–16	. . .
Insurance	3 253	. .	–179	–255	–203	–162	–143	114	–146	. . .
Financial	3 260	. .	–89	–130	–103	–74	–109	–186	–191	. . .
Computer and information	3 262	. .	–73	–93	–76	–66	–90	–69	–92	. . .
Royalties and licence fees	3 266	. .	–1,720	–2,385	–2,431	–2,414	–2,369	–2,661	–3,221	. . .
Other business services	3 268	. .	–4,058	–5,807	–7,806	–8,022	–7,716	–8,275	–10,539	. . .
Personal, cultural, and recreational	3 287	. .	–57	–98	–121	–137	–92	–153	–160	. . .
Government, n.i.e.	3 291	. .	–358	–412	–434	–465	–429	–407	–425	. . .

Table 2 (Continued). STANDARD PRESENTATION, 1994–2001
(Millions of U.S. dollars)

	Code		1994	1995	1996	1997	1998	1999	2000	2001
C. INCOME	4 300	. .	–487	–1,302	–1,816	–2,455	–5,638	–5,159	–2,421	–886
Total credit	2 300	. .	*2,836*	*3,486*	*3,666*	*3,878*	*2,675*	*3,245*	*6,375*	*7,040*
Total debit	3 300	. .	*–3,322*	*–4,787*	*–5,482*	*–6,333*	*–8,313*	*–8,404*	*–8,797*	*–7,926*
Compensation of employees, credit	2 310	. .	**785**	**774**	**745**	**706**	**446**	**527**	**582**	**535**
Compensation of employees, debit	3 310	. .	**–96**	**–132**	**–180**	**–6**	**–42**	**–42**	**–51**	**–53**
Investment income, credit	2 320	. .	**2,051**	**2,712**	**2,922**	**3,172**	**2,229**	**2,718**	**5,794**	**6,505**
Direct investment income	2 330	. .	562	541	374	378	–966	–790	449	581
Dividends and distributed branch profits	2 332	. .	562	506	331	378	126	91	648	740
Reinvested earnings and undistributed branch profits	2 333	. .	. . .	35	43	. . .	–1,111	–931	–248	–167
Income on debt (interest)	2 334	. .	. . .	. . .	. . .	. . .	20	51	49	8
Portfolio investment income	2 339	. .	758	1,021	1,309	1,365	897	2,240	3,446	4,188
Income on equity	2 340	. .	. . .	. . .	. . .	. . .	. . .	. . .	. . .	. . .
Income on bonds and notes	2 350	. .	. . .	. . .	. . .	. . .	. . .	. . .	. . .	. . .
Income on money market instruments	2 360	. .	. . .	. . .	. . .	. . .	. . .	. . .	. . .	. . .
Other investment income	2 370	. .	730	1,151	1,238	1,429	2,298	1,267	1,899	1,736
Investment income, debit	3 320	. .	**–3,226**	**–4,655**	**–5,302**	**–6,327**	**–8,271**	**–8,361**	**–8,746**	**–7,873**
Direct investment income	3 330	. .	–245	–383	–356	–405	–397	–823	–1,194	–1,244
Dividends and distributed branch profits	3 332	. .	–217	–374	–335	–399	–385	–783	–1,157	. . .
Reinvested earnings and undistributed branch profits	3 333	. .	–28	–9	–21	–6	–7	. . .	. . .	. . .
Income on debt (interest)	3 334	. .	. . .	. . .	. . .	. . .	–5	–40	–37	. . .
Portfolio investment income	3 339	. .	–780	–998	–1,504	–1,460	–2,275	–3,133	–3,126	–2,909
Income on equity	3 340	. .	. . .	. . .	. . .	. . .	. . .	. . .	. . .	. . .
Income on bonds and notes	3 350	. .	. . .	. . .	. . .	. . .	. . .	. . .	. . .	. . .
Income on money market instruments	3 360	. .	. . .	. . .	. . .	. . .	. . .	. . .	. . .	. . .
Other investment income	3 370	. .	–2,201	–3,274	–3,442	–4,461	–5,599	–4,405	–4,427	–3,721
D. CURRENT TRANSFERS	4 379	. .	1,280	218	–46	667	3,352	1,916	680	–363
Credit	2 379	. .	**3,672**	**4,104**	**4,279**	**5,288**	**6,737**	**6,421**	**6,500**	**6,548**
General government	2 380	. .	89	90	32	47	43	64	47	253
Other sectors	2 390	. .	3,583	4,014	4,247	5,241	6,694	6,357	6,453	6,295
Workers' remittances	2 391	. .	245	291	183	129	90	54	63	49
Other current transfers	2 392	. .	3,338	3,723	4,065	5,112	6,604	6,303	6,390	6,246
Debit	3 379	. .	**–2,392**	**–3,886**	**–4,325**	**–4,621**	**–3,384**	**–4,506**	**–5,820**	**–6,911**
General government	3 380	. .	–318	–348	–402	–421	–446	–376	–446	–496
Other sectors	3 390	. .	–2,074	–3,538	–3,923	–4,200	–2,939	–4,130	–5,374	–6,415
Workers' remittances	3 391	. .	. . .	. . .	. . .	–235	–169	–184	–227	–215
Other current transfers	3 392	. .	–2,074	–3,538	–3,923	–3,965	–2,769	–3,945	–5,147	–6,200
CAPITAL AND FINANCIAL ACCOUNT	4 996	. .	**5,683**	**9,746**	**21,911**	**13,177**	**–34,140**	**–20,941**	**–11,680**	**–11,315**
CAPITAL ACCOUNT	4 994	. .	**–437**	**–488**	**–598**	**–608**	**171**	**–389**	**–615**	**–443**
Total credit	2 994	. .	*8*	*15*	*19*	*17*	*464*	*95*	*98*	*29*
Total debit	3 994	. .	*–445*	*–502*	*–617*	*–624*	*–293*	*–484*	*–713*	*–471*
Capital transfers, credit	2 400	. .	**8**	**15**	**19**	**17**	**6**	**85**	**90**	**27**
General government	2 401	. .	. . .	. . .	. . .	. . .	. . .	. . .	. . .	. . .
Debt forgiveness	2 402	. .	. . .	. . .	. . .	. . .	. . .	. . .	. . .	. . .
Other capital transfers	2 410	. .	. . .	. . .	. . .	. . .	. . .	. . .	. . .	. . .
Other sectors	2 430	. .	8	15	19	17	6	85	90	27
Migrants' transfers	2 431	. .	8	15	19	17	6	85	90	27
Debt forgiveness	2 432	. .	. . .	. . .	. . .	. . .	. . .	. . .	. . .	. . .
Other capital transfers	2 440	. .	. . .	. . .	. . .	. . .	. . .	. . .	. . .	. . .
Capital transfers, debit	3 400	. .	**–445**	**–502**	**–617**	**–624**	**–275**	**–459**	**–694**	**–434**
General government	3 401	. .	. . .	. . .	. . .	. . .	. . .	. . .	. . .	. . .
Debt forgiveness	3 402	. .	. . .	. . .	. . .	. . .	. . .	. . .	. . .	. . .
Other capital transfers	3 410	. .	. . .	. . .	. . .	. . .	. . .	. . .	. . .	. . .
Other sectors	3 430	. .	–445	–502	–617	–624	–275	–459	–694	–434
Migrants' transfers	3 431	. .	–445	–502	–617	–624	–275	–459	–694	–434
Debt forgiveness	3 432	. .	. . .	. . .	. . .	. . .	. . .	. . .	. . .	. . .
Other capital transfers	3 440	. .	. . .	. . .	. . .	. . .	. . .	. . .	. . .	. . .
Nonproduced nonfinancial assets, credit	2 480	. .	**. . .**	**. . .**	**. . .**	**. . .**	**458**	**10**	**8**	**2**
Nonproduced nonfinancial assets, debit	3 480	. .	**. . .**	**. . .**	**. . .**	**. . .**	**–18**	**–25**	**–19**	**–38**

Table 2 (Continued). STANDARD PRESENTATION, 1994–2001
(Millions of U.S. dollars)

	Code	1994	1995	1996	1997	1998	1999	2000	2001
FINANCIAL ACCOUNT	4 995 . .	**6,119**	**10,234**	**22,509**	**13,784**	**-34,311**	**-20,551**	**-11,065**	**-10,873**
A. DIRECT INVESTMENT	4 500 . .	-1,651	-1,776	-2,345	-1,605	673	5,136	4,285	598
Direct investment abroad	4 505 . .	**-2,461**	**-3,552**	**-4,671**	**-4,449**	**-4,740**	**-4,198**	**-4,999**	**-2,600**
Equity capital	4 510 . .	-2,322	-3,262	-4,373	-4,258	-3,823	-4,004	-4,617	-2,012
Claims on affiliated enterprises	4 515 . .	-2,322	-3,262	-4,373	-4,258	-3,823	-4,004	-4,617	-2,012
Liabilities to affiliated enterprises	4 520 . .	...	...	...	...	...	...	...	...
Reinvested earnings	4 525 . .	...	-35	-43	...	1,111	931	248	167
Other capital	4 530 . .	-139	-255	-255	-191	-2,028	-1,125	-630	-755
Claims on affiliated enterprises	4 535 . .	-139	-255	-255	-191	-2,028	-1,125	-630	-755
Liabilities to affiliated enterprises	4 540 . .	...	...	...	...	...	...	...	...
Direct investment in Korea	4 555 . .	**810**	**1,776**	**2,326**	**2,844**	**5,412**	**9,333**	**9,283**	**3,198**
Equity capital	4 560 . .	782	1,767	2,305	2,778	4,889	8,889	8,282	2,979
Claims on direct investors	4 565 . .	...	...	...	...	...	...	...	...
Liabilities to direct investors	4 570 . .	782	1,767	2,305	2,778	4,889	8,889	8,282	2,979
Reinvested earnings	4 575 . .	28	9	21	6	7	...	...	...
Other capital	4 580 . .	...	...	...	61	517	444	1,001	219
Claims on direct investors	4 585 . .	...	...	...	...	...	...	...	...
Liabilities to direct investors	4 590 . .	...	...	...	61	517	444	1,001	219
B. PORTFOLIO INVESTMENT	4 600 . .	6,232	11,712	15,102	14,384	-1,224	9,190	12,177	6,357
Assets	4 602 . .	**-2,481**	**-2,907**	**-6,413**	**1,076**	**-1,999**	**1,282**	**-520**	**-5,499**
Equity securities	4 610 . .	-382	-238	-653	-320	42	-271	-480	-273
Monetary authorities	4 611 . .	...	...	...	...	...	...	...	...
General government	4 612 . .	...	...	...	...	...	...	...	...
Banks	4 613 . .	-87	-71	-32	89	-30	68	16	14
Other sectors	4 614 . .	-295	-168	-621	-409	71	-338	-496	-287
Debt securities	4 619 . .	-2,098	-2,669	-5,760	1,395	-2,041	1,553	-40	-5,226
Bonds and notes	4 620 . .	-1,902	-2,356	-4,558	745	-1,864	911	5	-4,016
Monetary authorities	4 621 . .	...	...	...	...	...	...	...	...
General government	4 622 . .	-892	-1,169	-1,305	...	...	...	...	...
Banks	4 623 . .	-1,010	-1,187	-3,252	717	-519	1,602	144	-560
Other sectors	4 624 . .	...	...	...	28	-1,346	-692	-140	-3,455
Money market instruments	4 630 . .	-197	-314	-1,202	651	-176	642	-45	-1,211
Monetary authorities	4 631 . .	...	...	...	...	...	...	...	...
General government	4 632 . .	...	...	...	...	...	...	...	...
Banks	4 633 . .	-136	-195	-203	186	-108	199	37	-1,147
Other sectors	4 634 . .	-61	-118	-999	465	-68	443	-82	-64
Liabilities	4 652 . .	**8,713**	**14,619**	**21,514**	**13,308**	**775**	**7,908**	**12,697**	**11,856**
Equity securities	4 660 . .	3,614	4,219	5,954	2,525	3,856	12,072	13,094	10,165
Banks	4 663 . .	...	...	...	...	...	...	...	...
Other sectors	4 664 . .	...	...	...	...	...	...	...	...
Debt securities	4 669 . .	5,099	10,400	15,561	10,783	-3,081	-4,164	-397	1,691
Bonds and notes	4 670 . .	5,099	10,402	15,543	10,801	-2,855	-3,612	-1,649	2,186
Monetary authorities	4 671 . .	...	...	...	...	4,000	...	...	...
General government	4 672 . .	300	-199	113	744	-312	-20	...	...
Banks	4 673 . .	617	3,021	6,043	676	-2,181	-3,072	199	-1,740
Other sectors	4 674 . .	4,182	7,580	9,387	9,380	-4,361	-520	-1,848	3,926
Money market instruments	4 680 . .	...	-2	18	-18	-227	-552	1,252	-495
Monetary authorities	4 681 . .	...	...	...	...	...	...	...	...
General government	4 682 . .	...	...	...	...	...	...	...	...
Banks	4 683 . .	...	-2	18	-18	-300	-228	1,200	-363
Other sectors	4 684 . .	...	...	...	...	73	-324	52	-132
C. FINANCIAL DERIVATIVES	4 910 . .	-112	-121	83	-89	-654	-514	-179	-106
Monetary authorities	4 911 . .	...	...	...	...	...	...	...	...
General government	4 912 . .	...	...	...	...	...	...	...	...
Banks	4 913 . .	-112	-96	58	-107	-529	-483	-180	-80
Other sectors	4 914 . .	...	-25	25	18	-125	-31	...	-27
Assets	4 900 . .	**452**	**623**	**414**	**932**	**412**	**401**	**532**	**272**
Monetary authorities	4 901 . .	...	...	...	...	...	...	...	...
General government	4 902 . .	...	...	...	...	...	...	...	...
Banks	4 903 . .	452	622	425	921	410	435	532	301
Other sectors	4 904 . .	...	1	-11	11	3	-34	...	-29
Liabilities	4 905 . .	**-565**	**-744**	**-331**	**-1,021**	**-1,066**	**-915**	**-711**	**-378**
Monetary authorities	4 906 . .	...	...	...	...	...	...	...	...
General government	4 907 . .	...	...	...	...	...	...	...	...
Banks	4 908 . .	-565	-718	-367	-1,028	-939	-918	-711	-380
Other sectors	4 909 . .	...	-27	36	8	-128	4	...	2

Table 2 (Concluded). STANDARD PRESENTATION, 1994–2001
(Millions of U.S. dollars)

	Code	1994	1995	1996	1997	1998	1999	2000	2001
D. OTHER INVESTMENT	4 700 . .	6,264	7,459	11,085	–10,781	–2,137	–11,374	–3,557	–9,997
Assets	4 703 . .	**–7,369**	**–13,991**	**–13,487**	**–13,568**	**6,693**	**–2,606**	**–2,289**	**7,458**
Trade credits	4 706 . .	–130	–1,011	–822	–3,306	915	–1,759	–634	–845
General government	4 707 . .	. . .	. . .	. . .	. . .	. . .	. . .	. . .	. . .
of which: Short-term	4 709 . .	. . .	. . .	. . .	. . .	. . .	. . .	. . .	. . .
Other sectors	4 710 . .	–130	–1,011	–822	–3,306	915	–1,759	–634	–845
of which: Short-term	4 712 . .	*–79*	*–168*	*–150*	*–2,023*	*–438*	*–602*	*–885*	*–506*
Loans	4 714 . .	–2,048	–4,954	–5,556	–11,866	3,604	4,834	–2,239	4,340
Monetary authorities	4 715 . .	–45	–13	5	–5	. . .	8	10	5
of which: Short-term	4 718 . .	. . .	. . .	. . .	. . .	. . .	. . .	. . .	. . .
General government	4 719 . .	–38	–44	–79	–69	–81	–103	–81	–117
of which: Short-term	4 721 . .	. . .	. . .	. . .	. . .	. . .	. . .	. . .	. . .
Banks	4 722 . .	–1,070	–3,172	–3,384	–11,127	3,659	3,295	–1,865	3,995
of which: Short-term	4 724 . .	*–1,056*	*–3,107*	*–3,339*	*–11,174*	*7,833*	*2,682*	*–2,422*	*3,564*
Other sectors	4 725 . .	–895	–1,725	–2,099	–666	26	1,633	–303	456
of which: Short-term	4 727 . .	*–857*	*–1,553*	*–1,922*	*–434*	*–701*	*582*	*–1,303*	*1,061*
Currency and deposits	4 730 . .	–1,559	–2,656	–2,631	762	886	–2,270	1,390	1,501
Monetary authorities	4 731 . .	. . .	. . .	. . .	. . .	. . .	. . .	. . .	. . .
General government	4 732 . .	–258	–112	–464	–80	34	–65	–74	–369
Banks	4 733 . .	–440	–842	–811	–56	189	–1,580	–67	1,746
Other sectors	4 734 . .	–861	–1,702	–1,356	898	663	–624	1,530	124
Other assets	4 736 . .	–3,632	–5,371	–4,478	842	1,287	–3,410	–807	2,462
Monetary authorities	4 737 . .	–27	–24	–5	–82	–36	–172	–54	–61
of which: Short-term	4 739 . .	. . .	. . .	. . .	. . .	. . .	. . .	. . .	. . .
General government	4 740 . .	. . .	. . .	. . .	. . .	. . .	. . .	. . .	. . .
of which: Short-term	4 742 . .	. . .	. . .	. . .	. . .	. . .	. . .	. . .	. . .
Banks	4 743 . .	–3,551	–5,185	–3,979	2,846	3,122	–1,918	712	3,307
of which: Short-term	4 745 . .	. . .	. . .	. . .	. . .	. . .	. . .	. . .	. . .
Other sectors	4 746 . .	–54	–162	–494	–1,922	–1,798	–1,320	–1,465	–784
of which: Short-term	4 748 . .	. . .	. . .	. . .	. . .	. . .	. . .	. . .	. . .
Liabilities	4 753 . .	**13,632**	**21,450**	**24,571**	**2,787**	**–8,830**	**–8,768**	**–1,268**	**–17,456**
Trade credits	4 756 . .	2,858	4,141	4,547	–2,296	–7,096	4,591	4,282	–2,685
General government	4 757 . .	. . .	. . .	. . .	. . .	. . .	. . .	. . .	. . .
of which: Short-term	4 759 . .	. . .	. . .	. . .	. . .	. . .	. . .	. . .	. . .
Other sectors	4 760 . .	2,858	4,141	4,547	–2,296	–7,096	4,591	4,282	–2,685
of which: Short-term	4 762 . .	*3,188*	*4,332*	*4,024*	*–2,563*	*–7,133*	*4,488*	*4,323*	*–2,401*
Loans	4 764 . .	10,817	16,239	19,347	3,772	–1,483	–13,446	–4,858	–13,921
Monetary authorities	4 765 . .	. . .	. . .	. . .	11,104	5,038	–10,271	. . .	–5,692
of which: Use of Fund credit and loans from the Fund	4 766 . .	. . .	. . .	. . .	*11,104*	*5,038*	*–10,271*	. . .	*–5,692*
of which: Short-term	4 768 . .	. . .	. . .	. . .	. . .	. . .	. . .	. . .	. . .
General government	4 769 . .	–335	–593	–493	4,671	4,628	3,309	110	–400
of which: Short-term	4 771 . .	. . .	. . .	. . .	. . .	. . .	. . .	. . .	. . .
Banks	4 772 . .	7,561	10,552	9,684	–9,699	–6,569	1,438	–4,992	–4,228
of which: Short-term	4 774 . .	*5,378*	*8,517*	*7,192*	*–12,085*	*–12,250*	*5,528*	*–1,804*	*–3,354*
Other sectors	4 775 . .	3,591	6,281	10,156	–2,304	–4,580	–7,922	23	–3,601
of which: Short-term	4 777 . .	*2,268*	*3,921*	*7,358*	*–5,907*	*–8,365*	*–2,890*	*844*	*–575*
Currency and deposits	4 780 . .	–7	970	21	–596	678	–648	–869	–755
Monetary authorities	4 781 . .	. . .	. . .	. . .	. . .	. . .	. . .	. . .	. . .
General government	4 782 . .	. . .	. . .	. . .	. . .	. . .	. . .	. . .	. . .
Banks	4 783 . .	–136	800	–169	–398	507	40	324	–1,106
Other sectors	4 784 . .	129	169	190	–198	171	–689	–1,193	350
Other liabilities	4 786 . .	–36	100	656	1,907	–930	736	177	–95
Monetary authorities	4 787 . .	–2	–10	–29	23	25	148	28	63
of which: Short-term	4 789 . .	. . .	. . .	. . .	. . .	. . .	. . .	. . .	. . .
General government	4 790 . .	. . .	. . .	. . .	. . .	. . .	. . .	. . .	. . .
of which: Short-term	4 792 . .	. . .	. . .	. . .	. . .	. . .	. . .	. . .	. . .
Banks	4 793 . .	–57	37	436	313	–171	–60	130	19
of which: Short-term	4 795 . .	. . .	. . .	. . .	. . .	. . .	. . .	. . .	. . .
Other sectors	4 796 . .	23	73	250	1,571	–784	647	19	–176
of which: Short-term	4 798 . .	. . .	. . .	. . .	. . .	. . .	. . .	. . .	. . .
E. RESERVE ASSETS	4 802 . .	–4,614	–7,039	–1,416	11,875	–30,968	–22,989	–23,790	–7,724
Monetary gold	4 812 . .	. . .	–1	–2	–1	–1	–1	–1	–1
Special drawing rights	4 811 . .	–14	–20	–24	52	54	6	–7	. . .
Reserve position in the Fund	4 810 . .	–35	–116	–52	42	599	–288	. . .	. . .
Foreign exchange	4 803 . .	–4,564	–6,902	–1,338	11,782	–31,621	–22,707	–23,783	–7,723
Other claims	4 813 . .	. . .	. . .	. . .	. . .	. . .	. . .	. . .	. . .
NET ERRORS AND OMISSIONS	4 998 . .	**–1,816**	**–1,240**	**1,095**	**–5,010**	**–6,225**	**–3,536**	**–561**	**2,698**

Part 3 of the *Yearbook* contains descriptions of the methodologies, compilation practices, and sources used to compile these data.

Table 1. ANALYTIC PRESENTATION, 1994–2001

(Millions of U.S. dollars)

	Code	1994	1995	1996	1997	1998	1999	2000	2001
A. Current Account[1]	4 993 Z.	**3,227**	**5,016**	**7,107**	**7,934**	**2,215**	**5,062**	**14,670**	**8,562**
Goods: exports f.o.b.	2 100 ..	11,284	12,833	14,946	14,281	9,618	12,276	19,478	16,167
Goods: imports f.o.b.	3 100 ..	–6,616	–7,254	–7,949	–7,747	–7,715	–6,708	–6,451	–6,929
Balance on Goods	4 100 ..	*4,669*	*5,579*	*6,997*	*6,533*	*1,903*	*5,568*	*13,027*	*9,238*
Services: credit	2 200 ..	1,415	1,401	1,520	1,760	1,762	1,560	1,822	1,787
Services: debit	3 200 ..	–4,531	–5,381	–5,100	–5,129	–5,542	–5,171	–4,923	–5,338
Balance on Goods and Services	4 991 ..	*1,553*	*1,598*	*3,417*	*3,164*	*–1,877*	*1,958*	*9,926*	*5,686*
Income: credit	2 300 ..	4,174	6,125	6,409	7,744	7,163	6,094	7,315	5,481
Income: debit	3 300 ..	–1,004	–1,243	–1,229	–1,467	–1,296	–985	–616	–525
Balance on Goods, Services, and Income	4 992 ..	*4,723*	*6,480*	*8,597*	*9,441*	*3,990*	*7,066*	*16,626*	*10,643*
Current transfers: credit	2 379 Z.	94	54	53	79	98	99	85	52
Current transfers: debit	3 379 ..	–1,590	–1,518	–1,543	–1,586	–1,874	–2,102	–2,041	–2,133
B. Capital Account[1]	4 994 Z.	**–205**	**–194**	**–204**	**–96**	**79**	**703**	**2,217**	**2,931**
Capital account: credit	2 994 Z.	...	...	3	115	289	716	2,236	2,951
Capital account: debit	3 994 ..	–205	–194	–207	–211	–210	–13	–20	–20
Total, Groups A Plus B	4 981 ..	*3,022*	*4,822*	*6,904*	*7,839*	*2,293*	*5,765*	*16,886*	*11,494*
C. Financial Account[1]	4 995 W.	**3,304**	**157**	**–7,632**	**–6,211**	**–2,920**	**–5,706**	**–13,307**	**–6,036**
Direct investment abroad	4 505 ..	1,519	1,022	–1,740	969	1,867	–23	303	–323
Direct investment in Kuwait	4 555 Z.	...	7	347	20	59	72	16	–39
Portfolio investment assets	4 602 ..	394	–2,064	–788	–6,926	–4,768	–2,638	–12,923	–7,372
Equity securities	4 610 ..	...	...	...	...	...	...	...	...
Debt securities	4 619 ..	394	–2,064	–788	–6,926	–4,768	–2,638	–12,923	–7,372
Portfolio investment liabilities	4 652 Z.	...	–50	27	...	...	79	254	–78
Equity securities	4 660 ..	...	...	...	...	...	...	...	...
Debt securities	4 669 Z.	...	–50	27	...	...	79	254	–78
Financial derivatives	4 910 ..	...	...	...	...	...	...	...	...
Financial derivatives assets	4 900 ..	...	...	...	...	...	...	...	...
Financial derivatives liabilities	4 905 ..	...	...	...	...	...	...	...	...
Other investment assets	4 703 ..	529	–221	–745	3,356	646	–3,512	–1,108	430
Monetary authorities	4 701 ..	...	...	...	...	...	...	...	...
General government	4 704 ..	825	724	–1,122	2,993	–10	–3,288	–284	916
Banks	4 705 ..	–401	–734	–23	260	929	–161	–1,004	238
Other sectors	4 728 ..	104	–211	401	102	–272	–62	179	–724
Other investment liabilities	4 753 W.	862	1,464	–4,733	–3,629	–725	315	150	1,347
Monetary authorities	4 753 WA	–3	–54	–17	3	–10	...	7	...
General government	4 753 ZB	525	1,541	–5,371	–6,290	–1,316	–115	–372	7
Banks	4 753 ZC	589	–97	304	1,523	–456	302	–297	1,301
Other sectors	4 753 ZD	–249	74	351	1,134	1,057	128	812	39
Total, Groups A Through C	4 983 ..	*6,326*	*4,979*	*–728*	*1,628*	*–627*	*59*	*3,579*	*5,458*
D. Net Errors and Omissions	4 998 ..	**–6,276**	**–5,120**	**704**	**–1,622**	**885**	**859**	**–1,311**	**–2,553**
Total, Groups A Through D	4 984 ..	*50*	*–141*	*–25*	*6*	*258*	*918*	*2,268*	*2,905*
E. Reserves and Related Items	4 802 A.	**–50**	**141**	**25**	**–6**	**–258**	**–918**	**–2,268**	**–2,905**
Reserve assets	4 802 ..	–50	141	25	–6	–258	–918	–2,268	–2,905
Use of Fund credit and loans	4 766 ..	...	...	...	...	...	...	...	...
Exceptional financing	4 920 ..	...	...	...	...	...	...	...	...
Conversion rates: Kuwaiti dinar per U.S. dollar	0 101 ..	**.2969**	**.2984**	**.2994**	**.3033**	**.3048**	**.3044**	**.3068**	**.3067**

[1] Excludes components that have been classified in the categories of Group E.

Table 2. STANDARD PRESENTATION, 1994–2001
(Millions of U.S. dollars)

	Code	1994	1995	1996	1997	1998	1999	2000	2001
CURRENT ACCOUNT	4 993 . .	**3,227**	**5,016**	**7,107**	**7,934**	**2,215**	**5,062**	**14,670**	**8,562**
A. GOODS	4 100 . .	4,669	5,579	6,997	6,533	1,903	5,568	13,027	9,238
Credit	2 100 . .	**11,284**	**12,833**	**14,946**	**14,281**	**9,618**	**12,276**	**19,478**	**16,167**
General merchandise: exports f.o.b.	2 110 . .	11,284	12,833	14,946	14,281	9,618	12,276	19,478	16,167
Goods for processing: exports f.o.b.	2 150 . .	. . .	. . .	. . .	. . .	. . .	. . .	. . .	. . .
Repairs on goods	2 160 . .	. . .	. . .	. . .	. . .	. . .	. . .	. . .	. . .
Goods procured in ports by carriers	2 170 . .	. . .	. . .	. . .	. . .	. . .	. . .	. . .	. . .
Nonmonetary gold	2 180 . .	. . .	. . .	. . .	. . .	. . .	. . .	. . .	. . .
Debit	3 100 . .	**–6,616**	**–7,254**	**–7,949**	**–7,747**	**–7,715**	**–6,708**	**–6,451**	**–6,929**
General merchandise: imports f.o.b.	3 110 . .	–6,616	–7,254	–7,949	–7,747	–7,715	–6,708	–6,451	–6,929
Goods for processing: imports f.o.b.	3 150 . .	. . .	. . .	. . .	. . .	. . .	. . .	. . .	. . .
Repairs on goods	3 160 . .	. . .	. . .	. . .	. . .	. . .	. . .	. . .	. . .
Goods procured in ports by carriers	3 170 . .	. . .	. . .	. . .	. . .	. . .	. . .	. . .	. . .
Nonmonetary gold	3 180 . .	. . .	. . .	. . .	. . .	. . .	. . .	. . .	. . .
B. SERVICES	4 200 . .	–3,116	–3,981	–3,580	–3,369	–3,780	–3,610	–3,101	–3,551
Total credit	2 200 . .	*1,415*	*1,401*	*1,520*	*1,760*	*1,762*	*1,560*	*1,822*	*1,787*
Total debit	3 200 . .	*–4,531*	*–5,381*	*–5,100*	*–5,129*	*–5,542*	*–5,171*	*–4,923*	*–5,338*
Transportation services, credit	2 205 . .	**1,031**	**945**	**985**	**1,220**	**1,198**	**1,120**	**1,382**	**1,327**
Passenger	2 850 . .	*205*	*188*	*207*	*211*	*249*	*250*	*297*	*303*
Freight	2 851 . .	*805*	*727*	*751*	*992*	*932*	*854*	*1,066*	*1,004*
Other	2 852 . .	*20*	*30*	*27*	*16*	*16*	*16*	*20*	*20*
Sea transport, passenger	2 207 . .	. . .	. . .	. . .	. . .	. . .	. . .	. . .	. . .
Sea transport, freight	2 208 . .	805	727	751	992	932	854	1,066	1,004
Sea transport, other	2 209 . .	. . .	. . .	. . .	. . .	. . .	. . .	. . .	. . .
Air transport, passenger	2 211 . .	205	188	207	211	249	250	297	303
Air transport, freight	2 212 . .	. . .	. . .	. . .	. . .	. . .	. . .	. . .	. . .
Air transport, other	2 213 . .	. . .	. . .	. . .	. . .	. . .	. . .	. . .	. . .
Other transport, passenger	2 215 . .	. . .	. . .	. . .	. . .	. . .	. . .	. . .	. . .
Other transport, freight	2 216 . .	. . .	. . .	. . .	. . .	. . .	. . .	. . .	. . .
Other transport, other	2 217 . .	. . .	. . .	. . .	. . .	. . .	. . .	. . .	. . .
Transportation services, debit	3 205 . .	**–1,411**	**–1,504**	**–1,627**	**–1,572**	**–1,624**	**–1,498**	**–1,539**	**–1,556**
Passenger	3 850 . .	*–222*	*–265*	*–287*	*–307*	*–305*	*–302*	*–359*	*–365*
Freight	3 851 . .	*–1,058*	*–1,203*	*–1,279*	*–1,203*	*–1,250*	*–1,130*	*–1,131*	*–1,141*
Other	3 852 . .	*–131*	*–37*	*–60*	*–63*	*–69*	*–66*	*–49*	*–49*
Sea transport, passenger	3 207 . .	. . .	. . .	. . .	. . .	. . .	. . .	. . .	. . .
Sea transport, freight	3 208 . .	–1,058	–1,203	–1,279	–1,203	–1,250	–1,130	–1,131	–1,141
Sea transport, other	3 209 . .	. . .	. . .	. . .	. . .	. . .	. . .	. . .	. . .
Air transport, passenger	3 211 . .	–222	–265	–287	–307	–305	–302	–359	–365
Air transport, freight	3 212 . .	. . .	. . .	. . .	. . .	. . .	. . .	. . .	. . .
Air transport, other	3 213 . .	. . .	. . .	. . .	. . .	. . .	. . .	. . .	. . .
Other transport, passenger	3 215 . .	. . .	. . .	. . .	. . .	. . .	. . .	. . .	. . .
Other transport, freight	3 216 . .	. . .	. . .	. . .	. . .	. . .	. . .	. . .	. . .
Other transport, other	3 217 . .	. . .	. . .	. . .	. . .	. . .	. . .	. . .	. . .
Travel, credit	2 236 . .	**101**	**121**	**184**	**188**	**207**	**92**	**98**	**104**
Business travel	2 237 . .	101	121	184	188	207	92	98	104
Personal travel	2 240 . .	. . .	. . .	. . .	. . .	. . .	. . .	. . .	. . .
Travel, debit	3 236 . .	**–2,146**	**–2,248**	**–2,492**	**–2,377**	**–2,517**	**–2,270**	**–2,494**	**–2,843**
Business travel	3 237 . .	–2,146	–2,248	–2,492	–2,377	–2,517	–2,270	–2,494	–2,843
Personal travel	3 240 . .	. . .	. . .	. . .	. . .	. . .	. . .	. . .	. . .
Other services, credit	2 200 BA	**283**	**335**	**351**	**353**	**358**	**348**	**342**	**355**
Communications	2 245 . .	. . .	. . .	. . .	. . .	. . .	. . .	. . .	. . .
Construction	2 249 . .	. . .	. . .	. . .	. . .	. . .	. . .	. . .	. . .
Insurance	2 253 . .	57	64	70	69	72	66	72	72
Financial	2 260 . .	. . .	. . .	. . .	. . .	. . .	. . .	. . .	. . .
Computer and information	2 262 . .	. . .	. . .	. . .	. . .	. . .	. . .	. . .	. . .
Royalties and licence fees	2 266 . .	. . .	. . .	. . .	. . .	. . .	. . .	. . .	. . .
Other business services	2 268 . .	. . .	13	23	30	20	20	20	20
Personal, cultural, and recreational	2 287 . .	. . .	. . .	. . .	. . .	. . .	. . .	. . .	. . .
Government, n.i.e.	2 291 . .	226	258	257	254	266	263	251	264
Other services, debit	3 200 BA	**–973**	**–1,628**	**–982**	**–1,180**	**–1,401**	**–1,403**	**–890**	**–939**
Communications	3 245 . .	. . .	. . .	. . .	. . .	. . .	. . .	. . .	. . .
Construction	3 249 . .	. . .	. . .	. . .	. . .	. . .	. . .	. . .	. . .
Insurance	3 253 . .	–54	–64	–67	–66	–69	–62	–59	–65
Financial	3 260 . .	. . .	. . .	. . .	. . .	. . .	. . .	. . .	. . .
Computer and information	3 262 . .	. . .	. . .	. . .	. . .	. . .	. . .	. . .	. . .
Royalties and licence fees	3 266 . .	. . .	. . .	. . .	. . .	. . .	. . .	. . .	. . .
Other business services	3 268 . .	–30	–30	–30	–40	–33	–36	–26	–39
Personal, cultural, and recreational	3 287 . .	. . .	. . .	. . .	. . .	. . .	. . .	. . .	. . .
Government, n.i.e.	3 291 . .	–889	–1,535	–885	–1,075	–1,299	–1,304	–805	–835

Table 2 (Continued). STANDARD PRESENTATION, 1994–2001
(Millions of U.S. dollars)

	Code	1994	1995	1996	1997	1998	1999	2000	2001
C. INCOME	4 300	3,170	4,882	5,180	6,277	5,867	5,108	6,699	4,956
Total credit	2 300	*4,174*	*6,125*	*6,409*	*7,744*	*7,163*	*6,094*	*7,315*	*5,481*
Total debit	3 300	*-1,004*	*-1,243*	*-1,229*	*-1,467*	*-1,296*	*-985*	*-616*	*-525*
Compensation of employees, credit	2 310	**...**	**...**	**...**	**...**	**...**	**...**	**...**	**...**
Compensation of employees, debit	3 310	**...**	**...**	**...**	**...**	**...**	**...**	**...**	**...**
Investment income, credit	2 320	**4,174**	**6,125**	**6,409**	**7,744**	**7,163**	**6,094**	**7,315**	**5,481**
Direct investment income	2 330	...	...	...	...	...	...	...	...
Dividends and distributed branch profits	2 332	...	...	...	...	...	...	...	...
Reinvested earnings and undistributed branch profits	2 333	...	...	...	...	...	...	...	...
Income on debt (interest)	2 334	...	...	...	...	...	...	...	...
Portfolio investment income	2 339	...	...	...	...	...	...	...	...
Income on equity	2 340	...	...	...	...	...	...	...	...
Income on bonds and notes	2 350	...	...	...	...	...	...	...	...
Income on money market instruments	2 360	...	...	...	...	...	...	...	...
Other investment income	2 370	4,174	6,125	6,409	7,744	7,163	6,094	7,315	5,481
Investment income, debit	3 320	**-1,004**	**-1,243**	**-1,229**	**-1,467**	**-1,296**	**-985**	**-616**	**-525**
Direct investment income	3 330	...	...	...	...	...	...	...	...
Dividends and distributed branch profits	3 332	...	...	...	...	...	...	...	...
Reinvested earnings and undistributed branch profits	3 333	...	...	...	...	...	...	...	...
Income on debt (interest)	3 334	...	...	...	...	...	...	...	...
Portfolio investment income	3 339	...	...	...	...	...	...	...	...
Income on equity	3 340	...	...	...	...	...	...	...	...
Income on bonds and notes	3 350	...	...	...	...	...	...	...	...
Income on money market instruments	3 360	...	...	...	...	...	...	...	...
Other investment income	3 370	-1,004	-1,243	-1,229	-1,467	-1,296	-985	-616	-525
D. CURRENT TRANSFERS	4 379	-1,496	-1,464	-1,490	-1,507	-1,775	-2,004	-1,956	-2,080
Credit	2 379	**94**	**54**	**53**	**79**	**98**	**99**	**85**	**52**
General government	2 380	94	54	53	79	98	99	85	52
Other sectors	2 390	...	...	...	...	...	...	...	...
Workers' remittances	2 391	...	...	...	...	...	...	...	...
Other current transfers	2 392	...	...	...	...	...	...	...	...
Debit	3 379	**-1,590**	**-1,518**	**-1,543**	**-1,586**	**-1,874**	**-2,102**	**-2,041**	**-2,133**
General government	3 380	-239	-144	-137	-178	-217	-171	-225	-261
Other sectors	3 390	-1,351	-1,374	-1,406	-1,408	-1,657	-1,932	-1,816	-1,872
Workers' remittances	3 391	-1,331	-1,354	-1,376	-1,375	-1,611	-1,731	-1,734	-1,784
Other current transfers	3 392	-20	-20	-30	-33	-46	-200	-81	-88
CAPITAL AND FINANCIAL ACCOUNT	4 996	**3,049**	**104**	**-7,811**	**-6,312**	**-3,100**	**-5,921**	**-13,359**	**-6,009**
CAPITAL ACCOUNT	4 994	**-205**	**-194**	**-204**	**-96**	**79**	**703**	**2,217**	**2,931**
Total credit	2 994	*...*	*...*	*3*	*115*	*289*	*716*	*2,236*	*2,951*
Total debit	3 994	*-205*	*-194*	*-207*	*-211*	*-210*	*-13*	*-20*	*-20*
Capital transfers, credit	2 400	**...**	**...**	**3**	**115**	**289**	**716**	**2,236**	**2,951**
General government	2 401	...	...	...	...	...	...	...	...
Debt forgiveness	2 402	...	...	...	...	...	...	...	...
Other capital transfers	2 410	...	...	...	...	...	...	...	...
Other sectors	2 430	...	...	3	115	289	716	2,236	2,951
Migrants' transfers	2 431	...	...	...	...	...	...	...	...
Debt forgiveness	2 432	...	...	...	...	...	...	...	...
Other capital transfers	2 440	...	...	3	115	289	716	2,236	2,951
Capital transfers, debit	3 400	**-205**	**-194**	**-207**	**-211**	**-210**	**-13**	**-20**	**-20**
General government	3 401	-205	-194	-207	-211	-210	-13	-20	-20
Debt forgiveness	3 402	...	...	...	...	...	...	...	...
Other capital transfers	3 410	-205	-194	-207	-211	-210	-13	-20	-20
Other sectors	3 430	...	...	...	...	...	...	...	...
Migrants' transfers	3 431	...	...	...	...	...	...	...	...
Debt forgiveness	3 432	...	...	...	...	...	...	...	...
Other capital transfers	3 440	...	...	...	...	...	...	...	...
Nonproduced nonfinancial assets, credit	2 480	**...**	**...**	**...**	**...**	**...**	**...**	**...**	**...**
Nonproduced nonfinancial assets, debit	3 480	**...**	**...**	**...**	**...**	**...**	**...**	**...**	**...**

Table 2 (Continued). STANDARD PRESENTATION, 1994–2001
(Millions of U.S. dollars)

	Code		1994	1995	1996	1997	1998	1999	2000	2001
FINANCIAL ACCOUNT	4 995	. .	**3,254**	**299**	**–7,607**	**–6,217**	**–3,178**	**–6,624**	**–15,575**	**–8,940**
A. DIRECT INVESTMENT	4 500	. .	1,519	1,029	–1,393	989	1,926	49	319	–362
Direct investment abroad	4 505	. .	**1,519**	**1,022**	**–1,740**	**969**	**1,867**	**–23**	**303**	**–323**
Equity capital	4 510	. .	1,519	1,022	–1,740	969	1,867	–23	303	–323
Claims on affiliated enterprises	4 515	. .	. . .	. . .	–1,763	–7	. . .	–36	. . .	–323
Liabilities to affiliated enterprises	4 520	. .	1,519	1,022	23	976	1,867	13	303	. . .
Reinvested earnings	4 525	. .	. . .	. . .	. . .	. . .	. . .	. . .	. . .	. . .
Other capital	4 530	. .	. . .	. . .	. . .	. . .	. . .	. . .	. . .	. . .
Claims on affiliated enterprises	4 535	. .	. . .	. . .	. . .	. . .	. . .	. . .	. . .	. . .
Liabilities to affiliated enterprises	4 540	. .	. . .	. . .	. . .	. . .	. . .	. . .	. . .	. . .
Direct investment in Kuwait	4 555	. .	**. . .**	**7**	**347**	**20**	**59**	**72**	**16**	**–39**
Equity capital	4 560	. .	. . .	7	347	20	59	72	16	–39
Claims on direct investors	4 565	. .	. . .	7	347	20	59	72	16	–39
Liabilities to direct investors	4 570	. .	. . .	. . .	. . .	. . .	. . .	. . .	. . .	. . .
Reinvested earnings	4 575	. .	. . .	. . .	. . .	. . .	. . .	. . .	. . .	. . .
Other capital	4 580	. .	. . .	. . .	. . .	. . .	. . .	. . .	. . .	. . .
Claims on direct investors	4 585	. .	. . .	. . .	. . .	. . .	. . .	. . .	. . .	. . .
Liabilities to direct investors	4 590	. .	. . .	. . .	. . .	. . .	. . .	. . .	. . .	. . .
B. PORTFOLIO INVESTMENT	4 600	. .	394	–2,114	–762	–6,926	–4,768	–2,559	–12,668	–7,451
Assets	4 602	. .	**394**	**–2,064**	**–788**	**–6,926**	**–4,768**	**–2,638**	**–12,923**	**–7,372**
Equity securities	4 610	. .	. . .	. . .	. . .	. . .	. . .	. . .	. . .	. . .
Monetary authorities	4 611	. .	. . .	. . .	. . .	. . .	. . .	. . .	. . .	. . .
General government	4 612	. .	. . .	. . .	. . .	. . .	. . .	. . .	. . .	. . .
Banks	4 613	. .	. . .	. . .	. . .	. . .	. . .	. . .	. . .	. . .
Other sectors	4 614	. .	. . .	. . .	. . .	. . .	. . .	. . .	. . .	. . .
Debt securities	4 619	. .	394	–2,064	–788	–6,926	–4,768	–2,638	–12,923	–7,372
Bonds and notes	4 620	. .	394	–2,064	–788	–6,926	–4,768	–2,638	–12,923	–7,372
Monetary authorities	4 621	. .	. . .	. . .	. . .	. . .	. . .	. . .	. . .	. . .
General government	4 622	. .	573	–2,426	–324	–5,835	–4,046	–2,299	–12,006	–7,878
Banks	4 623	. .	–115	50	–100	–92	154	168	411	–434
Other sectors	4 624	. .	–64	312	–364	–999	–876	–506	–1,327	939
Money market instruments	4 630	. .	. . .	. . .	. . .	. . .	. . .	. . .	. . .	. . .
Monetary authorities	4 631	. .	. . .	. . .	. . .	. . .	. . .	. . .	. . .	. . .
General government	4 632	. .	. . .	. . .	. . .	. . .	. . .	. . .	. . .	. . .
Banks	4 633	. .	. . .	. . .	. . .	. . .	. . .	. . .	. . .	. . .
Other sectors	4 634	. .	. . .	. . .	. . .	. . .	. . .	. . .	. . .	. . .
Liabilities	4 652	. .	**. . .**	**–50**	**27**	**. . .**	**. . .**	**79**	**254**	**–78**
Equity securities	4 660	. .	. . .	. . .	. . .	. . .	. . .	. . .	. . .	. . .
Banks	4 663	. .	. . .	. . .	. . .	. . .	. . .	. . .	. . .	. . .
Other sectors	4 664	. .	. . .	. . .	. . .	. . .	. . .	. . .	. . .	. . .
Debt securities	4 669	. .	. . .	–50	27	. . .	. . .	79	254	–78
Bonds and notes	4 670	. .	. . .	–50	27	. . .	. . .	79	254	–78
Monetary authorities	4 671	. .	. . .	. . .	. . .	. . .	. . .	. . .	. . .	. . .
General government	4 672	. .	. . .	. . .	. . .	. . .	. . .	. . .	. . .	. . .
Banks	4 673	. .	. . .	–50	. . .	. . .	. . .	. . .	. . .	. . .
Other sectors	4 674	. .	. . .	. . .	27	. . .	. . .	79	254	–78
Money market instruments	4 680	. .	. . .	. . .	. . .	. . .	. . .	. . .	. . .	. . .
Monetary authorities	4 681	. .	. . .	. . .	. . .	. . .	. . .	. . .	. . .	. . .
General government	4 682	. .	. . .	. . .	. . .	. . .	. . .	. . .	. . .	. . .
Banks	4 683	. .	. . .	. . .	. . .	. . .	. . .	. . .	. . .	. . .
Other sectors	4 684	. .	. . .	. . .	. . .	. . .	. . .	. . .	. . .	. . .
C. FINANCIAL DERIVATIVES	4 910	. .	. . .	. . .	. . .	. . .	. . .	. . .	. . .	. . .
Monetary authorities	4 911	. .	. . .	. . .	. . .	. . .	. . .	. . .	. . .	. . .
General government	4 912	. .	. . .	. . .	. . .	. . .	. . .	. . .	. . .	. . .
Banks	4 913	. .	. . .	. . .	. . .	. . .	. . .	. . .	. . .	. . .
Other sectors	4 914	. .	. . .	. . .	. . .	. . .	. . .	. . .	. . .	. . .
Assets	4 900	. .	**. . .**	**. . .**	**. . .**	**. . .**	**. . .**	**. . .**	**. . .**	**. . .**
Monetary authorities	4 901	. .	. . .	. . .	. . .	. . .	. . .	. . .	. . .	. . .
General government	4 902	. .	. . .	. . .	. . .	. . .	. . .	. . .	. . .	. . .
Banks	4 903	. .	. . .	. . .	. . .	. . .	. . .	. . .	. . .	. . .
Other sectors	4 904	. .	. . .	. . .	. . .	. . .	. . .	. . .	. . .	. . .
Liabilities	4 905	. .	**. . .**	**. . .**	**. . .**	**. . .**	**. . .**	**. . .**	**. . .**	**. . .**
Monetary authorities	4 906	. .	. . .	. . .	. . .	. . .	. . .	. . .	. . .	. . .
General government	4 907	. .	. . .	. . .	. . .	. . .	. . .	. . .	. . .	. . .
Banks	4 908	. .	. . .	. . .	. . .	. . .	. . .	. . .	. . .	. . .
Other sectors	4 909	. .	. . .	. . .	. . .	. . .	. . .	. . .	. . .	. . .

Table 2 (Concluded). STANDARD PRESENTATION, 1994–2001
(Millions of U.S. dollars)

	Code	1994	1995	1996	1997	1998	1999	2000	2001
D. OTHER INVESTMENT	4 700	1,391	1,243	–5,477	–274	–79	–3,196	–958	1,777
Assets	4 703	**529**	**–221**	**–745**	**3,356**	**646**	**–3,512**	**–1,108**	**430**
Trade credits	4 706	–199	–1,260	–287	287	538	–736	–130	470
General government	4 707	–199	–1,260	–287	287	538	–736	–130	470
of which: Short-term	4 709	*–199*	*–1,260*	*–287*	*287*	*538*	*–736*	*–130*	*470*
Other sectors	4 710	...	...	...	...	...	...	...	...
of which: Short-term	4 712	...	...	...	...	...	...	...	...
Loans	4 714	–98	–596	271	–386	–289	–463	–313	176
Monetary authorities	4 715	...	...	...	...	...	...	...	...
of which: Short-term	4 718	...	...	...	...	...	...	...	...
General government	4 719	57	–472	150	–392	–39	–493	–535	–476
of which: Short-term	4 721	...	...	...	...	...	...	...	...
Banks	4 722	–185	–188	167	–23	33	89	114	551
of which: Short-term	4 724	*–185*	*–188*	*167*	*–23*	*33*	*89*	*114*	*551*
Other sectors	4 725	30	64	–47	30	–282	–59	108	101
of which: Short-term	4 727	...	...	...	...	...	...	...	...
Currency and deposits	4 730	296	1,223	2,772	–1,559	715	–2,152	–711	496
Monetary authorities	4 731	...	...	...	...	...	...	...	...
General government	4 732	431	2,151	2,525	–1,938	–236	–1,945	329	1,050
Banks	4 733	–202	–560	–217	287	902	–309	–1,115	–297
Other sectors	4 734	67	–369	464	92	49	102	75	–258
Other assets	4 736	529	412	–3,500	5,014	–318	–161	46	–711
Monetary authorities	4 737	...	...	...	...	...	...	...	...
of which: Short-term	4 739	...	...	...	...	...	...	...	...
General government	4 740	536	305	–3,510	5,037	–272	–115	52	–127
of which: Short-term	4 742	...	...	...	...	...	...	...	...
Banks	4 743	–13	13	27	–3	–7	59	–3	–16
of which: Short-term	4 745	...	...	...	...	...	...	...	...
Other sectors	4 746	7	94	–17	–20	–39	–105	–3	–567
of which: Short-term	4 748	...	...	...	...	...	...	...	...
Liabilities	4 753	**862**	**1,464**	**–4,733**	**–3,629**	**–725**	**315**	**150**	**1,347**
Trade credits	4 756	243	134	–57	–333	–187	–105	–143	...
General government	4 757	243	134	–57	–333	–187	–105	–143	...
of which: Short-term	4 759	*243*	*134*	*–57*	*–333*	*–187*	*–105*	*–143*	...
Other sectors	4 760	...	...	...	...	...	...	...	...
of which: Short-term	4 762	...	...	...	...	...	...	...	...
Loans	4 764	–286	657	–4,045	–4,592	–246	181	290	179
Monetary authorities	4 765	...	...	...	...	...	...	...	...
of which: Use of Fund credit and loans from the Fund	4 766	...	...	...	...	...	...	...	...
of which: Short-term	4 768	...	...	...	...	...	...	...	...
General government	4 769	–7	546	–4,295	–5,769	–1,125	–36	–385	7
of which: Short-term	4 771	...	...	...	...	...	...	...	...
Banks	4 772	...	...	...	...	...	...	...	...
of which: Short-term	4 774	...	...	...	...	...	...	...	...
Other sectors	4 775	–280	111	250	1,177	879	217	675	173
of which: Short-term	4 777	...	...	...	...	...	...	...	...
Currency and deposits	4 780	606	–23	311	1,523	–446	302	–329	1,295
Monetary authorities	4 781	...	...	...	...	...	...	...	...
General government	4 782	...	...	...	...	...	...	...	...
Banks	4 783	606	–23	311	1,523	–446	302	–329	1,295
Other sectors	4 784	...	...	...	...	...	...	...	...
Other liabilities	4 786	300	697	–942	–227	154	–62	333	–127
Monetary authorities	4 787	–3	–54	–17	3	–10	...	7	...
of which: Short-term	4 789	*–3*	*–54*	*–17*	*3*	*–10*	...	*7*	...
General government	4 790	290	861	–1,019	–188	–3	26	156	...
of which: Short-term	4 792	*290*	*861*	*–1,019*	*–188*	*–3*	*26*	*156*	...
Banks	4 793	–17	–74	–7	...	–10	...	33	7
of which: Short-term	4 795	*–17*	*–74*	*–7*	...	*–10*	...	*33*	*7*
Other sectors	4 796	30	–37	100	–43	177	–89	137	–134
of which: Short-term	4 798	*30*	*–37*	*100*	*–43*	*177*	*–89*	*137*	*–134*
E. RESERVE ASSETS	4 802	–50	141	25	–6	–258	–918	–2,268	–2,905
Monetary gold	4 812	...	...	...	...	...	...	...	...
Special drawing rights	4 811	–9	–9	–10	–8	–11	40	–21	–21
Reserve position in the Fund	4 810	36	6	4	–42	–107	–170	–8	–129
Foreign exchange	4 803	–78	145	31	44	–140	–788	–2,240	–2,755
Other claims	4 813	...	...	...	...	...	...	...	...
NET ERRORS AND OMISSIONS	4 998	**–6,276**	**–5,120**	**704**	**–1,622**	**885**	**859**	**–1,311**	**–2,553**

Part 3 of the *Yearbook* contains descriptions of the methodologies, compilation practices, and sources used to compile these data.

Table 1. ANALYTIC PRESENTATION, 1994–2001
(Millions of U.S. dollars)

	Code	1994	1995	1996	1997	1998	1999	2000	2001
A. Current Account [1]	4 993 Z.	**–84.0**	**–234.7**	**–424.8**	**–138.5**	**–412.5**	**–252.4**	**–125.8**	**–52.6**
Goods: exports f.o.b	2 100 . .	340.0	408.9	531.2	630.8	535.1	462.6	510.9	480.3
Goods: imports f.o.b	3 100 . .	–426.1	–531.0	–782.9	–646.1	–755.7	–551.1	–506.4	–441.2
Balance on Goods	4 100 . .	*–86.1*	*–122.0*	*–251.7*	*–15.3*	*–220.7*	*–88.5*	*4.6*	*39.1*
Services: credit	2 200 . .	32.7	39.2	31.5	45.0	62.8	65.0	61.8	80.5
Services: debit	3 200 . .	–71.1	–195.1	–249.0	–171.2	–175.7	–154.4	–148.8	–125.1
Balance on Goods and Services	4 991 . .	*–124.6*	*–278.0*	*–469.2*	*–141.4*	*–333.6*	*–177.9*	*–82.4*	*–5.5*
Income: credit	2 300 . .	. . .	3.7	4.4	6.8	12.6	10.9	17.0	11.9
Income: debit	3 300 . .	–22.0	–39.2	–43.9	–71.4	–91.7	–85.4	–100.9	–77.4
Balance on Goods, Services, and Income	4 992 . .	*–146.6*	*–313.4*	*–508.7*	*–206.1*	*–412.7*	*–252.4*	*–166.3*	*–71.0*
Current transfers: credit	2 379 Z.	63.4	80.4	85.9	69.8	2.2	1.2	43.0	21.6
Current transfers: debit	3 379 . .	–.8	–1.7	–1.9	–2.2	–2.0	–1.2	–2.4	–3.2
B. Capital Account [1]	4 994 Z.	**–62.4**	**–29.0**	**–15.9**	**–8.4**	**–8.1**	**–15.2**	**–11.3**	**–32.0**
Capital account: credit	2 994 Z.	.3	2.2	9.0	6.2	3.9	14.6	22.8	9.2
Capital account: debit	3 994 . .	–62.7	–31.3	–25.0	–14.6	–12.0	–29.8	–34.2	–41.2
Total, Groups A Plus B	4 981 . .	*–146.3*	*–263.8*	*–440.7*	*–146.9*	*–420.7*	*–267.5*	*–137.1*	*–84.6*
C. Financial Account [1]	4 995 W.	**103.4**	**259.9**	**362.5**	**250.7**	**284.6**	**220.8**	**56.9**	**31.4**
Direct investment abroad	4 505 . .	. . .	. . .	. . .	. . .	–22.6	–6.1	–4.5	–6.1
Direct investment in Kyrgyz Republic	4 555 Z.	38.2	96.1	47.2	83.8	109.2	44.4	–2.4	5.0
Portfolio investment assets	4 602 . .	. . .	–.1	.1	.6	–.2	. . .	–1.6	1.2
Equity securities	4 610 . .	. . .	. . .	. . .	. . .	. . .	. . .	. . .	. . .
Debt securities	4 619 . .	. . .	–.1	.1	.6	–.2	. . .	–1.6	1.2
Portfolio investment liabilities	4 652 Z.	. . .	1.8	–1.8	5.0	–4.1	.1	.3	. . .
Equity securities	4 660 . .	. . .	. . .	. . .	. . .	. . .	.2	.3	. . .
Debt securities	4 669 Z.	. . .	1.8	–1.8	5.0	–4.1	–.1	. . .	. . .
Financial derivatives	4 910 . .	. . .	. . .	. . .	19.0	30.6	26.4	25.8	17.6
Financial derivatives assets	4 900 . .	. . .	. . .	. . .	19.0	30.6	26.4	25.8	17.6
Financial derivatives liabilities	4 905 . .	. . .	. . .	. . .	. . .	. . .	. . .	. . .	. . .
Other investment assets	4 703 . .	–43.2	11.9	1.9	–43.1	–84.1	–.7	–27.3	–4.3
Monetary authorities	4 701 . .	. . .	–1.0	. . .	–3.0	–2.0	. . .	. . .	. . .
General government	4 704 . .	–1.7	–2.1	13.3	. . .	–57.4	–6.9	–31.9	–6.7
Banks	4 705 . .	1.3	–1.2	1.6	–18.7	9.6	–1.4	1.6	–16.5
Other sectors	4 728 . .	–42.9	16.2	–13.0	–21.5	–34.3	7.6	6.1	18.9
Other investment liabilities	4 753 W.	108.5	150.2	315.1	185.4	255.8	156.6	66.6	17.9
Monetary authorities	4 753 WA	–17.7	.2	.2	. . .	. . .	. . .	. . .	. . .
General government	4 753 ZB	110.9	102.0	104.7	137.5	177.1	224.5	96.8	86.5
Banks	4 753 ZC	3.6	–3.3	–2.1	14.0	1.0	–2.8	–.4	3.9
Other sectors	4 753 ZD	11.7	51.2	212.2	33.9	77.7	–65.0	–29.8	–72.4
Total, Groups A Through C	4 983 . .	*–43.0*	*–3.9*	*–78.2*	*103.8*	*–136.1*	*–46.7*	*–80.2*	*–53.3*
D. Net Errors and Omissions	4 998 . .	**48.0**	**–76.9**	**58.4**	**–57.7**	**63.4**	**–3.0**	**9.8**	**21.3**
Total, Groups A Through D	4 984 . .	*5.0*	*–80.7*	*–19.8*	*46.2*	*–72.7*	*–49.7*	*–70.4*	*–32.0*
E. Reserves and Related Items	4 802 A.	**–5.0**	**80.7**	**19.8**	**–46.2**	**72.7**	**49.7**	**70.4**	**32.0**
Reserve assets	4 802 . .	–31.9	.1	–18.6	–82.8	5.9	–61.3	–21.3	–17.7
Use of Fund credit and loans	4 766 . .	13.8	46.3	19.6	34.1	2.8	19.4	7.4	–2.1
Exceptional financing	4 920 . .	13.1	34.4	18.8	2.6	64.1	91.7	84.3	51.8
Conversion rates: soms per U.S. dollar	0 101 . .	**10.842**	**10.822**	**12.810**	**17.362**	**20.838**	**39.008**	**47.704**	**48.378**

[1] Excludes components that have been classified in the categories of Group E.

Table 2. STANDARD PRESENTATION, 1994–2001

(Millions of U.S. dollars)

	Code	1994	1995	1996	1997	1998	1999	2000	2001
CURRENT ACCOUNT	4 993 . .	**-84.0**	**-234.7**	**-424.8**	**-138.5**	**-364.0**	**-184.4**	**-79.0**	**-19.9**
A. GOODS	4 100 . .	-86.1	-122.0	-251.7	-15.3	-220.7	-88.5	4.6	39.1
Credit	2 100 . .	**340.0**	**408.9**	**531.2**	**630.8**	**535.1**	**462.6**	**510.9**	**480.3**
General merchandise: exports f.o.b.	2 110 . .	340.0	408.9	505.4	629.6	338.0	278.9	446.0	255.7
Goods for processing: exports f.o.b.	2 150 . .	...	...	...	...	...	...	...	...
Repairs on goods	2 160 . .	...	...	...	...	...	...	...	...
Goods procured in ports by carriers	2 170 . .	...	...	.5	1.2	1.3	.6	-86.9	...
Nonmonetary gold	2 180 . .	...	...	25.3	...	195.8	183.1	151.9	224.6
Debit	3 100 . .	**-426.1**	**-531.0**	**-782.9**	**-646.1**	**-755.7**	**-551.1**	**-506.4**	**-441.2**
General merchandise: imports f.o.b.	3 110 . .	-426.1	-528.5	-779.5	-639.4	-752.2	-549.5	-504.7	-440.3
Goods for processing: imports f.o.b.	3 150 . .	...	...	...	...	...	...	...	...
Repairs on goods	3 160 . .	...	...	...	...	...	...	...	...
Goods procured in ports by carriers	3 170 . .	...	-2.4	-3.4	-6.7	-3.5	-1.6	-1.6	-.9
Nonmonetary gold	3 180 . .	...	...	...	...	...	...	...	...
B. SERVICES	4 200 . .	-38.4	-156.0	-217.5	-126.2	-112.9	-89.4	-87.0	-44.6
Total credit	2 200 . .	*32.7*	*39.2*	*31.5*	*45.0*	*62.8*	*65.0*	*61.8*	*80.5*
Total debit	3 200 . .	*-71.1*	*-195.1*	*-249.0*	*-171.2*	*-175.7*	*-154.4*	*-148.8*	*-125.1*
Transportation services, credit	2 205 . .	**14.3**	**15.5**	**7.2**	**8.8**	**19.1**	**19.9**	**16.7**	**18.8**
Passenger	2 850 . .	...	...	...	...	...	...	*5.3*	*6.5*
Freight	2 851 . .	*14.3*	*15.5*	*6.7*	*7.6*	*16.7*	*17.4*	*5.5*	*4.1*
Other	2 852 . .	...	...	*.6*	*1.2*	*2.5*	*2.6*	*5.9*	*8.1*
Sea transport, passenger	2 207 . .	...	...	...	...	...	...	...	...
Sea transport, freight	2 208 . .	...	...	...	...	...	...	...	...
Sea transport, other	2 209 . .	...	...	...	...	...	...	...	...
Air transport, passenger	2 211 . .	...	...	...	...	...	...	1.6	3.1
Air transport, freight	2 212 . .	9.0	8.1	5.6	7.2	14.6	9.1	3.0	.9
Air transport, other	2 213 . .	...	...	...	...	...	...	3.1	5.3
Other transport, passenger	2 215 . .	...	...	...	...	...	...	3.7	3.5
Other transport, freight	2 216 . .	5.4	7.4	1.1	.5	2.0	8.3	2.5	3.2
Other transport, other	2 217 . .	...	...	.6	1.2	2.5	2.6	2.8	2.8
Transportation services, debit	3 205 . .	**-26.5**	**-52.4**	**-103.4**	**-91.2**	**-93.2**	**-77.7**	**-69.9**	**-50.2**
Passenger	3 850 . .	...	...	*-.7*	*-7.1*	*-5.0*	*-4.8*	*-8.6*	*-8.9*
Freight	3 851 . .	*-26.5*	*-50.5*	*-95.0*	*-71.8*	*-81.4*	*-57.8*	*-48.8*	*-38.7*
Other	3 852 . .	...	*-1.9*	*-7.6*	*-12.3*	*-6.9*	*-15.2*	*-12.6*	*-2.5*
Sea transport, passenger	3 207 . .	...	...	...	...	...	...	...	...
Sea transport, freight	3 208 . .	...	...	...	-1.3	...	...	...	...
Sea transport, other	3 209 . .	...	...	...	...	...	...	...	...
Air transport, passenger	3 211 . .	...	...	-.7	-7.1	-5.0	-4.8	-4.3	-5.7
Air transport, freight	3 212 . .	-.1	...	...	-1.1	-3.4	-3.2	-7.7	-7.7
Air transport, other	3 213 . .	...	...	...	-2.5	...	...	-3.7	...
Other transport, passenger	3 215 . .	...	...	...	...	...	...	-4.3	-3.2
Other transport, freight	3 216 . .	-26.4	-50.5	-95.0	-69.5	-78.0	-54.6	-41.0	-31.0
Other transport, other	3 217 . .	...	-1.9	-7.6	-9.8	-6.9	-15.2	-8.8	-2.5
Travel, credit	2 236 . .	**2.6**	**4.7**	**4.2**	**7.1**	**8.4**	**14.1**	**15.3**	**24.4**
Business travel	2 237 . .	2.6	4.7	4.2	7.1	3.8	6.4	4.0	13.1
Personal travel	2 240 . .	...	...	...	...	4.6	7.8	11.2	11.3
Travel, debit	3 236 . .	**-2.2**	**-6.5**	**-5.7**	**-3.7**	**-3.5**	**-10.7**	**-15.6**	**-11.9**
Business travel	3 237 . .	...	...	...	...	-1.7	-5.1	-8.5	-8.3
Personal travel	3 240 . .	-2.2	-6.5	-5.7	-3.7	-1.8	-5.6	-7.1	-3.6
Other services, credit	2 200 BA	**15.7**	**19.0**	**20.0**	**29.1**	**35.3**	**31.0**	**29.9**	**37.4**
Communications	2 245 . .	6.4	9.5	9.0	9.4	9.8	10.3	9.3	8.7
Construction	2 249 . .	3.6	1.6	1.2	4.9	6.7	3.9	3.1	4.4
Insurance	2 253 . .	.2	...	...	...	.9	.7	.5	.2
Financial	2 260 . .	...	...	...	.3	1.4	.3	1.0	1.7
Computer and information	2 262 . .	...	...	...	...	.1	.2	.5	.5
Royalties and licence fees	2 266 . .	...	...	...	...	.5	.6	.7	1.0
Other business services	2 268 . .	4.4	4.8	8.1	8.6	5.2	6.6	7.4	9.4
Personal, cultural, and recreational	2 287 . .	1.1	3.1	1.7	1.0	5.8	3.7	2.5	3.3
Government, n.i.e.	2 291 . .	...	...	...	4.9	4.8	4.6	4.9	8.2
Other services, debit	3 200 BA	**-42.4**	**-136.2**	**-139.9**	**-76.3**	**-79.0**	**-66.0**	**-63.3**	**-63.0**
Communications	3 245 . .	...	-8.4	-8.2	-8.5	-8.3	-8.2	-7.0	-7.9
Construction	3 249 . .	-2.8	-48.1	-50.7	-7.0	-9.7	-3.2	-6.0	-6.7
Insurance	3 253 . .	-2.9	-7.8	-10.7	-12.8	-11.6	-10.1	-8.0	-7.4
Financial	3 260 . .	...	-.5	-.1	-.2	-6.9	-5.3	-4.2	-3.6
Computer and information	3 262 . .	...	...	-.1	-.2	-2.4	-.7	-.9	-1.2
Royalties and licence fees	3 266 . .	...	...	...	...	-1.6	-.9	-.7	-1.8
Other business services	3 268 . .	-34.1	-69.7	-67.7	-44.6	-33.4	-32.0	-29.7	-28.9
Personal, cultural, and recreational	3 287 . .	...	...	-.2	-.4	-2.0	-2.8	-3.0	-2.2
Government, n.i.e.	3 291 . .	-2.4	-1.7	-2.3	-2.7	-3.1	-2.7	-3.9	-3.4

Table 2 (Continued). STANDARD PRESENTATION, 1994–2001

(Millions of U.S. dollars)

	Code	1994	1995	1996	1997	1998	1999	2000	2001
C. INCOME	4 300	–22.0	–35.4	–39.5	–64.7	–79.1	–74.4	–83.9	–65.5
Total credit	2 300	*. . .*	*3.7*	*4.4*	*6.8*	*12.6*	*10.9*	*17.0*	*11.9*
Total debit	3 300	*–22.0*	*–39.2*	*–43.9*	*–71.4*	*–91.7*	*–85.4*	*–100.9*	*–77.4*
Compensation of employees, credit	2 310	**. . .**	**. . .**	**. . .**	**. . .**	**. . .**	**. . .**	**. . .**	**. . .**
Compensation of employees, debit	3 310	**–3.5**	**–9.4**	**–7.2**	**–13.4**	**–14.7**	**–11.5**	**–10.3**	**–10.3**
Investment income, credit	2 320	**. . .**	**3.7**	**4.4**	**6.8**	**12.6**	**10.9**	**17.0**	**11.9**
Direct investment income	2 330	. . .	. . .	. . .	. . .	. . .	. . .	. . .	. . .
Dividends and distributed branch profits	2 332	. . .	. . .	. . .	. . .	. . .	. . .	. . .	. . .
Reinvested earnings and undistributed branch profits	2 333	. . .	. . .	. . .	. . .	. . .	. . .	. . .	. . .
Income on debt (interest)	2 334	. . .	. . .	. . .	. . .	. . .	. . .	. . .	. . .
Portfolio investment income	2 339	. . .	. . .	.3	. . .	. . .	. . .	. . .	. . .
Income on equity	2 340	. . .	. . .	. . .	. . .	. . .	. . .	. . .	. . .
Income on bonds and notes	2 350	. . .	. . .	. . .	. . .	. . .	. . .	. . .	. . .
Income on money market instruments	2 360	. . .	. . .	.3	. . .	. . .	. . .	. . .	. . .
Other investment income	2 370	. . .	3.7	4.1	6.8	12.5	10.9	16.9	11.9
Investment income, debit	3 320	**–18.5**	**–29.7**	**–36.7**	**–58.0**	**–77.0**	**–73.9**	**–90.5**	**–67.1**
Direct investment income	3 330	. . .	. . .	–2.1	–.8	–8.3	–4.8	–39.1	–27.4
Dividends and distributed branch profits	3 332	. . .	. . .	–1.6	–.1	–.8	–.9	–1.3	–.5
Reinvested earnings and undistributed branch profits	3 333	. . .	. . .	–.5	–.8	–7.6	–3.9	–8.0	–13.5
Income on debt (interest)	3 334	. . .	. . .	. . .	. . .	. . .	. . .	–29.8	–13.5
Portfolio investment income	3 339	. . .	. . .	–.3	. . .	–2.1	–.9	. . .	–.1
Income on equity	3 340	. . .	. . .	. . .	. . .	. . .	. . .	. . .	. . .
Income on bonds and notes	3 350	. . .	. . .	. . .	. . .	–2.1	–.4	. . .	–.1
Income on money market instruments	3 360	. . .	. . .	–.3	. . .	. . .	–.4	. . .	. . .
Other investment income	3 370	–18.5	–29.7	–34.3	–57.2	–66.5	–68.2	–51.4	–39.6
D. CURRENT TRANSFERS	4 379	62.6	78.7	84.0	67.6	48.7	68.0	87.3	51.1
Credit	2 379	**63.4**	**80.4**	**85.9**	**69.8**	**50.8**	**69.1**	**89.8**	**54.3**
General government	2 380	62.4	79.1	83.4	67.1	48.6	68.0	46.8	32.7
Other sectors	2 390	1.0	1.2	2.4	2.7	2.2	1.2	43.0	21.6
Workers' remittances	2 391	1.0	1.2	2.4	2.7	2.2	1.2	43.0	21.6
Other current transfers	2 392	. . .	. . .	. . .	. . .	. . .	. . .	. . .	. . .
Debit	3 379	**–.8**	**–1.7**	**–1.9**	**–2.2**	**–2.0**	**–1.2**	**–2.4**	**–3.2**
General government	3 380	–.6	–1.3	–1.3	–1.6	–1.5	–.8	–1.4	–1.1
Other sectors	3 390	–.2	–.4	–.6	–.6	–.6	–.4	–1.1	–2.1
Workers' remittances	3 391	–.2	–.4	–.6	–.6	–.6	–.4	–1.1	–2.1
Other current transfers	3 392	. . .	. . .	. . .	. . .	. . .	. . .	. . .	. . .
CAPITAL AND FINANCIAL ACCOUNT	4 996	**36.0**	**311.6**	**366.4**	**196.2**	**300.6**	**187.4**	**69.2**	**–1.4**
CAPITAL ACCOUNT	4 994	**–62.4**	**–29.0**	**–15.9**	**–8.4**	**–8.1**	**–15.2**	**–11.3**	**–32.0**
Total credit	2 994	*.3*	*2.2*	*9.0*	*6.2*	*3.9*	*14.6*	*22.8*	*9.2*
Total debit	3 994	*–62.7*	*–31.3*	*–25.0*	*–14.6*	*–12.0*	*–29.8*	*–34.2*	*–41.2*
Capital transfers, credit	2 400	**.3**	**2.2**	**9.0**	**6.2**	**3.9**	**14.6**	**22.8**	**9.2**
General government	2 401	.3	2.2	9.0	6.2	3.9	6.7	10.1	2.6
Debt forgiveness	2 402	. . .	. . .	. . .	. . .	. . .	. . .	. . .	. . .
Other capital transfers	2 410	.3	2.2	9.0	6.2	3.9	6.7	10.1	2.6
Other sectors	2 430	. . .	. . .	. . .	. . .	. . .	7.9	12.7	6.6
Migrants' transfers	2 431	. . .	. . .	. . .	. . .	. . .	7.9	6.6	6.6
Debt forgiveness	2 432	. . .	. . .	. . .	. . .	. . .	. . .	6.1	. . .
Other capital transfers	2 440	. . .	. . .	. . .	. . .	. . .	. . .	. . .	. . .
Capital transfers, debit	3 400	**–62.7**	**–31.3**	**–25.0**	**–14.6**	**–12.0**	**–29.8**	**–34.2**	**–41.2**
General government	3 401	. . .	. . .	. . .	. . .	. . .	. . .	. . .	. . .
Debt forgiveness	3 402	. . .	. . .	. . .	. . .	. . .	. . .	. . .	. . .
Other capital transfers	3 410	. . .	. . .	. . .	. . .	. . .	. . .	. . .	. . .
Other sectors	3 430	–62.7	–31.3	–25.0	–14.6	–12.0	–29.8	–34.2	–41.2
Migrants' transfers	3 431	–62.7	–31.3	–25.0	–14.6	–12.0	–29.8	–34.2	–41.2
Debt forgiveness	3 432	. . .	. . .	. . .	. . .	. . .	. . .	. . .	. . .
Other capital transfers	3 440	. . .	. . .	. . .	. . .	. . .	. . .	. . .	. . .
Nonproduced nonfinancial assets, credit	2 480	. . .	. . .	. . .	. . .	. . .	. . .	. . .	. . .
Nonproduced nonfinancial assets, debit	3 480	. . .	. . .	. . .	. . .	. . .	. . .	. . .	. . .

Table 2 (Continued). STANDARD PRESENTATION, 1994–2001

(Millions of U.S. dollars)

	Code		1994	1995	1996	1997	1998	1999	2000	2001
FINANCIAL ACCOUNT	4 995	. .	**98.4**	**340.6**	**382.3**	**204.5**	**308.8**	**202.5**	**80.5**	**30.6**
A. DIRECT INVESTMENT	4 500	. .	38.2	96.1	47.2	83.8	86.6	38.4	–6.9	–1.1
Direct investment abroad	4 505	. .	**. . .**	**. . .**	**. . .**	**. . .**	**–22.6**	**–6.1**	**–4.5**	**–6.1**
Equity capital	4 510	. .	. . .	. . .	. . .	. . .	–22.6	–6.1	–4.5	–6.1
Claims on affiliated enterprises	4 515	. .	. . .	. . .	. . .	. . .	–22.6	–6.1	–4.5	–6.1
Liabilities to affiliated enterprises	4 520	. .	. . .	. . .	. . .	. . .	. . .	. . .	. . .	. . .
Reinvested earnings	4 525	. .	. . .	. . .	. . .	. . .	. . .	. . .	. . .	. . .
Other capital	4 530	. .	. . .	. . .	. . .	. . .	. . .	. . .	. . .	. . .
Claims on affiliated enterprises	4 535	. .	. . .	. . .	. . .	. . .	. . .	. . .	. . .	. . .
Liabilities to affiliated enterprises	4 540	. .	. . .	. . .	. . .	. . .	. . .	. . .	. . .	. . .
Direct investment in Kyrgyz Republic	4 555	. .	**38.2**	**96.1**	**47.2**	**83.8**	**109.2**	**44.4**	**–2.4**	**5.0**
Equity capital	4 560	. .	38.2	16.4	49.0	53.1	86.9	11.2	17.6	12.3
Claims on direct investors	4 565	. .	. . .	. . .	. . .	. . .	. . .	. . .	. . .	. . .
Liabilities to direct investors	4 570	. .	38.2	16.4	49.0	53.1	86.9	11.2	17.6	12.3
Reinvested earnings	4 575	. .	. . .	. . .	.5	.8	7.6	3.9	8.0	13.5
Other capital	4 580	. .	. . .	79.7	–2.3	30.0	14.7	29.4	–28.0	–20.8
Claims on direct investors	4 585	. .	. . .	. . .	. . .	. . .	. . .	. . .	. . .	. . .
Liabilities to direct investors	4 590	. .	. . .	79.7	–2.3	30.0	14.7	29.4	–28.0	–20.8
B. PORTFOLIO INVESTMENT	4 600	. .	. . .	1.7	–1.7	5.7	–4.3	.2	–1.3	1.2
Assets	4 602	. .	**. . .**	**–.1**	**.1**	**.6**	**–.2**	**. . .**	**–1.6**	**1.2**
Equity securities	4 610	. .	. . .	. . .	. . .	. . .	. . .	. . .	. . .	. . .
Monetary authorities	4 611	. .	. . .	. . .	. . .	. . .	. . .	. . .	. . .	. . .
General government	4 612	. .	. . .	. . .	. . .	. . .	. . .	. . .	. . .	. . .
Banks	4 613	. .	. . .	. . .	. . .	. . .	. . .	. . .	. . .	. . .
Other sectors	4 614	. .	. . .	. . .	. . .	. . .	. . .	. . .	. . .	. . .
Debt securities	4 619	. .	. . .	–.1	.1	.6	–.2	. . .	–1.6	1.2
Bonds and notes	4 620	. .	. . .	. . .	. . .	.6	–.2	. . .	–1.6	1.2
Monetary authorities	4 621	. .	. . .	. . .	. . .	. . .	. . .	. . .	. . .	. . .
General government	4 622	. .	. . .	. . .	. . .	. . .	. . .	. . .	. . .	. . .
Banks	4 623	. .	. . .	. . .	. . .	.6	–.2	. . .	–1.6	1.2
Other sectors	4 624	. .	. . .	. . .	. . .	. . .	. . .	. . .	. . .	. . .
Money market instruments	4 630	. .	. . .	–.1	.1	. . .	. . .	. . .	. . .	. . .
Monetary authorities	4 631	. .	. . .	. . .	. . .	. . .	. . .	. . .	. . .	. . .
General government	4 632	. .	. . .	. . .	. . .	. . .	. . .	. . .	. . .	. . .
Banks	4 633	. .	. . .	. . .	.1	. . .	. . .	. . .	. . .	. . .
Other sectors	4 634	. .	. . .	. . .	. . .	. . .	. . .	. . .	. . .	. . .
Liabilities	4 652	. .	**. . .**	**1.8**	**–1.8**	**5.0**	**–4.1**	**.1**	**.3**	**. . .**
Equity securities	4 660	. .	. . .	. . .	. . .	. . .	. . .	.2	.3	. . .
Banks	4 663	. .	. . .	. . .	. . .	. . .	. . .	.2	.2	. . .
Other sectors	4 664	. .	. . .	. . .	. . .	. . .	. . .	.1	.1	. . .
Debt securities	4 669	. .	. . .	1.8	–1.8	5.0	–4.1	–.1	. . .	. . .
Bonds and notes	4 670	. .	. . .	. . .	. . .	. . .	. . .	. . .	. . .	. . .
Monetary authorities	4 671	. .	. . .	. . .	. . .	. . .	. . .	. . .	. . .	. . .
General government	4 672	. .	. . .	. . .	. . .	. . .	. . .	. . .	. . .	. . .
Banks	4 673	. .	. . .	. . .	. . .	. . .	. . .	. . .	. . .	. . .
Other sectors	4 674	. .	. . .	. . .	. . .	. . .	. . .	. . .	. . .	. . .
Money market instruments	4 680	. .	. . .	1.8	–1.8	5.0	–4.1	–.1	. . .	. . .
Monetary authorities	4 681	. .	. . .	. . .	. . .	. . .	–4.1	–.1	. . .	. . .
General government	4 682	. .	. . .	1.8	–1.8	4.0	. . .	. . .	. . .	. . .
Banks	4 683	. .	. . .	. . .	. . .	1.1	. . .	. . .	. . .	. . .
Other sectors	4 684	. .	. . .	. . .	. . .	. . .	. . .	. . .	. . .	. . .
C. FINANCIAL DERIVATIVES	4 910	. .	. . .	. . .	. . .	19.0	30.6	26.4	25.8	17.6
Monetary authorities	4 911	. .	. . .	. . .	. . .	. . .	. . .	. . .	. . .	. . .
General government	4 912	. .	. . .	. . .	. . .	. . .	. . .	. . .	. . .	. . .
Banks	4 913	. .	. . .	. . .	. . .	. . .	. . .	. . .	. . .	. . .
Other sectors	4 914	. .	. . .	. . .	. . .	19.0	30.6	26.4	25.8	17.6
Assets	4 900	. .	**. . .**	**. . .**	**. . .**	**19.0**	**30.6**	**26.4**	**25.8**	**17.6**
Monetary authorities	4 901	. .	. . .	. . .	. . .	. . .	. . .	. . .	. . .	. . .
General government	4 902	. .	. . .	. . .	. . .	. . .	. . .	. . .	. . .	. . .
Banks	4 903	. .	. . .	. . .	. . .	. . .	. . .	. . .	. . .	. . .
Other sectors	4 904	. .	. . .	. . .	. . .	19.0	30.6	26.4	25.8	17.6
Liabilities	4 905	. .	**. . .**	**. . .**	**. . .**	**. . .**	**. . .**	**. . .**	**. . .**	**. . .**
Monetary authorities	4 906	. .	. . .	. . .	. . .	. . .	. . .	. . .	. . .	. . .
General government	4 907	. .	. . .	. . .	. . .	. . .	. . .	. . .	. . .	. . .
Banks	4 908	. .	. . .	. . .	. . .	. . .	. . .	. . .	. . .	. . .
Other sectors	4 909	. .	. . .	. . .	. . .	. . .	. . .	. . .	. . .	. . .

Table 2 (Concluded). STANDARD PRESENTATION, 1994–2001
(Millions of U.S. dollars)

	Code	1994	1995	1996	1997	1998	1999	2000	2001
D. OTHER INVESTMENT	4 700 . .	92.1	242.8	355.4	178.9	190.0	199.0	84.2	30.6
Assets	4 703 . .	**–43.2**	**11.9**	**1.9**	**–43.1**	**–84.1**	**–.7**	**–27.3**	**–4.3**
Trade credits	4 706 . .	–42.9	19.8	–12.7	14.7	–100.5	–9.2	–32.8	–2.8
General government	4 707 . .	. . .	. . .	. . .	. . .	–57.1	–6.6	–31.8	–6.6
of which: Short-term	4 709 . .	. . .	. . .	. . .	. . .	*–14.8*	*–2.2*	*–10.5*	*–2.2*
Other sectors	4 710 . .	–42.9	19.8	–12.7	14.7	–43.4	–2.6	–1.0	3.8
of which: Short-term	4 712 . .	. . .	. . .	. . .	. . .	*–11.3*	*–1.0*	*–.5*	*1.0*
Loans	4 714 . .	. . .	. . .	. . .	. . .	.7	.2	–.2	–.3
Monetary authorities	4 715 . .	. . .	. . .	. . .	. . .	. . .	. . .	. . .	. . .
of which: Short-term	4 718 . .	. . .	. . .	. . .	. . .	. . .	. . .	. . .	. . .
General government	4 719 . .	. . .	. . .	. . .	. . .	. . .	. . .	. . .	. . .
of which: Short-term	4 721 . .	. . .	. . .	. . .	. . .	. . .	. . .	. . .	. . .
Banks	4 722 . .	. . .	. . .	. . .	. . .	.7	.2	–.2	–.3
of which: Short-term	4 724 . .	. . .	. . .	. . .	. . .	*.7*	*.2*	*–.2*	*–.3*
Other sectors	4 725 . .	. . .	. . .	. . .	. . .	. . .	. . .	. . .	. . .
of which: Short-term	4 727 . .	. . .	. . .	. . .	. . .	. . .	. . .	. . .	. . .
Currency and deposits	4 730 . .	1.3	–1.2	1.6	–18.7	18.1	7.5	–2.8	–1.3
Monetary authorities	4 731 . .	. . .	. . .	. . .	. . .	. . .	. . .	. . .	. . .
General government	4 732 . .	. . .	. . .	. . .	. . .	. . .	. . .	. . .	. . .
Banks	4 733 . .	1.3	–1.2	1.6	–18.7	8.9	–1.6	–1.4	–16.1
Other sectors	4 734 . .	. . .	. . .	. . .	. . .	9.1	9.1	–1.5	14.9
Other assets	4 736 . .	–1.7	–6.7	13.1	–39.2	–2.4	.8	8.5	.2
Monetary authorities	4 737 . .	. . .	–1.0	. . .	–3.0	–2.0	. . .	. . .	. . .
of which: Short-term	4 739 . .	. . .	. . .	. . .	. . .	. . .	. . .	. . .	. . .
General government	4 740 . .	–1.7	–2.1	13.3	. . .	–.3	–.3	–.1	–.1
of which: Short-term	4 742 . .	. . .	. . .	. . .	. . .	. . .	. . .	. . .	. . .
Banks	4 743 . .	. . .	. . .	. . .	. . .	. . .	. . .	. . .	. . .
of which: Short-term	4 745 . .	. . .	. . .	. . .	. . .	. . .	. . .	. . .	. . .
Other sectors	4 746 . .	. . .	–3.6	–.2	–36.2	–.1	1.0	8.6	.3
of which: Short-term	4 748 . .	. . .	*–3.6*	*–.2*	*–36.2*	*–.1*	*1.0*	*8.6*	*.3*
Liabilities	4 753 . .	**135.3**	**230.8**	**353.5**	**222.0**	**274.1**	**199.7**	**111.5**	**34.9**
Trade credits	4 756 . .	11.7	–38.5	8.9	23.3	149.0	26.2	26.0	.7
General government	4 757 . .	. . .	. . .	. . .	. . .	47.5	47.6	3.9	19.3
of which: Short-term	4 759 . .	. . .	. . .	. . .	. . .	*10.9*	*15.8*	*1.2*	*6.0*
Other sectors	4 760 . .	11.7	–38.5	8.9	23.3	101.5	–21.5	22.2	–18.6
of which: Short-term	4 762 . .	. . .	. . .	. . .	. . .	*23.4*	*–4.3*	*7.7*	*–6.7*
Loans	4 764 . .	124.8	240.6	385.8	194.7	108.4	149.5	55.0	14.1
Monetary authorities	4 765 . .	13.8	46.3	19.6	34.1	2.8	19.4	7.4	–2.1
of which: Use of Fund credit and loans from the Fund	4 766 . .	*13.8*	*46.3*	*19.6*	*34.1*	*2.8*	*19.4*	*7.4*	*–2.1*
of which: Short-term	4 768 . .	. . .	. . .	. . .	. . .	. . .	. . .	. . .	. . .
General government	4 769 . .	111.1	104.6	162.8	141.9	129.6	176.8	92.9	67.2
of which: Short-term	4 771 . .	. . .	. . .	. . .	. . .	. . .	. . .	. . .	. . .
Banks	4 772 . .	. . .	. . .	. . .	8.1	. . .	–3.2	6.6	2.9
of which: Short-term	4 774 . .	. . .	. . .	. . .	*8.1*	. . .	*–3.2*	*6.6*	*2.9*
Other sectors	4 775 . .	. . .	89.7	203.3	10.6	–24.0	–43.5	–52.0	–53.8
of which: Short-term	4 777 . .	. . .	. . .	. . .	. . .	. . .	. . .	*.4*	*.3*
Currency and deposits	4 780 . .	3.6	–3.3	–2.1	5.9	1.0	.4	–1.0	1.0
Monetary authorities	4 781 . .	. . .	. . .	. . .	. . .	. . .	. . .	. . .	. . .
General government	4 782 . .	. . .	. . .	. . .	. . .	. . .	. . .	. . .	. . .
Banks	4 783 . .	3.6	–3.3	–2.1	5.9	1.0	.4	–1.0	1.0
Other sectors	4 784 . .	. . .	. . .	. . .	. . .	. . .	. . .	. . .	. . .
Other liabilities	4 786 . .	–4.8	32.0	–39.2	–1.8	15.7	23.7	31.5	19.1
Monetary authorities	4 787 . .	–17.7	.2	.2	. . .	. . .	. . .	. . .	. . .
of which: Short-term	4 789 . .	*–17.7*	*.2*	*.2*	. . .	. . .	. . .	. . .	. . .
General government	4 790 . .	12.9	31.8	–39.4	–1.8	15.4	22.1	27.8	15.6
of which: Short-term	4 792 . .	*12.9*	*31.8*	*–39.4*	*–1.8*	*15.4*	*22.1*	*27.8*	*15.6*
Banks	4 793 . .	. . .	. . .	. . .	. . .	. . .	. . .	. . .	. . .
of which: Short-term	4 795 . .	. . .	. . .	. . .	. . .	. . .	. . .	. . .	. . .
Other sectors	4 796 . .	. . .	. . .	. . .	. . .	.4	1.6	3.7	3.5
of which: Short-term	4 798 . .	. . .	. . .	. . .	. . .	*.2*	*1.6*	*3.7*	*3.5*
E. RESERVE ASSETS	4 802 . .	–31.9	.1	–18.6	–82.8	5.9	–61.3	–21.3	–17.7
Monetary gold	4 812 . .	. . .	. . .	. . .	. . .	. . .	. . .	. . .	. . .
Special drawing rights	4 811 . .	12.1	–14.6	6.5	6.2	.6	–4.9	4.2	–.8
Reserve position in the Fund	4 810 . .	. . .	. . .	. . .	. . .	. . .	. . .	. . .	. . .
Foreign exchange	4 803 . .	–43.9	14.6	–25.1	–89.0	5.3	–56.5	–25.5	–16.9
Other claims	4 813 . .	. . .	. . .	. . .	. . .	. . .	. . .	. . .	. . .
NET ERRORS AND OMISSIONS	4 998 . .	**48.0**	**–76.9**	**58.4**	**–57.7**	**63.4**	**–3.0**	**9.8**	**21.3**

Part 3 of the *Yearbook* contains descriptions of the methodologies, compilation practices, and sources used to compile these data.

Table 3. INTERNATIONAL INVESTMENT POSITION (End–period stocks), 1994–2001
(Millions of U.S. dollars)

	Code	1994	1995	1996	1997	1998	1999	2000	2001
ASSETS	8 995 C.	190.1	202.4	203.9	341.3	366.2	405.2	479.6	519.4
Direct investment abroad	8 505	**. . .**	**. . .**	**. . .**	**. . .**	**22.6**	**28.7**	**33.2**	**39.3**
Equity capital and reinvested earnings	8 506	. . .	. . .	. . .	. . .	22.6	28.7	33.2	39.3
Claims on affiliated enterprises	8 507	. . .	. . .	. . .	. . .	22.6	28.7	33.2	39.3
Liabilities to affiliated enterprises	8 508	. . .	. . .	. . .	. . .	. . .	. . .	. . .	. . .
Other capital	8 530	. . .	. . .	. . .	. . .	. . .	. . .	. . .	. . .
Claims on affiliated enterprises	8 535	. . .	. . .	. . .	. . .	. . .	. . .	. . .	. . .
Liabilities to affiliated enterprises	8 540	. . .	. . .	. . .	. . .	. . .	. . .	. . .	. . .
Portfolio investment	8 602	**. . .**	**.1**	**.6**	**. . .**	**.2**	**.2**	**1.6**	**3.7**
Equity securities	8 610	. . .	. . .	. . .	. . .	. . .	. . .	. . .	. . .
Monetary authorities	8 611	. . .	. . .	. . .	. . .	. . .	. . .	. . .	. . .
General government	8 612	. . .	. . .	. . .	. . .	. . .	. . .	. . .	. . .
Banks	8 613	. . .	. . .	. . .	. . .	. . .	. . .	. . .	. . .
Other sectors	8 614	. . .	. . .	. . .	. . .	. . .	. . .	. . .	. . .
Debt securities	8 619	. . .	.1	.6	. . .	.2	.2	1.6	3.7
Bonds and notes	8 620	. . .	.1	.6	. . .	.2	.2	1.6	3.7
Monetary authorities	8 621	. . .	. . .	. . .	. . .	. . .	. . .	. . .	. . .
General government	8 622	. . .	. . .	. . .	. . .	. . .	. . .	. . .	. . .
Banks	8 623	. . .	. . .	. . .	. . .	. . .	. . .	. . .	. . .
Other sectors	8 624	. . .	.1	.6	. . .	.2	.2	1.6	3.7
Money market instruments	8 630	. . .	. . .	. . .	. . .	. . .	. . .	. . .	. . .
Monetary authorities	8 631	. . .	. . .	. . .	. . .	. . .	. . .	. . .	. . .
General government	8 632	. . .	. . .	. . .	. . .	. . .	. . .	. . .	. . .
Banks	8 633	. . .	. . .	. . .	. . .	. . .	. . .	. . .	. . .
Other sectors	8 634	. . .	. . .	. . .	. . .	. . .	. . .	. . .	. . .
Financial derivatives	8 900	**. . .**	**. . .**	**. . .**	**31.7**	**7.8**	**7.3**	**19.5**	**17.2**
Monetary authorities	8 901	. . .	. . .	. . .	. . .	. . .	. . .	. . .	. . .
General government	8 902	. . .	. . .	. . .	. . .	. . .	. . .	. . .	. . .
Banks	8 903	. . .	. . .	. . .	. . .	. . .	. . .	. . .	. . .
Other sectors	8 904	. . .	. . .	. . .	31.7	7.8	7.3	19.5	17.2
Other investment	8 703	**92.2**	**88.6**	**75.8**	**113.7**	**146.9**	**120.3**	**164.1**	**174.1**
Trade credits	8 706	70.7	62.9	49.9	66.2	105.9	78.5	99.3	105.4
General government	8 707	70.7	62.9	49.9	33.3	57.3	42.2	70.2	78.0
of which: Short-term	8 709	*24.0*	*21.4*	*17.0*	*11.3*	*19.5*	*14.3*	*23.9*	*26.5*
Other sectors	8 710	. . .	. . .	. . .	32.9	48.7	36.3	29.1	27.4
of which: Short-term	8 712	. . .	. . .	. . .	*11.2*	*16.5*	*12.4*	*12.2*	*11.4*
Loans	8 714	. . .	. . .	. . .	. . .	. . .	. . .	2.6	2.8
Monetary authorities	8 715	. . .	. . .	. . .	. . .	. . .	. . .	. . .	. . .
of which: Short-term	8 718	. . .	. . .	. . .	. . .	. . .	. . .	. . .	. . .
General government	8 719	. . .	. . .	. . .	. . .	. . .	. . .	2.4	2.3
of which: Short-term	8 721	. . .	. . .	. . .	. . .	. . .	. . .	. . .	. . .
Banks	8 722	. . .	. . .	. . .	. . .	. . .	. . .	.2	.5
of which: Short-term	8 724	. . .	. . .	. . .	. . .	. . .	. . .	*.2*	*.5*
Other sectors	8 725	. . .	. . .	. . .	. . .	. . .	. . .	. . .	. . .
of which: Short-term	8 727	. . .	. . .	. . .	. . .	. . .	. . .	. . .	. . .
Currency and deposits	8 730	19.9	20.9	19.5	38.1	29.2	30.8	59.7	63.8
Monetary authorities	8 731	. . .	. . .	. . .	. . .	. . .	. . .	. . .	. . .
General government	8 732	. . .	. . .	. . .	. . .	. . .	. . .	. . .	. . .
Banks	8 733	19.9	20.9	19.5	38.1	29.2	30.8	59.7	63.8
Other sectors	8 734	. . .	. . .	. . .	. . .	. . .	. . .	. . .	. . .
Other assets	8 736	1.7	4.8	6.5	9.4	11.8	11.1	2.6	2.1
Monetary authorities	8 737	. . .	. . .	. . .	. . .	. . .	. . .	. . .	. . .
of which: Short-term	8 739	. . .	. . .	. . .	. . .	. . .	. . .	. . .	. . .
General government	8 740	1.7	4.8	6.5	9.4	11.8	11.1	2.6	2.1
of which: Short-term	8 742	. . .	. . .	. . .	. . .	. . .	. . .	. . .	. . .
Banks	8 743	. . .	. . .	. . .	. . .	. . .	. . .	. . .	. . .
of which: Short-term	8 745	. . .	. . .	. . .	. . .	. . .	. . .	. . .	. . .
Other sectors	8 746	. . .	. . .	. . .	. . .	. . .	. . .	. . .	. . .
of which: Short-term	8 748	. . .	. . .	. . .	. . .	. . .	. . .	. . .	. . .
Reserve assets	8 802	**97.9**	**113.7**	**127.5**	**195.9**	**188.6**	**248.8**	**261.1**	**285.2**
Monetary gold	8 812	30.5	47.7	43.2	29.1	25.2	24.2	22.8	23.0
Special drawing rights	8 811	1.0	14.3	7.4	.9	.3	5.1	.7	1.3
Reserve position in the Fund	8 810	. . .	. . .	. . .	. . .	. . .	. . .	. . .	. . .
Foreign exchange	8 803	66.5	51.8	76.9	165.9	163.1	219.5	237.6	260.9
Other claims	8 813	. . .	. . .	. . .	. . .	. . .	. . .	. . .	. . .

Table 3 (Concluded). INTERNATIONAL INVESTMENT POSITION (End–period stocks), 1994–2001
(Millions of U.S. dollars)

	Code	1994	1995	1996	1997	1998	1999	2000	2001
LIABILITIES	8 995 D.	528.4	913.8	1,301.3	1,711.7	1,962.5	2,125.9	2,134.5	2,125.0
Direct investment in Kyrgyz Republic	8 555 . .	**48.2**	**144.3**	**191.0**	**274.1**	**383.3**	**427.7**	**438.6**	**427.3**
Equity capital and reinvested earnings	8 556 . .	30.4	90.9	120.4	172.7	241.5	269.5	276.3	269.2
Claims on direct investors	8 557 . .	. . .	. . .	. . .	. . .	. . .	. . .	. . .	. . .
Liabilities to direct investors	8 558 . .	30.4	90.9	120.4	172.7	241.5	269.5	276.3	269.2
Other capital	8 580 . .	17.8	53.4	70.7	101.4	141.8	158.3	162.3	158.1
Claims on direct investors	8 585 . .	. . .	. . .	. . .	. . .	. . .	. . .	. . .	. . .
Liabilities to direct investors	8 590 . .	17.8	53.4	70.7	101.4	141.8	158.3	162.3	158.1
Portfolio investment	8 652 . .	**. . .**	**1.8**	**. . .**	**5.0**	**.9**	**.8**	**1.2**	**2.3**
Equity securities	8 660 . .	. . .	. . .	. . .	. . .	. . .	. . .	. . .	. . .
Banks	8 663 . .	. . .	. . .	. . .	. . .	. . .	. . .	. . .	. . .
Other sectors	8 664 . .	. . .	. . .	. . .	. . .	. . .	. . .	. . .	. . .
Debt securities	8 669 . .	. . .	1.8	. . .	5.0	.9	.8	1.2	2.3
Bonds and notes	8 670 . .	. . .	1.8	. . .	5.0	.9	.8	1.2	2.3
Monetary authorities	8 671 . .	. . .	. . .	. . .	. . .	. . .	. . .	. . .	. . .
General government	8 672 . .	. . .	. . .	. . .	. . .	. . .	. . .	. . .	. . .
Banks	8 673 . .	. . .	. . .	. . .	. . .	. . .	. . .	. . .	. . .
Other sectors	8 674 . .	. . .	1.8	. . .	5.0	.9	.8	1.2	2.3
Money market instruments	8 680 . .	. . .	. . .	. . .	. . .	. . .	. . .	. . .	. . .
Monetary authorities	8 681 . .	. . .	. . .	. . .	. . .	. . .	. . .	. . .	. . .
General government	8 682 . .	. . .	. . .	. . .	. . .	. . .	. . .	. . .	. . .
Banks	8 683 . .	. . .	. . .	. . .	. . .	. . .	. . .	. . .	. . .
Other sectors	8 684 . .	. . .	. . .	. . .	. . .	. . .	. . .	. . .	. . .
Financial derivatives	8 905 . .	**. . .**	**. . .**	**. . .**	**. . .**	**. . .**	**. . .**	**. . .**	**. . .**
Monetary authorities	8 906 . .	. . .	. . .	. . .	. . .	. . .	. . .	. . .	. . .
General government	8 907 . .	. . .	. . .	. . .	. . .	. . .	. . .	. . .	. . .
Banks	8 908 . .	. . .	. . .	. . .	. . .	. . .	. . .	. . .	. . .
Other sectors	8 909 . .	. . .	. . .	. . .	. . .	. . .	. . .	. . .	. . .
Other investment	8 753 . .	**480.2**	**767.8**	**1,110.3**	**1,432.6**	**1,578.3**	**1,697.3**	**1,694.8**	**1,695.3**
Trade credits	8 756 . .	33.0	43.1	32.3	167.1	186.3	143.1	128.5	131.1
General government	8 757 . .	33.0	43.1	32.3	54.4	61.2	73.0	72.3	92.3
of which: Short-term	8 759 . .	*10.9*	*14.2*	*10.7*	*17.9*	*20.2*	*24.1*	*23.9*	*30.5*
Other sectors	8 760 . .	. . .	. . .	. . .	112.7	125.2	70.0	56.2	38.8
of which: Short-term	8 762 . .	. . .	. . .	. . .	*37.2*	*41.3*	*23.1*	*–5.6*	*–9.3*
Loans	8 764 . .	437.9	718.8	1,074.0	1,255.6	1,381.2	1,543.0	1,559.7	1,560.9
Monetary authorities	8 765 . .	77.8	124.3	139.6	164.9	175.2	190.3	188.0	179.3
of which: Use of Fund credit and loans from the Fund	8 766 . .	*77.8*	*124.3*	*139.6*	*164.9*	*175.2*	*190.3*	*188.0*	*179.3*
of which: Short-term	8 768 . .	. . .	. . .	. . .	. . .	. . .	. . .	. . .	. . .
General government	8 769 . .	360.1	504.7	641.4	785.5	918.2	1,122.2	1,207.5	1,262.1
of which: Short-term	8 771 . .	. . .	. . .	. . .	. . .	. . .	. . .	. . .	. . .
Banks	8 772 . .	. . .	. . .	. . .	8.1	8.1	4.9	1.6	4.5
of which: Short-term	8 774 . .	. . .	. . .	. . .	*8.1*	*8.1*	*4.9*	*1.6*	*4.5*
Other sectors	8 775 . .	. . .	89.7	293.0	297.2	279.7	225.6	162.6	114.9
of which: Short-term	8 777 . .	. . .	. . .	. . .	. . .	. . .	. . .	. . .	. . .
Currency and deposits	8 780 . .	9.3	6.0	4.0	9.9	10.8	11.2	.1	1.1
Monetary authorities	8 781 . .	. . .	. . .	. . .	. . .	. . .	. . .	. . .	. . .
General government	8 782 . .	. . .	. . .	. . .	. . .	. . .	. . .	. . .	. . .
Banks	8 783 . .	9.3	6.0	4.0	9.9	10.8	11.2	.1	1.1
Other sectors	8 784 . .	. . .	. . .	. . .	. . .	. . .	. . .	. . .	. . .
Other liabilities	8 786 . .	. . .	. . .	. . .	. . .	. . .	. . .	6.5	2.2
Monetary authorities	8 787 . .	. . .	. . .	. . .	. . .	. . .	. . .	. . .	. . .
of which: Short-term	8 789 . .	. . .	. . .	. . .	. . .	. . .	. . .	. . .	. . .
General government	8 790 . .	. . .	. . .	. . .	. . .	. . .	. . .	. . .	. . .
of which: Short-term	8 792 . .	. . .	. . .	. . .	. . .	. . .	. . .	. . .	. . .
Banks	8 793 . .	. . .	. . .	. . .	. . .	. . .	. . .	. . .	. . .
of which: Short-term	8 795 . .	. . .	. . .	. . .	. . .	. . .	. . .	. . .	. . .
Other sectors	8 796 . .	. . .	. . .	. . .	. . .	. . .	. . .	6.5	2.2
of which: Short-term	8 798 . .	. . .	. . .	. . .	. . .	. . .	. . .	*6.5*	*2.2*
NET INTERNATIONAL INVESTMENT POSITION	8 995 . .	**–338.3**	**–711.4**	**–1,097.4**	**–1,370.4**	**–1,596.4**	**–1,720.6**	**–1,655.0**	**–1,605.6**
Conversion rates: soms per U.S. dollar (end of period)	0 102 . .	**10.650**	**11.200**	**16.700**	**17.375**	**29.376**	**45.429**	**48.304**	**47.719**

Table 1. ANALYTIC PRESENTATION, 1994–2001
(Millions of U.S. dollars)

	Code	1994	1995	1996	1997	1998	1999	2000	2001
A. Current Account[1]	4 993 Z.	**–284.0**	**–346.2**	**–346.8**	**–305.5**	**–150.1**	**–121.1**	**–8.5**	**–82.4**
Goods: exports f.o.b.	2 100 . .	305.5	310.9	322.8	318.3	342.1	338.2	330.3	311.1
Goods: imports f.o.b.	3 100 . .	–519.2	–626.8	–643.7	–601.3	–506.8	–527.7	–535.3	–527.9
Balance on Goods	4 100 . .	*–213.7*	*–315.9*	*–320.9*	*–283.0*	*–164.7*	*–189.5*	*–205.0*	*–216.8*
Services: credit	2 200 . .	87.0	96.8	104.4	105.8	145.0	130.0	175.7	166.1
Services: debit	3 200 . .	–152.1	–121.6	–126.0	–110.5	–95.5	–51.8	–43.1	–31.6
Balance on Goods and Services	4 991 . .	*–278.8*	*–340.7*	*–342.5*	*–287.7*	*–115.2*	*–111.3*	*–72.4*	*–82.3*
Income: credit	2 300 . .	7.2	7.4	9.2	11.1	6.9	10.5	7.3	5.8
Income: debit	3 300 . .	–9.2	–12.9	–13.5	–28.9	–41.8	–49.9	–59.7	–39.6
Balance on Goods, Services, and Income	4 992 . .	*–280.8*	*–346.2*	*–346.8*	*–305.5*	*–150.1*	*–150.7*	*–124.7*	*–116.1*
Current transfers: credit	2 379 Z.	. . .	. . .	. . .	. . .	. . .	80.2	116.3	33.7
Current transfers: debit	3 379 . .	–3.2	. . .	. . .	. . .	. . .	–50.6	. . .	. . .
B. Capital Account[1]	4 994 Z.	**9.5**	**13.2**	**35.0**	**33.4**	**43.1**	**. . .**	**. . .**	**. . .**
Capital account: credit	2 994 Z.	9.5	21.7	44.9	40.3	49.4	. . .	. . .	. . .
Capital account: debit	3 994 . .	. . .	–8.5	–9.9	–6.9	–6.3	. . .	. . .	. . .
Total, Groups A Plus B	4 981 . .	*–274.5*	*–333.0*	*–311.8*	*–272.1*	*–107.0*	*–121.1*	*–8.5*	*–82.4*
C. Financial Account[1]	4 995 W.	**24.3**	**90.0**	**135.7**	**3.5**	**–43.4**	**–46.9**	**126.1**	**135.7**
Direct investment abroad	4 505 . .	. . .	. . .	. . .	. . .	. . .	. . .	. . .	. . .
Direct investment in Lao PDR	4 555 Z.	59.2	95.1	159.8	. . .	. . .	. . .	33.9	23.9
Portfolio investment assets	4 602 . .	. . .	. . .	. . .	. . .	. . .	. . .	. . .	. . .
Equity securities	4 610 . .	. . .	. . .	. . .	. . .	. . .	. . .	. . .	. . .
Debt securities	4 619 . .	. . .	. . .	. . .	. . .	. . .	. . .	. . .	. . .
Portfolio investment liabilities	4 652 Z.	. . .	. . .	. . .	. . .	. . .	. . .	. . .	. . .
Equity securities	4 660 . .	. . .	. . .	. . .	. . .	. . .	. . .	. . .	. . .
Debt securities	4 669 Z.	. . .	. . .	. . .	. . .	. . .	. . .	. . .	. . .
Financial derivatives	4 910 . .	. . .	. . .	. . .	. . .	. . .	. . .	. . .	. . .
Financial derivatives assets	4 900 . .	. . .	. . .	. . .	. . .	. . .	. . .	. . .	. . .
Financial derivatives liabilities	4 905 . .	. . .	. . .	. . .	. . .	. . .	. . .	. . .	. . .
Other investment assets	4 703 . .	–9.6	–1.5	–14.1	39.5	–22.8	–43.2	18.8	25.2
Monetary authorities	4 701 . .	. . .	. . .	. . .	. . .	. . .	. . .	. . .	. . .
General government	4 704 . .	. . .	. . .	. . .	. . .	. . .	. . .	. . .	. . .
Banks	4 705 . .	–9.6	–1.5	–14.1	39.5	–22.8	–43.2	18.8	25.2
Other sectors	4 728 . .	. . .	. . .	. . .	. . .	. . .	. . .	. . .	. . .
Other investment liabilities	4 753 W.	–25.3	–3.6	–10.0	–36.0	–20.6	–3.7	73.3	86.6
Monetary authorities	4 753 WA	. . .	–15.4	–17.5	–18.2	–25.3	. . .	. . .	. . .
General government	4 753 ZB	–8.3	. . .	. . .	. . .	. . .	. . .	67.2	79.0
Banks	4 753 ZC	–17.0	11.8	7.5	–17.8	4.7	–3.7	6.2	7.6
Other sectors	4 753 ZD	. . .	. . .	. . .	. . .	. . .	. . .	. . .	. . .
Total, Groups A Through C	4 983 . .	*–250.2*	*–243.0*	*–176.1*	*–268.6*	*–150.4*	*–168.0*	*117.6*	*53.3*
D. Net Errors and Omissions	4 998 . .	**71.8**	**92.4**	**17.7**	**–100.5**	**–103.8**	**–165.1**	**–74.2**	**–57.2**
Total, Groups A Through D	4 984 . .	*–178.4*	*–150.6*	*–158.4*	*–369.1*	*–254.2*	*–333.1*	*43.4*	*–3.9*
E. Reserves and Related Items	4 802 A.	**178.4**	**150.6**	**158.4**	**369.1**	**254.2**	**333.1**	**–43.4**	**3.9**
Reserve assets	4 802 . .	–5.6	–73.0	–70.7	25.4	28.1	12.4	–35.7	7.4
Use of Fund credit and loans	4 766 . .	8.1	15.6	5.5	3.3	–6.4	–8.0	–7.7	–3.6
Exceptional financing	4 920 . .	175.9	208.0	223.6	340.4	232.5	328.7	. . .	. . .
Conversion rates: kip per U.S. dollar	0 101 . .	**717.7**	**804.7**	**921.0**	**1,260.0**	**3,298.3**	**7,102.0**	**7,887.6**	**8,954.6**

[1] Excludes components that have been classified in the categories of Group E.

Table 2. STANDARD PRESENTATION, 1994–2001

(Millions of U.S. dollars)

	Code		1994	1995	1996	1997	1998	1999	2000	2001
CURRENT ACCOUNT	4 993	. .	**–160.3**	**–236.7**	**–265.1**	**–206.0**	**–76.5**	**89.7**	**–8.5**	**–82.4**
A. GOODS	4 100	. .	–213.7	–315.9	–320.9	–283.0	–164.7	–189.5	–205.0	–216.8
Credit	2 100	. .	**305.5**	**310.9**	**322.8**	**318.3**	**342.1**	**338.2**	**330.3**	**311.1**
General merchandise: exports f.o.b.	2 110	. .	177.4	194.2	230.6	146.7	185.9	162.0	330.3	311.1
Goods for processing: exports f.o.b.	2 150	. .	104.4	94.4	76.6	20.8	66.5	92.9	. . .	. . .
Repairs on goods	2 160	. .	. . .	. . .	. . .	108.9	88.0	82.5	. . .	. . .
Goods procured in ports by carriers	2 170	. .	4.9	.4	.4	.4	.4	.8	. . .	. . .
Nonmonetary gold	2 180	. .	18.8	21.9	15.2	41.5	1.3	. . .	. . .	. . .
Debit	3 100	. .	**–519.2**	**–626.8**	**–643.7**	**–601.3**	**–506.8**	**–527.7**	**–535.3**	**–527.9**
General merchandise: imports f.o.b.	3 110	. .	–391.2	–514.2	–541.7	–447.9	–414.8	–388.3	–535.3	–527.9
Goods for processing: imports f.o.b.	3 150	. .	–79.0	–79.6	–82.0	–3.2	–5.8	–83.5	. . .	. . .
Repairs on goods	3 160	. .	. . .	. . .	. . .	–98.6	–83.8	–51.8	. . .	. . .
Goods procured in ports by carriers	3 170	. .	–6.0	–3.5	–1.2	–1.2	–1.7	–2.0	. . .	. . .
Nonmonetary gold	3 180	. .	–43.0	–29.5	–18.8	–50.4	–.7	–2.1	. . .	. . .
B. SERVICES	4 200	. .	–65.1	–24.8	–21.6	–4.7	49.5	78.2	132.6	134.5
Total credit	2 200	. .	*87.0*	*96.8*	*104.4*	*105.8*	*145.0*	*130.0*	*175.7*	*166.1*
Total debit	3 200	. .	*–152.1*	*–121.6*	*–126.0*	*–110.5*	*–95.5*	*–51.8*	*–43.1*	*–31.6*
Transportation services, credit	2 205	. .	**11.3**	**15.4**	**16.1**	**19.3**	**19.1**	**18.1**	**19.7**	**22.7**
Passenger	2 850	. .	*1.9*	*1.2*	*1.4*	*2.5*	*2.2*	*3.9*	. . .	. . .
Freight	2 851	. .	*1.0*	*3.9*	*3.3*	*6.2*	*5.1*	*2.8*	. . .	. . .
Other	2 852	. .	*8.4*	*10.3*	*11.4*	*10.6*	*11.8*	*11.4*	. . .	. . .
Sea transport, passenger	2 207	. .	. . .	. . .	. . .	. . .	. . .	. . .	. . .	. . .
Sea transport, freight	2 208	. .	. . .	3.9	3.3	6.2	5.1	2.8	. . .	. . .
Sea transport, other	2 209	. .	. . .	. . .	. . .	. . .	. . .	. . .	. . .	. . .
Air transport, passenger	2 211	. .	1.9	1.2	1.4	2.5	2.2	3.9	. . .	. . .
Air transport, freight	2 212	. .	. . .	. . .	. . .	. . .	. . .	. . .	. . .	. . .
Air transport, other	2 213	. .	8.4	. . .	. . .	. . .	. . .	. . .	. . .	. . .
Other transport, passenger	2 215	. .	. . .	. . .	. . .	. . .	. . .	. . .	. . .	. . .
Other transport, freight	2 216	. .	1.0	. . .	. . .	. . .	. . .	. . .	. . .	. . .
Other transport, other	2 217	. .	. . .	10.3	11.4	10.6	11.8	11.4	. . .	. . .
Transportation services, debit	3 205	. .	**–43.2**	**–51.4**	**–48.0**	**–45.0**	**–37.9**	**–5.2**	**–4.9**	**–4.9**
Passenger	3 850	. .	*–4.6*	*–4.0*	*–6.3*	*–6.3*	*–5.6*	*–5.2*	. . .	. . .
Freight	3 851	. .	*–38.6*	*–47.4*	*–40.9*	*–38.7*	*–32.3*	. . .	. . .	. . .
Other	3 852	. .	. . .	. . .	*–.8*	. . .	. . .	. . .	. . .	. . .
Sea transport, passenger	3 207	. .	. . .	. . .	. . .	. . .	. . .	. . .	. . .	. . .
Sea transport, freight	3 208	. .	–35.3	–47.4	–40.9	–38.7	–32.3	. . .	. . .	. . .
Sea transport, other	3 209	. .	. . .	. . .	. . .	. . .	. . .	. . .	. . .	. . .
Air transport, passenger	3 211	. .	–4.6	–3.3	–6.3	–5.4	–4.8	–4.4	. . .	. . .
Air transport, freight	3 212	. .	. . .	. . .	. . .	. . .	. . .	. . .	. . .	. . .
Air transport, other	3 213	. .	. . .	. . .	. . .	. . .	. . .	. . .	. . .	. . .
Other transport, passenger	3 215	. .	. . .	–.7	. . .	–.9	–.8	–.8	. . .	. . .
Other transport, freight	3 216	. .	–3.3	. . .	. . .	. . .	. . .	. . .	. . .	. . .
Other transport, other	3 217	. .	. . .	. . .	–.8	. . .	. . .	. . .	. . .	. . .
Travel, credit	2 236	. .	**42.7**	**51.4**	**62.3**	**57.8**	**95.0**	**81.8**	**113.9**	**103.8**
Business travel	2 237	. .	. . .	. . .	. . .	. . .	. . .	. . .	. . .	. . .
Personal travel	2 240	. .	42.7	51.4	62.3	57.8	95.0	81.8	. . .	. . .
Travel, debit	3 236	. .	**–18.0**	**–29.6**	**–22.2**	**–21.0**	**–23.2**	**–11.8**	**–8.1**	**–.1**
Business travel	3 237	. .	. . .	. . .	. . .	. . .	. . .	. . .	. . .	. . .
Personal travel	3 240	. .	–18.0	–29.6	–22.2	–21.0	–23.2	–11.8	. . .	. . .
Other services, credit	2 200	BA	**33.0**	**30.0**	**26.0**	**28.7**	**30.9**	**30.1**	**42.1**	**39.6**
Communications	2 245	. .	1.0	.4	.4	.6	.7	.6	. . .	. . .
Construction	2 249	. .	. . .	. . .	. . .	. . .	. . .	. . .	. . .	. . .
Insurance	2 253	. .	.4	.4	.4	.5	.8	.8	. . .	. . .
Financial	2 260	. .	. . .	. . .	. . .	. . .	. . .	. . .	. . .	. . .
Computer and information	2 262	. .	. . .	. . .	. . .	. . .	. . .	. . .	. . .	. . .
Royalties and licence fees	2 266	. .	. . .	. . .	. . .	. . .	. . .	. . .	. . .	. . .
Other business services	2 268	. .	.4	. . .	. . .	. . .	. . .	. . .	. . .	. . .
Personal, cultural, and recreational	2 287	. .	. . .	. . .	. . .	. . .	. . .	. . .	. . .	. . .
Government, n.i.e.	2 291	. .	31.2	29.2	25.2	27.6	29.4	28.7	42.1	39.6
Other services, debit	3 200	BA	**–90.9**	**–40.6**	**–55.8**	**–44.5**	**–34.4**	**–34.8**	**–30.1**	**–26.7**
Communications	3 245	. .	–.8	–.4	–.6	–.7	–.8	–.6	. . .	. . .
Construction	3 249	. .	–10.8	–24.0	–36.1	–35.2	–25.8	–18.1	. . .	. . .
Insurance	3 253	. .	–1.0	–4.7	–5.8	–5.0	–4.5	. . .	. . .	. . .
Financial	3 260	. .	. . .	. . .	. . .	. . .	. . .	. . .	. . .	. . .
Computer and information	3 262	. .	. . .	. . .	. . .	. . .	. . .	. . .	. . .	. . .
Royalties and licence fees	3 266	. .	. . .	. . .	. . .	. . .	. . .	. . .	. . .	. . .
Other business services	3 268	. .	–75.6	–8.5	–9.9	. . .	. . .	–13.0	. . .	. . .
Personal, cultural, and recreational	3 287	. .	. . .	. . .	. . .	. . .	. . .	. . .	. . .	. . .
Government, n.i.e.	3 291	. .	–2.7	–3.0	–3.4	–3.6	–3.3	–3.1	–30.1	–26.7

Table 2 (Continued). STANDARD PRESENTATION, 1994–2001
(Millions of U.S. dollars)

	Code	1994	1995	1996	1997	1998	1999	2000	2001
C. INCOME	4 300	–2.0	–5.5	–4.3	–17.8	–34.9	–39.4	–52.4	–33.8
Total credit	2 300	*7.2*	*7.4*	*9.2*	*11.1*	*6.9*	*10.5*	*7.3*	*5.8*
Total debit	3 300	*–9.2*	*–12.9*	*–13.5*	*–28.9*	*–41.8*	*–49.9*	*–59.7*	*–39.6*
Compensation of employees, credit	2 310	**.5**	**.4**	**.5**	**.5**	**.6**	**.6**	**.7**	**.7**
Compensation of employees, debit	3 310	**–.5**	**–.4**	**–.4**	**–.4**	**–.4**	**–.4**	**–.4**	**–.5**
Investment income, credit	2 320	**6.7**	**7.0**	**8.7**	**10.6**	**6.3**	**9.9**	**6.6**	**5.1**
Direct investment income	2 330	...	...	...	...	...	...	...	...
Dividends and distributed branch profits	2 332	...	...	...	...	...	...	...	...
Reinvested earnings and undistributed branch profits	2 333	...	...	...	...	...	...	...	...
Income on debt (interest)	2 334	...	...	...	...	...	...	...	...
Portfolio investment income	2 339	...	...	...	...	...	...	...	...
Income on equity	2 340	...	...	...	...	...	...	...	...
Income on bonds and notes	2 350	...	...	...	...	...	...	...	...
Income on money market instruments	2 360	...	...	...	...	...	...	...	...
Other investment income	2 370	6.7	7.0	8.7	10.6	6.3	9.9	...	...
Investment income, debit	3 320	**–8.7**	**–12.5**	**–13.1**	**–28.5**	**–41.4**	**–49.5**	**–59.2**	**–39.2**
Direct investment income	3 330	...	–5.8	–6.2	–10.5	–13.6	–12.9	...	...
Dividends and distributed branch profits	3 332	...	–5.8	–6.2	–10.5	–13.6	–12.9	...	...
Reinvested earnings and undistributed branch profits	3 333	...	...	...	...	...	...	...	...
Income on debt (interest)	3 334	...	...	...	...	...	...	...	...
Portfolio investment income	3 339	...	...	...	...	...	...	...	...
Income on equity	3 340	...	...	...	...	...	...	...	...
Income on bonds and notes	3 350	...	...	...	...	...	...	...	...
Income on money market instruments	3 360	...	...	...	...	...	...	...	...
Other investment income	3 370	–8.7	–6.7	–6.9	–18.0	–27.8	–36.6	...	...
D. CURRENT TRANSFERS	4 379	120.5	109.5	81.7	99.5	73.6	240.4	116.3	33.7
Credit	2 379	**123.7**	**109.5**	**81.7**	**99.5**	**73.6**	**291.0**	**116.3**	**33.7**
General government	2 380	123.7	109.5	81.7	99.5	73.6	210.8	115.6	23.0
Other sectors	2 390	...	...	...	...	...	80.2	.6	10.7
Workers' remittances	2 391	...	...	...	...	...	...	...	...
Other current transfers	2 392	...	...	...	...	...	80.2	...	...
Debit	3 379	**–3.2**	**...**	**...**	**...**	**...**	**–50.6**	**...**	**...**
General government	3 380	–3.2	...	...	...	...	...	...	...
Other sectors	3 390	...	...	...	...	...	–50.6	...	...
Workers' remittances	3 391	...	...	...	...	...	...	...	...
Other current transfers	3 392	...	...	...	...	...	–50.6	...	...
CAPITAL AND FINANCIAL ACCOUNT	4 996	**88.5**	**144.3**	**247.4**	**306.5**	**180.3**	**75.4**	**82.7**	**139.6**
CAPITAL ACCOUNT	4 994	**9.5**	**13.2**	**35.0**	**33.4**	**43.1**	**...**	**...**	**...**
Total credit	2 994	*9.5*	*21.7*	*44.9*	*40.3*	*49.4*	...	...	...
Total debit	3 994	...	*–8.5*	*–9.9*	*–6.9*	*–6.3*	...	...	...
Capital transfers, credit	2 400	**9.5**	**21.7**	**44.9**	**40.3**	**49.4**	**...**	**...**	**...**
General government	2 401	...	...	...	...	...	...	...	...
Debt forgiveness	2 402	...	...	...	...	...	...	...	...
Other capital transfers	2 410	...	...	...	...	...	...	...	...
Other sectors	2 430	9.5	21.7	44.9	40.3	49.4	...	...	...
Migrants' transfers	2 431	9.5	21.7	44.9	40.3	49.4	...	...	...
Debt forgiveness	2 432	...	...	...	...	...	...	...	...
Other capital transfers	2 440	...	...	...	...	...	...	...	...
Capital transfers, debit	3 400	**...**	**–8.5**	**–9.9**	**–6.9**	**–6.3**	**...**	**...**	**...**
General government	3 401	...	...	...	...	...	...	...	...
Debt forgiveness	3 402	...	...	...	...	...	...	...	...
Other capital transfers	3 410	...	...	...	...	...	...	...	...
Other sectors	3 430	...	–8.5	–9.9	–6.9	–6.3	...	...	...
Migrants' transfers	3 431	...	–8.5	–9.9	–6.9	–6.3	...	...	...
Debt forgiveness	3 432	...	...	...	...	...	...	...	...
Other capital transfers	3 440	...	...	...	...	...	...	...	...
Nonproduced nonfinancial assets, credit	2 480	**...**	**...**	**...**	**...**	**...**	**...**	**...**	**...**
Nonproduced nonfinancial assets, debit	3 480	**...**	**...**	**...**	**...**	**...**	**...**	**...**	**...**

Table 2 (Continued). STANDARD PRESENTATION, 1994–2001

(Millions of U.S. dollars)

	Code	1994	1995	1996	1997	1998	1999	2000	2001
FINANCIAL ACCOUNT	4 995 . .	**79.0**	**131.1**	**212.4**	**273.1**	**137.2**	**75.4**	**82.7**	**139.6**
A. DIRECT INVESTMENT	4 500 . .	59.2	95.1	159.8	91.0	45.9	78.9	33.9	23.9
Direct investment abroad	4 505 . .	**. . .**	**. . .**	**. . .**	**. . .**	**. . .**	**. . .**	**. . .**	**. . .**
Equity capital	4 510 . .	. . .	. . .	. . .	. . .	. . .	. . .	. . .	. . .
Claims on affiliated enterprises	4 515 . .	. . .	. . .	. . .	. . .	. . .	. . .	. . .	. . .
Liabilities to affiliated enterprises	4 520 . .	. . .	. . .	. . .	. . .	. . .	. . .	. . .	. . .
Reinvested earnings	4 525 . .	. . .	. . .	. . .	. . .	. . .	. . .	. . .	. . .
Other capital	4 530 . .	. . .	. . .	. . .	. . .	. . .	. . .	. . .	. . .
Claims on affiliated enterprises	4 535 . .	. . .	. . .	. . .	. . .	. . .	. . .	. . .	. . .
Liabilities to affiliated enterprises	4 540 . .	. . .	. . .	. . .	. . .	. . .	. . .	. . .	. . .
Direct investment in Lao PDR	4 555 . .	**59.2**	**95.1**	**159.8**	**91.0**	**45.9**	**78.9**	**33.9**	**23.9**
Equity capital	4 560 . .	. . .	95.1	159.8	91.0	45.9	78.9	33.9	23.9
Claims on direct investors	4 565 . .	. . .	. . .	. . .	. . .	. . .	. . .	. . .	. . .
Liabilities to direct investors	4 570 . .	. . .	95.1	159.8	91.0	45.9	78.9	. . .	. . .
Reinvested earnings	4 575 . .	. . .	. . .	. . .	. . .	. . .	. . .	. . .	. . .
Other capital	4 580 . .	59.2	. . .	. . .	. . .	. . .	. . .	. . .	. . .
Claims on direct investors	4 585 . .	. . .	. . .	. . .	. . .	. . .	. . .	. . .	. . .
Liabilities to direct investors	4 590 . .	59.2	. . .	. . .	. . .	. . .	. . .	. . .	. . .
B. PORTFOLIO INVESTMENT	4 600 . .	. . .	. . .	. . .	. . .	. . .	. . .	. . .	. . .
Assets	4 602 . .	**. . .**	**. . .**	**. . .**	**. . .**	**. . .**	**. . .**	**. . .**	**. . .**
Equity securities	4 610 . .	. . .	. . .	. . .	. . .	. . .	. . .	. . .	. . .
Monetary authorities	4 611 . .	. . .	. . .	. . .	. . .	. . .	. . .	. . .	. . .
General government	4 612 . .	. . .	. . .	. . .	. . .	. . .	. . .	. . .	. . .
Banks	4 613 . .	. . .	. . .	. . .	. . .	. . .	. . .	. . .	. . .
Other sectors	4 614 . .	. . .	. . .	. . .	. . .	. . .	. . .	. . .	. . .
Debt securities	4 619 . .	. . .	. . .	. . .	. . .	. . .	. . .	. . .	. . .
Bonds and notes	4 620 . .	. . .	. . .	. . .	. . .	. . .	. . .	. . .	. . .
Monetary authorities	4 621 . .	. . .	. . .	. . .	. . .	. . .	. . .	. . .	. . .
General government	4 622 . .	. . .	. . .	. . .	. . .	. . .	. . .	. . .	. . .
Banks	4 623 . .	. . .	. . .	. . .	. . .	. . .	. . .	. . .	. . .
Other sectors	4 624 . .	. . .	. . .	. . .	. . .	. . .	. . .	. . .	. . .
Money market instruments	4 630 . .	. . .	. . .	. . .	. . .	. . .	. . .	. . .	. . .
Monetary authorities	4 631 . .	. . .	. . .	. . .	. . .	. . .	. . .	. . .	. . .
General government	4 632 . .	. . .	. . .	. . .	. . .	. . .	. . .	. . .	. . .
Banks	4 633 . .	. . .	. . .	. . .	. . .	. . .	. . .	. . .	. . .
Other sectors	4 634 . .	. . .	. . .	. . .	. . .	. . .	. . .	. . .	. . .
Liabilities	4 652 . .	**. . .**	**. . .**	**. . .**	**. . .**	**. . .**	**. . .**	**. . .**	**. . .**
Equity securities	4 660 . .	. . .	. . .	. . .	. . .	. . .	. . .	. . .	. . .
Banks	4 663 . .	. . .	. . .	. . .	. . .	. . .	. . .	. . .	. . .
Other sectors	4 664 . .	. . .	. . .	. . .	. . .	. . .	. . .	. . .	. . .
Debt securities	4 669 . .	. . .	. . .	. . .	. . .	. . .	. . .	. . .	. . .
Bonds and notes	4 670 . .	. . .	. . .	. . .	. . .	. . .	. . .	. . .	. . .
Monetary authorities	4 671 . .	. . .	. . .	. . .	. . .	. . .	. . .	. . .	. . .
General government	4 672 . .	. . .	. . .	. . .	. . .	. . .	. . .	. . .	. . .
Banks	4 673 . .	. . .	. . .	. . .	. . .	. . .	. . .	. . .	. . .
Other sectors	4 674 . .	. . .	. . .	. . .	. . .	. . .	. . .	. . .	. . .
Money market instruments	4 680 . .	. . .	. . .	. . .	. . .	. . .	. . .	. . .	. . .
Monetary authorities	4 681 . .	. . .	. . .	. . .	. . .	. . .	. . .	. . .	. . .
General government	4 682 . .	. . .	. . .	. . .	. . .	. . .	. . .	. . .	. . .
Banks	4 683 . .	. . .	. . .	. . .	. . .	. . .	. . .	. . .	. . .
Other sectors	4 684 . .	. . .	. . .	. . .	. . .	. . .	. . .	. . .	. . .
C. FINANCIAL DERIVATIVES	4 910 . .	. . .	. . .	. . .	. . .	. . .	. . .	. . .	. . .
Monetary authorities	4 911 . .	. . .	. . .	. . .	. . .	. . .	. . .	. . .	. . .
General government	4 912 . .	. . .	. . .	. . .	. . .	. . .	. . .	. . .	. . .
Banks	4 913 . .	. . .	. . .	. . .	. . .	. . .	. . .	. . .	. . .
Other sectors	4 914 . .	. . .	. . .	. . .	. . .	. . .	. . .	. . .	. . .
Assets	4 900 . .	**. . .**	**. . .**	**. . .**	**. . .**	**. . .**	**. . .**	**. . .**	**. . .**
Monetary authorities	4 901 . .	. . .	. . .	. . .	. . .	. . .	. . .	. . .	. . .
General government	4 902 . .	. . .	. . .	. . .	. . .	. . .	. . .	. . .	. . .
Banks	4 903 . .	. . .	. . .	. . .	. . .	. . .	. . .	. . .	. . .
Other sectors	4 904 . .	. . .	. . .	. . .	. . .	. . .	. . .	. . .	. . .
Liabilities	4 905 . .	**. . .**	**. . .**	**. . .**	**. . .**	**. . .**	**. . .**	**. . .**	**. . .**
Monetary authorities	4 906 . .	. . .	. . .	. . .	. . .	. . .	. . .	. . .	. . .
General government	4 907 . .	. . .	. . .	. . .	. . .	. . .	. . .	. . .	. . .
Banks	4 908 . .	. . .	. . .	. . .	. . .	. . .	. . .	. . .	. . .
Other sectors	4 909 . .	. . .	. . .	. . .	. . .	. . .	. . .	. . .	. . .

Table 2 (Concluded). STANDARD PRESENTATION, 1994–2001

(Millions of U.S. dollars)

	Code	1994	1995	1996	1997	1998	1999	2000	2001
D. OTHER INVESTMENT	4 700	25.4	109.0	123.3	156.7	63.2	–15.9	84.5	108.2
Assets	4 703	**–9.6**	**–1.5**	**–14.1**	**39.5**	**–22.8**	**–43.2**	**18.8**	**25.2**
Trade credits	4 706	...	...	...	...	...	...	...	...
General government	4 707	...	...	...	...	...	...	...	...
of which: Short-term	4 709	...	...	...	...	...	...	...	...
Other sectors	4 710	...	...	...	...	...	...	...	...
of which: Short-term	4 712	...	...	...	...	...	...	...	...
Loans	4 714	...	...	...	...	...	...	18.8	25.2
Monetary authorities	4 715	...	...	...	...	...	...	...	...
of which: Short-term	4 718	...	...	...	...	...	...	...	...
General government	4 719	...	...	...	...	...	...	...	...
of which: Short-term	4 721	...	...	...	...	...	...	...	...
Banks	4 722	...	...	...	...	...	...	18.8	25.2
of which: Short-term	4 724	...	...	...	...	...	...	...	...
Other sectors	4 725	...	...	...	...	...	...	...	...
of which: Short-term	4 727	...	...	...	...	...	...	...	...
Currency and deposits	4 730	–9.6	–1.5	–14.1	39.5	–22.8	–43.2	...	...
Monetary authorities	4 731	...	...	...	...	...	...	...	...
General government	4 732	...	...	...	...	...	...	...	...
Banks	4 733	–9.6	–1.5	–14.1	39.5	–22.8	–43.2	...	...
Other sectors	4 734	...	...	...	...	...	...	...	...
Other assets	4 736	...	...	...	...	...	...	...	...
Monetary authorities	4 737	...	...	...	...	...	...	...	...
of which: Short-term	4 739	...	...	...	...	...	...	...	...
General government	4 740	...	...	...	...	...	...	...	...
of which: Short-term	4 742	...	...	...	...	...	...	...	...
Banks	4 743	...	...	...	...	...	...	...	...
of which: Short-term	4 745	...	...	...	...	...	...	...	...
Other sectors	4 746	...	...	...	...	...	...	...	...
of which: Short-term	4 748	...	...	...	...	...	...	...	...
Liabilities	4 753	**35.0**	**110.5**	**137.4**	**117.2**	**86.0**	**27.3**	**65.6**	**83.1**
Trade credits	4 756	...	...	...	...	...	...	67.2	79.0
General government	4 757	...	...	...	...	...	...	67.2	79.0
of which: Short-term	4 759	...	...	...	...	...	...	...	...
Other sectors	4 760	...	...	...	...	...	...	...	...
of which: Short-term	4 762	...	...	...	...	...	...	...	...
Loans	4 764	62.4	82.8	124.5	131.3	90.0	34.6	–1.5	4.1
Monetary authorities	4 765	8.1	82.8	124.5	131.3	90.0	34.6	–7.7	–3.6
of which: Use of Fund credit and loans from the Fund	4 766	*8.1*	*15.6*	*5.5*	*3.3*	*–6.4*	*–8.0*	*–7.7*	*–3.6*
of which: Short-term	4 768	...	...	...	...	...	...	...	...
General government	4 769	54.3	...	...	...	...	...	...	...
of which: Short-term	4 771	...	...	...	...	...	...	...	...
Banks	4 772	...	...	...	...	...	...	6.2	7.6
of which: Short-term	4 774	...	...	...	...	...	...	...	...
Other sectors	4 775	...	...	...	...	...	...	...	...
of which: Short-term	4 777	...	...	...	...	...	...	...	...
Currency and deposits	4 780	–17.0	11.8	7.5	–17.8	4.7	–3.7	...	...
Monetary authorities	4 781	...	...	...	...	...	...	...	...
General government	4 782	...	...	...	...	...	...	...	...
Banks	4 783	–17.0	11.8	7.5	–17.8	4.7	–3.7	...	...
Other sectors	4 784	...	...	...	...	...	...	...	...
Other liabilities	4 786	–10.4	15.9	5.4	3.7	–8.7	–3.6	...	...
Monetary authorities	4 787	–10.4	15.9	5.4	3.7	–8.7	–3.6	...	...
of which: Short-term	4 789	*–10.4*	*15.9*	*5.4*	*3.7*	*–8.7*	*–3.6*	...	...
General government	4 790	...	...	...	...	...	...	...	...
of which: Short-term	4 792	...	...	...	...	...	...	...	...
Banks	4 793	...	...	...	...	...	...	...	...
of which: Short-term	4 795	...	...	...	...	...	...	...	...
Other sectors	4 796	...	...	...	...	...	...	...	...
of which: Short-term	4 798	...	...	...	...	...	...	...	...
E. RESERVE ASSETS	4 802	–5.6	–73.0	–70.7	25.4	28.1	12.4	–35.7	7.4
Monetary gold	4 812	...	...	...	...	...	...	3.5	–1.8
Special drawing rights	4 811	–7.7	–3.0	3.4	–3.0	6.8	5.8	–.1	–3.4
Reserve position in the Fund	4 810	...	...	...	...	...	...	...	...
Foreign exchange	4 803	2.1	–70.0	–74.1	28.4	21.3	6.6	–39.1	12.7
Other claims	4 813	...	...	...	...	...	...	...	...
NET ERRORS AND OMISSIONS	4 998	**71.8**	**92.4**	**17.7**	**–100.5**	**–103.8**	**–165.1**	**–74.2**	**–57.2**

Part 3 of the *Yearbook* contains descriptions of the methodologies, compilation practices, and sources used to compile these data.

Table 1. ANALYTIC PRESENTATION, 1994–2001
(Millions of U.S. dollars)

	Code	1994	1995	1996	1997	1998	1999	2000	2001
A. Current Account[1]	4 993 Z.	**201**	**–16**	**–280**	**–345**	**–650**	**–654**	**–494**	**–734**
Goods: exports f.o.b	2 100 . .	1,022	1,368	1,488	1,838	2,011	1,889	2,058	2,216
Goods: imports f.o.b	3 100 . .	–1,322	–1,947	–2,286	–2,686	–3,141	–2,916	–3,116	–3,566
Balance on Goods	4 100 . .	*–301*	*–580*	*–798*	*–848*	*–1,130*	*–1,027*	*–1,058*	*–1,351*
Services: credit	2 200 . .	657	720	1,126	1,033	1,108	1,024	1,212	1,187
Services: debit	3 200 . .	–297	–246	–742	–662	–806	–689	–770	–692
Balance on Goods and Services	4 991 . .	*60*	*–106*	*–414*	*–477*	*–827*	*–691*	*–616*	*–856*
Income: credit	2 300 . .	51	71	140	177	207	158	215	278
Income: debit	3 300 . .	–42	–53	–99	–122	–154	–214	–191	–235
Balance on Goods, Services, and Income	4 992 . .	*68*	*–87*	*–373*	*–422*	*–774*	*–747*	*–592*	*–813*
Current transfers: credit	2 379 Z.	136	75	98	91	137	114	203	221
Current transfers: debit	3 379 . .	–3	–5	–5	–14	–13	–21	–105	–143
B. Capital Account[1]	4 994 Z.	**. . .**	**. . .**	**. . .**	**14**	**14**	**13**	**30**	**44**
Capital account: credit	2 994 Z.	. . .	. . .	. . .	14	14	13	39	56
Capital account: debit	3 994 . .	. . .	. . .	. . .	. . .	. . .	. . .	–9	–12
Total, Groups A Plus B	4 981 . .	*201*	*–16*	*–280*	*–331*	*–635*	*–642*	*–465*	*–691*
C. Financial Account[1]	4 995 W.	**363**	**636**	**537**	**347**	**601**	**768**	**519**	**956**
Direct investment abroad	4 505 . .	65	65	–3	–6	–54	–17	–9	–7
Direct investment in Latvia	4 555 Z.	214	180	382	521	357	348	410	177
Portfolio investment assets	4 602 . .	–22	–37	–165	–539	–33	58	–346	–57
Equity securities	4 610 . .	–12	–7	12	–113	7	77	–40	7
Debt securities	4 619 . .	–10	–30	–177	–426	–40	–19	–306	–64
Portfolio investment liabilities	4 652 Z.	. . .	. . .	24	–32	27	215	25	189
Equity securities	4 660 . .	. . .	. . .	–2	6	30	7	–7	6
Debt securities	4 669 Z.	. . .	. . .	26	–39	–3	209	32	183
Financial derivatives	4 910 . .	. . .	. . .	. . .	. . .	. . .	. . .	2	1
Financial derivatives assets	4 900 . .	. . .	. . .	. . .	. . .	. . .	. . .	2	3
Financial derivatives liabilities	4 905 . .	. . .	. . .	. . .	. . .	. . .	. . .	. . .	–3
Other investment assets	4 703 . .	–387	–31	–214	–326	75	–214	–336	–66
Monetary authorities	4 701 . .	5	1	–1	. . .	. . .	36	25	. . .
General government	4 704 . .	. . .	. . .	. . .	. . .	. . .	. . .	. . .	–7
Banks	4 705 . .	–400	99	–261	–253	67	–275	–370	–107
Other sectors	4 728 . .	8	–130	48	–73	9	25	10	47
Other investment liabilities	4 753 W.	493	458	513	730	229	379	773	719
Monetary authorities	4 753 WA	–5	. . .	. . .	. . .	. . .	6	. . .	1
General government	4 753 ZB	54	55	45	20	45	14	–8	7
Banks	4 753 ZC	272	88	385	558	69	354	719	529
Other sectors	4 753 ZD	172	315	84	152	115	4	62	182
Total, Groups A Through C	4 983 . .	*565*	*619*	*257*	*16*	*–34*	*127*	*54*	*265*
D. Net Errors and Omissions	4 998 . .	**–508**	**–653**	**–46**	**87**	**97**	**38**	**–26**	**49**
Total, Groups A Through D	4 984 . .	*57*	*–33*	*211*	*102*	*63*	*165*	*28*	*314*
E. Reserves and Related Items	4 802 A.	**–57**	**33**	**–211**	**–102**	**–63**	**–165**	**–28**	**–314**
Reserve assets	4 802 . .	–103	36	–186	–65	–38	–150	–18	–305
Use of Fund credit and loans	4 766 . .	47	–3	–25	–37	–25	–15	–10	–10
Exceptional financing	4 920 . .	. . .	. . .	. . .	. . .	. . .	. . .	. . .	. . .
Conversion rates: lats per U.S. dollar	0 101 . .	**.5598**	**.5276**	**.5508**	**.5809**	**.5898**	**.5852**	**.6065**	**.6279**

[1] Excludes components that have been classified in the categories of Group E.

Table 2. STANDARD PRESENTATION, 1994–2001
(Millions of U.S. dollars)

	Code	1994	1995	1996	1997	1998	1999	2000	2001
CURRENT ACCOUNT	4 993 . .	**201**	**–16**	**–280**	**–345**	**–650**	**–654**	**–494**	**–734**
A. GOODS	4 100 . .	–301	–580	–798	–848	–1,130	–1,027	–1,058	–1,351
Credit	2 100 . .	**1,022**	**1,368**	**1,488**	**1,838**	**2,011**	**1,889**	**2,058**	**2,216**
General merchandise: exports f.o.b.	2 110 . .	1,022	1,368	1,221	1,425	1,549	1,437	1,584	1,736
Goods for processing: exports f.o.b.	2 150 . .	. . .	. . .	222	336	372	377	423	406
Repairs on goods	2 160 . .	. . .	. . .	44	56	48	40	35	35
Goods procured in ports by carriers	2 170 . .	. . .	. . .	. . .	22	42	36	16	39
Nonmonetary gold	2 180 . .	. . .	. . .	. . .	. . .	. . .	. . .	. . .	. . .
Debit	3 100 . .	**–1,322**	**–1,947**	**–2,286**	**–2,686**	**–3,141**	**–2,916**	**–3,116**	**–3,566**
General merchandise: imports f.o.b.	3 110 . .	–1,282	–1,897	–2,033	–2,337	–2,748	–2,572	–2,718	–3,204
Goods for processing: imports f.o.b.	3 150 . .	. . .	. . .	–207	–282	–316	–265	–342	–296
Repairs on goods	3 160 . .	. . .	. . .	–4	–3	–18	–21	–12	–15
Goods procured in ports by carriers	3 170 . .	–40	–51	–41	–64	–59	–58	–43	–51
Nonmonetary gold	3 180 . .	. . .	. . .	. . .	. . .	. . .	. . .	. . .	. . .
B. SERVICES	4 200 . .	360	474	384	371	303	336	442	494
Total credit	2 200 . .	*657*	*720*	*1,126*	*1,033*	*1,108*	*1,024*	*1,212*	*1,187*
Total debit	3 200 . .	*–297*	*–246*	*–742*	*–662*	*–806*	*–689*	*–770*	*–692*
Transportation services, credit	2 205 . .	**600**	**659**	**706**	**716**	**728**	**713**	**796**	**769**
Passenger	2 850 . .	*8*	*17*	*16*	*43*	*40*	*35*	*42*	*34*
Freight	2 851 . .	*320*	*417*	*311*	*193*	*269*	*266*	*327*	*413*
Other	2 852 . .	*273*	*225*	*380*	*481*	*419*	*412*	*428*	*322*
Sea transport, passenger	2 207 . .	. . .	. . .	. . .	. . .	1	1	1	1
Sea transport, freight	2 208 . .	211	168	143	106	96	98	144	179
Sea transport, other	2 209 . .	106	149	286	303	230	225	321	260
Air transport, passenger	2 211 . .	5	12	13	35	35	33	36	27
Air transport, freight	2 212 . .	. . .	. . .	. . .	3	1	2	3	4
Air transport, other	2 213 . .	4	6	7	22	19	20	22	23
Other transport, passenger	2 215 . .	3	6	3	8	4	1	5	7
Other transport, freight	2 216 . .	109	248	168	84	172	167	180	230
Other transport, other	2 217 . .	163	70	86	156	170	167	84	39
Transportation services, debit	3 205 . .	**–136**	**–153**	**–173**	**–201**	**–221**	**–191**	**–236**	**–208**
Passenger	3 850 . .	*–34*	*–38*	*–34*	*–53*	*–50*	*–53*	*–34*	*–32*
Freight	3 851 . .	*–34*	*–48*	*–60*	*–78*	*–83*	*–68*	*–110*	*–85*
Other	3 852 . .	*–68*	*–67*	*–79*	*–70*	*–89*	*–70*	*–93*	*–91*
Sea transport, passenger	3 207 . .	. . .	. . .	. . .	. . .	. . .	. . .	–1	–1
Sea transport, freight	3 208 . .	. . .	. . .	. . .	. . .	–18	–14	–26	–16
Sea transport, other	3 209 . .	–58	–53	–41	–30	–4	–3	–35	–46
Air transport, passenger	3 211 . .	–34	–38	–34	–53	–49	–53	–32	–30
Air transport, freight	3 212 . .	. . .	. . .	. . .	. . .	–7	–6	–10	–11
Air transport, other	3 213 . .	–3	–5	. . .	–8	–9	–7	–24	–21
Other transport, passenger	3 215 . .	. . .	. . .	. . .	. . .	. . .	. . .	–2	–1
Other transport, freight	3 216 . .	–34	–48	–60	–78	–58	–47	–74	–58
Other transport, other	3 217 . .	–7	–9	–37	–32	–76	–60	–33	–25
Travel, credit	2 236 . .	**18**	**20**	**215**	**192**	**182**	**118**	**131**	**119**
Business travel	2 237 . .	. . .	. . .	50	43	42	50	79	60
Personal travel	2 240 . .	18	20	165	149	140	68	52	59
Travel, debit	3 236 . .	**–31**	**–24**	**–373**	**–326**	**–305**	**–268**	**–248**	**–224**
Business travel	3 237 . .	–2	–4	–99	–80	–67	–52	–55	–42
Personal travel	3 240 . .	–29	–21	–274	–246	–239	–216	–193	–182
Other services, credit	2 200 BA	**39**	**41**	**204**	**124**	**199**	**194**	**286**	**298**
Communications	2 245 . .	5	5	29	31	30	33	46	26
Construction	2 249 . .	12	8	7	11	6	4	14	13
Insurance	2 253 . .	. . .	. . .	. . .	. . .	. . .	7	8	13
Financial	2 260 . .	6	17	36	40	39	34	35	48
Computer and information	2 262 . .	. . .	. . .	2	8	10	19	20	22
Royalties and licence fees	2 266 . .	. . .	. . .	. . .	. . .	2	10	2	3
Other business services	2 268 . .	10	8	126	28	107	82	140	155
Personal, cultural, and recreational	2 287 . .	. . .	. . .	. . .	. . .	1	. . .	1	1
Government, n.i.e.	2 291 . .	6	2	4	6	5	4	19	18
Other services, debit	3 200 BA	**–130**	**–68**	**–195**	**–136**	**–279**	**–229**	**–286**	**–260**
Communications	3 245 . .	–5	–4	–22	–23	–26	–23	–26	–10
Construction	3 249 . .	–1	–13	–21	–31	–8	–9	–28	–17
Insurance	3 253 . .	–14	–10	–15	–6	–59	–46	–54	–42
Financial	3 260 . .	–13	–6	–16	–15	–17	–11	–12	–37
Computer and information	3 262 . .	. . .	. . .	–2	–2	–7	–6	–14	–16
Royalties and licence fees	3 266 . .	. . .	. . .	–1	–1	–7	–10	–12	–7
Other business services	3 268 . .	–11	–15	–81	–32	–68	–64	–77	–118
Personal, cultural, and recreational	3 287 . .	. . .	. . .	. . .	. . .	. . .	. . .	–4	–5
Government, n.i.e.	3 291 . .	–86	–21	–39	–25	–89	–60	–61	–9

Table 2 (Continued). STANDARD PRESENTATION, 1994–2001

(Millions of U.S. dollars)

	Code	1994	1995	1996	1997	1998	1999	2000	2001
C. INCOME	4 300 . .	9	19	41	55	53	–56	24	44
Total credit	2 300 . .	*51*	*71*	*140*	*177*	*207*	*158*	*215*	*278*
Total debit	3 300 . .	*–42*	*–53*	*–99*	*–122*	*–154*	*–214*	*–191*	*–235*
Compensation of employees, credit	2 310 . .	**. . .**	**. . .**	**41**	**44**	**46**	**46**	**70**	**110**
Compensation of employees, debit	3 310 . .	**–2**	**–1**	**–2**	**–4**	**–5**	**–5**	**–4**	**–5**
Investment income, credit	2 320 . .	**51**	**71**	**100**	**133**	**161**	**112**	**146**	**168**
Direct investment income	2 330 . .	. . .	. . .	1	2	9	. . .	1	3
Dividends and distributed branch profits	2 332 . .	. . .	. . .	1	. . .	. . .	. . .	. . .	. . .
Reinvested earnings and undistributed branch profits	2 333 . .	. . .	. . .	. . .	1	8	. . .	. . .	2
Income on debt (interest)	2 334 . .	. . .	. . .	. . .	. . .	. . .	. . .	1	1
Portfolio investment income	2 339 . .	9	38	32	82	96	61	65	92
Income on equity	2 340 . .	. . .	38	1	. . .	1	. . .	1	. . .
Income on bonds and notes	2 350 . .	8	. . .	31	81	95	55	59	87
Income on money market instruments	2 360 . .	. . .	. . .	. . .	. . .	1	6	6	5
Other investment income	2 370 . .	42	33	67	50	57	51	79	73
Investment income, debit	3 320 . .	**–40**	**–51**	**–97**	**–119**	**–149**	**–209**	**–187**	**–230**
Direct investment income	3 330 . .	. . .	. . .	–50	–70	–82	–124	–84	–111
Dividends and distributed branch profits	3 332 . .	. . .	. . .	–8	–4	–11	–20	–12	–21
Reinvested earnings and undistributed branch profits	3 333 . .	. . .	. . .	–35	–53	–60	–89	–57	–64
Income on debt (interest)	3 334 . .	. . .	. . .	–7	–13	–11	–14	–16	–26
Portfolio investment income	3 339 . .	. . .	. . .	. . .	–1	–2	–11	–16	–17
Income on equity	3 340 . .	. . .	. . .	. . .	–1	. . .	–1	. . .	–1
Income on bonds and notes	3 350 . .	. . .	. . .	. . .	. . .	–1	–10	–14	–15
Income on money market instruments	3 360 . .	. . .	. . .	. . .	. . .	. . .	. . .	–1	–1
Other investment income	3 370 . .	–40	–51	–47	–48	–65	–75	–87	–101
D. CURRENT TRANSFERS	4 379 . .	133	71	93	77	125	93	97	78
Credit	2 379 . .	**136**	**75**	**98**	**91**	**137**	**114**	**203**	**221**
General government	2 380 . .	110	40	56	37	88	68	45	36
Other sectors	2 390 . .	26	36	42	54	50	46	158	185
Workers' remittances	2 391 . .	. . .	. . .	. . .	2	3	3	61	96
Other current transfers	2 392 . .	26	36	42	52	47	44	97	89
Debit	3 379 . .	**–3**	**–5**	**–5**	**–14**	**–13**	**–21**	**–105**	**–143**
General government	3 380 . .	–3	–5	–5	–4	–6	–7	–10	–12
Other sectors	3 390 . .	. . .	. . .	. . .	–9	–7	–14	–96	–130
Workers' remittances	3 391 . .	. . .	. . .	. . .	–1	–3	–3	–31	–48
Other current transfers	3 392 . .	. . .	. . .	. . .	–8	–4	–12	–65	–83
CAPITAL AND FINANCIAL ACCOUNT	4 996 . .	**307**	**669**	**326**	**259**	**553**	**616**	**521**	**685**
CAPITAL ACCOUNT	4 994 . .	**. . .**	**. . .**	**. . .**	**14**	**14**	**13**	**30**	**44**
Total credit	2 994 . .	. . .	. . .	. . .	*14*	*14*	*13*	*39*	*56*
Total debit	3 994 . .	. . .	. . .	. . .	. . .	. . .	. . .	*–9*	*–12*
Capital transfers, credit	2 400 . .	**. . .**	**. . .**	**. . .**	**14**	**14**	**13**	**37**	**53**
General government	2 401 . .	. . .	. . .	. . .	14	14	13	26	38
Debt forgiveness	2 402 . .	. . .	. . .	. . .	. . .	. . .	. . .	. . .	. . .
Other capital transfers	2 410 . .	. . .	. . .	. . .	14	14	13	26	38
Other sectors	2 430 . .	. . .	. . .	. . .	. . .	. . .	. . .	12	15
Migrants' transfers	2 431 . .	. . .	. . .	. . .	. . .	. . .	. . .	. . .	. . .
Debt forgiveness	2 432 . .	. . .	. . .	. . .	. . .	. . .	. . .	. . .	. . .
Other capital transfers	2 440 . .	. . .	. . .	. . .	. . .	. . .	. . .	12	15
Capital transfers, debit	3 400 . .	**. . .**	**. . .**	**. . .**	**. . .**	**. . .**	**. . .**	**–8**	**–10**
General government	3 401 . .	. . .	. . .	. . .	. . .	. . .	. . .	–1	. . .
Debt forgiveness	3 402 . .	. . .	. . .	. . .	. . .	. . .	. . .	. . .	. . .
Other capital transfers	3 410 . .	. . .	. . .	. . .	. . .	. . .	. . .	–1	. . .
Other sectors	3 430 . .	. . .	. . .	. . .	. . .	. . .	. . .	–7	–10
Migrants' transfers	3 431 . .	. . .	. . .	. . .	. . .	. . .	. . .	. . .	. . .
Debt forgiveness	3 432 . .	. . .	. . .	. . .	. . .	. . .	. . .	. . .	. . .
Other capital transfers	3 440 . .	. . .	. . .	. . .	. . .	. . .	. . .	–7	–10
Nonproduced nonfinancial assets, credit	2 480 . .	**. . .**	**. . .**	**. . .**	**. . .**	**. . .**	**. . .**	**1**	**3**
Nonproduced nonfinancial assets, debit	3 480 . .	**. . .**	**. . .**	**. . .**	**. . .**	**. . .**	**. . .**	**–1**	**–2**

Table 2 (Continued). STANDARD PRESENTATION, 1994–2001
(Millions of U.S. dollars)

	Code	1994	1995	1996	1997	1998	1999	2000	2001
FINANCIAL ACCOUNT	4 995 . .	**307**	**669**	**326**	**245**	**538**	**603**	**491**	**642**
A. DIRECT INVESTMENT	4 500 . .	279	245	379	515	303	331	401	170
Direct investment abroad	4 505 . .	**65**	**65**	**–3**	**–6**	**–54**	**–17**	**–9**	**–7**
Equity capital	4 510 . .	26	2	–9	–10	–12	1	–2	–8
Claims on affiliated enterprises	4 515 . .	1	2	–9	–10	–12	1	–1	–8
Liabilities to affiliated enterprises	4 520 . .	25	. . .	. . .	. . .	. . .	. . .	–1	. . .
Reinvested earnings	4 525 . .	. . .	. . .	. . .	–1	–8	. . .	. . .	–2
Other capital	4 530 . .	38	63	6	5	–34	–18	–4	3
Claims on affiliated enterprises	4 535 . .	–9	1	3	5	–33	–19	–3	1
Liabilities to affiliated enterprises	4 540 . .	47	62	3	. . .	–1	1	–1	2
Direct investment in Latvia	4 555 . .	**214**	**180**	**382**	**521**	**357**	**348**	**410**	**177**
Equity capital	4 560 . .	214	180	219	357	209	178	213	213
Claims on direct investors	4 565 . .	4	–3	. . .	28	–6	2	5	–79
Liabilities to direct investors	4 570 . .	210	182	219	329	215	176	208	291
Reinvested earnings	4 575 . .	. . .	. . .	35	53	60	89	57	64
Other capital	4 580 . .	. . .	. . .	128	112	88	80	140	–100
Claims on direct investors	4 585 . .	. . .	. . .	54	19	–10	–2	–2	–4
Liabilities to direct investors	4 590 . .	. . .	. . .	74	93	97	82	142	–96
B. PORTFOLIO INVESTMENT	4 600 . .	–22	–37	–141	–572	–6	273	–321	132
Assets	4 602 . .	**–22**	**–37**	**–165**	**–539**	**–33**	**58**	**–346**	**–57**
Equity securities	4 610 . .	–12	–7	12	–113	7	77	–40	7
Monetary authorities	4 611 . .	. . .	. . .	. . .	. . .	. . .	. . .	. . .	. . .
General government	4 612 . .	. . .	. . .	. . .	. . .	. . .	. . .	. . .	. . .
Banks	4 613 . .	–12	–6	12	–112	21	75	–29	7
Other sectors	4 614 . .	. . .	–1	. . .	–1	–13	2	–11	. . .
Debt securities	4 619 . .	–10	–30	–177	–426	–40	–19	–306	–64
Bonds and notes	4 620 . .	–10	–30	–177	–346	–90	–28	–335	–55
Monetary authorities	4 621 . .	. . .	. . .	. . .	. . .	. . .	. . .	. . .	. . .
General government	4 622 . .	. . .	. . .	. . .	. . .	. . .	. . .	. . .	. . .
Banks	4 623 . .	–9	–30	–177	–346	–87	–29	–341	–56
Other sectors	4 624 . .	–1	. . .	. . .	. . .	–3	. . .	5	1
Money market instruments	4 630 . .	. . .	. . .	. . .	–81	49	9	29	–9
Monetary authorities	4 631 . .	. . .	. . .	. . .	. . .	. . .	. . .	. . .	. . .
General government	4 632 . .	. . .	. . .	. . .	. . .	. . .	. . .	. . .	. . .
Banks	4 633 . .	. . .	. . .	. . .	–81	50	9	24	–9
Other sectors	4 634 . .	. . .	. . .	. . .	. . .	–1	. . .	6	1
Liabilities	4 652 . .	**. . .**	**. . .**	**24**	**–32**	**27**	**215**	**25**	**189**
Equity securities	4 660 . .	. . .	. . .	–2	6	30	7	–7	6
Banks	4 663 . .	. . .	. . .	. . .	. . .	26	–3	–9	–1
Other sectors	4 664 . .	. . .	. . .	–3	6	4	10	2	6
Debt securities	4 669 . .	. . .	. . .	26	–39	–3	209	32	183
Bonds and notes	4 670 . .	. . .	. . .	26	–39	–3	209	38	182
Monetary authorities	4 671 . .	. . .	. . .	. . .	. . .	. . .	. . .	. . .	. . .
General government	4 672 . .	. . .	. . .	26	–37	–3	211	37	183
Banks	4 673 . .	. . .	. . .	. . .	. . .	. . .	. . .	. . .	. . .
Other sectors	4 674 . .	. . .	. . .	. . .	–2	–1	–2	. . .	–1
Money market instruments	4 680 . .	. . .	. . .	. . .	. . .	. . .	. . .	–6	1
Monetary authorities	4 681 . .	. . .	. . .	. . .	. . .	. . .	. . .	. . .	. . .
General government	4 682 . .	. . .	. . .	. . .	. . .	. . .	. . .	–3	. . .
Banks	4 683 . .	. . .	. . .	. . .	. . .	. . .	. . .	. . .	. . .
Other sectors	4 684 . .	. . .	. . .	. . .	. . .	. . .	. . .	–3	1
C. FINANCIAL DERIVATIVES	4 910 . .	. . .	. . .	. . .	. . .	. . .	. . .	2	1
Monetary authorities	4 911 . .	. . .	. . .	. . .	. . .	. . .	. . .	. . .	. . .
General government	4 912 . .	. . .	. . .	. . .	. . .	. . .	. . .	. . .	. . .
Banks	4 913 . .	. . .	. . .	. . .	. . .	. . .	. . .	. . .	. . .
Other sectors	4 914 . .	. . .	. . .	. . .	. . .	. . .	. . .	2	. . .
Assets	4 900 . .	**. . .**	**. . .**	**. . .**	**. . .**	**. . .**	**. . .**	**2**	**3**
Monetary authorities	4 901 . .	. . .	. . .	. . .	. . .	. . .	. . .	. . .	3
General government	4 902 . .	. . .	. . .	. . .	. . .	. . .	. . .	. . .	. . .
Banks	4 903 . .	. . .	. . .	. . .	. . .	. . .	. . .	. . .	. . .
Other sectors	4 904 . .	. . .	. . .	. . .	. . .	. . .	. . .	2	. . .
Liabilities	4 905 . .	**. . .**	**. . .**	**. . .**	**. . .**	**. . .**	**. . .**	**. . .**	**–3**
Monetary authorities	4 906 . .	. . .	. . .	. . .	. . .	. . .	. . .	. . .	–3
General government	4 907 . .	. . .	. . .	. . .	. . .	. . .	. . .	. . .	. . .
Banks	4 908 . .	. . .	. . .	. . .	. . .	. . .	. . .	. . .	. . .
Other sectors	4 909 . .	. . .	. . .	. . .	. . .	. . .	. . .	. . .	. . .

Table 2 (Concluded). STANDARD PRESENTATION, 1994–2001
(Millions of U.S. dollars)

	Code	1994	1995	1996	1997	1998	1999	2000	2001
D. OTHER INVESTMENT	4 700 . .	153	425	274	367	280	149	428	644
Assets	4 703 . .	**-387**	**-31**	**-214**	**-326**	**75**	**-214**	**-336**	**-66**
Trade credits	4 706 . .	39	-23	54	-59	4	20	-18	-20
General government	4 707 . .	...	...	...	...	...	...	...	...
of which: Short-term	4 709 . .	...	...	...	...	...	...	...	...
Other sectors	4 710 . .	39	-23	54	-59	4	20	-18	-20
of which: Short-term	4 712 . .	...	*-23*	*54*	*-59*	*4*	*20*	*-18*	*-25*
Loans	4 714 . .	-180	161	-44	-118	-67	-36	102	-10
Monetary authorities	4 715 . .	1	...	...	...	...	...	...	...
of which: Short-term	4 718 . .	...	...	...	...	...	...	...	...
General government	4 719 . .	...	...	...	...	...	...	...	-2
of which: Short-term	4 721 . .	...	...	...	...	...	...	...	...
Banks	4 722 . .	-180	165	-45	-134	-69	-22	74	-25
of which: Short-term	4 724 . .	...	*146*	*-38*	*-99*	*-13*	*-3*	*61*	*22*
Other sectors	4 725 . .	-1	-4	2	16	2	-14	27	16
of which: Short-term	4 727 . .	*-1*	*-4*	*3*	*16*	...	*-7*	*-14*	*13*
Currency and deposits	4 730 . .	-197	-65	-225	-127	152	-191	-424	-42
Monetary authorities	4 731 . .	4	1	-1	...	...	36	25	...
General government	4 732 . .	...	...	...	...	...	...	...	-5
Banks	4 733 . .	-217	-59	-213	-104	160	-245	-454	-88
Other sectors	4 734 . .	15	-7	-11	-23	-8	18	5	51
Other assets	4 736 . .	-49	-104	1	-23	-14	-7	5	6
Monetary authorities	4 737 . .	...	...	...	...	...	...	...	...
of which: Short-term	4 739 . .	...	...	...	...	...	...	...	...
General government	4 740 . .	...	...	...	...	...	...	...	...
of which: Short-term	4 742 . .	...	...	...	...	...	...	...	...
Banks	4 743 . .	-3	-8	-3	-15	-24	-8	9	6
of which: Short-term	4 745 . .	*-3*	*-8*	*-3*	*-15*	*-24*	*-8*	*9*	*6*
Other sectors	4 746 . .	-45	-96	4	-7	11	1	-4	...
of which: Short-term	4 748 . .	*-45*	*-96*	*4*	*-7*	*11*	*1*	*-4*	*-1*
Liabilities	4 753 . .	**540**	**456**	**488**	**693**	**204**	**364**	**763**	**710**
Trade credits	4 756 . .	51	139	67	-12	...	-5	17	22
General government	4 757 . .	...	...	...	...	...	...	...	...
of which: Short-term	4 759 . .	...	...	...	...	...	...	...	...
Other sectors	4 760 . .	51	139	67	-12	...	-5	17	22
of which: Short-term	4 762 . .	*51*	*139*	*67*	*-12*	...	*-5*	*17*	*16*
Loans	4 764 . .	221	50	99	182	274	6	32	343
Monetary authorities	4 765 . .	47	-3	-25	-37	-25	-15	-10	-10
of which: Use of Fund credit and loans from the Fund	4 766 . .	*47*	*-3*	*-25*	*-37*	*-25*	*-15*	*-10*	*-10*
of which: Short-term	4 768 . .	...	...	...	...	...	...	...	...
General government	4 769 . .	54	55	45	20	45	14	-8	7
of which: Short-term	4 771 . .	...	...	...	...	...	...	...	...
Banks	4 772 . .	75	-74	55	45	137	-10	10	201
of which: Short-term	4 774 . .	*75*	*-74*	*50*	...	...	...	...	*141*
Other sectors	4 775 . .	45	72	25	153	116	17	39	145
of which: Short-term	4 777 . .	*45*	*72*	*8*	*19*	*67*	*19*	*24*	*23*
Currency and deposits	4 780 . .	178	90	241	329	-44	416	587	337
Monetary authorities	4 781 . .	-5	...	...	...	...	...	...	1
General government	4 782 . .	...	...	...	...	...	...	...	...
Banks	4 783 . .	183	90	242	329	-44	416	588	337
Other sectors	4 784 . .	...	...	...	...	...	...	...	...
Other liabilities	4 786 . .	90	176	80	195	-25	-53	127	7
Monetary authorities	4 787 . .	...	...	...	...	...	6	...	1
of which: Short-term	4 789 . .	...	...	...	...	...	*6*	...	*1*
General government	4 790 . .	...	...	...	...	...	...	...	...
of which: Short-term	4 792 . .	...	...	...	...	...	...	...	...
Banks	4 793 . .	13	72	88	184	-24	-51	121	-9
of which: Short-term	4 795 . .	*13*	*72*	*88*	*184*	*-24*	*-51*	*121*	*-9*
Other sectors	4 796 . .	76	104	-8	11	-1	-8	6	15
of which: Short-term	4 798 . .	*76*	*104*	*-8*	*11*	*-1*	*-8*	*6*	*15*
E. RESERVE ASSETS	4 802 . .	-103	36	-186	-65	-38	-150	-18	-305
Monetary gold	4 812 . .	...	...	...	...	...	...	...	...
Special drawing rights	4 811 . .	103	-2	...	...	2	-3	3	...
Reserve position in the Fund	4 810 . .	...	...	...	...	...	...	...	...
Foreign exchange	4 803 . .	-208	39	-145	-62	-13	-147	-21	-305
Other claims	4 813 . .	2	-1	-40	-4	-27	...	...	...
NET ERRORS AND OMISSIONS	4 998 . .	**-508**	**-653**	**-46**	**87**	**97**	**38**	**-26**	**49**

Part 3 of the *Yearbook* contains descriptions of the methodologies, compilation practices, and sources used to compile these data.

Table 3. INTERNATIONAL INVESTMENT POSITION (End-period stocks), 1994–2001

(Millions of U.S. dollars)

	Code	1994	1995	1996	1997	1998	1999	2000	2001
ASSETS	8 995 C.	...	1,851	2,366	3,244	3,050	3,262	3,964	4,063
Direct investment abroad	8 505 . .	**...**	**231**	**209**	**222**	**281**	**215**	**242**	**42**
Equity capital and reinvested earnings	8 506 . .	...	171	174	197	227	148	172	34
Claims on affiliated enterprises	8 507 . .	...	171	174	197	227	148	172	34
Liabilities to affiliated enterprises	8 508 . .	...	...	...	...	...	...	...	–1
Other capital	8 530 . .	...	60	35	26	54	68	70	8
Claims on affiliated enterprises	8 535 . .	...	63	40	29	57	72	79	23
Liabilities to affiliated enterprises	8 540 . .	...	–3	–5	–4	–3	–4	–9	–15
Portfolio investment	8 602 . .	**...**	**62**	**227**	**755**	**590**	**533**	**854**	**665**
Equity securities	8 610 . .	...	21	9	122	113	37	63	55
Monetary authorities	8 611 . .	...	2	2	2	2	2	2	2
General government	8 612 . .	...	...	...	...	...	...	...	...
Banks	8 613 . .	...	18	6	118	95	20	49	42
Other sectors	8 614 . .	...	1	1	3	16	16	12	12
Debt securities	8 619 . .	...	41	218	633	477	495	791	610
Bonds and notes	8 620 . .	...	41	218	380	400	428	751	560
Monetary authorities	8 621 . .	...	...	...	...	...	...	...	...
General government	8 622 . .	...	...	...	...	...	...	...	...
Banks	8 623 . .	...	39	215	380	395	418	748	558
Other sectors	8 624 . .	...	2	3	...	4	10	3	2
Money market instruments	8 630 . .	...	...	...	253	78	67	41	50
Monetary authorities	8 631 . .	...	...	...	...	...	...	...	...
General government	8 632 . .	...	...	...	...	...	...	...	...
Banks	8 633 . .	...	...	...	253	77	64	40	49
Other sectors	8 634 . .	...	...	...	...	1	4	1	1
Financial derivatives	8 900 . .	**...**	**...**	**...**	**...**	**...**	**...**	**...**	**3**
Monetary authorities	8 901 . .	...	...	...	...	...	...	...	2
General government	8 902 . .	...	...	...	...	...	...	...	...
Banks	8 903 . .	...	...	...	...	...	...	...	...
Other sectors	8 904 . .	...	...	...	...	...	...	...	...
Other investment	8 703 . .	**...**	**972**	**1,158**	**1,442**	**1,298**	**1,602**	**1,950**	**2,135**
Trade credits	8 706 . .	...	349	262	320	350	341	340	419
General government	8 707 . .	...	...	...	...	...	...	...	...
of which: Short-term	8 709 . .	...	...	...	...	...	...	...	...
Other sectors	8 710 . .	...	349	262	320	350	341	340	419
of which: Short-term	8 712 . .	...	*349*	*262*	*320*	*350*	*341*	*340*	*411*
Loans	8 714 . .	...	74	116	232	298	331	281	707
Monetary authorities	8 715 . .	...	...	...	...	...	...	...	...
of which: Short-term	8 718 . .	...	...	...	...	...	...	...	...
General government	8 719 . .	...	...	...	...	...	...	...	2
of which: Short-term	8 721 . .	...	...	...	...	...	...	...	...
Banks	8 722 . .	...	48	93	227	292	313	252	681
of which: Short-term	8 724 . .	...	*34*	*71*	*170*	*181*	*183*	*120*	*504*
Other sectors	8 725 . .	...	26	24	5	6	18	29	25
of which: Short-term	8 727 . .	...	*26*	*22*	*5*	*5*	*9*	*29*	*19*
Currency and deposits	8 730 . .	...	522	755	849	615	886	1,290	982
Monetary authorities	8 731 . .	...	2	3	2	1	36	1	1
General government	8 732 . .	...	...	...	...	...	...	3	7
Banks	8 733 . .	...	483	693	792	547	783	1,233	916
Other sectors	8 734 . .	...	38	60	55	68	66	53	58
Other assets	8 736 . .	...	27	25	41	35	45	39	27
Monetary authorities	8 737 . .	...	...	...	...	...	...	...	...
of which: Short-term	8 739 . .	...	...	...	...	...	...	...	...
General government	8 740 . .	...	...	...	...	...	...	...	...
of which: Short-term	8 742 . .	...	...	...	...	...	...	...	...
Banks	8 743 . .	...	11	14	29	33	40	30	19
of which: Short-term	8 745 . .	...	*11*	*14*	*29*	*33*	*40*	*30*	*19*
Other sectors	8 746 . .	...	15	11	12	2	5	8	8
of which: Short-term	8 748 . .	...	*15*	*11*	*12*	*2*	*5*	*8*	*8*
Reserve assets	8 802 . .	**...**	**586**	**772**	**825**	**881**	**913**	**919**	**1,218**
Monetary gold	8 812 . .	...	75	75	74	...	...	...	...
Special drawing rights	8 811 . .	...	2	2	2	...	3	...	...
Reserve position in the Fund	8 810 . .	...	...	...	...	...	...	...	...
Foreign exchange	8 803 . .	...	506	652	702	804	910	919	1,218
Other claims	8 813 . .	...	3	43	47	77	...	...	...

Table 3 (Concluded). INTERNATIONAL INVESTMENT POSITION (End–period stocks), 1994–2001
(Millions of U.S. dollars)

	Code	1994	1995	1996	1997	1998	1999	2000	2001
LIABILITIES	8 995 D.	...	1,932	2,717	3,707	4,250	5,235	6,109	7,162
Direct investment in Latvia	8 555 . .	**...**	**616**	**936**	**1,272**	**1,558**	**1,885**	**2,081**	**2,343**
Equity capital and reinvested earnings	8 556 . .	...	510	687	967	1,149	1,338	1,415	1,628
Claims on direct investors	8 557 . .	...	...	...	–1	–7	–9	–3	–84
Liabilities to direct investors	8 558 . .	...	510	687	968	1,155	1,347	1,417	1,712
Other capital	8 580 . .	...	106	249	305	409	546	666	714
Claims on direct investors	8 585 . .	...	–119	–61	–21	–35	–58	–47	–83
Liabilities to direct investors	8 590 . .	...	225	310	326	444	604	714	797
Portfolio investment	8 652 . .	**...**	**23**	**46**	**13**	**43**	**275**	**259**	**434**
Equity securities	8 660 . .	...	7	5	9	42	51	40	46
Banks	8 663 . .	...	...	...	...	28	24	13	12
Other sectors	8 664 . .	...	7	5	9	14	27	27	34
Debt securities	8 669 . .	...	16	41	4	1	224	219	389
Bonds and notes	8 670 . .	...	16	41	4	1	224	218	386
Monetary authorities	8 671 . .	...	...	...	...	...	...	...	...
General government	8 672 . .	...	16	41	3	...	224	216	386
Banks	8 673 . .	...	...	...	...	...	...	...	...
Other sectors	8 674 . .	...	...	...	1	1	...	1	...
Money market instruments	8 680 . .	...	...	...	...	...	...	2	3
Monetary authorities	8 681 . .	...	...	...	...	...	...	...	...
General government	8 682 . .	...	...	...	...	...	...	1	1
Banks	8 683 . .	...	...	...	...	...	...	...	...
Other sectors	8 684 . .	...	...	...	...	...	...	1	2
Financial derivatives	8 905 . .	**...**	**...**	**...**	**...**	**...**	**...**	**...**	**7**
Monetary authorities	8 906 . .	...	...	...	...	...	...	...	7
General government	8 907 . .	...	...	...	...	...	...	...	...
Banks	8 908 . .	...	...	...	...	...	...	...	...
Other sectors	8 909 . .	...	...	...	...	...	...	...	...
Other investment	8 753 . .	**...**	**1,294**	**1,735**	**2,422**	**2,650**	**3,076**	**3,769**	**4,378**
Trade credits	8 756 . .	...	259	309	350	456	480	502	519
General government	8 757 . .	...	...	...	...	...	...	...	...
of which: Short-term	8 759 . .	...	...	...	...	...	...	...	...
Other sectors	8 760 . .	...	259	309	350	456	480	502	519
of which: Short-term	8 762 . .	...	*259*	*309*	*350*	*456*	*480*	*502*	*509*
Loans	8 764 . .	...	642	727	776	1,094	1,150	1,117	2,176
Monetary authorities	8 765 . .	...	160	130	86	64	47	35	24
of which: Use of Fund credit and loans from the Fund	8 766 . .	*160*	*160*	*130*	*86*	*64*	*47*	*35*	*24*
of which: Short-term	8 768 . .	...	...	...	...	...	...	...	...
General government	8 769 . .	...	242	279	284	343	346	326	324
of which: Short-term	8 771 . .	...	...	...	...	...	...	...	...
Banks	8 772 . .	...	60	114	69	206	196	201	971
of which: Short-term	8 774 . .	...	*42*	*91*	...	...	...	...	*646*
Other sectors	8 775 . .	...	180	204	337	481	561	555	857
of which: Short-term	8 777 . .	...	*48*	*58*	*74*	*147*	*163*	*188*	*195*
Currency and deposits	8 780	...	287	527	945	833	1,240	1,824	1,622
Monetary authorities	8 781 . .	...	1	1	1	1	1	...	1
General government	8 782 . .	...	...	...	...	...	...	...	...
Banks	8 783 . .	...	286	527	944	832	1,240	1,824	1,621
Other sectors	8 784 . .	...	...	...	...	...	...	...	...
Other liabilities	8 786 . .	...	106	172	352	267	206	327	62
Monetary authorities	8 787 . .	...	...	...	...	...	6	1	2
of which: Short-term	8 789 . .	...	...	...	...	...	*6*	*1*	*2*
General government	8 790 . .	...	...	...	...	...	...	...	...
of which: Short-term	8 792 . .	...	...	...	...	...	...	...	...
Banks	8 793 . .	...	53	141	320	239	183	303	24
of which: Short-term	8 795 . .	...	*53*	*141*	*320*	*239*	*183*	*303*	*24*
Other sectors	8 796 . .	...	53	32	32	28	17	22	36
of which: Short-term	8 798 . .	...	*53*	*32*	*32*	*28*	*17*	*22*	*36*
NET INTERNATIONAL INVESTMENT POSITION	8 995 . .	**...**	**–80**	**–351**	**–463**	**–1,200**	**–1,973**	**–2,145**	**–3,099**
Conversion rates: lats per U.S. dollar (end of period)	0 102 . .	**.5480**	**.5370**	**.5560**	**.5900**	**.5690**	**.5830**	**.6130**	**.6380**

Lesotho
666

Table 1. ANALYTIC PRESENTATION, 1994–2001

(Millions of U.S. dollars)

	Code		1994	1995	1996	1997	1998	1999	2000	2001
A. Current Account[1]	4 993	Z.	**108.1**	**–323.0**	**–302.5**	**–269.2**	**–280.2**	**–220.8**	**–151.4**	**–95.0**
Goods: exports f.o.b.	2 100	. .	143.5	160.0	186.9	196.1	193.4	172.5	211.1	278.6
Goods: imports f.o.b.	3 100	. .	–810.2	–985.2	–998.6	–1,024.4	–866.0	–779.2	–727.6	–678.6
Balance on Goods	4 100	. .	*–666.7*	*–825.2*	*–811.8*	*–828.3*	*–672.5*	*–606.7*	*–516.5*	*–400.0*
Services: credit	2 200	. .	37.8	39.0	42.6	86.9	53.6	43.7	42.7	40.5
Services: debit	3 200	. .	–64.2	–61.1	–55.9	–67.6	–52.2	–50.1	–42.5	–48.8
Balance on Goods and Services	4 991	. .	*–693.2*	*–847.3*	*–825.1*	*–809.0*	*–671.2*	*–613.1*	*–516.4*	*–408.3*
Income: credit	2 300	. .	369.6	471.6	453.0	447.4	357.7	325.0	288.8	235.3
Income: debit	3 300	. .	–39.4	–157.4	–119.5	–110.0	–123.6	–80.6	–62.6	–56.7
Balance on Goods, Services, and Income	4 992	. .	*–363.0*	*–533.2*	*–491.6*	*–471.6*	*–437.1*	*–368.6*	*–290.2*	*–229.7*
Current transfers: credit	2 379	Z.	472.1	211.3	190.2	202.9	158.0	149.4	139.8	137.2
Current transfers: debit	3 379	. .	–.9	–1.2	–1.1	–.5	–1.2	–1.6	–1.0	–2.5
B. Capital Account[1]	4 994	Z.	**. . .**	**43.7**	**45.5**	**44.5**	**22.9**	**15.2**	**22.0**	**16.8**
Capital account: credit	2 994	Z.	. . .	43.7	45.5	44.5	22.9	15.2	22.0	16.8
Capital account: debit	3 994	. .	. . .	. . .	. . .	. . .	. . .	. . .	. . .	. . .
Total, Groups A Plus B	4 981	. .	*108.1*	*–279.4*	*–257.0*	*–224.7*	*–257.4*	*–205.6*	*–129.4*	*–78.2*
C. Financial Account[1]	4 995	W.	**33.0**	**349.1**	**350.6**	**323.7**	**316.1**	**135.8**	**85.2**	**89.1**
Direct investment abroad	4 505	. .	. . .	. . .	. . .	. . .	. . .	. . .	. . .	. . .
Direct investment in Lesotho	4 555	Z.	18.7	275.3	287.5	268.1	264.8	163.3	117.8	117.0
Portfolio investment assets	4 602	. .	. . .	. . .	. . .	. . .	. . .	. . .	. . .	. . .
Equity securities	4 610	. .	. . .	. . .	. . .	. . .	. . .	. . .	. . .	. . .
Debt securities	4 619	. .	. . .	. . .	. . .	. . .	. . .	. . .	. . .	. . .
Portfolio investment liabilities	4 652	Z.	. . .	. . .	. . .	. . .	. . .	. . .	. . .	. . .
Equity securities	4 660	. .	. . .	. . .	. . .	. . .	. . .	. . .	. . .	. . .
Debt securities	4 669	Z.	. . .	. . .	. . .	. . .	. . .	. . .	. . .	. . .
Financial derivatives	4 910	. .	. . .	. . .	. . .	. . .	. . .	. . .	. . .	. . .
Financial derivatives assets	4 900	. .	. . .	. . .	. . .	. . .	. . .	. . .	. . .	. . .
Financial derivatives liabilities	4 905	. .	. . .	. . .	. . .	. . .	. . .	. . .	. . .	. . .
Other investment assets	4 703	. .	–13.4	18.8	–7.0	–5.0	–1.7	–11.0	–19.1	–20.2
Monetary authorities	4 701	. .	. . .	. . .	. . .	. . .	. . .	. . .	. . .	. . .
General government	4 704	. .	. . .	. . .	. . .	. . .	. . .	. . .	. . .	. . .
Banks	4 705	. .	–13.4	18.8	–7.0	–5.0	–1.7	–11.0	–19.1	–20.2
Other sectors	4 728	. .	. . .	. . .	. . .	. . .	. . .	. . .	. . .	. . .
Other investment liabilities	4 753	W.	27.6	55.0	70.1	60.5	53.0	–16.6	–13.5	–7.7
Monetary authorities	4 753	WA	.3	6.3	–.2	. . .	.1	–5.4	–3.5	16.0
General government	4 753	ZB	26.0	49.2	71.8	68.6	59.8	–9.3	–15.1	–19.0
Banks	4 753	ZC	1.9	. . .	. . .	–7.2	–6.7	–1.2	5.2	–4.8
Other sectors	4 753	ZD	–.5	–.5	–1.4	–.9	–.1	–.6	–.1	. . .
Total, Groups A Through C	4 983	. .	*141.1*	*69.7*	*93.6*	*99.0*	*58.8*	*–69.8*	*–44.3*	*11.0*
D. Net Errors and Omissions	4 998	. .	**–20.3**	**28.1**	**23.3**	**42.1**	**56.8**	**29.0**	**62.1**	**154.7**
Total, Groups A Through D	4 984	. .	*120.9*	*97.8*	*116.9*	*141.0*	*115.6*	*–40.8*	*17.8*	*165.7*
E. Reserves and Related Items	4 802	A.	**–120.9**	**–97.8**	**–116.9**	**–141.0**	**–115.6**	**40.8**	**–17.8**	**–165.7**
Reserve assets	4 802	. .	–124.6	–95.1	–113.5	–136.8	–110.7	46.7	–12.6	–170.2
Use of Fund credit and loans	4 766	. .	3.8	–2.7	–3.4	–4.3	–4.9	–5.9	–5.2	4.5
Exceptional financing	4 920	. .	. . .	. . .	. . .	. . .	. . .	. . .	. . .	. . .
Conversion rates: maloti per U.S. dollar	0 101	. .	**3.5508**	**3.6271**	**4.2993**	**4.6080**	**5.5283**	**6.1095**	**6.9398**	**8.6092**

[1] Excludes components that have been classified in the categories of Group E.

Table 2. STANDARD PRESENTATION, 1994–2001
(Millions of U.S. dollars)

	Code	1994	1995	1996	1997	1998	1999	2000	2001
CURRENT ACCOUNT	4 993 . .	**108.1**	**–323.0**	**–302.5**	**–269.2**	**–280.2**	**–220.8**	**–151.4**	**–95.0**
A. GOODS	4 100 . .	–666.7	–825.2	–811.8	–828.3	–672.5	–606.7	–516.5	–400.0
Credit	2 100 . .	**143.5**	**160.0**	**186.9**	**196.1**	**193.4**	**172.5**	**211.1**	**278.6**
General merchandise: exports f.o.b.	2 110 . .	143.5	160.0	186.9	196.1	193.4	172.5	211.1	278.6
Goods for processing: exports f.o.b.	2 150 . .	. . .	. . .	. . .	. . .	. . .	. . .	. . .	. . .
Repairs on goods	2 160 . .	. . .	. . .	. . .	. . .	. . .	. . .	. . .	. . .
Goods procured in ports by carriers	2 170 . .	. . .	. . .	. . .	. . .	. . .	. . .	. . .	. . .
Nonmonetary gold	2 180 . .	. . .	. . .	. . .	. . .	. . .	. . .	. . .	. . .
Debit	3 100 . .	**–810.2**	**–985.2**	**–998.6**	**–1,024.4**	**–866.0**	**–779.2**	**–727.6**	**–678.6**
General merchandise: imports f.o.b.	3 110 . .	–810.2	–985.2	–998.6	–1,024.4	–866.0	–779.2	–727.6	–678.6
Goods for processing: imports f.o.b.	3 150 . .	. . .	. . .	. . .	. . .	. . .	. . .	. . .	. . .
Repairs on goods	3 160 . .	. . .	. . .	. . .	. . .	. . .	. . .	. . .	. . .
Goods procured in ports by carriers	3 170 . .	. . .	. . .	. . .	. . .	. . .	. . .	. . .	. . .
Nonmonetary gold	3 180 . .	. . .	. . .	. . .	. . .	. . .	. . .	. . .	. . .
B. SERVICES	4 200 . .	–26.4	–22.1	–13.3	19.3	1.4	–6.4	.1	–8.4
Total credit	2 200 . .	*37.8*	*39.0*	*42.6*	*86.9*	*53.6*	*43.7*	*42.7*	*40.5*
Total debit	3 200 . .	*–64.2*	*–61.1*	*–55.9*	*–67.6*	*–52.2*	*–50.1*	*–42.5*	*–48.8*
Transportation services, credit	2 205 . .	**3.1**	**2.1**	**1.9**	**2.4**	**1.3**	**.6**	**.5**	**.4**
Passenger	2 850 . .	*2.9*	*2.0*	*1.7*	*1.7*	*.7*	*.1*	. . .	. . .
Freight	2 851 . .	. . .	. . .	. . .	. . .	. . .	. . .	. . .	. . .
Other	2 852 . .	*.2*	*.1*	*.1*	*.7*	*.6*	*.6*	*.5*	*.4*
Sea transport, passenger	2 207 . .	. . .	. . .	. . .	. . .	. . .	. . .	. . .	. . .
Sea transport, freight	2 208 . .	. . .	. . .	. . .	. . .	. . .	. . .	. . .	. . .
Sea transport, other	2 209 . .	. . .	. . .	. . .	. . .	. . .	. . .	. . .	. . .
Air transport, passenger	2 211 . .	. . .	. . .	. . .	. . .	. . .	.1	. . .	. . .
Air transport, freight	2 212 . .	. . .	. . .	. . .	. . .	. . .	. . .	. . .	. . .
Air transport, other	2 213 . .	. . .	. . .	. . .	. . .	. . .	.6	.5	.4
Other transport, passenger	2 215 . .	. . .	. . .	. . .	. . .	. . .	. . .	. . .	. . .
Other transport, freight	2 216 . .	. . .	. . .	. . .	. . .	. . .	. . .	. . .	. . .
Other transport, other	2 217 . .	. . .	. . .	. . .	. . .	. . .	. . .	. . .	. . .
Transportation services, debit	3 205 . .	**–32.6**	**–43.8**	**–41.9**	**–43.3**	**–36.7**	**–33.4**	**–31.5**	**–28.6**
Passenger	3 850 . .	*–3.5*	*–4.1*	*–3.7*	*–3.0*	*–2.7*	*–3.2*	*–3.2*	*–2.5*
Freight	3 851 . .	*–29.1*	*–39.0*	*–37.7*	*–39.9*	*–33.5*	*–30.2*	*–28.3*	*–26.1*
Other	3 852 . .	. . .	*–.6*	*–.5*	*–.4*	*–.4*	. . .	. . .	. . .
Sea transport, passenger	3 207 . .	. . .	. . .	. . .	. . .	. . .	. . .	. . .	. . .
Sea transport, freight	3 208 . .	. . .	. . .	. . .	. . .	. . .	. . .	. . .	. . .
Sea transport, other	3 209 . .	. . .	. . .	. . .	. . .	. . .	. . .	. . .	. . .
Air transport, passenger	3 211 . .	. . .	. . .	. . .	. . .	. . .	–3.2	–3.2	–2.5
Air transport, freight	3 212 . .	. . .	. . .	. . .	. . .	. . .	. . .	. . .	. . .
Air transport, other	3 213 . .	. . .	. . .	. . .	. . .	. . .	. . .	. . .	. . .
Other transport, passenger	3 215 . .	. . .	. . .	. . .	. . .	. . .	. . .	. . .	. . .
Other transport, freight	3 216 . .	. . .	. . .	. . .	. . .	. . .	–30.2	–28.3	–26.1
Other transport, other	3 217 . .	. . .	. . .	. . .	. . .	. . .	. . .	. . .	. . .
Travel, credit	2 236 . .	**17.4**	**27.3**	**32.4**	**32.1**	**24.5**	**23.0**	**24.2**	**22.8**
Business travel	2 237 . .	. . .	. . .	. . .	. . .	. . .	9.1	9.8	8.6
Personal travel	2 240 . .	. . .	27.3	32.4	32.1	24.5	13.9	14.4	14.1
Travel, debit	3 236 . .	**–6.8**	**–13.2**	**–12.4**	**–13.7**	**–12.6**	**–13.7**	**–9.4**	**–9.1**
Business travel	3 237 . .	. . .	–.2	–.2	–.2	–.4	–.6	–.6	–.2
Personal travel	3 240 . .	. . .	–13.0	–12.2	–13.5	–12.3	–13.1	–8.8	–8.9
Other services, credit	2 200 BA	**17.3**	**9.5**	**8.4**	**52.4**	**27.7**	**20.1**	**18.0**	**17.3**
Communications	2 245 . .	. . .	. . .	. . .	. . .	. . .	. . .	. . .	. . .
Construction	2 249 . .	. . .	. . .	. . .	. . .	. . .	. . .	. . .	. . .
Insurance	2 253 . .	. . .	.4	. . .	. . .	. . .	–.4	–.5	. . .
Financial	2 260 . .	. . .	. . .	. . .	. . .	. . .	. . .	. . .	. . .
Computer and information	2 262 . .	. . .	. . .	. . .	. . .	. . .	. . .	. . .	. . .
Royalties and licence fees	2 266 . .	. . .	. . .	. . .	44.2	20.4	13.1	11.7	11.5
Other business services	2 268 . .	9.1	.2	.2	.1	.1	.2	. . .	. . .
Personal, cultural, and recreational	2 287 . .	. . .	. . .	. . .	. . .	. . .	. . .	. . .	. . .
Government, n.i.e.	2 291 . .	8.2	8.9	8.2	8.1	7.2	7.1	6.7	5.8
Other services, debit	3 200 BA	**–24.8**	**–4.1**	**–1.6**	**–10.7**	**–2.8**	**–3.0**	**–1.7**	**–11.1**
Communications	3 245 . .	. . .	. . .	. . .	. . .	. . .	. . .	. . .	. . .
Construction	3 249 . .	. . .	. . .	. . .	. . .	. . .	. . .	. . .	. . .
Insurance	3 253 . .	–3.2	–.1	–.1	. . .	.5	. . .	. . .	–.5
Financial	3 260 . .	. . .	. . .	. . .	. . .	. . .	. . .	. . .	. . .
Computer and information	3 262 . .	. . .	. . .	. . .	. . .	. . .	. . .	. . .	. . .
Royalties and licence fees	3 266 . .	. . .	–1.4	–.3	–1.1	–1.4	. . .	. . .	. . .
Other business services	3 268 . .	. . .	. . .	–.1	–.1	–.1	. . .	. . .	. . .
Personal, cultural, and recreational	3 287 . .	. . .	. . .	. . .	. . .	. . .	. . .	. . .	. . .
Government, n.i.e.	3 291 . .	–21.6	–2.6	–1.1	–9.4	–1.9	–3.0	–1.6	–10.6

Table 2 (Continued). STANDARD PRESENTATION, 1994–2001
(Millions of U.S. dollars)

	Code	1994	1995	1996	1997	1998	1999	2000	2001
C. INCOME	4 300 . .	330.2	314.2	333.5	337.5	234.0	244.4	226.1	178.6
Total credit	2 300 . .	*369.6*	*471.6*	*453.0*	*447.4*	*357.7*	*325.0*	*288.8*	*235.3*
Total debit	3 300 . .	*–39.4*	*–157.4*	*–119.5*	*–110.0*	*–123.6*	*–80.6*	*–62.6*	*–56.7*
Compensation of employees, credit	2 310 . .	**319.7**	**409.7**	**387.1**	**377.9**	**293.5**	**275.2**	**252.1**	**208.1**
Compensation of employees, debit	3 310 . .	**. . .**	**–75.4**	**–60.5**	**–56.3**	**–55.6**	**–34.1**	**–27.5**	**–24.7**
Investment income, credit	2 320 . .	**49.9**	**61.9**	**65.9**	**69.5**	**64.2**	**49.8**	**36.7**	**27.1**
Direct investment income	2 330 . .	. . .	. . .	. . .	. . .	. . .	. . .	. . .	. . .
Dividends and distributed branch profits	2 332 . .	. . .	. . .	. . .	. . .	. . .	. . .	. . .	. . .
Reinvested earnings and undistributed branch profits	2 333 . .	. . .	. . .	. . .	. . .	. . .	. . .	. . .	. . .
Income on debt (interest)	2 334 . .	. . .	. . .	. . .	. . .	. . .	. . .	. . .	. . .
Portfolio investment income	2 339 . .	. . .	. . .	. . .	. . .	. . .	. . .	. . .	. . .
Income on equity	2 340 . .	. . .	. . .	. . .	. . .	. . .	. . .	. . .	. . .
Income on bonds and notes	2 350 . .	. . .	. . .	. . .	. . .	. . .	. . .	. . .	. . .
Income on money market instruments	2 360 . .	. . .	. . .	. . .	. . .	. . .	. . .	. . .	. . .
Other investment income	2 370 . .	49.9	61.9	65.9	69.5	64.2	49.8	36.7	27.1
Investment income, debit	3 320 . .	**–39.4**	**–82.1**	**–59.0**	**–53.7**	**–68.0**	**–46.5**	**–35.1**	**–31.9**
Direct investment income	3 330 . .	–26.9	–71.4	–45.0	–40.6	–51.3	–28.5	–15.0	–16.0
Dividends and distributed branch profits	3 332 . .	–26.9	–71.4	–45.0	–40.6	–51.3	–28.5	–15.0	–16.0
Reinvested earnings and undistributed branch profits	3 333 . .	. . .	. . .	. . .	. . .	. . .	. . .	. . .	. . .
Income on debt (interest)	3 334 . .	. . .	. . .	. . .	. . .	. . .	. . .	. . .	. . .
Portfolio investment income	3 339 . .	. . .	. . .	. . .	. . .	. . .	. . .	. . .	. . .
Income on equity	3 340 . .	. . .	. . .	. . .	. . .	. . .	. . .	. . .	. . .
Income on bonds and notes	3 350 . .	. . .	. . .	. . .	. . .	. . .	. . .	. . .	. . .
Income on money market instruments	3 360 . .	. . .	. . .	. . .	. . .	. . .	. . .	. . .	. . .
Other investment income	3 370 . .	–12.5	–10.7	–14.0	–13.1	–16.7	–18.0	–20.1	–15.9
D. CURRENT TRANSFERS	4 379 . .	471.2	210.1	189.1	202.4	156.9	147.8	138.8	134.7
Credit	2 379 . .	**472.1**	**211.3**	**190.2**	**202.9**	**158.0**	**149.4**	**139.8**	**137.2**
General government	2 380 . .	459.4	207.7	187.4	200.5	155.0	147.5	137.4	133.6
Other sectors	2 390 . .	12.7	3.6	2.8	2.4	3.0	2.0	2.4	3.6
Workers' remittances	2 391 . .	. . .	.8	.6	.8	1.1	.7	.1	1.3
Other current transfers	2 392 . .	12.7	2.9	2.2	1.6	1.9	1.3	2.3	2.3
Debit	3 379 . .	**–.9**	**–1.2**	**–1.1**	**–.5**	**–1.2**	**–1.6**	**–1.0**	**–2.5**
General government	3 380 . .	–.9	–1.1	–1.0	–.3	–1.0	–1.5	–1.0	–2.5
Other sectors	3 390 . .	–.1	–.1	. . .	–.1	–.1	–.1	. . .	. . .
Workers' remittances	3 391 . .	. . .	. . .	. . .	. . .	. . .	. . .	. . .	. . .
Other current transfers	3 392 . .	–.1	–.1	. . .	–.1	–.1	–.1	. . .	. . .
CAPITAL AND FINANCIAL ACCOUNT	4 996 . .	–87.9	294.9	279.3	227.1	223.4	191.8	89.4	–59.7
CAPITAL ACCOUNT	4 994 . .	. . .	43.7	45.5	44.5	22.9	15.2	22.0	16.8
Total credit	2 994 . .	. . .	*43.7*	*45.5*	*44.5*	*22.9*	*15.2*	*22.0*	*16.8*
Total debit	3 994 . .	. . .	. . .	. . .	. . .	. . .	. . .	. . .	. . .
Capital transfers, credit	2 400 . .	**. . .**	**43.7**	**45.5**	**44.5**	**22.9**	**15.2**	**22.0**	**16.8**
General government	2 401 . .	. . .	43.7	45.5	44.5	22.9	15.2	22.0	16.8
Debt forgiveness	2 402 . .	. . .	. . .	. . .	. . .	. . .	. . .	. . .	. . .
Other capital transfers	2 410 . .	. . .	. . .	. . .	. . .	. . .	15.2	22.0	16.8
Other sectors	2 430 . .	. . .	. . .	. . .	. . .	. . .	. . .	. . .	. . .
Migrants' transfers	2 431 . .	. . .	. . .	. . .	. . .	. . .	. . .	. . .	. . .
Debt forgiveness	2 432 . .	. . .	. . .	. . .	. . .	. . .	. . .	. . .	. . .
Other capital transfers	2 440 . .	. . .	. . .	. . .	. . .	. . .	. . .	. . .	. . .
Capital transfers, debit	3 400 . .	**. . .**	**. . .**	**. . .**	**. . .**	**. . .**	**. . .**	**. . .**	**. . .**
General government	3 401 . .	. . .	. . .	. . .	. . .	. . .	. . .	. . .	. . .
Debt forgiveness	3 402 . .	. . .	. . .	. . .	. . .	. . .	. . .	. . .	. . .
Other capital transfers	3 410 . .	. . .	. . .	. . .	. . .	. . .	. . .	. . .	. . .
Other sectors	3 430 . .	. . .	. . .	. . .	. . .	. . .	. . .	. . .	. . .
Migrants' transfers	3 431 . .	. . .	. . .	. . .	. . .	. . .	. . .	. . .	. . .
Debt forgiveness	3 432 . .	. . .	. . .	. . .	. . .	. . .	. . .	. . .	. . .
Other capital transfers	3 440 . .	. . .	. . .	. . .	. . .	. . .	. . .	. . .	. . .
Nonproduced nonfinancial assets, credit	2 480 . .	**. . .**	**. . .**	**. . .**	**. . .**	**. . .**	**. . .**	**. . .**	**. . .**
Nonproduced nonfinancial assets, debit	3 480 . .	**. . .**	**. . .**	**. . .**	**. . .**	**. . .**	**. . .**	**. . .**	**. . .**

Table 2 (Continued). STANDARD PRESENTATION, 1994–2001

(Millions of U.S. dollars)

	Code	1994	1995	1996	1997	1998	1999	2000	2001
FINANCIAL ACCOUNT	4 995 . .	**–87.9**	**251.3**	**233.8**	**182.6**	**200.6**	**176.6**	**67.4**	**–76.6**
A. DIRECT INVESTMENT	4 500 . .	18.7	275.3	287.5	268.1	264.8	163.3	117.8	117.0
Direct investment abroad	4 505 . .	**. . .**	**. . .**	**. . .**	**. . .**	**. . .**	**. . .**	**. . .**	**. . .**
Equity capital	4 510 . .	. . .	. . .	. . .	. . .	. . .	. . .	. . .	. . .
Claims on affiliated enterprises	4 515 . .	. . .	. . .	. . .	. . .	. . .	. . .	. . .	. . .
Liabilities to affiliated enterprises	4 520 . .	. . .	. . .	. . .	. . .	. . .	. . .	. . .	. . .
Reinvested earnings	4 525 . .	. . .	. . .	. . .	. . .	. . .	. . .	. . .	. . .
Other capital	4 530 . .	. . .	. . .	. . .	. . .	. . .	. . .	. . .	. . .
Claims on affiliated enterprises	4 535 . .	. . .	. . .	. . .	. . .	. . .	. . .	. . .	. . .
Liabilities to affiliated enterprises	4 540 . .	. . .	. . .	. . .	. . .	. . .	. . .	. . .	. . .
Direct investment in Lesotho	4 555 . .	**18.7**	**275.3**	**287.5**	**268.1**	**264.8**	**163.3**	**117.8**	**117.0**
Equity capital	4 560 . .	18.7	23.4	28.3	31.8	26.9	32.7	31.5	28.5
Claims on direct investors	4 565 . .	. . .	. . .	. . .	. . .	. . .	. . .	. . .	. . .
Liabilities to direct investors	4 570 . .	. . .	23.4	28.3	. . .	. . .	32.7	31.5	28.5
Reinvested earnings	4 575 . .	. . .	. . .	. . .	. . .	. . .	. . .	. . .	. . .
Other capital	4 580 . .	. . .	251.9	259.2	236.4	237.9	130.6	86.3	88.5
Claims on direct investors	4 585 . .	. . .	. . .	. . .	. . .	. . .	. . .	. . .	. . .
Liabilities to direct investors	4 590 . .	. . .	251.9	259.2	236.4	237.9	130.6	86.3	88.5
B. PORTFOLIO INVESTMENT	4 600 . .	. . .	. . .	. . .	. . .	. . .	. . .	. . .	. . .
Assets	4 602 . .	**. . .**	**. . .**	**. . .**	**. . .**	**. . .**	**. . .**	**. . .**	**. . .**
Equity securities	4 610 . .	. . .	. . .	. . .	. . .	. . .	. . .	. . .	. . .
Monetary authorities	4 611 . .	. . .	. . .	. . .	. . .	. . .	. . .	. . .	. . .
General government	4 612 . .	. . .	. . .	. . .	. . .	. . .	. . .	. . .	. . .
Banks	4 613 . .	. . .	. . .	. . .	. . .	. . .	. . .	. . .	. . .
Other sectors	4 614 . .	. . .	. . .	. . .	. . .	. . .	. . .	. . .	. . .
Debt securities	4 619 . .	. . .	. . .	. . .	. . .	. . .	. . .	. . .	. . .
Bonds and notes	4 620 . .	. . .	. . .	. . .	. . .	. . .	. . .	. . .	. . .
Monetary authorities	4 621 . .	. . .	. . .	. . .	. . .	. . .	. . .	. . .	. . .
General government	4 622 . .	. . .	. . .	. . .	. . .	. . .	. . .	. . .	. . .
Banks	4 623 . .	. . .	. . .	. . .	. . .	. . .	. . .	. . .	. . .
Other sectors	4 624 . .	. . .	. . .	. . .	. . .	. . .	. . .	. . .	. . .
Money market instruments	4 630 . .	. . .	. . .	. . .	. . .	. . .	. . .	. . .	. . .
Monetary authorities	4 631 . .	. . .	. . .	. . .	. . .	. . .	. . .	. . .	. . .
General government	4 632 . .	. . .	. . .	. . .	. . .	. . .	. . .	. . .	. . .
Banks	4 633 . .	. . .	. . .	. . .	. . .	. . .	. . .	. . .	. . .
Other sectors	4 634 . .	. . .	. . .	. . .	. . .	. . .	. . .	. . .	. . .
Liabilities	4 652 . .	**. . .**	**. . .**	**. . .**	**. . .**	**. . .**	**. . .**	**. . .**	**. . .**
Equity securities	4 660 . .	. . .	. . .	. . .	. . .	. . .	. . .	. . .	. . .
Banks	4 663 . .	. . .	. . .	. . .	. . .	. . .	. . .	. . .	. . .
Other sectors	4 664 . .	. . .	. . .	. . .	. . .	. . .	. . .	. . .	. . .
Debt securities	4 669 . .	. . .	. . .	. . .	. . .	. . .	. . .	. . .	. . .
Bonds and notes	4 670 . .	. . .	. . .	. . .	. . .	. . .	. . .	. . .	. . .
Monetary authorities	4 671 . .	. . .	. . .	. . .	. . .	. . .	. . .	. . .	. . .
General government	4 672 . .	. . .	. . .	. . .	. . .	. . .	. . .	. . .	. . .
Banks	4 673 . .	. . .	. . .	. . .	. . .	. . .	. . .	. . .	. . .
Other sectors	4 674 . .	. . .	. . .	. . .	. . .	. . .	. . .	. . .	. . .
Money market instruments	4 680 . .	. . .	. . .	. . .	. . .	. . .	. . .	. . .	. . .
Monetary authorities	4 681 . .	. . .	. . .	. . .	. . .	. . .	. . .	. . .	. . .
General government	4 682 . .	. . .	. . .	. . .	. . .	. . .	. . .	. . .	. . .
Banks	4 683 . .	. . .	. . .	. . .	. . .	. . .	. . .	. . .	. . .
Other sectors	4 684 . .	. . .	. . .	. . .	. . .	. . .	. . .	. . .	. . .
C. FINANCIAL DERIVATIVES	4 910 . .	. . .	. . .	. . .	. . .	. . .	. . .	. . .	. . .
Monetary authorities	4 911 . .	. . .	. . .	. . .	. . .	. . .	. . .	. . .	. . .
General government	4 912 . .	. . .	. . .	. . .	. . .	. . .	. . .	. . .	. . .
Banks	4 913 . .	. . .	. . .	. . .	. . .	. . .	. . .	. . .	. . .
Other sectors	4 914 . .	. . .	. . .	. . .	. . .	. . .	. . .	. . .	. . .
Assets	4 900 . .	**. . .**	**. . .**	**. . .**	**. . .**	**. . .**	**. . .**	**. . .**	**. . .**
Monetary authorities	4 901 . .	. . .	. . .	. . .	. . .	. . .	. . .	. . .	. . .
General government	4 902 . .	. . .	. . .	. . .	. . .	. . .	. . .	. . .	. . .
Banks	4 903 . .	. . .	. . .	. . .	. . .	. . .	. . .	. . .	. . .
Other sectors	4 904 . .	. . .	. . .	. . .	. . .	. . .	. . .	. . .	. . .
Liabilities	4 905 . .	**. . .**	**. . .**	**. . .**	**. . .**	**. . .**	**. . .**	**. . .**	**. . .**
Monetary authorities	4 906 . .	. . .	. . .	. . .	. . .	. . .	. . .	. . .	. . .
General government	4 907 . .	. . .	. . .	. . .	. . .	. . .	. . .	. . .	. . .
Banks	4 908 . .	. . .	. . .	. . .	. . .	. . .	. . .	. . .	. . .
Other sectors	4 909 . .	. . .	. . .	. . .	. . .	. . .	. . .	. . .	. . .

Table 2 (Concluded). STANDARD PRESENTATION, 1994–2001
(Millions of U.S. dollars)

	Code	1994	1995	1996	1997	1998	1999	2000	2001
D. OTHER INVESTMENT	4 700 . .	18.0	71.0	59.8	51.3	46.4	–33.4	–37.8	–23.4
Assets	4 703 . .	**–13.4**	**18.8**	**–7.0**	**–5.0**	**–1.7**	**–11.0**	**–19.1**	**–20.2**
Trade credits	4 706 . .	...	...	...	...	...	...	...	...
General government	4 707 . .	...	...	...	...	...	...	...	...
of which: Short-term	4 709 . .	...	...	...	...	...	...	...	...
Other sectors	4 710 . .	...	...	...	...	...	...	...	...
of which: Short-term	4 712 . .	...	...	...	...	...	...	...	...
Loans	4 714 . .	...	...	...	...	...	...	...	...
Monetary authorities	4 715 . .	...	...	...	...	...	...	...	...
of which: Short-term	4 718 . .	...	...	...	...	...	...	...	...
General government	4 719 . .	...	...	...	...	...	...	...	...
of which: Short-term	4 721 . .	...	...	...	...	...	...	...	...
Banks	4 722 . .	...	...	...	...	...	...	...	...
of which: Short-term	4 724 . .	...	...	...	...	...	...	...	...
Other sectors	4 725 . .	...	...	...	...	...	...	...	...
of which: Short-term	4 727 . .	...	...	...	...	...	...	...	...
Currency and deposits	4 730 . .	–13.4	18.8	–7.0	–5.0	–1.7	–11.0	–19.1	–20.2
Monetary authorities	4 731 . .	...	...	...	...	...	...	...	...
General government	4 732 . .	...	...	...	...	...	...	...	...
Banks	4 733 . .	–13.4	18.8	–7.0	–5.0	–1.7	–11.0	–19.1	–20.2
Other sectors	4 734 . .	...	...	...	...	...	...	...	...
Other assets	4 736 . .	...	...	...	...	...	...	...	...
Monetary authorities	4 737 . .	...	...	...	...	...	...	...	...
of which: Short-term	4 739 . .	...	...	...	...	...	...	...	...
General government	4 740 . .	...	...	...	...	...	...	...	...
of which: Short-term	4 742 . .	...	...	...	...	...	...	...	...
Banks	4 743 . .	...	...	...	...	...	...	...	...
of which: Short-term	4 745 . .	...	...	...	...	...	...	...	...
Other sectors	4 746 . .	...	...	...	...	...	...	...	...
of which: Short-term	4 748 . .	...	...	...	...	...	...	...	...
Liabilities	4 753 . .	**31.4**	**52.3**	**66.7**	**56.2**	**48.1**	**–22.5**	**–18.7**	**–3.2**
Trade credits	4 756 . .	...	...	...	...	...	...	...	...
General government	4 757 . .	...	...	...	...	...	...	...	...
of which: Short-term	4 759 . .	...	...	...	...	...	...	...	...
Other sectors	4 760 . .	...	...	...	...	...	...	...	...
of which: Short-term	4 762 . .	...	...	...	...	...	...	...	...
Loans	4 764 . .	29.3	45.9	66.9	63.4	54.7	–15.8	–20.4	–14.4
Monetary authorities	4 765 . .	3.8	–2.7	–3.4	–4.3	–4.9	–5.9	–5.2	4.5
of which: Use of Fund credit and loans from the Fund	4 766 . .	*3.8*	*–2.7*	*–3.4*	*–4.3*	*–4.9*	*–5.9*	*–5.2*	*4.5*
of which: Short-term	4 768 . .	...	...	...	...	...	...	...	...
General government	4 769 . .	26.0	49.2	71.8	68.6	59.8	–9.3	–15.1	–19.0
of which: Short-term	4 771 . .	...	...	...	...	...	...	...	...
Banks	4 772 . .	...	...	...	...	...	...	...	...
of which: Short-term	4 774 . .	...	...	...	...	...	...	...	...
Other sectors	4 775 . .	–.5	–.5	–1.4	–.9	–.1	–.6	–.1	...
of which: Short-term	4 777 . .	...	...	...	...	...	...	...	...
Currency and deposits	4 780 . .	1.9	6.6	–.4	–7.2	–6.7	...	...	...
Monetary authorities	4 781 . .	...	6.6	–.4	...	...	...	...	...
General government	4 782 . .	...	...	...	...	...	...	...	...
Banks	4 783 . .	1.9	...	...	–7.2	–6.7	...	...	...
Other sectors	4 784 . .	...	...	...	...	...	...	...	...
Other liabilities	4 786 . .	.3	–.2	.2	...	.1	–6.6	1.7	11.2
Monetary authorities	4 787 . .	.3	–.2	.2	...	.1	–5.4	–3.5	16.0
of which: Short-term	4 789 . .	*.3*	...	...	...	*.1*	*–5.4*	*–3.5*	*16.0*
General government	4 790 . .	...	...	...	...	...	...	...	...
of which: Short-term	4 792 . .	...	...	...	...	...	...	...	...
Banks	4 793 . .	...	...	...	...	...	–1.2	5.2	–4.8
of which: Short-term	4 795 . .	...	...	...	...	...	*–1.2*	*5.2*	*–4.8*
Other sectors	4 796 . .	...	...	...	...	...	...	...	...
of which: Short-term	4 798 . .	...	...	...	...	...	...	...	...
E. RESERVE ASSETS	4 802 . .	–124.6	–95.1	–113.5	–136.8	–110.7	46.7	–12.6	–170.2
Monetary gold	4 812 . .	...	...	...	...	...	...	...	...
Special drawing rights	4 811 . .	.1	.1	–1.0	...	...	...	.5	.1
Reserve position in the Fund	4 810 . .	...	...	...	...	...	...	...	...
Foreign exchange	4 803 . .	–124.8	–95.2	–112.5	–136.8	–110.7	46.7	–13.1	–170.2
Other claims	4 813 . .	...	...	...	...	...	...	...	...
NET ERRORS AND OMISSIONS	4 998 . .	**–20.3**	**28.1**	**23.3**	**42.1**	**56.8**	**29.0**	**62.1**	**154.7**

Part 3 of the *Yearbook* contains descriptions of the methodologies, compilation practices, and sources used to compile these data.

Table 3. INTERNATIONAL INVESTMENT POSITION (End-period stocks), 1994–2001
(Millions of U.S. dollars)

	Code	1994	1995	1996	1997	1998	1999	2000	2001
ASSETS	8 995 C.	...	...	...	...	...	...	...	...
Direct investment abroad	8 505 . .	**...**	**...**	**...**	**...**	**...**	**...**	**...**	**...**
Equity capital and reinvested earnings	8 506 . .	...	...	...	...	...	...	...	...
Claims on affiliated enterprises	8 507 . .	...	...	...	...	...	...	...	...
Liabilities to affiliated enterprises	8 508 . .	...	...	...	...	...	...	...	...
Other capital	8 530 . .	...	...	...	...	...	...	...	...
Claims on affiliated enterprises	8 535 . .	...	...	...	...	...	...	...	...
Liabilities to affiliated enterprises	8 540 . .	...	...	...	...	...	...	...	...
Portfolio investment	8 602 . .	**...**	**...**	**...**	**...**	**...**	**...**	**...**	**...**
Equity securities	8 610 . .	...	...	...	...	...	...	...	...
Monetary authorities	8 611 . .	...	...	...	...	...	...	...	...
General government	8 612 . .	...	...	...	...	...	...	...	...
Banks	8 613 . .	...	...	...	...	...	...	...	...
Other sectors	8 614 . .	...	...	...	...	...	...	...	...
Debt securities	8 619 . .	...	...	...	...	...	...	...	...
Bonds and notes	8 620 . .	...	...	...	...	...	...	...	...
Monetary authorities	8 621 . .	...	...	...	...	...	...	...	...
General government	8 622 . .	...	...	...	...	...	...	...	...
Banks	8 623 . .	...	...	...	...	...	...	...	...
Other sectors	8 624 . .	...	...	...	...	...	...	...	...
Money market instruments	8 630 . .	...	...	...	...	...	...	...	...
Monetary authorities	8 631 . .	...	...	...	...	...	...	...	...
General government	8 632 . .	...	...	...	...	...	...	...	...
Banks	8 633 . .	...	...	...	...	...	...	...	...
Other sectors	8 634 . .	...	...	...	...	...	...	...	...
Financial derivatives	8 900 . .	**...**	**...**	**...**	**...**	**...**	**...**	**...**	**...**
Monetary authorities	8 901 . .	...	...	...	...	...	...	...	...
General government	8 902 . .	...	...	...	...	...	...	...	...
Banks	8 903 . .	...	...	...	...	...	...	...	...
Other sectors	8 904 . .	...	...	...	...	...	...	...	...
Other investment	8 703 . .	**...**	**71.8**	**61.9**	**114.5**	**83.8**	**79.6**	**80.5**	**65.1**
Trade credits	8 706 . .	...	...	...	...	...	...	...	...
General government	8 707 . .	...	...	...	...	...	...	...	...
of which: Short-term	8 709 . .	...	...	...	...	...	...	...	...
Other sectors	8 710 . .	...	...	...	...	...	...	...	...
of which: Short-term	8 712 . .	...	...	...	...	...	...	...	...
Loans	8 714 . .	...	...	...	...	...	...	...	...
Monetary authorities	8 715 . .	...	...	...	...	...	...	...	...
of which: Short-term	8 718 . .	...	...	...	...	...	...	...	...
General government	8 719 . .	...	...	...	...	...	...	...	...
of which: Short-term	8 721 . .	...	...	...	...	...	...	...	...
Banks	8 722 . .	...	...	...	...	...	...	...	...
of which: Short-term	8 724 . .	...	...	...	...	...	...	...	...
Other sectors	8 725 . .	...	...	...	...	...	...	...	...
of which: Short-term	8 727 . .	...	...	...	...	...	...	...	...
Currency and deposits	8 730 . .	...	6.9	3.7	2.6	2.0	79.6	80.5	65.1
Monetary authorities	8 731 . .	...	...	...	...	...	...	...	...
General government	8 732 . .	...	...	...	...	...	...	...	...
Banks	8 733 . .	...	6.9	3.7	2.6	2.0	79.6	80.5	65.1
Other sectors	8 734 . .	...	...	...	...	...	...	...	...
Other assets	8 736 . .	...	64.9	58.3	111.9	81.8	...	...	...
Monetary authorities	8 737 . .	...	...	...	...	...	...	...	...
of which: Short-term	8 739 . .	...	...	...	...	...	...	...	...
General government	8 740 . .	...	...	...	...	...	...	...	...
of which: Short-term	8 742 . .	...	...	...	...	...	...	...	...
Banks	8 743 . .	...	64.9	58.3	111.9	81.8	...	...	...
of which: Short-term	8 745 . .	...	*64.9*	*58.3*	*111.9*	*81.8*	...	...	...
Other sectors	8 746 . .	...	...	...	...	...	...	...	...
of which: Short-term	8 748 . .	...	...	...	...	...	...	...	...
Reserve assets	8 802 . .	**...**	**456.7**	**460.5**	**571.7**	**575.1**	**499.8**	**419.8**	**423.7**
Monetary gold	8 812 . .	...	...	...	...	...	...	...	...
Special drawing rights	8 811 . .	.5	.3	1.3	1.2	1.2	1.2	.7	.6
Reserve position in the Fund	8 810 . .	5.1	5.2	5.0	4.8	5.0	4.8	4.6	4.4
Foreign exchange	8 803 . .	...	211.6	307.3	422.7	411.9	493.8	414.6	418.7
Other claims	8 813 . .	...	239.6	146.9	143.1	157.0	...	...	...

Table 3 (Concluded). INTERNATIONAL INVESTMENT POSITION (End–period stocks), 1994–2001
(Millions of U.S. dollars)

	Code		1994	1995	1996	1997	1998	1999	2000	2001
LIABILITIES	8 995	D.	...	...	...	...	...	...	...	...
Direct investment in Lesotho	8 555	..	**...**	**...**	**...**	**...**	**...**	**...**	**...**	**...**
Equity capital and reinvested earnings	8 556	..	...	...	...	...	...	...	...	...
Claims on direct investors	8 557	..	...	...	...	...	...	...	...	...
Liabilities to direct investors	8 558	..	...	...	...	...	...	...	...	...
Other capital	8 580	..	...	...	...	...	...	...	...	...
Claims on direct investors	8 585	..	...	...	...	...	...	...	...	...
Liabilities to direct investors	8 590	..	...	...	...	...	...	...	...	...
Portfolio investment	8 652	..	**...**	**...**	**...**	**...**	**...**	**...**	**...**	**...**
Equity securities	8 660	..	...	...	...	...	...	...	...	...
Banks	8 663	..	...	...	...	...	...	...	...	...
Other sectors	8 664	..	...	...	...	...	...	...	...	...
Debt securities	8 669	..	...	...	...	...	...	...	...	...
Bonds and notes	8 670	..	...	...	...	...	...	...	...	...
Monetary authorities	8 671	..	...	...	...	...	...	...	...	...
General government	8 672	..	...	...	...	...	...	...	...	...
Banks	8 673	..	...	...	...	...	...	...	...	...
Other sectors	8 674	..	...	...	...	...	...	...	...	...
Money market instruments	8 680	..	...	...	...	...	...	...	...	...
Monetary authorities	8 681	..	...	...	...	...	...	...	...	...
General government	8 682	..	...	...	...	...	...	...	...	...
Banks	8 683	..	...	...	...	...	...	...	...	...
Other sectors	8 684	..	...	...	...	...	...	...	...	...
Financial derivatives	8 905	..	**...**	**...**	**...**	**...**	**...**	**...**	**...**	**...**
Monetary authorities	8 906	..	...	...	...	...	...	...	...	...
General government	8 907	..	...	...	...	...	...	...	...	...
Banks	8 908	..	...	...	...	...	...	...	...	...
Other sectors	8 909	..	...	...	...	...	...	...	...	...
Other investment	8 753	..	**...**	**566.8**	**535.6**	**512.6**	**590.7**	**559.5**	**600.9**	**580.9**
Trade credits	8 756	..	...	...	...	...	...	...	...	...
General government	8 757	..	...	...	...	...	...	...	...	...
of which: Short-term	8 759	..	...	...	...	...	...	...	...	...
Other sectors	8 760	..	...	...	...	...	...	...	...	...
of which: Short-term	8 762	..	...	...	...	...	...	...	...	...
Loans	8 764	..	...	548.7	521.5	502.8	567.1	17.1	11.1	530.4
Monetary authorities	8 765	..	...	38.4	33.8	27.5	23.6	17.1	11.1	15.2
of which: Use of Fund credit and loans from the Fund	8 766	..	*40.3*	*38.4*	*33.8*	*27.5*	*23.6*	*17.1*	*11.1*	*15.2*
of which: Short-term	8 768	..	...	...	...	...	...	...	...	...
General government	8 769	..	...	510.3	487.7	475.3	543.5	...	...	515.1
of which: Short-term	8 771	..	...	...	...	...	...	...	...	...
Banks	8 772	..	...	...	...	...	...	...	...	...
of which: Short-term	8 774	..	...	...	...	...	...	...	...	...
Other sectors	8 775	..	...	...	...	...	...	...	...	...
of which: Short-term	8 777	..	...	...	...	...	...	...	...	...
Currency and deposits	8 780	..	...	16.5	12.8	8.5	22.4	1.1	.6	8.5
Monetary authorities	8 781	..	...	...	...	...	...	1.1	.6	...
General government	8 782	..	...	...	...	...	...	...	...	...
Banks	8 783	..	...	16.5	12.8	8.5	22.4	...	...	8.5
Other sectors	8 784	..	...	...	...	...	...	...	...	...
Other liabilities	8 786	..	...	1.6	1.3	1.3	1.1	541.3	589.2	42.0
Monetary authorities	8 787	..	...	1.6	1.3	1.3	1.1	...	...	42.0
of which: Short-term	8 789	..	...	*1.6*	*1.3*	*1.3*	*1.1*	...	...	...
General government	8 790	..	...	...	...	...	...	534.8	570.7	...
of which: Short-term	8 792	..	...	...	...	...	...	...	...	...
Banks	8 793	..	...	...	...	...	...	6.5	18.5	...
of which: Short-term	8 795	..	...	...	...	...	...	...	...	...
Other sectors	8 796	..	...	...	...	...	...	...	...	...
of which: Short-term	8 798	..	...	...	...	...	...	...	...	...
NET INTERNATIONAL INVESTMENT POSITION	8 995	..	**...**	**...**	**...**	**...**	**...**	**...**	**...**	**...**
Conversion rates: maloti per U.S. dollar (end of period)	0 102	..	**3.5435**	**3.6475**	**4.6825**	**4.8675**	**5.8600**	**6.1545**	**7.5685**	**12.1265**

Table 1. ANALYTIC PRESENTATION, 1994–2001
(Millions of U.S. dollars)

	Code	1994	1995	1996	1997	1998	1999	2000	2001
A. Current Account [1]	4 993 Z.	**29**	**1,998**	**1,477**	**1,875**	**–391**	**1,984**	...	...
Goods: exports f.o.b	2 100 . .	8,365	9,038	9,578	9,876	6,328	6,758	...	...
Goods: imports f.o.b	3 100 . .	–7,339	–6,257	–7,059	–7,160	–5,857	–3,996	...	...
Balance on Goods	4 100 . .	*1,026*	*2,781*	*2,519*	*2,716*	*471*	*2,762*	...	...
Services: credit	2 200 . .	40	37	31	33	47	55	...	...
Services: debit	3 200 . .	–780	–716	–951	–920	–1,016	–918	...	...
Balance on Goods and Services	4 991 . .	*286*	*2,102*	*1,599*	*1,829*	*–498*	*1,899*	...	...
Income: credit	2 300 . .	487	526	573	640	633	507	...	...
Income: debit	3 300 . .	–438	–365	–356	–354	–259	–218	...	...
Balance on Goods, Services, and Income	4 992 . .	*335*	*2,263*	*1,816*	*2,115*	*–124*	*2,187*	...	...
Current transfers: credit	2 379 Z.	5	5	3	4	5	6	...	...
Current transfers: debit	3 379 . .	–311	–270	–342	–244	–272	–210	...	...
B. Capital Account [1]	4 994 Z.	...	...	...	...	...	...	...	...
Capital account: credit	2 994 Z.	...	...	...	...	...	...	...	...
Capital account: debit	3 994 . .	...	...	...	...	...	...	...	...
Total, Groups A Plus B	4 981 . .	*29*	*1,998*	*1,477*	*1,875*	*–391*	*1,984*	...	...
C. Financial Account [1]	4 995 W.	**160**	**–250**	**224**	**–884**	**–555**	**–971**	...	...
Direct investment abroad	4 505 . .	–28	–83	–63	–282	–304	–210	...	...
Direct investment in Libya	4 555 Z.	–79	–107	–135	–82	–152	–119	...	...
Portfolio investment assets	4 602 . .	–137	–128	...	–774	–212	–3	...	...
Equity securities	4 610 . .	–137	–128	...	–774	–212	–3	...	...
Debt securities	4 619 . .	...	...	...	...	...	...	...	...
Portfolio investment liabilities	4 652 Z.	...	...	...	...	...	...	...	...
Equity securities	4 660 . .	...	...	...	...	...	...	...	...
Debt securities	4 669 Z.	...	...	...	...	...	...	...	...
Financial derivatives	4 910 . .	...	...	...	...	...	...	...	...
Financial derivatives assets	4 900 . .	...	...	...	...	...	...	...	...
Financial derivatives liabilities	4 905 . .	...	...	...	...	...	...	...	...
Other investment assets	4 703 . .	–1,904	–1,646	–1,734	–1,040	–164	–293	...	...
Monetary authorities	4 701 . .	–10	46	–33	46	–7	–604	...	...
General government	4 704 . .	–1,876	–1,657	–1,540	–678	–591	461	...	...
Banks	4 705 . .	–18	–35	–161	–408	434	–150	...	...
Other sectors	4 728 . .	...	...	...	...	...	...	...	...
Other investment liabilities	4 753 W.	2,308	1,714	2,156	1,294	277	–346	...	...
Monetary authorities	4 753 WA	184	207	443	–219	–6	–72	...	...
General government	4 753 ZB	2,109	1,571	1,681	1,576	263	–214	...	...
Banks	4 753 ZC	15	–64	32	–63	20	–60	...	...
Other sectors	4 753 ZD	...	...	...	...	...	...	...	...
Total, Groups A Through C	4 983 . .	*189*	*1,748*	*1,701*	*991*	*–945*	*1,013*	...	...
D. Net Errors and Omissions	4 998 . .	**106**	**299**	**–234**	**878**	**432**	**–372**	...	...
Total, Groups A Through D	4 984 . .	*295*	*2,047*	*1,467*	*1,869*	*–513*	*641*	...	...
E. Reserves and Related Items	4 802 A.	**–295**	**–2,047**	**–1,467**	**–1,869**	**513**	**–641**	...	...
Reserve assets	4 802 . .	–295	–2,047	–1,467	–1,869	513	–641	...	...
Use of Fund credit and loans	4 766 . .	...	...	...	...	...	...	...	...
Exceptional financing	4 920 . .	...	...	...	...	...	...	...	...
Conversion rates: Libyan dinar per U.S. dollar	0 101 . .	**.3209**	**.3462**	**.3617**	**.3816**	**.3936**	**.4994**	**.5096**	**.5968**

[1] Excludes components that have been classified in the categories of Group E.

Table 2. STANDARD PRESENTATION, 1994–2001

(Millions of U.S. dollars)

	Code		1994	1995	1996	1997	1998	1999	2000	2001
CURRENT ACCOUNT	4 993	. .	**29**	**1,998**	**1,477**	**1,875**	**–391**	**1,984**	**. . .**	**. . .**
A. GOODS	4 100	. .	1,026	2,781	2,519	2,716	471	2,762	. . .	. . .
Credit	2 100	. .	**8,365**	**9,038**	**9,578**	**9,876**	**6,328**	**6,758**	**. . .**	**. . .**
General merchandise: exports f.o.b.	2 110	. .	8,365	9,038	9,578	9,876	6,328	6,758	. . .	. . .
Goods for processing: exports f.o.b.	2 150	. .	. . .	. . .	. . .	. . .	. . .	. . .	. . .	. . .
Repairs on goods	2 160	. .	. . .	. . .	. . .	. . .	. . .	. . .	. . .	. . .
Goods procured in ports by carriers	2 170	. .	. . .	. . .	. . .	. . .	. . .	. . .	. . .	. . .
Nonmonetary gold	2 180	. .	. . .	. . .	. . .	. . .	. . .	. . .	. . .	. . .
Debit	3 100	. .	**–7,339**	**–6,257**	**–7,059**	**–7,160**	**–5,857**	**–3,996**	**. . .**	**. . .**
General merchandise: imports f.o.b.	3 110	. .	–7,324	–6,242	–7,045	–7,146	–5,837	–3,996	. . .	. . .
Goods for processing: imports f.o.b.	3 150	. .	. . .	. . .	. . .	. . .	. . .	. . .	. . .	. . .
Repairs on goods	3 160	. .	. . .	. . .	. . .	. . .	. . .	. . .	. . .	. . .
Goods procured in ports by carriers	3 170	. .	. . .	. . .	. . .	. . .	. . .	. . .	. . .	. . .
Nonmonetary gold	3 180	. .	–15	–15	–14	–14	–20	. . .	. . .	. . .
B. SERVICES	4 200	. .	–740	–679	–920	–887	–969	–864	. . .	. . .
Total credit	2 200	. .	*40*	*37*	*31*	*33*	*47*	*55*	. . .	. . .
Total debit	3 200	. .	*–780*	*–716*	*–951*	*–920*	*–1,016*	*–918*	. . .	. . .
Transportation services, credit	2 205	. .	**17**	**15**	**13**	**13**	**25**	**18**	**. . .**	**. . .**
Passenger	2 850	. .	*2*	*2*	*2*	*1*	*19*	*11*	. . .	. . .
Freight	2 851	. .	. . .	. . .	. . .	. . .	. . .	. . .	. . .	. . .
Other	2 852	. .	*15*	*13*	*11*	*12*	*6*	*6*	. . .	. . .
Sea transport, passenger	2 207	. .	. . .	. . .	. . .	. . .	. . .	. . .	. . .	. . .
Sea transport, freight	2 208	. .	. . .	. . .	. . .	. . .	. . .	. . .	. . .	. . .
Sea transport, other	2 209	. .	. . .	. . .	. . .	. . .	. . .	. . .	. . .	. . .
Air transport, passenger	2 211	. .	. . .	. . .	. . .	. . .	. . .	. . .	. . .	. . .
Air transport, freight	2 212	. .	. . .	. . .	. . .	. . .	. . .	. . .	. . .	. . .
Air transport, other	2 213	. .	. . .	. . .	. . .	. . .	. . .	. . .	. . .	. . .
Other transport, passenger	2 215	. .	. . .	. . .	. . .	. . .	. . .	. . .	. . .	. . .
Other transport, freight	2 216	. .	. . .	. . .	. . .	. . .	. . .	. . .	. . .	. . .
Other transport, other	2 217	. .	. . .	. . .	. . .	. . .	. . .	. . .	. . .	. . .
Transportation services, debit	3 205	. .	**–455**	**–394**	**–682**	**–413**	**–459**	**–376**	**. . .**	**. . .**
Passenger	3 850	. .	*–31*	*–22*	*–18*	*–17*	*–142*	*–160*	. . .	. . .
Freight	3 851	. .	*–401*	*–361*	*–652*	*–382*	*–308*	*–200*	. . .	. . .
Other	3 852	. .	*–23*	*–11*	*–12*	*–14*	*–9*	*–17*	. . .	. . .
Sea transport, passenger	3 207	. .	. . .	. . .	. . .	. . .	. . .	. . .	. . .	. . .
Sea transport, freight	3 208	. .	. . .	. . .	. . .	. . .	. . .	. . .	. . .	. . .
Sea transport, other	3 209	. .	. . .	. . .	. . .	. . .	. . .	. . .	. . .	. . .
Air transport, passenger	3 211	. .	. . .	. . .	. . .	. . .	. . .	. . .	. . .	. . .
Air transport, freight	3 212	. .	. . .	. . .	. . .	. . .	. . .	. . .	. . .	. . .
Air transport, other	3 213	. .	. . .	. . .	. . .	. . .	. . .	. . .	. . .	. . .
Other transport, passenger	3 215	. .	–31	–22	–18	–17	–142	. . .	. . .	. . .
Other transport, freight	3 216	. .	. . .	. . .	. . .	. . .	. . .	. . .	. . .	. . .
Other transport, other	3 217	. .	. . .	. . .	. . .	. . .	. . .	. . .	. . .	. . .
Travel, credit	2 236	. .	**3**	**3**	**2**	**2**	**9**	**25**	**. . .**	**. . .**
Business travel	2 237	. .	. . .	. . .	. . .	. . .	. . .	. . .	. . .	. . .
Personal travel	2 240	. .	. . .	. . .	. . .	. . .	. . .	. . .	. . .	. . .
Travel, debit	3 236	. .	**–126**	**–92**	**–81**	**–325**	**–334**	**–373**	**. . .**	**. . .**
Business travel	3 237	. .	. . .	. . .	. . .	. . .	. . .	. . .	. . .	. . .
Personal travel	3 240	. .	. . .	. . .	. . .	. . .	. . .	. . .	. . .	. . .
Other services, credit	2 200	BA	**20**	**19**	**16**	**18**	**13**	**12**	**. . .**	**. . .**
Communications	2 245	. .	. . .	. . .	. . .	. . .	. . .	. . .	. . .	. . .
Construction	2 249	. .	. . .	. . .	. . .	. . .	. . .	. . .	. . .	. . .
Insurance	2 253	. .	. . .	. . .	. . .	. . .	. . .	. . .	. . .	. . .
Financial	2 260	. .	. . .	. . .	. . .	. . .	. . .	. . .	. . .	. . .
Computer and information	2 262	. .	. . .	. . .	. . .	. . .	. . .	. . .	. . .	. . .
Royalties and licence fees	2 266	. .	. . .	. . .	. . .	. . .	. . .	. . .	. . .	. . .
Other business services	2 268	. .	5	6	5	5	3	4	. . .	. . .
Personal, cultural, and recreational	2 287	. .	. . .	. . .	. . .	. . .	. . .	. . .	. . .	. . .
Government, n.i.e.	2 291	. .	15	13	11	13	10	8	. . .	. . .
Other services, debit	3 200	BA	**–199**	**–230**	**–188**	**–182**	**–223**	**–169**	**. . .**	**. . .**
Communications	3 245	. .	. . .	. . .	. . .	. . .	. . .	. . .	. . .	. . .
Construction	3 249	. .	. . .	. . .	. . .	. . .	. . .	. . .	. . .	. . .
Insurance	3 253	. .	. . .	. . .	. . .	. . .	. . .	. . .	. . .	. . .
Financial	3 260	. .	. . .	. . .	. . .	. . .	. . .	. . .	. . .	. . .
Computer and information	3 262	. .	. . .	. . .	. . .	. . .	. . .	. . .	. . .	. . .
Royalties and licence fees	3 266	. .	. . .	. . .	. . .	. . .	. . .	. . .	. . .	. . .
Other business services	3 268	. .	–124	–152	–116	–115	–122	–74	. . .	. . .
Personal, cultural, and recreational	3 287	. .	. . .	. . .	. . .	. . .	. . .	. . .	. . .	. . .
Government, n.i.e.	3 291	. .	–75	–78	–72	–67	–101	–95	. . .	. . .

Table 2 (Continued). STANDARD PRESENTATION, 1994–2001

(Millions of U.S. dollars)

	Code	1994	1995	1996	1997	1998	1999	2000	2001
C. INCOME	4 300 . .	49	161	217	286	374	289	...	...
Total credit	2 300 . .	*487*	*526*	*573*	*640*	*633*	*507*	...	...
Total debit	3 300 . .	*–438*	*–365*	*–356*	*–354*	*–259*	*–218*	...	...
Compensation of employees, credit	2 310 . .	**...**	**...**	**...**	**...**	**...**	**...**	**...**	**...**
Compensation of employees, debit	3 310 . .	**...**	**...**	**...**	**...**	**...**	**...**	**...**	**...**
Investment income, credit	2 320 . .	**487**	**526**	**573**	**640**	**633**	**507**	**...**	**...**
Direct investment income	2 330 . .	16	16	15	14	24	20	...	...
Dividends and distributed branch profits	2 332 . .	16	16	15	14	24	20	...	...
Reinvested earnings and undistributed branch profits	2 333 . .	...	...	...	...	...	...	...	...
Income on debt (interest)	2 334 . .	...	...	...	...	...	...	...	...
Portfolio investment income	2 339 . .	...	...	...	...	...	...	...	...
Income on equity	2 340 . .	...	...	...	...	...	...	...	...
Income on bonds and notes	2 350 . .	...	...	...	...	...	...	...	...
Income on money market instruments	2 360 . .	...	...	...	...	...	...	...	...
Other investment income	2 370 . .	471	510	558	626	609	487	...	...
Investment income, debit	3 320 . .	**–438**	**–365**	**–356**	**–354**	**–259**	**–218**	**...**	**...**
Direct investment income	3 330 . .	–383	–306	–234	–235	–168	–156	...	...
Dividends and distributed branch profits	3 332 . .	–383	–306	–234	–235	–168	–156	...	...
Reinvested earnings and undistributed branch profits	3 333 . .	...	...	...	...	...	...	...	...
Income on debt (interest)	3 334 . .	...	...	...	...	...	...	...	...
Portfolio investment income	3 339 . .	...	...	...	...	...	...	...	...
Income on equity	3 340 . .	...	...	...	...	...	...	...	...
Income on bonds and notes	3 350 . .	...	...	...	...	...	...	...	...
Income on money market instruments	3 360 . .	...	...	...	...	...	...	...	...
Other investment income	3 370 . .	–55	–59	–122	–119	–91	–62	...	...
D. CURRENT TRANSFERS	4 379 . .	–306	–265	–339	–240	–267	–203	...	...
Credit	2 379 . .	**5**	**5**	**3**	**4**	**5**	**6**	**...**	**...**
General government	2 380 . .	5	5	3	4	5	6	...	...
Other sectors	2 390 . .	...	...	...	...	...	...	...	...
Workers' remittances	2 391 . .	...	...	...	...	...	...	...	...
Other current transfers	2 392 . .	...	...	...	...	...	...	...	...
Debit	3 379 . .	**–311**	**–270**	**–342**	**–244**	**–272**	**–210**	**...**	**...**
General government	3 380 . .	–4	–2	–14	–12	–25	–12	...	...
Other sectors	3 390 . .	–307	–268	–328	–232	–247	–198	...	...
Workers' remittances	3 391 . .	–307	–268	–328	–232	–247	–198	...	...
Other current transfers	3 392 . .	...	...	...	...	...	...	...	...
CAPITAL AND FINANCIAL ACCOUNT	4 996 . .	**–135**	**–2,297**	**–1,243**	**–2,753**	**–42**	**–1,612**	**...**	**...**
CAPITAL ACCOUNT	4 994 . .	**...**	**...**	**...**	**...**	**...**	**...**	**...**	**...**
Total credit	2 994	...	...	...	...	...	...	...	...
Total debit	3 994 . .	...	...	...	...	...	...	...	...
Capital transfers, credit	2 400 . .	**...**	**...**	**...**	**...**	**...**	**...**	**...**	**...**
General government	2 401 . .	...	...	...	...	...	...	...	...
Debt forgiveness	2 402 . .	...	...	...	...	...	...	...	...
Other capital transfers	2 410 . .	...	...	...	...	...	...	...	...
Other sectors	2 430 . .	...	...	...	...	...	...	...	...
Migrants' transfers	2 431 . .	...	...	...	...	...	...	...	...
Debt forgiveness	2 432 . .	...	...	...	...	...	...	...	...
Other capital transfers	2 440 . .	...	...	...	...	...	...	...	...
Capital transfers, debit	3 400 . .	**...**	**...**	**...**	**...**	**...**	**...**	**...**	**...**
General government	3 401 . .	...	...	...	...	...	...	...	...
Debt forgiveness	3 402 . .	...	...	...	...	...	...	...	...
Other capital transfers	3 410 . .	...	...	...	...	...	...	...	...
Other sectors	3 430 . .	...	...	...	...	...	...	...	...
Migrants' transfers	3 431 . .	...	...	...	...	...	...	...	...
Debt forgiveness	3 432 . .	...	...	...	...	...	...	...	...
Other capital transfers	3 440 . .	...	...	...	...	...	...	...	...
Nonproduced nonfinancial assets, credit	2 480 . .	**...**	**...**	**...**	**...**	**...**	**...**	**...**	**...**
Nonproduced nonfinancial assets, debit	3 480 . .	**...**	**...**	**...**	**...**	**...**	**...**	**...**	**...**

Table 2 (Continued). STANDARD PRESENTATION, 1994–2001

(Millions of U.S. dollars)

	Code	1994	1995	1996	1997	1998	1999	2000	2001
FINANCIAL ACCOUNT	4 995	**–135**	**–2,297**	**–1,243**	**–2,753**	**–42**	**–1,612**	**...**	**...**
A. DIRECT INVESTMENT	4 500	–107	–190	–198	–364	–456	–329	...	...
Direct investment abroad	4 505	**–28**	**–83**	**–63**	**–282**	**–304**	**–210**	**...**	**...**
Equity capital	4 510	–28	–83	–63	–282	–304	–210	...	...
Claims on affiliated enterprises	4 515	...	...	...	...	...	...	...	...
Liabilities to affiliated enterprises	4 520	...	...	...	...	...	...	...	...
Reinvested earnings	4 525	...	...	...	...	...	...	...	...
Other capital	4 530	...	...	...	...	...	...	...	...
Claims on affiliated enterprises	4 535	...	...	...	...	...	...	...	...
Liabilities to affiliated enterprises	4 540	...	...	...	...	...	...	...	...
Direct investment in Libya	4 555	**–79**	**–107**	**–135**	**–82**	**–152**	**–119**	**...**	**...**
Equity capital	4 560	–79	–107	–135	–82	–152	–119	...	...
Claims on direct investors	4 565	...	...	...	...	...	...	...	...
Liabilities to direct investors	4 570	...	...	...	...	...	...	...	...
Reinvested earnings	4 575	...	...	...	...	...	...	...	...
Other capital	4 580	...	...	...	...	...	...	...	...
Claims on direct investors	4 585	...	...	...	...	...	...	...	...
Liabilities to direct investors	4 590	...	...	...	...	...	...	...	...
B. PORTFOLIO INVESTMENT	4 600	–137	–128	...	–774	–212	–3	...	...
Assets	4 602	**–137**	**–128**	**...**	**–774**	**–212**	**–3**	**...**	**...**
Equity securities	4 610	–137	–128	...	–774	–212	–3	...	...
Monetary authorities	4 611	...	...	...	...	...	...	...	...
General government	4 612	...	...	...	...	...	...	...	...
Banks	4 613	...	...	...	...	...	...	...	...
Other sectors	4 614	...	...	...	...	...	...	...	...
Debt securities	4 619	...	...	...	...	...	...	...	...
Bonds and notes	4 620	...	...	...	...	...	...	...	...
Monetary authorities	4 621	...	...	...	...	...	...	...	...
General government	4 622	...	...	...	...	...	...	...	...
Banks	4 623	...	...	...	...	...	...	...	...
Other sectors	4 624	...	...	...	...	...	...	...	...
Money market instruments	4 630	...	...	...	...	...	...	...	...
Monetary authorities	4 631	...	...	...	...	...	...	...	...
General government	4 632	...	...	...	...	...	...	...	...
Banks	4 633	...	...	...	...	...	...	...	...
Other sectors	4 634	...	...	...	...	...	...	...	...
Liabilities	4 652	**...**	**...**	**...**	**...**	**...**	**...**	**...**	**...**
Equity securities	4 660	...	...	...	...	...	...	...	...
Banks	4 663	...	...	...	...	...	...	...	...
Other sectors	4 664	...	...	...	...	...	...	...	...
Debt securities	4 669	...	...	...	...	...	...	...	...
Bonds and notes	4 670	...	...	...	...	...	...	...	...
Monetary authorities	4 671	...	...	...	...	...	...	...	...
General government	4 672	...	...	...	...	...	...	...	...
Banks	4 673	...	...	...	...	...	...	...	...
Other sectors	4 674	...	...	...	...	...	...	...	...
Money market instruments	4 680	...	...	...	...	...	...	...	...
Monetary authorities	4 681	...	...	...	...	...	...	...	...
General government	4 682	...	...	...	...	...	...	...	...
Banks	4 683	...	...	...	...	...	...	...	...
Other sectors	4 684	...	...	...	...	...	...	...	...
C. FINANCIAL DERIVATIVES	4 910	...	...	...	...	...	...	...	...
Monetary authorities	4 911	...	...	...	...	...	...	...	...
General government	4 912	...	...	...	...	...	...	...	...
Banks	4 913	...	...	...	...	...	...	...	...
Other sectors	4 914	...	...	...	...	...	...	...	...
Assets	4 900	**...**	**...**	**...**	**...**	**...**	**...**	**...**	**...**
Monetary authorities	4 901	...	...	...	...	...	...	...	...
General government	4 902	...	...	...	...	...	...	...	...
Banks	4 903	...	...	...	...	...	...	...	...
Other sectors	4 904	...	...	...	...	...	...	...	...
Liabilities	4 905	**...**	**...**	**...**	**...**	**...**	**...**	**...**	**...**
Monetary authorities	4 906	...	...	...	...	...	...	...	...
General government	4 907	...	...	...	...	...	...	...	...
Banks	4 908	...	...	...	...	...	...	...	...
Other sectors	4 909	...	...	...	...	...	...	...	...

Table 2 (Concluded). STANDARD PRESENTATION, 1994–2001

(Millions of U.S. dollars)

	Code	1994	1995	1996	1997	1998	1999	2000	2001
D. OTHER INVESTMENT	4 700 . .	404	68	422	254	113	–639	. . .	. . .
Assets	4 703 . .	**–1,904**	**–1,646**	**–1,734**	**–1,040**	**–164**	**–293**	**. . .**	**. . .**
Trade credits	4 706 . .	. . .	. . .	. . .	. . .	. . .	. . .	. . .	. . .
General government	4 707 . .	. . .	. . .	. . .	. . .	. . .	. . .	. . .	. . .
of which: Short-term	4 709 . .	. . .	. . .	. . .	. . .	. . .	. . .	. . .	. . .
Other sectors	4 710 . .	. . .	. . .	. . .	. . .	. . .	. . .	. . .	. . .
of which: Short-term	4 712 . .	. . .	. . .	. . .	. . .	. . .	. . .	. . .	. . .
Loans	4 714 . .	–729	–359	–116	–318	–548	–357	. . .	. . .
Monetary authorities	4 715 . .	–21	. . .	. . .	. . .	. . .	. . .	. . .	. . .
of which: Short-term	4 718 . .	. . .	. . .	. . .	. . .	. . .	. . .	. . .	. . .
General government	4 719 . .	–708	–359	–116	117	–548	–357	. . .	. . .
of which: Short-term	4 721 . .	*–222*	*9*	*–278*	*–158*	*–275*	*–206*	. . .	. . .
Banks	4 722 . .	. . .	. . .	. . .	–435	. . .	. . .	. . .	. . .
of which: Short-term	4 724 . .	. . .	. . .	. . .	*–435*	. . .	. . .	. . .	. . .
Other sectors	4 725 . .	. . .	. . .	. . .	. . .	. . .	. . .	. . .	. . .
of which: Short-term	4 727 . .	. . .	. . .	. . .	. . .	. . .	. . .	. . .	. . .
Currency and deposits	4 730 . .	. . .	. . .	. . .	. . .	. . .	. . .	. . .	. . .
Monetary authorities	4 731 . .	. . .	. . .	. . .	. . .	. . .	. . .	. . .	. . .
General government	4 732 . .	. . .	. . .	. . .	. . .	. . .	. . .	. . .	. . .
Banks	4 733 . .	. . .	. . .	. . .	. . .	. . .	. . .	. . .	. . .
Other sectors	4 734 . .	. . .	. . .	. . .	. . .	. . .	. . .	. . .	. . .
Other assets	4 736 . .	–1,175	–1,287	–1,618	–722	384	64	. . .	. . .
Monetary authorities	4 737 . .	11	46	–33	46	–7	–604	. . .	. . .
of which: Short-term	4 739 . .	*4*	*46*	*–33*	*46*	*31*	. . .	. . .	. . .
General government	4 740 . .	–1,168	–1,298	–1,424	–795	–43	817	. . .	. . .
of which: Short-term	4 742 . .	*–1,168*	*–1,298*	*–1,424*	*–795*	*–43*	*817*	. . .	. . .
Banks	4 743 . .	–18	–35	–161	27	434	–150	. . .	. . .
of which: Short-term	4 745 . .	*–19*	*–35*	*–137*	. . .	*438*	*–124*	. . .	. . .
Other sectors	4 746 . .	. . .	. . .	. . .	. . .	. . .	. . .	. . .	. . .
of which: Short-term	4 748 . .	. . .	. . .	. . .	. . .	. . .	. . .	. . .	. . .
Liabilities	4 753 . .	**2,308**	**1,714**	**2,156**	**1,294**	**277**	**–346**	**. . .**	**. . .**
Trade credits	4 756 . .	. . .	. . .	. . .	. . .	. . .	. . .	. . .	. . .
General government	4 757 . .	. . .	. . .	. . .	. . .	. . .	. . .	. . .	. . .
of which: Short-term	4 759 . .	. . .	. . .	. . .	. . .	. . .	. . .	. . .	. . .
Other sectors	4 760 . .	. . .	. . .	. . .	. . .	. . .	. . .	. . .	. . .
of which: Short-term	4 762 . .	. . .	. . .	. . .	. . .	. . .	. . .	. . .	. . .
Loans	4 764 . .	20	–72	86	15	–20	–72	. . .	. . .
Monetary authorities	4 765 . .	. . .	. . .	. . .	. . .	. . .	. . .	. . .	. . .
of which: Use of Fund credit and loans from the Fund	4 766 . .	. . .	. . .	. . .	. . .	. . .	. . .	. . .	. . .
of which: Short-term	4 768 . .	. . .	. . .	. . .	. . .	. . .	. . .	. . .	. . .
General government	4 769 . .	5	–8	39	15	–20	22	. . .	. . .
of which: Short-term	4 771 . .	*5*	*–8*	*39*	*15*	*–20*	*22*	. . .	. . .
Banks	4 772 . .	15	–64	47	. . .	. . .	–95	. . .	. . .
of which: Short-term	4 774 . .	. . .	. . .	. . .	. . .	. . .	. . .	. . .	. . .
Other sectors	4 775 . .	. . .	. . .	. . .	. . .	. . .	. . .	. . .	. . .
of which: Short-term	4 777 . .	. . .	. . .	. . .	. . .	. . .	. . .	. . .	. . .
Currency and deposits	4 780 . .	. . .	. . .	. . .	. . .	. . .	. . .	. . .	. . .
Monetary authorities	4 781 . .	. . .	. . .	. . .	. . .	. . .	. . .	. . .	. . .
General government	4 782 . .	. . .	. . .	. . .	. . .	. . .	. . .	. . .	. . .
Banks	4 783 . .	. . .	. . .	. . .	. . .	. . .	. . .	. . .	. . .
Other sectors	4 784 . .	. . .	. . .	. . .	. . .	. . .	. . .	. . .	. . .
Other liabilities	4 786 . .	2,288	1,786	2,070	1,279	297	–274	. . .	. . .
Monetary authorities	4 787 . .	184	207	443	–219	–6	–72	. . .	. . .
of which: Short-term	4 789 . .	*184*	*207*	*443*	*–219*	*–6*	*–72*	. . .	. . .
General government	4 790 . .	2,104	1,579	1,642	1,561	283	–236	. . .	. . .
of which: Short-term	4 792 . .	*2,104*	*1,579*	*1,642*	*1,561*	*283*	*–236*	. . .	. . .
Banks	4 793 . .	. . .	. . .	–15	–63	20	34	. . .	. . .
of which: Short-term	4 795 . .	. . .	. . .	*–15*	. . .	*–18*	*34*	. . .	. . .
Other sectors	4 796 . .	. . .	. . .	. . .	. . .	. . .	. . .	. . .	. . .
of which: Short-term	4 798 . .	. . .	. . .	. . .	. . .	. . .	. . .	. . .	. . .
E. RESERVE ASSETS	4 802 . .	–295	–2,047	–1,467	–1,869	513	–641	. . .	. . .
Monetary gold	4 812 . .	–14	–6	–2	–35	–2	. . .	. . .	. . .
Special drawing rights	4 811 . .	–31	–38	–35	–34	–37	74	. . .	. . .
Reserve position in the Fund	4 810 . .	. . .	. . .	. . .	. . .	. . .	–106	. . .	. . .
Foreign exchange	4 803 . .	–415	–3,191	40	–1,050	486	–272	. . .	. . .
Other claims	4 813 . .	165	1,188	–1,470	–750	66	–337	. . .	. . .
NET ERRORS AND OMISSIONS	4 998 . .	**106**	**299**	**–234**	**878**	**432**	**–372**	**. . .**	**. . .**

Table 1. ANALYTIC PRESENTATION, 1994–2001
(Millions of U.S. dollars)

	Code	1994	1995	1996	1997	1998	1999	2000	2001
A. Current Account [1]	4 993 Z.	**–94.0**	**–614.4**	**–722.6**	**–981.3**	**–1,298.2**	**–1,194.0**	**–674.9**	**–573.6**
Goods: exports f.o.b.	2 100 . .	2,029.2	2,706.1	3,413.2	4,192.4	3,961.6	3,146.7	4,050.4	4,889.0
Goods: imports f.o.b.	3 100 . .	–2,234.1	–3,404.0	–4,309.3	–5,339.9	–5,479.9	–4,551.2	–5,154.1	–5,997.0
Balance on Goods	4 100 . .	*–204.9*	*–697.9*	*–896.2*	*–1,147.5*	*–1,518.3*	*–1,404.6*	*–1,103.8*	*–1,108.0*
Services: credit	2 200 . .	321.9	485.2	797.5	1,031.8	1,109.0	1,091.5	1,058.8	1,157.0
Services: debit	3 200 . .	–376.5	–498.1	–676.7	–897.4	–868.5	–786.1	–678.7	–700.3
Balance on Goods and Services	4 991 . .	*–259.4*	*–710.8*	*–775.4*	*–1,013.0*	*–1,277.8*	*–1,099.1*	*–723.7*	*–651.4*
Income: credit	2 300 . .	21.4	50.9	52.0	80.4	124.6	114.8	185.5	205.7
Income: debit	3 300 . .	–12.8	–63.7	–143.0	–278.8	–380.0	–372.6	–379.3	–385.5
Balance on Goods, Services, and Income	4 992 . .	*–250.8*	*–723.7*	*–866.4*	*–1,211.4*	*–1,533.2*	*–1,356.8*	*–917.5*	*–831.1*
Current transfers: credit	2 379 Z.	161.6	112.3	149.4	237.0	240.4	167.4	246.8	262.0
Current transfers: debit	3 379 . .	–4.8	–3.0	–5.6	–7.0	–5.4	–4.6	–4.3	–4.5
B. Capital Account [1]	4 994 Z.	**12.9**	**–39.0**	**5.5**	**4.1**	**–1.7**	**–3.3**	**2.1**	**1.4**
Capital account: credit	2 994 Z.	12.9	3.3	5.5	4.5	.9	2.7	2.6	1.5
Capital account: debit	3 994 . .	. . .	–42.3	. . .	–.4	–2.6	–6.0	–.4	–.1
Total, Groups A Plus B	4 981 . .	*–81.1*	*–653.4*	*–717.1*	*–977.2*	*–1,299.9*	*–1,197.3*	*–672.8*	*–572.2*
C. Financial Account [1]	4 995 W.	**240.9**	**534.4**	**645.6**	**1,005.6**	**1,443.9**	**1,060.7**	**702.4**	**777.6**
Direct investment abroad	4 505 . .	. . .	–1.0	–.1	–26.9	–4.2	–8.6	–3.7	–7.1
Direct investment in Lithuania	4 555 Z.	31.3	72.6	152.4	354.5	925.5	486.5	378.9	445.8
Portfolio investment assets	4 602 . .	–.2	–10.5	–26.9	7.7	–10.1	–1.9	–141.4	26.2
Equity securities	4 610 . .	–.2	–3.0	.8	.1	–.3	–3.0	–1.4	1.1
Debt securities	4 619 . .	. . .	–7.5	–27.7	7.6	–9.8	1.1	–140.0	25.1
Portfolio investment liabilities	4 652 Z.	4.6	26.6	89.6	180.5	–42.7	507.5	405.9	238.0
Equity securities	4 660 . .	4.6	6.2	15.9	30.5	11.4	8.9	121.5	–16.3
Debt securities	4 669 Z.	. . .	20.4	73.7	150.1	–54.1	498.6	284.4	254.3
Financial derivatives	4 910 . .	. . .	. . .	. . .	. . .	. . .	. . .	. . .	–1.3
Financial derivatives assets	4 900 . .	. . .	. . .	. . .	. . .	. . .	. . .	. . .	18.3
Financial derivatives liabilities	4 905 . .	. . .	. . .	. . .	. . .	. . .	. . .	. . .	–19.6
Other investment assets	4 703 . .	–26.4	–36.1	–170.4	–219.3	–24.0	–182.5	39.9	–225.0
Monetary authorities	4 701 . .	. . .	67.0	.2	.1	. . .	. . .	. . .	. . .
General government	4 704 . .	. . .	. . .	. . .	. . .	. . .	. . .	. . .	–2.6
Banks	4 705 . .	–17.3	–18.0	–139.5	–88.1	57.2	–125.7	–142.2	–158.2
Other sectors	4 728 . .	–9.2	–85.0	–31.1	–131.3	–81.2	–56.7	182.1	–64.2
Other investment liabilities	4 753 W.	231.6	482.8	601.0	709.1	599.3	259.7	22.8	300.9
Monetary authorities	4 753 WA	–.9	–25.1	1.0	–1.0	. . .	–.1	–102.0	51.7
General government	4 753 ZB	85.5	178.5	228.5	42.9	129.3	212.0	. . .	–53.7
Banks	4 753 ZC	75.8	10.8	108.5	104.3	177.9	99.9	53.1	169.4
Other sectors	4 753 ZD	71.2	318.5	263.1	562.8	292.1	–52.1	71.7	133.5
Total, Groups A Through C	4 983 . .	*159.8*	*–118.9*	*–71.5*	*28.4*	*144.0*	*–136.6*	*29.6*	*205.4*
D. Net Errors and Omissions	4 998 . .	**–46.9**	**287.2**	**66.7**	**195.8**	**282.9**	**–42.1**	**128.3**	**153.6**
Total, Groups A Through D	4 984 . .	*112.8*	*168.3*	*–4.8*	*224.2*	*426.8*	*–178.7*	*158.0*	*359.0*
E. Reserves and Related Items	4 802 A.	**–112.8**	**–168.3**	**4.8**	**–224.2**	**–426.8**	**178.7**	**–158.0**	**–359.0**
Reserve assets	4 802 . .	–179.7	–231.3	–15.9	–238.2	–398.8	195.3	–130.7	–325.0
Use of Fund credit and loans	4 766 . .	66.9	63.0	20.7	14.1	–28.0	–16.6	–27.3	–34.0
Exceptional financing	4 920 . .	. . .	. . .	. . .	. . .	. . .	. . .	. . .	. . .
Conversion rates: litai per U.S. dollar	0 101 . .	**3.9778**	**4.0000**	**4.0000**	**4.0000**	**4.0000**	**4.0000**	**4.0000**	**4.0000**

[1] Excludes components that have been classified in the categories of Group E.

Table 2. STANDARD PRESENTATION, 1994–2001

(Millions of U.S. dollars)

	Code	1994	1995	1996	1997	1998	1999	2000	2001
CURRENT ACCOUNT	4 993 . .	**–94.0**	**–614.4**	**–722.6**	**–981.3**	**–1,298.2**	**–1,194.0**	**–674.9**	**–573.6**
A. GOODS	4 100 . .	–204.9	–697.9	–896.2	–1,147.5	–1,518.3	–1,404.6	–1,103.8	–1,108.0
Credit	2 100 . .	**2,029.2**	**2,706.1**	**3,413.2**	**4,192.4**	**3,961.6**	**3,146.7**	**4,050.4**	**4,889.0**
General merchandise: exports f.o.b.	2 110 . .	2,029.2	2,705.0	3,410.5	3,372.2	3,104.4	2,318.1	3,102.6	3,844.8
Goods for processing: exports f.o.b.	2 150 . .	. . .	. . .	. . .	813.2	850.0	821.9	937.5	1,033.6
Repairs on goods	2 160 . .	. . .	. . .	. . .	. . .	. . .	. . .	. . .	. . .
Goods procured in ports by carriers	2 170 . .	. . .	1.1	2.7	3.6	3.7	1.9	2.4	3.0
Nonmonetary gold	2 180 . .	. . .	. . .	. . .	3.5	3.6	4.7	7.9	7.5
Debit	3 100 . .	**–2,234.1**	**–3,404.0**	**–4,309.3**	**–5,339.9**	**–5,479.9**	**–4,551.2**	**–5,154.1**	**–5,997.0**
General merchandise: imports f.o.b.	3 110 . .	–2,234.1	–3,389.8	–4,291.3	–4,718.2	–4,833.2	–3,918.7	–4,440.9	–5,173.0
Goods for processing: imports f.o.b.	3 150 . .	. . .	. . .	. . .	–594.5	–609.0	–590.2	–652.6	–754.4
Repairs on goods	3 160 . .	. . .	. . .	. . .	. . .	. . .	. . .	. . .	. . .
Goods procured in ports by carriers	3 170 . .	. . .	–14.2	–18.0	–22.6	–30.1	–33.4	–50.1	–59.2
Nonmonetary gold	3 180 . .	. . .	. . .	. . .	–4.6	–7.7	–9.0	–10.5	–10.3
B. SERVICES	4 200 . .	–54.5	–12.9	120.8	134.5	240.5	305.5	380.1	456.7
Total credit	2 200 . .	*321.9*	*485.2*	*797.5*	*1,031.8*	*1,109.0*	*1,091.5*	*1,058.8*	*1,157.0*
Total debit	3 200 . .	*–376.5*	*–498.1*	*–676.7*	*–897.4*	*–868.5*	*–786.1*	*–678.7*	*–700.3*
Transportation services, credit	2 205 . .	**207.6**	**287.5**	**358.4**	**442.6**	**434.0**	**399.3**	**491.6**	**531.9**
Passenger	2 850 . .	*13.8*	*25.4*	*29.4*	*39.2*	*44.0*	*41.2*	*38.5*	*41.6*
Freight	2 851 . .	*161.4*	*187.3*	*248.4*	*317.8*	*304.8*	*268.2*	*321.9*	*358.1*
Other	2 852 . .	*32.4*	*74.9*	*80.7*	*85.7*	*85.2*	*89.9*	*131.3*	*132.2*
Sea transport, passenger	2 207 . .	1.6	3.8	6.4	2.9	2.9	3.0	2.8	4.7
Sea transport, freight	2 208 . .	95.6	88.9	93.4	94.2	81.3	68.0	65.7	65.9
Sea transport, other	2 209 . .	. . .	10.5	52.3	62.3	60.0	68.2	111.7	109.7
Air transport, passenger	2 211 . .	9.3	16.3	15.2	24.8	30.8	29.7	26.9	28.0
Air transport, freight	2 212 . .	.2	.8	1.2	1.4	1.6	2.0	3.6	3.8
Air transport, other	2 213 . .	2.3	4.4	20.6	13.4	14.4	15.1	13.1	14.4
Other transport, passenger	2 215 . .	3.0	5.2	7.7	11.4	10.3	8.5	8.8	9.0
Other transport, freight	2 216 . .	65.6	97.6	153.8	222.2	221.9	198.2	252.5	288.5
Other transport, other	2 217 . .	30.1	60.0	7.8	10.0	10.8	6.6	6.4	8.1
Transportation services, debit	3 205 . .	**–197.0**	**–292.2**	**–298.9**	**–360.2**	**–265.9**	**–213.3**	**–221.1**	**–236.6**
Passenger	3 850 . .	*–.9*	*–.5*	*–4.3*	*–12.3*	*–12.2*	*–8.8*	*–8.2*	*–8.3*
Freight	3 851 . .	*–152.6*	*–247.1*	*–242.4*	*–283.0*	*–146.5*	*–146.2*	*–161.4*	*–173.1*
Other	3 852 . .	*–43.5*	*–44.5*	*–52.2*	*–64.9*	*–107.2*	*–58.2*	*–51.5*	*–55.2*
Sea transport, passenger	3 207 . .	. . .	. . .	. . .	. . .	. . .	. . .	. . .	. . .
Sea transport, freight	3 208 . .	. . .	. . .	–42.6	–57.1	–32.7	–29.1	–31.5	–30.4
Sea transport, other	3 209 . .	–19.8	–19.8	–21.2	–24.3	–24.0	–18.8	–14.7	–10.9
Air transport, passenger	3 211 . .	. . .	. . .	–3.2	–6.9	–7.5	–5.4	–4.4	–3.3
Air transport, freight	3 212 . .	. . .	. . .	–12.2	–12.8	–8.8	–7.4	–5.6	–5.3
Air transport, other	3 213 . .	–20.7	–18.9	–20.2	–16.2	–18.0	–18.1	–15.9	–20.8
Other transport, passenger	3 215 . .	–.9	–.5	–1.2	–5.3	–4.7	–3.5	–3.8	–5.0
Other transport, freight	3 216 . .	–152.6	–247.1	–187.7	–213.1	–105.0	–109.7	–124.4	–137.4
Other transport, other	3 217 . .	–3.0	–5.8	–10.8	–24.4	–65.2	–21.3	–20.8	–23.6
Travel, credit	2 236 . .	**68.6**	**77.0**	**315.6**	**359.6**	**459.5**	**550.4**	**391.3**	**383.0**
Business travel	2 237 . .	. . .	. . .	. . .	170.6	77.2	112.1	106.8	82.1
Personal travel	2 240 . .	. . .	77.0	315.6	189.0	382.4	438.3	284.5	301.0
Travel, debit	3 236 . .	**–50.3**	**–106.3**	**–265.8**	**–277.4**	**–292.2**	**–340.9**	**–253.1**	**–218.5**
Business travel	3 237 . .	. . .	. . .	–2.1	–126.5	–49.0	–69.5	–69.4	–47.0
Personal travel	3 240 . .	. . .	–106.3	–263.8	–150.9	–243.2	–271.5	–183.7	–171.6
Other services, credit	2 200 BA	**45.7**	**120.7**	**123.6**	**229.6**	**215.5**	**141.9**	**175.8**	**242.1**
Communications	2 245 . .	9.7	23.9	26.4	40.6	26.6	35.3	35.4	37.0
Construction	2 249 . .	31.2	64.9	61.1	77.3	41.7	18.5	13.9	17.5
Insurance	2 253 . .	1.2	2.8	2.8	17.3	20.4	1.7	2.7	9.3
Financial	2 260 . .	.1	1.7	5.7	6.4	5.5	7.2	3.1	9.5
Computer and information	2 262 . .	. . .	.3	.1	2.8	7.2	9.0	15.5	24.2
Royalties and licence fees	2 266 . .	. . .	. . .	. . .	1.4	.1	.1	. . .	.5
Other business services	2 268 . .	3.5	24.1	16.2	70.4	98.3	60.6	87.3	123.6
Personal, cultural, and recreational	2 287 . .	. . .	. . .	. . .	1.4	3.1	1.2	11.3	10.4
Government, n.i.e.	2 291 . .	. . .	3.0	11.4	12.0	12.8	8.2	6.7	10.2
Other services, debit	3 200 BA	**–129.2**	**–99.6**	**–112.0**	**–259.8**	**–310.4**	**–231.9**	**–204.5**	**–245.2**
Communications	3 245 . .	–7.6	–20.8	–25.1	–43.1	–28.5	–35.5	–33.3	–38.2
Construction	3 249 . .	–1.7	–10.3	–6.6	–74.7	–109.7	–38.4	–9.2	–14.1
Insurance	3 253 . .	. . .	–2.5	–2.7	–18.0	–23.2	–4.9	–7.8	–20.5
Financial	3 260 . .	–.2	–2.4	–3.7	–5.9	–3.8	–3.4	–5.3	–6.9
Computer and information	3 262 . .	–.4	–.7	–1.8	–2.8	–3.3	–3.8	–13.0	–9.7
Royalties and licence fees	3 266 . .	–.2	–1.4	–4.3	–5.0	–6.0	–14.1	–12.3	–10.2
Other business services	3 268 . .	–8.3	–20.4	–30.5	–56.4	–77.5	–86.5	–96.0	–108.3
Personal, cultural, and recreational	3 287 . .	. . .	. . .	. . .	–6.8	–6.3	–6.4	–4.2	–5.8
Government, n.i.e.	3 291 . .	–110.7	–41.1	–37.4	–47.1	–52.2	–39.0	–23.5	–31.7

Table 2 (Continued). STANDARD PRESENTATION, 1994–2001

(Millions of U.S. dollars)

	Code	1994	1995	1996	1997	1998	1999	2000	2001
C. INCOME	4 300 . .	8.6	–12.9	–91.0	–198.4	–255.4	–257.7	–193.8	–179.8
Total credit	2 300 . .	*21.4*	*50.9*	*52.0*	*80.4*	*124.6*	*114.8*	*185.5*	*205.7*
Total debit	3 300 . .	*–12.8*	*–63.7*	*–143.0*	*–278.8*	*–380.0*	*–372.6*	*–379.3*	*–385.5*
Compensation of employees, credit	2 310 . .	**. . .**	**. . .**	**.7**	**1.1**	**1.4**	**1.5**	**47.7**	**76.1**
Compensation of employees, debit	3 310 . .	**–.3**	**–.4**	**–32.2**	**–57.0**	**–61.9**	**–45.1**	**–36.8**	**–28.2**
Investment income, credit	2 320 . .	**21.4**	**50.9**	**51.3**	**79.3**	**123.2**	**113.4**	**137.8**	**129.6**
Direct investment income	2 330 . .	. . .	. . .	.1	.4	16.9	14.1	15.4	4.9
Dividends and distributed branch profits	2 332 . .	. . .	. . .	.1	. . .	. . .	. . .	. . .	. . .
Reinvested earnings and undistributed branch profits	2 333 . .	. . .	. . .	. . .	.1	–.5	–.6	.2	–.5
Income on debt (interest)	2 334 . .	. . .	. . .	. . .	.2	17.4	14.6	15.1	5.3
Portfolio investment income	2 339 . .	. . .	28.1	20.0	29.1	60.1	61.7	59.5	60.7
Income on equity	2 340 . .	. . .	.2	.2	.3	.3	.2	. . .	.3
Income on bonds and notes	2 350 . .	. . .	27.9	19.8	2.1	1.0	3.2	59.5	60.4
Income on money market instruments	2 360 . .	. . .	. . .	. . .	26.7	58.8	58.3	. . .	. . .
Other investment income	2 370 . .	21.4	22.8	31.2	49.9	46.3	37.5	63.0	64.1
Investment income, debit	3 320 . .	**–12.5**	**–63.3**	**–110.8**	**–221.8**	**–318.1**	**–327.5**	**–342.5**	**–357.3**
Direct investment income	3 330 . .	–.5	–8.1	–27.4	–77.1	–148.5	–165.5	–123.5	–144.9
Dividends and distributed branch profits	3 332 . .	–.5	–1.0	–2.8	–28.1	–37.7	–12.2	–29.2	–53.4
Reinvested earnings and undistributed branch profits	3 333 . .	. . .	–7.1	–24.6	–43.5	–99.8	–146.5	–88.4	–85.7
Income on debt (interest)	3 334 . .	. . .	. . .	. . .	–5.5	–11.0	–6.8	–5.9	–5.8
Portfolio investment income	3 339 . .	. . .	–12.3	–18.7	–34.9	–35.5	–27.6	–63.7	–68.6
Income on equity	3 340 . .	. . .	. . .	. . .	–10.6	–9.8	–3.9	–7.1	–10.1
Income on bonds and notes	3 350 . .	. . .	–12.3	–18.7	–15.4	–14.3	–10.7	–56.7	–58.4
Income on money market instruments	3 360 . .	. . .	. . .	. . .	–8.9	–11.5	–13.1	. . .	. . .
Other investment income	3 370 . .	–12.0	–42.9	–64.7	–109.8	–134.2	–134.4	–155.2	–143.9
D. CURRENT TRANSFERS	4 379 . .	156.8	109.3	143.8	230.0	235.0	162.8	242.6	257.5
Credit	2 379 . .	**161.6**	**112.3**	**149.4**	**237.0**	**240.4**	**167.4**	**246.8**	**262.0**
General government	2 380 . .	122.7	63.7	77.4	106.1	107.0	61.2	66.1	38.4
Other sectors	2 390 . .	38.9	48.6	72.0	130.8	133.4	106.2	180.8	223.7
Workers' remittances	2 391 . .	.7	1.1	1.9	1.8	2.1	1.5	2.3	3.1
Other current transfers	2 392 . .	38.2	47.5	70.2	129.0	131.3	104.6	178.5	220.6
Debit	3 379 . .	**–4.8**	**–3.0**	**–5.6**	**–7.0**	**–5.4**	**–4.6**	**–4.3**	**–4.5**
General government	3 380 . .	–4.5	–2.3	–4.7	–5.7	–3.8	–2.9	–2.9	–3.1
Other sectors	3 390 . .	–.3	–.6	–1.0	–1.2	–1.6	–1.7	–1.4	–1.4
Workers' remittances	3 391 . .	–.3	–.6	–.9	–1.1	–1.5	–1.5	–1.3	–1.3
Other current transfers	3 392 . .	. . .	–.1	–.1	–.1	–.1	–.1	–.1	–.2
CAPITAL AND FINANCIAL ACCOUNT	4 996 . .	**140.9**	**327.1**	**655.9**	**785.5**	**1,015.4**	**1,236.1**	**546.6**	**420.0**
CAPITAL ACCOUNT	4 994 . .	**12.9**	**–39.0**	**5.5**	**4.1**	**–1.7**	**–3.3**	**2.1**	**1.4**
Total credit	2 994 . .	*12.9*	*3.3*	*5.5*	*4.5*	*.9*	*2.7*	*2.6*	*1.5*
Total debit	3 994 . .	. . .	*–42.3*	. . .	*–.4*	*–2.6*	*–6.0*	*–.4*	*–.1*
Capital transfers, credit	2 400 . .	**12.9**	**3.3**	**5.5**	**4.5**	**.9**	**2.7**	**2.6**	**1.5**
General government	2 401 . .	12.9	1.4	5.5	1.9	.3	.1	1.2	. . .
Debt forgiveness	2 402 . .	. . .	. . .	. . .	. . .	. . .	. . .	. . .	. . .
Other capital transfers	2 410 . .	12.9	1.4	5.5	1.9	.3	.1	1.2	. . .
Other sectors	2 430 . .	. . .	1.9	. . .	2.5	.7	2.6	1.4	1.5
Migrants' transfers	2 431 . .	. . .	. . .	. . .	. . .	. . .	. . .	. . .	. . .
Debt forgiveness	2 432 . .	. . .	. . .	. . .	.5	.5	2.6	.8	1.5
Other capital transfers	2 440 . .	. . .	1.9	. . .	2.1	.2	. . .	.5	. . .
Capital transfers, debit	3 400 . .	**. . .**	**–42.3**	**. . .**	**–.4**	**–2.6**	**–6.0**	**–.4**	**–.1**
General government	3 401 . .	. . .	–42.0	. . .	. . .	. . .	. . .	. . .	. . .
Debt forgiveness	3 402 . .	. . .	–42.0	. . .	. . .	. . .	. . .	. . .	. . .
Other capital transfers	3 410 . .	. . .	. . .	. . .	. . .	. . .	. . .	. . .	. . .
Other sectors	3 430 . .	. . .	–.3	. . .	–.4	–2.6	–6.0	–.4	–.1
Migrants' transfers	3 431 . .	. . .	. . .	. . .	. . .	. . .	. . .	. . .	. . .
Debt forgiveness	3 432 . .	. . .	–.3	. . .	–.4	–2.6	–6.0	–.4	–.1
Other capital transfers	3 440 . .	. . .	. . .	. . .	. . .	. . .	. . .	. . .	. . .
Nonproduced nonfinancial assets, credit	2 480 . .	**. . .**	**. . .**	**. . .**	**. . .**	**. . .**	**. . .**	**. . .**	**. . .**
Nonproduced nonfinancial assets, debit	3 480 . .	**. . .**	**. . .**	**. . .**	**. . .**	**. . .**	**. . .**	**. . .**	**. . .**

Table 2 (Continued). STANDARD PRESENTATION, 1994–2001
(Millions of U.S. dollars)

	Code	1994	1995	1996	1997	1998	1999	2000	2001
FINANCIAL ACCOUNT	4 995 . .	**128.1**	**366.1**	**650.4**	**781.4**	**1,017.0**	**1,239.4**	**544.4**	**418.6**
A. DIRECT INVESTMENT	4 500 . .	31.3	71.6	152.3	327.6	921.3	477.8	375.2	438.7
Direct investment abroad	4 505 . .	**. . .**	**–1.0**	**–.1**	**–26.9**	**–4.2**	**–8.6**	**–3.7**	**–7.1**
Equity capital	4 510 . .	. . .	–1.0	–.1	–1.5	–2.3	–11.2	–1.7	–5.4
Claims on affiliated enterprises	4 515 . .	. . .	–1.0	–.1	–1.5	–2.3	–11.2	–1.7	–5.4
Liabilities to affiliated enterprises	4 520 . .	. . .	. . .	. . .	. . .	. . .	. . .	. . .	. . .
Reinvested earnings	4 525 . .	. . .	. . .	. . .	–.1	.5	.6	–.2	.5
Other capital	4 530 . .	. . .	. . .	. . .	–25.3	–2.5	2.0	–1.8	–2.2
Claims on affiliated enterprises	4 535 . .	. . .	. . .	. . .	–27.4	–2.5	2.1	–1.8	–3.3
Liabilities to affiliated enterprises	4 540 . .	. . .	. . .	. . .	2.1	. . .	–.1	. . .	1.0
Direct investment in Lithuania	4 555 . .	**31.3**	**72.6**	**152.4**	**354.5**	**925.5**	**486.5**	**378.9**	**445.8**
Equity capital	4 560 . .	31.3	65.4	127.8	217.6	772.1	371.7	181.4	260.7
Claims on direct investors	4 565 . .	. . .	. . .	. . .	. . .	–.1	. . .	. . .	. . .
Liabilities to direct investors	4 570 . .	31.3	65.4	127.8	217.6	772.2	371.7	181.4	260.7
Reinvested earnings	4 575 . .	. . .	7.1	24.6	43.5	99.8	146.5	88.4	85.7
Other capital	4 580 . .	. . .	.1	. . .	93.4	53.6	–31.7	109.1	99.5
Claims on direct investors	4 585 . .	. . .	. . .	. . .	–5.6	6.8	–78.2	–1.4	4.5
Liabilities to direct investors	4 590 . .	. . .	.1	. . .	99.1	46.8	46.5	110.5	95.0
B. PORTFOLIO INVESTMENT	4 600 . .	4.4	16.2	62.7	188.2	–52.8	505.6	264.5	264.3
Assets	4 602 . .	**–.2**	**–10.5**	**–26.9**	**7.7**	**–10.1**	**–1.9**	**–141.4**	**26.2**
Equity securities	4 610 . .	–.2	–3.0	.8	.1	–.3	–3.0	–1.4	1.1
Monetary authorities	4 611 . .	. . .	–1.9	. . .	. . .	. . .	. . .	. . .	. . .
General government	4 612 . .	. . .	. . .	. . .	. . .	. . .	. . .	. . .	. . .
Banks	4 613 . .	. . .	–.8	.8	–.2	–.4	–.2	–1.4	1.1
Other sectors	4 614 . .	–.1	–.3	.1	.3	.1	–2.8	.1	. . .
Debt securities	4 619 . .	. . .	–7.5	–27.7	7.6	–9.8	1.1	–140.0	25.1
Bonds and notes	4 620 . .	. . .	–7.5	–27.7	.4	–15.3	1.2	–79.9	–18.5
Monetary authorities	4 621 . .	. . .	. . .	. . .	. . .	. . .	. . .	. . .	. . .
General government	4 622 . .	. . .	. . .	. . .	. . .	. . .	. . .	. . .	. . .
Banks	4 623 . .	. . .	–7.3	–26.2	.4	–15.3	1.2	–79.9	–18.5
Other sectors	4 624 . .	. . .	–.2	–1.5	.1	. . .	. . .	. . .	. . .
Money market instruments	4 630 . .	. . .	. . .	. . .	7.2	5.5	–.1	–60.1	43.6
Monetary authorities	4 631 . .	. . .	. . .	. . .	. . .	. . .	. . .	. . .	. . .
General government	4 632 . .	. . .	. . .	. . .	. . .	. . .	. . .	. . .	. . .
Banks	4 633 . .	. . .	. . .	. . .	8.0	5.3	–.1	–53.8	43.7
Other sectors	4 634 . .	. . .	. . .	. . .	–.9	.2	–.1	–6.4	–.1
Liabilities	4 652 . .	**4.6**	**26.6**	**89.6**	**180.5**	**–42.7**	**507.5**	**405.9**	**238.0**
Equity securities	4 660 . .	4.6	6.2	15.9	30.5	11.4	8.9	121.5	–16.3
Banks	4 663 . .	4.6	5.9	14.5	22.5	12.3	–5.3	–17.1	–4.4
Other sectors	4 664 . .	. . .	.3	1.5	8.0	–.9	14.2	138.7	–11.9
Debt securities	4 669 . .	. . .	20.4	73.7	150.1	–54.1	498.6	284.4	254.3
Bonds and notes	4 670 . .	. . .	20.4	73.7	165.0	–55.1	514.5	309.8	245.5
Monetary authorities	4 671 . .	. . .	. . .	. . .	. . .	. . .	. . .	. . .	. . .
General government	4 672 . .	. . .	20.4	73.7	90.0	23.9	545.6	306.4	165.3
Banks	4 673 . .	. . .	. . .	. . .	. . .	. . .	.8	–.3	2.7
Other sectors	4 674 . .	. . .	. . .	. . .	75.0	–79.0	–31.9	3.7	77.6
Money market instruments	4 680 . .	. . .	. . .	. . .	–14.9	1.0	–15.8	–25.4	8.8
Monetary authorities	4 681 . .	. . .	. . .	. . .	. . .	. . .	. . .	. . .	. . .
General government	4 682 . .	. . .	. . .	. . .	–89.7	18.5	–17.0	–22.0	–.6
Banks	4 683 . .	. . .	. . .	. . .	. . .	. . .	.2	–.2	9.4
Other sectors	4 684 . .	. . .	. . .	. . .	74.7	–17.5	1.0	–3.2	–.1
C. FINANCIAL DERIVATIVES	4 910 . .	. . .	. . .	. . .	. . .	. . .	. . .	. . .	–1.3
Monetary authorities	4 911 . .	. . .	. . .	. . .	. . .	. . .	. . .	. . .	. . .
General government	4 912 . .	. . .	. . .	. . .	. . .	. . .	. . .	. . .	. . .
Banks	4 913 . .	. . .	. . .	. . .	. . .	. . .	. . .	. . .	–1.3
Other sectors	4 914 . .	. . .	. . .	. . .	. . .	. . .	. . .	. . .	. . .
Assets	4 900 . .	**. . .**	**. . .**	**. . .**	**. . .**	**. . .**	**. . .**	**. . .**	**18.3**
Monetary authorities	4 901 . .	. . .	. . .	. . .	. . .	. . .	. . .	. . .	. . .
General government	4 902 . .	. . .	. . .	. . .	. . .	. . .	. . .	. . .	. . .
Banks	4 903 . .	. . .	. . .	. . .	. . .	. . .	. . .	. . .	18.3
Other sectors	4 904 . .	. . .	. . .	. . .	. . .	. . .	. . .	. . .	. . .
Liabilities	4 905 . .	**. . .**	**. . .**	**. . .**	**. . .**	**. . .**	**. . .**	**. . .**	**–19.6**
Monetary authorities	4 906 . .	. . .	. . .	. . .	. . .	. . .	. . .	. . .	. . .
General government	4 907 . .	. . .	. . .	. . .	. . .	. . .	. . .	. . .	. . .
Banks	4 908 . .	. . .	. . .	. . .	. . .	. . .	. . .	. . .	–19.6
Other sectors	4 909 . .	. . .	. . .	. . .	. . .	. . .	. . .	. . .	. . .

Table 2 (Concluded). STANDARD PRESENTATION, 1994–2001
(Millions of U.S. dollars)

	Code	1994	1995	1996	1997	1998	1999	2000	2001
D. OTHER INVESTMENT	4 700	272.1	509.7	451.3	503.8	547.2	60.7	35.4	41.9
Assets	4 703	**–26.4**	**–36.1**	**–170.4**	**–219.3**	**–24.0**	**–182.5**	**39.9**	**–225.0**
Trade credits	4 706	. . .	–64.3	–33.2	–66.7	–143.7	85.3	74.5	–79.9
General government	4 707	. . .	. . .	. . .	. . .	. . .	. . .	. . .	. . .
of which: Short-term	4 709	. . .	. . .	. . .	. . .	. . .	. . .	. . .	. . .
Other sectors	4 710	. . .	–64.3	–33.2	–66.7	–143.7	85.3	74.5	–79.9
of which: Short-term	4 712	. . .	*–64.3*	*–33.2*	*–66.7*	*–143.7*	*85.3*	*74.5*	*–79.9*
Loans	4 714	–11.6	–13.1	–9.5	13.5	–16.6	–37.0	22.8	–97.9
Monetary authorities	4 715	. . .	. . .	. . .	. . .	. . .	. . .	. . .	. . .
of which: Short-term	4 718	. . .	. . .	. . .	. . .	. . .	. . .	. . .	. . .
General government	4 719	. . .	. . .	. . .	. . .	. . .	. . .	. . .	. . .
of which: Short-term	4 721	. . .	. . .	. . .	. . .	. . .	. . .	. . .	. . .
Banks	4 722	–11.6	–13.2	–9.5	20.2	–15.5	–32.7	20.8	–96.0
of which: Short-term	4 724	*–11.6*	*–8.3*	*–13.1*	*25.6*	*–10.2*	*–29.8*	*22.0*	*–100.9*
Other sectors	4 725	. . .	.1	. . .	–6.7	–1.1	–4.3	2.0	–1.9
of which: Short-term	4 727	. . .	*–.1*	*–.1*	*–1.8*	*2.8*	*–3.1*	*1.8*	*–.5*
Currency and deposits	4 730	–7.2	43.3	–128.6	–152.1	144.4	–248.6	–51.6	–38.1
Monetary authorities	4 731	. . .	67.0	.2	.1	. . .	. . .	. . .	. . .
General government	4 732	. . .	. . .	. . .	. . .	. . .	. . .	. . .	–2.6
Banks	4 733	–5.7	–2.8	–130.9	–108.5	88.7	–108.3	–157.9	–57.6
Other sectors	4 734	–1.6	–20.8	2.2	–43.7	55.7	–140.3	106.3	22.2
Other assets	4 736	–7.6	–2.0	.8	–13.9	–8.1	17.9	–5.9	–9.2
Monetary authorities	4 737	. . .	. . .	. . .	. . .	. . .	. . .	. . .	. . .
of which: Short-term	4 739	. . .	. . .	. . .	. . .	. . .	. . .	. . .	. . .
General government	4 740	. . .	. . .	. . .	. . .	. . .	. . .	. . .	. . .
of which: Short-term	4 742	. . .	. . .	. . .	. . .	. . .	. . .	. . .	. . .
Banks	4 743	. . .	–2.0	.9	.2	–16.0	15.2	–5.1	–4.5
of which: Short-term	4 745	. . .	*–2.0*	*.9*	*.2*	*–16.0*	*15.2*	*–5.1*	*–4.5*
Other sectors	4 746	–7.6	. . .	–.1	–14.1	7.9	2.6	–.8	–4.7
of which: Short-term	4 748	*–7.6*	. . .	*–.1*	*–14.1*	*7.9*	*2.6*	*–.8*	*–4.7*
Liabilities	4 753	**298.5**	**545.7**	**621.7**	**723.1**	**571.3**	**243.2**	**–4.5**	**266.9**
Trade credits	4 756	. . .	195.1	41.4	218.1	110.0	–37.3	–2.5	143.4
General government	4 757	. . .	. . .	. . .	. . .	. . .	. . .	. . .	. . .
of which: Short-term	4 759	. . .	. . .	. . .	. . .	. . .	. . .	. . .	. . .
Other sectors	4 760	. . .	195.1	41.4	218.1	110.0	–37.3	–2.5	143.4
of which: Short-term	4 762	. . .	*195.1*	*41.4*	*218.1*	*110.0*	*–37.3*	*–2.5*	*143.4*
Loans	4 764	206.8	370.6	499.0	452.2	452.0	225.0	–85.0	–.5
Monetary authorities	4 765	66.9	63.0	20.7	14.1	–28.0	–16.6	–129.2	–34.0
of which: Use of Fund credit and loans from the Fund	4 766	*66.9*	*63.0*	*20.7*	*14.1*	*–28.0*	*–16.6*	*–27.3*	*–34.0*
of which: Short-term	4 768	. . .	. . .	. . .	. . .	. . .	. . .	*–25.0*	. . .
General government	4 769	85.5	178.5	228.5	42.9	129.3	212.0	. . .	–53.7
of which: Short-term	4 771	. . .	. . .	. . .	. . .	. . .	*25.0*	. . .	. . .
Banks	4 772	19.3	5.6	36.1	81.4	165.9	61.7	–6.4	90.7
of which: Short-term	4 774	*7.2*	*–.7*	*23.1*	*–30.4*	*20.1*	*–16.1*	*30.3*	*192.1*
Other sectors	4 775	35.1	123.5	213.8	313.9	184.8	–32.2	50.6	–3.5
of which: Short-term	4 777	. . .	*22.7*	*15.3*	*–13.1*	*117.9*	*–74.8*	*–14.6*	*13.2*
Currency and deposits	4 780	55.6	–21.0	69.0	39.1	–4.1	32.4	58.6	30.6
Monetary authorities	4 781	–.9	–25.1	1.0	–1.0	. . .	–.1	–.1	.1
General government	4 782	. . .	. . .	. . .	. . .	. . .	. . .	. . .	. . .
Banks	4 783	56.4	4.1	67.4	23.0	–4.1	32.5	58.7	30.5
Other sectors	4 784	. . .	. . .	.6	17.1	. . .	. . .	. . .	. . .
Other liabilities	4 786	36.1	1.1	12.3	13.7	13.4	23.1	24.5	93.4
Monetary authorities	4 787	. . .	. . .	. . .	. . .	. . .	. . .	. . .	51.6
of which: Short-term	4 789	. . .	. . .	. . .	. . .	. . .	. . .	. . .	*51.6*
General government	4 790	. . .	. . .	. . .	. . .	. . .	. . .	. . .	. . .
of which: Short-term	4 792	. . .	. . .	. . .	. . .	. . .	. . .	. . .	. . .
Banks	4 793	. . .	1.1	5.0	. . .	16.1	5.7	.8	48.2
of which: Short-term	4 795	. . .	*1.1*	*5.0*	. . .	*16.1*	*5.7*	*.8*	*48.2*
Other sectors	4 796	36.1	. . .	7.3	13.7	–2.6	17.4	23.7	–6.4
of which: Short-term	4 798	*36.1*	. . .	*7.3*	*13.7*	*–2.6*	*17.4*	*23.7*	*–6.4*
E. RESERVE ASSETS	4 802	–179.7	–231.3	–15.9	–238.2	–398.8	195.3	–130.7	–325.0
Monetary gold	4 812	. . .	–.1	–.1	. . .	.1	–.1	. . .	. . .
Special drawing rights	4 811	62.5	–2.7	7.4	–1.1	–5.1	11.3	2.9	–17.3
Reserve position in the Fund	4 810	. . .	. . .	. . .	. . .	. . .	. . .	. . .	. . .
Foreign exchange	4 803	–242.2	–228.6	–23.2	–237.2	–393.8	184.1	–133.6	–307.8
Other claims	4 813	. . .	. . .	. . .	. . .	. . .	. . .	. . .	. . .
NET ERRORS AND OMISSIONS	4 998	**–46.9**	**287.2**	**66.7**	**195.8**	**282.9**	**–42.1**	**128.3**	**153.6**

Part 3 of the *Yearbook* contains descriptions of the methodologies, compilation practices, and sources used to compile these data.

Table 3. INTERNATIONAL INVESTMENT POSITION (End–period stocks), 1994–2001

(Millions of U.S. dollars)

	Code	1994	1995	1996	1997	1998	1999	2000	2001
ASSETS	8 995 C.	997.6	1,274.6	1,692.7	2,148.6	2,472.2	2,452.7	2,677.7	3,126.3
Direct investment abroad	8 505 . .	**.2**	**1.2**	**2.8**	**26.0**	**16.5**	**25.9**	**29.3**	**47.9**
Equity capital and reinvested earnings	8 506 . .	.2	1.2	1.9	3.6	5.3	16.1	17.6	26.4
Claims on affiliated enterprises	8 507 . .	.2	1.2	1.9	3.6	5.3	16.1	17.6	26.4
Liabilities to affiliated enterprises	8 508 . .	...	...	...	...	...	...	...	...
Other capital	8 530 . .	...	...	.9	22.4	11.1	9.9	11.7	21.4
Claims on affiliated enterprises	8 535 . .	...	...	2.1	25.3	11.2	10.1	12.0	22.7
Liabilities to affiliated enterprises	8 540 . .	...	...	–1.2	–2.9	–.1	–.2	–.3	–1.3
Portfolio investment	8 602 . .	**.6**	**11.1**	**38.1**	**29.7**	**38.0**	**32.5**	**172.3**	**138.2**
Equity securities	8 610 . .	.2	3.1	2.6	2.9	2.9	5.9	6.0	4.9
Monetary authorities	8 611 . .	...	1.9	1.9	1.9	1.9	1.9	2.0	2.0
General government	8 612 . .	...	...	...	...	...	...	...	...
Banks	8 613 . .	...	.8	...	.2	.5	.6	2.0	.9
Other sectors	8 614 . .	.2	.4	.7	.8	.4	3.4	2.1	2.1
Debt securities	8 619 . .	.5	7.9	35.5	26.8	35.1	26.7	166.4	133.2
Bonds and notes	8 620 . .	.5	7.9	...	...	17.3	12.1	91.0	109.2
Monetary authorities	8 621 . .	...	...	...	...	...	...	...	...
General government	8 622 . .	...	...	...	...	...	...	...	...
Banks	8 623 . .	...	7.3	...	...	17.3	12.1	91.0	108.5
Other sectors	8 624 . .	.4	.6	...	...	...	...	...	.8
Money market instruments	8 630 . .	...	...	35.5	26.8	17.8	14.6	75.4	24.0
Monetary authorities	8 631 . .	...	...	...	...	...	...	...	...
General government	8 632 . .	...	...	...	...	...	...	...	...
Banks	8 633 . .	...	...	33.5	24.2	15.3	12.1	65.1	15.2
Other sectors	8 634 . .	...	...	1.9	2.5	2.5	2.5	10.3	8.8
Financial derivatives	8 900 . .	...	...	...	...	...	...	...	...
Monetary authorities	8 901 . .	...	...	...	...	...	...	...	...
General government	8 902 . .	...	...	...	...	...	...	...	...
Banks	8 903 . .	...	...	...	...	...	...	...	...
Other sectors	8 904 . .	...	...	...	...	...	...	...	...
Other investment	8 703 . .	**409.4**	**443.4**	**817.5**	**1,030.2**	**957.7**	**1,152.1**	**1,117.4**	**1,271.1**
Trade credits	8 706 . .	173.6	237.9	464.2	530.5	571.9	508.8	437.7	518.7
General government	8 707 . .	...	...	...	...	...	...	...	...
of which: *Short-term*	8 709 . .	...	...	...	...	...	...	...	...
Other sectors	8 710 . .	173.6	237.9	464.2	530.5	571.9	508.8	437.7	518.7
of which: *Short-term*	8 712 . .	*173.6*	*237.9*	*464.2*	*530.5*	*571.9*	*508.8*	*437.7*	*518.7*
Loans	8 714 . .	16.5	27.5	45.5	25.6	41.8	69.6	357.4	447.8
Monetary authorities	8 715 . .	...	...	...	...	...	...	...	...
of which: *Short-term*	8 718 . .	...	...	...	...	...	...	...	...
General government	8 719 . .	...	...	...	...	...	...	...	...
of which: *Short-term*	8 721 . .	...	...	...	...	...	...	...	...
Banks	8 722 . .	15.1	26.2	36.8	16.5	31.5	55.2	344.9	439.4
of which: *Short-term*	8 724 . .	...	...	*34.8*	*9.2*	*18.9*	*43.1*	*331.5*	*430.9*
Other sectors	8 725 . .	1.4	1.4	8.8	9.1	10.3	14.3	12.6	8.4
of which: *Short-term*	8 727 . .	*.2*	*.3*	*5.8*	*2.2*	*5.1*	*8.1*	*5.9*	*2.0*
Currency and deposits	8 730 . .	219.2	175.9	305.0	457.6	318.8	567.0	309.3	282.3
Monetary authorities	8 731 . .	67.2	.2	.1	...	...	...	...	...
General government	8 732 . .	...	...	...	...	...	...	...	...
Banks	8 733 . .	88.2	91.0	206.3	314.7	226.1	334.4	188.9	186.6
Other sectors	8 734 . .	63.9	84.7	98.7	142.9	92.7	232.6	120.4	95.6
Other assets	8 736 . .	...	2.0	2.8	16.5	25.2	6.7	12.9	22.3
Monetary authorities	8 737 . .	...	...	...	...	...	...	...	...
of which: *Short-term*	8 739 . .	...	...	...	...	...	...	...	...
General government	8 740 . .	...	...	...	...	...	...	...	...
of which: *Short-term*	8 742 . .	...	...	...	...	...	...	...	...
Banks	8 743 . .	...	2.0	.3	.1	16.1	.9	6.0	10.5
of which: *Short-term*	8 745 . .	...	*2.0*	*.3*	*.1*	*16.1*	*.9*	*6.0*	*10.5*
Other sectors	8 746 . .	...	...	2.5	16.4	9.1	5.9	7.0	11.8
of which: *Short-term*	8 748 . .	...	...	...	*16.4*	*9.1*	*5.9*	*7.0*	*11.8*
Reserve assets	8 802 . .	**587.4**	**819.0**	**834.3**	**1,062.7**	**1,460.0**	**1,242.1**	**1,358.7**	**1,669.2**
Monetary gold	8 812 . .	61.9	62.0	62.0	52.7	50.9	47.1	47.1	51.5
Special drawing rights	8 811 . .	15.1	18.2	10.2	10.7	16.2	4.4	1.3	18.4
Reserve position in the Fund	8 810 . .	...	...	...	...	...	...	...	...
Foreign exchange	8 803 . .	510.3	738.9	762.0	999.2	1,392.9	1,190.6	1,097.1	1,599.3
Other claims	8 813 . .	...	...	...	...	...	...	213.1	...

Table 3 (Concluded). INTERNATIONAL INVESTMENT POSITION (End–period stocks), 1994–2001

(Millions of U.S. dollars)

	Code		1994	1995	1996	1997	1998	1999	2000	2001
LIABILITIES	8 995	D.	1,115.8	1,795.8	2,813.2	3,964.8	4,928.8	6,114.1	6,693.3	7,331.4
Direct investment in Lithuania	8 555	. .	**262.2**	**353.9**	**700.3**	**1,040.6**	**1,625.3**	**2,063.0**	**2,334.3**	**2,665.5**
Equity capital and reinvested earnings	8 556	. .	262.2	353.9	412.7	666.7	1,133.7	1,626.6	1,809.5	2,069.5
Claims on direct investors	8 557	. .	. . .	. . .	–.3	–.1	–.2	–.1	–.1	–.1
Liabilities to direct investors	8 558	. .	262.2	353.9	413.0	666.9	1,133.9	1,626.7	1,809.6	2,069.6
Other capital	8 580	. .	. . .	. . .	287.7	373.9	491.6	436.4	524.8	596.0
Claims on direct investors	8 585	. .	. . .	. . .	–15.4	–21.0	–13.6	–95.0	–100.4	–100.7
Liabilities to direct investors	8 590	. .	. . .	. . .	303.1	394.9	505.2	531.4	625.2	696.7
Portfolio investment	8 652	. .	**12.9**	**40.5**	**306.8**	**416.1**	**368.2**	**833.6**	**1,140.4**	**1,312.6**
Equity securities	8 660	. .	5.8	12.4	31.5	61.3	67.1	62.0	128.1	95.6
Banks	8 663	. .	5.4	11.6	24.0	46.8	60.8	37.3	31.7	26.8
Other sectors	8 664	. .	.4	.7	7.6	14.5	6.3	24.6	96.3	68.8
Debt securities	8 669	. .	7.2	28.1	275.3	354.7	301.1	771.6	1,012.3	1,217.1
Bonds and notes	8 670	. .	7.2	28.1	185.0	275.0	277.1	742.0	1,008.1	1,204.5
Monetary authorities	8 671	. .	. . .	. . .	. . .	. . .	. . .	. . .	. . .	. . .
General government	8 672	. .	7.2	28.1	185.0	200.0	223.9	723.4	986.1	1,103.9
Banks	8 673	. .	. . .	. . .	. . .	. . .	. . .	.8	.4	3.0
Other sectors	8 674	. .	. . .	. . .	. . .	75.0	53.2	17.9	21.6	97.7
Money market instruments	8 680	. .	. . .	. . .	90.3	79.7	24.0	29.6	4.2	12.6
Monetary authorities	8 681	. .	. . .	. . .	. . .	. . .	. . .	. . .	. . .	. . .
General government	8 682	. .	. . .	. . .	90.3	5.0	23.9	25.0	4.2	2.9
Banks	8 683	. .	. . .	. . .	. . .	. . .	. . .	.2	. . .	9.6
Other sectors	8 684	. .	. . .	. . .	. . .	74.7	.1	4.4	.1	. . .
Financial derivatives	8 905	. .	. . .	. . .	. . .	. . .	. . .	. . .	. . .	. . .
Monetary authorities	8 906	. .	. . .	. . .	. . .	. . .	. . .	. . .	. . .	. . .
General government	8 907	. .	. . .	. . .	. . .	. . .	. . .	. . .	. . .	. . .
Banks	8 908	. .	. . .	. . .	. . .	. . .	. . .	. . .	. . .	. . .
Other sectors	8 909	. .	. . .	. . .	. . .	. . .	. . .	. . .	. . .	. . .
Other investment	8 753	. .	**840.7**	**1,401.4**	**1,806.1**	**2,508.1**	**2,935.3**	**3,217.5**	**3,218.6**	**3,353.3**
Trade credits	8 756	. .	188.2	383.3	453.2	670.9	647.9	691.6	732.3	862.3
General government	8 757	. .	. . .	. . .	. . .	. . .	. . .	. . .	. . .	. . .
of which: Short-term	8 759	. .	. . .	. . .	. . .	. . .	. . .	. . .	. . .	. . .
Other sectors	8 760	. .	188.2	383.3	453.2	670.9	647.9	691.6	732.3	862.3
of which: Short-term	8 762	. .	*188.2*	*383.3*	*453.2*	*670.9*	*647.9*	*691.6*	*732.3*	*862.3*
Loans	8 764	. .	562.1	947.7	1,196.2	1,644.0	2,101.8	2,286.9	2,261.5	2,149.3
Monetary authorities	8 765	. .	196.4	261.5	273.4	270.5	253.2	230.2	191.6	151.2
of which: Use of Fund credit and loans from the Fund	8 766	. .	*196.4*	*261.5*	*273.4*	*270.5*	*253.2*	*230.2*	*191.6*	*151.2*
of which: Short-term	8 768	. .	. . .	. . .	. . .	. . .	. . .	. . .	. . .	. . .
General government	8 769	. .	235.2	424.0	447.4	549.2	694.2	881.3	767.0	694.1
of which: Short-term	8 771	. .	. . .	. . .	. . .	. . .	. . .	*25.0*	. . .	. . .
Banks	8 772	. .	20.9	28.7	56.0	133.7	302.3	342.2	412.3	474.0
of which: Short-term	8 774	. .	. . .	. . .	*46.4*	*12.8*	*35.3*	*11.6*	*126.5*	*298.3*
Other sectors	8 775	. .	109.6	233.4	419.4	690.7	852.1	833.2	890.7	830.0
of which: Short-term	8 777	. .	*15.3*	*37.9*	*139.8*	*73.8*	*149.4*	*72.9*	*26.1*	*43.6*
Currency and deposits	8 780	. .	90.3	69.4	127.6	149.0	144.8	189.2	147.9	166.1
Monetary authorities	8 781	. .	25.2	.1	1.7	.4	.3	.3	.2	.3
General government	8 782	. .	. . .	. . .	. . .	. . .	. . .	. . .	. . .	. . .
Banks	8 783	. .	65.2	69.3	125.9	148.6	144.5	188.9	147.7	165.8
Other sectors	8 784	. .	. . .	. . .	. . .	. . .	. . .	. . .	. . .	. . .
Other liabilities	8 786	. .	. . .	1.1	29.1	44.2	40.8	49.8	76.9	175.6
Monetary authorities	8 787	. .	. . .	. . .	. . .	. . .	. . .	. . .	. . .	51.6
of which: Short-term	8 789	. .	. . .	. . .	. . .	. . .	. . .	. . .	. . .	*51.6*
General government	8 790	. .	. . .	. . .	. . .	. . .	. . .	. . .	. . .	. . .
of which: Short-term	8 792	. .	. . .	. . .	. . .	. . .	. . .	. . .	. . .	. . .
Banks	8 793	. .	. . .	1.1	.4	.5	16.5	8.6	8.2	51.3
of which: Short-term	8 795	. .	. . .	*1.1*	*.4*	*.5*	*16.5*	*8.6*	*8.2*	*51.3*
Other sectors	8 796	. .	. . .	. . .	28.7	43.8	24.2	41.2	68.7	72.8
of which: Short-term	8 798	. .	. . .	. . .	*28.7*	*43.8*	*24.2*	*41.2*	*68.7*	*72.8*
NET INTERNATIONAL INVESTMENT POSITION	8 995	. .	**–118.3**	**–521.2**	**–1,120.6**	**–1,816.2**	**–2,456.6**	**–3,661.4**	**–4,015.6**	**–4,205.1**
Conversion rates: litai per U.S. dollar (end of period)	0 102	. .	**4.0000**	**4.0000**	**4.0000**	**4.0000**	**4.0000**	**4.0000**	**4.0000**	**4.0000**

Table 1. ANALYTIC PRESENTATION, 1994–2001
(Millions of U.S. dollars)

	Code		1994	1995	1996	1997	1998	1999	2000	2001
A. Current Account[1]	4 993	Z.	...	**2,426**	**2,219**	**1,834**	**1,626**	**1,650**	**2,562**	**1,674**
Goods: exports f.o.b	2 100	..	...	8,578	7,944	7,745	8,557	8,565	8,635	8,996
Goods: imports f.o.b	3 100	..	...	–10,269	–9,872	–9,770	–10,881	–11,151	–11,056	–11,395
Balance on Goods	4 100	..	...	*–1,690*	*–1,928*	*–2,025*	*–2,324*	*–2,586*	*–2,420*	*–2,399*
Services: credit	2 200	..	...	10,619	11,930	12,583	14,084	17,134	20,301	19,945
Services: debit	3 200	..	...	–7,519	–8,483	–8,683	–9,947	–11,840	–13,581	–13,708
Balance on Goods and Services	4 991	..	...	*1,410*	*1,519*	*1,874*	*1,813*	*2,708*	*4,300*	*3,838*
Income: credit	2 300	..	...	48,798	40,476	38,439	46,814	47,931	50,400	52,302
Income: debit	3 300	..	...	–47,209	–39,220	–37,971	–46,578	–48,413	–51,678	–53,941
Balance on Goods, Services, and Income	4 992	..	...	*2,999*	*2,774*	*2,342*	*2,049*	*2,227*	*3,022*	*2,199*
Current transfers: credit	2 379	Z.	...	1,791	2,186	1,985	2,185	2,282	2,750	2,269
Current transfers: debit	3 379	..	...	–2,364	–2,741	–2,493	–2,608	–2,859	–3,211	–2,793
B. Capital Account[1]	4 994	Z.	...	...	...	...	...	...	...	...
Capital account: credit	2 994	Z.	...	...	...	...	...	...	...	...
Capital account: debit	3 994	..	...	...	...	...	...	...	...	...
Total, Groups A Plus B	4 981	..	...	*2,426*	*2,219*	*1,834*	*1,626*	*–2,586*	*–2,420*	*–2,399*
C. Financial Account[1]	4 995	W.	...	...	...	...	...	...	...	...
Direct investment abroad	4 505	..	...	...	...	...	...	...	...	...
Direct investment in Luxembourg	4 555	Z.	...	...	...	...	...	...	...	...
Portfolio investment assets	4 602	..	...	...	...	...	...	...	...	...
Equity securities	4 610	..	...	...	...	...	...	...	...	...
Debt securities	4 619	..	...	...	...	...	...	...	...	...
Portfolio investment liabilities	4 652	Z.	...	...	...	...	...	...	...	...
Equity securities	4 660	..	...	...	...	...	...	...	...	...
Debt securities	4 669	Z.	...	...	...	...	...	...	...	...
Financial derivatives	4 910	..	...	...	...	...	...	...	...	...
Financial derivatives assets	4 900	..	...	...	...	...	...	...	...	...
Financial derivatives liabilities	4 905	..	...	...	...	...	...	...	...	...
Other investment assets	4 703	..	...	...	...	...	...	...	...	...
Monetary authorities	4 701	..	...	...	...	...	...	...	...	...
General government	4 704	..	...	...	...	...	...	...	...	...
Banks	4 705	..	...	...	...	...	...	...	...	...
Other sectors	4 728	..	...	...	...	...	...	...	...	...
Other investment liabilities	4 753	W.	...	...	...	...	...	...	...	...
Monetary authorities	4 753	WA	...	...	...	...	...	...	...	...
General government	4 753	ZB	...	...	...	...	...	...	...	...
Banks	4 753	ZC	...	...	...	...	...	...	...	...
Other sectors	4 753	ZD	...	...	...	...	...	...	...	...
Total, Groups A Through C	4 983	..	...	*2,426*	*2,219*	*1,834*	*1,626*	*–2,586*	*–2,420*	*–2,399*
D. Net Errors and Omissions	4 998	..	...	...	...	...	...	...	...	...
Total, Groups A Through D	4 984	..	...	...	...	...	...	...	...	...
E. Reserves and Related Items	4 802	A.	...	...	...	...	...	...	...	...
Reserve assets	4 802	..	...	...	...	...	...	...	...	...
Use of Fund credit and loans	4 766	..	...	...	...	...	...	...	...	...
Exceptional financing	4 920	..	...	...	...	...	...	...	...	...
Conversion rates: Luxembourg francs per U.S. dollar	0 101	..	**33.4565**	**29.4800**	**30.9615**	**35.7739**	**36.2986**	...	...	...
Conversion rates: euros per U.S. dollar	0 103	..	...	...	...	...	...	**.9386**	**1.0854**	**1.1175**

[1] Excludes components that have been classified in the categories of Group E.

Table 2. STANDARD PRESENTATION, 1994–2001

(Millions of U.S. dollars)

	Code		1994	1995	1996	1997	1998	1999	2000	2001
CURRENT ACCOUNT	4 993	. .	...	**2,426**	**2,219**	**1,834**	**1,626**	**1,650**	**2,562**	**1,674**
A. GOODS	4 100	. .	...	–1,690	–1,928	–2,025	–2,324	–2,586	–2,420	–2,399
Credit	2 100	. .	...	**8,578**	**7,944**	**7,745**	**8,557**	**8,565**	**8,635**	**8,996**
General merchandise: exports f.o.b.	2 110	. .	...	...	...	...	...	...	...	...
Goods for processing: exports f.o.b.	2 150	. .	...	...	...	...	...	...	...	...
Repairs on goods	2 160	. .	...	...	...	...	...	...	...	...
Goods procured in ports by carriers	2 170	. .	...	...	...	...	...	...	...	...
Nonmonetary gold	2 180	. .	...	...	...	...	...	...	...	...
Debit	3 100	. .	...	**–10,269**	**–9,872**	**–9,770**	**–10,881**	**–11,151**	**–11,056**	**–11,395**
General merchandise: imports f.o.b.	3 110	. .	...	...	...	...	...	...	...	...
Goods for processing: imports f.o.b.	3 150	. .	...	...	...	...	...	...	...	...
Repairs on goods	3 160	. .	...	...	...	...	...	...	...	...
Goods procured in ports by carriers	3 170	. .	...	...	...	...	...	...	...	...
Nonmonetary gold	3 180	. .	...	...	...	...	...	...	...	...
B. SERVICES	4 200	. .	...	3,100	3,446	3,899	4,137	5,294	6,720	6,237
Total credit	2 200	. .	...	*10,619*	*11,930*	*12,583*	*14,084*	*17,134*	*20,301*	*19,945*
Total debit	3 200	. .	...	*–7,519*	*–8,483*	*–8,683*	*–9,947*	*–11,840*	*–13,581*	*–13,708*
Transportation services, credit	2 205	. .	...	**733**	**752**	**924**	**995**	**1,146**	**1,331**	**1,368**
Passenger	2 850	. .	...	...	...	...	...	...	...	...
Freight	2 851	. .	...	...	...	...	...	...	...	...
Other	2 852	. .	...	...	...	...	...	...	...	...
Sea transport, passenger	2 207	. .	...	...	...	...	...	...	...	...
Sea transport, freight	2 208	. .	...	...	...	...	...	...	...	...
Sea transport, other	2 209	. .	...	...	...	...	...	...	...	...
Air transport, passenger	2 211	. .	...	...	...	...	...	...	...	...
Air transport, freight	2 212	. .	...	...	...	...	...	...	...	...
Air transport, other	2 213	. .	...	...	...	...	...	...	...	...
Other transport, passenger	2 215	. .	...	...	...	...	...	...	...	...
Other transport, freight	2 216	. .	...	...	...	...	...	...	...	...
Other transport, other	2 217	. .	...	...	...	...	...	...	...	...
Transportation services, debit	3 205	. .	...	**–660**	**–719**	**–771**	**–746**	**–819**	**–834**	**–917**
Passenger	3 850	. .	...	...	...	...	...	...	...	...
Freight	3 851	. .	...	...	...	...	...	...	...	...
Other	3 852	. .	...	...	...	...	...	...	...	...
Sea transport, passenger	3 207	. .	...	...	...	...	...	...	...	...
Sea transport, freight	3 208	. .	...	...	...	...	...	...	...	...
Sea transport, other	3 209	. .	...	...	...	...	...	...	...	...
Air transport, passenger	3 211	. .	...	...	...	...	...	...	...	...
Air transport, freight	3 212	. .	...	...	...	...	...	...	...	...
Air transport, other	3 213	. .	...	...	...	...	...	...	...	...
Other transport, passenger	3 215	. .	...	...	...	...	...	...	...	...
Other transport, freight	3 216	. .	...	...	...	...	...	...	...	...
Other transport, other	3 217	. .	...	...	...	...	...	...	...	...
Travel, credit	2 236	. .	...	**1,695**	**1,640**	**1,639**	**1,634**	**1,697**	**1,686**	**1,780**
Business travel	2 237	. .	...	506	498	467	505	530	529	587
Personal travel	2 240	. .	...	1,189	1,142	1,172	1,129	1,167	1,157	1,194
Travel, debit	3 236	. .	...	**–1,192**	**–1,189**	**–1,115**	**–1,335**	**–1,316**	**–1,309**	**–1,464**
Business travel	3 237	. .	...	–149	–155	–151	–168	–174	–170	–220
Personal travel	3 240	. .	...	–1,043	–1,034	–964	–1,168	–1,143	–1,139	–1,244
Other services, credit	2 200	BA	...	**8,191**	**9,537**	**10,019**	**11,455**	**14,291**	**17,283**	**16,797**
Communications	2 245	. .	...	358	502	504	516	621	683	736
Construction	2 249	. .	...	20	35	58	27	35	32	45
Insurance	2 253	. .	...	613	700	723	740	896	955	807
Financial	2 260	. .	...	5,250	6,062	6,678	7,754	10,401	13,198	12,628
Computer and information	2 262	. .	...	126	146	142	144	167	172	172
Royalties and licence fees	2 266	. .	...	44	61	75	100	122	134	202
Other business services	2 268	. .	...	1,401	1,544	1,400	1,590	1,485	1,521	1,666
Personal, cultural, and recreational	2 287	. .	...	92	177	190	338	340	376	330
Government, n.i.e.	2 291	. .	...	288	310	249	244	224	212	211
Other services, debit	3 200	BA	...	**–5,667**	**–6,575**	**–6,797**	**–7,865**	**–9,705**	**–11,438**	**–11,327**
Communications	3 245	. .	...	–68	–49	–36	–45	–73	–138	–159
Construction	3 249	. .	...	–95	–161	–132	–120	–116	–113	–102
Insurance	3 253	. .	...	–477	–583	–529	–561	–654	–691	–559
Financial	3 260	. .	...	–2,974	–3,433	–3,851	–4,575	–6,272	–7,340	–7,103
Computer and information	3 262	. .	...	–68	–90	–106	–155	–186	–278	–283
Royalties and licence fees	3 266	. .	...	–51	–61	–100	–99	–107	–122	–243
Other business services	3 268	. .	...	–1,498	–1,761	–1,646	–1,825	–1,739	–2,238	–2,402
Personal, cultural, and recreational	3 287	. .	...	–424	–414	–370	–465	–509	–481	–435
Government, n.i.e.	3 291	. .	...	–14	–23	–28	–22	–50	–37	–40

Table 2 (Continued). STANDARD PRESENTATION, 1994–2001
(Millions of U.S. dollars)

	Code	1994	1995	1996	1997	1998	1999	2000	2001
C. INCOME	4 300 . .	...	1,589	1,255	468	236	-482	-1,278	-1,639
Total credit	2 300 . .	...	*48,798*	*40,476*	*38,439*	*46,814*	*47,931*	*50,400*	*52,302*
Total debit	3 300 . .	...	*-47,209*	*-39,220*	*-37,971*	*-46,578*	*-48,413*	*-51,678*	*-53,941*
Compensation of employees, credit	2 310 . .	...	**730**	**711**	**649**	**657**	**652**	**579**	**576**
Compensation of employees, debit	3 310 . .	...	**-2,215**	**-2,304**	**-2,219**	**-2,459**	**-2,695**	**-2,720**	**-3,138**
Investment income, credit	2 320 . .	...	**48,068**	**39,765**	**37,790**	**46,157**	**47,280**	**49,821**	**51,725**
Direct investment income	2 330 . .	...	...	...	...	...	...	...	...
Dividends and distributed branch profits	2 332 . .	...	...	...	...	...	...	...	...
Reinvested earnings and undistributed branch profits	2 333 . .	...	...	...	...	...	...	...	...
Income on debt (interest)	2 334 . .	...	...	...	...	...	...	...	...
Portfolio investment income	2 339 . .	...	...	...	...	...	...	...	...
Income on equity	2 340 . .	...	...	...	...	...	...	...	...
Income on bonds and notes	2 350 . .	...	...	...	...	...	...	...	...
Income on money market instruments	2 360 . .	...	...	...	...	...	...	...	...
Other investment income	2 370 . .	...	...	...	...	...	...	...	...
Investment income, debit	3 320 . .	...	**-44,994**	**-36,916**	**-35,752**	**-44,119**	**-45,718**	**-48,958**	**-50,803**
Direct investment income	3 330 . .	...	...	...	...	...	...	...	...
Dividends and distributed branch profits	3 332 . .	...	...	...	...	...	...	...	...
Reinvested earnings and undistributed branch profits	3 333 . .	...	...	...	...	...	...	...	...
Income on debt (interest)	3 334 . .	...	...	...	...	...	...	...	...
Portfolio investment income	3 339 . .	...	...	...	...	...	...	...	...
Income on equity	3 340 . .	...	...	...	...	...	...	...	...
Income on bonds and notes	3 350 . .	...	...	...	...	...	...	...	...
Income on money market instruments	3 360 . .	...	...	...	...	...	...	...	...
Other investment income	3 370 . .	...	...	...	...	...	...	...	...
D. CURRENT TRANSFERS	4 379 . .	...	-573	-555	-508	-423	-577	-461	-525
Credit	2 379 . .	...	**1,791**	**2,186**	**1,985**	**2,185**	**2,282**	**2,750**	**2,269**
General government	2 380 . .	...	764	836	774	802	884	876	958
Other sectors	2 390 . .	...	1,028	1,350	1,211	1,383	1,397	1,874	1,310
Workers' remittances	2 391 . .	...	...	...	...	...	...	...	...
Other current transfers	2 392 . .	...	...	...	...	...	...	...	...
Debit	3 379 . .	...	**-2,364**	**-2,741**	**-2,493**	**-2,608**	**-2,859**	**-3,211**	**-2,793**
General government	3 380 . .	...	-815	-818	-798	-927	-1,011	-901	-998
Other sectors	3 390 . .	...	-1,549	-1,924	-1,696	-1,681	-1,848	-2,309	-1,796
Workers' remittances	3 391 . .	...	...	...	...	...	...	...	...
Other current transfers	3 392 . .	...	...	...	...	...	...	...	...
CAPITAL AND FINANCIAL ACCOUNT	4 996 . .	...	...	...	...	...	...	...	...
CAPITAL ACCOUNT	4 994 . .	...	...	...	...	...	...	...	...
Total credit	2 994 . .	...	...	...	...	...	...	...	...
Total debit	3 994 . .	...	...	...	...	...	...	...	...
Capital transfers, credit	2 400 . .	...	...	...	...	...	...	...	...
General government	2 401 . .	...	...	...	...	...	...	...	...
Debt forgiveness	2 402 . .	...	...	...	...	...	...	...	...
Other capital transfers	2 410 . .	...	...	...	...	...	...	...	...
Other sectors	2 430 . .	...	...	...	...	...	...	...	...
Migrants' transfers	2 431 . .	...	...	...	...	...	...	...	...
Debt forgiveness	2 432 . .	...	...	...	...	...	...	...	...
Other capital transfers	2 440 . .	...	...	...	...	...	...	...	...
Capital transfers, debit	3 400 . .	...	...	...	...	...	...	...	...
General government	3 401 . .	...	...	...	...	...	...	...	...
Debt forgiveness	3 402 . .	...	...	...	...	...	...	...	...
Other capital transfers	3 410 . .	...	...	...	...	...	...	...	...
Other sectors	3 430 . .	...	...	...	...	...	...	...	...
Migrants' transfers	3 431 . .	...	...	...	...	...	...	...	...
Debt forgiveness	3 432 . .	...	...	...	...	...	...	...	...
Other capital transfers	3 440 . .	...	...	...	...	...	...	...	...
Nonproduced nonfinancial assets, credit	2 480 . .	...	...	...	...	...	...	...	...
Nonproduced nonfinancial assets, debit	3 480 . .	...	...	...	...	...	...	...	...

Table 2 (Continued). STANDARD PRESENTATION, 1994–2001
(Millions of U.S. dollars)

	Code	1994	1995	1996	1997	1998	1999	2000	2001
FINANCIAL ACCOUNT	4 995	...	...	...	...	...	...	...	...
A. DIRECT INVESTMENT	4 500	...	...	...	...	...	...	...	...
Direct investment abroad	4 505	...	...	...	...	...	...	...	...
Equity capital	4 510	...	...	...	...	...	...	...	...
Claims on affiliated enterprises	4 515	...	...	...	...	...	...	...	...
Liabilities to affiliated enterprises	4 520	...	...	...	...	...	...	...	...
Reinvested earnings	4 525	...	...	...	...	...	...	...	...
Other capital	4 530	...	...	...	...	...	...	...	...
Claims on affiliated enterprises	4 535	...	...	...	...	...	...	...	...
Liabilities to affiliated enterprises	4 540	...	...	...	...	...	...	...	...
Direct investment in Luxembourg	4 555	...	...	...	...	...	...	...	...
Equity capital	4 560	...	...	...	...	...	...	...	...
Claims on direct investors	4 565	...	...	...	...	...	...	...	...
Liabilities to direct investors	4 570	...	...	...	...	...	...	...	...
Reinvested earnings	4 575	...	...	...	...	...	...	...	...
Other capital	4 580	...	...	...	...	...	...	...	...
Claims on direct investors	4 585	...	...	...	...	...	...	...	...
Liabilities to direct investors	4 590	...	...	...	...	...	...	...	...
B. PORTFOLIO INVESTMENT	4 600	...	...	...	...	...	...	...	...
Assets	4 602	...	...	...	...	...	...	...	...
Equity securities	4 610	...	...	...	...	...	...	...	...
Monetary authorities	4 611	...	...	...	...	...	...	...	...
General government	4 612	...	...	...	...	...	...	...	...
Banks	4 613	...	...	...	...	...	...	...	...
Other sectors	4 614	...	...	...	...	...	...	...	...
Debt securities	4 619	...	...	...	...	...	...	...	...
Bonds and notes	4 620	...	...	...	...	...	...	...	...
Monetary authorities	4 621	...	...	...	...	...	...	...	...
General government	4 622	...	...	...	...	...	...	...	...
Banks	4 623	...	...	...	...	...	...	...	...
Other sectors	4 624	...	...	...	...	...	...	...	...
Money market instruments	4 630	...	...	...	...	...	...	...	...
Monetary authorities	4 631	...	...	...	...	...	...	...	...
General government	4 632	...	...	...	...	...	...	...	...
Banks	4 633	...	...	...	...	...	...	...	...
Other sectors	4 634	...	...	...	...	...	...	...	...
Liabilities	4 652	...	...	...	...	...	...	...	...
Equity securities	4 660	...	...	...	...	...	...	...	...
Banks	4 663	...	...	...	...	...	...	...	...
Other sectors	4 664	...	...	...	...	...	...	...	...
Debt securities	4 669	...	...	...	...	...	...	...	...
Bonds and notes	4 670	...	...	...	...	...	...	...	...
Monetary authorities	4 671	...	...	...	...	...	...	...	...
General government	4 672	...	...	...	...	...	...	...	...
Banks	4 673	...	...	...	...	...	...	...	...
Other sectors	4 674	...	...	...	...	...	...	...	...
Money market instruments	4 680	...	...	...	...	...	...	...	...
Monetary authorities	4 681	...	...	...	...	...	...	...	...
General government	4 682	...	...	...	...	...	...	...	...
Banks	4 683	...	...	...	...	...	...	...	...
Other sectors	4 684	...	...	...	...	...	...	...	...
C. FINANCIAL DERIVATIVES	4 910	...	...	...	...	...	...	...	...
Monetary authorities	4 911	...	...	...	...	...	...	...	...
General government	4 912	...	...	...	...	...	...	...	...
Banks	4 913	...	...	...	...	...	...	...	...
Other sectors	4 914	...	...	...	...	...	...	...	...
Assets	4 900	...	...	...	...	...	...	...	...
Monetary authorities	4 901	...	...	...	...	...	...	...	...
General government	4 902	...	...	...	...	...	...	...	...
Banks	4 903	...	...	...	...	...	...	...	...
Other sectors	4 904	...	...	...	...	...	...	...	...
Liabilities	4 905	...	...	...	...	...	...	...	...
Monetary authorities	4 906	...	...	...	...	...	...	...	...
General government	4 907	...	...	...	...	...	...	...	...
Banks	4 908	...	...	...	...	...	...	...	...
Other sectors	4 909	...	...	...	...	...	...	...	...

Table 2 (Concluded). STANDARD PRESENTATION, 1994–2001
(Millions of U.S. dollars)

	Code	1994	1995	1996	1997	1998	1999	2000	2001
D. OTHER INVESTMENT	4 700 . .	...	...	...	...	...	...	...	...
Assets	4 703 . .	...	...	...	...	...	...	...	...
Trade credits	4 706 . .	...	...	...	...	...	...	...	...
General government	4 707 . .	...	...	...	...	...	...	...	...
of which: Short-term	4 709 . .	...	...	...	...	...	...	...	...
Other sectors	4 710 . .	...	...	...	...	...	...	...	...
of which: Short-term	4 712 . .	...	...	...	...	...	...	...	...
Loans	4 714 . .	...	...	...	...	...	...	...	...
Monetary authorities	4 715 . .	...	...	...	...	...	...	...	...
of which: Short-term	4 718 . .	...	...	...	...	...	...	...	...
General government	4 719 . .	...	...	...	...	...	...	...	...
of which: Short-term	4 721 . .	...	...	...	...	...	...	...	...
Banks	4 722 . .	...	...	...	...	...	...	...	...
of which: Short-term	4 724 . .	...	...	...	...	...	...	...	...
Other sectors	4 725 . .	...	...	...	...	...	...	...	...
of which: Short-term	4 727 . .	...	...	...	...	...	...	...	...
Currency and deposits	4 730 . .	...	...	...	...	...	...	...	...
Monetary authorities	4 731 . .	...	...	...	...	...	...	...	...
General government	4 732 . .	...	...	...	...	...	...	...	...
Banks	4 733 . .	...	...	...	...	...	...	...	...
Other sectors	4 734 . .	...	...	...	...	...	...	...	...
Other assets	4 736 . .	...	...	...	...	...	...	...	...
Monetary authorities	4 737 . .	...	...	...	...	...	...	...	...
of which: Short-term	4 739 . .	...	...	...	...	...	...	...	...
General government	4 740 . .	...	...	...	...	...	...	...	...
of which: Short-term	4 742 . .	...	...	...	...	...	...	...	...
Banks	4 743 . .	...	...	...	...	...	...	...	...
of which: Short-term	4 745 . .	...	...	...	...	...	...	...	...
Other sectors	4 746 . .	...	...	...	...	...	...	...	...
of which: Short-term	4 748 . .	...	...	...	...	...	...	...	...
Liabilities	4 753 . .	...	...	...	...	...	...	...	...
Trade credits	4 756 . .	...	...	...	...	...	...	...	...
General government	4 757 . .	...	...	...	...	...	...	...	...
of which: Short-term	4 759 . .	...	...	...	...	...	...	...	...
Other sectors	4 760 . .	...	...	...	...	...	...	...	...
of which: Short-term	4 762 . .	...	...	...	...	...	...	...	...
Loans	4 764 . .	...	...	...	...	...	...	...	...
Monetary authorities	4 765 . .	...	...	...	...	...	...	...	...
of which: Use of Fund credit and loans from the Fund	4 766 . .	...	...	...	...	...	...	...	...
of which: Short-term	4 768 . .	...	...	...	...	...	...	...	...
General government	4 769 . .	...	...	...	...	...	...	...	...
of which: Short-term	4 771 . .	...	...	...	...	...	...	...	...
Banks	4 772 . .	...	...	...	...	...	...	...	...
of which: Short-term	4 774 . .	...	...	...	...	...	...	...	...
Other sectors	4 775 . .	...	...	...	...	...	...	...	...
of which: Short-term	4 777 . .	...	...	...	...	...	...	...	...
Currency and deposits	4 780 . .	...	...	...	...	...	...	...	...
Monetary authorities	4 781 . .	...	...	...	...	...	...	...	...
General government	4 782 . .	...	...	...	...	...	...	...	...
Banks	4 783 . .	...	...	...	...	...	...	...	...
Other sectors	4 784 . .	...	...	...	...	...	...	...	...
Other liabilities	4 786 . .	...	...	...	...	...	...	...	...
Monetary authorities	4 787 . .	...	...	...	...	...	...	...	...
of which: Short-term	4 789 . .	...	...	...	...	...	...	...	...
General government	4 790 . .	...	...	...	...	...	...	...	...
of which: Short-term	4 792 . .	...	...	...	...	...	...	...	...
Banks	4 793 . .	...	...	...	...	...	...	...	...
of which: Short-term	4 795 . .	...	...	...	...	...	...	...	...
Other sectors	4 796 . .	...	...	...	...	...	...	...	...
of which: Short-term	4 798 . .	...	...	...	...	...	...	...	...
E. RESERVE ASSETS	4 802 . .	...	...	...	...	...	...	...	...
Monetary gold	4 812 . .	...	...	...	...	...	...	...	...
Special drawing rights	4 811 . .	...	...	...	...	...	...	...	...
Reserve position in the Fund	4 810 . .	...	...	...	...	...	...	...	...
Foreign exchange	4 803 . .	...	...	...	...	...	...	...	...
Other claims	4 813 . .	...	...	...	...	...	...	...	...
NET ERRORS AND OMISSIONS	4 998 . .	...	...	...	...	...	...	...	...

Table 1. ANALYTIC PRESENTATION, 1994–2001
(Millions of U.S. dollars)

	Code		1994	1995	1996	1997	1998	1999	2000	2001
A. Current Account [1]	4 993	Z.	**...**	**...**	**–288.1**	**–275.5**	**–311.7**	**–109.3**	**–107.2**	**–324.3**
Goods: exports f.o.b	2 100	..	...	...	1,147.4	1,201.4	1,292.9	1,192.1	1,317.1	1,153.5
Goods: imports f.o.b	3 100	..	...	...	–1,464.0	–1,589.1	–1,713.2	–1,602.2	–1,875.2	–1,574.9
Balance on Goods	4 100	..	...	...	*–316.5*	*–387.6*	*–420.3*	*–410.1*	*–558.0*	*–421.4*
Services: credit	2 200	..	...	...	154.3	128.3	131.3	248.4	303.1	233.8
Services: debit	3 200	..	...	...	–309.3	–272.9	–304.3	–323.8	–357.8	–336.7
Balance on Goods and Services	4 991	..	...	...	*–471.5*	*–532.2*	*–593.3*	*–485.5*	*–612.7*	*–524.3*
Income: credit	2 300	..	...	...	45.3	39.0	23.5	22.5	42.2	48.1
Income: debit	3 300	..	...	...	–75.0	–72.6	–68.4	–66.3	–87.3	–88.6
Balance on Goods, Services, and Income	4 992	..	...	...	*–501.2*	*–565.8*	*–638.1*	*–529.4*	*–657.8*	*–564.8*
Current transfers: credit	2 379	Z.	...	...	475.4	535.0	692.6	750.3	923.1	872.5
Current transfers: debit	3 379	..	...	...	–262.3	–244.8	–366.2	–330.2	–372.4	–632.0
B. Capital Account [1]	4 994	Z.	**...**	**...**	**...**	**...**	**9.4**	**4.4**	**.3**	**1.3**
Capital account: credit	2 994	Z.	...	...	...	...	11.2	4.4	.3	3.6
Capital account: debit	3 994	..	...	...	...	...	–1.8	...	...	–2.3
Total, Groups A Plus B	4 981	..	...	...	*–288.1*	*–275.5*	*–302.3*	*–104.9*	*–106.8*	*–323.0*
C. Financial Account [1]	4 995	W.	**...**	**...**	**174.3**	**186.8**	**449.2**	**189.6**	**385.2**	**388.2**
Direct investment abroad	4 505	..	...	...	...	...	...	...	.6	–.9
Direct investment in Macedonia, FYR	4 555	Z.	...	...	11.2	15.7	117.7	30.1	175.6	443.2
Portfolio investment assets	4 602	..	...	...	–.5	–2.5	–.6	–.4	...	3.2
Equity securities	4 610	..	...	...	–.5	–2.5	–.6	–.4	...	...
Debt securities	4 619	..	...	...	...	...	...	...	...	3.2
Portfolio investment liabilities	4 652	Z.	...	...	.8	4.6	8.4	.5	–.1	...
Equity securities	4 660	..	...	...	.8	4.6	8.4	.5	–.1	...
Debt securities	4 669	Z.	...	...	...	...	...	...	...	...
Financial derivatives	4 910	..	...	...	...	...	...	...	...	...
Financial derivatives assets	4 900	..	...	...	...	...	...	...	...	...
Financial derivatives liabilities	4 905	..	...	...	...	...	...	...	...	...
Other investment assets	4 703	..	...	...	–133.2	–73.0	–77.2	–81.0	–81.1	8.8
Monetary authorities	4 701	..	...	...	...	...	...	...	...	–231.3
General government	4 704	..	...	...	...	...	...	–14.6	...	...
Banks	4 705	..	...	...	25.3	–57.5	–51.0	–66.4	–81.1	–237.7
Other sectors	4 728	..	...	...	–158.5	–15.6	–26.2	...	...	477.8
Other investment liabilities	4 753	W.	...	...	295.9	242.0	400.9	240.4	290.2	–66.1
Monetary authorities	4 753	WA	...	...	...	...	...	...	14.7	140.1
General government	4 753	ZB	...	...	59.9	–71.6	109.2	68.8	50.9	–66.4
Banks	4 753	ZC	...	...	–1.2	29.8	97.7	30.9	–35.1	–63.1
Other sectors	4 753	ZD	...	...	237.3	283.8	194.0	140.7	259.8	–76.7
Total, Groups A Through C	4 983	..	...	...	*–113.9*	*–88.7*	*146.9*	*84.7*	*278.4*	*65.2*
D. Net Errors and Omissions	4 998	..	**...**	**...**	**18.8**	**–29.9**	**–114.8**	**34.5**	**–46.0**	**25.9**
Total, Groups A Through D	4 984	..	...	...	*–95.1*	*–118.6*	*32.1*	*119.2*	*232.3*	*91.1*
E. Reserves and Related Items	4 802	A.	**...**	**...**	**95.1**	**118.6**	**–32.1**	**–119.2**	**–232.3**	**–91.1**
Reserve assets	4 802	..	...	...	7.6	–35.1	–42.0	–141.6	–234.7	–83.5
Use of Fund credit and loans	4 766	..	...	...	13.5	24.6	9.9	1.8	–15.6	–7.6
Exceptional financing	4 920	..	...	...	73.9	129.2	...	20.6	18.0	...
Conversion rates: denars per U.S. dollar	0 101	..	**43.263**	**37.882**	**39.981**	**50.004**	**54.462**	**56.902**	**65.904**	**68.037**

[1] Excludes components that have been classified in the categories of Group E.

Table 2. STANDARD PRESENTATION, 1994–2001
(Millions of U.S. dollars)

	Code	1994	1995	1996	1997	1998	1999	2000	2001
CURRENT ACCOUNT	4 993 . .	**. . .**	**. . .**	**–288.1**	**–275.5**	**–311.7**	**–109.3**	**–107.2**	**–324.3**
A. GOODS	4 100 . .	. . .	. . .	–316.5	–387.6	–420.3	–410.1	–558.0	–421.4
Credit	2 100 . .	**. . .**	**. . .**	**1,147.4**	**1,201.4**	**1,292.9**	**1,192.1**	**1,317.1**	**1,153.5**
General merchandise: exports f.o.b.	2 110 . .	. . .	. . .	775.9	764.9	696.4	671.8	678.8	601.0
Goods for processing: exports f.o.b.	2 150 . .	. . .	. . .	371.5	436.5	591.8	513.3	633.7	549.8
Repairs on goods	2 160 . .	. . .	. . .	. . .	. . .	3.7	2.6	.9	.6
Goods procured in ports by carriers	2 170 . .	. . .	. . .	. . .	. . .	1.1	4.3	3.7	2.1
Nonmonetary gold	2 180 . .	. . .	. . .	. . .	. . .	. . .	. . .	. . .	. . .
Debit	3 100 . .	**. . .**	**. . .**	**–1,464.0**	**–1,589.1**	**–1,713.2**	**–1,602.2**	**–1,875.2**	**–1,574.9**
General merchandise: imports f.o.b.	3 110 . .	. . .	. . .	–1,205.1	–1,197.5	–1,277.2	–1,222.2	–1,371.3	–1,193.8
Goods for processing: imports f.o.b.	3 150 . .	. . .	. . .	–258.9	–391.6	–432.9	–377.3	–502.3	–379.5
Repairs on goods	3 160 . .	. . .	. . .	. . .	. . .	–2.6	–2.7	–1.6	–1.4
Goods procured in ports by carriers	3 170 . .	. . .	. . .	. . .	. . .	. . .	. . .	. . .	. . .
Nonmonetary gold	3 180 . .	. . .	. . .	. . .	. . .	–.5	–.1	–.1	–.2
B. SERVICES	4 200 . .	. . .	. . .	–155.0	–144.6	–173.0	–75.4	–54.7	–102.9
Total credit	2 200 . .	. . .	. . .	*154.3*	*128.3*	*131.3*	*248.4*	*303.1*	*233.8*
Total debit	3 200 . .	. . .	. . .	*–309.3*	*–272.9*	*–304.3*	*–323.8*	*–357.8*	*–336.7*
Transportation services, credit	2 205 . .	**. . .**	**. . .**	**48.5**	**54.2**	**61.2**	**87.1**	**116.2**	**74.7**
Passenger	2 850 . .	. . .	. . .	*13.6*	*14.8*	*12.8*	*39.6*	*49.6*	*23.4*
Freight	2 851 . .	. . .	. . .	*27.3*	*27.6*	*32.6*	*32.4*	*47.5*	*33.5*
Other	2 852 . .	. . .	. . .	*7.5*	*11.8*	*15.8*	*15.2*	*19.1*	*17.8*
Sea transport, passenger	2 207 . .	. . .	. . .	. . .	. . .	. . .	. . .	. . .	. . .
Sea transport, freight	2 208 . .	. . .	. . .	1.7	3.9	2.5	.1	. . .	.1
Sea transport, other	2 209 . .	. . .	. . .	. . .	1.4	1.6	. . .	. . .	.4
Air transport, passenger	2 211 . .	. . .	. . .	12.5	14.0	12.0	38.5	48.4	22.8
Air transport, freight	2 212 . .	. . .	. . .	.4	.2	.4	.5	.6	.3
Air transport, other	2 213 . .	. . .	. . .	7.1	10.2	13.9	14.0	18.7	17.2
Other transport, passenger	2 215 . .	. . .	. . .	1.2	.8	.8	1.1	1.2	.6
Other transport, freight	2 216 . .	. . .	. . .	25.2	23.5	29.7	31.8	46.9	33.1
Other transport, other	2 217 . .	. . .	. . .	.4	.2	.3	1.2	.4	.2
Transportation services, debit	3 205 . .	**. . .**	**. . .**	**–148.8**	**–131.7**	**–144.4**	**–152.7**	**–170.1**	**–141.0**
Passenger	3 850 . .	. . .	. . .	*–4.0*	*–6.4*	*–7.1*	*–9.9*	*–23.6*	*–20.5*
Freight	3 851 . .	. . .	. . .	*–121.5*	*–101.3*	*–107.8*	*–110.2*	*–114.3*	*–101.8*
Other	3 852 . .	. . .	. . .	*–23.4*	*–24.1*	*–29.5*	*–32.6*	*–32.2*	*–18.7*
Sea transport, passenger	3 207 . .	. . .	. . .	–.1	. . .	. . .	. . .	. . .	. . .
Sea transport, freight	3 208 . .	. . .	. . .	–8.8	–8.4	–4.1	–4.2	–3.4	–4.9
Sea transport, other	3 209 . .	. . .	. . .	–4.4	–6.7	–9.1	–6.9	–4.0	–3.1
Air transport, passenger	3 211 . .	. . .	. . .	–3.0	–5.7	–6.5	–8.4	–22.9	–19.8
Air transport, freight	3 212 . .	. . .	. . .	–3.1	–2.9	–1.2	–1.3	–2.9	–6.2
Air transport, other	3 213 . .	. . .	. . .	–4.2	–2.5	–4.9	–12.7	–14.9	–3.8
Other transport, passenger	3 215 . .	. . .	. . .	–.8	–.7	–.6	–1.6	–.7	–.7
Other transport, freight	3 216 . .	. . .	. . .	–109.6	–90.0	–102.5	–104.7	–107.9	–90.7
Other transport, other	3 217 . .	. . .	. . .	–14.8	–14.9	–15.5	–13.0	–13.3	–11.8
Travel, credit	2 236 . .	**. . .**	**. . .**	**20.6**	**14.0**	**14.7**	**37.0**	**37.4**	**25.1**
Business travel	2 237 . .	. . .	. . .	. . .	. . .	. . .	. . .	. . .	. . .
Personal travel	2 240 . .	. . .	. . .	20.6	14.0	14.7	37.0	37.4	25.1
Travel, debit	3 236 . .	**. . .**	**. . .**	**–26.3**	**–26.8**	**–30.7**	**–32.1**	**–34.3**	**–38.5**
Business travel	3 237 . .	. . .	. . .	–23.4	–19.8	–20.0	–20.0	–20.9	–21.3
Personal travel	3 240 . .	. . .	. . .	–2.8	–7.0	–10.7	–12.1	–13.4	–17.2
Other services, credit	2 200 BA	**. . .**	**. . .**	**85.2**	**60.1**	**55.4**	**124.4**	**149.5**	**134.0**
Communications	2 245 . .	. . .	. . .	17.3	15.9	18.5	30.7	39.0	32.5
Construction	2 249 . .	. . .	. . .	12.5	7.7	4.5	10.7	15.4	13.7
Insurance	2 253 . .	. . .	. . .	1.6	1.3	1.7	2.3	2.8	2.4
Financial	2 260 . .	. . .	. . .	3.9	1.7	3.1	1.0	1.8	1.2
Computer and information	2 262 . .	. . .	. . .	.5	.5	.3	1.3	1.0	1.6
Royalties and licence fees	2 266 . .	. . .	. . .	.8	1.6	1.4	2.2	2.8	3.3
Other business services	2 268 . .	. . .	. . .	42.8	28.7	22.7	52.6	63.4	32.4
Personal, cultural, and recreational	2 287 . .	. . .	. . .	2.9	1.1	2.1	1.6	1.4	1.8
Government, n.i.e.	2 291 . .	. . .	. . .	3.0	1.7	1.1	21.8	21.9	45.1
Other services, debit	3 200 BA	**. . .**	**. . .**	**–134.2**	**–114.4**	**–129.2**	**–139.0**	**–153.4**	**–157.2**
Communications	3 245 . .	. . .	. . .	–2.4	–2.4	–5.1	–6.5	–6.5	–7.5
Construction	3 249 . .	. . .	. . .	–8.6	–5.2	–6.3	–10.6	–.3	–1.1
Insurance	3 253 . .	. . .	. . .	–57.0	–43.5	–47.9	–47.6	–52.1	–43.9
Financial	3 260 . .	. . .	. . .	–5.0	–2.8	–2.9	–2.2	–2.6	–2.2
Computer and information	3 262 . .	. . .	. . .	–.7	–1.2	–1.0	–.9	–1.6	–8.2
Royalties and licence fees	3 266 . .	. . .	. . .	–2.8	–2.3	–2.4	–2.5	–5.7	–5.6
Other business services	3 268 . .	. . .	. . .	–46.9	–48.6	–54.0	–59.8	–75.2	–80.4
Personal, cultural, and recreational	3 287 . .	. . .	. . .	–1.4	–1.8	–2.1	–1.2	–1.8	–2.6
Government, n.i.e.	3 291 . .	. . .	. . .	–9.4	–6.8	–7.5	–7.7	–7.7	–5.7

Table 2 (Continued). STANDARD PRESENTATION, 1994–2001
(Millions of U.S. dollars)

	Code	1994	1995	1996	1997	1998	1999	2000	2001
C. INCOME	4 300	...	...	–29.7	–33.6	–44.8	–43.9	–45.1	–40.5
Total credit	2 300	...	...	*45.3*	*39.0*	*23.5*	*22.5*	*42.2*	*48.1*
Total debit	3 300	...	...	*–75.0*	*–72.6*	*–68.4*	*–66.3*	*–87.3*	*–88.6*
Compensation of employees, credit	2 310	...	...	**22.5**	**21.7**	...	...	**.4**	**1.1**
Compensation of employees, debit	3 310	...	...	**–.9**	**–.4**	...	...	...	...
Investment income, credit	2 320	...	...	**22.8**	**17.3**	**23.5**	**22.5**	**41.8**	**47.0**
Direct investment income	2 330	...	...	.1	...	...	.3	...	...
Dividends and distributed branch profits	2 332	...	...	.1	...	...	.3	...	...
Reinvested earnings and undistributed branch profits	2 333	...	...	...	...	...	...	...	...
Income on debt (interest)	2 334	...	...	...	...	...	...	...	...
Portfolio investment income	2 339	...	...	5.0	...	...	...	...	...
Income on equity	2 340	...	...	...	...	...	...	...	...
Income on bonds and notes	2 350	...	...	5.0	...	...	...	...	...
Income on money market instruments	2 360	...	...	...	...	...	...	...	...
Other investment income	2 370	...	...	17.7	17.3	23.5	22.2	41.7	47.0
Investment income, debit	3 320	...	...	**–74.2**	**–72.2**	**–68.3**	**–66.3**	**–87.3**	**–88.6**
Direct investment income	3 330	...	...	...	...	–.5	–1.3	–6.9	–8.1
Dividends and distributed branch profits	3 332	...	...	...	...	–.5	–1.3	–6.9	–8.1
Reinvested earnings and undistributed branch profits	3 333	...	...	...	...	...	...	...	...
Income on debt (interest)	3 334	...	...	...	...	...	...	...	...
Portfolio investment income	3 339	...	...	...	...	...	...	...	...
Income on equity	3 340	...	...	...	...	...	...	...	...
Income on bonds and notes	3 350	...	...	...	...	...	...	...	...
Income on money market instruments	3 360	...	...	...	...	...	...	...	...
Other investment income	3 370	...	...	–74.2	–72.2	–67.9	–65.0	–80.3	–80.5
D. CURRENT TRANSFERS	4 379	...	...	213.1	290.3	326.4	420.1	550.7	240.5
Credit	2 379	...	...	**475.4**	**535.0**	**692.6**	**750.3**	**923.1**	**872.5**
General government	2 380	...	...	53.3	7.5	28.0	93.7	97.0	54.9
Other sectors	2 390	...	...	422.1	527.5	664.6	656.6	826.2	817.6
Workers' remittances	2 391	...	...	45.3	56.0	63.3	70.8	80.5	68.1
Other current transfers	2 392	...	...	376.8	471.6	601.4	585.9	745.7	749.5
Debit	3 379	...	...	**–262.3**	**–244.8**	**–366.2**	**–330.2**	**–372.4**	**–632.0**
General government	3 380	...	...	–1.7	...	–.7	–.1	–.4	–6.7
Other sectors	3 390	...	...	–260.6	–244.7	–365.5	–330.1	–372.1	–625.3
Workers' remittances	3 391	...	...	...	...	–13.9	–7.3	–4.0	–16.6
Other current transfers	3 392	...	...	–260.6	–244.7	–351.6	–322.8	–368.1	–608.7
CAPITAL AND FINANCIAL ACCOUNT	4 996	...	...	**269.3**	**305.4**	**426.5**	**74.8**	**153.2**	**298.4**
CAPITAL ACCOUNT	4 994	...	...	...	...	**9.4**	**4.4**	**.3**	**1.3**
Total credit	2 994	...	...	...	...	*11.2*	*4.4*	*.3*	*3.6*
Total debit	3 994	...	...	...	...	*–1.8*	...	...	*–2.3*
Capital transfers, credit	2 400	...	...	...	...	**11.2**	**4.4**	**.3**	**3.6**
General government	2 401	...	...	...	...	11.2	4.4	...	3.6
Debt forgiveness	2 402	...	...	...	...	...	...	...	...
Other capital transfers	2 410	...	...	...	...	11.2	4.4	...	3.6
Other sectors	2 430	...	...	...	...	...	...	.3	...
Migrants' transfers	2 431	...	...	...	...	...	...	...	...
Debt forgiveness	2 432	...	...	...	...	...	...	...	...
Other capital transfers	2 440	...	...	...	...	...	...	.3	...
Capital transfers, debit	3 400	...	...	...	...	...	...	...	...
General government	3 401	...	...	...	...	...	...	...	...
Debt forgiveness	3 402	...	...	...	...	...	...	...	...
Other capital transfers	3 410	...	...	...	...	...	...	...	...
Other sectors	3 430	...	...	...	...	...	...	...	...
Migrants' transfers	3 431	...	...	...	...	...	...	...	...
Debt forgiveness	3 432	...	...	...	...	...	...	...	...
Other capital transfers	3 440	...	...	...	...	...	...	...	...
Nonproduced nonfinancial assets, credit	2 480	...	...	...	...	...	...	...	...
Nonproduced nonfinancial assets, debit	3 480	...	...	...	...	**–1.8**	...	...	**–2.3**

Table 2 (Continued). STANDARD PRESENTATION, 1994–2001

(Millions of U.S. dollars)

	Code	1994	1995	1996	1997	1998	1999	2000	2001
FINANCIAL ACCOUNT	4 995	**. . .**	**. . .**	**269.3**	**305.4**	**417.0**	**70.5**	**152.9**	**297.1**
A. DIRECT INVESTMENT	4 500	. . .	. . .	11.2	15.7	117.7	30.1	176.2	442.3
Direct investment abroad	4 505	**. . .**	**. . .**	**. . .**	**. . .**	**. . .**	**. . .**	**.6**	**–.9**
Equity capital	4 510	. . .	. . .	. . .	. . .	. . .	. . .	.6	–.9
Claims on affiliated enterprises	4 515	. . .	. . .	. . .	. . .	. . .	. . .	.6	–.9
Liabilities to affiliated enterprises	4 520	. . .	. . .	. . .	. . .	. . .	. . .	. . .	. . .
Reinvested earnings	4 525	. . .	. . .	. . .	. . .	. . .	. . .	. . .	. . .
Other capital	4 530	. . .	. . .	. . .	. . .	. . .	. . .	. . .	. . .
Claims on affiliated enterprises	4 535	. . .	. . .	. . .	. . .	. . .	. . .	. . .	. . .
Liabilities to affiliated enterprises	4 540	. . .	. . .	. . .	. . .	. . .	. . .	. . .	. . .
Direct investment in Macedonia, FYR	4 555	**. . .**	**. . .**	**11.2**	**15.7**	**117.7**	**30.1**	**175.6**	**443.2**
Equity capital	4 560	. . .	. . .	6.8	6.9	117.7	30.1	175.6	443.2
Claims on direct investors	4 565	. . .	. . .	. . .	. . .	. . .	. . .	. . .	. . .
Liabilities to direct investors	4 570	. . .	. . .	6.8	6.9	117.7	30.1	175.6	443.2
Reinvested earnings	4 575	. . .	. . .	. . .	. . .	. . .	. . .	. . .	. . .
Other capital	4 580	. . .	. . .	4.4	8.9	. . .	. . .	. . .	. . .
Claims on direct investors	4 585	. . .	. . .	. . .	. . .	. . .	. . .	. . .	. . .
Liabilities to direct investors	4 590	. . .	. . .	4.4	8.9	. . .	. . .	. . .	. . .
B. PORTFOLIO INVESTMENT	4 600	. . .	. . .	.3	2.1	7.8	.1	–.1	3.2
Assets	4 602	**. . .**	**. . .**	**–.5**	**–2.5**	**–.6**	**–.4**	**. . .**	**3.2**
Equity securities	4 610	. . .	. . .	–.5	–2.5	–.6	–.4	. . .	. . .
Monetary authorities	4 611	. . .	. . .	. . .	. . .	. . .	. . .	. . .	. . .
General government	4 612	. . .	. . .	. . .	. . .	. . .	. . .	. . .	. . .
Banks	4 613	. . .	. . .	. . .	. . .	. . .	. . .	. . .	. . .
Other sectors	4 614	. . .	. . .	. . .	. . .	. . .	. . .	. . .	. . .
Debt securities	4 619	. . .	. . .	. . .	. . .	. . .	. . .	. . .	3.2
Bonds and notes	4 620	. . .	. . .	. . .	. . .	. . .	. . .	. . .	3.2
Monetary authorities	4 621	. . .	. . .	. . .	. . .	. . .	. . .	. . .	. . .
General government	4 622	. . .	. . .	. . .	. . .	. . .	. . .	. . .	. . .
Banks	4 623	. . .	. . .	. . .	. . .	. . .	. . .	. . .	3.2
Other sectors	4 624	. . .	. . .	. . .	. . .	. . .	. . .	. . .	. . .
Money market instruments	4 630	. . .	. . .	. . .	. . .	. . .	. . .	. . .	. . .
Monetary authorities	4 631	. . .	. . .	. . .	. . .	. . .	. . .	. . .	. . .
General government	4 632	. . .	. . .	. . .	. . .	. . .	. . .	. . .	. . .
Banks	4 633	. . .	. . .	. . .	. . .	. . .	. . .	. . .	. . .
Other sectors	4 634	. . .	. . .	. . .	. . .	. . .	. . .	. . .	. . .
Liabilities	4 652	**. . .**	**. . .**	**.8**	**4.6**	**8.4**	**.5**	**–.1**	**. . .**
Equity securities	4 660	. . .	. . .	.8	4.6	8.4	.5	–.1	. . .
Banks	4 663	. . .	. . .	. . .	. . .	. . .	. . .	. . .	. . .
Other sectors	4 664	. . .	. . .	. . .	. . .	. . .	. . .	–.1	. . .
Debt securities	4 669	. . .	. . .	. . .	. . .	. . .	. . .	. . .	. . .
Bonds and notes	4 670	. . .	. . .	. . .	. . .	. . .	. . .	. . .	. . .
Monetary authorities	4 671	. . .	. . .	. . .	. . .	. . .	. . .	. . .	. . .
General government	4 672	. . .	. . .	. . .	. . .	. . .	. . .	. . .	. . .
Banks	4 673	. . .	. . .	. . .	. . .	. . .	. . .	. . .	. . .
Other sectors	4 674	. . .	. . .	. . .	. . .	. . .	. . .	. . .	. . .
Money market instruments	4 680	. . .	. . .	. . .	. . .	. . .	. . .	. . .	. . .
Monetary authorities	4 681	. . .	. . .	. . .	. . .	. . .	. . .	. . .	. . .
General government	4 682	. . .	. . .	. . .	. . .	. . .	. . .	. . .	. . .
Banks	4 683	. . .	. . .	. . .	. . .	. . .	. . .	. . .	. . .
Other sectors	4 684	. . .	. . .	. . .	. . .	. . .	. . .	. . .	. . .
C. FINANCIAL DERIVATIVES	4 910	. . .	. . .	. . .	. . .	. . .	. . .	. . .	. . .
Monetary authorities	4 911	. . .	. . .	. . .	. . .	. . .	. . .	. . .	. . .
General government	4 912	. . .	. . .	. . .	. . .	. . .	. . .	. . .	. . .
Banks	4 913	. . .	. . .	. . .	. . .	. . .	. . .	. . .	. . .
Other sectors	4 914	. . .	. . .	. . .	. . .	. . .	. . .	. . .	. . .
Assets	4 900	**. . .**	**. . .**	**. . .**	**. . .**	**. . .**	**. . .**	**. . .**	**. . .**
Monetary authorities	4 901	. . .	. . .	. . .	. . .	. . .	. . .	. . .	. . .
General government	4 902	. . .	. . .	. . .	. . .	. . .	. . .	. . .	. . .
Banks	4 903	. . .	. . .	. . .	. . .	. . .	. . .	. . .	. . .
Other sectors	4 904	. . .	. . .	. . .	. . .	. . .	. . .	. . .	. . .
Liabilities	4 905	**. . .**	**. . .**	**. . .**	**. . .**	**. . .**	**. . .**	**. . .**	**. . .**
Monetary authorities	4 906	. . .	. . .	. . .	. . .	. . .	. . .	. . .	. . .
General government	4 907	. . .	. . .	. . .	. . .	. . .	. . .	. . .	. . .
Banks	4 908	. . .	. . .	. . .	. . .	. . .	. . .	. . .	. . .
Other sectors	4 909	. . .	. . .	. . .	. . .	. . .	. . .	. . .	. . .

Table 2 (Concluded). STANDARD PRESENTATION, 1994–2001

(Millions of U.S. dollars)

	Code	1994	1995	1996	1997	1998	1999	2000	2001
D. OTHER INVESTMENT	4 700 . .	...	...	250.1	322.7	333.6	181.8	211.4	–64.9
Assets	4 703 . .	**...**	**...**	**–133.2**	**–73.0**	**–77.2**	**–81.0**	**–81.1**	**8.8**
Trade credits	4 706 . .	...	...	–158.5	–15.6	...	...	...	...
General government	4 707 . .	...	...	...	...	...	...	...	...
of which: Short-term	4 709 . .	...	...	...	...	...	...	...	...
Other sectors	4 710 . .	...	...	–158.5	–15.6	...	...	...	...
of which: Short-term	4 712 . .	...	...	*–158.5*	*–15.6*	...	...	...	...
Loans	4 714 . .	...	...	...	...	...	...	3.1	–10.3
Monetary authorities	4 715 . .	...	...	...	...	...	...	...	...
of which: Short-term	4 718 . .	...	...	...	...	...	...	...	...
General government	4 719 . .	...	...	...	...	...	...	...	...
of which: Short-term	4 721 . .	...	...	...	...	...	...	...	...
Banks	4 722 . .	...	...	...	...	...	...	3.1	–10.3
of which: Short-term	4 724 . .	...	...	...	...	...	...	*3.1*	*–13.5*
Other sectors	4 725 . .	...	...	...	...	...	...	...	...
of which: Short-term	4 727 . .	...	...	...	...	...	...	...	...
Currency and deposits	4 730 . .	...	...	25.3	–57.5	–77.2	–81.0	–81.4	18.1
Monetary authorities	4 731 . .	...	...	...	...	...	...	...	–231.3
General government	4 732 . .	...	...	...	...	...	–14.6	...	...
Banks	4 733 . .	...	...	25.3	–57.5	–51.0	–66.4	–81.4	–228.4
Other sectors	4 734 . .	...	...	...	...	–26.2	...	...	477.8
Other assets	4 736 . .	...	...	...	...	...	...	–2.9	1.0
Monetary authorities	4 737 . .	...	...	...	...	...	...	...	...
of which: Short-term	4 739 . .	...	...	...	...	...	...	...	...
General government	4 740 . .	...	...	...	...	...	...	...	...
of which: Short-term	4 742 . .	...	...	...	...	...	...	...	...
Banks	4 743 . .	...	...	...	...	...	...	–2.9	1.0
of which: Short-term	4 745 . .	...	...	...	...	...	...	*–2.9*	*1.0*
Other sectors	4 746 . .	...	...	...	...	...	...	...	...
of which: Short-term	4 748 . .	...	...	...	...	...	...	...	...
Liabilities	4 753 . .	**...**	**...**	**383.3**	**395.7**	**410.8**	**262.9**	**292.6**	**–73.7**
Trade credits	4 756 . .	...	...	237.3	283.8	158.0	108.5	232.6	–105.7
General government	4 757 . .	...	...	...	...	...	...	...	...
of which: Short-term	4 759 . .	...	...	...	...	...	...	...	...
Other sectors	4 760 . .	...	...	237.3	283.8	158.0	108.5	232.6	–105.7
of which: Short-term	4 762 . .	...	...	*237.3*	*283.8*	*158.0*	*108.5*	*232.6*	*–105.7*
Loans	4 764 . .	...	...	73.1	189.2	232.9	94.6	10.1	–72.2
Monetary authorities	4 765 . .	...	...	13.5	24.6	9.9	1.8	–.9	–21.7
of which: Use of Fund credit and loans from the Fund	4 766 . .	...	...	*13.5*	*24.6*	*9.9*	*1.8*	*–15.6*	*–7.6*
of which: Short-term	4 768 . .	...	...	...	...	...	...	*14.7*	*–14.1*
General government	4 769 . .	...	...	96.9	163.2	109.1	64.4	49.8	–64.9
of which: Short-term	4 771 . .	...	...	...	...	...	...	...	...
Banks	4 772 . .	...	...	–37.3	1.5	77.9	–3.8	–66.0	–14.6
of which: Short-term	4 774 . .	...	...	...	...	...	...	*–11.3*	*22.8*
Other sectors	4 775 . .	...	...	...	...	36.0	32.2	27.2	29.0
of which: Short-term	4 777 . .	...	...	...	...	...	...	...	...
Currency and deposits	4 780 . .	...	...	36.1	28.3	19.8	26.3	10.2	93.1
Monetary authorities	4 781 . .	...	...	...	...	...	...	...	154.2
General government	4 782 . .	...	...	...	...	...	...	...	...
Banks	4 783 . .	...	...	36.1	28.3	19.8	26.3	10.2	–61.1
Other sectors	4 784 . .	...	...	...	...	...	...	...	...
Other liabilities	4 786 . .	...	...	36.9	–105.6	.1	33.5	39.6	11.1
Monetary authorities	4 787 . .	...	...	...	...	...	...	...	...
of which: Short-term	4 789 . .	...	...	...	...	...	...	...	...
General government	4 790 . .	...	...	–28.1	–105.6	.1	25.0	19.0	–1.5
of which: Short-term	4 792 . .	...	...	*–28.1*	*–105.6*	*.1*	*25.0*	*19.0*	*–1.5*
Banks	4 793 . .	...	...	65.0	...	...	8.4	20.6	12.6
of which: Short-term	4 795 . .	...	...	*65.0*	...	...	*8.4*	*20.6*	*12.4*
Other sectors	4 796 . .	...	...	...	...	...	...	...	...
of which: Short-term	4 798 . .	...	...	...	...	...	...	...	...
E. RESERVE ASSETS	4 802 . .	...	...	7.6	–35.1	–42.0	–141.6	–234.7	–83.5
Monetary gold	4 812 . .	...	...	...	...	...	...	–1.0	...
Special drawing rights	4 811 . .	...	...	.2	–.4	–.6	–.2	.4	–1.7
Reserve position in the Fund	4 810 . .	...	...	...	...	...	...	...	...
Foreign exchange	4 803 . .	...	...	7.5	–34.7	–41.4	–141.4	–234.1	–81.8
Other claims	4 813 . .	...	...	...	...	...	...	...	...
NET ERRORS AND OMISSIONS	4 998 . .	**...**	**...**	**18.8**	**–29.9**	**–114.8**	**34.5**	**–46.0**	**25.9**

Part 3 of the *Yearbook* contains descriptions of the methodologies, compilation practices, and sources used to compile these data.

Table 3. INTERNATIONAL INVESTMENT POSITION (End–period stocks), 1994–2001
(Millions of U.S. dollars)

	Code	1994	1995	1996	1997	1998	1999	2000	2001
ASSETS	8 995 C.	...	...	...	...	...	...	...	...
Direct investment abroad	8 505 . .	...	...	...	...	...	...	...	...
Equity capital and reinvested earnings	8 506 . .	...	...	...	...	...	...	...	...
Claims on affiliated enterprises	8 507 . .	...	...	...	...	...	...	...	...
Liabilities to affiliated enterprises	8 508 . .	...	...	...	...	...	...	...	...
Other capital	8 530 . .	...	...	...	...	...	...	...	...
Claims on affiliated enterprises	8 535 . .	...	...	...	...	...	...	...	...
Liabilities to affiliated enterprises	8 540 . .	...	...	...	...	...	...	...	...
Portfolio investment	8 602 . .	...	...	...	...	...	...	...	...
Equity securities	8 610 . .	...	...	...	...	...	...	...	...
Monetary authorities	8 611 . .	...	...	...	...	...	...	...	...
General government	8 612 . .	...	...	...	...	...	...	...	...
Banks	8 613 . .	...	...	...	...	...	...	...	...
Other sectors	8 614 . .	...	...	...	...	...	...	...	...
Debt securities	8 619 . .	...	...	...	...	...	...	...	...
Bonds and notes	8 620 . .	...	...	...	...	...	...	...	...
Monetary authorities	8 621 . .	...	...	...	...	...	...	...	...
General government	8 622 . .	...	...	...	...	...	...	...	...
Banks	8 623 . .	...	...	...	...	...	...	...	...
Other sectors	8 624 . .	...	...	...	...	...	...	...	...
Money market instruments	8 630 . .	...	...	...	...	...	...	...	...
Monetary authorities	8 631 . .	...	...	...	...	...	...	...	...
General government	8 632 . .	...	...	...	...	...	...	...	...
Banks	8 633 . .	...	...	...	...	...	...	...	...
Other sectors	8 634 . .	...	...	...	...	...	...	...	...
Financial derivatives	8 900 . .	...	...	...	...	...	...	...	...
Monetary authorities	8 901 . .	...	...	...	...	...	...	...	...
General government	8 902 . .	...	...	...	...	...	...	...	...
Banks	8 903 . .	...	...	...	...	...	...	...	...
Other sectors	8 904 . .	...	...	...	...	...	...	...	...
Other investment	8 703 . .	...	...	**229.3**	**286.8**	**337.8**	**425.4**	**458.8**	**895.7**
Trade credits	8 706 . .	...	...	...	...	...	...	...	...
General government	8 707 . .	...	...	...	...	...	...	...	...
of which: Short-term	8 709 . .	...	...	...	...	...	...	...	...
Other sectors	8 710 . .	...	...	...	...	...	...	...	...
of which: Short-term	8 712 . .	...	...	...	...	...	...	...	...
Loans	8 714 . .	...	...	...	...	...	...	...	...
Monetary authorities	8 715 . .	...	...	...	...	...	...	...	...
of which: Short-term	8 718 . .	...	...	...	...	...	...	...	...
General government	8 719 . .	...	...	...	...	...	...	...	...
of which: Short-term	8 721 . .	...	...	...	...	...	...	...	...
Banks	8 722 . .	...	...	...	...	...	...	...	...
of which: Short-term	8 724 . .	...	...	...	...	...	...	...	...
Other sectors	8 725 . .	...	...	...	...	...	...	...	...
of which: Short-term	8 727 . .	...	...	...	...	...	...	...	...
Currency and deposits	8 730 . .	...	...	229.3	286.8	337.8	425.4	458.8	895.7
Monetary authorities	8 731 . .	...	...	...	...	...	21.2	21.4	252.7
General government	8 732 . .	...	...	...	...	...	...	...	...
Banks	8 733 . .	...	...	229.3	286.8	337.8	404.2	437.4	643.0
Other sectors	8 734 . .	...	...	...	...	...	...	...	...
Other assets	8 736 . .	...	...	...	...	...	...	...	...
Monetary authorities	8 737 . .	...	...	...	...	...	...	...	...
of which: Short-term	8 739 . .	...	...	...	...	...	...	...	...
General government	8 740 . .	...	...	...	...	...	...	...	...
of which: Short-term	8 742 . .	...	...	...	...	...	...	...	...
Banks	8 743 . .	...	...	...	...	...	...	...	...
of which: Short-term	8 745 . .	...	...	...	...	...	...	...	...
Other sectors	8 746 . .	...	...	...	...	...	...	...	...
of which: Short-term	8 748 . .	...	...	...	...	...	...	...	...
Reserve assets	8 802 . .	...	...	**267.5**	**280.4**	**367.2**	**478.3**	**712.6**	**775.2**
Monetary gold	8 812 . .	...	...	28.0	23.5	28.5	29.7	30.7	53.7
Special drawing rights	8 811 . .	...	.2	...	.4	1.1	1.2	.7	2.2
Reserve position in the Fund	8 810 . .	...	...	...	...	...	...	...	...
Foreign exchange	8 803 . .	...	...	239.5	256.6	337.6	447.4	681.3	719.3
Other claims	8 813 . .	...	...	...	...	...	...	...	...

Table 3 (Concluded). INTERNATIONAL INVESTMENT POSITION (End–period stocks), 1994–2001
(Millions of U.S. dollars)

	Code	1994	1995	1996	1997	1998	1999	2000	2001
LIABILITIES	8 995 D.	...	...	...	...	...	...	...	...
Direct investment in Macedonia, FYR	8 555 . .	...	...	...	...	...	...	...	...
Equity capital and reinvested earnings	8 556 . .	...	...	...	...	...	...	...	...
Claims on direct investors	8 557 . .	...	...	...	...	...	...	...	...
Liabilities to direct investors	8 558 . .	...	...	...	...	...	...	...	...
Other capital	8 580 . .	...	...	...	...	...	...	...	...
Claims on direct investors	8 585 . .	...	...	...	...	...	...	...	...
Liabilities to direct investors	8 590 . .	...	...	...	...	...	...	...	...
Portfolio investment	8 652 . .	...	...	...	...	...	...	...	...
Equity securities	8 660 . .	...	...	...	...	...	...	...	...
Banks	8 663 . .	...	...	...	...	...	...	...	...
Other sectors	8 664 . .	...	...	...	...	...	...	...	...
Debt securities	8 669 . .	...	...	...	...	...	...	...	...
Bonds and notes	8 670 . .	...	...	...	...	...	...	...	...
Monetary authorities	8 671 . .	...	...	...	...	...	...	...	...
General government	8 672 . .	...	...	...	...	...	...	...	...
Banks	8 673 . .	...	...	...	...	...	...	...	...
Other sectors	8 674 . .	...	...	...	...	...	...	...	...
Money market instruments	8 680 . .	...	...	...	...	...	...	...	...
Monetary authorities	8 681 . .	...	...	...	...	...	...	...	...
General government	8 682 . .	...	...	...	...	...	...	...	...
Banks	8 683 . .	...	...	...	...	...	...	...	...
Other sectors	8 684 . .	...	...	...	...	...	...	...	...
Financial derivatives	8 905 . .	...	...	...	...	...	...	...	...
Monetary authorities	8 906 . .	...	...	...	...	...	...	...	...
General government	8 907 . .	...	...	...	...	...	...	...	...
Banks	8 908 . .	...	...	...	...	...	...	...	...
Other sectors	8 909 . .	...	...	...	...	...	...	...	...
Other investment	8 753 . .	...	...	**1,243.1**	**1,259.7**	**1,545.0**	**1,603.7**	**1,603.0**	**1,654.3**
Trade credits	8 756 . .	...	...	...	...	...	...	...	...
General government	8 757 . .	...	...	...	...	...	...	...	...
of which: Short-term	8 759 . .	...	...	...	...	...	...	...	...
Other sectors	8 760 . .	...	...	...	...	...	...	...	...
of which: Short-term	8 762 . .	...	...	...	...	...	...	...	...
Loans	8 764 . .	...	...	1,242.0	1,258.8	1,544.0	1,600.8	1,600.6	1,493.5
Monetary authorities	8 765 . .	...	...	68.2	88.1	102.4	101.7	95.4	70.8
of which: Use of Fund credit and loans from the Fund	8 766 . .	*20.5*	*56.6*	*68.2*	*88.1*	*102.4*	*101.7*	*81.2*	*70.8*
of which: Short-term	8 768 . .	...	...	...	...	...	...	*14.2*	...
General government	8 769 . .	...	...	1,041.2	999.3	1,126.2	1,156.3	1,216.3	1,147.8
of which: Short-term	8 771 . .	...	...	...	...	...	...	...	...
Banks	8 772 . .	...	...	120.2	155.3	288.6	318.3	215.0	170.7
of which: Short-term	8 774 . .	...	...	*115.9*	*144.4*	*164.1*	*188.5*	*172.4*	*138.5*
Other sectors	8 775 . .	...	...	12.4	16.0	26.8	24.5	73.9	104.2
of which: Short-term	8 777 . .	...	...	...	...	...	...	...	...
Currency and deposits	8 780 . .	...	...	1.1	.9	1.0	2.9	2.4	160.8
Monetary authorities	8 781 . .	...	...	...	...	...	...	...	154.2
General government	8 782 . .	...	...	...	...	...	...	...	...
Banks	8 783 . .	...	...	1.1	.9	1.0	2.9	2.4	6.6
Other sectors	8 784 . .	...	...	...	...	...	...	...	...
Other liabilities	8 786 . .	...	...	...	...	...	...	...	...
Monetary authorities	8 787 . .	...	...	...	...	...	...	...	...
of which: Short-term	8 789 . .	...	...	...	...	...	...	...	...
General government	8 790 . .	...	...	...	...	...	...	...	...
of which: Short-term	8 792 . .	...	...	...	...	...	...	...	...
Banks	8 793 . .	...	...	...	...	...	...	...	...
of which: Short-term	8 795 . .	...	...	...	...	...	...	...	...
Other sectors	8 796 . .	...	...	...	...	...	...	...	...
of which: Short-term	8 798 . .	...	...	...	...	...	...	...	...
NET INTERNATIONAL INVESTMENT POSITION	8 995 . .	...	...	...	...	...	...	...	...
Conversion rates: denars per U.S. dollar (end of period)	0 102 . .	**40.596**	**37.980**	**41.411**	**55.421**	**51.836**	**60.339**	**66.328**	**69.172**

Table 1. ANALYTIC PRESENTATION, 1994–2001

(Millions of U.S. dollars)

	Code			1994	1995	1996	1997	1998	1999	2000	2001
A. Current Account [1]	4	993	Z.	**–277**	**–276**	**–291**	**–266**	**–301**	**–252**	**–283**	**–20**
Goods: exports f.o.b	2	100	. .	450	507	509	516	538	584	824	111
Goods: imports f.o.b	3	100	. .	–546	–628	–629	–694	–693	–742	–997	–114
Balance on Goods	4	100	. .	*–96*	*–122*	*–120*	*–178*	*–154*	*–158*	*–174*	*–3*
Services: credit	2	200	. .	206	242	293	272	291	326	364	42
Services: debit	3	200	. .	–328	–359	–373	–386	–436	–456	–522	–61
Balance on Goods and Services	4	991	. .	*–218*	*–238*	*–200*	*–292*	*–299*	*–289*	*–332*	*–22*
Income: credit	2	300	. .	2	7	6	20	25	21	22	3
Income: debit	3	300	. .	–158	–174	–169	–115	–103	–63	–64	–13
Balance on Goods, Services, and Income	4	992	. .	*–374*	*–405*	*–363*	*–387*	*–377*	*–331*	*–373*	*–32*
Current transfers: credit	2	379	Z.	114	141	94	156	109	111	122	14
Current transfers: debit	3	379	. .	–17	–12	–23	–35	–33	–32	–31	–2
B. Capital Account [1]	4	994	Z.	**62**	**45**	**5**	**115**	**103**	**129**	**115**	**13**
Capital account: credit	2	994	Z.	62	45	5	115	103	129	115	13
Capital account: debit	3	994	. .	. . .	. . .	. . .	. . .	. . .	. . .	. . .	. . .
Total, Groups A Plus B	4	981	. .	*–215*	*–231*	*–286*	*–150*	*–198*	*–123*	*–168*	*–7*
C. Financial Account [1]	4	995	W.	**–122**	**–198**	**133**	**110**	**–76**	**–14**	**–31**	**–17**
Direct investment abroad	4	505	. .	. . .	. . .	. . .	. . .	. . .	. . .	. . .	. . .
Direct investment in Madagascar	4	555	Z.	6	10	10	14	17	58	83	11
Portfolio investment assets	4	602	. .	. . .	. . .	. . .	. . .	. . .	. . .	. . .	. . .
Equity securities	4	610	. .	. . .	. . .	. . .	. . .	. . .	. . .	. . .	. . .
Debt securities	4	619	. .	. . .	. . .	. . .	. . .	. . .	. . .	. . .	. . .
Portfolio investment liabilities	4	652	Z.	. . .	. . .	. . .	. . .	. . .	. . .	. . .	. . .
Equity securities	4	660	. .	. . .	. . .	. . .	. . .	. . .	. . .	. . .	. . .
Debt securities	4	669	Z.	. . .	. . .	. . .	. . .	. . .	. . .	. . .	. . .
Financial derivatives	4	910	. .	. . .	. . .	. . .	. . .	. . .	. . .	. . .	. . .
Financial derivatives assets	4	900	. .	. . .	. . .	. . .	. . .	. . .	. . .	. . .	. . .
Financial derivatives liabilities	4	905	. .	. . .	. . .	. . .	. . .	. . .	. . .	. . .	. . .
Other investment assets	4	703	. .	19	–62	37	135	–68	–73	–87	–15
Monetary authorities	4	701	. .	38	–45	. . .	157	–84	–71	–40	–17
General government	4	704	. .	. . .	. . .	. . .	. . .	. . .	. . .	. . .	. . .
Banks	4	705	. .	–18	–12	37	–22	16	2	–48	2
Other sectors	4	728	. .	–1	–5	. . .	. . .	. . .	. . .	. . .	. . .
Other investment liabilities	4	753	W.	–147	–145	86	–39	–25	1	–26	–12
Monetary authorities	4	753	WA	–235	–230	. . .	. . .	. . .	. . .	–1	. . .
General government	4	753	ZB	79	91	–167	–28	–26	–3	–28	–10
Banks	4	753	ZC	6	–8	. . .	–4	9	6	15	–1
Other sectors	4	753	ZD	3	3	253	–8	–7	–2	–12	–1
Total, Groups A Through C	4	983	. .	*–338*	*–428*	*–152*	*–41*	*–274*	*–137*	*–199*	*–23*
D. Net Errors and Omissions	4	998	. .	**61**	**98**	**59**	**25**	**–25**	**32**	**39**	**–31**
Total, Groups A Through D	4	984	. .	*–276*	*–330*	*–94*	*–16*	*–299*	*–104*	*–160*	*–54*
E. Reserves and Related Items	4	802	A.	**276**	**330**	**94**	**16**	**299**	**104**	**160**	**54**
Reserve assets	4	802	. .	–14	–2	–137	–214	205	11	–30	2
Use of Fund credit and loans	4	766	. .	–12	–15	3	1	–14	6	45	27
Exceptional financing	4	920	. .	303	347	228	229	108	88	145	25
Conversion rates: Malagasy francs per U.S. dollar	0	101	. .	**3,067.3**	**4,265.6**	**4,061.3**	**5,090.9**	**5,441.4**	**6,283.8**	**6,767.5**	**6,588.5**

[1] Excludes components that have been classified in the categories of Group E.

Table 2. STANDARD PRESENTATION, 1994–2001

(Millions of U.S. dollars)

	Code		1994	1995	1996	1997	1998	1999	2000	2001
CURRENT ACCOUNT	4 993	. .	**–277**	**–276**	**–153**	**–202**	**–289**	**–225**	**–260**	**–17**
A. GOODS	4 100	. .	–96	–122	–120	–178	–154	–158	–174	–3
Credit	2 100	. .	**450**	**507**	**509**	**516**	**538**	**584**	**824**	**111**
General merchandise: exports f.o.b.	2 110	. .	447	502	488	323	334	391	414	63
Goods for processing: exports f.o.b.	2 150	. .	. . .	. . .	22	190	200	190	407	47
Repairs on goods	2 160	. .	. . .	2	. . .	. . .	1	. . .	. . .	. . .
Goods procured in ports by carriers	2 170	. .	2	3	. . .	2	2	2	2	. . .
Nonmonetary gold	2 180	. .	. . .	. . .	. . .	. . .	. . .	. . .	. . .	. . .
Debit	3 100	. .	**–546**	**–628**	**–629**	**–694**	**–693**	**–742**	**–997**	**–114**
General merchandise: imports f.o.b.	3 110	. .	–491	–528	–566	–546	–535	–562	–633	–82
Goods for processing: imports f.o.b.	3 150	. .	–54	–100	–63	–148	–157	–180	–365	–31
Repairs on goods	3 160	. .	. . .	. . .	. . .	. . .	. . .	. . .	. . .	. . .
Goods procured in ports by carriers	3 170	. .	. . .	. . .	. . .	. . .	. . .	. . .	. . .	. . .
Nonmonetary gold	3 180	. .	. . .	. . .	. . .	. . .	. . .	. . .	. . .	. . .
B. SERVICES	4 200	. .	–123	–116	–80	–114	–145	–130	–158	–19
Total credit	2 200	. .	*206*	*242*	*293*	*272*	*291*	*326*	*364*	*42*
Total debit	3 200	. .	*–328*	*–359*	*–373*	*–386*	*–436*	*–456*	*–522*	*–61*
Transportation services, credit	2 205	. .	**58**	**65**	**79**	**56**	**61**	**55**	**51**	**7**
Passenger	2 850	. .	*39*	*48*	*37*	*36*	*44*	*37*	*31*	*4*
Freight	2 851	. .	*4*	*5*	*5*	*5*	*5*	*6*	*8*	*1*
Other	2 852	. .	*15*	*13*	*38*	*16*	*12*	*13*	*12*	*2*
Sea transport, passenger	2 207	. .	. . .	. . .	. . .	. . .	. . .	. . .	. . .	. . .
Sea transport, freight	2 208	. .	4	5	5	5	5	6	8	1
Sea transport, other	2 209	. .	12	9	17	11	8	9	7	1
Air transport, passenger	2 211	. .	39	48	37	36	44	37	31	4
Air transport, freight	2 212	. .	. . .	. . .	. . .	. . .	. . .	. . .	. . .	. . .
Air transport, other	2 213	. .	3	3	21	4	4	4	5	1
Other transport, passenger	2 215	. .	. . .	. . .	. . .	. . .	. . .	. . .	. . .	. . .
Other transport, freight	2 216	. .	. . .	. . .	. . .	. . .	. . .	. . .	. . .	. . .
Other transport, other	2 217	. .	. . .	. . .	. . .	. . .	. . .	. . .	. . .	. . .
Transportation services, debit	3 205	. .	**–134**	**–154**	**–174**	**–152**	**–142**	**–149**	**–191**	**–25**
Passenger	3 850	. .	*–17*	*–20*	*–17*	*–21*	*–21*	*–22*	*–24*	*–6*
Freight	3 851	. .	*–88*	*–102*	*–102*	*–111*	*–110*	*–115*	*–148*	*–17*
Other	3 852	. .	*–29*	*–32*	*–56*	*–20*	*–11*	*–12*	*–19*	*–2*
Sea transport, passenger	3 207	. .	. . .	. . .	. . .	. . .	. . .	. . .	. . .	. . .
Sea transport, freight	3 208	. .	–88	–102	–102	–111	–110	–115	–148	–17
Sea transport, other	3 209	. .	–9	–10	–3	–2	. . .	. . .	–3	. . .
Air transport, passenger	3 211	. .	–17	–20	–17	–21	–21	–22	–24	–6
Air transport, freight	3 212	. .	. . .	. . .	. . .	. . .	. . .	. . .	. . .	. . .
Air transport, other	3 213	. .	–20	–22	–53	–18	–11	–12	–16	–2
Other transport, passenger	3 215	. .	. . .	. . .	. . .	. . .	. . .	. . .	. . .	. . .
Other transport, freight	3 216	. .	. . .	. . .	. . .	. . .	. . .	. . .	. . .	. . .
Other transport, other	3 217	. .	. . .	. . .	. . .	. . .	. . .	. . .	. . .	. . .
Travel, credit	2 236	. .	**46**	**58**	**65**	**74**	**92**	**100**	**121**	**14**
Business travel	2 237	. .	. . .	. . .	. . .	. . .	. . .	. . .	. . .	. . .
Personal travel	2 240	. .	46	58	65	74	92	100	121	14
Travel, debit	3 236	. .	**–47**	**–59**	**–72**	**–80**	**–119**	**–111**	**–115**	**–15**
Business travel	3 237	. .	–1	–3	–48	–4	–13	–8	–9	–1
Personal travel	3 240	. .	–46	–56	–24	–76	–105	–103	–106	–14
Other services, credit	2 200	BA	**101**	**120**	**149**	**141**	**139**	**171**	**192**	**21**
Communications	2 245	. .	6	4	5	8	8	7	6	1
Construction	2 249	. .	. . .	. . .	. . .	10	22	23	20	2
Insurance	2 253	. .	3	4	5	3	5	3	3	. . .
Financial	2 260	. .	1	1	. . .	1	1	1	1	. . .
Computer and information	2 262	. .	. . .	. . .	. . .	. . .	. . .	. . .	. . .	. . .
Royalties and licence fees	2 266	. .	1	1	1	1	1	1	1	. . .
Other business services	2 268	. .	67	86	98	90	75	101	109	9
Personal, cultural, and recreational	2 287	. .	. . .	. . .	. . .	. . .	. . .	. . .	. . .	. . .
Government, n.i.e.	2 291	. .	22	24	40	29	27	36	50	9
Other services, debit	3 200	BA	**–147**	**–146**	**–127**	**–154**	**–175**	**–196**	**–216**	**–20**
Communications	3 245	. .	–1	–5	–21	–1	–3	–2	–2	. . .
Construction	3 249	. .	. . .	. . .	. . .	–15	–19	–29	–37	–6
Insurance	3 253	. .	–4	–7	–3	–5	–5	–5	–5	. . .
Financial	3 260	. .	–2	–3	. . .	–2	. . .	–1	–1	. . .
Computer and information	3 262	. .	. . .	. . .	. . .	. . .	. . .	. . .	. . .	. . .
Royalties and licence fees	3 266	. .	–9	–9	–3	–11	–10	–10	–11	–1
Other business services	3 268	. .	–52	–40	–5	–22	–28	–28	–33	–3
Personal, cultural, and recreational	3 287	. .	. . .	. . .	. . .	. . .	. . .	. . .	. . .	. . .
Government, n.i.e.	3 291	. .	–79	–81	–94	–97	–109	–120	–127	–10

Table 2 (Continued). STANDARD PRESENTATION, 1994–2001
(Millions of U.S. dollars)

	Code		1994	1995	1996	1997	1998	1999	2000	2001
C. INCOME	4 300	. .	–155	–167	–163	–95	–78	–42	–42	–10
Total credit	2 300	. .	*2*	*7*	*6*	*20*	*25*	*21*	*22*	*3*
Total debit	3 300	. .	*–158*	*–174*	*–169*	*–115*	*–103*	*–63*	*–64*	*–13*
Compensation of employees, credit	2 310	. .	**. . .**	**. . .**	**. . .**	**12**	**11**	**12**	**11**	**1**
Compensation of employees, debit	3 310	. .	**. . .**	**. . .**	**–2**	**–2**	**–2**	**. . .**	**–1**	**–1**
Investment income, credit	2 320	. .	**2**	**7**	**6**	**8**	**13**	**9**	**11**	**2**
Direct investment income	2 330	. .	. . .	. . .	. . .	. . .	. . .	. . .	. . .	. . .
Dividends and distributed branch profits	2 332	. .	. . .	. . .	. . .	. . .	. . .	. . .	. . .	. . .
Reinvested earnings and undistributed branch profits	2 333	. .	. . .	. . .	. . .	. . .	. . .	. . .	. . .	. . .
Income on debt (interest)	2 334	. .	. . .	. . .	. . .	. . .	. . .	. . .	. . .	. . .
Portfolio investment income	2 339	. .	. . .	. . .	. . .	. . .	. . .	. . .	. . .	. . .
Income on equity	2 340	. .	. . .	. . .	. . .	. . .	. . .	. . .	. . .	. . .
Income on bonds and notes	2 350	. .	. . .	. . .	. . .	. . .	. . .	. . .	. . .	. . .
Income on money market instruments	2 360	. .	. . .	. . .	. . .	. . .	. . .	. . .	. . .	. . .
Other investment income	2 370	. .	2	7	6	8	13	9	11	2
Investment income, debit	3 320	. .	**–158**	**–174**	**–167**	**–113**	**–101**	**–63**	**–63**	**–11**
Direct investment income	3 330	. .	–1	–3	. . .	–7	–7	–9	–4	–5
Dividends and distributed branch profits	3 332	. .	–1	–3	. . .	–7	–7	–9	–4	–5
Reinvested earnings and undistributed branch profits	3 333	. .	. . .	. . .	. . .	. . .	. . .	. . .	. . .	. . .
Income on debt (interest)	3 334	. .	. . .	. . .	. . .	. . .	. . .	. . .	. . .	. . .
Portfolio investment income	3 339	. .	. . .	. . .	. . .	. . .	. . .	. . .	. . .	. . .
Income on equity	3 340	. .	. . .	. . .	. . .	. . .	. . .	. . .	. . .	. . .
Income on bonds and notes	3 350	. .	. . .	. . .	. . .	. . .	. . .	. . .	. . .	. . .
Income on money market instruments	3 360	. .	. . .	. . .	. . .	. . .	. . .	. . .	. . .	. . .
Other investment income	3 370	. .	–156	–170	–167	–106	–94	–54	–58	–7
D. CURRENT TRANSFERS	4 379	. .	97	129	210	185	88	107	113	15
Credit	2 379	. .	**114**	**141**	**233**	**220**	**121**	**138**	**144**	**17**
General government	2 380	. .	64	63	138	103	39	33	42	4
Other sectors	2 390	. .	49	78	94	117	81	105	102	14
Workers' remittances	2 391	. .	11	9	6	. . .	. . .	. . .	. . .	. . .
Other current transfers	2 392	. .	38	69	88	117	81	105	102	14
Debit	3 379	. .	**–17**	**–12**	**–23**	**–35**	**–33**	**–32**	**–31**	**–2**
General government	3 380	. .	–9	–2	–1	–22	–22	–21	–21	–2
Other sectors	3 390	. .	–8	–11	–22	–13	–11	–11	–10	. . .
Workers' remittances	3 391	. .	–8	–11	–11	–13	–11	–11	–10	. . .
Other current transfers	3 392	. .	. . .	. . .	–11	. . .	. . .	. . .	. . .	. . .
CAPITAL AND FINANCIAL ACCOUNT	4 996	. .	**216**	**178**	**94**	**177**	**314**	**192**	**222**	**47**
CAPITAL ACCOUNT	4 994	. .	**62**	**45**	**5**	**115**	**103**	**129**	**115**	**13**
Total credit	2 994	. .	*62*	*45*	*5*	*115*	*103*	*129*	*115*	*13*
Total debit	3 994	. .	. . .	. . .	. . .	. . .	. . .	. . .	. . .	. . .
Capital transfers, credit	2 400	. .	**62**	**45**	**5**	**115**	**103**	**129**	**115**	**13**
General government	2 401	. .	60	40	. . .	115	103	129	115	13
Debt forgiveness	2 402	. .	. . .	. . .	. . .	. . .	. . .	. . .	. . .	. . .
Other capital transfers	2 410	. .	60	40	. . .	115	103	129	115	13
Other sectors	2 430	. .	2	5	5	. . .	. . .	. . .	. . .	. . .
Migrants' transfers	2 431	. .	2	5	5	. . .	. . .	. . .	. . .	. . .
Debt forgiveness	2 432	. .	. . .	. . .	. . .	. . .	. . .	. . .	. . .	. . .
Other capital transfers	2 440	. .	. . .	. . .	. . .	. . .	. . .	. . .	. . .	. . .
Capital transfers, debit	3 400	. .	**. . .**	**. . .**	**. . .**	**. . .**	**. . .**	**. . .**	**. . .**	**. . .**
General government	3 401	. .	. . .	. . .	. . .	. . .	. . .	. . .	. . .	. . .
Debt forgiveness	3 402	. .	. . .	. . .	. . .	. . .	. . .	. . .	. . .	. . .
Other capital transfers	3 410	. .	. . .	. . .	. . .	. . .	. . .	. . .	. . .	. . .
Other sectors	3 430	. .	. . .	. . .	. . .	. . .	. . .	. . .	. . .	. . .
Migrants' transfers	3 431	. .	. . .	. . .	. . .	. . .	. . .	. . .	. . .	. . .
Debt forgiveness	3 432	. .	. . .	. . .	. . .	. . .	. . .	. . .	. . .	. . .
Other capital transfers	3 440	. .	. . .	. . .	. . .	. . .	. . .	. . .	. . .	. . .
Nonproduced nonfinancial assets, credit	2 480	. .	**. . .**	**. . .**	**. . .**	**. . .**	**. . .**	**. . .**	**. . .**	**. . .**
Nonproduced nonfinancial assets, debit	3 480	. .	**. . .**	**. . .**	**. . .**	**. . .**	**. . .**	**. . .**	**. . .**	**. . .**

Table 2 (Continued). STANDARD PRESENTATION, 1994–2001

(Millions of U.S. dollars)

	Code	1994	1995	1996	1997	1998	1999	2000	2001
FINANCIAL ACCOUNT	4 995	**154**	**132**	**89**	**62**	**212**	**63**	**107**	**34**
A. DIRECT INVESTMENT	4 500	6	10	10	14	17	58	83	11
Direct investment abroad	4 505	...	...	...	...	...	...	...	...
Equity capital	4 510	...	...	...	...	...	...	...	...
Claims on affiliated enterprises	4 515	...	...	...	...	...	...	...	...
Liabilities to affiliated enterprises	4 520	...	...	...	...	...	...	...	...
Reinvested earnings	4 525	...	...	...	...	...	...	...	...
Other capital	4 530	...	...	...	...	...	...	...	...
Claims on affiliated enterprises	4 535	...	...	...	...	...	...	...	...
Liabilities to affiliated enterprises	4 540	...	...	...	...	...	...	...	...
Direct investment in Madagascar	4 555	**6**	**10**	**10**	**14**	**17**	**58**	**83**	**11**
Equity capital	4 560	6	10	10	14	17	58	83	11
Claims on direct investors	4 565	...	...	...	...	...	...	...	...
Liabilities to direct investors	4 570	...	...	...	14	17	58	83	11
Reinvested earnings	4 575	...	...	...	...	...	...	...	...
Other capital	4 580	...	...	...	...	...	...	...	...
Claims on direct investors	4 585	...	...	...	...	...	...	...	...
Liabilities to direct investors	4 590	...	...	...	...	...	...	...	...
B. PORTFOLIO INVESTMENT	4 600	...	...	...	...	...	...	...	...
Assets	4 602	...	...	...	...	...	...	...	...
Equity securities	4 610	...	...	...	...	...	...	...	...
Monetary authorities	4 611	...	...	...	...	...	...	...	...
General government	4 612	...	...	...	...	...	...	...	...
Banks	4 613	...	...	...	...	...	...	...	...
Other sectors	4 614	...	...	...	...	...	...	...	...
Debt securities	4 619	...	...	...	...	...	...	...	...
Bonds and notes	4 620	...	...	...	...	...	...	...	...
Monetary authorities	4 621	...	...	...	...	...	...	...	...
General government	4 622	...	...	...	...	...	...	...	...
Banks	4 623	...	...	...	...	...	...	...	...
Other sectors	4 624	...	...	...	...	...	...	...	...
Money market instruments	4 630	...	...	...	...	...	...	...	...
Monetary authorities	4 631	...	...	...	...	...	...	...	...
General government	4 632	...	...	...	...	...	...	...	...
Banks	4 633	...	...	...	...	...	...	...	...
Other sectors	4 634	...	...	...	...	...	...	...	...
Liabilities	4 652	...	...	...	...	...	...	...	...
Equity securities	4 660	...	...	...	...	...	...	...	...
Banks	4 663	...	...	...	...	...	...	...	...
Other sectors	4 664	...	...	...	...	...	...	...	...
Debt securities	4 669	...	...	...	...	...	...	...	...
Bonds and notes	4 670	...	...	...	...	...	...	...	...
Monetary authorities	4 671	...	...	...	...	...	...	...	...
General government	4 672	...	...	...	...	...	...	...	...
Banks	4 673	...	...	...	...	...	...	...	...
Other sectors	4 674	...	...	...	...	...	...	...	...
Money market instruments	4 680	...	...	...	...	...	...	...	...
Monetary authorities	4 681	...	...	...	...	...	...	...	...
General government	4 682	...	...	...	...	...	...	...	...
Banks	4 683	...	...	...	...	...	...	...	...
Other sectors	4 684	...	...	...	...	...	...	...	...
C. FINANCIAL DERIVATIVES	4 910	...	...	...	...	...	...	...	...
Monetary authorities	4 911	...	...	...	...	...	...	...	...
General government	4 912	...	...	...	...	...	...	...	...
Banks	4 913	...	...	...	...	...	...	...	...
Other sectors	4 914	...	...	...	...	...	...	...	...
Assets	4 900	...	...	...	...	...	...	...	...
Monetary authorities	4 901	...	...	...	...	...	...	...	...
General government	4 902	...	...	...	...	...	...	...	...
Banks	4 903	...	...	...	...	...	...	...	...
Other sectors	4 904	...	...	...	...	...	...	...	...
Liabilities	4 905	...	...	...	...	...	...	...	...
Monetary authorities	4 906	...	...	...	...	...	...	...	...
General government	4 907	...	...	...	...	...	...	...	...
Banks	4 908	...	...	...	...	...	...	...	...
Other sectors	4 909	...	...	...	...	...	...	...	...

Table 2 (Concluded). STANDARD PRESENTATION, 1994–2001
(Millions of U.S. dollars)

	Code	1994	1995	1996	1997	1998	1999	2000	2001
D. OTHER INVESTMENT	4 700 . .	163	125	216	262	–10	–6	54	21
Assets	4 703 . .	**19**	**–62**	**37**	**135**	**–68**	**–73**	**–87**	**–15**
Trade credits	4 706 . .	...	...	...	...	...	...	...	...
General government	4 707 . .	...	...	...	...	...	...	...	...
of which: Short-term	4 709 . .	...	...	...	...	...	...	...	...
Other sectors	4 710 . .	...	...	...	...	...	...	...	...
of which: Short-term	4 712 . .	...	...	...	...	...	...	...	...
Loans	4 714 . .	...	...	...	–10	2	–13	–52	...
Monetary authorities	4 715 . .	...	...	...	...	...	...	...	...
of which: Short-term	4 718 . .	...	...	...	...	...	...	...	...
General government	4 719 . .	...	...	...	...	...	...	...	...
of which: Short-term	4 721 . .	...	...	...	...	...	...	...	...
Banks	4 722 . .	...	...	...	–10	2	–13	–52	...
of which: Short-term	4 724 . .	...	...	...	...	...	...	...	...
Other sectors	4 725 . .	...	...	...	...	...	...	...	...
of which: Short-term	4 727 . .	...	...	...	...	...	...	...	...
Currency and deposits	4 730 . .	–26	–6	37	–10	16	7	17	1
Monetary authorities	4 731 . .	...	...	...	...	...	...	...	...
General government	4 732 . .	...	...	...	...	...	...	...	...
Banks	4 733 . .	–26	–6	37	–10	16	7	17	1
Other sectors	4 734 . .	...	...	...	...	...	...	...	...
Other assets	4 736 . .	46	–57	...	155	–86	–67	–53	–16
Monetary authorities	4 737 . .	38	–45	...	157	–84	–71	–40	–17
of which: Short-term	4 739 . .	*38*	*–45*	...	*9*	*1*	*3*	*–30*	*3*
General government	4 740 . .	...	...	...	...	...	...	...	...
of which: Short-term	4 742 . .	...	...	...	...	...	...	...	...
Banks	4 743 . .	9	–6	...	–3	–2	3	–13	1
of which: Short-term	4 745 . .	...	...	...	*–3*	*–2*	*3*	*–13*	*1*
Other sectors	4 746 . .	–1	–5	...	...	...	...	...	...
of which: Short-term	4 748 . .	*–1*	*–5*	...	...	...	...	...	...
Liabilities	4 753 . .	**143**	**187**	**179**	**127**	**58**	**67**	**142**	**36**
Trade credits	4 756 . .	...	...	...	...	...	...	...	...
General government	4 757 . .	...	...	...	...	...	...	...	...
of which: Short-term	4 759 . .	...	...	...	...	...	...	...	...
Other sectors	4 760 . .	...	...	...	...	...	...	...	...
of which: Short-term	4 762 . .	...	...	...	...	...	...	...	...
Loans	4 764 . .	–166	–155	–74	1,227	32	57	135	37
Monetary authorities	4 765 . .	–246	–246	3	1	–14	6	45	27
of which: Use of Fund credit and loans from the Fund	4 766 . .	*–12*	*–15*	*3*	*1*	*–14*	*6*	*45*	*27*
of which: Short-term	4 768 . .	...	...	...	...	...	...	...	...
General government	4 769 . .	79	91	–77	1,234	54	53	102	11
of which: Short-term	4 771 . .	...	...	...	...	...	...	...	...
Banks	4 772 . .	...	...	...	...	...	...	...	...
of which: Short-term	4 774 . .	...	...	...	...	...	...	...	...
Other sectors	4 775 . .	...	...	...	–8	–7	–2	–12	–1
of which: Short-term	4 777 . .	...	...	...	...	...	...	...	...
Currency and deposits	4 780 . .	4	–7	...	2	...	...	–1	...
Monetary authorities	4 781 . .	–2	1	...	...	...	...	–1	...
General government	4 782 . .	...	...	...	...	...	...	...	...
Banks	4 783 . .	6	–8	...	–2	...	–1	...	...
Other sectors	4 784 . .	...	...	...	...	...	...	...	...
Other liabilities	4 786 . .	306	349	253	–1,098	25	10	8	–2
Monetary authorities	4 787 . .	...	...	...	...	...	...	...	...
of which: Short-term	4 789 . .	...	...	...	...	...	...	...	...
General government	4 790 . .	303	347	...	–1,097	17	4	–8	...
of which: Short-term	4 792 . .	*303*	*347*	...	*–1,097*	*17*	*4*	*–8*	...
Banks	4 793 . .	...	...	...	–2	9	6	15	–2
of which: Short-term	4 795 . .	...	...	...	*–2*	*9*	*6*	*15*	*–2*
Other sectors	4 796 . .	3	3	253	...	...	...	...	...
of which: Short-term	4 798 . .	*3*	*3*	*253*	...	...	...	...	...
E. RESERVE ASSETS	4 802 . .	–14	–2	–137	–214	205	11	–30	2
Monetary gold	4 812 . .	...	...	...	...	...	...	...	...
Special drawing rights	4 811 . .	...	...	...	...	...	...	...	...
Reserve position in the Fund	4 810 . .	...	...	...	...	...	...	...	...
Foreign exchange	4 803 . .	–14	–2	–137	–214	205	11	–30	2
Other claims	4 813 . .	...	...	...	...	...	...	...	...
NET ERRORS AND OMISSIONS	4 998 . .	**61**	**98**	**59**	**25**	**–25**	**32**	**39**	**–31**

Table 1. ANALYTIC PRESENTATION, 1994–2001
(Millions of U.S. dollars)

	Code	1994	1995	1996	1997	1998	1999	2000	2001
A. Current Account [1]	4 993 Z.	**–4,520**	**–8,644**	**–4,462**	**–5,935**	**9,529**	**12,603**	**8,409**	**. . .**
Goods: exports f.o.b.	2 100 . .	56,897	71,767	76,985	77,538	71,883	84,098	98,429	. . .
Goods: imports f.o.b.	3 100 . .	–55,320	–71,871	–73,137	–74,029	–54,378	–61,453	–77,576	. . .
Balance on Goods	4 100 . .	*1,577*	*–103*	*3,848*	*3,510*	*17,505*	*22,644*	*20,854*	. . .
Services: credit	2 200 . .	9,320	11,602	15,135	15,727	11,517	11,919	13,775	. . .
Services: debit	3 200 . .	–12,052	–14,981	–17,573	–18,297	–13,127	–14,736	–16,726	. . .
Balance on Goods and Services	4 991 . .	*–1,155*	*–3,483*	*1,411*	*940*	*15,895*	*19,828*	*17,903*	. . .
Income: credit	2 300 . .	2,308	2,623	2,693	2,485	1,542	2,003	2,098	. . .
Income: debit	3 300 . .	–5,903	–6,767	–7,383	–7,851	–5,446	–7,499	–9,612	. . .
Balance on Goods, Services, and Income	4 992 . .	*–4,750*	*–7,626*	*–3,279*	*–4,426*	*11,991*	*14,332*	*10,388*	. . .
Current transfers: credit	2 379 Z.	411	700	766	944	728	801	720	. . .
Current transfers: debit	3 379 . .	–182	–1,717	–1,948	–2,453	–3,190	–2,529	–2,699	. . .
B. Capital Account [1]	4 994 Z.	**–82**	**. . .**	**. . .**	**. . .**	**. . .**	**. . .**	**. . .**	**. . .**
Capital account: credit	2 994 Z.	. . .	. . .	. . .	. . .	. . .	. . .	. . .	. . .
Capital account: debit	3 994 . .	–82	. . .	. . .	. . .	. . .	. . .	. . .	. . .
Total, Groups A Plus B	4 981 . .	*–4,602*	*–8,644*	*–4,462*	*–5,935*	*9,529*	*12,603*	*8,409*	. . .
C. Financial Account [1]	4 995 W.	**1,288**	**7,643**	**9,477**	**2,198**	**–2,550**	**–6,619**	**–6,276**	**. . .**
Direct investment abroad	4 505 . .	. . .	. . .	. . .	. . .	. . .	–1,422	–2,026	. . .
Direct investment in Malaysia	4 555 Z.	4,342	4,178	5,078	5,137	2,163	3,895	3,788	. . .
Portfolio investment assets	4 602 . .	. . .	. . .	. . .	. . .	. . .	. . .	. . .	. . .
Equity securities	4 610 . .	. . .	. . .	. . .	. . .	. . .	. . .	. . .	. . .
Debt securities	4 619 . .	. . .	. . .	. . .	. . .	. . .	. . .	. . .	. . .
Portfolio investment liabilities	4 652 Z.	–1,649	–436	–268	–248	283	–1,156	–2,472	. . .
Equity securities	4 660 . .	. . .	. . .	. . .	. . .	. . .	. . .	. . .	. . .
Debt securities	4 669 Z.	–1,649	–436	–268	–248	283	. . .	. . .	. . .
Financial derivatives	4 910 . .	. . .	. . .	. . .	. . .	. . .	. . .	. . .	. . .
Financial derivatives assets	4 900 . .	. . .	. . .	. . .	. . .	. . .	. . .	. . .	. . .
Financial derivatives liabilities	4 905 . .	. . .	. . .	. . .	. . .	. . .	. . .	. . .	. . .
Other investment assets	4 703 . .	504	1,015	4,134	–4,604	–5,269	–7,936	–5,565	. . .
Monetary authorities	4 701 . .	. . .	. . .	. . .	. . .	. . .	. . .	. . .	. . .
General government	4 704 . .	–52	5	33	–14	–11	. . .	. . .	. . .
Banks	4 705 . .	–1,281	28	3,339	–979	–2,677	. . .	. . .	. . .
Other sectors	4 728 . .	1,837	982	762	–3,611	–2,581	. . .	. . .	. . .
Other investment liabilities	4 753 W.	–1,909	2,885	533	1,912	272	. . .	. . .	. . .
Monetary authorities	4 753 WA	–3	. . .	. . .	. . .	. . .	. . .	. . .	. . .
General government	4 753 ZB	–163	–216	–597	–350	180	. . .	. . .	. . .
Banks	4 753 ZC	–3,789	. . .	. . .	. . .	. . .	. . .	. . .	. . .
Other sectors	4 753 ZD	2,047	3,102	1,130	2,263	92	. . .	. . .	. . .
Total, Groups A Through C	4 983 . .	*–3,314*	*–1,001*	*5,015*	*–3,738*	*6,979*	*5,984*	*2,133*	. . .
D. Net Errors and Omissions	4 998 . .	**154**	**–762**	**–2,502**	**–137**	**3,039**	**–1,273**	**–3,142**	**. . .**
Total, Groups A Through D	4 984 . .	*–3,160*	*–1,763*	*2,513*	*–3,875*	*10,018*	*4,712*	*–1,009*	. . .
E. Reserves and Related Items	4 802 A.	**3,160**	**1,763**	**–2,513**	**3,875**	**–10,018**	**–4,712**	**1,009**	**. . .**
Reserve assets	4 802 . .	3,160	1,763	–2,513	3,875	–10,018	–4,712	1,009	. . .
Use of Fund credit and loans	4 766 . .	. . .	. . .	. . .	. . .	. . .	. . .	. . .	. . .
Exceptional financing	4 920 . .	. . .	. . .	. . .	. . .	. . .	. . .	. . .	. . .
Conversion rates: ringgit per U.S. dollar	0 101 . .	**2.6243**	**2.5044**	**2.5159**	**2.8132**	**3.9244**	**3.8000**	**3.8000**	**3.8000**

[1] Excludes components that have been classified in the categories of Group E.

Table 2. STANDARD PRESENTATION, 1994–2001

(Millions of U.S. dollars)

	Code	1994	1995	1996	1997	1998	1999	2000	2001
CURRENT ACCOUNT	4 993 . .	**–4,520**	**–8,644**	**–4,462**	**–5,935**	**9,529**	**12,603**	**8,409**	**. . .**
A. GOODS	4 100 . .	1,577	–103	3,848	3,510	17,505	22,644	20,854	. . .
Credit	2 100 . .	**56,897**	**71,767**	**76,985**	**77,538**	**71,883**	**84,098**	**98,429**	**. . .**
General merchandise: exports f.o.b.	2 110 . .	56,590	71,629	76,820	77,231	71,692	83,861	98,092	. . .
Goods for processing: exports f.o.b.	2 150 . .	. . .	. . .	. . .	. . .	. . .	45	93	. . .
Repairs on goods	2 160 . .	. . .	. . .	. . .	. . .	. . .	. . .	. . .	. . .
Goods procured in ports by carriers	2 170 . .	308	97	130	148	109	119	128	. . .
Nonmonetary gold	2 180 . .	. . .	41	35	159	83	72	116	. . .
Debit	3 100 . .	**–55,320**	**–71,871**	**–73,137**	**–74,029**	**–54,378**	**–61,453**	**–77,576**	**. . .**
General merchandise: imports f.o.b.	3 110 . .	–53,341	–69,745	–71,003	–72,250	–53,674	–60,237	–76,223	. . .
Goods for processing: imports f.o.b.	3 150 . .	. . .	. . .	. . .	. . .	. . .	–48	–83	. . .
Repairs on goods	3 160 . .	. . .	. . .	. . .	. . .	. . .	. . .	. . .	. . .
Goods procured in ports by carriers	3 170 . .	–468	–239	–291	–291	–241	–244	–323	. . .
Nonmonetary gold	3 180 . .	–1,511	–1,886	–1,842	–1,488	–463	–924	–947	. . .
B. SERVICES	4 200 . .	–2,732	–3,379	–2,437	–2,569	–1,610	–2,817	–2,951	. . .
Total credit	2 200 . .	*9,320*	*11,602*	*15,135*	*15,727*	*11,517*	*11,919*	*13,775*	. . .
Total debit	3 200 . .	*–12,052*	*–14,981*	*–17,573*	*–18,297*	*–13,127*	*–14,736*	*–16,726*	. . .
Transportation services, credit	2 205 . .	**1,871**	**2,466**	**2,822**	**2,861**	**2,271**	**2,493**	**2,926**	**. . .**
Passenger	2 850 . .	*830*	*1,075*	*1,255*	*1,184*	*856*	*814*	*991*	. . .
Freight	2 851 . .	*776*	*1,012*	*1,105*	*1,165*	*1,055*	*1,301*	*1,483*	. . .
Other	2 852 . .	*265*	*379*	*463*	*513*	*360*	*378*	*452*	. . .
Sea transport, passenger	2 207 . .	. . .	. . .	. . .	. . .	. . .	. . .	. . .	. . .
Sea transport, freight	2 208 . .	. . .	. . .	. . .	. . .	. . .	1,142	1,270	. . .
Sea transport, other	2 209 . .	. . .	. . .	. . .	. . .	. . .	282	357	. . .
Air transport, passenger	2 211 . .	. . .	. . .	. . .	. . .	. . .	814	991	. . .
Air transport, freight	2 212 . .	. . .	. . .	. . .	. . .	. . .	159	213	. . .
Air transport, other	2 213 . .	. . .	. . .	. . .	. . .	. . .	96	94	. . .
Other transport, passenger	2 215 . .	. . .	. . .	. . .	. . .	. . .	. . .	. . .	. . .
Other transport, freight	2 216 . .	. . .	. . .	. . .	. . .	. . .	. . .	. . .	. . .
Other transport, other	2 217 . .	. . .	. . .	. . .	. . .	. . .	. . .	. . .	. . .
Transportation services, debit	3 205 . .	**–4,356**	**–5,609**	**–5,433**	**–5,549**	**–4,088**	**–4,720**	**–5,913**	**. . .**
Passenger	3 850 . .	*–365*	*–408*	*–463*	*–568*	*–375*	*–409*	*–468*	. . .
Freight	3 851 . .	*–3,590*	*–4,624*	*–4,372*	*–4,400*	*–3,213*	*–3,790*	*–4,848*	. . .
Other	3 852 . .	*–402*	*–578*	*–597*	*–582*	*–501*	*–521*	*–597*	. . .
Sea transport, passenger	3 207 . .	. . .	. . .	. . .	. . .	. . .	. . .	. . .	. . .
Sea transport, freight	3 208 . .	. . .	. . .	. . .	. . .	. . .	–3,790	–4,848	. . .
Sea transport, other	3 209 . .	. . .	. . .	. . .	. . .	. . .	–240	–286	. . .
Air transport, passenger	3 211 . .	. . .	. . .	. . .	. . .	. . .	–409	–468	. . .
Air transport, freight	3 212 . .	. . .	. . .	. . .	. . .	. . .	. . .	. . .	. . .
Air transport, other	3 213 . .	. . .	. . .	. . .	. . .	. . .	–281	–311	. . .
Other transport, passenger	3 215 . .	. . .	. . .	. . .	. . .	. . .	. . .	. . .	. . .
Other transport, freight	3 216 . .	. . .	. . .	. . .	. . .	. . .	. . .	. . .	. . .
Other transport, other	3 217 . .	. . .	. . .	. . .	. . .	. . .	. . .	. . .	. . .
Travel, credit	2 236 . .	**3,367**	**3,969**	**4,477**	**3,741**	**2,381**	**3,588**	**4,681**	**. . .**
Business travel	2 237 . .	. . .	. . .	. . .	. . .	. . .	. . .	. . .	. . .
Personal travel	2 240 . .	. . .	. . .	. . .	. . .	. . .	3,588	4,681	. . .
Travel, debit	3 236 . .	**–1,994**	**–2,314**	**–2,569**	**–2,590**	**–1,785**	**–1,973**	**–2,052**	**. . .**
Business travel	3 237 . .	. . .	. . .	. . .	. . .	. . .	. . .	. . .	. . .
Personal travel	3 240 . .	. . .	. . .	. . .	. . .	. . .	–1,973	–2,052	. . .
Other services, credit	2 200 BA	**4,082**	**5,167**	**7,836**	**9,126**	**6,865**	**5,838**	**6,168**	**. . .**
Communications	2 245 . .	. . .	. . .	. . .	. . .	. . .	131	181	. . .
Construction	2 249 . .	. . .	. . .	. . .	. . .	. . .	480	314	. . .
Insurance	2 253 . .	6	. . .	. . .	. . .	. . .	175	156	. . .
Financial	2 260 . .	. . .	. . .	. . .	. . .	. . .	113	160	. . .
Computer and information	2 262 . .	. . .	. . .	. . .	. . .	. . .	60	82	. . .
Royalties and licence fees	2 266 . .	. . .	. . .	. . .	. . .	. . .	15	18	. . .
Other business services	2 268 . .	3,955	5,004	7,667	8,967	6,749	4,714	5,098	. . .
Personal, cultural, and recreational	2 287 . .	. . .	. . .	. . .	. . .	. . .	32	33	. . .
Government, n.i.e.	2 291 . .	120	163	169	159	116	119	126	. . .
Other services, debit	3 200 BA	**–5,702**	**–7,057**	**–9,571**	**–10,158**	**–7,254**	**–8,042**	**–8,761**	**. . .**
Communications	3 245 . .	. . .	. . .	. . .	. . .	. . .	–184	–231	. . .
Construction	3 249 . .	. . .	. . .	. . .	. . .	. . .	–1,259	–1,091	. . .
Insurance	3 253 . .	. . .	. . .	. . .	. . .	. . .	–253	–289	. . .
Financial	3 260 . .	. . .	. . .	. . .	. . .	. . .	–186	–175	. . .
Computer and information	3 262 . .	. . .	. . .	. . .	. . .	. . .	–156	–201	. . .
Royalties and licence fees	3 266 . .	. . .	. . .	. . .	. . .	. . .	–481	–546	. . .
Other business services	3 268 . .	–5,568	–6,898	–9,404	–9,976	–7,099	–5,342	–6,046	. . .
Personal, cultural, and recreational	3 287 . .	. . .	. . .	. . .	. . .	. . .	–68	–70	. . .
Government, n.i.e.	3 291 . .	–134	–159	–167	–182	–154	–114	–112	. . .

Table 2 (Continued). STANDARD PRESENTATION, 1994–2001
(Millions of U.S. dollars)

	Code	1994	1995	1996	1997	1998	1999	2000	2001
C. INCOME	4 300 . .	–3,595	–4,144	–4,690	–5,366	–3,904	–5,496	–7,514	. . .
Total credit	2 300 . .	*2,308*	*2,623*	*2,693*	*2,485*	*1,542*	*2,003*	*2,098*	. . .
Total debit	3 300 . .	*–5,903*	*–6,767*	*–7,383*	*–7,851*	*–5,446*	*–7,499*	*–9,612*	. . .
Compensation of employees, credit	2 310 . .	**119**	**116**	**164**	**194**	**190**	**323**	**327**	**. . .**
Compensation of employees, debit	3 310 . .	**–106**	**–131**	**–233**	**–357**	**–318**	**–484**	**–490**	**. . .**
Investment income, credit	2 320 . .	**2,189**	**2,508**	**2,529**	**2,290**	**1,353**	**1,680**	**1,771**	**. . .**
Direct investment income	2 330 . .	103	82	127	73	–98	112	–125	. . .
Dividends and distributed branch profits	2 332 . .	89	68	110	54	–110	. . .	. . .	. . .
Reinvested earnings and undistributed branch profits	2 333 . .	. . .	. . .	. . .	. . .	. . .	. . .	. . .	. . .
Income on debt (interest)	2 334 . .	14	14	17	19	12	57	47	. . .
Portfolio investment income	2 339 . .	366	498	664	564	148	72	77	. . .
Income on equity	2 340 . .	366	498	664	564	148	41	33	. . .
Income on bonds and notes	2 350 . .	. . .	. . .	. . .	. . .	. . .	31	44	. . .
Income on money market instruments	2 360 . .	. . .	. . .	. . .	. . .	. . .	. . .	. . .	. . .
Other investment income	2 370 . .	1,720	1,928	1,738	1,653	1,303	1,496	1,819	. . .
Investment income, debit	3 320 . .	**–5,797**	**–6,636**	**–7,151**	**–7,494**	**–5,128**	**–7,016**	**–9,122**	**. . .**
Direct investment income	3 330 . .	–3,938	–4,144	–4,459	–5,075	–2,796	–5,402	–7,172	. . .
Dividends and distributed branch profits	3 332 . .	–3,777	–3,960	–4,345	–4,899	–2,663	. . .	. . .	. . .
Reinvested earnings and undistributed branch profits	3 333 . .	. . .	. . .	. . .	. . .	. . .	. . .	. . .	. . .
Income on debt (interest)	3 334 . .	–160	–184	–113	–175	–133	–213	–148	. . .
Portfolio investment income	3 339 . .	–595	–904	–1,128	–544	–585	–224	–262	. . .
Income on equity	3 340 . .	–595	–904	–1,128	–544	–585	–171	–211	. . .
Income on bonds and notes	3 350 . .	. . .	. . .	. . .	. . .	. . .	–53	–51	. . .
Income on money market instruments	3 360 . .	. . .	. . .	. . .	. . .	. . .	. . .	. . .	. . .
Other investment income	3 370 . .	–1,265	–1,588	–1,564	–1,875	–1,748	–1,391	–1,689	. . .
D. CURRENT TRANSFERS	4 379 . .	229	–1,017	–1,182	–1,509	–2,463	–1,728	–1,979	. . .
Credit	2 379 . .	**411**	**700**	**766**	**944**	**728**	**801**	**720**	**. . .**
General government	2 380 . .	75	100	73	64	61	82	81	. . .
Other sectors	2 390 . .	336	600	693	880	666	719	639	. . .
Workers' remittances	2 391 . .	. . .	. . .	. . .	. . .	. . .	. . .	. . .	. . .
Other current transfers	2 392 . .	336	600	693	880	666	719	639	. . .
Debit	3 379 . .	**–182**	**–1,717**	**–1,948**	**–2,453**	**–3,190**	**–2,529**	**–2,699**	**. . .**
General government	3 380 . .	–24	–55	–97	–42	–65	–70	–58	. . .
Other sectors	3 390 . .	–158	–1,662	–1,851	–2,411	–3,125	–2,459	–2,642	. . .
Workers' remittances	3 391 . .	. . .	–1,198	–1,192	–1,717	–2,606	. . .	. . .	. . .
Other current transfers	3 392 . .	–158	–464	–659	–694	–519	–2,459	–2,642	. . .
CAPITAL AND FINANCIAL ACCOUNT	4 996 . .	**4,366**	**9,405**	**6,964**	**6,072**	**–12,567**	**–11,331**	**–5,267**	**. . .**
CAPITAL ACCOUNT	4 994 . .	**–82**	**. . .**	**. . .**	**. . .**	**. . .**	**. . .**	**. . .**	**. . .**
Total credit	2 994 . .	. . .	. . .	. . .	. . .	. . .	. . .	. . .	. . .
Total debit	3 994 . .	*–82*	. . .	. . .	. . .	. . .	. . .	. . .	. . .
Capital transfers, credit	2 400 . .	**. . .**	**. . .**	**. . .**	**. . .**	**. . .**	**. . .**	**. . .**	**. . .**
General government	2 401 . .	. . .	. . .	. . .	. . .	. . .	. . .	. . .	. . .
Debt forgiveness	2 402 . .	. . .	. . .	. . .	. . .	. . .	. . .	. . .	. . .
Other capital transfers	2 410 . .	. . .	. . .	. . .	. . .	. . .	. . .	. . .	. . .
Other sectors	2 430 . .	. . .	. . .	. . .	. . .	. . .	. . .	. . .	. . .
Migrants' transfers	2 431 . .	. . .	. . .	. . .	. . .	. . .	. . .	. . .	. . .
Debt forgiveness	2 432 . .	. . .	. . .	. . .	. . .	. . .	. . .	. . .	. . .
Other capital transfers	2 440 . .	. . .	. . .	. . .	. . .	. . .	. . .	. . .	. . .
Capital transfers, debit	3 400 . .	**–82**	**. . .**	**. . .**	**. . .**	**. . .**	**. . .**	**. . .**	**. . .**
General government	3 401 . .	. . .	. . .	. . .	. . .	. . .	. . .	. . .	. . .
Debt forgiveness	3 402 . .	. . .	. . .	. . .	. . .	. . .	. . .	. . .	. . .
Other capital transfers	3 410 . .	. . .	. . .	. . .	. . .	. . .	. . .	. . .	. . .
Other sectors	3 430 . .	–82	. . .	. . .	. . .	. . .	. . .	. . .	. . .
Migrants' transfers	3 431 . .	–82	. . .	. . .	. . .	. . .	. . .	. . .	. . .
Debt forgiveness	3 432 . .	. . .	. . .	. . .	. . .	. . .	. . .	. . .	. . .
Other capital transfers	3 440 . .	. . .	. . .	. . .	. . .	. . .	. . .	. . .	. . .
Nonproduced nonfinancial assets, credit	2 480 . .	**. . .**	**. . .**	**. . .**	**. . .**	**. . .**	**. . .**	**. . .**	**. . .**
Nonproduced nonfinancial assets, debit	3 480 . .	**. . .**	**. . .**	**. . .**	**. . .**	**. . .**	**. . .**	**. . .**	**. . .**

Table 2 (Continued). STANDARD PRESENTATION, 1994–2001
(Millions of U.S. dollars)

	Code	1994	1995	1996	1997	1998	1999	2000	2001
FINANCIAL ACCOUNT	4 995 . .	**4,448**	**9,405**	**6,964**	**6,072**	**-12,567**	**-11,331**	**-5,267**	**. . .**
A. DIRECT INVESTMENT	4 500 . .	4,342	4,178	5,078	5,137	2,163	2,473	1,762	. . .
Direct investment abroad	4 505 . .	**. . .**	**. . .**	**. . .**	**. . .**	**. . .**	**-1,422**	**-2,026**	**. . .**
Equity capital	4 510 . .	. . .	. . .	. . .	. . .	. . .	. . .	. . .	. . .
Claims on affiliated enterprises	4 515 . .	. . .	. . .	. . .	. . .	. . .	. . .	. . .	. . .
Liabilities to affiliated enterprises	4 520 . .	. . .	. . .	. . .	. . .	. . .	. . .	. . .	. . .
Reinvested earnings	4 525 . .	. . .	. . .	. . .	. . .	. . .	. . .	. . .	. . .
Other capital	4 530 . .	. . .	. . .	. . .	. . .	. . .	. . .	. . .	. . .
Claims on affiliated enterprises	4 535 . .	. . .	. . .	. . .	. . .	. . .	. . .	. . .	. . .
Liabilities to affiliated enterprises	4 540 . .	. . .	. . .	. . .	. . .	. . .	. . .	. . .	. . .
Direct investment in Malaysia	4 555 . .	**4,342**	**4,178**	**5,078**	**5,137**	**2,163**	**3,895**	**3,788**	**. . .**
Equity capital	4 560 . .	. . .	. . .	. . .	. . .	. . .	. . .	. . .	. . .
Claims on direct investors	4 565 . .	. . .	. . .	. . .	. . .	. . .	. . .	. . .	. . .
Liabilities to direct investors	4 570 . .	. . .	. . .	. . .	. . .	. . .	. . .	. . .	. . .
Reinvested earnings	4 575 . .	. . .	. . .	. . .	. . .	. . .	. . .	. . .	. . .
Other capital	4 580 . .	4,342	4,178	5,078	5,137	2,163	. . .	. . .	. . .
Claims on direct investors	4 585 . .	. . .	. . .	. . .	. . .	. . .	. . .	. . .	. . .
Liabilities to direct investors	4 590 . .	. . .	. . .	. . .	. . .	. . .	. . .	. . .	. . .
B. PORTFOLIO INVESTMENT	4 600 . .	–1,649	–436	–268	–248	283	–1,156	–2,472	. . .
Assets	4 602 . .	**. . .**	**. . .**	**. . .**	**. . .**	**. . .**	**. . .**	**. . .**	**. . .**
Equity securities	4 610 . .	. . .	. . .	. . .	. . .	. . .	. . .	. . .	. . .
Monetary authorities	4 611 . .	. . .	. . .	. . .	. . .	. . .	. . .	. . .	. . .
General government	4 612 . .	. . .	. . .	. . .	. . .	. . .	. . .	. . .	. . .
Banks	4 613 . .	. . .	. . .	. . .	. . .	. . .	. . .	. . .	. . .
Other sectors	4 614 . .	. . .	. . .	. . .	. . .	. . .	. . .	. . .	. . .
Debt securities	4 619 . .	. . .	. . .	. . .	. . .	. . .	. . .	. . .	. . .
Bonds and notes	4 620 . .	. . .	. . .	. . .	. . .	. . .	. . .	. . .	. . .
Monetary authorities	4 621 . .	. . .	. . .	. . .	. . .	. . .	. . .	. . .	. . .
General government	4 622 . .	. . .	. . .	. . .	. . .	. . .	. . .	. . .	. . .
Banks	4 623 . .	. . .	. . .	. . .	. . .	. . .	. . .	. . .	. . .
Other sectors	4 624 . .	. . .	. . .	. . .	. . .	. . .	. . .	. . .	. . .
Money market instruments	4 630 . .	. . .	. . .	. . .	. . .	. . .	. . .	. . .	. . .
Monetary authorities	4 631 . .	. . .	. . .	. . .	. . .	. . .	. . .	. . .	. . .
General government	4 632 . .	. . .	. . .	. . .	. . .	. . .	. . .	. . .	. . .
Banks	4 633 . .	. . .	. . .	. . .	. . .	. . .	. . .	. . .	. . .
Other sectors	4 634 . .	. . .	. . .	. . .	. . .	. . .	. . .	. . .	. . .
Liabilities	4 652 . .	**–1,649**	**–436**	**–268**	**–248**	**283**	**–1,156**	**–2,472**	**. . .**
Equity securities	4 660 . .	. . .	. . .	. . .	. . .	. . .	. . .	. . .	. . .
Banks	4 663 . .	. . .	. . .	. . .	. . .	. . .	. . .	. . .	. . .
Other sectors	4 664 . .	. . .	. . .	. . .	. . .	. . .	. . .	. . .	. . .
Debt securities	4 669 . .	–1,649	–436	–268	–248	283	. . .	. . .	. . .
Bonds and notes	4 670 . .	–1,649	–436	–268	–248	283	. . .	. . .	. . .
Monetary authorities	4 671 . .	. . .	. . .	. . .	. . .	. . .	. . .	. . .	. . .
General government	4 672 . .	–1,649	–436	–268	–248	283	. . .	. . .	. . .
Banks	4 673 . .	. . .	. . .	. . .	. . .	. . .	. . .	. . .	. . .
Other sectors	4 674 . .	. . .	. . .	. . .	. . .	. . .	. . .	. . .	. . .
Money market instruments	4 680 . .	. . .	. . .	. . .	. . .	. . .	. . .	. . .	. . .
Monetary authorities	4 681 . .	. . .	. . .	. . .	. . .	. . .	. . .	. . .	. . .
General government	4 682 . .	. . .	. . .	. . .	. . .	. . .	. . .	. . .	. . .
Banks	4 683 . .	. . .	. . .	. . .	. . .	. . .	. . .	. . .	. . .
Other sectors	4 684 . .	. . .	. . .	. . .	. . .	. . .	. . .	. . .	. . .
C. FINANCIAL DERIVATIVES	4 910 . .	. . .	. . .	. . .	. . .	. . .	. . .	. . .	. . .
Monetary authorities	4 911 . .	. . .	. . .	. . .	. . .	. . .	. . .	. . .	. . .
General government	4 912 . .	. . .	. . .	. . .	. . .	. . .	. . .	. . .	. . .
Banks	4 913 . .	. . .	. . .	. . .	. . .	. . .	. . .	. . .	. . .
Other sectors	4 914 . .	. . .	. . .	. . .	. . .	. . .	. . .	. . .	. . .
Assets	4 900 . .	**. . .**	**. . .**	**. . .**	**. . .**	**. . .**	**. . .**	**. . .**	**. . .**
Monetary authorities	4 901 . .	. . .	. . .	. . .	. . .	. . .	. . .	. . .	. . .
General government	4 902 . .	. . .	. . .	. . .	. . .	. . .	. . .	. . .	. . .
Banks	4 903 . .	. . .	. . .	. . .	. . .	. . .	. . .	. . .	. . .
Other sectors	4 904 . .	. . .	. . .	. . .	. . .	. . .	. . .	. . .	. . .
Liabilities	4 905 . .	**. . .**	**. . .**	**. . .**	**. . .**	**. . .**	**. . .**	**. . .**	**. . .**
Monetary authorities	4 906 . .	. . .	. . .	. . .	. . .	. . .	. . .	. . .	. . .
General government	4 907 . .	. . .	. . .	. . .	. . .	. . .	. . .	. . .	. . .
Banks	4 908 . .	. . .	. . .	. . .	. . .	. . .	. . .	. . .	. . .
Other sectors	4 909 . .	. . .	. . .	. . .	. . .	. . .	. . .	. . .	. . .

Table 2 (Concluded). STANDARD PRESENTATION, 1994–2001
(Millions of U.S. dollars)

	Code	1994	1995	1996	1997	1998	1999	2000	2001
D. OTHER INVESTMENT	4 700	–1,405	3,900	4,667	–2,691	–4,996	–7,936	–5,565	
Assets	4 703	**504**	**1,015**	**4,134**	**–4,604**	**–5,269**	**–7,936**	**–5,565**	**. . .**
Trade credits	4 706	. . .	. . .	. . .	. . .	. . .	. . .	. . .	. . .
General government	4 707	. . .	. . .	. . .	. . .	. . .	. . .	. . .	. . .
of which: Short-term	4 709	. . .	. . .	. . .	. . .	. . .	. . .	. . .	. . .
Other sectors	4 710	. . .	. . .	. . .	. . .	. . .	. . .	. . .	. . .
of which: Short-term	4 712	. . .	. . .	. . .	. . .	. . .	. . .	. . .	. . .
Loans	4 714	. . .	. . .	. . .	. . .	. . .	. . .	. . .	. . .
Monetary authorities	4 715	. . .	. . .	. . .	. . .	. . .	. . .	. . .	. . .
of which: Short-term	4 718	. . .	. . .	. . .	. . .	. . .	. . .	. . .	. . .
General government	4 719	. . .	. . .	. . .	. . .	. . .	. . .	. . .	. . .
of which: Short-term	4 721	. . .	. . .	. . .	. . .	. . .	. . .	. . .	. . .
Banks	4 722	. . .	. . .	. . .	. . .	. . .	. . .	. . .	. . .
of which: Short-term	4 724	. . .	. . .	. . .	. . .	. . .	. . .	. . .	. . .
Other sectors	4 725	. . .	. . .	. . .	. . .	. . .	. . .	. . .	. . .
of which: Short-term	4 727	. . .	. . .	. . .	. . .	. . .	. . .	. . .	. . .
Currency and deposits	4 730	556	. . .	. . .	. . .	. . .	. . .	. . .	. . .
Monetary authorities	4 731	. . .	. . .	. . .	. . .	. . .	. . .	. . .	. . .
General government	4 732	. . .	. . .	. . .	. . .	. . .	. . .	. . .	. . .
Banks	4 733	–1,281	. . .	. . .	. . .	. . .	. . .	. . .	. . .
Other sectors	4 734	1,837	. . .	. . .	. . .	. . .	. . .	. . .	. . .
Other assets	4 736	–52	1,015	4,134	–4,604	–5,269	. . .	. . .	. . .
Monetary authorities	4 737	. . .	. . .	. . .	. . .	. . .	. . .	. . .	. . .
of which: Short-term	4 739	. . .	. . .	. . .	. . .	. . .	. . .	. . .	. . .
General government	4 740	–52	5	33	–14	–11	. . .	. . .	. . .
of which: Short-term	4 742	. . .	. . .	. . .	. . .	. . .	. . .	. . .	. . .
Banks	4 743	. . .	28	3,339	–979	–2,677	. . .	. . .	. . .
of which: Short-term	4 745	. . .	*28*	*3,339*	*–979*	*–2,677*	. . .	. . .	. . .
Other sectors	4 746	. . .	982	762	–3,611	–2,581	. . .	. . .	. . .
of which: Short-term	4 748	. . .	*982*	*762*	*–3,611*	*–2,581*	. . .	. . .	. . .
Liabilities	4 753	**–1,909**	**2,885**	**533**	**1,912**	**272**	**. . .**	**. . .**	**. . .**
Trade credits	4 756	. . .	. . .	. . .	. . .	. . .	. . .	. . .	. . .
General government	4 757	. . .	. . .	. . .	. . .	. . .	. . .	. . .	. . .
of which: Short-term	4 759	. . .	. . .	. . .	. . .	. . .	. . .	. . .	. . .
Other sectors	4 760	. . .	. . .	. . .	. . .	. . .	. . .	. . .	. . .
of which: Short-term	4 762	. . .	. . .	. . .	. . .	. . .	. . .	. . .	. . .
Loans	4 764	1,884	2,885	533	1,912	272	. . .	. . .	. . .
Monetary authorities	4 765	. . .	. . .	. . .	. . .	. . .	. . .	. . .	. . .
of which: Use of Fund credit and loans from the Fund	4 766	. . .	. . .	. . .	. . .	. . .	. . .	. . .	. . .
of which: Short-term	4 768	. . .	. . .	. . .	. . .	. . .	. . .	. . .	. . .
General government	4 769	–163	–216	–597	–350	180	. . .	. . .	. . .
of which: Short-term	4 771	. . .	. . .	. . .	. . .	. . .	. . .	. . .	. . .
Banks	4 772	. . .	. . .	. . .	. . .	. . .	. . .	. . .	. . .
of which: Short-term	4 774	. . .	. . .	. . .	. . .	. . .	. . .	. . .	. . .
Other sectors	4 775	2,047	3,102	1,130	2,263	92	. . .	. . .	. . .
of which: Short-term	4 777	. . .	. . .	. . .	. . .	. . .	. . .	. . .	. . .
Currency and deposits	4 780	–3,793	. . .	. . .	. . .	. . .	. . .	. . .	. . .
Monetary authorities	4 781	–3	. . .	. . .	. . .	. . .	. . .	. . .	. . .
General government	4 782	. . .	. . .	. . .	. . .	. . .	. . .	. . .	. . .
Banks	4 783	–3,789	. . .	. . .	. . .	. . .	. . .	. . .	. . .
Other sectors	4 784	. . .	. . .	. . .	. . .	. . .	. . .	. . .	. . .
Other liabilities	4 786	. . .	. . .	. . .	. . .	. . .	. . .	. . .	. . .
Monetary authorities	4 787	. . .	. . .	. . .	. . .	. . .	. . .	. . .	. . .
of which: Short-term	4 789	. . .	. . .	. . .	. . .	. . .	. . .	. . .	. . .
General government	4 790	. . .	. . .	. . .	. . .	. . .	. . .	. . .	. . .
of which: Short-term	4 792	. . .	. . .	. . .	. . .	. . .	. . .	. . .	. . .
Banks	4 793	. . .	. . .	. . .	. . .	. . .	. . .	. . .	. . .
of which: Short-term	4 795	. . .	. . .	. . .	. . .	. . .	. . .	. . .	. . .
Other sectors	4 796	. . .	. . .	. . .	. . .	. . .	. . .	. . .	. . .
of which: Short-term	4 798	. . .	. . .	. . .	. . .	. . .	. . .	. . .	. . .
E. RESERVE ASSETS	4 802	3,160	1,763	–2,513	3,875	–10,018	–4,712	1,009	. . .
Monetary gold	4 812	. . .	. . .	. . .	. . .	. . .	. . .	. . .	. . .
Special drawing rights	4 811	–7	–13	–20	–20	–22	118	–26	. . .
Reserve position in the Fund	4 810	–63	–278	–32	46	. . .	–226	. . .	. . .
Foreign exchange	4 803	3,231	2,054	–2,462	3,848	–9,996	–4,604	1,035	. . .
Other claims	4 813	. . .	. . .	. . .	. . .	. . .	. . .	. . .	. . .
NET ERRORS AND OMISSIONS	4 998	**154**	**–762**	**–2,502**	**–137**	**3,039**	**–1,273**	**–3,142**	**. . .**

Part 3 of the *Yearbook* contains descriptions of the methodologies, compilation practices, and sources used to compile these data.

Table 1. ANALYTIC PRESENTATION, 1994–2001
(Millions of U.S. dollars)

	Code			1994	1995	1996	1997	1998	1999	2000	2001
A. Current Account[1]	4	993	Z.	**–11.2**	**–18.3**	**–7.3**	**–34.2**	**–23.3**	**–81.7**	**–53.1**	**–61.0**
Goods: exports f.o.b	2	100	. .	75.4	85.0	80.0	93.0	95.6	91.4	108.7	110.2
Goods: imports f.o.b	3	100	. .	–195.1	–235.8	–265.5	–307.0	–311.5	–353.9	–342.0	–348.0
Balance on Goods	4	100	. .	*–119.7*	*–150.8*	*–185.5*	*–214.0*	*–215.9*	*–262.5*	*–233.3*	*–237.8*
Services: credit	2	200	. .	197.4	232.8	289.0	312.1	331.3	342.7	348.5	354.1
Services: debit	3	200	. .	–62.8	–76.8	–87.8	–94.2	–98.9	–108.2	–109.7	–109.3
Balance on Goods and Services	4	991	. .	*14.9*	*5.2*	*15.7*	*3.9*	*16.5*	*–28.0*	*5.5*	*7.0*
Income: credit	2	300	. .	3.8	4.5	5.9	7.5	8.6	9.1	10.3	6.9
Income: debit	3	300	. .	–24.0	–24.4	–27.8	–34.9	–36.7	–40.0	–40.4	–45.4
Balance on Goods, Services, and Income	4	992	. .	*–5.3*	*–14.7*	*–6.2*	*–23.5*	*–11.6*	*–58.9*	*–24.6*	*–31.5*
Current transfers: credit	2	379	Z.	16.3	23.0	26.2	17.2	18.9	17.7	17.7	20.1
Current transfers: debit	3	379	. .	–22.2	–26.6	–27.3	–27.9	–30.6	–40.5	–46.2	–49.6
B. Capital Account[1]	4	994	Z.	**. . .**	**. . .**	**. . .**	**. . .**	**. . .**	**. . .**	**. . .**	**. . .**
Capital account: credit	2	994	Z.	. . .	. . .	. . .	. . .	. . .	. . .	. . .	. . .
Capital account: debit	3	994	. .	. . .	. . .	. . .	. . .	. . .	. . .	. . .	. . .
Total, Groups A Plus B	4	981	. .	*–11.2*	*–18.3*	*–7.3*	*–34.2*	*–23.3*	*–81.7*	*–53.1*	*–61.0*
C. Financial Account[1]	4	995	W.	**27.4**	**67.6**	**52.2**	**71.0**	**60.3**	**76.1**	**40.0**	**35.1**
Direct investment abroad	4	505	. .	. . .	. . .	. . .	. . .	. . .	. . .	. . .	. . .
Direct investment in Maldives	4	555	Z.	8.7	7.2	9.3	11.4	11.5	12.3	13.0	11.7
Portfolio investment assets	4	602	. .	. . .	. . .	. . .	. . .	. . .	. . .	. . .	. . .
Equity securities	4	610	. .	. . .	. . .	. . .	. . .	. . .	. . .	. . .	. . .
Debt securities	4	619	. .	. . .	. . .	. . .	. . .	. . .	. . .	. . .	. . .
Portfolio investment liabilities	4	652	Z.	. . .	. . .	. . .	. . .	. . .	. . .	. . .	. . .
Equity securities	4	660	. .	. . .	. . .	. . .	. . .	. . .	. . .	. . .	. . .
Debt securities	4	669	Z.	. . .	. . .	. . .	. . .	. . .	. . .	. . .	. . .
Financial derivatives	4	910	. .	. . .	. . .	. . .	. . .	. . .	. . .	. . .	. . .
Financial derivatives assets	4	900	. .	. . .	. . .	. . .	. . .	. . .	. . .	. . .	. . .
Financial derivatives liabilities	4	905	. .	. . .	. . .	. . .	. . .	. . .	. . .	. . .	. . .
Other investment assets	4	703	. .	13.2	29.9	32.7	53.8	30.8	47.4	22.8	21.3
Monetary authorities	4	701	. .	. . .	. . .	. . .	. . .	. . .	. . .	. . .	. . .
General government	4	704	. .	. . .	. . .	. . .	. . .	. . .	. . .	. . .	. . .
Banks	4	705	. .	1.9	–3.8	–7.3	10.9	12.1	4.5	–2.8	–3.0
Other sectors	4	728	. .	11.3	33.7	40.0	42.9	42.9	42.9	25.6	24.3
Other investment liabilities	4	753	W.	5.5	30.5	10.2	5.8	18.0	16.4	4.2	2.1
Monetary authorities	4	753	WA	.7	.1	. . .	–15.3	. . .	. . .	. . .	.1
General government	4	753	ZB	8.2	24.7	17.3	21.9	14.7	5.1	–2.1	7.6
Banks	4	753	ZC	–3.4	5.7	–7.1	–.8	3.3	11.3	6.3	–5.4
Other sectors	4	753	ZD	. . .	. . .	. . .	. . .	. . .	. . .	. . .	. . .
Total, Groups A Through C	4	983	. .	*16.2*	*49.3*	*44.9*	*36.8*	*37.0*	*–5.6*	*–13.1*	*–25.9*
D. Net Errors and Omissions	4	998	. .	**–10.8**	**–32.2**	**–16.6**	**–14.6**	**–16.9**	**14.2**	**8.8**	**–3.8**
Total, Groups A Through D	4	984	. .	*5.4*	*17.1*	*28.3*	*22.2*	*20.1*	*8.6*	*–4.3*	*–29.7*
E. Reserves and Related Items	4	802	A.	**–5.4**	**–17.1**	**–28.3**	**–22.2**	**–20.1**	**–8.6**	**4.3**	**29.7**
Reserve assets	4	802	. .	–5.4	–17.1	–28.3	–22.2	–20.1	–8.6	4.3	29.7
Use of Fund credit and loans	4	766	. .	. . .	. . .	. . .	. . .	. . .	. . .	. . .	. . .
Exceptional financing	4	920	. .	. . .	. . .	. . .	. . .	. . .	. . .	. . .	. . .
Conversion rates: rufiyaa per U.S. dollar	0	101	. .	**11.586**	**11.770**	**11.770**	**11.770**	**11.770**	**11.770**	**11.770**	**12.242**

[1] Excludes components that have been classified in the categories of Group E.

Table 2. STANDARD PRESENTATION, 1994–2001

(Millions of U.S. dollars)

	Code	1994	1995	1996	1997	1998	1999	2000	2001
CURRENT ACCOUNT	4 993 . .	**–11.2**	**–18.3**	**–7.3**	**–34.2**	**–23.3**	**–81.7**	**–53.1**	**–61.0**
A. GOODS	4 100 . .	–119.7	–150.8	–185.5	–214.0	–215.9	–262.5	–233.3	–237.8
Credit	2 100 . .	**75.4**	**85.0**	**80.0**	**93.0**	**95.6**	**91.4**	**108.7**	**110.2**
General merchandise: exports f.o.b.	2 110 . .	60.7	67.7	63.8	76.5	77.1	71.2	80.6	82.1
Goods for processing: exports f.o.b.	2 150 . .	. . .	. . .	. . .	. . .	. . .	. . .	. . .	. . .
Repairs on goods	2 160 . .	. . .	. . .	. . .	. . .	. . .	. . .	. . .	. . .
Goods procured in ports by carriers	2 170 . .	14.7	17.3	16.2	16.5	18.5	20.2	28.1	28.1
Nonmonetary gold	2 180 . .	. . .	. . .	. . .	. . .	. . .	. . .	. . .	. . .
Debit	3 100 . .	**–195.1**	**–235.8**	**–265.5**	**–307.0**	**–311.5**	**–353.9**	**–342.0**	**–348.0**
General merchandise: imports f.o.b.	3 110 . .	–195.1	–235.8	–265.5	–307.0	–311.5	–353.9	–342.0	–348.0
Goods for processing: imports f.o.b.	3 150 . .	. . .	. . .	. . .	. . .	. . .	. . .	. . .	. . .
Repairs on goods	3 160 . .	. . .	. . .	. . .	. . .	. . .	. . .	. . .	. . .
Goods procured in ports by carriers	3 170 . .	. . .	. . .	. . .	. . .	. . .	. . .	. . .	. . .
Nonmonetary gold	3 180 . .	. . .	. . .	. . .	. . .	. . .	. . .	. . .	. . .
B. SERVICES	4 200 . .	134.6	156.0	201.2	217.9	232.4	234.5	238.8	244.8
Total credit	2 200 . .	*197.4*	*232.8*	*289.0*	*312.1*	*331.3*	*342.7*	*348.5*	*354.1*
Total debit	3 200 . .	*–62.8*	*–76.8*	*–87.8*	*–94.2*	*–98.9*	*–108.2*	*–109.7*	*–109.3*
Transportation services, credit	2 205 . .	**12.1**	**17.0**	**18.6**	**19.8**	**22.2**	**23.6**	**20.2**	**19.9**
Passenger	2 850 . .	. . .	. . .	. . .	. . .	. . .	. . .	. . .	. . .
Freight	2 851 . .	*3.3*	*7.2*	*6.3*	*6.6*	*6.1*	*6.7*	*6.9*	*3.6*
Other	2 852 . .	*8.8*	*9.8*	*12.3*	*13.2*	*16.1*	*16.9*	*13.3*	*16.3*
Sea transport, passenger	2 207 . .	. . .	. . .	. . .	. . .	. . .	. . .	. . .	. . .
Sea transport, freight	2 208 . .	. . .	. . .	. . .	. . .	. . .	. . .	. . .	. . .
Sea transport, other	2 209 . .	. . .	. . .	. . .	. . .	. . .	. . .	. . .	. . .
Air transport, passenger	2 211 . .	. . .	. . .	. . .	. . .	. . .	. . .	. . .	. . .
Air transport, freight	2 212 . .	. . .	. . .	. . .	. . .	. . .	. . .	. . .	. . .
Air transport, other	2 213 . .	8.8	9.8	12.3	13.2	16.1	16.9	13.3	16.3
Other transport, passenger	2 215 . .	. . .	. . .	. . .	. . .	. . .	. . .	. . .	. . .
Other transport, freight	2 216 . .	. . .	. . .	. . .	. . .	. . .	. . .	. . .	. . .
Other transport, other	2 217 . .	. . .	. . .	. . .	. . .	. . .	. . .	. . .	. . .
Transportation services, debit	3 205 . .	**–29.5**	**–36.3**	**–39.9**	**–44.2**	**–46.1**	**–51.4**	**–53.6**	**–53.0**
Passenger	3 850 . .	*–8.7*	*–10.1*	*–10.4*	*–11.4*	*–12.5*	*–13.3*	*–14.1*	*–13.7*
Freight	3 851 . .	*–18.6*	*–24.4*	*–27.4*	*–31.7*	*–32.5*	*–36.9*	*–35.7*	*–36.3*
Other	3 852 . .	*–2.2*	*–1.8*	*–2.1*	*–1.1*	*–1.1*	*–1.2*	*–3.8*	*–3.0*
Sea transport, passenger	3 207 . .	. . .	. . .	. . .	. . .	. . .	. . .	. . .	. . .
Sea transport, freight	3 208 . .	. . .	. . .	. . .	. . .	. . .	. . .	. . .	. . .
Sea transport, other	3 209 . .	–1.2	–.9	–1.0	–1.1	–1.1	–1.2	–2.6	–1.3
Air transport, passenger	3 211 . .	–8.7	–10.1	–10.4	–11.4	–12.5	–13.3	–14.1	–13.7
Air transport, freight	3 212 . .	. . .	. . .	. . .	. . .	. . .	. . .	. . .	. . .
Air transport, other	3 213 . .	–1.0	–.9	–1.1	. . .	. . .	. . .	–1.2	–1.7
Other transport, passenger	3 215 . .	. . .	. . .	. . .	. . .	. . .	. . .	. . .	. . .
Other transport, freight	3 216 . .	. . .	. . .	. . .	. . .	. . .	. . .	. . .	. . .
Other transport, other	3 217 . .	. . .	. . .	. . .	. . .	. . .	. . .	. . .	. . .
Travel, credit	2 236 . .	**180.7**	**210.7**	**265.6**	**286.0**	**303.0**	**313.5**	**320.7**	**327.1**
Business travel	2 237 . .	. . .	. . .	. . .	. . .	. . .	. . .	. . .	. . .
Personal travel	2 240 . .	180.7	210.7	265.6	286.0	303.0	313.5	320.7	327.1
Travel, debit	3 236 . .	**–27.8**	**–31.4**	**–38.0**	**–39.4**	**–42.2**	**–45.1**	**–46.1**	**–45.2**
Business travel	3 237 . .	–.7	–2.0	–.8	–3.0	–2.3	–1.7	–1.5	–1.4
Personal travel	3 240 . .	–27.1	–29.4	–37.2	–36.4	–39.9	–43.4	–44.6	–43.8
Other services, credit	2 200 BA	**4.6**	**5.1**	**4.8**	**6.3**	**6.1**	**5.6**	**7.6**	**7.1**
Communications	2 245 . .	. . .	. . .	. . .	. . .	. . .	. . .	. . .	. . .
Construction	2 249 . .	. . .	. . .	. . .	. . .	. . .	. . .	. . .	. . .
Insurance	2 253 . .	.4	.8	.7	.7	.7	.7	.8	.4
Financial	2 260 . .	. . .	. . .	. . .	. . .	. . .	. . .	. . .	. . .
Computer and information	2 262 . .	. . .	. . .	. . .	. . .	. . .	. . .	. . .	. . .
Royalties and licence fees	2 266 . .	1.5	1.4	1.1	2.7	2.6	2.0	3.7	3.6
Other business services	2 268 . .	.1	.2	.1	. . .	.1	. . .	. . .	. . .
Personal, cultural, and recreational	2 287 . .	. . .	. . .	. . .	. . .	. . .	. . .	. . .	. . .
Government, n.i.e.	2 291 . .	2.6	2.7	2.9	2.9	2.7	2.9	3.1	3.1
Other services, debit	3 200 BA	**–5.5**	**–9.1**	**–9.9**	**–10.6**	**–10.6**	**–11.7**	**–10.0**	**–11.1**
Communications	3 245 . .	. . .	. . .	. . .	. . .	. . .	. . .	. . .	. . .
Construction	3 249 . .	. . .	. . .	. . .	. . .	. . .	. . .	. . .	. . .
Insurance	3 253 . .	–2.1	–2.7	–3.0	–3.5	–3.6	–4.1	–4.0	–4.0
Financial	3 260 . .	. . .	. . .	. . .	. . .	. . .	. . .	. . .	. . .
Computer and information	3 262 . .	. . .	. . .	. . .	. . .	. . .	. . .	. . .	. . .
Royalties and licence fees	3 266 . .	. . .	. . .	. . .	. . .	. . .	. . .	. . .	. . .
Other business services	3 268 . .	–2.3	–5.1	–5.4	–5.7	–5.7	–6.2	–4.2	–5.4
Personal, cultural, and recreational	3 287 . .	. . .	. . .	. . .	. . .	. . .	. . .	. . .	. . .
Government, n.i.e.	3 291 . .	–1.1	–1.3	–1.5	–1.4	–1.3	–1.4	–1.8	–1.7

Table 2 (Continued). STANDARD PRESENTATION, 1994–2001
(Millions of U.S. dollars)

	Code		1994	1995	1996	1997	1998	1999	2000	2001
C. INCOME	4 300	. .	–20.2	–19.9	–21.9	–27.4	–28.1	–30.9	–30.1	–38.5
Total credit	2 300	. .	*3.8*	*4.5*	*5.9*	*7.5*	*8.6*	*9.1*	*10.3*	*6.9*
Total debit	3 300	. .	*–24.0*	*–24.4*	*–27.8*	*–34.9*	*–36.7*	*–40.0*	*–40.4*	*–45.4*
Compensation of employees, credit	2 310	. .	**2.2**	**2.4**	**2.7**	**2.5**	**2.5**	**2.2**	**2.2**	**1.8**
Compensation of employees, debit	3 310	. .	**–.3**	**–.2**	**–.2**	**–.2**	**–.2**	**–.4**	**–.1**	**–.4**
Investment income, credit	2 320	. .	**1.6**	**2.1**	**3.2**	**5.0**	**6.1**	**6.9**	**8.1**	**5.1**
Direct investment income	2 330	. .	. . .	. . .	. . .	. . .	. . .	. . .	. . .	. . .
Dividends and distributed branch profits	2 332	. .	. . .	. . .	. . .	. . .	. . .	. . .	. . .	. . .
Reinvested earnings and undistributed branch profits	2 333	. .	. . .	. . .	. . .	. . .	. . .	. . .	. . .	. . .
Income on debt (interest)	2 334	. .	. . .	. . .	. . .	. . .	. . .	. . .	. . .	. . .
Portfolio investment income	2 339	. .	. . .	. . .	. . .	. . .	. . .	. . .	. . .	. . .
Income on equity	2 340	. .	. . .	. . .	. . .	. . .	. . .	. . .	. . .	. . .
Income on bonds and notes	2 350	. .	. . .	. . .	. . .	. . .	. . .	. . .	. . .	. . .
Income on money market instruments	2 360	. .	. . .	. . .	. . .	. . .	. . .	. . .	. . .	. . .
Other investment income	2 370	. .	1.6	2.1	3.2	5.0	6.1	6.9	8.1	5.1
Investment income, debit	3 320	. .	**–23.7**	**–24.2**	**–27.6**	**–34.7**	**–36.5**	**–39.6**	**–40.3**	**–45.0**
Direct investment income	3 330	. .	–20.3	–19.8	–23.0	–29.8	–31.7	–34.2	–34.4	–39.5
Dividends and distributed branch profits	3 332	. .	–11.6	–12.6	–13.7	–18.4	–20.2	–21.9	–21.4	–27.8
Reinvested earnings and undistributed branch profits	3 333	. .	–8.7	–7.2	–9.3	–11.4	–11.5	–12.3	–13.0	–11.7
Income on debt (interest)	3 334	. .	. . .	. . .	. . .	. . .	. . .	. . .	. . .	. . .
Portfolio investment income	3 339	. .	. . .	. . .	. . .	. . .	. . .	. . .	. . .	. . .
Income on equity	3 340	. .	. . .	. . .	. . .	. . .	. . .	. . .	. . .	. . .
Income on bonds and notes	3 350	. .	. . .	. . .	. . .	. . .	. . .	. . .	. . .	. . .
Income on money market instruments	3 360	. .	. . .	. . .	. . .	. . .	. . .	. . .	. . .	. . .
Other investment income	3 370	. .	–3.4	–4.4	–4.6	–4.9	–4.8	–5.4	–5.9	–5.5
D. CURRENT TRANSFERS	4 379	. .	–5.9	–3.6	–1.1	–10.7	–11.7	–22.8	–28.5	–29.5
Credit	2 379	. .	**16.3**	**23.0**	**26.2**	**17.2**	**18.9**	**17.7**	**17.7**	**20.1**
General government	2 380	. .	16.3	23.0	26.2	17.2	18.9	17.7	17.7	20.1
Other sectors	2 390	. .	. . .	. . .	. . .	. . .	. . .	. . .	. . .	. . .
Workers' remittances	2 391	. .	. . .	. . .	. . .	. . .	. . .	. . .	. . .	. . .
Other current transfers	2 392	. .	. . .	. . .	. . .	. . .	. . .	. . .	. . .	. . .
Debit	3 379	. .	**–22.2**	**–26.6**	**–27.3**	**–27.9**	**–30.6**	**–40.5**	**–46.2**	**–49.6**
General government	3 380	. .	. . .	. . .	. . .	. . .	. . .	. . .	. . .	. . .
Other sectors	3 390	. .	–22.2	–26.6	–27.3	–27.9	–30.6	–40.5	–46.2	–49.6
Workers' remittances	3 391	. .	–22.2	–26.6	–27.3	–27.9	–30.6	–40.5	–46.2	–49.6
Other current transfers	3 392	. .	. . .	. . .	. . .	. . .	. . .	. . .	. . .	. . .
CAPITAL AND FINANCIAL ACCOUNT	4 996	. .	**22.0**	**50.5**	**23.9**	**48.8**	**40.2**	**67.5**	**44.3**	**64.8**
CAPITAL ACCOUNT	4 994	. .	. . .	. . .	. . .	. . .	. . .	. . .	. . .	. . .
Total credit	2 994	. .	. . .	. . .	. . .	. . .	. . .	. . .	. . .	. . .
Total debit	3 994	. .	. . .	. . .	. . .	. . .	. . .	. . .	. . .	. . .
Capital transfers, credit	2 400	. .	**. . .**	**. . .**	**. . .**	**. . .**	**. . .**	**. . .**	**. . .**	**. . .**
General government	2 401	. .	. . .	. . .	. . .	. . .	. . .	. . .	. . .	. . .
Debt forgiveness	2 402	. .	. . .	. . .	. . .	. . .	. . .	. . .	. . .	. . .
Other capital transfers	2 410	. .	. . .	. . .	. . .	. . .	. . .	. . .	. . .	. . .
Other sectors	2 430	. .	. . .	. . .	. . .	. . .	. . .	. . .	. . .	. . .
Migrants' transfers	2 431	. .	. . .	. . .	. . .	. . .	. . .	. . .	. . .	. . .
Debt forgiveness	2 432	. .	. . .	. . .	. . .	. . .	. . .	. . .	. . .	. . .
Other capital transfers	2 440	. .	. . .	. . .	. . .	. . .	. . .	. . .	. . .	. . .
Capital transfers, debit	3 400	. .	**. . .**	**. . .**	**. . .**	**. . .**	**. . .**	**. . .**	**. . .**	**. . .**
General government	3 401	. .	. . .	. . .	. . .	. . .	. . .	. . .	. . .	. . .
Debt forgiveness	3 402	. .	. . .	. . .	. . .	. . .	. . .	. . .	. . .	. . .
Other capital transfers	3 410	. .	. . .	. . .	. . .	. . .	. . .	. . .	. . .	. . .
Other sectors	3 430	. .	. . .	. . .	. . .	. . .	. . .	. . .	. . .	. . .
Migrants' transfers	3 431	. .	. . .	. . .	. . .	. . .	. . .	. . .	. . .	. . .
Debt forgiveness	3 432	. .	. . .	. . .	. . .	. . .	. . .	. . .	. . .	. . .
Other capital transfers	3 440	. .	. . .	. . .	. . .	. . .	. . .	. . .	. . .	. . .
Nonproduced nonfinancial assets, credit	2 480	. .	**. . .**	**. . .**	**. . .**	**. . .**	**. . .**	**. . .**	**. . .**	**. . .**
Nonproduced nonfinancial assets, debit	3 480	. .	**. . .**	**. . .**	**. . .**	**. . .**	**. . .**	**. . .**	**. . .**	**. . .**

Table 2 (Continued). STANDARD PRESENTATION, 1994–2001

(Millions of U.S. dollars)

	Code	1994	1995	1996	1997	1998	1999	2000	2001
FINANCIAL ACCOUNT	4 995 . .	**22.0**	**50.5**	**23.9**	**48.8**	**40.2**	**67.5**	**44.3**	**64.8**
A. DIRECT INVESTMENT	4 500 . .	8.7	7.2	9.3	11.4	11.5	12.3	13.0	11.7
Direct investment abroad	4 505 . .	...	...	...	...	...	...	...	...
Equity capital	4 510 . .	...	...	...	...	...	...	...	...
Claims on affiliated enterprises	4 515 . .	...	...	...	...	...	...	...	...
Liabilities to affiliated enterprises	4 520 . .	...	...	...	...	...	...	...	...
Reinvested earnings	4 525 . .	...	...	...	...	...	...	...	...
Other capital	4 530 . .	...	...	...	...	...	...	...	...
Claims on affiliated enterprises	4 535 . .	...	...	...	...	...	...	...	...
Liabilities to affiliated enterprises	4 540 . .	...	...	...	...	...	...	...	...
Direct investment in Maldives	4 555 . .	**8.7**	**7.2**	**9.3**	**11.4**	**11.5**	**12.3**	**13.0**	**11.7**
Equity capital	4 560 . .	...	...	...	...	...	...	...	...
Claims on direct investors	4 565 . .	...	...	...	...	...	...	...	...
Liabilities to direct investors	4 570 . .	...	...	...	...	...	...	...	...
Reinvested earnings	4 575 . .	8.7	7.2	9.3	11.4	11.5	12.3	13.0	11.7
Other capital	4 580 . .	...	...	...	...	...	...	...	...
Claims on direct investors	4 585 . .	...	...	...	...	...	...	...	...
Liabilities to direct investors	4 590 . .	...	...	...	...	...	...	...	...
B. PORTFOLIO INVESTMENT	4 600 . .	...	...	...	...	...	...	...	...
Assets	4 602 . .	...	...	...	...	...	...	...	...
Equity securities	4 610 . .	...	...	...	...	...	...	...	...
Monetary authorities	4 611 . .	...	...	...	...	...	...	...	...
General government	4 612 . .	...	...	...	...	...	...	...	...
Banks	4 613 . .	...	...	...	...	...	...	...	...
Other sectors	4 614 . .	...	...	...	...	...	...	...	...
Debt securities	4 619 . .	...	...	...	...	...	...	...	...
Bonds and notes	4 620 . .	...	...	...	...	...	...	...	...
Monetary authorities	4 621 . .	...	...	...	...	...	...	...	...
General government	4 622 . .	...	...	...	...	...	...	...	...
Banks	4 623 . .	...	...	...	...	...	...	...	...
Other sectors	4 624 . .	...	...	...	...	...	...	...	...
Money market instruments	4 630 . .	...	...	...	...	...	...	...	...
Monetary authorities	4 631 . .	...	...	...	...	...	...	...	...
General government	4 632 . .	...	...	...	...	...	...	...	...
Banks	4 633 . .	...	...	...	...	...	...	...	...
Other sectors	4 634 . .	...	...	...	...	...	...	...	...
Liabilities	4 652 . .	...	...	...	...	...	...	...	...
Equity securities	4 660 . .	...	...	...	...	...	...	...	...
Banks	4 663 . .	...	...	...	...	...	...	...	...
Other sectors	4 664 . .	...	...	...	...	...	...	...	...
Debt securities	4 669 . .	...	...	...	...	...	...	...	...
Bonds and notes	4 670 . .	...	...	...	...	...	...	...	...
Monetary authorities	4 671 . .	...	...	...	...	...	...	...	...
General government	4 672 . .	...	...	...	...	...	...	...	...
Banks	4 673 . .	...	...	...	...	...	...	...	...
Other sectors	4 674 . .	...	...	...	...	...	...	...	...
Money market instruments	4 680 . .	...	...	...	...	...	...	...	...
Monetary authorities	4 681 . .	...	...	...	...	...	...	...	...
General government	4 682 . .	...	...	...	...	...	...	...	...
Banks	4 683 . .	...	...	...	...	...	...	...	...
Other sectors	4 684 . .	...	...	...	...	...	...	...	...
C. FINANCIAL DERIVATIVES	4 910 . .	...	...	...	...	...	...	...	...
Monetary authorities	4 911 . .	...	...	...	...	...	...	...	...
General government	4 912 . .	...	...	...	...	...	...	...	...
Banks	4 913 . .	...	...	...	...	...	...	...	...
Other sectors	4 914 . .	...	...	...	...	...	...	...	...
Assets	4 900 . .	...	...	...	...	...	...	...	...
Monetary authorities	4 901 . .	...	...	...	...	...	...	...	...
General government	4 902 . .	...	...	...	...	...	...	...	...
Banks	4 903 . .	...	...	...	...	...	...	...	...
Other sectors	4 904 . .	...	...	...	...	...	...	...	...
Liabilities	4 905 . .	...	...	...	...	...	...	...	...
Monetary authorities	4 906 . .	...	...	...	...	...	...	...	...
General government	4 907 . .	...	...	...	...	...	...	...	...
Banks	4 908 . .	...	...	...	...	...	...	...	...
Other sectors	4 909 . .	...	...	...	...	...	...	...	...

Table 2 (Concluded). STANDARD PRESENTATION, 1994–2001
(Millions of U.S. dollars)

	Code	1994	1995	1996	1997	1998	1999	2000	2001
D. OTHER INVESTMENT	4 700 . .	18.7	60.4	42.9	59.6	48.8	63.8	27.0	23.4
Assets	4 703 . .	**13.2**	**29.9**	**32.7**	**53.8**	**30.8**	**47.4**	**22.8**	**21.3**
Trade credits	4 706 . .	11.3	33.7	40.0	42.9	42.9	42.9	25.6	24.3
General government	4 707 . .	. . .	. . .	. . .	. . .	. . .	. . .	. . .	. . .
of which: Short-term	4 709 . .	. . .	. . .	. . .	. . .	. . .	. . .	. . .	. . .
Other sectors	4 710 . .	11.3	33.7	40.0	42.9	42.9	42.9	25.6	24.3
of which: Short-term	4 712 . .	. . .	. . .	. . .	. . .	. . .	. . .	. . .	. . .
Loans	4 714 . .	. . .	. . .	. . .	.1	–.5	.9	1.4	–.6
Monetary authorities	4 715 . .	. . .	. . .	. . .	. . .	. . .	. . .	. . .	. . .
of which: Short-term	4 718 . .	. . .	. . .	. . .	. . .	. . .	. . .	. . .	. . .
General government	4 719 . .	. . .	. . .	. . .	. . .	. . .	. . .	. . .	. . .
of which: Short-term	4 721 . .	. . .	. . .	. . .	. . .	. . .	. . .	. . .	. . .
Banks	4 722 . .	. . .	. . .	. . .	.1	–.5	.9	1.4	–.6
of which: Short-term	4 724 . .	. . .	. . .	. . .	. . .	. . .	. . .	. . .	. . .
Other sectors	4 725 . .	. . .	. . .	. . .	. . .	. . .	. . .	. . .	. . .
of which: Short-term	4 727 . .	. . .	. . .	. . .	. . .	. . .	. . .	. . .	. . .
Currency and deposits	4 730 . .	1.9	–3.8	–7.3	10.8	–11.6	3.6	–4.2	–2.4
Monetary authorities	4 731 . .	. . .	. . .	. . .	. . .	. . .	. . .	. . .	. . .
General government	4 732 . .	. . .	. . .	. . .	. . .	. . .	. . .	. . .	. . .
Banks	4 733 . .	1.9	–3.8	–7.3	10.8	–11.6	3.6	–4.2	–2.4
Other sectors	4 734 . .	. . .	. . .	. . .	. . .	. . .	. . .	. . .	. . .
Other assets	4 736 . .	. . .	. . .	. . .	. . .	. . .	. . .	. . .	. . .
Monetary authorities	4 737 . .	. . .	. . .	. . .	. . .	. . .	. . .	. . .	. . .
of which: Short-term	4 739 . .	. . .	. . .	. . .	. . .	. . .	. . .	. . .	. . .
General government	4 740 . .	. . .	. . .	. . .	. . .	. . .	. . .	. . .	. . .
of which: Short-term	4 742 . .	. . .	. . .	. . .	. . .	. . .	. . .	. . .	. . .
Banks	4 743 . .	. . .	. . .	. . .	. . .	. . .	. . .	. . .	. . .
of which: Short-term	4 745 . .	. . .	. . .	. . .	. . .	. . .	. . .	. . .	. . .
Other sectors	4 746 . .	. . .	. . .	. . .	. . .	. . .	. . .	. . .	. . .
of which: Short-term	4 748 . .	. . .	. . .	. . .	. . .	. . .	. . .	. . .	. . .
Liabilities	4 753 . .	**5.5**	**30.5**	**10.2**	**5.8**	**18.0**	**16.4**	**4.2**	**2.1**
Trade credits	4 756 . .	. . .	. . .	. . .	. . .	. . .	. . .	. . .	. . .
General government	4 757 . .	. . .	. . .	. . .	. . .	. . .	. . .	. . .	. . .
of which: Short-term	4 759 . .	. . .	. . .	. . .	. . .	. . .	. . .	. . .	. . .
Other sectors	4 760 . .	. . .	. . .	. . .	. . .	. . .	. . .	. . .	. . .
of which: Short-term	4 762 . .	. . .	. . .	. . .	. . .	. . .	. . .	. . .	. . .
Loans	4 764 . .	5.8	30.1	11.0	21.1	17.5	17.3	3.4	2.0
Monetary authorities	4 765 . .	. . .	. . .	. . .	. . .	. . .	. . .	. . .	. . .
of which: Use of Fund credit and loans from the Fund	4 766 . .	. . .	. . .	. . .	. . .	. . .	. . .	. . .	. . .
of which: Short-term	4 768 . .	. . .	. . .	. . .	. . .	. . .	. . .	. . .	. . .
General government	4 769 . .	8.2	24.7	17.3	21.9	14.7	5.1	–2.1	7.6
of which: Short-term	4 771 . .	. . .	. . .	. . .	. . .	. . .	. . .	. . .	. . .
Banks	4 772 . .	–2.4	5.4	–6.3	–.8	2.8	12.2	5.5	–5.6
of which: Short-term	4 774 . .	. . .	. . .	. . .	. . .	. . .	. . .	. . .	. . .
Other sectors	4 775 . .	. . .	. . .	. . .	. . .	. . .	. . .	. . .	. . .
of which: Short-term	4 777 . .	. . .	. . .	. . .	. . .	. . .	. . .	. . .	. . .
Currency and deposits	4 780 . .	–1.0	.3	–.8	. . .	.5	.9	.8	.2
Monetary authorities	4 781 . .	. . .	. . .	. . .	. . .	. . .	. . .	. . .	. . .
General government	4 782 . .	. . .	. . .	. . .	. . .	. . .	. . .	. . .	. . .
Banks	4 783 . .	–1.0	.3	–.8	. . .	.5	–.9	.8	.2
Other sectors	4 784 . .	. . .	. . .	. . .	. . .	. . .	. . .	. . .	. . .
Other liabilities	4 786 . .	.7	.1	. . .	–15.3	. . .	. . .	. . .	–.1
Monetary authorities	4 787 . .	.7	.1	. . .	–15.3	. . .	. . .	. . .	–.1
of which: Short-term	4 789 . .	*.7*	*.1*	. . .	*–15.3*	. . .	. . .	. . .	*–.1*
General government	4 790 . .	. . .	. . .	. . .	. . .	. . .	. . .	. . .	. . .
of which: Short-term	4 792 . .	. . .	. . .	. . .	. . .	. . .	. . .	. . .	. . .
Banks	4 793 . .	. . .	. . .	. . .	. . .	. . .	. . .	. . .	. . .
of which: Short-term	4 795 . .	. . .	. . .	. . .	. . .	. . .	. . .	. . .	. . .
Other sectors	4 796 . .	. . .	. . .	. . .	. . .	. . .	. . .	. . .	. . .
of which: Short-term	4 798 . .	. . .	. . .	. . .	. . .	. . .	. . .	. . .	. . .
E. RESERVE ASSETS	4 802 . .	–5.4	–17.1	–28.3	–22.2	–20.1	–8.6	4.3	29.7
Monetary gold	4 812 . .	–.3	. . .	–.1	. . .	. . .	. . .	.1	. . .
Special drawing rights	4 811 . .	. . .	. . .	. . .	. . .	. . .	. . .	–.1	–.1
Reserve position in the Fund	4 810 . .	. . .	. . .	. . .	. . .	. . .	–.9	. . .	. . .
Foreign exchange	4 803 . .	–4.5	–17.1	–28.2	–22.2	–20.1	–7.6	4.3	29.7
Other claims	4 813 . .	–.6	. . .	. . .	. . .	. . .	. . .	. . .	.1
NET ERRORS AND OMISSIONS	4 998 . .	**–10.8**	**–32.2**	**–16.6**	**–14.6**	**–16.9**	**14.2**	**8.8**	**–3.8**

Part 3 of the *Yearbook* contains descriptions of the methodologies, compilation practices, and sources used to compile these data.

Table 3. INTERNATIONAL INVESTMENT POSITION (End-period stocks), 1994–2001
(Millions of U.S. dollars)

	Code		1994	1995	1996	1997	1998	1999	2000	2001
ASSETS	8 995	C	...	...	...	...	...	...	...	...
Direct investment abroad	8 505	..	...	...	...	...	...	...	...	...
Equity capital and reinvested earnings	8 506	..	...	...	...	...	...	...	...	...
Claims on affiliated enterprises	8 507	..	...	...	...	...	...	...	...	...
Liabilities to affiliated enterprises	8 508	..	...	...	...	...	...	...	...	...
Other capital	8 530	..	...	...	...	...	...	...	...	...
Claims on affiliated enterprises	8 535	..	...	...	...	...	...	...	...	...
Liabilities to affiliated enterprises	8 540	..	...	...	...	...	...	...	...	...
Portfolio investment	8 602	..	...	...	...	...	...	...	...	...
Equity securities	8 610	..	...	...	...	...	...	...	...	...
Monetary authorities	8 611	..	...	...	...	...	...	...	...	...
General government	8 612	..	...	...	...	...	...	...	...	...
Banks	8 613	..	...	...	...	...	...	...	...	...
Other sectors	8 614	..	...	...	...	...	...	...	...	...
Debt securities	8 619	..	...	...	...	...	...	...	...	...
Bonds and notes	8 620	..	...	...	...	...	...	...	...	...
Monetary authorities	8 621	..	...	...	...	...	...	...	...	...
General government	8 622	..	...	...	...	...	...	...	...	...
Banks	8 623	..	...	...	...	...	...	...	...	...
Other sectors	8 624	..	...	...	...	...	...	...	...	...
Money market instruments	8 630	..	...	...	...	...	...	...	...	...
Monetary authorities	8 631	..	...	...	...	...	...	...	...	...
General government	8 632	..	...	...	...	...	...	...	...	...
Banks	8 633	..	...	...	...	...	...	...	...	...
Other sectors	8 634	..	...	...	...	...	...	...	...	...
Financial derivatives	8 900	..	...	...	...	...	...	...	...	...
Monetary authorities	8 901	..	...	...	...	...	...	...	...	...
General government	8 902	..	...	...	...	...	...	...	...	...
Banks	8 903	..	...	...	...	...	...	...	...	...
Other sectors	8 904	..	...	...	...	...	...	...	...	...
Other investment	8 703	..	**10.2**	**14.0**	**22.3**	**11.5**	**23.7**	**19.1**	**21.9**	**24.9**
Trade credits	8 706	..	...	...	...	...	...	...	...	...
General government	8 707	..	...	...	...	...	...	...	...	...
of which: Short-term	8 709	..	...	...	...	...	...	...	...	...
Other sectors	8 710	..	...	...	...	...	...	...	...	...
of which: Short-term	8 712	..	...	...	...	...	...	...	...	...
Loans	8 714	..	2.4	2.4	3.4	3.3	3.9	2.9	1.5	2.1
Monetary authorities	8 715	..	...	...	...	...	...	...	...	...
of which: Short-term	8 718	..	...	...	...	...	...	...	...	...
General government	8 719	..	...	...	...	...	...	...	...	...
of which: Short-term	8 721	..	...	...	...	...	...	...	...	...
Banks	8 722	..	2.4	2.4	3.4	3.3	3.9	2.9	1.5	2.1
of which: Short-term	8 724	..	...	...	...	...	...	...	...	...
Other sectors	8 725	..	...	...	...	...	...	...	...	...
of which: Short-term	8 727	..	...	...	...	...	...	...	...	...
Currency and deposits	8 730	..	7.8	11.6	18.9	8.2	19.8	16.2	20.4	22.8
Monetary authorities	8 731	..	...	...	...	...	...	...	...	...
General government	8 732	..	...	...	...	...	...	...	...	...
Banks	8 733	..	7.8	11.6	18.9	8.2	19.8	16.2	20.4	22.8
Other sectors	8 734	..	...	...	...	...	...	...	...	...
Other assets	8 736	..	...	...	...	...	...	...	...	...
Monetary authorities	8 737	..	...	...	...	...	...	...	...	...
of which: Short-term	8 739	..	...	...	...	...	...	...	...	...
General government	8 740	..	...	...	...	...	...	...	...	...
of which: Short-term	8 742	..	...	...	...	...	...	...	...	...
Banks	8 743	..	...	...	...	...	...	...	...	...
of which: Short-term	8 745	..	...	...	...	...	...	...	...	...
Other sectors	8 746	..	...	...	...	...	...	...	...	...
of which: Short-term	8 748	..	...	...	...	...	...	...	...	...
Reserve assets	8 802	..	**32.0**	**49.3**	**77.6**	**99.7**	**120.0**	**128.5**	**124.0**	**94.4**
Monetary gold	8 812	..	.5	.5	.6	.6	.6	.6	.4	.5
Special drawing rights	8 811	..	...	.1	.1	.1	.1	.2	.3	.3
Reserve position in the Fund	8 810	..	1.3	1.3	1.3	1.2	1.2	2.1	2.0	2.0
Foreign exchange	8 803	..	29.4	46.6	74.8	97.0	117.2	124.8	120.5	90.8
Other claims	8 813	..	.8	.8	.8	.8	.8	.8	.8	.8

Table 3 (Concluded). INTERNATIONAL INVESTMENT POSITION (End–period stocks), 1994–2001
(Millions of U.S. dollars)

	Code	1994	1995	1996	1997	1998	1999	2000	2001
LIABILITIES	8 995 D.	...	...	...	...	...	...	...	...
Direct investment in Maldives	8 555 . .	...	...	...	...	...	...	...	...
Equity capital and reinvested earnings	8 556 . .	...	...	...	...	...	...	...	...
Claims on direct investors	8 557 . .	...	...	...	...	...	...	...	...
Liabilities to direct investors	8 558 . .	...	...	...	...	...	...	...	...
Other capital	8 580 . .	...	...	...	...	...	...	...	...
Claims on direct investors	8 585 . .	...	...	...	...	...	...	...	...
Liabilities to direct investors	8 590 . .	...	...	...	...	...	...	...	...
Portfolio investment	8 652 . .	...	...	...	...	...	...	...	...
Equity securities	8 660 . .	...	...	...	...	...	...	...	...
Banks	8 663 . .	...	...	...	...	...	...	...	...
Other sectors	8 664 . .	...	...	...	...	...	...	...	...
Debt securities	8 669 . .	...	...	...	...	...	...	...	...
Bonds and notes	8 670 . .	...	...	...	...	...	...	...	...
Monetary authorities	8 671 . .	...	...	...	...	...	...	...	...
General government	8 672 . .	...	...	...	...	...	...	...	...
Banks	8 673 . .	...	...	...	...	...	...	...	...
Other sectors	8 674 . .	...	...	...	...	...	...	...	...
Money market instruments	8 680 . .	...	...	...	...	...	...	...	...
Monetary authorities	8 681 . .	...	...	...	...	...	...	...	...
General government	8 682 . .	...	...	...	...	...	...	...	...
Banks	8 683 . .	...	...	...	...	...	...	...	...
Other sectors	8 684 . .	...	...	...	...	...	...	...	...
Financial derivatives	8 905 . .	...	...	...	...	...	...	...	...
Monetary authorities	8 906 . .	...	...	...	...	...	...	...	...
General government	8 907 . .	...	...	...	...	...	...	...	...
Banks	8 908 . .	...	...	...	...	...	...	...	...
Other sectors	8 909 . .	...	...	...	...	...	...	...	...
Other investment	8 753 . .	**141.8**	**173.0**	**178.2**	**179.0**	**201.7**	**213.8**	**212.5**	**210.2**
Trade credits	8 756 . .	...	...	...	...	...	...	...	...
General government	8 757 . .	...	...	...	...	...	...	...	...
of which: Short-term	8 759 . .	...	...	...	...	...	...	...	...
Other sectors	8 760 . .	...	...	...	...	...	...	...	...
of which: Short-term	8 762 . .	...	...	...	...	...	...	...	...
Loans	8 764 . .	139.4	170.3	176.1	176.9	199.1	212.2	210.1	207.9
Monetary authorities	8 765 . .	15.3	15.4	15.3	...	...	...	...	...
of which: Use of Fund credit and loans from the Fund	8 766 . .	...	...	...	...	...	...	...	...
of which: Short-term	8 768 . .	...	...	...	...	...	...	...	...
General government	8 769 . .	110.8	136.2	148.4	165.3	184.7	185.6	178.0	181.3
of which: Short-term	8 771 . .	...	...	...	...	...	...	...	...
Banks	8 772 . .	13.3	18.7	12.4	11.6	14.4	26.6	32.1	26.6
of which: Short-term	8 774 . .	...	...	...	...	...	...	...	...
Other sectors	8 775 . .	...	...	...	...	...	...	...	...
of which: Short-term	8 777 . .	...	...	...	...	...	...	...	...
Currency and deposits	8 780 . .	1.6	1.9	1.2	1.2	1.7	.7	1.5	1.5
Monetary authorities	8 781 . .	...	...	...	...	...	...	...	...
General government	8 782 . .	...	...	...	...	...	...	...	...
Banks	8 783 . .	1.6	1.9	1.2	1.2	1.7	.7	1.5	1.5
Other sectors	8 784 . .	...	...	...	...	...	...	...	...
Other liabilities	8 786 . .	.8	.8	.9	.9	.9	.9	.9	.8
Monetary authorities	8 787 . .	.8	.8	.9	.9	.9	.9	.9	.8
of which: Short-term	8 789 . .	*.8*	*.8*	*.9*	*.9*	*.9*	*.9*	*.9*	*.8*
General government	8 790 . .	...	...	...	...	...	...	...	...
of which: Short-term	8 792 . .	...	...	...	...	...	...	...	...
Banks	8 793 . .	...	...	...	...	...	...	...	...
of which: Short-term	8 795 . .	...	...	...	...	...	...	...	...
Other sectors	8 796 . .	...	...	...	...	...	...	...	...
of which: Short-term	8 798 . .	...	...	...	...	...	...	...	...
NET INTERNATIONAL INVESTMENT POSITION	8 995 . .	...	...	...	...	...	...	...	...
Conversion rates: rufiyaa per U.S. dollar (end of period)	0 102 . .	**11.770**	**11.770**	**11.770**	**11.770**	**11.770**	**11.770**	**11.770**	**12.800**

Table 1. ANALYTIC PRESENTATION, 1994–2001
(Millions of U.S. dollars)

	Code	1994	1995	1996	1997	1998	1999	2000	2001
A. Current Account [1]	4 993 Z.	**–162.6**	**–283.8**	**–273.2**	**–178.4**	...	...	...	...
Goods: exports f.o.b	2 100 ..	334.9	441.8	433.5	561.6	...	...	...	...
Goods: imports f.o.b	3 100 ..	–449.2	–556.8	–551.5	–551.9	...	...	...	...
Balance on Goods	4 100 ..	*–114.3*	*–115.0*	*–118.0*	*9.7*	...	...	...	...
Services: credit	2 200 ..	69.0	87.6	87.6	82.1	...	...	...	...
Services: debit	3 200 ..	–317.0	–434.5	–382.8	–345.6	...	...	...	...
Balance on Goods and Services	4 991 ..	*–362.3*	*–461.9*	*–413.2*	*–253.8*	...	...	...	...
Income: credit	2 300 ..	9.3	8.3	10.9	10.6	...	...	...	...
Income: debit	3 300 ..	–49.7	–48.9	–67.1	–61.7	...	...	...	...
Balance on Goods, Services, and Income	4 992 ..	*–402.7*	*–502.6*	*–469.3*	*–304.8*	...	...	...	...
Current transfers: credit	2 379 Z.	281.3	266.8	246.1	170.0	...	...	...	...
Current transfers: debit	3 379 ..	–41.2	–48.0	–50.0	–43.5	...	...	...	...
B. Capital Account [1]	4 994 Z.	**99.1**	**126.2**	**136.4**	**108.6**	...	...	...	...
Capital account: credit	2 994 Z.	99.1	126.2	136.4	108.6	...	...	...	...
Capital account: debit	3 994 ..	...	...	...	...	...	...	...	...
Total, Groups A Plus B	4 981 ..	*–63.6*	*–157.6*	*–136.8*	*–69.8*	...	...	...	...
C. Financial Account [1]	4 995 W.	**–7.0**	**118.6**	**174.6**	**52.7**	...	...	...	...
Direct investment abroad	4 505 ..	...	...	...	...	...	...	...	...
Direct investment in Mali	4 555 Z.	17.4	111.4	84.1	39.4	...	...	...	...
Portfolio investment assets	4 602 ..	...	...	...	...	...	...	...	...
Equity securities	4 610 ..	...	...	...	...	...	...	...	...
Debt securities	4 619 ..	...	...	...	...	...	...	...	...
Portfolio investment liabilities	4 652 Z.	...	...	...	...	...	...	...	...
Equity securities	4 660 ..	...	...	...	...	...	...	...	...
Debt securities	4 669 Z.	...	...	...	...	...	...	...	...
Financial derivatives	4 910 ..	...	...	...	...	...	...	...	...
Financial derivatives assets	4 900 ..	...	...	...	...	...	...	...	...
Financial derivatives liabilities	4 905 ..	...	...	...	...	...	...	...	...
Other investment assets	4 703 ..	–104.0	–52.3	4.1	–12.4	...	...	...	...
Monetary authorities	4 701 ..	...	...	...	...	...	...	...	...
General government	4 704 ..	...	...	...	...	...	...	...	...
Banks	4 705 ..	–100.3	–33.2	16.8	2.0	...	...	...	...
Other sectors	4 728 ..	–3.7	–19.2	–12.7	–14.4	...	...	...	...
Other investment liabilities	4 753 W.	79.6	59.6	86.4	25.7	...	...	...	...
Monetary authorities	4 753 WA	...	...	...	...	...	...	...	...
General government	4 753 ZB	33.1	89.8	80.5	57.7	...	...	...	...
Banks	4 753 ZC	11.9	–1.4	–10.6	6.7	...	...	...	...
Other sectors	4 753 ZD	34.5	–28.7	16.5	–38.7	...	...	...	...
Total, Groups A Through C	4 983 ..	*–70.6*	*–39.0*	*37.8*	*–17.1*	...	...	...	...
D. Net Errors and Omissions	4 998 ..	**5.6**	**–13.0**	**–8.8**	**7.9**	...	...	...	...
Total, Groups A Through D	4 984 ..	*–65.0*	*–52.0*	*29.0*	*–9.2*	...	...	...	...
E. Reserves and Related Items	4 802 A.	**65.0**	**52.0**	**–29.0**	**9.2**	...	...	...	...
Reserve assets	4 802 ..	–37.6	–80.2	–131.6	–38.3	...	...	...	...
Use of Fund credit and loans	4 766 ..	32.7	38.4	22.4	21.3	...	...	...	...
Exceptional financing	4 920 ..	69.9	93.8	80.1	26.2	...	...	...	...
Conversion rates: CFA francs per U.S. dollar	0 101 ..	**555.20**	**499.15**	**511.55**	**583.67**	**589.95**	**615.70**	**711.98**	**733.04**

[1] Excludes components that have been classified in the categories of Group E.

Table 2. STANDARD PRESENTATION, 1994–2001
(Millions of U.S. dollars)

	Code	1994	1995	1996	1997	1998	1999	2000	2001
CURRENT ACCOUNT	4 993 . .	**–162.6**	**–283.8**	**–273.2**	**–178.4**	...	...	...	...
A. GOODS	4 100 . .	–114.3	–115.0	–118.0	9.7	...	...	...	...
Credit	2 100 . .	**334.9**	**441.8**	**433.5**	**561.6**	...	...	...	...
General merchandise: exports f.o.b.	2 110 . .	285.9	370.5	355.8	360.9	...	...	...	...
Goods for processing: exports f.o.b.	2 150 . .	...	...	...	...	...	...	...	...
Repairs on goods	2 160 . .	...	...	...	...	...	...	...	...
Goods procured in ports by carriers	2 170 . .	...	...	...	...	...	...	...	...
Nonmonetary gold	2 180 . .	49.0	71.3	77.7	200.7	...	...	...	...
Debit	3 100 . .	**–449.2**	**–556.8**	**–551.5**	**–551.9**	...	...	...	...
General merchandise: imports f.o.b.	3 110 . .	–449.2	–556.8	–551.5	–551.9	...	...	...	...
Goods for processing: imports f.o.b.	3 150 . .	...	...	...	...	...	...	...	...
Repairs on goods	3 160 . .	...	...	...	...	...	...	...	...
Goods procured in ports by carriers	3 170 . .	...	...	...	...	...	...	...	...
Nonmonetary gold	3 180 . .	...	...	...	...	...	...	...	...
B. SERVICES	4 200 . .	–248.0	–347.0	–295.2	–263.5	...	...	...	...
Total credit	2 200 . .	*69.0*	*87.6*	*87.6*	*82.1*	...	...	...	...
Total debit	3 200 . .	*–317.0*	*–434.5*	*–382.8*	*–345.6*	...	...	...	...
Transportation services, credit	2 205 . .	**17.0**	**22.1**	**25.4**	**22.8**	...	...	...	...
Passenger	2 850 . .	*1.0*	*1.2*	*1.3*	*1.2*	...	...	...	...
Freight	2 851 . .	*4.2*	*5.7*	*6.6*	*6.0*	...	...	...	...
Other	2 852 . .	*11.8*	*15.2*	*17.5*	*15.6*	...	...	...	...
Sea transport, passenger	2 207 . .	...	...	...	...	...	...	...	...
Sea transport, freight	2 208 . .	...	...	...	...	...	...	...	...
Sea transport, other	2 209 . .	...	...	...	...	...	...	...	...
Air transport, passenger	2 211 . .	...	...	...	...	...	...	...	...
Air transport, freight	2 212 . .	...	...	...	...	...	...	...	...
Air transport, other	2 213 . .	...	...	...	...	...	...	...	...
Other transport, passenger	2 215 . .	1.0	1.2	1.3	1.2	...	...	...	...
Other transport, freight	2 216 . .	4.2	5.7	6.6	6.0	...	...	...	...
Other transport, other	2 217 . .	...	...	...	...	...	...	...	...
Transportation services, debit	3 205 . .	**–205.9**	**–245.8**	**–248.9**	**–223.9**	...	...	...	...
Passenger	3 850 . .	*–20.6*	*–24.7*	*–24.4*	*–21.8*	...	...	...	...
Freight	3 851 . .	*–180.1*	*–215.3*	*–218.4*	*–197.0*	...	...	...	...
Other	3 852 . .	*–5.3*	*–5.9*	*–6.1*	*–5.1*	...	...	...	...
Sea transport, passenger	3 207 . .	...	...	...	...	...	...	...	...
Sea transport, freight	3 208 . .	–72.0	–86.1	–87.3	–78.8	...	...	...	...
Sea transport, other	3 209 . .	...	...	...	...	...	...	...	...
Air transport, passenger	3 211 . .	...	...	...	...	...	...	...	...
Air transport, freight	3 212 . .	...	...	...	...	...	...	...	...
Air transport, other	3 213 . .	...	...	...	...	...	...	...	...
Other transport, passenger	3 215 . .	–20.6	–24.7	–24.4	–21.8	...	...	...	...
Other transport, freight	3 216 . .	–108.0	–129.2	–131.0	–118.2	...	...	...	...
Other transport, other	3 217 . .	...	...	...	...	...	...	...	...
Travel, credit	2 236 . .	**23.8**	**25.4**	**29.3**	**26.4**	...	...	...	...
Business travel	2 237 . .	...	...	...	...	...	...	...	...
Personal travel	2 240 . .	...	...	...	...	...	...	...	...
Travel, debit	3 236 . .	**–42.3**	**–49.2**	**–45.7**	**–42.5**	...	...	...	...
Business travel	3 237 . .	...	...	...	...	...	...	...	...
Personal travel	3 240 . .	...	...	...	...	...	...	...	...
Other services, credit	2 200 BA	**28.2**	**40.0**	**32.8**	**32.9**	...	...	...	...
Communications	2 245 . .	...	...	...	...	...	...	...	...
Construction	2 249 . .	...	...	...	...	...	...	...	...
Insurance	2 253 . .	2.9	3.4	3.5	3.3	...	...	...	...
Financial	2 260 . .	...	...	...	...	...	...	...	...
Computer and information	2 262 . .	...	...	...	...	...	...	...	...
Royalties and licence fees	2 266 . .	...	...	...	...	...	...	...	...
Other business services	2 268 . .	7.0	17.2	8.0	9.6	...	...	...	...
Personal, cultural, and recreational	2 287 . .	...	...	...	...	...	...	...	...
Government, n.i.e.	2 291 . .	18.3	19.4	21.3	20.0	...	...	...	...
Other services, debit	3 200 BA	**–68.8**	**–139.5**	**–88.2**	**–79.2**	...	...	...	...
Communications	3 245 . .	...	...	...	...	...	...	...	...
Construction	3 249 . .	...	...	...	...	...	...	...	...
Insurance	3 253 . .	–4.4	–5.6	–5.5	–5.0	...	...	...	...
Financial	3 260 . .	...	...	...	...	...	...	...	...
Computer and information	3 262 . .	...	...	...	...	...	...	...	...
Royalties and licence fees	3 266 . .	...	...	...	...	...	...	...	...
Other business services	3 268 . .	–43.4	–111.6	–60.4	–52.9	...	...	...	...
Personal, cultural, and recreational	3 287 . .	...	...	...	...	...	...	...	...
Government, n.i.e.	3 291 . .	–21.0	–22.3	–22.3	–21.2	...	...	...	...

Table 2 (Continued). STANDARD PRESENTATION, 1994–2001
(Millions of U.S. dollars)

	Code	1994	1995	1996	1997	1998	1999	2000	2001
C. INCOME	4 300	–40.4	–40.6	–56.1	–51.1	...	...	...	...
Total credit	2 300	*9.3*	*8.3*	*10.9*	*10.6*	...	...	...	...
Total debit	3 300	*–49.7*	*–48.9*	*–67.1*	*–61.7*	...	...	...	...
Compensation of employees, credit	2 310	...	...	...	...	...	...	...	...
Compensation of employees, debit	3 310	...	...	...	...	...	...	...	...
Investment income, credit	2 320	**9.3**	**8.3**	**10.9**	**10.6**	...	...	...	...
Direct investment income	2 330	...	...	...	...	...	...	...	...
Dividends and distributed branch profits	2 332	...	...	...	...	...	...	...	...
Reinvested earnings and undistributed branch profits	2 333	...	...	...	...	...	...	...	...
Income on debt (interest)	2 334	...	...	...	...	...	...	...	...
Portfolio investment income	2 339	...	...	...	...	...	...	...	...
Income on equity	2 340	...	...	...	...	...	...	...	...
Income on bonds and notes	2 350	...	...	...	...	...	...	...	...
Income on money market instruments	2 360	...	...	...	...	...	...	...	...
Other investment income	2 370	9.3	8.3	10.9	10.6	...	...	...	...
Investment income, debit	3 320	**–49.7**	**–48.9**	**–67.1**	**–61.7**	...	...	...	...
Direct investment income	3 330	...	–5.5	–5.9	–10.3	...	...	...	...
Dividends and distributed branch profits	3 332	–2.2	–.4	...	...	...	...	...	...
Reinvested earnings and undistributed branch profits	3 333	2.2	–5.1	–5.9	–10.3	...	...	...	...
Income on debt (interest)	3 334	...	...	...	...	...	...	...	...
Portfolio investment income	3 339	...	...	...	...	...	...	...	...
Income on equity	3 340	...	...	...	...	...	...	...	...
Income on bonds and notes	3 350	...	...	...	...	...	...	...	...
Income on money market instruments	3 360	...	...	...	...	...	...	...	...
Other investment income	3 370	–49.7	–43.5	–61.2	–51.4	...	...	...	...
D. CURRENT TRANSFERS	4 379	240.1	218.8	196.1	126.4	...	...	...	...
Credit	2 379	**281.3**	**266.8**	**246.1**	**170.0**	...	...	...	...
General government	2 380	158.0	126.3	109.7	57.6	...	...	...	...
Other sectors	2 390	123.3	140.5	136.4	112.4	...	...	...	...
Workers' remittances	2 391	103.2	112.1	107.1	90.5	...	...	...	...
Other current transfers	2 392	20.1	28.4	29.3	21.9	...	...	...	...
Debit	3 379	**–41.2**	**–48.0**	**–50.0**	**–43.5**	...	...	...	...
General government	3 380	–2.7	–3.4	–3.5	–3.1	...	...	...	...
Other sectors	3 390	–38.5	–44.7	–46.5	–40.4	...	...	...	...
Workers' remittances	3 391	–36.6	–42.2	–43.9	–36.6	...	...	...	...
Other current transfers	3 392	–1.9	–2.4	–2.6	–3.9	...	...	...	...
CAPITAL AND FINANCIAL ACCOUNT	4 996	**157.1**	**296.8**	**282.0**	**170.5**	...	...	...	...
CAPITAL ACCOUNT	4 994	**111.3**	**130.2**	**136.4**	**108.6**	...	...	...	...
Total credit	2 994	*111.3*	*130.2*	*136.4*	*108.6*	...	...	...	...
Total debit	3 994	...	...	...	...	...	...	...	...
Capital transfers, credit	2 400	**111.3**	**130.2**	**136.4**	**108.6**	...	...	...	...
General government	2 401	111.3	130.2	136.4	108.6	...	...	...	...
Debt forgiveness	2 402	12.2	4.0	...	...	...	...	...	...
Other capital transfers	2 410	99.1	126.2	136.4	108.6	...	...	...	...
Other sectors	2 430	...	...	...	...	...	...	...	...
Migrants' transfers	2 431	...	...	...	...	...	...	...	...
Debt forgiveness	2 432	...	...	...	...	...	...	...	...
Other capital transfers	2 440	...	...	...	...	...	...	...	...
Capital transfers, debit	3 400	...	...	...	...	...	...	...	...
General government	3 401	...	...	...	...	...	...	...	...
Debt forgiveness	3 402	...	...	...	...	...	...	...	...
Other capital transfers	3 410	...	...	...	...	...	...	...	...
Other sectors	3 430	...	...	...	...	...	...	...	...
Migrants' transfers	3 431	...	...	...	...	...	...	...	...
Debt forgiveness	3 432	...	...	...	...	...	...	...	...
Other capital transfers	3 440	...	...	...	...	...	...	...	...
Nonproduced nonfinancial assets, credit	2 480	...	...	...	...	...	...	...	...
Nonproduced nonfinancial assets, debit	3 480	...	...	...	...	...	...	...	...

Table 2 (Continued). STANDARD PRESENTATION, 1994–2001

(Millions of U.S. dollars)

	Code	1994	1995	1996	1997	1998	1999	2000	2001
FINANCIAL ACCOUNT	4 995 . .	**45.7**	**166.6**	**145.6**	**61.9**	**. . .**	**. . .**	**. . .**	**. . .**
A. DIRECT INVESTMENT	4 500 . .	17.4	111.4	84.1	39.4	. . .	. . .	. . .	. . .
Direct investment abroad	4 505 . .	**. . .**	**. . .**	**. . .**	**. . .**	**. . .**	**. . .**	**. . .**	**. . .**
Equity capital	4 510 . .	. . .	. . .	. . .	. . .	. . .	. . .	. . .	. . .
Claims on affiliated enterprises	4 515 . .	. . .	. . .	. . .	. . .	. . .	. . .	. . .	. . .
Liabilities to affiliated enterprises	4 520 . .	. . .	. . .	. . .	. . .	. . .	. . .	. . .	. . .
Reinvested earnings	4 525 . .	. . .	. . .	. . .	. . .	. . .	. . .	. . .	. . .
Other capital	4 530 . .	. . .	. . .	. . .	. . .	. . .	. . .	. . .	. . .
Claims on affiliated enterprises	4 535 . .	. . .	. . .	. . .	. . .	. . .	. . .	. . .	. . .
Liabilities to affiliated enterprises	4 540 . .	. . .	. . .	. . .	. . .	. . .	. . .	. . .	. . .
Direct investment in Mali	4 555 . .	**17.4**	**111.4**	**84.1**	**39.4**	**. . .**	**. . .**	**. . .**	**. . .**
Equity capital	4 560 . .	. . .	. . .	. . .	. . .	. . .	. . .	. . .	. . .
Claims on direct investors	4 565 . .	. . .	. . .	. . .	. . .	. . .	. . .	. . .	. . .
Liabilities to direct investors	4 570 . .	. . .	. . .	. . .	. . .	. . .	. . .	. . .	. . .
Reinvested earnings	4 575 . .	–2.2	5.1	5.9	10.3	. . .	. . .	. . .	. . .
Other capital	4 580 . .	19.7	106.3	78.2	29.1	. . .	. . .	. . .	. . .
Claims on direct investors	4 585 . .	. . .	. . .	. . .	. . .	. . .	. . .	. . .	. . .
Liabilities to direct investors	4 590 . .	19.7	106.3	78.2	29.1	. . .	. . .	. . .	. . .
B. PORTFOLIO INVESTMENT	4 600 . .	. . .	. . .	. . .	. . .	. . .	. . .	. . .	. . .
Assets	4 602 . .	**. . .**	**. . .**	**. . .**	**. . .**	**. . .**	**. . .**	**. . .**	**. . .**
Equity securities	4 610 . .	. . .	. . .	. . .	. . .	. . .	. . .	. . .	. . .
Monetary authorities	4 611 . .	. . .	. . .	. . .	. . .	. . .	. . .	. . .	. . .
General government	4 612 . .	. . .	. . .	. . .	. . .	. . .	. . .	. . .	. . .
Banks	4 613 . .	. . .	. . .	. . .	. . .	. . .	. . .	. . .	. . .
Other sectors	4 614 . .	. . .	. . .	. . .	. . .	. . .	. . .	. . .	. . .
Debt securities	4 619 . .	. . .	. . .	. . .	. . .	. . .	. . .	. . .	. . .
Bonds and notes	4 620 . .	. . .	. . .	. . .	. . .	. . .	. . .	. . .	. . .
Monetary authorities	4 621 . .	. . .	. . .	. . .	. . .	. . .	. . .	. . .	. . .
General government	4 622 . .	. . .	. . .	. . .	. . .	. . .	. . .	. . .	. . .
Banks	4 623 . .	. . .	. . .	. . .	. . .	. . .	. . .	. . .	. . .
Other sectors	4 624 . .	. . .	. . .	. . .	. . .	. . .	. . .	. . .	. . .
Money market instruments	4 630 . .	. . .	. . .	. . .	. . .	. . .	. . .	. . .	. . .
Monetary authorities	4 631 . .	. . .	. . .	. . .	. . .	. . .	. . .	. . .	. . .
General government	4 632 . .	. . .	. . .	. . .	. . .	. . .	. . .	. . .	. . .
Banks	4 633 . .	. . .	. . .	. . .	. . .	. . .	. . .	. . .	. . .
Other sectors	4 634 . .	. . .	. . .	. . .	. . .	. . .	. . .	. . .	. . .
Liabilities	4 652 . .	**. . .**	**. . .**	**. . .**	**. . .**	**. . .**	**. . .**	**. . .**	**. . .**
Equity securities	4 660 . .	. . .	. . .	. . .	. . .	. . .	. . .	. . .	. . .
Banks	4 663 . .	. . .	. . .	. . .	. . .	. . .	. . .	. . .	. . .
Other sectors	4 664 . .	. . .	. . .	. . .	. . .	. . .	. . .	. . .	. . .
Debt securities	4 669 . .	. . .	. . .	. . .	. . .	. . .	. . .	. . .	. . .
Bonds and notes	4 670 . .	. . .	. . .	. . .	. . .	. . .	. . .	. . .	. . .
Monetary authorities	4 671 . .	. . .	. . .	. . .	. . .	. . .	. . .	. . .	. . .
General government	4 672 . .	. . .	. . .	. . .	. . .	. . .	. . .	. . .	. . .
Banks	4 673 . .	. . .	. . .	. . .	. . .	. . .	. . .	. . .	. . .
Other sectors	4 674 . .	. . .	. . .	. . .	. . .	. . .	. . .	. . .	. . .
Money market instruments	4 680 . .	. . .	. . .	. . .	. . .	. . .	. . .	. . .	. . .
Monetary authorities	4 681 . .	. . .	. . .	. . .	. . .	. . .	. . .	. . .	. . .
General government	4 682 . .	. . .	. . .	. . .	. . .	. . .	. . .	. . .	. . .
Banks	4 683 . .	. . .	. . .	. . .	. . .	. . .	. . .	. . .	. . .
Other sectors	4 684 . .	. . .	. . .	. . .	. . .	. . .	. . .	. . .	. . .
C. FINANCIAL DERIVATIVES	4 910 . .	. . .	. . .	. . .	. . .	. . .	. . .	. . .	. . .
Monetary authorities	4 911 . .	. . .	. . .	. . .	. . .	. . .	. . .	. . .	. . .
General government	4 912 . .	. . .	. . .	. . .	. . .	. . .	. . .	. . .	. . .
Banks	4 913 . .	. . .	. . .	. . .	. . .	. . .	. . .	. . .	. . .
Other sectors	4 914 . .	. . .	. . .	. . .	. . .	. . .	. . .	. . .	. . .
Assets	4 900 . .	**. . .**	**. . .**	**. . .**	**. . .**	**. . .**	**. . .**	**. . .**	**. . .**
Monetary authorities	4 901 . .	. . .	. . .	. . .	. . .	. . .	. . .	. . .	. . .
General government	4 902 . .	. . .	. . .	. . .	. . .	. . .	. . .	. . .	. . .
Banks	4 903 . .	. . .	. . .	. . .	. . .	. . .	. . .	. . .	. . .
Other sectors	4 904 . .	. . .	. . .	. . .	. . .	. . .	. . .	. . .	. . .
Liabilities	4 905 . .	**. . .**	**. . .**	**. . .**	**. . .**	**. . .**	**. . .**	**. . .**	**. . .**
Monetary authorities	4 906 . .	. . .	. . .	. . .	. . .	. . .	. . .	. . .	. . .
General government	4 907 . .	. . .	. . .	. . .	. . .	. . .	. . .	. . .	. . .
Banks	4 908 . .	. . .	. . .	. . .	. . .	. . .	. . .	. . .	. . .
Other sectors	4 909 . .	. . .	. . .	. . .	. . .	. . .	. . .	. . .	. . .

Table 2 (Concluded). STANDARD PRESENTATION, 1994–2001
(Millions of U.S. dollars)

	Code	1994	1995	1996	1997	1998	1999	2000	2001
D. OTHER INVESTMENT	4 700	65.9	135.4	193.1	60.8	...	...	...	...
Assets	4 703	**–104.0**	**–52.3**	**4.1**	**–12.4**	...	...	...	...
Trade credits	4 706	–1.8	–21.5	–17.2	11.3	...	...	...	...
General government	4 707	...	...	...	...	...	...	...	...
of which: Short-term	4 709	...	...	...	...	...	...	...	...
Other sectors	4 710	–1.8	–21.5	–17.2	11.3	...	...	...	...
of which: Short-term	4 712	*–1.8*	*–21.5*	*–17.2*	*11.3*	...	...	...	...
Loans	4 714	...	...	...	...	...	...	...	...
Monetary authorities	4 715	...	...	...	...	...	...	...	...
of which: Short-term	4 718	...	...	...	...	...	...	...	...
General government	4 719	...	...	...	...	...	...	...	...
of which: Short-term	4 721	...	...	...	...	...	...	...	...
Banks	4 722	...	...	...	...	...	...	...	...
of which: Short-term	4 724	...	...	...	...	...	...	...	...
Other sectors	4 725	...	...	...	...	...	...	...	...
of which: Short-term	4 727	...	...	...	...	...	...	...	...
Currency and deposits	4 730	–100.3	–33.2	16.8	2.0	...	...	...	...
Monetary authorities	4 731	...	...	...	...	...	...	...	...
General government	4 732	...	...	...	...	...	...	...	...
Banks	4 733	–100.3	–33.2	16.8	2.0	...	...	...	...
Other sectors	4 734	...	...	...	...	...	...	...	...
Other assets	4 736	–1.9	2.3	4.5	–25.7	...	...	...	...
Monetary authorities	4 737	...	...	...	...	...	...	...	...
of which: Short-term	4 739	...	...	...	...	...	...	...	...
General government	4 740	...	...	...	...	...	...	...	...
of which: Short-term	4 742	...	...	...	...	...	...	...	...
Banks	4 743	...	...	...	...	...	...	...	...
of which: Short-term	4 745	...	...	...	...	...	...	...	...
Other sectors	4 746	–1.9	2.3	4.5	–25.7	...	...	...	...
of which: Short-term	4 748	*–1.9*	*2.3*	*4.5*	*–25.7*	...	...	...	...
Liabilities	4 753	**169.9**	**187.7**	**189.0**	**73.2**	...	...	...	...
Trade credits	4 756	9.7	–7.1	11.7	–13.0	...	...	...	...
General government	4 757	...	...	...	...	...	...	...	...
of which: Short-term	4 759	...	...	...	...	...	...	...	...
Other sectors	4 760	9.7	–7.1	11.7	–13.0	...	...	...	...
of which: Short-term	4 762	*9.7*	*–7.1*	*11.7*	*–13.0*	...	...	...	...
Loans	4 764	159.1	217.9	183.1	105.2	...	...	...	...
Monetary authorities	4 765	32.7	38.4	22.4	21.3	...	...	...	...
of which: Use of Fund credit and loans from the Fund	4 766	*32.7*	*38.4*	*22.4*	*21.3*	...	...	...	...
of which: Short-term	4 768	...	...	...	...	...	...	...	...
General government	4 769	126.4	179.5	160.7	84.0	...	...	...	...
of which: Short-term	4 771	...	...	...	...	...	...	...	...
Banks	4 772	...	...	...	...	...	...	...	...
of which: Short-term	4 774	...	...	...	...	...	...	...	...
Other sectors	4 775	...	...	...	...	...	...	...	...
of which: Short-term	4 777	...	...	...	...	...	...	...	...
Currency and deposits	4 780	11.9	–1.4	–10.6	6.7	...	...	...	...
Monetary authorities	4 781	...	...	...	...	...	...	...	...
General government	4 782	...	...	...	...	...	...	...	...
Banks	4 783	11.9	–1.4	–10.6	6.7	...	...	...	...
Other sectors	4 784	...	...	...	...	...	...	...	...
Other liabilities	4 786	–10.9	–21.6	4.7	–25.7	...	...	...	...
Monetary authorities	4 787	...	...	...	...	...	...	...	...
of which: Short-term	4 789	...	...	...	...	...	...	...	...
General government	4 790	–35.7	...	...	...	...	...	...	...
of which: Short-term	4 792	*–35.7*	...	...	...	...	...	...	...
Banks	4 793	...	...	...	...	...	...	...	...
of which: Short-term	4 795	...	...	...	...	...	...	...	...
Other sectors	4 796	24.8	–21.6	4.7	–25.7	...	...	...	...
of which: Short-term	4 798	*24.8*	*–21.6*	*4.7*	*–25.7*	...	...	...	...
E. RESERVE ASSETS	4 802	–37.6	–80.2	–131.6	–38.3	...	...	...	...
Monetary gold	4 812	...	...	...	...	...	...	...	...
Special drawing rights	4 811	–.1	–.3	.1	.2	...	...	...	...
Reserve position in the Fund	4 810	...	...	...	...	...	...	...	...
Foreign exchange	4 803	–30.7	–80.5	–132.1	–37.8	...	...	...	...
Other claims	4 813	–6.8	.6	.4	–.7	...	...	...	...
NET ERRORS AND OMISSIONS	4 998	**5.6**	**–13.0**	**–8.8**	**7.9**	...	...	...	...

Part 3 of the *Yearbook* contains descriptions of the methodologies, compilation practices, and sources used to compile these data.

Table 1. ANALYTIC PRESENTATION, 1994–2001
(Millions of U.S. dollars)

	Code	1994	1995	1996	1997	1998	1999	2000	2001
A. Current Account [1]	4 993 Z.	**–131.5**	**–360.8**	**–404.0**	**–200.9**	**–221.5**	**–121.7**	**–470.5**	**–172.4**
Goods: exports f.o.b	2 100 . .	1,618.5	1,949.4	1,772.8	1,663.2	1,824.3	2,016.9	2,478.3	2,002.8
Goods: imports f.o.b	3 100 . .	–2,221.0	–2,673.1	–2,536.2	–2,320.7	–2,417.0	–2,588.4	–3,096.2	–2,492.4
Balance on Goods	4 100 . .	*–602.5*	*–723.7*	*–763.4*	*–657.4*	*–592.7*	*–571.4*	*–617.9*	*–489.6*
Services: credit	2 200 . .	994.6	1,047.5	1,070.7	1,111.5	1,181.4	1,218.9	1,108.6	1,106.8
Services: debit	3 200 . .	–686.5	–750.8	–754.1	–719.7	–800.4	–845.5	–873.9	–791.1
Balance on Goods and Services	4 991 . .	*–294.5*	*–427.0*	*–446.8*	*–265.5*	*–211.7*	*–198.1*	*–383.3*	*–173.8*
Income: credit	2 300 . .	219.4	287.7	309.7	360.4	510.6	1,234.9	895.7	815.2
Income: debit	3 300 . .	–150.6	–247.7	–298.0	–351.2	–578.4	–1,200.7	–1,008.4	–821.2
Balance on Goods, Services, and Income	4 992 . .	*–225.7*	*–387.0*	*–435.0*	*–256.3*	*–279.5*	*–163.9*	*–496.0*	*–179.9*
Current transfers: credit	2 379 Z.	101.2	80.5	87.1	122.4	114.9	120.1	101.7	190.2
Current transfers: debit	3 379 . .	–7.1	–54.3	–56.1	–66.9	–56.9	–77.8	–76.1	–182.7
B. Capital Account [1]	4 994 Z.	**. . .**	**12.5**	**58.1**	**8.4**	**28.5**	**25.5**	**18.2**	**1.6**
Capital account: credit	2 994 Z.	. . .	16.8	64.2	32.9	33.1	31.0	23.8	4.4
Capital account: debit	3 994 . .	. . .	–4.3	–6.1	–24.5	–4.6	–5.5	–5.6	–2.9
Total, Groups A Plus B	4 981 . .	*–131.5*	*–348.3*	*–345.9*	*–192.5*	*–193.0*	*–96.1*	*–452.3*	*–170.9*
C. Financial Account [1]	4 995 W.	**480.9**	**25.0**	**205.9**	**107.5**	**294.8**	**401.9**	**157.0**	**252.0**
Direct investment abroad	4 505 . .	1.0	–5.0	–6.1	–16.2	–14.4	–44.5	–25.7	–6.5
Direct investment in Malta	4 555 Z.	151.7	131.7	276.8	80.8	273.3	814.6	604.4	293.3
Portfolio investment assets	4 602 . .	304.4	–459.7	–120.1	107.9	–141.3	–471.4	–744.5	–445.8
Equity securities	4 610 . .	247.2	. . .	–.9	–10.1	6.3	–11.7	–17.5	–37.0
Debt securities	4 619 . .	57.2	–459.7	–119.2	118.0	–147.6	–459.7	–727.1	–408.8
Portfolio investment liabilities	4 652 Z.	. . .	1.9	3.3	.3	58.9	–32.8	–8.5	–6.7
Equity securities	4 660 . .	. . .	–4.2	3.1	.3	–1.5	–7.5•	1.3	–1.8
Debt securities	4 669 Z.	. . .	6.1	.3	. . .	60.5	–25.3	–9.8	–4.9
Financial derivatives	4 910 . .	. . .	. . .	. . .	. . .	. . .	. . .	. . .	. . .
Financial derivatives assets	4 900 . .	. . .	. . .	. . .	. . .	. . .	. . .	. . .	. . .
Financial derivatives liabilities	4 905 . .	. . .	. . .	. . .	. . .	. . .	. . .	. . .	. . .
Other investment assets	4 703 . .	103.4	–286.0	–619.1	–1,003.0	–2,052.2	–1,593.5	–928.6	1,823.3
Monetary authorities	4 701 . .	. . .	. . .	. . .	. . .	. . .	. . .	. . .	. . .
General government	4 704 . .	–.5	. . .	. . .	. . .	. . .	. . .	. . .	. . .
Banks	4 705 . .	79.6	–280.5	–581.5	–934.3	–2,077.4	–1,606.0	–965.5	1,825.2
Other sectors	4 728 . .	24.4	–5.5	–37.6	–68.7	25.2	12.5	36.9	–1.9
Other investment liabilities	4 753 W.	–79.7	642.0	671.1	937.8	2,170.5	1,729.5	1,259.9	–1,405.7
Monetary authorities	4 753 WA	. . .	. . .	. . .	. . .	. . .	. . .	. . .	. . .
General government	4 753 ZB	6.0	40.8	51.8	–26.3	–9.4	222.8	–23.1	12.5
Banks	4 753 ZC	–274.6	680.6	597.5	903.4	2,183.7	1,807.4	1,267.5	–1,416.9
Other sectors	4 753 ZD	188.8	2.2	21.7	60.7	–3.9	–300.6	15.5	–1.3
Total, Groups A Through C	4 983 . .	*349.3*	*–323.4*	*–140.0*	*–85.0*	*101.8*	*305.7*	*–295.3*	*81.1*
D. Net Errors and Omissions	4 998 . .	**33.4**	**16.3**	**55.1**	**91.8**	**89.1**	**–67.3**	**73.7**	**173.9**
Total, Groups A Through D	4 984 . .	*382.8*	*–307.1*	*–84.9*	*6.8*	*190.9*	*238.4*	*–221.6*	*255.1*
E. Reserves and Related Items	4 802 A.	**–382.8**	**307.1**	**84.9**	**–6.8**	**–190.9**	**–238.4**	**221.6**	**–255.1**
Reserve assets	4 802 . .	–382.8	307.1	84.9	–6.8	–190.9	–238.4	221.6	–255.1
Use of Fund credit and loans	4 766 . .	. . .	. . .	. . .	. . .	. . .	. . .	. . .	. . .
Exceptional financing	4 920 . .	. . .	. . .	. . .	. . .	. . .	. . .	. . .	. . .
Conversion rates: Maltese lira per U.S. dollar	0 101 . .	**.3779**	**.3531**	**.3605**	**.3860**	**.3885**	**.3989**	**.4382**	**.4501**

[1] Excludes components that have been classified in the categories of Group E.

Table 2. STANDARD PRESENTATION, 1994–2001

(Millions of U.S. dollars)

	Code		1994	1995	1996	1997	1998	1999	2000	2001
CURRENT ACCOUNT	4 993	. .	**–131.5**	**–360.8**	**–404.0**	**–200.9**	**–221.5**	**–121.7**	**–470.5**	**–172.4**
A. GOODS	4 100	. .	–602.5	–723.7	–763.4	–657.4	–592.7	–571.4	–617.9	–489.6
Credit	2 100	. .	**1,618.5**	**1,949.4**	**1,772.8**	**1,663.2**	**1,824.3**	**2,016.9**	**2,478.3**	**2,002.8**
General merchandise: exports f.o.b.	2 110	. .	1,569.9	1,898.3	1,705.9	1,587.9	1,773.3	1,939.8	2,347.1	1,879.4
Goods for processing: exports f.o.b.	2 150	. .	. . .	. . .	. . .	. . .	. . .	. . .	. . .	. . .
Repairs on goods	2 160	. .	4.8	4.5	2.8	1.8	. . .	.3	. . .	. . .
Goods procured in ports by carriers	2 170	. .	43.7	46.5	64.1	73.5	51.1	76.9	131.2	123.4
Nonmonetary gold	2 180	. .	. . .	. . .	. . .	. . .	. . .	. . .	. . .	. . .
Debit	3 100	. .	**–2,221.0**	**–2,673.1**	**–2,536.2**	**–2,320.7**	**–2,417.0**	**–2,588.4**	**–3,096.2**	**–2,492.4**
General merchandise: imports f.o.b.	3 110	. .	–2,175.1	–2,624.2	–2,475.4	–2,267.3	–2,375.6	–2,537.1	–3,034.6	–2,427.8
Goods for processing: imports f.o.b.	3 150	. .	. . .	. . .	. . .	. . .	. . .	. . .	. . .	. . .
Repairs on goods	3 160	. .	–9.5	–12.5	–14.2	–12.4	–10.8	–20.0	–20.7	–25.3
Goods procured in ports by carriers	3 170	. .	–13.0	–13.6	–16.9	–16.7	–10.0	–12.2	–18.4	–16.2
Nonmonetary gold	3 180	. .	–23.5	–22.8	–29.7	–24.2	–20.6	–19.0	–22.5	–23.1
B. SERVICES	4 200	. .	308.0	296.7	316.6	391.9	381.0	373.3	234.7	315.8
Total credit	2 200	. .	*994.6*	*1,047.5*	*1,070.7*	*1,111.5*	*1,181.4*	*1,218.9*	*1,108.6*	*1,106.8*
Total debit	3 200	. .	*–686.5*	*–750.8*	*–754.1*	*–719.7*	*–800.4*	*–845.5*	*–873.9*	*–791.1*
Transportation services, credit	2 205	. .	**221.7**	**260.3**	**257.9**	**276.6**	**314.7**	**331.8**	**303.6**	**324.5**
Passenger	2 850	. .	*148.2*	*157.1*	*148.3*	*154.2*	*164.8*	*173.6*	*144.3*	*142.6*
Freight	2 851	. .	*12.4*	*11.1*	*11.9*	*25.1*	*31.3*	*28.8*	*27.5*	*25.6*
Other	2 852	. .	*61.2*	*92.2*	*97.6*	*97.3*	*118.6*	*129.4*	*131.8*	*156.2*
Sea transport, passenger	2 207	. .	. . .	. . .	. . .	. . .	. . .	. . .	. . .	. . .
Sea transport, freight	2 208	. .	. . .	. . .	. . .	. . .	. . .	. . .	. . .	. . .
Sea transport, other	2 209	. .	. . .	. . .	. . .	. . .	. . .	. . .	. . .	. . .
Air transport, passenger	2 211	. .	. . .	. . .	. . .	. . .	. . .	. . .	. . .	. . .
Air transport, freight	2 212	. .	. . .	. . .	. . .	. . .	. . .	. . .	. . .	. . .
Air transport, other	2 213	. .	. . .	. . .	. . .	. . .	. . .	. . .	. . .	. . .
Other transport, passenger	2 215	. .	. . .	. . .	. . .	. . .	. . .	. . .	. . .	. . .
Other transport, freight	2 216	. .	. . .	. . .	. . .	. . .	. . .	. . .	. . .	. . .
Other transport, other	2 217	. .	. . .	. . .	. . .	. . .	. . .	. . .	. . .	. . .
Transportation services, debit	3 205	. .	**–309.5**	**–368.5**	**–364.7**	**–345.5**	**–375.9**	**–413.6**	**–446.4**	**–384.1**
Passenger	3 850	. .	*–23.3*	*–23.5*	*–25.5*	*–25.9*	*–28.3*	*–30.1*	*–24.0*	*–22.0*
Freight	3 851	. .	*–208.0*	*–250.5*	*–241.6*	*–219.0*	*–229.1*	*–244.4*	*–301.2*	*–239.6*
Other	3 852	. .	*–78.3*	*–94.5*	*–97.6*	*–100.6*	*–118.4*	*–139.1*	*–121.3*	*–122.5*
Sea transport, passenger	3 207	. .	. . .	. . .	. . .	. . .	. . .	. . .	. . .	. . .
Sea transport, freight	3 208	. .	. . .	. . .	. . .	. . .	. . .	. . .	. . .	. . .
Sea transport, other	3 209	. .	. . .	. . .	. . .	. . .	. . .	. . .	. . .	. . .
Air transport, passenger	3 211	. .	. . .	. . .	. . .	. . .	. . .	. . .	. . .	. . .
Air transport, freight	3 212	. .	. . .	. . .	. . .	. . .	. . .	. . .	. . .	. . .
Air transport, other	3 213	. .	. . .	. . .	. . .	. . .	. . .	. . .	. . .	. . .
Other transport, passenger	3 215	. .	. . .	. . .	. . .	. . .	. . .	. . .	. . .	. . .
Other transport, freight	3 216	. .	. . .	. . .	. . .	. . .	. . .	. . .	. . .	. . .
Other transport, other	3 217	. .	. . .	. . .	. . .	. . .	. . .	. . .	. . .	. . .
Travel, credit	2 236	. .	**640.0**	**660.9**	**634.5**	**644.8**	**656.4**	**678.5**	**609.6**	**578.2**
Business travel	2 237	. .	. . .	. . .	. . .	. . .	. . .	. . .	. . .	. . .
Personal travel	2 240	. .	. . .	. . .	. . .	. . .	. . .	. . .	. . .	. . .
Travel, debit	3 236	. .	**–177.3**	**–214.3**	**–218.5**	**–189.9**	**–193.1**	**–200.7**	**–200.0**	**–180.3**
Business travel	3 237	. .	. . .	. . .	. . .	. . .	. . .	. . .	. . .	. . .
Personal travel	3 240	. .	. . .	. . .	. . .	. . .	. . .	. . .	. . .	. . .
Other services, credit	2 200	BA	**132.8**	**126.3**	**178.4**	**190.1**	**210.2**	**208.6**	**195.4**	**204.2**
Communications	2 245	. .	16.3	15.6	19.4	14.5	15.2	21.8	23.9	22.4
Construction	2 249	. .	. . .	. . .	. . .	. . .	. . .	. . .	. . .	. . .
Insurance	2 253	. .	31.0	17.0	17.8	18.4	19.1	19.3	19.0	19.8
Financial	2 260	. .	. . .	. . .	. . .	. . .	. . .	. . .	. . .	. . .
Computer and information	2 262	. .	. . .	. . .	1.1	. . .	. . .	. . .	3.4	1.8
Royalties and licence fees	2 266	. .	.1	. . .	.8	. . .	1.0	. . .	1.6	.7
Other business services	2 268	. .	65.8	71.6	120.1	134.8	150.5	147.9	129.4	139.6
Personal, cultural, and recreational	2 287	. .	. . .	. . .	. . .	. . .	. . .	. . .	. . .	. . .
Government, n.i.e.	2 291	. .	19.6	22.1	19.1	22.4	24.4	19.6	18.1	20.0
Other services, debit	3 200	BA	**–199.7**	**–168.0**	**–170.9**	**–184.3**	**–231.4**	**–231.3**	**–227.5**	**–226.6**
Communications	3 245	. .	–21.3	–16.4	–13.9	–11.5	–9.8	–12.5	–13.9	–13.3
Construction	3 249	. .	. . .	. . .	. . .	. . .	. . .	. . .	. . .	. . .
Insurance	3 253	. .	–87.0	–50.7	–56.6	–49.9	–68.2	–53.6	–59.6	–59.3
Financial	3 260	. .	. . .	. . .	. . .	. . .	. . .	. . .	. . .	. . .
Computer and information	3 262	. .	. . .	–4.5	–2.5	–1.0	–2.1	–2.8	–1.8	–2.0
Royalties and licence fees	3 266	. .	–5.5	–8.5	–10.8	–13.2	–11.6	–13.5	–9.8	–10.4
Other business services	3 268	. .	–62.6	–67.4	–69.1	–76.1	–101.1	–105.4	–113.5	–113.1
Personal, cultural, and recreational	3 287	. .	–4.7	–2.3	–1.9	–4.7	–4.9	–3.8	–3.7	–3.8
Government, n.i.e.	3 291	. .	–18.6	–18.1	–16.1	–27.9	–33.8	–39.7	–25.1	–24.7

Table 2 (Continued). STANDARD PRESENTATION, 1994–2001
(Millions of U.S. dollars)

	Code	1994	1995	1996	1997	1998	1999	2000	2001
C. INCOME	4 300 . .	68.9	40.0	11.8	9.2	–67.8	34.2	–112.7	–6.1
Total credit	2 300 . .	*219.4*	*287.7*	*309.7*	*360.4*	*510.6*	*1,234.9*	*895.7*	*815.2*
Total debit	3 300 . .	*–150.6*	*–247.7*	*–298.0*	*–351.2*	*–578.4*	*–1,200.7*	*–1,008.4*	*–821.2*
Compensation of employees, credit	2 310 . .	**18.2**	**13.6**	**11.4**	**6.2**	**11.1**	**9.8**	**10.0**	**5.8**
Compensation of employees, debit	3 310 . .	**–.5**	**–7.9**	**–7.8**	**–8.3**	**–6.2**	**–8.3**	**–7.3**	**–6.4**
Investment income, credit	2 320 . .	**201.2**	**274.1**	**298.4**	**354.2**	**499.5**	**1,225.2**	**885.7**	**809.4**
Direct investment income	2 330 . .	201.2	274.1	298.4	354.2	499.5	1,225.2	885.7	809.4
Dividends and distributed branch profits	2 332 . .	.1	12.2	11.7	10.9	28.6	10.8	6.1	8.0
Reinvested earnings and undistributed branch profits	2 333 . .	. . .	. . .	–.6	–2.1	–3.1	.7	6.8	.4
Income on debt (interest)	2 334 . .	201.1	261.9	287.2	345.4	474.0	1,213.7	872.7	800.9
Portfolio investment income	2 339 . .	. . .	. . .	. . .	. . .	. . .	. . .	. . .	. . .
Income on equity	2 340 . .	. . .	. . .	. . .	. . .	. . .	. . .	. . .	. . .
Income on bonds and notes	2 350 . .	. . .	. . .	. . .	. . .	. . .	. . .	. . .	. . .
Income on money market instruments	2 360 . .	. . .	. . .	. . .	. . .	. . .	. . .	. . .	. . .
Other investment income	2 370 . .	. . .	. . .	. . .	. . .	. . .	. . .	. . .	. . .
Investment income, debit	3 320 . .	**–150.1**	**–239.8**	**–290.2**	**–342.9**	**–572.2**	**–1,192.5**	**–1,001.1**	**–814.8**
Direct investment income	3 330 . .	–149.4	–239.5	–290.2	–342.6	–572.0	–1,191.0	–997.6	–813.7
Dividends and distributed branch profits	3 332 . .	–26.4	–51.7	–61.9	–76.2	–97.5	–60.2	–54.6	–53.4
Reinvested earnings and undistributed branch profits	3 333 . .	–57.5	–76.2	–95.1	–43.8	–93.5	–91.8	–261.7	–88.3
Income on debt (interest)	3 334 . .	–65.5	–111.7	–133.2	–222.6	–380.9	–1,039.0	–681.3	–671.9
Portfolio investment income	3 339 . .	. . .	. . .	. . .	. . .	. . .	. . .	. . .	. . .
Income on equity	3 340 . .	. . .	. . .	. . .	. . .	. . .	. . .	. . .	. . .
Income on bonds and notes	3 350 . .	. . .	. . .	. . .	. . .	. . .	. . .	. . .	. . .
Income on money market instruments	3 360 . .	. . .	. . .	. . .	. . .	. . .	. . .	. . .	. . .
Other investment income	3 370 . .	–.7	–.3	. . .	–.3	–.3	–1.5	–3.5	–1.1
D. CURRENT TRANSFERS	4 379 . .	94.1	26.2	31.0	55.5	58.0	42.2	25.5	7.5
Credit	2 379 . .	**101.2**	**80.5**	**87.1**	**122.4**	**114.9**	**120.1**	**101.7**	**190.2**
General government	2 380 . .	34.9	.8	1.1	11.9	14.7	8.1	25.9	62.6
Other sectors	2 390 . .	66.3	79.6	86.0	110.5	100.3	112.0	75.7	127.6
Workers' remittances	2 391 . .	5.3	2.6	3.6	3.1	1.8	3.8	1.1	.7
Other current transfers	2 392 . .	61.0	77.1	82.4	107.4	98.5	108.2	74.6	127.0
Debit	3 379 . .	**–7.1**	**–54.3**	**–56.1**	**–66.9**	**–56.9**	**–77.8**	**–76.1**	**–182.7**
General government	3 380 . .	–2.7	–2.8	–1.9	–7.2	–11.9	–16.8	–24.9	–54.8
Other sectors	3 390 . .	–4.4	–51.5	–54.1	–59.7	–45.0	–61.1	–51.2	–127.9
Workers' remittances	3 391 . .	–2.4	–.9	–1.4	–.8	–1.0	–1.5	–1.4	–1.3
Other current transfers	3 392 . .	–2.0	–50.7	–52.7	–58.9	–44.0	–59.6	–49.9	–126.6
CAPITAL AND FINANCIAL ACCOUNT	4 996 . .	**98.1**	**344.5**	**348.9**	**109.0**	**132.4**	**189.0**	**396.8**	**–1.5**
CAPITAL ACCOUNT	4 994 . .	**. . .**	**12.5**	**58.1**	**8.4**	**28.5**	**25.5**	**18.2**	**1.6**
Total credit	2 994 . .	. . .	*16.8*	*64.2*	*32.9*	*33.1*	*31.0*	*23.8*	*4.4*
Total debit	3 994 . .	. . .	*–4.3*	*–6.1*	*–24.5*	*–4.6*	*–5.5*	*–5.6*	*–2.9*
Capital transfers, credit	2 400 . .	**. . .**	**16.8**	**64.2**	**32.9**	**33.1**	**31.0**	**23.8**	**4.4**
General government	2 401 . .	. . .	12.8	57.3	25.4	25.5	24.1	21.5	3.1
Debt forgiveness	2 402 . .	. . .	. . .	. . .	. . .	. . .	. . .	. . .	. . .
Other capital transfers	2 410 . .	. . .	12.8	57.3	25.4	25.5	24.1	21.5	3.1
Other sectors	2 430 . .	. . .	4.0	6.9	7.5	7.7	6.9	2.3	1.3
Migrants' transfers	2 431 . .	. . .	4.0	6.9	7.5	7.7	6.9	2.3	1.3
Debt forgiveness	2 432 . .	. . .	. . .	. . .	. . .	. . .	. . .	. . .	. . .
Other capital transfers	2 440 . .	. . .	. . .	. . .	. . .	. . .	. . .	. . .	. . .
Capital transfers, debit	3 400 . .	**. . .**	**–4.3**	**–6.1**	**–24.5**	**–4.6**	**–5.5**	**–5.6**	**–2.9**
General government	3 401 . .	. . .	. . .	. . .	. . .	. . .	. . .	. . .	. . .
Debt forgiveness	3 402 . .	. . .	. . .	. . .	. . .	. . .	. . .	. . .	. . .
Other capital transfers	3 410 . .	. . .	. . .	. . .	. . .	. . .	. . .	. . .	. . .
Other sectors	3 430 . .	. . .	–4.3	–6.1	–24.5	–4.6	–5.5	–5.6	–2.9
Migrants' transfers	3 431 . .	. . .	–4.3	–6.1	–4.1	–4.6	–5.5	–5.6	–2.9
Debt forgiveness	3 432 . .	. . .	. . .	. . .	–20.4	. . .	. . .	. . .	. . .
Other capital transfers	3 440 . .	. . .	. . .	. . .	. . .	. . .	. . .	. . .	. . .
Nonproduced nonfinancial assets, credit	2 480 . .	**. . .**	**. . .**	**. . .**	**. . .**	**. . .**	**. . .**	**. . .**	**. . .**
Nonproduced nonfinancial assets, debit	3 480 . .	**. . .**	**. . .**	**. . .**	**. . .**	**. . .**	**. . .**	**. . .**	**. . .**

Table 2 (Continued). STANDARD PRESENTATION, 1994–2001
(Millions of U.S. dollars)

	Code		1994	1995	1996	1997	1998	1999	2000	2001
FINANCIAL ACCOUNT	4 995	. .	**98.1**	**332.1**	**290.8**	**100.7**	**103.9**	**163.4**	**378.6**	**–3.1**
A. DIRECT INVESTMENT	4 500	. .	152.7	126.7	270.7	64.6	258.9	770.0	578.7	286.9
Direct investment abroad	4 505	. .	**1.0**	**–5.0**	**–6.1**	**–16.2**	**–14.4**	**–44.5**	**–25.7**	**–6.5**
Equity capital	4 510	. .	–3.1	–5.0	–6.7	–18.3	–17.5	–43.8	–22.2	–6.0
Claims on affiliated enterprises	4 515	. .	–3.1	–5.0	–6.7	–18.3	–17.5	–43.8	–22.2	–6.0
Liabilities to affiliated enterprises	4 520	. .	. . .	. . .	. . .	. . .	. . .	. . .	. . .	. . .
Reinvested earnings	4 525	. .	. . .	. . .	.6	2.1	3.1	–.7	–6.8	–.4
Other capital	4 530	. .	4.1	. . .	. . .	. . .	. . .	. . .	3.3	. . .
Claims on affiliated enterprises	4 535	. .	4.1	. . .	. . .	. . .	. . .	. . .	–1.0	. . .
Liabilities to affiliated enterprises	4 540	. .	. . .	. . .	. . .	. . .	. . .	. . .	4.3	. . .
Direct investment in Malta	4 555	. .	**151.7**	**131.7**	**276.8**	**80.8**	**273.3**	**814.6**	**604.4**	**293.3**
Equity capital	4 560	. .	61.1	64.0	35.8	11.3	11.2	251.9	119.0	119.3
Claims on direct investors	4 565	. .	. . .	. . .	. . .	. . .	. . .	. . .	. . .	. . .
Liabilities to direct investors	4 570	. .	61.1	64.0	35.8	11.3	11.2	251.9	119.0	119.3
Reinvested earnings	4 575	. .	57.5	76.2	95.1	43.8	93.5	91.8	261.7	88.3
Other capital	4 580	. .	33.1	–8.4	145.9	25.7	168.6	470.9	223.7	85.8
Claims on direct investors	4 585	. .	. . .	–260.9	–36.5	–55.7	–52.8	169.3	–137.4	–160.8
Liabilities to direct investors	4 590	. .	33.1	252.5	182.4	81.4	221.4	301.6	361.1	246.6
B. PORTFOLIO INVESTMENT	4 600	. .	304.4	–457.8	–116.8	108.2	–82.4	–504.2	–753.0	–452.5
Assets	4 602	. .	**304.4**	**–459.7**	**–120.1**	**107.9**	**–141.3**	**–471.4**	**–744.5**	**–445.8**
Equity securities	4 610	. .	247.2	. . .	–.9	–10.1	6.3	–11.7	–17.5	–37.0
Monetary authorities	4 611	. .	. . .	. . .	. . .	. . .	. . .	. . .	. . .	. . .
General government	4 612	. .	. . .	–.3	–.6	. . .	. . .	. . .	. . .	. . .
Banks	4 613	. .	. . .	.3	–.3	–10.1	6.3	–11.7	12.8	. . .
Other sectors	4 614	. .	247.2	. . .	. . .	. . .	. . .	. . .	–30.2	–37.0
Debt securities	4 619	. .	57.2	–459.7	–119.2	118.0	–147.6	–459.7	–727.1	–408.8
Bonds and notes	4 620	. .	57.2	–507.2	–68.3	84.5	–160.4	–396.8	–777.2	190.5
Monetary authorities	4 621	. .	. . .	. . .	. . .	. . .	. . .	. . .	. . .	. . .
General government	4 622	. .	. . .	. . .	. . .	. . .	. . .	. . .	. . .	. . .
Banks	4 623	. .	57.2	–514.9	–81.9	77.5	–165.3	–408.8	–798.6	185.6
Other sectors	4 624	. .	. . .	7.6	13.6	7.0	4.9	12.0	21.4	4.9
Money market instruments	4 630	. .	. . .	47.5	–50.9	33.5	12.8	–62.9	50.1	–599.3
Monetary authorities	4 631	. .	. . .	. . .	. . .	. . .	. . .	. . .	. . .	. . .
General government	4 632	. .	. . .	. . .	. . .	. . .	. . .	. . .	. . .	. . .
Banks	4 633	. .	. . .	42.4	–49.8	35.4	13.2	–56.9	54.2	–610.1
Other sectors	4 634	. .	. . .	5.1	–1.2	–1.9	–.4	–6.0	–4.0	10.8
Liabilities	4 652	. .	**. . .**	**1.9**	**3.3**	**.3**	**58.9**	**–32.8**	**–8.5**	**–6.7**
Equity securities	4 660	. .	. . .	–4.2	3.1	.3	–1.5	–7.5	1.3	–1.8
Banks	4 663	. .	. . .	. . .	. . .	. . .	. . .	. . .	. . .	. . .
Other sectors	4 664	. .	. . .	–4.2	3.1	.3	–1.5	–7.5	1.3	–1.8
Debt securities	4 669	. .	. . .	6.1	.3	. . .	60.5	–25.3	–9.8	–4.9
Bonds and notes	4 670	. .	. . .	. . .	. . .	. . .	1.6	–2.5	–.5	–12.8
Monetary authorities	4 671	. .	. . .	. . .	. . .	. . .	. . .	. . .	. . .	. . .
General government	4 672	. .	. . .	. . .	. . .	. . .	. . .	. . .	. . .	. . .
Banks	4 673	. .	. . .	. . .	. . .	. . .	1.6	–2.5	–.5	–12.8
Other sectors	4 674	. .	. . .	. . .	. . .	. . .	. . .	. . .	. . .	. . .
Money market instruments	4 680	. .	. . .	6.1	.3	. . .	58.9	–22.7	–9.3	8.0
Monetary authorities	4 681	. .	. . .	. . .	. . .	. . .	. . .	. . .	. . .	. . .
General government	4 682	. .	. . .	. . .	. . .	. . .	. . .	. . .	. . .	. . .
Banks	4 683	. .	. . .	. . .	. . .	. . .	8.5	–.3	.2	9.7
Other sectors	4 684	. .	. . .	6.1	.3	. . .	50.4	–22.5	–9.5	–1.7
C. FINANCIAL DERIVATIVES	4 910	. .	. . .	. . .	. . .	. . .	. . .	. . .	. . .	. . .
Monetary authorities	4 911	. .	. . .	. . .	. . .	. . .	. . .	. . .	. . .	. . .
General government	4 912	. .	. . .	. . .	. . .	. . .	. . .	. . .	. . .	. . .
Banks	4 913	. .	. . .	. . .	. . .	. . .	. . .	. . .	. . .	. . .
Other sectors	4 914	. .	. . .	. . .	. . .	. . .	. . .	. . .	. . .	. . .
Assets	4 900	. .	**. . .**	**. . .**	**. . .**	**. . .**	**. . .**	**. . .**	**. . .**	**. . .**
Monetary authorities	4 901	. .	. . .	. . .	. . .	. . .	. . .	. . .	. . .	. . .
General government	4 902	. .	. . .	. . .	. . .	. . .	. . .	. . .	. . .	. . .
Banks	4 903	. .	. . .	. . .	. . .	. . .	. . .	. . .	. . .	. . .
Other sectors	4 904	. .	. . .	. . .	. . .	. . .	. . .	. . .	. . .	. . .
Liabilities	4 905	. .	**. . .**	**. . .**	**. . .**	**. . .**	**. . .**	**. . .**	**. . .**	**. . .**
Monetary authorities	4 906	. .	. . .	. . .	. . .	. . .	. . .	. . .	. . .	. . .
General government	4 907	. .	. . .	. . .	. . .	. . .	. . .	. . .	. . .	. . .
Banks	4 908	. .	. . .	. . .	. . .	. . .	. . .	. . .	. . .	. . .
Other sectors	4 909	. .	. . .	. . .	. . .	. . .	. . .	. . .	. . .	. . .

Table 2 (Concluded). STANDARD PRESENTATION, 1994–2001
(Millions of U.S. dollars)

	Code	1994	1995	1996	1997	1998	1999	2000	2001
D. OTHER INVESTMENT	4 700 . .	23.7	356.1	52.0	–65.3	118.3	136.0	331.3	417.6
Assets	4 703 . .	**103.4**	**–286.0**	**–619.1**	**–1,003.0**	**–2,052.2**	**–1,593.5**	**–928.6**	**1,823.3**
Trade credits	4 706 . .	–46.4	–14.5	5.1	–24.1	27.1	–44.4	23.1	12.5
General government	4 707 . .	. . .	. . .	. . .	. . .	. . .	. . .	. . .	. . .
of which: Short-term	4 709 . .	. . .	. . .	. . .	. . .	. . .	. . .	. . .	. . .
Other sectors	4 710 . .	–46.4	–14.5	5.1	–24.1	27.1	–44.4	23.1	12.5
of which: Short-term	4 712 . .	–46.4	–14.5	5.1	–24.1	27.1	–44.4	23.1	12.5
Loans	4 714 . .	134.4	–204.6	–502.4	–551.9	–377.6	–522.4	–880.9	55.8
Monetary authorities	4 715 . .	. . .	. . .	. . .	. . .	. . .	. . .	. . .	. . .
of which: Short-term	4 718 . .	. . .	. . .	. . .	. . .	. . .	. . .	. . .	. . .
General government	4 719 . .	. . .	. . .	. . .	. . .	. . .	. . .	. . .	. . .
of which: Short-term	4 721 . .	. . .	. . .	. . .	. . .	. . .	. . .	. . .	. . .
Banks	4 722 . .	134.4	–207.1	–443.5	–527.4	–375.3	–525.1	–880.0	61.8
of which: Short-term	4 724 . .	. . .	. . .	. . .	. . .	. . .	. . .	. . .	. . .
Other sectors	4 725 . .	. . .	2.6	–58.9	–24.5	–2.3	2.8	–.9	–6.0
of which: Short-term	4 727 . .	. . .	1.1	–5.0	–1.0	–4.9	–5.0	–1.3	–2.7
Currency and deposits	4 730 . .	–30.1	–36.3	–110.3	–366.5	–1,674.8	–113.4	1,215.4	168.2
Monetary authorities	4 731 . .	. . .	. . .	. . .	. . .	. . .	. . .	. . .	. . .
General government	4 732 . .	. . .	. . .	. . .	. . .	. . .	. . .	. . .	. . .
Banks	4 733 . .	–54.9	–47.9	–131.8	–362.8	–1,680.5	–175.0	1,177.4	162.5
Other sectors	4 734 . .	24.8	11.6	21.5	–3.7	5.7	61.6	38.0	5.7
Other assets	4 736 . .	45.5	–30.5	–11.4	–60.5	–26.9	–913.3	–1,286.2	1,586.9
Monetary authorities	4 737 . .	. . .	. . .	. . .	. . .	. . .	. . .	. . .	. . .
of which: Short-term	4 739 . .	. . .	. . .	. . .	. . .	. . .	. . .	. . .	. . .
General government	4 740 . .	–.5	. . .	. . .	. . .	. . .	. . .	. . .	. . .
of which: Short-term	4 742 . .	. . .	. . .	. . .	. . .	. . .	. . .	. . .	. . .
Banks	4 743 . .	. . .	–25.4	–6.1	–44.1	–21.6	–905.9	–1,262.9	1,600.9
of which: Short-term	4 745 . .	. . .	–25.4	–6.1	–44.1	–21.6	–905.9	–1,262.9	1,600.9
Other sectors	4 746 . .	46.0	–5.1	–5.3	–16.4	–5.3	–7.5	–23.3	–14.1
of which: Short-term	4 748 . .	46.0	3.4	4.4	–2.1	1.1	1.6	–9.5	–4.7
Liabilities	4 753 . .	**–79.7**	**642.0**	**671.1**	**937.8**	**2,170.5**	**1,729.5**	**1,259.9**	**–1,405.7**
Trade credits	4 756 . .	24.1	–7.6	–15.8	15.0	28.2	–9.3	7.6	16.4
General government	4 757 . .	. . .	. . .	. . .	. . .	. . .	. . .	. . .	. . .
of which: Short-term	4 759 . .	. . .	. . .	. . .	. . .	. . .	. . .	. . .	. . .
Other sectors	4 760 . .	24.1	–7.6	–15.8	15.0	28.2	–9.3	7.6	16.4
of which: Short-term	4 762 . .	24.1	–7.6	–15.8	15.0	28.2	–9.3	7.6	16.4
Loans	4 764 . .	13.2	51.7	214.4	116.0	414.2	193.3	–32.0	–291.9
Monetary authorities	4 765 . .	. . .	. . .	. . .	. . .	. . .	. . .	. . .	. . .
of which: Use of Fund credit and loans from the Fund	4 766 . .	. . .	. . .	. . .	. . .	. . .	. . .	. . .	. . .
of which: Short-term	4 768 . .	. . .	. . .	. . .	. . .	. . .	. . .	. . .	. . .
General government	4 769 . .	6.0	–40.8	51.8	–26.3	–9.4	222.8	–23.1	12.5
of which: Short-term	4 771 . .	. . .	. . .	. . .	. . .	. . .	. . .	. . .	. . .
Banks	4 772 . .	. . .	82.9	112.5	93.8	454.6	264.7	–15.1	–285.7
of which: Short-term	4 774 . .	. . .	. . .	. . .	3.8	. . .	. . .	. . .	. . .
Other sectors	4 775 . .	7.2	9.6	50.1	48.5	–31.0	–294.1	6.2	–18.8
of which: Short-term	4 777 . .	7.2	1.1	20.0	30.8	–51.7	3.5	.5	. . .
Currency and deposits	4 780 . .	–127.1	309.4	587.9	748.1	1,619.6	924.1	959.2	127.9
Monetary authorities	4 781 . .	. . .	. . .	. . .	. . .	. . .	. . .	. . .	. . .
General government	4 782 . .	. . .	. . .	. . .	. . .	. . .	. . .	. . .	. . .
Banks	4 783 . .	–274.6	309.4	587.9	748.1	1,619.6	924.1	–959.2	–127.9
Other sectors	4 784 . .	147.5	. . .	. . .	. . .	. . .	. . .	. . .	. . .
Other liabilities	4 786 . .	10.1	288.5	–115.4	58.6	108.6	621.4	2,243.5	–1,002.3
Monetary authorities	4 787 . .	. . .	. . .	. . .	. . .	. . .	. . .	. . .	. . .
of which: Short-term	4 789 . .	. . .	. . .	. . .	. . .	. . .	. . .	. . .	. . .
General government	4 790 . .	. . .	. . .	. . .	. . .	. . .	. . .	. . .	. . .
of which: Short-term	4 792 . .	. . .	. . .	. . .	. . .	. . .	. . .	. . .	. . .
Banks	4 793 . .	. . .	288.2	–102.9	61.5	109.6	618.7	2,241.8	–1,003.4
of which: Short-term	4 795 . .	. . .	288.2	–102.9	61.5	109.6	618.7	2,241.8	–1,003.4
Other sectors	4 796 . .	10.1	.2	–12.5	–2.9	–1.0	2.8	1.7	1.1
of which: Short-term	4 798 . .	10.1	.2	–12.5	–2.9	–1.0	2.8	1.7	1.1
E. RESERVE ASSETS	4 802 . .	–382.8	307.1	84.9	–6.8	–190.9	–238.4	221.6	–255.1
Monetary gold	4 812 . .	6.4	9.2	–.3	5.3	1.6	. . .	.9	–.5
Special drawing rights	4 811 . .	–.5	–3.1	–3.1	–3.0	–3.3	30.0	–2.6	–2.4
Reserve position in the Fund	4 810 . .	–.3	–2.9	–5.0	–1.3	. . .	–11.9	. . .	. . .
Foreign exchange	4 803 . .	–235.7	302.8	11.8	–81.1	–238.9	–218.8	227.2	–254.0
Other claims	4 813 . .	–152.7	1.1	81.3	73.2	49.7	–37.7	–3.8	1.8
NET ERRORS AND OMISSIONS	4 998 . .	**33.4**	**16.3**	**55.1**	**91.8**	**89.1**	**–67.3**	**73.7**	**173.9**

Part 3 of the *Yearbook* contains descriptions of the methodologies, compilation practices, and sources used to compile these data.

Table 3. INTERNATIONAL INVESTMENT POSITION (End–period stocks), 1994–2001

(Millions of U.S. dollars)

	Code	1994	1995	1996	1997	1998	1999	2000	2001
ASSETS	8 995 C.	3,479.5	4,102.2	4,754.5	5,296.6	8,018.2	9,726.1	10,729.7	...
Direct investment abroad	8 505 . .	**28.3**	**32.3**	**107.6**	**140.0**	**170.4**	**185.2**	**203.1**	...
Equity capital and reinvested earnings	8 506 . .	28.3	34.3	40.0	53.5	70.5	105.3	128.4	...
Claims on affiliated enterprises	8 507 . .	28.3	34.3	40.0	53.5	70.5	105.3	128.4	...
Liabilities to affiliated enterprises	8 508 . .	...	...	...	...	...	...	...	...
Other capital	8 530 . .	...	–2.0	67.6	86.5	99.9	79.8	74.7	...
Claims on affiliated enterprises	8 535 . .	4.6	7.7	75.6	99.8	115.3	87.6	83.6	...
Liabilities to affiliated enterprises	8 540 . .	–4.6	–9.6	–8.1	–13.3	–15.4	–7.8	–8.9	...
Portfolio investment	8 602 . .	**886.4**	**1,394.4**	**1,505.2**	**1,286.1**	**1,496.0**	**1,911.3**	**2,595.2**	...
Equity securities	8 610 . .	2.4	4.0	4.7	15.1	6.6	24.5	40.4	...
Monetary authorities	8 611 . .	...	...	...	...	...	...	...	...
General government	8 612 . .	...	...	...	...	...	...	...	...
Banks	8 613 . .	1.1	.9	1.1	11.0	5.0	15.8	2.5	...
Other sectors	8 614 . .	1.4	3.1	3.6	4.1	1.6	8.7	37.9	...
Debt securities	8 619 . .	884.0	1,390.5	1,500.5	1,271.0	1,489.3	1,886.8	2,554.8	...
Bonds and notes	8 620 . .	828.8	1,378.6	1,440.1	1,247.7	1,472.6	1,815.0	2,534.4	...
Monetary authorities	8 621 . .	...	...	...	...	...	...	...	...
General government	8 622 . .	...	...	...	...	...	...	...	...
Banks	8 623 . .	816.3	1,369.2	1,424.3	1,232.4	1,457.0	1,798.9	2,519.4	...
Other sectors	8 624 . .	12.5	9.4	15.8	15.4	15.6	16.0	15.1	...
Money market instruments	8 630 . .	55.1	11.9	60.3	23.3	16.7	71.8	20.3	...
Monetary authorities	8 631 . .	...	...	...	...	...	...	...	...
General government	8 632 . .	...	...	...	...	...	...	...	...
Banks	8 633 . .	43.5	3.4	52.3	13.3	...	55.1	...	...
Other sectors	8 634 . .	11.7	8.5	8.1	10.0	16.7	16.7	20.3	...
Financial derivatives	8 900 . .	...	...	...	...	...	...	...	...
Monetary authorities	8 901 . .	...	...	...	...	...	...	...	...
General government	8 902 . .	...	...	...	...	...	...	...	...
Banks	8 903 . .	...	...	...	...	...	...	...	...
Other sectors	8 904 . .	...	...	...	...	...	...	...	...
Other investment	8 703 . .	**689.2**	**1,027.5**	**1,600.8**	**2,433.5**	**4,656.1**	**5,833.2**	**6,459.8**	...
Trade credits	8 706 . .	201.6	224.7	215.2	222.4	202.4	228.6	192.8	...
General government	8 707 . .	...	...	...	...	...	...	...	...
of which: Short-term	8 709 . .	...	...	...	...	...	...	...	...
Other sectors	8 710 . .	201.6	224.7	215.2	222.4	202.4	228.6	192.8	...
of which: Short-term	8 712 . .	*201.6*	*224.7*	*215.2*	*222.4*	*202.4*	*228.6*	*192.8*	...
Loans	8 714 . .	84.5	291.7	735.5	1,195.5	1,638.0	2,017.6	2,822.7	...
Monetary authorities	8 715 . .	...	...	...	...	...	...	...	...
of which: Short-term	8 718 . .	...	...	...	...	...	...	...	...
General government	8 719 . .	...	...	...	...	...	...	...	...
of which: Short-term	8 721 . .	...	...	...	...	...	...	...	...
Banks	8 722 . .	75.0	284.6	723.0	1,183.0	1,619.2	1,998.9	2,804.2	...
of which: Short-term	8 724 . .	...	...	...	...	...	...	...	...
Other sectors	8 725 . .	9.5	7.1	12.5	12.5	18.8	18.7	18.5	...
of which: Short-term	8 727 . .	*5.4*	*4.3*	*9.2*	*9.2*	*14.6*	*18.2*	*18.5*	...
Currency and deposits	8 730 . .	365.9	450.3	588.4	924.2	2,699.1	2,599.3	1,199.9	...
Monetary authorities	8 731 . .	...	...	...	...	...	...	...	...
General government	8 732 . .	...	...	...	...	...	...	...	...
Banks	8 733 . .	301.5	362.9	487.7	810.1	2,574.1	2,512.7	1,154.7	...
Other sectors	8 734 . .	64.4	87.4	100.7	114.1	125.1	86.6	45.2	...
Other assets	8 736 . .	37.2	60.7	61.7	91.4	116.6	987.7	2,244.3	...
Monetary authorities	8 737 . .	...	...	...	...	...	...	...	...
of which: Short-term	8 739 . .	...	...	...	...	...	...	...	...
General government	8 740 . .	2.7	2.0	2.5	2.6	2.6	2.4	2.3	...
of which: Short-term	8 742 . .	...	...	...	...	...	...	...	...
Banks	8 743 . .	19.6	46.5	51.7	80.1	106.0	979.4	2,227.4	...
of which: Short-term	8 745 . .	*19.6*	*46.5*	*51.7*	*80.1*	*106.0*	*979.4*	*2,227.4*	...
Other sectors	8 746 . .	14.9	12.2	7.5	8.7	7.9	5.8	14.6	...
of which: Short-term	8 748 . .	*14.9*	*12.2*	*7.5*	*8.7*	*7.9*	*5.8*	*14.6*	...
Reserve assets	8 802 . .	**1,875.6**	**1,647.8**	**1,540.8**	**1,437.0**	**1,695.7**	**1,796.5**	**1,471.6**	...
Monetary gold	8 812 . .	19.8	10.2	10.0	3.3	1.9	1.7	1.1	...
Special drawing rights	8 811 . .	52.0	56.0	57.2	56.6	62.5	30.9	31.9	...
Reserve position in the Fund	8 810 . .	37.1	40.5	44.1	42.7	44.5	55.3	52.5	...
Foreign exchange	8 803 . .	1,766.6	1,541.2	1,429.6	1,334.5	1,586.8	1,708.7	1,386.1	...
Other claims	8 813 . .	...	...	...	...	...	...	...	...

Table 3 (Concluded). INTERNATIONAL INVESTMENT POSITION (End–period stocks), 1994–2001

(Millions of U.S. dollars)

	Code	1994	1995	1996	1997	1998	1999	2000	2001
LIABILITIES	8 995 D.	2,126.0	2,947.2	3,877.4	4,578.3	7,295.4	9,139.9	10,554.8	...
Direct investment in Malta	8 555 ..	**415.9**	**562.1**	**844.2**	**857.9**	**1,174.3**	**1,860.6**	**2,373.8**	**...**
Equity capital and reinvested earnings	8 556 ..	484.6	645.0	762.5	755.8	888.1	1,149.8	1,466.7	...
Claims on direct investors	8 557 ..	...	...	...	...	...	...	...	...
Liabilities to direct investors	8 558 ..	484.6	645.0	762.5	755.8	888.1	1,149.8	1,466.7	...
Other capital	8 580 ..	–68.7	–82.9	81.8	102.1	286.2	710.8	907.1	...
Claims on direct investors	8 585 ..	–207.5	–475.3	–486.9	–495.8	–556.7	–362.8	–475.8	...
Liabilities to direct investors	8 590 ..	138.8	392.5	568.7	597.9	842.8	1,073.6	1,382.9	...
Portfolio investment	8 652 ..	**17.4**	**24.1**	**23.9**	**65.0**	**129.8**	**94.4**	**95.5**	**...**
Equity securities	8 660 ..	...	...	...	...	...	...	...	...
Banks	8 663 ..	...	...	...	...	...	...	...	...
Other sectors	8 664 ..	...	...	...	...	...	...	...	...
Debt securities	8 669 ..	17.4	24.1	23.9	65.0	129.8	94.4	95.5	...
Bonds and notes	8 670 ..	...	...	...	43.0	46.1	39.8	37.0	...
Monetary authorities	8 671 ..	...	...	...	...	...	...	...	...
General government	8 672 ..	...	...	...	...	...	...	...	...
Banks	8 673 ..	...	...	...	43.0	46.1	39.8	37.0	...
Other sectors	8 674 ..	...	...	...	...	...	...	...	...
Money market instruments	8 680 ..	17.4	24.1	23.9	22.0	83.7	54.6	58.5	...
Monetary authorities	8 681 ..	...	...	...	...	...	...	...	...
General government	8 682 ..	...	...	...	...	...	...	...	...
Banks	8 683 ..	...	...	...	...	8.7	7.8	7.5	...
Other sectors	8 684 ..	17.4	24.1	23.9	22.0	75.0	46.8	50.9	...
Financial derivatives	8 905 ..	**...**	**...**	**...**	**...**	**...**	**...**	**...**	**...**
Monetary authorities	8 906 ..	...	...	...	...	...	...	...	...
General government	8 907 ..	...	...	...	...	...	...	...	...
Banks	8 908 ..	...	...	...	...	...	...	...	...
Other sectors	8 909 ..	...	...	...	...	...	...	...	...
Other investment	8 753 ..	**1,692.7**	**2,361.0**	**3,009.3**	**3,655.3**	**5,991.3**	**7,184.9**	**8,085.5**	**...**
Trade credits	8 756 ..	171.7	170.8	152.1	154.8	190.5	166.0	162.2	...
General government	8 757 ..	...	...	...	...	...	...	...	...
of which: Short-term	8 759 ..	...	...	...	...	...	...	...	...
Other sectors	8 760 ..	171.7	170.8	152.1	154.8	190.5	166.0	162.2	...
of which: Short-term	8 762 ..	*171.7*	*170.8*	*152.1*	*154.8*	*190.5*	*166.0*	*162.2*	...
Loans	8 764 ..	811.2	888.8	1,093.4	1,095.9	1,538.4	1,649.0	1,546.7	...
Monetary authorities	8 765 ..	...	...	...	...	...	...	...	...
of which: Use of Fund credit and loans from the Fund	8 766 ..	...	...	...	...	...	...	...	...
of which: Short-term	8 768 ..	...	...	...	...	...	...	...	...
General government	8 769 ..	152.9	151.5	144.0	129.0	123.2	107.5	89.8	...
of which: Short-term	8 771 ..	...	...	...	...	...	...	...	...
Banks	8 772 ..	3.0	86.0	196.6	231.1	700.8	896.9	857.1	...
of which: Short-term	8 774 ..	...	...	...	...	...	...	...	...
Other sectors	8 775 ..	655.2	651.3	752.7	735.8	714.3	644.5	599.9	...
of which: Short-term	8 777 ..	*27.2*	*29.5*	*48.9*	*75.5*	*26.2*	*27.7*	*26.3*	...
Currency and deposits	8 780 ..	658.8	956.9	1,526.0	2,138.4	3,873.7	4,410.1	3,178.8	...
Monetary authorities	8 781 ..	...	...	...	...	...	...	...	...
General government	8 782 ..	...	...	...	...	...	...	...	...
Banks	8 783 ..	658.8	956.9	1,526.0	2,138.4	3,873.7	4,410.1	3,178.8	...
Other sectors	8 784 ..	...	...	...	...	...	...	...	...
Other liabilities	8 786 ..	51.1	344.5	237.7	266.2	388.7	959.8	3,197.8	...
Monetary authorities	8 787 ..	...	...	...	...	...	...	...	...
of which: Short-term	8 789 ..	...	...	...	...	...	...	...	...
General government	8 790 ..	...	...	...	...	...	...	...	...
of which: Short-term	8 792 ..	...	...	...	...	...	...	...	...
Banks	8 793 ..	40.2	333.1	225.2	257.2	380.5	949.6	3,186.1	...
of which: Short-term	8 795 ..	*40.2*	*333.1*	*225.2*	*257.2*	*380.5*	*949.6*	*3,186.1*	...
Other sectors	8 796 ..	10.9	11.4	12.5	9.0	8.2	10.2	11.6	...
of which: Short-term	8 798 ..	*10.9*	*11.4*	*12.5*	*9.0*	*8.2*	*10.2*	*11.6*	...
NET INTERNATIONAL INVESTMENT POSITION	8 995 ..	**1,353.4**	**1,154.9**	**877.1**	**718.4**	**722.8**	**586.3**	**174.8**	**...**
Conversion rates: Maltese lira per U.S. dollar (end of period)	0 102 ..	**.3681**	**.3524**	**.3596**	**.3907**	**.3774**	**.4121**	**.4378**	**.4521**

Table 1. ANALYTIC PRESENTATION, 1994–2001
(Millions of U.S. dollars)

	Code	1994	1995	1996	1997	1998	1999	2000	2001
A. Current Account [1]	4 993 Z.	**–69.9**	**22.1**	**91.3**	**47.8**	**77.2**	**. . .**	**. . .**	**. . .**
Goods: exports f.o.b	2 100 . .	399.7	476.4	480.0	423.6	358.6	. . .	. . .	. . .
Goods: imports f.o.b	3 100 . .	–352.3	–292.6	–346.1	–316.5	–318.7	. . .	. . .	. . .
Balance on Goods	4 100 . .	*47.4*	*183.8*	*133.9*	*107.2*	*40.0*	. . .	. . .	. . .
Services: credit	2 200 . .	26.0	27.9	31.6	34.9	34.0	. . .	. . .	. . .
Services: debit	3 200 . .	–181.1	–217.0	–231.3	–200.0	–152.5	. . .	. . .	. . .
Balance on Goods and Services	4 991 . .	*–107.7*	*–5.3*	*–65.8*	*–57.9*	*–78.6*	. . .	. . .	. . .
Income: credit	2 300 . .	1.1	1.3	.9	1.4	2.5	. . .	. . .	. . .
Income: debit	3 300 . .	–47.7	–49.5	–45.9	–40.3	–34.0	. . .	. . .	. . .
Balance on Goods, Services, and Income	4 992 . .	*–154.3*	*–53.5*	*–110.8*	*–96.8*	*–110.2*	. . .	. . .	. . .
Current transfers: credit	2 379 Z.	113.3	94.7	217.5	157.9	198.3	. . .	. . .	. . .
Current transfers: debit	3 379 . .	–28.9	–19.2	–15.5	–13.3	–10.8	. . .	. . .	. . .
B. Capital Account [1]	4 994 Z.	**. . .**	**. . .**	**. . .**	**. . .**	**. . .**	**. . .**	**. . .**	**. . .**
Capital account: credit	2 994 Z.	. . .	. . .	. . .	. . .	. . .	. . .	. . .	. . .
Capital account: debit	3 994 . .	. . .	. . .	. . .	. . .	. . .	. . .	. . .	. . .
Total, Groups A Plus B	4 981 . .	*–69.9*	*22.1*	*91.3*	*47.8*	*77.2*	. . .	. . .	. . .
C. Financial Account [1]	4 995 W.	**–11.4**	**–10.2**	**–86.1**	**–17.3**	**–25.9**	**. . .**	**. . .**	**. . .**
Direct investment abroad	4 505 . .	. . .	. . .	. . .	. . .	. . .	. . .	. . .	. . .
Direct investment in Mauritania	4 555 Z.	2.1	7.0	. . .	. . .	.1	. . .	. . .	. . .
Portfolio investment assets	4 602 . .	. . .	. . .	. . .	. . .	. . .	. . .	. . .	. . .
Equity securities	4 610 . .	. . .	. . .	. . .	. . .	. . .	. . .	. . .	. . .
Debt securities	4 619 . .	. . .	. . .	. . .	. . .	. . .	. . .	. . .	. . .
Portfolio investment liabilities	4 652 Z.	–.2	–.5	–.4	. . .	–.4	. . .	. . .	. . .
Equity securities	4 660 . .	. . .	. . .	. . .	. . .	. . .	. . .	. . .	. . .
Debt securities	4 669 Z.	–.2	–.5	–.4	. . .	–.4	. . .	. . .	. . .
Financial derivatives	4 910 . .	. . .	. . .	. . .	. . .	. . .	. . .	. . .	. . .
Financial derivatives assets	4 900 . .	. . .	. . .	. . .	. . .	. . .	. . .	. . .	. . .
Financial derivatives liabilities	4 905 . .	. . .	. . .	. . .	. . .	. . .	. . .	. . .	. . .
Other investment assets	4 703 . .	169.3	211.5	236.0	191.1	190.1	. . .	. . .	. . .
Monetary authorities	4 701 . .	. . .	. . .	. . .	. . .	. . .	. . .	. . .	. . .
General government	4 704 . .	–2.2	–.4	–.2	. . .	. . .	. . .	. . .	. . .
Banks	4 705 . .	. . .	. . .	. . .	. . .	. . .	. . .	. . .	. . .
Other sectors	4 728 . .	171.5	211.9	236.2	191.1	190.1	. . .	. . .	. . .
Other investment liabilities	4 753 W.	–182.6	–228.2	–321.6	–208.4	–215.7	. . .	. . .	. . .
Monetary authorities	4 753 WA	. . .	. . .	. . .	. . .	. . .	. . .	. . .	. . .
General government	4 753 ZB	–7.0	.2	–.2	5.3	.7	. . .	. . .	. . .
Banks	4 753 ZC	. . .	. . .	. . .	. . .	. . .	. . .	. . .	. . .
Other sectors	4 753 ZD	–175.5	–228.4	–321.4	–213.7	–216.4	. . .	. . .	. . .
Total, Groups A Through C	4 983 . .	*–81.2*	*11.9*	*5.2*	*30.5*	*51.3*	. . .	. . .	. . .
D. Net Errors and Omissions	4 998 . .	**–23.5**	**–18.1**	**–1.0**	**–3.0**	**–8.1**	**. . .**	**. . .**	**. . .**
Total, Groups A Through D	4 984 . .	*–104.7*	*–6.2*	*4.2*	*27.6*	*43.2*	. . .	. . .	. . .
E. Reserves and Related Items	4 802 A.	**104.7**	**6.2**	**–4.2**	**–27.6**	**–43.2**	**. . .**	**. . .**	**. . .**
Reserve assets	4 802 . .	46.9	–42.9	–58.3	–58.8	–46.3	. . .	. . .	. . .
Use of Fund credit and loans	4 766 . .	17.9	12.2	10.9	12.0	–6.9	. . .	. . .	. . .
Exceptional financing	4 920 . .	40.0	36.9	43.3	19.3	10.0	. . .	. . .	. . .
Conversion rates: ouguiyas per U.S. dollar	0 101 . .	**123.58**	**129.77**	**137.22**	**151.85**	**188.48**	**209.51**	**238.92**	**255.63**

[1] Excludes components that have been classified in the categories of Group E.

Table 2. STANDARD PRESENTATION, 1994–2001

(Millions of U.S. dollars)

	Code	1994	1995	1996	1997	1998	1999	2000	2001
CURRENT ACCOUNT	4 993 . .	**–69.9**	**22.1**	**91.3**	**47.8**	**77.2**	**...**	**...**	**...**
A. GOODS	4 100 . .	47.4	183.8	133.9	107.2	40.0	...	...	...
Credit	2 100 . .	**399.7**	**476.4**	**480.0**	**423.6**	**358.6**	**...**	**...**	**...**
General merchandise: exports f.o.b.	2 110 . .	399.7	476.4	480.0	423.6	358.6	...	...	...
Goods for processing: exports f.o.b.	2 150 . .	...	...	...	...	...	...	...	...
Repairs on goods	2 160 . .	...	...	...	...	...	...	...	...
Goods procured in ports by carriers	2 170 . .	...	...	...	...	...	...	...	...
Nonmonetary gold	2 180 . .	...	...	...	...	...	...	...	...
Debit	3 100 . .	**–352.3**	**–292.6**	**–346.1**	**–316.5**	**–318.7**	**...**	**...**	**...**
General merchandise: imports f.o.b.	3 110 . .	–352.3	–292.6	–346.1	–316.5	–318.7	...	...	...
Goods for processing: imports f.o.b.	3 150 . .	...	...	...	...	...	...	...	...
Repairs on goods	3 160 . .	...	...	...	...	...	...	...	...
Goods procured in ports by carriers	3 170 . .	...	...	...	...	...	...	...	...
Nonmonetary gold	3 180 . .	...	...	...	...	...	...	...	...
B. SERVICES	4 200 . .	–155.1	–189.1	–199.7	–165.0	–118.6	...	...	...
Total credit	2 200 . .	*26.0*	*27.9*	*31.6*	*34.9*	*34.0*	...	...	...
Total debit	3 200 . .	*–181.1*	*–217.0*	*–231.3*	*–200.0*	*–152.5*	...	...	...
Transportation services, credit	2 205 . .	**1.7**	**1.8**	**.7**	**.7**	**.6**	**...**	**...**	**...**
Passenger	2 850 . .	*.6*	...	...	*.1*	*.1*	...	...	...
Freight	2 851 . .	...	...	...	...	...	...	...	...
Other	2 852 . .	*1.1*	*1.7*	*.7*	*.6*	*.5*	...	...	...
Sea transport, passenger	2 207 . .	...	...	...	...	...	...	...	...
Sea transport, freight	2 208 . .	...	...	...	...	...	...	...	...
Sea transport, other	2 209 . .	...	...	...	...	...	...	...	...
Air transport, passenger	2 211 . .	...	...	...	...	...	...	...	...
Air transport, freight	2 212 . .	...	...	...	...	...	...	...	...
Air transport, other	2 213 . .	...	...	...	...	...	...	...	...
Other transport, passenger	2 215 . .	...	...	...	...	...	...	...	...
Other transport, freight	2 216 . .	...	...	...	...	...	...	...	...
Other transport, other	2 217 . .	...	...	...	...	...	...	...	...
Transportation services, debit	3 205 . .	**–93.8**	**–120.9**	**–134.2**	**–97.9**	**–48.5**	**...**	**...**	**...**
Passenger	3 850 . .	*–5.9*	*–7.1*	*–4.9*	*–5.1*	*–5.3*	...	...	...
Freight	3 851 . .	*–31.5*	*–25.4*	*–32.9*	*–31.4*	*–30.5*	...	...	...
Other	3 852 . .	*–56.4*	*–88.4*	*–96.4*	*–61.4*	*–12.7*	...	...	...
Sea transport, passenger	3 207 . .	...	...	...	...	...	...	...	...
Sea transport, freight	3 208 . .	...	...	...	...	...	...	...	...
Sea transport, other	3 209 . .	...	...	...	...	...	...	...	...
Air transport, passenger	3 211 . .	...	...	...	...	...	...	...	...
Air transport, freight	3 212 . .	...	...	...	...	...	...	...	...
Air transport, other	3 213 . .	...	...	...	...	...	...	...	...
Other transport, passenger	3 215 . .	...	...	...	...	...	...	...	...
Other transport, freight	3 216 . .	...	...	...	...	...	...	...	...
Other transport, other	3 217 . .	...	...	...	...	...	...	...	...
Travel, credit	2 236 . .	**10.8**	**11.2**	**19.2**	**21.2**	**20.2**	**...**	**...**	**...**
Business travel	2 237 . .	...	...	...	...	...	...	...	...
Personal travel	2 240 . .	...	...	...	...	...	...	...	...
Travel, debit	3 236 . .	**–17.9**	**–22.9**	**–35.7**	**–47.6**	**–42.5**	**...**	**...**	**...**
Business travel	3 237 . .	...	...	...	...	...	...	...	...
Personal travel	3 240 . .	...	...	...	...	...	...	...	...
Other services, credit	2 200 BA	**13.5**	**14.9**	**11.7**	**13.0**	**13.1**	**...**	**...**	**...**
Communications	2 245 . .	...	...	...	...	...	...	...	...
Construction	2 249 . .	...	...	...	...	...	...	...	...
Insurance	2 253 . .	...	...	...	...	...	...	...	...
Financial	2 260 . .	...	...	...	...	...	...	...	...
Computer and information	2 262 . .	...	...	...	...	...	...	...	...
Royalties and licence fees	2 266 . .	...	...	...	...	...	...	...	...
Other business services	2 268 . .	4.1	6.4	3.6	3.4	3.6	...	...	...
Personal, cultural, and recreational	2 287 . .	...	...	...	...	...	...	...	...
Government, n.i.e.	2 291 . .	9.4	8.6	8.1	9.6	9.6	...	...	...
Other services, debit	3 200 BA	**–69.4**	**–73.2**	**–61.4**	**–54.5**	**–61.6**	**...**	**...**	**...**
Communications	3 245 . .	...	...	...	...	...	...	...	...
Construction	3 249 . .	...	...	...	...	...	...	...	...
Insurance	3 253 . .	–3.5	–2.8	...	...	...	...	...	...
Financial	3 260 . .	...	...	...	...	...	...	...	...
Computer and information	3 262 . .	...	...	...	...	...	...	...	...
Royalties and licence fees	3 266 . .	...	...	...	...	...	...	...	...
Other business services	3 268 . .	–46.7	–50.0	–37.6	–34.7	–38.5	...	...	...
Personal, cultural, and recreational	3 287 . .	...	...	...	...	...	...	...	...
Government, n.i.e.	3 291 . .	–19.2	–20.4	–23.8	–19.8	–23.0	...	...	...

Table 2 (Continued). STANDARD PRESENTATION, 1994–2001

(Millions of U.S. dollars)

	Code	1994	1995	1996	1997	1998	1999	2000	2001
C. INCOME	4 300 . .	–46.6	–48.2	–45.0	–38.9	–31.6	. . .	. . .	. . .
Total credit	2 300 . .	*1.1*	*1.3*	*.9*	*1.4*	*2.5*	. . .	. . .	. . .
Total debit	3 300 . .	*–47.7*	*–49.5*	*–45.9*	*–40.3*	*–34.0*	. . .	. . .	. . .
Compensation of employees, credit	2 310 . .	**. . .**	**. . .**	**. . .**	**. . .**	**. . .**	**. . .**	**. . .**	**. . .**
Compensation of employees, debit	3 310 . .	**. . .**	**. . .**	**. . .**	**. . .**	**. . .**	**. . .**	**. . .**	**. . .**
Investment income, credit	2 320 . .	**1.1**	**1.3**	**.9**	**1.4**	**2.5**	**. . .**	**. . .**	**. . .**
Direct investment income	2 330 . .	. . .	. . .	. . .	. . .	. . .	. . .	. . .	. . .
Dividends and distributed branch profits	2 332 . .	. . .	. . .	. . .	. . .	. . .	. . .	. . .	. . .
Reinvested earnings and undistributed branch profits	2 333 . .	. . .	. . .	. . .	. . .	. . .	. . .	. . .	. . .
Income on debt (interest)	2 334 . .	. . .	. . .	. . .	. . .	. . .	. . .	. . .	. . .
Portfolio investment income	2 339 . .	. . .	. . .	. . .	. . .	. . .	. . .	. . .	. . .
Income on equity	2 340 . .	. . .	. . .	. . .	. . .	. . .	. . .	. . .	. . .
Income on bonds and notes	2 350 . .	. . .	. . .	. . .	. . .	. . .	. . .	. . .	. . .
Income on money market instruments	2 360 . .	. . .	. . .	. . .	. . .	. . .	. . .	. . .	. . .
Other investment income	2 370 . .	1.1	1.3	.9	1.4	2.5	. . .	. . .	. . .
Investment income, debit	3 320 . .	**–47.7**	**–49.5**	**–45.9**	**–40.3**	**–34.0**	**. . .**	**. . .**	**. . .**
Direct investment income	3 330 . .	–2.3	–4.5	. . .	–1.5	–1.3	. . .	. . .	. . .
Dividends and distributed branch profits	3 332 . .	–2.3	–4.5	. . .	–1.5	–1.3	. . .	. . .	. . .
Reinvested earnings and undistributed branch profits	3 333 . .	. . .	. . .	. . .	. . .	. . .	. . .	. . .	. . .
Income on debt (interest)	3 334 . .	. . .	. . .	. . .	. . .	. . .	. . .	. . .	. . .
Portfolio investment income	3 339 . .	. . .	. . .	. . .	. . .	. . .	. . .	. . .	. . .
Income on equity	3 340 . .	. . .	. . .	. . .	. . .	. . .	. . .	. . .	. . .
Income on bonds and notes	3 350 . .	. . .	. . .	. . .	. . .	. . .	. . .	. . .	. . .
Income on money market instruments	3 360 . .	. . .	. . .	. . .	. . .	. . .	. . .	. . .	. . .
Other investment income	3 370 . .	–45.3	–45.0	–45.9	–38.8	–32.8	. . .	. . .	. . .
D. CURRENT TRANSFERS	4 379 . .	84.4	75.6	202.1	144.6	187.4	. . .	. . .	. . .
Credit	2 379 . .	**113.3**	**94.7**	**217.5**	**157.9**	**198.3**	**. . .**	**. . .**	**. . .**
General government	2 380 . .	101.8	82.3	206.0	111.9	114.2	. . .	. . .	. . .
Other sectors	2 390 . .	11.6	12.4	11.6	46.0	84.1	. . .	. . .	. . .
Workers' remittances	2 391 . .	4.9	5.4	4.4	2.7	2.2	. . .	. . .	. . .
Other current transfers	2 392 . .	6.7	7.0	7.2	43.3	81.9	. . .	. . .	. . .
Debit	3 379 . .	**–28.9**	**–19.2**	**–15.5**	**–13.3**	**–10.8**	**. . .**	**. . .**	**. . .**
General government	3 380 . .	–2.2	–3.1	–2.4	–1.4	–1.1	. . .	. . .	. . .
Other sectors	3 390 . .	–26.7	–16.0	–13.1	–11.8	–9.8	. . .	. . .	. . .
Workers' remittances	3 391 . .	–24.9	–14.4	–12.2	–11.6	–9.6	. . .	. . .	. . .
Other current transfers	3 392 . .	–1.8	–1.6	–.9	–.3	–.2	. . .	. . .	. . .
CAPITAL AND FINANCIAL ACCOUNT	4 996 . .	**93.3**	**–4.0**	**–90.3**	**–44.9**	**–69.1**	**. . .**	**. . .**	**. . .**
CAPITAL ACCOUNT	4 994 . .	**. . .**	**. . .**	**. . .**	**. . .**	**. . .**	**. . .**	**. . .**	**. . .**
Total credit	2 994 . .	. . .	. . .	. . .	. . .	. . .	. . .	. . .	. . .
Total debit	3 994 . .	. . .	. . .	. . .	. . .	. . .	. . .	. . .	. . .
Capital transfers, credit	2 400 . .	**. . .**	**. . .**	**. . .**	**. . .**	**. . .**	**. . .**	**. . .**	**. . .**
General government	2 401 . .	. . .	. . .	. . .	. . .	. . .	. . .	. . .	. . .
Debt forgiveness	2 402 . .	. . .	. . .	. . .	. . .	. . .	. . .	. . .	. . .
Other capital transfers	2 410 . .	. . .	. . .	. . .	. . .	. . .	. . .	. . .	. . .
Other sectors	2 430 . .	. . .	. . .	. . .	. . .	. . .	. . .	. . .	. . .
Migrants' transfers	2 431 . .	. . .	. . .	. . .	. . .	. . .	. . .	. . .	. . .
Debt forgiveness	2 432 . .	. . .	. . .	. . .	. . .	. . .	. . .	. . .	. . .
Other capital transfers	2 440 . .	. . .	. . .	. . .	. . .	. . .	. . .	. . .	. . .
Capital transfers, debit	3 400 . .	**. . .**	**. . .**	**. . .**	**. . .**	**. . .**	**. . .**	**. . .**	**. . .**
General government	3 401 . .	. . .	. . .	. . .	. . .	. . .	. . .	. . .	. . .
Debt forgiveness	3 402 . .	. . .	. . .	. . .	. . .	. . .	. . .	. . .	. . .
Other capital transfers	3 410 . .	. . .	. . .	. . .	. . .	. . .	. . .	. . .	. . .
Other sectors	3 430 . .	. . .	. . .	. . .	. . .	. . .	. . .	. . .	. . .
Migrants' transfers	3 431 . .	. . .	. . .	. . .	. . .	. . .	. . .	. . .	. . .
Debt forgiveness	3 432 . .	. . .	. . .	. . .	. . .	. . .	. . .	. . .	. . .
Other capital transfers	3 440 . .	. . .	. . .	. . .	. . .	. . .	. . .	. . .	. . .
Nonproduced nonfinancial assets, credit	2 480 . .	**. . .**	**. . .**	**. . .**	**. . .**	**. . .**	**. . .**	**. . .**	**. . .**
Nonproduced nonfinancial assets, debit	3 480 . .	**. . .**	**. . .**	**. . .**	**. . .**	**. . .**	**. . .**	**. . .**	**. . .**

Table 2 (Continued). STANDARD PRESENTATION, 1994–2001
(Millions of U.S. dollars)

	Code	1994	1995	1996	1997	1998	1999	2000	2001
FINANCIAL ACCOUNT	4 995 . .	**93.3**	**–4.0**	**–90.3**	**–44.9**	**–69.1**	...	...	...
A. DIRECT INVESTMENT	4 500 . .	2.1	7.0	...	...	.1	...	...	...
Direct investment abroad	4 505 . .	...	...	...	...	...	...	...	...
Equity capital	4 510 . .	...	...	...	...	...	...	...	...
Claims on affiliated enterprises	4 515 . .	...	...	...	...	...	...	...	...
Liabilities to affiliated enterprises	4 520 . .	...	...	...	...	...	...	...	...
Reinvested earnings	4 525 . .	...	...	...	...	...	...	...	...
Other capital	4 530 . .	...	...	...	...	...	...	...	...
Claims on affiliated enterprises	4 535 . .	...	...	...	...	...	...	...	...
Liabilities to affiliated enterprises	4 540 . .	...	...	...	...	...	...	...	...
Direct investment in Mauritania	4 555 . .	**2.1**	**7.0**	...	...	**.1**	...	...	...
Equity capital	4 560 . .	2.1	7.0	...	...	.1	...	...	...
Claims on direct investors	4 565 . .	...	...	...	...	...	...	...	...
Liabilities to direct investors	4 570 . .	...	...	...	...	...	...	...	...
Reinvested earnings	4 575 . .	...	...	...	...	...	...	...	...
Other capital	4 580 . .	...	...	...	...	...	...	...	...
Claims on direct investors	4 585 . .	...	...	...	...	...	...	...	...
Liabilities to direct investors	4 590 . .	...	...	...	...	...	...	...	...
B. PORTFOLIO INVESTMENT	4 600 . .	–.2	–.5	–.4	...	–.4	...	...	...
Assets	4 602 . .	...	...	...	...	...	...	...	...
Equity securities	4 610 . .	...	...	...	...	...	...	...	...
Monetary authorities	4 611 . .	...	...	...	...	...	...	...	...
General government	4 612 . .	...	...	...	...	...	...	...	...
Banks	4 613 . .	...	...	...	...	...	...	...	...
Other sectors	4 614 . .	...	...	...	...	...	...	...	...
Debt securities	4 619 . .	...	...	...	...	...	...	...	...
Bonds and notes	4 620 . .	...	...	...	...	...	...	...	...
Monetary authorities	4 621 . .	...	...	...	...	...	...	...	...
General government	4 622 . .	...	...	...	...	...	...	...	...
Banks	4 623 . .	...	...	...	...	...	...	...	...
Other sectors	4 624 . .	...	...	...	...	...	...	...	...
Money market instruments	4 630 . .	...	...	...	...	...	...	...	...
Monetary authorities	4 631 . .	...	...	...	...	...	...	...	...
General government	4 632 . .	...	...	...	...	...	...	...	...
Banks	4 633 . .	...	...	...	...	...	...	...	...
Other sectors	4 634 . .	...	...	...	...	...	...	...	...
Liabilities	4 652 . .	**–.2**	**–.5**	**–.4**	...	**–.4**	...	...	...
Equity securities	4 660 . .	...	...	...	...	...	...	...	...
Banks	4 663 . .	...	...	...	...	...	...	...	...
Other sectors	4 664 . .	...	...	...	...	...	...	...	...
Debt securities	4 669 . .	–.2	–.5	–.4	...	–.4	...	...	...
Bonds and notes	4 670 . .	–.2	–.5	–.4	...	–.4	...	...	...
Monetary authorities	4 671 . .	...	...	...	...	...	...	...	...
General government	4 672 . .	–.2	–.5	–.4	...	–.4	...	...	...
Banks	4 673 . .	...	...	...	...	...	...	...	...
Other sectors	4 674 . .	...	...	...	...	...	...	...	...
Money market instruments	4 680 . .	...	...	...	...	...	...	...	...
Monetary authorities	4 681 . .	...	...	...	...	...	...	...	...
General government	4 682 . .	...	...	...	...	...	...	...	...
Banks	4 683 . .	...	...	...	...	...	...	...	...
Other sectors	4 684 . .	...	...	...	...	...	...	...	...
C. FINANCIAL DERIVATIVES	4 910 . .	...	...	...	...	...	...	...	...
Monetary authorities	4 911 . .	...	...	...	...	...	...	...	...
General government	4 912 . .	...	...	...	...	...	...	...	...
Banks	4 913 . .	...	...	...	...	...	...	...	...
Other sectors	4 914 . .	...	...	...	...	...	...	...	...
Assets	4 900 . .	...	...	...	...	...	...	...	...
Monetary authorities	4 901 . .	...	...	...	...	...	...	...	...
General government	4 902 . .	...	...	...	...	...	...	...	...
Banks	4 903 . .	...	...	...	...	...	...	...	...
Other sectors	4 904 . .	...	...	...	...	...	...	...	...
Liabilities	4 905 . .	...	...	...	...	...	...	...	...
Monetary authorities	4 906 . .	...	...	...	...	...	...	...	...
General government	4 907 . .	...	...	...	...	...	...	...	...
Banks	4 908 . .	...	...	...	...	...	...	...	...
Other sectors	4 909 . .	...	...	...	...	...	...	...	...

Table 2 (Concluded). STANDARD PRESENTATION, 1994–2001
(Millions of U.S. dollars)

	Code	1994	1995	1996	1997	1998	1999	2000	2001
D. OTHER INVESTMENT	4 700	44.6	32.4	–31.5	13.9	–22.5	. . .	. . .	. . .
Assets	4 703	**169.3**	**211.5**	**236.0**	**191.1**	**190.1**	**. . .**	**. . .**	**. . .**
Trade credits	4 706	. . .	. . .	. . .	. . .	. . .	. . .	. . .	. . .
General government	4 707	. . .	. . .	. . .	. . .	. . .	. . .	. . .	. . .
of which: Short-term	4 709	. . .	. . .	. . .	. . .	. . .	. . .	. . .	. . .
Other sectors	4 710	. . .	. . .	. . .	. . .	. . .	. . .	. . .	. . .
of which: Short-term	4 712	. . .	. . .	. . .	. . .	. . .	. . .	. . .	. . .
Loans	4 714	. . .	. . .	. . .	. . .	. . .	. . .	. . .	. . .
Monetary authorities	4 715	. . .	. . .	. . .	. . .	. . .	. . .	. . .	. . .
of which: Short-term	4 718	. . .	. . .	. . .	. . .	. . .	. . .	. . .	. . .
General government	4 719	. . .	. . .	. . .	. . .	. . .	. . .	. . .	. . .
of which: Short-term	4 721	. . .	. . .	. . .	. . .	. . .	. . .	. . .	. . .
Banks	4 722	. . .	. . .	. . .	. . .	. . .	. . .	. . .	. . .
of which: Short-term	4 724	. . .	. . .	. . .	. . .	. . .	. . .	. . .	. . .
Other sectors	4 725	. . .	. . .	. . .	. . .	. . .	. . .	. . .	. . .
of which: Short-term	4 727	. . .	. . .	. . .	. . .	. . .	. . .	. . .	. . .
Currency and deposits	4 730	171.5	211.9	236.2	191.1	190.1	. . .	. . .	. . .
Monetary authorities	4 731	. . .	. . .	. . .	. . .	. . .	. . .	. . .	. . .
General government	4 732	. . .	. . .	. . .	. . .	. . .	. . .	. . .	. . .
Banks	4 733	. . .	. . .	. . .	. . .	. . .	. . .	. . .	. . .
Other sectors	4 734	171.5	211.9	236.2	191.1	190.1	. . .	. . .	. . .
Other assets	4 736	–2.2	–.4	–.2	. . .	. . .	. . .	. . .	. . .
Monetary authorities	4 737	. . .	. . .	. . .	. . .	. . .	. . .	. . .	. . .
of which: Short-term	4 739	. . .	. . .	. . .	. . .	. . .	. . .	. . .	. . .
General government	4 740	–2.2	–.4	–.2	. . .	. . .	. . .	. . .	. . .
of which: Short-term	4 742	. . .	. . .	. . .	. . .	. . .	. . .	. . .	. . .
Banks	4 743	. . .	. . .	. . .	. . .	. . .	. . .	. . .	. . .
of which: Short-term	4 745	. . .	. . .	. . .	. . .	. . .	. . .	. . .	. . .
Other sectors	4 746	. . .	. . .	. . .	. . .	. . .	. . .	. . .	. . .
of which: Short-term	4 748	. . .	. . .	. . .	. . .	. . .	. . .	. . .	. . .
Liabilities	4 753	**–124.7**	**–179.1**	**–267.5**	**–177.1**	**–212.6**	**. . .**	**. . .**	**. . .**
Trade credits	4 756	. . .	. . .	. . .	. . .	. . .	. . .	. . .	. . .
General government	4 757	. . .	. . .	. . .	. . .	. . .	. . .	. . .	. . .
of which: Short-term	4 759	. . .	. . .	. . .	. . .	. . .	. . .	. . .	. . .
Other sectors	4 760	. . .	. . .	. . .	. . .	. . .	. . .	. . .	. . .
of which: Short-term	4 762	. . .	. . .	. . .	. . .	. . .	. . .	. . .	. . .
Loans	4 764	60.8	48.0	46.2	26.2	–4.9	. . .	. . .	. . .
Monetary authorities	4 765	17.9	12.2	10.9	12.0	–6.9	. . .	. . .	. . .
of which: Use of Fund credit and loans from the Fund	4 766	*17.9*	*12.2*	*10.9*	*12.0*	*–6.9*	. . .	. . .	. . .
of which: Short-term	4 768	. . .	. . .	. . .	. . .	. . .	. . .	. . .	. . .
General government	4 769	25.2	32.9	39.7	23.1	10.1	. . .	. . .	. . .
of which: Short-term	4 771	. . .	. . .	. . .	. . .	. . .	. . .	. . .	. . .
Banks	4 772	. . .	. . .	. . .	. . .	. . .	. . .	. . .	. . .
of which: Short-term	4 774	. . .	. . .	. . .	. . .	. . .	. . .	. . .	. . .
Other sectors	4 775	17.7	2.8	–4.4	–8.8	–8.1	. . .	. . .	. . .
of which: Short-term	4 777	. . .	. . .	. . .	. . .	. . .	. . .	. . .	. . .
Currency and deposits	4 780	. . .	. . .	. . .	. . .	. . .	. . .	. . .	. . .
Monetary authorities	4 781	. . .	. . .	. . .	. . .	. . .	. . .	. . .	. . .
General government	4 782	. . .	. . .	. . .	. . .	. . .	. . .	. . .	. . .
Banks	4 783	. . .	. . .	. . .	. . .	. . .	. . .	. . .	. . .
Other sectors	4 784	. . .	. . .	. . .	. . .	. . .	. . .	. . .	. . .
Other liabilities	4 786	–185.5	–227.1	–313.6	–203.3	–207.7	. . .	. . .	. . .
Monetary authorities	4 787	. . .	. . .	. . .	. . .	. . .	. . .	. . .	. . .
of which: Short-term	4 789	. . .	. . .	. . .	. . .	. . .	. . .	. . .	. . .
General government	4 790	. . .	. . .	. . .	. . .	. . .	. . .	. . .	. . .
of which: Short-term	4 792	. . .	. . .	. . .	. . .	. . .	. . .	. . .	. . .
Banks	4 793	. . .	. . .	. . .	. . .	. . .	. . .	. . .	. . .
of which: Short-term	4 795	. . .	. . .	. . .	. . .	. . .	. . .	. . .	. . .
Other sectors	4 796	–185.5	–227.1	–313.6	–203.3	–207.7	. . .	. . .	. . .
of which: Short-term	4 798	*–185.5*	*–227.1*	*–313.6*	*–203.3*	*–207.7*	. . .	. . .	. . .
E. RESERVE ASSETS	4 802	46.9	–42.9	–58.3	–58.8	–46.3	. . .	. . .	. . .
Monetary gold	4 812	. . .	. . .	. . .	. . .	. . .	. . .	. . .	. . .
Special drawing rights	4 811	.1	–.1	–1.4	1.0	.3	. . .	. . .	. . .
Reserve position in the Fund	4 810	. . .	. . .	. . .	. . .	. . .	. . .	. . .	. . .
Foreign exchange	4 803	46.8	–42.8	–56.9	–59.8	–46.6	. . .	. . .	. . .
Other claims	4 813	. . .	. . .	. . .	. . .	. . .	. . .	. . .	. . .
NET ERRORS AND OMISSIONS	4 998	**–23.5**	**–18.1**	**–1.0**	**–3.0**	**–8.1**	**. . .**	**. . .**	**. . .**

Table 1. ANALYTIC PRESENTATION, 1994–2001
(Millions of U.S. dollars)

	Code			1994	1995	1996	1997	1998	1999	2000	2001
A. Current Account [1]	4	993	Z.	**–232.1**	**–21.9**	**34.0**	**–88.9**	**3.3**	**–131.1**	**–33.3**	**. . .**
Goods: exports f.o.b	2	100	. .	1,376.9	1,571.7	1,810.6	1,600.1	1,669.3	1,589.2	1,559.4	. . .
Goods: imports f.o.b	3	100	. .	–1,773.9	–1,812.2	–2,136.3	–2,036.1	–1,933.3	–2,107.9	–1,953.3	. . .
Balance on Goods	4	100	. .	*–397.0*	*–240.5*	*–325.7*	*–436.0*	*–264.0*	*–518.7*	*–393.9*	. . .
Services: credit	2	200	. .	632.7	777.7	960.8	893.7	916.9	1,035.6	1,071.0	. . .
Services: debit	3	200	. .	–546.4	–641.3	–672.9	–656.3	–718.0	–728.1	–746.0	. . .
Balance on Goods and Services	4	991	. .	*–310.6*	*–104.2*	*–37.9*	*–198.6*	*–65.1*	*–211.2*	*–69.0*	. . .
Income: credit	2	300	. .	31.7	52.2	31.1	47.0	47.8	35.1	36.0	. . .
Income: debit	3	300	. .	–56.4	–71.3	–75.1	–64.6	–74.4	–58.6	–64.1	. . .
Balance on Goods, Services, and Income	4	992	. .	*–335.3*	*–123.3*	*–81.8*	*–216.3*	*–91.7*	*–234.8*	*–97.1*	. . .
Current transfers: credit	2	379	Z.	129.6	146.8	182.8	206.4	186.8	196.4	167.6	. . .
Current transfers: debit	3	379	. .	–26.3	–45.4	–67.0	–79.0	–91.8	–92.7	–103.8	. . .
B. Capital Account [1]	4	994	Z.	**–1.3**	**–1.1**	**–.8**	**–.5**	**–.8**	**–.5**	**–.6**	**. . .**
Capital account: credit	2	994	Z.	. . .	. . .	. . .	. . .	. . .	. . .	. . .	. . .
Capital account: debit	3	994	. .	–1.3	–1.1	–.8	–.5	–.8	–.5	–.6	. . .
Total, Groups A Plus B	4	981	. .	*–233.4*	*–22.9*	*33.2*	*–89.5*	*2.5*	*–131.5*	*–33.9*	. . .
C. Financial Account [1]	4	995	W.	**41.4**	**25.1**	**91.9**	**–18.6**	**–26.0**	**134.0**	**182.0**	**. . .**
Direct investment abroad	4	505	. .	–1.1	–3.6	–2.7	–3.2	–13.7	–6.4	–13.0	. . .
Direct investment in Mauritius	4	555	Z.	20.0	18.7	36.7	55.3	12.2	49.4	265.6	. . .
Portfolio investment assets	4	602	. .	–.3	. . .	–2.0	–96.8	43.6	59.1	23.1	. . .
Equity securities	4	610	. .	. . .	. . .	. . .	. . .	–3.3	59.1	23.1	. . .
Debt securities	4	619	. .	–.3	. . .	–2.0	–96.8	46.9	. . .	. . .	. . .
Portfolio investment liabilities	4	652	Z.	2.1	175.9	36.8	30.6	–28.7	–61.4	–143.1	. . .
Equity securities	4	660	. .	2.1	22.0	36.8	30.6	5.0	–61.4	–143.1	. . .
Debt securities	4	669	Z.	. . .	154.0	. . .	. . .	–33.7	. . .	. . .	. . .
Financial derivatives	4	910	. .	. . .	. . .	. . .	. . .	. . .	. . .	. . .	. . .
Financial derivatives assets	4	900	. .	. . .	. . .	. . .	. . .	. . .	. . .	. . .	. . .
Financial derivatives liabilities	4	905	. .	. . .	. . .	. . .	. . .	. . .	. . .	. . .	. . .
Other investment assets	4	703	. .	–64.6	–136.4	17.9	–115.7	–66.7	–245.9	–288.6	. . .
Monetary authorities	4	701	. .	. . .	. . .	. . .	. . .	. . .	. . .	. . .	. . .
General government	4	704	. .	. . .	. . .	. . .	. . .	. . .	. . .	. . .	. . .
Banks	4	705	. .	11.5	–85.2	–3.9	–121.2	–69.1	–32.9	–51.5	. . .
Other sectors	4	728	. .	–53.1	–51.2	21.8	5.5	2.4	–213.1	–237.0	. . .
Other investment liabilities	4	753	W.	85.2	–29.5	5.1	111.2	27.3	339.4	337.9	. . .
Monctary authoritics	4	753	WA	. . .	. . .	. . .	. . .	. . .	. . .	. . .	. . .
General government	4	753	ZB	–14.1	–18.8	–20.4	9.0	–14.2	–11.4	–22.7	. . .
Banks	4	753	ZC	9.2	27.7	–6.9	–10.1	96.4	–20.4	13.7	. . .
Other sectors	4	753	ZD	90.1	–38.5	32.5	112.3	–54.9	371.2	346.8	. . .
Total, Groups A Through C	4	983	. .	*–192.0*	*2.1*	*125.1*	*–108.0*	*–23.5*	*2.5*	*148.1*	. . .
D. Net Errors and Omissions	4	998	. .	**148.5**	**106.7**	**–76.8**	**73.4**	**–41.9**	**187.3**	**82.5**	**. . .**
Total, Groups A Through D	4	984	. .	*–43.5*	*108.8*	*48.3*	*–34.6*	*–65.4*	*189.7*	*230.6*	. . .
E. Reserves and Related Items	4	802	A.	**43.5**	**–108.8**	**–48.3**	**34.6**	**65.4**	**–189.7**	**–230.6**	**. . .**
Reserve assets	4	802	. .	43.5	–108.8	–48.3	34.6	65.4	–189.7	–230.6	. . .
Use of Fund credit and loans	4	766	. .	. . .	. . .	. . .	. . .	. . .	. . .	. . .	. . .
Exceptional financing	4	920	. .	. . .	. . .	. . .	. . .	. . .	. . .	. . .	. . .
Conversion rates: Mauritian rupees per U.S. dollar	0	101	. .	**17.960**	**17.386**	**17.948**	**21.057**	**23.993**	**25.186**	**26.250**	**29.129**

[1] Excludes components that have been classified in the categories of Group E.

Table 2. STANDARD PRESENTATION, 1994–2001
(Millions of U.S. dollars)

	Code	1994	1995	1996	1997	1998	1999	2000	2001
CURRENT ACCOUNT	4 993 . .	**–232.1**	**–21.9**	**34.0**	**–88.9**	**3.3**	**–131.1**	**–33.3**	**. . .**
A. GOODS	4 100 . .	–397.0	–240.5	–325.7	–436.0	–264.0	–518.7	–393.9	. . .
Credit	2 100 . .	**1,376.9**	**1,571.7**	**1,810.6**	**1,600.1**	**1,669.3**	**1,589.2**	**1,559.4**	**. . .**
General merchandise: exports f.o.b.	2 110 . .	1,343.5	1,538.9	1,775.1	1,568.0	1,639.2	1,554.8	1,492.3	. . .
Goods for processing: exports f.o.b.	2 150 . .	. . .	. . .	. . .	. . .	. . .	. . .	. . .	. . .
Repairs on goods	2 160 . .	. . .	. . .	. . .	. . .	. . .	. . .	. . .	. . .
Goods procured in ports by carriers	2 170 . .	33.4	32.8	35.4	32.1	30.1	34.3	67.1	. . .
Nonmonetary gold	2 180 . .	. . .	. . .	. . .	. . .	. . .	. . .	. . .	. . .
Debit	3 100 . .	**–1,773.9**	**–1,812.2**	**–2,136.3**	**–2,036.1**	**–1,933.3**	**–2,107.9**	**–1,953.3**	**. . .**
General merchandise: imports f.o.b.	3 110 . .	–1,759.5	–1,797.2	–2,117.3	–2,015.5	–1,916.1	–2,091.0	–1,926.8	. . .
Goods for processing: imports f.o.b.	3 150 . .	. . .	. . .	. . .	. . .	. . .	. . .	. . .	. . .
Repairs on goods	3 160 . .	. . .	. . .	. . .	. . .	. . .	. . .	. . .	. . .
Goods procured in ports by carriers	3 170 . .	–14.4	–15.1	–19.0	–20.7	–17.2	–16.9	–26.5	. . .
Nonmonetary gold	3 180 . .	. . .	. . .	. . .	. . .	. . .	. . .	. . .	. . .
B. SERVICES	4 200 . .	86.4	136.4	287.8	237.4	198.9	307.5	325.0	. . .
Total credit	2 200 . .	*632.7*	*777.7*	*960.8*	*893.7*	*916.9*	*1,035.6*	*1,071.0*	. . .
Total debit	3 200 . .	*–546.4*	*–641.3*	*–672.9*	*–656.3*	*–718.0*	*–728.1*	*–746.0*	. . .
Transportation services, credit	2 205 . .	**170.7**	**199.7**	**217.6**	**210.1**	**200.2**	**203.7**	**223.2**	**. . .**
Passenger	2 850 . .	*157.3*	*185.5*	*200.5*	*188.1*	*176.3*	*175.1*	*189.6*	. . .
Freight	2 851 . .	*.8*	*.9*	*1.0*	*1.0*	*1.3*	*1.0*	*8.4*	. . .
Other	2 852 . .	*12.5*	*13.3*	*16.0*	*20.9*	*22.6*	*27.7*	*25.1*	. . .
Sea transport, passenger	2 207 . .	. . .	. . .	. . .	. . .	. . .	. . .	. . .	. . .
Sea transport, freight	2 208 . .	. . .	. . .	. . .	. . .	. . .	. . .	. . .	. . .
Sea transport, other	2 209 . .	. . .	. . .	. . .	. . .	. . .	. . .	. . .	. . .
Air transport, passenger	2 211 . .	. . .	. . .	. . .	. . .	. . .	. . .	. . .	. . .
Air transport, freight	2 212 . .	. . .	. . .	. . .	. . .	. . .	. . .	. . .	. . .
Air transport, other	2 213 . .	. . .	. . .	. . .	. . .	. . .	. . .	. . .	. . .
Other transport, passenger	2 215 . .	. . .	. . .	. . .	. . .	. . .	. . .	. . .	. . .
Other transport, freight	2 216 . .	. . .	. . .	. . .	. . .	. . .	. . .	. . .	. . .
Other transport, other	2 217 . .	. . .	. . .	. . .	. . .	. . .	. . .	. . .	. . .
Transportation services, debit	3 205 . .	**–233.5**	**–251.7**	**–249.8**	**–245.4**	**–244.5**	**–251.0**	**–246.2**	**. . .**
Passenger	3 850 . .	*–23.7*	*–25.0*	*–26.1*	*–20.8*	*–17.9*	*–22.6*	*–20.9*	. . .
Freight	3 851 . .	*–135.6*	*–149.3*	*–151.7*	*–143.0*	*–136.5*	*–135.5*	*–125.9*	. . .
Other	3 852 . .	*–74.2*	*–77.4*	*–72.0*	*–81.6*	*–90.1*	*–92.9*	*–99.4*	. . .
Sea transport, passenger	3 207 . .	. . .	. . .	. . .	. . .	. . .	. . .	. . .	. . .
Sea transport, freight	3 208 . .	. . .	. . .	. . .	. . .	. . .	. . .	. . .	. . .
Sea transport, other	3 209 . .	. . .	. . .	. . .	. . .	. . .	. . .	. . .	. . .
Air transport, passenger	3 211 . .	. . .	. . .	. . .	. . .	. . .	. . .	. . .	. . .
Air transport, freight	3 212 . .	. . .	. . .	. . .	. . .	. . .	. . .	. . .	. . .
Air transport, other	3 213 . .	. . .	. . .	. . .	. . .	. . .	. . .	. . .	. . .
Other transport, passenger	3 215 . .	. . .	. . .	. . .	. . .	. . .	. . .	. . .	. . .
Other transport, freight	3 216 . .	. . .	. . .	. . .	. . .	. . .	. . .	. . .	. . .
Other transport, other	3 217 . .	. . .	. . .	. . .	. . .	. . .	. . .	. . .	. . .
Travel, credit	2 236 . .	**357.2**	**429.8**	**504.2**	**478.1**	**495.6**	**542.7**	**542.0**	**. . .**
Business travel	2 237 . .	. . .	. . .	. . .	. . .	. . .	. . .	. . .	. . .
Personal travel	2 240 . .	. . .	. . .	. . .	. . .	. . .	. . .	. . .	. . .
Travel, debit	3 236 . .	**–142.9**	**–159.0**	**–178.8**	**–173.1**	**–184.6**	**–187.1**	**–181.6**	**. . .**
Business travel	3 237 . .	. . .	. . .	. . .	. . .	. . .	. . .	. . .	. . .
Personal travel	3 240 . .	. . .	. . .	. . .	. . .	. . .	. . .	. . .	. . .
Other services, credit	2 200 BA	**104.9**	**148.2**	**239.0**	**205.4**	**221.1**	**289.2**	**305.8**	**. . .**
Communications	2 245 . .	. . .	. . .	. . .	. . .	. . .	. . .	16.0	. . .
Construction	2 249 . .	. . .	. . .	. . .	. . .	. . .	. . .	9.3	. . .
Insurance	2 253 . .	.1	.1	.1	.1	.1	46.1	43.0	. . .
Financial	2 260 . .	. . .	. . .	. . .	. . .	. . .	. . .	21.4	. . .
Computer and information	2 262 . .	. . .	. . .	. . .	. . .	. . .	. . .	2.8	. . .
Royalties and licence fees	2 266 . .	. . .	. . .	. . .	. . .	. . .	. . .	. . .	. . .
Other business services	2 268 . .	101.1	143.1	233.5	200.9	214.7	237.5	207.3	. . .
Personal, cultural, and recreational	2 287 . .	. . .	. . .	. . .	. . .	. . .	. . .	2.0	. . .
Government, n.i.e.	2 291 . .	3.7	5.0	5.4	4.5	6.3	5.6	4.0	. . .
Other services, debit	3 200 BA	**–170.0**	**–230.6**	**–244.4**	**–237.7**	**–288.9**	**–290.0**	**–318.2**	**. . .**
Communications	3 245 . .	. . .	. . .	. . .	. . .	. . .	. . .	–16.2	. . .
Construction	3 249 . .	. . .	. . .	. . .	. . .	. . .	. . .	–.4	. . .
Insurance	3 253 . .	–22.7	–28.9	–25.1	–24.2	–26.5	–26.8	–44.3	. . .
Financial	3 260 . .	. . .	. . .	. . .	. . .	. . .	. . .	–21.5	. . .
Computer and information	3 262 . .	. . .	. . .	. . .	. . .	. . .	. . .	–5.3	. . .
Royalties and licence fees	3 266 . .	. . .	. . .	. . .	. . .	. . .	. . .	–1.2	. . .
Other business services	3 268 . .	–126.8	–190.9	–212.6	–213.6	–250.5	–253.9	–211.1	. . .
Personal, cultural, and recreational	3 287 . .	. . .	. . .	. . .	. . .	. . .	. . .	–4.1	. . .
Government, n.i.e.	3 291 . .	–20.4	–10.8	–6.7	. . .	–11.9	–9.4	–14.1	. . .

Table 2 (Continued). STANDARD PRESENTATION, 1994–2001
(Millions of U.S. dollars)

	Code	1994	1995	1996	1997	1998	1999	2000	2001
C. INCOME	4 300 . .	–24.7	–19.1	–44.0	–17.7	–26.5	–23.6	–28.1	. . .
Total credit	2 300 . .	*31.7*	*52.2*	*31.1*	*47.0*	*47.8*	*35.1*	*36.0*	. . .
Total debit	3 300 . .	*–56.4*	*–71.3*	*–75.1*	*–64.6*	*–74.4*	*–58.6*	*–64.1*	. . .
Compensation of employees, credit	2 310 . .	. . .	. . .	. . .	. . .	. . .	. . .	. . .	. . .
Compensation of employees, debit	3 310 . .	. . .	. . .	. . .	. . .	. . .	. . .	. . .	. . .
Investment income, credit	2 320 . .	**31.7**	**52.2**	**31.1**	**47.0**	**47.8**	**35.1**	**36.0**	. . .
Direct investment income	2 330 . .	1.1	1.6	1.9	1.9	2.1	.5	.9	. . .
Dividends and distributed branch profits	2 332 . .	1.1	1.6	1.9	1.9	2.1	.5	.9	. . .
Reinvested earnings and undistributed branch profits	2 333 . .	. . .	. . .	. . .	. . .	. . .	. . .	. . .	. . .
Income on debt (interest)	2 334 . .	. . .	. . .	. . .	. . .	. . .	. . .	. . .	. . .
Portfolio investment income	2 339 . .	. . .	. . .	. . .	. . .	. . .	.6	1.4	. . .
Income on equity	2 340 . .	. . .	. . .	. . .	. . .	. . .	.6	1.4	. . .
Income on bonds and notes	2 350 . .	. . .	. . .	. . .	. . .	. . .	. . .	. . .	. . .
Income on money market instruments	2 360 . .	. . .	. . .	. . .	. . .	. . .	. . .	. . .	. . .
Other investment income	2 370 . .	30.6	50.7	29.3	45.1	45.7	33.9	33.6	. . .
Investment income, debit	3 320 . .	**–56.4**	**–71.3**	**–75.1**	**–64.6**	**–74.4**	**–58.6**	**–64.1**	. . .
Direct investment income	3 330 . .	–11.6	–15.5	–9.7	–7.5	–13.4	–4.4	–8.1	. . .
Dividends and distributed branch profits	3 332 . .	–11.6	–15.5	–9.7	–7.5	–13.4	–4.4	–8.1	. . .
Reinvested earnings and undistributed branch profits	3 333 . .	. . .	. . .	. . .	. . .	. . .	. . .	. . .	. . .
Income on debt (interest)	3 334 . .	. . .	. . .	. . .	. . .	. . .	. . .	. . .	. . .
Portfolio investment income	3 339 . .	. . .	. . .	. . .	. . .	. . .	–.8	–3.8	. . .
Income on equity	3 340 . .	. . .	. . .	. . .	. . .	. . .	–.8	–3.8	. . .
Income on bonds and notes	3 350 . .	. . .	. . .	. . .	. . .	. . .	. . .	. . .	. . .
Income on money market instruments	3 360 . .	. . .	. . .	. . .	. . .	. . .	. . .	. . .	. . .
Other investment income	3 370 . .	–44.8	–55.8	–65.4	–57.1	–61.0	–53.5	–52.2	. . .
D. CURRENT TRANSFERS	4 379 . .	103.2	101.4	115.8	127.4	94.9	103.7	63.8	. . .
Credit	2 379 . .	**129.6**	**146.8**	**182.8**	**206.4**	**186.8**	**196.4**	**167.6**	. . .
General government	2 380 . .	12.0	9.6	9.0	8.1	6.4	11.6	8.0	. . .
Other sectors	2 390 . .	117.5	137.2	173.8	198.3	180.4	184.7	159.6	. . .
Workers' remittances	2 391 . .	. . .	. . .	. . .	. . .	. . .	. . .	. . .	. . .
Other current transfers	2 392 . .	117.5	137.2	173.8	198.3	180.4	184.7	159.6	. . .
Debit	3 379 . .	**–26.3**	**–45.4**	**–67.0**	**–79.0**	**–91.8**	**–92.7**	**–103.8**	. . .
General government	3 380 . .	–3.3	–3.3	–4.2	–1.0	–1.0	–.8	–.8	. . .
Other sectors	3 390 . .	–23.0	–42.1	–62.7	–78.0	–90.8	–91.8	–103.0	. . .
Workers' remittances	3 391 . .	. . .	. . .	. . .	. . .	. . .	. . .	. . .	. . .
Other current transfers	3 392 . .	–23.0	–42.1	–62.7	–78.0	–90.8	–91.8	–103.0	. . .
CAPITAL AND FINANCIAL ACCOUNT	4 996 . .	**83.5**	**–84.8**	**42.8**	**15.5**	**38.6**	**–56.2**	**–49.2**	. . .
CAPITAL ACCOUNT	4 994 . .	**–1.3**	**–1.1**	**–.8**	**–.5**	**–.8**	**–.5**	**–.6**	. . .
Total credit	2 994 . .	. . .	. . .	. . .	. . .	. . .	. . .	. . .	. . .
Total debit	3 994 . .	*–1.3*	*–1.1*	*–.8*	*–.5*	*–.8*	*–.5*	*–.6*	. . .
Capital transfers, credit	2 400 . .	. . .	. . .	. . .	. . .	. . .	. . .	. . .	. . .
General government	2 401 . .	. . .	. . .	. . .	. . .	. . .	. . .	. . .	. . .
Debt forgiveness	2 402 . .	. . .	. . .	. . .	. . .	. . .	. . .	. . .	. . .
Other capital transfers	2 410 . .	. . .	. . .	. . .	. . .	. . .	. . .	. . .	. . .
Other sectors	2 430 . .	. . .	. . .	. . .	. . .	. . .	. . .	. . .	. . .
Migrants' transfers	2 431 . .	. . .	. . .	. . .	. . .	. . .	. . .	. . .	. . .
Debt forgiveness	2 432 . .	. . .	. . .	. . .	. . .	. . .	. . .	. . .	. . .
Other capital transfers	2 440 . .	. . .	. . .	. . .	. . .	. . .	. . .	. . .	. . .
Capital transfers, debit	3 400 . .	**–1.3**	**–1.1**	**–.8**	**–.5**	**–.8**	**–.5**	**–.6**	. . .
General government	3 401 . .	. . .	. . .	. . .	. . .	. . .	. . .	. . .	. . .
Debt forgiveness	3 402 . .	. . .	. . .	. . .	. . .	. . .	. . .	. . .	. . .
Other capital transfers	3 410 . .	. . .	. . .	. . .	. . .	. . .	. . .	. . .	. . .
Other sectors	3 430 . .	–1.3	–1.1	–.8	–.5	–.8	–.5	–.6	. . .
Migrants' transfers	3 431 . .	–1.3	–1.1	–.8	–.5	–.8	–.5	–.6	. . .
Debt forgiveness	3 432 . .	. . .	. . .	. . .	. . .	. . .	. . .	. . .	. . .
Other capital transfers	3 440 . .	. . .	. . .	. . .	. . .	. . .	. . .	. . .	. . .
Nonproduced nonfinancial assets, credit	2 480 . .	. . .	. . .	. . .	. . .	. . .	. . .	. . .	. . .
Nonproduced nonfinancial assets, debit	3 480 . .	. . .	. . .	. . .	. . .	. . .	. . .	. . .	. . .

Table 2 (Continued). STANDARD PRESENTATION, 1994–2001
(Millions of U.S. dollars)

	Code	1994	1995	1996	1997	1998	1999	2000	2001
FINANCIAL ACCOUNT	4 995	**84.9**	**–83.7**	**43.6**	**16.0**	**39.4**	**–55.7**	**–48.6**	**. . .**
A. DIRECT INVESTMENT	4 500	18.9	15.1	34.0	52.1	–1.5	42.9	252.7	. . .
Direct investment abroad	4 505	**–1.1**	**–3.6**	**–2.7**	**–3.2**	**–13.7**	**–6.4**	**–13.0**	**. . .**
Equity capital	4 510	–1.1	–3.6	–2.7	–3.2	–13.7	. . .	. . .	. . .
Claims on affiliated enterprises	4 515	. . .	. . .	. . .	. . .	. . .	. . .	. . .	. . .
Liabilities to affiliated enterprises	4 520	. . .	. . .	. . .	. . .	. . .	. . .	. . .	. . .
Reinvested earnings	4 525	. . .	. . .	. . .	. . .	. . .	. . .	. . .	. . .
Other capital	4 530	. . .	. . .	. . .	. . .	. . .	–6.4	–13.0	. . .
Claims on affiliated enterprises	4 535	. . .	. . .	. . .	. . .	. . .	. . .	. . .	. . .
Liabilities to affiliated enterprises	4 540	. . .	. . .	. . .	. . .	. . .	. . .	. . .	. . .
Direct investment in Mauritius	4 555	**20.0**	**18.7**	**36.7**	**55.3**	**12.2**	**49.4**	**265.6**	**. . .**
Equity capital	4 560	20.0	18.7	36.7	55.3	12.2	49.4	265.6	. . .
Claims on direct investors	4 565	. . .	. . .	. . .	. . .	. . .	. . .	. . .	. . .
Liabilities to direct investors	4 570	. . .	. . .	. . .	. . .	. . .	. . .	. . .	. . .
Reinvested earnings	4 575	. . .	. . .	. . .	. . .	. . .	. . .	. . .	. . .
Other capital	4 580	. . .	. . .	. . .	. . .	. . .	. . .	. . .	. . .
Claims on direct investors	4 585	. . .	. . .	. . .	. . .	. . .	. . .	. . .	. . .
Liabilities to direct investors	4 590	. . .	. . .	. . .	. . .	. . .	. . .	. . .	. . .
B. PORTFOLIO INVESTMENT	4 600	1.8	175.9	34.8	–66.2	14.9	–2.3	–120.0	. . .
Assets	4 602	**–.3**	**. . .**	**–2.0**	**–96.8**	**43.6**	**59.1**	**23.1**	**. . .**
Equity securities	4 610	. . .	. . .	. . .	. . .	–3.3	59.1	23.1	. . .
Monetary authorities	4 611	. . .	. . .	. . .	. . .	. . .	. . .	. . .	. . .
General government	4 612	. . .	. . .	. . .	. . .	. . .	. . .	. . .	. . .
Banks	4 613	. . .	. . .	. . .	. . .	. . .	. . .	. . .	. . .
Other sectors	4 614	. . .	. . .	. . .	. . .	–3.3	59.1	23.1	. . .
Debt securities	4 619	–.3	. . .	–2.0	–96.8	46.9	. . .	. . .	. . .
Bonds and notes	4 620	–.3	. . .	–2.0	–96.8	46.9	. . .	. . .	. . .
Monetary authorities	4 621	. . .	. . .	. . .	. . .	. . .	. . .	. . .	. . .
General government	4 622	. . .	. . .	. . .	. . .	. . .	. . .	. . .	. . .
Banks	4 623	. . .	. . .	. . .	. . .	. . .	. . .	. . .	. . .
Other sectors	4 624	. . .	. . .	. . .	. . .	. . .	. . .	. . .	. . .
Money market instruments	4 630	. . .	. . .	. . .	. . .	. . .	. . .	. . .	. . .
Monetary authorities	4 631	. . .	. . .	. . .	. . .	. . .	. . .	. . .	. . .
General government	4 632	. . .	. . .	. . .	. . .	. . .	. . .	. . .	. . .
Banks	4 633	. . .	. . .	. . .	. . .	. . .	. . .	. . .	. . .
Other sectors	4 634	. . .	. . .	. . .	. . .	. . .	. . .	. . .	. . .
Liabilities	4 652	**2.1**	**175.9**	**36.8**	**30.6**	**–28.7**	**–61.4**	**–143.1**	**. . .**
Equity securities	4 660	2.1	22.0	36.8	30.6	5.0	–61.4	–143.1	. . .
Banks	4 663	. . .	. . .	. . .	. . .	. . .	. . .	. . .	. . .
Other sectors	4 664	. . .	22.0	36.8	30.6	5.0	–61.4	–143.1	. . .
Debt securities	4 669	. . .	154.0	. . .	. . .	–33.7	. . .	. . .	. . .
Bonds and notes	4 670	. . .	154.0	. . .	. . .	–33.7	. . .	. . .	. . .
Monetary authorities	4 671	. . .	. . .	. . .	. . .	. . .	. . .	. . .	. . .
General government	4 672	. . .	154.0	. . .	. . .	–33.7	. . .	. . .	. . .
Banks	4 673	. . .	. . .	. . .	. . .	. . .	. . .	. . .	. . .
Other sectors	4 674	. . .	. . .	. . .	. . .	. . .	. . .	. . .	. . .
Money market instruments	4 680	. . .	. . .	. . .	. . .	. . .	. . .	. . .	. . .
Monetary authorities	4 681	. . .	. . .	. . .	. . .	. . .	. . .	. . .	. . .
General government	4 682	. . .	. . .	. . .	. . .	. . .	. . .	. . .	. . .
Banks	4 683	. . .	. . .	. . .	. . .	. . .	. . .	. . .	. . .
Other sectors	4 684	. . .	. . .	. . .	. . .	. . .	. . .	. . .	. . .
C. FINANCIAL DERIVATIVES	4 910	. . .	. . .	. . .	. . .	. . .	. . .	. . .	. . .
Monetary authorities	4 911	. . .	. . .	. . .	. . .	. . .	. . .	. . .	. . .
General government	4 912	. . .	. . .	. . .	. . .	. . .	. . .	. . .	. . .
Banks	4 913	. . .	. . .	. . .	. . .	. . .	. . .	. . .	. . .
Other sectors	4 914	. . .	. . .	. . .	. . .	. . .	. . .	. . .	. . .
Assets	4 900	**. . .**	**. . .**	**. . .**	**. . .**	**. . .**	**. . .**	**. . .**	**. . .**
Monetary authorities	4 901	. . .	. . .	. . .	. . .	. . .	. . .	. . .	. . .
General government	4 902	. . .	. . .	. . .	. . .	. . .	. . .	. . .	. . .
Banks	4 903	. . .	. . .	. . .	. . .	. . .	. . .	. . .	. . .
Other sectors	4 904	. . .	. . .	. . .	. . .	. . .	. . .	. . .	. . .
Liabilities	4 905	**. . .**	**. . .**	**. . .**	**. . .**	**. . .**	**. . .**	**. . .**	**. . .**
Monetary authorities	4 906	. . .	. . .	. . .	. . .	. . .	. . .	. . .	. . .
General government	4 907	. . .	. . .	. . .	. . .	. . .	. . .	. . .	. . .
Banks	4 908	. . .	. . .	. . .	. . .	. . .	. . .	. . .	. . .
Other sectors	4 909	. . .	. . .	. . .	. . .	. . .	. . .	. . .	. . .

Table 2 (Concluded). STANDARD PRESENTATION, 1994–2001
(Millions of U.S. dollars)

	Code	1994	1995	1996	1997	1998	1999	2000	2001
D. OTHER INVESTMENT	4 700 . .	20.6	–165.9	23.1	–4.5	–39.4	93.4	49.3	. . .
Assets	4 703 . .	**–64.6**	**–136.4**	**17.9**	**–115.7**	**–66.7**	**–245.9**	**–288.6**	**. . .**
Trade credits	4 706 . .	. . .	. . .	. . .	. . .	. . .	. . .	. . .	. . .
General government	4 707 . .	. . .	. . .	. . .	. . .	. . .	. . .	. . .	. . .
of which: Short-term	4 709 . .	. . .	. . .	. . .	. . .	. . .	. . .	. . .	. . .
Other sectors	4 710 . .	. . .	. . .	. . .	. . .	. . .	. . .	. . .	. . .
of which: Short-term	4 712 . .	. . .	. . .	. . .	. . .	. . .	. . .	. . .	. . .
Loans	4 714 . .	.2	–23.0	–12.5	4.3	2.4	23.0	26.6	. . .
Monetary authorities	4 715 . .	. . .	. . .	. . .	. . .	. . .	. . .	. . .	. . .
of which: Short-term	4 718 . .	. . .	. . .	. . .	. . .	. . .	. . .	. . .	. . .
General government	4 719 . .	. . .	. . .	. . .	. . .	. . .	. . .	. . .	. . .
of which: Short-term	4 721 . .	. . .	. . .	. . .	. . .	. . .	. . .	. . .	. . .
Banks	4 722 . .	. . .	. . .	. . .	. . .	. . .	. . .	. . .	. . .
of which: Short-term	4 724 . .	. . .	. . .	. . .	. . .	. . .	. . .	. . .	. . .
Other sectors	4 725 . .	.2	–23.0	–12.5	4.3	2.4	23.0	26.6	. . .
of which: Short-term	4 727 . .	*.2*	*–23.0*	*–12.5*	*4.3*	*2.4*	*23.0*	*26.6*	. . .
Currency and deposits	4 730 . .	–49.2	–98.1	28.6	–120.1	–69.1	–268.9	–315.2	. . .
Monetary authorities	4 731 . .	. . .	. . .	. . .	. . .	. . .	. . .	. . .	. . .
General government	4 732 . .	. . .	. . .	. . .	. . .	. . .	. . .	. . .	. . .
Banks	4 733 . .	–11.5	–85.2	–3.9	–121.2	–69.1	–32.9	–51.5	. . .
Other sectors	4 734 . .	–37.7	–12.8	32.5	1.1	. . .	–236.0	–263.6	. . .
Other assets	4 736 . .	–15.5	–15.4	1.8	. . .	. . .	. . .	. . .	. . .
Monetary authorities	4 737 . .	. . .	. . .	. . .	. . .	. . .	. . .	. . .	. . .
of which: Short-term	4 739 . .	. . .	. . .	. . .	. . .	. . .	. . .	. . .	. . .
General government	4 740 . .	. . .	. . .	. . .	. . .	. . .	. . .	. . .	. . .
of which: Short-term	4 742 . .	. . .	. . .	. . .	. . .	. . .	. . .	. . .	. . .
Banks	4 743 . .	. . .	. . .	. . .	. . .	. . .	. . .	. . .	. . .
of which: Short-term	4 745 . .	. . .	. . .	. . .	. . .	. . .	. . .	. . .	. . .
Other sectors	4 746 . .	–15.5	–15.4	1.8	. . .	. . .	. . .	. . .	. . .
of which: Short-term	4 748 . .	. . .	. . .	. . .	. . .	. . .	. . .	. . .	. . .
Liabilities	4 753 . .	**85.2**	**–29.5**	**5.1**	**111.2**	**27.3**	**339.4**	**337.9**	**. . .**
Trade credits	4 756 . .	. . .	. . .	. . .	. . .	. . .	. . .	. . .	. . .
General government	4 757 . .	. . .	. . .	. . .	. . .	. . .	. . .	. . .	. . .
of which: Short-term	4 759 . .	. . .	. . .	. . .	. . .	. . .	. . .	. . .	. . .
Other sectors	4 760 . .	. . .	. . .	. . .	. . .	. . .	. . .	. . .	. . .
of which: Short-term	4 762 . .	. . .	. . .	. . .	. . .	. . .	. . .	. . .	. . .
Loans	4 764 . .	76.3	–57.2	12.0	121.3	–69.1	29.5	–1.8	. . .
Monetary authorities	4 765 . .	. . .	. . .	. . .	. . .	. . .	. . .	. . .	. . .
of which: Use of Fund credit and loans from the Fund	4 766 . .	. . .	. . .	. . .	. . .	. . .	. . .	. . .	. . .
of which: Short-term	4 768 . .	. . .	. . .	. . .	. . .	. . .	. . .	. . .	. . .
General government	4 769 . .	–14.1	–18.8	–20.4	9.0	–14.2	–11.4	–22.7	. . .
of which: Short-term	4 771 . .	. . .	. . .	. . .	. . .	. . .	. . .	. . .	. . .
Banks	4 772 . .	. . .	. . .	. . .	. . .	. . .	. . .	. . .	. . .
of which: Short-term	4 774 . .	. . .	. . .	. . .	. . .	. . .	. . .	. . .	. . .
Other sectors	4 775 . .	90.4	–38.5	32.5	112.3	–54.9	40.9	20.8	. . .
of which: Short-term	4 777 . .	. . .	. . .	. . .	. . .	. . .	. . .	. . .	. . .
Currency and deposits	4 780 . .	9.2	27.7	–6.9	–10.1	96.4	309.9	339.7	. . .
Monetary authorities	4 781 . .	. . .	. . .	. . .	. . .	. . .	. . .	. . .	. . .
General government	4 782 . .	. . .	. . .	. . .	. . .	. . .	. . .	. . .	. . .
Banks	4 783 . .	9.2	27.7	–6.9	–10.1	96.4	–20.4	13.7	. . .
Other sectors	4 784 . .	. . .	. . .	. . .	. . .	. . .	330.2	326.0	. . .
Other liabilities	4 786 . .	–.3	. . .	. . .	. . .	. . .	. . .	. . .	. . .
Monetary authorities	4 787 . .	. . .	. . .	. . .	. . .	. . .	. . .	. . .	. . .
of which: Short-term	4 789 . .	. . .	. . .	. . .	. . .	. . .	. . .	. . .	. . .
General government	4 790 . .	. . .	. . .	. . .	. . .	. . .	. . .	. . .	. . .
of which: Short-term	4 792 . .	. . .	. . .	. . .	. . .	. . .	. . .	. . .	. . .
Banks	4 793 . .	. . .	. . .	. . .	. . .	. . .	. . .	. . .	. . .
of which: Short-term	4 795 . .	. . .	. . .	. . .	. . .	. . .	. . .	. . .	. . .
Other sectors	4 796 . .	–.3	. . .	. . .	. . .	. . .	. . .	. . .	. . .
of which: Short-term	4 798 . .	*–.3*	. . .	. . .	. . .	. . .	. . .	. . .	. . .
E. RESERVE ASSETS	4 802 . .	43.5	–108.8	–48.3	34.6	65.4	–189.7	–230.6	. . .
Monetary gold	4 812 . .	. . .	. . .	. . .	. . .	. . .	. . .	. . .	. . .
Special drawing rights	4 811 . .	–.4	–.5	–.7	–.4	–.5	9.4	–.5	. . .
Reserve position in the Fund	4 810 . .	. . .	. . .	. . .	. . .	. . .	–9.8	. . .	. . .
Foreign exchange	4 803 . .	44.0	–108.3	–47.6	35.1	65.9	–189.3	–230.1	. . .
Other claims	4 813 . .	–.1	. . .	. . .	. . .	. . .	. . .	. . .	. . .
NET ERRORS AND OMISSIONS	4 998 . .	**148.5**	**106.7**	**–76.8**	**73.4**	**–41.9**	**187.3**	**82.5**	**. . .**

Part 3 of the *Yearbook* contains descriptions of the methodologies, compilation practices, and sources used to compile these data.

Table 3. INTERNATIONAL INVESTMENT POSITION (End–period stocks), 1994–2001

(Millions of U.S. dollars)

	Code		1994	1995	1996	1997	1998	1999	2000	2001
ASSETS	8 995	C.	...	...	...	...	...	...	...	...
Direct investment abroad	8 505	. .	**...**	**...**	**...**	**...**	**...**	**...**	**...**	**...**
Equity capital and reinvested earnings	8 506	. .	...	...	...	...	...	...	...	...
Claims on affiliated enterprises	8 507	. .	...	...	...	...	...	...	...	...
Liabilities to affiliated enterprises	8 508	. .	...	...	...	...	...	...	...	...
Other capital	8 530	. .	...	...	...	...	...	...	...	...
Claims on affiliated enterprises	8 535	. .	...	...	...	...	...	...	...	...
Liabilities to affiliated enterprises	8 540	. .	...	...	...	...	...	...	...	...
Portfolio investment	8 602	. .	**...**	**...**	**...**	**...**	**...**	**...**	**...**	**...**
Equity securities	8 610	. .	...	...	...	...	...	...	...	...
Monetary authorities	8 611	. .	...	...	...	...	...	...	...	...
General government	8 612	. .	...	...	...	...	...	...	...	...
Banks	8 613	. .	...	...	...	...	...	...	...	...
Other sectors	8 614	. .	...	...	...	...	...	...	...	...
Debt securities	8 619	. .	...	...	...	...	...	...	...	...
Bonds and notes	8 620	. .	...	...	...	...	...	...	...	...
Monetary authorities	8 621	. .	...	...	...	...	...	...	...	...
General government	8 622	. .	...	...	...	...	...	...	...	...
Banks	8 623	. .	...	...	...	...	...	...	...	...
Other sectors	8 624	. .	...	...	...	...	...	...	...	...
Money market instruments	8 630	. .	...	...	...	...	...	...	...	...
Monetary authorities	8 631	. .	...	...	...	...	...	...	...	...
General government	8 632	. .	...	...	...	...	...	...	...	...
Banks	8 633	. .	...	...	...	...	...	...	...	...
Other sectors	8 634	. .	...	...	...	...	...	...	...	...
Financial derivatives	8 900	. .	**...**	**...**	**...**	**...**	**...**	**...**	**...**	**...**
Monetary authorities	8 901	. .	...	...	...	...	...	...	...	...
General government	8 902	. .	...	...	...	...	...	...	...	...
Banks	8 903	. .	...	...	...	...	...	...	...	...
Other sectors	8 904	. .	...	...	...	...	...	...	...	...
Other investment	8 703	. .	**243.0**	**364.8**	**342.9**	**386.1**	**394.7**	**652.3**	**887.2**	**...**
Trade credits	8 706	. .	...	...	...	...	...	...	...	...
General government	8 707	. .	...	...	...	...	...	...	...	...
of which: Short-term	8 709	. .	...	...	...	...	...	...	...	...
Other sectors	8 710	. .	...	...	...	...	...	...	...	...
of which: Short-term	8 712	. .	...	...	...	...	...	...	...	...
Loans	8 714	. .	25.1	48.0	59.7	44.1	35.3	21.4	19.9	...
Monetary authorities	8 715	. .	...	...	...	...	...	...	...	...
of which: Short-term	8 718	. .	...	...	...	...	...	...	...	...
General government	8 719	. .	...	...	...	...	...	...	...	...
of which: Short-term	8 721	. .	...	...	...	...	...	...	...	...
Banks	8 722	. .	...	...	...	...	...	...	...	...
of which: Short-term	8 724	. .	...	...	...	...	...	...	...	...
Other sectors	8 725	. .	25.1	48.0	59.7	44.1	35.3	21.4	19.9	...
of which: Short-term	8 727	. .	*25.1*	*48.0*	*59.7*	*44.1*	*35.3*	*21.4*	*19.9*	...
Currency and deposits	8 730	. .	217.9	316.8	283.2	342.0	359.4	630.9	867.3	...
Monetary authorities	8 731	. .	...	...	...	...	...	...	...	...
General government	8 732	. .	...	...	...	...	...	...	...	...
Banks	8 733	. .	142.5	227.9	228.4	298.8	335.1	383.8	400.2	...
Other sectors	8 734	. .	75.4	88.9	54.9	43.2	24.3	247.1	467.1	...
Other assets	8 736	. .	...	...	...	...	...	...	...	...
Monetary authorities	8 737	. .	...	...	...	...	...	...	...	...
of which: Short-term	8 739	. .	...	...	...	...	...	...	...	...
General government	8 740	. .	...	...	...	...	...	...	...	...
of which: Short-term	8 742	. .	...	...	...	...	...	...	...	...
Banks	8 743	. .	...	...	...	...	...	...	...	...
of which: Short-term	8 745	. .	...	...	...	...	...	...	...	...
Other sectors	8 746	. .	...	...	...	...	...	...	...	...
of which: Short-term	8 748	. .	...	...	...	...	...	...	...	...
Reserve assets	8 802	. .	**751.8**	**867.5**	**900.2**	**699.5**	**571.0**	**743.3**	**909.8**	**...**
Monetary gold	8 812	. .	4.0	4.1	4.0	6.2	11.9	12.3	12.3	...
Special drawing rights	8 811	. .	31.2	32.2	31.9	30.3	32.2	22.1	21.4	21.1
Reserve position in the Fund	8 810	. .	10.7	10.9	10.6	9.9	10.4	19.9	18.9	18.2
Foreign exchange	8 803	. .	705.8	820.2	853.7	653.0	516.5	689.1	857.2	...
Other claims	8 813	. .	.1	.1	.1	...	...	...	...	...

Table 3 (Concluded). INTERNATIONAL INVESTMENT POSITION (End–period stocks), 1994–2001
(Millions of U.S. dollars)

	Code	1994	1995	1996	1997	1998	1999	2000	2001
LIABILITIES	8 995 D.	...	...	...	...	...	...	...	...
Direct investment in Mauritius	8 555 . .	**...**	**...**	**...**	**...**	**...**	**...**	**...**	**...**
Equity capital and reinvested earnings	8 556 . .	...	...	...	...	...	...	...	...
Claims on direct investors	8 557 . .	...	...	...	...	...	...	...	...
Liabilities to direct investors	8 558 . .	...	...	...	...	...	...	...	...
Other capital	8 580 . .	...	...	...	...	...	...	...	...
Claims on direct investors	8 585 . .	...	...	...	...	...	...	...	...
Liabilities to direct investors	8 590 . .	...	...	...	...	...	...	...	...
Portfolio investment	8 652 . .	**...**	**156.3**	**167.2**	**150.9**	**117.7**	**117.8**	**...**	**...**
Equity securities	8 660 . .	...	...	...	...	...	...	...	...
Banks	8 663 . .	...	...	...	...	...	...	...	...
Other sectors	8 664 . .	...	...	...	...	...	...	...	...
Debt securities	8 669 . .	...	156.3	167.2	150.9	117.7	117.8	...	...
Bonds and notes	8 670 . .	...	156.3	167.2	150.9	117.7	117.8	...	...
Monetary authorities	8 671 . .	...	...	...	...	...	...	...	...
General government	8 672 . .	...	156.3	167.2	150.9	117.7	117.8	...	...
Banks	8 673 . .	...	...	...	...	...	...	...	...
Other sectors	8 674 . .	...	...	...	...	...	...	...	...
Money market instruments	8 680 . .	...	...	...	...	...	...	...	...
Monetary authorities	8 681 . .	...	...	...	...	...	...	...	...
General government	8 682 . .	...	...	...	...	...	...	...	...
Banks	8 683 . .	...	...	...	...	...	...	...	...
Other sectors	8 684 . .	...	...	...	...	...	...	...	...
Financial derivatives	8 905 . .	**...**	**...**	**...**	**...**	**...**	**...**	**...**	**...**
Monetary authorities	8 906 . .	...	...	...	...	...	...	...	...
General government	8 907 . .	...	...	...	...	...	...	...	...
Banks	8 908 . .	...	...	...	...	...	...	...	...
Other sectors	8 909 . .	...	...	...	...	...	...	...	...
Other investment	8 753 . .	**1,128.3**	**1,189.2**	**1,259.9**	**1,167.2**	**1,202.3**	**1,483.6**	**1,722.5**	**...**
Trade credits	8 756 . .	...	...	...	...	...	...	...	...
General government	8 757 . .	...	...	...	...	...	...	...	...
of which: Short-term	8 759 . .	...	...	...	...	...	...	...	...
Other sectors	8 760 . .	...	...	...	...	...	...	...	...
of which: Short-term	8 762 . .	...	...	...	...	...	...	...	...
Loans	8 764 . .	1,088.5	1,121.7	1,200.5	1,128.8	1,074.4	1,052.8	1,006.3	...
Monetary authorities	8 765 . .	...	...	...	...	...	...	...	...
of which: Use of Fund credit and loans from the Fund	8 766 . .	...	...	...	...	...	...	...	...
of which: Short-term	8 768 . .	...	...	...	...	...	...	...	...
General government	8 769 . .	324.8	328.3	352.6	300.1	294.1	273.4	246.2	...
of which: Short-term	8 771 . .	...	...	...	...	...	...	...	...
Banks	8 772 . .	...	...	...	...	...	...	...	...
of which: Short-term	8 774 . .	...	...	...	...	...	...	...	...
Other sectors	8 775 . .	763.7	793.4	847.9	828.7	780.3	779.4	760.1	...
of which: Short-term	8 777 . .	...	...	...	...	...	...	...	...
Currency and deposits	8 780 . .	39.8	67.5	59.5	38.4	127.9	430.8	716.1	...
Monetary authorities	8 781 . .	...	...	...	...	...	...	...	...
General government	8 782 . .	...	...	...	...	...	...	...	...
Banks	8 783 . .	39.8	67.5	59.5	38.4	127.9	104.3	106.6	...
Other sectors	8 784 . .	...	...	...	...	...	326.5	609.5	...
Other liabilities	8 786 . .	...	...	...	...	...	...	...	...
Monetary authorities	8 787 . .	...	...	...	...	...	...	...	...
of which: Short-term	8 789 . .	...	...	...	...	...	...	...	...
General government	8 790 . .	...	...	...	...	...	...	...	...
of which: Short-term	8 792 . .	...	...	...	...	...	...	...	...
Banks	8 793 . .	...	...	...	...	...	...	...	...
of which: Short-term	8 795 . .	...	...	...	...	...	...	...	...
Other sectors	8 796 . .	...	...	...	...	...	...	...	...
of which: Short-term	8 798 . .	...	...	...	...	...	...	...	...
NET INTERNATIONAL INVESTMENT POSITION	8 995 . .	**...**	**...**	**...**	**...**	**...**	**...**	**...**	**...**
Conversion rates: Mauritian rupees per U.S. dollar (end of period)	0 102 . .	**17.863**	**17.664**	**17.972**	**22.265**	**24.784**	**25.468**	**27.882**	**30.394**

Table 1. ANALYTIC PRESENTATION, 1994–2001

(Millions of U.S. dollars)

	Code			1994	1995	1996	1997	1998	1999	2000	2001
A. Current Account [1]	4	993	Z.	**–29,662**	**–1,576**	**–2,529**	**–7,696**	**–16,097**	**–14,017**	**–17,764**	**–17,708**
Goods: exports f.o.b.	2	100	..	60,882	79,542	96,002	110,431	117,459	136,392	166,456	158,443
Goods: imports f.o.b.	3	100	..	–79,346	–72,453	–89,469	–109,808	–125,374	–141,975	–174,457	–168,398
Balance on Goods	4	100	..	*–18,464*	*7,089*	*6,533*	*623*	*–7,915*	*–5,583*	*–8,001*	*–9,955*
Services: credit	2	200	..	10,321	9,780	10,723	11,182	11,662	11,737	13,752	12,699
Services: debit	3	200	..	–13,043	–9,715	–10,817	–12,615	–13,012	–14,473	–17,363	–17,194
Balance on Goods and Services	4	991	..	*–21,185*	*7,153*	*6,439*	*–810*	*–9,265*	*–8,319*	*–11,612*	*–14,450*
Income: credit	2	300	..	3,347	3,713	4,033	4,431	4,911	4,476	6,049	5,098
Income: debit	3	300	..	–15,605	–16,402	–17,506	–16,537	–17,731	–16,462	–19,173	–17,672
Balance on Goods, Services, and Income	4	992	..	*–33,444*	*–5,536*	*–7,034*	*–12,916*	*–22,085*	*–20,305*	*–24,736*	*–27,024*
Current transfers: credit	2	379	Z.	3,822	3,995	4,535	5,245	6,016	6,315	7,001	9,338
Current transfers: debit	3	379	..	–40	–35	–30	–25	–28	–27	–29	–22
B. Capital Account [1]	4	994	Z.	**...**	**...**	**...**	**...**	**...**	**...**	**...**	**...**
Capital account: credit	2	994	Z.	...	...	...	...	...	...	...	...
Capital account: debit	3	994	..	...	...	...	...	...	...	...	...
Total, Groups A Plus B	4	981	..	*–29,662*	*–1,576*	*–2,529*	*–7,696*	*–16,097*	*–14,017*	*–17,764*	*–17,708*
C. Financial Account [1]	4	995	W.	**15,787**	**–10,487**	**4,248**	**25,745**	**12,194**	**14,445**	**25,547**	**22,267**
Direct investment abroad	4	505	..	...	...	...	...	...	...	...	–3,708
Direct investment in Mexico	4	555	Z.	10,973	9,526	9,186	12,831	11,897	12,478	14,192	24,731
Portfolio investment assets	4	602	..	–767	–662	544	–708	–768	–836	1,290	3,857
Equity securities	4	610	..	...	...	...	...	...	...	...	...
Debt securities	4	619	..	–767	–662	544	–708	–768	–836	1,290	3,857
Portfolio investment liabilities	4	652	Z.	8,182	–9,715	3,537	6,002	–206	6,285	4,269	986
Equity securities	4	660	..	4,084	519	2,801	3,215	–665	3,769	447	150
Debt securities	4	669	Z.	4,099	–10,234	736	2,787	459	2,516	3,822	836
Financial derivatives	4	910	..	...	...	...	...	...	...	...	...
Financial derivatives assets	4	900	..	...	...	...	...	...	...	...	...
Financial derivatives liabilities	4	905	..	...	...	...	...	...	...	...	...
Other investment assets	4	703	..	–4,903	–6,694	–6,886	7,425	1,201	–3,170	5,808	–3,588
Monetary authorities	4	701	..	...	...	...	...	...	...	...	...
General government	4	704	..	–1,400	–3,619	–22	57	26	...	...	...
Banks	4	705	..	–885	–1,510	–1,018	5,112	–1,209	–1,895	44	–4,666
Other sectors	4	728	..	–2,618	–1,565	–5,846	2,256	2,384	–1,275	5,764	1,078
Other investment liabilities	4	753	W.	2,302	–2,942	–2,133	195	70	–312	–12	–11
Monetary authorities	4	753	WA	...	–788	–1,459	...	...	...	...	...
General government	4	753	ZB	–986	210	–659	206	75	–300	...	...
Banks	4	753	ZC	2,799	–5,297	...	...	...	...	...	...
Other sectors	4	753	ZD	488	2,933	–15	–11	–5	–12	–12	–11
Total, Groups A Through C	4	983	..	*–13,875*	*–12,064*	*1,719*	*18,049*	*–3,903*	*428*	*7,783*	*4,559*
D. Net Errors and Omissions	4	998	..	**–3,323**	**–4,248**	**229**	**2,411**	**402**	**735**	**3,673**	**2,317**
Total, Groups A Through D	4	984	..	*–17,199*	*–16,312*	*1,948*	*20,460*	*–3,501*	*1,163*	*11,456*	*6,876*
E. Reserves and Related Items	4	802	A.	**17,199**	**16,312**	**–1,948**	**–20,460**	**3,501**	**–1,163**	**–11,456**	**–6,876**
Reserve assets	4	802	..	18,398	–9,648	–1,805	–10,513	–2,118	–598	–2,862	–7,339
Use of Fund credit and loans	4	766	..	–1,199	11,950	–2,057	–3,485	–1,075	–3,681	–4,288	...
Exceptional financing	4	920	..	...	14,010	1,913	–6,463	6,694	3,115	–4,306	463
Conversion rates: Mexican pesos per U.S. dollar	0	101	..	**3.3751**	**6.4194**	**7.5994**	**7.9185**	**9.1360**	**9.5604**	**9.4556**	**9.3423**

[1] Excludes components that have been classified in the categories of Group E.

Table 2. STANDARD PRESENTATION, 1994–2001

(Millions of U.S. dollars)

	Code	1994	1995	1996	1997	1998	1999	2000	2001
CURRENT ACCOUNT	4 993 . .	**–29,662**	**–1,576**	**–2,500**	**–7,666**	**–16,073**	**–13,990**	**–17,740**	**–17,683**
A. GOODS	4 100 . .	–18,464	7,089	6,533	623	–7,915	–5,583	–8,001	–9,955
Credit	2 100 . .	**60,882**	**79,542**	**96,002**	**110,431**	**117,459**	**136,392**	**166,456**	**158,443**
General merchandise: exports f.o.b.	2 110 . .	34,613	48,438	59,081	65,265	64,376	72,538	86,988	81,562
Goods for processing: exports f.o.b.	2 150 . .	26,269	31,103	36,921	45,166	53,083	63,854	79,468	76,881
Repairs on goods	2 160 . .	. . .	. . .	. . .	. . .	. . .	. . .	. . .	. . .
Goods procured in ports by carriers	2 170 . .	. . .	. . .	. . .	. . .	. . .	. . .	. . .	. . .
Nonmonetary gold	2 180 . .	. . .	. . .	. . .	. . .	. . .	. . .	. . .	. . .
Debit	3 100 . .	**–79,346**	**–72,453**	**–89,469**	**–109,808**	**–125,374**	**–141,975**	**–174,457**	**–168,398**
General merchandise: imports f.o.b.	3 110 . .	–58,880	–46,274	–58,964	–73,476	–82,817	–91,565	–112,749	–110,798
Goods for processing: imports f.o.b.	3 150 . .	–20,466	–26,179	–30,505	–36,332	–42,557	–50,410	–61,708	–57,600
Repairs on goods	3 160 . .	. . .	. . .	. . .	. . .	. . .	. . .	. . .	. . .
Goods procured in ports by carriers	3 170 . .	. . .	. . .	. . .	. . .	. . .	. . .	. . .	. . .
Nonmonetary gold	3 180 . .	. . .	. . .	. . .	. . .	. . .	. . .	. . .	. . .
B. SERVICES	4 200 . .	–2,721	64	–94	–1,433	–1,350	–2,736	–3,611	–4,495
Total credit	2 200 . .	*10,321*	*9,780*	*10,723*	*11,182*	*11,662*	*11,737*	*13,752*	*12,699*
Total debit	3 200 . .	*–13,043*	*–9,715*	*–10,817*	*–12,615*	*–13,012*	*–14,473*	*–17,363*	*–17,194*
Transportation services, credit	2 205 . .	**1,066**	**1,164**	**1,413**	**1,416**	**1,434**	**1,343**	**1,369**	**1,282**
Passenger	2 850 . .	*619*	*668*	*775*	*808*	*815*	*912*	*840*	*789*
Freight	2 851 . .	. . .	. . .	. . .	. . .	. . .	. . .	. . .	. . .
Other	2 852 . .	*447*	*497*	*638*	*608*	*619*	*431*	*529*	*493*
Sea transport, passenger	2 207 . .	. . .	. . .	. . .	. . .	. . .	. . .	. . .	. . .
Sea transport, freight	2 208 . .	. . .	. . .	. . .	. . .	. . .	. . .	. . .	. . .
Sea transport, other	2 209 . .	236	314	358	388	330	139	105	113
Air transport, passenger	2 211 . .	619	668	775	808	815	912	840	789
Air transport, freight	2 212 . .	. . .	. . .	. . .	. . .	. . .	. . .	. . .	. . .
Air transport, other	2 213 . .	211	182	280	220	289	292	424	380
Other transport, passenger	2 215 . .	. . .	. . .	. . .	. . .	. . .	. . .	. . .	. . .
Other transport, freight	2 216 . .	. . .	. . .	. . .	. . .	. . .	. . .	. . .	. . .
Other transport, other	2 217 . .	. . .	. . .	. . .	. . .	. . .	. . .	. . .	. . .
Transportation services, debit	3 205 . .	**–4,286**	**–3,424**	**–1,668**	**–1,694**	**–1,604**	**–1,665**	**–1,982**	**–2,104**
Passenger	3 850 . .	*–542*	*–416*	*–576*	*–662*	*–624*	*–651*	*–866*	*–982*
Freight	3 851 . .	*–3,222*	*–2,347*	*–412*	*–289*	*–306*	*–336*	*–273*	*–282*
Other	3 852 . .	*–522*	*–660*	*–680*	*–743*	*–674*	*–678*	*–843*	*–840*
Sea transport, passenger	3 207 . .	. . .	. . .	. . .	. . .	. . .	. . .	. . .	. . .
Sea transport, freight	3 208 . .	–2,770	–2,018	–69	–68	–31	–16	–10	–10
Sea transport, other	3 209 . .	–137	–156	–181	–173	–95	–17	–9	–5
Air transport, passenger	3 211 . .	–542	–416	–576	–662	–624	–651	–866	–982
Air transport, freight	3 212 . .	–453	–330	–343	–221	–275	–320	–263	–272
Air transport, other	3 213 . .	–385	–504	–499	–570	–579	–661	–834	–835
Other transport, passenger	3 215 . .	. . .	. . .	. . .	. . .	. . .	. . .	. . .	. . .
Other transport, freight	3 216 . .	. . .	. . .	. . .	. . .	. . .	. . .	. . .	. . .
Other transport, other	3 217 . .	. . .	. . .	. . .	. . .	. . .	. . .	. . .	. . .
Travel, credit	2 236 . .	**6,363**	**6,179**	**6,756**	**7,375**	**7,493**	**7,224**	**8,293**	**8,400**
Business travel	2 237 . .	568	469	495	491	348	312	383	449
Personal travel	2 240 . .	5,795	5,710	6,261	6,884	7,145	6,912	7,910	7,951
Travel, debit	3 236 . .	**–5,338**	**–3,171**	**–3,388**	**–3,893**	**–4,210**	**–4,542**	**–5,500**	**–5,702**
Business travel	3 237 . .	–314	–297	–452	–420	–307	–425	–329	–442
Personal travel	3 240 . .	5,024	–2,873	–2,936	–3,473	–3,903	–4,117	–5,171	–5,260
Other services, credit	2 200 BA	**2,891**	**2,436**	**2,554**	**2,391**	**2,735**	**3,170**	**4,090**	**3,017**
Communications	2 245 . .	1,389	860	846	1,159	1,043	1,168	1,212	787
Construction	2 249 . .	. . .	. . .	. . .	. . .	. . .	. . .	. . .	. . .
Insurance	2 253 . .	662	641	818	350	840	1,073	1,799	1,351
Financial	2 260 . .	. . .	. . .	. . .	. . .	. . .	. . .	. . .	. . .
Computer and information	2 262 . .	. . .	. . .	. . .	. . .	. . .	. . .	. . .	. . .
Royalties and licence fees	2 266 . .	20	114	122	131	139	42	42	40
Other business services	2 268 . .	570	622	557	561	582	549	520	370
Personal, cultural, and recreational	2 287 . .	5	5	4	4	4	209	328	317
Government, n.i.e.	2 291 . .	246	195	207	186	127	129	189	152
Other services, debit	3 200 BA	**–3,419**	**–3,121**	**–5,761**	**–7,028**	**–7,198**	**–8,266**	**–9,881**	**–9,388**
Communications	3 245 . .	. . .	. . .	. . .	–401	–361	–436	–365	–331
Construction	3 249 . .	. . .	. . .	. . .	. . .	. . .	. . .	. . .	. . .
Insurance	3 253 . .	–1,270	–895	–3,474	–4,044	–4,748	–5,235	–6,295	–6,488
Financial	3 260 . .	–104	–231	–228	–313	–127	–427	–918	–557
Computer and information	3 262 . .	. . .	. . .	. . .	. . .	. . .	. . .	. . .	. . .
Royalties and licence fees	3 266 . .	–668	–484	–360	–502	–454	–554	–407	–419
Other business services	3 268 . .	–719	–812	–872	–980	–1,065	–976	–1,008	–721
Personal, cultural, and recreational	3 287 . .	–5	–5	–4	–4	–4	–227	–245	–198
Government, n.i.e.	3 291 . .	–652	–695	–823	–784	–439	–411	–643	–674

Table 2 (Continued). STANDARD PRESENTATION, 1994–2001

(Millions of U.S. dollars)

	Code	1994	1995	1996	1997	1998	1999	2000	2001
C. INCOME	4 300	−12,259	−12,689	−13,473	−12,106	−12,820	−11,986	−13,124	−12,574
Total credit	2 300	*3,347*	*3,713*	*4,033*	*4,431*	*4,911*	*4,476*	*6,049*	*5,098*
Total debit	3 300	*−15,605*	*−16,402*	*−17,506*	*−16,537*	*−17,731*	*−16,462*	*−19,173*	*−17,672*
Compensation of employees, credit	2 310	**647**	**695**	**726**	**681**	**876**	**740**	**1,024**	**1,024**
Compensation of employees, debit	3 310	...	...	...	...	...	...	...	...
Investment income, credit	2 320	**2,700**	**3,018**	**3,307**	**3,750**	**4,035**	**3,736**	**5,025**	**4,074**
Direct investment income	2 330	...	...	...	...	...	...	...	...
Dividends and distributed branch profits	2 332	...	...	...	...	...	...	...	...
Reinvested earnings and undistributed branch profits	2 333	...	...	...	...	...	...	...	...
Income on debt (interest)	2 334	...	...	...	...	...	...	...	...
Portfolio investment income	2 339	...	...	...	...	...	...	...	...
Income on equity	2 340	...	...	...	...	...	...	...	...
Income on bonds and notes	2 350	...	...	...	...	...	...	...	...
Income on money market instruments	2 360	...	...	...	...	...	...	...	...
Other investment income	2 370	2,700	3,018	3,307	3,750	4,035	3,736	5,025	4,074
Investment income, debit	3 320	**−15,605**	**−16,402**	**−17,506**	**−16,537**	**−17,731**	**−16,462**	**−19,173**	**−17,672**
Direct investment income	3 330	−4,793	−4,259	−4,022	−3,777	−5,251	−3,517	−5,634	−5,092
Dividends and distributed branch profits	3 332	−1,260	−1,199	−1,432	−1,626	−2,387	−1,214	−2,038	−1,505
Reinvested earnings and undistributed branch profits	3 333	−2,367	−1,572	−2,590	−2,151	−2,864	−2,303	−3,596	−3,587
Income on debt (interest)	3 334	−1,166	−1,488	...	...	...	...	...	...
Portfolio investment income	3 339	−4,488	−4,224	−997	−797	−490	−367	−140	−163
Income on equity	3 340	−171	−56	−124	−325	...	...	...	...
Income on bonds and notes	3 350	−1,879	−2,308	...	...	...	...	...	...
Income on money market instruments	3 360	−2,438	−1,860	−873	−472	−490	−367	−140	−163
Other investment income	3 370	−6,325	−7,919	−12,487	−11,963	−11,990	−12,578	−13,399	−12,417
D. CURRENT TRANSFERS	4 379	3,782	3,960	4,534	5,250	6,012	6,315	6,996	9,341
Credit	2 379	**3,822**	**3,995**	**4,564**	**5,275**	**6,040**	**6,342**	**7,025**	**9,363**
General government	2 380	102	99	68	70	64	67	64	65
Other sectors	2 390	3,720	3,896	4,496	5,205	5,976	6,275	6,961	9,298
Workers' remittances	2 391	3,475	3,673	4,224	4,865	5,627	5,909	6,572	8,896
Other current transfers	2 392	245	223	272	340	349	366	389	402
Debit	3 379	**−40**	**−35**	**−30**	**−25**	**−28**	**−27**	**−29**	**−22**
General government	3 380	−40	−35	...	...	...	...	...	...
Other sectors	3 390	...	...	−30	−25	−28	−27	−29	−22
Workers' remittances	3 391	...	...	...	...	...	...	...	...
Other current transfers	3 392	...	...	−30	−25	−28	−27	−29	−22
CAPITAL AND FINANCIAL ACCOUNT	4 996	**32,986**	**5,824**	**2,271**	**5,255**	**15,671**	**13,255**	**14,067**	**15,366**
CAPITAL ACCOUNT	4 994	...	...	...	...	...	...	...	...
Total credit	2 994	...	...	...	...	...	...	...	...
Total debit	3 994	...	...	...	...	...	...	...	...
Capital transfers, credit	2 400	...	...	...	...	...	...	...	...
General government	2 401	...	...	...	...	...	...	...	...
Debt forgiveness	2 402	...	...	...	...	...	...	...	...
Other capital transfers	2 410	...	...	...	...	...	...	...	...
Other sectors	2 430	...	...	...	...	...	...	...	...
Migrants' transfers	2 431	...	...	...	...	...	...	...	...
Debt forgiveness	2 432	...	...	...	...	...	...	...	...
Other capital transfers	2 440	...	...	...	...	...	...	...	...
Capital transfers, debit	3 400	...	...	...	...	...	...	...	...
General government	3 401	...	...	...	...	...	...	...	...
Debt forgiveness	3 402	...	...	...	...	...	...	...	...
Other capital transfers	3 410	...	...	...	...	...	...	...	...
Other sectors	3 430	...	...	...	...	...	...	...	...
Migrants' transfers	3 431	...	...	...	...	...	...	...	...
Debt forgiveness	3 432	...	...	...	...	...	...	...	...
Other capital transfers	3 440	...	...	...	...	...	...	...	...
Nonproduced nonfinancial assets, credit	2 480	...	...	...	...	...	...	...	...
Nonproduced nonfinancial assets, debit	3 480	...	...	...	...	...	...	...	...

Table 2 (Continued). STANDARD PRESENTATION, 1994–2001
(Millions of U.S. dollars)

	Code	1994	1995	1996	1997	1998	1999	2000	2001
FINANCIAL ACCOUNT	4 995 . .	**32,986**	**5,824**	**2,271**	**5,255**	**15,671**	**13,255**	**14,067**	**15,366**
A. DIRECT INVESTMENT	4 500 . .	10,973	9,526	9,186	12,831	11,897	12,478	14,192	21,023
Direct investment abroad	4 505 . .	**. . .**	**. . .**	**. . .**	**. . .**	**. . .**	**. . .**	**. . .**	**–3,708**
Equity capital	4 510 . .	. . .	. . .	. . .	. . .	. . .	. . .	. . .	. . .
Claims on affiliated enterprises	4 515 . .	. . .	. . .	. . .	. . .	. . .	. . .	. . .	. . .
Liabilities to affiliated enterprises	4 520 . .	. . .	. . .	. . .	. . .	. . .	. . .	. . .	. . .
Reinvested earnings	4 525 . .	. . .	. . .	. . .	. . .	. . .	. . .	. . .	. . .
Other capital	4 530 . .	. . .	. . .	. . .	. . .	. . .	. . .	. . .	. . .
Claims on affiliated enterprises	4 535 . .	. . .	. . .	. . .	. . .	. . .	. . .	. . .	. . .
Liabilities to affiliated enterprises	4 540 . .	. . .	. . .	. . .	. . .	. . .	. . .	. . .	. . .
Direct investment in Mexico	4 555 . .	**10,973**	**9,526**	**9,186**	**12,831**	**11,897**	**12,478**	**14,192**	**24,731**
Equity capital	4 560 . .	5,672	6,838	5,529	9,116	5,743	4,974	5,701	18,394
Claims on direct investors	4 565 . .	. . .	. . .	. . .	. . .	. . .	. . .	. . .	. . .
Liabilities to direct investors	4 570 . .	5,672	6,838	5,529	9,116	5,743	4,974	5,701	18,394
Reinvested earnings	4 575 . .	2,367	1,572	2,590	2,151	2,864	2,303	3,596	3,587
Other capital	4 580 . .	2,934	1,116	1,067	1,564	3,290	5,201	4,895	2,750
Claims on direct investors	4 585 . .	. . .	. . .	. . .	. . .	. . .	. . .	. . .	. . .
Liabilities to direct investors	4 590 . .	2,934	1,116	1,067	1,564	3,290	5,201	4,895	2,750
B. PORTFOLIO INVESTMENT	4 600 . .	7,415	–10,377	13,961	4,329	–1,505	9,080	720	6,856
Assets	4 602 . .	**–767**	**–662**	**544**	**–708**	**–768**	**–836**	**1,290**	**3,857**
Equity securities	4 610 . .	. . .	. . .	. . .	. . .	. . .	. . .	. . .	. . .
Monetary authorities	4 611 . .	. . .	. . .	. . .	. . .	. . .	. . .	. . .	. . .
General government	4 612 . .	. . .	. . .	. . .	. . .	. . .	. . .	. . .	. . .
Banks	4 613 . .	. . .	. . .	. . .	. . .	. . .	. . .	. . .	. . .
Other sectors	4 614 . .	. . .	. . .	. . .	. . .	. . .	. . .	. . .	. . .
Debt securities	4 619 . .	–767	–662	544	–708	–768	–836	1,290	3,857
Bonds and notes	4 620 . .	–767	–662	544	–708	–768	–836	1,290	3,857
Monetary authorities	4 621 . .	. . .	. . .	. . .	. . .	. . .	. . .	. . .	. . .
General government	4 622 . .	–615	–662	544	–708	–768	–836	1,290	3,857
Banks	4 623 . .	–152	. . .	. . .	. . .	. . .	. . .	. . .	. . .
Other sectors	4 624 . .	. . .	. . .	. . .	. . .	. . .	. . .	. . .	. . .
Money market instruments	4 630 . .	. . .	. . .	. . .	. . .	. . .	. . .	. . .	. . .
Monetary authorities	4 631 . .	. . .	. . .	. . .	. . .	. . .	. . .	. . .	. . .
General government	4 632 . .	. . .	. . .	. . .	. . .	. . .	. . .	. . .	. . .
Banks	4 633 . .	. . .	. . .	. . .	. . .	. . .	. . .	. . .	. . .
Other sectors	4 634 . .	. . .	. . .	. . .	. . .	. . .	. . .	. . .	. . .
Liabilities	4 652 . .	**8,182**	**–9,715**	**13,417**	**5,037**	**–737**	**9,916**	**–570**	**2,999**
Equity securities	4 660 . .	4,084	519	2,801	3,215	–665	3,769	447	150
Banks	4 663 . .	. . .	. . .	. . .	. . .	. . .	. . .	. . .	. . .
Other sectors	4 664 . .	. . .	. . .	2,801	3,215	–665	3,769	447	150
Debt securities	4 669 . .	4,099	–10,234	10,616	1,822	–72	6,147	–1,017	2,849
Bonds and notes	4 670 . .	6,041	3,557	9,668	1,331	–202	7,089	–992	1,909
Monetary authorities	4 671 . .	. . .	. . .	. . .	. . .	. . .	. . .	. . .	. . .
General government	4 672 . .	134	4,061	9,192	–1,299	554	5,589	–3,086	1,849
Banks	4 673 . .	3,153	–29	–839	–1,062	–1,749	–1,186	–1,748	–122
Other sectors	4 674 . .	2,754	–475	1,315	3,692	993	2,686	3,842	182
Money market instruments	4 680 . .	–1,942	–13,791	948	491	130	–942	–25	940
Monetary authorities	4 681 . .	. . .	. . .	. . .	. . .	. . .	. . .	. . .	. . .
General government	4 682 . .	–1,942	–13,791	948	491	130	–942	–25	940
Banks	4 683 . .	. . .	. . .	. . .	. . .	. . .	. . .	. . .	. . .
Other sectors	4 684 . .	. . .	. . .	. . .	. . .	. . .	. . .	. . .	. . .
C. FINANCIAL DERIVATIVES	4 910 . .	. . .	. . .	. . .	. . .	. . .	. . .	. . .	. . .
Monetary authorities	4 911 . .	. . .	. . .	. . .	. . .	. . .	. . .	. . .	. . .
General government	4 912 . .	. . .	. . .	. . .	. . .	. . .	. . .	. . .	. . .
Banks	4 913 . .	. . .	. . .	. . .	. . .	. . .	. . .	. . .	. . .
Other sectors	4 914 . .	. . .	. . .	. . .	. . .	. . .	. . .	. . .	. . .
Assets	4 900 . .	**. . .**	**. . .**	**. . .**	**. . .**	**. . .**	**. . .**	**. . .**	**. . .**
Monetary authorities	4 901 . .	. . .	. . .	. . .	. . .	. . .	. . .	. . .	. . .
General government	4 902 . .	. . .	. . .	. . .	. . .	. . .	. . .	. . .	. . .
Banks	4 903 . .	. . .	. . .	. . .	. . .	. . .	. . .	. . .	. . .
Other sectors	4 904 . .	. . .	. . .	. . .	. . .	. . .	. . .	. . .	. . .
Liabilities	4 905 . .	**. . .**	**. . .**	**. . .**	**. . .**	**. . .**	**. . .**	**. . .**	**. . .**
Monetary authorities	4 906 . .	. . .	. . .	. . .	. . .	. . .	. . .	. . .	. . .
General government	4 907 . .	. . .	. . .	. . .	. . .	. . .	. . .	. . .	. . .
Banks	4 908 . .	. . .	. . .	. . .	. . .	. . .	. . .	. . .	. . .
Other sectors	4 909 . .	. . .	. . .	. . .	. . .	. . .	. . .	. . .	. . .

Table 2 (Concluded). STANDARD PRESENTATION, 1994–2001
(Millions of U.S. dollars)

	Code	1994	1995	1996	1997	1998	1999	2000	2001
D. OTHER INVESTMENT	4 700 . .	–3,800	16,323	–19,072	–1,393	7,397	–7,706	2,017	–5,174
Assets	4 703 . .	**–4,903**	**–6,694**	**–6,886**	**7,425**	**1,201**	**–3,170**	**5,808**	**–3,588**
Trade credits	4 706 . .	–41	–276	–625	–113	331	425	412	. . .
General government	4 707 . .	. . .	–26	–22	57	26	. . .	. . .	. . .
of which: Short-term	4 709 . .	. . .	. . .	. . .	. . .	. . .	. . .	. . .	. . .
Other sectors	4 710 . .	–41	–250	–603	–170	305	425	412	. . .
of which: Short-term	4 712 . .	*–41*	*–250*	*–603*	*–170*	*305*	*425*	*412*	. . .
Loans	4 714 . .	–265	. . .	. . .	. . .	. . .	. . .	. . .	. . .
Monetary authorities	4 715 . .	. . .	. . .	. . .	. . .	. . .	. . .	. . .	. . .
of which: Short-term	4 718 . .	. . .	. . .	. . .	. . .	. . .	. . .	. . .	. . .
General government	4 719 . .	. . .	. . .	. . .	. . .	. . .	. . .	. . .	. . .
of which: Short-term	4 721 . .	. . .	. . .	. . .	. . .	. . .	. . .	. . .	. . .
Banks	4 722 . .	–265	. . .	. . .	. . .	. . .	. . .	. . .	. . .
of which: Short-term	4 724 . .	. . .	. . .	. . .	. . .	. . .	. . .	. . .	. . .
Other sectors	4 725 . .	. . .	. . .	. . .	. . .	. . .	. . .	. . .	. . .
of which: Short-term	4 727 . .	. . .	. . .	. . .	. . .	. . .	. . .	. . .	. . .
Currency and deposits	4 730 . .	–3,198	–2,825	–6,055	4,861	156	–3,038	3,549	–1,812
Monetary authorities	4 731 . .	. . .	. . .	. . .	. . .	. . .	. . .	. . .	. . .
General government	4 732 . .	. . .	. . .	. . .	. . .	. . .	. . .	. . .	. . .
Banks	4 733 . .	–621	–1,510	–812	2,435	–1,923	–1,338	–1,803	–2,890
Other sectors	4 734 . .	–2,577	–1,315	–5,243	2,426	2,079	–1,700	5,352	1,078
Other assets	4 736 . .	–1,400	–3,593	–206	2,677	714	–557	1,847	–1,776
Monetary authorities	4 737 . .	. . .	. . .	. . .	. . .	. . .	. . .	. . .	. . .
of which: Short-term	4 739 . .	. . .	. . .	. . .	. . .	. . .	. . .	. . .	. . .
General government	4 740 . .	–1,400	–3,593	. . .	. . .	. . .	. . .	. . .	. . .
of which: Short-term	4 742 . .	*–1,400*	*–3,593*	. . .	. . .	. . .	. . .	. . .	. . .
Banks	4 743 . .	. . .	. . .	–206	2,677	714	–557	1,847	–1,776
of which: Short-term	4 745 . .	. . .	. . .	*–206*	*2,677*	*714*	*–557*	*1,847*	*–1,776*
Other sectors	4 746 . .	. . .	. . .	. . .	. . .	. . .	. . .	. . .	. . .
of which: Short-term	4 748 . .	. . .	. . .	. . .	. . .	. . .	. . .	. . .	. . .
Liabilities	4 753 . .	**1,103**	**23,017**	**–12,186**	**–8,818**	**6,196**	**–4,536**	**–3,791**	**–1,586**
Trade credits	4 756 . .	25	–20	–15	–11	–5	–12	–12	–11
General government	4 757 . .	. . .	. . .	. . .	. . .	. . .	. . .	. . .	. . .
of which: Short-term	4 759 . .	. . .	. . .	. . .	. . .	. . .	. . .	. . .	. . .
Other sectors	4 760 . .	25	–20	–15	–11	–5	–12	–12	–11
of which: Short-term	4 762 . .	. . .	. . .	. . .	. . .	. . .	. . .	. . .	. . .
Loans	4 764 . .	1,742	24,955	–12,171	–8,807	6,201	–4,524	–3,779	–1,575
Monetary authorities	4 765 . .	–1,199	13,399	–3,516	–3,485	–1,075	–3,681	–4,288	. . .
of which: Use of Fund credit and loans from the Fund	4 766 . .	*–1,199*	*11,950*	*–2,057*	*–3,485*	*–1,075*	*–3,681*	*–4,288*	. . .
of which: Short-term	4 768 . .	. . .	. . .	. . .	. . .	. . .	. . .	. . .	. . .
General government	4 769 . .	–986	10,710	–8,595	–3,994	1,356	–4,294	–2,896	–603
of which: Short-term	4 771 . .	. . .	*670*	*–659*	*206*	*75*	*–300*	. . .	. . .
Banks	4 772 . .	3,463	–2,106	–2,965	–2,999	97	–2,311	–882	–4,150
of which: Short-term	4 774 . .	*3,053*	*209*	*–1,678*	*–1,081*	*496*	*–24*	*–178*	*–1,655*
Other sectors	4 775 . .	463	2,953	2,905	1,671	5,823	5,762	4,287	3,178
of which: Short-term	4 777 . .	*–530*	*1,359*	*1,343*	*119*	*2,058*	*2,941*	*1,838*	*309*
Currency and deposits	4 780 . .	–664	–1,918	. . .	. . .	. . .	. . .	. . .	. . .
Monetary authorities	4 781 . .	. . .	. . .	. . .	. . .	. . .	. . .	. . .	. . .
General government	4 782 . .	. . .	. . .	. . .	. . .	. . .	. . .	. . .	. . .
Banks	4 783 . .	–664	–1,918	. . .	. . .	. . .	. . .	. . .	. . .
Other sectors	4 784 . .	. . .	. . .	. . .	. . .	. . .	. . .	. . .	. . .
Other liabilities	4 786 . .	. . .	. . .	. . .	. . .	. . .	. . .	. . .	. . .
Monetary authorities	4 787 . .	. . .	. . .	. . .	. . .	. . .	. . .	. . .	. . .
of which: Short-term	4 789 . .	. . .	. . .	. . .	. . .	. . .	. . .	. . .	. . .
General government	4 790 . .	. . .	. . .	. . .	. . .	. . .	. . .	. . .	. . .
of which: Short-term	4 792 . .	. . .	. . .	. . .	. . .	. . .	. . .	. . .	. . .
Banks	4 793 . .	. . .	. . .	. . .	. . .	. . .	. . .	. . .	. . .
of which: Short-term	4 795 . .	. . .	. . .	. . .	. . .	. . .	. . .	. . .	. . .
Other sectors	4 796 . .	. . .	. . .	. . .	. . .	. . .	. . .	. . .	. . .
of which: Short-term	4 798 . .	. . .	. . .	. . .	. . .	. . .	. . .	. . .	. . .
E. RESERVE ASSETS	4 802 . .	18,398	–9,648	–1,805	–10,513	–2,118	–598	–2,862	–7,339
Monetary gold	4 812 . .	27	–35	104	39	–8	17	–22	5
Special drawing rights	4 811 . .	55	–1,475	1,303	–423	341	–450	382	–3
Reserve position in the Fund	4 810 . .	. . .	. . .	. . .	. . .	. . .	–4	. . .	. . .
Foreign exchange	4 803 . .	18,788	–9,145	–3,933	–8,956	–3,263	477	–4,077	–9,347
Other claims	4 813 . .	–472	1,007	722	–1,173	812	–638	855	2,006
NET ERRORS AND OMISSIONS	4 998 . .	**–3,323**	**–4,248**	**229**	**2,411**	**402**	**735**	**3,673**	**2,317**

Part 3 of the *Yearbook* contains descriptions of the methodologies, compilation practices, and sources used to compile these data.

Table 1. ANALYTIC PRESENTATION, 1994–2001

(Millions of U.S. dollars)

	Code	1994	1995	1996	1997	1998	1999	2000	2001
A. Current Account [1]	4 993 Z.	**–82.0**	**–87.8**	**–194.8**	**–274.9**	**–334.7**	**–65.6**	**–116.2**	**–108.8**
Goods: exports f.o.b	2 100 . .	618.5	739.0	822.9	889.6	643.6	474.1	476.5	569.5
Goods: imports f.o.b	3 100 . .	–672.4	–809.2	–1,082.5	–1,237.6	–1,031.7	–609.8	–768.3	–882.3
Balance on Goods	4 100 . .	*–53.9*	*–70.2*	*–259.7*	*–348.0*	*–388.1*	*–135.7*	*–291.8*	*–312.8*
Services: credit	2 200 . .	32.8	144.5	106.0	167.7	152.0	140.9	167.9	170.4
Services: debit	3 200 . .	–79.0	–196.3	–166.4	–196.1	–198.6	–171.0	–203.2	–218.7
Balance on Goods and Services	4 991 . .	*–100.0*	*–122.0*	*–320.0*	*–376.4*	*–434.6*	*–165.8*	*–327.1*	*–361.1*
Income: credit	2 300 . .	10.8	14.2	99.3	132.7	136.8	120.4	167.3	233.5
Income: debit	3 300 . .	–26.1	–32.4	–44.2	–85.3	–102.3	–95.2	–104.2	–124.1
Balance on Goods, Services, and Income	4 992 . .	*–115.4*	*–140.2*	*–264.9*	*–329.0*	*–400.1*	*–140.6*	*–263.9*	*–251.7*
Current transfers: credit	2 379 Z.	36.9	66.6	72.9	104.1	110.9	114.7	162.9	160.9
Current transfers: debit	3 379 . .	–3.6	–14.1	–2.8	–50.0	–45.5	–39.6	–15.2	–18.0
B. Capital Account [1]	4 994 Z.	**–1.0**	**–.4**	**–.1**	**–.2**	**–.4**	**1.1**	**1.9**	**–1.9**
Capital account: credit	2 994 Z.	. . .	. . .	.1	.1	2.1	1.5	2.8	1.1
Capital account: debit	3 994 . .	–1.0	–.4	–.1	–.3	–2.5	–.4	–.9	–3.0
Total, Groups A Plus B	4 981 . .	*–83.0*	*–88.2*	*–194.8*	*–275.1*	*–335.1*	*–64.4*	*–114.3*	*–110.7*
C. Financial Account [1]	4 995 W.	**211.1**	**–68.8**	**76.6**	**95.2**	**5.2**	**–35.9**	**144.9**	**31.3**
Direct investment abroad	4 505 . .	. . .	–.5	–.6	–.5	.7	–.1	–.1	. . .
Direct investment in Moldova	4 555 Z.	11.6	25.9	23.7	78.7	75.5	40.4	142.8	93.5
Portfolio investment assets	4 602 . .	–.4	. . .	. . .	. . .	. . .	. . .	. . .	–3.1
Equity securities	4 610 . .	–.4	. . .	. . .	. . .	. . .	. . .	. . .	. . .
Debt securities	4 619 . .	. . .	. . .	. . .	. . .	. . .	. . .	. . .	–3.1
Portfolio investment liabilities	4 652 Z.	.6	–.5	30.8	18.6	–59.1	–7.1	2.5	3.6
Equity securities	4 660 . .	.6	–.5	.8	3.7	6.5	5.5	2.6	3.6
Debt securities	4 669 Z.	. . .	. . .	30.0	14.9	–65.6	–12.5	–.1	. . .
Financial derivatives	4 910 . .	. . .	. . .	. . .	. . .	. . .	. . .	. . .	. . .
Financial derivatives assets	4 900 . .	. . .	. . .	. . .	. . .	. . .	. . .	. . .	. . .
Financial derivatives liabilities	4 905 . .	. . .	. . .	. . .	. . .	. . .	. . .	. . .	. . .
Other investment assets	4 703 . .	–81.7	–116.4	–51.4	1.8	–86.8	–110.9	–39.4	–39.4
Monetary authorities	4 701 . .	–1.3	2.9	.3	3.7	2.9	. . .	.1	. . .
General government	4 704 . .	–4.1	11.9	12.2	1.6	–.6	–4.3	. . .	8.3
Banks	4 705 . .	–10.1	–13.5	–6.5	10.6	–10.9	–15.4	–16.5	1.2
Other sectors	4 728 . .	–66.2	–117.7	–57.4	–14.2	–78.2	–91.3	–23.1	–48.9
Other investment liabilities	4 753 W.	281.0	22.7	74.0	–3.4	74.8	41.7	39.2	–23.3
Monetary authorities	4 753 WA	3.1	1.8	–1.9	–2.7	5.2	–2.4	1.6	1.0
General government	4 753 ZB	147.0	–19.7	43.2	–59.2	9.7	–22.2	–4.9	–21.7
Banks	4 753 ZC	–.8	11.4	21.9	11.8	6.9	–20.3	2.6	–1.0
Other sectors	4 753 ZD	131.6	29.2	10.7	46.6	53.1	86.6	39.9	.4
Total, Groups A Through C	4 983 . .	*128.1*	*–157.0*	*–118.2*	*–179.9*	*–329.9*	*–100.3*	*30.6*	*–79.4*
D. Net Errors and Omissions	4 998 . .	**–115.2**	**–18.4**	**15.5**	**–7.9**	**–22.8**	**–20.1**	**–4.8**	**44.6**
Total, Groups A Through D	4 984 . .	*12.9*	*–175.4*	*–102.7*	*–187.8*	*–352.8*	*–120.4*	*25.8*	*–34.8*
E. Reserves and Related Items	4 802 A.	**–12.9**	**175.4**	**102.7**	**187.8**	**352.8**	**120.4**	**–25.8**	**34.8**
Reserve assets	4 802 . .	–103.1	–76.7	–56.9	–50.2	225.7	–48.8	–46.8	–9.7
Use of Fund credit and loans	4 766 . .	71.5	64.8	25.2	.8	–64.4	4.0	–12.7	–2.3
Exceptional financing	4 920 . .	18.7	187.3	134.4	237.2	191.4	165.1	33.7	46.9
Conversion rates: lei per U.S. dollar	0 101 . .	**. . .**	**4.4958**	**4.6045**	**4.6236**	**5.3707**	**10.5158**	**12.4342**	**12.8651**

[1] Excludes components that have been classified in the categories of Group E.

Moldova
921

Table 2. STANDARD PRESENTATION, 1994–2001

(Millions of U.S. dollars)

	Code	1994	1995	1996	1997	1998	1999	2000	2001
CURRENT ACCOUNT	4 993 . .	**–82.0**	**–84.6**	**–191.8**	**–274.9**	**–334.7**	**–54.9**	**–106.1**	**–98.6**
A. GOODS	4 100 . .	–53.9	–70.2	–259.7	–348.0	–388.1	–135.7	–291.8	–312.8
Credit	2 100 . .	**618.5**	**739.0**	**822.9**	**889.6**	**643.6**	**474.1**	**476.5**	**569.5**
General merchandise: exports f.o.b.	2 110 . .	618.5	739.0	822.9	833.7	575.0	400.3	375.6	447.0
Goods for processing: exports f.o.b.	2 150 . .	. . .	. . .	. . .	56.0	68.6	73.8	100.9	122.5
Repairs on goods	2 160 . .	. . .	. . .	. . .	. . .	. . .	. . .	. . .	. . .
Goods procured in ports by carriers	2 170 . .	. . .	. . .	. . .	. . .	. . .	. . .	. . .	. . .
Nonmonetary gold	2 180 . .	. . .	. . .	. . .	. . .	. . .	. . .	. . .	. . .
Debit	3 100 . .	**–672.4**	**–809.2**	**–1,082.5**	**–1,237.6**	**–1,031.7**	**–609.8**	**–768.3**	**–882.3**
General merchandise: imports f.o.b.	3 110 . .	–672.4	–809.2	–1,082.5	–1,187.4	–975.4	–550.6	–685.4	–780.9
Goods for processing: imports f.o.b.	3 150 . .	. . .	. . .	. . .	–50.2	–56.2	–58.5	–81.0	–100.9
Repairs on goods	3 160 . .	. . .	. . .	. . .	. . .	. . .	–.6	–1.6	–.5
Goods procured in ports by carriers	3 170 . .	. . .	. . .	. . .	. . .	. . .	. . .	. . .	. . .
Nonmonetary gold	3 180 . .	. . .	. . .	. . .	. . .	. . .	–.2	–.2	. . .
B. SERVICES	4 200 . .	–46.1	–51.8	–60.4	–28.4	–46.5	–30.1	–35.3	–48.3
Total credit	2 200 . .	*32.8*	*144.5*	*106.0*	*167.7*	*152.0*	*140.9*	*167.9*	*170.4*
Total debit	3 200 . .	*–79.0*	*–196.3*	*–166.4*	*–196.1*	*–198.6*	*–171.0*	*–203.2*	*–218.7*
Transportation services, credit	2 205 . .	**10.2**	**42.3**	**55.4**	**84.4**	**74.3**	**65.9**	**82.5**	**77.1**
Passenger	2 850 . .	*3.1*	*13.5*	*17.0*	*24.2*	*23.9*	*20.4*	*16.8*	*16.3*
Freight	2 851 . .	*6.1*	*27.7*	*32.1*	*56.6*	*50.2*	*44.8*	*64.6*	*59.1*
Other	2 852 . .	*1.0*	*1.1*	*6.3*	*3.6*	*.2*	*.7*	*1.1*	*1.7*
Sea transport, passenger	2 207 . .	. . .	. . .	. . .	. . .	. . .	. . .	. . .	. . .
Sea transport, freight	2 208 . .	. . .	. . .	. . .	. . .	. . .	. . .	. . .	. . .
Sea transport, other	2 209 . .	. . .	. . .	. . .	. . .	. . .	. . .	. . .	. . .
Air transport, passenger	2 211 . .	.9	12.5	5.7	19.5	19.2	17.5	14.2	13.1
Air transport, freight	2 212 . .	1.8	1.6	11.4	1.6	2.0	1.7	1.5	2.9
Air transport, other	2 213 . .	.3	. . .	1.9	. . .	.1	.1	.1	.2
Other transport, passenger	2 215 . .	2.1	1.0	11.3	4.7	4.7	2.9	2.7	3.2
Other transport, freight	2 216 . .	4.3	26.1	20.7	55.1	48.2	43.1	63.1	56.2
Other transport, other	2 217 . .	.7	1.1	4.4	3.6	.2	.6	1.0	1.5
Transportation services, debit	3 205 . .	**–51.0**	**–99.4**	**–80.9**	**–94.9**	**–77.9**	**–52.5**	**–57.6**	**–62.0**
Passenger	3 850 . .	*–15.3*	*–16.6*	*–24.8*	*–9.8*	*–13.6*	*–9.3*	*–10.5*	*–13.6*
Freight	3 851 . .	*–30.6*	*–74.6*	*–48.9*	*–78.7*	*–64.0*	*–42.1*	*–45.2*	*–46.3*
Other	3 852 . .	*–5.1*	*–8.2*	*–7.2*	*–6.4*	*–.4*	*–1.1*	*–1.9*	*–2.1*
Sea transport, passenger	3 207 . .	. . .	. . .	. . .	. . .	. . .	. . .	. . .	. . .
Sea transport, freight	3 208 . .	. . .	. . .	. . .	. . .	–.1	–.3	–.8	–.5
Sea transport, other	3 209 . .	. . .	. . .	. . .	. . .	. . .	. . .	. . .	. . .
Air transport, passenger	3 211 . .	–4.6	–9.1	–8.3	–3.6	–7.7	–6.1	–8.0	–11.3
Air transport, freight	3 212 . .	–9.2	–4.9	–16.7	–6.4	–4.7	–2.5	–3.4	–2.0
Air transport, other	3 213 . .	–1.5	–2.9	–2.8	–.5	–.2	–.3	–.6	–.5
Other transport, passenger	3 215 . .	–10.7	–7.6	–16.4	–6.2	–5.9	–3.2	–2.5	–2.3
Other transport, freight	3 216 . .	–21.4	–69.7	–32.3	–72.3	–59.2	–39.3	–41.0	–43.8
Other transport, other	3 217 . .	–3.6	–5.3	–4.5	–5.9	–.2	–.8	–1.2	–1.6
Travel, credit	2 236 . .	**7.5**	**56.9**	**33.5**	**49.8**	**40.2**	**37.6**	**46.2**	**46.0**
Business travel	2 237 . .	. . .	17.1	10.0	20.2	9.7	10.4	12.9	11.2
Personal travel	2 240 . .	. . .	39.9	23.4	29.6	30.5	27.3	33.3	34.8
Travel, debit	3 236 . .	**–10.3**	**–56.4**	**–52.4**	**–65.0**	**–59.5**	**–57.8**	**–80.2**	**–88.4**
Business travel	3 237 . .	. . .	–16.9	–24.1	–30.2	–27.1	–26.8	–34.7	–38.5
Personal travel	3 240 . .	. . .	–39.5	–28.3	–34.7	–32.4	–31.1	–45.6	–49.9
Other services, credit	2 200 BA	**15.1**	**45.3**	**17.2**	**33.6**	**37.6**	**37.4**	**39.2**	**47.3**
Communications	2 245 . .	.9	3.7	5.2	8.3	14.5	16.2	16.5	16.6
Construction	2 249 . .	1.0	.3	2.6	1.6	3.7	1.2	.8	.6
Insurance	2 253 . .	.1	.6	.6	.8	.5	.5	1.1	2.0
Financial	2 260 . .	1.0	16.1	1.4	.7	3.3	2.2	1.9	2.8
Computer and information	2 262 . .	1.3	.2	.2	.6	.6	1.1	.7	.3
Royalties and licence fees	2 266 . .	. . .	. . .	.5	. . .	.2	.1	.7	1.2
Other business services	2 268 . .	10.8	23.1	4.0	16.7	10.7	9.6	11.6	16.6
Personal, cultural, and recreational	2 287 . .	. . .	. . .	. . .	. . .	. . .	.3	.3	.7
Government, n.i.e.	2 291 . .	. . .	1.3	2.8	4.9	4.1	6.2	5.6	6.5
Other services, debit	3 200 BA	**–17.7**	**–40.5**	**–33.2**	**–36.3**	**–61.2**	**–60.7**	**–65.3**	**–68.3**
Communications	3 245 . .	–.8	–1.7	–2.9	–2.0	–8.4	–8.9	–7.6	–7.6
Construction	3 249 . .	–.1	–.8	–1.7	–3.5	–6.9	–12.8	–11.2	–4.2
Insurance	3 253 . .	–.3	–.9	–.9	–.7	–1.4	–2.4	–2.7	–3.8
Financial	3 260 . .	–3.0	–17.0	–2.1	–2.4	–4.4	–4.8	–2.1	–3.6
Computer and information	3 262 . .	–.3	–.4	–.3	–.5	–3.8	–2.0	–3.0	–2.4
Royalties and licence fees	3 266 . .	. . .	. . .	–2.0	–.1	–.3	–.3	–1.8	–1.0
Other business services	3 268 . .	–8.7	–16.3	–12.6	–21.9	–26.9	–22.5	–29.2	–36.3
Personal, cultural, and recreational	3 287 . .	. . .	. . .	. . .	. . .	–.2	–.2	. . .	. . .
Government, n.i.e.	3 291 . .	–4.5	–3.5	–10.6	–5.2	–8.9	–6.7	–7.8	–9.4

Table 2 (Continued). STANDARD PRESENTATION, 1994–2001
(Millions of U.S. dollars)

	Code		1994	1995	1996	1997	1998	1999	2000	2001
C. INCOME	4 300	. .	–15.3	–18.2	55.1	47.4	34.5	25.2	63.2	109.4
Total credit	2 300	. .	*10.8*	*14.2*	*99.3*	*132.7*	*136.8*	*120.4*	*167.3*	*233.5*
Total debit	3 300	. .	*–26.1*	*–32.4*	*–44.2*	*–85.3*	*–102.3*	*–95.2*	*–104.2*	*–124.1*
Compensation of employees, credit	2 310	. .	**. . .**	**. . .**	**84.0**	**113.0**	**121.0**	**109.8**	**153.4**	**221.2**
Compensation of employees, debit	3 310	. .	**–9.5**	**. . .**	**–5.1**	**–19.8**	**–21.3**	**–19.8**	**–27.1**	**–37.5**
Investment income, credit	2 320	. .	**10.8**	**14.2**	**15.3**	**19.7**	**15.8**	**10.6**	**14.0**	**12.3**
Direct investment income	2 330	. .	. . .	. . .	. . .	. . .	. . .	. . .	. . .	. . .
Dividends and distributed branch profits	2 332	. .	. . .	. . .	. . .	. . .	. . .	. . .	. . .	. . .
Reinvested earnings and undistributed branch profits	2 333	. .	. . .	. . .	. . .	. . .	. . .	. . .	. . .	. . .
Income on debt (interest)	2 334	. .	. . .	. . .	. . .	. . .	. . .	. . .	. . .	. . .
Portfolio investment income	2 339	. .	.9	. . .	. . .	. . .	. . .	. . .	5.5	3.3
Income on equity	2 340	. .	. . .	. . .	. . .	. . .	. . .	. . .	. . .	. . .
Income on bonds and notes	2 350	. .	. . .	. . .	. . .	. . .	. . .	. . .	5.5	3.3
Income on money market instruments	2 360	. .	. . .	. . .	. . .	. . .	. . .	. . .	. . .	. . .
Other investment income	2 370	. .	9.9	14.2	15.3	19.7	15.8	10.6	8.4	9.0
Investment income, debit	3 320	. .	**–16.6**	**–32.4**	**–39.1**	**–65.5**	**–81.0**	**–75.4**	**–77.0**	**–86.6**
Direct investment income	3 330	. .	. . .	–.1	–.8	–1.9	–7.0	–13.9	–18.7	–18.2
Dividends and distributed branch profits	3 332	. . .	. . .	–.1	–.8	–.9	–.6	–6.0	–2.7	–4.5
Reinvested earnings and undistributed branch profits	3 333	. .	. . .	. . .	. . .	–.9	–5.8	–5.7	–11.7	–8.3
Income on debt (interest)	3 334	. .	. . .	. . .	. . .	. . .	–.5	–2.2	–4.3	–5.4
Portfolio investment income	3 339	. .	. . .	–.6	–2.6	–24.7	–28.3	–12.8	–11.1	–14.0
Income on equity	3 340	. .	. . .	. . .	. . .	. . .	–.9	–.2	–.3	. . .
Income on bonds and notes	3 350	. .	. . .	. . .	–1.2	–14.3	–20.7	–11.4	–10.8	–14.0
Income on money market instruments	3 360	. .	. . .	–.6	–1.4	–10.4	–6.7	–1.2	. . .	. . .
Other investment income	3 370	. .	–16.6	–31.7	–35.6	–39.0	–45.7	–48.8	–47.2	–54.4
D. CURRENT TRANSFERS	4 379	. .	33.3	55.6	73.1	54.1	65.4	85.8	157.8	153.1
Credit	2 379	. .	**36.9**	**69.7**	**75.9**	**104.1**	**110.9**	**125.4**	**173.0**	**171.1**
General government	2 380	. .	. . .	25.4	35.8	50.6	50.9	58.3	83.4	87.7
Other sectors	2 390	. .	. . .	44.3	40.0	53.5	60.1	67.0	89.7	83.4
Workers' remittances	2 391	. .	. . .	1.0	3.1	1.3	1.2	1.2	3.3	1.1
Other current transfers	2 392	. .	. . .	43.3	36.9	52.2	58.9	65.9	86.4	82.3
Debit	3 379	. .	**–3.6**	**–14.1**	**–2.8**	**–50.0**	**–45.5**	**–39.6**	**–15.2**	**–18.0**
General government	3 380	. .	. . .	–4.6	–2.0	–10.7	–7.2	–5.7	–8.0	–9.2
Other sectors	3 390	. .	. . .	–9.6	–.8	–39.3	–38.3	–33.9	–7.2	–8.8
Workers' remittances	3 391	. .	. . .	–.3	–.8	–.2	–.1	–.3	–.2	–.3
Other current transfers	3 392	. .	. . .	–9.3	. . .	–39.1	–38.2	–33.6	–7.0	–8.5
CAPITAL AND FINANCIAL ACCOUNT	4 996	. .	**197.3**	**103.0**	**176.4**	**282.8**	**357.6**	**75.0**	**111.0**	**54.0**
CAPITAL ACCOUNT	4 994	. .	**–1.0**	**–.4**	**–.1**	**–.2**	**.3**	**116.7**	**4.3**	**–1.9**
Total credit	2 994	. .	. . .	. . .	*.1*	*.1*	*2.8*	*117.0*	*5.2*	*1.1*
Total debit	3 994	. .	*–1.0*	*–.4*	*–.1*	*–.3*	*–2.5*	*–.4*	*–.9*	*–3.0*
Capital transfers, credit	2 400	. .	**. . .**	**. . .**	**.1**	**.1**	**2.8**	**117.0**	**5.2**	**1.1**
General government	2 401	. .	. . .	. . .	. . .	. . .	.7	115.5	4.0	. . .
Debt forgiveness	2 402	. .	. . .	. . .	. . .	. . .	.7	115.5	2.4	. . .
Other capital transfers	2 410	. .	. . .	. . .	. . .	. . .	. . .	. . .	1.6	. . .
Other sectors	2 430	. .	. . .	. . .	.1	.1	2.1	1.5	1.1	1.1
Migrants' transfers	2 431	. .	. . .	. . .	.1	.1	2.1	1.5	1.1	1.1
Debt forgiveness	2 432	. .	. . .	. . .	. . .	. . .	. . .	. . .	. . .	. . .
Other capital transfers	2 440	. .	. . .	. . .	. . .	. . .	. . .	. . .	. . .	. . .
Capital transfers, debit	3 400	. .	**–1.0**	**–.4**	**–.1**	**–.3**	**–2.5**	**–.4**	**–.9**	**–3.0**
General government	3 401	. .	. . .	. . .	. . .	. . .	. . .	. . .	. . .	. . .
Debt forgiveness	3 402	. .	. . .	. . .	. . .	. . .	. . .	. . .	. . .	. . .
Other capital transfers	3 410	. .	. . .	. . .	. . .	. . .	. . .	. . .	. . .	. . .
Other sectors	3 430	. .	. . .	–.4	–.1	–.3	–2.5	–.4	–.9	–3.0
Migrants' transfers	3 431	. .	. . .	–.4	–.1	–.3	–2.5	–.4	–.9	–.1
Debt forgiveness	3 432	. .	. . .	. . .	. . .	. . .	. . .	. . .	. . .	. . .
Other capital transfers	3 440	. .	. . .	. . .	. . .	. . .	. . .	. . .	. . .	–2.9
Nonproduced nonfinancial assets, credit	2 480	. .	**. . .**	**. . .**	**. . .**	**. . .**	**. . .**	**. . .**	**. . .**	**. . .**
Nonproduced nonfinancial assets, debit	3 480	. .	**. . .**	**. . .**	**. . .**	**. . .**	**. . .**	**. . .**	**. . .**	**. . .**

Table 2 (Continued). STANDARD PRESENTATION, 1994–2001

(Millions of U.S. dollars)

	Code	1994	1995	1996	1997	1998	1999	2000	2001
FINANCIAL ACCOUNT	4 995 . .	**198.2**	**103.4**	**176.4**	**283.1**	**357.2**	**–41.7**	**106.7**	**55.9**
A. DIRECT INVESTMENT	4 500 . .	11.6	66.4	23.2	78.3	76.2	40.4	142.7	148.7
Direct investment abroad	4 505 . .	**. . .**	**–.5**	**–.6**	**–.5**	**.7**	**–.1**	**–.1**	**. . .**
Equity capital	4 510 . .	. . .	. . .	. . .	–.4	. . .	–.1	–.1	. . .
Claims on affiliated enterprises	4 515 . .	. . .	. . .	. . .	–.4	. . .	–.1	–.1	. . .
Liabilities to affiliated enterprises	4 520 . .	. . .	. . .	. . .	. . .	. . .	. . .	. . .	. . .
Reinvested earnings	4 525 . .	. . .	. . .	. . .	. . .	. . .	. . .	. . .	. . .
Other capital	4 530 . .	. . .	–.5	–.6	–.1	.8	. . .	. . .	. . .
Claims on affiliated enterprises	4 535 . .	. . .	–.5	–.6	–.1	.8	. . .	. . .	. . .
Liabilities to affiliated enterprises	4 540 . .	. . .	. . .	. . .	. . .	. . .	. . .	. . .	. . .
Direct investment in Moldova	4 555 . .	**11.6**	**66.9**	**23.7**	**78.7**	**75.5**	**40.4**	**142.8**	**148.7**
Equity capital	4 560 . .	. . .	65.2	21.1	69.5	54.2	36.6	83.6	114.6
Claims on direct investors	4 565 . .	. . .	. . .	. . .	. . .	. . .	. . .	. . .	. . .
Liabilities to direct investors	4 570 . .	. . .	65.2	21.1	69.5	54.2	36.6	83.6	114.6
Reinvested earnings	4 575 . .	. . .	. . .	. . .	.9	5.8	5.7	11.7	8.3
Other capital	4 580 . .	. . .	1.7	2.7	8.3	15.5	–1.9	47.5	25.8
Claims on direct investors	4 585 . .	. . .	. . .	. . .	. . .	. . .	. . .	. . .	. . .
Liabilities to direct investors	4 590 . .	. . .	1.7	2.7	8.3	15.5	–1.9	47.5	25.8
B. PORTFOLIO INVESTMENT	4 600 . .	.3	–.5	60.8	233.6	–59.1	–140.1	92.5	–25.3
Assets	4 602 . .	**–.4**	**. . .**	**. . .**	**. . .**	**. . .**	**. . .**	**. . .**	**–3.1**
Equity securities	4 610 . .	–.4	. . .	. . .	. . .	. . .	. . .	. . .	. . .
Monetary authorities	4 611 . .	. . .	. . .	. . .	. . .	. . .	. . .	. . .	. . .
General government	4 612 . .	–.4	. . .	. . .	. . .	. . .	. . .	. . .	. . .
Banks	4 613 . .	. . .	. . .	. . .	. . .	. . .	. . .	. . .	. . .
Other sectors	4 614 . .	. . .	. . .	. . .	. . .	. . .	. . .	. . .	. . .
Debt securities	4 619 . .	. . .	. . .	. . .	. . .	. . .	. . .	. . .	–3.1
Bonds and notes	4 620 . .	. . .	. . .	. . .	. . .	. . .	. . .	. . .	–3.1
Monetary authorities	4 621 . .	. . .	. . .	. . .	. . .	. . .	. . .	. . .	. . .
General government	4 622 . .	. . .	. . .	. . .	. . .	. . .	. . .	. . .	. . .
Banks	4 623 . .	. . .	. . .	. . .	. . .	. . .	. . .	. . .	–3.0
Other sectors	4 624 . .	. . .	. . .	. . .	. . .	. . .	. . .	. . .	–.1
Money market instruments	4 630 . .	. . .	. . .	. . .	. . .	. . .	. . .	. . .	. . .
Monetary authorities	4 631 . .	. . .	. . .	. . .	. . .	. . .	. . .	. . .	. . .
General government	4 632 . .	. . .	. . .	. . .	. . .	. . .	. . .	. . .	. . .
Banks	4 633 . .	. . .	. . .	. . .	. . .	. . .	. . .	. . .	. . .
Other sectors	4 634 . .	. . .	. . .	. . .	. . .	. . .	. . .	. . .	. . .
Liabilities	4 652 . .	**.6**	**–.5**	**60.8**	**233.6**	**–59.1**	**–140.1**	**92.5**	**–22.2**
Equity securities	4 660 . .	.6	–.5	.8	3.7	6.5	5.5	2.6	3.6
Banks	4 663 . .	. . .	. . .	.7	3.0	–.7	1.3	2.6	.6
Other sectors	4 664 . .	.6	–.5	.1	.7	7.2	4.1	. . .	3.0
Debt securities	4 669 . .	. . .	. . .	60.0	229.9	–65.6	–145.5	89.9	–25.8
Bonds and notes	4 670 . .	. . .	. . .	30.0	218.8	–30.2	–141.0	89.9	–25.8
Monetary authorities	4 671 . .	. . .	. . .	. . .	. . .	. . .	. . .	. . .	. . .
General government	4 672 . .	. . .	. . .	30.0	218.8	–30.2	–141.0	89.9	–25.8
Banks	4 673 . .	. . .	. . .	. . .	. . .	. . .	. . .	. . .	. . .
Other sectors	4 674 . .	. . .	. . .	. . .	. . .	. . .	. . .	. . .	. . .
Money market instruments	4 680 . .	. . .	. . .	30.0	11.2	–35.4	–4.6	. . .	. . .
Monetary authorities	4 681 . .	. . .	. . .	. . .	. . .	. . .	. . .	. . .	. . .
General government	4 682 . .	. . .	. . .	30.0	11.2	–35.4	–4.6	. . .	. . .
Banks	4 683 . .	. . .	. . .	. . .	. . .	. . .	. . .	. . .	. . .
Other sectors	4 684 . .	. . .	. . .	. . .	. . .	. . .	. . .	. . .	. . .
C. FINANCIAL DERIVATIVES	4 910 . .	. . .	. . .	. . .	. . .	. . .	. . .	. . .	. . .
Monetary authorities	4 911 . .	. . .	. . .	. . .	. . .	. . .	. . .	. . .	. . .
General government	4 912 . .	. . .	. . .	. . .	. . .	. . .	. . .	. . .	. . .
Banks	4 913 . .	. . .	. . .	. . .	. . .	. . .	. . .	. . .	. . .
Other sectors	4 914 . .	. . .	. . .	. . .	. . .	. . .	. . .	. . .	. . .
Assets	4 900 . .	**. . .**	**. . .**	**. . .**	**. . .**	**. . .**	**. . .**	**. . .**	**. . .**
Monetary authorities	4 901 . .	. . .	. . .	. . .	. . .	. . .	. . .	. . .	. . .
General government	4 902 . .	. . .	. . .	. . .	. . .	. . .	. . .	. . .	. . .
Banks	4 903 . .	. . .	. . .	. . .	. . .	. . .	. . .	. . .	. . .
Other sectors	4 904 . .	. . .	. . .	. . .	. . .	. . .	. . .	. . .	. . .
Liabilities	4 905 . .	**. . .**	**. . .**	**. . .**	**. . .**	**. . .**	**. . .**	**. . .**	**. . .**
Monetary authorities	4 906 . .	. . .	. . .	. . .	. . .	. . .	. . .	. . .	. . .
General government	4 907 . .	. . .	. . .	. . .	. . .	. . .	. . .	. . .	. . .
Banks	4 908 . .	. . .	. . .	. . .	. . .	. . .	. . .	. . .	. . .
Other sectors	4 909 . .	. . .	. . .	. . .	. . .	. . .	. . .	. . .	. . .

Table 2 (Concluded). STANDARD PRESENTATION, 1994–2001
(Millions of U.S. dollars)

	Code	1994	1995	1996	1997	1998	1999	2000	2001
D. OTHER INVESTMENT	4 700 . .	289.5	114.2	149.3	21.4	114.4	106.8	–81.7	–57.7
Assets	4 703 . .	**–81.7**	**–116.4**	**–51.4**	**1.8**	**–86.8**	**–110.9**	**–39.4**	**–39.4**
Trade credits	4 706 . .	–65.8	–122.1	–44.5	–4.0	–71.7	–75.6	–18.2	–41.0
General government	4 707 . .	–.3	.6	–6.4	4.8	2.6	. . .	. . .	. . .
of which: Short-term	4 709 . .	*–.3*	*.6*	*–6.4*	*4.8*	*2.6*	. . .	. . .	. . .
Other sectors	4 710 . .	–65.6	–122.7	–38.1	–8.7	–74.3	–75.6	–18.2	–41.0
of which: Short-term	4 712 . .	*–65.6*	*–122.7*	*–38.1*	*–8.7*	*–74.3*	*–75.6*	*–18.2*	*–41.0*
Loans	4 714 . .	9.2	9.5	2.4	. . .	. . .	. . .	. . .	. . .
Monetary authorities	4 715 . .	. . .	. . .	. . .	. . .	. . .	. . .	. . .	. . .
of which: Short-term	4 718 . .	. . .	. . .	. . .	. . .	. . .	. . .	. . .	. . .
General government	4 719 . .	9.5	9.5	2.4	. . .	. . .	. . .	. . .	. . .
of which: Short-term	4 721 . .	. . .	. . .	. . .	. . .	. . .	. . .	. . .	. . .
Banks	4 722 . .	–.2	. . .	. . .	. . .	. . .	. . .	. . .	. . .
of which: Short-term	4 724 . .	*–.2*	. . .	. . .	. . .	. . .	. . .	. . .	. . .
Other sectors	4 725 . .	. . .	. . .	. . .	. . .	. . .	. . .	. . .	. . .
of which: Short-term	4 727 . .	. . .	. . .	. . .	. . .	. . .	. . .	. . .	. . .
Currency and deposits	4 730 . .	–11.3	–5.4	–25.3	5.8	–15.6	–35.3	–21.3	1.6
Monetary authorities	4 731 . .	–1.3	2.9	.3	3.7	2.9	. . .	.1	. . .
General government	4 732 . .	. . .	. . .	. . .	–3.1	–3.2	–4.3	. . .	8.3
Banks	4 733 . .	–9.9	–13.5	–6.5	10.6	–10.9	–15.4	–16.5	1.2
Other sectors	4 734 . .	–.1	5.2	–19.1	–5.4	–4.4	–15.7	–4.9	–7.9
Other assets	4 736 . .	–13.8	1.6	16.1	–.1	.5	. . .	. . .	. . .
Monetary authorities	4 737 . .	. . .	. . .	. . .	. . .	. . .	. . .	. . .	. . .
of which: Short-term	4 739 . .	. . .	. . .	. . .	. . .	. . .	. . .	. . .	. . .
General government	4 740 . .	–13.3	1.7	16.2	–.1	. . .	. . .	. . .	. . .
of which: Short-term	4 742 . .	. . .	*1.7*	*16.2*	*–.1*	. . .	. . .	. . .	. . .
Banks	4 743 . .	. . .	. . .	. . .	. . .	. . .	. . .	. . .	. . .
of which: Short-term	4 745 . .	. . .	. . .	. . .	. . .	. . .	. . .	. . .	. . .
Other sectors	4 746 . .	–.5	–.2	–.2	. . .	.5	. . .	. . .	. . .
of which: Short-term	4 748 . .	. . .	*–.2*	*–.2*	. . .	*.5*	. . .	. . .	. . .
Liabilities	4 753 . .	**371.2**	**230.6**	**200.7**	**19.5**	**201.2**	**217.7**	**–42.2**	**–18.3**
Trade credits	4 756 . .	123.2	15.4	–1.3	5.7	63.3	21.8	–8.8	–11.4
General government	4 757 . .	–3.6	.5	. . .	. . .	. . .	. . .	. . .	. . .
of which: Short-term	4 759 . .	*–3.6*	*.5*	. . .	. . .	. . .	. . .	. . .	. . .
Other sectors	4 760 . .	126.8	14.9	–1.3	5.7	63.3	21.8	–8.8	–11.4
of which: Short-term	4 762 . .	*126.8*	*14.9*	*–1.3*	*5.7*	*63.3*	*21.8*	*–8.8*	*–11.4*
Loans	4 764 . .	223.2	137.0	173.4	19.3	–2.4	79.6	151.7	–2.9
Monetary authorities	4 765 . .	71.5	64.8	25.2	.8	–64.4	4.0	–12.7	–2.3
of which: Use of Fund credit and loans from the Fund	4 766 . .	*71.5*	*64.8*	*25.2*	*.8*	*–64.4*	*4.0*	*–12.7*	*–2.3*
of which: Short-term	4 768 . .	. . .	. . .	. . .	. . .	. . .	. . .	. . .	. . .
General government	4 769 . .	151.5	55.2	109.0	–23.4	54.5	32.6	134.7	–15.3
of which: Short-term	4 771 . .	. . .	. . .	. . .	*3.3*	*–3.3*	. . .	. . .	. . .
Banks	4 772 . .	.2	5.8	19.8	1.0	17.5	–20.0	–6.1	1.1
of which: Short-term	4 774 . .	*.2*	*–.2*	. . .	*4.7*	*5.0*	*–8.2*	*.3*	*–.2*
Other sectors	4 775 . .	.1	11.3	19.4	40.9	–10.0	63.0	35.9	13.6
of which: Short-term	4 777 . .	*.1*	*.5*	*.3*	*2.0*	*–.5*	*2.1*	*2.1*	*6.3*
Currency and deposits	4 780 . .	2.2	7.2	.4	8.1	–5.5	–2.7	10.3	–3.1
Monetary authorities	4 781 . .	3.1	1.8	–1.9	–2.7	5.2	–2.4	1.6	–1.0
General government	4 782 . .	. . .	. . .	. . .	. . .	. . .	. . .	. . .	. . .
Banks	4 783 . .	–1.0	5.4	2.3	10.8	–10.6	–.3	8.7	–2.1
Other sectors	4 784 . .	. . .	. . .	. . .	. . .	. . .	. . .	. . .	. . .
Other liabilities	4 786 . .	22.6	71.0	28.2	–13.6	145.7	118.9	–195.4	–.9
Monetary authorities	4 787 . .	. . .	. . .	. . .	. . .	. . .	. . .	. . .	. . .
of which: Short-term	4 789 . .	. . .	. . .	. . .	. . .	. . .	. . .	. . .	. . .
General government	4 790 . .	17.5	21.1	–34.5	34.6	42.5	37.6	–113.9	4.8
of which: Short-term	4 792 . .	*17.5*	*21.1*	*–34.5*	*34.6*	*42.5*	*37.6*	*–113.9*	*4.8*
Banks	4 793 . .	. . .	.2	–.1	. . .	. . .	. . .	. . .	. . .
of which: Short-term	4 795 . .	. . .	*.2*	*–.1*	. . .	. . .	. . .	. . .	. . .
Other sectors	4 796 . .	5.0	49.7	62.8	–48.1	103.3	81.3	–81.6	–5.7
of which: Short-term	4 798 . .	*5.0*	*49.7*	*62.8*	*–48.1*	*103.3*	*81.3*	*–81.6*	*–5.7*
E. RESERVE ASSETS	4 802 . .	–103.1	–76.7	–56.9	–50.2	225.7	–48.8	–46.8	–9.7
Monetary gold	4 812 . .	. . .	. . .	. . .	. . .	. . .	. . .	. . .	. . .
Special drawing rights	4 811 . .	14.6	8.8	4.9	6.3	.6	.3	. . .	–.4
Reserve position in the Fund	4 810 . .	. . .	. . .	. . .	. . .	. . .	. . .	. . .	. . .
Foreign exchange	4 803 . .	–117.7	–85.5	–61.8	–56.4	225.2	–49.0	–46.8	–9.3
Other claims	4 813 . .	. . .	. . .	. . .	. . .	. . .	. . .	. . .	. . .
NET ERRORS AND OMISSIONS	4 998 . .	**–115.2**	**–18.4**	**15.5**	**–7.9**	**–22.8**	**–20.1**	**–4.8**	**44.6**

Part 3 of the *Yearbook* contains descriptions of the methodologies, compilation practices, and sources used to compile these data.

Table 3. INTERNATIONAL INVESTMENT POSITION (End–period stocks), 1994–2001

(Millions of U.S. dollars)

	Code	1994	1995	1996	1997	1998	1999	2000	2001
ASSETS	8 995 C.	303.3	499.8	612.4	657.9	463.9	594.2	668.4	705.8
Direct investment abroad	8 505 . .	**17.8**	**18.3**	**18.9**	**19.3**	**18.6**	**18.6**	**18.7**	**18.8**
Equity capital and reinvested earnings	8 506 . .	17.8	17.8	17.8	18.2	18.2	18.3	18.3	18.4
Claims on affiliated enterprises	8 507 . .	17.8	17.8	17.8	18.2	18.2	18.3	18.3	18.4
Liabilities to affiliated enterprises	8 508 . .	...	...	...	...	...	...	...	...
Other capital	8 530 . .	...	.5	1.1	1.2	.4	.4	.4	.4
Claims on affiliated enterprises	8 535 . .	...	.5	1.1	1.2	.4	.4	.4	.4
Liabilities to affiliated enterprises	8 540 . .	...	...	...	...	...	...	...	...
Portfolio investment	8 602 . .	**.4**	**.4**	**.4**	**.4**	**.4**	**.4**	**.4**	**3.6**
Equity securities	8 610 . .	.4	.4	.4	.4	.4	.4	.4	.4
Monetary authorities	8 611 . .	...	...	...	...	...	...	...	...
General government	8 612 . .	.4	.4	.4	.4	.4	.4	.4	.4
Banks	8 613 . .	...	...	...	...	...	...	...	...
Other sectors	8 614 . .	...	...	...	...	...	...	...	...
Debt securities	8 619 . .	...	...	...	...	...	...	...	3.2
Bonds and notes	8 620 . .	...	...	...	...	...	...	...	3.2
Monetary authorities	8 621 . .	...	...	...	...	...	...	...	...
General government	8 622 . .	...	...	...	...	...	...	...	...
Banks	8 623 . .	...	...	...	...	...	...	...	3.1
Other sectors	8 624 . .	...	...	...	...	...	...	...	.1
Money market instruments	8 630 . .	...	...	...	...	...	...	...	...
Monetary authorities	8 631 . .	...	...	...	...	...	...	...	...
General government	8 632 . .	...	...	...	...	...	...	...	...
Banks	8 633 . .	...	...	...	...	...	...	...	...
Other sectors	8 634 . .	...	...	...	...	...	...	...	...
Financial derivatives	8 900 . .	**...**	**...**	**...**	**...**	**...**	**...**	**...**	**...**
Monetary authorities	8 901 . .	...	...	...	...	...	...	...	...
General government	8 902 . .	...	...	...	...	...	...	...	...
Banks	8 903 . .	...	...	...	...	...	...	...	...
Other sectors	8 904 . .	...	...	...	...	...	...	...	...
Other investment	8 703 . .	**105.3**	**224.0**	**279.6**	**276.0**	**308.1**	**394.8**	**426.7**	**454.8**
Trade credits	8 706 . .	34.2	155.4	194.1	198.1	217.9	272.7	283.8	314.5
General government	8 707 . .	1.9	1.3	7.6	2.9	.3	.3	.3	.3
of which: Short-term	8 709 . .	*1.9*	*1.3*	*7.6*	*2.9*	*.3*	*.3*	*.3*	*.3*
Other sectors	8 710 . .	32.3	154.1	186.4	195.2	217.6	272.4	283.5	314.2
of which: Short-term	8 712 . .	*32.3*	*154.1*	*186.4*	*195.2*	*217.6*	*272.4*	*283.5*	*314.2*
Loans	8 714 . .	11.9	2.4	...	...	...	...	...	...
Monetary authorities	8 715 . .	...	...	...	...	...	...	...	...
of which: Short-term	8 718 . .	...	...	...	...	...	...	...	...
General government	8 719 . .	11.9	2.4	...	...	...	...	...	...
of which: Short-term	8 721 . .	...	...	...	...	...	...	...	...
Banks	8 722 . .	...	...	...	...	...	...	...	...
of which: Short-term	8 724 . .	...	...	...	...	...	...	...	...
Other sectors	8 725 . .	...	...	...	...	...	...	...	...
of which: Short-term	8 727 . .	...	...	...	...	...	...	...	...
Currency and deposits	8 730 . .	40.8	49.5	74.8	67.1	79.8	111.7	132.5	129.9
Monetary authorities	8 731 . .	9.9	7.1	6.8	3.1	.1	.1	...	...
General government	8 732 . .	...	...	...	3.3	6.5	9.8	9.6	1.3
Banks	8 733 . .	27.4	40.8	47.3	36.7	44.9	58.1	74.4	72.7
Other sectors	8 734 . .	3.5	1.6	20.7	24.0	28.4	43.8	48.5	55.9
Other assets	8 736 . .	18.5	16.9	10.8	10.8	10.4	10.4	10.4	10.4
Monetary authorities	8 737 . .	...	...	...	...	...	...	...	...
of which: Short-term	8 739 . .	...	...	...	...	...	...	...	...
General government	8 740 . .	18.0	16.2	...	...	...	...	...	...
of which: Short-term	8 742 . .	*18.0*	*16.2*	...	...	...	...	...	...
Banks	8 743 . .	...	...	...	...	...	...	...	...
of which: Short-term	8 745 . .	...	...	...	...	...	...	...	...
Other sectors	8 746 . .	.5	.6	10.8	10.8	10.4	10.4	10.4	10.4
of which: Short-term	8 748 . .	*.5*	*.6*	*10.8*	*10.8*	*10.4*	*10.4*	*10.4*	*10.4*
Reserve assets	8 802 . .	**179.8**	**257.0**	**313.6**	**362.2**	**136.9**	**180.4**	**222.6**	**228.6**
Monetary gold	8 812 . .	...	...	...	...	...	...	...	...
Special drawing rights	8 811 . .	21.3	13.1	7.8	1.2	.7	.3	.3	.7
Reserve position in the Fund	8 810 . .	...	...	...	...	...	...	...	...
Foreign exchange	8 803 . .	158.4	243.9	305.7	361.0	136.2	180.1	222.3	227.8
Other claims	8 813 . .	...	...	...	...	...	...	...	...

Table 3 (Concluded). INTERNATIONAL INVESTMENT POSITION (End–period stocks), 1994–2001

(Millions of U.S. dollars)

	Code	1994	1995	1996	1997	1998	1999	2000	2001
LIABILITIES	8 995 D.	720.0	1,022.2	1,289.5	1,594.6	1,822.6	1,943.0	2,102.2	2,168.9
Direct investment in Moldova	8 555 . .	**28.6**	**93.2**	**116.9**	**192.7**	**255.3**	**317.8**	**461.9**	**608.5**
Equity capital and reinvested earnings	8 556 . .	28.6	91.5	112.5	180.0	227.1	291.6	388.2	509.0
Claims on direct investors	8 557 . .	. . .	. . .	. . .	. . .	. . .	. . .	. . .	. . .
Liabilities to direct investors	8 558 . .	28.6	91.5	112.5	180.0	227.1	291.6	388.2	509.0
Other capital	8 580 . .	. . .	1.7	4.4	12.7	28.2	26.3	73.7	99.5
Claims on direct investors	8 585 . .	. . .	. . .	. . .	. . .	. . .	. . .	. . .	. . .
Liabilities to direct investors	8 590 . .	. . .	1.7	4.4	12.7	28.2	26.3	73.7	99.5
Portfolio investment	8 652 . .	**.7**	**.4**	**60.7**	**296.3**	**232.3**	**86.6**	**176.2**	**144.1**
Equity securities	8 660 . .	.7	.4	.8	6.0	10.4	11.5	11.2	14.4
Banks	8 663 . .	. . .	.3	.6	5.1	4.2	3.2	3.5	3.9
Other sectors	8 664 . .	.7	.1	.2	.9	6.2	8.3	7.7	10.5
Debt securities	8 669 . .	. . .	.1	59.9	290.3	221.9	75.1	165.0	129.7
Bonds and notes	8 670 . .	. . .	. . .	30.2	247.3	216.5	75.1	165.0	129.7
Monetary authorities	8 671 . .	. . .	. . .	. . .	. . .	. . .	. . .	. . .	. . .
General government	8 672 . .	. . .	. . .	30.2	247.3	216.5	75.1	165.0	129.7
Banks	8 673 . .	. . .	. . .	. . .	. . .	. . .	. . .	. . .	. . .
Other sectors	8 674 . .	. . .	. . .	. . .	. . .	. . .	. . .	. . .	. . .
Money market instruments	8 680 . .	. . .	.1	29.8	43.0	5.4	. . .	. . .	. . .
Monetary authorities	8 681 . .	. . .	. . .	. . .	. . .	. . .	. . .	. . .	. . .
General government	8 682 . .	. . .	.1	29.8	43.0	5.4	. . .	. . .	. . .
Banks	8 683 . .	. . .	. . .	. . .	. . .	. . .	. . .	. . .	. . .
Other sectors	8 684 . .	. . .	. . .	. . .	. . .	. . .	. . .	. . .	. . .
Financial derivatives	8 905 . .	**. . .**	**. . .**	**. . .**	**. . .**	**. . .**	**. . .**	**. . .**	**. . .**
Monetary authorities	8 906 . .	. . .	. . .	. . .	. . .	. . .	. . .	. . .	. . .
General government	8 907 . .	. . .	. . .	. . .	. . .	. . .	. . .	. . .	. . .
Banks	8 908 . .	. . .	. . .	. . .	. . .	. . .	. . .	. . .	. . .
Other sectors	8 909 . .	. . .	. . .	. . .	. . .	. . .	. . .	. . .	. . .
Other investment	8 753 . .	**690.7**	**928.6**	**1,111.9**	**1,105.7**	**1,335.1**	**1,538.6**	**1,464.1**	**1,416.3**
Trade credits	8 756 . .	18.2	33.6	31.8	37.6	95.6	116.0	106.9	92.0
General government	8 757 . .	. . .	.5	. . .	. . .	. . .	. . .	. . .	. . .
of which: Short-term	8 759 . .	. . .	*.5*	. . .	. . .	. . .	. . .	. . .	. . .
Other sectors	8 760 . .	18.2	33.1	31.8	37.6	95.6	116.0	106.9	92.0
of which: Short-term	8 762 . .	*18.2*	*33.1*	*31.8*	*37.6*	*95.6*	*116.0*	*106.9*	*92.0*
Loans	8 764 . .	493.2	632.9	790.5	755.3	778.3	836.3	956.9	926.7
Monetary authorities	8 765 . .	164.2	230.2	247.7	233.0	176.8	175.3	154.1	146.1
of which: Use of Fund credit and loans from the Fund	8 766 . .	*164.2*	*230.2*	*247.7*	*233.0*	*176.8*	*175.3*	*154.1*	*146.1*
of which: Short-term	8 768 . .	. . .	. . .	. . .	. . .	. . .	. . .	. . .	. . .
General government	8 769 . .	324.8	380.0	481.5	427.7	494.9	515.3	627.1	591.7
of which: Short-term	8 771 . .	. . .	. . .	. . .	*3.3*	. . .	. . .	. . .	. . .
Banks	8 772 . .	.2	6.0	24.1	22.7	43.1	22.1	15.6	16.7
of which: Short-term	8 774 . .	*.2*	. . .	. . .	*2.8*	*10.4*	*2.0*	*2.3*	*2.1*
Other sectors	8 775 . .	4.0	16.7	37.2	71.9	63.5	123.6	160.1	172.2
of which: Short-term	8 777 . .	. . .	*.1*	*1.1*	*3.3*	*1.9*	*3.9*	*5.9*	*11.0*
Currency and deposits	8 780 . .	7.4	14.6	15.0	23.1	12.7	9.0	19.1	15.9
Monetary authorities	8 781 . .	6.5	8.3	6.4	3.7	4.4	1.1	2.6	1.5
General government	8 782 . .	. . .	. . .	. . .	. . .	. . .	. . .	. . .	. . .
Banks	8 783 . .	.9	6.4	8.6	19.4	8.3	7.9	16.5	14.4
Other sectors	8 784 . .	. . .	. . .	. . .	. . .	. . .	. . .	. . .	. . .
Other liabilities	8 786 . .	171.9	247.4	274.6	289.7	448.5	577.4	381.2	381.7
Monetary authorities	8 787 . .	. . .	. . .	. . .	. . .	. . .	. . .	. . .	. . .
of which: Short-term	8 789 . .	. . .	. . .	. . .	. . .	. . .	. . .	. . .	. . .
General government	8 790 . .	17.5	38.6	4.1	41.0	83.5	121.1	7.0	11.9
of which: Short-term	8 792 . .	*17.5*	*38.6*	*4.1*	*41.0*	*83.5*	*121.1*	*7.0*	*11.9*
Banks	8 793 . .	. . .	.1	. . .	. . .	. . .	. . .	. . .	. . .
of which: Short-term	8 795 . .	. . .	*.1*	. . .	. . .	. . .	. . .	. . .	. . .
Other sectors	8 796 . .	154.4	208.7	270.6	248.7	365.0	456.3	374.2	369.8
of which: Short-term	8 798 . .	*154.4*	*208.7*	*270.6*	*248.7*	*365.0*	*456.3*	*374.2*	*369.8*
NET INTERNATIONAL INVESTMENT POSITION	8 995 . .	**-416.7**	**-522.4**	**-677.1**	**-936.7**	**-1,358.7**	**-1,348.8**	**-1,433.8**	**-1,463.2**
Conversion rates: lei per U.S. dollar (end of period)	0 102 . .	**4.2700**	**4.4990**	**4.6743**	**4.6605**	**8.3226**	**11.5902**	**12.3833**	**13.0909**

Table 1. ANALYTIC PRESENTATION, 1994–2001
(Millions of U.S. dollars)

	Code	1994	1995	1996	1997	1998	1999	2000	2001
A. Current Account [1]	4 993 Z.	**46.4**	**38.9**	**–100.5**	**55.2**	**–128.5**	**–112.2**	**–156.1**	**–150.6**
Goods: exports f.o.b	2 100 ..	367.0	451.0	423.4	568.5	462.4	454.3	535.8	460.0
Goods: imports f.o.b	3 100 ..	–333.3	–425.7	–459.7	–453.1	–524.2	–510.7	–608.4	–549.3
Balance on Goods	4 100 ..	*33.7*	*25.3*	*–36.3*	*115.4*	*–61.8*	*–56.4*	*–72.6*	*–89.3*
Services: credit	2 200 ..	45.4	57.3	55.7	52.7	77.8	75.8	77.7	86.4
Services: debit	3 200 ..	–91.2	–95.4	–112.8	–105.1	–146.8	–145.7	–162.8	–173.8
Balance on Goods and Services	4 991 ..	*–12.1*	*–12.8*	*–93.4*	*63.0*	*–130.8*	*–126.3*	*–157.7*	*–176.7*
Income: credit	2 300 ..	3.2	3.0	13.4	6.1	10.1	6.7	13.0	20.8
Income: debit	3 300 ..	–22.5	–28.4	–26.7	–18.1	–9.7	–6.6	–19.5	–16.5
Balance on Goods, Services, and Income	4 992 ..	*–31.4*	*–38.2*	*–106.7*	*51.0*	*–130.4*	*–126.2*	*–164.2*	*–172.4*
Current transfers: credit	2 379 Z.	77.8	77.1	6.2	4.2	5.5	17.6	25.0	41.2
Current transfers: debit	3 379 ..	...	...	...	...	–3.6	–3.6	–16.9	–19.4
B. Capital Account [1]	4 994 Z.	**...**	**...**	**...**	**...**	**...**	**...**	**...**	**...**
Capital account: credit	2 994 Z.	...	...	...	...	...	...	...	...
Capital account: debit	3 994 ..	...	...	...	...	...	...	...	...
Total, Groups A Plus B	4 981 ..	*46.4*	*38.9*	*–100.5*	*55.2*	*–128.5*	*–112.2*	*–156.1*	*–150.6*
C. Financial Account [1]	4 995 W.	**–39.0**	**–15.9**	**41.3**	**27.0**	**126.2**	**69.6**	**89.9**	**121.3**
Direct investment abroad	4 505 ..	...	...	...	...	...	...	...	...
Direct investment in Mongolia	4 555 Z.	6.9	9.8	15.9	25.0	18.9	30.4	53.7	63.0
Portfolio investment assets	4 602 ..	...	...	...	...	...	...	...	...
Equity securities	4 610 ..	...	...	...	...	...	...	...	...
Debt securities	4 619 ..	...	...	...	...	...	...	...	...
Portfolio investment liabilities	4 652 Z.	...	1.0	...	...	...	...	...	...
Equity securities	4 660 ..	...	...	...	...	...	...	...	...
Debt securities	4 669 Z.	...	1.0	...	...	...	...	...	...
Financial derivatives	4 910 ..	...	...	...	...	...	...	...	...
Financial derivatives assets	4 900 ..	...	...	...	...	...	...	...	...
Financial derivatives liabilities	4 905 ..	...	...	...	...	...	...	...	...
Other investment assets	4 703 ..	–51.0	–49.2	–76.4	–108.1	–54.8	–51.8	–44.3	–14.4
Monetary authorities	4 701 ..	...	...	...	...	...	...	...	...
General government	4 704 ..	...	...	...	...	...	...	...	...
Banks	4 705 ..	–15.3	–15.3	–9.3	–18.1	...	–14.8	–10.7	.9
Other sectors	4 728 ..	–35.7	–33.9	–67.1	–90.0	–54.8	–37.0	–33.6	–15.3
Other investment liabilities	4 753 W.	5.1	22.5	101.8	110.1	162.1	91.0	80.5	72.7
Monetary authorities	4 753 WA	...	...	...	...	–5.2	...	...	...
General government	4 753 ZB	7.9	22.5	56.1	79.3	80.8	91.4	60.5	63.3
Banks	4 753 ZC	...	...	...	...	40.0	–4.8	–2.3	.5
Other sectors	4 753 ZD	–2.8	...	45.7	30.8	46.5	4.4	22.3	8.9
Total, Groups A Through C	4 983 ..	*7.4*	*23.0*	*–59.2*	*82.2*	*–2.3*	*–42.6*	*–66.2*	*–29.3*
D. Net Errors and Omissions	4 998 ..	**–1.0**	**9.1**	**–28.1**	**–75.6**	**–50.2**	**23.6**	**–19.3**	**–53.9**
Total, Groups A Through D	4 984 ..	*6.4*	*32.1*	*–87.3*	*6.6*	*–52.5*	*–19.0*	*–85.5*	*–83.2*
E. Reserves and Related Items	4 802 A.	**–6.4**	**–32.1**	**87.3**	**–6.6**	**52.5**	**19.0**	**85.5**	**83.2**
Reserve assets	4 802 ..	–27.4	–22.6	19.6	–61.2	–6.3	–40.6	–2.5	12.7
Use of Fund credit and loans	4 766 ..	21.1	–9.5	–1.8	6.7	–1.3	4.2	1.8	–1.6
Exceptional financing	4 920 ..	...	...	69.5	47.9	60.2	55.5	86.2	72.1
Conversion rates: togrogs per U.S. dollar	0 101 ..	**412.72**	**448.61**	**548.40**	**789.99**	**840.83**	**1,021.87**	**1,076.67**	**1,097.70**

[1] Excludes components that have been classified in the categories of Group E.

Table 2. STANDARD PRESENTATION, 1994–2001
(Millions of U.S. dollars)

	Code	1994	1995	1996	1997	1998	1999	2000	2001
CURRENT ACCOUNT	4 993 . .	**46.4**	**38.9**	**-36.9**	**102.9**	**-74.7**	**-51.9**	**-69.9**	**-78.5**
A. GOODS	4 100 . .	33.7	25.3	-36.3	115.4	-61.8	-56.4	-72.6	-89.3
Credit	2 100 . .	**367.0**	**451.0**	**423.4**	**568.5**	**462.4**	**454.3**	**535.8**	**460.0**
General merchandise: exports f.o.b.	2 110 . .	367.0	451.0	371.0	451.5	345.2	358.4	466.1	385.3
Goods for processing: exports f.o.b.	2 150 . .	. . .	. . .	. . .	. . .	. . .	. . .	. . .	. . .
Repairs on goods	2 160 . .	. . .	. . .	. . .	. . .	. . .	. . .	. . .	. . .
Goods procured in ports by carriers	2 170 . .	. . .	. . .	. . .	. . .	. . .	. . .	. . .	. . .
Nonmonetary gold	2 180 . .	. . .	. . .	52.4	117.0	117.2	95.9	69.7	74.7
Debit	3 100 . .	**-333.3**	**-425.7**	**-459.7**	**-453.1**	**-524.2**	**-510.7**	**-608.4**	**-549.3**
General merchandise: imports f.o.b.	3 110 . .	-333.3	-425.7	-459.7	-453.1	-524.2	-507.7	-608.4	-549.3
Goods for processing: imports f.o.b.	3 150 . .	. . .	. . .	. . .	. . .	. . .	. . .	. . .	. . .
Repairs on goods	3 160 . .	. . .	. . .	. . .	. . .	. . .	. . .	. . .	. . .
Goods procured in ports by carriers	3 170 . .	. . .	. . .	. . .	. . .	. . .	. . .	. . .	. . .
Nonmonetary gold	3 180 . .	. . .	. . .	. . .	. . .	. . .	-3.0	. . .	. . .
B. SERVICES	4 200 . .	-45.8	-38.1	-57.1	-52.4	-69.0	-69.9	-85.1	-87.4
Total credit	2 200 . .	*45.4*	*57.3*	*55.7*	*52.7*	*77.8*	*75.8*	*77.7*	*86.4*
Total debit	3 200 . .	*-91.2*	*-95.4*	*-112.8*	*-105.1*	*-146.8*	*-145.7*	*-162.8*	*-173.8*
Transportation services, credit	2 205 . .	**20.7**	**15.0**	**27.7**	**29.2**	**32.2**	**28.9**	**30.2**	**35.4**
Passenger	2 850 . .	*8.1*	*12.0*	*9.7*	*12.3*	*11.8*	*7.2*	*7.3*	*10.2*
Freight	2 851 . .	*5.5*	. . .	. . .	. . .	. . .	. . .	. . .	. . .
Other	2 852 . .	*7.1*	*3.0*	*18.0*	*16.9*	*20.4*	*21.7*	*22.9*	*25.2*
Sea transport, passenger	2 207 . .	. . .	. . .	. . .	. . .	. . .	. . .	. . .	. . .
Sea transport, freight	2 208 . .	. . .	. . .	. . .	. . .	. . .	. . .	. . .	. . .
Sea transport, other	2 209 . .	. . .	. . .	. . .	. . .	. . .	. . .	. . .	. . .
Air transport, passenger	2 211 . .	6.4	8.0	4.5	6.0	5.8	5.0	5.4	6.4
Air transport, freight	2 212 . .	. . .	. . .	. . .	. . .	. . .	. . .	. . .	. . .
Air transport, other	2 213 . .	. . .	. . .	14.0	12.8	18.2	21.2	22.3	24.8
Other transport, passenger	2 215 . .	1.7	4.0	5.2	6.3	6.0	2.2	1.9	3.8
Other transport, freight	2 216 . .	5.5	. . .	. . .	. . .	. . .	. . .	. . .	. . .
Other transport, other	2 217 . .	7.1	3.0	4.0	4.1	2.2	.5	.6	.4
Transportation services, debit	3 205 . .	**-60.7**	**-60.8**	**-75.0**	**-72.3**	**-81.3**	**-85.9**	**-85.1**	**-91.6**
Passenger	3 850 . .	*-4.9*	*-1.5*	*-18.0*	*-5.0*	*-4.6*	*-3.6*	*-3.4*	*-4.6*
Freight	3 851 . .	*-37.1*	*-47.3*	*-51.1*	*-50.3*	*-58.2*	*-56.4*	*-67.6*	*-61.0*
Other	3 852 . .	*-18.7*	*-12.0*	*-5.9*	*-17.0*	*-18.5*	*-25.9*	*-14.1*	*-26.0*
Sea transport, passenger	3 207 . .	. . .	. . .	. . .	. . .	. . .	. . .	. . .	. . .
Sea transport, freight	3 208 . .	. . .	. . .	. . .	. . .	. . .	. . .	. . .	. . .
Sea transport, other	3 209 . .	. . .	. . .	. . .	. . .	. . .	. . .	. . .	. . .
Air transport, passenger	3 211 . .	. . .	. . .	-9.4	-2.3	-2.5	-2.4	-2.3	-3.4
Air transport, freight	3 212 . .	. . .	. . .	. . .	. . .	. . .	. . .	. . .	. . .
Air transport, other	3 213 . .	. . .	. . .	-5.9	-11.0	-15.9	-13.6	-9.1	-14.9
Other transport, passenger	3 215 . .	-4.9	-1.5	-8.6	-2.7	-2.1	-1.2	-1.1	-1.2
Other transport, freight	3 216 . .	-37.1	-47.3	-51.1	-50.3	-58.2	-56.4	-67.6	-61.0
Other transport, other	3 217 . .	-18.7	-12.0	. . .	-6.0	-2.6	-12.3	-5.0	-11.1
Travel, credit	2 236 . .	**6.6**	**20.6**	**10.0**	**12.5**	**35.0**	**35.6**	**35.9**	**39.3**
Business travel	2 237 . .	. . .	. . .	10.0	12.5	35.0	. . .	. . .	. . .
Personal travel	2 240 . .	. . .	. . .	. . .	. . .	. . .	. . .	. . .	. . .
Travel, debit	3 236 . .	**-3.4**	**-19.5**	**-19.4**	**-13.5**	**-45.1**	**-40.9**	**-51.3**	**-55.3**
Business travel	3 237 . .	. . .	. . .	-19.4	-13.5	-45.1	. . .	. . .	. . .
Personal travel	3 240 . .	. . .	. . .	. . .	. . .	. . .	. . .	. . .	. . .
Other services, credit	2 200 BA	**18.1**	**21.7**	**18.0**	**11.0**	**10.6**	**11.3**	**11.6**	**11.7**
Communications	2 245 . .	3.8	5.0	4.8	6.8	7.2	7.5	7.7	6.6
Construction	2 249 . .	. . .	. . .	. . .	. . .	. . .	. . .	. . .	. . .
Insurance	2 253 . .	. . .	. . .	.6	1.7	.3	.3	.2	.9
Financial	2 260 . .	3.1	2.5	. . .	. . .	. . .	. . .	. . .	. . .
Computer and information	2 262 . .	. . .	. . .	. . .	. . .	. . .	. . .	. . .	. . .
Royalties and licence fees	2 266 . .	. . .	. . .	. . .	. . .	. . .	1.0	. . .	. . .
Other business services	2 268 . .	.3	4.2	. . .	. . .	. . .	. . .	. . .	. . .
Personal, cultural, and recreational	2 287 . .	. . .	. . .	. . .	. . .	. . .	. . .	. . .	. . .
Government, n.i.e.	2 291 . .	10.9	10.0	12.6	2.5	3.1	2.5	3.7	4.2
Other services, debit	3 200 BA	**-27.1**	**-15.1**	**-18.4**	**-19.3**	**-20.4**	**-18.9**	**-26.4**	**-26.9**
Communications	3 245 . .	-4.1	-4.0	-3.0	-4.7	-6.0	-4.3	-4.4	-3.8
Construction	3 249 . .	. . .	. . .	. . .	. . .	. . .	. . .	. . .	. . .
Insurance	3 253 . .	. . .	. . .	-2.0	-1.0	-3.4	-.9	-.8	-1.1
Financial	3 260 . .	. . .	. . .	. . .	. . .	. . .	. . .	-.3	. . .
Computer and information	3 262 . .	. . .	. . .	. . .	. . .	. . .	. . .	. . .	. . .
Royalties and licence fees	3 266 . .	. . .	. . .	. . .	. . .	. . .	. . .	. . .	. . .
Other business services	3 268 . .	-20.0	-3.1	-9.0	-9.0	-6.5	-8.1	-15.6	-16.8
Personal, cultural, and recreational	3 287 . .	. . .	. . .	. . .	. . .	. . .	. . .	. . .	. . .
Government, n.i.e.	3 291 . .	-3.0	-8.0	-4.4	-4.6	-4.5	-5.6	-5.3	-5.2

Table 2 (Continued). STANDARD PRESENTATION, 1994–2001

(Millions of U.S. dollars)

	Code	1994	1995	1996	1997	1998	1999	2000	2001
C. INCOME	4 300	–19.3	–25.4	–13.3	–12.0	.4	.1	–6.5	4.3
Total credit	2 300	*3.2*	*3.0*	*13.4*	*6.1*	*10.1*	*6.7*	*13.0*	*20.8*
Total debit	3 300	*–22.5*	*–28.4*	*–26.7*	*–18.1*	*–9.7*	*–6.6*	*–19.5*	*–16.5*
Compensation of employees, credit	2 310	...	...	...	...	...	...	...	...
Compensation of employees, debit	3 310	...	...	...	...	...	...	...	...
Investment income, credit	2 320	**3.2**	**3.0**	**13.4**	**6.1**	**10.1**	**6.7**	**13.0**	**20.8**
Direct investment income	2 330	...	...	...	...	...	...	...	...
Dividends and distributed branch profits	2 332	...	...	...	...	...	...	...	...
Reinvested earnings and undistributed branch profits	2 333	...	...	...	...	...	...	...	...
Income on debt (interest)	2 334	...	...	...	...	...	...	...	...
Portfolio investment income	2 339	...	...	...	...	...	...	...	...
Income on equity	2 340	...	...	...	...	...	...	...	...
Income on bonds and notes	2 350	...	...	...	...	...	...	...	...
Income on money market instruments	2 360	...	...	...	...	...	...	...	...
Other investment income	2 370	3.2	3.0	13.4	6.1	10.1	6.7	13.0	20.8
Investment income, debit	3 320	**–22.5**	**–28.4**	**–26.7**	**–18.1**	**–9.7**	**–6.6**	**–19.5**	**–16.5**
Direct investment income	3 330	–8.2	–17.8	–16.1	–7.6	–.5	–.4	–8.8	–5.9
Dividends and distributed branch profits	3 332	...	...	...	...	...	–.4	–8.8	–5.9
Reinvested earnings and undistributed branch profits	3 333	...	...	...	...	...	...	...	...
Income on debt (interest)	3 334	...	...	...	...	...	...	...	...
Portfolio investment income	3 339	...	...	...	...	...	...	...	...
Income on equity	3 340	...	...	...	...	...	...	...	...
Income on bonds and notes	3 350	...	...	...	...	...	...	...	...
Income on money market instruments	3 360	...	...	...	...	...	...	...	...
Other investment income	3 370	–14.3	–10.6	–10.6	–10.5	–9.2	–6.2	–10.7	–10.6
D. CURRENT TRANSFERS	4 379	77.8	77.1	69.8	51.9	55.7	74.3	94.3	93.9
Credit	2 379	**77.8**	**77.1**	**69.8**	**51.9**	**59.3**	**77.9**	**111.2**	**113.3**
General government	2 380	77.7	77.1	63.6	47.7	53.8	67.2	98.6	87.5
Other sectors	2 390	.1	...	6.2	4.2	5.5	10.7	12.6	25.8
Workers' remittances	2 391	...	...	...	...	5.5	7.2	12.0	24.0
Other current transfers	2 392	.1	...	6.2	4.2	...	3.5	.6	1.8
Debit	3 379	...	...	...	...	**–3.6**	**–3.6**	**–16.9**	**–19.4**
General government	3 380	...	...	...	...	–.6	...	...	...
Other sectors	3 390	...	...	...	...	–3.0	–3.6	–16.9	–19.4
Workers' remittances	3 391	...	...	...	...	–3.0	–3.2	–3.0	–3.4
Other current transfers	3 392	...	...	...	...	...	–.4	–13.9	–16.0
CAPITAL AND FINANCIAL ACCOUNT	4 996	**–45.4**	**–48.0**	**65.0**	**–27.3**	**124.9**	**28.3**	**89.2**	**132.4**
CAPITAL ACCOUNT	4 994	...	...	...	...	...	...	...	...
Total credit	2 994	...	...	...	...	...	...	...	...
Total debit	3 994	...	...	...	...	...	...	...	...
Capital transfers, credit	2 400	...	...	...	...	...	...	...	...
General government	2 401	...	...	...	...	...	...	...	...
Debt forgiveness	2 402	...	...	...	...	...	...	...	...
Other capital transfers	2 410	...	...	...	...	...	...	...	...
Other sectors	2 430	...	...	...	...	...	...	...	...
Migrants' transfers	2 431	...	...	...	...	...	...	...	...
Debt forgiveness	2 432	...	...	...	...	...	...	...	...
Other capital transfers	2 440	...	...	...	...	...	...	...	...
Capital transfers, debit	3 400	...	...	...	...	...	...	...	...
General government	3 401	...	...	...	...	...	...	...	...
Debt forgiveness	3 402	...	...	...	...	...	...	...	...
Other capital transfers	3 410	...	...	...	...	...	...	...	...
Other sectors	3 430	...	...	...	...	...	...	...	...
Migrants' transfers	3 431	...	...	...	...	...	...	...	...
Debt forgiveness	3 432	...	...	...	...	...	...	...	...
Other capital transfers	3 440	...	...	...	...	...	...	...	...
Nonproduced nonfinancial assets, credit	2 480	...	...	...	...	...	...	...	...
Nonproduced nonfinancial assets, debit	3 480	...	...	...	...	...	...	...	...

Table 2 (Continued). STANDARD PRESENTATION, 1994–2001
(Millions of U.S. dollars)

	Code		1994	1995	1996	1997	1998	1999	2000	2001
FINANCIAL ACCOUNT	4 995	. .	**–45.4**	**–48.0**	**65.0**	**–27.3**	**124.9**	**28.3**	**89.2**	**132.4**
A. DIRECT INVESTMENT	4 500	. .	6.9	9.8	15.9	25.0	18.9	30.4	53.7	63.0
Direct investment abroad	4 505	. .	**. . .**	**. . .**	**. . .**	**. . .**	**. . .**	**. . .**	**. . .**	**. . .**
Equity capital	4 510	. .	. . .	. . .	. . .	. . .	. . .	. . .	. . .	. . .
Claims on affiliated enterprises	4 515	. .	. . .	. . .	. . .	. . .	. . .	. . .	. . .	. . .
Liabilities to affiliated enterprises	4 520	. .	. . .	. . .	. . .	. . .	. . .	. . .	. . .	. . .
Reinvested earnings	4 525	. .	. . .	. . .	. . .	. . .	. . .	. . .	. . .	. . .
Other capital	4 530	. .	. . .	. . .	. . .	. . .	. . .	. . .	. . .	. . .
Claims on affiliated enterprises	4 535	. .	. . .	. . .	. . .	. . .	. . .	. . .	. . .	. . .
Liabilities to affiliated enterprises	4 540	. .	. . .	. . .	. . .	. . .	. . .	. . .	. . .	. . .
Direct investment in Mongolia	4 555	. .	**6.9**	**9.8**	**15.9**	**25.0**	**18.9**	**30.4**	**53.7**	**63.0**
Equity capital	4 560	. .	6.9	9.8	15.9	25.0	18.9	30.4	53.7	63.0
Claims on direct investors	4 565	. .	. . .	. . .	. . .	. . .	. . .	. . .	. . .	. . .
Liabilities to direct investors	4 570	. .	. . .	. . .	. . .	. . .	. . .	30.4	53.7	63.0
Reinvested earnings	4 575	. .	. . .	. . .	. . .	. . .	. . .	. . .	. . .	. . .
Other capital	4 580	. .	. . .	. . .	. . .	. . .	. . .	. . .	. . .	. . .
Claims on direct investors	4 585	. .	. . .	. . .	. . .	. . .	. . .	. . .	. . .	. . .
Liabilities to direct investors	4 590	. .	. . .	. . .	. . .	. . .	. . .	. . .	. . .	. . .
B. PORTFOLIO INVESTMENT	4 600	. .	. . .	1.0	. . .	. . .	. . .	. . .	. . .	. . .
Assets	4 602	. .	**. . .**	**. . .**	**. . .**	**. . .**	**. . .**	**. . .**	**. . .**	**. . .**
Equity securities	4 610	. .	. . .	. . .	. . .	. . .	. . .	. . .	. . .	. . .
Monetary authorities	4 611	. .	. . .	. . .	. . .	. . .	. . .	. . .	. . .	. . .
General government	4 612	. .	. . .	. . .	. . .	. . .	. . .	. . .	. . .	. . .
Banks	4 613	. .	. . .	. . .	. . .	. . .	. . .	. . .	. . .	. . .
Other sectors	4 614	. .	. . .	. . .	. . .	. . .	. . .	. . .	. . .	. . .
Debt securities	4 619	. .	. . .	. . .	. . .	. . .	. . .	. . .	. . .	. . .
Bonds and notes	4 620	. .	. . .	. . .	. . .	. . .	. . .	. . .	. . .	. . .
Monetary authorities	4 621	. .	. . .	. . .	. . .	. . .	. . .	. . .	. . .	. . .
General government	4 622	. .	. . .	. . .	. . .	. . .	. . .	. . .	. . .	. . .
Banks	4 623	. .	. . .	. . .	. . .	. . .	. . .	. . .	. . .	. . .
Other sectors	4 624	. .	. . .	. . .	. . .	. . .	. . .	. . .	. . .	. . .
Money market instruments	4 630	. .	. . .	. . .	. . .	. . .	. . .	. . .	. . .	. . .
Monetary authorities	4 631	. .	. . .	. . .	. . .	. . .	. . .	. . .	. . .	. . .
General government	4 632	. .	. . .	. . .	. . .	. . .	. . .	. . .	. . .	. . .
Banks	4 633	. .	. . .	. . .	. . .	. . .	. . .	. . .	. . .	. . .
Other sectors	4 634	. .	. . .	. . .	. . .	. . .	. . .	. . .	. . .	. . .
Liabilities	4 652	. .	**. . .**	**1.0**	**. . .**	**. . .**	**. . .**	**. . .**	**. . .**	**. . .**
Equity securities	4 660	. .	. . .	. . .	. . .	. . .	. . .	. . .	. . .	. . .
Banks	4 663	. .	. . .	. . .	. . .	. . .	. . .	. . .	. . .	. . .
Other sectors	4 664	. .	. . .	. . .	. . .	. . .	. . .	. . .	. . .	. . .
Debt securities	4 669	. .	. . .	1.0	. . .	. . .	. . .	. . .	. . .	. . .
Bonds and notes	4 670	. .	. . .	. . .	. . .	. . .	. . .	. . .	. . .	. . .
Monetary authorities	4 671	. .	. . .	. . .	. . .	. . .	. . .	. . .	. . .	. . .
General government	4 672	. .	. . .	. . .	. . .	. . .	. . .	. . .	. . .	. . .
Banks	4 673	. .	. . .	. . .	. . .	. . .	. . .	. . .	. . .	. . .
Other sectors	4 674	. .	. . .	. . .	. . .	. . .	. . .	. . .	. . .	. . .
Money market instruments	4 680	. .	. . .	. . .	. . .	. . .	. . .	. . .	. . .	. . .
Monetary authorities	4 681	. .	. . .	. . .	. . .	. . .	. . .	. . .	. . .	. . .
General government	4 682	. .	. . .	. . .	. . .	. . .	. . .	. . .	. . .	. . .
Banks	4 683	. .	. . .	. . .	. . .	. . .	. . .	. . .	. . .	. . .
Other sectors	4 684	. .	. . .	. . .	. . .	. . .	. . .	. . .	. . .	. . .
C. FINANCIAL DERIVATIVES	4 910	. .	. . .	. . .	. . .	. . .	. . .	. . .	. . .	. . .
Monetary authorities	4 911	. .	. . .	. . .	. . .	. . .	. . .	. . .	. . .	. . .
General government	4 912	. .	. . .	. . .	. . .	. . .	. . .	. . .	. . .	. . .
Banks	4 913	. .	. . .	. . .	. . .	. . .	. . .	. . .	. . .	. . .
Other sectors	4 914	. .	. . .	. . .	. . .	. . .	. . .	. . .	. . .	. . .
Assets	4 900	. .	**. . .**	**. . .**	**. . .**	**. . .**	**. . .**	**. . .**	**. . .**	**. . .**
Monetary authorities	4 901	. .	. . .	. . .	. . .	. . .	. . .	. . .	. . .	. . .
General government	4 902	. .	. . .	. . .	. . .	. . .	. . .	. . .	. . .	. . .
Banks	4 903	. .	. . .	. . .	. . .	. . .	. . .	. . .	. . .	. . .
Other sectors	4 904	. .	. . .	. . .	. . .	. . .	. . .	. . .	. . .	. . .
Liabilities	4 905	. .	**. . .**	**. . .**	**. . .**	**. . .**	**. . .**	**. . .**	**. . .**	**. . .**
Monetary authorities	4 906	. .	. . .	. . .	. . .	. . .	. . .	. . .	. . .	. . .
General government	4 907	. .	. . .	. . .	. . .	. . .	. . .	. . .	. . .	. . .
Banks	4 908	. .	. . .	. . .	. . .	. . .	. . .	. . .	. . .	. . .
Other sectors	4 909	. .	. . .	. . .	. . .	. . .	. . .	. . .	. . .	. . .

Table 2 (Concluded). STANDARD PRESENTATION, 1994–2001
(Millions of U.S. dollars)

	Code	1994	1995	1996	1997	1998	1999	2000	2001
D. OTHER INVESTMENT	4 700 ..	–24.8	–36.2	29.5	8.9	112.4	38.6	38.0	56.7
Assets	4 703 ..	**–51.0**	**–49.2**	**–76.4**	**–108.1**	**–54.8**	**–51.8**	**–44.3**	**–14.4**
Trade credits	4 706 ..	–35.7	–33.9	–67.1	–90.0	–54.8	–37.0	–33.6	–15.3
General government	4 707 ..	...	...	...	...	...	...	...	...
of which: Short-term	4 709 ..	...	...	...	...	...	...	...	...
Other sectors	4 710 ..	–35.7	–33.9	–67.1	–90.0	–54.8	–37.0	–33.6	–15.3
of which: Short-term	4 712 ..	*–35.7*	*–33.9*	*–67.1*	*–90.0*	*–54.8*	*–37.0*	*–33.6*	*–15.3*
Loans	4 714 ..	...	...	...	...	...	...	...	...
Monetary authorities	4 715 ..	...	...	...	...	...	...	...	...
of which: Short-term	4 718 ..	...	...	...	...	...	...	...	...
General government	4 719 ..	...	...	...	...	...	...	...	...
of which: Short-term	4 721 ..	...	...	...	...	...	...	...	...
Banks	4 722 ..	...	...	...	...	...	...	...	...
of which: Short-term	4 724 ..	...	...	...	...	...	...	...	...
Other sectors	4 725 ..	...	...	...	...	...	...	...	...
of which: Short-term	4 727 ..	...	...	...	...	...	...	...	...
Currency and deposits	4 730 ..	–15.3	–15.3	–9.3	–18.1	...	–14.8	–10.7	.9
Monetary authorities	4 731 ..	...	...	...	...	...	...	...	...
General government	4 732 ..	...	...	...	...	...	...	...	...
Banks	4 733 ..	–15.3	–15.3	–9.3	–18.1	...	–14.8	–10.7	.9
Other sectors	4 734 ..	...	...	...	...	...	...	...	...
Other assets	4 736 ..	...	...	...	...	...	...	...	...
Monetary authorities	4 737 ..	...	...	...	...	...	...	...	...
of which: Short-term	4 739 ..	...	...	...	...	...	...	...	...
General government	4 740 ..	...	...	...	...	...	...	...	...
of which: Short-term	4 742 ..	...	...	...	...	...	...	...	...
Banks	4 743 ..	...	...	...	...	...	...	...	...
of which: Short-term	4 745 ..	...	...	...	...	...	...	...	...
Other sectors	4 746 ..	...	...	...	...	...	...	...	...
of which: Short-term	4 748 ..	...	...	...	...	...	...	...	...
Liabilities	4 753 ..	**26.2**	**13.0**	**105.9**	**117.0**	**167.2**	**90.4**	**82.3**	**71.1**
Trade credits	4 756 ..	–2.8	...	45.7	30.8	19.3	...	...	...
General government	4 757 ..	...	...	...	...	...	...	...	...
of which: Short-term	4 759 ..	...	...	...	...	...	...	...	...
Other sectors	4 760 ..	–2.8	...	45.7	30.8	19.3	...	...	...
of which: Short-term	4 762 ..	*–2.8*	...	*45.7*	*30.8*	*19.3*	...	...	...
Loans	4 764 ..	29.0	13.0	54.3	86.0	103.9	98.0	84.6	70.6
Monetary authorities	4 765 ..	21.1	–9.5	–1.8	6.7	–4.1	4.2	1.8	–1.6
of which: Use of Fund credit and loans from the Fund	4 766 ..	*21.1*	*–9.5*	*–1.8*	*6.7*	*–1.3*	*4.2*	*1.8*	*–1.6*
of which: Short-term	4 768 ..	...	...	...	...	...	...	...	...
General government	4 769 ..	7.9	22.5	56.1	79.3	80.8	91.4	60.5	63.3
of which: Short-term	4 771 ..	...	...	...	...	...	...	...	...
Banks	4 772 ..	...	...	...	...	...	–2.0	...	...
of which: Short-term	4 774 ..	...	...	...	...	...	...	...	...
Other sectors	4 775 ..	...	...	...	...	27.2	4.4	22.3	8.9
of which: Short-term	4 777 ..	...	...	...	...	...	...	...	...
Currency and deposits	4 780 ..	...	...	...	...	40.0	–2.8	–2.3	.5
Monetary authorities	4 781 ..	...	...	...	...	...	...	...	...
General government	4 782 ..	...	...	...	...	...	...	...	...
Banks	4 783 ..	...	...	...	...	40.0	–2.8	–2.3	.5
Other sectors	4 784 ..	...	...	...	...	...	...	...	...
Other liabilities	4 786 ..	...	...	5.9	.2	4.0	–4.8	...	...
Monetary authorities	4 787 ..	...	...	5.9	.2	4.0	...	...	...
of which: Short-term	4 789 ..	...	...	*5.9*	*.2*	*4.0*	...	...	...
General government	4 790 ..	...	...	...	...	...	–4.8	...	...
of which: Short-term	4 792 ..	...	...	...	...	...	*–4.8*	...	...
Banks	4 793 ..	...	...	...	...	...	...	...	...
of which: Short-term	4 795 ..	...	...	...	...	...	...	...	...
Other sectors	4 796 ..	...	...	...	...	...	...	...	...
of which: Short-term	4 798 ..	...	...	...	...	...	...	...	...
E. RESERVE ASSETS	4 802 ..	–27.4	–22.6	19.6	–61.2	–6.3	–40.6	–2.5	12.7
Monetary gold	4 812 ..	–5.7	–23.5	...	...	...	...	...	...
Special drawing rights	4 811 ..	–2.8	.4	2.0	–.3	.3	.3	.1	...
Reserve position in the Fund	4 810 ..	...	...	...	...	...	...	...	...
Foreign exchange	4 803 ..	–18.9	.5	17.6	–60.9	–9.0	–41.7	–2.6	12.7
Other claims	4 813 ..	...	...	...	...	2.4	.8	...	...
NET ERRORS AND OMISSIONS	4 998 ..	**–1.0**	**9.1**	**–28.1**	**–75.6**	**–50.2**	**23.6**	**–19.3**	**–53.9**

Part 3 of the *Yearbook* contains descriptions of the methodologies, compilation practices, and sources used to compile these data.

Table 1. ANALYTIC PRESENTATION, 1994–2001
(Millions of U.S. dollars)

	Code		1994	1995	1996	1997	1998	1999	2000	2001
A. Current Account [1]	4 993	Z .	**-12.24**	**-1.96**	**15.71**	**-1.97**	**1.83**	**-1.48**	**-9.03**	. . .
Goods: exports f.o.b	2 100	. .	2.92	12.14	41.34	8.20	1.20	1.26	1.12	. . .
Goods: imports f.o.b	3 100	. .	-30.04	-33.90	-35.97	-28.11	-19.35	-19.27	-19.02	. . .
Balance on Goods	4 100	. .	*-27.12*	*-21.76*	*5.38*	*-19.91*	*-18.15*	*-18.00*	*-17.90*	. . .
Services: credit	2 200	. .	27.16	24.61	15.54	13.88	13.00	20.30	15.70	. . .
Services: debit	3 200	. .	-14.32	-14.77	-17.39	-12.92	-22.29	-21.64	-18.66	. . .
Balance on Goods and Services	4 991	. .	*-14.28*	*-11.92*	*3.53*	*-18.95*	*-27.44*	*-19.34*	*-20.87*	. . .
Income: credit	2 300	. .	-.01	.66	.54	.97	.77	1.19	1.48	. . .
Income: debit	3 300	. .	-4.44	-2.93	-2.00	-3.29	-2.55	-7.13	-4.16	. . .
Balance on Goods, Services, and Income	4 992	. .	*-18.73*	*-14.19*	*2.08*	*-21.27*	*-29.22*	*-25.29*	*-23.56*	. . .
Current transfers: credit	2 379	Z .	10.61	13.55	14.90	20.38	33.24	26.49	18.86	. . .
Current transfers: debit	3 379	. .	-4.12	-1.33	-1.26	-1.08	-2.19	-2.69	-4.33	. . .
B. Capital Account [1]	4 994	Z .	**10.10**	**5.16**	**-12.50**	**3.56**	**3.59**	**1.33**	**2.42**	. . .
Capital account: credit	2 994	Z .	10.10	6.67	2.32	7.19	7.22	4.96	5.31	. . .
Capital account: debit	3 994	. .	. . .	-1.51	-14.81	-3.63	-3.63	-3.63	-2.89	. . .
Total, Groups A Plus B	4 981	. .	*-2.13*	*3.20*	*3.22*	*1.59*	*5.43*	*-.15*	*-6.61*	. . .
C. Financial Account [1]	4 995	W.	**.73**	**1.93**	**-5.90**	**-8.94**	**3.95**	**-5.90**	**3.52**	. . .
Direct investment abroad	4 505	. .	. . .	. . .	. . .	. . .	. . .	. . .	. . .	. . .
Direct investment in Montserrat	4 555	Z .	7.16	3.03	-.32	2.57	2.57	8.21	3.46	. . .
Portfolio investment assets	4 602	. .	-.03	-.03	. . .	. . .	. . .	. . .	. . .	. . .
Equity securities	4 610	. .	. . .	. . .	. . .	. . .	. . .	. . .	. . .	. . .
Debt securities	4 619	. .	. . .	. . .	. . .	. . .	. . .	. . .	. . .	. . .
Portfolio investment liabilities	4 652	Z .	. . .	.06	. . .	.06	.09	-.03	.55	. . .
Equity securities	4 660	. .	. . .	. . .	. . .	. . .	. . .	. . .	. . .	. . .
Debt securities	4 669	Z .	. . .	. . .	. . .	. . .	. . .	. . .	. . .	. . .
Financial derivatives	4 910	. .	. . .	. . .	. . .	. . .	. . .	. . .	. . .	. . .
Financial derivatives assets	4 900	. .	. . .	. . .	. . .	. . .	. . .	. . .	. . .	. . .
Financial derivatives liabilities	4 905	. .	. . .	. . .	. . .	. . .	. . .	. . .	. . .	. . .
Other investment assets	4 703	. .	-3.60	-4.20	-5.25	-10.48	-1.35	-12.18	-4.61	. . .
Monetary authorities	4 701	. .	. . .	. . .	. . .	. . .	. . .	. . .	. . .	. . .
General government	4 704	. .	. . .	. . .	. . .	. . .	. . .	. . .	. . .	. . .
Banks	4 705	. .	. . .	. . .	. . .	. . .	. . .	. . .	. . .	. . .
Other sectors	4 728	. .	. . .	. . .	. . .	. . .	. . .	. . .	. . .	. . .
Other investment liabilities	4 753	W.	-2.81	3.06	-.33	-1.09	2.65	-1.91	4.12	. . .
Monetary authorities	4 753	WA	. . .	. . .	. . .	. . .	. . .	. . .	. . .	. . .
General government	4 753	ZB	. . .	. . .	. . .	. . .	. . .	. . .	. . .	. . .
Banks	4 753	ZC	. . .	. . .	. . .	. . .	. . .	. . .	. . .	. . .
Other sectors	4 753	ZD	. . .	. . .	. . .	. . .	. . .	. . .	. . .	. . .
Total, Groups A Through C	4 983	. .	*-1.40*	*5.13*	*-2.68*	*-7.36*	*9.38*	*-6.05*	*-3.09*	. . .
D. Net Errors and Omissions	4 998	. .	**2.97**	**-3.94**	**2.53**	**9.99**	**4.09**	**-4.56**	**-.54**	. . .
Total, Groups A Through D	4 984	. .	*1.57*	*1.19*	*-.15*	*2.64*	*13.47*	*-10.61*	*-3.62*	. . .
E. Reserves and Related Items	4 802	A .	**-1.57**	**-1.19**	**.15**	**-2.64**	**-13.48**	**10.61**	**3.62**	. . .
Reserve assets	4 802	. .	-1.57	-1.19	.15	-2.64	-13.48	10.61	3.62	. . .
Use of Fund credit and loans	4 766	. .	. . .	. . .	. . .	. . .	. . .	. . .	. . .	. . .
Exceptional financing	4 920	. .	. . .	. . .	. . .	. . .	. . .	. . .	. . .	. . .
Conversion rates: Eastern Caribbean dollars per U.S. dollar	0 101	. .	**2.7000**	**2.7000**	**2.7000**	**2.7000**	**2.7000**	**2.7000**	**2.7000**	. . .

[1] Excludes components that have been classified in the categories of Group E.

Table 2. STANDARD PRESENTATION, 1994–2001
(Millions of U.S. dollars)

	Code	1994	1995	1996	1997	1998	1999	2000	2001
CURRENT ACCOUNT	4 993 . .	**–12.24**	**–1.96**	**15.71**	**–1.97**	**1.83**	**–1.48**	**–9.03**	**. . .**
A. GOODS	4 100 . .	–27.12	–21.76	5.38	–19.91	–18.15	–18.00	–17.90	. . .
Credit	2 100 . .	**2.92**	**12.14**	**41.34**	**8.20**	**1.20**	**1.26**	**1.12**	**. . .**
General merchandise: exports f.o.b.	2 110 . .	2.91	12.13	41.33	8.18	1.20	1.26	1.11	. . .
Goods for processing: exports f.o.b.	2 150 . .	. . .	. . .	. . .	. . .	. . .	. . .	. . .	. . .
Repairs on goods	2 160 . .	. . .	. . .	. . .	. . .	. . .	. . .	. . .	. . .
Goods procured in ports by carriers	2 170 . .	.01	.01	.01	.01	. . .	. . .	. . .	. . .
Nonmonetary gold	2 180 . .	. . .	. . .	. . .	. . .	. . .	. . .	. . .	. . .
Debit	3 100 . .	**–30.04**	**–33.90**	**–35.97**	**–28.11**	**–19.35**	**–19.27**	**–19.02**	**. . .**
General merchandise: imports f.o.b.	3 110 . .	–29.93	–33.79	–35.85	–28.11	–19.35	–19.27	–19.02	. . .
Goods for processing: imports f.o.b.	3 150 . .	. . .	. . .	. . .	. . .	. . .	. . .	. . .	. . .
Repairs on goods	3 160 . .	. . .	. . .	. . .	. . .	. . .	. . .	. . .	. . .
Goods procured in ports by carriers	3 170 . .	–.11	–.11	–.11	. . .	. . .	. . .	. . .	. . .
Nonmonetary gold	3 180 . .	. . .	. . .	. . .	. . .	. . .	. . .	. . .	. . .
B. SERVICES	4 200 . .	12.84	9.84	–1.84	.96	–9.29	–1.34	–2.97	. . .
Total credit	2 200 . .	*27.16*	*24.61*	*15.54*	*13.88*	*13.00*	*20.30*	*15.70*	. . .
Total debit	3 200 . .	*–14.32*	*–14.77*	*–17.39*	*–12.92*	*–22.29*	*–21.64*	*–18.66*	. . .
Transportation services, credit	2 205 . .	**2.34**	**2.24**	**2.55**	**2.11**	**.28**	**1.24**	**.98**	**. . .**
Passenger	2 850 . .	. . .	. . .	. . .	. . .	. . .	. . .	. . .	. . .
Freight	2 851 . .	. . .	. . .	. . .	. . .	. . .	. . .	. . .	. . .
Other	2 852 . .	. . .	. . .	. . .	. . .	. . .	. . .	. . .	. . .
Sea transport, passenger	2 207 . .	. . .	. . .	. . .	. . .	. . .	. . .	. . .	. . .
Sea transport, freight	2 208 . .	. . .	. . .	. . .	. . .	. . .	. . .	. . .	. . .
Sea transport, other	2 209 . .	. . .	. . .	. . .	. . .	. . .	. . .	. . .	. . .
Air transport, passenger	2 211 . .	. . .	. . .	. . .	. . .	. . .	. . .	. . .	. . .
Air transport, freight	2 212 . .	. . .	. . .	. . .	. . .	. . .	. . .	. . .	. . .
Air transport, other	2 213 . .	. . .	. . .	. . .	. . .	. . .	. . .	. . .	. . .
Other transport, passenger	2 215 . .	. . .	. . .	. . .	. . .	. . .	. . .	. . .	. . .
Other transport, freight	2 216 . .	. . .	. . .	. . .	. . .	. . .	. . .	. . .	. . .
Other transport, other	2 217 . .	. . .	. . .	. . .	. . .	. . .	. . .	. . .	. . .
Transportation services, debit	3 205 . .	**–6.55**	**–6.99**	**–6.62**	**–4.09**	**–3.09**	**–3.59**	**–3.67**	**. . .**
Passenger	3 850 . .	. . .	. . .	. . .	. . .	. . .	. . .	. . .	. . .
Freight	3 851 . .	. . .	. . .	. . .	. . .	. . .	. . .	. . .	. . .
Other	3 852 . .	. . .	. . .	. . .	. . .	. . .	. . .	. . .	. . .
Sea transport, passenger	3 207 . .	. . .	. . .	. . .	. . .	. . .	. . .	. . .	. . .
Sea transport, freight	3 208 . .	. . .	. . .	. . .	. . .	. . .	. . .	. . .	. . .
Sea transport, other	3 209 . .	. . .	. . .	. . .	. . .	. . .	. . .	. . .	. . .
Air transport, passenger	3 211 . .	. . .	. . .	. . .	. . .	. . .	. . .	. . .	. . .
Air transport, freight	3 212 . .	. . .	. . .	. . .	. . .	. . .	. . .	. . .	. . .
Air transport, other	3 213 . .	. . .	. . .	. . .	. . .	. . .	. . .	. . .	. . .
Other transport, passenger	3 215 . .	. . .	. . .	. . .	. . .	. . .	. . .	. . .	. . .
Other transport, freight	3 216 . .	. . .	. . .	. . .	. . .	. . .	. . .	. . .	. . .
Other transport, other	3 217 . .	. . .	. . .	. . .	. . .	. . .	. . .	. . .	. . .
Travel, credit	2 236 . .	**20.07**	**17.39**	**8.40**	**4.74**	**5.59**	**8.07**	**8.96**	**. . .**
Business travel	2 237 . .	. . .	. . .	. . .	. . .	. . .	. . .	. . .	. . .
Personal travel	2 240 . .	. . .	. . .	. . .	. . .	. . .	. . .	. . .	. . .
Travel, debit	3 236 . .	**–3.22**	**–3.81**	**–3.70**	**–1.32**	**–1.32**	**–1.36**	**–1.73**	**. . .**
Business travel	3 237 . .	. . .	. . .	. . .	. . .	. . .	. . .	. . .	. . .
Personal travel	3 240 . .	. . .	. . .	. . .	. . .	. . .	. . .	. . .	. . .
Other services, credit	2 200 BA	**4.76**	**4.98**	**4.60**	**7.03**	**7.13**	**10.98**	**5.76**	**. . .**
Communications	2 245 . .	. . .	. . .	. . .	. . .	. . .	. . .	. . .	. . .
Construction	2 249 . .	. . .	. . .	. . .	. . .	. . .	. . .	. . .	. . .
Insurance	2 253 . .	.59	.70	.47	.18	.09	.43	.23	. . .
Financial	2 260 . .	. . .	. . .	. . .	. . .	. . .	.18	.19	. . .
Computer and information	2 262 . .	. . .	. . .	. . .	. . .	. . .	. . .	. . .	. . .
Royalties and licence fees	2 266 . .	. . .	. . .	. . .	. . .	. . .	.04	.08	. . .
Other business services	2 268 . .	4.16	4.28	4.13	6.85	7.04	10.33	5.26	. . .
Personal, cultural, and recreational	2 287 . .	. . .	. . .	. . .	. . .	. . .	. . .	. . .	. . .
Government, n.i.e.	2 291 . .	. . .	. . .	. . .	. . .	. . .	. . .	. . .	. . .
Other services, debit	3 200 BA	**–4.55**	**–3.97**	**–7.06**	**–7.51**	**–17.88**	**–16.69**	**–13.26**	**. . .**
Communications	3 245 . .	. . .	. . .	. . .	. . .	. . .	. . .	. . .	. . .
Construction	3 249 . .	–.16	. . .	. . .	. . .	. . .	. . .	. . .	. . .
Insurance	3 253 . .	–.86	–1.03	–.96	–1.30	–.46	–.73	–.62	. . .
Financial	3 260 . .	. . .	. . .	. . .	. . .	. . .	. . .	. . .	. . .
Computer and information	3 262 . .	. . .	. . .	. . .	. . .	. . .	. . .	. . .	. . .
Royalties and licence fees	3 266 . .	. . .	. . .	. . .	. . .	. . .	. . .	. . .	. . .
Other business services	3 268 . .	–2.20	–2.22	–1.80	–3.69	–3.68	–6.82	–4.34	. . .
Personal, cultural, and recreational	3 287 . .	. . .	. . .	. . .	. . .	. . .	. . .	. . .	. . .
Government, n.i.e.	3 291 . .	–1.33	–.72	–4.30	–2.52	–13.74	–9.13	–8.30	. . .

Table 2 (Continued). STANDARD PRESENTATION, 1994–2001
(Millions of U.S. dollars)

	Code	1994	1995	1996	1997	1998	1999	2000	2001
C. INCOME	4 300	–4.45	–2.27	–1.46	–2.32	–1.78	–5.94	–2.69	. . .
Total credit	2 300	*–.01*	*.66*	*.54*	*.97*	*.77*	*1.19*	*1.48*	. . .
Total debit	3 300	*–4.44*	*–2.93*	*–2.00*	*–3.29*	*–2.55*	*–7.13*	*–4.16*	. . .
Compensation of employees, credit	2 310	**.07**	**.07**	. . .	. . .	. . .	. . .	. . .	. . .
Compensation of employees, debit	3 310	. . .	. . .	. . .	. . .	. . .	. . .	. . .	. . .
Investment income, credit	2 320	**–.09**	**.59**	**.54**	**.97**	**.77**	**1.19**	**1.48**	. . .
Direct investment income	2 330	. . .	. . .	. . .	. . .	. . .	. . .	. . .	. . .
Dividends and distributed branch profits	2 332	. . .	. . .	. . .	. . .	. . .	. . .	. . .	. . .
Reinvested earnings and undistributed branch profits	2 333	. . .	. . .	. . .	. . .	. . .	. . .	. . .	. . .
Income on debt (interest)	2 334	. . .	. . .	. . .	. . .	. . .	. . .	. . .	. . .
Portfolio investment income	2 339	–.28	.38	.17	.23	.23	.23	.66	. . .
Income on equity	2 340	–.28	.38	.17	.23	.23	.23	.66	. . .
Income on bonds and notes	2 350	. . .	. . .	. . .	. . .	. . .	. . .	. . .	. . .
Income on money market instruments	2 360	. . .	. . .	. . .	. . .	. . .	. . .	. . .	. . .
Other investment income	2 370	.19	.21	.37	.74	.54	.96	.81	. . .
Investment income, debit	3 320	**–4.44**	**–2.93**	**–2.00**	**–3.29**	**–2.55**	**–7.13**	**–4.16**	. . .
Direct investment income	3 330	–3.86	–2.25	–.77	–1.92	–1.92	–6.09	–3.32	. . .
Dividends and distributed branch profits	3 332	–2.02	–1.16	–.74	. . .	. . .	. . .	–1.19	. . .
Reinvested earnings and undistributed branch profits	3 333	–1.47	–.74	. . .	–1.92	–1.92	–6.07	–2.11	. . .
Income on debt (interest)	3 334	–.36	–.36	–.03	. . .	. . .	–.03	–.02	. . .
Portfolio investment income	3 339	. . .	. . .	. . .	. . .	. . .	. . .	. . .	. . .
Income on equity	3 340	. . .	. . .	. . .	. . .	. . .	. . .	. . .	. . .
Income on bonds and notes	3 350	. . .	. . .	. . .	. . .	. . .	. . .	. . .	. . .
Income on money market instruments	3 360	. . .	. . .	. . .	. . .	. . .	. . .	. . .	. . .
Other investment income	3 370	–.58	–.67	–1.22	–1.36	–.63	–1.04	–.84	. . .
D. CURRENT TRANSFERS	4 379	6.49	12.23	13.64	19.30	31.05	23.80	14.53	. . .
Credit	2 379	**10.61**	**13.55**	**14.90**	**20.38**	**33.24**	**26.49**	**18.86**	. . .
General government	2 380	1.55	1.47	8.75	14.03	32.87	21.57	17.65	. . .
Other sectors	2 390	9.06	12.08	6.15	6.34	.37	4.92	1.21	. . .
Workers' remittances	2 391	. . .	. . .	. . .	. . .	. . .	. . .	. . .	. . .
Other current transfers	2 392	. . .	. . .	. . .	. . .	. . .	. . .	. . .	. . .
Debit	3 379	**–4.12**	**–1.33**	**–1.26**	**–1.08**	**–2.19**	**–2.69**	**–4.33**	. . .
General government	3 380	–.62	–.54	. . .	–1.08	–1.08	–1.57	–3.12	. . .
Other sectors	3 390	–3.50	–.78	–1.26	. . .	–1.11	–1.11	–1.21	. . .
Workers' remittances	3 391	. . .	. . .	. . .	. . .	. . .	. . .	. . .	. . .
Other current transfers	3 392	. . .	. . .	. . .	. . .	. . .	. . .	. . .	. . .
CAPITAL AND FINANCIAL ACCOUNT	4 996	**9.26**	**5.90**	**–18.24**	**–8.02**	**–5.93**	**6.04**	**9.56**	. . .
CAPITAL ACCOUNT	4 994	**10.10**	**5.16**	**–12.50**	**3.56**	**3.59**	**1.33**	**2.42**	. . .
Total credit	2 994	*10.10*	*6.67*	*2.32*	*7.19*	*7.22*	*4.96*	*5.31*	. . .
Total debit	3 994	. . .	*–1.51*	*–14.81*	*–3.63*	*–3.63*	*–3.63*	*–2.89*	. . .
Capital transfers, credit	2 400	**10.10**	**6.67**	**2.32**	**7.19**	**7.22**	**4.96**	**5.31**	. . .
General government	2 401	10.10	6.67	2.32	7.19	7.22	4.96	4.94	. . .
Debt forgiveness	2 402	. . .	. . .	. . .	. . .	. . .	. . .	. . .	. . .
Other capital transfers	2 410	10.10	6.67	2.32	7.19	7.22	4.96	4.94	. . .
Other sectors	2 430	. . .	. . .	. . .	. . .	. . .	. . .	.37	. . .
Migrants' transfers	2 431	. . .	. . .	. . .	. . .	. . .	. . .	.37	. . .
Debt forgiveness	2 432	. . .	. . .	. . .	. . .	. . .	. . .	. . .	. . .
Other capital transfers	2 440	. . .	. . .	. . .	. . .	. . .	. . .	. . .	. . .
Capital transfers, debit	3 400	. . .	**–1.51**	**–14.81**	**–3.63**	**–3.63**	**–3.63**	**–2.89**	. . .
General government	3 401	. . .	. . .	. . .	. . .	. . .	. . .	. . .	. . .
Debt forgiveness	3 402	. . .	. . .	. . .	. . .	. . .	. . .	. . .	. . .
Other capital transfers	3 410	. . .	. . .	. . .	. . .	. . .	. . .	. . .	. . .
Other sectors	3 430	. . .	–1.51	–14.81	–3.63	–3.63	–3.63	–2.89	. . .
Migrants' transfers	3 431	. . .	–1.51	–14.81	–3.63	–3.63	–3.63	–2.89	. . .
Debt forgiveness	3 432	. . .	. . .	. . .	. . .	. . .	. . .	. . .	. . .
Other capital transfers	3 440	. . .	. . .	. . .	. . .	. . .	. . .	. . .	. . .
Nonproduced nonfinancial assets, credit	2 480	. . .	. . .	. . .	. . .	. . .	. . .	. . .	. . .
Nonproduced nonfinancial assets, debit	3 480	. . .	. . .	. . .	. . .	. . .	. . .	. . .	. . .

Table 2 (Continued). STANDARD PRESENTATION, 1994–2001
(Millions of U.S. dollars)

	Code	1994	1995	1996	1997	1998	1999	2000	2001
FINANCIAL ACCOUNT	4 995	**–.84**	**.74**	**–5.75**	**–11.58**	**–9.52**	**4.71**	**7.14**	...
A. DIRECT INVESTMENT	4 500	7.16	3.03	–.32	2.57	2.57	8.21	3.46	...
Direct investment abroad	4 505	...	...	...	...	...	...	...	...
Equity capital	4 510	...	...	...	...	...	...	...	...
Claims on affiliated enterprises	4 515	...	...	...	...	...	...	...	...
Liabilities to affiliated enterprises	4 520	...	...	...	...	...	...	...	...
Reinvested earnings	4 525	...	...	...	...	...	...	...	...
Other capital	4 530	...	...	...	...	...	...	...	...
Claims on affiliated enterprises	4 535	...	...	...	...	...	...	...	...
Liabilities to affiliated enterprises	4 540	...	...	...	...	...	...	...	...
Direct investment in Montserrat	4 555	**7.16**	**3.03**	**–.32**	**2.57**	**2.57**	**8.21**	**3.46**	...
Equity capital	4 560	5.92	2.53	...	.64	.64	2.20	1.41	...
Claims on direct investors	4 565	...	...	...	...	...	...	...	...
Liabilities to direct investors	4 570	5.92	2.53	...	.64	.64	2.20	1.41	...
Reinvested earnings	4 575	1.47	.74	...	1.92	1.92	6.07	2.11	...
Other capital	4 580	–.23	–.23	–.32	...	...	–.06	–.06	...
Claims on direct investors	4 585	...	...	...	...	...	...	...	...
Liabilities to direct investors	4 590	–.23	–.23	–.32	...	...	–.06	–.06	...
B. PORTFOLIO INVESTMENT	4 600	–.03	.03	...	.06	.09	–.03	.55	...
Assets	4 602	**–.03**	**–.03**	...	...	...	...	...	...
Equity securities	4 610	...	...	...	...	...	...	...	...
Monetary authorities	4 611	...	...	...	...	...	...	...	...
General government	4 612	...	...	...	...	...	...	...	...
Banks	4 613	...	...	...	...	...	...	...	...
Other sectors	4 614	...	...	...	...	...	...	...	...
Debt securities	4 619	...	...	...	...	...	...	...	...
Bonds and notes	4 620	...	...	...	...	...	...	...	...
Monetary authorities	4 621	...	...	...	...	...	...	...	...
General government	4 622	...	...	...	...	...	...	...	...
Banks	4 623	...	...	...	...	...	...	...	...
Other sectors	4 624	...	...	...	...	...	...	...	...
Money market instruments	4 630	...	...	...	...	...	...	...	...
Monetary authorities	4 631	...	...	...	...	...	...	...	...
General government	4 632	...	...	...	...	...	...	...	...
Banks	4 633	...	...	...	...	...	...	...	...
Other sectors	4 634	...	...	...	...	...	...	...	...
Liabilities	4 652	...	**.06**	...	**.06**	**.09**	**–.03**	**.55**	...
Equity securities	4 660	...	...	...	...	...	...	...	...
Banks	4 663	...	...	...	...	...	...	...	...
Other sectors	4 664	...	...	...	...	...	...	...	...
Debt securities	4 669	...	...	...	...	...	...	...	...
Bonds and notes	4 670	...	...	...	...	...	...	...	...
Monetary authorities	4 671	...	...	...	...	...	...	...	...
General government	4 672	...	...	...	...	...	...	...	...
Banks	4 673	...	...	...	...	...	...	...	...
Other sectors	4 674	...	...	...	...	...	...	...	...
Money market instruments	4 680	...	...	...	...	...	...	...	...
Monetary authorities	4 681	...	...	...	...	...	...	...	...
General government	4 682	...	...	...	...	...	...	...	...
Banks	4 683	...	...	...	...	...	...	...	...
Other sectors	4 684	...	...	...	...	...	...	...	...
C. FINANCIAL DERIVATIVES	4 910	...	...	...	...	...	...	...	...
Monetary authorities	4 911	...	...	...	...	...	...	...	...
General government	4 912	...	...	...	...	...	...	...	...
Banks	4 913	...	...	...	...	...	...	...	...
Other sectors	4 914	...	...	...	...	...	...	...	...
Assets	4 900	...	...	...	...	...	...	...	...
Monetary authorities	4 901	...	...	...	...	...	...	...	...
General government	4 902	...	...	...	...	...	...	...	...
Banks	4 903	...	...	...	...	...	...	...	...
Other sectors	4 904	...	...	...	...	...	...	...	...
Liabilities	4 905	...	...	...	...	...	...	...	...
Monetary authorities	4 906	...	...	...	...	...	...	...	...
General government	4 907	...	...	...	...	...	...	...	...
Banks	4 908	...	...	...	...	...	...	...	...
Other sectors	4 909	...	...	...	...	...	...	...	...

Table 2 (Concluded). STANDARD PRESENTATION, 1994–2001
(Millions of U.S. dollars)

	Code	1994	1995	1996	1997	1998	1999	2000	2001
D. OTHER INVESTMENT	4 700	−6.41	−1.14	−5.58	−11.57	1.30	−14.09	−.49	. . .
Assets	4 703	**−3.60**	**−4.20**	**−5.25**	**−10.48**	**−1.35**	**−12.18**	**−4.61**	**. . .**
Trade credits	4 706	. . .	. . .	. . .	. . .	. . .	. . .	. . .	. . .
General government	4 707	. . .	. . .	. . .	. . .	. . .	. . .	. . .	. . .
of which: Short-term	4 709	. . .	. . .	. . .	. . .	. . .	. . .	. . .	. . .
Other sectors	4 710	. . .	. . .	. . .	. . .	. . .	. . .	. . .	. . .
of which: Short-term	4 712	. . .	. . .	. . .	. . .	. . .	. . .	. . .	. . .
Loans	4 714	. . .	. . .	. . .	. . .	. . .	. . .	. . .	. . .
Monetary authorities	4 715	. . .	. . .	. . .	. . .	. . .	. . .	. . .	. . .
of which: Short-term	4 718	. . .	. . .	. . .	. . .	. . .	. . .	. . .	. . .
General government	4 719	. . .	. . .	. . .	. . .	. . .	. . .	. . .	. . .
of which: Short-term	4 721	. . .	. . .	. . .	. . .	. . .	. . .	. . .	. . .
Banks	4 722	. . .	. . .	. . .	. . .	. . .	. . .	. . .	. . .
of which: Short-term	4 724	. . .	. . .	. . .	. . .	. . .	. . .	. . .	. . .
Other sectors	4 725	. . .	. . .	. . .	. . .	. . .	. . .	. . .	. . .
of which: Short-term	4 727	. . .	. . .	. . .	. . .	. . .	. . .	. . .	. . .
Currency and deposits	4 730	. . .	. . .	. . .	. . .	. . .	. . .	. . .	. . .
Monetary authorities	4 731	. . .	. . .	. . .	. . .	. . .	. . .	. . .	. . .
General government	4 732	. . .	. . .	. . .	. . .	. . .	. . .	. . .	. . .
Banks	4 733	. . .	. . .	. . .	. . .	. . .	. . .	. . .	. . .
Other sectors	4 734	. . .	. . .	. . .	. . .	. . .	. . .	. . .	. . .
Other assets	4 736	. . .	. . .	. . .	. . .	. . .	. . .	. . .	. . .
Monetary authorities	4 737	. . .	. . .	. . .	. . .	. . .	. . .	. . .	. . .
of which: Short-term	4 739	. . .	. . .	. . .	. . .	. . .	. . .	. . .	. . .
General government	4 740	. . .	. . .	. . .	. . .	. . .	. . .	. . .	. . .
of which: Short-term	4 742	. . .	. . .	. . .	. . .	. . .	. . .	. . .	. . .
Banks	4 743	. . .	. . .	. . .	. . .	. . .	. . .	. . .	. . .
of which: Short-term	4 745	. . .	. . .	. . .	. . .	. . .	. . .	. . .	. . .
Other sectors	4 746	. . .	. . .	. . .	. . .	. . .	. . .	. . .	. . .
of which: Short-term	4 748	. . .	. . .	. . .	. . .	. . .	. . .	. . .	. . .
Liabilities	4 753	**−2.81**	**3.06**	**−.33**	**−1.09**	**2.65**	**−1.91**	**4.12**	**. . .**
Trade credits	4 756	. . .	. . .	. . .	. . .	. . .	. . .	. . .	. . .
General government	4 757	. . .	. . .	. . .	. . .	. . .	. . .	. . .	. . .
of which: Short-term	4 759	. . .	. . .	. . .	. . .	. . .	. . .	. . .	. . .
Other sectors	4 760	. . .	. . .	. . .	. . .	. . .	. . .	. . .	. . .
of which: Short-term	4 762	. . .	. . .	. . .	. . .	. . .	. . .	. . .	. . .
Loans	4 764	. . .	. . .	. . .	. . .	. . .	. . .	. . .	. . .
Monetary authorities	4 765	. . .	. . .	. . .	. . .	. . .	. . .	. . .	. . .
of which: Use of Fund credit and loans from the Fund	4 766	. . .	. . .	. . .	. . .	. . .	. . .	. . .	. . .
of which: Short-term	4 768	. . .	. . .	. . .	. . .	. . .	. . .	. . .	. . .
General government	4 769	. . .	. . .	. . .	. . .	. . .	. . .	. . .	. . .
of which: Short-term	4 771	. . .	. . .	. . .	. . .	. . .	. . .	. . .	. . .
Banks	4 772	. . .	. . .	. . .	. . .	. . .	. . .	. . .	. . .
of which: Short-term	4 774	. . .	. . .	. . .	. . .	. . .	. . .	. . .	. . .
Other sectors	4 775	. . .	. . .	. . .	. . .	. . .	. . .	. . .	. . .
of which: Short-term	4 777	. . .	. . .	. . .	. . .	. . .	. . .	. . .	. . .
Currency and deposits	4 780	. . .	. . .	. . .	. . .	. . .	. . .	. . .	. . .
Monetary authorities	4 781	. . .	. . .	. . .	. . .	. . .	. . .	. . .	. . .
General government	4 782	. . .	. . .	. . .	. . .	. . .	. . .	. . .	. . .
Banks	4 783	. . .	. . .	. . .	. . .	. . .	. . .	. . .	. . .
Other sectors	4 784	. . .	. . .	. . .	. . .	. . .	. . .	. . .	. . .
Other liabilities	4 786	. . .	. . .	. . .	. . .	. . .	. . .	. . .	. . .
Monetary authorities	4 787	. . .	. . .	. . .	. . .	. . .	. . .	. . .	. . .
of which: Short-term	4 789	. . .	. . .	. . .	. . .	. . .	. . .	. . .	. . .
General government	4 790	. . .	. . .	. . .	. . .	. . .	. . .	. . .	. . .
of which: Short-term	4 792	. . .	. . .	. . .	. . .	. . .	. . .	. . .	. . .
Banks	4 793	. . .	. . .	. . .	. . .	. . .	. . .	. . .	. . .
of which: Short-term	4 795	. . .	. . .	. . .	. . .	. . .	. . .	. . .	. . .
Other sectors	4 796	. . .	. . .	. . .	. . .	. . .	. . .	. . .	. . .
of which: Short-term	4 798	. . .	. . .	. . .	. . .	. . .	. . .	. . .	. . .
E. RESERVE ASSETS	4 802	−1.57	−1.19	.15	−2.64	−13.48	10.61	3.62	. . .
Monetary gold	4 812	. . .	. . .	. . .	. . .	. . .	. . .	. . .	. . .
Special drawing rights	4 811	. . .	. . .	. . .	. . .	. . .	. . .	. . .	. . .
Reserve position in the Fund	4 810	. . .	. . .	. . .	. . .	. . .	. . .	. . .	. . .
Foreign exchange	4 803	−1.46	−1.19	.15	−2.64	−13.48	10.75	3.62	. . .
Other claims	4 813	−.10	. . .	. . .	. . .	. . .	−.14	. . .	. . .
NET ERRORS AND OMISSIONS	4 998	**2.97**	**−3.94**	**2.53**	**9.99**	**4.09**	**−4.56**	**−.54**	**. . .**

Part 3 of the *Yearbook* contains descriptions of the methodologies, compilation practices, and sources used to compile these data.

Table 1. ANALYTIC PRESENTATION, 1994–2001

(Millions of U.S. dollars)

	Code	1994	1995	1996	1997	1998	1999	2000	2001
A. Current Account [1]	4 993 Z.	**–723**	**–1,296**	**–58**	**–169**	**–146**	**–171**	**–501**	**1,606**
Goods: exports f.o.b	2 100 . .	5,541	6,871	6,886	7,039	7,144	7,509	7,419	7,142
Goods: imports f.o.b	3 100 . .	–7,648	–9,353	–9,080	–8,903	–9,463	–9,957	–10,654	–10,164
Balance on Goods	4 100 . .	*–2,107*	*–2,482*	*–2,193*	*–1,864*	*–2,319*	*–2,448*	*–3,235*	*–3,022*
Services: credit	2 200 . .	2,014	2,173	2,743	2,471	2,827	3,115	3,034	4,029
Services: debit	3 200 . .	–1,730	–1,890	–1,782	–1,724	–1,963	–2,003	–1,892	–2,119
Balance on Goods and Services	4 991 . .	*–1,822*	*–2,199*	*–1,233*	*–1,117*	*–1,455*	*–1,335*	*–2,093*	*–1,111*
Income: credit	2 300 . .	224	251	189	172	194	187	276	326
Income: debit	3 300 . .	–1,394	–1,569	–1,498	–1,348	–1,227	–1,172	–1,140	–1,159
Balance on Goods, Services, and Income	4 992 . .	*–2,992*	*–3,516*	*–2,541*	*–2,292*	*–2,489*	*–2,321*	*–2,958*	*–1,944*
Current transfers: credit	2 379 Z.	2,355	2,298	2,565	2,204	2,438	2,246	2,574	3,670
Current transfers: debit	3 379 . .	–86	–78	–82	–81	–95	–96	–118	–120
B. Capital Account [1]	4 994 Z.	**–3**	**–6**	**73**	**–5**	**–10**	**–9**	**–6**	**–9**
Capital account: credit	2 994 Z.	. . .	. . .	78	1	. . .	. . .	. . .	. . .
Capital account: debit	3 994 . .	–4	–6	–5	–5	–10	–9	–6	–9
Total, Groups A Plus B	4 981 . .	*–726*	*–1,302*	*15*	*–173*	*–156*	*–179*	*–507*	*1,597*
C. Financial Account [1]	4 995 W.	**1,248**	**–984**	**–897**	**–990**	**–644**	**–13**	**–774**	**–967**
Direct investment abroad	4 505 . .	–24	–15	–30	–9	–20	–18	–59	–97
Direct investment in Morocco	4 555 Z.	551	92	76	4	12	3	221	144
Portfolio investment assets	4 602 . .	. . .	. . .	. . .	. . .	. . .	. . .	. . .	. . .
Equity securities	4 610 . .	. . .	. . .	. . .	. . .	. . .	. . .	. . .	. . .
Debt securities	4 619 . .	. . .	. . .	. . .	. . .	. . .	. . .	. . .	. . .
Portfolio investment liabilities	4 652 Z.	238	20	142	38	24	6	17	–8
Equity securities	4 660 . .	238	20	142	38	24	6	17	–8
Debt securities	4 669 Z.	. . .	. . .	. . .	. . .	. . .	. . .	. . .	. . .
Financial derivatives	4 910 . .	. . .	. . .	. . .	. . .	. . .	. . .	. . .	. . .
Financial derivatives assets	4 900 . .	. . .	. . .	. . .	. . .	. . .	. . .	. . .	. . .
Financial derivatives liabilities	4 905 . .	. . .	. . .	. . .	. . .	. . .	. . .	. . .	. . .
Other investment assets	4 703 . .	344	. . .	. . .	. . .	. . .	. . .	. . .	. . .
Monetary authorities	4 701 . .	. . .	. . .	. . .	. . .	. . .	. . .	. . .	. . .
General government	4 704 . .	. . .	. . .	. . .	. . .	. . .	. . .	. . .	. . .
Banks	4 705 . .	. . .	. . .	. . .	. . .	. . .	. . .	. . .	. . .
Other sectors	4 728 . .	344	. . .	. . .	. . .	. . .	. . .	. . .	. . .
Other investment liabilities	4 753 W.	139	–1,083	–1,085	–1,022	–660	–4	–954	–1,006
Monetary authorities	4 753 WA	19	. . .	. . .	. . .	. . .	. . .	. . .	. . .
General government	4 753 ZB	–421	–967	–867	–1,232	–954	–1,293	–1,208	–1,215
Banks	4 753 ZC	–48	–132	–167	–123	–197	–152	–80	–93
Other sectors	4 753 ZD	588	16	–50	333	492	1,441	335	302
Total, Groups A Through C	4 983 . .	*521*	*–2,286*	*–882*	*–1,163*	*–800*	*–192*	*–1,281*	*630*
D. Net Errors and Omissions	4 998 . .	**–39**	**391**	**209**	**175**	**160**	**123**	**114**	**230**
Total, Groups A Through D	4 984 . .	*483*	*–1,895*	*–673*	*–988*	*–640*	*–69*	*–1,167*	*860*
E. Reserves and Related Items	4 802 A.	**–483**	**1,895**	**673**	**988**	**640**	**69**	**1,167**	**–860**
Reserve assets	4 802 . .	–362	984	–274	–553	–248	–1,636	416	–3,842
Use of Fund credit and loans	4 766 . .	–152	–101	–47	–3	. . .	. . .	. . .	. . .
Exceptional financing	4 920 . .	31	1,013	995	1,544	887	1,705	751	2,982
Conversion rates: Moroccan dirhams per U.S. dollar	0 101 . .	**9.2027**	**8.5402**	**8.7159**	**9.5271**	**9.6044**	**9.8044**	**10.6256**	**11.3030**

[1] Excludes components that have been classified in the categories of Group E.

Table 2. STANDARD PRESENTATION, 1994–2001
(Millions of U.S. dollars)

	Code	1994	1995	1996	1997	1998	1999	2000	2001
CURRENT ACCOUNT	4 993 . .	**–723**	**–1,186**	**35**	**–87**	**–144**	**–167**	**–475**	**1,611**
A. GOODS	4 100 . .	–2,107	–2,482	–2,193	–1,864	–2,319	–2,448	–3,235	–3,022
Credit	2 100 . .	**5,541**	**6,871**	**6,886**	**7,039**	**7,144**	**7,509**	**7,419**	**7,142**
General merchandise: exports f.o.b.	2 110 . .	3,957	4,687	4,734	4,657	4,638	4,844	4,843	4,668
Goods for processing: exports f.o.b.	2 150 . .	1,567	2,158	2,140	2,362	2,477	2,644	2,558	2,438
Repairs on goods	2 160 . .	. . .	. . .	. . .	. . .	. . .	. . .	. . .	. . .
Goods procured in ports by carriers	2 170 . .	17	26	12	21	29	21	18	36
Nonmonetary gold	2 180 . .	. . .	. . .	. . .	. . .	. . .	. . .	. . .	. . .
Debit	3 100 . .	**–7,648**	**–9,353**	**–9,080**	**–8,903**	**–9,463**	**–9,957**	**–10,654**	**–10,164**
General merchandise: imports f.o.b.	3 110 . .	–6,531	–7,858	–7,620	–7,247	–7,762	–8,140	–9,043	–8,531
Goods for processing: imports f.o.b.	3 150 . .	–1,097	–1,478	–1,451	–1,647	–1,690	–1,807	–1,602	–1,623
Repairs on goods	3 160 . .	. . .	. . .	. . .	. . .	. . .	. . .	. . .	. . .
Goods procured in ports by carriers	3 170 . .	–19	–17	–8	–9	–10	–10	–9	–9
Nonmonetary gold	3 180 . .	. . .	. . .	. . .	. . .	. . .	. . .	. . .	. . .
B. SERVICES	4 200 . .	285	284	961	747	864	1,112	1,142	1,910
Total credit	2 200 . .	*2,014*	*2,173*	*2,743*	*2,471*	*2,827*	*3,115*	*3,034*	*4,029*
Total debit	3 200 . .	*–1,730*	*–1,890*	*–1,782*	*–1,724*	*–1,963*	*–2,003*	*–1,892*	*–2,119*
Transportation services, credit	2 205 . .	**342**	**410**	**416**	**440**	**446**	**478**	**485**	**660**
Passenger	2 850 . .	*142*	*173*	*182*	*203*	*190*	*228*	*245*	*397*
Freight	2 851 . .	*200*	*237*	*234*	*237*	*256*	*250*	*240*	*263*
Other	2 852 . .	. . .	. . .	. . .	. . .	. . .	. . .	. . .	. . .
Sea transport, passenger	2 207 . .	. . .	. . .	. . .	. . .	. . .	. . .	6	4
Sea transport, freight	2 208 . .	194	224	217	218	228	228	205	221
Sea transport, other	2 209 . .	. . .	. . .	. . .	. . .	. . .	. . .	. . .	. . .
Air transport, passenger	2 211 . .	141	173	181	201	189	226	237	392
Air transport, freight	2 212 . .	. . .	. . .	1	1	1	4	6	8
Air transport, other	2 213 . .	. . .	. . .	. . .	. . .	. . .	. . .	. . .	. . .
Other transport, passenger	2 215 . .	1	. . .	1	1	1	1	2	1
Other transport, freight	2 216 . .	6	13	16	19	28	18	29	33
Other transport, other	2 217 . .	. . .	. . .	. . .	. . .	. . .	. . .	. . .	. . .
Transportation services, debit	3 205 . .	**–625**	**–650**	**–598**	**–571**	**–567**	**–627**	**–620**	**–782**
Passenger	3 850 . .	*–43*	*–54*	*–53*	*–48*	*–73*	*–126*	*–85*	*–214*
Freight	3 851 . .	*–581*	*–596*	*–545*	*–523*	*–494*	*–501*	*–535*	*–568*
Other	3 852 . .	. . .	. . .	. . .	. . .	. . .	. . .	. . .	. . .
Sea transport, passenger	3 207 . .	–7	–1	–2	–5	–2	–9	–3	–6
Sea transport, freight	3 208 . .	–523	–572	–515	–504	–474	–475	–449	–485
Sea transport, other	3 209 . .	. . .	. . .	. . .	. . .	. . .	. . .	. . .	. . .
Air transport, passenger	3 211 . .	–37	–51	–47	–41	–70	–117	–80	–208
Air transport, freight	3 212 . .	–19	–9	–4	–5	–5	–7	–21	–15
Air transport, other	3 213 . .	. . .	. . .	. . .	. . .	. . .	. . .	. . .	. . .
Other transport, passenger	3 215 . .	. . .	–3	–5	–2	–2	. . .	–2	–1
Other transport, freight	3 216 . .	–40	–14	–25	–14	–14	–20	–64	–68
Other transport, other	3 217 . .	. . .	. . .	. . .	. . .	. . .	. . .	. . .	. . .
Travel, credit	2 236 . .	**1,231**	**1,296**	**1,675**	**1,446**	**1,744**	**1,949**	**2,039**	**2,583**
Business travel	2 237 . .	. . .	. . .	. . .	. . .	. . .	. . .	. . .	. . .
Personal travel	2 240 . .	. . .	1,296	1,675	1,446	1,744	1,949	2,039	2,583
Travel, debit	3 236 . .	**–302**	**–302**	**–300**	**–315**	**–423**	**–452**	**–425**	**–389**
Business travel	3 237 . .	–33	–51	–54	–50	–81	–83	–86	–75
Personal travel	3 240 . .	–269	–251	–246	–265	–342	–369	–340	–314
Other services, credit	2 200 BA	**441**	**467**	**653**	**585**	**636**	**688**	**510**	**786**
Communications	2 245 . .	47	54	50	89	85	113	113	169
Construction	2 249 . .	. . .	. . .	. . .	. . .	. . .	. . .	. . .	. . .
Insurance	2 253 . .	39	27	43	30	27	25	30	29
Financial	2 260 . .	. . .	. . .	. . .	. . .	. . .	. . .	. . .	. . .
Computer and information	2 262 . .	. . .	. . .	. . .	. . .	. . .	. . .	. . .	. . .
Royalties and licence fees	2 266 . .	2	3	5	4	7	6	38	22
Other business services	2 268 . .	215	229	244	193	248	232	147	324
Personal, cultural, and recreational	2 287 . .	. . .	. . .	. . .	. . .	. . .	. . .	. . .	. . .
Government, n.i.e.	2 291 . .	138	153	310	268	269	312	181	242
Other services, debit	3 200 BA	**–803**	**–938**	**–884**	**–838**	**–972**	**–924**	**–847**	**–947**
Communications	3 245 . .	–22	–14	–17	–28	–36	–29	–17	–17
Construction	3 249 . .	. . .	. . .	. . .	. . .	. . .	. . .	. . .	. . .
Insurance	3 253 . .	–84	–48	–42	–40	–38	–37	–29	–38
Financial	3 260 . .	. . .	. . .	. . .	. . .	. . .	. . .	. . .	. . .
Computer and information	3 262 . .	. . .	. . .	. . .	. . .	. . .	. . .	. . .	. . .
Royalties and licence fees	3 266 . .	–100	–125	–133	–123	–172	–201	–210	–256
Other business services	3 268 . .	–75	–211	–211	–190	–245	–191	–219	–222
Personal, cultural, and recreational	3 287 . .	. . .	. . .	. . .	. . .	. . .	. . .	. . .	. . .
Government, n.i.e.	3 291 . .	–522	–540	–481	–457	–481	–466	–372	–414

Table 2 (Continued). STANDARD PRESENTATION, 1994–2001
(Millions of U.S. dollars)

	Code	1994	1995	1996	1997	1998	1999	2000	2001
C. INCOME	4 300	–1,170	–1,318	–1,309	–1,175	–1,033	–986	–864	–833
Total credit	2 300	*224*	*251*	*189*	*172*	*194*	*187*	*276*	*326*
Total debit	3 300	*–1,394*	*–1,569*	*–1,498*	*–1,348*	*–1,227*	*–1,172*	*–1,140*	*–1,159*
Compensation of employees, credit	2 310	...	...	...	...	...	...	...	...
Compensation of employees, debit	3 310	...	...	...	...	...	...	...	...
Investment income, credit	2 320	**224**	**251**	**189**	**172**	**194**	**187**	**276**	**326**
Direct investment income	2 330	14	11	12	3	5	10	13	13
Dividends and distributed branch profits	2 332	2	1	4	1	3	6	8	9
Reinvested earnings and undistributed branch profits	2 333	...	3	3	...	...	...	1	...
Income on debt (interest)	2 334	13	7	5	2	2	3	4	4
Portfolio investment income	2 339	...	...	...	...	1	...	...	...
Income on equity	2 340	...	...	...	...	1	...	...	...
Income on bonds and notes	2 350	...	...	...	...	...	...	...	...
Income on money market instruments	2 360	...	...	...	...	...	...	...	...
Other investment income	2 370	210	240	177	169	188	177	263	312
Investment income, debit	3 320	**–1,394**	**–1,569**	**–1,498**	**–1,348**	**–1,227**	**–1,172**	**–1,140**	**–1,159**
Direct investment income	3 330	–94	–100	–116	–160	–143	–186	–269	–401
Dividends and distributed branch profits	3 332	–67	–85	–88	–150	–119	–154	–154	–278
Reinvested earnings and undistributed branch profits	3 333	–25	–5	–19	–4	–12	–3	–10	–3
Income on debt (interest)	3 334	–2	–11	–9	–6	–12	–30	–105	–120
Portfolio investment income	3 339	–11	–14	–13	–14	–21	–40	–13	–2
Income on equity	3 340	...	–14	–13	–14	–21	–40	–13	–2
Income on bonds and notes	3 350	–11	...	...	...	...	...	...	...
Income on money market instruments	3 360	...	...	...	...	...	...	...	...
Other investment income	3 370	–1,290	–1,454	–1,369	–1,175	–1,063	–946	–859	–756
D. CURRENT TRANSFERS	4 379	2,270	2,330	2,576	2,205	2,345	2,154	2,483	3,555
Credit	2 379	**2,355**	**2,408**	**2,659**	**2,286**	**2,440**	**2,250**	**2,600**	**3,675**
General government	2 380	232	110	93	81	92	47	142	65
Other sectors	2 390	2,123	2,298	2,565	2,204	2,347	2,203	2,458	3,610
Workers' remittances	2 391	1,827	1,970	2,165	1,893	2,011	1,938	2,161	3,261
Other current transfers	2 392	296	328	400	311	337	265	297	349
Debit	3 379	**–86**	**–78**	**–82**	**–81**	**–95**	**–96**	**–118**	**–120**
General government	3 380	–59	–41	–43	–34	–41	–38	–42	–45
Other sectors	3 390	–27	–37	–39	–47	–54	–58	–76	–75
Workers' remittances	3 391	–13	–15	–14	–15	–22	–20	–23	–27
Other current transfers	3 392	–14	–23	–25	–32	–32	–39	–53	–48
CAPITAL AND FINANCIAL ACCOUNT	4 996	**762**	**795**	**–244**	**–88**	**–17**	**43**	**361**	**–1,841**
CAPITAL ACCOUNT	4 994	**–3**	**–6**	**73**	**–5**	**–10**	**–9**	**–6**	**–9**
Total credit	2 994	...	...	*78*	*1*	...	...	...	...
Total debit	3 994	*–4*	*–6*	*–5*	*–5*	*–10*	*–9*	*–6*	*–9*
Capital transfers, credit	2 400	...	...	**78**	**1**	...	...	...	...
General government	2 401	...	...	78	...	...	...	...	...
Debt forgiveness	2 402	...	...	78	...	...	...	...	...
Other capital transfers	2 410	...	...	...	...	...	...	...	...
Other sectors	2 430	...	...	...	1	...	...	...	...
Migrants' transfers	2 431	...	...	...	1	...	...	...	...
Debt forgiveness	2 432	...	...	...	...	...	...	...	...
Other capital transfers	2 440	...	...	...	...	...	...	...	...
Capital transfers, debit	3 400	**–4**	**–6**	**–5**	**–5**	**–10**	**–9**	**–6**	**–9**
General government	3 401	...	...	...	...	...	...	...	...
Debt forgiveness	3 402	...	...	...	...	...	...	...	...
Other capital transfers	3 410	...	...	...	...	...	...	...	...
Other sectors	3 430	–4	–6	–5	–5	–10	–9	–6	–9
Migrants' transfers	3 431	–4	–6	–5	–5	–10	–9	–6	–9
Debt forgiveness	3 432	...	...	...	...	...	...	...	...
Other capital transfers	3 440	...	...	...	...	...	...	...	...
Nonproduced nonfinancial assets, credit	2 480	...	...	...	...	...	...	...	...
Nonproduced nonfinancial assets, debit	3 480	...	...	...	...	...	...	...	...

Table 2 (Continued). STANDARD PRESENTATION, 1994–2001
(Millions of U.S. dollars)

	Code	1994	1995	1996	1997	1998	1999	2000	2001
FINANCIAL ACCOUNT	4 995 . .	**765**	**801**	**–317**	**–83**	**–7**	**52**	**367**	**–1,832**
A. DIRECT INVESTMENT	4 500 . .	527	320	327	1,071	313	831	368	2,728
Direct investment abroad	4 505 . .	**–24**	**–15**	**–30**	**–9**	**–20**	**–18**	**–59**	**–97**
Equity capital	4 510 . .	–24	–12	–27	–9	–20	–18	–58	–97
Claims on affiliated enterprises	4 515 . .	–24	–12	–27	–9	4	4	–58	–97
Liabilities to affiliated enterprises	4 520 . .	. . .	. . .	. . .	. . .	–24	–23	. . .	. . .
Reinvested earnings	4 525 . .	. . .	–3	–3	. . .	. . .	. . .	–1	. . .
Other capital	4 530 . .	. . .	. . .	. . .	. . .	. . .	. . .	. . .	. . .
Claims on affiliated enterprises	4 535 . .	. . .	. . .	. . .	. . .	. . .	. . .	. . .	. . .
Liabilities to affiliated enterprises	4 540 . .	. . .	. . .	. . .	. . .	. . .	. . .	. . .	. . .
Direct investment in Morocco	4 555 . .	**551**	**335**	**357**	**1,079**	**333**	**850**	**427**	**2,825**
Equity capital	4 560 . .	192	330	338	1,076	321	847	206	2,681
Claims on direct investors	4 565 . .	. . .	. . .	. . .	. . .	. . .	. . .	. . .	. . .
Liabilities to direct investors	4 570 . .	192	330	338	1,076	321	847	206	2,681
Reinvested earnings	4 575 . .	25	5	19	4	12	3	10	3
Other capital	4 580 . .	334	. . .	. . .	. . .	. . .	. . .	211	141
Claims on direct investors	4 585 . .	. . .	. . .	. . .	. . .	. . .	. . .	. . .	. . .
Liabilities to direct investors	4 590 . .	. . .	. . .	. . .	. . .	. . .	. . .	211	141
B. PORTFOLIO INVESTMENT	4 600 . .	238	20	142	38	24	6	17	–8
Assets	4 602 . .	**. . .**	**. . .**	**. . .**	**. . .**	**. . .**	**. . .**	**. . .**	**. . .**
Equity securities	4 610 . .	. . .	. . .	. . .	. . .	. . .	. . .	. . .	. . .
Monetary authorities	4 611 . .	. . .	. . .	. . .	. . .	. . .	. . .	. . .	. . .
General government	4 612 . .	. . .	. . .	. . .	. . .	. . .	. . .	. . .	. . .
Banks	4 613 . .	. . .	. . .	. . .	. . .	. . .	. . .	. . .	. . .
Other sectors	4 614 . .	. . .	. . .	. . .	. . .	. . .	. . .	. . .	. . .
Debt securities	4 619 . .	. . .	. . .	. . .	. . .	. . .	. . .	. . .	. . .
Bonds and notes	4 620 . .	. . .	. . .	. . .	. . .	. . .	. . .	. . .	. . .
Monetary authorities	4 621 . .	. . .	. . .	. . .	. . .	. . .	. . .	. . .	. . .
General government	4 622 . .	. . .	. . .	. . .	. . .	. . .	. . .	. . .	. . .
Banks	4 623 . .	. . .	. . .	. . .	. . .	. . .	. . .	. . .	. . .
Other sectors	4 624 . .	. . .	. . .	. . .	. . .	. . .	. . .	. . .	. . .
Money market instruments	4 630 . .	. . .	. . .	. . .	. . .	. . .	. . .	. . .	. . .
Monetary authorities	4 631 . .	. . .	. . .	. . .	. . .	. . .	. . .	. . .	. . .
General government	4 632 . .	. . .	. . .	. . .	. . .	. . .	. . .	. . .	. . .
Banks	4 633 . .	. . .	. . .	. . .	. . .	. . .	. . .	. . .	. . .
Other sectors	4 634 . .	. . .	. . .	. . .	. . .	. . .	. . .	. . .	. . .
Liabilities	4 652 . .	**238**	**20**	**142**	**38**	**24**	**6**	**17**	**–8**
Equity securities	4 660 . .	238	20	142	38	24	6	17	–8
Banks	4 663 . .	. . .	. . .	. . .	. . .	. . .	. . .	. . .	. . .
Other sectors	4 664 . .	238	20	142	38	24	6	17	–8
Debt securities	4 669 . .	. . .	. . .	. . .	. . .	. . .	. . .	. . .	. . .
Bonds and notes	4 670 . .	. . .	. . .	. . .	. . .	. . .	. . .	. . .	. . .
Monetary authorities	4 671 . .	. . .	. . .	. . .	. . .	. . .	. . .	. . .	. . .
General government	4 672 . .	. . .	. . .	. . .	. . .	. . .	. . .	. . .	. . .
Banks	4 673 . .	. . .	. . .	. . .	. . .	. . .	. . .	. . .	. . .
Other sectors	4 674 . .	. . .	. . .	. . .	. . .	. . .	. . .	. . .	. . .
Money market instruments	4 680 . .	. . .	. . .	. . .	. . .	. . .	. . .	. . .	. . .
Monetary authorities	4 681 . .	. . .	. . .	. . .	. . .	. . .	. . .	. . .	. . .
General government	4 682 . .	. . .	. . .	. . .	. . .	. . .	. . .	. . .	. . .
Banks	4 683 . .	. . .	. . .	. . .	. . .	. . .	. . .	. . .	. . .
Other sectors	4 684 . .	. . .	. . .	. . .	. . .	. . .	. . .	. . .	. . .
C. FINANCIAL DERIVATIVES	4 910 . .	. . .	. . .	. . .	. . .	. . .	. . .	. . .	. . .
Monetary authorities	4 911 . .	. . .	. . .	. . .	. . .	. . .	. . .	. . .	. . .
General government	4 912 . .	. . .	. . .	. . .	. . .	. . .	. . .	. . .	. . .
Banks	4 913 . .	. . .	. . .	. . .	. . .	. . .	. . .	. . .	. . .
Other sectors	4 914 . .	. . .	. . .	. . .	. . .	. . .	. . .	. . .	. . .
Assets	4 900 . .	**. . .**	**. . .**	**. . .**	**. . .**	**. . .**	**. . .**	**. . .**	**. . .**
Monetary authorities	4 901 . .	. . .	. . .	. . .	. . .	. . .	. . .	. . .	. . .
General government	4 902 . .	. . .	. . .	. . .	. . .	. . .	. . .	. . .	. . .
Banks	4 903 . .	. . .	. . .	. . .	. . .	. . .	. . .	. . .	. . .
Other sectors	4 904 . .	. . .	. . .	. . .	. . .	. . .	. . .	. . .	. . .
Liabilities	4 905 . .	**. . .**	**. . .**	**. . .**	**. . .**	**. . .**	**. . .**	**. . .**	**. . .**
Monetary authorities	4 906 . .	. . .	. . .	. . .	. . .	. . .	. . .	. . .	. . .
General government	4 907 . .	. . .	. . .	. . .	. . .	. . .	. . .	. . .	. . .
Banks	4 908 . .	. . .	. . .	. . .	. . .	. . .	. . .	. . .	. . .
Other sectors	4 909 . .	. . .	. . .	. . .	. . .	. . .	. . .	. . .	. . .

Table 2 (Concluded). STANDARD PRESENTATION, 1994–2001
(Millions of U.S. dollars)

	Code		1994	1995	1996	1997	1998	1999	2000	2001
D. OTHER INVESTMENT	4 700	. .	362	–524	–512	–638	–96	850	–434	–709
Assets	4 703	. .	**344**	**. . .**	**. . .**	**. . .**	**. . .**	**. . .**	**. . .**	**. . .**
Trade credits	4 706	. .	. . .	. . .	. . .	. . .	. . .	. . .	. . .	. . .
General government	4 707	. .	. . .	. . .	. . .	. . .	. . .	. . .	. . .	. . .
of which: Short-term	4 709	. .	. . .	. . .	. . .	. . .	. . .	. . .	. . .	. . .
Other sectors	4 710	. .	. . .	. . .	. . .	. . .	. . .	. . .	. . .	. . .
of which: Short-term	4 712	. .	. . .	. . .	. . .	. . .	. . .	. . .	. . .	. . .
Loans	4 714	. .	. . .	. . .	. . .	. . .	. . .	. . .	. . .	. . .
Monetary authorities	4 715	. .	. . .	. . .	. . .	. . .	. . .	. . .	. . .	. . .
of which: Short-term	4 718	. .	. . .	. . .	. . .	. . .	. . .	. . .	. . .	. . .
General government	4 719	. .	. . .	. . .	. . .	. . .	. . .	. . .	. . .	. . .
of which: Short-term	4 721	. .	. . .	. . .	. . .	. . .	. . .	. . .	. . .	. . .
Banks	4 722	. .	. . .	. . .	. . .	. . .	. . .	. . .	. . .	. . .
of which: Short-term	4 724	. .	. . .	. . .	. . .	. . .	. . .	. . .	. . .	. . .
Other sectors	4 725	. .	. . .	. . .	. . .	. . .	. . .	. . .	. . .	. . .
of which: Short-term	4 727	. .	. . .	. . .	. . .	. . .	. . .	. . .	. . .	. . .
Currency and deposits	4 730	. .	344	. . .	. . .	. . .	. . .	. . .	. . .	. . .
Monetary authorities	4 731	. .	. . .	. . .	. . .	. . .	. . .	. . .	. . .	. . .
General government	4 732	. .	. . .	. . .	. . .	. . .	. . .	. . .	. . .	. . .
Banks	4 733	. .	. . .	. . .	. . .	. . .	. . .	. . .	. . .	. . .
Other sectors	4 734	. .	344	. . .	. . .	. . .	. . .	. . .	. . .	. . .
Other assets	4 736	. .	. . .	. . .	. . .	. . .	. . .	. . .	. . .	. . .
Monetary authorities	4 737	. .	. . .	. . .	. . .	. . .	. . .	. . .	. . .	. . .
of which: Short-term	4 739	. .	. . .	. . .	. . .	. . .	. . .	. . .	. . .	. . .
General government	4 740	. .	. . .	. . .	. . .	. . .	. . .	. . .	. . .	. . .
of which: Short-term	4 742	. .	. . .	. . .	. . .	. . .	. . .	. . .	. . .	. . .
Banks	4 743	. .	. . .	. . .	. . .	. . .	. . .	. . .	. . .	. . .
of which: Short-term	4 745	. .	. . .	. . .	. . .	. . .	. . .	. . .	. . .	. . .
Other sectors	4 746	. .	. . .	. . .	. . .	. . .	. . .	. . .	. . .	. . .
of which: Short-term	4 748	. .	. . .	. . .	. . .	. . .	. . .	. . .	. . .	. . .
Liabilities	4 753	. .	**18**	**–524**	**–512**	**–638**	**–96**	**850**	**–434**	**–709**
Trade credits	4 756	. .	62	–527	–580	–507	–165	–183	416	318
General government	4 757	. .	–538	–518	–487	–750	–421	–738	. . .	. . .
of which: Short-term	4 759	. .	. . .	. . .	. . .	. . .	. . .	. . .	. . .	. . .
Other sectors	4 760	. .	600	–8	–93	243	256	555	416	318
of which: Short-term	4 762	. .	*249*	*–101*	*–114*	*182*	*286*	*516*	*416*	*318*
Loans	4 764	. .	–63	–1	57	–188	58	1,058	–874	–1,110
Monetary authorities	4 765	. .	–152	–101	–47	–3	. . .	. . .	. . .	. . .
of which: Use of Fund credit and loans from the Fund	4 766	. .	*–152*	*–101*	*–47*	*–3*	. . .	. . .	. . .	. . .
of which: Short-term	4 768	. .	. . .	. . .	. . .	. . .	. . .	. . .	. . .	. . .
General government	4 769	. .	118	196	138	–171	–22	274	–689	–919
of which: Short-term	4 771	. .	. . .	. . .	. . .	. . .	. . .	. . .	. . .	. . .
Banks	4 772	. .	–17	–120	–75	–103	–156	–102	–80	–93
of which: Short-term	4 774	. .	. . .	. . .	. . .	. . .	. . .	. . .	. . .	. . .
Other sectors	4 775	. .	–12	25	42	89	236	886	–105	–99
of which: Short-term	4 777	. .	. . .	. . .	. . .	. . .	. . .	. . .	. . .	. . .
Currency and deposits	4 780	. .	. . .	4	11	56	11	–25	24	83
Monetary authorities	4 781	. .	. . .	. . .	. . .	. . .	. . .	. . .	. . .	. . .
General government	4 782	. .	. . .	. . .	. . .	. . .	. . .	. . .	. . .	. . .
Banks	4 783	. .	. . .	4	11	56	11	–25	. . .	. . .
Other sectors	4 784	. .	. . .	. . .	. . .	. . .	. . .	. . .	24	83
Other liabilities	4 786	. .	19	. . .	. . .	. . .	. . .	. . .	. . .	. . .
Monetary authorities	4 787	. .	19	. . .	. . .	. . .	. . .	. . .	. . .	. . .
of which: Short-term	4 789	. .	. . .	. . .	. . .	. . .	. . .	. . .	. . .	. . .
General government	4 790	. .	. . .	. . .	. . .	. . .	. . .	. . .	. . .	. . .
of which: Short-term	4 792	. .	. . .	. . .	. . .	. . .	. . .	. . .	. . .	. . .
Banks	4 793	. .	. . .	. . .	. . .	. . .	. . .	. . .	. . .	. . .
of which: Short-term	4 795	. .	. . .	. . .	. . .	. . .	. . .	. . .	. . .	. . .
Other sectors	4 796	. .	. . .	. . .	. . .	. . .	. . .	. . .	. . .	. . .
of which: Short-term	4 798	. .	. . .	. . .	. . .	. . .	. . .	. . .	. . .	. . .
E. RESERVE ASSETS	4 802	. .	–362	984	–274	–553	–248	–1,636	416	–3,842
Monetary gold	4 812	. .	. . .	. . .	. . .	. . .	. . .	. . .	. . .	. . .
Special drawing rights	4 811	. .	10	1	18	6	–2	–81	–38	–9
Reserve position in the Fund	4 810	. .	. . .	. . .	. . .	. . .	. . .	–55	. . .	. . .
Foreign exchange	4 803	. .	–611	982	–292	–682	–326	–1,544	474	–3,798
Other claims	4 813	. .	239	. . .	. . .	123	81	44	–20	–36
NET ERRORS AND OMISSIONS	4 998	. .	**–39**	**391**	**209**	**175**	**160**	**123**	**114**	**230**

Part 3 of the *Yearbook* contains descriptions of the methodologies, compilation practices, and sources used to compile these data.

Table 1. ANALYTIC PRESENTATION, 1994–2001

(Millions of U.S. dollars)

	Code	1994	1995	1996	1997	1998	1999	2000	2001
A. Current Account [1]	4 993 Z.	**–467.2**	**–444.7**	**–420.5**	**–295.6**	**–429.3**	**–912.0**	**–763.6**	**–1,603.9**
Goods: exports f.o.b	2 100 . .	149.5	168.9	226.1	230.0	244.6	283.8	364.0	1,713.6
Goods: imports f.o.b	3 100 . .	–916.7	–705.2	–704.4	–684.0	–735.6	–1,090.0	–1,046.0	–2,438.3
Balance on Goods	4 100 . .	*–767.2*	*–536.3*	*–478.3*	*–454.0*	*–491.0*	*–806.2*	*–682.0*	*–724.7*
Services: credit	2 200 . .	191.1	242.4	253.2	278.7	286.2	295.2	325.4	590.1
Services: debit	3 200 . .	–323.3	–350.0	–319.0	–328.6	–396.2	–405.7	–445.8	–1,466.4
Balance on Goods and Services	4 991 . .	*–899.4*	*–643.9*	*–544.1*	*–503.9*	*–601.0*	*–916.7*	*–802.4*	*–1,601.0*
Income: credit	2 300 . .	54.8	59.1	61.0	63.6	46.3	57.8	79.3	129.9
Income: debit	3 300 . .	–187.2	–199.1	–162.1	–168.2	–187.8	–214.8	–271.4	–704.1
Balance on Goods, Services, and Income	4 992 . .	*–1,031.8*	*–783.9*	*–645.2*	*–608.5*	*–742.5*	*–1,073.7*	*–994.5*	*–2,175.2*
Current transfers: credit	2 379 Z.	564.6	339.2	224.7	312.9	313.2	256.3	337.3	657.5
Current transfers: debit	3 379 . .	. . .	. . .	. . .	. . .	. . .	–94.6	–106.4	–86.2
B. Capital Account [1]	4 994 Z.	**. . .**	**. . .**	**. . .**	**. . .**	**. . .**	**180.3**	**226.8**	**584.6**
Capital account: credit	2 994 Z.	. . .	. . .	. . .	. . .	. . .	180.3	226.8	584.6
Capital account: debit	3 994 . .	. . .	. . .	. . .	. . .	. . .	. . .	. . .	. . .
Total, Groups A Plus B	4 981 . .	*–467.2*	*–444.7*	*–420.5*	*–295.6*	*–429.3*	*–731.7*	*–536.8*	*–1,019.3*
C. Financial Account [1]	4 995 W.	**344.4**	**366.7**	**235.0**	**182.2**	**300.4**	**403.9**	**83.2**	**–271.6**
Direct investment abroad	4 505 . .	. . .	. . .	. . .	. . .	. . .	. . .	. . .	. . .
Direct investment in Mozambique	4 555 Z.	35.0	45.0	72.5	64.4	212.7	381.7	139.2	479.9
Portfolio investment assets	4 602 . .	. . .	. . .	. . .	. . .	. . .	. . .	. . .	. . .
Equity securities	4 610 . .	. . .	. . .	. . .	. . .	. . .	. . .	. . .	. . .
Debt securities	4 619 . .	. . .	. . .	. . .	. . .	. . .	. . .	. . .	. . .
Portfolio investment liabilities	4 652 Z.	. . .	. . .	. . .	. . .	. . .	. . .	. . .	. . .
Equity securities	4 660 . .	. . .	. . .	. . .	. . .	. . .	. . .	. . .	. . .
Debt securities	4 669 Z.	. . .	. . .	. . .	. . .	. . .	. . .	. . .	. . .
Financial derivatives	4 910 . .	. . .	. . .	. . .	. . .	. . .	. . .	. . .	. . .
Financial derivatives assets	4 900 . .	. . .	. . .	. . .	. . .	. . .	. . .	. . .	. . .
Financial derivatives liabilities	4 905 . .	. . .	. . .	. . .	. . .	. . .	. . .	. . .	. . .
Other investment assets	4 703 . .	. . .	. . .	. . .	. . .	19.0	2.6	–145.0	–61.7
Monetary authorities	4 701 . .	. . .	. . .	. . .	. . .	1.3	1.7	. . .	–2.4
General government	4 704 . .	. . .	. . .	. . .	. . .	. . .	. . .	. . .	. . .
Banks	4 705 . .	. . .	. . .	. . .	. . .	17.7	13.9	–124.0	–41.1
Other sectors	4 728 . .	. . .	. . .	. . .	. . .	. . .	–13.0	–21.0	–18.2
Other investment liabilities	4 753 W.	309.4	321.7	162.5	117.8	68.7	19.6	89.0	–689.8
Monetary authorities	4 753 WA	. . .	. . .	. . .	. . .	. . .	–5.8	–40.8	. . .
General government	4 753 ZB	309.4	321.7	86.2	48.8	–.8	–261.7	–171.4	–744.4
Banks	4 753 ZC	. . .	. . .	. . .	. . .	20.3	–33.6	16.6	63.0
Other sectors	4 753 ZD	. . .	. . .	76.3	69.0	49.2	320.7	284.6	–8.4
Total, Groups A Through C	4 983 . .	*–122.8*	*–78.0*	*–185.5*	*–113.4*	*–128.9*	*–327.8*	*–453.6*	*–1,290.9*
D. Net Errors and Omissions	4 998 . .	**–443.2**	**–308.6**	**–238.3**	**–364.8**	**–263.8**	**1.5**	**37.5**	**–134.5**
Total, Groups A Through D	4 984 . .	*–566.0*	*–386.6*	*–423.8*	*–478.2*	*–392.7*	*–326.3*	*–416.1*	*–1,425.4*
E. Reserves and Related Items	4 802 A.	**566.0**	**386.6**	**423.8**	**478.2**	**392.7**	**326.3**	**416.1**	**1,425.4**
Reserve assets	4 802 . .	–12.0	16.4	161.0	162.3	91.5	–44.0	–76.8	113.6
Use of Fund credit and loans	4 766 . .	10.4	–14.4	–14.4	19.9	9.6	–2.9	31.1	–15.8
Exceptional financing	4 920 . .	567.6	384.6	277.1	296.0	291.6	373.2	461.8	1,327.6
Conversion rates: meticais per U.S. dollar	0 101 . .	**6,158.4**	**9,203.4**	**11,517.8**	**11,772.6**	**12,110.2**	**13,028.6**	**15,447.1**	**20,703.6**

[1] Excludes components that have been classified in the categories of Group E.

Table 2. STANDARD PRESENTATION, 1994–2001

(Millions of U.S. dollars)

	Code		1994	1995	1996	1997	1998	1999	2000	2001
CURRENT ACCOUNT	4 993	. .	**–467.2**	**–444.7**	**–420.5**	**–295.6**	**–429.3**	**–912.0**	**–763.6**	**–1,603.9**
A. GOODS	4 100	. .	–767.2	–536.3	–478.3	–454.0	–491.0	–806.2	–682.0	–724.7
Credit	2 100	. .	**149.5**	**168.9**	**226.1**	**230.0**	**244.6**	**283.8**	**364.0**	**1,713.6**
General merchandise: exports f.o.b.	2 110	. .	149.5	168.9	226.1	230.0	244.6	283.8	364.0	1,713.6
Goods for processing: exports f.o.b.	2 150	. .	. . .	. . .	. . .	. . .	. . .	. . .	. . .	. . .
Repairs on goods	2 160	. .	. . .	. . .	. . .	. . .	. . .	. . .	. . .	. . .
Goods procured in ports by carriers	2 170	. .	. . .	. . .	. . .	. . .	. . .	. . .	. . .	. . .
Nonmonetary gold	2 180	. .	. . .	. . .	. . .	. . .	. . .	. . .	. . .	. . .
Debit	3 100	. .	**–916.7**	**–705.2**	**–704.4**	**–684.0**	**–735.6**	**–1,090.0**	**–1,046.0**	**–2,438.3**
General merchandise: imports f.o.b.	3 110	. .	–916.7	–705.2	–704.4	–684.0	–735.6	–1,090.0	–1,046.0	–2,438.3
Goods for processing: imports f.o.b.	3 150	. .	. . .	. . .	. . .	. . .	. . .	. . .	. . .	. . .
Repairs on goods	3 160	. .	. . .	. . .	. . .	. . .	. . .	. . .	. . .	. . .
Goods procured in ports by carriers	3 170	. .	. . .	. . .	. . .	. . .	. . .	. . .	. . .	. . .
Nonmonetary gold	3 180	. .	. . .	. . .	. . .	. . .	. . .	. . .	. . .	. . .
B. SERVICES	4 200	. .	–132.2	–107.6	–65.8	–49.9	–110.0	–110.5	–120.4	–876.3
Total credit	2 200	. .	*191.1*	*242.4*	*253.2*	*278.7*	*286.2*	*295.2*	*325.4*	*590.1*
Total debit	3 200	. .	*–323.3*	*–350.0*	*–319.0*	*–328.6*	*–396.2*	*–405.7*	*–445.8*	*–1,466.4*
Transportation services, credit	2 205	. .	**67.1**	**60.0**	**59.1**	**62.8**	**58.3**	**99.3**	**97.6**	**147.3**
Passenger	2 850	. .	. . .	. . .	. . .	. . .	. . .	. . .	. . .	. . .
Freight	2 851	. .	*67.1*	*60.0*	*59.1*	*62.8*	*58.3*	*99.3*	*95.7*	*18.2*
Other	2 852	. .	. . .	. . .	. . .	. . .	. . .	. . .	*1.9*	*129.1*
Sea transport, passenger	2 207	. .	. . .	. . .	. . .	. . .	. . .	. . .	. . .	. . .
Sea transport, freight	2 208	. .	. . .	. . .	. . .	. . .	. . .	. . .	. . .	17.9
Sea transport, other	2 209	. .	. . .	. . .	. . .	. . .	. . .	. . .	. . .	89.0
Air transport, passenger	2 211	. .	. . .	. . .	. . .	. . .	. . .	. . .	. . .	. . .
Air transport, freight	2 212	. .	. . .	. . .	. . .	. . .	. . .	.1	.2	.3
Air transport, other	2 213	. .	. . .	. . .	. . .	. . .	. . .	. . .	1.9	. . .
Other transport, passenger	2 215	. .	. . .	. . .	. . .	. . .	. . .	. . .	. . .	. . .
Other transport, freight	2 216	. .	. . .	. . .	. . .	. . .	. . .	99.2	95.5	. . .
Other transport, other	2 217	. .	. . .	. . .	. . .	. . .	. . .	. . .	. . .	40.1
Transportation services, debit	3 205	. .	**–139.8**	**–114.5**	**–103.9**	**–98.6**	**–107.0**	**–142.7**	**–165.3**	**–420.4**
Passenger	3 850	. .	. . .	. . .	. . .	. . .	. . .	*–4.1*	*–14.1*	*–57.4*
Freight	3 851	. .	*–91.6*	*–70.5*	*–70.4*	*–68.4*	*–73.6*	*–114.2*	*–114.3*	*–267.3*
Other	3 852	. .	*–48.2*	*–44.0*	*–33.5*	*–30.2*	*–33.4*	*–24.4*	*–36.9*	*–95.7*
Sea transport, passenger	3 207	. .	. . .	. . .	. . .	. . .	. . .	. . .	. . .	. . .
Sea transport, freight	3 208	. .	. . .	. . .	. . .	. . .	. . .	. . .	. . .	–255.4
Sea transport, other	3 209	. .	. . .	. . .	. . .	. . .	. . .	. . .	. . .	–16.5
Air transport, passenger	3 211	. .	. . .	. . .	. . .	. . .	. . .	–4.1	–14.1	–57.4
Air transport, freight	3 212	. .	. . .	. . .	. . .	. . .	. . .	–3.0	–4.4	–11.9
Air transport, other	3 213	. .	. . .	. . .	. . .	. . .	. . .	–5.8	–.6	–2.4
Other transport, passenger	3 215	. .	. . .	. . .	. . .	. . .	. . .	. . .	. . .	. . .
Other transport, freight	3 216	. .	. . .	. . .	. . .	. . .	. . .	–111.2	–109.9	. . .
Other transport, other	3 217	. .	. . .	. . .	. . .	. . .	. . .	–18.6	–36.3	–76.8
Travel, credit	2 236	. .	**. . .**	**. . .**	**. . .**	**. . .**	**. . .**	**61.2**	**74.1**	**136.5**
Business travel	2 237	. .	. . .	. . .	. . .	. . .	. . .	. . .	. . .	. . .
Personal travel	2 240	. .	. . .	. . .	. . .	. . .	. . .	61.2	74.1	136.5
Travel, debit	3 236	. .	**. . .**	**. . .**	**. . .**	**. . .**	**. . .**	**–135.8**	**–107.6**	**–283.4**
Business travel	3 237	. .	. . .	. . .	. . .	. . .	. . .	. . .	. . .	. . .
Personal travel	3 240	. .	. . .	. . .	. . .	. . .	. . .	–135.8	–107.6	–283.4
Other services, credit	2 200	BA	**124.0**	**182.4**	**194.1**	**215.9**	**227.9**	**134.7**	**153.7**	**306.3**
Communications	2 245	. .	. . .	. . .	. . .	. . .	. . .	7.8	7.7	30.4
Construction	2 249	. .	. . .	. . .	. . .	. . .	. . .	1.1	.2	3.5
Insurance	2 253	. .	. . .	. . .	. . .	. . .	. . .	. . .	. . .	. . .
Financial	2 260	. .	. . .	. . .	. . .	. . .	. . .	. . .	. . .	. . .
Computer and information	2 262	. .	. . .	. . .	. . .	. . .	. . .	. . .	. . .	. . .
Royalties and licence fees	2 266	. .	. . .	. . .	. . .	. . .	. . .	. . .	. . .	. . .
Other business services	2 268	. .	124.0	182.4	194.1	215.9	227.9	125.8	145.8	269.7
Personal, cultural, and recreational	2 287	. .	. . .	. . .	. . .	. . .	. . .	. . .	. . .	. . .
Government, n.i.e.	2 291	. .	. . .	. . .	. . .	. . .	. . .	. . .	. . .	2.7
Other services, debit	3 200	BA	**–183.5**	**–235.5**	**–215.1**	**–230.0**	**–289.2**	**–127.2**	**–172.9**	**–762.6**
Communications	3 245	. .	. . .	. . .	. . .	. . .	. . .	–2.4	–1.6	–44.6
Construction	3 249	. .	. . .	. . .	. . .	. . .	. . .	–1.0	–28.2	–108.3
Insurance	3 253	. .	–10.2	–7.8	–7.8	–7.6	–8.2	–13.6	–17.6	–40.2
Financial	3 260	. .	. . .	. . .	. . .	. . .	. . .	–3.9	–9.1	–3.9
Computer and information	3 262	. .	. . .	. . .	. . .	. . .	. . .	. . .	. . .	. . .
Royalties and licence fees	3 266	. .	. . .	. . .	. . .	. . .	. . .	. . .	–.1	. . .
Other business services	3 268	. .	–173.3	–227.7	–207.3	–222.4	–281.0	–92.2	–109.1	–538.5
Personal, cultural, and recreational	3 287	. .	. . .	. . .	. . .	. . .	. . .	. . .	. . .	. . .
Government, n.i.e.	3 291	. .	. . .	. . .	. . .	. . .	. . .	–14.1	–7.2	–27.1

Table 2 (Continued). STANDARD PRESENTATION, 1994–2001
(Millions of U.S. dollars)

	Code	1994	1995	1996	1997	1998	1999	2000	2001
C. INCOME	4 300 . .	–132.4	–140.0	–101.1	–104.6	–141.5	–157.0	–192.1	–574.2
Total credit	2 300 . .	*54.8*	*59.1*	*61.0*	*63.6*	*46.3*	*57.8*	*79.3*	*129.9*
Total debit	3 300 . .	*–187.2*	*–199.1*	*–162.1*	*–168.2*	*–187.8*	*–214.8*	*–271.4*	*–704.1*
Compensation of employees, credit	2 310 . .	**54.8**	**59.1**	**61.0**	**63.6**	**46.3**	**38.0**	**36.8**	**3.2**
Compensation of employees, debit	3 310 . .	**–19.4**	**–20.6**	**–15.7**	**–22.9**	**–31.1**	**–50.0**	**–53.4**	**–84.8**
Investment income, credit	2 320 . .	**. . .**	**. . .**	**. . .**	**. . .**	**. . .**	**19.8**	**42.5**	**126.7**
Direct investment income	2 330 . .	. . .	. . .	. . .	. . .	. . .	. . .	. . .	. . .
Dividends and distributed branch profits	2 332 . .	. . .	. . .	. . .	. . .	. . .	. . .	. . .	. . .
Reinvested earnings and undistributed branch profits	2 333 . .	. . .	. . .	. . .	. . .	. . .	. . .	. . .	. . .
Income on debt (interest)	2 334 . .	. . .	. . .	. . .	. . .	. . .	. . .	. . .	. . .
Portfolio investment income	2 339 . .	. . .	. . .	. . .	. . .	. . .	. . .	. . .	. . .
Income on equity	2 340 . .	. . .	. . .	. . .	. . .	. . .	. . .	. . .	. . .
Income on bonds and notes	2 350 . .	. . .	. . .	. . .	. . .	. . .	. . .	. . .	. . .
Income on money market instruments	2 360 . .	. . .	. . .	. . .	. . .	. . .	. . .	. . .	. . .
Other investment income	2 370 . .	. . .	. . .	. . .	. . .	. . .	19.8	42.5	126.7
Investment income, debit	3 320 . .	**–167.8**	**–178.5**	**–146.4**	**–145.3**	**–156.7**	**–164.8**	**–218.0**	**–619.3**
Direct investment income	3 330 . .	. . .	. . .	. . .	. . .	. . .	–5.8	–.3	–41.8
Dividends and distributed branch profits	3 332 . .	. . .	. . .	. . .	. . .	. . .	–5.8	–.3	–41.8
Reinvested earnings and undistributed branch profits	3 333 . .	. . .	. . .	. . .	. . .	. . .	. . .	. . .	. . .
Income on debt (interest)	3 334 . .	. . .	. . .	. . .	. . .	. . .	. . .	. . .	. . .
Portfolio investment income	3 339 . .	. . .	. . .	. . .	. . .	. . .	–56.4	–43.9	. . .
Income on equity	3 340 . .	. . .	. . .	. . .	. . .	. . .	. . .	. . .	. . .
Income on bonds and notes	3 350 . .	. . .	. . .	. . .	. . .	. . .	–56.4	–43.9	. . .
Income on money market instruments	3 360 . .	. . .	. . .	. . .	. . .	. . .	. . .	. . .	. . .
Other investment income	3 370 . .	–167.8	–178.5	–146.4	–145.3	–156.7	–102.6	–173.8	–577.5
D. CURRENT TRANSFERS	4 379 . .	564.6	339.2	224.7	312.9	313.2	161.7	230.9	571.3
Credit	2 379 . .	**564.6**	**339.2**	**224.7**	**312.9**	**313.2**	**256.3**	**337.3**	**657.5**
General government	2 380 . .	564.6	339.2	224.7	312.9	313.2	253.8	336.9	539.1
Other sectors	2 390 . .	. . .	. . .	. . .	. . .	. . .	2.5	.4	118.4
Workers' remittances	2 391 . .	. . .	. . .	. . .	. . .	. . .	. . .	. . .	116.2
Other current transfers	2 392 . .	. . .	. . .	. . .	. . .	. . .	2.5	.4	2.2
Debit	3 379 . .	**. . .**	**. . .**	**. . .**	**. . .**	**. . .**	**–94.6**	**–106.4**	**–86.2**
General government	3 380 . .	. . .	. . .	. . .	. . .	. . .	–4.8	–3.6	–12.9
Other sectors	3 390 . .	. . .	. . .	. . .	. . .	. . .	–89.8	–102.8	–73.3
Workers' remittances	3 391 . .	. . .	. . .	. . .	. . .	. . .	–89.8	–102.8	–73.3
Other current transfers	3 392 . .	. . .	. . .	. . .	. . .	. . .	. . .	. . .	. . .
CAPITAL AND FINANCIAL ACCOUNT	4 996 . .	**910.4**	**753.3**	**658.8**	**660.4**	**693.1**	**910.5**	**726.1**	**1,738.4**
CAPITAL ACCOUNT	4 994 . .	**33.9**	**39.9**	**49.5**	**56.8**	**11.1**	**212.0**	**305.8**	**584.6**
Total credit	2 994 . .	*33.9*	*39.9*	*49.5*	*56.8*	*11.1*	*212.0*	*305.8*	*584.6*
Total debit	3 994 . .	. . .	. . .	. . .	. . .	. . .	. . .	. . .	. . .
Capital transfers, credit	2 400 . .	**33.9**	**39.9**	**49.5**	**56.8**	**11.1**	**212.0**	**305.8**	**584.6**
General government	2 401 . .	33.9	39.9	49.5	56.8	11.1	212.0	305.8	584.6
Debt forgiveness	2 402 . .	33.9	39.9	49.5	56.8	11.1	31.7	79.0	. . .
Other capital transfers	2 410 . .	. . .	. . .	. . .	. . .	. . .	180.3	226.8	584.6
Other sectors	2 430 . .	. . .	. . .	. . .	. . .	. . .	. . .	. . .	. . .
Migrants' transfers	2 431 . .	. . .	. . .	. . .	. . .	. . .	. . .	. . .	. . .
Debt forgiveness	2 432 . .	. . .	. . .	. . .	. . .	. . .	. . .	. . .	. . .
Other capital transfers	2 440 . .	. . .	. . .	. . .	. . .	. . .	. . .	. . .	. . .
Capital transfers, debit	3 400 . .	**. . .**	**. . .**	**. . .**	**. . .**	**. . .**	**. . .**	**. . .**	**. . .**
General government	3 401 . .	. . .	. . .	. . .	. . .	. . .	. . .	. . .	. . .
Debt forgiveness	3 402 . .	. . .	. . .	. . .	. . .	. . .	. . .	. . .	. . .
Other capital transfers	3 410 . .	. . .	. . .	. . .	. . .	. . .	. . .	. . .	. . .
Other sectors	3 430 . .	. . .	. . .	. . .	. . .	. . .	. . .	. . .	. . .
Migrants' transfers	3 431 . .	. . .	. . .	. . .	. . .	. . .	. . .	. . .	. . .
Debt forgiveness	3 432 . .	. . .	. . .	. . .	. . .	. . .	. . .	. . .	. . .
Other capital transfers	3 440 . .	. . .	. . .	. . .	. . .	. . .	. . .	. . .	. . .
Nonproduced nonfinancial assets, credit	2 480 . .	**. . .**	**. . .**	**. . .**	**. . .**	**. . .**	**. . .**	**. . .**	**. . .**
Nonproduced nonfinancial assets, debit	3 480 . .	**. . .**	**. . .**	**. . .**	**. . .**	**. . .**	**. . .**	**. . .**	**. . .**

Table 2 (Continued). STANDARD PRESENTATION, 1994–2001

(Millions of U.S. dollars)

	Code		1994	1995	1996	1997	1998	1999	2000	2001
FINANCIAL ACCOUNT	4 995	. .	**876.5**	**713.4**	**609.3**	**603.6**	**682.0**	**698.5**	**420.3**	**1,153.8**
A. DIRECT INVESTMENT	4 500	. .	35.0	45.0	72.5	64.4	212.7	381.7	139.2	479.9
Direct investment abroad	4 505	. .	**. . .**	**. . .**	**. . .**	**. . .**	**. . .**	**. . .**	**. . .**	**. . .**
Equity capital	4 510	. .	. . .	. . .	. . .	. . .	. . .	. . .	. . .	. . .
Claims on affiliated enterprises	4 515	. .	. . .	. . .	. . .	. . .	. . .	. . .	. . .	. . .
Liabilities to affiliated enterprises	4 520	. .	. . .	. . .	. . .	. . .	. . .	. . .	. . .	. . .
Reinvested earnings	4 525	. .	. . .	. . .	. . .	. . .	. . .	. . .	. . .	. . .
Other capital	4 530	. .	. . .	. . .	. . .	. . .	. . .	. . .	. . .	. . .
Claims on affiliated enterprises	4 535	. .	. . .	. . .	. . .	. . .	. . .	. . .	. . .	. . .
Liabilities to affiliated enterprises	4 540	. .	. . .	. . .	. . .	. . .	. . .	. . .	. . .	. . .
Direct investment in Mozambique	4 555	. .	**35.0**	**45.0**	**72.5**	**64.4**	**212.7**	**381.7**	**139.2**	**479.9**
Equity capital	4 560	. .	35.0	45.0	72.5	64.4	212.7	381.7	139.2	479.9
Claims on direct investors	4 565	. .	. . .	. . .	. . .	. . .	. . .	. . .	. . .	. . .
Liabilities to direct investors	4 570	. .	. . .	. . .	. . .	. . .	. . .	381.7	139.2	479.9
Reinvested earnings	4 575	. .	. . .	. . .	. . .	. . .	. . .	. . .	. . .	. . .
Other capital	4 580	. .	. . .	. . .	. . .	. . .	. . .	. . .	. . .	. . .
Claims on direct investors	4 585	. .	. . .	. . .	. . .	. . .	. . .	. . .	. . .	. . .
Liabilities to direct investors	4 590	. .	. . .	. . .	. . .	. . .	. . .	. . .	. . .	. . .
B. PORTFOLIO INVESTMENT	4 600	. .	. . .	. . .	. . .	. . .	. . .	. . .	. . .	. . .
Assets	4 602	. .	**. . .**	**. . .**	**. . .**	**. . .**	**. . .**	**. . .**	**. . .**	**. . .**
Equity securities	4 610	. .	. . .	. . .	. . .	. . .	. . .	. . .	. . .	. . .
Monetary authorities	4 611	. .	. . .	. . .	. . .	. . .	. . .	. . .	. . .	. . .
General government	4 612	. .	. . .	. . .	. . .	. . .	. . .	. . .	. . .	. . .
Banks	4 613	. .	. . .	. . .	. . .	. . .	. . .	. . .	. . .	. . .
Other sectors	4 614	. .	. . .	. . .	. . .	. . .	. . .	. . .	. . .	. . .
Debt securities	4 619	. .	. . .	. . .	. . .	. . .	. . .	. . .	. . .	. . .
Bonds and notes	4 620	. .	. . .	. . .	. . .	. . .	. . .	. . .	. . .	. . .
Monetary authorities	4 621	. .	. . .	. . .	. . .	. . .	. . .	. . .	. . .	. . .
General government	4 622	. .	. . .	. . .	. . .	. . .	. . .	. . .	. . .	. . .
Banks	4 623	. .	. . .	. . .	. . .	. . .	. . .	. . .	. . .	. . .
Other sectors	4 624	. .	. . .	. . .	. . .	. . .	. . .	. . .	. . .	. . .
Money market instruments	4 630	. .	. . .	. . .	. . .	. . .	. . .	. . .	. . .	. . .
Monetary authorities	4 631	. .	. . .	. . .	. . .	. . .	. . .	. . .	. . .	. . .
General government	4 632	. .	. . .	. . .	. . .	. . .	. . .	. . .	. . .	. . .
Banks	4 633	. .	. . .	. . .	. . .	. . .	. . .	. . .	. . .	. . .
Other sectors	4 634	. .	. . .	. . .	. . .	. . .	. . .	. . .	. . .	. . .
Liabilities	4 652	. .	**. . .**	**. . .**	**. . .**	**. . .**	**. . .**	**. . .**	**. . .**	**. . .**
Equity securities	4 660	. .	. . .	. . .	. . .	. . .	. . .	. . .	. . .	. . .
Banks	4 663	. .	. . .	. . .	. . .	. . .	. . .	. . .	. . .	. . .
Other sectors	4 664	. .	. . .	. . .	. . .	. . .	. . .	. . .	. . .	. . .
Debt securities	4 669	. .	. . .	. . .	. . .	. . .	. . .	. . .	. . .	. . .
Bonds and notes	4 670	. .	. . .	. . .	. . .	. . .	. . .	. . .	. . .	. . .
Monetary authorities	4 671	. .	. . .	. . .	. . .	. . .	. . .	. . .	. . .	. . .
General government	4 672	. .	. . .	. . .	. . .	. . .	. . .	. . .	. . .	. . .
Banks	4 673	. .	. . .	. . .	. . .	. . .	. . .	. . .	. . .	. . .
Other sectors	4 674	. .	. . .	. . .	. . .	. . .	. . .	. . .	. . .	. . .
Money market instruments	4 680	. .	. . .	. . .	. . .	. . .	. . .	. . .	. . .	. . .
Monetary authorities	4 681	. .	. . .	. . .	. . .	. . .	. . .	. . .	. . .	. . .
General government	4 682	. .	. . .	. . .	. . .	. . .	. . .	. . .	. . .	. . .
Banks	4 683	. .	. . .	. . .	. . .	. . .	. . .	. . .	. . .	. . .
Other sectors	4 684	. .	. . .	. . .	. . .	. . .	. . .	. . .	. . .	. . .
C. FINANCIAL DERIVATIVES	4 910	. .	. . .	. . .	. . .	. . .	. . .	. . .	. . .	. . .
Monetary authorities	4 911	. .	. . .	. . .	. . .	. . .	. . .	. . .	. . .	. . .
General government	4 912	. .	. . .	. . .	. . .	. . .	. . .	. . .	. . .	. . .
Banks	4 913	. .	. . .	. . .	. . .	. . .	. . .	. . .	. . .	. . .
Other sectors	4 914	. .	. . .	. . .	. . .	. . .	. . .	. . .	. . .	. . .
Assets	4 900	. .	**. . .**	**. . .**	**. . .**	**. . .**	**. . .**	**. . .**	**. . .**	**. . .**
Monetary authorities	4 901	. .	. . .	. . .	. . .	. . .	. . .	. . .	. . .	. . .
General government	4 902	. .	. . .	. . .	. . .	. . .	. . .	. . .	. . .	. . .
Banks	4 903	. .	. . .	. . .	. . .	. . .	. . .	. . .	. . .	. . .
Other sectors	4 904	. .	. . .	. . .	. . .	. . .	. . .	. . .	. . .	. . .
Liabilities	4 905	. .	**. . .**	**. . .**	**. . .**	**. . .**	**. . .**	**. . .**	**. . .**	**. . .**
Monetary authorities	4 906	. .	. . .	. . .	. . .	. . .	. . .	. . .	. . .	. . .
General government	4 907	. .	. . .	. . .	. . .	. . .	. . .	. . .	. . .	. . .
Banks	4 908	. .	. . .	. . .	. . .	. . .	. . .	. . .	. . .	. . .
Other sectors	4 909	. .	. . .	. . .	. . .	. . .	. . .	. . .	. . .	. . .

Table 2 (Concluded). STANDARD PRESENTATION, 1994–2001
(Millions of U.S. dollars)

	Code	1994	1995	1996	1997	1998	1999	2000	2001
D. OTHER INVESTMENT	4 700 . .	853.5	652.0	375.7	376.9	377.8	360.8	357.9	560.3
Assets	4 703 . .	**...**	**...**	**...**	**...**	**19.0**	**2.6**	**–145.0**	**–61.7**
Trade credits	4 706 . .	...	...	...	...	...	–12.9	–21.0	–18.2
General government	4 707 . .	...	...	...	...	...	...	...	...
of which: Short-term	4 709 . .	...	...	...	...	...	...	...	...
Other sectors	4 710 . .	...	...	...	...	...	–12.9	–21.0	–18.2
of which: Short-term	4 712 . .	...	...	...	...	...	*–12.9*	*–21.0*	*–18.2*
Loans	4 714 . .	...	...	...	...	...	...	...	...
Monetary authorities	4 715 . .	...	...	...	...	...	...	...	...
of which: Short-term	4 718 . .	...	...	...	...	...	...	...	...
General government	4 719 . .	...	...	...	...	...	...	...	...
of which: Short-term	4 721 . .	...	...	...	...	...	...	...	...
Banks	4 722 . .	...	...	...	...	...	...	...	...
of which: Short-term	4 724 . .	...	...	...	...	...	...	...	...
Other sectors	4 725 . .	...	...	...	...	...	...	...	...
of which: Short-term	4 727 . .	...	...	...	...	...	...	...	...
Currency and deposits	4 730 . .	...	...	...	...	19.0	13.9	–124.0	–41.1
Monetary authorities	4 731 . .	...	...	...	...	1.3	...	...	...
General government	4 732 . .	...	...	...	...	...	...	...	...
Banks	4 733 . .	...	...	...	...	17.7	13.9	–124.0	–41.1
Other sectors	4 734 . .	...	...	...	...	...	...	...	...
Other assets	4 736 . .	...	...	...	...	...	1.6	...	–2.4
Monetary authorities	4 737 . .	...	...	...	...	...	1.7	...	–2.4
of which: Short-term	4 739 . .	...	...	...	...	...	*1.7*	...	*–2.4*
General government	4 740 . .	...	...	...	...	...	...	...	...
of which: Short-term	4 742 . .	...	...	...	...	...	...	...	...
Banks	4 743 . .	...	...	...	...	...	...	...	...
of which: Short-term	4 745 . .	...	...	...	...	...	...	...	...
Other sectors	4 746 . .	...	...	...	...	...	–.1	...	...
of which: Short-term	4 748 . .	...	...	...	...	...	*–.1*	...	...
Liabilities	4 753 . .	**853.5**	**652.0**	**375.7**	**376.9**	**358.8**	**358.2**	**502.9**	**622.0**
Trade credits	4 756 . .	...	...	...	...	...	...	...	...
General government	4 757 . .	...	...	...	...	...	...	...	...
of which: Short-term	4 759 . .	...	...	...	...	...	...	...	...
Other sectors	4 760 . .	...	...	...	...	...	...	...	...
of which: Short-term	4 762 . .	...	...	...	...	...	...	...	...
Loans	4 764 . .	685.9	608.7	437.2	4,312.0	320.4	397.6	527.1	559.0
Monetary authorities	4 765 . .	10.4	–14.4	–14.4	19.9	9.6	–2.9	31.1	–15.8
of which: Use of Fund credit and loans from the Fund	4 766 . .	*10.4*	*–14.4*	*–14.4*	*19.9*	*9.6*	*–2.9*	*31.1*	*–15.8*
of which: Short-term	4 768 . .	...	...	...	...	...	...	...	...
General government	4 769 . .	675.5	623.1	375.3	4,223.1	261.6	79.8	211.4	583.2
of which: Short-term	4 771 . .	...	...	...	...	...	...	...	...
Banks	4 772 . .	...	...	...	...	...	...	...	...
of which: Short-term	4 774 . .	...	...	...	...	...	...	...	...
Other sectors	4 775 . .	...	...	76.3	69.0	49.2	320.7	284.6	–8.4
of which: Short-term	4 777 . .	...	...	...	...	...	...	...	...
Currency and deposits	4 780 . .	...	...	...	...	...	...	...	63.0
Monetary authorities	4 781 . .	...	...	...	...	...	...	...	...
General government	4 782 . .	...	...	...	...	...	...	...	...
Banks	4 783 . .	...	...	...	...	...	...	...	63.0
Other sectors	4 784 . .	...	...	...	...	...	...	...	...
Other liabilities	4 786 . .	167.6	43.3	–61.5	–3,935.1	38.4	–39.4	–24.2	...
Monetary authorities	4 787 . .	...	...	...	...	...	–5.8	–40.8	...
of which: Short-term	4 789 . .	...	...	...	...	...	...	...	...
General government	4 790 . .	167.6	43.3	–61.5	–3,935.1	18.1	...	...	...
of which: Short-term	4 792 . .	*167.6*	*43.3*	*–61.5*	*–3,935.1*	*18.1*	...	...	...
Banks	4 793 . .	...	...	...	...	20.3	–33.6	16.6	...
of which: Short-term	4 795 . .	...	...	...	...	*2.8*	*–33.6*	*16.6*	...
Other sectors	4 796 . .	...	...	...	...	...	...	...	...
of which: Short-term	4 798 . .	...	...	...	...	...	...	...	...
E. RESERVE ASSETS	4 802 . .	–12.0	16.4	161.0	162.3	91.5	–44.0	–76.8	113.6
Monetary gold	4 812 . .	–1.1	...	–.3	–5.8	.4	3.1	–5.3	7.4
Special drawing rights	4 811 . .	...	...	...	...	...	...	...	...
Reserve position in the Fund	4 810 . .	...	...	...	...	...	...	...	...
Foreign exchange	4 803 . .	–10.9	16.4	161.3	168.1	91.1	–70.9	–96.3	106.2
Other claims	4 813 . .	...	...	...	...	...	23.8	24.8	...
NET ERRORS AND OMISSIONS	4 998 . .	**–443.2**	**–308.6**	**–238.3**	**–364.8**	**–263.8**	**1.5**	**37.5**	**–134.5**

Part 3 of the *Yearbook* contains descriptions of the methodologies, compilation practices, and sources used to compile these data.

Table 1. ANALYTIC PRESENTATION, 1994–2001
(Millions of U.S. dollars)

	Code	1994	1995	1996	1997	1998	1999	2000	2001
A. Current Account [1]	4 993 Z.	**–129.9**	**–258.5**	**–279.8**	**–412.0**	**–494.2**	**–281.9**	**–210.1**	**–305.5**
Goods: exports f.o.b.	2 100 ..	857.4	933.2	937.9	974.5	1,065.1	1,281.1	1,638.4	2,294.5
Goods: imports f.o.b.	3 100 ..	–1,466.7	–1,756.3	–1,869.1	–2,106.6	–2,451.2	–2,159.6	–2,136.9	–2,563.0
Balance on Goods	4 100 ..	*–609.4*	*–823.0*	*–931.2*	*–1,132.1*	*–1,386.1*	*–878.5*	*–498.5*	*–268.5*
Services: credit	2 200 ..	270.7	360.9	427.7	521.7	626.1	507.1	471.3	419.6
Services: debit	3 200 ..	–128.9	–243.8	–302.0	–443.4	–364.8	–288.2	–323.7	–376.6
Balance on Goods and Services	4 991 ..	*–467.6*	*–705.9*	*–805.4*	*–1,053.8*	*–1,124.7*	*–659.7*	*–350.8*	*–225.5*
Income: credit	2 300 ..	7.1	15.4	9.1	6.5	10.9	51.1	35.0	35.6
Income: debit	3 300 ..	–74.1	–124.2	–53.1	–20.3	–11.3	–54.0	–166.2	–398.7
Balance on Goods, Services, and Income	4 992 ..	*–534.5*	*–814.7*	*–849.4*	*–1,067.5*	*–1,125.1*	*–662.6*	*–482.0*	*–588.6*
Current transfers: credit	2 379 Z.	405.2	564.2	598.4	685.1	631.2	381.0	285.8	295.7
Current transfers: debit	3 379 ..	–.6	–8.0	–28.8	–29.7	–.3	–.3	–13.9	–12.6
B. Capital Account [1]	4 994 Z.	**...**	**...**	**...**	**...**	**...**	**...**	**...**	**...**
Capital account: credit	2 994 Z.	...	...	...	...	...	...	...	...
Capital account: debit	3 994 ..	...	...	...	...	...	...	...	...
Total, Groups A Plus B	4 981 ..	*–129.9*	*–258.5*	*–279.8*	*–412.0*	*–494.2*	*–281.9*	*–210.1*	*–305.5*
C. Financial Account [1]	4 995 W.	**185.2**	**242.8**	**266.8**	**469.1**	**535.1**	**248.8**	**210.2**	**395.1**
Direct investment abroad	4 505 ..	...	...	...	...	...	...	...	...
Direct investment in Myanmar	4 555 Z.	126.1	277.2	310.4	387.2	314.5	253.1	254.8	208.3
Portfolio investment assets	4 602 ..	...	...	...	...	...	...	...	...
Equity securities	4 610 ..	...	...	...	...	...	...	...	...
Debt securities	4 619 ..	...	...	...	...	...	...	...	...
Portfolio investment liabilities	4 652 Z.	...	...	...	...	...	...	...	...
Equity securities	4 660 ..	...	...	...	...	...	...	...	...
Debt securities	4 669 Z.	...	...	...	...	...	...	...	...
Financial derivatives	4 910 ..	...	...	...	...	...	...	...	...
Financial derivatives assets	4 900 ..	...	...	...	...	...	...	...	...
Financial derivatives liabilities	4 905 ..	...	...	...	...	...	...	...	...
Other investment assets	4 703 ..	...	...	...	...	...	...	...	...
Monetary authorities	4 701 ..	...	...	...	...	...	...	...	...
General government	4 704 ..	...	...	...	...	...	...	...	...
Banks	4 705 ..	...	...	...	...	...	...	...	...
Other sectors	4 728 ..	...	...	...	...	...	...	...	...
Other investment liabilities	4 753 W.	59.1	–34.4	–43.6	81.9	220.7	–4.3	–44.5	186.8
Monetary authorities	4 753 WA	2.6	2.3	–3.1	–5.6	–2.6	1.1	7.2	198.7
General government	4 753 ZB	56.5	–36.7	–40.6	87.5	226.9	–4.1	–55.7	–11.8
Banks	4 753 ZC	...	...	...	...	–3.6	–1.3	4.0	–.1
Other sectors	4 753 ZD	...	...	...	...	...	...	...	...
Total, Groups A Through C	4 983 ..	*55.3*	*–15.7*	*–13.0*	*57.0*	*40.9*	*–33.1*	*.1*	*89.6*
D. Net Errors and Omissions	4 998 ..	**–10.3**	**–16.2**	**–11.7**	**–26.0**	**18.8**	**–12.3**	**–23.4**	**88.4**
Total, Groups A Through D	4 984 ..	*45.0*	*–31.8*	*–24.7*	*31.0*	*59.7*	*–45.4*	*–23.3*	*178.0*
E. Reserves and Related Items	4 802 A.	**–45.0**	**31.8**	**24.7**	**–31.0**	**–59.7**	**45.4**	**23.3**	**–178.0**
Reserve assets	4 802 ..	–45.0	31.8	24.7	–31.0	–59.7	45.4	23.3	–178.0
Use of Fund credit and loans	4 766 ..	...	...	...	...	...	...	...	...
Exceptional financing	4 920 ..	...	...	...	...	...	...	...	...
Conversion rates: kyats per U.S. dollar	0 101 ..	**5.9749**	**5.6670**	**5.9176**	**6.2418**	**6.3432**	**6.2858**	**6.5167**	**6.7489**

[1] Excludes components that have been classified in the categories of Group E.

Table 2. STANDARD PRESENTATION, 1994–2001
(Millions of U.S. dollars)

	Code		1994	1995	1996	1997	1998	1999	2000	2001
CURRENT ACCOUNT	4 993	. .	**–129.9**	**–258.5**	**–279.8**	**–412.0**	**–494.2**	**–281.9**	**–210.1**	**–305.5**
A. GOODS	4 100	. .	–609.4	–823.0	–931.2	–1,132.1	–1,386.1	–878.5	–498.5	–268.5
Credit	2 100	. .	**857.4**	**933.2**	**937.9**	**974.5**	**1,065.1**	**1,281.1**	**1,638.4**	**2,294.5**
General merchandise: exports f.o.b.	2 110	. .	857.4	933.2	937.9	974.5	1,065.1	1,281.1	1,195.1	1,869.7
Goods for processing: exports f.o.b.	2 150	. .	. . .	. . .	. . .	. . .	. . .	. . .	443.3	424.8
Repairs on goods	2 160	. .	. . .	. . .	. . .	. . .	. . .	. . .	. . .	. . .
Goods procured in ports by carriers	2 170	. .	. . .	. . .	. . .	. . .	. . .	. . .	. . .	. . .
Nonmonetary gold	2 180	. .	. . .	. . .	. . .	. . .	. . .	. . .	. . .	. . .
Debit	3 100	. .	**–1,466.7**	**–1,756.3**	**–1,869.1**	**–2,106.6**	**–2,451.2**	**–2,159.6**	**–2,136.9**	**–2,563.0**
General merchandise: imports f.o.b.	3 110	. .	–1,466.7	–1,756.3	–1,869.1	–2,106.6	–2,451.2	–2,159.6	–2,136.9	–2,563.0
Goods for processing: imports f.o.b.	3 150	. .	. . .	. . .	. . .	. . .	. . .	. . .	. . .	. . .
Repairs on goods	3 160	. .	. . .	. . .	. . .	. . .	. . .	. . .	. . .	. . .
Goods procured in ports by carriers	3 170	. .	. . .	. . .	. . .	. . .	. . .	. . .	. . .	. . .
Nonmonetary gold	3 180	. .	. . .	. . .	. . .	. . .	. . .	. . .	. . .	. . .
B. SERVICES	4 200	. .	141.8	117.1	125.8	78.3	261.3	218.9	147.7	43.0
Total credit	2 200	. .	*270.7*	*360.9*	*427.7*	*521.7*	*626.1*	*507.1*	*471.3*	*419.6*
Total debit	3 200	. .	*–128.9*	*–243.8*	*–302.0*	*–443.4*	*–364.8*	*–288.2*	*–323.7*	*–376.6*
Transportation services, credit	2 205	. .	**2.5**	**22.6**	**40.1**	**36.3**	**33.3**	**81.1**	**74.9**	**79.2**
Passenger	2 850	. .	. . .	*17.6*	*33.3*	*27.8*	*24.5*	*33.1*	*32.5*	*24.5*
Freight	2 851	. .	*2.5*	*5.0*	*6.8*	*8.6*	*8.8*	*12.4*	*8.1*	*21.7*
Other	2 852	. .	. . .	. . .	. . .	. . .	. . .	*35.7*	*34.3*	*33.0*
Sea transport, passenger	2 207	. .	. . .	. . .	. . .	. . .	. . .	. . .	. . .	. . .
Sea transport, freight	2 208	. .	. . .	. . .	. . .	. . .	. . .	. . .	. . .	. . .
Sea transport, other	2 209	. .	. . .	. . .	. . .	. . .	. . .	. . .	. . .	. . .
Air transport, passenger	2 211	. .	. . .	. . .	. . .	. . .	. . .	. . .	. . .	. . .
Air transport, freight	2 212	. .	. . .	. . .	. . .	. . .	. . .	. . .	. . .	. . .
Air transport, other	2 213	. .	. . .	. . .	. . .	. . .	. . .	. . .	. . .	. . .
Other transport, passenger	2 215	. .	. . .	. . .	. . .	. . .	. . .	. . .	. . .	. . .
Other transport, freight	2 216	. .	. . .	. . .	. . .	. . .	. . .	. . .	. . .	. . .
Other transport, other	2 217	. .	. . .	. . .	. . .	. . .	. . .	. . .	. . .	. . .
Transportation services, debit	3 205	. .	**–17.2**	**–25.4**	**–36.2**	**–110.0**	**–161.6**	**–223.1**	**–250.5**	**–296.3**
Passenger	3 850	. .	. . .	. . .	. . .	*–4.8*	*–3.8*	*–4.9*	*–5.3*	*–5.0*
Freight	3 851	. .	*–17.2*	*–25.4*	*–36.2*	*–105.2*	*–157.8*	*–218.2*	*–245.2*	*–291.3*
Other	3 852	. .	. . .	. . .	. . .	. . .	. . .	. . .	. . .	. . .
Sea transport, passenger	3 207	. .	. . .	. . .	. . .	. . .	. . .	. . .	. . .	. . .
Sea transport, freight	3 208	. .	. . .	. . .	. . .	. . .	. . .	. . .	. . .	. . .
Sea transport, other	3 209	. .	. . .	. . .	. . .	. . .	. . .	. . .	. . .	. . .
Air transport, passenger	3 211	. .	. . .	. . .	. . .	. . .	. . .	. . .	. . .	. . .
Air transport, freight	3 212	. .	. . .	. . .	. . .	. . .	. . .	. . .	. . .	. . .
Air transport, other	3 213	. .	. . .	. . .	. . .	. . .	. . .	. . .	. . .	. . .
Other transport, passenger	3 215	. .	. . .	. . .	. . .	. . .	. . .	. . .	. . .	. . .
Other transport, freight	3 216	. .	. . .	. . .	. . .	. . .	. . .	. . .	. . .	. . .
Other transport, other	3 217	. .	. . .	. . .	. . .	. . .	. . .	. . .	. . .	. . .
Travel, credit	2 236	. .	**132.9**	**149.1**	**179.7**	**153.5**	**169.5**	**187.5**	**160.2**	**124.3**
Business travel	2 237	. .	. . .	. . .	. . .	. . .	. . .	. . .	. . .	. . .
Personal travel	2 240	. .	. . .	. . .	. . .	. . .	. . .	. . .	. . .	. . .
Travel, debit	3 236	. .	**–12.4**	**–17.6**	**–27.6**	**–32.7**	**–26.6**	**–21.3**	**–24.9**	**–27.3**
Business travel	3 237	. .	. . .	. . .	. . .	. . .	. . .	. . .	. . .	. . .
Personal travel	3 240	. .	. . .	. . .	. . .	. . .	. . .	. . .	. . .	. . .
Other services, credit	2 200	BA	**135.3**	**189.2**	**207.9**	**331.9**	**423.3**	**238.5**	**236.3**	**216.0**
Communications	2 245	. .	. . .	. . .	. . .	. . .	. . .	.2	.2	.2
Construction	2 249	. .	. . .	. . .	. . .	. . .	. . .	. . .	. . .	. . .
Insurance	2 253	. .	. . .	. . .	. . .	. . .	. . .	. . .	. . .	. . .
Financial	2 260	. .	. . .	. . .	. . .	. . .	. . .	. . .	. . .	. . .
Computer and information	2 262	. .	. . .	. . .	. . .	. . .	. . .	. . .	. . .	. . .
Royalties and licence fees	2 266	. .	. . .	. . .	. . .	. . .	. . .	1.8	.1	. . .
Other business services	2 268	. .	120.9	177.8	197.3	318.5	408.6	220.4	217.4	197.0
Personal, cultural, and recreational	2 287	. .	. . .	. . .	. . .	. . .	. . .	. . .	. . .	. . .
Government, n.i.e.	2 291	. .	14.4	11.4	10.6	13.4	14.8	16.1	18.5	18.8
Other services, debit	3 200	BA	**–99.3**	**–200.8**	**–238.2**	**–300.7**	**–176.6**	**–43.8**	**–48.3**	**–53.1**
Communications	3 245	. .	. . .	. . .	. . .	. . .	. . .	. . .	. . .	. . .
Construction	3 249	. .	. . .	. . .	. . .	. . .	. . .	. . .	. . .	. . .
Insurance	3 253	. .	–7.3	–1.2	. . .	. . .	. . .	. . .	. . .	. . .
Financial	3 260	. .	. . .	. . .	. . .	. . .	. . .	. . .	. . .	. . .
Computer and information	3 262	. .	. . .	. . .	. . .	. . .	. . .	. . .	. . .	. . .
Royalties and licence fees	3 266	. .	. . .	. . .	. . .	. . .	. . .	. . .	. . .	. . .
Other business services	3 268	. .	–80.6	–186.1	–224.8	–286.8	–161.0	–30.0	–30.5	–37.0
Personal, cultural, and recreational	3 287	. .	. . .	. . .	. . .	. . .	. . .	–.2	–.2	–.1
Government, n.i.e.	3 291	. .	–11.4	–13.5	–13.4	–13.9	–15.6	–13.6	–17.7	–15.9

Table 2 (Continued). STANDARD PRESENTATION, 1994–2001
(Millions of U.S. dollars)

	Code		1994	1995	1996	1997	1998	1999	2000	2001
C. INCOME	4 300	. .	–67.0	–108.8	–44.0	–13.7	–.4	–2.9	–131.2	–363.1
Total credit	2 300	. .	*7.1*	*15.4*	*9.1*	*6.5*	*10.9*	*51.1*	*35.0*	*35.6*
Total debit	3 300	. .	*–74.1*	*–124.2*	*–53.1*	*–20.3*	*–11.3*	*–54.0*	*–166.2*	*–398.7*
Compensation of employees, credit	2 310	. .	**. . .**	**. . .**	**. . .**	**. . .**	**. . .**	**38.7**	**26.5**	**30.5**
Compensation of employees, debit	3 310	. .	**. . .**	**. . .**	**. . .**	**. . .**	**. . .**	**. . .**	**. . .**	**. . .**
Investment income, credit	2 320	. .	**7.1**	**15.4**	**9.1**	**6.5**	**10.9**	**12.4**	**8.4**	**5.1**
Direct investment income	2 330	. .	. . .	. . .	. . .	. . .	. . .	. . .	. . .	. . .
Dividends and distributed branch profits	2 332	. .	. . .	. . .	. . .	. . .	. . .	. . .	. . .	. . .
Reinvested earnings and undistributed branch profits	2 333	. .	. . .	. . .	. . .	. . .	. . .	. . .	. . .	. . .
Income on debt (interest)	2 334	. .	. . .	. . .	. . .	. . .	. . .	. . .	. . .	. . .
Portfolio investment income	2 339	. .	. . .	. . .	. . .	. . .	. . .	. . .	. . .	. . .
Income on equity	2 340	. .	. . .	. . .	. . .	. . .	. . .	. . .	. . .	. . .
Income on bonds and notes	2 350	. .	. . .	. . .	. . .	. . .	. . .	. . .	. . .	. . .
Income on money market instruments	2 360	. .	. . .	. . .	. . .	. . .	. . .	. . .	. . .	. . .
Other investment income	2 370	. .	7.1	15.4	9.1	6.5	10.9	12.4	8.4	5.1
Investment income, debit	3 320	. .	**–74.1**	**–124.2**	**–53.1**	**–20.3**	**–11.3**	**–54.0**	**–166.2**	**–398.7**
Direct investment income	3 330	. .	. . .	. . .	. . .	. . .	. . .	–34.8	–135.1	–377.4
Dividends and distributed branch profits	3 332	. .	. . .	. . .	. . .	. . .	. . .	. . .	. . .	. . .
Reinvested earnings and undistributed branch profits	3 333	. .	. . .	. . .	. . .	. . .	. . .	. . .	. . .	. . .
Income on debt (interest)	3 334	. .	. . .	. . .	. . .	. . .	. . .	. . .	. . .	. . .
Portfolio investment income	3 339	. .	. . .	. . .	. . .	. . .	. . .	. . .	. . .	. . .
Income on equity	3 340	. .	. . .	. . .	. . .	. . .	. . .	. . .	. . .	. . .
Income on bonds and notes	3 350	. .	. . .	. . .	. . .	. . .	. . .	. . .	. . .	. . .
Income on money market instruments	3 360	. .	. . .	. . .	. . .	. . .	. . .	. . .	. . .	. . .
Other investment income	3 370	. .	–74.1	–124.2	–53.1	–20.3	–11.3	–19.2	–31.1	–21.3
D. CURRENT TRANSFERS	4 379	. .	404.7	556.2	569.6	655.4	630.9	380.7	271.9	283.0
Credit	2 379	. .	**405.2**	**564.2**	**598.4**	**685.1**	**631.2**	**381.0**	**285.8**	**295.7**
General government	2 380	. .	120.4	109.4	124.9	214.3	136.3	43.9	35.8	62.9
Other sectors	2 390	. .	284.9	454.9	473.4	470.8	495.0	337.2	250.1	232.7
Workers' remittances	2 391	. .	41.6	80.6	122.5	147.2	135.8	96.4	75.6	85.6
Other current transfers	2 392	. .	243.3	374.3	351.0	323.6	359.2	240.8	174.5	147.1
Debit	3 379	. .	**–.6**	**–8.0**	**–28.8**	**–29.7**	**–.3**	**–.3**	**–13.9**	**–12.6**
General government	3 380	. .	–.3	–.4	–.3	–.3	–.3	–.3	–.1	–.1
Other sectors	3 390	. .	–.2	–7.7	–28.5	–29.4	. . .	. . .	–13.8	–12.5
Workers' remittances	3 391	. .	. . .	. . .	. . .	. . .	. . .	. . .	–13.8	–12.5
Other current transfers	3 392	. .	–.2	–7.7	–28.5	–29.4	. . .	. . .	. . .	. . .
CAPITAL AND FINANCIAL ACCOUNT	4 996	. .	**140.2**	**274.6**	**291.6**	**438.0**	**475.4**	**294.2**	**233.6**	**217.1**
CAPITAL ACCOUNT	4 994	. .	. . .	. . .	. . .	. . .	. . .	. . .	. . .	. . .
Total credit	2 994	. .	. . .	. . .	. . .	. . .	. . .	. . .	. . .	. . .
Total debit	3 994	. .	. . .	. . .	. . .	. . .	. . .	. . .	. . .	. . .
Capital transfers, credit	2 400	. .	**. . .**	**. . .**	**. . .**	**. . .**	**. . .**	**. . .**	**. . .**	**. . .**
General government	2 401	. .	. . .	. . .	. . .	. . .	. . .	. . .	. . .	. . .
Debt forgiveness	2 402	. .	. . .	. . .	. . .	. . .	. . .	. . .	. . .	. . .
Other capital transfers	2 410	. .	. . .	. . .	. . .	. . .	. . .	. . .	. . .	. . .
Other sectors	2 430	. .	. . .	. . .	. . .	. . .	. . .	. . .	. . .	. . .
Migrants' transfers	2 431	. .	. . .	. . .	. . .	. . .	. . .	. . .	. . .	. . .
Debt forgiveness	2 432	. .	. . .	. . .	. . .	. . .	. . .	. . .	. . .	. . .
Other capital transfers	2 440	. .	. . .	. . .	. . .	. . .	. . .	. . .	. . .	. . .
Capital transfers, debit	3 400	. .	**. . .**	**. . .**	**. . .**	**. . .**	**. . .**	**. . .**	**. . .**	**. . .**
General government	3 401	. .	. . .	. . .	. . .	. . .	. . .	. . .	. . .	. . .
Debt forgiveness	3 402	. .	. . .	. . .	. . .	. . .	. . .	. . .	. . .	. . .
Other capital transfers	3 410	. .	. . .	. . .	. . .	. . .	. . .	. . .	. . .	. . .
Other sectors	3 430	. .	. . .	. . .	. . .	. . .	. . .	. . .	. . .	. . .
Migrants' transfers	3 431	. .	. . .	. . .	. . .	. . .	. . .	. . .	. . .	. . .
Debt forgiveness	3 432	. .	. . .	. . .	. . .	. . .	. . .	. . .	. . .	. . .
Other capital transfers	3 440	. .	. . .	. . .	. . .	. . .	. . .	. . .	. . .	. . .
Nonproduced nonfinancial assets, credit	2 480	. .	**. . .**	**. . .**	**. . .**	**. . .**	**. . .**	**. . .**	**. . .**	**. . .**
Nonproduced nonfinancial assets, debit	3 480	. .	**. . .**	**. . .**	**. . .**	**. . .**	**. . .**	**. . .**	**. . .**	**. . .**

Table 2 (Continued). STANDARD PRESENTATION, 1994–2001

(Millions of U.S. dollars)

	Code	1994	1995	1996	1997	1998	1999	2000	2001
FINANCIAL ACCOUNT	4 995 . .	**140.2**	**274.6**	**291.6**	**438.0**	**475.4**	**294.2**	**233.6**	**217.1**
A. DIRECT INVESTMENT	4 500 . .	126.1	277.2	310.4	387.2	314.5	253.1	254.8	208.3
Direct investment abroad	4 505 . .	...	...	...	...	...	...	...	...
Equity capital	4 510 . .	...	...	...	...	...	...	...	...
Claims on affiliated enterprises	4 515 . .	...	...	...	...	...	...	...	...
Liabilities to affiliated enterprises	4 520 . .	...	...	...	...	...	...	...	...
Reinvested earnings	4 525 . .	...	...	...	...	...	...	...	...
Other capital	4 530 . .	...	...	...	...	...	...	...	...
Claims on affiliated enterprises	4 535 . .	...	...	...	...	...	...	...	...
Liabilities to affiliated enterprises	4 540 . .	...	...	...	...	...	...	...	...
Direct investment in Myanmar	4 555 . .	**126.1**	**277.2**	**310.4**	**387.2**	**314.5**	**253.1**	**254.8**	**208.3**
Equity capital	4 560 . .	126.1	277.2	310.4	387.2	314.5	253.1	254.8	208.3
Claims on direct investors	4 565 . .	...	...	...	...	...	...	...	...
Liabilities to direct investors	4 570 . .	...	...	...	...	...	...	...	...
Reinvested earnings	4 575 . .	...	...	...	...	...	...	...	...
Other capital	4 580 . .	...	...	...	...	...	...	...	...
Claims on direct investors	4 585 . .	...	...	...	...	...	...	...	...
Liabilities to direct investors	4 590 . .	...	...	...	...	...	...	...	...
B. PORTFOLIO INVESTMENT	4 600 . .	...	...	...	...	...	...	...	...
Assets	4 602 . .	...	...	...	...	...	...	...	...
Equity securities	4 610 . .	...	...	...	...	...	...	...	...
Monetary authorities	4 611 . .	...	...	...	...	...	...	...	...
General government	4 612 . .	...	...	...	...	...	...	...	...
Banks	4 613 . .	...	...	...	...	...	...	...	...
Other sectors	4 614 . .	...	...	...	...	...	...	...	...
Debt securities	4 619 . .	...	...	...	...	...	...	...	...
Bonds and notes	4 620 . .	...	...	...	...	...	...	...	...
Monetary authorities	4 621 . .	...	...	...	...	...	...	...	...
General government	4 622 . .	...	...	...	...	...	...	...	...
Banks	4 623 . .	...	...	...	...	...	...	...	...
Other sectors	4 624 . .	...	...	...	...	...	...	...	...
Money market instruments	4 630 . .	...	...	...	...	...	...	...	...
Monetary authorities	4 631 . .	...	...	...	...	...	...	...	...
General government	4 632 . .	...	...	...	...	...	...	...	...
Banks	4 633 . .	...	...	...	...	...	...	...	...
Other sectors	4 634 . .	...	...	...	...	...	...	...	...
Liabilities	4 652 . .	...	...	...	...	...	...	...	...
Equity securities	4 660 . .	...	...	...	...	...	...	...	...
Banks	4 663 . .	...	...	...	...	...	...	...	...
Other sectors	4 664 . .	...	...	...	...	...	...	...	...
Debt securities	4 669 . .	...	...	...	...	...	...	...	...
Bonds and notes	4 670 . .	...	...	...	...	...	...	...	...
Monetary authorities	4 671 . .	...	...	...	...	...	...	...	...
General government	4 672 . .	...	...	...	...	...	...	...	...
Banks	4 673 . .	...	...	...	...	...	...	...	...
Other sectors	4 674 . .	...	...	...	...	...	...	...	...
Money market instruments	4 680 . .	...	...	...	...	...	...	...	...
Monetary authorities	4 681 . .	...	...	...	...	...	...	...	...
General government	4 682 . .	...	...	...	...	...	...	...	...
Banks	4 683 . .	...	...	...	...	...	...	...	...
Other sectors	4 684 . .	...	...	...	...	...	...	...	...
C. FINANCIAL DERIVATIVES	4 910 . .	...	...	...	...	...	...	...	...
Monetary authorities	4 911 . .	...	...	...	...	...	...	...	...
General government	4 912 . .	...	...	...	...	...	...	...	...
Banks	4 913 . .	...	...	...	...	...	...	...	...
Other sectors	4 914 . .	...	...	...	...	...	...	...	...
Assets	4 900 . .	...	...	...	...	...	...	...	...
Monetary authorities	4 901 . .	...	...	...	...	...	...	...	...
General government	4 902 . .	...	...	...	...	...	...	...	...
Banks	4 903 . .	...	...	...	...	...	...	...	...
Other sectors	4 904 . .	...	...	...	...	...	...	...	...
Liabilities	4 905 . .	...	...	...	...	...	...	...	...
Monetary authorities	4 906 . .	...	...	...	...	...	...	...	...
General government	4 907 . .	...	...	...	...	...	...	...	...
Banks	4 908 . .	...	...	...	...	...	...	...	...
Other sectors	4 909 . .	...	...	...	...	...	...	...	...

Table 2 (Concluded). STANDARD PRESENTATION, 1994–2001
(Millions of U.S. dollars)

	Code	1994	1995	1996	1997	1998	1999	2000	2001
D. OTHER INVESTMENT	4 700	59.1	–34.4	–43.6	81.9	220.7	–4.3	–44.5	186.8
Assets	4 703	...	...	...	...	...	...	...	...
Trade credits	4 706	...	...	...	...	...	...	...	...
General government	4 707	...	...	...	...	...	...	...	...
of which: Short-term	4 709	...	...	...	...	...	...	...	...
Other sectors	4 710	...	...	...	...	...	...	...	...
of which: Short-term	4 712	...	...	...	...	...	...	...	...
Loans	4 714	...	...	...	...	...	...	...	...
Monetary authorities	4 715	...	...	...	...	...	...	...	...
of which: Short-term	4 718	...	...	...	...	...	...	...	...
General government	4 719	...	...	...	...	...	...	...	...
of which: Short-term	4 721	...	...	...	...	...	...	...	...
Banks	4 722	...	...	...	...	...	...	...	...
of which: Short-term	4 724	...	...	...	...	...	...	...	...
Other sectors	4 725	...	...	...	...	...	...	...	...
of which: Short-term	4 727	...	...	...	...	...	...	...	...
Currency and deposits	4 730	...	...	...	...	...	...	...	...
Monetary authorities	4 731	...	...	...	...	...	...	...	...
General government	4 732	...	...	...	...	...	...	...	...
Banks	4 733	...	...	...	...	...	...	...	...
Other sectors	4 734	...	...	...	...	...	...	...	...
Other assets	4 736	...	...	...	...	...	...	...	...
Monetary authorities	4 737	...	...	...	...	...	...	...	...
of which: Short-term	4 739	...	...	...	...	...	...	...	...
General government	4 740	...	...	...	...	...	...	...	...
of which: Short-term	4 742	...	...	...	...	...	...	...	...
Banks	4 743	...	...	...	...	...	...	...	...
of which: Short-term	4 745	...	...	...	...	...	...	...	...
Other sectors	4 746	...	...	...	...	...	...	...	...
of which: Short-term	4 748	...	...	...	...	...	...	...	...
Liabilities	4 753	**59.1**	**–34.4**	**–43.6**	**81.9**	**220.7**	**–4.3**	**–44.5**	**186.8**
Trade credits	4 756	–14.3	–47.9	–62.1	...	...	...	...	...
General government	4 757	–14.3	–47.9	–62.1	...	...	...	...	...
of which: Short-term	4 759	...	...	...	...	...	...	...	...
Other sectors	4 760	...	...	...	...	...	...	...	...
of which: Short-term	4 762	...	...	...	...	...	...	...	...
Loans	4 764	70.8	11.2	21.6	87.5	226.9	–4.1	–55.7	–11.8
Monetary authorities	4 765	...	...	...	...	...	...	...	...
of which: Use of Fund credit and loans from the Fund	4 766	...	...	...	...	...	...	...	...
of which: Short-term	4 768	...	...	...	...	...	...	...	...
General government	4 769	70.8	11.2	21.6	87.5	226.9	–4.1	–55.7	–11.8
of which: Short-term	4 771	*–1.0*	*–26.2*	*50.0*	*53.5*	...	...	...	...
Banks	4 772	...	...	...	...	...	...	...	...
of which: Short-term	4 774	...	...	...	...	...	...	...	...
Other sectors	4 775	...	...	...	...	...	...	...	...
of which: Short-term	4 777	...	...	...	...	...	...	...	...
Currency and deposits	4 780	...	...	...	...	...	...	1.0	–.1
Monetary authorities	4 781	...	...	...	...	...	...	...	...
General government	4 782	...	...	...	...	...	...	...	...
Banks	4 783	...	...	...	...	...	...	1.0	–.1
Other sectors	4 784	...	...	...	...	...	...	...	...
Other liabilities	4 786	2.6	2.3	–3.1	–5.6	–6.2	–.3	10.2	198.7
Monetary authorities	4 787	2.6	2.3	–3.1	–5.6	–2.6	1.1	7.2	198.7
of which: Short-term	4 789	*2.6*	*2.3*	*–3.1*	*–5.6*	...	...	...	...
General government	4 790	...	...	...	...	...	...	...	...
of which: Short-term	4 792	...	...	...	...	...	...	...	...
Banks	4 793	...	...	...	...	–3.6	–1.3	3.0	...
of which: Short-term	4 795	...	...	...	...	...	...	...	...
Other sectors	4 796	...	...	...	...	...	...	...	...
of which: Short-term	4 798	...	...	...	...	...	...	...	...
E. RESERVE ASSETS	4 802	–45.0	31.8	24.7	–31.0	–59.7	45.4	23.3	–178.0
Monetary gold	4 812	7.7	8.5	1.3	...	...	...	...	...
Special drawing rights	4 811	.2	...	...	...	–.2	.2	...	–.4
Reserve position in the Fund	4 810	...	...	...	...	...	...	...	...
Foreign exchange	4 803	–52.8	23.3	23.4	–31.0	–59.5	22.5	.7	–178.7
Other claims	4 813	...	...	...	...	...	22.7	22.6	1.1
NET ERRORS AND OMISSIONS	4 998	**–10.3**	**–16.2**	**–11.7**	**–26.0**	**18.8**	**–12.3**	**–23.4**	**88.4**

Part 3 of the *Yearbook* contains descriptions of the methodologies, compilation practices, and sources used to compile these data.

Table 3. INTERNATIONAL INVESTMENT POSITION (End–period stocks), 1994–2001

(Millions of U.S. dollars)

	Code	1994	1995	1996	1997	1998	1999	2000	2001
ASSETS	8 995 C.	...	...	...	...	...	...	...	...
Direct investment abroad	8 505 . .	...	...	...	...	...	...	...	...
Equity capital and reinvested earnings	8 506 . .	...	...	...	...	...	...	...	...
Claims on affiliated enterprises	8 507 . .	...	...	...	...	...	...	...	...
Liabilities to affiliated enterprises	8 508 . .	...	...	...	...	...	...	...	...
Other capital	8 530 . .	...	...	...	...	...	...	...	...
Claims on affiliated enterprises	8 535 . .	...	...	...	...	...	...	...	...
Liabilities to affiliated enterprises	8 540 . .	...	...	...	...	...	...	...	...
Portfolio investment	8 602 . .	...	...	...	...	...	...	...	...
Equity securities	8 610 . .	...	...	...	...	...	...	...	...
Monetary authorities	8 611 . .	...	...	...	...	...	...	...	...
General government	8 612 . .	...	...	...	...	...	...	...	...
Banks	8 613 . .	...	...	...	...	...	...	...	...
Other sectors	8 614 . .	...	...	...	...	...	...	...	...
Debt securities	8 619 . .	...	...	...	...	...	...	...	...
Bonds and notes	8 620 . .	...	...	...	...	...	...	...	...
Monetary authorities	8 621 . .	...	...	...	...	...	...	...	...
General government	8 622 . .	...	...	...	...	...	...	...	...
Banks	8 623 . .	...	...	...	...	...	...	...	...
Other sectors	8 624 . .	...	...	...	...	...	...	...	...
Money market instruments	8 630 . .	...	...	...	...	...	...	...	...
Monetary authorities	8 631 . .	...	...	...	...	...	...	...	...
General government	8 632 . .	...	...	...	...	...	...	...	...
Banks	8 633 . .	...	...	...	...	...	...	...	...
Other sectors	8 634 . .	...	...	...	...	...	...	...	...
Financial derivatives	8 900 . .	...	...	...	...	...	...	...	...
Monetary authorities	8 901 . .	...	...	...	...	...	...	...	...
General government	8 902 . .	...	...	...	...	...	...	...	...
Banks	8 903 . .	...	...	...	...	...	...	...	...
Other sectors	8 904 . .	...	...	...	...	...	...	...	...
Other investment	8 703 . .	...	...	...	...	...	...	...	...
Trade credits	8 706 . .	...	...	...	...	...	...	...	...
General government	8 707 . .	...	...	...	...	...	...	...	...
of which: Short-term	8 709 . .	...	...	...	...	...	...	...	...
Other sectors	8 710 . .	...	...	...	...	...	...	...	...
of which: Short-term	8 712 . .	...	...	...	...	...	...	...	...
Loans	8 714 . .	...	...	...	...	...	...	...	...
Monetary authorities	8 715 . .	...	...	...	...	...	...	...	...
of which: Short-term	8 718 . .	...	...	...	...	...	...	...	...
General government	8 719 . .	...	...	...	...	...	...	...	...
of which: Short-term	8 721 . .	...	...	...	...	...	...	...	...
Banks	8 722 . .	...	...	...	...	...	...	...	...
of which: Short-term	8 724 . .	...	...	...	...	...	...	...	...
Other sectors	8 725 . .	...	...	...	...	...	...	...	...
of which: Short-term	8 727 . .	...	...	...	...	...	...	...	...
Currency and deposits	8 730 . .	...	...	...	...	...	...	...	...
Monetary authorities	8 731 . .	...	...	...	...	...	...	...	...
General government	8 732 . .	...	...	...	...	...	...	...	...
Banks	8 733 . .	...	...	...	...	...	...	...	...
Other sectors	8 734 . .	...	...	...	...	...	...	...	...
Other assets	8 736 . .	...	...	...	...	...	...	...	...
Monetary authorities	8 737 . .	...	...	...	...	...	...	...	...
of which: Short-term	8 739 . .	...	...	...	...	...	...	...	...
General government	8 740 . .	...	...	...	...	...	...	...	...
of which: Short-term	8 742 . .	...	...	...	...	...	...	...	...
Banks	8 743 . .	...	...	...	...	...	...	...	...
of which: Short-term	8 745 . .	...	...	...	...	...	...	...	...
Other sectors	8 746 . .	...	...	...	...	...	...	...	...
of which: Short-term	8 748 . .	...	...	...	...	...	...	...	...
Reserve assets	8 802 . .	...	...	...	...	...	**328.0**	**287.4**	**455.0**
Monetary gold	8 812 . .	...	...	...	...	...	66.4	63.3	62.8
Special drawing rights	8 811 . .	.1	.1	.1	.1	.3	.2	.1	.6
Reserve position in the Fund	8 810 . .	...	...	...	...	...	...	...	...
Foreign exchange	8 803 . .	...	...	...	...	...	26.7	24.6	200.2
Other claims	8 813 . .	...	...	...	...	...	234.8	199.3	191.5

Table 3 (Concluded). INTERNATIONAL INVESTMENT POSITION (End–period stocks), 1994–2001

(Millions of U.S. dollars)

	Code	1994	1995	1996	1997	1998	1999	2000	2001
LIABILITIES	8 995 D.	...	...	...	...	...	...	...	...
Direct investment in Myanmar	8 555 . .	...	...	...	...	...	**3,096.2**	**3,177.9**	**3,266.2**
Equity capital and reinvested earnings	8 556 . .	...	...	...	...	...	3,096.2	3,177.9	3,266.2
Claims on direct investors	8 557 . .	...	...	...	...	...	...	...	...
Liabilities to direct investors	8 558 . .	...	...	...	...	...	3,096.2	3,177.9	3,266.2
Other capital	8 580 . .	...	...	...	...	...	...	...	...
Claims on direct investors	8 585 . .	...	...	...	...	...	...	...	...
Liabilities to direct investors	8 590 . .	...	...	...	...	...	...	...	...
Portfolio investment	8 652 . .	...	...	...	...	...	...	...	...
Equity securities	8 660 . .	...	...	...	...	...	...	...	...
Banks	8 663 . .	...	...	...	...	...	...	...	...
Other sectors	8 664 . .	...	...	...	...	...	...	...	...
Debt securities	8 669 . .	...	...	...	...	...	...	...	...
Bonds and notes	8 670 . .	...	...	...	...	...	...	...	...
Monetary authorities	8 671 . .	...	...	...	...	...	...	...	...
General government	8 672 . .	...	...	...	...	...	...	...	...
Banks	8 673 . .	...	...	...	...	...	...	...	...
Other sectors	8 674 . .	...	...	...	...	...	...	...	...
Money market instruments	8 680 . .	...	...	...	...	...	...	...	...
Monetary authorities	8 681 . .	...	...	...	...	...	...	...	...
General government	8 682 . .	...	...	...	...	...	...	...	...
Banks	8 683 . .	...	...	...	...	...	...	...	...
Other sectors	8 684 . .	...	...	...	...	...	...	...	...
Financial derivatives	8 905 . .	...	...	...	...	...	...	...	...
Monetary authorities	8 906 . .	...	...	...	...	...	...	...	...
General government	8 907 . .	...	...	...	...	...	...	...	...
Banks	8 908 . .	...	...	...	...	...	...	...	...
Other sectors	8 909 . .	...	...	...	...	...	...	...	...
Other investment	8 753 . .	...	...	...	...	...	**5,370.5**	**5,057.1**	**5,056.1**
Trade credits	8 756 . .	...	...	...	...	...	...	...	...
General government	8 757 . .	...	...	...	...	...	...	...	...
of which: Short-term	8 759 . .	...	...	...	...	...	...	...	...
Other sectors	8 760 . .	...	...	...	...	...	...	...	...
of which: Short-term	8 762 . .	...	...	...	...	...	...	...	...
Loans	8 764 . .	...	...	...	...	...	5,267.7	4,948.3	4,755.2
Monetary authorities	8 765 . .	...	...	...	...	...	...	...	...
of which: Use of Fund credit and loans from the Fund	8 766 . .	...	...	...	...	...	...	...	...
of which: Short-term	8 768 . .	...	...	...	...	...	...	...	...
General government	8 769 . .	...	...	...	...	...	...	...	...
of which: Short-term	8 771 . .	...	...	...	...	...	...	...	...
Banks	8 772 . .	...	...	...	...	...	...	...	...
of which: Short-term	8 774 . .	...	...	...	...	...	...	...	...
Other sectors	8 775 . .	...	...	...	...	...	...	...	...
of which: Short-term	8 777 . .	...	...	...	...	...	...	...	...
Currency and deposits	8 780 . .	...	...	...	...	...	...	1.1	1.0
Monetary authorities	8 781 . .	...	...	...	...	...	...	...	...
General government	8 782 . .	...	...	...	...	...	...	...	...
Banks	8 783 . .	...	...	...	...	...	...	1.1	1.0
Other sectors	8 784 . .	...	...	...	...	...	...	...	...
Other liabilities	8 786 . .	...	...	...	...	...	102.8	107.7	300.0
Monetary authorities	8 787 . .	...	...	...	...	...	98.8	101.0	293.6
of which: Short-term	8 789 . .	...	...	...	...	...	...	...	...
General government	8 790 . .	...	...	...	...	...	...	...	...
of which: Short-term	8 792 . .	...	...	...	...	...	...	...	...
Banks	8 793 . .	...	...	...	...	...	4.0	6.7	6.4
of which: Short-term	8 795 . .	...	...	...	...	...	...	...	...
Other sectors	8 796 . .	...	...	...	...	...	...	...	...
of which: Short-term	8 798 . .	...	...	...	...	...	...	...	...
NET INTERNATIONAL INVESTMENT POSITION	8 995 . .	...	...	...	...	...	...	...	...
Conversion rates: kyats per U.S. dollar (end of period)	0 102 . .	**5.9030**	**5.7810**	**5.9877**	**6.3627**	**6.1087**	**6.2683**	**6.5985**	**6.8503**

Table 1. ANALYTIC PRESENTATION, 1994–2001
(Millions of U.S. dollars)

	Code	1994	1995	1996	1997	1998	1999	2000	2001
A. Current Account [1]	4 993 Z.	**85.3**	**175.9**	**115.8**	**90.4**	**161.8**	...	...	...
Goods: exports f.o.b	2 100 ..	1,320.4	1,418.4	1,403.7	1,343.3	1,278.3	...	...	...
Goods: imports f.o.b	3 100 ..	–1,406.3	–1,548.2	–1,530.9	–1,615.0	–1,450.9	...	...	...
Balance on Goods	4 100 ..	*–85.8*	*–129.7*	*–127.1*	*–271.7*	*–172.6*	...	...	...
Services: credit	2 200 ..	259.0	315.3	337.4	380.1	327.0	...	...	...
Services: debit	3 200 ..	–468.3	–551.5	–580.9	–533.7	–456.9	...	...	...
Balance on Goods and Services	4 991 ..	*–295.1*	*–365.9*	*–370.7*	*–425.2*	*–302.4*	...	...	...
Income: credit	2 300 ..	213.8	374.0	319.2	252.0	226.7	...	...	...
Income: debit	3 300 ..	–159.8	–235.1	–249.0	–180.6	–165.9	...	...	...
Balance on Goods, Services, and Income	4 992 ..	*–241.1*	*–227.1*	*–300.5*	*–353.8*	*–241.6*	...	...	...
Current transfers: credit	2 379 Z.	349.2	426.9	437.3	462.2	418.2	...	...	...
Current transfers: debit	3 379 ..	–22.7	–23.9	–21.0	–18.0	–14.7	...	...	...
B. Capital Account [1]	4 994 Z.	**43.2**	**40.1**	**42.1**	**33.5**	**23.8**	...	...	...
Capital account: credit	2 994 Z.	43.8	40.7	42.5	33.9	24.2	...	...	...
Capital account: debit	3 994 ..	–.6	–.6	–.5	–.4	–.4	...	...	...
Total, Groups A Plus B	4 981 ..	*128.6*	*216.0*	*157.8*	*123.9*	*185.7*	...	...	...
C. Financial Account [1]	4 995 W.	**–102.1**	**–205.3**	**–174.0**	**–71.4**	**–145.6**	...	...	...
Direct investment abroad	4 505 ..	6.1	3.5	21.7	–.7	2.2	...	...	...
Direct investment in Namibia	4 555 Z.	98.0	153.0	128.7	91.0	96.2	...	...	...
Portfolio investment assets	4 602 ..	–17.0	–5.1	–8.1	–14.6	–11.1	...	...	...
Equity securities	4 610 ..	–5.0	–3.8	–7.9	–14.6	–7.4	...	...	...
Debt securities	4 619 ..	–12.0	–1.3	–.3	...	–3.6	...	...	...
Portfolio investment liabilities	4 652 Z.	64.2	82.2	31.2	26.0	–4.4	...	...	...
Equity securities	4 660 ..	37.5	45.7	51.2	28.8	18.1	...	...	...
Debt securities	4 669 Z.	26.7	36.5	–20.0	–2.8	–22.4	...	...	...
Financial derivatives	4 910 ..	...	...	...	...	...	...	...	...
Financial derivatives assets	4 900 ..	...	...	...	...	...	...	...	...
Financial derivatives liabilities	4 905 ..	...	...	...	...	...	...	...	...
Other investment assets	4 703 ..	–301.0	–428.0	–411.2	–289.9	–175.5	...	...	...
Monetary authorities	4 701 ..	...	...	...	...	...	...	...	...
General government	4 704 ..	9.5	–1.4	–1.2	–1.1	–.9	...	...	...
Banks	4 705 ..	.1	14.8	–48.6	–40.6	–2.1	...	...	...
Other sectors	4 728 ..	–310.7	–441.5	–361.4	–248.2	–172.6	...	...	...
Other investment liabilities	4 753 W.	47.6	–10.9	63.8	116.7	–53.1	...	...	...
Monetary authorities	4 753 WA	...	...	...	...	...	...	...	...
General government	4 753 ZB	4.9	21.8	27.7	17.4	16.9	...	...	...
Banks	4 753 ZC	66.8	4.9	–49.0	116.5	–28.5	...	...	...
Other sectors	4 753 ZD	–24.1	–37.7	85.0	–17.1	–41.4	...	...	...
Total, Groups A Through C	4 983 ..	*26.5*	*10.7*	*–16.1*	*52.5*	*40.1*	...	...	...
D. Net Errors and Omissions	4 998 ..	**48.5**	**13.4**	**39.1**	**15.3**	**15.7**	...	...	...
Total, Groups A Through D	4 984 ..	*75.0*	*24.2*	*22.9*	*67.8*	*55.8*	...	...	...
E. Reserves and Related Items	4 802 A.	**–75.0**	**–24.2**	**–22.9**	**–67.8**	**–55.8**	...	...	...
Reserve assets	4 802 ..	–75.0	–24.2	–22.9	–67.8	–55.8	...	...	...
Use of Fund credit and loans	4 766 ..	...	...	...	...	...	...	...	...
Exceptional financing	4 920 ..	...	...	...	...	...	...	...	...
Conversion rates: Namibia dollars per U.S. dollar	0 101 ..	**3.5508**	**3.6271**	**4.2993**	**4.6080**	**5.5283**	**6.1095**	**6.9398**	**8.6092**

[1] Excludes components that have been classified in the categories of Group E.

Table 2. STANDARD PRESENTATION, 1994–2001

(Millions of U.S. dollars)

	Code	1994	1995	1996	1997	1998	1999	2000	2001
CURRENT ACCOUNT	4 993 . .	**85.3**	**175.9**	**115.8**	**90.4**	**161.8**	**. . .**	**. . .**	**. . .**
A. GOODS	4 100 . .	−85.8	−129.7	−127.1	−271.7	−172.6	. . .	. . .	. . .
Credit	2 100 . .	**1,320.4**	**1,418.4**	**1,403.7**	**1,343.3**	**1,278.3**	**. . .**	**. . .**	**. . .**
General merchandise: exports f.o.b.	2 110 . .	1,320.4	1,418.4	1,403.7	1,343.3	1,278.3	. . .	. . .	. . .
Goods for processing: exports f.o.b.	2 150 . .	. . .	. . .	. . .	. . .	. . .	. . .	. . .	. . .
Repairs on goods	2 160 . .	. . .	. . .	. . .	. . .	. . .	. . .	. . .	. . .
Goods procured in ports by carriers	2 170 . .	. . .	. . .	. . .	. . .	. . .	. . .	. . .	. . .
Nonmonetary gold	2 180 . .	. . .	. . .	. . .	. . .	. . .	. . .	. . .	. . .
Debit	3 100 . .	**−1,406.3**	**−1,548.2**	**−1,530.9**	**−1,615.0**	**−1,450.9**	**. . .**	**. . .**	**. . .**
General merchandise: imports f.o.b.	3 110 . .	−1,406.3	−1,548.2	−1,530.9	−1,615.0	−1,450.9	. . .	. . .	. . .
Goods for processing: imports f.o.b.	3 150 . .	. . .	. . .	. . .	. . .	. . .	. . .	. . .	. . .
Repairs on goods	3 160 . .	. . .	. . .	. . .	. . .	. . .	. . .	. . .	. . .
Goods procured in ports by carriers	3 170 . .	. . .	. . .	. . .	. . .	. . .	. . .	. . .	. . .
Nonmonetary gold	3 180 . .	. . .	. . .	. . .	. . .	. . .	. . .	. . .	. . .
B. SERVICES	4 200 . .	−209.3	−236.2	−243.6	−153.6	−129.8	. . .	. . .	. . .
Total credit	2 200 . .	*259.0*	*315.3*	*337.4*	*380.1*	*327.0*	. . .	. . .	. . .
Total debit	3 200 . .	*−468.3*	*−551.5*	*−580.9*	*−533.7*	*−456.9*	. . .	. . .	. . .
Transportation services, credit	2 205 . .	**. . .**	**. . .**	**. . .**	**. . .**	**. . .**	**. . .**	**. . .**	**. . .**
Passenger	2 850 . .	. . .	. . .	. . .	. . .	. . .	. . .	. . .	. . .
Freight	2 851 . .	. . .	. . .	. . .	. . .	. . .	. . .	. . .	. . .
Other	2 852 . .	. . .	. . .	. . .	. . .	. . .	. . .	. . .	. . .
Sea transport, passenger	2 207 . .	. . .	. . .	. . .	. . .	. . .	. . .	. . .	. . .
Sea transport, freight	2 208 . .	. . .	. . .	. . .	. . .	. . .	. . .	. . .	. . .
Sea transport, other	2 209 . .	. . .	. . .	. . .	. . .	. . .	. . .	. . .	. . .
Air transport, passenger	2 211 . .	. . .	. . .	. . .	. . .	. . .	. . .	. . .	. . .
Air transport, freight	2 212 . .	. . .	. . .	. . .	. . .	. . .	. . .	. . .	. . .
Air transport, other	2 213 . .	. . .	. . .	. . .	. . .	. . .	. . .	. . .	. . .
Other transport, passenger	2 215 . .	. . .	. . .	. . .	. . .	. . .	. . .	. . .	. . .
Other transport, freight	2 216 . .	. . .	. . .	. . .	. . .	. . .	. . .	. . .	. . .
Other transport, other	2 217 . .	. . .	. . .	. . .	. . .	. . .	. . .	. . .	. . .
Transportation services, debit	3 205 . .	**−192.8**	**−196.5**	**−197.5**	**−178.1**	**−149.9**	**. . .**	**. . .**	**. . .**
Passenger	3 850 . .	. . .	. . .	. . .	. . .	. . .	. . .	. . .	. . .
Freight	3 851 . .	*−110.7*	*−127.6*	*−126.2*	*−127.2*	*−117.4*	. . .	. . .	. . .
Other	3 852 . .	*−82.2*	*−69.0*	*−71.4*	*−50.9*	*−32.6*	. . .	. . .	. . .
Sea transport, passenger	3 207 . .	. . .	. . .	. . .	. . .	. . .	. . .	. . .	. . .
Sea transport, freight	3 208 . .	. . .	. . .	. . .	. . .	. . .	. . .	. . .	. . .
Sea transport, other	3 209 . .	. . .	. . .	. . .	. . .	. . .	. . .	. . .	. . .
Air transport, passenger	3 211 . .	. . .	. . .	. . .	. . .	. . .	. . .	. . .	. . .
Air transport, freight	3 212 . .	. . .	. . .	. . .	. . .	. . .	. . .	. . .	. . .
Air transport, other	3 213 . .	. . .	. . .	. . .	. . .	. . .	. . .	. . .	. . .
Other transport, passenger	3 215 . .	. . .	. . .	. . .	. . .	. . .	. . .	. . .	. . .
Other transport, freight	3 216 . .	. . .	. . .	. . .	. . .	. . .	. . .	. . .	. . .
Other transport, other	3 217 . .	. . .	. . .	. . .	. . .	. . .	. . .	. . .	. . .
Travel, credit	2 236 . .	**225.9**	**277.9**	**293.2**	**333.3**	**288.2**	**. . .**	**. . .**	**. . .**
Business travel	2 237 . .	. . .	. . .	. . .	. . .	. . .	. . .	. . .	. . .
Personal travel	2 240 . .	. . .	. . .	. . .	. . .	. . .	. . .	. . .	. . .
Travel, debit	3 236 . .	**−77.1**	**−89.6**	**−89.0**	**−99.2**	**−88.3**	**. . .**	**. . .**	**. . .**
Business travel	3 237 . .	. . .	. . .	. . .	. . .	. . .	. . .	. . .	. . .
Personal travel	3 240 . .	. . .	. . .	. . .	. . .	. . .	. . .	. . .	. . .
Other services, credit	2 200 BA	**33.1**	**37.4**	**44.1**	**46.8**	**38.9**	**. . .**	**. . .**	**. . .**
Communications	2 245 . .	8.6	9.0	7.9	7.6	6.0	. . .	. . .	. . .
Construction	2 249 . .	1.1	.4	.1	2.4	1.4	. . .	. . .	. . .
Insurance	2 253 . .	3.9	1.8	.7	1.1	.7	. . .	. . .	. . .
Financial	2 260 . .	.3	2.7	8.4	2.7	3.8	. . .	. . .	. . .
Computer and information	2 262 . .	.2	.1	.2	.2	.2	. . .	. . .	. . .
Royalties and licence fees	2 266 . .	.3	. . .	7.0	6.6	6.0	. . .	. . .	. . .
Other business services	2 268 . .	4.3	9.0	7.1	12.8	8.9	. . .	. . .	. . .
Personal, cultural, and recreational	2 287 . .	. . .	. . .	. . .	. . .	. . .	. . .	. . .	. . .
Government, n.i.e.	2 291 . .	14.3	14.3	12.7	13.3	11.9	. . .	. . .	. . .
Other services, debit	3 200 BA	**−198.4**	**−265.3**	**−294.4**	**−256.3**	**−218.7**	**. . .**	**. . .**	**. . .**
Communications	3 245 . .	−.1	−.2	−.2	−.2	−.1	. . .	. . .	. . .
Construction	3 249 . .	−5.9	−9.2	−11.6	−14.6	−11.6	. . .	. . .	. . .
Insurance	3 253 . .	−34.8	−49.4	−56.5	−72.8	−53.5	. . .	. . .	. . .
Financial	3 260 . .	−.6	−1.5	−1.4	−1.8	−1.8	. . .	. . .	. . .
Computer and information	3 262 . .	−11.8	−16.4	−13.6	−10.0	−8.7	. . .	. . .	. . .
Royalties and licence fees	3 266 . .	−4.7	−2.8	−3.1	−3.4	−2.5	. . .	. . .	. . .
Other business services	3 268 . .	−127.5	−172.1	−195.7	−141.5	−132.4	. . .	. . .	. . .
Personal, cultural, and recreational	3 287 . .	. . .	. . .	. . .	. . .	. . .	. . .	. . .	. . .
Government, n.i.e.	3 291 . .	−13.0	−13.6	−12.4	−12.0	−8.0	. . .	. . .	. . .

Table 2 (Continued). STANDARD PRESENTATION, 1994–2001
(Millions of U.S. dollars)

	Code	1994	1995	1996	1997	1998	1999	2000	2001
C. INCOME	4 300 . .	54.0	138.9	70.2	71.4	60.8	. . .	. . .	. . .
Total credit	2 300 . .	*213.8*	*374.0*	*319.2*	*252.0*	*226.7*	. . .	. . .	. . .
Total debit	3 300 . .	*–159.8*	*–235.1*	*–249.0*	*–180.6*	*–165.9*	. . .	. . .	. . .
Compensation of employees, credit	2 310 . .	**6.3**	**6.6**	**5.9**	**6.0**	**5.1**	. . .	. . .	. . .
Compensation of employees, debit	3 310 . .	**–6.1**	**–6.5**	**–6.8**	**–12.9**	**–7.4**	. . .	. . .	. . .
Investment income, credit	2 320 . .	**207.5**	**367.4**	**313.3**	**246.0**	**221.7**	. . .	. . .	. . .
Direct investment income	2 330 . .	–3.5	3.9	–1.3	.7	.2	. . .	. . .	. . .
Dividends and distributed branch profits	2 332 . .	1.2	5.4	.8	1.0	.5	. . .	. . .	. . .
Reinvested earnings and undistributed branch profits	2 333 . .	–4.8	–1.5	–3.0	–.2	–.4	. . .	. . .	. . .
Income on debt (interest)	2 334 . .	.2	. . .	.9	. . .	. . .	. . .	. . .	. . .
Portfolio investment income	2 339 . .	9.3	12.7	11.3	9.8	7.1	. . .	. . .	. . .
Income on equity	2 340 . .	2.8	3.2	3.7	5.3	2.9	. . .	. . .	. . .
Income on bonds and notes	2 350 . .	6.5	9.5	7.5	4.5	4.2	. . .	. . .	. . .
Income on money market instruments	2 360 . .	. . .	. . .	. . .	. . .	. . .	. . .	. . .	. . .
Other investment income	2 370 . .	201.7	350.8	303.3	235.5	214.4	. . .	. . .	. . .
Investment income, debit	3 320 . .	**–153.7**	**–228.7**	**–242.2**	**–167.7**	**–158.5**	. . .	. . .	. . .
Direct investment income	3 330 . .	–113.9	–186.5	–201.9	–136.5	–134.2	. . .	. . .	. . .
Dividends and distributed branch profits	3 332 . .	–62.5	–86.0	–119.0	–123.0	–98.9	. . .	. . .	. . .
Reinvested earnings and undistributed branch profits	3 333 . .	–51.1	–98.9	–79.2	–13.7	–35.3	. . .	. . .	. . .
Income on debt (interest)	3 334 . .	–.2	–1.6	–3.7	.2	. . .	. . .	. . .	. . .
Portfolio investment income	3 339 . .	–25.7	–20.4	–23.0	–16.4	–13.1	. . .	. . .	. . .
Income on equity	3 340 . .	. . .	. . .	. . .	. . .	. . .	. . .	. . .	. . .
Income on bonds and notes	3 350 . .	–25.5	–19.5	–22.5	–16.3	–13.0	. . .	. . .	. . .
Income on money market instruments	3 360 . .	–.3	–.8	–.4	–.2	–.1	. . .	. . .	. . .
Other investment income	3 370 . .	–14.1	–21.8	–17.3	–14.8	–11.2	. . .	. . .	. . .
D. CURRENT TRANSFERS	4 379 . .	326.5	403.0	416.3	444.2	403.5	. . .	. . .	. . .
Credit	2 379 . .	**349.2**	**426.9**	**437.3**	**462.2**	**418.2**	. . .	. . .	. . .
General government	2 380 . .	321.4	390.5	399.9	430.7	398.9	. . .	. . .	. . .
Other sectors	2 390 . .	27.8	36.4	37.4	31.4	19.3	. . .	. . .	. . .
Workers' remittances	2 391 . .	8.6	9.0	7.6	7.3	6.2	. . .	. . .	. . .
Other current transfers	2 392 . .	19.2	27.4	29.8	24.1	13.2	. . .	. . .	. . .
Debit	3 379 . .	**–22.7**	**–23.9**	**–21.0**	**–18.0**	**–14.7**	. . .	. . .	. . .
General government	3 380 . .	–14.6	–16.2	–14.5	–11.9	–9.7	. . .	. . .	. . .
Other sectors	3 390 . .	–8.2	–7.7	–6.5	–6.1	–5.1	. . .	. . .	. . .
Workers' remittances	3 391 . .	–5.1	–4.7	–4.0	–3.7	–3.1	. . .	. . .	. . .
Other current transfers	3 392 . .	–3.1	–3.0	–2.6	–2.4	–2.0	. . .	. . .	. . .
CAPITAL AND FINANCIAL ACCOUNT	4 996 . .	**–133.8**	**–189.4**	**–154.8**	**–105.7**	**–177.6**	. . .	. . .	. . .
CAPITAL ACCOUNT	4 994 . .	**43.2**	**40.1**	**42.1**	**33.5**	**23.8**	. . .	. . .	. . .
Total credit	2 994 . .	*43.8*	*40.7*	*42.5*	*33.9*	*24.2*	. . .	. . .	. . .
Total debit	3 994 . .	*–.6*	*–.6*	*–.5*	*–.4*	*–.4*	. . .	. . .	. . .
Capital transfers, credit	2 400 . .	**43.8**	**40.7**	**42.5**	**33.9**	**24.2**	. . .	. . .	. . .
General government	2 401 . .	41.3	39.8	41.4	32.2	23.1	. . .	. . .	. . .
Debt forgiveness	2 402 . .	. . .	. . .	. . .	. . .	. . .	. . .	. . .	. . .
Other capital transfers	2 410 . .	41.3	39.8	41.4	32.2	23.1	. . .	. . .	. . .
Other sectors	2 430 . .	2.5	.8	1.2	1.7	1.1	. . .	. . .	. . .
Migrants' transfers	2 431 . .	. . .	. . .	. . .	. . .	. . .	. . .	. . .	. . .
Debt forgiveness	2 432 . .	. . .	. . .	. . .	. . .	. . .	. . .	. . .	. . .
Other capital transfers	2 440 . .	2.5	.8	1.2	1.7	1.1	. . .	. . .	. . .
Capital transfers, debit	3 400 . .	**–.6**	**–.6**	**–.5**	**–.4**	**–.4**	. . .	. . .	. . .
General government	3 401 . .	. . .	. . .	. . .	. . .	. . .	. . .	. . .	. . .
Debt forgiveness	3 402 . .	. . .	. . .	. . .	. . .	. . .	. . .	. . .	. . .
Other capital transfers	3 410 . .	. . .	. . .	. . .	. . .	. . .	. . .	. . .	. . .
Other sectors	3 430 . .	–.6	–.6	–.5	–.4	–.4	. . .	. . .	. . .
Migrants' transfers	3 431 . .	. . .	. . .	. . .	. . .	. . .	. . .	. . .	. . .
Debt forgiveness	3 432 . .	. . .	. . .	. . .	. . .	. . .	. . .	. . .	. . .
Other capital transfers	3 440 . .	–.6	–.6	–.5	–.4	–.4	. . .	. . .	. . .
Nonproduced nonfinancial assets, credit	2 480 . .	. . .	. . .	. . .	. . .	. . .	. . .	. . .	. . .
Nonproduced nonfinancial assets, debit	3 480 . .	. . .	. . .	. . .	. . .	. . .	. . .	. . .	. . .

Table 2 (Continued). STANDARD PRESENTATION, 1994–2001
(Millions of U.S. dollars)

	Code	1994	1995	1996	1997	1998	1999	2000	2001
FINANCIAL ACCOUNT	4 995	**–177.1**	**–229.5**	**–196.9**	**–139.1**	**–201.4**	...	...	...
A. DIRECT INVESTMENT	4 500	104.1	156.5	150.4	90.3	98.4	...	...	...
Direct investment abroad	4 505	**6.1**	**3.5**	**21.7**	**–.7**	**2.2**	...	...	...
Equity capital	4 510	.7	.3	...	...	...	...	...	...
Claims on affiliated enterprises	4 515	...	...	...	...	...	...	...	...
Liabilities to affiliated enterprises	4 520	...	...	...	...	...	...	...	...
Reinvested earnings	4 525	4.8	1.5	3.0	.2	.4	...	...	...
Other capital	4 530	.6	1.7	18.7	–.9	1.8	...	...	...
Claims on affiliated enterprises	4 535	.6	1.7	18.7	–.9	1.8	...	...	...
Liabilities to affiliated enterprises	4 540	...	...	...	...	...	...	...	...
Direct investment in Namibia	4 555	**98.0**	**153.0**	**128.7**	**91.0**	**96.2**	...	...	...
Equity capital	4 560	27.1	31.1	73.9	77.6	72.7	...	...	...
Claims on direct investors	4 565	...	...	...	...	...	...	...	...
Liabilities to direct investors	4 570	...	...	...	...	...	...	...	...
Reinvested earnings	4 575	51.1	98.9	79.2	13.7	35.3	...	...	...
Other capital	4 580	19.7	23.0	–24.4	–.3	–11.8	...	...	...
Claims on direct investors	4 585	...	...	...	...	...	...	...	...
Liabilities to direct investors	4 590	...	...	...	...	...	...	...	...
B. PORTFOLIO INVESTMENT	4 600	47.3	77.1	23.1	11.5	–15.4	...	...	...
Assets	4 602	**–17.0**	**–5.1**	**–8.1**	**–14.6**	**–11.1**	...	...	...
Equity securities	4 610	–5.0	–3.8	–7.9	–14.6	–7.4	...	...	...
Monetary authorities	4 611	...	...	...	...	...	...	...	...
General government	4 612	–2.9	...	–.5	–4.4	–3.6	...	...	...
Banks	4 613	...	...	...	...	...	...	...	...
Other sectors	4 614	–2.0	–3.8	–7.4	–10.2	–3.8	...	...	...
Debt securities	4 619	–12.0	–1.3	–.3	...	–3.6	...	...	...
Bonds and notes	4 620	–12.0	–1.3	–.3	...	–3.6	...	...	...
Monetary authorities	4 621	...	...	...	...	...	...	...	...
General government	4 622	.2	.2	.2	...	...	...	...	...
Banks	4 623	2.9	...	...	...	...	...	...	...
Other sectors	4 624	–15.1	–1.5	–.4	...	–3.6	...	...	...
Money market instruments	4 630	...	...	...	...	...	...	...	...
Monetary authorities	4 631	...	...	...	...	...	...	...	...
General government	4 632	...	...	...	...	...	...	...	...
Banks	4 633	...	...	...	...	...	...	...	...
Other sectors	4 634	...	...	...	...	...	...	...	...
Liabilities	4 652	**64.2**	**82.2**	**31.2**	**26.0**	**–4.4**	...	...	...
Equity securities	4 660	37.5	45.7	51.2	28.8	18.1	...	...	...
Banks	4 663	...	...	...	...	...	...	...	...
Other sectors	4 664	37.5	45.7	51.2	28.8	18.1	...	...	...
Debt securities	4 669	26.7	36.5	–20.0	–2.8	–22.4	...	...	...
Bonds and notes	4 670	29.6	52.7	–9.5	–2.8	–22.4	...	...	...
Monetary authorities	4 671	...	...	...	...	...	...	...	...
General government	4 672	29.6	52.7	–9.5	–2.8	–22.4	...	...	...
Banks	4 673	...	...	...	...	...	...	...	...
Other sectors	4 674	...	...	...	...	...	...	...	...
Money market instruments	4 680	–2.9	–16.2	–10.5	...	...	...	...	...
Monetary authorities	4 681	...	...	...	...	...	...	...	...
General government	4 682	–2.9	–16.2	–10.5	...	...	...	...	...
Banks	4 683	...	...	...	...	...	...	...	...
Other sectors	4 684	...	...	...	...	...	...	...	...
C. FINANCIAL DERIVATIVES	4 910	...	...	...	...	...	...	...	...
Monetary authorities	4 911	...	...	...	...	...	...	...	...
General government	4 912	...	...	...	...	...	...	...	...
Banks	4 913	...	...	...	...	...	...	...	...
Other sectors	4 914	...	...	...	...	...	...	...	...
Assets	4 900	...	...	...	...	...	...	...	...
Monetary authorities	4 901	...	...	...	...	...	...	...	...
General government	4 902	...	...	...	...	...	...	...	...
Banks	4 903	...	...	...	...	...	...	...	...
Other sectors	4 904	...	...	...	...	...	...	...	...
Liabilities	4 905	...	...	...	...	...	...	...	...
Monetary authorities	4 906	...	...	...	...	...	...	...	...
General government	4 907	...	...	...	...	...	...	...	...
Banks	4 908	...	...	...	...	...	...	...	...
Other sectors	4 909	...	...	...	...	...	...	...	...

Table 2 (Concluded). STANDARD PRESENTATION, 1994–2001
(Millions of U.S. dollars)

	Code	1994	1995	1996	1997	1998	1999	2000	2001
D. OTHER INVESTMENT	4 700 . .	−253.4	−438.9	−347.4	−173.2	−228.6	...	...	...
Assets	4 703 . .	**−301.0**	**−428.0**	**−411.2**	**−289.9**	**−175.5**	**...**	**...**	**...**
Trade credits	4 706 . .	...	...	...	...	...	...	...	...
General government	4 707 . .	...	...	...	...	...	...	...	...
of which: Short-term	4 709 . .	...	...	...	...	...	...	...	...
Other sectors	4 710 . .	...	...	...	...	...	...	...	...
of which: Short-term	4 712 . .	...	...	...	...	...	...	...	...
Loans	4 714 . .	...	...	...	...	...	...	...	...
Monetary authorities	4 715 . .	...	...	...	...	...	...	...	...
of which: Short-term	4 718 . .	...	...	...	...	...	...	...	...
General government	4 719 . .	...	...	...	...	...	...	...	...
of which: Short-term	4 721 . .	...	...	...	...	...	...	...	...
Banks	4 722 . .	...	...	...	...	...	...	...	...
of which: Short-term	4 724 . .	...	...	...	...	...	...	...	...
Other sectors	4 725 . .	...	...	...	...	...	...	...	...
of which: Short-term	4 727 . .	...	...	...	...	...	...	...	...
Currency and deposits	4 730 . .	−13.3	18.0	−54.2	−44.1	−4.6	...	...	...
Monetary authorities	4 731 . .	...	...	...	...	...	...	...	...
General government	4 732 . .	...	...	...	...	...	...	...	...
Banks	4 733 . .	.1	14.8	−48.6	−40.6	−2.1	...	...	...
Other sectors	4 734 . .	−13.5	3.2	−5.6	−3.5	−2.5	...	...	...
Other assets	4 736 . .	−287.7	−446.0	−357.0	−245.8	−170.9	...	...	...
Monetary authorities	4 737 . .	...	...	...	...	...	...	...	...
of which: Short-term	4 739 . .	...	...	...	...	...	...	...	...
General government	4 740 . .	9.5	−1.4	−1.2	−1.1	−.9	...	...	...
of which: Short-term	4 742 . .	*11.0*	...	...	...	...	...	...	...
Banks	4 743 . .	...	...	...	...	...	...	...	...
of which: Short-term	4 745 . .	...	...	...	...	...	...	...	...
Other sectors	4 746 . .	−297.2	−444.6	−355.8	−244.7	−170.0	...	...	...
of which: Short-term	4 748 . .	...	...	...	...	...	...	...	...
Liabilities	4 753 . .	**47.6**	**−10.9**	**63.8**	**116.7**	**−53.1**	**...**	**...**	**...**
Trade credits	4 756 . .	...	...	...	...	...	...	...	...
General government	4 757 . .	...	...	...	...	...	...	...	...
of which: Short-term	4 759 . .	...	...	...	...	...	...	...	...
Other sectors	4 760 . .	...	...	...	...	...	...	...	...
of which: Short-term	4 762 . .	...	...	...	...	...	...	...	...
Loans	4 764 . .	4.9	21.8	27.7	17.4	16.9	...	...	...
Monetary authorities	4 765 . .	...	...	...	...	...	...	...	...
of which: Use of Fund credit and loans from the Fund	4 766 . .	...	...	...	...	...	...	...	...
of which: Short-term	4 768 . .	...	...	...	...	...	...	...	...
General government	4 769 . .	4.9	21.8	27.7	17.4	16.9	...	...	...
of which: Short-term	4 771 . .	...	...	...	...	...	...	...	...
Banks	4 772 . .	...	...	...	...	...	...	...	...
of which: Short-term	4 774 . .	...	...	...	...	...	...	...	...
Other sectors	4 775 . .	...	...	...	...	...	...	...	...
of which: Short-term	4 777 . .	...	...	...	...	...	...	...	...
Currency and deposits	4 780 . .	...	...	...	...	...	...	...	...
Monetary authorities	4 781 . .	...	...	...	...	...	...	...	...
General government	4 782 . .	...	...	...	...	...	...	...	...
Banks	4 783 . .	...	...	...	...	...	...	...	...
Other sectors	4 784 . .	...	...	...	...	...	...	...	...
Other liabilities	4 786 . .	42.7	−32.7	36.0	99.4	−70.0	...	...	...
Monetary authorities	4 787 . .	...	...	...	...	...	...	...	...
of which: Short-term	4 789 . .	...	...	...	...	...	...	...	...
General government	4 790 . .	...	...	...	...	...	...	...	...
of which: Short-term	4 792 . .	...	...	...	...	...	...	...	...
Banks	4 793 . .	66.8	4.9	−49.0	116.5	−28.5	...	...	...
of which: Short-term	4 795 . .	...	...	...	...	...	...	...	...
Other sectors	4 796 . .	−24.1	−37.7	85.0	−17.1	−41.4	...	...	...
of which: Short-term	4 798 . .	*29.9*	*−10.5*	*80.3*	*−37.4*	*−9.0*	...	...	...
E. RESERVE ASSETS	4 802 . .	−75.0	−24.2	−22.9	−67.8	−55.8	...	...	...
Monetary gold	4 812 . .	...	...	...	...	...	...	...	...
Special drawing rights	4 811 . .	...	...	...	...	...	...	...	...
Reserve position in the Fund	4 810 . .	...	...	...	...	...	...	...	...
Foreign exchange	4 803 . .	−75.0	−24.2	−22.9	−67.8	−55.8	...	...	...
Other claims	4 813 . .	...	...	...	...	...	...	...	...
NET ERRORS AND OMISSIONS	4 998 . .	**48.5**	**13.4**	**39.1**	**15.3**	**15.7**	**...**	**...**	**...**

Part 3 of the *Yearbook* contains descriptions of the methodologies, compilation practices, and sources used to compile these data.

Table 3. INTERNATIONAL INVESTMENT POSITION (End–period stocks), 1994–2001

(Millions of U.S. dollars)

	Code		1994	1995	1996	1997	1998	1999	2000	2001
ASSETS	8 995	C.	...	...	...	...	...	...	1,213.5	...
Direct investment abroad	8 505	. .	**15.8**	**14.8**	**13.0**	**...**	**...**	**...**	**44.9**	**...**
Equity capital and reinvested earnings	8 506	. .	11.0	10.1	9.0	...	...	...	7.6	...
Claims on affiliated enterprises	8 507	. .	...	...	...	...	...	...	...	...
Liabilities to affiliated enterprises	8 508	. .	...	...	...	...	...	...	...	...
Other capital	8 530	. .	4.8	4.7	4.1	...	...	...	37.4	...
Claims on affiliated enterprises	8 535	. .	...	...	...	...	...	...	...	...
Liabilities to affiliated enterprises	8 540	. .	...	...	...	...	...	...	...	...
Portfolio investment	8 602	. .	**165.1**	**164.8**	**128.8**	**...**	**...**	**...**	**610.5**	**...**
Equity securities	8 610	. .	85.2	90.2	72.8	...	...	...	603.7	...
Monetary authorities	8 611	. .	...	...	...	...	...	...	...	...
General government	8 612	. .	27.1	28.8	24.8	...	...	...	...	...
Banks	8 613	. .	...	...	...	...	...	...	...	...
Other sectors	8 614	. .	58.1	61.4	48.1	...	...	...	...	...
Debt securities	8 619	. .	79.9	74.6	56.0	...	...	...	6.8	...
Bonds and notes	8 620	. .	79.9	74.6	56.0	...	...	...	5.5	...
Monetary authorities	8 621	. .	...	...	...	...	...	...	...	...
General government	8 622	. .	5.1	4.7	3.6	...	...	...	...	...
Banks	8 623	. .	...	...	...	...	...	...	...	...
Other sectors	8 624	. .	74.8	69.9	52.3	...	...	...	...	...
Money market instruments	8 630	. .	...	...	...	...	...	...	1.3	...
Monetary authorities	8 631	. .	...	...	...	...	...	...	...	...
General government	8 632	. .	...	...	...	...	...	...	...	...
Banks	8 633	. .	...	...	...	...	...	...	...	...
Other sectors	8 634	. .	...	...	...	...	...	...	...	...
Financial derivatives	8 900	. .	**...**	**...**	**...**	**...**	**...**	**...**	**...**	**...**
Monetary authorities	8 901	. .	...	...	...	...	...	...	...	...
General government	8 902	. .	...	...	...	...	...	...	...	...
Banks	8 903	. .	...	...	...	...	...	...	...	...
Other sectors	8 904	. .	...	...	...	...	...	...	...	...
Other investment	8 703	. .	**2,404.1**	**2,291.4**	**1,760.6**	**...**	**...**	**...**	**295.1**	**...**
Trade credits	8 706	. .	...	...	...	...	...	...	5.0	...
General government	8 707	. .	...	...	...	...	...	...	...	...
of which: Short-term	8 709	. .	...	...	...	...	...	...	...	...
Other sectors	8 710	. .	...	...	...	...	...	...	5.0	...
of which: Short-term	8 712	. .	...	...	...	...	...	...	*5.0*	...
Loans	8 714	. .	...	...	...	...	...	...	132.7	...
Monetary authorities	8 715	. .	...	...	...	...	...	...	...	...
of which: Short-term	8 718	. .	...	...	...	...	...	...	...	...
General government	8 719	. .	...	...	...	...	...	...	...	...
of which: Short-term	8 721	. .	...	...	...	...	...	...	...	...
Banks	8 722	. .	...	...	...	...	...	...	51.3	...
of which: Short-term	8 724	. .	...	...	...	...	...	...	...	...
Other sectors	8 725	. .	...	...	...	...	...	...	81.4	...
of which: Short-term	8 727	. .	...	...	...	...	...	...	*55.9*	...
Currency and deposits	8 730	. .	46.0	38.1	74.3	...	...	...	.4	...
Monetary authorities	8 731	. .	...	...	...	...	...	...	...	...
General government	8 732	. .	...	...	...	...	...	...	...	...
Banks	8 733	. .	38.1	29.9	67.5	...	...	...	.4	...
Other sectors	8 734	. .	7.9	8.2	6.8	...	...	...	...	...
Other assets	8 736	. .	2,358.1	2,253.3	1,686.3	...	...	...	157.0	...
Monetary authorities	8 737	. .	...	...	...	...	...	...	...	...
of which: Short-term	8 739	. .	...	...	...	...	...	...	...	...
General government	8 740	. .	7.3	8.5	7.7	...	...	...	...	...
of which: Short-term	8 742	. .	...	...	...	...	...	...	...	...
Banks	8 743	. .	...	...	...	...	...	...	...	...
of which: Short-term	8 745	. .	...	...	...	...	...	...	...	...
Other sectors	8 746	. .	2,350.8	2,244.8	1,678.6	...	...	...	157.0	...
of which: Short-term	8 748	. .	*116.3*	*99.2*	*82.4*	...	...	...	...	...
Reserve assets	8 802	. .	**202.9**	**221.6**	**193.5**	**...**	**...**	**...**	**262.9**	**...**
Monetary gold	8 812	. .	...	...	...	...	...	...	...	...
Special drawing rights	8 811	. .	...	...	...	...	...	...	...	...
Reserve position in the Fund	8 810	. .	...	...	...	...	.1	.1	...	...
Foreign exchange	8 803	. .	202.9	221.5	193.5	...	...	...	262.8	...
Other claims	8 813	. .	...	...	...	...	...	...	...	...

Table 3 (Concluded). INTERNATIONAL INVESTMENT POSITION (End-period stocks), 1994–2001

(Millions of U.S. dollars)

	Code	1994	1995	1996	1997	1998	1999	2000	2001
LIABILITIES	8 995 D.	...	...	...	...	...	...	1,807.3	...
Direct investment in Namibia	8 555 . .	**1,601.2**	**1,707.7**	**1,492.2**	...	...	...	**1,276.3**	...
Equity capital and reinvested earnings	8 556 . .	1,377.2	1,506.5	1,333.3	...	...	...	1,105.7	...
Claims on direct investors	8 557 . .	...	...	...	...	...	...	...	...
Liabilities to direct investors	8 558 . .	...	...	...	...	...	...	...	...
Other capital	8 580 . .	224.1	201.2	158.9	...	...	...	170.6	...
Claims on direct investors	8 585 . .	...	...	...	...	...	...	...	...
Liabilities to direct investors	8 590 . .	...	...	...	...	...	...	...	...
Portfolio investment	8 652 . .	**289.8**	**390.4**	**334.9**	...	...	...	**75.0**	...
Equity securities	8 660 . .	69.1	119.0	141.8	...	...	...	1.7	...
Banks	8 663 . .	...	...	...	...	...	...	...	...
Other sectors	8 664 . .	...	...	...	...	...	...	...	...
Debt securities	8 669 . .	220.7	271.4	193.1	...	...	...	73.3	...
Bonds and notes	8 670 . .	219.6	259.1	193.1	...	...	...	...	...
Monetary authorities	8 671 . .	...	...	...	...	...	...	...	...
General government	8 672 . .	219.6	259.1	193.1	...	...	...	...	...
Banks	8 673 . .	...	...	...	...	...	...	...	...
Other sectors	8 674 . .	...	...	...	...	...	...	...	...
Money market instruments	8 680 . .	1.1	12.3	...	...	...	...	...	...
Monetary authorities	8 681 . .	...	...	...	...	...	...	...	...
General government	8 682 . .	1.1	12.3	...	...	...	...	...	...
Banks	8 683 . .	...	...	...	...	...	...	...	...
Other sectors	8 684 . .	...	...	...	...	...	...	...	...
Financial derivatives	8 905 . .	...	...	...	...	...	...	...	...
Monetary authorities	8 906 . .	...	...	...	...	...	...	...	...
General government	8 907 . .	...	...	...	...	...	...	...	...
Banks	8 908 . .	...	...	...	...	...	...	...	...
Other sectors	8 909 . .	...	...	...	...	...	...	...	...
Other investment	8 753 . .	**529.1**	**587.0**	**528.1**	...	...	...	**455.9**	...
Trade credits	8 756 . .	...	...	...	...	...	...	11.3	...
General government	8 757 . .	...	...	...	...	...	...	1.4	...
of which: Short-term	8 759 . .	...	...	...	...	...	...	*1.4*	...
Other sectors	8 760 . .	...	...	...	...	...	...	9.9	...
of which: Short-term	8 762 . .	...	...	...	...	...	...	*9.9*	...
Loans	8 764 . .	29.9	51.5	46.8	...	...	...	372.0	...
Monetary authorities	8 765 . .	...	...	...	...	...	...	...	...
of which: Use of Fund credit and loans from the Fund	8 766 . .	...	...	...	...	...	...	...	...
of which: Short-term	8 768 . .	...	...	...	...	...	...	...	...
General government	8 769 . .	29.9	51.5	46.8	...	...	...	127.9	...
of which: Short-term	8 771 . .	...	...	...	...	...	...	...	...
Banks	8 772	...	...	...	...	...	...	70.1	...
of which: Short-term	8 774 . .	...	...	...	...	...	...	*66.6*	...
Other sectors	8 775 . .	...	...	...	...	...	...	174.0	...
of which: Short-term	8 777 . .	...	...	...	...	...	...	*89.8*	...
Currency and deposits	8 780 . .	...	...	...	...	...	...	...	...
Monetary authorities	8 781 . .	...	...	...	...	...	...	...	...
General government	8 782 . .	...	...	...	...	...	...	...	...
Banks	8 783 . .	...	...	...	...	...	...	...	...
Other sectors	8 784 . .	...	...	...	...	...	...	...	...
Other liabilities	8 786 . .	499.2	535.4	481.4	...	...	...	72.6	...
Monetary authorities	8 787 . .	203.2	214.9	183.0	...	...	...	...	...
of which: Short-term	8 789 . .	...	...	...	...	...	...	...	...
General government	8 790 . .	...	...	...	...	...	...	...	...
of which: Short-term	8 792 . .	...	...	...	...	...	...	...	...
Banks	8 793 . .	143.9	134.1	136.0	...	...	...	...	...
of which: Short-term	8 795 . .	*127.3*	*125.8*	*130.7*	...	...	...	...	...
Other sectors	8 796 . .	152.1	186.4	162.3	...	...	...	72.6	...
of which: Short-term	8 798 . .	*128.1*	*160.9*	*131.8*	...	...	...	*72.6*	...
NET INTERNATIONAL INVESTMENT POSITION	8 995 . .	...	...	...	...	...	...	**–593.8**	...
Conversion rates: Namibia dollars per U.S. dollar (end of period)	0 102 . .	**3.5435**	**3.6475**	**4.6825**	**4.8675**	**5.8600**	**6.1545**	**7.5685**	**12.1265**

Table 1. ANALYTIC PRESENTATION, 1994–2001
(Millions of U.S. dollars)

	Code	1994	1995	1996	1997	1998	1999	2000	2001
A. Current Account [1]	4 993 Z.	**–351.9**	**–356.4**	**–326.6**	**–388.1**	**–67.2**	**–256.5**	**–298.7**	**–339.3**
Goods: exports f.o.b	2 100 . .	368.7	349.9	388.7	413.8	482.0	612.3	776.1	720.5
Goods: imports f.o.b	3 100 . .	–1,158.9	–1,310.8	–1,494.7	–1,691.9	–1,239.1	–1,494.2	–1,590.1	–1,485.7
Balance on Goods	4 100 . .	*–790.3*	*–961.0*	*–1,105.9*	*–1,278.1*	*–757.1*	*–881.9*	*–814.0*	*–765.2*
Services: credit	2 200 . .	579.2	679.0	757.5	865.7	565.1	655.1	505.9	413.3
Services: debit	3 200 . .	–296.6	–313.3	–242.8	–224.5	–196.2	–212.5	–199.9	–214.7
Balance on Goods and Services	4 991 . .	*–507.6*	*–595.2*	*–591.3*	*–637.0*	*–388.1*	*–439.2*	*–508.0*	*–566.6*
Income: credit	2 300 . .	34.6	43.6	33.1	31.9	45.4	55.8	72.2	70.3
Income: debit	3 300 . .	–30.8	–34.9	–32.0	–28.6	–26.5	–28.4	–35.2	–58.8
Balance on Goods, Services, and Income	4 992 . .	*–503.9*	*–586.5*	*–590.2*	*–633.7*	*–369.2*	*–411.9*	*–471.0*	*–555.2*
Current transfers: credit	2 379 Z.	160.7	239.2	281.6	267.4	326.0	182.3	189.0	240.2
Current transfers: debit	3 379 . .	–8.7	–9.1	–18.0	–21.8	–24.1	–26.9	–16.7	–24.3
B. Capital Account [1]	4 994 Z.	**. . .**	**. . .**	**. . .**	**. . .**	**. . .**	**. . .**	**. . .**	**. . .**
Capital account: credit	2 994 Z.	. . .	. . .	. . .	. . .	. . .	. . .	. . .	. . .
Capital account: debit	3 994 . .	. . .	. . .	. . .	. . .	. . .	. . .	. . .	. . .
Total, Groups A Plus B	4 981 . .	*–351.9*	*–356.4*	*–326.6*	*–388.1*	*–67.2*	*–256.5*	*–298.7*	*–339.3*
C. Financial Account [1]	4 995 W.	**407.3**	**368.5**	**275.2**	**340.3**	**212.9**	**–24.5**	**76.1**	**–216.9**
Direct investment abroad	4 505 . .	. . .	. . .	. . .	. . .	. . .	. . .	. . .	. . .
Direct investment in Nepal	4 555 Z.	. . .	. . .	19.2	23.1	12.0	. . .	. . .	. . .
Portfolio investment assets	4 602 . .	. . .	. . .	. . .	. . .	. . .	. . .	. . .	. . .
Equity securities	4 610 . .	. . .	. . .	. . .	. . .	. . .	. . .	. . .	. . .
Debt securities	4 619 . .	. . .	. . .	. . .	. . .	. . .	. . .	. . .	. . .
Portfolio investment liabilities	4 652 Z.	. . .	. . .	. . .	. . .	. . .	. . .	. . .	. . .
Equity securities	4 660 . .	. . .	. . .	. . .	. . .	. . .	. . .	. . .	. . .
Debt securities	4 669 Z.	. . .	. . .	. . .	. . .	. . .	. . .	. . .	. . .
Financial derivatives	4 910 . .	. . .	. . .	. . .	. . .	. . .	. . .	. . .	. . .
Financial derivatives assets	4 900 . .	. . .	. . .	. . .	. . .	. . .	. . .	. . .	. . .
Financial derivatives liabilities	4 905 . .	. . .	. . .	. . .	. . .	. . .	. . .	. . .	. . .
Other investment assets	4 703 . .	159.2	264.4	91.6	89.4	90.8	48.2	128.6	11.2
Monetary authorities	4 701 . .	. . .	. . .	. . .	. . .	. . .	. . .	. . .	. . .
General government	4 704 . .	. . .	. . .	. . .	. . .	. . .	. . .	. . .	. . .
Banks	4 705 . .	. . .	. . .	. . .	. . .	. . .	. . .	. . .	. . .
Other sectors	4 728 . .	159.2	264.4	91.6	89.4	90.8	48.2	128.6	11.2
Other investment liabilities	4 753 W.	248.0	104.1	164.5	227.8	110.0	–72.8	–52.6	–228.0
Monetary authorities	4 753 WA	4.3	.1	–3.3	1.0	.4	–2.0	4.5	–3.5
General government	4 753 ZB	237.5	106.8	128.4	165.9	151.8	–56.2	–61.0	–63.5
Banks	4 753 ZC	5.4	–4.5	38.2	68.8	17.0	13.2	67.4	3.2
Other sectors	4 753 ZD	.8	1.7	1.2	–7.8	–59.1	–27.8	–63.5	–164.3
Total, Groups A Through C	4 983 . .	*55.4*	*12.1*	*–51.4*	*–47.8*	*145.7*	*–281.0*	*–222.7*	*–556.1*
D. Net Errors and Omissions	4 998 . .	**7.1**	**2.8**	**82.3**	**216.6**	**134.0**	**58.3**	**145.7**	**256.5**
Total, Groups A Through D	4 984 . .	*62.5*	*15.0*	*30.9*	*168.8*	*279.7*	*–222.7*	*–77.0*	*–299.6*
E. Reserves and Related Items	4 802 A.	**–62.5**	**–15.0**	**–30.9**	**–168.8**	**–279.7**	**222.7**	**77.0**	**299.6**
Reserve assets	4 802 . .	–65.0	–7.0	–23.4	–161.7	–273.0	–144.4	–291.0	–5.2
Use of Fund credit and loans	4 766 . .	2.5	–8.0	–7.5	–7.2	–6.6	–5.9	–4.4	–4.3
Exceptional financing	4 920 . .	. . .	. . .	. . .	. . .	. . .	373.0	372.4	309.1
Conversion rates: Nepalese rupees per U.S. dollar	0 101 . .	**49.398**	**51.890**	**56.692**	**58.010**	**65.976**	**68.239**	**71.094**	**74.949**

[1] Excludes components that have been classified in the categories of Group E.

Table 2. STANDARD PRESENTATION, 1994–2001
(Millions of U.S. dollars)

	Code		1994	1995	1996	1997	1998	1999	2000	2001
CURRENT ACCOUNT	4 993	. .	**–351.9**	**–356.4**	**–326.6**	**–388.1**	**–67.2**	**–78.7**	**–130.6**	**–164.7**
A. GOODS	4 100	. .	–790.3	–961.0	–1,105.9	–1,278.1	–757.1	–881.9	–814.0	–765.2
Credit	2 100	. .	**368.7**	**349.9**	**388.7**	**413.8**	**482.0**	**612.3**	**776.1**	**720.5**
General merchandise: exports f.o.b.	2 110	. .	368.7	349.9	388.7	413.8	482.0	612.3	776.1	720.5
Goods for processing: exports f.o.b.	2 150	. .	. . .	. . .	. . .	. . .	. . .	. . .	. . .	. . .
Repairs on goods	2 160	. .	. . .	. . .	. . .	. . .	. . .	. . .	. . .	. . .
Goods procured in ports by carriers	2 170	. .	. . .	. . .	. . .	. . .	. . .	. . .	. . .	. . .
Nonmonetary gold	2 180	. .	. . .	. . .	. . .	. . .	. . .	. . .	. . .	. . .
Debit	3 100	. .	**–1,158.9**	**–1,310.8**	**–1,494.7**	**–1,691.9**	**–1,239.1**	**–1,494.2**	**–1,590.1**	**–1,485.7**
General merchandise: imports f.o.b.	3 110	. .	–1,158.9	–1,310.8	–1,494.7	–1,691.9	–1,239.1	–1,494.2	–1,590.1	–1,485.7
Goods for processing: imports f.o.b.	3 150	. .	. . .	. . .	. . .	. . .	. . .	. . .	. . .	. . .
Repairs on goods	3 160	. .	. . .	. . .	. . .	. . .	. . .	. . .	. . .	. . .
Goods procured in ports by carriers	3 170	. .	. . .	. . .	. . .	. . .	. . .	. . .	. . .	. . .
Nonmonetary gold	3 180	. .	. . .	. . .	. . .	. . .	. . .	. . .	. . .	. . .
B. SERVICES	4 200	. .	282.6	365.8	514.6	641.2	369.0	442.6	306.0	198.6
Total credit	2 200	. .	*579.2*	*679.0*	*757.5*	*865.7*	*565.1*	*655.1*	*505.9*	*413.3*
Total debit	3 200	. .	*–296.6*	*–313.3*	*–242.8*	*–224.5*	*–196.2*	*–212.5*	*–199.9*	*–214.7*
Transportation services, credit	2 205	. .	**46.1**	**55.3**	**76.0**	**54.9**	**59.4**	**56.0**	**61.4**	**47.3**
Passenger	2 850	. .	*46.1*	*55.3*	*76.0*	*54.9*	*59.4*	*56.0*	*61.4*	*47.3*
Freight	2 851	. .	. . .	. . .	. . .	. . .	. . .	. . .	. . .	. . .
Other	2 852	. .	. . .	. . .	. . .	. . .	. . .	. . .	. . .	. . .
Sea transport, passenger	2 207	. .	. . .	. . .	. . .	. . .	. . .	. . .	. . .	. . .
Sea transport, freight	2 208	. .	. . .	. . .	. . .	. . .	. . .	. . .	. . .	. . .
Sea transport, other	2 209	. .	. . .	. . .	. . .	. . .	. . .	. . .	. . .	. . .
Air transport, passenger	2 211	. .	. . .	. . .	. . .	. . .	. . .	. . .	. . .	. . .
Air transport, freight	2 212	. .	. . .	. . .	. . .	. . .	. . .	. . .	. . .	. . .
Air transport, other	2 213	. .	. . .	. . .	. . .	. . .	. . .	. . .	. . .	. . .
Other transport, passenger	2 215	. .	. . .	. . .	. . .	. . .	. . .	. . .	. . .	. . .
Other transport, freight	2 216	. .	. . .	. . .	. . .	. . .	. . .	. . .	. . .	. . .
Other transport, other	2 217	. .	. . .	. . .	. . .	. . .	. . .	. . .	. . .	. . .
Transportation services, debit	3 205	. .	**–95.9**	**–110.7**	**–55.6**	**–62.2**	**–56.0**	**–73.7**	**–64.8**	**–71.6**
Passenger	3 850	. .	*–22.9*	*–31.1*	*–29.7*	*–37.5*	*–29.0*	*–44.7*	*–35.9*	*–47.7*
Freight	3 851	. .	*–73.0*	*–79.6*	*–25.9*	*–24.7*	*–27.1*	*–29.0*	*–28.9*	*–24.0*
Other	3 852	. .	. . .	. . .	. . .	. . .	. . .	. . .	. . .	. . .
Sea transport, passenger	3 207	. .	. . .	. . .	. . .	. . .	. . .	. . .	. . .	. . .
Sea transport, freight	3 208	. .	. . .	. . .	. . .	. . .	. . .	. . .	. . .	. . .
Sea transport, other	3 209	. .	. . .	. . .	. . .	. . .	. . .	. . .	. . .	. . .
Air transport, passenger	3 211	. .	. . .	. . .	. . .	. . .	. . .	. . .	. . .	. . .
Air transport, freight	3 212	. .	. . .	. . .	. . .	. . .	. . .	. . .	. . .	. . .
Air transport, other	3 213	. .	. . .	. . .	. . .	. . .	. . .	. . .	. . .	. . .
Other transport, passenger	3 215	. .	. . .	. . .	. . .	. . .	. . .	. . .	. . .	. . .
Other transport, freight	3 216	. .	. . .	. . .	. . .	. . .	. . .	. . .	. . .	. . .
Other transport, other	3 217	. .	. . .	. . .	. . .	. . .	. . .	. . .	. . .	. . .
Travel, credit	2 236	. .	**172.1**	**177.4**	**160.6**	**145.6**	**189.1**	**173.0**	**157.8**	**143.8**
Business travel	2 237	. .	. . .	. . .	. . .	. . .	. . .	. . .	. . .	. . .
Personal travel	2 240	. .	. . .	. . .	. . .	. . .	. . .	. . .	. . .	. . .
Travel, debit	3 236	. .	**–112.4**	**–136.3**	**–124.9**	**–103.3**	**–77.7**	**–71.4**	**–73.3**	**–79.7**
Business travel	3 237	. .	. . .	. . .	. . .	. . .	. . .	. . .	. . .	. . .
Personal travel	3 240	. .	. . .	. . .	. . .	. . .	. . .	. . .	. . .	. . .
Other services, credit	2 200	BA	**361.0**	**446.4**	**520.9**	**665.2**	**316.7**	**426.0**	**286.7**	**222.2**
Communications	2 245	. .	. . .	. . .	. . .	. . .	. . .	. . .	. . .	. . .
Construction	2 249	. .	. . .	. . .	. . .	. . .	. . .	. . .	. . .	. . .
Insurance	2 253	. .	. . .	. . .	. . .	. . .	. . .	. . .	. . .	. . .
Financial	2 260	. .	. . .	. . .	. . .	. . .	. . .	. . .	. . .	. . .
Computer and information	2 262	. .	. . .	. . .	. . .	. . .	. . .	. . .	. . .	. . .
Royalties and licence fees	2 266	. .	. . .	. . .	. . .	. . .	. . .	. . .	. . .	. . .
Other business services	2 268	. .	308.5	359.2	442.9	594.7	184.4	224.9	190.8	111.6
Personal, cultural, and recreational	2 287	. .	. . .	. . .	. . .	. . .	. . .	. . .	. . .	. . .
Government, n.i.e.	2 291	. .	52.5	87.1	78.0	70.6	132.2	201.1	96.0	110.6
Other services, debit	3 200	BA	**–88.3**	**–66.2**	**–62.3**	**–59.0**	**–62.4**	**–67.3**	**–61.9**	**–63.3**
Communications	3 245	. .	. . .	. . .	. . .	. . .	. . .	. . .	. . .	. . .
Construction	3 249	. .	. . .	. . .	. . .	. . .	. . .	. . .	. . .	. . .
Insurance	3 253	. .	–8.1	–9.2	. . .	. . .	. . .	. . .	. . .	. . .
Financial	3 260	. .	. . .	. . .	. . .	. . .	. . .	. . .	. . .	. . .
Computer and information	3 262	. .	. . .	. . .	. . .	. . .	. . .	. . .	. . .	. . .
Royalties and licence fees	3 266	. .	. . .	. . .	. . .	. . .	. . .	. . .	. . .	. . .
Other business services	3 268	. .	–73.1	–48.5	–54.5	–50.3	–55.0	–56.9	–55.2	–54.0
Personal, cultural, and recreational	3 287	. .	. . .	. . .	. . .	. . .	. . .	. . .	. . .	. . .
Government, n.i.e.	3 291	. .	–7.1	–8.5	–7.8	–8.7	–7.4	–10.4	–6.7	–9.4

Table 2 (Continued). STANDARD PRESENTATION, 1994–2001

(Millions of U.S. dollars)

	Code		1994	1995	1996	1997	1998	1999	2000	2001
C. INCOME	4 300	..	3.8	8.7	1.1	3.3	18.9	27.4	37.0	11.5
Total credit	2 300	..	*34.6*	*43.6*	*33.1*	*31.9*	*45.4*	*55.8*	*72.2*	*70.3*
Total debit	3 300	..	*–30.8*	*–34.9*	*–32.0*	*–28.6*	*–26.5*	*–28.4*	*–35.2*	*–58.8*
Compensation of employees, credit	2 310	..	...	...	...	...	...	...	...	...
Compensation of employees, debit	3 310	..	...	...	...	...	...	...	...	...
Investment income, credit	2 320	..	**34.6**	**43.6**	**33.1**	**31.9**	**45.4**	**55.8**	**72.2**	**70.3**
Direct investment income	2 330	..	...	...	...	...	...	...	...	...
Dividends and distributed branch profits	2 332	..	...	...	...	...	...	...	...	...
Reinvested earnings and undistributed branch profits	2 333	..	...	...	...	...	...	...	...	...
Income on debt (interest)	2 334	..	...	...	...	...	...	...	...	...
Portfolio investment income	2 339	..	...	...	...	...	...	...	...	...
Income on equity	2 340	..	...	...	...	...	...	...	...	...
Income on bonds and notes	2 350	..	...	...	...	...	...	...	...	...
Income on money market instruments	2 360	..	...	...	...	...	...	...	...	...
Other investment income	2 370	..	34.6	43.6	33.1	31.9	45.4	55.8	72.2	70.3
Investment income, debit	3 320	..	**–30.8**	**–34.9**	**–32.0**	**–28.6**	**–26.5**	**–28.4**	**–35.2**	**–58.8**
Direct investment income	3 330	..	...	...	...	...	...	...	...	...
Dividends and distributed branch profits	3 332	..	...	...	...	...	...	...	...	...
Reinvested earnings and undistributed branch profits	3 333	..	...	...	...	...	...	...	...	...
Income on debt (interest)	3 334	..	...	...	...	...	...	...	...	...
Portfolio investment income	3 339	..	...	...	...	...	...	...	...	...
Income on equity	3 340	..	...	...	...	...	...	...	...	...
Income on bonds and notes	3 350	..	...	...	...	...	...	...	...	...
Income on money market instruments	3 360	..	...	...	...	...	...	...	...	...
Other investment income	3 370	..	–30.8	–34.9	–32.0	–28.6	–26.5	–28.4	–35.2	–58.8
D. CURRENT TRANSFERS	4 379	..	152.0	230.1	263.6	245.6	302.0	333.2	340.3	390.5
Credit	2 379	..	**160.7**	**239.2**	**281.6**	**267.4**	**326.0**	**360.1**	**357.1**	**414.8**
General government	2 380	..	80.9	145.8	187.2	185.9	186.8	177.8	168.1	174.6
Other sectors	2 390	..	79.8	93.4	94.4	81.5	139.3	182.3	189.0	240.2
Workers' remittances	2 391	..	50.1	56.8	44.2	49.5	67.5	83.5	111.5	147.0
Other current transfers	2 392	..	29.7	36.5	50.3	32.1	71.8	98.9	77.5	93.2
Debit	3 379	..	**–8.7**	**–9.1**	**–18.0**	**–21.8**	**–24.1**	**–26.9**	**–16.7**	**–24.3**
General government	3 380	..	...	...	...	...	...	...	...	...
Other sectors	3 390	..	–8.7	–9.1	–18.0	–21.8	–24.1	–26.9	–16.7	–24.3
Workers' remittances	3 391	..	–8.7	–9.1	–18.0	–21.8	–24.1	–26.9	–16.7	–24.3
Other current transfers	3 392	..	...	...	...	...	...	...	...	...
CAPITAL AND FINANCIAL ACCOUNT	4 996	..	**344.7**	**353.5**	**244.3**	**171.5**	**–66.8**	**20.4**	**–15.1**	**–91.9**
CAPITAL ACCOUNT	4 994	..	...	...	...	...	...	...	...	...
Total credit	2 994	..	...	...	...	...	...	...	...	...
Total debit	3 994	..	...	...	...	...	...	...	...	...
Capital transfers, credit	2 400	..	...	...	...	...	...	...	...	...
General government	2 401	..	...	...	...	...	...	...	...	...
Debt forgiveness	2 402	..	...	...	...	...	...	...	...	...
Other capital transfers	2 410	..	...	...	...	...	...	...	...	...
Other sectors	2 430	..	...	...	...	...	...	...	...	...
Migrants' transfers	2 431	..	...	...	...	...	...	...	...	...
Debt forgiveness	2 432	..	...	...	...	...	...	...	...	...
Other capital transfers	2 440	..	...	...	...	...	...	...	...	...
Capital transfers, debit	3 400	..	...	...	...	...	...	...	...	...
General government	3 401	..	...	...	...	...	...	...	...	...
Debt forgiveness	3 402	..	...	...	...	...	...	...	...	...
Other capital transfers	3 410	..	...	...	...	...	...	...	...	...
Other sectors	3 430	..	...	...	...	...	...	...	...	...
Migrants' transfers	3 431	..	...	...	...	...	...	...	...	...
Debt forgiveness	3 432	..	...	...	...	...	...	...	...	...
Other capital transfers	3 440	..	...	...	...	...	...	...	...	...
Nonproduced nonfinancial assets, credit	2 480	..	...	...	...	...	...	...	...	...
Nonproduced nonfinancial assets, debit	3 480	..	...	...	...	...	...	...	...	...

Table 2 (Continued). STANDARD PRESENTATION, 1994–2001

(Millions of U.S. dollars)

	Code	1994	1995	1996	1997	1998	1999	2000	2001
FINANCIAL ACCOUNT	4 995 . .	**344.7**	**353.5**	**244.3**	**171.5**	**–66.8**	**20.4**	**–15.1**	**–91.9**
A. DIRECT INVESTMENT	4 500 . .	. . .	. . .	19.2	23.1	12.0	4.4	–.5	. . .
Direct investment abroad	4 505 . .	. . .	. . .	. . .	. . .	. . .	. . .	. . .	. . .
Equity capital	4 510 . .	. . .	. . .	. . .	. . .	. . .	. . .	. . .	. . .
Claims on affiliated enterprises	4 515 . .	. . .	. . .	. . .	. . .	. . .	. . .	. . .	. . .
Liabilities to affiliated enterprises	4 520 . .	. . .	. . .	. . .	. . .	. . .	. . .	. . .	. . .
Reinvested earnings	4 525 . .	. . .	. . .	. . .	. . .	. . .	. . .	. . .	. . .
Other capital	4 530 . .	. . .	. . .	. . .	. . .	. . .	. . .	. . .	. . .
Claims on affiliated enterprises	4 535 . .	. . .	. . .	. . .	. . .	. . .	. . .	. . .	. . .
Liabilities to affiliated enterprises	4 540 . .	. . .	. . .	. . .	. . .	. . .	. . .	. . .	. . .
Direct investment in Nepal	4 555 . .	. . .	. . .	**19.2**	**23.1**	**12.0**	**4.4**	**–.5**	. . .
Equity capital	4 560 . .	. . .	. . .	19.2	23.1	12.0	4.4	–.5	. . .
Claims on direct investors	4 565 . .	. . .	. . .	. . .	. . .	. . .	. . .	. . .	. . .
Liabilities to direct investors	4 570 . .	. . .	. . .	. . .	. . .	. . .	4.4	–.5	. . .
Reinvested earnings	4 575 . .	. . .	. . .	. . .	. . .	. . .	. . .	. . .	. . .
Other capital	4 580 . .	. . .	. . .	. . .	. . .	. . .	. . .	. . .	. . .
Claims on direct investors	4 585 . .	. . .	. . .	. . .	. . .	. . .	. . .	. . .	. . .
Liabilities to direct investors	4 590 . .	. . .	. . .	. . .	. . .	. . .	. . .	. . .	. . .
B. PORTFOLIO INVESTMENT	4 600 . .	. . .	. . .	. . .	. . .	. . .	. . .	. . .	. . .
Assets	4 602 . .	. . .	. . .	. . .	. . .	. . .	. . .	. . .	. . .
Equity securities	4 610 . .	. . .	. . .	. . .	. . .	. . .	. . .	. . .	. . .
Monetary authorities	4 611 . .	. . .	. . .	. . .	. . .	. . .	. . .	. . .	. . .
General government	4 612 . .	. . .	. . .	. . .	. . .	. . .	. . .	. . .	. . .
Banks	4 613 . .	. . .	. . .	. . .	. . .	. . .	. . .	. . .	. . .
Other sectors	4 614 . .	. . .	. . .	. . .	. . .	. . .	. . .	. . .	. . .
Debt securities	4 619 . .	. . .	. . .	. . .	. . .	. . .	. . .	. . .	. . .
Bonds and notes	4 620 . .	. . .	. . .	. . .	. . .	. . .	. . .	. . .	. . .
Monetary authorities	4 621 . .	. . .	. . .	. . .	. . .	. . .	. . .	. . .	. . .
General government	4 622 . .	. . .	. . .	. . .	. . .	. . .	. . .	. . .	. . .
Banks	4 623 . .	. . .	. . .	. . .	. . .	. . .	. . .	. . .	. . .
Other sectors	4 624 . .	. . .	. . .	. . .	. . .	. . .	. . .	. . .	. . .
Money market instruments	4 630 . .	. . .	. . .	. . .	. . .	. . .	. . .	. . .	. . .
Monetary authorities	4 631 . .	. . .	. . .	. . .	. . .	. . .	. . .	. . .	. . .
General government	4 632 . .	. . .	. . .	. . .	. . .	. . .	. . .	. . .	. . .
Banks	4 633 . .	. . .	. . .	. . .	. . .	. . .	. . .	. . .	. . .
Other sectors	4 634 . .	. . .	. . .	. . .	. . .	. . .	. . .	. . .	. . .
Liabilities	4 652 . .	. . .	. . .	. . .	. . .	. . .	. . .	. . .	. . .
Equity securities	4 660 . .	. . .	. . .	. . .	. . .	. . .	. . .	. . .	. . .
Banks	4 663 . .	. . .	. . .	. . .	. . .	. . .	. . .	. . .	. . .
Other sectors	4 664 . .	. . .	. . .	. . .	. . .	. . .	. . .	. . .	. . .
Debt securities	4 669 . .	. . .	. . .	. . .	. . .	. . .	. . .	. . .	. . .
Bonds and notes	4 670 . .	. . .	. . .	. . .	. . .	. . .	. . .	. . .	. . .
Monetary authorities	4 671 . .	. . .	. . .	. . .	. . .	. . .	. . .	. . .	. . .
General government	4 672 . .	. . .	. . .	. . .	. . .	. . .	. . .	. . .	. . .
Banks	4 673 . .	. . .	. . .	. . .	. . .	. . .	. . .	. . .	. . .
Other sectors	4 674 . .	. . .	. . .	. . .	. . .	. . .	. . .	. . .	. . .
Money market instruments	4 680 . .	. . .	. . .	. . .	. . .	. . .	. . .	. . .	. . .
Monetary authorities	4 681 . .	. . .	. . .	. . .	. . .	. . .	. . .	. . .	. . .
General government	4 682 . .	. . .	. . .	. . .	. . .	. . .	. . .	. . .	. . .
Banks	4 683 . .	. . .	. . .	. . .	. . .	. . .	. . .	. . .	. . .
Other sectors	4 684 . .	. . .	. . .	. . .	. . .	. . .	. . .	. . .	. . .
C. FINANCIAL DERIVATIVES	4 910 . .	. . .	. . .	. . .	. . .	. . .	. . .	. . .	. . .
Monetary authorities	4 911 . .	. . .	. . .	. . .	. . .	. . .	. . .	. . .	. . .
General government	4 912 . .	. . .	. . .	. . .	. . .	. . .	. . .	. . .	. . .
Banks	4 913 . .	. . .	. . .	. . .	. . .	. . .	. . .	. . .	. . .
Other sectors	4 914 . .	. . .	. . .	. . .	. . .	. . .	. . .	. . .	. . .
Assets	4 900 . .	. . .	. . .	. . .	. . .	. . .	. . .	. . .	. . .
Monetary authorities	4 901 . .	. . .	. . .	. . .	. . .	. . .	. . .	. . .	. . .
General government	4 902 . .	. . .	. . .	. . .	. . .	. . .	. . .	. . .	. . .
Banks	4 903 . .	. . .	. . .	. . .	. . .	. . .	. . .	. . .	. . .
Other sectors	4 904 . .	. . .	. . .	. . .	. . .	. . .	. . .	. . .	. . .
Liabilities	4 905 . .	. . .	. . .	. . .	. . .	. . .	. . .	. . .	. . .
Monetary authorities	4 906 . .	. . .	. . .	. . .	. . .	. . .	. . .	. . .	. . .
General government	4 907 . .	. . .	. . .	. . .	. . .	. . .	. . .	. . .	. . .
Banks	4 908 . .	. . .	. . .	. . .	. . .	. . .	. . .	. . .	. . .
Other sectors	4 909 . .	. . .	. . .	. . .	. . .	. . .	. . .	. . .	. . .

Table 2 (Concluded). STANDARD PRESENTATION, 1994–2001
(Millions of U.S. dollars)

	Code	1994	1995	1996	1997	1998	1999	2000	2001
D. OTHER INVESTMENT	4 700 . .	409.7	360.5	248.5	310.1	194.2	160.4	276.4	–86.6
Assets	4 703 . .	**159.2**	**264.4**	**91.6**	**89.4**	**90.8**	**48.2**	**128.6**	**11.2**
Trade credits	4 706 . .	...	...	91.6	89.4	90.8	48.2	128.6	11.2
General government	4 707 . .	...	...	...	...	...	...	...	...
of which: Short-term	4 709 . .	...	...	...	...	...	...	...	...
Other sectors	4 710 . .	...	...	91.6	89.4	90.8	48.2	128.6	11.2
of which: Short-term	4 712 . .	...	...	...	...	...	*48.2*	*128.6*	*11.2*
Loans	4 714 . .	159.2	264.4	...	...	...	...	...	...
Monetary authorities	4 715 . .	...	...	...	...	...	...	...	...
of which: Short-term	4 718 . .	...	...	...	...	...	...	...	...
General government	4 719 . .	...	...	...	...	...	...	...	...
of which: Short-term	4 721 . .	...	...	...	...	...	...	...	...
Banks	4 722 . .	...	...	...	...	...	...	...	...
of which: Short-term	4 724 . .	...	...	...	...	...	...	...	...
Other sectors	4 725 . .	159.2	264.4	...	...	...	...	...	...
of which: Short-term	4 727 . .	*159.2*	*264.4*	...	...	...	...	...	...
Currency and deposits	4 730 . .	...	...	...	...	...	...	...	...
Monetary authorities	4 731 . .	...	...	...	...	...	...	...	...
General government	4 732 . .	...	...	...	...	...	...	...	...
Banks	4 733 . .	...	...	...	...	...	...	...	...
Other sectors	4 734 . .	...	...	...	...	...	...	...	...
Other assets	4 736 . .	...	...	...	...	...	...	...	...
Monetary authorities	4 737 . .	...	...	...	...	...	...	...	...
of which: Short-term	4 739 . .	...	...	...	...	...	...	...	...
General government	4 740 . .	...	...	...	...	...	...	...	...
of which: Short-term	4 742 . .	...	...	...	...	...	...	...	...
Banks	4 743 . .	...	...	...	...	...	...	...	...
of which: Short-term	4 745 . .	...	...	...	...	...	...	...	...
Other sectors	4 746 . .	...	...	...	...	...	...	...	...
of which: Short-term	4 748 . .	...	...	...	...	...	...	...	...
Liabilities	4 753 . .	**250.5**	**96.1**	**156.9**	**220.7**	**103.4**	**112.2**	**147.8**	**–97.8**
Trade credits	4 756 . .	...	...	...	–9.0	–59.4	–17.1	–60.1	–162.6
General government	4 757 . .	...	...	...	...	...	...	...	...
of which: Short-term	4 759 . .	...	...	...	...	...	...	...	...
Other sectors	4 760 . .	...	...	...	–9.0	–59.4	–17.1	–60.1	–162.6
of which: Short-term	4 762 . .	...	...	...	...	...	*–17.1*	*–60.1*	*–162.6*
Loans	4 764 . .	240.0	98.9	120.9	158.7	145.2	117.7	135.3	64.5
Monetary authorities	4 765 . .	2.5	–8.0	–7.5	–7.2	–6.6	–5.9	–4.4	–4.3
of which: Use of Fund credit and loans from the Fund	4 766 . .	*2.5*	*–8.0*	*–7.5*	*–7.2*	*–6.6*	*–5.9*	*–4.4*	*–4.3*
of which: Short-term	4 768 . .	...	...	...	...	...	...	...	...
General government	4 769 . .	237.5	106.8	128.4	165.9	151.8	113.5	132.0	71.1
of which: Short-term	4 771 . .	...	...	...	...	...	...	...	...
Banks	4 772 . .	...	...	...	...	...	...	...	...
of which: Short-term	4 774 . .	...	...	...	...	...	...	...	...
Other sectors	4 775 . .	...	...	...	...	...	10.1	7.7	–2.3
of which: Short-term	4 777 . .	...	...	...	...	...	...	...	...
Currency and deposits	4 780 . .	5.4	–4.5	38.2	68.8	17.0	13.2	67.4	3.2
Monetary authorities	4 781 . .	...	...	...	...	...	...	...	...
General government	4 782 . .	...	...	...	...	...	...	...	...
Banks	4 783 . .	5.4	–4.5	38.2	68.8	17.0	13.2	67.4	3.2
Other sectors	4 784 . .	...	...	...	...	...	...	...	...
Other liabilities	4 786 . .	5.1	1.7	–2.2	2.2	.7	–1.6	5.2	–2.9
Monetary authorities	4 787 . .	4.3	.1	–3.3	1.0	.4	–2.0	4.5	–3.5
of which: Short-term	4 789 . .	*4.3*	*.1*	*–3.3*	*1.0*	*.4*	*–2.0*	*4.5*	*–3.5*
General government	4 790 . .	...	...	...	...	...	...	...	...
of which: Short-term	4 792 . .	...	...	...	...	...	...	...	...
Banks	4 793 . .	...	...	...	...	...	...	...	...
of which: Short-term	4 795 . .	...	...	...	...	...	...	...	...
Other sectors	4 796 . .	.8	1.7	1.2	1.2	.3	.4	.7	.6
of which: Short-term	4 798 . .	*.8*	*1.7*	*1.2*	*1.2*	*.3*	*.4*	*.7*	*.6*
E. RESERVE ASSETS	4 802 . .	–65.0	–7.0	–23.4	–161.7	–273.0	–144.4	–291.0	–5.2
Monetary gold	4 812 . .	–.1	–.8	–.1	–.7	–.4	–.1	–.5	–.2
Special drawing rights	4 811 . .	–.1	.1	...	–.1	.1	–.3	.3	–.1
Reserve position in the Fund	4 810 . .	...	...	...	...	...	...	...	...
Foreign exchange	4 803 . .	–64.8	–6.3	–23.3	–160.9	–272.7	–144.0	–290.8	–5.0
Other claims	4 813 . .	...	...	...	...	...	...	...	...
NET ERRORS AND OMISSIONS	4 998 . .	**7.1**	**2.8**	**82.3**	**216.6**	**134.0**	**58.3**	**145.7**	**256.5**

Part 3 of the *Yearbook* contains descriptions of the methodologies, compilation practices, and sources used to compile these data.

Table 1. ANALYTIC PRESENTATION, 1994–2001
(Millions of U.S. dollars)

	Code	1994	1995	1996	1997	1998	1999	2000	2001
A. Current Account [1]	4 993 Z.	**17,294**	**25,552**	**21,228**	**24,594**	**13,449**	**15,540**	**7,458**	**3,743**
Goods: exports f.o.b	2 100 . .	141,810	195,600	195,079	188,988	196,041	195,691	204,411	202,947
Goods: imports f.o.b	3 100 . .	–123,124	–171,788	–172,312	–168,051	–175,611	–179,657	–186,848	–183,082
Balance on Goods	4 100 . .	*18,686*	*23,812*	*22,767*	*20,937*	*20,430*	*16,034*	*17,563*	*19,865*
Services: credit	2 200 . .	41,523	46,920	48,495	50,155	51,661	54,102	52,404	52,928
Services: debit	3 200 . .	–41,303	–45,768	–46,535	–46,883	–49,185	–51,583	–53,172	–54,902
Balance on Goods and Services	4 991 . .	*18,905*	*24,964*	*24,726*	*24,209*	*22,907*	*18,553*	*16,796*	*17,892*
Income: credit	2 300 . .	29,466	35,548	36,026	38,729	35,697	43,356	42,666	37,983
Income: debit	3 300 . .	–25,799	–28,527	–32,755	–32,224	–37,973	–40,017	–45,752	–45,505
Balance on Goods, Services, and Income	4 992 . .	*22,571*	*31,986*	*27,998*	*30,713*	*20,631*	*21,891*	*13,709*	*10,369*
Current transfers: credit	2 379 Z.	4,197	4,725	4,319	4,346	3,799	4,566	4,366	4,586
Current transfers: debit	3 379 . .	–9,474	–11,159	–11,089	–10,465	–10,981	–10,918	–10,617	–11,213
B. Capital Account [1]	4 994 Z.	**–1,006**	**–1,099**	**–2,024**	**–1,297**	**–420**	**–214**	**606**	**–566**
Capital account: credit	2 994 Z.	564	856	1,267	1,099	1,037	1,688	2,856	1,118
Capital account: debit	3 994 . .	–1,569	–1,955	–3,291	–2,396	–1,457	–1,902	–2,249	–1,684
Total, Groups A Plus B	4 981 . .	*16,288*	*24,453*	*19,204*	*23,296*	*13,029*	*15,325*	*8,065*	*3,177*
C. Financial Account [1]	4 995 W.	**–9,969**	**–18,614**	**–5,198**	**–13,839**	**–14,537**	**–12,422**	**–8,023**	**–11,180**
Direct investment abroad	4 505 . .	–17,581	–19,981	–31,666	–24,046	–36,842	–56,993	–69,519	–39,659
Direct investment in the Netherlands	4 555 Z.	7,127	12,225	16,609	11,052	37,609	41,205	57,363	51,239
Portfolio investment assets	4 602 . .	–9,570	–16,498	–25,013	–38,942	–69,292	–94,489	–65,635	–76,809
Equity securities	4 610 . .	–6,595	–8,730	–2,895	–12,140	–19,890	–52,668	–23,449	–29,513
Debt securities	4 619 . .	–2,975	–7,768	–22,119	–26,802	–49,402	–41,821	–42,186	–47,296
Portfolio investment liabilities	4 652 Z.	–834	6,123	13,432	17,752	30,012	100,213	55,416	73,109
Equity securities	4 660 . .	–1,385	–743	3,280	774	3,826	30,491	16,970	12,934
Debt securities	4 669 Z.	551	6,865	10,152	16,979	26,186	69,722	38,446	60,175
Financial derivatives	4 910 . .	–368	–1,744	–749	–446	976	4,213	–3,964	–5,768
Financial derivatives assets	4 900 . .	11,888	18,454	23,385	31,899	53,364	63,425	83,002	87,504
Financial derivatives liabilities	4 905 . .	–12,256	–20,198	–24,134	–32,346	–52,388	–59,211	–86,966	–93,272
Other investment assets	4 703 . .	7,270	–8,127	1,582	–37,217	–56,475	–2,648	–31,906	–69,672
Monetary authorities	4 701 . .	. . .	. . .	. . .	. . .	–235	107	–2,877	794
General government	4 704 . .	–44	7	–270	146	181	–1,442	532	–837
Banks	4 705 . .	9,437	–3,474	2,926	–31,241	–49,373	9,488	–18,042	–60,706
Other sectors	4 728 . .	–2,124	–4,660	–1,075	–6,122	–7,047	–10,802	–11,519	–8,923
Other investment liabilities	4 753 W.	3,988	9,389	20,607	58,009	79,475	–3,923	50,221	56,379
Monetary authorities	4 753 WA	91	–137	–42	41	930	–410	7	8
General government	4 753 ZB	1,151	24	–131	536	284	640	329	2,829
Banks	4 753 ZC	–493	4,174	15,697	52,519	60,697	–1,541	18,367	57,759
Other sectors	4 753 ZD	3,239	5,327	5,083	5,984	17,564	–2,612	31,518	–4,216
Total, Groups A Through C	4 983 . .	*6,319*	*5,839*	*14,005*	*9,458*	*–1,507*	*2,904*	*41*	*–8,003*
D. Net Errors and Omissions	4 998 . .	**–5,819**	**–7,752**	**–19,696**	**–12,165**	**–832**	**–7,515**	**179**	**7,653**
Total, Groups A Through D	4 984 . .	*500*	*–1,913*	*–5,691*	*–2,708*	*–2,339*	*–4,611*	*220*	*–350*
E. Reserves and Related Items	4 802 A.	**–500**	**1,913**	**5,691**	**2,708**	**2,339**	**4,611**	**–220**	**350**
Reserve assets	4 802 . .	–500	1,913	5,691	2,708	2,339	4,611	–220	350
Use of Fund credit and loans	4 766 . .	. . .	. . .	. . .	. . .	. . .	. . .	. . .	. . .
Exceptional financing	4 920 . .	. . .	. . .	. . .	. . .	. . .	. . .	. . .	. . .
Conversion rates: Netherlands guilders per U.S. dollar	0 101 . .	**1.8200**	**1.6057**	**1.6859**	**1.9513**	**1.9837**	**. . .**	**. . .**	**. . .**
Conversion rates: euros per U.S. dollar	0 103 . .	**. . .**	**. . .**	**. . .**	**. . .**	**. . .**	**.9386**	**1.0854**	**1.1175**

[1] Excludes components that have been classified in the categories of Group E.

Table 2. STANDARD PRESENTATION, 1994–2001

(Millions of U.S. dollars)

	Code			1994	1995	1996	1997	1998	1999	2000	2001
CURRENT ACCOUNT	4	993	. .	**17,294**	**25,552**	**21,228**	**24,594**	**13,449**	**15,540**	**7,458**	**3,743**
A. GOODS	4	100	. .	18,686	23,812	22,767	20,937	20,430	16,034	17,563	19,865
Credit	2	100	. .	**141,810**	**195,600**	**195,079**	**188,988**	**196,041**	**195,691**	**204,411**	**202,947**
General merchandise: exports f.o.b.	2	110	. .	134,049	186,840	185,671	179,577	188,363	188,509	194,182	194,718
Goods for processing: exports f.o.b.	2	150	. .	6,345	6,785	7,287	7,619	6,152	5,741	8,622	6,898
Repairs on goods	2	160	. .	180	450	419	327	370	341	260	245
Goods procured in ports by carriers	2	170	. .	1,087	1,372	1,471	1,344	1,091	1,044	1,318	1,031
Nonmonetary gold	2	180	. .	149	152	231	121	65	56	28	55
Debit	3	100	. .	**–123,124**	**–171,788**	**–172,312**	**–168,051**	**–175,611**	**–179,657**	**–186,848**	**–183,082**
General merchandise: imports f.o.b.	3	110	. .	–116,903	–163,817	–163,904	–159,533	–168,834	–173,013	–178,411	–175,884
Goods for processing: imports f.o.b.	3	150	. .	–5,990	–6,503	–6,879	–7,090	–5,526	–5,449	–7,144	–6,051
Repairs on goods	3	160	. .	. . .	–221	–139	–117	–123	–100	–81	–107
Goods procured in ports by carriers	3	170	. .	. . .	–1,025	–1,197	–1,134	–984	–979	–1,171	–942
Nonmonetary gold	3	180	. .	–231	–223	–195	–177	–144	–117	–41	–97
B. SERVICES	4	200	. .	219	1,152	1,959	3,272	2,476	2,519	–768	–1,973
Total credit	2	200	. .	*41,523*	*46,920*	*48,495*	*50,155*	*51,661*	*54,102*	*52,404*	*52,928*
Total debit	3	200	. .	*–41,303*	*–45,768*	*–46,535*	*–46,883*	*–49,185*	*–51,583*	*–53,172*	*–54,902*
Transportation services, credit	2	205	. .	**16,590**	**19,019**	**20,000**	**20,775**	**20,994**	**21,194**	**19,786**	**19,642**
Passenger	2	850	. .	*3,566*	*4,753*	*5,832*	*6,302*	*6,496*	*6,993*	*5,922*	*5,573*
Freight	2	851	. .	*9,070*	*10,101*	*9,901*	*10,160*	*10,411*	*10,257*	*10,407*	*10,658*
Other	2	852	. .	*3,954*	*4,165*	*4,266*	*4,314*	*4,087*	*3,944*	*3,457*	*3,411*
Sea transport, passenger	2	207	. .	15	17	17	16	16	15	16	15
Sea transport, freight	2	208	. .	4,604	4,985	4,588	4,893	5,227	4,910	5,176	5,286
Sea transport, other	2	209	. .	. . .	. . .	. . .	. . .	. . .	. . .	. . .	. . .
Air transport, passenger	2	211	. .	3,482	4,685	5,769	6,253	6,447	6,954	5,887	5,540
Air transport, freight	2	212	. .	807	1,092	1,344	1,449	1,485	1,602	1,351	1,271
Air transport, other	2	213	. .	. . .	. . .	. . .	. . .	. . .	. . .	. . .	. . .
Other transport, passenger	2	215	. .	69	50	46	33	32	24	19	18
Other transport, freight	2	216	. .	3,660	4,024	3,969	3,818	3,699	3,745	3,880	4,100
Other transport, other	2	217	. .	3,954	4,165	4,266	4,314	4,087	3,944	3,457	3,411
Transportation services, debit	3	205	. .	**–13,224**	**–13,588**	**–13,510**	**–13,550**	**–14,805**	**–15,060**	**–14,646**	**–14,088**
Passenger	3	850	. .	*–2,080*	*–2,376*	*–2,564*	*–2,394*	*–3,179*	*–3,337*	*–3,032*	*–2,256*
Freight	3	851	. .	*–9,212*	*–9,781*	*–9,417*	*–9,326*	*–10,186*	*–10,041*	*–9,933*	*–10,004*
Other	3	852	. .	*–1,932*	*–1,431*	*–1,529*	*–1,830*	*–1,441*	*–1,682*	*–1,682*	*–1,828*
Sea transport, passenger	3	207	. .	–82	–97	–102	–93	–95	–95	–103	–99
Sea transport, freight	3	208	. .	–6,794	–7,110	–6,638	–6,552	–7,132	–6,872	–6,939	–6,837
Sea transport, other	3	209	. .	. . .	. . .	. . .	. . .	. . .	. . .	. . .	. . .
Air transport, passenger	3	211	. .	–1,865	–2,171	–2,347	–2,213	–2,992	–3,171	–2,875	–2,110
Air transport, freight	3	212	. .	–237	–271	–295	–280	–387	–410	–372	–274
Air transport, other	3	213	. .	. . .	. . .	. . .	. . .	. . .	. . .	. . .	. . .
Other transport, passenger	3	215	. .	–133	–108	–116	–88	–91	–71	–54	–47
Other transport, freight	3	216	. .	–2,181	–2,401	–2,484	–2,494	–2,667	–2,760	–2,622	–2,893
Other transport, other	3	217	. .	–1,932	–1,431	–1,529	–1,830	–1,441	–1,682	–1,682	–1,828
Travel, credit	2	236	. .	**5,435**	**6,578**	**6,568**	**6,299**	**6,796**	**6,979**	**7,196**	**6,710**
Business travel	2	237	. .	. . .	. . .	. . .	. . .	. . .	. . .	. . .	. . .
Personal travel	2	240	. .	. . .	. . .	. . .	. . .	. . .	. . .	. . .	. . .
Travel, debit	3	236	. .	**–9,371**	**–11,674**	**–12,276**	**–11,227**	**–12,005**	**–12,027**	**–12,191**	**–11,993**
Business travel	3	237	. .	. . .	. . .	. . .	. . .	. . .	. . .	. . .	. . .
Personal travel	3	240	. .	. . .	. . .	. . .	. . .	. . .	. . .	. . .	. . .
Other services, credit	2	200	BA	**19,498**	**21,323**	**21,927**	**23,081**	**23,871**	**25,930**	**25,423**	**26,577**
Communications	2	245	. .	618	634	648	652	906	1,377	1,419	1,835
Construction	2	249	. .	3,435	3,274	3,024	3,291	2,809	2,990	2,581	3,182
Insurance	2	253	. .	. . .	171	207	190	118	254	204	231
Financial	2	260	. .	303	355	499	490	521	618	735	790
Computer and information	2	262	. .	. . .	620	638	816	977	1,141	1,167	865
Royalties and licence fees	2	266	. .	2,211	2,370	2,427	2,199	2,515	2,435	2,172	1,723
Other business services	2	268	. .	11,893	12,160	12,965	13,738	14,367	15,389	15,634	16,461
Personal, cultural, and recreational	2	287	. .	. . .	467	501	456	468	537	554	535
Government, n.i.e.	2	291	. .	1,037	1,272	1,018	1,247	1,190	1,188	957	956
Other services, debit	3	200	BA	**–18,708**	**–20,506**	**–20,749**	**–22,106**	**–22,374**	**–24,495**	**–26,335**	**–28,821**
Communications	3	245	. .	–417	–681	–667	–667	–898	–1,424	–1,417	–1,738
Construction	3	249	. .	–1,893	–1,620	–1,515	–1,847	–1,122	–1,128	–979	–1,130
Insurance	3	253	. .	–523	–906	–903	–669	–647	–582	–564	–534
Financial	3	260	. .	–283	–423	–422	–527	–685	–726	–960	–1,181
Computer and information	3	262	. .	. . .	–536	–651	–688	–810	–1,004	–1,187	–1,313
Royalties and licence fees	3	266	. .	–2,674	–3,006	–2,945	–2,655	–3,061	–3,463	–2,568	–2,319
Other business services	3	268	. .	–11,932	–11,670	–11,975	–13,134	–13,623	–14,332	–16,664	–18,438
Personal, cultural, and recreational	3	287	. .	. . .	–513	–520	–534	–496	–499	–599	–579
Government, n.i.e.	3	291	. .	–988	–1,152	–1,151	–1,385	–1,033	–1,337	–1,398	–1,589

Table 2 (Continued). STANDARD PRESENTATION, 1994–2001

(Millions of U.S. dollars)

	Code	1994	1995	1996	1997	1998	1999	2000	2001
C. INCOME	4 300 . .	3,667	7,022	3,271	6,505	–2,276	3,338	–3,086	–7,522
Total credit	2 300 . .	*29,466*	*35,548*	*36,026*	*38,729*	*35,697*	*43,356*	*42,666*	*37,983*
Total debit	3 300 . .	*–25,799*	*–28,527*	*–32,755*	*–32,224*	*–37,973*	*–40,017*	*–45,752*	*–45,505*
Compensation of employees, credit	2 310 . .	**511**	**665**	**697**	**661**	**631**	**485**	**428**	**478**
Compensation of employees, debit	3 310 . .	**–760**	**–1,083**	**–1,009**	**–962**	**–985**	**–972**	**–925**	**–978**
Investment income, credit	2 320 . .	**28,955**	**34,884**	**35,329**	**38,068**	**35,066**	**42,871**	**42,239**	**37,505**
Direct investment income	2 330 . .	10,078	13,454	13,473	15,719	10,001	17,634	17,303	11,427
Dividends and distributed branch profits	2 332 . .	6,670	6,952	9,245	8,993	9,514	13,620	16,678	12,248
Reinvested earnings and undistributed branch profits	2 333 . .	2,205	5,196	2,867	5,065	–1,298	1,885	–2,024	–4,036
Income on debt (interest)	2 334 . .	1,204	1,306	1,361	1,662	1,785	2,129	2,648	3,214
Portfolio investment income	2 339 . .	5,297	7,839	8,849	9,207	10,199	10,813	10,867	10,259
Income on equity	2 340 . .	1,006	1,522	1,700	2,131	2,724	2,921	1,741	1,439
Income on bonds and notes	2 350 . .	4,291	6,317	7,149	7,076	7,475	7,891	9,127	8,821
Income on money market instruments	2 360 . .	. . .	. . .	. . .	. . .	. . .	. . .	. . .	. . .
Other investment income	2 370 . .	13,580	13,590	13,007	13,141	14,866	14,425	14,069	15,818
Investment income, debit	3 320 . .	**–25,039**	**–27,444**	**–31,746**	**–31,262**	**–36,987**	**–39,045**	**–44,828**	**–44,527**
Direct investment income	3 330 . .	–6,047	–6,084	–10,623	–9,341	–11,542	–10,890	–13,999	–11,894
Dividends and distributed branch profits	3 332 . .	–3,955	–4,248	–5,325	–5,216	–4,541	–4,399	–5,285	–5,851
Reinvested earnings and undistributed branch profits	3 333 . .	–857	–351	–3,733	–2,840	–5,695	–4,995	–7,031	–3,562
Income on debt (interest)	3 334 . .	–1,235	–1,485	–1,565	–1,285	–1,306	–1,496	–1,683	–2,482
Portfolio investment income	3 339 . .	–7,518	–9,923	–9,452	–8,811	–10,784	–13,074	–15,106	–15,759
Income on equity	3 340 . .	–1,952	–3,262	–3,154	–3,243	–4,395	–5,088	–5,429	–5,358
Income on bonds and notes	3 350 . .	–5,565	–6,661	–6,298	–5,568	–6,389	–7,986	–9,676	–10,401
Income on money market instruments	3 360 . .	–1	. . .	. . .	. . .	. . .	. . .	. . .	. . .
Other investment income	3 370 . .	–11,474	–11,436	–11,671	–13,110	–14,662	–15,081	–15,724	–16,873
D. CURRENT TRANSFERS	4 379 . .	–5,277	–6,434	–6,770	–6,120	–7,182	–6,352	–6,251	–6,626
Credit	2 379 . .	**4,197**	**4,725**	**4,319**	**4,346**	**3,799**	**4,566**	**4,366**	**4,586**
General government	2 380 . .	3,056	3,468	2,922	2,997	2,490	3,094	2,876	3,024
Other sectors	2 390 . .	1,141	1,257	1,397	1,348	1,309	1,472	1,490	1,562
Workers' remittances	2 391 . .	. . .	. . .	. . .	. . .	. . .	. . .	. . .	. . .
Other current transfers	2 392 . .	1,141	1,257	1,397	1,348	1,309	1,472	1,490	1,562
Debit	3 379 . .	**–9,474**	**–11,159**	**–11,089**	**–10,465**	**–10,981**	**–10,918**	**–10,617**	**–11,213**
General government	3 380 . .	–7,292	–8,760	–8,539	–7,991	–8,518	–8,211	–7,845	–8,331
Other sectors	3 390 . .	–2,182	–2,399	–2,550	–2,475	–2,463	–2,707	–2,772	–2,881
Workers' remittances	3 391 . .	–403	–423	–434	–429	–438	–534	–522	–547
Other current transfers	3 392 . .	–1,779	–1,976	–2,116	–2,046	–2,024	–2,173	–2,250	–2,334
CAPITAL AND FINANCIAL ACCOUNT	4 996 . .	**–11,475**	**–17,800**	**–1,532**	**–12,428**	**–12,617**	**–8,025**	**–7,637**	**–11,396**
CAPITAL ACCOUNT	4 994 . .	**–1,006**	**–1,099**	**–2,024**	**–1,297**	**–420**	**–214**	**606**	**–566**
Total credit	2 994 . .	*564*	*856*	*1,267*	*1,099*	*1,037*	*1,688*	*2,856*	*1,118*
Total debit	3 994 . .	*–1,569*	*–1,955*	*–3,291*	*–2,396*	*–1,457*	*–1,902*	*–2,249*	*–1,684*
Capital transfers, credit	2 400 . .	**564**	**856**	**1,267**	**1,099**	**1,037**	**1,688**	**1,066**	**1,109**
General government	2 401 . .	5	100	118	215	148	111	232	145
Debt forgiveness	2 402 . .	. . .	. . .	. . .	. . .	. . .	. . .	. . .	. . .
Other capital transfers	2 410 . .	. . .	. . .	. . .	. . .	. . .	. . .	. . .	. . .
Other sectors	2 430 . .	559	755	1,149	884	889	1,577	834	963
Migrants' transfers	2 431 . .	473	694	1,057	834	833	1,493	730	875
Debt forgiveness	2 432 . .	. . .	. . .	. . .	. . .	. . .	. . .	. . .	. . .
Other capital transfers	2 440 . .	85	61	93	51	57	84	104	89
Capital transfers, debit	3 400 . .	**–1,569**	**–1,955**	**–3,291**	**–2,396**	**–1,457**	**–1,902**	**–1,787**	**–1,489**
General government	3 401 . .	–140	–160	–112	–516	–24	–13	–8	–62
Debt forgiveness	3 402 . .	. . .	. . .	. . .	. . .	. . .	. . .	. . .	. . .
Other capital transfers	3 410 . .	. . .	. . .	. . .	. . .	. . .	. . .	. . .	. . .
Other sectors	3 430 . .	–1,429	–1,795	–3,179	–1,881	–1,433	–1,889	–1,779	–1,427
Migrants' transfers	3 431 . .	–1,349	–1,296	–2,817	–1,786	–1,392	–1,767	–1,673	–1,298
Debt forgiveness	3 432 . .	. . .	. . .	. . .	. . .	. . .	. . .	. . .	. . .
Other capital transfers	3 440 . .	–81	–499	–362	–94	–42	–122	–107	–129
Nonproduced nonfinancial assets, credit	2 480 . .	**. . .**	**. . .**	**. . .**	**. . .**	**. . .**	**. . .**	**1,790**	**9**
Nonproduced nonfinancial assets, debit	3 480 . .	**. . .**	**. . .**	**. . .**	**. . .**	**. . .**	**. . .**	**–462**	**–194**

Table 2 (Continued). STANDARD PRESENTATION, 1994–2001
(Millions of U.S. dollars)

	Code	1994	1995	1996	1997	1998	1999	2000	2001
FINANCIAL ACCOUNT	4 995	**-10,469**	**-16,701**	**492**	**-11,131**	**-12,198**	**-7,811**	**-8,244**	**-10,830**
A. DIRECT INVESTMENT	4 500	-10,455	-7,756	-15,057	-12,995	767	-15,788	-12,156	11,580
Direct investment abroad	4 505	**-17,581**	**-19,981**	**-31,666**	**-24,046**	**-36,842**	**-56,993**	**-69,519**	**-39,659**
Equity capital	4 510	-8,352	-13,827	-15,318	-10,846	-21,075	-29,609	-41,010	-13,298
Claims on affiliated enterprises	4 515	...	...	...	...	...	...	...	...
Liabilities to affiliated enterprises	4 520	...	...	...	...	...	...	...	...
Reinvested earnings	4 525	-2,205	-5,196	-2,867	-5,065	1,298	-1,885	2,024	4,036
Other capital	4 530	-7,024	-958	-13,482	-8,136	-17,064	-25,498	-30,533	-30,396
Claims on affiliated enterprises	4 535	...	...	...	...	...	...	...	...
Liabilities to affiliated enterprises	4 540	...	...	...	...	...	...	...	...
Direct investment in the Netherlands	4 555	**7,127**	**12,225**	**16,609**	**11,052**	**37,609**	**41,205**	**57,363**	**51,239**
Equity capital	4 560	2,259	4,189	6,909	5,287	16,671	11,122	10,887	7,620
Claims on direct investors	4 565	...	...	...	...	...	...	...	...
Liabilities to direct investors	4 570	...	...	...	...	...	...	...	...
Reinvested earnings	4 575	857	351	3,733	2,840	5,695	4,995	7,031	3,562
Other capital	4 580	4,011	7,685	5,967	2,924	15,242	25,088	39,445	40,057
Claims on direct investors	4 585	...	...	...	...	...	...	...	...
Liabilities to direct investors	4 590	...	...	...	...	...	...	...	...
B. PORTFOLIO INVESTMENT	4 600	-10,404	-10,375	-11,581	-21,190	-39,280	5,724	-10,219	-3,699
Assets	4 602	**-9,570**	**-16,498**	**-25,013**	**-38,942**	**-69,292**	**-94,489**	**-65,635**	**-76,809**
Equity securities	4 610	-6,595	-8,730	-2,895	-12,140	-19,890	-52,668	-23,449	-29,513
Monetary authorities	4 611	...	...	...	...	...	...	...	...
General government	4 612	...	...	...	...	...	...	...	...
Banks	4 613	...	...	...	...	...	...	...	...
Other sectors	4 614	...	...	...	...	...	...	...	...
Debt securities	4 619	-2,975	-7,768	-22,119	-26,802	-49,402	-41,821	-42,186	-47,296
Bonds and notes	4 620	-5,494	-9,647	-23,777	-25,249	-47,867	-34,795	-47,386	-49,662
Monetary authorities	4 621	...	...	...	...	...	...	...	...
General government	4 622	...	...	...	...	...	...	...	...
Banks	4 623	...	...	...	...	...	...	...	...
Other sectors	4 624	...	...	...	...	...	...	...	...
Money market instruments	4 630	2,519	1,879	1,658	-1,553	-1,535	-7,026	5,200	2,366
Monetary authorities	4 631	...	...	...	...	...	...	...	...
General government	4 632	...	...	...	...	...	...	...	...
Banks	4 633	...	...	...	...	...	...	...	...
Other sectors	4 634	...	...	...	...	...	...	...	...
Liabilities	4 652	**-834**	**6,123**	**13,432**	**17,752**	**30,012**	**100,213**	**55,416**	**73,109**
Equity securities	4 660	-1,385	-743	3,280	774	3,826	30,491	16,970	12,934
Banks	4 663	...	...	...	...	...	...	...	...
Other sectors	4 664	...	...	...	...	...	...	...	...
Debt securities	4 669	551	6,865	10,152	16,979	26,186	69,722	38,446	60,175
Bonds and notes	4 670	-594	6,638	7,153	13,491	25,099	63,770	41,820	54,320
Monetary authorities	4 671	...	...	...	...	...	...	...	...
General government	4 672	-12,041	-4,697	-6,363	414	6,279	16,615	5,144	13,038
Banks	4 673	7,412	8,372	10,448	10,327	9,651	29,285	15,664	23,285
Other sectors	4 674	4,035	2,962	3,068	2,750	9,169	17,870	21,012	17,997
Money market instruments	4 680	1,145	227	2,999	3,488	1,087	5,952	-3,374	5,856
Monetary authorities	4 681	...	...	...	...	25	1	-2	-43
General government	4 682	231	715	2,037	174	88	-155	122	735
Banks	4 683	1,085	-96	960	1,606	833	5,671	-2,456	1,935
Other sectors	4 684	-171	-391	2	1,708	142	435	-1,038	3,229
C. FINANCIAL DERIVATIVES	4 910	-368	-1,744	-749	-446	976	4,213	-3,964	-5,768
Monetary authorities	4 911	...	...	...	...	...	19	40	...
General government	4 912	...	...	...	...	...	1	...	...
Banks	4 913	-318	-1,649	-934	-166	702	3,876	-3,541	-5,550
Other sectors	4 914	-50	-95	185	-281	274	318	-462	-218
Assets	4 900	**11,888**	**18,454**	**23,385**	**31,899**	**53,364**	**63,425**	**83,002**	**87,504**
Monetary authorities	4 901	...	...	...	...	...	19	40	...
General government	4 902	...	...	...	...	...	1	...	...
Banks	4 903	10,982	17,693	22,635	31,296	52,759	62,284	82,566	85,493
Other sectors	4 904	907	760	750	603	605	1,121	396	2,010
Liabilities	4 905	**-12,256**	**-20,198**	**-24,134**	**-32,346**	**-52,388**	**-59,211**	**-86,966**	**-93,272**
Monetary authorities	4 906	...	...	...	...	...	...	...	...
General government	4 907	...	...	...	...	...	...	...	...
Banks	4 908	-11,300	-19,342	-23,569	-31,462	-52,057	-58,408	-86,107	-91,043
Other sectors	4 909	-956	-856	-565	-884	-331	-803	-858	-2,229

Table 2 (Concluded). STANDARD PRESENTATION, 1994–2001
(Millions of U.S. dollars)

	Code	1994	1995	1996	1997	1998	1999	2000	2001
D. OTHER INVESTMENT	4 700 . .	11,257	1,262	22,189	20,792	23,000	–6,571	18,315	–13,293
Assets	4 703 . .	**7,270**	**–8,127**	**1,582**	**–37,217**	**–56,475**	**–2,648**	**–31,906**	**–69,672**
Trade credits	4 706 . .	–482	–2,620	344	–2,310	–699	–1,127	–3,178	1,165
General government	4 707 . .	–38	–119	–379	–151	. . .	. . .	. . .	. . .
of which: Short-term	4 709 . .	. . .	. . .	. . .	. . .	. . .	. . .	. . .	. . .
Other sectors	4 710 . .	–444	–2,502	723	–2,159	–699	–1,127	–3,178	1,165
of which: Short-term	4 712 . .	*–630*	*–2,539*	*–1,400*	*–2,175*	*–684*	*–1,838*	*–3,178*	*1,165*
Loans	4 714 . .	4,586	–4,227	–117	–4,682	–8,128	–9,661	–11,314	–7,728
Monetary authorities	4 715 . .	. . .	. . .	. . .	. . .	. . .	–2,414	. . .	. . .
of which: Short-term	4 718 . .	. . .	. . .	. . .	. . .	. . .	. . .	. . .	. . .
General government	4 719 . .	340	419	375	375	341	–1,388	709	–672
of which: Short-term	4 721 . .	. . .	. . .	. . .	. . .	*30*	*–1,691*	*546*	*–874*
Banks	4 722 . .	4,000	–4,697	–711	–4,285	–5,872	–4,433	–10,192	–7,222
of which: Short-term	4 724 . .	. . .	. . .	. . .	. . .	. . .	. . .	. . .	. . .
Other sectors	4 725 . .	246	52	219	–771	–2,598	–1,426	–1,831	167
of which: Short-term	4 727 . .	*–6*	*–118*	*135*	*–357*	*–2,496*	*–1,250*	*–1,350*	*603*
Currency and deposits	4 730 . .	4,044	–586	1,827	–29,957	–47,019	8,541	–15,990	–59,222
Monetary authorities	4 731 . .	. . .	. . .	. . .	. . .	. . .	2,521	–2,877	794
General government	4 732 . .	. . .	. . .	. . .	. . .	. . .	. . .	. . .	. . .
Banks	4 733 . .	5,437	1,224	3,638	–26,956	–43,501	13,921	–7,850	–53,483
Other sectors	4 734 . .	–1,393	–1,810	–1,811	–3,001	–3,517	–7,901	–5,263	–6,533
Other assets	4 736 . .	–878	–694	–472	–268	–629	–402	–1,424	–3,887
Monetary authorities	4 737 . .	. . .	. . .	. . .	. . .	–235	. . .	. . .	. . .
of which: Short-term	4 739 . .	. . .	. . .	. . .	. . .	. . .	. . .	. . .	. . .
General government	4 740 . .	–346	–293	–265	–77	–160	–54	–177	–165
of which: Short-term	4 742 . .	. . .	. . .	. . .	. . .	. . .	. . .	. . .	. . .
Banks	4 743 . .	. . .	. . .	. . .	. . .	. . .	. . .	. . .	. . .
of which: Short-term	4 745 . .	. . .	. . .	. . .	. . .	. . .	. . .	. . .	. . .
Other sectors	4 746 . .	–533	–401	–207	–191	–234	–347	–1,247	–3,722
of which: Short-term	4 748 . .	*–513*	*–472*	*–291*	*–276*	*–332*	*–1,041*	*–1,544*	*–3,585*
Liabilities	4 753 . .	**3,988**	**9,389**	**20,607**	**58,009**	**79,475**	**–3,923**	**50,221**	**56,379**
Trade credits	4 756 . .	657	1,738	906	1,284	442	1,822	1,902	–1,171
General government	4 757 . .	. . .	. . .	. . .	. . .	. . .	. . .	. . .	. . .
of which: Short-term	4 759 . .	. . .	. . .	. . .	. . .	. . .	. . .	. . .	. . .
Other sectors	4 760 . .	657	1,738	906	1,284	442	1,822	1,902	–1,171
of which: Short-term	4 762 . .	*829*	*1,730*	*946*	*1,266*	*466*	*1,869*	*1,909*	*–1,171*
Loans	4 764 . .	731	–3,634	3,187	1,777	9,423	16,538	21,335	6,197
Monetary authorities	4 765 . .	. . .	. . .	. . .	. . .	–4	. . .	. . .	. . .
of which: Use of Fund credit and loans from the Fund	4 766 . .	. . .	. . .	. . .	. . .	. . .	. . .	. . .	. . .
of which: Short-term	4 768 . .	. . .	. . .	. . .	. . .	*–4*	. . .	. . .	. . .
General government	4 769 . .	271	39	232	25	. . .	908	78	2,539
of which: Short-term	4 771 . .	*271*	*39*	*160*	. . .	. . .	*366*	*77*	*2,497*
Banks	4 772 . .	–653	–4,715	546	883	4,514	11,740	51	–885
of which: Short-term	4 774 . .	. . .	. . .	. . .	. . .	. . .	. . .	. . .	. . .
Other sectors	4 775 . .	1,113	1,042	2,409	869	4,913	3,889	21,308	4,543
of which: Short-term	4 777 . .	*–503*	*–300*	*934*	*–327*	*1,186*	*1,461*	*3,622*	*–210*
Currency and deposits	4 780 . .	983	8,845	14,965	51,630	73,251	–21,862	21,519	53,724
Monetary authorities	4 781 . .	91	–137	–42	41	934	–410	7	8
General government	4 782 . .	777	–4	–284	–392	430	23	332	302
Banks	4 783 . .	159	8,890	15,148	51,636	56,183	–13,282	18,418	58,643
Other sectors	4 784 . .	–44	96	143	345	15,703	–8,192	2,762	–5,229
Other liabilities	4 786 . .	1,617	2,439	1,549	3,317	–3,640	–422	5,465	–2,371
Monetary authorities	4 787 . .	. . .	. . .	. . .	. . .	. . .	. . .	. . .	. . .
of which: Short-term	4 789 . .	. . .	. . .	. . .	. . .	. . .	. . .	. . .	. . .
General government	4 790 . .	103	–10	–79	–169	–147	–291	–81	–13
of which: Short-term	4 792 . .	*103*	*–10*	*–79*	*–169*	*–147*	*–291*	*–81*	*–13*
Banks	4 793 . .	1	–1	3	. . .	. . .	1	. . .	1
of which: Short-term	4 795 . .	*1*	*–1*	*3*	. . .	. . .	*1*	. . .	*1*
Other sectors	4 796 . .	1,513	2,450	1,625	3,486	–3,494	–132	5,546	–2,360
of which: Short-term	4 798 . .	*414*	*–558*	*–465*	*22*	*–87*	*18*	*321*	*402*
E. RESERVE ASSETS	4 802 . .	–500	1,913	5,691	2,708	2,339	4,611	–220	350
Monetary gold	4 812 . .	61	. . .	. . .	3,198	–1,959	640	671	237
Special drawing rights	4 811 . .	–25	–255	74	–26	–76	–132	323	–123
Reserve position in the Fund	4 810 . .	–8	–557	–155	–472	–663	316	474	–447
Foreign exchange	4 803 . .	–528	2,724	5,771	8	5,037	3,788	–1,689	683
Other claims	4 813 . .	. . .	. . .	. . .	. . .	. . .	. . .	. . .	. . .
NET ERRORS AND OMISSIONS	4 998 . .	**–5,819**	**–7,752**	**–19,696**	**–12,165**	**–832**	**–7,515**	**179**	**7,653**

Part 3 of the *Yearbook* contains descriptions of the methodologies, compilation practices, and sources used to compile these data.

Table 3. INTERNATIONAL INVESTMENT POSITION (End–period stocks), 1994–2001

(Millions of U.S. dollars)

	Code	1994	1995	1996	1997	1998	1999	2000	2001
ASSETS	8 995 C.	547,619	651,023	696,816	746,983	957,873	1,077,477	1,141,931	...
Direct investment abroad	8 505 . .	**142,953**	**172,672**	**194,026**	**198,554**	**229,000**	**264,638**	**309,708**	**...**
Equity capital and reinvested earnings	8 506 . .	104,358	130,045	143,053	143,249	155,089	168,546	189,412	...
Claims on affiliated enterprises	8 507 . .	...	...	...	...	...	...	...	...
Liabilities to affiliated enterprises	8 508 . .	...	...	...	...	...	...	...	...
Other capital	8 530 . .	38,595	42,627	50,973	55,306	73,911	96,092	120,296	...
Claims on affiliated enterprises	8 535 . .	...	...	...	...	...	...	...	...
Liabilities to affiliated enterprises	8 540 . .	...	...	...	...	...	...	...	...
Portfolio investment	8 602 . .	**119,467**	**164,012**	**204,757**	**242,157**	**363,140**	**453,076**	**474,224**	**...**
Equity securities	8 610 . .	67,258	91,747	107,708	124,066	173,149	249,426	253,589	...
Monetary authorities	8 611 . .	288	374	402	494	417	475	518	...
General government	8 612 . .	...	...	...	...	...	...	...	...
Banks	8 613 . .	461	685	631	1,311	1,891	482	2,201	...
Other sectors	8 614 . .	66,509	90,688	106,676	122,262	170,841	248,469	250,870	...
Debt securities	8 619 . .	52,209	72,265	97,049	118,091	189,991	203,649	220,635	...
Bonds and notes	8 620 . .	50,661	71,428	96,409	115,840	185,386	192,827	216,137	...
Monetary authorities	8 621 . .	231	250	172	187	223	6,464	7,240	...
General government	8 622 . .	...	...	...	...	...	...	...	...
Banks	8 623 . .	20,518	24,806	33,838	42,950	74,003	59,708	65,628	...
Other sectors	8 624 . .	29,912	46,372	62,399	72,703	111,160	126,655	143,269	...
Money market instruments	8 630 . .	1,548	837	640	2,250	4,605	10,823	4,497	...
Monetary authorities	8 631 . .	...	...	...	...	...	...	...	...
General government	8 632 . .	...	...	...	...	...	...	...	...
Banks	8 633 . .	...	...	...	...	...	...	...	...
Other sectors	8 634 . .	...	...	...	...	...	...	...	...
Financial derivatives	8 900 . .	**...**	**...**	**...**	**...**	**...**	**39,731**	**29,220**	**...**
Monetary authorities	8 901 . .	...	...	...	...	...	...	...	...
General government	8 902 . .	...	...	...	...	...	...	...	...
Banks	8 903 . .	...	...	...	...	...	38,451	28,583	...
Other sectors	8 904 . .	...	...	...	...	...	1,280	637	...
Other investment	8 703 . .	**237,295**	**267,157**	**258,385**	**273,551**	**336,186**	**300,753**	**312,323**	**...**
Trade credits	8 706 . .	15,133	17,402	17,465	19,125	20,873	21,068	22,555	...
General government	8 707 . .	908	1,029	1,391	1,517	1,527	1,500	1,490	...
of which: Short-term	8 709 . .	...	...	...	...	...	...	...	...
Other sectors	8 710 . .	14,225	16,373	16,074	17,607	19,345	19,569	21,066	...
of which: Short-term	8 712 . .	*13,683*	*15,855*	*15,526*	*17,107*	*18,808*	*18,377*	*19,946*	...
Loans	8 714 . .	40,964	45,739	43,392	43,606	50,809	53,007	61,542	...
Monetary authorities	8 715 . .	...	...	...	...	...	3,013	2,327	...
of which: Short-term	8 718 . .	...	...	...	...	...	...	...	...
General government	8 719 . .	8,085	8,435	7,576	6,701	7,451	5,881	5,334	...
of which: Short-term	8 721 . .	...	...	...	...	...	...	...	...
Banks	8 722 . .	22,865	26,774	26,102	27,348	30,790	31,203	39,817	...
of which: Short-term	8 724 . .	...	...	...	...	...	...	...	...
Other sectors	8 725 . .	10,013	10,530	9,714	9,557	12,568	12,910	14,065	...
of which: Short-term	8 727 . .	*359*	*497*	*335*	*652*	*3,164*	*4,279*	*5,469*	...
Currency and deposits	8 730 . .	148,595	168,307	163,592	180,420	231,741	194,293	196,379	...
Monetary authorities	8 731 . .	...	...	...	...	...	...	...	...
General government	8 732 . .	...	...	...	...	...	...	...	...
Banks	8 733 . .	136,187	153,055	147,948	163,545	210,473	165,906	163,828	...
Other sectors	8 734 . .	12,409	15,252	15,644	16,875	21,268	28,387	32,552	...
Other assets	8 736 . .	32,603	35,709	33,935	30,401	32,764	32,385	31,846	...
Monetary authorities	8 737 . .	...	...	...	...	252	217	201	...
of which: Short-term	8 739 . .	...	...	...	...	...	...	...	...
General government	8 740 . .	13,448	14,520	14,157	13,036	13,619	14,911	14,095	...
of which: Short-term	8 742 . .	...	...	...	...	...	...	...	...
Banks	8 743 . .	...	...	...	...	...	...	...	...
of which: Short-term	8 745 . .	...	...	...	...	...	...	...	...
Other sectors	8 746 . .	19,155	21,190	19,779	17,365	18,893	17,257	17,550	...
of which: Short-term	8 748 . .	*19,197*	*21,235*	*19,820*	*17,401*	*18,931*	*17,290*	*17,581*	...
Reserve assets	8 802 . .	**47,904**	**47,182**	**39,649**	**32,721**	**29,547**	**19,280**	**16,456**	**...**
Monetary gold	8 812 . .	13,306	13,452	12,856	7,833	9,726	9,183	7,364	...
Special drawing rights	8 811 . .	645	916	814	791	907	1,019	653	752
Reserve position in the Fund	8 810 . .	1,171	1,738	1,834	2,193	2,975	2,580	1,986	2,352
Foreign exchange	8 803 . .	32,782	31,075	24,145	21,903	15,940	6,498	6,453	...
Other claims	8 813 . .	...	...	...	...	...	...	...	...

Table 3 (Concluded). INTERNATIONAL INVESTMENT POSITION (End–period stocks), 1994–2001

(Millions of U.S. dollars)

	Code	1994	1995	1996	1997	1998	1999	2000	2001
LIABILITIES	8 995 D.	484,362	586,112	658,739	721,135	984,336	1,085,946	1,183,646	. . .
Direct investment in the Netherlands	8 555 . .	**93,409**	**116,049**	**126,543**	**122,193**	**175,757**	**189,234**	**238,329**	. . .
Equity capital and reinvested earnings	8 556 . .	61,101	73,585	79,707	77,970	101,960	109,004	127,028	. . .
Claims on direct investors	8 557 . .	. . .	. . .	. . .	. . .	. . .	. . .	. . .	. . .
Liabilities to direct investors	8 558 . .	. . .	. . .	. . .	. . .	. . .	. . .	. . .	. . .
Other capital	8 580 . .	32,308	42,464	46,836	44,223	62,513	80,230	111,301	. . .
Claims on direct investors	8 585 . .	. . .	. . .	. . .	. . .	. . .	. . .	. . .	. . .
Liabilities to direct investors	8 590 . .	. . .	. . .	. . .	. . .	. . .	. . .	. . .	. . .
Portfolio investment	8 652 . .	**176,410**	**225,266**	**276,532**	**318,336**	**445,573**	**527,482**	**562,790**	. . .
Equity securities	8 660 . .	105,239	129,955	179,628	224,692	308,671	372,914	369,572	. . .
Banks	8 663 . .	. . .	. . .	. . .	. . .	. . .	. . .	. . .	. . .
Other sectors	8 664 . .	. . .	. . .	. . .	. . .	. . .	. . .	. . .	. . .
Debt securities	8 669 . .	71,171	95,311	96,903	93,645	136,902	154,569	193,217	. . .
Bonds and notes	8 670 . .	68,700	92,371	91,247	90,815	132,803	144,285	184,900	. . .
Monetary authorities	8 671 . .	. . .	. . .	. . .	. . .	. . .	. . .	. . .	. . .
General government	8 672 . .	46,049	62,390	52,019	50,815	54,800	58,175	68,699	. . .
Banks	8 673 . .	. . .	. . .	. . .	21,390	54,455	60,866	79,458	. . .
Other sectors	8 674 . .	22,651	29,980	39,228	18,610	23,548	25,244	36,743	. . .
Money market instruments	8 680 . .	2,472	2,941	5,656	2,829	4,100	10,284	8,318	. . .
Monetary authorities	8 681 . .	. . .	. . .	. . .	. . .	. . .	. . .	. . .	. . .
General government	8 682 . .	. . .	. . .	. . .	. . .	. . .	. . .	. . .	. . .
Banks	8 683 . .	. . .	. . .	. . .	. . .	. . .	. . .	. . .	. . .
Other sectors	8 684 . .	. . .	. . .	. . .	. . .	. . .	. . .	. . .	. . .
Financial derivatives	8 905 . .	**. . .**	**. . .**	**. . .**	**. . .**	**. . .**	**30,543**	**24,440**	. . .
Monetary authorities	8 906 . .	. . .	. . .	. . .	. . .	. . .	. . .	. . .	. . .
General government	8 907 . .	. . .	. . .	. . .	. . .	. . .	. . .	. . .	. . .
Banks	8 908 . .	. . .	. . .	. . .	. . .	. . .	29,695	24,042	. . .
Other sectors	8 909 . .	. . .	. . .	. . .	. . .	. . .	848	397	. . .
Other investment	8 753 . .	**214,543**	**244,796**	**255,665**	**280,606**	**363,006**	**338,687**	**358,088**	. . .
Trade credits	8 756 . .	9,532	10,865	10,601	11,578	12,828	12,738	13,658	. . .
General government	8 757 . .	. . .	. . .	. . .	. . .	. . .	. . .	. . .	. . .
of which: Short-term	8 759 . .	. . .	. . .	. . .	. . .	. . .	. . .	. . .	. . .
Other sectors	8 760 . .	9,532	10,865	10,601	11,578	12,828	12,738	13,658	. . .
of which: Short-term	8 762 . .	*8,945*	*10,240*	*10,045*	*11,050*	*12,307*	*12,300*	*13,244*	. . .
Loans	8 764 . .	37,889	40,353	41,330	41,260	45,908	66,891	84,420	. . .
Monetary authorities	8 765 . .	. . .	. . .	. . .	. . .	. . .	. . .	. . .	. . .
of which: Use of Fund credit and loans from the Fund	8 766 . .	. . .	. . .	. . .	. . .	. . .	. . .	. . .	. . .
of which: Short-term	8 768 . .	. . .	. . .	. . .	. . .	. . .	. . .	. . .	. . .
General government	8 769 . .	304	367	561	510	545	1,344	1,372	. . .
of which: Short-term	8 771 . .	*279*	*341*	*469*	*405*	*433*	*723*	*791*	. .
Banks	8 772 . .	10,225	9,977	9,825	11,446	9,777	29,260	28,187	. . .
of which: Short-term	8 774 . .	. . .	. . .	. . .	. . .	. . .	. . .	. . .	. . .
Other sectors	8 775 . .	27,360	30,009	30,944	29,304	35,586	36,287	54,860	. . .
of which: Short-term	8 777 . .	*5,572*	*5,669*	*6,308*	*5,588*	*6,690*	*7,552*	*10,895*	. . .
Currency and deposits	8 780 . .	149,722	175,786	187,470	213,175	289,375	243,141	244,799	. . .
Monetary authorities	8 781 . .	263	141	80	64	725	3,271	115	. . .
General government	8 782 . .	803	890	543	334	627	990	1,360	. . .
Banks	8 783 . .	147,961	174,150	186,044	211,914	287,137	236,077	240,396	. . .
Other sectors	8 784 . .	695	604	803	862	887	2,804	2,927	. . .
Other liabilities	8 786 . .	17,400	17,793	16,264	14,593	14,895	15,916	15,212	. . .
Monetary authorities	8 787 . .	. . .	. . .	. . .	. . .	. . .	. . .	. . .	. . .
of which: Short-term	8 789 . .	. . .	. . .	. . .	. . .	. . .	. . .	. . .	. . .
General government	8 790 . .	9,758	10,280	9,866	9,047	9,061	10,755	10,052	. . .
of which: Short-term	8 792 . .	. . .	. . .	. . .	. . .	. . .	. . .	. . .	. . .
Banks	8 793 . .	103	110	105	91	97	83	77	. . .
of which: Short-term	8 795 . .	*103*	*110*	*105*	*91*	*97*	*83*	*77*	. . .
Other sectors	8 796 . .	7,539	7,403	6,293	5,456	5,737	5,077	5,082	. . .
of which: Short-term	8 798 . .	*7,539*	*7,403*	*6,293*	*5,456*	*5,737*	*5,077*	*5,082*	. . .
NET INTERNATIONAL INVESTMENT POSITION	8 995 . .	**63,258**	**64,911**	**38,077**	**25,848**	**–26,463**	**–8,469**	**–41,716**	. . .
Conversion rates: Netherlands guilders per U.S. dollar (end of period)	0 102 . .	**1.7351**	**1.6044**	**1.7436**	**2.0172**	**1.8888**	. . .	. . .	. . .
Conversion rates: euros per U.S. dollar (end of period)	0 104 . .	. . .	. . .	. . .	. . .	. . .	**.9954**	**1.0747**	**1.1347**

Netherlands Antilles
353

Table 1. ANALYTIC PRESENTATION, 1994–2001

(Millions of U.S. dollars)

	Code		1994	1995	1996	1997	1998	1999	2000	2001
A. Current Account [1]	4 993	Z .	**–97.9**	**127.6**	**–253.8**	**–65.1**	**–136.9**	**–331.0**	**–113.6**	**–119.8**
Goods: exports f.o.b	2 100	. .	351.1	586.5	614.6	501.4	465.6	467.0	614.7	548.9
Goods: imports f.o.b	3 100	. .	–1,271.6	–1,621.5	–1,743.7	–1,476.6	–1,513.2	–1,584.2	–1,619.2	–1,548.4
Balance on Goods	4 100	. .	*–920.5*	*–1,034.9*	*–1,129.1*	*–975.3*	*–1,047.7*	*–1,117.3*	*–1,004.5*	*–999.6*
Services: credit	2 200	. .	1,414.2	1,491.6	1,405.9	1,425.0	1,508.9	1,464.9	1,622.7	1,667.0
Services: debit	3 200	. .	–670.5	–563.3	–624.0	–574.7	–611.3	–662.0	–791.1	–823.3
Balance on Goods and Services	4 991	. .	*–176.8*	*–106.6*	*–347.3*	*–125.0*	*–150.0*	*–314.3*	*–172.9*	*–155.9*
Income: credit	2 300	. .	133.7	117.4	135.4	100.8	146.2	100.9	126.3	104.7
Income: debit	3 300	. .	–99.4	–99.4	–71.7	–54.1	–109.3	–121.4	–104.8	–88.3
Balance on Goods, Services, and Income	4 992	. .	*–142.5*	*–88.5*	*–283.5*	*–78.3*	*–113.1*	*–334.7*	*–151.5*	*–139.4*
Current transfers: credit	2 379	Z .	217.9	365.8	174.7	165.3	137.2	179.6	242.5	219.1
Current transfers: debit	3 379	. .	–173.3	–149.6	–145.0	–152.1	–160.9	–175.8	–204.6	–199.6
B. Capital Account [1]	4 994	Z .	**–.7**	**61.9**	**71.3**	**75.1**	**86.9**	**108.4**	**29.8**	**37.2**
Capital account: credit	2 994	Z .	1.0	66.8	71.9	76.9	91.3	109.8	31.3	37.8
Capital account: debit	3 994	. .	–1.7	–4.9	–.6	–1.7	–4.4	–1.5	–1.5	–.6
Total, Groups A Plus B	4 981	. .	*–98.5*	*189.5*	*–182.5*	*10.0*	*–50.0*	*–222.6*	*–83.8*	*–82.6*
C. Financial Account [1]	4 995	W .	**–2.3**	**–142.5**	**95.8**	**–31.2**	**58.0**	**123.2**	**–72.4**	**298.4**
Direct investment abroad	4 505	. .	–1.0	–1.3	.8	6.5	2.0	1.2	2.2	–.9
Direct investment in the Netherlands Antilles	4 555	Z .	21.5	–150.0	–59.8	–88.5	–52.6	–21.8	–63.1	–.4
Portfolio investment assets	4 602	. .	–69.1	–18.0	–22.3	9.2	–21.2	–7.1	–37.9	–26.3
Equity securities	4 610	. .	. . .	–15.7	–19.2	–5.4	–3.9	–3.0	–33.9	–7.2
Debt securities	4 619	. .	–69.1	–2.3	–3.1	14.6	–17.3	–4.1	–4.0	–19.1
Portfolio investment liabilities	4 652	Z .	10.9	1.1	–8.2	–.2	–.2	–3.1	.1	–.2
Equity securities	4 660	. .	. . .	. . .	. . .	. . .	. . .	. . .	. . .	. . .
Debt securities	4 669	Z .	10.9	1.1	–8.2	–.2	–.2	–3.1	.1	–.2
Financial derivatives	4 910	. .	. . .	. . .	. . .	. . .	. . .	. . .	–.1	.1
Financial derivatives assets	4 900	. .	. . .	. . .	. . .	. . .	. . .	. . .	. . .	.1
Financial derivatives liabilities	4 905	. .	. . .	. . .	. . .	. . .	. . .	. . .	–.1	. . .
Other investment assets	4 703	. .	15.3	67.1	84.6	46.1	111.7	87.9	–12.3	165.5
Monetary authorities	4 701	. .	. . .	–.8	5.1	2.8	3.9	2.6	–.1	. . .
General government	4 704	. .	. . .	2.2	7.2	2.0	4.4	. . .	–.9	. . .
Banks	4 705	. .	–55.8	–3.4	42.8	19.3	21.7	57.2	1.6	13.9
Other sectors	4 728	. .	71.1	69.1	29.4	21.9	81.7	28.1	–13.0	151.6
Other investment liabilities	4 753	W .	20.1	–41.3	100.7	–4.4	18.4	66.3	38.7	160.8
Monetary authorities	4 753	WA	. . .	. . .	. . .	. . .	. . .	. . .	1.3	. . .
General government	4 753	ZB	–38.3	–19.9	–19.9	–38.2	–51.2	–67.8	–19.1	–.2
Banks	4 753	ZC	59.7	–5.8	45.8	–5.7	–.1	3.0	40.0	93.7
Other sectors	4 753	ZD	–1.3	–15.6	74.8	39.5	69.7	131.1	16.5	67.2
Total, Groups A Through C	4 983	. .	*–100.8*	*47.0*	*–86.7*	*–21.2*	*8.0*	*–99.4*	*–156.2*	*215.8*
D. Net Errors and Omissions	4 998	. .	**24.9**	**13.4**	**14.8**	**14.9**	**17.4**	**24.6**	**38.7**	**15.0**
Total, Groups A Through D	4 984	. .	*–75.9*	*60.4*	*–71.9*	*–6.3*	*25.5*	*–74.7*	*–117.5*	*230.8*
E. Reserves and Related Items	4 802	A .	**75.9**	**–60.4**	**71.9**	**6.3**	**–25.5**	**74.7**	**117.5**	**–230.8**
Reserve assets	4 802	. .	75.9	–60.4	53.8	–27.8	–75.6	8.3	47.8	–231.9
Use of Fund credit and loans	4 766	. .	. . .	. . .	. . .	. . .	. . .	. . .	. . .	. . .
Exceptional financing	4 920	. .	. . .	. . .	18.1	34.1	50.2	66.5	69.7	1.1
Conversion rates: Netherlands Antillean guilders per U.S. dollar	0 101	. .	**1.7900**	**1.7900**	**1.7900**	**1.7900**	**1.7900**	**1.7900**	**1.7900**	**1.7900**

[1] Excludes components that have been classified in the categories of Group E.

Table 2. STANDARD PRESENTATION, 1994–2001
(Millions of U.S. dollars)

	Code	1994	1995	1996	1997	1998	1999	2000	2001
CURRENT ACCOUNT	4 993 . .	**–97.9**	**127.6**	**–253.8**	**–65.1**	**–136.9**	**–331.0**	**–113.6**	**–119.8**
A. GOODS	4 100 . .	–920.5	–1,034.9	–1,129.1	–975.3	–1,047.7	–1,117.3	–1,004.5	–999.6
Credit	2 100 . .	**351.1**	**586.5**	**614.6**	**501.4**	**465.6**	**467.0**	**614.7**	**548.9**
General merchandise: exports f.o.b.	2 110 . .	245.2	443.2	441.8	331.5	319.1	298.3	360.2	307.5
Goods for processing: exports f.o.b.	2 150 . .	. . .	4.2	3.9	3.7	6.9	11.1	6.6	9.2
Repairs on goods	2 160 . .	. . .	35.9	35.3	42.0	39.0	32.4	39.8	38.9
Goods procured in ports by carriers	2 170 . .	105.9	103.2	133.6	124.3	100.6	125.1	208.0	193.2
Nonmonetary gold	2 180 . .	. . .	. . .	. . .	. . .	. . .	. . .	. . .	. . .
Debit	3 100 . .	**–1,271.6**	**–1,621.5**	**–1,743.7**	**–1,476.6**	**–1,513.2**	**–1,584.2**	**–1,619.2**	**–1,548.4**
General merchandise: imports f.o.b.	3 110 . .	–1,271.6	–1,570.3	–1,699.9	–1,440.5	–1,486.0	–1,549.4	–1,573.4	–1,511.7
Goods for processing: imports f.o.b.	3 150 . .	. . .	–40.2	–32.1	–23.4	–17.0	–19.7	–36.6	–29.7
Repairs on goods	3 160 . .	. . .	–5.8	–5.2	–6.4	–5.6	–8.5	–1.1	. . .
Goods procured in ports by carriers	3 170 . .	. . .	–5.1	–6.5	–6.4	–4.6	–6.6	–8.1	–7.1
Nonmonetary gold	3 180 . .	. . .	. . .	. . .	. . .	. . .	. . .	. . .	. . .
B. SERVICES	4 200 . .	743.7	928.3	781.8	850.2	897.7	803.0	831.6	843.7
Total credit	2 200 . .	*1,414.2*	*1,491.6*	*1,405.9*	*1,425.0*	*1,508.9*	*1,464.9*	*1,622.7*	*1,667.0*
Total debit	3 200 . .	*–670.5*	*–563.3*	*–624.0*	*–574.7*	*–611.3*	*–662.0*	*–791.1*	*–823.3*
Transportation services, credit	2 205 . .	**219.7**	**175.0**	**174.8**	**173.4**	**177.7**	**168.6**	**162.6**	**176.6**
Passenger	2 850 . .	*65.9*	*49.4*	*58.3*	*54.7*	*57.7*	*65.9*	*63.0*	*69.0*
Freight	2 851 . .	. . .	*3.6*	*2.8*	*3.4*	*2.8*	*3.5*	*2.1*	*3.5*
Other	2 852 . .	*153.8*	*122.0*	*113.7*	*115.3*	*117.2*	*99.2*	*97.4*	*104.1*
Sea transport, passenger	2 207 . .	. . .	1.1	1.6	3.1	4.0	4.7	.8	2.1
Sea transport, freight	2 208 . .	. . .	. . .	. . .	. . .	. . .	. . .	. . .	. . .
Sea transport, other	2 209 . .	. . .	121.4	113.6	115.0	116.4	97.7	90.7	98.5
Air transport, passenger	2 211 . .	. . .	48.3	56.8	51.7	53.6	61.2	62.2	66.9
Air transport, freight	2 212 . .	. . .	3.6	2.8	3.4	2.8	3.5	2.1	3.5
Air transport, other	2 213 . .	. . .	.6	.1	.3	.8	1.5	6.8	5.6
Other transport, passenger	2 215 . .	. . .	. . .	. . .	. . .	. . .	. . .	. . .	. . .
Other transport, freight	2 216 . .	. . .	. . .	. . .	. . .	. . .	. . .	. . .	. . .
Other transport, other	2 217 . .	. . .	. . .	. . .	. . .	. . .	. . .	. . .	. . .
Transportation services, debit	3 205 . .	**–203.2**	**–69.2**	**–84.3**	**–78.4**	**–94.3**	**–102.3**	**–104.7**	**–104.8**
Passenger	3 850 . .	*–8.0*	*–10.4*	*–19.6*	*–21.3*	*–19.9*	*–19.6*	*–39.4*	*–47.7*
Freight	3 851 . .	*–135.6*	*–40.4*	*–43.8*	*–37.1*	*–38.3*	*–53.5*	*–40.6*	*–38.9*
Other	3 852 . .	*–59.7*	*–18.4*	*–20.9*	*–20.0*	*–36.1*	*–29.3*	*–24.6*	*–18.2*
Sea transport, passenger	3 207 . .	. . .	–.7	–1.1	–.5	–.4	–.4	–2.1	–.2
Sea transport, freight	3 208 . .	. . .	–36.4	–39.4	–33.4	–34.4	–43.1	–36.5	–35.0
Sea transport, other	3 209 . .	. . .	–13.5	–14.7	–9.7	–19.2	–14.9	–9.2	–8.2
Air transport, passenger	3 211 . .	. . .	–9.7	–18.4	–20.8	–19.6	–19.1	–37.4	–47.5
Air transport, freight	3 212 . .	. . .	–4.0	–4.4	–3.7	–3.9	–10.4	–4.1	–3.9
Air transport, other	3 213 . .	. . .	–4.9	–6.2	–10.3	–16.9	–14.4	–15.4	–10.0
Other transport, passenger	3 215 . .	. . .	. . .	. . .	. . .	. . .	. . .	. . .	. . .
Other transport, freight	3 216 . .	. . .	. . .	. . .	. . .	. . .	. . .	. . .	. . .
Other transport, other	3 217 . .	. . .	. . .	. . .	. . .	. . .	. . .	. . .	. . .
Travel, credit	2 236 . .	**637.8**	**693.5**	**631.3**	**711.8**	**814.6**	**703.5**	**764.3**	**764.0**
Business travel	2 237 . .	637.8	. . .	. . .	. . .	. . .	. . .	. . .	. . .
Personal travel	2 240 . .	. . .	693.5	631.3	711.8	814.6	703.5	764.3	764.0
Travel, debit	3 236 . .	**–206.0**	**–221.9**	**–254.7**	**–254.6**	**–258.7**	**–306.5**	**–304.8**	**–306.8**
Business travel	3 237 . .	–206.0	. . .	. . .	. . .	. . .	. . .	. . .	. . .
Personal travel	3 240 . .	. . .	–221.9	–254.7	254.6	–258.7	–306.5	–304.8	–306.8
Other services, credit	2 200 BA	**556.7**	**623.2**	**599.7**	**539.8**	**516.7**	**592.8**	**695.9**	**726.4**
Communications	2 245 . .	. . .	33.0	17.9	12.1	8.3	12.1	17.7	20.6
Construction	2 249 . .	. . .	14.6	14.6	15.6	19.8	40.6	34.0	50.2
Insurance	2 253 . .	. . .	1.9	2.5	2.9	4.2	3.9	3.9	7.8
Financial	2 260 . .	. . .	6.5	7.7	5.8	5.3	4.4	14.4	8.7
Computer and information	2 262 . .	. . .	8.1	6.2	4.8	3.5	4.2	1.9	1.5
Royalties and licence fees	2 266 . .	.1	2.8	4.5	4.1	5.0	6.2	6.4	2.7
Other business services	2 268 . .	524.2	528.0	516.6	458.5	454.5	506.6	594.6	588.3
Personal, cultural, and recreational	2 287 . .	. . .	1.5	1.7	2.0	1.9	2.2	1.6	.6
Government, n.i.e.	2 291 . .	32.5	26.8	28.0	34.0	14.2	12.6	21.3	46.1
Other services, debit	3 200 BA	**–261.3**	**–272.2**	**–285.0**	**–241.7**	**–258.3**	**–253.1**	**–381.6**	**–411.7**
Communications	3 245 . .	. . .	–15.5	–2.9	–5.9	–8.0	–2.5	–16.8	–18.7
Construction	3 249 . .	. . .	–1.7	–.9	–4.4	–1.7	–4.5	–31.7	–55.1
Insurance	3 253 . .	–15.1	–19.3	–19.7	–17.2	–18.4	–17.8	–18.2	–31.1
Financial	3 260 . .	. . .	–4.3	–5.3	–4.7	–3.8	–1.8	–5.6	–6.1
Computer and information	3 262 . .	. . .	–2.4	–4.7	–2.5	–3.0	–4.2	–13.5	–5.0
Royalties and licence fees	3 266 . .	–.8	–3.9	–5.1	–5.4	–6.8	–5.6	–4.1	–4.7
Other business services	3 268 . .	–239.5	–224.0	–245.0	–199.4	–214.5	–213.4	–286.9	–287.1
Personal, cultural, and recreational	3 287 . .	. . .	–1.1	–1.3	–2.2	–2.2	–2.8	–1.1	–.6
Government, n.i.e.	3 291 . .	–5.9	. . .	–.1	. . .	. . .	–.3	–3.8	–3.2

Table 2 (Continued). STANDARD PRESENTATION, 1994–2001

(Millions of U.S. dollars)

	Code	1994	1995	1996	1997	1998	1999	2000	2001
C. INCOME	4 300 . .	34.2	18.0	63.7	46.7	36.9	–20.4	21.5	16.5
Total credit	2 300 . .	*133.7*	*117.4*	*135.4*	*100.8*	*146.2*	*100.9*	*126.3*	*104.7*
Total debit	3 300 . .	*–99.4*	*–99.4*	*–71.7*	*–54.1*	*–109.3*	*–121.4*	*–104.8*	*–88.3*
Compensation of employees, credit	2 310 . .	**8.3**	**6.5**	**13.0**	**5.8**	**5.3**	**3.9**	**6.8**	**8.0**
Compensation of employees, debit	3 310 . .	**–16.8**	**–3.4**	**–5.7**	**–7.0**	**–42.6**	**–69.8**	**–37.5**	**–36.8**
Investment income, credit	2 320 . .	**125.4**	**110.9**	**122.4**	**95.0**	**140.9**	**97.0**	**119.5**	**96.8**
Direct investment income	2 330 . .	14.5	2.9	13.4	5.9	19.8	4.6	1.8	6.2
Dividends and distributed branch profits	2 332 . .	13.7	2.3	13.0	5.7	19.7	4.5	.8	3.7
Reinvested earnings and undistributed branch profits	2 333 . .	.8	.6	.3	.1	. . .	. . .	.1	.4
Income on debt (interest)	2 334 . .	. . .	.1	.1	.1	.1	.1	.9	2.1
Portfolio investment income	2 339 . .	. . .	78.4	73.5	64.2	89.6	72.3	70.8	68.5
Income on equity	2 340 . .	. . .	10.9	10.1	12.8	31.7	27.4	14.5	15.3
Income on bonds and notes	2 350 . .	. . .	. . .	. . .	. . .	. . .	. . .	. . .	. . .
Income on money market instruments	2 360 . .	. . .	67.5	63.5	51.3	57.9	45.0	56.3	53.2
Other investment income	2 370 . .	110.8	29.6	35.5	24.9	31.5	20.1	46.9	22.0
Investment income, debit	3 320 . .	**–82.7**	**–96.0**	**–66.0**	**–47.0**	**–66.8**	**–51.6**	**–67.3**	**–51.5**
Direct investment income	3 330 . .	–41.8	–47.7	–27.7	–24.9	–23.6	–27.0	–4.0	–4.3
Dividends and distributed branch profits	3 332 . .	–20.7	–47.3	–27.7	–24.1	–22.7	–25.8	–.9	–.5
Reinvested earnings and undistributed branch profits	3 333 . .	–21.1	. . .	. . .	. . .	–.8	–1.1	–.5	–.9
Income on debt (interest)	3 334 . .	. . .	–.3	–.1	–.8	–.1	–.2	–2.6	–2.8
Portfolio investment income	3 339 . .	. . .	–14.9	–15.4	–9.1	–21.3	–16.1	–25.3	–23.2
Income on equity	3 340 . .	. . .	–12.0	–13.7	–6.9	–15.3	–9.2	–24.5	–21.6
Income on bonds and notes	3 350 . .	. . .	. . .	. . .	. . .	. . .	. . .	. . .	. . .
Income on money market instruments	3 360 . .	. . .	–3.0	–1.7	–2.1	–6.0	–6.9	–.8	–1.6
Other investment income	3 370 . .	–40.9	–33.4	–22.8	–13.1	–21.8	–8.5	–38.0	–24.0
D. CURRENT TRANSFERS	4 379 . .	44.6	216.1	29.7	13.2	–23.8	3.7	37.9	19.6
Credit	2 379 . .	**217.9**	**365.8**	**174.7**	**165.3**	**137.2**	**179.6**	**242.5**	**219.1**
General government	2 380 . .	127.2	142.7	93.0	82.4	65.5	70.4	76.3	59.4
Other sectors	2 390 . .	90.7	223.1	81.7	82.9	71.7	109.1	166.2	159.7
Workers' remittances	2 391 . .	. . .	3.6	9.0	11.6	9.6	15.9	5.6	12.2
Other current transfers	2 392 . .	90.7	219.5	72.7	71.3	62.1	93.2	160.6	147.5
Debit	3 379 . .	**–173.3**	**–149.6**	**–145.0**	**–152.1**	**–160.9**	**–175.8**	**–204.6**	**–199.6**
General government	3 380 . .	. . .	–28.2	–24.8	–19.9	–23.4	–20.1	–10.4	–9.6
Other sectors	3 390 . .	–173.3	–121.4	–120.2	–132.2	–137.5	–155.7	–194.2	–189.9
Workers' remittances	3 391 . .	. . .	–5.6	–7.5	–11.7	–12.6	–19.3	–8.9	–11.7
Other current transfers	3 392 . .	–173.3	–115.8	–112.7	–120.5	–124.9	–136.4	–185.3	–178.2
CAPITAL AND FINANCIAL ACCOUNT	4 996 . .	**73.0**	**–141.0**	**239.0**	**50.2**	**119.5**	**306.4**	**74.9**	**104.8**
CAPITAL ACCOUNT	4 994 . .	**–.7**	**61.9**	**71.3**	**75.1**	**86.9**	**108.4**	**29.8**	**37.2**
Total credit	2 994 . .	*1.0*	*66.8*	*71.9*	*76.9*	*91.3*	*109.8*	*31.3*	*37.8*
Total debit	3 994 . .	*–1.7*	*–4.9*	*–.6*	*–1.7*	*–4.4*	*–1.5*	*–1.5*	*–.6*
Capital transfers, credit	2 400 . .	**1.0**	**66.8**	**71.9**	**76.9**	**91.3**	**109.8**	**31.3**	**37.8**
General government	2 401 . .	. . .	65.4	69.7	74.6	89.3	107.7	31.1	33.7
Debt forgiveness	2 402 . .	. . .	. . .	. . .	. . .	. . .	. . .	. . .	33.7
Other capital transfers	2 410 . .	. . .	65.4	69.7	74.6	89.3	107.7	31.1	. . .
Other sectors	2 430 . .	1.0	1.3	2.2	2.2	2.0	2.2	.2	4.1
Migrants' transfers	2 431 . .	1.0	1.3	2.2	1.2	2.0	2.0	.1	3.9
Debt forgiveness	2 432 . .	. . .	. . .	. . .	. . .	. . .	. . .	. . .	. . .
Other capital transfers	2 440 . .	. . .	. . .	. . .	1.0	. . .	.2	.1	.2
Capital transfers, debit	3 400 . .	**–1.7**	**–4.9**	**–.6**	**–1.7**	**–4.4**	**–1.5**	**–1.5**	**–.6**
General government	3 401 . .	. . .	–2.7	–.1	. . .	. . .	. . .	. . .	. . .
Debt forgiveness	3 402 . .	. . .	. . .	. . .	. . .	. . .	. . .	. . .	. . .
Other capital transfers	3 410 . .	. . .	–2.7	–.1	. . .	. . .	. . .	. . .	. . .
Other sectors	3 430 . .	–1.7	–2.2	–.4	–1.7	–4.4	–1.5	–1.5	–.6
Migrants' transfers	3 431 . .	–1.7	–2.2	–.4	–1.7	–4.4	–1.5	–1.2	–.3
Debt forgiveness	3 432 . .	. . .	. . .	. . .	. . .	. . .	. . .	. . .	. . .
Other capital transfers	3 440 . .	. . .	. . .	. . .	. . .	. . .	. . .	–.3	–.3
Nonproduced nonfinancial assets, credit	2 480 . .	**. . .**	**. . .**	**. . .**	**. . .**	**. . .**	**. . .**	**. . .**	**. . .**
Nonproduced nonfinancial assets, debit	3 480 . .	**. . .**	**. . .**	**. . .**	**. . .**	**. . .**	**. . .**	**. . .**	**. . .**

Table 2 (Continued). STANDARD PRESENTATION, 1994–2001

(Millions of U.S. dollars)

	Code	1994	1995	1996	1997	1998	1999	2000	2001
FINANCIAL ACCOUNT	4 995 . .	**73.6**	**–202.9**	**167.7**	**–24.9**	**32.6**	**198.0**	**45.1**	**67.6**
A. DIRECT INVESTMENT	4 500 . .	20.5	–151.3	–59.0	–82.0	–50.6	–20.7	–60.9	–1.3
Direct investment abroad	4 505 . .	**–1.0**	**–1.3**	**.8**	**6.5**	**2.0**	**1.2**	**2.2**	**–.9**
Equity capital	4 510 . .	–.2	.4	1.1	4.9	.5	1.0	. . .	. . .
Claims on affiliated enterprises	4 515 . .	. . .	.8	1.7	5.5	.9	1.3	. . .	.1
Liabilities to affiliated enterprises	4 520 . .	. . .	–.4	–.6	–.6	–.4	–.3	. . .	–.1
Reinvested earnings	4 525 . .	–.8	–.6	–.3	–.1	. . .	. . .	–.1	–.4
Other capital	4 530 . .	. . .	–1.2	. . .	1.7	1.5	.2	2.2	–.4
Claims on affiliated enterprises	4 535 . .	. . .	.8	. . .	1.7	1.5	.2	2.5	. . .
Liabilities to affiliated enterprises	4 540 . .	. . .	–2.1	. . .	. . .	. . .	. . .	–.2	–.4
Direct investment in the Netherlands Antilles	4 555 . .	**21.5**	**–150.0**	**–59.8**	**–88.5**	**–52.6**	**–21.8**	**–63.1**	**–.4**
Equity capital	4 560 . .	7.8	–.1	5.8	9.2	7.7	7.5	8.4	33.2
Claims on direct investors	4 565 . .	. . .	10.4	10.8	11.6	11.3	11.7	17.3	42.7
Liabilities to direct investors	4 570 . .	. . .	–10.6	–5.0	–2.5	–3.7	–4.1	–8.8	–9.6
Reinvested earnings	4 575 . .	21.1	. . .	. . .	. . .	.8	1.1	.5	.9
Other capital	4 580 . .	–7.4	–149.9	–65.6	–97.7	–61.1	–30.4	–72.0	–34.6
Claims on direct investors	4 585 . .	. . .	46.9	75.6	59.3	66.0	67.4	76.4	84.0
Liabilities to direct investors	4 590 . .	. . .	–196.8	–141.3	–157.0	–127.1	–97.9	–148.4	–118.5
B. PORTFOLIO INVESTMENT	4 600 . .	–58.2	–16.9	–30.6	9.0	–21.4	–10.2	–37.9	–26.5
Assets	4 602 . .	**–69.1**	**–18.0**	**–22.3**	**9.2**	**–21.2**	**–7.1**	**–37.9**	**–26.3**
Equity securities	4 610 . .	. . .	–15.7	–19.2	–5.4	–3.9	–3.0	–33.9	–7.2
Monetary authorities	4 611 . .	. . .	. . .	. . .	. . .	. . .	. . .	. . .	. . .
General government	4 612 . .	. . .	. . .	. . .	. . .	. . .	. . .	. . .	. . .
Banks	4 613 . .	. . .	. . .	. . .	. . .	. . .	. . .	–.1	. . .
Other sectors	4 614 . .	. . .	–15.7	–19.2	–5.4	–3.9	–3.0	–33.9	–7.2
Debt securities	4 619 . .	–69.1	–2.3	–3.1	14.6	–17.3	–4.1	–4.0	–19.1
Bonds and notes	4 620 . .	–69.1	3.6	3.9	2.0	3.1	2.5	6.7	–7.8
Monetary authorities	4 621 . .	. . .	. . .	. . .	. . .	. . .	. . .	. . .	. . .
General government	4 622 . .	. . .	. . .	. . .	. . .	. . .	. . .	. . .	. . .
Banks	4 623 . .	. . .	. . .	. . .	. . .	. . .	. . .	–.5	. . .
Other sectors	4 624 . .	. . .	3.6	3.9	2.0	3.1	2.5	7.2	–7.8
Money market instruments	4 630 . .	. . .	–5.9	–7.0	12.6	–20.4	–6.6	–10.7	–11.3
Monetary authorities	4 631 . .	. . .	. . .	. . .	. . .	. . .	. . .	. . .	. . .
General government	4 632 . .	. . .	. . .	. . .	. . .	. . .	. . .	. . .	. . .
Banks	4 633 . .	. . .	. . .	. . .	. . .	. . .	. . .	. . .	–.1
Other sectors	4 634 . .	. . .	–5.9	–7.0	12.6	–20.4	–6.6	–10.7	–11.2
Liabilities	4 652 . .	**10.9**	**1.1**	**–8.2**	**–.2**	**–.2**	**–3.1**	**.1**	**–.2**
Equity securities	4 660 . .	. . .	. . .	. . .	. . .	. . .	. . .	. . .	. . .
Banks	4 663 . .	. . .	. . .	. . .	. . .	. . .	. . .	. . .	. . .
Other sectors	4 664 . .	. . .	. . .	. . .	. . .	. . .	. . .	. . .	. . .
Debt securities	4 669 . .	10.9	1.1	–8.2	–.2	–.2	–3.1	.1	–.2
Bonds and notes	4 670 . .	10.9	. . .	. . .	. . .	. . .	. . .	–1.3	–.4
Monetary authorities	4 671 . .	. . .	. . .	. . .	. . .	. . .	. . .	. . .	. . .
General government	4 672 . .	. . .	. . .	. . .	. . .	. . .	. . .	–1.3	–.6
Banks	4 673 . .	. . .	. . .	. . .	. . .	. . .	. . .	. . .	.2
Other sectors	4 674 . .	10.9	. . .	. . .	. . .	. . .	. . .	. . .	. . .
Money market instruments	4 680 . .	. . .	1.1	–8.2	–.2	–.2	–3.1	1.4	.2
Monetary authorities	4 681 . .	. . .	. . .	. . .	. . .	. . .	. . .	. . .	. . .
General government	4 682 . .	. . .	1.7	. . .	. . .	. . .	. . .	.1	.1
Banks	4 683 . .	. . .	. . .	. . .	. . .	. . .	. . .	. . .	. . .
Other sectors	4 684 . .	. . .	–.6	–8.2	–.2	–.2	–3.1	1.3	.1
C. FINANCIAL DERIVATIVES	4 910 . .	. . .	. . .	. . .	. . .	. . .	. . .	–.1	.1
Monetary authorities	4 911 . .	. . .	. . .	. . .	. . .	. . .	. . .	. . .	. . .
General government	4 912 . .	. . .	. . .	. . .	. . .	. . .	. . .	. . .	. . .
Banks	4 913 . .	. . .	. . .	. . .	. . .	. . .	. . .	–.1	. . .
Other sectors	4 914 . .	. . .	. . .	. . .	. . .	. . .	. . .	. . .	.1
Assets	4 900 . .	**. . .**	**. . .**	**. . .**	**. . .**	**. . .**	**. . .**	**. . .**	**.1**
Monetary authorities	4 901 . .	. . .	. . .	. . .	. . .	. . .	. . .	. . .	. . .
General government	4 902 . .	. . .	. . .	. . .	. . .	. . .	. . .	. . .	. . .
Banks	4 903 . .	. . .	. . .	. . .	. . .	. . .	. . .	. . .	. . .
Other sectors	4 904 . .	. . .	. . .	. . .	. . .	. . .	. . .	. . .	.1
Liabilities	4 905 . .	**. . .**	**. . .**	**. . .**	**. . .**	**. . .**	**. . .**	**–.1**	**. . .**
Monetary authorities	4 906 . .	. . .	. . .	. . .	. . .	. . .	. . .	. . .	. . .
General government	4 907 . .	. . .	. . .	. . .	. . .	. . .	. . .	. . .	. . .
Banks	4 908 . .	. . .	. . .	. . .	. . .	. . .	. . .	–.1	. . .
Other sectors	4 909 . .	. . .	. . .	. . .	. . .	. . .	. . .	. . .	. . .

Table 2 (Concluded). STANDARD PRESENTATION, 1994–2001

(Millions of U.S. dollars)

	Code	1994	1995	1996	1997	1998	1999	2000	2001
D. OTHER INVESTMENT	4 700 . .	35.4	25.8	203.4	75.8	180.2	220.6	96.1	327.3
Assets	4 703 . .	**15.3**	**67.1**	**84.6**	**46.1**	**111.7**	**87.9**	**–12.3**	**165.5**
Trade credits	4 706 . .	. . .	11.8	18.7	25.0	35.2	27.1	–13.7	115.9
General government	4 707 . .	. . .	. . .	. . .	. . .	. . .	. . .	. . .	. . .
of which: Short-term	4 709 . .	. . .	. . .	. . .	. . .	. . .	. . .	. . .	. . .
Other sectors	4 710 . .	. . .	11.8	18.7	25.0	35.2	27.1	–13.7	115.9
of which: Short-term	4 712 . .	. . .	*13.7*	*19.4*	*26.4*	*40.7*	*25.4*	*–14.5*	*114.4*
Loans	4 714 . .	1.3	–1.6	2.3	3.2	2.4	2.8	3.2	8.1
Monetary authorities	4 715 . .	. . .	. . .	. . .	. . .	. . .	. . .	–.1	. . .
of which: Short-term	4 718 . .	. . .	. . .	. . .	. . .	. . .	. . .	. . .	. . .
General government	4 719 . .	. . .	. . .	. . .	. . .	. . .	. . .	. . .	. . .
of which: Short-term	4 721 . .	. . .	. . .	. . .	. . .	. . .	. . .	. . .	. . .
Banks	4 722 . .	. . .	. . .	. . .	. . .	. . .	. . .	–.1	5.9
of which: Short-term	4 724 . .	. . .	. . .	. . .	. . .	. . .	. . .	. . .	. . .
Other sectors	4 725 . .	1.3	–1.6	2.3	3.2	2.4	2.8	3.3	2.2
of which: Short-term	4 727 . .	. . .	*–1.6*	*2.3*	*3.2*	*2.4*	*2.8*	*.3*	*.1*
Currency and deposits	4 730 . .	14.0	27.0	23.2	22.0	11.3	–13.9	11.8	10.7
Monetary authorities	4 731 . .	. . .	. . .	. . .	. . .	. . .	. . .	. . .	. . .
General government	4 732 . .	. . .	. . .	. . .	. . .	. . .	. . .	. . .	. . .
Banks	4 733 . .	–55.8	. . .	. . .	. . .	. . .	. . .	. . .	. . .
Other sectors	4 734 . .	69.8	27.0	23.2	22.0	11.3	–13.9	11.8	10.7
Other assets	4 736 . .	. . .	29.9	40.5	–4.1	62.7	71.8	–13.5	30.8
Monetary authorities	4 737 . .	. . .	–.8	5.1	2.8	3.9	2.6	. . .	. . .
of which: Short-term	4 739 . .	. . .	*–.8*	*5.1*	*2.8*	*3.9*	*2.6*	. . .	. . .
General government	4 740 . .	. . .	2.2	7.2	2.0	4.4	. . .	–.9	. . .
of which: Short-term	4 742 . .	. . .	*2.2*	*7.2*	*2.0*	*4.4*	. . .	*–.9*	. . .
Banks	4 743 . .	. . .	–3.4	42.8	19.3	21.7	57.2	1.7	8.0
of which: Short-term	4 745 . .	. . .	*–3.4*	*42.8*	*19.3*	*21.7*	*57.2*	*3.7*	*7.0*
Other sectors	4 746 . .	. . .	31.9	–14.7	–28.3	32.8	12.1	–14.3	22.8
of which: Short-term	4 748 . .	. . .	*17.7*	*–29.2*	*–32.8*	*10.8*	*2.5*	*–2.9*	*20.3*
Liabilities	4 753 . .	**20.1**	**–41.3**	**118.8**	**29.7**	**68.5**	**132.7**	**108.4**	**161.8**
Trade credits	4 756 . .	. . .	1.8	40.4	11.2	75.5	74.2	–6.4	–25.1
General government	4 757 . .	. . .	. . .	. . .	. . .	. . .	. . .	. . .	. . .
of which: Short-term	4 759 . .	. . .	. . .	. . .	. . .	. . .	. . .	. . .	. . .
Other sectors	4 760 . .	. . .	1.8	40.4	11.2	75.5	74.2	–6.4	–25.1
of which: Short-term	4 762 . .	. . .	*9.3*	*32.1*	*16.8*	*66.9*	*89.2*	*–5.7*	*–25.3*
Loans	4 764 . .	–38.1	–45.7	31.5	–24.7	–46.6	–62.1	63.8	39.2
Monetary authorities	4 765 . .	. . .	. . .	. . .	. . .	. . .	. . .	1.3	. . .
of which: Use of Fund credit and loans from the Fund	4 766 . .	. . .	. . .	. . .	. . .	. . .	. . .	. . .	. . .
of which: Short-term	4 768 . .	. . .	. . .	. . .	. . .	. . .	. . .	*1.3*	. . .
General government	4 769 . .	–38.3	–19.9	–19.9	–38.2	–51.2	–67.8	63.6	–.2
of which: Short-term	4 771 . .	. . .	. . .	. . .	. . .	. . .	. . .	. . .	. . .
Banks	4 772 . .	3.9	–5.8	45.8	–5.7	–.1	3.0	35.0	32.1
of which: Short-term	4 774 . .	. . .	. . .	. . .	. . .	. . .	. . .	. . .	. . .
Other sectors	4 775 . .	–3.7	–20.0	5.6	19.2	4.6	2.7	–36.1	7.3
of which: Short-term	4 777 . .	. . .	. . .	. . .	. . .	. . .	. . .	*–3.9*	*–12.7*
Currency and deposits	4 780 . .	55.8	. . .	. . .	. . .	. . .	. . .	. . .	. . .
Monetary authorities	4 781 . .	. . .	. . .	. . .	. . .	. . .	. . .	. . .	. . .
General government	4 782 . .	. . .	. . .	. . .	. . .	. . .	. . .	. . .	. . .
Banks	4 783 . .	55.8	. . .	. . .	. . .	. . .	. . .	. . .	. . .
Other sectors	4 784 . .	. . .	. . .	. . .	. . .	. . .	. . .	. . .	. . .
Other liabilities	4 786 . .	2.5	2.6	46.9	43.2	39.7	120.7	51.1	147.7
Monetary authorities	4 787 . .	. . .	. . .	. . .	. . .	. . .	. . .	. . .	. . .
of which: Short-term	4 789 . .	. . .	. . .	. . .	. . .	. . .	. . .	. . .	. . .
General government	4 790 . .	. . .	. . .	18.1	34.1	50.2	66.5	–13.0	1.1
of which: Short-term	4 792 . .	. . .	. . .	*18.1*	*34.1*	*50.2*	*66.5*	*6.6*	*1.1*
Banks	4 793 . .	. . .	. . .	. . .	. . .	. . .	. . .	5.0	61.7
of which: Short-term	4 795 . .	. . .	. . .	. . .	. . .	. . .	. . .	*4.2*	*–2.0*
Other sectors	4 796 . .	2.5	2.6	28.8	9.2	–10.4	54.2	59.0	85.0
of which: Short-term	4 798 . .	. . .	*5.0*	*30.9*	*13.7*	*–10.3*	*47.3*	*65.5*	*98.4*
E. RESERVE ASSETS	4 802 . .	75.9	–60.4	53.8	–27.8	–75.6	8.3	47.8	–231.9
Monetary gold	4 812 . .	. . .	. . .	. . .	. . .	. . .	. . .	. . .	. . .
Special drawing rights	4 811 . .	. . .	. . .	. . .	. . .	. . .	. . .	. . .	. . .
Reserve position in the Fund	4 810 . .	. . .	. . .	. . .	. . .	. . .	. . .	. . .	. . .
Foreign exchange	4 803 . .	55.2	–60.4	53.8	–27.8	–75.6	8.3	47.8	–231.9
Other claims	4 813 . .	20.7	. . .	. . .	. . .	. . .	. . .	. . .	. . .
NET ERRORS AND OMISSIONS	4 998 . .	**24.9**	**13.4**	**14.8**	**14.9**	**17.4**	**24.6**	**38.7**	**15.0**

Part 3 of the *Yearbook* contains descriptions of the methodologies, compilation practices, and sources used to compile these data.

Table 1. ANALYTIC PRESENTATION, 1994–2001

(Millions of U.S. dollars)

	Code	1994	1995	1996	1997	1998	1999	2000	2001
A. Current Account [1]	4 993 Z.	**–2,384**	**–3,003**	**–3,883**	**–4,301**	**–2,110**	**–3,488**	**–2,675**	**–1,403**
Goods: exports f.o.b	2 100 . .	12,176	13,554	14,338	14,282	12,246	12,657	13,530	13,920
Goods: imports f.o.b	3 100 . .	–10,769	–12,584	–13,815	–13,380	–11,333	–13,028	–12,848	–12,446
Balance on Goods	4 100 . .	*1,408*	*971*	*523*	*903*	*912*	*–371*	*681*	*1,474*
Services: credit	2 200 . .	3,667	4,481	4,519	4,072	3,572	4,194	4,359	4,344
Services: debit	3 200 . .	–4,101	–4,694	–4,755	–4,718	–4,323	–4,387	–4,467	–4,217
Balance on Goods and Services	4 991 . .	*973*	*757*	*288*	*257*	*161*	*–564*	*574*	*1,601*
Income: credit	2 300 . .	358	940	372	393	880	919	601	569
Income: debit	3 300 . .	–4,045	–4,895	–5,085	–5,249	–3,493	–4,037	–4,074	–3,714
Balance on Goods, Services, and Income	4 992 . .	*–2,713*	*–3,198*	*–4,426*	*–4,599*	*–2,452*	*–3,683*	*–2,900*	*–1,544*
Current transfers: credit	2 379 Z.	638	558	897	680	681	609	634	576
Current transfers: debit	3 379 . .	–309	–363	–354	–383	–339	–415	–409	–435
B. Capital Account [1]	4 994 Z.	**617**	**1,224**	**1,335**	**236**	**–183**	**–218**	**–182**	**439**
Capital account: credit	2 994 Z.	995	1,652	1,838	777	260	259	236	818
Capital account: debit	3 994 . .	–379	–427	–502	–541	–444	–477	–418	–379
Total, Groups A Plus B	4 981 . .	*–1,768*	*–1,779*	*–2,548*	*–4,065*	*–2,293*	*–3,707*	*–2,857*	*–964*
C. Financial Account [1]	4 995 W.	**2,220**	**4,665**	**3,571**	**4,045**	**1,580**	**1,974**	**3,274**	**1,927**
Direct investment abroad	4 505 . .	–1,725	337	1,533	45	–928	–803	–904	–297
Direct investment in New Zealand	4 555 Z.	2,543	3,659	2,231	2,624	1,191	1,412	3,330	1,731
Portfolio investment assets	4 602 . .	–72	–284	–430	–1,612	–467	–666	–2,185	–1,146
Equity securities	4 610 . .	–152	–216	–339	–925	114	–893	–1,667	–868
Debt securities	4 619 . .	81	–68	–90	–687	–581	227	–518	–278
Portfolio investment liabilities	4 652 Z.	614	96	–104	403	425	–2,285	1,926	–355
Equity securities	4 660 . .	23	–100	175	88	22	172	–498	184
Debt securities	4 669 Z.	591	197	–279	315	402	–2,458	2,425	–539
Financial derivatives	4 910 . .	. . .	. . .	. . .	. . .	. . .	. . .	. . .	. . .
Financial derivatives assets	4 900 . .	. . .	. . .	. . .	. . .	. . .	. . .	. . .	. . .
Financial derivatives liabilities	4 905 . .	. . .	. . .	. . .	. . .	. . .	. . .	. . .	. . .
Other investment assets	4 703 . .	–78	–392	–920	991	–305	–1,282	–838	–3,297
Monetary authorities	4 701 . .	. . .	. . .	. . .	. . .	. . .	. . .	. . .	. . .
General government	4 704 . .	–82	–57	–94	238	55	212	–947	–3,688
Banks	4 705 . .	66	–346	–932	819	–285	–1,591	. . .	. . .
Other sectors	4 728 . .	–61	11	106	–65	–75	97	108	391
Other investment liabilities	4 753 W.	937	1,249	1,262	1,595	1,665	5,597	1,945	5,291
Monetary authorities	4 753 WA	. . .	. . .	. . .	. . .	. . .	. . .	. . .	. . .
General government	4 753 ZB	–290	–144	–135	–73	68	13	. . .	4,423
Banks	4 753 ZC	767	1,096	964	1,131	1,559	5,446	. . .	. . .
Other sectors	4 753 ZD	460	297	432	537	38	138	. . .	868
Total, Groups A Through C	4 983 . .	*452*	*2,886*	*1,023*	*–20*	*–713*	*–1,733*	*417*	*963*
D. Net Errors and Omissions	4 998 . .	**281**	**–2,502**	**749**	**–1,423**	**227**	**1,921**	**–560**	**–1,150**
Total, Groups A Through D	4 984 . .	*733*	*384*	*1,772*	*–1,442*	*–486*	*188*	*–143*	*–187*
E. Reserves and Related Items	4 802 A.	**–733**	**–384**	**–1,772**	**1,442**	**486**	**–188**	**143**	**187**
Reserve assets	4 802 . .	–733	–384	–1,772	1,442	486	–188	143	187
Use of Fund credit and loans	4 766 . .	. . .	. . .	. . .	. . .	. . .	. . .	. . .	. . .
Exceptional financing	4 920 . .	. . .	. . .	. . .	. . .	. . .	. . .	. . .	. . .
Conversion rates: New Zealand dollars per U.S. dollar	0 101 . .	**1.6865**	**1.5239**	**1.4548**	**1.5124**	**1.8682**	**1.8896**	**2.2011**	**2.3788**

[1] Excludes components that have been classified in the categories of Group E.

Table 2. STANDARD PRESENTATION, 1994–2001

(Millions of U.S. dollars)

	Code	1994	1995	1996	1997	1998	1999	2000	2001
CURRENT ACCOUNT	4 993 ..	**–2,384**	**–3,003**	**–3,883**	**–4,301**	**–2,110**	**–3,488**	**–2,675**	**–1,403**
A. GOODS	4 100 ..	1,408	971	523	903	912	–371	681	1,474
Credit	2 100 ..	**12,176**	**13,554**	**14,338**	**14,282**	**12,246**	**12,657**	**13,530**	**13,920**
General merchandise: exports f.o.b.	2 110 ..	12,176	13,554	14,211	14,128	12,162	12,574	13,426	13,824
Goods for processing: exports f.o.b.	2 150 ..	...	...	...	...	...	...	...	...
Repairs on goods	2 160 ..	...	...	...	...	...	...	...	...
Goods procured in ports by carriers	2 170 ..	...	...	...	...	...	...	...	...
Nonmonetary gold	2 180 ..	...	...	126	154	84	83	103	95
Debit	3 100 ..	**–10,769**	**–12,584**	**–13,815**	**–13,380**	**–11,333**	**–13,028**	**–12,848**	**–12,446**
General merchandise: imports f.o.b.	3 110 ..	–10,769	–12,584	–13,806	–13,370	–11,324	–13,020	–12,841	–12,439
Goods for processing: imports f.o.b.	3 150 ..	...	...	...	...	...	...	...	...
Repairs on goods	3 160 ..	...	...	...	...	...	...	...	...
Goods procured in ports by carriers	3 170 ..	...	...	...	...	...	...	...	...
Nonmonetary gold	3 180 ..	...	...	–8	–10	–9	–8	–7	–6
B. SERVICES	4 200 ..	–434	–214	–235	–646	–751	–193	–108	127
Total credit	2 200 ..	*3,667*	*4,481*	*4,519*	*4,072*	*3,572*	*4,194*	*4,359*	*4,344*
Total debit	3 200 ..	*–4,101*	*–4,694*	*–4,755*	*–4,718*	*–4,323*	*–4,387*	*–4,467*	*–4,217*
Transportation services, credit	2 205 ..	**1,433**	**1,525**	**1,425**	**1,284**	**1,114**	**1,296**	**1,223**	**1,145**
Passenger	2 850 ..	*761*	...	...	...	...	...	...	...
Freight	2 851 ..	*235*	...	...	...	...	...	...	...
Other	2 852 ..	*438*	...	...	...	...	...	...	...
Sea transport, passenger	2 207 ..	...	...	...	...	...	...	...	...
Sea transport, freight	2 208 ..	...	...	...	...	...	...	...	...
Sea transport, other	2 209 ..	...	...	...	...	...	...	...	...
Air transport, passenger	2 211 ..	...	...	...	...	...	...	...	...
Air transport, freight	2 212 ..	...	...	...	...	...	...	...	...
Air transport, other	2 213 ..	...	...	...	...	...	...	...	...
Other transport, passenger	2 215 ..	...	...	...	...	...	...	...	...
Other transport, freight	2 216 ..	...	...	...	...	...	...	...	...
Other transport, other	2 217 ..	...	...	...	...	...	...	...	...
Transportation services, debit	3 205 ..	**–1,590**	**–1,881**	**–1,768**	**–1,666**	**–1,458**	**–1,484**	**–1,428**	**–1,439**
Passenger	3 850 ..	*–385*	...	...	...	...	...	...	...
Freight	3 851 ..	*–735*	...	...	...	...	...	...	...
Other	3 852 ..	*–470*	...	...	...	...	...	...	...
Sea transport, passenger	3 207 ..	...	...	...	...	...	...	...	...
Sea transport, freight	3 208 ..	...	...	...	...	...	...	...	...
Sea transport, other	3 209 ..	...	...	...	...	...	...	...	...
Air transport, passenger	3 211 ..	...	...	...	...	...	...	...	...
Air transport, freight	3 212 ..	...	...	...	...	...	...	...	...
Air transport, other	3 213 ..	...	...	...	...	...	...	...	...
Other transport, passenger	3 215 ..	...	...	...	...	...	...	...	...
Other transport, freight	3 216 ..	...	...	...	...	...	...	...	...
Other transport, other	3 217 ..	...	...	...	...	...	...	...	...
Travel, credit	2 236 ..	**1,663**	**2,318**	**2,553**	**2,211**	**1,863**	**2,229**	**2,276**	**2,343**
Business travel	2 237 ..	...	...	...	280	251	286	250	272
Personal travel	2 240 ..	...	...	...	1,932	1,613	1,943	2,026	2,071
Travel, debit	3 236 ..	**–1,194**	**–1,289**	**–1,510**	**–1,515**	**–1,447**	**–1,505**	**–1,533**	**–1,332**
Business travel	3 237 ..	...	...	...	...	...	...	–409	–442
Personal travel	3 240 ..	...	...	...	...	...	...	–1,125	–890
Other services, credit	2 200 BA	**571**	**637**	**542**	**577**	**595**	**670**	**860**	**857**
Communications	2 245 ..	...	...	...	...	...	...	...	165
Construction	2 249 ..	...	...	...	...	1	4	6	13
Insurance	2 253 ..	–11	–11	2	8	10	12	13	19
Financial	2 260 ..	...	15	25	32	38	32	42	24
Computer and information	2 262 ..	...	20	29	45	54	74	76	82
Royalties and licence fees	2 266 ..	...	11	15	27	50	49	47	61
Other business services	2 268 ..	515	500	371	357	331	342	494	353
Personal, cultural, and recreational	2 287 ..	...	22	21	34	48	98	129	82
Government, n.i.e.	2 291 ..	68	81	78	74	62	59	53	58
Other services, debit	3 200 BA	**–1,318**	**–1,525**	**–1,477**	**–1,537**	**–1,419**	**–1,399**	**–1,505**	**–1,446**
Communications	3 245 ..	...	...	...	...	...	...	...	–143
Construction	3 249 ..	...	...	...	...	–1	–6	–3	–6
Insurance	3 253 ..	–186	–230	–149	–124	–118	–114	–82	–99
Financial	3 260 ..	...	–9	–17	–23	–22	–42	–45	–41
Computer and information	3 262 ..	...	–40	–58	–78	–96	–103	–97	–91
Royalties and licence fees	3 266 ..	...	–200	–291	–351	–293	–317	–308	–297
Other business services	3 268 ..	–1,064	–949	–858	–861	–803	–724	–878	–688
Personal, cultural, and recreational	3 287 ..	...	–3	–10	–13	–14	–20	–30	–19
Government, n.i.e.	3 291 ..	–67	–94	–94	–86	–72	–71	–62	–61

Table 2 (Continued). STANDARD PRESENTATION, 1994–2001

(Millions of U.S. dollars)

	Code	1994	1995	1996	1997	1998	1999	2000	2001
C. INCOME	4 300 ..	–3,686	–3,955	–4,714	–4,855	–2,612	–3,118	–3,473	–3,146
Total credit	2 300 ..	*358*	*940*	*372*	*393*	*880*	*919*	*601*	*569*
Total debit	3 300 ..	*–4,045*	*–4,895*	*–5,085*	*–5,249*	*–3,493*	*–4,037*	*–4,074*	*–3,714*
Compensation of employees, credit	2 310 ..	...	...	...	...	...	...	...	...
Compensation of employees, debit	3 310 ..	...	...	...	...	...	...	...	...
Investment income, credit	2 320 ..	**358**	**940**	**372**	**393**	**880**	**919**	**601**	**569**
Direct investment income	2 330 ..	127	619	–58	–102	401	449	–10	–211
Dividends and distributed branch profits	2 332 ..	–138	...	...	...	...	...	...	...
Reinvested earnings and undistributed branch profits	2 333 ..	265	...	...	...	...	...	...	...
Income on debt (interest)	2 334 ..	...	–170	–489	...	...	...	...	...
Portfolio investment income	2 339 ..	...	...	92	199	144	160	366	451
Income on equity	2 340 ..	...	...	...	...	...	...	...	...
Income on bonds and notes	2 350 ..	...	...	...	...	...	...	...	...
Income on money market instruments	2 360 ..	...	...	...	...	...	...	...	...
Other investment income	2 370 ..	231	321	338	296	335	310	245	329
Investment income, debit	3 320 ..	**–4,045**	**–4,895**	**–5,085**	**–5,249**	**–3,493**	**–4,037**	**–4,074**	**–3,714**
Direct investment income	3 330 ..	–2,335	–3,017	–3,246	–3,203	–1,766	–2,560	–1,988	–1,761
Dividends and distributed branch profits	3 332 ..	–1,256	...	...	...	...	...	...	...
Reinvested earnings and undistributed branch profits	3 333 ..	–1,079	...	...	...	...	...	...	...
Income on debt (interest)	3 334 ..	...	–435	–596	–609	–398	–425	–321	...
Portfolio investment income	3 339 ..	...	...	–54	–25	–3	–1	–957	–1,073
Income on equity	3 340 ..	...	...	...	...	...	...	...	...
Income on bonds and notes	3 350 ..	...	...	...	...	...	...	...	...
Income on money market instruments	3 360 ..	...	...	...	...	...	...	...	...
Other investment income	3 370 ..	–1,710	–1,878	–1,785	–2,021	–1,724	–1,476	–1,128	–881
D. CURRENT TRANSFERS	4 379 ..	329	195	543	297	342	194	225	141
Credit	2 379 ..	**638**	**558**	**897**	**680**	**681**	**609**	**634**	**576**
General government	2 380 ..	379	283	631	453	455	377	410	368
Other sectors	2 390 ..	259	275	266	228	226	232	224	208
Workers' remittances	2 391 ..	...	206	269	233	223	226	215	216
Other current transfers	2 392 ..	259	69	–3	–5	3	6	9	–8
Debit	3 379 ..	**–309**	**–363**	**–354**	**–383**	**–339**	**–415**	**–409**	**–435**
General government	3 380 ..	–217	–185	–173	–199	–196	–207	–242	–273
Other sectors	3 390 ..	–92	–177	–181	–184	–143	–209	–167	–163
Workers' remittances	3 391 ..	...	–157	–152	–142	–115	–180	–124	–98
Other current transfers	3 392 ..	–92	–20	–29	–42	–28	–28	–43	–65
CAPITAL AND FINANCIAL ACCOUNT	4 996 ..	**2,104**	**5,505**	**3,134**	**5,724**	**1,883**	**1,567**	**3,235**	**2,553**
CAPITAL ACCOUNT	4 994 ..	**617**	**1,224**	**1,335**	**236**	**–183**	**–218**	**–182**	**439**
Total credit	2 994 ..	*995*	*1,652*	*1,838*	*777*	*260*	*259*	*236*	*818*
Total debit	3 994 ..	*–379*	*–427*	*–502*	*–541*	*–444*	*–477*	*–418*	*–379*
Capital transfers, credit	2 400 ..	**995**	**1,652**	**1,838**	**777**	**259**	**258**	**236**	**818**
General government	2 401 ..	...	...	...	...	...	...	...	...
Debt forgiveness	2 402 ..	...	...	...	...	...	...	...	...
Other capital transfers	2 410 ..	...	...	...	...	...	...	...	...
Other sectors	2 430 ..	995	1,652	1,838	777	259	258	236	818
Migrants' transfers	2 431 ..	995	1,652	1,838	777	259	258	236	818
Debt forgiveness	2 432 ..	...	...	...	...	...	...	...	...
Other capital transfers	2 440 ..	...	...	...	...	...	...	...	...
Capital transfers, debit	3 400 ..	**–379**	**–427**	**–502**	**–541**	**–436**	**–469**	**–418**	**–377**
General government	3 401 ..	...	...	...	...	...	...	...	...
Debt forgiveness	3 402 ..	...	...	...	...	...	...	...	...
Other capital transfers	3 410 ..	...	...	...	...	...	...	...	...
Other sectors	3 430 ..	–379	–427	–502	–541	–436	–469	–418	–377
Migrants' transfers	3 431 ..	–379	–427	–502	–541	–436	–469	–418	–377
Debt forgiveness	3 432 ..	...	...	...	...	...	...	...	...
Other capital transfers	3 440 ..	...	...	...	...	...	...	...	...
Nonproduced nonfinancial assets, credit	2 480 ..	...	...	...	...	**1**	**1**	...	...
Nonproduced nonfinancial assets, debit	3 480 ..	...	...	...	...	**–7**	**–8**	...	**–2**

Table 2 (Continued). STANDARD PRESENTATION, 1994–2001

(Millions of U.S. dollars)

	Code	1994	1995	1996	1997	1998	1999	2000	2001
FINANCIAL ACCOUNT	4 995	**1,487**	**4,281**	**1,799**	**5,488**	**2,066**	**1,785**	**3,417**	**2,114**
A. DIRECT INVESTMENT	4 500	818	3,995	3,764	2,669	263	609	2,426	1,434
Direct investment abroad	4 505	**–1,725**	**337**	**1,533**	**45**	**–928**	**–803**	**–904**	**–297**
Equity capital	4 510	–619	–452	–695	–383	–3,757	–2,248	4,495	...
Claims on affiliated enterprises	4 515	...	...	...	...	–3,757	–2,248	...	...
Liabilities to affiliated enterprises	4 520	...	...	...	...	...	...	...	...
Reinvested earnings	4 525	–265	...	...	...	...	...	...	...
Other capital	4 530	–840	789	2,229	428	2,829	1,445	–5,399	...
Claims on affiliated enterprises	4 535	–81	–491	190	–172	–292	59	...	...
Liabilities to affiliated enterprises	4 540	–759	1,280	2,038	600	3,121	1,385	...	...
Direct investment in New Zealand	4 555	**2,543**	**3,659**	**2,231**	**2,624**	**1,191**	**1,412**	**3,330**	**1,731**
Equity capital	4 560	792	3,143	811	2,326	506	628	1,827	2,854
Claims on direct investors	4 565	...	...	...	...	...	...	...	...
Liabilities to direct investors	4 570	...	...	...	...	506	628	1,827	2,854
Reinvested earnings	4 575	1,079	...	...	...	...	...	...	...
Other capital	4 580	671	515	1,419	298	685	783	1,503	–1,123
Claims on direct investors	4 585	202	54	216	261	–106	–578	...	...
Liabilities to direct investors	4 590	469	461	1,203	36	791	1,361	...	...
B. PORTFOLIO INVESTMENT	4 600	542	–187	–534	–1,209	–43	–2,951	–259	–1,501
Assets	4 602	**–72**	**–284**	**–430**	**–1,612**	**–467**	**–666**	**–2,185**	**–1,146**
Equity securities	4 610	–152	–216	–339	–925	114	–893	–1,667	–868
Monetary authorities	4 611	...	...	...	...	...	...	...	...
General government	4 612	–19	–7	–5	–22	–64	–44	...	...
Banks	4 613	–110	–126	–128	149	53	–39	...	...
Other sectors	4 614	–23	–84	–206	–1,053	124	–810	...	...
Debt securities	4 619	81	–68	–90	–687	–581	227	–518	–278
Bonds and notes	4 620	79	–70	–96	–619	–569	118	–476	–402
Monetary authorities	4 621	...	...	...	...	...	...	...	...
General government	4 622	...	...	...	...	–21	–127	...	...
Banks	4 623	...	...	...	...	–35	3	...	...
Other sectors	4 624	...	...	...	...	–513	242	...	...
Money market instruments	4 630	1	3	5	–68	–12	109	–42	124
Monetary authorities	4 631	...	...	...	...	...	...	...	...
General government	4 632	...	...	...	...	...	...	...	...
Banks	4 633	...	...	...	...	...	...	...	...
Other sectors	4 634	...	...	...	...	–12	109	...	...
Liabilities	4 652	**614**	**96**	**–104**	**403**	**425**	**–2,285**	**1,926**	**–355**
Equity securities	4 660	23	–100	175	88	22	172	–498	184
Banks	4 663	...	...	...	...	...	...	...	...
Other sectors	4 664	23	–100	175	88	22	172	...	...
Debt securities	4 669	591	197	–279	315	402	–2,458	2,425	–539
Bonds and notes	4 670	–81	130	–789	183	484	–269	1,680	–147
Monetary authorities	4 671	...	...	...	...	...	...	...	...
General government	4 672	–637	–463	–297	–518	–915	–920	...	...
Banks	4 673	...	...	...	...	1,248	489	...	...
Other sectors	4 674	556	593	–492	702	150	162	...	...
Money market instruments	4 680	672	66	510	132	–81	–2,189	745	–392
Monetary authorities	4 681	...	...	...	...	...	...	...	...
General government	4 682	...	...	...	...	–333	–103	...	...
Banks	4 683	...	...	...	...	443	–1,668	...	...
Other sectors	4 684	...	...	...	...	–191	–418	...	...
C. FINANCIAL DERIVATIVES	4 910	...	...	...	...	...	...	...	...
Monetary authorities	4 911	...	...	...	...	...	...	...	...
General government	4 912	...	...	...	...	...	...	...	...
Banks	4 913	...	...	...	...	...	...	...	...
Other sectors	4 914	...	...	...	...	...	...	...	...
Assets	4 900	**...**	**...**	**...**	**...**	**...**	**...**	**...**	**...**
Monetary authorities	4 901	...	...	...	...	...	...	...	...
General government	4 902	...	...	...	...	...	...	...	...
Banks	4 903	...	...	...	...	...	...	...	...
Other sectors	4 904	...	...	...	...	...	...	...	...
Liabilities	4 905	**...**	**...**	**...**	**...**	**...**	**...**	**...**	**...**
Monetary authorities	4 906	...	...	...	...	...	...	...	...
General government	4 907	...	...	...	...	...	...	...	...
Banks	4 908	...	...	...	...	...	...	...	...
Other sectors	4 909	...	...	...	...	...	...	...	...

Table 2 (Concluded). STANDARD PRESENTATION, 1994–2001

(Millions of U.S. dollars)

	Code	1994	1995	1996	1997	1998	1999	2000	2001
D. OTHER INVESTMENT	4 700	860	857	342	2,586	1,360	4,316	1,107	1,994
Assets	4 703	**–78**	**–392**	**–920**	**991**	**–305**	**–1,282**	**–838**	**–3,297**
Trade credits	4 706	–122	–78	–109	201	–15	264	–129	–136
General government	4 707	–83	–95	–97	220	47	208	...	...
of which: Short-term	4 709	*–2*	*–1*	*1*	*1*	...	...	...	...
Other sectors	4 710	–39	16	–12	–19	–62	56	–129	–136
of which: Short-term	4 712	*–39*	*16*	*–12*	*–19*	*–62*	*56*	...	...
Loans	4 714	–100	–313	–696	711	–329	–1,559	–947	–3,688
Monetary authorities	4 715	...	...	...	...	...	...	...	...
of which: Short-term	4 718	...	...	...	...	...	...	...	...
General government	4 719	...	...	...	...	5	2	–947	–3,688
of which: Short-term	4 721	...	...	...	...	*5*	*2*	...	*–1,136*
Banks	4 722	–85	–323	–700	713	–353	–1,317	...	...
of which: Short-term	4 724	...	...	...	...	*–249*	*–537*	...	...
Other sectors	4 725	–16	9	4	–2	19	–243	...	...
of which: Short-term	4 727	...	...	...	...	*–13*	*–197*	...	...
Currency and deposits	4 730	144	18	–187	102	115	–253	–628	351
Monetary authorities	4 731	...	...	...	...	...	...	...	...
General government	4 732	...	42	1	16	3	3	...	...
Banks	4 733	151	–26	–234	106	69	–273	...	...
Other sectors	4 734	–8	1	47	–20	43	17	–628	351
Other assets	4 736	1	–18	72	–23	–76	266	866	176
Monetary authorities	4 737	...	...	...	...	...	...	...	...
of which: Short-term	4 739	...	...	...	...	...	...	...	...
General government	4 740	...	–4	2	1	...	...	...	...
of which: Short-term	4 742	...	...	...	...	...	...	...	...
Banks	4 743	...	2	2	1	–1	...	...	...
of which: Short-term	4 745	...	...	...	...	*–1*	...	...	...
Other sectors	4 746	1	–16	68	–25	–75	267	866	176
of which: Short-term	4 748	...	...	...	...	*–76*	*266*	...	...
Liabilities	4 753	**937**	**1,249**	**1,262**	**1,595**	**1,665**	**5,597**	**1,945**	**5,291**
Trade credits	4 756	50	–12	13	131	75	58	15	–17
General government	4 757	–4	–1	–1	53	5	–5	...	...
of which: Short-term	4 759	*–4*	*–1*	*–1*	*53*	*5*	*–5*	...	...
Other sectors	4 760	54	–11	13	79	70	63	...	–17
of which: Short-term	4 762	*54*	*–11*	*13*	*79*	*70*	*63*	...	...
Loans	4 764	171	165	582	1,051	233	137	–7	4,423
Monetary authorities	4 765	...	...	...	...	...	...	...	...
of which: Use of Fund credit and loans from the Fund	4 766	...	...	...	...	...	...	...	...
of which: Short-term	4 768	...	...	...	...	...	...	...	...
General government	4 769	–273	–137	–132	–125	63	18	...	4,423
of which: Short-term	4 771	...	...	...	...	*–51*	*–21*	...	*129*
Banks	4 772	34	–11	325	668	172	53	...	...
of which: Short-term	4 774	...	...	...	...	*230*	*73*	...	...
Other sectors	4 775	410	313	389	508	–2	66	...	...
of which: Short-term	4 777	...	...	...	...	*269*	*–89*	...	...
Currency and deposits	4 780	846	1,087	669	421	1,720	5,508	1,955	816
Monetary authorities	4 781	...	...	...	...	...	...	...	...
General government	4 782	...	...	...	...	...	...	...	...
Banks	4 783	849	1,087	627	460	1,699	5,501	...	...
Other sectors	4 784	–3	...	42	–39	22	7	...	816
Other liabilities	4 786	–130	10	–2	–9	–363	–106	–18	68
Monetary authorities	4 787	...	...	...	...	...	...	...	...
of which: Short-term	4 789	...	...	...	...	...	...	...	...
General government	4 790	–13	–5	–2	–1	...	...	...	...
of which: Short-term	4 792	...	...	...	...	...	...	...	...
Banks	4 793	–116	20	12	3	–311	–108	...	...
of which: Short-term	4 795	...	...	...	...	*–311*	*–108*	...	...
Other sectors	4 796	–1	–5	–12	–11	–52	1	...	68
of which: Short-term	4 798	...	...	...	...	*–13*	*15*	...	...
E. RESERVE ASSETS	4 802	–733	–384	–1,772	1,442	486	–188	143	187
Monetary gold	4 812	...	...	...	...	...	...	...	...
Special drawing rights	4 811	...	–1	...	...	–1	–5	–7	–4
Reserve position in the Fund	4 810	4	–14	–24	–7	–163	–77	82	–79
Foreign exchange	4 803	–736	–369	–1,749	1,449	651	–107	355	21
Other claims	4 813	...	...	...	...	...	...	–288	249
NET ERRORS AND OMISSIONS	4 998	**281**	**–2,502**	**749**	**–1,423**	**227**	**1,921**	**–560**	**–1,150**

Part 3 of the *Yearbook* contains descriptions of the methodologies, compilation practices, and sources used to compile these data.

Table 3. INTERNATIONAL INVESTMENT POSITION (End–March stocks through 1999)

(Millions of U.S. dollars)

	Code	1994	1995	1996	1997	1998	1999	2000	2001
ASSETS	8 995 C.	13,206	16,201	23,573	23,023	19,348	20,126	30,676	32,161
Direct investment abroad	8 505 . .	**5,163**	**7,630**	**8,928**	**6,749**	**5,775**	**6,746**	**6,431**	**6,637**
Equity capital and reinvested earnings	8 506 . .	7,449	9,321	12,760	13,098	10,718	15,048	7,050	5,043
Claims on affiliated enterprises	8 507 . .	. . .	. . .	. . .	. . .	. . .	15,048	. . .	. . .
Liabilities to affiliated enterprises	8 508 . .	. . .	. . .	. . .	. . .	. . .	. . .	. . .	. . .
Other capital	8 530 . .	–2,286	–1,690	–3,832	–6,349	–4,943	–8,302	–619	1,593
Claims on affiliated enterprises	8 535 . .	1,418	1,911	1,954	1,714	1,618	1,833	. . .	. . .
Liabilities to affiliated enterprises	8 540 . .	–3,704	–3,602	–5,785	–8,063	–6,561	–10,136	. . .	. . .
Portfolio investment	8 602 . .	**1,362**	**1,707**	**5,815**	**6,434**	**6,476**	**6,374**	**11,247**	**11,675**
Equity securities	8 610 . .	834	1,226	4,407	4,895	4,620	4,193	6,706	7,024
Monetary authorities	8 611 . .	. . .	. . .	. . .	. . .	. . .	. . .	. . .	. . .
General government	8 612 . .	. . .	. . .	. . .	. . .	. . .	133	. . .	. . .
Banks	8 613 . .	. . .	. . .	. . .	. . .	. . .	1	. . .	. . .
Other sectors	8 614 . .	. . .	. . .	. . .	. . .	. . .	4,059	. . .	. . .
Debt securities	8 619 . .	529	481	1,408	1,539	1,855	2,181	4,541	4,651
Bonds and notes	8 620 . .	. . .	. . .	. . .	. . .	. . .	2,044	. . .	. . .
Monetary authorities	8 621 . .	. . .	. . .	. . .	. . .	. . .	. . .	. . .	. . .
General government	8 622 . .	. . .	. . .	. . .	. . .	. . .	61	. . .	. . .
Banks	8 623 . .	. . .	. . .	. . .	. . .	. . .	151	. . .	. . .
Other sectors	8 624 . .	. . .	. . .	. . .	. . .	. . .	1,832	. . .	. . .
Money market instruments	8 630 . .	. . .	. . .	. . .	. . .	. . .	136	. . .	. . .
Monetary authorities	8 631 . .	. . .	. . .	. . .	. . .	. . .	. . .	. . .	. . .
General government	8 632 . .	. . .	. . .	. . .	. . .	. . .	. . .	. . .	. . .
Banks	8 633 . .	. . .	. . .	. . .	. . .	. . .	. . .	. . .	. . .
Other sectors	8 634 . .	. . .	. . .	. . .	. . .	. . .	136	. . .	. . .
Financial derivatives	8 900 . .	**. . .**	**. . .**	**. . .**	**. . .**	**. . .**	**. . .**	**4,289**	**2,462**
Monetary authorities	8 901 . .	. . .	. . .	. . .	. . .	. . .	. . .	. . .	. . .
General government	8 902 . .	. . .	. . .	. . .	. . .	. . .	. . .	. . .	. . .
Banks	8 903 . .	. . .	. . .	. . .	. . .	. . .	. . .	. . .	. . .
Other sectors	8 904 . .	. . .	. . .	. . .	. . .	. . .	. . .	. . .	. . .
Other investment	8 703 . .	**2,793**	**2,898**	**4,245**	**5,313**	**2,804**	**3,352**	**4,756**	**7,821**
Trade credits	8 706 . .	. . .	1,359	1,430	1,557	903	898	745	869
General government	8 707 . .	. . .	. . .	. . .	. . .	. . .	176	. . .	. . .
of which: Short-term	8 709 . .	. . .	. . .	. . .	. . .	. . .	*1*	. . .	. . .
Other sectors	8 710 . .	. . .	. . .	. . .	. . .	. . .	722	. . .	. . .
of which: Short-term	8 712 . .	. . .	. . .	. . .	. . .	. . .	*722*	. . .	. . .
Loans	8 714 . .	. . .	1,128	1,820	2,601	1,083	1,737	2,547	6,142
Monetary authorities	8 715 . .	. . .	. . .	. . .	. . .	. . .	. . .	. . .	. . .
of which: Short-term	8 718 . .	. . .	. . .	. . .	. . .	. . .	. . .	. . .	. . .
General government	8 719 . .	. . .	. . .	. . .	. . .	. . .	. . .	. . .	. . .
of which: Short-term	8 721 . .	. . .	. . .	. . .	. . .	. . .	. . .	. . .	. . .
Banks	8 722 . .	. . .	. . .	. . .	. . .	. . .	1,696	. . .	. . .
of which: Short-term	8 724 . .	. . .	. . .	. . .	. . .	. . .	*1,094*	. . .	. . .
Other sectors	8 725 . .	. . .	. . .	. . .	. . .	. . .	41	. . .	. . .
of which: Short-term	8 727 . .	. . .	. . .	. . .	. . .	. . .	*17*	. . .	. . .
Currency and deposits	8 730 . .	. . .	403	544	795	476	337	1,161	693
Monetary authorities	8 731 . .	. . .	. . .	. . .	. . .	. . .	. . .	. . .	. . .
General government	8 732 . .	. . .	. . .	. . .	. . .	. . .	8	. . .	. . .
Banks	8 733 . .	. . .	. . .	. . .	. . .	. . .	281	. . .	. . .
Other sectors	8 734 . .	. . .	. . .	. . .	. . .	. . .	49	. . .	. . .
Other assets	8 736 . .	. . .	8	452	361	341	380	303	118
Monetary authorities	8 737 . .	. . .	. . .	. . .	. . .	. . .	. . .	. . .	. . .
of which: Short-term	8 739 . .	. . .	. . .	. . .	. . .	. . .	. . .	. . .	. . .
General government	8 740 . .	. . .	. . .	. . .	. . .	. . .	3	. . .	. . .
of which: Short-term	8 742 . .	. . .	. . .	. . .	. . .	. . .	. . .	. . .	. . .
Banks	8 743 . .	. . .	. . .	. . .	. . .	. . .	3	. . .	. . .
of which: Short-term	8 745 . .	. . .	. . .	. . .	. . .	. . .	*3*	. . .	. . .
Other sectors	8 746 . .	. . .	. . .	. . .	. . .	. . .	374	. . .	. . .
of which: Short-term	8 748 . .	. . .	. . .	. . .	. . .	. . .	*365*	. . .	. . .
Reserve assets	8 802 . .	**3,888**	**3,967**	**4,584**	**4,528**	**4,293**	**3,654**	**3,952**	**3,566**
Monetary gold	8 812 . .	. . .	. . .	. . .	. . .	. . .	. . .	. . .	. . .
Special drawing rights	8 811 . .	. . .	. . .	1	. . .	2	7	13	16
Reserve position in the Fund	8 810 . .	147	164	182	178	356	424	320	388
Foreign exchange	8 803 . .	3,741	3,802	4,401	4,349	3,935	3,223	3,025	2,815
Other claims	8 813 . .	. . .	. . .	. . .	. . .	. . .	. . .	594	347

Table 3 (Continued). INTERNATIONAL INVESTMENT POSITION (End–March stocks through 1999)
(Millions of U.S. dollars)

	Code	1994	1995	1996	1997	1998	1999	2000	2001
LIABILITIES	8 995 D.	51,100	62,339	71,631	78,547	68,752	63,782	70,272	70,909
Direct investment in New Zealand	8 555 . .	**19,315**	**25,574**	**33,381**	**37,491**	**34,889**	**31,636**	**21,673**	**20,408**
Equity capital and reinvested earnings	8 556 . .	15,311	20,759	27,603	30,344	28,053	25,377	16,564	16,547
Claims on direct investors	8 557 . .	. . .	. . .	. . .	. . .	. . .	. . .	. . .	. . .
Liabilities to direct investors	8 558 . .	. . .	. . .	. . .	. . .	. . .	25,377	. . .	. . .
Other capital	8 580 . .	4,004	4,815	5,778	7,147	6,836	6,259	5,109	3,861
Claims on direct investors	8 585 . .	–1,326	–1,262	–1,197	–933	–370	–675	. . .	. . .
Liabilities to direct investors	8 590 . .	5,330	6,077	6,974	8,080	7,206	6,934	. . .	. . .
Portfolio investment	8 652 . .	**17,595**	**19,809**	**19,361**	**20,166**	**17,581**	**16,697**	**25,482**	**23,804**
Equity securities	8 660 . .	816	1,483	288	1,045	208	227	4,540	4,151
Banks	8 663 . .	. . .	. . .	. . .	. . .	. . .	. . .	. . .	. . .
Other sectors	8 664 . .	. . .	. . .	. . .	. . .	. . .	227	. . .	. . .
Debt securities	8 669 . .	16,779	18,327	19,072	19,121	17,373	16,470	20,942	19,653
Bonds and notes	8 670 . .	13,811	14,518	15,203	14,586	12,608	12,148	. . .	. . .
Monetary authorities	8 671 . .	. . .	. . .	. . .	. . .	. . .	. . .	. . .	. . .
General government	8 672 . .	. . .	. . .	. . .	. . .	. . .	7,446	. . .	. . .
Banks	8 673 . .	. . .	. . .	. . .	. . .	. . .	2,334	. . .	. . .
Other sectors	8 674 . .	. . .	. . .	. . .	. . .	. . .	2,369	. . .	. . .
Money market instruments	8 680 . .	2,968	3,809	3,870	4,535	4,764	4,322	. . .	. . .
Monetary authorities	8 681 . .	. . .	. . .	. . .	. . .	. . .	. . .	. . .	. . .
General government	8 682 . .	. . .	. . .	. . .	. . .	. . .	874	. . .	. . .
Banks	8 683 . .	. . .	. . .	. . .	. . .	. . .	2,310	. . .	. . .
Other sectors	8 684 . .	. . .	. . .	. . .	. . .	. . .	1,138	. . .	. . .
Financial derivatives	8 905 . .	**. . .**	**. . .**	**. . .**	**. . .**	**. . .**	**. . .**	**3,256**	**2,640**
Monetary authorities	8 906 . .	. . .	. . .	. . .	. . .	. . .	. . .	. . .	. . .
General government	8 907 . .	. . .	. . .	. . .	. . .	. . .	. . .	. . .	. . .
Banks	8 908 . .	. . .	. . .	. . .	. . .	. . .	. . .	. . .	. . .
Other sectors	8 909 . .	. . .	. . .	. . .	. . .	. . .	. . .	. . .	. . .
Other investment	8 753 . .	**14,189**	**16,955**	**18,889**	**20,890**	**16,282**	**15,450**	**19,861**	**24,057**
Trade credits	8 756 . .	584	674	648	740	688	567	619	583
General government	8 758 . .	. . .	. . .	. . .	. . .	. . .	. . .	. . .	. . .
of which: Short-term	8 759 . .	. . .	. . .	. . .	. . .	. . .	*3*	. . .	. . .
Other sectors	8 760 . .	. . .	. . .	. . .	. . .	. . .	564	. . .	. . .
of which: Short-term	8 762 . .	. . .	. . .	. . .	. . .	. . .	*564*	. . .	. . .
Loans	8 764 . .	5,943	6,402	6,706	7,068	6,650	5,901	15,188	18,873
Monetary authorities	8 765 . .	. . .	. . .	. . .	. . .	. . .	. . .	. . .	. . .
of which: Use of Fund credit and loans from the Fund	8 766 . .	. . .	. . .	. . .	. . .	. . .	. . .	. . .	. . .
of which: Short-term	8 768 . .	. . .	. . .	. . .	. . .	. . .	. . .	. . .	. . .
General government	8 769 . .	. . .	. . .	. . .	. . .	. . .	400	. . .	. . .
of which: Short-term	8 771 . .	. . .	. . .	. . .	. . .	. . .	*88*	. . .	. . .
Banks	8 772 . .	. . .	. . .	. . .	. . .	. . .	1,416	. . .	. . .
of which: Short-term	8 774 . .	. . .	. . .	. . .	. . .	. . .	*1,215*	. . .	. . .
Other sectors	8 775 . .	. . .	. . .	. . .	. . .	. . .	4,085	. . .	. . .
of which: Short-term	8 777 . .	. . .	. . .	. . .	. . .	. . .	*1,152*	. . .	. . .
Currency and deposits	8 780 . .	7,431	9,790	11,456	12,734	8,382	8,916	3,930	4,445
Monetary authorities	8 781 . .	. . .	. . .	. . .	. . .	. . .	. . .	. . .	. . .
General government	8 782 . .	. . .	. . .	. . .	. . .	. . .	. . .	. . .	. . .
Banks	8 783 . .	. . .	. . .	. . .	. . .	. . .	8,878	. . .	. . .
Other sectors	8 784 . .	. . .	. . .	. . .	. . .	. . .	39	. . .	. . .
Other liabilities	8 786 . .	231	88	78	348	562	65	124	155
Monetary authorities	8 787 . .	. . .	. . .	. . .	. . .	. . .	. . .	. . .	. . .
of which: Short-term	8 789 . .	. . .	. . .	. . .	. . .	. . .	. . .	. . .	. . .
General government	8 790 . .	. . .	. . .	. . .	. . .	. . .	. . .	. . .	. . .
of which: Short-term	8 792 . .	. . .	. . .	. . .	. . .	. . .	. . .	. . .	. . .
Banks	8 793 . .	. . .	. . .	. . .	. . .	. . .	6	. . .	. . .
of which: Short-term	8 795 . .	. . .	. . .	. . .	. . .	. . .	*6*	. . .	. . .
Other sectors	8 796 . .	. . .	. . .	. . .	. . .	. . .	59	. . .	. . .
of which: Short-term	8 798 . .	. . .	. . .	. . .	. . .	. . .	*59*	. . .	. . .
NET INTERNATIONAL INVESTMENT POSITION	8 995 . .	**–37,894**	**–46,137**	**–48,058**	**–55,523**	**–49,404**	**–43,657**	**–39,596**	**–38,748**
Conversion rates: New Zealand dollars per U.S. dollar (end of period)	0 102 . .	**1.7778**	**1.5399**	**1.4743**	**1.4382**	**1.8044**	**1.9952**	**2.2717**	**2.4067**

Table 1. ANALYTIC PRESENTATION, 1994–2001
(Millions of U.S. dollars)

	Code	1994	1995	1996	1997	1998	1999	2000	2001
A. Current Account[1]	4 993 Z.	**–714.3**	**–576.6**	**–627.8**	**–670.6**	**–501.1**	**–693.9**	**–486.3**	**–561.1**
Goods: exports f.o.b.	2 100 ..	338.6	470.5	470.2	581.6	580.1	552.4	652.8	601.9
Goods: imports f.o.b.	3 100 ..	–781.4	–882.3	–1,044.3	–1,371.2	–1,397.1	–1,698.2	–1,647.3	–1,629.5
Balance on Goods	4 100 ..	*–442.8*	*–411.8*	*–574.1*	*–789.6*	*–817.0*	*–1,145.8*	*–994.5*	*–1,027.6*
Services: credit	2 200 ..	125.2	142.3	173.2	215.7	250.9	286.9	303.5	331.8
Services: debit	3 200 ..	–172.9	–220.5	–252.8	–239.4	–267.8	–334.7	–343.4	–353.5
Balance on Goods and Services	4 991 ..	*–490.5*	*–490.0*	*–653.7*	*–813.3*	*–833.9*	*–1,193.6*	*–1,034.4*	*–1,049.3*
Income: credit	2 300 ..	6.7	7.1	10.5	14.7	26.0	30.7	30.7	14.7
Income: debit	3 300 ..	–478.9	–379.2	–334.8	–279.4	–211.2	–227.5	–232.5	–263.2
Balance on Goods, Services, and Income	4 992 ..	*–962.7*	*–862.1*	*–978.0*	*–1,078.0*	*–1,019.1*	*–1,390.4*	*–1,236.2*	*–1,297.8*
Current transfers: credit	2 379 Z.	248.4	285.5	350.2	407.4	518.0	696.5	749.9	736.7
Current transfers: debit	3 379 ..	...	...	...	...	...	...	...	...
B. Capital Account[1]	4 994 Z.	**...**	**...**	**...**	**...**	**...**	**...**	**...**	**...**
Capital account: credit	2 994 Z.	...	...	...	...	...	...	...	...
Capital account: debit	3 994 ..	...	...	...	...	...	...	...	...
Total, Groups A Plus B	4 981 ..	*–714.3*	*–576.6*	*–627.8*	*–670.6*	*–501.1*	*–693.9*	*–486.3*	*–561.1*
C. Financial Account[1]	4 995 W.	**–901.9**	**–625.0**	**–355.0**	**3.2**	**197.1**	**488.2**	**60.8**	**40.4**
Direct investment abroad	4 505 ..	...	...	...	...	...	...	...	...
Direct investment in Nicaragua	4 555 Z.	40.0	75.4	97.0	173.1	183.7	300.0	265.0	132.3
Portfolio investment assets	4 602 ..	...	...	...	...	...	...	...	...
Equity securities	4 610 ..	...	...	...	...	...	...	...	...
Debt securities	4 619 ..	...	...	...	...	...	...	...	...
Portfolio investment liabilities	4 652 Z.	...	...	...	...	...	...	...	...
Equity securities	4 660 ..	...	...	...	...	...	...	...	...
Debt securities	4 669 Z.	...	...	...	...	...	...	...	...
Financial derivatives	4 910 ..	...	...	...	...	...	...	...	...
Financial derivatives assets	4 900 ..	...	...	...	...	...	...	...	...
Financial derivatives liabilities	4 905 ..	...	...	...	...	...	...	...	...
Other investment assets	4 703 ..	–1.3	–32.0	–54.3	–70.8	55.2	22.2	79.9	–60.4
Monetary authorities	4 701 ..	...	...	...	...	...	...	...	...
General government	4 704 ..	...	...	...	...	...	...	...	...
Banks	4 705 ..	–1.3	–32.0	–54.3	–70.8	55.2	22.2	79.9	–60.4
Other sectors	4 728 ..	...	...	...	...	...	...	...	...
Other investment liabilities	4 753 W.	–940.6	–668.4	–397.7	–99.1	–41.8	166.0	–284.1	–31.5
Monetary authorities	4 753 WA	–544.3	–221.7	–126.1	–106.0	–18.1	62.4	–39.4	–19.5
General government	4 753 ZB	–418.7	–381.2	–295.4	–103.1	–154.8	–63.9	–73.6	–83.1
Banks	4 753 ZC	14.3	5.8	6.0	25.1	.3	63.6	–19.2	38.4
Other sectors	4 753 ZD	8.1	–71.3	17.8	84.9	130.8	103.9	–151.9	32.7
Total, Groups A Through C	4 983 ..	*–1,616.2*	*–1,201.6*	*–982.8*	*–667.4*	*–304.0*	*–205.7*	*–425.5*	*–520.7*
D. Net Errors and Omissions	4 998 ..	**50.4**	**157.8**	**172.7**	**352.8**	**–105.6**	**–254.6**	**–42.2**	**–13.3**
Total, Groups A Through D	4 984 ..	*–1,565.8*	*–1,043.8*	*–810.1*	*–314.6*	*–409.6*	*–460.3*	*–467.7*	*–534.0*
E. Reserves and Related Items	4 802 A.	**1,565.8**	**1,043.8**	**810.1**	**314.6**	**409.6**	**460.3**	**467.7**	**534.0**
Reserve assets	4 802 ..	–84.6	11.5	–53.1	–173.2	30.3	–156.5	16.8	113.9
Use of Fund credit and loans	4 766 ..	26.1	–12.9	–9.3	...	22.6	105.3	20.9	–5.0
Exceptional financing	4 920 ..	1,624.3	1,045.2	872.5	487.8	356.7	511.5	430.0	425.1
Conversion rates: córdobas per U.S. dollar	0 101 ..	**6.723**	**7.546**	**8.436**	**9.448**	**10.582**	**11.809**	**12.684**	**13.372**

[1] Excludes components that have been classified in the categories of Group E.

Table 2. STANDARD PRESENTATION, 1994–2001

(Millions of U.S. dollars)

	Code	1994	1995	1996	1997	1998	1999	2000	2001
CURRENT ACCOUNT	4 993 . .	**-667.3**	**-497.1**	**-565.9**	**-649.1**	**-493.4**	**-628.8**	**-474.4**	**-557.4**
A. GOODS	4 100 . .	-442.8	-411.8	-574.1	-789.6	-817.0	-1,145.8	-994.5	-1,027.6
Credit	2 100 . .	**338.6**	**470.5**	**470.2**	**581.6**	**580.1**	**552.4**	**652.8**	**601.9**
General merchandise: exports f.o.b.	2 110 . .	330.4	456.2	458.8	569.1	541.7	516.1	621.4	562.3
Goods for processing: exports f.o.b.	2 150 . .	...	...	...	...	...	...	...	...
Repairs on goods	2 160 . .	...	...	...	...	...	...	...	...
Goods procured in ports by carriers	2 170 . .	4.0	3.8	4.5	5.0	6.2	6.2	7.1	9.7
Nonmonetary gold	2 180 . .	4.2	10.5	6.9	7.5	32.2	30.1	24.3	29.9
Debit	3 100 . .	**-781.4**	**-882.3**	**-1,044.3**	**-1,371.2**	**-1,397.1**	**-1,698.2**	**-1,647.3**	**-1,629.5**
General merchandise: imports f.o.b.	3 110 . .	-781.4	-882.3	-1,044.3	-1,371.2	-1,397.1	-1,698.2	-1,647.3	-1,629.5
Goods for processing: imports f.o.b.	3 150 . .	...	...	...	...	...	...	...	...
Repairs on goods	3 160 . .	...	...	...	...	...	...	...	...
Goods procured in ports by carriers	3 170 . .	...	...	...	...	...	...	...	...
Nonmonetary gold	3 180 . .	...	...	...	...	...	...	...	...
B. SERVICES	4 200 . .	-47.7	-78.2	-79.6	-23.7	-16.9	-47.8	-39.9	-21.7
Total credit	2 200 . .	*125.2*	*142.3*	*173.2*	*215.7*	*250.9*	*286.9*	*303.5*	*331.8*
Total debit	3 200 . .	*-172.9*	*-220.5*	*-252.8*	*-239.4*	*-267.8*	*-334.7*	*-343.4*	*-353.5*
Transportation services, credit	2 205 . .	**12.2**	**15.7**	**17.2**	**22.3**	**24.3**	**27.4**	**30.1**	**25.7**
Passenger	2 850 . .	*1.0*	*1.0*	*1.4*	*2.3*	*2.7*	*3.4*	*3.8*	*3.1*
Freight	2 851 . .	*5.5*	*7.5*	*7.3*	*9.3*	*9.2*	*8.6*	*10.2*	*9.5*
Other	2 852 . .	*5.7*	*7.2*	*8.5*	*10.7*	*12.4*	*15.4*	*16.1*	*13.1*
Sea transport, passenger	2 207 . .	...	...	...	...	...	...	...	...
Sea transport, freight	2 208 . .	...	...	...	...	...	...	...	...
Sea transport, other	2 209 . .	4.0	4.7	4.7	5.8	6.9	7.7	6.7	6.3
Air transport, passenger	2 211 . .	1.0	1.0	1.4	2.3	2.7	3.4	3.8	3.1
Air transport, freight	2 212 . .	1.1	1.5	1.4	1.8	1.8	1.7	2.0	1.9
Air transport, other	2 213 . .	1.7	2.5	3.8	4.9	5.5	7.7	9.4	6.8
Other transport, passenger	2 215 . .	...	...	...	...	...	...	...	...
Other transport, freight	2 216 . .	4.4	6.0	5.9	7.5	7.4	6.9	8.2	7.6
Other transport, other	2 217 . .	...	...	...	...	...	...	...	...
Transportation services, debit	3 205 . .	**-74.4**	**-81.1**	**-93.7**	**-74.9**	**-88.2**	**-146.4**	**-151.7**	**-167.2**
Passenger	3 850 . .	*-15.5*	*-16.0*	*-19.0*	*-20.9*	*-23.8*	*-35.7*	*-48.0*	*-51.8*
Freight	3 851 . .	*-58.9*	*-65.1*	*-74.7*	*-54.0*	*-64.4*	*-110.7*	*-103.7*	*-115.4*
Other	3 852 . .	...	...	...	...	...	...	...	...
Sea transport, passenger	3 207 . .	...	...	...	...	...	...	...	...
Sea transport, freight	3 208 . .	-20.6	-22.7	-26.1	-18.9	-22.5	-38.8	-36.3	-32.3
Sea transport, other	3 209 . .	...	...	...	...	...	...	...	...
Air transport, passenger	3 211 . .	-15.5	-16.0	-19.0	-20.9	-23.8	-35.7	-48.0	-51.8
Air transport, freight	3 212 . .	-8.9	-9.7	-11.2	-8.1	-9.7	-16.5	-15.7	-12.7
Air transport, other	3 213 . .	...	...	...	...	...	...	...	...
Other transport, passenger	3 215 . .	...	...	...	...	...	...	...	...
Other transport, freight	3 216 . .	-29.4	-32.7	-37.4	-27.0	-32.2	-55.4	-51.7	-70.4
Other transport, other	3 217 . .	...	...	...	...	...	...	...	...
Travel, credit	2 236 . .	**40.2**	**49.5**	**54.2**	**79.8**	**100.1**	**125.2**	**128.6**	**135.3**
Business travel	2 237 . .	...	...	...	...	...	...	...	...
Personal travel	2 240 . .	40.2	49.5	54.2	79.8	100.1	125.2	128.6	135.3
Travel, debit	3 236 . .	**-30.1**	**-40.0**	**-60.0**	**-65.0**	**-70.0**	**-77.8**	**-78.4**	**-76.0**
Business travel	3 237 . .	...	...	...	...	...	...	...	...
Personal travel	3 240 . .	-30.1	-40.0	-60.0	-65.0	-70.0	-77.8	-78.4	-76.0
Other services, credit	2 200 BA	**72.8**	**77.1**	**101.8**	**113.6**	**126.5**	**134.3**	**144.8**	**170.8**
Communications	2 245 . .	25.3	25.8	25.7	19.6	24.0	24.0	25.1	24.3
Construction	2 249 . .	...	...	...	...	...	...	...	...
Insurance	2 253 . .	1.4	1.9	1.8	2.3	2.3	2.1	2.5	2.4
Financial	2 260 . .	...	...	...	...	...	...	...	...
Computer and information	2 262 . .	...	...	...	...	...	...	...	...
Royalties and licence fees	2 266 . .	...	...	...	...	...	...	...	...
Other business services	2 268 . .	13.4	27.1	46.0	60.6	69.0	74.6	82.4	108.5
Personal, cultural, and recreational	2 287 . .	...	...	...	...	...	...	...	...
Government, n.i.e.	2 291 . .	32.7	22.3	28.3	31.1	31.2	33.6	34.8	35.6
Other services, debit	3 200 BA	**-68.4**	**-99.4**	**-99.1**	**-99.5**	**-109.6**	**-110.5**	**-113.3**	**-110.3**
Communications	3 245 . .	-4.3	-5.1	-3.8	-3.3	-3.3	-2.9	-3.1	-3.6
Construction	3 249 . .	...	...	...	...	...	...	...	...
Insurance	3 253 . .	-6.2	-6.8	-8.0	-5.7	-6.9	-11.7	-11.0	-12.2
Financial	3 260 . .	...	...	...	...	...	...	...	...
Computer and information	3 262 . .	...	...	...	...	...	...	...	...
Royalties and licence fees	3 266 . .	...	...	...	...	...	...	...	...
Other business services	3 268 . .	-44.4	-74.3	-73.5	-77.8	-84.6	-79.9	-82.6	-77.0
Personal, cultural, and recreational	3 287 . .	...	...	...	...	...	...	...	...
Government, n.i.e.	3 291 . .	-13.5	-13.2	-13.8	-12.7	-14.8	-16.0	-16.6	-17.5

Table 2 (Continued). STANDARD PRESENTATION, 1994–2001
(Millions of U.S. dollars)

	Code	1994	1995	1996	1997	1998	1999	2000	2001
C. INCOME	4 300	-472.2	-372.1	-324.3	-264.7	-185.2	-196.8	-201.8	-248.5
Total credit	2 300	*6.7*	*7.1*	*10.5*	*14.7*	*26.0*	*30.7*	*30.7*	*14.7*
Total debit	3 300	*-478.9*	*-379.2*	*-334.8*	*-279.4*	*-211.2*	*-227.5*	*-232.5*	*-263.2*
Compensation of employees, credit	2 310	...	...	...	...	...	...	...	...
Compensation of employees, debit	3 310	...	...	...	...	...	...	...	...
Investment income, credit	2 320	**6.7**	**7.1**	**10.5**	**14.7**	**26.0**	**30.7**	**30.7**	**14.7**
Direct investment income	2 330	...	...	...	...	...	...	...	...
Dividends and distributed branch profits	2 332	...	...	...	...	...	...	...	...
Reinvested earnings and undistributed branch profits	2 333	...	...	...	...	...	...	...	...
Income on debt (interest)	2 334	...	...	...	...	...	...	...	...
Portfolio investment income	2 339	...	...	...	...	...	...	...	...
Income on equity	2 340	...	...	...	...	...	...	...	...
Income on bonds and notes	2 350	...	...	...	...	...	...	...	...
Income on money market instruments	2 360	...	...	...	...	...	...	...	...
Other investment income	2 370	6.7	7.1	10.5	14.7	26.0	30.7	30.7	14.7
Investment income, debit	3 320	**-478.9**	**-379.2**	**-334.8**	**-279.4**	**-211.2**	**-227.5**	**-232.5**	**-263.2**
Direct investment income	3 330	-16.7	-28.5	-45.0	-53.4	-58.2	-62.3	-69.4	-84.4
Dividends and distributed branch profits	3 332	-6.7	-13.5	-23.0	-30.3	-34.5	-37.3	-41.2	-54.4
Reinvested earnings and undistributed branch profits	3 333	-10.0	-15.0	-22.0	-23.1	-23.7	-25.0	-28.2	-30.0
Income on debt (interest)	3 334	...	...	...	...	...	...	...	...
Portfolio investment income	3 339	...	...	...	...	...	...	...	...
Income on equity	3 340	...	...	...	...	...	...	...	...
Income on bonds and notes	3 350	...	...	...	...	...	...	...	...
Income on money market instruments	3 360	...	...	...	...	...	...	...	...
Other investment income	3 370	-462.2	-350.7	-289.8	-226.0	-153.0	-165.2	-163.1	-178.8
D. CURRENT TRANSFERS	4 379	295.4	365.0	412.1	428.9	525.7	761.6	761.8	740.4
Credit	2 379	**295.4**	**365.0**	**412.1**	**428.9**	**525.7**	**761.6**	**761.8**	**740.4**
General government	2 380	139.4	158.1	135.1	86.5	64.9	163.1	147.6	95.8
Other sectors	2 390	156.0	206.9	277.0	342.4	460.8	598.5	614.2	644.6
Workers' remittances	2 391	50.0	75.0	95.0	150.0	200.0	300.0	320.0	335.7
Other current transfers	2 392	106.0	131.9	182.0	192.4	260.8	298.5	294.2	308.9
Debit	3 379	...	...	...	...	...	...	...	...
General government	3 380	...	...	...	...	...	...	...	...
Other sectors	3 390	...	...	...	...	...	...	...	...
Workers' remittances	3 391	...	...	...	...	...	...	...	...
Other current transfers	3 392	...	...	...	...	...	...	...	...
CAPITAL AND FINANCIAL ACCOUNT	4 996	**616.9**	**339.3**	**393.2**	**296.3**	**599.0**	**883.4**	**516.6**	**570.7**
CAPITAL ACCOUNT	4 994	**144.1**	**1,479.8**	**4,219.3**	**123.7**	**147.4**	**102.6**	**25.5**	**511.6**
Total credit	2 994	*144.1*	*1,479.8*	*4,219.3*	*123.7*	*147.4*	*102.6*	*25.5*	*511.6*
Total debit	3 994	...	...	...	...	...	...	...	...
Capital transfers, credit	2 400	**144.1**	**1,479.8**	**4,219.3**	**123.7**	**147.4**	**102.6**	**25.5**	**511.6**
General government	2 401	144.1	1,479.8	4,219.3	123.7	147.4	102.6	25.5	511.6
Debt forgiveness	2 402	144.1	1,479.8	4,219.3	123.7	147.4	102.6	25.5	511.6
Other capital transfers	2 410	...	...	...	...	...	...	...	...
Other sectors	2 430	...	...	...	...	...	...	...	...
Migrants' transfers	2 431	...	...	...	...	...	...	...	...
Debt forgiveness	2 432	...	...	...	...	...	...	...	...
Other capital transfers	2 440	...	...	...	...	...	...	...	...
Capital transfers, debit	3 400	...	...	...	...	...	...	...	...
General government	3 401	...	...	...	...	...	...	...	...
Debt forgiveness	3 402	...	...	...	...	...	...	...	...
Other capital transfers	3 410	...	...	...	...	...	...	...	...
Other sectors	3 430	...	...	...	...	...	...	...	...
Migrants' transfers	3 431	...	...	...	...	...	...	...	...
Debt forgiveness	3 432	...	...	...	...	...	...	...	...
Other capital transfers	3 440	...	...	...	...	...	...	...	...
Nonproduced nonfinancial assets, credit	2 480	...	...	...	...	...	...	...	...
Nonproduced nonfinancial assets, debit	3 480	...	...	...	...	...	...	...	...

Table 2 (Continued). STANDARD PRESENTATION, 1994–2001
(Millions of U.S. dollars)

	Code	1994	1995	1996	1997	1998	1999	2000	2001
FINANCIAL ACCOUNT	4 995 . .	**472.8**	**–1,140.5**	**–3,826.1**	**172.6**	**451.6**	**780.8**	**491.1**	**59.1**
A. DIRECT INVESTMENT	4 500 . .	40.0	75.4	97.0	173.1	183.7	300.0	265.0	132.3
Direct investment abroad	4 505 . .	**. . .**	**. . .**	**. . .**	**. . .**	**. . .**	**. . .**	**. . .**	**. . .**
Equity capital	4 510 . .	. . .	. . .	. . .	. . .	. . .	. . .	. . .	. . .
Claims on affiliated enterprises	4 515 . .	. . .	. . .	. . .	. . .	. . .	. . .	. . .	. . .
Liabilities to affiliated enterprises	4 520 . .	. . .	. . .	. . .	. . .	. . .	. . .	. . .	. . .
Reinvested earnings	4 525 . .	. . .	. . .	. . .	. . .	. . .	. . .	. . .	. . .
Other capital	4 530 . .	. . .	. . .	. . .	. . .	. . .	. . .	. . .	. . .
Claims on affiliated enterprises	4 535 . .	. . .	. . .	. . .	. . .	. . .	. . .	. . .	. . .
Liabilities to affiliated enterprises	4 540 . .	. . .	. . .	. . .	. . .	. . .	. . .	. . .	. . .
Direct investment in Nicaragua	4 555 . .	**40.0**	**75.4**	**97.0**	**173.1**	**183.7**	**300.0**	**265.0**	**132.3**
Equity capital	4 560 . .	30.0	60.4	75.0	150.0	160.0	275.0	236.8	102.3
Claims on direct investors	4 565 . .	. . .	. . .	. . .	. . .	. . .	. . .	. . .	. . .
Liabilities to direct investors	4 570 . .	30.0	60.4	75.0	150.0	160.0	275.0	236.8	102.3
Reinvested earnings	4 575 . .	10.0	15.0	22.0	23.1	23.7	25.0	28.2	30.0
Other capital	4 580 . .	. . .	. . .	. . .	. . .	. . .	. . .	. . .	. . .
Claims on direct investors	4 585 . .	. . .	. . .	. . .	. . .	. . .	. . .	. . .	. . .
Liabilities to direct investors	4 590 . .	. . .	. . .	. . .	. . .	. . .	. . .	. . .	. . .
B. PORTFOLIO INVESTMENT	4 600 . .	. . .	5.3	18.0	160.7	–128.2	–19.9	34.6	52.0
Assets	4 602 . .	**. . .**	**. . .**	**. . .**	**. . .**	**. . .**	**. . .**	**. . .**	**. . .**
Equity securities	4 610 . .	. . .	. . .	. . .	. . .	. . .	. . .	. . .	. . .
Monetary authorities	4 611 . .	. . .	. . .	. . .	. . .	. . .	. . .	. . .	. . .
General government	4 612 . .	. . .	. . .	. . .	. . .	. . .	. . .	. . .	. . .
Banks	4 613 . .	. . .	. . .	. . .	. . .	. . .	. . .	. . .	. . .
Other sectors	4 614 . .	. . .	. . .	. . .	. . .	. . .	. . .	. . .	. . .
Debt securities	4 619 . .	. . .	. . .	. . .	. . .	. . .	. . .	. . .	. . .
Bonds and notes	4 620 . .	. . .	. . .	. . .	. . .	. . .	. . .	. . .	. . .
Monetary authorities	4 621 . .	. . .	. . .	. . .	. . .	. . .	. . .	. . .	. . .
General government	4 622 . .	. . .	. . .	. . .	. . .	. . .	. . .	. . .	. . .
Banks	4 623 . .	. . .	. . .	. . .	. . .	. . .	. . .	. . .	. . .
Other sectors	4 624 . .	. . .	. . .	. . .	. . .	. . .	. . .	. . .	. . .
Money market instruments	4 630 . .	. . .	. . .	. . .	. . .	. . .	. . .	. . .	. . .
Monetary authorities	4 631 . .	. . .	. . .	. . .	. . .	. . .	. . .	. . .	. . .
General government	4 632 . .	. . .	. . .	. . .	. . .	. . .	. . .	. . .	. . .
Banks	4 633 . .	. . .	. . .	. . .	. . .	. . .	. . .	. . .	. . .
Other sectors	4 634 . .	. . .	. . .	. . .	. . .	. . .	. . .	. . .	. . .
Liabilities	4 652 . .	**. . .**	**5.3**	**18.0**	**160.7**	**–128.2**	**–19.9**	**34.6**	**52.0**
Equity securities	4 660 . .	. . .	. . .	. . .	. . .	. . .	. . .	. . .	. . .
Banks	4 663 . .	. . .	. . .	. . .	. . .	. . .	. . .	. . .	. . .
Other sectors	4 664 . .	. . .	. . .	. . .	. . .	. . .	. . .	. . .	. . .
Debt securities	4 669 . .	. . .	5.3	18.0	160.7	–128.2	–19.9	34.6	52.0
Bonds and notes	4 670 . .	. . .	. . .	. . .	. . .	. . .	. . .	. . .	. . .
Monetary authorities	4 671 . .	. . .	. . .	. . .	. . .	. . .	. . .	. . .	. . .
General government	4 672 . .	. . .	. . .	. . .	. . .	. . .	. . .	. . .	. . .
Banks	4 673 . .	. . .	. . .	. . .	. . .	. . .	. . .	. . .	. . .
Other sectors	4 674 . .	. . .	. . .	. . .	. . .	. . .	. . .	. . .	. . .
Money market instruments	4 680 . .	. . .	5.3	18.0	160.7	–128.2	–19.9	34.6	52.0
Monetary authorities	4 681 . .	. . .	5.3	18.0	160.7	–128.2	–19.9	34.6	52.0
General government	4 682 . .	. . .	. . .	. . .	. . .	. . .	. . .	. . .	. . .
Banks	4 683 . .	. . .	. . .	. . .	. . .	. . .	. . .	. . .	. . .
Other sectors	4 684 . .	. . .	. . .	. . .	. . .	. . .	. . .	. . .	. . .
C. FINANCIAL DERIVATIVES	4 910 . .	. . .	. . .	. . .	. . .	. . .	. . .	. . .	. . .
Monetary authorities	4 911 . .	. . .	. . .	. . .	. . .	. . .	. . .	. . .	. . .
General government	4 912 . .	. . .	. . .	. . .	. . .	. . .	. . .	. . .	. . .
Banks	4 913 . .	. . .	. . .	. . .	. . .	. . .	. . .	. . .	. . .
Other sectors	4 914 . .	. . .	. . .	. . .	. . .	. . .	. . .	. . .	. . .
Assets	4 900 . .	**. . .**	**. . .**	**. . .**	**. . .**	**. . .**	**. . .**	**. . .**	**. . .**
Monetary authorities	4 901 . .	. . .	. . .	. . .	. . .	. . .	. . .	. . .	. . .
General government	4 902 . .	. . .	. . .	. . .	. . .	. . .	. . .	. . .	. . .
Banks	4 903 . .	. . .	. . .	. . .	. . .	. . .	. . .	. . .	. . .
Other sectors	4 904 . .	. . .	. . .	. . .	. . .	. . .	. . .	. . .	. . .
Liabilities	4 905 . .	**. . .**	**. . .**	**. . .**	**. . .**	**. . .**	**. . .**	**. . .**	**. . .**
Monetary authorities	4 906 . .	. . .	. . .	. . .	. . .	. . .	. . .	. . .	. . .
General government	4 907 . .	. . .	. . .	. . .	. . .	. . .	. . .	. . .	. . .
Banks	4 908 . .	. . .	. . .	. . .	. . .	. . .	. . .	. . .	. . .
Other sectors	4 909 . .	. . .	. . .	. . .	. . .	. . .	. . .	. . .	. . .

Table 2 (Concluded). STANDARD PRESENTATION, 1994–2001
(Millions of U.S. dollars)

	Code	1994	1995	1996	1997	1998	1999	2000	2001
D. OTHER INVESTMENT	4 700 . .	517.4	-1,232.7	-3,888.0	12.0	365.8	657.2	174.7	-239.1
Assets	4 703 . .	**-1.3**	**-32.0**	**-54.3**	**-70.8**	**55.2**	**22.2**	**79.9**	**-60.4**
Trade credits	4 706 . .	...	...	...	...	...	...	...	...
General government	4 707 . .	...	...	...	...	...	...	...	...
of which: Short-term	4 709 . .	...	...	...	...	...	...	...	...
Other sectors	4 710 . .	...	...	...	...	...	...	...	...
of which: Short-term	4 712 . .	...	...	...	...	...	...	...	...
Loans	4 714 . .	...	...	...	...	...	...	...	...
Monetary authorities	4 715 . .	...	...	...	...	...	...	...	...
of which: Short-term	4 718 . .	...	...	...	...	...	...	...	...
General government	4 719 . .	...	...	...	...	...	...	...	...
of which: Short-term	4 721 . .	...	...	...	...	...	...	...	...
Banks	4 722 . .	...	...	...	...	...	...	...	...
of which: Short-term	4 724 . .	...	...	...	...	...	...	...	...
Other sectors	4 725 . .	...	...	...	...	...	...	...	...
of which: Short-term	4 727 . .	...	...	...	...	...	...	...	...
Currency and deposits	4 730 . .	-1.3	5.3	-46.4	-30.1	13.5	13.8	38.8	-60.2
Monetary authorities	4 731 . .	...	...	...	...	...	...	...	...
General government	4 732 . .	...	...	...	...	...	...	...	...
Banks	4 733 . .	-1.3	5.3	-46.4	-30.1	13.5	13.8	38.8	-60.2
Other sectors	4 734 . .	...	...	...	...	...	...	...	...
Other assets	4 736 . .	...	-37.3	-7.9	-40.7	41.7	8.4	41.1	-.2
Monetary authorities	4 737 . .	...	...	...	...	...	...	...	...
of which: Short-term	4 739 . .	...	...	...	...	...	...	...	...
General government	4 740 . .	...	...	...	...	...	...	...	...
of which: Short-term	4 742 . .	...	...	...	...	...	...	...	...
Banks	4 743 . .	...	-37.3	-7.9	-40.7	41.7	8.4	41.1	-.2
of which: Short-term	4 745 . .	...	*-37.3*	*-7.9*	*-40.7*	*41.7*	*8.4*	*41.1*	*-.2*
Other sectors	4 746 . .	...	...	...	...	...	...	...	...
of which: Short-term	4 748 . .	...	...	...	...	...	...	...	...
Liabilities	4 753 . .	**518.7**	**-1,200.7**	**-3,833.7**	**82.8**	**310.6**	**635.0**	**94.8**	**-178.7**
Trade credits	4 756 . .	28.1	-50.2	59.9	106.9	173.5	144.1	-99.8	69.7
General government	4 757 . .	...	...	...	...	...	...	...	...
of which: Short-term	4 759 . .	...	...	...	...	...	...	...	...
Other sectors	4 760 . .	28.1	-50.2	59.9	106.9	173.5	144.1	-99.8	69.7
of which: Short-term	4 762 . .	*28.1*	*-50.2*	*59.9*	*106.9*	*173.5*	*144.1*	*-99.8*	*69.7*
Loans	4 764 . .	-272.8	-47.0	615.2	434.6	197.9	326.2	140.3	114.5
Monetary authorities	4 765 . .	-437.7	-190.9	-108.9	-51.3	5.8	72.8	-39.5	-18.4
of which: Use of Fund credit and loans from the Fund	4 766 . .	*26.1*	*-12.9*	*-9.3*	...	*22.6*	*105.3*	*20.9*	*-5.0*
of which: Short-term	4 768 . .	...	...	...	...	...	...	...	...
General government	4 769 . .	123.1	99.5	665.2	429.3	199.9	245.5	187.9	135.6
of which: Short-term	4 771 . .	...	...	...	...	...	...	...	...
Banks	4 772 . .	...	25.5	15.2	30.4	1.4	7.1	13.5	18.7
of which: Short-term	4 774 . .	...	...	...	...	...	...	...	...
Other sectors	4 775 . .	41.8	18.9	43.7	26.2	-9.2	.8	-21.6	-21.4
of which: Short-term	4 777 . .	...	...	...	...	...	...	...	...
Currency and deposits	4 780 . .	14.3	5.8	.6	9.7	-1.1	56.5	-32.7	19.7
Monetary authorities	4 781 . .	...	...	...	...	...	...	...	...
General government	4 782 . .	...	...	...	...	...	...	...	...
Banks	4 783 . .	14.3	5.8	.6	9.7	-1.1	56.5	-32.7	19.7
Other sectors	4 784 . .	...	...	...	...	...	...	...	...
Other liabilities	4 786 . .	749.1	-1,109.3	-4,509.4	-468.4	-59.7	108.2	87.0	-382.6
Monetary authorities	4 787 . .	640.2	134.3	104.5	-222.6	5.3	149.0	53.8	-404.5
of which: Short-term	4 789 . .	*640.2*	*134.3*	*104.5*	*-222.6*	*5.3*	*149.0*	*53.8*	*-404.5*
General government	4 790 . .	108.9	-1,243.6	-4,613.9	-245.8	-65.0	-40.8	33.2	21.9
of which: Short-term	4 792 . .	*108.9*	*-1,243.6*	*-4,613.9*	*-245.8*	*-65.0*	*-40.8*	*33.2*	*21.9*
Banks	4 793 . .	...	...	...	...	...	...	...	...
of which: Short-term	4 795 . .	...	...	...	...	...	...	...	...
Other sectors	4 796 . .	...	...	...	...	...	...	...	...
of which: Short-term	4 798 . .	...	...	...	...	...	...	...	...
E. RESERVE ASSETS	4 802 . .	-84.6	11.5	-53.1	-173.2	30.3	-156.5	16.8	113.9
Monetary gold	4 812 . .	-1.2	-.6	...	...	-.1	5.2	-5.3	5.0
Special drawing rights	4 811 . .	...	...	...	...	-.2	...	.1	-.3
Reserve position in the Fund	4 810 . .	...	...	...	...	...	...	...	...
Foreign exchange	4 803 . .	-86.0	4.8	-61.1	-180.6	27.7	-159.5	21.1	108.8
Other claims	4 813 . .	2.6	7.3	8.0	7.4	2.9	-2.2	.9	.4
NET ERRORS AND OMISSIONS	4 998 . .	**50.4**	**157.8**	**172.7**	**352.8**	**-105.6**	**-254.6**	**-42.2**	**-13.3**

Part 3 of the *Yearbook* contains descriptions of the methodologies, compilation practices, and sources used to compile these data.

Table 1. ANALYTIC PRESENTATION, 1994–2001
(Millions of U.S. dollars)

	Code		1994	1995	1996	1997	1998	1999	2000	2001
A. Current Account [1]	4 993	Z.	**–126.1**	**–151.7**	...	...	...	...	...	...
Goods: exports f.o.b	2 100	..	226.8	288.1	...	...	...	...	...	...
Goods: imports f.o.b	3 100	..	–271.3	–305.6	...	...	...	...	...	...
Balance on Goods	4 100	..	*–44.5*	*–17.6*	...	...	...	...	...	...
Services: credit	2 200	..	30.4	33.3	...	...	...	...	...	...
Services: debit	3 200	..	–149.1	–151.8	...	...	...	...	...	...
Balance on Goods and Services	4 991	..	*–163.2*	*–136.0*	...	...	...	...	...	...
Income: credit	2 300	..	15.6	5.8	...	...	...	...	...	...
Income: debit	3 300	..	–45.2	–52.9	...	...	...	...	...	...
Balance on Goods, Services, and Income	4 992	..	*–192.8*	*–183.2*	...	...	...	...	...	...
Current transfers: credit	2 379	Z.	115.1	60.6	...	...	...	...	...	...
Current transfers: debit	3 379	..	–48.5	–29.1	...	...	...	...	...	...
B. Capital Account [1]	4 994	Z.	**88.2**	**65.3**	...	...	...	...	...	...
Capital account: credit	2 994	Z.	88.2	65.3	...	...	...	...	...	...
Capital account: debit	3 994	..	...	...	...	...	...	...	...	...
Total, Groups A Plus B	4 981	..	*–37.9*	*–86.3*	...	...	...	...	...	...
C. Financial Account [1]	4 995	W.	**29.9**	**–46.1**	...	...	...	...	...	...
Direct investment abroad	4 505	..	1.8	–7.1	...	...	...	...	...	...
Direct investment in Niger	4 555	Z.	–11.3	7.2	...	...	...	...	...	...
Portfolio investment assets	4 602	..	...	...	...	...	...	...	...	...
Equity securities	4 610	..	...	...	...	...	...	...	...	...
Debt securities	4 619	..	...	...	...	...	...	...	...	...
Portfolio investment liabilities	4 652	Z.	...	...	...	...	...	...	...	...
Equity securities	4 660	..	...	...	...	...	...	...	...	...
Debt securities	4 669	Z.	...	...	...	...	...	...	...	...
Financial derivatives	4 910	..	...	...	...	...	...	...	...	...
Financial derivatives assets	4 900	..	...	...	...	...	...	...	...	...
Financial derivatives liabilities	4 905	..	...	...	...	...	...	...	...	...
Other investment assets	4 703	..	22.3	–18.4	...	...	...	...	...	...
Monetary authorities	4 701	..	...	...	...	...	...	...	...	...
General government	4 704	..	.3	...	...	...	...	...	...	...
Banks	4 705	..	...	...	...	...	...	...	...	...
Other sectors	4 728	..	22.0	–18.4	...	...	...	...	...	...
Other investment liabilities	4 753	W.	17.1	–27.8	...	...	...	...	...	...
Monetary authorities	4 753	WA	–22.3	–2.3	...	...	...	...	...	...
General government	4 753	ZB	6.7	–14.8	...	...	...	...	...	...
Banks	4 753	ZC	19.4	–10.8	...	...	...	...	...	...
Other sectors	4 753	ZD	13.3	.1	...	...	...	...	...	...
Total, Groups A Through C	4 983	..	*–8.0*	*–132.5*	...	...	...	...	...	...
D. Net Errors and Omissions	4 998	..	**–67.8**	**114.4**	...	...	...	...	...	...
Total, Groups A Through D	4 984	..	*–75.8*	*–18.1*	...	...	...	...	...	...
E. Reserves and Related Items	4 802	A.	**75.8**	**18.1**	...	...	...	...	...	...
Reserve assets	4 802	..	28.7	–25.8	...	...	...	...	...	...
Use of Fund credit and loans	4 766	..	5.4	–10.2	...	...	...	...	...	...
Exceptional financing	4 920	..	41.7	54.1	...	...	...	...	...	...
Conversion rates: CFA francs per U.S. dollar	0 101	..	**555.20**	**499.15**	**511.55**	**583.67**	**589.95**	**615.70**	**711.98**	**733.04**

[1] Excludes components that have been classified in the categories of Group E.

Table 2. STANDARD PRESENTATION, 1994–2001
(Millions of U.S. dollars)

	Code	1994	1995	1996	1997	1998	1999	2000	2001
CURRENT ACCOUNT	4 993 . .	**–126.1**	**–151.7**	...	...	...	...	...	...
A. GOODS	4 100 . .	–44.5	–17.6	...	...	...	...	...	...
Credit	2 100 . .	**226.8**	**288.1**	...	...	...	...	...	...
General merchandise: exports f.o.b.	2 110 . .	225.4	286.5	...	...	...	...	...	...
Goods for processing: exports f.o.b.	2 150 . .	...	...	...	...	...	...	...	...
Repairs on goods	2 160 . .	...	...	...	...	...	...	...	...
Goods procured in ports by carriers	2 170 . .	1.4	1.5	...	...	...	...	...	...
Nonmonetary gold	2 180 . .	...	...	...	...	...	...	...	...
Debit	3 100 . .	**–271.3**	**–305.6**	...	...	...	...	...	...
General merchandise: imports f.o.b.	3 110 . .	–262.9	–297.3	...	...	...	...	...	...
Goods for processing: imports f.o.b.	3 150 . .	...	...	...	...	...	...	...	...
Repairs on goods	3 160 . .	...	...	...	...	...	...	...	...
Goods procured in ports by carriers	3 170 . .	–8.1	–8.1	...	...	...	...	...	...
Nonmonetary gold	3 180 . .	–.3	–.3	...	...	...	...	...	...
B. SERVICES	4 200 . .	–118.8	–118.5	...	...	...	...	...	...
Total credit	2 200 . .	*30.4*	*33.3*	...	...	...	...	...	...
Total debit	3 200 . .	*–149.1*	*–151.8*	...	...	...	...	...	...
Transportation services, credit	2 205 . .	**.4**	**.4**	...	...	...	...	...	...
Passenger	2 850 . .	...	...	...	...	...	...	...	...
Freight	2 851 . .	*.4*	*.4*	...	...	...	...	...	...
Other	2 852 . .	...	...	...	...	...	...	...	...
Sea transport, passenger	2 207 . .	...	...	...	...	...	...	...	...
Sea transport, freight	2 208 . .	...	...	...	...	...	...	...	...
Sea transport, other	2 209 . .	...	...	...	...	...	...	...	...
Air transport, passenger	2 211 . .	...	...	...	...	...	...	...	...
Air transport, freight	2 212 . .	...	...	...	...	...	...	...	...
Air transport, other	2 213 . .	...	...	...	...	...	...	...	...
Other transport, passenger	2 215 . .	...	...	...	...	...	...	...	...
Other transport, freight	2 216 . .	.4	.4	...	...	...	...	...	...
Other transport, other	2 217 . .	...	...	...	...	...	...	...	...
Transportation services, debit	3 205 . .	**–77.3**	**–89.5**	...	...	...	...	...	...
Passenger	3 850 . .	*–12.2*	*–13.1*	...	...	...	...	...	...
Freight	3 851 . .	*–65.1*	*–76.4*	...	...	...	...	...	...
Other	3 852 . .	...	...	...	...	...	...	...	...
Sea transport, passenger	3 207 . .	...	...	...	...	...	...	...	...
Sea transport, freight	3 208 . .	...	...	...	...	...	...	...	...
Sea transport, other	3 209 . .	...	...	...	...	...	...	...	...
Air transport, passenger	3 211 . .	–10.5	–12.1	...	...	...	...	...	...
Air transport, freight	3 212 . .	...	...	...	...	...	...	...	...
Air transport, other	3 213 . .	...	...	...	...	...	...	...	...
Other transport, passenger	3 215 . .	–1.7	–1.0	...	...	...	...	...	...
Other transport, freight	3 216 . .	–65.1	–76.4	...	...	...	...	...	...
Other transport, other	3 217 . .	...	...	...	...	...	...	...	...
Travel, credit	2 236 . .	**4.6**	**7.1**	...	...	...	...	...	...
Business travel	2 237 . .	...	...	...	...	...	...	...	...
Personal travel	2 240 . .	4.6	7.1	...	...	...	...	...	...
Travel, debit	3 236 . .	**–19.6**	**–13.3**	...	...	...	...	...	...
Business travel	3 237 . .	–.8	–.9	...	...	...	...	...	...
Personal travel	3 240 . .	–18.7	–12.4	...	...	...	...	...	...
Other services, credit	2 200 BA	**25.4**	**25.8**	...	...	...	...	...	...
Communications	2 245 . .	.1	.1	...	...	...	...	...	...
Construction	2 249 . .	...	...	...	...	...	...	...	...
Insurance	2 253 . .	...	...	...	...	...	...	...	...
Financial	2 260 . .	...	...	...	...	...	...	...	...
Computer and information	2 262 . .	...	...	...	...	...	...	...	...
Royalties and licence fees	2 266 . .	...	...	...	...	...	...	...	...
Other business services	2 268 . .	2.6	4.7	...	...	...	...	...	...
Personal, cultural, and recreational	2 287 . .	...	...	...	...	...	...	...	...
Government, n.i.e.	2 291 . .	22.7	21.0	...	...	...	...	...	...
Other services, debit	3 200 BA	**–52.2**	**–49.0**	...	...	...	...	...	...
Communications	3 245 . .	...	...	...	...	...	...	...	...
Construction	3 249 . .	...	...	...	...	...	...	...	...
Insurance	3 253 . .	–2.3	–3.1	...	...	...	...	...	...
Financial	3 260 . .	...	...	...	...	...	...	...	...
Computer and information	3 262 . .	–.1	...	...	...	...	...	...	...
Royalties and licence fees	3 266 . .	–.5	–.6	...	...	...	...	...	...
Other business services	3 268 . .	–14.6	–13.8	...	...	...	...	...	...
Personal, cultural, and recreational	3 287 . .	...	...	...	...	...	...	...	...
Government, n.i.e.	3 291 . .	–34.7	–31.5	...	...	...	...	...	...

Table 2 (Continued). STANDARD PRESENTATION, 1994–2001
(Millions of U.S. dollars)

	Code	1994	1995	1996	1997	1998	1999	2000	2001
C. INCOME	4 300	–29.6	–47.1	...	...	...	...	...	...
Total credit	2 300	*15.6*	*5.8*	...	...	...	...	...	...
Total debit	3 300	*–45.2*	*–52.9*	...	...	...	...	...	...
Compensation of employees, credit	2 310	**1.2**	**1.4**	...	...	...	...	...	...
Compensation of employees, debit	3 310	...	...	...	...	...	...	...	...
Investment income, credit	2 320	**14.4**	**4.4**	...	...	...	...	...	...
Direct investment income	2 330	11.0	.5	...	...	...	...	...	...
Dividends and distributed branch profits	2 332	.3	...	...	...	...	...	...	...
Reinvested earnings and undistributed branch profits	2 333	9.8	...	...	...	...	...	...	...
Income on debt (interest)	2 334	.9	.5	...	...	...	...	...	...
Portfolio investment income	2 339	...	...	...	...	...	...	...	...
Income on equity	2 340	...	...	...	...	...	...	...	...
Income on bonds and notes	2 350	...	...	...	...	...	...	...	...
Income on money market instruments	2 360	...	...	...	...	...	...	...	...
Other investment income	2 370	3.4	3.9	...	...	...	...	...	...
Investment income, debit	3 320	**–45.2**	**–52.9**	...	...	...	...	...	...
Direct investment income	3 330	–7.8	–3.8	...	...	...	...	...	...
Dividends and distributed branch profits	3 332	–7.4	–.9	...	...	...	...	...	...
Reinvested earnings and undistributed branch profits	3 333	4.2	.4	...	...	...	...	...	...
Income on debt (interest)	3 334	–4.6	–3.3	...	...	...	...	...	...
Portfolio investment income	3 339	–33.3	–42.3	...	...	...	...	...	...
Income on equity	3 340	...	...	...	...	...	...	...	...
Income on bonds and notes	3 350	–33.3	–42.3	...	...	...	...	...	...
Income on money market instruments	3 360	...	...	...	...	...	...	...	...
Other investment income	3 370	–4.0	–6.8	...	...	...	...	...	...
D. CURRENT TRANSFERS	4 379	66.7	31.5	...	...	...	...	...	...
Credit	2 379	**115.1**	**60.6**	...	...	...	...	...	...
General government	2 380	109.5	54.2	...	...	...	...	...	...
Other sectors	2 390	5.7	6.3	...	...	...	...	...	...
Workers' remittances	2 391	5.7	6.3	...	...	...	...	...	...
Other current transfers	2 392	...	...	...	...	...	...	...	...
Debit	3 379	**–48.5**	**–29.1**	...	...	...	...	...	...
General government	3 380	–1.9	–.4	...	...	...	...	...	...
Other sectors	3 390	–46.5	–28.6	...	...	...	...	...	...
Workers' remittances	3 391	–46.5	–28.6	...	...	...	...	...	...
Other current transfers	3 392	...	...	...	...	...	...	...	...
CAPITAL AND FINANCIAL ACCOUNT	4 996	**194.0**	**37.3**	...	...	...	...	...	...
CAPITAL ACCOUNT	4 994	**158.9**	**65.3**	...	...	...	...	...	...
Total credit	2 994	*158.9*	*65.3*	...	...	...	...	...	...
Total debit	3 994	...	...	...	...	...	...	...	...
Capital transfers, credit	2 400	**158.9**	**65.3**	...	...	...	...	...	...
General government	2 401	158.9	65.3	...	...	...	...	...	...
Debt forgiveness	2 402	70.7	...	...	...	...	...	...	...
Other capital transfers	2 410	88.2	65.3	...	...	...	...	...	...
Other sectors	2 430	...	...	...	...	...	...	...	...
Migrants' transfers	2 431	...	...	...	...	...	...	...	...
Debt forgiveness	2 432	...	...	...	...	...	...	...	...
Other capital transfers	2 440	...	...	...	...	...	...	...	...
Capital transfers, debit	3 400	...	...	...	...	...	...	...	...
General government	3 401	...	...	...	...	...	...	...	...
Debt forgiveness	3 402	...	...	...	...	...	...	...	...
Other capital transfers	3 410	...	...	...	...	...	...	...	...
Other sectors	3 430	...	...	...	...	...	...	...	...
Migrants' transfers	3 431	...	...	...	...	...	...	...	...
Debt forgiveness	3 432	...	...	...	...	...	...	...	...
Other capital transfers	3 440	...	...	...	...	...	...	...	...
Nonproduced nonfinancial assets, credit	2 480	...	...	...	...	...	...	...	...
Nonproduced nonfinancial assets, debit	3 480	...	...	...	...	...	...	...	...

Table 2 (Continued). STANDARD PRESENTATION, 1994–2001

(Millions of U.S. dollars)

	Code	1994	1995	1996	1997	1998	1999	2000	2001
FINANCIAL ACCOUNT	4 995	**35.0**	**–28.1**	...	...	...	...	...	...
A. DIRECT INVESTMENT	4 500	–9.5	...	...	...	...	...	...	...
Direct investment abroad	4 505	**1.8**	**–7.1**	...	...	...	...	...	...
Equity capital	4 510	...	...	...	...	...	...	...	...
Claims on affiliated enterprises	4 515	...	...	...	...	...	...	...	...
Liabilities to affiliated enterprises	4 520	...	...	...	...	...	...	...	...
Reinvested earnings	4 525	–9.8	...	...	...	...	...	...	...
Other capital	4 530	11.6	–7.1	...	...	...	...	...	...
Claims on affiliated enterprises	4 535	–2.3	–.1	...	...	...	...	...	...
Liabilities to affiliated enterprises	4 540	14.0	–7.0	...	...	...	...	...	...
Direct investment in Niger	4 555	**–11.3**	**7.2**	...	...	...	...	...	...
Equity capital	4 560	...	...	...	...	...	...	...	...
Claims on direct investors	4 565	...	...	...	...	...	...	...	...
Liabilities to direct investors	4 570	...	...	...	...	...	...	...	...
Reinvested earnings	4 575	–4.2	–.4	...	...	...	...	...	...
Other capital	4 580	–7.0	7.6	...	...	...	...	...	...
Claims on direct investors	4 585	–1.4	–2.1	...	...	...	...	...	...
Liabilities to direct investors	4 590	–5.7	9.7	...	...	...	...	...	...
B. PORTFOLIO INVESTMENT	4 600	...	...	...	...	...	...	...	...
Assets	4 602	...	...	...	...	...	...	...	...
Equity securities	4 610	...	...	...	...	...	...	...	...
Monetary authorities	4 611	...	...	...	...	...	...	...	...
General government	4 612	...	...	...	...	...	...	...	...
Banks	4 613	...	...	...	...	...	...	...	...
Other sectors	4 614	...	...	...	...	...	...	...	...
Debt securities	4 619	...	...	...	...	...	...	...	...
Bonds and notes	4 620	...	...	...	...	...	...	...	...
Monetary authorities	4 621	...	...	...	...	...	...	...	...
General government	4 622	...	...	...	...	...	...	...	...
Banks	4 623	...	...	...	...	...	...	...	...
Other sectors	4 624	...	...	...	...	...	...	...	...
Money market instruments	4 630	...	...	...	...	...	...	...	...
Monetary authorities	4 631	...	...	...	...	...	...	...	...
General government	4 632	...	...	...	...	...	...	...	...
Banks	4 633	...	...	...	...	...	...	...	...
Other sectors	4 634	...	...	...	...	...	...	...	...
Liabilities	4 652	...	...	...	...	...	...	...	...
Equity securities	4 660	...	...	...	...	...	...	...	...
Banks	4 663	...	...	...	...	...	...	...	...
Other sectors	4 664	...	...	...	...	...	...	...	...
Debt securities	4 669	...	...	...	...	...	...	...	...
Bonds and notes	4 670	...	...	...	...	...	...	...	...
Monetary authorities	4 671	...	...	...	...	...	...	...	...
General government	4 672	...	...	...	...	...	...	...	...
Banks	4 673	...	...	...	...	...	...	...	...
Other sectors	4 674	...	...	...	...	...	...	...	...
Money market instruments	4 680	...	...	...	...	...	...	...	...
Monetary authorities	4 681	...	...	...	...	...	...	...	...
General government	4 682	...	...	...	...	...	...	...	...
Banks	4 683	...	...	...	...	...	...	...	...
Other sectors	4 684	...	...	...	...	...	...	...	...
C. FINANCIAL DERIVATIVES	4 910	...	...	...	...	...	...	...	...
Monetary authorities	4 911	...	...	...	...	...	...	...	...
General government	4 912	...	...	...	...	...	...	...	...
Banks	4 913	...	...	...	...	...	...	...	...
Other sectors	4 914	...	...	...	...	...	...	...	...
Assets	4 900	...	...	...	...	...	...	...	...
Monetary authorities	4 901	...	...	...	...	...	...	...	...
General government	4 902	...	...	...	...	...	...	...	...
Banks	4 903	...	...	...	...	...	...	...	...
Other sectors	4 904	...	...	...	...	...	...	...	...
Liabilities	4 905	...	...	...	...	...	...	...	...
Monetary authorities	4 906	...	...	...	...	...	...	...	...
General government	4 907	...	...	...	...	...	...	...	...
Banks	4 908	...	...	...	...	...	...	...	...
Other sectors	4 909	...	...	...	...	...	...	...	...

Table 2 (Concluded). STANDARD PRESENTATION, 1994–2001
(Millions of U.S. dollars)

	Code	1994	1995	1996	1997	1998	1999	2000	2001
D. OTHER INVESTMENT	4 700 . .	15.8	–2.3	. . .	. . .	. . .	. . .	. . .	. . .
Assets	4 703 . .	**22.3**	**–18.4**	**. . .**	**. . .**	**. . .**	**. . .**	**. . .**	**. . .**
Trade credits	4 706 . .	22.2	–18.0	. . .	. . .	. . .	. . .	. . .	. . .
General government	4 707 . .	. . .	. . .	. . .	. . .	. . .	. . .	. . .	. . .
of which: Short-term	4 709 . .	. . .	. . .	. . .	. . .	. . .	. . .	. . .	. . .
Other sectors	4 710 . .	22.2	–18.0	. . .	. . .	. . .	. . .	. . .	. . .
of which: Short-term	4 712 . .	*22.2*	*–18.0*	. . .	. . .	. . .	. . .	. . .	. . .
Loans	4 714 . .	. . .	. . .	. . .	. . .	. . .	. . .	. . .	. . .
Monetary authorities	4 715 . .	. . .	. . .	. . .	. . .	. . .	. . .	. . .	. . .
of which: Short-term	4 718 . .	. . .	. . .	. . .	. . .	. . .	. . .	. . .	. . .
General government	4 719 . .	. . .	. . .	. . .	. . .	. . .	. . .	. . .	. . .
of which: Short-term	4 721 . .	. . .	. . .	. . .	. . .	. . .	. . .	. . .	. . .
Banks	4 722 . .	. . .	. . .	. . .	. . .	. . .	. . .	. . .	. . .
of which: Short-term	4 724 . .	. . .	. . .	. . .	. . .	. . .	. . .	. . .	. . .
Other sectors	4 725 . .	. . .	. . .	. . .	. . .	. . .	. . .	. . .	. . .
of which: Short-term	4 727 . .	. . .	. . .	. . .	. . .	. . .	. . .	. . .	. . .
Currency and deposits	4 730 . .	. . .	. . .	. . .	. . .	. . .	. . .	. . .	. . .
Monetary authorities	4 731 . .	. . .	. . .	. . .	. . .	. . .	. . .	. . .	. . .
General government	4 732 . .	. . .	. . .	. . .	. . .	. . .	. . .	. . .	. . .
Banks	4 733 . .	. . .	. . .	. . .	. . .	. . .	. . .	. . .	. . .
Other sectors	4 734 . .	. . .	. . .	. . .	. . .	. . .	. . .	. . .	. . .
Other assets	4 736 . .	.1	–.4	. . .	. . .	. . .	. . .	. . .	. . .
Monetary authorities	4 737 . .	. . .	. . .	. . .	. . .	. . .	. . .	. . .	. . .
of which: Short-term	4 739 . .	. . .	. . .	. . .	. . .	. . .	. . .	. . .	. . .
General government	4 740 . .	.3	. . .	. . .	. . .	. . .	. . .	. . .	. . .
of which: Short-term	4 742 . .	. . .	. . .	. . .	. . .	. . .	. . .	. . .	. . .
Banks	4 743 . .	. . .	. . .	. . .	. . .	. . .	. . .	. . .	. . .
of which: Short-term	4 745 . .	. . .	. . .	. . .	. . .	. . .	. . .	. . .	. . .
Other sectors	4 746 . .	–.2	–.4	. . .	. . .	. . .	. . .	. . .	. . .
of which: Short-term	4 748 . .	*–.2*	*–.6*	. . .	. . .	. . .	. . .	. . .	. . .
Liabilities	4 753 . .	**–6.5**	**16.1**	**. . .**	**. . .**	**. . .**	**. . .**	**. . .**	**. . .**
Trade credits	4 756 . .	15.3	–6.8	. . .	. . .	. . .	. . .	. . .	. . .
General government	4 757 . .	. . .	. . .	. . .	. . .	. . .	. . .	. . .	. . .
of which: Short-term	4 759 . .	. . .	. . .	. . .	. . .	. . .	. . .	. . .	. . .
Other sectors	4 760 . .	15.3	–6.8	. . .	. . .	. . .	. . .	. . .	. . .
of which: Short-term	4 762 . .	*15.3*	*–6.8*	. . .	. . .	. . .	. . .	. . .	. . .
Loans	4 764 . .	106.3	–18.8	. . .	. . .	. . .	. . .	. . .	. . .
Monetary authorities	4 765 . .	5.4	–10.2	. . .	. . .	. . .	. . .	. . .	. . .
of which: Use of Fund credit and loans from the Fund	4 766 . .	*5.4*	*–10.2*	. . .	. . .	. . .	. . .	. . .	. . .
of which: Short-term	4 768 . .	. . .	. . .	. . .	. . .	. . .	. . .	. . .	. . .
General government	4 769 . .	97.5	–14.8	. . .	. . .	. . .	. . .	. . .	. . .
of which: Short-term	4 771 . .	. . .	. . .	. . .	. . .	. . .	. . .	. . .	. . .
Banks	4 772 . .	. . .	. . .	. . .	. . .	. . .	. . .	. . .	. . .
of which: Short-term	4 774 . .	. . .	. . .	. . .	. . .	. . .	. . .	. . .	. . .
Other sectors	4 775 . .	3.4	6.2	. . .	. . .	. . .	. . .	. . .	. . .
of which: Short-term	4 777 . .	. . .	. . .	. . .	. . .	. . .	. . .	. . .	. . .
Currency and deposits	4 780 . .	–4.7	–9.2	. . .	. . .	. . .	. . .	. . .	. . .
Monetary authorities	4 781 . .	–22.3	–2.3	. . .	. . .	. . .	. . .	. . .	. . .
General government	4 782 . .	. . .	. . .	. . .	. . .	. . .	. . .	. . .	. . .
Banks	4 783 . .	17.5	–6.9	. . .	. . .	. . .	. . .	. . .	. . .
Other sectors	4 784 . .	. . .	. . .	. . .	. . .	. . .	. . .	. . .	. . .
Other liabilities	4 786 . .	–123.3	50.9	. . .	. . .	. . .	. . .	. . .	. . .
Monetary authorities	4 787 . .	. . .	. . .	. . .	. . .	. . .	. . .	. . .	. . .
of which: Short-term	4 789 . .	. . .	. . .	. . .	. . .	. . .	. . .	. . .	. . .
General government	4 790 . .	–119.8	54.1	. . .	. . .	. . .	. . .	. . .	. . .
of which: Short-term	4 792 . .	*–119.8*	*54.1*	. . .	. . .	. . .	. . .	. . .	. . .
Banks	4 793 . .	1.9	–3.9	. . .	. . .	. . .	. . .	. . .	. . .
of which: Short-term	4 795 . .	*1.9*	*–3.9*	. . .	. . .	. . .	. . .	. . .	. . .
Other sectors	4 796 . .	–5.4	.7	. . .	. . .	. . .	. . .	. . .	. . .
of which: Short-term	4 798 . .	*–5.4*	*.7*	. . .	. . .	. . .	. . .	. . .	. . .
E. RESERVE ASSETS	4 802 . .	28.7	–25.8	. . .	. . .	. . .	. . .	. . .	. . .
Monetary gold	4 812 . .	. . .	. . .	. . .	. . .	. . .	. . .	. . .	. . .
Special drawing rights	4 811 . .	.1	.1	. . .	. . .	. . .	. . .	. . .	. . .
Reserve position in the Fund	4 810 . .	. . .	. . .	. . .	. . .	. . .	. . .	. . .	. . .
Foreign exchange	4 803 . .	12.5	–19.3	. . .	. . .	. . .	. . .	. . .	. . .
Other claims	4 813 . .	16.1	–6.6	. . .	. . .	. . .	. . .	. . .	. . .
NET ERRORS AND OMISSIONS	4 998 . .	**–67.8**	**114.4**	**. . .**	**. . .**	**. . .**	**. . .**	**. . .**	**. . .**

Part 3 of the *Yearbook* contains descriptions of the methodologies, compilation practices, and sources used to compile these data.

Table 1. ANALYTIC PRESENTATION, 1994–2001
(Millions of U.S. dollars)

	Code		1994	1995	1996	1997	1998	1999	2000	2001
A. Current Account [1]	4 993	Z.	**–2,128**	**–2,578**	**3,507**	**552**	**–4,244**	**506**	**. . .**	**. . .**
Goods: exports f.o.b	2 100	. .	9,459	11,734	16,117	15,207	8,971	12,876	. . .	. . .
Goods: imports f.o.b	3 100	. .	–6,511	–8,222	–6,438	–9,501	–9,211	–8,588	. . .	. . .
Balance on Goods	4 100	. .	*2,948*	*3,513*	*9,679*	*5,706*	*–240*	*4,288*	. . .	. . .
Services: credit	2 200	. .	371	608	733	786	884	980	. . .	. . .
Services: debit	3 200	. .	–3,007	–4,619	–4,827	–4,712	–4,166	–3,476	. . .	. . .
Balance on Goods and Services	4 991	. .	*312*	*–499*	*5,584*	*1,781*	*–3,522*	*1,792*	. . .	. . .
Income: credit	2 300	. .	49	101	115	258	333	240	. . .	. . .
Income: debit	3 300	. .	–2,986	–2,979	–3,137	–3,404	–2,624	–2,818	. . .	. . .
Balance on Goods, Services, and Income	4 992	. .	*–2,626*	*–3,377*	*2,562*	*–1,365*	*–5,813*	*–786*	. . .	. . .
Current transfers: credit	2 379	Z.	550	804	947	1,920	1,574	1,301	. . .	. . .
Current transfers: debit	3 379	. .	–52	–5	–2	–4	–5	–9	. . .	. . .
B. Capital Account [1]	4 994	Z.	**. . .**	**–66**	**–68**	**–49**	**–54**	**–48**	**. . .**	**. . .**
Capital account: credit	2 994	Z.	. . .	. . .	. . .	. . .	. . .	. . .	. . .	. . .
Capital account: debit	3 994	. .	. . .	–66	–68	–49	–54	–48	. . .	. . .
Total, Groups A Plus B	4 981	. .	*–2,128*	*–2,645*	*3,439*	*502*	*–4,298*	*458*	. . .	. . .
C. Financial Account [1]	4 995	W.	**329**	**–46**	**–4,155**	**–425**	**1,502**	**–4,002**	**. . .**	**. . .**
Direct investment abroad	4 505	. .	. . .	. . .	. . .	. . .	. . .	. . .	. . .	. . .
Direct investment in Nigeria	4 555	Z.	1,959	1,079	1,593	1,539	1,051	1,005	. . .	. . .
Portfolio investment assets	4 602	. .	. . .	. . .	. . .	9	51	50	. . .	. . .
Equity securities	4 610	. .	. . .	. . .	. . .	. . .	. . .	. . .	. . .	. . .
Debt securities	4 619	. .	. . .	. . .	. . .	9	51	50	. . .	. . .
Portfolio investment liabilities	4 652	Z.	–27	–82	–173	–76	–59	–39	. . .	. . .
Equity securities	4 660	. .	. . .	. . .	. . .	. . .	. . .	. . .	. . .	. . .
Debt securities	4 669	Z.	–27	–82	–173	–76	–59	–39	. . .	. . .
Financial derivatives	4 910	. .	. . .	. . .	. . .	. . .	. . .	. . .	. . .	. . .
Financial derivatives assets	4 900	. .	. . .	. . .	. . .	. . .	. . .	. . .	. . .	. . .
Financial derivatives liabilities	4 905	. .	. . .	. . .	. . .	. . .	. . .	. . .	. . .	. . .
Other investment assets	4 703	. .	–1,286	–3,295	–4,320	–2,183	–332	–3,319	. . .	. . .
Monetary authorities	4 701	. .	. . .	. . .	. . .	. . .	. . .	. . .	. . .	. . .
General government	4 704	. .	–969	–1,030	. . .	. . .	. . .	. . .	. . .	. . .
Banks	4 705	. .	320	–560	138	–80	–284	–651	. . .	. . .
Other sectors	4 728	. .	–637	–1,705	–4,458	–2,103	–48	–2,668	. . .	. . .
Other investment liabilities	4 753	W.	–317	2,251	–1,256	286	792	–1,699	. . .	. . .
Monetary authorities	4 753	WA	. . .	. . .	. . .	. . .	. . .	. . .	. . .	. . .
General government	4 753	ZB	–1,885	–1,535	–3,039	–2,883	–1,637	–1,659	. . .	. . .
Banks	4 753	ZC	–1	. . .	–4	1	21	34	. . .	. . .
Other sectors	4 753	ZD	1,570	3,787	1,787	3,167	2,407	–74	. . .	. . .
Total, Groups A Through C	4 983	. .	*–1,799*	*–2,691*	*–716*	*77*	*–2,795*	*–3,544*	. . .	. . .
D. Net Errors and Omissions	4 998	. .	**–139**	**–83**	**–45**	**–62**	**–77**	**7**	**. . .**	**. . .**
Total, Groups A Through D	4 984	. .	*–1,938*	*–2,774*	*–761*	*15*	*–2,873*	*–3,538*	. . .	. . .
E. Reserves and Related Items	4 802	A.	**1,938**	**2,774**	**761**	**–15**	**2,873**	**3,538**	**. . .**	**. . .**
Reserve assets	4 802	. .	–327	217	–2,634	–3,507	481	1,650	. . .	. . .
Use of Fund credit and loans	4 766	. .	. . .	. . .	. . .	. . .	. . .	. . .	. . .	. . .
Exceptional financing	4 920	. .	2,265	2,557	3,395	3,491	2,392	1,887	. . .	. . .
Conversion rates: naira per U.S. dollar	0 101	. .	**21.996**	**70.363**	**69.845**	**71.751**	**76.809**	**92.338**	**. . .**	**. . .**

[1] Excludes components that have been classified in the categories of Group E.

Table 2. STANDARD PRESENTATION, 1994–2001

(Millions of U.S. dollars)

	Code		1994	1995	1996	1997	1998	1999	2000	2001
CURRENT ACCOUNT	4 993	. .	**–2,128**	**–2,578**	**3,507**	**552**	**–4,244**	**506**	**...**	**...**
A. GOODS	4 100	. .	2,948	3,513	9,679	5,706	–240	4,288	...	...
Credit	2 100	. .	**9,459**	**11,734**	**16,117**	**15,207**	**8,971**	**12,876**	**...**	**...**
General merchandise: exports f.o.b.	2 110	. .	9,459	11,734	16,117	15,207	8,971	12,876	...	...
Goods for processing: exports f.o.b.	2 150	. .	...	...	...	...	...	...	...	...
Repairs on goods	2 160	. .	...	...	...	...	...	...	...	...
Goods procured in ports by carriers	2 170	. .	...	...	...	...	...	...	...	...
Nonmonetary gold	2 180	. .	...	...	...	...	...	...	...	...
Debit	3 100	. .	**–6,511**	**–8,222**	**–6,438**	**–9,501**	**–9,211**	**–8,588**	**...**	**...**
General merchandise: imports f.o.b.	3 110	. .	–6,511	–8,222	–6,438	–9,501	–9,211	–8,588	...	...
Goods for processing: imports f.o.b.	3 150	. .	...	...	...	...	...	...	...	...
Repairs on goods	3 160	. .	...	...	...	...	...	...	...	...
Goods procured in ports by carriers	3 170	. .	...	...	...	...	...	...	...	...
Nonmonetary gold	3 180	. .	...	...	...	...	...	...	...	...
B. SERVICES	4 200	. .	–2,636	–4,012	–4,094	–3,925	–3,282	–2,496	...	...
Total credit	2 200	. .	*371*	*608*	*733*	*786*	*884*	*980*	...	...
Total debit	3 200	. .	*–3,007*	*–4,619*	*–4,827*	*–4,712*	*–4,166*	*–3,476*	...	...
Transportation services, credit	2 205	. .	**51**	**100**	**76**	**91**	**113**	**118**	**...**	**...**
Passenger	2 850	. .	*15*	*30*	*23*	*28*	*34*	*45*	...	...
Freight	2 851	. .	*14*	*24*	*17*	*26*	*28*	*26*	...	...
Other	2 852	. .	*21*	*46*	*37*	*37*	*51*	*47*	...	...
Sea transport, passenger	2 207	. .	...	...	...	...	...	...	...	...
Sea transport, freight	2 208	. .	...	...	...	...	...	...	...	...
Sea transport, other	2 209	. .	...	...	...	...	...	...	...	...
Air transport, passenger	2 211	. .	...	...	...	...	...	...	...	...
Air transport, freight	2 212	. .	...	...	...	...	...	...	...	...
Air transport, other	2 213	. .	...	...	...	...	...	...	...	...
Other transport, passenger	2 215	. .	...	...	...	...	...	...	...	...
Other transport, freight	2 216	. .	...	...	...	...	...	...	...	...
Other transport, other	2 217	. .	...	...	...	...	...	...	...	...
Transportation services, debit	3 205	. .	**–754**	**–987**	**–454**	**–744**	**–704**	**–657**	**...**	**...**
Passenger	3 850	. .	*–24*	*–32*	*–14*	*–24*	*–22*	*–20*	...	...
Freight	3 851	. .	*–692*	*–906*	*–422*	*–683*	*–649*	*–607*	...	...
Other	3 852	. .	*–38*	*–49*	*–18*	*–37*	*–33*	*–30*	...	...
Sea transport, passenger	3 207	. .	...	...	...	...	...	...	...	...
Sea transport, freight	3 208	. .	...	...	...	...	...	...	...	...
Sea transport, other	3 209	. .	...	...	...	...	...	...	...	...
Air transport, passenger	3 211	. .	...	...	...	...	...	...	...	...
Air transport, freight	3 212	. .	...	...	...	...	...	...	...	...
Air transport, other	3 213	. .	...	...	...	...	...	...	...	...
Other transport, passenger	3 215	. .	...	...	...	...	...	...	...	...
Other transport, freight	3 216	. .	...	...	...	...	...	...	...	...
Other transport, other	3 217	. .	...	...	...	...	...	...	...	...
Travel, credit	2 236	. .	**10**	**17**	**35**	**55**	**47**	**54**	**...**	**...**
Business travel	2 237	.	...	...	...	...	...	...	...	...
Personal travel	2 240	. .	...	...	...	...	...	...	...	...
Travel, debit	3 236	. .	**–858**	**–906**	**–1,304**	**–1,816**	**–1,567**	**–620**	**...**	**...**
Business travel	3 237	. .	...	...	...	...	...	...	...	...
Personal travel	3 240	. .	...	...	...	...	...	...	...	...
Other services, credit	2 200	BA	**310**	**491**	**621**	**641**	**723**	**808**	**...**	**...**
Communications	2 245	. .	...	...	...	...	...	...	...	...
Construction	2 249	. .	...	...	...	...	...	...	...	...
Insurance	2 253	. .	2	4	2	3	4	8	...	...
Financial	2 260	. .	...	...	...	...	...	...	...	...
Computer and information	2 262	. .	...	...	...	...	...	...	...	...
Royalties and licence fees	2 266	. .	...	...	...	...	...	...	...	...
Other business services	2 268	. .	309	488	619	637	719	800	...	...
Personal, cultural, and recreational	2 287	. .	...	...	...	...	...	...	...	...
Government, n.i.e.	2 291	. .	...	...	...	...	...	...	...	...
Other services, debit	3 200	BA	**–1,395**	**–2,726**	**–3,069**	**–2,152**	**–1,894**	**–2,198**	**...**	**...**
Communications	3 .									.
Government, n.i.e.	2 291	. .	...	...	...	...	...	...	...	...
Other services, debit	3 200	BA	**–1,395**	**–2,726**	**–3,069**	**–2,152**	**–1,894**	**–2,198**	**...**	**...**
Communications	3 5 3	. .	–77	–112	–47	–110	–85	–93	...	...
Financial	3 260	. .	...	...	...	...	...	...	...	...
Computer and information	3 262	. .	...	...	...	...	...	...	...	...
Royalties and licence fees	3 266	. .	...	...	...	...	...	...	...	...
Other business services	3 268	. .	–1,292	–2,393	–2,736	–2,024	–1,697	–1,940	...	...
Personal, cultural, and recreational	3 287	. .	...	...	...	...	...	...	...	...
Government, n.i.e.	3 291	. .	–26	–221	–286	–17	–112	–165	...	...

Table 2 (Continued). STANDARD PRESENTATION, 1994–2001
(Millions of U.S. dollars)

	Code	1994	1995	1996	1997	1998	1999	2000	2001
C. INCOME	4 300	–2,938	–2,878	–3,022	–3,145	–2,291	–2,578	...	...
Total credit	2 300	*49*	*101*	*115*	*258*	*333*	*240*	...	...
Total debit	3 300	*–2,986*	*–2,979*	*–3,137*	*–3,404*	*–2,624*	*–2,818*	...	...
Compensation of employees, credit	2 310	**...**	**...**	**...**	**...**	**...**	**...**	**...**	**...**
Compensation of employees, debit	3 310	**...**	**...**	**...**	**...**	**...**	**...**	**...**	**...**
Investment income, credit	2 320	**49**	**101**	**115**	**258**	**333**	**240**	**...**	**...**
Direct investment income	2 330	...	...	...	...	...	...	...	...
Dividends and distributed branch profits	2 332	...	...	...	...	...	...	...	...
Reinvested earnings and undistributed branch profits	2 333	...	...	...	...	...	...	...	...
Income on debt (interest)	2 334	...	...	...	...	...	...	...	...
Portfolio investment income	2 339	...	...	...	...	...	...	...	...
Income on equity	2 340	...	...	...	...	...	...	...	...
Income on bonds and notes	2 350	...	...	...	...	...	...	...	...
Income on money market instruments	2 360	...	...	...	...	...	...	...	...
Other investment income	2 370	49	101	115	258	333	240	...	...
Investment income, debit	3 320	**–2,986**	**–2,979**	**–3,137**	**–3,404**	**–2,624**	**–2,818**	**...**	**...**
Direct investment income	3 330	–1,334	–1,330	–1,598	–1,477	–1,427	–1,621	...	...
Dividends and distributed branch profits	3 332	–1,334	–1,330	–1,598	–1,477	–1,427	–1,621	...	...
Reinvested earnings and undistributed branch profits	3 333	...	...	...	...	...	...	...	...
Income on debt (interest)	3 334	...	...	...	...	...	...	...	...
Portfolio investment income	3 339	...	...	...	...	...	...	...	...
Income on equity	3 340	...	...	...	...	...	...	...	...
Income on bonds and notes	3 350	...	...	...	...	...	...	...	...
Income on money market instruments	3 360	...	...	...	...	...	...	...	...
Other investment income	3 370	–1,653	–1,649	–1,539	–1,927	–1,197	–1,197	...	...
D. CURRENT TRANSFERS	4 379	498	799	945	1,916	1,570	1,292	...	...
Credit	2 379	**550**	**804**	**947**	**1,920**	**1,574**	**1,301**	**...**	**...**
General government	2 380	...	...	...	...	...	...	...	...
Other sectors	2 390	550	804	947	1,920	1,574	1,301	...	...
Workers' remittances	2 391	550	804	947	1,920	1,574	1,301	...	...
Other current transfers	2 392	...	...	...	...	...	...	...	...
Debit	3 379	**–52**	**–5**	**–2**	**–4**	**–5**	**–9**	**...**	**...**
General government	3 380	–48	...	...	...	...	...	...	...
Other sectors	3 390	–4	–5	–2	–4	–5	–9	...	...
Workers' remittances	3 391	–4	–5	–2	–4	–5	–9	...	...
Other current transfers	3 392	...	...	...	...	...	...	...	...
CAPITAL AND FINANCIAL ACCOUNT	4 996	**2,267**	**2,661**	**–3,462**	**–489**	**4,321**	**–512**	**...**	**...**
CAPITAL ACCOUNT	4 994	**...**	**–66**	**–68**	**–49**	**–54**	**–48**	**...**	**...**
Total credit	2 994	...	...	...	...	...	...	...	...
Total debit	3 994	...	*–66*	*–68*	*–49*	*–54*	*–48*	...	...
Capital transfers, credit	2 400	**...**	**...**	**...**	**...**	**...**	**...**	**...**	**...**
General government	2 401	...	...	...	...	...	...	...	...
Debt forgiveness	2 402	...	...	...	...	...	...	...	...
Other capital transfers	2 410	...	...	...	...	...	...	...	...
Other sectors	2 430	...	...	...	...	...	...	...	...
Migrants' transfers	2 431	...	...	...	...	...	...	...	...
Debt forgiveness	2 432	...	...	...	...	...	...	...	...
Other capital transfers	2 440	...	...	...	...	...	...	...	...
Capital transfers, debit	3 400	**...**	**–66**	**–68**	**–49**	**–54**	**–48**	**...**	**...**
General government	3 401	...	...	...	...	...	...	...	...
Debt forgiveness	3 402	...	...	...	...	...	...	...	...
Other capital transfers	3 410	...	...	...	...	...	...	...	...
Other sectors	3 430	...	...	...	...	...	...	...	...
Migrants' transfers	3 431	...	...	...	...	...	...	...	...
Debt forgiveness	3 432	...	...	...	...	...	...	...	...
Other capital transfers	3 440	...	...	...	...	...	...	...	...
Nonproduced nonfinancial assets, credit	2 480	**...**	**...**	**...**	**...**	**...**	**...**	**...**	**...**
Nonproduced nonfinancial assets, debit	3 480	**...**	**...**	**...**	**...**	**...**	**...**	**...**	**...**

Table 2 (Continued). STANDARD PRESENTATION, 1994–2001
(Millions of U.S. dollars)

	Code	1994	1995	1996	1997	1998	1999	2000	2001
FINANCIAL ACCOUNT	4 995 . .	**2,267**	**2,727**	**–3,394**	**–440**	**4,375**	**–465**	**. . .**	**. . .**
A. DIRECT INVESTMENT	4 500 . .	1,959	1,079	1,593	1,539	1,051	1,005	. . .	. . .
Direct investment abroad	4 505 . .	**. . .**	**. . .**	**. . .**	**. . .**	**. . .**	**. . .**	**. . .**	**. . .**
Equity capital	4 510 . .	. . .	. . .	. . .	. . .	. . .	. . .	. . .	. . .
Claims on affiliated enterprises	4 515 . .	. . .	. . .	. . .	. . .	. . .	. . .	. . .	. . .
Liabilities to affiliated enterprises	4 520 . .	. . .	. . .	. . .	. . .	. . .	. . .	. . .	. . .
Reinvested earnings	4 525 . .	. . .	. . .	. . .	. . .	. . .	. . .	. . .	. . .
Other capital	4 530 . .	. . .	. . .	. . .	. . .	. . .	. . .	. . .	. . .
Claims on affiliated enterprises	4 535 . .	. . .	. . .	. . .	. . .	. . .	. . .	. . .	. . .
Liabilities to affiliated enterprises	4 540 . .	. . .	. . .	. . .	. . .	. . .	. . .	. . .	. . .
Direct investment in Nigeria	4 555 . .	**1,959**	**1,079**	**1,593**	**1,539**	**1,051**	**1,005**	**. . .**	**. . .**
Equity capital	4 560 . .	. . .	. . .	. . .	. . .	. . .	. . .	. . .	. . .
Claims on direct investors	4 565 . .	. . .	. . .	. . .	. . .	. . .	. . .	. . .	. . .
Liabilities to direct investors	4 570 . .	. . .	. . .	. . .	. . .	. . .	. . .	. . .	. . .
Reinvested earnings	4 575 . .	. . .	. . .	. . .	. . .	. . .	. . .	. . .	. . .
Other capital	4 580 . .	1,959	1,079	1,593	1,539	1,051	1,005	. . .	. . .
Claims on direct investors	4 585 . .	. . .	. . .	. . .	. . .	. . .	. . .	. . .	. . .
Liabilities to direct investors	4 590 . .	. . .	. . .	. . .	. . .	. . .	. . .	. . .	. . .
B. PORTFOLIO INVESTMENT	4 600 . .	–27	–82	–173	–67	–8	11	. . .	. . .
Assets	4 602 . .	**. . .**	**. . .**	**. . .**	**9**	**51**	**50**	**. . .**	**. . .**
Equity securities	4 610 . .	. . .	. . .	. . .	. . .	. . .	. . .	. . .	. . .
Monetary authorities	4 611 . .	. . .	. . .	. . .	. . .	. . .	. . .	. . .	. . .
General government	4 612 . .	. . .	. . .	. . .	. . .	. . .	. . .	. . .	. . .
Banks	4 613 . .	. . .	. . .	. . .	. . .	. . .	. . .	. . .	. . .
Other sectors	4 614 . .	. . .	. . .	. . .	. . .	. . .	. . .	. . .	. . .
Debt securities	4 619 . .	. . .	. . .	. . .	9	51	50	. . .	. . .
Bonds and notes	4 620 . .	. . .	. . .	. . .	. . .	. . .	. . .	. . .	. . .
Monetary authorities	4 621 . .	. . .	. . .	. . .	. . .	. . .	. . .	. . .	. . .
General government	4 622 . .	. . .	. . .	. . .	. . .	. . .	. . .	. . .	. . .
Banks	4 623 . .	. . .	. . .	. . .	. . .	. . .	. . .	. . .	. . .
Other sectors	4 624 . .	. . .	. . .	. . .	. . .	. . .	. . .	. . .	. . .
Money market instruments	4 630 . .	. . .	. . .	. . .	. . .	. . .	. . .	. . .	. . .
Monetary authorities	4 631 . .	. . .	. . .	. . .	. . .	. . .	. . .	. . .	. . .
General government	4 632 . .	. . .	. . .	. . .	. . .	. . .	. . .	. . .	. . .
Banks	4 633 . .	. . .	. . .	. . .	. . .	. . .	. . .	. . .	. . .
Other sectors	4 634 . .	. . .	. . .	. . .	. . .	. . .	. . .	. . .	. . .
Liabilities	4 652 . .	**–27**	**–82**	**–173**	**–76**	**–59**	**–39**	**. . .**	**. . .**
Equity securities	4 660 . .	. . .	. . .	. . .	. . .	. . .	. . .	. . .	. . .
Banks	4 663 . .	. . .	. . .	. . .	. . .	. . .	. . .	. . .	. . .
Other sectors	4 664 . .	. . .	. . .	. . .	. . .	. . .	. . .	. . .	. . .
Debt securities	4 669 . .	–27	–82	–173	–76	–59	–39	. . .	. . .
Bonds and notes	4 670 . .	–27	–82	–173	–76	–59	–39	. . .	. . .
Monetary authorities	4 671 . .	. . .	. . .	. . .	. . .	. . .	. . .	. . .	. . .
General government	4 672 . .	–27	–82	–173	–76	–59	–39	. . .	. . .
Banks	4 673 . .	. . .	. . .	. . .	. . .	. . .	. . .	. . .	. . .
Other sectors	4 674 . .	. . .	. . .	. . .	. . .	. . .	. . .	. . .	. . .
Money market instruments	4 680 . .	. . .	. . .	. . .	. . .	. . .	. . .	. . .	. . .
Monetary authorities	4 681 . .	. . .	. . .	. . .	. . .	. . .	. . .	. . .	. . .
General government	4 682 . .	. . .	. . .	. . .	. . .	. . .	. . .	. . .	. . .
Banks	4 683 . .	. . .	. . .	. . .	. . .	. . .	. . .	. . .	. . .
Other sectors	4 684 . .	. . .	. . .	. . .	. . .	. . .	. . .	. . .	. . .
C. FINANCIAL DERIVATIVES	4 910 . .	. . .	. . .	. . .	. . .	. . .	. . .	. . .	. . .
Monetary authorities	4 911 . .	. . .	. . .	. . .	. . .	. . .	. . .	. . .	. . .
General government	4 912 . .	. . .	. . .	. . .	. . .	. . .	. . .	. . .	. . .
Banks	4 913 . .	. . .	. . .	. . .	. . .	. . .	. . .	. . .	. . .
Other sectors	4 914 . .	. . .	. . .	. . .	. . .	. . .	. . .	. . .	. . .
Assets	4 900 . .	**. . .**	**. . .**	**. . .**	**. . .**	**. . .**	**. . .**	**. . .**	**. . .**
Monetary authorities	4 901 . .	. . .	. . .	. . .	. . .	. . .	. . .	. . .	. . .
General government	4 902 . .	. . .	. . .	. . .	. . .	. . .	. . .	. . .	. . .
Banks	4 903 . .	. . .	. . .	. . .	. . .	. . .	. . .	. . .	. . .
Other sectors	4 904 . .	. . .	. . .	. . .	. . .	. . .	. . .	. . .	. . .
Liabilities	4 905 . .	**. . .**	**. . .**	**. . .**	**. . .**	**. . .**	**. . .**	**. . .**	**. . .**
Monetary authorities	4 906 . .	. . .	. . .	. . .	. . .	. . .	. . .	. . .	. . .
General government	4 907 . .	. . .	. . .	. . .	. . .	. . .	. . .	. . .	. . .
Banks	4 908 . .	. . .	. . .	. . .	. . .	. . .	. . .	. . .	. . .
Other sectors	4 909 . .	. . .	. . .	. . .	. . .	. . .	. . .	. . .	. . .

Table 2 (Concluded). STANDARD PRESENTATION, 1994–2001
(Millions of U.S. dollars)

	Code	1994	1995	1996	1997	1998	1999	2000	2001
D. OTHER INVESTMENT	4 700	662	1,513	–2,181	1,594	2,851	–3,131	...	...
Assets	4 703	**–1,286**	**–3,295**	**–4,320**	**–2,183**	**–332**	**–3,319**	...	...
Trade credits	4 706	...	...	...	...	...	...	...	...
General government	4 707	...	...	...	...	...	...	...	...
of which: Short-term	4 709	...	...	...	...	...	...	...	...
Other sectors	4 710	...	...	...	...	...	...	...	...
of which: Short-term	4 712	...	...	...	...	...	...	...	...
Loans	4 714	...	...	...	...	...	...	...	...
Monetary authorities	4 715	...	...	...	...	...	...	...	...
of which: Short-term	4 718	...	...	...	...	...	...	...	...
General government	4 719	...	...	...	...	...	...	...	...
of which: Short-term	4 721	...	...	...	...	...	...	...	...
Banks	4 722	...	...	...	...	...	...	...	...
of which: Short-term	4 724	...	...	...	...	...	...	...	...
Other sectors	4 725	...	...	...	...	...	...	...	...
of which: Short-term	4 727	...	...	...	...	...	...	...	...
Currency and deposits	4 730	–1,286	–3,295	–4,320	–2,183	–332	–3,319	...	...
Monetary authorities	4 731	...	...	...	...	...	...	...	...
General government	4 732	–969	–1,030	...	...	...	...	...	...
Banks	4 733	320	–560	138	–80	–284	–651	...	...
Other sectors	4 734	–637	–1,705	–4,458	–2,103	–48	–2,668	...	...
Other assets	4 736	...	...	...	...	...	...	...	...
Monetary authorities	4 737	...	...	...	...	...	...	...	...
of which: Short-term	4 739	...	...	...	...	...	...	...	...
General government	4 740	...	...	...	...	...	...	...	...
of which: Short-term	4 742	...	...	...	...	...	...	...	...
Banks	4 743	...	...	...	...	...	...	...	...
of which: Short-term	4 745	...	...	...	...	...	...	...	...
Other sectors	4 746	...	...	...	...	...	...	...	...
of which: Short-term	4 748	...	...	...	...	...	...	...	...
Liabilities	4 753	**1,948**	**4,808**	**2,139**	**3,777**	**3,183**	**188**	...	...
Trade credits	4 756	...	...	...	...	...	...	...	...
General government	4 757	...	...	...	...	...	...	...	...
of which: Short-term	4 759	...	...	...	...	...	...	...	...
Other sectors	4 760	...	...	...	...	...	...	...	...
of which: Short-term	4 762	...	...	...	...	...	...	...	...
Loans	4 764	–1,885	–1,535	–3,039	–2,883	–1,637	–1,659	...	...
Monetary authorities	4 765	...	...	...	...	...	...	...	...
of which: Use of Fund credit and loans from the Fund	4 766	...	...	...	...	...	...	...	...
of which: Short-term	4 768	...	...	...	...	...	...	...	...
General government	4 769	–1,885	–1,535	–3,039	–2,883	–1,637	–1,659	...	...
of which: Short-term	4 771	...	...	...	...	...	...	...	...
Banks	4 772	...	...	...	...	...	...	...	...
of which: Short-term	4 774	...	...	...	...	...	...	...	...
Other sectors	4 775	...	...	...	...	...	...	...	...
of which: Short-term	4 777	...	...	...	...	...	...	...	...
Currency and deposits	4 780	–1	...	–4	1	21	34	...	...
Monetary authorities	4 781	...	...	...	...	...	...	...	...
General government	4 782	...	...	...	...	...	...	...	...
Banks	4 783	–1	...	–4	1	21	34	...	...
Other sectors	4 784	...	...	...	...	...	...	...	...
Other liabilities	4 786	3,835	6,343	5,182	6,659	4,799	1,813	...	...
Monetary authorities	4 787	2,265	2,557	3,395	3,491	2,392	1,887	...	...
of which: Short-term	4 789	*2,265*	*2,557*	*3,395*	*3,491*	*2,392*	*1,887*	...	...
General government	4 790	...	...	...	...	...	...	...	...
of which: Short-term	4 792	...	...	...	...	...	...	...	...
Banks	4 793	...	...	...	...	...	...	...	...
of which: Short-term	4 795	...	...	...	...	...	...	...	...
Other sectors	4 796	1,570	3,787	1,787	3,167	2,407	–74	...	...
of which: Short-term	4 798	*1,570*	*3,787*	*1,787*	*3,167*	*2,407*	*–74*	...	...
E. RESERVE ASSETS	4 802	–327	217	–2,634	–3,507	481	1,650	...	...
Monetary gold	4 812	...	...	...	...	...	...	...	...
Special drawing rights	4 811	...	–1	...	...	...	...	...	...
Reserve position in the Fund	4 810	...	...	...	...	...	...	...	...
Foreign exchange	4 803	–327	218	–2,634	–3,506	481	1,650	...	...
Other claims	4 813	...	...	...	...	...	...	...	...
NET ERRORS AND OMISSIONS	4 998	**–139**	**–83**	**–45**	**–62**	**–77**	**7**	...	...

Part 3 of the *Yearbook* contains descriptions of the methodologies, compilation practices, and sources used to compile these data.

Table 1. ANALYTIC PRESENTATION, 1994–2001
(Millions of U.S. dollars)

	Code	1994	1995	1996	1997	1998	1999	2000	2001
A. Current Account [1]	4 993 Z.	**3,760**	**5,233**	**10,969**	**10,036**	**6**	**8,378**	**24,807**	**25,960**
Goods: exports f.o.b	2 100 . .	35,016	42,385	50,081	49,375	40,888	46,224	60,463	59,699
Goods: imports f.o.b	3 100 . .	-27,520	-33,701	-37,109	-37,727	-38,827	-35,501	-34,520	-33,681
Balance on Goods	4 100 . .	*7,496*	*8,685*	*12,972*	*11,648*	*2,061*	*10,723*	*25,942*	*26,018*
Services: credit	2 200 . .	12,247	13,672	14,819	15,708	15,542	15,878	17,331	17,958
Services: debit	3 200 . .	-12,065	-13,147	-13,435	-14,233	-14,820	-14,882	-15,422	-15,392
Balance on Goods and Services	4 991 . .	*7,678*	*9,210*	*14,356*	*13,123*	*2,783*	*11,719*	*27,851*	*28,584*
Income: credit	2 300 . .	3,415	4,590	5,164	5,590	6,809	6,100	6,641	7,590
Income: debit	3 300 . .	-5,589	-6,509	-7,046	-7,284	-8,053	-7,998	-8,295	-8,530
Balance on Goods, Services, and Income	4 992 . .	*5,504*	*7,291*	*12,475*	*11,429*	*1,539*	*9,821*	*26,197*	*27,644*
Current transfers: credit	2 379 Z.	1,291	1,280	1,329	1,468	1,500	1,681	1,321	1,473
Current transfers: debit	3 379 . .	-3,035	-3,339	-2,835	-2,861	-3,034	-3,124	-2,712	-3,157
B. Capital Account [1]	4 994 Z.	**-157**	**-170**	**-127**	**-184**	**-116**	**-116**	**-186**	**-93**
Capital account: credit	2 994 Z.	93	86	65	30	44	40	34	105
Capital account: debit	3 994 . .	-250	-255	-192	-214	-160	-156	-220	-197
Total, Groups A Plus B	4 981 . .	*3,603*	*5,063*	*10,842*	*9,852*	*-110*	*8,262*	*24,620*	*25,867*
C. Financial Account [1]	4 995 W.	**-1,363**	**-542**	**-1,462**	**-6,607**	**61**	**431**	**-13,155**	**-23,877**
Direct investment abroad	4 505 . .	-2,166	-2,859	-5,886	-5,003	-3,200	-6,018	-8,511	1,086
Direct investment in Norway	4 555 Z.	2,736	2,393	3,179	3,886	4,354	8,056	5,806	2,166
Portfolio investment assets	4 602 . .	992	-3,531	-9,833	-12,618	-9,348	-7,228	-25,144	-29,420
Equity securities	4 610 . .	213	-379	-1,177	-2,644	-9,066	-2,378	-11,034	-12,291
Debt securities	4 619 . .	780	-3,151	-8,657	-9,974	-282	-4,850	-14,109	-17,129
Portfolio investment liabilities	4 652 Z.	-518	655	100	2,500	7,289	4,238	9,844	2,756
Equity securities	4 660 . .	654	636	-237	-1,190	. . .	-1,033	1,630	2,732
Debt securities	4 669 Z.	-1,172	19	337	3,691	7,289	5,271	8,214	24
Financial derivatives	4 910 . .	. . .	. . .	59	142	-87	243	-460	-1,139
Financial derivatives assets	4 900 . .	. . .	. . .	-43	17	-162	152	-329	-1,228
Financial derivatives liabilities	4 905 . .	. . .	. . .	101	125	74	92	-131	88
Other investment assets	4 703 . .	154	961	-67	-1,403	-3,632	-7,663	-14,148	-2,261
Monetary authorities	4 701 . .	. . .	. . .	. . .	. . .	. . .	. . .	. . .	. . .
General government	4 704 . .	-13	-156	71	91	-1,167	-1,099	-2,072	1,758
Banks	4 705 . .	-638	435	-1,216	-1,465	-1,062	-969	-1,806	434
Other sectors	4 728 . .	804	682	1,077	-29	1,403	-5,595	-10,271	-4,453
Other investment liabilities	4 753 W.	-2,562	1,840	10,987	5,888	4,685	8,802	19,459	2,935
Monetary authorities	4 753 WA	139	-624	1,505	-803	19	-19	3	44
General government	4 753 ZB	-164	3	. . .	94	1,346	3,460	9,657	-432
Banks	4 753 ZC	-604	247	8,677	4,126	-856	1,789	1,321	2,290
Other sectors	4 753 ZD	-1,933	2,214	806	2,472	4,176	3,573	8,478	1,033
Total, Groups A Through C	4 983 . .	*2,240*	*4,521*	*9,380*	*3,245*	*-49*	*8,693*	*11,466*	*1,990*
D. Net Errors and Omissions	4 998 . .	**-1,987**	**-3,947**	**-2,910**	**-4,443**	**-6,335**	**-2,710**	**-7,780**	**-4,104**
Total, Groups A Through D	4 984 . .	*253*	*575*	*6,470*	*-1,198*	*-6,384*	*5,984*	*3,686*	*-2,114*
E. Reserves and Related Items	4 802 A.	**-253**	**-575**	**-6,470**	**1,198**	**6,384**	**-5,984**	**-3,686**	**2,114**
Reserve assets	4 802 . .	-253	-575	-6,470	1,198	6,384	-5,984	-3,686	2,114
Use of Fund credit and loans	4 766 . .	. . .	. . .	. . .	. . .	. . .	. . .	. . .	. . .
Exceptional financing	4 920 . .	. . .	. . .	. . .	. . .	. . .	. . .	. . .	. . .
Conversion rates: Norwegian kroner per U.S. dollar	0 101 . .	**7.0576**	**6.3352**	**6.4498**	**7.0734**	**7.5451**	**7.7992**	**8.8018**	**8.9917**

[1] Excludes components that have been classified in the categories of Group E.

Table 2. STANDARD PRESENTATION, 1994–2001

(Millions of U.S. dollars)

	Code	1994	1995	1996	1997	1998	1999	2000	2001
CURRENT ACCOUNT	4 993 . .	**3,760**	**5,233**	**10,969**	**10,036**	**6**	**8,378**	**24,807**	**25,960**
A. GOODS	4 100 . .	7,496	8,685	12,972	11,648	2,061	10,723	25,942	26,018
Credit	2 100 . .	**35,016**	**42,385**	**50,081**	**49,375**	**40,888**	**46,224**	**60,463**	**59,699**
General merchandise: exports f.o.b.	2 110 . .	34,795	42,001	49,688	48,847	40,483	45,903	60,106	59,244
Goods for processing: exports f.o.b.	2 150 . .	...	...	...	...	...	...	...	...
Repairs on goods	2 160 . .	91	187	165	304	238	204	209	301
Goods procured in ports by carriers	2 170 . .	131	198	228	224	167	117	147	154
Nonmonetary gold	2 180 . .	...	...	...	...	...	...	...	...
Debit	3 100 . .	**–27,520**	**–33,701**	**–37,109**	**–37,727**	**–38,827**	**–35,501**	**–34,520**	**–33,681**
General merchandise: imports f.o.b.	3 110 . .	–26,431	–32,250	–35,523	–35,966	–37,333	–33,973	–33,021	–32,227
Goods for processing: imports f.o.b.	3 150 . .	...	...	...	...	...	...	...	...
Repairs on goods	3 160 . .	–540	–807	–771	–934	–868	–906	–924	–892
Goods procured in ports by carriers	3 170 . .	–549	–644	–815	–827	–625	–623	–575	–561
Nonmonetary gold	3 180 . .	...	...	...	...	...	...	...	...
B. SERVICES	4 200 . .	182	525	1,384	1,474	722	996	1,908	2,566
Total credit	2 200 . .	*12,247*	*13,672*	*14,819*	*15,708*	*15,542*	*15,878*	*17,331*	*17,958*
Total debit	3 200 . .	*–12,065*	*–13,147*	*–13,435*	*–14,233*	*–14,820*	*–14,882*	*–15,422*	*–15,392*
Transportation services, credit	2 205 . .	**7,450**	**8,516**	**8,779**	**9,007**	**8,566**	**8,659**	**10,083**	**10,790**
Passenger	2 850 . .	*405*	*492*	*514*	*435*	*429*	*473*	*454*	*384*
Freight	2 851 . .	*5,145*	*5,635*	*6,097*	*6,471*	*6,087*	*5,991*	*6,632*	*7,033*
Other	2 852 . .	*1,900*	*2,388*	*2,168*	*2,102*	*2,050*	*2,195*	*2,997*	*3,373*
Sea transport, passenger	2 207 . .	141	195	209	205	213	206	183	179
Sea transport, freight	2 208 . .	4,732	5,155	5,455	5,798	5,297	5,110	5,843	6,213
Sea transport, other	2 209 . .	1,330	1,663	1,497	1,566	1,462	1,709	2,313	2,567
Air transport, passenger	2 211 . .	236	281	292	218	203	256	261	197
Air transport, freight	2 212 . .	41	42	45	53	51	42	65	49
Air transport, other	2 213 . .	90	90	89	72	75	60	115	87
Other transport, passenger	2 215 . .	28	17	13	12	12	11	10	9
Other transport, freight	2 216 . .	372	439	596	620	739	838	723	770
Other transport, other	2 217 . .	480	636	582	463	513	426	569	720
Transportation services, debit	3 205 . .	**–4,648**	**–4,992**	**–5,039**	**–5,218**	**–5,038**	**–5,065**	**–5,841**	**–5,733**
Passenger	3 850 . .	*–263*	*–249*	*–268*	*–308*	*–346*	*–291*	*–292*	*–304*
Freight	3 851 . .	*–1,412*	*–1,255*	*–1,120*	*–1,040*	*–791*	*–802*	*–555*	*–702*
Other	3 852 . .	*–2,972*	*–3,488*	*–3,651*	*–3,870*	*–3,901*	*–3,972*	*–4,994*	*–4,727*
Sea transport, passenger	3 207 . .	–13	–8	–12	–21	–38	–39	–15	–36
Sea transport, freight	3 208 . .	–700	–841	–797	–468	–523	–391	–322	–418
Sea transport, other	3 209 . .	–2,560	–3,048	–3,183	–3,417	–3,395	–3,479	–4,493	–4,207
Air transport, passenger	3 211 . .	–228	–224	–245	–276	–295	–240	–269	–260
Air transport, freight	3 212 . .	–25	–30	–28	–55	–42	–50	–56	–71
Air transport, other	3 213 . .	–338	–367	–427	–419	–469	–461	–477	–491
Other transport, passenger	3 215 . .	–22	–17	–12	–12	–13	–11	–8	–8
Other transport, freight	3 216 . .	–687	–385	–294	–517	–226	–361	–178	–212
Other transport, other	3 217 . .	–75	–73	–41	–33	–38	–32	–23	–29
Travel, credit	2 236 . .	**2,128**	**2,238**	**2,256**	**2,135**	**2,116**	**2,277**	**1,944**	**1,928**
Business travel	2 237 . .	...	...	...	...	...	...	...	...
Personal travel	2 240 . .	2,128	2,238	2,256	2,135	2,116	2,277	1,944	1,928
Travel, debit	3 236 . .	**–3,723**	**–4,232**	**–4,491**	**–4,448**	**–4,723**	**–4,857**	**–4,423**	**–4,280**
Business travel	3 237 . .	–1,229	–1,397	–1,458	–1,422	–1,511	–1,556	–1,460	–1,413
Personal travel	3 240 . .	–2,495	–2,835	–3,033	–3,027	–3,212	–3,301	–2,963	–2,868
Other services, credit	2 200 BA	**2,668**	**2,919**	**3,783**	**4,566**	**4,860**	**4,942**	**5,304**	**5,240**
Communications	2 245 . .	162	178	216	201	258	289	286	293
Construction	2 249 . .	82	43	53	57	71	83	68	87
Insurance	2 253 . .	446	418	519	296	266	161	436	415
Financial	2 260 . .	44	81	150	182	265	279	208	307
Computer and information	2 262 . .	79	105	122	153	357	366	319	247
Royalties and licence fees	2 266 . .	115	111	118	103	89	149	161	155
Other business services	2 268 . .	1,330	1,682	2,281	3,260	3,288	3,326	3,511	3,362
Personal, cultural, and recreational	2 287 . .	78	87	104	111	104	113	165	221
Government, n.i.e.	2 291 . .	332	215	219	205	163	176	150	153
Other services, debit	3 200 BA	**–3,694**	**–3,923**	**–3,905**	**–4,567**	**–5,060**	**–4,960**	**–5,159**	**–5,379**
Communications	3 245 . .	–157	–156	–172	–168	–213	–166	–169	–196
Construction	3 249 . .	–16	–35	–26	–14	–96	–45	–27	–23
Insurance	3 253 . .	–713	–652	–735	–522	–526	–393	–545	–594
Financial	3 260 . .	–66	–84	–73	–57	–125	–103	–106	–140
Computer and information	3 262 . .	–224	–279	–149	–118	–185	–211	–243	–156
Royalties and licence fees	3 266 . .	–297	–375	–290	–364	–348	–342	–439	–329
Other business services	3 268 . .	–1,990	–2,169	–2,229	–3,054	–3,260	–3,382	–3,157	–3,470
Personal, cultural, and recreational	3 287 . .	–72	–78	–108	–149	–148	–168	–314	–340
Government, n.i.e.	3 291 . .	–159	–95	–123	–121	–159	–150	–159	–131

Table 2 (Continued). STANDARD PRESENTATION, 1994–2001
(Millions of U.S. dollars)

	Code	1994	1995	1996	1997	1998	1999	2000	2001
C. INCOME	4 300	–2,174	–1,919	–1,881	–1,694	–1,244	–1,898	–1,654	–940
Total credit	2 300	*3,415*	*4,590*	*5,164*	*5,590*	*6,809*	*6,100*	*6,641*	*7,590*
Total debit	3 300	*–5,589*	*–6,509*	*–7,046*	*–7,284*	*–8,053*	*–7,998*	*–8,295*	*–8,530*
Compensation of employees, credit	2 310	**170**	**239**	**309**	**289**	**301**	**262**	**246**	**254**
Compensation of employees, debit	3 310	**–475**	**–603**	**–647**	**–703**	**–746**	**–730**	**–735**	**–677**
Investment income, credit	2 320	**3,244**	**4,352**	**4,855**	**5,301**	**6,508**	**5,839**	**6,395**	**7,336**
Direct investment income	2 330	528	902	1,270	1,247	1,587	1,622	1,479	1,558
Dividends and distributed branch profits	2 332	97	270	319	470	506	562	593	802
Reinvested earnings and undistributed branch profits	2 333	431	632	952	777	1,080	1,060	887	756
Income on debt (interest)	2 334	...	...	...	...	...	...	...	...
Portfolio investment income	2 339	317	501	666	616	553	677	884	986
Income on equity	2 340	...	...	...	...	...	...	...	...
Income on bonds and notes	2 350	317	501	666	616	553	677	884	986
Income on money market instruments	2 360	...	...	...	...	...	...	...	...
Other investment income	2 370	2,399	2,949	2,919	3,438	4,368	3,540	4,032	4,791
Investment income, debit	3 320	**–5,114**	**–5,906**	**–6,398**	**–6,580**	**–7,307**	**–7,268**	**–7,560**	**–7,853**
Direct investment income	3 330	–1,647	–2,073	–2,845	–2,576	–2,835	–2,714	–2,418	–2,577
Dividends and distributed branch profits	3 332	–1,069	–1,267	–1,710	–1,671	–1,814	–1,343	–2,790	–3,160
Reinvested earnings and undistributed branch profits	3 333	–578	–805	–1,135	–905	–1,021	–1,371	372	583
Income on debt (interest)	3 334	...	...	...	...	...	...	...	...
Portfolio investment income	3 339	–160	–206	–279	–458	–417	–427	–433	–528
Income on equity	3 340	...	...	...	...	...	...	...	...
Income on bonds and notes	3 350	–160	–206	–279	–458	–417	–427	–433	–528
Income on money market instruments	3 360	...	...	...	...	...	...	...	...
Other investment income	3 370	–3,306	–3,628	–3,275	–3,547	–4,055	–4,128	–4,709	–4,748
D. CURRENT TRANSFERS	4 379	–1,744	–2,059	–1,506	–1,393	–1,533	–1,444	–1,391	–1,684
Credit	2 379	**1,291**	**1,280**	**1,329**	**1,468**	**1,500**	**1,681**	**1,321**	**1,473**
General government	2 380	...	55	98	49	63	101	123	112
Other sectors	2 390	1,291	1,225	1,232	1,419	1,437	1,580	1,198	1,361
Workers' remittances	2 391	...	...	...	...	...	...	...	...
Other current transfers	2 392	...	...	...	...	...	...	...	...
Debit	3 379	**–3,035**	**–3,339**	**–2,835**	**–2,861**	**–3,034**	**–3,124**	**–2,712**	**–3,157**
General government	3 380	–1,054	–1,255	–1,117	–1,033	–1,111	–1,040	–1,086	–1,233
Other sectors	3 390	–1,981	–2,084	–1,719	–1,828	–1,922	–2,084	–1,626	–1,923
Workers' remittances	3 391	...	...	...	...	...	...	...	...
Other current transfers	3 392	...	...	...	...	...	...	...	...
CAPITAL AND FINANCIAL ACCOUNT	4 996	**–1,773**	**–1,286**	**–8,059**	**–5,593**	**6,329**	**–5,668**	**–17,027**	**–21,856**
CAPITAL ACCOUNT	4 994	**–157**	**–170**	**–127**	**–184**	**–116**	**–116**	**–186**	**–93**
Total credit	2 994	*93*	*86*	*65*	*30*	*44*	*40*	*34*	*105*
Total debit	3 994	*–250*	*–255*	*–192*	*–214*	*–160*	*–156*	*–220*	*–197*
Capital transfers, credit	2 400	**93**	**86**	**65**	**30**	**44**	**40**	**34**	**105**
General government	2 401	...	...	...	...	...	...	...	...
Debt forgiveness	2 402	...	...	...	...	...	...	...	...
Other capital transfers	2 410	...	...	...	...	...	...	...	...
Other sectors	2 430	93	86	65	30	44	40	34	105
Migrants' transfers	2 431	...	...	...	...	...	...	...	...
Debt forgiveness	2 432	...	...	...	...	...	...	...	...
Other capital transfers	2 440	...	...	...	...	...	...	...	...
Capital transfers, debit	3 400	**–250**	**–255**	**–192**	**–214**	**–160**	**–156**	**–220**	**–197**
General government	3 401	–136	–130	–131	–143	–106	–98	–85	–115
Debt forgiveness	3 402	...	...	...	...	...	...	...	...
Other capital transfers	3 410	...	...	...	...	...	...	...	...
Other sectors	3 430	–114	–125	–61	–71	–54	–58	–134	–83
Migrants' transfers	3 431	...	...	...	...	...	...	...	...
Debt forgiveness	3 432	...	...	...	...	...	...	...	...
Other capital transfers	3 440	...	...	...	...	...	...	...	...
Nonproduced nonfinancial assets, credit	2 480	...	...	...	...	...	...	...	...
Nonproduced nonfinancial assets, debit	3 480	...	...	...	...	...	...	...	...

Table 2 (Continued). STANDARD PRESENTATION, 1994–2001

(Millions of U.S. dollars)

	Code	1994	1995	1996	1997	1998	1999	2000	2001
FINANCIAL ACCOUNT	4 995 . .	**–1,616**	**–1,116**	**–7,932**	**–5,409**	**6,445**	**–5,552**	**–16,840**	**–21,763**
A. DIRECT INVESTMENT	4 500 . .	571	–466	–2,707	–1,117	1,154	2,038	–2,705	3,252
Direct investment abroad	4 505 . .	**–2,166**	**–2,859**	**–5,886**	**–5,003**	**–3,200**	**–6,018**	**–8,511**	**1,086**
Equity capital	4 510 . .	–1,020	–1,931	–3,758	–2,012	–1,388	–1,995	–8,237	828
Claims on affiliated enterprises	4 515 . .	. . .	. . .	. . .	. . .	. . .	. . .	. . .	. . .
Liabilities to affiliated enterprises	4 520 . .	. . .	. . .	. . .	. . .	. . .	. . .	. . .	. . .
Reinvested earnings	4 525 . .	–431	–632	–952	–777	–1,080	–1,060	–887	–756
Other capital	4 530 . .	–714	–296	–1,176	–2,214	–731	–2,962	613	1,015
Claims on affiliated enterprises	4 535 . .	–714	–296	–1,867	–2,430	–1,476	–2,141	–317	715
Liabilities to affiliated enterprises	4 540 . .	. . .	. . .	691	216	745	–821	930	300
Direct investment in Norway	4 555 . .	**2,736**	**2,393**	**3,179**	**3,886**	**4,354**	**8,056**	**5,806**	**2,166**
Equity capital	4 560 . .	139	475	2,468	2,861	552	5,285	7,169	814
Claims on direct investors	4 565 . .	. . .	. . .	. . .	. . .	. . .	. . .	. . .	. . .
Liabilities to direct investors	4 570 . .	. . .	. . .	. . .	. . .	. . .	. . .	. . .	. . .
Reinvested earnings	4 575 . .	578	805	1,135	905	1,021	1,371	–372	–583
Other capital	4 580 . .	2,019	1,113	–423	120	2,781	1,400	–991	1,935
Claims on direct investors	4 585 . .	. . .	. . .	42	–413	–547	133	–440	353
Liabilities to direct investors	4 590 . .	2,019	1,113	–465	533	3,329	1,267	–550	1,582
B. PORTFOLIO INVESTMENT	4 600 . .	474	–2,875	–9,733	–10,118	–2,059	–2,990	–15,300	–26,664
Assets	4 602 . .	**992**	**–3,531**	**–9,833**	**–12,618**	**–9,348**	**–7,228**	**–25,144**	**–29,420**
Equity securities	4 610 . .	213	–379	–1,177	–2,644	–9,066	–2,378	–11,034	–12,291
Monetary authorities	4 611 . .	. . .	. . .	. . .	. . .	. . .	. . .	. . .	–2,597
General government	4 612 . .	1	. . .	. . .	–1	–10	–8	–11	–120
Banks	4 613 . .	–62	–42	52	2	–23	55	–8	–55
Other sectors	4 614 . .	274	–337	–1,229	–2,646	–9,033	–2,425	–11,016	–9,520
Debt securities	4 619 . .	780	–3,151	–8,657	–9,974	–282	–4,850	–14,109	–17,129
Bonds and notes	4 620 . .	1,630	–2,931	–9,549	–10,179	766	–4,675	–14,223	–18,184
Monetary authorities	4 621 . .	. . .	. . .	. . .	. . .	. . .	. . .	. . .	. . .
General government	4 622 . .	. . .	. . .	–7,018	–8,463	2,199	–3,986	–11,532	–12,708
Banks	4 623 . .	387	–97	–491	–585	–950	211	–1,429	–695
Other sectors	4 624 . .	1,243	–2,834	–2,039	–1,131	–483	–900	–1,263	–4,781
Money market instruments	4 630 . .	–850	–220	892	205	–1,048	–175	114	1,055
Monetary authorities	4 631 . .	. . .	. . .	. . .	. . .	. . .	. . .	. . .	. . .
General government	4 632 . .	. . .	. . .	. . .	170	–11	18	17	–94
Banks	4 633 . .	–232	–223	–182	546	23	–3	–42	32
Other sectors	4 634 . .	–618	3	1,074	–511	–1,060	–190	139	1,117
Liabilities	4 652 . .	**–518**	**655**	**100**	**2,500**	**7,289**	**4,238**	**9,844**	**2,756**
Equity securities	4 660 . .	654	636	–237	–1,190	. . .	–1,033	1,630	2,732
Banks	4 663 . .	16	199	221	–57	76	–279	–658	119
Other sectors	4 664 . .	638	437	–458	–1,133	–75	–754	2,288	2,613
Debt securities	4 669 . .	–1,172	19	337	3,691	7,289	5,271	8,214	24
Bonds and notes	4 670 . .	–1,165	–1,110	1,362	3,357	6,625	6,853	6,307	1,474
Monetary authorities	4 671 . .	. . .	. . .	. . .	. . .	. . .	. . .	1	–54
General government	4 672 . .	–586	–247	–1,734	–2,191	–1,131	1,218	2,224	–1,536
Banks	4 673 . .	–654	–423	1,185	3,073	3,297	1,207	2,561	2,282
Other sectors	4 674 . .	76	–441	1,911	2,475	4,459	4,427	1,521	782
Money market instruments	4 680 . .	–7	1,130	–1,026	333	664	–1,582	1,907	–1,450
Monetary authorities	4 681 . .	. . .	. . .	. . .	. . .	. . .	. . .	. . .	. . .
General government	4 682 . .	107	523	–657	518	–931	–459	–196	70
Banks	4 683 . .	–21	9	–5	–5	1,282	27	2,332	–572
Other sectors	4 684 . .	–93	598	–364	–180	312	–1,150	–229	–948
C. FINANCIAL DERIVATIVES	4 910 . .	. . .	. . .	59	142	–87	243	–460	–1,139
Monetary authorities	4 911 . .	. . .	. . .	34	28	1	. . .	. . .	. . .
General government	4 912 . .	. . .	. . .	1	34	–25	41	–9	–233
Banks	4 913 . .	. . .	. . .	64	–2	–30	111	–79	–29
Other sectors	4 914 . .	. . .	. . .	–40	82	–33	91	–372	–878
Assets	4 900 . .	**. . .**	**. . .**	**–43**	**17**	**–162**	**152**	**–329**	**–1,228**
Monetary authorities	4 901 . .	. . .	. . .	. . .	. . .	. . .	. . .	. . .	. . .
General government	4 902 . .	. . .	. . .	1	34	–25	41	–9	–231
Banks	4 903 . .	. . .	. . .	9	–65	–95	43	–142	–140
Other sectors	4 904 . .	. . .	. . .	–52	48	–42	67	–178	–857
Liabilities	4 905 . .	**. . .**	**. . .**	**101**	**125**	**74**	**92**	**–131**	**88**
Monetary authorities	4 906 . .	. . .	. . .	34	28	1	. . .	. . .	. . .
General government	4 907 . .	. . .	. . .	. . .	. . .	. . .	. . .	. . .	–2
Banks	4 908 . .	. . .	. . .	55	63	65	68	64	111
Other sectors	4 909 . .	. . .	. . .	12	34	9	24	–195	–21

Table 2 (Concluded). STANDARD PRESENTATION, 1994–2001
(Millions of U.S. dollars)

	Code		1994	1995	1996	1997	1998	1999	2000	2001
D. OTHER INVESTMENT	4 700	. .	–2,408	2,800	10,920	4,486	1,053	1,140	5,310	674
Assets	4 703	. .	**154**	**961**	**–67**	**–1,403**	**–3,632**	**–7,663**	**–14,148**	**–2,261**
Trade credits	4 706	. .	2,505	1,786	1,392	1,499	1,960	22	486	2,375
General government	4 707	. .	. . .	. . .	. . .	. . .	. . .	. . .	. . .	. . .
of which: Short-term	4 709	. .	. . .	. . .	. . .	. . .	. . .	. . .	. . .	. . .
Other sectors	4 710	. .	2,505	1,786	1,392	1,499	1,960	22	486	2,375
of which: Short-term	4 712	. .	*2,446*	*1,825*	*985*	*946*	*1,789*	*–376*	*486*	*2,077*
Loans	4 714	. .	–218	–935	–719	–1,589	–1,562	–3,493	–6,462	–5,721
Monetary authorities	4 715	. .	. . .	. . .	. . .	. . .	. . .	. . .	. . .	. . .
of which: Short-term	4 718	. .	. . .	. . .	. . .	. . .	. . .	. . .	. . .	. . .
General government	4 719	. .	–3	–161	–9	. . .	1	. . .	. . .	. . .
of which: Short-term	4 721	. .	. . .	. . .	. . .	. . .	. . .	. . .	. . .	. . .
Banks	4 722	. .	–2	–476	–1,243	–752	–66	–920	484	–293
of which: Short-term	4 724	. .	*84*	*74*	*–64*	*–752*	. . .	. . .	. . .	. . .
Other sectors	4 725	. .	–212	–298	532	–837	–1,497	–2,573	–6,946	–5,428
of which: Short-term	4 727	. .	*–170*	*–229*	*275*	. . .	. . .	. . .	. . .	. . .
Currency and deposits	4 730	. .	–757	480	–192	206	–3,723	–1,070	–6,269	1,911
Monetary authorities	4 731	. .	. . .	. . .	. . .	. . .	. . .	. . .	. . .	. . .
General government	4 732	. .	–38	1	79	90	–1,167	–1,093	–2,059	1,767
Banks	4 733	. .	–572	816	87	–446	–996	–49	–2,289	727
Other sectors	4 734	. .	–147	–337	–358	563	–1,560	72	–1,920	–583
Other assets	4 736	. .	–1,376	–370	–548	–1,519	–308	–3,121	–1,904	–826
Monetary authorities	4 737	. .	. . .	. . .	. . .	. . .	. . .	. . .	. . .	. . .
of which: Short-term	4 739	. .	. . .	. . .	. . .	. . .	. . .	. . .	. . .	. . .
General government	4 740	. .	29	4	1	1	–1	–6	–13	–9
of which: Short-term	4 742	. .	. . .	. . .	. . .	. . .	. . .	. . .	. . .	. . .
Banks	4 743	. .	–64	95	–60	–267	. . .	. . .	. . .	. . .
of which: Short-term	4 745	. .	. . .	. . .	. . .	. . .	. . .	. . .	. . .	. . .
Other sectors	4 746	. .	–1,341	–469	–489	–1,253	–307	–3,116	–1,891	–817
of which: Short-term	4 748	. .	. . .	. . .	. . .	. . .	. . .	. . .	. . .	. . .
Liabilities	4 753	. .	**–2,562**	**1,840**	**10,987**	**5,888**	**4,685**	**8,802**	**19,459**	**2,935**
Trade credits	4 756	. .	–964	33	258	440	180	–334	354	–223
General government	4 757	. .	. . .	. . .	. . .	. . .	. . .	. . .	. . .	. . .
of which: Short-term	4 759	. .	. . .	. . .	. . .	. . .	. . .	. . .	. . .	. . .
Other sectors	4 760	. .	–964	33	258	440	180	–334	354	–223
of which: Short-term	4 762	. .	*–843*	*271*	*286*	*387*	*180*	*–334*	*354*	*–223*
Loans	4 764	. .	–1,227	1,932	2,128	1,886	5,750	6,429	17,424	1,580
Monetary authorities	4 765	. .	208	–318	1,481	–684	. . .	. . .	. . .	. . .
of which: Use of Fund credit and loans from the Fund	4 766	. .	. . .	. . .	. . .	. . .	. . .	. . .	. . .	. . .
of which: Short-term	4 768	. .	*208*	*–318*	*1,481*	*–684*	. . .	. . .	. . .	. . .
General government	4 769	. .	–169	2	. . .	94	1,346	3,460	9,658	–432
of which: Short-term	4 771	. .	. . .	. . .	. . .	*94*	*1,346*	*3,460*	*9,658*	*–432*
Banks	4 772	. .	–198	–83	–57	245	462	71	330	654
of which: Short-term	4 774	. .	*–58*	*–77*	*–57*	*245*	. . .	. . .	. . .	. . .
Other sectors	4 775	. .	–1,068	2,330	705	2,231	3,942	2,899	7,435	1,358
of which: Short-term	4 777	. .	. . .	. . .	. . .	. . .	. . .	. . .	. . .	. . .
Currency and deposits	4 780	. .	–463	325	8,679	3,635	–1,298	1,699	994	1,680
Monetary authorities	4 781	. .	–8	33	7	–19	19	–19	3	44
General government	4 782	. .	. . .	. . .	. . .	. . .	. . .	. . .	. . .	. . .
Banks	4 783	. .	–455	292	8,672	3,654	–1,317	1,718	991	1,636
Other sectors	4 784	. .	. . .	. . .	. . .	. . .	. . .	. . .	. . .	. . .
Other liabilities	4 786	. .	92	–450	–78	–73	53	1,009	687	–101
Monetary authorities	4 787	. .	–61	–339	17	–100	. . .	. . .	. . .	. . .
of which: Short-term	4 789	. .	. . .	*–339*	. . .	. . .	. . .	. . .	. . .	. . .
General government	4 790	. .	5	1	. . .	. . .	. . .	. . .	–2	. . .
of which: Short-term	4 792	. .	. . .	. . .	. . .	. . .	. . .	. . .	. . .	. . .
Banks	4 793	. .	49	37	62	227	. . .	. . .	. . .	. . .
of which: Short-term	4 795	. .	. . .	. . .	. . .	. . .	. . .	. . .	. . .	. . .
Other sectors	4 796	. .	99	–149	–157	–199	53	1,009	689	–101
of which: Short-term	4 798	. .	. . .	. . .	. . .	. . .	. . .	. . .	. . .	. . .
E. RESERVE ASSETS	4 802	. .	–253	–575	–6,470	1,198	6,384	–5,984	–3,686	2,114
Monetary gold	4 812	. .	. . .	. . .	. . .	. . .	. . .	. . .	. . .	. . .
Special drawing rights	4 811	. .	29	–60	94	–13	–49	–5	85	–57
Reserve position in the Fund	4 810	. .	–22	–292	–11	–111	–235	380	228	–163
Foreign exchange	4 803	. .	–1,520	–1,929	–878	–2,886	6,153	–4,520	–1,798	5,926
Other claims	4 813	. .	1,259	1,706	–5,675	4,208	515	–1,839	–2,200	–3,591
NET ERRORS AND OMISSIONS	4 998	. .	**–1,987**	**–3,947**	**–2,910**	**–4,443**	**–6,335**	**–2,710**	**–7,780**	**–4,104**

Part 3 of the *Yearbook* contains descriptions of the methodologies, compilation practices, and sources used to compile these data.

Table 1. ANALYTIC PRESENTATION, 1994–2001
(Millions of U.S. dollars)

	Code	1994	1995	1996	1997	1998	1999	2000	2001
A. Current Account [1]	4 993 Z.	**–805**	**–801**	**338**	**–78**	**–2,950**	**–291**	**3,423**	**2,315**
Goods: exports f.o.b	2 100 . .	5,542	6,065	7,373	7,657	5,521	7,239	11,319	11,074
Goods: imports f.o.b	3 100 . .	–3,693	–4,050	–4,231	–4,645	–5,215	–4,300	–4,593	–5,311
Balance on Goods	4 100 . .	*1,849*	*2,015*	*3,142*	*3,012*	*307*	*2,939*	*6,726*	*5,763*
Services: credit	2 200 . .	13	13	237	268	369	401	424	349
Services: debit	3 200 . .	–900	–985	–1,233	–1,467	–1,683	–1,511	–1,566	–1,678
Balance on Goods and Services	4 991 . .	*962*	*1,043*	*2,146*	*1,813*	*–1,007*	*1,829*	*5,584*	*4,434*
Income: credit	2 300 . .	257	325	257	385	338	187	291	309
Income: debit	3 300 . .	–724	–699	–694	–775	–814	–869	–1,001	–897
Balance on Goods, Services, and Income	4 992 . .	*495*	*669*	*1,709*	*1,423*	*–1,483*	*1,147*	*4,874*	*3,847*
Current transfers: credit	2 379 Z.	65	68	. . .	. . .	. . .	. . .	. . .	. . .
Current transfers: debit	3 379 . .	–1,365	–1,537	–1,371	–1,501	–1,467	–1,438	–1,451	–1,532
B. Capital Account [1]	4 994 Z.	**. . .**	**. . .**	**10**	**31**	**–5**	**–3**	**8**	**–10**
Capital account: credit	2 994 Z.	. . .	. . .	29	55	21	16	34	8
Capital account: debit	3 994 . .	. . .	. . .	–18	–23	–26	–18	–26	–18
Total, Groups A Plus B	4 981 . .	*–805*	*–801*	*349*	*–47*	*–2,955*	*–294*	*3,430*	*2,304*
C. Financial Account [1]	4 995 W.	**230**	**–19**	**260**	**52**	**1,488**	**109**	**–494**	**–887**
Direct investment abroad	4 505 . .	. . .	. . .	. . .	. . .	. . .	. . .	. . .	. . .
Direct investment in Oman	4 555 Z.	76	46	60	65	101	21	70	42
Portfolio investment assets	4 602 . .	. . .	. . .	. . .	. . .	. . .	. . .	. . .	. . .
Equity securities	4 610 . .	. . .	. . .	. . .	. . .	. . .	. . .	. . .	. . .
Debt securities	4 619 . .	. . .	. . .	. . .	. . .	. . .	. . .	. . .	. . .
Portfolio investment liabilities	4 652 Z.	. . .	. . .	8	18	185	26	–36	13
Equity securities	4 660 . .	. . .	. . .	10	86	239	13	–10	–3
Debt securities	4 669 Z.	. . .	. . .	–3	–68	–55	13	–26	16
Financial derivatives	4 910 . .	. . .	. . .	. . .	. . .	. . .	. . .	. . .	. . .
Financial derivatives assets	4 900 . .	. . .	. . .	. . .	. . .	. . .	. . .	. . .	. . .
Financial derivatives liabilities	4 905 . .	. . .	. . .	. . .	. . .	. . .	. . .	. . .	. . .
Other investment assets	4 703 . .	–174	–52	–237	–715	642	–307	–356	229
Monetary authorities	4 701 . .	. . .	. . .	. . .	. . .	. . .	. . .	. . .	. . .
General government	4 704 . .	–104	–88	–291	117	88	–538	–133	10
Banks	4 705 . .	–10	62	55	–832	554	231	–224	218
Other sectors	4 728 . .	–60	–26	. . .	. . .	. . .	. . .	. . .	. . .
Other investment liabilities	4 753 W.	328	–13	429	684	559	369	–172	–1,170
Monetary authorities	4 753 WA	. . .	. . .	. . .	. . .	. . .	. . .	. . .	. . .
General government	4 753 ZB	325	–18	140	–112	–26	101	–114	–447
Banks	4 753 ZC	3	5	213	676	195	143	–21	–112
Other sectors	4 753 ZD	. . .	. . .	75	120	390	125	–36	–611
Total, Groups A Through C	4 983 . .	*–575*	*–819*	*609*	*5*	*–1,467*	*–185*	*2,936*	*1,417*
D. Net Errors and Omissions	4 998 . .	**–86**	**388**	**–420**	**526**	**702**	**399**	**–674**	**–384**
Total, Groups A Through D	4 984 . .	*–661*	*–432*	*189*	*531*	*–765*	*215*	*2,262*	*1,034*
E. Reserves and Related Items	4 802 A.	**661**	**432**	**–189**	**–531**	**765**	**–215**	**–2,262**	**–1,034**
Reserve assets	4 802 . .	661	432	–189	–531	765	–215	–2,262	–1,034
Use of Fund credit and loans	4 766 . .	. . .	. . .	. . .	. . .	. . .	. . .	. . .	. . .
Exceptional financing	4 920 . .	. . .	. . .	. . .	. . .	. . .	. . .	. . .	. . .
Conversion rates: rial Omani per U.S. dollar	0 101 . .	**.3845**	**.3845**	**.3845**	**.3845**	**.3845**	**.3845**	**.3845**	**.3845**

[1] Excludes components that have been classified in the categories of Group E.

Table 2. STANDARD PRESENTATION, 1994–2001

(Millions of U.S. dollars)

	Code	1994	1995	1996	1997	1998	1999	2000	2001
CURRENT ACCOUNT	4 993 . .	**–805**	**–801**	**338**	**–78**	**–2,950**	**–291**	**3,423**	**2,315**
A. GOODS	4 100 . .	1,849	2,015	3,142	3,012	307	2,939	6,726	5,763
Credit	2 100 . .	**5,542**	**6,065**	**7,373**	**7,657**	**5,521**	**7,239**	**11,319**	**11,074**
General merchandise: exports f.o.b.	2 110 . .	5,542	6,065	7,373	7,657	5,521	7,239	11,319	11,074
Goods for processing: exports f.o.b.	2 150 . .	. . .	. . .	. . .	. . .	. . .	. . .	. . .	. . .
Repairs on goods	2 160 . .	. . .	. . .	. . .	. . .	. . .	. . .	. . .	. . .
Goods procured in ports by carriers	2 170 . .	. . .	. . .	. . .	. . .	. . .	. . .	. . .	. . .
Nonmonetary gold	2 180 . .	. . .	. . .	. . .	. . .	. . .	. . .	. . .	. . .
Debit	3 160 . .	**–3,693**	**–4,050**	. . .	. . .	. . .	. . .	. . .	. . .
Goods procured in ports by carriers	3 170 . .	. . .	. . .	. . .	. . .	. . .	. . .	. . .	. . .
Nonmonetary gold	3 180 . .	. . .	. . .	. . .	. . .	. . .	. . .	. . .	. . .
B. SERVICES	4 200 . .	–887	–972	–996	–1,199	–1,314	–1,111	–1,142	–1,329
Total credit	2 200 . .	*13*	*13*	*237*	*268*	*369*	*401*	*424*	*349*
Total debit	3 200 . .	*–900*	*–985*	*–1,233*	*–1,467*	*–1,683*	*–1,511*	*–1,566*	*–1,678*
Transportation services, credit	2 205 . .	**13**	**13**	**18**	**18**	**112**	**146**	**153**	**159**
Passenger	2 850 . .	. . .	. . .	. . .	. . .	*68*	*83*	*75*	*73*
Freight	2 851 . .	. . .	. . .	. . .	. . .	. . .	. . .	. . .	. . .
Other	2 852 . .	*13*	*13*	*18*	*18*	*44*	*62*	*78*	*86*
Sea transport, passenger	2 207 . .	. . .	. . .	. . .	. . .	. . .	. . .	. . .	. . .
Sea transport, freight	2 208 . .	. . .	. . .	. . .	. . .	. . .	. . .	. . .	. . .
Sea transport, other	2 209 . .	. . .	. . .	. . .	. . .	. . .	. . .	. . .	. . .
Air transport, passenger	2 211 . .	. . .	. . .	. . .	. . .	68	83	75	73
Air transport, freight	2 212 . .	. . .	. . .	. . .	. . .	. . .	. . .	. . .	. . .
Air transport, other	2 213 . .	. . .	. . .	. . .	18	44	62	78	86
Other transport, passenger	2 215 . .	. . .	. . .	. . .	. . .	. . .	. . .	. . .	. . .
Other transport, freight	2 216 . .	. . .	. . .	. . .	. . .	. . .	. . .	. . .	. . .
Other transport, other	2 217 . .	. . .	. . .	. . .	. . .	. . .	. . .	. . .	. . .
Transportation services, debit	3 205 . .	**–377**	**–411**	**–450**	**–494**	**–598**	**–499**	**–546**	**–622**
Passenger	3 850 . .	. . .	. . .	. . .	. . .	*–44*	*–42*	*–57*	*–57*
Freight	3 851 . .	*–377*	*–411*	*–450*	*–494*	*–554*	*–455*	*–486*	*–564*
Other	3 852 . .	. . .	. . .	. . .	. . .	. . .	*–3*	*–3*	. . .
Sea transport, passenger	3 207 . .	. . .	. . .	. . .	. . .	. . .	. . .	. . .	. . .
Sea transport, freight	3 208 . .	. . .	. . .	. . .	. . .	. . .	. . .	. . .	. . .
Sea transport, other	3 209 . .	. . .	. . .	. . .	. . .	. . .	. . .	. . .	. . .
Air transport, passenger	3 211 . .	. . .	. . .	. . .	. . .	–44	–42	–57	–57
Air transport, freight	3 212 . .	. . .	. . .	. . .	–494	–554	–455	–486	–564
Air transport, other	3 213 . .	. . .	. . .	. . .	. . .	. . .	–3	–3	. . .
Other transport, passenger	3 215 . .	. . .	. . .	. . .	. . .	. . .	. . .	. . .	. . .
Other transport, freight	3 216 . .	. . .	. . .	. . .	. . .	. . .	. . .	. . .	. . .
Other transport, other	3 217 . .	. . .	. . .	. . .	. . .	. . .	. . .	. . .	. . .
Travel, credit	2 236 . .	**. . .**	**. . .**	**192**	**192**	**205**	**205**	**221**	**143**
Business travel	2 237 . .	. . .	. . .	. . .	. . .	. . .	. . .	. . .	. . .
Personal travel	2 240 . .	. . .	. . .	192	192	205	205	221	143
Travel, debit	3 236 . .	**–47**	**–47**	**–255**	**–257**	**–294**	**–328**	**–351**	**–367**
Business travel	3 237 . .	. . .	. . .	. . .	. . .	. . .	. . .	. . .	. . .
Personal travel	3 240 . .	. . .	. . .	–255	–257	–294	–328	–351	367
Other services, credit	2 200 BA	**. . .**	**. . .**	**26**	**57**	**52**	**49**	**49**	**47**
Communications	2 245 . .	. . .	. . .	23	52	44	42	36	31
Construction	2 249 . .	. . .	. . .	. . .	. . .	. . .	. . .	. . .	. . .
Insurance	2 253 . .	. . .	. . .	3	5	8	8	13	16
Financial	2 260 . .	. . .	. . .	. . .	. . .	. . .	. . .	. . .	. . .
Computer and information	2 262 . .	. . .	. . .	. . .	. . .	. . .	. . .	. . .	. . .
Royalties and licence fees	2 266 . .	. . .	. . .	. . .	. . .	. . .	. . .	. . .	. . .
Other business services	2 268 . .	. . .	. . .	. . .	. . .	. . .	. . .	. . .	. . .
Personal, cultural, and recreational	2 287 . .	. . .	. . .	. . .	. . .	. . .	. . .	. . .	. . .
Government, n.i.e.	2 291 . .	. . .	. . .	. . .	. . .	. . .	. . .	. . .	. . .
Other services, debit	3 200 BA	**–476**	**–527**	**–528**	**–715**	**–791**	**–684**	**–668**	**–689**
Communications	3 245 . .	. . .	. . .	–34	–73	–47	–57	–68	–73
Construction	3 249 . .	. . .	. . .	. . .	. . .	. . .	. . .	. . .	. . .
Insurance	3 253 . .	–42	–46	–60	–65	–83	–104	–114	–120
Financial	3 260 . .	. . .	. . .	. . .	. . .	. . .	. . .	. . .	. . .
Computer and information	3 262 . .	. . .	. . .	. . .	. . .	. . .	. . .	. . .	. . .
Royalties and licence fees	3 266 . .	. . .	. . .	. . .	. . .	. . .	. . .	. . .	. . .
Other business services	3 268 . .	–434	–481	–434	–577	–661	–523	–486	–497
Personal, cultural, and recreational	3 287 . .	. . .	. . .	. . .	. . .	. . .	. . .	. . .	. . .
Government, n.i.e.	3 291 . .	. . .	. . .	. . .	. . .	. . .	. . .	. . .	. . .

Table 2 (Continued). STANDARD PRESENTATION, 1994–2001
(Millions of U.S. dollars)

	Code	1994	1995	1996	1997	1998	1999	2000	2001
C. INCOME	4 300	–467	–374	–437	–390	–476	–681	–710	–588
Total credit	2 300	*257*	*325*	*257*	*385*	*338*	*187*	*291*	*309*
Total debit	3 300	*–724*	*–699*	*–694*	*–775*	*–814*	*–869*	*–1,001*	*–897*
Compensation of employees, credit	2 310	**. . .**	**. . .**	**39**	**39**	**39**	**39**	**39**	**39**
Compensation of employees, debit	3 310	**. . .**	**. . .**	**. . .**	**. . .**	**. . .**	**. . .**	**. . .**	**. . .**
Investment income, credit	2 320	**257**	**325**	**218**	**346**	**299**	**148**	**252**	**270**
Direct investment income	2 330	. . .	. . .	. . .	. . .	. . .	. . .	. . .	. . .
Dividends and distributed branch profits	2 332	. . .	. . .	. . .	. . .	. . .	. . .	. . .	. . .
Reinvested earnings and undistributed branch profits	2 333	. . .	. . .	. . .	. . .	. . .	. . .	. . .	. . .
Income on debt (interest)	2 334	. . .	. . .	. . .	. . .	. . .	. . .	. . .	. . .
Portfolio investment income	2 339	. . .	. . .	. . .	. . .	. . .	. . .	. . .	. . .
Income on equity	2 340	. . .	. . .	. . .	. . .	. . .	. . .	. . .	. . .
Income on bonds and notes	2 350	. . .	. . .	. . .	. . .	. . .	. . .	. . .	. . .
Income on money market instruments	2 360	. . .	. . .	. . .	. . .	. . .	. . .	. . .	. . .
Other investment income	2 370	257	325	218	346	299	148	252	270
Investment income, debit	3 320	**–724**	**–699**	**–694**	**–775**	**–814**	**–869**	**–1,001**	**–897**
Direct investment income	3 330	–524	–507	–507	–601	–616	–567	–674	–614
Dividends and distributed branch profits	3 332	–507	–489	–501	–590	–606	–564	–661	–611
Reinvested earnings and undistributed branch profits	3 333	–17	–18	–6	–10	–10	–3	–13	–3
Income on debt (interest)	3 334	. . .	. . .	. . .	. . .	. . .	. . .	. . .	. . .
Portfolio investment income	3 339	. . .	. . .	. . .	. . .	. . .	. . .	. . .	. . .
Income on equity	3 340	. . .	. . .	. . .	. . .	. . .	. . .	. . .	. . .
Income on bonds and notes	3 350	. . .	. . .	. . .	. . .	. . .	. . .	. . .	. . .
Income on money market instruments	3 360	. . .	. . .	. . .	. . .	. . .	. . .	. . .	. . .
Other investment income	3 370	–200	–192	–187	–174	–198	–302	–328	–283
D. CURRENT TRANSFERS	4 379	–1,300	–1,469	–1,371	–1,501	–1,467	–1,438	–1,451	–1,532
Credit	2 379	**65**	**68**	**. . .**	**. . .**	**. . .**	**. . .**	**. . .**	**. . .**
General government	2 380	26	29	. . .	. . .	. . .	. . .	. . .	. . .
Other sectors	2 390	39	39	. . .	. . .	. . .	. . .	. . .	. . .
Workers' remittances	2 391	39	39	. . .	. . .	. . .	. . .	. . .	. . .
Other current transfers	2 392	. . .	. . .	. . .	. . .	. . .	. . .	. . .	. . .
Debit	3 379	**–1,365**	**–1,537**	**–1,371**	**–1,501**	**–1,467**	**–1,438**	**–1,451**	**–1,532**
General government	3 380	. . .	. . .	. . .	. . .	. . .	. . .	. . .	. . .
Other sectors	3 390	–1,365	–1,537	–1,371	–1,501	–1,467	–1,438	–1,451	–1,532
Workers' remittances	3 391	–1,365	–1,537	–1,371	–1,501	–1,467	–1,438	–1,451	–1,532
Other current transfers	3 392	. . .	. . .	. . .	. . .	. . .	. . .	. . .	. . .
CAPITAL AND FINANCIAL ACCOUNT	4 996	**891**	**413**	**82**	**–448**	**2,248**	**–108**	**–2,749**	**–1,931**
CAPITAL ACCOUNT	4 994	**. . .**	**. . .**	**10**	**31**	**–5**	**–3**	**8**	**–10**
Total credit	2 994	. . .	. . .	*29*	*55*	*21*	*16*	*34*	*8*
Total debit	3 994	. . .	. . .	*–18*	*–23*	*–26*	*–18*	*–26*	*–18*
Capital transfers, credit	2 400	**. . .**	**. . .**	**29**	**55**	**21**	**16**	**34**	**8**
General government	2 401	. . .	. . .	29	55	21	16	34	8
Debt forgiveness	2 402	. . .	. . .	. . .	. . .	. . .	. . .	. . .	. . .
Other capital transfers	2 410	. . .	. . .	. . .	55	21	16	34	8
Other sectors	2 430	. . .	. . .	. . .	. . .	. . .	. . .	. . .	. . .
Migrants' transfers	2 431	. . .	. . .	. . .	. . .	. . .	. . .	. . .	. . .
Debt forgiveness	2 432	. . .	. . .	. . .	. . .	. . .	. . .	. . .	. . .
Other capital transfers	2 440	. . .	. . .	. . .	. . .	. . .	. . .	. . .	. . .
Capital transfers, debit	3 400	**. . .**	**. . .**	**–18**	**–23**	**–26**	**–18**	**–26**	**–18**
General government	3 401	. . .	. . .	–18	–23	–26	–18	–26	–18
Debt forgiveness	3 402	. . .	. . .	. . .	. . .	. . .	. . .	. . .	. . .
Other capital transfers	3 410	. . .	. . .	. . .	–23	–26	–18	–26	–18
Other sectors	3 430	. . .	. . .	. . .	. . .	. . .	. . .	. . .	. . .
Migrants' transfers	3 431	. . .	. . .	. . .	. . .	. . .	. . .	. . .	. . .
Debt forgiveness	3 432	. . .	. . .	. . .	. . .	. . .	. . .	. . .	. . .
Other capital transfers	3 440	. . .	. . .	. . .	. . .	. . .	. . .	. . .	. . .
Nonproduced nonfinancial assets, credit	2 480	**. . .**	**. . .**	**. . .**	**. . .**	**. . .**	**. . .**	**. . .**	**. . .**
Nonproduced nonfinancial assets, debit	3 480	**. . .**	**. . .**	**. . .**	**. . .**	**. . .**	**. . .**	**. . .**	**. . .**

Table 2 (Continued). STANDARD PRESENTATION, 1994–2001
(Millions of U.S. dollars)

	Code	1994	1995	1996	1997	1998	1999	2000	2001
FINANCIAL ACCOUNT	4 995 . .	**891**	**413**	**72**	**–479**	**2,253**	**–105**	**–2,757**	**–1,920**
A. DIRECT INVESTMENT	4 500 . .	76	46	60	65	101	21	70	42
Direct investment abroad	4 505 . .	**. . .**	**. . .**	**. . .**	**. . .**	**. . .**	**. . .**	**. . .**	**. . .**
Equity capital	4 510 . .	. . .	. . .	. . .	. . .	. . .	. . .	. . .	. . .
Claims on affiliated enterprises	4 515 . .	. . .	. . .	. . .	. . .	. . .	. . .	. . .	. . .
Liabilities to affiliated enterprises	4 520 . .	. . .	. . .	. . .	. . .	. . .	. . .	. . .	. . .
Reinvested earnings	4 525 . .	. . .	. . .	. . .	. . .	. . .	. . .	. . .	. . .
Other capital	4 530 . .	. . .	. . .	. . .	. . .	. . .	. . .	. . .	. . .
Claims on affiliated enterprises	4 535 . .	. . .	. . .	. . .	. . .	. . .	. . .	. . .	. . .
Liabilities to affiliated enterprises	4 540 . .	. . .	. . .	. . .	. . .	. . .	. . .	. . .	. . .
Direct investment in Oman	4 555 . .	**76**	**46**	**60**	**65**	**101**	**21**	**70**	**42**
Equity capital	4 560 . .	60	29	54	55	91	18	57	39
Claims on direct investors	4 565 . .	. . .	. . .	54	. . .	. . .	. . .	. . .	. . .
Liabilities to direct investors	4 570 . .	. . .	. . .	. . .	55	91	18	57	39
Reinvested earnings	4 575 . .	17	18	6	10	10	3	13	3
Other capital	4 580 . .	. . .	. . .	. . .	. . .	. . .	. . .	. . .	. . .
Claims on direct investors	4 585 . .	. . .	. . .	. . .	. . .	. . .	. . .	. . .	. . .
Liabilities to direct investors	4 590 . .	. . .	. . .	. . .	. . .	. . .	. . .	. . .	. . .
B. PORTFOLIO INVESTMENT	4 600 . .	. . .	. . .	8	18	185	26	–36	13
Assets	4 602 . .	**. . .**	**. . .**	**. . .**	**. . .**	**. . .**	**. . .**	**. . .**	**. . .**
Equity securities	4 610 . .	. . .	. . .	. . .	. . .	. . .	. . .	. . .	. . .
Monetary authorities	4 611 . .	. . .	. . .	. . .	. . .	. . .	. . .	. . .	. . .
General government	4 612 . .	. . .	. . .	. . .	. . .	. . .	. . .	. . .	. . .
Banks	4 613 . .	. . .	. . .	. . .	. . .	. . .	. . .	. . .	. . .
Other sectors	4 614 . .	. . .	. . .	. . .	. . .	. . .	. . .	. . .	. . .
Debt securities	4 619 . .	. . .	. . .	. . .	. . .	. . .	. . .	. . .	. . .
Bonds and notes	4 620 . .	. . .	. . .	. . .	. . .	. . .	. . .	. . .	. . .
Monetary authorities	4 621 . .	. . .	. . .	. . .	. . .	. . .	. . .	. . .	. . .
General government	4 622 . .	. . .	. . .	. . .	. . .	. . .	. . .	. . .	. . .
Banks	4 623 . .	. . .	. . .	. . .	. . .	. . .	. . .	. . .	. . .
Other sectors	4 624 . .	. . .	. . .	. . .	. . .	. . .	. . .	. . .	. . .
Money market instruments	4 630 . .	. . .	. . .	. . .	. . .	. . .	. . .	. . .	. . .
Monetary authorities	4 631 . .	. . .	. . .	. . .	. . .	. . .	. . .	. . .	. . .
General government	4 632 . .	. . .	. . .	. . .	. . .	. . .	. . .	. . .	. . .
Banks	4 633 . .	. . .	. . .	. . .	. . .	. . .	. . .	. . .	. . .
Other sectors	4 634 . .	. . .	. . .	. . .	. . .	. . .	. . .	. . .	. . .
Liabilities	4 652 . .	**. . .**	**. . .**	**8**	**18**	**185**	**26**	**–36**	**13**
Equity securities	4 660 . .	. . .	. . .	10	86	239	13	–10	–3
Banks	4 663 . .	. . .	. . .	3	10	23	8	8	3
Other sectors	4 664 . .	. . .	. . .	8	75	216	5	–18	–5
Debt securities	4 669 . .	. . .	. . .	–3	–68	–55	13	–26	16
Bonds and notes	4 670 . .	. . .	. . .	–3	–68	–55	13	–26	16
Monetary authorities	4 671 . .	. . .	. . .	. . .	. . .	. . .	. . .	. . .	. . .
General government	4 672 . .	. . .	. . .	–3	–68	–55	13	–26	16
Banks	4 673 . .	. . .	. . .	. . .	. . .	. . .	. . .	. . .	. . .
Other sectors	4 674 . .	. . .	. . .	. . .	. . .	. . .	. . .	. . .	. . .
Money market instruments	4 680 . .	. . .	. . .	. . .	. . .	. . .	. . .	. . .	. . .
Monetary authorities	4 681 . .	. . .	. . .	. . .	. . .	. . .	. . .	. . .	. . .
General government	4 682 . .	. . .	. . .	. . .	. . .	. . .	. . .	. . .	. . .
Banks	4 683 . .	. . .	. . .	. . .	. . .	. . .	. . .	. . .	. . .
Other sectors	4 684 . .	. . .	. . .	. . .	. . .	. . .	. . .	. . .	. . .
C. FINANCIAL DERIVATIVES	4 910 . .	. . .	. . .	. . .	. . .	. . .	. . .	. . .	. . .
Monetary authorities	4 911 . .	. . .	. . .	. . .	. . .	. . .	. . .	. . .	. . .
General government	4 912 . .	. . .	. . .	. . .	. . .	. . .	. . .	. . .	. . .
Banks	4 913 . .	. . .	. . .	. . .	. . .	. . .	. . .	. . .	. . .
Other sectors	4 914 . .	. . .	. . .	. . .	. . .	. . .	. . .	. . .	. . .
Assets	4 900 . .	**. . .**	**. . .**	**. . .**	**. . .**	**. . .**	**. . .**	**. . .**	**. . .**
Monetary authorities	4 901 . .	. . .	. . .	. . .	. . .	. . .	. . .	. . .	. . .
General government	4 902 . .	. . .	. . .	. . .	. . .	. . .	. . .	. . .	. . .
Banks	4 903 . .	. . .	. . .	. . .	. . .	. . .	. . .	. . .	. . .
Other sectors	4 904 . .	. . .	. . .	. . .	. . .	. . .	. . .	. . .	. . .
Liabilities	4 905 . .	**. . .**	**. . .**	**. . .**	**. . .**	**. . .**	**. . .**	**. . .**	**. . .**
Monetary authorities	4 906 . .	. . .	. . .	. . .	. . .	. . .	. . .	. . .	. . .
General government	4 907 . .	. . .	. . .	. . .	. . .	. . .	. . .	. . .	. . .
Banks	4 908 . .	. . .	. . .	. . .	. . .	. . .	. . .	. . .	. . .
Other sectors	4 909 . .	. . .	. . .	. . .	. . .	. . .	. . .	. . .	. . .

Table 2 (Concluded). STANDARD PRESENTATION, 1994–2001
(Millions of U.S. dollars)

	Code	1994	1995	1996	1997	1998	1999	2000	2001
D. OTHER INVESTMENT	4 700	153	–65	192	–31	1,202	62	–528	–941
Assets	4 703	**–174**	**–52**	**–237**	**–715**	**642**	**–307**	**–356**	**229**
Trade credits	4 706	...	...	–187	198	156	–424	16	138
General government	4 707	...	...	–187	198	156	–424	16	138
of which: Short-term	4 709	...	...	*–187*	*198*	*156*	*–424*	*16*	*138*
Other sectors	4 710	...	...	...	...	...	...	...	...
of which: Short-term	4 712	...	...	...	...	...	...	...	...
Loans	4 714	–60	–26	...	...	...	...	...	...
Monetary authorities	4 715	...	...	...	...	...	...	...	...
of which: Short-term	4 718	...	...	...	...	...	...	...	...
General government	4 719	...	...	...	...	...	...	...	...
of which: Short-term	4 721	...	...	...	...	...	...	...	...
Banks	4 722	...	...	...	...	...	...	...	...
of which: Short-term	4 724	...	...	...	...	...	...	...	...
Other sectors	4 725	–60	–26	...	...	...	...	...	...
of which: Short-term	4 727	*–60*	*–26*	...	...	...	...	...	...
Currency and deposits	4 730	–10	62	55	–832	554	231	–224	218
Monetary authorities	4 731	...	...	...	...	...	...	...	...
General government	4 732	...	...	...	...	...	...	...	...
Banks	4 733	–10	62	55	–832	554	231	–224	218
Other sectors	4 734	...	...	...	...	...	...	...	...
Other assets	4 736	–104	–88	–104	–81	–68	–114	–148	–127
Monetary authorities	4 737	...	...	...	...	...	...	...	...
of which: Short-term	4 739	...	...	...	...	...	...	...	...
General government	4 740	–104	–88	–104	–81	–68	–114	–148	–127
of which: Short-term	4 742	...	...	...	...	...	...	...	...
Banks	4 743	...	...	...	...	...	...	...	...
of which: Short-term	4 745	...	...	...	...	...	...	...	...
Other sectors	4 746	...	...	...	...	...	...	...	...
of which: Short-term	4 748	...	...	...	...	...	...	...	...
Liabilities	4 753	**328**	**–13**	**429**	**684**	**559**	**369**	**–172**	**–1,170**
Trade credits	4 756	...	...	...	...	...	...	...	...
General government	4 757	...	...	...	...	...	...	...	...
of which: Short-term	4 759	...	...	...	...	...	...	...	...
Other sectors	4 760	...	...	...	...	...	...	...	...
of which: Short-term	4 762	...	...	...	...	...	...	...	...
Loans	4 764	421	–140	216	8	364	226	–151	–1,059
Monetary authorities	4 765	...	...	...	...	...	...	...	...
of which: Use of Fund credit and loans from the Fund	4 766	...	...	...	...	...	...	...	...
of which: Short-term	4 768	...	...	...	...	...	...	...	...
General government	4 769	421	–140	140	–112	–26	101	–114	–447
of which: Short-term	4 771	*135*	*–153*	*31*	*–31*	*299*	*–299*	...	*10*
Banks	4 772	...	...	...	...	...	...	...	...
of which: Short-term	4 774	...	...	...	...	...	...	...	...
Other sectors	4 775	...	...	75	120	390	125	–36	–611
of which: Short-term	4 777	...	...	...	...	...	...	...	...
Currency and deposits	4 780	3	5	213	676	195	143	–21	–112
Monetary authorities	4 781	...	...	...	...	...	...	...	...
General government	4 782	...	...	...	...	...	...	...	...
Banks	4 783	3	5	213	676	195	143	–21	–112
Other sectors	4 784	...	...	...	...	...	...	...	...
Other liabilities	4 786	–96	122	...	...	...	...	...	...
Monetary authorities	4 787	...	...	...	...	...	...	...	...
of which: Short-term	4 789	...	...	...	...	...	...	...	...
General government	4 790	–96	122	...	...	...	...	...	...
of which: Short-term	4 792	...	...	...	...	...	...	...	...
Banks	4 793	...	...	...	...	...	...	...	...
of which: Short-term	4 795	...	...	...	...	...	...	...	...
Other sectors	4 796	...	...	...	...	...	...	...	...
of which: Short-term	4 798	...	...	...	...	...	...	...	...
E. RESERVE ASSETS	4 802	661	432	–189	–531	765	–215	–2,262	–1,034
Monetary gold	4 812	...	...	...	...	...	...	...	...
Special drawing rights	4 811	–2	–2	–2	–2	–2	14	–2	–2
Reserve position in the Fund	4 810	3	2	1	4	...	–26	...	–19
Foreign exchange	4 803	236	–157	–179	–195	172	–879	346	–21
Other claims	4 813	424	588	–8	–338	596	676	–2,606	–991
NET ERRORS AND OMISSIONS	4 998	**–86**	**388**	**–420**	**526**	**702**	**399**	**–674**	**–384**

Part 3 of the *Yearbook* contains descriptions of the methodologies, compilation practices, and sources used to compile these data.

Table 1. ANALYTIC PRESENTATION, 1994–2001
(Millions of U.S. dollars)

	Code	1994	1995	1996	1997	1998	1999	2000	2001
A. Current Account[1]	4 993 Z.	**–1,812**	**–3,349**	**–4,436**	**–1,712**	**–2,248**	**–920**	**–85**	**1,880**
Goods: exports f.o.b	2 100 . .	7,117	8,356	8,507	8,351	7,850	7,673	8,739	9,131
Goods: imports f.o.b	3 100 . .	–9,355	–11,248	–12,164	–10,750	–9,834	–9,520	–9,896	–9,739
Balance on Goods	4 100 . .	*–2,239*	*–2,891*	*–3,656*	*–2,399*	*–1,984*	*–1,847*	*–1,157*	*–608*
Services: credit	2 200 . .	1,753	1,857	2,016	1,625	1,404	1,373	1,380	1,459
Services: debit	3 200 . .	–2,529	–2,938	–3,459	–2,658	–2,261	–2,146	–2,252	–2,330
Balance on Goods and Services	4 991 . .	*–3,015*	*–3,972*	*–5,099*	*–3,433*	*–2,841*	*–2,620*	*–2,029*	*–1,479*
Income: credit	2 300 . .	149	187	175	147	83	119	118	113
Income: debit	3 300 . .	–1,830	–2,125	–2,198	–2,366	–2,263	–1,959	–2,336	–2,192
Balance on Goods, Services, and Income	4 992 . .	*–4,695*	*–5,910*	*–7,121*	*–5,652*	*–5,021*	*–4,460*	*–4,247*	*–3,558*
Current transfers: credit	2 379 Z.	2,919	2,611	2,739	3,981	2,801	3,582	4,200	5,499
Current transfers: debit	3 379 . .	–35	–49	–54	–40	–28	–42	–38	–61
B. Capital Account[1]	4 994 Z.	**. . .**	**. . .**	**. . .**	**. . .**	**. . .**	**. . .**	**. . .**	**. . .**
Capital account: credit	2 994 Z.	. . .	. . .	. . .	. . .	. . .	. . .	. . .	. . .
Capital account: debit	3 994 . .	. . .	. . .	. . .	. . .	. . .	. . .	. . .	. . .
Total, Groups A Plus B	4 981 . .	*–1,812*	*–3,349*	*–4,436*	*–1,712*	*–2,248*	*–920*	*–85*	*1,880*
C. Financial Account[1]	4 995 W.	**2,977**	**2,449**	**3,496**	**2,321**	**–1,873**	**–2,364**	**–3,099**	**–399**
Direct investment abroad	4 505 . .	–1	. . .	–7	24	–50	–21	–11	–31
Direct investment in Pakistan	4 555 Z.	421	723	922	716	506	532	308	383
Portfolio investment assets	4 602 . .	. . .	. . .	. . .	. . .	. . .	. . .	. . .	. . .
Equity securities	4 610 . .	. . .	. . .	. . .	. . .	. . .	. . .	. . .	. . .
Debt securities	4 619 . .	. . .	. . .	. . .	. . .	. . .	. . .	. . .	. . .
Portfolio investment liabilities	4 652 Z.	1,471	4	261	279	–57	46	–451	–192
Equity securities	4 660 . .	1,254	10	285	330	–22	66	35	–130
Debt securities	4 669 Z.	217	–6	–24	–51	–35	–20	–486	–62
Financial derivatives	4 910 . .	. . .	. . .	. . .	. . .	. . .	. . .	. . .	. . .
Financial derivatives assets	4 900 . .	. . .	. . .	. . .	. . .	. . .	. . .	. . .	. . .
Financial derivatives liabilities	4 905 . .	. . .	. . .	. . .	. . .	. . .	. . .	. . .	. . .
Other investment assets	4 703 . .	–283	–196	–164	–21	44	–523	–437	54
Monetary authorities	4 701 . .	. . .	. . .	. . .	. . .	. . .	. . .	. . .	. . .
General government	4 704 . .	–19	6	116	96	247	–358	–15	45
Banks	4 705 . .	–108	–116	8	–40	172	–25	–18	–17
Other sectors	4 728 . .	–157	–85	–288	–77	–375	–140	–404	26
Other investment liabilities	4 753 W.	1,369	1,919	2,484	1,323	–2,316	–2,398	–2,508	–613
Monetary authorities	4 753 WA	–282	–50	474	71	91	–262	–168	–13
General government	4 753 ZB	1,132	1,034	700	1,878	–795	2	–729	–38
Banks	4 753 ZC	313	613	310	–1,044	–663	–1,292	–1,160	–14
Other sectors	4 753 ZD	205	321	1,000	559	–949	–846	–451	–548
Total, Groups A Through C	4 983 . .	*1,165*	*–899*	*–940*	*609*	*–4,121*	*–3,284*	*–3,184*	*1,481*
D. Net Errors and Omissions	4 998 . .	**178**	**–304**	**160**	**–72**	**1,011**	**768**	**557**	**716**
Total, Groups A Through D	4 984 . .	*1,343*	*–1,204*	*–780*	*538*	*–3,110*	*–2,516*	*–2,627*	*2,197*
E. Reserves and Related Items	4 802 A.	**–1,343**	**1,204**	**780**	**–538**	**3,110**	**2,516**	**2,627**	**–2,197**
Reserve assets	4 802 . .	–1,744	1,180	946	–511	222	–842	7	–2,716
Use of Fund credit and loans	4 766 . .	401	23	–166	–27	20	391	–101	327
Exceptional financing	4 920 . .	. . .	. . .	. . .	. . .	2,868	2,966	2,721	192
Conversion rates: Pakistan rupees per U.S. dollar	0 101 . .	**30.4226**	**31.4937**	**35.9088**	**40.9179**	**44.9428**	**49.1183**	**53.6482**	**61.9272**

[1] Excludes components that have been classified in the categories of Group E.

Table 2. STANDARD PRESENTATION, 1994–2001

(Millions of U.S. dollars)

	Code	1994	1995	1996	1997	1998	1999	2000	2001
CURRENT ACCOUNT	4 993 . .	**–1,812**	**–3,349**	**–4,436**	**–1,712**	**–2,248**	**–920**	**–85**	**1,880**
A. GOODS	4 100 . .	–2,239	–2,891	–3,656	–2,399	–1,984	–1,847	–1,157	–608
Credit	2 100 . .	**7,117**	**8,356**	**8,507**	**8,351**	**7,850**	**7,673**	**8,739**	**9,131**
General merchandise: exports f.o.b.	2 110 . .	7,117	8,356	8,507	8,351	7,850	7,673	8,739	9,131
Goods for processing: exports f.o.b.	2 150 . .	. . .	. . .	. . .	. . .	. . .	. . .	. . .	. . .
Repairs on goods	2 160 . .	. . .	. . .	. . .	. . .	. . .	. . .	. . .	. . .
Goods procured in ports by carriers	2 170 . .	. . .	. . .	. . .	. . .	. . .	. . .	. . .	. . .
Nonmonetary gold	2 180 . .	. . .	. . .	. . .	. . .	. . .	. . .	. . .	. . .
Debit	3 100 . .	**–9,355**	**–11,248**	**–12,164**	**–10,750**	**–9,834**	**–9,520**	**–9,896**	**–9,739**
General merchandise: imports f.o.b.	3 110 . .	–9,355	–11,248	–12,164	–10,750	–9,834	–9,520	–9,896	–9,739
Goods for processing: imports f.o.b.	3 150 . .	. . .	. . .	. . .	. . .	. . .	. . .	. . .	. . .
Repairs on goods	3 160 . .	. . .	. . .	. . .	. . .	. . .	. . .	. . .	. . .
Goods procured in ports by carriers	3 170 . .	. . .	. . .	. . .	. . .	. . .	. . .	. . .	. . .
Nonmonetary gold	3 180 . .	. . .	. . .	. . .	. . .	. . .	. . .	. . .	. . .
B. SERVICES	4 200 . .	–777	–1,080	–1,443	–1,033	–857	–773	–872	–871
Total credit	2 200 . .	*1,753*	*1,857*	*2,016*	*1,625*	*1,404*	*1,373*	*1,380*	*1,459*
Total debit	3 200 . .	*–2,529*	*–2,938*	*–3,459*	*–2,658*	*–2,261*	*–2,146*	*–2,252*	*–2,330*
Transportation services, credit	2 205 . .	**869**	**830**	**782**	**825**	**715**	**746**	**840**	**818**
Passenger	2 850 . .	*523*	*472*	*485*	*515*	*469*	*418*	*470*	*445*
Freight	2 851 . .	*61*	*66*	*65*	*64*	*54*	*66*	*77*	*83*
Other	2 852 . .	*285*	*292*	*232*	*246*	*192*	*262*	*293*	*290*
Sea transport, passenger	2 207 . .	. . .	. . .	. . .	. . .	. . .	. . .	. . .	. . .
Sea transport, freight	2 208 . .	16	27	26	23	14	25	30	36
Sea transport, other	2 209 . .	155	158	96	99	71	96	94	99
Air transport, passenger	2 211 . .	523	472	485	515	469	418	470	445
Air transport, freight	2 212 . .	45	39	39	42	40	41	47	47
Air transport, other	2 213 . .	130	134	136	147	121	166	199	191
Other transport, passenger	2 215 . .	. . .	. . .	. . .	. . .	. . .	. . .	. . .	. . .
Other transport, freight	2 216 . .	. . .	. . .	. . .	. . .	. . .	. . .	. . .	. . .
Other transport, other	2 217 . .	. . .	. . .	. . .	. . .	. . .	. . .	. . .	. . .
Transportation services, debit	3 205 . .	**–1,489**	**–1,628**	**–1,751**	**–1,735**	**–1,394**	**–1,416**	**–1,517**	**–1,553**
Passenger	3 850 . .	*–193*	*–208*	*–223*	*–238*	*–208*	*–263*	*–324*	*–303*
Freight	3 851 . .	*–815*	*–972*	*–1,027*	*–939*	*–851*	*–810*	*–808*	*–820*
Other	3 852 . .	*–480*	*–449*	*–501*	*–558*	*–335*	*–343*	*–385*	*–430*
Sea transport, passenger	3 207 . .	. . .	. . .	. . .	. . .	. . .	. . .	. . .	. . .
Sea transport, freight	3 208 . .	–815	–972	–1,027	–939	–851	–810	–808	–820
Sea transport, other	3 209 . .	–86	–90	–82	–77	–17	–12	–15	–26
Air transport, passenger	3 211 . .	–193	–208	–223	–238	–208	–263	–324	–303
Air transport, freight	3 212 . .	. . .	. . .	. . .	. . .	. . .	. . .	. . .	. . .
Air transport, other	3 213 . .	–394	–359	–419	–481	–318	–331	–370	–404
Other transport, passenger	3 215 . .	. . .	. . .	. . .	. . .	. . .	. . .	. . .	. . .
Other transport, freight	3 216 . .	. . .	. . .	. . .	. . .	. . .	. . .	. . .	. . .
Other transport, other	3 217 . .	. . .	. . .	. . .	. . .	. . .	. . .	. . .	. . .
Travel, credit	2 236 . .	**124**	**110**	**105**	**103**	**87**	**74**	**81**	**88**
Business travel	2 237 . .	1	1	4	. . .	. . .	. . .	. . .	. . .
Personal travel	2 240 . .	123	109	102	103	87	74	81	88
Travel, debit	3 236 . .	**–412**	**–446**	**–795**	**–353**	**–357**	**–184**	**–250**	**–252**
Business travel	3 237 . .	–12	–16	–20	–9	–9	–4	–6	–8
Personal travel	3 240 . .	–400	–430	–774	–344	–348	–180	–244	–244
Other services, credit	2 200 BA	**760**	**918**	**1,129**	**697**	**602**	**553**	**459**	**553**
Communications	2 245 . .	249	269	379	282	307	282	190	202
Construction	2 249 . .	. . .	. . .	. . .	. . .	. . .	. . .	. . .	. . .
Insurance	2 253 . .	6	4	12	8	5	4	5	18
Financial	2 260 . .	15	11	28	33	13	12	10	11
Computer and information	2 262 . .	. . .	. . .	. . .	2	4	9	22	19
Royalties and licence fees	2 266 . .	2	6	18	2	1	6	. . .	2
Other business services	2 268 . .	157	178	196	169	171	131	136	144
Personal, cultural, and recreational	2 287 . .	22	26	26	22	. . .	. . .	. . .	. . .
Government, n.i.e.	2 291 . .	309	426	470	179	101	109	96	157
Other services, debit	3 200 BA	**–629**	**–863**	**–913**	**–570**	**–510**	**–546**	**–485**	**–525**
Communications	3 245 . .	–6	–3	–7	–21	–19	–34	–15	–19
Construction	3 249 . .	. . .	. . .	. . .	. . .	. . .	. . .	. . .	. . .
Insurance	3 253 . .	–43	–45	–44	–43	–33	–37	–34	–54
Financial	3 260 . .	–52	–60	–71	–61	–43	–36	–45	–46
Computer and information	3 262 . .	. . .	. . .	. . .	. . .	. . .	. . .	. . .	. . .
Royalties and licence fees	3 266 . .	–12	–21	–14	–19	–11	–22	–28	–19
Other business services	3 268 . .	–159	–214	–221	–179	–187	–165	–220	–273
Personal, cultural, and recreational	3 287 . .	–10	–12	–11	–12	. . .	. . .	. . .	. . .
Government, n.i.e.	3 291 . .	–348	–507	–546	–234	–217	–252	–143	–114

Table 2 (Continued). STANDARD PRESENTATION, 1994–2001
(Millions of U.S. dollars)

	Code		1994	1995	1996	1997	1998	1999	2000	2001
C. INCOME	4 300	. .	−1,680	−1,939	−2,022	−2,220	−2,180	−1,840	−2,218	−2,079
Total credit	2 300	. .	*149*	*187*	*175*	*147*	*83*	*119*	*118*	*113*
Total debit	3 300	. .	*−1,830*	*−2,125*	*−2,198*	*−2,366*	*−2,263*	*−1,959*	*−2,336*	*−2,192*
Compensation of employees, credit	2 310	. .	**. . .**	**. . .**	**. . .**	**. . .**	**. . .**	**. . .**	**. . .**	**. . .**
Compensation of employees, debit	3 310	. .	**. . .**	**. . .**	**. . .**	**. . .**	**. . .**	**. . .**	**. . .**	**. . .**
Investment income, credit	2 320	. .	**149**	**187**	**175**	**147**	**83**	**119**	**118**	**113**
Direct investment income	2 330	. .	30	8	21	14	4	12	2	3
Dividends and distributed branch profits	2 332	. .	30	8	21	14	4	12	2	3
Reinvested earnings and undistributed branch profits	2 333	. .	. . .	. . .	. . .	. . .	. . .	. . .	. . .	. . .
Income on debt (interest)	2 334	. .	. . .	. . .	. . .	. . .	. . .	. . .	. . .	. . .
Portfolio investment income	2 339	. .	. . .	. . .	. . .	. . .	. . .	. . .	. . .	. . .
Income on equity	2 340	. .	. . .	. . .	. . .	. . .	. . .	. . .	. . .	. . .
Income on bonds and notes	2 350	. .	. . .	. . .	. . .	. . .	. . .	. . .	. . .	. . .
Income on money market instruments	2 360	. .	. . .	. . .	. . .	. . .	. . .	. . .	. . .	. . .
Other investment income	2 370	. .	120	178	154	133	79	107	116	110
Investment income, debit	3 320	. .	**−1,830**	**−2,125**	**−2,198**	**−2,366**	**−2,263**	**−1,959**	**−2,336**	**−2,192**
Direct investment income	3 330	. .	−248	−300	−180	−283	−307	−269	−429	−470
Dividends and distributed branch profits	3 332	. .	−170	−191	−131	−211	−250	−202	−330	−371
Reinvested earnings and undistributed branch profits	3 333	. .	−78	−109	−49	−71	−57	−67	−99	−99
Income on debt (interest)	3 334	. .	. . .	. . .	. . .	. . .	. . .	. . .	. . .	. . .
Portfolio investment income	3 339	. .	−34	−53	−80	−105	−432	−252	−372	−400
Income on equity	3 340	. .	. . .	. . .	. . .	. . .	−291	−94	−149	−206
Income on bonds and notes	3 350	. .	. . .	. . .	. . .	. . .	−121	−141	−206	−179
Income on money market instruments	3 360	. .	−34	−53	−80	−105	−20	−17	−17	−15
Other investment income	3 370	. .	−1,547	−1,772	−1,938	−1,979	−1,524	−1,438	−1,535	−1,322
D. CURRENT TRANSFERS	4 379	. .	2,883	2,562	2,685	3,941	2,773	3,540	4,162	5,438
Credit	2 379	. .	**2,919**	**2,611**	**2,739**	**3,981**	**2,801**	**3,582**	**4,200**	**5,499**
General government	2 380	. .	369	291	238	250	400	730	1,005	1,352
Other sectors	2 390	. .	2,550	2,319	2,501	3,730	2,401	2,852	3,195	4,147
Workers' remittances	2 391	. .	1,749	1,712	1,284	1,707	1,172	996	1,075	1,461
Other current transfers	2 392	. .	801	607	1,217	2,023	1,229	1,856	2,120	2,686
Debit	3 379	. .	**−35**	**−49**	**−54**	**−40**	**−28**	**−42**	**−38**	**−61**
General government	3 380	. .	−12	−16	−25	−9	−3	−14	−4	−4
Other sectors	3 390	. .	−23	−33	−30	−31	−25	−28	−34	−57
Workers' remittances	3 391	. .	−2	−4	−4	−2	−5	−3	−2	−3
Other current transfers	3 392	. .	−22	−28	−26	−29	−20	−25	−32	−54
CAPITAL AND FINANCIAL ACCOUNT	4 996	. .	**1,634**	**3,653**	**4,276**	**1,783**	**1,237**	**152**	**−472**	**−2,596**
CAPITAL ACCOUNT	4 994	. .	**. . .**	**. . .**	**. . .**	**. . .**	**. . .**	**. . .**	**. . .**	**. . .**
Total credit	2 994	. .	. . .	. . .	. . .	. . .	. . .	. . .	. . .	. . .
Total debit	3 994	. .	. . .	. . .	. . .	. . .	. . .	. . .	. . .	. . .
Capital transfers, credit	2 400	. .	**. . .**	**. . .**	**. . .**	**. . .**	**. . .**	**. . .**	**. . .**	**. . .**
General government	2 401	. .	. . .	. . .	. . .	. . .	. . .	. . .	. . .	. . .
Debt forgiveness	2 402	. .	. . .	. . .	. . .	. . .	. . .	. . .	. . .	. . .
Other capital transfers	2 410	. .	. . .	. . .	. . .	. . .	. . .	. . .	. . .	. . .
Other sectors	2 430	. .	. . .	. . .	. . .	. . .	. . .	. . .	. . .	. . .
Migrants' transfers	2 431	. .	. . .	. . .	. . .	. . .	. . .	. . .	. . .	. . .
Debt forgiveness	2 432	. .	. . .	. . .	. . .	. . .	. . .	. . .	. . .	. . .
Other capital transfers	2 440	. .	. . .	. . .	. . .	. . .	. . .	. . .	. . .	. . .
Capital transfers, debit	3 400	. .	**. . .**	**. . .**	**. . .**	**. . .**	**. . .**	**. . .**	**. . .**	**. . .**
General government	3 401	. .	. . .	. . .	. . .	. . .	. . .	. . .	. . .	. . .
Debt forgiveness	3 402	. .	. . .	. . .	. . .	. . .	. . .	. . .	. . .	. . .
Other capital transfers	3 410	. .	. . .	. . .	. . .	. . .	. . .	. . .	. . .	. . .
Other sectors	3 430	. .	. . .	. . .	. . .	. . .	. . .	. . .	. . .	. . .
Migrants' transfers	3 431	. .	. . .	. . .	. . .	. . .	. . .	. . .	. . .	. . .
Debt forgiveness	3 432	. .	. . .	. . .	. . .	. . .	. . .	. . .	. . .	. . .
Other capital transfers	3 440	. .	. . .	. . .	. . .	. . .	. . .	. . .	. . .	. . .
Nonproduced nonfinancial assets, credit	2 480	. .	**. . .**	**. . .**	**. . .**	**. . .**	**. . .**	**. . .**	**. . .**	**. . .**
Nonproduced nonfinancial assets, debit	3 480	. .	**. . .**	**. . .**	**. . .**	**. . .**	**. . .**	**. . .**	**. . .**	**. . .**

Table 2 (Continued). STANDARD PRESENTATION, 1994–2001
(Millions of U.S. dollars)

	Code	1994	1995	1996	1997	1998	1999	2000	2001
FINANCIAL ACCOUNT	4 995	**1,634**	**3,653**	**4,276**	**1,783**	**1,237**	**152**	**–472**	**–2,596**
A. DIRECT INVESTMENT	4 500	420	722	915	741	456	511	297	352
Direct investment abroad	4 505	**–1**	**...**	**–7**	**24**	**–50**	**–21**	**–11**	**–31**
Equity capital	4 510	–1	...	–7	24	...	...	...	...
Claims on affiliated enterprises	4 515	...	...	...	...	...	...	...	...
Liabilities to affiliated enterprises	4 520	...	...	...	...	...	...	...	...
Reinvested earnings	4 525	...	...	...	...	...	...	...	...
Other capital	4 530	...	...	...	...	–50	–21	–11	–31
Claims on affiliated enterprises	4 535	...	...	...	...	–50	–21	–11	–31
Liabilities to affiliated enterprises	4 540	...	...	...	...	...	...	...	...
Direct investment in Pakistan	4 555	**421**	**723**	**922**	**716**	**506**	**532**	**308**	**383**
Equity capital	4 560	274	399	570	406	449	465	209	284
Claims on direct investors	4 565	...	...	...	...	...	...	...	...
Liabilities to direct investors	4 570	...	...	...	...	449	465	209	284
Reinvested earnings	4 575	78	109	49	71	57	67	99	99
Other capital	4 580	69	214	303	239	...	...	...	...
Claims on direct investors	4 585	...	...	...	...	...	...	...	...
Liabilities to direct investors	4 590	...	...	...	...	...	...	...	...
B. PORTFOLIO INVESTMENT	4 600	1,471	4	261	279	19	120	9	–192
Assets	4 602	**...**	**...**	**...**	**...**	**...**	**...**	**...**	**...**
Equity securities	4 610	...	...	...	...	...	...	...	...
Monetary authorities	4 611	...	...	...	...	...	...	...	...
General government	4 612	...	...	...	...	...	...	...	...
Banks	4 613	...	...	...	...	...	...	...	...
Other sectors	4 614	...	...	...	...	...	...	...	...
Debt securities	4 619	...	...	...	...	...	...	...	...
Bonds and notes	4 620	...	...	...	...	...	...	...	...
Monetary authorities	4 621	...	...	...	...	...	...	...	...
General government	4 622	...	...	...	...	...	...	...	...
Banks	4 623	...	...	...	...	...	...	...	...
Other sectors	4 624	...	...	...	...	...	...	...	...
Money market instruments	4 630	...	...	...	...	...	...	...	...
Monetary authorities	4 631	...	...	...	...	...	...	...	...
General government	4 632	...	...	...	...	...	...	...	...
Banks	4 633	...	...	...	...	...	...	...	...
Other sectors	4 634	...	...	...	...	...	...	...	...
Liabilities	4 652	**1,471**	**4**	**261**	**279**	**19**	**120**	**9**	**–192**
Equity securities	4 660	1,254	10	285	330	–22	66	35	–130
Banks	4 663	...	...	...	...	...	...	...	...
Other sectors	4 664	...	...	...	...	–22	66	35	–130
Debt securities	4 669	217	–6	–24	–51	41	54	–26	–62
Bonds and notes	4 670	217	–6	–24	–51	–35	130	–26	–62
Monetary authorities	4 671	...	...	...	...	...	...	...	...
General government	4 672	217	–6	–24	–51	–35	130	–26	–62
Banks	4 673	...	...	...	...	...	...	...	...
Other sectors	4 674	...	...	...	...	...	...	...	...
Money market instruments	4 680	...	...	...	...	76	–76	...	...
Monetary authorities	4 681	...	...	...	...	...	...	...	...
General government	4 682	...	...	...	...	...	...	...	...
Banks	4 683	...	...	...	...	...	...	...	...
Other sectors	4 684	...	...	...	...	76	–76	...	...
C. FINANCIAL DERIVATIVES	4 910	...	...	...	...	...	...	...	...
Monetary authorities	4 911	...	...	...	...	...	...	...	...
General government	4 912	...	...	...	...	...	...	...	...
Banks	4 913	...	...	...	...	...	...	...	...
Other sectors	4 914	...	...	...	...	...	...	...	...
Assets	4 900	**...**	**...**	**...**	**...**	**...**	**...**	**...**	**...**
Monetary authorities	4 901	...	...	...	...	...	...	...	...
General government	4 902	...	...	...	...	...	...	...	...
Banks	4 903	...	...	...	...	...	...	...	...
Other sectors	4 904	...	...	...	...	...	...	...	...
Liabilities	4 905	**...**	**...**	**...**	**...**	**...**	**...**	**...**	**...**
Monetary authorities	4 906	...	...	...	...	...	...	...	...
General government	4 907	...	...	...	...	...	...	...	...
Banks	4 908	...	...	...	...	...	...	...	...
Other sectors	4 909	...	...	...	...	...	...	...	...

Table 2 (Concluded). STANDARD PRESENTATION, 1994–2001
(Millions of U.S. dollars)

	Code	1994	1995	1996	1997	1998	1999	2000	2001
D. OTHER INVESTMENT	4 700 . .	1,487	1,747	2,154	1,275	540	362	–785	–40
Assets	4 703 . .	**–283**	**–196**	**–164**	**–21**	**44**	**–523**	**–437**	**54**
Trade credits	4 706 . .	–15	–10	–19	11	. . .	. . .	. . .	. . .
General government	4 707 . .	–15	–10	–19	11	. . .	. . .	. . .	. . .
of which: Short-term	4 709 . .	. . .	. . .	. . .	. . .	. . .	. . .	. . .	. . .
Other sectors	4 710 . .	. . .	. . .	. . .	. . .	. . .	. . .	. . .	. . .
of which: Short-term	4 712 . .	. . .	. . .	. . .	. . .	. . .	. . .	. . .	. . .
Loans	4 714 . .	. . .	. . .	. . .	. . .	. . .	. . .	. . .	. . .
Monetary authorities	4 715 . .	. . .	. . .	. . .	. . .	. . .	. . .	. . .	. . .
of which: Short-term	4 718 . .	. . .	. . .	. . .	. . .	. . .	. . .	. . .	. . .
General government	4 719 . .	. . .	. . .	. . .	. . .	. . .	. . .	. . .	. . .
of which: Short-term	4 721 . .	. . .	. . .	. . .	. . .	. . .	. . .	. . .	. . .
Banks	4 722 . .	. . .	. . .	. . .	. . .	. . .	. . .	. . .	. . .
of which: Short-term	4 724 . .	. . .	. . .	. . .	. . .	. . .	. . .	. . .	. . .
Other sectors	4 725 . .	. . .	. . .	. . .	. . .	. . .	. . .	. . .	. . .
of which: Short-term	4 727 . .	. . .	. . .	. . .	. . .	. . .	. . .	. . .	. . .
Currency and deposits	4 730 . .	. . .	. . .	. . .	. . .	. . .	. . .	. . .	. . .
Monetary authorities	4 731 . .	. . .	. . .	. . .	. . .	. . .	. . .	. . .	. . .
General government	4 732 . .	. . .	. . .	. . .	. . .	. . .	. . .	. . .	. . .
Banks	4 733 . .	. . .	. . .	. . .	. . .	. . .	. . .	. . .	. . .
Other sectors	4 734 . .	. . .	. . .	. . .	. . .	. . .	. . .	. . .	. . .
Other assets	4 736 . .	–268	–186	–145	–32	44	–523	–437	54
Monetary authorities	4 737 . .	. . .	. . .	. . .	. . .	. . .	. . .	. . .	. . .
of which: Short-term	4 739 . .	. . .	. . .	. . .	. . .	. . .	. . .	. . .	. . .
General government	4 740 . .	–4	16	135	85	247	–358	–15	45
of which: Short-term	4 742 . .	*1*	*22*	*15*	*–3*	*–99*	*–8*	*–15*	. . .
Banks	4 743 . .	–108	–116	8	–40	172	–25	–18	–17
of which: Short-term	4 745 . .	*–108*	*–116*	*8*	*–40*	*172*	*–25*	*–18*	*–17*
Other sectors	4 746 . .	–157	–85	–288	–77	–375	–140	–404	26
of which: Short-term	4 748 . .	*–157*	*–85*	*–288*	*–77*	*–375*	*–140*	*–404*	*26*
Liabilities	4 753 . .	**1,771**	**1,942**	**2,318**	**1,296**	**496**	**885**	**–348**	**–94**
Trade credits	4 756 . .	. . .	. . .	. . .	. . .	. . .	. . .	. . .	. . .
General government	4 757 . .	. . .	. . .	. . .	. . .	. . .	. . .	. . .	. . .
of which: Short-term	4 759 . .	. . .	. . .	. . .	. . .	. . .	. . .	. . .	. . .
Other sectors	4 760 . .	. . .	. . .	. . .	. . .	. . .	. . .	. . .	. . .
of which: Short-term	4 762 . .	. . .	. . .	. . .	. . .	. . .	. . .	. . .	. . .
Loans	4 764 . .	1,658	1,365	670	1,945	679	1,494	–112	567
Monetary authorities	4 765 . .	401	23	–166	–27	20	391	–101	327
of which: Use of Fund credit and loans from the Fund	4 766 . .	*401*	*23*	*–166*	*–27*	*20*	*391*	*–101*	*327*
of which: Short-term	4 768 . .	. . .	. . .	. . .	. . .	. . .	. . .	. . .	. . .
General government	4 769 . .	1,150	1,050	717	1,894	408	1,622	348	558
of which: Short-term	4 771 . .	*104*	*281*	*–67*	*1,157*	*–299*	*54*	*–153*	*–195*
Banks	4 772 . .	39	13	–31	1	13	. . .	. . .	. . .
of which: Short-term	4 774 . .	*2*	. . .	. . .	. . .	. . .	. . .	. . .	. . .
Other sectors	4 775 . .	68	279	150	77	238	–519	–359	–318
of which: Short-term	4 777 . .	. . .	. . .	*55*	*–30*	*–25*	. . .	*7*	*21*
Currency and deposits	4 780 . .	. . .	. . .	. . .	. . .	. . .	. . .	. . .	. . .
Monetary authorities	4 781 . .	. . .	. . .	. . .	. . .	. . .	. . .	. . .	. . .
General government	4 782 . .	. . .	. . .	. . .	. . .	. . .	. . .	. . .	. . .
Banks	4 783 . .	. . .	. . .	. . .	. . .	. . .	. . .	. . .	. . .
Other sectors	4 784 . .	. . .	. . .	. . .	. . .	. . .	. . .	. . .	. . .
Other liabilities	4 786 . .	113	577	1,647	–649	–183	–609	–236	–661
Monetary authorities	4 787 . .	–282	–50	474	–71	241	38	82	–13
of which: Short-term	4 789 . .	*–282*	*37*	*474*	*–71*	*–9*	*38*	*332*	*–13*
General government	4 790 . .	–17	–16	–17	–16	–10	307	–10	–21
of which: Short-term	4 792 . .	. . .	. . .	. . .	. . .	*21*	*–21*	. . .	. . .
Banks	4 793 . .	275	601	341	–1,045	–58	–583	–326	–340
of which: Short-term	4 795 . .	*264*	*614*	*333*	*–1,045*	*–57*	*–583*	*–322*	*–338*
Other sectors	4 796 . .	137	42	850	483	–356	–371	18	–287
of which: Short-term	4 798 . .	*150*	*105*	*669*	*795*	*–319*	*–650*	*–3*	*–285*
E. RESERVE ASSETS	4 802 . .	–1,744	1,180	946	–511	222	–842	7	–2,716
Monetary gold	4 812 . .	. . .	. . .	. . .	. . .	. . .	. . .	. . .	. . .
Special drawing rights	4 811 . .	1	–15	1	2	10	1	–13	9
Reserve position in the Fund	4 810 . .	. . .	. . .	. . .	. . .	. . .	. . .	. . .	. . .
Foreign exchange	4 803 . .	–1,756	1,243	965	–662	386	–415	43	–2,115
Other claims	4 813 . .	10	–48	–20	149	–174	–427	–23	–610
NET ERRORS AND OMISSIONS	4 998 . .	**178**	**–304**	**160**	**–72**	**1,011**	**768**	**557**	**716**

Part 3 of the *Yearbook* contains descriptions of the methodologies, compilation practices, and sources used to compile these data.

Table 1. ANALYTIC PRESENTATION, 1994–2001
(Millions of U.S. dollars)

	Code	1994	1995	1996	1997	1998	1999	2000	2001
A. Current Account[1]	4 993 Z.	**15.9**	**–470.6**	**–200.6**	**–506.7**	**–1,182.3**	**–1,320.2**	**–933.2**	**–499.5**
Goods: exports f.o.b	2 100 . .	6,044.8	6,090.9	5,822.9	6,669.7	6,350.1	5,303.3	5,836.7	5,883.7
Goods: imports f.o.b	3 100 . .	–6,294.9	–6,679.8	–6,467.0	–7,354.9	–7,714.6	–6,689.4	–7,026.6	–6,709.5
Balance on Goods	4 100 . .	*–250.1*	*–588.9*	*–644.1*	*–685.2*	*–1,364.5*	*–1,386.1*	*–1,189.9*	*–825.8*
Services: credit	2 200 . .	1,403.7	1,519.4	1,592.0	1,720.7	1,836.8	1,793.2	1,829.6	1,816.9
Services: debit	3 200 . .	–1,064.3	–1,087.8	–1,034.0	–1,293.2	–1,222.5	–1,143.1	–1,137.8	–1,144.0
Balance on Goods and Services	4 991 . .	*89.3*	*–157.3*	*–86.1*	*–257.7*	*–750.2*	*–736.0*	*–498.1*	*–152.9*
Income: credit	2 300 . .	1,202.9	1,644.1	1,422.1	1,436.0	1,679.7	1,503.3	1,580.4	1,398.7
Income: debit	3 300 . .	–1,425.2	–2,110.0	–1,671.3	–1,835.6	–2,270.4	–2,258.6	–2,192.4	–1,944.0
Balance on Goods, Services, and Income	4 992 . .	*–133.0*	*–623.2*	*–335.3*	*–657.3*	*–1,340.9*	*–1,491.3*	*–1,110.1*	*–698.2*
Current transfers: credit	2 379 Z.	185.5	184.1	167.7	185.2	195.2	202.7	208.6	226.8
Current transfers: debit	3 379 . .	–36.6	–31.5	–33.0	–34.6	–36.6	–31.6	–31.7	–28.1
B. Capital Account[1]	4 994 Z.	**. . .**	**8.5**	**2.5**	**72.7**	**50.9**	**3.0**	**1.7**	**1.6**
Capital account: credit	2 994 Z.	. . .	8.5	2.5	72.7	50.9	3.0	1.7	1.6
Capital account: debit	3 994 . .	. . .	. . .	. . .	. . .	. . .	. . .	. . .	. . .
Total, Groups A Plus B	4 981 . .	*15.9*	*–462.1*	*–198.1*	*–434.0*	*–1,131.4*	*–1,317.2*	*–931.5*	*–497.9*
C. Financial Account[1]	4 995 W.	**–288.2**	**115.6**	**561.2**	**972.3**	**1,076.8**	**1,398.2**	**2.1**	**587.1**
Direct investment abroad	4 505 . .	. . .	. . .	. . .	. . .	. . .	. . .	. . .	. . .
Direct investment in Panama	4 555 Z.	401.5	223.0	415.5	1,299.3	1,296.0	652.4	603.4	512.6
Portfolio investment assets	4 602 . .	–48.4	318.5	487.8	–1,036.5	431.7	–550.2	–109.3	–778.3
Equity securities	4 610 . .	. . .	.2	–10.2	–.8	–5.1	–28.7	–.6	–.2
Debt securities	4 619 . .	–48.4	318.3	498.0	–1,035.7	436.8	–521.5	–108.7	–778.1
Portfolio investment liabilities	4 652 Z.	–.4	–.3	–67.1	–80.3	–65.5	–99.2	–86.8	–66.2
Equity securities	4 660 . .	.4	.2	–.1	–.1	. . .	. . .	. . .	. . .
Debt securities	4 669 Z.	–.8	–.5	–67.0	–80.2	–65.5	–99.2	–86.8	–66.2
Financial derivatives	4 910 . .	. . .	. . .	. . .	. . .	. . .	. . .	. . .	. . .
Financial derivatives assets	4 900 . .	. . .	. . .	. . .	. . .	. . .	. . .	. . .	. . .
Financial derivatives liabilities	4 905 . .	. . .	. . .	. . .	. . .	. . .	. . .	. . .	. . .
Other investment assets	4 703 . .	–5,277.7	–371.3	406.2	–478.7	776.7	1,983.0	358.5	856.3
Monetary authorities	4 701 . .	. . .	. . .	. . .	. . .	. . .	–5.2	5.2	. . .
General government	4 704 . .	. . .	–1.0	–38.2	–2.3	–263.3	266.6	–4.0	–2.1
Banks	4 705 . .	–5,254.4	–176.3	533.1	–276.1	1,284.6	1,968.7	189.1	1,020.8
Other sectors	4 728 . .	–23.3	–194.0	–88.7	–200.3	–244.6	–247.1	168.2	–162.4
Other investment liabilities	4 753 W.	4,636.8	–54.3	–681.2	1,268.5	–1,362.1	–587.8	–763.7	62.7
Monetary authorities	4 753 WA	–1.3	54.6	–1.7	6.8	–1.0	–.7	–6.4	3.7
General government	4 753 ZB	–198.8	–36.1	–50.5	130.4	85.6	33.7	–2.6	3.5
Banks	4 753 ZC	4,915.5	–122.8	–793.7	1,033.2	–1,446.8	–550.8	–418.4	57.1
Other sectors	4 753 ZD	–78.6	50.0	164.7	98.1	.1	–70.0	–336.3	–1.6
Total, Groups A Through C	4 983 . .	*–272.3*	*–346.5*	*363.1*	*538.3*	*–54.6*	*81.0*	*–929.4*	*89.2*
D. Net Errors and Omissions	4 998 . .	**–89.5**	**15.2**	**–96.3**	**–195.0**	**–325.1**	**–228.7**	**602.4**	**–387.7**
Total, Groups A Through D	4 984 . .	*–361.8*	*–331.3*	*266.8*	*343.3*	*–379.7*	*–147.7*	*–327.0*	*–298.5*
E. Reserves and Related Items	4 802 A.	**361.8**	**331.3**	**–266.8**	**–343.3**	**379.7**	**147.7**	**327.0**	**298.5**
Reserve assets	4 802 . .	–105.7	–77.7	–297.7	–611.1	19.8	–184.5	108.1	–484.4
Use of Fund credit and loans	4 766 . .	12.5	–25.9	24.2	19.6	27.3	–23.5	–51.7	–33.3
Exceptional financing	4 920 . .	454.9	434.9	6.8	248.2	332.6	355.7	270.6	816.2
Conversion rates: balboa per U.S. dollar	0 101 . .	**1.0000**	**1.0000**	**1.0000**	**1.0000**	**1.0000**	**1.0000**	**1.0000**	**1.0000**

[1] Excludes components that have been classified in the categories of Group E.

Table 2. STANDARD PRESENTATION, 1994–2001
(Millions of U.S. dollars)

	Code	1994	1995	1996	1997	1998	1999	2000	2001
CURRENT ACCOUNT	4 993 . .	**15.9**	**–470.6**	**–200.6**	**–506.7**	**–1,182.3**	**–1,320.2**	**–933.2**	**–499.5**
A. GOODS	4 100 . .	–250.1	–588.9	–644.1	–685.2	–1,364.5	–1,386.1	–1,189.9	–825.8
Credit	2 100 . .	**6,044.8**	**6,090.9**	**5,822.9**	**6,669.7**	**6,350.1**	**5,303.3**	**5,836.7**	**5,883.7**
General merchandise: exports f.o.b.	2 110 . .	5,946.3	5,958.2	5,666.7	6,509.8	6,246.1	5,189.5	5,596.5	5,677.6
Goods for processing: exports f.o.b.	2 150 . .	. . .	. . .	. . .	18.8	7.7	6.1	13.4	4.6
Repairs on goods	2 160 . .	.6	1.2	1.8	1.3	1.4	2.0	2.2	2.2
Goods procured in ports by carriers	2 170 . .	97.9	131.5	154.4	139.8	94.9	105.7	224.6	199.3
Nonmonetary gold	2 180 . .	. . .	. . .	. . .	. . .	. . .	. . .	. . .	. . .
Debit	3 100 . .	**–6,294.9**	**–6,679.8**	**–6,467.0**	**–7,354.9**	**–7,714.6**	**–6,689.4**	**–7,026.6**	**–6,709.5**
General merchandise: imports f.o.b.	3 110 . .	–6,285.0	–6,667.0	–6,457.1	–7,330.9	–7,693.6	–6,667.2	–7,006.9	–6,687.0
Goods for processing: imports f.o.b.	3 150 . .	. . .	. . .	. . .	–9.9	–5.4	–5.6	–4.6	–3.0
Repairs on goods	3 160 . .	–.2	–1.6	–1.3	–2.2	–5.2	–4.2	–4.3	–4.6
Goods procured in ports by carriers	3 170 . .	–9.7	–11.2	–8.6	–11.9	–10.4	–12.4	–10.8	–15.1
Nonmonetary gold	3 180 . .	. . .	. . .	. . .	. . .	. . .	. . .	. . .	.2
B. SERVICES	4 200 . .	339.4	431.6	558.0	427.5	614.3	650.1	691.8	672.9
Total credit	2 200 . .	*1,403.7*	*1,519.4*	*1,592.0*	*1,720.7*	*1,836.8*	*1,793.2*	*1,829.6*	*1,816.9*
Total debit	3 200 . .	*–1,064.3*	*–1,087.8*	*–1,034.0*	*–1,293.2*	*–1,222.5*	*–1,143.1*	*–1,137.8*	*–1,144.0*
Transportation services, credit	2 205 . .	**704.5**	**783.7**	**811.3**	**909.0**	**971.5**	**983.0**	**1,023.3**	**962.5**
Passenger	2 850 . .	*48.3*	*63.4*	*72.4*	*93.5*	*110.3*	*109.5*	*116.6*	*129.0*
Freight	2 851 . .	*26.8*	*24.8*	*13.8*	*4.1*	*5.6*	*6.9*	*7.0*	*5.6*
Other	2 852 . .	*629.4*	*695.5*	*725.1*	*811.4*	*855.6*	*866.6*	*899.7*	*827.9*
Sea transport, passenger	2 207 . .	. . .	. . .	. . .	. . .	. . .	. . .	. . .	. . .
Sea transport, freight	2 208 . .	. . .	. . .	. . .	. . .	. . .	. . .	. . .	. . .
Sea transport, other	2 209 . .	606.3	670.9	700.6	780.2	822.5	834.2	863.4	790.3
Air transport, passenger	2 211 . .	48.3	63.4	72.4	93.5	110.3	109.5	116.6	129.0
Air transport, freight	2 212 . .	3.3	2.8	2.9	4.1	5.6	6.9	7.0	5.6
Air transport, other	2 213 . .	23.1	24.6	24.5	31.2	33.1	32.4	36.3	37.6
Other transport, passenger	2 215 . .	. . .	. . .	. . .	. . .	. . .	. . .	. . .	. . .
Other transport, freight	2 216 . .	23.5	22.0	10.9	. . .	. . .	. . .	. . .	. . .
Other transport, other	2 217 . .	. . .	. . .	. . .	. . .	. . .	. . .	. . .	. . .
Transportation services, debit	3 205 . .	**–750.2**	**–744.8**	**–677.5**	**–786.3**	**–636.2**	**–612.6**	**–626.7**	**–614.8**
Passenger	3 850 . .	*–56.4*	*–59.7*	*–69.9*	*–78.3*	*–64.4*	*–68.8*	*–80.2*	*–78.2*
Freight	3 851 . .	*–686.7*	*–678.1*	*–600.1*	*–698.8*	*–557.4*	*–530.8*	*–535.7*	*–522.2*
Other	3 852 . .	*–7.1*	*–7.0*	*–7.5*	*–9.2*	*–14.4*	*–13.0*	*–10.8*	*–14.4*
Sea transport, passenger	3 207 . .	. . .	. . .	. . .	. . .	. . .	. . .	. . .	. . .
Sea transport, freight	3 208 . .	–686.7	–678.1	–600.1	–698.8	–557.4	–530.8	–535.7	–522.2
Sea transport, other	3 209 . .	. . .	. . .	. . .	. . .	. . .	. . .	. . .	. . .
Air transport, passenger	3 211 . .	–56.4	–59.7	–69.9	–78.3	–64.4	–68.8	–80.2	–78.2
Air transport, freight	3 212 . .	. . .	. . .	. . .	. . .	. . .	. . .	. . .	. . .
Air transport, other	3 213 . .	–7.1	–7.0	–7.5	–9.2	–14.4	–13.0	–10.8	–14.4
Other transport, passenger	3 215 . .	. . .	. . .	. . .	. . .	. . .	. . .	. . .	. . .
Other transport, freight	3 216 . .	. . .	. . .	. . .	. . .	. . .	. . .	. . .	. . .
Other transport, other	3 217 . .	. . .	. . .	. . .	. . .	. . .	. . .	. . .	. . .
Travel, credit	2 236 . .	**261.6**	**309.4**	**359.9**	**376.8**	**382.0**	**387.2**	**453.2**	**486.0**
Business travel	2 237 . .	57.7	60.7	56.9	85.0	85.8	88.3	86.9	90.2
Personal travel	2 240 . .	203.9	248.7	303.0	291.8	296.2	298.9	366.3	395.8
Travel, debit	3 236 . .	**–122.6**	**–120.7**	**–140.3**	**–165.1**	**–180.6**	**–184.5**	**–186.6**	**–176.0**
Business travel	3 237 . .	–10.7	–10.1	–17.0	–19.6	–21.2	–22.9	–22.5	–21.1
Personal travel	3 240 . .	–111.9	–110.6	–123.3	–145.5	–159.4	–161.6	–164.1	–154.9
Other services, credit	2 200 BA	**437.6**	**426.3**	**420.8**	**434.9**	**483.3**	**423.0**	**353.1**	**368.4**
Communications	2 245 . .	38.9	33.7	37.7	38.5	52.8	39.3	33.5	43.7
Construction	2 249 . .	. . .	. . .	. . .	. . .	. . .	. . .	. . .	. . .
Insurance	2 253 . .	13.2	16.9	18.0	17.4	19.0	31.6	41.6	36.8
Financial	2 260 . .	47.1	62.8	71.3	78.1	140.0	142.5	140.4	127.7
Computer and information	2 262 . .	. . .	. . .	. . .	. . .	. . .	. . .	. . .	. . .
Royalties and licence fees	2 266 . .	. . .	. . .	. . .	. . .	. . .	. . .	. . .	. . .
Other business services	2 268 . .	107.1	91.2	91.5	94.8	137.2	109.3	113.6	134.2
Personal, cultural, and recreational	2 287 . .	. . .	. . .	. . .	. . .	. . .	. . .	. . .	. . .
Government, n.i.e.	2 291 . .	231.3	221.7	202.3	206.1	134.3	100.3	24.0	26.0
Other services, debit	3 200 BA	**–191.5**	**–222.3**	**–216.2**	**–341.8**	**–405.7**	**–346.0**	**–324.5**	**–353.2**
Communications	3 245 . .	–.5	–.6	–.5	–1.7	–32.5	–21.0	–14.7	–18.7
Construction	3 249 . .	. . .	. . .	. . .	. . .	. . .	. . .	. . .	. . .
Insurance	3 253 . .	–44.8	–58.0	–53.2	–78.1	–79.4	–73.8	–80.6	–74.4
Financial	3 260 . .	–32.0	–34.5	–32.0	–79.8	–101.9	–63.2	–36.4	–58.7
Computer and information	3 262 . .	. . .	. . .	. . .	. . .	. . .	. . .	. . .	. . .
Royalties and licence fees	3 266 . .	–12.4	–16.0	–17.3	–16.4	–26.4	–30.0	–29.7	–30.5
Other business services	3 268 . .	–67.9	–74.6	–79.7	–119.6	–123.1	–114.0	–123.1	–125.1
Personal, cultural, and recreational	3 287 . .	. . .	. . .	. . .	. . .	. . .	. . .	. . .	. . .
Government, n.i.e.	3 291 . .	–33.9	–38.6	–33.5	–46.2	–42.4	–44.0	–40.0	–45.8

Table 2 (Continued). STANDARD PRESENTATION, 1994–2001
(Millions of U.S. dollars)

	Code	1994	1995	1996	1997	1998	1999	2000	2001
C. INCOME	4 300	–222.3	–465.9	–249.2	–399.6	–590.7	–755.3	–612.0	–545.3
Total credit	2 300	*1,202.9*	*1,644.1*	*1,422.1*	*1,436.0*	*1,679.7*	*1,503.3*	*1,580.4*	*1,398.7*
Total debit	3 300	*–1,425.2*	*–2,110.0*	*–1,671.3*	*–1,835.6*	*–2,270.4*	*–2,258.6*	*–2,192.4*	*–1,944.0*
Compensation of employees, credit	2 310	**94.9**	**95.7**	**70.4**	**48.1**	**42.3**	**32.3**	**. . .**	**. . .**
Compensation of employees, debit	3 310	**. . .**	**. . .**	**. . .**	**. . .**	**. . .**	**. . .**	**. . .**	**. . .**
Investment income, credit	2 320	**1,108.0**	**1,548.4**	**1,351.7**	**1,387.9**	**1,637.4**	**1,471.0**	**1,580.4**	**1,398.7**
Direct investment income	2 330	. . .	. . .	. . .	. . .	. . .	. . .	. . .	. . .
Dividends and distributed branch profits	2 332	. . .	. . .	. . .	. . .	. . .	. . .	. . .	. . .
Reinvested earnings and undistributed branch profits	2 333	. . .	. . .	. . .	. . .	. . .	. . .	. . .	. . .
Income on debt (interest)	2 334	. . .	. . .	. . .	. . .	. . .	. . .	. . .	. . .
Portfolio investment income	2 339	161.3	141.1	147.7	149.7	175.3	159.7	241.4	279.1
Income on equity	2 340	. . .	. . .	. . .	. . .	. . .	. . .	. . .	. . .
Income on bonds and notes	2 350	161.3	141.1	147.7	149.7	175.3	159.7	241.4	279.1
Income on money market instruments	2 360	. . .	. . .	. . .	. . .	. . .	. . .	. . .	. . .
Other investment income	2 370	946.7	1,407.3	1,204.0	1,238.2	1,462.1	1,311.3	1,339.0	1,119.6
Investment income, debit	3 320	**–1,425.2**	**–2,110.0**	**–1,671.3**	**–1,835.6**	**–2,270.4**	**–2,258.6**	**–2,192.4**	**–1,944.0**
Direct investment income	3 330	–276.9	–396.4	–408.6	–515.8	–711.9	–791.0	–614.9	–547.6
Dividends and distributed branch profits	3 332	–182.4	–260.6	–275.2	–293.7	–549.3	–416.2	–327.5	–354.9
Reinvested earnings and undistributed branch profits	3 333	–87.0	–131.5	–132.7	–222.1	–162.6	–374.8	–287.4	–192.7
Income on debt (interest)	3 334	–7.5	–4.3	–.7	. . .	. . .	. . .	. . .	. . .
Portfolio investment income	3 339	–35.7	–31.9	–29.5	–196.6	–230.6	–260.5	–293.2	–349.1
Income on equity	3 340	–.7	–.6	–.7	. . .	. . .	. . .	. . .	. . .
Income on bonds and notes	3 350	–35.0	–31.3	–28.8	–196.6	–230.6	–260.5	–293.2	–349.1
Income on money market instruments	3 360	. . .	. . .	. . .	. . .	. . .	. . .	. . .	. . .
Other investment income	3 370	–1,112.6	–1,681.7	–1,233.2	–1,123.2	–1,327.9	–1,207.1	–1,284.3	–1,047.3
D. CURRENT TRANSFERS	4 379	148.9	152.6	134.7	150.6	158.6	171.1	176.9	198.7
Credit	2 379	**185.5**	**184.1**	**167.7**	**185.2**	**195.2**	**202.7**	**208.6**	**226.8**
General government	2 380	75.6	75.0	57.8	71.4	79.9	83.0	69.3	85.9
Other sectors	2 390	109.9	109.1	109.9	113.8	115.3	119.7	139.3	140.9
Workers' remittances	2 391	17.1	16.3	15.8	16.2	15.9	16.0	16.4	21.2
Other current transfers	2 392	92.8	92.8	94.1	97.6	99.4	103.7	122.9	119.7
Debit	3 379	**–36.6**	**–31.5**	**–33.0**	**–34.6**	**–36.6**	**–31.6**	**–31.7**	**–28.1**
General government	3 380	–8.3	–7.4	–9.0	–9.9	–11.4	–5.5	–5.1	–5.2
Other sectors	3 390	–28.3	–24.1	–24.0	–24.7	–25.2	–26.1	–26.6	–22.9
Workers' remittances	3 391	–24.8	–20.4	–20.0	–21.3	–20.6	–21.2	–22.0	–18.4
Other current transfers	3 392	–3.5	–3.7	–4.0	–3.4	–4.6	–4.9	–4.6	–4.5
CAPITAL AND FINANCIAL ACCOUNT	4 996	**73.6**	**455.4**	**296.9**	**701.7**	**1,507.4**	**1,548.9**	**330.8**	**887.2**
CAPITAL ACCOUNT	4 994	**. . .**	**8.5**	**2.5**	**72.7**	**50.9**	**3.0**	**1.7**	**1.6**
Total credit	2 994	. . .	*8.5*	*2.5*	*72.7*	*50.9*	*3.0*	*1.7*	*1.6*
Total debit	3 994	. . .	. . .	. . .	. . .	. . .	. . .	. . .	. . .
Capital transfers, credit	2 400	**. . .**	**8.5**	**2.5**	**72.7**	**50.9**	**3.0**	**1.7**	**1.6**
General government	2 401	. . .	8.5	2.5	72.7	50.9	3.0	1.7	1.6
Debt forgiveness	2 402	. . .	. . .	. . .	. . .	. . .	. . .	. . .	. . .
Other capital transfers	2 410	. . .	8.5	2.5	72.7	50.9	3.0	1.7	1.6
Other sectors	2 430	. . .	. . .	. . .	. . .	. . .	. . .	. . .	. . .
Migrants' transfers	2 431	. . .	. . .	. . .	. . .	. . .	. . .	. . .	. . .
Debt forgiveness	2 432	. . .	. . .	. . .	. . .	. . .	. . .	. . .	. . .
Other capital transfers	2 440	. . .	. . .	. . .	. . .	. . .	. . .	. . .	. . .
Capital transfers, debit	3 400	**. . .**	**. . .**	**. . .**	**. . .**	**. . .**	**. . .**	**. . .**	**. . .**
General government	3 401	. . .	. . .	. . .	. . .	. . .	. . .	. . .	. . .
Debt forgiveness	3 402	. . .	. . .	. . .	. . .	. . .	. . .	. . .	. . .
Other capital transfers	3 410	. . .	. . .	. . .	. . .	. . .	. . .	. . .	. . .
Other sectors	3 430	. . .	. . .	. . .	. . .	. . .	. . .	. . .	. . .
Migrants' transfers	3 431	. . .	. . .	. . .	. . .	. . .	. . .	. . .	. . .
Debt forgiveness	3 432	. . .	. . .	. . .	. . .	. . .	. . .	. . .	. . .
Other capital transfers	3 440	. . .	. . .	. . .	. . .	. . .	. . .	. . .	. . .
Nonproduced nonfinancial assets, credit	2 480	**. . .**	**. . .**	**. . .**	**. . .**	**. . .**	**. . .**	**. . .**	**. . .**
Nonproduced nonfinancial assets, debit	3 480	**. . .**	**. . .**	**. . .**	**. . .**	**. . .**	**. . .**	**. . .**	**. . .**

Table 2 (Continued). STANDARD PRESENTATION, 1994–2001
(Millions of U.S. dollars)

	Code	1994	1995	1996	1997	1998	1999	2000	2001
FINANCIAL ACCOUNT	4 995	**73.6**	**446.9**	**294.4**	**629.0**	**1,456.5**	**1,545.9**	**329.1**	**885.6**
A. DIRECT INVESTMENT	4 500	401.5	223.0	415.5	1,299.3	1,296.0	652.4	603.4	512.6
Direct investment abroad	4 505	**. . .**	**. . .**	**. . .**	**. . .**	**. . .**	**. . .**	**. . .**	**. . .**
Equity capital	4 510	. . .	. . .	. . .	. . .	. . .	. . .	. . .	. . .
Claims on affiliated enterprises	4 515	. . .	. . .	. . .	. . .	. . .	. . .	. . .	. . .
Liabilities to affiliated enterprises	4 520	. . .	. . .	. . .	. . .	. . .	. . .	. . .	. . .
Reinvested earnings	4 525	. . .	. . .	. . .	. . .	. . .	. . .	. . .	. . .
Other capital	4 530	. . .	. . .	. . .	. . .	. . .	. . .	. . .	. . .
Claims on affiliated enterprises	4 535	. . .	. . .	. . .	. . .	. . .	. . .	. . .	. . .
Liabilities to affiliated enterprises	4 540	. . .	. . .	. . .	. . .	. . .	. . .	. . .	. . .
Direct investment in Panama	4 555	**401.5**	**223.0**	**415.5**	**1,299.3**	**1,296.0**	**652.4**	**603.4**	**512.6**
Equity capital	4 560	256.1	42.7	172.7	982.7	979.4	175.5	174.4	337.6
Claims on direct investors	4 565	. . .	. . .	. . .	. . .	. . .	. . .	. . .	. . .
Liabilities to direct investors	4 570	256.1	42.7	172.7	982.7	979.4	175.5	174.4	337.6
Reinvested earnings	4 575	87.0	131.5	132.7	222.1	162.6	374.8	287.4	192.7
Other capital	4 580	58.4	48.8	110.1	94.5	154.0	102.1	141.6	–17.7
Claims on direct investors	4 585	. . .	–58.3	–12.8	–12.9	–84.9	–56.4	–51.3	–49.4
Liabilities to direct investors	4 590	58.4	107.1	122.9	107.4	238.9	158.5	192.9	31.7
B. PORTFOLIO INVESTMENT	4 600	373.3	318.2	3,648.4	–875.2	660.0	–293.7	74.2	–28.4
Assets	4 602	**–48.4**	**318.5**	**487.8**	**–1,036.5**	**431.7**	**–550.2**	**–109.3**	**–778.3**
Equity securities	4 610	. . .	.2	–10.2	–.8	–5.1	–28.7	–.6	–.2
Monetary authorities	4 611	. . .	. . .	. . .	. . .	. . .	. . .	. . .	. . .
General government	4 612	. . .	. . .	. . .	. . .	. . .	. . .	. . .	. . .
Banks	4 613	. . .	. . .	. . .	. . .	. . .	. . .	. . .	. . .
Other sectors	4 614	. . .	.2	–10.2	–.8	–5.1	–28.7	–.6	–.2
Debt securities	4 619	–48.4	318.3	498.0	–1,035.7	436.8	–521.5	–108.7	–778.1
Bonds and notes	4 620	–48.4	318.3	498.0	–1,035.7	436.8	–521.5	–108.7	–778.1
Monetary authorities	4 621	. . .	. . .	. . .	. . .	. . .	. . .	. . .	. . .
General government	4 622	. . .	. . .	–57.1	9.1	3.6	–4.0	–4.0	–4.4
Banks	4 623	–48.4	318.1	570.7	–1,044.8	445.2	–543.7	–102.2	–775.2
Other sectors	4 624	. . .	.2	–15.6	. . .	–12.0	26.2	–2.5	1.5
Money market instruments	4 630	. . .	. . .	. . .	. . .	. . .	. . .	. . .	. . .
Monetary authorities	4 631	. . .	. . .	. . .	. . .	. . .	. . .	. . .	. . .
General government	4 632	. . .	. . .	. . .	. . .	. . .	. . .	. . .	. . .
Banks	4 633	. . .	. . .	. . .	. . .	. . .	. . .	. . .	. . .
Other sectors	4 634	. . .	. . .	. . .	. . .	. . .	. . .	. . .	. . .
Liabilities	4 652	**421.7**	**–.3**	**3,160.6**	**161.3**	**228.3**	**256.5**	**183.5**	**749.9**
Equity securities	4 660	.4	.2	–.1	–.1	. . .	. . .	. . .	. . .
Banks	4 663	. . .	. . .	. . .	. . .	. . .	. . .	. . .	. . .
Other sectors	4 664	.4	.2	–.1	–.1	. . .	. . .	. . .	. . .
Debt securities	4 669	421.3	–.5	3,160.7	161.4	228.3	256.5	183.5	749.9
Bonds and notes	4 670	421.3	–.5	3,160.7	161.4	228.3	256.5	183.5	749.9
Monetary authorities	4 671	. . .	. . .	. . .	. . .	. . .	. . .	. . .	. . .
General government	4 672	421.3	–.5	3,160.7	161.4	228.3	256.5	183.5	749.9
Banks	4 673	. . .	. . .	. . .	. . .	. . .	. . .	. . .	. . .
Other sectors	4 674	. . .	. . .	. . .	. . .	. . .	. . .	. . .	. . .
Money market instruments	4 680	. . .	. . .	. . .	. . .	. . .	. . .	. . .	. . .
Monetary authorities	4 681	. . .	. . .	. . .	. . .	. . .	. . .	. . .	. . .
General government	4 682	. . .	. . .	. . .	. . .	. . .	. . .	. . .	. . .
Banks	4 683	. . .	. . .	. . .	. . .	. . .	. . .	. . .	. . .
Other sectors	4 684	. . .	. . .	. . .	. . .	. . .	. . .	. . .	. . .
C. FINANCIAL DERIVATIVES	4 910	. . .	. . .	. . .	. . .	. . .	. . .	. . .	. . .
Monetary authorities	4 911	. . .	. . .	. . .	. . .	. . .	. . .	. . .	. . .
General government	4 912	. . .	. . .	. . .	. . .	. . .	. . .	. . .	. . .
Banks	4 913	. . .	. . .	. . .	. . .	. . .	. . .	. . .	. . .
Other sectors	4 914	. . .	. . .	. . .	. . .	. . .	. . .	. . .	. . .
Assets	4 900	**. . .**	**. . .**	**. . .**	**. . .**	**. . .**	**. . .**	**. . .**	**. . .**
Monetary authorities	4 901	. . .	. . .	. . .	. . .	. . .	. . .	. . .	. . .
General government	4 902	. . .	. . .	. . .	. . .	. . .	. . .	. . .	. . .
Banks	4 903	. . .	. . .	. . .	. . .	. . .	. . .	. . .	. . .
Other sectors	4 904	. . .	. . .	. . .	. . .	. . .	. . .	. . .	. . .
Liabilities	4 905	**. . .**	**. . .**	**. . .**	**. . .**	**. . .**	**. . .**	**. . .**	**. . .**
Monetary authorities	4 906	. . .	. . .	. . .	. . .	. . .	. . .	. . .	. . .
General government	4 907	. . .	. . .	. . .	. . .	. . .	. . .	. . .	. . .
Banks	4 908	. . .	. . .	. . .	. . .	. . .	. . .	. . .	. . .
Other sectors	4 909	. . .	. . .	. . .	. . .	. . .	. . .	. . .	. . .

Table 2 (Concluded). STANDARD PRESENTATION, 1994–2001

(Millions of U.S. dollars)

	Code	1994	1995	1996	1997	1998	1999	2000	2001
D. OTHER INVESTMENT	4 700	–595.6	–16.6	–3,471.7	816.0	–519.3	1,371.7	–456.6	885.8
Assets	4 703	**–5,277.7**	**–371.3**	**406.2**	**–478.7**	**776.7**	**1,983.0**	**358.5**	**856.3**
Trade credits	4 706	–12.2	–164.8	–159.0	–207.2	–214.7	–194.3	–134.2	–86.4
General government	4 707	...	...	...	...	...	...	...	...
of which: Short-term	4 709	...	...	...	...	...	...	...	...
Other sectors	4 710	–12.2	–164.8	–159.0	–207.2	–214.7	–194.3	–134.2	–86.4
of which: Short-term	4 712	*–12.2*	*–164.8*	*–159.1*	*–207.7*	*–181.2*	*–199.2*	*–128.9*	*–85.6*
Loans	4 714	–2,379.4	–1,535.9	776.1	146.6	–331.1	2,389.3	815.3	158.5
Monetary authorities	4 715	...	...	...	...	...	–5.0	5.0	...
of which: Short-term	4 718	...	...	...	...	...	*–5.0*	*5.0*	...
General government	4 719	...	...	...	...	–257.5	257.5	...	...
of which: Short-term	4 721	...	...	...	...	...	...	...	...
Banks	4 722	–2,379.4	–1,535.9	776.1	146.6	–73.6	2,136.8	810.3	158.5
of which: Short-term	4 724	*–2,379.4*	*–1,535.9*	*776.1*	*146.6*	*–73.6*	*2,136.8*	*810.3*	*158.5*
Other sectors	4 725	...	...	...	...	...	...	...	...
of which: Short-term	4 727	...	...	...	...	...	...	...	...
Currency and deposits	4 730	–2,145.9	1,209.7	–131.4	–1,010.2	1,363.7	–257.2	–475.0	697.7
Monetary authorities	4 731	...	...	...	...	...	...	...	...
General government	4 732	...	...	–37.2	–1.8	–3.8	9.1	–4.0	–2.1
Banks	4 733	–2,145.9	1,209.7	–94.2	–1,008.4	1,367.5	–266.3	–471.0	699.8
Other sectors	4 734	...	...	...	...	...	...	...	...
Other assets	4 736	–740.2	119.7	–79.5	592.1	–41.2	45.2	152.4	86.5
Monetary authorities	4 737	...	...	...	...	...	–.2	.2	...
of which: Short-term	4 739	...	...	...	...	...	*–.2*	*.2*	...
General government	4 740	...	–1.0	–1.0	–.5	–2.0	...	...	...
of which: Short-term	4 742	...	...	...	...	...	...	...	...
Banks	4 743	–729.1	149.9	–148.8	585.7	–9.3	98.2	–150.2	162.5
of which: Short-term	4 745	*–729.1*	*149.9*	*–148.8*	*585.7*	*–9.3*	*98.2*	*–150.2*	*162.5*
Other sectors	4 746	–11.1	–29.2	70.3	6.9	–29.9	–52.8	302.4	–76.0
of which: Short-term	4 748	*–11.1*	*–29.2*	*70.3*	*6.9*	*–29.9*	*–52.8*	*302.4*	*–76.0*
Liabilities	4 753	**4,682.1**	**354.7**	**–3,877.9**	**1,294.7**	**–1,296.0**	**–611.3**	**–815.1**	**29.5**
Trade credits	4 756	...	6.2	143.2	89.9	–94.9	–53.8	–.3	–1.8
General government	4 757	...	...	...	...	...	...	...	...
of which: Short-term	4 759	...	...	...	...	...	...	...	...
Other sectors	4 760	...	6.2	143.2	89.9	–94.9	–53.8	–.3	–1.8
of which: Short-term	4 762	...	*8.3*	*142.0*	*92.1*	*–95.8*	*–57.9*	*–2.3*	*–3.3*
Loans	4 764	778.7	450.8	804.4	424.2	741.3	–104.1	536.7	317.6
Monetary authorities	4 765	9.4	26.1	20.0	20.2	25.4	–25.1	–51.7	–33.3
of which: Use of Fund credit and loans from the Fund	4 766	*12.5*	*–25.9*	*24.2*	*19.6*	*27.3*	*–23.5*	*–51.7*	*–33.3*
of which: Short-term	4 768	*–.7*	*.3*	*–.8*	*–1.6*	*–1.6*	*–1.6*	...	...
General government	4 769	–176.3	–33.4	60.8	195.7	146.0	33.7	–2.6	3.5
of which: Short-term	4 771	...	...	...	...	...	...	...	...
Banks	4 772	1,016.1	415.4	661.2	193.4	475.5	–95.2	583.8	347.1
of which: Short-term	4 774	*841.6*	*356.1*	*–162.4*	*–232.0*	*653.8*	*–176.6*	*213.4*	*–361.1*
Other sectors	4 775	–70.5	42.7	62.4	14.9	94.4	–17.5	7.2	.3
of which: Short-term	4 777	*12.6*	*96.5*	*70.5*	*60.8*	*112.5*	*–4.4*	*17.5*	*8.8*
Currency and deposits	4 780	3,487.5	–697.5	–1,215.4	1,215.2	–1,894.4	–585.6	–1,026.0	–272.7
Monetary authorities	4 781	...	...	1.9	2.9	.9	.9	–6.4	3.7
General government	4 782	...	...	...	...	...	...	...	...
Banks	4 783	3,487.5	–697.5	–1,217.3	1,212.3	–1,895.3	–586.5	–1,019.6	–276.4
Other sectors	4 784	...	...	...	...	...	...	...	...
Other liabilities	4 786	415.9	595.2	–3,610.1	–434.6	–48.0	132.2	–325.5	–13.6
Monetary authorities	4 787	1.8	2.6	–93.5	3.3	...	...	...	...
of which: Short-term	4 789	*1.8*	*2.6*	*–93.5*	*3.3*	...	...	...	...
General government	4 790	–27.7	440.1	–2,900.3	–58.7	–21.6	...	.3	.1
of which: Short-term	4 792	*–27.7*	*440.1*	*–2,900.3*	*–58.7*	*–21.6*	...	*.3*	*.1*
Banks	4 793	411.9	159.3	–237.6	–372.5	–27.0	130.9	17.4	–13.6
of which: Short-term	4 795	*411.9*	*159.3*	*–237.6*	*–372.5*	*–27.0*	*130.9*	*17.4*	*–13.6*
Other sectors	4 796	29.9	–6.8	–378.7	–6.7	.6	1.3	–343.2	–.1
of which: Short-term	4 798	*29.9*	*–6.8*	*–378.7*	*–6.7*	*.6*	*1.3*	*–343.2*	*–.1*
E. RESERVE ASSETS	4 802	–105.7	–77.7	–297.7	–611.1	19.8	–184.5	108.1	–484.4
Monetary gold	4 812	...	...	...	...	...	...	...	...
Special drawing rights	4 811	.2	–1.4	.9	–.8	.3	–1.6	1.1	–1.0
Reserve position in the Fund	4 810	...	...	...	...	...	...	...	...
Foreign exchange	4 803	–105.8	–76.3	–238.6	–59.7	76.3	145.8	–41.3	–1,183.0
Other claims	4 813	...	...	–60.0	–550.6	–56.8	–328.7	148.3	699.6
NET ERRORS AND OMISSIONS	4 998	**–89.5**	**15.2**	**–96.3**	**–195.0**	**–325.1**	**–228.7**	**602.4**	**–387.7**

Part 3 of the *Yearbook* contains descriptions of the methodologies, compilation practices, and sources used to compile these data.

Table 3. INTERNATIONAL INVESTMENT POSITION (End-period stocks), 1994–2001

(Millions of U.S. dollars)

	Code	1994	1995	1996	1997	1998	1999	2000	2001
ASSETS	8 995 C.	...	25,275.7	24,677.0	26,871.0	25,643.3	24,394.5	24,036.1	24,441.9
Direct investment abroad	8 505 . .	...	...	...	...	...	...	...	...
Equity capital and reinvested earnings	8 506 . .	...	...	...	...	...	...	...	...
Claims on affiliated enterprises	8 507 . .	...	...	...	...	...	...	...	...
Liabilities to affiliated enterprises	8 508 . .	...	...	...	...	...	...	...	...
Other capital	8 530 . .	...	...	...	...	...	...	...	...
Claims on affiliated enterprises	8 535 . .	...	...	...	...	...	...	...	...
Liabilities to affiliated enterprises	8 540 . .	...	...	...	...	...	...	...	...
Portfolio investment	8 602 . .	...	**1,889.4**	**1,401.6**	**2,438.1**	**2,006.4**	**2,556.6**	**2,665.9**	**3,444.2**
Equity securities	8 610 . .	...	7.6	17.8	18.6	23.7	52.4	53.0	53.2
Monetary authorities	8 611 . .	...	...	...	...	...	...	...	...
General government	8 612 . .	...	...	...	...	...	...	...	...
Banks	8 613 . .	...	...	...	...	...	...	...	...
Other sectors	8 614 . .	...	7.6	17.8	18.6	23.7	52.4	53.0	53.2
Debt securities	8 619 . .	...	1,881.8	1,383.8	2,419.5	1,982.7	2,504.2	2,612.9	3,391.0
Bonds and notes	8 620 . .	...	1,881.8	1,383.8	2,419.5	1,982.7	2,504.2	2,612.9	3,391.0
Monetary authorities	8 621 . .	...	...	...	...	...	...	...	...
General government	8 622 . .	...	...	57.1	48.0	44.4	48.4	52.4	56.8
Banks	8 623 . .	...	1,855.5	1,284.8	2,329.6	1,884.4	2,428.1	2,530.3	3,305.5
Other sectors	8 624 . .	...	26.3	41.9	41.9	53.9	27.7	30.2	28.7
Money market instruments	8 630 . .	...	...	...	...	...	...	...	...
Monetary authorities	8 631 . .	...	...	...	...	...	...	...	...
General government	8 632 . .	...	...	...	...	...	...	...	...
Banks	8 633 . .	...	...	...	...	...	...	...	...
Other sectors	8 634 . .	...	...	...	...	...	...	...	...
Financial derivatives	8 900 . .	...	...	...	...	...	...	...	...
Monetary authorities	8 901 . .	...	...	...	...	...	...	...	...
General government	8 902 . .	...	...	...	...	...	...	...	...
Banks	8 903 . .	...	...	...	...	...	...	...	...
Other sectors	8 904 . .	...	...	...	...	...	...	...	...
Other investment	8 703 . .	...	**22,605.0**	**22,196.8**	**22,675.5**	**21,898.7**	**19,915.7**	**19,557.1**	**18,700.7**
Trade credits	8 706 . .	...	1,363.0	1,522.0	1,729.2	1,943.8	2,138.1	2,272.2	2,358.6
General government	8 707 . .	...	...	...	...	...	...	...	...
of which: Short-term	8 709 . .	...	...	...	...	...	...	...	...
Other sectors	8 710 . .	...	1,363.0	1,522.0	1,729.2	1,943.8	2,138.1	2,272.2	2,358.6
of which: Short-term	8 712 . .	...	*1,353.7*	*1,512.8*	*1,720.5*	*1,901.6*	*2,100.8*	*2,229.7*	*2,315.3*
Loans	8 714 . .	...	13,785.3	13,009.2	12,862.6	13,193.7	10,804.4	9,989.1	9,830.6
Monetary authorities	8 715 . .	...	...	...	...	...	5.0	...	...
of which: Short-term	8 718 . .	...	...	...	...	...	*5.0*	...	...
General government	8 719 . .	...	...	...	...	257.5	...	...	...
of which: Short-term	8 721 . .	...	...	...	...	...	...	...	...
Banks	8 722 . .	...	13,785.3	13,009.2	12,862.6	12,936.2	10,799.4	9,989.1	9,830.6
of which: Short-term	8 724 . .	...	*13,785.3*	*13,009.2*	*12,862.6*	*12,936.2*	*10,799.4*	*9,989.1*	*9,830.6*
Other sectors	8 725 . .	...	...	...	...	...	...	...	...
of which: Short-term	8 727 . .	...	...	...	...	...	...	...	...
Currency and deposits	8 730 . .	...	5,812.1	5,943.5	6,953.7	5,590.0	5,847.2	6,322.2	5,624.5
Monetary authorities	8 731 . .	...	...	...	...	...	...	...	...
General government	8 732 . .	...	...	37.2	39.0	42.8	33.7	37.7	39.8
Banks	8 733 . .	...	5,812.1	5,906.3	6,914.7	5,547.2	5,813.5	6,284.5	5,584.7
Other sectors	8 734 . .	...	...	...	...	...	...	...	...
Other assets	8 736 . .	...	1,644.6	1,722.1	1,130.0	1,171.2	1,126.0	973.6	887.0
Monetary authorities	8 737 . .	...	...	...	...	...	.2	...	...
of which: Short-term	8 739 . .	...	...	...	...	...	*.2*	...	...
General government	8 740 . .	...	27.7	26.7	27.2	29.2	29.2	29.2	29.2
of which: Short-term	8 742 . .	...	...	...	...	...	...	...	...
Banks	8 743 . .	...	1,171.4	1,320.2	734.5	743.8	645.6	795.8	633.3
of which: Short-term	8 745 . .	...	*1,171.4*	*1,320.2*	*734.5*	*743.8*	*645.6*	*795.8*	*633.3*
Other sectors	8 746 . .	...	445.5	375.2	368.3	398.2	451.0	148.6	224.5
of which: Short-term	8 748 . .	...	*445.5*	*375.2*	*368.3*	*398.2*	*451.0*	*148.6*	*224.5*
Reserve assets	8 802 . .	...	**781.3**	**1,078.6**	**1,757.4**	**1,738.2**	**1,922.2**	**1,813.1**	**2,297.0**
Monetary gold	8 812 . .	...	...	...	...	...	...	...	...
Special drawing rights	8 811 . .	...	.8	...	.5	.1	1.6	.3	1.4
Reserve position in the Fund	8 810 . .	17.3	17.6	17.1	16.0	16.7	16.3	15.5	14.9
Foreign exchange	8 803 . .	...	762.9	1,001.5	1,130.3	1,054.0	908.2	949.5	2,132.5
Other claims	8 813 . .	...	...	60.0	610.6	667.4	996.1	847.8	148.2

Table 3 (Concluded). INTERNATIONAL INVESTMENT POSITION (End–period stocks), 1994–2001

(Millions of U.S. dollars)

	Code	1994	1995	1996	1997	1998	1999	2000	2001
LIABILITIES	8 995 D.	...	31,056.1	30,081.7	32,548.8	32,766.1	33,029.9	32,098.5	33,337.7
Direct investment in Panama	8 555 ..	...	**3,244.6**	**3,660.1**	**4,959.4**	**6,308.0**	**6,960.4**	**6,744.0**	**7,256.6**
Equity capital and reinvested earnings	8 556 ..	...	2,885.0	3,190.4	4,395.2	5,589.8	6,140.1	5,645.9	6,176.2
Claims on direct investors	8 557 ..	...	...	...	...	...	...	...	...
Liabilities to direct investors	8 558 ..	...	2,885.0	3,190.4	4,395.2	5,589.8	6,140.1	5,645.9	6,176.2
Other capital	8 580 ..	...	359.6	469.7	564.2	718.2	820.3	1,098.1	1,080.4
Claims on direct investors	8 585 ..	...	–58.3	–71.1	–84.0	–168.9	–225.3	–276.6	–326.0
Liabilities to direct investors	8 590 ..	...	417.9	540.8	648.2	887.1	1,045.6	1,374.7	1,406.4
Portfolio investment	8 652 ..	...	**432.7**	**3,593.9**	**3,528.5**	**3,733.8**	**3,948.2**	**4,097.6**	**4,820.6**
Equity securities	8 660 ..	...	.1	...	...	...	...	...	...
Banks	8 663 ..	...	...	...	...	...	...	...	...
Other sectors	8 664 ..	...	.1	...	...	...	...	...	...
Debt securities	8 669 ..	...	432.6	3,593.9	3,528.5	3,733.8	3,948.2	4,097.6	4,820.6
Bonds and notes	8 670 ..	...	432.6	3,593.9	3,528.5	3,733.8	3,948.2	4,097.6	4,820.6
Monetary authorities	8 671 ..	...	...	...	...	...	...	...	...
General government	8 672 ..	...	432.6	3,593.9	3,528.5	3,733.8	3,948.2	4,097.6	4,820.6
Banks	8 673 ..	...	...	...	...	...	...	...	...
Other sectors	8 674 ..	...	...	...	...	...	...	...	...
Money market instruments	8 680 ..	...	...	...	...	...	...	...	...
Monetary authorities	8 681 ..	...	...	...	...	...	...	...	...
General government	8 682 ..	...	...	...	...	...	...	...	...
Banks	8 683 ..	...	...	...	...	...	...	...	...
Other sectors	8 684 ..	...	...	...	...	...	...	...	...
Financial derivatives	8 905 ..	...	...	...	...	...	...	...	...
Monetary authorities	8 906 ..	...	...	...	...	...	...	...	...
General government	8 907 ..	...	...	...	...	...	...	...	...
Banks	8 908 ..	...	...	...	...	...	...	...	...
Other sectors	8 909 ..	...	...	...	...	...	...	...	...
Other investment	8 753 ..	...	**27,378.8**	**22,827.7**	**24,060.9**	**22,724.3**	**22,121.3**	**21,256.9**	**21,260.5**
Trade credits	8 756 ..	...	814.0	957.2	1,047.1	952.1	898.3	897.9	896.1
General government	8 757 ..	...	...	...	...	...	...	...	...
of which: Short-term	8 759 ..	...	...	...	...	...	...	...	...
Other sectors	8 760 ..	...	814.0	957.2	1,047.1	952.1	898.3	897.9	896.1
of which: Short-term	8 762 ..	...	*808.8*	*950.8*	*1,042.9*	*947.1*	*889.2*	*886.9*	*883.6*
Loans	8 764 ..	...	4,536.0	5,204.1	5,568.0	6,286.0	6,190.2	6,677.7	6,969.4
Monetary authorities	8 765 ..	...	202.0	218.1	231.7	264.4	234.7	176.0	139.9
of which: Use of Fund credit and loans from the Fund	8 766 ..	*133.2*	*110.5*	*130.8*	*142.2*	*176.8*	*148.7*	*90.0*	*53.9*
of which: Short-term	8 768 ..	...	*4.0*	*3.2*	*3.2*	*1.6*	...	...	...
General government	8 769 ..	...	1,037.7	985.8	1,136.8	1,336.9	1,395.6	1,350.8	1,331.2
of which: Short-term	8 771 ..	...	...	...	...	...	...	...	...
Banks	8 772 ..	...	2,796.4	3,457.6	3,651.0	4,126.5	4,031.3	4,615.1	4,962.2
of which: Short-term	8 774 ..	...	*2,391.5*	*2,229.1*	*1,997.1*	*2,650.9*	*2,474.3*	*2,687.7*	*2,326.6*
Other sectors	8 775 ..	...	499.9	542.6	548.5	558.2	528.6	535.8	536.1
of which: Short-term	8 777 ..	...	*209.5*	*280.0*	*340.8*	*453.3*	*448.9*	*466.4*	*475.2*
Currency and deposits	8 780 ..	...	16,640.4	15,425.0	16,640.2	14,745.8	14,160.2	13,134.2	12,861.5
Monetary authorities	8 781 ..	...	42.2	44.1	47.0	47.9	48.8	42.4	46.1
General government	8 782 ..	...	...	...	...	...	...	...	...
Banks	8 783 ..	...	16,598.2	15,380.9	16,593.2	14,697.9	14,111.4	13,091.8	12,815.4
Other sectors	8 784 ..	...	...	...	...	...	...	...	...
Other liabilities	8 786 ..	...	5,388.4	1,241.4	805.6	740.4	872.6	547.1	533.5
Monetary authorities	8 787 ..	...	27.3	27.9	31.2	31.2	31.2	31.2	31.2
of which: Short-term	8 789 ..	...	*27.3*	*27.9*	*31.2*	*31.2*	*31.2*	*31.2*	*31.2*
General government	8 790 ..	...	3,599.7	101.0	41.2	2.4	2.5	2.8	2.9
of which: Short-term	8 792 ..	...	*3,599.7*	*101.0*	*41.2*	*2.4*	*2.5*	*2.8*	*2.9*
Banks	8 793 ..	...	1,315.8	1,078.2	705.7	678.7	809.6	827.0	813.4
of which: Short-term	8 795 ..	...	*1,315.8*	*1,078.2*	*705.7*	*678.7*	*809.6*	*827.0*	*813.4*
Other sectors	8 796 ..	...	445.6	34.3	27.5	28.1	29.3	–313.9	–314.0
of which: Short-term	8 798 ..	...	*445.6*	*34.3*	*27.5*	*28.1*	*29.3*	*–313.9*	*–314.0*
NET INTERNATIONAL INVESTMENT POSITION	8 995 ..	...	**–5,780.4**	**–5,404.7**	**–5,677.8**	**–7,122.7**	**–8,635.4**	**–8,062.4**	**–8,895.8**
Conversion rates: balboa per U.S. dollar (end of period)	0 102 ..	**1.0000**	**1.0000**	**1.0000**	**1.0000**	**1.0000**	**1.0000**	**1.0000**	**1.0000**

Table 1. ANALYTIC PRESENTATION, 1994–2001
(Millions of U.S. dollars)

	Code	1994	1995	1996	1997	1998	1999	2000	2001
A. Current Account [1]	4 993 Z.	**402.1**	**491.9**	**188.9**	**–192.2**	**–28.9**	**94.7**	**345.4**	**282.1**
Goods: exports f.o.b	2 100 . .	2,651.0	2,670.4	2,529.8	2,160.1	1,773.3	1,927.4	2,094.1	1,812.9
Goods: imports f.o.b	3 100 . .	–1,324.9	–1,262.4	–1,513.3	–1,483.3	–1,078.3	–1,071.4	–998.8	–932.4
Balance on Goods	4 100 . .	*1,326.1*	*1,408.0*	*1,016.6*	*676.8*	*695.0*	*856.0*	*1,095.3*	*880.5*
Services: credit	2 200 . .	235.4	321.3	432.2	396.9	318.0	247.5	242.7	285.1
Services: debit	3 200 . .	–608.0	–642.1	–778.5	–923.6	–793.8	–727.9	–772.3	–662.0
Balance on Goods and Services	4 991 . .	*953.5*	*1,087.2*	*670.2*	*150.1*	*219.2*	*375.6*	*565.7*	*503.7*
Income: credit	2 300 . .	22.4	22.5	32.1	35.1	20.9	18.6	32.0	20.0
Income: debit	3 300 . .	–423.4	–510.7	–461.2	–344.8	–279.7	–291.1	–242.1	–250.2
Balance on Goods, Services, and Income	4 992 . .	*552.5*	*599.1*	*241.1*	*–159.5*	*–39.6*	*103.1*	*355.6*	*273.4*
Current transfers: credit	2 379 Z.	58.8	66.7	252.1	69.9	82.4	60.3	62.4	75.9
Current transfers: debit	3 379 . .	–209.3	–173.9	–304.2	–102.6	–71.6	–68.7	–72.7	–67.3
B. Capital Account [1]	4 994 Z.	**. . .**	**. . .**	**. . .**	**. . .**	**. . .**	**. . .**	**. . .**	**. . .**
Capital account: credit	2 994 Z.	19.9	15.7	15.2	13.9	9.7	7.8	7.2	5.9
Capital account: debit	3 994 . .	–19.9	–15.7	–15.2	–13.9	–9.7	–7.8	–7.2	–5.9
Total, Groups A Plus B	4 981 . .	*402.1*	*491.9*	*188.9*	*–192.2*	*–28.9*	*94.7*	*345.4*	*282.1*
C. Financial Account [1]	4 995 W.	**–609.2**	**–444.7**	**46.6**	**8.0**	**–179.7**	**16.0**	**–254.1**	**–151.9**
Direct investment abroad	4 505 . .	. . .	. . .	. . .	. . .	. . .	. . .	. . .	. . .
Direct investment in Papua New Guinea	4 555 Z.	57.0	454.6	111.3	28.6	109.6	296.5	95.9	62.5
Portfolio investment assets	4 602 . .	–2.1	–48.7	69.9	–25.5	87.0	89.0	–123.8	–72.7
Equity securities	4 610 . .	. . .	. . .	. . .	. . .	. . .	. . .	. . .	. . .
Debt securities	4 619 . .	–2.1	–48.7	69.9	–25.5	87.0	89.0	–123.8	–72.7
Portfolio investment liabilities	4 652 Z.	. . .	. . .	. . .	. . .	. . .	. . .	. . .	. . .
Equity securities	4 660 . .	. . .	. . .	. . .	. . .	. . .	. . .	. . .	. . .
Debt securities	4 669 Z.	. . .	. . .	. . .	. . .	. . .	. . .	. . .	. . .
Financial derivatives	4 910 . .	. . .	. . .	. . .	. . .	. . .	. . .	. . .	. . .
Financial derivatives assets	4 900 . .	. . .	. . .	. . .	. . .	. . .	. . .	. . .	. . .
Financial derivatives liabilities	4 905 . .	. . .	. . .	. . .	. . .	. . .	. . .	. . .	. . .
Other investment assets	4 703 . .	58.8	–283.8	180.0	29.6	–55.0	10.7	–41.0	–66.9
Monetary authorities	4 701 . .	. . .	. . .	. . .	. . .	. . .	. . .	. . .	. . .
General government	4 704 . .	. . .	. . .	. . .	. . .	. . .	. . .	. . .	. . .
Banks	4 705 . .	. . .	. . .	. . .	. . .	. . .	–2.1	–21.2	–26.7
Other sectors	4 728 . .	58.8	–283.8	180.0	29.6	–55.0	12.8	–19.8	–40.2
Other investment liabilities	4 753 W.	–722.9	–566.8	–314.6	–24.7	–321.2	–380.2	–185.2	–74.7
Monetary authorities	4 753 WA	. . .	. . .	–68.2	. . .	. . .	. . .	. . .	. . .
General government	4 753 ZB	–102.1	–23.5	10.0	–62.7	–44.2	39.4	.2	49.0
Banks	4 753 ZC	–26.9	27.4	–34.0	–42.3	16.4	. . .	. . .	. . .
Other sectors	4 753 ZD	–593.9	–570.7	–222.4	80.3	–293.4	–419.6	–185.4	–123.7
Total, Groups A Through C	4 983 . .	*–207.1*	*47.2*	*235.6*	*–184.3*	*–208.5*	*110.7*	*91.3*	*130.2*
D. Net Errors and Omissions	4 998 . .	**37.1**	**–86.6**	**–33.1**	**7.3**	**–12.5**	**14.3**	**13.1**	**–1.6**
Total, Groups A Through D	4 984 . .	*–170.1*	*–39.5*	*202.5*	*–177.0*	*–221.0*	*125.0*	*104.5*	*128.6*
E. Reserves and Related Items	4 802 A.	**170.1**	**39.5**	**–202.5**	**177.0**	**221.0**	**–125.0**	**–104.5**	**–128.6**
Reserve assets	4 802 . .	33.8	–177.4	–329.7	83.7	149.1	–49.7	–127.9	–203.6
Use of Fund credit and loans	4 766 . .	–30.6	35.0	2.9	. . .	–4.2	–22.8	18.1	70.9
Exceptional financing	4 920 . .	166.8	181.9	124.4	93.2	76.1	–52.5	5.3	4.1
Conversion rates: kina per U.S. dollar	0 101 . .	**1.0113**	**1.2798**	**1.3191**	**1.4380**	**2.0736**	**2.5708**	**2.7822**	**3.3887**

[1] Excludes components that have been classified in the categories of Group E.

Table 2. STANDARD PRESENTATION, 1994–2001

(Millions of U.S. dollars)

	Code	1994	1995	1996	1997	1998	1999	2000	2001
CURRENT ACCOUNT	4 993 . .	**568.9**	**673.8**	**313.3**	**–99.0**	**47.3**	**120.0**	**350.7**	**286.1**
A. GOODS	4 100 . .	1,326.1	1,408.0	1,016.6	676.8	695.0	856.0	1,095.3	880.5
Credit	2 100 . .	**2,651.0**	**2,670.4**	**2,529.8**	**2,160.1**	**1,773.3**	**1,927.4**	**2,094.1**	**1,812.9**
General merchandise: exports f.o.b.	2 110 . .	2,651.0	2,670.4	2,529.8	2,160.1	1,773.3	1,927.4	2,094.1	1,812.9
Goods for processing: exports f.o.b.	2 150 . .	...	...	...	...	...	...	...	...
Repairs on goods	2 160 . .	...	...	...	...	...	...	...	...
Goods procured in ports by carriers	2 170 . .	...	...	...	...	...	...	...	...
Nonmonetary gold	2 180 . .	...	...	...	...	...	...	...	...
Debit	3 100 . .	**–1,324.9**	**–1,262.4**	**–1,513.3**	**–1,483.3**	**–1,078.3**	**–1,071.4**	**–998.8**	**–932.4**
General merchandise: imports f.o.b.	3 110 . .	–1,324.9	–1,262.4	–1,513.3	–1,483.3	–1,078.3	–1,071.4	–998.8	–932.4
Goods for processing: imports f.o.b.	3 150 . .	...	...	...	...	...	...	...	...
Repairs on goods	3 160 . .	...	...	...	...	...	...	...	...
Goods procured in ports by carriers	3 170 . .	...	...	...	...	...	...	...	...
Nonmonetary gold	3 180 . .	...	...	...	...	...	...	...	...
B. SERVICES	4 200 . .	–372.6	–320.8	–346.4	–526.6	–475.8	–480.3	–529.6	–376.9
Total credit	2 200 . .	*235.4*	*321.3*	*432.2*	*396.9*	*318.0*	*247.5*	*242.7*	*285.1*
Total debit	3 200 . .	*–608.0*	*–642.1*	*–778.5*	*–923.6*	*–793.8*	*–727.9*	*–772.3*	*–662.0*
Transportation services, credit	2 205 . .	**37.4**	**34.7**	**33.8**	**21.8**	**11.5**	**10.7**	**11.8**	**21.3**
Passenger	2 850 . .	...	...	...	...	...	...	...	...
Freight	2 851 . .	*37.4*	*34.7*	*33.8*	*21.8*	*11.5*	*10.7*	*11.8*	*21.3*
Other	2 852 . .	...	...	...	...	...	...	...	...
Sea transport, passenger	2 207 . .	...	...	...	...	...	...	...	...
Sea transport, freight	2 208 . .	37.4	34.7	33.8	21.8	11.5	10.7	11.8	21.3
Sea transport, other	2 209 . .	...	...	...	...	...	...	...	...
Air transport, passenger	2 211 . .	...	...	...	...	...	...	...	...
Air transport, freight	2 212 . .	...	...	...	...	...	...	...	...
Air transport, other	2 213 . .	...	...	...	...	...	...	...	...
Other transport, passenger	2 215 . .	...	...	...	...	...	...	...	...
Other transport, freight	2 216 . .	...	...	...	...	...	...	...	...
Other transport, other	2 217 . .	...	...	...	...	...	...	...	...
Transportation services, debit	3 205 . .	**–174.3**	**–161.7**	**–179.9**	**–221.6**	**–160.9**	**–181.0**	**–162.9**	**–172.9**
Passenger	3 850 . .	...	...	...	...	...	...	...	...
Freight	3 851 . .	*–174.3*	*–161.7*	*–179.9*	*–221.6*	*–160.9*	*–181.0*	*–162.9*	*–172.9*
Other	3 852 . .	...	...	...	...	...	...	...	...
Sea transport, passenger	3 207 . .	...	...	...	...	...	...	...	...
Sea transport, freight	3 208 . .	–174.3	–161.7	–179.9	–221.6	–160.9	–181.0	–162.9	–172.9
Sea transport, other	3 209 . .	...	...	...	...	...	...	...	...
Air transport, passenger	3 211 . .	...	...	...	...	...	...	...	...
Air transport, freight	3 212 . .	...	...	...	...	...	...	...	...
Air transport, other	3 213 . .	...	...	...	...	...	...	...	...
Other transport, passenger	3 215 . .	...	...	...	...	...	...	...	...
Other transport, freight	3 216 . .	...	...	...	...	...	...	...	...
Other transport, other	3 217 . .	...	...	...	...	...	...	...	...
Travel, credit	2 236 . .	**30.0**	**25.2**	**13.6**	**8.1**	**15.1**	**5.9**	**7.2**	**5.2**
Business travel	2 237 . .	...	...	...	...	...	5.1	6.2	4.4
Personal travel	2 240 . .	30.0	25.2	13.6	8.1	15.1	.8	1.0	.7
Travel, debit	3 236 . .	**–70.5**	**–58.2**	**–72.0**	**–77.6**	**–51.8**	**–53.0**	**–50.3**	**–38.2**
Business travel	3 237 . .	...	...	...	...	...	–42.5	–40.6	–29.7
Personal travel	3 240 . .	–70.5	–58.2	–72.0	–77.6	–51.8	–10.5	–9.7	–8.5
Other services, credit	2 200 BA	**168.0**	**261.5**	**384.8**	**367.1**	**291.5**	**230.9**	**223.6**	**258.6**
Communications	2 245 . .	...	...	...	...	...	...	...	...
Construction	2 249 . .	...	...	...	...	...	...	...	...
Insurance	2 253 . .	4.2	3.9	13.5	15.3	7.1	9.4	4.5	5.3
Financial	2 260 . .	...	...	...	...	...	...	...	...
Computer and information	2 262 . .	...	...	...	...	...	...	...	...
Royalties and licence fees	2 266 . .	...	...	...	...	...	...	...	...
Other business services	2 268 . .	163.9	257.6	371.3	351.7	284.4	221.5	219.2	253.4
Personal, cultural, and recreational	2 287 . .	...	...	...	...	...	...	...	...
Government, n.i.e.	2 291 . .	...	...	...	...	...	...	...	...
Other services, debit	3 200 BA	**–363.2**	**–422.3**	**–526.6**	**–624.3**	**–581.2**	**–493.9**	**–559.1**	**–450.9**
Communications	3 245 . .	...	...	...	...	...	...	...	...
Construction	3 249 . .	...	...	...	...	...	...	...	...
Insurance	3 253 . .	–19.4	–18.0	–59.0	–63.3	–48.9	–46.6	–40.2	–48.3
Financial	3 260 . .	...	...	...	...	...	...	...	...
Computer and information	3 262 . .	...	...	...	...	...	...	...	...
Royalties and licence fees	3 266 . .	...	...	...	...	...	...	...	...
Other business services	3 268 . .	–343.8	–404.3	–467.5	–561.0	–532.3	–447.2	–518.9	–402.6
Personal, cultural, and recreational	3 287 . .	...	...	...	...	...	...	...	...
Government, n.i.e.	3 291 . .	...	...	...	...	...	...	...	...

Table 2 (Continued). STANDARD PRESENTATION, 1994–2001
(Millions of U.S. dollars)

	Code	1994	1995	1996	1997	1998	1999	2000	2001
C. INCOME	4 300	–401.0	–488.1	–429.1	–309.7	–258.8	–272.5	–210.1	–230.3
Total credit	2 300	*22.4*	*22.5*	*32.1*	*35.1*	*20.9*	*18.6*	*32.0*	*20.0*
Total debit	3 300	*–423.4*	*–510.7*	*–461.2*	*–344.8*	*–279.7*	*–291.1*	*–242.1*	*–250.2*
Compensation of employees, credit	2 310	**. . .**	**. . .**	**. . .**	**. . .**	**. . .**	**. . .**	**. . .**	**. . .**
Compensation of employees, debit	3 310	**. . .**	**. . .**	**. . .**	**. . .**	**. . .**	**. . .**	**. . .**	**. . .**
Investment income, credit	2 320	**22.4**	**22.5**	**32.1**	**35.1**	**20.9**	**18.6**	**32.0**	**20.0**
Direct investment income	2 330	.1	3.9	.1	.9	.8	5.4	1.2	1.6
Dividends and distributed branch profits	2 332	.1	3.9	.1	.9	.8	5.4	1.2	1.6
Reinvested earnings and undistributed branch profits	2 333	. . .	. . .	. . .	. . .	. . .	. . .	. . .	. . .
Income on debt (interest)	2 334	. . .	. . .	. . .	. . .	. . .	. . .	. . .	. . .
Portfolio investment income	2 339	. . .	. . .	. . .	. . .	. . .	3.4	10.1	5.8
Income on equity	2 340	. . .	. . .	. . .	. . .	. . .	. . .	. . .	. . .
Income on bonds and notes	2 350	. . .	. . .	. . .	. . .	. . .	3.4	10.1	5.8
Income on money market instruments	2 360	. . .	. . .	. . .	. . .	. . .	. . .	. . .	. . .
Other investment income	2 370	22.3	18.6	32.0	34.2	20.2	9.8	20.7	12.6
Investment income, debit	3 320	**–423.4**	**–510.7**	**–461.2**	**–344.8**	**–279.7**	**–291.1**	**–242.1**	**–250.2**
Direct investment income	3 330	–247.7	–408.9	–369.7	–248.3	–176.2	–239.4	–197.7	–205.7
Dividends and distributed branch profits	3 332	–188.0	–361.9	–324.2	–206.4	–147.1	–161.9	–125.9	–154.3
Reinvested earnings and undistributed branch profits	3 333	–59.7	–47.0	–45.5	–41.8	–29.1	–23.5	–21.7	–17.8
Income on debt (interest)	3 334	. . .	. . .	. . .	. . .	. . .	–53.9	–50.1	–33.6
Portfolio investment income	3 339	. . .	. . .	. . .	. . .	. . .	. . .	. . .	. . .
Income on equity	3 340	. . .	. . .	. . .	. . .	. . .	. . .	. . .	. . .
Income on bonds and notes	3 350	. . .	. . .	. . .	. . .	. . .	. . .	. . .	. . .
Income on money market instruments	3 360	. . .	. . .	. . .	. . .	. . .	. . .	. . .	. . .
Other investment income	3 370	–175.7	–101.7	–91.5	–96.5	–103.5	–51.7	–44.4	–44.6
D. CURRENT TRANSFERS	4 379	16.4	74.7	72.2	60.5	86.9	16.9	–4.9	12.8
Credit	2 379	**225.7**	**248.6**	**376.4**	**163.1**	**158.5**	**85.6**	**67.7**	**80.0**
General government	2 380	166.8	181.9	124.4	93.2	76.1	25.3	5.3	4.1
Other sectors	2 390	58.8	66.7	252.1	69.9	82.4	60.3	62.4	75.9
Workers' remittances	2 391	. . .	. . .	. . .	. . .	. . .	. . .	. . .	. . .
Other current transfers	2 392	58.8	66.7	252.1	69.9	82.4	60.3	62.4	75.9
Debit	3 379	**–209.3**	**–173.9**	**–304.2**	**–102.6**	**–71.6**	**–68.7**	**–72.7**	**–67.3**
General government	3 380	. . .	. . .	. . .	. . .	. . .	. . .	. . .	. . .
Other sectors	3 390	–209.3	–173.9	–304.2	–102.6	–71.6	–68.7	–72.7	–67.3
Workers' remittances	3 391	. . .	. . .	–3.3	–12.3	–5.9	–8.3	–11.2	–10.7
Other current transfers	3 392	–209.3	–173.9	–301.0	–90.3	–65.7	–60.4	–61.4	–56.5
CAPITAL AND FINANCIAL ACCOUNT	4 996	**–605.9**	**–587.2**	**–280.2**	**91.7**	**–34.8**	**–134.3**	**–363.8**	**–284.5**
CAPITAL ACCOUNT	4 994	. . .	. . .	. . .	. . .	. . .	. . .	. . .	. . .
Total credit	2 994	*19.9*	*15.7*	*15.2*	*13.9*	*9.7*	*7.8*	*7.2*	*5.9*
Total debit	3 994	*–19.9*	*–15.7*	*–15.2*	*–13.9*	*–9.7*	*–7.8*	*–7.2*	*–5.9*
Capital transfers, credit	2 400	**19.9**	**15.7**	**15.2**	**13.9**	**9.7**	**7.8**	**7.2**	**5.9**
General government	2 401	. . .	. . .	. . .	. . .	. . .	. . .	. . .	. . .
Debt forgiveness	2 402	. . .	. . .	. . .	. . .	. . .	. . .	. . .	. . .
Other capital transfers	2 410	. . .	. . .	. . .	. . .	. . .	. . .	. . .	. . .
Other sectors	2 430	19.9	15.7	15.2	13.9	9.7	7.8	7.2	5.9
Migrants' transfers	2 431	19.9	15.7	15.2	13.9	9.7	7.8	7.2	5.9
Debt forgiveness	2 432	. . .	. . .	. . .	. . .	. . .	. . .	. . .	. . .
Other capital transfers	2 440	. . .	. . .	. . .	. . .	. . .	. . .	. . .	. . .
Capital transfers, debit	3 400	**–19.9**	**–15.7**	**–15.2**	**–13.9**	**–9.7**	**–7.8**	**–7.2**	**–5.9**
General government	3 401	. . .	. . .	. . .	. . .	. . .	. . .	. . .	. . .
Debt forgiveness	3 402	. . .	. . .	. . .	. . .	. . .	. . .	. . .	. . .
Other capital transfers	3 410	. . .	. . .	. . .	. . .	. . .	. . .	. . .	. . .
Other sectors	3 430	–19.9	–15.7	–15.2	–13.9	–9.7	–7.8	–7.2	–5.9
Migrants' transfers	3 431	–19.9	–15.7	–15.2	–13.9	–9.7	–7.8	–7.2	–5.9
Debt forgiveness	3 432	. . .	. . .	. . .	. . .	. . .	. . .	. . .	. . .
Other capital transfers	3 440	. . .	. . .	. . .	. . .	. . .	. . .	. . .	. . .
Nonproduced nonfinancial assets, credit	2 480	**. . .**	**. . .**	**. . .**	**. . .**	**. . .**	**. . .**	**. . .**	**. . .**
Nonproduced nonfinancial assets, debit	3 480	**. . .**	**. . .**	**. . .**	**. . .**	**. . .**	**. . .**	**. . .**	**. . .**

Table 2 (Continued). STANDARD PRESENTATION, 1994–2001

(Millions of U.S. dollars)

	Code	1994	1995	1996	1997	1998	1999	2000	2001
FINANCIAL ACCOUNT	4 995 . .	**–605.9**	**–587.2**	**–280.2**	**91.7**	**–34.8**	**–134.3**	**–363.8**	**–284.5**
A. DIRECT INVESTMENT	4 500 . .	57.0	454.6	111.3	28.6	109.6	296.5	95.9	62.5
Direct investment abroad	4 505 . .	**. . .**	**. . .**	**. . .**	**. . .**	**. . .**	**. . .**	**. . .**	**. . .**
Equity capital	4 510 . .	. . .	. . .	. . .	. . .	. . .	. . .	. . .	. . .
Claims on affiliated enterprises	4 515 . .	. . .	. . .	. . .	. . .	. . .	. . .	. . .	. . .
Liabilities to affiliated enterprises	4 520 . .	. . .	. . .	. . .	. . .	. . .	. . .	. . .	. . .
Reinvested earnings	4 525 . .	. . .	. . .	. . .	. . .	. . .	. . .	. . .	. . .
Other capital	4 530 . .	. . .	. . .	. . .	. . .	. . .	. . .	. . .	. . .
Claims on affiliated enterprises	4 535 . .	. . .	. . .	. . .	. . .	. . .	. . .	. . .	. . .
Liabilities to affiliated enterprises	4 540 . .	. . .	. . .	. . .	. . .	. . .	. . .	. . .	. . .
Direct investment in Papua New Guinea	4 555 . .	**57.0**	**454.6**	**111.3**	**28.6**	**109.6**	**296.5**	**95.9**	**62.5**
Equity capital	4 560 . .	. . .	407.6	69.1	–8.1	82.9	274.3	74.6	45.3
Claims on direct investors	4 565 . .	. . .	. . .	. . .	. . .	. . .	. . .	. . .	. . .
Liabilities to direct investors	4 570 . .	. . .	407.6	69.1	–8.1	82.9	274.3	74.6	45.3
Reinvested earnings	4 575 . .	59.7	47.0	45.5	41.8	29.1	23.5	21.7	17.8
Other capital	4 580 . .	–2.8	. . .	–3.3	–5.1	–2.4	–1.4	–.4	–.5
Claims on direct investors	4 585 . .	–2.8	. . .	1.5	.3	.2	–1.5	–.6	–.6
Liabilities to direct investors	4 590 . .	. . .	. . .	–4.8	–5.4	–2.6	.1	.2	.1
B. PORTFOLIO INVESTMENT	4 600 . .	–2.1	–48.7	69.9	–25.5	87.0	11.3	–123.8	–72.7
Assets	4 602 . .	**–2.1**	**–48.7**	**69.9**	**–25.5**	**87.0**	**89.0**	**–123.8**	**–72.7**
Equity securities	4 610 . .	. . .	. . .	. . .	. . .	. . .	. . .	. . .	. . .
Monetary authorities	4 611 . .	. . .	. . .	. . .	. . .	. . .	. . .	. . .	. . .
General government	4 612 . .	. . .	. . .	. . .	. . .	. . .	. . .	. . .	. . .
Banks	4 613 . .	. . .	. . .	. . .	. . .	. . .	. . .	. . .	. . .
Other sectors	4 614 . .	. . .	. . .	. . .	. . .	. . .	. . .	. . .	. . .
Debt securities	4 619 . .	–2.1	–48.7	69.9	–25.5	87.0	89.0	–123.8	–72.7
Bonds and notes	4 620 . .	. . .	. . .	97.9	–74.6	–27.5	–33.0	–10.8	.7
Monetary authorities	4 621 . .	. . .	. . .	. . .	. . .	. . .	. . .	. . .	. . .
General government	4 622 . .	. . .	. . .	. . .	. . .	. . .	. . .	. . .	. . .
Banks	4 623 . .	. . .	. . .	. . .	. . .	. . .	. . .	. . .	. . .
Other sectors	4 624 . .	. . .	. . .	97.9	–74.6	–27.5	–33.0	–10.8	.7
Money market instruments	4 630 . .	–2.1	–48.7	–28.0	49.1	114.5	122.0	–113.0	–73.4
Monetary authorities	4 631 . .	. . .	. . .	. . .	. . .	. . .	. . .	. . .	. . .
General government	4 632 . .	. . .	. . .	. . .	. . .	. . .	. . .	. . .	. . .
Banks	4 633 . .	. . .	. . .	. . .	. . .	. . .	. . .	. . .	. . .
Other sectors	4 634 . .	–2.1	–48.7	–28.0	49.1	114.5	122.0	–113.0	–73.4
Liabilities	4 652 . .	**. . .**	**. . .**	**. . .**	**. . .**	**. . .**	**–77.7**	**. . .**	**. . .**
Equity securities	4 660 . .	. . .	. . .	. . .	. . .	. . .	. . .	. . .	. . .
Banks	4 663 . .	. . .	. . .	. . .	. . .	. . .	. . .	. . .	. . .
Other sectors	4 664 . .	. . .	. . .	. . .	. . .	. . .	. . .	. . .	. . .
Debt securities	4 669 . .	. . .	. . .	. . .	. . .	. . .	–77.7	. . .	. . .
Bonds and notes	4 670 . .	. . .	. . .	. . .	. . .	. . .	. . .	. . .	. . .
Monetary authorities	4 671 . .	. . .	. . .	. . .	. . .	. . .	. . .	. . .	. . .
General government	4 672 . .	. . .	. . .	. . .	. . .	. . .	. . .	. . .	. . .
Banks	4 673 . .	. . .	. . .	. . .	. . .	. . .	. . .	. . .	. . .
Other sectors	4 674 . .	. . .	. . .	. . .	. . .	. . .	. . .	. . .	. . .
Money market instruments	4 680 . .	. . .	. . .	. . .	. . .	. . .	–77.7	. . .	. . .
Monetary authorities	4 681 . .	. . .	. . .	. . .	. . .	. . .	. . .	. . .	. . .
General government	4 682 . .	. . .	. . .	. . .	. . .	. . .	–77.7	. . .	. . .
Banks	4 683 . .	. . .	. . .	. . .	. . .	. . .	. . .	. . .	. . .
Other sectors	4 684 . .	. . .	. . .	. . .	. . .	. . .	. . .	. . .	. . .
C. FINANCIAL DERIVATIVES	4 910 . .	. . .	. . .	. . .	. . .	. . .	. . .	. . .	. . .
Monetary authorities	4 911 . .	. . .	. . .	. . .	. . .	. . .	. . .	. . .	. . .
General government	4 912 . .	. . .	. . .	. . .	. . .	. . .	. . .	. . .	. . .
Banks	4 913 . .	. . .	. . .	. . .	. . .	. . .	. . .	. . .	. . .
Other sectors	4 914 . .	. . .	. . .	. . .	. . .	. . .	. . .	. . .	. . .
Assets	4 900 . .	**. . .**	**. . .**	**. . .**	**. . .**	**. . .**	**. . .**	**. . .**	**. . .**
Monetary authorities	4 901 . .	. . .	. . .	. . .	. . .	. . .	. . .	. . .	. . .
General government	4 902 . .	. . .	. . .	. . .	. . .	. . .	. . .	. . .	. . .
Banks	4 903 . .	. . .	. . .	. . .	. . .	. . .	. . .	. . .	. . .
Other sectors	4 904 . .	. . .	. . .	. . .	. . .	. . .	. . .	. . .	. . .
Liabilities	4 905 . .	**. . .**	**. . .**	**. . .**	**. . .**	**. . .**	**. . .**	**. . .**	**. . .**
Monetary authorities	4 906 . .	. . .	. . .	. . .	. . .	. . .	. . .	. . .	. . .
General government	4 907 . .	. . .	. . .	. . .	. . .	. . .	. . .	. . .	. . .
Banks	4 908 . .	. . .	. . .	. . .	. . .	. . .	. . .	. . .	. . .
Other sectors	4 909 . .	. . .	. . .	. . .	. . .	. . .	. . .	. . .	. . .

Table 2 (Concluded). STANDARD PRESENTATION, 1994–2001

(Millions of U.S. dollars)

	Code	1994	1995	1996	1997	1998	1999	2000	2001
D. OTHER INVESTMENT	4 700	–694.7	–815.6	–131.7	4.9	–380.5	–392.4	–208.1	–70.8
Assets	4 703	**58.8**	**–283.8**	**180.0**	**29.6**	**–55.0**	**10.7**	**–41.0**	**–66.9**
Trade credits	4 706	...	...	...	...	...	...	...	...
General government	4 707	...	...	...	...	...	...	...	...
of which: Short-term	4 709	...	...	...	...	...	...	...	...
Other sectors	4 710	...	...	...	...	...	...	...	...
of which: Short-term	4 712	...	...	...	...	...	...	...	...
Loans	4 714	...	...	...	...	...	...	...	...
Monetary authorities	4 715	...	...	...	...	...	...	...	...
of which: Short-term	4 718	...	...	...	...	...	...	...	...
General government	4 719	...	...	...	...	...	...	...	...
of which: Short-term	4 721	...	...	...	...	...	...	...	...
Banks	4 722	...	...	...	...	...	...	...	...
of which: Short-term	4 724	...	...	...	...	...	...	...	...
Other sectors	4 725	...	...	...	...	...	...	...	...
of which: Short-term	4 727	...	...	...	...	...	...	...	...
Currency and deposits	4 730	58.8	–283.8	180.0	29.6	–55.0	10.7	–41.0	–66.9
Monetary authorities	4 731	...	...	...	...	...	...	...	...
General government	4 732	...	...	...	...	...	...	...	...
Banks	4 733	...	...	...	...	...	–2.1	–21.2	–26.7
Other sectors	4 734	58.8	–283.8	180.0	29.6	–55.0	12.8	–19.8	–40.2
Other assets	4 736	...	...	...	...	...	...	...	...
Monetary authorities	4 737	...	...	...	...	...	...	...	...
of which: Short-term	4 739	...	...	...	...	...	...	...	...
General government	4 740	...	...	...	...	...	...	...	...
of which: Short-term	4 742	...	...	...	...	...	...	...	...
Banks	4 743	...	...	...	...	...	...	...	...
of which: Short-term	4 745	...	...	...	...	...	...	...	...
Other sectors	4 746	...	...	...	...	...	...	...	...
of which: Short-term	4 748	...	...	...	...	...	...	...	...
Liabilities	4 753	**–753.5**	**–531.8**	**–311.7**	**–24.7**	**–325.5**	**–403.0**	**–167.1**	**–3.8**
Trade credits	4 756	...	...	...	...	...	...	...	...
General government	4 757	...	...	...	...	...	...	...	...
of which: Short-term	4 759	...	...	...	...	...	...	...	...
Other sectors	4 760	...	...	...	...	...	...	...	...
of which: Short-term	4 762	...	...	...	...	...	...	...	...
Loans	4 764	–617.6	–313.0	–177.4	203.2	–179.3	–353.3	–159.4	–67.8
Monetary authorities	4 765	–30.6	35.0	–65.3	...	–4.2	–22.8	18.1	70.9
of which: Use of Fund credit and loans from the Fund	4 766	*–30.6*	*35.0*	*2.9*	...	*–4.2*	*–22.8*	*18.1*	*70.9*
of which: Short-term	4 768	...	...	...	...	...	...	...	...
General government	4 769	–102.1	–23.5	10.0	–62.7	–44.2	39.4	.2	49.0
of which: Short-term	4 771	...	...	...	...	...	...	...	...
Banks	4 772	...	...	...	...	...	...	...	...
of which: Short-term	4 774	...	...	...	...	...	...	...	...
Other sectors	4 775	–484.9	–324.5	–122.1	266.0	–130.9	–369.9	–177.7	–187.7
of which: Short-term	4 777	...	...	...	...	...	...	...	...
Currency and deposits	4 780	–26.9	27.4	–34.0	–42.3	16.4	...	...	...
Monetary authorities	4 781	...	...	...	...	...	...	...	...
General government	4 782	...	...	...	...	...	...	...	...
Banks	4 783	–26.9	27.4	–34.0	–42.3	16.4	...	...	...
Other sectors	4 784	...	...	...	...	...	...	...	...
Other liabilities	4 786	–109.0	–246.2	–100.3	–185.7	–162.5	–49.7	–7.7	64.0
Monetary authorities	4 787	...	...	...	...	...	...	...	...
of which: Short-term	4 789	...	...	...	...	...	...	...	...
General government	4 790	...	...	...	...	...	...	...	...
of which: Short-term	4 792	...	...	...	...	...	...	...	...
Banks	4 793	...	...	...	...	...	...	...	...
of which: Short-term	4 795	...	...	...	...	...	...	...	...
Other sectors	4 796	–109.0	–246.2	–100.3	–185.7	–162.5	–49.7	–7.7	64.0
of which: Short-term	4 798	*–109.0*	*–246.2*	*–100.3*	*–185.7*	*–162.5*	*–49.7*	*–7.7*	*64.0*
E. RESERVE ASSETS	4 802	33.8	–177.4	–329.7	83.7	149.1	–49.7	–127.9	–203.6
Monetary gold	4 812	6.7	...	–19.0	...	...	...	...	...
Special drawing rights	4 811	...	–.6	.6	...	...	–.7	–11.8	3.1
Reserve position in the Fund	4 810	...	...	...	...	...	...	–.2	–.2
Foreign exchange	4 803	27.2	–176.8	–311.4	81.7	152.8	–49.0	–115.9	–209.7
Other claims	4 813	...	...	...	2.1	–3.7	...	...	3.2
NET ERRORS AND OMISSIONS	4 998	**37.1**	**–86.6**	**–33.1**	**7.3**	**–12.5**	**14.3**	**13.1**	**–1.6**

Part 3 of the *Yearbook* contains descriptions of the methodologies, compilation practices, and sources used to compile these data.

Table 1. ANALYTIC PRESENTATION, 1994–2001
(Millions of U.S. dollars)

	Code	1994	1995	1996	1997	1998	1999	2000	2001
A. Current Account[1]	4 993 Z.	**-274.1**	**-92.3**	**-352.9**	**-650.4**	**-160.0**	**-165.4**	**-290.5**	**-207.0**
Goods: exports f.o.b.	2 100 . .	3,360.1	4,218.6	3,796.9	3,327.5	3,548.6	2,312.4	2,225.8	2,408.5
Goods: imports f.o.b.	3 100 . .	-3,603.5	-4,489.0	-4,383.4	-4,192.4	-3,941.5	-2,752.9	-2,904.0	-2,954.2
Balance on Goods	4 100 . .	*-243.4*	*-270.4*	*-586.5*	*-864.9*	*-392.9*	*-440.5*	*-678.2*	*-545.7*
Services: credit	2 200 . .	426.2	583.8	600.5	655.0	625.5	575.4	618.5	580.1
Services: debit	3 200 . .	-593.4	-710.7	-658.8	-654.6	-575.9	-493.0	-436.1	-409.7
Balance on Goods and Services	4 991 . .	*-410.6*	*-397.3*	*-644.8*	*-864.5*	*-343.3*	*-358.1*	*-495.8*	*-375.3*
Income: credit	2 300 . .	247.9	272.6	280.9	278.1	266.3	212.5	247.9	218.2
Income: debit	3 300 . .	-134.1	-162.9	-171.2	-244.9	-260.3	-195.0	-219.4	-216.3
Balance on Goods, Services, and Income	4 992 . .	*-296.8*	*-287.6*	*-535.1*	*-831.3*	*-337.3*	*-340.6*	*-467.3*	*-373.4*
Current transfers: credit	2 379 Z.	25.6	199.7	183.0	182.2	178.3	176.7	178.3	168.0
Current transfers: debit	3 379 . .	-2.9	-4.4	-.8	-1.3	-1.0	-1.5	-1.5	-1.6
B. Capital Account[1]	4 994 Z.	**8.8**	**10.6**	**14.2**	**7.5**	**5.4**	**19.6**	**3.0**	**15.2**
Capital account: credit	2 994 Z.	8.8	10.6	14.2	7.5	5.4	19.6	3.0	15.2
Capital account: debit	3 994 . .	...	...	...	...	...	...	...	...
Total, Groups A Plus B	4 981 . .	*-265.3*	*-81.7*	*-338.7*	*-642.9*	*-154.6*	*-145.8*	*-287.5*	*-191.8*
	4 Z.	*8.8*	*10.6*	*14.2*	*7.5*	*5.4*	*19.6*	*3.0*	*15.2*
Capital account: debit	*3 994* . .	...	...	...	...	...	...	...	...
Total, Groups A Plus B	4 981 . .	*-265.3*	*-81.7*	*-338.7*	*-642.9*	*-154.6*	*-145.8*	*-287.5*	*-191.8*
nt assets	*4 602* . .	...	*-.8*	*-3.6*	*-4.3*	*9.0*	*-9.0*	*2.0*	*.4*
Equity securities	*4 610* . .	...	...	...	...	*-.7*	*-6.8*	*1.4*	...
Debt securities	*4 619* . .	...	*-.8*	*-3.6*	*-4.3*	*9.7*	*-2.2*	*.6*	*.4*
Portfolio investment liabilities	*4 652 Z.*	...	...	*-.1*	...	...	...	*.5*	*-.1*
Equity securities	*4 660* . .	...	...	...	...	...	...	...	...
Debt securities	*4 669 Z.*	...	...	*-.1*	...	...	...	*.5*	*-.1*
Financial derivatives	*4 910* . .	...	...	...	...	...	...	...	...
Financial derivatives assets	*4 900* . .	...	...	...	...	...	...	...	...
Financial derivatives liabilities	*4 905* . .	...	...	...	...	...	...	...	...
Other investment assets	*4 703* . .	*-89.8*	*-58.5*	*-31.9*	*72.9*	*-5.0*	*-117.7*	*-209.1*	*190.4*
Monetary authorities	*4 701* . .	*.1*	...	...	...	...	...	...	...
General government	*4 704* . .	*23.1*	*-43.1*	*-59.0*	*-45.8*	*60.7*	*-63.6*	*-81.2*	*78.8*
Banks	*4 705* . .	*-1.5*	*-169.7*	*3.5*	*100.5*	*-42.7*	*-1.9*	*-69.3*	*68.2*
Other sectors	*4 728* . .	*-111.5*	*154.3*	*23.6*	*18.2*	*-23.0*	*-52.2*	*-58.6*	*43.4*
Other investment liabilities	*4 753 W.*	*165.6*	*193.7*	*43.8*	*122.6*	*-27.4*	*127.0*	*121.1*	*13.9*
Monetary authorities	*4 753 WA*	*-1.6*	*-8.7*	*-3.5*	*-5.0*	*-4.3*	*-3.8*	*-3.3*	*-3.6*
General government	*4 753 ZB*	*29.8*	*101.6*	*122.5*	*137.1*	*112.3*	*97.6*	*90.4*	*41.9*
Banks	*4 753 ZC*	*97.3*	*118.6*	*-188.4*	*71.6*	*-50.7*	*-101.5*	*-8.9*	*-30.8*
Other sectors	*4 753 ZD*	*40.1*	*-17.8*	*113.2*	*-81.1*	*-84.7*	*134.7*	*42.9*	*6.4*
Total, Groups A Through C	4 983 . .	*-52.4*	*150.8*	*-186.3*	*-221.6*	*158.3*	*-56.6*	*-260.1*	*86.2*
D. Net Errors and Omissions	4 998 . .	**353.0**	**-106.0**	**139.8**	**5.8**	**-141.6**	**-244.3**	**-79.3**	**-136.4**
Total, Groups A Through D	4 984 . .	*300.6*	*44.8*	*-46.5*	*-215.8*	*16.7*	*-300.9*	*-339.4*	*-50.2*
E. Reserves and Related Items	4 802 A.	**-300.6**	**-44.8**	**46.5**	**215.8**	**-16.7**	**300.9**	**339.4**	**50.2**
Reserve assets	4 802 . .	-339.3	-60.2	39.4	205.8	-23.4	-116.7	210.2	45.4
Use of Fund credit and loans	4 766 . .	...	...	...	...	...	...	...	...
Exceptional financing	4 920 . .	38.7	15.4	7.1	10.0	6.7	417.6	129.2	4.8
Conversion rates: guaranies per U.S. dollar	0 101 . .	**1,904.8**	**1,963.0**	**2,056.8**	**2,177.9**	**2,726.5**	**3,119.1**	**3,486.4**	**4,105.9**

[1] Excludes components that have been classified in the categories of Group E.

Table 2. STANDARD PRESENTATION, 1994–2001
(Millions of U.S. dollars)

	Code	1994	1995	1996	1997	1998	1999	2000	2001
CURRENT ACCOUNT	4 993 . . .	**–274.1**	**–92.3**	**–352.9**	**–650.4**	**–160.0**	**–165.4**	**–290.5**	**–207.0**
A. GOODS	4 100 . .	–243.4	–270.4	–586.5	–864.9	–392.9	–440.5	–678.2	–545.7
Credit	2 100 . .	**3,360.1**	**4,218.6**	**3,796.9**	**3,327.5**	**3,548.6**	**2,312.4**	**2,225.8**	**2,408.5**
General merchandise: exports f.o.b.	2 110 . .	3,359.7	4,217.4	3,793.7	3,324.0	3,544.4	2,307.1	2,219.2	2,401.3
Goods for processing: exports f.o.b.	2 150 . .	. . .	. . .	. . .	. . .	. . .	. . .	. . .	. . .
Repairs on goods	2 160 . .	. . .	. . .	. . .	. . .	. . .	.9	. . .	.4
Goods procured in ports by carriers	2 170 . .	.4	1.2	3.2	3.5	4.2	4.4	6.6	6.8
Nonmonetary gold	2 180 . .	. . .	. . .	. . .	. . .	. . .	. . .	. . .	. . .
Debit	3 100 . .	**–3,603.5**	**–4,489.0**	**–4,383.4**	**–4,192.4**	**–3,941.5**	**–2,752.9**	**–2,904.0**	**–2,954.2**
General merchandise: imports f.o.b.	3 110 . .	–3,602.6	–4,487.3	–4,382.7	–4,191.8	–3,940.8	–2,750.2	–2,901.5	–2,950.6
Goods for processing: imports f.o.b.	3 150 . .	. . .	. . .	. . .	. . .	. . .	. . .	. . .	. . .
Repairs on goods	3 160 . .	. . .	. . .	. . .	. . .	. . .	–.8	–.6	–.8
Goods procured in ports by carriers	3 170 . .	–.9	–1.7	–.7	–.6	–.7	–1.9	–1.9	–2.8
Nonmonetary gold	3 180 . .	. . .	. . .	. . .	. . .	. . .	. . .	. . .	. . .
B. SERVICES	4 200 . .	–167.2	–126.9	–58.3	.4	49.6	82.4	182.4	170.4
Total credit	2 200 . .	*426.2*	*583.8*	*600.5*	*655.0*	*625.5*	*575.4*	*618.5*	*580.1*
Total debit	3 200 . .	*–593.4*	*–710.7*	*–658.8*	*–654.6*	*–575.9*	*–493.0*	*–436.1*	*–409.7*
Transportation services, credit	2 205 . .	**26.2**	**75.1**	**69.9**	**74.8**	**66.0**	**60.8**	**69.4**	**86.9**
Passenger	2 850 . .	*5.3*	*25.2*	*19.1*	*16.6*	*17.1*	*14.2*	*14.9*	*21.6*
Freight	2 851 . .	*17.9*	*44.3*	*44.4*	*48.6*	*39.7*	*37.4*	*45.3*	*55.5*
Other	2 852 . .	*3.0*	*5.6*	*6.4*	*9.6*	*9.2*	*9.2*	*9.2*	*9.8*
Sea transport, passenger	2 207 . .	. . .	. . .	. . .	. . .	. . .	. . .	. . .	. . .
Sea transport, freight	2 208 . .	. . .	. . .	. . .	. . .	. . .	. . .	. . .	. . .
Sea transport, other	2 209 . .	. . .	. . .	. . .	. . .	. . .	. . .	. . .	. . .
Air transport, passenger	2 211 . .	. . .	20.0	13.8	8.2	10.5	9.0	9.0	15.2
Air transport, freight	2 212 . .	. . .	. . .	. . .	. . .	. . .	. . .	1.3	. . .
Air transport, other	2 213 . .	. . .	. . .	. . .	. . .	. . .	. . .	. . .	. . .
Other transport, passenger	2 215 . .	5.3	5.2	5.3	8.4	6.6	5.2	5.9	6.4
Other transport, freight	2 216 . .	17.9	44.3	44.4	48.6	39.7	37.4	44.0	55.5
Other transport, other	2 217 . .	3.0	5.6	6.4	9.6	9.2	9.2	9.2	9.8
Transportation services, debit	3 205 . .	**–389.4**	**–448.7**	**–389.2**	**–397.3**	**–324.4**	**–275.7**	**–236.5**	**–214.0**
Passenger	3 850 . .	*–30.8*	*–40.0*	*–45.9*	*–71.8*	*–80.2*	*–72.2*	*–72.6*	*–58.4*
Freight	3 851 . .	*–357.7*	*–405.4*	*–338.8*	*–320.5*	*–241.3*	*–200.0*	*–160.4*	*–151.2*
Other	3 852 . .	*–.9*	*–3.3*	*–4.5*	*–5.0*	*–2.9*	*–3.5*	*–3.5*	*–4.4*
Sea transport, passenger	3 207 . .	. . .	. . .	. . .	. . .	. . .	. . .	. . .	. . .
Sea transport, freight	3 208 . .	. . .	–162.2	–153.8	–127.2	–93.8	–73.7	–32.2	–43.5
Sea transport, other	3 209 . .	. . .	. . .	. . .	. . .	. . .	. . .	. . .	. . .
Air transport, passenger	3 211 . .	. . .	–34.0	–39.6	–64.3	–72.0	–64.8	–64.8	–50.0
Air transport, freight	3 212 . .	. . .	–60.8	–30.1	–41.8	–42.6	–40.5	–29.7	–21.7
Air transport, other	3 213 . .	. . .	. . .	. . .	. . .	. . .	. . .	. . .	. . .
Other transport, passenger	3 215 . .	–30.8	–6.0	–6.3	–7.5	–8.2	–7.4	–7.8	–8.4
Other transport, freight	3 216 . .	–357.7	–182.4	–154.9	–151.5	–104.9	–85.8	–98.5	–86.0
Other transport, other	3 217 . .	–.9	–3.3	–4.5	–5.0	–2.9	–3.5	–3.5	–4.4
Travel, credit	2 236 . .	**115.9**	**137.3**	**140.0**	**128.3**	**111.4**	**80.8**	**100.6**	**77.2**
Business travel	2 237 . .	. . .	. . .	. . .	. . .	. . .	. . .	. . .	. . .
Personal travel	2 240 . .	115.9	137.3	140.0	128.3	111.4	80.8	100.6	77.2
Travel, debit	3 236 . .	**–112.3**	**–133.3**	**–138.6**	**–139.2**	**–142.5**	**–109.1**	**–96.5**	**–90.8**
Business travel	3 237 . .	. . .	. . .	. . .	. . .	. . .	. . .	. . .	. . .
Personal travel	3 240 . .	–112.3	–133.3	–138.6	–139.2	–142.5	–109.1	–96.5	–90.8
Other services, credit	2 200 BA	**284.1**	**371.4**	**390.6**	**451.9**	**448.1**	**433.8**	**448.5**	**416.0**
Communications	2 245 . .	49.0	15.4	11.0	14.0	10.0	11.5	10.3	11.7
Construction	2 249 . .	. . .	. . .	. . .	. . .	. . .	. . .	. . .	. . .
Insurance	2 253 . .	11.9	18.5	20.6	26.0	20.6	11.7	22.0	22.4
Financial	2 260 . .	1.6	10.0	12.0	19.6	29.9	12.5	6.1	4.7
Computer and information	2 262 . .	.1	.1	.2	.2	.3	.3	.3	.4
Royalties and licence fees	2 266 . .	114.1	139.8	156.6	181.8	182.8	191.6	202.6	180.1
Other business services	2 268 . .	89.7	169.4	170.6	189.2	184.5	185.2	185.0	166.1
Personal, cultural, and recreational	2 287 . .	2.7	. . .	. . .	. . .	. . .	. . .	. . .	. . .
Government, n.i.e.	2 291 . .	15.0	18.2	19.6	21.1	20.0	21.0	22.2	30.6
Other services, debit	3 200 BA	**–91.7**	**–128.7**	**–131.0**	**–118.1**	**–109.0**	**–108.2**	**–103.1**	**–104.9**
Communications	3 245 . .	–.3	–6.8	. . .	. . .	. . .	–.2	–.2	–.4
Construction	3 249 . .	. . .	. . .	. . .	. . .	. . .	. . .	. . .	. . .
Insurance	3 253 . .	–62.1	–80.3	–82.1	–74.8	–63.3	–56.6	–51.4	–52.9
Financial	3 260 . .	–.4	–3.8	–4.4	–5.9	–11.4	–10.4	–5.5	–3.9
Computer and information	3 262 . .	. . .	–.6	–.7	–.8	–.8	–2.0	–.4	–4.9
Royalties and licence fees	3 266 . .	–.1	–1.2	–1.2	–1.6	–2.4	–3.4	–8.2	–7.2
Other business services	3 268 . .	–.3	–1.0	–7.6	–10.0	–4.1	–5.1	–6.9	–7.6
Personal, cultural, and recreational	3 287 . .	–3.8	. . .	. . .	. . .	. . .	. . .	. . .	. . .
Government, n.i.e.	3 291 . .	–24.7	–35.0	–35.0	–25.0	–27.0	–30.5	–30.5	–28.0

Table 2 (Continued). STANDARD PRESENTATION, 1994–2001

(Millions of U.S. dollars)

	Code	1994	1995	1996	1997	1998	1999	2000	2001
C. INCOME	4 300 . .	113.8	109.7	109.7	33.2	6.0	17.5	28.5	1.9
Total credit	2 300 . .	*247.9*	*272.6*	*280.9*	*278.1*	*266.3*	*212.5*	*247.9*	*218.2*
Total debit	3 300 . .	*–134.1*	*–162.9*	*–171.2*	*–244.9*	*–260.3*	*–195.0*	*–219.4*	*–216.3*
Compensation of employees, credit	2 310 . .	**147.9**	**151.9**	**160.4**	**157.4**	**143.4**	**119.5**	**113.2**	**112.0**
Compensation of employees, debit	3 310 . .	**. . .**	**. . .**	**. . .**	**. . .**	**. . .**	**. . .**	**. . .**	**. . .**
Investment income, credit	2 320 . .	**100.0**	**120.7**	**120.5**	**120.7**	**122.9**	**93.0**	**134.7**	**106.2**
Direct investment income	2 330 . .	. . .	11.5	11.9	11.9	12.4	12.1	12.4	23.0
Dividends and distributed branch profits	2 332 . .	. . .	6.4	6.7	6.1	6.0	6.0	6.0	17.0
Reinvested earnings and undistributed branch profits	2 333 . .	. . .	5.1	5.2	5.7	5.6	5.6	5.7	5.8
Income on debt (interest)	2 334 . .	. . .	. . .	. . .	.1	.8	.5	.7	.2
Portfolio investment income	2 339 . .	. . .	. . .	.6	.3	1.1	1.0	.2	. . .
Income on equity	2 340 . .	. . .	. . .	. . .	. . .	. . .	. . .	. . .	. . .
Income on bonds and notes	2 350 . .	. . .	. . .	.6	.3	1.1	1.0	.2	. . .
Income on money market instruments	2 360 . .	. . .	. . .	. . .	. . .	. . .	. . .	. . .	. . .
Other investment income	2 370 . .	100.0	109.2	108.0	108.5	109.4	79.9	122.1	83.2
Investment income, debit	3 320 . .	**–134.1**	**–162.9**	**–171.2**	**–244.9**	**–260.3**	**–195.0**	**–219.4**	**–216.3**
Direct investment income	3 330 . .	–39.2	–62.0	–78.1	–150.4	–178.3	–104.6	–84.3	–88.9
Dividends and distributed branch profits	3 332 . .	–8.9	–20.6	–36.1	–67.9	–80.7	–121.0	–71.0	–91.4
Reinvested earnings and undistributed branch profits	3 333 . .	–22.5	–41.4	–42.0	–82.5	–96.7	19.7	–7.4	4.1
Income on debt (interest)	3 334 . .	–7.8	. . .	. . .	. . .	–.9	–3.3	–5.9	–1.6
Portfolio investment income	3 339 . .	. . .	. . .	–1.3	–4.6	–4.6	–6.4	. . .	. . .
Income on equity	3 340 . .	. . .	. . .	. . .	. . .	. . .	. . .	. . .	. . .
Income on bonds and notes	3 350 . .	. . .	. . .	–1.3	–4.6	–4.6	–6.4	. . .	. . .
Income on money market instruments	3 360 . .	. . .	. . .	. . .	. . .	. . .	. . .	. . .	. . .
Other investment income	3 370 . .	–94.9	–100.9	–91.8	–89.9	–77.4	–84.0	–135.1	–127.4
D. CURRENT TRANSFERS	4 379 . .	22.7	195.3	182.2	180.9	177.3	175.2	176.8	166.4
Credit	2 379 . .	**25.6**	**199.7**	**183.0**	**182.2**	**178.3**	**176.7**	**178.3**	**168.0**
General government	2 380 . .	19.2	60.3	42.2	36.9	30.2	20.9	18.8	20.0
Other sectors	2 390 . .	6.4	139.4	140.8	145.3	148.1	155.8	159.5	148.0
Workers' remittances	2 391 . .	. . .	134.9	136.9	141.2	142.6	148.0	151.7	140.0
Other current transfers	2 392 . .	6.4	4.5	3.9	4.1	5.5	7.8	7.8	8.0
Debit	3 379 . .	**–2.9**	**–4.4**	**–.8**	**–1.3**	**–1.0**	**–1.5**	**–1.5**	**–1.6**
General government	3 380 . .	–2.9	–4.4	–.8	–1.3	–1.0	–1.5	–1.5	–1.6
Other sectors	3 390 . .	. . .	. . .	. . .	. . .	. . .	. . .	. . .	. . .
Workers' remittances	3 391 . .	. . .	. . .	. . .	. . .	. . .	. . .	. . .	. . .
Other current transfers	3 392 . .	. . .	. . .	. . .	. . .	. . .	. . .	. . .	. . .
CAPITAL AND FINANCIAL ACCOUNT	4 996 . .	**–78.9**	**198.3**	**213.1**	**644.6**	**301.6**	**409.7**	**369.8**	**343.4**
CAPITAL ACCOUNT	4 994 . .	**8.8**	**10.6**	**14.2**	**7.5**	**5.4**	**19.6**	**3.0**	**15.2**
Total credit	2 994 . .	*8.8*	*10.6*	*14.2*	*7.5*	*5.4*	*19.6*	*3.0*	*15.2*
Total debit	3 994 . .	. . .	. . .	. . .	. . .	. . .	. . .	. . .	. . .
Capital transfers, credit	2 400 . .	**8.8**	**10.6**	**14.2**	**7.5**	**5.4**	**19.6**	**3.0**	**15.2**
General government	2 401 . .	5.6	10.6	14.2	7.5	5.4	19.6	3.0	15.2
Debt forgiveness	2 402 . .	. . .	. . .	. . .	. . .	. . .	. . .	. . .	. . .
Other capital transfers	2 410 . .	5.6	10.6	14.2	7.5	5.4	19.6	3.0	15.2
Other sectors	2 430 . .	3.2	. . .	. . .	. . .	. . .	. . .	. . .	. . .
Migrants' transfers	2 431 . .	. . .	. . .	. . .	. . .	. . .	. . .	. . .	. . .
Debt forgiveness	2 432 . .	. . .	. . .	. . .	. . .	. . .	. . .	. . .	. . .
Other capital transfers	2 440 . .	3.2	. . .	. . .	. . .	. . .	. . .	. . .	. . .
Capital transfers, debit	3 400 . .	**. . .**	**. . .**	**. . .**	**. . .**	**. . .**	**. . .**	**. . .**	**. . .**
General government	3 401 . .	. . .	. . .	. . .	. . .	. . .	. . .	. . .	. . .
Debt forgiveness	3 402 . .	. . .	. . .	. . .	. . .	. . .	. . .	. . .	. . .
Other capital transfers	3 410 . .	. . .	. . .	. . .	. . .	. . .	. . .	. . .	. . .
Other sectors	3 430 . .	. . .	. . .	. . .	. . .	. . .	. . .	. . .	. . .
Migrants' transfers	3 431 . .	. . .	. . .	. . .	. . .	. . .	. . .	. . .	. . .
Debt forgiveness	3 432 . .	. . .	. . .	. . .	. . .	. . .	. . .	. . .	. . .
Other capital transfers	3 440 . .	. . .	. . .	. . .	. . .	. . .	. . .	. . .	. . .
Nonproduced nonfinancial assets, credit	2 480 . .	**. . .**	**. . .**	**. . .**	**. . .**	**. . .**	**. . .**	**. . .**	**. . .**
Nonproduced nonfinancial assets, debit	3 480 . .	**. . .**	**. . .**	**. . .**	**. . .**	**. . .**	**. . .**	**. . .**	**. . .**

Table 2 (Continued). STANDARD PRESENTATION, 1994–2001

(Millions of U.S. dollars)

	Code	1994	1995	1996	1997	1998	1999	2000	2001
FINANCIAL ACCOUNT	4 995	**–87.7**	**187.7**	**198.9**	**637.1**	**296.2**	**390.1**	**366.8**	**328.2**
A. DIRECT INVESTMENT	4 500	137.1	98.1	144.2	230.1	336.3	88.9	112.9	73.4
Direct investment abroad	4 505	**. . .**	**–5.1**	**–5.2**	**–5.7**	**–5.6**	**–5.6**	**–5.7**	**–5.8**
Equity capital	4 510	. . .	. . .	. . .	. . .	. . .	. . .	. . .	. . .
Claims on affiliated enterprises	4 515	. . .	. . .	. . .	. . .	. . .	. . .	. . .	. . .
Liabilities to affiliated enterprises	4 520	. . .	. . .	. . .	. . .	. . .	. . .	. . .	. . .
Reinvested earnings	4 525	. . .	–5.1	–5.2	–5.7	–5.6	–5.6	–5.7	–5.8
Other capital	4 530	. . .	. . .	. . .	. . .	. . .	. . .	. . .	. . .
Claims on affiliated enterprises	4 535	. . .	. . .	. . .	. . .	. . .	. . .	. . .	. . .
Liabilities to affiliated enterprises	4 540	. . .	. . .	. . .	. . .	. . .	. . .	. . .	. . .
Direct investment in Paraguay	4 555	**137.1**	**103.2**	**149.4**	**235.8**	**341.9**	**94.5**	**118.6**	**79.2**
Equity capital	4 560	97.9	61.8	99.6	121.7	133.6	89.5	119.5	119.7
Claims on direct investors	4 565	. . .	. . .	. . .	. . .	. . .	. . .	. . .	. . .
Liabilities to direct investors	4 570	97.9	61.8	99.6	121.7	133.6	89.5	119.5	119.7
Reinvested earnings	4 575	22.5	41.4	42.0	82.5	96.7	–19.7	7.4	–4.1
Other capital	4 580	16.7	. . .	7.8	31.6	111.6	24.7	–8.3	–36.4
Claims on direct investors	4 585	. . .	. . .	–.3	–5.2	–7.4	–.5	–9.9	–23.2
Liabilities to direct investors	4 590	16.7	. . .	8.1	36.8	119.0	25.2	1.6	–13.2
B. PORTFOLIO INVESTMENT	4 600	. . .	–.8	–3.7	–4.3	9.0	–9.0	2.5	.3
Assets	4 602	**. . .**	**–.8**	**–3.6**	**–4.3**	**9.0**	**–9.0**	**2.0**	**.4**
Equity securities	4 610	. . .	. . .	. . .	. . .	–.7	–6.8	1.4	. . .
Monetary authorities	4 611	. . .	. . .	. . .	. . .	. . .	. . .	. . .	. . .
General government	4 612	. . .	. . .	. . .	. . .	. . .	. . .	. . .	. . .
Banks	4 613	. . .	. . .	. . .	. . .	. . .	. . .	. . .	. . .
Other sectors	4 614	. . .	. . .	. . .	. . .	–.7	–6.8	1.4	. . .
Debt securities	4 619	. . .	–.8	–3.6	–4.3	9.7	–2.2	.6	.4
Bonds and notes	4 620	. . .	–.8	–3.6	–4.3	9.7	–2.2	.6	.4
Monetary authorities	4 621	. . .	. . .	. . .	. . .	. . .	. . .	. . .	. . .
General government	4 622	. . .	. . .	. . .	. . .	. . .	. . .	. . .	. . .
Banks	4 623	. . .	–.8	–3.6	–4.3	10.8	–2.2	2.2	. . .
Other sectors	4 624	. . .	. . .	. . .	. . .	–1.1	. . .	–1.6	.4
Money market instruments	4 630	. . .	. . .	. . .	. . .	. . .	. . .	. . .	. . .
Monetary authorities	4 631	. . .	. . .	. . .	. . .	. . .	. . .	. . .	. . .
General government	4 632	. . .	. . .	. . .	. . .	. . .	. . .	. . .	. . .
Banks	4 633	. . .	. . .	. . .	. . .	. . .	. . .	. . .	. . .
Other sectors	4 634	. . .	. . .	. . .	. . .	. . .	. . .	. . .	. . .
Liabilities	4 652	**. . .**	**. . .**	**–.1**	**. . .**	**. . .**	**. . .**	**.5**	**–.1**
Equity securities	4 660	. . .	. . .	. . .	. . .	. . .	. . .	. . .	. . .
Banks	4 663	. . .	. . .	. . .	. . .	. . .	. . .	. . .	. . .
Other sectors	4 664	. . .	. . .	. . .	. . .	. . .	. . .	. . .	. . .
Debt securities	4 669	. . .	. . .	–.1	. . .	. . .	. . .	.5	–.1
Bonds and notes	4 670	. . .	. . .	–.1	. . .	. . .	. . .	.5	–.1
Monetary authorities	4 671	. . .	. . .	. . .	. . .	. . .	. . .	. . .	. . .
General government	4 672	. . .	. . .	. . .	. . .	. . .	. . .	. . .	. . .
Banks	4 673	. . .	. . .	–.1	. . .	. . .	. . .	. . .	. . .
Other sectors	4 674	. . .	. . .	. . .	. . .	. . .	. . .	.5	–.1
Money market instruments	4 680	. . .	. . .	. . .	. . .	. . .	. . .	. . .	. . .
Monetary authorities	4 681	. . .	. . .	. . .	. . .	. . .	. . .	. . .	. . .
General government	4 682	. . .	. . .	. . .	. . .	. . .	. . .	. . .	. . .
Banks	4 683	. . .	. . .	. . .	. . .	. . .	. . .	. . .	. . .
Other sectors	4 684	. . .	. . .	. . .	. . .	. . .	. . .	. . .	. . .
C. FINANCIAL DERIVATIVES	4 910	. . .	. . .	. . .	. . .	. . .	. . .	. . .	. . .
Monetary authorities	4 911	. . .	. . .	. . .	. . .	. . .	. . .	. . .	. . .
General government	4 912	. . .	. . .	. . .	. . .	. . .	. . .	. . .	. . .
Banks	4 913	. . .	. . .	. . .	. . .	. . .	. . .	. . .	. . .
Other sectors	4 914	. . .	. . .	. . .	. . .	. . .	. . .	. . .	. . .
Assets	4 900	**. . .**	**. . .**	**. . .**	**. . .**	**. . .**	**. . .**	**. . .**	**. . .**
Monetary authorities	4 901	. . .	. . .	. . .	. . .	. . .	. . .	. . .	. . .
General government	4 902	. . .	. . .	. . .	. . .	. . .	. . .	. . .	. . .
Banks	4 903	. . .	. . .	. . .	. . .	. . .	. . .	. . .	. . .
Other sectors	4 904	. . .	. . .	. . .	. . .	. . .	. . .	. . .	. . .
Liabilities	4 905	**. . .**	**. . .**	**. . .**	**. . .**	**. . .**	**. . .**	**. . .**	**. . .**
Monetary authorities	4 906	. . .	. . .	. . .	. . .	. . .	. . .	. . .	. . .
General government	4 907	. . .	. . .	. . .	. . .	. . .	. . .	. . .	. . .
Banks	4 908	. . .	. . .	. . .	. . .	. . .	. . .	. . .	. . .
Other sectors	4 909	. . .	. . .	. . .	. . .	. . .	. . .	. . .	. . .

Table 2 (Concluded). STANDARD PRESENTATION, 1994–2001
(Millions of U.S. dollars)

	Code	1994	1995	1996	1997	1998	1999	2000	2001
D. OTHER INVESTMENT	4 700 . .	114.5	150.6	19.0	205.5	–25.7	426.9	41.2	209.1
Assets	4								. . .
of which: Short-term	4 709 . .	*30.7*	. . .	. . .	. . .	. . .	. . .	. . .	. . .
Other sectors	4 710 . .	. . .	. . .	–7.0	25.1	–10.9	11.4	–21.7	15.3
of which: Short-term	4 712 . .	. . .	. . .	*–7.0*	*25.1*	*–10.9*	*11.4*	*–21.7*	*15.3*
Loans	4 714 . .	. . .	–62.3	–148.5	64.8	19.0	–138.0	–235.9	1.2
Monetary authorities	4 715 . .	. . .	. . .	. . .	. . .	. . .	. . .	. . .	. . .
of which: Short-term	4 718 . .	. . .	. . .	. . .	. . .	. . .	. . .	. . .	. . .
General government	4 719 . .	. . .	–13.0	–21.4	–27.5	–7.3	–32.3	–34.9	–29.6
of which: Short-term	4 721 . .	. . .	. . .	. . .	. . .	. . .	. . .	. . .	. . .
Banks	4 722 . .	. . .	–48.7	–126.1	93.8	28.0	–34.3	–176.0	40.2
of which: Short-term	4 724 . .	. . .	*–48.7*	*–126.1*	*93.8*	*28.0*	*–34.3*	*–176.0*	*40.2*
Other sectors	4 725 . .	. . .	–.6	–1.0	–1.5	–1.7	–71.4	–25.0	–9.4
of which: Short-term	4 727 . .	. . .	. . .	. . .	. . .	. . .	*–.5*	*–.5*	*–2.6*
Currency and deposits	4 730 . .	–101.5	47.6	193.8	–16.0	–97.1	48.0	100.2	43.7
Monetary authorities	4 731 . .	. . .	. . .	. . .	. . .	. . .	. . .	. . .	. . .
General government	4 732 . .	. . .	. . .	. . .	. . .	. . .	. . .	. . .	. . .
Banks	4 733 . .	10.0	–118.4	151.2	20.0	–91.7	40.5	101.7	14.7
Other sectors	4 734 . .	–111.5	166.0	42.6	–36.0	–5.4	7.5	–1.5	29.0
Other assets	4 736 . .	–11.4	–43.8	–70.2	–1.0	84.0	–39.1	–51.7	130.2
Monetary authorities	4 737 . .	.1	. . .	. . .	. . .	. . .	. . .	. . .	. . .
of which: Short-term	4 739 . .	. . .	. . .	. . .	. . .	. . .	. . .	. . .	. . .
General government	4 740 . .	. . .	–30.1	–37.6	–18.3	68.0	–31.3	–46.3	108.4
of which: Short-term	4 742 . .	. . .	*–30.1*	*–37.6*	*–18.3*	*68.0*	*–31.3*	*–46.3*	*108.4*
Banks	4 743 . .	–11.5	–2.6	–21.6	–13.3	21.0	–8.1	5.0	13.3
of which: Short-term	4 745 . .	*–11.5*	*–2.6*	*–21.6*	*–13.3*	*21.0*	*–8.1*	*5.0*	*13.3*
Other sectors	4 746 . .	. . .	–11.1	–11.0	30.6	–5.0	.3	–10.4	8.5
of which: Short-term	4 748 . .	. . .	*–10.1*	*–11.4*	*30.9*	*–4.9*	*–.9*	*–9.6*	*7.3*
Liabilities	4 753 . .	**204.3**	**209.1**	**50.9**	**132.6**	**–20.7**	**544.6**	**250.3**	**18.7**
Trade credits	4 756 . .	. . .	25.2	153.6	–114.2	–79.3	89.6	70.5	13.7
General government	4 757 . .	. . .	. . .	. . .	. . .	. . .	. . .	. . .	. . .
of which: Short-term	4 759 . .	. . .	. . .	. . .	. . .	. . .	. . .	. . .	. . .
Other sectors	4 760 . .	. . .	25.2	153.6	–114.2	–79.3	89.6	70.5	13.7
of which: Short-term	4 762 . .	. . .	*25.2*	*153.6*	*–114.2*	*–79.3*	*89.6*	*70.5*	*13.7*
Loans	4 764 . .	33.6	77.9	74.1	165.0	126.2	501.9	143.5	19.5
Monetary authorities	4 765 . .	–3.4	–3.3	–3.3	–3.3	–3.3	–3.4	–3.4	–3.2
of which: Use of Fund credit and loans from the Fund	4 766 . .	. . .	. . .	. . .	. . .	. . .	. . .	. . .	. . .
of which: Short-term	4 768 . .	. . .	. . .	. . .	. . .	. . .	*–.1*	*–.1*	. . .
General government	4 769 . .	29.8	101.6	122.5	137.1	112.3	497.6	180.4	41.9
of which: Short-term	4 771 . .	*–.6*	. . .	. . .	. . .	. . .	. . .	. . .	. . .
Banks	4 772 . .	32.8	17.2	–10.8	6.1	14.0	–45.0	–7.2	–10.5
of which: Short-term	4 774 . .	*35.8*	*19.4*	*–8.9*	*8.7*	*15.3*	*–43.7*	*–6.0*	*–9.3*
Other sectors	4 775 . .	–25.6	–37.6	–34.3	25.1	3.2	52.7	–26.3	–8.7
of which: Short-term	4 777 . .	*–16.3*	*5.6*	. . .	*–.1*	*9.9*	*3.8*	*14.5*	*–1.0*
Currency and deposits	4 780 . .	21.0	83.6	–206.7	22.0	–.2	–55.4	–12.4	9.9
Monetary authorities	4 781 . .	. . .	. . .	. . .	. . .	. . .	. . .	. . .	. . .
General government	4 782 . .	. . .	. . .	. . .	. . .	. . .	. . .	. . .	. . .
Banks	4 783 . .	21.0	84.2	–202.1	13.1	7.6	–51.5	–12.4	10.0
Other sectors	4 784 . .	. . .	–.6	–4.6	8.9	–7.8	–3.9	. . .	–.1
Other liabilities	4 786 . .	149.7	22.4	29.9	59.8	–67.4	8.5	48.7	–24.4
Monetary authorities	4 787 . .	1.8	–5.4	–.2	–1.7	–1.0	–.4	.1	–.4
of which: Short-term	4 789 . .	*1.8*	*–5.4*	*–.2*	*–1.7*	*–1.0*	*–.4*	*.1*	*–.4*
General government	4 790 . .	2.0	9.1	4.8	3.1	3.4	15.9	33.0	3.3
of which: Short-term	4 792 . .	*2.0*	*9.1*	*4.8*	*3.1*	*3.4*	*15.9*	*33.0*	*3.3*
Banks	4 793 . .	43.5	17.2	24.5	52.4	–72.0	–5.4	10.9	–30.3
of which: Short-term	4 795 . .	*43.5*	*17.2*	*24.5*	*52.4*	*–72.0*	*–5.4*	*10.9*	*–30.3*
Other sectors	4 796 . .	102.4	1.5	.8	6.0	2.2	–1.6	4.7	3.0
of which: Short-term	4 798 . .	*102.5*	*–.7*	*2.3*	*6.9*	*3.0*	*–.6*	*5.7*	*1.8*
E. RESERVE ASSETS	4 802 . .	–339.3	–60.2	39.4	205.8	–23.4	–116.7	210.2	45.4
Monetary gold	4 812 . .	.3	. . .	. . .	. . .	. . .	. . .	. . .	. . .
Special drawing rights	4 811 . .	–3.7	–4.5	–4.0	–3.8	–4.1	6.0	–4.8	–3.6
Reserve position in the Fund	4 810 . .	2.8	. . .	. . .	. . .	. . .	–9.6	. . .	. . .
Foreign exchange	4 803 . .	–378.0	–4.0	157.3	170.4	–70.0	–162.2	177.4	49.1
Other claims	4 813 . .	39.3	–51.7	–113.9	39.2	50.7	49.1	37.6	–.1
NET ERRORS AND OMISSIONS	4 998 . .	**353.0**	**–106.0**	**139.8**	**5.8**	**–141.6**	**–244.3**	**–79.3**	**–136.4**

Part 3 of the *Yearbook* contains descriptions of the methodologies, compilation practices, and sources used to compile these data.

Table 3. INTERNATIONAL INVESTMENT POSITION (End–period stocks), 1994–2001

(Millions of U.S. dollars)

	Code	1994	1995	1996	1997	1998	1999	2000	2001
ASSETS	8 995 C.	...	2,569.4	2,566.7	2,284.6	2,311.9	2,576.7	2,596.5	2,375.6
Direct investment abroad	8 505 . .	**...**	**178.6**	**186.0**	**194.1**	**201.3**	**208.2**	**213.9**	**219.7**
Equity capital and reinvested earnings	8 506 . .	...	178.6	186.0	194.1	201.3	208.2	213.9	219.7
Claims on affiliated enterprises	8 507 . .	...	178.6	186.0	194.1	201.3	208.2	213.9	219.7
Liabilities to affiliated enterprises	8 508 . .	...	...	...	...	...	...	...	...
Other capital	8 530 . .	...	...	...	...	...	...	...	...
Claims on affiliated enterprises	8 535 . .	...	...	...	...	...	...	...	...
Liabilities to affiliated enterprises	8 540 . .	...	...	...	...	...	...	...	...
Portfolio investment	8 602 . .	**...**	**6.3**	**9.9**	**14.2**	**8.9**	**20.1**	**11.9**	**11.0**
Equity securities	8 610 . .	...	3.4	3.4	3.4	7.8	16.8	10.3	10.3
Monetary authorities	8 611 . .	...	3.4	3.4	3.4	7.1	9.8	9.8	9.8
General government	8 612 . .	...	...	...	...	...	...	...	...
Banks	8 613 . .	...	...	...	...	...	...	...	...
Other sectors	8 614 . .	...	...	...	...	.7	7.0	.5	.5
Debt securities	8 619 . .	...	2.9	6.5	10.8	1.1	3.3	1.6	.7
Bonds and notes	8 620 . .	...	2.9	6.5	10.8	1.1	3.3	1.6	.7
Monetary authorities	8 621 . .	...	...	...	...	...	...	...	...
General government	8 622 . .	...	...	...	...	...	...	...	...
Banks	8 623 . .	...	2.9	6.5	10.8	...	2.2	...	...
Other sectors	8 624 . .	...	...	...	...	1.1	1.1	1.6	.7
Money market instruments	8 630 . .	...	...	...	...	...	...	...	...
Monetary authorities	8 631 . .	...	...	...	...	...	...	...	...
General government	8 632 . .	...	...	...	...	...	...	...	...
Banks	8 633 . .	...	...	...	...	...	...	...	...
Other sectors	8 634 . .	...	...	...	...	...	...	...	...
Financial derivatives	8 900 . .	**...**	**...**	**...**	**...**	**...**	**...**	**...**	**...**
Monetary authorities	8 901 . .	...	...	...	...	...	...	...	...
General government	8 902 . .	...	...	...	...	...	...	...	...
Banks	8 903 . .	...	...	...	...	...	...	...	...
Other sectors	8 904 . .	...	...	...	...	...	...	...	...
Other investment	8 703 . .	**...**	**1,278.1**	**1,308.5**	**1,230.5**	**1,226.9**	**1,360.2**	**1,598.9**	**1,422.9**
Trade credits	8 706 . .	...	36.3	42.4	16.5	25.8	12.8	59.7	33.1
General government	8 707 . .	...	...	...	...	...	...	...	...
of which: Short-term	8 709 . .	...	...	...	...	...	...	...	...
Other sectors	8 710 . .	...	36.3	42.4	16.5	25.8	12.8	59.7	33.1
of which: Short-term	8 712 . .	...	*36.3*	*42.4*	*16.5*	*25.8*	*12.8*	*59.7*	*33.1*
Loans	8 714 . .	...	301.8	450.3	385.5	366.6	502.7	732.2	728.2
Monetary authorities	8 715 . .	...	...	...	...	...	...	...	...
of which: Short-term	8 718 . .	...	...	...	...	...	...	...	...
General government	8 719 . .	...	154.3	175.7	203.2	210.6	242.9	277.8	307.4
of which: Short-term	8 721 . .	...	...	...	...	...	...	...	...
Banks	8 722 . .	...	146.8	272.9	179.1	151.1	185.4	361.3	321.1
of which: Short-term	8 724 . .	...	*146.8*	*272.9*	*179.1*	*151.1*	*185.4*	*361.3*	*321.1*
Other sectors	8 725 . .	...	.7	1.7	3.2	4.9	74.4	93.1	99.7
of which: Short-term	8 727 . .	...	...	...	...	...	*.8*	*1.3*	*3.9*
Currency and deposits	8 730 . .	...	858.9	664.9	679.4	773.8	745.8	676.8	628.0
Monetary authorities	8 731 . .	...	...	...	...	...	...	...	...
General government	8 732 . .	...	...	...	...	...	...	...	...
Banks	8 733 . .	...	356.9	205.6	185.6	277.4	236.8	135.0	120.4
Other sectors	8 734 . .	...	502.0	459.3	493.8	496.4	509.0	541.8	507.6
Other assets	8 736 . .	...	81.1	150.9	149.1	60.7	98.9	130.2	33.6
Monetary authorities	8 737 . .	...	...	...	...	...	...	...	...
of which: Short-term	8 739 . .	...	...	...	...	...	...	...	...
General government	8 740 . .	...	34.0	71.6	89.9	22.0	53.3	99.6	25.3
of which: Short-term	8 742 . .	...	*34.0*	*71.6*	*89.9*	*22.0*	*53.3*	*99.6*	*25.3*
Banks	8 743 . .	...	7.9	29.1	39.5	14.0	21.2	16.5	3.1
of which: Short-term	8 745 . .	...	*7.9*	*29.1*	*39.5*	*14.0*	*21.2*	*16.5*	*3.1*
Other sectors	8 746 . .	...	39.2	50.2	19.7	24.7	24.4	14.1	5.2
of which: Short-term	8 748 . .	...	*36.3*	*47.7*	*16.9*	*21.8*	*22.7*	*11.6*	*3.9*
Reserve assets	8 802 . .	**...**	**1,106.4**	**1,062.3**	**845.8**	**874.8**	**988.2**	**771.8**	**722.0**
Monetary gold	8 812 . .	...	13.5	12.9	10.1	10.0	10.1	9.6	9.7
Special drawing rights	8 811 . .	98.7	104.9	105.4	102.7	111.4	102.7	102.3	102.2
Reserve position in the Fund	8 810 . .	21.2	21.6	20.9	19.6	20.5	29.5	28.0	27.0
Foreign exchange	8 803 . .	...	900.1	742.8	572.4	642.4	804.6	626.9	577.3
Other claims	8 813 . .	...	66.3	180.3	141.0	90.5	41.3	5.1	5.8

Table 3 (Concluded). INTERNATIONAL INVESTMENT POSITION (End–period stocks), 1994–2001
(Millions of U.S. dollars)

	Code	1994	1995	1996	1997	1998	1999	2000	2001
LIABILITIES	8 995 D.	...	2,877.1	2,954.2	3,132.1	3,385.5	3,982.3	4,340.1	4,075.2
Direct investment in Paraguay	8 555 . .	**...**	**705.2**	**829.3**	**977.7**	**1,196.1**	**1,215.7**	**1,311.2**	**1,141.6**
Equity capital and reinvested earnings	8 556 . .	...	637.7	758.4	885.1	1,011.5	1,006.1	1,142.2	1,023.9
Claims on direct investors	8 557 . .	...	...	...	...	...	...	...	...
Liabilities to direct investors	8 558 . .	...	637.7	758.4	885.1	1,011.5	1,006.1	1,142.2	1,023.9
Other capital	8 580 . .	...	67.5	70.9	92.6	184.6	209.6	169.0	117.7
Claims on direct investors	8 585 . .	...	...	–.3	–5.0	–11.5	–19.7	–51.4	–68.3
Liabilities to direct investors	8 590 . .	...	67.5	71.2	97.6	196.1	229.3	220.4	186.0
Portfolio investment	8 652 . .	**...**	**.1**	**...**	**...**	**...**	**...**	**.5**	**.4**
Equity securities	8 660 . .	...	...	...	...	...	...	...	...
Banks	8 663 . .	...	...	...	...	...	...	...	...
Other sectors	8 664 . .	...	...	...	...	...	...	...	...
Debt securities	8 669 . .	...	.1	...	...	...	...	.5	.4
Bonds and notes	8 670 . .	...	.1	...	...	...	...	.5	.4
Monetary authorities	8 671 . .	...	...	...	...	...	...	...	...
General government	8 672 . .	...	...	...	...	...	...	...	...
Banks	8 673 . .	...	.1	...	...	...	...	...	...
Other sectors	8 674 . .	...	...	...	...	...	...	.5	.4
Money market instruments	8 680 . .	...	...	...	...	...	...	...	...
Monetary authorities	8 681 . .	...	...	...	...	...	...	...	...
General government	8 682 . .	...	...	...	...	...	...	...	...
Banks	8 683 . .	...	...	...	...	...	...	...	...
Other sectors	8 684 . .	...	...	...	...	...	...	...	...
Financial derivatives	8 905 . .	**...**	**...**	**...**	**...**	**...**	**...**	**...**	**...**
Monetary authorities	8 906 . .	...	...	...	...	...	...	...	...
General government	8 907 . .	...	...	...	...	...	...	...	...
Banks	8 908 . .	...	...	...	...	...	...	...	...
Other sectors	8 909 . .	...	...	...	...	...	...	...	...
Other investment	8 753 . .	**...**	**2,171.8**	**2,124.9**	**2,154.4**	**2,189.4**	**2,766.6**	**3,028.4**	**2,933.2**
Trade credits	8 756 . .	...	230.1	382.6	237.6	156.3	255.2	412.5	415.6
General government	8 757 . .	...	...	...	...	...	...	...	...
of which: Short-term	8 759 . .	...	...	...	...	...	...	...	...
Other sectors	8 760 . .	...	230.1	382.6	237.6	156.3	255.2	412.5	415.6
of which: Short-term	8 762 . .	...	*230.1*	*382.6*	*237.6*	*156.3*	*255.2*	*412.5*	*415.6*
Loans	8 764 . .	...	1,537.5	1,515.2	1,608.4	1,792.9	2,311.3	2,393.5	2,331.0
Monetary authorities	8 765 . .	...	47.1	43.8	40.5	37.2	33.9	30.5	27.3
of which: Use of Fund credit and loans from the Fund	8 766 . .	...	...	...	...	...	...	...	...
of which: Short-term	8 768 . .	...	...	...	...	...	...	...	...
General government	8 769 . .	...	995.5	1,041.2	1,129.3	1,297.7	1,818.0	1,941.4	1,922.9
of which: Short-term	8 771 . .	...	...	...	...	...	...	...	...
Banks	8 772 . .	...	83.1	72.4	78.7	92.8	47.6	40.4	30.2
of which: Short-term	8 774 . .	...	*61.8*	*52.9*	*61.6*	*77.0*	*33.3*	*27.3*	*18.4*
Other sectors	8 775 . .	...	411.8	357.8	359.9	365.2	411.8	381.2	350.6
of which: Short-term	8 777 . .	...	...	...	...	*9.5*	*17.8*	*31.0*	*26.9*
Currency and deposits	8 780 . .	...	280.4	73.6	95.5	95.0	42.0	23.0	32.8
Monetary authorities	8 781 . .	...	...	...	...	...	...	...	...
General government	8 782 . .	...	...	...	...	...	...	...	...
Banks	8 783 . .	...	268.5	66.3	79.3	86.6	35.1	22.6	32.4
Other sectors	8 784 . .	...	11.9	7.3	16.2	8.4	6.9	.4	.4
Other liabilities	8 786 . .	...	123.8	153.5	212.9	145.2	158.1	199.4	153.8
Monetary authorities	8 787 . .	...	3.7	3.5	1.8	.8	.4	2.2	3.6
of which: Short-term	8 789 . .	...	*3.7*	*3.5*	*1.8*	*.8*	*.4*	*2.2*	*3.6*
General government	8 790 . .	...	9.1	13.6	16.7	20.4	36.3	60.4	40.7
of which: Short-term	8 792 . .	...	*9.1*	*13.6*	*16.7*	*20.4*	*36.3*	*60.4*	*40.7*
Banks	8 793 . .	...	54.9	79.4	131.5	59.0	53.9	64.6	34.4
of which: Short-term	8 795 . .	...	*54.9*	*79.4*	*131.5*	*59.0*	*53.8*	*64.5*	*34.3*
Other sectors	8 796 . .	...	56.1	57.0	62.9	65.0	67.5	72.2	75.1
of which: Short-term	8 798 . .	...	*46.0*	*48.4*	*55.2*	*58.1*	*61.5*	*67.2*	*69.1*
NET INTERNATIONAL INVESTMENT POSITION	8 995 . .	**...**	**–307.7**	**–387.5**	**–847.5**	**–1,073.6**	**–1,405.6**	**–1,743.6**	**–1,699.6**
Conversion rates: guaranies per U.S. dollar (end of period)	0 102 . .	**1,924.7**	**1,979.7**	**2,109.7**	**2,360.0**	**2,840.2**	**3,328.9**	**3,526.9**	**4,682.0**

Table 1. ANALYTIC PRESENTATION, 1994–2001
(Millions of U.S. dollars)

	Code	1994	1995	1996	1997	1998	1999	2000	2001
A. Current Account [1]	4 993 Z.	**–2,741**	**–4,618**	**–3,681**	**–3,413**	**–3,357**	**–1,483**	**–1,568**	**–1,098**
Goods: exports f.o.b	2 100 . .	4,597	5,587	5,898	6,831	5,757	6,116	7,033	7,106
Goods: imports f.o.b	3 100 . .	–5,595	–7,755	–7,884	–8,554	–8,219	–6,748	–7,350	–7,198
Balance on Goods	4 100 . .	*–998*	*–2,168*	*–1,986*	*–1,723*	*–2,462*	*–632*	*–317*	*–92*
Services: credit	2 200 . .	1,063	1,131	1,413	1,555	1,773	1,589	1,578	1,491
Services: debit	3 200 . .	–1,565	–1,879	–2,086	–2,342	–2,434	–2,258	–2,374	–2,291
Balance on Goods and Services	4 991 . .	*–1,500*	*–2,916*	*–2,659*	*–2,510*	*–3,123*	*–1,301*	*–1,113*	*–892*
Income: credit	2 300 . .	338	574	612	726	785	650	739	634
Income: debit	3 300 . .	–2,330	–3,085	–2,524	–2,550	–1,997	–1,798	–2,190	–1,837
Balance on Goods, Services, and Income	4 992 . .	*–3,492*	*–5,427*	*–4,571*	*–4,334*	*–4,335*	*–2,449*	*–2,564*	*–2,095*
Current transfers: credit	2 379 Z.	758	814	898	929	989	993	1,004	1,006
Current transfers: debit	3 379 . .	–7	–5	–8	–8	–11	–27	–8	–9
B. Capital Account [1]	4 994 Z.	**–57**	**33**	**23**	**–49**	**–57**	**–54**	**–68**	**–67**
Capital account: credit	2 994 Z.	32	66	52	25	21	25	24	32
Capital account: debit	3 994 . .	–89	–33	–29	–74	–78	–79	–92	–99
Total, Groups A Plus B	4 981 . .	*–2,798*	*–4,585*	*–3,658*	*–3,462*	*–3,414*	*–1,537*	*–1,636*	*–1,165*
C. Financial Account [1]	4 995 W.	**4,200**	**3,510**	**3,640**	**5,867**	**1,832**	**532**	**879**	**1,031**
Direct investment abroad	4 505 . .	. . .	–8	16	–84	–64	–128	. . .	. . .
Direct investment in Peru	4 555 Z.	3,289	2,558	3,471	2,140	1,644	1,939	662	1,064
Portfolio investment assets	4 602 . .	–55	–5	–105	–251	–137	–228	–539	–298
Equity securities	4 610 . .	–31	13	–90	–91	–133	–172	–375	–265
Debt securities	4 619 . .	–24	–18	–15	–160	–4	–56	–164	–33
Portfolio investment liabilities	4 652 Z.	548	163	288	407	–224	–125	75	–6
Equity securities	4 660 . .	465	171	295	157	–346	–107	123	42
Debt securities	4 669 Z.	83	–8	–7	250	122	–18	–48	–48
Financial derivatives	4 910 . .	. . .	. . .	. . .	. . .	. . .	. . .	. . .	. . .
Financial derivatives assets	4 900 . .	. . .	. . .	. . .	. . .	. . .	. . .	. . .	. . .
Financial derivatives liabilities	4 905 . .	. . .	. . .	. . .	. . .	. . .	. . .	. . .	. . .
Other investment assets	4 703 . .	–264	–576	–666	560	65	130	198	66
Monetary authorities	4 701 . .	–2	–5	–32	–104	20	–6	–34	–15
General government	4 704 . .	. . .	. . .	. . .	. . .	. . .	. . .	. . .	. . .
Banks	4 705 . .	–272	–428	–463	869	24	–101	233	48
Other sectors	4 728 . .	10	–143	–171	–205	21	237	–1	33
Other investment liabilities	4 753 W.	682	1,378	636	3,095	548	–1,056	483	205
Monetary authorities	4 753 WA	37	–23	–87	–8	–38	–33	24	–10
General government	4 753 ZB	98	–213	–438	713	–22	–71	666	549
Banks	4 753 ZC	–247	801	223	1,667	–223	–1,001	–245	–466
Other sectors	4 753 ZD	794	813	938	723	831	49	38	132
Total, Groups A Through C	4 983 . .	*1,402*	*–1,075*	*–18*	*2,405*	*–1,582*	*–1,005*	*–757*	*–134*
D. Net Errors and Omissions	4 998 . .	**150**	**483**	**715**	**–350**	**341**	**138**	**628**	**533**
Total, Groups A Through D	4 984 . .	*1,552*	*–592*	*697*	*2,055*	*–1,241*	*–867*	*–129*	*399*
E. Reserves and Related Items	4 802 A.	**–1,552**	**592**	**–697**	**–2,055**	**1,241**	**867**	**129**	**–399**
Reserve assets	4 802 . .	–3,059	–921	–1,784	–1,493	1,142	985	329	–275
Use of Fund credit and loans	4 766 . .	. . .	. . .	. . .	149	–145	–147	–141	–154
Exceptional financing	4 920 . .	1,507	1,513	1,087	–711	244	29	–59	31
Conversion rates: nuevos soles per U.S. dollar	0 101 . .	**2.1950**	**2.2533**	**2.4533**	**2.6642**	**2.9300**	**3.3833**	**3.4900**	**3.5068**

[1] Excludes components that have been classified in the categories of Group E.

Table 2. STANDARD PRESENTATION, 1994–2001
(Millions of U.S. dollars)

	Code	1994	1995	1996	1997	1998	1999	2000	2001
CURRENT ACCOUNT	4 993 . .	**–2,741**	**–4,618**	**–3,681**	**–3,413**	**–3,357**	**–1,483**	**–1,568**	**–1,098**
A. GOODS	4 100 . .	–998	–2,168	–1,986	–1,723	–2,462	–632	–317	–92
Credit	2 100 . .	**4,597**	**5,587**	**5,898**	**6,831**	**5,757**	**6,116**	**7,033**	**7,106**
General merchandise: exports f.o.b.	2 110 . .	4,213	5,068	5,245	6,259	4,751	4,855	5,804	5,859
Goods for processing: exports f.o.b.	2 150 . .	. . .	. . .	. . .	. . .	. . .	. . .	. . .	. . .
Repairs on goods	2 160 . .	1	. . .	. . .	1	1	1	1	. . .
Goods procured in ports by carriers	2 170 . .	46	56	73	72	77	68	84	81
Nonmonetary gold	2 180 . .	337	463	580	499	928	1,192	1,144	1,166
Debit	3 100 . .	**–5,595**	**–7,755**	**–7,884**	**–8,554**	**–8,219**	**–6,748**	**–7,350**	**–7,198**
General merchandise: imports f.o.b.	3 110 . .	–5,311	–7,398	–7,659	–8,238	–7,820	–6,476	–7,014	–6,854
Goods for processing: imports f.o.b.	3 150 . .	–242	–306	–172	–278	–325	–246	–306	–306
Repairs on goods	3 160 . .	–8	–12	–9	–11	–21	–14	–6	–5
Goods procured in ports by carriers	3 170 . .	–26	–31	–28	–16	–12	–6	–16	–28
Nonmonetary gold	3 180 . .	–8	–8	–16	–11	–41	–6	–8	–5
B. SERVICES	4 200 . .	–502	–748	–673	–787	–661	–669	–796	–800
Total credit	2 200 . .	*1,063*	*1,131*	*1,413*	*1,555*	*1,773*	*1,589*	*1,578*	*1,491*
Total debit	3 200 . .	*–1,565*	*–1,879*	*–2,086*	*–2,342*	*–2,434*	*–2,258*	*–2,374*	*–2,291*
Transportation services, credit	2 205 . .	**305**	**339**	**324**	**294**	**305**	**236**	**243**	**257**
Passenger	2 850 . .	*79*	*93*	*103*	*95*	*102*	*21*	*24*	*30*
Freight	2 851 . .	*55*	*55*	*50*	*24*	*18*	*9*	*10*	*13*
Other	2 852 . .	*171*	*191*	*171*	*175*	*185*	*206*	*209*	*214*
Sea transport, passenger	2 207 . .	. . .	. . .	. . .	. . .	. . .	. . .	. . .	. . .
Sea transport, freight	2 208 . .	49	49	45	18	10	8	6	4
Sea transport, other	2 209 . .	77	86	77	74	68	68	75	75
Air transport, passenger	2 211 . .	79	93	103	95	102	21	24	30
Air transport, freight	2 212 . .	6	6	5	6	8	1	4	9
Air transport, other	2 213 . .	94	105	94	101	117	138	134	139
Other transport, passenger	2 215 . .	. . .	. . .	. . .	. . .	. . .	. . .	. . .	. . .
Other transport, freight	2 216 . .	. . .	. . .	. . .	. . .	. . .	. . .	. . .	. . .
Other transport, other	2 217 . .	. . .	. . .	. . .	. . .	. . .	. . .	. . .	. . .
Transportation services, debit	3 205 . .	**–735**	**–904**	**–843**	**–903**	**–957**	**–793**	**–860**	**–915**
Passenger	3 850 . .	*–114*	*–131*	*–141*	*–174*	*–189*	*–209*	*–218*	*–229*
Freight	3 851 . .	*–499*	*–625*	*–577*	*–642*	*–647*	*–522*	*–568*	*–601*
Other	3 852 . .	*–122*	*–148*	*–125*	*–87*	*–121*	*–62*	*–74*	*–85*
Sea transport, passenger	3 207 . .	. . .	. . .	. . .	. . .	. . .	. . .	. . .	. . .
Sea transport, freight	3 208 . .	–455	–563	–516	–563	–579	–463	–505	–538
Sea transport, other	3 209 . .	–58	–63	–54	–21	–28	–25	–25	–25
Air transport, passenger	3 211 . .	–114	–131	–141	–174	–189	–209	–218	–229
Air transport, freight	3 212 . .	–44	–62	–61	–79	–68	–59	–63	–63
Air transport, other	3 213 . .	–64	–85	–71	–66	–93	–37	–49	–60
Other transport, passenger	3 215 . .	. . .	. . .	. . .	. . .	. . .	. . .	. . .	. . .
Other transport, freight	3 216 . .	. . .	. . .	. . .	. . .	. . .	. . .	. . .	. . .
Other transport, other	3 217 . .	. . .	. . .	. . .	. . .	. . .	. . .	. . .	. . .
Travel, credit	2 236 . .	**331**	**428**	**670**	**817**	**845**	**889**	**911**	**817**
Business travel	2 237 . .	. . .	. . .	. . .	. . .	. . .	. . .	. . .	. . .
Personal travel	2 240 . .	331	428	670	817	845	889	911	817
Travel, debit	3 236 . .	**–266**	**–296**	**–350**	**–434**	**–453**	**–444**	**–531**	**–592**
Business travel	3 237 . .	. . .	. . .	. . .	. . .	. . .	. . .	. . .	. . .
Personal travel	3 240 . .	–266	–296	–350	–434	–453	–444	–531	–592
Other services, credit	2 200 BA	**427**	**364**	**419**	**444**	**623**	**464**	**424**	**417**
Communications	2 245 . .	165	173	174	169	126	105	85	85
Construction	2 249 . .	. . .	. . .	. . .	. . .	. . .	. . .	. . .	. . .
Insurance	2 253 . .	117	74	114	114	304	133	110	116
Financial	2 260 . .	. . .	. . .	. . .	. . .	. . .	. . .	. . .	. . .
Computer and information	2 262 . .	. . .	. . .	. . .	. . .	. . .	. . .	. . .	. . .
Royalties and licence fees	2 266 . .	. . .	. . .	. . .	8	. . .	. . .	. . .	. . .
Other business services	2 268 . .	32	28	40	57	92	120	120	103
Personal, cultural, and recreational	2 287 . .	. . .	. . .	. . .	. . .	. . .	. . .	. . .	. . .
Government, n.i.e.	2 291 . .	113	89	91	96	101	106	109	113
Other services, debit	3 200 BA	**–564**	**–679**	**–893**	**–1,005**	**–1,024**	**–1,021**	**–983**	**–784**
Communications	3 245 . .	–67	–69	–69	–66	–58	–53	–63	–63
Construction	3 249 . .	. . .	. . .	. . .	. . .	. . .	. . .	. . .	. . .
Insurance	3 253 . .	–146	–129	–156	–160	–156	–163	–149	–173
Financial	3 260 . .	–38	–54	–56	–58	–52	–35	–31	–16
Computer and information	3 262 . .	. . .	. . .	. . .	. . .	. . .	. . .	. . .	. . .
Royalties and licence fees	3 266 . .	–36	–48	–80	–56	–64	–60	–57	–46
Other business services	3 268 . .	–198	–295	–436	–558	–561	–603	–556	–363
Personal, cultural, and recreational	3 287 . .	. . .	. . .	. . .	. . .	. . .	. . .	. . .	. . .
Government, n.i.e.	3 291 . .	–79	–84	–96	–107	–133	–107	–127	–123

Table 2 (Continued). STANDARD PRESENTATION, 1994–2001
(Millions of U.S. dollars)

	Code	1994	1995	1996	1997	1998	1999	2000	2001
C. INCOME	4 300 . .	–1,992	–2,511	–1,912	–1,824	–1,212	–1,148	–1,451	–1,203
Total credit	2 300 . .	*338*	*574*	*612*	*726*	*785*	*650*	*739*	*634*
Total debit	3 300 . .	*–2,330*	*–3,085*	*–2,524*	*–2,550*	*–1,997*	*–1,798*	*–2,190*	*–1,837*
Compensation of employees, credit	2 310 . .	...	...	...	...	...	...	...	...
Compensation of employees, debit	3 310 . .	...	...	...	...	...	...	...	...
Investment income, credit	2 320 . .	**338**	**574**	**612**	**726**	**785**	**650**	**739**	**634**
Direct investment income	2 330 . .	...	...	...	...	...	...	...	...
Dividends and distributed branch profits	2 332 . .	...	...	...	...	...	...	...	...
Reinvested earnings and undistributed branch profits	2 333 . .	...	...	...	...	...	...	...	...
Income on debt (interest)	2 334 . .	...	...	...	...	...	...	...	...
Portfolio investment income	2 339 . .	...	...	...	...	...	...	...	...
Income on equity	2 340 . .	...	...	...	...	...	...	...	...
Income on bonds and notes	2 350 . .	...	...	...	...	...	...	...	...
Income on money market instruments	2 360 . .	...	...	...	...	...	...	...	...
Other investment income	2 370 . .	338	574	612	726	785	650	739	634
Investment income, debit	3 320 . .	**–2,330**	**–3,085**	**–2,524**	**–2,550**	**–1,997**	**–1,798**	**–2,190**	**–1,837**
Direct investment income	3 330 . .	–372	–862	–683	–930	–221	–38	–381	–250
Dividends and distributed branch profits	3 332 . .	–136	–257	–338	–505	–380	–309	–330	–325
Reinvested earnings and undistributed branch profits	3 333 . .	–236	–605	–345	–425	159	271	–51	75
Income on debt (interest)	3 334 . .	...	...	...	...	...	...	...	...
Portfolio investment income	3 339 . .	–181	–298	–298	–436	–614	–515	–471	–354
Income on equity	3 340 . .	...	...	...	...	...	...	...	...
Income on bonds and notes	3 350 . .	–181	–298	–298	–436	–614	–515	–471	–354
Income on money market instruments	3 360 . .	...	...	...	...	...	...	...	...
Other investment income	3 370 . .	–1,777	–1,925	–1,543	–1,184	–1,162	–1,245	–1,338	–1,233
D. CURRENT TRANSFERS	4 379 . .	751	809	890	921	978	966	996	997
Credit	2 379 . .	**758**	**814**	**898**	**929**	**989**	**993**	**1,004**	**1,006**
General government	2 380 . .	69	30	25	9	4	41	26	6
Other sectors	2 390 . .	689	784	873	920	985	952	978	1,000
Workers' remittances	2 391 . .	472	600	596	636	648	672	718	716
Other current transfers	2 392 . .	217	184	277	284	337	280	260	284
Debit	3 379 . .	**–7**	**–5**	**–8**	**–8**	**–11**	**–27**	**–8**	**–9**
General government	3 380 . .	–7	–5	–8	–8	–11	–27	–8	–9
Other sectors	3 390 . .	...	...	...	...	...	...	...	...
Workers' remittances	3 391 . .	...	...	...	...	...	...	...	...
Other current transfers	3 392 . .	...	...	...	...	...	...	...	...
CAPITAL AND FINANCIAL ACCOUNT	4 996 . .	**2,591**	**4,135**	**2,966**	**3,763**	**3,016**	**1,345**	**940**	**565**
CAPITAL ACCOUNT	4 994 . .	**–24**	**61**	**65**	**75**	**–21**	**–10**	**–68**	**–34**
Total credit	2 994 . .	*65*	*94*	*94*	*149*	*57*	*69*	*24*	*65*
Total debit	3 994 . .	*–89*	*–33*	*–29*	*–74*	*–78*	*–79*	*–92*	*–99*
Capital transfers, credit	2 400 . .	**65**	**94**	**94**	**149**	**57**	**69**	**24**	**65**
General government	2 401 . .	59	86	86	142	41	56	13	45
Debt forgiveness	2 402 . .	33	28	42	124	36	44	...	33
Other capital transfers	2 410 . .	26	58	44	18	5	12	13	12
Other sectors	2 430 . .	6	8	8	7	16	13	11	20
Migrants' transfers	2 431 . .	...	...	...	...	...	...	...	...
Debt forgiveness	2 432 . .	...	...	...	...	...	...	...	...
Other capital transfers	2 440 . .	6	8	8	7	16	13	11	20
Capital transfers, debit	3 400 . .	**–89**	**–33**	**–29**	**–74**	**–78**	**–79**	**–92**	**–99**
General government	3 401 . .	...	...	...	...	...	...	...	...
Debt forgiveness	3 402 . .	...	...	...	...	...	...	...	...
Other capital transfers	3 410 . .	...	...	...	...	...	...	...	...
Other sectors	3 430 . .	–89	–33	–29	–74	–78	–79	–92	–99
Migrants' transfers	3 431 . .	–89	–33	–29	–74	–78	–79	–92	–99
Debt forgiveness	3 432 . .	...	...	...	...	...	...	...	...
Other capital transfers	3 440 . .	...	...	...	...	...	...	...	...
Nonproduced nonfinancial assets, credit	2 480 . .	...	...	...	...	...	...	...	...
Nonproduced nonfinancial assets, debit	3 480 . .	...	...	...	...	...	...	...	...

Table 2 (Continued). STANDARD PRESENTATION, 1994–2001
(Millions of U.S. dollars)

	Code	1994	1995	1996	1997	1998	1999	2000	2001
FINANCIAL ACCOUNT	4 995	**2,615**	**4,074**	**2,901**	**3,688**	**3,037**	**1,355**	**1,008**	**599**
A. DIRECT INVESTMENT	4 500	3,289	2,550	3,487	2,056	1,580	1,811	662	1,064
Direct investment abroad	4 505	**. . .**	**–8**	**16**	**–84**	**–64**	**–128**	**. . .**	**. . .**
Equity capital	4 510	. . .	–8	16	–84	–64	–128	. . .	. . .
Claims on affiliated enterprises	4 515	. . .	–8	16	–84	–64	–128	. . .	. . .
Liabilities to affiliated enterprises	4 520	. . .	. . .	. . .	. . .	. . .	. . .	. . .	. . .
Reinvested earnings	4 525	. . .	. . .	. . .	. . .	. . .	. . .	. . .	. . .
Other capital	4 530	. . .	. . .	. . .	. . .	. . .	. . .	. . .	. . .
Claims on affiliated enterprises	4 535	. . .	. . .	. . .	. . .	. . .	. . .	. . .	. . .
Liabilities to affiliated enterprises	4 540	. . .	. . .	. . .	. . .	. . .	. . .	. . .	. . .
Direct investment in Peru	4 555	**3,289**	**2,558**	**3,471**	**2,140**	**1,644**	**1,939**	**662**	**1,064**
Equity capital	4 560	3,053	1,953	3,126	1,715	1,803	2,210	611	1,139
Claims on direct investors	4 565	. . .	. . .	. . .	. . .	. . .	. . .	. . .	. . .
Liabilities to direct investors	4 570	3,053	1,953	3,126	1,715	1,803	2,210	611	1,139
Reinvested earnings	4 575	236	605	345	425	–159	–271	51	–75
Other capital	4 580	. . .	. . .	. . .	. . .	. . .	. . .	. . .	. . .
Claims on direct investors	4 585	. . .	. . .	. . .	. . .	. . .	. . .	. . .	. . .
Liabilities to direct investors	4 590	. . .	. . .	. . .	. . .	. . .	. . .	. . .	. . .
B. PORTFOLIO INVESTMENT	4 600	493	158	183	5,029	–361	–353	–464	–304
Assets	4 602	**–55**	**–5**	**–105**	**–251**	**–137**	**–228**	**–539**	**–298**
Equity securities	4 610	–31	13	–90	–91	–133	–172	–375	–265
Monetary authorities	4 611	. . .	. . .	. . .	. . .	. . .	. . .	. . .	. . .
General government	4 612	. . .	. . .	. . .	. . .	. . .	. . .	. . .	. . .
Banks	4 613	–41	65	–38	–38	–44	–41	–143	–117
Other sectors	4 614	10	–52	–52	–53	–89	–131	–232	–148
Debt securities	4 619	–24	–18	–15	–160	–4	–56	–164	–33
Bonds and notes	4 620	–24	–18	–15	–160	–4	–56	–164	–33
Monetary authorities	4 621	. . .	. . .	. . .	. . .	. . .	. . .	. . .	. . .
General government	4 622	–24	–21	–23	–156	–21	–20	–129	–33
Banks	4 623	. . .	. . .	. . .	. . .	. . .	. . .	. . .	. . .
Other sectors	4 624	. . .	3	8	–4	17	–36	–35	. . .
Money market instruments	4 630	. . .	. . .	. . .	. . .	. . .	. . .	. . .	. . .
Monetary authorities	4 631	. . .	. . .	. . .	. . .	. . .	. . .	. . .	. . .
General government	4 632	. . .	. . .	. . .	. . .	. . .	. . .	. . .	. . .
Banks	4 633	. . .	. . .	. . .	. . .	. . .	. . .	. . .	. . .
Other sectors	4 634	. . .	. . .	. . .	. . .	. . .	. . .	. . .	. . .
Liabilities	4 652	**548**	**163**	**288**	**5,280**	**–224**	**–125**	**75**	**–6**
Equity securities	4 660	465	171	295	157	–346	–107	123	42
Banks	4 663	. . .	. . .	. . .	. . .	. . .	. . .	. . .	. . .
Other sectors	4 664	465	171	295	157	–346	–107	123	42
Debt securities	4 669	83	–8	–7	5,123	122	–18	–48	–48
Bonds and notes	4 670	83	–8	–7	5,123	122	–18	–48	–48
Monetary authorities	4 671	. . .	. . .	. . .	. . .	. . .	. . .	. . .	. . .
General government	4 672	. . .	. . .	. . .	4,873	. . .	. . .	. . .	. . .
Banks	4 673	. . .	. . .	. . .	. . .	. . .	. . .	. . .	. . .
Other sectors	4 674	83	–8	–7	250	122	–18	–48	–48
Money market instruments	4 680	. . .	. . .	. . .	. . .	. . .	. . .	. . .	. . .
Monetary authorities	4 681	. . .	. . .	. . .	. . .	. . .	. . .	. . .	. . .
General government	4 682	. . .	. . .	. . .	. . .	. . .	. . .	. . .	. . .
Banks	4 683	. . .	. . .	. . .	. . .	. . .	. . .	. . .	. . .
Other sectors	4 684	. . .	. . .	. . .	. . .	. . .	. . .	. . .	. . .
C. FINANCIAL DERIVATIVES	4 910	. . .	. . .	. . .	. . .	. . .	. . .	. . .	. . .
Monetary authorities	4 911	. . .	. . .	. . .	. . .	. . .	. . .	. . .	. . .
General government	4 912	. . .	. . .	. . .	. . .	. . .	. . .	. . .	. . .
Banks	4 913	. . .	. . .	. . .	. . .	. . .	. . .	. . .	. . .
Other sectors	4 914	. . .	. . .	. . .	. . .	. . .	. . .	. . .	. . .
Assets	4 900	**. . .**	**. . .**	**. . .**	**. . .**	**. . .**	**. . .**	**. . .**	**. . .**
Monetary authorities	4 901	. . .	. . .	. . .	. . .	. . .	. . .	. . .	. . .
General government	4 902	. . .	. . .	. . .	. . .	. . .	. . .	. . .	. . .
Banks	4 903	. . .	. . .	. . .	. . .	. . .	. . .	. . .	. . .
Other sectors	4 904	. . .	. . .	. . .	. . .	. . .	. . .	. . .	. . .
Liabilities	4 905	**. . .**	**. . .**	**. . .**	**. . .**	**. . .**	**. . .**	**. . .**	**. . .**
Monetary authorities	4 906	. . .	. . .	. . .	. . .	. . .	. . .	. . .	. . .
General government	4 907	. . .	. . .	. . .	. . .	. . .	. . .	. . .	. . .
Banks	4 908	. . .	. . .	. . .	. . .	. . .	. . .	. . .	. . .
Other sectors	4 909	. . .	. . .	. . .	. . .	. . .	. . .	. . .	. . .

Table 2 (Concluded). STANDARD PRESENTATION, 1994–2001
(Millions of U.S. dollars)

	Code		1994	1995	1996	1997	1998	1999	2000	2001
D. OTHER INVESTMENT	4 700	. .	1,892	2,287	1,015	–1,904	676	–1,088	481	115
Assets	4 703	. .	**–264**	**–576**	**–666**	**560**	**65**	**130**	**198**	**66**
Trade credits	4 706	. .	. . .	. . .	. . .	. . .	. . .	. . .	. . .	. . .
General government	4 707	. .	. . .	. . .	. . .	. . .	. . .	. . .	. . .	. . .
of which: Short-term	4 709	. .	. . .	. . .	. . .	. . .	. . .	. . .	. . .	. . .
Other sectors	4 710	. .	. . .	. . .	. . .	. . .	. . .	. . .	. . .	. . .
of which: Short-term	4 712	. .	. . .	. . .	. . .	. . .	. . .	. . .	. . .	. . .
Loans	4 714	. .	. . .	. . .	. . .	. . .	. . .	. . .	. . .	. . .
Monetary authorities	4 715	. .	. . .	. . .	. . .	. . .	. . .	. . .	. . .	. . .
of which: Short-term	4 718	. .	. . .	. . .	. . .	. . .	. . .	. . .	. . .	. . .
General government	4 719	. .	. . .	. . .	. . .	. . .	. . .	. . .	. . .	. . .
of which: Short-term	4 721	. .	. . .	. . .	. . .	. . .	. . .	. . .	. . .	. . .
Banks	4 722	. .	. . .	. . .	. . .	. . .	. . .	. . .	. . .	. . .
of which: Short-term	4 724	. .	. . .	. . .	. . .	. . .	. . .	. . .	. . .	. . .
Other sectors	4 725	. .	. . .	. . .	. . .	. . .	. . .	. . .	. . .	. . .
of which: Short-term	4 727	. .	. . .	. . .	. . .	. . .	. . .	. . .	. . .	. . .
Currency and deposits	4 730	. .	–262	–572	–632	837	27	–37	231	81
Monetary authorities	4 731	. .	. . .	. . .	. . .	. . .	. . .	. . .	. . .	. . .
General government	4 732	. .	. . .	. . .	. . .	. . .	. . .	. . .	. . .	. . .
Banks	4 733	. .	–272	–429	–461	1,042	6	–274	232	48
Other sectors	4 734	. .	10	–143	–171	–205	21	237	–1	33
Other assets	4 736	. .	–2	–4	–34	–277	38	167	–33	–15
Monetary authorities	4 737	. .	–2	–5	–32	–104	20	–6	–34	–15
of which: Short-term	4 739	. .	*–2*	*–5*	*–32*	*–104*	*20*	*–6*	*–34*	*–15*
General government	4 740	. .	. . .	. . .	. . .	. . .	. . .	. . .	. . .	. . .
of which: Short-term	4 742	. .	. . .	. . .	. . .	. . .	. . .	. . .	. . .	. . .
Banks	4 743	. .	. . .	1	–2	–173	18	173	1	. . .
of which: Short-term	4 745	. .	. . .	. . .	. . .	. . .	. . .	. . .	. . .	. . .
Other sectors	4 746	. .	. . .	. . .	. . .	. . .	. . .	. . .	. . .	. . .
of which: Short-term	4 748	. .	. . .	. . .	. . .	. . .	. . .	. . .	. . .	. . .
Liabilities	4 753	. .	**2,156**	**2,863**	**1,681**	**–2,464**	**611**	**–1,218**	**283**	**49**
Trade credits	4 756	. .	. . .	. . .	. . .	. . .	. . .	. . .	. . .	. . .
General government	4 757	. .	. . .	. . .	. . .	. . .	. . .	. . .	. . .	. . .
of which: Short-term	4 759	. .	. . .	. . .	. . .	. . .	. . .	. . .	. . .	. . .
Other sectors	4 760	. .	. . .	. . .	. . .	. . .	. . .	. . .	. . .	. . .
of which: Short-term	4 762	. .	. . .	. . .	. . .	. . .	. . .	. . .	. . .	. . .
Loans	4 764	. .	1,395	2,054	1,225	3,678	622	–1,203	342	105
Monetary authorities	4 765	. .	37	–23	–87	141	–183	–180	–117	–164
of which: Use of Fund credit and loans from the Fund	4 766	. .	. . .	. . .	. . .	*149*	*–145*	*–147*	*–141*	*–154*
of which: Short-term	4 768	. .	*37*	*–23*	*–87*	*–8*	*–38*	*–33*	*24*	*–10*
General government	4 769	. .	803	463	148	1,144	195	–71	666	603
of which: Short-term	4 771	. .	*435*	. . .	. . .	. . .	. . .	. . .	. . .	. . .
Banks	4 772	. .	–239	801	226	1,670	–221	1,001	–245	–466
of which: Short-term	4 774	. .	*–299*	*683*	*192*	*1,466*	*–141*	*–1,046*	*–316*	*–332*
Other sectors	4 775	. .	794	813	938	723	831	49	38	132
of which: Short-term	4 777	. .	*562*	*526*	*266*	*337*	*–314*	*–593*	*–270*	*–235*
Currency and deposits	4 780	. .	. . .	. . .	. . .	. . .	. . .	. . .	. . .	. . .
Monetary authorities	4 781	. .	. . .	. . .	. . .	. . .	. . .	. . .	. . .	. . .
General government	4 782	. .	. . .	. . .	. . .	. . .	. . .	. . .	. . .	. . .
Banks	4 783	. .	. . .	. . .	. . .	. . .	. . .	. . .	. . .	. . .
Other sectors	4 784	. .	. . .	. . .	. . .	. . .	. . .	. . .	. . .	. . .
Other liabilities	4 786	. .	761	809	456	–6,142	–11	–15	–59	–56
Monetary authorities	4 787	. .	. . .	. . .	. . .	. . .	. . .	. . .	. . .	. . .
of which: Short-term	4 789	. .	. . .	. . .	. . .	. . .	. . .	. . .	. . .	. . .
General government	4 790	. .	769	809	459	–6,139	–9	–15	–59	–56
of which: Short-term	4 792	. .	*769*	*809*	*459*	*–6,139*	*–9*	*–15*	*–59*	*–56*
Banks	4 793	. .	–8	. . .	–3	–3	–2	. . .	. . .	. . .
of which: Short-term	4 795	. .	. . .	. . .	. . .	. . .	. . .	. . .	. . .	. . .
Other sectors	4 796	. .	. . .	. . .	. . .	. . .	. . .	. . .	. . .	. . .
of which: Short-term	4 798	. .	. . .	. . .	. . .	. . .	. . .	. . .	. . .	. . .
E. RESERVE ASSETS	4 802	. .	–3,059	–921	–1,784	–1,493	1,142	985	329	–275
Monetary gold	4 812	. .	71	–3	17	77	. . .	–4	50	–3
Special drawing rights	4 811	. .	1	. . .	. . .	. . .	–2	2	–2	. . .
Reserve position in the Fund	4 810	. .	. . .	. . .	. . .	. . .	. . .	. . .	. . .	. . .
Foreign exchange	4 803	. .	–3,086	–916	–1,849	–1,574	1,150	1,021	264	–265
Other claims	4 813	. .	–45	–2	48	4	–6	–34	17	–7
NET ERRORS AND OMISSIONS	4 998	. .	**150**	**483**	**715**	**–350**	**341**	**138**	**628**	**533**

Part 3 of the *Yearbook* contains descriptions of the methodologies, compilation practices, and sources used to compile these data.

Table 3. INTERNATIONAL INVESTMENT POSITION (End-period stocks), 1994–2001

(Millions of U.S. dollars)

	Code	1994	1995	1996	1997	1998	1999	2000	2001
ASSETS	8 995 C.	10,711	12,341	14,856	16,034	14,977	14,280	14,214	14,771
Direct investment abroad	8 505 . .	**109**	**567**	**543**	**602**	**438**	**651**	**505**	**574**
Equity capital and reinvested earnings	8 506 . .	109	567	543	602	438	651	505	574
Claims on affiliated enterprises	8 507 . .	109	567	543	602	438	651	505	574
Liabilities to affiliated enterprises	8 508 . .	. . .	. . .	. . .	. . .	. . .	. . .	. . .	. . .
Other capital	8 530 . .	. . .	. . .	. . .	. . .	. . .	. . .	. . .	. . .
Claims on affiliated enterprises	8 535 . .	. . .	. . .	. . .	. . .	. . .	. . .	. . .	. . .
Liabilities to affiliated enterprises	8 540 . .	. . .	. . .	. . .	. . .	. . .	. . .	. . .	. . .
Portfolio investment	8 602 . .	**313**	**294**	**416**	**720**	**1,013**	**1,224**	**1,870**	**2,161**
Equity securities	8 610 . .	313	294	416	582	867	1,070	1,647	1,953
Monetary authorities	8 611 . .	. . .	. . .	. . .	. . .	. . .	. . .	. . .	. . .
General government	8 612 . .	. . .	. . .	. . .	. . .	. . .	. . .	. . .	. . .
Banks	8 613 . .	133	67	105	143	187	228	371	488
Other sectors	8 614 . .	180	227	311	439	680	842	1,276	1,465
Debt securities	8 619 . .	. . .	. . .	. . .	138	146	154	223	208
Bonds and notes	8 620 . .	. . .	. . .	. . .	138	146	154	223	208
Monetary authorities	8 621 . .	. . .	. . .	. . .	. . .	. . .	. . .	. . .	. . .
General government	8 622 . .	. . .	. . .	. . .	138	146	154	223	208
Banks	8 623 . .	. . .	. . .	. . .	. . .	. . .	. . .	. . .	. . .
Other sectors	8 624 . .	. . .	. . .	. . .	. . .	. . .	. . .	. . .	. . .
Money market instruments	8 630 . .	. . .	. . .	. . .	. . .	. . .	. . .	. . .	. . .
Monetary authorities	8 631 . .	. . .	. . .	. . .	. . .	. . .	. . .	. . .	. . .
General government	8 632 . .	. . .	. . .	. . .	. . .	. . .	. . .	. . .	. . .
Banks	8 633 . .	. . .	. . .	. . .	. . .	. . .	. . .	. . .	. . .
Other sectors	8 634 . .	. . .	. . .	. . .	. . .	. . .	. . .	. . .	. . .
Financial derivatives	8 900 . .	**. . .**	**. . .**	**. . .**	**. . .**	**. . .**	**. . .**	**. . .**	**. . .**
Monetary authorities	8 901 . .	. . .	. . .	. . .	. . .	. . .	. . .	. . .	. . .
General government	8 902 . .	. . .	. . .	. . .	. . .	. . .	. . .	. . .	. . .
Banks	8 903 . .	. . .	. . .	. . .	. . .	. . .	. . .	. . .	. . .
Other sectors	8 904 . .	. . .	. . .	. . .	. . .	. . .	. . .	. . .	. . .
Other investment	8 703 . .	**3,476**	**3,745**	**4,379**	**3,701**	**3,657**	**3,522**	**3,286**	**3,206**
Trade credits	8 706 . .	. . .	. . .	. . .	. . .	. . .	. . .	. . .	. . .
General government	8 707 . .	. . .	. . .	. . .	. . .	. . .	. . .	. . .	. . .
of which: Short-term	8 709 . .	. . .	. . .	. . .	. . .	. . .	. . .	. . .	. . .
Other sectors	8 710 . .	. . .	. . .	. . .	. . .	. . .	. . .	. . .	. . .
of which: Short-term	8 712 . .	. . .	. . .	. . .	. . .	. . .	. . .	. . .	. . .
Loans	8 714 . .	. . .	. . .	. . .	. . .	. . .	. . .	. . .	. . .
Monetary authorities	8 715 . .	. . .	. . .	. . .	. . .	. . .	. . .	. . .	. . .
of which: Short-term	8 718 . .	. . .	. . .	. . .	. . .	. . .	. . .	. . .	. . .
General government	8 719 . .	. . .	. . .	. . .	. . .	. . .	. . .	. . .	. . .
of which: Short-term	8 721 . .	. . .	. . .	. . .	. . .	. . .	. . .	. . .	. . .
Banks	8 722 . .	. . .	. . .	. . .	. . .	. . .	. . .	. . .	. . .
of which: Short-term	8 724 . .	. . .	. . .	. . .	. . .	. . .	. . .	. . .	. . .
Other sectors	8 725 . .	. . .	. . .	. . .	. . .	. . .	. . .	. . .	. . .
of which: Short-term	8 727 . .	. . .	. . .	. . .	. . .	. . .	. . .	. . .	. . .
Currency and deposits	8 730 . .	3,367	3,639	4,271	3,434	3,407	3,444	3,213	3,132
Monetary authorities	8 731 . .	. . .	. . .	. . .	. . .	. . .	. . .	. . .	. . .
General government	8 732 . .	. . .	. . .	. . .	. . .	. . .	. . .	. . .	. . .
Banks	8 733 . .	1,017	1,446	1,907	865	859	1,133	901	853
Other sectors	8 734 . .	2,350	2,193	2,364	2,569	2,548	2,311	2,312	2,279
Other assets	8 736 . .	109	106	108	267	250	78	73	74
Monetary authorities	8 737 . .	64	62	62	48	49	50	46	47
of which: Short-term	8 739 . .	*64*	*62*	*62*	*48*	*49*	*50*	*46*	*47*
General government	8 740 . .	. . .	. . .	. . .	. . .	. . .	. . .	. . .	. . .
of which: Short-term	8 742 . .	. . .	. . .	. . .	. . .	. . .	. . .	. . .	. . .
Banks	8 743 . .	45	44	46	219	201	28	27	27
of which: Short-term	8 745 . .	. . .	. . .	. . .	. . .	. . .	. . .	. . .	. . .
Other sectors	8 746 . .	. . .	. . .	. . .	. . .	. . .	. . .	. . .	. . .
of which: Short-term	8 748 . .	. . .	. . .	. . .	. . .	. . .	. . .	. . .	. . .
Reserve assets	8 802 . .	**6,813**	**7,735**	**9,518**	**11,011**	**9,869**	**8,883**	**8,553**	**8,830**
Monetary gold	8 812 . .	395	398	381	304	304	308	258	262
Special drawing rights	8 811 . .	. . .	1	. . .	. . .	2	. . .	1	2
Reserve position in the Fund	8 810 . .	. . .	. . .	. . .	. . .	. . .	. . .	. . .	. . .
Foreign exchange	8 803 . .	6,071	6,987	8,836	10,410	9,260	8,239	7,975	8,240
Other claims	8 813 . .	347	349	301	297	303	336	319	326

Table 3 (Concluded). INTERNATIONAL INVESTMENT POSITION (End-period stocks), 1994–2001

(Millions of U.S. dollars)

	Code		1994	1995	1996	1997	1998	1999	2000	2001
LIABILITIES	8 995	D.	36,200	40,485	43,628	40,590	41,563	41,518	41,139	40,789
Direct investment in Peru	8 555	. .	**4,451**	**5,510**	**6,720**	**7,804**	**8,436**	**9,829**	**10,503**	**10,669**
Equity capital and reinvested earnings	8 556	. .	4,451	5,510	6,720	7,804	8,436	9,829	10,503	10,669
Claims on direct investors	8 557	. .	. . .	. . .	. . .	. . .	. . .	. . .	. . .	. . .
Liabilities to direct investors	8 558	. .	4,451	5,510	6,720	7,804	8,436	9,829	10,503	10,669
Other capital	8 580	. .	. . .	. . .	. . .	. . .	. . .	. . .	. . .	. . .
Claims on direct investors	8 585	. .	. . .	. . .	. . .	. . .	. . .	. . .	. . .	. . .
Liabilities to direct investors	8 590	. .	. . .	. . .	. . .	. . .	. . .	. . .	. . .	. . .
Portfolio investment	8 652	. .	**1,636**	**1,680**	**3,184**	**8,138**	**7,312**	**7,013**	**6,384**	**6,486**
Equity securities	8 660	. .	1,547	1,599	3,111	3,685	2,737	2,859	2,278	2,427
Banks	8 663	. .	. . .	. . .	. . .	. . .	. . .	. . .	. . .	. . .
Other sectors	8 664	. .	1,547	1,599	3,111	3,685	2,737	2,859	2,278	2,427
Debt securities	8 669	. .	89	81	73	4,453	4,575	4,154	4,106	4,059
Bonds and notes	8 670	. .	89	81	73	4,453	4,575	4,154	4,106	4,059
Monetary authorities	8 671	. .	. . .	. . .	. . .	. . .	. . .	. . .	. . .	. . .
General government	8 672	. .	. . .	. . .	. . .	4,130	4,130	3,727	3,727	3,727
Banks	8 673	. .	. . .	. . .	. . .	. . .	. . .	. . .	. . .	. . .
Other sectors	8 674	. .	89	81	73	323	445	427	379	332
Money market instruments	8 680	. .	. . .	. . .	. . .	. . .	. . .	. . .	. . .	. . .
Monetary authorities	8 681	. .	. . .	. . .	. . .	. . .	. . .	. . .	. . .	. . .
General government	8 682	. .	. . .	. . .	. . .	. . .	. . .	. . .	. . .	. . .
Banks	8 683	. .	. . .	. . .	. . .	. . .	. . .	. . .	. . .	. . .
Other sectors	8 684	. .	. . .	. . .	. . .	. . .	. . .	. . .	. . .	. . .
Financial derivatives	8 905	. .	**. . .**	**. . .**	**. . .**	**. . .**	**. . .**	**. . .**	**. . .**	**. . .**
Monetary authorities	8 906	. .	. . .	. . .	. . .	. . .	. . .	. . .	. . .	. . .
General government	8 907	. .	. . .	. . .	. . .	. . .	. . .	. . .	. . .	. . .
Banks	8 908	. .	. . .	. . .	. . .	. . .	. . .	. . .	. . .	. . .
Other sectors	8 909	. .	. . .	. . .	. . .	. . .	. . .	. . .	. . .	. . .
Other investment	8 753	. .	**30,113**	**33,295**	**33,724**	**24,648**	**25,815**	**24,676**	**24,252**	**23,634**
Trade credits	8 756	. .	. . .	. . .	. . .	. . .	. . .	. . .	. . .	. . .
General government	8 757	. .	. . .	. . .	. . .	. . .	. . .	. . .	. . .	. . .
of which: Short-term	8 759	. .	. . .	. . .	. . .	. . .	. . .	. . .	. . .	. . .
Other sectors	8 760	. .	. . .	. . .	. . .	. . .	. . .	. . .	. . .	. . .
of which: Short-term	8 762	. .	. . .	. . .	. . .	. . .	. . .	. . .	. . .	. . .
Loans	8 764	. .	30,113	33,295	33,724	24,648	25,815	24,676	24,252	23,634
Monetary authorities	8 765	. .	1,137	1,131	1,013	1,092	948	745	592	410
of which: Use of Fund credit and loans from the Fund	8 766	. .	*938*	*955*	*924*	*1,011*	*905*	*735*	*558*	*387*
of which: Short-term	8 768	. .	*199*	*176*	*89*	*81*	*43*	*10*	*34*	*23*
General government	8 769	. .	24,978	26,612	26,039	14,657	14,888	14,963	14,970	14,868
of which: Short-term	8 771	. .	*998*	*960*	*843*	. . .	. . .	. . .	. . .	. . .
Banks	8 772	. .	797	1,598	1,824	3,494	3,273	2,272	2,026	1,560
of which: Short-term	8 774	. .	*710*	*1,393*	*1,585*	*3,051*	*2,909*	*1,863*	*1,547*	*1,215*
Other sectors	8 775	. .	3,201	3,954	4,848	5,405	6,706	6,696	6,664	6,796
of which: Short-term	8 777	. .	*2,210*	*2,736*	*3,002*	*3,299*	*2,985*	*2,392*	*2,122*	*1,887*
Currency and deposits	8 780	. .	. . .	. . .	. . .	. . .	. . .	. . .	. . .	. . .
Monetary authorities	8 781	. .	. . .	. . .	. . .	. . .	. . .	. . .	. . .	. . .
General government	8 782	. .	. . .	. . .	. . .	. . .	. . .	. . .	. . .	. . .
Banks	8 783	. .	. . .	. . .	. . .	. . .	. . .	. . .	. . .	. . .
Other sectors	8 784	. .	. . .	. . .	. . .	. . .	. . .	. . .	. . .	. . .
Other liabilities	8 786	. .	. . .	. . .	. . .	. . .	. . .	. . .	. . .	. . .
Monetary authorities	8 787	. .	. . .	. . .	. . .	. . .	. . .	. . .	. . .	. . .
of which: Short-term	8 789	. .	. . .	. . .	. . .	. . .	. . .	. . .	. . .	. . .
General government	8 790	. .	. . .	. . .	. . .	. . .	. . .	. . .	. . .	. . .
of which: Short-term	8 792	. .	. . .	. . .	. . .	. . .	. . .	. . .	. . .	. . .
Banks	8 793	. .	. . .	. . .	. . .	. . .	. . .	. . .	. . .	. . .
of which: Short-term	8 795	. .	. . .	. . .	. . .	. . .	. . .	. . .	. . .	. . .
Other sectors	8 796	. .	. . .	. . .	. . .	. . .	. . .	. . .	. . .	. . .
of which: Short-term	8 798	. .	. . .	. . .	. . .	. . .	. . .	. . .	. . .	. . .
NET INTERNATIONAL INVESTMENT POSITION	8 995	. .	**–25,489**	**–28,145**	**–28,772**	**–24,556**	**–26,586**	**–27,237**	**–26,925**	**–26,018**
Conversion rates: nuevos soles per U.S. dollar (end of period)	0 102	. .	**2.1800**	**2.3100**	**2.6000**	**2.7300**	**3.1600**	**3.5100**	**3.5270**	**3.4440**

Table 1. ANALYTIC PRESENTATION, 1994–2001
(Millions of U.S. dollars)

	Code	1994	1995	1996	1997	1998	1999	2000	2001
A. Current Account[1]	4 993 Z.	**–2,950**	**–1,980**	**–3,953**	**–4,351**	**1,546**	**7,910**	**8,459**	**4,503**
Goods: exports f.o.b.	2 100 . .	13,483	17,447	20,543	25,228	29,496	34,210	37,295	31,242
Goods: imports f.o.b.	3 100 . .	–21,333	–26,391	–31,885	–36,355	–29,524	–29,252	–30,377	–28,496
Balance on Goods	4 100 . .	*–7,850*	*–8,944*	*–11,342*	*–11,127*	*–28*	*4,958*	*6,918*	*2,746*
Services: credit	2 200 . .	6,768	9,348	12,947	15,137	7,477	4,802	3,972	3,151
Services: debit	3 200 . .	–4,654	–6,926	–9,429	–14,122	–10,107	–7,515	–6,084	–5,090
Balance on Goods and Services	4 991 . .	*–5,736*	*–6,522*	*–7,824*	*–10,112*	*–2,658*	*2,245*	*4,806*	*807*
Income: credit	2 300 . .	3,782	6,067	6,059	7,698	6,440	8,081	7,804	7,348
Income: debit	3 300 . .	–1,932	–2,405	–2,777	–3,017	–2,671	–2,910	–4,588	–4,096
Balance on Goods, Services, and Income	4 992 . .	*–3,886*	*–2,860*	*–4,542*	*–5,431*	*1,111*	*7,416*	*8,022*	*4,059*
Current transfers: credit	2 379 Z.	1,041	1,147	1,185	1,670	758	610	552	515
Current transfers: debit	3 379 . .	–105	–267	–596	–590	–323	–116	–115	–71
B. Capital Account[1]	4 994 Z.	**. . .**	**. . .**	**. . .**	**. . .**	**. . .**	**–9**	**38**	**–12**
Capital account: credit	2 994 Z.	. . .	. . .	. . .	. . .	. . .	44	74	12
Capital account: debit	3 994 . .	. . .	. . .	. . .	. . .	. . .	–53	–36	–24
Total, Groups A Plus B	4 981 . .	*–2,950*	*–1,980*	*–3,953*	*–4,351*	*1,546*	*7,901*	*8,497*	*4,491*
C. Financial Account[1]	4 995 W.	**5,120**	**5,309**	**11,277**	**6,498**	**483**	**–935**	**–6,497**	**–4,317**
Direct investment abroad	4 505 . .	–302	–399	–182	–136	–160	59	107	161
Direct investment in the Philippines	4 555 Z.	1,591	1,478	1,517	1,222	2,287	573	1,241	1,792
Portfolio investment assets	4 602 . .	–632	–1,429	191	–9	–603	–278	–806	234
Equity securities	4 610 . .	. . .	. . .	21	30	–184	–55	–42	–4
Debt securities	4 619 . .	–632	–1,429	170	–39	–419	–223	–764	238
Portfolio investment liabilities	4 652 Z.	901	2,619	5,126	600	–325	5,094	693	178
Equity securities	4 660 . .	. . .	. . .	2,101	–406	264	512	–183	383
Debt securities	4 669 Z.	901	2,619	3,025	1,006	–589	4,582	876	–205
Financial derivatives	4 910 . .	. . .	. . .	. . .	. . .	. . .	. . .	. . .	. . .
Financial derivatives assets	4 900 . .	. . .	. . .	. . .	. . .	. . .	. . .	. . .	. . .
Financial derivatives liabilities	4 905 . .	. . .	. . .	. . .	. . .	. . .	. . .	. . .	. . .
Other investment assets	4 703 . .	. . .	. . .	–1,745	425	809	–5,669	–15,311	–13,893
Monetary authorities	4 701 . .	. . .	. . .	. . .	. . .	. . .	. . .	. . .	. . .
General government	4 704 . .	. . .	. . .	. . .	. . .	. . .	. . .	. . .	. . .
Banks	4 705 . .	. . .	. . .	–1,745	425	809	–949	2,267	466
Other sectors	4 728 . .	. . .	. . .	. . .	. . .	. . .	–4,720	–17,578	–14,359
Other investment liabilities	4 753 W.	3,562	3,040	6,370	4,396	–1,525	–714	7,579	7,211
Monetary authorities	4 753 WA	. . .	. . .	199	–98	5	75	61	668
General government	4 753 ZB	–1,121	–408	–808	–218	–207	181	–125	–78
Banks	4 753 ZC	1,694	1,648	5,036	1,668	–1,118	–1,343	–192	–1,207
Other sectors	4 753 ZD	2,989	1,800	1,943	3,044	–205	373	7,835	7,828
Total, Groups A Through C	4 983 . .	*2,170*	*3,329*	*7,324*	*2,147*	*2,029*	*6,966*	*2,000*	*174*
D. Net Errors and Omissions	4 998 . .	**157**	**–2,094**	**–2,986**	**–5,241**	**–750**	**–3,307**	**–2,481**	**–854**
Total, Groups A Through D	4 984 . .	*2,327*	*1,235*	*4,338*	*–3,094*	*1,279*	*3,659*	*–481*	*–680*
E. Reserves and Related Items	4 802 A.	**–2,327**	**–1,235**	**–4,338**	**3,094**	**–1,279**	**–3,659**	**481**	**680**
Reserve assets	4 802 . .	–2,107	–873	–4,037	2,610	–1,938	–3,947	73	–476
Use of Fund credit and loans	4 766 . .	–220	–362	–301	485	659	288	303	–8
Exceptional financing	4 920 . .	. . .	. . .	. . .	. . .	. . .	. . .	105	1,164
Conversion rates: Philippine pesos per U.S. dollar	0 101 . .	**26.417**	**25.714**	**26.216**	**29.471**	**40.893**	**39.089**	**44.192**	**50.993**

[1] Excludes components that have been classified in the categories of Group E.

Table 2. STANDARD PRESENTATION, 1994–2001
(Millions of U.S. dollars)

	Code	1994	1995	1996	1997	1998	1999	2000	2001
CURRENT ACCOUNT	4 993 . .	**–2,950**	**–1,980**	**–3,953**	**–4,351**	**1,546**	**7,910**	**8,459**	**4,503**
A. GOODS	4 100 . .	–7,850	–8,944	–11,342	–11,127	–28	4,958	6,918	2,746
Credit	2 100 . .	**13,483**	**17,447**	**20,543**	**25,228**	**29,496**	**34,210**	**37,295**	**31,242**
General merchandise: exports f.o.b.	2 110 . .	13,418	17,381	20,488	25,179	29,462	17,071	20,638	18,349
Goods for processing: exports f.o.b.	2 150 . .	. . .	. . .	. . .	. . .	. . .	16,927	16,015	12,332
Repairs on goods	2 160 . .	. . .	. . .	. . .	. . .	. . .	. . .	455	467
Goods procured in ports by carriers	2 170 . .	. . .	. . .	. . .	. . .	. . .	. . .	. . .	. . .
Nonmonetary gold	2 180 . .	65	66	55	49	34	212	187	94
Debit	3 100 . .	**–21,333**	**–26,391**	**–31,885**	**–36,355**	**–29,524**	**–29,252**	**–30,377**	**–28,496**
General merchandise: imports f.o.b.	3 110 . .	–21,333	–26,391	–31,885	–36,355	–29,524	–23,887	–25,432	–24,062
Goods for processing: imports f.o.b.	3 150 . .	. . .	. . .	. . .	. . .	. . .	–5,345	–4,845	–4,320
Repairs on goods	3 160 . .	. . .	. . .	. . .	. . .	. . .	. . .	–80	–109
Goods procured in ports by carriers	3 170 . .	. . .	. . .	. . .	. . .	. . .	. . .	. . .	. . .
Nonmonetary gold	3 180 . .	. . .	. . .	. . .	. . .	. . .	–20	–20	–5
B. SERVICES	4 200 . .	2,114	2,422	3,518	1,015	–2,630	–2,713	–2,112	–1,939
Total credit	2 200 . .	*6,768*	*9,348*	*12,947*	*15,137*	*7,477*	*4,802*	*3,972*	*3,151*
Total debit	3 200 . .	*–4,654*	*–6,926*	*–9,429*	*–14,122*	*–10,107*	*–7,515*	*–6,084*	*–5,090*
Transportation services, credit	2 205 . .	**233**	**274**	**358**	**357**	**324**	**575**	**891**	**659**
Passenger	2 850 . .	*29*	*5*	*5*	*6*	*13*	*15*	*243*	*99*
Freight	2 851 . .	*179*	*242*	*324*	*321*	*285*	*428*	*481*	*380*
Other	2 852 . .	*25*	*27*	*29*	*30*	*26*	*132*	*167*	*180*
Sea transport, passenger	2 207 . .	. . .	. . .	. . .	. . .	. . .	. . .	. . .	. . .
Sea transport, freight	2 208 . .	. . .	. . .	. . .	. . .	. . .	. . .	. . .	. . .
Sea transport, other	2 209 . .	. . .	. . .	. . .	. . .	. . .	. . .	. . .	. . .
Air transport, passenger	2 211 . .	. . .	. . .	. . .	. . .	. . .	. . .	. . .	. . .
Air transport, freight	2 212 . .	. . .	. . .	. . .	. . .	. . .	. . .	. . .	. . .
Air transport, other	2 213 . .	. . .	. . .	. . .	. . .	. . .	. . .	. . .	. . .
Other transport, passenger	2 215 . .	. . .	. . .	. . .	. . .	. . .	. . .	. . .	. . .
Other transport, freight	2 216 . .	. . .	. . .	. . .	. . .	. . .	. . .	. . .	. . .
Other transport, other	2 217 . .	. . .	. . .	. . .	. . .	. . .	. . .	. . .	. . .
Transportation services, debit	3 205 . .	**–1,457**	**–2,051**	**–2,287**	**–2,673**	**–1,983**	**–1,944**	**–2,676**	**–2,325**
Passenger	3 850 . .	*–176*	*–129*	*–21*	*–34*	*–72*	*–132*	*–316*	*–335*
Freight	3 851 . .	*–1,276*	*–1,917*	*–2,247*	*–2,560*	*–1,874*	*–1,595*	*–2,119*	*–1,741*
Other	3 852 . .	*–5*	*–5*	*–19*	*–79*	*–37*	*–217*	*–241*	*–249*
Sea transport, passenger	3 207 . .	. . .	. . .	. . .	. . .	. . .	. . .	. . .	. . .
Sea transport, freight	3 208 . .	. . .	. . .	. . .	. . .	. . .	. . .	. . .	. . .
Sea transport, other	3 209 . .	. . .	. . .	. . .	. . .	. . .	. . .	. . .	. . .
Air transport, passenger	3 211 . .	. . .	. . .	. . .	. . .	. . .	. . .	. . .	. . .
Air transport, freight	3 212 . .	. . .	. . .	. . .	. . .	. . .	. . .	. . .	. . .
Air transport, other	3 213 . .	. . .	. . .	. . .	. . .	. . .	. . .	. . .	. . .
Other transport, passenger	3 215 . .	. . .	. . .	. . .	. . .	. . .	. . .	. . .	. . .
Other transport, freight	3 216 . .	. . .	. . .	. . .	. . .	. . .	. . .	. . .	. . .
Other transport, other	3 217 . .	. . .	. . .	. . .	. . .	. . .	. . .	. . .	. . .
Travel, credit	2 236 . .	**973**	**1,136**	**1,546**	**2,341**	**1,418**	**2,553**	**2,134**	**1,723**
Business travel	2 237 . .	. . .	. . .	. . .	. . .	. . .	. . .	. . .	. . .
Personal travel	2 240 . .	. . .	. . .	. . .	. . .	. . .	. . .	. . .	. . .
Travel, debit	3 236 . .	**–196**	**–422**	**–1,266**	**–1,935**	**–1,950**	**–1,308**	**–1,005**	**–1,224**
Business travel	3 237 . .	. . .	. . .	. . .	. . .	. . .	. . .	. . .	. . .
Personal travel	3 240 . .	. . .	. . .	. . .	. . .	. . .	. . .	. . .	. . .
Other services, credit	2 200 BA	**5,562**	**7,938**	**11,043**	**12,439**	**5,735**	**1,674**	**947**	**769**
Communications	2 245 . .	. . .	. . .	. . .	. . .	. . .	424	182	330
Construction	2 249 . .	6	10	18	27	37	58	97	64
Insurance	2 253 . .	10	62	28	24	24	51	66	48
Financial	2 260 . .	. . .	. . .	. . .	. . .	. . .	67	80	34
Computer and information	2 262 . .	. . .	. . .	. . .	. . .	. . .	57	76	22
Royalties and licence fees	2 266 . .	. . .	2	5	18	. . .	6	7	1
Other business services	2 268 . .	5,527	7,839	10,974	12,363	5,662	929	359	219
Personal, cultural, and recreational	2 287 . .	. . .	. . .	. . .	. . .	. . .	58	43	15
Government, n.i.e.	2 291 . .	19	25	18	7	12	24	37	36
Other services, debit	3 200 BA	**–3,001**	**–4,453**	**–5,876**	**–9,514**	**–6,174**	**–4,263**	**–2,403**	**–1,541**
Communications	3 245 . .	. . .	. . .	. . .	. . .	. . .	–731	–261	–215
Construction	3 249 . .	–23	–58	–1,186	–511	–218	–166	–124	–298
Insurance	3 253 . .	–101	–109	–80	–110	–43	–81	–156	–116
Financial	3 260 . .	. . .	. . .	. . .	. . .	. . .	–317	–469	–75
Computer and information	3 262 . .	. . .	. . .	. . .	. . .	. . .	–95	–94	–83
Royalties and licence fees	3 266 . .	–95	–99	–82	–158	–70	–110	–197	–158
Other business services	3 268 . .	–2,767	–4,167	–4,491	–8,686	–5,823	–2,601	–954	–537
Personal, cultural, and recreational	3 287 . .	. . .	. . .	. . .	. . .	. . .	–139	–130	–57
Government, n.i.e.	3 291 . .	–15	–20	–37	–49	–20	–23	–18	–2

Table 2 (Continued). STANDARD PRESENTATION, 1994–2001
(Millions of U.S. dollars)

	Code	1994	1995	1996	1997	1998	1999	2000	2001
C. INCOME	4 300	1,850	3,662	3,282	4,681	3,769	5,171	3,216	3,252
Total credit	2 300	*3,782*	*6,067*	*6,059*	*7,698*	*6,440*	*8,081*	*7,804*	*7,348*
Total debit	3 300	*-1,932*	*-2,405*	*-2,777*	*-3,017*	*-2,671*	*-2,910*	*-4,588*	*-4,096*
Compensation of employees, credit	2 310	**3,009**	**4,928**	**4,306**	**5,742**	**4,926**	**6,794**	**6,050**	**6,235**
Compensation of employees, debit	3 310	**-13**	**-15**	**-57**	**...**	**...**	**...**	**...**	**...**
Investment income, credit	2 320	**773**	**1,139**	**1,753**	**1,956**	**1,514**	**1,287**	**1,754**	**1,113**
Direct investment income	2 330	116	342	700	589	303	63	163	10
Dividends and distributed branch profits	2 332	116	342	700	589	303	35	57	10
Reinvested earnings and undistributed branch profits	2 333	...	...	...	...	...	...	...	...
Income on debt (interest)	2 334	...	...	...	...	...	28	106	...
Portfolio investment income	2 339	...	...	...	...	...	763	645	633
Income on equity	2 340	...	...	...	...	...	16	8	6
Income on bonds and notes	2 350	...	...	...	...	...	164	621	584
Income on money market instruments	2 360	...	...	...	...	...	583	16	43
Other investment income	2 370	657	797	1,053	1,367	1,211	461	946	470
Investment income, debit	3 320	**-1,919**	**-2,390**	**-2,720**	**-3,017**	**-2,671**	**-2,910**	**-4,588**	**-4,096**
Direct investment income	3 330	-340	-515	-514	-450	-414	-301	-965	-1,160
Dividends and distributed branch profits	3 332	-340	-515	-514	-450	-414	-219	-297	-664
Reinvested earnings and undistributed branch profits	3 333	...	...	...	...	...	...	-579	-489
Income on debt (interest)	3 334	...	...	...	...	...	-82	-89	-7
Portfolio investment income	3 339	...	...	...	...	...	-923	-1,090	-1,179
Income on equity	3 340	...	...	...	...	...	-38	-16	-29
Income on bonds and notes	3 350	...	...	...	...	...	-820	-1,050	-1,138
Income on money market instruments	3 360	...	...	...	...	...	-65	-24	-12
Other investment income	3 370	-1,579	-1,875	-2,206	-2,567	-2,257	-1,686	-2,533	-1,757
D. CURRENT TRANSFERS	4 379	936	880	589	1,080	435	494	437	444
Credit	2 379	**1,041**	**1,147**	**1,185**	**1,670**	**758**	**610**	**552**	**515**
General government	2 380	72	77	77	51	54	76	183	132
Other sectors	2 390	969	1,070	1,108	1,619	704	534	369	383
Workers' remittances	2 391	443	432	569	1,057	204	102	125	122
Other current transfers	2 392	526	638	539	562	500	432	244	261
Debit	3 379	**-105**	**-267**	**-596**	**-590**	**-323**	**-116**	**-115**	**-71**
General government	3 380	...	...	-48	-36	-36	-38	-19	-21
Other sectors	3 390	-105	-267	-548	-554	-287	-78	-96	-50
Workers' remittances	3 391	-76	-136	...	...	...	-57	-72	-32
Other current transfers	3 392	-29	-131	-548	-554	-287	-21	-24	-18
CAPITAL AND FINANCIAL ACCOUNT	4 996	**2,793**	**4,074**	**6,939**	**9,592**	**-796**	**-4,603**	**-5,978**	**-3,649**
CAPITAL ACCOUNT	4 994	**...**	**...**	**...**	**...**	**...**	**-9**	**38**	**-12**
Total credit	2 994	...	...	...	...	...	*44*	*74*	*12*
Total debit	3 994	...	...	...	...	...	*-53*	*-36*	*-24*
Capital transfers, credit	2 400	**...**	**...**	**...**	**...**	**...**	**44**	**74**	**12**
General government	2 401	...	...	...	...	...	...	28	3
Debt forgiveness	2 402	...	...	...	...	...	...	...	...
Other capital transfers	2 410	...	...	...	...	...	...	28	3
Other sectors	2 430	...	...	...	...	...	44	46	9
Migrants' transfers	2 431	...	...	...	...	...	22	37	9
Debt forgiveness	2 432	...	...	...	...	...	...	...	...
Other capital transfers	2 440	...	...	...	...	...	22	9	...
Capital transfers, debit	3 400	**...**	**...**	**...**	**...**	**...**	**-52**	**-30**	**-24**
General government	3 401	...	...	...	...	...	...	...	...
Debt forgiveness	3 402	...	...	...	...	...	...	...	...
Other capital transfers	3 410	...	...	...	...	...	...	...	...
Other sectors	3 430	...	...	...	...	...	-52	-30	-24
Migrants' transfers	3 431	...	...	...	...	...	-25	-21	-24
Debt forgiveness	3 432	...	...	...	...	...	...	...	...
Other capital transfers	3 440	...	...	...	...	...	-27	-9	...
Nonproduced nonfinancial assets, credit	2 480	**...**	**...**	**...**	**...**	**...**	**...**	**...**	**...**
Nonproduced nonfinancial assets, debit	3 480	**...**	**...**	**...**	**...**	**...**	**-1**	**-6**	**...**

Table 2 (Continued). STANDARD PRESENTATION, 1994–2001
(Millions of U.S. dollars)

	Code	1994	1995	1996	1997	1998	1999	2000	2001
FINANCIAL ACCOUNT	4 995 . .	**2,793**	**4,074**	**6,939**	**9,592**	**–796**	**–4,594**	**–6,016**	**–3,637**
A. DIRECT INVESTMENT	4 500 . .	1,289	1,079	1,335	1,086	2,127	632	1,348	1,953
Direct investment abroad	4 505 . .	**–302**	**–399**	**–182**	**–136**	**–160**	**59**	**107**	**161**
Equity capital	4 510 . .	–302	–399	–182	–136	–160	59	95	162
Claims on affiliated enterprises	4 515 . .	–302	–399	–182	–136	–160	59	95	162
Liabilities to affiliated enterprises	4 520 . .	. . .	. . .	. . .	. . .	. . .	. . .	. . .	. . .
Reinvested earnings	4 525 . .	. . .	. . .	. . .	. . .	. . .	. . .	. . .	. . .
Other capital	4 530 . .	. . .	. . .	. . .	. . .	. . .	. . .	12	–1
Claims on affiliated enterprises	4 535 . .	. . .	. . .	. . .	. . .	. . .	. . .	12	–1
Liabilities to affiliated enterprises	4 540 . .	. . .	. . .	. . .	. . .	. . .	. . .	. . .	. . .
Direct investment in the Philippines	4 555 . .	**1,591**	**1,478**	**1,517**	**1,222**	**2,287**	**573**	**1,241**	**1,792**
Equity capital	4 560 . .	1,591	1,478	1,517	1,249	1,752	746	1,024	628
Claims on direct investors	4 565 . .	. . .	. . .	. . .	. . .	. . .	. . .	. . .	. . .
Liabilities to direct investors	4 570 . .	1,591	1,478	1,517	1,249	1,752	746	1,024	628
Reinvested earnings	4 575 . .	. . .	. . .	. . .	. . .	. . .	. . .	579	488
Other capital	4 580 . .	. . .	. . .	. . .	–27	535	–173	–362	676
Claims on direct investors	4 585 . .	. . .	. . .	. . .	. . .	. . .	. . .	. . .	. . .
Liabilities to direct investors	4 590 . .	. . .	. . .	. . .	–27	535	–173	–362	676
B. PORTFOLIO INVESTMENT	4 600 . .	269	1,190	5,317	591	–928	4,816	–113	1,399
Assets	4 602 . .	**–632**	**–1,429**	**191**	**–9**	**–603**	**–278**	**–806**	**234**
Equity securities	4 610 . .	. . .	. . .	21	30	–184	–55	–42	–4
Monetary authorities	4 611 . .	. . .	. . .	. . .	. . .	. . .	. . .	. . .	. . .
General government	4 612 . .	. . .	. . .	. . .	. . .	. . .	. . .	. . .	. . .
Banks	4 613 . .	. . .	. . .	. . .	. . .	. . .	. . .	. . .	. . .
Other sectors	4 614 . .	. . .	. . .	21	30	–184	–55	–42	–4
Debt securities	4 619 . .	–632	–1,429	170	–39	–419	–223	–764	238
Bonds and notes	4 620 . .	–632	–1,429	170	–39	–419	–223	–764	238
Monetary authorities	4 621 . .	. . .	. . .	. . .	. . .	. . .	. . .	. . .	. . .
General government	4 622 . .	. . .	. . .	. . .	. . .	. . .	. . .	. . .	. . .
Banks	4 623 . .	. . .	. . .	113	–64	–419	–113	–357	292
Other sectors	4 624 . .	. . .	. . .	57	25	. . .	–110	–407	–54
Money market instruments	4 630 . .	. . .	. . .	. . .	. . .	. . .	. . .	. . .	. . .
Monetary authorities	4 631 . .	. . .	. . .	. . .	. . .	. . .	. . .	. . .	. . .
General government	4 632 . .	. . .	. . .	. . .	. . .	. . .	. . .	. . .	. . .
Banks	4 633 . .	. . .	. . .	. . .	. . .	. . .	. . .	. . .	. . .
Other sectors	4 634 . .	. . .	. . .	. . .	. . .	. . .	. . .	. . .	. . .
Liabilities	4 652 . .	**901**	**2,619**	**5,126**	**600**	**–325**	**5,094**	**693**	**1,165**
Equity securities	4 660 . .	. . .	. . .	2,101	–406	264	512	–183	383
Banks	4 663 . .	. . .	. . .	. . .	. . .	. . .	. . .	. . .	. . .
Other sectors	4 664 . .	. . .	. . .	2,101	–406	264	512	–183	383
Debt securities	4 669 . .	901	2,619	3,025	1,006	–589	4,582	876	782
Bonds and notes	4 670 . .	901	2,619	3,025	1,006	–589	4,582	876	782
Monetary authorities	4 671 . .	. . .	. . .	591	–122	–38	1,158	88	–47
General government	4 672 . .	. . .	. . .	. . .	–28	440	2,912	2,223	944
Banks	4 673 . .	. . .	. . .	1,103	–450	–657	316	. . .	. . .
Other sectors	4 674 . .	901	2,619	1,331	1,606	–334	196	–1,435	–115
Money market instruments	4 680 . .	. . .	. . .	. . .	. . .	. . .	. . .	. . .	. . .
Monetary authorities	4 681 . .	. . .	. . .	. . .	. . .	. . .	. . .	. . .	. . .
General government	4 682 . .	. . .	. . .	. . .	. . .	. . .	. . .	. . .	. . .
Banks	4 683 . .	. . .	. . .	. . .	. . .	. . .	. . .	. . .	. . .
Other sectors	4 684 . .	. . .	. . .	. . .	. . .	. . .	. . .	. . .	. . .
C. FINANCIAL DERIVATIVES	4 910 . .	. . .	. . .	. . .	. . .	. . .	. . .	. . .	. . .
Monetary authorities	4 911 . .	. . .	. . .	. . .	. . .	. . .	. . .	. . .	. . .
General government	4 912 . .	. . .	. . .	. . .	. . .	. . .	. . .	. . .	. . .
Banks	4 913 . .	. . .	. . .	. . .	. . .	. . .	. . .	. . .	. . .
Other sectors	4 914 . .	. . .	. . .	. . .	. . .	. . .	. . .	. . .	. . .
Assets	4 900 . .	**. . .**	**. . .**	**. . .**	**. . .**	**. . .**	**. . .**	**. . .**	**. . .**
Monetary authorities	4 901 . .	. . .	. . .	. . .	. . .	. . .	. . .	. . .	. . .
General government	4 902 . .	. . .	. . .	. . .	. . .	. . .	. . .	. . .	. . .
Banks	4 903 . .	. . .	. . .	. . .	. . .	. . .	. . .	. . .	. . .
Other sectors	4 904 . .	. . .	. . .	. . .	. . .	. . .	. . .	. . .	. . .
Liabilities	4 905 . .	**. . .**	**. . .**	**. . .**	**. . .**	**. . .**	**. . .**	**. . .**	**. . .**
Monetary authorities	4 906 . .	. . .	. . .	. . .	. . .	. . .	. . .	. . .	. . .
General government	4 907 . .	. . .	. . .	. . .	. . .	. . .	. . .	. . .	. . .
Banks	4 908 . .	. . .	. . .	. . .	. . .	. . .	. . .	. . .	. . .
Other sectors	4 909 . .	. . .	. . .	. . .	. . .	. . .	. . .	. . .	. . .

Table 2 (Concluded). STANDARD PRESENTATION, 1994–2001
(Millions of U.S. dollars)

	Code	1994	1995	1996	1997	1998	1999	2000	2001
D. OTHER INVESTMENT	4 700	3,342	2,678	4,324	5,306	–57	–6,095	–7,324	–6,513
Assets	4 703	**. . .**	**. . .**	**–1,745**	**425**	**809**	**–5,669**	**–15,311**	**–13,893**
Trade credits	4 706	. . .	. . .	. . .	. . .	. . .	–4,720	–17,401	–13,770
General government	4 707	. . .	. . .	. . .	. . .	. . .	. . .	. . .	. . .
of which: Short-term	4 709	. . .	. . .	. . .	. . .	. . .	. . .	. . .	. . .
Other sectors	4 710	. . .	. . .	. . .	. . .	. . .	–4,720	–17,401	–13,770
of which: Short-term	4 712	. . .	. . .	. . .	. . .	. . .	*–4,720*	*–17,401*	*–13,770*
Loans	4 714	. . .	. . .	–145	15	184	130	1,309	–830
Monetary authorities	4 715	. . .	. . .	. . .	. . .	. . .	. . .	. . .	. . .
of which: Short-term	4 718	. . .	. . .	. . .	. . .	. . .	. . .	. . .	. . .
General government	4 719	. . .	. . .	. . .	. . .	. . .	. . .	. . .	. . .
of which: Short-term	4 721	. . .	. . .	. . .	. . .	. . .	. . .	. . .	. . .
Banks	4 722	. . .	. . .	–145	15	184	130	1,309	–830
of which: Short-term	4 724	. . .	. . .	*–145*	*15*	*184*	*130*	*1,309*	*–830*
Other sectors	4 725	. . .	. . .	. . .	. . .	. . .	. . .	. . .	. . .
of which: Short-term	4 727	. . .	. . .	. . .	. . .	. . .	. . .	. . .	. . .
Currency and deposits	4 730	. . .	. . .	–1,542	484	605	–981	757	508
Monetary authorities	4 731	. . .	. . .	. . .	. . .	. . .	. . .	. . .	. . .
General government	4 732	. . .	. . .	. . .	. . .	. . .	. . .	. . .	. . .
Banks	4 733	. . .	. . .	–1,542	484	605	–981	934	1,097
Other sectors	4 734	. . .	. . .	. . .	. . .	. . .	. . .	–177	–589
Other assets	4 736	. . .	. . .	–58	–74	20	–98	24	199
Monetary authorities	4 737	. . .	. . .	. . .	. . .	. . .	. . .	. . .	. . .
of which: Short-term	4 739	. . .	. . .	. . .	. . .	. . .	. . .	. . .	. . .
General government	4 740	. . .	. . .	. . .	. . .	. . .	. . .	. . .	. . .
of which: Short-term	4 742	. . .	. . .	. . .	. . .	. . .	. . .	. . .	. . .
Banks	4 743	. . .	. . .	–58	–74	20	–98	24	199
of which: Short-term	4 745	. . .	. . .	*–58*	*–74*	*20*	*–98*	*17*	*199*
Other sectors	4 746	. . .	. . .	. . .	. . .	. . .	. . .	. . .	. . .
of which: Short-term	4 748	. . .	. . .	. . .	. . .	. . .	. . .	. . .	. . .
Liabilities	4 753	**3,342**	**2,678**	**6,069**	**4,881**	**–866**	**–426**	**7,987**	**7,380**
Trade credits	4 756	. . .	. . .	. . .	. . .	. . .	. . .	7,157	7,499
General government	4 757	. . .	. . .	. . .	. . .	. . .	. . .	. . .	. . .
of which: Short-term	4 759	. . .	. . .	. . .	. . .	. . .	. . .	. . .	. . .
Other sectors	4 760	. . .	. . .	. . .	. . .	. . .	. . .	7,157	7,499
of which: Short-term	4 762	. . .	. . .	. . .	. . .	. . .	. . .	*7,157*	*7,499*
Loans	4 764	1,610	1,030	2,370	2,995	291	1,228	772	441
Monetary authorities	4 765	–220	–362	–102	387	664	363	469	837
of which: Use of Fund credit and loans from the Fund	4 766	*–220*	*–362*	*–301*	*485*	*659*	*288*	*303*	*–8*
of which: Short-term	4 768	. . .	. . .	*199*	*–98*	*5*	*75*	*115*	*674*
General government	4 769	–1,121	–408	–808	–218	–207	181	–125	–78
of which: Short-term	4 771	*–446*	*344*	. . .	. . .	. . .	. . .	. . .	. . .
Banks	4 772	. . .	. . .	1,337	–218	39	311	–250	–647
of which: Short-term	4 774	. . .	. . .	*1,014*	*–472*	*–84*	*311*	*–250*	*–647*
Other sectors	4 775	2,951	1,800	1,943	3,044	–205	373	678	329
of which: Short-term	4 777	*1,002*	*–56*	*540*	*495*	*–1,521*	*103*	*–274*	*–357*
Currency and deposits	4 780	1,694	1,648	3,417	1,568	–560	–1,785	–120	–340
Monetary authorities	4 781	. . .	. . .	. . .	. . .	. . .	. . .	. . .	. . .
General government	4 782	. . .	. . .	. . .	. . .	. . .	. . .	. . .	. . .
Banks	4 783	1,694	1,648	3,417	1,568	–560	–1,785	–120	–340
Other sectors	4 784	. . .	. . .	. . .	. . .	. . .	. . .	. . .	. . .
Other liabilities	4 786	38	. . .	282	318	–597	131	178	–220
Monetary authorities	4 787	. . .	. . .	. . .	. . .	. . .	. . .	. . .	. . .
of which: Short-term	4 789	. . .	. . .	. . .	. . .	. . .	. . .	. . .	. . .
General government	4 790	. . .	. . .	. . .	. . .	. . .	. . .	. . .	. . .
of which: Short-term	4 792	. . .	. . .	. . .	. . .	. . .	. . .	. . .	. . .
Banks	4 793	. . .	. . .	282	318	–597	131	178	–220
of which: Short-term	4 795	. . .	. . .	*282*	*318*	*–597*	*131*	*178*	*–220*
Other sectors	4 796	38	. . .	. . .	. . .	. . .	. . .	. . .	. . .
of which: Short-term	4 798	. . .	. . .	. . .	. . .	. . .	. . .	. . .	. . .
E. RESERVE ASSETS	4 802	–2,107	–873	–4,037	2,610	–1,938	–3,947	73	–476
Monetary gold	4 812	295	–109	–204	14	–18	14	–22	1
Special drawing rights	4 811	–14	17	5	1	. . .	–5	4	–13
Reserve position in the Fund	4 810	. . .	. . .	. . .	. . .	. . .	. . .	. . .	. . .
Foreign exchange	4 803	–2,388	–781	–3,838	2,595	–1,920	–3,956	91	–464
Other claims	4 813	. . .	. . .	. . .	. . .	. . .	. . .	. . .	. . .
NET ERRORS AND OMISSIONS	4 998	**157**	**–2,094**	**–2,986**	**–5,241**	**–750**	**–3,307**	**–2,481**	**–854**

Part 3 of the *Yearbook* contains descriptions of the methodologies, compilation practices, and sources used to compile these data.

Table 1. ANALYTIC PRESENTATION, 1994–2001
(Millions of U.S. dollars)

	Code	1994	1995	1996	1997	1998	1999	2000	2001
A. Current Account [1]	4 993 Z.	**954**	**854**	**–3,264**	**–5,744**	**–6,901**	**–12,487**	**–9,998**	**–5,357**
Goods: exports f.o.b	2 100 . .	18,355	25,041	27,557	30,731	32,467	30,060	35,902	41,664
Goods: imports f.o.b	3 100 . .	–18,930	–26,687	–34,844	–40,553	–45,303	–45,132	–48,210	–49,324
Balance on Goods	4 100 . .	*–575*	*–1,646*	*–7,287*	*–9,822*	*–12,836*	*–15,072*	*–12,308*	*–7,660*
Services: credit	2 200 . .	6,699	10,675	9,747	8,915	10,840	8,363	10,387	9,755
Services: debit	3 200 . .	–3,859	–7,138	–6,343	–5,743	–6,624	–6,982	–8,994	–8,951
Balance on Goods and Services	4 991 . .	*2,265*	*1,891*	*–3,883*	*–6,650*	*–8,620*	*–13,691*	*–10,915*	*–6,856*
Income: credit	2 300 . .	546	1,089	1,527	1,467	2,226	1,837	2,250	2,625
Income: debit	3 300 . .	–3,109	–3,084	–2,602	–2,596	–3,404	–2,847	–3,713	–4,015
Balance on Goods, Services, and Income	4 992 . .	*–298*	*–104*	*–4,958*	*–7,779*	*–9,798*	*–14,701*	*–12,378*	*–8,246*
Current transfers: credit	2 379 Z.	2,174	2,459	2,825	2,700	3,520	2,898	3,008	3,737
Current transfers: debit	3 379 . .	–922	–1,501	–1,131	–665	–623	–684	–628	–848
B. Capital Account [1]	4 994 Z.	**9,215**	**285**	**94**	**66**	**63**	**55**	**32**	**75**
Capital account: credit	2 994 Z.	9,215	285	5,833	91	117	95	109	112
Capital account: debit	3 994 . .	. . .	. . .	–5,739	–25	–54	–40	–77	–37
Total, Groups A Plus B	4 981 . .	*10,169*	*1,139*	*–3,170*	*–5,678*	*–6,838*	*–12,432*	*–9,966*	*–5,282*
C. Financial Account [1]	4 995 W.	**–9,065**	**9,260**	**6,673**	**7,410**	**13,282**	**10,462**	**10,204**	**3,172**
Direct investment abroad	4 505 . .	–29	–42	–53	–45	–316	–31	–17	89
Direct investment in Poland	4 555 Z.	1,875	3,659	4,498	4,908	6,365	7,270	9,341	5,713
Portfolio investment assets	4 602 . .	–624	1	282	815	–130	–548	–89	46
Equity securities	4 610 . .	. . .	127	–17	56	1	–172	–23	–68
Debt securities	4 619 . .	–624	–126	299	759	–131	–376	–66	114
Portfolio investment liabilities	4 652 Z.	. . .	1,176	22	1,295	1,827	691	3,422	1,067
Equity securities	4 660 . .	. . .	219	749	599	1,734	14	447	–307
Debt securities	4 669 Z.	. . .	957	–727	696	93	677	2,975	1,374
Financial derivatives	4 910 . .	. . .	. . .	–3	–12	. . .	569	269	–336
Financial derivatives assets	4 900 . .	. . .	. . .	. . .	. . .	. . .	579	269	. . .
Financial derivatives liabilities	4 905 . .	. . .	. . .	–3	–12	. . .	–10	. . .	–336
Other investment assets	4 703 . .	–1,841	3,356	6,191	–754	2,107	–3,339	–3,870	–4,071
Monetary authorities	4 701 . .	194	65	37	. . .	1	1	1	1
General government	4 704 . .	34	46	5,767	41	53	–6	–49	–36
Banks	4 705 . .	–1,718	1,057	453	–1,076	2,207	–2,694	–3,014	3,398
Other sectors	4 728 . .	–351	2,188	–66	281	–154	–640	–808	–638
Other investment liabilities	4 753 W.	–8,446	1,110	–4,264	1,203	3,429	5,850	1,148	664
Monetary authorities	4 753 WA	15	14	102	–561	199	380	–1,392	118
General government	4 753 ZB	–8,709	–3	6,033	–52	–370	–224	–291	–3,045
Banks	4 753 ZC	170	575	314	719	1,483	2,013	–475	283
Other sectors	4 753 ZD	78	524	1,353	1,097	2,117	3,681	3,306	3,308
Total, Groups A Through C	4 983 . .	*1,104*	*10,399*	*3,503*	*1,732*	*6,444*	*–1,970*	*238*	*–2,110*
D. Net Errors and Omissions	4 998 . .	**–98**	**–564**	**321**	**1,309**	**–520**	**2,126**	**387**	**1,682**
Total, Groups A Through D	4 984 . .	*1,006*	*9,835*	*3,824*	*3,041*	*5,924*	*156*	*625*	*–428*
E. Reserves and Related Items	4 802 A.	**–1,006**	**–9,835**	**–3,824**	**–3,041**	**–5,924**	**–156**	**–625**	**428**
Reserve assets	4 802 . .	–1,514	–8,431	–3,828	–3,044	–5,926	–156	–625	428
Use of Fund credit and loans	4 766 . .	603	–1,408	. . .	. . .	. . .	. . .	. . .	. . .
Exceptional financing	4 920 . .	–96	4	4	3	2	. . .	. . .	. . .
Conversion rates: zlotys per U.S. dollar	0 101 . .	**2.2723**	**2.4250**	**2.6961**	**3.2793**	**3.4754**	**3.9671**	**4.3461**	**4.0939**

[1] Excludes components that have been classified in the categories of Group E.

Table 2. STANDARD PRESENTATION, 1994–2001
(Millions of U.S. dollars)

	Code	1994	1995	1996	1997	1998	1999	2000	2001
CURRENT ACCOUNT	4 993 . .	**954**	**854**	**–3,264**	**–5,744**	**–6,901**	**–12,487**	**–9,998**	**–5,357**
A. GOODS	4 100 . .	–575	–1,646	–7,287	–9,822	–12,836	–15,072	–12,308	–7,660
Credit	2 100 . .	**18,355**	**25,041**	**27,557**	**30,731**	**32,467**	**30,060**	**35,902**	**41,664**
General merchandise: exports f.o.b.	2 110 . .	18,355	25,041	27,557	30,731	32,467	30,060	26,032	30,163
Goods for processing: exports f.o.b.	2 150 . .	. . .	. . .	. . .	. . .	. . .	. . .	9,795	11,420
Repairs on goods	2 160 . .	. . .	. . .	. . .	. . .	. . .	. . .	17	25
Goods procured in ports by carriers	2 170 . .	. . .	. . .	. . .	. . .	. . .	. . .	56	56
Nonmonetary gold	2 180 . .	. . .	. . .	. . .	. . .	. . .	. . .	2	. . .
Debit	3 100 . .	**–18,930**	**–26,687**	**–34,844**	**–40,553**	**–45,303**	**–45,132**	**–48,210**	**–49,324**
General merchandise: imports f.o.b.	3 110 . .	–18,930	–26,687	–34,844	–40,553	–45,303	–45,132	–43,628	–43,959
Goods for processing: imports f.o.b.	3 150 . .	. . .	. . .	. . .	. . .	. . .	. . .	–4,539	–5,330
Repairs on goods	3 160 . .	. . .	. . .	. . .	. . .	. . .	. . .	–42	–33
Goods procured in ports by carriers	3 170 . .	. . .	. . .	. . .	. . .	. . .	. . .	. . .	. . .
Nonmonetary gold	3 180 . .	. . .	. . .	. . .	. . .	. . .	. . .	–1	–2
B. SERVICES	4 200 . .	2,840	3,537	3,404	3,172	4,216	1,381	1,393	804
Total credit	2 200 . .	*6,699*	*10,675*	*9,747*	*8,915*	*10,840*	*8,363*	*10,387*	*9,755*
Total debit	3 200 . .	*–3,859*	*–7,138*	*–6,343*	*–5,743*	*–6,624*	*–6,982*	*–8,994*	*–8,951*
Transportation services, credit	2 205 . .	**2,438**	**3,041**	**2,752**	**3,112**	**2,874**	**2,419**	**2,434**	**2,685**
Passenger	2 850 . .	*282*	*313*	*320*	*374*	*375*	*398*	*449*	*477*
Freight	2 851 . .	*1,705*	*2,093*	*1,809*	*2,000*	*1,993*	*1,616*	*1,719*	*1,966*
Other	2 852 . .	*451*	*635*	*623*	*738*	*506*	*405*	*266*	*242*
Sea transport, passenger	2 207 . .	13	12	9	9	9	10	4	7
Sea transport, freight	2 208 . .	1,101	1,331	1,039	1,123	1,043	797	799	811
Sea transport, other	2 209 . .	231	259	227	209	109	–32	55	52
Air transport, passenger	2 211 . .	233	247	283	337	338	378	404	410
Air transport, freight	2 212 . .	18	22	28	28	31	26	20	30
Air transport, other	2 213 . .	82	91	93	89	95	265	72	43
Other transport, passenger	2 215 . .	36	54	28	28	28	10	41	60
Other transport, freight	2 216 . .	586	740	742	849	919	793	900	1,125
Other transport, other	2 217 . .	138	285	303	440	302	172	139	147
Transportation services, debit	3 205 . .	**–1,365**	**–1,768**	**–1,690**	**–1,590**	**–1,663**	**–1,524**	**–1,535**	**–1,580**
Passenger	3 850 . .	*–109*	*–365*	*–117*	*–105*	*–94*	*–210*	*–103*	*–100*
Freight	3 851 . .	*–345*	*–488*	*–640*	*–602*	*–681*	*–820*	*–905*	*–950*
Other	3 852 . .	*–911*	*–915*	*–933*	*–883*	*–888*	*–494*	*–527*	*–530*
Sea transport, passenger	3 207 . .	–3	–3	–3	–4	–3	–2	–5	–4
Sea transport, freight	3 208 . .	–124	–152	–189	–204	–209	–267	–226	–276
Sea transport, other	3 209 . .	–717	–609	–488	–445	–437	–158	–173	–156
Air transport, passenger	3 211 . .	–88	–342	–92	–82	–75	–189	–79	–76
Air transport, freight	3 212 . .	–10	–13	–15	–13	–12	–42	–16	–18
Air transport, other	3 213 . .	–108	–65	–214	–214	–221	–219	–280	–290
Other transport, passenger	3 215 . .	–18	–20	–22	–19	–16	–19	–19	–20
Other transport, freight	3 216 . .	–211	–323	–436	–385	–460	–511	–663	–656
Other transport, other	3 217 . .	–86	–241	–231	–224	–230	–117	–74	–84
Travel, credit	2 236 . .	**2,325**	**2,306**	**3,158**	**2,297**	**4,292**	**3,173**	**5,678**	**4,645**
Business travel	2 237 . .	65	67	75	68	68	61	. . .	. . .
Personal travel	2 240 . .	2,260	2,239	3,083	2,229	4,224	3,112	. . .	. . .
Travel, debit	3 236 . .	**–320**	**–410**	**–583**	**–589**	**–773**	**–859**	**–3,313**	**–3,495**
Business travel	3 237 . .	–257	–359	–422	–387	–401	–370	. . .	. . .
Personal travel	3 240 . .	–63	–51	–161	–202	–372	–489	. . .	. . .
Other services, credit	2 200 BA	**1,936**	**5,328**	**3,837**	**3,506**	**3,674**	**2,771**	**2,275**	**2,425**
Communications	2 245 . .	209	302	315	386	431	376	234	201
Construction	2 249 . .	618	2,799	1,534	700	358	333	297	431
Insurance	2 253 . .	152	738	514	807	1,343	570	208	185
Financial	2 260 . .	69	145	224	121	172	155	104	173
Computer and information	2 262 . .	2	12	28	20	29	31	60	82
Royalties and licence fees	2 266 . .	1	4	24	27	22	25	34	48
Other business services	2 268 . .	827	1,263	1,115	1,380	1,197	1,189	1,285	1,228
Personal, cultural, and recreational	2 287 . .	14	27	36	48	92	60	51	69
Government, n.i.e.	2 291 . .	44	38	47	17	30	32	2	8
Other services, debit	3 200 BA	**–2,174**	**–4,960**	**–4,070**	**–3,564**	**–4,188**	**–4,599**	**–4,146**	**–3,876**
Communications	3 245 . .	–160	–195	–203	–234	–354	–566	–423	–278
Construction	3 249 . .	–406	–2,056	–1,109	–378	–273	–374	–316	–324
Insurance	3 253 . .	–236	–727	–701	–840	–963	–741	–320	–287
Financial	3 260 . .	–127	–228	–226	–188	–247	–210	–220	–432
Computer and information	3 262 . .	–35	–58	–135	–86	–124	–145	–218	–264
Royalties and licence fees	3 266 . .	–18	–44	–144	–175	–195	–491	–555	–508
Other business services	3 268 . .	–1,066	–1,496	–1,396	–1,473	–1,821	–1,826	–1,822	–1,554
Personal, cultural, and recreational	3 287 . .	–13	–26	–41	–57	–66	–101	–139	–120
Government, n.i.e.	3 291 . .	–113	–130	–115	–133	–145	–145	–133	–109

Table 2 (Continued). STANDARD PRESENTATION, 1994–2001
(Millions of U.S. dollars)

	Code	1994	1995	1996	1997	1998	1999	2000	2001
C. INCOME	4 300	–2,563	–1,995	–1,075	–1,129	–1,178	–1,010	–1,463	–1,390
Total credit	2 300	*546*	*1,089*	*1,527*	*1,467*	*2,226*	*1,837*	*2,250*	*2,625*
Total debit	3 300	*–3,109*	*–3,084*	*–2,602*	*–2,596*	*–3,404*	*–2,847*	*–3,713*	*–4,015*
Compensation of employees, credit	2 310	**23**	**28**	**51**	**51**	**132**	**127**	**192**	**193**
Compensation of employees, debit	3 310	**–130**	**–251**	**–230**	**–176**	**–161**	**–156**	**–213**	**–250**
Investment income, credit	2 320	**523**	**1,061**	**1,476**	**1,416**	**2,094**	**1,710**	**2,058**	**2,432**
Direct investment income	2 330	12	20	26	7	6	–13	24	32
Dividends and distributed branch profits	2 332	2	7	5	8	33	19	17	18
Reinvested earnings and undistributed branch profits	2 333	10	13	21	–3	–31	–40	–12	9
Income on debt (interest)	2 334	...	...	...	2	4	8	19	5
Portfolio investment income	2 339	191	516	689	716	1,016	1,065	1,050	1,442
Income on equity	2 340	...	6	22	4	5	3	17	8
Income on bonds and notes	2 350	171	372	664	709	965	937	882	1,431
Income on money market instruments	2 360	20	138	3	3	46	125	151	3
Other investment income	2 370	320	525	761	693	1,072	658	984	958
Investment income, debit	3 320	**–2,979**	**–2,833**	**–2,372**	**–2,420**	**–3,243**	**–2,691**	**–3,500**	**–3,765**
Direct investment income	3 330	–389	–1,048	–549	–639	–610	–396	–701	–714
Dividends and distributed branch profits	3 332	–7	–155	–217	–362	–466	–430	–559	–982
Reinvested earnings and undistributed branch profits	3 333	–382	–888	–244	–25	264	453	400	1,040
Income on debt (interest)	3 334	...	–5	–88	–252	–408	–419	–542	–772
Portfolio investment income	3 339	–18	–391	–556	–574	–948	–846	–931	–1,057
Income on equity	3 340	...	–2	–19	–54	–139	–127	–140	–234
Income on bonds and notes	3 350	–18	–363	–536	–513	–704	–671	–693	–821
Income on money market instruments	3 360	...	–26	–1	–7	–105	–48	–98	–2
Other investment income	3 370	–2,572	–1,394	–1,267	–1,207	–1,685	–1,449	–1,868	–1,994
D. CURRENT TRANSFERS	4 379	1,252	958	1,694	2,035	2,897	2,214	2,380	2,889
Credit	2 379	**2,174**	**2,459**	**2,825**	**2,700**	**3,520**	**2,898**	**3,008**	**3,737**
General government	2 380	128	244	82	120	458	269	361	406
Other sectors	2 390	2,046	2,215	2,743	2,580	3,062	2,629	2,647	3,331
Workers' remittances	2 391	558	696	723	797	938	698	639	938
Other current transfers	2 392	1,488	1,519	2,020	1,783	2,124	1,931	2,008	2,393
Debit	3 379	**–922**	**–1,501**	**–1,131**	**–665**	**–623**	**–684**	**–628**	**–848**
General government	3 380	...	...	...	...	–20	–52	–58	–124
Other sectors	3 390	–922	–1,501	–1,131	–665	–603	–632	–570	–724
Workers' remittances	3 391	–25	–11	–13	–5	–15	–35	–11	–14
Other current transfers	3 392	–897	–1,490	–1,118	–660	–588	–597	–559	–710
CAPITAL AND FINANCIAL ACCOUNT	4 996	**–856**	**–290**	**2,943**	**4,435**	**7,421**	**10,361**	**9,611**	**3,675**
CAPITAL ACCOUNT	4 994	**9,215**	**285**	**94**	**66**	**63**	**55**	**32**	**75**
Total credit	2 994	*9,215*	*285*	*5,833*	*91*	*117*	*95*	*109*	*112*
Total debit	3 994	...	...	*–5,739*	*25*	*–54*	*–40*	*–77*	*–37*
Capital transfers, credit	2 400	**9,215**	**285**	**5,825**	**91**	**116**	**93**	**109**	**111**
General government	2 401	9,215	285	5,821	90	94	70	55	27
Debt forgiveness	2 402	9,215	285	5,799	64	90	57	32	22
Other capital transfers	2 410	...	...	22	26	4	13	23	5
Other sectors	2 430	...	...	4	1	22	23	54	84
Migrants' transfers	2 431	...	...	...	...	...	...	...	...
Debt forgiveness	2 432	...	...	4	1	3	8	22	76
Other capital transfers	2 440	...	...	...	...	19	15	32	8
Capital transfers, debit	3 400	**...**	**...**	**–5,732**	**–10**	**–42**	**–4**	**–61**	**–4**
General government	3 401	...	...	–5,732	–9	–38	–1	–20	...
Debt forgiveness	3 402	...	...	–5,730	...	–37	...	...	...
Other capital transfers	3 410	...	...	–2	–9	–1	–1	–20	...
Other sectors	3 430	...	...	...	–1	–4	–3	–41	–4
Migrants' transfers	3 431	...	...	...	...	...	...	...	...
Debt forgiveness	3 432	...	...	...	–1	–1	–2	–36	–3
Other capital transfers	3 440	...	...	...	...	–3	–1	–5	–1
Nonproduced nonfinancial assets, credit	2 480	**...**	**...**	**8**	**...**	**1**	**2**	**...**	**1**
Nonproduced nonfinancial assets, debit	3 480	**...**	**...**	**–7**	**–15**	**–12**	**–36**	**–16**	**–33**

Table 2 (Continued). STANDARD PRESENTATION, 1994–2001
(Millions of U.S. dollars)

	Code	1994	1995	1996	1997	1998	1999	2000	2001
FINANCIAL ACCOUNT	4 995	**–10,071**	**–575**	**2,849**	**4,369**	**7,358**	**10,306**	**9,579**	**3,600**
A. DIRECT INVESTMENT	4 500	1,846	3,617	4,445	4,863	6,049	7,239	9,324	5,802
Direct investment abroad	4 505	**–29**	**–42**	**–53**	**–45**	**–316**	**–31**	**–17**	**89**
Equity capital	4 510	–19	–29	–12	–24	–117	–99	–111	48
Claims on affiliated enterprises	4 515	–19	–29	–12	–24	–117	–99	–111	48
Liabilities to affiliated enterprises	4 520	. . .	. . .	. . .	. . .	. . .	. . .	. . .	. . .
Reinvested earnings	4 525	–10	–13	–21	3	31	40	12	–9
Other capital	4 530	. . .	. . .	–20	–24	–230	28	82	50
Claims on affiliated enterprises	4 535	. . .	. . .	–20	–24	–230	1	73	54
Liabilities to affiliated enterprises	4 540	. . .	. . .	. . .	. . .	. . .	27	9	–4
Direct investment in Poland	4 555	**1,875**	**3,659**	**4,498**	**4,908**	**6,365**	**7,270**	**9,341**	**5,713**
Equity capital	4 560	1,096	2,105	3,159	3,116	4,604	6,467	8,812	5,300
Claims on direct investors	4 565	. . .	. . .	. . .	. . .	. . .	. . .	. . .	. . .
Liabilities to direct investors	4 570	1,096	2,105	3,159	3,116	4,604	6,467	8,812	5,300
Reinvested earnings	4 575	382	888	244	25	–264	–453	–400	–1,040
Other capital	4 580	397	666	1,095	1,767	2,025	1,256	929	1,453
Claims on direct investors	4 585	. . .	. . .	–2	–2	–18	–110	18	34
Liabilities to direct investors	4 590	397	666	1,097	1,769	2,043	1,366	911	1,419
B. PORTFOLIO INVESTMENT	4 600	–624	1,177	304	2,110	1,697	143	3,333	1,113
Assets	4 602	**–624**	**1**	**282**	**815**	**–130**	**–548**	**–89**	**46**
Equity securities	4 610	. . .	127	–17	56	1	–172	–23	–68
Monetary authorities	4 611	. . .	. . .	. . .	. . .	. . .	. . .	. . .	. . .
General government	4 612	. . .	. . .	. . .	. . .	. . .	–1	–1	–1
Banks	4 613	. . .	127	–17	59	. . .	–18	–5	2
Other sectors	4 614	. . .	. . .	. . .	–3	1	–153	–17	–69
Debt securities	4 619	–624	–126	299	759	–131	–376	–66	114
Bonds and notes	4 620	–624	–86	286	675	–103	–315	–9	125
Monetary authorities	4 621	. . .	. . .	. . .	. . .	. . .	. . .	. . .	. . .
General government	4 622	–624	45	. . .	289	. . .	–25	10	195
Banks	4 623	. . .	–131	286	383	–102	–297	22	–35
Other sectors	4 624	. . .	. . .	. . .	3	–1	7	–41	–35
Money market instruments	4 630	. . .	–40	13	84	–28	–61	–57	–11
Monetary authorities	4 631	. . .	. . .	. . .	. . .	. . .	. . .	. . .	. . .
General government	4 632	. . .	. . .	. . .	. . .	. . .	. . .	–3	. . .
Banks	4 633	. . .	–40	13	64	–22	–8	–26	–19
Other sectors	4 634	. . .	. . .	. . .	20	–6	–53	–28	8
Liabilities	4 652	**. . .**	**1,176**	**22**	**1,295**	**1,827**	**691**	**3,422**	**1,067**
Equity securities	4 660	. . .	219	749	599	1,734	14	447	–307
Banks	4 663	. . .	25	129	126	211	–355	–213	187
Other sectors	4 664	. . .	194	620	473	1,523	369	660	–494
Debt securities	4 669	. . .	957	–727	696	93	677	2,975	1,374
Bonds and notes	4 670	. . .	418	–387	760	302	719	2,888	1,365
Monetary authorities	4 671	. . .	. . .	. . .	. . .	. . .	. . .	. . .	. . .
General government	4 672	. . .	418	245	154	–610	142	2,205	789
Banks	4 673	. . .	. . .	–632	562	–91	–160	100	60
Other sectors	4 674	. . .	. . .	. . .	44	1,003	737	583	516
Money market instruments	4 680	. . .	539	–340	–64	–209	–42	87	9
Monetary authorities	4 681	. . .	. . .	. . .	. . .	. . .	. . .	. . .	. . .
General government	4 682	. . .	533	–400	26	–112	–61	13	15
Banks	4 683	. . .	. . .	. . .	67	–163	17	. . .	. . .
Other sectors	4 684	. . .	6	60	–157	66	2	74	–6
C. FINANCIAL DERIVATIVES	4 910	. . .	. . .	–3	–12	. . .	569	269	–336
Monetary authorities	4 911	. . .	. . .	. . .	. . .	. . .	. . .	. . .	. . .
General government	4 912	. . .	. . .	. . .	. . .	. . .	. . .	. . .	. . .
Banks	4 913	. . .	. . .	–3	–12	. . .	554	378	–186
Other sectors	4 914	. . .	. . .	. . .	. . .	. . .	15	–109	–150
Assets	4 900	**. . .**	**. . .**	**. . .**	**. . .**	**. . .**	**579**	**269**	**. . .**
Monetary authorities	4 901	. . .	. . .	. . .	. . .	. . .	. . .	. . .	. . .
General government	4 902	. . .	. . .	. . .	. . .	. . .	. . .	. . .	. . .
Banks	4 903	. . .	. . .	. . .	. . .	. . .	561	378	. . .
Other sectors	4 904	. . .	. . .	. . .	. . .	. . .	18	–109	. . .
Liabilities	4 905	**. . .**	**. . .**	**–3**	**–12**	**. . .**	**–10**	**. . .**	**–336**
Monetary authorities	4 906	. . .	. . .	. . .	. . .	. . .	. . .	. . .	. . .
General government	4 907	. . .	. . .	. . .	. . .	. . .	. . .	. . .	. . .
Banks	4 908	. . .	. . .	–3	–12	. . .	–7	. . .	. . .
Other sectors	4 909	. . .	. . .	. . .	. . .	. . .	–3	. . .	. . .

Table 2 (Concluded). STANDARD PRESENTATION, 1994–2001
(Millions of U.S. dollars)

	Code	1994	1995	1996	1997	1998	1999	2000	2001
D. OTHER INVESTMENT	4 700	–9,780	3,062	1,931	452	5,538	2,511	–2,722	–3,407
Assets	4 703	**–1,841**	**3,356**	**6,191**	**–754**	**2,107**	**–3,339**	**–3,870**	**–4,071**
Trade credits	4 706	126	–119	–224	170	–94	–573	–542	–744
General government	4 707	. . .	. . .	. . .	. . .	. . .	. . .	. . .	. . .
of which: Short-term	4 709	. . .	. . .	. . .	. . .	. . .	. . .	. . .	. . .
Other sectors	4 710	126	–119	–224	170	–94	–573	–542	–744
of which: Short-term	4 712	*126*	*–119*	*–224*	*170*	*–94*	*–573*	*–542*	*–744*
Loans	4 714	–21	–59	–27	–188	–83	19	67	81
Monetary authorities	4 715	. . .	. . .	. . .	. . .	1	1	1	1
of which: Short-term	4 718	. . .	. . .	. . .	. . .	. . .	. . .	. . .	. . .
General government	4 719	. . .	44	25	7	5	3	–15	–18
of which: Short-term	4 721	. . .	. . .	. . .	. . .	. . .	. . .	. . .	. . .
Banks	4 722	. . .	–83	–29	–219	–87	19	83	95
of which: Short-term	4 724	. . .	*–112*	*2*	*–80*	*–5*	*13*	*47*	*14*
Other sectors	4 725	–21	–20	–23	24	–2	–4	–2	3
of which: Short-term	4 727	. . .	*–22*	*–8*	*3*	*4*	*–3*	*–1*	. . .
Currency and deposits	4 730	–1,853	3,793	685	–768	2,229	–2,776	–3,366	–3,348
Monetary authorities	4 731	194	65	37	. . .	. . .	. . .	. . .	. . .
General government	4 732	. . .	. . .	. . .	. . .	. . .	. . .	–5	. . .
Banks	4 733	–1,582	1,146	474	–857	2,294	–2,713	–3,097	–3,493
Other sectors	4 734	–465	2,582	174	89	–65	–63	–264	145
Other assets	4 736	–93	–259	5,757	32	55	–9	–29	–60
Monetary authorities	4 737	. . .	. . .	. . .	. . .	. . .	. . .	. . .	. . .
of which: Short-term	4 739	. . .	. . .	. . .	. . .	. . .	. . .	. . .	. . .
General government	4 740	34	2	5,742	34	48	–9	–29	–18
of which: Short-term	4 742	*34*	*2*	*5,742*	*34*	*48*	*–9*	*–29*	*–18*
Banks	4 743	–136	–6	8	. . .	. . .	. . .	. . .	. . .
of which: Short-term	4 745	*–136*	*–6*	*8*	. . .	. . .	. . .	. . .	. . .
Other sectors	4 746	9	–255	7	–2	7	. . .	. . .	–42
of which: Short-term	4 748	*9*	*–255*	*7*	*–2*	*7*	. . .	. . .	*–42*
Liabilities	4 753	**–7,939**	**–294**	**–4,260**	**1,206**	**3,431**	**5,850**	**1,148**	**664**
Trade credits	4 756	–174	223	703	–159	–51	1,726	722	479
General government	4 757	. . .	. . .	. . .	. . .	. . .	. . .	. . .	. . .
of which: Short-term	4 759	. . .	. . .	. . .	. . .	. . .	. . .	. . .	. . .
Other sectors	4 760	–174	223	703	–159	–51	1,726	722	479
of which: Short-term	4 762	*–174*	*223*	*703*	*–159*	*–51*	*1,726*	*722*	*479*
Loans	4 764	–7,792	–1,019	–5,432	1,757	2,651	3,401	2,110	–598
Monetary authorities	4 765	616	–1,394	–85	–14	–30	–9	–6	–7
of which: Use of Fund credit and loans from the Fund	4 766	*603*	*–1,408*	. . .	. . .	. . .	. . .	. . .	. . .
of which: Short-term	4 768	. . .	. . .	. . .	. . .	. . .	. . .	. . .	. . .
General government	4 769	–8,621	8	–6,013	–49	–368	–224	–291	–3,045
of which: Short-term	4 771	*–50*	. . .	. . .	*221*	*–215*	. . .	. . .	. . .
Banks	4 772	–39	66	16	564	881	1,795	7	–30
of which: Short-term	4 774	*–1*	. . .	*11*	*66*	*44*	*147*	*–143*	*–67*
Other sectors	4 775	252	301	650	1,256	2,168	1,839	2,414	2,484
of which: Short-term	4 777	*–20*	*–8*	*–23*	*33*	*190*	*175*	*–155*	*120*
Currency and deposits	4 780	193	508	463	–392	831	607	–1,854	438
Monetary authorities	4 781	2	. . .	187	–547	229	389	–1,386	125
General government	4 782	. . .	. . .	. . .	. . .	. . .	. . .	. . .	. . .
Banks	4 783	191	508	276	155	602	218	–468	313
Other sectors	4 784	. . .	. . .	. . .	. . .	. . .	. . .	. . .	. . .
Other liabilities	4 786	–166	–6	6	. . .	. . .	116	170	345
Monetary authorities	4 787	. . .	. . .	. . .	. . .	. . .	. . .	. . .	. . .
of which: Short-term	4 789	. . .	. . .	. . .	. . .	. . .	. . .	. . .	. . .
General government	4 790	–184	–7	–16	. . .	. . .	. . .	. . .	. . .
of which: Short-term	4 792	*–184*	*–7*	*–16*	. . .	. . .	. . .	. . .	. . .
Banks	4 793	18	1	22	. . .	. . .	. . .	. . .	. . .
of which: Short-term	4 795	*18*	*1*	*22*	. . .	. . .	. . .	. . .	. . .
Other sectors	4 796	. . .	. . .	. . .	. . .	. . .	116	170	345
of which: Short-term	4 798	. . .	. . .	. . .	. . .	. . .	*116*	*170*	*345*
E. RESERVE ASSETS	4 802	–1,514	–8,431	–3,828	–3,044	–5,926	–156	–625	428
Monetary gold	4 812	. . .	. . .	. . .	–100	–710	. . .	. . .	–1
Special drawing rights	4 811	–1	–1	–2	–1	–1	–4	–7	–9
Reserve position in the Fund	4 810	. . .	. . .	. . .	. . .	. . .	–131	. . .	–247
Foreign exchange	4 803	–1,513	–8,430	–658	19	–9,814	–362	–1,409	1,237
Other claims	4 813	. . .	. . .	–3,168	–2,962	4,599	342	791	–552
NET ERRORS AND OMISSIONS	4 998	**–98**	**–564**	**321**	**1,309**	**–520**	**2,126**	**387**	**1,682**

Part 3 of the *Yearbook* contains descriptions of the methodologies, compilation practices, and sources used to compile these data.

Table 3. INTERNATIONAL INVESTMENT POSITION (End–period stocks), 1994–2001
(Millions of U.S. dollars)

	Code	1994	1995	1996	1997	1998	1999	2000	2001
ASSETS	8 995 C.	23,506	31,966	28,746	31,908	38,399	40,101	44,672	47,654
Direct investment abroad	8 505 . .	**461**	**539**	**735**	**678**	**1,165**	**1,024**	**1,018**	**1,107**
Equity capital and reinvested earnings	8 506 . .	461	539	715	635	898	812	870	986
Claims on affiliated enterprises	8 507 . .	461	539	715	635	898	812	870	986
Liabilities to affiliated enterprises	8 508 . .	...	...	...	...	...	...	...	...
Other capital	8 530 . .	...	...	20	43	267	212	148	121
Claims on affiliated enterprises	8 535 . .	...	...	20	43	267	240	163	132
Liabilities to affiliated enterprises	8 540 . .	...	...	...	...	...	–28	–15	–11
Portfolio investment	8 602 . .	**1,287**	**1,937**	**1,338**	**839**	**1,093**	**1,143**	**1,575**	**1,311**
Equity securities	8 610 . .	...	...	38	2	9	28	47	108
Monetary authorities	8 611 . .	...	...	...	2	2	2	2	10
General government	8 612 . .	...	...	...	...	...	...	...	...
Banks	8 613 . .	...	...	38	...	...	21	31	33
Other sectors	8 614 . .	...	...	...	...	7	5	14	65
Debt securities	8 619 . .	...	...	1,300	837	1,084	1,115	1,528	1,203
Bonds and notes	8 620 . .	...	...	1,242	831	1,059	1,099	1,467	1,185
Monetary authorities	8 621 . .	...	...	...	...	...	...	...	...
General government	8 622 . .	...	...	...	666	781	596	857	415
Banks	8 623 . .	...	...	842	165	278	475	562	548
Other sectors	8 624 . .	...	...	400	...	...	28	48	222
Money market instruments	8 630 . .	...	...	58	6	25	16	61	18
Monetary authorities	8 631 . .	...	...	...	...	...	...	...	...
General government	8 632 . .	...	...	44	...	...	...	...	...
Banks	8						...	3	2
Financial derivatives	8 900 . .	...	...	...	...	...	...	...	...
Monetary authorities	8 901 . .	...	...	...	...	...	...	...	...
General government	8 902 . .	...	...	...	...	...	...	...	...
Banks	8 903 . .	...	...	...	...	...	...	...	...
Other sectors	8 904 . .	...	...	...	...	...	...	...	...
Other investment	8 703 . .	**15,727**	**14,527**	**8,454**	**8,988**	**7,866**	**10,619**	**14,615**	**18,682**
Trade credits	8 706 . .	1,154	1,424	2,036	1,781	2,325	2,521	3,151	3,895
General government	8 707 . .	...	...	...	...	...	...	...	...
of which: Short-term	8 709 . .	...	...	...	...	...	...	...	...
Other sectors	8 710 . .	1,154	1,424	2,036	1,781	2,325	2,521	3,151	3,895
of which: Short-term	8 712 . .	*1,154*	*1,424*	*2,036*	*1,781*	*2,325*	*2,521*	*3,151*	*3,895*
Loans	8 714 . .	1,397	880	912	1,156	1,343	1,286	1,259	1,153
Monetary authorities	8 715 . .	6	6	6	5	4	2	1	...
of which: Short-term	8 718 . .	...	...	...	...	...	...	...	...
General government	8 719 . .	1,051	829	800	786	773	770	780	783
of which: Short-term	8 721 . .	...	...	...	...	...	...	...	...
Banks	8 722 . .	69	14	54	338	537	487	458	354
of which: Short-term	8 724 . .	*36*	*5*	*32*	*120*	*207*	*139*	*100*	*109*
Other sectors	8 725 . .	271	31	52	27	29	27	20	16
of which: Short-term	8 727 . .	...	*1*	*11*	*8*	*4*	*8*	*1*	*1*
Currency and deposits	8 730 . .	7,252	6,319	5,394	5,980	4,170	6,551	9,906	13,273
Monetary authorities	8 731 . .	246	181	144	...	...	...	...	...
General government	8 732 . .	...	...	...	...	...	...	...	...
Banks	8 733 . .	6,598	5,651	4,938	5,823	3,882	6,210	9,300	12,853
Other sectors	8 734 . .	408	487	312	157	288	341	606	420
Other assets	8 736 . .	5,924	5,904	112	71	28	261	299	361
Monetary authorities	8 737 . .	...	...	...	...	...	...	...	...
of which: Short-term	8 739 . .	...	...	...	...	...	...	...	...
General government	8 740 . .	5,919	5,891	81	43	28	261	296	313
of which: Short-term	8 742 . .	*5,919*	*5,891*	*81*	*43*	*28*	*27*	*7*	*7*
Banks	8 743 . .	5	13	5	...	...	...	...	...
of which: Short-term	8 745 . .	...	...	...	...	...	...	...	...
Other sectors	8 746 . .	...	...	26	28	...	...	3	48
of which: Short-term	8 748 . .	...	...	*26*	*28*	...	...	*3*	*48*
Reserve assets	8 802 . .	**6,031**	**14,963**	**18,219**	**21,403**	**28,275**	**27,315**	**27,464**	**26,554**
Monetary gold	8 812 . .	189	189	189	263	950	960	901	915
Special drawing rights	8 811 . .	1	2	4	5	7	11	18	26
Reserve position in the Fund	8 810 . .	113	115	111	104	109	236	224	461
Foreign exchange	8 803 . .	5,728	14,657	14,747	14,900	25,501	24,288	25,318	23,631
Other claims	8 813 . .	...	...	3,168	6,131	1,708	1,819	1,003	1,521

Table 3 (Concluded). INTERNATIONAL INVESTMENT POSITION (End-period stocks), 1994–2001

(Millions of U.S. dollars)

	Code		1994	1995	1996	1997	1998	1999	2000	2001
LIABILITIES	8 995	D.	53,075	59,304	58,515	62,439	80,205	89,257	99,999	106,210
Direct investment in Poland	8 555	. .	**3,789**	**7,843**	**11,463**	**14,587**	**22,479**	**26,075**	**34,227**	**41,031**
Equity capital and reinvested earnings	8 556	. .	2,840	6,130	8,697	10,125	16,063	18,986	25,353	30,970
Claims on direct investors	8 557	. .	. . .	. . .	. . .	. . .	. . .	. . .	. . .	. . .
Liabilities to direct investors	8 558	. .	2,840	6,130	8,697	10,125	16,063	18,986	25,353	30,970
Other capital	8 580	. .	949	1,713	2,766	4,462	6,416	7,089	8,874	10,061
Claims on direct investors	8 585	. .	. . .	. . .	–2	–5	–22	–125	–154	–98
Liabilities to direct investors	8 590	. .	. . .	. . .	2,768	4,467	6,438	7,214	9,028	10,159
Portfolio investment	8 652	. .	**8,431**	**9,375**	**10,148**	**11,325**	**13,658**	**14,617**	**18,057**	**18,895**
Equity securities	8 660	. .	443	663	2,279	2,672	4,969	4,980	5,350	4,301
Banks	8 663	. .	. . .	. . .	. . .	. . .	. . .	. . .	. . .	. . .
Other sectors	8 664	. .	. . .	. . .	. . .	. . .	. . .	. . .	. . .	. . .
Debt securities	8 669	. .	7,988	8,712	7,869	8,653	8,689	9,637	12,707	14,594
Bonds and notes	8 670	. .	7,988	7,777	7,115	7,974	8,215	9,469	12,448	14,347
Monetary authorities	8 671	. .	. . .	. . .	. . .	. . .	. . .	. . .	. . .	. . .
General government	8 672	. .	7,988	7,777	6,884	7,343	6,672	6,777	9,073	10,014
Banks	8 673	. .	. . .	. . .	200	306	215	10	110	167
Other sectors	8 674	. .	. . .	. . .	31	325	1,328	2,682	3,265	4,166
Money market instruments	8 680	. .	. . .	935	754	679	474	168	259	247
Monetary authorities	8 681	. .	. . .	. . .	. . .	. . .	. . .	. . .	. . .	. . .
General government	8 682	. .	. . .	924	678	475	365	145	158	234
Banks	8 683	. .	. . .	. . .	. . .	182	21	. . .	. . .	. . .
Other sectors	8 684	. .	. . .	11	76	22	88	23	101	13
Financial derivatives	8 905	. .	**. . .**	**. . .**	**. . .**	**. . .**	**. . .**	**. . .**	**. . .**	**. . .**
Monetary authorities	8 906	. .	. . .	. . .	. . .	. . .	. . .	. . .	. . .	. . .
General government	8 907	. .	. . .	. . .	. . .	. . .	. . .	. . .	. . .	. . .
Banks	8 908	. .	. . .	. . .	. . .	. . .	. . .	. . .	. . .	. . .
Other sectors	8 909	. .	. . .	. . .	. . .	. . .	. . .	. . .	. . .	. . .
Other investment	8 753	. .	**40,855**	**42,086**	**36,904**	**36,527**	**44,068**	**48,565**	**47,715**	**46,284**
Trade credits	8 756	. .	995	1,276	2,197	1,862	3,560	5,225	5,612	6,106
General government	8 757	. .	. . .	. . .	. . .	. . .	. . .	. . .	. . .	. . .
of which: Short-term	8 759	. .	. . .	. . .	. . .	. . .	. . .	. . .	. . .	. . .
Other sectors	8 760	. .	995	1,276	2,197	1,862	3,560	5,225	5,612	6,106
of which: Short-term	8 762	. .	*995*	*1,276*	*2,197*	*1,862*	*3,560*	*5,225*	*5,612*	*6,106*
Loans	8 764	. .	38,939	39,409	32,776	31,982	36,964	38,678	39,241	36,767
Monetary authorities	8 765	. .	1,493	174	78	58	32	23	15	8
of which: Use of Fund credit and loans from the Fund	8 766	. .	*1,341*	. . .	. . .	. . .	. . .	. . .	. . .	. . .
of which: Short-term	8 768	. .	. . .	. . .	. . .	. . .	. . .	. . .	. . .	. . .
General government	8 769	. .	34,482	35,936	28,708	26,584	27,061	25,197	23,747	18,987
of which: Short-term	8 771	. .	. . .	. . .	. . .	*217*	. . .	. . .	. . .	. . .
Banks	8 772	. .	498	452	488	1,104	2,084	3,681	3,595	3,679
of which: Short-term	8 774	. .	*59*	. . .	*15*	*278*	*120*	*277*	*78*	*8*
Other sectors	8 775	. .	2,466	2,847	3,502	4,236	7,787	9,777	11,884	14,093
of which: Short-term	8 777	. .	*45*	*88*	*72*	*105*	*279*	*457*	*243*	*255*
Currency and deposits	8 780	. .	863	1,346	1,872	2,683	3,544	4,544	2,638	3,043
Monetary authorities	8 781	. .	. . .	. . .	187	733	893	1,821	421	420
General government	8 782	. .	. . .	. . .	. . .	. . .	. . .	. . .	. . .	. . .
Banks	8 783	. .	863	1,346	1,685	1,950	2,651	2,723	2,217	2,623
Other sectors	8 784	. .	. . .	. . .	. . .	. . .	. . .	. . .	. . .	. . .
Other liabilities	8 786	. .	58	55	59	. . .	. . .	118	224	368
Monetary authorities	8 787	. .	. . .	. . .	. . .	. . .	. . .	. . .	. . .	. . .
of which: Short-term	8 789	. .	. . .	. . .	. . .	. . .	. . .	. . .	. . .	. . .
General government	8 790	. .	25	19	1	. . .	. . .	2	2	2
of which: Short-term	8 792	. .	*25*	*19*	*1*	. . .	. . .	*2*	*2*	*2*
Banks	8 793	. .	33	36	58	. . .	. . .	. . .	. . .	. . .
of which: Short-term	8 795	. .	*33*	*36*	*58*	. . .	. . .	. . .	. . .	. . .
Other sectors	8 796	. .	. . .	. . .	. . .	. . .	. . .	116	222	366
of which: Short-term	8 798	. .	. . .	. . .	. . .	. . .	. . .	*116*	*222*	*366*
NET INTERNATIONAL INVESTMENT POSITION	8 995	. .	**–29,569**	**–27,338**	**–29,769**	**–30,531**	**–41,806**	**–49,156**	**–55,327**	**–58,556**
Conversion rates: zlotys per U.S. dollar (end of period)	0 102	. .	**2.4372**	**2.4680**	**2.8755**	**3.5180**	**3.5040**	**4.1483**	**4.1432**	**3.9863**

Table 1. ANALYTIC PRESENTATION, 1994–2001
(Millions of U.S. dollars)

	Code	1994	1995	1996	1997	1998	1999	2000	2001
A. Current Account [1]	4 993 Z.	**–2,196**	**–132**	**–5,216**	**–6,465**	**–7,833**	**–9,764**	**–10,962**	**–9,959**
Goods: exports f.o.b	2 100 . .	18,645	24,024	25,623	25,379	25,618	25,468	25,219	25,795
Goods: imports f.o.b	3 100 . .	–26,966	–32,934	–35,345	–35,721	–37,829	–39,227	–39,155	–38,774
Balance on Goods	4 100 . .	*–8,321*	*–8,910*	*–9,722*	*–10,342*	*–12,211*	*–13,758*	*–13,936*	*–12,979*
Services: credit	2 200 . .	6,755	8,236	8,040	8,002	8,829	8,659	8,472	8,787
Services: debit	3 200 . .	–5,486	–6,611	–6,636	–6,572	–6,903	–6,801	–6,593	–6,193
Balance on Goods and Services	4 991 . .	*–7,052*	*–7,285*	*–8,317*	*–8,912*	*–10,285*	*–11,900*	*–12,057*	*–10,385*
Income: credit	2 300 . .	2,232	4,095	4,250	4,238	4,496	4,261	4,793	5,128
Income: debit	3 300 . .	–2,797	–4,074	–5,420	–5,744	–6,135	–6,029	–7,101	–8,182
Balance on Goods, Services, and Income	4 992 . .	*–7,616*	*–7,264*	*–9,488*	*–10,418*	*–11,924*	*–13,669*	*–14,365*	*–13,439*
Current transfers: credit	2 379 Z.	7,410	9,046	6,515	5,985	6,170	6,048	5,386	5,626
Current transfers: debit	3 379 . .	–1,989	–1,914	–2,243	–2,031	–2,080	–2,143	–1,983	–2,145
B. Capital Account [1]	4 994 Z.	**. . .**	**. . .**	**2,695**	**2,704**	**2,546**	**2,459**	**1,512**	**1,067**
Capital account: credit	2 994 Z.	. . .	. . .	2,836	2,893	2,724	2,642	1,681	1,276
Capital account: debit	3 994 . .	. . .	. . .	–141	–189	–179	–183	–169	–209
Total, Groups A Plus B	4 981 . .	*–2,196*	*–132*	*–2,521*	*–3,761*	*–5,288*	*–7,306*	*–9,450*	*–8,892*
C. Financial Account [1]	4 995 W.	**1,052**	**3,025**	**3,835**	**6,662**	**5,980**	**9,098**	**11,184**	**10,386**
Direct investment abroad	4 505 . .	–287	–688	–972	–2,187	–3,851	–3,019	–7,749	–7,874
Direct investment in Portugal	4 555 Z.	1,270	685	1,703	2,542	3,151	1,235	6,518	5,945
Portfolio investment assets	4 602 . .	–3,456	–3,148	–5,549	–8,697	–5,997	–6,737	–4,583	–6,430
Equity securities	4 610 . .	–66	–159	–602	–568	–975	–2,110	–1,044	–1,755
Debt securities	4 619 . .	–3,390	–2,989	–4,947	–8,129	–5,022	–4,626	–3,539	–4,676
Portfolio investment liabilities	4 652 Z.	3,934	2,066	2,383	8,790	5,385	9,945	2,792	8,405
Equity securities	4 660 . .	562	–179	1,669	3,821	2,165	691	415	424
Debt securities	4 669 Z.	3,372	2,244	714	4,970	3,221	9,254	2,376	7,981
Financial derivatives	4 910 . .	. . .	. . .	–36	–19	131	197	323	256
Financial derivatives assets	4 900 . .	. . .	. . .	93	341	1,116	2,682	3,673	3,086
Financial derivatives liabilities	4 905 . .	. . .	. . .	–130	–360	–985	–2,485	–3,351	–2,830
Other investment assets	4 703 . .	–7,098	–7,568	–3,368	–5,346	–7,100	421	–10,262	–4,743
Monetary authorities	4 701 . .	. . .	–26	–3	1	–94	–1,005	11	21
General government	4 704 . .	. . .	. . .	1	11	. . .	–20	–12	–42
Banks	4 705 . .	–4,741	–6,679	–2,945	–3,116	–3,813	973	–7,201	–1,034
Other sectors	4 728 . .	–2,358	–863	–422	–2,241	–3,192	473	–3,059	–3,687
Other investment liabilities	4 753 W.	6,689	11,678	9,675	11,579	14,260	7,055	24,146	14,827
Monetary authorities	4 753 WA	299	–99	731	1,343	837	–3	4,862	88
General government	4 753 ZB	–139	144	–312	–40	–73	–43	–179	–151
Banks	4 753 ZC	7,069	11,189	8,595	8,936	12,245	6,999	18,231	14,481
Other sectors	4 753 ZD	–540	444	661	1,339	1,250	102	1,232	409
Total, Groups A Through C	4 983 . .	*–1,144*	*2,893*	*1,314*	*2,901*	*692*	*1,793*	*1,734*	*1,494*
D. Net Errors and Omissions	4 998 . .	**–287**	**–3,193**	**–767**	**–1,928**	**–184**	**–1,577**	**–1,363**	**–642**
Total, Groups A Through D	4 984 . .	*–1,430*	*–300*	*547*	*974*	*508*	*216*	*371*	*852*
E. Reserves and Related Items	4 802 A.	**1,430**	**300**	**–547**	**–974**	**–508**	**–216**	**–371**	**–852**
Reserve assets	4 802 . .	1,430	300	–547	–974	–508	–216	–371	–852
Use of Fund credit and loans	4 766 . .	. . .	. . .	. . .	. . .	. . .	. . .	. . .	. . .
Exceptional financing	4 920 . .	. . .	. . .	. . .	. . .	. . .	. . .	. . .	. . .
Conversion rates: Portuguese escudos per U.S. dollar	0 101 . .	**165.99**	**151.11**	**154.24**	**175.31**	**180.10**	**. . .**	**. . .**	**. . .**
Conversion rates: euros per U.S. dollar	0 103 . .	**. . .**	**. . .**	**. . .**	**. . .**	**. . .**	**.9386**	**1.0854**	**1.1175**

[1] Excludes components that have been classified in the categories of Group E.

Table 2. STANDARD PRESENTATION, 1994–2001

(Millions of U.S. dollars)

	Code			1994	1995	1996	1997	1998	1999	2000	2001
CURRENT ACCOUNT	4	993	. .	**–2,196**	**–132**	**–5,216**	**–6,465**	**–7,833**	**–9,764**	**–10,962**	**–9,959**
A. GOODS	4	100	. .	–8,321	–8,910	–9,722	–10,342	–12,211	–13,758	–13,936	–12,979
Credit	2	100	. .	**18,645**	**24,024**	**25,623**	**25,379**	**25,618**	**25,468**	**25,219**	**25,795**
General merchandise: exports f.o.b.	2	110	. .	18,344	23,734	25,290	25,029	25,218	25,186	24,940	25,560
Goods for processing: exports f.o.b.	2	150	. .	52	41	70	99	94	89	89	76
Repairs on goods	2	160	. .	145	149	174	162	215	104	105	81
Goods procured in ports by carriers	2	170	. .	102	100	88	90	91	89	85	78
Nonmonetary gold	2	180	. .	2	. . .	. . .	. . .	. . .	1	. . .	. . .
Debit	3	100	. .	**–26,966**	**–32,934**	**–35,345**	**–35,721**	**–37,829**	**–39,227**	**–39,155**	**–38,774**
General merchandise: imports f.o.b.	3	110	. .	–26,806	–32,764	–35,191	–35,593	–37,698	–39,132	–39,010	–38,625
Goods for processing: imports f.o.b.	3	150	. .	–11	–7	–5	–5	–3	–1	–1	. . .
Repairs on goods	3	160	. .	–10	–11	–10	–18	–29	–13	–10	–10
Goods procured in ports by carriers	3	170	. .	–62	–67	–66	–74	–71	–50	–65	–72
Nonmonetary gold	3	180	. .	–76	–85	–72	–32	–27	–30	–69	–67
B. SERVICES	4	200	. .	1,269	1,625	1,404	1,430	1,926	1,858	1,879	2,593
Total credit	2	200	. .	*6,755*	*8,236*	*8,040*	*8,002*	*8,829*	*8,659*	*8,472*	*8,787*
Total debit	3	200	. .	*–5,486*	*–6,611*	*–6,636*	*–6,572*	*–6,903*	*–6,801*	*–6,593*	*–6,193*
Transportation services, credit	2	205	. .	**1,028**	**1,515**	**1,440**	**1,475**	**1,619**	**1,457**	**1,457**	**1,577**
Passenger	2	850	. .	*482*	*815*	*795*	*843*	*920*	*786*	*784*	*765*
Freight	2	851	. .	*277*	*327*	*310*	*341*	*371*	*387*	*418*	*447*
Other	2	852	. .	*270*	*373*	*336*	*291*	*328*	*283*	*255*	*365*
Sea transport, passenger	2	207	. .	2	. . .	3	. . .	1	. . .	. . .	. . .
Sea transport, freight	2	208	. .	107	114	101	120	117	104	109	97
Sea transport, other	2	209	. .	106	128	125	93	105	76	76	133
Air transport, passenger	2	211	. .	472	806	784	834	910	775	777	759
Air transport, freight	2	212	. .	45	50	37	43	47	50	61	71
Air transport, other	2	213	. .	146	215	171	156	171	177	145	179
Other transport, passenger	2	215	. .	7	9	8	10	10	11	7	6
Other transport, freight	2	216	. .	125	163	172	179	208	234	248	279
Other transport, other	2	217	. .	18	30	40	41	52	30	33	53
Transportation services, debit	3	205	. .	**–1,438**	**–1,700**	**–1,780**	**–1,811**	**–1,913**	**–1,894**	**–1,936**	**–1,981**
Passenger	3	850	. .	*–341*	*–440*	*–426*	*–432*	*–447*	*–497*	*–526*	*–486*
Freight	3	851	. .	*–937*	*–1,140*	*–1,217*	*–1,249*	*–1,335*	*–1,283*	*–1,296*	*–1,303*
Other	3	852	. .	*–159*	*–120*	*–136*	*–131*	*–130*	*–114*	*–115*	*–192*
Sea transport, passenger	3	207	. .	–2	–3	–1	. . .	–1	–1	–3	–3
Sea transport, freight	3	208	. .	–589	–717	–765	–772	–819	–716	–712	–707
Sea transport, other	3	209	. .	–74	–64	–49	–37	–45	–38	–36	–51
Air transport, passenger	3	211	. .	–331	–424	–412	–420	–433	–487	–517	–477
Air transport, freight	3	212	. .	–86	–105	–112	–113	–120	–100	–100	–99
Air transport, other	3	213	. .	–78	–48	–80	–84	–80	–67	–69	–130
Other transport, passenger	3	215	. .	–9	–14	–13	–11	–14	–8	–6	–6
Other transport, freight	3	216	. .	–262	–318	–340	–365	–396	–467	–485	–497
Other transport, other	3	217	. .	–8	–8	–7	–9	–6	–9	–10	–11
Travel, credit	2	236	. .	**4,142**	**4,831**	**4,823**	**4,824**	**5,471**	**5,260**	**5,243**	**5,464**
Business travel	2	237	. .	. . .	. . .	. . .	. . .	. . .	. . .	. . .	. . .
Personal travel	2	240	. .	. . .	. . .	. . .	. . .	. . .	. . .	. . .	. . .
Travel, debit	3	236	. .	**–1,707**	**–2,099**	**–2,287**	**–2,174**	**–2,329**	**–2,261**	**–2,228**	**–2,102**
Business travel	3	237	. .	. . .	. . .	. . .	. . .	. . .	. . .	. . .	. . .
Personal travel	3	240	. .	. . .	. . .	. . .	. . .	. . .	. . .	. . .	. . .
Other services, credit	2	200	BA	**1,586**	**1,890**	**1,776**	**1,703**	**1,739**	**1,942**	**1,772**	**1,746**
Communications	2	245	. .	336	327	294	270	212	182	173	188
Construction	2	249	. .	153	232	299	251	193	176	150	184
Insurance	2	253	. .	92	110	54	49	81	70	60	56
Financial	2	260	. .	116	258	244	214	178	258	241	128
Computer and information	2	262	. .	22	41	45	48	52	73	75	60
Royalties and licence fees	2	266	. .	29	19	19	28	43	25	29	25
Other business services	2	268	. .	667	707	651	644	747	956	805	850
Personal, cultural, and recreational	2	287	. .	117	121	95	120	139	110	136	142
Government, n.i.e.	2	291	. .	54	75	76	80	94	93	102	113
Other services, debit	3	200	BA	**–2,341**	**–2,812**	**–2,569**	**–2,587**	**–2,661**	**–2,647**	**–2,428**	**–2,111**
Communications	3	245	. .	–165	–204	–179	–178	–168	–134	–157	–177
Construction	3	249	. .	–81	–207	–261	–135	–107	–127	–59	–70
Insurance	3	253	. .	–248	–307	–98	–87	–93	–102	–101	–94
Financial	3	260	. .	–162	–259	–193	–189	–147	–198	–252	–157
Computer and information	3	262	. .	–49	–77	–113	–125	–142	–195	–162	–152
Royalties and licence fees	3	266	. .	–206	–237	–303	–285	–304	–303	–276	–234
Other business services	3	268	. .	–1,070	–1,085	–991	–1,124	–1,173	–1,102	–937	–789
Personal, cultural, and recreational	3	287	. .	–128	–165	–155	–184	–246	–226	–239	–256
Government, n.i.e.	3	291	. .	–231	–272	–276	–279	–280	–259	–244	–182

Table 2 (Continued). STANDARD PRESENTATION, 1994–2001
(Millions of U.S. dollars)

	Code	1994	1995	1996	1997	1998	1999	2000	2001
C. INCOME	4 300 . .	–564	21	–1,170	–1,506	–1,639	–1,768	–2,309	–3,054
Total credit	2 300 . .	*2,232*	*4,095*	*4,250*	*4,238*	*4,496*	*4,261*	*4,793*	*5,128*
Total debit	3 300 . .	*–2,797*	*–4,074*	*–5,420*	*–5,744*	*–6,135*	*–6,029*	*–7,101*	*–8,182*
Compensation of employees, credit	2 310 . .	**137**	**160**	**150**	**141**	**170**	**157**	**152**	**149**
Compensation of employees, debit	3 310 . .	**–66**	**–84**	**–106**	**–116**	**–94**	**–127**	**–127**	**–145**
Investment income, credit	2 320 . .	**2,096**	**3,935**	**4,099**	**4,098**	**4,326**	**4,104**	**4,641**	**4,979**
Direct investment income	2 330 . .	62	43	331	441	611	619	717	1,078
Dividends and distributed branch profits	2 332 . .	62	42	266	103	252	173	162	251
Reinvested earnings and undistributed branch profits	2 333 . .	. . .	1	55	312	316	414	503	734
Income on debt (interest)	2 334 . .	. . .	. . .	10	25	42	32	52	92
Portfolio investment income	2 339 . .	599	1,404	990	890	997	1,649	1,678	1,589
Income on equity	2 340 . .	. . .	. . .	270	101	78	133	126	136
Income on bonds and notes	2 350 . .	. . .	. . .	638	763	891	1,360	1,235	1,246
Income on money market instruments	2 360 . .	. . .	. . .	82	26	28	157	317	207
Other investment income	2 370 . .	1,435	2,488	2,778	2,767	2,719	1,836	2,246	2,312
Investment income, debit	3 320 . .	**–2,731**	**–3,990**	**–5,314**	**–5,628**	**–6,041**	**–5,902**	**–6,974**	**–8,037**
Direct investment income	3 330 . .	–231	–308	–1,101	–1,218	–1,447	–1,603	–1,717	–1,924
Dividends and distributed branch profits	3 332 . .	–231	–308	–361	–368	–509	–416	–922	–948
Reinvested earnings and undistributed branch profits	3 333 . .	. . .	. . .	–718	–796	–809	–1,059	–639	–828
Income on debt (interest)	3 334 . .	. . .	. . .	–22	–53	–130	–128	–156	–149
Portfolio investment income	3 339 . .	–726	–815	–944	–1,479	–1,628	–1,843	–2,114	–1,971
Income on equity	3 340 . .	. . .	. . .	–71	–126	–189	–192	–374	–412
Income on bonds and notes	3 350 . .	. . .	. . .	–870	–1,314	–1,363	–1,528	–1,626	–1,494
Income on money market instruments	3 360 . .	. . .	. . .	–3	–39	–77	–122	–115	–65
Other investment income	3 370 . .	–1,774	–2,867	–3,269	–2,931	–2,965	–2,456	–3,142	–4,143
D. CURRENT TRANSFERS	4 379 . .	5,421	7,132	4,272	3,954	4,090	3,904	3,403	3,480
Credit	2 379 . .	**7,410**	**9,046**	**6,515**	**5,985**	**6,170**	**6,048**	**5,386**	**5,626**
General government	2 380 . .	3,511	5,172	2,375	2,082	2,212	2,072	1,517	1,449
Other sectors	2 390 . .	3,899	3,874	4,139	3,904	3,958	3,975	3,869	4,177
Workers' remittances	2 391 . .	3,669	3,793	3,575	3,436	3,361	3,320	3,179	3,337
Other current transfers	2 392 . .	230	81	564	467	597	655	691	840
Debit	3 379 . .	**–1,989**	**–1,914**	**–2,243**	**–2,031**	**–2,080**	**–2,143**	**–1,983**	**–2,145**
General government	3 380 . .	–1,569	–1,422	–1,559	–1,486	–1,453	–1,506	–1,347	–1,272
Other sectors	3 390 . .	–420	–491	–684	–545	–627	–637	–636	–874
Workers' remittances	3 391 . .	–321	–443	–178	–106	–113	–142	–173	–353
Other current transfers	3 392 . .	–100	–48	–506	–439	–513	–496	–463	–521
CAPITAL AND FINANCIAL ACCOUNT	4 996 . .	2,483	3,325	5,983	8,392	8,018	11,341	12,325	10,601
CAPITAL ACCOUNT	4 994 . .	. . .	. . .	2,695	2,704	2,546	2,459	1,512	1,067
Total credit	2 994 . .	. . .	. . .	*2,836*	*2,893*	*2,724*	*2,642*	*1,681*	*1,276*
Total debit	3 994 . .	. . .	. . .	*–141*	*–189*	*–179*	*–183*	*–169*	*–209*
Capital transfers, credit	2 400 . .	. . .	. . .	**2,829**	**2,821**	**2,674**	**2,600**	**1,625**	**1,248**
General government	2 401 . .	. . .	. . .	2,698	2,656	2,524	2,460	1,513	1,123
Debt forgiveness	2 402 . .	. . .	. . .	. . .	. . .	. . .	. . .	. . .	. . .
Other capital transfers	2 410 . .	. . .	. . .	2,698	2,656	2,524	2,460	1,513	1,123
Other sectors	2 430 . .	. . .	. . .	132	164	150	139	112	125
Migrants' transfers	2 431 . .	. . .	. . .	84	100	97	92	75	87
Debt forgiveness	2 432 . .	. . .	. . .	3	1	. . .	. . .	. . .	. . .
Other capital transfers	2 440 . .	. . .	. . .	45	64	53	47	36	38
Capital transfers, debit	3 400 . .	. . .	. . .	**–130**	**–148**	**–144**	**–132**	**–130**	**–164**
General government	3 401 . .	. . .	. . .	–5	–15	–18	–9	–21	–47
Debt forgiveness	3 402 . .	. . .	. . .	. . .	. . .	. . .	. . .	. . .	. . .
Other capital transfers	3 410 . .	. . .	. . .	–5	–15	–18	–9	–21	–47
Other sectors	3 430 . .	. . .	. . .	–125	–133	–126	–123	–109	–117
Migrants' transfers	3 431 . .	. . .	. . .	–61	–74	–92	–86	–78	–90
Debt forgiveness	3 432 . .	. . .	. . .	–3	–28	–4	. . .	. . .	. . .
Other capital transfers	3 440 . .	. . .	. . .	–61	–32	–29	–37	–30	–28
Nonproduced nonfinancial assets, credit	2 480 . .	. . .	. . .	**7**	**72**	**50**	**42**	**56**	**28**
Nonproduced nonfinancial assets, debit	3 480 . .	. . .	. . .	**–11**	**–41**	**–35**	**–51**	**–39**	**–45**

Table 2 (Continued). STANDARD PRESENTATION, 1994–2001
(Millions of U.S. dollars)

	Code		1994	1995	1996	1997	1998	1999	2000	2001
FINANCIAL ACCOUNT	4 995	. .	**2,483**	**3,325**	**3,288**	**5,689**	**5,472**	**8,883**	**10,813**	**9,534**
A. DIRECT INVESTMENT	4 500	. .	983	–4	731	355	–700	–1,783	–1,232	–1,929
Direct investment abroad	4 505	. .	**–287**	**–688**	**–972**	**–2,187**	**–3,851**	**–3,019**	**–7,749**	**–7,874**
Equity capital	4 510	. .	–185	–476	–694	–1,865	–3,148	–2,598	–7,682	–4,662
Claims on affiliated enterprises	4 515	. .	. . .	. . .	–691	–1,861	–3,142	–2,596	–7,675	–4,662
Liabilities to affiliated enterprises	4 520	. .	. . .	. . .	–3	–4	–7	–2	–6	. . .
Reinvested earnings	4 525	. .	. . .	–1	–55	–312	–316	–414	–503	–734
Other capital	4 530	. .	–102	–211	–223	–9	–387	–7	435	–2,477
Claims on affiliated enterprises	4 535	. .	. . .	. . .	–216	–514	27,285	847	–1,018	–2,505
Liabilities to affiliated enterprises	4 540	. .	. . .	. . .	–8	505	–27,672	–854	1,453	28
Direct investment in Portugal	4 555	. .	**1,270**	**685**	**1,703**	**2,542**	**3,151**	**1,235**	**6,518**	**5,945**
Equity capital	4 560	. .	989	150	1,117	810	1,356	–576	5,310	1,345
Claims on direct investors	4 565	. .	. . .	. . .	. . .	–6	–4	1	–11	25
Liabilities to direct investors	4 570	. .	**1,270**	**685**	**1,703**	**2,542**	**3,151**	**1,235**	**6,518**	**5,945**
Equity capital	4 560	. .	989	150	1,117	810	1,356	–576	5,310	1,345
Claims on direct investors	4 565	. .	. . .	. . .	. . .	–6	–4	1	–11	25
Liabilities to direct investors	4 570	. .	**1,270**	**685**	**1,703**	**2,542**	**3,151**	**1,235**	**6,518**	**5,945**
Equity capital	4 560	. .	989	150	1,117	810	1,356	–576	5,310	1,345
Claims on direct investors	4 565	. .	. . .	. . .	. . .	–6	–4	1	–11	25
Liabilities to direct investors	4 570	. .	**1,270**	**685**	**1,703**	**2,542**	**3,151**	**1,235**	**6,518**	**5,945**
Equity capital	4 560	. .	989	150	1,117	810	1,356	–576	5,310	1,345
Claims on direct investors	4 565	. .	. . .	. . .	. . .	–6	–4	1	–11	25
Liabilities to direct investors	4 570	. .	. . .	. . .	–287	–270	–457	–384	–196	–142
Liabilities to direct investors	4 590	. .	. . .	. . .	155	1,205	1,444	1,136	765	3,914
B. PORTFOLIO INVESTMENT	4 600	. .	478	–1,082	–3,166	93	–611	3,209	–1,791	1,975
Assets	4 602	. .	**–3,456**	**–3,148**	**–5,549**	**–8,697**	**–5,997**	**–6,737**	**–4,583**	**–6,430**
Equity securities	4 610	. .	–66	–159	–602	–568	–975	–2,110	–1,044	–1,755
Monetary authorities	4 611	. .	. . .	. . .	. . .	. . .	. . .	. . .	. . .	. . .
General government	4 612	. .	. . .	. . .	. . .	. . .	–1	–13	–126	–248
Banks	4 613	. .	–28	–39	–630	–211	–487	–772	–30	–28
Other sectors	4 614	. .	–37	–121	29	–357	–487	–1,325	–888	–1,479
Debt securities	4 619	. .	–3,390	–2,989	–4,947	–8,129	–5,022	–4,626	–3,539	–4,676
Bonds and notes	4 620	. .	–1,607	–4,745	–6,463	–8,860	–4,751	–3,706	–4,088	–4,863
Monetary authorities	4 621	. .	. . .	. . .	. . .	. . .	. . .	731	–47	357
General government	4 622	. .	. . .	. . .	3	–2	–10	–214	–295	–387
Banks	4 623	. .	–540	–1,702	–3,637	–2,933	–722	809	1,031	–893
Other sectors	4 624	. .	–1,067	–3,043	–2,829	–5,925	–4,020	–5,032	–4,776	–3,940
Money market instruments	4 630	. .	–1,783	1,756	1,515	731	–271	–920	549	187
Monetary authorities	4 631	. .	. . .	. . .	. . .	. . .	. . .	–390	–488	47
General government	4 632	. .	. . .	. . .	. . .	. . .	. . .	. . .	. . .	–43
Banks	4 633	. .	–337	–551	220	134	–158	–257	–13	22
Other sectors	4 634	. .	–1,446	2,307	1,295	597	–112	–273	1,051	161
Liabilities	4 652	. .	**3,934**	**2,066**	**2,383**	**8,790**	**5,385**	**9,945**	**2,792**	**8,405**
Equity securities	4 660	. .	562	–179	1,669	3,821	2,165	691	415	424
Banks	4 663	. .	. . .	. . .	213	930	871	–184	52	154
Other sectors	4 664	. .	. . .	. . .	1,456	2,891	1,294	875	364	270
Debt securities	4 669	. .	3,372	2,244	714	4,970	3,221	9,254	2,376	7,981
Bonds and notes	4 670	. .	3,372	1,587	383	3,359	4,213	7,048	2,151	6,085
Monetary authorities	4 671	. .	. . .	. . .	. . .	. . .	. . .	. . .	. . .	. . .
General government	4 672	. .	. . .	. . .	403	3,743	5,417	7,024	2,744	2,326
Banks	4 673	. .	. . .	. . .	44	–509	–1,123	–1,070	–289	2,834
Other sectors	4 674	. .	. . .	. . .	–65	124	–81	1,094	–304	925
Money market instruments	4 680	. .	. . .	657	331	1,611	–992	2,206	225	1,896
Monetary authorities	4 681	. .	. . .	. . .	. . .	. . .	. . .	. . .	. . .	. . .
General government	4 682	. .	. . .	. . .	302	35	–300	621	–141	1,554
Banks	4 683	. .	. . .	. . .	. . .	1,423	–675	1,618	366	–336
Other sectors	4 684	. .	. . .	. . .	29	153	–17	–33	. . .	678
C. FINANCIAL DERIVATIVES	4 910	. .	. . .	. . .	–36	–19	131	197	323	256
Monetary authorities	4 911	. .	. . .	. . .	. . .	. . .	. . .	. . .	1	–3
General government	4 912	. .	. . .	. . .	. . .	9	55	. . .	185	96
Banks	4 913	. .	. . .	. . .	–37	12	80	254	224	263
Other sectors	4 914	. .	1	. . .	1	–40	–3	–57	–88	–100
Assets	4 900	. .	**. . .**	**. . .**	**93**	**341**	**1,116**	**2,682**	**3,673**	**3,086**
Monetary authorities	4 901	. .	. . .	. . .	. . .	. . .	. . .	. . .	5	3
General government	4 902	. .	. . .	. . .	. . .	9	55	. . .	286	672
Banks	4 903	. .	. . .	. . .	90	325	992	2,438	3,150	2,122
Other sectors	4 904	. .	1	. . .	3	7	70	244	232	290
Liabilities	4 905	. .	**. . .**	**. . .**	**–130**	**–360**	**–985**	**–2,485**	**–3,351**	**–2,830**
Monetary authorities	4 906	. .	. . .	. . .	. . .	. . .	. . .	. . .	–3	–5
General government	4 907	. .	. . .	. . .	. . .	. . .	. . .	. . .	–101	–576
Banks	4 908	. .	. . .	. . .	–127	–313	–912	–2,184	–2,926	–1,859
Other sectors	4 909	. .	. . .	. . .	–3	–48	–73	–301	–320	–390

Table 2 (Concluded). STANDARD PRESENTATION, 1994–2001
(Millions of U.S. dollars)

	Code	1994	1995	1996	1997	1998	1999	2000	2001
D. OTHER INVESTMENT	4 700 . .	–410	4,111	6,306	6,233	7,160	7,475	13,884	10,084
Assets	4 703 . .	**–7,098**	**–7,568**	**–3,368**	**–5,346**	**–7,100**	**421**	**–10,262**	**–4,743**
Trade credits	4 706 . .	. . .	. . .	–170	–779	–112	–304	–757	–30
General government	4 707 . .	. . .	. . .	. . .	. . .	. . .	. . .	. . .	. . .
of which: Short-term	4 709 . .	. . .	. . .	. . .	. . .	. . .	. . .	. . .	. . .
Other sectors	4 710 . .	. . .	. . .	–170	–779	–112	–304	–757	–30
of which: Short-term	4 712 . .	. . .	. . .	. . .	. . .	. . .	. . .	. . .	. . .
Loans	4 714 . .	–51	–311	–333	–4,081	–300	–1,822	–2,880	–1,025
Monetary authorities	4 715 . .	. . .	. . .	. . .	. . .	. . .	. . .	. . .	. . .
of which: Short-term	4 718 . .	. . .	. . .	. . .	. . .	. . .	. . .	. . .	. . .
General government	4 719 . .	. . .	. . .	12	12	–1	–14	–2	5
of which: Short-term	4 721 . .	. . .	. . .	. . .	. . .	*–1*	*–8*	. . .	. . .
Banks	4 722 . .	7	79	–302	–4,088	–293	–1,795	–2,844	–1,003
of which: Short-term	4 724 . .	. . .	. . .	. . .	. . .	. . .	. . .	. . .	. . .
Other sectors	4 725 . .	–58	–391	–43	–4	–7	–13	–35	–28
of which: Short-term	4 727 . .	*–37*	*–223*	*–1*	*–3*	*–11*	*–5*	*–19*	*–26*
Currency and deposits	4 730 . .	–6,685	–7,176	–2,850	–505	–6,586	2,546	–6,621	–3,688
Monetary authorities	4 731 . .	. . .	. . .	–3	1	. . .	–1,005	11	21
General government	4 732 . .	. . .	. . .	–1	–1	1	–6	–10	–48
Banks	4 733 . .	–4,747	–6,758	–2,655	969	–3,506	2,769	–4,358	–31
Other sectors	4 734 . .	–1,937	–418	–191	–1,474	–3,081	788	–2,264	–3,631
Other assets	4 736 . .	–363	–80	–16	20	–100	. . .	–3	1
Monetary authorities	4 737 . .	. . .	–26	. . .	. . .	–94	. . .	. . .	. . .
of which: Short-term	4 739 . .	. . .	*–12*	. . .	. . .	. . .	. . .	. . .	. . .
General government	4 740 . .	. . .	. . .	–10	. . .	. . .	. . .	–1	. . .
of which: Short-term	4 742 . .	. . .	. . .	*–10*	. . .	. . .	. . .	. . .	. . .
Banks	4 743 . .	. . .	. . .	12	3	–15	–2	. . .	. . .
of which: Short-term	4 745 . .	. . .	. . .	*12*	*3*	*–15*	*–2*	. . .	. . .
Other sectors	4 746 . .	–362	–54	–18	16	8	1	–2	1
of which: Short-term	4 748 . .	*–362*	*–54*	*–19*	*14*	*4*	*–3*	*1*	. . .
Liabilities	4 753 . .	**6,689**	**11,678**	**9,675**	**11,579**	**14,260**	**7,055**	**24,146**	**14,827**
Trade credits	4 756 . .	. . .	. . .	273	809	565	598	514	–105
General government	4 757 . .	. . .	. . .	. . .	. . .	. . .	. . .	. . .	. . .
of which: Short-term	4 759 . .	. . .	. . .	. . .	. . .	. . .	. . .	. . .	. . .
Other sectors	4 760 . .	. . .	. . .	273	809	565	598	514	–105
of which: Short-term	4 762 . .	. . .	. . .	. . .	. . .	. . .	. . .	. . .	. . .
Loans	4 764 . .	–834	406	2,426	4,287	3,186	5,713	6,175	9,206
Monetary authorities	4 765 . .	. . .	. . .	709	1,386	922	491	7	–53
of which: Use of Fund credit and loans from the Fund	4 766 . .	. . .	. . .	. . .	. . .	. . .	. . .	. . .	. . .
of which: Short-term	4 768 . .	. . .	. . .	*709*	*1,386*	*922*	*213*	*–232*	*300*
General government	4 769 . .	–139	144	–312	–40	–73	–43	–179	–151
of which: Short-term	4 771 . .	. . .	. . .	. . .	. . .	. . .	*–11*	*–50*	*24*
Banks	4 772 . .	–136	–201	1,623	2,418	1,679	5,766	5,619	8,910
of which: Short-term	4 774 . .	. . .	. . .	. . .	. . .	. . .	. . .	. . .	. . .
Other sectors	4 775 . .	–559	463	406	524	658	–501	727	499
of which: Short-term	4 777 . .	*–79*	*307*	*–482*	*397*	*168*	*–656*	*184*	*–159*
Currency and deposits	4 780 . .	7,205	11,391	6,982	6,469	10,391	740	17,470	5,710
Monetary authorities	4 781 . .	. . .	. . .	21	–42	–85	–494	4,859	138
General government	4 782 . .	. . .	. . .	. . .	. . .	. . .	. . .	. . .	. . .
Banks	4 783 . .	7,205	11,391	6,960	6,511	10,476	1,233	12,611	5,571
Other sectors	4 784 . .	. . .	. . .	. . .	. . .	. . .	. . .	. . .	. . .
Other liabilities	4 786 . .	318	–118	–6	14	117	4	–12	17
Monetary authorities	4 787 . .	299	–99	. . .	. . .	. . .	. . .	–5	3
of which: Short-term	4 789 . .	*299*	*–99*	. . .	. . .	. . .	. . .	. . .	*1*
General government	4 790 . .	. . .	. . .	. . .	. . .	. . .	. . .	. . .	. . .
of which: Short-term	4 792 . .	. . .	. . .	. . .	. . .	. . .	. . .	. . .	. . .
Banks	4 793 . .	. . .	. . .	12	8	91	–1	. . .	. . .
of which: Short-term	4 795 . .	. . .	. . .	*12*	*8*	*91*	*–1*	. . .	. . .
Other sectors	4 796 . .	19	–19	–18	6	27	5	–8	14
of which: Short-term	4 798 . .	*19*	*–19*	*–25*	*–1*	*20*	*3*	. . .	. . .
E. RESERVE ASSETS	4 802 . .	1,430	300	–547	–974	–508	–216	–371	–852
Monetary gold	4 812 . .	–1	. . .	–1	–1	–1,172	161	. . .	. . .
Special drawing rights	4 811 . .	–9	–13	–16	–15	–22	88	–12	–10
Reserve position in the Fund	4 810 . .	–16	–110	–25	10	–173	230	42	–72
Foreign exchange	4 803 . .	1,456	423	–505	–967	859	–695	–401	–769
Other claims	4 813 . .	. . .	. . .	. . .	. . .	. . .	. . .	. . .	. . .
NET ERRORS AND OMISSIONS	4 998 . .	**–287**	**–3,193**	**–767**	**–1,928**	**–184**	**–1,577**	**–1,363**	**–642**

Part 3 of the *Yearbook* contains descriptions of the methodologies, compilation practices, and sources used to compile these data.

Table 3. INTERNATIONAL INVESTMENT POSITION (End–period stocks), 1994–2001

(Millions of U.S. dollars)

	Code	1994	1995	1996	1997	1998	1999	2000	2001
ASSETS	8 995 C.	...	...	86,425	99,344	128,461	122,341	140,791	153,300
Direct investment abroad	8 505 . .	...	...	**4,726**	**5,932**	**9,622**	**10,330**	**17,781**	**24,881**
Equity capital and reinvested earnings	8 506 . .	...	...	3,993	5,127	8,532	9,567	17,501	22,222
Claims on affiliated enterprises	8 507 . .	...	...	3,993	5,127	8,533	9,570	17,505	22,226
Liabilities to affiliated enterprises	8 508 . .	...	...	...	...	–1	–3	–4	–4
Other capital	8 530 . .	...	...	733	805	1,089	763	280	2,659
Claims on affiliated enterprises	8 535 . .	...	...	790	996	4,534	3,217	4,001	6,211
Liabilities to affiliated enterprises	8 540 . .	...	...	–57	–191	–3,445	–2,453	–3,721	–3,553
Portfolio investment	8 602 . .	...	...	**17,502**	**20,368**	**28,489**	**36,459**	**39,096**	**42,531**
Equity securities	8 610 . .	...	...	4,997	4,765	6,008	7,227	7,587	7,761
Monetary authorities	8 611 . .	...	...	...	...	...	...	...	...
General government	8 612 . .	...	...	...	...	...	13	133	359
Banks	8 613 . .	...	...	1,415	1,361	1,935	1,551	1,440	1,263
Other sectors	8 614 . .	...	...	3,582	3,404	4,073	5,663	6,014	6,139
Debt securities	8 619 . .	...	...	12,505	15,602	22,480	29,232	31,509	34,770
Bonds and notes	8 620 . .	...	...	10,401	15,232	21,784	23,282	26,489	30,036
Monetary authorities	8 621 . .	...	...	...	...	...	2,347	2,236	1,759
General government	8 622 . .	...	...	14	1	11	219	509	870
Banks	8 623 . .	...	...	5,060	6,269	7,827	5,880	4,644	5,338
Other sectors	8 624 . .	...	...	5,327	8,962	13,946	14,836	19,099	22,070
Money market instruments	8 630 . .	...	...	2,104	370	696	5,950	5,020	4,733
Monetary authorities	8 631 . .	...	...	...	...	...	3,700	3,926	3,696
General government	8 632 . .	...	...	...	...	...	...	...	48
Banks	8 633 . .	...	...	362	50	216	74	93	84
Other sectors	8 634 . .	...	...	1,742	321	480	2,176	1,001	905
Financial derivatives	8 900 . .	...	...	**422**	**381**	**355**	**2,054**	**2,758**	**1,929**
Monetary authorities	8 901 . .	...	...	...	...	...	...	1	1
General government	8 902 . .	...	...	...	–3	...	374	328	378
Banks	8 903 . .	...	...	415	376	355	1,681	2,428	1,548
Other sectors	8 904 . .	...	...	7	8	...	...	1	2
Other investment	8 703 . .	**32,543**	**37,810**	**42,030**	**52,341**	**68,409**	**59,397**	**66,930**	**68,877**
Trade credits	8 706 . .	...	...	1,343	1,269	6,496	5,915	6,282	5,994
General government	8 707 . .	...	...	...	...	...	...	...	...
of which: Short-term	8 709 . .	...	...	...	...	...	...	...	...
Other sectors	8 710 . .	...	...	1,343	1,269	6,496	5,915	6,282	5,994
of which: Short-term	8 712 . .	...	...	*1,343*	*1,269*	*6,496*	*5,915*	*6,282*	*5,994*
Loans	8 714 . .	901	926	881	845	44,381	39,698	45,130	44,563
Monetary authorities	8 715 . .	...	...	...	...	...	...	...	...
of which: Short-term	8 718 . .	...	...	...	...	...	...	...	...
General government	8 719 . .	...	...	...	...	11	16	18	12
of which: Short-term	8 721 . .	...	...	...	...	*1*	*1*	*1*	*1*
Banks	8 722 . .	901	926	...	...	44,306	39,608	45,005	44,419
of which: Short-term	8 724 . .	*901*	*926*	...	...	*35,710*	*29,871*	*33,154*	*32,017*
Other sectors	8 725 . .	...	...	881	845	64	73	107	131
of which: Short-term	8 727 . .	...	...	*423*	*428*	*17*	*20*	*38*	*63*
Currency and deposits	8 730 . .	27,598	31,208	38,931	49,455	16,993	13,304	15,065	17,885
Monetary authorities	8 731 . .	...	...	...	...	1	1,369	1,265	1,184
General government	8 732 . .	...	...	3	5	4	22	30	75
Banks	8 733 . .	20,220	23,714	29,900	38,718	...	...	...	...
Other sectors	8 734 . .	7,379	7,494	9,028	10,731	16,988	11,913	13,770	16,626
Other assets	8 736 . .	4,044	5,676	875	772	539	480	453	435
Monetary authorities	8 737 . .	...	...	47	28	127	110	101	96
of which: Short-term	8 739 . .	...	...	*17*	*1*	...	...	...	...
General government	8 740 . .	15	28	77	73	32	28	26	25
of which: Short-term	8 742 . .	*15*	*28*	*77*	*73*	*32*	*28*	*26*	*25*
Banks	8 743 . .	4,028	5,647	...	...	83	80	77	77
of which: Short-term	8 745 . .	...	...	...	...	*83*	*80*	*77*	*76*
Other sectors	8 746 . .	...	...	752	671	297	262	248	238
of which: Short-term	8 748 . .	...	...	*752*	*671*	*285*	*256*	*239*	*231*
Reserve assets	8 802 . .	**21,669**	**21,954**	**21,745**	**20,321**	**21,586**	**14,100**	**14,227**	**15,082**
Monetary gold	8 812 . .	6,161	6,180	5,936	4,669	5,774	5,673	5,318	5,415
Special drawing rights	8 811 . .	71	85	98	107	135	44	54	62
Reserve position in the Fund	8 810 . .	337	450	461	423	623	377	316	376
Foreign exchange	8 803 . .	15,101	15,239	15,250	15,123	15,054	8,006	8,539	9,229
Other claims	8 813 . .	...	...	...	...	...	...	...	...

Table 3 (Concluded). INTERNATIONAL INVESTMENT POSITION (End–period stocks), 1994–2001
(Millions of U.S. dollars)

	Code	1994	1995	1996	1997	1998	1999	2000	2001
LIABILITIES	8 995 D.	...	...	93,951	113,075	154,894	157,753	182,039	197,400
Direct investment in Portugal	8 555 ..	**...**	**...**	**18,947**	**18,605**	**24,465**	**23,520**	**28,161**	**32,671**
Equity capital and reinvested earnings	8 556 ..	...	...	15,636	14,822	21,883	19,897	24,417	25,341
Claims on direct investors	8 557 ..	...	...	–77	–66	–258	–1	–1	–1
Liabilities to direct investors	8 558 ..	...	...	15,713	14,888	22,141	19,898	24,418	25,342
Other capital	8 580 ..	...	...	3,311	3,783	2,582	3,623	3,743	7,330
Claims on direct investors	8 585 ..	...	...	–455	–579	–1,129	–1,651	–1,910	–1,955
Liabilities to direct investors	8 590 ..	...	...	3,766	4,363	3,711	5,273	5,654	9,284
Portfolio investment	8 652 ..	**13,656**	**16,430**	**21,327**	**36,207**	**46,933**	**51,719**	**51,249**	**52,899**
Equity securities	8 660 ..	3,597	3,651	6,573	12,663	18,806	19,487	18,408	13,563
Banks	8 663 ..	1,769	1,275	1,716	3,046	5,606	4,790	4,175	3,211
Other sectors	8 664 ..	1,828	2,376	4,857	9,616	13,200	14,697	14,233	10,353
Debt securities	8 669 ..	10,059	12,779	14,755	23,544	28,127	32,232	32,841	39,336
Bonds and notes	8 670 ..	10,059	12,125	14,553	22,220	27,740	29,754	30,906	35,560
Monetary authorities	8 671 ..	...	...	...	...	...	...	...	...
General government	8 672 ..	9,765	11,828	13,733	15,849	22,436	25,316	26,622	27,739
Banks	8 673 ..	42	104	517	6,039	4,797	3,107	3,340	6,038
Other sectors	8 674 ..	251	194	303	332	507	1,331	944	1,783
Money market instruments	8 680 ..	...	653	201	1,324	388	2,477	1,935	3,776
Monetary authorities	8 681 ..	...	...	...	...	...	...	...	...
General government	8 682 ..	...	628	169	303	3	605	429	1,956
Banks	8 683 ..	...	...	...	853	217	1,768	1,414	1,058
Other sectors	8 684 ..	...	25	32	167	167	104	92	761
Financial derivatives	8 905 ..	**...**	**...**	**...**	**...**	**63**	**1,412**	**2,223**	**1,184**
Monetary authorities	8 906 ..	...	...	...	...	...	...	1	3
General government	8 907 ..	...	...	...	...	60	...	...	...
Banks	8 908 ..	...	...	...	...	...	1,412	2,222	1,182
Other sectors	8 909 ..	...	...	...	...	3	...	...	...
Other investment	8 753 ..	**37,266**	**49,532**	**53,677**	**58,263**	**83,432**	**81,102**	**100,407**	**110,645**
Trade credits	8 756 ..	...	...	1,457	1,351	6,650	6,345	6,135	5,709
General government	8 757 ..	...	...	...	...	...	...	...	...
of which: Short-term	8 759 ..	...	...	...	...	...	...	...	...
Other sectors	8 760 ..	...	...	1,457	1,351	6,650	6,345	6,135	5,709
of which: Short-term	8 762 ..	...	...	*1,457*	*1,351*	*6,650*	*6,345*	*6,135*	*5,709*
Loans	8 764 ..	17,328	19,684	15,542	14,326	76,338	75,215	90,058	100,845
Monetary authorities	8 765 ..	...	...	228	1,893	2,813	3,396	3,448	3,392
of which: Use of Fund credit and loans from the Fund	8 766 ..	...	...	...	...	...	...	...	...
of which: Short-term	8 768 ..	...	...	*228*	*1,893*	*2,813*	*3,334*	*3,094*	*3,392*
General government	8 769 ..	1,973	2,229	1,675	1,613	2,057	2,114	1,926	1,670
of which: Short-term	8 771 ..	...	...	...	...	...	*89*	*33*	*51*
Banks	8 772 ..	1,952	2,863	...	...	56,470	57,717	72,811	83,970
of which: Short-term	8 774 ..	*1,106*	*2,178*	...	...	*49,769*	*46,063*	*56,235*	*59,252*
Other sectors	8 775 ..	13,403	14,592	13,639	10,820	14,997	11,989	11,873	11,813
of which: Short-term	8 777 ..	*2,275*	*2,652*	*2,202*	*525*	*1,526*	*650*	*837*	*654*
Currency and deposits	8 780 ..	17,571	26,253	36,320	42,261	118	–663	4,023	3,890
Monetary authorities	8 781 ..	...	...	...	...	118	–663	4,023	3,890
General government	8 782 ..	...	...	...	...	...	...	...	...
Banks	8 783 ..	17,571	26,253	36,320	42,261	...	...	...	...
Other sectors	8 784 ..	...	...	...	...	...	...	...	...
Other liabilities	8 786 ..	2,367	3,594	357	326	326	205	192	201
Monetary authorities	8 787 ..	362	278	212	191	118	...	...	...
of which: Short-term	8 789 ..	*362*	*278*	*212*	*191*	...	...	...	...
General government	8 790 ..	...	...	1	1	...	...	...	...
of which: Short-term	8 792 ..	...	...	*1*	*1*	...	...	...	...
Banks	8 793 ..	2,004	3,316	...	...	108	106	105	104
of which: Short-term	8 795 ..	...	...	...	...	*108*	*105*	*104*	*103*
Other sectors	8 796 ..	...	...	144	134	100	98	87	97
of which: Short-term	8 798 ..	...	...	*144*	*134*	*91*	*88*	*84*	*80*
NET INTERNATIONAL INVESTMENT POSITION	8 995 ..	**...**	**...**	**–7,526**	**–13,732**	**–26,433**	**–35,413**	**–41,248**	**–44,100**
Conversion rates: Portuguese escudos per U.S. dollar (end of period)	0 102 ..	**159.09**	**149.41**	**156.38**	**183.33**	**171.83**	**...**	**...**	**...**
Conversion rates: euros per U.S. dollar (end of period)	0 104 ..	**...**	**...**	**...**	**...**	**...**	**.9954**	**1.0747**	**1.1347**

Table 1. ANALYTIC PRESENTATION, 1994–2001
(Millions of U.S. dollars)

	Code	1994	1995	1996	1997	1998	1999	2000	2001
A. Current Account [1]	4 993 Z.	**–455**	**–1,780**	**–2,579**	**–2,137**	**–2,918**	**–1,297**	**–1,359**	**–2,317**
Goods: exports f.o.b	2 100 . .	6,151	7,910	8,085	8,431	8,302	8,503	10,366	11,385
Goods: imports f.o.b	3 100 . .	–6,562	–9,487	–10,555	–10,411	–10,927	–9,595	–12,050	–14,354
Balance on Goods	4 100 . .	*–411*	*–1,577*	*–2,470*	*–1,980*	*–2,625*	*–1,092*	*–1,684*	*–2,969*
Services: credit	2 200 . .	1,044	1,494	1,563	1,524	1,217	1,365	1,767	1,994
Services: debit	3 200 . .	–1,215	–1,819	–1,948	–1,938	–1,871	–1,785	–2,021	–2,203
Balance on Goods and Services	4 991 . .	*–582*	*–1,902*	*–2,855*	*–2,394*	*–3,279*	*–1,512*	*–1,938*	*–3,178*
Income: credit	2 300 . .	116	81	78	204	313	152	325	455
Income: debit	3 300 . .	–245	–322	–387	–526	–705	–563	–606	–737
Balance on Goods, Services, and Income	4 992 . .	*–711*	*–2,143*	*–3,164*	*–2,716*	*–3,671*	*–1,923*	*–2,219*	*–3,460*
Current transfers: credit	2 379 Z.	317	473	667	731	886	804	1,079	1,417
Current transfers: debit	3 379 . .	–61	–110	–82	–152	–133	–178	–219	–274
B. Capital Account [1]	4 994 Z.	**. . .**	**32**	**152**	**43**	**39**	**45**	**36**	**95**
Capital account: credit	2 994 Z.	. . .	32	152	43	39	46	37	108
Capital account: debit	3 994 . .	. . .	. . .	. . .	. . .	. . .	–1	–1	–13
Total, Groups A Plus B	4 981 . .	*–455*	*–1,748*	*–2,427*	*–2,094*	*–2,879*	*–1,252*	*–1,323*	*–2,222*
C. Financial Account [1]	4 995 W.	**535**	**812**	**1,486**	**2,458**	**2,042**	**697**	**1,943**	**2,938**
Direct investment abroad	4 505 . .	. . .	–2	. . .	9	9	–16	11	17
Direct investment in Romania	4 555 Z.	341	419	263	1,215	2,031	1,041	1,025	1,157
Portfolio investment assets	4 602 . .	75	–22	. . .	–6	1	9	28	–8
Equity securities	4 610 . .	. . .	–4	. . .	–6	1	9	31	–7
Debt securities	4 619 . .	75	–18	. . .	. . .	. . .	. . .	–3	–1
Portfolio investment liabilities	4 652 Z.	. . .	54	193	540	129	–724	74	583
Equity securities	4 660 . .	. . .	. . .	. . .	195	95	68	58	8
Debt securities	4 669 Z.	. . .	54	193	345	34	–792	16	575
Financial derivatives	4 910 . .	. . .	. . .	. . .	. . .	. . .	. . .	. . .	. . .
Financial derivatives assets	4 900 . .	. . .	. . .	. . .	. . .	. . .	. . .	. . .	. . .
Financial derivatives liabilities	4 905 . .	. . .	. . .	. . .	. . .	. . .	. . .	. . .	. . .
Other investment assets	4 703 . .	–671	186	–271	–6	208	246	–407	–44
Monetary authorities	4 701 . .	. . .	. . .	. . .	. . .	. . .	. . .	. . .	. . .
General government	4 704 . .	–24	–62	–9	10	–10	9	–82	–44
Banks	4 705 . .	–621	254	–315	–140	179	236	–354	–102
Other sectors	4 728 . .	–26	–6	53	124	39	1	29	102
Other investment liabilities	4 753 W.	790	177	1,301	706	–336	141	1,212	1,233
Monetary authorities	4 753 WA	. . .	. . .	–150	. . .	. . .	73	–14	. . .
General government	4 753 ZB	75	–27	209	547	–7	40	681	320
Banks	4 753 ZC	190	–57	536	–132	–260	–54	–74	159
Other sectors	4 753 ZD	525	261	706	291	–69	82	619	754
Total, Groups A Through C	4 983 . .	*80*	*–936*	*–941*	*364*	*–837*	*–555*	*620*	*716*
D. Net Errors and Omissions	4 998 . .	**91**	**456**	**359**	**1,095**	**194**	**794**	**286**	**819**
Total, Groups A Through D	4 984 . .	*171*	*–480*	*–582*	*1,459*	*–643*	*239*	*906*	*1,535*
E. Reserves and Related Items	4 802 A.	**–171**	**480**	**582**	**–1,459**	**643**	**–239**	**–906**	**–1,535**
Reserve assets	4 802 . .	–616	259	–218	–1,664	844	–173	–926	–1,484
Use of Fund credit and loans	4 766 . .	217	–316	–356	29	–126	–66	20	–51
Exceptional financing	4 920 . .	228	536	1,157	176	–75	. . .	. . .	. . .
Conversion rates: lei per U.S. dollar	0 101 . .	**1,655.1**	**2,033.3**	**3,084.2**	**7,167.9**	**8,875.6**	**15,332.8**	**21,708.7**	**29,060.8**

[1] Excludes components that have been classified in the categories of Group E.

Table 2. STANDARD PRESENTATION, 1994–2001
(Millions of U.S. dollars)

	Code	1994	1995	1996	1997	1998	1999	2000	2001
CURRENT ACCOUNT	4 993 . .	**–428**	**–1,774**	**–2,571**	**–2,137**	**–2,918**	**–1,297**	**–1,359**	**–2,317**
A. GOODS	4 100 . .	–411	–1,577	–2,470	–1,980	–2,625	–1,092	–1,684	–2,969
Credit	2 100 . .	**6,151**	**7,910**	**8,085**	**8,431**	**8,302**	**8,503**	**10,366**	**11,385**
General merchandise: exports f.o.b.	2 110 . .	6,146	7,900	8,066	8,402	8,188	8,309	10,127	11,007
Goods for processing: exports f.o.b.	2 150 . .	. . .	1	13	11	86	166	202	334
Repairs on goods	2 160 . .	5	9	4	17	27	26	36	44
Goods procured in ports by carriers	2 170 . .	. . .	. . .	2	1	1	2	1	. . .
Nonmonetary gold	2 180 . .	. . .	. . .	. . .	. . .	. . .	. . .	. . .	. . .
Debit	3 100 . .	**–6,562**	**–9,487**	**–10,555**	**–10,411**	**–10,927**	**–9,595**	**–12,050**	**–14,354**
General merchandise: imports f.o.b.	3 110 . .	–6,544	–9,451	–10,521	–10,371	–10,902	–9,581	–12,034	–14,339
Goods for processing: imports f.o.b.	3 150 . .	–2	–8	–8	–8	–7	–3	–2	–3
Repairs on goods	3 160 . .	–5	–6	–3	–7	–7	–3	–5	–4
Goods procured in ports by carriers	3 170 . .	–11	–22	–23	–25	–11	–8	–9	–8
Nonmonetary gold	3 180 . .	. . .	. . .	. . .	. . .	. . .	. . .	. . .	. . .
B. SERVICES	4 200 . .	–171	–325	–385	–414	–654	–420	–254	–209
Total credit	2 200 . .	*1,044*	*1,494*	*1,563*	*1,524*	*1,217*	*1,365*	*1,767*	*1,994*
Total debit	3 200 . .	*–1,215*	*–1,819*	*–1,948*	*–1,938*	*–1,871*	*–1,785*	*–2,021*	*–2,203*
Transportation services, credit	2 205 . .	**381**	**471**	**572**	**588**	**504**	**534**	**652**	**789**
Passenger	2 850 . .	*114*	*99*	*141*	*77*	*91*	*54*	*35*	*57*
Freight	2 851 . .	*200*	*264*	*256*	*368*	*350*	*362*	*440*	*528*
Other	2 852 . .	*67*	*108*	*175*	*143*	*63*	*118*	*177*	*204*
Sea transport, passenger	2 207 . .	. . .	. . .	. . .	. . .	. . .	. . .	. . .	. . .
Sea transport, freight	2 208 . .	67	95	108	41	40	37	44	35
Sea transport, other	2 209 . .	6	16	27	30	29	33	63	62
Air transport, passenger	2 211 . .	113	96	139	74	88	44	23	35
Air transport, freight	2 212 . .	. . .	4	4	3	3	4	5	4
Air transport, other	2 213 . .	52	75	130	64	12	69	94	122
Other transport, passenger	2 215 . .	1	3	2	3	3	10	12	22
Other transport, freight	2 216 . .	133	165	144	324	307	321	391	489
Other transport, other	2 217 . .	9	17	18	49	22	16	20	20
Transportation services, debit	3 205 . .	**–403**	**–604**	**–692**	**–565**	**–633**	**–570**	**–655**	**–788**
Passenger	3 850 . .	*–52*	*–52*	*–51*	*–18*	*–46*	*–26*	*–22*	*–26*
Freight	3 851 . .	*–324*	*–524*	*–611*	*–505*	*–536*	*–464*	*–514*	*–704*
Other	3 852 . .	*–27*	*–28*	*–30*	*–42*	*–51*	*–80*	*–119*	*–58*
Sea transport, passenger	3 207 . .	. . .	. . .	. . .	. . .	. . .	–1	. . .	. . .
Sea transport, freight	3 208 . .	–78	–214	–308	–138	–122	–111	–83	–148
Sea transport, other	3 209 . .	–9	–6	–8	–10	–10	–10	–21	–11
Air transport, passenger	3 211 . .	–48	–44	–41	–8	–40	–23	–19	–13
Air transport, freight	3 212 . .	. . .	–12	–17	–33	–34	–26	–26	–31
Air transport, other	3 213 . .	–7	–9	–16	–28	–33	–62	–23	–34
Other transport, passenger	3 215 . .	–4	–8	–10	–10	–6	–2	–3	–13
Other transport, freight	3 216 . .	–246	–298	–286	–334	–380	–327	–405	–525
Other transport, other	3 217 . .	–11	–13	–6	–4	–8	–8	–75	–13
Travel, credit	2 236 . .	**414**	**590**	**529**	**526**	**260**	**252**	**359**	**362**
Business travel	2 237 . .	. . .	. . .	. . .	. . .	. . .	12	116	59
Personal travel	2 240 . .	414	590	529	526	260	240	243	303
Travel, debit	3 236 . .	**–449**	**–697**	**–665**	**–681**	**–458**	**–402**	**–425**	**–449**
Business travel	3 237 . .	–134	–175	–215	–214	–180	–214	–241	–245
Personal travel	3 240 . .	–315	–522	–450	–467	–278	–188	–184	–204
Other services, credit	2 200 BA	**249**	**433**	**462**	**410**	**453**	**579**	**756**	**843**
Communications	2 245 . .	44	66	75	86	97	92	145	135
Construction	2 249 . .	28	137	52	35	40	33	30	59
Insurance	2 253 . .	17	30	21	29	29	22	21	37
Financial	2 260 . .	52	50	53	47	39	34	110	94
Computer and information	2 262 . .	2	2	3	3	10	24	44	50
Royalties and licence fees	2 266 . .	2	3	101	. . .	3	4	3	16
Other business services	2 268 . .	54	87	92	126	145	280	300	360
Personal, cultural, and recreational	2 287 . .	29	40	54	60	65	65	76	67
Government, n.i.e.	2 291 . .	21	18	11	24	25	25	27	25
Other services, debit	3 200 BA	**–363**	**–518**	**–591**	**–692**	**–780**	**–813**	**–941**	**–966**
Communications	3 245 . .	–11	–28	–30	–23	–44	–83	–82	–91
Construction	3 249 . .	–3	–20	–15	–21	–20	–9	–28	–24
Insurance	3 253 . .	–20	–24	–29	–36	–45	–37	–41	–49
Financial	3 260 . .	–46	–72	–59	–60	–49	–59	–98	–76
Computer and information	3 262 . .	–5	–2	–4	–11	–20	–25	–29	–34
Royalties and licence fees	3 266 . .	–3	–8	–12	–29	–21	–38	–45	–60
Other business services	3 268 . .	–212	–321	–379	–411	–475	–428	–499	–509
Personal, cultural, and recreational	3 287 . .	–14	–25	–39	–62	–73	–108	–74	–83
Government, n.i.e.	3 291 . .	–49	–18	–24	–39	–33	–26	–45	–40

Table 2 (Continued). STANDARD PRESENTATION, 1994–2001

(Millions of U.S. dollars)

	Code	1994	1995	1996	1997	1998	1999	2000	2001
C. INCOME	4 300 . .	–129	–241	–309	–322	–392	–411	–281	–282
Total credit	2 300 . .	*116*	*81*	*78*	*204*	*313*	*152*	*325*	*455*
Total debit	3 300 . .	*–245*	*–322*	*–387*	*–526*	*–705*	*–563*	*–606*	*–737*
Compensation of employees, credit	2 310 . .	**7**	**5**	**8**	**14**	**45**	**92**	**94**	**112**
Compensation of employees, debit	3 310 . .	**. . .**	**–1**	**–2**	**–1**	**–6**	**–7**	**–5**	**–4**
Investment income, credit	2 320 . .	**109**	**76**	**70**	**190**	**268**	**60**	**231**	**343**
Direct investment income	2 330 . .	2	6	5	4	13	2	8	15
Dividends and distributed branch profits	2 332 . .	2	6	5	4	13	2	6	14
Reinvested earnings and undistributed branch profits	2 333 . .	. . .	. . .	. . .	. . .	. . .	. . .	. . .	. . .
Income on debt (interest)	2 334 . .	. . .	. . .	. . .	. . .	. . .	. . .	2	1
Portfolio investment income	2 339 . .	. . .	6	. . .	. . .	1	9	103	178
Income on equity	2 340 . .	. . .	. . .	. . .	. . .	1	. . .	5	3
Income on bonds and notes	2 350 . .	. . .	6	. . .	. . .	. . .	. . .	. . .	152
Income on money market instruments	2 360 . .	. . .	. . .	. . .	. . .	. . .	9	98	23
Other investment income	2 370 . .	107	64	65	186	254	49	120	150
Investment income, debit	3 320 . .	**–245**	**–321**	**–385**	**–525**	**–699**	**–556**	**–601**	**–733**
Direct investment income	3 330 . .	–12	–28	–24	–30	–154	–52	–72	–117
Dividends and distributed branch profits	3 332 . .	–12	–28	–24	–30	–154	–49	–59	–108
Reinvested earnings and undistributed branch profits	3 333 . .	. . .	. . .	. . .	. . .	. . .	. . .	. . .	. . .
Income on debt (interest)	3 334 . .	. . .	. . .	. . .	. . .	. . .	–3	–13	–9
Portfolio investment income	3 339 . .	. . .	. . .	–16	–76	–121	–89	–74	–105
Income on equity	3 340 . .	. . .	. . .	–1	–15	. . .	–2	. . .	–4
Income on bonds and notes	3 350 . .	. . .	. . .	–15	–61	–121	–87	–69	–101
Income on money market instruments	3 360 . .	. . .	. . .	. . .	. . .	. . .	. . .	–5	. . .
Other investment income	3 370 . .	–233	–293	–345	–419	–424	–415	–455	–511
D. CURRENT TRANSFERS	4 379 . .	283	369	593	579	753	626	860	1,143
Credit	2 379 . .	**344**	**479**	**675**	**731**	**886**	**804**	**1,079**	**1,417**
General government	2 380 . .	117	92	70	82	73	79	99	252
Other sectors	2 390 . .	227	387	605	649	813	725	980	1,165
Workers' remittances	2 391 . .	4	4	10	2	4	4	2	4
Other current transfers	2 392 . .	223	383	595	647	809	721	978	1,161
Debit	3 379 . .	**–61**	**–110**	**–82**	**–152**	**–133**	**–178**	**–219**	**–274**
General government	3 380 . .	–16	–29	–23	–18	–21	–22	–29	–31
Other sectors	3 390 . .	–45	–81	–59	–134	–112	–156	–190	–243
Workers' remittances	3 391 . .	–5	–1	. . .	. . .	. . .	–1	–1	–1
Other current transfers	3 392 . .	–40	–80	–59	–134	–112	–155	–189	–242
CAPITAL AND FINANCIAL ACCOUNT	4 996 . .	**337**	**1,318**	**2,212**	**1,042**	**2,724**	**503**	**1,073**	**1,498**
CAPITAL ACCOUNT	4 994 . .	**12**	**242**	**152**	**43**	**39**	**45**	**36**	**95**
Total credit	2 994 . .	*12*	*242*	*152*	*43*	*39*	*46*	*37*	*108*
Total debit	3 994 . .	. . .	. . .	. . .	. . .	. . .	*–1*	*–1*	*–13*
Capital transfers, credit	2 400 . .	**12**	**242**	**152**	**43**	**39**	**46**	**37**	**108**
General government	2 401 . .	12	242	152	43	39	44	35	95
Debt forgiveness	2 402 . .	12	228	. . .	. . .	. . .	. . .	. . .	23
Other capital transfers	2 410 . .	. . .	14	152	43	39	44	35	72
Other sectors	2 430 . .	. . .	. . .	. . .	. . .	. . .	2	2	13
Migrants' transfers	2 431 . .	. . .	. . .	. . .	. . .	. . .	. . .	. . .	. . .
Debt forgiveness	2 432 . .	. . .	. . .	. . .	. . .	. . .	. . .	. . .	12
Other capital transfers	2 440 . .	. . .	. . .	. . .	. . .	. . .	2	2	1
Capital transfers, debit	3 400 . .	**. . .**	**. . .**	**. . .**	**. . .**	**. . .**	**–1**	**–1**	**–13**
General government	3 401 . .	. . .	. . .	. . .	. . .	. . .	. . .	. . .	–11
Debt forgiveness	3 402 . .	. . .	. . .	. . .	. . .	. . .	. . .	. . .	–11
Other capital transfers	3 410 . .	. . .	. . .	. . .	. . .	. . .	. . .	. . .	. . .
Other sectors	3 430 . .	. . .	. . .	. . .	. . .	. . .	–1	–1	–2
Migrants' transfers	3 431 . .	. . .	. . .	. . .	. . .	. . .	. . .	. . .	. . .
Debt forgiveness	3 432 . .	. . .	. . .	. . .	. . .	. . .	. . .	. . .	. . .
Other capital transfers	3 440 . .	. . .	. . .	. . .	. . .	. . .	–1	–1	–2
Nonproduced nonfinancial assets, credit	2 480 . .	**. . .**	**. . .**	**. . .**	**. . .**	**. . .**	**. . .**	**. . .**	**. . .**
Nonproduced nonfinancial assets, debit	3 480 . .	**. . .**	**. . .**	**. . .**	**. . .**	**. . .**	**. . .**	**. . .**	**. . .**

Table 2 (Continued). STANDARD PRESENTATION, 1994–2001
(Millions of U.S. dollars)

	Code	1994	1995	1996	1997	1998	1999	2000	2001
FINANCIAL ACCOUNT	4 995 . .	**325**	**1,076**	**2,060**	**999**	**2,685**	**458**	**1,037**	**1,403**
A. DIRECT INVESTMENT	4 500 . .	341	417	263	1,224	2,040	1,025	1,036	1,174
Direct investment abroad	4 505 . .	**. . .**	**–2**	**. . .**	**9**	**9**	**–16**	**11**	**17**
Equity capital	4 510 . .	. . .	–2	. . .	9	9	–16	11	17
Claims on affiliated enterprises	4 515 . .	. . .	. . .	. . .	9	9	–16	11	17
Liabilities to affiliated enterprises	4 520 . .	. . .	. . .	. . .	. . .	. . .	. . .	. . .	. . .
Reinvested earnings	4 525 . .	. . .	. . .	. . .	. . .	. . .	. . .	. . .	. . .
Other capital	4 530 . .	. . .	. . .	. . .	. . .	. . .	. . .	. . .	. . .
Claims on affiliated enterprises	4 535 . .	. . .	. . .	. . .	. . .	. . .	. . .	. . .	. . .
Liabilities to affiliated enterprises	4 540 . .	. . .	. . .	. . .	. . .	. . .	. . .	. . .	. . .
Direct investment in Romania	4 555 . .	**341**	**419**	**263**	**1,215**	**2,031**	**1,041**	**1,025**	**1,157**
Equity capital	4 560 . .	341	419	263	1,215	2,031	1,041	932	1,023
Claims on direct investors	4 565 . .	. . .	. . .	. . .	. . .	. . .	. . .	. . .	. . .
Liabilities to direct investors	4 570 . .	341	419	263	1,215	2,031	1,041	932	1,023
Reinvested earnings	4 575 . .	. . .	. . .	. . .	. . .	. . .	. . .	. . .	. . .
Other capital	4 580 . .	. . .	. . .	. . .	. . .	. . .	. . .	93	134
Claims on direct investors	4 585 . .	. . .	. . .	. . .	. . .	. . .	. . .	. . .	. . .
Liabilities to direct investors	4 590 . .	. . .	. . .	. . .	. . .	. . .	. . .	93	134
B. PORTFOLIO INVESTMENT	4 600 . .	75	32	1,222	883	130	–715	102	575
Assets	4 602 . .	**75**	**–22**	**. . .**	**–6**	**1**	**9**	**28**	**–8**
Equity securities	4 610 . .	. . .	–4	. . .	–6	1	9	31	–7
Monetary authorities	4 611 . .	. . .	. . .	. . .	. . .	. . .	. . .	. . .	. . .
General government	4 612 . .	. . .	. . .	. . .	. . .	. . .	–11	. . .	. . .
Banks	4 613 . .	. . .	. . .	. . .	–13	–11	23	6	–2
Other sectors	4 614 . .	. . .	. . .	. . .	7	12	–3	25	–5
Debt securities	4 619 . .	75	–18	. . .	. . .	. . .	. . .	–3	–1
Bonds and notes	4 620 . .	75	–18	. . .	. . .	. . .	. . .	–3	–1
Monetary authorities	4 621 . .	. . .	. . .	. . .	. . .	. . .	. . .	. . .	. . .
General government	4 622 . .	. . .	. . .	. . .	. . .	. . .	. . .	–3	–1
Banks	4 623 . .	81	. . .	. . .	. . .	. . .	. . .	. . .	. . .
Other sectors	4 624 . .	–6	. . .	. . .	. . .	. . .	. . .	. . .	. . .
Money market instruments	4 630 . .	. . .	. . .	. . .	. . .	. . .	. . .	. . .	. . .
Monetary authorities	4 631 . .	. . .	. . .	. . .	. . .	. . .	. . .	. . .	. . .
General government	4 632 . .	. . .	. . .	. . .	. . .	. . .	. . .	. . .	. . .
Banks	4 633 . .	. . .	. . .	. . .	. . .	. . .	. . .	. . .	. . .
Other sectors	4 634 . .	. . .	. . .	. . .	. . .	. . .	. . .	. . .	. . .
Liabilities	4 652 . .	**. . .**	**54**	**1,222**	**889**	**129**	**–724**	**74**	**583**
Equity securities	4 660 . .	. . .	. . .	. . .	195	95	68	58	8
Banks	4 663 . .	. . .	. . .	. . .	. . .	. . .	. . .	. . .	. . .
Other sectors	4 664 . .	. . .	. . .	. . .	195	95	68	58	8
Debt securities	4 669 . .	. . .	54	1,222	694	34	–792	16	575
Bonds and notes	4 670 . .	. . .	1	1,029	640	–13	–765	21	582
Monetary authorities	4 671 . .	. . .	. . .	1,029	. . .	. . .	–678	. . .	–275
General government	4 672 . .	. . .	. . .	. . .	349	. . .	. . .	259	655
Banks	4 673 . .	. . .	1	. . .	75	–13	–43	–34	–2
Other sectors	4 674 . .	. . .	. . .	. . .	216	. . .	–44	–204	204
Money market instruments	4 680 . .	. . .	53	193	54	47	–27	–5	–7
Monetary authorities	4 681 . .	. . .	. . .	. . .	. . .	. . .	. . .	. . .	. . .
General government	4 682 . .	. . .	. . .	. . .	. . .	. . .	. . .	. . .	. . .
Banks	4 683 . .	. . .	53	193	. . .	. . .	. . .	. . .	. . .
Other sectors	4 684 . .	. . .	. . .	. . .	54	47	–27	–5	–7
C. FINANCIAL DERIVATIVES	4 910 . .	. . .	. . .	. . .	. . .	. . .	. . .	. . .	. . .
Monetary authorities	4 911 . .	. . .	. . .	. . .	. . .	. . .	. . .	. . .	. . .
General government	4 912 . .	. . .	. . .	. . .	. . .	. . .	. . .	. . .	. . .
Banks	4 913 . .	. . .	. . .	. . .	. . .	. . .	. . .	. . .	. . .
Other sectors	4 914 . .	. . .	. . .	. . .	. . .	. . .	. . .	. . .	. . .
Assets	4 900 . .	**. . .**	**. . .**	**. . .**	**. . .**	**. . .**	**. . .**	**. . .**	**. . .**
Monetary authorities	4 901 . .	. . .	. . .	. . .	. . .	. . .	. . .	. . .	. . .
General government	4 902 . .	. . .	. . .	. . .	. . .	. . .	. . .	. . .	. . .
Banks	4 903 . .	. . .	. . .	. . .	. . .	. . .	. . .	. . .	. . .
Other sectors	4 904 . .	. . .	. . .	. . .	. . .	. . .	. . .	. . .	. . .
Liabilities	4 905 . .	**. . .**	**. . .**	**. . .**	**. . .**	**. . .**	**. . .**	**. . .**	**. . .**
Monetary authorities	4 906 . .	. . .	. . .	. . .	. . .	. . .	. . .	. . .	. . .
General government	4 907 . .	. . .	. . .	. . .	. . .	. . .	. . .	. . .	. . .
Banks	4 908 . .	. . .	. . .	. . .	. . .	. . .	. . .	. . .	. . .
Other sectors	4 909 . .	. . .	. . .	. . .	. . .	. . .	. . .	. . .	. . .

Table 2 (Concluded). STANDARD PRESENTATION, 1994–2001
(Millions of U.S. dollars)

	Code	1994	1995	1996	1997	1998	1999	2000	2001
D. OTHER INVESTMENT	4 700 . .	525	367	794	556	–329	321	825	1,138
Assets	4 703 . .	**–671**	**186**	**–271**	**–6**	**208**	**246**	**–407**	**–44**
Trade credits	4 706 . .	. . .	–110	35	106	35	10	–67	50
General government	4 707 . .	. . .	–63	–16	–22	–8	6	–81	–50
of which: Short-term	4 709 . .	. . .	. . .	. . .	. . .	. . .	. . .	. . .	. . .
Other sectors	4 710 . .	. . .	–47	51	128	43	4	14	100
of which: Short-term	4 712 . .	. . .	*–106*	*40*	*95*	*13*	*–16*	*20*	*98*
Loans	4 714 . .	–103	–3	–8	–22	36	–19	1	–1
Monetary authorities	4 715 . .	. . .	. . .	. . .	. . .	. . .	. . .	. . .	. . .
of which: Short-term	4 718 . .	. . .	. . .	. . .	. . .	. . .	. . .	. . .	. . .
General government	4 719 . .	–24	. . .	. . .	. . .	. . .	. . .	. . .	. . .
of which: Short-term	4 721 . .	. . .	. . .	. . .	. . .	. . .	. . .	. . .	. . .
Banks	4 722 . .	. . .	–3	–8	–22	36	–19	–14	–3
of which: Short-term	4 724 . .	. . .	*–9*	*–4*	*–24*	*37*	*–21*	*14*	*–4*
Other sectors	4 725 . .	–79	. . .	. . .	. . .	. . .	. . .	15	2
of which: Short-term	4 727 . .	*–100*	. . .	. . .	. . .	. . .	. . .	. . .	. . .
Currency and deposits	4 730 . .	–500	274	–280	–256	112	230	–311	–134
Monetary authorities	4 731 . .	. . .	. . .	. . .	. . .	. . .	. . .	. . .	. . .
General government	4 732 . .	. . .	. . .	. . .	. . .	. . .	. . .	. . .	. . .
Banks	4 733 . .	–500	274	–280	–256	112	230	–311	–134
Other sectors	4 734 . .	. . .	. . .	. . .	. . .	. . .	. . .	. . .	. . .
Other assets	4 736 . .	–68	25	–18	166	25	25	–30	41
Monetary authorities	4 737 . .	. . .	. . .	. . .	. . .	. . .	. . .	. . .	. . .
of which: Short-term	4 739 . .	. . .	. . .	. . .	. . .	. . .	. . .	. . .	. . .
General government	4 740 . .	. . .	1	7	32	–2	3	–1	6
of which: Short-term	4 742 . .	. . .	*1*	*7*	*32*	*–2*	*3*	*–1*	*6*
Banks	4 743 . .	–121	–17	–27	138	31	25	–29	35
of which: Short-term	4 745 . .	*–121*	*–17*	*–27*	*138*	*31*	*25*	*–29*	*35*
Other sectors	4 746 . .	53	41	2	–4	–4	–3	. . .	. . .
of which: Short-term	4 748 . .	*53*	*41*	*2*	*–4*	*–4*	*–3*	. . .	. . .
Liabilities	4 753 . .	**1,196**	**181**	**1,065**	**562**	**–537**	**75**	**1,232**	**1,182**
Trade credits	4 756 . .	. . .	713	830	523	416	–380	–26	73
General government	4 757 . .	. . .	399	167	220	240	. . .	–12	–16
of which: Short-term	4 759 . .	. . .	. . .	. . .	. . .	. . .	. . .	. . .	. . .
Other sectors	4 760 . .	. . .	314	663	303	176	–380	–14	89
of which: Short-term	4 762 . .	. . .	*–73*	*219*	*–149*	*–324*	*–213*	*–6*	*33*
Loans	4 764 . .	1,204	102	–66	241	–869	454	1,249	970
Monetary authorities	4 765 . .	217	4	–386	–144	–201	7	6	–51
of which: Use of Fund credit and loans from the Fund	4 766 . .	*217*	*–316*	*–356*	*29*	*–126*	*–66*	*20*	*–51*
of which: Short-term	4 768 . .	. . .	*150*	*–150*	. . .	. . .	*114*	*–14*	. . .
General government	4 769 . .	264	80	103	351	–247	46	702	366
of which: Short-term	4 771 . .	. . .	. . .	. . .	. . .	. . .	. . .	. . .	. . .
Banks	4 772 . .	86	18	217	34	–203	–78	–85	–2
of which: Short-term	4 774 . .	*48*	*–44*	*67*	*–68*	*–18*	*10*	*–7*	*3*
Other sectors	4 775 . .	637	. . .	. . .	. . .	–218	479	626	657
of which: Short-term	4 777 . .	*27*	. . .	. . .	. . .	*–218*	*20*	*–11*	*58*
Currency and deposits	4 780 . .	104	–75	319	–166	–57	24	11	143
Monetary authorities	4 781 . .	. . .	. . .	. . .	. . .	. . .	. . .	. . .	. . .
General government	4 782 . .	. . .	. . .	. . .	. . .	. . .	. . .	. . .	. . .
Banks	4 783 . .	104	–75	319	–166	–57	24	11	143
Other sectors	4 784 . .	. . .	. . .	. . .	. . .	. . .	. . .	. . .	. . .
Other liabilities	4 786 . .	–112	–559	–18	–36	–27	–23	–2	–4
Monetary authorities	4 787 . .	. . .	. . .	. . .	. . .	. . .	. . .	. . .	. . .
of which: Short-term	4 789 . .	. . .	. . .	. . .	. . .	. . .	. . .	. . .	. . .
General government	4 790 . .	. . .	–506	–61	–24	. . .	–6	–9	–30
of which: Short-term	4 792 . .	. . .	*–506*	*–61*	*–24*	. . .	*–6*	*–9*	. . .
Banks	4 793 . .	. . .	. . .	. . .	. . .	. . .	. . .	. . .	18
of which: Short-term	4 795 . .	. . .	. . .	. . .	. . .	. . .	. . .	. . .	. . .
Other sectors	4 796 . .	–112	–53	43	–12	–27	–17	7	8
of which: Short-term	4 798 . .	*–112*	*–53*	*43*	*–12*	*–27*	*–17*	*7*	*8*
E. RESERVE ASSETS	4 802 . .	–616	259	–218	–1,664	844	–173	–926	–1,484
Monetary gold	4 812 . .	–69	. . .	. . .	. . .	. . .	–5	. . .	–5
Special drawing rights	4 811 . .	–51	1	51	–101	103	–9	9	–6
Reserve position in the Fund	4 810 . .	. . .	. . .	. . .	. . .	. . .	. . .	. . .	. . .
Foreign exchange	4 803 . .	–496	258	–269	–1,563	741	–159	–935	–1,473
Other claims	4 813 . .	. . .	. . .	. . .	. . .	. . .	. . .	. . .	. . .
NET ERRORS AND OMISSIONS	4 998 . .	**91**	**456**	**359**	**1,095**	**194**	**794**	**286**	**819**

Part 3 of the *Yearbook* contains descriptions of the methodologies, compilation practices, and sources used to compile these data.

Table 3. INTERNATIONAL INVESTMENT POSITION (End–period stocks), 1994–2001

(Millions of U.S. dollars)

	Code	1994	1995	1996	1997	1998	1999	2000	2001
ASSETS	8 995 C.	8,847	8,492	9,084	10,164	9,546	9,718	10,935	12,377
Direct investment abroad	8 505 . .	**107**	**121**	**120**	**114**	**123**	**133**	**142**	**127**
Equity capital and reinvested earnings	8 506 . .	107	121	120	114	123	133	142	127
Claims on affiliated enterprises	8 507 . .	107	121	120	114	123	133	142	127
Liabilities to affiliated enterprises	8 508 . .	...	...	...	...	...	...	...	...
Other capital	8 530 . .	...	...	...	...	...	...	...	...
Claims on affiliated enterprises	8 535 . .	...	...	...	...	...	...	...	...
Liabilities to affiliated enterprises	8 540 . .	...	...	...	...	...	...	...	...
Portfolio investment	8 602 . .	**1,179**	**1,224**	**1,252**	**1,115**	**1,190**	**1,545**	**1,480**	**1,429**
Equity securities	8 610 . .	1,176	1,211	1,239	1,103	1,167	1,541	1,480	1,429
Monetary authorities	8 611 . .	1,102	1,132	1,160	1,028	1,071	1,411	1,351	1,302
General government	8 612 . .	74	79	78	75	96	131	128	127
Banks	8 613 . .	...	...	...	...	...	...	...	...
Other sectors	8 614 . .	...	...	...	...	...	...	...	...
Debt securities	8 619 . .	3	13	13	11	23	4	...	...
Bonds and notes	8 620 . .	3	11	11	11	23	4	...	...
Monetary authorities	8 621 . .	...	...	...	...	...	...	...	...
General government	8 622 . .	...	...	...	...	...	...	...	...
Banks	8 623 . .	3	11	11	11	23	4	...	...
Other sectors	8 624 . .	...	...	...	...	...	...	...	...
Money market instruments	8 630 . .	...	2	2	...	...	...	...	...
Monetary authorities	8 631 . .	...	...	...	...	...	...	...	...
General government	8 632 . .	...	...	...	...	...	...	...	...
Banks	8 633 . .	...	...	...	...	...	...	...	...
Other sectors	8 634 . .	...	2	2	...	...	...	...	...
Financial derivatives	8 900 . .	**...**	**...**	**...**	**...**	**...**	**...**	**...**	**...**
Monetary authorities	8 901 . .	...	...	...	...	...	...	...	...
General government	8 902 . .	...	...	...	...	...	...	...	...
Banks	8 903 . .	...	...	...	...	...	...	...	...
Other sectors	8 904 . .	...	...	...	...	...	...	...	...
Other investment	8 703 . .	**5,964**	**5,768**	**6,120**	**5,874**	**5,935**	**5,547**	**5,924**	**5,960**
Trade credits	8 706 . .	4,119	4,178	4,106	3,826	4,039	3,987	4,054	4,025
General government	8 707 . .	2,720	2,714	2,734	2,597	2,723	3,343	3,422	3,494
of which: Short-term	8 709 . .	...	...	...	...	...	...	...	...
Other sectors	8 710 . .	1,399	1,464	1,371	1,230	1,316	645	632	531
of which: Short-term	8 712 . .	*501*	*607*	*567*	*472*	*459*	*474*	*455*	*359*
Loans	8 714 . .	1	10	15	37	2	21	35	38
Monetary authorities	8 715 . .	...	...	...	...	...	...	...	...
of which: Short-term	8 718 . .	...	...	...	...	...	...	...	...
General government	8 719 . .	...	...	...	...	...	...	...	...
of which: Short-term	8 721 . .	...	...	...	...	...	...	...	...
Banks	8 722 . .	1	10	15	37	2	21	35	38
of which: Short-term	8 724 . .	*1*	*10*	*10*	*34*	...	*21*	*7*	*11*
Other sectors	8 725 . .	...	...	...	...	...	...	...	...
of which: Short-term	8 727 . .	...	...	...	...	...	...	...	...
Currency and deposits	8 730 . .	1,542	1,265	1,586	1,630	1,501	1,186	1,483	1,552
Monetary authorities	8 731 . .	...	...	...	...	...	...	...	...
General government	8 732 . .	7	4	15	3	4	2	3	5
Banks	8 733 . .	1,491	1,234	1,541	1,599	1,470	1,157	1,452	1,519
Other sectors	8 734 . .	44	26	30	27	27	27	27	27
Other assets	8 736 . .	302	315	414	381	393	352	353	345
Monetary authorities	8 737 . .	...	...	...	...	...	...	...	...
of which: Short-term	8 739 . .	...	...	...	...	...	...	...	...
General government	8 740 . .	277	288	383	350	355	352	353	345
of which: Short-term	8 742 . .	*176*	*184*	*282*	*251*	*254*	*252*	*253*	*247*
Banks	8 743 . .	...	...	...	...	...	...	...	...
of which: Short-term	8 745 . .	...	...	...	...	...	...	...	...
Other sectors	8 746 . .	25	26	30	31	38	...	...	...
of which: Short-term	8 748 . .	*25*	*26*	*30*	*31*	*38*	...	...	...
Reserve assets	8 802 . .	**1,598**	**1,380**	**1,592**	**3,061**	**2,299**	**2,493**	**3,390**	**4,861**
Monetary gold	8 812 . .	1,006	1,046	1,042	868	924	967	920	939
Special drawing rights	8 811 . .	56	56	4	104	1	10	1	7
Reserve position in the Fund	8 810 . .	...	...	...	...	...	...	...	...
Foreign exchange	8 803 . .	536	278	547	2,090	1,374	1,516	2,469	3,916
Other claims	8 813 . .	...	...	...	...	...	...	...	...

Table 3 (Concluded). INTERNATIONAL INVESTMENT POSITION (End-period stocks), 1994–2001

(Millions of U.S. dollars)

	Code	1994	1995	1996	1997	1998	1999	2000	2001
LIABILITIES	8 995 D.	7,500	7,976	11,468	13,864	16,045	16,761	19,299	21,940
Direct investment in Romania	8 555 . .	**402**	**421**	**1,097**	**2,352**	**4,418**	**5,469**	**6,480**	**7,613**
Equity capital and reinvested earnings	8 556 . .	401	418	1,081	2,305	4,335	5,297	6,229	7,252
Claims on direct investors	8 557 . .	401	418	1,081	2,305	4,335	5,297	6,229	7,252
Liabilities to direct investors	8 558 . .	...	...	...	...	...	...	...	...
Other capital	8 580 . .	1	3	16	47	83	172	251	361
Claims on direct investors	8 585 . .	1	3	16	47	83	172	251	361
Liabilities to direct investors	8 590 . .	...	...	...	...	...	...	...	...
Portfolio investment	8 652 . .	**719**	**785**	**2,408**	**3,069**	**3,338**	**3,025**	**3,032**	**3,526**
Equity securities	8 660 . .	719	732	1,178	1,312	1,459	1,867	1,865	1,824
Banks	8 663 . .	...	...	...	...	...	...	...	...
Other sectors	8 664 . .	719	732	1,178	1,312	1,459	1,867	1,865	1,824
Debt securities	8 669 . .	...	54	1,229	1,757	1,879	1,158	1,167	1,702
Bonds and notes	8 670 . .	...	54	1,229	1,757	1,879	1,158	1,154	1,696
Monetary authorities	8 671 . .	...	...	994	906	996	318	286	...
General government	8 672 . .	...	...	...	335	358	309	565	1,197
Banks	8 673 . .	...	1	1	75	64	37	4	2
Other sectors	8 674 . .	...	53	234	440	461	494	300	497
Money market instruments	8 680 . .	...	...	...	...	...	...	13	7
Monetary authorities	8 681 . .	...	...	...	...	...	...	...	...
General government	8 682 . .	...	...	...	...	...	...	...	...
Banks	8 683 . .	...	...	...	...	...	...	...	...
Other sectors	8 684 . .	...	...	...	...	...	...	13	7
Financial derivatives	8 905 . .	...	...	...	...	...	...	...	...
Monetary authorities	8 906 . .	...	...	...	...	...	...	...	...
General government	8 907 . .	...	...	...	...	...	...	...	...
Banks	8 908 . .	...	...	...	...	...	...	...	...
Other sectors	8 909 . .	...	...	...	...	...	...	...	...
Other investment	8 753 . .	**6,379**	**6,770**	**7,963**	**8,443**	**8,289**	**8,267**	**9,787**	**10,801**
Trade credits	8 756 . .	1,145	1,437	1,804	1,544	1,171	805	836	835
General government	8 757 . .	128	341	291	248	263	228	188	125
of which: Short-term	8 759 . .	...	...	...	...	...	...	...	...
Other sectors	8 760 . .	1,017	1,096	1,513	1,296	908	577	648	710
of which: Short-term	8 762 . .	*885*	*815*	*1,106*	*966*	*578*	*367*	*358*	*390*
Loans	8 764 . .	4,382	5,051	5,541	6,583	6,889	7,130	8,447	9,328
Monetary authorities	8 765 . .	1,383	1,358	941	858	580	470	453	387
of which: Use of Fund credit and loans from the Fund	8 766 . .	*1,323*	*1,038*	*651*	*641*	*539*	*458*	*453*	*387*
of which: Short-term	8 768 . .	*60*	*150*	...	*100*	...	*12*	...	...
General government	8 769 . .	1,576	1,893	2,154	2,625	2,684	2,682	3,403	3,696
of which: Short-term	8 771 . .	...	...	...	...	...	...	...	...
Banks	8 772 . .	430	567	772	703	403	370	253	244
of which: Short-term	8 774 . .	*22*	*35*	*109*	*37*	*15*	*24*	*18*	*21*
Other sectors	8 775 . .	993	1,233	1,673	2,397	3,222	3,608	4,339	5,001
of which: Short-term	8 777 . .	...	...	...	*134*	*15*	*35*	*24*	*82*
Currency and deposits	8 780 . .	251	177	496	230	173	299	353	510
Monetary authorities	8 781 . .	...	...	...	...	...	...	...	...
General government	8 782 . .	...	...	...	100	...	102	100	100
Banks	8 783 . .	251	177	496	130	173	197	253	410
Other sectors	8 784 . .	...	...	...	...	...	...	...	...
Other liabilities	8 786 . .	601	105	123	87	56	33	151	128
Monetary authorities	8 787 . .	...	...	...	...	...	...	...	...
of which: Short-term	8 789 . .	...	...	...	...	...	...	...	...
General government	8 790 . .	594	101	39	15	16	10	121	91
of which: Short-term	8 792 . .	*594*	*101*	*39*	*15*	*16*	*10*	*1*	*1*
Banks	8 793 . .	...	...	...	...	...	...	...	...
of which: Short-term	8 795 . .	...	...	...	...	...	...	...	...
Other sectors	8 796 . .	7	4	84	72	41	23	30	38
of which: Short-term	8 798 . .	*7*	*4*	*84*	*72*	*41*	*23*	*30*	*38*
NET INTERNATIONAL INVESTMENT POSITION	8 995 . .	**1,347**	**516**	**–2,384**	**–3,700**	**–6,498**	**–7,044**	**–8,364**	**–9,563**
Conversion rates: lei per U.S. dollar (end of period)	0 102 . .	**1,767.0**	**2,578.0**	**4,035.0**	**8,023.0**	**10,951.0**	**18,255.0**	**25,926.0**	**31,597.0**

Table 1. ANALYTIC PRESENTATION, 1994–2001
(Millions of U.S. dollars)

	Code	1994	1995	1996	1997	1998	1999	2000	2001
A. Current Account [1]	4 993 Z.	**8,292**	**7,457**	**11,725**	**2,032**	**659**	**24,730**	**47,293**	**34,621**
Goods: exports f.o.b.	2 100 . .	67,826	82,913	90,563	89,008	74,884	75,666	105,565	101,603
Goods: imports f.o.b.	3 100 . .	-50,452	-62,604	-68,092	-71,983	-58,015	-39,537	-44,862	-53,764
Balance on Goods	4 100 . .	*17,374*	*20,310*	*22,471*	*17,025*	*16,869*	*36,129*	*60,703*	*47,839*
Services: credit	2 200 . .	8,424	10,568	13,282	14,080	12,373	9,067	9,975	10,904
Services: debit	3 200 . .	-15,435	-20,206	-18,665	-20,025	-16,456	-13,351	-16,718	-19,405
Balance on Goods and Services	4 991 . .	*10,363*	*10,672*	*17,088*	*11,080*	*12,786*	*31,845*	*53,961*	*39,338*
Income: credit	2 300 . .	3,500	4,278	4,333	4,367	4,301	3,882	4,753	6,800
Income: debit	3 300 . .	-5,340	-7,650	-9,768	-13,058	-16,091	-11,597	-11,489	-10,759
Balance on Goods, Services, and Income	4 992 . .	*8,523*	*7,300*	*11,653*	*2,388*	*996*	*24,129*	*47,224*	*35,379*
Current transfers: credit	2 379 Z.	312	894	773	410	308	1,183	807	381
Current transfers: debit	3 379 . .	-543	-738	-700	-766	-644	-582	-738	-1,140
B. Capital Account [1]	4 994 Z.	**2,410**	**-347**	**-463**	**-797**	**-382**	**-328**	**10,676**	**-9,378**
Capital account: credit	2 994 Z.	5,882	3,122	3,066	2,137	1,704	885	11,543	2,125
Capital account: debit	3 994 . .	-3,472	-3,469	-3,529	-2,934	-2,087	-1,213	-867	-11,503
Total, Groups A Plus B	4 981 . .	*10,702*	*7,109*	*11,262*	*1,235*	*277*	*24,402*	*57,969*	*25,243*
C. Financial Account [1]	4 995 W.	**-30,220**	**-7,468**	**-23,581**	**-2,902**	**-12,582**	**-19,073**	**-34,290**	**-4,738**
Direct investment abroad	4 505 . .	-281	-605	-922	-3,185	-1,270	-2,208	-3,177	-2,533
Direct investment in Russia	4 555 Z.	690	2,065	2,579	4,865	2,761	3,310	2,714	2,469
Portfolio investment assets	4 602 . .	114	-1,705	-172	-156	-257	254	-411	77
Equity securities	4 610 . .	-19	-42	-117	33	-10	5	-40	-60
Debt securities	4 619 . .	133	-1,663	-56	-189	-247	249	-371	137
Portfolio investment liabilities	4 652 Z.	-93	-738	4,583	17,795	6,293	-1,882	-12,808	-730
Equity securities	4 660 . .	45	47	2,152	1,265	714	-287	150	543
Debt securities	4 669 Z.	-137	-785	2,430	16,530	5,579	-1,595	-12,959	-1,272
Financial derivatives	4 910 . .	. . .	. . .	. . .	. . .	. . .	. . .	. . .	. . .
Financial derivatives assets	4 900 . .	. . .	. . .	. . .	. . .	. . .	. . .	. . .	. . .
Financial derivatives liabilities	4 905 . .	. . .	. . .	. . .	. . .	. . .	. . .	. . .	. . .
Other investment assets	4 703 . .	-20,436	-1,789	-31,357	-26,703	-15,636	-14,857	-17,520	-577
Monetary authorities	4 701 . .	. . .	. . .	. . .	. . .	. . .	. . .	. . .	. . .
General government	4 704 . .	-3,117	-1,042	-317	7,158	-1,150	-1,348	-1,617	10,099
Banks	4 705 . .	-3,117	4,317	-1,972	-1,082	501	-3,625	-3,332	-1,917
Other sectors	4 728 . .	-14,202	-5,064	-29,068	-32,779	-14,987	-9,884	-12,572	-8,758
Other investment liabilities	4 753 W.	-10,214	-4,696	1,709	4,483	-4,474	-3,690	-3,088	-3,444
Monetary authorities	4 753 WA	-325	391	-230	-38	65	3	155	49
General government	4 753 ZB	-11,746	-8,716	-6,033	-10,764	-3,176	-1,975	-2,876	-7,480
Banks	4 753 ZC	1,305	2,449	4,259	8,649	-6,360	-1,270	568	3,697
Other sectors	4 753 ZD	551	1,182	3,713	6,636	4,997	-448	-935	289
Total, Groups A Through C	4 983 . .	*-19,518*	*-358*	*-12,319*	*-1,667*	*-12,305*	*5,329*	*23,679*	*20,505*
D. Net Errors and Omissions	4 998 . .	**406**	**-7,967**	**-4,898**	**-4,852**	**-9,073**	**-7,032**	**-9,756**	**-9,239**
Total, Groups A Through D	4 984 . .	*-19,112*	*-8,326*	*-17,217*	*-6,519*	*-21,378*	*-1,704*	*13,923*	*11,266*
E. Reserves and Related Items	4 802 A.	**19,112**	**8,326**	**17,217**	**6,519**	**21,378**	**1,704**	**-13,923**	**-11,266**
Reserve assets	4 802 . .	1,935	-10,382	2,840	-1,930	5,306	-1,772	-16,009	-8,211
Use of Fund credit and loans	4 766 . .	1,514	5,473	3,237	1,526	5,206	-3,603	-2,899	-3,829
Exceptional financing	4 920 . .	15,662	13,235	11,140	6,923	10,866	7,078	4,985	773
Conversion rates: rubles per U.S. dollar	0 101 . .	**2.191**	**4.559**	**5.121**	**5.785**	**9.705**	**24.620**	**28.129**	**29.169**

[1] Excludes components that have been classified in the categories of Group E.

Table 2. STANDARD PRESENTATION, 1994–2001
(Millions of U.S. dollars)

	Code	1994	1995	1996	1997	1998	1999	2000	2001
CURRENT ACCOUNT	4 993 . .	**8,292**	**7,457**	**11,725**	**2,032**	**659**	**24,730**	**47,293**	**34,621**
A. GOODS	4 100 . .	17,374	20,310	22,471	17,025	16,869	36,129	60,703	47,839
Credit	2 100 . .	**67,826**	**82,913**	**90,563**	**89,008**	**74,884**	**75,666**	**105,565**	**101,603**
General merchandise: exports f.o.b.	2 110 . .	67,717	82,824	90,256	88,517	74,419	75,360	105,109	101,239
Goods for processing: exports f.o.b.	2 150 . .	. . .	. . .	. . .	. . .	. . .	. . .	. . .	. . .
Repairs on goods	2 160 . .	. . .	. . .	. . .	. . .	88	85	148	69
Goods procured in ports by carriers	2 170 . .	110	90	307	491	377	220	309	296
Nonmonetary gold	2 180 . .	. . .	. . .	. . .	. . .	. . .	. . .	. . .	. . .
Debit	3 100 . .	**–50,452**	**–62,604**	**–68,092**	**–71,983**	**–58,015**	**–39,537**	**–44,862**	**–53,764**
General merchandise: imports f.o.b.	3 110 . .	–49,710	–61,727	–67,170	–71,109	–57,024	–38,681	–43,774	–52,757
Goods for processing: imports f.o.b.	3 150 . .	. . .	. . .	. . .	. . .	. . .	. . .	. . .	. . .
Repairs on goods	3 160 . .	. . .	. . .	. . .	. . .	–119	–92	–169	–191
Goods procured in ports by carriers	3 170 . .	–742	–876	–923	–874	–872	–765	–919	–815
Nonmonetary gold	3 180 . .	. . .	. . .	. . .	. . .	. . .	. . .	. . .	. . .
B. SERVICES	4 200 . .	–7,011	–9,638	–5,383	–5,945	–4,083	–4,284	–6,743	–8,501
Total credit	2 200 . .	*8,424*	*10,568*	*13,282*	*14,080*	*12,373*	*9,067*	*9,975*	*10,904*
Total debit	3 200 . .	*–15,435*	*–20,206*	*–18,665*	*–20,025*	*–16,456*	*–13,351*	*–16,718*	*–19,405*
Transportation services, credit	2 205 . .	**3,863**	**3,781**	**3,630**	**3,649**	**3,171**	**3,006**	**3,555**	**4,655**
Passenger	2 850 . .	. . .	. . .	. . .	. . .	. . .	. . .	. . .	*1,154*
Freight	2 851 . .	. . .	. . .	. . .	. . .	. . .	. . .	. . .	*2,017*
Other	2 852 . .	. . .	. . .	. . .	. . .	. . .	. . .	. . .	*1,484*
Sea transport, passenger	2 207 . .	. . .	. . .	. . .	. . .	. . .	. . .	. . .	1
Sea transport, freight	2 208 . .	. . .	. . .	. . .	. . .	. . .	. . .	. . .	746
Sea transport, other	2 209 . .	. . .	. . .	. . .	. . .	. . .	. . .	. . .	831
Air transport, passenger	2 211 . .	. . .	. . .	. . .	. . .	. . .	. . .	. . .	1,052
Air transport, freight	2 212 . .	. . .	. . .	. . .	. . .	. . .	. . .	. . .	411
Air transport, other	2 213 . .	. . .	. . .	. . .	. . .	. . .	. . .	. . .	349
Other transport, passenger	2 215 . .	. . .	. . .	. . .	. . .	. . .	. . .	. . .	102
Other transport, freight	2 216 . .	. . .	. . .	. . .	. . .	. . .	. . .	. . .	860
Other transport, other	2 217 . .	. . .	. . .	. . .	. . .	. . .	. . .	. . .	304
Transportation services, debit	3 205 . .	**–3,028**	**–3,307**	**–2,592**	**–2,991**	**–2,763**	**–2,221**	**–2,330**	**–2,985**
Passenger	3 850 . .	. . .	. . .	. . .	. . .	. . .	. . .	. . .	*–476*
Freight	3 851 . .	. . .	. . .	. . .	. . .	. . .	. . .	. . .	*–1,502*
Other	3 852 . .	. . .	. . .	. . .	. . .	. . .	. . .	. . .	*–1,007*
Sea transport, passenger	3 207 . .	. . .	. . .	. . .	. . .	. . .	. . .	. . .	–1
Sea transport, freight	3 208 . .	. . .	. . .	. . .	. . .	. . .	. . .	. . .	–624
Sea transport, other	3 209 . .	. . .	. . .	. . .	. . .	. . .	. . .	. . .	–454
Air transport, passenger	3 211 . .	. . .	. . .	. . .	. . .	. . .	. . .	. . .	–347
Air transport, freight	3 212 . .	. . .	. . .	. . .	. . .	. . .	. . .	. . .	–569
Air transport, other	3 213 . .	. . .	. . .	. . .	. . .	. . .	. . .	. . .	–342
Other transport, passenger	3 215 . .	. . .	. . .	. . .	. . .	. . .	. . .	. . .	–128
Other transport, freight	3 216 . .	. . .	. . .	. . .	. . .	. . .	. . .	. . .	–309
Other transport, other	3 217 . .	. . .	. . .	. . .	. . .	. . .	. . .	. . .	–211
Travel, credit	2 236 . .	**2,412**	**4,312**	7,102	7,164	6,508	**3,723**	**3,839**	**3,750**
Business travel	2 237 . .	. . .	. . .	. . .	. . .	. . .	1,480	1,428	1,386
Personal travel	2 240 . .	. . .	. . .	. . .	. . .	. . .	2,243	2,411	2,364
Travel, debit	3 236 . .	**–7,092**	**–11,599**	**–10,011**	**–10,113**	**–8,677**	–7,097	**–9,336**	**–10,360**
Business travel	3 237 . .	. . .	. . .	. . .	. . .	. . .	–1,834	–1,830	–2,048
Personal travel	3 240 . .	. . .	. . .	. . .	. . .	. . .	–5,263	–7,506	–8,312
Other services, credit	2 200 BA	**2,150**	**2,475**	**2,550**	**3,268**	**2,694**	**2,338**	**2,580**	**2,498**
Communications	2 245 . .	294	483	563	627	551	464	385	365
Construction	2 249 . .	131	103	91	94	142	126	170	93
Insurance	2 253 . .	. . .	. . .	. . .	. . .	14	22	35	59
Financial	2 260 . .	92	68	84	142	98	101	100	128
Computer and information	2 262 . .	. . .	. . .	. . .	. . .	. . .	34	59	128
Royalties and licence fees	2 266 . .	4	4	159	176	27	43	91	60
Other business services	2 268 . .	1,630	1,817	1,651	2,229	1,863	1,549	1,740	1,354
Personal, cultural, and recreational	2 287 . .	. . .	. . .	. . .	. . .	. . .	. . .	. . .	85
Government, n.i.e.	2 291 . .	. . .	. . .	. . .	. . .	. . .	. . .	. . .	227
Other services, debit	3 200 BA	**–5,315**	**–5,299**	**–6,062**	**–6,921**	**–5,016**	**–4,033**	**–5,052**	**–6,060**
Communications	3 245 . .	–190	–309	–364	–353	–355	–309	–288	–274
Construction	3 249 . .	–1,969	–1,670	–1,085	–805	–548	–261	–406	–336
Insurance	3 253 . .	. . .	. . .	. . .	. . .	–163	–261	–412	–379
Financial	3 260 . .	–127	–72	–124	–390	–239	–81	–36	–211
Computer and information	3 262 . .	. . .	. . .	. . .	. . .	. . .	–7	–474	–557
Royalties and licence fees	3 266 . .	–24	–4	–44	–11	–3	–8	–69	–343
Other business services	3 268 . .	–3,005	–3,243	–4,445	–5,361	–3,710	–3,106	–3,367	–3,041
Personal, cultural, and recreational	3 287 . .	. . .	. . .	. . .	. . .	. . .	. . .	. . .	–166
Government, n.i.e.	3 291 . .	. . .	. . .	. . .	. . .	. . .	. . .	. . .	–754

Table 2 (Continued). STANDARD PRESENTATION, 1994–2001
(Millions of U.S. dollars)

	Code	1994	1995	1996	1997	1998	1999	2000	2001
C. INCOME	4 300	–1,840	–3,372	–5,435	–8,692	–11,790	–7,716	–6,737	–3,959
Total credit	2 300	*3,500*	*4,278*	*4,333*	*4,367*	*4,301*	*3,882*	*4,753*	*6,800*
Total debit	3 300	*–5,340*	*–7,650*	*–9,768*	*–13,058*	*–16,091*	*–11,597*	*–11,489*	*–10,759*
Compensation of employees, credit	2 310	**108**	**166**	**102**	**227**	**301**	**425**	**500**	**624**
Compensation of employees, debit	3 310	**–222**	**–469**	**–508**	**–568**	**–465**	**–204**	**–232**	**–494**
Investment income, credit	2 320	**3,392**	**4,112**	**4,232**	**4,140**	**4,000**	**3,456**	**4,253**	**6,176**
Direct investment income	2 330	104	100	146	22	27	15	62	599
Dividends and distributed branch profits	2 332	104	100	146	21	8	8	60	534
Reinvested earnings and undistributed branch profits	2 333	. . .	. . .	. . .	1	5	2	1	65
Income on debt (interest)	2 334	. . .	. . .	. . .	. . .	14	5	. . .	. . .
Portfolio investment income	2 339	28	116	154	141	84	73	120	106
Income on equity	2 340	12	9	10	3	4	. . .	1	3
Income on bonds and notes	2 350	16	107	144	139	80	73	119	104
Income on money market instruments	2 360	. . .	. . .	. . .	. . .	. . .	. . .	. . .	. . .
Other investment income	2 370	3,260	3,896	3,932	3,976	3,890	3,368	4,071	5,471
Investment income, debit	3 320	**–5,118**	**–7,181**	**–9,260**	**–12,490**	**–15,626**	**–11,393**	**–11,257**	**–10,265**
Direct investment income	3 330	–67	–197	–227	–924	–856	–617	–887	–1,214
Dividends and distributed branch profits	3 332	–67	–197	–227	–207	–290	–214	–365	–586
Reinvested earnings and undistributed branch profits	3 333	. . .	. . .	. . .	. . .	–137	–115	–95	–151
Income on debt (interest)	3 334	. . .	. . .	. . .	–716	–429	–288	–428	–477
Portfolio investment income	3 339	–171	–143	–806	–4,222	–7,697	–4,581	–3,896	–2,988
Income on equity	3 340	–25	–9	–10	–4	–1	. . .	. . .	–5
Income on bonds and notes	3 350	–147	–134	–796	–4,218	–7,695	–4,581	–3,896	–2,983
Income on money market instruments	3 360	. . .	. . .	. . .	. . .	. . .	. . .	. . .	. . .
Other investment income	3 370	–4,880	–6,841	–8,227	–7,344	–7,074	–6,194	–6,474	–6,063
D. CURRENT TRANSFERS	4 379	–232	157	72	–356	–337	601	69	–759
Credit	2 379	**312**	**894**	**773**	**410**	**308**	**1,183**	**807**	**381**
General government	2 380	27	83	44	36	44	21	22	121
Other sectors	2 390	284	811	729	374	263	1,162	785	260
Workers' remittances	2 391	. . .	. . .	. . .	. . .	. . .	. . .	. . .	. . .
Other current transfers	2 392	284	811	729	374	263	1,162	785	260
Debit	3 379	**–543**	**–738**	**–700**	**–766**	**–644**	**–582**	**–738**	**–1,140**
General government	3 380	–531	–617	–505	–422	–262	–299	–284	–361
Other sectors	3 390	–13	–120	–196	–344	–382	–283	–455	–779
Workers' remittances	3 391	. . .	. . .	. . .	. . .	. . .	. . .	. . .	. . .
Other current transfers	3 392	–13	–120	–196	–344	–382	–283	–455	–779
CAPITAL AND FINANCIAL ACCOUNT	4 996	**–8,698**	**511**	**–6,827**	**2,820**	**8,414**	**–17,698**	**–37,538**	**–25,382**
CAPITAL ACCOUNT	4 994	**2,410**	**–347**	**–463**	**–797**	**–382**	**–328**	**10,955**	**–9,356**
Total credit	2 994	*5,882*	*3,122*	*3,066*	*2,137*	*1,704*	*885*	*11,822*	*2,147*
Total debit	3 994	*–3,472*	*–3,469*	*–3,529*	*–2,934*	*–2,087*	*–1,213*	*–867*	*–11,503*
Capital transfers, credit	2 400	**5,882**	**3,122**	**3,066**	**2,137**	**1,704**	**885**	**11,822**	**2,147**
General government	2 401	1,427	786	397	96	80	20	11,047	1,731
Debt forgiveness	2 402	. . .	. . .	. . .	. . .	. . .	. . .	11,035	1,722
Other capital transfers	2 410	1,427	786	397	96	80	20	12	8
Other sectors	2 430	4,455	2,336	2,668	2,041	1,624	865	775	417
Migrants' transfers	2 431	4,455	2,336	2,668	2,041	1,624	865	775	417
Debt forgiveness	2 432	. . .	. . .	. . .	. . .	. . .	. . .	. . .	. . .
Other capital transfers	2 440	. . .	. . .	. . .	. . .	. . .	. . .	. . .	. . .
Capital transfers, debit	3 400	**–3,472**	**–3,469**	**–3,529**	**–2,934**	**–2,087**	**–1,213**	**–867**	**–11,503**
General government	3 401	. . .	. . .	. . .	. . .	. . .	–9	. . .	–10,595
Debt forgiveness	3 402	. . .	. . .	. . .	. . .	. . .	–9	. . .	–10,595
Other capital transfers	3 410	. . .	. . .	. . .	. . .	. . .	. . .	. . .	. . .
Other sectors	3 430	–3,472	–3,469	–3,529	–2,934	–2,087	–1,204	–867	–908
Migrants' transfers	3 431	–3,472	–3,469	–3,529	–2,934	–2,087	–1,204	–867	–908
Debt forgiveness	3 432	. . .	. . .	. . .	. . .	. . .	. . .	. . .	. . .
Other capital transfers	3 440	. . .	. . .	. . .	. . .	. . .	. . .	. . .	. . .
Nonproduced nonfinancial assets, credit	2 480	**. . .**	**. . .**	**. . .**	**. . .**	**. . .**	**. . .**	**. . .**	**. . .**
Nonproduced nonfinancial assets, debit	3 480	**. . .**	**. . .**	**. . .**	**. . .**	**. . .**	**. . .**	**. . .**	**. . .**

Table 2 (Continued). STANDARD PRESENTATION, 1994–2001
(Millions of U.S. dollars)

	Code	1994	1995	1996	1997	1998	1999	2000	2001
FINANCIAL ACCOUNT	4 995 . .	**–11,108**	**858**	**–6,364**	**3,617**	**8,796**	**–17,370**	**–48,492**	**–16,026**
A. DIRECT INVESTMENT	4 500 . .	409	1,460	1,657	1,680	1,492	1,102	–463	–64
Direct investment abroad	4 505 . .	**–281**	**–605**	**–922**	**–3,185**	**–1,270**	**–2,208**	**–3,177**	**–2,533**
Equity capital	4 510 . .	–281	–605	–922	–3,161	–1,295	–1,866	–2,140	–2,111
Claims on affiliated enterprises	4 515 . .	. . .	. . .	. . .	–3,161	–1,295	–1,866	–2,140	–2,111
Liabilities to affiliated enterprises	4 520 . .	. . .	. . .	. . .	. . .	. . .	. . .	. . .	. . .
Reinvested earnings	4 525 . .	. . .	. . .	. . .	–1	–5	–2	–1	–65
Other capital	4 530 . .	. . .	. . .	. . .	–23	30	–340	–1,035	–357
Claims on affiliated enterprises	4 535 . .	. . .	. . .	. . .	–23	30	–340	–1,035	–357
Liabilities to affiliated enterprises	4 540 . .	. . .	. . .	. . .	. . .	. . .	. . .	. . .	. . .
Direct investment in Russia	4 555 . .	**690**	**2,065**	**2,579**	**4,865**	**2,761**	**3,310**	**2,714**	**2,469**
Equity capital	4 560 . .	690	2,065	2,579	3,804	2,008	2,318	948	1,232
Claims on direct investors	4 565 . .	. . .	. . .	. . .	. . .	. . .	. . .	. . .	. . .
Liabilities to direct investors	4 570 . .	. . .	. . .	. . .	3,804	2,008	2,318	948	1,232
Reinvested earnings	4 575 . .	. . .	. . .	. . .	. . .	137	115	95	151
Other capital	4 580 . .	. . .	. . .	. . .	1,061	616	876	1,672	1,085
Claims on direct investors	4 585 . .	. . .	. . .	. . .	. . .	. . .	. . .	. . .	. . .
Liabilities to direct investors	4 590 . .	. . .	. . .	. . .	1,061	616	876	1,672	1,085
B. PORTFOLIO INVESTMENT	4 600 . .	22	–2,443	4,410	45,775	8,618	–946	–10,334	–653
Assets	4 602 . .	**114**	**–1,705**	**–172**	**–156**	**–257**	**254**	**–411**	**77**
Equity securities	4 610 . .	–19	–42	–117	33	–10	5	–40	–60
Monetary authorities	4 611 . .	. . .	. . .	. . .	. . .	. . .	. . .	. . .	. . .
General government	4 612 . .	. . .	. . .	. . .	. . .	. . .	. . .	. . .	. . .
Banks	4 613 . .	–19	–42	–117	33	–10	5	–9	2
Other sectors	4 614 . .	. . .	. . .	. . .	. . .	. . .	. . .	–31	–62
Debt securities	4 619 . .	133	–1,663	–56	–189	–247	249	–371	137
Bonds and notes	4 620 . .	133	–1,663	–56	–189	–247	249	–371	92
Monetary authorities	4 621 . .	. . .	. . .	. . .	. . .	. . .	. . .	. . .	. . .
General government	4 622 . .	. . .	. . .	. . .	. . .	. . .	. . .	. . .	. . .
Banks	4 623 . .	133	–263	–644	–173	–247	249	151	164
Other sectors	4 624 . .	. . .	–1,400	588	–16	. . .	. . .	–522	–72
Money market instruments	4 630 . .	. . .	. . .	. . .	. . .	. . .	. . .	. . .	45
Monetary authorities	4 631 . .	. . .	. . .	. . .	. . .	. . .	. . .	. . .	. . .
General government	4 632 . .	. . .	. . .	. . .	. . .	. . .	. . .	. . .	. . .
Banks	4 633 . .	. . .	. . .	. . .	. . .	. . .	. . .	. . .	45
Other sectors	4 634 . .	. . .	. . .	. . .	. . .	. . .	. . .	. . .	. . .
Liabilities	4 652 . .	**–93**	**–738**	**4,583**	**45,931**	**8,876**	**–1,199**	**–9,923**	**–730**
Equity securities	4 660 . .	45	47	2,152	1,265	714	–287	150	543
Banks	4 663 . .	45	36	50	93	33	–10	2	14
Other sectors	4 664 . .	. . .	12	2,102	1,172	681	–277	148	529
Debt securities	4 669 . .	–137	–785	2,430	44,667	8,162	–913	–10,073	–1,272
Bonds and notes	4 670 . .	–137	–785	2,430	44,667	8,162	–913	–10,073	–1,963
Monetary authorities	4 671 . .	. . .	. . .	. . .	. . .	. . .	. . .	. . .	. . .
General government	4 672 . .	–48	–820	2,270	44,449	8,273	–868	–10,761	–2,252
Banks	4 673 . .	–89	7	76	110	–262	–97	527	72
Other sectors	4 674 . .	. . .	28	84	107	150	52	161	217
Money market instruments	4 680 . .	. . .	. . .	. . .	. . .	. . .	. . .	. . .	691
Monetary authorities	4 681 . .	. . .	. . .	. . .	. . .	. . .	. . .	. . .	. . .
General government	4 682 . .	. . .	. . .	. . .	. . .	. . .	. . .	. . .	18
Banks	4 683 . .	. . .	. . .	. . .	. . .	. . .	. . .	. . .	673
Other sectors	4 684 . .	. . .	. . .	. . .	. . .	. . .	. . .	. . .	. . .
C. FINANCIAL DERIVATIVES	4 910 . .	. . .	. . .	. . .	. . .	. . .	. . .	. . .	. . .
Monetary authorities	4 911 . .	. . .	. . .	. . .	. . .	. . .	. . .	. . .	. . .
General government	4 912 . .	. . .	. . .	. . .	. . .	. . .	. . .	. . .	. . .
Banks	4 913 . .	. . .	. . .	. . .	. . .	. . .	. . .	. . .	. . .
Other sectors	4 914 . .	. . .	. . .	. . .	. . .	. . .	. . .	. . .	. . .
Assets	4 900 . .	**. . .**	**. . .**	**. . .**	**. . .**	**. . .**	**. . .**	**. . .**	**. . .**
Monetary authorities	4 901 . .	. . .	. . .	. . .	. . .	. . .	. . .	. . .	. . .
General government	4 902 . .	. . .	. . .	. . .	. . .	. . .	. . .	. . .	. . .
Banks	4 903 . .	. . .	. . .	. . .	. . .	. . .	. . .	. . .	. . .
Other sectors	4 904 . .	. . .	. . .	. . .	. . .	. . .	. . .	. . .	. . .
Liabilities	4 905 . .	**. . .**	**. . .**	**. . .**	**. . .**	**. . .**	**. . .**	**. . .**	**. . .**
Monetary authorities	4 906 . .	. . .	. . .	. . .	. . .	. . .	. . .	. . .	. . .
General government	4 907 . .	. . .	. . .	. . .	. . .	. . .	. . .	. . .	. . .
Banks	4 908 . .	. . .	. . .	. . .	. . .	. . .	. . .	. . .	. . .
Other sectors	4 909 . .	. . .	. . .	. . .	. . .	. . .	. . .	. . .	. . .

Table 2 (Concluded). STANDARD PRESENTATION, 1994–2001
(Millions of U.S. dollars)

	Code	1994	1995	1996	1997	1998	1999	2000	2001
D. OTHER INVESTMENT	4 700	-13,474	12,223	-15,271	-41,908	-6,620	-15,754	-21,687	-7,099
Assets	4 703	**-20,436**	**-1,789**	**-31,357**	**-26,703**	**-15,636**	**-14,857**	**-17,520**	**-577**
Trade credits	4 706	-4,396	476	-9,839	-6,598	-6,497	-4,913	-4,179	-6
General government	4 707	171	215	74	168	65	46	1	352
of which: Short-term	4 709	...	...	...	...	...	...	...	...
Other sectors	4 710	-4,566	261	-9,913	-6,766	-6,562	-4,959	-4,180	-357
of which: Short-term	4 712	*-4,566*	*261*	*-9,913*	*-6,766*	*-6,562*	*-4,959*	*-4,180*	*-357*
Loans	4 714	9,536	8,641	9,499	7,004	5,346	4,855	5,366	-739
Monetary authorities	4 715	...	...	...	...	...	...	...	...
of which: Short-term	4 718	...	...	...	...	...	...	...	...
General government	4 719	10,621	9,001	9,139	9,643	5,679	4,576	5,806	302
of which: Short-term	4 721	...	...	...	...	...	...	...	...
Banks	4 722	-1,085	-357	444	-2,164	40	409	-395	-673
of which: Short-term	4 724	...	...	...	...	*839*	*325*	*-221*	*-402*
Other sectors	4 725	...	-4	-83	-475	-374	-129	-45	-368
of which: Short-term	4 727	...	...	...	...	...	...	...	*-312*
Currency and deposits	4 730	-7,405	5,511	-11,251	-12,476	1,974	-3,164	-4,464	-654
Monetary authorities	4 731	...	...	...	...	...	...	...	...
General government	4 732	-1,167	294	-73	656	221	-224	141	229
Banks	4 733	-896	4,695	-2,231	269	970	-3,995	-3,182	-881
Other sectors	4 734	-5,342	522	-8,948	-13,401	784	1,056	-1,424	-2
Other assets	4 736	-18,171	-16,416	-19,766	-14,633	-16,459	-11,636	-14,243	822
Monetary authorities	4 737	...	...	...	...	...	...	...	...
of which: Short-term	4 739	...	...	...	...	...	...	...	...
General government	4 740	-12,742	-10,552	-9,457	-3,308	-7,114	-5,745	-7,564	9,216
of which: Short-term	4 742	*-12,742*	*-10,552*	*-9,447*	*-3,074*	*-7,117*	*-5,720*	*-7,541*	*9,238*
Banks	4 743	-1,135	-22	-185	813	-509	-39	245	-364
of which: Short-term	4 745	...	...	...	...	*-524*	*-32*	*249*	*-377*
Other sectors	4 746	-4,294	-5,842	-10,124	-12,137	-8,836	-5,851	-6,923	-8,031
of which: Short-term	4 748	...	...	...	...	*-1*	*-436*	*-575*	*-907*
Liabilities	4 753	**6,962**	**14,012**	**16,086**	**-15,204**	**9,016**	**-897**	**-4,166**	**-6,522**
Trade credits	4 756	...	...	...	...	...	...	...	...
General government	4 757	...	...	...	...	...	...	...	...
of which: Short-term	4 759	...	...	...	...	...	...	...	...
Other sectors	4 760	...	...	...	...	...	...	...	...
of which: Short-term	4 762	...	...	...	...	...	...	...	...
Loans	4 764	1,975	9,075	11,158	13,317	7,313	-2,888	-3,597	-5,932
Monetary authorities	4 765	1,514	5,473	3,237	1,526	5,206	-3,603	-2,899	-3,829
of which: Use of Fund credit and loans from the Fund	4 766	*1,514*	*5,473*	*3,237*	*1,526*	*5,206*	*-3,603*	*-2,899*	*-3,829*
of which: Short-term	4 768	...	...	...	...	...	...	...	...
General government	4 769	-256	1,802	2,826	1,316	516	2,680	634	-5,268
of which: Short-term	4 771	...	...	...	...	...	...	...	...
Banks	4 772	426	661	1,705	3,840	-3,407	-1,517	-397	2,395
of which: Short-term	4 774	...	...	...	...	*-3,944*	*-1,783*	*581*	*2,042*
Other sectors	4 775	291	1,139	3,390	6,636	4,997	-448	-935	769
of which: Short-term	4 777	...	...	...	...	...	...	...	*393*
Currency and deposits	4 780	1,361	2,855	1,317	-4,732	-2,985	164	880	1,529
Monetary authorities	4 781	-325	391	-230	-38	65	3	155	49
General government	4 782	887	1,076	-110	-8,972	-75	51	-2	-1
Banks	4 783	799	1,388	1,657	4,278	-2,975	111	727	1,481
Other sectors	4 784	...	...	...	...	...	...	...	...
Other liabilities	4 786	3,625	2,082	3,611	-23,790	4,688	1,827	-1,449	-2,118
Monetary authorities	4 787	...	...	...	...	...	...	...	...
of which: Short-term	4 789	...	...	...	...	...	...	...	...
General government	4 790	3,285	1,641	2,391	-24,321	4,667	1,690	-1,688	-1,460
of which: Short-term	4 792	*3,285*	*1,641*	*2,391*	*-24,321*	*4,759*	*1,690*	*-1,688*	*-1,460*
Banks	4 793	80	399	897	531	21	136	238	-179
of which: Short-term	4 795	...	...	...	...	*20*	*47*	*173*	*-107*
Other sectors	4 796	260	42	323	...	...	...	...	-480
of which: Short-term	4 798	...	...	...	...	...	...	...	*-480*
E. RESERVE ASSETS	4 802	1,935	-10,382	2,840	-1,930	5,306	-1,772	-16,009	-8,211
Monetary gold	4 812	...	...	...	...	...	...	...	...
Special drawing rights	4 811	41	-118	109	-118	120	11	...	-2
Reserve position in the Fund	4 810	...	...	...	...	...	...	...	...
Foreign exchange	4 803	1,894	-10,264	2,731	-1,812	5,186	-1,783	-16,009	-8,208
Other claims	4 813	...	...	...	...	...	...	...	...
NET ERRORS AND OMISSIONS	4 998	**406**	**-7,967**	**-4,898**	**-4,852**	**-9,073**	**-7,032**	**-9,756**	**-9,239**

Part 3 of the *Yearbook* contains descriptions of the methodologies, compilation practices, and sources used to compile these data.

Table 3. INTERNATIONAL INVESTMENT POSITION (End–period stocks), 1994–2001

(Millions of U.S. dollars)

	Code	1994	1995	1996	1997	1998	1999	2000	2001
ASSETS	8 995 C.	22,245	28,645	29,041	33,440	25,557	28,392	246,661	250,321
Direct investment abroad	8 505 . .	**2,272**	**2,420**	**2,685**	**2,789**	**2,703**	**1,076**	**12,394**	**14,734**
Equity capital and reinvested earnings	8 506 . .	1,116	1,215	1,530	1,515	1,491	672	10,723	12,625
Claims on affiliated enterprises	8 507 . .	1,116	1,215	1,530	1,515	1,491	672	10,723	12,625
Liabilities to affiliated enterprises	8 508 . .	. . .	. . .	. . .	. . .	. . .	. . .	. . .	. . .
Other capital	8 530 . .	1,156	1,205	1,155	1,274	1,212	404	1,671	2,110
Claims on affiliated enterprises	8 535 . .	1,156	1,205	1,155	1,274	1,212	404	1,671	2,110
Liabilities to affiliated enterprises	8 540 . .	. . .	. . .	. . .	. . .	. . .	. . .	. . .	. . .
Portfolio investment	8 602 . .	**486**	**764**	**1,230**	**1,383**	**1,308**	**861**	**1,258**	**1,292**
Equity securities	8 610 . .	7	27	43	12	18	6	46	101
Monetary authorities	8 611 . .	. . .	. . .	. . .	. . .	. . .	. . .	. . .	. . .
General government	8 612 . .	. . .	. . .	. . .	. . .	. . .	. . .	. . .	. . .
Banks	8 613 . .	7	27	43	12	18	6	15	11
Other sectors	8 614 . .	. . .	. . .	. . .	. . .	. . .	. . .	31	90
Debt securities	8 619 . .	479	737	1,187	1,371	1,290	855	1,212	1,191
Bonds and notes	8 620 . .	479	737	1,187	746	748	713	897	953
Monetary authorities	8 621 . .	. . .	. . .	. . .	. . .	. . .	. . .	. . .	. . .
General government	8 622 . .	. . .	. . .	. . .	. . .	. . .	. . .	. . .	. . .
Banks	8 623 . .	479	737	1,187	746	748	713	354	342
Other sectors	8 624 . .	. . .	. . .	. . .	. . .	. . .	. . .	544	611
Money market instruments	8 630 . .	. . .	. . .	. . .	625	542	142	315	238
Monetary authorities	8 631 . .	. . .	. . .	. . .	. . .	. . .	. . .	. . .	. . .
General government	8 632 . .	. . .	. . .	. . .	. . .	. . .	. . .	. . .	. . .
Banks	8 633 . .	. . .	. . .	. . .	625	542	142	315	231
Other sectors	8 634 . .	. . .	. . .	. . .	. . .	. . .	. . .	. . .	7
Financial derivatives	8 900 . .	. . .	. . .	. . .	. . .	. . .	. . .	. . .	. . .
Monetary authorities	8 901 . .	. . .	. . .	. . .	. . .	. . .	. . .	. . .	. . .
General government	8 902 . .	. . .	. . .	. . .	. . .	. . .	. . .	. . .	. . .
Banks	8 903 . .	. . .	. . .	. . .	. . .	. . .	. . .	. . .	. . .
Other sectors	8 904 . .	. . .	. . .	. . .	. . .	. . .	. . .	. . .	. . .
Other investment	8 703 . .	**12,982**	**8,254**	**9,802**	**11,484**	**9,323**	**14,000**	**205,037**	**197,672**
Trade credits	8 706 . .	. . .	. . .	. . .	. . .	. . .	. . .	17,813	17,595
General government	8 707 . .	. . .	. . .	. . .	. . .	. . .	. . .	4,555	4,095
of which: Short-term	8 709 . .	. . .	. . .	. . .	. . .	. . .	. . .	*4*	*4*
Other sectors	8 710 . .	. . .	. . .	. . .	. . .	. . .	. . .	13,258	13,500
of which: Short-term	8 712 . .	. . .	. . .	. . .	. . .	. . .	. . .	*13,258*	*13,500*
Loans	8 714 . .	1,274	1,727	1,218	3,638	2,890	2,179	23,416	23,815
Monetary authorities	8 715 . .	. . .	. . .	. . .	. . .	. . .	. . .	. . .	. . .
of which: Short-term	8 718 . .	. . .	. . .	. . .	. . .	. . .	. . .	. . .	. . .
General government	8 719 . .	. . .	. . .	. . .	. . .	. . .	. . .	19,770	19,210
of which: Short-term	8 721 . .	. . .	. . .	. . .	. . .	. . .	. . .	. . .	. . .
Banks	8 722 . .	1,274	1,727	1,218	3,638	2,890	2,179	2,536	3,129
of which: Short-term	8 724 . .	*765*	*1,183*	*918*	*2,854*	*1,408*	*1,026*	*1,223*	*1,552*
Other sectors	8 725 . .	. . .	. . .	. . .	. . .	. . .	. . .	1,110	1,476
of which: Short-term	8 727 . .	. . .	. . .	. . .	. . .	. . .	. . .	. . .	*312*
Currency and deposits	8 730 . .	9,606	4,864	6,991	7,371	5,840	11,160	55,876	56,331
Monetary authorities	8 731 . .	. . .	. . .	. . .	. . .	. . .	. . .	. . .	. . .
General government	8 732 . .	. . .	. . .	. . .	. . .	. . .	. . .	5,556	5,326
Banks	8 733 . .	9,606	4,864	6,991	7,371	5,840	11,160	14,107	14,790
Other sectors	8 734 . .	. . .	. . .	. . .	. . .	. . .	. . .	36,213	36,214
Other assets	8 736 . .	2,102	1,663	1,593	475	593	661	107,932	99,932
Monetary authorities	8 737 . .	. . .	. . .	. . .	. . .	. . .	. . .	. . .	. . .
of which: Short-term	8 739 . .	. . .	. . .	. . .	. . .	. . .	. . .	. . .	. . .
General government	8 740 . .	. . .	. . .	. . .	. . .	. . .	. . .	102,206	92,237
of which: Short-term	8 742 . .	. . .	. . .	. . .	. . .	. . .	. . .	*101,971*	*91,987*
Banks	8 743 . .	2,102	1,663	1,593	475	593	661	378	705
of which: Short-term	8 745 . .	*1,803*	*1,289*	*1,306*	*401*	*550*	*602*	*315*	*656*
Other sectors	8 746 . .	. . .	. . .	. . .	. . .	. . .	. . .	5,348	6,990
of which: Short-term	8 748 . .	. . .	. . .	. . .	. . .	. . .	. . .	*1,022*	*1,926*
Reserve assets	8 802 . .	**6,505**	**17,207**	**15,324**	**17,784**	**12,223**	**12,455**	**27,972**	**36,622**
Monetary gold	8 812 . .	2,525	2,824	4,047	4,889	4,422	3,998	3,708	4,080
Special drawing rights	8 811 . .	3	117	5	122	. . .	1	1	3
Reserve position in the Fund	8 810 . .	1	1	1	1	1	1	1	1
Foreign exchange	8 803 . .	3,976	14,265	11,271	12,771	7,800	8,455	24,263	32,538
Other claims	8 813 . .	. . .	. . .	. . .	. . .	. . .	. . .	. . .	. . .

Table 3 (Concluded). INTERNATIONAL INVESTMENT POSITION (End–period stocks), 1994–2001

(Millions of U.S. dollars)

	Code	1994	1995	1996	1997	1998	1999	2000	2001
LIABILITIES	8 995 D.	7,380	15,492	22,162	32,829	29,925	24,087	165,735	164,797
Direct investment in Russia	8 555 . .	**332**	**345**	**426**	**970**	**373**	**731**	**17,956**	**20,142**
Equity capital and reinvested earnings	8 556 . .	332	345	426	970	373	564	12,321	13,468
Claims on direct investors	8 557 . .	. . .	. . .	. . .	. . .	. . .	. . .	. . .	. . .
Liabilities to direct investors	8 558 . .	332	345	426	970	373	564	12,321	13,468
Other capital	8 580 . .	. . .	. . .	. . .	. . .	. . .	167	5,636	6,674
Claims on direct investors	8 585 . .	. . .	. . .	. . .	. . .	. . .	. . .	. . .	. . .
Liabilities to direct investors	8 590 . .	. . .	. . .	. . .	. . .	. . .	167	5,636	6,674
Portfolio investment	8 652 . .	**369**	**437**	**567**	**1,032**	**495**	**346**	**26,169**	**30,818**
Equity securities	8 660 . .	79	132	122	241	36	40	4,678	5,354
Banks	8 663 . .	79	132	122	241	36	40	52	53
Other sectors	8 664 . .	. . .	. . .	. . .	. . .	. . .	. . .	4,626	5,301
Debt securities	8 669 . .	290	305	445	791	459	306	21,491	25,465
Bonds and notes	8 670 . .	290	305	445	217	146	121	21,166	24,454
Monetary authorities	8 671 . .	. . .	. . .	. . .	. . .	. . .	. . .	. . .	. . .
General government	8 672 . .	. . .	. . .	. . .	. . .	. . .	. . .	19,556	22,572
Banks	8 673 . .	290	305	445	217	146	121	504	560
Other sectors	8 674 . .	. . .	. . .	. . .	. . .	. . .	. . .	1,107	1,322
Money market instruments	8 680 . .	. . .	. . .	. . .	574	313	185	325	1,011
Monetary authorities	8 681 . .	. . .	. . .	. . .	. . .	. . .	. . .	. . .	. . .
General government	8 682 . .	. . .	. . .	. . .	. . .	. . .	. . .	23	36
Banks	8 683 . .	. . .	. . .	. . .	574	313	185	302	975
Other sectors	8 684 . .	. . .	. . .	. . .	. . .	. . .	. . .	. . .	. . .
Financial derivatives	8 905 . .	. . .	. . .	. . .	. . .	. . .	. . .	. . .	. . .
Monetary authorities	8 906 . .	. . .	. . .	. . .	. . .	. . .	. . .	. . .	. . .
General government	8 907 . .	. . .	. . .	. . .	. . .	. . .	. . .	. . .	. . .
Banks	8 908 . .	. . .	. . .	. . .	. . .	. . .	. . .	. . .	. . .
Other sectors	8 909 . .	. . .	. . .	. . .	. . .	. . .	. . .	. . .	. . .
Other investment	8 753 . .	**6,679**	**14,710**	**21,169**	**30,827**	**29,057**	**23,010**	**121,609**	**113,837**
Trade credits	8 756 . .	. . .	. . .	. . .	. . .	. . .	. . .	. . .	. . .
General government	8 757 . .	. . .	. . .	. . .	. . .	. . .	. . .	. . .	. . .
of which: Short-term	8 759 . .	. . .	. . .	. . .	. . .	. . .	. . .	. . .	. . .
Other sectors	8 760 . .	. . .	. . .	. . .	. . .	. . .	. . .	. . .	. . .
of which: Short-term	8 762 . .	. . .	. . .	. . .	. . .	. . .	. . .	. . .	. . .
Loans	8 764 . .	4,642	10,747	15,252	22,747	24,332	18,377	100,999	92,323
Monetary authorities	8 765 . .	4,198	9,617	12,508	13,231	19,335	15,238	11,613	7,433
of which: Use of Fund credit and loans from the Fund	8 766 . .	*4,198*	*9,617*	*12,508*	*13,231*	*19,335*	*15,238*	*11,613*	*7,433*
of which: Short-term	8 768 . .	. . .	. . .	. . .	. . .	. . .	. . .	. . .	. . .
General government	8 769 . .	. . .	. . .	. . .	. . .	. . .	. . .	69,786	62,511
of which: Short-term	8 771 . .	. . .	. . .	. . .	. . .	. . .	. . .	. . .	. . .
Banks	8 772 . .	444	1,130	2,744	9,516	4,997	3,139	2,663	5,004
of which: Short-term	8 774 . .	*347*	*830*	*2,358*	*7,911*	*3,221*	*1,355*	*1,862*	*3,832*
Other sectors	8 775 . .	. . .	. . .	. . .	. . .	. . .	. . .	16,938	17,375
of which: Short-term	8 777 . .	. . .	. . .	. . .	. . .	. . .	. . .	*1,835*	*2,228*
Currency and deposits	8 780 . .	1,168	2,847	4,100	7,466	3,751	3,577	8,659	10,008
Monetary authorities	8 781 . .	. . .	. . .	. . .	. . .	. . .	. . .	162	198
General government	8 782 . .	. . .	. . .	. . .	. . .	. . .	. . .	4,332	4,293
Banks	8 783 . .	1,168	2,847	4,100	7,466	3,751	3,577	4,166	5,517
Other sectors	8 784 . .	. . .	. . .	. . .	. . .	. . .	. . .	. . .	. . .
Other liabilities	8 786 . .	869	1,116	1,817	614	974	1,056	11,951	11,506
Monetary authorities	8 787 . .	. . .	. . .	. . .	. . .	. . .	. . .	. . .	. . .
of which: Short-term	8 789 . .	. . .	. . .	. . .	. . .	. . .	. . .	. . .	. . .
General government	8 790 . .	. . .	. . .	. . .	. . .	. . .	. . .	10,625	10,152
of which: Short-term	8 792 . .	. . .	. . .	. . .	. . .	. . .	. . .	*10,625*	*10,152*
Banks	8 793 . .	869	1,116	1,817	614	974	1,056	1,326	1,289
of which: Short-term	8 795 . .	*867*	*1,112*	*1,817*	*609*	*970*	*963*	*1,169*	*1,207*
Other sectors	8 796 . .	. . .	. . .	. . .	. . .	. . .	. . .	. . .	65
of which: Short-term	8 798 . .	. . .	. . .	. . .	. . .	. . .	. . .	. . .	*65*
NET INTERNATIONAL INVESTMENT POSITION	8 995 . .	**14,865**	**13,153**	**6,879**	**611**	**–4,368**	**4,305**	**80,926**	**85,524**
Conversion rates: rubles per U.S. dollar (end of period)	0 102 . .	**3.550**	**4.640**	**5.560**	**5.960**	**20.650**	**27.000**	**28.160**	**30.140**

Table 1. ANALYTIC PRESENTATION, 1994–2001
(Millions of U.S. dollars)

	Code	1994	1995	1996	1997	1998	1999	2000	2001
A. Current Account [1]	4 993 Z.	**–46.2**	**57.5**	**–8.5**	**–62.2**	**–83.1**	**–143.0**	**–114.5**	**–118.1**
Goods: exports f.o.b	2 100 . .	32.2	56.7	61.7	93.2	64.5	62.3	69.1	93.3
Goods: imports f.o.b	3 100 . .	–367.4	–219.1	–218.5	–278.2	–234.0	–249.7	–225.3	–245.1
Balance on Goods	4 100 . .	*–335.2*	*–162.5*	*–156.8*	*–185.0*	*–169.5*	*–187.5*	*–156.2*	*–151.8*
Services: credit	2 200 . .	. . .	17.9	21.5	51.2	48.5	51.3	40.6	50.2
Services: debit	3 200 . .	–109.6	–154.7	–149.7	–198.3	–190.6	–195.5	–202.1	–189.1
Balance on Goods and Services	4 991 . .	*–444.8*	*–299.2*	*–284.9*	*–332.2*	*–311.6*	*–331.7*	*–317.7*	*–290.7*
Income: credit	2 300 . .	. . .	24.3	5.4	8.0	8.8	7.9	13.9	14.1
Income: debit	3 300 . .	. . .	–17.5	–18.8	–24.8	–15.9	–18.7	–28.7	–34.0
Balance on Goods, Services, and Income	4 992 . .	*–444.8*	*–292.5*	*–298.3*	*–348.9*	*–318.8*	*–342.5*	*–332.4*	*–310.7*
Current transfers: credit	2 379 Z.	398.6	354.9	293.9	311.6	252.6	212.3	235.1	210.4
Current transfers: debit	3 379 . .	. . .	–4.9	–4.1	–24.9	–16.9	–12.8	–17.2	–17.9
B. Capital Account [1]	4 994 Z.	**. . .**	**. . .**	**. . .**	**. . .**	**. . .**	**71.0**	**62.7**	**50.2**
Capital account: credit	2 994 Z.	. . .	. . .	. . .	. . .	. . .	71.0	62.7	50.2
Capital account: debit	3 994 . .	. . .	. . .	. . .	. . .	. . .	. . .	. . .	. . .
Total, Groups A Plus B	4 981 . .	*–46.2*	*57.5*	*–8.5*	*–62.2*	*–83.1*	*–72.1*	*–51.8*	*–67.9*
C. Financial Account [1]	4 995 W.	**–12.5**	**–10.7**	**24.8**	**46.8**	**–16.8**	**–33.6**	**10.8**	**–44.0**
Direct investment abroad	4 505 . .	. . .	. . .	. . .	. . .	. . .	. . .	. . .	. . .
Direct investment in Rwanda	4 555 Z.	. . .	2.2	2.2	2.6	7.1	1.7	8.4	4.6
Portfolio investment assets	4 602 . .	. . .	. . .	–.1	. . .	–.1	.8	.1	. . .
Equity securities	4 610 . .	. . .	. . .	–.1	. . .	–.1	.8	.1	. . .
Debt securities	4 619 . .	. . .	. . .	. . .	. . .	. . .	. . .	. . .	. . .
Portfolio investment liabilities	4 652 Z.	. . .	. . .	. . .	. . .	. . .	. . .	. . .	. . .
Equity securities	4 660 . .	. . .	. . .	. . .	. . .	. . .	. . .	. . .	. . .
Debt securities	4 669 Z.	. . .	. . .	. . .	. . .	. . .	. . .	. . .	. . .
Financial derivatives	4 910 . .	. . .	. . .	. . .	. . .	. . .	. . .	. . .	. . .
Financial derivatives assets	4 900 . .	. . .	. . .	. . .	. . .	. . .	. . .	. . .	. . .
Financial derivatives liabilities	4 905 . .	. . .	. . .	. . .	. . .	. . .	. . .	. . .	. . .
Other investment assets	4 703 . .	. . .	–52.0	–13.6	1.2	–.8	–10.4	23.4	–.5
Monetary authorities	4 701 . .	. . .	. . .	. . .	. . .	. . .	. . .	. . .	. . .
General government	4 704 . .	. . .	. . .	. . .	. . .	. . .	. . .	. . .	. . .
Banks	4 705 . .	. . .	–38.6	–13.6	1.2	–.8	–10.4	17.3	–4.9
Other sectors	4 728 . .	. . .	–13.4	. . .	. . .	. . .	. . .	6.0	4.4
Other investment liabilities	4 753 W.	–12.5	39.1	36.3	43.0	–23.0	–25.7	–21.0	–48.2
Monetary authorities	4 753 WA	. . .	. . .	. . .	. . .	. . .	. . .	. . .	. . .
General government	4 753 ZB	–12.5	39.1	37.2	43.0	–22.5	–24.1	–23.0	–50.3
Banks	4 753 ZC	. . .	. . .	. . .	. . .	. . .	. . .	. . .	. . .
Other sectors	4 753 ZD	. . .	. . .	–.9	. . .	–.5	–1.6	2.1	2.1
Total, Groups A Through C	4 983 . .	*–58.7*	*46.8*	*16.3*	*–15.4*	*–99.8*	*–105.6*	*–41.0*	*–112.0*
D. Net Errors and Omissions	4 998 . .	**62.4**	**5.8**	**4.1**	**46.0**	**92.8**	**33.0**	**–91.1**	**42.3**
Total, Groups A Through D	4 984 . .	*3.7*	*52.6*	*20.3*	*30.5*	*–7.0*	*–72.6*	*–132.1*	*–69.6*
E. Reserves and Related Items	4 802 A.	**–3.7**	**–52.6**	**–20.3**	**–30.5**	**7.0**	**72.6**	**132.1**	**69.6**
Reserve assets	4 802 . .	–3.7	–66.0	–19.1	–48.4	–21.2	38.1	78.8	10.9
Use of Fund credit and loans	4 766 . .	. . .	13.3	–1.3	17.9	13.5	20.8	13.6	.9
Exceptional financing	4 920 . .	. . .	. . .	. . .	. . .	14.7	13.7	39.6	57.8
Conversion rates: Rwanda francs per U.S. dollar	0 101 . .	**220.00**	**262.20**	**306.82**	**301.53**	**312.31**	**333.94**	**389.70**	**442.99**

[1] Excludes components that have been classified in the categories of Group E.

Table 2. STANDARD PRESENTATION, 1994–2001

(Millions of U.S. dollars)

	Code	1994	1995	1996	1997	1998	1999	2000	2001
CURRENT ACCOUNT	4 993 . .	**–46.2**	**57.5**	**–8.5**	**–62.2**	**–83.1**	**–143.0**	**–114.5**	**–118.1**
A. GOODS	4 100 . .	–335.2	–162.5	–156.8	–185.0	–169.5	–187.5	–156.2	–151.8
Credit	2 100 . .	**32.2**	**56.7**	**61.7**	**93.2**	**64.5**	**62.3**	**69.1**	**93.3**
General merchandise: exports f.o.b.	2 110 . .	32.2	56.7	61.7	93.2	64.5	62.3	69.1	93.3
Goods for processing: exports f.o.b.	2 150 . .	. . .	. . .	. . .	. . .	. . .	. . .	. . .	. . .
Repairs on goods	2 160 . .	. . .	. . .	. . .	. . .	. . .	. . .	. . .	. . .
Goods procured in ports by carriers	2 170 . .	. . .	. . .	. . .	. . .	. . .	. . .	. . .	. . .
Nonmonetary gold	2 180 . .	. . .	. . .	. . .	. . .	. . .	. . .	. . .	. . .
Debit	3 100 . .	**–367.4**	**–219.1**	**–218.5**	**–278.2**	**–234.0**	**–249.7**	**–225.3**	**–245.1**
General merchandise: imports f.o.b.	3 110 . .	–367.4	–219.1	–218.5	–278.2	–234.0	–249.7	–225.3	–245.1
Goods for processing: imports f.o.b.	3 150 . .	. . .	. . .	. . .	. . .	. . .	. . .	. . .	. . .
Repairs on goods	3 160 . .	. . .	. . .	. . .	. . .	. . .	. . .	. . .	. . .
Goods procured in ports by carriers	3 170 . .	. . .	. . .	. . .	. . .	. . .	. . .	. . .	. . .
Nonmonetary gold	3 180 . .	. . .	. . .	. . .	. . .	. . .	. . .	. . .	. . .
B. SERVICES	4 200 . .	–109.6	–136.8	–128.1	–147.2	–142.1	–144.2	–161.4	–138.9
Total credit	2 200 . .	. . .	*17.9*	*21.5*	*51.2*	*48.5*	*51.3*	*40.6*	*50.2*
Total debit	3 200 . .	*–109.6*	*–154.7*	*–149.7*	*–198.3*	*–190.6*	*–195.5*	*–202.1*	*–189.1*
Transportation services, credit	2 205 . .	**. . .**	**6.4**	**7.1**	**9.1**	**9.0**	**15.2**	**14.2**	**16.2**
Passenger	2 850 . .	. . .	*1.5*	*1.6*	*1.7*	*1.4*	*3.7*	*3.8*	*4.1*
Freight	2 851 . .	. . .	*2.7*	*3.2*	*4.8*	*5.5*	*5.8*	*5.6*	*5.4*
Other	2 852 . .	. . .	*2.3*	*2.3*	*2.5*	*2.1*	*5.6*	*4.8*	*6.7*
Sea transport, passenger	2 207 . .	. . .	. . .	. . .	. . .	. . .	. . .	. . .	. . .
Sea transport, freight	2 208 . .	. . .	. . .	. . .	. . .	. . .	. . .	. . .	. . .
Sea transport, other	2 209 . .	. . .	. . .	. . .	. . .	. . .	. . .	. . .	. . .
Air transport, passenger	2 211 . .	. . .	. . .	. . .	. . .	. . .	. . .	. . .	. . .
Air transport, freight	2 212 . .	. . .	. . .	. . .	. . .	. . .	. . .	. . .	. . .
Air transport, other	2 213 . .	. . .	. . .	. . .	. . .	. . .	. . .	. . .	. . .
Other transport, passenger	2 215 . .	. . .	. . .	. . .	. . .	. . .	. . .	. . .	. . .
Other transport, freight	2 216 . .	. . .	. . .	. . .	. . .	. . .	. . .	. . .	. . .
Other transport, other	2 217 . .	. . .	. . .	. . .	. . .	. . .	. . .	. . .	. . .
Transportation services, debit	3 205 . .	**. . .**	**–42.0**	**–45.1**	**–69.8**	**–67.9**	**–73.5**	**–83.6**	**–81.5**
Passenger	3 850 . .	. . .	*–3.0*	*–5.7*	*–9.3*	*–8.5*	*–10.0*	*–12.8*	*–13.4*
Freight	3 851 . .	. . .	*–34.6*	*–31.0*	*–46.6*	*–46.6*	*–48.4*	*–58.6*	*–54.7*
Other	3 852 . .	. . .	*–4.4*	*–8.5*	*–13.9*	*–12.8*	*–15.1*	*–12.1*	*–13.4*
Sea transport, passenger	3 207 . .	. . .	. . .	. . .	. . .	. . .	. . .	. . .	. . .
Sea transport, freight	3 208 . .	. . .	. . .	. . .	. . .	. . .	. . .	. . .	. . .
Sea transport, other	3 209 . .	. . .	. . .	. . .	. . .	. . .	. . .	. . .	. . .
Air transport, passenger	3 211 . .	. . .	. . .	. . .	. . .	. . .	. . .	. . .	. . .
Air transport, freight	3 212 . .	. . .	. . .	. . .	. . .	. . .	. . .	. . .	. . .
Air transport, other	3 213 . .	. . .	. . .	. . .	. . .	. . .	. . .	. . .	. . .
Other transport, passenger	3 215 . .	. . .	. . .	. . .	. . .	. . .	. . .	. . .	. . .
Other transport, freight	3 216 . .	. . .	. . .	. . .	. . .	. . .	. . .	. . .	. . .
Other transport, other	3 217 . .	. . .	. . .	. . .	. . .	. . .	. . .	. . .	. . .
Travel, credit	2 236 . .	**. . .**	**2.3**	**3.5**	**17.0**	**19.1**	**17.1**	**4.3**	**9.0**
Business travel	2 237 . .	. . .	. . .	. . .	. . .	. . .	. . .	. . .	. . .
Personal travel	2 240 . .	. . .	. . .	. . .	. . .	. . .	. . .	. . .	. . .
Travel, debit	3 236 . .	**. . .**	**–9.8**	**–12.5**	**–12.9**	**–16.5**	**–18.3**	**–21.9**	**–20.1**
Business travel	3 237 . .	. . .	. . .	. . .	. . .	. . .	. . .	. . .	. . .
Personal travel	3 240 . .	. . .	. . .	. . .	. . .	. . .	. . .	. . .	. . .
Other services, credit	2 200 BA	**. . .**	**9.1**	**10.9**	**25.1**	**20.4**	**19.1**	**22.2**	**24.9**
Communications	2 245 . .	. . .	. . .	. . .	. . .	. . .	. . .	. . .	. . .
Construction	2 249 . .	. . .	. . .	. . .	. . .	. . .	. . .	. . .	. . .
Insurance	2 253 . .	. . .	. . .	. . .	. . .	. . .	. . .	. . .	. . .
Financial	2 260 . .	. . .	. . .	. . .	. . .	. . .	. . .	. . .	. . .
Computer and information	2 262 . .	. . .	. . .	. . .	. . .	. . .	. . .	. . .	. . .
Royalties and licence fees	2 266 . .	. . .	. . .	.1	. . .	1.2	. . .	. . .	. . .
Other business services	2 268 . .	. . .	1.9	2.1	8.3	2.7	4.3	3.4	4.1
Personal, cultural, and recreational	2 287 . .	. . .	. . .	. . .	. . .	. . .	. . .	. . .	. . .
Government, n.i.e.	2 291 . .	. . .	7.3	8.7	16.8	16.4	14.7	18.7	20.8
Other services, debit	3 200 BA	**. . .**	**–102.8**	**–92.0**	**–115.7**	**–106.1**	**–103.6**	**–96.5**	**–87.5**
Communications	3 245 . .	. . .	. . .	. . .	. . .	. . .	. . .	. . .	. . .
Construction	3 249 . .	. . .	. . .	. . .	. . .	. . .	. . .	. . .	. . .
Insurance	3 253 . .	. . .	. . .	. . .	. . .	. . .	. . .	. . .	. . .
Financial	3 260 . .	. . .	. . .	. . .	. . .	. . .	. . .	. . .	. . .
Computer and information	3 262 . .	. . .	. . .	. . .	. . .	. . .	. . .	. . .	. . .
Royalties and licence fees	3 266 . .	. . .	. . .	–.6	–1.2	–1.1	–.6	–.6	–.4
Other business services	3 268 . .	. . .	–5.8	–4.5	–15.5	–14.3	–14.2	–8.2	–11.3
Personal, cultural, and recreational	3 287 . .	. . .	. . .	. . .	. . .	. . .	. . .	. . .	. . .
Government, n.i.e.	3 291 . .	. . .	–97.0	–86.9	–98.9	–90.7	–88.8	–87.7	–75.8

Table 2 (Continued). STANDARD PRESENTATION, 1994–2001
(Millions of U.S. dollars)

	Code	1994	1995	1996	1997	1998	1999	2000	2001
C. INCOME	4 300 . .	...	6.7	-13.4	-16.7	-7.2	-10.8	-14.8	-19.9
Total credit	2 300 . .	...	*24.3*	*5.4*	*8.0*	*8.8*	*7.9*	*13.9*	*14.1*
Total debit	3 300 . .	...	*-17.5*	*-18.8*	*-24.8*	*-15.9*	*-18.7*	*-28.7*	*-34.0*
Compensation of employees, credit	2 310 . .	**...**	**21.1**	**...**	**...**	**...**	**...**	**3.0**	**2.4**
Compensation of employees, debit	3 310 . .	**...**	**-1.1**	**-3.2**	**-6.2**	**-2.8**	**-4.1**	**-12.2**	**-16.8**
Investment income, credit	2 320 . .	**...**	**3.1**	**5.4**	**8.0**	**8.8**	**7.9**	**10.8**	**11.7**
Direct investment income	2 330 . .	...	...	...	...	...	...	...	...
Dividends and distributed branch profits	2 332 . .	...	...	...	...	...	...	...	...
Reinvested earnings and undistributed branch profits	2 333 . .	...	...	...	...	...	...	...	...
Income on debt (interest)	2 334 . .	...	...	...	...	...	...	...	...
Portfolio investment income	2 339 . .	...	...	...	...	...	...	...	...
Income on equity	2 340 . .	...	...	...	...	...	...	...	...
Income on bonds and notes	2 350 . .	...	...	...	...	...	...	...	...
Income on money market instruments	2 360 . .	...	...	...	...	...	...	...	...
Other investment income	2 370 . .	...	3.1	5.4	8.0	8.8	7.9	10.8	11.7
Investment income, debit	3 320 . .	**...**	**-16.4**	**-15.6**	**-18.6**	**-13.1**	**-14.6**	**-16.5**	**-17.2**
Direct investment income	3 330 . .	...	-1.5	-2.2	-4.0	-.2	-.8	-3.1	-3.4
Dividends and distributed branch profits	3 332 . .	...	-1.5	-2.2	-4.0	-.2	-.8	-2.8	-3.4
Reinvested earnings and undistributed branch profits	3 333 . .	...	...	...	...	...	...	-.3	...
Income on debt (interest)	3 334 . .	...	...	...	...	...	...	...	...
Portfolio investment income	3 339 . .	...	...	...	...	...	...	...	...
Income on equity	3 340 . .	...	...	...	...	...	...	...	...
Income on bonds and notes	3 350 . .	...	...	...	...	...	...	...	...
Income on money market instruments	3 360 . .	...	...	...	...	...	...	...	...
Other investment income	3 370 . .	...	-15.0	-13.5	-14.6	-12.9	-13.8	-13.4	-13.9
D. CURRENT TRANSFERS	4 379 . .	398.6	350.0	289.8	286.7	235.7	199.5	217.9	192.5
Credit	2 379 . .	**398.6**	**354.9**	**293.9**	**311.6**	**252.6**	**212.3**	**235.1**	**210.4**
General government	2 380 . .	354.1	337.5	265.1	263.3	218.7	182.5	207.8	172.2
Other sectors	2 390 . .	44.5	17.4	28.9	48.3	33.9	29.8	27.3	38.1
Workers' remittances	2 391 . .	...	...	...	5.2	...	...	3.7	5.4
Other current transfers	2 392 . .	...	...	...	43.1	33.9	29.8	23.7	32.7
Debit	3 379 . .	**...**	**-4.9**	**-4.1**	**-24.9**	**-16.9**	**-12.8**	**-17.2**	**-17.9**
General government	3 380 . .	...	-4.9	-1.7	-1.4	-1.4	-1.3	-.9	-1.5
Other sectors	3 390 . .	...	...	-2.4	-23.6	-15.5	-11.6	-16.3	-16.4
Workers' remittances	3 391 . .	...	...	...	-22.0	...	...	-16.1	-15.9
Other current transfers	3 392 . .	...	...	...	-1.6	-15.5	-11.6	-.2	-.5
CAPITAL AND FINANCIAL ACCOUNT	4 996 . .	**-16.2**	**-63.3**	**4.4**	**16.3**	**-9.7**	**110.0**	**205.6**	**75.8**
CAPITAL ACCOUNT	4 994 . .	**...**	**...**	**...**	**...**	**16.4**	**74.0**	**63.6**	**62.4**
Total credit	2 994 . .	...	...	...	...	*16.4*	*74.0*	*63.6*	*62.4*
Total debit	3 994 . .	...	...	...	...	...	...	...	...
Capital transfers, credit	2 400 . .	**...**	**...**	**...**	**...**	**16.4**	**74.0**	**63.6**	**62.4**
General government	2 401 . .	...	...	...	...	16.4	74.0	63.6	62.4
Debt forgiveness	2 402 . .	...	...	...	...	16.4	3.0	.9	12.2
Other capital transfers	2 410 . .	...	...	...	...	...	71.0	62.7	50.2
Other sectors	2 430 . .	...	...	...	...	...	...	...	...
Migrants' transfers	2 431 . .	...	...	...	...	...	...	...	...
Debt forgiveness	2 432 . .	...	...	...	...	...	...	...	...
Other capital transfers	2 440 . .	...	...	...	...	...	...	...	...
Capital transfers, debit	3 400 . .	**...**	**...**	**...**	**...**	**...**	**...**	**...**	**...**
General government	3 401 . .	...	...	...	...	...	...	...	...
Debt forgiveness	3 402 . .	...	...	...	...	...	...	...	...
Other capital transfers	3 410 . .	...	...	...	...	...	...	...	...
Other sectors	3 430 . .	...	...	...	...	...	...	...	...
Migrants' transfers	3 431 . .	...	...	...	...	...	...	...	...
Debt forgiveness	3 432 . .	...	...	...	...	...	...	...	...
Other capital transfers	3 440 . .	...	...	...	...	...	...	...	...
Nonproduced nonfinancial assets, credit	2 480 . .	**...**	**...**	**...**	**...**	**...**	**...**	**...**	**...**
Nonproduced nonfinancial assets, debit	3 480 . .	**...**	**...**	**...**	**...**	**...**	**...**	**...**	**...**

Table 2 (Continued). STANDARD PRESENTATION, 1994–2001
(Millions of U.S. dollars)

	Code	1994	1995	1996	1997	1998	1999	2000	2001
FINANCIAL ACCOUNT	4 995	**–16.2**	**–63.3**	**4.4**	**16.3**	**–26.1**	**36.0**	**142.0**	**13.4**
A. DIRECT INVESTMENT	4 500	...	2.2	2.2	2.6	7.1	1.7	8.4	4.6
Direct investment abroad	4 505	...	...	...	...	...	...	...	...
Equity capital	4 510	...	...	...	...	...	...	...	...
Claims on affiliated enterprises	4 515	...	...	...	...	...	...	...	...
Liabilities to affiliated enterprises	4 520	...	...	...	...	...	...	...	...
Reinvested earnings	4 525	...	...	...	...	...	...	...	...
Other capital	4 530	...	...	...	...	...	...	...	...
Claims on affiliated enterprises	4 535	...	...	...	...	...	...	...	...
Liabilities to affiliated enterprises	4 540	...	...	...	...	...	...	...	...
Direct investment in Rwanda	4 555	...	**2.2**	**2.2**	**2.6**	**7.1**	**1.7**	**8.4**	**4.6**
Equity capital	4 560	...	...	...	...	7.1	1.7	8.1	4.6
Claims on direct investors	4 565	...	...	...	...	...	...	...	...
Liabilities to direct investors	4 570	...	...	...	...	7.1	1.7	8.1	4.6
Reinvested earnings	4 575	...	...	...	...	...	...	.3	...
Other capital	4 580	...	2.2	2.2	2.6	...	...	...	...
Claims on direct investors	4 585	...	...	...	...	...	...	...	...
Liabilities to direct investors	4 590	...	...	...	...	...	...	...	...
B. PORTFOLIO INVESTMENT	4 600	...	...	–.1	...	–.1	.8	.1	...
Assets	4 602	...	...	**–.1**	...	**–.1**	**.8**	**.1**	...
Equity securities	4 610	...	...	–.1	...	–.1	.8	.1	...
Monetary authorities	4 611	...	...	...	...	...	...	...	...
General government	4 612	...	...	...	...	–.1	.8	.1	...
Banks	4 613	...	...	...	...	...	...	...	...
Other sectors	4 614	...	...	...	...	...	...	...	...
Debt securities	4 619	...	...	...	...	...	...	...	...
Bonds and notes	4 620	...	...	...	...	...	...	...	...
Monetary authorities	4 621	...	...	...	...	...	...	...	...
General government	4 622	...	...	...	...	...	...	...	...
Banks	4 623	...	...	...	...	...	...	...	...
Other sectors	4 624	...	...	...	...	...	...	...	...
Money market instruments	4 630	...	...	...	...	...	...	...	...
Monetary authorities	4 631	...	...	...	...	...	...	...	...
General government	4 632	...	...	...	...	...	...	...	...
Banks	4 633	...	...	...	...	...	...	...	...
Other sectors	4 634	...	...	...	...	...	...	...	...
Liabilities	4 652	...	...	...	...	...	...	...	...
Equity securities	4 660	...	...	...	...	...	...	...	...
Banks	4 663	...	...	...	...	...	...	...	...
Other sectors	4 664	...	...	...	...	...	...	...	...
Debt securities	4 669	...	...	...	...	...	...	...	...
Bonds and notes	4 670	...	...	...	...	...	...	...	...
Monetary authorities	4 671	...	...	...	...	...	...	...	...
General government	4 672	...	...	...	...	...	...	...	...
Banks	4 673	...	...	...	...	...	...	...	...
Other sectors	4 674	...	...	...	...	...	...	...	...
Money market instruments	4 680	...	...	...	...	...	...	...	...
Monetary authorities	4 681	...	...	...	...	...	...	...	...
General government	4 682	...	...	...	...	...	...	...	...
Banks	4 683	...	...	...	...	...	...	...	...
Other sectors	4 684	...	...	...	...	...	...	...	...
C. FINANCIAL DERIVATIVES	4 910	...	...	...	...	...	...	...	...
Monetary authorities	4 911	...	...	...	...	...	...	...	...
General government	4 912	...	...	...	...	...	...	...	...
Banks	4 913	...	...	...	...	...	...	...	...
Other sectors	4 914	...	...	...	...	...	...	...	...
Assets	4 900	...	...	...	...	...	...	...	...
Monetary authorities	4 901	...	...	...	...	...	...	...	...
General government	4 902	...	...	...	...	...	...	...	...
Banks	4 903	...	...	...	...	...	...	...	...
Other sectors	4 904	...	...	...	...	...	...	...	...
Liabilities	4 905	...	...	...	...	...	...	...	...
Monetary authorities	4 906	...	...	...	...	...	...	...	...
General government	4 907	...	...	...	...	...	...	...	...
Banks	4 908	...	...	...	...	...	...	...	...
Other sectors	4 909	...	...	...	...	...	...	...	...

Table 2 (Concluded). STANDARD PRESENTATION, 1994–2001
(Millions of U.S. dollars)

	Code	1994	1995	1996	1997	1998	1999	2000	2001
D. OTHER INVESTMENT	4 700 . .	-12.5	.4	21.4	62.1	-12.0	-4.6	54.7	-2.1
Assets	4 703 . .	**. . .**	**-52.0**	**-13.6**	**1.2**	**-.8**	**-10.4**	**23.4**	**-.5**
Trade credits	4 706 . .	. . .	-13.4	. . .	. . .	. . .	. . .	6.0	4.4
General government	4 707 . .	. . .	. . .	. . .	. . .	. . .	. . .	. . .	. . .
of which: Short-term	4 709 . .	. . .	. . .	. . .	. . .	. . .	. . .	. . .	. . .
Other sectors	4 710 . .	. . .	-13.4	. . .	. . .	. . .	. . .	6.0	4.4
of which: Short-term	4 712 . .	. . .	*-13.4*	. . .	. . .	. . .	. . .	*6.0*	*4.4*
Loans	4 714 . .	. . .	-38.6	-13.6	1.2	-.8	-10.4	17.3	-4.9
Monetary authorities	4 715 . .	. . .	. . .	. . .	. . .	. . .	. . .	. . .	. . .
of which: Short-term	4 718 . .	. . .	. . .	. . .	. . .	. . .	. . .	. . .	. . .
General government	4 719 . .	. . .	. . .	. . .	. . .	. . .	. . .	. . .	. . .
of which: Short-term	4 721 . .	. . .	. . .	. . .	. . .	. . .	. . .	. . .	. . .
Banks	4 722 . .	. . .	-38.6	-13.6	1.2	-.8	-10.4	17.3	-4.9
of which: Short-term	4 724 . .	. . .	*-38.6*	*-13.6*	*1.2*	*-.8*	*-10.4*	*17.3*	*-4.9*
Other sectors	4 725 . .	. . .	. . .	. . .	. . .	. . .	. . .	. . .	. . .
of which: Short-term	4 727 . .	. . .	. . .	. . .	. . .	. . .	. . .	. . .	. . .
Currency and deposits	4 730 . .	. . .	. . .	. . .	. . .	. . .	. . .	. . .	. . .
Monetary authorities	4 731 . .	. . .	. . .	. . .	. . .	. . .	. . .	. . .	. . .
General government	4 732 . .	. . .	. . .	. . .	. . .	. . .	. . .	. . .	. . .
Banks	4 733 . .	. . .	. . .	. . .	. . .	. . .	. . .	. . .	. . .
Other sectors	4 734 . .	. . .	. . .	. . .	. . .	. . .	. . .	. . .	. . .
Other assets	4 736 . .	. . .	. . .	. . .	. . .	. . .	. . .	. . .	. . .
Monetary authorities	4 737 . .	. . .	. . .	. . .	. . .	. . .	. . .	. . .	. . .
of which: Short-term	4 739 . .	. . .	. . .	. . .	. . .	. . .	. . .	. . .	. . .
General government	4 740 . .	. . .	. . .	. . .	. . .	. . .	. . .	. . .	. . .
of which: Short-term	4 742 . .	. . .	. . .	. . .	. . .	. . .	. . .	. . .	. . .
Banks	4 743 . .	. . .	. . .	. . .	. . .	. . .	. . .	. . .	. . .
of which: Short-term	4 745 . .	. . .	. . .	. . .	. . .	. . .	. . .	. . .	. . .
Other sectors	4 746 . .	. . .	. . .	. . .	. . .	. . .	. . .	. . .	. . .
of which: Short-term	4 748 . .	. . .	. . .	. . .	. . .	. . .	. . .	. . .	. . .
Liabilities	4 753 . .	**-12.5**	**52.4**	**35.0**	**60.9**	**-11.2**	**5.7**	**31.4**	**-1.7**
Trade credits	4 756 . .	. . .	. . .	. . .	. . .	. . .	. . .	. . .	. . .
General government	4 757 . .	. . .	. . .	. . .	. . .	. . .	. . .	. . .	. . .
of which: Short-term	4 759 . .	. . .	. . .	. . .	. . .	. . .	. . .	. . .	. . .
Other sectors	4 760 . .	. . .	. . .	. . .	. . .	. . .	. . .	. . .	. . .
of which: Short-term	4 762 . .	. . .	. . .	. . .	. . .	. . .	. . .	. . .	. . .
Loans	4 764 . .	-12.5	52.4	35.0	60.9	78.0	83.2	47.3	45.3
Monetary authorities	4 765 . .	. . .	13.3	-1.3	17.9	13.5	20.8	13.6	.9
of which: Use of Fund credit and loans from the Fund	4 766 . .	. . .	*13.3*	*-1.3*	*17.9*	*13.5*	*20.8*	*13.6*	*.9*
of which: Short-term	4 768 . .	. . .	. . .	. . .	. . .	. . .	. . .	. . .	. . .
General government	4 769 . .	-12.5	39.1	37.2	43.0	65.0	64.1	31.6	42.3
of which: Short-term	4 771 . .	. . .	. . .	. . .	. . .	. . .	. . .	. . .	. . .
Banks	4 772 . .	. . .	. . .	. . .	. . .	. . .	. . .	. . .	. . .
of which: Short-term	4 774 . .	. . .	. . .	. . .	. . .	. . .	. . .	. . .	. . .
Other sectors	4 775 . .	. . .	. . .	-.9	. . .	-.5	-1.6	2.1	2.1
of which: Short-term	4 777 . .	. . .	. . .	. . .	. . .	. . .	. . .	*3.0*	*2.1*
Currency and deposits	4 780 . .	. . .	. . .	. . .	. . .	. . .	. . .	. . .	. . .
Monetary authorities	4 781 . .	. . .	. . .	. . .	. . .	. . .	. . .	. . .	. . .
General government	4 782 . .	. . .	. . .	. . .	. . .	. . .	. . .	. . .	. . .
Banks	4 783 . .	. . .	. . .	. . .	. . .	. . .	. . .	. . .	. . .
Other sectors	4 784 . .	. . .	. . .	. . .	. . .	. . .	. . .	. . .	. . .
Other liabilities	4 786 . .	. . .	. . .	. . .	. . .	-89.2	-77.5	-15.9	-47.0
Monetary authorities	4 787 . .	. . .	. . .	. . .	. . .	. . .	. . .	. . .	. . .
of which: Short-term	4 789 . .	. . .	. . .	. . .	. . .	. . .	. . .	. . .	. . .
General government	4 790 . .	. . .	. . .	. . .	. . .	-89.2	-77.5	-15.9	-47.0
of which: Short-term	4 792 . .	. . .	. . .	. . .	. . .	*-89.2*	*-77.5*	*-15.9*	*-47.0*
Banks	4 793 . .	. . .	. . .	. . .	. . .	. . .	. . .	. . .	. . .
of which: Short-term	4 795 . .	. . .	. . .	. . .	. . .	. . .	. . .	. . .	. . .
Other sectors	4 796 . .	. . .	. . .	. . .	. . .	. . .	. . .	. . .	. . .
of which: Short-term	4 798 . .	. . .	. . .	. . .	. . .	. . .	. . .	. . .	. . .
E. RESERVE ASSETS	4 802 . .	-3.7	-66.0	-19.1	-48.4	-21.2	38.1	78.8	10.9
Monetary gold	4 812 . .	. . .	. . .	. . .	. . .	. . .	. . .	. . .	. . .
Special drawing rights	4 811 . .	.5	-17.7	1.4	-9.5	3.1	9.4	12.7	-11.4
Reserve position in the Fund	4 810 . .	. . .	14.5	. . .	. . .	. . .	. . .	. . .	. . .
Foreign exchange	4 803 . .	-4.2	-62.8	-20.4	-38.9	-24.3	28.7	66.1	22.3
Other claims	4 813 . .	. . .	. . .	. . .	. . .	. . .	. . .	. . .	. . .
NET ERRORS AND OMISSIONS	4 998 . .	**62.4**	**5.8**	**4.1**	**46.0**	**92.8**	**33.0**	**-91.1**	**42.3**

Part 3 of the *Yearbook* contains descriptions of the methodologies, compilation practices, and sources used to compile these data.

Table 3. INTERNATIONAL INVESTMENT POSITION (End–period stocks), 1994–2001

(Millions of U.S. dollars)

	Code	1994	1995	1996	1997	1998	1999	2000	2001
ASSETS	8 995 C.	...	...	...	...	244.0	231.3	267.8	286.5
Direct investment abroad	8 505 ..	**...**	**...**	**...**	**...**	**...**	**...**	**...**	**...**
Equity capital and reinvested earnings	8 506 ..	...	...	...	...	...	...	...	...
Claims on affiliated enterprises	8 507 ..	...	...	...	...	...	...	...	...
Liabilities to affiliated enterprises	8 508 ..	...	...	...	...	...	...	...	...
Other capital	8 530 ..	...	...	...	...	...	...	...	...
Claims on affiliated enterprises	8 535 ..	...	...	...	...	...	...	...	...
Liabilities to affiliated enterprises	8 540 ..	...	...	...	...	...	...	...	...
Portfolio investment	8 602 ..	**...**	**...**	**...**	**...**	**.1**	**.8**	**.7**	**.6**
Equity securities	8 610 ..	...	...	...	...	.1	.8	.7	.6
Monetary authorities	8 611 ..	...	...	...	...	...	...	...	...
General government	8 612 ..	...	...	...	...	.1	.8	.7	.6
Banks	8 613 ..	...	...	...	...	...	...	...	...
Other sectors	8 614 ..	...	...	...	...	...	...	...	...
Debt securities	8 619 ..	...	...	...	...	...	...	...	...
Bonds and notes	8 620 ..	...	...	...	...	...	...	...	...
Monetary authorities	8 621 ..	...	...	...	...	...	...	...	...
General government	8 622 ..	...	...	...	...	...	...	...	...
Banks	8 623 ..	...	...	...	...	...	...	...	...
Other sectors	8 624 ..	...	...	...	...	...	...	...	...
Money market instruments	8 630 ..	...	...	...	...	...	...	...	...
Monetary authorities	8 631 ..	...	...	...	...	...	...	...	...
General government	8 632 ..	...	...	...	...	...	...	...	...
Banks	8 633 ..	...	...	...	...	...	...	...	...
Other sectors	8 634 ..	...	...	...	...	...	...	...	...
Financial derivatives	8 900 ..	**...**	**...**	**...**	**...**	**...**	**...**	**...**	**...**
Monetary authorities	8 901 ..	...	...	...	...	...	...	...	...
General government	8 902 ..	...	...	...	...	...	...	...	...
Banks	8 903 ..	...	...	...	...	...	...	...	...
Other sectors	8 904 ..	...	...	...	...	...	...	...	...
Other investment	8 703 ..	**...**	**...**	**...**	**...**	**75.2**	**56.3**	**76.5**	**73.7**
Trade credits	8 706 ..	...	...	...	...	...	...	...	...
1 General government	8 700 ..	...	...	...	...	...	...	...	...
of which: Short-term	8 712 ..	...	...	...	...	...	...	...	...
Loans	8 714 ..	...	...	...	...	75.2	56.3	76.5	73.7
Monetary authorities	8 715 ..	...	...	...	...	...	...	...	...
of which: Short-term	8 718 ..	...	...	...	...	...	...	...	...
General government	8 719 ..	...	...	...	...	...	...	...	...
of which: Short-term	8 721 ..	...	...	...	...	...	...	...	...
Banks	8 722 ..	...	...	...	...	75.2	56.3	76.5	73.7
of which: Short-term	8 724 ..	...	...	...	...	*75.2*	*56.3*	*76.5*	*73.7*
Other sectors	8 725 ..	...	...	...	...	...	...	...	...
of which: Short-term	8 727 ..	...	...	...	...	...	...	...	...
Currency and deposits	8 730 ..	...	...	...	...	...	...	...	...
Monetary authorities	8 731 ..	...	...	...	...	...	...	...	...
General government	8 732 ..	...	...	...	...	...	...	...	...
Banks	8 733 ..	...	...	...	...	...	...	...	...
Other sectors	8 734 ..	...	...	...	...	...	...	...	...
Other assets	8 736 ..	...	...	...	...	...	...	...	...
Monetary authorities	8 737 ..	...	...	...	...	...	...	...	...
of which: Short-term	8 739 ..	...	...	...	...	...	...	...	...
General government	8 740 ..	...	...	...	...	...	...	...	...
of which: Short-term	8 742 ..	...	...	...	...	...	...	...	...
Banks	8 743 ..	...	...	...	...	...	...	...	...
of which: Short-term	8 745 ..	...	...	...	...	...	...	...	...
Other sectors	8 746 ..	...	...	...	...	...	...	...	...
of which: Short-term	8 748 ..	...	...	...	...	...	...	...	...
Reserve assets	8 802 ..	**...**	**...**	**...**	**...**	**168.8**	**174.2**	**190.6**	**212.1**
Monetary gold	8 812 ..	...	...	...	...	...	...	...	...
Special drawing rights	8 811 ..	2.6	20.3	18.3	26.5	24.4	14.5	1.1	12.3
Reserve position in the Fund	8 810 ..	14.3	...	...	...	...	...	...	...
Foreign exchange	8 803 ..	...	...	...	...	144.3	159.7	189.5	199.8
Other claims	8 813 ..	...	...	...	...	...	...	...	...

Table 3 (Concluded). INTERNATIONAL INVESTMENT POSITION (End-period stocks), 1994–2001

(Millions of U.S. dollars)

	Code	1994	1995	1996	1997	1998	1999	2000	2001
LIABILITIES	8 995 D.	...	...	...	...	1,373.0	1,373.0	1,354.7	1,347.3
Direct investment in Rwanda	8 555 ..	**...**	**...**	**...**	**...**	**62.5**	**59.0**	**55.2**	**56.4**
Equity capital and reinvested earnings	8 556 ..	...	...	...	...	62.5	59.0	55.2	56.4
Claims on direct investors	8 557 ..	...	...	...	...	...	...	...	...
Liabilities to direct investors	8 558 ..	...	...	...	...	62.5	59.0	55.2	56.4
Other capital	8 580 ..	...	...	...	...	...	...	...	...
Claims on direct investors	8 585 ..	...	...	...	...	...	...	...	...
Liabilities to direct investors	8 590 ..	...	...	...	...	...	...	...	...
Portfolio investment	8 652 ..	**...**	**...**	**...**	**...**	**.1**	**.1**	**.1**	**.1**
Equity securities	8 660 ..	...	...	...	...	.1	.1	.1	.1
Banks	8 663 ..	...	...	...	...	...	...	...	...
Other sectors	8 664 ..	...	...	...	...	...	...	...	...
Debt securities	8 669 ..	...	...	...	...	...	...	...	...
Bonds and notes	8 670 ..	...	...	...	...	...	...	...	...
Monetary authorities	8 671 ..	...	...	...	...	...	...	...	...
General government	8 672 ..	...	...	...	...	...	...	...	...
Banks	8 673 ..	...	...	...	...	...	...	...	...
Other sectors	8 674 ..	...	...	...	...	...	...	...	...
Money market instruments	8 680 ..	...	...	...	...	...	...	...	...
Monetary authorities	8 681 ..	...	...	...	...	...	...	...	...
General government	8 682 ..	...	...	...	...	...	...	...	...
Banks	8 683 ..	...	...	...	...	...	...	...	...
Other sectors	8 684 ..	...	...	...	...	...	...	...	...
Financial derivatives	8 905 ..	**...**	**...**	**...**	**...**	**...**	**...**	**...**	**...**
Monetary authorities	8 906 ..	...	...	...	...	...	...	...	...
General government	8 907 ..	...	...	...	...	...	...	...	...
Banks	8 908 ..	...	...	...	...	...	...	...	...
Other sectors	8 909 ..	...	...	...	...	...	...	...	...
Other investment	8 753 ..	**...**	**...**	**...**	**...**	**1,310.4**	**1,313.9**	**1,299.4**	**1,290.8**
Trade credits	8 756 ..	...	...	...	...	12.9	11.2	10.6	10.3
General government	8 757 ..	...	...	...	...	12.9	11.2	10.6	10.3
of which: Short-term	8 759 ..	...	...	...	...	*12.9*	*11.2*	*10.6*	*10.3*
Other sectors	8 760 ..	...	...	...	...	...	...	...	...
of which: Short-term	8 762 ..	...	...	...	...	...	...	...	...
Loans	8 764 ..	...	...	...	...	1,273.4	1,281.5	1,270.9	1,264.4
Monetary authorities	8 765 ..	...	...	...	...	58.2	75.8	85.8	84.3
of which: Use of Fund credit and loans from the Fund	8 766 ..	*12.8*	*26.3*	*24.2*	*40.4*	*56.4*	*75.9*	*85.8*	*83.7*
of which: Short-term	8 768 ..	...	...	...	...	...	...	...	...
General government	8 769 ..	...	...	...	...	1,187.4	1,185.4	1,164.1	1,158.5
of which: Short-term	8 771 ..	...	...	...	...	...	...	...	...
Banks	8 772 ..	...	...	...	...	11.9	5.3	8.1	10.1
of which: Short-term	8 774 ..	...	...	...	...	*11.9*	*5.3*	*8.1*	*10.1*
Other sectors	8 775 ..	...	...	...	...	15.9	15.0	12.9	11.4
of which: Short-term	8 777 ..	...	...	...	...	...	...	...	...
Currency and deposits	8 780 ..	...	...	...	...	...	...	...	...
Monetary authorities	8 781 ..	...	...	...	...	...	...	...	...
General government	8 782 ..	...	...	...	...	...	...	...	...
Banks	8 783 ..	...	...	...	...	...	...	...	...
Other sectors	8 784 ..	...	...	...	...	...	...	...	...
Other liabilities	8 786 ..	...	...	...	...	24.1	21.2	17.9	16.1
Monetary authorities	8 787 ..	...	...	...	...	24.1	21.2	17.9	16.1
of which: Short-term	8 789 ..	...	...	...	...	*24.1*	*21.2*	*17.9*	*16.1*
General government	8 790 ..	...	...	...	...	...	...	...	...
of which: Short-term	8 792 ..	...	...	...	...	...	...	...	...
Banks	8 793 ..	...	...	...	...	...	...	...	...
of which: Short-term	8 795 ..	...	...	...	...	...	...	...	...
Other sectors	8 796 ..	...	...	...	...	...	...	...	...
of which: Short-term	8 798 ..	...	...	...	...	...	...	...	...
NET INTERNATIONAL INVESTMENT POSITION	8 995 ..	**...**	**...**	**...**	**...**	**–1,129.0**	**–1,141.7**	**–1,086.9**	**–1,060.8**
Conversion rates: Rwanda francs per U.S. dollar (end of period)	0 102 ..	**138.33**	**299.81**	**304.16**	**304.67**	**320.34**	**349.53**	**430.49**	**457.90**

Table 1. ANALYTIC PRESENTATION, 1994–2001
(Millions of U.S. dollars)

	Code		1994	1995	1996	1997	1998	1999	2000	2001
A. Current Account [1]	4 993	Z.	**–24.30**	**–45.46**	**–65.95**	**–53.98**	**–41.50**	**–82.96**	**–62.33**	**. . .**
Goods: exports f.o.b	2 100	. .	28.57	36.56	39.07	51.35	44.80	44.94	54.56	. . .
Goods: imports f.o.b	3 100	. .	–98.27	–117.12	–131.51	–129.72	–131.10	–135.19	–172.56	. . .
Balance on Goods	4 100	. .	*–69.70*	*–80.56*	*–92.44*	*–78.37*	*–86.30*	*–90.24*	*–118.00*	. . .
Services: credit	2 200	. .	92.38	81.95	87.24	95.47	105.30	99.51	96.66	. . .
Services: debit	3 200	. .	–44.86	–55.07	–61.30	–65.04	–61.94	–85.33	–74.33	. . .
Balance on Goods and Services	4 991	. .	*–22.18*	*–53.68*	*–66.49*	*–47.94*	*–42.94*	*–76.06*	*–95.68*	. . .
Income: credit	2 300	. .	2.91	6.77	3.14	2.89	4.84	6.45	5.54	. . .
Income: debit	3 300	. .	–15.91	–17.73	–18.76	–24.01	–30.48	–33.84	–34.83	. . .
Balance on Goods, Services, and Income	4 992	. .	*–35.19*	*–64.64*	*–82.12*	*–69.07*	*–68.59*	*–103.46*	*–124.97*	. . .
Current transfers: credit	2 379	Z.	16.56	23.26	20.80	21.76	33.66	24.05	69.89	. . .
Current transfers: debit	3 379	. .	–5.67	–4.08	–4.63	–6.67	–6.58	–3.56	–7.25	. . .
B. Capital Account [1]	4 994	Z.	**1.73**	**7.26**	**5.45**	**4.17**	**8.25**	**5.81**	**12.24**	**. . .**
Capital account: credit	2 994	Z.	2.61	7.41	5.63	4.36	8.43	5.99	12.43	. . .
Capital account: debit	3 994	. .	–.88	–.16	–.19	–.19	–.19	–.19	–.19	. . .
Total, Groups A Plus B	4 981	. .	*–22.57*	*–38.21*	*–60.50*	*–49.81*	*–33.26*	*–77.16*	*–50.09*	. . .
C. Financial Account [1]	4 995	W.	**23.74**	**24.79**	**48.37**	**43.36**	**35.82**	**94.80**	**66.60**	**. . .**
Direct investment abroad	4 505	. .	. . .	. . .	. . .	. . .	. . .	. . .	. . .	. . .
Direct investment in St. Kitts and Nevis	4 555	Z.	15.35	20.47	35.17	19.67	31.93	57.74	96.21	. . .
Portfolio investment assets	4 602	. .	. . .	2.59	.88	.01	.01	.02	.03	. . .
Equity securities	4 610	. .	. . .	. . .	. . .	. . .	. . .	. . .	. . .	. . .
Debt securities	4 619	. .	. . .	. . .	. . .	. . .	. . .	. . .	. . .	. . .
Portfolio investment liabilities	4 652	Z.	.23	.15	7.09	.44	–.13	.01	1.12	. . .
Equity securities	4 660	. .	. . .	. . .	. . .	. . .	. . .	. . .	. . .	. . .
Debt securities	4 669	Z.	. . .	. . .	. . .	. . .	. . .	. . .	. . .	. . .
Financial derivatives	4 910	. .	. . .	. . .	. . .	. . .	. . .	. . .	. . .	. . .
Financial derivatives assets	4 900	. .	. . .	. . .	. . .	. . .	. . .	. . .	. . .	. . .
Financial derivatives liabilities	4 905	. .	. . .	. . .	. . .	. . .	. . .	. . .	. . .	. . .
Other investment assets	4 703	. .	–10.04	–3.70	–13.10	–36.39	–4.99	1.47	–10.74	. . .
Monetary authorities	4 701	. .	. . .	. . .	. . .	. . .	. . .	. . .	. . .	. . .
General government	4 704	. .	. . .	. . .	. . .	. . .	. . .	. . .	. . .	. . .
Banks	4 705	. .	. . .	. . .	. . .	. . .	. . .	. . .	. . .	. . .
Other sectors	4 728	. .	. . .	. . .	. . .	. . .	. . .	. . .	. . .	. . .
Other investment liabilities	4 753	W.	18.20	5.28	18.33	59.63	9.00	35.56	–20.02	. . .
Monetary authorities	4 753	WA	. . .	. . .	. . .	. . .	. . .	. . .	. . .	. . .
General government	4 753	ZB	. . .	. . .	. . .	. . .	. . .	. . .	. . .	. . .
Banks	4 753	ZC	. . .	. . .	. . .	. . .	. . .	. . .	. . .	. . .
Other sectors	4 753	ZD	. . .	. . .	. . .	. . .	. . .	. . .	. . .	. . .
Total, Groups A Through C	4 983	. .	*1.16*	*–13.42*	*–12.13*	*–6.46*	*2.57*	*17.64*	*16.51*	. . .
D. Net Errors and Omissions	4 998	. .	**–1.77**	**15.71**	**11.24**	**9.48**	**8.43**	**–14.90**	**–20.84**	**. . .**
Total, Groups A Through D	4 984	. .	*–.61*	*2.29*	*–.89*	*3.02*	*10.99*	*2.74*	*–4.33*	. . .
E. Reserves and Related Items	4 802	A.	**.61**	**–2.29**	**.89**	**–3.02**	**–10.99**	**–2.74**	**4.33**	**. . .**
Reserve assets	4 802	. .	.61	–2.29	.89	–3.02	–13.27	–2.74	4.33	. . .
Use of Fund credit and loans	4 766	. .	. . .	. . .	. . .	. . .	2.28	. . .	. . .	. . .
Exceptional financing	4 920	. .	. . .	. . .	. . .	. . .	. . .	. . .	. . .	. . .
Conversion rates: Eastern Caribbean dollars per U.S. dollar	0 101	. .	**2.7000**	**2.7000**	**2.7000**	**2.7000**	**2.7000**	**2.7000**	**2.7000**	**2.7000**

[1] Excludes components that have been classified in the categories of Group E.

Table 2. STANDARD PRESENTATION, 1994–2001
(Millions of U.S. dollars)

	Code		1994	1995	1996	1997	1998	1999	2000	2001
CURRENT ACCOUNT	4 993	. .	**–24.30**	**–45.46**	**–65.95**	**–53.98**	**–41.50**	**–82.96**	**–62.33**	. . .
A. GOODS	4 100	. .	–69.70	–80.56	–92.44	–78.37	–86.30	–90.24	–118.00	. . .
Credit	2 100	. .	**28.57**	**36.56**	**39.07**	**51.35**	**44.80**	**44.94**	**54.56**	. . .
General merchandise: exports f.o.b.	2 110	. .	27.85	35.88	38.00	50.17	42.23	44.31	52.45	. . .
Goods for processing: exports f.o.b.	2 150	. .	. . .	. . .	. . .	. . .	. . .	. . .	. . .	. . .
Repairs on goods	2 160	. .	. . .	. . .	. . .	. . .	. . .	. . .	. . .	. . .
Goods procured in ports by carriers	2 170	. .	.72	.68	1.07	1.18	2.57	.64	2.11	. . .
Nonmonetary gold	2 180	. .	. . .	. . .	. . .	. . .	. . .	. . .	. . .	. . .
Debit	3 100	. .	**–98.27**	**–117.12**	**–131.51**	**–129.72**	**–131.10**	**–135.19**	**–172.56**	. . .
General merchandise: imports f.o.b.	3 110	. .	–98.27	–117.12	–131.30	–129.51	–130.89	–135.12	–172.46	. . .
Goods for processing: imports f.o.b.	3 150	. .	. . .	. . .	. . .	. . .	. . .	. . .	. . .	. . .
Repairs on goods	3 160	. .	. . .	. . .	. . .	. . .	. . .	. . .	. . .	. . .
Goods procured in ports by carriers	3 170	. .	. . .	. . .	–.21	–.21	–.21	–.07	–.10	. . .
Nonmonetary gold	3 180	. .	. . .	. . .	. . .	. . .	. . .	. . .	. . .	. . .
B. SERVICES	4 200	. .	47.51	26.88	25.94	30.43	43.36	14.18	22.33	. . .
Total credit	2 200	. .	*92.38*	*81.95*	*87.24*	*95.47*	*105.30*	*99.51*	*96.66*	. . .
Total debit	3 200	. .	*–44.86*	*–55.07*	*–61.30*	*–65.04*	*–61.94*	*–85.33*	*–74.33*	. . .
Transportation services, credit	2 205	. .	**4.81**	**5.08**	**6.58**	**7.04**	**7.99**	**7.77**	**9.42**	. . .
Passenger	2 850	. .	. . .	. . .	. . .	. . .	. . .	. . .	. . .	. . .
Freight	2 851	. .	. . .	. . .	. . .	. . .	. . .	. . .	. . .	. . .
Other	2 852	. .	. . .	. . .	. . .	. . .	. . .	. . .	. . .	. . .
Sea transport, passenger	2 207	. .	. . .	. . .	. . .	. . .	. . .	. . .	. . .	. . .
Sea transport, freight	2 208	. .	. . .	. . .	. . .	. . .	. . .	. . .	. . .	. . .
Sea transport, other	2 209	. .	. . .	. . .	. . .	. . .	. . .	. . .	. . .	. . .
Air transport, passenger	2 211	. .	. . .	. . .	. . .	. . .	. . .	. . .	. . .	. . .
Air transport, freight	2 212	. .	. . .	. . .	. . .	. . .	. . .	. . .	. . .	. . .
Air transport, other	2 213	. .	. . .	. . .	. . .	. . .	. . .	. . .	. . .	. . .
Other transport, passenger	2 215	. .	. . .	. . .	. . .	. . .	. . .	. . .	. . .	. . .
Other transport, freight	2 216	. .	. . .	. . .	. . .	. . .	. . .	. . .	. . .	. . .
Other transport, other	2 217	. .	. . .	. . .	. . .	. . .	. . .	. . .	. . .	. . .
Transportation services, debit	3 205	. .	**–16.78**	**–20.80**	**–23.11**	**–25.47**	**–26.57**	**–28.82**	**–30.28**	. . .
Passenger	3 850	. .	. . .	. . .	. . .	. . .	. . .	. . .	. . .	. . .
Freight	3 851	. .	. . .	. . .	. . .	. . .	. . .	. . .	. . .	. . .
Other	3 852	. .	. . .	. . .	. . .	. . .	. . .	. . .	. . .	. . .
Sea transport, passenger	3 207	. .	. . .	. . .	. . .	. . .	. . .	. . .	. . .	. . .
Sea transport, freight	3 208	. .	. . .	. . .	. . .	. . .	. . .	. . .	. . .	. . .
Sea transport, other	3 209	. .	. . .	. . .	. . .	. . .	. . .	. . .	. . .	. . .
Air transport, passenger	3 211	. .	. . .	. . .	. . .	. . .	. . .	. . .	. . .	. . .
Air transport, freight	3 212	. .	. . .	. . .	. . .	. . .	. . .	. . .	. . .	. . .
Air transport, other	3 213	. .	. . .	. . .	. . .	. . .	. . .	. . .	. . .	. . .
Other transport, passenger	3 215	. .	. . .	. . .	. . .	. . .	. . .	. . .	. . .	. . .
Other transport, freight	3 216	. .	. . .	. . .	. . .	. . .	. . .	. . .	. . .	. . .
Other transport, other	3 217	. .	. . .	. . .	. . .	. . .	. . .	. . .	. . .	. . .
Travel, credit	2 236	. .	**76.86**	**63.04**	**66.81**	**72.44**	**76.03**	**67.66**	**58.23**	. . .
Business travel	2 237	. .	. . .	. . .	. . .	. . .	. . .	. . .	. . .	. . .
Personal travel	2 240	. .	. . .	. . .	. . .	. . .	. . .	. . .	. . .	. . .
Travel, debit	3 236	. .	**–5.79**	**–5.11**	**–5.47**	**–5.91**	**–6.17**	**–6.80**	**–8.77**	. . .
Business travel	3 237	. .	. . .	. . .	. . .	. . .	. . .	. . .	. . .	. . .
Personal travel	3 240	. .	. . .	. . .	. . .	. . .	. . .	. . .	. . .	. . .
Other services, credit	2 200	BA	**10.71**	**13.83**	**13.85**	**15.99**	**21.29**	**24.08**	**29.00**	. . .
Communications	2 245	. .	. . .	. . .	. . .	. . .	. . .	. . .	. . .	. . .
Construction	2 249	. .	. . .	. . .	. . .	.02	.07	. . .	1.00	. . .
Insurance	2 253	. .	1.46	1.57	1.27	1.67	3.44	1.31	3.19	. . .
Financial	2 260	. .	. . .	. . .	. . .	. . .	5.33	6.18	6.86	. . .
Computer and information	2 262	. .	. . .	. . .	. . .	. . .	. . .	. . .	. . .	. . .
Royalties and licence fees	2 266	. .	. . .	. . .	. . .	. . .	. . .	. . .	. . .	. . .
Other business services	2 268	. .	8.57	10.26	11.30	12.47	9.83	13.62	14.50	. . .
Personal, cultural, and recreational	2 287	. .	. . .	. . .	. . .	. . .	. . .	. . .	. . .	. . .
Government, n.i.e.	2 291	. .	.68	2.00	1.28	1.82	2.63	2.97	3.47	. . .
Other services, debit	3 200	BA	**–22.30**	**–29.16**	**–32.72**	**–33.66**	**–29.21**	**–49.71**	**–35.28**	. . .
Communications	3 245	. .	. . .	. . .	. . .	. . .	. . .	. . .	. . .	. . .
Construction	3 249	. .	. . .	–2.89	–2.30	–2.55	–.48	–2.91	–5.12	. . .
Insurance	3 253	. .	–5.82	–5.80	–6.07	–5.74	–5.86	–6.77	–8.52	. . .
Financial	3 260	. .	. . .	. . .	. . .	. . .	. . .	. . .	. . .	. . .
Computer and information	3 262	. .	. . .	. . .	. . .	. . .	. . .	. . .	. . .	. . .
Royalties and licence fees	3 266	. .	–.01	. . .	–.30	–.31	–.30	–.82	–.77	. . .
Other business services	3 268	. .	–14.18	–16.77	–20.63	–21.27	–18.27	–35.15	–17.18	. . .
Personal, cultural, and recreational	3 287	. .	. . .	. . .	. . .	. . .	. . .	. . .	. . .	. . .
Government, n.i.e.	3 291	. .	–2.28	–3.70	–3.42	–3.78	–4.30	–4.07	–3.68	. . .

Table 2 (Continued). STANDARD PRESENTATION, 1994–2001
(Millions of U.S. dollars)

	Code	1994	1995	1996	1997	1998	1999	2000	2001
C. INCOME	4 300	-13.01	-10.96	-15.63	-21.12	-25.64	-27.40	-29.29	...
Total credit	2 300	*2.91*	*6.77*	*3.14*	*2.89*	*4.84*	*6.45*	*5.54*	...
Total debit	3 300	*-15.91*	*-17.73*	*-18.76*	*-24.01*	*-30.48*	*-33.84*	*-34.83*	...
Compensation of employees, credit	2 310	**.11**	**.07**	**.09**	**.08**	**.75**	**1.22**	**.96**	...
Compensation of employees, debit	3 310	**-.87**	**-.86**	**-1.68**	**-2.46**	**-1.05**	**-1.23**	**-3.09**	...
Investment income, credit	2 320	**2.79**	**6.70**	**3.05**	**2.81**	**4.09**	**5.23**	**4.59**	...
Direct investment income	2 330	...	...	...	...	...	...	.01	...
Dividends and distributed branch profits	2 332	...	...	...	...	...	...	...	...
Reinvested earnings and undistributed branch profits	2 333	...	...	...	...	...	...	...	...
Income on debt (interest)	2 334	...	...	...	...	...	...	.01	...
Portfolio investment income	2 339	.81	2.49	.81	.16	.85	.44	.61	...
Income on equity	2 340	.81	2.49	.81	.16	.85	.44	.61	...
Income on bonds and notes	2 350	...	...	...	...	...	...	...	...
Income on money market instruments	2 360	...	...	...	...	...	...	...	...
Other investment income	2 370	1.99	4.20	2.24	2.65	3.24	4.78	3.96	...
Investment income, debit	3 320	**-15.04**	**-16.87**	**-17.09**	**-21.56**	**-29.43**	**-32.62**	**-31.75**	...
Direct investment income	3 330	-12.60	-14.39	-13.74	-16.73	-21.29	-22.22	-21.22	...
Dividends and distributed branch profits	3 332	-4.20	-3.71	-4.88	-7.66	-8.36	-12.93	-13.06	...
Reinvested earnings and undistributed branch profits	3 333	-3.25	-4.97	-4.99	-6.73	-6.02	-3.84	-3.66	...
Income on debt (interest)	3 334	-5.16	-5.70	-3.87	-2.34	-6.91	-5.46	-4.50	...
Portfolio investment income	3 339	...	...	...	...	...	...	...	...
Income on equity	3 340	...	...	...	...	...	...	...	...
Income on bonds and notes	3 350	...	...	...	...	...	...	...	...
Income on money market instruments	3 360	...	...	...	...	...	...	...	...
Other investment income	3 370	-2.44	-2.48	-3.35	-4.82	-8.14	-10.40	-10.53	...
D. CURRENT TRANSFERS	4 379	10.89	19.18	16.17	15.09	27.08	20.50	62.64	...
Credit	2 379	**16.56**	**23.26**	**20.80**	**21.76**	**33.66**	**24.05**	**69.89**	...
General government	2 380	1.06	2.79	1.73	1.81	3.71	1.97	1.52	...
Other sectors	2 390	15.50	20.47	19.08	19.94	29.95	22.09	68.37	...
Workers' remittances	2 391	...	...	...	...	...	...	...	...
Other current transfers	2 392	...	...	...	...	...	...	...	...
Debit	3 379	**-5.67**	**-4.08**	**-4.63**	**-6.67**	**-6.58**	**-3.56**	**-7.25**	...
General government	3 380	-3.97	-3.75	-3.58	-3.68	-4.46	-2.27	-3.00	...
Other sectors	3 390	-1.70	-.33	-1.05	-3.00	-2.12	-1.28	-4.25	...
Workers' remittances	3 391	...	...	...	...	...	...	...	...
Other current transfers	3 392	...	...	...	...	...	...	...	...
CAPITAL AND FINANCIAL ACCOUNT	4 996	**26.07**	**29.76**	**54.71**	**44.50**	**33.08**	**97.86**	**83.17**	...
CAPITAL ACCOUNT	4 994	**1.73**	**7.26**	**5.45**	**4.17**	**8.25**	**5.81**	**12.24**	...
Total credit	2 994	*2.61*	*7.41*	*5.63*	*4.36*	*8.43*	*5.99*	*12.43*	...
Total debit	3 994	*-.88*	*-.16*	*-.19*	*-.19*	*-.19*	*-.19*	*-.19*	...
Capital transfers, credit	2 400	**2.61**	**7.41**	**5.63**	**4.36**	**8.43**	**5.99**	**12.43**	...
General government	2 401	.62	5.71	3.42	1.63	5.29	3.07	9.60	...
Debt forgiveness	2 402	...	...	...	...	...	...	...	...
Other capital transfers	2 410	.62	5.71	3.42	1.63	5.29	3.07	9.60	...
Other sectors	2 430	1.99	1.70	2.21	2.72	3.15	2.92	2.82	...
Migrants' transfers	2 431	1.99	1.70	2.21	2.72	3.15	2.92	2.82	...
Debt forgiveness	2 432	...	...	...	...	...	...	...	...
Other capital transfers	2 440	...	...	...	...	...	...	...	...
Capital transfers, debit	3 400	**-.29**	**-.16**	**-.19**	**-.19**	**-.19**	**-.19**	**-.19**	...
General government	3 401	...	...	...	...	...	...	...	...
Debt forgiveness	3 402	...	...	...	...	...	...	...	...
Other capital transfers	3 410	...	...	...	...	...	...	...	...
Other sectors	3 430	-.29	-.16	-.19	-.19	-.19	-.19	-.19	...
Migrants' transfers	3 431	-.29	-.16	-.19	-.19	-.19	-.19	-.19	...
Debt forgiveness	3 432	...	...	...	...	...	...	...	...
Other capital transfers	3 440	...	...	...	...	...	...	...	...
Nonproduced nonfinancial assets, credit	2 480	...	...	...	...	...	...	...	...
Nonproduced nonfinancial assets, debit	3 480	**-.59**	...	...	...	...	...	...	...

Table 2 (Continued). STANDARD PRESENTATION, 1994–2001

(Millions of U.S. dollars)

	Code	1994	1995	1996	1997	1998	1999	2000	2001
FINANCIAL ACCOUNT	4 995 . .	**24.35**	**22.50**	**49.26**	**40.33**	**24.83**	**92.06**	**70.93**	**. . .**
A. DIRECT INVESTMENT	4 500 . .	15.35	20.47	35.17	19.67	31.93	57.74	96.21	. . .
Direct investment abroad	4 505 . .	**. . .**	**. . .**	**. . .**	**. . .**	**. . .**	**. . .**	**. . .**	**. . .**
Equity capital	4 510 . .	. . .	. . .	. . .	. . .	. . .	. . .	. . .	. . .
Claims on affiliated enterprises	4 515 . .	. . .	. . .	. . .	. . .	. . .	. . .	. . .	. . .
Liabilities to affiliated enterprises	4 520 . .	. . .	. . .	. . .	. . .	. . .	. . .	. . .	. . .
Reinvested earnings	4 525 . .	. . .	. . .	. . .	. . .	. . .	. . .	. . .	. . .
Other capital	4 530 . .	. . .	. . .	. . .	. . .	. . .	. . .	. . .	. . .
Claims on affiliated enterprises	4 535 . .	. . .	. . .	. . .	. . .	. . .	. . .	. . .	. . .
Liabilities to affiliated enterprises	4 540 . .	. . .	. . .	. . .	. . .	. . .	. . .	. . .	. . .
Direct investment in St. Kitts and Nevis	4 555 . .	**15.35**	**20.47**	**35.17**	**19.67**	**31.93**	**57.74**	**96.21**	**. . .**
Equity capital	4 560 . .	11.31	17.69	26.18	18.73	27.39	40.48	64.48	. . .
Claims on direct investors	4 565 . .	. . .	. . .	. . .	. . .	. . .	. . .	. . .	. . .
Liabilities to direct investors	4 570 . .	11.31	17.69	26.18	18.73	27.39	40.48	64.48	. . .
Reinvested earnings	4 575 . .	3.25	4.97	4.99	6.73	6.02	3.84	3.66	. . .
Other capital	4 580 . .	.79	–2.19	4.00	–5.80	–1.49	13.42	28.07	. . .
Claims on direct investors	4 585 . .	. . .	. . .	. . .	. . .	. . .	. . .	. . .	. . .
Liabilities to direct investors	4 590 . .	.79	–2.19	4.00	–5.80	–1.49	13.42	28.07	. . .
B. PORTFOLIO INVESTMENT	4 600 . .	.23	2.74	7.97	.44	–.12	.03	1.15	. . .
Assets	4 602 . .	**. . .**	**2.59**	**.88**	**.01**	**.01**	**.02**	**.03**	**. . .**
Equity securities	4 610 . .	. . .	. . .	. . .	. . .	. . .	. . .	. . .	. . .
Monetary authorities	4 611 . .	. . .	. . .	. . .	. . .	. . .	. . .	. . .	. . .
General government	4 612 . .	. . .	. . .	. . .	. . .	. . .	. . .	. . .	. . .
Banks	4 613 . .	. . .	. . .	. . .	. . .	. . .	. . .	. . .	. . .
Other sectors	4 614 . .	. . .	. . .	. . .	. . .	. . .	. . .	. . .	. . .
Debt securities	4 619 . .	. . .	. . .	. . .	. . .	. . .	. . .	. . .	. . .
Bonds and notes	4 620 . .	. . .	. . .	. . .	. . .	. . .	. . .	. . .	. . .
Monetary authorities	4 621 . .	. . .	. . .	. . .	. . .	. . .	. . .	. . .	. . .
General government	4 622 . .	. . .	. . .	. . .	. . .	. . .	. . .	. . .	. . .
Banks	4 623 . .	. . .	. . .	. . .	. . .	. . .	. . .	. . .	. . .
Other sectors	4 624 . .	. . .	. . .	. . .	. . .	. . .	. . .	. . .	. . .
Money market instruments	4 630 . .	. . .	. . .	. . .	. . .	. . .	. . .	. . .	. . .
Monetary authorities	4 631 . .	. . .	. . .	. . .	. . .	. . .	. . .	. . .	. . .
General government	4 632 . .	. . .	. . .	. . .	. . .	. . .	. . .	. . .	. . .
Banks	4 633 . .	. . .	. . .	. . .	. . .	. . .	. . .	. . .	. . .
Other sectors	4 634 . .	. . .	. . .	. . .	. . .	. . .	. . .	. . .	. . .
Liabilities	4 652 . .	**.23**	**.15**	**7.09**	**.44**	**–.13**	**.01**	**1.12**	**. . .**
Equity securities	4 660 . .	. . .	. . .	. . .	. . .	. . .	. . .	. . .	. . .
Banks	4 663 . .	. . .	. . .	. . .	. . .	. . .	. . .	. . .	. . .
Other sectors	4 664 . .	. . .	. . .	. . .	. . .	. . .	. . .	. . .	. . .
Debt securities	4 669 . .	. . .	. . .	. . .	. . .	. . .	. . .	. . .	. . .
Bonds and notes	4 670 . .	. . .	. . .	. . .	. . .	. . .	. . .	. . .	. . .
Monetary authorities	4 671 . .	. . .	. . .	. . .	. . .	. . .	. . .	. . .	. . .
General government	4 672 . .	. . .	. . .	. . .	. . .	. . .	. . .	. . .	. . .
Banks	4 673 . .	. . .	. . .	. . .	. . .	. . .	. . .	. . .	. . .
Other sectors	4 674 . .	. . .	. . .	. . .	. . .	. . .	. . .	. . .	. . .
Money market instruments	4 680 . .	. . .	. . .	. . .	. . .	. . .	. . .	. . .	. . .
Monetary authorities	4 681 . .	. . .	. . .	. . .	. . .	. . .	. . .	. . .	. . .
General government	4 682 . .	. . .	. . .	. . .	. . .	. . .	. . .	. . .	. . .
Banks	4 683 . .	. . .	. . .	. . .	. . .	. . .	. . .	. . .	. . .
Other sectors	4 684 . .	. . .	. . .	. . .	. . .	. . .	. . .	. . .	. . .
C. FINANCIAL DERIVATIVES	4 910 . .	. . .	. . .	. . .	. . .	. . .	. . .	. . .	. . .
Monetary authorities	4 911 . .	. . .	. . .	. . .	. . .	. . .	. . .	. . .	. . .
General government	4 912 . .	. . .	. . .	. . .	. . .	. . .	. . .	. . .	. . .
Banks	4 913 . .	. . .	. . .	. . .	. . .	. . .	. . .	. . .	. . .
Other sectors	4 914 . .	. . .	. . .	. . .	. . .	. . .	. . .	. . .	. . .
Assets	4 900 . .	**. . .**	**. . .**	**. . .**	**. . .**	**. . .**	**. . .**	**. . .**	**. . .**
Monetary authorities	4 901 . .	. . .	. . .	. . .	. . .	. . .	. . .	. . .	. . .
General government	4 902 . .	. . .	. . .	. . .	. . .	. . .	. . .	. . .	. . .
Banks	4 903 . .	. . .	. . .	. . .	. . .	. . .	. . .	. . .	. . .
Other sectors	4 904 . .	. . .	. . .	. . .	. . .	. . .	. . .	. . .	. . .
Liabilities	4 905 . .	**. . .**	**. . .**	**. . .**	**. . .**	**. . .**	**. . .**	**. . .**	**. . .**
Monetary authorities	4 906 . .	. . .	. . .	. . .	. . .	. . .	. . .	. . .	. . .
General government	4 907 . .	. . .	. . .	. . .	. . .	. . .	. . .	. . .	. . .
Banks	4 908 . .	. . .	. . .	. . .	. . .	. . .	. . .	. . .	. . .
Other sectors	4 909 . .	. . .	. . .	. . .	. . .	. . .	. . .	. . .	. . .

Table 2 (Concluded). STANDARD PRESENTATION, 1994–2001
(Millions of U.S. dollars)

	Code	1994	1995	1996	1997	1998	1999	2000	2001
D. OTHER INVESTMENT	4 700	8.16	1.58	5.23	23.24	6.29	37.03	–30.76	. . .
Assets	4 703	**–10.04**	**–3.70**	**–13.10**	**–36.39**	**–4.99**	**1.47**	**–10.74**	**. . .**
Trade credits	4 706	. . .	. . .	. . .	. . .	. . .	. . .	. . .	. . .
General government	4 707	. . .	. . .	. . .	. . .	. . .	. . .	. . .	. . .
of which: Short-term	4 709	. . .	. . .	. . .	. . .	. . .	. . .	. . .	. . .
Other sectors	4 710	. . .	. . .	. . .	. . .	. . .	. . .	. . .	. . .
of which: Short-term	4 712	. . .	. . .	. . .	. . .	. . .	. . .	. . .	. . .
Loans	4 714	. . .	. . .	. . .	. . .	. . .	. . .	. . .	. . .
Monetary authorities	4 715	. . .	. . .	. . .	. . .	. . .	. . .	. . .	. . .
of which: Short-term	4 718	. . .	. . .	. . .	. . .	. . .	. . .	. . .	. . .
General government	4 719	. . .	. . .	. . .	. . .	. . .	. . .	. . .	. . .
of which: Short-term	4 721	. . .	. . .	. . .	. . .	. . .	. . .	. . .	. . .
Banks	4 722	. . .	. . .	. . .	. . .	. . .	. . .	. . .	. . .
of which: Short-term	4 724	. . .	. . .	. . .	. . .	. . .	. . .	. . .	. . .
Other sectors	4 725	. . .	. . .	. . .	. . .	. . .	. . .	. . .	. . .
of which: Short-term	4 727	. . .	. . .	. . .	. . .	. . .	. . .	. . .	. . .
Currency and deposits	4 730	. . .	. . .	. . .	. . .	. . .	. . .	. . .	. . .
Monetary authorities	4 731	. . .	. . .	. . .	. . .	. . .	. . .	. . .	. . .
General government	4 732	. . .	. . .	. . .	. . .	. . .	. . .	. . .	. . .
Banks	4 733	. . .	. . .	. . .	. . .	. . .	. . .	. . .	. . .
Other sectors	4 734	. . .	. . .	. . .	. . .	. . .	. . .	. . .	. . .
Other assets	4 736	. . .	. . .	. . .	. . .	. . .	. . .	. . .	. . .
Monetary authorities	4 737	. . .	. . .	. . .	. . .	. . .	. . .	. . .	. . .
of which: Short-term	4 739	. . .	. . .	. . .	. . .	. . .	. . .	. . .	. . .
General government	4 740	. . .	. . .	. . .	. . .	. . .	. . .	. . .	. . .
of which: Short-term	4 742	. . .	. . .	. . .	. . .	. . .	. . .	. . .	. . .
Banks	4 743	. . .	. . .	. . .	. . .	. . .	. . .	. . .	. . .
of which: Short-term	4 745	. . .	. . .	. . .	. . .	. . .	. . .	. . .	. . .
Other sectors	4 746	. . .	. . .	. . .	. . .	. . .	. . .	. . .	. . .
of which: Short-term	4 748	. . .	. . .	. . .	. . .	. . .	. . .	. . .	. . .
Liabilities	4 753	**18.20**	**5.28**	**18.33**	**59.63**	**11.28**	**35.56**	**–20.02**	**. . .**
Trade credits	4 756	. . .	. . .	. . .	. . .	. . .	. . .	. . .	. . .
General government	4 757	. . .	. . .	. . .	. . .	. . .	. . .	. . .	. . .
of which: Short-term	4 759	. . .	. . .	. . .	. . .	. . .	. . .	. . .	. . .
Other sectors	4 760	. . .	. . .	. . .	. . .	. . .	. . .	. . .	. . .
of which: Short-term	4 762	. . .	. . .	. . .	. . .	. . .	. . .	. . .	. . .
Loans	4 764	. . .	. . .	. . .	. . .	2.28	. . .	. . .	. . .
Monetary authorities	4 765	. . .	. . .	. . .	. . .	2.28	. . .	. . .	. . .
of which: Use of Fund credit and loans from the Fund	4 766	. . .	. . .	. . .	. . .	*2.28*	. . .	. . .	. . .
of which: Short-term	4 768	. . .	. . .	. . .	. . .	. . .	. . .	. . .	. . .
General government	4 769	. . .	. . .	. . .	. . .	. . .	. . .	. . .	. . .
of which: Short-term	4 771	. . .	. . .	. . .	. . .	. . .	. . .	. . .	. . .
Banks	4 772	. . .	. . .	. . .	. . .	. . .	. . .	. . .	. . .
of which: Short-term	4 774	. . .	. . .	. . .	. . .	. . .	. . .	. . .	. . .
Other sectors	4 775	. . .	. . .	. . .	. . .	. . .	. . .	. . .	. . .
of which: Short-term	4 777	. . .	. . .	. . .	. . .	. . .	. . .	. . .	. . .
Currency and deposits	4 780	. . .	. . .	. . .	. . .	. . .	. . .	. . .	. . .
Monetary authorities	4 781	. . .	. . .	. . .	. . .	. . .	. . .	. . .	. . .
General government	4 782	. . .	. . .	. . .	. . .	. . .	. . .	. . .	. . .
Banks	4 783	. . .	. . .	. . .	. . .	. . .	. . .	. . .	. . .
Other sectors	4 784	. . .	. . .	. . .	. . .	. . .	. . .	. . .	. . .
Other liabilities	4 786	. . .	. . .	. . .	. . .	. . .	. . .	. . .	. . .
Monetary authorities	4 787	. . .	. . .	. . .	. . .	. . .	. . .	. . .	. . .
of which: Short-term	4 789	. . .	. . .	. . .	. . .	. . .	. . .	. . .	. . .
General government	4 790	. . .	. . .	. . .	. . .	. . .	. . .	. . .	. . .
of which: Short-term	4 792	. . .	. . .	. . .	. . .	. . .	. . .	. . .	. . .
Banks	4 793	. . .	. . .	. . .	. . .	. . .	. . .	. . .	. . .
of which: Short-term	4 795	. . .	. . .	. . .	. . .	. . .	. . .	. . .	. . .
Other sectors	4 796	. . .	. . .	. . .	. . .	. . .	. . .	. . .	. . .
of which: Short-term	4 798	. . .	. . .	. . .	. . .	. . .	. . .	. . .	. . .
E. RESERVE ASSETS	4 802	.61	–2.29	.89	–3.02	–13.27	–2.74	4.33	. . .
Monetary gold	4 812	. . .	. . .	. . .	. . .	. . .	. . .	. . .	. . .
Special drawing rights	4 811	. . .	. . .	. . .	. . .	. . .	. . .	. . .	. . .
Reserve position in the Fund	4 810	. . .	. . .	. . .	. . .	. . .	–.08	–.01	. . .
Foreign exchange	4 803	–2.32	–1.69	.74	–3.34	–10.73	–2.70	4.39	. . .
Other claims	4 813	2.93	–.59	.15	.32	–2.54	.04	–.04	. . .
NET ERRORS AND OMISSIONS	4 998	**–1.77**	**15.71**	**11.24**	**9.48**	**8.43**	**–14.90**	**–20.84**	**. . .**

Part 3 of the *Yearbook* contains descriptions of the methodologies, compilation practices, and sources used to compile these data.

Table 1. ANALYTIC PRESENTATION, 1994–2001
(Millions of U.S. dollars)

	Code	1994	1995	1996	1997	1998	1999	2000	2001
A. Current Account [1]	4 993 Z.	**–48.38**	**–33.09**	**–54.40**	**–78.39**	**–65.97**	**–79.21**	**–82.41**	**. . .**
Goods: exports f.o.b.	2 100 . .	99.92	114.65	86.33	70.25	70.37	60.93	54.76	. . .
Goods: imports f.o.b.	3 100 . .	–265.62	–269.38	–267.40	–292.37	–295.06	–312.01	–307.99	. . .
Balance on Goods	4 100 . .	*–165.70*	*–154.73*	*–181.08*	*–222.12*	*–224.69*	*–251.08*	*–253.23*	. . .
Services: credit	2 200 . .	237.69	265.03	266.79	288.42	313.81	321.07	308.52	. . .
Services: debit	3 200 . .	–104.16	–123.55	–119.53	–119.01	–129.27	–133.14	–118.25	. . .
Balance on Goods and Services	4 991 . .	*–32.18*	*–13.24*	*–33.81*	*–52.71*	*–40.14*	*–63.15*	*–62.96*	. . .
Income: credit	2 300 . .	4.97	5.75	3.36	3.29	3.39	2.38	3.90	. . .
Income: debit	3 300 . .	–38.33	–44.53	–37.13	–41.95	–48.71	–40.45	–41.38	. . .
Balance on Goods, Services, and Income	4 992 . .	*–65.54*	*–52.02*	*–67.58*	*–91.37*	*–85.47*	*–101.22*	*–100.44*	. . .
Current transfers: credit	2 379 Z.	25.46	28.42	28.53	24.60	29.56	31.64	29.40	. . .
Current transfers: debit	3 379 . .	–8.30	–9.50	–15.35	–11.61	–10.06	–9.63	–11.38	. . .
B. Capital Account [1]	4 994 Z.	**10.71**	**13.21**	**10.40**	**9.66**	**22.54**	**26.06**	**17.79**	**. . .**
Capital account: credit	2 994 Z.	11.83	13.58	11.14	10.42	23.31	26.80	20.12	. . .
Capital account: debit	3 994 . .	–1.12	–.37	–.74	–.76	–.78	–.74	–2.33	. . .
Total, Groups A Plus B	4 981 . .	*–37.67*	*–19.88*	*–44.01*	*–68.73*	*–43.43*	*–53.15*	*–64.63*	. . .
C. Financial Account [1]	4 995 W.	**41.71**	**27.62**	**41.43**	**86.62**	**55.76**	**57.36**	**66.07**	**. . .**
Direct investment abroad	4 505 . .	. . .	. . .	. . .	. . .	. . .	. . .	. . .	. . .
Direct investment in St. Lucia	4 555 Z.	32.52	32.75	18.41	49.90	83.40	83.06	48.94	. . .
Portfolio investment assets	4 602 . .	–.47	–.47	–.06	–.06	–.11	. . .	–.64	. . .
Equity securities	4 610 . .	. . .	. . .	. . .	. . .	. . .	. . .	. . .	. . .
Debt securities	4 619 . .	. . .	. . .	. . .	. . .	. . .	. . .	. . .	. . .
Portfolio investment liabilities	4 652 Z.	.77	.71	1.73	2.99	3.44	–2.90	5.51	. . .
Equity securities	4 660 . .	. . .	. . .	. . .	. . .	. . .	. . .	. . .	. . .
Debt securities	4 669 Z.	. . .	. . .	. . .	. . .	. . .	. . .	. . .	. . .
Financial derivatives	4 910 . .	. . .	. . .	. . .	. . .	. . .	. . .	. . .	. . .
Financial derivatives assets	4 900 . .	. . .	. . .	. . .	. . .	. . .	. . .	. . .	. . .
Financial derivatives liabilities	4 905 . .	. . .	. . .	. . .	. . .	. . .	. . .	. . .	. . .
Other investment assets	4 703 . .	1.47	–15.34	–9.31	1.00	–31.96	–20.54	–15.00	. . .
Monetary authorities	4 701 . .	. . .	. . .	. . .	. . .	. . .	. . .	. . .	. . .
General government	4 704 . .	. . .	. . .	. . .	. . .	. . .	. . .	. . .	. . .
Banks	4 705 . .	. . .	. . .	. . .	. . .	. . .	. . .	. . .	. . .
Other sectors	4 728 . .	. . .	. . .	. . .	. . .	. . .	. . .	. . .	. . .
Other investment liabilities	4 753 W.	7.41	9.97	30.66	32.80	.99	–2.26	27.26	. . .
Monetary authorities	4 753 WA	. . .	. . .	. . .	. . .	. . .	. . .	. . .	. . .
General government	4 753 ZB	. . .	. . .	. . .	. . .	. . .	. . .	. . .	. . .
Banks	4 753 ZC	. . .	. . .	. . .	. . .	. . .	. . .	. . .	. . .
Other sectors	4 753 ZD	. . .	. . .	. . .	. . .	. . .	. . .	. . .	. . .
Total, Groups A Through C	4 983 . .	*4.04*	*7.74*	*–2.58*	*17.90*	*12.33*	*4.21*	*1.44*	. . .
D. Net Errors and Omissions	4 998 . .	**–7.49**	**–2.01**	**–3.71**	**–12.93**	**2.78**	**3.58**	**6.70**	**. . .**
Total, Groups A Through D	4 984 . .	*–3.45*	*5.72*	*–6.29*	*4.97*	*15.11*	*7.79*	*8.14*	. . .
E. Reserves and Related Items	4 802 A.	**3.45**	**–5.72**	**6.29**	**–4.97**	**–15.11**	**–7.79**	**–8.14**	**. . .**
Reserve assets	4 802 . .	3.45	–5.72	6.29	–4.97	–15.11	–7.79	–8.14	. . .
Use of Fund credit and loans	4 766 . .	. . .	. . .	. . .	. . .	. . .	. . .	. . .	. . .
Exceptional financing	4 920 . .	. . .	. . .	. . .	. . .	. . .	. . .	. . .	. . .
Conversion rates: Eastern Caribbean dollars per U.S. dollar	0 101 . .	**2.7000**	**2.7000**	**2.7000**	**2.7000**	**2.7000**	**2.7000**	**2.7000**	**2.7000**

[1] Excludes components that have been classified in the categories of Group E.

Table 2. STANDARD PRESENTATION, 1994–2001

(Millions of U.S. dollars)

	Code		1994	1995	1996	1997	1998	1999	2000	2001
CURRENT ACCOUNT	4 993	. .	**–48.38**	**–33.09**	**–54.40**	**–78.39**	**–65.97**	**–79.21**	**–82.41**	**. . .**
A. GOODS	4 100	. .	–165.70	–154.73	–181.08	–222.12	–224.69	–251.08	–253.23	. . .
Credit	2 100	. .	**99.92**	**114.65**	**86.33**	**70.25**	**70.37**	**60.93**	**54.76**	**. . .**
General merchandise: exports f.o.b.	2 110	. .	94.85	108.97	79.50	61.26	62.19	55.68	45.16	. . .
Goods for processing: exports f.o.b.	2 150	. .	. . .	. . .	. . .	. . .	. . .	. . .	. . .	. . .
Repairs on goods	2 160	. .	.02	.01	.01	.03	.01	. . .	.01	. . .
Goods procured in ports by carriers	2 170	. .	5.05	5.67	6.82	8.96	8.17	5.24	9.59	. . .
Nonmonetary gold	2 180	. .	. . .	. . .	. . .	. . .	. . .	. . .	. . .	. . .
Debit	3 100	. .	**–265.62**	**–269.38**	**–267.40**	**–292.37**	**–295.06**	**–312.01**	**–307.99**	**. . .**
General merchandise: imports f.o.b.	3 110	. .	–265.56	–269.31	–267.34	–292.31	–294.99	–312.01	–307.99	. . .
Goods for processing: imports f.o.b.	3 150	. .	. . .	. . .	. . .	. . .	. . .	. . .	. . .	. . .
Repairs on goods	3 160	. .	. . .	. . .	. . .	. . .	. . .	. . .	. . .	. . .
Goods procured in ports by carriers	3 170	. .	–.06	–.07	–.06	–.06	–.06	. . .	. . .	. . .
Nonmonetary gold	3 180	. .	. . .	. . .	. . .	. . .	. . .	. . .	. . .	. . .
B. SERVICES	4 200	. .	133.53	141.49	147.26	169.41	184.54	187.93	190.27	. . .
Total credit	2 200	. .	*237.69*	*265.03*	*266.79*	*288.42*	*313.81*	*321.07*	*308.52*	. . .
Total debit	3 200	. .	*–104.16*	*–123.55*	*–119.53*	*–119.01*	*–129.27*	*–133.14*	*–118.25*	. . .
Transportation services, credit	2 205	. .	**14.41**	**14.15**	**12.02**	**13.56**	**17.22**	**10.97**	**10.33**	**. . .**
Passenger	2 850	. .	. . .	. . .	. . .	. . .	. . .	. . .	. . .	. . .
Freight	2 851	. .	. . .	. . .	. . .	. . .	. . .	. . .	. . .	. . .
Other	2 852	. .	. . .	. . .	. . .	. . .	. . .	. . .	. . .	. . .
Sea transport, passenger	2 207	. .	. . .	. . .	. . .	. . .	. . .	. . .	. . .	. . .
Sea transport, freight	2 208	. .	. . .	. . .	. . .	. . .	. . .	. . .	. . .	. . .
Sea transport, other	2 209	. .	. . .	. . .	. . .	. . .	. . .	. . .	. . .	. . .
Air transport, passenger	2 211	. .	. . .	. . .	. . .	. . .	. . .	. . .	. . .	. . .
Air transport, freight	2 212	. .	. . .	. . .	. . .	. . .	. . .	. . .	. . .	. . .
Air transport, other	2 213	. .	. . .	. . .	. . .	. . .	. . .	. . .	. . .	. . .
Other transport, passenger	2 215	. .	. . .	. . .	. . .	. . .	. . .	. . .	. . .	. . .
Other transport, freight	2 216	. .	. . .	. . .	. . .	. . .	. . .	. . .	. . .	. . .
Other transport, other	2 217	. .	. . .	. . .	. . .	. . .	. . .	. . .	. . .	. . .
Transportation services, debit	3 205	. .	**–41.19**	**–42.31**	**–41.90**	**–44.16**	**–41.83**	**–44.77**	**–44.40**	**. . .**
Passenger	3 850	. .	. . .	. . .	. . .	. . .	. . .	. . .	. . .	. . .
Freight	3 851	. .	. . .	. . .	. . .	. . .	. . .	. . .	. . .	. . .
Other	3 852	. .	. . .	. . .	. . .	. . .	. . .	. . .	. . .	. . .
Sea transport, passenger	3 207	. .	. . .	. . .	. . .	. . .	. . .	. . .	. . .	. . .
Sea transport, freight	3 208	. .	. . .	. . .	. . .	. . .	. . .	. . .	. . .	. . .
Sea transport, other	3 209	. .	. . .	. . .	. . .	. . .	. . .	. . .	. . .	. . .
Air transport, passenger	3 211	. .	. . .	. . .	. . .	. . .	. . .	. . .	. . .	. . .
Air transport, freight	3 212	. .	. . .	. . .	. . .	. . .	. . .	. . .	. . .	. . .
Air transport, other	3 213	. .	. . .	. . .	. . .	. . .	. . .	. . .	. . .	. . .
Other transport, passenger	3 215	. .	. . .	. . .	. . .	. . .	. . .	. . .	. . .	. . .
Other transport, freight	3 216	. .	. . .	. . .	. . .	. . .	. . .	. . .	. . .	. . .
Other transport, other	3 217	. .	. . .	. . .	. . .	. . .	. . .	. . .	. . .	. . .
Travel, credit	2 236	. .	**207.15**	**229.50**	**236.58**	**253.30**	**277.64**	**278.56**	**276.67**	**. . .**
Business travel	2 237	. .	. . .	. . .	. . .	. . .	. . .	. . .	. . .	. . .
Personal travel	2 240	. .	. . .	. . .	. . .	. . .	. . .	. . .	. . .	. . .
Travel, debit	3 236	. .	**–22.51**	**–25.26**	**–28.78**	**–29.49**	**–31.19**	**–32.97**	**–33.30**	**. . .**
Business travel	3 237	. .	. . .	. . .	. . .	. . .	. . .	. . .	. . .	. . .
Personal travel	3 240	. .	. . .	. . .	. . .	. . .	. . .	. . .	. . .	. . .
Other services, credit	2 200	BA	**16.12**	**21.38**	**18.19**	**21.56**	**18.95**	**31.54**	**21.52**	**. . .**
Communications	2 245	. .	. . .	. . .	. . .	. . .	. . .	. . .	. . .	. . .
Construction	2 249	. .	. . .	. . .	. . .	. . .	. . .	. . .	. . .	. . .
Insurance	2 253	. .	2.80	3.30	3.69	3.51	3.15	3.18	4.09	. . .
Financial	2 260	. .	. . .	. . .	. . .	. . .	. . .	. . .	. . .	. . .
Computer and information	2 262	. .	. . .	. . .	. . .	. . .	. . .	. . .	. . .	. . .
Royalties and licence fees	2 266	. .	. . .	. . .	. . .	. . .	. . .	. . .	. . .	. . .
Other business services	2 268	. .	12.27	17.11	13.44	16.84	14.51	26.99	16.07	. . .
Personal, cultural, and recreational	2 287	. .	. . .	. . .	. . .	. . .	. . .	. . .	. . .	. . .
Government, n.i.e.	2 291	. .	1.05	.97	1.07	1.20	1.29	1.36	1.37	. . .
Other services, debit	3 200	BA	**–40.46**	**–55.98**	**–48.86**	**–45.36**	**–56.26**	**–55.41**	**–40.54**	**. . .**
Communications	3 245	. .	. . .	. . .	. . .	. . .	. . .	. . .	. . .	. . .
Construction	3 249	. .	–4.60	–.74	. . .	. . .	–.06	. . .	. . .	. . .
Insurance	3 253	. .	–7.19	–7.39	–7.47	–8.03	–7.83	–8.23	–8.52	. . .
Financial	3 260	. .	. . .	. . .	. . .	. . .	. . .	. . .	. . .	. . .
Computer and information	3 262	. .	. . .	. . .	. . .	. . .	. . .	. . .	. . .	. . .
Royalties and licence fees	3 266	. .	–1.22	–1.56	–1.46	–1.37	–1.96	–1.57	–1.57	. . .
Other business services	3 268	. .	–21.60	–40.47	–33.14	–30.90	–37.89	–40.81	–23.83	. . .
Personal, cultural, and recreational	3 287	. .	. . .	. . .	. . .	. . .	. . .	. . .	. . .	. . .
Government, n.i.e.	3 291	. .	–5.86	–5.82	–6.79	–5.06	–8.52	–4.80	–6.63	. . .

Table 2 (Continued). STANDARD PRESENTATION, 1994–2001
(Millions of U.S. dollars)

	Code	1994	1995	1996	1997	1998	1999	2000	2001
C. INCOME	4 300 . .	–33.36	–38.77	–33.77	–38.66	–45.32	–38.07	–37.48	. . .
Total credit	2 300 . .	*4.97*	*5.75*	*3.36*	*3.29*	*3.39*	*2.38*	*3.90*	. . .
Total debit	3 300 . .	*–38.33*	*–44.53*	*–37.13*	*–41.95*	*–48.71*	*–40.45*	*–41.38*	. . .
Compensation of employees, credit	2 310 . .	**.37**	**.24**	**.16**	**.16**	**.16**	**.20**	**.26**	. . .
Compensation of employees, debit	3 310 . .	. . .	. . .	. . .	. . .	. . .	. . .	. . .	. . .
Investment income, credit	2 320 . .	**4.60**	**5.51**	**3.20**	**3.13**	**3.23**	**2.18**	**3.64**	. . .
Direct investment income	2 330 . .	. . .	.02	. . .	. . .	. . .	. . .	. . .	. . .
Dividends and distributed branch profits	2 332 . .	. . .	. . .	. . .	. . .	. . .	. . .	. . .	. . .
Reinvested earnings and undistributed branch profits	2 333 . .	. . .	. . .	. . .	. . .	. . .	. . .	. . .	. . .
Income on debt (interest)	2 334 . .	. . .	.02	. . .	. . .	. . .	. . .	. . .	. . .
Portfolio investment income	2 339 . .	1.31	2.39	1.81	1.68	1.74	.96	1.29	. . .
Income on equity	2 340 . .	1.31	2.39	1.81	1.68	1.74	.96	1.29	. . .
Income on bonds and notes	2 350 . .	. . .	. . .	. . .	. . .	. . .	. . .	. . .	. . .
Income on money market instruments	2 360 . .	. . .	. . .	. . .	. . .	. . .	. . .	. . .	. . .
Other investment income	2 370 . .	3.29	3.10	1.40	1.46	1.49	1.23	2.35	. . .
Investment income, debit	3 320 . .	**–38.33**	**–44.53**	**–37.13**	**–41.95**	**–48.71**	**–40.45**	**–41.38**	. . .
Direct investment income	3 330 . .	–29.35	–35.31	–26.65	–28.48	–31.91	–27.08	–26.63	. . .
Dividends and distributed branch profits	3 332 . .	–12.24	–7.91	–8.84	–11.73	–13.54	–15.14	–15.39	. . .
Reinvested earnings and undistributed branch profits	3 333 . .	–16.01	–25.07	–15.61	–14.73	–16.10	–11.89	–11.18	. . .
Income on debt (interest)	3 334 . .	–1.10	–2.33	–2.21	–2.01	–2.27	–.06	–.06	. . .
Portfolio investment income	3 339 . .	. . .	. . .	. . .	. . .	. . .	. . .	. . .	. . .
Income on equity	3 340 . .	. . .	. . .	. . .	. . .	. . .	. . .	. . .	. . .
Income on bonds and notes	3 350 . .	. . .	. . .	. . .	. . .	. . .	. . .	. . .	. . .
Income on money market instruments	3 360 . .	. . .	. . .	. . .	. . .	. . .	. . .	. . .	. . .
Other investment income	3 370 . .	–8.98	–9.22	–10.47	–13.47	–16.80	–13.37	–14.76	. . .
D. CURRENT TRANSFERS	4 379 . .	17.16	18.93	13.18	12.98	19.50	22.01	18.02	. . .
Credit	2 379 . .	**25.46**	**28.42**	**28.53**	**24.60**	**29.56**	**31.64**	**29.40**	. . .
General government	2 380 . .	1.85	1.83	3.30	1.60	6.07	7.89	4.70	. . .
Other sectors	2 390 . .	23.61	26.59	25.23	22.99	23.50	23.76	24.70	. . .
Workers' remittances	2 391 . .	. . .	. . .	. . .	. . .	. . .	. . .	. . .	. . .
Other current transfers	2 392 . .	. . .	. . .	. . .	. . .	. . .	. . .	. . .	. . .
Debit	3 379 . .	**–8.30**	**–9.50**	**–15.35**	**–11.61**	**–10.06**	**–9.63**	**–11.38**	. . .
General government	3 380 . .	–1.58	–1.60	–1.72	–1.82	–1.76	–1.81	–1.74	. . .
Other sectors	3 390 . .	–6.72	–7.90	–13.63	–9.80	–8.30	–7.82	–9.63	. . .
Workers' remittances	3 391 . .	. . .	. . .	. . .	. . .	. . .	. . .	. . .	. . .
Other current transfers	3 392 . .	. . .	. . .	. . .	. . .	. . .	. . .	. . .	. . .
CAPITAL AND FINANCIAL ACCOUNT	4 996 . .	**55.87**	**35.10**	**58.11**	**91.32**	**63.18**	**75.62**	**75.71**	. . .
CAPITAL ACCOUNT	4 994 . .	**10.71**	**13.21**	**10.40**	**9.66**	**22.54**	**26.06**	**17.79**	. . .
Total credit	2 994 . .	*11.83*	*13.58*	*11.14*	*10.42*	*23.31*	*26.80*	*20.12*	. . .
Total debit	3 994 . .	*–1.12*	*–.37*	*–.74*	*–.76*	*–.78*	*–.74*	*–2.33*	. . .
Capital transfers, credit	2 400 . .	**8.54**	**8.49**	**11.14**	**10.42**	**23.31**	**26.80**	**20.12**	. . .
General government	2 401 . .	6.69	6.64	8.91	8.12	20.96	24.20	17.53	. . .
Debt forgiveness	2 402 . .	. . .	. . .	. . .	. . .	. . .	. . .	. . .	. . .
Other capital transfers	2 410 . .	6.69	6.64	8.91	8.12	20.96	24.20	17.53	. . .
Other sectors	2 430 . .	1.86	1.85	2.22	2.30	2.36	2.59	2.59	. . .
Migrants' transfers	2 431 . .	1.86	1.85	2.22	2.30	2.36	2.59	2.59	. . .
Debt forgiveness	2 432 . .	. . .	. . .	. . .	. . .	. . .	. . .	. . .	. . .
Other capital transfers	2 440 . .	. . .	. . .	. . .	. . .	. . .	. . .	. . .	. . .
Capital transfers, debit	3 400 . .	**–.38**	**–.37**	**–.74**	**–.76**	**–.78**	**–.74**	**–.74**	. . .
General government	3 401 . .	. . .	. . .	. . .	. . .	. . .	. . .	. . .	. . .
Debt forgiveness	3 402 . .	. . .	. . .	. . .	. . .	. . .	. . .	. . .	. . .
Other capital transfers	3 410 . .	. . .	. . .	. . .	. . .	. . .	. . .	. . .	. . .
Other sectors	3 430 . .	–.38	–.37	–.74	–.76	–.78	–.74	–.74	. . .
Migrants' transfers	3 431 . .	–.38	–.37	–.74	–.76	–.78	–.74	–.74	. . .
Debt forgiveness	3 432 . .	. . .	. . .	. . .	. . .	. . .	. . .	. . .	. . .
Other capital transfers	3 440 . .	. . .	. . .	. . .	. . .	. . .	. . .	. . .	. . .
Nonproduced nonfinancial assets, credit	2 480 . .	**3.29**	**5.10**	. . .	. . .	. . .	. . .	. . .	. . .
Nonproduced nonfinancial assets, debit	3 480 . .	**–.74**	. . .	. . .	. . .	. . .	. . .	**–1.59**	. . .

Table 2 (Continued). STANDARD PRESENTATION, 1994–2001
(Millions of U.S. dollars)

	Code	1994	1995	1996	1997	1998	1999	2000	2001
FINANCIAL ACCOUNT	4 995	**45.16**	**21.89**	**47.72**	**81.66**	**40.65**	**49.57**	**57.93**	...
A. DIRECT INVESTMENT	4 500	32.52	32.75	18.41	49.90	83.40	83.06	48.94	...
Direct investment abroad	4 505	...	...	...	...	...	...	...	...
Equity capital	4 510	...	...	...	...	...	...	...	...
Claims on affiliated enterprises	4 515	...	...	...	...	...	...	...	...
Liabilities to affiliated enterprises	4 520	...	...	...	...	...	...	...	...
Reinvested earnings	4 525	...	...	...	...	...	...	...	...
Other capital	4 530	...	...	...	...	...	...	...	...
Claims on affiliated enterprises	4 535	...	...	...	...	...	...	...	...
Liabilities to affiliated enterprises	4 540	...	...	...	...	...	...	...	...
Direct investment in St. Lucia	4 555	**32.52**	**32.75**	**18.41**	**49.90**	**83.40**	**83.06**	**48.94**	...
Equity capital	4 560	6.19	6.58	4.14	4.01	3.17	72.72	30.45	...
Claims on direct investors	4 565	...	...	...	...	...	...	...	...
Liabilities to direct investors	4 570	6.19	6.58	4.14	4.01	3.17	72.72	30.45	...
Reinvested earnings	4 575	16.01	25.07	15.61	14.73	16.10	11.89	11.18	...
Other capital	4 580	10.32	1.10	–1.33	31.16	64.12	–1.54	7.32	...
Claims on direct investors	4 585	...	...	...	...	...	...	...	...
Liabilities to direct investors	4 590	10.32	1.10	–1.33	31.16	64.12	–1.54	7.32	...
B. PORTFOLIO INVESTMENT	4 600	.30	.24	1.67	2.93	3.32	–2.90	4.87	...
Assets	4 602	**–.47**	**–.47**	**–.06**	**–.06**	**–.11**	...	**–.64**	...
Equity securities	4 610	...	...	...	...	...	...	...	...
Monetary authorities	4 611	...	...	...	...	...	...	...	...
General government	4 612	...	...	...	...	...	...	...	...
Banks	4 613	...	...	...	...	...	...	...	...
Other sectors	4 614	...	...	...	...	...	...	...	...
Debt securities	4 619	...	...	...	...	...	...	...	...
Bonds and notes	4 620	...	...	...	...	...	...	...	...
Debt securities	4 619	...	...	...	...	...	...	...	...
Bonds and notes	4 620	...	...	...	...	...	...	...	...
Banks	4 623	...	...	...	...	...	...	...	...
Other sectors	4 624	...	...	...	...	...	...	...	...
Money market instruments	4 630	...	...	...	...	...	...	...	...
Monetary authorities	4 631	...	...	...	...	...	...	...	...
General government	4 632	...	...	...	...	...	...	...	...
Banks	4 633	...	...	...	...	...	...	...	...
Other sectors	4 634	...	...	...	...	...	...	...	...
Liabilities	4 652	**.77**	**.71**	**1.73**	**2.99**	**3.44**	**–2.90**	**5.51**	...
Equity securities	4 660	...	...	...	...	...	...	...	...
Banks	4 663	...	...	...	...	...	...	...	...
Other sectors	4 664	...	...	...	...	...	...	...	...
Debt securities	4 669	...	...	...	...	...	...	...	...
Bonds and notes	4 670	...	...	...	...	...	...	...	...
Monetary authorities	4 671	...	...	...	...	...	...	...	...
General government	4 672	...	...	...	...	...	...	...	...
Banks	4 673	...	...	...	...	...	...	...	...
Other sectors	4 674	...	...	...	...	...	...	...	...
Money market instruments	4 680	...	...	...	...	...	...	...	...
Monetary authorities	4 681	...	...	...	...	...	...	...	...
General government	4 682	...	...	...	...	...	...	...	...
Banks	4 683	...	...	...	...	...	...	...	...
Other sectors	4 684	...	...	...	...	...	...	...	...
C. FINANCIAL DERIVATIVES	4 910	...	...	...	...	...	...	...	...
Monetary authorities	4 911	...	...	...	...	...	...	...	...
General government	4 912	...	...	...	...	...	...	...	...
Banks	4 913	...	...	...	...	...	...	...	...
Other sectors	4 914	...	...	...	...	...	...	...	...
Assets	4 900	...	...	...	...	...	...	...	...
Monetary authorities	4 901	...	...	...	...	...	...	...	...
General government	4 902	...	...	...	...	...	...	...	...
Banks	4 903	...	...	...	...	...	...	...	...
Other sectors	4 904	...	...	...	...	...	...	...	...
Liabilities	4 905	...	...	...	...	...	...	...	...
Monetary authorities	4 906	...	...	...	...	...	...	...	...
General government	4 907	...	...	...	...	...	...	...	...
Banks	4 908	...	...	...	...	...	...	...	...
Other sectors	4 909	...	...	...	...	...	...	...	...

Table 2 (Concluded). STANDARD PRESENTATION, 1994–2001
(Millions of U.S. dollars)

	Code	1994	1995	1996	1997	1998	1999	2000	2001
D. OTHER INVESTMENT	4 700	8.88	–5.37	21.35	33.80	–30.97	–22.80	12.26	...
Assets	4 703	**1.47**	**–15.34**	**–9.31**	**1.00**	**–31.96**	**–20.54**	**–15.00**	...
Trade credits	4 706	...	...	...	...	...	...	...	...
General government	4 707	...	...	...	...	...	...	...	...
of which: Short-term	4 709	...	...	...	...	...	...	...	...
Other sectors	4 710	...	...	...	...	...	...	...	...
of which: Short-term	4 712	...	...	...	...	...	...	...	...
Loans	4 714	...	...	...	...	...	...	...	...
Monetary authorities	4 715	...	...	...	...	...	...	...	...
of which: Short-term	4 718	...	...	...	...	...	...	...	...
General government	4 719	...	...	...	...	...	...	...	...
of which: Short-term	4 721	...	...	...	...	...	...	...	...
Banks	4 722	...	...	...	...	...	...	...	...
of which: Short-term	4 724	...	...	...	...	...	...	...	...
Other sectors	4 725	...	...	...	...	...	...	...	...
of which: Short-term	4 727	...	...	...	...	...	...	...	...
Currency and deposits	4 730	...	...	...	...	...	...	...	...
Monetary authorities	4 731	...	...	...	...	...	...	...	...
General government	4 732	...	...	...	...	...	...	...	...
Banks	4 733	...	...	...	...	...	...	...	...
Other sectors	4 734	...	...	...	...	...	...	...	...
Other assets	4 736	...	...	...	...	...	...	...	...
Monetary authorities	4 737	...	...	...	...	...	...	...	...
of which: Short-term	4 739	...	...	...	...	...	...	...	...
General government	4 740	...	...	...	...	...	...	...	...
of which: Short-term	4 742	...	...	...	...	...	...	...	...
Banks	4 743	...	...	...	...	...	...	...	...
of which: Short-term	4 745	...	...	...	...	...	...	...	...
Other sectors	4 746	...	...	...	...	...	...	...	...
of which: Short-term	4 748	...	...	...	...	...	...	...	...
Liabilities	4 753	**7.41**	**9.97**	**30.66**	**32.80**	**.99**	**–2.26**	**27.26**	...
Trade credits	4 756	...	...	...	...	...	...	...	...
General government	4 757	...	...	...	...	...	...	...	...
of which: Short-term	4 759	...	...	...	...	...	...	...	...
Other sectors	4 760	...	...	...	...	...	...	...	...
of which: Short-term	4 762	...	...	...	...	...	...	...	...
Loans	4 764	...	...	...	...	...	...	...	...
Monetary authorities	4 765	...	...	...	...	...	...	...	...
of which: Use of Fund credit and loans from the Fund	4 766	...	...	...	...	...	...	...	...
of which: Short-term	4 768	...	...	...	...	...	...	...	...
General government	4 769	...	...	...	...	...	...	...	...
of which: Short-term	4 771	...	...	...	...	...	...	...	...
Banks	4 772	...	...	...	...	...	...	...	...
of which: Short-term	4 774	...	...	...	...	...	...	...	...
Other sectors	4 775	...	...	...	...	...	...	...	...
of which: Short-term	4 777	...	...	...	...	...	...	...	...
Currency and deposits	4 780	...	...	...	...	...	...	...	...
Monetary authorities	4 781	...	...	...	...	...	...	...	...
General government	4 782	...	...	...	...	...	...	...	...
Banks	4 783	...	...	...	...	...	...	...	...
Other sectors	4 784	...	...	...	...	...	...	...	...
Other liabilities	4 786	...	...	...	...	...	...	...	...
Monetary authorities	4 787	...	...	...	...	...	...	...	...
of which: Short-term	4 789	...	...	...	...	...	...	...	...
General government	4 790	...	...	...	...	...	...	...	...
of which: Short-term	4 792	...	...	...	...	...	...	...	...
Banks	4 793	...	...	...	...	...	...	...	...
of which: Short-term	4 795	...	...	...	...	...	...	...	...
Other sectors	4 796	...	...	...	...	...	...	...	...
of which: Short-term	4 798	...	...	...	...	...	...	...	...
E. RESERVE ASSETS	4 802	3.45	–5.72	6.29	–4.97	–15.11	–7.79	–8.14	...
Monetary gold	4 812	...	...	...	...	...	...	...	...
Special drawing rights	4 811	–.03	–.04	–.04	–.04	–.04	–.04	.09	...
Reserve position in the Fund	4 810	...	...	...	...	...	...	...	...
Foreign exchange	4 803	3.49	–5.68	6.33	–4.93	–9.51	–3.93	–4.51	...
Other claims	4 813	...	...	...	...	–5.56	–3.83	–3.72	...
NET ERRORS AND OMISSIONS	4 998	**–7.49**	**–2.01**	**–3.71**	**–12.93**	**2.78**	**3.58**	**6.70**	...

Part 3 of the *Yearbook* contains descriptions of the methodologies, compilation practices, and sources used to compile these data.

Table 1. ANALYTIC PRESENTATION, 1994–2001

(Millions of U.S. dollars)

	Code	1994	1995	1996	1997	1998	1999	2000	2001
A. Current Account [1]	4 993 Z.	**–57.43**	**–40.68**	**–35.74**	**–84.12**	**–94.22**	**–72.34**	**–26.28**	**. . .**
Goods: exports f.o.b	2 100 . .	48.86	61.94	52.56	47.33	50.24	49.61	51.75	. . .
Goods: imports f.o.b	3 100 . .	–115.43	–119.37	–128.07	–152.61	–169.96	–177.05	–142.92	. . .
Balance on Goods	4 100 . .	*–66.57*	*–57.43*	*–75.51*	*–105.29*	*–119.71*	*–127.44*	*–91.17*	. . .
Services: credit	2 200 . .	63.40	74.37	96.68	99.41	107.19	125.76	126.23	. . .
Services: debit	3 200 . .	–54.64	–55.14	–58.22	–76.33	–79.05	–66.47	–59.83	. . .
Balance on Goods and Services	4 991 . .	*–57.81*	*–38.20*	*–37.06*	*–82.21*	*–91.57*	*–68.15*	*–24.77*	. . .
Income: credit	2 300 . .	3.46	4.01	4.02	2.67	3.04	3.16	3.14	. . .
Income: debit	3 300 . .	–15.27	–15.67	–13.15	–15.34	–16.66	–22.78	–23.43	. . .
Balance on Goods, Services, and Income	4 992 . .	*–69.63*	*–49.86*	*–46.18*	*–94.89*	*–105.19*	*–87.77*	*–45.05*	. . .
Current transfers: credit	2 379 Z.	19.42	16.81	19.72	20.83	21.60	23.39	25.43	. . .
Current transfers: debit	3 379 . .	–7.23	–7.63	–9.28	–10.06	–10.63	–7.96	–6.67	. . .
B. Capital Account [1]	4 994 Z.	**4.01**	**5.87**	**3.83**	**5.89**	**13.33**	**7.82**	**12.07**	**. . .**
Capital account: credit	2 994 Z.	5.37	6.92	4.94	7.00	14.60	9.12	13.40	. . .
Capital account: debit	3 994 . .	–1.36	–1.05	–1.11	–1.12	–1.27	–1.30	–1.33	. . .
Total, Groups A Plus B	4 981 . .	*–53.42*	*–34.81*	*–31.91*	*–78.24*	*–80.89*	*–64.53*	*–14.21*	. . .
C. Financial Account [1]	4 995 W.	**39.90**	**35.11**	**35.94**	**81.75**	**91.23**	**55.46**	**14.33**	**. . .**
Direct investment abroad	4 505 . .	. . .	. . .	. . .	. . .	. . .	. . .	. . .	. . .
Direct investment in St. Vincent and the Grenadines	4 555 Z.	46.91	30.64	42.64	92.47	88.95	56.09	28.17	. . .
Portfolio investment assets	4 602 . .	.24	. . .	–.37	.08	–.37	–.22	–.52	. . .
Equity securities	4 610 . .	. . .	. . .	. . .	. . .	. . .	. . .	. . .	. . .
Debt securities	4 619 . .	. . .	. . .	. . .	. . .	. . .	. . .	. . .	. . .
Portfolio investment liabilities	4 652 Z.	.06	. . .	–2.37	1.61	.26	.11	1.96	. . .
Equity securities	4 660 . .	. . .	. . .	. . .	. . .	. . .	. . .	. . .	. . .
Debt securities	4 669 Z.	. . .	. . .	. . .	. . .	. . .	. . .	. . .	. . .
Financial derivatives	4 910 . .	. . .	. . .	. . .	. . .	. . .	. . .	. . .	. . .
Financial derivatives assets	4 900 . .	. . .	. . .	. . .	. . .	. . .	. . .	. . .	. . .
Financial derivatives liabilities	4 905 . .	. . .	. . .	. . .	. . .	. . .	. . .	. . .	. . .
Other investment assets	4 703 . .	–8.92	2.06	–2.33	–5.78	–8.54	–44.83	–8.84	. . .
Monetary authorities	4 701 . .	. . .	. . .	. . .	. . .	. . .	. . .	. . .	. . .
General government	4 704 . .	. . .	. . .	. . .	. . .	. . .	. . .	. . .	. . .
Banks	4 705 . .	. . .	. . .	. . .	. . .	. . .	. . .	. . .	. . .
Other sectors	4 728 . .	. . .	. . .	. . .	. . .	. . .	. . .	. . .	. . .
Other investment liabilities	4 753 W.	1.60	2.41	–1.63	–6.63	10.94	44.32	–6.44	. . .
Monetary authorities	4 753 WA	. . .	. . .	. . .	. . .	. . .	. . .	. . .	. . .
General government	4 753 ZB	. . .	. . .	. . .	. . .	. . .	. . .	. . .	. . .
Banks	4 753 ZC	. . .	. . .	. . .	. . .	. . .	. . .	. . .	. . .
Other sectors	4 753 ZD	. . .	. . .	. . .	. . .	. . .	. . .	. . .	. . .
Total, Groups A Through C	4 983 . .	*–13.52*	*.30*	*4.03*	*3.51*	*10.35*	*–9.07*	*.12*	. . .
D. Net Errors and Omissions	4 998 . .	**13.71**	**–1.68**	**–3.66**	**–2.45**	**–1.61**	**12.29**	**11.93**	**. . .**
Total, Groups A Through D	4 984 . .	*.18*	*–1.38*	*.37*	*1.06*	*8.74*	*3.23*	*12.05*	. . .
E. Reserves and Related Items	4 802 A.	**–.18**	**1.38**	**–.37**	**–1.06**	**–8.74**	**–3.23**	**–12.05**	**. . .**
Reserve assets	4 802 . .	–.18	1.38	–.37	–1.06	–8.74	–3.23	–12.05	. . .
Use of Fund credit and loans	4 766 . .	. . .	. . .	. . .	. . .	. . .	. . .	. . .	. . .
Exceptional financing	4 920 . .	. . .	. . .	. . .	. . .	. . .	. . .	. . .	. . .
Conversion rates: Eastern Caribbean dollars per U.S. dollar	0 101 . .	**2.7000**	**2.7000**	**2.7000**	**2.7000**	**2.7000**	**2.7000**	**2.7000**	**2.7000**

[1] Excludes components that have been classified in the categories of Group E.

Table 2. STANDARD PRESENTATION, 1994–2001
(Millions of U.S. dollars)

	Code	1994	1995	1996	1997	1998	1999	2000	2001
CURRENT ACCOUNT	4 993 . .	**–57.43**	**–40.68**	**–35.74**	**–84.12**	**–94.22**	**–72.34**	**–26.28**	. . .
A. GOODS	4 100 . .	–66.57	–57.43	–75.51	–105.29	–119.71	–127.44	–91.17	. . .
Credit	2 100 . .	**48.86**	**61.94**	**52.56**	**47.33**	**50.24**	**49.61**	**51.75**	. . .
General merchandise: exports f.o.b.	2 110 . .	46.20	59.41	51.65	46.10	49.80	49.41	50.59	. . .
Goods for processing: exports f.o.b.	2 150 . .	. . .	. . .	. . .	. . .	. . .	. . .	. . .	. . .
Repairs on goods	2 160 . .	. . .	. . .	. . .	. . .	. . .	. . .	. . .	. . .
Goods procured in ports by carriers	2 170 . .	2.66	2.53	.91	1.22	.44	.20	1.16	. . .
Nonmonetary gold	2 180 . .	. . .	. . .	. . .	. . .	. . .	. . .	. . .	. . .
Debit	3 100 . .	**–115.43**	**–119.37**	**–128.07**	**–152.61**	**–169.96**	**–177.05**	**–142.92**	. . .
General merchandise: imports f.o.b.	3 110 . .	–114.41	–118.36	–126.90	–151.44	–169.09	–176.70	–142.28	. . .
Goods for processing: imports f.o.b.	3 150 . .	. . .	. . .	. . .	. . .	. . .	. . .	. . .	. . .
Repairs on goods	3 160 . .	. . .	. . .	. . .	. . .	. . .	. . .	. . .	. . .
Goods procured in ports by carriers	3 170 . .	–1.03	–1.01	–1.17	–1.17	–.87	–.35	–.64	. . .
Nonmonetary gold	3 180 . .	. . .	. . .	. . .	. . .	. . .	. . .	. . .	. . .
B. SERVICES	4 200 . .	8.76	19.23	38.46	23.07	28.14	59.29	66.40	. . .
Total credit	2 200 . .	*63.40*	*74.37*	*96.68*	*99.41*	*107.19*	*125.76*	*126.23*	. . .
Total debit	3 200 . .	*–54.64*	*–55.14*	*–58.22*	*–76.33*	*–79.05*	*–66.47*	*–59.83*	. . .
Transportation services, credit	2 205 . .	**4.38**	**5.32**	**5.09**	**6.28**	**9.86**	**10.41**	**10.51**	. . .
Passenger	2 850 . .	. . .	. . .	. . .	. . .	. . .	. . .	. . .	. . .
Freight	2 851 . .	. . .	. . .	. . .	. . .	. . .	. . .	. . .	. . .
Other	2 852 . .	. . .	. . .	. . .	. . .	. . .	. . .	. . .	. . .
Sea transport, passenger	2 207 . .	. . .	. . .	. . .	. . .	. . .	. . .	. . .	. . .
Sea transport, freight	2 208 . .	. . .	. . .	. . .	. . .	. . .	. . .	. . .	. . .
Sea transport, other	2 209 . .	. . .	. . .	. . .	. . .	. . .	. . .	. . .	. . .
Air transport, passenger	2 211 . .	. . .	. . .	. . .	. . .	. . .	. . .	. . .	. . .
Air transport, freight	2 212 . .	. . .	. . .	. . .	. . .	. . .	. . .	. . .	. . .
Air transport, other	2 213 . .	. . .	. . .	. . .	. . .	. . .	. . .	. . .	. . .
Other transport, passenger	2 215 . .	. . .	. . .	. . .	. . .	. . .	. . .	. . .	. . .
Other transport, freight	2 216 . .	. . .	. . .	. . .	. . .	. . .	. . .	. . .	. . .
Other transport, other	2 217 . .	. . .	. . .	. . .	. . .	. . .	. . .	. . .	. . .
Transportation services, debit	3 205 . .	**–18.10**	**–19.74**	**–20.10**	**–22.68**	**–27.25**	**–28.81**	**–24.69**	. . .
Passenger	3 850 . .	. . .	. . .	. . .	. . .	. . .	. . .	. . .	. . .
Freight	3 851 . .	. . .	. . .	. . .	. . .	. . .	. . .	. . .	. . .
Other	3 852 . .	. . .	. . .	. . .	. . .	. . .	. . .	. . .	. . .
Sea transport, passenger	3 207 . .	. . .	. . .	. . .	. . .	. . .	. . .	. . .	. . .
Sea transport, freight	3 208 . .	. . .	. . .	. . .	. . .	. . .	. . .	. . .	. . .
Sea transport, other	3 209 . .	. . .	. . .	. . .	. . .	. . .	. . .	. . .	. . .
Air transport, passenger	3 211 . .	. . .	. . .	. . .	. . .	. . .	. . .	. . .	. . .
Air transport, freight	3 212 . .	. . .	. . .	. . .	. . .	. . .	. . .	. . .	. . .
Air transport, other	3 213 . .	. . .	. . .	. . .	. . .	. . .	. . .	. . .	. . .
Other transport, passenger	3 215 . .	. . .	. . .	. . .	. . .	. . .	. . .	. . .	. . .
Other transport, freight	3 216 . .	. . .	. . .	. . .	. . .	. . .	. . .	. . .	. . .
Other transport, other	3 217 . .	. . .	. . .	. . .	. . .	. . .	. . .	. . .	. . .
Travel, credit	2 236 . .	**44.01**	**52.89**	**64.03**	**69.14**	**73.22**	**76.50**	**75.34**	. . .
Business travel	2 237 . .	. . .	. . .	. . .	. . .	. . .	. . .	. . .	. . .
Personal travel	2 240 . .	. . .	. . .	. . .	. . .	. . .	. . .	. . .	. . .
Travel, debit	3 236 . .	**–6.00**	**–6.53**	**–7.57**	**–7.34**	**–7.50**	**–9.24**	**–9.45**	. . .
Business travel	3 237 . .	. . .	. . .	. . .	. . .	. . .	. . .	. . .	. . .
Personal travel	3 240 . .	. . .	. . .	. . .	. . .	. . .	. . .	. . .	. . .
Other services, credit	2 200 BA	**15.00**	**16.16**	**27.56**	**23.99**	**24.12**	**38.85**	**40.37**	. . .
Communications	2 245 . .	. . .	. . .	. . .	. . .	. . .	. . .	. . .	. . .
Construction	2 249 . .	. . .	. . .	. . .	. . .	. . .	. . .	. . .	. . .
Insurance	2 253 . .	.99	.81	.91	.87	1.01	1.23	1.53	. . .
Financial	2 260 . .	. . .	. . .	3.51	5.76	8.44	12.97	14.87	. . .
Computer and information	2 262 . .	. . .	. . .	. . .	. . .	. . .	. . .	. . .	. . .
Royalties and licence fees	2 266 . .	. . .	. . .	.30	. . .	. . .	. . .	. . .	. . .
Other business services	2 268 . .	11.42	13.03	22.03	16.18	13.19	22.75	21.82	. . .
Personal, cultural, and recreational	2 287 . .	. . .	. . .	. . .	. . .	. . .	. . .	. . .	. . .
Government, n.i.e.	2 291 . .	2.60	2.32	.82	1.17	1.47	1.89	2.14	. . .
Other services, debit	3 200 BA	**–30.54**	**–28.88**	**–30.55**	**–46.31**	**–44.30**	**–28.42**	**–25.68**	. . .
Communications	3 245 . .	. . .	. . .	. . .	. . .	. . .	. . .	. . .	. . .
Construction	3 249 . .	. . .	. . .	–3.72	–13.07	–12.90	–2.41	. . .	. . .
Insurance	3 253 . .	–2.94	–3.76	–4.14	–4.36	–4.93	–5.14	–4.48	. . .
Financial	3 260 . .	. . .	. . .	. . .	. . .	. . .	. . .	. . .	. . .
Computer and information	3 262 . .	. . .	. . .	. . .	. . .	. . .	. . .	. . .	. . .
Royalties and licence fees	3 266 . .	–.39	–.42	–.28	–.33	–.29	–.56	–.54	. . .
Other business services	3 268 . .	–21.91	–22.84	–19.21	–24.16	–21.00	–15.40	–16.89	. . .
Personal, cultural, and recreational	3 287 . .	. . .	. . .	. . .	. . .	. . .	. . .	. . .	. . .
Government, n.i.e.	3 291 . .	–5.29	–1.85	–3.20	–4.41	–5.17	–4.90	–3.77	. . .

Table 2 (Continued). STANDARD PRESENTATION, 1994–2001

(Millions of U.S. dollars)

	Code	1994	1995	1996	1997	1998	1999	2000	2001
C. INCOME	4 300	-11.81	-11.66	-9.13	-12.67	-13.62	-19.62	-20.28	...
Total credit	2 300	*3.46*	*4.01*	*4.02*	*2.67*	*3.04*	*3.16*	*3.14*	...
Total debit	3 300	*-15.27*	*-15.67*	*-13.15*	*-15.34*	*-16.66*	*-22.78*	*-23.43*	...
Compensation of employees, credit	2 310	**.31**	**.31**	**.18**	**.07**	**.07**	**.12**	**.13**	...
Compensation of employees, debit	3 310	**-.03**	...	...	...	...	...	...	...
Investment income, credit	2 320	**3.15**	**3.70**	**3.84**	**2.60**	**2.97**	**3.04**	**3.01**	...
Direct investment income	2 330	.01	.04	.05	.05	.05	...	...	...
Dividends and distributed branch profits	2 332	...	...	...	...	.05	...	...	...
Reinvested earnings and undistributed branch profits	2 333	...	...	...	...	...	...	...	...
Income on debt (interest)	2 334	.01	.04	.05	.05	...	...	...	...
Portfolio investment income	2 339	.25	1.19	.81	.93	1.02	.82	1.15	...
Income on equity	2 340	.25	1.19	.81	.93	1.02	.82	1.15	...
Income on bonds and notes	2 350	...	...	...	...	...	...	...	...
Income on money market instruments	2 360	...	...	...	...	...	...	...	...
Other investment income	2 370	2.89	2.47	2.99	1.61	1.90	2.22	1.86	...
Investment income, debit	3 320	**-15.24**	**-15.67**	**-13.15**	**-15.34**	**-16.66**	**-22.78**	**-23.43**	...
Direct investment income	3 330	-11.40	-11.05	-9.17	-10.34	-10.84	-14.80	-13.69	...
Dividends and distributed branch profits	3 332	-5.46	-3.65	-1.79	-2.13	-3.32	-4.04	-3.16	...
Reinvested earnings and undistributed branch profits	3 333	-5.90	-7.40	-7.36	-7.84	-7.40	-10.64	-10.31	...
Income on debt (interest)	3 334	-.04	...	-.02	-.37	-.12	-.12	-.21	...
Portfolio investment income	3 339	...	...	...	...	...	...	...	...
Income on equity	3 340	...	...	...	...	...	...	...	...
Income on bonds and notes	3 350	...	...	...	...	...	...	...	...
Income on money market instruments	3 360	...	...	...	...	...	...	...	...
Other investment income	3 370	-3.84	-4.62	-3.97	-5.00	-5.82	-7.98	-9.74	...
D. CURRENT TRANSFERS	4 379	12.19	9.18	10.44	10.77	10.97	15.43	18.77	...
Credit	2 379	**19.42**	**16.81**	**19.72**	**20.83**	**21.60**	**23.39**	**25.43**	...
General government	2 380	3.81	1.11	2.94	3.41	3.24	3.53	5.12	...
Other sectors	2 390	15.61	15.70	16.78	17.41	18.36	19.85	20.31	...
Workers' remittances	2 391	...	...	...	...	...	...	...	...
Other current transfers	2 392	...	...	...	...	...	...	...	...
Debit	3 379	**-7.23**	**-7.63**	**-9.28**	**-10.06**	**-10.63**	**-7.96**	**-6.67**	...
General government	3 380	-2.47	-3.19	-3.12	-2.80	-2.97	-2.61	-2.35	...
Other sectors	3 390	-4.76	-4.44	-6.16	-7.26	-7.65	-5.34	-4.31	...
Workers' remittances	3 391	...	...	...	...	...	...	...	...
Other current transfers	3 392	...	...	...	...	...	...	...	...
CAPITAL AND FINANCIAL ACCOUNT	4 996	**43.73**	**42.36**	**39.40**	**86.57**	**95.83**	**60.05**	**14.35**	...
CAPITAL ACCOUNT	4 994	**4.01**	**5.87**	**3.83**	**5.89**	**13.33**	**7.82**	**12.07**	...
Total credit	2 994	*5.37*	*6.92*	*4.94*	*7.00*	*14.60*	*9.12*	*13.40*	...
Total debit	3 994	*-1.36*	*-1.05*	*-1.11*	*-1.12*	*-1.27*	*-1.30*	*-1.33*	...
Capital transfers, credit	2 400	**5.37**	**5.11**	**4.94**	**7.00**	**14.60**	**9.12**	**13.40**	...
General government	2 401	3.52	3.26	2.71	4.76	12.07	6.53	10.76	...
Debt forgiveness	2 402	...	...	...	...	...	...	...	...
Other capital transfers	2 410	3.52	3.26	2.71	4.76	12.07	6.53	10.76	...
Other sectors	2 430	1.85	1.85	2.22	2.24	2.53	2.59	2.64	...
Migrants' transfers	2 431	1.85	1.85	2.22	2.24	2.53	2.59	2.64	...
Debt forgiveness	2 432	...	...	...	...	...	...	...	...
Other capital transfers	2 440	...	...	...	...	...	...	...	...
Capital transfers, debit	3 400	**-.74**	**-.74**	**-1.11**	**-1.12**	**-1.27**	**-1.30**	**-1.33**	...
General government	3 401	...	...	...	...	...	...	...	...
Debt forgiveness	3 402	...	...	...	...	...	...	...	...
Other capital transfers	3 410	...	...	...	...	...	...	...	...
Other sectors	3 430	-.74	-.74	-1.11	-1.12	-1.27	-1.30	-1.33	...
Migrants' transfers	3 431	-.74	-.74	-1.11	-1.12	-1.27	-1.30	-1.33	...
Debt forgiveness	3 432	...	...	...	...	...	...	...	...
Other capital transfers	3 440	...	...	...	...	...	...	...	...
Nonproduced nonfinancial assets, credit	2 480	...	**1.80**	...	...	...	...	...	...
Nonproduced nonfinancial assets, debit	3 480	**-.62**	**-.31**	...	...	...	...	...	...

Table 2 (Continued). STANDARD PRESENTATION, 1994–2001

(Millions of U.S. dollars)

	Code	1994	1995	1996	1997	1998	1999	2000	2001
FINANCIAL ACCOUNT	4 995 . .	**39.72**	**36.49**	**35.58**	**80.69**	**82.49**	**52.23**	**2.28**	**...**
A. DIRECT INVESTMENT	4 500 . .	46.91	30.64	42.64	92.47	88.95	56.09	28.17	...
Direct investment abroad	4 505 . .	**...**	**...**	**...**	**...**	**...**	**...**	**...**	**...**
Equity capital	4 510 . .	...	...	...	...	...	...	...	...
Claims on affiliated enterprises	4 515 . .	...	...	...	...	...	...	...	...
Liabilities to affiliated enterprises	4 520 . .	...	...	...	...	...	...	...	...
Reinvested earnings	4 525 . .	...	...	...	...	...	...	...	...
Other capital	4 530 . .	...	...	...	...	...	...	...	...
Claims on affiliated enterprises	4 535 . .	...	...	...	...	...	...	...	...
Liabilities to affiliated enterprises	4 540 . .	...	...	...	...	...	...	...	...
Direct investment in St. Vincent and the Grenadines	4 555 . .	**46.91**	**30.64**	**42.64**	**92.47**	**88.95**	**56.09**	**28.17**	**...**
Equity capital	4 560 . .	11.81	4.60	10.51	6.76	3.64	3.57	11.52	...
Claims on direct investors	4 565 . .	...	...	...	...	...	...	...	...
Liabilities to direct investors	4 570 . .	11.81	4.60	10.51	6.76	3.64	3.57	11.52	...
Reinvested earnings	4 575 . .	5.90	7.40	7.36	7.84	7.40	10.64	10.31	...
Other capital	4 580 . .	29.21	18.64	24.77	77.87	77.91	41.88	6.33	...
Claims on direct investors	4 585 . .	...	...	...	...	...	...	...	...
Liabilities to direct investors	4 590 . .	29.21	18.64	24.77	77.87	77.91	41.88	6.33	...
B. PORTFOLIO INVESTMENT	4 600 . .	.30	...	–2.74	1.69	–.11	–.11	1.44	...
Assets	4 602 . .	**.24**	**...**	**–.37**	**.08**	**–.37**	**–.22**	**–.52**	**...**
Equity securities	4 610 . .	...	...	...	...	...	...	...	...
Monetary authorities	4 611 . .	...	...	...	...	...	...	...	...
General government	4 612 . .	...	...	...	...	...	...	...	...
Banks	4 613 . .	...	...	...	...	...	...	...	...
Other sectors	4 614 . .	...	...	...	...	...	...	...	...
Debt securities	4 619 . .	...	...	...	...	...	...	...	...
Bonds and notes	4 620 . .	...	...	...	...	...	...	...	...
Monetary authorities	4 621 . .	...	...	...	...	...	...	...	...
General government	4 622 . .	...	...	...	...	...	...	...	...
Banks	4 623 . .	...	...	...	...	...	...	...	...
Other sectors	4 624 . .	...	...	...	...	...	...	...	...
Money market instruments	4 630 . .	...	...	...	...	...	...	...	...
Monetary authorities	4 631 . .	...	...	...	...	...	...	...	...
General government	4 632 . .	...	...	...	...	...	...	...	...
Banks	4 633 . .	...	...	...	...	...	...	...	...
Other sectors	4 634 . .	...	...	...	...	...	...	...	...
Liabilities	4 652 . .	**.06**	**...**	**–2.37**	**1.61**	**.26**	**.11**	**1.96**	**...**
Equity securities	4 660 . .	...	...	...	...	...	...	...	...
Banks	4 663 . .	...	...	...	...	...	...	...	...
Other sectors	4 664 . .	...	...	...	...	...	...	...	...
Debt securities	4 669 . .	...	...	...	...	...	...	...	...
Bonds and notes	4 670 . .	...	...	...	...	...	...	...	...
Monetary authorities	4 671 . .	...	...	...	...	...	...	...	...
General government	4 672 . .	...	...	...	...	...	...	...	...
Banks	4 673 . .	...	...	...	...	...	...	...	...
Other sectors	4 674 . .	...	...	...	...	...	...	...	...
Money market instruments	4 680 . .	...	...	...	...	...	...	...	...
Monetary authorities	4 681 . .	...	...	...	...	...	...	...	...
General government	4 682 . .	...	...	...	...	...	...	...	...
Banks	4 683 . .	...	...	...	...	...	...	...	...
Other sectors	4 684 . .	...	...	...	...	...	...	...	...
C. FINANCIAL DERIVATIVES	4 910 . .	...	...	...	...	...	...	...	...
Monetary authorities	4 911 . .	...	...	...	...	...	...	...	...
General government	4 912 . .	...	...	...	...	...	...	...	...
Banks	4 913 . .	...	...	...	...	...	...	...	...
Other sectors	4 914 . .	...	...	...	...	...	...	...	...
Assets	4 900 . .	**...**	**...**	**...**	**...**	**...**	**...**	**...**	**...**
Monetary authorities	4 901 . .	...	...	...	...	...	...	...	...
General government	4 902 . .	...	...	...	...	...	...	...	...
Banks	4 903 . .	...	...	...	...	...	...	...	...
Other sectors	4 904 . .	...	...	...	...	...	...	...	...
Liabilities	4 905 . .	**...**	**...**	**...**	**...**	**...**	**...**	**...**	**...**
Monetary authorities	4 906 . .	...	...	...	...	...	...	...	...
General government	4 907 . .	...	...	...	...	...	...	...	...
Banks	4 908 . .	...	...	...	...	...	...	...	...
Other sectors	4 909 . .	...	...	...	...	...	...	...	...

Table 2 (Concluded). STANDARD PRESENTATION, 1994–2001

(Millions of U.S. dollars)

	Code	1994	1995	1996	1997	1998	1999	2000	2001
D. OTHER INVESTMENT	4 700	–7.32	4.47	–3.96	–12.41	2.40	–.51	–15.28	...
Assets	4 703	**–8.92**	**2.06**	**–2.33**	**–5.78**	**–8.54**	**–44.83**	**–8.84**	...
Trade credits	4 706	...	...	...	...	...	...	...	...
General government	4 707	...	...	...	...	...	...	...	...
of which: Short-term	4 709	...	...	...	...	...	...	...	...
Other sectors	4 710	...	...	...	...	...	...	...	...
of which: Short-term	4 712	...	...	...	...	...	...	...	...
Loans	4 714	...	...	...	...	...	...	...	...
Monetary authorities	4 715	...	...	...	...	...	...	...	...
of which: Short-term	4 718	...	...	...	...	...	...	...	...
General government	4 719	...	...	...	...	...	...	...	...
of which: Short-term	4 721	...	...	...	...	...	...	...	...
Banks	4 722	...	...	...	...	...	...	...	...
of which: Short-term	4 724	...	...	...	...	...	...	...	...
Other sectors	4 725	...	...	...	...	...	...	...	...
of which: Short-term	4 727	...	...	...	...	...	...	...	...
Currency and deposits	4 730	...	...	...	...	...	...	...	...
Monetary authorities	4 731	...	...	...	...	...	...	...	...
General government	4 732	...	...	...	...	...	...	...	...
Banks	4 733	...	...	...	...	...	...	...	...
Other sectors	4 734	...	...	...	...	...	...	...	...
Other assets	4 736	...	...	...	...	...	...	...	...
Monetary authorities	4 737	...	...	...	...	...	...	...	...
of which: Short-term	4 739	...	...	...	...	...	...	...	...
General government	4 740	...	...	...	...	...	...	...	...
of which: Short-term	4 742	...	...	...	...	...	...	...	...
Banks	4 743	...	...	...	...	...	...	...	...
of which: Short-term	4 745	...	...	...	...	...	...	...	...
Other sectors	4 746	...	...	...	...	...	...	...	...
of which: Short-term	4 748	...	...	...	...	...	...	...	...
Liabilities	4 753	**1.60**	**2.41**	**–1.63**	**–6.63**	**10.94**	**44.32**	**–6.44**	...
Trade credits	4 756	...	...	...	...	...	...	...	...
General government	4 757	...	...	...	...	...	...	...	...
of which: Short-term	4 759	...	...	...	...	...	...	...	...
Other sectors	4 760	...	...	...	...	...	...	...	...
of which: Short-term	4 762	...	...	...	...	...	...	...	...
Loans	4 764	...	...	...	...	...	...	...	...
Monetary authorities	4 765	...	...	...	...	...	...	...	...
of which: Use of Fund credit and loans from the Fund	4 766	...	...	...	...	...	...	...	...
of which: Short-term	4 768	...	...	...	...	...	...	...	...
General government	4 769	...	...	...	...	...	...	...	...
of which: Short-term	4 771	...	...	...	...	...	...	...	...
Banks	4 772	...	...	...	...	...	...	...	...
of which: Short-term	4 774	...	...	...	...	...	...	...	...
Other sectors	4 775	...	...	...	...	...	...	...	...
of which: Short-term	4 777	...	...	...	...	...	...	...	...
Currency and deposits	4 780	...	...	...	...	...	...	...	...
Monetary authorities	4 781	...	...	...	...	...	...	...	...
General government	4 782	...	...	...	...	...	...	...	...
Banks	4 783	...	...	...	...	...	...	...	...
Other sectors	4 784	...	...	...	...	...	...	...	...
Other liabilities	4 786	...	...	...	...	...	...	...	...
Monetary authorities	4 787	...	...	...	...	...	...	...	...
of which: Short-term	4 789	...	...	...	...	...	...	...	...
General government	4 790	...	...	...	...	...	...	...	...
of which: Short-term	4 792	...	...	...	...	...	...	...	...
Banks	4 793	...	...	...	...	...	...	...	...
of which: Short-term	4 795	...	...	...	...	...	...	...	...
Other sectors	4 796	...	...	...	...	...	...	...	...
of which: Short-term	4 798	...	...	...	...	...	...	...	...
E. RESERVE ASSETS	4 802	–.18	1.38	–.37	–1.06	–8.74	–3.23	–12.05	...
Monetary gold	4 812	...	...	...	...	...	...	...	...
Special drawing rights	4 811	.01	.01	.01	.01	.01	...	.01	...
Reserve position in the Fund	4 810	...	...	...	...	...	...	...	...
Foreign exchange	4 803	–.19	1.37	–.38	–1.07	–7.54	–3.84	–12.64	...
Other claims	4 813	...	...	...	...	–1.20	.61	.58	...
NET ERRORS AND OMISSIONS	4 998	**13.71**	**–1.68**	**–3.66**	**–2.45**	**–1.61**	**12.29**	**11.93**	...

Part 3 of the *Yearbook* contains descriptions of the methodologies, compilation practices, and sources used to compile these data.

Table 1. ANALYTIC PRESENTATION, 1994–2001
(Millions of U.S. dollars)

	Code	1994	1995	1996	1997	1998	1999	2000	2001
A. Current Account[1]	4 993 Z.	**5.76**	**9.33**	**12.28**	**9.13**	**20.09**	**–18.79**	**. . .**	**. . .**
Goods: exports f.o.b	2 100 . .	3.52	8.76	10.08	14.63	20.40	18.15	. . .	. . .
Goods: imports f.o.b	3 100 . .	–68.81	–80.29	–90.76	–100.11	–96.91	–115.66	. . .	. . .
Balance on Goods	4 100 . .	*–65.29*	*–71.53*	*–80.67*	*–85.48*	*–76.51*	*–97.51*	. . .	. . .
Services: credit	2 200 . .	43.00	55.70	65.15	65.24	62.56	61.31	. . .	. . .
Services: debit	3 200 . .	–28.17	–35.19	–34.33	–40.08	–29.09	–24.55	. . .	. . .
Balance on Goods and Services	4 991 . .	*–50.46*	*–51.02*	*–49.85*	*–60.32*	*–43.04*	*–60.74*	. . .	. . .
Income: credit	2 300 . .	4.03	4.66	5.45	5.52	5.97	2.75	. . .	. . .
Income: debit	3 300 . .	–4.45	–4.42	–2.43	–4.14	–2.39	–2.36	. . .	. . .
Balance on Goods, Services, and Income	4 992 . .	*–50.88*	*–50.79*	*–46.84*	*–58.94*	*–39.47*	*–60.34*	. . .	. . .
Current transfers: credit	2 379 Z.	62.75	66.74	66.89	73.71	64.12	44.67	. . .	. . .
Current transfers: debit	3 379 . .	–6.11	–6.62	–7.77	–5.65	–4.56	–3.12	. . .	. . .
B. Capital Account[1]	4 994 Z.	**. . .**	**. . .**	**. . .**	**. . .**	**. . .**	**24.46**	**. . .**	**. . .**
Capital account: credit	2 994 Z.	. . .	. . .	. . .	. . .	. . .	27.11	. . .	. . .
Capital account: debit	3 994 . .	. . .	. . .	. . .	. . .	. . .	–2.66	. . .	. . .
Total, Groups A Plus B	4 981 . .	*5.76*	*9.33*	*12.28*	*9.13*	*20.09*	*5.67*	. . .	. . .
C. Financial Account[1]	4 995 W.	**–5.46**	**–5.60**	**–3.60**	**–5.93**	**–4.99**	**–.73**	**. . .**	**. . .**
Direct investment abroad	4 505 . .	. . .	. . .	. . .	. . .	. . .	. . .	. . .	. . .
Direct investment in Samoa	4 555 Z.	. . .	. . .	. . .	. . .	. . .	. . .	. . .	. . .
Portfolio investment assets	4 602 . .	. . .	. . .	. . .	. . .	. . .	. . .	. . .	. . .
Equity securities	4 610 . .	. . .	. . .	. . .	. . .	. . .	. . .	. . .	. . .
Debt securities	4 619 . .	. . .	. . .	. . .	. . .	. . .	. . .	. . .	. . .
Portfolio investment liabilities	4 652 Z.	. . .	. . .	. . .	. . .	. . .	. . .	. . .	. . .
Equity securities	4 660 . .	. . .	. . .	. . .	. . .	. . .	. . .	. . .	. . .
Debt securities	4 669 Z.	. . .	. . .	. . .	. . .	. . .	. . .	. . .	. . .
Financial derivatives	4 910 . .	. . .	. . .	. . .	. . .	. . .	. . .	. . .	. . .
Financial derivatives assets	4 900 . .	. . .	. . .	. . .	. . .	. . .	. . .	. . .	. . .
Financial derivatives liabilities	4 905 . .	. . .	. . .	. . .	. . .	. . .	. . .	. . .	. . .
Other investment assets	4 703 . .	. . .	. . .	. . .	. . .	. . .	. . .	. . .	. . .
Monetary authorities	4 701 . .	. . .	. . .	. . .	. . .	. . .	. . .	. . .	. . .
General government	4 704 . .	. . .	. . .	. . .	. . .	. . .	. . .	. . .	. . .
Banks	4 705 . .	. . .	. . .	. . .	. . .	. . .	. . .	. . .	. . .
Other sectors	4 728 . .	. . .	. . .	. . .	. . .	. . .	. . .	. . .	. . .
Other investment liabilities	4 753 W.	–5.46	–5.60	–3.60	–5.93	–4.99	–.73	. . .	. . .
Monetary authorities	4 753 WA	–.13	.01	–.01	–.01	.16	. . .	. . .	. . .
General government	4 753 ZB	6.82	3.80	.20	–1.48	–1.04	–2.79	. . .	. . .
Banks	4 753 ZC	.03	–1.12	1.65	1.05	–.54	5.42	. . .	. . .
Other sectors	4 753 ZD	–12.18	–8.29	–5.44	–5.49	–3.57	–3.36	. . .	. . .
Total, Groups A Through C	4 983 . .	*.31*	*3.74*	*8.68*	*3.20*	*15.10*	*4.94*	. . .	. . .
D. Net Errors and Omissions	4 998 . .	**–4.17**	**–1.70**	**–1.30**	**7.89**	**–9.59**	**2.10**	**. . .**	**. . .**
Total, Groups A Through D	4 984 . .	*–3.86*	*2.04*	*7.38*	*11.09*	*5.51*	*7.04*	. . .	. . .
E. Reserves and Related Items	4 802 A.	**3.86**	**–2.04**	**–7.38**	**–11.09**	**–5.51**	**–7.04**	**. . .**	**. . .**
Reserve assets	4 802 . .	3.86	–2.04	–7.38	–11.09	–5.51	–7.04	. . .	. . .
Use of Fund credit and loans	4 766 . .	. . .	. . .	. . .	. . .	. . .	. . .	. . .	. . .
Exceptional financing	4 920 . .	. . .	. . .	. . .	. . .	. . .	. . .	. . .	. . .
Conversion rates: tala per U.S. dollar	0 101 . .	**2.5350**	**2.4734**	**2.4622**	**2.5594**	**2.9477**	**3.0132**	**3.2864**	**3.4780**

[1] Excludes components that have been classified in the categories of Group E.

Table 2. STANDARD PRESENTATION, 1994–2001

(Millions of U.S. dollars)

	Code	1994	1995	1996	1997	1998	1999	2000	2001
CURRENT ACCOUNT	4 993 . .	**5.76**	**9.33**	**12.28**	**9.13**	**20.09**	**–18.79**	**. . .**	**. . .**
A. GOODS	4 100 . .	–65.29	–71.53	–80.67	–85.48	–76.51	–97.51	. . .	. . .
Credit	2 100 . .	**3.52**	**8.76**	**10.08**	**14.63**	**20.40**	**18.15**	**. . .**	**. . .**
General merchandise: exports f.o.b.	2 110 . .	3.52	8.76	10.08	14.63	20.40	18.15	. . .	. . .
Goods for processing: exports f.o.b.	2 150 . .	. . .	. . .	. . .	. . .	. . .	. . .	. . .	. . .
Repairs on goods	2 160 . .	. . .	. . .	. . .	. . .	. . .	. . .	. . .	. . .
Goods procured in ports by carriers	2 170 . .	. . .	. . .	. . .	. . .	. . .	. . .	. . .	. . .
Nonmonetary gold	2 180 . .	. . .	. . .	. . .	. . .	. . .	. . .	. . .	. . .
Debit	3 100 . .	**–68.81**	**–80.29**	**–90.76**	**–100.11**	**–96.91**	**–115.66**	**. . .**	**. . .**
General merchandise: imports f.o.b.	3 110 . .	–68.81	–80.29	–90.76	–100.11	–96.91	–115.66	. . .	. . .
Goods for processing: imports f.o.b.	3 150 . .	. . .	. . .	. . .	. . .	. . .	. . .	. . .	. . .
Repairs on goods	3 160 . .	. . .	. . .	. . .	. . .	. . .	. . .	. . .	. . .
Goods procured in ports by carriers	3 170 . .	. . .	. . .	. . .	. . .	. . .	. . .	. . .	. . .
Nonmonetary gold	3 180 . .	. . .	. . .	. . .	. . .	. . .	. . .	. . .	. . .
B. SERVICES	4 200 . .	14.83	20.51	30.82	25.16	33.47	36.77	. . .	. . .
Total credit	2 200 . .	*43.00*	*55.70*	*65.15*	*65.24*	*62.56*	*61.31*	. . .	. . .
Total debit	3 200 . .	*–28.17*	*–35.19*	*–34.33*	*–40.08*	*–29.09*	*–24.55*	. . .	. . .
Transportation services, credit	2 205 . .	**2.17**	**1.69**	**1.84**	**1.89**	**2.01**	**.86**	**. . .**	**. . .**
Passenger	2 850 . .	*.98*	*.70*	*.40*	*.51*	*.60*	*.51*	. . .	. . .
Freight	2 851 . .	*.35*	*.42*	*.48*	*.51*	*.51*	*.35*	. . .	. . .
Other	2 852 . .	*.84*	*.57*	*.96*	*.87*	*.91*	. . .	. . .	. . .
Sea transport, passenger	2 207 . .	. . .	.21	.04	.04	.04	.03	. . .	. . .
Sea transport, freight	2 208 . .	. . .	.30	.34	.30	.26	.23	. . .	. . .
Sea transport, other	2 209 . .	. . .	.57	.96	.87	.91	. . .	. . .	. . .
Air transport, passenger	2 211 . .	. . .	.49	.36	.48	.56	.48	. . .	. . .
Air transport, freight	2 212 . .	. . .	.13	.15	.20	.24	.12	. . .	. . .
Air transport, other	2 213 . .	. . .	. . .	. . .	. . .	. . .	. . .	. . .	. . .
Other transport, passenger	2 215 . .	. . .	. . .	. . .	. . .	. . .	. . .	. . .	. . .
Other transport, freight	2 216 . .	. . .	. . .	. . .	. . .	. . .	. . .	. . .	. . .
Other transport, other	2 217 . .	. . .	. . .	. . .	. . .	. . .	. . .	. . .	. . .
Transportation services, debit	3 205 . .	**–14.67**	**–15.58**	**–14.24**	**–19.00**	**–21.22**	**–4.12**	**. . .**	**. . .**
Passenger	3 850 . .	*–3.42*	*–3.57*	*–5.23*	*–6.94*	*–7.75*	*–.44*	. . .	. . .
Freight	3 851 . .	*–11.25*	*–12.01*	*–8.37*	*–11.19*	*–12.50*	*–3.68*	. . .	. . .
Other	3 852 . .	. . .	. . .	*–.64*	*–.88*	*–.97*	. . .	. . .	. . .
Sea transport, passenger	3 207 . .	. . .	–.18	–.26	–.33	–.37	–.29	. . .	. . .
Sea transport, freight	3 208 . .	. . .	–8.41	–5.86	–7.85	–8.76	–2.59	. . .	. . .
Sea transport, other	3 209 . .	. . .	. . .	. . .	. . .	. . .	. . .	. . .	. . .
Air transport, passenger	3 211 . .	. . .	–3.39	–4.97	–6.61	–7.38	–.15	. . .	. . .
Air transport, freight	3 212 . .	. . .	–3.60	–2.51	–3.34	–3.75	–1.09	. . .	. . .
Air transport, other	3 213 . .	. . .	. . .	–.64	–.88	–.97	. . .	. . .	. . .
Other transport, passenger	3 215 . .	. . .	. . .	. . .	. . .	. . .	. . .	. . .	. . .
Other transport, freight	3 216 . .	. . .	. . .	. . .	. . .	. . .	. . .	. . .	. . .
Other transport, other	3 217 . .	. . .	. . .	. . .	. . .	. . .	. . .	. . .	. . .
Travel, credit	2 236 . .	**24.69**	**34.78**	**39.89**	**38.39**	**39.06**	**41.75**	**. . .**	**. . .**
Business travel	2 237 . .	. . .	. . .	. . .	. . .	. . .	. . .	. . .	. . .
Personal travel	2 240 . .	. . .	. . .	. . .	. . .	. . .	41.75	. . .	. . .
Travel, debit	3 236 . .	**–3.70**	**–3.18**	**–3.66**	**–4.75**	**–3.52**	**–3.85**	**. . .**	**. . .**
Business travel	3 237 . .	. . .	–.83	–.89	–.86	–.62	. . .	. . .	. . .
Personal travel	3 240 . .	. . .	–2.35	–2.77	–3.88	–2.90	–3.85	. . .	. . .
Other services, credit	2 200 BA	**16.13**	**19.23**	**23.41**	**24.96**	**21.48**	**18.70**	**. . .**	**. . .**
Communications	2 245 . .	. . .	. . .	. . .	. . .	. . .	. . .	. . .	. . .
Construction	2 249 . .	. . .	. . .	. . .	. . .	. . .	. . .	. . .	. . .
Insurance	2 253 . .	1.06	.13	.06	.11	.06	.10	. . .	. . .
Financial	2 260 . .	. . .	. . .	. . .	. . .	. . .	. . .	. . .	. . .
Computer and information	2 262 . .	. . .	. . .	. . .	. . .	. . .	. . .	. . .	. . .
Royalties and licence fees	2 266 . .	.15	. . .	. . .	. . .	. . .	. . .	. . .	. . .
Other business services	2 268 . .	5.20	16.34	20.04	18.31	16.62	4.27	. . .	. . .
Personal, cultural, and recreational	2 287 . .	6.37	. . .	. . .	. . .	. . .	. . .	. . .	. . .
Government, n.i.e.	2 291 . .	3.35	2.76	3.32	6.54	4.80	14.33	. . .	. . .
Other services, debit	3 200 BA	**–9.79**	**–16.43**	**–16.43**	**–16.33**	**–4.35**	**–16.58**	**. . .**	**. . .**
Communications	3 245 . .	. . .	–.69	–1.24	–1.78	–1.00	–1.39	. . .	. . .
Construction	3 249 . .	. . .	–.16	–.07	–.15	. . .	–2.99	. . .	. . .
Insurance	3 253 . .	–1.21	–1.42	–1.81	–1.15	–.81	–1.43	. . .	. . .
Financial	3 260 . .	. . .	. . .	. . .	. . .	. . .	. . .	. . .	. . .
Computer and information	3 262 . .	. . .	. . .	. . .	. . .	. . .	. . .	. . .	. . .
Royalties and licence fees	3 266 . .	. . .	. . .	–.06	–.12	.19	–.20	. . .	. . .
Other business services	3 268 . .	–7.93	–12.75	–12.07	–11.74	–2.47	–5.20	. . .	. . .
Personal, cultural, and recreational	3 287 . .	. . .	. . .	. . .	. . .	. . .	. . .	. . .	. . .
Government, n.i.e.	3 291 . .	–.65	–1.43	–1.18	–1.39	–.25	–5.38	. . .	. . .

Table 2 (Continued). STANDARD PRESENTATION, 1994–2001
(Millions of U.S. dollars)

	Code	1994	1995	1996	1997	1998	1999	2000	2001
C. INCOME	4 300 . .	–.42	.23	3.01	1.38	3.58	.40	. . .	. . .
Total credit	2 300 . .	*4.03*	*4.66*	*5.45*	*5.52*	*5.97*	*2.75*	. . .	. . .
Total debit	3 300 . .	*–4.45*	*–4.42*	*–2.43*	*–4.14*	*–2.39*	*–2.36*	. . .	. . .
Compensation of employees, credit	2 310 . .	**1.08**	**1.27**	**1.67**	**1.52**	**1.78**	. . .	. . .	. . .
Compensation of employees, debit	3 310 . .	**–.06**	. . .	. . .	. . .	. . .	. . .	. . .	. . .
Investment income, credit	2 320 . .	**2.95**	**3.38**	**3.77**	**4.00**	**4.18**	**2.75**	. . .	. . .
Direct investment income	2 330 . .	. . .	. . .	. . .	. . .	. . .	.03	. . .	. . .
Dividends and distributed branch profits	2 332 . .	. . .	. . .	. . .	. . .	. . .	.03	. . .	. . .
Reinvested earnings and undistributed branch profits	2 333 . .	. . .	. . .	. . .	. . .	. . .	. . .	. . .	. . .
Income on debt (interest)	2 334 . .	. . .	. . .	. . .	. . .	. . .	. . .	. . .	. . .
Portfolio investment income	2 339 . .	. . .	. . .	. . .	. . .	. . .	. . .	. . .	. . .
Income on equity	2 340 . .	. . .	. . .	. . .	. . .	. . .	. . .	. . .	. . .
Income on bonds and notes	2 350 . .	. . .	. . .	. . .	. . .	. . .	. . .	. . .	. . .
Income on money market instruments	2 360 . .	. . .	. . .	. . .	. . .	. . .	. . .	. . .	. . .
Other investment income	2 370 . .	2.95	3.38	3.77	4.00	4.18	2.72	. . .	. . .
Investment income, debit	3 320 . .	**–4.39**	**–4.42**	**–2.43**	**–4.14**	**–2.39**	**–2.36**	. . .	. . .
Direct investment income	3 330 . .	. . .	. . .	. . .	. . .	. . .	–.63	. . .	. . .
Dividends and distributed branch profits	3 332 . .	. . .	. . .	. . .	. . .	. . .	–.63	. . .	. . .
Reinvested earnings and undistributed branch profits	3 333 . .	. . .	. . .	. . .	. . .	. . .	. . .	. . .	. . .
Income on debt (interest)	3 334 . .	. . .	. . .	. . .	. . .	. . .	. . .	. . .	. . .
Portfolio investment income	3 339 . .	. . .	. . .	. . .	. . .	. . .	–.20	. . .	. . .
Income on equity	3 340 . .	. . .	. . .	. . .	. . .	. . .	–.20	. . .	. . .
Income on bonds and notes	3 350 . .	. . .	. . .	. . .	. . .	. . .	. . .	. . .	. . .
Income on money market instruments	3 360 . .	. . .	. . .	. . .	. . .	. . .	. . .	. . .	. . .
Other investment income	3 370 . .	–4.39	–4.42	–2.43	–4.14	–2.39	–1.53	. . .	. . .
D. CURRENT TRANSFERS	4 379 . .	56.64	60.12	59.12	68.06	59.56	41.55	. . .	. . .
Credit	2 379 . .	**62.75**	**66.74**	**66.89**	**73.71**	**64.12**	**44.67**	. . .	. . .
General government	2 380 . .	26.35	27.49	24.29	28.64	23.90	. . .	. . .	. . .
Other sectors	2 390 . .	36.40	39.25	42.60	45.07	40.22	44.67	. . .	. . .
Workers' remittances	2 391 . .	36.40	39.25	42.60	45.07	40.22	44.67	. . .	. . .
Other current transfers	2 392 . .	. . .	. . .	. . .	. . .	. . .	. . .	. . .	. . .
Debit	3 379 . .	**–6.11**	**–6.62**	**–7.77**	**–5.65**	**–4.56**	**–3.12**	. . .	. . .
General government	3 380 . .	–2.60	–2.51	–1.91	–2.54	–1.63	. . .	. . .	. . .
Other sectors	3 390 . .	–3.50	–4.12	–5.86	–3.11	–2.93	–3.12	. . .	. . .
Workers' remittances	3 391 . .	–3.50	–4.12	–5.86	–3.11	–2.93	–3.12	. . .	. . .
Other current transfers	3 392 . .	. . .	. . .	. . .	. . .	. . .	. . .	. . .	. . .
CAPITAL AND FINANCIAL ACCOUNT	4 996 . .	**–1.59**	**–7.63**	**–10.98**	**–17.02**	**–10.50**	**16.69**	. . .	. . .
CAPITAL ACCOUNT	4 994 . .	. . .	. . .	. . .	. . .	. . .	**24.46**	. . .	. . .
Total credit	2 994 . .	. . .	. . .	. . .	. . .	. . .	*27.11*	. . .	. . .
Total debit	3 994 . .	. . .	. . .	. . .	. . .	. . .	*–2.66*	. . .	. . .
Capital transfers, credit	2 400 . .	. . .	. . .	. . .	. . .	. . .	**27.11**	. . .	. . .
General government	2 401 . .	. . .	. . .	. . .	. . .	. . .	27.11	. . .	. . .
Debt forgiveness	2 402 . .	. . .	. . .	. . .	. . .	. . .	. . .	. . .	. . .
Other capital transfers	2 410 . .	. . .	. . .	. . .	. . .	. . .	27.11	. . .	. . .
Other sectors	2 430 . .	. . .	. . .	. . .	. . .	. . .	. . .	. . .	. . .
Migrants' transfers	2 431 . .	. . .	. . .	. . .	. . .	. . .	. . .	. . .	. . .
Debt forgiveness	2 432 . .	. . .	. . .	. . .	. . .	. . .	. . .	. . .	. . .
Other capital transfers	2 440 . .	. . .	. . .	. . .	. . .	. . .	. . .	. . .	. . .
Capital transfers, debit	3 400 . .	. . .	. . .	. . .	. . .	. . .	**–2.66**	. . .	. . .
General government	3 401 . .	. . .	. . .	. . .	. . .	. . .	–2.66	. . .	. . .
Debt forgiveness	3 402 . .	. . .	. . .	. . .	. . .	. . .	. . .	. . .	. . .
Other capital transfers	3 410 . .	. . .	. . .	. . .	. . .	. . .	–2.66	. . .	. . .
Other sectors	3 430 . .	. . .	. . .	. . .	. . .	. . .	. . .	. . .	. . .
Migrants' transfers	3 431 . .	. . .	. . .	. . .	. . .	. . .	. . .	. . .	. . .
Debt forgiveness	3 432 . .	. . .	. . .	. . .	. . .	. . .	. . .	. . .	. . .
Other capital transfers	3 440 . .	. . .	. . .	. . .	. . .	. . .	. . .	. . .	. . .
Nonproduced nonfinancial assets, credit	2 480 . .	. . .	. . .	. . .	. . .	. . .	. . .	. . .	. . .
Nonproduced nonfinancial assets, debit	3 480 . .	. . .	. . .	. . .	. . .	. . .	. . .	. . .	. . .

Table 2 (Continued). STANDARD PRESENTATION, 1994–2001
(Millions of U.S. dollars)

	Code		1994	1995	1996	1997	1998	1999	2000	2001
FINANCIAL ACCOUNT	4 995	. .	**-1.59**	**-7.63**	**-10.98**	**-17.02**	**-10.50**	**-7.77**	**. . .**	**. . .**
A. DIRECT INVESTMENT	4 500	. .	. . .	. . .	. . .	. . .	. . .	. . .	. . .	. . .
Direct investment abroad	4 505	. .	**. . .**	**. . .**	**. . .**	**. . .**	**. . .**	**. . .**	**. . .**	**. . .**
Equity capital	4 510	. .	. . .	. . .	. . .	. . .	. . .	. . .	. . .	. . .
Claims on affiliated enterprises	4 515	. .	. . .	. . .	. . .	. . .	. . .	. . .	. . .	. . .
Liabilities to affiliated enterprises	4 520	. .	. . .	. . .	. . .	. . .	. . .	. . .	. . .	. . .
Reinvested earnings	4 525	. .	. . .	. . .	. . .	. . .	. . .	. . .	. . .	. . .
Other capital	4 530	. .	. . .	. . .	. . .	. . .	. . .	. . .	. . .	. . .
Claims on affiliated enterprises	4 535	. .	. . .	. . .	. . .	. . .	. . .	. . .	. . .	. . .
Liabilities to affiliated enterprises	4 540	. .	. . .	. . .	. . .	. . .	. . .	. . .	. . .	. . .
Direct investment in Samoa	4 555	. .	**. . .**	**. . .**	**. . .**	**. . .**	**. . .**	**. . .**	**. . .**	**. . .**
Equity capital	4 560	. .	. . .	. . .	. . .	. . .	. . .	. . .	. . .	. . .
Claims on direct investors	4 565	. .	. . .	. . .	. . .	. . .	. . .	. . .	. . .	. . .
Liabilities to direct investors	4 570	. .	. . .	. . .	. . .	. . .	. . .	. . .	. . .	. . .
Reinvested earnings	4 575	. .	. . .	. . .	. . .	. . .	. . .	. . .	. . .	. . .
Other capital	4 580	. .	. . .	. . .	. . .	. . .	. . .	. . .	. . .	. . .
Claims on direct investors	4 585	. .	. . .	. . .	. . .	. . .	. . .	. . .	. . .	. . .
Liabilities to direct investors	4 590	. .	. . .	. . .	. . .	. . .	. . .	. . .	. . .	. . .
B. PORTFOLIO INVESTMENT	4 600	. .	. . .	. . .	. . .	. . .	. . .	. . .	. . .	. . .
Assets	4 602	. .	**. . .**	**. . .**	**. . .**	**. . .**	**. . .**	**. . .**	**. . .**	**. . .**
Equity securities	4 610	. .	. . .	. . .	. . .	. . .	. . .	. . .	. . .	. . .
Monetary authorities	4 611	. .	. . .	. . .	. . .	. . .	. . .	. . .	. . .	. . .
General government	4 612	. .	. . .	. . .	. . .	. . .	. . .	. . .	. . .	. . .
Banks	4 613	. .	. . .	. . .	. . .	. . .	. . .	. . .	. . .	. . .
Other sectors	4 614	. .	. . .	. . .	. . .	. . .	. . .	. . .	. . .	. . .
Debt securities	4 619	. .	. . .	. . .	. . .	. . .	. . .	. . .	. . .	. . .
Bonds and notes	4 620	. .	. . .	. . .	. . .	. . .	. . .	. . .	. . .	. . .
Monetary authorities	4 621	. .	. . .	. . .	. . .	. . .	. . .	. . .	. . .	. . .
General government	4 622	. .	. . .	. . .	. . .	. . .	. . .	. . .	. . .	. . .
Banks	4 623	. .	. . .	. . .	. . .	. . .	. . .	. . .	. . .	. . .
Other sectors	4 624	. .	. . .	. . .	. . .	. . .	. . .	. . .	. . .	. . .
Money market instruments	4 630	. .	. . .	. . .	. . .	. . .	. . .	. . .	. . .	. . .
Monetary authorities	4 631	. .	. . .	. . .	. . .	. . .	. . .	. . .	. . .	. . .
General government	4 632	. .	. . .	. . .	. . .	. . .	. . .	. . .	. . .	. . .
Banks	4 633	. .	. . .	. . .	. . .	. . .	. . .	. . .	. . .	. . .
Other sectors	4 634	. .	. . .	. . .	. . .	. . .	. . .	. . .	. . .	. . .
Liabilities	4 652	. .	**. . .**	**. . .**	**. . .**	**. . .**	**. . .**	**. . .**	**. . .**	**. . .**
Equity securities	4 660	. .	. . .	. . .	. . .	. . .	. . .	. . .	. . .	. . .
Banks	4 663	. .	. . .	. . .	. . .	. . .	. . .	. . .	. . .	. . .
Other sectors	4 664	. .	. . .	. . .	. . .	. . .	. . .	. . .	. . .	. . .
Debt securities	4 669	. .	. . .	. . .	. . .	. . .	. . .	. . .	. . .	. . .
Bonds and notes	4 670	. .	. . .	. . .	. . .	. . .	. . .	. . .	. . .	. . .
Monetary authorities	4 671	. .	. . .	. . .	. . .	. . .	. . .	. . .	. . .	. . .
General government	4 672	. .	. . .	. . .	. . .	. . .	. . .	. . .	. . .	. . .
Banks	4 673	. .	. . .	. . .	. . .	. . .	. . .	. . .	. . .	. . .
Other sectors	4 674	. .	. . .	. . .	. . .	. . .	. . .	. . .	. . .	. . .
Money market instruments	4 680	. .	. . .	. . .	. . .	. . .	. . .	. . .	. . .	. . .
Monetary authorities	4 681	. .	. . .	. . .	. . .	. . .	. . .	. . .	. . .	. . .
General government	4 682	. .	. . .	. . .	. . .	. . .	. . .	. . .	. . .	. . .
Banks	4 683	. .	. . .	. . .	. . .	. . .	. . .	. . .	. . .	. . .
Other sectors	4 684	. .	. . .	. . .	. . .	. . .	. . .	. . .	. . .	. . .
C. FINANCIAL DERIVATIVES	4 910	. .	. . .	. . .	. . .	. . .	. . .	. . .	. . .	. . .
Monetary authorities	4 911	. .	. . .	. . .	. . .	. . .	. . .	. . .	. . .	. . .
General government	4 912	. .	. . .	. . .	. . .	. . .	. . .	. . .	. . .	. . .
Banks	4 913	. .	. . .	. . .	. . .	. . .	. . .	. . .	. . .	. . .
Other sectors	4 914	. .	. . .	. . .	. . .	. . .	. . .	. . .	. . .	. . .
Assets	4 900	. .	**. . .**	**. . .**	**. . .**	**. . .**	**. . .**	**. . .**	**. . .**	**. . .**
Banks	4 903	. .	. . .	. . .	. . .	. . .	. . .	. . .	. . .	. . .
Other sectors	4 904	. .	. . .	. . .	. . .	. . .	. . .	. . .	. . .	. . .
Liabilities	4 905	. .	**. . .**	**. . .**	**. . .**	**. . .**	**. . .**	**. . .**	**. . .**	**. . .**
Monetary authorities	4 906	. .	. . .	. . .	. . .	. . .	. . .	. . .	. . .	. . .
General government	4 907	. .	. . .	. . .	. . .	. . .	. . .	. . .	. . .	. . .
Banks	4 908	. .	. . .	. . .	. . .	. . .	. . .	. . .	. . .	. . .
Other sectors	4 909	. .	. . .	. . .	. . .	. . .	. . .	. . .	. . .	. . .

Table 2 (Concluded). STANDARD PRESENTATION, 1994–2001

(Millions of U.S. dollars)

	Code	1994	1995	1996	1997	1998	1999	2000	2001
D. OTHER INVESTMENT	4 700 . .	–5.46	–5.60	–3.60	–5.93	–4.99	–.73	...	...
Assets	4 703 . .	**...**	**...**	**...**	**...**	**...**	**...**	**...**	**...**
Trade credits	4 706 . .	...	...	...	...	...	...	...	...
General government	4 707 . .	...	...	...	...	...	...	...	...
of which: Short-term	4 709 . .	...	...	...	...	...	...	...	...
Other sectors	4 710 . .	...	...	...	...	...	...	...	...
of which: Short-term	4 712 . .	...	...	...	...	...	...	...	...
Loans	4 714 . .	...	...	...	...	...	...	...	...
Monetary authorities	4 715 . .	...	...	...	...	...	...	...	...
of which: Short-term	4 718 . .	...	...	...	...	...	...	...	...
General government	4 719 . .	...	...	...	...	...	...	...	...
of which: Short-term	4 721 . .	...	...	...	...	...	...	...	...
Banks	4 722 . .	...	...	...	...	...	...	...	...
of which: Short-term	4 724 . .	...	...	...	...	...	...	...	...
Other sectors	4 725 . .	...	...	...	...	...	...	...	...
of which: Short-term	4 727 . .	...	...	...	...	...	...	...	...
Currency and deposits	4 730 . .	...	...	...	...	...	...	...	...
Monetary authorities	4 731 . .	...	...	...	...	...	...	...	...
General government	4 732 . .	...	...	...	...	...	...	...	...
Banks	4 733 . .	...	...	...	...	...	...	...	...
Other sectors	4 734 . .	...	...	...	...	...	...	...	...
Other assets	4 736 . .	...	...	...	...	...	...	...	...
Monetary authorities	4 737 . .	...	...	...	...	...	...	...	...
of which: Short-term	4 739 . .	...	...	...	...	...	...	...	...
General government	4 740 . .	...	...	...	...	...	...	...	...
of which: Short-term	4 742 . .	...	...	...	...	...	...	...	...
Banks	4 743 . .	...	...	...	...	...	...	...	...
of which: Short-term	4 745 . .	...	...	...	...	...	...	...	...
Other sectors	4 746 . .	...	...	...	...	...	...	...	...
of which: Short-term	4 748 . .	...	...	...	...	...	...	...	...
Liabilities	4 753 . .	**–5.46**	**–5.60**	**–3.60**	**–5.93**	**–4.99**	**–.73**	**...**	**...**
Trade credits	4 756 . .	...	...	...	...	...	...	...	...
General government	4 757 . .	...	...	...	...	...	...	...	...
of which: Short-term	4 759 . .	...	...	...	...	...	...	...	...
Other sectors	4 760 . .	...	...	...	...	...	...	...	...
of which: Short-term	4 762 . .	...	...	...	...	...	...	...	...
Loans	4 764 . .	–7.57	–4.49	–5.24	–6.96	–4.61	–6.15	...	...
Monetary authorities	4 765 . .	...	...	...	...	...	...	...	...
of which: Use of Fund credit and loans from the Fund	4 766 . .	...	...	...	...	...	...	...	...
of which: Short-term	4 768 . .	...	...	...	...	...	...	...	...
General government	4 769 . .	6.82	3.80	.20	–1.48	–1.04	–2.79	...	...
of which: Short-term	4 771 . .	...	...	...	...	...	...	...	...
Banks	4 772 . .	...	...	...	...	...	...	...	...
of which: Short-term	4 774 . .	...	...	...	...	...	...	...	...
Other sectors	4 775 . .	–14.40	–8.29	–5.44	–5.49	–3.57	–3.36	...	...
of which: Short-term	4 777 . .	...	...	...	...	...	...	...	...
Currency and deposits	4 780 . .	1.72	–1.11	1.64	1.04	–.38	...	...	...
Monetary authorities	4 781 . .	–.13	.01	–.01	.01	.16	...	...	...
General government	4 782 . .	...	...	...	...	...	...	...	...
Banks	4 783 . .	.03	–1.12	1.65	1.05	–.54	...	...	...
Other sectors	4 784 . .	1.81	...	...	...	...	...	...	...
Other liabilities	4 786 . .	.40	...	...	...	...	5.42	...	...
Monetary authorities	4 787 . .	...	...	...	...	...	...	...	...
of which: Short-term	4 789 . .	...	...	...	...	...	...	...	...
General government	4 790 . .	...	...	...	...	...	...	...	...
of which: Short-term	4 792 . .	...	...	...	...	...	...	...	...
Banks	4 793 . .	...	...	...	...	...	5.42	...	...
of which: Short-term	4 795 . .	...	...	...	...	...	*5.42*	...	...
Other sectors	4 796 . .	.40	...	...	...	...	...	...	...
of which: Short-term	4 798 . .	*.40*	...	...	...	...	...	...	...
E. RESERVE ASSETS	4 802 . .	3.86	–2.04	–7.38	–11.09	–5.51	–7.04	...	...
Monetary gold	4 812 . .	...	...	...	...	...	...	...	...
Special drawing rights	4 811 . .	–.06	–.07	–.09	–.06	–.07	–.06	...	...
Reserve position in the Fund	4 810 . .	...	–.01	...	–.02	...	...	...	...
Foreign exchange	4 803 . .	3.92	–1.96	–7.29	–11.01	–5.44	–6.99	...	...
Other claims	4 813 . .	...	...	...	...	...	...	...	...
NET ERRORS AND OMISSIONS	4 998 . .	**–4.17**	**–1.70**	**–1.30**	**7.89**	**–9.59**	**2.10**	**...**	**...**

Part 3 of the *Yearbook* contains descriptions of the methodologies, compilation practices, and sources used to compile these data.

Table 1. ANALYTIC PRESENTATION, 1994–2001

(Millions of U.S. dollars)

	Code	1994	1995	1996	1997	1998	1999	2000	2001
A. Current Account [1]	4 993 Z.	**. . .**	**. . .**	**. . .**	**. . .**	**. . .**	**. . .**	**. . .**	**–21.43**
Goods: exports f.o.b	2 100 . .	. . .	. . .	. . .	. . .	. . .	. . .	. . .	3.28
Goods: imports f.o.b	3 100 . .	. . .	. . .	. . .	. . .	. . .	. . .	. . .	–24.43
Balance on Goods	4 100 . .	. . .	. . .	. . .	. . .	. . .	. . .	. . .	*–21.15*
Services: credit	2 200 . .	. . .	. . .	. . .	. . .	. . .	. . .	. . .	13.56
Services: debit	3 200 . .	. . .	. . .	. . .	. . .	. . .	. . .	. . .	–15.21
Balance on Goods and Services	4 991 . .	. . .	. . .	. . .	. . .	. . .	. . .	. . .	*–22.80*
Income: credit	2 300 . .	. . .	. . .	. . .	. . .	. . .	. . .	. . .	. . .
Income: debit	3 300 . .	. . .	. . .	. . .	. . .	. . .	. . .	. . .	–3.70
Balance on Goods, Services, and Income	4 992 . .	. . .	. . .	. . .	. . .	. . .	. . .	. . .	*–26.50*
Current transfers: credit	2 379 Z.	. . .	. . .	. . .	. . .	. . .	. . .	. . .	5.07
Current transfers: debit	3 379 . .	. . .	. . .	. . .	. . .	. . .	. . .	. . .	. . .
B. Capital Account [1]	4 994 Z.	**. . .**	**. . .**	**. . .**	**. . .**	**. . .**	**. . .**	**. . .**	**11.41**
Capital account: credit	2 994 Z.	. . .	. . .	. . .	. . .	. . .	. . .	. . .	11.41
Capital account: debit	3 994 . .	. . .	. . .	. . .	. . .	. . .	. . .	. . .	. . .
Total, Groups A Plus B	4 981 . .	. . .	. . .	. . .	. . .	. . .	. . .	. . .	*–10.02*
C. Financial Account [1]	4 995 W.	**. . .**	**. . .**	**. . .**	**. . .**	**. . .**	**. . .**	**. . .**	**8.93**
Direct investment abroad	4 505 . .	. . .	. . .	. . .	. . .	. . .	. . .	. . .	. . .
Direct investment in Sao Tome and Principe	4 555 Z.	. . .	. . .	. . .	. . .	. . .	. . .	. . .	5.50
Portfolio investment assets	4 602 . .	. . .	. . .	. . .	. . .	. . .	. . .	. . .	. . .
Equity securities	4 610 . .	. . .	. . .	. . .	. . .	. . .	. . .	. . .	. . .
Debt securities	4 619 . .	. . .	. . .	. . .	. . .	. . .	. . .	. . .	. . .
Portfolio investment liabilities	4 652 Z.	. . .	. . .	. . .	. . .	. . .	. . .	. . .	. . .
Equity securities	4 660 . .	. . .	. . .	. . .	. . .	. . .	. . .	. . .	. . .
Debt securities	4 669 Z.	. . .	. . .	. . .	. . .	. . .	. . .	. . .	. . .
Financial derivatives	4 910 . .	. . .	. . .	. . .	. . .	. . .	. . .	. . .	. . .
Financial derivatives assets	4 900 . .	. . .	. . .	. . .	. . .	. . .	. . .	. . .	. . .
Financial derivatives liabilities	4 905 . .	. . .	. . .	. . .	. . .	. . .	. . .	. . .	. . .
Other investment assets	4 703 . .	. . .	. . .	. . .	. . .	. . .	. . .	. . .	. . .
Monetary authorities	4 701 . .	. . .	. . .	. . .	. . .	. . .	. . .	. . .	. . .
General government	4 704 . .	. . .	. . .	. . .	. . .	. . .	. . .	. . .	. . .
Banks	4 705 . .	. . .	. . .	. . .	. . .	. . .	. . .	. . .	. . .
Other sectors	4 728 . .	. . .	. . .	. . .	. . .	. . .	. . .	. . .	. . .
Other investment liabilities	4 753 W.	. . .	. . .	. . .	. . .	. . .	. . .	. . .	3.43
Monetary authorities	4 753 WA	. . .	. . .	. . .	. . .	. . .	. . .	. . .	. . .
General government	4 753 ZB	. . .	. . .	. . .	. . .	. . .	. . .	. . .	3.43
Banks	4 753 ZC	. . .	. . .	. . .	. . .	. . .	. . .	. . .	. . .
Other sectors	4 753 ZD	. . .	. . .	. . .	. . .	. . .	. . .	. . .	. . .
Total, Groups A Through C	4 983 . .	. . .	. . .	. . .	. . .	. . .	. . .	. . .	*–1.09*
D. Net Errors and Omissions	4 998 . .	**. . .**	**. . .**	**. . .**	**. . .**	**. . .**	**. . .**	**. . .**	**3.71**
Total, Groups A Through D	4 984 . .	. . .	. . .	. . .	. . .	. . .	. . .	. . .	*2.62*
E. Reserves and Related Items	4 802 A.	**. . .**	**. . .**	**. . .**	**. . .**	**. . .**	**. . .**	**. . .**	**–2.62**
Reserve assets	4 802 . .	. . .	. . .	. . .	. . .	. . .	. . .	. . .	–4.32
Use of Fund credit and loans	4 766 . .	. . .	. . .	. . .	. . .	. . .	. . .	. . .	. . .
Exceptional financing	4 920 . .	. . .	. . .	. . .	. . .	. . .	. . .	. . .	1.70
Conversion rates: dobras per U.S. dollar	0 101 . .	**732.63**	**1,420.34**	**2,203.16**	**4,552.51**	**6,883.24**	**7,118.96**	**7,978.17**	**8,842.11**

[1] Excludes components that have been classified in the categories of Group E.

Table 2. STANDARD PRESENTATION, 1994–2001

(Millions of U.S. dollars)

	Code	1994	1995	1996	1997	1998	1999	2000	2001
CURRENT ACCOUNT	4 993 . .	...	...	...	...	...	...	...	**–21.43**
A. GOODS	4 100 . .	...	...	...	...	...	...	...	–21.15
Credit	2 100 . .	...	...	...	...	...	...	...	**3.28**
General merchandise: exports f.o.b.	2 110 . .	...	...	...	...	...	...	...	3.28
Goods for processing: exports f.o.b.	2 150 . .	...	...	...	...	...	...	...	...
Repairs on goods	2 160 . .	...	...	...	...	...	...	...	...
Goods procured in ports by carriers	2 170 . .	...	...	...	...	...	...	...	...
Nonmonetary gold	2 180 . .	...	...	...	...	...	...	...	...
Debit	3 100 . .	...	...	...	...	...	...	...	**–24.43**
General merchandise: imports f.o.b.	3 110 . .	...	...	...	...	...	...	...	–24.43
Goods for processing: imports f.o.b.	3 150 . .	...	...	...	...	...	...	...	...
Repairs on goods	3 160 . .	...	...	...	...	...	...	...	...
Goods procured in ports by carriers	3 170 . .	...	...	...	...	...	...	...	...
Nonmonetary gold	3 180 . .	...	...	...	...	...	...	...	...
B. SERVICES	4 200 . .	...	...	...	...	...	...	...	–1.65
Total credit	2 200 . .	...	...	...	...	...	...	...	*13.56*
Total debit	3 200 . .	...	...	...	...	...	...	...	*–15.21*
Transportation services, credit	2 205 . .	...	...	...	...	...	...	...	**2.22**
Passenger	2 850 . .	...	...	...	...	...	...	...	*1.92*
Freight	2 851 . .	...	...	...	...	...	...	...	...
Other	2 852 . .	...	...	...	...	...	...	...	*.30*
Sea transport, passenger	2 207 . .	...	...	...	...	...	...	...	...
Sea transport, freight	2 208 . .	...	...	...	...	...	...	...	...
Sea transport, other	2 209 . .	...	...	...	...	...	...	...	.15
Air transport, passenger	2 211 . .	...	...	...	...	...	...	...	1.92
Air transport, freight	2 212 . .	...	...	...	...	...	...	...	...
Air transport, other	2 213 . .	...	...	...	...	...	...	...	.15
Other transport, passenger	2 215 . .	...	...	...	...	...	...	...	...
Other transport, freight	2 216 . .	...	...	...	...	...	...	...	...
Other transport, other	2 217 . .	...	...	...	...	...	...	...	...
Transportation services, debit	3 205 . .	...	...	...	...	...	...	...	**–5.77**
Passenger	3 850 . .	...	...	...	...	...	...	...	*–1.14*
Freight	3 851 . .	...	...	...	...	...	...	...	*–4.31*
Other	3 852 . .	...	...	...	...	...	...	...	*–.32*
Sea transport, passenger	3 207 . .	...	...	...	...	...	...	...	...
Sea transport, freight	3 208 . .	...	...	...	...	...	...	...	–3.88
Sea transport, other	3 209 . .	...	...	...	...	...	...	...	–.16
Air transport, passenger	3 211 . .	...	...	...	...	...	...	...	–1.14
Air transport, freight	3 212 . .	...	...	...	...	...	...	...	–.43
Air transport, other	3 213 . .	...	...	...	...	...	...	...	–.16
Other transport, passenger	3 215 . .	...	...	...	...	...	...	...	...
Other transport, freight	3 216 . .	...	...	...	...	...	...	...	...
Other transport, other	3 217 . .	...	...	...	...	...	...	...	...
Travel, credit	2 236 . .	...	...	...	...	...	...	...	**7.68**
Business travel	2 237 . .	...	...	...	...	...	...	...	1.54
Personal travel	2 240 . .	...	...	...	...	...	...	...	6.14
Travel, debit	3 236 . .	...	...	...	...	...	...	...	**–3.68**
Business travel	3 237 . .	...	...	...	...	...	...	...	–1.77
Personal travel	3 240 . .	...	...	...	...	...	...	...	–1.91
Other services, credit	2 200 BA	...	...	...	...	...	...	...	**3.66**
Communications	2 245 . .	...	...	...	...	...	...	...	1.67
Construction	2 249 . .	...	...	...	...	...	...	...	...
Insurance	2 253 . .	...	...	...	...	...	...	...	.40
Financial	2 260 . .	...	...	...	...	...	...	...	.28
Computer and information	2 262 . .	...	...	...	...	...	...	...	...
Royalties and licence fees	2 266 . .	...	...	...	...	...	...	...	.77
Other business services	2 268 . .	...	...	...	...	...	...	...	.32
Personal, cultural, and recreational	2 287 . .	...	...	...	...	...	...	...	...
Government, n.i.e.	2 291 . .	...	...	...	...	...	...	...	.22
Other services, debit	3 200 BA	...	...	...	...	...	...	...	**–5.76**
Communications	3 245 . .	...	...	...	...	...	...	...	–.41
Construction	3 249 . .	...	...	...	...	...	...	...	...
Insurance	3 253 . .	...	...	...	...	...	...	...	–1.50
Financial	3 260 . .	...	...	...	...	...	...	...	–.37
Computer and information	3 262 . .	...	...	...	...	...	...	...	...
Royalties and licence fees	3 266 . .	...	...	...	...	...	...	...	...
Other business services	3 268 . .	...	...	...	...	...	...	...	–1.04
Personal, cultural, and recreational	3 287 . .	...	...	...	...	...	...	...	...
Government, n.i.e.	3 291 . .	...	...	...	...	...	...	...	–2.44

Table 2 (Continued). STANDARD PRESENTATION, 1994–2001

(Millions of U.S. dollars)

	Code	1994	1995	1996	1997	1998	1999	2000	2001
C. INCOME	4 300	...	...	...	...	...	...	...	–3.70
Total credit	2 300	...	...	...	...	...	...	...	...
Total debit	3 300	...	...	...	...	...	...	...	*–3.70*
Compensation of employees, credit	2 310	...	...	...	...	...	...	...	...
Compensation of employees, debit	3 310	...	...	...	...	...	...	...	...
Investment income, credit	2 320	...	...	...	...	...	...	...	...
Direct investment income	2 330	...	...	...	...	...	...	...	...
Dividends and distributed branch profits	2 332	...	...	...	...	...	...	...	...
Reinvested earnings and undistributed branch profits	2 333	...	...	...	...	...	...	...	...
Income on debt (interest)	2 334	...	...	...	...	...	...	...	...
Portfolio investment income	2 339	...	...	...	...	...	...	...	...
Income on equity	2 340	...	...	...	...	...	...	...	...
Income on bonds and notes	2 350	...	...	...	...	...	...	...	...
Income on money market instruments	2 360	...	...	...	...	...	...	...	...
Other investment income	2 370	...	...	...	...	...	...	...	...
Investment income, debit	3 320	...	...	...	...	...	...	...	**–3.70**
Direct investment income	3 330	...	...	...	...	...	...	...	...
Dividends and distributed branch profits	3 332	...	...	...	...	...	...	...	...
Reinvested earnings and undistributed branch profits	3 333	...	...	...	...	...	...	...	...
Income on debt (interest)	3 334	...	...	...	...	...	...	...	...
Portfolio investment income	3 339	...	...	...	...	...	...	...	...
Income on equity	3 340	...	...	...	...	...	...	...	...
Income on bonds and notes	3 350	...	...	...	...	...	...	...	...
Income on money market instruments	3 360	...	...	...	...	...	...	...	...
Other investment income	3 370	...	...	...	...	...	...	...	–3.70
D. CURRENT TRANSFERS	4 379	...	...	...	...	...	...	...	5.07
Credit	2 379	...	...	...	...	...	...	...	**5.07**
General government	2 380	...	...	...	...	...	...	...	4.47
Other sectors	2 390	...	...	...	...	...	...	...	.60
Workers' remittances	2 391	...	...	...	...	...	...	...	.60
Other current transfers	2 392	...	...	...	...	...	...	...	...
Debit	3 379	...	...	...	...	...	...	...	...
General government	3 380	...	...	...	...	...	...	...	...
Other sectors	3 390	...	...	...	...	...	...	...	...
Workers' remittances	3 391	...	...	...	...	...	...	...	...
Other current transfers	3 392	...	...	...	...	...	...	...	...
CAPITAL AND FINANCIAL ACCOUNT	4 996	...	...	...	...	...	...	...	**17.72**
CAPITAL ACCOUNT	4 994	...	...	...	...	...	...	...	**14.31**
Total credit	2 994	...	...	...	...	...	...	...	*14.31*
Total debit	3 994	...	...	...	...	...	...	...	...
Capital transfers, credit	2 400	...	...	...	...	...	...	...	**14.31**
General government	2 401	...	...	...	...	...	...	...	2.90
Debt forgiveness	2 402	...	...	...	...	...	...	...	2.90
Other capital transfers	2 410	...	...	...	...	...	...	...	...
Other sectors	2 430	...	...	...	...	...	...	...	11.41
Migrants' transfers	2 431	...	...	...	...	...	...	...	...
Debt forgiveness	2 432	...	...	...	...	...	...	...	...
Other capital transfers	2 440	...	...	...	...	...	...	...	11.41
Capital transfers, debit	3 400	...	...	...	...	...	...	...	...
General government	3 401	...	...	...	...	...	...	...	...
Debt forgiveness	3 402	...	...	...	...	...	...	...	...
Other capital transfers	3 410	...	...	...	...	...	...	...	...
Other sectors	3 430	...	...	...	...	...	...	...	...
Migrants' transfers	3 431	...	...	...	...	...	...	...	...
Debt forgiveness	3 432	...	...	...	...	...	...	...	...
Other capital transfers	3 440	...	...	...	...	...	...	...	...
Nonproduced nonfinancial assets, credit	2 480	...	...	...	...	...	...	...	...
Nonproduced nonfinancial assets, debit	3 480	...	...	...	...	...	...	...	...

Table 2 (Continued). STANDARD PRESENTATION, 1994–2001
(Millions of U.S. dollars)

	Code	1994	1995	1996	1997	1998	1999	2000	2001
FINANCIAL ACCOUNT	4 995	...	...	...	...	...	...	...	**3.41**
A. DIRECT INVESTMENT	4 500	...	...	...	...	...	...	...	5.50
Direct investment abroad	4 505	...	...	...	...	...	...	...	...
Equity capital	4 510	...	...	...	...	...	...	...	...
Claims on affiliated enterprises	4 515	...	...	...	...	...	...	...	...
Liabilities to affiliated enterprises	4 520	...	...	...	...	...	...	...	...
Reinvested earnings	4 525	...	...	...	...	...	...	...	...
Other capital	4 530	...	...	...	...	...	...	...	...
Claims on affiliated enterprises	4 535	...	...	...	...	...	...	...	...
Liabilities to affiliated enterprises	4 540	...	...	...	...	...	...	...	...
Direct investment in Sao Tome and Principe	4 555	...	...	...	...	...	...	...	**5.50**
Equity capital	4 560	...	...	...	...	...	...	...	5.50
Claims on direct investors	4 565	...	...	...	...	...	...	...	...
Liabilities to direct investors	4 570	...	...	...	...	...	...	...	5.50
Reinvested earnings	4 575	...	...	...	...	...	...	...	...
Other capital	4 580	...	...	...	...	...	...	...	...
Claims on direct investors	4 585	...	...	...	...	...	...	...	...
Liabilities to direct investors	4 590	...	...	...	...	...	...	...	...
B. PORTFOLIO INVESTMENT	4 600	...	...	...	...	...	...	...	...
Assets	4 602	...	...	...	...	...	...	...	...
Equity securities	4 610	...	...	...	...	...	...	...	...
Monetary authorities	4 611	...	...	...	...	...	...	...	...
General government	4 612	...	...	...	...	...	...	...	...
Banks	4 613	...	...	...	...	...	...	...	...
Other sectors	4 614	...	...	...	...	...	...	...	...
Debt securities	4 619	...	...	...	...	...	...	...	...
Bonds and notes	4 620	...	...	...	...	...	...	...	...
Monetary authorities	4 621	...	...	...	...	...	...	...	...
General government	4 622	...	...	...	...	...	...	...	...
Banks	4 623	...	...	...	...	...	...	...	...
Other sectors	4 624	...	...	...	...	...	...	...	...
Money market instruments	4 630	...	...	...	...	...	...	...	...
Monetary authorities	4 631	...	...	...	...	...	...	...	...
General government	4 632	...	...	...	...	...	...	...	...
Banks	4 633	...	...	...	...	...	...	...	...
Other sectors	4 634	...	...	...	...	...	...	...	...
Liabilities	4 652	...	...	...	...	...	...	...	...
Equity securities	4 660	...	...	...	...	...	...	...	...
Banks	4 663	...	...	...	...	...	...	...	...
Other sectors	4 664	...	...	...	...	...	...	...	...
Debt securities	4 669	...	...	...	...	...	...	...	...
Bonds and notes	4 670	...	...	...	...	...	...	...	...
Monetary authorities	4 671	...	...	...	...	...	...	...	...
General government	4 672	...	...	...	...	...	...	...	...
Banks	4 673	...	...	...	...	...	...	...	...
Other sectors	4 674	...	...	...	...	...	...	...	...
Money market instruments	4 680	...	...	...	...	...	...	...	...
Monetary authorities	4 681	...	...	...	...	...	...	...	...
General government	4 682	...	...	...	...	...	...	...	...
Banks	4 683	...	...	...	...	...	...	...	...
Other sectors	4 684	...	...	...	...	...	...	...	...
C. FINANCIAL DERIVATIVES	4 910	...	...	...	...	...	...	...	...
Monetary authorities	4 911	...	...	...	...	...	...	...	...
General government	4 912	...	...	...	...	...	...	...	...
Banks	4 913	...	...	...	...	...	...	...	...
Other sectors	4 914	...	...	...	...	...	...	...	...
Assets	4 900	...	...	...	...	...	...	...	...
Monetary authorities	4 901	...	...	...	...	...	...	...	...
General government	4 902	...	...	...	...	...	...	...	...
Banks	4 903	...	...	...	...	...	...	...	...
Other sectors	4 904	...	...	...	...	...	...	...	...
Liabilities	4 905	...	...	...	...	...	...	...	...
Monetary authorities	4 906	...	...	...	...	...	...	...	...
General government	4 907	...	...	...	...	...	...	...	...
Banks	4 908	...	...	...	...	...	...	...	...
Other sectors	4 909	...	...	...	...	...	...	...	...

Table 2 (Concluded). STANDARD PRESENTATION, 1994–2001
(Millions of U.S. dollars)

	Code	1994	1995	1996	1997	1998	1999	2000	2001
D. OTHER INVESTMENT	4 700	...	...	...	...	...	...	...	2.23
Assets	4 703	**...**	**...**	**...**	**...**	**...**	**...**	**...**	**...**
Trade credits	4 706	...	...	...	...	...	...	...	...
General government	4 707	...	...	...	...	...	...	...	...
of which: Short-term	4 709	...	...	...	...	...	...	...	...
Other sectors	4 710	...	...	...	...	...	...	...	...
of which: Short-term	4 712	...	...	...	...	...	...	...	...
Loans	4 714	...	...	...	...	...	...	...	...
Monetary authorities	4 715	...	...	...	...	...	...	...	...
of which: Short-term	4 718	...	...	...	...	...	...	...	...
General government	4 719	...	...	...	...	...	...	...	...
of which: Short-term	4 721	...	...	...	...	...	...	...	...
Banks	4 722	...	...	...	...	...	...	...	...
of which: Short-term	4 724	...	...	...	...	...	...	...	...
Other sectors	4 725	...	...	...	...	...	...	...	...
of which: Short-term	4 727	...	...	...	...	...	...	...	...
Currency and deposits	4 730	...	...	...	...	...	...	...	...
Monetary authorities	4 731	...	...	...	...	...	...	...	...
General government	4 732	...	...	...	...	...	...	...	...
Banks	4 733	...	...	...	...	...	...	...	...
Other sectors	4 734	...	...	...	...	...	...	...	...
Other assets	4 736	...	...	...	...	...	...	...	...
Monetary authorities	4 737	...	...	...	...	...	...	...	...
of which: Short-term	4 739	...	...	...	...	...	...	...	...
General government	4 740	...	...	...	...	...	...	...	...
of which: Short-term	4 742	...	...	...	...	...	...	...	...
Banks	4 743	...	...	...	...	...	...	...	...
of which: Short-term	4 745	...	...	...	...	...	...	...	...
Other sectors	4 746	...	...	...	...	...	...	...	...
of which: Short-term	4 748	...	...	...	...	...	...	...	...
Liabilities	4 753	**...**	**...**	**...**	**...**	**...**	**...**	**...**	**2.23**
Trade credits	4 756	...	...	...	...	...	...	...	...
General government	4 757	...	...	...	...	...	...	...	...
of which: Short-term	4 759	...	...	...	...	...	...	...	...
Other sectors	4 760	...	...	...	...	...	...	...	...
of which: Short-term	4 762	...	...	...	...	...	...	...	...
Loans	4 764	...	...	...	...	...	...	...	3.43
Monetary authorities	4 765	...	...	...	...	...	...	...	...
of which: Use of Fund credit and loans from the Fund	4 766	...	...	...	...	...	...	...	...
of which: Short-term	4 768	...	...	...	...	...	...	...	...
General government	4 769	...	...	...	...	...	...	...	3.43
of which: Short-term	4 771	...	...	...	...	...	...	...	...
Banks	4 772	...	...	...	...	...	...	...	...
of which: Short-term	4 774	...	...	...	...	...	...	...	...
Other sectors	4 775	...	...	...	...	...	...	...	...
of which: Short-term	4 777	...	...	...	...	...	...	...	...
Currency and deposits	4 780	...	...	...	...	...	...	...	...
Monetary authorities	4 781	...	...	...	...	...	...	...	...
General government	4 782	...	...	...	...	...	...	...	...
Banks	4 783	...	...	...	...	...	...	...	...
Other sectors	4 784	...	...	...	...	...	...	...	...
Other liabilities	4 786	...	...	...	...	...	...	...	–1.20
Monetary authorities	4 787	...	...	...	...	...	...	...	...
of which: Short-term	4 789	...	...	...	...	...	...	...	...
General government	4 790	...	...	...	...	...	...	...	–1.20
of which: Short-term	4 792	...	...	...	...	...	...	...	*–1.20*
									...
Other sectors	4 796	...	...	...	...	...	...	...	...
of which: Short-term	4 798	...	...	...	...	...	...	...	...
E. RESERVE ASSETS	4 802	...	...	...	...	...	...	...	–4.32
Monetary gold	4 812	...	...	...	...	...	...	...	...
Special drawing rights	4 811	...	...	...	...	...	...	...	...
Reserve position in the Fund	4 810	...	...	...	...	...	...	...	...
Foreign exchange	4 803	...	...	...	...	...	...	...	–4.32
Other claims	4 813	...	...	...	...	...	...	...	...
NET ERRORS AND OMISSIONS	4 998	**...**	**...**	**...**	**...**	**...**	**...**	**...**	**3.71**

Table 1. ANALYTIC PRESENTATION, 1994–2001
(Millions of U.S. dollars)

	Code	1994	1995	1996	1997	1998	1999	2000	2001
A. Current Account [1]	4 993 Z.	**–10,487**	**–5,325**	**681**	**305**	**–13,150**	**412**	**14,336**	**14,502**
Goods: exports f.o.b	2 100 . .	42,614	50,041	60,729	60,731	38,822	50,757	77,584	73,032
Goods: imports f.o.b	3 100 . .	–21,325	–25,650	–25,358	–26,370	–27,535	–25,717	–27,741	–28,645
Balance on Goods	4 100 . .	*21,289*	*24,390*	*35,370*	*34,362*	*11,287*	*25,039*	*49,843*	*44,387*
Services: credit	2 200 . .	3,347	3,480	2,772	4,257	4,730	5,380	4,785	5,182
Services: debit	3 200 . .	–17,893	–19,083	–24,295	–25,963	–16,882	–18,855	–25,262	–19,307
Balance on Goods and Services	4 991 . .	*6,743*	*8,787*	*13,848*	*12,655*	*–865*	*11,564*	*29,367*	*30,262*
Income: credit	2 300 . .	4,032	4,987	5,127	5,756	5,810	5,811	3,349	4,130
Income: debit	3 300 . .	–2,560	–2,184	–2,681	–2,971	–3,041	–2,887	–2,869	–4,650
Balance on Goods, Services, and Income	4 992 . .	*8,215*	*11,591*	*16,294*	*15,440*	*1,903*	*14,489*	*29,847*	*29,742*
Current transfers: credit	2 379 Z.	. . .	. . .	. . .	. . .	. . .	. . .	. . .	. . .
Current transfers: debit	3 379 . .	–18,702	–16,916	–15,613	–15,134	–15,053	–14,077	–15,511	–15,240
B. Capital Account [1]	4 994 Z.	**. . .**	**. . .**	**. . .**	**. . .**	**. . .**	**. . .**	**. . .**	**. . .**
Capital account: credit	2 994 Z.	. . .	. . .	. . .	. . .	. . .	. . .	. . .	. . .
Capital account: debit	3 994 . .	. . .	. . .	. . .	. . .	. . .	. . .	. . .	. . .
Total, Groups A Plus B	4 981 . .	*–10,487*	*–5,325*	*681*	*305*	*–13,150*	*412*	*14,336*	*14,502*
C. Financial Account [1]	4 995 W.	**10,341**	**6,542**	**5,069**	**343**	**12,431**	**2,403**	**–11,672**	**–16,411**
Direct investment abroad	4 505 . .	. . .	. . .	. . .	. . .	. . .	. . .	. . .	. . .
Direct investment in Saudi Arabia	4 555 Z.	350	–1,877	–1,129	3,044	4,289	–780	–1,884	20
Portfolio investment assets	4 602 . .	–2,527	4,057	–2,642	–7,362	6,941	11,712	–9,394	–2,798
Equity securities	4 610 . .	. . .	. . .	. . .	. . .	. . .	. . .	. . .	. . .
Debt securities	4 619 . .	–2,527	4,057	–2,642	–7,362	6,941	11,712	–9,394	–2,798
Portfolio investment liabilities	4 652 Z.	. . .	. . .	. . .	. . .	. . .	. . .	. . .	. . .
Equity securities	4 660 . .	. . .	. . .	. . .	. . .	. . .	. . .	. . .	. . .
Debt securities	4 669 Z.	. . .	. . .	. . .	. . .	. . .	. . .	. . .	. . .
Financial derivatives	4 910 . .	. . .	. . .	. . .	. . .	. . .	. . .	. . .	. . .
Financial derivatives assets	4 900 . .	. . .	. . .	. . .	. . .	. . .	. . .	. . .	. . .
Financial derivatives liabilities	4 905 . .	. . .	. . .	. . .	. . .	. . .	. . .	. . .	. . .
Other investment assets	4 703 . .	12,022	4,221	9,115	2,688	1,983	–10,678	–3,943	–12,343
Monetary authorities	4 701 . .	. . .	. . .	. . .	. . .	. . .	. . .	. . .	. . .
General government	4 704 . .	. . .	. . .	. . .	. . .	. . .	. . .	. . .	. . .
Banks	4 705 . .	3,588	46	–2,188	1,777	3,621	–1,480	–2,595	491
Other sectors	4 728 . .	8,434	4,175	11,303	911	–1,639	–9,198	–1,348	–12,834
Other investment liabilities	4 753 W.	497	142	–275	1,973	–782	2,149	3,549	–1,289
Monetary authorities	4 753 WA	. . .	. . .	. . .	. . .	. . .	. . .	. . .	. . .
General government	4 753 ZB	. . .	. . .	. . .	. . .	. . .	. . .	. . .	. . .
Banks	4 753 ZC	497	142	–275	1,973	–782	2,149	3,549	–1,289
Other sectors	4 753 ZD	. . .	. . .	. . .	. . .	. . .	. . .	. . .	. . .
Total, Groups A Through C	4 983 . .	*–146*	*1,217*	*5,749*	*649*	*–719*	*2,815*	*2,664*	*–1,909*
D. Net Errors and Omissions	4 998 . .	**. . .**	**. . .**	**. . .**	**. . .**	**. . .**	**. . .**	**. . .**	**. . .**
Total, Groups A Through D	4 984 . .	*–146*	*1,217*	*5,749*	*648*	*–719*	*2,815*	*2,665*	*–1,909*
E. Reserves and Related Items	4 802 A.	**146**	**–1,217**	**–5,749**	**–648**	**719**	**–2,815**	**–2,665**	**1,909**
Reserve assets	4 802 . .	146	–1,217	–5,749	–648	719	–2,815	–2,665	1,909
Use of Fund credit and loans	4 766 . .	. . .	. . .	. . .	. . .	. . .	. . .	. . .	. . .
Exceptional financing	4 920 . .	. . .	. . .	. . .	. . .	. . .	. . .	. . .	. . .
Conversion rates: riyals per U.S. dollar	0 101 . .	**3.7450**	**3.7450**	**3.7450**	**3.7450**	**3.7450**	**3.7450**	**3.7450**	**3.7450**

[1] Excludes components that have been classified in the categories of Group E.

Table 2. STANDARD PRESENTATION, 1994–2001

(Millions of U.S. dollars)

	Code		1994	1995	1996	1997	1998	1999	2000	2001
CURRENT ACCOUNT	4 993	. .	**–10,487**	**–5,325**	**681**	**305**	**–13,150**	**412**	**14,336**	**14,502**
A. GOODS	4 100	. .	...	...	...	...	...	...	...	...
Repairs on goods	2 160	. .	...	...	...	...	...	...	...	...
Goods procured in ports by carriers	2 170	. .	114	131	163	160	97	135	213	194
Nonmonetary gold	2 180	. .	...	...	...	...	...	...	...	...
Debit	3 100	. .	**–21,325**	**–25,650**	**–25,358**	**–26,370**	**–27,535**	**–25,717**	**–27,741**	**–28,645**
General merchandise: imports f.o.b.	3 110	. .	–21,325	–25,650	–25,358	–26,370	–27,535	–25,717	–27,741	–28,645
Goods for processing: imports f.o.b.	3 150	. .	...	...	...	...	...	...	...	...
Repairs on goods	3 160	. .	...	...	...	...	...	...	...	...
Goods procured in ports by carriers	3 170	. .	...	...	...	...	...	...	...	...
Nonmonetary gold	3 180	. .	...	...	...	...	...	...	...	...
B. SERVICES	4 200	. .	–14,546	–15,603	–21,523	–21,706	–12,152	–13,475	–20,476	–14,124
Total credit	2 200	. .	*3,347*	*3,480*	*2,772*	*4,257*	*4,730*	*5,380*	*4,785*	*5,182*
Total debit	3 200	. .	*–17,893*	*–19,083*	*–24,295*	*–25,963*	*–16,882*	*–18,855*	*–25,262*	*–19,307*
Transportation services, credit	2 205	. .	**...**	**...**	**...**	**...**	**...**	**...**	**...**	**...**
Passenger	2 850	. .	...	...	...	...	...	...	...	...
Freight	2 851	. .	...	...	...	...	...	...	...	...
Other	2 852	. .	...	...	...	...	...	...	...	...
Sea transport, passenger	2 207	. .	...	...	...	...	...	...	...	...
Sea transport, freight	2 208	. .	...	...	...	...	...	...	...	...
Sea transport, other	2 209	. .	...	...	...	...	...	...	...	...
Air transport, passenger	2 211	. .	...	...	...	...	...	...	...	...
Air transport, freight	2 212	. .	...	...	...	...	...	...	...	...
Air transport, other	2 213	. .	...	...	...	...	...	...	...	...
Other transport, passenger	2 215	. .	...	...	...	...	...	...	...	...
Other transport, freight	2 216	. .	...	...	...	...	...	...	...	...
Other transport, other	2 217	. .	...	...	...	...	...	...	...	...
Transportation services, debit	3 205	. .	**–1,823**	**–2,193**	**–2,166**	**–2,136**	**–2,230**	**–2,083**	**–2,247**	**–2,320**
Passenger	3 850	. .	...	...	...	...	...	...	...	...
Freight	3 851	. .	*–1,823*	*–2,193*	*–2,166*	*–2,136*	*–2,230*	*–2,083*	*–2,247*	*–2,320*
Other	3 852	. .	...	...	...	...	...	...	...	...
Sea transport, passenger	3 207	. .	...	...	...	...	...	...	...	...
Sea transport, freight	3 208	. .	–1,823	–2,193	–2,166	–2,136	–2,230	–2,083	–2,247	–2,320
Sea transport, other	3 209	. .	...	...	...	...	...	...	...	...
Air transport, passenger	3 211	. .	...	...	...	...	...	...	...	...
Air transport, freight	3 212	. .	...	...	...	...	...	...	...	...
Air transport, other	3 213	. .	...	...	...	...	...	...	...	...
Other transport, passenger	3 215	. .	...	...	...	...	...	...	...	...
Other transport, freight	3 216	. .	...	...	...	...	...	...	...	...
Other transport, other	3 217	. .	...	...	...	...	...	...	...	...
Travel, credit	2 236	. .	**...**	**...**	**...**	**...**	**...**	**...**	**...**	**...**
Business travel	2 237	. .	...	...	...	...	...	...	...	...
Personal travel	2 240	. .	...	...	...	...	...	...	...	...
Travel, debit	3 236	. .	**...**	**...**	**...**	**...**	**...**	**...**	**...**	**...**
Business travel	3 237	. .	...	...	...	...	...	...	...	...
Personal travel	3 240	. .	...	...	...	...	...	...	...	...
Other services, credit	2 200	BA	**3,347**	**3,480**	**2,772**	**4,257**	**4,730**	**5,380**	**4,785**	**5,182**
Communications	2 245	. .	...	...	...	...	...	...	...	...
Construction	2 249	. .	...	...	...	...	...	...	...	...
Insurance	2 253	. .	...	...	...	...	...	...	...	...
Financial	2 260	. .	...	...	...	...	...	...	...	...
Computer and information	2 262	. .	...	...	...	...	...	...	...	...
Royalties and licence fees	2 266	. .	...	...	...	...	...	...	...	...
Other business services	2 268	. .	3,347	3,480	2,772	4,257	4,730	5,380	4,785	5,182
Personal, cultural, and recreational	2 287	. .	...	...	...	...	...	...	...	...
Government, n.i.e.	2 291	. .	...	...	...	...	...	...	...	...
Other services, debit	3 200	BA	**–16,070**	**–16,890**	**–22,129**	**–23,827**	**–14,652**	**–16,772**	**–23,015**	**–16,986**
Communications	3 245	. .	...	...	...	...	...	...	...	...
Construction	3 249	. .	...	...	...	...	...	...	...	...
Insurance	3 253	. .	–203	–244	–241	–235	–248	–232	–250	–258
Financial	3 260	. .	...	...	...	...	...	...	...	...
Computer and information	3 262	. .	...	...	...	...	...	...	...	...
Royalties and licence fees	3 266	. .	...	...	...	...	...	...	...	...
Other business services	3 268	. .	–6,902	–6,244	–10,186	–12,039	–6,181	–7,124	–8,445	–4,586
Personal, cultural, and recreational	3 287	. .	...	...	...	...	...	...	...	...
Government, n.i.e.	3 291	. .	–8,965	–10,402	–11,703	–11,553	–8,223	–9,417	–14,320	–12,142

Table 2 (Continued). STANDARD PRESENTATION, 1994–2001
(Millions of U.S. dollars)

	Code	1994	1995	1996	1997	1998	1999	2000	2001
C. INCOME	4 300 . .	1,472	2,803	2,446	2,785	2,768	2,925	480	–520
Total credit	2 300 . .	*4,032*	*4,987*	*5,127*	*5,756*	*5,810*	*5,811*	*3,349*	*4,130*
Total debit	3 300 . .	*–2,560*	*–2,184*	*–2,681*	*–2,971*	*–3,041*	*–2,887*	*–2,869*	*–4,650*
Compensation of employees, credit	2 310 . .	...	...	...	...	...	...	...	...
Compensation of employees, debit	3 310 . .	...	...	...	...	...	...	...	...
Investment income, credit	2 320 . .	**4,032**	**4,987**	**5,127**	**5,756**	**5,810**	**5,811**	**3,349**	**4,130**
Direct investment income	2 330 . .	...	...	...	...	...	...	...	...
Dividends and distributed branch profits	2 332 . .	...	...	...	...	...	...	...	...
Reinvested earnings and undistributed branch profits	2 333 . .	...	...	...	...	...	...	...	...
Income on debt (interest)	2 334 . .	...	...	...	...	...	...	...	...
Portfolio investment income	2 339 . .	...	...	...	...	...	...	...	...
Income on equity	2 340 . .	...	...	...	...	...	...	...	...
Income on bonds and notes	2 350 . .	...	...	...	...	...	...	...	...
Income on money market instruments	2 360 . .	...	...	...	...	...	...	...	...
Other investment income	2 370 . .	4,032	4,987	5,127	5,756	5,810	5,811	3,349	4,130
Investment income, debit	3 320 . .	**–2,560**	**–2,184**	**–2,681**	**–2,971**	**–3,041**	**–2,887**	**–2,869**	**–4,650**
Direct investment income	3 330 . .	–2,560	–2,184	–2,681	–2,971	–3,041	–2,887	–2,869	–4,650
Dividends and distributed branch profits	3 332 . .	–2,560	–2,184	–2,681	–2,971	–3,041	–2,887	–2,869	–4,650
Reinvested earnings and undistributed branch profits	3 333 . .	...	...	...	...	...	...	...	...
Income on debt (interest)	3 334 . .	...	...	...	...	...	...	...	...
Portfolio investment income	3 339 . .	...	...	...	...	...	...	...	...
Income on equity	3 340 . .	...	...	...	...	...	...	...	...
Income on bonds and notes	3 350 . .	...	...	...	...	...	...	...	...
Income on money market instruments	3 360 . .	...	...	...	...	...	...	...	...
Other investment income	3 370 . .	...	...	...	...	...	...	...	...
D. CURRENT TRANSFERS	4 379 . .	–18,702	–16,916	–15,613	–15,134	–15,053	–14,077	–15,511	–15,240
Credit	2 379 . .	...	...	...	...	...	...	...	...
General government	2 380 . .	...	...	...	...	...	...	...	...
Other sectors	2 390 . .	...	...	...	...	...	...	...	...
Workers' remittances	2 391 . .	...	...	...	...	...	...	...	...
Other current transfers	2 392 . .	...	...	...	...	...	...	...	...
Debit	3 379 . .	**–18,702**	**–16,916**	**–15,613**	**–15,134**	**–15,053**	**–14,077**	**–15,511**	**–15,240**
General government	3 380 . .	–600	–300	–100	–100	–99	–100	–100	–100
Other sectors	3 390 . .	–18,102	–16,616	–15,513	–15,034	–14,954	–13,977	–15,411	–15,140
Workers' remittances	3 391 . .	–18,102	–16,616	–15,513	–15,034	–14,954	–13,977	–15,411	–15,140
Other current transfers	3 392 . .	...	...	...	...	...	...	...	...
CAPITAL AND FINANCIAL ACCOUNT	4 996 . .	**10,486**	**5,325**	**–680**	**–305**	**13,150**	**–412**	**–14,336**	**–14,502**
CAPITAL ACCOUNT	4 994 . .	...	...	...	...	...	...	...	...
Total credit	2 994 . .	...	...	...	...	...	...	...	...
Total debit	3 994 . .	...	...	...	...	...	...	...	...
Capital transfers, credit	2 400 . .	...	...	...	...	...	...	...	...
General government	2 401 . .	...	...	...	...	...	...	...	...
Debt forgiveness	2 402 . .	...	...	...	...	...	...	...	...
Other capital transfers	2 410 . .	...	...	...	...	...	...	...	...
Other sectors	2 430 . .	...	...	...	...	...	...	...	...
Migrants' transfers	2 431 . .	...	...	...	...	...	...	...	...
Debt forgiveness	2 432 . .	...	...	...	...	...	...	...	...
Other capital transfers	2 440 . .	...	...	...	...	...	...	...	...
Capital transfers, debit	3 400 . .	...	...	...	...	...	...	...	...
General government	3 401 . .	...	...	...	...	...	...	...	...
Debt forgiveness	3 402 . .	...	...	...	...	...	...	...	...
Other capital transfers	3 410 . .	...	...	...	...	...	...	...	...
Other sectors	3 430 . .	...	...	...	...	...	...	...	...
Migrants' transfers	3 431 . .	...	...	...	...	...	...	...	...
Debt forgiveness	3 432 . .	...	...	...	...	...	...	...	...
Other capital transfers	3 440 . .	...	...	...	...	...	...	...	...
Nonproduced nonfinancial assets, credit	2 480 . .	...	...	...	...	...	...	...	...
Nonproduced nonfinancial assets, debit	3 480 . .	...	...	...	...	...	...	...	...

Table 2 (Continued). STANDARD PRESENTATION, 1994–2001

(Millions of U.S. dollars)

	Code	1994	1995	1996	1997	1998	1999	2000	2001
FINANCIAL ACCOUNT	4 995	**10,486**	**5,325**	**–680**	**–305**	**13,150**	**–412**	**–14,336**	**–14,502**
A. DIRECT INVESTMENT	4 500	350	–1,877	–1,129	3,044	4,289	–780	–1,884	20
Direct investment abroad	4 505	**...**	**...**	**...**	**...**	**...**	**...**	**...**	**...**
Equity capital	4 510	...	...	...	...	...	...	...	...
Claims on affiliated enterprises	4 515	...	...	...	...	...	...	...	...
Liabilities to affiliated enterprises	4 520	...	...	...	...	...	...	...	...
Reinvested earnings	4 525	...	...	...	...	...	...	...	...
Other capital	4 530	...	...	...	...	...	...	...	...
Claims on affiliated enterprises	4 535	...	...	...	...	...	...	...	...
Liabilities to affiliated enterprises	4 540	...	...	...	...	...	...	...	...
Direct investment in Saudi Arabia	4 555	**350**	**–1,877**	**–1,129**	**3,044**	**4,289**	**–780**	**–1,884**	**20**
Equity capital	4 560	...	...	...	...	...	...	...	...
Claims on direct investors	4 565	...	...	...	...	...	...	...	...
Liabilities to direct investors	4 570	...	...	...	...	...	...	...	...
Reinvested earnings	4 575	...	...	...	...	...	...	...	...
Other capital	4 580	350	–1,877	–1,129	3,044	4,289	–780	–1,884	20
Claims on direct investors	4 585	...	...	...	...	...	...	...	...
Liabilities to direct investors	4 590	...	...	...	...	...	...	...	...
B. PORTFOLIO INVESTMENT	4 600	–2,527	4,057	–2,642	–7,362	6,941	11,712	–9,394	–2,798
Assets	4 602	**–2,527**	**4,057**	**–2,642**	**–7,362**	**6,941**	**11,712**	**–9,394**	**–2,798**
Equity securities	4 610	...	...	...	...	...	...	...	...
Monetary authorities	4 611	...	...	...	...	...	...	...	...
General government	4 612	...	...	...	...	...	...	...	...
Banks	4 613	...	...	...	...	...	...	...	...
Other sectors	4 614	...	...	...	...	...	...	...	...
Debt securities	4 619	–2,527	4,057	–2,642	–7,362	6,941	11,712	–9,394	–2,798
Bonds and notes	4 620	–2,527	4,057	–2,642	–7,362	6,941	11,712	–9,394	–2,798
Monetary authorities	4 621	...	...	...	...	...	...	...	...
General government	4 622	–2,527	4,057	–2,642	–7,362	6,941	11,712	–9,394	–2,798
Banks	4 623	...	...	...	...	...	...	...	...
Other sectors	4 624	...	...	...	...	...	...	...	...
Money market instruments	4 630	...	...	...	...	...	...	...	...
Monetary authorities	4 631	...	...	...	...	...	...	...	...
General government	4 632	...	...	...	...	...	...	...	...
Banks	4 633	...	...	...	...	...	...	...	...
Other sectors	4 634	...	...	...	...	...	...	...	...
Liabilities	4 652	**...**	**...**	**...**	**...**	**...**	**...**	**...**	**...**
Equity securities	4 660	...	...	...	...	...	...	...	...
Banks	4 663	...	...	...	...	...	...	...	...
Other sectors	4 664	...	...	...	...	...	...	...	...
Debt securities	4 669	...	...	...	...	...	...	...	...
Bonds and notes	4 670	...	...	...	...	...	...	...	...
Monetary authorities	4 671	...	...	...	...	...	...	...	...
General government	4 672	...	...	...	...	...	...	...	...
Banks	4 673	...	...	...	...	...	...	...	...
Other sectors	4 674	...	...	...	...	...	...	...	...
Money market instruments	4 680	...	...	...	...	...	...	...	...
Monetary authorities	4 681	...	...	...	...	...	...	...	...
General government	4 682	...	...	...	...	...	...	...	...
Banks	4 683	...	...	...	...	...	...	...	...
Other sectors	4 684	...	...	...	...	...	...	...	...
C. FINANCIAL DERIVATIVES	4 910	...	...	...	...	...	...	...	...
Monetary authorities	4 911	...	...	...	...	...	...	...	...
General government	4 912	...	...	...	...	...	...	...	...
Banks	4 913	...	...	...	...	...	...	...	...
Other sectors	4 914	...	...	...	...	...	...	...	...
Assets	4 900	**...**	**...**	**...**	**...**	**...**	**...**	**...**	**...**
Monetary authorities	4 901	...	...	...	...	...	...	...	...
General government	4 902	...	...	...	...	...	...	...	...
Banks	4 903	...	...	...	...	...	...	...	...
Other sectors	4 904	...	...	...	...	...	...	...	...
Liabilities	4 905	**...**	**...**	**...**	**...**	**...**	**...**	**...**	**...**
Monetary authorities	4 906	...	...	...	...	...	...	...	...
General government	4 907	...	...	...	...	...	...	...	...
Banks	4 908	...	...	...	...	...	...	...	...
Other sectors	4 909	...	...	...	...	...	...	...	...

Table 2 (Concluded). STANDARD PRESENTATION, 1994–2001
(Millions of U.S. dollars)

	Code		1994	1995	1996	1997	1998	1999	2000	2001
D. OTHER INVESTMENT	4 700	. .	12,518	4,363	8,840	4,661	1,200	–8,529	–394	–13,632
Assets	4 703	. .	**12,022**	**4,221**	**9,115**	**2,688**	**1,983**	**–10,678**	**–3,943**	**–12,343**
Trade credits	4 706	. .	. . .	. . .	. . .	. . .	. . .	. . .	. . .	. . .
General government	4 707	. .	. . .	. . .	. . .	. . .	. . .	. . .	. . .	. . .
of which: Short-term	4 709	. .	. . .	. . .	. . .	. . .	. . .	. . .	. . .	. . .
Other sectors	4 710	. .	. . .	. . .	. . .	. . .	. . .	. . .	. . .	. . .
of which: Short-term	4 712	. .	. . .	. . .	. . .	. . .	. . .	. . .	. . .	. . .
Loans	4 714	. .	. . .	. . .	. . .	. . .	. . .	. . .	. . .	. . .
Monetary authorities	4 715	. .	. . .	. . .	. . .	. . .	. . .	. . .	. . .	. . .
of which: Short-term	4 718	. .	. . .	. . .	. . .	. . .	. . .	. . .	. . .	. . .
General government	4 719	. .	. . .	. . .	. . .	. . .	. . .	. . .	. . .	. . .
of which: Short-term	4 721	. .	. . .	. . .	. . .	. . .	. . .	. . .	. . .	. . .
Banks	4 722	. .	. . .	. . .	. . .	. . .	. . .	. . .	. . .	. . .
of which: Short-term	4 724	. .	. . .	. . .	. . .	. . .	. . .	. . .	. . .	. . .
Other sectors	4 725	. .	. . .	. . .	. . .	. . .	. . .	. . .	. . .	. . .
of which: Short-term	4 727	. .	. . .	. . .	. . .	. . .	. . .	. . .	. . .	. . .
Currency and deposits	4 730	. .	12,022	4,221	9,115	2,688	1,983	–10,678	–3,943	–12,343
Monetary authorities	4 731	. .	. . .	. . .	. . .	. . .	. . .	. . .	. . .	. . .
General government	4 732	. .	. . .	. . .	. . .	. . .	. . .	. . .	. . .	. . .
Banks	4 733	. .	3,588	46	–2,188	1,777	3,621	–1,480	–2,595	491
Other sectors	4 734	. .	8,434	4,175	11,303	911	–1,639	–9,198	–1,348	–12,834
Other assets	4 736	. .	. . .	. . .	. . .	. . .	. . .	. . .	. . .	. . .
Monetary authorities	4 737	. .	. . .	. . .	. . .	. . .	. . .	. . .	. . .	. . .
of which: Short-term	4 739	. .	. . .	. . .	. . .	. . .	. . .	. . .	. . .	. . .
General government	4 740	. .	. . .	. . .	. . .	. . .	. . .	. . .	. . .	. . .
of which: Short-term	4 742	. .	. . .	. . .	. . .	. . .	. . .	. . .	. . .	. . .
Banks	4 743	. .	. . .	. . .	. . .	. . .	. . .	. . .	. . .	. . .
of which: Short-term	4 745	. .	. . .	. . .	. . .	. . .	. . .	. . .	. . .	. . .
Other sectors	4 746	. .	. . .	. . .	. . .	. . .	. . .	. . .	. . .	. . .
of which: Short-term	4 748	. .	. . .	. . .	. . .	. . .	. . .	. . .	. . .	. . .
Liabilities	4 753	. .	**497**	**142**	**–275**	**1,973**	**–782**	**2,149**	**3,549**	**–1,289**
Trade credits	4 756	. .	. . .	. . .	. . .	. . .	. . .	. . .	. . .	. . .
General government	4 757	. .	. . .	. . .	. . .	. . .	. . .	. . .	. . .	. . .
of which: Short-term	4 759	. .	. . .	. . .	. . .	. . .	. . .	. . .	. . .	. . .
Other sectors	4 760	. .	. . .	. . .	. . .	. . .	. . .	. . .	. . .	. . .
of which: Short-term	4 762	. .	. . .	. . .	. . .	. . .	. . .	. . .	. . .	. . .
Loans	4 764	. .	. . .	. . .	. . .	. . .	. . .	. . .	. . .	. . .
Monetary authorities	4 765	. .	. . .	. . .	. . .	. . .	. . .	. . .	. . .	. . .
of which: Use of Fund credit and loans from the Fund	4 766	. .	. . .	. . .	. . .	. . .	. . .	. . .	. . .	. . .
of which: Short-term	4 768	. .	. . .	. . .	. . .	. . .	. . .	. . .	. . .	. . .
General government	4 769	. .	. . .	. . .	. . .	. . .	. . .	. . .	. . .	. . .
of which: Short-term	4 771	. .	. . .	. . .	. . .	. . .	. . .	. . .	. . .	. . .
Banks	4 772	. .	. . .	. . .	. . .	. . .	. . .	. . .	. . .	. . .
of which: Short-term	4 774	. .	. . .	. . .	. . .	. . .	. . .	. . .	. . .	. . .
Other sectors	4 775	. .	. . .	. . .	. . .	. . .	. . .	. . .	. . .	. . .
of which: Short-term	4 777	. .	. . .	. . .	. . .	. . .	. . .	. . .	. . .	. . .
Currency and deposits	4 780	. .	497	142	–275	1,973	–782	2,149	3,549	–1,289
Monetary authorities	4 781	. .	. . .	. . .	. . .	. . .	. . .	. . .	. . .	. . .
General government	4 782	. .	. . .	. . .	. . .	. . .	. . .	. . .	. . .	. . .
Banks	4 783	. .	497	142	–275	1,973	–782	2,149	3,549	–1,289
Other sectors	4 784	. .	. . .	. . .	. . .	. . .	. . .	. . .	. . .	. . .
Other liabilities	4 786	. .	. . .	. . .	. . .	. . .	. . .	. . .	. . .	. . .
Monetary authorities	4 787	. .	. . .	. . .	. . .	. . .	. . .	. . .	. . .	. . .
of which: Short-term	4 789	. .	. . .	. . .	. . .	. . .	. . .	. . .	. . .	. . .
General government	4 790	. .	. . .	. . .	. . .	. . .	. . .	. . .	. . .	. . .
of which: Short-term	4 792	. .	. . .	. . .	. . .	. . .	. . .	. . .	. . .	. . .
Banks	4 793	. .	. . .	. . .	. . .	. . .	. . .	. . .	. . .	. . .
of which: Short-term	4 795	. .	. . .	. . .	. . .	. . .	. . .	. . .	. . .	. . .
Other sectors	4 796	. .	. . .	. . .	. . .	. . .	. . .	. . .	. . .	. . .
of which: Short-term	4 798	. .	. . .	. . .	. . .	. . .	. . .	. . .	. . .	. . .
E. RESERVE ASSETS	4 802	. .	146	–1,217	–5,749	–648	719	–2,815	–2,665	1,909
Monetary gold	4 812	. .	. . .	. . .	. . .	. . .	. . .	. . .	. . .	. . .
Special drawing rights	4 811	. .	–21	–49	–48	–42	–46	602	–47	–58
Reserve position in the Fund	4 810	. .	373	45	20	39	12	–640	–71	–1,273
Foreign exchange	4 803	. .	–206	–1,213	–5,721	–645	753	–2,776	–2,546	3,240
Other claims	4 813	. .	. . .	. . .	. . .	. . .	. . .	. . .	. . .	. . .
NET ERRORS AND OMISSIONS	4 998	. .	. . .	. . .	. . .	. . .	. . .	. . .	. . .	. . .

Part 3 of the *Yearbook* contains descriptions of the methodologies, compilation practices, and sources used to compile these data.

Table 1. ANALYTIC PRESENTATION, 1994–2001
(Millions of U.S. dollars)

	Code		1994	1995	1996	1997	1998	1999	2000	2001
A. Current Account [1]	4 993	Z.	**–187.5**	**–244.5**	**–199.5**	**–184.8**	**–247.5**	**–320.2**	**...**	**...**
Goods: exports f.o.b	2 100	..	818.8	993.3	988.0	904.6	967.7	1,027.1	...	...
Goods: imports f.o.b	3 100	..	–1,022.0	–1,242.9	–1,264.0	–1,176.0	–1,280.6	–1,372.8	...	...
Balance on Goods	4 100	..	*–203.2*	*–249.6*	*–275.9*	*–271.5*	*–312.9*	*–345.8*	...	...
Services: credit	2 200	..	412.3	512.5	378.6	371.7	425.1	416.1	...	...
Services: debit	3 200	..	–492.7	–578.2	–395.9	–391.7	–442.9	–430.4	...	...
Balance on Goods and Services	4 991	..	*–283.6*	*–315.3*	*–293.2*	*–291.5*	*–330.6*	*–360.0*	...	...
Income: credit	2 300	..	63.3	87.2	81.3	67.9	76.6	83.3	...	...
Income: debit	3 300	..	–164.5	–211.5	–154.1	–139.8	–164.6	–202.5	...	...
Balance on Goods, Services, and Income	4 992	..	*–384.7*	*–439.6*	*–366.0*	*–363.4*	*–418.6*	*–479.2*	...	...
Current transfers: credit	2 379	Z.	267.0	284.7	244.3	258.8	254.7	225.4	...	...
Current transfers: debit	3 379	..	–69.7	–89.6	–77.8	–80.3	–83.6	–66.3	...	...
B. Capital Account [1]	4 994	Z.	**190.6**	**187.0**	**169.2**	**96.0**	**98.3**	**98.6**	**...**	**...**
Capital account: credit	2 994	Z.	200.5	201.2	169.3	96.3	98.8	99.0	...	...
Capital account: debit	3 994	..	–9.9	–14.2	–.1	–.3	–.4	–.5	...	...
Total, Groups A Plus B	4 981	..	*3.2*	*–57.5*	*–30.4*	*–88.9*	*–149.1*	*–221.6*	...	...
C. Financial Account [1]	4 995	W.	**48.5**	**44.2**	**–179.1**	**3.5**	**–109.7**	**–54.8**	**...**	**...**
Direct investment abroad	4 505	..	–17.4	3.3	–3.0	.5	–10.5	–14.5	...	...
Direct investment in Senegal	4 555	Z.	66.9	31.7	8.4	176.4	70.8	156.6	...	...
Portfolio investment assets	4 602	..	–1.5	–.4	–25.8	–18.9	–21.9	–31.3	...	...
Equity securities	4 610	..	–1.5	–.4	–2.4	.9	–9.8	–6.2	...	...
Debt securities	4 619	..	...	...	–23.4	–19.9	–12.1	–25.1	...	...
Portfolio investment liabilities	4 652	Z.	.5	4.0	–4.8	–8.1	–3.9	...	...	...
Equity securities	4 660	..	.5	4.1	...	8.4	2.6	3.4	...	...
Debt securities	4 669	Z.	...	–.1	–4.8	–16.4	–6.5	–3.4	...	...
Financial derivatives	4 910	..	...	...	...	–.7	.1	–.7	...	...
Financial derivatives assets	4 900	..	...	...	...	–.7	...	–.7	...	...
Financial derivatives liabilities	4 905	..	...	...	...	...	.1	...	...	...
Other investment assets	4 703	..	–92.5	–6.2	–70.7	–22.1	–58.8	–62.3	...	...
Monetary authorities	4 701	..	...	...	...	...	...	...	...	...
General government	4 704	..	...	...	–3.1	–.9	–.4	...	...	...
Banks	4 705	..	–108.8	10.9	30.9	–24.5	–42.4	–54.8	...	...
Other sectors	4 728	..	16.3	–17.1	–98.5	3.3	–15.9	–7.6	...	...
Other investment liabilities	4 753	W.	92.6	11.8	–83.2	–123.7	–85.5	–102.6	...	...
Monetary authorities	4 753	WA	–76.2	–35.7	1.5	.3	.7	2.5	...	...
General government	4 753	ZB	90.7	83.9	–140.4	–132.6	–112.9	–114.8	...	...
Banks	4 753	ZC	9.8	–27.1	–4.3	23.6	23.5	5.9	...	...
Other sectors	4 753	ZD	68.3	–9.3	60.0	–14.9	3.3	3.7	...	...
Total, Groups A Through C	4 983	..	*51.6*	*–13.3*	*–209.4*	*–85.4*	*–258.8*	*–276.4*	...	...
D. Net Errors and Omissions	4 998	..	**–28.9**	**–19.6**	**7.6**	**–9.3**	**10.7**	**8.2**	**...**	**...**
Total, Groups A Through D	4 984	..	*22.8*	*–32.9*	*–201.9*	*–94.7*	*–248.1*	*–268.2*	...	...
E. Reserves and Related Items	4 802	A.	**–22.8**	**32.9**	**201.9**	**94.7**	**248.1**	**268.2**	**...**	**...**
Reserve assets	4 802	..	–170.1	–74.8	–34.8	–137.4	–20.7	–31.6	...	...
Use of Fund credit and loans	4 766	..	38.9	42.9	–9.8	–12.8	–11.6	–13.4	...	...
Exceptional financing	4 920	..	108.4	64.9	246.5	244.8	280.4	313.2	...	...
Conversion rates: CFA francs per U.S. dollar	0 101	..	**555.20**	**499.15**	**511.55**	**583.67**	**589.95**	**615.70**	**711.98**	**733.04**

[1] Excludes components that have been classified in the categories of Group E.

Table 2. STANDARD PRESENTATION, 1994–2001

(Millions of U.S. dollars)

	Code	1994	1995	1996	1997	1998	1999	2000	2001
CURRENT ACCOUNT	4 993 . .	**–187.5**	**–244.5**	**–199.5**	**–184.8**	**–247.5**	**–320.2**	**. . .**	**. . .**
A. GOODS	4 100 . .	–203.2	–249.6	–275.9	–271.5	–312.9	–345.8	. . .	. . .
Credit	2 100 . .	**818.8**	**993.3**	**988.0**	**904.6**	**967.7**	**1,027.1**	**. . .**	**. . .**
General merchandise: exports f.o.b.	2 110 . .	790.9	968.6	963.2	880.7	945.9	1,002.7	. . .	. . .
Goods for processing: exports f.o.b.	2 150 . .	. . .	. . .	. . .	. . .	.2	. . .	. . .	. . .
Repairs on goods	2 160 . .	. . .	. . .	.1	.2	.1	.1	. . .	. . .
Goods procured in ports by carriers	2 170 . .	27.9	24.7	24.8	23.6	21.5	24.2	. . .	. . .
Nonmonetary gold	2 180 . .	. . .	. . .	. . .	. . .	. . .	. . .	. . .	. . .
Debit	3 100 . .	**–1,022.0**	**–1,242.9**	**–1,264.0**	**–1,176.0**	**–1,280.6**	**–1,372.8**	**. . .**	**. . .**
General merchandise: imports f.o.b.	3 110 . .	–1,022.0	–1,242.9	–1,263.7	–1,174.5	–1,279.0	–1,372.8	. . .	. . .
Goods for processing: imports f.o.b.	3 150 . .	. . .	. . .	. . .	. . .	. . .	. . .	. . .	. . .
Repairs on goods	3 160 . .	. . .	. . .	–.2	–1.6	–1.5	. . .	. . .	. . .
Goods procured in ports by carriers	3 170 . .	. . .	. . .	. . .	. . .	. . .	. . .	. . .	. . .
Nonmonetary gold	3 180 . .	. . .	. . .	. . .	. . .	. . .	. . .	. . .	. . .
B. SERVICES	4 200 . .	–80.4	–65.7	–17.2	–20.0	–17.8	–14.2	. . .	. . .
Total credit	2 200 . .	*412.3*	*512.5*	*378.6*	*371.7*	*425.1*	*416.1*	. . .	. . .
Total debit	3 200 . .	*–492.7*	*–578.2*	*–395.9*	*–391.7*	*–442.9*	*–430.4*	. . .	. . .
Transportation services, credit	2 205 . .	**41.8**	**56.2**	**72.1**	**52.8**	**49.6**	**35.7**	**. . .**	**. . .**
Passenger	2 850 . .	*.2*	*.2*	*8.2*	*9.0*	*8.9*	*9.4*	. . .	. . .
Freight	2 851 . .	*15.4*	*18.6*	*1.5*	*1.5*	*1.5*	*1.5*	. . .	. . .
Other	2 852 . .	*26.3*	*37.4*	*62.3*	*42.3*	*39.2*	*24.7*	. . .	. . .
Sea transport, passenger	2 207 . .	. . .	. . .	. . .	. . .	. . .	. . .	. . .	. . .
Sea transport, freight	2 208 . .	15.4	18.6	. . .	. . .	. . .	. . .	. . .	. . .
Sea transport, other	2 209 . .	. . .	. . .	42.2	21.4	17.8	12.2	. . .	. . .
Air transport, passenger	2 211 . .	.2	.2	.2	.2	.1	.1	. . .	. . .
Air transport, freight	2 212 . .	. . .	. . .	. . .	. . .	. . .	. . .	. . .	. . .
Air transport, other	2 213 . .	. . .	. . .	3.9	7.0	7.7	6.7	. . .	. . .
Other transport, passenger	2 215 . .	. . .	. . .	8.0	8.9	8.8	9.3	. . .	. . .
Other transport, freight	2 216 . .	. . .	. . .	1.5	1.5	1.5	1.5	. . .	. . .
Other transport, other	2 217 . .	26.3	37.4	16.2	13.9	13.7	5.8	. . .	. . .
Transportation services, debit	3 205 . .	**–181.0**	**–231.0**	**–246.3**	**–236.8**	**–248.4**	**–253.2**	**. . .**	**. . .**
Passenger	3 850 . .	*–57.9*	*–82.0*	*–74.0*	*–74.7*	*–81.0*	*–82.1*	. . .	. . .
Freight	3 851 . .	*–116.1*	*–141.2*	*–160.6*	*–151.6*	*–157.0*	*–159.5*	. . .	. . .
Other	3 852 . .	*–6.9*	*–7.7*	*–11.7*	*–10.5*	*–10.4*	*–11.6*	. . .	. . .
Sea transport, passenger	3 207 . .	. . .	. . .	. . .	. . .	. . .	. . .	. . .	. . .
Sea transport, freight	3 208 . .	–116.1	–141.2	–143.6	–133.5	–97.4	–108.1	. . .	. . .
Sea transport, other	3 209 . .	. . .	. . .	. . .	. . .	. . .	. . .	. . .	. . .
Air transport, passenger	3 211 . .	–57.9	–82.0	–73.4	–74.2	–80.4	–81.6	. . .	. . .
Air transport, freight	3 212 . .	. . .	. . .	–16.9	–17.7	–59.1	–50.2	. . .	. . .
Air transport, other	3 213 . .	. . .	. . .	–11.6	–10.4	–10.3	–11.4	. . .	. . .
Other transport, passenger	3 215 . .	. . .	. . .	–.6	–.6	–.6	–.5	. . .	. . .
Other transport, freight	3 216 . .	. . .	. . .	–.1	–.4	–.5	–1.2	. . .	. . .
Other transport, other	3 217 . .	–6.9	–7.7	–.1	–.1	–.1	–.1	. . .	. . .
Travel, credit	2 236 . .	**129.6**	**167.9**	**156.2**	**162.4**	**171.6**	**173.6**	**. . .**	**. . .**
Business travel	2 237 . .	66.0	85.5	58.1	60.6	64.3	69.2	. . .	. . .
Personal travel	2 240 . .	63.6	82.3	98.1	101.8	107.3	104.4	. . .	. . .
Travel, debit	3 236 . .	**–47.7**	**–71.7**	**–53.3**	**–52.7**	**–53.9**	**–53.9**	**. . .**	**. . .**
Business travel	3 237 . .	–24.3	–36.5	–5.9	–5.0	–4.5	–5.5	. . .	. . .
Personal travel	3 240 . .	–23.4	–35.2	–47.4	–47.7	–49.4	–48.4	. . .	. . .
Other services, credit	2 200 BA	**240.9**	**288.4**	**150.4**	**156.5**	**203.9**	**206.9**	**. . .**	**. . .**
Communications	2 245 . .	. . .	. . .	36.4	45.1	50.7	48.8	. . .	. . .
Construction	2 249 . .	. . .	. . .	1.9	3.4	12.7	7.9	. . .	. . .
Insurance	2 253 . .	1.7	2.1	1.0	1.3	8.9	2.6	. . .	. . .
Financial	2 260 . .	. . .	. . .	.5	.7	2.5	4.8	. . .	. . .
Computer and information	2 262 . .	. . .	. . .	.1	. . .	. . .	.7	. . .	. . .
Royalties and licence fees	2 266 . .	.7	1.1	.1	. . .	.1	1.6	. . .	. . .
Other business services	2 268 . .	135.6	136.8	47.0	63.2	70.0	75.7	. . .	. . .
Personal, cultural, and recreational	2 287 . .	. . .	. . .	–.1	. . .	. . .	. . .	. . .	. . .
Government, n.i.e.	2 291 . .	102.9	148.5	63.4	42.8	58.9	64.8	. . .	. . .
Other services, debit	3 200 BA	**–264.0**	**–275.5**	**–96.2**	**–102.2**	**–140.7**	**–123.3**	**. . .**	**. . .**
Communications	3 245 . .	. . .	. . .	–3.6	–4.4	–3.0	–4.7	. . .	. . .
Construction	3 249 . .	. . .	. . .	–2.3	–12.9	–.5	–.5	. . .	. . .
Insurance	3 253 . .	–23.3	–28.3	–35.1	–32.2	–40.3	–38.5	. . .	. . .
Financial	3 260 . .	. . .	. . .	–2.6	–4.2	–7.0	–3.1	. . .	. . .
Computer and information	3 262 . .	. . .	. . .	–1.3	–2.8	–.9	–3.5	. . .	. . .
Royalties and licence fees	3 266 . .	–.1	–.1	–.5	–2.2	–3.6	–5.2	. . .	. . .
Other business services	3 268 . .	–80.7	–73.5	–39.9	–40.6	–74.7	–56.4	. . .	. . .
Personal, cultural, and recreational	3 287 . .	. . .	. . .	–.4	–.4	. . .	–.2	. . .	. . .
Government, n.i.e.	3 291 . .	–159.8	–173.6	–10.4	–2.4	–10.5	–11.1	. . .	. . .

Table 2 (Continued). STANDARD PRESENTATION, 1994–2001
(Millions of U.S. dollars)

	Code	1994	1995	1996	1997	1998	1999	2000	2001
C. INCOME	4 300 . .	−101.2	−124.3	−72.9	−71.9	−87.9	−119.2	. . .	. . .
Total credit	2 300 . .	*63.3*	*87.2*	*81.3*	*67.9*	*76.6*	*83.3*	. . .	. . .
Total debit	3 300 . .	*−164.5*	*−211.5*	*−154.1*	*−139.8*	*−164.6*	*−202.5*	. . .	. . .
Compensation of employees, credit	2 310 . .	**40.8**	**59.5**	**68.0**	**58.0**	**56.5**	**56.4**	**. . .**	**. . .**
Compensation of employees, debit	3 310 . .	**. . .**	**. . .**	**−7.8**	**−5.3**	**−5.8**	**−6.8**	**. . .**	**. . .**
Investment income, credit	2 320 . .	**22.6**	**27.7**	**13.3**	**9.9**	**20.2**	**26.9**	**. . .**	**. . .**
Direct investment income	2 330 . .	3.6	8.8	1.5	.5	1.8	5.2	. . .	. . .
Dividends and distributed branch profits	2 332 . .	3.6	8.8	.5	.1	1.5	1.5	. . .	. . .
Reinvested earnings and undistributed branch profits	2 333 . .	. . .	. . .	1.0	.4	.2	3.5	. . .	. . .
Income on debt (interest)	2 334 . .	. . .	. . .	. . .	. . .	. . .	.2	. . .	. . .
Portfolio investment income	2 339 . .	. . .	. . .	.6	.5	1.3	2.5	. . .	. . .
Income on equity	2 340 . .	. . .	. . .	.1	.1	. . .	.3	. . .	. . .
Income on bonds and notes	2 350 . .	. . .	. . .	.6	.4	1.2	1.6	. . .	. . .
Income on money market instruments	2 360 . .	. . .	. . .	. . .	. . .	. . .	.6	. . .	. . .
Other investment income	2 370 . .	18.9	18.9	11.1	8.9	17.1	19.2	. . .	. . .
Investment income, debit	3 320 . .	**−164.5**	**−211.5**	**−146.3**	**−134.5**	**−158.8**	**−195.7**	**. . .**	**. . .**
Direct investment income	3 330 . .	−34.4	−61.8	−14.4	−16.8	−45.1	−73.7	. . .	. . .
Dividends and distributed branch profits	3 332 . .	−15.3	−47.5	−14.0	−11.6	−38.4	−48.1	. . .	. . .
Reinvested earnings and undistributed branch profits	3 333 . .	−19.1	−14.3	−.3	−4.4	−6.2	−24.9	. . .	. . .
Income on debt (interest)	3 334 . .	. . .	. . .	−.1	−.8	−.5	−.7	. . .	. . .
Portfolio investment income	3 339 . .	. . .	. . .	−13.5	−12.4	−15.4	−18.3	. . .	. . .
Income on equity	3 340 . .	. . .	. . .	−3.9	−5.7	−7.9	−11.1	. . .	. . .
Income on bonds and notes	3 350 . .	. . .	. . .	−9.6	−6.7	−7.4	−7.0	. . .	. . .
Income on money market instruments	3 360 . .	. . .	. . .	. . .	. . .	. . .	−.2	. . .	. . .
Other investment income	3 370 . .	−130.1	−149.7	−118.4	−105.3	−98.2	−103.7	. . .	. . .
D. CURRENT TRANSFERS	4 379 . .	197.3	195.1	166.5	178.5	171.1	159.1	. . .	. . .
Credit	2 379 . .	**267.0**	**284.7**	**244.3**	**258.8**	**254.7**	**225.4**	**. . .**	**. . .**
General government	2 380 . .	166.3	166.2	139.5	153.8	148.3	82.7	. . .	. . .
Other sectors	2 390 . .	100.6	118.4	104.9	105.1	106.4	142.7	. . .	. . .
Workers' remittances	2 391 . .	73.1	86.5	82.5	92.5	91.0	129.7	. . .	. . .
Other current transfers	2 392 . .	27.6	32.0	22.4	12.6	15.4	13.0	. . .	. . .
Debit	3 379 . .	**−69.7**	**−89.6**	**−77.8**	**−80.3**	**−83.6**	**−66.3**	**. . .**	**. . .**
General government	3 380 . .	−6.0	−9.0	−12.9	−10.3	−13.4	−6.1	. . .	. . .
Other sectors	3 390 . .	−63.7	−80.5	−65.0	−70.0	−70.2	−60.2	. . .	. . .
Workers' remittances	3 391 . .	−59.9	−76.4	−60.2	−64.5	−60.7	−54.0	. . .	. . .
Other current transfers	3 392 . .	−3.9	−4.2	−4.8	−5.6	−9.4	−6.2	. . .	. . .
CAPITAL AND FINANCIAL ACCOUNT	4 996 . .	**216.3**	**264.1**	**192.0**	**194.1**	**236.7**	**312.0**	**. . .**	**. . .**
CAPITAL ACCOUNT	4 994 . .	**218.9**	**208.8**	**169.2**	**96.0**	**98.3**	**98.6**	**. . .**	**. . .**
Total credit	2 994 . .	*228.8*	*223.0*	*169.3*	*96.3*	*98.8*	*99.0*	. . .	. . .
Total debit	3 994 . .	*−9.9*	*−14.2*	*−.1*	*−.3*	*−.4*	*−.5*	. . .	. . .
Capital transfers, credit	2 400 . .	**228.8**	**223.0**	**169.3**	**96.3**	**98.8**	**99.0**	**. . .**	**. . .**
General government	2 401 . .	224.3	217.7	164.4	92.2	95.3	95.1	. . .	. . .
Debt forgiveness	2 402 . .	28.3	21.8	. . .	. . .	. . .	. . .	. . .	. . .
Other capital transfers	2 410 . .	196.0	195.9	164.4	92.2	95.3	95.1	. . .	. . .
Other sectors	2 430 . .	4.5	5.3	4.9	4.1	3.5	4.0	. . .	. . .
Migrants' transfers	2 431 . .	. . .	. . .	. . .	. . .	. . .	. . .	. . .	. . .
Debt forgiveness	2 432 . .	. . .	. . .	. . .	. . .	. . .	. . .	. . .	. . .
Other capital transfers	2 440 . .	4.5	5.3	4.9	4.1	3.5	4.0	. . .	. . .
Capital transfers, debit	3 400 . .	**−9.9**	**−14.2**	**. . .**	**. . .**	**. . .**	**. . .**	**. . .**	**. . .**
General government	3 401 . .	−7.0	−10.6	. . .	. . .	. . .	. . .	. . .	. . .
Debt forgiveness	3 402 . .	. . .	. . .	. . .	. . .	. . .	. . .	. . .	. . .
Other capital transfers	3 410 . .	−7.0	−10.6	. . .	. . .	. . .	. . .	. . .	. . .
Other sectors	3 430 . .	−2.8	−3.6	. . .	. . .	. . .	. . .	. . .	. . .
Migrants' transfers	3 431 . .	. . .	. . .	. . .	. . .	. . .	. . .	. . .	. . .
Debt forgiveness	3 432 . .	. . .	. . .	. . .	. . .	. . .	. . .	. . .	. . .
Other capital transfers	3 440 . .	−2.8	−3.6	. . .	. . .	. . .	. . .	. . .	. . .
Nonproduced nonfinancial assets, credit	2 480 . .	**. . .**	**. . .**	**. . .**	**. . .**	**. . .**	**. . .**	**. . .**	**. . .**
Nonproduced nonfinancial assets, debit	3 480 . .	**. . .**	**. . .**	**−.1**	**−.3**	**−.4**	**−.5**	**. . .**	**. . .**

Table 2 (Continued). STANDARD PRESENTATION, 1994–2001

(Millions of U.S. dollars)

	Code	1994	1995	1996	1997	1998	1999	2000	2001
FINANCIAL ACCOUNT	4 995 . .	**–2.6**	**55.3**	**22.8**	**98.2**	**138.4**	**213.4**	**...**	**...**
A. DIRECT INVESTMENT	4 500 . .	49.5	35.0	5.4	176.9	60.3	142.2	...	...
Direct investment abroad	4 505 . .	**–17.4**	**3.3**	**–3.0**	**.5**	**–10.5**	**–14.5**	**...**	**...**
Equity capital	4 510 . .	–5.9	12.5	.2	–.5	–7.3	–8.1	...	...
Claims on affiliated enterprises	4 515 . .	...	...	...	...	...	...	...	...
Liabilities to affiliated enterprises	4 520 . .	...	...	...	...	...	...	...	...
Reinvested earnings	4 525 . .	...	...	–1.0	–.4	–.2	–3.5	...	...
Other capital	4 530 . .	–11.5	–9.2	–2.2	1.3	–3.0	–2.9	...	...
Claims on affiliated enterprises	4 535 . .	...	...	–6.0	–1.5	–2.6	–1.9	...	...
Liabilities to affiliated enterprises	4 540 . .	...	...	3.8	2.8	–.4	–1.0	...	...
Direct investment in Senegal	4 555 . .	**66.9**	**31.7**	**8.4**	**176.4**	**70.8**	**156.6**	**...**	**...**
Equity capital	4 560 . .	–.4	–.2	1.0	156.7	63.8	124.4	...	...
Claims on direct investors	4 565 . .	...	...	...	...	...	...	...	...
Liabilities to direct investors	4 570 . .	...	...	...	...	...	...	...	...
Reinvested earnings	4 575 . .	19.1	14.3	.3	4.4	6.2	24.9	...	...
Other capital	4 580 . .	48.3	17.6	7.1	15.3	.9	7.4	...	...
Claims on direct investors	4 585 . .	...	...	–1.4	...	–.9	–9.4	...	...
Liabilities to direct investors	4 590 . .	...	...	8.5	15.3	1.8	16.7	...	...
B. PORTFOLIO INVESTMENT	4 600 . .	–1.1	3.7	–30.6	–27.0	–25.8	–31.3	...	...
Assets	4 602 . .	**–1.5**	**–.4**	**–25.8**	**–18.9**	**–21.9**	**–31.3**	**...**	**...**
Equity securities	4 610 . .	–1.5	–.4	–2.4	.9	–9.8	–6.2	...	...
Monetary authorities	4 611 . .	...	...	...	...	...	...	...	...
General government	4 612 . .	...	...	...	...	...	...	...	...
Banks	4 613 . .	...	...	–2.1	...	–2.7	.7	...	...
Other sectors	4 614 . .	–1.5	–.4	–.4	.9	–7.1	–6.9	...	...
Debt securities	4 619 . .	...	...	–23.4	–19.9	–12.1	–25.1	...	...
Bonds and notes	4 620 . .	...	...	–22.9	–20.3	–.2	–17.8	...	...
Monetary authorities	4 621 . .	...	...	...	...	...	...	...	...
General government	4 622 . .	...	...	.1	...	...	...	...	...
Banks	4 623 . .	...	...	–23.0	–19.7	.1	–17.2	...	...
Other sectors	4 624 . .	...	...	...	–.6	–.3	–.6	...	...
Money market instruments	4 630 . .	...	...	–.5	.4	–11.9	–7.3	...	...
Monetary authorities	4 631 . .	...	...	...	...	...	...	...	...
General government	4 632 . .	...	...	...	...	...	...	...	...
Banks	4 633 . .	...	...	...	...	...	...	...	...
Other sectors	4 634 . .	...	...	–.5	.4	–11.9	–7.3	...	...
Liabilities	4 652 . .	**.5**	**4.0**	**–4.8**	**–8.1**	**–3.9**	**...**	**...**	**...**
Equity securities	4 660 . .	.5	4.1	...	8.4	2.6	3.4	...	...
Banks	4 663 . .	...	...	...	...	...	.3	...	...
Other sectors	4 664 . .	.5	4.1	...	8.4	2.6	3.1	...	...
Debt securities	4 669 . .	...	–.1	–4.8	–16.4	–6.5	–3.4	...	...
Bonds and notes	4 670 . .	...	–.1	–7.5	–25.0	–2.5	–6.7	...	...
Monetary authorities	4 671 . .	...	...	...	...	...	...	...	...
General government	4 672 . .	...	–.1	–20.1	–13.9	–2.5	–7.1	...	...
Banks	4 673 . .	...	...	...	...	...	.8	...	...
Other sectors	4 674 . .	...	...	12.7	–11.1	...	–.4	...	...
Money market instruments	4 680 . .	...	...	2.6	8.6	–4.0	3.3	...	...
Monetary authorities	4 681 . .	...	...	...	...	...	...	...	...
General government	4 682 . .	...	...	...	...	...	...	...	...
Banks	4 683 . .	...	...	...	...	...	...	...	...
Other sectors	4 684 . .	...	...	2.6	8.6	–4.0	3.3	...	...
C. FINANCIAL DERIVATIVES	4 910 . .	...	...	...	–.7	.1	–.7	...	...
Monetary authorities	4 911 . .	...	...	...	...	...	...	...	...
General government	4 912 . .	...	...	...	...	...	...	...	...
Banks	4 913 . .	...	...	...	...	...	...	...	...
Other sectors	4 914 . .	...	...	...	–.7	.1	–.7	...	...
Assets	4 900 . .	**...**	**...**	**...**	**–.7**	**...**	**–.7**	**...**	**...**
Monetary authorities	4 901 . .	...	...	...	...	...	...	...	...
General government	4 902 . .	...	...	...	...	...	...	...	...
Banks	4 903 . .	...	...	...	...	...	...	...	...
Other sectors	4 904 . .	...	...	...	–.7	...	–.7	...	...
Liabilities	4 905 . .	**...**	**...**	**...**	**...**	**.1**	**...**	**...**	**...**
Monetary authorities	4 906 . .	...	...	...	...	...	...	...	...
General government	4 907 . .	...	...	...	...	...	...	...	...
Banks	4 908 . .	...	...	...	...	...	...	...	...
Other sectors	4 909 . .	...	...	...	...	.1	...	...	...

Table 2 (Concluded). STANDARD PRESENTATION, 1994–2001
(Millions of U.S. dollars)

	Code	1994	1995	1996	1997	1998	1999	2000	2001
D. OTHER INVESTMENT	4 700 . .	119.2	91.5	82.8	86.4	124.5	134.8	. . .	. . .
Assets	4 703 . .	**–92.5**	**–6.2**	**–70.7**	**–22.1**	**–58.8**	**–62.3**	**. . .**	**. . .**
Trade credits	4 706 . .	. . .	. . .	–12.0	–5.5	–9.1	–15.2	. . .	. . .
General government	4 707 . .	. . .	. . .	. . .	. . .	. . .	. . .	. . .	. . .
of which: Short-term	4 709 . .	. . .	. . .	. . .	. . .	. . .	. . .	. . .	. . .
Other sectors	4 710 . .	. . .	. . .	–12.0	–5.5	–9.1	–15.2	. . .	. . .
of which: Short-term	4 712 . .	. . .	. . .	. . .	. . .	. . .	. . .	. . .	. . .
Loans	4 714 . .	–24.3	4.4	28.6	–8.7	–28.1	–12.5	. . .	. . .
Monetary authorities	4 715 . .	. . .	. . .	. . .	. . .	. . .	. . .	. . .	. . .
of which: Short-term	4 718 . .	. . .	. . .	. . .	. . .	. . .	. . .	. . .	. . .
General government	4 719 . .	. . .	. . .	. . .	. . .	. . .	. . .	. . .	. . .
of which: Short-term	4 721 . .	. . .	. . .	. . .	. . .	. . .	. . .	. . .	. . .
Banks	4 722 . .	. . .	. . .	30.5	–7.3	–26.6	–12.5	. . .	. . .
of which: Short-term	4 724 . .	. . .	. . .	*2.8*	*–3.3*	*–18.5*	*–5.5*	. . .	. . .
Other sectors	4 725 . .	–24.3	4.4	–2.0	–1.3	–1.5	. . .	. . .	. . .
of which: Short-term	4 727 . .	*–24.3*	*4.4*	. . .	. . .	. . .	. . .	. . .	. . .
Currency and deposits	4 730 . .	–48.6	–21.9	–37.7	–41.4	–13.6	–34.1	. . .	. . .
Monetary authorities	4 731 . .	. . .	. . .	. . .	. . .	. . .	. . .	. . .	. . .
General government	4 732 . .	. . .	. . .	–3.1	–.6	–.4	. . .	. . .	. . .
Banks	4 733 . .	–88.5	–1.6	–2.0	–17.4	–15.8	–39.4	. . .	. . .
Other sectors	4 734 . .	39.9	–20.4	–32.6	–23.4	2.6	5.3	. . .	. . .
Other assets	4 736 . .	–19.6	11.3	–49.5	33.5	–7.9	–.5	. . .	. . .
Monetary authorities	4 737 . .	. . .	. . .	. . .	. . .	. . .	. . .	. . .	. . .
of which: Short-term	4 739 . .	. . .	. . .	. . .	. . .	. . .	. . .	. . .	. . .
General government	4 740 . .	. . .	. . .	. . .	–.3	. . .	. . .	. . .	. . .
of which: Short-term	4 742 . .	. . .	. . .	. . .	. . .	. . .	. . .	. . .	. . .
Banks	4 743 . .	–20.3	12.5	2.4	.3	. . .	–2.9	. . .	. . .
of which: Short-term	4 745 . .	. . .	. . .	*2.4*	*.3*	. . .	*–2.9*	. . .	. . .
Other sectors	4 746 . .	.6	–1.1	–52.0	33.6	–7.9	2.4	. . .	. . .
of which: Short-term	4 748 . .	. . .	. . .	. . .	. . .	. . .	. . .	. . .	. . .
Liabilities	4 753 . .	**211.7**	**97.7**	**153.5**	**108.4**	**183.3**	**197.2**	**. . .**	**. . .**
Trade credits	4 756 . .	. . .	. . .	49.3	8.4	–15.3	18.0	. . .	. . .
General government	4 757 . .	. . .	. . .	. . .	. . .	. . .	. . .	. . .	. . .
of which: Short-term	4 759 . .	. . .	. . .	. . .	. . .	. . .	. . .	. . .	. . .
Other sectors	4 760 . .	. . .	. . .	49.3	8.4	–15.3	18.0	. . .	. . .
of which: Short-term	4 762 . .	. . .	. . .	. . .	. . .	. . .	. . .	. . .	. . .
Loans	4 764 . .	443.0	275.6	71.6	75.3	133.8	173.9	. . .	. . .
Monetary authorities	4 765 . .	38.9	42.9	–9.8	–12.8	–11.6	–13.4	. . .	. . .
of which: Use of Fund credit and loans from the Fund	4 766 . .	*38.9*	*42.9*	*–9.8*	*–12.8*	*–11.6*	*–13.4*	. . .	. . .
of which: Short-term	4 768 . .	. . .	. . .	. . .	. . .	. . .	. . .	. . .	. . .
General government	4 769 . .	402.6	229.3	92.9	83.5	124.3	73.0	. . .	. . .
of which: Short-term	4 771 . .	*.4*	. . .	*–9.3*	*–3.7*	*–5.4*	*17.3*	. . .	. . .
Other sectors	4 775 . .	–6.8	6.4	–5.2	14.1	31.5	81.0	. . .	. . .
of which: Short-term	4 777 . .	*21.1*	*24.2*	*.5*	*1.1*	*2.8*	*3.9*	. . .	. . .
Currency and deposits	4 780 . .	37.2	5.3	6.2	33.4	32.8	10.3	. . .	. . .
Monetary authorities	4 781 . .	48.8	.1	1.9	–1.1	1.0	4.1	. . .	. . .
General government	4 782 . .	. . .	. . .	. . .	. . .	. . .	. . .	. . .	. . .
Banks	4 783 . .	–11.6	5.2	4.4	34.5	31.9	6.2	. . .	. . .
Other sectors	4 784 . .	. . .	. . .	. . .	. . .	. . .	. . .	. . .	. . .
Other liabilities	4 786 . .	–268.5	–183.2	26.3	–8.8	31.9	–5.0	. . .	. . .
Monetary authorities	4 787 . .	–125.0	–35.8	–.3	1.4	–.3	–1.5	. . .	. . .
of which: Short-term	4 789 . .	*–125.0*	*–35.8*	*–.3*	*1.4*	. . .	. . .	. . .	. . .
General government	4 790 . .	–231.8	–102.4	.4	. . .	. . .	. . .	. . .	. . .
of which: Short-term	4 792 . .	*–231.8*	*–102.4*	*.4*	. . .	. . .	. . .	. . .	. . .
Banks	4 793 . .	13.3	–29.3	.7	–.4	2.2	. . .	. . .	. . .
of which: Short-term	4 795 . .	. . .	. . .	*.3*	*–.4*	*2.2*	. . .	. . .	. . .
Other sectors	4 796 . .	75.1	–15.7	25.5	–9.7	29.9	–3.4	. . .	. . .
of which: Short-term	4 798 . .	*4.5*	*.4*	. . .	. . .	. . .	. . .	. . .	. . .
E. RESERVE ASSETS	4 802 . .	–170.1	–74.8	–34.8	–137.4	–20.7	–31.6	. . .	. . .
Monetary gold	4 812 . .	. . .	. . .	. . .	. . .	. . .	. . .	. . .	. . .
Special drawing rights	4 811 . .	–.6	–2.8	1.9	1.1	. . .	–2.1	. . .	. . .
Reserve position in the Fund	4 810 . .	–.1	–.1	–.1	–.1	. . .	. . .	. . .	. . .
Foreign exchange	4 803 . .	–169.5	–71.9	–36.6	–138.4	–20.7	–29.5	. . .	. . .
Other claims	4 813 . .	. . .	. . .	. . .	. . .	. . .	. . .	. . .	. . .
NET ERRORS AND OMISSIONS	4 998 . .	**–28.9**	**–19.6**	**7.6**	**–9.3**	**10.7**	**8.2**	**. . .**	**. . .**

Part 3 of the *Yearbook* contains descriptions of the methodologies, compilation practices, and sources used to compile these data.

Table 3. INTERNATIONAL INVESTMENT POSITION (End–period stocks), 1994–2001
(Millions of U.S. dollars)

	Code	1994	1995	1996	1997	1998	1999	2000	2001
ASSETS	8 995 C .	...	561.4	640.7	711.7	860.1	889.8	...	...
Direct investment abroad	8 505 . .	**...**	**9.9**	**10.2**	**2.6**	**8.9**	**18.3**	**...**	**...**
Equity capital and reinvested earnings	8 506 . .	...	6.8	6.1	4.3	10.4	20.3	...	...
Claims on affiliated enterprises	8 507 . .	...	...	...	...	...	...	...	...
Liabilities to affiliated enterprises	8 508 . .	...	...	...	...	...	...	...	...
Other capital	8 530 . .	...	3.2	4.1	–1.7	–1.5	–2.0	...	...
Claims on affiliated enterprises	8 535 . .	...	...	...	...	...	...	...	...
Liabilities to affiliated enterprises	8 540 . .	...	...	...	...	...	...	...	...
Portfolio investment	8 602 . .	**...**	**8.6**	**33.2**	**52.2**	**78.2**	**93.7**	**...**	**...**
Equity securities	8 610 . .	...	.9	3.2	.7	20.8	14.2	...	...
Monetary authorities	8 611 . .	...	...	...	...	...	...	...	...
General government	8 612 . .	...	...	...	...	...	...	...	...
Banks	8 613 . .	...	...	2.1	.2	12.9	1.0	...	...
Other sectors	8 614 . .	...	...	...	...	...	...	...	...
Debt securities	8 619 . .	...	7.6	30.0	51.5	57.4	79.5	...	...
Bonds and notes	8 620 . .	...	5.2	27.2	37.1	32.2	62.1	...	...
Monetary authorities	8 621 . .	...	...	...	...	...	...	...	...
General government	8 622 . .	...	...	...	...	...	...	...	...
Banks	8 623 . .	...	...	26.9	34.6	29.8	60.3	...	...
Other sectors	8 624 . .	...	...	...	...	...	...	...	...
Money market instruments	8 630 . .	...	2.4	2.8	14.3	25.2	17.4	...	...
Monetary authorities	8 631 . .	...	...	...	...	...	...	...	...
General government	8 632 . .	...	...	...	...	...	...	...	...
Banks	8 633 . .	...	...	...	11.6	10.5	...	...	...
Other sectors	8 634 . .	...	...	...	...	...	...	...	...
Financial derivatives	8 900 . .	**...**	**.1**	**.1**	**.8**	**...**	**.7**	**...**	**...**
Monetary authorities	8 901 . .	...	...	...	...	...	...	...	...
General government	8 902 . .	...	...	...	...	...	...	...	...
Banks	8 903 . .	...	...	...	...	...	...	...	...
Other sectors	8 904 . .	...	...	...	...	...	...	...	...
Other investment	8 703 . .	**197.0**	**271.0**	**308.9**	**269.8**	**339.9**	**374.1**	**...**	**...**
Trade credits	8 706 . .	...	60.8	66.0	68.3	78.3	111.3	...	...
General government	8 707 . .	...	...	...	...	...	...	...	...
of which: Short-term	8 709 . .	...	...	...	...	...	...	...	...
Other sectors	8 710 . .	...	...	...	...	...	...	...	...
of which: Short-term	8 712 . .	...	...	...	...	...	...	...	...
Loans	8 714 . .	...	44.0	13.3	20.1	50.8	54.5	...	...
Monetary authorities	8 715 . .	...	...	...	...	...	...	...	...
of which: Short-term	8 718 . .	...	...	...	...	...	...	...	...
General government	8 719 . .	...	...	...	...	...	...	...	...
of which: Short-term	8 721 . .	...	...	...	...	...	...	...	...
Banks	8 722 . .	...	43.6	11.0	16.8	45.8	51.2	...	...
of which: Short-term	8 724 . .	...	*4.7*	*1.7*	*4.8*	*24.4*	*25.9*	...	...
Other sectors	8 725 . .	...	.4	2.3	3.3	5.0	3.4	...	...
of which: Short-term	8 727 . .	...	...	...	...	...	...	...	...
Currency and deposits	8 730 . .	162.2	134.3	151.4	145.8	164.9	169.0	...	...
Monetary authorities	8 731 . .	...	...	...	...	...	...	...	...
General government	8 732 . .	...	.4	3.4	3.6	3.5	3.0	...	...
Banks	8 733 . .	162.2	96.4	92.2	97.6	120.5	140.9	...	...
Other sectors	8 734 . .	...	37.5	55.8	44.7	40.9	25.1	...	...
Other assets	8 736 . .	34.8	31.9	78.2	35.6	45.8	39.2	...	...
Monetary authorities	8 737 . .	...	...	...	...	...	...	...	...
of which: Short-term	8 739 . .	...	...	...	...	...	...	...	...
General government	8 740 . .	...	...	...	.3	...	...	...	...
of which: Short-term	8 742 . .	...	...	...	...	...	...	...	...
Banks	8 743 . .	34.8	4.4	1.7	1.2	1.3	3.8	...	...
of which: Short-term	8 745 . .	...	*4.4*	*1.7*	*1.2*	*1.3*	*3.8*	...	...
Other sectors	8 746 . .	...	27.5	76.5	34.1	44.6	35.4	...	...
of which: Short-term	8 842 . .	...	...	...	...	...	...	...	...
Special drawing rights	8 811 . .	1.1	3.8	1.7	.5	.5	2.5	.9	...
Reserve position in the Fund	8 810 . .	1.7	1.8	1.8	1.8	1.9	1.9	1.8	...
Foreign exchange	8 803 . .	176.9	266.2	284.8	384.0	430.7	398.6	...	...
Other claims	8 813 . .	...	...	...	...	...	...	...	...

Table 3 (Concluded). INTERNATIONAL INVESTMENT POSITION (End–period stocks), 1994–2001
(Millions of U.S. dollars)

	Code		1994	1995	1996	1997	1998	1999	2000	2001
LIABILITIES	8 995	D.	...	4,261.8	4,100.6	4,072.1	4,721.1	4,223.1	...	...
Direct investment in Senegal	8 555	..	**...**	**78.6**	**76.4**	**256.2**	**372.1**	**329.4**	**...**	**...**
Equity capital and reinvested earnings	8 556	..	...	70.9	61.7	228.5	359.2	302.0	...	...
Claims on direct investors	8 557	..	...	...	...	...	...	...	...	...
Liabilities to direct investors	8 558	..	...	...	...	...	...	...	...	...
Other capital	8 580	..	...	7.7	14.7	27.6	12.9	27.4	...	...
Claims on direct investors	8 585	..	...	...	...	...	...	...	...	...
Liabilities to direct investors	8 590	..	...	...	...	...	...	...	...	...
Portfolio investment	8 652	..	**...**	**83.3**	**73.0**	**56.8**	**96.2**	**92.9**	**...**	**...**
Equity securities	8 660	..	...	10.3	9.4	17.2	66.8	63.5	...	...
Banks	8 663	..	...	2.9	2.7	2.4	2.2	2.2	...	...
Other sectors	8 664	..	...	7.4	6.7	14.9	64.5	61.3	...	...
Debt securities	8 669	..	...	73.0	63.6	39.6	29.4	29.4	...	...
Bonds and notes	8 670	..	...	69.0	57.2	25.6	24.7	22.3	...	...
Monetary authorities	8 671	..	...	...	...	...	...	...	...	...
General government	8 672	..	...	...	44.8	25.6	24.7	19.1	...	...
Banks	8 673	..	...	...	...	...	...	.8	...	...
Other sectors	8 674	..	...	...	12.4	...	...	2.4	...	...
Money market instruments	8 680	..	...	4.1	6.4	13.9	4.7	7.1	...	...
Monetary authorities	8 681	..	...	...	...	...	...	...	...	...
General government	8 682	..	...	...	...	...	...	...	...	...
Banks	8 683	..	...	...	6.4	...	...	...	...	...
Other sectors	8 684	..	...	...	...	...	...	...	...	...
Financial derivatives	8 905	..	**...**	**...**	**...**	**...**	**.1**	**...**	**...**	**...**
Monetary authorities	8 906	..	...	...	...	...	...	...	...	...
General government	8 907	..	...	...	...	...	...	...	...	...
Banks	8 908	..	...	...	...	...	...	...	...	...
Other sectors	8 909	..	...	...	...	...	...	...	...	...
Other investment	8 753	..	**3,443.6**	**4,099.9**	**3,951.2**	**3,759.1**	**4,252.7**	**3,800.8**	**...**	**...**
Trade credits	8 756	..	4.1	128.6	163.5	160.0	142.1	168.9	...	...
General government	8 757	..	4.1	128.6	...	...	...	...	...	...
of which: Short-term	8 759	..	...	...	...	...	...	...	...	...
Other sectors	8 760	..	...	...	163.5	160.0	142.1	168.9	...	...
of which: Short-term	8 762	..	...	...	...	...	...	...	...	...
Loans	8 764	..	3,123.8	3,688.0	3,491.5	3,308.8	3,743.6	3,348.9	...	...
Monetary authorities	8 765	..	299.9	346.8	325.6	292.1	292.5	272.0	...	...
of which: Use of Fund credit and loans from the Fund	8 766	..	*299.9*	*346.8*	*325.6*	*292.1*	*292.5*	*272.0*	*254.6*	*257.3*
of which: Short-term	8 768	..	...	...	...	...	...	...	...	...
General government	8 769	..	2,793.5	3,193.7	3,033.8	2,863.0	3,231.2	2,850.9	...	...
of which: Short-term	8 771	..	...	...	...	...	...	...	...	...
Banks	8 772	..	30.4	43.2	34.3	20.8	11.2	41.1	...	...
of which: Short-term	8 774	..	...	*24.0*	*13.4*	*8.1*	*2.9*	*18.9*	...	...
Other sectors	8 775	..	...	104.3	97.8	132.9	208.6	184.9	...	...
of which: Short-term	8 777	..	...	...	...	...	...	...	...	...
Currency and deposits	8 780	..	144.9	263.9	253.2	256.2	307.1	274.1	...	...
Monetary authorities	8 781	..	110.6	122.3	116.2	100.6	108.1	96.9	...	...
General government	8 782	..	...	...	...	...	...	...	...	...
Banks	8 783	..	34.3	141.7	137.0	155.7	198.9	177.2	...	...
Other sectors	8 784	..	...	...	...	...	...	...	...	...
Other liabilities	8 786	..	170.8	19.3	43.1	34.1	60.1	8.8	...	...
Monetary authorities	8 787	..	35.6	1.0	.7	1.9	1.7	.1	...	...
of which: Short-term	8 789	..	*35.6*	*1.0*	...	...	...	...	...	...
General government	8 790	..	85.1	1.3	1.7	1.5	1.6	1.4	...	...
of which: Short-term	8 792	..	*85.1*	*1.3*	*1.7*	*1.5*	...	...	...	...
Banks	8 793	..	50.1	...	...	...	...	...	...	...
of which: Short-term	8 795	..	...	...	...	...	...	...	...	...
Other sectors	8 796	..	...	17.0	40.8	30.8	56.7	7.4	...	...
of which: Short-term	8 798	..	...	...	...	...	...	...	...	...
NET INTERNATIONAL INVESTMENT POSITION	8 995	..	**...**	**–3,700.3**	**–3,459.9**	**–3,360.4**	**–3,861.0**	**–3,333.3**	**...**	**...**
Conversion rates: CFA francs per U.S. dollar (end of period)	0 102	..	**534.60**	**490.00**	**523.70**	**598.81**	**562.21**	**652.95**	**704.95**	**744.31**

Table 1. ANALYTIC PRESENTATION, 1994–2001
(Millions of U.S. dollars)

	Code		1994	1995	1996	1997	1998	1999	2000	2001
A. Current Account [1]	4 993	Z.	**-23.46**	**-53.75**	**-59.28**	**-72.84**	**-119.10**	**-135.38**	**-51.98**	**-100.06**
Goods: exports f.o.b	2 100	..	52.99	53.51	96.66	113.56	122.84	145.66	194.76	215.26
Goods: imports f.o.b	3 100	..	-188.06	-214.26	-266.98	-303.50	-334.63	-374.59	-304.12	-386.94
Balance on Goods	4 100	..	*-135.07*	*-160.75*	*-170.32*	*-189.94*	*-211.79*	*-228.93*	*-109.37*	*-171.68*
Services: credit	2 200	..	200.28	224.65	237.04	255.81	247.48	275.86	269.29	283.19
Services: debit	3 200	..	-77.42	-100.24	-114.07	-127.63	-132.17	-156.70	-178.01	-192.88
Balance on Goods and Services	4 991	..	*-12.21*	*-36.34*	*-47.35*	*-61.75*	*-96.49*	*-109.77*	*-18.08*	*-81.36*
Income: credit	2 300	..	8.09	12.56	10.48	9.65	5.43	8.46	10.50	8.93
Income: debit	3 300	..	-19.84	-32.21	-25.53	-21.92	-26.38	-33.34	-42.55	-27.98
Balance on Goods, Services, and Income	4 992	..	*-23.96*	*-56.00*	*-62.40*	*-74.03*	*-117.43*	*-134.65*	*-50.13*	*-100.41*
Current transfers: credit	2 379	Z.	13.85	13.52	15.19	14.24	9.77	10.09	8.14	10.52
Current transfers: debit	3 379	..	-13.35	-11.28	-12.07	-13.05	-11.44	-10.82	-9.99	-10.16
B. Capital Account [1]	4 994	Z.	**4.27**	**1.05**	**5.65**	**6.76**	**21.66**	**16.47**	**8.75**	**9.39**
Capital account: credit	2 994	Z.	4.27	1.05	5.65	6.76	21.66	16.47	8.75	9.39
Capital account: debit	3 994	..	...	...	...	...	...	...	...	...
Total, Groups A Plus B	4 981	..	*-19.19*	*-52.70*	*-53.63*	*-66.07*	*-97.44*	*-118.91*	*-43.23*	*-90.67*
C. Financial Account [1]	4 995	W.	**21.06**	**30.93**	**21.27**	**48.74**	**56.10**	**50.18**	**-.70**	**125.15**
Direct investment abroad	4 505	..	-13.33	-16.97	-12.47	-9.87	-3.00	-8.98	-10.54	-11.10
Direct investment in Seychelles	4 555	Z.	30.74	45.88	28.81	53.40	53.21	55.22	25.20	59.43
Portfolio investment assets	4 602	..	-.93	-5.75	6.66	.08	-.78	-.02	-.09	-.07
Equity securities	4 610	..	...	...	...	...	...	...	...	...
Debt securities	4 619	..	-.93	-5.75	6.66	.08	-.78	-.02	-.09	-.07
Portfolio investment liabilities	4 652	Z.	.16	-.17	...	2.94	2.83	.56	1.05	1.09
Equity securities	4 660	..	...	...	...	...	...	...	...	...
Debt securities	4 669	Z.	.16	-.17	...	2.94	2.83	.56	1.05	1.09
Financial derivatives	4 910	..	...	...	...	...	...	...	...	...
Financial derivatives assets	4 900	..	...	...	...	...	...	...	...	...
Financial derivatives liabilities	4 905	..	...	...	...	...	...	...	...	...
Other investment assets	4 703	..	1.60	-2.56	-11.79	-12.73	-5.66	-12.97	-14.86	-8.76
Monetary authorities	4 701	..	...	...	...	...	...	...	...	...
General government	4 704	..	...	...	...	...	...	...	...	...
Banks	4 705	..	...	...	...	...	...	...	...	...
Other sectors	4 728	..	1.60	-2.56	-11.79	-12.73	-5.66	-12.97	-14.86	-8.76
Other investment liabilities	4 753	W.	2.83	10.50	10.06	14.92	9.50	16.38	-1.47	84.56
Monetary authorities	4 753	WA	...	...	...	...	...	...	...	...
General government	4 753	ZB	2.83	...	...	...	...	...	...	...
Banks	4 753	ZC	...	...	...	...	...	...	...	...
Other sectors	4 753	ZD	...	10.50	10.06	14.92	9.50	16.38	-1.47	84.56
Total, Groups A Through C	4 983	..	*1.88*	*-21.77*	*-32.36*	*-17.33*	*-41.34*	*-68.72*	*-43.93*	*34.49*
D. Net Errors and Omissions	4 998	..	**-20.16**	**10.01**	**7.07**	**11.61**	**-2.81**	**11.37**	**-18.78**	**-12.62**
Total, Groups A Through D	4 984	..	*-18.29*	*-11.76*	*-25.29*	*-5.72*	*-44.15*	*-57.35*	*-62.71*	*21.86*
E. Reserves and Related Items	4 802	A.	**18.29**	**11.76**	**25.29**	**5.72**	**44.15**	**57.35**	**62.71**	**-21.86**
Reserve assets	4 802	..	7.43	3.42	4.86	-5.12	3.26	-8.42	-19.39	10.32
Use of Fund credit and loans	4 766	..	...	...	...	...	...	...	...	...
Exceptional financing	4 920	..	10.86	8.34	20.42	10.84	40.90	65.77	82.10	-32.18
Conversion rates: Seychelles rupees per U.S. dollar	0 101	..	**5.0559**	**4.7620**	**4.9700**	**5.0263**	**5.2622**	**5.3426**	**5.7138**	**5.8575**

[1] Excludes components that have been classified in the categories of Group E.

Table 2. STANDARD PRESENTATION, 1994–2001

(Millions of U.S. dollars)

	Code	1994	1995	1996	1997	1998	1999	2000	2001
CURRENT ACCOUNT	4 993 . .	**-15.91**	**-49.38**	**-52.46**	**-66.05**	**-107.81**	**-129.87**	**-47.57**	**-97.03**
A. GOODS	4 100 . .	-135.07	-160.75	-170.32	-189.94	-211.79	-228.93	-109.37	-171.68
Credit	2 100 . .	**52.99**	**53.51**	**96.66**	**113.56**	**122.84**	**145.66**	**194.76**	**215.26**
General merchandise: exports f.o.b.	2 110 . .	28.42	26.88	63.40	71.78	93.29	111.67	129.65	161.84
Goods for processing: exports f.o.b.	2 150 . .	. . .	. . .	. . .	. . .	. . .	. . .	. . .	. . .
Repairs on goods	2 160 . .	. . .	.27	.34	.30	.53	.52	.67	.65
Goods procured in ports by carriers	2 170 . .	24.57	26.35	32.92	41.48	29.02	33.47	64.44	52.77
Nonmonetary gold	2 180 . .	. . .	. . .	. . .	. . .	. . .	. . .	. . .	. . .
Debit	3 100 . .	**-188.06**	**-214.26**	**-266.98**	**-303.50**	**-334.63**	**-374.59**	**-304.12**	**-386.94**
General merchandise: imports f.o.b.	3 110 . .	-175.24	-197.99	-249.20	-289.38	-325.57	-361.44	-290.30	-374.56
Goods for processing: imports f.o.b.	3 150 . .	. . .	. . .	. . .	. . .	. . .	. . .	. . .	. . .
Repairs on goods	3 160 . .	-7.71	-6.13	-5.90	-2.29	. . .	-1.07	-2.66	-1.74
Goods procured in ports by carriers	3 170 . .	-5.10	-10.14	-11.89	-11.84	-9.06	-12.09	-11.17	-10.64
Nonmonetary gold	3 180 . .	. . .	. . .	. . .	. . .	. . .	. . .	. . .	. . .
B. SERVICES	4 200 . .	122.86	124.41	122.97	128.18	115.31	119.16	91.28	90.31
Total credit	2 200 . .	*200.28*	*224.65*	*237.04*	*255.81*	*247.48*	*275.86*	*269.29*	*283.19*
Total debit	3 200 . .	*-77.42*	*-100.24*	*-114.07*	*-127.63*	*-132.17*	*-156.70*	*-178.01*	*-192.88*
Transportation services, credit	2 205 . .	**65.05**	**71.34**	**75.57**	**74.57**	**90.80**	**114.25**	**112.94**	**124.92**
Passenger	2 850 . .	*43.71*	*47.48*	*47.99*	*43.37*	*61.97*	*71.43*	*67.19*	*74.64*
Freight	2 851 . .	*2.77*	*3.15*	*5.51*	*8.95*	*11.04*	*19.17*	*24.27*	*30.64*
Other	2 852 . .	*18.57*	*20.71*	*22.07*	*22.24*	*17.79*	*23.66*	*21.47*	*19.63*
Sea transport, passenger	2 207 . .	. . .	. . .	. . .	. . .	. . .	. . .	. . .	. . .
Sea transport, freight	2 208 . .	2.77	3.15	5.51	8.95	11.04	19.17	24.27	30.64
Sea transport, other	2 209 . .	12.22	14.15	15.65	14.05	12.96	18.23	16.36	14.77
Air transport, passenger	2 211 . .	43.71	47.48	47.99	43.37	61.97	71.43	67.19	74.64
Air transport, freight	2 212 . .	. . .	. . .	. . .	. . .	. . .	. . .	. . .	. . .
Air transport, other	2 213 . .	6.35	6.55	6.42	8.20	4.83	5.43	5.11	4.87
Other transport, passenger	2 215 . .	. . .	. . .	. . .	. . .	. . .	. . .	. . .	. . .
Other transport, freight	2 216 . .	. . .	. . .	. . .	. . .	. . .	. . .	. . .	. . .
Other transport, other	2 217 . .	. . .	. . .	. . .	. . .	. . .	. . .	. . .	. . .
Transportation services, debit	3 205 . .	**-29.49**	**-34.36**	**-44.53**	**-50.12**	**-52.24**	**-67.81**	**-56.35**	**-57.69**
Passenger	3 850 . .	*-2.77*	*-3.23*	*-3.24*	*-3.24*	*-2.64*	*-6.87*	*-7.67*	*-7.90*
Freight	3 851 . .	*-25.77*	*-29.11*	*-36.14*	*-40.01*	*-44.34*	*-53.16*	*-42.69*	*-44.25*
Other	3 852 . .	*-.95*	*-2.02*	*-5.15*	*-6.86*	*-5.26*	*-7.79*	*-6.00*	*-5.53*
Sea transport, passenger	3 207 . .	. . .	. . .	. . .	. . .	. . .	. . .	. . .	. . .
Sea transport, freight	3 208 . .	-25.77	-29.11	-36.14	-40.01	-44.34	-53.16	-42.69	-44.25
Sea transport, other	3 209 . .	. . .	. . .	. . .	. . .	. . .	-.21	-.11	-.02
Air transport, passenger	3 211 . .	-2.77	-3.23	-3.24	-3.24	-2.64	-6.87	-7.67	-7.90
Air transport, freight	3 212 . .	. . .	. . .	. . .	. . .	. . .	. . .	. . .	. . .
Air transport, other	3 213 . .	-.95	-2.02	-5.15	-6.86	-5.26	-7.58	-5.90	-5.51
Other transport, passenger	3 215 . .	. . .	. . .	. . .	. . .	. . .	. . .	. . .	. . .
Other transport, freight	3 216 . .	. . .	. . .	. . .	. . .	. . .	. . .	. . .	. . .
Other transport, other	3 217 . .	. . .	. . .	. . .	. . .	. . .	. . .	. . .	. . .
Travel, credit	2 236 . .	**121.30**	**129.15**	**140.70**	**156.60**	**134.73**	**135.51**	**133.24**	**132.72**
Business travel	2 237 . .	. . .	. . .	. . .	. . .	. . .	. . .	. . .	. . .
Personal travel	2 240 . .	121.30	129.15	140.70	156.60	134.73	135.51	133.24	132.72
Travel, debit	3 236 . .	**-26.43**	**-28.38**	**-28.30**	**-27.71**	**-25.53**	**-21.09**	**-25.14**	**-30.44**
Business travel	3 237 . .	. . .	. . .	. . .	. . .	. . .	. . .	. . .	. . .
Personal travel	3 240 . .	-26.43	-28.38	-28.30	-27.71	-25.53	-21.09	-25.14	-30.44
Other services, credit	2 200 BA	**13.92**	**24.17**	**20.76**	**24.65**	**21.95**	**26.09**	**23.12**	**25.56**
Communications	2 245 . .	. . .	3.15	3.50	5.03	5.32	7.41	7.14	7.17
Construction	2 249 . .	. . .	. . .	. . .	. . .	. . .	. . .	. . .	. . .
Insurance	2 253 . .	1.80	2.10	3.08	7.96	3.91	1.14	1.16	2.99
Financial	2 260 . .	. . .	. . .	. . .	. . .	. . .	. . .	. . .	. . .
Computer and information	2 262 . .	. . .	. . .	. . .	. . .	. . .	. . .	. . .	. . .
Royalties and licence fees	2 266 . .	. . .	. . .	. . .	. . .	. . .	. . .	. . .	. . .
Other business services	2 268 . .	. . .	1.05	.24	1.07	2.07	1.27	1.23	1.81
Personal, cultural, and recreational	2 287 . .	. . .	. . .	. . .	. . .	. . .	. . .	. . .	. . .
Government, n.i.e.	2 291 . .	12.12	17.87	13.94	10.58	10.64	16.27	13.60	13.59
Other services, debit	3 200 BA	**-21.50**	**-37.51**	**-41.25**	**-49.80**	**-54.41**	**-67.79**	**-96.52**	**-104.75**
Communications	3 245 . .	. . .	. . .	. . .	. . .	. . .	. . .	. . .	. . .
Construction	3 249 . .	. . .	. . .	. . .	. . .	-1.88	-22.42	-34.43	-35.56
Insurance	3 253 . .	-6.96	-9.07	-9.80	-15.34	-13.25	-4.57	-4.50	-5.00
Financial	3 260 . .	. . .	. . .	. . .	. . .	. . .	. . .	. . .	. . .
Computer and information	3 262 . .	. . .	. . .	. . .	. . .	. . .	. . .	. . .	. . .
Royalties and licence fees	3 266 . .	. . .	-.42	-.62	-.60	-.38	-.47	-.44	-.43
Other business services	3 268 . .	-11.79	-24.86	-25.15	-29.84	-34.09	-36.22	-52.50	-59.75
Personal, cultural, and recreational	3 287 . .	. . .	. . .	. . .	. . .	. . .	. . .	. . .	. . .
Government, n.i.e.	3 291 . .	-2.75	-3.15	-5.67	-4.02	-4.81	-4.12	-4.66	-4.01

Table 2 (Continued). STANDARD PRESENTATION, 1994–2001

(Millions of U.S. dollars)

	Code	1994	1995	1996	1997	1998	1999	2000	2001
C. INCOME	4 300 . .	-11.75	-19.66	-15.05	-12.28	-20.94	-24.88	-32.05	-19.05
Total credit	2 300 . .	*8.09*	*12.56*	*10.48*	*9.65*	*5.43*	*8.46*	*10.50*	*8.93*
Total debit	3 300 . .	*-19.84*	*-32.21*	*-25.53*	*-21.92*	*-26.38*	*-33.34*	*-42.55*	*-27.98*
Compensation of employees, credit	2 310 . .	**.30**	**.50**	**.70**	**.22**	**.11**	**.19**	**.18**	**.17**
Compensation of employees, debit	3 310 . .	**-.08**	**-.27**	**-.36**	**-.36**	**-1.56**	**-1.31**	**-3.45**	**-3.11**
Investment income, credit	2 320 . .	**7.79**	**12.05**	**9.78**	**9.43**	**5.32**	**8.27**	**10.33**	**8.76**
Direct investment income	2 330 . .	6.67	8.48	6.24	4.95	1.50	4.49	6.30	5.12
Dividends and distributed branch profits	2 332 . .	...	...	...	...	...	...	...	...
Reinvested earnings and undistributed branch profits	2 333 . .	6.67	8.48	6.24	4.95	1.50	4.49	6.30	5.12
Income on debt (interest)	2 334 . .	...	...	...	...	...	...	...	...
Portfolio investment income	2 339 . .	...	...	...	...	...	...	...	...
Income on equity	2 340 . .	...	...	...	...	...	...	...	...
Income on bonds and notes	2 350 . .	...	...	...	...	...	...	...	...
Income on money market instruments	2 360 . .	...	...	...	...	...	...	...	...
Other investment income	2 370 . .	1.13	3.57	3.54	4.48	3.82	3.78	4.03	3.64
Investment income, debit	3 320 . .	**-19.76**	**-31.94**	**-25.17**	**-21.57**	**-24.82**	**-32.03**	**-39.10**	**-24.87**
Direct investment income	3 330 . .	-8.03	-14.11	-9.58	-6.15	-6.02	-7.56	-6.98	-6.01
Dividends and distributed branch profits	3 332 . .	-1.98	-2.52	-3.02	-2.17	-2.22	-3.82	-1.73	-.03
Reinvested earnings and undistributed branch profits	3 333 . .	-6.05	-11.59	-6.56	-3.98	-3.80	-3.74	-5.25	-5.98
Income on debt (interest)	3 334 . .	...	...	...	...	...	...	...	...
Portfolio investment income	3 339 . .	...	...	...	...	...	...	...	...
Income on equity	3 340 . .	...	...	...	...	...	...	...	...
Income on bonds and notes	3 350 . .	...	...	...	...	...	...	...	...
Income on money market instruments	3 360 . .	...	...	...	...	...	...	...	...
Other investment income	3 370 . .	-11.73	-17.83	-15.59	-15.42	-18.79	-24.46	-32.12	-18.86
D. CURRENT TRANSFERS	4 379 . .	8.05	6.61	9.94	7.98	9.62	4.77	2.56	3.38
Credit	2 379 . .	**21.40**	**17.89**	**22.01**	**21.03**	**21.06**	**15.59**	**12.55**	**13.54**
General government	2 380 . .	15.43	11.97	17.10	15.08	17.41	11.64	8.75	9.46
Other sectors	2 390 . .	5.97	5.92	4.91	5.95	3.65	3.95	3.80	4.08
Workers' remittances	2 391 . .	...	...	...	...	...	...	...	...
Other current transfers	2 392 . .	5.97	5.92	4.91	5.95	3.65	3.95	3.80	4.08
Debit	3 379 . .	**-13.35**	**-11.28**	**-12.07**	**-13.05**	**-11.44**	**-10.82**	**-9.99**	**-10.16**
General government	3 380 . .	-.40	-.38	-1.05	-.70	-.06	-.02	-.09	-.36
Other sectors	3 390 . .	-12.96	-10.90	-11.03	-12.35	-11.38	-10.80	-9.91	-9.80
Workers' remittances	3 391 . .	...	...	...	...	...	...	...	...
Other current transfers	3 392 . .	-12.96	-10.90	-11.03	-12.35	-11.38	-10.80	-9.91	-9.80
CAPITAL AND FINANCIAL ACCOUNT	4 996 . .	**36.07**	**39.37**	**45.39**	**54.45**	**110.63**	**118.50**	**66.35**	**109.66**
CAPITAL ACCOUNT	4 994 . .	**4.27**	**1.05**	**5.65**	**6.76**	**21.66**	**16.47**	**8.75**	**9.39**
Total credit	2 994 . .	*4.27*	*1.05*	*5.65*	*6.76*	*21.66*	*16.47*	*8.75*	*9.39*
Total debit	3 994 . .	...	...	...	...	...	...	...	...
Capital transfers, credit	2 400 . .	**4.27**	**1.05**	**5.65**	**6.76**	**21.66**	**16.47**	**8.75**	**9.39**
General government	2 401 . .	4.27	1.05	5.65	6.76	21.66	16.47	8.75	9.39
Debt forgiveness	2 402 . .	...	...	...	...	...	...	...	...
Other capital transfers	2 410 . .	4.27	1.05	5.65	6.76	21.66	16.47	8.75	9.39
Other sectors	2 430 . .	...	...	...	...	...	...	...	...
Migrants' transfers	2 431 . .	...	...	...	...	...	...	...	...
Debt forgiveness	2 432 . .	...	...	...	...	...	...	...	...
Other capital transfers	2 440 . .	...	...	...	...	...	...	...	...
Capital transfers, debit	3 400 . .	...	...	...	...	...	...	...	...
General government	3 401 . .	...	...	...	...	...	...	...	...
Debt forgiveness	3 402 . .	...	...	...	...	...	...	...	...
Other capital transfers	3 410 . .	...	...	...	...	...	...	...	...
Other sectors	3 430 . .	...	...	...	...	...	...	...	...
Migrants' transfers	3 431 . .	...	...	...	...	...	...	...	...
Debt forgiveness	3 432 . .	...	...	...	...	...	...	...	...
Other capital transfers	3 440 . .	...	...	...	...	...	...	...	...
Nonproduced nonfinancial assets, credit	2 480 . .	...	...	...	...	...	...	...	...
Nonproduced nonfinancial assets, debit	3 480 . .	...	...	...	...	...	...	...	...

Table 2 (Continued). STANDARD PRESENTATION, 1994–2001
(Millions of U.S. dollars)

	Code	1994	1995	1996	1997	1998	1999	2000	2001
FINANCIAL ACCOUNT	4 995 . .	**31.79**	**38.32**	**39.73**	**47.68**	**88.96**	**102.03**	**57.60**	**100.27**
A. DIRECT INVESTMENT	4 500 . .	17.41	28.92	16.34	43.53	50.21	46.23	14.67	48.33
Direct investment abroad	4 505 . .	**–13.33**	**–16.97**	**–12.47**	**–9.87**	**–3.00**	**–8.98**	**–10.54**	**–11.10**
Equity capital	4 510 . .	–6.67	–8.48	–6.24	–4.93	–1.50	–4.49	–4.24	–5.98
Claims on affiliated enterprises	4 515 . .	–6.67	–8.48	–6.24	–4.93	–1.50	–4.49	–4.24	–5.98
Liabilities to affiliated enterprises	4 520 . .	. . .	. . .	. . .	. . .	. . .	. . .	. . .	. . .
Reinvested earnings	4 525 . .	–6.67	–8.48	–6.24	–4.93	–1.50	–4.49	–6.30	–5.12
Other capital	4 530 . .	. . .	. . .	. . .	. . .	. . .	. . .	. . .	. . .
Claims on affiliated enterprises	4 535 . .	. . .	. . .	. . .	. . .	. . .	. . .	. . .	. . .
Liabilities to affiliated enterprises	4 540 . .	. . .	. . .	. . .	. . .	. . .	. . .	. . .	. . .
Direct investment in Seychelles	4 555 . .	**30.74**	**45.88**	**28.81**	**53.40**	**53.21**	**55.22**	**25.20**	**59.43**
Equity capital	4 560 . .	8.98	15.75	17.61	49.32	49.41	51.47	19.95	53.45
Claims on direct investors	4 565 . .	. . .	. . .	. . .	. . .	. . .	. . .	. . .	. . .
Liabilities to direct investors	4 570 . .	8.98	15.75	17.61	49.32	49.41	51.47	19.95	53.45
Reinvested earnings	4 575 . .	6.05	11.59	6.56	3.98	3.80	3.74	5.25	5.98
Other capital	4 580 . .	15.70	18.54	4.65	.10	. . .	. . .	. . .	. . .
Claims on direct investors	4 585 . .	. . .	. . .	. . .	. . .	. . .	. . .	. . .	. . .
Liabilities to direct investors	4 590 . .	15.70	18.54	4.65	.10	. . .	. . .	. . .	. . .
B. PORTFOLIO INVESTMENT	4 600 . .	–.77	–5.92	6.66	3.02	2.05	.54	.96	1.02
Assets	4 602 . .	**–.93**	**–5.75**	**6.66**	**.08**	**–.78**	**–.02**	**–.09**	**–.07**
Equity securities	4 610 . .	. . .	. . .	. . .	. . .	. . .	. . .	. . .	. . .
Monetary authorities	4 611 . .	. . .	. . .	. . .	. . .	. . .	. . .	. . .	. . .
General government	4 612 . .	. . .	. . .	. . .	. . .	. . .	. . .	. . .	. . .
Banks	4 613 . .	. . .	. . .	. . .	. . .	. . .	. . .	. . .	. . .
Other sectors	4 614 . .	. . .	. . .	. . .	. . .	. . .	. . .	. . .	. . .
Debt securities	4 619 . .	–.93	–5.75	6.66	.08	–.78	–.02	–.09	–.07
Bonds and notes	4 620 . .	. . .	. . .	. . .	. . .	–.78	–.02	–.09	–.07
Monetary authorities	4 621 . .	. . .	. . .	. . .	. . .	. . .	. . .	. . .	. . .
General government	4 622 . .	. . .	. . .	. . .	. . .	. . .	. . .	. . .	. . .
Banks	4 623 . .	. . .	. . .	. . .	. . .	–.78	–.02	–.09	–.07
Other sectors	4 624 . .	. . .	. . .	. . .	. . .	. . .	. . .	. . .	. . .
Money market instruments	4 630 . .	–.93	–5.75	6.66	.08	. . .	. . .	. . .	. . .
Monetary authorities	4 631 . .	. . .	. . .	. . .	. . .	. . .	. . .	. . .	. . .
General government	4 632 . .	. . .	. . .	. . .	. . .	. . .	. . .	. . .	. . .
Banks	4 633 . .	–.93	–5.75	6.66	.08	. . .	. . .	. . .	. . .
Other sectors	4 634 . .	. . .	. . .	. . .	. . .	. . .	. . .	. . .	. . .
Liabilities	4 652 . .	**.16**	**–.17**	**. . .**	**2.94**	**2.83**	**.56**	**1.05**	**1.09**
Equity securities	4 660 . .	. . .	. . .	. . .	. . .	. . .	. . .	. . .	. . .
Banks	4 663 . .	. . .	. . .	. . .	. . .	. . .	. . .	. . .	. . .
Other sectors	4 664 . .	. . .	. . .	. . .	. . .	. . .	. . .	. . .	. . .
Debt securities	4 669 . .	.16	–.17	. . .	2.94	2.83	.56	1.05	1.09
Bonds and notes	4 670 . .	.16	–.17	. . .	2.94	2.83	.56	1.05	1.09
Monetary authorities	4 671 . .	. . .	. . .	. . .	. . .	. . .	. . .	. . .	. . .
General government	4 672 . .	. . .	. . .	. . .	. . .	. . .	. . .	. . .	. . .
Banks	4 673 . .	.16	–.17	. . .	2.94	2.83	.56	1.05	1.09
Other sectors	4 674 . .	. . .	. . .	. . .	. . .	. . .	. . .	. . .	. . .
Money market instruments	4 680 . .	. . .	. . .	. . .	. . .	. . .	. . .	. . .	. . .
Monetary authorities	4 681 . .	. . .	. . .	. . .	. . .	. . .	. . .	. . .	. . .
General government	4 682 . .	. . .	. . .	. . .	. . .	. . .	. . .	. . .	. . .
Banks	4 683 . .	. . .	. . .	. . .	. . .	. . .	. . .	. . .	. . .
Other sectors	4 684 . .	. . .	. . .	. . .	. . .	. . .	. . .	. . .	. . .
C. FINANCIAL DERIVATIVES	4 910 . .	. . .	. . .	. . .	. . .	. . .	. . .	. . .	. . .
Monetary authorities	4 911 . .	. . .	. . .	. . .	. . .	. . .	. . .	. . .	. . .
General government	4 912 . .	. . .	. . .	. . .	. . .	. . .	. . .	. . .	. . .
Banks	4 913 . .	. . .	. . .	. . .	. . .	. . .	. . .	. . .	. . .
Other sectors	4 914 . .	. . .	. . .	. . .	. . .	. . .	. . .	. . .	. . .
Assets	4 900 . .	**. . .**	**. . .**	**. . .**	**. . .**	**. . .**	**. . .**	**. . .**	**. . .**
Monetary authorities	4 901 . .	. . .	. . .	. . .	. . .	. . .	. . .	. . .	. . .
General government	4 902 . .	. . .	. . .	. . .	. . .	. . .	. . .	. . .	. . .
Banks	4 903 . .	. . .	. . .	. . .	. . .	. . .	. . .	. . .	. . .
Other sectors	4 904 . .	. . .	. . .	. . .	. . .	. . .	. . .	. . .	. . .
Liabilities	4 905 . .	**. . .**	**. . .**	**. . .**	**. . .**	**. . .**	**. . .**	**. . .**	**. . .**
Monetary authorities	4 906 . .	. . .	. . .	. . .	. . .	. . .	. . .	. . .	. . .
General government	4 907 . .	. . .	. . .	. . .	. . .	. . .	. . .	. . .	. . .
Banks	4 908 . .	. . .	. . .	. . .	. . .	. . .	. . .	. . .	. . .
Other sectors	4 909 . .	. . .	. . .	. . .	. . .	. . .	. . .	. . .	. . .

Table 2 (Concluded). STANDARD PRESENTATION, 1994–2001
(Millions of U.S. dollars)

	Code	1994	1995	1996	1997	1998	1999	2000	2001
D. OTHER INVESTMENT	4 700 . .	7.73	11.91	11.87	6.25	33.45	63.68	61.36	40.60
Assets	4 703 . .	**1.60**	**–2.56**	**–11.79**	**–12.73**	**–5.66**	**–12.97**	**–14.86**	**–8.76**
Trade credits	4 706 . .	. . .	. . .	. . .	. . .	. . .	. . .	. . .	. . .
General government	4 707 . .	. . .	. . .	. . .	. . .	. . .	. . .	. . .	. . .
of which: Short-term	4 709 . .	. . .	. . .	. . .	. . .	. . .	. . .	. . .	. . .
Other sectors	4 710 . .	. . .	. . .	. . .	. . .	. . .	. . .	. . .	. . .
of which: Short-term	4 712 . .	. . .	. . .	. . .	. . .	. . .	. . .	. . .	. . .
Loans	4 714 . .	. . .	. . .	. . .	. . .	. . .	. . .	. . .	. . .
Monetary authorities	4 715 . .	. . .	. . .	. . .	. . .	. . .	. . .	. . .	. . .
of which: Short-term	4 718 . .	. . .	. . .	. . .	. . .	. . .	. . .	. . .	. . .
General government	4 719 . .	. . .	. . .	. . .	. . .	. . .	. . .	. . .	. . .
of which: Short-term	4 721 . .	. . .	. . .	. . .	. . .	. . .	. . .	. . .	. . .
Banks	4 722 . .	. . .	. . .	. . .	. . .	. . .	. . .	. . .	. . .
of which: Short-term	4 724 . .	. . .	. . .	. . .	. . .	. . .	. . .	. . .	. . .
Other sectors	4 725 . .	. . .	. . .	. . .	. . .	. . .	. . .	. . .	. . .
of which: Short-term	4 727 . .	. . .	. . .	. . .	. . .	. . .	. . .	. . .	. . .
Currency and deposits	4 730 . .	1.60	–2.56	–11.79	–12.73	–5.66	–12.97	–14.86	–8.76
Monetary authorities	4 731 . .	. . .	. . .	. . .	. . .	. . .	. . .	. . .	. . .
General government	4 732 . .	. . .	. . .	. . .	. . .	. . .	. . .	. . .	. . .
Banks	4 733 . .	. . .	. . .	. . .	. . .	. . .	. . .	. . .	. . .
Other sectors	4 734 . .	1.60	–2.56	–11.79	–12.73	–5.66	–12.97	–14.86	–8.76
Other assets	4 736 . .	. . .	. . .	. . .	. . .	. . .	. . .	. . .	. . .
Monetary authorities	4 737 . .	. . .	. . .	. . .	. . .	. . .	. . .	. . .	. . .
of which: Short-term	4 739 . .	. . .	. . .	. . .	. . .	. . .	. . .	. . .	. . .
General government	4 740 . .	. . .	. . .	. . .	. . .	. . .	. . .	. . .	. . .
of which: Short-term	4 742 . .	. . .	. . .	. . .	. . .	. . .	. . .	. . .	. . .
Banks	4 743 . .	. . .	. . .	. . .	. . .	. . .	. . .	. . .	. . .
of which: Short-term	4 745 . .	. . .	. . .	. . .	. . .	. . .	. . .	. . .	. . .
Other sectors	4 746 . .	. . .	. . .	. . .	. . .	. . .	. . .	. . .	. . .
of which: Short-term	4 748 . .	. . .	. . .	. . .	. . .	. . .	. . .	. . .	. . .
Liabilities	4 753 . .	**6.13**	**14.47**	**23.66**	**18.98**	**39.11**	**76.65**	**76.22**	**49.36**
Trade credits	4 756 . .	2.83	. . .	. . .	. . .	. . .	. . .	. . .	. . .
General government	4 757 . .	2.83	. . .	. . .	. . .	. . .	. . .	. . .	. . .
of which: Short-term	4 759 . .	*2.83*	. . .	. . .	. . .	. . .	. . .	. . .	. . .
Other sectors	4 760 . .	. . .	. . .	. . .	. . .	. . .	. . .	. . .	. . .
of which: Short-term	4 762 . .	. . .	. . .	. . .	. . .	. . .	. . .	. . .	. . .
Loans	4 764 . .	–8.74	2.39	11.61	6.92	28.30	64.11	75.69	–44.20
Monetary authorities	4 765 . .	–2.06	–2.86	–3.14	–10.19	20.58	11.36	41.79	8.45
of which: Use of Fund credit and loans from the Fund	4 766 . .	. . .	. . .	. . .	. . .	. . .	. . .	. . .	. . .
of which: Short-term	4 768 . .	*–2.06*	*–2.86*	*–3.14*	*–10.19*	*20.58*	*11.36*	*41.79*	*8.45*
General government	4 769 . .	–6.82	–10.14	–3.50	–5.33	–5.51	29.87	24.41	–31.84
of which: Short-term	4 771 . .	*–6.82*	*–10.14*	*–3.50*	*–5.33*	*–5.51*	*29.87*	*24.41*	*–31.84*
Banks	4 772 . .	. . .	5.73	9.90	8.12	2.30	7.00	7.63	–2.34
of which: Short-term	4 774 . .	. . .	*5.73*	*9.90*	*8.12*	*2.30*	*7.00*	*7.63*	*–2.34*
Other sectors	4 775 . .	.14	9.66	8.35	14.32	10.93	15.87	1.86	–18.47
of which: Short-term	4 777 . .	*.14*	*9.66*	*8.35*	*14.32*	*10.93*	*15.87*	*1.86*	*–18.47*
Currency and deposits	4 780 . .	. . .	. . .	. . .	. . .	. . .	. . .	. . .	. . .
Monetary authorities	4 781 . .	. . .	. . .	. . .	. . .	. . .	. . .	. . .	. . .
General government	4 782 . .	. . .	. . .	. . .	. . .	. . .	. . .	. . .	. . .
Banks	4 783 . .	. . .	. . .	. . .	. . .	. . .	. . .	. . .	. . .
Other sectors	4 784 . .	. . .	. . .	. . .	. . .	. . .	. . .	. . .	. . .
Other liabilities	4 786 . .	12.05	12.07	12.05	12.06	10.81	12.54	.53	93.55
Monetary authorities	4 787 . .	. . .	. . .	. . .	. . .	. . .	. . .	. . .	. . .
of which: Short-term	4 789 . .	. . .	. . .	. . .	. . .	. . .	. . .	. . .	. . .
General government	4 790 . .	. . .	. . .	. . .	. . .	. . .	. . .	. . .	. . .
of which: Short-term	4 792 . .	. . .	. . .	. . .	. . .	. . .	. . .	. . .	. . .
Banks	4 793 . .	. . .	. . .	. . .	. . .	. . .	. . .	. . .	. . .
of which: Short-term	4 795 . .	. . .	. . .	. . .	. . .	. . .	. . .	. . .	. . .
Other sectors	4 796 . .	12.05	12.07	12.05	12.06	10.81	12.54	.53	93.55
of which: Short-term	4 798 . .	*12.05*	*12.07*	*12.05*	*12.06*	*10.81*	*12.54*	*.53*	*6.88*
E. RESERVE ASSETS	4 802 . .	7.43	3.42	4.86	–5.12	3.26	–8.42	–19.39	10.32
Monetary gold	4 812 . .	. . .	. . .	. . .	. . .	. . .	. . .	. . .	. . .
Special drawing rights	4 811 . .	–.01	. . .	. . .	–.01	. . .	. . .	.02	–.01
Reserve position in the Fund	4 810 . .	. . .	. . .	. . .	. . .	1.07	. . .	. . .	. . .
Foreign exchange	4 803 . .	7.44	3.42	4.87	–5.11	2.19	–8.42	–19.41	10.33
Other claims	4 813 . .	. . .	. . .	. . .	. . .	. . .	. . .	. . .	. . .
NET ERRORS AND OMISSIONS	4 998 . .	**–20.16**	**10.01**	**7.07**	**11.61**	**–2.81**	**11.37**	**–18.78**	**–12.62**

Part 3 of the *Yearbook* contains descriptions of the methodologies, compilation practices, and sources used to compile these data.

Table 1. ANALYTIC PRESENTATION, 1994–2001
(Millions of U.S. dollars)

	Code		1994	1995	1996	1997	1998	1999	2000	2001
A. Current Account [1]	4 993	Z.	**-89.1**	**-126.5**	**...**	**...**	**...**	**...**	**...**	**...**
Goods: exports f.o.b	2 100	. .	116.0	41.5	...	...	...	...	...	...
Goods: imports f.o.b	3 100	. .	-188.7	-168.1	...	...	...	...	...	...
Balance on Goods	4 100	. .	*-72.7*	*-126.7*	...	...	...	...	...	...
Services: credit	2 200	. .	100.2	86.8	...	...	...	...	...	...
Services: debit	3 200	. .	-107.6	-91.8	...	...	...	...	...	...
Balance on Goods and Services	4 991	. .	*-80.1*	*-131.7*	...	...	...	...	...	...
Income: credit	2 300	. .	1.5	.7	...	...	...	...	...	...
Income: debit	3 300	. .	-57.0	-21.4	...	...	...	...	...	...
Balance on Goods, Services, and Income	4 992	. .	*-135.7*	*-152.3*	...	...	...	...	...	...
Current transfers: credit	2 379	Z.	47.5	35.3	...	...	...	...	...	...
Current transfers: debit	3 379	. .	-.9	-9.5	...	...	...	...	...	...
B. Capital Account [1]	4 994	Z.	**.1**	**...**	**...**	**...**	**...**	**...**	**...**	**...**
Capital account: credit	2 994	Z.	.1	...	...	...	...	...	...	...
Capital account: debit	3 994	. .	...	...	...	...	...	...	...	...
Total, Groups A Plus B	4 981	. .	*-89.1*	*-126.5*	...	...	...	...	...	...
C. Financial Account [1]	4 995	W.	**-25.5**	**61.6**	**...**	**...**	**...**	**...**	**...**	**...**
Direct investment abroad	4 505	. .	...	...	...	...	...	...	...	...
Direct investment in Sierra Leone	4 555	Z.	-2.9	-1.7	...	...	...	...	...	...
Portfolio investment assets	4 602	. .	...	...	...	...	...	...	...	...
Equity securities	4 610	. .	...	...	...	...	...	...	...	...
Debt securities	4 619	. .	...	...	...	...	...	...	...	...
Portfolio investment liabilities	4 652	Z.	...	...	...	...	...	...	...	...
Equity securities	4 660	. .	...	...	...	...	...	...	...	...
Debt securities	4 669	Z.	...	...	...	...	...	...	...	...
Financial derivatives	4 910	. .	...	...	...	...	...	...	...	...
Financial derivatives assets	4 900	. .	...	...	...	...	...	...	...	...
Financial derivatives liabilities	4 905	. .	...	...	...	...	...	...	...	...
Other investment assets	4 703	. .	-.8	15.6	...	...	...	...	...	...
Monetary authorities	4 701	. .	...	...	...	...	...	...	...	...
General government	4 704	. .	...	...	...	...	...	...	...	...
Banks	4 705	. .	4.4	15.9	...	...	...	...	...	...
Other sectors	4 728	. .	-5.2	-.4	...	...	...	...	...	...
Other investment liabilities	4 753	W.	-21.8	47.8	...	...	...	...	...	...
Monetary authorities	4 753	WA	...	...	...	...	...	...	...	...
General government	4 753	ZB	-15.2	41.9	...	...	...	...	...	...
Banks	4 753	ZC	2.8	-1.5	...	...	...	...	...	...
Other sectors	4 753	ZD	-9.5	7.4	...	...	...	...	...	...
Total, Groups A Through C	4 983	. .	*-114.6*	*-64.8*	...	...	...	...	...	...
D. Net Errors and Omissions	4 998	. .	**55.1**	**19.3**	**...**	**...**	**...**	**...**	**...**	**...**
Total, Groups A Through D	4 984	. .	*-59.5*	*-45.6*	...	...	...	...	...	...
E. Reserves and Related Items	4 802	A.	**59.5**	**45.6**	**...**	**...**	**...**	**...**	**...**	**...**
Reserve assets	4 802	. .	-18.6	2.4	...	...	...	...	...	...
Use of Fund credit and loans	4 766	. .	55.1	15.9	...	...	...	...	...	...
Exceptional financing	4 920	. .	22.9	27.3	...	...	...	...	...	...
Conversion rates: leones per U.S. dollar	0 101	. .	**586.74**	**755.22**	**920.73**	**981.48**	**1,563.62**	**1,804.20**	**2,092.13**	**1,986.15**

[1] Excludes components that have been classified in the categories of Group E.

Table 2. STANDARD PRESENTATION, 1994–2001
(Millions of U.S. dollars)

	Code	1994	1995	1996	1997	1998	1999	2000	2001
CURRENT ACCOUNT	4 993 . .	**-89.1**	**-126.5**	...	...	...	...	...	...
A. GOODS	4 100 . .	-72.7	-126.7	...	...	...	...	...	...
Credit	2 100 . .	**116.0**	**41.5**	...	...	...	...	...	...
General merchandise: exports f.o.b.	2 110 . .	112.6	39.4	...	...	...	...	...	...
Goods for processing: exports f.o.b.	2 150 . .	...	...	...	...	...	...	...	...
Repairs on goods	2 160 . .	...	...	...	...	...	...	...	...
Goods procured in ports by carriers	2 170 . .	3.4	2.1	...	...	...	...	...	...
Nonmonetary gold	2 180 . .	...	...	...	...	...	...	...	...
Debit	3 100 . .	**-188.7**	**-168.1**	...	...	...	...	...	...
General merchandise: imports f.o.b.	3 110 . .	-188.7	-168.1	...	...	...	...	...	...
Goods for processing: imports f.o.b.	3 150 . .	...	...	...	...	...	...	...	...
Repairs on goods	3 160 . .	...	...	...	...	...	...	...	...
Goods procured in ports by carriers	3 170 . .	...	...	...	...	...	...	...	...
Nonmonetary gold	3 180 . .	...	...	...	...	...	...	...	...
B. SERVICES	4 200 . .	-7.4	-5.0	...	...	...	...	...	...
Total credit	2 200 . .	*100.2*	*86.8*	...	...	...	...	...	...
Total debit	3 200 . .	*-107.6*	*-91.8*	...	...	...	...	...	...
Transportation services, credit	2 205 . .	**12.4**	**9.7**	...	...	...	...	...	...
Passenger	2 850 . .	...	...	...	...	...	...	...	...
Freight	2 851 . .	...	...	...	...	...	...	...	...
Other	2 852 . .	*12.4*	*9.7*	...	...	...	...	...	...
Sea transport, passenger	2 207 . .	...	...	...	...	...	...	...	...
Sea transport, freight	2 208 . .	...	...	...	...	...	...	...	...
Sea transport, other	2 209 . .	...	...	...	...	...	...	...	...
Air transport, passenger	2 211 . .	...	...	...	...	...	...	...	...
Air transport, freight	2 212 . .	...	...	...	...	...	...	...	...
Air transport, other	2 213 . .	...	...	...	...	...	...	...	...
Other transport, passenger	2 215 . .	...	...	...	...	...	...	...	...
Other transport, freight	2 216 . .	...	...	...	...	...	...	...	...
Other transport, other	2 217 . .	...	...	...	...	...	...	...	...
Transportation services, debit	3 205 . .	**-15.6**	**-13.8**	...	...	...	...	...	...
Passenger	3 850 . .	*-.6*	*-.5*	...	...	...	...	...	...
Freight	3 851 . .	*-15.1*	*-13.3*	...	...	...	...	...	...
Other	3 852 . .	...	...	...	...	...	...	...	...
Sea transport, passenger	3 207 . .	...	...	...	...	...	...	...	...
Sea transport, freight	3 208 . .	...	...	...	...	...	...	...	...
Sea transport, other	3 209 . .	...	...	...	...	...	...	...	...
Air transport, passenger	3 211 . .	...	...	...	...	...	...	...	...
Air transport, freight	3 212 . .	...	...	...	...	...	...	...	...
Air transport, other	3 213 . .	...	...	...	...	...	...	...	...
Other transport, passenger	3 215 . .	...	...	...	...	...	...	...	...
Other transport, freight	3 216 . .	...	...	...	...	...	...	...	...
Other transport, other	3 217 . .	...	...	...	...	...	...	...	...
Travel, credit	2 236 . .	**69.1**	**57.2**	...	...	...	...	...	...
Business travel	2 237 . .	...	...	...	...	...	...	...	...
Personal travel	2 240 . .	...	...	...	...	...	...	...	...
Travel, debit	3 236 . .	**-61.8**	**-49.5**	...	...	...	...	...	...
Business travel	3 237 . .	...	...	...	...	...	...	...	...
Personal travel	3 240 . .	...	...	...	...	...	...	...	...
Other services, credit	2 200 BA	**18.7**	**19.9**	...	...	...	...	...	...
Communications	2 245 . .	...	...	...	...	...	...	...	...
Construction	2 249 . .	...	...	...	...	...	...	...	...
Insurance	2 253 . .	.2	.2	...	...	...	...	...	...
Financial	2 260 . .	...	...	...	...	...	...	...	...
Computer and information	2 262 . .	...	...	...	...	...	...	...	...
Royalties and licence fees	2 266 . .	...	...	...	...	...	...	...	...
Other business services	2 268 . .	4.3	3.9	...	...	...	...	...	...
Personal, cultural, and recreational	2 287 . .	...	...	...	...	...	...	...	...
Government, n.i.e.	2 291 . .	14.2	15.8	...	...	...	...	...	...
Other services, debit	3 200 BA	**-30.1**	**-28.5**	...	...	...	...	...	...
Communications	3 245 . .	...	...	...	...	...	...	...	...
Construction	3 249 . .	...	...	...	...	...	...	...	...
Insurance	3 253 . .	-3.4	-3.0	...	...	...	...	...	...
Financial	3 260 . .	...	...	...	...	...	...	...	...
Computer and information	3 262 . .	...	...	...	...	...	...	...	...
Royalties and licence fees	3 266 . .	...	...	...	...	...	...	...	...
Other business services	3 268 . .	-12.5	-12.9	...	...	...	...	...	...
Personal, cultural, and recreational	3 287 . .	...	...	...	...	...	...	...	...
Government, n.i.e.	3 291 . .	-14.2	-12.6	...	...	...	...	...	...

Table 2 (Continued). STANDARD PRESENTATION, 1994–2001
(Millions of U.S. dollars)

	Code	1994	1995	1996	1997	1998	1999	2000	2001
C. INCOME	4 300	–55.6	–20.6	...	...	...	...	...	...
Total credit	2 300	*1.5*	*.7*	...	...	...	...	...	...
Total debit	3 300	*–57.0*	*–21.4*	...	...	...	...	...	...
Compensation of employees, credit	2 310	**...**	**...**	**...**	**...**	**...**	**...**	**...**	**...**
Compensation of employees, debit	3 310	**...**	**...**	**...**	**...**	**...**	**...**	**...**	**...**
Investment income, credit	2 320	**1.5**	**.7**	**...**	**...**	**...**	**...**	**...**	**...**
Direct investment income	2 330	.3	...	...	...	...	...	...	...
Dividends and distributed branch profits	2 332	.3	...	...	...	...	...	...	...
Reinvested earnings and undistributed branch profits	2 333	...	...	...	...	...	...	...	...
Income on debt (interest)	2 334	...	...	...	...	...	...	...	...
Portfolio investment income	2 339	...	...	...	...	...	...	...	...
Income on equity	2 340	...	...	...	...	...	...	...	...
Income on bonds and notes	2 350	...	...	...	...	...	...	...	...
Income on money market instruments	2 360	...	...	...	...	...	...	...	...
Other investment income	2 370	1.1	.7	...	...	...	...	...	...
Investment income, debit	3 320	**–57.0**	**–21.4**	**...**	**...**	**...**	**...**	**...**	**...**
Direct investment income	3 330	.2	–2.3	...	...	...	...	...	...
Dividends and distributed branch profits	3 332	–2.9	–7.0	...	...	...	...	...	...
Reinvested earnings and undistributed branch profits	3 333	3.2	4.7	...	...	...	...	...	...
Income on debt (interest)	3 334	...	...	...	...	...	...	...	...
Portfolio investment income	3 339	...	...	...	...	...	...	...	...
Income on equity	3 340	...	...	...	...	...	...	...	...
Income on bonds and notes	3 350	...	...	...	...	...	...	...	...
Income on money market instruments	3 360	...	...	...	...	...	...	...	...
Other investment income	3 370	–57.3	–19.1	...	...	...	...	...	...
D. CURRENT TRANSFERS	4 379	46.6	25.8	...	...	...	...	...	...
Credit	2 379	**47.5**	**35.3**	**...**	**...**	**...**	**...**	**...**	**...**
General government	2 380	46.3	11.1	...	...	...	...	...	...
Other sectors	2 390	1.1	24.2	...	...	...	...	...	...
Workers' remittances	2 391	...	...	...	...	...	...	...	...
Other current transfers	2 392	1.1	24.2	...	...	...	...	...	...
Debit	3 379	**–.9**	**–9.5**	**...**	**...**	**...**	**...**	**...**	**...**
General government	3 380	–.8	–9.5	...	...	...	...	...	...
Other sectors	3 390	–.1	...	...	...	...	...	...	...
Workers' remittances	3 391	...	...	...	...	...	...	...	...
Other current transfers	3 392	–.1	...	...	...	...	...	...	...
CAPITAL AND FINANCIAL ACCOUNT	4 996	**34.0**	**107.2**	**...**	**...**	**...**	**...**	**...**	**...**
CAPITAL ACCOUNT	4 994	**.1**	**...**	**...**	**...**	**...**	**...**	**...**	**...**
Total credit	2 994	*.1*	...	...	...	...	...	...	...
Total debit	3 994	...	...	...	...	...	...	...	...
Capital transfers, credit	2 400	**.1**	**...**	**...**	**...**	**...**	**...**	**...**	**...**
General government	2 401	...	...	...	...	...	...	...	...
Debt forgiveness	2 402	...	...	...	...	...	...	...	...
Other capital transfers	2 410	...	...	...	...	...	...	...	...
Other sectors	2 430	.1	...	...	...	...	...	...	...
Migrants' transfers	2 431	.1	...	...	...	...	...	...	...
Debt forgiveness	2 432	...	...	...	...	...	...	...	...
Other capital transfers	2 440	...	...	...	...	...	...	...	...
Capital transfers, debit	3 400	**...**	**...**	**...**	**...**	**...**	**...**	**...**	**...**
General government	3 401	...	...	...	...	...	...	...	...
Debt forgiveness	3 402	...	...	...	...	...	...	...	...
Other capital transfers	3 410	...	...	...	...	...	...	...	...
Other sectors	3 430	...	...	...	...	...	...	...	...
Migrants' transfers	3 431	...	...	...	...	...	...	...	...
Debt forgiveness	3 432	...	...	...	...	...	...	...	...
Other capital transfers	3 440	...	...	...	...	...	...	...	...
Nonproduced nonfinancial assets, credit	2 480	**...**	**...**	**...**	**...**	**...**	**...**	**...**	**...**
Nonproduced nonfinancial assets, debit	3 480	**...**	**...**	**...**	**...**	**...**	**...**	**...**	**...**

Table 2 (Continued). STANDARD PRESENTATION, 1994–2001
(Millions of U.S. dollars)

	Code		1994	1995	1996	1997	1998	1999	2000	2001
FINANCIAL ACCOUNT	4 995	. .	**33.9**	**107.2**	...	...	...	...	...	...
A. DIRECT INVESTMENT	4 500	. .	–2.9	–1.7	...	...	...	...	...	...
Direct investment abroad	4 505	. .	...	...	...	...	...	...	...	...
Equity capital	4 510	. .	...	...	...	...	...	...	...	...
Claims on affiliated enterprises	4 515	. .	...	...	...	...	...	...	...	...
Liabilities to affiliated enterprises	4 520	. .	...	...	...	...	...	...	...	...
Reinvested earnings	4 525	. .	...	...	...	...	...	...	...	...
Other capital	4 530	. .	...	...	...	...	...	...	...	...
Claims on affiliated enterprises	4 535	. .	...	...	...	...	...	...	...	...
Liabilities to affiliated enterprises	4 540	. .	...	...	...	...	...	...	...	...
Direct investment in Sierra Leone	4 555	. .	**–2.9**	**–1.7**	...	...	...	...	...	...
Equity capital	4 560	. .	...	...	...	...	...	...	...	...
Claims on direct investors	4 565	. .	...	...	...	...	...	...	...	...
Liabilities to direct investors	4 570	. .	...	...	...	...	...	...	...	...
Reinvested earnings	4 575	. .	–3.2	–4.7	...	...	...	...	...	...
Other capital	4 580	. .	.3	3.0	...	...	...	...	...	...
Claims on direct investors	4 585	. .	...	...	...	...	...	...	...	...
Liabilities to direct investors	4 590	. .	...	...	...	...	...	...	...	...
B. PORTFOLIO INVESTMENT	4 600	. .	...	...	...	...	...	...	...	...
Assets	4 602	. .	...	...	...	...	...	...	...	...
Equity securities	4 610	. .	...	...	...	...	...	...	...	...
Monetary authorities	4 611	. .	...	...	...	...	...	...	...	...
General government	4 612	. .	...	...	...	...	...	...	...	...
Banks	4 613	. .	...	...	...	...	...	...	...	...
Other sectors	4 614	. .	...	...	...	...	...	...	...	...
Debt securities	4 619	. .	...	...	...	...	...	...	...	...
Bonds and notes	4 620	. .	...	...	...	...	...	...	...	...
Monetary authorities	4 621	. .	...	...	...	...	...	...	...	...
General government	4 622	. .	...	...	...	...	...	...	...	...
Banks	4 623	. .	...	...	...	...	...	...	...	...
Other sectors	4 624	. .	...	...	...	...	...	...	...	...
Money market instruments	4 630	. .	...	...	...	...	...	...	...	...
Monetary authorities	4 631	. .	...	...	...	...	...	...	...	...
General government	4 632	. .	...	...	...	...	...	...	...	...
Banks	4 633	. .	...	...	...	...	...	...	...	...
Other sectors	4 634	. .	...	...	...	...	...	...	...	...
Liabilities	4 652	. .	...	...	...	...	...	...	...	...
Equity securities	4 660	. .	...	...	...	...	...	...	...	...
Banks	4 663	. .	...	...	...	...	...	...	...	...
Other sectors	4 664	. .	...	...	...	...	...	...	...	...
Debt securities	4 669	. .	...	...	...	...	...	...	...	...
Bonds and notes	4 670	. .	...	...	...	...	...	...	...	...
Monetary authorities	4 671	. .	...	...	...	...	...	...	...	...
General government	4 672	. .	...	...	...	...	...	...	...	...
Banks	4 673	. .	...	...	...	...	...	...	...	...
Other sectors	4 674	. .	...	...	...	...	...	...	...	...
Money market instruments	4 680	. .	...	...	...	...	...	...	...	...
Monetary authorities	4 681	. .	...	...	...	...	...	...	...	...
General government	4 682	. .	...	...	...	...	...	...	...	...
Banks	4 683	. .	...	...	...	...	...	...	...	...
Other sectors	4 684	. .	...	...	...	...	...	...	...	...
C. FINANCIAL DERIVATIVES	4 910	. .	...	...	...	...	...	...	...	...
Monetary authorities	4 911	. .	...	...	...	...	...	...	...	...
General government	4 912	. .	...	...	...	...	...	...	...	...
Banks	4 913	. .	...	...	...	...	...	...	...	...
Other sectors	4 914	. .	...	...	...	...	...	...	...	...
Assets	4 900	. .	...	...	...	...	...	...	...	...
Monetary authorities	4 901	. .	...	...	...	...	...	...	...	...
General government	4 902	. .	...	...	...	...	...	...	...	...
Banks	4 903	. .	...	...	...	...	...	...	...	...
Other sectors	4 904	. .	...	...	...	...	...	...	...	...
Liabilities	4 905	. .	...	...	...	...	...	...	...	...
Monetary authorities	4 906	. .	...	...	...	...	...	...	...	...
General government	4 907	. .	...	...	...	...	...	...	...	...
Banks	4 908	. .	...	...	...	...	...	...	...	...
Other sectors	4 909	. .	...	...	...	...	...	...	...	...

Table 2 (Concluded). STANDARD PRESENTATION, 1994–2001
(Millions of U.S. dollars)

	Code	1994	1995	1996	1997	1998	1999	2000	2001
D. OTHER INVESTMENT	4 700	55.4	106.5	...	...	...	...	...	...
Assets	4 703	**–.8**	**15.6**	**...**	**...**	**...**	**...**	**...**	**...**
Trade credits	4 706	1.0	–1.0	...	...	...	...	...	...
General government	4 707	...	...	...	...	...	...	...	...
of which: Short-term	4 709	...	...	...	...	...	...	...	...
Other sectors	4 710	1.0	–1.0	...	...	...	...	...	...
of which: Short-term	4 712	*1.0*	*–1.0*	...	...	...	...	...	...
Loans	4 714	...	...	...	...	...	...	...	...
Monetary authorities	4 715	...	...	...	...	...	...	...	...
of which: Short-term	4 718	...	...	...	...	...	...	...	...
General government	4 719	...	...	...	...	...	...	...	...
of which: Short-term	4 721	...	...	...	...	...	...	...	...
Banks	4 722	...	...	...	...	...	...	...	...
of which: Short-term	4 724	...	...	...	...	...	...	...	...
Other sectors	4 725	...	...	...	...	...	...	...	...
of which: Short-term	4 727	...	...	...	...	...	...	...	...
Currency and deposits	4 730	–1.8	16.6	...	...	...	...	...	...
Monetary authorities	4 731	...	...	...	...	...	...	...	...
General government	4 732	...	...	...	...	...	...	...	...
Banks	4 733	4.4	15.9	...	...	...	...	...	...
Other sectors	4 734	–6.1	.6	...	...	...	...	...	...
Other assets	4 736	...	...	...	...	...	...	...	...
Monetary authorities	4 737	...	...	...	...	...	...	...	...
of which: Short-term	4 739	...	...	...	...	...	...	...	...
General government	4 740	...	...	...	...	...	...	...	...
of which: Short-term	4 742	...	...	...	...	...	...	...	...
Banks	4 743	...	...	...	...	...	...	...	...
of which: Short-term	4 745	...	...	...	...	...	...	...	...
Other sectors	4 746	...	...	...	...	...	...	...	...
of which: Short-term	4 748	...	...	...	...	...	...	...	...
Liabilities	4 753	**56.2**	**90.9**	**...**	**...**	**...**	**...**	**...**	**...**
Trade credits	4 756	.2	–.3	...	...	...	...	...	...
General government	4 757	...	...	...	...	...	...	...	...
of which: Short-term	4 759	...	...	...	...	...	...	...	...
Other sectors	4 760	.2	–.3	...	...	...	...	...	...
of which: Short-term	4 762	*.2*	*–.3*	...	...	...	...	...	...
Loans	4 764	96.4	78.3	...	...	...	...	...	...
Monetary authorities	4 765	55.1	15.9	...	...	...	...	...	...
of which: Use of Fund credit and loans from the Fund	4 766	*55.1*	*15.9*	...	...	...	...	...	...
of which: Short-term	4 768	...	...	...	...	...	...	...	...
General government	4 769	40.6	63.1	...	...	...	...	...	...
of which: Short-term	4 771	...	*–41.8*	...	...	...	...	...	...
Banks	4 772	...	...	...	...	...	...	...	...
of which: Short-term	4 774	...	...	...	...	...	...	...	...
Other sectors	4 775	.7	–.7	...	...	...	...	...	...
of which: Short-term	4 777	*.7*	*–.4*	...	...	...	...	...	...
Currency and deposits	4 780	2.8	–1.5	...	...	...	...	...	...
Monetary authorities	4 781	...	...	...	...	...	...	...	...
General government	4 782	...	...	...	...	...	...	...	...
Banks	4 783	2.8	–1.5	...	...	...	...	...	...
Other sectors	4 784	...	...	...	...	...	...	...	...
Other liabilities	4 786	–43.3	14.5	...	...	...	...	...	...
Monetary authorities	4 787	...	...	...	...	...	...	...	...
of which: Short-term	4 789	...	...	...	...	...	...	...	...
General government	4 790	–32.9	6.1	...	...	...	...	...	...
of which: Short-term	4 792	*38.3*	*28.4*	...	...	...	...	...	...
Banks	4 793	...	...	...	...	...	...	...	...
of which: Short-term	4 795	...	...	...	...	...	...	...	...
Other sectors	4 796	–10.4	8.4	...	...	...	...	...	...
of which: Short-term	4 798	...	...	...	...	...	...	...	...
E. RESERVE ASSETS	4 802	–18.6	2.4	...	...	...	...	...	...
Monetary gold	4 812	...	...	...	...	...	...	...	...
Special drawing rights	4 811	–4.6	–7.7	...	...	...	...	...	...
Reserve position in the Fund	4 810	...	...	...	...	...	...	...	...
Foreign exchange	4 803	–13.9	10.2	...	...	...	...	...	...
Other claims	4 813	...	...	...	...	...	...	...	...
NET ERRORS AND OMISSIONS	4 998	**55.1**	**19.3**	**...**	**...**	**...**	**...**	**...**	**...**

Part 3 of the *Yearbook* contains descriptions of the methodologies, compilation practices, and sources used to compile these data.

Table 1. ANALYTIC PRESENTATION, 1994–2001
(Millions of U.S. dollars)

	Code	1994	1995	1996	1997	1998	1999	2000	2001
A. Current Account [1]	4 993 Z.	**11,400**	**14,900**	**12,571**	**18,122**	**19,706**	**16,527**	**15,921**	**17,884**
Goods: exports f.o.b	2 100 . .	97,919	118,456	126,012	125,732	110,591	115,514	139,054	122,478
Goods: imports f.o.b	3 100 . .	−96,565	−117,480	−123,819	−124,701	−95,685	−104,287	−127,483	−109,605
Balance on Goods	4 100 . .	*1,354*	*976*	*2,193*	*1,031*	*14,907*	*11,227*	*11,571*	*12,872*
Services: credit	2 200 . .	23,044	29,649	29,838	30,871	18,125	23,690	26,761	26,168
Services: debit	3 200 . .	−13,898	−17,367	−19,726	−18,748	−17,071	−19,235	−21,694	−20,443
Balance on Goods and Services	4 991 . .	*10,500*	*13,258*	*12,305*	*13,154*	*15,961*	*15,682*	*16,639*	*18,598*
Income: credit	2 300 . .	9,783	12,958	12,379	13,575	12,665	16,184	16,295	14,920
Income: debit	3 300 . .	−8,222	−10,430	−11,041	−7,398	−7,733	−14,156	−15,700	−14,257
Balance on Goods, Services, and Income	4 992 . .	*12,061*	*15,786*	*13,642*	*19,330*	*20,893*	*17,710*	*17,234*	*19,262*
Current transfers: credit	2 379 Z.	145	156	161	153	130	134	127	123
Current transfers: debit	3 379 . .	−806	−1,042	−1,232	−1,361	−1,317	−1,317	−1,441	−1,501
B. Capital Account [1]	4 994 Z.	**−84**	**−71**	**−139**	**−173**	**−226**	**−191**	**−163**	**−161**
Capital account: credit	2 994 Z.	. . .	. . .	. . .	. . .	. . .	. . .	. . .	. . .
Capital account: debit	3 994 . .	−84	−71	−139	−173	−226	−191	−163	−161
Total, Groups A Plus B	4 981 . .	*11,316*	*14,829*	*12,432*	*17,949*	*19,480*	*16,336*	*15,758*	*17,723*
C. Financial Account [1]	4 995 W.	**−8,841**	**−878**	**−8,771**	**−13,642**	**−21,009**	**−11,359**	**−10,836**	**−18,768**
Direct investment abroad	4 505 . .	−4,577	−3,442	−6,827	−9,465	−795	−4,277	−4,966	−10,216
Direct investment in Singapore	4 555 Z.	8,550	8,788	8,608	10,746	6,389	11,803	5,407	8,609
Portfolio investment assets	4 602 . .	−7,840	−7,769	−12,783	−14,910	−10,860	−7,938	−7,867	−5,256
Equity securities	4 610 . .	−7,414	−7,972	−10,098	−12,492	−6,937	−9,034	−5,579	−4,477
Debt securities	4 619 . .	−426	203	−2,685	−2,418	−3,923	1,096	−2,288	−779
Portfolio investment liabilities	4 652 Z.	114	410	983	−55	929	2,311	−2,034	720
Equity securities	4 660 . .	169	462	1,004	−67	938	2,313	−2,034	718
Debt securities	4 669 Z.	−55	−52	−21	12	−8	−2	−1	2
Financial derivatives	4 910 . .	. . .	. . .	. . .	. . .	. . .	. . .	. . .	. . .
Financial derivatives assets	4 900 . .	. . .	. . .	. . .	. . .	. . .	. . .	. . .	. . .
Financial derivatives liabilities	4 905 . .	. . .	. . .	. . .	. . .	. . .	. . .	. . .	. . .
Other investment assets	4 703 . .	−10,999	−12,150	−13,868	−37,868	127	−20,002	−5,974	−15,472
Monetary authorities	4 701 . .	. . .	. . .	. . .	. . .	. . .	. . .	. . .	. . .
General government	4 704 . .	. . .	−7	. . .	. . .	. . .	. . .	. . .	−5
Banks	4 705 . .	−4,291	1,154	−3,533	−12,382	2,217	−10,665	1,466	−10,259
Other sectors	4 728 . .	−6,708	13,297	−10,335	−25,486	−2,090	−9,337	−7,439	−5,209
Other investment liabilities	4 753 W.	5,911	13,285	15,116	37,910	−16,800	6,743	4,598	2,847
Monetary authorities	4 753 WA	. . .	. . .	. . .	. . .	. . .	. . .	. . .	. . .
General government	4 753 ZB	−4	. . .	. . .	. . .	. . .	. . .	. . .	. . .
Banks	4 753 ZC	5,409	4,423	8,032	18,687	−12,787	3,210	7,416	7,059
Other sectors	4 753 ZD	506	8,863	7,084	19,223	−4,013	3,533	−2,818	−4,212
Total, Groups A Through C	4 983 . .	*2,475*	*13,951*	*3,661*	*4,308*	*−1,528*	*4,977*	*4,922*	*−1,045*
D. Net Errors and Omissions	4 998 . .	**2,261**	**−5,352**	**3,734**	**3,632**	**4,494**	**−783**	**1,884**	**184**
Total, Groups A Through D	4 984 . .	*4,736*	*8,599*	*7,396*	*7,940*	*2,965*	*4,194*	*6,806*	*−861*
E. Reserves and Related Items	4 802 A.	**−4,736**	**−8,599**	**−7,396**	**−7,940**	**−2,965**	**−4,194**	**−6,806**	**861**
Reserve assets	4 802 . .	−4,736	−8,599	−7,396	−7,940	−2,965	−4,194	−6,806	861
Use of Fund credit and loans	4 766 . .	. . .	. . .	. . .	. . .	. . .	. . .	. . .	. . .
Exceptional financing	4 920 . .	. . .	. . .	. . .	. . .	. . .	. . .	. . .	. . .
Conversion rates: Singapore dollars per U.S. dollar	0 101 . .	**1.5274**	**1.4174**	**1.4100**	**1.4848**	**1.6736**	**1.6950**	**1.7240**	**1.7917**

[1] Excludes components that have been classified in the categories of Group E.

Table 2. STANDARD PRESENTATION, 1994–2001
(Millions of U.S. dollars)

	Code		1994	1995	1996	1997	1998	1999	2000	2001
CURRENT ACCOUNT	4 993	..	**11,400**	**14,900**	**12,571**	**18,122**	**19,706**	**16,527**	**15,921**	**17,884**
A. GOODS	4 100	..	1,354	976	2,193	1,031	14,907	11,227	11,571	12,872
Credit	2 100	..	**97,919**	**118,456**	**126,012**	**125,732**	**110,591**	**115,514**	**139,054**	**122,478**
General merchandise: exports f.o.b.	2 110	..	96,165	116,620	123,802	123,418	108,722	113,379	135,646	118,890
Goods for processing: exports f.o.b.	2 150	..	...	...	...	...	...	...	...	...
Repairs on goods	2 160	..	...	...	...	...	...	...	...	...
Goods procured in ports by carriers	2 170	..	1,754	1,836	2,210	2,314	1,870	2,135	3,408	3,587
Nonmonetary gold	2 180	..	...	...	...	...	...	...	...	...
Debit	3 100	..	**–96,565**	**–117,480**	**–123,819**	**–124,701**	**–95,685**	**–104,287**	**–127,483**	**–109,605**
General merchandise: imports f.o.b.	3 110	..	–96,140	–116,933	–123,194	–124,074	–95,231	–103,745	–126,591	–108,851
Goods for processing: imports f.o.b.	3 150	..	...	...	...	...	...	...	...	...
Repairs on goods	3 160	..	...	...	...	...	...	...	...	...
Goods procured in ports by carriers	3 170	..	–425	–547	–625	–627	–454	–542	–892	–754
Nonmonetary gold	3 180	..	...	...	...	...	...	...	...	...
B. SERVICES	4 200	..	9,146	12,281	10,112	12,123	1,054	4,455	5,068	5,726
Total credit	2 200	..	*23,044*	*29,649*	*29,838*	*30,871*	*18,125*	*23,690*	*26,761*	*26,168*
Total debit	3 200	..	*–13,898*	*–17,367*	*–19,726*	*–18,748*	*–17,071*	*–19,235*	*–21,694*	*–20,443*
Transportation services, credit	2 205	..	**4,042**	**4,957**	**5,203**	**5,158**	**4,456**	**4,577**	**5,336**	**4,720**
Passenger	2 850	..	...	...	...	...	...	...	...	...
Freight	2 851	..	*2,894*	*3,546*	*3,750*	*3,750*	*3,294*	*3,439*	*4,139*	*3,651*
Other	2 852	..	*1,149*	*1,411*	*1,453*	*1,407*	*1,162*	*1,138*	*1,197*	*1,069*
Sea transport, passenger	2 207	..	...	...	...	...	...	...	...	...
Sea transport, freight	2 208	..	...	...	...	...	...	...	...	...
Sea transport, other	2 209	..	...	...	...	...	...	...	...	...
Air transport, passenger	2 211	..	...	...	...	...	...	...	...	...
Air transport, freight	2 212	..	...	...	...	...	...	...	...	...
Air transport, other	2 213	..	...	...	...	...	...	...	...	...
Other transport, passenger	2 215	..	...	...	...	...	...	...	...	...
Other transport, freight	2 216	..	...	...	...	...	...	...	...	...
Other transport, other	2 217	..	...	...	...	...	...	...	...	...
Transportation services, debit	3 205	..	**–4,797**	**–5,927**	**–6,278**	**–6,359**	**–5,783**	**–6,357**	**–8,054**	**–7,029**
Passenger	3 850	..	...	...	...	...	...	...	...	...
Freight	3 851	..	*–3,880*	*–4,888*	*–5,168*	*–5,230*	*–3,840*	*–4,257*	*–5,227*	*–4,579*
Other	3 852	..	*–917*	*–1,040*	*–1,110*	*–1,129*	*–1,943*	*–2,100*	*–2,827*	*–2,450*
Sea transport, passenger	3 207	..	...	...	...	...	...	...	...	...
Sea transport, freight	3 208	..	...	...	...	...	...	...	...	...
Sea transport, other	3 209	..	...	...	...	...	...	...	...	...
Air transport, passenger	3 211	..	...	...	...	...	...	...	...	...
Air transport, freight	3 212	..	...	...	...	...	...	...	...	...
Air transport, other	3 213	..	...	...	...	...	...	...	...	...
Other transport, passenger	3 215	..	...	...	...	...	...	...	...	...
Other transport, freight	3 216	..	...	...	...	...	...	...	...	...
Other transport, other	3 217	..	...	...	...	...	...	...	...	...
Travel, credit	2 236	..	**6,781**	**7,744**	**7,354**	**6,303**	**4,764**	**5,084**	**5,394**	**5,111**
Business travel	2 237	..	...	...	...	...	...	...	...	...
Personal travel	2 240	..	...	...	...	...	...	...	...	...
Travel, debit	3 236	..	**–3,868**	**–4,631**	**–5,769**	**–4,892**	**–4,438**	**–4,814**	**–5,159**	**–5,181**
Business travel	3 237	..	...	...	...	...	...	...	...	...
Personal travel	3 240	..	...	...	...	...	...	...	...	...
Other services, credit	2 200	BA	**12,220**	**16,948**	**17,281**	**19,410**	**8,905**	**14,030**	**16,032**	**16,338**
Communications	2 245	..	...	...	...	...	...	...	...	...
Construction	2 249	..	...	...	...	...	...	...	...	...
Insurance	2 253	..	330	354	402	863	435	501	957	1,119
Financial	2 260	..	...	...	...	...	...	...	...	...
Computer and information	2 262	..	...	...	...	...	...	...	...	...
Royalties and licence fees	2 266	..	...	...	...	...	...	...	...	...
Other business services	2 268	..	11,786	16,500	16,781	18,454	8,372	13,447	14,995	15,142
Personal, cultural, and recreational	2 287	..	...	...	...	...	...	...	...	...
Government, n.i.e.	2 291	..	105	93	98	93	97	81	80	77
Other services, debit	3 200	BA	**–5,233**	**–6,809**	**–7,679**	**–7,497**	**–6,849**	**–8,063**	**–8,480**	**–8,233**
Communications	3 245	..	...	...	...	...	...	...	...	...
Construction	3 249	..	...	...	...	...	...	...	...	...
Insurance	3 253	..	–771	–974	–1,002	–997	–733	–803	–965	–827
Financial	3 260	..	...	...	...	...	...	...	...	...
Computer and information	3 262	..	...	...	...	...	...	...	...	...
Royalties and licence fees	3 266	..	...	...	...	...	...	...	...	...
Other business services	3 268	..	–4,363	–5,717	–6,576	–6,382	–6,001	–7,147	–7,401	–7,271
Personal, cultural, and recreational	3 287	..	...	...	...	...	...	...	...	...
Government, n.i.e.	3 291	..	–98	–118	–101	–119	–116	–113	–114	–135

Table 2 (Continued). STANDARD PRESENTATION, 1994–2001
(Millions of U.S. dollars)

	Code	1994	1995	1996	1997	1998	1999	2000	2001
C. INCOME	4 300 . .	1,561	2,528	1,338	6,177	4,932	2,028	595	664
Total credit	2 300 . .	*9,783*	*12,958*	*12,379*	*13,575*	*12,665*	*16,184*	*16,295*	*14,920*
Total debit	3 300 . .	*–8,222*	*–10,430*	*–11,041*	*–7,398*	*–7,733*	*–14,156*	*–15,700*	*–14,257*
Compensation of employees, credit	2 310 . .	**. . .**	**. . .**	**. . .**	**. . .**	**. . .**	**. . .**	**. . .**	**. . .**
Compensation of employees, debit	3 310 . .	**. . .**	**. . .**	**. . .**	**. . .**	**. . .**	**. . .**	**. . .**	**. . .**
Investment income, credit	2 320 . .	**9,783**	**12,958**	**. . .**	**. . .**	**. . .**	**. . .**	**. . .**	**. . .**
Direct investment income	2 330 . .	. . .	. . .	. . .	. . .	. . .	. . .	. . .	. . .
Dividends and distributed branch profits	2 332 . .	. . .	. . .	. . .	. . .	. . .	. . .	. . .	. . .
Reinvested earnings and undistributed branch profits	2 333 . .	. . .	. . .	. . .	. . .	. . .	. . .	. . .	. . .
Income on debt (interest)	2 334 . .	. . .	. . .	. . .	. . .	. . .	. . .	. . .	. . .
Portfolio investment income	2 339 . .	. . .	. . .	. . .	. . .	. . .	. . .	. . .	. . .
Income on equity	2 340 . .	. . .	. . .	. . .	. . .	. . .	. . .	. . .	. . .
Income on bonds and notes	2 350 . .	. . .	. . .	. . .	. . .	. . .	. . .	. . .	. . .
Income on money market instruments	2 360 . .	. . .	. . .	. . .	. . .	. . .	. . .	. . .	. . .
Other investment income	2 370 . .	9,783	12,958	. . .	. . .	. . .	. . .	. . .	. . .
Investment income, debit	3 320 . .	**–8,222**	**–10,430**	**. . .**	**. . .**	**. . .**	**. . .**	**. . .**	**. . .**
Direct investment income	3 330 . .	. . .	. . .	. . .	. . .	. . .	. . .	. . .	. . .
Dividends and distributed branch profits	3 332 . .	. . .	. . .	. . .	. . .	. . .	. . .	. . .	. . .
Reinvested earnings and undistributed branch profits	3 333 . .	. . .	. . .	. . .	. . .	. . .	. . .	. . .	. . .
Income on debt (interest)	3 334 . .	. . .	. . .	. . .	. . .	. . .	. . .	. . .	. . .
Portfolio investment income	3 339 . .	. . .	. . .	. . .	. . .	. . .	. . .	. . .	. . .
Income on equity	3 340 . .	. . .	. . .	. . .	. . .	. . .	. . .	. . .	. . .
Income on bonds and notes	3 350 . .	. . .	. . .	. . .	. . .	. . .	. . .	. . .	. . .
Income on money market instruments	3 360 . .	. . .	. . .	. . .	. . .	. . .	. . .	. . .	. . .
Other investment income	3 370 . .	–8,222	–10,430	. . .	. . .	. . .	. . .	. . .	. . .
D. CURRENT TRANSFERS	4 379 . .	–661	–886	–1,071	–1,208	–1,187	–1,183	–1,313	–1,377
Credit	2 379 . .	**145**	**156**	**161**	**153**	**130**	**134**	**127**	**123**
General government	2 380 . .	6	7	11	10	4	10	5	5
Other sectors	2 390 . .	139	149	150	142	126	125	123	118
Workers' remittances	2 391 . .	. . .	. . .	. . .	. . .	. . .	. . .	. . .	. . .
Other current transfers	2 392 . .	139	149	150	142	126	125	123	118
Debit	3 379 . .	**–806**	**–1,042**	**–1,232**	**–1,361**	**–1,317**	**–1,317**	**–1,441**	**–1,501**
General government	3 380 . .	–139	–228	–245	–284	–237	–250	–325	–347
Other sectors	3 390 . .	–667	–814	–987	–1,077	–1,079	–1,067	–1,116	–1,154
Workers' remittances	3 391 . .	. . .	. . .	. . .	. . .	. . .	. . .	. . .	. . .
Other current transfers	3 392 . .	–667	–814	–987	–1,077	–1,079	–1,067	–1,116	–1,154
CAPITAL AND FINANCIAL ACCOUNT	4 996 . .	**–13,661**	**–9,548**	**–16,305**	**–21,755**	**–24,200**	**–15,744**	**–17,805**	**–18,068**
CAPITAL ACCOUNT	4 994 . .	**–84**	**–71**	**–139**	**–173**	**–226**	**–191**	**–163**	**–161**
Total credit	2 994 . .	. . .	. . .	. . .	. . .	. . .	. . .	. . .	. . .
Total debit	3 994 . .	*–84*	*–71*	*–139*	*–173*	*–226*	*–191*	*–163*	*–161*
Capital transfers, credit	2 400 . .	**. . .**	**. . .**	**. . .**	**. . .**	**. . .**	**. . .**	**. . .**	**. . .**
General government	2 401 . .	. . .	. . .	. . .	. . .	. . .	. . .	. . .	. . .
Debt forgiveness	2 402 . .	. . .	. . .	. . .	. . .	. . .	. . .	. . .	. . .
Other capital transfers	2 410 . .	. . .	. . .	. . .	. . .	. . .	. . .	. . .	. . .
Other sectors	2 430 . .	. . .	. . .	. . .	. . .	. . .	. . .	. . .	. . .
Migrants' transfers	2 431 . .	. . .	. . .	. . .	. . .	. . .	. . .	. . .	. . .
Debt forgiveness	2 432 . .	. . .	. . .	. . .	. . .	. . .	. . .	. . .	. . .
Other capital transfers	2 440 . .	. . .	. . .	. . .	. . .	. . .	. . .	. . .	. . .
Capital transfers, debit	3 400 . .	**–84**	**–71**	**–139**	**–173**	**–226**	**–191**	**–163**	**–161**
General government	3 401 . .	. . .	. . .	. . .	. . .	. . .	. . .	. . .	. . .
Debt forgiveness	3 402 . .	. . .	. . .	. . .	. . .	. . .	. . .	. . .	. . .
Other capital transfers	3 410 . .	. . .	. . .	. . .	. . .	. . .	. . .	. . .	. . .
Other sectors	3 430 . .	. . .	. . .	. . .	. . .	. . .	. . .	. . .	. . .
Migrants' transfers	3 431 . .	. . .	. . .	. . .	. . .	. . .	. . .	. . .	. . .
Debt forgiveness	3 432 . .	. . .	. . .	. . .	. . .	. . .	. . .	. . .	. . .
Other capital transfers	3 440 . .	. . .	. . .	. . .	. . .	. . .	. . .	. . .	. . .
Nonproduced nonfinancial assets, credit	2 480 . .	**. . .**	**. . .**	**. . .**	**. . .**	**. . .**	**. . .**	**. . .**	**. . .**
Nonproduced nonfinancial assets, debit	3 480 . .	**. . .**	**. . .**	**. . .**	**. . .**	**. . .**	**. . .**	**. . .**	**. . .**

Table 2 (Continued). STANDARD PRESENTATION, 1994–2001
(Millions of U.S. dollars)

	Code	1994	1995	1996	1997	1998	1999	2000	2001
FINANCIAL ACCOUNT	4 995	**-13,577**	**-9,477**	**-16,167**	**-21,581**	**-23,974**	**-15,553**	**-17,642**	**-17,907**
A. DIRECT INVESTMENT	4 500	3,973	5,346	1,781	1,281	5,594	7,527	440	-1,607
Direct investment abroad	4 505	**-4,577**	**-3,442**	**-6,827**	**-9,465**	**-795**	**-4,277**	**-4,966**	**-10,216**
Equity capital	4 510	-4,577	-3,442	...	...	...	...	...	...
Claims on affiliated enterprises	4 515	...	...	...	...	...	...	...	...
Liabilities to affiliated enterprises	4 520	...	...	...	...	...	...	...	...
Reinvested earnings	4 525	...	...	...	...	...	...	...	...
Other capital	4 530	...	...	...	...	...	...	...	...
Claims on affiliated enterprises	4 535	...	...	...	...	...	...	...	...
Liabilities to affiliated enterprises	4 540	...	...	...	...	...	...	...	...
Direct investment in Singapore	4 555	**8,550**	**8,788**	**8,608**	**10,746**	**6,389**	**11,803**	**5,407**	**8,609**
Equity capital	4 560	8,550	8,788	...	...	...	...	...	...
Claims on direct investors	4 565	...	...	...	...	...	...	...	...
Liabilities to direct investors	4 570	...	...	...	...	...	...	...	...
Reinvested earnings	4 575	...	...	...	...	...	...	...	...
Other capital	4 580	...	...	...	...	...	...	...	...
Claims on direct investors	4 585	...	...	...	...	...	...	...	...
Liabilities to direct investors	4 590	...	...	...	...	...	...	...	...
B. PORTFOLIO INVESTMENT	4 600	-7,726	-7,359	-11,800	-14,965	-9,930	-5,627	-9,901	-4,536
Assets	4 602	**-7,840**	**-7,769**	**-12,783**	**-14,910**	**-10,860**	**-7,938**	**-7,867**	**-5,256**
Equity securities	4 610	-7,414	-7,972	-10,098	-12,492	-6,937	-9,034	-5,579	-4,477
Monetary authorities	4 611	...	...	...	...	...	...	...	...
General government	4 612	...	...	...	...	...	...	...	...
Banks	4 613	...	...	...	...	...	...	...	...
Other sectors	4 614	-7,414	-7,972	-10,098	-12,492	-6,937	-9,034	-5,579	-4,477
Debt securities	4 619	-426	203	-2,685	-2,418	-3,923	1,096	-2,288	-779
Bonds and notes	4 620	-426	203	-2,685	-2,418	-3,923	1,096	-2,288	-779
Monetary authorities	4 621	...	...	...	...	...	...	...	...
General government	4 622	...	...	...	...	...	...	...	...
Banks	4 623	...	...	...	...	...	...	...	...
Other sectors	4 624	-426	203	-2,685	-2,418	-3,923	1,096	-2,288	-779
Money market instruments	4 630	...	...	...	...	...	...	...	...
Monetary authorities	4 631	...	...	...	...	...	...	...	...
General government	4 632	...	...	...	...	...	...	...	...
Banks	4 633	...	...	...	...	...	...	...	...
Other sectors	4 634	...	...	...	...	...	...	...	...
Liabilities	4 652	**114**	**410**	**983**	**-55**	**929**	**2,311**	**-2,034**	**720**
Equity securities	4 660	169	462	1,004	-67	938	2,313	-2,034	718
Banks	4 663	...	...	...	...	...	...	...	...
Other sectors	4 664	169	462	1,004	-67	938	2,313	-2,034	718
Debt securities	4 669	-55	-52	-21	12	-8	-2	-1	2
Bonds and notes	4 670	-55	-52	-21	12	-8	-2	-1	2
Monetary authorities	4 671	...	...	...	...	...	...	...	...
General government	4 672	...	...	...	...	...	...	...	...
Banks	4 673	...	...	...	...	...	...	...	...
Other sectors	4 674	...	-52	-21	12	-8	-2	-1	2
Money market instruments	4 680	...	...	...	...	...	...	...	...
Monetary authorities	4 681	...	...	...	...	...	...	...	...
General government	4 682	...	...	...	...	...	...	...	...
Banks	4 683	...	...	...	...	...	...	...	...
Other sectors	4 684	...	...	...	...	...	...	...	...
C. FINANCIAL DERIVATIVES	4 910	...	...	...	...	...	...	...	...
Monetary authorities	4 911	...	...	...	...	...	...	...	...
General government	4 912	...	...	...	...	...	...	...	...
Banks	4 913	...	...	...	...	...	...	...	...
Other sectors	4 914	...	...	...	...	...	...	...	...
Assets	4 900	**...**	**...**	**...**	**...**	**...**	**...**	**...**	**...**
Monetary authorities	4 901	...	...	...	...	...	...	...	...
General government	4 902	...	...	...	...	...	...	...	...
Banks	4 903	...	...	...	...	...	...	...	...
Other sectors	4 904	...	...	...	...	...	...	...	...
Liabilities	4 905	**...**	**...**	**...**	**...**	**...**	**...**	**...**	**...**
Monetary authorities	4 906	...	...	...	...	...	...	...	...
General government	4 907	...	...	...	...	...	...	...	...
Banks	4 908	...	...	...	...	...	...	...	...
Other sectors	4 909	...	...	...	...	...	...	...	...

Table 2 (Concluded). STANDARD PRESENTATION, 1994–2001
(Millions of U.S. dollars)

	Code	1994	1995	1996	1997	1998	1999	2000	2001
D. OTHER INVESTMENT	4 700 . .	–5,088	1,135	1,248	42	–16,672	–13,259	–1,375	–12,625
Assets	4 703 . .	**–10,999**	**–12,150**	**–13,868**	**–37,868**	**127**	**–20,002**	**–5,974**	**–15,472**
Trade credits	4 706 . .	. . .	. . .	. . .	. . .	. . .	. . .	. . .	. . .
General government	4 707 . .	. . .	. . .	. . .	. . .	. . .	. . .	. . .	. . .
of which: Short-term	4 709 . .	. . .	. . .	. . .	. . .	. . .	. . .	. . .	. . .
Other sectors	4 710 . .	. . .	. . .	. . .	. . .	. . .	. . .	. . .	. . .
of which: Short-term	4 712 . .	. . .	. . .	. . .	. . .	. . .	. . .	. . .	. . .
Loans	4 714 . .	–775	–2,248	–5,433	–4,370	–454	–3,072	–664	–3,459
Monetary authorities	4 715 . .	. . .	. . .	. . .	. . .	. . .	. . .	. . .	. . .
of which: Short-term	4 718 . .	. . .	. . .	. . .	. . .	. . .	. . .	. . .	. . .
General government	4 719 . .	. . .	. . .	. . .	. . .	. . .	. . .	. . .	. . .
of which: Short-term	4 721 . .	. . .	. . .	. . .	. . .	. . .	. . .	. . .	. . .
Banks	4 722 . .	. . .	. . .	. . .	. . .	. . .	. . .	. . .	. . .
of which: Short-term	4 724 . .	. . .	. . .	. . .	. . .	. . .	. . .	. . .	. . .
Other sectors	4 725 . .	–775	–2,248	–5,433	–4,370	–454	–3,072	–664	–3,459
of which: Short-term	4 727 . .	. . .	. . .	. . .	. . .	. . .	. . .	. . .	. . .
Currency and deposits	4 730 . .	–3,856	–2,986	–4,076	–24,625	4,949	–10,646	–824	–9,598
Monetary authorities	4 731 . .	. . .	. . .	. . .	. . .	. . .	. . .	. . .	. . .
General government	4 732 . .	. . .	. . .	. . .	. . .	. . .	. . .	. . .	. . .
Banks	4 733 . .	–3,295	1,906	–2,241	–11,195	3,391	–8,822	2,788	–8,756
Other sectors	4 734 . .	–561	–4,892	–1,836	–13,430	1,558	–1,824	–3,612	–842
Other assets	4 736 . .	–6,368	–6,916	–4,358	–8,873	–4,368	–6,284	–4,486	–2,415
Monetary authorities	4 737 . .	. . .	. . .	. . .	. . .	. . .	. . .	. . .	. . .
of which: Short-term	4 739 . .	. . .	. . .	. . .	. . .	. . .	. . .	. . .	. . .
General government	4 740 . .	. . .	–7	. . .	. . .	. . .	. . .	. . .	–5
of which: Short-term	4 742 . .	. . .	. . .	. . .	. . .	. . .	. . .	. . .	. . .
Banks	4 743 . .	–996	–752	–1,292	–1,187	–1,173	–1,843	–1,322	–1,503
of which: Short-term	4 745 . .	. . .	. . .	. . .	. . .	. . .	. . .	. . .	. . .
Other sectors	4 746 . .	–5,371	–6,157	–3,066	–7,686	–3,195	–4,441	–3,164	–907
of which: Short-term	4 748 . .	*–943*	*–1,134*	*1,013*	*–2,089*	*–965*	*–2,002*	*–693*	*–770*
Liabilities	4 753 . .	**5,911**	**13,285**	**15,116**	**37,910**	**–16,800**	**6,743**	**4,598**	**2,847**
Trade credits	4 756 . .	. . .	. . .	. . .	. . .	. . .	. . .	. . .	. . .
General government	4 757 . .	. . .	. . .	. . .	. . .	. . .	. . .	. . .	. . .
of which: Short-term	4 759 . .	. . .	. . .	. . .	. . .	. . .	. . .	. . .	. . .
Other sectors	4 760 . .	. . .	. . .	. . .	. . .	. . .	. . .	. . .	. . .
of which: Short-term	4 762 . .	. . .	. . .	. . .	. . .	. . .	. . .	. . .	. . .
Loans	4 764 . .	1,853	5,157	5,314	15,218	–3,526	3,460	–1,491	–3,149
Monetary authorities	4 765 . .	. . .	. . .	. . .	. . .	. . .	. . .	. . .	. . .
of which: Use of Fund credit and loans from the Fund	4 766 . .	. . .	. . .	. . .	. . .	. . .	. . .	. . .	. . .
of which: Short-term	4 768 . .	. . .	. . .	. . .	. . .	. . .	. . .	. . .	. . .
General government	4 769 . .	–4	. . .	. . .	. . .	. . .	. . .	. . .	. . .
of which: Short-term	4 771 . .	. . .	. . .	. . .	. . .	. . .	. . .	. . .	. . .
Banks	4 772 . .	. . .	. . .	. . .	. . .	. . .	. . .	. . .	. . .
of which: Short-term	4 774 . .	. . .	. . .	. . .	. . .	. . .	. . .	. . .	. . .
Other sectors	4 775 . .	1,858	5,157	5,314	15,218	–3,526	3,460	–1,491	–3,149
of which: Short-term	4 777 . .	. . .	. . .	. . .	. . .	. . .	. . .	. . .	. . .
Currency and deposits	4 780 . .	5,454	3,966	8,121	18,512	–11,489	2,857	6,917	1,265
Monetary authorities	4 781 . .	. . .	. . .	. . .	. . .	. . .	. . .	. . .	. . .
General government	4 782 . .	. . .	. . .	. . .	. . .	. . .	. . .	. . .	. . .
Banks	4 783 . .	5,454	3,966	8,121	18,512	–11,489	2,857	6,917	1,265
Other sectors	4 784 . .	. . .	. . .	. . .	. . .	. . .	. . .	. . .	. . .
Other liabilities	4 786 . .	–1,397	4,163	1,680	4,181	–1,785	425	–828	4,732
Monetary authorities	4 787 . .	. . .	. . .	. . .	. . .	. . .	. . .	. . .	. . .
of which: Short-term	4 789 . .	. . .	. . .	. . .	. . .	. . .	. . .	. . .	. . .
General government	4 790 . .	. . .	. . .	. . .	. . .	. . .	. . .	. . .	. . .
of which: Short-term	4 792 . .	. . .	. . .	. . .	. . .	. . .	. . .	. . .	. . .
Banks	4 793 . .	–46	457	–90	175	–1,298	353	500	5,795
of which: Short-term	4 795 . .	. . .	. . .	. . .	. . .	. . .	. . .	. . .	. . .
Other sectors	4 796 . .	–1,351	3,706	1,770	4,006	–487	73	–1,327	–1,063
of which: Short-term	4 798 . .	*–1,741*	*2,821*	*656*	*620*	*172*	*–141*	*–215*	*–138*
E. RESERVE ASSETS	4 802 . .	–4,736	–8,599	–7,396	–7,940	–2,965	–4,194	–6,806	861
Monetary gold	4 812 . .	. . .	. . .	. . .	. . .	. . .	. . .	. . .	. . .
Special drawing rights	4 811 . .	46	–14	–14	–13	–17	–33	–21	–18
Reserve position in the Fund	4 810 . .	–22	–42	–7	–59	–69	–8	87	–75
Foreign exchange	4 803 . .	–4,761	–8,544	–7,375	–7,868	–2,879	–4,153	–6,872	955
Other claims	4 813 . .	. . .	. . .	. . .	. . .	. . .	. . .	. . .	. . .
NET ERRORS AND OMISSIONS	4 998 . .	**2,261**	**–5,352**	**3,734**	**3,632**	**4,494**	**–783**	**1,884**	**184**

Part 3 of the *Yearbook* contains descriptions of the methodologies, compilation practices, and sources used to compile these data.

Table 3. INTERNATIONAL INVESTMENT POSITION (End–period stocks), 1994–2001
(Millions of U.S. dollars)

	Code	1994	1995	1996	1997	1998	1999	2000	2001
ASSETS	8 995 C.	...	...	...	...	...	...	...	337,762
Direct investment abroad	8 505 . .	...	...	...	...	...	...	...	**67,254**
Equity capital and reinvested earnings	8 506 . .	...	...	...	...	...	...	...	...
Claims on affiliated enterprises	8 507 . .	...	...	...	...	...	...	...	...
Liabilities to affiliated enterprises	8 508 . .	...	...	...	...	...	...	...	...
Other capital	8 530 . .	...	...	...	...	...	...	...	...
Claims on affiliated enterprises	8 535 . .	...	...	...	...	...	...	...	...
Liabilities to affiliated enterprises	8 540 . .	...	...	...	...	...	...	...	...
Portfolio investment	8 602 . .	...	...	...	...	...	...	...	**55,637**
Equity securities	8 610 . .	...	...	...	...	...	...	...	...
Monetary authorities	8 611 . .	...	...	...	...	...	...	...	...
General government	8 612 . .	...	...	...	...	...	...	...	...
Banks	8 613 . .	...	...	...	...	...	...	...	...
Other sectors	8 614 . .	...	...	...	...	...	...	...	...
Debt securities	8 619 . .	...	...	...	...	...	...	...	...
Bonds and notes	8 620 . .	...	...	...	...	...	...	...	...
Monetary authorities	8 621 . .	...	...	...	...	...	...	...	...
General government	8 622 . .	...	...	...	...	...	...	...	...
Banks	8 623 . .	...	...	...	...	...	...	...	...
Other sectors	8 624 . .	...	...	...	...	...	...	...	...
Money market instruments	8 630 . .	...	...	...	...	...	...	...	...
Monetary authorities	8 631 . .	...	...	...	...	...	...	...	...
General government	8 632 . .	...	...	...	...	...	...	...	...
Banks	8 633 . .	...	...	...	...	...	...	...	...
Other sectors	8 634 . .	...	...	...	...	...	...	...	...
Financial derivatives	8 900 . .	...	...	...	...	...	...	...	...
Monetary authorities	8 901 . .	...	...	...	...	...	...	...	...
General government	8 902 . .	...	...	...	...	...	...	...	...
Banks	8 903 . .	...	...	...	...	...	...	...	...
Other sectors	8 904 . .	...	...	...	...	...	...	...	...
Other investment	8 703 . .	...	...	...	...	...	...	...	**139,266**
Trade credits	8 706 . .	...	...	...	...	...	...	...	...
General government	8 707 . .	...	...	...	...	...	...	...	...
of which: Short-term	8 709 . .	...	...	...	...	...	...	...	...
Other sectors	8 710 . .	...	...	...	...	...	...	...	...
of which: Short-term	8 712 . .	...	...	...	...	...	...	...	...
Loans	8 714 . .	...	...	...	...	...	...	...	...
Monetary authorities	8 715 . .	...	...	...	...	...	...	...	...
of which: Short-term	8 718 . .	...	...	...	...	...	...	...	...
General government	8 719 . .	...	...	...	...	...	...	...	...
of which: Short-term	8 721 . .	...	...	...	...	...	...	...	...
Banks	8 722 . .	...	...	...	...	...	...	...	...
of which: Short-term	8 724 . .	...	...	...	...	...	...	...	...
Other sectors	8 725 . .	...	...	...	...	...	...	...	...
of which: Short-term	8 727 . .	...	...	...	...	...	...	...	...
Currency and deposits	8 730 . .	...	...	...	...	...	...	...	...
Monetary authorities	8 731 . .	...	...	...	...	...	...	...	...
General government	8 732 . .	...	...	...	...	...	...	...	...
Banks	8 733 . .	...	...	...	...	...	...	...	...
Other sectors	8 734 . .	...	...	...	...	...	...	...	...
Other assets	8 736 . .	...	...	...	...	...	...	...	...
Monetary authorities	8 737 . .	...	...	...	...	...	...	...	...
of which: Short-term	8 739 . .	...	...	...	...	...	...	...	...
General government	8 740 . .	...	...	...	...	...	...	...	...
of which: Short-term	8 742 . .	...	...	...	...	...	...	...	...
Banks	8 743 . .	...	...	...	...	...	...	...	...
of which: Short-term	8 745 . .	...	...	...	...	...	...	...	...
Other sectors	8 746 . .	...	...	...	...	...	...	...	...
of which: Short-term	8 748 . .	...	...	...	...	...	...	...	...
Reserve assets	8 802 . .	...	...	...	...	...	...	...	**75,603**
Monetary gold	8 812 . .	...	...	...	...	...	...	...	...
Special drawing rights	8 811 . .	35	49	61	70	91	122	137	150
Reserve position in the Fund	8 810 . .	252	297	294	335	419	416	310	374
Foreign exchange	8 803 . .	...	...	...	...	...	...	...	...
Other claims	8 813 . .	...	...	...	...	...	...	...	...

Table 3 (Concluded). INTERNATIONAL INVESTMENT POSITION (End–period stocks), 1994–2001

(Millions of U.S. dollars)

	Code	1994	1995	1996	1997	1998	1999	2000	2001
LIABILITIES	8 995 D.	...	...	...	...	...	...	...	284,405
Direct investment in Singapore	8 555 . .	...	...	...	...	...	...	...	**116,428**
Equity capital and reinvested earnings	8 556 . .	...	...	...	...	...	...	...	...
Claims on direct investors	8 557 . .	...	...	...	...	...	...	...	...
Liabilities to direct investors	8 558 . .	...	...	...	...	...	...	...	...
Other capital	8 580 . .	...	...	...	...	...	...	...	...
Claims on direct investors	8 585 . .	...	...	...	...	...	...	...	...
Liabilities to direct investors	8 590 . .	...	...	...	...	...	...	...	...
Portfolio investment	8 652 . .	...	...	...	...	...	...	...	**45,348**
Equity securities	8 660 . .	...	...	...	...	...	...	...	...
Banks	8 663 . .	...	...	...	...	...	...	...	...
Other sectors	8 664 . .	...	...	...	...	...	...	...	...
Debt securities	8 669 . .	...	...	...	...	...	...	...	...
Bonds and notes	8 670 . .	...	...	...	...	...	...	...	...
Monetary authorities	8 671 . .	...	...	...	...	...	...	...	...
General government	8 672 . .	...	...	...	...	...	...	...	...
Banks	8 673 . .	...	...	...	...	...	...	...	...
Other sectors	8 674 . .	...	...	...	...	...	...	...	...
Money market instruments	8 680 . .	...	...	...	...	...	...	...	...
Monetary authorities	8 681 . .	...	...	...	...	...	...	...	...
General government	8 682 . .	...	...	...	...	...	...	...	...
Banks	8 683 . .	...	...	...	...	...	...	...	...
Other sectors	8 684 . .	...	...	...	...	...	...	...	...
Financial derivatives	8 905 . .	...	...	...	...	...	...	...	...
Monetary authorities	8 906 . .	...	...	...	...	...	...	...	...
General government	8 907 . .	...	...	...	...	...	...	...	...
Banks	8 908 . .	...	...	...	...	...	...	...	...
Other sectors	8 909 . .	...	...	...	...	...	...	...	...
Other investment	8 753 . .	...	...	...	...	...	...	...	**122,629**
Trade credits	8 756 . .	...	...	...	...	...	...	...	...
General government	8 757 . .	...	...	...	...	...	...	...	...
of which: Short-term	8 759 . .	...	...	...	...	...	...	...	...
Other sectors	8 760 . .	...	...	...	...	...	...	...	...
of which: Short-term	8 762 . .	...	...	...	...	...	...	...	...
Loans	8 764 . .	...	...	...	...	...	...	...	...
Monetary authorities	8 765 . .	...	...	...	...	...	...	...	...
of which: Use of Fund credit and loans from the Fund	8 766 . .	...	...	...	...	...	...	...	...
of which: Short-term	8 768 . .	...	...	...	...	...	...	...	...
General government	8 769 . .	...	...	...	...	...	...	...	...
of which: Short-term	8 771 . .	...	...	...	...	...	...	...	...
Banks	8 772 . .	...	...	...	...	...	...	...	...
of which: Short-term	8 774 . .	...	...	...	...	...	...	...	...
Other sectors	8 775 . .	...	...	...	...	...	...	...	...
of which: Short-term	8 777 . .	...	...	...	...	...	...	...	...
Currency and deposits	8 780 . .	...	...	...	...	...	...	...	...
Monetary authorities	8 781 . .	...	...	...	...	...	...	...	...
General government	8 782 . .	...	...	...	...	...	...	...	...
Banks	8 783 . .	...	...	...	...	...	...	...	...
Other sectors	8 784 . .	...	...	...	...	...	...	...	...
Other liabilities	8 786 . .	...	...	...	...	...	...	...	...
Monetary authorities	8 787 . .	...	...	...	...	...	...	...	...
of which: Short-term	8 789 . .	...	...	...	...	...	...	...	...
General government	8 790 . .	...	...	...	...	...	...	...	...
of which: Short-term	8 792 . .	...	...	...	...	...	...	...	...
Banks	8 793 . .	...	...	...	...	...	...	...	...
of which: Short-term	8 795 . .	...	...	...	...	...	...	...	...
Other sectors	8 796 . .	...	...	...	...	...	...	...	...
of which: Short-term	8 798 . .	...	...	...	...	...	...	...	...
NET INTERNATIONAL INVESTMENT POSITION	8 995 . .	...	...	...	...	...	...	...	**53,357**
Conversion rates: Singapore dollars per U.S. dollar (end of period)	0 102 . .	**1.4607**	**1.4143**	**1.3998**	**1.6755**	**1.6605**	**1.6660**	**1.7315**	**1.8510**

Table 1. ANALYTIC PRESENTATION, 1994–2001

(Millions of U.S. dollars)

	Code	1994	1995	1996	1997	1998	1999	2000	2001
A. Current Account [1]	4 993 Z.	**671**	**390**	**–2,090**	**–1,961**	**–2,126**	**–1,155**	**–694**	**. . .**
Goods: exports f.o.b.	2 100 . .	6,706	8,591	8,824	9,641	10,720	10,201	11,896	. . .
Goods: imports f.o.b.	3 100 . .	–6,645	–8,820	–11,106	–11,725	–13,071	–11,310	–12,791	. . .
Balance on Goods	4 100 . .	*61*	*–229*	*–2,283*	*–2,084*	*–2,351*	*–1,109*	*–895*	. . .
Services: credit	2 200 . .	2,261	2,378	2,066	2,167	2,292	1,899	2,241	. . .
Services: debit	3 200 . .	–1,600	–1,838	–2,028	–2,094	–2,276	–1,844	–1,805	. . .
Balance on Goods and Services	4 991 . .	*722*	*311*	*–2,245*	*–2,011*	*–2,334*	*–1,054*	*–459*	. . .
Income: credit	2 300 . .	155	250	224	315	437	268	268	. . .
Income: debit	3 300 . .	–275	–263	–270	–438	–595	–568	–623	. . .
Balance on Goods, Services, and Income	4 992 . .	*602*	*297*	*–2,291*	*–2,135*	*–2,492*	*–1,353*	*–814*	. . .
Current transfers: credit	2 379 Z.	166	243	483	540	645	466	344	. . .
Current transfers: debit	3 379 . .	–98	–150	–282	–367	–279	–268	–224	. . .
B. Capital Account [1]	4 994 Z.	**84**	**46**	**30**	**. . .**	**70**	**158**	**91**	**. . .**
Capital account: credit	2 994 Z.	84	46	30	. . .	83	171	106	. . .
Capital account: debit	3 994 . .	. . .	. . .	. . .	. . .	–12	–13	–15	. . .
Total, Groups A Plus B	4 981 . .	*755*	*436*	*–2,060*	*–1,961*	*–2,056*	*–998*	*–603*	. . .
C. Financial Account [1]	4 995 W.	**71**	**1,211**	**2,268**	**1,780**	**1,912**	**1,789**	**1,472**	**. . .**
Direct investment abroad	4 505 . .	–14	–10	–48	–95	–145	376	–22	. . .
Direct investment in Slovak Republic	4 555 Z.	270	236	351	174	562	354	2,052	. . .
Portfolio investment assets	4 602 . .	–26	157	–12	–81	–57	247	–195	. . .
Equity securities	4 610 . .	–26	174	69	86	33	2	11	. . .
Debt securities	4 619 . .	. . .	–17	–81	–167	–91	246	–206	. . .
Portfolio investment liabilities	4 652 Z.	304	53	29	93	841	405	1,016	. . .
Equity securities	4 660 . .	111	–16	28	102	–35	47	–53	. . .
Debt securities	4 669 Z.	193	69	1	–10	876	358	1,069	. . .
Financial derivatives	4 910 . .	. . .	. . .	. . .	. . .	. . .	. . .	1	. . .
Financial derivatives assets	4 900 . .	. . .	. . .	. . .	. . .	. . .	. . .	. . .	. . .
Financial derivatives liabilities	4 905 . .	. . .	. . .	. . .	. . .	. . .	. . .	1	. . .
Other investment assets	4 703 . .	–548	–116	–334	–1,028	190	1,713	–973	. . .
Monetary authorities	4 701 . .	. . .	. . .	. . .	. . .	. . .	. . .	. . .	. . .
General government	4 704 . .	–211	140	337	61	117	9	1	. . .
Banks	4 705 . .	–344	–248	–662	–1,122	110	1,878	–748	. . .
Other sectors	4 728 . .	7	–8	–10	33	–37	–174	–226	. . .
Other investment liabilities	4 753 W.	84	891	2,282	2,718	520	–1,307	–407	. . .
Monetary authorities	4 753 WA	38	42	52	153	55	14	–26	. . .
General government	4 753 ZB	–52	–173	–124	184	–321	55	149	. . .
Banks	4 753 ZC	38	463	1,440	1,084	–138	–1,882	30	. . .
Other sectors	4 753 ZD	60	559	914	1,298	924	506	–561	. . .
Total, Groups A Through C	4 983 . .	*825*	*1,647*	*208*	*–181*	*–144*	*791*	*869*	. . .
D. Net Errors and Omissions	4 998 . .	**380**	**144**	**162**	**280**	**–333**	**–14**	**51**	**. . .**
Total, Groups A Through D	4 984 . .	*1,205*	*1,791*	*370*	*99*	*–478*	*777*	*920*	. . .
E. Reserves and Related Items	4 802 A.	**–1,205**	**–1,791**	**–370**	**–99**	**478**	**–777**	**–920**	**. . .**
Reserve assets	4 802 . .	–1,256	–1,590	–245	–47	545	–725	–794	. . .
Use of Fund credit and loans	4 766 . .	51	–201	–125	–52	–67	–52	–125	. . .
Exceptional financing	4 920 . .	. . .	. . .	. . .	. . .	. . .	. . .	. . .	. . .
Conversion rates: Slovak koruny per U.S. dollar	0 101 . .	**32.045**	**29.713**	**30.654**	**33.616**	**35.233**	**41.363**	**46.035**	**48.355**

[1] Excludes components that have been classified in the categories of Group E.

Table 2. STANDARD PRESENTATION, 1994–2001
(Millions of U.S. dollars)

	Code		1994	1995	1996	1997	1998	1999	2000	2001
CURRENT ACCOUNT	4 993	. .	**671**	**390**	**–2,090**	**–1,961**	**–2,126**	**–1,155**	**–694**	. . .
A. GOODS	4 100	. .	61	–229	–2,283	–2,084	–2,351	–1,109	–895	. . .
Credit	2 100	. .	**6,706**	**8,591**	**8,824**	**9,641**	**10,720**	**10,201**	**11,896**	. . .
General merchandise: exports f.o.b.	2 110	. .	. . .	. . .	. . .	. . .	. . .	. . .	. . .	. . .
Goods for processing: exports f.o.b.	2 150	. .	. . .	. . .	. . .	. . .	. . .	. . .	. . .	. . .
Repairs on goods	2 160	. .	. . .	. . .	. . .	. . .	. . .	. . .	. . .	. . .
Goods procured in ports by carriers	2 170	. .	. . .	. . .	. . .	. . .	. . .	. . .	. . .	. . .
Nonmonetary gold	2 180	. .	. . .	. . .	. . .	. . .	. . .	. . .	. . .	. . .
Debit	3 100	. .	**–6,645**	**–8,820**	**–11,106**	**–11,725**	**–13,071**	**–11,310**	**–12,791**	. . .
General merchandise: imports f.o.b.	3 110	. .	. . .	. . .	. . .	. . .	. . .	. . .	. . .	. . .
Goods for processing: imports f.o.b.	3 150	. .	. . .	. . .	. . .	. . .	. . .	. . .	. . .	. . .
Repairs on goods	3 160	. .	. . .	. . .	. . .	. . .	. . .	. . .	. . .	. . .
Goods procured in ports by carriers	3 170	. .	. . .	. . .	. . .	. . .	. . .	. . .	. . .	. . .
Nonmonetary gold	3 180	. .	. . .	. . .	. . .	. . .	. . .	. . .	. . .	. . .
B. SERVICES	4 200	. .	662	540	38	73	16	55	436	. . .
Total credit	2 200	. .	*2,261*	*2,378*	*2,066*	*2,167*	*2,292*	*1,899*	*2,241*	. . .
Total debit	3 200	. .	*–1,600*	*–1,838*	*–2,028*	*–2,094*	*–2,276*	*–1,844*	*–1,805*	. . .
Transportation services, credit	2 205	. .	**539**	**616**	**643**	**740**	**766**	**694**	**995**	. . .
Passenger	2 850	. .	*7*	*7*	*8*	*10*	*5*	*4*	*8*	. . .
Freight	2 851	. .	*523*	*605*	*628*	*721*	*752*	*683*	*983*	. . .
Other	2 852	. .	*9*	*4*	*6*	*9*	*9*	*6*	*4*	. . .
Sea transport, passenger	2 207	. .	. . .	. . .	. . .	1	. . .	. . .	. . .	. . .
Sea transport, freight	2 208	. .	6	1	3	8	6	6	3	. . .
Sea transport, other	2 209	. .	. . .	. . .	. . .	. . .	. . .	. . .	. . .	. . .
Air transport, passenger	2 211	. .	3	5	6	4	2	2	5	. . .
Air transport, freight	2 212	. .	. . .	2	7	18	17	8	2	. . .
Air transport, other	2 213	. .	. . .	. . .	. . .	. . .	. . .	. . .	. . .	. . .
Other transport, passenger	2 215	. .	4	2	2	5	3	2	3	. . .
Other transport, freight	2 216	. .	517	601	619	696	729	670	977	. . .
Other transport, other	2 217	. .	9	4	6	9	9	6	4	. . .
Transportation services, debit	3 205	. .	**–162**	**–307**	**–394**	**–342**	**–444**	**–379**	**–434**	. . .
Passenger	3 850	. .	*–12*	*–17*	*–35*	*–45*	*–52*	*–48*	*–45*	. . .
Freight	3 851	. .	*–143*	*–278*	*–349*	*–287*	*–388*	*–328*	*–387*	. . .
Other	3 852	. .	*–8*	*–11*	*–10*	*–10*	*–4*	*–3*	*–2*	. . .
Sea transport, passenger	3 207	. .	. . .	. . .	–1	–1	. . .	. . .	. . .	. . .
Sea transport, freight	3 208	. .	–10	–13	–18	–14	–15	–20	–22	. . .
Sea transport, other	3 209	. .	. . .	. . .	. . .	. . .	. . .	. . .	. . .	. . .
Air transport, passenger	3 211	. .	–9	–15	–32	–42	–49	–43	–42	. . .
Air transport, freight	3 212	. .	–2	–5	–4	–5	–5	–4	–4	. . .
Air transport, other	3 213	. .	. . .	. . .	. . .	. . .	. . .	. . .	. . .	. . .
Other transport, passenger	3 215	. .	–2	–1	–3	–2	–3	–5	–2	. . .
Other transport, freight	3 216	. .	–131	–260	–328	–268	–369	–303	–361	. . .
Other transport, other	3 217	. .	–8	–11	–10	–10	–4	–3	2	. . .
Travel, credit	2 236	. .	**568**	**623**	**673**	**545**	**488**	**461**	**433**	. . .
Business travel	2 237	. .	. . .	. . .	. . .	. . .	. . .	. . .	. . .	. . .
Personal travel	2 240	. .	568	623	673	545	488	461	433	. . .
Travel, debit	3 236	. .	**–282**	**–321**	**–482**	**–439**	**–475**	**–339**	**–296**	. . .
Business travel	3 237	. .	–88	–173	–149	–139	–108	–65	–30	. . .
Personal travel	3 240	. .	–194	–148	–333	–300	–367	–274	–266	. . .
Other services, credit	2 200	BA	**1,154**	**1,140**	**750**	**883**	**1,037**	**745**	**813**	. . .
Communications	2 245	. .	274	265	20	29	37	52	51	. . .
Construction	2 249	. .	74	109	103	133	106	62	68	. . .
Insurance	2 253	. .	16	2	6	14	13	7	12	. . .
Financial	2 260	. .	64	114	106	91	52	43	36	. . .
Computer and information	2 262	. .	. . .	. . .	8	13	24	35	52	. . .
Royalties and licence fees	2 266	. .	7	11	18	17	14	15	16	. . .
Other business services	2 268	. .	679	638	464	533	712	474	501	. . .
Personal, cultural, and recreational	2 287	. .	. . .	. . .	19	38	61	44	54	. . .
Government, n.i.e.	2 291	. .	40	. . .	6	16	17	13	23	. . .
Other services, debit	3 200	BA	**–1,156**	**–1,210**	**–1,152**	**–1,314**	**–1,357**	**–1,127**	**–1,076**	. . .
Communications	3 245	. .	–304	–279	–19	–27	–36	–29	–25	. . .
Construction	3 249	. .	–24	–31	–89	–102	–123	–92	–77	. . .
Insurance	3 253	. .	–33	–24	–46	–39	–23	–22	–21	. . .
Financial	3 260	. .	–38	–65	–135	–89	–63	–74	–66	. . .
Computer and information	3 262	. .	. . .	. . .	–16	–29	–62	–51	–57	. . .
Royalties and licence fees	3 266	. .	–64	–79	–83	–85	–55	–54	–58	. . .
Other business services	3 268	. .	–642	–695	–700	–870	–931	–722	–693	. . .
Personal, cultural, and recreational	3 287	. .	. . .	. . .	–32	–40	–60	–51	–53	. . .
Government, n.i.e.	3 291	. .	–51	–38	–31	–32	–4	–32	–26	. . .

Table 2 (Continued). STANDARD PRESENTATION, 1994–2001

(Millions of U.S. dollars)

	Code	1994	1995	1996	1997	1998	1999	2000	2001
C. INCOME	4 300 . .	–120	–14	–47	–123	–158	–299	–355	. . .
Total credit	2 300 . .	*155*	*250*	*224*	*315*	*437*	*268*	*268*	. . .
Total debit	3 300 . .	*–275*	*–263*	*–270*	*–438*	*–595*	*–568*	*–623*	. . .
Compensation of employees, credit	2 310 . .	**48**	**26**	**17**	**22**	**23**	**19**	**18**	**. . .**
Compensation of employees, debit	3 310 . .	**–6**	**–3**	**–9**	**–9**	**–8**	**–7**	**–7**	**. . .**
Investment income, credit	2 320 . .	**107**	**224**	**207**	**293**	**414**	**249**	**250**	**. . .**
Direct investment income	2 330 . .	. . .	. . .	1	1	17	12	27	. . .
Dividends and distributed branch profits	2 332 . .	. . .	. . .	1	. . .	9	12	26	. . .
Reinvested earnings and undistributed branch profits	2 333 . .	. . .	. . .	. . .	. . .	. . .	. . .	. . .	. . .
Income on debt (interest)	2 334 . .	. . .	. . .	. . .	. . .	8	. . .	1	. . .
Portfolio investment income	2 339 . .	25	46	112	109	132	132	139	. . .
Income on equity	2 340 . .	27	10	9	10	2	. . .	. . .	. . .
Income on bonds and notes	2 350 . .	–2	18	68	96	125	129	137	. . .
Income on money market instruments	2 360 . .	. . .	18	35	3	5	2	2	. . .
Other investment income	2 370 . .	82	178	94	184	265	105	84	. . .
Investment income, debit	3 320 . .	**–269**	**–261**	**–261**	**–429**	**–588**	**–561**	**–616**	**. . .**
Direct investment income	3 330 . .	. . .	. . .	–4	–3	–60	–51	–43	. . .
Dividends and distributed branch profits	3 332 . .	. . .	. . .	–3	–2	–50	–41	–36	. . .
Reinvested earnings and undistributed branch profits	3 333 . .	. . .	. . .	–1	–1	. . .	. . .	. . .	. . .
Income on debt (interest)	3 334 . .	. . .	. . .	. . .	. . .	–9	–10	–6	. . .
Portfolio investment income	3 339 . .	–27	–75	–74	–86	–78	–147	–182	. . .
Income on equity	3 340 . .	–33	–18	–17	–33	–2	–1	. . .	. . .
Income on bonds and notes	3 350 . .	6	–58	–54	–46	–75	–141	–177	. . .
Income on money market instruments	3 360 . .	. . .	. . .	–2	–7	–1	–6	–4	. . .
Other investment income	3 370 . .	–243	–186	–184	–340	–450	–362	–392	. . .
D. CURRENT TRANSFERS	4 379 . .	68	93	201	173	366	198	120	. . .
Credit	2 379 . .	**166**	**243**	**483**	**540**	**645**	**466**	**344**	**. . .**
General government	2 380 . .	14	43	13	28	. . .	1	1	. . .
Other sectors	2 390 . .	151	199	470	512	645	465	343	. . .
Workers' remittances	2 391 . .	. . .	. . .	4	7	. . .	. . .	. . .	. . .
Other current transfers	2 392 . .	151	199	466	505	645	465	343	. . .
Debit	3 379 . .	**–98**	**–150**	**–282**	**–367**	**–279**	**–268**	**–224**	**. . .**
General government	3 380 . .	–8	–27	–4	–18	–1	–2	–6	. . .
Other sectors	3 390 . .	–89	–123	–278	–349	–279	–266	–218	. . .
Workers' remittances	3 391 . .	. . .	. . .	–4	–5	. . .	. . .	. . .	. . .
Other current transfers	3 392 . .	–89	–123	–274	–344	–279	–266	–218	. . .
CAPITAL AND FINANCIAL ACCOUNT	4 996 . .	**–1,050**	**–534**	**1,928**	**1,681**	**2,460**	**1,169**	**644**	**. . .**
CAPITAL ACCOUNT	4 994 . .	**84**	**46**	**30**	**. . .**	**70**	**158**	**91**	**. . .**
Total credit	2 994 . .	*84*	*46*	*30*	. . .	*83*	*171*	*106*	. . .
Total debit	3 994 . .	. . .	. . .	. . .	. . .	*–12*	*–13*	*–15*	. . .
Capital transfers, credit	2 400 . .	**84**	**46**	**30**	**. . .**	**83**	**171**	**106**	**. . .**
General government	2 401 . .	. . .	. . .	. . .	. . .	25	15	2	. . .
Debt forgiveness	2 402 . .	. . .	. . .	. . .	. . .	. . .	. . .	. . .	. . .
Other capital transfers	2 410 . .	. . .	. . .	. . .	. . .	25	15	2	. . .
Other sectors	2 430 . .	84	46	30	. . .	58	156	104	. . .
Migrants' transfers	2 431 . .	. . .	. . .	. . .	. . .	1	1	. . .	. . .
Debt forgiveness	2 432 . .	84	46	30	. . .	. . .	. . .	. . .	. . .
Other capital transfers	2 440 . .	. . .	. . .	. . .	. . .	57	155	104	. . .
Capital transfers, debit	3 400 . .	**. . .**	**. . .**	**. . .**	**. . .**	**–12**	**–13**	**–15**	**. . .**
General government	3 401 . .	. . .	. . .	. . .	. . .	–2	–2	–1	. . .
Debt forgiveness	3 402 . .	. . .	. . .	. . .	. . .	. . .	. . .	. . .	. . .
Other capital transfers	3 410 . .	. . .	. . .	. . .	. . .	–2	–2	–1	. . .
Other sectors	3 430 . .	. . .	. . .	. . .	. . .	–11	–11	–14	. . .
Migrants' transfers	3 431 . .	. . .	. . .	. . .	. . .	–1	–1	–1	. . .
Debt forgiveness	3 432 . .	. . .	. . .	. . .	. . .	. . .	. . .	. . .	. . .
Other capital transfers	3 440 . .	. . .	. . .	. . .	. . .	–9	–10	–13	. . .
Nonproduced nonfinancial assets, credit	2 480 . .	**. . .**	**. . .**	**. . .**	**. . .**	**. . .**	**. . .**	**. . .**	**. . .**
Nonproduced nonfinancial assets, debit	3 480 . .	**. . .**	**. . .**	**. . .**	**. . .**	**. . .**	**. . .**	**. . .**	**. . .**

Table 2 (Continued). STANDARD PRESENTATION, 1994–2001
(Millions of U.S. dollars)

	Code	1994	1995	1996	1997	1998	1999	2000	2001
FINANCIAL ACCOUNT	4 995 . .	**–1,134**	**–580**	**1,898**	**1,681**	**2,389**	**1,012**	**553**	**. . .**
A. DIRECT INVESTMENT	4 500 . .	256	226	303	78	417	730	2,031	. . .
Direct investment abroad	4 505 . .	**–14**	**–10**	**–48**	**–95**	**–145**	**376**	**–22**	**. . .**
Equity capital	4 510 . .	–14	–9	–52	–94	–137	395	–15	. . .
Claims on affiliated enterprises	4 515 . .	–14	–9	–52	–94	–137	395	–15	. . .
Liabilities to affiliated enterprises	4 520 . .	. . .	. . .	. . .	. . .	. . .	. . .	. . .	. . .
Reinvested earnings	4 525 . .	. . .	. . .	. . .	. . .	. . .	. . .	. . .	. . .
Other capital	4 530 . .	. . .	–1	4	–1	–8	–19	–7	. . .
Claims on affiliated enterprises	4 535 . .	. . .	. . .	. . .	. . .	–11	–18	–5	. . .
Liabilities to affiliated enterprises	4 540 . .	. . .	. . .	. . .	–1	3	–1	–2	. . .
Direct investment in Slovak Republic	4 555 . .	**270**	**236**	**351**	**174**	**562**	**354**	**2,052**	**. . .**
Equity capital	4 560 . .	270	225	328	157	386	330	1,960	. . .
Claims on direct investors	4 565 . .	. . .	. . .	. . .	–2	. . .	. . .	. . .	. . .
Liabilities to direct investors	4 570 . .	270	225	328	159	386	330	1,960	. . .
Reinvested earnings	4 575 . .	. . .	. . .	1	1	. . .	. . .	. . .	. . .
Other capital	4 580 . .	. . .	11	23	16	176	24	92	. . .
Claims on direct investors	4 585 . .	. . .	. . .	. . .	–2	–81	14	–132	. . .
Liabilities to direct investors	4 590 . .	. . .	. . .	. . .	18	257	10	224	. . .
B. PORTFOLIO INVESTMENT	4 600 . .	278	210	17	12	784	652	821	. . .
Assets	4 602 . .	**–26**	**157**	**–12**	**–81**	**–57**	**247**	**–195**	**. . .**
Equity securities	4 610 . .	–26	174	69	86	33	2	11	. . .
Monetary authorities	4 611 . .	. . .	. . .	. . .	. . .	. . .	. . .	. . .	. . .
General government	4 612 . .	. . .	. . .	. . .	. . .	. . .	. . .	. . .	. . .
Banks	4 613 . .	. . .	. . .	2	3	–2	1	9	. . .
Other sectors	4 614 . .	–26	174	68	82	35	. . .	2	. . .
Debt securities	4 619 . .	. . .	–17	–81	–167	–91	246	–206	. . .
Bonds and notes	4 620 . .	. . .	–17	–36	–62	–104	102	–129	. . .
Monetary authorities	4 621 . .	. . .	. . .	. . .	. . .	. . .	. . .	. . .	. . .
General government	4 622 . .	. . .	. . .	. . .	. . .	. . .	. . .	. . .	. . .
Banks	4 623 . .	. . .	–17	–36	–62	–105	102	–118	. . .
Other sectors	4 624 . .	. . .	. . .	1	1	1	. . .	–10	. . .
Money market instruments	4 630 . .	. . .	. . .	–46	–105	13	143	–77	. . .
Monetary authorities	4 631 . .	. . .	. . .	. . .	. . .	. . .	. . .	. . .	. . .
General government	4 632 . .	. . .	. . .	. . .	. . .	. . .	. . .	. . .	. . .
Banks	4 633 . .	. . .	. . .	–45	–106	13	144	–5	. . .
Other sectors	4 634 . .	. . .	. . .	–1	1	. . .	. . .	–72	. . .
Liabilities	4 652 . .	**304**	**53**	**29**	**93**	**841**	**405**	**1,016**	**. . .**
Equity securities	4 660 . .	111	–16	28	102	–35	47	–53	. . .
Banks	4 663 . .	. . .	. . .	. . .	. . .	. . .	. . .	. . .	. . .
Other sectors	4 664 . .	111	–16	28	102	–35	47	–53	. . .
Debt securities	4 669 . .	193	69	1	–10	876	358	1,069	. . .
Bonds and notes	4 670 . .	193	70	. . .	–8	861	321	1,071	. . .
Monetary authorities	4 671	193	. . .	. . .	–11	–110	206	74	. . .
General government	4 672 . .	. . .	. . .	. . .	. . .	964	531	683	. . .
Banks	4 673 . .	. . .	. . .	. . .	. . .	. . .	. . .	–12	. . .
Other sectors	4 674 . .	. . .	70	. . .	2	7	–5	475	. . .
Money market instruments	4 680 . .	. . .	. . .	1	–1	16	37	–2	. . .
Monetary authorities	4 681 . .	. . .	. . .	. . .	. . .	. . .	. . .	. . .	. . .
General government	4 682 . .	. . .	. . .	. . .	. . .	. . .	. . .	. . .	. . .
Banks	4 683 . .	. . .	. . .	. . .	. . .	. . .	. . .	. . .	. . .
Other sectors	4 684 . .	. . .	. . .	1	–1	16	37	–2	. . .
C. FINANCIAL DERIVATIVES	4 910 . .	. . .	. . .	. . .	. . .	. . .	. . .	1	. . .
Monetary authorities	4 911 . .	. . .	. . .	. . .	. . .	. . .	. . .	. . .	. . .
General government	4 912 . .	. . .	. . .	. . .	. . .	. . .	. . .	. . .	. . .
Banks	4 913 . .	. . .	. . .	. . .	. . .	. . .	. . .	. . .	. . .
Other sectors	4 914 . .	. . .	. . .	. . .	. . .	. . .	. . .	1	. . .
Assets	4 900 . .	**. . .**	**. . .**	**. . .**	**. . .**	**. . .**	**. . .**	**. . .**	**. . .**
Monetary authorities	4 901 . .	. . .	. . .	. . .	. . .	. . .	. . .	. . .	. . .
General government	4 902 . .	. . .	. . .	. . .	. . .	. . .	. . .	. . .	. . .
Banks	4 903 . .	. . .	. . .	. . .	. . .	. . .	. . .	. . .	. . .
Other sectors	4 904 . .	. . .	. . .	. . .	. . .	. . .	. . .	. . .	. . .
Liabilities	4 905 . .	**. . .**	**. . .**	**. . .**	**. . .**	**. . .**	**. . .**	**1**	**. . .**
Monetary authorities	4 906 . .	. . .	. . .	. . .	. . .	. . .	. . .	. . .	. . .
General government	4 907 . .	. . .	. . .	. . .	. . .	. . .	. . .	. . .	. . .
Banks	4 908 . .	. . .	. . .	. . .	. . .	. . .	. . .	. . .	. . .
Other sectors	4 909 . .	. . .	. . .	. . .	. . .	. . .	. . .	1	. . .

Table 2 (Concluded). STANDARD PRESENTATION, 1994–2001

(Millions of U.S. dollars)

	Code	1994	1995	1996	1997	1998	1999	2000	2001
D. OTHER INVESTMENT	4 700	–412	574	1,823	1,638	643	354	–1,506	...
Assets	4 703	**–548**	**–116**	**–334**	**–1,028**	**190**	**1,713**	**–973**	...
Trade credits	4 706	–10	60	–11	26	–33	–177	–139	...
General government	4 707	...	...	...	...	...	...	...	...
of which: Short-term	4 709	...	...	...	...	...	...	...	...
Other sectors	4 710	–10	60	–11	26	–33	–177	–139	...
of which: Short-term	4 712	*–34*	*2*	*–4*	*10*	*–48*	*–178*	*–139*	...
Loans	4 714	76	46	99	–114	–87	350	31	...
Monetary authorities	4 715	...	...	...	...	...	...	...	...
of which: Short-term	4 718	...	...	...	...	...	...	...	...
General government	4 719	159	57	337	61	117	9	1	...
of which: Short-term	4 721	...	...	...	...	...	...	...	...
Banks	4 722	–83	41	–239	–171	–203	340	120	...
of which: Short-term	4 724	*–77*	*51*	*–115*	*–195*	*–198*	*319*	*88*	...
Other sectors	4 725	...	–52	...	–3	–1	...	–90	...
of which: Short-term	4 727	...	...	...	*–1*	*–1*	...	*1*	...
Currency and deposits	4 730	–226	–291	–427	–927	341	1,412	–754	...
Monetary authorities	4 731	...	...	...	...	...	...	...	...
General government	4 732	...	...	...	...	...	...	...	...
Banks	4 733	–244	–275	–428	–937	344	1,409	–756	...
Other sectors	4 734	17	–17	1	10	–3	4	2	...
Other assets	4 736	–387	69	5	–14	–30	129	–112	...
Monetary authorities	4 737	...	...	...	...	...	...	...	...
of which: Short-term	4 739	...	...	...	...	...	...	...	...
General government	4 740	–370	84	...	...	...	...	...	...
of which: Short-term	4 742	*–370*	*84*	...	...	...	...	...	...
Banks	4 743	–17	–14	5	–14	–30	129	–112	...
of which: Short-term	4 745	*–15*	*–26*	*5*	*–14*	*–30*	*129*	*–112*	...
Other sectors	4 746	...	...	...	...	...	...	...	...
of which: Short-term	4 748	...	...	...	...	...	...	...	...
Liabilities	4 753	**135**	**689**	**2,158**	**2,666**	**453**	**–1,359**	**–533**	...
Trade credits	4 756	–92	–16	79	305	323	156	–5	...
General government	4 757	...	...	...	...	...	...	...	...
of which: Short-term	4 759	...	...	...	...	...	...	...	...
Other sectors	4 760	–92	–16	79	305	323	156	–5	...
of which: Short-term	4 762	*–84*	*84*	*122*	*191*	*242*	*177*	*6*	...
Loans	4 764	331	482	1,100	1,374	276	–598	–626	...
Monetary authorities	4 765	87	–159	–78	100	–17	–46	–134	...
of which: Use of Fund credit and loans from the Fund	4 766	*51*	*–201*	*–125*	*–52*	*–67*	*–52*	*–125*	...
of which: Short-term	4 768	...	...	...	...	...	...	...	...
General government	4 769	–15	–173	–124	184	–321	55	149	...
of which: Short-term	4 771	...	...	...	*187*	*–180*	...	...	...
Banks	4 772	108	240	468	97	14	–958	–85	...
of which: Short-term	4 774	*16*	*30*	*441*	*177*	*96*	*–818*	*–45*	...
Other sectors	4 775	151	574	835	993	601	350	–556	...
of which: Short-term	4 777	*–19*	*56*	*39*	*106*	*–80*	*2*	*–186*	...
Currency and deposits	4 780	–43	161	449	763	–282	–950	71	...
Monetary authorities	4 781	3	...	6	1	5	7	–17	...
General government	4 782	...	...	...	...	...	...	...	...
Banks	4 783	–46	162	443	762	–287	–957	88	...
Other sectors	4 784	...	...	...	...	...	...	...	...
Other liabilities	4 786	–61	61	528	224	135	33	27	...
Monetary authorities	4 787	...	...	...	...	...	...	...	...
of which: Short-term	4 789	...	...	...	...	...	...	...	...
General government	4 790	–37	...	...	...	...	...	...	...
of which: Short-term	4 792	*–37*	...	...	...	...	...	...	...
Banks	4 793	–24	61	528	224	135	33	27	...
of which: Short-term	4 795	...	*16*	*339*	*209*	*145*	*–10*	*17*	...
Other sectors	4 796	...	...	...	...	...	...	...	...
of which: Short-term	4 798	...	...	...	...	...	...	...	...
E. RESERVE ASSETS	4 802	–1,256	–1,590	–245	–47	545	–725	–794	...
Monetary gold	4 812	94	–2	–81	116	–3	6	...	...
Special drawing rights	4 811	–85	33	41	–11	25	1	...	...
Reserve position in the Fund	4 810	...	...	...	...	...	...	...	...
Foreign exchange	4 803	–1,265	–1,621	–205	–152	523	–732	–794	...
Other claims	4 813	...	...	...	...	...	...	...	...
NET ERRORS AND OMISSIONS	4 998	**380**	**144**	**162**	**280**	**–333**	**–14**	**51**	...

Part 3 of the *Yearbook* contains descriptions of the methodologies, compilation practices, and sources used to compile these data.

Table 3. INTERNATIONAL INVESTMENT POSITION (End–period stocks), 1994–2001

(Millions of U.S. dollars)

	Code	1994	1995	1996	1997	1998	1999	2000	2001
ASSETS	8 995 C.	8,421	10,156	10,311	10,648	10,322	8,652	10,089	. . .
Direct investment abroad	8 505 . .	**166**	**139**	**182**	**234**	**404**	**342**	**364**	**. . .**
Equity capital and reinvested earnings	8 506 . .	142	111	158	212	375	299	310	. . .
Claims on affiliated enterprises	8 507 . .	142	111	158	213	377	300	311	. . .
Liabilities to affiliated enterprises	8 508 . .	. . .	. . .	–1	. . .	–2	–1	–1	. . .
Other capital	8 530 . .	25	27	25	22	29	43	54	. . .
Claims on affiliated enterprises	8 535 . .	. . .	. . .	26	22	33	45	54	. . .
Liabilities to affiliated enterprises	8 540 . .	. . .	. . .	–1	. . .	–4	–2	. . .	. . .
Portfolio investment	8 602 . .	**429**	**259**	**282**	**330**	**406**	**146**	**336**	**. . .**
Equity securities	8 610 . .	424	234	171	71	35	28	15	. . .
Monetary authorities	8 611 . .	. . .	. . .	. . .	. . .	. . .	. . .	. . .	. . .
General government	8 612 . .	. . .	. . .	. . .	. . .	. . .	. . .	. . .	. . .
Banks	8 613 . .	3	32	25	20	23	19	8	. . .
Other sectors	8 614 . .	421	202	146	51	12	9	7	. . .
Debt securities	8 619 . .	5	25	111	259	371	118	321	. . .
Bonds and notes	8 620 . .	3	24	60	112	231	116	241	. . .
Monetary authorities	8 621 . .	. . .	. . .	. . .	. . .	. . .	. . .	. . .	. . .
General government	8 622 . .	. . .	. . .	. . .	. . .	. . .	. . .	. . .	. . .
Banks	8 623 . .	. . .	20	57	110	230	116	231	. . .
Other sectors	8 624 . .	3	4	3	2	. . .	. . .	11	. . .
Money market instruments	8 630 . .	1	1	51	147	141	1	80	. . .
Monetary authorities	8 631 . .	. . .	. . .	. . .	. . .	. . .	. . .	. . .	. . .
General government	8 632 . .	. . .	. . .	. . .	. . .	. . .	. . .	. . .	. . .
Banks	8 633 . .	. . .	. . .	51	147	141	1	5	. . .
Other sectors	8 634 . .	1	1	1	. . .	. . .	. . .	75	. . .
Financial derivatives	8 900 . .	**. . .**	**. . .**	**. . .**	**. . .**	**. . .**	**. . .**	**. . .**	**. . .**
Monetary authorities	8 901 . .	. . .	. . .	. . .	. . .	. . .	. . .	. . .	. . .
General government	8 902 . .	. . .	. . .	. . .	. . .	. . .	. . .	. . .	. . .
Banks	8 903 . .	. . .	. . .	. . .	. . .	. . .	. . .	. . .	. . .
Other sectors	8 904 . .	. . .	. . .	. . .	. . .	. . .	. . .	. . .	. . .
Other investment	8 703 . .	**5,633**	**5,896**	**5,948**	**6,461**	**6,267**	**4,419**	**5,006**	**. . .**
Trade credits	8 706 . .	1,231	1,236	1,246	1,159	1,132	1,129	1,140	. . .
General government	8 707 . .	. . .	. . .	. . .	. . .	. . .	. . .	. . .	. . .
of which: Short-term	8 709 . .	. . .	. . .	. . .	. . .	. . .	. . .	. . .	. . .
Other sectors	8 710 . .	1,231	1,236	1,246	1,159	1,132	1,129	1,140	. . .
of which: Short-term	8 712 . .	*1,121*	*1,181*	*1,190*	*1,120*	*1,107*	*1,103*	*1,113*	. . .
Loans	8 714 . .	2,906	2,939	2,699	2,577	2,650	2,092	1,871	. . .
Monetary authorities	8 715 . .	. . .	. . .	. . .	. . .	. . .	. . .	. . .	. . .
of which: Short-term	8 718 . .	. . .	. . .	. . .	. . .	. . .	. . .	. . .	. . .
General government	8 719 . .	2,779	2,883	2,383	2,127	1,893	1,654	1,484	. . .
of which: Short-term	8 721 . .	. . .	. . .	. . .	. . .	. . .	. . .	. . .	. . .
Banks	8 722 . .	126	29	290	427	728	338	196	. . .
of which: Short-term	8 724 . .	*94*	*28*	*147*	*318*	*561*	*211*	*108*	. . .
Other sectors	8 725 . .	. . .	27	25	24	28	101	191	. . .
of which: Short-term	8 727 . .	. . .	. . .	. . .	*1*	*2*	*1*	*1*	. . .
Currency and deposits	8 730 . .	1,187	1,537	1,869	2,588	2,306	1,156	1,849	. . .
Monetary authorities	8 731 . .	. . .	. . .	. . .	. . .	. . .	. . .	. . .	. . .
General government	8 732 . .	. . .	. . .	. . .	. . .	. . .	. . .	. . .	. . .
Banks	8 733 . .	1,184	1,509	1,860	2,586	2,299	1,150	1,845	. . .
Other sectors	8 734 . .	3	28	9	2	7	6	4	. . .
Other assets	8 736 . .	309	184	135	137	179	42	145	. . .
Monetary authorities	8 737 . .	. . .	. . .	. . .	. . .	. . .	. . .	. . .	. . .
of which: Short-term	8 739 . .	. . .	. . .	. . .	. . .	. . .	. . .	. . .	. . .
General government	8 740 . .	168	45	10	9	3	4	. . .	. . .
of which: Short-term	8 742 . .	*168*	*45*	*10*	*9*	*3*	*4*	. . .	. . .
Banks	8 743 . .	141	138	125	128	175	38	145	. . .
of which: Short-term	8 745 . .	*130*	*138*	*125*	*128*	*175*	*38*	*145*	. . .
Other sectors	8 746 . .	. . .	. . .	. . .	. . .	. . .	. . .	. . .	. . .
of which: Short-term	8 748 . .	. . .	. . .	. . .	. . .	. . .	. . .	. . .	. . .
Reserve assets	8 802 . .	**2,192**	**3,862**	**3,898**	**3,623**	**3,244**	**3,745**	**4,384**	**. . .**
Monetary gold	8 812 . .	379	379	434	230	207	201	188	. . .
Special drawing rights	8 811 . .	86	58	16	26	2	1	. . .	. . .
Reserve position in the Fund	8 810 . .	. . .	. . .	. . .	. . .	. . .	. . .	. . .	. . .
Foreign exchange	8 803 . .	1,727	3,426	3,448	3,367	3,035	3,544	4,195	. . .
Other claims	8 813 . .	. . .	. . .	. . .	. . .	. . .	. . .	. . .	. . .

Table 3 (Concluded). INTERNATIONAL INVESTMENT POSITION (End–period stocks), 1994–2001

(Millions of U.S. dollars)

	Code	1994	1995	1996	1997	1998	1999	2000	2001
LIABILITIES	8 995 D.	6,137	7,316	9,769	11,848	14,656	13,200	14,368	...
Direct investment in Slovak Republic	8 555 ..	**897**	**1,297**	**2,046**	**2,083**	**2,890**	**3,188**	**4,504**	**...**
Equity capital and reinvested earnings	8 556 ..	778	1,162	1,592	1,650	2,099	2,233	3,562	...
Claims on direct investors	8 557 ..	...	...	...	–2	...	...	...	...
Liabilities to direct investors	8 558 ..	778	1,162	1,592	1,652	2,099	2,233	3,562	...
Other capital	8 580 ..	119	136	453	433	791	955	942	...
Claims on direct investors	8 585 ..	...	...	–69	–66	–123	–125	–235	...
Liabilities to direct investors	8 590 ..	...	...	523	499	914	1,081	1,177	...
Portfolio investment	8 652 ..	**583**	**608**	**563**	**595**	**1,549**	**2,039**	**2,830**	**...**
Equity securities	8 660 ..	56	43	62	157	102	341	260	...
Banks	8 663 ..	...	...	...	...	...	...	...	...
Other sectors	8 664 ..	56	43	62	157	102	341	260	...
Debt securities	8 669 ..	527	565	500	438	1,447	1,698	2,570	...
Bonds and notes	8 670 ..	527	565	499	438	1,428	1,675	2,555	...
Monetary authorities	8 671 ..	515	501	443	386	304	98	...	...
General government	8 672 ..	...	...	...	...	1,059	1,492	2,100	...
Banks	8 673 ..	...	...	...	...	...	13	...	...
Other sectors	8 674 ..	12	63	56	53	66	72	456	...
Money market instruments	8 680 ..	...	...	1	...	19	22	15	...
Monetary authorities	8 681 ..	...	...	...	...	...	...	...	...
General government	8 682 ..	...	...	...	...	...	...	...	...
Banks	8 683 ..	...	...	...	...	...	...	...	...
Other sectors	8 684 ..	...	...	1	...	19	22	15	...
Financial derivatives	8 905 ..	**...**	**...**	**...**	**...**	**...**	**...**	**...**	**...**
Monetary authorities	8 906 ..	...	...	...	...	...	...	...	...
General government	8 907 ..	...	...	...	...	...	...	...	...
Banks	8 908 ..	...	...	...	...	...	...	...	...
Other sectors	8 909 ..	...	...	...	...	...	...	...	...
Other investment	8 753 ..	**4,657**	**5,411**	**7,161**	**9,170**	**10,217**	**7,974**	**7,034**	**...**
Trade credits	8 756 ..	1,522	1,582	1,677	1,832	1,865	1,773	1,600	...
General government	8 757 ..	...	...	...	...	...	...	...	...
of which: Short-term	8 759 ..	...	...	...	...	...	...	...	...
Other sectors	8 760 ..	1,522	1,582	1,677	1,832	1,865	1,773	1,600	...
of which: Short-term	8 762 ..	*1,207*	*1,358*	*1,508*	*1,563*	*1,721*	*1,669*	*1,515*	...
Loans	8 764 ..	2,928	3,512	4,211	5,258	6,545	5,679	4,831	...
Monetary authorities	8 765 ..	679	533	433	499	523	503	324	...
of which: Use of Fund credit and loans from the Fund	8 766 ..	*642*	*457*	*319*	*249*	*190*	*132*	...	...
of which: Short-term	8 768 ..	...	...	...	...	...	...	...	...
General government	8 769 ..	1,101	958	786	912	621	671	788	...
of which: Short-term	8 771 ..	...	...	...	*186*	...	...	...	...
Banks	8 772 ..	333	588	1,026	1,037	1,158	177	85	...
of which: Short-term	8 774 ..	*111*	*166*	*606*	*727*	*873*	*59*	*10*	...
Other sectors	8 775 ..	815	1,433	1,965	2,810	4,244	4,328	3,635	...
of which: Short-term	8 777 ..	*23*	*77*	*116*	*192*	*300*	*292*	*97*	...
Currency and deposits	8 780 ..	132	289	726	1,369	1,254	276	338	...
Monetary authorities	8 781 ..	3	4	9	8	14	19	...	...
General government	8 782 ..	...	...	...	...	...	...	...	...
Banks	8 783 ..	129	285	717	1,361	1,240	258	338	...
Other sectors	8 784 ..	...	...	...	...	...	...	...	...
Other liabilities	8 786 ..	74	29	546	711	552	245	265	...
Monetary authorities	8 787 ..	...	...	...	...	...	...	...	...
of which: Short-term	8 789 ..	...	...	...	...	...	...	...	...
General government	8 790 ..	...	...	...	...	...	...	...	...
of which: Short-term	8 792 ..	...	...	...	...	...	...	...	...
Banks	8 793 ..	74	29	546	711	552	245	265	...
of which: Short-term	8 795 ..	*7*	*29*	*351*	*517*	*357*	*38*	*54*	...
Other sectors	8 796 ..	...	...	...	...	...	...	...	...
of which: Short-term	8 798 ..	...	...	...	...	...	...	...	...
NET INTERNATIONAL INVESTMENT POSITION	8 995 ..	**2,284**	**2,840**	**542**	**–1,200**	**–4,334**	**–4,548**	**–4,279**	**...**
Conversion rates: Slovak koruny per U.S. dollar (end of period)	0 102 ..	**31.277**	**29.569**	**31.895**	**34.782**	**36.913**	**42.266**	**47.389**	**48.467**

Table 1. ANALYTIC PRESENTATION, 1994–2001
(Millions of U.S. dollars)

	Code	1994	1995	1996	1997	1998	1999	2000	2001
A. Current Account [1]	4 993 Z.	**574.8**	**–74.8**	**55.4**	**50.4**	**–118.0**	**–698.3**	**–547.7**	**30.9**
Goods: exports f.o.b.	2 100 . .	6,831.7	8,350.2	8,352.6	8,405.9	9,090.9	8,623.2	8,807.9	9,342.8
Goods: imports f.o.b.	3 100 . .	–7,168.2	–9,304.2	–9,178.7	–9,180.7	–9,882.9	–9,858.3	–9,946.9	–9,962.3
Balance on Goods	4 100 . .	*–336.5*	*–953.9*	*–826.1*	*–774.8*	*–792.0*	*–1,235.1*	*–1,138.9*	*–619.5*
Services: credit	2 200 . .	1,808.1	2,026.9	2,134.7	2,040.5	2,024.6	1,875.3	1,887.6	1,959.6
Services: debit	3 200 . .	–1,164.7	–1,444.2	–1,494.2	–1,404.8	–1,523.8	–1,521.8	–1,437.9	–1,457.5
Balance on Goods and Services	4 991 . .	*306.9*	*–371.3*	*–185.6*	*–139.2*	*–291.2*	*–881.6*	*–689.2*	*–117.4*
Income: credit	2 300 . .	324.7	405.6	413.1	391.8	412.9	426.9	434.0	462.6
Income: debit	3 300 . .	–153.3	–204.3	–259.9	–316.4	–357.0	–363.2	–407.8	–443.4
Balance on Goods, Services, and Income	4 992 . .	*478.2*	*–170.0*	*–32.4*	*–63.8*	*–235.4*	*–817.9*	*–663.0*	*–98.2*
Current transfers: credit	2 379 Z.	237.2	247.7	250.9	259.5	299.8	334.9	340.8	390.0
Current transfers: debit	3 379 . .	–140.6	–152.4	–163.1	–145.3	–182.4	–215.3	–225.4	–260.8
B. Capital Account [1]	4 994 Z.	**–3.2**	**–7.0**	**–1.9**	**1.1**	**–1.5**	**–.7**	**3.5**	**–3.6**
Capital account: credit	2 994 Z.	2.7	3.1	5.5	5.0	3.5	3.3	6.8	3.3
Capital account: debit	3 994 . .	–5.8	–10.1	–7.4	–3.9	–5.0	–4.0	–3.3	–6.9
Total, Groups A Plus B	4 981 . .	*571.6*	*–81.7*	*53.6*	*51.5*	*–119.5*	*–699.0*	*–544.2*	*27.3*
C. Financial Account [1]	4 995 W.	**138.6**	**516.3**	**534.5**	**1,162.9**	**215.8**	**576.1**	**680.4**	**1,204.3**
Direct investment abroad	4 505 . .	12.7	10.0	–7.0	–31.0	5.5	–47.6	–65.3	–132.8
Direct investment in Slovenia	4 555 Z.	116.7	150.5	173.5	334.3	215.5	106.5	135.9	503.3
Portfolio investment assets	4 602 . .	–32.5	–28.9	6.4	–.2	–30.2	–7.8	–58.4	–107.5
Equity securities	4 610 . .	. . .	. . .	. . .	. . .	. . .	–.5	–14.5	–23.3
Debt securities	4 619 . .	–32.5	–28.9	6.4	–.2	–30.2	–7.3	–43.9	–84.2
Portfolio investment liabilities	4 652 Z.	. . .	15.5	630.5	236.1	119.8	361.6	246.0	188.9
Equity securities	4 660 . .	. . .	. . .	. . .	52.2	7.2	–3.2	25.4	–2.3
Debt securities	4 669 Z.	. . .	15.5	630.5	184.0	112.6	364.8	220.6	191.2
Financial derivatives	4 910 . .	. . .	. . .	. . .	. . .	. . .	. . .	. . .	. . .
Financial derivatives assets	4 900 . .	. . .	. . .	. . .	. . .	. . .	. . .	. . .	. . .
Financial derivatives liabilities	4 905 . .	. . .	. . .	. . .	. . .	. . .	. . .	. . .	. . .
Other investment assets	4 703 . .	–211.5	–242.8	–442.0	262.3	–464.6	–568.5	–519.2	206.6
Monetary authorities	4 701 . .	–98.3	–66.8	131.4	–7.6	–5.4	–5.6	–5.9	–6.2
General government	4 704 . .	–.4	–2.2	–1.4	–1.3	–1.8	–1.6	–1.1	–.5
Banks	4 705 . .	–353.1	–302.3	–321.8	479.2	–51.8	–7.8	–253.7	–303.1
Other sectors	4 728 . .	240.3	128.4	–250.2	–208.0	–405.6	–553.5	–258.5	516.4
Other investment liabilities	4 753 W.	253.1	612.1	173.1	361.4	369.8	732.0	941.3	545.7
Monetary authorities	4 753 WA	.1	.1	.2	. . .	.1	–.4	.1	. . .
General government	4 753 ZB	92.2	137.6	–67.6	–25.7	–18.3	–3.2	79.6	–27.8
Banks	4 753 ZC	40.6	267.3	–19.8	4.7	90.6	260.5	290.8	230.6
Other sectors	4 753 ZD	120.3	207.1	260.4	382.5	297.3	474.9	570.9	343.0
Total, Groups A Through C	4 983 . .	*710.2*	*434.6*	*588.1*	*1,214.4*	*96.3*	*–122.9*	*136.2*	*1,231.6*
D. Net Errors and Omissions	4 998 . .	**–63.7**	**–194.6**	**2.0**	**74.0**	**61.4**	**41.5**	**42.1**	**53.0**
Total, Groups A Through D	4 984 . .	*646.5*	*240.0*	*590.0*	*1,288.4*	*157.8*	*–81.4*	*178.3*	*1,284.6*
E. Reserves and Related Items	4 802 A.	**–646.5**	**–240.0**	**–590.0**	**–1,288.4**	**–157.8**	**81.4**	**–178.3**	**–1,284.6**
Reserve assets	4 802 . .	–641.3	–236.5	–587.4	–1,287.2	–157.8	81.4	–178.3	–1,284.6
Use of Fund credit and loans	4 766 . .	–5.2	–3.4	–2.6	–1.2	. . .	. . .	. . .	. . .
Exceptional financing	4 920 . .	. . .	. . .	. . .	. . .	. . .	. . .	. . .	. . .
Conversion rates: tolars per U.S. dollar	0 101 . .	**128.81**	**118.52**	**135.36**	**159.69**	**166.13**	**181.77**	**222.66**	**242.75**

[1] Excludes components that have been classified in the categories of Group E.

Table 2. STANDARD PRESENTATION, 1994–2001

(Millions of U.S. dollars)

	Code	1994	1995	1996	1997	1998	1999	2000	2001
CURRENT ACCOUNT	4 993 . .	**574.8**	**–74.8**	**55.4**	**50.4**	**–118.0**	**–698.3**	**–547.7**	**30.9**
A. GOODS	4 100 . .	–336.5	–953.9	–826.1	–774.8	–792.0	–1,235.1	–1,138.9	–619.5
Credit	2 100 . .	**6,831.7**	**8,350.2**	**8,352.6**	**8,405.9**	**9,090.9**	**8,623.2**	**8,807.9**	**9,342.8**
General merchandise: exports f.o.b.	2 110 . .	5,916.6	7,333.5	7,367.7	7,516.4	8,209.2	7,857.1	8,757.4	9,284.0
Goods for processing: exports f.o.b.	2 150 . .	912.1	1,012.8	982.9	887.6	879.6	764.1	47.3	56.0
Repairs on goods	2 160 . .	. . .	. . .	. . .	. . .	. . .	. . .	. . .	. . .
Goods procured in ports by carriers	2 170 . .	2.6	3.5	1.5	1.3	1.2	1.5	2.1	2.0
Nonmonetary gold	2 180 . .	.4	.4	.5	.6	.9	.5	1.1	.9
Debit	3 100 . .	**–7,168.2**	**–9,304.2**	**–9,178.7**	**–9,180.7**	**–9,882.9**	**–9,858.3**	**–9,946.9**	**–9,962.3**
General merchandise: imports f.o.b.	3 110 . .	–6,521.1	–8,580.9	–8,513.7	–8,551.6	–9,264.7	–9,320.1	–9,885.3	–9,884.2
Goods for processing: imports f.o.b.	3 150 . .	–642.1	–718.8	–656.6	–621.4	–608.0	–526.6	–49.5	–66.1
Repairs on goods	3 160 . .	. . .	. . .	. . .	. . .	. . .	. . .	. . .	. . .
Goods procured in ports by carriers	3 170 . .	. . .	. . .	. . .	. . .	. . .	. . .	. . .	. . .
Nonmonetary gold	3 180 . .	–5.1	–4.5	–8.4	–7.8	–10.2	–11.6	–12.0	–12.0
B. SERVICES	4 200 . .	643.3	582.6	640.5	635.7	500.8	353.5	449.7	502.1
Total credit	2 200 . .	*1,808.1*	*2,026.9*	*2,134.7*	*2,040.5*	*2,024.6*	*1,875.3*	*1,887.6*	*1,959.6*
Total debit	3 200 . .	*–1,164.7*	*–1,444.2*	*–1,494.2*	*–1,404.8*	*–1,523.8*	*–1,521.8*	*–1,437.9*	*–1,457.5*
Transportation services, credit	2 205 . .	**486.7**	**505.3**	**480.8**	**464.5**	**540.0**	**520.7**	**492.4**	**499.8**
Passenger	2 850 . .	*42.0*	*44.2*	*39.9*	*44.3*	*47.3*	*52.7*	*55.0*	*58.3*
Freight	2 851 . .	*274.9*	*262.7*	*247.5*	*254.6*	*297.4*	*289.6*	*281.6*	*296.7*
Other	2 852 . .	*169.8*	*198.5*	*193.4*	*165.6*	*195.3*	*178.4*	*155.8*	*144.8*
Sea transport, passenger	2 207 . .	.1	.1	.2	.6	.4	.2	.6	.4
Sea transport, freight	2 208 . .	55.5	56.6	45.6	38.9	29.9	28.6	23.3	22.0
Sea transport, other	2 209 . .	.4	24.9	29.3	35.9	46.6	41.6	36.8	37.0
Air transport, passenger	2 211 . .	35.0	37.6	33.0	37.7	40.3	46.7	48.6	52.8
Air transport, freight	2 212 . .	2.4	2.6	2.6	2.8	4.0	4.6	5.6	5.9
Air transport, other	2 213 . .	.3	1.5	1.5	1.4	.9	1.7	2.1	5.4
Other transport, passenger	2 215 . .	6.9	6.5	6.8	6.0	6.6	5.8	5.8	5.2
Other transport, freight	2 216 . .	217.1	203.5	199.3	212.8	263.6	256.4	252.7	268.8
Other transport, other	2 217 . .	169.1	172.0	162.6	128.3	147.8	135.1	117.0	102.4
Transportation services, debit	3 205 . .	**–420.5**	**–437.9**	**–409.0**	**–368.7**	**–411.8**	**–380.0**	**–353.7**	**–318.2**
Passenger	3 850 . .	*–21.7*	*–30.6*	*–33.4*	*–35.7*	*–40.0*	*–36.7*	*–32.9*	*–31.8*
Freight	3 851 . .	*–246.0*	*–245.6*	*–235.7*	*–220.0*	*–259.7*	*–238.5*	*–218.5*	*–192.0*
Other	3 852 . .	*–152.8*	*–161.7*	*–139.9*	*–113.0*	*–112.2*	*–104.8*	*–102.3*	*–94.4*
Sea transport, passenger	3 207 . .	–.5	–.9	–1.6	–1.6	–1.7	–1.0	–1.0	–1.2
Sea transport, freight	3 208 . .	–27.5	–27.9	–24.3	–22.8	–23.3	–32.0	–29.8	–32.5
Sea transport, other	3 209 . .	–.5	–15.9	–10.0	–10.6	–8.6	–7.0	–7.8	–6.0
Air transport, passenger	3 211 . .	–15.9	–24.3	–27.3	–30.7	–34.6	–32.6	–28.9	–27.3
Air transport, freight	3 212 . .	–4.2	–4.1	–5.4	–4.9	–5.8	–5.3	–6.9	–7.2
Air transport, other	3 213 . .	–.2	–.8	–1.1	–.7	–2.8	–2.1	–2.6	–2.3
Other transport, passenger	3 215 . .	–5.3	–5.4	–4.6	–3.4	–3.7	–3.0	–3.0	–3.3
Other transport, freight	3 216 . .	–214.4	–213.6	–206.0	–192.3	–230.6	–201.1	–181.8	–152.3
Other transport, other	3 217 . .	–152.1	–145.1	–128.7	–101.8	–100.8	–95.7	–91.9	–86.1
Travel, credit	2 236 . .	**913.0**	**1,084.0**	**1,239.7**	**1,180.5**	**1,088.4**	**957.6**	**960.8**	**1,001.0**
Business travel	2 237 . .	. . .	. . .	. . .	. . .	. . .	. . .	. . .	. . .
Personal travel	2 240 . .	913.0	1,084.0	1,239.7	1,180.5	1,088.4	957.6	960.8	1,001.0
Travel, debit	3 236 . .	**–389.4**	**–574.9**	**–603.6**	**–517.7**	**–560.6**	**–541.4**	**–511.4**	**–528.0**
Business travel	3 237 . .	–59.9	–64.2	–64.3	–60.4	–60.7	–60.1	–59.7	–64.8
Personal travel	3 240 . .	–329.5	–510.7	–539.3	–457.4	–500.0	–481.2	–451.7	–463.2
Other services, credit	2 200 BA	**408.4**	**437.5**	**414.1**	**395.5**	**396.2**	**397.1**	**434.4**	**458.8**
Communications	2 245 . .	12.7	11.8	13.9	21.4	24.8	24.1	24.7	33.8
Construction	2 249 . .	124.0	134.8	92.2	79.4	72.7	57.5	65.9	70.4
Insurance	2 253 . .	2.9	3.1	4.2	4.5	5.2	4.8	7.0	7.5
Financial	2 260 . .	6.5	8.0	10.7	10.6	8.4	8.5	8.1	10.9
Computer and information	2 262 . .	5.4	12.0	29.3	32.6	47.6	54.5	53.9	64.1
Royalties and licence fees	2 266 . .	3.2	4.0	6.3	5.1	8.7	8.0	11.8	14.4
Other business services	2 268 . .	244.7	247.1	242.4	225.6	213.7	220.2	244.1	238.2
Personal, cultural, and recreational	2 287 . .	6.3	5.5	9.0	10.6	12.3	16.4	13.6	16.2
Government, n.i.e.	2 291 . .	2.7	11.2	6.1	5.7	2.8	3.2	5.2	3.4
Other services, debit	3 200 BA	**–354.8**	**–431.4**	**–481.6**	**–518.4**	**–551.4**	**–600.5**	**–572.9**	**–611.4**
Communications	3 245 . .	–5.5	–11.4	–16.4	–27.0	–31.0	–37.3	–50.9	–59.8
Construction	3 249 . .	–3.3	–23.7	–43.9	–52.8	–35.4	–62.4	–51.8	–46.4
Insurance	3 253 . .	–7.1	–9.8	–10.8	–10.4	–12.8	–10.4	–8.5	–10.0
Financial	3 260 . .	–12.3	–15.4	–19.7	–22.0	–32.3	–23.1	–26.3	–25.0
Computer and information	3 262 . .	–19.0	–27.2	–31.2	–51.2	–46.7	–52.9	–57.4	–57.6
Royalties and licence fees	3 266 . .	–16.2	–23.0	–27.1	–32.6	–38.9	–47.1	–49.4	–60.4
Other business services	3 268 . .	–261.3	–286.1	–295.7	–279.9	–306.0	–315.0	–277.8	–300.0
Personal, cultural, and recreational	3 287 . .	–13.4	–19.2	–22.6	–29.1	–33.1	–36.3	–36.0	–36.8
Government, n.i.e.	3 291 . .	–16.8	–15.8	–14.4	–13.4	–15.2	–16.0	–14.9	–15.5

Table 2 (Continued). STANDARD PRESENTATION, 1994–2001

(Millions of U.S. dollars)

	Code	1994	1995	1996	1997	1998	1999	2000	2001
C. INCOME	4 300 . .	171.4	201.3	153.2	75.4	55.9	63.7	26.2	19.1
Total credit	2 300 . .	*324.7*	*405.6*	*413.1*	*391.8*	*412.9*	*426.9*	*434.0*	*462.6*
Total debit	3 300 . .	*–153.3*	*–204.3*	*–259.9*	*–316.4*	*–357.0*	*–363.2*	*–407.8*	*–443.4*
Compensation of employees, credit	2 310 . .	**217.3**	**215.8**	**233.7**	**205.6**	**205.9**	**207.4**	**188.1**	**181.6**
Compensation of employees, debit	3 310 . .	**–16.1**	**–25.3**	**–24.0**	**–26.3**	**–27.2**	**–24.9**	**–27.0**	**–26.6**
Investment income, credit	2 320 . .	**107.4**	**189.8**	**179.4**	**186.2**	**207.0**	**219.6**	**246.0**	**281.0**
Direct investment income	2 330 . .	–1.9	–1.5	5.4	10.8	–12.5	6.7	22.7	4.5
Dividends and distributed branch profits	2 332 . .	8.0	13.8	4.8	7.4	5.5	4.0	7.1	9.2
Reinvested earnings and undistributed branch profits	2 333 . .	–9.8	–15.2	.6	3.4	–18.0	2.8	15.6	–4.7
Income on debt (interest)	2 334 . .	. . .	. . .	. . .	. . .	. . .	. . .	. . .	. . .
Portfolio investment income	2 339 . .	. . .	13.8	19.8	30.9	82.8	123.2	118.5	150.9
Income on equity	2 340 . .	. . .	. . .	. . .	. . .	. . .	. . .	. . .	. . .
Income on bonds and notes	2 350 . .	. . .	13.7	19.7	30.8	82.8	107.3	80.7	103.8
Income on money market instruments	2 360 . .	. . .	.2	.1	. . .	. . .	15.9	37.9	47.1
Other investment income	2 370 . .	109.3	177.4	154.3	144.6	136.7	89.6	104.7	125.6
Investment income, debit	3 320 . .	**–137.3**	**–179.0**	**–235.9**	**–290.0**	**–329.8**	**–338.4**	**–380.8**	**–416.8**
Direct investment income	3 330 . .	4.9	4.1	–13.4	–49.8	–73.4	–82.3	–89.6	–20.9
Dividends and distributed branch profits	3 332 . .	–6.4	–21.1	–18.1	–20.8	–27.1	–56.8	–41.0	–46.5
Reinvested earnings and undistributed branch profits	3 333 . .	11.4	25.2	4.7	–29.0	–46.2	–25.5	–48.6	25.6
Income on debt (interest)	3 334 . .	. . .	. . .	. . .	. . .	. . .	. . .	. . .	. . .
Portfolio investment income	3 339 . .	. . .	–7.7	–27.2	–30.7	–50.5	–77.9	–93.7	–136.5
Income on equity	3 340 . .	. . .	. . .	. . .	. . .	. . .	. . .	. . .	. . .
Income on bonds and notes	3 350 . .	. . .	–7.7	–27.1	–30.7	–50.5	–77.9	–92.7	–133.1
Income on money market instruments	3 360 . .	. . .	. . .	–.1	. . .	. . .	. . .	–1.0	–3.4
Other investment income	3 370 . .	–142.2	–175.3	–195.3	–209.6	–205.9	–178.2	–197.5	–259.5
D. CURRENT TRANSFERS	4 379 . .	96.6	95.2	87.8	114.2	117.3	119.5	115.3	129.1
Credit	2 379 . .	**237.2**	**247.7**	**250.9**	**259.5**	**299.8**	**334.9**	**340.8**	**390.0**
General government	2 380 . .	11.3	18.7	16.4	29.5	21.6	24.0	41.1	55.2
Other sectors	2 390 . .	226.0	229.0	234.5	230.0	278.1	310.9	299.7	334.8
Workers' remittances	2 391 . .	55.5	54.2	41.7	32.4	18.7	15.4	14.1	16.6
Other current transfers	2 392 . .	170.4	174.8	192.8	197.6	259.5	295.5	285.6	318.2
Debit	3 379 . .	**–140.6**	**–152.4**	**–163.1**	**–145.3**	**–182.4**	**–215.3**	**–225.4**	**–260.8**
General government	3 380 . .	–120.1	–101.2	–96.7	–95.7	–105.9	–108.6	–101.7	–122.1
Other sectors	3 390 . .	–20.5	–51.2	–66.4	–49.6	–76.5	–106.7	–123.7	–138.7
Workers' remittances	3 391 . .	. . .	–1.7	–1.1	–.8	–.2	–.1	–.2	. . .
Other current transfers	3 392 . .	–20.5	–49.5	–65.3	–48.8	–76.3	–106.6	–123.6	–138.7
CAPITAL AND FINANCIAL ACCOUNT	4 996 . .	**–511.1**	**269.3**	**–57.4**	**–124.4**	**56.6**	**656.8**	**505.6**	**–83.9**
CAPITAL ACCOUNT	4 994 . .	**–3.2**	**–7.0**	**–1.9**	**1.1**	**–1.5**	**–.7**	**3.5**	**–3.6**
Total credit	2 994 . .	*2.7*	*3.1*	*5.5*	*5.0*	*3.5*	*3.3*	*6.8*	*3.3*
Total debit	3 994 . .	*–5.8*	*–10.1*	*–7.4*	*–3.9*	*–5.0*	*–4.0*	*–3.3*	*–6.9*
Capital transfers, credit	2 400 . .	**2.1**	**2.9**	**5.1**	**4.8**	**3.3**	**2.9**	**3.1**	**2.2**
General government	2 401 . .	. . .	1.0	1.1	1.4	.2	.1	. . .	. . .
Debt forgiveness	2 402 . .	. . .	. . .	. . .	. . .	. . .	. . .	. . .	. . .
Other capital transfers	2 410 . .	. . .	1.0	1.1	1.4	.2	.1	. . .	. . .
Other sectors	2 430 . .	2.1	2.0	4.0	3.4	3.2	2.8	3.1	2.2
Migrants' transfers	2 431 . .	.4	2.0	4.0	3.4	3.2	2.8	3.1	2.2
Debt forgiveness	2 432 . .	. . .	. . .	. . .	. . .	. . .	. . .	. . .	. . .
Other capital transfers	2 440 . .	1.8	. . .	. . .	. . .	. . .	. . .	. . .	. . .
Capital transfers, debit	3 400 . .	**–3.7**	**–7.6**	**–4.4**	**–2.7**	**–3.7**	**–2.9**	**–2.4**	**–1.6**
General government	3 401 . .	. . .	–4.0	. . .	–.1	. . .	. . .	–.2	. . .
Debt forgiveness	3 402 . .	. . .	. . .	. . .	. . .	. . .	. . .	. . .	. . .
Other capital transfers	3 410 . .	. . .	–4.0	. . .	–.1	. . .	. . .	–.2	. . .
Other sectors	3 430 . .	–3.7	–3.6	–4.3	–2.6	–3.7	–2.9	–2.3	–1.6
Migrants' transfers	3 431 . .	–3.7	–3.6	–4.3	–2.6	–3.7	–2.9	–2.3	–1.6
Debt forgiveness	3 432 . .	. . .	. . .	. . .	. . .	. . .	. . .	. . .	. . .
Other capital transfers	3 440 . .	. . .	. . .	. . .	. . .	. . .	. . .	. . .	. . .
Nonproduced nonfinancial assets, credit	2 480 . .	**.5**	**.2**	**.4**	**.2**	**.2**	**.4**	**3.8**	**1.1**
Nonproduced nonfinancial assets, debit	3 480 . .	**–2.1**	**–2.5**	**–3.0**	**–1.2**	**–1.3**	**–1.1**	**–.9**	**–5.3**

Table 2 (Continued). STANDARD PRESENTATION, 1994–2001
(Millions of U.S. dollars)

	Code	1994	1995	1996	1997	1998	1999	2000	2001
FINANCIAL ACCOUNT	4 995 . .	**–507.9**	**276.3**	**–55.6**	**–125.5**	**58.1**	**657.5**	**502.1**	**–80.3**
A. DIRECT INVESTMENT	4 500 . .	129.5	160.5	166.5	303.3	221.0	58.9	70.6	370.5
Direct investment abroad	4 505 . .	**12.7**	**10.0**	**–7.0**	**–31.0**	**5.5**	**–47.6**	**–65.3**	**–132.8**
Equity capital	4 510 . .	2.9	–5.2	–6.4	–27.6	–12.5	–44.8	–49.7	–92.0
Claims on affiliated enterprises	4 515 . .	...	...	...	...	...	...	...	...
Liabilities to affiliated enterprises	4 520 . .	...	...	...	...	...	...	...	...
Reinvested earnings	4 525 . .	9.8	15.2	–.6	–3.4	18.0	–2.8	–15.6	4.7
Other capital	4 530 . .	...	...	...	...	...	...	...	–45.5
Claims on affiliated enterprises	4 535 . .	...	...	...	...	...	...	...	–34.4
Liabilities to affiliated enterprises	4 540 . .	...	...	...	...	...	...	...	–11.1
Direct investment in Slovenia	4 555 . .	**116.7**	**150.5**	**173.5**	**334.3**	**215.5**	**106.5**	**135.9**	**503.3**
Equity capital	4 560 . .	128.1	175.6	178.2	305.3	169.3	81.1	87.4	354.5
Claims on direct investors	4 565 . .	...	...	...	...	...	...	...	...
Liabilities to direct investors	4 570 . .	...	...	...	...	...	...	...	...
Reinvested earnings	4 575 . .	–11.4	–25.2	–4.7	29.0	46.2	25.5	48.6	–25.6
Other capital	4 580 . .	...	...	...	...	...	...	...	174.5
Claims on direct investors	4 585 . .	...	...	...	...	...	...	...	–8.9
Liabilities to direct investors	4 590 . .	...	...	...	...	...	...	...	183.4
B. PORTFOLIO INVESTMENT	4 600 . .	–32.5	–13.5	636.9	236.0	89.6	353.8	187.6	81.4
Assets	4 602 . .	**–32.5**	**–28.9**	**6.4**	**–.2**	**–30.2**	**–7.8**	**–58.4**	**–107.5**
Equity securities	4 610 . .	...	...	...	...	...	–.5	–14.5	–23.3
Monetary authorities	4 611 . .	...	...	...	...	...	...	...	...
General government	4 612 . .	...	...	...	...	...	...	...	...
Banks	4 613 . .	...	...	...	...	...	–.2	–3.6	–18.6
Other sectors	4 614 . .	...	...	...	...	...	–.4	–10.9	–4.6
Debt securities	4 619 . .	–32.5	–28.9	6.4	–.2	–30.2	–7.3	–43.9	–84.2
Bonds and notes	4 620 . .	–32.5	–33.2	.6	–.1	–32.0	–2.3	–44.2	–87.0
Monetary authorities	4 621 . .	...	...	...	...	...	...	...	...
General government	4 622 . .	–.1	...	...	...	...	.1	...	...
Banks	4 623 . .	–37.8	–33.4	.5	–1.6	–32.0	–2.4	–38.9	–76.6
Other sectors	4 624 . .	5.3	.2	.1	1.4	...	...	–5.2	–10.3
Money market instruments	4 630 . .	...	4.3	5.8	–.1	1.8	–5.0	.2	2.7
Monetary authorities	4 631 . .	...	...	...	...	...	...	...	...
General government	4 632 . .	...	...	...	...	...	...	...	...
Banks	4 633 . .	...	3.9	5.8	...	...	–5.0	...	...
Other sectors	4 634 . .	...	.4	...	–.1	1.8	...	.2	2.7
Liabilities	4 652 . .	**...**	**15.5**	**630.5**	**236.1**	**119.8**	**361.6**	**246.0**	**188.9**
Equity securities	4 660 . .	...	...	...	52.2	7.2	–3.2	25.4	–2.3
Banks	4 663 . .	...	...	...	...	...	...	...	...
Other sectors	4 664 . .	...	...	...	52.2	7.2	–3.2	25.4	–2.3
Debt securities	4 669 . .	...	15.5	630.5	184.0	112.6	364.8	220.6	191.2
Bonds and notes	4 670 . .	...	15.8	632.4	184.0	113.5	364.8	220.7	178.6
Monetary authorities	4 671 . .	...	...	...	...	...	...	...	...
General government	4 672 . .	...	...	628.3	195.0	95.1	427.9	358.0	164.5
Banks	4 673 . .	...	15.9	4.5	–11.4	9.3	–60.4	–65.5	–4.4
Other sectors	4 674 . .	...	...	–.4	.3	9.1	–2.7	–71.9	18.5
Money market instruments	4 680 . .	...	–.4	–1.9	...	–.9	...	–.1	12.6
Monetary authorities	4 681 . .	...	...	...	...	...	...	...	...
General government	4 682 . .	...	...	...	...	...	...	...	...
Banks	4 683 . .	...	–.4	–2.0	...	–.9	...	–.1	...
Other sectors	4 684 . .	...	...	.1	...	...	...	...	12.6
C. FINANCIAL DERIVATIVES	4 910 . .	...	...	...	...	...	...	...	...
Monetary authorities	4 911 . .	...	...	...	...	...	...	...	...
General government	4 912 . .	...	...	...	...	...	...	...	...
Banks	4 913 . .	...	...	...	...	...	...	...	...
Other sectors	4 914 . .	...	...	...	...	...	...	...	...
Assets	4 900 . .	**...**	**...**	**...**	**...**	**...**	**...**	**...**	**...**
Monetary authorities	4 901 . .	...	...	...	...	...	...	...	...
General government	4 902 . .	...	...	...	...	...	...	...	...
Banks	4 903 . .	...	...	...	...	...	...	...	...
Other sectors	4 904 . .	...	...	...	...	...	...	...	...
Liabilities	4 905 . .	**...**	**...**	**...**	**...**	**...**	**...**	**...**	**...**
Monetary authorities	4 906 . .	...	...	...	...	...	...	...	...
General government	4 907 . .	...	...	...	...	...	...	...	...
Banks	4 908 . .	...	...	...	...	...	...	...	...
Other sectors	4 909 . .	...	...	...	...	...	...	...	...

Table 2 (Concluded). STANDARD PRESENTATION, 1994–2001
(Millions of U.S. dollars)

	Code	1994	1995	1996	1997	1998	1999	2000	2001
D. OTHER INVESTMENT	4 700	36.5	365.8	−271.4	622.4	−94.8	163.4	422.2	752.3
Assets	4 703	**−211.5**	**−242.8**	**−442.0**	**262.3**	**−464.6**	**−568.5**	**−519.2**	**206.6**
Trade credits	4 706	−9.0	−5.4	−306.8	−363.3	−471.0	−296.7	−162.7	−198.1
General government	4 707	...	...	...	...	...	...	...	...
of which: Short-term	4 709	...	...	...	...	...	...	...	...
Other sectors	4 710	−9.0	−5.4	−306.8	−363.3	−471.0	−296.7	−162.7	−198.1
of which: Short-term	4 712	*−8.5*	*−18.8*	*−315.8*	*−372.0*	*−453.6*	*−271.6*	*−164.3*	*−233.7*
Loans	4 714	−10.7	−17.0	−5.0	−64.5	−54.7	−41.2	−65.3	10.6
Monetary authorities	4 715	...	...	...	...	...	...	...	...
of which: Short-term	4 718	...	...	...	...	...	...	...	...
General government	4 719	...	...	...	...	...	...	...	...
of which: Short-term	4 721	...	...	...	...	...	...	...	...
Banks	4 722	−11.2	−14.2	−3.6	−69.2	−31.3	−8.8	10.6	−6.1
of which: Short-term	4 724	*−1.0*	*−5.4*	*.1*	*−32.2*	*7.0*	*−12.4*	*16.7*	*2.1*
Other sectors	4 725	.6	−2.7	−1.4	4.7	−23.3	−32.4	−75.9	16.7
of which: Short-term	4 727	*−.3*	...	*−1.7*	*1.6*	*−10.5*	*−.2*	*−11.3*	*−4.6*
Currency and deposits	4 730	−80.2	−65.2	−281.7	747.3	54.6	−197.5	−261.0	423.3
Monetary authorities	4 731	...	...	...	...	...	...	...	...
General government	4 732	...	...	...	...	...	...	...	...
Banks	4 733	−328.4	−201.4	−339.3	598.6	−29.6	29.5	−240.8	−276.2
Other sectors	4 734	248.3	136.2	57.6	148.7	84.2	−227.1	−20.2	699.5
Other assets	4 736	−111.7	−155.2	151.5	−57.3	6.5	−33.1	−30.2	−29.2
Monetary authorities	4 737	−98.3	−66.8	131.4	−7.6	−5.4	−5.6	−5.9	−6.2
of which: Short-term	4 739	*−98.3*	*−66.8*	*131.4*	*−7.6*	*−5.4*	*−5.6*	*−5.9*	*−6.2*
General government	4 740	−.4	−2.2	−1.4	−1.3	−1.8	−1.6	−1.1	−.5
of which: Short-term	4 742	...	...	...	...	...	...	...	...
Banks	4 743	−13.5	−86.6	21.1	−50.2	9.2	−28.5	−23.4	−20.7
of which: Short-term	4 745	*−13.3*	*−86.3*	*24.0*	*−52.7*	*8.4*	*−29.5*	*−23.4*	*−15.5*
Other sectors	4 746	.4	.4	.4	1.8	4.6	2.6	.3	−1.7
of which: Short-term	4 748	*.4*	*.4*	*.4*	*1.8*	*4.6*	*2.6*	*.3*	*−1.7*
Liabilities	4 753	**247.9**	**608.6**	**170.5**	**360.1**	**369.8**	**732.0**	**941.3**	**545.7**
Trade credits	4 756	−10.6	−4.0	21.4	8.8	44.9	−19.6	−19.3	−5.2
General government	4 757	−4.0	−2.5	−1.0	−3.0	−1.0	−.4	−.3	−.1
of which: Short-term	4 759	...	...	...	...	...	...	...	...
Other sectors	4 760	−6.5	−1.6	22.4	11.8	45.8	−19.2	−19.0	−5.1
of which: Short-term	4 762	...	...	...	...	...	...	...	...
Loans	4 764	325.8	565.5	−7.8	331.4	272.4	748.9	943.6	416.4
Monetary authorities	4 765	−5.2	−3.4	−2.6	−1.2	...	...	...	...
of which: Use of Fund credit and loans from the Fund	4 766	*−5.2*	*−3.4*	*−2.6*	*−1.2*	...	...	...	...
of which: Short-term	4 768	...	...	...	...	...	...	...	...
General government	4 769	96.3	140.1	−68.8	−23.8	−22.1	−3.3	79.2	−28.3
of which: Short-term	4 771	*−3.4*	...	*5.0*	*.1*	*−.6*	*−4.6*	...	*−6.9*
Banks	4 772	106.3	215.7	−174.6	−15.1	40.8	255.5	272.1	90.7
of which: Short-term	4 774	*.2*	*3.3*	*−3.2*	...	*.5*	*7.0*	*−4.6*	*−1.1*
Other sectors	4 775	128.4	213.2	238.2	371.4	253.7	496.7	592.3	353.9
of which: Short-term	4 777	*−5.9*	*−49.4*	*4.9*	*68.9*	*−19.8*	*21.3*	*−22.2*	*−8.3*
Currency and deposits	4 780	−.1	39.3	161.4	19.5	47.1	−3.5	30.1	136.2
Monetary authorities	4 781	.1	.1	.2	...	.1	−.4	.1	...
General government	4 782	...	...	...	...	...	...	...	...
Banks	4 783	−.2	39.2	161.3	19.5	47.0	−3.2	30.1	136.2
Other sectors	4 784	...	...	...	...	...	...	...	...
Other liabilities	4 786	−67.2	7.9	−4.6	.6	5.5	6.2	−13.1	−1.6
Monetary authorities	4 787	...	...	...	...	...	...	...	...
of which: Short-term	4 789	...	...	...	...	...	...	...	...
General government	4 790	...	...	2.1	1.1	4.9	.5	.7	.5
of which: Short-term	4 792	...	...	...	...	...	...	...	...
Banks	4 793	−65.5	12.4	−6.5	.2	2.9	8.2	−11.4	3.6
of which: Short-term	4 795	*−65.5*	*12.4*	*−6.5*	*.2*	*2.9*	*8.2*	*−11.4*	*3.6*
Other sectors	4 796	−1.7	−4.5	−.2	−.7	−2.3	−2.5	−2.4	−5.8
of which: Short-term	4 798	...	...	...	...	...	...	...	...
E. RESERVE ASSETS	4 802	−641.3	−236.5	−587.4	−1,287.2	−157.8	81.4	−178.3	−1,284.6
Monetary gold	4 812	...	...	...	...	...	.1	−.1	−.2
Special drawing rights	4 811	...	...	−.1	...	−.2	−1.4	−2.2	−1.5
Reserve position in the Fund	4 810	...	...	...	...	−45.8	−43.8	20.0	−1.2
Foreign exchange	4 803	−641.4	−236.5	−587.4	−1,287.2	−111.8	126.4	−196.0	−1,281.7
Other claims	4 813	...	...	...	...	...	...	...	...
NET ERRORS AND OMISSIONS	4 998	**−63.7**	**−194.6**	**2.0**	**74.0**	**61.4**	**41.5**	**42.1**	**53.0**

Part 3 of the *Yearbook* contains descriptions of the methodologies, compilation practices, and sources used to compile these data.

Table 3. INTERNATIONAL INVESTMENT POSITION (End–period stocks), 1994–2001
(Millions of U.S. dollars)

	Code	1994	1995	1996	1997	1998	1999	2000	2001
ASSETS	8 995 C.	5,864.3	6,841.5	7,155.4	7,668.1	8,450.3	7,856.1	8,300.2	9,837.2
Direct investment abroad	8 505 . .	**354.0**	**489.9**	**459.5**	**459.4**	**636.2**	**626.5**	**767.6**	**949.5**
Equity capital and reinvested earnings	8 506 . .	342.4	366.2	342.9	324.7	381.5	379.1	464.0	584.2
Claims on affiliated enterprises	8 507 . .	342.4	366.2	342.9	324.7	381.5	379.1	464.0	584.2
Liabilities to affiliated enterprises	8 508 . .	. . .	. . .	. . .	. . .	. . .	. . .	. . .	. . .
Other capital	8 530 . .	11.7	123.7	116.6	134.7	254.7	247.4	303.6	365.3
Claims on affiliated enterprises	8 535 . .	265.4	351.6	346.7	402.6	431.8	412.1	467.5	497.8
Liabilities to affiliated enterprises	8 540 . .	–253.7	–227.8	–230.1	–267.9	–177.1	–164.7	–163.9	–132.5
Portfolio investment	8 602 . .	**62.1**	**106.4**	**93.9**	**55.9**	**39.7**	**130.4**	**175.4**	**251.1**
Equity securities	8 610 . .	15.0	17.1	15.8	15.4	16.7	32.4	36.8	21.6
Monetary authorities	8 611 . .	. . .	. . .	. . .	. . .	. . .	. . .	. . .	. . .
General government	8 612 . .	. . .	. . .	. . .	. . .	. . .	. . .	. . .	. . .
Banks	8 613 . .	4.0	6.2	6.4	6.0	7.3	6.2	5.3	4.3
Other sectors	8 614 . .	11.0	10.9	9.4	9.5	9.5	26.2	31.5	17.3
Debt securities	8 619 . .	47.0	89.3	78.1	40.4	22.9	98.0	138.6	229.6
Bonds and notes	8 620 . .	47.0	89.3	78.1	40.4	22.9	98.0	138.6	229.6
Monetary authorities	8 621 . .	. . .	. . .	. . .	. . .	. . .	. . .	. . .	. . .
General government	8 622 . .	. . .	. . .	. . .	. . .	. . .	. . .	. . .	. . .
Banks	8 623 . .	47.0	89.3	78.1	40.4	22.9	98.0	130.8	198.9
Other sectors	8 624 . .	. . .	. . .	. . .	. . .	. . .	. . .	7.8	30.7
Money market instruments	8 630 . .	. . .	. . .	. . .	. . .	. . .	. . .	. . .	. . .
Monetary authorities	8 631 . .	. . .	. . .	. . .	. . .	. . .	. . .	. . .	. . .
General government	8 632 . .	. . .	. . .	. . .	. . .	. . .	. . .	. . .	. . .
Banks	8 633 . .	. . .	. . .	. . .	. . .	. . .	. . .	. . .	. . .
Other sectors	8 634 . .	. . .	. . .	. . .	. . .	. . .	. . .	. . .	. . .
Financial derivatives	8 900 . .	**. . .**	**. . .**	**. . .**	**. . .**	**. . .**	**. . .**	**. . .**	**. . .**
Monetary authorities	8 901 . .	. . .	. . .	. . .	. . .	. . .	. . .	. . .	. . .
General government	8 902 . .	. . .	. . .	. . .	. . .	. . .	. . .	. . .	. . .
Banks	8 903 . .	. . .	. . .	. . .	. . .	. . .	. . .	. . .	. . .
Other sectors	8 904 . .	. . .	. . .	. . .	. . .	. . .	. . .	. . .	. . .
Other investment	8 703 . .	**3,949.2**	**4,424.3**	**4,304.6**	**3,838.1**	**4,135.9**	**3,931.1**	**4,161.1**	**4,239.4**
Trade credits	8 706 . .	1,659.3	1,809.7	1,737.9	1,880.0	2,104.9	2,002.0	2,037.1	1,816.2
General government	8 707 . .	. . .	. . .	. . .	. . .	. . .	. . .	. . .	. . .
of which: Short-term	8 709 . .	. . .	. . .	. . .	. . .	. . .	. . .	. . .	. . .
Other sectors	8 710 . .	1,659.3	1,809.7	1,737.9	1,880.0	2,104.9	2,002.0	2,037.1	1,816.2
of which: Short-term	8 712 . .	*1,475.9*	*1,630.2*	*1,569.2*	*1,724.6*	*1,924.8*	*1,802.6*	*1,844.0*	*1,662.1*
Loans	8 714 . .	28.3	43.4	45.8	104.8	138.3	145.3	179.1	174.2
Monetary authorities	8 715 . .	. . .	. . .	. . .	. . .	. . .	. . .	. . .	. . .
of which: Short-term	8 718 . .	. . .	. . .	. . .	. . .	. . .	. . .	. . .	. . .
General government	8 719 . .	. . .	. . .	. . .	. . .	. . .	. . .	. . .	. . .
of which: Short-term	8 721 . .	. . .	. . .	. . .	. . .	. . .	. . .	. . .	. . .
Banks	8 722 . .	22.9	37.4	39.1	100.0	124.9	119.0	99.8	111.6
of which: Short-term	8 724 . .	*8.0*	*13.7*	*12.6*	*42.9*	*37.9*	*45.0*	*25.7*	*23.0*
Other sectors	8 725 . .	5.4	6.0	6.7	4.8	13.4	26.3	79.4	62.6
of which: Short-term	8 727 . .	*1.4*	*1.5*	*3.2*	*1.4*	*7.9*	*4.9*	*7.5*	*6.1*
Currency and deposits	8 730 . .	1,749.1	2,090.5	2,247.1	1,537.5	1,563.7	1,465.9	1,625.6	1,910.3
Monetary authorities	8 731 . .	. . .	. . .	. . .	. . .	. . .	. . .	. . .	. . .
General government	8 732 . .	. . .	. . .	. . .	. . .	. . .	. . .	. . .	. . .
Banks	8 733 . .	1,276.9	1,561.4	1,786.7	1,022.5	1,103.1	957.2	1,155.5	1,379.1
Other sectors	8 734 . .	472.1	529.1	460.4	514.9	460.6	508.7	470.0	531.2
Other assets	8 736 . .	512.6	480.6	273.8	315.9	329.1	317.9	319.4	338.7
Monetary authorities	8 737 . .	103.3	170.1	33.3	40.7	46.3	51.8	57.9	76.0
of which: Short-term	8 739 . .	*103.3*	*170.1*	*33.3*	*40.7*	*46.3*	*51.8*	*57.8*	*63.5*
General government	8 740 . .	. . .	. . .	. . .	. . .	. . .	. . .	. . .	. . .
of which: Short-term	8 742 . .	. . .	. . .	. . .	. . .	. . .	. . .	. . .	. . .
Banks	8 743 . .	409.3	310.5	240.5	275.1	282.8	266.1	261.4	262.7
of which: Short-term	8 745 . .	*409.3*	*310.5*	*239.3*	*273.2*	*281.7*	*266.1*	*261.4*	*262.0*
Other sectors	8 746 . .	. . .	. . .	. . .	. . .	. . .	. . .	. . .	. . .
of which: Short-term	8 748 . .	. . .	. . .	. . .	. . .	. . .	. . .	. . .	. . .
Reserve assets	8 802 . .	**1,499.1**	**1,820.9**	**2,297.5**	**3,314.8**	**3,638.6**	**3,168.1**	**3,196.1**	**4,397.2**
Monetary gold	8 812 . .	.1	.1	.1	.1	.1	.1	.1	67.2
Special drawing rights	8 811 . .	.1	.1	.1	.1	.2	1.6	3.7	5.0
Reserve position in the Fund	8 810 . .	18.8	19.1	18.5	17.4	65.4	107.6	82.3	80.6
Foreign exchange	8 803 . .	1,480.1	1,801.6	2,278.7	3,297.2	3,572.9	3,058.8	3,110.0	4,244.3
Other claims	8 813 . .	. . .	. . .	. . .	. . .	. . .	. . .	. . .	. . .

Table 3 (Concluded). INTERNATIONAL INVESTMENT POSITION (End-period stocks), 1994–2001

(Millions of U.S. dollars)

	Code	1994	1995	1996	1997	1998	1999	2000	2001
LIABILITIES	8 995 D.	5,088.1	6,379.7	7,674.7	8,067.0	9,437.4	9,832.1	10,668.0	11,177.1
Direct investment in Slovenia	8 555 . .	**1,325.9**	**1,763.4**	**1,998.1**	**2,207.4**	**2,777.0**	**2,682.4**	**2,892.7**	**3,209.0**
Equity capital and reinvested earnings	8 556 . .	966.5	1,203.5	1,274.9	1,559.4	2,016.2	1,910.1	1,969.1	2,185.6
Claims on direct investors	8 557 . .	. . .	. . .	. . .	. . .	. . .	. . .	. . .	. . .
Liabilities to direct investors	8 558 . .	966.5	1,203.5	1,274.9	1,559.4	2,016.2	1,910.1	1,969.1	2,185.6
Other capital	8 580 . .	359.4	559.9	723.2	647.9	760.8	772.4	923.6	1,023.4
Claims on direct investors	8 585 . .	–116.2	–137.6	–174.7	–187.0	–110.9	–111.1	–133.2	–201.8
Liabilities to direct investors	8 590 . .	475.7	697.5	897.9	834.9	871.7	883.5	1,056.8	1,225.2
Portfolio investment	8 652 . .	**88.9**	**104.1**	**1,138.2**	**1,276.6**	**1,421.5**	**1,661.0**	**1,793.4**	**1,877.6**
Equity securities	8 660 . .	45.9	62.7	133.8	156.7	139.4	163.0	167.8	167.9
Banks	8 663 . .	17.9	27.5	30.2	15.6	18.0	14.0	24.5	10.5
Other sectors	8 664 . .	28.0	35.2	103.6	141.1	121.5	149.0	143.3	157.5
Debt securities	8 669 . .	43.0	41.4	1,004.4	1,119.9	1,282.1	1,497.9	1,625.6	1,709.7
Bonds and notes	8 670 . .	43.0	41.4	1,004.4	1,119.9	1,282.1	1,497.9	1,625.6	1,709.7
Monetary authorities	8 671 . .	. . .	. . .	. . .	. . .	. . .	. . .	. . .	. . .
General government	8 672 . .	. . .	. . .	944.2	1,062.8	1,218.4	1,434.7	1,570.2	1,686.9
Banks	8 673 . .	. . .	17.0	25.3	22.0	23.5	20.2	18.7	.2
Other sectors	8 674 . .	43.0	24.4	35.0	35.1	40.2	43.1	36.7	22.6
Money market instruments	8 680 . .	. . .	. . .	. . .	. . .	. . .	. . .	. . .	. . .
Monetary authorities	8 681 . .	. . .	. . .	. . .	. . .	. . .	. . .	. . .	. . .
General government	8 682 . .	. . .	. . .	. . .	. . .	. . .	. . .	. . .	. . .
Banks	8 683 . .	. . .	. . .	. . .	. . .	. . .	. . .	. . .	. . .
Other sectors	8 684 . .	. . .	. . .	. . .	. . .	. . .	. . .	. . .	. . .
Financial derivatives	8 905 . .	**. . .**	**. . .**	**. . .**	**. . .**	**. . .**	**. . .**	**. . .**	**. . .**
Monetary authorities	8 906 . .	. . .	. . .	. . .	. . .	. . .	. . .	. . .	. . .
General government	8 907 . .	. . .	. . .	. . .	. . .	. . .	. . .	. . .	. . .
Banks	8 908 . .	. . .	. . .	. . .	. . .	. . .	. . .	. . .	. . .
Other sectors	8 909 . .	. . .	. . .	. . .	. . .	. . .	. . .	. . .	. . .
Other investment	8 753 . .	**3,673.2**	**4,512.2**	**4,538.5**	**4,583.0**	**5,238.9**	**5,488.7**	**5,981.9**	**6,090.5**
Trade credits	8 756 . .	1,442.6	1,738.0	1,585.7	1,681.8	1,814.9	1,765.4	1,787.0	1,559.5
General government	8 757 . .	7.3	6.9	5.4	1.8	.9	.4	.1	. . .
of which: Short-term	8 759 . .	. . .	. . .	. . .	. . .	. . .	. . .	. . .	. . .
Other sectors	8 760 . .	1,435.4	1,731.1	1,580.2	1,680.0	1,814.0	1,765.0	1,787.0	1,559.5
of which: Short-term	8 762 . .	*1,357.0*	*1,653.0*	*1,484.5*	*1,584.4*	*1,678.8*	*1,663.3*	*1,706.1*	*1,490.6*
Loans	8 764 . .	1,887.3	2,382.7	2,441.9	2,452.1	2,918.3	3,221.9	3,748.8	3,964.1
Monetary authorities	8 765 . .	7.2	4.0	1.3	. . .	. . .	. . .	. . .	. . .
of which: Use of Fund credit and loans from the Fund	8 766 . .	*7.2*	*4.0*	*1.3*	. . .	. . .	. . .	. . .	. . .
of which: Short-term	8 768 . .	. . .	. . .	. . .	. . .	. . .	. . .	. . .	. . .
General government	8 769 . .	570.2	780.0	728.6	685.0	822.5	701.7	752.8	706.1
of which: Short-term	8 771 . .	. . .	. . .	. . .	. . .	. . .	. . .	. . .	. . .
Banks	8 772 . .	324.2	388.5	611.6	566.6	537.1	690.9	858.3	988.4
of which: Short-term	8 774 . .	*1.5*	*3.4*	. . .	. . .	*.5*	*7.3*	*1.9*	*.9*
Other sectors	8 775 . .	985.7	1,210.3	1,100.5	1,200.5	1,558.7	1,829.4	2,137.7	2,269.7
of which: Short-term	8 777 . .	*50.0*	*8.3*	*14.9*	*78.0*	*67.2*	*72.0*	*41.9*	*32.6*
Currency and deposits	8 780 . .	171.7	219.1	363.8	345.0	407.7	364.9	373.3	492.2
Monetary authorities	8 781 . .	.1	.2	.3	.2	.4	.3	. . .	. . .
General government	8 782 . .	. . .	. . .	. . .	. . .	. . .	. . .	. . .	. . .
Banks	8 783 . .	171.6	218.9	363.5	344.8	407.4	364.6	373.3	492.2
Other sectors	8 784 . .	. . .	. . .	. . .	. . .	. . .	. . .	. . .	. . .
Other liabilities	8 786 . .	171.6	172.4	147.1	104.1	98.0	136.5	72.8	74.7
Monetary authorities	8 787 . .	. . .	. . .	. . .	. . .	. . .	. . .	. . .	. . .
of which: Short-term	8 789 . .	. . .	. . .	. . .	. . .	. . .	. . .	. . .	. . .
General government	8 790 . .	. . .	. . .	. . .	. . .	. . .	. . .	. . .	. . .
of which: Short-term	8 792 . .	. . .	. . .	. . .	. . .	. . .	. . .	. . .	. . .
Banks	8 793 . .	65.6	78.7	70.9	69.4	73.3	122.9	66.7	69.7
of which: Short-term	8 795 . .	*.1*	*.6*	*.4*	*.4*	*.6*	*54.1*	*.4*	*5.0*
Other sectors	8 796 . .	106.0	93.7	76.3	34.8	24.7	13.6	6.1	5.0
of which: Short-term	8 798 . .	. . .	. . .	. . .	. . .	. . .	. . .	. . .	. . .
NET INTERNATIONAL INVESTMENT POSITION	8 995 . .	**776.3**	**461.9**	**–519.3**	**–398.9**	**–987.1**	**–1,976.0**	**–2,367.8**	**–1,339.9**
Conversion rates: tolars per U.S. dollar (end of period)	0 102 . .	**126.46**	**125.99**	**141.48**	**169.18**	**161.20**	**196.77**	**227.38**	**250.95**

Table 1. ANALYTIC PRESENTATION, 1994–2001

(Millions of U.S. dollars)

	Code	1994	1995	1996	1997	1998	1999	2000	2001
A. Current Account [1]	4 993 Z.	**-3.43**	**8.34**	**14.58**	**-37.91**	**8.12**	**21.48**	**. . .**	**. . .**
Goods: exports f.o.b	2 100 . .	142.16	168.30	161.51	156.45	141.83	164.57	. . .	. . .
Goods: imports f.o.b	3 100 . .	-142.22	-154.53	-150.55	-184.53	-159.90	-110.04	. . .	. . .
Balance on Goods	4 100 . .	*-.06*	*13.77*	*10.96*	*-28.09*	*-18.07*	*54.53*	. . .	. . .
Services: credit	2 200 . .	49.95	41.81	53.14	70.35	55.07	56.30	. . .	. . .
Services: debit	3 200 . .	-105.94	-76.93	-85.47	-107.18	-54.53	-87.49	. . .	. . .
Balance on Goods and Services	4 991 . .	*-56.06*	*-21.35*	*-21.37*	*-64.92*	*-17.53*	*23.34*	. . .	. . .
Income: credit	2 300 . .	1.52	1.20	2.36	2.69	2.12	5.46	. . .	. . .
Income: debit	3 300 . .	-4.44	-7.96	-9.42	-11.17	-10.01	-22.38	. . .	. . .
Balance on Goods, Services, and Income	4 992 . .	*-58.97*	*-28.10*	*-28.43*	*-73.39*	*-25.42*	*6.41*	. . .	. . .
Current transfers: credit	2 379 Z.	66.60	53.17	57.48	52.57	56.44	41.54	. . .	. . .
Current transfers: debit	3 379 . .	-11.06	-16.74	-14.47	-17.08	-22.90	-26.48	. . .	. . .
B. Capital Account [1]	4 994 Z.	**2.70**	**.65**	**-2.19**	**-1.00**	**6.65**	**9.16**	**. . .**	**. . .**
Capital account: credit	2 994 Z.	2.86	1.50	.50	.30	6.91	9.16	. . .	. . .
Capital account: debit	3 994 . .	-.15	-.85	-2.69	-1.29	-.27	. . .	. . .	. . .
Total, Groups A Plus B	4 981 . .	*-.73*	*8.98*	*12.39*	*-38.90*	*14.76*	*30.63*	. . .	. . .
C. Financial Account [1]	4 995 W.	**1.49**	**-8.31**	**-1.37**	**45.68**	**16.88**	**-33.77**	**. . .**	**. . .**
Direct investment abroad	4 505 . .	. . .	. . .	. . .	. . .	. . .	. . .	. . .	. . .
Direct investment in Solomon Islands	4 555 Z.	2.10	2.03	5.94	33.85	8.80	9.90	. . .	. . .
Portfolio investment assets	4 602 . .	. . .	. . .	. . .	. . .	. . .	. . .	. . .	. . .
Equity securities	4 610 . .	. . .	. . .	. . .	. . .	. . .	. . .	. . .	. . .
Debt securities	4 619 . .	. . .	. . .	. . .	. . .	. . .	. . .	. . .	. . .
Portfolio investment liabilities	4 652 Z.	. . .	. . .	. . .	. . .	. . .	. . .	. . .	. . .
Equity securities	4 660 . .	. . .	. . .	. . .	. . .	. . .	. . .	. . .	. . .
Debt securities	4 669 Z.	. . .	. . .	. . .	. . .	. . .	. . .	. . .	. . .
Financial derivatives	4 910 . .	. . .	. . .	. . .	. . .	. . .	. . .	. . .	. . .
Financial derivatives assets	4 900 . .	. . .	. . .	. . .	. . .	. . .	. . .	. . .	. . .
Financial derivatives liabilities	4 905 . .	. . .	. . .	. . .	. . .	. . .	. . .	. . .	. . .
Other investment assets	4 703 . .	. . .	. . .	. . .	. . .	. . .	.04	. . .	. . .
Monetary authorities	4 701 . .	. . .	. . .	. . .	. . .	. . .	. . .	. . .	. . .
General government	4 704 . .	. . .	. . .	. . .	. . .	. . .	. . .	. . .	. . .
Banks	4 705 . .	. . .	. . .	. . .	. . .	. . .	. . .	. . .	. . .
Other sectors	4 728 . .	. . .	. . .	. . .	. . .	. . .	.04	. . .	. . .
Other investment liabilities	4 753 W.	-.61	-10.34	-7.32	11.84	8.08	-43.72	. . .	. . .
Monetary authorities	4 753 WA	-1.25	.03	.08	-.62	-.37	. . .	. . .	. . .
General government	4 753 ZB	-1.34	6.20	5.72	5.17	8.60	-11.02	. . .	. . .
Banks	4 753 ZC	3.31	-2.85	2.30	-.62	-1.23	-.27	. . .	. . .
Other sectors	4 753 ZD	-1.34	-13.71	-15.42	7.91	1.08	-32.43	. . .	. . .
Total, Groups A Through C	4 983 . .	*.76*	*.68*	*11.02*	*6.78*	*31.65*	*-3.14*	. . .	. . .
D. Net Errors and Omissions	4 998 . .	**-2.80**	**-1.45**	**6.96**	**2.31**	**-14.41**	**-1.58**	**. . .**	**. . .**
Total, Groups A Through D	4 984 . .	*-2.04*	*-.77*	*17.98*	*9.09*	*17.24*	*-4.72*	. . .	. . .
E. Reserves and Related Items	4 802 A.	**2.04**	**.77**	**-17.98**	**-9.09**	**-17.24**	**4.72**	**. . .**	**. . .**
Reserve assets	4 802 . .	2.04	.77	-17.98	-9.09	-17.24	4.72	. . .	. . .
Use of Fund credit and loans	4 766 . .	. . .	. . .	. . .	. . .	. . .	. . .	. . .	. . .
Exceptional financing	4 920 . .	. . .	. . .	. . .	. . .	. . .	. . .	. . .	. . .
Conversion rates: Solomon Islands dollars per U.S. dollar	0 101 . .	**3.2914**	**3.4059**	**3.5664**	**3.7169**	**4.8156**	**4.8381**	**5.0889**	**. . .**

[1] Excludes components that have been classified in the categories of Group E.

Table 2. STANDARD PRESENTATION, 1994–2001
(Millions of U.S. dollars)

	Code	1994	1995	1996	1997	1998	1999	2000	2001
CURRENT ACCOUNT	4 993 . .	**–3.43**	**8.34**	**14.58**	**–37.91**	**8.12**	**21.48**	**. . .**	**. . .**
A. GOODS	4 100 . .	–.06	13.77	10.96	–28.09	–18.07	54.53	. . .	. . .
Credit	2 100 . .	**142.16**	**168.30**	**161.51**	**156.45**	**141.83**	**164.57**	**. . .**	**. . .**
General merchandise: exports f.o.b.	2 110 . .	142.16	168.30	161.51	156.45	141.83	164.46	. . .	. . .
Goods for processing: exports f.o.b.	2 150 . .	. . .	. . .	. . .	. . .	. . .	. . .	. . .	. . .
Repairs on goods	2 160 . .	. . .	. . .	. . .	. . .	. . .	.02	. . .	. . .
Goods procured in ports by carriers	2 170 . .	. . .	. . .	. . .	. . .	. . .	.08	. . .	. . .
Nonmonetary gold	2 180 . .	. . .	. . .	. . .	. . .	. . .	. . .	. . .	. . .
Debit	3 100 . .	**–142.22**	**–154.53**	**–150.55**	**–184.53**	**–159.90**	**–110.04**	**. . .**	**. . .**
General merchandise: imports f.o.b.	3 110 . .	–142.22	–154.53	–150.55	–184.53	–159.90	–110.04	. . .	. . .
Goods for processing: imports f.o.b.	3 150 . .	. . .	. . .	. . .	. . .	. . .	. . .	. . .	. . .
Repairs on goods	3 160 . .	. . .	. . .	. . .	. . .	. . .	. . .	. . .	. . .
Goods procured in ports by carriers	3 170 . .	. . .	. . .	. . .	. . .	. . .	. . .	. . .	. . .
Nonmonetary gold	3 180 . .	. . .	. . .	. . .	. . .	. . .	. . .	. . .	. . .
B. SERVICES	4 200 . .	–56.00	–35.12	–32.33	–36.83	.54	–31.19	. . .	. . .
Total credit	2 200 . .	*49.95*	*41.81*	*53.14*	*70.35*	*55.07*	*56.30*	. . .	. . .
Total debit	3 200 . .	*–105.94*	*–76.93*	*–85.47*	*–107.18*	*–54.53*	*–87.49*	. . .	. . .
Transportation services, credit	2 205 . .	**2.55**	**1.38**	**2.05**	**2.58**	**1.74**	**4.82**	**. . .**	**. . .**
Passenger	2 850 . .	*2.55*	*1.38*	*2.05*	*2.58*	*.54*	*3.97*	. . .	. . .
Freight	2 851 . .	. . .	. . .	. . .	. . .	*1.06*	*.27*	. . .	. . .
Other	2 852 . .	. . .	. . .	. . .	. . .	*.15*	*.58*	. . .	. . .
Sea transport, passenger	2 207 . .	. . .	. . .	. . .	. . .	. . .	.02	. . .	. . .
Sea transport, freight	2 208 . .	. . .	. . .	. . .	. . .	.73	.17	. . .	. . .
Sea transport, other	2 209 . .	. . .	. . .	. . .	. . .	. . .	.48	. . .	. . .
Air transport, passenger	2 211 . .	. . .	. . .	. . .	. . .	.54	3.95	. . .	. . .
Air transport, freight	2 212 . .	. . .	. . .	. . .	. . .	.33	.10	. . .	. . .
Air transport, other	2 213 . .	. . .	. . .	. . .	. . .	.15	.10	. . .	. . .
Other transport, passenger	2 215 . .	. . .	. . .	. . .	. . .	. . .	. . .	. . .	. . .
Other transport, freight	2 216 . .	. . .	. . .	. . .	. . .	. . .	. . .	. . .	. . .
Other transport, other	2 217 . .	. . .	. . .	. . .	. . .	. . .	. . .	. . .	. . .
Transportation services, debit	3 205 . .	**–2.80**	**–3.90**	**–3.28**	**–5.78**	**–8.53**	**–54.59**	**. . .**	**. . .**
Passenger	3 850 . .	*–2.80*	*–3.90*	*–3.28*	*–5.78*	*–4.38*	*–4.22*	. . .	. . .
Freight	3 851 . .	. . .	. . .	. . .	. . .	*–4.15*	*–49.67*	. . .	. . .
Other	3 852 . .	. . .	. . .	. . .	. . .	. . .	*–.70*	. . .	. . .
Sea transport, passenger	3 207 . .	. . .	. . .	. . .	. . .	. . .	–.02	. . .	. . .
Sea transport, freight	3 208 . .	. . .	. . .	. . .	. . .	–3.45	–41.17	. . .	. . .
Sea transport, other	3 209 . .	. . .	. . .	. . .	. . .	. . .	–.33	. . .	. . .
Air transport, passenger	3 211 . .	. . .	. . .	. . .	. . .	–4.38	–4.20	. . .	. . .
Air transport, freight	3 212 . .	. . .	. . .	. . .	. . .	–.71	–8.49	. . .	. . .
Air transport, other	3 213 . .	. . .	. . .	. . .	. . .	. . .	–.37	. . .	. . .
Other transport, passenger	3 215 . .	. . .	. . .	. . .	. . .	. . .	. . .	. . .	. . .
Other transport, freight	3 216 . .	. . .	. . .	. . .	. . .	. . .	. . .	. . .	. . .
Other transport, other	3 217 . .	. . .	. . .	. . .	. . .	. . .	. . .	. . .	. . .
Travel, credit	2 236 . .	**16.89**	**15.71**	**13.85**	**7.08**	**6.62**	**5.68**	**. . .**	**. . .**
Business travel	2 237 . .	. . .	. . .	. . .	. . .	2.55	.35	. . .	. . .
Personal travel	2 240 . .	. . .	. . .	. . .	. . .	4.07	5.33	. . .	. . .
Travel, debit	3 236 . .	**–12.82**	**–13.48**	**–15.20**	**–8.99**	**–5.79**	**–7.17**	**. . .**	**. . .**
Business travel	3 237 . .	. . .	. . .	. . .	. . .	–1.35	–2.73	. . .	. . .
Personal travel	3 240 . .	. . .	. . .	. . .	. . .	–4.44	–4.44	. . .	. . .
Other services, credit	2 200 BA	**30.50**	**24.72**	**37.24**	**60.70**	**46.70**	**45.80**	**. . .**	**. . .**
Communications	2 245 . .	. . .	. . .	. . .	. . .	2.37	2.27	. . .	. . .
Construction	2 249 . .	. . .	. . .	. . .	. . .	.50	.31	. . .	. . .
Insurance	2 253 . .	.18	.09	.39	.05	.12	.04	. . .	. . .
Financial	2 260 . .	. . .	. . .	. . .	. . .	11.34	19.28	. . .	. . .
Computer and information	2 262 . .	. . .	. . .	. . .	. . .	.06	.02	. . .	. . .
Royalties and licence fees	2 266 . .	. . .	. . .	. . .	. . .	.10	.06	. . .	. . .
Other business services	2 268 . .	22.54	18.17	30.23	54.51	28.49	17.96	. . .	. . .
Personal, cultural, and recreational	2 287 . .	. . .	. . .	. . .	. . .	.64	.29	. . .	. . .
Government, n.i.e.	2 291 . .	7.78	6.46	6.62	6.13	3.07	5.56	. . .	. . .
Other services, debit	3 200 BA	**–90.33**	**–59.54**	**–66.99**	**–92.41**	**–40.20**	**–25.73**	**. . .**	**. . .**
Communications	3 245 . .	. . .	. . .	. . .	. . .	–4.65	–5.39	. . .	. . .
Construction	3 249 . .	. . .	. . .	. . .	. . .	–.25	–.06	. . .	. . .
Insurance	3 253 . .	–2.37	–2.26	–1.77	–2.72	–1.12	5.06	. . .	. . .
Financial	3 260 . .	. . .	. . .	. . .	. . .	–8.66	–5.19	. . .	. . .
Computer and information	3 262 . .	. . .	. . .	. . .	. . .	–2.16	–1.63	. . .	. . .
Royalties and licence fees	3 266 . .	–.06	–.12	–.08	–.05	–.10	–.06	. . .	. . .
Other business services	3 268 . .	–86.26	–56.17	–59.19	–85.23	–22.30	–16.76	. . .	. . .
Personal, cultural, and recreational	3 287 . .	. . .	. . .	. . .	. . .	. . .	–.21	. . .	. . .
Government, n.i.e.	3 291 . .	–1.64	–1.00	–5.94	–4.41	–.96	–1.49	. . .	. . .

Table 2 (Continued). STANDARD PRESENTATION, 1994–2001

(Millions of U.S. dollars)

	Code		1994	1995	1996	1997	1998	1999	2000	2001
C. INCOME	4 300	. .	–2.92	–6.75	–7.07	–8.47	–7.89	–16.93	. . .	. . .
Total credit	2 300	. .	*1.52*	*1.20*	*2.36*	*2.69*	*2.12*	*5.46*	. . .	. . .
Total debit	3 300	. .	*–4.44*	*–7.96*	*–9.42*	*–11.17*	*–10.01*	*–22.38*	. . .	. . .
Compensation of employees, credit	2 310	. .	**. . .**	**. . .**	**. . .**	**. . .**	**. . .**	**2.36**	**. . .**	**. . .**
Compensation of employees, debit	3 310	. .	**. . .**	**. . .**	**. . .**	**. . .**	**. . .**	**–5.73**	**. . .**	**. . .**
Investment income, credit	2 320	. .	**1.52**	**1.20**	**2.36**	**2.69**	**2.12**	**3.10**	**. . .**	**. . .**
Direct investment income	2 330	. .	.49	.23	.64	.30	.39	.33	. . .	. . .
Dividends and distributed branch profits	2 332	. .	.49	.23	.64	.30	.39	. . .	. . .	. . .
Reinvested earnings and undistributed branch profits	2 333	. .	. . .	. . .	. . .	. . .	. . .	. . .	. . .	. . .
Income on debt (interest)	2 334	. .	. . .	. . .	. . .	. . .	. . .	.33	. . .	. . .
Portfolio investment income	2 339	. .	. . .	. . .	. . .	. . .	. . .	. . .	. . .	. . .
Income on equity	2 340	. .	. . .	. . .	. . .	. . .	. . .	. . .	. . .	. . .
Income on bonds and notes	2 350	. .	. . .	. . .	. . .	. . .	. . .	. . .	. . .	. . .
Income on money market instruments	2 360	. .	. . .	. . .	. . .	. . .	. . .	. . .	. . .	. . .
Other investment income	2 370	. .	1.03	.97	1.71	2.39	1.72	2.77	. . .	. . .
Investment income, debit	3 320	. .	**–4.44**	**–7.96**	**–9.42**	**–11.17**	**–10.01**	**–16.66**	**. . .**	**. . .**
Direct investment income	3 330	. .	–3.49	–6.81	–7.51	–8.58	–7.81	–10.60	. . .	. . .
Dividends and distributed branch profits	3 332	. .	–3.49	–6.81	–7.51	–8.58	–2.70	–3.22	. . .	. . .
Reinvested earnings and undistributed branch profits	3 333	. .	. . .	. . .	. . .	. . .	–5.11	–4.94	. . .	. . .
Income on debt (interest)	3 334	. .	. . .	. . .	. . .	. . .	. . .	–2.44	. . .	. . .
Portfolio investment income	3 339	. .	. . .	. . .	. . .	. . .	. . .	. . .	. . .	. . .
Income on equity	3 340	. .	. . .	. . .	. . .	. . .	. . .	. . .	. . .	. . .
Income on bonds and notes	3 350	. .	. . .	. . .	. . .	. . .	. . .	. . .	. . .	. . .
Income on money market instruments	3 360	. .	. . .	. . .	. . .	. . .	. . .	. . .	. . .	. . .
Other investment income	3 370	. .	–.94	–1.15	–1.91	–2.58	–2.20	–6.06	. . .	. . .
D. CURRENT TRANSFERS	4 379	. .	55.54	36.44	43.01	35.49	33.54	15.07	. . .	. . .
Credit	2 379	. .	**66.60**	**53.17**	**57.48**	**52.57**	**56.44**	**41.54**	**. . .**	**. . .**
General government	2 380	. .	54.35	35.23	38.98	31.15	31.04	21.31	. . .	. . .
Other sectors	2 390	. .	12.24	17.94	18.51	21.42	25.40	20.24	. . .	. . .
Workers' remittances	2 391	. .	. . .	. . .	. . .	. . .	. . .	. . .	. . .	. . .
Other current transfers	2 392	. .	12.24	17.94	18.51	21.42	25.40	20.24	. . .	. . .
Debit	3 379	. .	**–11.06**	**–16.74**	**–14.47**	**–17.08**	**–22.90**	**–26.48**	**. . .**	**. . .**
General government	3 380	. .	. . .	. . .	. . .	. . .	. . .	–3.58	. . .	. . .
Other sectors	3 390	. .	–11.06	–16.74	–14.47	–17.08	–22.90	–22.90	. . .	. . .
Workers' remittances	3 391	. .	–5.77	–8.07	–8.47	–2.85	–2.49	. . .	. . .	. . .
Other current transfers	3 392	. .	–5.29	–8.66	–6.00	–14.23	–20.41	–22.90	. . .	. . .
CAPITAL AND FINANCIAL ACCOUNT	4 996	. .	**6.23**	**–6.89**	**–21.54**	**35.60**	**6.29**	**–19.90**	**. . .**	**. . .**
CAPITAL ACCOUNT	4 994	. .	**2.70**	**.65**	**–2.19**	**–1.00**	**6.65**	**9.16**	**. . .**	**. . .**
Total credit	2 994	. .	*2.86*	*1.50*	*.50*	*.30*	*6.91*	*9.16*	. . .	. . .
Total debit	3 994	. .	*–.15*	*–.85*	*–2.69*	*–1.29*	*–.27*	. . .	. . .	. . .
Capital transfers, credit	2 400	. .	**2.86**	**1.50**	**.50**	**.30**	**6.91**	**9.16**	**. . .**	**. . .**
General government	2 401	. .	2.86	1.50	.50	.30	6.91	8.39	. . .	. . .
Debt forgiveness	2 402	. .	. . .	. . .	. . .	. . .	. . .	. . .	. . .	. . .
Other capital transfers	2 410	. .	. . .	. . .	. . .	. . .	. . .	8.39	. . .	. . .
Other sectors	2 430	. .	. . .	. . .	. . .	. . .	. . .	.76	. . .	. . .
Migrants' transfers	2 431	. .	. . .	. . .	. . .	. . .	. . .	. . .	. . .	. . .
Debt forgiveness	2 432	. .	. . .	. . .	. . .	. . .	. . .	. . .	. . .	. . .
Other capital transfers	2 440	. .	. . .	. . .	. . .	. . .	. . .	.76	. . .	. . .
Capital transfers, debit	3 400	. .	**–.15**	**–.85**	**–2.69**	**–1.29**	**–.27**	**. . .**	**. . .**	**. . .**
General government	3 401	. .	. . .	. . .	. . .	. . .	. . .	. . .	. . .	. . .
Debt forgiveness	3 402	. .	. . .	. . .	. . .	. . .	. . .	. . .	. . .	. . .
Other capital transfers	3 410	. .	. . .	. . .	. . .	. . .	. . .	. . .	. . .	. . .
Other sectors	3 430	. .	–.15	–.85	–2.69	–1.29	–.27	. . .	. . .	. . .
Migrants' transfers	3 431	. .	–.15	–.85	–2.69	–1.29	–.27	. . .	. . .	. . .
Debt forgiveness	3 432	. .	. . .	. . .	. . .	. . .	. . .	. . .	. . .	. . .
Other capital transfers	3 440	. .	. . .	. . .	. . .	. . .	. . .	. . .	. . .	. . .
Nonproduced nonfinancial assets, credit	2 480	. .	**. . .**	**. . .**	**. . .**	**. . .**	**. . .**	**. . .**	**. . .**	**. . .**
Nonproduced nonfinancial assets, debit	3 480	. .	**. . .**	**. . .**	**. . .**	**. . .**	**. . .**	**. . .**	**. . .**	**. . .**

Table 2 (Continued). STANDARD PRESENTATION, 1994–2001
(Millions of U.S. dollars)

	Code	1994	1995	1996	1997	1998	1999	2000	2001
FINANCIAL ACCOUNT	4 995 . .	**3.53**	**-7.54**	**-19.35**	**36.59**	**-.35**	**-29.05**	**. . .**	**. . .**
A. DIRECT INVESTMENT	4 500 . .	2.10	2.03	5.94	33.85	8.80	9.90	. . .	. . .
Direct investment abroad	4 505 . .	**. . .**	**. . .**	**. . .**	**. . .**	**. . .**	**. . .**	**. . .**	**. . .**
Equity capital	4 510 . .	. . .	. . .	. . .	. . .	. . .	. . .	. . .	. . .
Claims on affiliated enterprises	4 515 . .	. . .	. . .	. . .	. . .	. . .	. . .	. . .	. . .
Liabilities to affiliated enterprises	4 520 . .	. . .	. . .	. . .	. . .	. . .	. . .	. . .	. . .
Reinvested earnings	4 525 . .	. . .	. . .	. . .	. . .	. . .	. . .	. . .	. . .
Other capital	4 530 . .	. . .	. . .	. . .	. . .	. . .	. . .	. . .	. . .
Claims on affiliated enterprises	4 535 . .	. . .	. . .	. . .	. . .	. . .	. . .	. . .	. . .
Liabilities to affiliated enterprises	4 540 . .	. . .	. . .	. . .	. . .	. . .	. . .	. . .	. . .
Direct investment in Solomon Islands	4 555 . .	**2.10**	**2.03**	**5.94**	**33.85**	**8.80**	**9.90**	**. . .**	**. . .**
Equity capital	4 560 . .	.52	1.35	.45	34.54	4.92	-1.57	. . .	. . .
Claims on direct investors	4 565 . .	. . .	. . .	. . .	. . .	. . .	. . .	. . .	. . .
Liabilities to direct investors	4 570 . .	. . .	. . .	. . .	. . .	. . .	-1.57	. . .	. . .
Reinvested earnings	4 575 . .	. . .	. . .	. . .	. . .	5.11	4.94	. . .	. . .
Other capital	4 580 . .	1.58	.68	5.50	-.70	-1.23	6.53	. . .	. . .
Claims on direct investors	4 585 . .	. . .	. . .	. . .	. . .	. . .	. . .	. . .	. . .
Liabilities to direct investors	4 590 . .	. . .	. . .	. . .	. . .	. . .	6.53	. . .	. . .
B. PORTFOLIO INVESTMENT	4 600 . .	. . .	. . .	. . .	. . .	. . .	. . .	. . .	. . .
Assets	4 602 . .	**. . .**	**. . .**	**. . .**	**. . .**	**. . .**	**. . .**	**. . .**	**. . .**
Equity securities	4 610 . .	. . .	. . .	. . .	. . .	. . .	. . .	. . .	. . .
Monetary authorities	4 611 . .	. . .	. . .	. . .	. . .	. . .	. . .	. . .	. . .
General government	4 612 . .	. . .	. . .	. . .	. . .	. . .	. . .	. . .	. . .
Banks	4 613 . .	. . .	. . .	. . .	. . .	. . .	. . .	. . .	. . .
Other sectors	4 614 . .	. . .	. . .	. . .	. . .	. . .	. . .	. . .	. . .
Debt securities	4 619 . .	. . .	. . .	. . .	. . .	. . .	. . .	. . .	. . .
Bonds and notes	4 620 . .	. . .	. . .	. . .	. . .	. . .	. . .	. . .	. . .
Monetary authorities	4 621 . .	. . .	. . .	. . .	. . .	. . .	. . .	. . .	. . .
General government	4 622 . .	. . .	. . .	. . .	. . .	. . .	. . .	. . .	. . .
Banks	4 623 . .	. . .	. . .	. . .	. . .	. . .	. . .	. . .	. . .
Other sectors	4 624 . .	. . .	. . .	. . .	. . .	. . .	. . .	. . .	. . .
Money market instruments	4 630 . .	. . .	. . .	. . .	. . .	. . .	. . .	. . .	. . .
Monetary authorities	4 631 . .	. . .	. . .	. . .	. . .	. . .	. . .	. . .	. . .
General government	4 632 . .	. . .	. . .	. . .	. . .	. . .	. . .	. . .	. . .
Banks	4 633 . .	. . .	. . .	. . .	. . .	. . .	. . .	. . .	. . .
Other sectors	4 634 . .	. . .	. . .	. . .	. . .	. . .	. . .	. . .	. . .
Liabilities	4 652 . .	**. . .**	**. . .**	**. . .**	**. . .**	**. . .**	**. . .**	**. . .**	**. . .**
Equity securities	4 660 . .	. . .	. . .	. . .	. . .	. . .	. . .	. . .	. . .
Banks	4 663 . .	. . .	. . .	. . .	. . .	. . .	. . .	. . .	. . .
Other sectors	4 664 . .	. . .	. . .	. . .	. . .	. . .	. . .	. . .	. . .
Debt securities	4 669 . .	. . .	. . .	. . .	. . .	. . .	. . .	. . .	. . .
Bonds and notes	4 670 . .	. . .	. . .	. . .	. . .	. . .	. . .	. . .	. . .
Monetary authorities	4 671 . .	. . .	. . .	. . .	. . .	. . .	. . .	. . .	. . .
General government	4 672 . .	. . .	. . .	. . .	. . .	. . .	. . .	. . .	. . .
Banks	4 673 . .	. . .	. . .	. . .	. . .	. . .	. . .	. . .	. . .
Other sectors	4 674 . .	. . .	. . .	. . .	. . .	. . .	. . .	. . .	. . .
Money market instruments	4 680 . .	. . .	. . .	. . .	. . .	. . .	. . .	. . .	. . .
Monetary authorities	4 681 . .	. . .	. . .	. . .	. . .	. . .	. . .	. . .	. . .
General government	4 682 . .	. . .	. . .	. . .	. . .	. . .	. . .	. . .	. . .
Banks	4 683 . .	. . .	. . .	. . .	. . .	. . .	. . .	. . .	. . .
Other sectors	4 684 . .	. . .	. . .	. . .	. . .	. . .	. . .	. . .	. . .
C. FINANCIAL DERIVATIVES	4 910 . .	. . .	. . .	. . .	. . .	. . .	. . .	. . .	. . .
Monetary authorities	4 911 . .	. . .	. . .	. . .	. . .	. . .	. . .	. . .	. . .
General government	4 912 . .	. . .	. . .	. . .	. . .	. . .	. . .	. . .	. . .
Banks	4 913 . .	. . .	. . .	. . .	. . .	. . .	. . .	. . .	. . .
Other sectors	4 914 . .	. . .	. . .	. . .	. . .	. . .	. . .	. . .	. . .
Assets	4 900 . .	**. . .**	**. . .**	**. . .**	**. . .**	**. . .**	**. . .**	**. . .**	**. . .**
Monetary authorities	4 901 . .	. . .	. . .	. . .	. . .	. . .	. . .	. . .	. . .
General government	4 902 . .	. . .	. . .	. . .	. . .	. . .	. . .	. . .	. . .
Banks	4 903 . .	. . .	. . .	. . .	. . .	. . .	. . .	. . .	. . .
Other sectors	4 904 . .	. . .	. . .	. . .	. . .	. . .	. . .	. . .	. . .
Liabilities	4 905 . .	**. . .**	**. . .**	**. . .**	**. . .**	**. . .**	**. . .**	**. . .**	**. . .**
Monetary authorities	4 906 . .	. . .	. . .	. . .	. . .	. . .	. . .	. . .	. . .
General government	4 907 . .	. . .	. . .	. . .	. . .	. . .	. . .	. . .	. . .
Banks	4 908 . .	. . .	. . .	. . .	. . .	. . .	. . .	. . .	. . .
Other sectors	4 909 . .	. . .	. . .	. . .	. . .	. . .	. . .	. . .	. . .

Table 2 (Concluded). STANDARD PRESENTATION, 1994–2001
(Millions of U.S. dollars)

	Code	1994	1995	1996	1997	1998	1999	2000	2001
D. OTHER INVESTMENT	4 700 . .	–.61	–10.34	–7.32	11.84	8.08	–43.67	...	...
Assets	4 703 . .	**...**	**...**	**...**	**...**	**...**	**.04**	**...**	**...**
Trade credits	4 706 . .	...	...	...	...	...	...	...	...
General government	4 707 . .	...	...	...	...	...	...	...	...
of which: Short-term	4 709 . .	...	...	...	...	...	...	...	...
Other sectors	4 710 . .	...	...	...	...	...	...	...	...
of which: Short-term	4 712 . .	...	...	...	...	...	...	...	...
Loans	4 714 . .	...	...	...	...	...	...	...	...
Monetary authorities	4 715 . .	...	...	...	...	...	...	...	...
of which: Short-term	4 718 . .	...	...	...	...	...	...	...	...
General government	4 719 . .	...	...	...	...	...	...	...	...
of which: Short-term	4 721 . .	...	...	...	...	...	...	...	...
Banks	4 722 . .	...	...	...	...	...	...	...	...
of which: Short-term	4 724 . .	...	...	...	...	...	...	...	...
Other sectors	4 725 . .	...	...	...	...	...	...	...	...
of which: Short-term	4 727 . .	...	...	...	...	...	...	...	...
Currency and deposits	4 730 . .	...	...	...	...	...	...	...	...
Monetary authorities	4 731 . .	...	...	...	...	...	...	...	...
General government	4 732 . .	...	...	...	...	...	...	...	...
Banks	4 733 . .	...	...	...	...	...	...	...	...
Other sectors	4 734 . .	...	...	...	...	...	...	...	...
Other assets	4 736 . .	...	...	...	...	...	.04	...	...
Monetary authorities	4 737 . .	...	...	...	...	...	...	...	...
of which: Short-term	4 739 . .	...	...	...	...	...	...	...	...
General government	4 740 . .	...	...	...	...	...	...	...	...
of which: Short-term	4 742 . .	...	...	...	...	...	...	...	...
Banks	4 743 . .	...	...	...	...	...	...	...	...
of which: Short-term	4 745 . .	...	...	...	...	...	...	...	...
Other sectors	4 746 . .	...	...	...	...	...	.04	...	...
of which: Short-term	4 748 . .	...	...	...	...	...	...	...	...
Liabilities	4 753 . .	**–.61**	**–10.34**	**–7.32**	**11.84**	**8.08**	**–43.72**	**...**	**...**
Trade credits	4 756 . .	...	...	...	...	...	–18.85	...	...
General government	4 757 . .	...	...	...	...	...	7.23	...	...
of which: Short-term	4 759 . .	...	...	...	...	...	*7.23*	...	...
Other sectors	4 760 . .	...	...	...	...	...	–26.08	...	...
of which: Short-term	4 762 . .	...	...	...	...	...	...	...	...
Loans	4 764 . .	–2.67	–7.52	–9.70	13.08	9.68	–24.55	...	...
Monetary authorities	4 765 . .	...	...	...	...	...	...	...	...
of which: Use of Fund credit and loans from the Fund	4 766 . .	...	...	...	...	...	...	...	...
of which: Short-term	4 768 . .	...	...	...	...	...	...	...	...
General government	4 769 . .	–1.34	6.20	5.72	5.17	8.60	–18.25	...	...
of which: Short-term	4 771 . .	...	*2.73*	*7.82*	*10.25*	*–3.57*	*–2.87*	...	...
Banks	4 772 . .	...	...	...	...	...	.04	...	...
of which: Short-term	4 774 . .	...	...	...	...	...	*.04*	...	...
Other sectors	4 775 . .	–1.34	–13.71	–15.42	7.91	1.08	–6.35	...	...
of which: Short-term	4 777 . .	...	...	...	...	...	*–.06*	...	...
Currency and deposits	4 780 . .	2.07	–2.82	2.38	–1.24	–1.60	.33	...	...
Monetary authorities	4 781 . .	–1.25	.03	.08	–.62	–.37	...	...	...
General government	4 782 . .	...	...	...	...	...	...	...	...
Banks	4 783 . .	3.31	–2.85	2.30	–.62	–1.23	.33	...	...
Other sectors	4 784 . .	...	...	...	...	...	...	...	...
Other liabilities	4 786 . .	...	...	...	...	...	–.64	...	...
Monetary authorities	4 787 . .	...	...	...	...	...	...	...	...
of which: Short-term	4 789 . .	...	...	...	...	...	...	...	...
General government	4 790 . .	...	...	...	...	...	...	...	...
of which: Short-term	4 792 . .	...	...	...	...	...	...	...	...
Banks	4 793 . .	...	...	...	...	...	–.64	...	...
of which: Short-term	4 795 . .	...	...	...	...	...	*–.64*	...	...
Other sectors	4 796 . .	...	...	...	...	...	...	...	...
of which: Short-term	4 798 . .	...	...	...	...	...	...	...	...
E. RESERVE ASSETS	4 802 . .	2.04	.77	–17.98	–9.09	–17.24	4.72	...	...
Monetary gold	4 812 . .	...	...	...	...	...	...	...	...
Special drawing rights	4 811 . .	.04	.01	...	.01	...	–.01	...	...
Reserve position in the Fund	4 810 . .	...	...	...	...	...	...	...	...
Foreign exchange	4 803 . .	2.01	.76	–17.97	–9.09	–17.24	4.59	...	...
Other claims	4 813 . .	...	...	...	...	...	.14	...	...
NET ERRORS AND OMISSIONS	4 998 . .	**–2.80**	**–1.45**	**6.96**	**2.31**	**–14.41**	**–1.58**	**...**	**...**

Part 3 of the *Yearbook* contains descriptions of the methodologies, compilation practices, and sources used to compile these data.

Table 1. ANALYTIC PRESENTATION, 1994–2001
(Millions of U.S. dollars)

	Code	1994	1995	1996	1997	1998	1999	2000	2001
A. Current Account [1]	4 993 Z.	**112**	**–2,205**	**–1,880**	**–2,273**	**–2,157**	**–640**	**–575**	**–166**
Goods: exports f.o.b.	2 100 . .	26,333	30,071	30,263	31,171	29,264	28,627	31,636	30,642
Goods: imports f.o.b.	3 100 . .	–21,852	–27,404	–27,568	–28,848	–27,208	–24,554	–27,320	–25,677
Balance on Goods	4 100 . .	*4,481*	*2,667*	*2,695*	*2,324*	*2,056*	*4,073*	*4,316*	*4,966*
Services: credit	2 200 . .	3,749	4,618	5,028	5,334	5,281	5,074	4,895	4,662
Services: debit	3 200 . .	–5,087	–5,969	–5,733	–6,002	–5,595	–5,707	–5,719	–5,208
Balance on Goods and Services	4 991 . .	*3,143*	*1,315*	*1,990*	*1,655*	*1,742*	*3,440*	*3,492*	*4,419*
Income: credit	2 300 . .	972	1,136	1,077	1,298	1,307	1,568	2,261	2,168
Income: debit	3 300 . .	–3,394	–4,011	–4,194	–4,502	–4,463	–4,721	–5,401	–6,014
Balance on Goods, Services, and Income	4 992 . .	*721*	*–1,560*	*–1,127*	*–1,549*	*–1,414*	*287*	*351*	*573*
Current transfers: credit	2 379 Z.	143	196	54	138	60	66	106	126
Current transfers: debit	3 379 . .	–752	–841	–807	–862	–804	–993	–1,033	–865
B. Capital Account [1]	4 994 Z.	**–67**	**–40**	**–47**	**–193**	**–56**	**–62**	**–52**	**–32**
Capital account: credit	2 994 Z.	20	22	25	29	24	20	19	15
Capital account: debit	3 994 . .	–87	–62	–72	–222	–80	–82	–71	–47
Total, Groups A Plus B	4 981 . .	*45*	*–2,245*	*–1,927*	*–2,466*	*–2,213*	*–701*	*–627*	*–197*
C. Financial Account [1]	4 995 W.	**1,087**	**4,003**	**3,018**	**8,131**	**4,852**	**5,305**	**99**	**501**
Direct investment abroad	4 505 . .	–1,261	–2,494	–1,048	–2,324	–1,634	–1,584	–277	3,686
Direct investment in South Africa	4 555 Z.	374	1,248	816	3,811	550	1,503	969	7,162
Portfolio investment assets	4 602 . .	–82	–447	–2,000	–4,587	–5,575	–5,113	–3,672	–5,331
Equity securities	4 610 . .	–29	–387	–1,698	–3,891	–4,768	–4,050	–3,019	–4,864
Debt securities	4 619 . .	–53	–61	–302	–696	–807	–1,064	–652	–467
Portfolio investment liabilities	4 652 Z.	2,918	2,937	4,446	11,274	9,869	13,799	1,807	–2,971
Equity securities	4 660 . .	88	2,914	2,318	5,473	8,632	9,001	4,169	–962
Debt securities	4 669 Z.	2,830	23	2,127	5,802	1,237	4,798	–2,361	–2,009
Financial derivatives	4 910 . .	. . .	. . .	. . .	53	97	–122	–142	. . .
Financial derivatives assets	4 900 . .	. . .	. . .	. . .	. . .	. . .	–46	–144	. . .
Financial derivatives liabilities	4 905 . .	. . .	. . .	. . .	53	97	–76	2	. . .
Other investment assets	4 703 . .	–298	–525	–599	–1,983	–694	–1,644	59	–1,432
Monetary authorities	4 701 . .	44	75	12	206	. . .	6	. . .	. . .
General government	4 704 . .	–1	1	. . .	2	1	. . .	. . .	–407
Banks	4 705 . .	–85	62	–127	–122	–135	–61	–244	–334
Other sectors	4 728 . .	–255	–663	–484	–2,069	–560	–1,589	303	–691
Other investment liabilities	4 753 W.	–565	3,285	1,403	1,887	2,237	–1,535	1,354	–614
Monetary authorities	4 753 WA	–105	–1,414	–89	2,186	1,172	105	–410	1,582
General government	4 753 ZB	–467	118	469	–120	–73	–270	6	134
Banks	4 753 ZC	360	2,945	1,044	–283	784	–945	1,196	–787
Other sectors	4 753 ZD	–353	1,636	–21	105	355	–425	563	–1,543
Total, Groups A Through C	4 983 . .	*1,132*	*1,758*	*1,091*	*5,665*	*2,639*	*4,604*	*–528*	*303*
D. Net Errors and Omissions	4 998 . .	**–449**	**–852**	**–2,363**	**–1,070**	**–1,719**	**–389**	**928**	**1,855**
Total, Groups A Through D	4 984 . .	*683*	*907*	*–1,272*	*4,595*	*920*	*4,215*	*400*	*2,158*
E. Reserves and Related Items	4 802 A.	**–683**	**–907**	**1,272**	**–4,595**	**–920**	**–4,215**	**–400**	**–2,158**
Reserve assets	4 802 . .	–683	–907	1,272	–4,174	–502	–4,215	–400	–2,158
Use of Fund credit and loans	4 766 . .	. . .	. . .	. . .	–421	–418	. . .	. . .	. . .
Exceptional financing	4 920 . .	. . .	. . .	. . .	. . .	. . .	. . .	. . .	. . .
Conversion rates: rand per U.S. dollar	0 101 . .	**3.5508**	**3.6271**	**4.2993**	**4.6080**	**5.5283**	**6.1095**	**6.9398**	**8.6092**

[1] Excludes components that have been classified in the categories of Group E.

Table 2. STANDARD PRESENTATION, 1994–2001

(Millions of U.S. dollars)

	Code	1994	1995	1996	1997	1998	1999	2000	2001
CURRENT ACCOUNT	4 993 . .	**112**	**–2,205**	**–1,880**	**–2,273**	**–2,157**	**–640**	**–575**	**–166**
A. GOODS	4 100 . .	4,481	2,667	2,695	2,324	2,056	4,073	4,316	4,966
Credit	2 100 . .	**26,333**	**30,071**	**30,263**	**31,171**	**29,264**	**28,627**	**31,636**	**30,642**
General merchandise: exports f.o.b.	2 110 . .	19,319	23,695	23,845	25,053	24,229	24,296	27,200	26,682
Goods for processing: exports f.o.b.	2 150 . .	. . .	. . .	. . .	. . .	. . .	. . .	. . .	. . .
Repairs on goods	2 160 . .	. . .	. . .	. . .	. . .	. . .	. . .	. . .	. . .
Goods procured in ports by carriers	2 170 . .	344	161	280	512	332	357	552	548
Nonmonetary gold	2 180 . .	6,669	6,215	6,139	5,607	4,703	3,974	3,884	3,413
Debit	3 100 . .	**–21,852**	**–27,404**	**–27,568**	**–28,848**	**–27,208**	**–24,554**	**–27,320**	**–25,677**
General merchandise: imports f.o.b.	3 110 . .	–21,756	–27,298	–27,468	–28,746	–27,117	–24,460	–27,213	–25,578
Goods for processing: imports f.o.b.	3 150 . .	. . .	. . .	. . .	. . .	. . .	. . .	. . .	. . .
Repairs on goods	3 160 . .	–10	–12	–12	–10	–11	–16	–23	–24
Goods procured in ports by carriers	3 170 . .	–86	–95	–88	–92	–80	–78	–84	–74
Nonmonetary gold	3 180 . .	. . .	. . .	. . .	. . .	. . .	. . .	. . .	. . .
B. SERVICES	4 200 . .	–1,338	–1,351	–705	–669	–314	–633	–824	–547
Total credit	2 200 . .	*3,749*	*4,618*	*5,028*	*5,334*	*5,281*	*5,074*	*4,895*	*4,662*
Total debit	3 200 . .	*–5,087*	*–5,969*	*–5,733*	*–6,002*	*–5,595*	*–5,707*	*–5,719*	*–5,208*
Transportation services, credit	2 205 . .	**900**	**1,069**	**1,003**	**1,090**	**1,094**	**1,085**	**1,183**	**1,185**
Passenger	2 850 . .	*369*	*527*	*521*	*570*	*565*	*607*	*661*	*687*
Freight	2 851 . .	*343*	*302*	*230*	*266*	*292*	*206*	*255*	*235*
Other	2 852 . .	*188*	*239*	*252*	*254*	*237*	*273*	*267*	*263*
Sea transport, passenger	2 207 . .	. . .	. . .	. . .	. . .	. . .	. . .	. . .	. . .
Sea transport, freight	2 208 . .	. . .	. . .	. . .	. . .	. . .	. . .	. . .	. . .
Sea transport, other	2 209 . .	. . .	. . .	. . .	. . .	. . .	. . .	. . .	. . .
Air transport, passenger	2 211 . .	. . .	. . .	. . .	. . .	. . .	. . .	. . .	. . .
Air transport, freight	2 212 . .	. . .	. . .	. . .	. . .	. . .	. . .	. . .	. . .
Air transport, other	2 213 . .	. . .	. . .	. . .	. . .	. . .	. . .	. . .	. . .
Other transport, passenger	2 215 . .	. . .	. . .	. . .	. . .	. . .	. . .	. . .	. . .
Other transport, freight	2 216 . .	. . .	. . .	. . .	. . .	. . .	. . .	. . .	. . .
Other transport, other	2 217 . .	. . .	. . .	. . .	. . .	. . .	. . .	. . .	. . .
Transportation services, debit	3 205 . .	**–1,910**	**–2,295**	**–2,343**	**–2,479**	**–2,299**	**–2,380**	**–2,442**	**–2,257**
Passenger	3 850 . .	*–585*	*–565*	*–566*	*–596*	*–592*	*–688*	*–599*	*–520*
Freight	3 851 . .	*–1,210*	*–1,573*	*–1,616*	*–1,700*	*–1,529*	*–1,522*	*–1,658*	*–1,622*
Other	3 852 . .	*–115*	*–157*	*–160*	*–184*	*–178*	*–170*	*–184*	*–115*
Sea transport, passenger	3 207 . .	. . .	. . .	. . .	. . .	. . .	. . .	. . .	. . .
Sea transport, freight	3 208 . .	. . .	. . .	. . .	. . .	. . .	. . .	. . .	. . .
Sea transport, other	3 209 . .	. . .	. . .	. . .	. . .	. . .	. . .	. . .	. . .
Air transport, passenger	3 211 . .	. . .	. . .	. . .	. . .	. . .	. . .	. . .	. . .
Air transport, freight	3 212 . .	. . .	. . .	. . .	. . .	. . .	. . .	. . .	. . .
Air transport, other	3 213 . .	. . .	. . .	. . .	. . .	. . .	. . .	. . .	. . .
Other transport, passenger	3 215 . .	. . .	. . .	. . .	. . .	. . .	. . .	. . .	. . .
Other transport, freight	3 216 . .	. . .	. . .	. . .	. . .	. . .	. . .	. . .	. . .
Other transport, other	3 217 . .	. . .	. . .	. . .	. . .	. . .	. . .	. . .	. . .
Travel, credit	2 236 . .	**2,064**	**2,126**	**2,575**	**2,769**	**2,717**	**2,637**	**2,513**	**2,501**
Business travel	2 237 . .	848	493	600	605	541	455	420	421
Personal travel	2 240 . .	1,216	1,633	1,975	2,164	2,176	2,182	2,092	2,081
Travel, debit	3 236 . .	**–1,861**	**–1,849**	**–1,754**	**–1,961**	**–1,908**	**–2,028**	**–2,085**	**–1,917**
Business travel	3 237 . .	–529	–574	–571	–652	–627	–656	–738	–632
Personal travel	3 240 . .	–1,332	–1,275	–1,183	–1,309	–1,281	–1,372	–1,347	–1,285
Other services, credit	2 200 BA	**785**	**1,423**	**1,450**	**1,475**	**1,471**	**1,352**	**1,199**	**975**
Communications	2 245 . .	35	44	86	78	74	69	57	54
Construction	2 249 . .	. . .	. . .	. . .	. . .	. . .	. . .	. . .	. . .
Insurance	2 253 . .	282	439	463	460	544	503	451	370
Financial	2 260 . .	. . .	. . .	. . .	. . .	. . .	. . .	. . .	. . .
Computer and information	2 262 . .	. . .	. . .	. . .	. . .	. . .	. . .	. . .	. . .
Royalties and licence fees	2 266 . .	51	45	67	73	72	71	62	51
Other business services	2 268 . .	223	691	614	680	599	540	472	383
Personal, cultural, and recreational	2 287 . .	. . .	. . .	. . .	. . .	. . .	. . .	. . .	. . .
Government, n.i.e.	2 291 . .	194	204	221	184	183	169	158	117
Other services, debit	3 200 BA	**–1,316**	**–1,825**	**–1,635**	**–1,562**	**–1,388**	**–1,299**	**–1,193**	**–1,034**
Communications	3 245 . .	–179	–124	–126	–123	–105	–95	–83	–70
Construction	3 249 . .	. . .	. . .	. . .	. . .	. . .	. . .	. . .	. . .
Insurance	3 253 . .	–437	–814	–496	–505	–409	–398	–380	–340
Financial	3 260 . .	. . .	. . .	. . .	. . .	. . .	. . .	. . .	. . .
Computer and information	3 262 . .	. . .	. . .	. . .	. . .	. . .	. . .	. . .	. . .
Royalties and licence fees	3 266 . .	–114	–293	–309	–258	–165	–162	–142	–115
Other business services	3 268 . .	–385	–380	–476	–482	–515	–466	–421	–386
Personal, cultural, and recreational	3 287 . .	. . .	. . .	. . .	. . .	. . .	. . .	. . .	. . .
Government, n.i.e.	3 291 . .	–200	–215	–227	–194	–193	–178	–166	–124

Table 2 (Continued). STANDARD PRESENTATION, 1994–2001

(Millions of U.S. dollars)

	Code		1994	1995	1996	1997	1998	1999	2000	2001
C. INCOME	4 300	. .	–2,422	–2,875	–3,118	–3,204	–3,156	–3,153	–3,140	–3,846
Total credit	2 300	. .	*972*	*1,136*	*1,077*	*1,298*	*1,307*	*1,568*	*2,261*	*2,168*
Total debit	3 300	. .	*–3,394*	*–4,011*	*–4,194*	*–4,502*	*–4,463*	*–4,721*	*–5,401*	*–6,014*
Compensation of employees, credit	2 310	. .	**79**	**83**	**75**	**75**	**91**	**83**	**74**	**61**
Compensation of employees, debit	3 310	. .	**–572**	**–567**	**–518**	**–492**	**–419**	**–363**	**–319**	**–262**
Investment income, credit	2 320	. .	**894**	**1,053**	**1,002**	**1,223**	**1,216**	**1,484**	**2,187**	**2,106**
Direct investment income	2 330	. .	646	720	705	756	667	696	878	668
Dividends and distributed branch profits	2 332	. .	567	655	638	617	445	590	756	567
Reinvested earnings and undistributed branch profits	2 333	. .	. . .	. . .	. . .	. . .	. . .	. . .	. . .	. . .
Income on debt (interest)	2 334	. .	79	65	67	139	222	106	122	101
Portfolio investment income	2 339	. .	248	333	297	467	549	789	1,309	1,438
Income on equity	2 340	. .	99	73	75	65	44	146	526	726
Income on bonds and notes	2 350	. .	. . .	. . .	. . .	. . .	. . .	. . .	. . .	. . .
Income on money market instruments	2 360	. .	. . .	. . .	. . .	. . .	. . .	. . .	. . .	. . .
Other investment income	2 370	. .	. . .	. . .	. . .	. . .	. . .	. . .	. . .	. . .
Investment income, debit	3 320	. .	**–2,823**	**–3,444**	**–3,676**	**–4,010**	**–4,043**	**–4,358**	**–5,081**	**–5,752**
Direct investment income	3 330	. .	–659	–535	–682	–803	–805	–1,111	–2,329	–2,883
Dividends and distributed branch profits	3 332	. .	–583	–437	–542	–566	–569	–919	–2,180	–2,763
Reinvested earnings and undistributed branch profits	3 333	. .	. . .	. . .	. . .	. . .	. . .	. . .	. . .	. . .
Income on debt (interest)	3 334	. .	–75	–98	–140	–238	–236	–192	–150	–120
Portfolio investment income	3 339	. .	–2,164	–2,910	–2,994	–3,207	–3,238	–3,247	–2,752	–2,869
Income on equity	3 340	. .	–243	–393	–567	–439	–476	–423	–492	–1,002
Income on bonds and notes	3 350	. .	. . .	. . .	. . .	. . .	. . .	. . .	. . .	. . .
Income on money market instruments	3 360	. .	. . .	. . .	. . .	. . .	. . .	. . .	. . .	. . .
Other investment income	3 370	. .	. . .	. . .	. . .	. . .	. . .	. . .	. . .	. . .
D. CURRENT TRANSFERS	4 379	. .	–609	–645	–753	–724	–744	–926	–926	–738
Credit	2 379	. .	**143**	**196**	**54**	**138**	**60**	**66**	**106**	**126**
General government	2 380	. .	120	165	31	105	26	28	69	92
Other sectors	2 390	. .	23	30	23	34	34	38	38	34
Workers' remittances	2 391	. .	. . .	. . .	. . .	. . .	. . .	. . .	. . .	. . .
Other current transfers	2 392	. .	23	30	23	34	34	38	38	34
Debit	3 379	. .	**–752**	**–841**	**–807**	**–862**	**–804**	**–993**	**–1,033**	**–865**
General government	3 380	. .	–717	–794	–761	–831	–777	–957	–1,003	–837
Other sectors	3 390	. .	–36	–47	–46	–31	–27	–35	–30	–28
Workers' remittances	3 391	. .	. . .	. . .	. . .	. . .	. . .	. . .	. . .	. . .
Other current transfers	3 392	. .	–36	–47	–46	–31	–27	–35	–30	–28
CAPITAL AND FINANCIAL ACCOUNT	4 996	. .	**337**	**3,057**	**4,243**	**3,343**	**3,876**	**1,028**	**–353**	**–1,690**
CAPITAL ACCOUNT	4 994	. .	**–67**	**–40**	**–47**	**–193**	**–56**	**–62**	**–52**	**–32**
Total credit	2 994	. .	*20*	*22*	*25*	*29*	*24*	*20*	*19*	*15*
Total debit	3 994	. .	*–87*	*–62*	*–72*	*–222*	*–80*	*–82*	*–71*	*–47*
Capital transfers, credit	2 400	. .	**20**	**22**	**25**	**29**	**24**	**20**	**19**	**15**
General government	2 401	. .	. . .	. . .	. . .	. . .	. . .	. . .	. . .	. . .
Debt forgiveness	2 402	. .	. . .	. . .	. . .	. . .	. . .	. . .	. . .	. . .
Other capital transfers	2 410	. .	. . .	. . .	. . .	. . .	. . .	. . .	. . .	. . .
Other sectors	2 430	. .	20	22	25	29	24	20	19	15
Migrants' transfers	2 431	. .	20	22	25	29	24	20	19	15
Debt forgiveness	2 432	. .	. . .	. . .	. . .	. . .	. . .	. . .	. . .	. . .
Other capital transfers	2 440	. .	. . .	. . .	. . .	. . .	. . .	. . .	. . .	. . .
Capital transfers, debit	3 400	. .	**–87**	**–62**	**–72**	**–222**	**–80**	**–82**	**–71**	**–47**
General government	3 401	. .	. . .	. . .	. . .	–135	. . .	. . .	. . .	. . .
Debt forgiveness	3 402	. .	. . .	. . .	. . .	–135	. . .	. . .	. . .	. . .
Other capital transfers	3 410	. .	. . .	. . .	. . .	. . .	. . .	. . .	. . .	. . .
Other sectors	3 430	. .	–87	–62	–72	–88	–80	–82	–71	–47
Migrants' transfers	3 431	. .	–87	–62	–72	–88	–80	–82	–71	–47
Debt forgiveness	3 432	. .	. . .	. . .	. . .	. . .	. . .	. . .	. . .	. . .
Other capital transfers	3 440	. .	. . .	. . .	. . .	. . .	. . .	. . .	. . .	. . .
Nonproduced nonfinancial assets, credit	2 480	. .	. . .	. . .	. . .	. . .	. . .	. . .	. . .	. . .
Nonproduced nonfinancial assets, debit	3 480	. .	. . .	. . .	. . .	. . .	. . .	. . .	. . .	. . .

Table 2 (Continued). STANDARD PRESENTATION, 1994–2001
(Millions of U.S. dollars)

	Code	1994	1995	1996	1997	1998	1999	2000	2001
FINANCIAL ACCOUNT	4 995 . .	**404**	**3,097**	**4,290**	**3,536**	**3,932**	**1,090**	**–301**	**–1,658**
A. DIRECT INVESTMENT	4 500 . .	–886	–1,245	–232	1,487	–1,084	–81	692	10,848
Direct investment abroad	4 505 . .	**–1,261**	**–2,494**	**–1,048**	**–2,324**	**–1,634**	**–1,584**	**–277**	**3,686**
Equity capital	4 510 . .	–1,358	–2,306	–1,264	–2,178	–1,554	–836	154	4,450
Claims on affiliated enterprises	4 515 . .	. . .	. . .	. . .	. . .	–1,554	–836	154	4,450
Liabilities to affiliated enterprises	4 520 . .	. . .	. . .	. . .	. . .	. . .	. . .	. . .	. . .
Reinvested earnings	4 525 . .	. . .	. . .	. . .	. . .	. . .	. . .	. . .	. . .
Other capital	4 530 . .	97	–187	216	–145	–80	–749	–432	–763
Claims on affiliated enterprises	4 535 . .	. . .	. . .	. . .	. . .	–80	–749	–432	–763
Liabilities to affiliated enterprises	4 540 . .	. . .	. . .	. . .	. . .	. . .	. . .	. . .	. . .
Direct investment in South Africa	4 555 . .	**374**	**1,248**	**816**	**3,811**	**550**	**1,503**	**969**	**7,162**
Equity capital	4 560 . .	4	288	582	3,595	484	1,075	913	7,032
Claims on direct investors	4 565 . .	. . .	. . .	. . .	. . .	. . .	. . .	. . .	. . .
Liabilities to direct investors	4 570 . .	. . .	. . .	. . .	. . .	484	1,075	913	7,032
Reinvested earnings	4 575 . .	. . .	. . .	. . .	. . .	. . .	. . .	. . .	. . .
Other capital	4 580 . .	371	961	235	216	66	429	56	131
Claims on direct investors	4 585 . .	. . .	. . .	. . .	. . .	. . .	. . .	. . .	. . .
Liabilities to direct investors	4 590 . .	. . .	. . .	. . .	. . .	66	429	56	131
B. PORTFOLIO INVESTMENT	4 600 . .	2,836	2,490	2,445	6,687	4,294	8,686	–1,864	–8,302
Assets	4 602 . .	**–82**	**–447**	**–2,000**	**–4,587**	**–5,575**	**–5,113**	**–3,672**	**–5,331**
Equity securities	4 610 . .	–29	–387	–1,698	–3,891	–4,768	–4,050	–3,019	–4,864
Monetary authorities	4 611 . .	. . .	. . .	. . .	. . .	. . .	. . .	. . .	. . .
General government	4 612 . .	. . .	. . .	. . .	. . .	. . .	. . .	. . .	. . .
Banks	4 613 . .	5	–44	14	83	34	–37	–84	6
Other sectors	4 614 . .	–35	–342	–1,712	–3,974	–4,802	–4,013	–2,935	–4,869
Debt securities	4 619 . .	–53	–61	–302	–696	–807	–1,064	–652	–467
Bonds and notes	4 620 . .	–59	–61	–302	–696	–807	–1,064	–652	–467
Monetary authorities	4 621 . .	. . .	. . .	. . .	. . .	. . .	. . .	. . .	. . .
General government	4 622 . .	. . .	. . .	. . .	. . .	. . .	. . .	. . .	. . .
Banks	4 623 . .	. . .	. . .	. . .	. . .	. . .	. . .	. . .	. . .
Other sectors	4 624 . .	–59	–61	–302	–696	–807	–1,064	–652	–467
Money market instruments	4 630 . .	6	. . .	. . .	. . .	. . .	. . .	. . .	. . .
Monetary authorities	4 631 . .	. . .	. . .	. . .	. . .	. . .	. . .	. . .	. . .
General government	4 632 . .	. . .	. . .	. . .	. . .	. . .	. . .	. . .	. . .
Banks	4 633 . .	6	. . .	. . .	. . .	. . .	. . .	. . .	. . .
Other sectors	4 634 . .	. . .	. . .	. . .	. . .	. . .	. . .	. . .	. . .
Liabilities	4 652 . .	**2,918**	**2,937**	**4,446**	**11,274**	**9,869**	**13,799**	**1,807**	**–2,971**
Equity securities	4 660 . .	88	2,914	2,318	5,473	8,632	9,001	4,169	–962
Banks	4 663 . .	–470	867	62	651	524	731	274	255
Other sectors	4 664 . .	558	2,047	2,256	4,822	8,108	8,270	3,895	–1,217
Debt securities	4 669 . .	2,830	23	2,127	5,802	1,237	4,798	–2,361	–2,009
Bonds and notes	4 670 . .	1,703	2,120	1,976	5,469	1,225	4,745	–2,072	–2,156
Monetary authorities	4 671 . .	. . .	. . .	. . .	. . .	. . .	. . .	. . .	. . .
General government	4 672 . .	1,451	1,005	1,966	5,278	1,152	4,704	–1,958	–1,389
Banks	4 673 . .	. . .	. . .	. . .	21	–71	. . .	. . .	. . .
Other sectors	4 674 . .	252	1,115	9	170	144	41	–114	–768
Money market instruments	4 680 . .	1,127	–2,097	152	333	12	54	–289	147
Monetary authorities	4 681 . .	. . .	. . .	. . .	. . .	. . .	. . .	. . .	. . .
General government	4 682 . .	486	–472	. . .	. . .	. . .	. . .	. . .	. . .
Banks	4 683 . .	641	–1,625	152	333	12	54	–289	147
Other sectors	4 684 . .	. . .	. . .	. . .	. . .	. . .	. . .	. . .	. . .
C. FINANCIAL DERIVATIVES	4 910 . .	. . .	. . .	. . .	53	97	–122	–142	. . .
Monetary authorities	4 911 . .	. . .	. . .	. . .	. . .	. . .	. . .	. . .	. . .
General government	4 912 . .	. . .	. . .	. . .	. . .	. . .	. . .	. . .	. . .
Banks	4 913 . .	. . .	. . .	. . .	12	65	–122	–142	. . .
Other sectors	4 914 . .	. . .	. . .	. . .	41	33	. . .	. . .	. . .
Assets	4 900 . .	**. . .**	**. . .**	**. . .**	**. . .**	**. . .**	**–46**	**–144**	**. . .**
Monetary authorities	4 901 . .	. . .	. . .	. . .	. . .	. . .	. . .	. . .	. . .
General government	4 902 . .	. . .	. . .	. . .	. . .	. . .	. . .	. . .	. . .
Banks	4 903 . .	. . .	. . .	. . .	. . .	. . .	–46	–144	. . .
Other sectors	4 904 . .	. . .	. . .	. . .	. . .	. . .	. . .	. . .	. . .
Liabilities	4 905 . .	**. . .**	**. . .**	**. . .**	**53**	**97**	**–76**	**2**	**. . .**
Monetary authorities	4 906 . .	. . .	. . .	. . .	. . .	. . .	. . .	. . .	. . .
General government	4 907 . .	. . .	. . .	. . .	. . .	. . .	. . .	. . .	. . .
Banks	4 908 . .	. . .	. . .	. . .	12	65	–76	2	. . .
Other sectors	4 909 . .	. . .	. . .	. . .	41	33	. . .	. . .	. . .

Table 2 (Concluded). STANDARD PRESENTATION, 1994–2001
(Millions of U.S. dollars)

	Code	1994	1995	1996	1997	1998	1999	2000	2001
D. OTHER INVESTMENT	4 700 . .	–862	2,759	804	–517	1,125	–3,178	1,413	–2,046
Assets	4 703 . .	**–298**	**–525**	**–599**	**–1,983**	**–694**	**–1,644**	**59**	**–1,432**
Trade credits	4 706 . .	. . .	. . .	. . .	. . .	. . .	–182	–622	–765
General government	4 707 . .	. . .	. . .	. . .	. . .	. . .	. . .	. . .	–407
of which: Short-term	4 709 . .	. . .	. . .	. . .	. . .	. . .	. . .	. . .	. . .
Other sectors	4 710 . .	. . .	. . .	. . .	. . .	. . .	–182	–622	–358
of which: Short-term	4 712 . .	. . .	. . .	. . .	. . .	. . .	*–182*	*–622*	*–358*
Loans	4 714 . .	44	–588	–472	–1,760	–143	–675	547	–337
Monetary authorities	4 715 . .	44	75	12	206	. . .	6	. . .	. . .
of which: Short-term	4 718 . .	. . .	. . .	. . .	. . .	. . .	. . .	. . .	. . .
General government	4 719 . .	. . .	. . .	. . .	2	1	. . .	. . .	. . .
of which: Short-term	4 721 . .	. . .	. . .	. . .	. . .	. . .	. . .	. . .	. . .
Banks	4 722 . .	. . .	. . .	. . .	. . .	. . .	. . .	. . .	. . .
of which: Short-term	4 724 . .	. . .	. . .	. . .	. . .	. . .	. . .	. . .	. . .
Other sectors	4 725 . .	. . .	–663	–484	–1,968	–144	–681	547	–337
of which: Short-term	4 727 . .	. . .	*–117*	*–147*	*–1,381*	*–55*	*–342*	*546*	*–455*
Currency and deposits	4 730 . .	–85	62	–127	–122	–135	–532	400	–10
Monetary authorities	4 731 . .	. . .	. . .	. . .	. . .	. . .	. . .	. . .	. . .
General government	4 732 . .	. . .	. . .	. . .	. . .	. . .	. . .	. . .	. . .
Banks	4 733 . .	–85	62	–127	–122	–135	–52	–235	–346
Other sectors	4 734 . .	. . .	. . .	. . .	. . .	. . .	–480	635	336
Other assets	4 736 . .	–256	1	. . .	–101	–416	–255	–267	–320
Monetary authorities	4 737 . .	. . .	. . .	. . .	. . .	. . .	. . .	. . .	. . .
of which: Short-term	4 739 . .	. . .	. . .	. . .	. . .	. . .	. . .	. . .	. . .
General government	4 740 . .	–1	1	. . .	. . .	. . .	. . .	. . .	. . .
of which: Short-term	4 742 . .	. . .	. . .	. . .	. . .	. . .	. . .	. . .	. . .
Banks	4 743 . .	. . .	. . .	. . .	. . .	. . .	–8	–9	12
of which: Short-term	4 745 . .	. . .	. . .	. . .	. . .	. . .	*–8*	*–9*	*12*
Other sectors	4 746 . .	–255	. . .	. . .	–101	–416	–247	–258	–332
of which: Short-term	4 748 . .	*–255*	. . .	. . .	. . .	. . .	. . .	*–30*	*–17*
Liabilities	4 753 . .	**–565**	**3,285**	**1,403**	**1,466**	**1,819**	**–1,535**	**1,354**	**–614**
Trade credits	4 756 . .	–28	–28	–19	. . .	. . .	–107	38	–3
General government	4 757 . .	. . .	. . .	. . .	. . .	. . .	. . .	. . .	. . .
of which: Short-term	4 759 . .	. . .	. . .	. . .	. . .	. . .	. . .	. . .	. . .
Other sectors	4 760 . .	–28	–28	–19	. . .	. . .	–107	38	–3
of which: Short-term	4 762 . .	*–28*	*–28*	*–19*	. . .	. . .	*–107*	*38*	*–3*
Loans	4 764 . .	–1,253	379	–473	19	1,511	–991	940	586
Monetary authorities	4 765 . .	–117	–1,465	4	1,707	795	–10	–315	1,584
of which: Use of Fund credit and loans from the Fund	4 766 . .	. . .	. . .	. . .	*–421*	*–418*	. . .	. . .	. . .
of which: Short-term	4 768 . .	*–117*	*–1,465*	*4*	*2,128*	*1,213*	*–10*	*–315*	*1,584*
General government	4 769 . .	–467	118	469	–120	–73	–270	6	134
of which: Short-term	4 771 . .	. . .	. . .	. . .	. . .	. . .	. . .	. . .	. . .
Banks	4 772 . .	–603	603	–1,000	–1,843	–1,491	–675	382	–186
of which: Short-term	4 774 . .	*–196*	*513*	*–736*	*–1,607*	*–1,490*	*–577*	*434*	*–110*
Other sectors	4 775 . .	66	1,123	54	275	2,281	–36	868	–947
of which: Short-term	4 777 . .	*–66*	*–33*	*–21*	*483*	*2,650*	*–1,140*	*682*	*–206*
Currency and deposits	4 780 . .	975	2,392	1,951	1,631	2,143	–102	737	–604
Monetary authorities	4 781 . .	12	51	–93	57	–41	116	–95	–2
General government	4 782 . .	. . .	. . .	. . .	. . .	. . .	. . .	. . .	. . .
Banks	4 783 . .	963	2,342	2,044	1,573	2,184	–218	833	–602
Other sectors	4 784 . .	. . .	. . .	. . .	. . .	. . .	. . .	. . .	. . .
Other liabilities	4 786 . .	–259	541	–56	–183	–1,836	–335	–362	–593
Monetary authorities	4 787 . .	. . .	. . .	. . .	. . .	. . .	. . .	. . .	. . .
of which: Short-term	4 789 . .	. . .	. . .	. . .	. . .	. . .	. . .	. . .	. . .
General government	4 790 . .	. . .	. . .	. . .	. . .	. . .	. . .	. . .	. . .
of which: Short-term	4 792 . .	. . .	. . .	. . .	. . .	. . .	. . .	. . .	. . .
Banks	4 793 . .	. . .	. . .	. . .	–13	90	–52	–19	1
of which: Short-term	4 795 . .	. . .	. . .	. . .	*–13*	*90*	*–52*	*–19*	*1*
Other sectors	4 796 . .	–259	541	–56	–170	–1,926	–283	–343	–594
of which: Short-term	4 798 . .	*–93*	*541*	*–56*	*–170*	*–1,926*	*–283*	*–343*	*–594*
E. RESERVE ASSETS	4 802 . .	–683	–907	1,272	–4,174	–502	–4,215	–400	–2,158
Monetary gold	4 812 . .	191	–31	156	–58	–10	69	–430	1
Special drawing rights	4 811 . .	11	–5	4	–8	–167	–106	–17	. . .
Reserve position in the Fund	4 810 . .	. . .	. . .	. . .	. . .	. . .	. . .	. . .	. . .
Foreign exchange	4 803 . .	–657	–1,163	1,765	–3,884	485	–2,027	72	–63
Other claims	4 813 . .	–229	292	–652	–224	–811	–2,152	–25	–2,096
NET ERRORS AND OMISSIONS	4 998 . .	**–449**	**–852**	**–2,363**	**–1,070**	**–1,719**	**–389**	**928**	**1,855**

Part 3 of the *Yearbook* contains descriptions of the methodologies, compilation practices, and sources used to compile these data.

Table 3. INTERNATIONAL INVESTMENT POSITION (End-period stocks), 1994–2001

(Millions of U.S. dollars)

	Code	1994	1995	1996	1997	1998	1999	2000	2001
ASSETS	8 995 C.	27,559	33,893	35,056	47,869	56,855	92,532	95,596	...
Direct investment abroad	8 505 . .	**19,105**	**23,301**	**24,349**	**23,250**	**26,858**	**32,990**	**32,325**	**...**
Equity capital and reinvested earnings	8 506 . .	17,022	21,096	22,892	22,128	26,284	31,925	31,069	...
Claims on affiliated enterprises	8 507 . .	...	...	...	...	...	...	...	...
Liabilities to affiliated enterprises	8 508 . .	...	...	...	...	...	...	...	...
Other capital	8 530 . .	2,082	2,205	1,457	1,122	573	1,065	1,256	...
Claims on affiliated enterprises	8 535 . .	...	...	...	...	...	...	...	...
Liabilities to affiliated enterprises	8 540 . .	...	...	...	...	...	...	...	...
Portfolio investment	8 602 . .	**98**	**632**	**2,605**	**12,060**	**18,231**	**41,961**	**45,264**	**...**
Equity securities	8 610 . .	61	569	2,237	10,895	15,833	38,349	41,675	...
Monetary authorities	8 611 . .	...	...	...	...	...	...	...	...
General government	8 612 . .	...	...	...	...	...	...	...	...
Banks	8 613 . .	6	144	85	7	6	18	92	...
Other sectors	8 614 . .	54	425	2,151	10,889	15,827	38,331	41,584	...
Debt securities	8 619 . .	38	63	368	1,164	2,398	3,612	3,589	...
Bonds and notes	8 620 . .	38	63	368	1,164	2,398	3,612	3,589	...
Monetary authorities	8 621 . .	...	...	...	...	...	...	...	...
General government	8 622 . .	...	...	...	...	...	...	...	...
Banks	8 623 . .	...	...	...	...	...	...	...	...
Other sectors	8 624 . .	38	63	368	1,164	2,398	3,612	3,589	...
Money market instruments	8 630 . .	...	...	...	...	...	...	...	...
Monetary authorities	8 631 . .	...	...	...	...	...	...	...	...
General government	8 632 . .	...	...	...	...	...	...	...	...
Banks	8 633 . .	...	...	...	...	...	...	...	...
Other sectors	8 634 . .	...	...	...	...	...	...	...	...
Financial derivatives	8 900 . .	**...**	**...**	**...**	**...**	**...**	**...**	**...**	**...**
Monetary authorities	8 901 . .	...	...	...	...	...	...	...	...
General government	8 902 . .	...	...	...	...	...	...	...	...
Banks	8 903 . .	...	...	...	...	...	...	...	...
Other sectors	8 904 . .	...	...	...	...	...	...	...	...
Other investment	8 703 . .	**4,349**	**4,985**	**4,657**	**5,297**	**4,565**	**6,308**	**6,720**	**...**
Trade credits	8 706 . .	...	...	...	...	...	...	...	...
General government	8 707 . .	...	...	...	...	...	...	...	...
of which: Short-term	8 709 . .	...	...	...	...	...	...	...	...
Other sectors	8 710 . .	...	...	...	...	...	...	...	...
of which: Short-term	8 712 . .	...	...	...	...	...	...	...	...
Loans	8 714 . .	4,245	4,946	4,507	5,039	4,265	5,971	6,224	...
Monetary authorities	8 715 . .	392	306	227	24	19	12	10	...
of which: Short-term	8 718 . .	...	...	...	...	...	...	...	...
General government	8 719 . .	2,040	2,371	2,148	1,839	1,596	2,512	2,703	...
of which: Short-term	8 721 . .	*1*	*2*	*1*	*2*	*1*	*1*	*1*	...
Banks	8 722 . .	...	...	...	...	...	...	...	...
of which: Short-term	8 724 . .	...	...	...	...	...	...	...	...
Other sectors	8 725 . .	1,813	2,269	2,132	3,176	2,650	3,447	3,511	...
of which: Short-term	8 727 . .	*1,607*	*2,033*	*1,978*	*3,033*	*2,467*	*2,977*	*2,917*	...
Currency and deposits	8 730 . .	104	39	150	258	300	338	496	...
Monetary authorities	8 731 . .	...	...	...	...	...	...	...	...
General government	8 732 . .	...	...	...	...	...	...	...	...
Banks	8 733 . .	104	39	150	258	300	338	496	...
Other sectors	8 734 . .	...	...	...	...	...	...	...	...
Other assets	8 736 . .	...	...	...	...	...	...	...	...
Monetary authorities	8 737 . .	...	...	...	...	...	...	...	...
of which: Short-term	8 739 . .	...	...	...	...	...	...	...	...
General government	8 740 . .	...	...	...	...	...	...	...	...
of which: Short-term	8 742 . .	...	...	...	...	...	...	...	...
Banks	8 743 . .	...	...	...	...	...	...	...	...
of which: Short-term	8 745 . .	...	...	...	...	...	...	...	...
Other sectors	8 746 . .	...	...	...	...	...	...	...	...
of which: Short-term	8 748 . .	...	...	...	...	...	...	...	...
Reserve assets	8 802 . .	**4,008**	**4,975**	**3,445**	**7,262**	**7,201**	**11,273**	**11,287**	**...**
Monetary gold	8 812 . .	1,445	1,481	1,261	1,048	1,034	1,020	1,451	...
Special drawing rights	8 811 . .	1	5	1	9	185	288	290	280
Reserve position in the Fund	8 810 . .	...	...	...	...	...	...	...	...
Foreign exchange	8 803 . .	1,683	2,813	939	4,788	4,170	6,064	5,791	...
Other claims	8 813 . .	879	676	1,244	1,416	1,812	3,901	3,754	...

Table 3 (Concluded). INTERNATIONAL INVESTMENT POSITION (End–period stocks), 1994–2001
(Millions of U.S. dollars)

	Code		1994	1995	1996	1997	1998	1999	2000	2001
LIABILITIES	8 995	D.	52,197	62,610	60,449	68,546	69,835	116,962	102,231	...
Direct investment in South Africa	8 555	..	**12,615**	**15,014**	**13,236**	**16,736**	**15,676**	**51,772**	**43,451**	...
Equity capital and reinvested earnings	8 556	..	9,538	11,380	10,202	13,232	12,394	48,111	39,980	...
Claims on direct investors	8 557	..	...	...	...	...	...	...	...	...
Liabilities to direct investors	8 558	..	...	...	...	...	...	...	...	...
Other capital	8 580	..	3,077	3,634	3,033	3,504	3,283	3,661	3,471	...
Claims on direct investors	8 585	..	...	...	...	...	...	...	...	...
Liabilities to direct investors	8 590	..	...	...	...	...	...	...	...	...
Portfolio investment	8 652	..	**18,998**	**23,446**	**23,804**	**28,143**	**30,547**	**42,249**	**36,529**	...
Equity securities	8 660	..	9,246	12,492	13,366	13,144	17,519	26,461	22,599	...
Banks	8 663	..	399	559	565	1,326	1,664	2,638	2,565	...
Other sectors	8 664	..	8,847	11,933	12,800	11,818	15,854	23,823	20,034	...
Debt securities	8 669	..	9,752	10,953	10,439	14,999	13,028	15,789	13,930	...
Bonds and notes	8 670	..	8,537	10,953	10,308	14,564	12,641	15,368	13,838	...
Monetary authorities	8 671	..	...	...	...	...	...	...	...	...
General government	8 672	..	3,614	4,274	5,329	9,288	8,214	11,036	8,779	...
Banks	8 673	..	...	382	270	290	201	200	200	...
Other sectors	8 674	..	4,923	6,297	4,709	4,986	4,227	4,131	4,859	...
Money market instruments	8 680	..	1,215	...	131	436	387	421	92	...
Monetary authorities	8 681	..	...	...	...	...	...	...	...	...
General government	8 682	..	...	...	...	...	...	...	...	...
Banks	8 683	..	1,215	...	131	436	387	421	92	...
Other sectors	8 684	..	...	...	...	...	...	...	...	...
Financial derivatives	8 905	..	**4**	**10**	**14**	**66**	**119**	**43**	**35**	...
Monetary authorities	8 906	..	...	...	...	...	...	...	...	...
General government	8 907	..	...	...	...	...	...	...	...	...
Banks	8 908	..	1	4	5	15	79	...	...	...
Other sectors	8 909	..	3	6	9	51	41	43	35	...
Other investment	8 753	..	**20,580**	**24,140**	**23,395**	**23,601**	**23,492**	**22,898**	**22,216**	...
Trade credits	8 756	..	...	...	...	...	...	...	...	...
General government	8 757	..	...	...	...	...	...	...	...	...
of which: Short-term	8 759	..	...	...	...	...	...	...	...	...
Other sectors	8 760	..	...	...	...	...	...	...	...	...
of which: Short-term	8 762	..	...	...	...	...	...	...	...	...
Loans	8 764	..	19,453	21,310	20,892	19,623	17,842	17,572	16,762	...
Monetary authorities	8 765	..	2,332	913	884	2,430	3,084	3,050	2,595	...
of which: Use of Fund credit and loans from the Fund	8 766	..	*897*	*913*	*884*	*415*	...	...	...	...
of which: Short-term	8 768	..	*1,435*	...	...	*2,015*	*3,084*	*3,050*	*2,595*	...
General government	8 769	..	3,108	3,072	3,244	2,776	2,537	3,125	3,023	...
of which: Short-term	8 771	..	*2,500*	*2,347*	*2,127*	*1,820*	*1,581*	*2,498*	*2,434*	...
Banks	8 772	..	5,020	6,435	6,903	5,032	3,601	2,882	3,259	...
of which: Short-term	8 774	..	*3,640*	*5,348*	*6,253*	*4,603*	*3,370*	*2,764*	*3,173*	...
Other sectors	8 775	..	8,993	10,889	9,861	9,386	8,620	8,515	7,885	...
of which: Short-term	8 777	..	*2,886*	*3,629*	*3,188*	*3,341*	*2,766*	*2,201*	*1,878*	...
Currency and deposits	8 780	..	1,126	2,831	2,503	3,978	5,650	5,326	5,454	...
Monetary authorities	8 781	..	203	229	96	148	97	211	86	...
General government	8 782	..	...	...	...	...	...	...	...	...
Banks	8 783	..	924	2,602	2,407	3,829	5,553	5,115	5,368	...
Other sectors	8 784	..	...	...	...	...	...	...	...	...
Other liabilities	8 786	..	...	...	...	...	...	...	...	...
Monetary authorities	8 787	..	...	...	...	...	...	...	...	...
of which: Short-term	8 789	..	...	...	...	...	...	...	...	...
General government	8 790	..	...	...	...	...	...	...	...	...
of which: Short-term	8 792	..	...	...	...	...	...	...	...	...
Banks	8 793	..	...	...	...	...	...	...	...	...
of which: Short-term	8 795	..	...	...	...	...	...	...	...	...
Other sectors	8 796	..	...	...	...	...	...	...	...	...
of which: Short-term	8 798	..	...	...	...	...	...	...	...	...
NET INTERNATIONAL INVESTMENT POSITION	8 995	..	**–24,637**	**–28,717**	**–25,393**	**–20,677**	**–12,980**	**–24,430**	**–6,635**	...
Conversion rates: rand per U.S. dollar (end of period)	0 102	..	**3.5435**	**3.6475**	**4.6825**	**4.8675**	**5.8600**	**6.1545**	**7.5685**	**12.1265**

Table 1. ANALYTIC PRESENTATION, 1994–2001
(Millions of U.S. dollars)

	Code	1994	1995	1996	1997	1998	1999	2000	2001
A. Current Account [1]	4 993 Z.	**-6,389**	**792**	**407**	**2,512**	**-3,135**	**-13,761**	**-19,237**	**-15,082**
Goods: exports f.o.b	2 100 . .	73,925	93,439	102,735	106,926	111,986	112,664	116,205	117,561
Goods: imports f.o.b	3 100 . .	-88,817	-111,854	-119,017	-120,333	-132,744	-143,002	-151,025	-149,061
Balance on Goods	4 100 . .	*-14,892*	*-18,415*	*-16,283*	*-13,407*	*-20,758*	*-30,339*	*-34,820*	*-31,500*
Services: credit	2 200 . .	33,859	40,209	44,387	44,161	49,308	53,418	53,540	57,775
Services: debit	3 200 . .	-18,865	-21,509	-23,979	-24,315	-27,421	-30,532	-31,283	-33,516
Balance on Goods and Services	4 991 . .	*102*	*284*	*4,126*	*6,439*	*1,129*	*-7,452*	*-12,564*	*-7,242*
Income: credit	2 300 . .	8,687	13,689	14,095	13,162	14,621	12,636	15,017	19,796
Income: debit	3 300 . .	-16,457	-17,817	-20,207	-19,911	-22,134	-22,087	-23,268	-29,342
Balance on Goods, Services, and Income	4 992 . .	*-7,668*	*-3,843*	*-1,986*	*-310*	*-6,385*	*-16,903*	*-20,815*	*-16,787*
Current transfers: credit	2 379 Z.	9,171	12,055	11,112	11,738	12,690	13,435	11,629	12,567
Current transfers: debit	3 379 . .	-7,893	-7,420	-8,718	-8,916	-9,441	-10,292	-10,050	-10,862
B. Capital Account [1]	4 994 Z.	**2,305**	**6,004**	**6,589**	**6,437**	**6,330**	**6,967**	**4,792**	**4,960**
Capital account: credit	2 994 Z.	3,571	7,374	7,713	7,275	7,160	8,060	5,806	5,833
Capital account: debit	3 994 . .	-1,266	-1,370	-1,124	-837	-830	-1,094	-1,014	-872
Total, Groups A Plus B	4 981 . .	*-4,084*	*6,796*	*6,997*	*8,949*	*3,195*	*-6,794*	*-14,444*	*-10,122*
C. Financial Account [1]	4 995 W.	**4,491**	**-7,951**	**20,138**	**8,547**	**-14,156**	**-10,997**	**16,942**	**15,886**
Direct investment abroad	4 505 . .	-4,051	-4,206	-5,577	-12,423	-19,065	-41,754	-53,865	-27,704
Direct investment in Spain	4 555 Z.	9,216	6,297	6,796	6,384	11,905	15,541	36,931	21,540
Portfolio investment assets	4 602 . .	-1,492	-490	-3,653	-16,450	-44,193	-47,397	-59,320	-43,528
Equity securities	4 610 . .	-1,039	-534	-776	-5,272	-10,120	-17,279	-36,136	-366
Debt securities	4 619 . .	-453	44	-2,877	-11,178	-34,073	-30,118	-23,185	-43,162
Portfolio investment liabilities	4 652 Z.	-20,856	21,653	3,128	11,772	16,736	45,549	58,146	27,569
Equity securities	4 660 . .	1,154	4,215	147	-294	10,072	9,975	19,692	7,350
Debt securities	4 669 Z.	-22,010	17,438	2,981	12,066	6,664	35,574	38,455	20,219
Financial derivatives	4 910 . .	158	-557	-875	41	-2,776	260	2,025	47
Financial derivatives assets	4 900 . .	...	...	...	...	...	...	...	...
Financial derivatives liabilities	4 905 . .	158	-557	-875	41	-2,776	260	2,025	47
Other investment assets	4 703 . .	9,152	-36,816	2,469	-1,415	-21,604	-24,624	-18,640	10,196
Monetary authorities	4 701 . .	3	-71	-4	8	-422	-39,311	-7,837	14,992
General government	4 704 . .	-620	-402	-502	-377	-427	-209	-253	-287
Banks	4 705 . .	14,437	-26,899	9,969	13,175	-1,960	5,298	-7,588	-3,512
Other sectors	4 728 . .	-4,668	-9,446	-6,993	-14,220	-18,795	9,599	-2,962	-996
Other investment liabilities	4 753 W.	12,363	6,168	17,849	20,638	44,841	41,427	51,666	27,766
Monetary authorities	4 753 WA	27	23	461	-466	-2	-11	-141	-185
General government	4 753 ZB	3,007	1,493	-226	4	1,043	-296	902	572
Banks	4 753 ZC	10,572	4,049	18,646	20,490	38,957	26,039	36,510	14,937
Other sectors	4 753 ZD	-1,242	604	-1,032	611	4,843	15,695	14,395	12,441
Total, Groups A Through C	4 983 . .	*407*	*-1,154*	*27,135*	*17,497*	*-10,961*	*-17,791*	*2,498*	*5,764*
D. Net Errors and Omissions	4 998 . .	**-371**	**-5,260**	**-2,856**	**-5,741**	**-3,395**	**-5,059**	**-5,379**	**-7,104**
Total, Groups A Through D	4 984 . .	*36*	*-6,414*	*24,279*	*11,756*	*-14,355*	*-22,850*	*-2,881*	*-1,340*
E. Reserves and Related Items	4 802 A.	**-36**	**6,414**	**-24,279**	**-11,756**	**14,355**	**22,850**	**2,881**	**1,340**
Reserve assets	4 802 . .	-36	6,414	-24,279	-11,756	14,355	22,850	2,881	1,340
Use of Fund credit and loans	4 766 . .	...	...	...	...	...	...	...	...
Exceptional financing	4 920 . .	...	...	...	...	...	...	...	...
Conversion rates: pesetas per U.S. dollar	0 101 . .	**133.96**	**124.69**	**126.66**	**146.41**	**149.40**	**...**	**...**	**...**
Conversion rates: euros per U.S. dollar	0 103 . .	**...**	**...**	**...**	**...**	**...**	**.9386**	**1.0854**	**1.1175**

[1] Excludes components that have been classified in the categories of Group E.

Table 2. STANDARD PRESENTATION, 1994–2001
(Millions of U.S. dollars)

	Code	1994	1995	1996	1997	1998	1999	2000	2001
CURRENT ACCOUNT	4 993 . .	**–6,389**	**792**	**407**	**2,512**	**–3,135**	**–13,761**	**–19,237**	**–15,082**
A. GOODS	4 100 . .	–14,892	–18,415	–16,283	–13,407	–20,758	–30,339	–34,820	–31,500
Credit	2 100 . .	**73,925**	**93,439**	**102,735**	**106,926**	**111,986**	**112,664**	**116,205**	**117,561**
General merchandise: exports f.o.b.	2 110 . .	. . .	. . .	. . .	. . .	. . .	110,208	113,444	114,590
Goods for processing: exports f.o.b.	2 150 . .	. . .	. . .	. . .	. . .	. . .	971	1,015	1,294
Repairs on goods	2 160 . .	. . .	. . .	. . .	. . .	. . .	252	193	199
Goods procured in ports by carriers	2 170 . .	. . .	. . .	. . .	. . .	. . .	1,054	1,471	1,409
Nonmonetary gold	2 180 . .	. . .	. . .	. . .	. . .	. . .	179	83	69
Debit	3 100 . .	**–88,817**	**–111,854**	**–119,017**	**–120,333**	**–132,744**	**–143,002**	**–151,025**	**–149,061**
General merchandise: imports f.o.b.	3 110 . .	. . .	. . .	. . .	. . .	. . .	–140,719	–148,369	–146,009
Goods for processing: imports f.o.b.	3 150 . .	. . .	. . .	. . .	. . .	. . .	–1,025	–1,219	–1,615
Repairs on goods	3 160 . .	. . .	. . .	. . .	. . .	. . .	–315	–218	–221
Goods procured in ports by carriers	3 170 . .	. . .	. . .	. . .	. . .	. . .	–604	–722	–719
Nonmonetary gold	3 180 . .	. . .	. . .	. . .	. . .	. . .	–340	–498	–499
B. SERVICES	4 200 . .	14,994	18,699	20,409	19,846	21,887	22,886	22,257	24,258
Total credit	2 200 . .	*33,859*	*40,209*	*44,387*	*44,161*	*49,308*	*53,418*	*53,540*	*57,775*
Total debit	3 200 . .	*–18,865*	*–21,509*	*–23,979*	*–24,315*	*–27,421*	*–30,532*	*–31,283*	*–33,516*
Transportation services, credit	2 205 . .	**5,060**	**5,943**	**6,771**	**6,868**	**7,332**	**7,486**	**7,843**	**8,275**
Passenger	2 850 . .	*1,504*	*2,000*	*2,581*	*2,465*	*2,476*	*2,570*	*2,854*	*3,287*
Freight	2 851 . .	*2,152*	*2,303*	*2,530*	*2,643*	*2,771*	*2,674*	*2,791*	*2,857*
Other	2 852 . .	*1,403*	*1,640*	*1,660*	*1,760*	*2,085*	*2,242*	*2,198*	*2,131*
Sea transport, passenger	2 207 . .	29	21	26	26	52	64	29	30
Sea transport, freight	2 208 . .	801	1,027	1,130	1,195	1,254	1,269	1,314	1,361
Sea transport, other	2 209 . .	520	330	375	418	482	495	452	482
Air transport, passenger	2 211 . .	1,454	1,957	2,530	2,412	2,394	2,467	2,795	3,227
Air transport, freight	2 212 . .	441	109	126	161	171	163	198	211
Air transport, other	2 213 . .	779	1,228	1,252	1,314	1,567	1,698	1,657	1,575
Other transport, passenger	2 215 . .	22	22	25	27	30	39	29	30
Other transport, freight	2 216 . .	910	1,166	1,275	1,286	1,346	1,241	1,279	1,285
Other transport, other	2 217 . .	104	83	33	28	36	49	89	74
Transportation services, debit	3 205 . .	**–4,848**	**–5,641**	**–6,450**	**–6,586**	**–7,187**	**–7,729**	**–8,172**	**–8,185**
Passenger	3 850 . .	*–916*	*–1,289*	*–1,276*	*–1,483*	*–1,832*	*–1,941*	*–1,788*	*–1,705*
Freight	3 851 . .	*–2,826*	*–3,536*	*–3,741*	*–3,846*	*–4,230*	*–4,445*	*–4,758*	*–4,703*
Other	3 852 . .	*–1,106*	*–816*	*–1,433*	*–1,257*	*–1,125*	*–1,343*	*–1,626*	*–1,776*
Sea transport, passenger	3 207 . .	–22	–29	–31	–47	–55	–62	–60	–47
Sea transport, freight	3 208 . .	–1,843	–2,327	–2,474	–2,517	–2,771	–3,007	–3,180	–3,172
Sea transport, other	3 209 . .	–271	–219	–243	–222	–207	–244	–283	–311
Air transport, passenger	3 211 . .	–857	–1,253	–1,235	–1,428	–1,766	–1,866	–1,714	–1,643
Air transport, freight	3 212 . .	–110	–116	–124	–124	–137	–148	–157	–153
Air transport, other	3 213 . .	–643	–539	–1,114	–967	–843	–1,005	–1,267	–1,373
Other transport, passenger	3 215 . .	–38	–7	–9	–9	–11	–13	–14	–15
Other transport, freight	3 216 . .	–873	–1,092	–1,144	–1,204	–1,322	–1,290	–1,420	–1,378
Other transport, other	3 217 . .	–191	–58	–76	–68	–75	–93	–76	–93
Travel, credit	2 236 . .	**21,648**	**25,510**	**27,525**	**26,754**	**29,905**	**32,302**	**30,978**	**32,718**
Business travel	2 237 . .	. . .	. . .	. . .	. . .	. . .	. . .	. . .	. . .
Personal travel	2 240 . .	. . .	. . .	. . .	. . .	. . .	. . .	. . .	. . .
Travel, debit	3 236 . .	**–4,160**	**–4,479**	**–4,922**	**–4,497**	**–5,016**	**–5,489**	**–5,476**	**–5,961**
Business travel	3 237 . .	. . .	. . .	. . .	. . .	. . .	. . .	. . .	. . .
Personal travel	3 240 . .	. . .	. . .	. . .	. . .	. . .	. . .	. . .	. . .
Other services, credit	2 200 BA	**7,152**	**8,756**	**10,091**	**10,539**	**12,072**	**13,631**	**14,718**	**16,782**
Communications	2 245 . .	478	543	642	550	532	581	668	791
Construction	2 249 . .	434	464	475	532	540	491	534	698
Insurance	2 253 . .	914	954	909	731	733	828	713	908
Financial	2 260 . .	601	613	752	936	1,330	1,346	1,394	1,394
Computer and information	2 262 . .	606	1,031	1,278	1,437	1,720	2,094	2,043	2,189
Royalties and licence fees	2 266 . .	220	196	214	211	242	343	421	365
Other business services	2 268 . .	3,302	4,287	5,171	5,462	6,204	7,156	8,070	9,459
Personal, cultural, and recreational	2 287 . .	202	220	249	347	439	444	535	619
Government, n.i.e.	2 291 . .	394	449	402	332	331	349	340	359
Other services, debit	3 200 BA	**–9,857**	**–11,390**	**–12,607**	**–13,231**	**–15,218**	**–17,314**	**–17,636**	**–19,370**
Communications	3 245 . .	–326	–399	–442	–458	–541	–577	–744	–952
Construction	3 249 . .	–143	–264	–211	–229	–297	–142	–109	–101
Insurance	3 253 . .	–947	–1,075	–1,079	–907	–930	–962	–832	–989
Financial	3 260 . .	–584	–574	–536	–639	–1,013	–1,313	–1,082	–1,180
Computer and information	3 262 . .	–636	–729	–976	–856	–1,021	–1,162	–1,227	–1,559
Royalties and licence fees	3 266 . .	–1,061	–1,267	–1,449	–1,644	–1,877	–1,864	–1,681	–1,678
Other business services	3 268 . .	–4,604	–5,774	–6,415	–6,816	–7,883	–9,613	–10,202	–11,356
Personal, cultural, and recreational	3 287 . .	–598	–767	–1,041	–1,271	–1,272	–1,250	–1,425	–1,276
Government, n.i.e.	3 291 . .	–959	–539	–458	–412	–383	–431	–333	–279

Table 2 (Continued). STANDARD PRESENTATION, 1994–2001
(Millions of U.S. dollars)

	Code	1994	1995	1996	1997	1998	1999	2000	2001
C. INCOME	4 300	-7,770	-4,128	-6,112	-6,750	-7,513	-9,451	-8,252	-9,545
Total credit	2 300	*8,687*	*13,689*	*14,095*	*13,162*	*14,621*	*12,636*	*15,017*	*19,796*
Total debit	3 300	*-16,457*	*-17,817*	*-20,207*	*-19,911*	*-22,134*	*-22,087*	*-23,268*	*-29,342*
Compensation of employees, credit	2 310	**104**	**158**	**175**	**240**	**310**	**344**	**356**	**389**
Compensation of employees, debit	3 310	**-101**	**-163**	**-201**	**-243**	**-307**	**-343**	**-414**	**-409**
Investment income, credit	2 320	**8,583**	**13,531**	**13,920**	**12,922**	**14,311**	**12,292**	**14,661**	**19,407**
Direct investment income	2 330	527	587	574	712	1,174	1,310	1,931	4,582
Dividends and distributed branch profits	2 332	...	...	...	...	...	...	...	...
Reinvested earnings and undistributed branch profits	2 333	...	...	...	...	...	...	...	...
Income on debt (interest)	2 334	106	158	168	101	129	145	343	370
Portfolio investment income	2 339	842	1,066	1,273	1,143	1,802	2,958	4,371	5,932
Income on equity	2 340	56	123	100	138	239	493	750	752
Income on bonds and notes	2 350	...	...	...	...	...	2,417	3,470	4,876
Income on money market instruments	2 360	...	...	...	...	...	49	152	304
Other investment income	2 370	7,213	11,878	12,072	11,067	11,335	8,024	8,358	8,893
Investment income, debit	3 320	**-16,356**	**-17,654**	**-20,006**	**-19,668**	**-21,827**	**-21,744**	**-22,854**	**-28,932**
Direct investment income	3 330	-2,142	-1,879	-2,971	-3,507	-4,151	-4,043	-4,064	-5,481
Dividends and distributed branch profits	3 332	...	...	...	...	...	...	...	...
Reinvested earnings and undistributed branch profits	3 333	...	...	...	...	...	...	...	...
Income on debt (interest)	3 334	-713	-933	-893	-586	-593	-469	-601	-957
Portfolio investment income	3 339	-7,150	-7,211	-8,685	-7,338	-7,855	-8,202	-8,544	-10,289
Income on equity	3 340	-1,109	-1,350	-1,659	-1,530	-1,801	-1,864	-2,075	-2,645
Income on bonds and notes	3 350	...	...	...	...	...	-6,327	-6,453	-7,632
Income on money market instruments	3 360	...	...	...	...	...	-11	-16	-13
Other investment income	3 370	-7,064	-8,564	-8,350	-8,823	-9,820	-9,499	-10,246	-13,162
D. CURRENT TRANSFERS	4 379	1,279	4,635	2,393	2,822	3,249	3,143	1,578	1,705
Credit	2 379	**9,171**	**12,055**	**11,112**	**11,738**	**12,690**	**13,435**	**11,629**	**12,567**
General government	2 380	800	2,454	2,056	2,501	2,541	2,717	1,277	1,461
Other sectors	2 390	8,371	9,601	9,056	9,237	10,149	10,718	10,352	11,106
Workers' remittances	2 391	2,176	2,605	2,749	2,661	2,944	3,305	3,417	3,665
Other current transfers	2 392	6,195	6,996	6,307	6,576	7,205	7,413	6,935	7,441
Debit	3 379	**-7,893**	**-7,420**	**-8,718**	**-8,916**	**-9,441**	**-10,292**	**-10,050**	**-10,862**
General government	3 380	-6,371	-5,764	-6,846	-7,015	-7,241	-7,590	-6,961	-6,965
Other sectors	3 390	-1,522	-1,656	-1,873	-1,901	-2,200	-2,702	-3,089	-3,897
Workers' remittances	3 391	-389	-482	-553	-590	-710	-968	-1,325	-1,805
Other current transfers	3 392	-1,132	-1,174	-1,320	-1,311	-1,491	-1,734	-1,764	-2,091
CAPITAL AND FINANCIAL ACCOUNT	4 996	**6,760**	**4,467**	**2,449**	**3,229**	**6,530**	**18,820**	**24,616**	**22,186**
CAPITAL ACCOUNT	4 994	**2,305**	**6,004**	**6,589**	**6,437**	**6,330**	**6,967**	**4,792**	**4,960**
Total credit	2 994	*3,571*	*7,374*	*7,713*	*7,275*	*7,160*	*8,060*	*5,806*	*5,833*
Total debit	3 994	*-1,266*	*-1,370*	*-1,124*	*-837*	*-830*	*-1,094*	*-1,014*	*-872*
Capital transfers, credit	2 400	**3,509**	**7,303**	**7,623**	**7,216**	**7,049**	**7,882**	**5,509**	**5,709**
General government	2 401	3,092	6,651	6,862	5,240	6,228	7,110	4,626	4,831
Debt forgiveness	2 402	324	524	666	682	534	456	419	473
Other capital transfers	2 410	2,767	6,127	6,196	4,559	5,694	6,654	4,207	4,358
Other sectors	2 430	417	652	762	1,976	821	772	882	878
Migrants' transfers	2 431	351	472	570	628	681	665	745	638
Debt forgiveness	2 432	...	84	51	1,234	41	3	2	173
Other capital transfers	2 440	66	96	140	114	99	104	136	67
Capital transfers, debit	3 400	**-1,176**	**-1,265**	**-980**	**-676**	**-713**	**-717**	**-740**	**-461**
General government	3 401	-888	-1,009	-667	-376	-424	-316	-329	-155
Debt forgiveness	3 402	-743	-802	-479	-226	-214	-210	-220	-111
Other capital transfers	3 410	-145	-208	-188	-150	-210	-106	-109	-44
Other sectors	3 430	-288	-255	-314	-300	-289	-401	-411	-305
Migrants' transfers	3 431	-226	-224	-268	-251	-227	-301	-319	-252
Debt forgiveness	3 432	...	...	...	...	-2	-25	-2	...
Other capital transfers	3 440	-63	-31	-46	-48	-60	-75	-90	-54
Nonproduced nonfinancial assets, credit	2 480	**63**	**71**	**90**	**58**	**111**	**178**	**297**	**124**
Nonproduced nonfinancial assets, debit	3 480	**-90**	**-105**	**-143**	**-162**	**-116**	**-377**	**-274**	**-412**

Table 2 (Continued). STANDARD PRESENTATION, 1994–2001
(Millions of U.S. dollars)

	Code		1994	1995	1996	1997	1998	1999	2000	2001
FINANCIAL ACCOUNT	4 995	. .	**4,455**	**–1,537**	**–4,141**	**–3,208**	**200**	**11,853**	**19,823**	**17,226**
A. DIRECT INVESTMENT	4 500	. .	5,165	2,091	1,219	–6,039	–7,160	–26,212	–16,935	–6,164
Direct investment abroad	4 505	. .	**–4,051**	**–4,206**	**–5,577**	**–12,423**	**–19,065**	**–41,754**	**–53,865**	**–27,704**
Equity capital	4 510	. .	–4,346	–3,580	–5,002	–10,887	–15,915	–40,452	–48,031	–21,281
Claims on affiliated enterprises	4 515	. .	...	...	...	...	...	–40,452	–48,031	–21,281
Liabilities to affiliated enterprises	4 520	. .	...	...	...	...	...	...	...	...
Reinvested earnings	4 525	. .	...	...	...	...	...	...	...	...
Other capital	4 530	. .	295	–626	–575	–1,536	–3,149	–1,302	–5,834	–6,423
Claims on affiliated enterprises	4 535	. .	38	–676	–551	–1,458	–3,527	–1,533	–6,815	–6,588
Liabilities to affiliated enterprises	4 540	. .	257	49	–24	–78	378	231	981	165
Direct investment in Spain	4 555	. .	**9,216**	**6,297**	**6,796**	**6,384**	**11,905**	**15,541**	**36,931**	**21,540**
Equity capital	4 560	. .	8,652	5,472	5,623	6,231	7,075	13,852	30,995	13,325
Claims on direct investors	4 565	. .	...	...	...	...	...	...	...	...
Liabilities to direct investors	4 570	. .	...	...	...	...	...	13,852	30,995	13,325
Reinvested earnings	4 575	. .	...	...	...	...	...	...	...	...
Other capital	4 580	. .	564	825	1,173	153	4,829	1,689	5,936	8,216
Claims on direct investors	4 585	. .	700	–145	–202	–575	–1,056	–838	–675	–511
Liabilities to direct investors	4 590	. .	–136	970	1,375	729	5,885	2,527	6,611	8,726
B. PORTFOLIO INVESTMENT	4 600	. .	–22,347	21,163	–525	–4,678	–27,457	–1,848	–1,174	–15,959
Assets	4 602	. .	**–1,492**	**–490**	**–3,653**	**–16,450**	**–44,193**	**–47,397**	**–59,320**	**–43,528**
Equity securities	4 610	. .	–1,039	–534	–776	–5,272	–10,120	–17,279	–36,136	–366
Monetary authorities	4 611	. .	...	...	...	...	...	...	...	...
General government	4 612	. .	...	...	...	...	...	...	...	...
Banks	4 613	. .	–150	–195	–74	–549	–887	–2,935	–291	1,746
Other sectors	4 614	. .	–889	–339	–702	–4,723	–9,233	–14,344	–35,844	–2,112
Debt securities	4 619	. .	–453	44	–2,877	–11,178	–34,073	–30,118	–23,185	–43,162
Bonds and notes	4 620	. .	–459	–168	–2,832	–11,035	–32,129	–30,066	–18,636	–38,614
Monetary authorities	4 621	. .	...	...	...	...	...	...	...	...
General government	4 622	. .	...	...	...	...	...	...	...	...
Banks	4 623	. .	–574	–567	–1,931	–5,741	–9,554	–12,824	–3,567	–18,618
Other sectors	4 624	. .	115	399	–901	–5,293	–22,575	–17,241	–15,068	–19,996
Money market instruments	4 630	. .	5	212	–45	–144	–1,944	–52	–4,549	–4,548
Monetary authorities	4 631	. .	...	...	...	...	...	...	...	...
General government	4 632	. .	...	...	...	...	...	...	...	...
Banks	4 633	. .	–37	269	–75	...	–481	–779	–1,039	–4,708
Other sectors	4 634	. .	42	–57	30	–143	–1,463	727	–3,510	160
Liabilities	4 652	. .	**–20,856**	**21,653**	**3,128**	**11,772**	**16,736**	**45,549**	**58,146**	**27,569**
Equity securities	4 660	. .	1,154	4,215	147	–294	10,072	9,975	19,692	7,350
Banks	4 663	. .	...	...	...	...	...	...	...	...
Other sectors	4 664	. .	...	...	...	...	...	...	...	...
Debt securities	4 669	. .	–22,010	17,438	2,981	12,066	6,664	35,574	38,455	20,219
Bonds and notes	4 670	. .	–21,046	15,677	2,349	12,150	8,721	33,150	37,127	22,083
Monetary authorities	4 671	. .	...	...	...	...	...	...	...	...
General government	4 672	. .	–22,987	16,107	1,473	10,790	6,617	24,882	30,382	10,804
Banks	4 673	. .	1,008	–567	723	1,028	2,609	6,784	4,083	5,574
Other sectors	4 674	. .	932	136	154	333	–505	1,484	2,662	5,704
Money market instruments	4 680	. .	–964	1,762	632	–84	–2,057	2,424	1,328	–1,864
Monetary authorities	4 681	. .	...	...	...	...	...	...	...	...
General government	4 682	. .	–962	1,792	594	–184	–2,041	1,173	1,156	–1,810
Banks	4 683	. .	–13	...	–1	65	–78	22	1	–22
Other sectors	4 684	. .	11	–31	39	35	62	1,229	170	–31
C. FINANCIAL DERIVATIVES	4 910	. .	158	–557	–875	41	–2,776	260	2,025	47
Monetary authorities	4 911	. .	...	...	...	...	...	...	...	...
General government	4 912	. .	58	–94	–64	27	212	115	165	–6
Banks	4 913	. .	8	4	–114	1,348	–859	1,845	2,958	52
Other sectors	4 914	. .	92	–467	–697	–1,334	–2,129	–1,701	–1,099	1
Assets	4 900	. .	**...**	**...**	**...**	**...**	**...**	**...**	**...**	**...**
Monetary authorities	4 901	. .	...	...	...	...	...	...	...	...
General government	4 902	. .	...	...	...	...	...	...	...	...
Banks	4 903	. .	...	...	...	...	...	...	...	...
Other sectors	4 904	. .	...	...	...	...	...	...	...	...
Liabilities	4 905	. .	**158**	**–557**	**–875**	**41**	**–2,776**	**260**	**2,025**	**47**
Monetary authorities	4 906	. .	...	...	...	...	...	...	...	...
General government	4 907	. .	58	–94	–64	27	212	115	165	–6
Banks	4 908	. .	8	4	–114	1,348	–859	1,845	2,958	52
Other sectors	4 909	. .	92	–467	–697	–1,334	–2,129	–1,701	–1,099	1

Table 2 (Concluded). STANDARD PRESENTATION, 1994–2001
(Millions of U.S. dollars)

	Code	1994	1995	1996	1997	1998	1999	2000	2001
D. OTHER INVESTMENT	4 700	21,515	–30,648	20,319	19,224	23,237	16,803	33,026	37,962
Assets	4 703	**9,152**	**–36,816**	**2,469**	**–1,415**	**–21,604**	**–24,624**	**–18,640**	**10,196**
Trade credits	4 706	–14	–30	–14	2	–4	–10	1	1
General government	4 707	. . .	. . .	. . .	. . .	. . .	. . .	. . .	. . .
of which: Short-term	4 709	. . .	. . .	. . .	. . .	. . .	. . .	. . .	. . .
Other sectors	4 710	–14	–30	–14	2	–4	–10	1	1
of which: Short-term	4 712	. . .	. . .	. . .	. . .	. . .	. . .	. . .	. . .
Loans	4 714	2,590	–3,292	289	–3,592	–2,832	–789	–3,042	–4,953
Monetary authorities	4 715	3	–3	–4	8	3	11	1	4
of which: Short-term	4 718	. . .	. . .	. . .	. . .	. . .	. . .	. . .	. . .
General government	4 719	–585	–279	–330	–246	–214	–178	–154	–111
of which: Short-term	4 721	. . .	. . .	. . .	. . .	. . .	. . .	. . .	. . .
Banks	4 722	3,250	–2,840	572	–3,938	–2,681	–729	–2,844	–4,829
of which: Short-term	4 724	*4,134*	*–3,143*	*2,262*	*–1,606*	*–1,819*	*962*	*–859*	*–2,306*
Other sectors	4 725	–78	–169	51	584	60	108	–45	–16
of which: Short-term	4 727	*–83*	*–99*	*165*	*569*	*184*	*76*	*50*	*101*
Currency and deposits	4 730	6,789	–33,122	2,466	2,454	–18,098	–23,609	–15,240	15,403
Monetary authorities	4 731	. . .	. . .	. . .	. . .	. . .	–39,316	–7,838	14,988
General government	4 732	4	–5	–71	–47	–111	33	–32	–34
Banks	4 733	11,187	–24,058	9,397	17,113	721	6,020	–4,708	1,385
Other sectors	4 734	–4,402	–9,058	–6,859	–14,612	–18,708	9,654	–2,663	–936
Other assets	4 736	–212	–373	–272	–279	–670	–215	–358	–255
Monetary authorities	4 737	–1	–67	. . .	. . .	–425	–6	. . .	. . .
of which: Short-term	4 739	. . .	. . .	. . .	. . .	. . .	. . .	. . .	. . .
General government	4 740	–38	–117	–101	–84	–102	–64	–67	–141
of which: Short-term	4 742	. . .	. . .	. . .	. . .	. . .	. . .	. . .	. . .
Banks	4 743	. . .	. . .	. . .	–1	. . .	7	–36	–68
of which: Short-term	4 745	. . .	. . .	. . .	. . .	. . .	*7*	*–36*	*–68*
Other sectors	4 746	–174	–188	–171	–194	–143	–153	–255	–46
of which: Short-term	4 748	. . .	. . .	. . .	. . .	. . .	*–4*	*–107*	*78*
Liabilities	4 753	**12,363**	**6,168**	**17,849**	**20,638**	**44,841**	**41,427**	**51,666**	**27,766**
Trade credits	4 756	27	–74	–80	–23	–51	107	–35	–115
General government	4 757	. . .	. . .	. . .	. . .	. . .	. . .	. . .	. . .
of which: Short-term	4 759	. . .	. . .	. . .	. . .	. . .	. . .	. . .	. . .
Other sectors	4 760	27	–74	–80	–23	–51	107	–35	–115
of which: Short-term	4 762	. . .	. . .	. . .	. . .	. . .	. . .	. . .	. . .
Loans	4 764	1,738	2,171	–1,178	637	5,936	15,292	15,332	13,129
Monetary authorities	4 765	. . .	. . .	. . .	. . .	. . .	. . .	. . .	. . .
of which: Use of Fund credit and loans from the Fund	4 766	. . .	. . .	. . .	. . .	. . .	. . .	. . .	. . .
of which: Short-term	4 768	. . .	. . .	. . .	. . .	. . .	. . .	. . .	. . .
General government	4 769	3,007	1,493	–226	4	1,043	–296	902	572
of which: Short-term	4 771	*1,196*	*514*	*–878*	*144*	*385*	*–142*	*917*	*34*
Banks	4 772	. . .	. . .	. . .	. . .	. . .	. . .	. . .	. . .
of which: Short-term	4 774	. . .	. . .	. . .	. . .	. . .	. . .	. . .	. . .
Other sectors	4 775	–1,269	678	–952	634	4,893	15,587	14,430	12,557
of which: Short-term	4 777	*–533*	*711*	*795*	*339*	*1,810*	*9,657*	*3,818*	*647*
Currency and deposits	4 780	10,569	4,074	19,110	20,022	38,942	25,708	36,534	14,536
Monetary authorities	4 781	27	23	461	–466	–2	–11	–141	–185
General government	4 782	. . .	. . .	. . .	. . .	. . .	. . .	. . .	. . .
Banks	4 783	10,542	4,051	18,648	20,488	38,944	25,719	36,676	14,721
Other sectors	4 784	. . .	. . .	. . .	. . .	. . .	. . .	. . .	. . .
Other liabilities	4 786	30	–2	–2	2	13	320	–165	216
Monetary authorities	4 787	. . .	. . .	. . .	. . .	. . .	. . .	. . .	. . .
of which: Short-term	4 789	. . .	. . .	. . .	. . .	. . .	. . .	. . .	. . .
General government	4 790	. . .	. . .	. . .	. . .	. . .	. . .	. . .	. . .
of which: Short-term	4 792	. . .	. . .	. . .	. . .	. . .	. . .	. . .	. . .
Banks	4 793	30	–2	–2	2	13	320	–165	216
of which: Short-term	4 795	*30*	*–2*	*–2*	*2*	*13*	*320*	*–165*	*216*
Other sectors	4 796	. . .	. . .	. . .	. . .	. . .	. . .	. . .	. . .
of which: Short-term	4 798	. . .	. . .	. . .	. . .	. . .	. . .	. . .	. . .
E. RESERVE ASSETS	4 802	–36	6,414	–24,279	–11,756	14,355	22,850	2,881	1,340
Monetary gold	4 812	. . .	–6	. . .	. . .	–1,081	752	. . .	. . .
Special drawing rights	4 811	–25	–152	–54	–51	–77	302	–43	–73
Reserve position in the Fund	4 810	–13	–462	–66	–406	–202	610	269	–186
Foreign exchange	4 803	–3	7,025	–24,167	–11,315	15,669	21,131	2,655	1,599
Other claims	4 813	4	9	8	17	46	55	. . .	. . .
NET ERRORS AND OMISSIONS	4 998	**–371**	**–5,260**	**–2,856**	**–5,741**	**–3,395**	**–5,059**	**–5,379**	**–7,104**

Part 3 of the *Yearbook* contains descriptions of the methodologies, compilation practices, and sources used to compile these data.

Table 3. INTERNATIONAL INVESTMENT POSITION (End–period stocks), 1994–2001
(Millions of U.S. dollars)

	Code	1994	1995	1996	1997	1998	1999	2000	2001
ASSETS	8 995 C.	221,860	268,762	289,787	311,244	397,987	454,034	564,031	596,647
Direct investment abroad	8 505 . .	**30,052**	**36,225**	**40,548**	**50,322**	**70,130**	**112,746**	**165,894**	**190,593**
Equity capital and reinvested earnings	8 506 . .	28,101	33,605	37,562	46,842	63,433	105,289	152,722	171,467
Claims on affiliated enterprises	8 507 . .	...	...	...	...	...	...	...	...
Liabilities to affiliated enterprises	8 508 . .	...	...	...	...	...	...	...	...
Other capital	8 530 . .	1,951	2,619	2,986	3,481	6,697	7,457	13,172	19,127
Claims on affiliated enterprises	8 535 . .	2,346	3,097	3,405	3,797	7,419	8,388	15,038	21,148
Liabilities to affiliated enterprises	8 540 . .	–395	–478	–419	–316	–722	–931	–1,866	–2,021
Portfolio investment	8 602 . .	**17,284**	**18,244**	**21,108**	**34,858**	**81,237**	**117,868**	**171,599**	**202,139**
Equity securities	8 610 . .	3,454	3,764	4,441	9,235	19,978	33,060	70,953	67,960
Monetary authorities	8 611 . .	...	...	...	...	...	...	...	...
General government	8 612 . .	...	...	...	...	...	...	...	...
Banks	8 613 . .	600	404	556	1,074	1,977	2,810	6,183	3,789
Other sectors	8 614 . .	2,854	3,361	3,885	8,161	18,001	30,251	64,770	64,171
Debt securities	8 619 . .	13,830	14,480	16,667	25,623	61,259	84,807	100,646	134,180
Bonds and notes	8 620 . .	13,132	13,912	16,073	24,937	58,749	80,329	94,297	127,857
Monetary authorities	8 621 . .	...	...	...	...	...	...	...	...
General government	8 622 . .	...	...	...	...	...	...	...	...
Banks	8 623 . .	6,809	7,915	7,336	10,151	17,839	26,666	29,441	49,486
Other sectors	8 624 . .	6,323	5,996	8,737	14,786	40,910	53,663	64,856	78,371
Money market instruments	8 630 . .	698	568	594	686	2,510	4,479	6,349	6,322
Monetary authorities	8 631 . .	...	...	...	...	...	...	...	...
General government	8 632 . .	...	...	...	...	...	...	...	...
Banks	8 633 . .	569	338	396	356	708	3,558	1,994	2,263
Other sectors	8 634 . .	129	231	198	330	1,802	920	4,355	4,059
Financial derivatives	8 900 . .	**...**	**...**	**...**	**...**	**...**	**...**	**...**	**...**
Monetary authorities	8 901 . .	...	...	...	...	...	...	...	...
General government	8 902 . .	...	...	...	...	...	...	...	...
Banks	8 903 . .	...	...	...	...	...	...	...	...
Other sectors	8 904 . .	...	...	...	...	...	...	...	...
Other investment	8 703 . .	**130,690**	**176,931**	**167,717**	**155,680**	**185,832**	**185,410**	**190,962**	**169,660**
Trade credits	8 706 . .	...	...	...	...	...	...	...	...
General government	8 707 . .	...	...	...	...	...	...	...	...
of which: Short-term	8 709 . .	...	...	...	...	...	...	...	...
Other sectors	8 710 . .	...	...	...	...	...	...	...	...
of which: Short-term	8 712 . .	...	...	...	...	...	...	...	...
Loans	8 714 . .	19,091	23,697	22,274	23,968	26,717	24,403	25,820	29,045
Monetary authorities	8 715 . .	...	...	...	...	...	...	...	...
of which: Short-term	8 718 . .	...	...	...	...	...	...	...	...
General government	8 719 . .	4,266	4,596	4,837	4,918	5,147	5,199	5,278	5,325
of which: Short-term	8 721 . .	...	...	...	...	...	...	...	...
Banks	8 722 . .	14,324	18,392	16,690	18,286	20,679	18,449	19,690	22,745
of which: Short-term	8 724 . .	...	...	...	...	...	...	...	...
Other sectors	8 725 . .	501	708	747	765	891	754	852	975
of which: Short-term	8 727 . .	...	...	...	...	...	...	...	...
Currency and deposits	8 730 . .	108,328	149,396	141,687	128,199	154,551	156,743	161,072	136,704
Monetary authorities	8 731 . .	159	173	160	138	63	36,205	42,143	25,675
General government	8 732 . .	46	66	122	152	280	223	236	242
Banks	8 733 . .	82,762	112,479	100,065	76,670	80,059	66,380	68,116	63,932
Other sectors	8 734 . .	25,361	36,678	41,341	51,239	74,148	53,935	50,576	46,854
Other assets	8 736 . .	3,272	3,838	3,755	3,513	4,565	4,265	4,069	3,911
Monetary authorities	8 737 . .	...	74	69	59	519	447	414	392
of which: Short-term	8 739 . .	...	...	...	...	...	...	...	...
General government	8 740 . .	1,154	1,367	1,364	1,259	1,445	1,295	1,274	1,330
of which: Short-term	8 742 . .	...	...	...	...	...	...	...	...
Banks	8 743 . .	...	...	8	...	...	11	30	93
of which: Short-term	8 745 . .	...	...	...	...	...	...	...	...
Other sectors	8 746 . .	2,118	2,397	2,316	2,195	2,602	2,512	2,351	2,096
of which: Short-term	8 748 . .	...	...	...	...	...	...	...	...
Reserve assets	8 802 . .	**43,834**	**37,362**	**60,414**	**70,384**	**60,788**	**38,010**	**35,576**	**34,254**
Monetary gold	8 812 . .	2,558	2,784	2,575	2,182	5,617	4,895	4,588	4,672
Special drawing rights	8 811 . .	255	411	451	474	575	260	290	351
Reserve position in the Fund	8 810 . .	1,109	1,583	1,597	1,902	2,193	1,525	1,182	1,326
Foreign exchange	8 803 . .	39,601	32,279	55,502	65,569	52,185	31,329	29,515	27,905
Other claims	8 813 . .	311	305	289	257	217	...	...	...

Table 3 (Concluded). INTERNATIONAL INVESTMENT POSITION (End–period stocks), 1994–2001

(Millions of U.S. dollars)

	Code	1994	1995	1996	1997	1998	1999	2000	2001
LIABILITIES	8 995 D.	322,228	383,415	400,206	410,687	528,172	571,105	672,855	717,313
Direct investment in Spain	8 555 . .	**96,312**	**109,185**	**107,880**	**100,025**	**118,115**	**116,680**	**144,718**	**163,986**
Equity capital and reinvested earnings	8 556 . .	80,720	91,723	90,855	85,833	98,004	97,868	120,898	132,435
Claims on direct investors	8 557 . .	...	...	...	...	...	...	...	...
Liabilities to direct investors	8 558 . .	...	...	...	...	...	...	...	...
Other capital	8 580 . .	15,591	17,462	17,025	14,192	20,111	18,812	23,820	31,551
Claims on direct investors	8 585 . .	–774	–1,021	–1,074	–1,516	–2,728	–3,343	–3,779	–4,195
Liabilities to direct investors	8 590 . .	16,366	18,483	18,099	15,708	22,839	22,155	27,599	35,746
Portfolio investment	8 652 . .	**83,764**	**118,426**	**126,696**	**137,322**	**183,995**	**209,710**	**243,155**	**252,039**
Equity securities	8 660 . .	24,146	32,461	39,162	46,974	75,775	86,820	90,918	88,187
Banks	8 663 . .	7,348	11,993	15,433	21,766	32,411	35,126	45,032	39,968
Other sectors	8 664 . .	16,798	20,468	23,729	25,207	43,364	51,694	45,887	48,219
Debt securities	8 669 . .	59,618	85,966	87,534	90,348	108,221	122,891	152,237	163,852
Bonds and notes	8 670 . .	57,826	82,300	83,458	86,868	106,538	119,079	147,434	160,945
Monetary authorities	8 671 . .	...	...	...	...	...	...	...	...
General government	8 672 . .	51,071	75,497	75,871	78,661	95,788	101,502	124,117	127,635
Banks	8 673 . .	2,596	2,191	3,138	3,981	6,788	12,420	15,839	20,593
Other sectors	8 674 . .	4,160	4,613	4,449	4,225	3,962	5,158	7,478	12,716
Money market instruments	8 680 . .	1,791	3,665	4,075	3,481	1,683	3,811	4,803	2,907
Monetary authorities	8 681 . .	...	...	...	...	...	...	...	...
General government	8 682 . .	1,359	3,229	3,634	2,999	1,199	2,209	3,162	1,408
Banks	8 683 . .	182	198	183	224	147	152	142	113
Other sectors	8 684 . .	250	239	259	257	337	1,451	1,499	1,386
Financial derivatives	8 905 . .	...	...	...	...	...	...	...	...
Monetary authorities	8 906 . .	...	...	...	...	...	...	...	...
General government	8 907 . .	...	...	...	...	...	...	...	...
Banks	8 908 . .	...	...	...	...	...	...	...	...
Other sectors	8 909 . .	...	...	...	...	...	...	...	...
Other investment	8 753 . .	**142,152**	**155,804**	**165,629**	**173,340**	**226,062**	**244,715**	**284,981**	**301,287**
Trade credits	8 756 . .	...	...	...	...	...	...	...	...
General government	8 757 . .	...	...	...	...	...	...	...	...
of which: Short-term	8 759 . .	...	...	...	...	...	...	...	...
Other sectors	8 760 . .	...	...	...	...	...	...	...	...
of which: Short-term	8 762 . .	...	...	...	...	...	...	...	...
Loans	8 764 . .	36,754	40,582	36,930	34,541	42,487	53,014	65,167	74,809
Monetary authorities	8 765 . .	...	...	...	...	...	...	...	...
of which: Use of Fund credit and loans from the Fund	8 766 . .	...	...	...	...	...	...	...	...
of which: Short-term	8 768 . .	...	...	...	...	...	...	...	...
General government	8 769 . .	9,989	12,355	11,503	10,158	11,725	10,158	10,419	10,349
of which: Short-term	8 771 . .	...	...	...	...	...	...	...	...
Banks	8 772 . .	...	...	...	...	...	...	...	...
of which: Short-term	8 774 . .	...	...	...	...	...	...	...	...
Other sectors	8 775 . .	26,765	28,227	25,428	24,383	30,763	42,856	54,748	64,460
of which: Short-term	8 777 . .	...	...	...	...	...	...	...	...
Currency and deposits	8 780 . .	104,988	114,613	128,326	138,403	183,147	191,124	219,630	226,072
Monetary authorities	8 781 . .	76	107	556	53	63	34	422	263
General government	8 782 . .	...	...	...	...	...	...	...	...
Banks	8 783 . .	104,912	114,506	127,770	138,350	183,084	191,090	219,207	225,809
Other sectors	8 784 . .	...	...	...	...	...	...	...	...
Other liabilities	8 786 . .	410	610	373	396	428	577	185	406
Monetary authorities	8 787 . .	...	...	...	...	...	...	...	...
of which: Short-term	8 789 . .	...	...	...	...	...	...	...	...
General government	8 790 . .	...	...	...	...	...	...	...	...
of which: Short-term	8 792 . .	...	...	...	...	...	...	...	...
Banks	8 793 . .	...	...	...	...	...	...	...	...
of which: Short-term	8 795 . .	...	...	...	...	...	...	...	...
Other sectors	8 796 . .	410	610	373	396	428	577	185	406
of which: Short-term	8 798 . .	...	...	...	...	...	...	...	...
NET INTERNATIONAL INVESTMENT POSITION	8 995 . .	**–100,368**	**–114,653**	**–110,418**	**–99,442**	**–130,185**	**–117,071**	**–108,823**	**–120,666**
Conversion rates: pesetas per U.S. dollar (end of period)	0 102 . .	**131.74**	**121.41**	**131.28**	**151.70**	**142.61**	...	...	...
Conversion rates: euros per U.S. dollar (end of period)	0 104 . .	...	...	...	...	...	**.9954**	**1.0747**	**1.1347**

Table 1. ANALYTIC PRESENTATION, 1994–2001

(Millions of U.S. dollars)

	Code		1994	1995	1996	1997	1998	1999	2000	2001
A. Current Account [1]	4 993	Z.	**–757.4**	**–769.9**	**–682.7**	**–394.7**	**–227.7**	**–561.3**	**–1,043.6**	**–264.7**
Goods: exports f.o.b	2 100	. .	3,208.3	3,797.9	4,095.2	4,638.7	4,808.0	4,596.2	5,439.6	4,821.1
Goods: imports f.o.b	3 100	. .	–4,293.4	–4,782.6	–4,895.0	–5,278.3	–5,313.4	–5,365.5	–6,483.6	–5,374.6
Balance on Goods	4 100	. .	*–1,085.0*	*–984.7*	*–799.7*	*–639.6*	*–505.4*	*–769.3*	*–1,044.0*	*–553.5*
Services: credit	2 200	. .	753.9	819.2	765.5	875.3	916.6	964.3	938.7	1,365.9
Services: debit	3 200	. .	–1,052.3	–1,199.1	–1,204.3	–1,302.6	–1,361.6	–1,413.7	–1,621.4	–1,755.6
Balance on Goods and Services	4 991	. .	*–1,383.4*	*–1,364.6*	*–1,238.6*	*–1,066.9*	*–950.5*	*–1,218.6*	*–1,726.7*	*–943.1*
Income: credit	2 300	. .	143.9	223.3	175.1	233.3	214.2	166.7	149.0	93.4
Income: debit	3 300	. .	–312.0	–360.6	–378.2	–392.9	–394.5	–419.3	–448.9	–373.9
Balance on Goods, Services, and Income	4 992	. .	*–1,551.6*	*–1,501.9*	*–1,441.6*	*–1,226.5*	*–1,130.8*	*–1,471.2*	*–2,026.6*	*–1,223.6*
Current transfers: credit	2 379	Z.	882.3	846.7	881.4	966.5	1,054.5	1,078.1	1,165.7	1,145.7
Current transfers: debit	3 379	. .	–88.1	–114.7	–122.4	–134.7	–151.3	–168.2	–182.7	–186.8
B. Capital Account [1]	4 994	Z.	**. . .**	**120.6**	**95.9**	**87.1**	**79.9**	**80.0**	**49.4**	**49.1**
Capital account: credit	2 994	Z.	. . .	124.2	99.7	91.3	84.6	85.2	55.0	54.9
Capital account: debit	3 994	. .	. . .	–3.5	–3.8	–4.2	–4.7	–5.2	–5.7	–5.8
Total, Groups A Plus B	4 981	. .	*–757.4*	*–649.3*	*–586.8*	*–307.6*	*–147.7*	*–481.3*	*–994.2*	*–215.6*
C. Financial Account [1]	4 995	W.	**958.8**	**730.1**	**452.2**	**466.7**	**345.1**	**413.4**	**447.2**	**380.2**
Direct investment abroad	4 505	. .	–8.3	. . .	. . .	. . .	. . .	. . .	. . .	. . .
Direct investment in Sri Lanka	4 555	Z.	166.4	56.0	119.9	430.1	193.4	176.4	173.0	171.7
Portfolio investment assets	4 602	. .	292.9	105.3	76.8	139.9	88.9	71.8	19.1	23.6
Equity securities	4 610	. .	. . .	. . .	. . .	. . .	. . .	. . .	. . .	. . .
Debt securities	4 619	. .	292.9	105.3	76.8	139.9	88.9	71.8	19.1	23.6
Portfolio investment liabilities	4 652	Z.	–265.9	–107.3	–70.2	–126.8	–112.9	–84.6	–63.4	–34.7
Equity securities	4 660	. .	. . .	. . .	. . .	. . .	. . .	. . .	. . .	. . .
Debt securities	4 669	Z.	–265.9	–107.3	–70.2	–126.8	–112.9	–84.6	–63.4	–34.7
Financial derivatives	4 910	. .	. . .	. . .	. . .	. . .	. . .	. . .	. . .	. . .
Financial derivatives assets	4 900	. .	. . .	. . .	. . .	. . .	. . .	. . .	. . .	. . .
Financial derivatives liabilities	4 905	. .	. . .	. . .	. . .	. . .	. . .	. . .	. . .	. . .
Other investment assets	4 703	. .	–134.0	41.7	–27.9	–392.9	75.9	23.2	–243.7	13.0
Monetary authorities	4 701	. .	. . .	. . .	. . .	. . .	. . .	. . .	. . .	. . .
General government	4 704	. .	9.4	3.6	–6.4	1.7	–2.9	–1.1	–4.4	–10.7
Banks	4 705	. .	–143.4	38.1	–21.5	–394.6	78.8	24.3	–239.4	23.8
Other sectors	4 728	. .	. . .	. . .	. . .	. . .	. . .	. . .	. . .	. . .
Other investment liabilities	4 753	W.	907.6	634.4	353.6	416.5	99.7	226.6	562.3	206.6
Monetary authorities	4 753	WA	9.6	14.4	11.6	30.3	17.5	65.8	75.8	20.1
General government	4 753	ZB	246.9	448.4	218.0	144.5	203.6	62.5	46.6	248.1
Banks	4 753	ZC	73.4	86.7	95.8	209.4	–130.7	–88.4	258.3	213.3
Other sectors	4 753	ZD	577.7	85.0	28.2	32.3	9.3	186.8	181.5	–274.9
Total, Groups A Through C	4 983	. .	*201.3*	*80.8*	*–134.6*	*159.2*	*197.3*	*–67.9*	*–547.0*	*164.6*
D. Net Errors and Omissions	4 998	. .	**106.3**	**157.9**	**143.6**	**148.0**	**26.3**	**–27.3**	**186.2**	**164.7**
Total, Groups A Through D	4 984	. .	*307.7*	*238.7*	*9.0*	*307.2*	*223.6*	*–95.2*	*–360.8*	*329.3*
E. Reserves and Related Items	4 802	A.	**–307.7**	**–238.7**	**–9.0**	**–307.2**	**–223.6**	**95.2**	**360.8**	**–329.3**
Reserve assets	4 802	. .	–373.5	–204.7	36.3	–241.4	–141.0	194.8	446.5	–389.0
Use of Fund credit and loans	4 766	. .	65.9	–34.1	–45.2	–65.7	–82.6	–99.7	–85.7	59.8
Exceptional financing	4 920	. .	. . .	. . .	. . .	. . .	. . .	. . .	. . .	. . .
Conversion rates: Sri Lanka rupees per U.S. dollar	0 101	. .	**49.415**	**51.252**	**55.271**	**58.995**	**64.450**	**70.635**	**77.005**	**89.383**

[1] Excludes components that have been classified in the categories of Group E.

Table 2. STANDARD PRESENTATION, 1994–2001

(Millions of U.S. dollars)

	Code		1994	1995	1996	1997	1998	1999	2000	2001
CURRENT ACCOUNT	4 993	. .	**–757.4**	**–769.9**	**–682.7**	**–394.7**	**–227.7**	**–561.3**	**–1,043.6**	**–264.7**
A. GOODS	4 100	. .	–1,085.0	–984.7	–799.7	–639.6	–505.4	–769.3	–1,044.0	–553.5
Credit	2 100	. .	**3,208.3**	**3,797.9**	**4,095.2**	**4,638.7**	**4,808.0**	**4,596.2**	**5,439.6**	**4,821.1**
General merchandise: exports f.o.b.	2 110	. .	3,208.3	3,797.9	4,095.2	4,638.7	4,808.0	4,596.2	5,439.6	4,821.1
Goods for processing: exports f.o.b.	2 150	. .	. . .	. . .	. . .	. . .	. . .	. . .	. . .	. . .
Repairs on goods	2 160	. .	. . .	. . .	. . .	. . .	. . .	. . .	. . .	. . .
Goods procured in ports by carriers	2 170	. .	. . .	. . .	. . .	. . .	. . .	. . .	. . .	. . .
Nonmonetary gold	2 180	. .	. . .	. . .	. . .	. . .	. . .	. . .	. . .	. . .
Debit	3 100	. .	**–4,293.4**	**–4,782.6**	**–4,895.0**	**–5,278.3**	**–5,313.4**	**–5,365.5**	**–6,483.6**	**–5,374.6**
General merchandise: imports f.o.b.	3 110	. .	–4,293.4	–4,782.6	–4,895.0	–5,278.3	–5,313.4	–5,365.5	–6,483.6	–5,374.6
Goods for processing: imports f.o.b.	3 150	. .	. . .	. . .	. . .	. . .	. . .	. . .	. . .	. . .
Repairs on goods	3 160	. .	. . .	. . .	. . .	. . .	. . .	. . .	. . .	. . .
Goods procured in ports by carriers	3 170	. .	. . .	. . .	. . .	. . .	. . .	. . .	. . .	. . .
Nonmonetary gold	3 180	. .	. . .	. . .	. . .	. . .	. . .	. . .	. . .	. . .
B. SERVICES	4 200	. .	–298.4	–379.9	–438.8	–427.3	–445.0	–449.4	–682.7	–389.7
Total credit	2 200	. .	*753.9*	*819.2*	*765.5*	*875.3*	*916.6*	*964.3*	*938.7*	*1,365.9*
Total debit	3 200	. .	*–1,052.3*	*–1,199.1*	*–1,204.3*	*–1,302.6*	*–1,361.6*	*–1,413.7*	*–1,621.4*	*–1,755.6*
Transportation services, credit	2 205	. .	**293.1**	**335.1**	**339.2**	**389.0**	**402.9**	**403.3**	**399.8**	**398.4**
Passenger	2 850	. .	*124.4*	*140.7*	*115.9*	*141.8*	*139.4*	*141.3*	*139.8*	*136.1*
Freight	2 851	. .	*26.1*	*26.8*	*28.5*	*33.3*	*34.3*	*36.5*	*42.3*	*41.5*
Other	2 852	. .	*142.6*	*167.6*	*194.8*	*213.9*	*229.2*	*225.5*	*217.6*	*220.8*
Sea transport, passenger	2 207	. .	. . .	. . .	. . .	. . .	. . .	. . .	. . .	. . .
Sea transport, freight	2 208	. .	. . .	. . .	. . .	. . .	. . .	. . .	. . .	. . .
Sea transport, other	2 209	. .	. . .	. . .	. . .	. . .	. . .	. . .	. . .	. . .
Air transport, passenger	2 211	. .	. . .	. . .	. . .	. . .	. . .	. . .	. . .	. . .
Air transport, freight	2 212	. .	. . .	. . .	. . .	. . .	. . .	. . .	. . .	. . .
Air transport, other	2 213	. .	. . .	. . .	. . .	. . .	. . .	. . .	. . .	. . .
Other transport, passenger	2 215	. .	. . .	. . .	. . .	. . .	. . .	. . .	. . .	. . .
Other transport, freight	2 216	. .	. . .	. . .	. . .	. . .	. . .	. . .	. . .	. . .
Other transport, other	2 217	. .	. . .	. . .	. . .	. . .	. . .	. . .	. . .	. . .
Transportation services, debit	3 205	. .	**–583.2**	**–678.7**	**–690.4**	**–761.0**	**–794.8**	**–818.3**	**–980.0**	**–845.9**
Passenger	3 850	. .	*–62.0*	*–93.0*	*–91.0*	*–100.4*	*–123.9*	*–122.8*	*–143.2*	*–152.0*
Freight	3 851	. .	*–465.2*	*–520.5*	*–534.3*	*–581.8*	*–588.5*	*–601.7*	*–723.9*	*–600.3*
Other	3 852	. .	*–56.0*	*–65.2*	*–65.1*	*–78.8*	*–82.3*	*–93.8*	*–112.9*	*–93.6*
Sea transport, passenger	3 207	. .	. . .	. . .	. . .	. . .	. . .	. . .	. . .	. . .
Sea transport, freight	3 208	. .	. . .	. . .	. . .	. . .	. . .	. . .	. . .	. . .
Sea transport, other	3 209	. .	. . .	. . .	. . .	. . .	. . .	. . .	. . .	. . .
Air transport, passenger	3 211	. .	. . .	. . .	. . .	. . .	. . .	. . .	. . .	. . .
Air transport, freight	3 212	. .	. . .	. . .	. . .	. . .	. . .	. . .	. . .	. . .
Air transport, other	3 213	. .	. . .	. . .	. . .	. . .	. . .	. . .	. . .	. . .
Other transport, passenger	3 215	. .	. . .	. . .	. . .	. . .	. . .	. . .	. . .	. . .
Other transport, freight	3 216	. .	. . .	. . .	. . .	. . .	. . .	. . .	. . .	. . .
Other transport, other	3 217	. .	. . .	. . .	. . .	. . .	. . .	. . .	. . .	. . .
Travel, credit	2 236	. .	**230.2**	**225.9**	**166.2**	**208.8**	**230.2**	**273.2**	**247.8**	**212.6**
Business travel	2 237	. .	. . .	. . .	. . .	. . .	. . .	. . .	. . .	. . .
Personal travel	2 240	. .	. . .	. . .	. . .	. . .	. . .	. . .	. . .	. . .
Travel, debit	3 236	. .	**–169.6**	**–186.4**	**–175.8**	**–179.6**	**–202.0**	**–218.0**	**–240.3**	**–245.0**
Business travel	3 237	. .	. . .	. . .	. . .	. . .	. . .	. . .	. . .	. . .
Personal travel	3 240	. .	. . .	. . .	. . .	. . .	. . .	. . .	. . .	. . .
Other services, credit	2 200	BA	**230.6**	**258.2**	**260.1**	**277.6**	**283.6**	**287.8**	**291.1**	**755.0**
Communications	2 245	. .	. . .	. . .	. . .	. . .	. . .	. . .	45.3	39.4
Construction	2 249	. .	. . .	. . .	. . .	. . .	. . .	. . .	. . .	33.6
Insurance	2 253	. .	20.4	26.9	27.5	29.8	33.9	37.0	40.6	423.3
Financial	2 260	. .	. . .	. . .	. . .	. . .	. . .	. . .	. . .	. . .
Computer and information	2 262	. .	. . .	. . .	. . .	. . .	. . .	. . .	. . .	66.0
Royalties and licence fees	2 266	. .	. . .	. . .	. . .	. . .	. . .	. . .	. . .	. . .
Other business services	2 268	. .	185.4	212.0	208.3	222.8	224.6	226.1	181.7	170.4
Personal, cultural, and recreational	2 287	. .	. . .	. . .	. . .	. . .	. . .	. . .	. . .	. . .
Government, n.i.e.	2 291	. .	24.8	19.3	24.3	25.0	25.1	24.8	23.6	22.3
Other services, debit	3 200	BA	**–299.4**	**–334.0**	**–338.2**	**–362.0**	**–364.8**	**–377.4**	**–401.2**	**–664.8**
Communications	3 245	. .	. . .	. . .	. . .	. . .	. . .	. . .	–46.9	–44.4
Construction	3 249	. .	. . .	. . .	. . .	. . .	. . .	. . .	. . .	. . .
Insurance	3 253	. .	–60.0	–63.4	–72.4	–78.6	–77.3	–79.5	–93.9	–374.4
Financial	3 260	. .	. . .	. . .	. . .	. . .	. . .	. . .	. . .	. . .
Computer and information	3 262	. .	. . .	. . .	. . .	. . .	. . .	. . .	. . .	. . .
Royalties and licence fees	3 266	. .	. . .	. . .	. . .	. . .	. . .	. . .	. . .	. . .
Other business services	3 268	. .	–207.1	–240.1	–235.0	–251.9	–253.9	–272.6	–230.6	–219.5
Personal, cultural, and recreational	3 287	. .	. . .	. . .	. . .	. . .	. . .	. . .	. . .	. . .
Government, n.i.e.	3 291	. .	–32.3	–30.5	–30.9	–31.5	–33.6	–25.2	–29.9	–26.6

Table 2 (Continued). STANDARD PRESENTATION, 1994–2001
(Millions of U.S. dollars)

	Code	1994	1995	1996	1997	1998	1999	2000	2001
C. INCOME	4 300 . .	–168.1	–137.3	–203.1	–159.6	–180.3	–252.6	–299.9	–280.5
Total credit	2 300 . .	*143.9*	*223.3*	*175.1*	*233.3*	*214.2*	*166.7*	*149.0*	*93.4*
Total debit	3 300 . .	*–312.0*	*–360.6*	*–378.2*	*–392.9*	*–394.5*	*–419.3*	*–448.9*	*–373.9*
Compensation of employees, credit	2 310 . .	**. . .**	**11.2**	**11.0**	**11.7**	**11.8**	**11.9**	**12.0**	**14.6**
Compensation of employees, debit	3 310 . .	**. . .**	**–12.6**	**–12.4**	**–13.3**	**–13.4**	**–13.5**	**–14.0**	**–16.7**
Investment income, credit	2 320 . .	**143.9**	**212.2**	**164.2**	**221.6**	**202.3**	**154.8**	**137.1**	**78.8**
Direct investment income	2 330 . .	.7	1.1	1.4	2.0	2.0	2.1	2.1	1.5
Dividends and distributed branch profits	2 332 . .	.7	1.1	1.4	2.0	2.0	2.1	2.1	1.5
Reinvested earnings and undistributed branch profits	2 333 . .	. . .	. . .	. . .	. . .	. . .	. . .	. . .	. . .
Income on debt (interest)	2 334 . .	. . .	. . .	. . .	. . .	. . .	. . .	. . .	. . .
Portfolio investment income	2 339 . .	. . .	. . .	. . .	. . .	. . .	. . .	. . .	. . .
Income on equity	2 340 . .	. . .	. . .	. . .	. . .	. . .	. . .	. . .	. . .
Income on bonds and notes	2 350 . .	. . .	. . .	. . .	. . .	. . .	. . .	. . .	. . .
Income on money market instruments	2 360 . .	. . .	. . .	. . .	. . .	. . .	. . .	. . .	. . .
Other investment income	2 370 . .	143.2	211.1	162.7	219.5	200.3	152.8	135.0	77.3
Investment income, debit	3 320 . .	**–312.0**	**–348.0**	**–365.8**	**–379.6**	**–381.2**	**–405.8**	**–434.9**	**–357.2**
Direct investment income	3 330 . .	–74.8	–71.7	–64.3	–76.9	–91.2	–110.9	–108.6	–103.5
Dividends and distributed branch profits	3 332 . .	–67.3	–64.5	–57.8	–69.2	–82.1	–99.8	–97.7	–93.1
Reinvested earnings and undistributed branch profits	3 333 . .	–7.5	–7.2	–6.4	–7.7	–9.1	–11.1	–10.9	–10.3
Income on debt (interest)	3 334 . .	. . .	. . .	. . .	. . .	. . .	. . .	. . .	. . .
Portfolio investment income	3 339 . .	. . .	. . .	. . .	. . .	. . .	. . .	. . .	. . .
Income on equity	3 340 . .	. . .	. . .	. . .	. . .	. . .	. . .	. . .	. . .
Income on bonds and notes	3 350 . .	. . .	. . .	. . .	. . .	. . .	. . .	. . .	. . .
Income on money market instruments	3 360 . .	. . .	. . .	. . .	. . .	. . .	. . .	. . .	. . .
Other investment income	3 370 . .	–237.2	–276.3	–301.6	–302.7	–289.9	–294.9	–326.3	–253.7
D. CURRENT TRANSFERS	4 379 . .	794.1	731.9	759.0	831.8	903.2	909.9	983.0	958.9
Credit	2 379 . .	**882.3**	**846.7**	**881.4**	**966.5**	**1,054.5**	**1,078.1**	**1,165.7**	**1,145.7**
General government	2 380 . .	167.1	56.8	49.1	44.5	53.0	25.7	23.4	21.5
Other sectors	2 390 . .	715.2	789.8	832.2	922.0	1,001.5	1,052.4	1,142.3	1,124.2
Workers' remittances	2 391 . .	715.2	789.8	832.2	922.0	1,001.5	1,052.4	1,142.3	1,124.2
Other current transfers	2 392 . .	. . .	. . .	. . .	. . .	. . .	. . .	. . .	. . .
Debit	3 379 . .	**–88.1**	**–114.7**	**–122.4**	**–134.7**	**–151.3**	**–168.2**	**–182.7**	**–186.8**
General government	3 380 . .	. . .	. . .	. . .	. . .	. . .	. . .	. . .	. . .
Other sectors	3 390 . .	–88.1	–114.7	–122.4	–134.7	–151.3	–168.2	–182.7	–186.8
Workers' remittances	3 391 . .	. . .	. . .	. . .	. . .	. . .	. . .	. . .	. . .
Other current transfers	3 392 . .	–88.1	–114.7	–122.4	–134.7	–151.3	–168.2	–182.7	–186.8
CAPITAL AND FINANCIAL ACCOUNT	4 996 . .	**651.1**	**612.0**	**539.1**	**246.7**	**201.4**	**588.6**	**857.4**	**100.1**
CAPITAL ACCOUNT	4 994 . .	**. . .**	**120.6**	**95.9**	**87.1**	**79.9**	**80.0**	**49.4**	**49.1**
Total credit	2 994 . .	*. . .*	*124.2*	*99.7*	*91.3*	*84.6*	*85.2*	*55.0*	*54.9*
Total debit	3 994 . .	*. . .*	*–3.5*	*–3.8*	*–4.2*	*–4.7*	*–5.2*	*–5.7*	*–5.8*
Capital transfers, credit	2 400 . .	**. . .**	**124.2**	**99.7**	**91.3**	**84.6**	**85.2**	**55.0**	**54.9**
General government	2 401 . .	. . .	116.2	91.3	82.6	74.5	77.1	43.5	40.0
Debt forgiveness	2 402 . .	. . .	. . .	. . .	. . .	. . .	. . .	. . .	. . .
Other capital transfers	2 410 . .	. . .	. . .	. . .	. . .	. . .	. . .	. . .	. . .
Other sectors	2 430 . .	. . .	8.0	8.4	8.7	10.1	8.1	11.5	14.9
Migrants' transfers	2 431 . .	. . .	8.0	8.4	8.7	10.1	8.1	11.5	14.9
Debt forgiveness	2 432 . .	. . .	. . .	. . .	. . .	. . .	. . .	. . .	. . .
Other capital transfers	2 440 . .	. . .	. . .	. . .	. . .	. . .	. . .	. . .	. . .
Capital transfers, debit	3 400 . .	**. . .**	**–3.5**	**–3.8**	**–4.2**	**–4.7**	**–5.2**	**–5.7**	**–5.8**
General government	3 401 . .	. . .	. . .	. . .	. . .	. . .	. . .	. . .	. . .
Debt forgiveness	3 402 . .	. . .	. . .	. . .	. . .	. . .	. . .	. . .	. . .
Other capital transfers	3 410 . .	. . .	. . .	. . .	. . .	. . .	. . .	. . .	. . .
Other sectors	3 430 . .	. . .	–3.5	–3.8	–4.2	–4.7	–5.2	–5.7	–5.8
Migrants' transfers	3 431 . .	. . .	–3.5	–3.8	–4.2	–4.7	–5.2	–5.7	–5.8
Debt forgiveness	3 432 . .	. . .	. . .	. . .	. . .	. . .	. . .	. . .	. . .
Other capital transfers	3 440 . .	. . .	. . .	. . .	. . .	. . .	. . .	. . .	. . .
Nonproduced nonfinancial assets, credit	2 480 . .	**. . .**	**. . .**	**. . .**	**. . .**	**. . .**	**. . .**	**. . .**	**. . .**
Nonproduced nonfinancial assets, debit	3 480 . .	**. . .**	**. . .**	**. . .**	**. . .**	**. . .**	**. . .**	**. . .**	**. . .**

Table 2 (Continued). STANDARD PRESENTATION, 1994–2001

(Millions of U.S. dollars)

	Code	1994	1995	1996	1997	1998	1999	2000	2001
FINANCIAL ACCOUNT	4 995 . .	**651.1**	**491.4**	**443.2**	**159.6**	**121.5**	**508.6**	**808.0**	**50.9**
A. DIRECT INVESTMENT	4 500 . .	158.2	56.0	119.9	430.1	193.4	176.4	173.0	171.7
Direct investment abroad	4 505 . .	**-8.3**	**. . .**	**. . .**	**. . .**	**. . .**	**. . .**	**. . .**	**. . .**
Equity capital	4 510 . .	-8.3	. . .	. . .	. . .	. . .	. . .	. . .	. . .
Claims on affiliated enterprises	4 515 . .	. . .	. . .	. . .	. . .	. . .	. . .	. . .	. . .
Liabilities to affiliated enterprises	4 520 . .	. . .	. . .	. . .	. . .	. . .	. . .	. . .	. . .
Reinvested earnings	4 525 . .	. . .	. . .	. . .	. . .	. . .	. . .	. . .	. . .
Other capital	4 530 . .	. . .	. . .	. . .	. . .	. . .	. . .	. . .	. . .
Claims on affiliated enterprises	4 535 . .	. . .	. . .	. . .	. . .	. . .	. . .	. . .	. . .
Liabilities to affiliated enterprises	4 540 . .	. . .	. . .	. . .	. . .	. . .	. . .	. . .	. . .
Direct investment in Sri Lanka	4 555 . .	**166.4**	**56.0**	**119.9**	**430.1**	**193.4**	**176.4**	**173.0**	**171.7**
Equity capital	4 560 . .	158.9	56.1	126.7	427.2	197.7	189.6	164.1	161.4
Claims on direct investors	4 565 . .	. . .	. . .	. . .	. . .	. . .	. . .	. . .	. . .
Liabilities to direct investors	4 570 . .	. . .	. . .	. . .	. . .	. . .	. . .	. . .	. . .
Reinvested earnings	4 575 . .	7.5	7.2	6.4	7.7	9.1	11.1	10.9	10.3
Other capital	4 580 . .	. . .	-7.3	-13.3	-4.8	-13.4	-24.3	-2.0	. . .
Claims on direct investors	4 585 . .	. . .	. . .	. . .	. . .	. . .	. . .	. . .	. . .
Liabilities to direct investors	4 590 . .	. . .	-7.3	-13.3	-4.8	-13.4	-24.3	-2.0	. . .
B. PORTFOLIO INVESTMENT	4 600 . .	27.0	-2.0	6.7	13.1	-24.0	-12.8	-44.3	-11.1
Assets	4 602 . .	**292.9**	**105.3**	**76.8**	**139.9**	**88.9**	**71.8**	**19.1**	**23.6**
Equity securities	4 610 . .	. . .	. . .	. . .	. . .	. . .	. . .	. . .	. . .
Monetary authorities	4 611 . .	. . .	. . .	. . .	. . .	. . .	. . .	. . .	. . .
General government	4 612 . .	. . .	. . .	. . .	. . .	. . .	. . .	. . .	. . .
Banks	4 613 . .	. . .	. . .	. . .	. . .	. . .	. . .	. . .	. . .
Other sectors	4 614 . .	. . .	. . .	. . .	. . .	. . .	. . .	. . .	. . .
Debt securities	4 619 . .	292.9	105.3	76.8	139.9	88.9	71.8	19.1	23.6
Bonds and notes	4 620 . .	292.9	105.3	76.8	139.9	88.9	71.8	19.1	23.6
Monetary authorities	4 621 . .	. . .	. . .	. . .	. . .	. . .	. . .	. . .	. . .
General government	4 622 . .	. . .	. . .	. . .	. . .	. . .	. . .	. . .	. . .
Banks	4 623 . .	. . .	. . .	. . .	. . .	. . .	. . .	. . .	. . .
Other sectors	4 624 . .	. . .	. . .	. . .	. . .	. . .	. . .	. . .	. . .
Money market instruments	4 630 . .	. . .	. . .	. . .	. . .	. . .	. . .	. . .	. . .
Monetary authorities	4 631 . .	. . .	. . .	. . .	. . .	. . .	. . .	. . .	. . .
General government	4 632 . .	. . .	. . .	. . .	. . .	. . .	. . .	. . .	. . .
Banks	4 633 . .	. . .	. . .	. . .	. . .	. . .	. . .	. . .	. . .
Other sectors	4 634 . .	. . .	. . .	. . .	. . .	. . .	. . .	. . .	. . .
Liabilities	4 652 . .	**-265.9**	**-107.3**	**-70.2**	**-126.8**	**-112.9**	**-84.6**	**-63.4**	**-34.7**
Equity securities	4 660 . .	. . .	. . .	. . .	. . .	. . .	. . .	. . .	. . .
Banks	4 663 . .	. . .	. . .	. . .	. . .	. . .	. . .	. . .	. . .
Other sectors	4 664 . .	. . .	. . .	. . .	. . .	. . .	. . .	. . .	. . .
Debt securities	4 669 . .	-265.9	-107.3	-70.2	-126.8	-112.9	-84.6	-63.4	-34.7
Bonds and notes	4 670 . .	-265.9	-107.3	-70.2	-126.8	-112.9	-84.6	-63.4	-34.7
Monetary authorities	4 671 . .	. . .	. . .	. . .	. . .	. . .	. . .	. . .	. . .
General government	4 672 . .	. . .	. . .	. . .	. . .	. . .	. . .	. . .	. . .
Banks	4 673 . .	. . .	. . .	. . .	. . .	. . .	. . .	. . .	. . .
Other sectors	4 674 . .	. . .	. . .	. . .	. . .	. . .	. . .	. . .	. . .
Money market instruments	4 680 . .	. . .	. . .	. . .	. . .	. . .	. . .	. . .	. . .
Monetary authorities	4 681 . .	. . .	. . .	. . .	. . .	. . .	. . .	. . .	. . .
General government	4 682 . .	. . .	. . .	. . .	. . .	. . .	. . .	. . .	. . .
Banks	4 683 . .	. . .	. . .	. . .	. . .	. . .	. . .	. . .	. . .
Other sectors	4 684 . .	. . .	. . .	. . .	. . .	. . .	. . .	. . .	. . .
C. FINANCIAL DERIVATIVES	4 910 . .	. . .	. . .	. . .	. . .	. . .	. . .	. . .	. . .
Monetary authorities	4 911 . .	. . .	. . .	. . .	. . .	. . .	. . .	. . .	. . .
General government	4 912 . .	. . .	. . .	. . .	. . .	. . .	. . .	. . .	. . .
Banks	4 913 . .	. . .	. . .	. . .	. . .	. . .	. . .	. . .	. . .
Other sectors	4 914 . .	. . .	. . .	. . .	. . .	. . .	. . .	. . .	. . .
Assets	4 900 . .	**. . .**	**. . .**	**. . .**	**. . .**	**. . .**	**. . .**	**. . .**	**. . .**
Monetary authorities	4 901 . .	. . .	. . .	. . .	. . .	. . .	. . .	. . .	. . .
General government	4 902 . .	. . .	. . .	. . .	. . .	. . .	. . .	. . .	. . .
Banks	4 903 . .	. . .	. . .	. . .	. . .	. . .	. . .	. . .	. . .
Other sectors	4 904 . .	. . .	. . .	. . .	. . .	. . .	. . .	. . .	. . .
Liabilities	4 905 . .	**. . .**	**. . .**	**. . .**	**. . .**	**. . .**	**. . .**	**. . .**	**. . .**
Monetary authorities	4 906 . .	. . .	. . .	. . .	. . .	. . .	. . .	. . .	. . .
General government	4 907 . .	. . .	. . .	. . .	. . .	. . .	. . .	. . .	. . .
Banks	4 908 . .	. . .	. . .	. . .	. . .	. . .	. . .	. . .	. . .
Other sectors	4 909 . .	. . .	. . .	. . .	. . .	. . .	. . .	. . .	. . .

Table 2 (Concluded). STANDARD PRESENTATION, 1994–2001
(Millions of U.S. dollars)

	Code	1994	1995	1996	1997	1998	1999	2000	2001
D. OTHER INVESTMENT	4 700 ..	839.4	642.1	280.4	–42.1	93.1	150.2	232.9	279.4
Assets	4 703 ..	**–134.0**	**41.7**	**–27.9**	**–392.9**	**75.9**	**23.2**	**–243.7**	**13.0**
Trade credits	4 706 ..	...	...	...	...	...	...	...	...
General government	4 707 ..	...	...	...	...	...	...	...	...
of which: Short-term	4 709 ..	...	...	...	...	...	...	...	...
Other sectors	4 710 ..	...	...	...	...	...	...	...	...
of which: Short-term	4 712 ..	...	...	...	...	...	...	...	...
Loans	4 714 ..	...	...	...	...	...	...	...	...
Monetary authorities	4 715 ..	...	...	...	...	...	...	...	...
of which: Short-term	4 718 ..	...	...	...	...	...	...	...	...
General government	4 719 ..	...	...	...	...	...	...	...	...
of which: Short-term	4 721 ..	...	...	...	...	...	...	...	...
Banks	4 722 ..	...	...	...	...	...	...	...	...
of which: Short-term	4 724 ..	...	...	...	...	...	...	...	...
Other sectors	4 725 ..	...	...	...	...	...	...	...	...
of which: Short-term	4 727 ..	...	...	...	...	...	...	...	...
Currency and deposits	4 730 ..	–134.0	41.7	–27.9	–392.9	75.9	23.2	–243.7	13.0
Monetary authorities	4 731 ..	...	...	...	...	...	...	...	...
General government	4 732 ..	9.4	3.6	–6.4	1.7	–2.9	–1.1	–4.4	–10.7
Banks	4 733 ..	–143.4	38.1	–21.5	–394.6	78.8	24.3	–239.4	23.8
Other sectors	4 734 ..	...	...	...	...	...	...	...	...
Other assets	4 736 ..	...	...	...	...	...	...	...	...
Monetary authorities	4 737 ..	...	...	...	...	...	...	...	...
of which: Short-term	4 739 ..	...	...	...	...	...	...	...	...
General government	4 740 ..	...	...	...	...	...	...	...	...
of which: Short-term	4 742 ..	...	...	...	...	...	...	...	...
Banks	4 743 ..	...	...	...	...	...	...	...	...
of which: Short-term	4 745 ..	...	...	...	...	...	...	...	...
Other sectors	4 746 ..	...	...	...	...	...	...	...	...
of which: Short-term	4 748 ..	...	...	...	...	...	...	...	...
Liabilities	4 753 ..	**973.4**	**600.3**	**308.4**	**350.8**	**17.1**	**127.0**	**476.6**	**266.4**
Trade credits	4 756 ..	...	...	...	...	...	...	...	...
General government	4 757 ..	...	...	...	...	...	...	...	...
of which: Short-term	4 759 ..	...	...	...	...	...	...	...	...
Other sectors	4 760 ..	...	...	...	...	...	...	...	...
of which: Short-term	4 762 ..	...	...	...	...	...	...	...	...
Loans	4 764 ..	1,199.1	907.7	872.3	356.6	305.8	196.7	309.3	712.6
Monetary authorities	4 765 ..	65.9	–34.1	–45.2	–65.7	–82.6	–99.7	–85.7	59.8
of which: Use of Fund credit and loans from the Fund	4 766 ..	*65.9*	*–34.1*	*–45.2*	*–65.7*	*–82.6*	*–99.7*	*–85.7*	*59.8*
of which: Short-term	4 768 ..	...	...	...	...	...	...	...	...
General government	4 769 ..	246.9	448.4	218.0	144.5	203.6	62.5	46.6	248.1
of which: Short-term	4 771 ..	...	...	...	...	...	...	...	...
Banks	4 772 ..	...	...	...	...	...	...	...	...
of which: Short-term	4 774 ..	...	...	...	...	...	...	...	...
Other sectors	4 775 ..	886.3	493.4	699.6	277.8	184.8	233.9	348.4	404.8
of which: Short-term	4 777 ..	*570.3*	*436.2*	*696.4*	*225.6*	*183.5*	*37.5*	*266.2*	*661.7*
Currency and deposits	4 780 ..	83.0	101.0	107.4	239.7	–113.2	–22.7	334.2	233.4
Monetary authorities	4 781 ..	9.6	14.4	11.6	30.3	17.5	65.8	75.8	20.1
General government	4 782 ..	...	...	...	...	...	...	...	...
Banks	4 783 ..	73.4	86.7	95.8	209.4	–130.7	–88.4	258.3	213.3
Other sectors	4 784 ..	...	...	...	...	...	...	...	...
Other liabilities	4 786 ..	–308.6	–408.4	–671.4	–245.5	–175.5	–47.1	–166.9	–679.7
Monetary authorities	4 787 ..	...	...	...	...	...	...	...	...
of which: Short-term	4 789 ..	...	...	...	...	...	...	...	...
General government	4 790 ..	...	...	...	...	...	...	...	...
of which: Short-term	4 792 ..	...	...	...	...	...	...	...	...
Banks	4 793 ..	...	...	...	...	...	...	...	...
of which: Short-term	4 795 ..	...	...	...	...	...	...	...	...
Other sectors	4 796 ..	–308.6	–408.4	–671.4	–245.5	–175.5	–47.1	–166.9	–679.7
of which: Short-term	4 798 ..	*–308.6*	*–408.4*	*–671.4*	*–245.5*	*–175.5*	*–47.1*	*–166.9*	*–679.7*
E. RESERVE ASSETS	4 802 ..	–373.5	–204.7	36.3	–241.4	–141.0	194.8	446.5	–389.0
Monetary gold	4 812 ..	...	...	...	...	...	...	...	...
Special drawing rights	4 811 ..	.1	–.3	–1.0	1.4	–.5	.3	.5	–.7
Reserve position in the Fund	4 810 ..	–.1	...	...	...	...	–37.9	...	–.1
Foreign exchange	4 803 ..	–373.6	–204.4	37.3	–242.9	–140.5	232.5	446.1	–388.3
Other claims	4 813 ..	...	...	...	...	...	...	...	...
NET ERRORS AND OMISSIONS	4 998 ..	**106.3**	**157.9**	**143.6**	**148.0**	**26.3**	**–27.3**	**186.2**	**164.7**

Part 3 of the *Yearbook* contains descriptions of the methodologies, compilation practices, and sources used to compile these data.

Table 1. ANALYTIC PRESENTATION, 1994–2001
(Millions of U.S. dollars)

	Code	1994	1995	1996	1997	1998	1999	2000	2001
A. Current Account [1]	4 993 Z.	**–601.7**	**–499.9**	**–826.8**	**–828.1**	**–956.5**	**–464.8**	**–556.8**	**–618.3**
Goods: exports f.o.b.	2 100 . .	523.9	555.7	620.3	594.2	595.7	780.1	1,806.7	1,698.7
Goods: imports f.o.b.	3 100 . .	–1,045.4	–1,066.0	–1,339.5	–1,421.9	–1,732.2	–1,256.0	–1,366.3	–1,395.1
Balance on Goods	4 100 . .	*–521.5*	*–510.3*	*–719.2*	*–827.7*	*–1,136.5*	*–475.9*	*440.4*	*303.6*
Services: credit	2 200 . .	76.2	125.3	50.7	31.5	15.8	81.6	27.4	14.6
Services: debit	3 200 . .	–223.7	–172.3	–200.8	–172.8	–204.0	–274.9	–647.6	–660.3
Balance on Goods and Services	4 991 . .	*–669.0*	*–557.3*	*–869.3*	*–969.0*	*–1,324.7*	*–669.2*	*–179.8*	*–342.1*
Income: credit	2 300 . .	1.6	1.9	6.3	16.9	13.7	19.1	4.6	17.8
Income: debit	3 300 . .	–15.9	–4.9	–.7	–5.3	–10.6	–123.2	–579.6	–571.9
Balance on Goods, Services, and Income	4 992 . .	*–683.3*	*–560.3*	*–863.7*	*–957.4*	*–1,321.6*	*–773.3*	*–754.8*	*–896.2*
Current transfers: credit	2 379 Z.	120.1	346.2	236.3	439.1	731.8	702.2	651.3	730.4
Current transfers: debit	3 379 . .	–38.5	–285.8	–199.4	–309.8	–366.7	–393.7	–453.3	–452.5
B. Capital Account [1]	4 994 Z.	**. . .**	**. . .**	**. . .**	**. . .**	**–54.2**	**–22.9**	**–119.3**	**–93.3**
Capital account: credit	2 994 Z.	. . .	. . .	. . .	. . .	13.0	45.8	16.5	11.9
Capital account: debit	3 994 . .	. . .	. . .	. . .	. . .	–67.2	–68.7	–135.8	–105.2
Total, Groups A Plus B	4 981 . .	*–601.7*	*–499.9*	*–826.8*	*–828.1*	*–1,010.7*	*–487.7*	*–676.1*	*–711.6*
C. Financial Account [1]	4 995 W.	**276.0**	**473.7**	**136.8**	**195.0**	**333.4**	**435.3**	**431.6**	**561.2**
Direct investment abroad	4 505 . .	. . .	. . .	. . .	. . .	. . .	. . .	. . .	. . .
Direct investment in Sudan	4 555 Z.	. . .	. . .	.4	97.9	370.7	370.8	392.2	574.0
Portfolio investment assets	4 602 . .	. . .	. . .	. . .	. . .	. . .	. . .	. . .	.7
Equity securities	4 610 . .	. . .	. . .	. . .	. . .	. . .	. . .	. . .	. . .
Debt securities	4 619 . .	. . .	. . .	. . .	. . .	. . .	. . .	. . .	.7
Portfolio investment liabilities	4 652 Z.	. . .	. . .	. . .	. . .	. . .	. . .	. . .	. . .
Equity securities	4 660 . .	. . .	. . .	. . .	. . .	. . .	. . .	. . .	. . .
Debt securities	4 669 Z.	. . .	. . .	. . .	. . .	. . .	. . .	. . .	. . .
Financial derivatives	4 910 . .	. . .	. . .	. . .	. . .	. . .	. . .	. . .	. . .
Financial derivatives assets	4 900 . .	. . .	. . .	. . .	. . .	. . .	. . .	. . .	. . .
Financial derivatives liabilities	4 905 . .	. . .	. . .	. . .	. . .	. . .	. . .	. . .	. . .
Other investment assets	4 703 . .	. . .	. . .	. . .	. . .	–78.5	–38.4	–53.4	–55.1
Monetary authorities	4 701 . .	. . .	. . .	. . .	. . .	. . .	. . .	. . .	. . .
General government	4 704 . .	. . .	. . .	. . .	. . .	. . .	. . .	. . .	. . .
Banks	4 705 . .	. . .	. . .	. . .	. . .	–78.5	–38.4	–53.4	–55.1
Other sectors	4 728 . .	. . .	. . .	. . .	. . .	. . .	. . .	. . .	. . .
Other investment liabilities	4 753 W.	276.0	473.7	136.4	97.1	41.2	102.9	92.8	41.6
Monetary authorities	4 753 WA	28.3	73.6	62.4	20.1	8.0	–3.7	14.0	40.6
General government	4 753 ZB	–3.1	9.8	–22.5	–45.1	–1.0	. . .	. . .	. . .
Banks	4 753 ZC	250.8	390.3	96.2	119.3	34.2	106.6	78.8	1.0
Other sectors	4 753 ZD	. . .	. . .	.3	2.8	. . .	. . .	. . .	. . .
Total, Groups A Through C	4 983 . .	*–325.7*	*–26.2*	*–690.0*	*–633.1*	*–677.3*	*–52.4*	*–244.5*	*–150.4*
D. Net Errors and Omissions	4 998 . .	**344.8**	**89.3**	**727.5**	**651.2**	**750.5**	**167.2**	**368.4**	**–.5**
Total, Groups A Through D	4 984 . .	*19.1*	*63.1*	*37.5*	*18.1*	*73.2*	*114.8*	*123.9*	*–150.9*
E. Reserves and Related Items	4 802 A.	**–19.1**	**–63.1**	**–37.5**	**–18.1**	**–73.2**	**–114.8**	**–123.9**	**150.9**
Reserve assets	4 802 . .	–19.1	–23.6	–2.0	24.0	–16.0	–110.0	–108.0	127.6
Use of Fund credit and loans	4 766 . .	. . .	–39.5	–35.5	–42.1	–57.2	–37.8	–54.0	–52.3
Exceptional financing	4 920 . .	. . .	. . .	. . .	. . .	. . .	33.0	38.1	75.6
Conversion rates: Sudanese dinars per U.S. dollar	0 101 . .	**28.96**	**58.09**	**125.08**	**157.57**	**200.80**	**252.55**	**257.12**	**258.70**

[1] Excludes components that have been classified in the categories of Group E.

Table 2. STANDARD PRESENTATION, 1994–2001
(Millions of U.S. dollars)

	Code		1994	1995	1996	1997	1998	1999	2000	2001
CURRENT ACCOUNT	4 993	. .	**–601.7**	**–499.9**	**–826.8**	**–828.1**	**–956.5**	**–431.1**	**–517.7**	**–521.9**
A. GOODS	4 100	. .	–521.5	–510.3	–719.2	–827.7	–1,136.5	–475.9	440.4	303.6
Credit	2 100	. .	**523.9**	**555.7**	**620.3**	**594.2**	**595.7**	**780.1**	**1,806.7**	**1,698.7**
General merchandise: exports f.o.b.	2 110	. .	523.9	555.7	620.3	594.2	595.7	780.1	1,806.7	1,698.7
Goods for processing: exports f.o.b.	2 150	. .	. . .	. . .	. . .	. . .	. . .	. . .	. . .	. . .
Repairs on goods	2 160	. .	. . .	. . .	. . .	. . .	. . .	. . .	. . .	. . .
Goods procured in ports by carriers	2 170	. .	. . .	. . .	. . .	. . .	. . .	. . .	. . .	. . .
Nonmonetary gold	2 180	. .	. . .	. . .	. . .	. . .	. . .	. . .	. . .	. . .
Debit	3 100	. .	**–1,045.4**	**–1,066.0**	**–1,339.5**	**–1,421.9**	**–1,732.2**	**–1,256.0**	**–1,366.3**	**–1,395.1**
General merchandise: imports f.o.b.	3 110	. .	–1,045.4	–1,066.0	–1,339.5	–1,421.9	–1,732.2	–1,256.0	–1,366.3	–1,395.1
Goods for processing: imports f.o.b.	3 150	. .	. . .	. . .	. . .	. . .	. . .	. . .	. . .	. . .
Repairs on goods	3 160	. .	. . .	. . .	. . .	. . .	. . .	. . .	. . .	. . .
Goods procured in ports by carriers	3 170	. .	. . .	. . .	. . .	. . .	. . .	. . .	. . .	. . .
Nonmonetary gold	3 180	. .	. . .	. . .	. . .	. . .	. . .	. . .	. . .	. . .
B. SERVICES	4 200	. .	–147.5	–47.0	–150.1	–141.3	–188.2	–193.3	–620.2	–645.7
Total credit	2 200	. .	*76.2*	*125.3*	*50.7*	*31.5*	*15.8*	*81.6*	*27.4*	*14.6*
Total debit	3 200	. .	*–223.7*	*–172.3*	*–200.8*	*–172.8*	*–204.0*	*–274.9*	*–647.6*	*–660.3*
Transportation services, credit	2 205	. .	**.6**	**.7**	**.8**	**1.1**	**5.7**	**3.4**	**15.2**	**6.0**
Passenger	2 850	. .	. . .	. . .	. . .	. . .	. . .	. . .	. . .	. . .
Freight	2 851	. .	. . .	. . .	. . .	. . .	*5.7*	*3.4*	*15.2*	*6.0*
Other	2 852	. .	*.6*	*.7*	*.8*	*1.1*	. . .	. . .	. . .	. . .
Sea transport, passenger	2 207	. .	. . .	. . .	. . .	. . .	. . .	. . .	. . .	. . .
Sea transport, freight	2 208	. .	. . .	. . .	. . .	. . .	. . .	. . .	. . .	. . .
Sea transport, other	2 209	. .	. . .	. . .	. . .	. . .	. . .	. . .	. . .	. . .
Air transport, passenger	2 211	. .	. . .	. . .	. . .	. . .	. . .	. . .	. . .	. . .
Air transport, freight	2 212	. .	. . .	. . .	. . .	. . .	. . .	. . .	. . .	. . .
Air transport, other	2 213	. .	. . .	. . .	. . .	. . .	. . .	. . .	. . .	. . .
Other transport, passenger	2 215	. .	. . .	. . .	. . .	. . .	. . .	. . .	. . .	. . .
Other transport, freight	2 216	. .	. . .	. . .	. . .	. . .	. . .	3.4	15.2	6.0
Other transport, other	2 217	. .	.6	.7	.8	1.1	. . .	. . .	. . .	. . .
Transportation services, debit	3 205	. .	**–97.9**	**–40.8**	**–128.5**	**–126.4**	**–161.2**	**–221.4**	**–555.3**	**–558.9**
Passenger	3 850	. .	. . .	. . .	. . .	. . .	. . .	. . .	. . .	. . .
Freight	3 851	. .	*–92.9*	*–36.5*	*–119.1*	*–126.4*	*–161.2*	*–221.4*	*–555.3*	*–558.9*
Other	3 852	. .	*–5.0*	*–4.3*	*–9.4*	. . .	. . .	. . .	. . .	. . .
Sea transport, passenger	3 207	. .	. . .	. . .	. . .	. . .	. . .	. . .	. . .	. . .
Sea transport, freight	3 208	. .	. . .	. . .	. . .	. . .	–161.2	. . .	. . .	. . .
Sea transport, other	3 209	. .	. . .	. . .	. . .	. . .	. . .	. . .	. . .	. . .
Air transport, passenger	3 211	. .	. . .	. . .	. . .	. . .	. . .	. . .	. . .	. . .
Air transport, freight	3 212	. .	. . .	. . .	. . .	. . .	. . .	. . .	. . .	. . .
Air transport, other	3 213	. .	. . .	. . .	. . .	. . .	. . .	. . .	. . .	. . .
Other transport, passenger	3 215	. .	. . .	. . .	. . .	. . .	. . .	. . .	. . .	. . .
Other transport, freight	3 216	. .	. . .	. . .	. . .	. . .	. . .	–221.4	–555.3	–558.9
Other transport, other	3 217	. .	–5.0	–4.3	–9.4	. . .	. . .	. . .	. . .	. . .
Travel, credit	2 236	. .	**4.4**	**7.9**	**8.4**	**4.3**	**2.0**	**1.7**	**5.4**	**3.1**
Business travel	2 237	. .	. . .	. . .	. . .	. . .	. . .	. . .	. . .	. . .
Personal travel	2 240	. .	. . .	. . .	. . .	. . .	2.0	1.7	5.4	3.1
Travel, debit	3 236	. .	**–46.9**	**–42.9**	**–27.7**	**–33.2**	**–29.4**	**–35.1**	**–55.4**	**–74.2**
Business travel	3 237	. .	. . .	. . .	. . .	. . .	. . .	. . .	. . .	. . .
Personal travel	3 240	. .	–46.9	–42.9	–27.7	–33.2	–29.4	–35.1	–55.4	–74.2
Other services, credit	2 200	BA	**71.2**	**116.7**	**41.5**	**26.1**	**8.1**	**76.5**	**6.8**	**5.5**
Communications	2 245	. .	. . .	. . .	. . .	1.2	1.6	2.2	2.6	3.2
Construction	2 249	. .	. . .	. . .	. . .	20.9	.1	2.9	.4	. . .
Insurance	2 253	. .	.7	3.0	. . .	. . .	. . .	. . .	. . .	1.1
Financial	2 260	. .	. . .	. . .	. . .	. . .	. . .	. . .	. . .	. . .
Computer and information	2 262	. .	. . .	. . .	. . .	. . .	. . .	. . .	. . .	. . .
Royalties and licence fees	2 266	. .	. . .	. . .	. . .	.2	.2	. . .	. . .	. . .
Other business services	2 268	. .	38.3	70.2	27.8	2.0	4.0	71.3	.1	.1
Personal, cultural, and recreational	2 287	. .	. . .	. . .	. . .	. . .	. . .	. . .	.5	. . .
Government, n.i.e.	2 291	. .	32.2	43.5	13.7	1.8	2.2	.1	3.2	1.1
Other services, debit	3 200	BA	**–78.9**	**–88.6**	**–44.6**	**–13.2**	**–13.4**	**–18.4**	**–36.9**	**–27.2**
Communications	3 245	. .	. . .	. . .	. . .	–1.7	–6.1	–5.7	–14.5	–4.4
Construction	3 249	. .	–4.2	–.2	. . .	–4.4	. . .	. . .	. . .	. . .
Insurance	3 253	. .	–6.5	–.5	. . .	–.4	.1	.2	–.1	. . .
Financial	3 260	. .	. . .	. . .	–1.1	. . .	–.2	. . .	–.1	. . .
Computer and information	3 262	. .	. . .	. . .	. . .	. . .	. . .	–.5	–.5	–.6
Royalties and licence fees	3 266	. .	. . .	. . .	. . .	–.4	.2	. . .	–.1	. . .
Other business services	3 268	. .	–43.7	–65.1	–11.5	–1.5	–3.8	–5.6	–6.0	. . .
Personal, cultural, and recreational	3 287	. .	. . .	. . .	. . .	–.1	. . .	–1.6	. . .	. . .
Government, n.i.e.	3 291	. .	–24.5	–22.8	–32.0	–4.7	–3.6	–5.2	–15.6	–22.2

Table 2 (Continued). STANDARD PRESENTATION, 1994–2001

(Millions of U.S. dollars)

	Code	1994	1995	1996	1997	1998	1999	2000	2001
C. INCOME	4 300	–14.3	–3.0	5.6	11.6	3.1	–104.1	–575.0	–554.1
Total credit	2 300	*1.6*	*1.9*	*6.3*	*16.9*	*13.7*	*19.1*	*4.6*	*17.8*
Total debit	3 300	*–15.9*	*–4.9*	*–.7*	*–5.3*	*–10.6*	*–123.2*	*–579.6*	*–571.9*
Compensation of employees, credit	2 310	**. . .**	**. . .**	**1.3**	**3.2**	**.1**	**1.0**	**2.6**	**9.2**
Compensation of employees, debit	3 310	**–.2**	**–.9**	**. . .**	**–.4**	**–4.6**	**–2.7**	**–4.4**	**–1.9**
Investment income, credit	2 320	**1.6**	**1.9**	**5.0**	**13.7**	**13.6**	**18.1**	**2.0**	**8.6**
Direct investment income	2 330	. . .	. . .	. . .	. . .	. . .	. . .	. . .	. . .
Dividends and distributed branch profits	2 332	. . .	. . .	. . .	. . .	. . .	. . .	. . .	. . .
Reinvested earnings and undistributed branch profits	2 333	. . .	. . .	. . .	. . .	. . .	. . .	. . .	. . .
Income on debt (interest)	2 334	. . .	. . .	. . .	. . .	. . .	. . .	. . .	. . .
Portfolio investment income	2 339	. . .	. . .	. . .	. . .	. . .	. . .	. . .	. . .
Income on equity	2 340	. . .	. . .	. . .	. . .	. . .	. . .	. . .	. . .
Income on bonds and notes	2 350	. . .	. . .	. . .	. . .	. . .	. . .	. . .	. . .
Income on money market instruments	2 360	. . .	. . .	. . .	. . .	. . .	. . .	. . .	. . .
Other investment income	2 370	1.6	1.9	5.0	13.7	13.6	18.1	2.0	8.6
Investment income, debit	3 320	**–15.7**	**–4.0**	**–.7**	**–4.9**	**–6.0**	**–120.5**	**–575.2**	**–570.0**
Direct investment income	3 330	. . .	. . .	. . .	. . .	. . .	. . .	. . .	. . .
Dividends and distributed branch profits	3 332	. . .	. . .	. . .	. . .	. . .	. . .	. . .	. . .
Reinvested earnings and undistributed branch profits	3 333	. . .	. . .	. . .	. . .	. . .	. . .	. . .	. . .
Income on debt (interest)	3 334	. . .	. . .	. . .	. . .	. . .	. . .	. . .	. . .
Portfolio investment income	3 339	. . .	. . .	. . .	. . .	. . .	. . .	. . .	. . .
Income on equity	3 340	. . .	. . .	. . .	. . .	. . .	. . .	. . .	. . .
Income on bonds and notes	3 350	. . .	. . .	. . .	. . .	. . .	. . .	. . .	. . .
Income on money market instruments	3 360	. . .	. . .	. . .	. . .	. . .	. . .	. . .	. . .
Other investment income	3 370	–15.7	–4.0	–.7	–4.9	–6.0	–120.5	–575.2	–570.0
D. CURRENT TRANSFERS	4 379	81.6	60.4	36.9	129.3	365.1	342.2	237.1	374.3
Credit	2 379	**120.1**	**346.2**	**236.3**	**439.1**	**731.8**	**735.9**	**690.4**	**826.8**
General government	2 380	12.6	. . .	16.1	22.7	45.3	71.8	52.2	96.4
Other sectors	2 390	107.5	346.2	220.2	416.4	686.5	664.1	638.2	730.4
Workers' remittances	2 391	107.2	346.2	220.2	416.4	686.5	664.1	638.2	730.4
Other current transfers	2 392	.3	. . .	. . .	. . .	. . .	. . .	. . .	. . .
Debit	3 379	**–38.5**	**–285.8**	**–199.4**	**–309.8**	**–366.7**	**–393.7**	**–453.3**	**–452.5**
General government	3 380	. . .	. . .	. . .	–9.0	–10.4	–17.1	–10.2	. . .
Other sectors	3 390	–38.5	–285.8	–199.4	–300.8	–356.3	–376.6	–443.1	–452.5
Workers' remittances	3 391	. . .	. . .	. . .	. . .	. . .	. . .	. . .	. . .
Other current transfers	3 392	–38.5	–285.8	–199.4	–300.8	–356.3	–376.6	–443.1	–452.5
CAPITAL AND FINANCIAL ACCOUNT	4 996	**256.9**	**410.6**	**99.3**	**176.9**	**206.0**	**263.9**	**149.3**	**522.4**
CAPITAL ACCOUNT	4 994	**. . .**	**. . .**	**. . .**	**. . .**	**–54.2**	**–22.9**	**–119.3**	**–93.3**
Total credit	2 994	. . .	. . .	. . .	. . .	*13.0*	*45.8*	*16.5*	*11.9*
Total debit	3 994	. . .	. . .	. . .	. . .	*–67.2*	*–68.7*	*–135.8*	*–105.2*
Capital transfers, credit	2 400	**. . .**	**. . .**	**. . .**	**. . .**	**13.0**	**45.8**	**16.5**	**11.9**
General government	2 401	. . .	. . .	. . .	. . .	13.0	45.8	16.5	11.9
Debt forgiveness	2 402	. . .	. . .	. . .	. . .	. . .	. . .	. . .	. . .
Other capital transfers	2 410	. . .	. . .	. . .	. . .	. . .	45.8	16.5	11.9
Other sectors	2 430	. . .	. . .	. . .	. . .	. . .	. . .	. . .	. . .
Migrants' transfers	2 431	. . .	. . .	. . .	. . .	. . .	. . .	. . .	. . .
Debt forgiveness	2 432	. . .	. . .	. . .	. . .	. . .	. . .	. . .	. . .
Other capital transfers	2 440	. . .	. . .	. . .	. . .	. . .	. . .	. . .	. . .
Capital transfers, debit	3 400	**. . .**	**. . .**	**. . .**	**. . .**	**–67.2**	**–68.7**	**–135.8**	**–105.2**
General government	3 401	. . .	. . .	. . .	. . .	–67.2	–68.7	–135.8	–105.2
Debt forgiveness	3 402	. . .	. . .	. . .	. . .	. . .	. . .	. . .	. . .
Other capital transfers	3 410	. . .	. . .	. . .	. . .	. . .	–68.7	–135.8	–105.2
Other sectors	3 430	. . .	. . .	. . .	. . .	. . .	. . .	. . .	. . .
Migrants' transfers	3 431	. . .	. . .	. . .	. . .	. . .	. . .	. . .	. . .
Debt forgiveness	3 432	. . .	. . .	. . .	. . .	. . .	. . .	. . .	. . .
Other capital transfers	3 440	. . .	. . .	. . .	. . .	. . .	. . .	. . .	. . .
Nonproduced nonfinancial assets, credit	2 480	**. . .**	**. . .**	**. . .**	**. . .**	**. . .**	**. . .**	**. . .**	**. . .**
Nonproduced nonfinancial assets, debit	3 480	**. . .**	**. . .**	**. . .**	**. . .**	**. . .**	**. . .**	**. . .**	**. . .**

Table 2 (Continued). STANDARD PRESENTATION, 1994–2001

(Millions of U.S. dollars)

	Code	1994	1995	1996	1997	1998	1999	2000	2001
FINANCIAL ACCOUNT	4 995 . .	**256.9**	**410.6**	**99.3**	**176.9**	**260.2**	**286.8**	**268.6**	**615.7**
A. DIRECT INVESTMENT	4 500 . .	...	...	.4	97.9	370.7	370.8	392.2	574.0
Direct investment abroad	4 505 . .	...	...	...	...	...	...	...	...
Equity capital	4 510 . .	...	...	...	...	...	...	...	...
Claims on affiliated enterprises	4 515 . .	...	...	...	...	...	...	...	...
Liabilities to affiliated enterprises	4 520 . .	...	...	...	...	...	...	...	...
Reinvested earnings	4 525 . .	...	...	...	...	...	...	...	...
Other capital	4 530 . .	...	...	...	...	...	...	...	...
Claims on affiliated enterprises	4 535 . .	...	...	...	...	...	...	...	...
Liabilities to affiliated enterprises	4 540 . .	...	...	...	...	...	...	...	...
Direct investment in Sudan	4 555 . .	...	...	**.4**	**97.9**	**370.7**	**370.8**	**392.2**	**574.0**
Equity capital	4 560 . .	...	...	.4	97.9	370.7	370.8	392.2	574.0
Claims on direct investors	4 565 . .	...	...	...	...	...	...	...	...
Liabilities to direct investors	4 570 . .	...	...	.4	97.9	370.7	370.8	392.2	574.0
Reinvested earnings	4 575 . .	...	...	...	...	...	...	...	...
Other capital	4 580 . .	...	...	...	...	...	...	...	...
Claims on direct investors	4 585 . .	...	...	...	...	...	...	...	...
Liabilities to direct investors	4 590 . .	...	...	...	...	...	...	...	...
B. PORTFOLIO INVESTMENT	4 600 . .	...	...	...	...	...	...	...	.7
Assets	4 602 . .	...	...	...	...	...	...	...	**.7**
Equity securities	4 610 . .	...	...	...	...	...	...	...	...
Monetary authorities	4 611 . .	...	...	...	...	...	...	...	...
General government	4 612 . .	...	...	...	...	...	...	...	...
Banks	4 613 . .	...	...	...	...	...	...	...	...
Other sectors	4 614 . .	...	...	...	...	...	...	...	...
Debt securities	4 619 . .	...	...	...	...	...	...	...	.7
Bonds and notes	4 620 . .	...	...	...	...	...	...	...	.7
Monetary authorities	4 621 . .	...	...	...	...	...	...	...	...
General government	4 622 . .	...	...	...	...	...	...	...	...
Banks	4 623 . .	...	...	...	...	...	...	...	...
Other sectors	4 624 . .	...	...	...	...	...	...	...	.7
Money market instruments	4 630 . .	...	...	...	...	...	...	...	...
Monetary authorities	4 631 . .	...	...	...	...	...	...	...	...
General government	4 632 . .	...	...	...	...	...	...	...	...
Banks	4 633 . .	...	...	...	...	...	...	...	...
Other sectors	4 634 . .	...	...	...	...	...	...	...	...
Liabilities	4 652 . .	...	...	...	...	...	...	...	...
Equity securities	4 660 . .	...	...	...	...	...	...	...	...
Banks	4 663 . .	...	...	...	...	...	...	...	...
Other sectors	4 664 . .	...	...	...	...	...	...	...	...
Debt securities	4 669 . .	...	...	...	...	...	...	...	...
Bonds and notes	4 670 . .	...	...	...	...	...	...	...	...
Monetary authorities	4 671 . .	...	...	...	...	...	...	...	...
General government	4 672 . .	...	...	...	...	...	...	...	...
Banks	4 673 . .	...	...	...	...	...	...	...	...
Other sectors	4 674 . .	...	...	...	...	...	...	...	...
Money market instruments	4 680 . .	...	...	...	...	...	...	...	...
Monetary authorities	4 681 . .	...	...	...	...	...	...	...	...
General government	4 682 . .	...	...	...	...	...	...	...	...
Banks	4 683 . .	...	...	...	...	...	...	...	...
Other sectors	4 684 . .	...	...	...	...	...	...	...	...
C. FINANCIAL DERIVATIVES	4 910 . .	...	...	...	...	...	...	...	...
Monetary authorities	4 911 . .	...	...	...	...	...	...	...	...
General government	4 912 . .	...	...	...	...	...	...	...	...
Banks	4 913 . .	...	...	...	...	...	...	...	...
Other sectors	4 914 . .	...	...	...	...	...	...	...	...
Assets	4 900 . .	...	...	...	...	...	...	...	...
Monetary authorities	4 901 . .	...	...	...	...	...	...	...	...
General government	4 902 . .	...	...	...	...	...	...	...	...
Banks	4 903 . .	...	...	...	...	...	...	...	...
Other sectors	4 904 . .	...	...	...	...	...	...	...	...
Liabilities	4 905 . .	...	...	...	...	...	...	...	...
Monetary authorities	4 906 . .	...	...	...	...	...	...	...	...
General government	4 907 . .	...	...	...	...	...	...	...	...
Banks	4 908 . .	...	...	...	...	...	...	...	...
Other sectors	4 909 . .	...	...	...	...	...	...	...	...

Table 2 (Concluded). STANDARD PRESENTATION, 1994–2001
(Millions of U.S. dollars)

	Code	1994	1995	1996	1997	1998	1999	2000	2001
D. OTHER INVESTMENT	4 700	276.0	434.2	100.9	55.0	−94.5	26.0	−15.6	−86.6
Assets	4 703	**. . .**	**. . .**	**. . .**	**. . .**	**−78.5**	**−38.4**	**−53.4**	**−55.1**
Trade credits	4 706	. . .	. . .	. . .	. . .	. . .	. . .	. . .	. . .
General government	4 707	. . .	. . .	. . .	. . .	. . .	. . .	. . .	. . .
of which: Short-term	4 709	. . .	. . .	. . .	. . .	. . .	. . .	. . .	. . .
Other sectors	4 710	. . .	. . .	. . .	. . .	. . .	. . .	. . .	. . .
of which: Short-term	4 712	. . .	. . .	. . .	. . .	. . .	. . .	. . .	. . .
Loans	4 714	. . .	. . .	. . .	. . .	−68.1	−31.5	−17.6	1.9
Monetary authorities	4 715	. . .	. . .	. . .	. . .	. . .	. . .	. . .	. . .
of which: Short-term	4 718	. . .	. . .	. . .	. . .	. . .	. . .	. . .	. . .
General government	4 719	. . .	. . .	. . .	. . .	. . .	. . .	. . .	. . .
of which: Short-term	4 721	. . .	. . .	. . .	. . .	. . .	. . .	. . .	. . .
Banks	4 722	. . .	. . .	. . .	. . .	−68.1	−31.5	−17.6	1.9
of which: Short-term	4 724	. . .	. . .	. . .	. . .	*−68.1*	*−31.5*	*−17.6*	*1.9*
Other sectors	4 725	. . .	. . .	. . .	. . .	. . .	. . .	. . .	. . .
of which: Short-term	4 727	. . .	. . .	. . .	. . .	. . .	. . .	. . .	. . .
Currency and deposits	4 730	. . .	. . .	. . .	. . .	−10.4	−6.9	−35.8	−57.0
Monetary authorities	4 731	. . .	. . .	. . .	. . .	. . .	. . .	. . .	. . .
General government	4 732	. . .	. . .	. . .	. . .	. . .	. . .	. . .	. . .
Banks	4 733	. . .	. . .	. . .	. . .	−10.4	−6.9	−35.8	−57.0
Other sectors	4 734	. . .	. . .	. . .	. . .	. . .	. . .	. . .	. . .
Other assets	4 736	. . .	. . .	. . .	. . .	. . .	. . .	. . .	. . .
Monetary authorities	4 737	. . .	. . .	. . .	. . .	. . .	. . .	. . .	. . .
of which: Short-term	4 739	. . .	. . .	. . .	. . .	. . .	. . .	. . .	. . .
General government	4 740	. . .	. . .	. . .	. . .	. . .	. . .	. . .	. . .
of which: Short-term	4 742	. . .	. . .	. . .	. . .	. . .	. . .	. . .	. . .
Banks	4 743	. . .	. . .	. . .	. . .	. . .	. . .	. . .	. . .
of which: Short-term	4 745	. . .	. . .	. . .	. . .	. . .	. . .	. . .	. . .
Other sectors	4 746	. . .	. . .	. . .	. . .	. . .	. . .	. . .	. . .
of which: Short-term	4 748	. . .	. . .	. . .	. . .	. . .	. . .	. . .	. . .
Liabilities	4 753	**276.0**	**434.2**	**100.9**	**55.0**	**−16.0**	**64.4**	**37.8**	**−31.5**
Trade credits	4 756	−11.8	−.1	−.2	. . .	−1.0	. . .	. . .	. . .
General government	4 757	−11.8	−.1	−.2	. . .	−1.0	. . .	. . .	. . .
of which: Short-term	4 759	. . .	. . .	. . .	. . .	. . .	. . .	. . .	. . .
Other sectors	4 760	. . .	. . .	. . .	. . .	. . .	. . .	. . .	. . .
of which: Short-term	4 762	. . .	. . .	. . .	. . .	. . .	. . .	. . .	. . .
Loans	4 764	198.0	361.9	97.3	60.1	−12.9	55.3	32.8	9.4
Monetary authorities	4 765	−11.9	21.5	26.9	−22.0	−49.2	−41.5	−40.0	−11.7
of which: Use of Fund credit and loans from the Fund	4 766	. . .	*−39.5*	*−35.5*	*−42.1*	*−57.2*	*−37.8*	*−54.0*	*−52.3*
of which: Short-term	4 768	*−11.9*	*61.0*	*62.4*	*20.1*	*8.0*	*−3.7*	*14.0*	*40.6*
General government	4 769	8.7	9.9	−22.3	−45.1	. . .	. . .	. . .	. . .
of which: Short-term	4 771	. . .	. . .	. . .	. . .	. . .	. . .	. . .	. . .
Banks	4 772	201.2	330.5	92.7	127.2	36.3	96.8	72.8	21.1
of which: Short-term	4 774	*201.2*	*330.7*	*92.7*	*127.2*	*36.3*	*96.8*	*72.8*	*21.1*
Other sectors	4 775	. . .	. . .	. . .	. . .	. . .	. . .	. . .	. . .
of which: Short-term	4 777	. . .	. . .	. . .	. . .	. . .	. . .	. . .	. . .
Currency and deposits	4 780	49.6	21.7	3.8	−5.1	−5.7	9.8	6.0	−20.1
Monetary authorities	4 781	. . .	. . .	. . .	. . .	. . .	. . .	. . .	. . .
General government	4 782	. . .	. . .	. . .	. . .	. . .	. . .	. . .	. . .
Banks	4 783	49.6	21.7	3.5	−7.9	−5.7	9.8	6.0	−20.1
Other sectors	4 784	. . .	. . .	.3	2.8	. . .	. . .	. . .	. . .
Other liabilities	4 786	40.2	50.7	. . .	. . .	3.6	−.7	−1.0	−20.8
Monetary authorities	4 787	40.2	12.6	. . .	. . .	. . .	. . .	. . .	. . .
of which: Short-term	4 789	*40.2*	*12.6*	. . .	. . .	. . .	. . .	. . .	. . .
General government	4 790	. . .	. . .	. . .	. . .	. . .	−.7	−1.0	−20.8
of which: Short-term	4 792	. . .	. . .	. . .	. . .	. . .	*−.7*	*−1.0*	*−20.8*
Banks	4 793	. . .	38.1	. . .	. . .	3.6	. . .	. . .	. . .
of which: Short-term	4 795	. . .	*38.1*	. . .	. . .	*3.6*	. . .	. . .	. . .
Other sectors	4 796	. . .	. . .	. . .	. . .	. . .	. . .	. . .	. . .
of which: Short-term	4 798	. . .	. . .	. . .	. . .	. . .	. . .	. . .	. . .
E. RESERVE ASSETS	4 802	−19.1	−23.6	−2.0	24.0	−16.0	−110.0	−108.0	127.6
Monetary gold	4 812	. . .	. . .	. . .	. . .	. . .	. . .	. . .	. . .
Special drawing rights	4 811	. . .	. . .	. . .	. . .	. . .	. . .	. . .	. . .
Reserve position in the Fund	4 810	. . .	. . .	. . .	. . .	. . .	. . .	. . .	. . .
Foreign exchange	4 803	−19.1	−23.6	−2.0	24.0	−16.0	−110.0	−108.0	127.6
Other claims	4 813	. . .	. . .	. . .	. . .	. . .	. . .	. . .	. . .
NET ERRORS AND OMISSIONS	4 998	**344.8**	**89.3**	**727.5**	**651.2**	**750.5**	**167.2**	**368.4**	**−.5**

Part 3 of the *Yearbook* contains descriptions of the methodologies, compilation practices, and sources used to compile these data.

Table 1. ANALYTIC PRESENTATION, 1994–2001
(Millions of U.S. dollars)

	Code	1994	1995	1996	1997	1998	1999	2000	2001
A. Current Account [1]	4 993 Z.	**58.6**	**62.8**	**–63.5**	**–67.7**	**–154.9**	**–29.1**	**32.3**	**–84.0**
Goods: exports f.o.b	2 100 ..	293.6	415.6	397.2	401.6	349.7	342.0	399.1	437.0
Goods: imports f.o.b	3 100 ..	–194.3	–292.6	–398.8	–365.5	–376.9	–297.9	–246.1	–297.2
Balance on Goods	4 100 ..	*99.3*	*123.0*	*–1.6*	*36.1*	*–27.2*	*44.1*	*153.0*	*139.8*
Services: credit	2 200 ..	72.6	104.1	103.8	91.6	72.0	79.1	90.9	59.4
Services: debit	3 200 ..	–113.5	–161.4	–169.5	–193.8	–196.9	–151.1	–215.5	–174.7
Balance on Goods and Services	4 991 ..	*58.4*	*65.7*	*–67.3*	*–66.1*	*–152.1*	*–27.9*	*28.4*	*24.5*
Income: credit	2 300 ..	.9	2.7	7.0	7.4	6.5	7.9	13.2	5.4
Income: debit	3 300 ..	–4.7	–5.3	–4.3	–10.0	–7.0	–7.6	–7.2	–113.0
Balance on Goods, Services, and Income	4 992 ..	*54.6*	*63.1*	*–64.6*	*–68.7*	*–152.6*	*–27.6*	*34.4*	*–83.1*
Current transfers: credit	2 379 Z.	6.2	2.0	3.6	4.0	1.3	1.8	1.2	2.1
Current transfers: debit	3 379 ..	–2.2	–2.3	–2.5	–3.0	–3.6	–3.3	–3.3	–3.0
B. Capital Account [1]	4 994 Z.	**–.2**	**22.1**	**41.6**	**14.6**	**6.6**	**3.5**	**2.3**	**1.5**
Capital account: credit	2 994 Z.	.2	22.1	41.6	14.6	6.6	3.5	2.3	1.5
Capital account: debit	3 994 ..	–.4	...	...	...	...	...	...	...
Total, Groups A Plus B	4 981 ..	*58.4*	*84.9*	*–21.9*	*–53.1*	*–148.3*	*–25.6*	*34.6*	*–82.5*
C. Financial Account [1]	4 995 W.	**–84.1**	**–6.7**	**27.7**	**26.9**	**30.5**	**–21.6**	**–139.1**	**104.5**
Direct investment abroad	4 505 ..	...	...	...	...	...	...	...	...
Direct investment in Suriname	4 555 Z.	–30.2	–20.6	19.1	–9.2	9.1	–61.5	–148.0	–26.8
Portfolio investment assets	4 602 ..	...	...	...	...	...	...	...	...
Equity securities	4 610 ..	...	...	...	...	...	...	...	...
Debt securities	4 619 ..	...	...	...	...	...	...	...	...
Portfolio investment liabilities	4 652 Z.	...	...	...	...	...	...	...	...
Equity securities	4 660 ..	...	...	...	...	...	...	...	...
Debt securities	4 669 Z.	...	...	...	...	...	...	...	...
Financial derivatives	4 910 ..	...	...	...	...	...	...	...	...
Financial derivatives assets	4 900 ..	...	...	...	...	...	...	...	...
Financial derivatives liabilities	4 905 ..	...	...	...	...	...	...	...	...
Other investment assets	4 703 ..	–19.1	15.7	25.5	15.2	18.6	27.1	24.6	40.7
Monetary authorities	4 701 ..	...	...	...	...	...	...	...	...
General government	4 704 ..	...	...	...	...	...	...	...	...
Banks	4 705 ..	–31.3	...	...	...	...	...	...	...
Other sectors	4 728 ..	12.2	15.7	25.5	15.2	18.6	27.1	24.6	40.7
Other investment liabilities	4 753 W.	–34.8	–1.8	–16.9	20.9	2.8	12.8	–15.7	90.6
Monetary authorities	4 753 WA	...	...	...	...	...	...	...	1.2
General government	4 753 ZB	2.1	4.2	–15.0	1.3	19.3	16.1	–21.4	50.7
Banks	4 753 ZC	–29.6	...	...	...	...	...	...	...
Other sectors	4 753 ZD	–7.3	–6.0	–1.9	19.6	–16.5	–3.3	5.7	38.7
Total, Groups A Through C	4 983 ..	*–25.7*	*78.2*	*5.8*	*–26.2*	*–117.8*	*–47.2*	*–104.5*	*22.0*
D. Net Errors and Omissions	4 998 ..	**60.0**	**41.6**	**–7.5**	**45.3**	**125.9**	**42.8**	**114.3**	**56.1**
Total, Groups A Through D	4 984 ..	*34.3*	*119.8*	*–1.7*	*19.1*	*8.1*	*–4.4*	*9.8*	*78.1*
E. Reserves and Related Items	4 802 A.	**–34.3**	**–119.8**	**1.7**	**–19.1**	**–8.1**	**4.4**	**–9.8**	**–78.1**
Reserve assets	4 802 ..	–34.3	–119.8	1.7	–19.1	–8.1	4.4	–9.8	–78.1
Use of Fund credit and loans	4 766 ..	...	...	...	...	...	...	...	...
Exceptional financing	4 920 ..	...	...	...	...	...	...	...	...
Conversion rates: Suriname guilders per U.S. dollar	0 101 ..	**1.00**	**442.23**	**401.26**	**401.00**	**401.00**	**859.44**	**1,322.47**	**2,178.50**

[1] Excludes components that have been classified in the categories of Group E.

Table 2. STANDARD PRESENTATION, 1994–2001
(Millions of U.S. dollars)

	Code		1994	1995	1996	1997	1998	1999	2000	2001
CURRENT ACCOUNT	4 993	. .	**58.6**	**62.8**	**–63.5**	**–67.7**	**–154.9**	**–29.1**	**32.3**	**–84.0**
A. GOODS	4 100	. .	99.3	123.0	–1.6	36.1	–27.2	44.1	153.0	139.8
Credit	2 100	. .	**293.6**	**415.6**	**397.2**	**401.6**	**349.7**	**342.0**	**399.1**	**437.0**
General merchandise: exports f.o.b.	2 110	. .	293.6	415.6	397.2	401.6	349.7	342.0	399.1	437.0
Goods for processing: exports f.o.b.	2 150	. .	. . .	. . .	. . .	. . .	. . .	. . .	. . .	. . .
Repairs on goods	2 160	. .	. . .	. . .	. . .	. . .	. . .	. . .	. . .	. . .
Goods procured in ports by carriers	2 170	. .	. . .	. . .	. . .	. . .	. . .	. . .	. . .	. . .
Nonmonetary gold	2 180	. .	. . .	. . .	. . .	. . .	. . .	. . .	. . .	. . .
Debit	3 100	. .	**–194.3**	**–292.6**	**–398.8**	**–365.5**	**–376.9**	**–297.9**	**–246.1**	**–297.2**
General merchandise: imports f.o.b.	3 110	. .	–194.3	–292.6	–398.8	–365.5	–376.9	–297.9	–246.1	–297.2
Goods for processing: imports f.o.b.	3 150	. .	. . .	. . .	. . .	. . .	. . .	. . .	. . .	. . .
Repairs on goods	3 160	. .	. . .	. . .	. . .	. . .	. . .	. . .	. . .	. . .
Goods procured in ports by carriers	3 170	. .	. . .	. . .	. . .	. . .	. . .	. . .	. . .	. . .
Nonmonetary gold	3 180	. .	. . .	. . .	. . .	. . .	. . .	. . .	. . .	. . .
B. SERVICES	4 200	. .	–40.9	–57.3	–65.7	–102.2	–124.9	–72.0	–124.6	–115.3
Total credit	2 200	. .	*72.6*	*104.1*	*103.8*	*91.6*	*72.0*	*79.1*	*90.9*	*59.4*
Total debit	3 200	. .	*–113.5*	*–161.4*	*–169.5*	*–193.8*	*–196.9*	*–151.1*	*–215.5*	*–174.7*
Transportation services, credit	2 205	. .	**35.2**	**41.4**	**36.8**	**37.0**	**45.9**	**48.9**	**37.1**	**19.0**
Passenger	2 850	. .	*25.2*	*31.3*	*30.4*	*29.0*	*34.1*	*35.5*	*26.1*	*12.0*
Freight	2 851	. .	*4.9*	*4.2*	*2.3*	*1.8*	*2.3*	*2.7*	*1.8*	*.6*
Other	2 852	. .	*5.1*	*5.9*	*4.1*	*6.2*	*9.5*	*10.7*	*9.2*	*6.4*
Sea transport, passenger	2 207	. .	. . .	. . .	. . .	. . .	. . .	. . .	. . .	. . .
Sea transport, freight	2 208	. .	. . .	. . .	. . .	. . .	. . .	. . .	. . .	. . .
Sea transport, other	2 209	. .	. . .	. . .	. . .	. . .	. . .	. . .	. . .	. . .
Air transport, passenger	2 211	. .	. . .	31.3	30.4	29.0	34.1	35.5	26.1	12.0
Air transport, freight	2 212	. .	. . .	4.2	2.3	1.8	2.3	2.7	1.8	.6
Air transport, other	2 213	. .	. . .	5.9	4.1	6.2	9.5	10.7	9.2	6.4
Other transport, passenger	2 215	. .	. . .	. . .	. . .	. . .	. . .	. . .	. . .	. . .
Other transport, freight	2 216	. .	. . .	. . .	. . .	. . .	. . .	. . .	. . .	. . .
Other transport, other	2 217	. .	. . .	. . .	. . .	. . .	. . .	. . .	. . .	. . .
Transportation services, debit	3 205	. .	**–56.9**	**–77.8**	**–71.3**	**–78.8**	**–91.5**	**–67.5**	**–88.7**	**–63.8**
Passenger	3 850	. .	*–21.6*	*–24.3*	*–29.8*	*–29.8*	*–37.8*	*–33.9*	*–43.8*	*–39.1*
Freight	3 851	. .	*–17.8*	*–26.9*	*–20.4*	*–23.7*	*–22.6*	*–20.6*	*–13.4*	*–19.6*
Other	3 852	. .	*–17.5*	*–26.6*	*–21.1*	*–25.3*	*–31.1*	*–13.0*	*–31.5*	*–5.1*
Sea transport, passenger	3 207	. .	. . .	. . .	. . .	. . .	. . .	. . .	. . .	. . .
Sea transport, freight	3 208	. .	. . .	. . .	. . .	. . .	. . .	. . .	. . .	. . .
Sea transport, other	3 209	. .	. . .	. . .	. . .	. . .	. . .	. . .	. . .	. . .
Air transport, passenger	3 211	. .	. . .	–24.3	–29.8	–29.8	–37.8	–33.9	–43.8	–39.1
Air transport, freight	3 212	. .	. . .	–26.9	–20.4	–23.7	–22.6	–20.6	–13.4	–19.6
Air transport, other	3 213	. .	. . .	–26.6	–21.1	–25.3	–31.1	–13.0	–31.5	–5.1
Other transport, passenger	3 215	. .	. . .	. . .	. . .	. . .	. . .	. . .	. . .	. . .
Other transport, freight	3 216	. .	. . .	. . .	. . .	. . .	. . .	. . .	. . .	. . .
Other transport, other	3 217	. .	. . .	. . .	. . .	. . .	. . .	. . .	. . .	. . .
Travel, credit	2 236	. .	**11.2**	**21.2**	**13.8**	**8.5**	**1.9**	**9.3**	**15.8**	**14.4**
Business travel	2 237	. .	. . .	. . .	. . .	. . .	. . .	. . .	. . .	. . .
Personal travel	2 240	. .	. . .	21.2	13.8	8.5	1.9	9.3	15.8	14.4
Travel, debit	3 236	. .	**–3.1**	**–3.4**	**–7.7**	**–11.1**	**–10.8**	**–12.9**	**–22.9**	**–29.4**
Business travel	3 237	. .	. . .	. . .	. . .	. . .	. . .	. . .	. . .	. . .
Personal travel	3 240	. .	. . .	–3.4	–7.7	–11.1	–10.8	–12.9	–22.9	–29.4
Other services, credit	2 200	BA	**26.2**	**41.5**	**53.3**	**46.1**	**24.3**	**20.9**	**38.0**	**26.0**
Communications	2 245	. .	. . .	. . .	. . .	. . .	. . .	. . .	. . .	. . .
Construction	2 249	. .	. . .	. . .	. . .	. . .	. . .	. . .	. . .	. . .
Insurance	2 253	. .	.5	.5	.3	.2	.3	.3	.2	. . .
Financial	2 260	. .	. . .	. . .	. . .	. . .	. . .	. . .	. . .	. . .
Computer and information	2 262	. .	. . .	. . .	. . .	. . .	. . .	. . .	. . .	. . .
Royalties and licence fees	2 266	. .	. . .	.1	. . .	. . .	. . .	. . .	. . .	. . .
Other business services	2 268	. .	22.6	37.9	45.2	38.9	19.2	14.3	32.1	22.8
Personal, cultural, and recreational	2 287	. .	. . .	. . .	. . .	. . .	. . .	. . .	. . .	. . .
Government, n.i.e.	2 291	. .	3.1	3.0	7.8	7.0	4.8	6.3	5.7	3.2
Other services, debit	3 200	BA	**–53.5**	**–80.2**	**–90.5**	**–103.9**	**–94.6**	**–70.7**	**–103.9**	**–81.5**
Communications	3 245	. .	. . .	. . .	. . .	. . .	. . .	. . .	. . .	. . .
Construction	3 249	. .	. . .	. . .	. . .	. . .	. . .	. . .	. . .	. . .
Insurance	3 253	. .	–2.0	–2.9	–2.3	–2.6	–2.5	–2.3	–1.9	–2.2
Financial	3 260	. .	. . .	. . .	. . .	. . .	. . .	. . .	. . .	. . .
Computer and information	3 262	. .	. . .	. . .	. . .	. . .	. . .	. . .	. . .	. . .
Royalties and licence fees	3 266	. .	. . .	–.3	. . .	. . .	. . .	. . .	. . .	. . .
Other business services	3 268	. .	–36.6	–61.2	–62.3	–81.8	–69.4	–53.3	–63.3	–68.9
Personal, cultural, and recreational	3 287	. .	. . .	. . .	. . .	. . .	. . .	. . .	. . .	. . .
Government, n.i.e.	3 291	. .	–14.9	–15.8	–25.9	–19.5	–22.7	–15.1	–38.7	–10.4

Table 2 (Continued). STANDARD PRESENTATION, 1994–2001
(Millions of U.S. dollars)

	Code	1994	1995	1996	1997	1998	1999	2000	2001
C. INCOME	4 300 . .	–3.8	–2.6	2.7	–2.6	–.5	.3	6.0	–107.6
Total credit	2 300 . .	*.9*	*2.7*	*7.0*	*7.4*	*6.5*	*7.9*	*13.2*	*5.4*
Total debit	3 300 . .	*–4.7*	*–5.3*	*–4.3*	*–10.0*	*–7.0*	*–7.6*	*–7.2*	*–113.0*
Compensation of employees, credit	2 310 . .	**. . .**	**. . .**	**. . .**	**.3**	**. . .**	**2.1**	**. . .**	**. . .**
Compensation of employees, debit	3 310 . .	**–1.0**	**–1.2**	**–1.3**	**–1.2**	**–.8**	**–1.0**	**–1.1**	**–1.2**
Investment income, credit	2 320 . .	**.9**	**2.7**	**7.0**	**7.1**	**6.5**	**5.8**	**13.2**	**5.4**
Direct investment income	2 330 . .	. . .	. . .	. . .	. . .	. . .	. . .	. . .	. . .
Dividends and distributed branch profits	2 332 . .	. . .	. . .	. . .	. . .	. . .	. . .	. . .	. . .
Reinvested earnings and undistributed branch profits	2 333 . .	. . .	. . .	. . .	. . .	. . .	. . .	. . .	. . .
Income on debt (interest)	2 334 . .	. . .	. . .	. . .	. . .	. . .	. . .	. . .	. . .
Portfolio investment income	2 339 . .	. . .	. . .	. . .	. . .	. . .	. . .	. . .	. . .
Income on equity	2 340 . .	. . .	. . .	. . .	. . .	. . .	. . .	. . .	. . .
Income on bonds and notes	2 350 . .	. . .	. . .	. . .	. . .	. . .	. . .	. . .	. . .
Income on money market instruments	2 360 . .	. . .	. . .	. . .	. . .	. . .	. . .	. . .	. . .
Other investment income	2 370 . .	.9	2.7	7.0	7.1	6.5	5.8	13.2	5.4
Investment income, debit	3 320 . .	**–3.7**	**–4.1**	**–3.0**	**–8.8**	**–6.2**	**–6.6**	**–6.1**	**–111.8**
Direct investment income	3 330 . .	. . .	. . .	. . .	. . .	. . .	. . .	. . .	. . .
Dividends and distributed branch profits	3 332 . .	. . .	. . .	. . .	. . .	. . .	. . .	. . .	. . .
Reinvested earnings and undistributed branch profits	3 333 . .	. . .	. . .	. . .	. . .	. . .	. . .	. . .	. . .
Income on debt (interest)	3 334 . .	. . .	. . .	. . .	. . .	. . .	. . .	. . .	. . .
Portfolio investment income	3 339 . .	. . .	. . .	. . .	. . .	. . .	. . .	. . .	. . .
Income on equity	3 340 . .	. . .	. . .	. . .	. . .	. . .	. . .	. . .	. . .
Income on bonds and notes	3 350 . .	. . .	. . .	. . .	. . .	. . .	. . .	. . .	. . .
Income on money market instruments	3 360 . .	. . .	. . .	. . .	. . .	. . .	. . .	. . .	. . .
Other investment income	3 370 . .	–3.7	–4.1	–3.0	–8.8	–6.2	–6.6	–6.1	–111.8
D. CURRENT TRANSFERS	4 379 . .	4.0	–.3	1.1	1.0	–2.3	–1.5	–2.1	–.9
Credit	2 379 . .	**6.2**	**2.0**	**3.6**	**4.0**	**1.3**	**1.8**	**1.2**	**2.1**
General government	2 380 . .	5.7	. . .	. . .	. . .	. . .	. . .	. . .	. . .
Other sectors	2 390 . .	.5	2.0	3.6	4.0	1.3	1.8	1.2	2.1
Workers' remittances	2 391 . .	. . .	. . .	. . .	.1	. . .	.2	. . .	.2
Other current transfers	2 392 . .	.5	2.0	3.6	3.9	1.3	1.6	1.2	1.9
Debit	3 379 . .	**–2.2**	**–2.3**	**–2.5**	**–3.0**	**–3.6**	**–3.3**	**–3.3**	**–3.0**
General government	3 380 . .	. . .	. . .	. . .	. . .	. . .	. . .	. . .	. . .
Other sectors	3 390 . .	–2.2	–2.3	–2.5	–3.0	–3.6	–3.3	–3.3	–3.0
Workers' remittances	3 391 . .	–1.1	–1.1	–1.6	–1.5	–1.5	–1.2	–.7	–.8
Other current transfers	3 392 . .	–1.1	–1.2	–.9	–1.5	–2.1	–2.1	–2.6	–2.2
CAPITAL AND FINANCIAL ACCOUNT	4 996 . .	**–118.6**	**–104.4**	**71.0**	**22.4**	**29.0**	**–13.7**	**–146.6**	**27.9**
CAPITAL ACCOUNT	4 994 . .	**–.2**	**22.1**	**41.6**	**14.6**	**6.6**	**3.5**	**2.3**	**1.5**
Total credit	2 994 . .	*.2*	*22.1*	*41.6*	*14.6*	*6.6*	*3.5*	*2.3*	*1.5*
Total debit	3 994 . .	*–.4*	. . .	. . .	. . .	. . .	. . .	. . .	. . .
Capital transfers, credit	2 400 . .	**.2**	**22.1**	**41.6**	**14.6**	**6.6**	**3.5**	**2.3**	**1.5**
General government	2 401 . .	. . .	22.1	41.6	14.6	6.6	3.5	2.3	1.5
Debt forgiveness	2 402 . .	. . .	. . .	. . .	. . .	. . .	. . .	. . .	. . .
Other capital transfers	2 410 . .	. . .	22.1	41.6	14.6	6.6	3.5	2.3	1.5
Other sectors	2 430 . .	.2	. . .	. . .	. . .	. . .	. . .	. . .	. . .
Migrants' transfers	2 431 . .	.2	. . .	. . .	. . .	. . .	. . .	. . .	. . .
Debt forgiveness	2 432 . .	. . .	. . .	. . .	. . .	. . .	. . .	. . .	. . .
Other capital transfers	2 440 . .	. . .	. . .	. . .	. . .	. . .	. . .	. . .	. . .
Capital transfers, debit	3 400 . .	**–.4**	**. . .**	**. . .**	**. . .**	**. . .**	**. . .**	**. . .**	**. . .**
General government	3 401 . .	. . .	. . .	. . .	. . .	. . .	. . .	. . .	. . .
Debt forgiveness	3 402 . .	. . .	. . .	. . .	. . .	. . .	. . .	. . .	. . .
Other capital transfers	3 410 . .	. . .	. . .	. . .	. . .	. . .	. . .	. . .	. . .
Other sectors	3 430 . .	–.4	. . .	. . .	. . .	. . .	. . .	. . .	. . .
Migrants' transfers	3 431 . .	–.4	. . .	. . .	. . .	. . .	. . .	. . .	. . .
Debt forgiveness	3 432 . .	. . .	. . .	. . .	. . .	. . .	. . .	. . .	. . .
Other capital transfers	3 440 . .	. . .	. . .	. . .	. . .	. . .	. . .	. . .	. . .
Nonproduced nonfinancial assets, credit	2 480 . .	**. . .**	**. . .**	**. . .**	**. . .**	**. . .**	**. . .**	**. . .**	**. . .**
Nonproduced nonfinancial assets, debit	3 480 . .	**. . .**	**. . .**	**. . .**	**. . .**	**. . .**	**. . .**	**. . .**	**. . .**

Table 2 (Continued). STANDARD PRESENTATION, 1994–2001

(Millions of U.S. dollars)

	Code	1994	1995	1996	1997	1998	1999	2000	2001
FINANCIAL ACCOUNT	4 995 . .	**–118.4**	**–126.5**	**29.4**	**7.8**	**22.4**	**–17.2**	**–148.9**	**26.4**
A. DIRECT INVESTMENT	4 500 . .	–30.2	–20.6	19.1	–9.2	9.1	–61.5	–148.0	–26.8
Direct investment abroad	4 505 . .	...	...	...	...	...	...	...	...
Equity capital	4 510 . .	...	...	...	...	...	...	...	...
Claims on affiliated enterprises	4 515 . .	...	...	...	...	...	...	...	...
Liabilities to affiliated enterprises	4 520 . .	...	...	...	...	...	...	...	...
Reinvested earnings	4 525 . .	...	...	...	...	...	...	...	...
Other capital	4 530 . .	...	...	...	...	...	...	...	...
Claims on affiliated enterprises	4 535 . .	...	...	...	...	...	...	...	...
Liabilities to affiliated enterprises	4 540 . .	...	...	...	...	...	...	...	...
Direct investment in Suriname	4 555 . .	**–30.2**	**–20.6**	**19.1**	**–9.2**	**9.1**	**–61.5**	**–148.0**	**–26.8**
Equity capital	4 560 . .	–.1	.8	.6	.6	...	...	...	...
Claims on direct investors	4 565 . .	...	...	...	...	...	...	...	...
Liabilities to direct investors	4 570 . .	...	.8	.6	.6	...	...	...	...
Reinvested earnings	4 575 . .	...	...	...	...	...	...	...	...
Other capital	4 580 . .	–30.1	–21.4	18.5	–9.8	9.1	–61.5	–148.0	–26.8
Claims on direct investors	4 585 . .	...	...	...	...	...	...	...	...
Liabilities to direct investors	4 590 . .	...	–21.4	18.5	–9.8	9.1	–61.5	–148.0	–26.8
B. PORTFOLIO INVESTMENT	4 600 . .	...	...	...	...	...	...	...	...
Assets	4 602 . .	...	...	...	...	...	...	...	...
Equity securities	4 610 . .	...	...	...	...	...	...	...	...
Monetary authorities	4 611 . .	...	...	...	...	...	...	...	...
General government	4 612 . .	...	...	...	...	...	...	...	...
Banks	4 613 . .	...	...	...	...	...	...	...	...
Other sectors	4 614 . .	...	...	...	...	...	...	...	...
Debt securities	4 619 . .	...	...	...	...	...	...	...	...
Bonds and notes	4 620 . .	...	...	...	...	...	...	...	...
Monetary authorities	4 621 . .	...	...	...	...	...	...	...	...
General government	4 622 . .	...	...	...	...	...	...	...	...
Banks	4 623 . .	...	...	...	...	...	...	...	...
Other sectors	4 624 . .	...	...	...	...	...	...	...	...
Money market instruments	4 630 . .	...	...	...	...	...	...	...	...
Monetary authorities	4 631 . .	...	...	...	...	...	...	...	...
General government	4 632 . .	...	...	...	...	...	...	...	...
Banks	4 633 . .	...	...	...	...	...	...	...	...
Other sectors	4 634 . .	...	...	...	...	...	...	...	...
Liabilities	4 652 . .	...	...	...	...	...	...	...	...
Equity securities	4 660 . .	...	...	...	...	...	...	...	...
Banks	4 663 . .	...	...	...	...	...	...	...	...
Other sectors	4 664 . .	...	...	...	...	...	...	...	...
Debt securities	4 669 . .	...	...	...	...	...	...	...	...
Bonds and notes	4 670 . .	...	...	...	...	...	...	...	...
Monetary authorities	4 671 . .	...	...	...	...	...	...	...	...
General government	4 672 . .	...	...	...	...	...	...	...	...
Banks	4 673 . .	...	...	...	...	...	...	...	...
Other sectors	4 674 . .	...	...	...	...	...	...	...	...
Money market instruments	4 680 . .	...	...	...	...	...	...	...	...
Monetary authorities	4 681 . .	...	...	...	...	...	...	...	...
General government	4 682 . .	...	...	...	...	...	...	...	...
Banks	4 683 . .	...	...	...	...	...	...	...	...
Other sectors	4 684 . .	...	...	...	...	...	...	...	...
C. FINANCIAL DERIVATIVES	4 910 . .	...	...	...	...	...	...	...	...
Monetary authorities	4 911 . .	...	...	...	...	...	...	...	...
General government	4 912 . .	...	...	...	...	...	...	...	...
Banks	4 913 . .	...	...	...	...	...	...	...	...
Other sectors	4 914 . .	...	...	...	...	...	...	...	...
Assets	4 900 . .	...	...	...	...	...	...	...	...
Monetary authorities	4 901 . .	...	...	...	...	...	...	...	...
General government	4 902 . .	...	...	...	...	...	...	...	...
Banks	4 903 . .	...	...	...	...	...	...	...	...
Other sectors	4 904 . .	...	...	...	...	...	...	...	...
Liabilities	4 905 . .	...	...	...	...	...	...	...	...
Monetary authorities	4 906 . .	...	...	...	...	...	...	...	...
General government	4 907 . .	...	...	...	...	...	...	...	...
Banks	4 908 . .	...	...	...	...	...	...	...	...
Other sectors	4 909 . .	...	...	...	...	...	...	...	...

Table 2 (Concluded). STANDARD PRESENTATION, 1994–2001
(Millions of U.S. dollars)

	Code	1994	1995	1996	1997	1998	1999	2000	2001
D. OTHER INVESTMENT	4 700 . .	–53.9	13.9	8.6	36.1	21.4	39.9	8.9	131.3
Assets	4 703 . .	**–19.1**	**15.7**	**25.5**	**15.2**	**18.6**	**27.1**	**24.6**	**40.7**
Trade credits	4 706 . .	. . .	. . .	. . .	. . .	. . .	. . .	. . .	. . .
General government	4 707 . .	. . .	. . .	. . .	. . .	. . .	. . .	. . .	. . .
of which: Short-term	4 709 . .	. . .	. . .	. . .	. . .	. . .	. . .	. . .	. . .
Other sectors	4 710 . .	. . .	. . .	. . .	. . .	. . .	. . .	. . .	. . .
of which: Short-term	4 712 . .	. . .	. . .	. . .	. . .	. . .	. . .	. . .	. . .
Loans	4 714 . .	. . .	. . .	. . .	. . .	. . .	. . .	. . .	. . .
Monetary authorities	4 715 . .	. . .	. . .	. . .	. . .	. . .	. . .	. . .	. . .
of which: Short-term	4 718 . .	. . .	. . .	. . .	. . .	. . .	. . .	. . .	. . .
General government	4 719 . .	. . .	. . .	. . .	. . .	. . .	. . .	. . .	. . .
of which: Short-term	4 721 . .	. . .	. . .	. . .	. . .	. . .	. . .	. . .	. . .
Banks	4 722 . .	. . .	. . .	. . .	. . .	. . .	. . .	. . .	. . .
of which: Short-term	4 724 . .	. . .	. . .	. . .	. . .	. . .	. . .	. . .	. . .
Other sectors	4 725 . .	. . .	. . .	. . .	. . .	. . .	. . .	. . .	. . .
of which: Short-term	4 727 . .	. . .	. . .	. . .	. . .	. . .	. . .	. . .	. . .
Currency and deposits	4 730 . .	–19.1	15.7	25.5	15.2	18.6	27.1	24.6	40.7
Monetary authorities	4 731 . .	. . .	. . .	. . .	. . .	. . .	. . .	. . .	. . .
General government	4 732 . .	. . .	. . .	. . .	. . .	. . .	. . .	. . .	. . .
Banks	4 733 . .	–31.3	. . .	. . .	. . .	. . .	. . .	. . .	. . .
Other sectors	4 734 . .	12.2	15.7	25.5	15.2	18.6	27.1	24.6	40.7
Other assets	4 736 . .	. . .	. . .	. . .	. . .	. . .	. . .	. . .	. . .
Monetary authorities	4 737 . .	. . .	. . .	. . .	. . .	. . .	. . .	. . .	. . .
of which: Short-term	4 739 . .	. . .	. . .	. . .	. . .	. . .	. . .	. . .	. . .
General government	4 740 . .	. . .	. . .	. . .	. . .	. . .	. . .	. . .	. . .
of which: Short-term	4 742 . .	. . .	. . .	. . .	. . .	. . .	. . .	. . .	. . .
Banks	4 743 . .	. . .	. . .	. . .	. . .	. . .	. . .	. . .	. . .
of which: Short-term	4 745 . .	. . .	. . .	. . .	. . .	. . .	. . .	. . .	. . .
Other sectors	4 746 . .	. . .	. . .	. . .	. . .	. . .	. . .	. . .	. . .
of which: Short-term	4 748 . .	. . .	. . .	. . .	. . .	. . .	. . .	. . .	. . .
Liabilities	4 753 . .	**–34.8**	**–1.8**	**–16.9**	**20.9**	**2.8**	**12.8**	**–15.7**	**90.6**
Trade credits	4 756 . .	. . .	. . .	. . .	. . .	. . .	. . .	. . .	. . .
General government	4 757 . .	. . .	. . .	. . .	. . .	. . .	. . .	. . .	. . .
of which: Short-term	4 759 . .	. . .	. . .	. . .	. . .	. . .	. . .	. . .	. . .
Other sectors	4 760 . .	. . .	. . .	. . .	. . .	. . .	. . .	. . .	. . .
of which: Short-term	4 762 . .	. . .	. . .	. . .	. . .	. . .	. . .	. . .	. . .
Loans	4 764 . .	–5.2	–1.8	–16.9	20.9	2.8	12.8	–15.7	89.4
Monetary authorities	4 765 . .	. . .	. . .	. . .	. . .	. . .	. . .	. . .	. . .
of which: Use of Fund credit and loans from the Fund	4 766 . .	. . .	. . .	. . .	. . .	. . .	. . .	. . .	. . .
of which: Short-term	4 768 . .	. . .	. . .	. . .	. . .	. . .	. . .	. . .	. . .
General government	4 769 . .	2.1	4.2	–15.0	1.3	19.3	16.1	–21.4	50.7
of which: Short-term	4 771 . .	. . .	. . .	. . .	. . .	. . .	. . .	. . .	. . .
Banks	4 772 . .	. . .	. . .	. . .	. . .	. . .	. . .	. . .	. . .
of which: Short-term	4 774 . .	. . .	. . .	. . .	. . .	. . .	. . .	. . .	. . .
Other sectors	4 775 . .	–7.3	–6.0	–1.9	19.6	–16.5	–3.3	5.7	38.7
of which: Short-term	4 777 . .	. . .	. . .	. . .	. . .	. . .	. . .	. . .	. . .
Currency and deposits	4 780 . .	–29.6	. . .	. . .	. . .	. . .	. . .	. . .	. . .
Monetary authorities	4 781 . .	. . .	. . .	. . .	. . .	. . .	. . .	. . .	. . .
General government	4 782 . .	. . .	. . .	. . .	. . .	. . .	. . .	. . .	. . .
Banks	4 783 . .	–29.6	. . .	. . .	. . .	. . .	. . .	. . .	. . .
Other sectors	4 784 . .	. . .	. . .	. . .	. . .	. . .	. . .	. . .	. . .
Other liabilities	4 786 . .	. . .	. . .	. . .	. . .	. . .	. . .	. . .	1.2
Monetary authorities	4 787 . .	. . .	. . .	. . .	. . .	. . .	. . .	. . .	1.2
of which: Short-term	4 789 . .	. . .	. . .	. . .	. . .	. . .	. . .	. . .	. . .
General government	4 790 . .	. . .	. . .	. . .	. . .	. . .	. . .	. . .	. . .
of which: Short-term	4 792 . .	. . .	. . .	. . .	. . .	. . .	. . .	. . .	. . .
Banks	4 793 . .	. . .	. . .	. . .	. . .	. . .	. . .	. . .	. . .
of which: Short-term	4 795 . .	. . .	. . .	. . .	. . .	. . .	. . .	. . .	. . .
Other sectors	4 796 . .	. . .	. . .	. . .	. . .	. . .	. . .	. . .	. . .
of which: Short-term	4 798 . .	. . .	. . .	. . .	. . .	. . .	. . .	. . .	. . .
E. RESERVE ASSETS	4 802 . .	–34.3	–119.8	1.7	–19.1	–8.1	4.4	–9.8	–78.1
Monetary gold	4 812 . .	. . .	–23.2	–17.1	3.7	–.3	18.9	–4.4	–2.2
Special drawing rights	4 811 . .	. . .	–11.5	–.7	. . .	. . .	8.6	.3	.3
Reserve position in the Fund	4 810 . .	. . .	. . .	. . .	. . .	. . .	–8.5	. . .	. . .
Foreign exchange	4 803 . .	–31.2	–85.1	19.5	–22.8	–7.8	–14.7	–5.7	–76.2
Other claims	4 813 . .	–3.1	. . .	. . .	. . .	. . .	. . .	. . .	. . .
NET ERRORS AND OMISSIONS	4 998 . .	**60.0**	**41.6**	**–7.5**	**45.3**	**125.9**	**42.8**	**114.3**	**56.1**

Part 3 of the *Yearbook* contains descriptions of the methodologies, compilation practices, and sources used to compile these data.

Table 1. ANALYTIC PRESENTATION, 1994–2001
(Millions of U.S. dollars)

	Code	1994	1995	1996	1997	1998	1999	2000	2001
A. Current Account [1]	4 993 Z.	**1.9**	**–29.7**	**–52.0**	**–2.7**	**–93.3**	**–21.7**	**–51.4**	**–52.7**
Goods: exports f.o.b	2 100 . .	790.9	867.8	850.5	961.3	967.8	936.7	905.0	809.3
Goods: imports f.o.b	3 100 . .	–841.0	–1,064.4	–1,054.4	–1,065.5	–1,073.8	–1,067.9	–1,040.9	–882.0
Balance on Goods	4 100 . .	*–50.1*	*–196.6*	*–203.9*	*–104.2*	*–106.0*	*–131.3*	*–135.8*	*–72.7*
Services: credit	2 200 . .	112.8	151.8	100.8	91.9	91.4	95.2	107.4	85.0
Services: debit	3 200 . .	–201.8	–209.5	–240.7	–244.8	–267.7	–204.5	–212.4	–179.1
Balance on Goods and Services	4 991 . .	*–139.1*	*–254.2*	*–343.9*	*–257.1*	*–282.2*	*–240.5*	*–240.9*	*–166.7*
Income: credit	2 300 . .	138.5	162.6	200.8	182.7	167.8	164.0	125.2	118.8
Income: debit	3 300 . .	–155.0	–82.0	–68.7	–44.6	–111.4	–76.3	–59.0	–84.3
Balance on Goods, Services, and Income	4 992 . .	*–155.6*	*–173.7*	*–211.8*	*–119.1*	*–225.8*	*–152.8*	*–174.6*	*–132.3*
Current transfers: credit	2 379 Z.	252.6	257.2	268.7	226.8	242.7	241.4	234.1	186.1
Current transfers: debit	3 379 . .	–95.1	–113.3	–108.9	–110.5	–110.3	–110.2	–110.9	–106.5
B. Capital Account [1]	4 994 Z.	**–.2**	**. . .**	**.1**	**.1**	**. . .**	**. . .**	**.1**	**.5**
Capital account: credit	2 994 Z.	.1	.3	.1	.1	. . .	. . .	.1	.2
Capital account: debit	3 994 . .	–.3	–.3	. . .	. . .	. . .	. . .	. . .	.4
Total, Groups A Plus B	4 981 . .	*1.8*	*–29.7*	*–51.8*	*–2.7*	*–93.3*	*–21.7*	*–51.3*	*–52.2*
C. Financial Account [1]	4 995 W.	**–63.1**	**–47.3**	**–8.6**	**31.4**	**117.0**	**37.7**	**36.1**	**–43.2**
Direct investment abroad	4 505 . .	–64.7	–20.6	6.4	12.0	–23.9	–13.2	–14.3	6.1
Direct investment in Swaziland	4 555 Z.	63.3	51.8	21.7	–15.3	152.7	100.4	34.5	20.8
Portfolio investment assets	4 602 . .	–3.9	–9.6	–2.0	–2.0	–2.8	3.2	–4.0	–.1
Equity securities	4 610 . .	. . .	–1.9	–.2	–1.9	–1.3	1.5	–.1	–.1
Debt securities	4 619 . .	–3.9	–7.6	–1.7	. . .	–1.5	1.7	–3.9	. . .
Portfolio investment liabilities	4 652 Z.	.1	.8	.4	–.1	3.4	2.7	1.4	. . .
Equity securities	4 660 . .	.1	.8	.4	–.1	3.4	2.7	1.4	. . .
Debt securities	4 669 Z.	. . .	. . .	. . .	. . .	. . .	. . .	. . .	. . .
Financial derivatives	4 910 . .	. . .	. . .	. . .	. . .	. . .	. . .	. . .	. . .
Financial derivatives assets	4 900 . .	. . .	. . .	. . .	. . .	. . .	. . .	. . .	. . .
Financial derivatives liabilities	4 905 . .	. . .	. . .	. . .	. . .	. . .	. . .	. . .	. . .
Other investment assets	4 703 . .	–80.5	–31.0	–120.0	–12.3	1.6	–86.6	–24.1	–39.8
Monetary authorities	4 701 . .	. . .	. . .	. . .	. . .	. . .	. . .	. . .	. . .
General government	4 704 . .	–17.9	–6.7	–2.7	13.4	–4.8	17.2	12.4	15.1
Banks	4 705 . .	5.7	–5.3	–77.0	11.1	–22.9	–41.7	27.7	–27.7
Other sectors	4 728 . .	–68.3	–19.0	–40.3	–36.7	29.2	–62.2	–64.2	–27.2
Other investment liabilities	4 753 W.	22.7	–38.7	84.8	49.0	–14.0	31.3	42.6	–30.2
Monetary authorities	4 753 WA	30.6	–9.8	3.8	–19.2	22.2	28.5	6.2	14.7
General government	4 753 ZB	–14.8	–17.9	–18.5	–14.0	–14.1	–16.1	–13.4	–11.6
Banks	4 753 ZC	.7	.4	41.5	–25.9	–13.8	.3	6.4	–9.5
Other sectors	4 753 ZD	6.2	–11.3	57.9	108.1	–8.3	18.6	43.4	–23.8
Total, Groups A Through C	4 983 . .	*–61.3*	*–77.1*	*–60.4*	*28.7*	*23.7*	*16.0*	*–15.2*	*–95.4*
D. Net Errors and Omissions	4 998 . .	**48.8**	**78.9**	**36.9**	**–16.8**	**4.1**	**10.0**	**9.5**	**12.1**
Total, Groups A Through D	4 984 . .	*–12.5*	*1.8*	*–23.5*	*11.9*	*27.8*	*26.0*	*–5.7*	*–83.3*
E. Reserves and Related Items	4 802 A.	**12.5**	**–1.8**	**23.5**	**–11.9**	**–27.8**	**–26.0**	**5.7**	**83.3**
Reserve assets	4 802 . .	12.5	–29.8	–15.4	–25.3	–50.5	–26.3	6.5	56.5
Use of Fund credit and loans	4 766 . .	. . .	. . .	. . .	. . .	. . .	. . .	. . .	. . .
Exceptional financing	4 920 . .	. . .	28.0	38.8	13.5	22.7	.2	–.7	26.8
Conversion rates: emalangeni per U.S. dollar	0 101 . .	**3.5508**	**3.6271**	**4.2993**	**4.6080**	**5.5283**	**6.1095**	**6.9398**	**8.6092**

[1] Excludes components that have been classified in the categories of Group E.

Table 2. STANDARD PRESENTATION, 1994–2001
(Millions of U.S. dollars)

	Code	1994	1995	1996	1997	1998	1999	2000	2001
CURRENT ACCOUNT	4 993 . .	**1.9**	**–29.7**	**–52.0**	**–2.7**	**–93.3**	**–21.7**	**–51.4**	**–52.7**
A. GOODS	4 100 . .	–50.1	–196.6	–203.9	–104.2	–106.0	–131.3	–135.8	–72.7
Credit	2 100 . .	**790.9**	**867.8**	**850.5**	**961.3**	**967.8**	**936.7**	**905.0**	**809.3**
General merchandise: exports f.o.b.	2 110 . .	790.7	867.4	849.2	959.9	965.9	934.8	903.3	807.6
Goods for processing: exports f.o.b.	2 150 . .	. . .	. . .	1.1	1.2	1.7	1.7	1.4	1.5
Repairs on goods	2 160 . .	. . .	. . .	. . .	. . .	. . .	. . .	. . .	. . .
Goods procured in ports by carriers	2 170 . .	.3	.4	.2	.2	.2	.2	.3	.2
Nonmonetary gold	2 180 . .	. . .	. . .	. . .	. . .	. . .	. . .	. . .	. . .
Debit	3 100 . .	**–841.0**	**–1,064.4**	**–1,054.4**	**–1,065.5**	**–1,073.8**	**–1,067.9**	**–1,040.9**	**–882.0**
General merchandise: imports f.o.b.	3 110 . .	–826.3	–1,027.7	–1,002.4	–1,013.2	–1,013.9	–1,002.1	–969.7	–826.2
Goods for processing: imports f.o.b.	3 150 . .	–12.2	–33.2	–46.7	–47.9	–54.7	–63.1	–67.2	–52.5
Repairs on goods	3 160 . .	–1.2	–1.3	–4.3	–3.1	–4.0	–2.3	–3.6	–3.0
Goods procured in ports by carriers	3 170 . .	–1.3	–2.3	–1.1	–1.3	–1.1	–.5	–.4	–.3
Nonmonetary gold	3 180 . .	. . .	. . .	. . .	. . .	. . .	. . .	. . .	. . .
B. SERVICES	4 200 . .	–89.0	–57.6	–140.0	–152.9	–176.2	–109.3	–105.0	–94.1
Total credit	2 200 . .	*112.8*	*151.8*	*100.8*	*91.9*	*91.4*	*95.2*	*107.4*	*85.0*
Total debit	3 200 . .	*–201.8*	*–209.5*	*–240.7*	*–244.8*	*–267.7*	*–204.5*	*–212.4*	*–179.1*
Transportation services, credit	2 205 . .	**22.1**	**27.3**	**21.0**	**20.1**	**19.9**	**16.6**	**17.7**	**13.5**
Passenger	2 850 . .	*5.7*	*6.4*	*3.8*	*3.7*	*4.3*	*2.8*	*2.6*	*2.1*
Freight	2 851 . .	*16.4*	*20.8*	*17.2*	*16.4*	*15.5*	*13.9*	*15.2*	*11.4*
Other	2 852 . .	. . .	. . .	. . .	. . .	. . .	. . .	. . .	. . .
Sea transport, passenger	2 207 . .	. . .	. . .	. . .	. . .	. . .	. . .	. . .	. . .
Sea transport, freight	2 208 . .	.1	.1	.2	.2	1.4	1.2	.4	.4
Sea transport, other	2 209 . .	. . .	. . .	. . .	. . .	. . .	. . .	. . .	. . .
Air transport, passenger	2 211 . .	5.7	6.4	3.8	3.7	4.3	2.8	2.6	2.1
Air transport, freight	2 212 . .	. . .	. . .	. . .	. . .	. . .	. . .	.1	.1
Air transport, other	2 213 . .	. . .	. . .	. . .	. . .	. . .	. . .	. . .	. . .
Other transport, passenger	2 215 . .	. . .	. . .	. . .	. . .	. . .	. . .	. . .	. . .
Other transport, freight	2 216 . .	16.4	20.7	17.0	16.2	14.1	12.7	14.7	11.0
Other transport, other	2 217 . .	. . .	. . .	. . .	. . .	. . .	. . .	. . .	. . .
Transportation services, debit	3 205 . .	**–25.9**	**–32.3**	**–14.7**	**–23.2**	**–24.3**	**–24.2**	**–27.5**	**–28.1**
Passenger	3 850 . .	*–2.4*	*–2.4*	*–2.0*	*–2.0*	*–1.7*	*–1.4*	*–1.3*	*–1.0*
Freight	3 851 . .	*–2.7*	*–1.1*	*–.9*	*–9.2*	*–9.0*	*–9.7*	*–9.1*	*–12.0*
Other	3 852 . .	*–20.8*	*–28.8*	*–11.9*	*–12.0*	*–13.6*	*–13.1*	*–17.1*	*–15.1*
Sea transport, passenger	3 207 . .	. . .	. . .	. . .	. . .	. . .	. . .	. . .	. . .
Sea transport, freight	3 208 . .	–2.6	–1.1	–.8	–9.1	–8.8	–9.6	–8.9	–11.9
Sea transport, other	3 209 . .	. . .	. . .	. . .	. . .	. . .	. . .	. . .	. . .
Air transport, passenger	3 211 . .	–2.4	–2.4	–2.0	–2.0	–1.7	–1.4	–1.3	–1.0
Air transport, freight	3 212 . .	–.1	–.1	–.1	–.1	–.1	–.1	–.1	–.1
Air transport, other	3 213 . .	–20.8	–28.8	–11.9	–12.0	–13.6	–13.1	–17.1	–15.1
Other transport, passenger	3 215 . .	. . .	. . .	. . .	. . .	. . .	. . .	. . .	. . .
Other transport, freight	3 216 . .	. . .	. . .	. . .	. . .	. . .	. . .	. . .	. . .
Other transport, other	3 217 . .	. . .	. . .	. . .	. . .	. . .	. . .	. . .	. . .
Travel, credit	2 236 . .	**35.1**	**48.2**	**37.5**	**39.7**	**46.7**	**49.9**	**35.4**	**28.3**
Business travel	2 237 . .	27.2	32.9	30.7	31.4	30.2	30.3	27.1	22.3
Personal travel	2 240 . .	7.9	15.3	6.8	8.4	16.6	19.6	8.2	6.0
Travel, debit	3 236 . .	**–38.3**	**–42.7**	**–42.0**	**–38.0**	**–58.4**	**–59.4**	**–52.9**	**–43.7**
Business travel	3 237 . .	–12.1	–12.7	–11.7	–13.1	–25.8	–27.2	–24.7	–19.2
Personal travel	3 240 . .	–26.3	–30.0	–30.2	–25.0	–32.6	–32.2	–28.2	–24.5
Other services, credit	2 200 BA	**55.6**	**76.4**	**42.2**	**32.1**	**24.8**	**28.7**	**54.3**	**43.2**
Communications	2 245 . .	2.7	2.3	1.8	1.3	1.7	1.6	1.6	1.3
Construction	2 249 . .	. . .	. . .	. . .	. . .	. . .	. . .	. . .	. . .
Insurance	2 253 . .	. . .	. . .	. . .	. . .	. . .	. . .	. . .	. . .
Financial	2 260 . .	. . .	. . .	. . .	. . .	. . .	. . .	. . .	. . .
Computer and information	2 262 . .	14.4	12.6	10.6	11.0	.9	1.8	1.9	1.6
Royalties and licence fees	2 266 . .	.3	.3	.2	.2	.2	.2	.2	.2
Other business services	2 268 . .	34.9	59.0	26.8	17.3	17.3	21.7	48.0	38.0
Personal, cultural, and recreational	2 287 . .	. . .	. . .	. . .	. . .	. . .	. . .	. . .	. . .
Government, n.i.e.	2 291 . .	3.2	2.2	2.7	2.1	4.7	3.3	2.6	2.1
Other services, debit	3 200 BA	**–137.6**	**–134.4**	**–184.0**	**–183.7**	**–184.9**	**–120.9**	**–132.0**	**–107.3**
Communications	3 245 . .	–3.0	–2.6	–2.1	–2.6	–1.5	–1.3	–2.3	–1.9
Construction	3 249 . .	–1.2	–1.2	–1.5	–4.2	–4.4	–.5	–.6	–.5
Insurance	3 253 . .	–1.4	–8.9	–7.9	–7.5	–7.5	–7.2	–6.4	–5.1
Financial	3 260 . .	–.1	–.1	–.1	–.1	–.1	–.1	–.1	–.1
Computer and information	3 262 . .	–.6	–.3	–1.2	–1.2	–1.3	–1.2	–1.6	–1.3
Royalties and licence fees	3 266 . .	–13.4	–15.6	–14.6	–39.3	–39.3	–39.9	–35.1	–46.0
Other business services	3 268 . .	–106.2	–102.3	–148.5	–120.2	–125.2	–66.8	–75.8	–50.5
Personal, cultural, and recreational	3 287 . .	. . .	. . .	. . .	. . .	. . .	. . .	. . .	. . .
Government, n.i.e.	3 291 . .	–11.8	–3.4	–8.1	–8.6	–5.7	–3.9	–10.1	–1.9

Table 2 (Continued). STANDARD PRESENTATION, 1994–2001
(Millions of U.S. dollars)

	Code	1994	1995	1996	1997	1998	1999	2000	2001
C. INCOME	4 300	–16.5	80.6	132.1	138.1	56.4	87.7	66.2	34.4
Total credit	2 300	*138.5*	*162.6*	*200.8*	*182.7*	*167.8*	*164.0*	*125.2*	*118.8*
Total debit	3 300	*–155.0*	*–82.0*	*–68.7*	*–44.6*	*–111.4*	*–76.3*	*–59.0*	*–84.3*
Compensation of employees, credit	2 310	**76.9**	**82.2**	**75.4**	**83.8**	**78.4**	**70.0**	**56.8**	**52.7**
Compensation of employees, debit	3 310	...	...	...	...	...	...	...	...
Investment income, credit	2 320	**61.6**	**80.4**	**125.4**	**98.9**	**89.5**	**94.0**	**68.4**	**66.1**
Direct investment income	2 330	9.2	4.9	7.7	1.5	1.3	1.7	1.4	1.2
Dividends and distributed branch profits	2 332	2.7	3.3	3.0	.4	.4	.9	.7	.6
Reinvested earnings and undistributed branch profits	2 333	6.4	1.6	4.7	1.1	.9	.8	.7	.6
Income on debt (interest)	2 334	...	...	...	...	...	...	...	...
Portfolio investment income	2 339	...	...	...	...	...	...	...	...
Income on equity	2 340	...	...	...	...	...	...	...	...
Income on bonds and notes	2 350	...	...	...	...	...	...	...	...
Income on money market instruments	2 360	...	...	...	...	...	...	...	...
Other investment income	2 370	52.4	75.4	117.7	97.5	88.2	92.3	67.0	64.9
Investment income, debit	3 320	**–155.0**	**–82.0**	**–68.7**	**–44.6**	**–111.4**	**–76.3**	**–59.0**	**–84.3**
Direct investment income	3 330	–138.3	–68.0	–50.4	–23.7	–96.6	–54.0	–27.3	–70.5
Dividends and distributed branch profits	3 332	–80.6	–69.1	–58.5	–48.9	–23.6	–17.5	–17.6	–41.2
Reinvested earnings and undistributed branch profits	3 333	–57.7	1.1	8.1	25.2	–73.0	–36.6	–9.6	–29.4
Income on debt (interest)	3 334	...	...	...	...	...	...	...	...
Portfolio investment income	3 339	...	...	...	...	...	...	...	...
Income on equity	3 340	...	...	...	...	...	...	...	...
Income on bonds and notes	3 350	...	...	...	...	...	...	...	...
Income on money market instruments	3 360	...	...	...	...	...	...	...	...
Other investment income	3 370	–16.7	–14.1	–18.2	–20.9	–14.8	–22.3	–31.8	–13.8
D. CURRENT TRANSFERS	4 379	157.5	144.0	159.8	116.3	132.5	131.1	123.2	79.6
Credit	2 379	**252.6**	**257.2**	**268.7**	**226.8**	**242.7**	**241.4**	**234.1**	**186.1**
General government	2 380	246.1	251.8	262.8	223.4	238.0	232.6	224.2	180.0
Other sectors	2 390	6.5	5.4	5.9	3.5	4.7	8.8	9.8	6.1
Workers' remittances	2 391	...	...	...	...	...	...	...	...
Other current transfers	2 392	6.5	5.4	5.9	3.5	4.7	8.8	9.8	6.1
Debit	3 379	**–95.1**	**–113.3**	**–108.9**	**–110.5**	**–110.3**	**–110.2**	**–110.9**	**–106.5**
General government	3 380	–88.1	–109.6	–105.1	–108.2	–108.0	–102.8	–102.5	–90.7
Other sectors	3 390	–7.0	–3.7	–3.8	–2.4	–2.2	–7.5	–8.4	–15.8
Workers' remittances	3 391	–5.9	–3.4	–3.7	–2.2	–1.6	–6.8	–6.3	–14.9
Other current transfers	3 392	–1.1	–.2	–.2	–.2	–.6	–.7	–2.0	–.9
CAPITAL AND FINANCIAL ACCOUNT	4 996	**–50.7**	**–49.2**	**15.0**	**19.5**	**89.3**	**11.7**	**41.9**	**40.6**
CAPITAL ACCOUNT	4 994	**–.2**	...	**.1**	**.1**	...	...	**.1**	**.5**
Total credit	2 994	*.1*	*.3*	*.1*	*.1*	...	...	*.1*	*.2*
Total debit	3 994	*–.3*	*–.3*	...	...	...	...	...	*.4*
Capital transfers, credit	2 400	**.1**	**.3**	**.1**	**.1**	...	...	**.1**	**.2**
General government	2 401	...	...	...	...	...	...	...	...
Debt forgiveness	2 402	...	...	...	...	...	...	...	...
Other capital transfers	2 410	...	...	...	...	...	...	...	...
Other sectors	2 430	.1	.3	.1	.1	...	...	.1	.2
Migrants' transfers	2 431	.1	.3	.1	.1	...	...	.1	.2
Debt forgiveness	2 432	...	...	...	...	...	...	...	...
Other capital transfers	2 440	...	...	...	...	...	...	...	...
Capital transfers, debit	3 400	**–.3**	**–.3**	...	...	...	...	...	**.4**
General government	3 401	–.3	–.2	...	...	...	...	...	...
Debt forgiveness	3 402	...	...	...	...	...	...	...	...
Other capital transfers	3 410	–.3	–.2	...	...	...	...	...	...
Other sectors	3 430	...	–.1	...	...	...	...	...	.4
Migrants' transfers	3 431	...	–.1	...	...	...	...	...	.4
Debt forgiveness	3 432	...	...	...	...	...	...	...	...
Other capital transfers	3 440	...	...	...	...	...	...	...	...
Nonproduced nonfinancial assets, credit	2 480	...	...	...	...	...	...	...	...
Nonproduced nonfinancial assets, debit	3 480	...	...	...	...	...	...	...	...

Table 2 (Continued). STANDARD PRESENTATION, 1994–2001

(Millions of U.S. dollars)

	Code		1994	1995	1996	1997	1998	1999	2000	2001
FINANCIAL ACCOUNT	4 995	. .	**–50.6**	**–49.2**	**14.9**	**19.5**	**89.2**	**11.7**	**41.8**	**40.1**
A. DIRECT INVESTMENT	4 500	. .	–1.4	31.2	28.2	–3.3	128.8	87.1	20.1	26.9
Direct investment abroad	4 505	. .	**–64.7**	**–20.6**	**6.4**	**12.0**	**–23.9**	**–13.2**	**–14.3**	**6.1**
Equity capital	4 510	. .	–.9	–3.4	–4.3	6.6	–.8	1.4	.7	. . .
Claims on affiliated enterprises	4 515	. .	–.9	–3.4	–4.3	6.6	–.8	1.4	.7	. . .
Liabilities to affiliated enterprises	4 520	. .	. . .	. . .	. . .	. . .	. . .	. . .	. . .	. . .
Reinvested earnings	4 525	. .	–6.4	–1.6	–4.7	–1.1	–.9	–.8	–.7	–.6
Other capital	4 530	. .	–57.4	–15.5	15.4	6.4	–22.2	–13.8	–14.3	6.7
Claims on affiliated enterprises	4 535	. .	–57.4	–15.5	15.4	6.4	–22.2	–13.8	–14.3	6.7
Liabilities to affiliated enterprises	4 540	. .	. . .	. . .	. . .	. . .	. . .	. . .	. . .	. . .
Direct investment in Swaziland	4 555	. .	**63.3**	**51.8**	**21.7**	**–15.3**	**152.7**	**100.4**	**34.5**	**20.8**
Equity capital	4 560	. .	10.3	31.6	27.1	3.9	9.3	1.4	–21.2	–.2
Claims on direct investors	4 565	. .	. . .	. . .	. . .	. . .	. . .	. . .	. . .	. . .
Liabilities to direct investors	4 570	. .	10.3	31.6	27.1	3.9	9.3	1.4	–21.2	–.2
Reinvested earnings	4 575	. .	57.7	–1.1	–8.1	–25.2	73.0	36.6	9.6	29.4
Other capital	4 580	. .	–4.7	21.3	2.7	6.0	70.4	62.4	46.1	–8.3
Claims on direct investors	4 585	. .	. . .	. . .	. . .	. . .	. . .	. . .	. . .	. . .
Liabilities to direct investors	4 590	. .	–4.7	21.3	2.7	6.0	70.4	62.4	46.1	–8.3
B. PORTFOLIO INVESTMENT	4 600	. .	–3.8	–8.8	–1.5	–2.0	.6	5.9	–2.6	–.1
Assets	4 602	. .	**–3.9**	**–9.6**	**–2.0**	**–2.0**	**–2.8**	**3.2**	**–4.0**	**–.1**
Equity securities	4 610	. .	. . .	–1.9	–.2	–1.9	–1.3	1.5	–.1	–.1
Monetary authorities	4 611	. .	. . .	. . .	. . .	. . .	. . .	. . .	. . .	. . .
General government	4 612	. .	. . .	. . .	. . .	. . .	. . .	. . .	. . .	. . .
Banks	4 613	. .	. . .	. . .	. . .	. . .	. . .	. . .	. . .	. . .
Other sectors	4 614	. .	. . .	–1.9	–.2	–1.9	–1.3	1.5	–.1	–.1
Debt securities	4 619	. .	–3.9	–7.6	–1.7	. . .	–1.5	1.7	–3.9	. . .
Bonds and notes	4 620	. .	. . .	–7.3	–1.5	. . .	–3.5	1.7	–3.9	.2
Monetary authorities	4 621	. .	. . .	. . .	. . .	. . .	. . .	. . .	. . .	. . .
General government	4 622	. .	. . .	. . .	. . .	. . .	. . .	. . .	. . .	. . .
Banks	4 623	. .	. . .	. . .	. . .	. . .	. . .	. . .	. . .	. . .
Other sectors	4 624	. .	. . .	–7.3	–1.5	. . .	–3.5	1.7	–3.9	.2
Money market instruments	4 630	. .	–3.9	–.3	–.2	. . .	2.0	. . .	. . .	–.1
Monetary authorities	4 631	. .	. . .	. . .	. . .	. . .	. . .	. . .	. . .	. . .
General government	4 632	. .	. . .	. . .	. . .	. . .	. . .	. . .	. . .	. . .
Banks	4 633	. .	. . .	. . .	. . .	. . .	. . .	. . .	. . .	. . .
Other sectors	4 634	. .	–3.9	–.3	–.2	. . .	2.0	. . .	. . .	–.1
Liabilities	4 652	. .	**.1**	**.8**	**.4**	**–.1**	**3.4**	**2.7**	**1.4**	**. . .**
Equity securities	4 660	. .	.1	.8	.4	–.1	3.4	2.7	1.4	. . .
Banks	4 663	. .	. . .	. . .	. . .	. . .	. . .	. . .	. . .	. . .
Other sectors	4 664	. .	.1	.8	.4	–.1	3.4	2.7	1.4	. . .
Debt securities	4 669	. .	. . .	. . .	. . .	. . .	. . .	. . .	. . .	. . .
Bonds and notes	4 670	. .	. . .	. . .	. . .	. . .	. . .	. . .	. . .	. . .
Monetary authorities	4 671	. .	. . .	. . .	. . .	. . .	. . .	. . .	. . .	. . .
General government	4 672	. .	. . .	. . .	. . .	. . .	. . .	. . .	. . .	. . .
Banks	4 673	. .	. . .	. . .	. . .	. . .	. . .	. . .	. . .	. . .
Other sectors	4 674	. .	. . .	. . .	. . .	. . .	. . .	. . .	. . .	. . .
Money market instruments	4 680	. .	. . .	. . .	. . .	. . .	. . .	. . .	. . .	. . .
Monetary authorities	4 681	. .	. . .	. . .	. . .	. . .	. . .	. . .	. . .	. . .
General government	4 682	. .	. . .	. . .	. . .	. . .	. . .	. . .	. . .	. . .
Banks	4 683	. .	. . .	. . .	. . .	. . .	. . .	. . .	. . .	. . .
Other sectors	4 684	. .	. . .	. . .	. . .	. . .	. . .	. . .	. . .	. . .
C. FINANCIAL DERIVATIVES	4 910	. .	. . .	. . .	. . .	. . .	. . .	. . .	. . .	. . .
Monetary authorities	4 911	. .	. . .	. . .	. . .	. . .	. . .	. . .	. . .	. . .
General government	4 912	. .	. . .	. . .	. . .	. . .	. . .	. . .	. . .	. . .
Banks	4 913	. .	. . .	. . .	. . .	. . .	. . .	. . .	. . .	. . .
Other sectors	4 914	. .	. . .	. . .	. . .	. . .	. . .	. . .	. . .	. . .
Assets	4 900	. .	**. . .**	**. . .**	**. . .**	**. . .**	**. . .**	**. . .**	**. . .**	**. . .**
Monetary authorities	4 901	. .	. . .	. . .	. . .	. . .	. . .	. . .	. . .	. . .
General government	4 902	. .	. . .	. . .	. . .	. . .	. . .	. . .	. . .	. . .
Banks	4 903	. .	. . .	. . .	. . .	. . .	. . .	. . .	. . .	. . .
Other sectors	4 904	. .	. . .	. . .	. . .	. . .	. . .	. . .	. . .	. . .
Liabilities	4 905	. .	**. . .**	**. . .**	**. . .**	**. . .**	**. . .**	**. . .**	**. . .**	**. . .**
Monetary authorities	4 906	. .	. . .	. . .	. . .	. . .	. . .	. . .	. . .	. . .
General government	4 907	. .	. . .	. . .	. . .	. . .	. . .	. . .	. . .	. . .
Banks	4 908	. .	. . .	. . .	. . .	. . .	. . .	. . .	. . .	. . .
Other sectors	4 909	. .	. . .	. . .	. . .	. . .	. . .	. . .	. . .	. . .

Table 2 (Concluded). STANDARD PRESENTATION, 1994–2001
(Millions of U.S. dollars)

	Code	1994	1995	1996	1997	1998	1999	2000	2001
D. OTHER INVESTMENT	4 700 . .	-57.9	-41.7	3.6	50.2	10.3	-55.1	17.8	-43.3
Assets	4 703 . .	**-80.5**	**-31.0**	**-120.0**	**-12.3**	**1.6**	**-86.6**	**-24.1**	**-39.8**
Trade credits	4 706 . .	14.7	-1.1	18.6	-7.3	-7.0	-26.8	-.8	-28.9
General government	4 707 . .	. . .	. . .	. . .	. . .	. . .	. . .	. . .	. . .
of which: Short-term	4 709 . .	. . .	. . .	. . .	. . .	. . .	. . .	. . .	. . .
Other sectors	4 710 . .	14.7	-1.1	18.6	-7.3	-7.0	-26.8	-.8	-28.9
of which: Short-term	4 712 . .	*14.7*	*-1.1*	*18.6*	*-7.3*	*-7.0*	*-26.8*	*-.8*	*-28.9*
Loans	4 714 . .	.7	.5	-1.0	.1	.1	.8	.2	. . .
Monetary authorities	4 715 . .	. . .	. . .	. . .	. . .	. . .	. . .	. . .	. . .
of which: Short-term	4 718 . .	. . .	. . .	. . .	. . .	. . .	. . .	. . .	. . .
General government	4 719 . .	. . .	. . .	. . .	. . .	. . .	. . .	. . .	. . .
of which: Short-term	4 721 . .	. . .	. . .	. . .	. . .	. . .	. . .	. . .	. . .
Banks	4 722 . .	. . .	. . .	. . .	. . .	. . .	. . .	. . .	. . .
of which: Short-term	4 724 . .	. . .	. . .	. . .	. . .	. . .	. . .	. . .	. . .
Other sectors	4 725 . .	.7	.5	-1.0	.1	.1	.8	.2	. . .
of which: Short-term	4 727 . .	. . .	. . .	. . .	. . .	. . .	. . .	. . .	. . .
Currency and deposits	4 730 . .	2.7	-15.4	-105.6	16.0	7.8	-44.5	3.6	-18.2
Monetary authorities	4 731 . .	. . .	. . .	. . .	. . .	. . .	. . .	. . .	. . .
General government	4 732 . .	. . .	. . .	. . .	. . .	. . .	. . .	. . .	. . .
Banks	4 733 . .	5.7	-5.3	-77.0	11.1	-22.9	-41.7	27.7	-27.7
Other sectors	4 734 . .	-3.0	-10.0	-28.7	4.9	30.7	-2.9	-24.1	9.5
Other assets	4 736 . .	-98.7	-15.2	-32.0	-21.1	.7	-16.2	-27.2	7.2
Monetary authorities	4 737 . .	. . .	. . .	. . .	. . .	. . .	. . .	. . .	. . .
of which: Short-term	4 739 . .	. . .	. . .	. . .	. . .	. . .	. . .	. . .	. . .
General government	4 740 . .	-17.9	-6.7	-2.7	13.4	-4.8	17.2	12.4	15.1
of which: Short-term	4 742 . .	*-15.7*	*-17.5*	*-2.2*	*13.8*	*-4.8*	*17.2*	*12.4*	*15.1*
Banks	4 743 . .	. . .	. . .	. . .	. . .	. . .	. . .	. . .	. . .
of which: Short-term	4 745 . .	. . .	. . .	. . .	. . .	. . .	. . .	. . .	. . .
Other sectors	4 746 . .	-80.7	-8.5	-29.3	-34.4	5.5	-33.4	-39.6	-7.9
of which: Short-term	4 748 . .	. . .	. . .	. . .	. . .	. . .	. . .	. . .	. . .
Liabilities	4 753 . .	**22.7**	**-10.7**	**123.6**	**62.5**	**8.8**	**31.5**	**41.9**	**-3.4**
Trade credits	4 756 . .	-9.0	-4.4	1.3	45.8	33.4	.9	-1.2	9.7
General government	4 757 . .	. . .	. . .	. . .	. . .	. . .	. . .	. . .	. . .
of which: Short-term	4 759 . .	. . .	. . .	. . .	. . .	. . .	. . .	. . .	. . .
Other sectors	4 760 . .	-9.0	-4.4	1.3	45.8	33.4	.9	-1.2	9.7
of which: Short-term	4 762 . .	*-9.0*	*-4.4*	*1.3*	*45.8*	*33.4*	*.9*	*-1.2*	*9.7*
Loans	4 764 . .	-9.0	6.1	23.4	-2.2	9.2	23.0	21.5	-12.3
Monetary authorities	4 765 . .	. . .	. . .	. . .	. . .	. . .	. . .	. . .	. . .
of which: Use of Fund credit and loans from the Fund	4 766 . .	. . .	. . .	. . .	. . .	. . .	. . .	. . .	. . .
of which: Short-term	4 768 . .	. . .	. . .	. . .	. . .	. . .	. . .	. . .	. . .
General government	4 769 . .	-14.8	-7.1	3.2	-.6	-.7	-4.6	-1.2	4.3
of which: Short-term	4 771 . .	. . .	. . .	. . .	. . .	. . .	. . .	. . .	. . .
Banks	4 772 . .	. . .	. . .	. . .	. . .	. . .	. . .	. . .	. . .
of which: Short-term	4 774 . .	. . .	. . .	. . .	. . .	. . .	. . .	. . .	. . .
Other sectors	4 775 . .	5.8	13.2	20.2	-1.6	9.8	27.5	22.7	-16.6
of which: Short-term	4 777 . .	. . .	. . .	. . .	. . .	. . .	. . .	. . .	. . .
Currency and deposits	4 780 . .	30.6	-9.8	3.8	-19.2	22.2	28.5	6.2	14.7
Monetary authorities	4 781 . .	30.6	-9.8	3.8	-19.2	22.2	28.5	6.2	14.7
General government	4 782 . .	. . .	. . .	. . .	. . .	. . .	. . .	. . .	. . .
Banks	4 783 . .	. . .	. . .	. . .	. . .	. . .	. . .	. . .	. . .
Other sectors	4 784 . .	. . .	. . .	. . .	. . .	. . .	. . .	. . .	. . .
Other liabilities	4 786 . .	10.1	-2.5	95.1	38.0	-56.1	-20.8	15.3	-15.5
Monetary authorities	4 787 . .	. . .	. . .	. . .	. . .	. . .	. . .	. . .	. . .
of which: Short-term	4 789 . .	. . .	. . .	. . .	. . .	. . .	. . .	. . .	. . .
General government	4 790 . .	. . .	. . .	. . .	. . .	. . .	. . .	. . .	. . .
of which: Short-term	4 792 . .	. . .	. . .	. . .	. . .	. . .	. . .	. . .	. . .
Banks	4 793 . .	.7	.4	41.5	-25.9	-13.8	.3	6.4	-9.5
of which: Short-term	4 795 . .	*.7*	*.4*	*41.5*	*-25.9*	*-13.8*	*.3*	*6.4*	*-9.5*
Other sectors	4 796 . .	9.3	-2.9	53.6	63.9	-42.3	-21.1	8.9	-6.1
of which: Short-term	4 798 . .	*9.3*	*-2.9*	*53.6*	*63.9*	*-42.3*	*-21.1*	*8.9*	*-6.1*
E. RESERVE ASSETS	4 802 . .	12.5	-29.8	-15.4	-25.3	-50.5	-26.3	6.5	56.5
Monetary gold	4 812 . .	. . .	. . .	. . .	. . .	. . .	. . .	. . .	. . .
Special drawing rights	4 811 . .	. . .	. . .	. . .	. . .	. . .	4.9	. . .	. . .
Reserve position in the Fund	4 810 . .	. . .	. . .	. . .	. . .	. . .	-4.9	. . .	. . .
Foreign exchange	4 803 . .	12.5	-29.9	-15.4	-25.3	-50.5	-26.2	6.5	56.5
Other claims	4 813 . .	. . .	. . .	. . .	. . .	. . .	. . .	. . .	. . .
NET ERRORS AND OMISSIONS	4 998 . .	**48.8**	**78.9**	**36.9**	**-16.8**	**4.1**	**10.0**	**9.5**	**12.1**

Part 3 of the *Yearbook* contains descriptions of the methodologies, compilation practices, and sources used to compile these data.

Table 3. INTERNATIONAL INVESTMENT POSITION (End-period stocks), 1994–2001

(Millions of U.S. dollars)

	Code	1994	1995	1996	1997	1998	1999	2000	2001
ASSETS	8 995 C.	838.2	982.9	965.1	956.6	958.5	1,151.6	1,078.8	756.6
Direct investment abroad	8 505 . .	**108.8**	**135.5**	**95.4**	**82.3**	**90.1**	**98.1**	**92.3**	**52.9**
Equity capital and reinvested earnings	8 506 . .	7.0	10.2	11.9	5.1	5.0	3.4	2.2	1.4
Claims on affiliated enterprises	8 507 . .	7.0	10.2	11.9	5.1	5.0	3.4	2.2	1.4
Liabilities to affiliated enterprises	8 508 . .	...	...	...	...	...	...	...	...
Other capital	8 530 . .	101.8	125.4	83.5	77.2	85.0	94.7	90.1	51.5
Claims on affiliated enterprises	8 535 . .	101.8	125.4	83.5	77.2	85.0	94.7	90.1	51.5
Liabilities to affiliated enterprises	8 540 . .	...	...	...	...	...	...	...	...
Portfolio investment	8 602 . .	**7.3**	**16.6**	**14.8**	**16.1**	**16.0**	**11.9**	**13.4**	**9.3**
Equity securities	8 610 . .	.8	2.7	2.3	4.0	4.6	2.8	2.4	1.6
Monetary authorities	8 611 . .	...	...	...	...	...	...	...	...
General government	8 612 . .	...	...	...	...	...	...	...	...
Banks	8 613 . .	...	...	...	...	...	...	...	...
Other sectors	8 614 . .	.8	2.7	2.3	4.0	4.6	2.8	2.4	1.6
Debt securities	8 619 . .	6.6	14.0	12.5	12.0	11.4	9.1	11.1	7.7
Bonds and notes	8 620 . .	.1	7.3	7.2	6.9	9.0	6.8	9.2	5.6
Monetary authorities	8 621 . .	...	...	...	...	...	...	...	...
General government	8 622 . .	...	...	...	...	...	...	...	...
Banks	8 623 . .	...	...	...	...	...	...	...	...
Other sectors	8 624 . .	.1	7.3	7.2	6.9	9.0	6.8	9.2	5.6
Money market instruments	8 630 . .	6.5	6.6	5.3	5.1	2.4	2.3	1.8	2.1
Monetary authorities	8 631 . .	...	...	...	...	...	...	...	...
General government	8 632 . .	...	...	...	...	...	...	...	...
Banks	8 633 . .	...	...	...	...	...	...	...	...
Other sectors	8 634 . .	6.5	6.6	5.3	5.1	2.4	2.3	1.8	2.1
Financial derivatives	8 900 . .	...	...	...	...	...	...	...	...
Monetary authorities	8 901 . .	...	...	...	...	...	...	...	...
General government	8 902 . .	...	...	...	...	...	...	...	...
Banks	8 903 . .	...	...	...	...	...	...	...	...
Other sectors	8 904 . .	...	...	...	...	...	...	...	...
Other investment	8 703 . .	**479.2**	**553.4**	**572.5**	**568.7**	**497.2**	**669.0**	**626.0**	**418.9**
Trade credits	8 706 . .	95.9	118.8	75.5	81.7	74.5	97.5	80.0	70.4
General government	8 707 . .	...	...	...	...	...	...	...	...
of which: Short-term	8 709 . .	...	...	...	...	...	...	...	...
Other sectors	8 710 . .	95.9	118.8	75.5	81.7	74.5	97.5	80.0	70.4
of which: Short-term	8 712 . .	*95.9*	*118.8*	*75.5*	*81.7*	*74.5*	*97.5*	*80.0*	*70.4*
Loans	8 714 . .	2.3	1.8	2.2	2.1	1.7	.8	.4	.3
Monetary authorities	8 715 . .	...	...	...	...	...	...	...	...
of which: Short-term	8 718 . .	...	...	...	...	...	...	...	...
General government	8 719 . .	...	...	...	...	...	...	...	...
of which: Short-term	8 721 . .	...	...	...	...	...	...	...	...
Banks	8 722 . .	...	...	...	...	...	...	...	...
of which: Short-term	8 724	...	...	...	...	...	...	...	...
Other sectors	8 725 . .	2.3	1.8	2.2	2.1	1.7	.8	.4	.3
of which: Short-term	8 727 . .	...	...	...	...	...	...	...	...
Currency and deposits	8 730 . .	88.6	101.3	175.9	154.1	146.2	183.4	172.3	120.4
Monetary authorities	8 731 . .	...	...	...	...	...	...	...	...
General government	8 732 . .	...	...	...	...	...	...	...	...
Banks	8 733 . .	46.9	50.8	110.3	95.6	101.0	137.5	86.4	73.6
Other sectors	8 734 . .	41.7	50.5	65.6	58.5	45.3	46.0	85.9	46.8
Other assets	8 736 . .	292.4	331.4	318.8	330.8	274.7	387.3	373.4	227.8
Monetary authorities	8 737 . .	...	...	...	...	...	...	...	...
of which: Short-term	8 739 . .	...	...	...	...	...	...	...	...
General government	8 740 . .	144.6	124.6	98.8	86.5	77.0	56.2	34.3	10.7
of which: Short-term	8 742 . .	*133.6*	*124.6*	*98.3*	*85.7*	*76.3*	*55.5*	*33.8*	*10.4*
Banks	8 743 . .	...	...	...	...	...	...	...	...
of which: Short-term	8 745 . .	...	...	...	...	...	...	...	...
Other sectors	8 746 . .	147.8	206.8	220.1	244.3	197.8	331.1	339.1	217.0
of which: Short-term	8 748 . .	...	...	...	...	...	...	...	...
Reserve assets	8 802 . .	**242.9**	**277.4**	**282.4**	**289.5**	**355.3**	**372.6**	**347.1**	**275.6**
Monetary gold	8 812 . .	.1	.1	.1	.1	.1	...	...	...
Special drawing rights	8 811 . .	8.6	8.8	8.5	8.0	8.4	3.3	3.2	3.1
Reserve position in the Fund	8 810 . .	4.4	4.5	4.3	4.1	4.2	9.0	8.5	8.2
Foreign exchange	8 803 . .	229.8	264.0	269.5	277.4	342.6	360.2	335.3	264.3
Other claims	8 813 . .	...	...	...	...	...	...	...	...

Table 3 (Concluded). INTERNATIONAL INVESTMENT POSITION (End–period stocks), 1994–2001
(Millions of U.S. dollars)

	Code	1994	1995	1996	1997	1998	1999	2000	2001
LIABILITIES	8 995 D.	881.0	925.0	894.5	846.3	929.3	1,053.8	925.6	600.8
Direct investment in Swaziland	8 555 . .	**506.8**	**535.6**	**437.2**	**406.4**	**481.6**	**558.2**	**485.2**	**334.1**
Equity capital and reinvested earnings	8 556 . .	395.4	414.5	340.5	307.8	333.3	355.1	278.1	210.8
Claims on direct investors	8 557 . .	395.4	. . .	. . .	. . .	. . .	. . .	. . .	. . .
Liabilities to direct investors	8 558 . .	. . .	414.5	340.5	307.8	333.3	355.1	278.1	210.8
Other capital	8 580 . .	111.4	121.1	96.8	98.6	148.3	203.2	207.1	123.3
Claims on direct investors	8 585 . .	111.4	. . .	. . .	. . .	. . .	. . .	. . .	. . .
Liabilities to direct investors	8 590 . .	. . .	121.1	96.8	98.6	148.3	203.2	207.1	123.3
Portfolio investment	8 652 . .	**.7**	**1.4**	**1.5**	**1.4**	**4.3**	**6.8**	**6.8**	**4.2**
Equity securities	8 660 . .	.7	1.4	1.5	1.4	4.3	6.8	6.8	4.2
Banks	8 663 . .	. . .	. . .	. . .	. . .	. . .	. . .	. . .	. . .
Other sectors	8 664 . .	.7	1.4	1.5	1.4	4.3	6.8	6.8	4.2
Debt securities	8 669 . .	. . .	. . .	. . .	. . .	. . .	. . .	. . .	. . .
Bonds and notes	8 670 . .	. . .	. . .	. . .	. . .	. . .	. . .	. . .	. . .
Monetary authorities	8 671 . .	. . .	. . .	. . .	. . .	. . .	. . .	. . .	. . .
General government	8 672 . .	. . .	. . .	. . .	. . .	. . .	. . .	. . .	. . .
Banks	8 673 . .	. . .	. . .	. . .	. . .	. . .	. . .	. . .	. . .
Other sectors	8 674 . .	. . .	. . .	. . .	. . .	. . .	. . .	. . .	. . .
Money market instruments	8 680 . .	. . .	. . .	. . .	. . .	. . .	. . .	. . .	. . .
Monetary authorities	8 681 . .	. . .	. . .	. . .	. . .	. . .	. . .	. . .	. . .
General government	8 682 . .	. . .	. . .	. . .	. . .	. . .	. . .	. . .	. . .
Banks	8 683 . .	. . .	. . .	. . .	. . .	. . .	. . .	. . .	. . .
Other sectors	8 684 . .	. . .	. . .	. . .	. . .	. . .	. . .	. . .	. . .
Financial derivatives	8 905 . .	**. . .**	**. . .**	**. . .**	**. . .**	**. . .**	**. . .**	**. . .**	**. . .**
Monetary authorities	8 906 . .	. . .	. . .	. . .	. . .	. . .	. . .	. . .	. . .
General government	8 907 . .	. . .	. . .	. . .	. . .	. . .	. . .	. . .	. . .
Banks	8 908 . .	. . .	. . .	. . .	. . .	. . .	. . .	. . .	. . .
Other sectors	8 909 . .	. . .	. . .	. . .	. . .	. . .	. . .	. . .	. . .
Other investment	8 753 . .	**373.6**	**388.0**	**455.7**	**438.5**	**443.4**	**488.8**	**433.6**	**262.4**
Trade credits	8 756 . .	67.9	61.5	49.1	53.9	50.7	49.1	38.9	22.9
General government	8 757 . .	. . .	. . .	. . .	. . .	. . .	. . .	. . .	. . .
of which: Short-term	8 759 . .	. . .	. . .	. . .	. . .	. . .	. . .	. . .	. . .
Other sectors	8 760 . .	67.9	61.5	49.1	53.9	50.7	49.1	38.9	22.9
of which: Short-term	8 762 . .	*67.9*	*61.5*	*49.1*	*53.9*	*50.7*	*49.1*	*38.9*	*22.9*
Loans	8 764 . .	226.1	261.6	265.3	245.7	309.3	352.7	304.2	183.7
Monetary authorities	8 765 . .	. . .	. . .	. . .	. . .	. . .	. . .	. . .	. . .
of which: Use of Fund credit and loans from the Fund	8 766 . .	. . .	. . .	. . .	. . .	. . .	. . .	. . .	. . .
of which: Short-term	8 768 . .	. . .	. . .	. . .	. . .	. . .	. . .	. . .	. . .
General government	8 769 . .	175.3	194.5	194.4	177.4	243.3	262.5	210.0	136.7
of which: Short-term	8 771 . .	. . .	. . .	. . .	. . .	. . .	. . .	. . .	. . .
Banks	8 772 . .	. . .	. . .	. . .	. . .	. . .	. . .	. . .	. . .
of which: Short-term	8 774 . .	. . .	. . .	. . .	. . .	. . .	. . .	. . .	. . .
Other sectors	8 775 . .	50.8	67.1	70.9	68.3	66.0	90.2	94.2	47.0
of which: Short-term	8 777 . .	. . .	. . .	. . .	. . .	. . .	. . .	. . .	. . .
Currency and deposits	8 780 . .	53.8	42.6	74.8	29.3	32.2	59.2	59.7	40.9
Monetary authorities	8 781 . .	32.0	21.1	19.9	1.0	21.8	48.9	45.5	38.8
General government	8 782 . .	. . .	. . .	. . .	. . .	. . .	. . .	. . .	. . .
Banks	8 783 . .	21.7	21.5	54.9	28.2	10.4	10.3	14.3	2.2
Other sectors	8 784 . .	. . .	. . .	. . .	. . .	. . .	. . .	. . .	. . .
Other liabilities	8 786 . .	25.9	22.2	66.5	109.6	51.2	27.8	30.7	14.9
Monetary authorities	8 787 . .	. . .	. . .	. . .	. . .	. . .	. . .	. . .	. . .
of which: Short-term	8 789 . .	. . .	. . .	. . .	. . .	. . .	. . .	. . .	. . .
General government	8 790 . .	. . .	. . .	. . .	. . .	. . .	. . .	. . .	. . .
of which: Short-term	8 792 . .	. . .	. . .	. . .	. . .	. . .	. . .	. . .	. . .
Banks	8 793 . .	. . .	. . .	. . .	. . .	. . .	. . .	. . .	. . .
of which: Short-term	8 795 . .	. . .	. . .	. . .	. . .	. . .	. . .	. . .	. . .
Other sectors	8 796 . .	25.9	22.2	66.5	109.6	51.2	27.8	30.7	14.9
of which: Short-term	8 798 . .	*25.9*	*22.2*	*66.5*	*109.6*	*51.2*	*27.8*	*30.7*	*14.9*
NET INTERNATIONAL INVESTMENT POSITION	8 995 . .	**–42.8**	**57.8**	**70.6**	**110.4**	**29.2**	**97.9**	**153.3**	**155.8**
Conversion rates: emalangeni per U.S. dollar (end of period)	0 102 . .	**3.5435**	**3.6475**	**4.6825**	**4.8675**	**5.8600**	**6.1545**	**7.5685**	**12.1265**

Table 1. ANALYTIC PRESENTATION, 1994–2001
(Millions of U.S. dollars)

	Code	1994	1995	1996	1997	1998	1999	2000	2001
A. Current Account [1]	4 993 Z.	**743**	**4,940**	**5,892**	**7,406**	**4,639**	**5,982**	**6,617**	**6,696**
Goods: exports f.o.b	2 100 . .	60,199	79,903	84,690	83,194	85,179	87,568	87,431	76,200
Goods: imports f.o.b	3 100 . .	-50,641	-63,926	-66,053	-65,195	-67,547	-71,854	-72,216	-62,368
Balance on Goods	4 100 . .	*9,558*	*15,978*	*18,636*	*17,999*	*17,632*	*15,714*	*15,215*	*13,832*
Services: credit	2 200 . .	13,674	15,622	16,930	17,769	17,952	19,904	20,252	21,997
Services: debit	3 200 . .	-14,690	-17,216	-18,755	-19,524	-21,721	-22,617	-23,440	-23,020
Balance on Goods and Services	4 991 . .	*8,542*	*14,384*	*16,811*	*16,245*	*13,862*	*13,001*	*12,027*	*12,809*
Income: credit	2 300 . .	9,611	14,906	14,338	14,404	16,564	19,871	20,074	17,934
Income: debit	3 300 . .	-15,530	-21,379	-22,641	-20,513	-22,349	-23,291	-22,137	-20,786
Balance on Goods, Services, and Income	4 992 . .	*2,623*	*7,910*	*8,508*	*10,135*	*8,077*	*9,581*	*9,964*	*9,957*
Current transfers: credit	2 379 Z.	544	1,555	2,524	2,319	2,266	2,341	2,602	2,578
Current transfers: debit	3 379 . .	-2,424	-4,525	-5,140	-5,048	-5,704	-5,940	-5,950	-5,839
B. Capital Account [1]	4 994 Z.	**23**	**14**	**9**	**-228**	**868**	**-2,143**	**384**	**509**
Capital account: credit	2 994 Z.	37	32	31	211	1,502	1,289	1,226	1,111
Capital account: debit	3 994 . .	-14	-18	-22	-439	-634	-3,432	-841	-601
Total, Groups A Plus B	4 981 . .	*766*	*4,954*	*5,901*	*7,178*	*5,508*	*3,839*	*7,001*	*7,205*
C. Financial Account [1]	4 995 W.	**6,078**	**-5,052**	**-10,046**	**-10,121**	**5,961**	**-1,413**	**-3,297**	**1,824**
Direct investment abroad	4 505 . .	-6,685	-11,399	-5,112	-12,119	-22,671	-19,554	-39,962	-6,959
Direct investment in Sweden	4 555 Z.	6,269	14,939	5,492	10,271	19,413	59,386	22,125	13,085
Portfolio investment assets	4 602 . .	-2,459	-10,765	-13,136	-13,818	-17,615	-36,749	-12,772	-23,041
Equity securities	4 610 . .	-2,509	-9,378	-7,518	-10,179	-7,427	-29,766	758	-22,642
Debt securities	4 619 . .	51	-1,386	-5,618	-3,640	-10,188	-6,983	-13,530	-400
Portfolio investment liabilities	4 652 Z.	721	8,201	1,661	-2,384	2,023	1,882	9,017	10,338
Equity securities	4 660 . .	6,795	1,853	4,047	-1,687	-328	-3,895	17,997	-2,336
Debt securities	4 669 Z.	-6,074	6,348	-2,386	-697	2,351	5,777	-8,980	12,674
Financial derivatives	4 910 . .	. . .	-832	1,557	1,964	-1,302	59	-314	-5,216
Financial derivatives assets	4 900 . .	. . .	20,264	24,800	31,244	30,125	22,982	31,481	33,678
Financial derivatives liabilities	4 905 . .	. . .	-21,096	-23,243	-29,280	-31,428	-22,923	-31,795	-38,894
Other investment assets	4 703 . .	-3,400	-12,197	-10,828	-9,670	-5,901	-10,333	-16,000	929
Monetary authorities	4 701 . .	. . .	. . .	. . .	. . .	. . .	. . .	. . .	. . .
General government	4 704 . .	-290	-483	-303	-322	-244	-642	-150	37
Banks	4 705 . .	2,902	-8,037	-10,239	-4,971	-1,135	-5,296	-13,279	1,672
Other sectors	4 728 . .	-6,012	3,677	-287	-4,377	-4,522	-4,396	-2,571	-779
Other investment liabilities	4 753 W.	11,633	6,999	10,320	15,635	32,015	3,897	34,609	12,689
Monetary authorities	4 753 WA	. . .	. . .	. . .	-39	88	-743	-556	-812
General government	4 753 ZB	5,075	8,842	1,817	-1,583	578	1,047	129	-32
Banks	4 753 ZC	-1,957	-1,055	2,935	9,269	20,205	-3,846	29,682	10,077
Other sectors	4 753 ZD	8,515	-788	5,569	7,988	11,144	6,938	5,354	3,455
Total, Groups A Through C	4 983 . .	*6,844*	*-98*	*-4,145*	*-2,943*	*11,468*	*2,426*	*3,704*	*9,030*
D. Net Errors and Omissions	4 998 . .	**-4,462**	**-1,566**	**-2,241**	**-3,769**	**-8,214**	**-545**	**-3,534**	**-10,078**
Total, Groups A Through D	4 984 . .	*2,381*	*-1,664*	*-6,386*	*-6,712*	*3,254*	*1,881*	*170*	*-1,048*
E. Reserves and Related Items	4 802 A.	**-2,381**	**1,664**	**6,386**	**6,712**	**-3,254**	**-1,881**	**-170**	**1,048**
Reserve assets	4 802 . .	-2,381	1,664	6,386	6,712	-3,254	-1,881	-170	1,048
Use of Fund credit and loans	4 766 . .	. . .	. . .	. . .	. . .	. . .	. . .	. . .	. . .
Exceptional financing	4 920 . .	. . .	. . .	. . .	. . .	. . .	. . .	. . .	. . .
Conversion rates: kronor per U.S. dollar	0 101 . .	**7.7160**	**7.1333**	**6.7060**	**7.6349**	**7.9499**	**8.2624**	**9.1622**	**10.3291**

[1] Excludes components that have been classified in the categories of Group E.

Table 2. STANDARD PRESENTATION, 1994–2001

(Millions of U.S. dollars)

	Code	1994	1995	1996	1997	1998	1999	2000	2001
CURRENT ACCOUNT	4 993 . .	**743**	**4,940**	**5,892**	**7,406**	**4,639**	**5,982**	**6,617**	**6,696**
A. GOODS	4 100 . .	9,558	15,978	18,636	17,999	17,632	15,714	15,215	13,832
Credit	2 100 . .	**60,199**	**79,903**	**84,690**	**83,194**	**85,179**	**87,568**	**87,431**	**76,200**
General merchandise: exports f.o.b.	2 110 . .	60,080	79,903	84,690	83,130	84,966	85,196	87,139	75,995
Goods for processing: exports f.o.b.	2 150 . .	...	...	...	...	...	...	...	...
Repairs on goods	2 160 . .	...	...	...	...	...	2,180	...	...
Goods procured in ports by carriers	2 170 . .	...	...	...	64	213	192	292	205
Nonmonetary gold	2 180 . .	119	...	...	...	...	...	...	...
Debit	3 100 . .	**–50,641**	**–63,926**	**–66,053**	**–65,195**	**–67,547**	**–71,854**	**–72,216**	**–62,368**
General merchandise: imports f.o.b.	3 110 . .	–50,622	–63,926	–66,053	–65,065	–67,165	–69,484	–71,849	–61,970
Goods for processing: imports f.o.b.	3 150 . .	...	...	...	...	...	...	...	...
Repairs on goods	3 160 . .	...	...	...	...	...	–2,054	...	...
Goods procured in ports by carriers	3 170 . .	...	...	...	–130	–382	–315	–367	–399
Nonmonetary gold	3 180 . .	–20	...	...	...	...	...	...	...
B. SERVICES	4 200 . .	–1,016	–1,594	–1,825	–1,754	–3,769	–2,713	–3,188	–1,023
Total credit	2 200 . .	*13,674*	*15,622*	*16,930*	*17,769*	*17,952*	*19,904*	*20,252*	*21,997*
Total debit	3 200 . .	*–14,690*	*–17,216*	*–18,755*	*–19,524*	*–21,721*	*–22,617*	*–23,440*	*–23,020*
Transportation services, credit	2 205 . .	**4,394**	**4,946**	**5,108**	**5,713**	**4,779**	**4,440**	**4,359**	**5,266**
Passenger	2 850 . .	*823*	*919*	*848*	*425*	*809*	*811*	*761*	*947*
Freight	2 851 . .	*2,459*	*2,794*	*3,021*	*3,378*	*3,341*	*2,988*	*2,992*	*3,696*
Other	2 852 . .	*1,113*	*1,232*	*1,238*	*1,911*	*629*	*641*	*606*	*623*
Sea transport, passenger	2 207 . .	...	...	...	258	141	116	77	83
Sea transport, freight	2 208 . .	...	...	...	3,157	2,522	2,142	2,137	2,875
Sea transport, other	2 209 . .	...	...	...	354	224	174	169	163
Air transport, passenger	2 211 . .	...	...	...	160	634	655	652	820
Air transport, freight	2 212 . .	...	...	...	24	79	121	94	79
Air transport, other	2 213 . .	...	...	...	3	18	23	22	23
Other transport, passenger	2 215 . .	...	...	...	7	34	40	32	44
Other transport, freight	2 216 . .	...	...	...	198	740	725	761	743
Other transport, other	2 217 . .	...	...	...	1,554	387	444	415	437
Transportation services, debit	3 205 . .	**–4,037**	**–4,853**	**–4,914**	**–4,758**	**–4,154**	**–3,553**	**–3,640**	**–3,593**
Passenger	3 850 . .	*–1,070*	*–1,368*	*–1,389*	*–332*	*–872*	*–905*	*–911*	*–995*
Freight	3 851 . .	*–723*	*–935*	*–920*	*–1,426*	*–2,048*	*–1,460*	*–1,713*	*–1,677*
Other	3 852 . .	*–2,245*	*–2,550*	*–2,606*	*–3,001*	*–1,234*	*–1,188*	*–1,017*	*–920*
Sea transport, passenger	3 207 . .	...	...	...	–75	–45	–18	–19	–18
Sea transport, freight	3 208 . .	...	...	...	–1,382	–1,911	–1,346	–1,576	–1,547
Sea transport, other	3 209 . .	...	...	...	–1,286	–733	–709	–540	–455
Air transport, passenger	3 211 . .	...	...	...	–245	–791	–853	–866	–956
Air transport, freight	3 212 . .	...	...	...	–17	–34	–22	–28	–17
Air transport, other	3 213 . .	...	...	...	–39	–152	–148	–123	–109
Other transport, passenger	3 215 . .	...	...	...	–12	–36	–34	–26	–21
Other transport, freight	3 216 . .	...	...	...	–26	–103	–92	–109	–113
Other transport, other	3 217 . .	...	...	...	–1,676	–349	–332	–354	–356
Travel, credit	2 236 . .	**2,823**	**3,471**	**3,686**	**3,600**	**4,188**	**4,132**	**4,064**	**4,253**
Business travel	2 237 . .	...	...	...	...	...	...	...	...
Personal travel	2 240 . .	...	...	...	...	...	...	...	...
Travel, debit	3 236 . .	**–4,874**	**–5,448**	**–6,253**	**–6,518**	**–7,719**	**–8,022**	**–8,048**	**–6,921**
Business travel	3 237 . .	...	...	...	...	–2,907	–3,169	–2,695	–2,317
Personal travel	3 240 . .	...	...	...	...	–4,812	–4,853	–5,353	–4,604
Other services, credit	2 200 BA	**6,457**	**7,205**	**8,137**	**8,457**	**8,984**	**11,333**	**11,829**	**12,478**
Communications	2 245 . .	590	762	902	918	490	523	644	716
Construction	2 249 . .	1,968	2,337	2,758	2,335	757	853	678	602
Insurance	2 253 . .	384	365	401	363	386	466	517	472
Financial	2 260 . .	...	...	...	100	376	492	691	565
Computer and information	2 262 . .	...	...	...	210	986	1,097	1,191	1,433
Royalties and licence fees	2 266 . .	1,153	889	997	1,003	1,114	1,386	1,275	1,427
Other business services	2 268 . .	2,070	2,566	2,818	3,243	4,495	6,184	6,482	6,912
Personal, cultural, and recreational	2 287 . .	...	...	...	22	102	119	113	111
Government, n.i.e.	2 291 . .	291	286	261	265	277	213	238	239
Other services, debit	3 200 BA	**–5,779**	**–6,915**	**–7,588**	**–8,248**	**–9,847**	**–11,042**	**–11,752**	**–12,506**
Communications	3 245 . .	–441	–584	–643	–764	–728	–736	–792	–685
Construction	3 249 . .	–1,968	–2,440	–2,801	–2,452	–471	–381	–322	–298
Insurance	3 253 . .	–366	–240	–261	–226	–181	–212	–311	–260
Financial	3 260 . .	...	...	...	–84	–294	–430	–599	–546
Computer and information	3 262 . .	...	...	...	–175	–911	–1,052	–1,067	–894
Royalties and licence fees	3 266 . .	–775	–1,004	–1,006	–957	–939	–1,147	–900	–860
Other business services	3 268 . .	–2,133	–2,542	–2,773	–3,477	–6,141	–6,898	–7,602	–8,777
Personal, cultural, and recreational	3 287 . .	...	...	...	–16	–81	–82	–88	–87
Government, n.i.e.	3 291 . .	–96	–104	–104	–97	–101	–105	–73	–100

Table 2 (Continued). STANDARD PRESENTATION, 1994–2001
(Millions of U.S. dollars)

	Code		1994	1995	1996	1997	1998	1999	2000	2001
C. INCOME	4 300	. .	-5,919	-6,473	-8,303	-6,109	-5,785	-3,420	-2,063	-2,852
Total credit	2 300	. .	*9,611*	*14,906*	*14,338*	*14,404*	*16,564*	*19,871*	*20,074*	*17,934*
Total debit	3 300	. .	*-15,530*	*-21,379*	*-22,641*	*-20,513*	*-22,349*	*-23,291*	*-22,137*	*-20,786*
Compensation of employees, credit	2 310	. .	**106**	**128**	**134**	**172**	**224**	**269**	**304**	**329**
Compensation of employees, debit	3 310	. .	**-202**	**-302**	**-387**	**-356**	**-541**	**-531**	**-488**	**-543**
Investment income, credit	2 320	. .	**9,505**	**14,778**	**14,204**	**14,232**	**16,340**	**19,602**	**19,770**	**17,604**
Direct investment income	2 330	. .	4,473	7,243	6,092	6,976	8,964	11,221	12,880	10,535
Dividends and distributed branch profits	2 332	. .	1,439	2,025	2,059	2,347	3,712	2,093	3,001	6,091
Reinvested earnings and undistributed branch profits	2 333	. .	3,034	5,219	4,033	4,283	3,963	7,596	7,944	2,632
Income on debt (interest)	2 334	. .	...	...	...	346	1,289	1,533	1,934	1,812
Portfolio investment income	2 339	. .	...	...	...	1,193	4,559	5,739	3,777	4,037
Income on equity	2 340	. .	...	...	...	139	654	1,226	1,495	1,591
Income on bonds and notes	2 350	. .	...	...	...	410	1,991	1,973	2,140	2,406
Income on money market instruments	2 360	. .	...	...	...	644	1,914	2,540	143	41
Other investment income	2 370	. .	5,032	7,535	8,112	6,063	2,817	2,642	3,113	3,032
Investment income, debit	3 320	. .	**-15,328**	**-21,077**	**-22,254**	**-20,158**	**-21,808**	**-22,759**	**-21,648**	**-20,243**
Direct investment income	3 330	. .	-2,266	-4,315	-3,727	-3,826	-5,365	-7,553	-8,867	-6,908
Dividends and distributed branch profits	3 332	. .	-792	-1,891	-2,559	-2,158	-1,930	-1,817	-4,388	-4,391
Reinvested earnings and undistributed branch profits	3 333	. .	-1,474	-2,424	-1,168	-1,272	-2,221	-4,357	-2,728	-939
Income on debt (interest)	3 334	. .	...	...	...	-395	-1,213	-1,378	-1,750	-1,578
Portfolio investment income	3 339	. .	...	...	...	-2,856	-12,071	-11,015	-7,873	-8,257
Income on equity	3 340	. .	...	...	...	-35	-1,408	-1,113	-1,640	-1,645
Income on bonds and notes	3 350	. .	...	...	...	-1,777	-6,785	-6,634	-5,595	-5,631
Income on money market instruments	3 360	. .	...	...	...	-1,044	-3,877	-3,268	-639	-981
Other investment income	3 370	. .	-13,062	-16,762	-18,527	-13,476	-4,373	-4,192	-4,909	-5,078
D. CURRENT TRANSFERS	4 379	. .	-1,880	-2,970	-2,616	-2,729	-3,438	-3,599	-3,348	-3,261
Credit	2 379	. .	**544**	**1,555**	**2,524**	**2,319**	**2,266**	**2,341**	**2,602**	**2,578**
General government	2 380	. .	117	225	355	352	318	344	462	480
Other sectors	2 390	. .	427	1,330	2,169	1,966	1,948	1,997	2,141	2,098
Workers' remittances	2 391	. .	105	127	136	144	143	146	161	185
Other current transfers	2 392	. .	322	1,202	2,033	1,822	1,805	1,851	1,980	1,913
Debit	3 379	. .	**-2,424**	**-4,525**	**-5,140**	**-5,048**	**-5,704**	**-5,940**	**-5,950**	**-5,839**
General government	3 380	. .	-1,791	-1,747	-1,919	-2,177	-3,707	-3,719	-3,645	-3,469
Other sectors	3 390	. .	-633	-2,778	-3,221	-2,871	-1,996	-2,221	-2,305	-2,370
Workers' remittances	3 391	. .	-14	-15	-19	-29	-53	-36	-34	-31
Other current transfers	3 392	. .	-619	-2,762	-3,201	-2,842	-1,943	-2,184	-2,271	-2,339
CAPITAL AND FINANCIAL ACCOUNT	4 996	. .	**3,720**	**-3,374**	**-3,652**	**-3,637**	**3,575**	**-5,438**	**-3,083**	**3,382**
CAPITAL ACCOUNT	4 994	. .	**23**	**14**	**9**	**-228**	**868**	**-2,143**	**384**	**509**
Total credit	2 994	. .	*37*	*32*	*31*	*211*	*1,502*	*1,289*	*1,226*	*1,111*
Total debit	3 994	. .	*-14*	*18*	*-22*	*-439*	*-634*	*-3,432*	*-841*	*-601*
Capital transfers, credit	2 400	. .	**37**	**32**	**31**	**156**	**1,101**	**1,138**	**1,057**	**862**
General government	2 401	. .	...	...	...	...	...	...	...	...
Debt forgiveness	2 402	. .	...	...	...	...	...	...	...	...
Other capital transfers	2 410	. .	...	...	...	...	...	...	...	...
Other sectors	2 430	. .	37	32	31	156	1,101	1,138	1,057	862
Migrants' transfers	2 431	. .	37	32	31	29	25	58	46	29
Debt forgiveness	2 432	. .	...	...	...	...	...	...	...	...
Other capital transfers	2 440	. .	...	...	...	127	1,075	1,080	1,012	833
Capital transfers, debit	3 400	. .	**-14**	**-18**	**-22**	**-304**	**-424**	**-494**	**-448**	**-412**
General government	3 401	. .	...	...	...	-246	-347	-367	-383	-361
Debt forgiveness	3 402	. .	...	...	...	-20	-27	-76	-54	-58
Other capital transfers	3 410	. .	...	...	...	-227	-320	-291	-329	-303
Other sectors	3 430	. .	-14	-18	-22	-58	-77	-127	-65	-50
Migrants' transfers	3 431	. .	-14	-18	-22	-26	-26	-79	-23	-16
Debt forgiveness	3 432	. .	...	...	...	...	...	...	-6	...
Other capital transfers	3 440	. .	...	...	...	-31	-50	-47	-37	-35
Nonproduced nonfinancial assets, credit	2 480	. .	**...**	**...**	**...**	**55**	**402**	**151**	**168**	**249**
Nonproduced nonfinancial assets, debit	3 480	. .	**...**	**...**	**...**	**-135**	**-210**	**-2,938**	**-393**	**-190**

Table 2 (Continued). STANDARD PRESENTATION, 1994–2001

(Millions of U.S. dollars)

	Code	1994	1995	1996	1997	1998	1999	2000	2001
FINANCIAL ACCOUNT	4 995	**3,696**	**–3,388**	**–3,661**	**–3,409**	**2,707**	**–3,294**	**–3,467**	**2,872**
A. DIRECT INVESTMENT	4 500	–417	3,541	380	–1,847	–3,258	39,832	–17,837	6,126
Direct investment abroad	4 505	**–6,685**	**–11,399**	**–5,112**	**–12,119**	**–22,671**	**–19,554**	**–39,962**	**–6,959**
Equity capital	4 510	...	...	...	–1,989	–15,198	–6,778	–24,854	–3,566
Claims on affiliated enterprises	4 515	...	...	...	...	...	...	...	...
Liabilities to affiliated enterprises	4 520	...	...	...	...	...	...	...	...
Reinvested earnings	4 525	–3,034	–5,219	–4,033	–4,283	–3,963	–7,596	–7,944	–2,632
Other capital	4 530	–3,651	–6,180	–1,079	–5,846	–3,510	–5,181	–7,164	–761
Claims on affiliated enterprises	4 535	...	...	...	...	...	...	...	...
Liabilities to affiliated enterprises	4 540	...	...	...	...	...	...	...	...
Direct investment in Sweden	4 555	**6,269**	**14,939**	**5,492**	**10,271**	**19,413**	**59,386**	**22,125**	**13,085**
Equity capital	4 560	...	...	...	1,308	14,801	45,232	11,572	7,896
Claims on direct investors	4 565	...	...	...	...	...	...	...	...
Liabilities to direct investors	4 570	...	...	...	...	...	...	...	...
Reinvested earnings	4 575	1,474	2,424	1,168	1,272	2,221	4,357	2,728	939
Other capital	4 580	4,794	12,515	4,323	7,691	2,391	9,797	7,825	4,250
Claims on direct investors	4 585	...	...	...	...	...	...	...	...
Liabilities to direct investors	4 590	...	...	...	...	...	...	...	...
B. PORTFOLIO INVESTMENT	4 600	–1,738	–2,564	–11,475	–16,202	–15,592	–34,867	–3,754	–12,704
Assets	4 602	**–2,459**	**–10,765**	**–13,136**	**–13,818**	**–17,615**	**–36,749**	**–12,772**	**–23,041**
Equity securities	4 610	–2,509	–9,378	–7,518	–10,179	–7,427	–29,766	758	–22,642
Monetary authorities	4 611	...	...	...	...	...	...	...	...
General government	4 612	...	...	...	...	...	...	...	...
Banks	4 613	...	...	...	...	...	...	...	...
Other sectors	4 614	...	...	...	...	...	...	...	...
Debt securities	4 619	51	–1,386	–5,618	–3,640	–10,188	–6,983	–13,530	–400
Bonds and notes	4 620	51	–1,386	–5,618	–3,250	–9,721	–4,357	–7,786	1,542
Monetary authorities	4 621	...	...	...	...	...	...	...	...
General government	4 622	...	...	...	...	–3,739	–1,219	85	–1,503
Banks	4 623	...	...	...	...	–3,187	–19	–828	243
Other sectors	4 624	...	...	...	...	–2,796	–3,119	–7,043	2,802
Money market instruments	4 630	...	...	...	–390	–467	–2,626	–5,744	–1,942
Monetary authorities	4 631	...	...	...	...	...	...	...	...
General government	4 632	...	...	...	...	–17	–697	277	35
Banks	4 633	...	...	...	...	–114	–622	–2,662	720
Other sectors	4 634	...	...	...	...	–336	–1,308	–3,359	–2,697
Liabilities	4 652	**721**	**8,201**	**1,661**	**–2,384**	**2,023**	**1,882**	**9,017**	**10,338**
Equity securities	4 660	6,795	1,853	4,047	–1,687	–328	–3,895	17,997	–2,336
Banks	4 663	...	...	...	...	...	...	...	...
Other sectors	4 664	...	...	...	...	–328	–3,895	17,997	–2,336
Debt securities	4 669	–6,074	6,348	–2,386	–697	2,351	5,777	–8,980	12,674
Bonds and notes	4 670	–6,074	6,348	–2,386	–780	703	5,125	–9,926	6,945
Monetary authorities	4 671	...	...	...	...	–56	...	...	...
General government	4 672	–20	7,872	...	...	–537	–7,216	–16,120	645
Banks	4 673	...	...	...	...	523	8,937	2,398	2,418
Other sectors	4 674	–6,054	–1,524	...	...	773	3,404	3,796	3,882
Money market instruments	4 680	...	...	...	82	1,648	652	946	5,729
Monetary authorities	4 681	...	...	...	–8	–68	–42	...	...
General government	4 682	...	...	...	428	–859	–3,149	–2,439	3,500
Banks	4 683	...	...	...	–262	2,728	2,322	2,515	4,571
Other sectors	4 684	...	...	...	–76	–153	1,521	870	–2,343
C. FINANCIAL DERIVATIVES	4 910	...	–832	1,557	1,964	–1,302	59	–314	–5,216
Monetary authorities	4 911	...	...	...	...	...	...	...	...
General government	4 912	...	...	...	...	–969	1,207	1,117	–1,633
Banks	4 913	...	...	...	...	106	–1,836	–661	–3,202
Other sectors	4 914	...	...	...	...	–440	688	–770	–381
Assets	4 900	**...**	**20,264**	**24,800**	**31,244**	**30,125**	**22,982**	**31,481**	**33,678**
Monetary authorities	4 901	...	...	...	...	...	...	...	...
General government	4 902	...	...	...	...	3,254	2,921	2,695	2,615
Banks	4 903	...	...	...	...	21,983	16,181	18,863	19,737
Other sectors	4 904	...	...	...	...	4,888	3,880	9,924	11,326
Liabilities	4 905	**...**	**–21,096**	**–23,243**	**–29,280**	**–31,428**	**–22,923**	**–31,795**	**–38,894**
Monetary authorities	4 906	...	...	...	...	...	...	...	...
General government	4 907	...	...	...	...	–4,223	–1,713	–1,578	–4,248
Banks	4 908	...	...	...	...	–21,876	–18,017	–19,524	–22,939
Other sectors	4 909	...	...	...	...	–5,328	–3,192	–10,694	–11,707

Table 2 (Concluded). STANDARD PRESENTATION, 1994–2001
(Millions of U.S. dollars)

	Code	1994	1995	1996	1997	1998	1999	2000	2001
D. OTHER INVESTMENT	4 700	8,233	–5,198	–508	5,965	26,113	–6,437	18,609	13,618
Assets	4 703	**–3,400**	**–12,197**	**–10,828**	**–9,670**	**–5,901**	**–10,333**	**–16,000**	**929**
Trade credits	4 706	–2,003	–1,456	2	–1,727	–198	–1,251	–1,612	997
General government	4 707	. . .	. . .	. . .	. . .	. . .	. . .	. . .	. . .
of which: Short-term	4 709	. . .	. . .	. . .	. . .	. . .	. . .	. . .	. . .
Other sectors	4 710	–2,003	–1,456	2	–1,727	–198	–1,251	–1,612	997
of which: Short-term	4 712	*–2,003*	*–1,456*	*2*	*–1,727*	*–198*	*–1,251*	*–1,612*	*997*
Loans	4 714	–690	–1,813	–1,059	–3,805	–6,101	–8,653	–14,139	927
Monetary authorities	4 715	. . .	. . .	. . .	. . .	. . .	. . .	. . .	. . .
of which: Short-term	4 718	. . .	. . .	. . .	. . .	. . .	. . .	. . .	. . .
General government	4 719	–102	22	69	–177	43	–301	–33	47
of which: Short-term	4 721	. . .	. . .	. . .	*12*	*133*	*–129*	*204*	*502*
Banks	4 722	680	839	110	–1,668	–1,021	–5,334	–13,640	2,437
of which: Short-term	4 724	. . .	. . .	. . .	*278*	*2,222*	*–5,399*	*–13,483*	*4,101*
Other sectors	4 725	–1,268	–2,674	–1,238	–1,959	–5,123	–3,018	–466	–1,558
of which: Short-term	4 727	*–993*	*–2,278*	*–863*	*–2,598*	*–3,845*	*–1,290*	*–614*	*–1,691*
Currency and deposits	4 730	2,222	–8,876	–10,349	–3,837	. . .	. . .	. . .	. . .
Monetary authorities	4 731	. . .	. . .	. . .	. . .	. . .	. . .	. . .	. . .
General government	4 732	. . .	. . .	. . .	. . .	. . .	. . .	. . .	. . .
Banks	4 733	2,222	–8,876	–10,349	–3,837	. . .	. . .	. . .	. . .
Other sectors	4 734	. . .	. . .	. . .	. . .	. . .	. . .	. . .	. . .
Other assets	4 736	–2,929	–51	578	–301	398	–429	–249	–995
Monetary authorities	4 737	. . .	. . .	. . .	. . .	. . .	. . .	. . .	. . .
of which: Short-term	4 739	. . .	. . .	. . .	. . .	. . .	. . .	. . .	. . .
General government	4 740	–188	–504	–372	–144	–287	–341	–118	–11
of which: Short-term	4 742	*9*	*–3*	*5*	*–1*	. . .	. . .	. . .	. . .
Banks	4 743	. . .	. . .	. . .	534	–114	38	361	–765
of which: Short-term	4 745	. . .	. . .	. . .	*534*	*–114*	*38*	*361*	*–765*
Other sectors	4 746	–2,741	453	949	–691	799	–126	–492	–219
of which: Short-term	4 748	*–1,409*	*918*	*988*	*–420*	. . .	. . .	. . .	. . .
Liabilities	4 753	**11,633**	**6,999**	**10,320**	**15,635**	**32,015**	**3,897**	**34,609**	**12,689**
Trade credits	4 756	1,471	901	848	1,465	–79	413	1,125	13
General government	4 757	. . .	. . .	. . .	. . .	. . .	. . .	. . .	. . .
of which: Short-term	4 759	. . .	. . .	. . .	. . .	. . .	. . .	. . .	. . .
Other sectors	4 760	1,471	901	848	1,465	–79	413	1,125	13
of which: Short-term	4 762	*1,471*	*901*	*848*	*1,465*	*–79*	*413*	*1,125*	*13*
Loans	4 764	10,252	5,872	4,700	5,885	30,707	1,226	32,278	13,421
Monetary authorities	4 765	. . .	. . .	. . .	–39	88	–243	–556	–812
of which: Use of Fund credit and loans from the Fund	4 766	. . .	. . .	. . .	. . .	. . .	. . .	. . .	. . .
of which: Short-term	4 768	. . .	. . .	. . .	*–39*	*88*	*–243*	*–556*	*–812*
General government	4 769	5,433	7,992	1,814	–1,060	371	730	–18	64
of which: Short-term	4 771	*–701*	*188*	*–126*	*–3,452*	*266*	*–196*	*–503*	*30*
Banks	4 772	–2,293	389	–2,449	505	19,025	–5,786	28,623	10,727
of which: Short-term	4 774	. . .	. . .	. . .	*1,250*	*17,039*	*–6,802*	*28,308*	*9,749*
Other sectors	4 775	7,112	–1,731	5,336	6,480	11,222	6,525	4,229	3,442
of which: Short-term	4 777	*2,244*	*1,690*	*1,636*	*6,946*	*9,269*	*3,585*	*2,878*	*2,602*
Currency and deposits	4 780	336	–666	5,384	8,953	. . .	. . .	. . .	. . .
Monetary authorities	4 781	. . .	. . .	. . .	. . .	. . .	. . .	. . .	. . .
General government	4 782	. . .	. . .	. . .	. . .	. . .	. . .	. . .	. . .
Banks	4 783	336	–666	5,384	8,953	. . .	. . .	. . .	. . .
Other sectors	4 784	. . .	. . .	. . .	. . .	. . .	. . .	. . .	. . .
Other liabilities	4 786	–426	892	–612	–669	1,387	2,258	1,206	–746
Monetary authorities	4 787	. . .	. . .	. . .	. . .	. . .	. . .	. . .	. . .
of which: Short-term	4 789	. . .	. . .	. . .	. . .	. . .	. . .	. . .	. . .
General government	4 790	–358	850	3	–523	206	318	147	–96
of which: Short-term	4 792	*–358*	*850*	*3*	*–523*	*206*	*318*	*147*	*–96*
Banks	4 793	. . .	. . .	. . .	–189	1,180	1,940	1,059	–650
of which: Short-term	4 795	. . .	. . .	. . .	*–189*	*1,180*	*1,940*	*1,059*	*–650*
Other sectors	4 796	–68	42	–615	43	. . .	. . .	. . .	. . .
of which: Short-term	4 798	*–68*	*42*	*151*	*43*	. . .	. . .	. . .	. . .
E. RESERVE ASSETS	4 802	–2,381	1,664	6,386	6,712	–3,254	–1,881	–170	1,048
Monetary gold	4 812	. . .	. . .	. . .	. . .	. . .	. . .	. . .	. . .
Special drawing rights	4 811	–6	–367	142	–107	–20	90	82	10
Reserve position in the Fund	4 810	. . .	. . .	. . .	–186	–422	49	239	–181
Foreign exchange	4 803	–2,375	2,031	6,243	7,090	–4,255	–2,019	–491	1,219
Other claims	4 813	. . .	. . .	. . .	–85	1,444	. . .	. . .	. . .
NET ERRORS AND OMISSIONS	4 998	**–4,462**	**–1,566**	**–2,241**	**–3,769**	**–8,214**	**–545**	**–3,534**	**–10,078**

Part 3 of the *Yearbook* contains descriptions of the methodologies, compilation practices, and sources used to compile these data.

Table 3. INTERNATIONAL INVESTMENT POSITION (End–period stocks), 1994–2001

(Millions of U.S. dollars)

	Code	1994	1995	1996	1997	1998	1999	2000	2001
ASSETS	8 995 C.	165,515	227,989	248,580	241,838	295,255	353,559	365,450	...
Direct investment abroad	8 505 . .	**59,237**	**69,088**	**71,751**	**79,099**	**94,674**	**104,948**	**115,582**	...
Equity capital and reinvested earnings	8 506 . .	59,237	69,088	71,751	65,918	90,638	100,880	111,694	...
Claims on affiliated enterprises	8 507 . .	...	...	...	...	...	...	...	...
Liabilities to affiliated enterprises	8 508 . .	...	...	...	...	...	...	...	...
Other capital	8 530 . .	...	...	...	13,180	4,037	4,068	3,888	...
Claims on affiliated enterprises	8 535 . .	...	...	...	29,829	9,227	7,402	7,723	...
Liabilities to affiliated enterprises	8 540 . .	...	...	...	–16,648	–5,190	–3,334	–3,835	...
Portfolio investment	8 602 . .	**22,114**	**36,947**	**50,357**	**69,478**	**100,589**	**142,802**	**133,506**	...
Equity securities	8 610 . .	18,227	29,738	38,859	51,248	71,207	108,387	89,546	...
Monetary authorities	8 611 . .	...	...	...	...	...	...	...	...
General government	8 612 . .	...	...	...	587	496	1,056	1,030	...
Banks	8 613 . .	...	...	...	33,711	47,141	52,082	42,895	...
Other sectors	8 614 . .	18,227	29,738	38,859	16,951	23,570	55,249	45,621	...
Debt securities	8 619 . .	3,887	7,209	11,498	18,230	29,382	34,415	43,960	...
Bonds and notes	8 620 . .	...	7,209	11,498	16,563	28,127	32,517	40,922	...
Monetary authorities	8 621 . .	...	...	...	...	...	...	...	...
General government	8 622 . .	...	...	...	1,661	6,905	6,236	5,879	...
Banks	8 623 . .	...	...	...	4,241	6,259	6,142	7,353	...
Other sectors	8 624 . .	...	...	...	10,661	14,963	20,140	27,690	...
Money market instruments	8 630 . .	...	...	...	1,667	1,255	1,898	3,038	...
Monetary authorities	8 631 . .	...	...	...	...	...	...	...	...
General government	8 632 . .	...	...	...	...	14	460	211	...
Banks	8 633 . .	...	...	...	246	78	741	2,201	...
Other sectors	8 634 . .	...	...	...	1,421	1,164	697	626	...
Financial derivatives	8 900 . .	...	**15,920**	**16,446**	**16,450**	**15,579**	**14,990**	**18,679**	...
Monetary authorities	8 901 . .	...	...	...	...	...	...	...	...
General government	8 902 . .	...	1,502	3,784	2,403	3,171	2,429	4,772	...
Banks	8 903 . .	...	11,565	9,315	12,379	10,381	9,297	10,617	...
Other sectors	8 904 . .	...	2,854	3,347	1,668	2,027	3,263	3,290	...
Other investment	8 703 . .	**60,310**	**80,352**	**89,652**	**65,265**	**67,529**	**72,855**	**81,368**	...
Trade credits	8 706 . .	11,794	14,869	15,718	7,311	7,507	6,978	8,538	...
General government	8 707 . .	...	...	...	...	...	...	...	...
of which: Short-term	8 709 . .	...	...	...	...	...	...	...	...
Other sectors	8 710 . .	11,794	14,869	15,718	7,311	7,507	6,978	8,538	...
of which: Short-term	8 712 . .	...	...	...	*7,311*	*7,507*	*6,978*	*8,538*	...
Loans	8 714 . .	23,722	27,785	28,089	50,428	52,275	57,798	64,833	...
Monetary authorities	8 715 . .	...	...	...	...	...	...	...	...
of which: Short-term	8 718 . .	...	...	...	...	...	...	...	...
General government	8 719 . .	2,010	2,103	1,892	2,148	2,319	2,215	1,977	...
of which: Short-term	8 721 . .	...	...	...	*366*	*399*	*233*	*159*	...
Banks	8 722 . .	7,639	7,059	6,986	46,071	45,589	47,544	55,610	...
of which: Short-term	8 724 . .	*1,876*	*1,952*	*2,038*	*29,768*	*27,157*	*30,999*	*40,442*	...
Other sectors	8 725 . .	14,072	18,624	19,211	2,209	4,368	8,040	7,246	...
of which: Short-term	8 727 . .	*8,443*	*11,865*	*12,371*	*1,944*	*2,801*	*4,793*	*3,309*	...
Currency and deposits	8 730 . .	21,577	33,643	41,479	...	...	...	...	...
Monetary authorities	8 731 . .	...	...	...	...	...	...	...	...
General government	8 732 . .	...	...	...	...	...	...	...	...
Banks	8 733 . .	17,021	29,287	37,695	...	...	...	...	...
Other sectors	8 734 . .	4,557	4,356	3,784	...	...	...	...	...
Other assets	8 736 . .	3,217	4,055	4,366	7,526	7,747	8,079	7,997	...
Monetary authorities	8 737 . .	...	...	...	...	...	...	...	...
of which: Short-term	8 739 . .	...	...	...	...	...	...	...	...
General government	8 740 . .	3,217	4,055	4,366	4,026	4,198	4,293	4,007	...
of which: Short-term	8 742 . .	...	...	...	...	...	...	...	...
Banks	8 743 . .	...	...	...	528	555	584	408	...
of which: Short-term	8 745 . .	...	...	...	*528*	*555*	*584*	*408*	...
Other sectors	8 746 . .	...	...	...	2,972	2,995	3,201	3,582	...
of which: Short-term	8 748 . .	...	...	...	...	...	...	...	...
Reserve assets	8 802 . .	**23,855**	**25,682**	**20,375**	**11,546**	**16,884**	**17,964**	**16,316**	...
Monetary gold	8 812 . .	310	245	237	116	1,716	1,622	1,549	...
Special drawing rights	8 811 . .	68	441	286	373	412	313	215	197
Reserve position in the Fund	8 810 . .	659	671	649	795	1,267	1,184	890	1,039
Foreign exchange	8 803 . .	22,818	24,325	19,202	8,917	13,490	14,845	13,661	...
Other claims	8 813 . .	...	...	...	1,346	...	...	...	...

Table 3 (Concluded). INTERNATIONAL INVESTMENT POSITION (End–period stocks), 1994–2001
(Millions of U.S. dollars)

	Code	1994	1995	1996	1997	1998	1999	2000	2001
LIABILITIES	8 995 D.	261,074	324,863	352,787	339,476	389,867	430,625	424,279	...
Direct investment in Sweden	8 555 ..	**23,454**	**33,042**	**34,056**	**42,399**	**53,792**	**68,053**	**77,009**	...
Equity capital and reinvested earnings	8 556 ..	23,454	33,042	34,056	29,260	53,792	68,856	77,609	...
Claims on direct investors	8 557 ..	...	...	...	...	...	...	...	...
Liabilities to direct investors	8 558 ..	...	...	...	...	...	...	...	...
Other capital	8 580 ..	...	...	...	13,140	...	–804	–600	...
Claims on direct investors	8 585 ..	...	...	...	–3,881	...	–3,431	–3,553	...
Liabilities to direct investors	8 590 ..	...	...	...	17,020	...	2,628	2,953	...
Portfolio investment	8 652 ..	**57,897**	**77,348**	**99,549**	**207,565**	**225,711**	**259,959**	**225,025**	...
Equity securities	8 660 ..	35,918	48,061	70,295	79,472	94,033	129,384	106,660	...
Banks	8 663 ..	...	...	...	...	...	...	...	...
Other sectors	8 664 ..	35,918	48,061	70,295	79,472	94,033	129,384	106,660	...
Debt securities	8 669 ..	21,979	29,287	29,253	128,093	131,678	130,575	118,365	...
Bonds and notes	8 670 ..	...	29,287	29,253	114,278	113,862	113,811	100,593	...
Monetary authorities	8 671 ..	...	...	...	...	–14	–13	–12	...
General government	8 672 ..	...	...	...	69,810	68,081	55,980	40,002	...
Banks	8 673 ..	...	...	...	41,370	40,345	47,783	46,921	...
Other sectors	8 674 ..	...	...	...	3,099	5,450	10,061	13,681	...
Money market instruments	8 680 ..	...	...	...	13,815	17,817	16,764	17,772	...
Monetary authorities	8 681 ..	...	...	...	...	...	...	...	...
General government	8 682 ..	...	...	...	9,111	10,548	6,850	3,683	...
Banks	8 683 ..	...	...	...	3,058	5,581	6,867	10,291	...
Other sectors	8 684 ..	...	...	...	1,645	1,687	3,046	3,799	...
Financial derivatives	8 905 ..	...	**16,821**	**17,610**	**16,420**	**15,936**	**14,095**	**15,276**	...
Monetary authorities	8 906 ..	...	...	...	...	...	...	...	...
General government	8 907 ..	...	3,304	5,094	3,302	3,930	2,863	3,893	...
Banks	8 908 ..	...	10,063	9,315	11,581	10,424	8,378	7,835	...
Other sectors	8 909 ..	...	3,454	3,202	1,537	1,582	2,854	3,548	...
Other investment	8 753 ..	**179,723**	**197,651**	**201,572**	**73,091**	**94,427**	**88,518**	**106,969**	...
Trade credits	8 756 ..	8,175	9,913	10,770	5,280	5,176	5,789	6,030	...
General government	8 757 ..	...	...	...	...	...	...	...	...
of which: Short-term	8 759 ..	...	...	...	...	...	...	...	...
Other sectors	8 760 ..	8,175	9,913	10,770	5,280	5,176	5,789	6,030	...
of which: Short-term	8 762 ..	...	...	...	*5,280*	*5,176*	*5,789*	*6,030*	...
Loans	8 764 ..	135,093	144,784	144,229	66,282	88,075	81,335	99,471	...
Monetary authorities	8 765 ..	...	...	146	...	...	...	...	...
of which: Use of Fund credit and loans from the Fund	8 766 ..	...	...	...	...	...	...	...	...
of which: Short-term	8 768 ..	...	...	*146*	...	...	...	...	...
General government	8 769 ..	56,423	65,033	63,455	1,247	1,599	2,097	1,321	...
of which: Short-term	8 771 ..	*10,186*	*10,664*	*10,188*	*138*	*463*	*238*	*253*	...
Banks	8 772 ..	15,278	13,217	10,915	50,306	67,700	59,343	79,890	...
of which: Short-term	8 774 ..	*8,175*	*6,008*	*6,404*	*47,549*	*63,131*	*54,171*	*75,244*	...
Other sectors	8 775 ..	63,392	66,534	69,713	14,729	18,776	19,894	18,260	...
of which: Short-term	8 777 ..	*21,175*	*25,683*	*27,361*	*5,945*	*7,947*	*7,633*	*7,060*	...
Currency and deposits	8 780 ..	42,753	49,263	50,211	...	...	...	...	...
Monetary authorities	8 781 ..	...	...	...	...	...	...	...	...
General government	8 782 ..	...	...	...	...	...	...	...	...
Banks	8 783 ..	42,753	49,263	50,211	...	...	...	...	...
Other sectors	8 784 ..	...	...	...	...	...	...	...	...
Other liabilities	8 786 ..	–6,299	–6,308	–3,638	1,530	1,177	1,395	1,467	...
Monetary authorities	8 787 ..	...	...	...	...	...	...	...	...
of which: Short-term	8 789 ..	...	...	...	...	...	...	...	...
General government	8 790 ..	804	901	873	589	639	760	601	...
of which: Short-term	8 792 ..	...	...	...	*589*	*639*	*760*	*601*	...
Banks	8 793 ..	–7,103	–7,209	–4,512	941	538	635	866	...
of which: Short-term	8 795 ..	...	...	...	...	...	*635*	*866*	...
Other sectors	8 796 ..	...	...	...	...	...	...	...	...
of which: Short-term	8 798 ..	...	...	...	...	...	...	...	...
NET INTERNATIONAL INVESTMENT POSITION	8 995 ..	**–95,558**	**–96,874**	**–104,207**	**–97,637**	**–94,612**	**–77,066**	**–58,829**	...
Conversion rates: kronor per U.S. dollar (end of period)	0 102 ..	**7.4615**	**6.6582**	**6.8710**	**7.8770**	**8.0610**	**8.5250**	**9.5350**	**10.6675**

Table 1. ANALYTIC PRESENTATION, 1994–2001
(Millions of U.S. dollars)

	Code	1994	1995	1996	1997	1998	1999	2000	2001
A. Current Account [1]	4 993 Z.	**17,587**	**21,804**	**21,054**	**26,678**	**26,774**	**29,611**	**33,638**	**22,624**
Goods: exports f.o.b.	2 100 . .	82,625	97,139	95,544	95,039	93,782	91,823	94,842	95,826
Goods: imports f.o.b.	3 100 . .	-79,279	-93,880	-93,676	-92,302	-92,849	-90,981	-92,738	-94,262
Balance on Goods	4 100 . .	*3,346*	*3,259*	*1,868*	*2,738*	*933*	*843*	*2,104*	*1,564*
Services: credit	2 200 . .	22,619	26,026	26,250	25,300	26,732	28,459	28,877	27,726
Services: debit	3 200 . .	-12,770	-15,036	-15,690	-14,100	-15,085	-15,888	-15,573	-15,269
Balance on Goods and Services	4 991 . .	*13,195*	*14,249*	*12,428*	*13,938*	*12,579*	*13,414*	*15,408*	*14,020*
Income: credit	2 300 . .	26,747	31,575	32,997	35,066	45,927	50,111	61,036	49,751
Income: debit	3 300 . .	-18,932	-19,778	-20,383	-18,924	-28,051	-29,800	-39,882	-37,074
Balance on Goods, Services, and Income	4 992 . .	*21,010*	*26,045*	*25,042*	*30,080*	*30,456*	*33,725*	*36,562*	*26,697*
Current transfers: credit	2 379 Z.	2,526	2,995	2,961	2,626	2,786	7,638	6,853	9,682
Current transfers: debit	3 379 . .	-5,949	-7,237	-6,949	-6,028	-6,467	-11,752	-9,777	-13,755
B. Capital Account [1]	4 994 Z.	**-496**	**-595**	**-337**	**-245**	**258**	**-302**	**-3,073**	**189**
Capital account: credit	2 994 Z.	-116	-122	-104	-43	664	-35	406	1,922
Capital account: debit	3 994 . .	-380	-473	-233	-203	-406	-267	-3,479	-1,733
Total, Groups A Plus B	4 981 . .	*17,091*	*21,210*	*20,717*	*26,433*	*27,032*	*29,309*	*30,565*	*22,813*
C. Financial Account [1]	4 995 W.	**-11,852**	**-8,644**	**-24,252**	**-22,759**	**-22,988**	**-34,077**	**-28,163**	**-30,691**
Direct investment abroad	4 505 . .	-10,793	-12,210	-16,152	-17,732	-18,768	-33,277	-42,738	-11,052
Direct investment in Switzerland	4 555 Z.	4,104	3,599	4,373	7,306	9,649	12,342	20,010	8,628
Portfolio investment assets	4 602 . .	-19,112	-8,884	-22,731	-19,739	-14,882	-46,839	-22,309	-42,840
Equity securities	4 610 . .	-8,073	-4,064	-14,686	-9,159	-2,529	-17,500	-20,323	-14,958
Debt securities	4 619 . .	-11,040	-4,820	-8,045	-10,580	-12,353	-29,339	-1,986	-27,882
Portfolio investment liabilities	4 652 Z.	911	4,960	12,895	9,033	10,247	5,894	10,547	1,896
Equity securities	4 660 . .	-1,573	5,851	11,677	6,945	8,632	5,489	9,080	1,847
Debt securities	4 669 Z.	2,484	-891	1,218	2,088	1,615	404	1,467	49
Financial derivatives	4 910 . .	. . .	. . .	. . .	. . .	. . .	. . .	. . .	. . .
Financial derivatives assets	4 900 . .	. . .	. . .	. . .	. . .	. . .	. . .	. . .	. . .
Financial derivatives liabilities	4 905 . .	. . .	. . .	. . .	. . .	. . .	. . .	. . .	. . .
Other investment assets	4 703 . .	-30,798	-368	-70,355	-55,264	-60,089	-80,612	-93,277	23,059
Monetary authorities	4 701 . .	. . .	. . .	. . .	. . .	. . .	. . .	. . .	. . .
General government	4 704 . .	-70	-15	40	197	203	203	36	49
Banks	4 705 . .	-19,166	-9,423	-59,915	-52,384	-45,489	-77,286	-83,137	27,526
Other sectors	4 728 . .	-11,562	9,070	-10,480	-3,078	-14,803	-3,528	-10,176	-4,515
Other investment liabilities	4 753 W.	43,837	4,259	67,719	53,637	50,855	108,416	99,604	-10,382
Monetary authorities	4 753 WA	-104	-3	-9	10	80	34	38	846
General government	4 753 ZB	40	266	32	121	-4	-58	-59	-23
Banks	4 753 ZC	34,808	5,676	52,185	53,517	42,173	95,594	89,669	-16,550
Other sectors	4 753 ZD	9,093	-1,680	15,511	-11	8,606	12,846	9,955	5,344
Total, Groups A Through C	4 983 . .	*5,239*	*12,566*	*-3,535*	*3,674*	*4,044*	*-4,768*	*2,402*	*-7,878*
D. Net Errors and Omissions	4 998 . .	**-4,230**	**-12,537**	**6,057**	**-1,520**	**-2,865**	**2,284**	**-6,407**	**8,516**
Total, Groups A Through D	4 984 . .	*1,009*	*29*	*2,521*	*2,154*	*1,179*	*-2,484*	*-4,005*	*638*
E. Reserves and Related Items	4 802 A.	**-1,009**	**-29**	**-2,521**	**-2,154**	**-1,179**	**2,484**	**4,005**	**-638**
Reserve assets	4 802 . .	-1,009	-29	-2,521	-2,154	-1,179	2,484	4,005	-638
Use of Fund credit and loans	4 766 . .	. . .	. . .	. . .	. . .	. . .	. . .	. . .	. . .
Exceptional financing	4 920 . .	. . .	. . .	. . .	. . .	. . .	. . .	. . .	. . .
Conversion rates: Swiss francs per U.S. dollar	0 101 . .	**1.3677**	**1.1825**	**1.2360**	**1.4513**	**1.4498**	**1.5022**	**1.6888**	**1.6876**

[1] Excludes components that have been classified in the categories of Group E.

Table 2. STANDARD PRESENTATION, 1994–2001
(Millions of U.S. dollars)

	Code			1994	1995	1996	1997	1998	1999	2000	2001
CURRENT ACCOUNT	4	993	. .	**17,587**	**21,804**	**21,054**	**26,678**	**26,774**	**29,611**	**33,638**	**22,624**
A. GOODS	4	100	. .	3,346	3,259	1,868	2,738	933	843	2,104	1,564
Credit	2	100	. .	**82,625**	**97,139**	**95,544**	**95,039**	**93,782**	**91,823**	**94,842**	**95,826**
General merchandise: exports f.o.b.	2	110	. .	71,298	82,812	81,161	77,163	79,964	81,154	81,923	83,207
Goods for processing: exports f.o.b.	2	150	. .	...	...	...	...	...	...	...	...
Repairs on goods	2	160	. .	...	...	...	...	...	...	...	...
Goods procured in ports by carriers	2	170	. .	...	...	...	...	...	...	...	...
Nonmonetary gold	2	180	. .	11,326	14,327	14,383	17,877	13,818	10,669	12,919	12,619
Debit	3	100	. .	**-79,279**	**-93,880**	**-93,676**	**-92,302**	**-92,849**	**-90,981**	**-92,738**	**-94,262**
General merchandise: imports f.o.b.	3	110	. .	-67,589	-79,381	-78,081	-75,177	-78,967	-79,023	-81,922	-83,324
Goods for processing: imports f.o.b.	3	150	. .	...	...	...	...	...	...	...	...
Repairs on goods	3	160	. .	...	...	...	...	...	...	...	...
Goods procured in ports by carriers	3	170	. .	...	...	...	...	...	...	...	...
Nonmonetary gold	3	180	. .	-11,690	-14,499	-15,595	-17,124	-13,882	-11,957	-10,816	-10,939
B. SERVICES	4	200	. .	9,849	10,990	10,560	11,200	11,647	12,571	13,304	12,457
Total credit	2	200	. .	*22,619*	*26,026*	*26,250*	*25,300*	*26,732*	*28,459*	*28,877*	*27,726*
Total debit	3	200	. .	*-12,770*	*-15,036*	*-15,690*	*-14,100*	*-15,085*	*-15,888*	*-15,573*	*-15,269*
Transportation services, credit	2	205	. .	**3,273**	**3,810**	**3,940**	**4,119**	**4,345**	**4,409**	**4,538**	**4,439**
Passenger	2	850	. .	*1,667*	*1,895*	*1,888*	*2,091*	*2,197*	*2,297*	*2,340*	*2,513*
Freight	2	851	. .	*540*	*625*	*587*	*724*	*773*	*720*	*806*	*638*
Other	2	852	. .	*1,066*	*1,290*	*1,464*	*1,304*	*1,375*	*1,392*	*1,392*	*1,288*
Sea transport, passenger	2	207	. .	...	...	...	...	...	...	...	...
Sea transport, freight	2	208	. .	...	...	...	...	...	...	...	...
Sea transport, other	2	209	. .	...	...	...	...	...	...	...	...
Air transport, passenger	2	211	. .	...	...	...	...	...	...	...	...
Air transport, freight	2	212	. .	...	...	...	...	...	...	...	...
Air transport, other	2	213	. .	...	...	...	...	...	...	...	...
Other transport, passenger	2	215	. .	...	...	...	...	...	...	...	...
Other transport, freight	2	216	. .	...	...	...	...	...	...	...	...
Other transport, other	2	217	. .	1,066	1,290	1,464	1,304	1,375	1,392	1,392	1,288
Transportation services, debit	3	205	. .	**-4,326**	**-5,247**	**-5,514**	**-4,895**	**-5,219**	**-5,167**	**-5,228**	**-4,985**
Passenger	3	850	. .	*-1,647*	*-2,058*	*-2,172*	*-1,958*	*-1,940*	*-1,880*	*-1,945*	*-1,942*
Freight	3	851	. .	*-1,463*	*-1,732*	*-1,728*	*-1,703*	*-1,713*	*-1,679*	*-1,711*	*-1,739*
Other	3	852	. .	*-1,215*	*-1,458*	*-1,614*	*-1,234*	*-1,566*	*-1,608*	*-1,572*	*-1,303*
Sea transport, passenger	3	207	. .	...	...	...	...	...	...	...	...
Sea transport, freight	3	208	. .	...	...	...	...	...	...	...	...
Sea transport, other	3	209	. .	...	...	...	...	...	...	...	...
Air transport, passenger	3	211	. .	...	...	...	...	...	...	...	...
Air transport, freight	3	212	. .	...	...	...	...	...	...	...	...
Air transport, other	3	213	. .	...	...	...	...	...	...	...	...
Other transport, passenger	3	215	. .	...	...	...	...	...	...	...	...
Other transport, freight	3	216	. .	...	...	...	...	...	...	...	...
Other transport, other	3	217	. .	-1,215	-1,458	-1,614	-1,234	-1,566	-1,608	-1,572	1,303
Travel, credit	2	236	. .	**8,359**	**9,459**	**8,891**	**7,945**	**7,991**	**7,833**	**7,772**	**7,509**
Business travel	2	237	. .	...	...	...	...	...	...	...	...
Personal travel	2	240	. .	...	...	...	...	...	...	...	...
Travel, debit	3	236	. .	**-6,417**	**-7,420**	**-7,625**	**-6,987**	**-6,814**	**-6,774**	**-6,346**	**-6,350**
Business travel	3	237	. .	...	...	...	...	...	...	...	...
Personal travel	3	240	. .	...	...	...	...	...	...	...	...
Other services, credit	2	200	BA	**10,987**	**12,757**	**13,419**	**13,236**	**14,395**	**16,217**	**16,567**	**15,778**
Communications	2	245	. .	466	526	516	489	623	843	879	761
Construction	2	249	. .	...	...	...	...	...	...	...	...
Insurance	2	253	. .	1,163	1,227	1,431	1,426	1,571	1,899	1,445	1,064
Financial	2	260	. .	4,796	5,627	6,307	6,075	6,880	7,974	8,649	7,629
Computer and information	2	262	. .	...	...	...	...	...	...	...	...
Royalties and licence fees	2	266	. .	...	...	...	...	...	...	...	...
Other business services	2	268	. .	3,825	4,375	4,244	4,422	4,371	4,372	4,339	4,692
Personal, cultural, and recreational	2	287	. .	17	16	10	5	10	7	7	5
Government, n.i.e.	2	291	. .	720	985	911	820	939	1,122	1,247	1,627
Other services, debit	3	200	BA	**-2,027**	**-2,369**	**-2,551**	**-2,218**	**-3,051**	**-3,948**	**-3,999**	**-3,935**
Communications	3	245	. .	-585	-721	-727	-681	-775	-818	-885	-917
Construction	3	249	. .	...	...	...	...	...	...	...	...
Insurance	3	253	. .	-140	-165	-183	-175	-211	-222	-216	-218
Financial	3	260	. .	...	...	...	...	-506	-563	-783	-651
Computer and information	3	262	. .	...	...	...	...	...	...	...	...
Royalties and licence fees	3	266	. .	...	...	...	...	...	...	...	...
Other business services	3	268	. .	-1,103	-1,262	-1,430	-1,160	-1,356	-2,152	-1,942	-1,973
Personal, cultural, and recreational	3	287	. .	-74	-84	-78	-80	-71	-69	-61	-65
Government, n.i.e.	3	291	. .	-124	-137	-133	-121	-133	-123	-113	-110

Table 2 (Continued). STANDARD PRESENTATION, 1994–2001
(Millions of U.S. dollars)

	Code	1994	1995	1996	1997	1998	1999	2000	2001
C. INCOME	4 300 . .	7,815	11,797	12,614	16,143	17,876	20,311	21,154	12,677
Total credit	2 300 . .	*26,747*	*31,575*	*32,997*	*35,066*	*45,927*	*50,111*	*61,036*	*49,751*
Total debit	3 300 . .	*–18,932*	*–19,778*	*–20,383*	*–18,924*	*–28,051*	*–29,800*	*–39,882*	*–37,074*
Compensation of employees, credit	2 310 . .	**1,060**	**1,296**	**1,221**	**1,064**	**1,082**	**1,080**	**994**	**1,131**
Compensation of employees, debit	3 310 . .	**–6,078**	**–7,054**	**–6,764**	**–5,565**	**–5,526**	**–5,390**	**–5,601**	**–6,243**
Investment income, credit	2 320 . .	**25,687**	**30,279**	**31,776**	**34,002**	**44,844**	**49,030**	**60,042**	**48,620**
Direct investment income	2 330 . .	5,379	5,591	7,900	9,570	18,026	23,254	25,538	15,332
Dividends and distributed branch profits	2 332 . .	2,852	2,452	2,670	2,756	13,058	11,085	16,145	16,086
Reinvested earnings and undistributed branch profits	2 333 . .	2,528	3,138	5,231	6,814	4,968	12,169	9,393	–754
Income on debt (interest)	2 334 . .	. . .	. . .	. . .	. . .	. . .	. . .	. . .	. . .
Portfolio investment income	2 339 . .	9,798	11,719	11,565	10,546	12,360	14,437	14,512	14,580
Income on equity	2 340 . .	1,921	2,215	2,213	2,188	2,558	4,000	4,616	5,231
Income on bonds and notes	2 350 . .	. . .	. . .	. . .	. . .	. . .	. . .	. . .	. . .
Income on money market instruments	2 360 . .	. . .	. . .	. . .	. . .	. . .	. . .	. . .	. . .
Other investment income	2 370 . .	10,510	12,969	12,311	13,887	14,458	11,339	19,992	18,709
Investment income, debit	3 320 . .	**–12,854**	**–12,724**	**–13,620**	**–13,359**	**–22,524**	**–24,410**	**–34,281**	**–30,831**
Direct investment income	3 330 . .	–2,764	–698	–2,371	–858	–8,052	–10,434	–10,717	–6,632
Dividends and distributed branch profits	3 332 . .	. . .	. . .	. . .	. . .	–3,567	–3,972	–4,012	–7,031
Reinvested earnings and undistributed branch profits	3 333 . .	–2,764	–698	–2,371	–858	–4,485	–6,463	–6,705	399
Income on debt (interest)	3 334 . .	. . .	. . .	. . .	. . .	. . .	. . .	. . .	. . .
Portfolio investment income	3 339 . .	–3,191	–3,851	–3,942	–3,943	–5,512	–6,601	–7,130	–8,132
Income on equity	3 340 . .	–2,668	–3,201	–3,341	–3,395	–4,130	–4,890	–5,545	–6,606
Income on bonds and notes	3 350 . .	. . .	. . .	. . .	. . .	. . .	. . .	. . .	. . .
Income on money market instruments	3 360 . .	. . .	. . .	. . .	. . .	. . .	. . .	. . .	. . .
Other investment income	3 370 . .	–6,899	–8,175	–7,307	–8,558	–8,960	–7,374	–16,433	–16,067
D. CURRENT TRANSFERS	4 379 . .	–3,423	–4,241	–3,988	–3,402	–3,681	–4,114	–2,924	–4,073
Credit	2 379 . .	**2,526**	**2,995**	**2,961**	**2,626**	**2,786**	**7,638**	**6,853**	**9,682**
General government	2 380 . .	2,231	2,652	2,632	2,346	2,506	2,532	2,664	2,656
Other sectors	2 390 . .	295	343	329	280	280	5,105	4,189	7,026
Workers' remittances	2 391 . .	152	178	170	145	145	140	124	124
Other current transfers	2 392 . .	143	166	159	135	135	4,966	4,064	6,901
Debit	3 379 . .	**–5,949**	**–7,237**	**–6,949**	**–6,028**	**–6,467**	**–11,752**	**–9,777**	**–13,755**
General government	3 380 . .	–3,244	–4,097	–4,019	–3,681	–4,082	–4,040	–3,662	–3,830
Other sectors	3 390 . .	–2,705	–3,140	–2,930	–2,346	–2,385	–7,712	–6,115	–9,925
Workers' remittances	3 391 . .	–2,311	–2,679	–2,480	–1,975	–1,939	–1,889	–1,703	–1,819
Other current transfers	3 392 . .	–394	–461	–450	–371	–446	–5,823	–4,412	–8,106
CAPITAL AND FINANCIAL ACCOUNT	4 996 . .	**–13,357**	**–9,267**	**–27,111**	**–25,158**	**–23,910**	**–31,895**	**–27,231**	**–31,141**
CAPITAL ACCOUNT	4 994 . .	**–496**	**–595**	**–337**	**–245**	**258**	**–302**	**–3,073**	**189**
Total credit	2 994 . .	*–116*	*–122*	*–104*	*–43*	*664*	*–35*	*406*	*1,922*
Total debit	3 994 . .	*–380*	*–473*	*–233*	*–203*	*–406*	*–267*	*–3,479*	*–1,733*
Capital transfers, credit	2 400 . .	**–146**	**–132**	**–123**	**–79**	**–90**	**–88**	**–83**	**–83**
General government	2 401 . .	. . .	. . .	. . .	. . .	. . .	. . .	. . .	. . .
Debt forgiveness	2 402 . .	. . .	. . .	. . .	. . .	. . .	. . .	. . .	. . .
Other capital transfers	2 410 . .	. . .	. . .	. . .	. . .	. . .	. . .	. . .	. . .
Other sectors	2 430 . .	–146	–132	–123	–79	–90	–88	–83	–83
Migrants' transfers	2 431 . .	. . .	. . .	. . .	. . .	. . .	. . .	. . .	. . .
Debt forgiveness	2 432 . .	. . .	. . .	. . .	. . .	. . .	. . .	. . .	. . .
Other capital transfers	2 440 . .	–146	–132	–123	–79	–90	–88	–83	–83
Capital transfers, debit	3 400 . .	**–146**	**–132**	**–123**	**–79**	**–90**	**–88**	**–83**	**–83**
General government	3 401 . .	–146	–132	–123	–79	–90	–88	–83	–83
Debt forgiveness	3 402 . .	. . .	. . .	. . .	. . .	. . .	. . .	. . .	. . .
Other capital transfers	3 410 . .	–146	–132	–123	–79	–90	–88	–83	–83
Other sectors	3 430 . .	. . .	. . .	. . .	. . .	. . .	. . .	. . .	. . .
Migrants' transfers	3 431 . .	. . .	. . .	. . .	. . .	. . .	. . .	. . .	. . .
Debt forgiveness	3 432 . .	. . .	. . .	. . .	. . .	. . .	. . .	. . .	. . .
Other capital transfers	3 440 . .	. . .	. . .	. . .	. . .	. . .	. . .	. . .	. . .
Nonproduced nonfinancial assets, credit	2 480 . .	**31**	**10**	**19**	**36**	**755**	**53**	**489**	**2,005**
Nonproduced nonfinancial assets, debit	3 480 . .	**–234**	**–341**	**–110**	**–124**	**–316**	**–179**	**–3,396**	**–1,650**

Table 2 (Continued). STANDARD PRESENTATION, 1994–2001

(Millions of U.S. dollars)

	Code	1994	1995	1996	1997	1998	1999	2000	2001
FINANCIAL ACCOUNT	4 995 . .	**–12,861**	**–8,673**	**–26,774**	**–24,913**	**–24,168**	**–31,593**	**–24,158**	**–31,330**
A. DIRECT INVESTMENT	4 500 . .	–6,689	–8,611	–11,779	–10,426	–9,119	–20,935	–22,729	–2,424
Direct investment abroad	4 505 . .	**–10,793**	**–12,210**	**–16,152**	**–17,732**	**–18,768**	**–33,277**	**–42,738**	**–11,052**
Equity capital	4 510 . .	–8,221	–8,151	–10,603	–9,312	–11,690	–15,867	–33,165	–10,900
Claims on affiliated enterprises	4 515 . .	–8,221	–8,151	–10,603	–9,312	–11,690	–15,867	–33,165	–10,900
Liabilities to affiliated enterprises	4 520 . .	. . .	. . .	. . .	. . .	. . .	. . .	. . .	. . .
Reinvested earnings	4 525 . .	–2,528	–3,138	–5,231	–6,814	–4,968	–12,169	–9,393	754
Other capital	4 530 . .	–45	–921	–318	–1,606	–2,109	–5,240	–180	–906
Claims on affiliated enterprises	4 535 . .	–45	–921	–318	–1,606	–2,109	–5,240	–180	–906
Liabilities to affiliated enterprises	4 540 . .	. . .	. . .	. . .	. . .	. . .	. . .	. . .	. . .
Direct investment in Switzerland	4 555 . .	**4,104**	**3,599**	**4,373**	**7,306**	**9,649**	**12,342**	**20,010**	**8,628**
Equity capital	4 560 . .	919	3,461	2,510	4,781	4,221	5,667	12,396	9,024
Claims on direct investors	4 565 . .	. . .	. . .	. . .	. . .	. . .	. . .	. . .	. . .
Liabilities to direct investors	4 570 . .	919	3,461	2,510	4,781	4,221	5,667	12,396	9,024
Reinvested earnings	4 575 . .	2,764	698	2,371	858	4,484	6,463	6,705	–399
Other capital	4 580 . .	421	–559	–507	1,667	944	212	908	3
Claims on direct investors	4 585 . .	. . .	. . .	. . .	. . .	. . .	. . .	. . .	. . .
Liabilities to direct investors	4 590 . .	421	–559	–507	1,667	944	212	908	3
B. PORTFOLIO INVESTMENT	4 600 . .	–18,201	–3,924	–9,836	–10,705	–4,635	–40,946	–11,761	–40,945
Assets	4 602 . .	**–19,112**	**–8,884**	**–22,731**	**–19,739**	**–14,882**	**–46,839**	**–22,309**	**–42,840**
Equity securities	4 610 . .	–8,073	–4,064	–14,686	–9,159	–2,529	–17,500	–20,323	–14,958
Monetary authorities	4 611 . .	. . .	. . .	. . .	. . .	. . .	. . .	. . .	. . .
General government	4 612 . .	. . .	. . .	. . .	. . .	. . .	. . .	. . .	. . .
Banks	4 613 . .	. . .	. . .	. . .	. . .	. . .	. . .	. . .	. . .
Other sectors	4 614 . .	. . .	. . .	. . .	. . .	. . .	. . .	. . .	. . .
Debt securities	4 619 . .	–11,040	–4,820	–8,045	–10,580	–12,353	–29,339	–1,986	–27,882
Bonds and notes	4 620 . .	–10,986	–4,792	–7,716	–11,800	–12,277	–26,512	–1,012	–23,280
Monetary authorities	4 621 . .	. . .	. . .	. . .	. . .	. . .	. . .	. . .	. . .
General government	4 622 . .	. . .	. . .	. . .	. . .	. . .	. . .	. . .	. . .
Banks	4 623 . .	. . .	. . .	. . .	. . .	. . .	. . .	. . .	. . .
Other sectors	4 624 . .	. . .	. . .	. . .	. . .	. . .	. . .	. . .	. . .
Money market instruments	4 630 . .	–54	–29	–329	1,220	–75	–2,827	–974	–4,602
Monetary authorities	4 631 . .	. . .	. . .	. . .	. . .	. . .	. . .	. . .	. . .
General government	4 632 . .	. . .	. . .	. . .	. . .	. . .	. . .	. . .	. . .
Banks	4 633 . .	. . .	. . .	. . .	. . .	. . .	. . .	. . .	. . .
Other sectors	4 634 . .	. . .	. . .	. . .	. . .	. . .	. . .	. . .	. . .
Liabilities	4 652 . .	**911**	**4,960**	**12,895**	**9,033**	**10,247**	**5,894**	**10,547**	**1,896**
Equity securities	4 660 . .	–1,573	5,851	11,677	6,945	8,632	5,489	9,080	1,847
Banks	4 663 . .	. . .	. . .	. . .	. . .	. . .	. . .	. . .	. . .
Other sectors	4 664 . .	. . .	. . .	. . .	. . .	. . .	. . .	. . .	. . .
Debt securities	4 669 . .	2,484	–891	1,218	2,088	1,615	404	1,467	49
Bonds and notes	4 670 . .	2,484	–891	1,218	2,088	1,615	334	1,346	–457
Monetary authorities	4 671 . .	. . .	. . .	. . .	. . .	. . .	. . .	. . .	. . .
General government	4 672 . .	529	596	864	1,636	1,018	. . .	. . .	. . .
Banks	4 673 . .	. . .	. . .	. . .	. . .	. . .	. . .	. . .	. . .
Other sectors	4 674 . .	1,955	–1,488	354	451	597	. . .	. . .	. . .
Money market instruments	4 680 . .	. . .	. . .	. . .	. . .	. . .	71	121	505
Monetary authorities	4 681 . .	. . .	. . .	. . .	. . .	. . .	. . .	. . .	. . .
General government	4 682 . .	. . .	. . .	. . .	. . .	. . .	. . .	. . .	. . .
Banks	4 683 . .	. . .	. . .	. . .	. . .	. . .	. . .	. . .	. . .
Other sectors	4 684 . .	. . .	. . .	. . .	. . .	. . .	. . .	. . .	. . .
C. FINANCIAL DERIVATIVES	4 910 . .	. . .	. . .	. . .	. . .	. . .	. . .	. . .	. . .
Monetary authorities	4 911 . .	. . .	. . .	. . .	. . .	. . .	. . .	. . .	. . .
General government	4 912 . .	. . .	. . .	. . .	. . .	. . .	. . .	. . .	. . .
Banks	4 913 . .	. . .	. . .	. . .	. . .	. . .	. . .	. . .	. . .
Other sectors	4 914 . .	. . .	. . .	. . .	. . .	. . .	. . .	. . .	. . .
Assets	4 900 . .	**. . .**	**. . .**	**. . .**	**. . .**	**. . .**	**. . .**	**. . .**	**. . .**
Monetary authorities	4 901 . .	. . .	. . .	. . .	. . .	. . .	. . .	. . .	. . .
General government	4 902 . .	. . .	. . .	. . .	. . .	. . .	. . .	. . .	. . .
Banks	4 903 . .	. . .	. . .	. . .	. . .	. . .	. . .	. . .	. . .
Other sectors	4 904 . .	. . .	. . .	. . .	. . .	. . .	. . .	. . .	. . .
Liabilities	4 905 . .	**. . .**	**. . .**	**. . .**	**. . .**	**. . .**	**. . .**	**. . .**	**. . .**
Monetary authorities	4 906 . .	. . .	. . .	. . .	. . .	. . .	. . .	. . .	. . .
General government	4 907 . .	. . .	. . .	. . .	. . .	. . .	. . .	. . .	. . .
Banks	4 908 . .	. . .	. . .	. . .	. . .	. . .	. . .	. . .	. . .
Other sectors	4 909 . .	. . .	. . .	. . .	. . .	. . .	. . .	. . .	. . .

Table 2 (Concluded). STANDARD PRESENTATION, 1994–2001
(Millions of U.S. dollars)

	Code	1994	1995	1996	1997	1998	1999	2000	2001
D. OTHER INVESTMENT	4 700	13,039	3,891	–2,637	–1,627	–9,234	27,804	6,327	12,677
Assets	4 703	**–30,798**	**–368**	**–70,355**	**–55,264**	**–60,089**	**–80,612**	**–93,277**	**23,059**
Trade credits	4 706	. . .	. . .	. . .	. . .	. . .	. . .	. . .	. . .
General government	4 707	. . .	. . .	. . .	. . .	. . .	. . .	. . .	. . .
of which: Short-term	4 709	. . .	. . .	. . .	. . .	. . .	. . .	. . .	. . .
Other sectors	4 710	. . .	. . .	. . .	. . .	. . .	. . .	. . .	. . .
of which: Short-term	4 712	. . .	. . .	. . .	. . .	. . .	. . .	. . .	. . .
Loans	4 714	–117	759	517	–3,773	–5,624	–13,422	–13,047	12,469
Monetary authorities	4 715	. . .	. . .	. . .	. . .	. . .	. . .	. . .	. . .
of which: Short-term	4 718	. . .	. . .	. . .	. . .	. . .	. . .	. . .	. . .
General government	4 719	–89	–15	36	197	203	203	36	49
of which: Short-term	4 721	. . .	. . .	. . .	. . .	. . .	. . .	. . .	. . .
Banks	4 722	–28	774	481	–3,970	–5,828	–13,625	–13,083	12,420
of which: Short-term	4 724	. . .	. . .	. . .	. . .	. . .	. . .	. . .	. . .
Other sectors	4 725	. . .	. . .	. . .	. . .	. . .	. . .	. . .	. . .
of which: Short-term	4 727	. . .	. . .	. . .	. . .	. . .	. . .	. . .	. . .
Currency and deposits	4 730	–15,100	–6,058	–45,837	–50,403	–32,050	–62,740	–71,972	15,854
Monetary authorities	4 731	. . .	. . .	. . .	. . .	. . .	. . .	. . .	. . .
General government	4 732	. . .	. . .	. . .	. . .	. . .	. . .	. . .	. . .
Banks	4 733	–15,100	–6,058	–45,837	–50,403	–32,050	–62,740	–71,972	15,854
Other sectors	4 734	. . .	. . .	. . .	. . .	. . .	. . .	. . .	. . .
Other assets	4 736	–15,581	4,931	–25,035	–1,088	–22,415	–4,450	–8,258	–5,264
Monetary authorities	4 737	. . .	. . .	. . .	. . .	. . .	. . .	. . .	. . .
of which: Short-term	4 739	. . .	. . .	. . .	. . .	. . .	. . .	. . .	. . .
General government	4 740	19	. . .	3	. . .	. . .	. . .	. . .	. . .
of which: Short-term	4 742	. . .	. . .	. . .	. . .	. . .	. . .	. . .	. . .
Banks	4 743	–4,038	–4,139	–14,558	1,990	–7,612	–921	1,917	–748
of which: Short-term	4 745	*–4,038*	*–4,139*	*–14,558*	*1,990*	*–7,612*	*–921*	*1,917*	*–748*
Other sectors	4 746	–11,562	9,070	–10,480	–3,078	–14,803	–3,528	–10,176	–4,515
of which: Short-term	4 748	. . .	. . .	. . .	. . .	. . .	. . .	. . .	. . .
Liabilities	4 753	**43,837**	**4,259**	**67,719**	**53,637**	**50,855**	**108,416**	**99,604**	**–10,382**
Trade credits	4 756	. . .	. . .	. . .	. . .	. . .	. . .	. . .	. . .
General government	4 757	. . .	. . .	. . .	. . .	. . .	. . .	. . .	. . .
of which: Short-term	4 759	. . .	. . .	. . .	. . .	. . .	. . .	. . .	. . .
Other sectors	4 760	. . .	. . .	. . .	. . .	. . .	. . .	. . .	. . .
of which: Short-term	4 762	. . .	. . .	. . .	. . .	. . .	. . .	. . .	. . .
Loans	4 764	5,203	5,225	4,002	4,080	14,045	9,426	–1,405	–8,971
Monetary authorities	4 765	. . .	. . .	. . .	. . .	. . .	. . .	. . .	. . .
of which: Use of Fund credit and loans from the Fund	4 766	. . .	. . .	. . .	. . .	. . .	. . .	. . .	. . .
of which: Short-term	4 768	. . .	. . .	. . .	. . .	. . .	. . .	. . .	. . .
General government	4 769	. . .	. . .	. . .	. . .	. . .	. . .	. . .	. . .
of which: Short-term	4 771	. . .	. . .	. . .	. . .	. . .	. . .	. . .	. . .
Banks	4 772	5,203	5,225	4,002	4,080	14,045	9,426	–1,405	–8,971
of which: Short-term	4 774	*4,546*	*4,068*	*3,064*	*1,954*	*8,173*	. . .	. . .	. . .
Other sectors	4 775	. . .	. . .	. . .	. . .	. . .	. . .	. . .	. . .
of which: Short-term	4 777	. . .	. . .	. . .	. . .	. . .	. . .	. . .	. . .
Currency and deposits	4 780	25,485	–4,002	44,150	44,403	19,641	85,953	91,809	–7,913
Monetary authorities	4 781	. . .	. . .	. . .	. . .	. . .	. . .	. . .	. . .
General government	4 782	. . .	. . .	. . .	. . .	. . .	. . .	. . .	. . .
Banks	4 783	25,485	–4,002	44,150	44,403	19,641	85,953	91,809	–7,913
Other sectors	4 784	. . .	. . .	. . .	. . .	. . .	. . .	. . .	. . .
Other liabilities	4 786	13,148	3,036	19,566	5,153	17,168	13,037	9,199	6,501
Monetary authorities	4 787	–104	–3	–9	10	80	34	38	846
of which: Short-term	4 789	*–104*	*–3*	*–9*	*10*	*80*	*34*	*38*	*846*
General government	4 790	40	266	32	121	–4	–58	–59	–23
of which: Short-term	4 792	. . .	. . .	. . .	. . .	. . .	. . .	. . .	. . .
Banks	4 793	4,119	4,453	4,032	5,033	8,487	216	–735	334
of which: Short-term	4 795	. . .	. . .	. . .	. . .	. . .	. . .	. . .	. . .
Other sectors	4 796	9,093	–1,680	15,511	–11	8,606	12,846	9,955	5,344
of which: Short-term	4 798	. . .	. . .	. . .	. . .	. . .	. . .	. . .	. . .
E. RESERVE ASSETS	4 802	–1,009	–29	–2,521	–2,154	–1,179	2,484	4,005	–638
Monetary gold	4 812	. . .	. . .	. . .	. . .	. . .	. . .	. . .	. . .
Special drawing rights	4 811	–76	–16	136	–113	–31	–208	295	–124
Reserve position in the Fund	4 810	–56	–512	–122	–465	–553	831	339	–375
Foreign exchange	4 803	–893	479	–2,510	–1,500	–282	1,554	3,343	–139
Other claims	4 813	17	20	–24	–76	–312	308	27	. . .
NET ERRORS AND OMISSIONS	4 998	**–4,230**	**–12,537**	**6,057**	**–1,520**	**–2,865**	**2,284**	**–6,407**	**8,516**

Part 3 of the *Yearbook* contains descriptions of the methodologies, compilation practices, and sources used to compile these data.

Table 3. INTERNATIONAL INVESTMENT POSITION (End–period stocks), 1994–2001

(Millions of U.S. dollars)

	Code	1994	1995	1996	1997	1998	1999	2000	2001
ASSETS	8 995 C.	745,816	860,214	924,274	1,009,487	1,196,819	1,242,638	1,360,726	1,320,044
Direct investment abroad	8 505 ..	**112,586**	**142,479**	**141,591**	**165,365**	**184,232**	**194,585**	**227,661**	**236,426**
Equity capital and reinvested earnings	8 506 ..	95,639	123,006	127,730	146,053	163,648	166,881	202,280	212,258
Claims on affiliated enterprises	8 507 ..	95,639	123,006	127,730	146,053	163,648	166,881	202,280	212,258
Liabilities to affiliated enterprises	8 508 ..	...	...	...	...	...	...	...	...
Other capital	8 530 ..	16,946	19,473	13,861	19,311	20,584	27,704	25,380	24,168
Claims on affiliated enterprises	8 535 ..	22,191	27,720	20,587	26,401	29,205	36,837	39,874	37,413
Liabilities to affiliated enterprises	8 540 ..	–5,245	–8,247	–6,725	–7,089	–8,620	–9,134	–14,493	–13,245
Portfolio investment	8 602 ..	**293,846**	**347,040**	**359,820**	**382,782**	**469,523**	**508,041**	**504,560**	**495,177**
Equity securities	8 610 ..	100,797	120,543	138,922	165,438	209,618	259,679	265,897	247,408
Monetary authorities	8 611 ..	...	...	...	...	...	...	...	...
General government	8 612 ..	...	...	...	...	...	...	...	...
Banks	8 613 ..	2,297	3,895	3,622	4,970	8,031	...	...	...
Other sectors	8 614 ..	98,499	116,648	135,300	160,468	201,587	259,679	265,897	247,408
Debt securities	8 619 ..	193,049	226,497	220,898	217,344	259,905	248,363	238,663	247,769
Bonds and notes	8 620 ..	192,030	223,945	217,848	215,587	254,020	241,285	233,143	233,711
Monetary authorities	8 621 ..	...	...	...	...	...	...	...	...
General government	8 622 ..	...	...	...	...	...	...	...	...
Banks	8 623 ..	15,510	15,827	17,193	17,022	22,163	22,973	16,494	29,839
Other sectors	8 624 ..	176,520	208,118	200,654	198,565	231,858	218,311	216,649	203,872
Money market instruments	8 630 ..	1,019	2,552	3,050	1,757	5,884	7,078	5,520	14,058
Monetary authorities	8 631 ..	...	...	...	...	...	...	...	...
General government	8 632 ..	...	...	...	...	...	...	...	...
Banks	8 633 ..	1,019	2,552	3,050	1,757	1,894	3,285	2,962	6,109
Other sectors	8 634 ..	...	...	...	...	3,991	3,793	2,559	7,948
Financial derivatives	8 900 ..	...	...	...	...	...	...	...	...
Monetary authorities	8 901 ..	...	...	...	...	...	...	...	...
General government	8 902 ..	...	...	...	...	...	...	...	...
Banks	8 903 ..	...	...	...	...	...	...	...	...
Other sectors	8 904 ..	...	...	...	...	...	...	...	...
Other investment	8 703 ..	**293,976**	**322,125**	**375,575**	**414,208**	**492,632**	**496,073**	**575,024**	**536,743**
Trade credits	8 706 ..	...	...	...	...	...	...	...	...
General government	8 707 ..	...	...	...	...	...	...	...	...
of which: Short-term	8 709 ..	...	...	...	...	...	...	...	...
Other sectors	8 710 ..	...	...	...	...	...	...	...	...
of which: Short-term	8 712 ..	...	...	...	...	...	...	...	...
Loans	8 714 ..	206,149	239,804	293,041	332,467	402,057	406,187	480,672	444,926
Monetary authorities	8 715 ..	...	...	...	...	...	...	...	...
of which: Short-term	8 718 ..	...	...	...	...	...	...	...	...
General government	8 719 ..	798	924	730	643	620	478	477	308
of which: Short-term	8 721 ..	*2*	*3*	...	...	...	...	...	...
Banks	8 722 ..	163,586	183,006	231,511	276,736	332,647	342,082	413,332	375,251
of which: Short-term	8 724 ..	*116,005*	*133,299*	*170,214*	*215,511*	*263,062*	*265,175*	*326,319*	*302,404*
Other sectors	8 725 ..	41,765	55,874	60,801	55,088	68,790	63,626	66,862	69,367
of which: Short-term	8 727 ..	*21,177*	*32,377*	*36,792*	*33,482*	*43,502*	*40,503*	*43,173*	*40,345*
Currency and deposits	8 730 ..	...	...	...	...	...	...	...	...
Monetary authorities	8 731 ..	...	...	...	...	...	...	...	...
General government	8 732 ..	...	...	...	...	...	...	...	...
Banks	8 733 ..	...	...	...	...	...	...	...	...
Other sectors	8 734 ..	...	...	...	...	...	...	...	...
Other assets	8 736 ..	87,827	82,322	82,533	81,741	90,575	89,886	94,353	91,817
Monetary authorities	8 737 ..	...	...	...	...	...	...	...	...
of which: Short-term	8 739 ..	...	...	...	...	...	...	...	...
General government	8 740 ..	239	326	322	303	323	278	278	276
of which: Short-term	8 742 ..	...	...	...	...	...	...	...	...
Banks	8 743 ..	4	...	...	...	...	...	...	...
of which: Short-term	8 745 ..	...	...	...	...	...	...	...	...
Other sectors	8 746 ..	87,584	81,996	82,212	81,438	90,252	89,608	94,075	91,541
of which: Short-term	8 748 ..	*58,303*	*56,065*	*55,041*	*51,899*	*56,321*	*52,851*	*63,042*	*58,103*
Reserve assets	8 802 ..	**45,409**	**48,569**	**47,288**	**47,132**	**50,432**	**43,939**	**53,480**	**51,697**
Monetary gold	8 812 ..	9,077	10,347	8,841	8,180	8,648	7,442	21,219	19,664
Special drawing rights	8 811 ..	236	269	126	230	271	473	162	283
Reserve position in the Fund	8 810 ..	939	1,459	1,531	1,899	2,574	1,672	1,256	1,582
Foreign exchange	8 803 ..	35,006	36,343	36,637	36,604	38,363	34,139	30,830	30,156
Other claims	8 813 ..	151	151	152	219	577	213	13	13

Table 3 (Concluded). INTERNATIONAL INVESTMENT POSITION (End–period stocks), 1994–2001
(Millions of U.S. dollars)

	Code	1994	1995	1996	1997	1998	1999	2000	2001
LIABILITIES	8 995 D.	472,873	556,487	587,559	700,952	838,861	883,036	1,055,030	983,439
Direct investment in Switzerland	8 555 ..	**61,690**	**73,324**	**69,002**	**74,142**	**88,201**	**90,510**	**96,783**	**105,464**
Equity capital and reinvested earnings	8 556 ..	60,692	72,686	68,356	70,953	87,481	89,410	94,417	99,285
Claims on direct investors	8 557 ..	...	...	...	...	...	...	...	...
Liabilities to direct investors	8 558 ..	60,692	72,686	68,356	70,953	87,481	89,410	94,417	99,285
Other capital	8 580 ..	998	638	645	3,189	720	1,100	2,366	6,180
Claims on direct investors	8 585 ..	–2,878	–3,671	–2,888	–2,936	–3,745	–5,244	–5,579	–933
Liabilities to direct investors	8 590 ..	3,876	4,309	3,534	6,125	4,465	6,344	7,945	7,113
Portfolio investment	8 652 ..	**162,400**	**208,583**	**203,380**	**272,805**	**353,572**	**341,057**	**411,445**	**349,731**
Equity securities	8 660 ..	134,721	179,290	176,566	246,515	323,809	309,597	382,038	321,678
Banks	8 663 ..	...	...	...	...	...	...	...	...
Other sectors	8 664 ..	134,721	179,290	176,566	246,515	323,809	309,597	382,038	321,678
Debt securities	8 669 ..	27,679	29,293	26,814	26,289	29,763	31,460	29,407	28,053
Bonds and notes	8 670 ..	27,679	29,293	26,814	26,289	29,329	31,087	28,832	27,706
Monetary authorities	8 671 ..	...	...	...	...	...	...	...	...
General government	8 672 ..	2,005	3,013	3,321	4,741	5,497	4,104	6,244	6,375
Banks	8 673 ..	1,364	791	518	404	480	369	348	360
Other sectors	8 674 ..	24,310	25,490	22,974	21,145	23,353	26,614	22,240	20,971
Money market instruments	8 680 ..	...	...	...	...	434	373	575	347
Monetary authorities	8 681 ..	...	...	...	...	...	...	...	...
General government	8 682 ..	...	...	...	...	...	...	...	...
Banks	8 683 ..	...	...	...	...	52	38	30	28
Other sectors	8 684 ..	...	...	...	...	382	334	545	319
Financial derivatives	8 905 ..	**...**	**...**	**...**	**...**	**...**	**...**	**...**	**...**
Monetary authorities	8 906 ..	...	...	...	...	...	...	...	...
General government	8 907 ..	...	...	...	...	...	...	...	...
Banks	8 908 ..	...	...	...	...	...	...	...	...
Other sectors	8 909 ..	...	...	...	...	...	...	...	...
Other investment	8 753 ..	**248,783**	**274,580**	**315,178**	**354,005**	**397,088**	**451,470**	**546,802**	**528,244**
Trade credits	8 756 ..	...	...	...	...	...	...	...	...
General government	8 757 ..	...	...	...	...	...	...	...	...
of which: Short-term	8 759 ..	...	...	...	...	...	...	...	...
Other sectors	8 760 ..	...	...	...	...	...	...	...	...
of which: Short-term	8 762 ..	...	...	...	...	...	...	...	...
Loans	8 764 ..	199,774	226,613	270,806	306,415	344,821	393,745	477,568	461,624
Monetary authorities	8 765 ..	36	37	25	32	119	356	393	1,251
of which: Use of Fund credit and loans from the Fund	8 766 ..	...	...	...	...	...	...	...	...
of which: Short-term	8 768 ..	*36*	*37*	*25*	*32*	*119*	*356*	*393*	*1,251*
General government	8 769 ..	258	568	514	596	625	484	412	380
of which: Short-term	8 771 ..	*258*	*568*	*514*	*596*	*625*	*484*	*412*	*380*
Banks	8 772 ..	168,268	180,343	217,171	257,602	289,765	342,709	422,205	397,643
of which: Short-term	8 774 ..	*155,019*	*163,186*	*199,828*	*238,466*	*261,867*	*309,905*	*392,447*	*376,125*
Other sectors	8 775 ..	31,213	45,664	53,096	48,185	54,312	50,197	54,558	62,350
of which: Short-term	8 777 ..	*9,555*	*20,812*	*23,376*	*20,299*	*21,263*	*20,418*	*24,567*	*27,616*
Currency and deposits	8 780 ..	...	...	...	...	...	...	...	...
Monetary authorities	8 781 ..	...	...	...	...	...	...	...	...
General government	8 782 ..	...	...	...	...	...	...	...	...
Banks	8 783 ..	...	...	...	...	...	...	...	...
Other sectors	8 784 ..	...	...	...	...	...	...	...	...
Other liabilities	8 786 ..	49,009	47,967	44,372	47,590	52,267	57,724	69,234	66,620
Monetary authorities	8 787 ..	...	...	...	...	...	...	...	...
of which: Short-term	8 789 ..	...	...	...	...	...	...	...	...
General government	8 790 ..	...	...	...	...	...	...	...	...
of which: Short-term	8 792 ..	...	...	...	...	...	...	...	...
Banks	8 793 ..	2,299	529	1,435	1,106	700	2,127	901	1,075
of which: Short-term	8 795 ..	...	...	...	...	...	...	...	...
Other sectors	8 796 ..	46,710	47,438	42,937	46,484	51,567	55,597	68,333	65,545
of which: Short-term	8 798 ..	*46,710*	*47,438*	*42,937*	*46,484*	*51,567*	*55,597*	*68,333*	*65,545*
NET INTERNATIONAL INVESTMENT POSITION	8 995 ..	**272,943**	**303,727**	**336,714**	**308,534**	**357,958**	**359,601**	**305,695**	**336,605**
Conversion rates: Swiss francs per U.S. dollar (end of period)	0 102 ..	**1.3115**	**1.1505**	**1.3464**	**1.4553**	**1.3765**	**1.5996**	**1.6365**	**1.6773**

Table 1. ANALYTIC PRESENTATION, 1994–2001
(Millions of U.S. dollars)

	Code			1994	1995	1996	1997	1998	1999	2000	2001
A. Current Account [1]	4	993	Z.	**–791**	**263**	**40**	**461**	**58**	**201**	**1,062**	**. . .**
Goods: exports f.o.b	2	100	. .	3,329	3,858	4,178	4,057	3,142	3,806	5,146	. . .
Goods: imports f.o.b	3	100	. .	–4,604	–4,004	–4,516	–3,603	–3,320	–3,590	–3,723	. . .
Balance on Goods	4	100	. .	*–1,275*	*–146*	*–338*	*454*	*–178*	*216*	*1,423*	. . .
Services: credit	2	200	. .	1,863	1,899	1,792	1,582	1,666	1,651	1,700	. . .
Services: debit	3	200	. .	–1,611	–1,537	–1,555	–1,489	–1,491	–1,612	–1,667	. . .
Balance on Goods and Services	4	991	. .	*–1,023*	*216*	*–101*	*547*	*–3*	*255*	*1,456*	. . .
Income: credit	2	300	. .	638	444	534	421	369	356	345	. . .
Income: debit	3	300	. .	–997	–1,004	–1,017	–1,006	–839	–899	–1,224	. . .
Balance on Goods, Services, and Income	4	992	. .	*–1,382*	*–344*	*–584*	*–38*	*–473*	*–288*	*577*	. . .
Current transfers: credit	2	379	Z.	597	610	630	504	533	491	495	. . .
Current transfers: debit	3	379	. .	–6	–3	–6	–5	–2	–2	–10	. . .
B. Capital Account [1]	4	994	Z.	**102**	**20**	**26**	**18**	**27**	**80**	**63**	**. . .**
Capital account: credit	2	994	Z.	102	20	26	18	27	80	63	. . .
Capital account: debit	3	994	. .	. . .	. . .	. . .	. . .	. . .	. . .	. . .	. . .
Total, Groups A Plus B	4	981	. .	*–689*	*283*	*66*	*479*	*85*	*281*	*1,125*	. . .
C. Financial Account [1]	4	995	W.	**1,159**	**521**	**782**	**65**	**196**	**173**	**–392**	**. . .**
Direct investment abroad	4	505	. .	. . .	100	89	80	82	263	270	. . .
Direct investment in Syrian Arab Republic	4	555	Z.	251	. . .	. . .	. . .	. . .	. . .	. . .	. . .
Portfolio investment assets	4	602	. .	. . .	. . .	. . .	. . .	. . .	. . .	. . .	. . .
Equity securities	4	610	. .	. . .	. . .	. . .	. . .	. . .	. . .	. . .	. . .
Debt securities	4	619	. .	. . .	. . .	. . .	. . .	. . .	. . .	. . .	. . .
Portfolio investment liabilities	4	652	Z.	. . .	. . .	. . .	. . .	. . .	. . .	. . .	. . .
Equity securities	4	660	. .	. . .	. . .	. . .	. . .	. . .	. . .	. . .	. . .
Debt securities	4	669	Z.	. . .	. . .	. . .	. . .	. . .	. . .	. . .	. . .
Financial derivatives	4	910	. .	. . .	. . .	. . .	. . .	. . .	. . .	. . .	. . .
Financial derivatives assets	4	900	. .	. . .	. . .	. . .	. . .	. . .	. . .	. . .	. . .
Financial derivatives liabilities	4	905	. .	. . .	. . .	. . .	. . .	. . .	. . .	. . .	. . .
Other investment assets	4	703	. .	–718	1,510	1,660	1,496	1,422	1,332	1,049	. . .
Monetary authorities	4	701	. .	. . .	. . .	. . .	. . .	. . .	. . .	. . .	. . .
General government	4	704	. .	. . .	. . .	. . .	. . .	. . .	. . .	. . .	. . .
Banks	4	705	. .	. . .	1,510	1,660	1,496	1,422	1,332	1,049	. . .
Other sectors	4	728	. .	–718	. . .	. . .	. . .	. . .	. . .	. . .	. . .
Other investment liabilities	4	753	W.	1,626	–1,089	–967	–1,511	–1,308	–1,422	–1,711	. . .
Monetary authorities	4	753	WA	20	. . .	. . .	. . .	. . .	. . .	. . .	. . .
General government	4	753	ZB	339	. . .	. . .	. . .	. . .	. . .	. . .	. . .
Banks	4	753	ZC	–147	–1,089	–967	–1,511	–1,308	–1,422	–1,711	. . .
Other sectors	4	753	ZD	1,414	. . .	. . .	. . .	. . .	. . .	. . .	. . .
Total, Groups A Through C	4	983	. .	*470*	*804*	*848*	*544*	*281*	*454*	*733*	. . .
D. Net Errors and Omissions	4	998	. .	**96**	**35**	**139**	**–95**	**153**	**–195**	**–192**	**. . .**
Total, Groups A Through D	4	984	. .	*566*	*839*	*987*	*449*	*434*	*259*	*541*	. . .
E. Reserves and Related Items	4	802	A.	**–566**	**–839**	**–987**	**–449**	**–434**	**–259**	**–541**	**. . .**
Reserve assets	4	802	. .	–566	–839	–987	–449	–434	–259	–541	. . .
Use of Fund credit and loans	4	766	. .	. . .	. . .	. . .	. . .	. . .	. . .	. . .	. . .
Exceptional financing	4	920	. .	. . .	. . .	. . .	. . .	. . .	. . .	. . .	. . .
Conversion rates: Syrian pounds per U.S. dollar	0	101	. .	**11.225**	**11.225**	**11.225**	**11.225**	**11.225**	**11.225**	**11.225**	**11.225**

[1] Excludes components that have been classified in the categories of Group E.

Table 2. STANDARD PRESENTATION, 1994–2001

(Millions of U.S. dollars)

	Code	1994	1995	1996	1997	1998	1999	2000	2001
CURRENT ACCOUNT	4 993 . .	**–791**	**263**	**40**	**461**	**58**	**201**	**1,062**	**. . .**
A. GOODS	4 100 . .	–1,275	–146	–338	454	–178	216	1,423	. . .
Credit	2 100 . .	**3,329**	**3,858**	**4,178**	**4,057**	**3,142**	**3,806**	**5,146**	**. . .**
General merchandise: exports f.o.b.	2 110 . .	3,329	3,858	4,178	4,057	3,142	3,806	5,146	. . .
Goods for processing: exports f.o.b.	2 150 . .	. . .	. . .	. . .	. . .	. . .	. . .	. . .	. . .
Repairs on goods	2 160 . .	. . .	. . .	. . .	. . .	. . .	. . .	. . .	. . .
Goods procured in ports by carriers	2 170 . .	. . .	. . .	. . .	. . .	. . .	. . .	. . .	. . .
Nonmonetary gold	2 180 . .	. . .	. . .	. . .	. . .	. . .	. . .	. . .	. . .
Debit	3 100 . .	**–4,604**	**–4,004**	**–4,516**	**–3,603**	**–3,320**	**–3,590**	**–3,723**	**. . .**
General merchandise: imports f.o.b.	3 110 . .	–4,604	–4,004	–4,516	–3,603	–3,320	–3,590	–3,723	. . .
Goods for processing: imports f.o.b.	3 150 . .	. . .	. . .	. . .	. . .	. . .	. . .	. . .	. . .
Repairs on goods	3 160 . .	. . .	. . .	. . .	. . .	. . .	. . .	. . .	. . .
Goods procured in ports by carriers	3 170 . .	. . .	. . .	. . .	. . .	. . .	. . .	. . .	. . .
Nonmonetary gold	3 180 . .	. . .	. . .	. . .	. . .	. . .	. . .	. . .	. . .
B. SERVICES	4 200 . .	252	362	237	93	175	39	33	. . .
Total credit	2 200 . .	*1,863*	*1,899*	*1,792*	*1,582*	*1,666*	*1,651*	*1,700*	. . .
Total debit	3 200 . .	*–1,611*	*–1,537*	*–1,555*	*–1,489*	*–1,491*	*–1,612*	*–1,667*	. . .
Transportation services, credit	2 205 . .	**342**	**237**	**245**	**214**	**257**	**240**	**246**	**. . .**
Passenger	2 850 . .	. . .	. . .	. . .	. . .	. . .	. . .	. . .	. . .
Freight	2 851 . .	*342*	*237*	*245*	*214*	*257*	*240*	*246*	. . .
Other	2 852 . .	. . .	. . .	. . .	. . .	. . .	. . .	. . .	. . .
Sea transport, passenger	2 207 . .	. . .	. . .	. . .	. . .	. . .	. . .	. . .	. . .
Sea transport, freight	2 208 . .	. . .	. . .	. . .	. . .	. . .	. . .	. . .	. . .
Sea transport, other	2 209 . .	. . .	. . .	. . .	. . .	. . .	. . .	. . .	. . .
Air transport, passenger	2 211 . .	. . .	. . .	. . .	. . .	. . .	. . .	. . .	. . .
Air transport, freight	2 212 . .	. . .	. . .	. . .	. . .	. . .	. . .	. . .	. . .
Air transport, other	2 213 . .	. . .	. . .	. . .	. . .	. . .	. . .	. . .	. . .
Other transport, passenger	2 215 . .	. . .	. . .	. . .	. . .	. . .	. . .	. . .	. . .
Other transport, freight	2 216 . .	. . .	. . .	. . .	. . .	. . .	. . .	. . .	. . .
Other transport, other	2 217 . .	. . .	. . .	. . .	. . .	. . .	. . .	. . .	. . .
Transportation services, debit	3 205 . .	**–879**	**–777**	**–798**	**–668**	**–634**	**–689**	**–698**	**. . .**
Passenger	3 850 . .	. . .	. . .	. . .	. . .	. . .	. . .	. . .	. . .
Freight	3 851 . .	*–879*	*–777*	*–798*	*–668*	*–634*	*–689*	*–698*	. . .
Other	3 852 . .	. . .	. . .	. . .	. . .	. . .	. . .	. . .	. . .
Sea transport, passenger	3 207 . .	. . .	. . .	. . .	. . .	. . .	. . .	. . .	. . .
Sea transport, freight	3 208 . .	. . .	. . .	. . .	. . .	. . .	. . .	. . .	. . .
Sea transport, other	3 209 . .	. . .	. . .	. . .	. . .	. . .	. . .	. . .	. . .
Air transport, passenger	3 211 . .	. . .	. . .	. . .	. . .	. . .	. . .	. . .	. . .
Air transport, freight	3 212 . .	. . .	. . .	. . .	. . .	. . .	. . .	. . .	. . .
Air transport, other	3 213 . .	. . .	. . .	. . .	. . .	. . .	. . .	. . .	. . .
Other transport, passenger	3 215 . .	. . .	. . .	. . .	. . .	. . .	. . .	. . .	. . .
Other transport, freight	3 216 . .	. . .	. . .	. . .	. . .	. . .	. . .	. . .	. . .
Other transport, other	3 217 . .	. . .	. . .	. . .	. . .	. . .	. . .	. . .	. . .
Travel, credit	2 236 . .	**1,149**	**1,258**	**1,165**	**1,013**	**1,017**	**1,031**	**1,082**	**. . .**
Business travel	2 237 . .	. . .	. . .	. . .	. . .	. . .	. . .	. . .	. . .
Personal travel	2 240 . .	. . .	. . .	. . .	. . .	. . .	. . .	. . .	. . .
Travel, debit	3 236 . .	**–512**	**–498**	**–513**	**–545**	**–583**	**–631**	**–669**	**. . .**
Business travel	3 237 . .	. . .	. . .	. . .	. . .	. . .	. . .	. . .	. . .
Personal travel	3 240 . .	. . .	. . .	. . .	. . .	. . .	. . .	. . .	. . .
Other services, credit	2 200 BA	**372**	**404**	**382**	**355**	**392**	**380**	**372**	**. . .**
Communications	2 245 . .	. . .	. . .	. . .	. . .	. . .	. . .	. . .	. . .
Construction	2 249 . .	. . .	. . .	. . .	. . .	. . .	. . .	. . .	. . .
Insurance	2 253 . .	. . .	. . .	. . .	. . .	. . .	. . .	. . .	. . .
Financial	2 260 . .	. . .	. . .	. . .	. . .	. . .	. . .	. . .	. . .
Computer and information	2 262 . .	. . .	. . .	. . .	. . .	. . .	. . .	. . .	. . .
Royalties and licence fees	2 266 . .	. . .	. . .	. . .	. . .	. . .	. . .	. . .	. . .
Other business services	2 268 . .	125	137	130	117	148	144	153	. . .
Personal, cultural, and recreational	2 287 . .	. . .	. . .	. . .	. . .	. . .	. . .	. . .	. . .
Government, n.i.e.	2 291 . .	247	267	252	238	244	236	219	. . .
Other services, debit	3 200 BA	**–220**	**–262**	**–244**	**–276**	**–274**	**–292**	**–300**	**. . .**
Communications	3 245 . .	. . .	. . .	. . .	. . .	. . .	. . .	. . .	. . .
Construction	3 249 . .	. . .	. . .	. . .	. . .	. . .	. . .	. . .	. . .
Insurance	3 253 . .	. . .	. . .	. . .	. . .	. . .	. . .	. . .	. . .
Financial	3 260 . .	. . .	. . .	. . .	. . .	. . .	. . .	. . .	. . .
Computer and information	3 262 . .	. . .	. . .	. . .	. . .	. . .	. . .	. . .	. . .
Royalties and licence fees	3 266 . .	. . .	. . .	. . .	. . .	. . .	. . .	. . .	. . .
Other business services	3 268 . .	–59	–83	–67	–89	–82	–96	–101	. . .
Personal, cultural, and recreational	3 287 . .	. . .	. . .	. . .	. . .	. . .	. . .	. . .	. . .
Government, n.i.e.	3 291 . .	–161	–179	–177	–187	–192	–196	–199	. . .

Table 2 (Continued). STANDARD PRESENTATION, 1994–2001
(Millions of U.S. dollars)

	Code		1994	1995	1996	1997	1998	1999	2000	2001
C. INCOME	4 300	. .	–359	–560	–483	–585	–470	–543	–879	. . .
Total credit	2 300	. .	*638*	*444*	*534*	*421*	*369*	*356*	*345*	. . .
Total debit	3 300	. .	*–997*	*–1,004*	*–1,017*	*–1,006*	*–839*	*–899*	*–1,224*	. . .
Compensation of employees, credit	2 310	. .	**535**	**339**	**313**	**238**	**220**	**198**	**180**	**. . .**
Compensation of employees, debit	3 310	. .	**–11**	**–15**	**–20**	**–25**	**–29**	**–28**	**–29**	**. . .**
Investment income, credit	2 320	. .	**103**	**105**	**221**	**183**	**149**	**158**	**165**	**. . .**
Direct investment income	2 330	. .	. . .	. . .	. . .	. . .	. . .	. . .	. . .	. . .
Dividends and distributed branch profits	2 332	. .	. . .	. . .	. . .	. . .	. . .	. . .	. . .	. . .
Reinvested earnings and undistributed branch profits	2 333	. .	. . .	. . .	. . .	. . .	. . .	. . .	. . .	. . .
Income on debt (interest)	2 334	. .	. . .	. . .	. . .	. . .	. . .	. . .	. . .	. . .
Portfolio investment income	2 339	. .	. . .	. . .	. . .	. . .	. . .	. . .	. . .	. . .
Income on equity	2 340	. .	. . .	. . .	. . .	. . .	. . .	. . .	. . .	. . .
Income on bonds and notes	2 350	. .	. . .	. . .	. . .	. . .	. . .	. . .	. . .	. . .
Income on money market instruments	2 360	. .	. . .	. . .	. . .	. . .	. . .	. . .	. . .	. . .
Other investment income	2 370	. .	103	105	221	183	149	158	165	. . .
Investment income, debit	3 320	. .	**–986**	**–989**	**–997**	**–981**	**–810**	**–871**	**–1,195**	**. . .**
Direct investment income	3 330	. .	–828	. . .	. . .	. . .	. . .	. . .	. . .	. . .
Dividends and distributed branch profits	3 332	. .	–828	. . .	. . .	. . .	. . .	. . .	. . .	. . .
Reinvested earnings and undistributed branch profits	3 333	. .	. . .	. . .	. . .	. . .	. . .	. . .	. . .	. . .
Income on debt (interest)	3 334	. .	. . .	. . .	. . .	. . .	. . .	. . .	. . .	. . .
Portfolio investment income	3 339	. .	. . .	. . .	. . .	. . .	. . .	. . .	. . .	. . .
Income on equity	3 340	. .	. . .	. . .	. . .	. . .	. . .	. . .	. . .	. . .
Income on bonds and notes	3 350	. .	. . .	. . .	. . .	. . .	. . .	. . .	. . .	. . .
Income on money market instruments	3 360	. .	. . .	. . .	. . .	. . .	. . .	. . .	. . .	. . .
Other investment income	3 370	. .	–158	–989	–997	–981	–810	–871	–1,195	. . .
D. CURRENT TRANSFERS	4 379	. .	591	607	624	499	531	489	485	. . .
Credit	2 379	. .	**597**	**610**	**630**	**504**	**533**	**491**	**495**	**. . .**
General government	2 380	. .	27	12	12	14	28	26	19	. . .
Other sectors	2 390	. .	570	598	618	490	505	465	476	. . .
Workers' remittances	2 391	. .	. . .	. . .	. . .	. . .	. . .	. . .	. . .	. . .
Other current transfers	2 392	. .	570	598	618	490	505	465	476	. . .
Debit	3 379	. .	**–6**	**–3**	**–6**	**–5**	**–2**	**–2**	**–10**	**. . .**
General government	3 380	. .	–6	–3	–6	–5	–2	–2	–10	. . .
Other sectors	3 390	. .	. . .	. . .	. . .	. . .	. . .	. . .	. . .	. . .
Workers' remittances	3 391	. .	. . .	. . .	. . .	. . .	. . .	. . .	. . .	. . .
Other current transfers	3 392	. .	. . .	. . .	. . .	. . .	. . .	. . .	. . .	. . .
CAPITAL AND FINANCIAL ACCOUNT	4 996	. .	**695**	**–298**	**–179**	**–366**	**–211**	**–6**	**–870**	**. . .**
CAPITAL ACCOUNT	4 994	. .	**102**	**20**	**26**	**18**	**27**	**80**	**63**	**. . .**
Total credit	2 994	. .	*102*	*20*	*26*	*18*	*27*	*80*	*63*	. . .
Total debit	3 994	. .	. . .	. . .	. . .	. . .	. . .	. . .	. . .	. . .
Capital transfers, credit	2 400	. .	**102**	**20**	**26**	**18**	**27**	**80**	**63**	**. . .**
General government	2 401	. .	. . .	. . .	. . .	. . .	. . .	. . .	. . .	. . .
Debt forgiveness	2 402	. .	. . .	. . .	. . .	. . .	. . .	. . .	. . .	. . .
Other capital transfers	2 410	. .	. . .	. . .	. . .	. . .	. . .	. . .	. . .	. . .
Other sectors	2 430	. .	102	20	26	18	27	80	63	. . .
Migrants' transfers	2 431	. .	. . .	. . .	. . .	. . .	. . .	. . .	. . .	. . .
Debt forgiveness	2 432	. .	. . .	. . .	. . .	. . .	. . .	. . .	. . .	. . .
Other capital transfers	2 440	. .	102	20	26	18	27	80	63	. . .
Capital transfers, debit	3 400	. .	**. . .**	**. . .**	**. . .**	**. . .**	**. . .**	**. . .**	**. . .**	**. . .**
General government	3 401	. .	. . .	. . .	. . .	. . .	. . .	. . .	. . .	. . .
Debt forgiveness	3 402	. .	. . .	. . .	. . .	. . .	. . .	. . .	. . .	. . .
Other capital transfers	3 410	. .	. . .	. . .	. . .	. . .	. . .	. . .	. . .	. . .
Other sectors	3 430	. .	. . .	. . .	. . .	. . .	. . .	. . .	. . .	. . .
Migrants' transfers	3 431	. .	. . .	. . .	. . .	. . .	. . .	. . .	. . .	. . .
Debt forgiveness	3 432	. .	. . .	. . .	. . .	. . .	. . .	. . .	. . .	. . .
Other capital transfers	3 440	. .	. . .	. . .	. . .	. . .	. . .	. . .	. . .	. . .
Nonproduced nonfinancial assets, credit	2 480	. .	**. . .**	**. . .**	**. . .**	**. . .**	**. . .**	**. . .**	**. . .**	**. . .**
Nonproduced nonfinancial assets, debit	3 480	. .	**. . .**	**. . .**	**. . .**	**. . .**	**. . .**	**. . .**	**. . .**	**. . .**

Table 2 (Continued). STANDARD PRESENTATION, 1994–2001

(Millions of U.S. dollars)

	Code	1994	1995	1996	1997	1998	1999	2000	2001
FINANCIAL ACCOUNT	4 995	**593**	**–318**	**–205**	**–384**	**–238**	**–86**	**–933**	...
A. DIRECT INVESTMENT	4 500	251	100	89	80	82	263	270	...
Direct investment abroad	4 505	...	**100**	**89**	**80**	**82**	**263**	**270**	...
Equity capital	4 510	...	...	...	...	...	...	...	...
Claims on affiliated enterprises	4 515	...	...	...	...	...	...	...	...
Liabilities to affiliated enterprises	4 520	...	...	...	...	...	...	...	...
Reinvested earnings	4 525	...	...	...	...	...	...	...	...
Other capital	4 530	...	100	89	80	82	263	270	...
Claims on affiliated enterprises	4 535	...	...	...	...	...	...	...	...
Liabilities to affiliated enterprises	4 540	...	...	...	...	...	...	...	...
Direct investment in Syrian Arab Republic	4 555	**251**	...	...	...	...	...	...	...
Equity capital	4 560	251	...	...	...	...	...	...	...
Claims on direct investors	4 565	...	...	...	...	...	...	...	...
Liabilities to direct investors	4 570	251	...	...	...	...	...	...	...
Reinvested earnings	4 575	...	...	...	...	...	...	...	...
Other capital	4 580	...	...	...	...	...	...	...	...
Claims on direct investors	4 585	...	...	...	...	...	...	...	...
Liabilities to direct investors	4 590	...	...	...	...	...	...	...	...
B. PORTFOLIO INVESTMENT	4 600	...	...	...	...	...	...	...	...
Assets	4 602	...	...	...	...	...	...	...	...
Equity securities	4 610	...	...	...	...	...	...	...	...
Monetary authorities	4 611	...	...	...	...	...	...	...	...
General government	4 612	...	...	...	...	...	...	...	...
Banks	4 613	...	...	...	...	...	...	...	...
Other sectors	4 614	...	...	...	...	...	...	...	...
Debt securities	4 619	...	...	...	...	...	...	...	...
Bonds and notes	4 620	...	...	...	...	...	...	...	...
Monetary authorities	4 621	...	...	...	...	...	...	...	...
General government	4 622	...	...	...	...	...	...	...	...
Banks	4 623	...	...	...	...	...	...	...	...
Other sectors	4 624	...	...	...	...	...	...	...	...
Money market instruments	4 630	...	...	...	...	...	...	...	...
Monetary authorities	4 631	...	...	...	...	...	...	...	...
General government	4 632	...	...	...	...	...	...	...	...
Banks	4 633	...	...	...	...	...	...	...	...
Other sectors	4 634	...	...	...	...	...	...	...	...
Liabilities	4 652	...	...	...	...	...	...	...	...
Equity securities	4 660	...	...	...	...	...	...	...	...
Banks	4 663	...	...	...	...	...	...	...	...
Other sectors	4 664	...	...	...	...	...	...	...	...
Debt securities	4 669	...	...	...	...	...	...	...	...
Bonds and notes	4 670	...	...	...	...	...	...	...	...
Monetary authorities	4 671	...	...	...	...	...	...	...	...
General government	4 672	...	...	...	...	...	...	...	...
Banks	4 673	...	...	...	...	...	...	...	...
Other sectors	4 674	...	...	...	...	...	...	...	...
Money market instruments	4 680	...	...	...	...	...	...	...	...
Monetary authorities	4 681	...	...	...	...	...	...	...	...
General government	4 682	...	...	...	...	...	...	...	...
Banks	4 683	...	...	...	...	...	...	...	...
Other sectors	4 684	...	...	...	...	...	...	...	...
C. FINANCIAL DERIVATIVES	4 910	...	...	...	...	...	...	...	...
Monetary authorities	4 911	...	...	...	...	...	...	...	...
General government	4 912	...	...	...	...	...	...	...	...
Banks	4 913	...	...	...	...	...	...	...	...
Other sectors	4 914	...	...	...	...	...	...	...	...
Assets	4 900	...	...	...	...	...	...	...	...
Monetary authorities	4 901	...	...	...	...	...	...	...	...
General government	4 902	...	...	...	...	...	...	...	...
Banks	4 903	...	...	...	...	...	...	...	...
Other sectors	4 904	...	...	...	...	...	...	...	...
Liabilities	4 905	...	...	...	...	...	...	...	...
Monetary authorities	4 906	...	...	...	...	...	...	...	...
General government	4 907	...	...	...	...	...	...	...	...
Banks	4 908	...	...	...	...	...	...	...	...
Other sectors	4 909	...	...	...	...	...	...	...	...

Table 2 (Concluded). STANDARD PRESENTATION, 1994–2001

(Millions of U.S. dollars)

	Code	1994	1995	1996	1997	1998	1999	2000	2001
D. OTHER INVESTMENT	4 700 . .	908	421	693	–15	114	–90	–662	. . .
Assets	4 703 . .	**–718**	**1,510**	**1,660**	**1,496**	**1,422**	**1,332**	**1,049**	**. . .**
Trade credits	4 706 . .	. . .	. . .	. . .	. . .	. . .	. . .	. . .	. . .
General government	4 707 . .	. . .	. . .	. . .	. . .	. . .	. . .	. . .	. . .
of which: Short-term	4 709 . .	. . .	. . .	. . .	. . .	. . .	. . .	. . .	. . .
Other sectors	4 710 . .	. . .	. . .	. . .	. . .	. . .	. . .	. . .	. . .
of which: Short-term	4 712 . .	. . .	. . .	. . .	. . .	. . .	. . .	. . .	. . .
Loans	4 714 . .	. . .	. . .	. . .	. . .	. . .	. . .	. . .	. . .
Monetary authorities	4 715 . .	. . .	. . .	. . .	. . .	. . .	. . .	. . .	. . .
of which: Short-term	4 718 . .	. . .	. . .	. . .	. . .	. . .	. . .	. . .	. . .
General government	4 719 . .	. . .	. . .	. . .	. . .	. . .	. . .	. . .	. . .
of which: Short-term	4 721 . .	. . .	. . .	. . .	. . .	. . .	. . .	. . .	. . .
Banks	4 722 . .	. . .	. . .	. . .	. . .	. . .	. . .	. . .	. . .
of which: Short-term	4 724 . .	. . .	. . .	. . .	. . .	. . .	. . .	. . .	. . .
Other sectors	4 725 . .	. . .	. . .	. . .	. . .	. . .	. . .	. . .	. . .
of which: Short-term	4 727 . .	. . .	. . .	. . .	. . .	. . .	. . .	. . .	. . .
Currency and deposits	4 730 . .	. . .	. . .	. . .	. . .	. . .	. . .	. . .	. . .
Monetary authorities	4 731 . .	. . .	. . .	. . .	. . .	. . .	. . .	. . .	. . .
General government	4 732 . .	. . .	. . .	. . .	. . .	. . .	. . .	. . .	. . .
Banks	4 733 . .	. . .	. . .	. . .	. . .	. . .	. . .	. . .	. . .
Other sectors	4 734 . .	. . .	. . .	. . .	. . .	. . .	. . .	. . .	. . .
Other assets	4 736 . .	–718	1,510	1,660	1,496	1,422	1,332	1,049	. . .
Monetary authorities	4 737 . .	. . .	. . .	. . .	. . .	. . .	. . .	. . .	. . .
of which: Short-term	4 739 . .	. . .	. . .	. . .	. . .	. . .	. . .	. . .	. . .
General government	4 740 . .	. . .	. . .	. . .	. . .	. . .	. . .	. . .	. . .
of which: Short-term	4 742 . .	. . .	. . .	. . .	. . .	. . .	. . .	. . .	. . .
Banks	4 743 . .	. . .	1,510	1,660	1,496	1,422	1,332	1,049	. . .
of which: Short-term	4 745 . .	. . .	*1,175*	*1,255*	*1,116*	*1,032*	*920*	*788*	. . .
Other sectors	4 746 . .	–718	. . .	. . .	. . .	. . .	. . .	. . .	. . .
of which: Short-term	4 748 . .	*–718*	. . .	. . .	. . .	. . .	. . .	. . .	. . .
Liabilities	4 753 . .	**1,626**	**–1,089**	**–967**	**–1,511**	**–1,308**	**–1,422**	**–1,711**	**. . .**
Trade credits	4 756 . .	. . .	. . .	. . .	. . .	. . .	. . .	. . .	. . .
General government	4 757 . .	. . .	. . .	. . .	. . .	. . .	. . .	. . .	. . .
of which: Short-term	4 759 . .	. . .	. . .	. . .	. . .	. . .	. . .	. . .	. . .
Other sectors	4 760 . .	. . .	. . .	. . .	. . .	. . .	. . .	. . .	. . .
of which: Short-term	4 762 . .	. . .	. . .	. . .	. . .	. . .	. . .	. . .	. . .
Loans	4 764 . .	1,753	. . .	. . .	. . .	. . .	. . .	. . .	. . .
Monetary authorities	4 765 . .	. . .	. . .	. . .	. . .	. . .	. . .	. . .	. . .
of which: Use of Fund credit and loans from the Fund	4 766 . .	. . .	. . .	. . .	. . .	. . .	. . .	. . .	. . .
of which: Short-term	4 768 . .	. . .	. . .	. . .	. . .	. . .	. . .	. . .	. . .
General government	4 769 . .	339	. . .	. . .	. . .	. . .	. . .	. . .	. . .
of which: Short-term	4 771 . .	. . .	. . .	. . .	. . .	. . .	. . .	. . .	. . .
Banks	4 772 . .	. . .	. . .	. . .	. . .	. . .	. . .	. . .	. . .
of which: Short-term	4 774 . .	. . .	. . .	. . .	. . .	. . .	. . .	. . .	. . .
Other sectors	4 775 . .	1,414	. . .	. . .	. . .	. . .	. . .	. . .	. . .
of which: Short-term	4 777 . .	*1,414*	. . .	. . .	. . .	. . .	. . .	. . .	. . .
Currency and deposits	4 780 . .	. . .	. . .	. . .	. . .	. . .	. . .	. . .	. . .
Monetary authorities	4 781 . .	. . .	. . .	. . .	. . .	. . .	. . .	. . .	. . .
General government	4 782 . .	. . .	. . .	. . .	. . .	. . .	. . .	. . .	. . .
Banks	4 783 . .	. . .	. . .	. . .	. . .	. . .	. . .	. . .	. . .
Other sectors	4 784 . .	. . .	. . .	. . .	. . .	. . .	. . .	. . .	. . .
Other liabilities	4 786 . .	–127	–1,089	–967	–1,511	–1,308	–1,422	–1,711	. . .
Monetary authorities	4 787 . .	20	. . .	. . .	. . .	. . .	. . .	. . .	. . .
of which: Short-term	4 789 . .	*20*	. . .	. . .	. . .	. . .	. . .	. . .	. . .
General government	4 790 . .	. . .	. . .	. . .	. . .	. . .	. . .	. . .	. . .
of which: Short-term	4 792 . .	. . .	. . .	. . .	. . .	. . .	. . .	. . .	. . .
Banks	4 793 . .	–147	–1,089	–967	–1,511	–1,308	–1,422	–1,711	. . .
of which: Short-term	4 795 . .	*–147*	*–787*	*–762*	*–997*	*–1,091*	*–1,197*	*–1,296*	. . .
Other sectors	4 796 . .	. . .	. . .	. . .	. . .	. . .	. . .	. . .	. . .
of which: Short-term	4 798 . .	. . .	. . .	. . .	. . .	. . .	. . .	. . .	. . .
E. RESERVE ASSETS	4 802 . .	–566	–839	–987	–449	–434	–259	–541	. . .
Monetary gold	4 812 . .	. . .	. . .	. . .	. . .	. . .	. . .	. . .	. . .
Special drawing rights	4 811 . .	. . .	. . .	. . .	. . .	. . .	. . .	. . .	. . .
Reserve position in the Fund	4 810 . .	. . .	. . .	. . .	. . .	. . .	. . .	. . .	. . .
Foreign exchange	4 803 . .	–566	–839	–987	–449	–434	–259	–541	. . .
Other claims	4 813 . .	. . .	. . .	. . .	. . .	. . .	. . .	. . .	. . .
NET ERRORS AND OMISSIONS	4 998 . .	**96**	**35**	**139**	**–95**	**153**	**–195**	**–192**	**. . .**

Part 3 of the *Yearbook* contains descriptions of the methodologies, compilation practices, and sources used to compile these data.

Table 1. ANALYTIC PRESENTATION, 1994–2001
(Millions of U.S. dollars)

	Code	1994	1995	1996	1997	1998	1999	2000	2001
A. Current Account [1]	4 993 Z.	**–710.9**	**–646.3**	**–510.9**	**–629.8**	**–956.5**	**–745.9**	**–480.3**	**. . .**
Goods: exports f.o.b	2 100 . .	519.4	682.5	764.1	715.3	589.5	542.9	665.7	. . .
Goods: imports f.o.b	3 100 . .	–1,309.3	–1,340.0	–1,213.1	–1,164.4	–1,365.3	–1,368.3	–1,339.8	. . .
Balance on Goods	4 100 . .	*–789.9*	*–657.5*	*–449.0*	*–449.1*	*–775.9*	*–825.4*	*–674.1*	. . .
Services: credit	2 200 . .	418.2	582.6	608.1	494.1	555.0	624.4	614.6	. . .
Services: debit	3 200 . .	–503.3	–799.4	–953.4	–797.3	–988.1	–762.3	–670.3	. . .
Balance on Goods and Services	4 991 . .	*–875.0*	*–874.2*	*–794.3*	*–752.4*	*–1,209.0*	*–963.3*	*–729.8*	. . .
Income: credit	2 300 . .	30.9	31.8	50.3	44.9	35.1	54.8	59.5	. . .
Income: debit	3 300 . .	–153.4	–142.0	–105.4	–168.2	–173.7	–127.6	–139.0	. . .
Balance on Goods, Services, and Income	4 992 . .	*–997.5*	*–984.5*	*–849.4*	*–875.7*	*–1,347.7*	*–1,036.0*	*–809.3*	. . .
Current transfers: credit	2 379 Z.	311.5	370.5	370.9	313.6	426.6	413.4	406.0	. . .
Current transfers: debit	3 379 . .	–25.0	–32.3	–32.3	–67.7	–35.5	–123.3	–77.0	. . .
B. Capital Account [1]	4 994 Z.	**262.6**	**190.9**	**191.0**	**360.6**	**422.9**	**322.5**	**331.7**	**. . .**
Capital account: credit	2 994 Z.	262.6	190.9	191.0	360.6	422.9	322.5	331.7	. . .
Capital account: debit	3 994 . .	. . .	. . .	. . .	. . .	. . .	. . .	. . .	. . .
Total, Groups A Plus B	4 981 . .	*–448.3*	*–455.4*	*–319.9*	*–269.2*	*–533.6*	*–423.5*	*–148.7*	. . .
C. Financial Account [1]	4 995 W.	**–91.7**	**66.7**	**–92.8**	**3.6**	**77.6**	**80.8**	**–123.8**	**. . .**
Direct investment abroad	4 505 . .	. . .	. . .	. . .	. . .	. . .	. . .	. . .	. . .
Direct investment in Tanzania	4 555 Z.	50.0	119.9	150.1	157.9	172.3	183.4	193.5	. . .
Portfolio investment assets	4 602 . .	. . .	. . .	. . .	. . .	. . .	. . .	. . .	. . .
Equity securities	4 610 . .	. . .	. . .	. . .	. . .	. . .	. . .	. . .	. . .
Debt securities	4 619 . .	. . .	. . .	. . .	. . .	. . .	. . .	. . .	. . .
Portfolio investment liabilities	4 652 Z.	. . .	. . .	. . .	. . .	. . .	. . .	. . .	. . .
Equity securities	4 660 . .	. . .	. . .	. . .	. . .	. . .	. . .	. . .	. . .
Debt securities	4 669 Z.	. . .	. . .	. . .	. . .	. . .	. . .	. . .	. . .
Financial derivatives	4 910 . .	. . .	. . .	. . .	. . .	. . .	. . .	. . .	. . .
Financial derivatives assets	4 900 . .	. . .	. . .	. . .	. . .	. . .	. . .	. . .	. . .
Financial derivatives liabilities	4 905 . .	. . .	. . .	. . .	. . .	. . .	. . .	. . .	. . .
Other investment assets	4 703 . .	11.9	–75.1	20.1	–85.0	–50.7	14.8	10.2	. . .
Monetary authorities	4 701 . .	. . .	. . .	. . .	. . .	. . .	. . .	. . .	. . .
General government	4 704 . .	. . .	. . .	. . .	. . .	. . .	. . .	. . .	. . .
Banks	4 705 . .	–75.6	–162.5	–19.6	–85.0	–50.7	14.8	10.2	. . .
Other sectors	4 728 . .	87.5	87.4	39.7	. . .	. . .	. . .	. . .	. . .
Other investment liabilities	4 753 W.	–153.6	21.8	–262.9	–69.3	–44.0	–117.5	–327.5	. . .
Monetary authorities	4 753 WA	11.9	5.9	14.9	24.6	–48.7	. . .	. . .	. . .
General government	4 753 ZB	–202.0	–71.2	–225.9	–32.4	. . .	–75.7	–320.6	. . .
Banks	4 753 ZC	6.7	22.9	–23.5	–67.6	–17.6	–1.4	29.2	. . .
Other sectors	4 753 ZD	29.8	64.2	–28.5	6.2	22.4	–40.4	–36.1	. . .
Total, Groups A Through C	4 983 . .	*–540.0*	*–388.8*	*–412.6*	*–265.6*	*–455.9*	*–342.7*	*–272.5*	. . .
D. Net Errors and Omissions	4 998 . .	**121.4**	**30.0**	**158.6**	**–31.9**	**–53.5**	**269.3**	**137.7**	**. . .**
Total, Groups A Through D	4 984 . .	*–418.6*	*–358.7*	*–254.0*	*–297.5*	*–509.4*	*–73.4*	*–134.8*	. . .
E. Reserves and Related Items	4 802 A.	**418.6**	**358.7**	**254.0**	**297.5**	**509.4**	**73.4**	**134.8**	**. . .**
Reserve assets	4 802 . .	–122.8	43.3	–195.4	–206.9	22.3	–280.6	–205.8	. . .
Use of Fund credit and loans	4 766 . .	–15.4	–19.6	15.7	53.2	9.6	51.5	27.6	. . .
Exceptional financing	4 920 . .	556.8	335.1	433.8	451.2	477.5	302.5	312.9	. . .
Conversion rates: Tanzania shillings per U.S. dollar	0 101 . .	**509.63**	**574.76**	**579.98**	**612.12**	**664.67**	**744.76**	**800.41**	**876.41**

[1] Excludes components that have been classified in the categories of Group E.

Table 2. STANDARD PRESENTATION, 1994–2001
(Millions of U.S. dollars)

	Code	1994	1995	1996	1997	1998	1999	2000	2001
CURRENT ACCOUNT	4 993 . .	**–637.4**	**–589.8**	**–412.8**	**–473.4**	**–787.8**	**–647.4**	**–298.4**	. . .
A. GOODS	4 100 . .	–789.9	–657.5	–449.0	–449.1	–775.9	–825.4	–674.1	. . .
Credit	2 100 . .	**519.4**	**682.5**	**764.1**	**715.3**	**589.5**	**542.9**	**665.7**	. . .
General merchandise: exports f.o.b.	2 110 . .	519.4	682.5	764.1	715.3	589.5	542.9	665.7	. . .
Goods for processing: exports f.o.b.	2 150 . .	. . .	. . .	. . .	. . .	. . .	. . .	. . .	. . .
Repairs on goods	2 160 . .	. . .	. . .	. . .	. . .	. . .	. . .	. . .	. . .
Goods procured in ports by carriers	2 170 . .	. . .	. . .	. . .	. . .	. . .	. . .	. . .	. . .
Nonmonetary gold	2 180 . .	. . .	. . .	. . .	. . .	. . .	. . .	. . .	. . .
Debit	3 100 . .	**–1,309.3**	**–1,340.0**	**–1,213.1**	**–1,164.4**	**–1,365.3**	**–1,368.3**	**–1,339.8**	. . .
General merchandise: imports f.o.b.	3 110 . .	–1,309.3	–1,340.0	–1,213.1	–1,164.4	–1,365.3	–1,368.3	–1,339.8	. . .
Goods for processing: imports f.o.b.	3 150 . .	. . .	. . .	. . .	. . .	. . .	. . .	. . .	. . .
Repairs on goods	3 160 . .	. . .	. . .	. . .	. . .	. . .	. . .	. . .	. . .
Goods procured in ports by carriers	3 170 . .	. . .	. . .	. . .	. . .	. . .	. . .	. . .	. . .
Nonmonetary gold	3 180 . .	. . .	. . .	. . .	. . .	. . .	. . .	. . .	. . .
B. SERVICES	4 200 . .	–85.1	–216.8	–345.3	–303.2	–433.1	–137.9	–55.7	. . .
Total credit	2 200 . .	*418.2*	*582.6*	*608.1*	*494.1*	*555.0*	*624.4*	*614.6*	. . .
Total debit	3 200 . .	*–503.3*	*–799.4*	*–953.4*	*–797.3*	*–988.1*	*–762.3*	*–670.3*	. . .
Transportation services, credit	2 205 . .	**6.7**	**1.7**	**69.7**	**59.5**	**60.3**	**54.5**	**56.8**	. . .
Passenger	2 850 . .	. . .	. . .	. . .	*3.7*	*5.1*	*2.6*	*4.2*	. . .
Freight	2 851 . .	*6.7*	*1.7*	*69.7*	*5.4*	*51.0*	*45.4*	*40.7*	. . .
Other	2 852 . .	. . .	. . .	. . .	*50.4*	*4.1*	*6.4*	*11.9*	. . .
Sea transport, passenger	2 207 . .	. . .	. . .	. . .	. . .	. . .	. . .	. . .	. . .
Sea transport, freight	2 208 . .	6.7	1.7	69.7	5.4	51.0	45.4	40.7	. . .
Sea transport, other	2 209 . .	. . .	. . .	. . .	. . .	. . .	. . .	. . .	. . .
Air transport, passenger	2 211 . .	. . .	. . .	. . .	3.7	5.1	2.6	4.2	. . .
Air transport, freight	2 212 . .	. . .	. . .	. . .	. . .	. . .	. . .	. . .	. . .
Air transport, other	2 213 . .	. . .	. . .	. . .	. . .	. . .	. . .	. . .	. . .
Other transport, passenger	2 215 . .	. . .	. . .	. . .	. . .	. . .	. . .	. . .	. . .
Other transport, freight	2 216 . .	. . .	. . .	. . .	. . .	. . .	. . .	. . .	. . .
Other transport, other	2 217 . .	. . .	. . .	. . .	50.4	4.1	6.4	11.9	. . .
Transportation services, debit	3 205 . .	**–176.1**	**–217.0**	**–220.7**	**–205.7**	**–209.1**	**–220.8**	**–224.6**	. . .
Passenger	3 850 . .	. . .	. . .	. . .	*–17.0*	*–28.5*	*–27.4*	*–32.4*	. . .
Freight	3 851 . .	*–176.1*	*–217.0*	*–220.7*	*–158.5*	*–172.1*	*–190.8*	*–186.2*	. . .
Other	3 852 . .	. . .	. . .	. . .	*–30.2*	*–8.6*	*–2.5*	*–5.9*	. . .
Sea transport, passenger	3 207 . .	. . .	. . .	. . .	. . .	. . .	. . .	. . .	. . .
Sea transport, freight	3 208 . .	–176.1	–217.0	–220.7	–158.5	–172.1	–190.8	–186.2	. . .
Sea transport, other	3 209 . .	. . .	. . .	. . .	. . .	. . .	. . .	. . .	. . .
Air transport, passenger	3 211 . .	. . .	. . .	. . .	–17.0	–28.5	–27.4	–32.4	. . .
Air transport, freight	3 212 . .	. . .	. . .	. . .	. . .	. . .	. . .	. . .	. . .
Air transport, other	3 213 . .	. . .	. . .	. . .	. . .	. . .	. . .	. . .	. . .
Other transport, passenger	3 215 . .	. . .	. . .	. . .	. . .	. . .	. . .	. . .	. . .
Other transport, freight	3 216 . .	. . .	. . .	. . .	. . .	. . .	. . .	. . .	. . .
Other transport, other	3 217 . .	. . .	. . .	. . .	–30.2	–8.6	–2.5	–5.9	. . .
Travel, credit	2 236 . .	**183.1**	**501.6**	**473.1**	**339.5**	**399.2**	**466.2**	**376.6**	. . .
Business travel	2 237 . .	. . .	. . .	. . .	. . .	. . .	. . .	. . .	. . .
Personal travel	2 240 . .	. . .	. . .	. . .	. . .	. . .	466.2	376.6	. . .
Travel, debit	3 236 . .	**–206.3**	**–360.3**	**–412.3**	**–407.4**	**–493.4**	**–367.5**	**–337.2**	. . .
Business travel	3 237 . .	. . .	. . .	. . .	. . .	. . .	–367.5	–337.2	. . .
Personal travel	3 240 . .	. . .	. . .	. . .	. . .	. . .	. . .	. . .	. . .
Other services, credit	2 200 BA	**228.4**	**79.3**	**65.2**	**95.2**	**95.5**	**103.8**	**181.2**	. . .
Communications	2 245 . .	. . .	16.5	19.3	23.7	16.9	22.2	26.7	. . .
Construction	2 249 . .	. . .	2.0	3.2	11.4	14.1	24.5	22.9	. . .
Insurance	2 253 . .	.8	.1	2.6	1.5	.3	6.5	13.0	. . .
Financial	2 260 . .	. . .	. . .	16.1	12.3	21.5	25.5	20.6	. . .
Computer and information	2 262 . .	. . .	. . .	. . .	. . .	–.3	2.7	.4	. . .
Royalties and licence fees	2 266 . .	. . .	.2	. . .	3.4	.9	.5	.3	. . .
Other business services	2 268 . .	219.9	44.3	17.8	18.5	18.0	21.0	97.2	. . .
Personal, cultural, and recreational	2 287 . .	. . .	. . .	. . .	. . .	2.8	1.0	.1	. . .
Government, n.i.e.	2 291 . .	7.7	16.3	6.2	24.5	21.2	. . .	. . .	. . .
Other services, debit	3 200 BA	**–121.0**	**–222.0**	**–320.4**	**–184.3**	**–285.5**	**–174.0**	**–108.5**	. . .
Communications	3 245 . .	. . .	–17.6	–17.9	–15.1	–9.0	–4.8	–6.2	. . .
Construction	3 249 . .	. . .	–3.1	–3.0	–3.7	–.3	–.8	–1.6	. . .
Insurance	3 253 . .	–19.6	–20.0	–32.9	–21.2	–23.1	–31.1	–36.5	. . .
Financial	3 260 . .	. . .	. . .	–.7	–.1	–20.9	–25.8	–17.0	. . .
Computer and information	3 262 . .	. . .	. . .	. . .	. . .	–1.7	–3.2	–1.6	. . .
Royalties and licence fees	3 266 . .	. . .	. . .	. . .	–.3	–4.7	–4.0	–3.7	. . .
Other business services	3 268 . .	–37.0	–110.7	–195.4	–55.4	–122.1	–104.2	–41.8	. . .
Personal, cultural, and recreational	3 287 . .	. . .	. . .	. . .	. . .	–.4	–.1	–.1	. . .
Government, n.i.e.	3 291 . .	–64.5	–70.5	–70.6	–88.5	–103.3	. . .	. . .	. . .

Table 2 (Continued). STANDARD PRESENTATION, 1994–2001
(Millions of U.S. dollars)

	Code	1994	1995	1996	1997	1998	1999	2000	2001
C. INCOME	4 300	-122.5	-110.3	-55.1	-123.3	-138.7	-72.7	-79.5	...
Total credit	2 300	*30.9*	*31.8*	*50.3*	*44.9*	*35.1*	*54.8*	*59.5*	...
Total debit	3 300	*-153.4*	*-142.0*	*-105.4*	*-168.2*	*-173.7*	*-127.6*	*-139.0*	...
Compensation of employees, credit	2 310	...	**.8**	**19.3**	**1.6**	**11.5**	**7.2**	**8.1**	...
Compensation of employees, debit	3 310	...	**-.5**	**-.8**	**-.6**	**-4.0**	**-2.7**	**-4.8**	...
Investment income, credit	2 320	**30.9**	**30.9**	**30.9**	**43.3**	**23.6**	**47.6**	**51.4**	...
Direct investment income	2 330	...	...	...	2.0	7.3	11.7	9.0	...
Dividends and distributed branch profits	2 332	...	...	...	...	...	...	...	...
Reinvested earnings and undistributed branch profits	2 333	...	...	...	...	...	...	...	...
Income on debt (interest)	2 334	...	...	...	...	...	11.7	9.0	...
Portfolio investment income	2 339	...	...	...	...	.1	...	...	...
Income on equity	2 340	...	...	...	...	.1	...	...	...
Income on bonds and notes	2 350	...	...	...	...	...	...	...	...
Income on money market instruments	2 360	...	...	...	...	...	...	...	...
Other investment income	2 370	30.9	30.9	30.9	41.3	16.2	35.9	42.5	...
Investment income, debit	3 320	**-153.4**	**-141.5**	**-104.6**	**-167.5**	**-169.7**	**-124.9**	**-134.2**	...
Direct investment income	3 330	...	-1.6	-2.0	-3.2	-8.2	-8.9	-13.3	...
Dividends and distributed branch profits	3 332	...	...	...	...	...	...	...	...
Reinvested earnings and undistributed branch profits	3 333	...	...	...	...	...	...	...	...
Income on debt (interest)	3 334	...	...	...	...	...	-8.9	-13.3	...
Portfolio investment income	3 339	...	...	...	...	-36.9	...	...	...
Income on equity	3 340	...	...	...	...	-36.9	...	...	...
Income on bonds and notes	3 350	...	...	...	...	...	...	...	...
Income on money market instruments	3 360	...	...	...	...	...	...	...	...
Other investment income	3 370	-153.4	-139.9	-102.6	-164.3	-124.6	-116.0	-120.9	...
D. CURRENT TRANSFERS	4 379	360.1	394.7	436.7	402.2	559.8	388.7	510.9	...
Credit	2 379	**385.1**	**427.0**	**469.0**	**470.0**	**595.3**	**511.9**	**587.9**	...
General government	2 380	288.6	292.4	334.2	371.3	426.6	350.1	440.2	...
Other sectors	2 390	96.5	134.6	134.7	98.6	168.7	161.8	147.7	...
Workers' remittances	2 391	...	...	...	...	...	...	...	...
Other current transfers	2 392	96.5	134.6	134.7	98.6	168.7	161.8	147.7	...
Debit	3 379	**-25.0**	**-32.3**	**-32.3**	**-67.7**	**-35.5**	**-123.3**	**-77.0**	...
General government	3 380	-10.0	-10.0	-10.0	-10.7	-8.7	...	...	...
Other sectors	3 390	-15.0	-22.3	-22.3	-57.0	-26.8	-123.3	-77.0	...
Workers' remittances	3 391	...	...	...	...	...	...	...	...
Other current transfers	3 392	-15.0	-22.3	-22.3	-57.0	-26.8	-123.3	-77.0	...
CAPITAL AND FINANCIAL ACCOUNT	4 996	**516.0**	**559.7**	**254.2**	**505.3**	**841.3**	**378.1**	**160.7**	...
CAPITAL ACCOUNT	4 994	**286.4**	**190.9**	**191.0**	**360.6**	**422.9**	**410.2**	**462.6**	...
Total credit	2 994	*286.4*	*190.9*	*191.0*	*360.6*	*422.9*	*410.2*	*462.6*	...
Total debit	3 994	...	...	...	...	...	...	...	...
Capital transfers, credit	2 400	**286.4**	**190.9**	**191.0**	**360.6**	**422.9**	**410.2**	**462.6**	...
General government	2 401	280.8	185.1	185.3	349.6	412.3	393.9	446.9	...
Debt forgiveness	2 402	280.8	185.1	185.3	193.7	147.4	87.7	131.0	...
Other capital transfers	2 410	...	...	...	155.9	264.9	306.2	315.9	...
Other sectors	2 430	5.6	5.7	5.7	11.0	10.6	16.3	15.8	...
Migrants' transfers	2 431	...	...	...	...	...	...	...	...
Debt forgiveness	2 432	...	...	...	...	...	...	...	...
Other capital transfers	2 440	5.6	5.7	5.7	11.0	10.6	16.3	15.8	...
Capital transfers, debit	3 400	...	...	...	...	...	...	...	...
General government	3 401	...	...	...	...	...	...	...	...
Debt forgiveness	3 402	...	...	...	...	...	...	...	...
Other capital transfers	3 410	...	...	...	...	...	...	...	...
Other sectors	3 430	...	...	...	...	...	...	...	...
Migrants' transfers	3 431	...	...	...	...	...	...	...	...
Debt forgiveness	3 432	...	...	...	...	...	...	...	...
Other capital transfers	3 440	...	...	...	...	...	...	...	...
Nonproduced nonfinancial assets, credit	2 480	...	...	...	...	...	...	...	...
Nonproduced nonfinancial assets, debit	3 480	...	...	...	...	...	...	...	...

Table 2 (Continued). STANDARD PRESENTATION, 1994–2001
(Millions of U.S. dollars)

	Code	1994	1995	1996	1997	1998	1999	2000	2001
FINANCIAL ACCOUNT	4 995 . .	**229.6**	**368.9**	**63.1**	**144.7**	**418.4**	**–32.1**	**–301.9**	**. . .**
A. DIRECT INVESTMENT	4 500 . .	50.0	119.9	150.1	157.9	172.3	183.4	193.5	. . .
Direct investment abroad	4 505 . .	**. . .**	**. . .**	**. . .**	**. . .**	**. . .**	**. . .**	**. . .**	**. . .**
Equity capital	4 510 . .	. . .	. . .	. . .	. . .	. . .	. . .	. . .	. . .
Claims on affiliated enterprises	4 515 . .	. . .	. . .	. . .	. . .	. . .	. . .	. . .	. . .
Liabilities to affiliated enterprises	4 520 . .	. . .	. . .	. . .	. . .	. . .	. . .	. . .	. . .
Reinvested earnings	4 525 . .	. . .	. . .	. . .	. . .	. . .	. . .	. . .	. . .
Other capital	4 530 . .	. . .	. . .	. . .	. . .	. . .	. . .	. . .	. . .
Claims on affiliated enterprises	4 535 . .	. . .	. . .	. . .	. . .	. . .	. . .	. . .	. . .
Liabilities to affiliated enterprises	4 540 . .	. . .	. . .	. . .	. . .	. . .	. . .	. . .	. . .
Direct investment in Tanzania	4 555 . .	**50.0**	**119.9**	**150.1**	**157.9**	**172.3**	**183.4**	**193.5**	**. . .**
Equity capital	4 560 . .	50.0	119.9	150.1	157.9	172.3	183.4	193.5	. . .
Claims on direct investors	4 565 . .	. . .	. . .	. . .	. . .	. . .	. . .	. . .	. . .
Liabilities to direct investors	4 570 . .	. . .	. . .	. . .	. . .	. . .	183.4	193.5	. . .
Reinvested earnings	4 575 . .	. . .	. . .	. . .	. . .	. . .	. . .	. . .	. . .
Other capital	4 580 . .	. . .	. . .	. . .	. . .	. . .	. . .	. . .	. . .
Claims on direct investors	4 585 . .	. . .	. . .	. . .	. . .	. . .	. . .	. . .	. . .
Liabilities to direct investors	4 590 . .	. . .	. . .	. . .	. . .	. . .	. . .	. . .	. . .
B. PORTFOLIO INVESTMENT	4 600 . .	. . .	. . .	. . .	. . .	. . .	. . .	. . .	. . .
Assets	4 602 . .	**. . .**	**. . .**	**. . .**	**. . .**	**. . .**	**. . .**	**. . .**	**. . .**
Equity securities	4 610 . .	. . .	. . .	. . .	. . .	. . .	. . .	. . .	. . .
Monetary authorities	4 611 . .	. . .	. . .	. . .	. . .	. . .	. . .	. . .	. . .
General government	4 612 . .	. . .	. . .	. . .	. . .	. . .	. . .	. . .	. . .
Banks	4 613 . .	. . .	. . .	. . .	. . .	. . .	. . .	. . .	. . .
Other sectors	4 614 . .	. . .	. . .	. . .	. . .	. . .	. . .	. . .	. . .
Debt securities	4 619 . .	. . .	. . .	. . .	. . .	. . .	. . .	. . .	. . .
Bonds and notes	4 620 . .	. . .	. . .	. . .	. . .	. . .	. . .	. . .	. . .
Monetary authorities	4 621 . .	. . .	. . .	. . .	. . .	. . .	. . .	. . .	. . .
General government	4 622 . .	. . .	. . .	. . .	. . .	. . .	. . .	. . .	. . .
Banks	4 623 . .	. . .	. . .	. . .	. . .	. . .	. . .	. . .	. . .
Other sectors	4 624 . .	. . .	. . .	. . .	. . .	. . .	. . .	. . .	. . .
Money market instruments	4 630 . .	. . .	. . .	. . .	. . .	. . .	. . .	. . .	. . .
Monetary authorities	4 631 . .	. . .	. . .	. . .	. . .	. . .	. . .	. . .	. . .
General government	4 632 . .	. . .	. . .	. . .	. . .	. . .	. . .	. . .	. . .
Banks	4 633 . .	. . .	. . .	. . .	. . .	. . .	. . .	. . .	. . .
Other sectors	4 634 . .	. . .	. . .	. . .	. . .	. . .	. . .	. . .	. . .
Liabilities	4 652 . .	**. . .**	**. . .**	**. . .**	**. . .**	**. . .**	**. . .**	**. . .**	**. . .**
Equity securities	4 660 . .	. . .	. . .	. . .	. . .	. . .	. . .	. . .	. . .
Banks	4 663 . .	. . .	. . .	. . .	. . .	. . .	. . .	. . .	. . .
Other sectors	4 664 . .	. . .	. . .	. . .	. . .	. . .	. . .	. . .	. . .
Debt securities	4 669 . .	. . .	. . .	. . .	. . .	. . .	. . .	. . .	. . .
Bonds and notes	4 670 . .	. . .	. . .	. . .	. . .	. . .	. . .	. . .	. . .
Monetary authorities	4 671 . .	. . .	. . .	. . .	. . .	. . .	. . .	. . .	. . .
General government	4 672 . .	. . .	. . .	. . .	. . .	. . .	. . .	. . .	. . .
Banks	4 673 . .	. . .	. . .	. . .	. . .	. . .	. . .	. . .	. . .
Other sectors	4 674 . .	. . .	. . .	. . .	. . .	. . .	. . .	. . .	. . .
Money market instruments	4 680 . .	. . .	. . .	. . .	. . .	. . .	. . .	. . .	. . .
Monetary authorities	4 681 . .	. . .	. . .	. . .	. . .	. . .	. . .	. . .	. . .
General government	4 682 . .	. . .	. . .	. . .	. . .	. . .	. . .	. . .	. . .
Banks	4 683 . .	. . .	. . .	. . .	. . .	. . .	. . .	. . .	. . .
Other sectors	4 684 . .	. . .	. . .	. . .	. . .	. . .	. . .	. . .	. . .
C. FINANCIAL DERIVATIVES	4 910 . .	. . .	. . .	. . .	. . .	. . .	. . .	. . .	. . .
Monetary authorities	4 911 . .	. . .	. . .	. . .	. . .	. . .	. . .	. . .	. . .
General government	4 912 . .	. . .	. . .	. . .	. . .	. . .	. . .	. . .	. . .
Banks	4 913 . .	. . .	. . .	. . .	. . .	. . .	. . .	. . .	. . .
Other sectors	4 914 . .	. . .	. . .	. . .	. . .	. . .	. . .	. . .	. . .
Assets	4 900 . .	**. . .**	**. . .**	**. . .**	**. . .**	**. . .**	**. . .**	**. . .**	**. . .**
Monetary authorities	4 901 . .	. . .	. . .	. . .	. . .	. . .	. . .	. . .	. . .
General government	4 902 . .	. . .	. . .	. . .	. . .	. . .	. . .	. . .	. . .
Banks	4 903 . .	. . .	. . .	. . .	. . .	. . .	. . .	. . .	. . .
Other sectors	4 904 . .	. . .	. . .	. . .	. . .	. . .	. . .	. . .	. . .
Liabilities	4 905 . .	**. . .**	**. . .**	**. . .**	**. . .**	**. . .**	**. . .**	**. . .**	**. . .**
Monetary authorities	4 906 . .	. . .	. . .	. . .	. . .	. . .	. . .	. . .	. . .
General government	4 907 . .	. . .	. . .	. . .	. . .	. . .	. . .	. . .	. . .
Banks	4 908 . .	. . .	. . .	. . .	. . .	. . .	. . .	. . .	. . .
Other sectors	4 909 . .	. . .	. . .	. . .	. . .	. . .	. . .	. . .	. . .

Table 2 (Concluded). STANDARD PRESENTATION, 1994–2001
(Millions of U.S. dollars)

	Code	1994	1995	1996	1997	1998	1999	2000	2001
D. OTHER INVESTMENT	4 700 . .	302.4	205.7	108.5	193.7	223.8	65.1	–289.7	. . .
Assets	4 703 . .	**11.9**	**–75.1**	**20.1**	**–85.0**	**–50.7**	**14.8**	**10.2**	. . .
Trade credits	4 706 . .	. . .	. . .	. . .	. . .	. . .	. . .	. . .	. . .
General government	4 707 . .	. . .	. . .	. . .	. . .	. . .	. . .	. . .	. . .
of which: Short-term	4 709 . .	. . .	. . .	. . .	. . .	. . .	. . .	. . .	. . .
Other sectors	4 710 . .	. . .	. . .	. . .	. . .	. . .	. . .	. . .	. . .
of which: Short-term	4 712 . .	. . .	. . .	. . .	. . .	. . .	. . .	. . .	. . .
Loans	4 714 . .	. . .	. . .	. . .	. . .	. . .	. . .	. . .	. . .
Monetary authorities	4 715 . .	. . .	. . .	. . .	. . .	. . .	. . .	. . .	. . .
of which: Short-term	4 718 . .	. . .	. . .	. . .	. . .	. . .	. . .	. . .	. . .
General government	4 719 . .	. . .	. . .	. . .	. . .	. . .	. . .	. . .	. . .
of which: Short-term	4 721 . .	. . .	. . .	. . .	. . .	. . .	. . .	. . .	. . .
Banks	4 722 . .	. . .	. . .	. . .	. . .	. . .	. . .	. . .	. . .
of which: Short-term	4 724 . .	. . .	. . .	. . .	. . .	. . .	. . .	. . .	. . .
Other sectors	4 725 . .	. . .	. . .	. . .	. . .	. . .	. . .	. . .	. . .
of which: Short-term	4 727 . .	. . .	. . .	. . .	. . .	. . .	. . .	. . .	. . .
Currency and deposits	4 730 . .	11.9	–75.1	20.1	–85.0	–50.7	14.8	10.2	. . .
Monetary authorities	4 731 . .	. . .	. . .	. . .	. . .	. . .	. . .	. . .	. . .
General government	4 732 . .	. . .	. . .	. . .	. . .	. . .	. . .	. . .	. . .
Banks	4 733 . .	–75.6	–162.5	–19.6	–85.0	–50.7	14.8	10.2	. . .
Other sectors	4 734 . .	87.5	87.4	39.7	. . .	. . .	. . .	. . .	. . .
Other assets	4 736 . .	. . .	. . .	. . .	. . .	. . .	. . .	. . .	. . .
Monetary authorities	4 737 . .	. . .	. . .	. . .	. . .	. . .	. . .	. . .	. . .
of which: Short-term	4 739 . .	. . .	. . .	. . .	. . .	. . .	. . .	. . .	. . .
General government	4 740 . .	. . .	. . .	. . .	. . .	. . .	. . .	. . .	. . .
of which: Short-term	4 742 . .	. . .	. . .	. . .	. . .	. . .	. . .	. . .	. . .
Banks	4 743 . .	. . .	. . .	. . .	. . .	. . .	. . .	. . .	. . .
of which: Short-term	4 745 . .	. . .	. . .	. . .	. . .	. . .	. . .	. . .	. . .
Other sectors	4 746 . .	. . .	. . .	. . .	. . .	. . .	. . .	. . .	. . .
of which: Short-term	4 748 . .	. . .	. . .	. . .	. . .	. . .	. . .	. . .	. . .
Liabilities	4 753 . .	**290.5**	**280.8**	**88.4**	**278.7**	**274.5**	**50.2**	**–299.9**	. . .
Trade credits	4 756 . .	16.0	25.6	11.6	11.6	12.0	12.6	12.8	. . .
General government	4 757 . .	. . .	. . .	. . .	. . .	. . .	. . .	. . .	. . .
of which: Short-term	4 759 . .	. . .	. . .	. . .	. . .	. . .	. . .	. . .	. . .
Other sectors	4 760 . .	16.0	25.6	11.6	11.6	12.0	12.6	12.8	. . .
of which: Short-term	4 762 . .	*16.0*	*25.6*	*11.6*	*11.6*	*12.0*	*12.6*	*12.8*	. . .
Loans	4 764 . .	–40.5	–21.8	–247.9	104.2	179.3	48.7	–343.4	. . .
Monetary authorities	4 765 . .	3.2	–10.3	39.0	53.2	9.6	167.7	27.6	. . .
of which: Use of Fund credit and loans from the Fund	4 766 . .	*–15.4*	*–19.6*	*15.7*	*53.2*	*9.6*	*51.5*	*27.6*	. . .
of which: Short-term	4 768 . .	*18.6*	*9.3*	*23.3*	. . .	. . .	. . .	. . .	. . .
General government	4 769 . .	–57.5	–71.2	–225.9	127.2	172.9	–68.7	–320.7	. . .
of which: Short-term	4 771 . .	. . .	. . .	. . .	. . .	. . .	. . .	. . .	. . .
Banks	4 772 . .	. . .	21.1	–20.9	–70.2	–13.2	.2	–.9	. . .
of which: Short-term	4 774 . .	. . .	. . .	. . .	*–70.2*	*–14.0*	. . .	. . .	. . .
Other sectors	4 775 . .	13.8	38.6	–40.1	–5.9	10.1	–50.5	–49.4	. . .
of which: Short-term	4 777 . .	. . .	. . .	. . .	*11.6*	*12.1*	. . .	. . .	. . .
Currency and deposits	4 780 . .	18.6	7.7	12.4	27.1	–53.1	–1.6	30.1	. . .
Monetary authorities	4 781 . .	11.9	5.9	14.9	24.6	–48.7	. . .	. . .	. . .
General government	4 782 . .	. . .	. . .	. . .	. . .	. . .	. . .	. . .	. . .
Banks	4 783 . .	6.7	1.8	–2.6	2.6	–4.4	–1.6	30.1	. . .
Other sectors	4 784 . .	. . .	. . .	. . .	. . .	. . .	. . .	. . .	. . .
Other liabilities	4 786 . .	296.4	269.2	312.3	135.7	136.2	–9.5	.6	. . .
Monetary authorities	4 787 . .	. . .	. . .	. . .	. . .	. . .	. . .	. . .	. . .
of which: Short-term	4 789 . .	. . .	. . .	. . .	. . .	. . .	. . .	. . .	. . .
General government	4 790 . .	264.1	250.7	275.4	135.2	136.0	–7.0	.1	. . .
of which: Short-term	4 792 . .	*264.1*	*250.7*	*275.4*	*135.2*	*136.0*	*–7.0*	*.1*	. . .
Banks	4 793 . .	. . .	. . .	. . .	. . .	. . .	. . .	. . .	. . .
of which: Short-term	4 795 . .	. . .	. . .	. . .	. . .	. . .	. . .	. . .	. . .
Other sectors	4 796 . .	32.3	18.5	36.9	.5	.2	–2.6	.4	. . .
of which: Short-term	4 798 . .	*32.3*	*18.5*	*36.9*	*.5*	*.2*	*–2.6*	*.4*	. . .
E. RESERVE ASSETS	4 802 . .	–122.8	43.3	–195.4	–206.9	22.3	–280.6	–205.8	. . .
Monetary gold	4 812 . .	7.7	7.0	–5.8	–.7	–2.8	–5.2	–.4	. . .
Special drawing rights	4 811 . .	. . .	–.1	–.1	. . .	–.2	.1	.1	. . .
Reserve position in the Fund	4 810 . .	. . .	. . .	. . .	. . .	. . .	. . .	. . .	. . .
Foreign exchange	4 803 . .	–133.4	36.6	–189.1	–206.1	24.5	–275.3	–205.5	. . .
Other claims	4 813 . .	2.8	–.3	–.4	–.1	.8	–.1	.1	. . .
NET ERRORS AND OMISSIONS	4 998 . .	**121.4**	**30.0**	**158.6**	**–31.9**	**–53.5**	**269.3**	**137.7**	. . .

Part 3 of the *Yearbook* contains descriptions of the methodologies, compilation practices, and sources used to compile these data.

Table 3. INTERNATIONAL INVESTMENT POSITION (End-period stocks), 1994–2001

(Millions of U.S. dollars)

	Code	1994	1995	1996	1997	1998	1999	2000	2001
ASSETS	8 995 C.	477.0	578.8	744.4	995.6	991.4	1,153.0	1,485.7	...
Direct investment abroad	8 505 . .	...	...	...	...	...	...	...	...
Equity capital and reinvested earnings	8 506 . .	...	...	...	...	...	...	...	...
Claims on affiliated enterprises	8 507 . .	...	...	...	...	...	...	...	...
Liabilities to affiliated enterprises	8 508 . .	...	...	...	...	...	...	...	...
Other capital	8 530 . .	...	...	...	...	...	...	...	...
Claims on affiliated enterprises	8 535 . .	...	...	...	...	...	...	...	...
Liabilities to affiliated enterprises	8 540 . .	...	...	...	...	...	...	...	...
Portfolio investment	8 602 . .	...	...	...	...	...	...	...	...
Equity securities	8 610 . .	...	...	...	...	...	...	...	...
Monetary authorities	8 611 . .	...	...	...	...	...	...	...	...
General government	8 612 . .	...	...	...	...	...	...	...	...
Banks	8 613 . .	...	...	...	...	...	...	...	...
Other sectors	8 614 . .	...	...	...	...	...	...	...	...
Debt securities	8 619 . .	...	...	...	...	...	...	...	...
Bonds and notes	8 620 . .	...	...	...	...	...	...	...	...
Monetary authorities	8 621 . .	...	...	...	...	...	...	...	...
General government	8 622 . .	...	...	...	...	...	...	...	...
Banks	8 623 . .	...	...	...	...	...	...	...	...
Other sectors	8 624 . .	...	...	...	...	...	...	...	...
Money market instruments	8 630 . .	...	...	...	...	...	...	...	...
Monetary authorities	8 631 . .	...	...	...	...	...	...	...	...
General government	8 632 . .	...	...	...	...	...	...	...	...
Banks	8 633 . .	...	...	...	...	...	...	...	...
Other sectors	8 634 . .	...	...	...	...	...	...	...	...
Financial derivatives	8 900 . .	...	...	...	...	...	...	...	...
Monetary authorities	8 901 . .	...	...	...	...	...	...	...	...
General government	8 902 . .	...	...	...	...	...	...	...	...
Banks	8 903 . .	...	...	...	...	...	...	...	...
Other sectors	8 904 . .	...	...	...	...	...	...	...	...
Other investment	8 703 . .	**146.6**	**309.2**	**304.8**	**373.9**	**392.4**	**377.6**	**511.7**	...
Trade credits	8 706 . .	...	...	...	...	...	...	...	...
General government	8 707 . .	...	...	...	...	...	...	...	...
of which: Short-term	8 709 . .	...	...	...	...	...	...	...	...
Other sectors	8 710 . .	...	...	...	...	...	...	...	...
of which: Short-term	8 712 . .	...	...	...	...	...	...	...	...
Loans	8 714 . .	...	...	...	...	...	...	...	...
Monetary authorities	8 715 . .	...	...	...	...	...	...	...	...
of which: Short-term	8 718 . .	...	...	...	...	...	...	...	...
General government	8 719 . .	...	...	...	...	...	...	...	...
of which: Short-term	8 721 . .	...	...	...	...	...	...	...	...
Banks	8 722 . .	...	...	...	...	...	...	...	...
of which: Short-term	8 724 . .	...	...	...	...	...	...	...	...
Other sectors	8 725 . .	...	...	...	...	...	...	...	...
of which: Short-term	8 727 . .	...	...	...	...	...	...	...	...
Currency and deposits	8 730 . .	146.6	309.2	304.8	373.9	392.4	377.6	511.7	...
Monetary authorities	8 731 . .	...	...	...	...	...	...	...	...
General government	8 732 . .	...	...	...	...	...	...	...	...
Banks	8 733 . .	146.6	309.2	304.8	373.9	392.4	377.6	511.7	...
Other sectors	8 734 . .	...	...	...	...	...	...	...	...
Other assets	8 736 . .	...	...	...	...	...	...	...	...
Monetary authorities	8 737 . .	...	...	...	...	...	...	...	...
of which: Short-term	8 739 . .	...	...	...	...	...	...	...	...
General government	8 740 . .	...	...	...	...	...	...	...	...
of which: Short-term	8 742 . .	...	...	...	...	...	...	...	...
Banks	8 743 . .	...	...	...	...	...	...	...	...
of which: Short-term	8 745 . .	...	...	...	...	...	...	...	...
Other sectors	8 746 . .	...	...	...	...	...	...	...	...
of which: Short-term	8 748 . .	...	...	...	...	...	...	...	...
Reserve assets	8 802 . .	**330.4**	**269.6**	**439.6**	**621.7**	**599.0**	**775.4**	**974.1**	...
Monetary gold	8 812 . .	37.3	28.1	31.6	30.9	31.0	31.4	31.6	...
Special drawing rights	8 811 . .	...	.1	.1	.1	.4	.3	.1	...
Reserve position in the Fund	8 810 . .	14.6	14.8	14.3	13.5	14.0	13.7	13.0	...
Foreign exchange	8 803 . .	278.5	226.6	393.5	577.2	553.3	729.7	929.2	...
Other claims	8 813 . .	...	...	...	...	.2	.3	.2	...

Table 3 (Concluded). INTERNATIONAL INVESTMENT POSITION (End–period stocks), 1994–2001

(Millions of U.S. dollars)

	Code	1994	1995	1996	1997	1998	1999	2000	2001
LIABILITIES	8 995 D.	9,037.5	9,645.7	9,965.9	7,271.3	7,229.0	7,648.1	7,614.6	...
Direct investment in Tanzania	8 555 ..	**71.0**	**224.2**	**351.7**	**490.2**	**619.0**	**700.0**	**887.7**	...
Equity capital and reinvested earnings	8 556 ..	71.0	224.2	351.7	490.2	619.0	700.0	887.7	...
Claims on direct investors	8 557 ..	...	...	...	...	...	...	...	...
Liabilities to direct investors	8 558 ..	71.0	224.2	351.7	490.2	619.0	700.0	887.7	...
Other capital	8 580 ..	...	...	...	...	...	...	...	...
Claims on direct investors	8 585 ..	...	...	...	...	...	...	...	...
Liabilities to direct investors	8 590 ..	...	...	...	...	...	...	...	...
Portfolio investment	8 652 ..	...	...	...	...	...	...	...	...
Equity securities	8 660 ..	...	...	...	...	...	...	...	...
Banks	8 663 ..	...	...	...	...	...	...	...	...
Other sectors	8 664 ..	...	...	...	...	...	...	...	...
Debt securities	8 669 ..	...	...	...	...	...	...	...	...
Bonds and notes	8 670 ..	...	...	...	...	...	...	...	...
Monetary authorities	8 671 ..	...	...	...	...	...	...	...	...
General government	8 672 ..	...	...	...	...	...	...	...	...
Banks	8 673 ..	...	...	...	...	...	...	...	...
Other sectors	8 674 ..	...	...	...	...	...	...	...	...
Money market instruments	8 680 ..	...	...	...	...	...	...	...	...
Monetary authorities	8 681 ..	...	...	...	...	...	...	...	...
General government	8 682 ..	...	...	...	...	...	...	...	...
Banks	8 683 ..	...	...	...	...	...	...	...	...
Other sectors	8 684 ..	...	...	...	...	...	...	...	...
Financial derivatives	8 905 ..	...	...	...	...	...	...	...	...
Monetary authorities	8 906 ..	...	...	...	...	...	...	...	...
General government	8 907 ..	...	...	...	...	...	...	...	...
Banks	8 908 ..	...	...	...	...	...	...	...	...
Other sectors	8 909 ..	...	...	...	...	...	...	...	...
Other investment	8 753 ..	**8,966.5**	**9,421.5**	**9,614.2**	**6,781.1**	**6,610.0**	**6,948.1**	**6,726.9**	...
Trade credits	8 756 ..	...	...	...	...	11.8	29.9	42.4	...
General government	8 757 ..	...	...	...	...	...	...	...	...
of which: Short-term	8 759 ..	...	...	...	...	...	...	...	...
Other sectors	8 760 ..	...	...	...	...	11.8	29.9	42.4	...
of which: Short-term	8 762 ..	...	...	...	...	*11.8*	*29.9*	*42.4*	...
Loans	8 764 ..	6,732.7	6,804.4	6,698.8	6,781.1	6,483.1	6,860.3	6,576.8	...
Monetary authorities	8 765 ..	212.4	197.2	206.2	246.0	267.9	312.4	323.6	...
of which: Use of Fund credit and loans from the Fund	8 766 ..	*212.4*	*197.2*	*206.2*	*246.0*	*267.9*	*312.4*	*323.6*	*327.7*
of which: Short-term	8 768 ..	...	...	...	...	...	...	...	...
General government	8 769 ..	6,374.8	6,422.8	6,293.9	6,337.2	6,152.9	6,050.4	5,771.7	...
of which: Short-term	8 771 ..	...	...	...	...	...	...	...	...
Banks	8 772 ..	...	...	...	...	...	.9	...	...
of which: Short-term	8 774 ..	...	...	...	...	...	*.9*	...	...
Other sectors	8 775 ..	145.5	184.4	198.6	197.8	62.4	496.5	481.5	...
of which: Short-term	8 777 ..	...	...	...	...	...	...	...	...
Currency and deposits	8 780 ..	...	...	...	...	50.9	57.9	107.7	...
Monetary authorities	8 781 ..	...	...	...	...	48.1	57.9	107.7	...
General government	8 782 ..	...	...	...	...	...	...	...	...
Banks	8 783 ..	...	...	...	...	2.9	...	...	...
Other sectors	8 784 ..	...	...	...	...	...	...	...	...
Other liabilities	8 786 ..	2,233.8	2,617.2	2,915.4	...	64.2	...	...	...
Monetary authorities	8 787 ..	...	...	...	...	...	...	...	...
of which: Short-term	8 789 ..	...	...	...	...	...	...	...	...
General government	8 790 ..	1,755.1	2,087.3	2,321.0	...	47.7	...	...	...
of which: Short-term	8 792 ..	...	...	...	...	*47.7*	...	...	...
Banks	8 793 ..	...	...	...	...	16.5	...	...	...
of which: Short-term	8 795 ..	...	...	...	...	*16.5*	...	...	...
Other sectors	8 796 ..	478.7	529.9	594.4	...	...	...	...	...
of which: Short-term	8 798 ..	...	...	...	...	...	...	...	...
NET INTERNATIONAL INVESTMENT POSITION	8 995 ..	**–8,560.5**	**–9,066.9**	**–9,221.5**	**–6,275.7**	**–6,237.6**	**–6,495.1**	**–6,128.9**	...
Conversion rates: Tanzania shillings per U.S. dollar (end of period)	0 102 ..	**523.45**	**550.36**	**595.64**	**624.57**	**681.00**	**797.33**	**803.26**	**916.30**

Table 1. ANALYTIC PRESENTATION, 1994–2001
(Millions of U.S. dollars)

	Code		1994	1995	1996	1997	1998	1999	2000	2001
A. Current Account [1]	4 993	Z.	**–8,085**	**–13,554**	**–14,691**	**–3,021**	**14,243**	**12,428**	**9,313**	**6,227**
Goods: exports f.o.b	2 100	. .	44,478	55,447	54,408	56,656	52,753	56,775	67,894	63,202
Goods: imports f.o.b	3 100	. .	–48,204	–63,415	–63,897	–55,084	–36,515	–42,762	–56,193	–54,620
Balance on Goods	4 100	. .	*–3,726*	*–7,968*	*–9,488*	*1,572*	*16,238*	*14,013*	*11,701*	*8,582*
Services: credit	2 200	. .	11,640	14,845	17,007	15,763	13,156	14,635	13,868	13,024
Services: debit	3 200	. .	–15,396	–18,804	–19,585	–17,355	–11,998	–13,583	–15,460	–14,619
Balance on Goods and Services	4 991	. .	*–7,482*	*–11,927*	*–12,066*	*–20*	*17,395*	*15,066*	*10,109*	*6,987*
Income: credit	2 300	. .	2,562	3,801	3,969	3,742	3,324	3,092	4,235	3,839
Income: debit	3 300	. .	–4,292	–5,915	–7,354	–7,223	–6,891	–6,083	–5,616	–5,200
Balance on Goods, Services, and Income	4 992	. .	*–9,213*	*–14,040*	*–15,451*	*–3,500*	*13,828*	*12,075*	*8,727*	*5,626*
Current transfers: credit	2 379	Z.	1,901	1,190	1,651	1,392	820	806	952	990
Current transfers: debit	3 379	. .	–774	–704	–891	–913	–405	–452	–366	–389
B. Capital Account [1]	4 994	Z.	**. . .**	**. . .**	**. . .**	**. . .**	**. . .**	**. . .**	**. . .**	**. . .**
Capital account: credit	2 994	Z.	. . .	. . .	. . .	. . .	. . .	. . .	. . .	. . .
Capital account: debit	3 994	. .	. . .	. . .	. . .	. . .	. . .	. . .	. . .	. . .
Total, Groups A Plus B	4 981	. .	*–8,085*	*–13,554*	*–14,691*	*–3,021*	*14,243*	*12,428*	*9,313*	*6,227*
C. Financial Account [1]	4 995	W.	**12,167**	**21,909**	**19,486**	**–12,056**	**–14,110**	**–11,073**	**–10,434**	**–3,908**
Direct investment abroad	4 505	. .	–493	–886	–931	–580	–130	–346	23	–162
Direct investment in Thailand	4 555	Z.	1,366	2,068	2,336	3,895	7,315	6,213	3,366	3,820
Portfolio investment assets	4 602	. .	–5	–2	–41	–70	18	–2	–160	–287
Equity securities	4 610	. .	–5	–2	–41	–40	21	–1	–154	–287
Debt securities	4 619	. .	. . .	. . .	. . .	–31	–3	–2	–6	1
Portfolio investment liabilities	4 652	Z.	2,486	4,083	3,585	4,598	338	77	–546	–932
Equity securities	4 660	. .	–389	2,123	1,164	3,899	292	946	900	18
Debt securities	4 669	Z.	2,875	1,960	2,421	699	45	–869	–1,446	–951
Financial derivatives	4 910	. .	. . .	. . .	. . .	. . .	. . .	. . .	. . .	. . .
Financial derivatives assets	4 900	. .	. . .	. . .	. . .	. . .	. . .	. . .	. . .	. . .
Financial derivatives liabilities	4 905	. .	. . .	. . .	. . .	. . .	. . .	. . .	. . .	. . .
Other investment assets	4 703	. .	–1,027	–2,738	2,661	–2,555	–3,407	–1,755	–2,203	250
Monetary authorities	4 701	. .	. . .	. . .	. . .	. . .	. . .	. . .	. . .	. . .
General government	4 704	. .	. . .	. . .	. . .	. . .	. . .	. . .	. . .	. . .
Banks	4 705	. .	–1,027	–2,737	2,741	–2,608	–3,460	–1,708	–2,189	240
Other sectors	4 728	. .	. . .	–1	–80	53	53	–47	–14	11
Other investment liabilities	4 753	W.	9,839	19,383	11,876	–17,343	–18,243	–15,261	–10,914	–6,597
Monetary authorities	4 753	WA	. . .	. . .	. . .	–5,262	658	2,731	43	894
General government	4 753	ZB	–705	46	–58	737	100	–70	93	243
Banks	4 753	ZC	14,295	13,218	2,909	–3,045	–11,783	–11,566	–4,799	–2,093
Other sectors	4 753	ZD	–3,751	6,118	9,025	–9,774	–7,218	–6,356	–6,251	–5,641
Total, Groups A Through C	4 983	. .	*4,082*	*8,355*	*4,795*	*–15,077*	*132*	*1,355*	*–1,121*	*2,319*
D. Net Errors and Omissions	4 998	. .	**87**	**–1,196**	**–2,627**	**–3,173**	**–2,828**	**33**	**–685**	**155**
Total, Groups A Through D	4 984	. .	*4,169*	*7,159*	*2,167*	*–18,250*	*–2,696*	*1,388*	*–1,806*	*2,475*
E. Reserves and Related Items	4 802	A.	**–4,169**	**–7,159**	**–2,167**	**18,250**	**2,696**	**–1,388**	**1,806**	**–2,475**
Reserve assets	4 802	. .	–4,169	–7,159	–2,167	9,900	–1,433	–4,556	1,608	–1,307
Use of Fund credit and loans	4 766	. .	. . .	. . .	. . .	2,437	679	269	–192	–1,288
Exceptional financing	4 920	. .	. . .	. . .	. . .	5,913	3,450	2,898	391	121
Conversion rates: baht per U.S. dollar	0 101	. .	**25.150**	**24.915**	**25.343**	**31.364**	**41.359**	**37.814**	**40.112**	**44.432**

[1] Excludes components that have been classified in the categories of Group E.

Table 2. STANDARD PRESENTATION, 1994–2001
(Millions of U.S. dollars)

	Code	1994	1995	1996	1997	1998	1999	2000	2001
CURRENT ACCOUNT	4 993 . .	**–8,085**	**–13,554**	**–14,691**	**–3,021**	**14,243**	**12,428**	**9,313**	**6,227**
A. GOODS	4 100 . .	–3,726	–7,968	–9,488	1,572	16,238	14,013	11,701	8,582
Credit	2 100 . .	**44,478**	**55,447**	**54,408**	**56,656**	**52,753**	**56,775**	**67,894**	**63,202**
General merchandise: exports f.o.b.	2 110 . .	44,478	55,447	54,408	56,656	52,753	56,775	67,894	63,202
Goods for processing: exports f.o.b.	2 150 . .	. . .	. . .	. . .	. . .	. . .	. . .	. . .	. . .
Repairs on goods	2 160 . .	. . .	. . .	. . .	. . .	. . .	. . .	. . .	. . .
Goods procured in ports by carriers	2 170 . .	. . .	. . .	. . .	. . .	. . .	. . .	. . .	. . .
Nonmonetary gold	2 180 . .	. . .	. . .	. . .	. . .	. . .	. . .	. . .	. . .
Debit	3 100 . .	**–48,204**	**–63,415**	**–63,897**	**–55,084**	**–36,515**	**–42,762**	**–56,193**	**–54,620**
General merchandise: imports f.o.b.	3 110 . .	–47,874	–63,044	–63,499	–54,798	–36,322	–42,528	–55,711	–53,877
Goods for processing: imports f.o.b.	3 150 . .	. . .	. . .	. . .	. . .	. . .	. . .	. . .	. . .
Repairs on goods	3 160 . .	. . .	. . .	. . .	. . .	. . .	. . .	. . .	. . .
Goods procured in ports by carriers	3 170 . .	. . .	. . .	. . .	. . .	. . .	. . .	. . .	. . .
Nonmonetary gold	3 180 . .	–330	–371	–398	–287	–193	–234	–482	–742
B. SERVICES	4 200 . .	–3,756	–3,959	–2,578	–1,591	1,157	1,052	–1,592	–1,595
Total credit	2 200 . .	*11,640*	*14,845*	*17,007*	*15,763*	*13,156*	*14,635*	*13,868*	*13,024*
Total debit	3 200 . .	*–15,396*	*–18,804*	*–19,585*	*–17,355*	*–11,998*	*–13,583*	*–15,460*	*–14,619*
Transportation services, credit	2 205 . .	**1,842**	**2,455**	**2,618**	**2,417**	**2,671**	**3,017**	**3,250**	**3,057**
Passenger	2 850 . .	*1,153*	*1,222*	*1,278*	*1,392*	*1,780*	*2,388*	*2,452*	*2,303*
Freight	2 851 . .	*448*	*584*	*664*	*628*	*467*	*512*	*605*	*610*
Other	2 852 . .	*241*	*649*	*675*	*397*	*423*	*117*	*193*	*143*
Sea transport, passenger	2 207 . .	. . .	. . .	. . .	. . .	. . .	. . .	. . .	. . .
Sea transport, freight	2 208 . .	. . .	. . .	. . .	. . .	. . .	. . .	. . .	. . .
Sea transport, other	2 209 . .	. . .	. . .	. . .	. . .	. . .	. . .	. . .	. . .
Air transport, passenger	2 211 . .	. . .	. . .	. . .	. . .	. . .	. . .	. . .	. . .
Air transport, freight	2 212 . .	. . .	. . .	. . .	. . .	. . .	. . .	. . .	. . .
Air transport, other	2 213 . .	. . .	. . .	. . .	. . .	. . .	. . .	. . .	. . .
Other transport, passenger	2 215 . .	. . .	. . .	. . .	. . .	. . .	. . .	. . .	. . .
Other transport, freight	2 216 . .	. . .	. . .	. . .	. . .	. . .	. . .	. . .	. . .
Other transport, other	2 217 . .	. . .	. . .	. . .	. . .	. . .	. . .	. . .	. . .
Transportation services, debit	3 205 . .	**–5,862**	**–7,780**	**–7,845**	**–6,890**	**–4,604**	**–5,305**	**–6,760**	**–6,838**
Passenger	3 850 . .	*–384*	*–520*	*–449*	*–336*	*–286*	*–396*	*–446*	*–410*
Freight	3 851 . .	*–5,375*	*–7,125*	*–7,252*	*–6,342*	*–4,160*	*–4,746*	*–6,096*	*–6,160*
Other	3 852 . .	*–103*	*–135*	*–144*	*–212*	*–157*	*–163*	*–218*	*–268*
Sea transport, passenger	3 207 . .	. . .	. . .	. . .	. . .	. . .	. . .	. . .	. . .
Sea transport, freight	3 208 . .	. . .	. . .	. . .	. . .	. . .	. . .	. . .	. . .
Sea transport, other	3 209 . .	. . .	. . .	. . .	. . .	. . .	. . .	. . .	. . .
Air transport, passenger	3 211 . .	. . .	. . .	. . .	. . .	. . .	. . .	. . .	. . .
Air transport, freight	3 212 . .	. . .	. . .	. . .	. . .	. . .	. . .	. . .	. . .
Air transport, other	3 213 . .	. . .	. . .	. . .	. . .	. . .	. . .	. . .	. . .
Other transport, passenger	3 215 . .	. . .	. . .	. . .	. . .	. . .	. . .	. . .	. . .
Other transport, freight	3 216 . .	. . .	. . .	. . .	. . .	. . .	. . .	. . .	. . .
Other transport, other	3 217 . .	. . .	. . .	. . .	. . .	. . .	. . .	. . .	. . .
Travel, credit	2 236 . .	**6,063**	**8,035**	**9,089**	**7,660**	**6,174**	**7,028**	**7,483**	**7,075**
Business travel	2 237 . .	. . .	. . .	. . .	. . .	. . .	. . .	. . .	. . .
Personal travel	2 240 . .	. . .	. . .	. . .	. . .	. . .	. . .	. . .	. . .
Travel, debit	3 236 . .	**–4,065**	**–4,271**	**–4,286**	**–3,416**	**–1,960**	**–2,474**	**–2,772**	**–2,924**
Business travel	3 237 . .	. . .	. . .	. . .	. . .	. . .	. . .	. . .	. . .
Personal travel	3 240 . .	. . .	. . .	. . .	. . .	. . .	. . .	. . .	. . .
Other services, credit	2 200 BA	**3,735**	**4,356**	**5,301**	**5,686**	**4,311**	**4,591**	**3,135**	**2,892**
Communications	2 245 . .	. . .	199	225	205	159	143	132	109
Construction	2 249 . .	. . .	19	26	40	94	236	230	296
Insurance	2 253 . .	55	99	111	71	51	56	82	88
Financial	2 260 . .	. . .	. . .	. . .	. . .	. . .	. . .	. . .	. . .
Computer and information	2 262 . .	. . .	. . .	. . .	. . .	. . .	. . .	. . .	. . .
Royalties and licence fees	2 266 . .	4	1	25	44	7	19	9	9
Other business services	2 268 . .	3,461	3,844	4,611	5,181	3,919	4,042	2,600	2,298
Personal, cultural, and recreational	2 287 . .	. . .	. . .	. . .	. . .	. . .	. . .	. . .	. . .
Government, n.i.e.	2 291 . .	215	194	304	144	81	93	83	93
Other services, debit	3 200 BA	**–5,469**	**–6,753**	**–7,454**	**–7,048**	**–5,435**	**–5,804**	**–5,928**	**–4,857**
Communications	3 245 . .	. . .	–121	–121	–128	–54	–29	–39	–145
Construction	3 249 . .	. . .	–163	–157	–257	–124	–82	–105	–110
Insurance	3 253 . .	–756	–961	–960	–892	–592	–654	–801	–805
Financial	3 260 . .	. . .	. . .	. . .	. . .	. . .	. . .	. . .	. . .
Computer and information	3 262 . .	. . .	. . .	. . .	. . .	. . .	. . .	. . .	. . .
Royalties and licence fees	3 266 . .	–452	–630	–717	–804	–514	–583	–710	–823
Other business services	3 268 . .	–4,096	–4,675	–5,227	–4,757	–4,026	–4,337	–4,142	–2,839
Personal, cultural, and recreational	3 287 . .	. . .	. . .	. . .	. . .	. . .	. . .	. . .	. . .
Government, n.i.e.	3 291 . .	–165	–203	–272	–211	–124	–119	–131	–135

Table 2 (Continued). STANDARD PRESENTATION, 1994–2001
(Millions of U.S. dollars)

	Code	1994	1995	1996	1997	1998	1999	2000	2001
C. INCOME	4 300 . .	–1,731	–2,114	–3,385	–3,480	–3,567	–2,991	–1,381	–1,361
Total credit	2 300 . .	*2,562*	*3,801*	*3,969*	*3,742*	*3,324*	*3,092*	*4,235*	*3,839*
Total debit	3 300 . .	*–4,292*	*–5,915*	*–7,354*	*–7,223*	*–6,891*	*–6,083*	*–5,616*	*–5,200*
Compensation of employees, credit	2 310 . .	**1,281**	**1,695**	**1,806**	**1,658**	**1,424**	**1,460**	**1,697**	**1,252**
Compensation of employees, debit	3 310 . .	...	...	...	...	...	...	...	...
Investment income, credit	2 320 . .	**1,281**	**2,106**	**2,163**	**2,084**	**1,899**	**1,632**	**2,538**	**2,586**
Direct investment income	2 330 . .	...	...	...	...	...	...	...	...
Dividends and distributed branch profits	2 332 . .	...	...	...	...	...	...	...	...
Reinvested earnings and undistributed branch profits	2 333 . .	...	...	...	...	...	...	...	...
Income on debt (interest)	2 334 . .	...	...	...	...	...	...	...	...
Portfolio investment income	2 339 . .	...	...	...	...	...	...	...	...
Income on equity	2 340 . .	...	...	...	...	...	...	...	...
Income on bonds and notes	2 350 . .	...	...	...	...	...	...	...	...
Income on money market instruments	2 360 . .	...	...	...	...	...	...	...	...
Other investment income	2 370 . .	1,281	2,106	2,163	2,084	1,899	1,632	...	...
Investment income, debit	3 320 . .	**–4,292**	**–5,915**	**–7,354**	**–7,223**	**–6,891**	**–6,083**	**–5,616**	**–5,200**
Direct investment income	3 330 . .	...	...	...	...	...	...	...	...
Dividends and distributed branch profits	3 332 . .	...	...	...	...	...	...	...	...
Reinvested earnings and undistributed branch profits	3 333 . .	...	...	...	...	...	...	...	...
Income on debt (interest)	3 334 . .	...	...	...	...	...	...	...	...
Portfolio investment income	3 339 . .	...	...	...	...	...	...	...	...
Income on equity	3 340 . .	...	...	...	...	...	...	...	...
Income on bonds and notes	3 350 . .	...	...	...	...	...	...	...	...
Income on money market instruments	3 360 . .	...	...	...	...	...	...	...	...
Other investment income	3 370 . .	–4,292	–5,915	–7,354	–7,223	–6,891	–6,083	...	...
D. CURRENT TRANSFERS	4 379 . .	1,128	487	760	479	414	353	586	601
Credit	2 379 . .	**1,901**	**1,190**	**1,651**	**1,392**	**820**	**806**	**952**	**990**
General government	2 380 . .	75	57	61	36	36	52	84	110
Other sectors	2 390 . .	1,826	1,133	1,590	1,356	784	754	867	880
Workers' remittances	2 391 . .	...	...	...	...	...	...	...	...
Other current transfers	2 392 . .	1,826	...	...	...	...	...	...	...
Debit	3 379 . .	**–774**	**–704**	**–891**	**–913**	**–405**	**–452**	**–366**	**–389**
General government	3 380 . .	–14	–15	–31	–19	–8	–9	–7	–6
Other sectors	3 390 . .	–760	–688	–861	–894	–398	–443	–359	–384
Workers' remittances	3 391 . .	...	...	...	...	...	...	...	...
Other current transfers	3 392 . .	–760	...	...	...	...	...	...	...
CAPITAL AND FINANCIAL ACCOUNT	4 996 . .	**7,998**	**14,750**	**17,319**	**6,194**	**–11,414**	**–12,461**	**–8,628**	**–6,382**
CAPITAL ACCOUNT	4 994 . .	...	...	...	...	...	...	...	...
Total credit	2 994 . .	...	...	...	...	...	...	...	...
Total debit	3 994 . .	...	...	...	...	...	...	...	...
Capital transfers, credit	2 400 . .	...	...	...	...	...	...	...	...
General government	2 401 . .	...	...	...	...	...	...	...	...
Debt forgiveness	2 402 . .	...	...	...	...	...	...	...	...
Other capital transfers	2 410 . .	...	...	...	...	...	...	...	...
Other sectors	2 430 . .	...	...	...	...	...	...	...	...
Migrants' transfers	2 431 . .	...	...	...	...	...	...	...	...
Debt forgiveness	2 432 . .	...	...	...	...	...	...	...	...
Other capital transfers	2 440 . .	...	...	...	...	...	...	...	...
Capital transfers, debit	3 400 . .	...	...	...	...	...	...	...	...
General government	3 401 . .	...	...	...	...	...	...	...	...
Debt forgiveness	3 402 . .	...	...	...	...	...	...	...	...
Other capital transfers	3 410 . .	...	...	...	...	...	...	...	...
Other sectors	3 430 . .	...	...	...	...	...	...	...	...
Migrants' transfers	3 431 . .	...	...	...	...	...	...	...	...
Debt forgiveness	3 432 . .	...	...	...	...	...	...	...	...
Other capital transfers	3 440 . .	...	...	...	...	...	...	...	...
Nonproduced nonfinancial assets, credit	2 480 . .	...	...	...	...	...	...	...	...
Nonproduced nonfinancial assets, debit	3 480 . .	...	...	...	...	...	...	...	...

Table 2 (Continued). STANDARD PRESENTATION, 1994–2001

(Millions of U.S. dollars)

	Code	1994	1995	1996	1997	1998	1999	2000	2001
FINANCIAL ACCOUNT	4 995 . .	**7,998**	**14,750**	**17,319**	**6,194**	**–11,414**	**–12,461**	**–8,628**	**–6,382**
A. DIRECT INVESTMENT	4 500 . .	873	1,182	1,405	3,315	7,185	5,867	3,389	3,658
Direct investment abroad	4 505 . .	**–493**	**–886**	**–931**	**–580**	**–130**	**–346**	**23**	**–162**
Equity capital	4 510 . .	–493	–886	–931	–580	–130	–346	23	–162
Claims on affiliated enterprises	4 515 . .	. . .	. . .	. . .	. . .	. . .	. . .	. . .	. . .
Liabilities to affiliated enterprises	4 520 . .	. . .	. . .	. . .	. . .	. . .	. . .	. . .	. . .
Reinvested earnings	4 525 . .	. . .	. . .	. . .	. . .	. . .	. . .	. . .	. . .
Other capital	4 530 . .	. . .	. . .	. . .	. . .	. . .	. . .	. . .	. . .
Claims on affiliated enterprises	4 535 . .	. . .	. . .	. . .	. . .	. . .	. . .	. . .	. . .
Liabilities to affiliated enterprises	4 540 . .	. . .	. . .	. . .	. . .	. . .	. . .	. . .	. . .
Direct investment in Thailand	4 555 . .	**1,366**	**2,068**	**2,336**	**3,895**	**7,315**	**6,213**	**3,366**	**3,820**
Equity capital	4 560 . .	1,290	1,959	2,450	3,753	6,711	6,170	3,402	2,626
Claims on direct investors	4 565 . .	. . .	. . .	. . .	. . .	. . .	. . .	. . .	. . .
Liabilities to direct investors	4 570 . .	. . .	. . .	. . .	. . .	. . .	. . .	. . .	. . .
Reinvested earnings	4 575 . .	. . .	. . .	. . .	. . .	. . .	. . .	. . .	. . .
Other capital	4 580 . .	76	109	–114	142	604	43	–36	1,194
Claims on direct investors	4 585 . .	. . .	. . .	. . .	. . .	. . .	. . .	. . .	. . .
Liabilities to direct investors	4 590 . .	. . .	. . .	. . .	. . .	. . .	. . .	. . .	. . .
B. PORTFOLIO INVESTMENT	4 600 . .	2,482	4,081	3,544	4,527	355	75	–706	–1,219
Assets	4 602 . .	**–5**	**–2**	**–41**	**–70**	**18**	**–2**	**–160**	**–287**
Equity securities	4 610 . .	–5	–2	–41	–40	21	–1	–154	–287
Monetary authorities	4 611 . .	. . .	. . .	. . .	. . .	. . .	. . .	. . .	. . .
General government	4 612 . .	. . .	. . .	. . .	. . .	. . .	. . .	. . .	. . .
Banks	4 613 . .	. . .	. . .	. . .	–40	21	–1	–154	–287
Other sectors	4 614 . .	–5	. . .	. . .	. . .	. . .	. . .	. . .	. . .
Debt securities	4 619 . .	. . .	. . .	. . .	–31	–3	–2	–6	1
Bonds and notes	4 620 . .	. . .	. . .	. . .	. . .	. . .	. . .	. . .	. . .
Monetary authorities	4 621 . .	. . .	. . .	. . .	. . .	. . .	. . .	. . .	. . .
General government	4 622 . .	. . .	. . .	. . .	. . .	. . .	. . .	. . .	. . .
Banks	4 623 . .	. . .	. . .	. . .	. . .	. . .	. . .	. . .	. . .
Other sectors	4 624 . .	. . .	. . .	. . .	. . .	. . .	. . .	. . .	. . .
Money market instruments	4 630 . .	. . .	. . .	. . .	. . .	. . .	. . .	. . .	. . .
Monetary authorities	4 631 . .	. . .	. . .	. . .	. . .	. . .	. . .	. . .	. . .
General government	4 632 . .	. . .	. . .	. . .	. . .	. . .	. . .	. . .	. . .
Banks	4 633 . .	. . .	. . .	. . .	. . .	. . .	. . .	. . .	. . .
Other sectors	4 634 . .	. . .	. . .	. . .	. . .	. . .	. . .	. . .	. . .
Liabilities	4 652 . .	**2,486**	**4,083**	**3,585**	**4,598**	**338**	**77**	**–546**	**–932**
Equity securities	4 660 . .	–389	2,123	1,164	3,899	292	946	900	18
Banks	4 663 . .	. . .	. . .	. . .	. . .	. . .	. . .	. . .	. . .
Other sectors	4 664 . .	–389	2,123	1,164	3,899	292	946	900	18
Debt securities	4 669 . .	2,875	1,960	2,421	699	45	–869	–1,446	–951
Bonds and notes	4 670 . .	2,875	1,960	2,421	699	45	–869	–1,446	–951
Monetary authorities	4 671 . .	. . .	. . .	. . .	. . .	. . .	. . .	. . .	. . .
General government	4 672 . .	672	246	463	417	–218	–466	–352	–46
Banks	4 673 . .	574	745	–603	–135	–83	–7	–87	. . .
Other sectors	4 674 . .	1,629	969	2,561	417	346	–396	–1,008	–905
Money market instruments	4 680 . .	. . .	. . .	. . .	. . .	. . .	. . .	. . .	. . .
Monetary authorities	4 681 . .	. . .	. . .	. . .	. . .	. . .	. . .	. . .	. . .
General government	4 682 . .	. . .	. . .	. . .	. . .	. . .	. . .	. . .	. . .
Banks	4 683 . .	. . .	. . .	. . .	. . .	. . .	. . .	. . .	. . .
Other sectors	4 684 . .	. . .	. . .	. . .	. . .	. . .	. . .	. . .	. . .
C. FINANCIAL DERIVATIVES	4 910 . .	. . .	. . .	. . .	. . .	. . .	. . .	. . .	. . .
Monetary authorities	4 911 . .	. . .	. . .	. . .	. . .	. . .	. . .	. . .	. . .
General government	4 912 . .	. . .	. . .	. . .	. . .	. . .	. . .	. . .	. . .
Banks	4 913 . .	. . .	. . .	. . .	. . .	. . .	. . .	. . .	. . .
Other sectors	4 914 . .	. . .	. . .	. . .	. . .	. . .	. . .	. . .	. . .
Assets	4 900 . .	**. . .**	**. . .**	**. . .**	**. . .**	**. . .**	**. . .**	**. . .**	**. . .**
Monetary authorities	4 901 . .	. . .	. . .	. . .	. . .	. . .	. . .	. . .	. . .
General government	4 902 . .	. . .	. . .	. . .	. . .	. . .	. . .	. . .	. . .
Banks	4 903 . .	. . .	. . .	. . .	. . .	. . .	. . .	. . .	. . .
Other sectors	4 904 . .	. . .	. . .	. . .	. . .	. . .	. . .	. . .	. . .
Liabilities	4 905 . .	**. . .**	**. . .**	**. . .**	**. . .**	**. . .**	**. . .**	**. . .**	**. . .**
Monetary authorities	4 906 . .	. . .	. . .	. . .	. . .	. . .	. . .	. . .	. . .
General government	4 907 . .	. . .	. . .	. . .	. . .	. . .	. . .	. . .	. . .
Banks	4 908 . .	. . .	. . .	. . .	. . .	. . .	. . .	. . .	. . .
Other sectors	4 909 . .	. . .	. . .	. . .	. . .	. . .	. . .	. . .	. . .

Table 2 (Concluded). STANDARD PRESENTATION, 1994–2001
(Millions of U.S. dollars)

	Code	1994	1995	1996	1997	1998	1999	2000	2001
D. OTHER INVESTMENT	4 700 . .	8,812	16,645	14,537	-11,548	-17,521	-13,847	-12,919	-7,515
Assets	4 703 . .	**-1,027**	**-2,738**	**2,661**	**-2,555**	**-3,407**	**-1,755**	**-2,203**	**250**
Trade credits	4 706 . .	...	...	...	...	...	...	...	...
General government	4 707 . .	...	...	...	...	...	...	...	...
of which: Short-term	4 709 . .	...	...	...	...	...	...	...	...
Other sectors	4 710 . .	...	...	...	...	...	...	...	...
of which: Short-term	4 712 . .	...	...	...	...	...	...	...	...
Loans	4 714 . .	-68	-1	-80	-459	-1,203	623	-214	207
Monetary authorities	4 715 . .	...	...	...	...	...	...	...	...
of which: Short-term	4 718 . .	...	...	...	...	...	...	...	...
General government	4 719 . .	...	...	...	...	...	...	...	...
of which: Short-term	4 721 . .	...	...	...	...	...	...	...	...
Banks	4 722 . .	-68	...	...	-512	-1,256	670	-200	196
of which: Short-term	4 724 . .	*-68*	...	...	...	...	...	...	...
Other sectors	4 725 . .	...	-1	-80	53	53	-47	-14	11
of which: Short-term	4 727 . .	...	...	...	...	...	...	...	...
Currency and deposits	4 730 . .	-959	-2,737	2,741	-2,477	-2,948	-2,494	-2,055	-112
Monetary authorities	4 731 . .	...	...	...	...	...	...	...	...
General government	4 732 . .	...	...	...	...	...	...	...	...
Banks	4 733 . .	-959	-2,737	2,741	-2,477	-2,948	-2,494	-2,055	-112
Other sectors	4 734 . .	...	...	...	...	...	...	...	...
Other assets	4 736 . .	...	...	...	381	744	117	66	156
Monetary authorities	4 737 . .	...	...	...	...	...	...	...	...
of which: Short-term	4 739 . .	...	...	...	...	...	...	...	...
General government	4 740 . .	...	...	...	...	...	...	...	...
of which: Short-term	4 742 . .	...	...	...	...	...	...	...	...
Banks	4 743 . .	...	...	...	381	744	117	66	156
of which: Short-term	4 745 . .	...	...	...	...	...	...	...	...
Other sectors	4 746 . .	...	...	...	...	...	...	...	...
of which: Short-term	4 748 . .	...	...	...	...	...	...	...	...
Liabilities	4 753 . .	**9,839**	**19,383**	**11,876**	**-8,993**	**-14,114**	**-12,093**	**-10,716**	**-7,765**
Trade credits	4 756 . .	256	207	-182	-431	-425	484	-837	-508
General government	4 757 . .	...	...	...	...	...	...	...	...
of which: Short-term	4 759 . .	...	...	...	...	...	...	...	...
Other sectors	4 760 . .	256	207	-182	-431	-425	484	-837	-508
of which: Short-term	4 762 . .	*695*	*405*	*-64*	*-422*	*-583*	*796*	*-694*	*-423*
Loans	4 764 . .	8,371	15,725	9,216	2,404	-9,755	-11,825	-9,227	-7,880
Monetary authorities	4 765 . .	...	...	...	7,627	3,466	1,271	-192	-3,119
of which: Use of Fund credit and loans from the Fund	4 766 . .	...	...	...	*2,437*	*679*	*269*	*-192*	*-1,288*
of which: Short-term	4 768 . .	...	...	...	...	...	...	...	...
General government	4 769 . .	-486	-155	79	978	819	1,976	607	399
of which: Short-term	4 771 . .	*180*	*-92*	*-45*	*-33*	*7*	...	...	...
Banks	4 772 . .	14,295	13,218	2,909	-2,599	-11,190	-11,211	-4,828	-1,992
of which: Short-term	4 774 . .	*14,295*	...	...	...	...	...	...	...
Other sectors	4 775 . .	-5,439	2,662	6,228	-3,603	-2,850	-3,861	-4,813	-3,168
of which: Short-term	4 777 . .	*-5,934*	*-1,363*	*196*	*-4,551*	*-3,511*	*-2,551*	*-1,053*	*-302*
Currency and deposits	4 780 . .	2,061	3,396	2,922	-11,048	-3,571	-439	-361	1,377
Monetary authorities	4 781 . .	...	...	...	-5,262	658	2,731	43	2,725
General government	4 782 . .	...	...	...	...	...	...	...	...
Banks	4 783 . .	...	...	...	48	-2	7	5	4
Other sectors	4 784 . .	2,061	3,396	2,922	-5,834	-4,226	-3,177	-409	-1,352
Other liabilities	4 786 . .	-849	55	-80	81	-364	-313	-290	-753
Monetary authorities	4 787 . .	...	...	...	...	...	...	...	...
of which: Short-term	4 789 . .	...	...	...	...	...	...	...	...
General government	4 790 . .	-220	201	-136	482	-55	-149	-123	-35
of which: Short-term	4 792 . .	*-220*	...	...	...	...	...	...	...
Banks	4 793 . .	...	...	...	-495	-591	-361	23	-106
of which: Short-term	4 795 . .	...	...	...	...	...	...	...	...
Other sectors	4 796 . .	-629	-146	56	94	283	198	-191	-612
of which: Short-term	4 798 . .	*-629*	...	...	...	...	...	...	...
E. RESERVE ASSETS	4 802 . .	-4,169	-7,159	-2,167	9,900	-1,433	-4,556	1,608	-1,307
Monetary gold	4 812 . .	...	...	...	...	...	...	31	-31
Special drawing rights	4 811 . .	-8	-13	-16	-428	108	123	163	76
Reserve position in the Fund	4 810 . .	-20	-52	-22	452	...	...	...	...
Foreign exchange	4 803 . .	-4,141	-7,094	-2,130	9,876	-1,541	-4,679	1,413	-1,352
Other claims	4 813 . .	...	...	...	...	...	...	...	...
NET ERRORS AND OMISSIONS	4 998 . .	**87**	**-1,196**	**-2,627**	**-3,173**	**-2,828**	**33**	**-685**	**155**

Part 3 of the *Yearbook* contains descriptions of the methodologies, compilation practices, and sources used to compile these data.

Table 3. INTERNATIONAL INVESTMENT POSITION (End-period stocks), 1994–2001
(Millions of U.S. dollars)

	Code	1994	1995	1996	1997	1998	1999	2000	2001
ASSETS	8 995 C.	...	46,982	46,005	35,007	41,368	48,360	53,450	54,231
Direct investment abroad	8 505 . .	**...**	**365**	**481**	**401**	**410**	**418**	**1,991**	**2,309**
Equity capital and reinvested earnings	8 506 . .	...	365	481	401	410	418	1,551	1,639
Claims on affiliated enterprises	8 507 . .	...	...	...	...	...	...	1,551	1,639
Liabilities to affiliated enterprises	8 508 . .	...	...	...	...	...	...	...	...
Other capital	8 530 . .	...	...	...	...	...	...	439	670
Claims on affiliated enterprises	8 535 . .	...	...	...	...	...	...	439	670
Liabilities to affiliated enterprises	8 540 . .	...	...	...	...	...	...	...	...
Portfolio investment	8 602 . .	**...**	**...**	**...**	**43**	**28**	**29**	**478**	**813**
Equity securities	8 610 . .	...	...	...	...	...	...	42	57
Monetary authorities	8 611 . .	...	...	...	...	...	...	...	...
General government	8 612 . .	...	...	...	...	...	...	...	...
Banks	8 613 . .	...	...	...	...	...	...	20	20
Other sectors	8 614 . .	...	...	...	...	...	...	22	37
Debt securities	8 619 . .	...	...	...	...	...	...	436	756
Bonds and notes	8 620 . .	...	...	...	...	...	...	258	405
Monetary authorities	8 621 . .	...	...	...	...	...	...	...	...
General government	8 622 . .	...	...	...	...	...	...	...	...
Banks	8 623 . .	...	...	...	...	...	...	115	224
Other sectors	8 624 . .	...	...	...	...	...	...	143	181
Money market instruments	8 630 . .	...	...	...	...	...	...	178	351
Monetary authorities	8 631 . .	...	...	...	...	...	...	...	...
General government	8 632 . .	...	...	...	...	...	...	...	...
Banks	8 633 . .	...	...	...	...	...	...	50	227
Other sectors	8 634 . .	...	...	...	...	...	...	128	124
Financial derivatives	8 900 . .	**...**	**...**	**...**	**...**	**...**	**...**	**510**	**141**
Monetary authorities	8 901 . .	...	...	...	...	...	...	...	...
General government	8 902 . .	...	...	...	...	...	...	...	...
Banks	8 903 . .	...	...	...	...	...	...	503	133
Other sectors	8 904 . .	...	...	...	...	...	...	7	8
Other investment	8 703 . .	**...**	**9,672**	**6,879**	**7,671**	**11,394**	**13,132**	**17,810**	**17,928**
Trade credits	8 706 . .	...	...	...	...	...	...	1,063	1,685
General government	8 707 . .	...	...	...	...	...	...	...	...
of which: Short-term	8 709 . .	...	...	...	...	...	...	...	...
Other sectors	8 710 . .	...	...	...	...	...	...	1,063	1,685
of which: Short-term	8 712 . .	...	...	...	...	...	...	*1,062*	*1,677*
Loans	8 714 . .	...	...	...	1,261	2,201	1,412	2,416	1,800
Monetary authorities	8 715 . .	...	...	...	...	...	...	...	...
of which: Short-term	8 718 . .	...	...	...	...	...	...	...	...
General government	8 719 . .	...	...	...	...	...	...	...	...
of which: Short-term	8 721 . .	...	...	...	...	...	...	...	...
Banks	8 722 . .	...	...	...	1,261	2,201	1,412	2,322	1,741
of which: Short-term	8 724 . .	...	...	...	...	...	...	*1,277*	*715*
Other sectors	8 725 . .	...	...	...	...	...	...	94	59
of which: Short-term	8 727 . .	...	...	...	...	...	...	*74*	*20*
Currency and deposits	8 730 . .	...	9,672	6,879	5,932	8,834	11,096	13,297	13,557
Monetary authorities	8 731 . .	...	...	...	...	...	...	...	...
General government	8 732 . .	...	...	...	...	...	...	4	...
Banks	8 733 . .	...	9,672	6,879	5,932	8,834	11,096	13,125	13,167
Other sectors	8 734 . .	...	...	...	...	...	...	168	390
Other assets	8 736 . .	...	...	...	478	359	624	1,034	886
Monetary authorities	8 737 . .	...	...	...	...	...	...	...	...
of which: Short-term	8 739 . .	...	...	...	...	...	...	...	...
General government	8 740 . .	...	...	...	...	...	...	123	158
of which: Short-term	8 742 . .	...	...	...	...	...	...	...	...
Banks	8 743 . .	...	...	...	478	359	624	895	704
of which: Short-term	8 745 . .	...	...	...	*478*	*359*	*624*	*885*	*691*
Other sectors	8 746 . .	...	...	...	...	...	...	16	24
of which: Short-term	8 748 . .	...	...	...	...	...	...	*15*	*23*
Reserve assets	8 802 . .	**...**	**36,945**	**38,645**	**26,892**	**29,536**	**34,781**	**32,661**	**33,040**
Monetary gold	8 812 . .	...	963	914	713	711	718	645	686
Special drawing rights	8 811 . .	32	45	60	482	391	258	83	5
Reserve position in the Fund	8 810 . .	416	474	480	...	...	...	...	...
Foreign exchange	8 803 . .	...	35,463	37,192	25,697	28,434	33,805	31,933	32,349
Other claims	8 813 . .	...	...	...	...	...	...	...	...

Table 3 (Concluded). INTERNATIONAL INVESTMENT POSITION (End–period stocks), 1994–2001

(Millions of U.S. dollars)

	Code	1994	1995	1996	1997	1998	1999	2000	2001
LIABILITIES	8 995 D.	...	100,832	108,742	109,276	105,061	95,051	112,072	103,819
Direct investment in Thailand	8 555 . .	**...**	**4,919**	**4,745**	**4,738**	**6,481**	**6,837**	**25,834**	**29,158**
Equity capital and reinvested earnings	8 556 . .	...	...	...	...	...	...	19,066	21,578
Claims on direct investors	8 557 . .	...	...	...	...	...	...	...	...
Liabilities to direct investors	8 558 . .	...	...	...	...	...	...	19,066	21,578
Other capital	8 580 . .	...	4,919	4,745	4,738	6,481	6,837	6,746	7,566
Claims on direct investors	8 585 . .	...	...	...	...	...	...	–1,009	–878
Liabilities to direct investors	8 590 . .	...	4,919	4,745	4,738	6,481	6,837	7,755	8,444
Portfolio investment	8 652 . .	**...**	**6,684**	**9,472**	**9,774**	**10,552**	**9,921**	**16,315**	**16,941**
Equity securities	8 660 . .	...	...	...	...	...	...	8,153	10,098
Banks	8 663 . .	...	...	...	...	...	...	1,435	1,804
Other sectors	8 664 . .	...	...	...	...	...	...	6,718	8,294
Debt securities	8 669 . .	...	6,684	9,472	9,774	10,552	9,921	8,162	6,843
Bonds and notes	8 670 . .	...	6,684	9,472	9,774	10,552	9,921	7,868	6,377
Monetary authorities	8 671 . .	...	...	...	...	...	...	...	...
General government	8 672 . .	...	1,750	2,158	2,379	2,179	1,786	1,513	1,291
Banks	8 673 . .	...	492	330	194	110	101	15	20
Other sectors	8 674 . .	...	4,442	6,984	7,201	8,263	8,034	6,340	5,066
Money market instruments	8 680 . .	...	...	...	...	...	...	294	466
Monetary authorities	8 681 . .	...	...	...	...	...	...	...	...
General government	8 682 . .	...	...	...	...	...	...	26	147
Banks	8 683 . .	...	...	...	...	...	...	...	...
Other sectors	8 684 . .	...	...	...	...	...	...	268	319
Financial derivatives	8 905 . .	**...**	**...**	**...**	**...**	**...**	**...**	**2,643**	**2,448**
Monetary authorities	8 906 . .	...	...	...	...	...	...	2,136	2,078
General government	8 907 . .	...	...	...	...	...	...	...	...
Banks	8 908 . .	...	...	...	...	...	...	480	244
Other sectors	8 909 . .	...	...	...	...	...	...	27	126
Other investment	8 753 . .	**...**	**89,229**	**94,525**	**94,764**	**88,028**	**78,293**	**67,280**	**55,272**
Trade credits	8 756 . .	...	4,572	4,760	4,350	4,008	4,624	3,464	2,885
General government	8 757 . .	...	...	...	...	...	...	...	...
of which: Short-term	8 759 . .	...	...	...	...	...	...	...	...
Other sectors	8 760 . .	...	4,572	4,760	4,350	4,008	4,624	3,464	2,885
of which: Short-term	8 762 . .	...	*4,131*	*4,296*	*3,919*	*3,342*	*4,119*	*3,125*	*2,654*
Loans	8 764 . .	...	84,657	89,765	89,476	83,241	72,926	62,360	51,275
Monetary authorities	8 765 . .	...	...	...	7,157	11,203	12,817	12,019	8,327
of which: Use of Fund credit and loans from the Fund	8 766 . .	...	...	...	*2,429*	*3,238*	*3,431*	*3,062*	*1,681*
of which: Short-term	8 768 . .	...	...	...	...	...	...	...	...
General government	8 769 . .	...	3,126	2,994	3,672	4,768	7,102	7,347	7,297
of which: Short-term	8 771 . .	...	*85*	*34*	...	...	...	...	...
Banks	8 772 . .	...	41,346	41,410	37,960	27,304	16,707	12,200	9,322
of which: Short-term	8 774 . .	...	...	...	*23,465*	*16,658*	*8,723*	*5,324*	*4,909*
Other sectors	8 775 . .	...	40,185	45,361	40,687	39,966	36,300	30,794	26,329
of which: Short-term	8 777 . .	...	*11,684*	*11,894*	*7,319*	*4,523*	*3,031*	*3,496*	*2,462*
Currency and deposits	8 780 . .	...	...	...	282	288	295	694	575
Monetary authorities	8 781 . .	...	...	...	...	...	...	...	...
General government	8 782 . .	...	...	...	...	...	...	...	...
Banks	8 783 . .	...	...	...	282	288	295	694	575
Other sectors	8 784 . .	...	...	...	...	...	...	...	...
Other liabilities	8 786 . .	...	...	...	656	491	448	762	537
Monetary authorities	8 787 . .	...	...	...	...	...	...	...	...
of which: Short-term	8 789 . .	...	...	...	...	...	...	...	...
General government	8 790 . .	...	...	...	...	...	...	...	...
of which: Short-term	8 792 . .	...	...	...	...	...	...	...	...
Banks	8 793 . .	...	...	...	656	491	448	762	537
of which: Short-term	8 795 . .	...	...	...	*656*	*491*	*448*	*641*	*446*
Other sectors	8 796 . .	...	...	...	...	...	...	...	...
of which: Short-term	8 798 . .	...	...	...	...	...	...	...	...
NET INTERNATIONAL INVESTMENT POSITION	8 995 . .	**...**	**–53,850**	**–62,737**	**–74,268**	**–63,693**	**–46,691**	**–58,622**	**–49,588**
Conversion rates: baht per U.S. dollar (end of period)	0 102 . .	**25.090**	**25.190**	**25.610**	**47.247**	**36.691**	**37.470**	**43.268**	**44.222**

Table 1. ANALYTIC PRESENTATION, 1994–2001
(Millions of U.S. dollars)

	Code	1994	1995	1996	1997	1998	1999	2000	2001
A. Current Account [1]	4 993 Z.	**–56.3**	**–122.0**	**–153.9**	**–116.9**	**–140.1**	**–127.1**	**–139.6**	**. . .**
Goods: exports f.o.b.	2 100 . .	328.4	377.4	440.6	422.5	420.3	391.5	361.8	. . .
Goods: imports f.o.b.	3 100 . .	–365.5	–506.5	–567.8	–530.6	–553.5	–489.4	–484.6	. . .
Balance on Goods	4 100 . .	*–37.1*	*–129.1*	*–127.2*	*–108.1*	*–133.2*	*–98.0*	*–122.8*	. . .
Services: credit	2 200 . .	70.9	87.3	116.2	88.5	76.0	68.4	61.8	. . .
Services: debit	3 200 . .	–125.3	–164.3	–201.4	–167.8	–149.2	–130.6	–117.5	. . .
Balance on Goods and Services	4 991 . .	*–91.6*	*–206.0*	*–212.3*	*–187.4*	*–206.4*	*–160.1*	*–178.5*	. . .
Income: credit	2 300 . .	9.1	8.8	45.6	35.0	44.4	40.2	32.9	. . .
Income: debit	3 300 . .	–54.0	–42.4	–72.0	–63.9	–67.7	–78.6	–62.0	. . .
Balance on Goods, Services, and Income	4 992 . .	*–136.5*	*–239.6*	*–238.8*	*–216.3*	*–229.7*	*–198.5*	*–207.6*	. . .
Current transfers: credit	2 379 Z.	91.3	129.7	106.8	120.2	101.8	73.6	73.3	. . .
Current transfers: debit	3 379 . .	–11.2	–12.1	–21.9	–20.8	–12.2	–2.2	–5.4	. . .
B. Capital Account [1]	4 994 Z.	**. . .**	**. . .**	**5.6**	**5.8**	**6.1**	**6.9**	**8.7**	**. . .**
Capital account: credit	2 994 Z.	. . .	. . .	5.6	5.8	6.1	6.9	8.7	. . .
Capital account: debit	3 994 . .	. . .	. . .	. . .	. . .	. . .	. . .	. . .	. . .
Total, Groups A Plus B	4 981 . .	*–56.3*	*–122.0*	*–148.3*	*–111.1*	*–134.0*	*–120.2*	*–131.0*	. . .
C. Financial Account [1]	4 995 W.	**–40.5**	**–52.8**	**151.3**	**126.9**	**114.1**	**155.5**	**162.8**	**. . .**
Direct investment abroad	4 505 . .	. . .	5.8	–2.8	–2.5	–10.6	–2.9	–.4	. . .
Direct investment in Togo	4 555 Z.	15.4	26.2	17.3	21.0	30.2	42.6	41.9	. . .
Portfolio investment assets	4 602 . .	.7	5.0	–16.1	6.7	–5.2	–1.3	.8	. . .
Equity securities	4 610 . .	1.1	5.0	–.3	7.0	–4.4	–2.8	.6	. . .
Debt securities	4 619 . .	–.4	. . .	–15.8	–.3	–.7	1.6	.2	. . .
Portfolio investment liabilities	4 652 Z.	. . .	. . .	20.1	9.4	11.4	8.6	6.1	. . .
Equity securities	4 660 . .	. . .	. . .	18.8	10.6	11.6	8.5	6.1	. . .
Debt securities	4 669 Z.	. . .	. . .	1.3	–1.2	–.2	.1	. . .	. . .
Financial derivatives	4 910 . .	. . .	20.6	1.9	–4.9	–.3	–.3	–.1	. . .
Financial derivatives assets	4 900 . .	. . .	20.6	.3	2.1	–.1	. . .	–.1	. . .
Financial derivatives liabilities	4 905 . .	. . .	. . .	1.6	–7.0	–.2	–.3	. . .	. . .
Other investment assets	4 703 . .	–1.5	12.1	–19.2	–1.6	16.2	13.0	8.8	. . .
Monetary authorities	4 701 . .	. . .	. . .	. . .	. . .	. . .	. . .	. . .	. . .
General government	4 704 . .	. . .	. . .	–3.7	12.2	5.3	7.8	7.5	. . .
Banks	4 705 . .	. . .	. . .	4.6	. . .	–.7	.5	–16.8	. . .
Other sectors	4 728 . .	–1.5	12.1	–20.1	–13.8	11.6	4.7	18.1	. . .
Other investment liabilities	4 753 W.	–55.2	–122.4	150.1	98.9	72.3	95.8	105.7	. . .
Monetary authorities	4 753 WA	. . .	. . .	3.8	4.8	5.8	–5.0	2.5	. . .
General government	4 753 ZB	–19.3	–133.5	67.8	62.0	45.0	33.2	41.6	. . .
Banks	4 753 ZC	–66.2	. . .	13.1	. . .	–6.4	1.6	1.4	. . .
Other sectors	4 753 ZD	30.3	11.0	65.4	32.0	28.0	65.9	60.1	. . .
Total, Groups A Through C	4 983 . .	*–96.8*	*–174.7*	*3.0*	*15.8*	*–19.9*	*35.3*	*31.8*	. . .
D. Net Errors and Omissions	4 998 . .	**–.2**	**–19.3**	**–27.9**	**–2.7**	**2.7**	**–3.7**	**5.0**	**. . .**
Total, Groups A Through D	4 984 . .	*–97.1*	*–194.0*	*–24.9*	*13.1*	*–17.2*	*31.6*	*36.8*	. . .
E. Reserves and Related Items	4 802 A.	**97.1**	**194.0**	**24.9**	**–13.1**	**17.2**	**–31.6**	**–36.8**	**. . .**
Reserve assets	4 802 . .	–7.7	–26.9	34.3	–26.2	8.8	–22.2	–27.5	. . .
Use of Fund credit and loans	4 766 . .	9.3	22.0	–11.4	3.4	3.0	–9.4	–9.3	. . .
Exceptional financing	4 920 . .	95.5	199.0	2.0	9.7	5.4	. . .	. . .	. . .
Conversion rates: CFA francs per U.S. dollar	0 101 . .	**555.20**	**499.15**	**511.55**	**583.67**	**589.95**	**615.70**	**711.98**	**733.04**

[1] Excludes components that have been classified in the categories of Group E.

Table 2. STANDARD PRESENTATION, 1994–2001
(Millions of U.S. dollars)

	Code	1994	1995	1996	1997	1998	1999	2000	2001
CURRENT ACCOUNT	4 993 . .	**–56.3**	**–122.0**	**–153.9**	**–116.9**	**–140.1**	**–127.1**	**–139.6**	**. . .**
A. GOODS	4 100 . .	–37.1	–129.1	–127.2	–108.1	–133.2	–98.0	–122.8	. . .
Credit	2 100 . .	**328.4**	**377.4**	**440.6**	**422.5**	**420.3**	**391.5**	**361.8**	**. . .**
General merchandise: exports f.o.b.	2 110 . .	328.4	377.4	431.9	413.3	412.1	383.3	354.9	. . .
Goods for processing: exports f.o.b.	2 150 . .	. . .	. . .	. . .	. . .	. . .	. . .	. . .	. . .
Repairs on goods	2 160 . .	. . .	. . .	. . .	. . .	. . .	. . .	. . .	. . .
Goods procured in ports by carriers	2 170 . .	. . .	. . .	8.7	9.2	8.2	8.2	6.9	. . .
Nonmonetary gold	2 180 . .	. . .	. . .	. . .	. . .	. . .	. . .	. . .	. . .
Debit	3 100 . .	**–365.5**	**–506.5**	**–567.8**	**–530.6**	**–553.5**	**–489.4**	**–484.6**	**. . .**
General merchandise: imports f.o.b.	3 110 . .	–365.5	–506.5	–567.8	–530.5	–553.2	–489.3	–484.3	. . .
Goods for processing: imports f.o.b.	3 150 . .	. . .	. . .	. . .	. . .	. . .	. . .	. . .	. . .
Repairs on goods	3 160 . .	. . .	. . .	. . .	. . .	. . .	. . .	–.2	. . .
Goods procured in ports by carriers	3 170 . .	. . .	. . .	. . .	. . .	–.2	–.1	–.2	. . .
Nonmonetary gold	3 180 . .	. . .	. . .	. . .	. . .	. . .	. . .	. . .	. . .
B. SERVICES	4 200 . .	–54.5	–76.9	–85.2	–79.3	–73.2	–62.2	–55.7	. . .
Total credit	2 200 . .	*70.9*	*87.3*	*116.2*	*88.5*	*76.0*	*68.4*	*61.8*	. . .
Total debit	3 200 . .	*–125.3*	*–164.3*	*–201.4*	*–167.8*	*–149.2*	*–130.6*	*–117.5*	. . .
Transportation services, credit	2 205 . .	**15.2**	**21.6**	**10.1**	**8.8**	**11.2**	**12.8**	**10.5**	**. . .**
Passenger	2 850 . .	. . .	. . .	. . .	. . .	*4.3*	*2.8*	*3.3*	. . .
Freight	2 851 . .	*1.9*	*1.8*	*2.8*	*2.4*	*3.2*	*2.8*	*1.7*	. . .
Other	2 852 . .	*13.2*	*19.8*	*7.3*	*6.4*	*3.7*	*7.1*	*5.6*	. . .
Sea transport, passenger	2 207 . .	. . .	. . .	. . .	. . .	. . .	. . .	. . .	. . .
Sea transport, freight	2 208 . .	1.9	1.8	. . .	. . .	. . .	. . .	. . .	. . .
Sea transport, other	2 209 . .	13.2	19.8	7.3	6.4	3.6	6.8	4.7	. . .
Air transport, passenger	2 211 . .	. . .	. . .	. . .	. . .	1.4	.4	.9	. . .
Air transport, freight	2 212 . .	. . .	. . .	. . .	. . .	.1	. . .	. . .	. . .
Air transport, other	2 213 . .	. . .	. . .	. . .	. . .	.1	.3	.9	. . .
Other transport, passenger	2 215 . .	. . .	. . .	. . .	. . .	3.0	2.5	2.3	. . .
Other transport, freight	2 216 . .	. . .	. . .	2.8	2.4	3.1	2.8	1.7	. . .
Other transport, other	2 217 . .	. . .	. . .	. . .	. . .	. . .	. . .	. . .	. . .
Transportation services, debit	3 205 . .	**–69.7**	**–104.8**	**–118.6**	**–103.4**	**–106.5**	**–95.2**	**–84.0**	**. . .**
Passenger	3 850 . .	*–18.5*	*–21.8*	*–16.4*	*–8.5*	*–12.7*	*–14.3*	*–13.4*	. . .
Freight	3 851 . .	*–45.1*	*–76.8*	*–97.6*	*–90.9*	*–92.9*	*–78.2*	*–68.9*	. . .
Other	3 852 . .	*–6.1*	*–6.2*	*–4.5*	*–4.0*	*–1.0*	*–2.7*	*–1.7*	. . .
Sea transport, passenger	3 207 . .	. . .	. . .	. . .	. . .	. . .	. . .	. . .	. . .
Sea transport, freight	3 208 . .	–45.1	–76.8	–97.5	–81.7	–83.6	–70.1	–61.9	. . .
Sea transport, other	3 209 . .	–6.1	–6.2	–3.4	–3.0	–.8	–1.4	–.4	. . .
Air transport, passenger	3 211 . .	–18.5	–21.8	–16.4	–6.0	–12.7	–14.3	–13.4	. . .
Air transport, freight	3 212 . .	. . .	. . .	–.1	–9.2	–9.3	–8.1	–7.0	. . .
Air transport, other	3 213 . .	. . .	. . .	–1.1	–1.0	–.2	–1.3	–1.3	. . .
Other transport, passenger	3 215 . .	. . .	. . .	. . .	–2.6	. . .	. . .	. . .	. . .
Other transport, freight	3 216 . .	. . .	. . .	. . .	. . .	. . .	. . .	. . .	. . .
Other transport, other	3 217 . .	. . .	. . .	. . .	. . .	. . .	. . .	. . .	. . .
Travel, credit	2 236 . .	**11.5**	**12.7**	**9.8**	**11.9**	**10.6**	**6.9**	**8.0**	**. . .**
Business travel	2 237 . .	. . .	. . .	7.7	7.3	1.0	1.0	3.9	. . .
Personal travel	2 240 . .	11.5	12.7	2.1	4.6	9.6	5.9	4.2	. . .
Travel, debit	3 236 . .	**–17.8**	**–18.5**	**–3.1**	**–4.8**	**–3.3**	**–2.6**	**–2.0**	**. . .**
Business travel	3 237 . .	. . .	. . .	–2.8	–4.8	–3.2	–2.6	–2.0	. . .
Personal travel	3 240 . .	–17.8	–18.5	–.3	. . .	. . .	–.1	. . .	. . .
Other services, credit	2 200 BA	**44.3**	**53.0**	**96.3**	**67.8**	**54.2**	**48.8**	**43.2**	**. . .**
Communications	2 245 . .	. . .	. . .	6.3	7.3	3.3	7.8	4.8	. . .
Construction	2 249 . .	. . .	. . .	8.2	8.7	. . .	. . .	. . .	. . .
Insurance	2 253 . .	.4	1.1	2.1	1.9	1.5	.9	.4	. . .
Financial	2 260 . .	. . .	. . .	.7	.8	.9	2.3	3.6	. . .
Computer and information	2 262 . .	. . .	. . .	. . .	. . .	. . .	. . .	. . .	. . .
Royalties and licence fees	2 266 . .	. . .	. . .	. . .	. . .	. . .	. . .	. . .	. . .
Other business services	2 268 . .	24.7	28.2	64.4	38.2	36.9	23.1	18.3	. . .
Personal, cultural, and recreational	2 287 . .	. . .	. . .	.1	.1	.5	. . .	. . .	. . .
Government, n.i.e.	2 291 . .	19.2	23.7	14.5	10.8	11.1	14.6	16.1	. . .
Other services, debit	3 200 BA	**–37.8**	**–41.0**	**–79.7**	**–59.7**	**–39.5**	**–32.7**	**–31.5**	**. . .**
Communications	3 245 . .	. . .	. . .	–3.9	–6.3	–2.7	–5.9	–2.2	. . .
Construction	3 249 . .	. . .	. . .	–8.0	–5.6	–1.9	–.7	–.6	. . .
Insurance	3 253 . .	–8.2	–6.5	–21.9	–12.9	–17.1	–14.5	–14.7	. . .
Financial	3 260 . .	. . .	. . .	–2.6	–2.4	–6.5	–3.7	–2.2	. . .
Computer and information	3 262 . .	. . .	. . .	–.6	–14.0	–1.0	–1.4	–1.1	. . .
Royalties and licence fees	3 266 . .	. . .	. . .	–.6	–1.5	–.3	–.8	–.6	. . .
Other business services	3 268 . .	–13.5	–18.2	–37.7	–16.7	–9.4	–5.6	–9.0	. . .
Personal, cultural, and recreational	3 287 . .	. . .	. . .	. . .	–.1	–.3	. . .	. . .	. . .
Government, n.i.e.	3 291 . .	–16.2	–16.2	–4.4	–.2	–.3	–.2	–1.1	. . .

Table 2 (Continued). STANDARD PRESENTATION, 1994–2001
(Millions of U.S. dollars)

	Code	1994	1995	1996	1997	1998	1999	2000	2001
C. INCOME	4 300	–44.9	–33.6	–26.4	–28.8	–23.3	–38.4	–29.1	...
Total credit	2 300	*9.1*	*8.8*	*45.6*	*35.0*	*44.4*	*40.2*	*32.9*	...
Total debit	3 300	*–54.0*	*–42.4*	*–72.0*	*–63.9*	*–67.7*	*–78.6*	*–62.0*	...
Compensation of employees, credit	2 310	...	...	**16.1**	**17.7**	**18.5**	**18.4**	**18.5**	...
Compensation of employees, debit	3 310	...	...	**–1.2**	**–5.2**	**–5.4**	**–5.0**	**–2.9**	...
Investment income, credit	2 320	**9.1**	**8.8**	**29.5**	**17.4**	**25.8**	**21.8**	**14.4**	...
Direct investment income	2 330	5.3	7.2	4.5	4.1	12.0	7.1	2.4	...
Dividends and distributed branch profits	2 332	5.3	7.2	...	.1	.1	.5	.3	...
Reinvested earnings and undistributed branch profits	2 333	...	...	4.5	4.0	11.9	6.6	2.1	...
Income on debt (interest)	2 334	...	...	...	...	.1	...	...	...
Portfolio investment income	2 339	...	...	6.0	1.4	1.1	1.2	1.1	...
Income on equity	2 340	...	...	4.9	...	...	...	...	...
Income on bonds and notes	2 350	...	...	.7	.8	.8	.5	.4	...
Income on money market instruments	2 360	...	...	.5	.6	.2	.7	.7	...
Other investment income	2 370	3.8	1.6	19.0	11.8	12.7	13.5	10.9	...
Investment income, debit	3 320	**–54.0**	**–42.4**	**–70.8**	**–58.7**	**–62.3**	**–73.5**	**–59.2**	...
Direct investment income	3 330	–4.1	–1.5	–5.9	–16.3	–18.5	–18.5	–17.2	...
Dividends and distributed branch profits	3 332	–4.1	–1.5	–4.4	–5.3	–3.4	–7.2	–7.8	...
Reinvested earnings and undistributed branch profits	3 333	...	...	–1.0	–10.3	–13.9	–10.9	–8.4	...
Income on debt (interest)	3 334	...	...	–.5	–.7	–1.2	–.4	–1.0	...
Portfolio investment income	3 339	.4	...	–26.6	–5.6	–8.1	–8.2	–6.2	...
Income on equity	3 340	.4	...	–23.4	–2.7	–.5	–1.6	–1.9	...
Income on bonds and notes	3 350	...	...	–3.2	–2.5	–7.4	–6.5	–4.2	...
Income on money market instruments	3 360	...	...	...	–.4	–.3	...	–.1	...
Other investment income	3 370	–50.3	–40.9	–38.3	–36.8	–35.7	–46.9	–35.8	...
D. CURRENT TRANSFERS	4 379	80.1	117.6	84.9	99.4	89.6	71.4	68.0	...
Credit	2 379	**91.3**	**129.7**	**106.8**	**120.2**	**101.8**	**73.6**	**73.3**	...
General government	2 380	76.0	114.7	90.7	103.6	85.4	50.7	39.2	...
Other sectors	2 390	15.3	15.0	16.1	16.6	16.4	22.9	34.2	...
Workers' remittances	2 391	15.3	15.0	13.3	8.6	...	4.5	15.7	...
Other current transfers	2 392	...	...	2.8	8.0	16.4	18.4	18.5	...
Debit	3 379	**–11.2**	**–12.1**	**–21.9**	**–20.8**	**–12.2**	**–2.2**	**–5.4**	...
General government	3 380	–6.8	–6.8	–15.4	–13.5	–6.7	...	...	...
Other sectors	3 390	–4.4	–5.2	–6.5	–7.4	–5.5	–2.2	–5.4	...
Workers' remittances	3 391	–4.1	–4.9	–5.6	–5.2	–.7	–1.0	–3.9	...
Other current transfers	3 392	–.3	–.3	–.9	–2.2	–4.8	–1.2	–1.5	...
CAPITAL AND FINANCIAL ACCOUNT	4 996	**56.6**	**141.3**	**181.8**	**119.6**	**137.4**	**130.9**	**134.7**	...
CAPITAL ACCOUNT	4 994	**5.8**	**2.8**	**7.6**	**15.5**	**11.5**	**6.9**	**8.7**	...
Total credit	2 994	*5.8*	*2.8*	*7.6*	*15.5*	*11.5*	*6.9*	*8.7*	...
Total debit	3 994	...	...	...	...	...	...	...	...
Capital transfers, credit	2 400	**5.8**	**2.8**	**7.6**	**15.5**	**11.5**	**6.9**	**8.7**	...
General government	2 401	5.8	2.8	7.2	15.2	10.8	4.7	6.0	...
Debt forgiveness	2 402	5.8	2.8	2.0	9.7	10.8	1.0	...	...
Other capital transfers	2 410	...	...	5.2	5.5	...	3.7	6.0	...
Other sectors	2 430	...	...	.4	.4	.8	2.2	2.6	...
Migrants' transfers	2 431	...	...	...	...	...	...	...	...
Debt forgiveness	2 432	...	...	...	...	...	...	...	...
Other capital transfers	2 440	...	...	.4	.4	.8	2.2	2.6	...
Capital transfers, debit	3 400	...	...	...	...	...	...	...	...
General government	3 401	...	...	...	...	...	...	...	...
Debt forgiveness	3 402	...	...	...	...	...	...	...	...
Other capital transfers	3 410	...	...	...	...	...	...	...	...
Other sectors	3 430	...	...	...	...	...	...	...	...
Migrants' transfers	3 431	...	...	...	...	...	...	...	...
Debt forgiveness	3 432	...	...	...	...	...	...	...	...
Other capital transfers	3 440	...	...	...	...	...	...	...	...
Nonproduced nonfinancial assets, credit	2 480	...	...	...	...	...	...	...	...
Nonproduced nonfinancial assets, debit	3 480	...	...	...	...	...	...	...	...

Table 2 (Continued). STANDARD PRESENTATION, 1994–2001
(Millions of U.S. dollars)

	Code	1994	1995	1996	1997	1998	1999	2000	2001
FINANCIAL ACCOUNT	4 995 . .	**50.8**	**138.5**	**174.3**	**104.1**	**125.9**	**123.9**	**126.0**	**...**
A. DIRECT INVESTMENT	4 500 . .	15.4	32.0	14.5	18.5	19.6	39.7	41.5	...
Direct investment abroad	4 505 . .	**...**	**5.8**	**–2.8**	**–2.5**	**–10.6**	**–2.9**	**–.4**	**...**
Equity capital	4 510 . .	...	...	–.1	–1.8	–1.5	3.6	2.9	...
Claims on affiliated enterprises	4 515 . .	...	...	–.1	–1.8	–1.5	3.6	2.9	...
Liabilities to affiliated enterprises	4 520 . .	...	...	...	...	...	...	–.1	...
Reinvested earnings	4 525 . .	...	...	–4.5	–4.0	–11.9	–6.6	–2.1	...
Other capital	4 530 . .	...	5.8	1.8	3.4	2.8	.1	–1.2	...
Claims on affiliated enterprises	4 535 . .	...	5.8	–3.1	3.2	6.4	–3.6	–3.9	...
Liabilities to affiliated enterprises	4 540 . .	...	...	4.9	.2	–3.6	3.7	2.7	...
Direct investment in Togo	4 555 . .	**15.4**	**26.2**	**17.3**	**21.0**	**30.2**	**42.6**	**41.9**	**...**
Equity capital	4 560 . .	4.7	23.0	20.0	8.9	15.4	26.8	19.2	...
Claims on direct investors	4 565 . .	4.7	23.0	20.0	8.9	15.4	26.8	–3.9	...
Liabilities to direct investors	4 570 . .	...	...	...	...	...	...	23.1	...
Reinvested earnings	4 575 . .	...	...	1.0	10.3	13.9	10.9	8.4	...
Other capital	4 580 . .	10.7	3.2	–3.7	1.8	.9	4.9	14.4	...
Claims on direct investors	4 585 . .	14.0	11.0	...	...	.1	4.4	–4.2	...
Liabilities to direct investors	4 590 . .	–3.3	–7.8	–3.7	1.8	.8	.5	18.6	...
B. PORTFOLIO INVESTMENT	4 600 . .	.7	5.0	4.0	16.0	6.2	7.3	6.9	...
Assets	4 602 . .	**.7**	**5.0**	**–16.1**	**6.7**	**–5.2**	**–1.3**	**.8**	**...**
Equity securities	4 610 . .	1.1	5.0	–.3	7.0	–4.4	–2.8	.6	...
Monetary authorities	4 611 . .	...	...	...	...	...	...	...	...
General government	4 612 . .	...	...	...	...	...	...	...	...
Banks	4 613 . .	...	...	–.3	7.0	.1	...	–1.0	...
Other sectors	4 614 . .	1.1	5.0	...	...	–4.5	–2.8	1.6	...
Debt securities	4 619 . .	–.4	...	–15.8	–.3	–.7	1.6	.2	...
Bonds and notes	4 620 . .	–.4	...	–5.3	–.5	–.1	.7	1.0	...
Monetary authorities	4 621 . .	...	...	...	...	...	...	...	...
General government	4 622 . .	–.4	...	...	...	...	...	...	...
Banks	4 623 . .	...	...	–1.2	.3	.3	–.8	...	...
Other sectors	4 624 . .	...	...	–4.1	–.7	–.4	1.5	1.0	...
Money market instruments	4 630 . .	...	...	–10.4	.2	–.6	.9	–.7	...
Monetary authorities	4 631 . .	...	...	...	...	...	...	...	...
General government	4 632 . .	...	...	...	...	...	...	...	...
Banks	4 633 . .	...	...	...	...	...	...	...	...
Other sectors	4 634 . .	...	...	–10.4	.2	–.6	.9	–.7	...
Liabilities	4 652 . .	**...**	**...**	**20.1**	**9.4**	**11.4**	**8.6**	**6.1**	**...**
Equity securities	4 660 . .	...	...	18.8	10.6	11.6	8.5	6.1	...
Banks	4 663 . .	...	...	.6	.2	...	.5	.1	...
Other sectors	4 664 . .	...	...	18.2	10.4	11.6	8.0	6.0	...
Debt securities	4 669 . .	...	...	1.3	–1.2	–.2	.1	...	...
Bonds and notes	4 670 . .	...	...	...	–1.2	.2	.1	...	...
Monetary authorities	4 671 . .	...	...	...	...	...	...	...	...
General government	4 672 . .	...	...	...	...	...	...	...	...
Banks	4 673 . .	...	...	...	–1.2	...	...	...	...
Other sectors	4 674 . .	...	...	...	...	.2	.1	...	...
Money market instruments	4 680 . .	...	...	1.3	...	–.3	...	...	...
Monetary authorities	4 681 . .	...	...	...	...	...	...	...	...
General government	4 682 . .	...	...	...	...	...	...	...	...
Banks	4 683 . .	...	...	...	...	...	...	...	...
Other sectors	4 684 . .	...	...	1.3	...	–.3	...	...	...
C. FINANCIAL DERIVATIVES	4 910 . .	...	20.6	1.9	–4.9	–.3	–.3	–.1	...
Monetary authorities	4 911 . .	...	...	...	...	...	...	...	...
General government	4 912 . .	...	...	...	...	...	...	...	...
Banks	4 913 . .	...	20.6	...	...	...	...	...	...
Other sectors	4 914 . .	...	...	1.9	–4.9	–.3	–.3	–.1	...
Assets	4 900 . .	**...**	**20.6**	**.3**	**2.1**	**–.1**	**...**	**–.1**	**...**
Monetary authorities	4 901 . .	...	...	...	...	...	...	...	...
General government	4 902 . .	...	...	...	...	...	...	...	...
Banks	4 903 . .	...	20.6	...	...	...	...	...	...
Other sectors	4 904 . .	...	...	.3	2.1	–.1	...	–.1	...
Liabilities	4 905 . .	**...**	**...**	**1.6**	**–7.0**	**–.2**	**–.3**	**...**	**...**
Monetary authorities	4 906 . .	...	...	...	...	...	...	...	...
General government	4 907 . .	...	...	...	...	...	...	...	...
Banks	4 908 . .	...	...	...	...	...	...	...	...
Other sectors	4 909 . .	...	...	1.6	–7.0	–.2	–.3	...	...

Table 2 (Concluded). STANDARD PRESENTATION, 1994–2001
(Millions of U.S. dollars)

	Code	1994	1995	1996	1997	1998	1999	2000	2001
D. OTHER INVESTMENT	4 700 . .	42.4	107.8	119.5	100.6	91.6	99.4	105.2	. . .
Assets	4 703 . .	**–1.5**	**12.1**	**–19.2**	**–1.6**	**16.2**	**13.0**	**8.8**	**. . .**
Trade credits	4 706 . .	. . .	. . .	–9.6	–5.1	1.1	–.4	9.6	. . .
General government	4 707 . .	. . .	. . .	. . .	. . .	. . .	. . .	. . .	. . .
of which: Short-term	4 709 . .	. . .	. . .	. . .	. . .	. . .	. . .	. . .	. . .
Other sectors	4 710 . .	. . .	. . .	–9.6	–5.1	1.1	–.4	9.6	. . .
of which: Short-term	4 712 . .	. . .	. . .	*–9.6*	*–5.1*	*1.1*	. . .	. . .	. . .
Loans	4 714 . .	–1.5	.4	4.5	.9	–2.6	–5.2	2.9	. . .
Monetary authorities	4 715 . .	. . .	. . .	. . .	. . .	. . .	. . .	. . .	. . .
of which: Short-term	4 718 . .	. . .	. . .	. . .	. . .	. . .	. . .	. . .	. . .
General government	4 719 . .	. . .	. . .	. . .	. . .	. . .	. . .	. . .	. . .
of which: Short-term	4 721 . .	. . .	. . .	. . .	. . .	. . .	. . .	. . .	. . .
Banks	4 722 . .	. . .	. . .	5.2	. . .	–2.8	–5.6	2.5	. . .
of which: Short-term	4 724 . .	. . .	. . .	*5.2*	. . .	*–2.8*	*–4.2*	*1.5*	. . .
Other sectors	4 725 . .	–1.5	.4	–.7	.9	.1	.4	.3	. . .
of which: Short-term	4 727 . .	*–1.5*	*.4*	*–.7*	*.9*	*.1*	. . .	. . .	. . .
Currency and deposits	4 730 . .	. . .	. . .	–8.5	2.7	12.1	9.9	–11.3	. . .
Monetary authorities	4 731 . .	. . .	. . .	. . .	. . .	. . .	. . .	. . .	. . .
General government	4 732 . .	. . .	. . .	–3.9	12.2	3.8	4.9	4.7	. . .
Banks	4 733 . .	. . .	. . .	–.5	. . .	2.0	–.3	–19.3	. . .
Other sectors	4 734 . .	. . .	. . .	–4.0	–9.5	6.3	5.2	3.3	. . .
Other assets	4 736 . .	. . .	11.6	–5.6	–.2	5.6	8.8	7.7	. . .
Monetary authorities	4 737 . .	. . .	. . .	. . .	. . .	. . .	. . .	. . .	. . .
of which: Short-term	4 739 . .	. . .	. . .	. . .	. . .	. . .	. . .	. . .	. . .
General government	4 740 . .	. . .	. . .	.2	. . .	1.5	2.9	2.9	. . .
of which: Short-term	4 742 . .	. . .	. . .	*.2*	. . .	*1.5*	. . .	. . .	. . .
Banks	4 743 . .	. . .	. . .	. . .	. . .	. . .	6.4	. . .	. . .
of which: Short-term	4 745 . .	. . .	. . .	. . .	. . .	. . .	. . .	. . .	. . .
Other sectors	4 746 . .	. . .	11.6	–5.8	–.2	4.1	–.5	4.9	. . .
of which: Short-term	4 748 . .	. . .	*11.6*	*–5.8*	*–.2*	*4.1*	. . .	. . .	. . .
Liabilities	4 753 . .	**43.9**	**95.8**	**138.7**	**102.2**	**75.4**	**86.4**	**96.4**	**. . .**
Trade credits	4 756 . .	30.3	. . .	20.6	23.8	1.0	11.5	19.3	. . .
General government	4 757 . .	. . .	. . .	. . .	. . .	. . .	. . .	. . .	. . .
of which: Short-term	4 759 . .	. . .	. . .	. . .	. . .	. . .	. . .	. . .	. . .
Other sectors	4 760 . .	30.3	. . .	20.6	23.8	1.0	11.5	19.3	. . .
of which: Short-term	4 762 . .	*12.9*	. . .	. . .	. . .	. . .	. . .	. . .	. . .
Loans	4 764 . .	–76.2	14.7	96.1	71.6	76.2	54.2	57.1	. . .
Monetary authorities	4 765 . .	9.3	22.0	–11.4	3.4	3.0	–9.4	–9.3	. . .
of which: Use of Fund credit and loans from the Fund	4 766 . .	*9.3*	*22.0*	*–11.4*	*3.4*	*3.0*	*–9.4*	*–9.3*	. . .
of which: Short-term	4 768 . .	. . .	. . .	. . .	. . .	. . .	. . .	. . .	. . .
General government	4 769 . .	–19.3	–18.3	67.8	62.0	45.0	33.2	41.6	. . .
of which: Short-term	4 771 . .	. . .	. . .	*5.9*	*8.6*	*31.5*	*56.5*	*56.6*	. . .
Banks	4 772 . .	–66.2	. . .	1.1	. . .	3.6	–8.2	4.9	. . .
of which: Short-term	4 774 . .	. . .	. . .	*.1*	. . .	*4.3*	*–8.9*	*16.9*	. . .
Other sectors	4 775 . .	. . .	11.0	38.6	6.2	24.6	38.6	19.9	. . .
of which: Short-term	4 777 . .	. . .	*6.6*	. . .	*5.1*	. . .	*8.1*	. . .	. . .
Currency and deposits	4 780 . .	. . .	. . .	13.7	3.8	–3.4	2.2	–3.1	. . .
Monetary authorities	4 781 . .	. . .	. . .	1.7	3.8	6.6	–4.6	.4	. . .
General government	4 782 . .	. . .	. . .	. . .	. . .	. . .	. . .	. . .	. . .
Banks	4 783 . .	. . .	. . .	12.0	. . .	–10.0	6.9	–3.5	. . .
Other sectors	4 784 . .	. . .	. . .	. . .	. . .	. . .	. . .	. . .	. . .
Other liabilities	4 786 . .	89.7	81.0	8.4	3.0	1.6	18.5	23.1	. . .
Monetary authorities	4 787 . .	. . .	. . .	2.1	1.1	–.8	–.4	2.1	. . .
of which: Short-term	4 789 . .	. . .	. . .	*2.1*	*1.1*	*–.8*	. . .	. . .	. . .
General government	4 790 . .	89.7	81.0	. . .	. . .	. . .	. . .	. . .	. . .
of which: Short-term	4 792 . .	*89.7*	*81.0*	. . .	. . .	. . .	. . .	. . .	. . .
Banks	4 793 . .	. . .	. . .	. . .	. . .	. . .	3.0	. . .	. . .
of which: Short-term	4 795 . .	. . .	. . .	. . .	. . .	. . .	*3.0*	. . .	. . .
Other sectors	4 796 . .	. . .	. . .	6.3	1.9	2.4	15.9	21.0	. . .
of which: Short-term	4 798 . .	. . .	. . .	*6.3*	*1.9*	*2.4*	. . .	. . .	. . .
E. RESERVE ASSETS	4 802 . .	–7.7	–26.9	34.3	–26.2	8.8	–22.2	–27.5	. . .
Monetary gold	4 812 . .	. . .	. . .	. . .	. . .	. . .	. . .	. . .	. . .
Special drawing rights	4 811 . .	. . .	–.4	. . .	.3	–.1	–.2	.2	. . .
Reserve position in the Fund	4 810 . .	. . .	. . .	. . .	. . .	. . .	. . .	. . .	. . .
Foreign exchange	4 803 . .	–7.7	–26.6	34.3	–26.5	8.8	–22.0	–27.7	. . .
Other claims	4 813 . .	. . .	. . .	. . .	. . .	. . .	. . .	. . .	. . .
NET ERRORS AND OMISSIONS	4 998 . .	**–.2**	**–19.3**	**–27.9**	**–2.7**	**2.7**	**–3.7**	**5.0**	**. . .**

Part 3 of the *Yearbook* contains descriptions of the methodologies, compilation practices, and sources used to compile these data.

Table 3. INTERNATIONAL INVESTMENT POSITION (End–period stocks), 1994–2001
(Millions of U.S. dollars)

	Code	1994	1995	1996	1997	1998	1999	2000	2001
ASSETS	8 995 C.	...	...	...	...	...	364.1	340.4	...
Direct investment abroad	8 505 . .	...	...	...	...	...	**–10.1**	**–9.9**	...
Equity capital and reinvested earnings	8 506 . .	...	...	...	...	...	5.3	3.8	...
Claims on affiliated enterprises	8 507 . .	...	...	...	...	...	5.3	3.8	...
Liabilities to affiliated enterprises	8 508 . .	...	...	...	...	...	...	...	...
Other capital	8 530 . .	...	...	...	...	...	–15.4	–13.7	...
Claims on affiliated enterprises	8 535 . .	...	...	...	...	...	...	...	...
Liabilities to affiliated enterprises	8 540 . .	...	...	...	...	...	–15.4	–13.7	...
Portfolio investment	8 602 . .	...	...	...	...	...	**14.3**	**13.8**	...
Equity securities	8 610 . .	...	...	...	...	...	6.6	7.3	...
Monetary authorities	8 611 . .	...	...	...	...	...	...	...	...
General government	8 612 . .	...	...	...	...	...	...	...	...
Banks	8 613 . .	...	...	...	...	...	...	...	...
Other sectors	8 614 . .	...	...	...	...	...	6.6	7.3	...
Debt securities	8 619 . .	...	...	...	...	...	7.7	6.5	...
Bonds and notes	8 620 . .	...	...	...	...	...	3.5	1.7	...
Monetary authorities	8 621 . .	...	...	...	...	...	...	...	...
General government	8 622 . .	...	...	...	...	...	...	...	...
Banks	8 623 . .	...	...	...	...	...	.8	.9	...
Other sectors	8 624 . .	...	...	...	...	...	2.7	.8	...
Money market instruments	8 630 . .	...	...	...	...	...	4.2	4.8	...
Monetary authorities	8 631 . .	...	...	...	...	...	...	...	...
General government	8 632 . .	...	...	...	...	...	...	...	...
Banks	8 633 . .	...	...	...	...	...	4.1	3.9	...
Other sectors	8 634 . .	...	...	...	...	...	.2	.9	...
Financial derivatives	8 900 . .	...	...	...	...	...	**.1**	**.1**	...
Monetary authorities	8 901 . .	...	...	...	...	...	...	...	...
General government	8 902 . .	...	...	...	...	...	...	...	...
Banks	8 903 . .	...	...	...	...	...	...	...	...
Other sectors	8 904 . .	...	...	...	...	...	.1	.1	...
Other investment	8 703 . .	...	...	...	...	...	**237.7**	**195.5**	...
Trade credits	8 706 . .	...	...	...	...	...	84.3	63.8	...
General government	8 707 . .	...	...	...	...	...	...	...	...
of which: Short-term	8 709 . .	...	...	...	...	...	...	...	...
Other sectors	8 710 . .	...	...	...	...	...	84.3	63.8	...
of which: Short-term	8 712 . .	...	...	...	...	...	*84.3*	*63.8*	...
Loans	8 714 . .	...	...	...	...	...	12.2	18.6	...
Monetary authorities	8 715 . .	...	...	...	...	...	...	...	...
of which: Short-term	8 718 . .	...	...	...	...	...	...	...	...
General government	8 719 . .	...	...	...	...	...	...	...	...
of which: Short-term	8 721 . .	...	...	...	...	...	...	...	...
Banks	8 722 . .	...	...	...	...	...	11.4	17.7	...
of which: Short-term	8 724 . .	...	...	...	...	...	*8.9*	*6.8*	...
Other sectors	8 725 . .	...	...	...	...	...	.9	.9	...
of which: Short-term	8 727 . .	...	...	...	...	...	*.9*	*.9*	...
Currency and deposits	8 730 . .	...	...	...	...	...	79.1	98.1	...
Monetary authorities	8 731 . .	...	...	...	...	...	...	...	...
General government	8 732 . .	...	...	...	...	...	26.5	17.0	...
Banks	8 733 . .	...	...	...	...	...	49.7	65.5	...
Other sectors	8 734 . .	...	...	...	...	...	2.9	15.5	...
Other assets	8 736 . .	...	...	...	...	...	62.0	15.1	...
Monetary authorities	8 737 . .	...	...	...	...	...	...	...	...
of which: Short-term	8 739 . .	...	...	...	...	...	...	...	...
General government	8 740 . .	...	...	...	...	...	9.2	4.3	...
of which: Short-term	8 742 . .	...	...	...	...	...	*9.2*	*4.3*	...
Banks	8 743 . .	...	...	...	...	...	6.0	...	...
of which: Short-term	8 745 . .	...	...	...	...	...	...	...	...
Other sectors	8 746 . .	...	...	...	...	...	46.7	10.8	...
of which: Short-term	8 748 . .	...	...	...	...	...	*46.7*	*10.8*	...
Reserve assets	8 802 . .	...	...	...	...	...	**122.1**	**140.9**	...
Monetary gold	8 812 . .	...	...	...	...	...	...	...	...
Special drawing rights	8 811 . .	.1	.4	.4	...	.1	.2	...	.2
Reserve position in the Fund	8 810 . .	.4	.4	.4	.3	.4	.3	.4	.4
Foreign exchange	8 803 . .	...	...	...	...	...	121.5	140.5	...
Other claims	8 813 . .	...	...	...	...	...	...	...	...

Table 3 (Concluded). INTERNATIONAL INVESTMENT POSITION (End–period stocks), 1994–2001
(Millions of U.S. dollars)

	Code	1994	1995	1996	1997	1998	1999	2000	2001
LIABILITIES	8 995 D.	...	...	...	...	...	1,728.8	1,775.7	...
Direct investment in Togo	8 555 . .	...	...	...	...	...	**47.5**	**86.8**	...
Equity capital and reinvested earnings	8 556 . .	...	...	...	...	...	45.2	62.3	...
Claims on direct investors	8 557 . .	...	...	...	...	...	45.2	62.3	...
Liabilities to direct investors	8 558 . .	...	...	...	...	...	...	...	...
Other capital	8 580 . .	...	...	...	...	...	2.3	24.5	...
Claims on direct investors	8 585 . .	...	...	...	...	...	...	...	...
Liabilities to direct investors	8 590 . .	...	...	...	...	...	2.3	24.5	...
Portfolio investment	8 652 . .	...	...	...	...	...	**24.2**	**30.1**	...
Equity securities	8 660 . .	...	...	...	...	...	24.2	30.1	...
Banks	8 663 . .	...	...	...	...	...	.5	.5	...
Other sectors	8 664 . .	...	...	...	...	...	23.7	29.5	...
Debt securities	8 669 . .	...	...	...	...	...	.1	...	...
Bonds and notes	8 670 . .	...	...	...	...	...	.1	...	...
Monetary authorities	8 671 . .	...	...	...	...	...	...	...	...
General government	8 672 . .	...	...	...	...	...	...	...	...
Banks	8 673 . .	...	...	...	...	...	...	...	...
Other sectors	8 674 . .	...	...	...	...	...	.1	...	...
Money market instruments	8 680 . .	...	...	...	...	...	...	...	...
Monetary authorities	8 681 . .	...	...	...	...	...	...	...	...
General government	8 682 . .	...	...	...	...	...	...	...	...
Banks	8 683 . .	...	...	...	...	...	...	...	...
Other sectors	8 684 . .	...	...	...	...	...	...	...	...
Financial derivatives	8 905 . .	...	...	...	...	...	.7	...	...
Monetary authorities	8 906 . .	...	...	...	...	...	...	...	...
General government	8 907 . .	...	...	...	...	...	...	...	...
Banks	8 908 . .	...	...	...	...	...	.7	...	...
Other sectors	8 909 . .	...	...	...	...	...	...	...	...
Other investment	8 753 . .	...	...	...	...	...	**1,656.5**	**1,658.8**	...
Trade credits	8 756 . .	...	...	...	...	...	117.7	106.2	...
General government	8 757 . .	...	...	...	...	...	...	...	...
of which: Short-term	8 759 . .	...	...	...	...	...	...	...	...
Other sectors	8 760 . .	...	...	...	...	...	117.7	106.2	...
of which: Short-term	8 762 . .	...	...	...	...	...	*117.7*	*106.2*	...
Loans	8 764 . .	...	...	...	...	...	1,466.3	1,468.2	...
Monetary authorities	8 765 . .	...	...	...	...	...	83.0	72.1	...
of which: Use of Fund credit and loans from the Fund	8 766 . .	*81.8*	*104.7*	*89.9*	*87.6*	*94.8*	*83.0*	*69.5*	*56.9*
of which: Short-term	8 768 . .	...	...	...	...	...	...	...	...
General government	8 769 . .	...	...	...	...	...	1,322.2	1,325.3	...
of which: Short-term	8 771 . .	...	...	...	...	...	...	...	...
Banks	8 772 . .	...	...	...	...	...	3.6	8.3	...
of which: Short-term	8 774 . .	...	...	...	...	...	*2.9*	*19.7*	...
Other sectors	8 775 . .	...	...	...	...	...	57.6	62.5	...
of which: Short-term	8 777 . .	...	...	...	...	...	*57.6*	*62.5*	...
Currency and deposits	8 780 . .	...	...	...	...	...	56.1	55.2	...
Monetary authorities	8 781 . .	...	...	...	...	...	3.7	9.7	...
General government	8 782 . .	...	...	...	...	...	...	...	...
Banks	8 783 . .	...	...	...	...	...	52.4	45.4	...
Other sectors	8 784 . .	...	...	...	...	...	...	...	...
Other liabilities	8 786 . .	...	...	...	...	...	16.4	29.3	...
Monetary authorities	8 787 . .	...	...	...	...	...	.3	2.4	...
of which: Short-term	8 789 . .	...	...	...	...	...	*.3*	*2.4*	...
General government	8 790 . .	...	...	...	...	...	.1	...	...
of which: Short-term	8 792 . .	...	...	...	...	...	*.1*	...	...
Banks	8 793 . .	...	...	...	...	...	...	...	...
of which: Short-term	8 795 . .	...	...	...	...	...	...	...	...
Other sectors	8 796 . .	...	...	...	...	...	16.0	26.9	...
of which: Short-term	8 798 . .	...	...	...	...	...	...	...	...
NET INTERNATIONAL INVESTMENT POSITION	8 995 . .	...	...	...	...	...	**–1,364.8**	**–1,435.3**	...
Conversion rates: CFA francs per U.S. dollar (end of period)	0 102 . .	**534.60**	**490.00**	**523.70**	**598.81**	**562.21**	**652.95**	**704.95**	**744.31**

Table 1. ANALYTIC PRESENTATION, 1994–2001
(Thousands of U.S. dollars)

	Code	1994	1995	1996	1997	1998	1999	2000	2001
A. Current Account [1]	4 993 Z.	...	...	...	...	...	...	...	**–12,858**
Goods: exports f.o.b.	2 100 ..	...	...	...	...	...	...	...	6,657
Goods: imports f.o.b.	3 100 ..	...	...	...	...	...	...	...	–63,688
Balance on Goods	4 100 ..	...	...	...	...	...	...	...	*–57,031*
Services: credit	2 200 ..	...	...	...	...	...	...	...	17,125
Services: debit	3 200 ..	...	...	...	...	...	...	...	–27,152
Balance on Goods and Services	4 991 ..	...	...	...	...	...	...	...	*–67,058*
Income: credit	2 300 ..	...	...	...	...	...	...	...	5,675
Income: debit	3 300 ..	...	...	...	...	...	...	...	–2,266
Balance on Goods, Services, and Income	4 992 ..	...	...	...	...	...	...	...	*–63,650*
Current transfers: credit	2 379 Z.	...	...	...	...	...	...	...	62,507
Current transfers: debit	3 379 ..	...	...	...	...	...	...	...	–11,716
B. Capital Account [1]	4 994 Z.	...	...	...	...	...	...	...	**9,152**
Capital account: credit	2 994 Z.	...	...	...	...	...	...	...	11,727
Capital account: debit	3 994 ..	...	...	...	...	...	...	...	–2,575
Total, Groups A Plus B	4 981 ..	...	...	...	...	...	...	...	*–3,706*
C. Financial Account [1]	4 995 W.	...	...	...	...	...	...	...	**1,001**
Direct investment abroad	4 505 ..	...	...	...	...	...	...	...	...
Direct investment in Tonga	4 555 Z.	...	...	...	...	...	...	...	1,001
Portfolio investment assets	4 602 ..	...	...	...	...	...	...	...	...
Equity securities	4 610 ..	...	...	...	...	...	...	...	...
Debt securities	4 619 ..	...	...	...	...	...	...	...	...
Portfolio investment liabilities	4 652 Z.	...	...	...	...	...	...	...	...
Equity securities	4 660 ..	...	...	...	...	...	...	...	...
Debt securities	4 669 Z.	...	...	...	...	...	...	...	...
Financial derivatives	4 910 ..	...	...	...	...	...	...	...	...
Financial derivatives assets	4 900 ..	...	...	...	...	...	...	...	...
Financial derivatives liabilities	4 905 ..	...	...	...	...	...	...	...	...
Other investment assets	4 703 ..	...	...	...	...	...	...	...	...
Monetary authorities	4 701 ..	...	...	...	...	...	...	...	...
General government	4 704 ..	...	...	...	...	...	...	...	...
Banks	4 705 ..	...	...	...	...	...	...	...	...
Other sectors	4 728 ..	...	...	...	...	...	...	...	...
Other investment liabilities	4 753 W.	...	...	...	...	...	...	...	...
Monetary authorities	4 753 WA	...	...	...	...	...	...	...	...
General government	4 753 ZB	...	...	...	...	...	...	...	...
Banks	4 753 ZC	...	...	...	...	...	...	...	...
Other sectors	4 753 ZD	...	...	...	...	...	...	...	...
Total, Groups A Through C	4 983 ..	...	...	...	...	...	...	...	*–2,705*
D. Net Errors and Omissions	4 998 ..	...	...	...	...	...	...	...	**4,349**
Total, Groups A Through D	4 984 ..	...	...	...	...	...	...	...	*1,645*
E. Reserves and Related Items	4 802 A.	...	...	...	...	...	...	...	**–1,645**
Reserve assets	4 802 ..	...	...	...	...	...	...	...	–1,645
Use of Fund credit and loans	4 766 ..	...	...	...	...	...	...	...	...
Exceptional financing	4 920 ..	...	...	...	...	...	...	...	...
Conversion rates: pa'anga per U.S. dollar	0 101 ..	**1.3202**	**1.2709**	**1.2323**	**1.2635**	**1.4921**	**1.5991**	**1.7585**	**2.1236**

[1] Excludes components that have been classified in the categories of Group E.

Table 2. STANDARD PRESENTATION, 1994–2001

(Thousands of U.S. dollars)

	Code	1994	1995	1996	1997	1998	1999	2000	2001
CURRENT ACCOUNT	4 993 . .	...	...	...	...	...	...	...	**–12,858**
A. GOODS	4 100 . .	...	...	...	...	...	...	...	–57,031
Credit	2 100 . .	...	...	...	...	...	...	...	**6,657**
General merchandise: exports f.o.b.	2 110 . .	...	...	...	...	...	...	...	6,657
Goods for processing: exports f.o.b.	2 150 . .	...	...	...	...	...	...	...	...
Repairs on goods	2 160 . .	...	...	...	...	...	...	...	...
Goods procured in ports by carriers	2 170 . .	...	...	...	...	...	...	...	...
Nonmonetary gold	2 180 . .	...	...	...	...	...	...	...	...
Debit	3 100 . .	...	...	...	...	...	...	...	**–63,688**
General merchandise: imports f.o.b.	3 110 . .	...	...	...	...	...	...	...	–63,688
Goods for processing: imports f.o.b.	3 150 . .	...	...	...	...	...	...	...	...
Repairs on goods	3 160 . .	...	...	...	...	...	...	...	...
Goods procured in ports by carriers	3 170 . .	...	...	...	...	...	...	...	...
Nonmonetary gold	3 180 . .	...	...	...	...	...	...	...	...
B. SERVICES	4 200 . .	...	...	...	...	...	...	...	–10,027
Total credit	2 200 . .	...	...	...	...	...	...	...	*17,125*
Total debit	3 200 . .	...	...	...	...	...	...	...	*–27,152*
Transportation services, credit	2 205 . .	...	...	...	...	...	...	...	**2,263**
Passenger	2 850 . .	...	...	...	...	...	...	...	...
Freight	2 851 . .	...	...	...	...	...	...	...	...
Other	2 852 . .	...	...	...	...	...	...	...	...
Sea transport, passenger	2 207 . .	...	...	...	...	...	...	...	...
Sea transport, freight	2 208 . .	...	...	...	...	...	...	...	...
Sea transport, other	2 209 . .	...	...	...	...	...	...	...	...
Air transport, passenger	2 211 . .	...	...	...	...	...	...	...	...
Air transport, freight	2 212 . .	...	...	...	...	...	...	...	...
Air transport, other	2 213 . .	...	...	...	...	...	...	...	...
Other transport, passenger	2 215 . .	...	...	...	...	...	...	...	...
Other transport, freight	2 216 . .	...	...	...	...	...	...	...	...
Other transport, other	2 217 . .	...	...	...	...	...	...	...	...
Transportation services, debit	3 205 . .	...	...	...	...	...	...	...	**–14,158**
Passenger	3 850 . .	...	...	...	...	...	...	...	...
Freight	3 851 . .	...	...	...	...	...	...	...	...
Other	3 852 . .	...	...	...	...	...	...	...	...
Sea transport, passenger	3 207 . .	...	...	...	...	...	...	...	...
Sea transport, freight	3 208 . .	...	...	...	...	...	...	...	...
Sea transport, other	3 209 . .	...	...	...	...	...	...	...	...
Air transport, passenger	3 211 . .	...	...	...	...	...	...	...	...
Air transport, freight	3 212 . .	...	...	...	...	...	...	...	...
Air transport, other	3 213 . .	...	...	...	...	...	...	...	...
Other transport, passenger	3 215 . .	...	...	...	...	...	...	...	...
Other transport, freight	3 216 . .	...	...	...	...	...	...	...	...
Other transport, other	3 217 . .	...	...	...	...	...	...	...	...
Travel, credit	2 236 . .	...	...	...	...	...	...	...	**6,771**
Business travel	2 237 . .	...	...	...	...	...	...	...	...
Personal travel	2 240 . .	...	...	...	...	...	...	...	...
Travel, debit	3 236 . .	...	...	...	...	...	...	...	**–3,147**
Business travel	3 237 . .	...	...	...	...	...	...	...	...
Personal travel	3 240 . .	...	...	...	...	...	...	...	...
Other services, credit	2 200 BA	...	...	...	...	...	...	...	**8,092**
Communications	2 245 . .	...	...	...	...	...	...	...	...
Construction	2 249 . .	...	...	...	...	...	...	...	...
Insurance	2 253 . .	...	...	...	...	...	...	...	...
Financial	2 260 . .	...	...	...	...	...	...	...	...
Computer and information	2 262 . .	...	...	...	...	...	...	...	...
Royalties and licence fees	2 266 . .	...	...	...	...	...	...	...	...
Other business services	2 268 . .	...	...	...	...	...	...	...	6,787
Personal, cultural, and recreational	2 287 . .	...	...	...	...	...	...	...	68
Government, n.i.e.	2 291 . .	...	...	...	...	...	...	...	1,237
Other services, debit	3 200 BA	...	...	...	...	...	...	...	**–9,847**
Communications	3 245 . .	...	...	...	...	...	...	...	...
Construction	3 249 . .	...	...	...	...	...	...	...	...
Insurance	3 253 . .	...	...	...	...	...	...	...	...
Financial	3 260 . .	...	...	...	...	...	...	...	...
Computer and information	3 262 . .	...	...	...	...	...	...	...	...
Royalties and licence fees	3 266 . .	...	...	...	...	...	...	...	...
Other business services	3 268 . .	...	...	...	...	...	...	...	–6,455
Personal, cultural, and recreational	3 287 . .	...	...	...	...	...	...	...	–24
Government, n.i.e.	3 291 . .	...	...	...	...	...	...	...	–3,368

Table 2 (Continued). STANDARD PRESENTATION, 1994–2001

(Thousands of U.S. dollars)

	Code	1994	1995	1996	1997	1998	1999	2000	2001
C. INCOME	4 300	...	...	...	...	...	...	...	3,409
Total credit	2 300	...	...	...	...	...	...	...	*5,675*
Total debit	3 300	...	...	...	...	...	...	...	*–2,266*
Compensation of employees, credit	2 310	...	...	...	...	...	...	...	...
Compensation of employees, debit	3 310	...	...	...	...	...	...	...	...
Investment income, credit	2 320	...	...	...	...	...	...	...	...
Direct investment income	2 330	...	...	...	...	...	...	...	...
Dividends and distributed branch profits	2 332	...	...	...	...	...	...	...	...
Reinvested earnings and undistributed branch profits	2 333	...	...	...	...	...	...	...	...
Income on debt (interest)	2 334	...	...	...	...	...	...	...	...
Portfolio investment income	2 339	...	...	...	...	...	...	...	...
Income on equity	2 340	...	...	...	...	...	...	...	...
Income on bonds and notes	2 350	...	...	...	...	...	...	...	...
Income on money market instruments	2 360	...	...	...	...	...	...	...	...
Other investment income	2 370	...	...	...	...	...	...	...	...
Investment income, debit	3 320	...	...	...	...	...	...	...	...
Direct investment income	3 330	...	...	...	...	...	...	...	...
Dividends and distributed branch profits	3 332	...	...	...	...	...	...	...	...
Reinvested earnings and undistributed branch profits	3 333	...	...	...	...	...	...	...	...
Income on debt (interest)	3 334	...	...	...	...	...	...	...	...
Portfolio investment income	3 339	...	...	...	...	...	...	...	...
Income on equity	3 340	...	...	...	...	...	...	...	...
Income on bonds and notes	3 350	...	...	...	...	...	...	...	...
Income on money market instruments	3 360	...	...	...	...	...	...	...	...
Other investment income	3 370	...	...	...	...	...	...	...	...
D. CURRENT TRANSFERS	4 379	...	...	...	...	...	...	...	50,792
Credit	2 379	...	...	...	...	...	...	...	**62,507**
General government	2 380	...	...	...	...	...	...	...	5,560
Other sectors	2 390	...	...	...	...	...	...	...	56,947
Workers' remittances	2 391	...	...	...	...	...	...	...	52,533
Other current transfers	2 392	...	...	...	...	...	...	...	4,415
Debit	3 379	...	...	...	...	...	...	...	**–11,716**
General government	3 380	...	...	...	...	...	...	...	–735
Other sectors	3 390	...	...	...	...	...	...	...	–10,981
Workers' remittances	3 391	...	...	...	...	...	...	...	–10,674
Other current transfers	3 392	...	...	...	...	...	...	...	–307
CAPITAL AND FINANCIAL ACCOUNT	4 996	...	...	...	...	...	...	...	**8,509**
CAPITAL ACCOUNT	4 994	...	...	...	...	...	...	...	**9,152**
Total credit	2 994	...	...	...	...	...	...	...	*11,727*
Total debit	3 994	...	...	...	...	...	...	...	*–2,575*
Capital transfers, credit	2 400	...	...	...	...	...	...	...	...
General government	2 401	...	...	...	...	...	...	...	...
Debt forgiveness	2 402	...	...	...	...	...	...	...	...
Other capital transfers	2 410	...	...	...	...	...	...	...	...
Other sectors	2 430	...	...	...	...	...	...	...	...
Migrants' transfers	2 431	...	...	...	...	...	...	...	...
Debt forgiveness	2 432	...	...	...	...	...	...	...	...
Other capital transfers	2 440	...	...	...	...	...	...	...	...
Capital transfers, debit	3 400	...	...	...	...	...	...	...	...
General government	3 401	...	...	...	...	...	...	...	...
Debt forgiveness	3 402	...	...	...	...	...	...	...	...
Other capital transfers	3 410	...	...	...	...	...	...	...	...
Other sectors	3 430	...	...	...	...	...	...	...	...
Migrants' transfers	3 431	...	...	...	...	...	...	...	...
Debt forgiveness	3 432	...	...	...	...	...	...	...	...
Other capital transfers	3 440	...	...	...	...	...	...	...	...
Nonproduced nonfinancial assets, credit	2 480	...	...	...	...	...	...	...	...
Nonproduced nonfinancial assets, debit	3 480	...	...	...	...	...	...	...	...

Table 2 (Continued). STANDARD PRESENTATION, 1994–2001

(Thousands of U.S. dollars)

	Code	1994	1995	1996	1997	1998	1999	2000	2001
FINANCIAL ACCOUNT	4 995	**...**	**...**	**...**	**...**	**...**	**...**	**...**	**–643**
A. DIRECT INVESTMENT	4 500	...	...	...	...	...	...	...	1,001
Direct investment abroad	4 505	**...**	**...**	**...**	**...**	**...**	**...**	**...**	**...**
Equity capital	4 510	...	...	...	...	...	...	...	...
Claims on affiliated enterprises	4 515	...	...	...	...	...	...	...	...
Liabilities to affiliated enterprises	4 520	...	...	...	...	...	...	...	...
Reinvested earnings	4 525	...	...	...	...	...	...	...	...
Other capital	4 530	...	...	...	...	...	...	...	...
Claims on affiliated enterprises	4 535	...	...	...	...	...	...	...	...
Liabilities to affiliated enterprises	4 540	...	...	...	...	...	...	...	...
Direct investment in Tonga	4 555	**...**	**...**	**...**	**...**	**...**	**...**	**...**	**1,001**
Equity capital	4 560	...	...	...	...	...	...	...	...
Claims on direct investors	4 565	...	...	...	...	...	...	...	...
Liabilities to direct investors	4 570	...	...	...	...	...	...	...	...
Reinvested earnings	4 575	...	...	...	...	...	...	...	...
Other capital	4 580	...	...	...	...	...	...	...	...
Claims on direct investors	4 585	...	...	...	...	...	...	...	...
Liabilities to direct investors	4 590	...	...	...	...	...	...	...	...
B. PORTFOLIO INVESTMENT	4 600	...	...	...	...	...	...	...	...
Assets	4 602	**...**	**...**	**...**	**...**	**...**	**...**	**...**	**...**
Equity securities	4 610	...	...	...	...	...	...	...	...
Monetary authorities	4 611	...	...	...	...	...	...	...	...
General government	4 612	...	...	...	...	...	...	...	...
Banks	4 613	...	...	...	...	...	...	...	...
Other sectors	4 614	...	...	...	...	...	...	...	...
Debt securities	4 619	...	...	...	...	...	...	...	...
Bonds and notes	4 620	...	...	...	...	...	...	...	...
Monetary authorities	4 621	...	...	...	...	...	...	...	...
General government	4 622	...	...	...	...	...	...	...	...
Banks	4 623	...	...	...	...	...	...	...	...
Other sectors	4 624	...	...	...	...	...	...	...	...
Money market instruments	4 630	...	...	...	...	...	...	...	...
Monetary authorities	4 631	...	...	...	...	...	...	...	...
General government	4 632	...	...	...	...	...	...	...	...
Banks	4 633	...	...	...	...	...	...	...	...
Other sectors	4 634	...	...	...	...	...	...	...	...
Liabilities	4 652	**...**	**...**	**...**	**...**	**...**	**...**	**...**	**...**
Equity securities	4 660	...	...	...	...	...	...	...	...
Banks	4 663	...	...	...	...	...	...	...	...
Other sectors	4 664	...	...	...	...	...	...	...	...
Debt securities	4 669	...	...	...	...	...	...	...	...
Bonds and notes	4 670	...	...	...	...	...	...	...	...
Monetary authorities	4 671	...	...	...	...	...	...	...	...
General government	4 672	...	...	...	...	...	...	...	...
Banks	4 673	...	...	...	...	...	...	...	...
Other sectors	4 674	...	...	...	...	...	...	...	...
Money market instruments	4 680	...	...	...	...	...	...	...	...
Monetary authorities	4 681	...	...	...	...	...	...	...	...
General government	4 682	...	...	...	...	...	...	...	...
Banks	4 683	...	...	...	...	...	...	...	...
Other sectors	4 684	...	...	...	...	...	...	...	...
C. FINANCIAL DERIVATIVES	4 910	...	...	...	...	...	...	...	...
Monetary authorities	4 911	...	...	...	...	...	...	...	...
General government	4 912	...	...	...	...	...	...	...	...
Banks	4 913	...	...	...	...	...	...	...	...
Other sectors	4 914	...	...	...	...	...	...	...	...
Assets	4 900	**...**	**...**	**...**	**...**	**...**	**...**	**...**	**...**
Monetary authorities	4 901	...	...	...	...	...	...	...	...
General government	4 902	...	...	...	...	...	...	...	...
Banks	4 903	...	...	...	...	...	...	...	...
Other sectors	4 904	...	...	...	...	...	...	...	...
Liabilities	4 905	**...**	**...**	**...**	**...**	**...**	**...**	**...**	**...**
Monetary authorities	4 906	...	...	...	...	...	...	...	...
General government	4 907	...	...	...	...	...	...	...	...
Banks	4 908	...	...	...	...	...	...	...	...
Other sectors	4 909	...	...	...	...	...	...	...	...

Table 2 (Concluded). STANDARD PRESENTATION, 1994–2001
(Thousands of U.S. dollars)

	Code	1994	1995	1996	1997	1998	1999	2000	2001
D. OTHER INVESTMENT	4 700	...	...	...	...	...	...	...	...
Assets	4 703	...	...	...	...	...	...	...	...
Trade credits	4 706	...	...	...	...	...	...	...	...
General government	4 707	...	...	...	...	...	...	...	...
of which: Short-term	4 709	...	...	...	...	...	...	...	...
Other sectors	4 710	...	...	...	...	...	...	...	...
of which: Short-term	4 712	...	...	...	...	...	...	...	...
Loans	4 714	...	...	...	...	...	...	...	...
Monetary authorities	4 715	...	...	...	...	...	...	...	...
of which: Short-term	4 718	...	...	...	...	...	...	...	...
General government	4 719	...	...	...	...	...	...	...	...
of which: Short-term	4 721	...	...	...	...	...	...	...	...
Banks	4 722	...	...	...	...	...	...	...	...
of which: Short-term	4 724	...	...	...	...	...	...	...	...
Other sectors	4 725	...	...	...	...	...	...	...	...
of which: Short-term	4 727	...	...	...	...	...	...	...	...
Currency and deposits	4 730	...	...	...	...	...	...	...	...
Monetary authorities	4 731	...	...	...	...	...	...	...	...
General government	4 732	...	...	...	...	...	...	...	...
Banks	4 733	...	...	...	...	...	...	...	...
Other sectors	4 734	...	...	...	...	...	...	...	...
Other assets	4 736	...	...	...	...	...	...	...	...
Monetary authorities	4 737	...	...	...	...	...	...	...	...
of which: Short-term	4 739	...	...	...	...	...	...	...	...
General government	4 740	...	...	...	...	...	...	...	...
of which: Short-term	4 742	...	...	...	...	...	...	...	...
Banks	4 743	...	...	...	...	...	...	...	...
of which: Short-term	4 745	...	...	...	...	...	...	...	...
Other sectors	4 746	...	...	...	...	...	...	...	...
of which: Short-term	4 748	...	...	...	...	...	...	...	...
Liabilities	4 753	...	...	...	...	...	...	...	...
Trade credits	4 756	...	...	...	...	...	...	...	...
General government	4 757	...	...	...	...	...	...	...	...
of which: Short-term	4 759	...	...	...	...	...	...	...	...
Other sectors	4 760	...	...	...	...	...	...	...	...
of which: Short-term	4 762	...	...	...	...	...	...	...	...
Loans	4 764	...	...	...	...	...	...	...	...
Monetary authorities	4 765	...	...	...	...	...	...	...	...
of which: Use of Fund credit and loans from the Fund	4 766	...	...	...	...	...	...	...	...
of which: Short-term	4 768	...	...	...	...	...	...	...	...
General government	4 769	...	...	...	...	...	...	...	...
of which: Short-term	4 771	...	...	...	...	...	...	...	...
Banks	4 772	...	...	...	...	...	...	...	...
of which: Short-term	4 774	...	...	...	...	...	...	...	...
Other sectors	4 775	...	...	...	...	...	...	...	...
of which: Short-term	4 777	...	...	...	...	...	...	...	...
Currency and deposits	4 780	...	...	...	...	...	...	...	...
Monetary authorities	4 781	...	...	...	...	...	...	...	...
General government	4 782	...	...	...	...	...	...	...	...
Banks	4 783	...	...	...	...	...	...	...	...
Other sectors	4 784	...	...	...	...	...	...	...	...
Other liabilities	4 786	...	...	...	...	...	...	...	...
Monetary authorities	4 787	...	...	...	...	...	...	...	...
of which: Short-term	4 789	...	...	...	...	...	...	...	...
General government	4 790	...	...	...	...	...	...	...	...
of which: Short-term	4 792	...	...	...	...	...	...	...	...
Banks	4 793	...	...	...	...	...	...	...	...
of which: Short-term	4 795	...	...	...	...	...	...	...	...
Other sectors	4 796	...	...	...	...	...	...	...	...
of which: Short-term	4 798	...	...	...	...	...	...	...	...
E. RESERVE ASSETS	4 802	...	...	...	...	...	...	...	–1,645
Monetary gold	4 812	...	...	...	...	...	...	...	...
Special drawing rights	4 811	...	...	...	...	...	...	...	–74
Reserve position in the Fund	4 810	...	...	...	...	...	...	...	...
Foreign exchange	4 803	...	...	...	...	...	...	...	–1,571
Other claims	4 813	...	...	...	...	...	...	...	...
NET ERRORS AND OMISSIONS	4 998	...	...	...	...	...	...	...	**4,349**

Table 1. ANALYTIC PRESENTATION, 1994–2001

(Millions of U.S. dollars)

	Code			1994	1995	1996	1997	1998	1999	2000	2001
A. Current Account [1]	4	993	Z.	**217.8**	**293.8**	**105.1**	**–613.6**	**–643.5**	**. . .**	**. . .**	**. . .**
Goods: exports f.o.b	2	100	. .	1,777.6	2,456.1	2,354.1	2,448.0	2,258.0	. . .	. . .	. . .
Goods: imports f.o.b	3	100	. .	–1,036.6	–1,868.5	–1,971.6	–2,976.6	–2,998.9	. . .	. . .	. . .
Balance on Goods	4	100	. .	*741.1*	*587.7*	*382.4*	*–528.6*	*–740.8*	. . .	. . .	. . .
Services: credit	2	200	. .	326.6	342.6	461.2	546.5	671.7	. . .	. . .	. . .
Services: debit	3	200	. .	–438.1	–241.9	–217.5	–254.1	–255.4	. . .	. . .	. . .
Balance on Goods and Services	4	991	. .	*629.5*	*688.4*	*626.2*	*–236.2*	*–324.5*	. . .	. . .	. . .
Income: credit	2	300	. .	56.7	76.6	39.1	63.8	64.0	. . .	. . .	. . .
Income: debit	3	300	. .	–468.7	–466.7	–553.1	–445.0	–405.3	. . .	. . .	. . .
Balance on Goods, Services, and Income	4	992	. .	*217.5*	*298.3*	*112.2*	*–617.4*	*–665.8*	. . .	. . .	. . .
Current transfers: credit	2	379	Z.	28.3	34.0	34.2	37.0	58.4	. . .	. . .	. . .
Current transfers: debit	3	379	. .	–27.9	–38.5	–41.3	–33.2	–36.2	. . .	. . .	. . .
B. Capital Account [1]	4	994	Z.	**–6.4**	**–11.9**	**. . .**	**. . .**	**. . .**	**. . .**	**. . .**	**. . .**
Capital account: credit	2	994	Z.	1.1	1.1	. . .	. . .	. . .	. . .	. . .	. . .
Capital account: debit	3	994	. .	–7.5	–13.0	. . .	. . .	. . .	. . .	. . .	. . .
Total, Groups A Plus B	4	981	. .	*211.4*	*281.9*	*105.1*	*–613.6*	*–643.5*	. . .	. . .	. . .
C. Financial Account [1]	4	995	W.	**–32.2**	**–214.7**	**43.0**	**697.2**	**471.5**	**. . .**	**. . .**	**. . .**
Direct investment abroad	4	505	. .	. . .	. . .	. . .	. . .	. . .	. . .	. . .	. . .
Direct investment in Trinidad and Tobago	4	555	Z.	516.2	298.9	355.4	999.3	729.8	. . .	. . .	. . .
Portfolio investment assets	4	602	. .	. . .	–7.9	. . .	. . .	–.4	. . .	. . .	. . .
Equity securities	4	610	. .	. . .	–7.9	. . .	. . .	–.4	. . .	. . .	. . .
Debt securities	4	619	. .	. . .	. . .	. . .	. . .	. . .	. . .	. . .	. . .
Portfolio investment liabilities	4	652	Z.	. . .	16.7	. . .	. . .	. . .	. . .	. . .	. . .
Equity securities	4	660	. .	. . .	16.7	. . .	. . .	. . .	. . .	. . .	. . .
Debt securities	4	669	Z.	. . .	. . .	. . .	. . .	. . .	. . .	. . .	. . .
Financial derivatives	4	910	. .	. . .	. . .	. . .	. . .	. . .	. . .	. . .	. . .
Financial derivatives assets	4	900	. .	. . .	. . .	. . .	. . .	. . .	. . .	. . .	. . .
Financial derivatives liabilities	4	905	. .	. . .	. . .	. . .	. . .	. . .	. . .	. . .	. . .
Other investment assets	4	703	. .	–233.5	–57.3	3.0	32.6	1.0	. . .	. . .	. . .
Monetary authorities	4	701	. .	. . .	. . .	. . .	. . .	. . .	. . .	. . .	. . .
General government	4	704	. .	–56.1	32.4	3.0	32.6	1.0	. . .	. . .	. . .
Banks	4	705	. .	–109.3	–23.7	. . .	. . .	. . .	. . .	. . .	. . .
Other sectors	4	728	. .	–68.2	–66.0	. . .	. . .	. . .	. . .	. . .	. . .
Other investment liabilities	4	753	W.	–314.9	–465.1	–315.4	–334.7	–258.8	. . .	. . .	. . .
Monetary authorities	4	753	WA	. . .	. . .	. . .	. . .	–1.4	. . .	. . .	. . .
General government	4	753	ZB	–7.2	–116.8	47.3	–245.4	–104.7	. . .	. . .	. . .
Banks	4	753	ZC	–10.2	–51.3	–27.3	–21.9	–49.6	. . .	. . .	. . .
Other sectors	4	753	ZD	–297.4	–297.0	–335.4	–67.4	–103.2	. . .	. . .	. . .
Total, Groups A Through C	4	983	. .	*179.2*	*67.2*	*148.1*	*83.6*	*–172.0*	. . .	. . .	. . .
D. Net Errors and Omissions	4	998	. .	**6.3**	**16.5**	**90.0**	**110.0**	**252.2**	**. . .**	**. . .**	**. . .**
Total, Groups A Through D	4	984	. .	*185.5*	*83.7*	*238.1*	*193.6*	*80.2*	. . .	. . .	. . .
E. Reserves and Related Items	4	802	A.	**–185.5**	**–83.7**	**–238.1**	**–193.6**	**–80.2**	**. . .**	**. . .**	**. . .**
Reserve assets	4	802	. .	–113.6	–40.1	–213.0	–175.3	–76.0	. . .	. . .	. . .
Use of Fund credit and loans	4	766	. .	–71.9	–43.6	–25.1	–18.4	–4.2	. . .	. . .	. . .
Exceptional financing	4	920	. .	. . .	. . .	. . .	. . .	. . .	. . .	. . .	. . .
Conversion rates: Trinidad and Tobago dollars per U.S. dollar	0	101	. .	**5.9249**	**5.9478**	**6.0051**	**6.2517**	**6.2983**	**6.2989**	**6.2998**	**6.2332**

[1] Excludes components that have been classified in the categories of Group E.

Table 2. STANDARD PRESENTATION, 1994–2001

(Millions of U.S. dollars)

	Code	1994	1995	1996	1997	1998	1999	2000	2001
CURRENT ACCOUNT	4 993 . .	**217.8**	**293.8**	**105.1**	**–613.6**	**–643.5**	**. . .**	**. . .**	**. . .**
A. GOODS	4 100 . .	741.1	587.7	382.4	–528.6	–740.8	. . .	. . .	. . .
Credit	2 100 . .	**1,777.6**	**2,456.1**	**2,354.1**	**2,448.0**	**2,258.0**	**. . .**	**. . .**	**. . .**
General merchandise: exports f.o.b.	2 110 . .	1,760.0	2,436.2	2,333.3	2,424.4	2,230.9	. . .	. . .	. . .
Goods for processing: exports f.o.b.	2 150 . .	. . .	. . .	. . .	. . .	. . .	. . .	. . .	. . .
Repairs on goods	2 160 . .	. . .	. . .	. . .	. . .	. . .	. . .	. . .	. . .
Goods procured in ports by carriers	2 170 . .	17.6	19.9	20.7	23.6	27.1	. . .	. . .	. . .
Nonmonetary gold	2 180 . .	. . .	. . .	. . .	. . .	. . .	. . .	. . .	. . .
Debit	3 100 . .	**–1,036.6**	**–1,868.5**	**–1,971.6**	**–2,976.6**	**–2,998.9**	**. . .**	**. . .**	**. . .**
General merchandise: imports f.o.b.	3 110 . .	–1,036.6	–1,868.5	–1,971.6	–2,976.6	–2,998.9	. . .	. . .	. . .
Goods for processing: imports f.o.b.	3 150 . .	. . .	. . .	. . .	. . .	. . .	. . .	. . .	. . .
Repairs on goods	3 160 . .	. . .	. . .	. . .	. . .	. . .	. . .	. . .	. . .
Goods procured in ports by carriers	3 170 . .	. . .	. . .	. . .	. . .	. . .	. . .	. . .	. . .
Nonmonetary gold	3 180 . .	. . .	. . .	. . .	. . .	. . .	. . .	. . .	. . .
B. SERVICES	4 200 . .	–111.5	100.7	243.8	292.4	416.4	. . .	. . .	. . .
Total credit	2 200 . .	*326.6*	*342.6*	*461.2*	*546.5*	*671.7*	. . .	. . .	. . .
Total debit	3 200 . .	*–438.1*	*–241.9*	*–217.5*	*–254.1*	*–255.4*	. . .	. . .	. . .
Transportation services, credit	2 205 . .	**176.4**	**193.8**	**196.4**	**197.2**	**201.8**	**. . .**	**. . .**	**. . .**
Passenger	2 850 . .	*145.5*	*155.2*	*153.5*	*151.3*	*154.8*	. . .	. . .	. . .
Freight	2 851 . .	*9.8*	*9.7*	*9.6*	*7.1*	*4.9*	. . .	. . .	. . .
Other	2 852 . .	*21.1*	*28.9*	*33.3*	*38.9*	*42.2*	. . .	. . .	. . .
Sea transport, passenger	2 207 . .	. . .	. . .	. . .	. . .	. . .	. . .	. . .	. . .
Sea transport, freight	2 208 . .	. . .	. . .	. . .	. . .	. . .	. . .	. . .	. . .
Sea transport, other	2 209 . .	. . .	. . .	. . .	. . .	. . .	. . .	. . .	. . .
Air transport, passenger	2 211 . .	. . .	. . .	. . .	. . .	. . .	. . .	. . .	. . .
Air transport, freight	2 212 . .	. . .	. . .	. . .	. . .	. . .	. . .	. . .	. . .
Air transport, other	2 213 . .	. . .	. . .	. . .	. . .	. . .	. . .	. . .	. . .
Other transport, passenger	2 215 . .	. . .	. . .	. . .	. . .	. . .	. . .	. . .	. . .
Other transport, freight	2 216 . .	. . .	. . .	. . .	. . .	. . .	. . .	. . .	. . .
Other transport, other	2 217 . .	. . .	. . .	. . .	. . .	. . .	. . .	. . .	. . .
Transportation services, debit	3 205 . .	**–235.2**	**–94.2**	**–93.5**	**–109.1**	**–123.8**	**. . .**	**. . .**	**. . .**
Passenger	3 850 . .	*–22.0*	*–22.2*	*–22.1*	*–25.0*	*–24.7*	. . .	. . .	. . .
Freight	3 851 . .	*–130.3*	*–47.2*	*–46.7*	*–53.8*	*–62.7*	. . .	. . .	. . .
Other	3 852 . .	*–82.9*	*–24.7*	*–24.6*	*–30.3*	*–36.4*	. . .	. . .	. . .
Sea transport, passenger	3 207 . .	. . .	. . .	. . .	. . .	. . .	. . .	. . .	. . .
Sea transport, freight	3 208 . .	. . .	. . .	. . .	. . .	. . .	. . .	. . .	. . .
Sea transport, other	3 209 . .	. . .	. . .	. . .	. . .	. . .	. . .	. . .	. . .
Air transport, passenger	3 211 . .	. . .	. . .	. . .	. . .	. . .	. . .	. . .	. . .
Air transport, freight	3 212 . .	. . .	. . .	. . .	. . .	. . .	. . .	. . .	. . .
Air transport, other	3 213 . .	. . .	. . .	. . .	. . .	. . .	. . .	. . .	. . .
Other transport, passenger	3 215 . .	. . .	. . .	. . .	. . .	. . .	. . .	. . .	. . .
Other transport, freight	3 216 . .	. . .	. . .	. . .	. . .	. . .	. . .	. . .	. . .
Other transport, other	3 217 . .	. . .	. . .	. . .	. . .	. . .	. . .	. . .	. . .
Travel, credit	2 236 . .	**86.5**	**77.4**	**107.8**	**192.6**	**200.6**	**. . .**	**. . .**	**. . .**
Business travel	2 237 . .	27.5	25.4	20.9	39.5	46.1	. . .	. . .	. . .
Personal travel	2 240 . .	59.0	52.0	86.9	153.1	154.5	. . .	. . .	. . .
Travel, debit	3 236 . .	**–89.5**	**–69.3**	**–75.7**	**–71.6**	**–67.0**	**. . .**	**. . .**	**. . .**
Business travel	3 237 . .	–11.4	–1.8	. . .	. . .	. . .	. . .	. . .	. . .
Personal travel	3 240 . .	–78.1	–67.5	–75.7	–71.6	–67.0	. . .	. . .	. . .
Other services, credit	2 200 BA	**63.7**	**71.4**	**157.0**	**156.7**	**269.3**	**. . .**	**. . .**	**. . .**
Communications	2 245 . .	. . .	. . .	87.3	83.7	97.0	. . .	. . .	. . .
Construction	2 249 . .	. . .	. . .	. . .	. . .	. . .	. . .	. . .	. . .
Insurance	2 253 . .	. . .	30.4	30.3	36.7	30.3	. . .	. . .	. . .
Financial	2 260 . .	. . .	. . .	. . .	. . .	. . .	. . .	. . .	. . .
Computer and information	2 262 . .	. . .	. . .	. . .	. . .	. . .	. . .	. . .	. . .
Royalties and licence fees	2 266 . .	. . .	. . .	. . .	. . .	. . .	. . .	. . .	. . .
Other business services	2 268 . .	54.4	29.1	25.4	25.2	44.2	. . .	. . .	. . .
Personal, cultural, and recreational	2 287 . .	. . .	. . .	. . .	. . .	. . .	. . .	. . .	. . .
Government, n.i.e.	2 291 . .	9.3	11.9	14.0	11.1	97.8	. . .	. . .	. . .
Other services, debit	3 200 BA	**–113.4**	**–78.4**	**–48.3**	**–73.4**	**–64.5**	**. . .**	**. . .**	**. . .**
Communications	3 245 . .	. . .	. . .	–2.7	–3.9	–5.4	. . .	. . .	. . .
Construction	3 249 . .	. . .	. . .	. . .	. . .	. . .	. . .	. . .	. . .
Insurance	3 253 . .	–43.8	–17.7	–4.7	–1.2	–.3	. . .	. . .	. . .
Financial	3 260 . .	. . .	. . .	. . .	. . .	. . .	. . .	. . .	. . .
Computer and information	3 262 . .	. . .	. . .	. . .	. . .	. . .	. . .	. . .	. . .
Royalties and licence fees	3 266 . .	–1.0	–.4	–.3	–.6	–.2	. . .	. . .	. . .
Other business services	3 268 . .	–54.3	–41.6	–21.6	–45.3	–38.1	. . .	. . .	. . .
Personal, cultural, and recreational	3 287 . .	. . .	. . .	. . .	. . .	. . .	. . .	. . .	. . .
Government, n.i.e.	3 291 . .	–14.3	–18.6	–19.0	–22.4	–20.5	. . .	. . .	. . .

Table 2 (Continued). STANDARD PRESENTATION, 1994–2001

(Millions of U.S. dollars)

	Code	1994	1995	1996	1997	1998	1999	2000	2001
C. INCOME	4 300	–412.1	–390.1	–514.0	–381.2	–341.3	. . .	. . .	. . .
Total credit	2 300	*56.7*	*76.6*	*39.1*	*63.8*	*64.0*	. . .	. . .	. . .
Total debit	3 300	*–468.7*	*–466.7*	*–553.1*	*–445.0*	*–405.3*	. . .	. . .	. . .
Compensation of employees, credit	2 310	**. . .**	**. . .**	**. . .**	**. . .**	**. . .**	**. . .**	**. . .**	**. . .**
Compensation of employees, debit	3 310	**–1.3**	**–1.3**	**. . .**	**. . .**	**. . .**	**. . .**	**. . .**	**. . .**
Investment income, credit	2 320	**56.7**	**76.6**	**39.1**	**63.8**	**64.0**	**. . .**	**. . .**	**. . .**
Direct investment income	2 330	. . .	. . .	. . .	. . .	. . .	. . .	. . .	. . .
Dividends and distributed branch profits	2 332	. . .	. . .	. . .	. . .	. . .	. . .	. . .	. . .
Reinvested earnings and undistributed branch profits	2 333	. . .	. . .	. . .	. . .	. . .	. . .	. . .	. . .
Income on debt (interest)	2 334	. . .	. . .	. . .	. . .	. . .	. . .	. . .	. . .
Portfolio investment income	2 339	. . .	. . .	. . .	. . .	. . .	. . .	. . .	. . .
Income on equity	2 340	. . .	. . .	. . .	. . .	. . .	. . .	. . .	. . .
Income on bonds and notes	2 350	. . .	. . .	. . .	. . .	. . .	. . .	. . .	. . .
Income on money market instruments	2 360	. . .	. . .	. . .	. . .	. . .	. . .	. . .	. . .
Other investment income	2 370	56.7	76.6	39.1	63.8	64.0	. . .	. . .	. . .
Investment income, debit	3 320	**–467.4**	**–465.4**	**–553.1**	**–445.0**	**–405.3**	**. . .**	**. . .**	**. . .**
Direct investment income	3 330	–269.6	–186.8	–274.6	–227.3	–188.1	. . .	. . .	. . .
Dividends and distributed branch profits	3 332	–80.5	–27.7	–105.7	–102.2	–87.2	. . .	. . .	. . .
Reinvested earnings and undistributed branch profits	3 333	–189.0	–159.1	–168.9	–125.1	–100.9	. . .	. . .	. . .
Income on debt (interest)	3 334	. . .	. . .	. . .	. . .	. . .	. . .	. . .	. . .
Portfolio investment income	3 339	. . .	. . .	. . .	. . .	. . .	. . .	. . .	. . .
Income on equity	3 340	. . .	. . .	. . .	. . .	. . .	. . .	. . .	. . .
Income on bonds and notes	3 350	. . .	. . .	. . .	. . .	. . .	. . .	. . .	. . .
Income on money market instruments	3 360	. . .	. . .	. . .	. . .	. . .	. . .	. . .	. . .
Other investment income	3 370	–197.8	–278.6	–278.5	–217.7	–217.2	. . .	. . .	. . .
D. CURRENT TRANSFERS	4 379	.3	–4.5	–7.1	3.8	22.2	. . .	. . .	. . .
Credit	2 379	**28.3**	**34.0**	**34.2**	**37.0**	**58.4**	**. . .**	**. . .**	**. . .**
General government	2 380	2.2	3.2	4.7	5.4	10.7	. . .	. . .	. . .
Other sectors	2 390	26.1	30.8	29.5	31.6	47.8	. . .	. . .	. . .
Workers' remittances	2 391	25.7	30.4	28.1	30.2	44.6	. . .	. . .	. . .
Other current transfers	2 392	.4	.4	1.4	1.4	3.2	. . .	. . .	. . .
Debit	3 379	**–27.9**	**–38.5**	**–41.3**	**–33.2**	**–36.2**	**. . .**	**. . .**	**. . .**
General government	3 380	–4.1	–6.3	–5.5	–5.1	–4.3	. . .	. . .	. . .
Other sectors	3 390	–23.9	–32.2	–35.8	–28.1	–31.9	. . .	. . .	. . .
Workers' remittances	3 391	. . .	. . .	. . .	. . .	. . .	. . .	. . .	. . .
Other current transfers	3 392	–23.9	–32.2	–35.8	–28.1	–31.9	. . .	. . .	. . .
CAPITAL AND FINANCIAL ACCOUNT	4 996	**–224.1**	**–310.4**	**–195.1**	**503.6**	**391.4**	**. . .**	**. . .**	**. . .**
CAPITAL ACCOUNT	4 994	**–6.4**	**–11.9**	**. . .**	**. . .**	**. . .**	**. . .**	**. . .**	**. . .**
Total credit	2 994	*1.1*	*1.1*	. . .	. . .	. . .	. . .	. . .	. . .
Total debit	3 994	*–7.5*	*–13.0*	. . .	. . .	. . .	. . .	. . .	. . .
Capital transfers, credit	2 400	**1.1**	**1.1**	**. . .**	**. . .**	**. . .**	**. . .**	**. . .**	**. . .**
General government	2 401	. . .	. . .	. . .	. . .	. . .	. . .	. . .	. . .
Debt forgiveness	2 402	. . .	. . .	. . .	. . .	. . .	. . .	. . .	. . .
Other capital transfers	2 410	. . .	. . .	. . .	. . .	. . .	. . .	. . .	. . .
Other sectors	2 430	1.1	1.1	. . .	. . .	. . .	. . .	. . .	. . .
Migrants' transfers	2 431	1.1	1.1	. . .	. . .	. . .	. . .	. . .	. . .
Debt forgiveness	2 432	. . .	. . .	. . .	. . .	. . .	. . .	. . .	. . .
Other capital transfers	2 440	. . .	. . .	. . .	. . .	. . .	. . .	. . .	. . .
Capital transfers, debit	3 400	**–7.5**	**–13.0**	**. . .**	**. . .**	**. . .**	**. . .**	**. . .**	**. . .**
General government	3 401	. . .	. . .	. . .	. . .	. . .	. . .	. . .	. . .
Debt forgiveness	3 402	. . .	. . .	. . .	. . .	. . .	. . .	. . .	. . .
Other capital transfers	3 410	. . .	. . .	. . .	. . .	. . .	. . .	. . .	. . .
Other sectors	3 430	–7.5	–13.0	. . .	. . .	. . .	. . .	. . .	. . .
Migrants' transfers	3 431	–7.5	–13.0	. . .	. . .	. . .	. . .	. . .	. . .
Debt forgiveness	3 432	. . .	. . .	. . .	. . .	. . .	. . .	. . .	. . .
Other capital transfers	3 440	. . .	. . .	. . .	. . .	. . .	. . .	. . .	. . .
Nonproduced nonfinancial assets, credit	2 480	**. . .**	**. . .**	**. . .**	**. . .**	**. . .**	**. . .**	**. . .**	**. . .**
Nonproduced nonfinancial assets, debit	3 480	**. . .**	**. . .**	**. . .**	**. . .**	**. . .**	**. . .**	**. . .**	**. . .**

Table 2 (Continued). STANDARD PRESENTATION, 1994–2001
(Millions of U.S. dollars)

	Code	1994	1995	1996	1997	1998	1999	2000	2001
FINANCIAL ACCOUNT	4 995 . .	**–217.7**	**–298.4**	**–195.1**	**503.6**	**391.4**	...	...	...
A. DIRECT INVESTMENT	4 500 . .	516.2	298.9	355.4	999.3	729.8	...	...	...
Direct investment abroad	4 505 . .	...	...	...	...	...	...	...	...
Equity capital	4 510 . .	...	...	...	...	...	...	...	...
Claims on affiliated enterprises	4 515 . .	...	...	...	...	...	...	...	...
Liabilities to affiliated enterprises	4 520 . .	...	...	...	...	...	...	...	...
Reinvested earnings	4 525 . .	...	...	...	...	...	...	...	...
Other capital	4 530 . .	...	...	...	...	...	...	...	...
Claims on affiliated enterprises	4 535 . .	...	...	...	...	...	...	...	...
Liabilities to affiliated enterprises	4 540 . .	...	...	...	...	...	...	...	...
Direct investment in Trinidad and Tobago	4 555 . .	**516.2**	**298.9**	**355.4**	**999.3**	**729.8**	...	...	...
Equity capital	4 560 . .	378.0	137.3	186.5	772.9	622.9	...	...	...
Claims on direct investors	4 565 . .	...	...	...	...	...	...	...	...
Liabilities to direct investors	4 570 . .	...	...	...	...	...	...	...	...
Reinvested earnings	4 575 . .	189.0	159.1	168.9	125.1	100.9	...	...	...
Other capital	4 580 . .	–50.9	2.5	...	101.4	6.0	...	...	...
Claims on direct investors	4 585 . .	...	...	...	...	...	...	...	...
Liabilities to direct investors	4 590 . .	...	...	...	...	...	...	...	...
B. PORTFOLIO INVESTMENT	4 600 . .	...	8.8	...	...	–.4	...	...	...
Assets	4 602 . .	...	**–7.9**	...	...	**–.4**	...	...	...
Equity securities	4 610 . .	...	–7.9	...	...	–.4	...	...	...
Monetary authorities	4 611 . .	...	...	...	...	...	...	...	...
General government	4 612 . .	...	...	...	...	...	...	...	...
Banks	4 613 . .	...	...	...	...	...	...	...	...
Other sectors	4 614 . .	...	–7.9	...	...	–.4	...	...	...
Debt securities	4 619 . .	...	...	...	...	...	...	...	...
Bonds and notes	4 620 . .	...	...	...	...	...	...	...	...
Monetary authorities	4 621 . .	...	...	...	...	...	...	...	...
General government	4 622 . .	...	...	...	...	...	...	...	...
Banks	4 623 . .	...	...	...	...	...	...	...	...
Other sectors	4 624 . .	...	...	...	...	...	...	...	...
Money market instruments	4 630 . .	...	...	...	...	...	...	...	...
Monetary authorities	4 631 . .	...	...	...	...	...	...	...	...
General government	4 632 . .	...	...	...	...	...	...	...	...
Banks	4 633 . .	...	...	...	...	...	...	...	...
Other sectors	4 634 . .	...	...	...	...	...	...	...	...
Liabilities	4 652 . .	...	**16.7**	...	...	...	...	...	...
Equity securities	4 660 . .	...	16.7	...	...	...	...	...	...
Banks	4 663 . .	...	16.7	...	...	...	...	...	...
Other sectors	4 664 . .	...	...	...	...	...	...	...	...
Debt securities	4 669 . .	...	...	...	...	...	...	...	...
Bonds and notes	4 670 . .	...	...	...	...	...	...	...	...
Monetary authorities	4 671 . .	...	...	...	...	...	...	...	...
General government	4 672 . .	...	...	...	...	...	...	...	...
Banks	4 673 . .	...	...	...	...	...	...	...	...
Other sectors	4 674 . .	...	...	...	...	...	...	...	...
Money market instruments	4 680 . .	...	...	...	...	...	...	...	...
Monetary authorities	4 681 . .	...	...	...	...	...	...	...	...
General government	4 682 . .	...	...	...	...	...	...	...	...
Banks	4 683 . .	...	...	...	...	...	...	...	...
Other sectors	4 684 . .	...	...	...	...	...	...	...	...
C. FINANCIAL DERIVATIVES	4 910 . .	...	...	...	...	...	...	...	...
Monetary authorities	4 911 . .	...	...	...	...	...	...	...	...
General government	4 912 . .	...	...	...	...	...	...	...	...
Banks	4 913 . .	...	...	...	...	...	...	...	...
Other sectors	4 914 . .	...	...	...	...	...	...	...	...
Assets	4 900 . .	...	...	...	...	...	...	...	...
Monetary authorities	4 901 . .	...	...	...	...	...	...	...	...
General government	4 902 . .	...	...	...	...	...	...	...	...
Banks	4 903 . .	...	...	...	...	...	...	...	...
Other sectors	4 904 . .	...	...	...	...	...	...	...	...
Liabilities	4 905 . .	...	...	...	...	...	...	...	...
Monetary authorities	4 906 . .	...	...	...	...	...	...	...	...
General government	4 907 . .	...	...	...	...	...	...	...	...
Banks	4 908 . .	...	...	...	...	...	...	...	...
Other sectors	4 909 . .	...	...	...	...	...	...	...	...

Table 2 (Concluded). STANDARD PRESENTATION, 1994–2001
(Millions of U.S. dollars)

	Code	1994	1995	1996	1997	1998	1999	2000	2001
D. OTHER INVESTMENT	4 700	–620.3	–566.0	–337.5	–320.5	–262.0	...	...	...
Assets	4 703	**–233.5**	**–57.3**	**3.0**	**32.6**	**1.0**	**...**	**...**	**...**
Trade credits	4 706	...	–26.0	...	...	...	...	...	...
General government	4 707	...	...	...	...	...	...	...	...
of which: Short-term	4 709	...	...	...	...	...	...	...	...
Other sectors	4 710	...	–26.0	...	...	...	...	...	...
of which: Short-term	4 712	...	*–26.0*	...	...	...	...	...	...
Loans	4 714	...	32.4	3.0	32.6	1.0	...	...	...
Monetary authorities	4 715	...	...	...	...	...	...	...	...
of which: Short-term	4 718	...	...	...	...	...	...	...	...
General government	4 719	...	32.4	3.0	32.6	1.0	...	...	...
of which: Short-term	4 721	...	...	...	...	...	...	...	...
Banks	4 722	...	...	...	...	...	...	...	...
of which: Short-term	4 724	...	...	...	...	...	...	...	...
Other sectors	4 725	...	...	...	...	...	...	...	...
of which: Short-term	4 727	...	...	...	...	...	...	...	...
Currency and deposits	4 730	–109.3	–23.7	...	...	...	...	...	...
Monetary authorities	4 731	...	...	...	...	...	...	...	...
General government	4 732	...	...	...	...	...	...	...	...
Banks	4 733	–109.3	–23.7	...	...	...	...	...	...
Other sectors	4 734	...	...	...	...	...	...	...	...
Other assets	4 736	–124.2	–40.1	...	...	...	...	...	...
Monetary authorities	4 737	...	...	...	...	...	...	...	...
of which: Short-term	4 739	...	...	...	...	...	...	...	...
General government	4 740	–56.1	...	...	...	...	...	...	...
of which: Short-term	4 742	...	...	...	...	...	...	...	...
Banks	4 743	...	...	...	...	...	...	...	...
of which: Short-term	4 745	...	...	...	...	...	...	...	...
Other sectors	4 746	–68.2	–40.1	...	...	...	...	...	...
of which: Short-term	4 748	...	...	...	...	...	...	...	...
Liabilities	4 753	**–386.8**	**–508.7**	**–340.5**	**–353.1**	**–263.0**	**...**	**...**	**...**
Trade credits	4 756	...	–133.1	–311.1	–49.8	–103.5	...	...	...
General government	4 757	...	...	...	...	...	...	...	...
of which: Short-term	4 759	...	...	...	...	...	...	...	...
Other sectors	4 760	...	–133.1	–311.1	–49.8	–103.5	...	...	...
of which: Short-term	4 762	...	*–133.1*	*–311.1*	*–49.8*	*–103.5*	...	...	...
Loans	4 764	–117.6	–200.8	–2.1	–276.8	–110.0	...	...	...
Monetary authorities	4 765	–71.9	–43.6	–25.1	–18.4	–5.6	...	...	...
of which: Use of Fund credit and loans from the Fund	4 766	*–71.9*	*–43.6*	*–25.1*	*–18.4*	*–4.2*	...	...	...
of which: Short-term	4 768	...	...	...	...	...	...	...	...
General government	4 769	–7.2	–116.8	47.3	–245.4	–104.7	...	...	...
of which: Short-term	4 771	...	...	...	...	...	...	...	...
Banks	4 772	...	...	...	...	...	...	...	...
of which: Short-term	4 774	...	...	...	...	...	...	...	...
Other sectors	4 775	–38.4	–40.4	–24.2	–13.0	.3	...	...	...
of which: Short-term	4 777	...	...	...	...	...	...	...	...
Currency and deposits	4 780	–10.2	–51.3	...	...	...	...	...	...
Monetary authorities	4 781	...	...	...	...	...	...	...	...
General government	4 782	...	...	...	...	...	...	...	...
Banks	4 783	–10.2	–51.3	...	...	...	...	...	...
Other sectors	4 784	...	...	...	...	...	...	...	...
Other liabilities	4 786	–259.0	–123.5	–27.3	–26.5	–49.6	...	...	...
Monetary authorities	4 787	...	...	...	...	...	...	...	...
of which: Short-term	4 789	...	...	...	...	...	...	...	...
General government	4 790	...	...	...	...	...	...	...	...
of which: Short-term	4 792	...	...	...	...	...	...	...	...
Banks	4 793	...	...	–27.3	–21.9	–49.6	...	...	...
of which: Short-term	4 795	...	...	...	...	...	...	...	...
Other sectors	4 796	–259.0	–123.5	...	–4.6	...	...	...	...
of which: Short-term	4 798	...	...	...	...	...	...	...	...
E. RESERVE ASSETS	4 802	–113.6	–40.1	–213.0	–175.3	–76.0	...	...	...
Monetary gold	4 812	...	...	...	...	...	...	...	...
Special drawing rights	4 811	.2	–.2	.2	–.1	...	...	...	...
Reserve position in the Fund	4 810	...	...	...	...	...	...	...	...
Foreign exchange	4 803	–113.6	–40.0	–212.9	–174.8	–75.7	...	...	...
Other claims	4 813	–.2	...	–.3	–.4	–.3	...	...	...
NET ERRORS AND OMISSIONS	4 998	**6.3**	**16.5**	**90.0**	**110.0**	**252.2**	**...**	**...**	**...**

Part 3 of the *Yearbook* contains descriptions of the methodologies, compilation practices, and sources used to compile these data.

Table 1. ANALYTIC PRESENTATION, 1994–2001
(Millions of U.S. dollars)

	Code	1994	1995	1996	1997	1998	1999	2000	2001
A. Current Account [1]	4 993 Z.	**–537**	**–774**	**–478**	**–595**	**–675**	**–442**	**–821**	**–863**
Goods: exports f.o.b	2 100 . .	4,643	5,470	5,519	5,559	5,724	5,873	5,840	6,606
Goods: imports f.o.b	3 100 . .	–6,210	–7,459	–7,280	–7,514	–7,875	–8,014	–8,093	–8,997
Balance on Goods	4 100 . .	*–1,567*	*–1,989*	*–1,761*	*–1,955*	*–2,152*	*–2,141*	*–2,253*	*–2,391*
Services: credit	2 200 . .	2,267	2,509	2,632	2,613	2,757	2,920	2,767	2,912
Services: debit	3 200 . .	–1,361	–1,352	–1,244	–1,182	–1,257	–1,234	–1,218	–1,425
Balance on Goods and Services	4 991 . .	*–661*	*–832*	*–373*	*–524*	*–651*	*–455*	*–705*	*–904*
Income: credit	2 300 . .	71	119	66	77	90	89	94	95
Income: debit	3 300 . .	–745	–835	–1,030	–939	–947	–978	–1,036	–1,036
Balance on Goods, Services, and Income	4 992 . .	*–1,336*	*–1,548*	*–1,338*	*–1,386*	*–1,507*	*–1,344*	*–1,647*	*–1,845*
Current transfers: credit	2 379 Z.	816	805	879	821	852	920	825	958
Current transfers: debit	3 379 . .	–17	–31	–20	–30	–20	–18	. . .	24
B. Capital Account [1]	4 994 Z.	**–3**	**32**	**37**	**77**	**61**	**59**	**3**	**53**
Capital account: credit	2 994 Z.	5	47	46	95	83	72	9	56
Capital account: debit	3 994 . .	–8	–15	–9	–18	–22	–13	–6	–3
Total, Groups A Plus B	4 981 . .	*–540*	*–742*	*–441*	*–518*	*–615*	*–383*	*–819*	*–810*
C. Financial Account [1]	4 995 W.	**1,144**	**958**	**816**	**699**	**489**	**1,083**	**646**	**1,125**
Direct investment abroad	4 505 . .	–6	5	–1	–6	1	–3	–1	–1
Direct investment in Tunisia	4 555 Z.	432	264	238	339	650	350	752	457
Portfolio investment assets	4 602 . .	–1	2	–5	–1	. . .	. . .	. . .	. . .
Equity securities	4 610 . .	1	. . .	. . .	–1	. . .	. . .	. . .	. . .
Debt securities	4 619 . .	–2	2	–5	. . .	. . .	. . .	. . .	. . .
Portfolio investment liabilities	4 652 Z.	16	23	67	109	33	10	–20	–15
Equity securities	4 660 . .	6	12	29	55	58	–3	–18	–15
Debt securities	4 669 Z.	10	12	38	54	–25	13	–3	. . .
Financial derivatives	4 910 . .	. . .	. . .	. . .	. . .	. . .	. . .	. . .	. . .
Financial derivatives assets	4 900 . .	. . .	. . .	. . .	. . .	. . .	. . .	. . .	. . .
Financial derivatives liabilities	4 905 . .	. . .	. . .	. . .	. . .	. . .	. . .	. . .	. . .
Other investment assets	4 703 . .	–326	–327	–705	–729	–508	–228	–624	–416
Monetary authorities	4 701 . .	86	88	95	14	. . .	. . .	. . .	. . .
General government	4 704 . .	. . .	. . .	. . .	. . .	. . .	. . .	. . .	. . .
Banks	4 705 . .	67	150	–305	–250	10	8	. . .	. . .
Other sectors	4 728 . .	–479	–565	–494	–493	–517	–236	–624	–416
Other investment liabilities	4 753 W.	1,029	990	1,221	987	313	954	540	1,099
Monetary authorities	4 753 WA	. . .	–1	–11	28	. . .	. . .	. . .	. . .
General government	4 753 ZB	411	546	517	324	–49	314	128	752
Banks	4 753 ZC	168	44	189	90	. . .	. . .	. . .	. . .
Other sectors	4 753 ZD	450	401	527	544	362	640	412	347
Total, Groups A Through C	4 983 . .	*604*	*216*	*375*	*181*	*–126*	*701*	*–172*	*316*
D. Net Errors and Omissions	4 998 . .	**–78**	**–119**	**67**	**206**	**–12**	**38**	**–33**	**–27**
Total, Groups A Through D	4 984 . .	*527*	*97*	*442*	*386*	*–138*	*738*	*–205*	*288*
E. Reserves and Related Items	4 802 A.	**–527**	**–97**	**–442**	**–386**	**138**	**–738**	**205**	**–288**
Reserve assets	4 802 . .	–527	–82	–395	–336	187	–688	245	–257
Use of Fund credit and loans	4 766 . .	. . .	–15	–47	–51	–50	–50	–40	–31
Exceptional financing	4 920 . .	. . .	. . .	. . .	. . .	. . .	. . .	. . .	. . .
Conversion rates: Tunisian dinars per U.S. dollar	0 101 . .	**1.0116**	**.9458**	**.9734**	**1.1059**	**1.1387**	**1.1862**	**1.3707**	**1.4387**

[1] Excludes components that have been classified in the categories of Group E.

Table 2. STANDARD PRESENTATION, 1994–2001

(Millions of U.S. dollars)

	Code	1994	1995	1996	1997	1998	1999	2000	2001
CURRENT ACCOUNT	4 993 . .	**–537**	**–774**	**–478**	**–595**	**–675**	**–442**	**–821**	**–863**
A. GOODS	4 100 . .	–1,567	–1,989	–1,761	–1,955	–2,152	–2,141	–2,253	–2,391
Credit	2 100 . .	**4,643**	**5,470**	**5,519**	**5,559**	**5,724**	**5,873**	**5,840**	**6,606**
General merchandise: exports f.o.b.	2 110 . .	4,643	5,470	5,519	5,559	5,724	5,873	5,840	6,606
Goods for processing: exports f.o.b.	2 150 . .	. . .	. . .	. . .	. . .	. . .	. . .	. . .	. . .
Repairs on goods	2 160 . .	. . .	. . .	. . .	. . .	. . .	. . .	. . .	. . .
Goods procured in ports by carriers	2 170 . .	. . .	. . .	. . .	. . .	. . .	. . .	. . .	. . .
Nonmonetary gold	2 180 . .	. . .	. . .	. . .	. . .	. . .	. . .	. . .	. . .
Debit	3 100 . .	**–6,210**	**–7,459**	**–7,280**	**–7,514**	**–7,875**	**–8,014**	**–8,093**	**–8,997**
General merchandise: imports f.o.b.	3 110 . .	–6,210	–7,459	–7,280	–7,514	–7,875	–8,014	–8,093	–8,997
Goods for processing: imports f.o.b.	3 150 . .	. . .	. . .	. . .	. . .	. . .	. . .	. . .	. . .
Repairs on goods	3 160 . .	. . .	. . .	. . .	. . .	. . .	. . .	. . .	. . .
Goods procured in ports by carriers	3 170 . .	. . .	. . .	. . .	. . .	. . .	. . .	. . .	. . .
Nonmonetary gold	3 180 . .	. . .	. . .	. . .	. . .	. . .	. . .	. . .	. . .
B. SERVICES	4 200 . .	906	1,157	1,388	1,431	1,501	1,686	1,548	1,487
Total credit	2 200 . .	*2,267*	*2,509*	*2,632*	*2,613*	*2,757*	*2,920*	*2,767*	*2,912*
Total debit	3 200 . .	*–1,361*	*–1,352*	*–1,244*	*–1,182*	*–1,257*	*–1,234*	*–1,218*	*–1,425*
Transportation services, credit	2 205 . .	**577**	**598**	**642**	**644**	**635**	**599**	**595**	**638**
Passenger	2 850 . .	*271*	*308*	*307*	*315*	*323*	*291*	*295*	*310*
Freight	2 851 . .	*116*	*75*	*77*	*71*	*73*	*73*	*179*	*195*
Other	2 852 . .	*191*	*216*	*258*	*258*	*239*	*234*	*120*	*133*
Sea transport, passenger	2 207 . .	. . .	. . .	. . .	. . .	. . .	. . .	36	44
Sea transport, freight	2 208 . .	. . .	. . .	. . .	. . .	. . .	. . .	17	22
Sea transport, other	2 209 . .	. . .	. . .	. . .	. . .	. . .	. . .	7	4
Air transport, passenger	2 211 . .	. . .	. . .	. . .	. . .	. . .	. . .	258	264
Air transport, freight	2 212 . .	. . .	. . .	. . .	. . .	. . .	. . .	33	33
Air transport, other	2 213 . .	. . .	. . .	. . .	. . .	. . .	. . .	89	86
Other transport, passenger	2 215 . .	. . .	. . .	. . .	. . .	. . .	. . .	2	2
Other transport, freight	2 216 . .	. . .	. . .	. . .	. . .	. . .	. . .	130	140
Other transport, other	2 217 . .	. . .	. . .	. . .	. . .	. . .	. . .	23	42
Transportation services, debit	3 205 . .	**–464**	**–564**	**–521**	**–504**	**–591**	**–575**	**–548**	**–654**
Passenger	3 850 . .	*–38*	*–43*	*–31*	*–31*	*–36*	*–37*	*–47*	*–49*
Freight	3 851 . .	*–293*	*–364*	*–362*	*–354*	*–411*	*–398*	*–374*	*–452*
Other	3 852 . .	*–133*	*–156*	*–128*	*–119*	*–144*	*–140*	*–127*	*–152*
Sea transport, passenger	3 207 . .	. . .	. . .	. . .	. . .	. . .	. . .	. . .	. . .
Sea transport, freight	3 208 . .	. . .	. . .	. . .	. . .	. . .	. . .	–344	–416
Sea transport, other	3 209 . .	. . .	. . .	. . .	. . .	. . .	. . .	–65	–81
Air transport, passenger	3 211 . .	. . .	. . .	. . .	. . .	. . .	. . .	–47	–49
Air transport, freight	3 212 . .	. . .	. . .	. . .	. . .	. . .	. . .	–9	–10
Air transport, other	3 213 . .	. . .	. . .	. . .	. . .	. . .	. . .	–41	–43
Other transport, passenger	3 215 . .	. . .	. . .	. . .	. . .	. . .	. . .	. . .	. . .
Other transport, freight	3 216 . .	. . .	. . .	. . .	. . .	. . .	. . .	–22	–27
Other transport, other	3 217 . .	. . .	. . .	. . .	. . .	. . .	. . .	–21	–28
Travel, credit	2 236 . .	**1,417**	**1,530**	**1,588**	**1,543**	**1,657**	**1,827**	**1,682**	**1,751**
Business travel	2 237 . .	104	119	121	110	134	164	31	33
Personal travel	2 240 . .	1,313	1,411	1,467	1,432	1,523	1,663	1,652	1,718
Travel, debit	3 236 . .	**–216**	**–251**	**–251**	**–235**	**–235**	**–239**	**–263**	**–273**
Business travel	3 237 . .	–18	–43	–42	–42	–47	–51	–23	–24
Personal travel	3 240 . .	–198	–207	–209	–194	–189	–189	–239	–249
Other services, credit	2 200 BA	**273**	**381**	**402**	**427**	**465**	**495**	**490**	**523**
Communications	2 245 . .	18	26	15	15	16	13	12	13
Construction	2 249 . .	. . .	11	8	5	19	17	50	71
Insurance	2 253 . .	14	16	20	16	18	17	15	22
Financial	2 260 . .	22	21	26	38	34	33	34	38
Computer and information	2 262 . .	. . .	2	3	3	4	11	20	21
Royalties and licence fees	2 266 . .	1	1	1	1	11	10	15	15
Other business services	2 268 . .	123	193	221	252	212	240	255	256
Personal, cultural, and recreational	2 287 . .	3	2	3	2	2	3	3	4
Government, n.i.e.	2 291 . .	93	108	105	95	150	151	87	83
Other services, debit	3 200 BA	**–682**	**–538**	**–473**	**–443**	**–430**	**–420**	**–408**	**–498**
Communications	3 245 . .	–5	–7	–2	–5	–5	–8	–10	–13
Construction	3 249 . .	. . .	–174	–124	–39	–11	–7	–112	–135
Insurance	3 253 . .	–53	–61	–64	–65	–68	–58	–47	–54
Financial	3 260 . .	–15	–19	–23	–36	–40	–38	–36	–41
Computer and information	3 262 . .	. . .	–2	–2	–2	–3	–5	–6	–8
Royalties and licence fees	3 266 . .	–2	–2	–3	–4	–3	–3	–3	–6
Other business services	3 268 . .	–439	–160	–131	–167	–151	–164	–86	–138
Personal, cultural, and recreational	3 287 . .	–5	–4	–10	–10	–14	–9	–9	–10
Government, n.i.e.	3 291 . .	–163	–108	–113	–116	–136	–128	–99	–92

Table 2 (Continued). STANDARD PRESENTATION, 1994–2001
(Millions of U.S. dollars)

	Code	1994	1995	1996	1997	1998	1999	2000	2001
C. INCOME	4 300 . .	–674	–716	–965	–863	–856	–889	–942	–940
Total credit	2 300 . .	*71*	*119*	*66*	*77*	*90*	*89*	*94*	*95*
Total debit	3 300 . .	*–745*	*–835*	*–1,030*	*–939*	*–947*	*–978*	*–1,036*	*–1,036*
Compensation of employees, credit	2 310 . .	**. . .**	**. . .**	**. . .**	**. . .**	**. . .**	**. . .**	**. . .**	**. . .**
Compensation of employees, debit	3 310 . .	**. . .**	**. . .**	**. . .**	**. . .**	**. . .**	**. . .**	**. . .**	**. . .**
Investment income, credit	2 320 . .	**71**	**119**	**66**	**77**	**90**	**89**	**94**	**95**
Direct investment income	2 330 . .	1	1	2	2	2	3	3	3
Dividends and distributed branch profits	2 332 . .	1	1	2	2	2	3	3	3
Reinvested earnings and undistributed branch profits	2 333 . .	. . .	. . .	. . .	. . .	. . .	. . .	. . .	. . .
Income on debt (interest)	2 334 . .	. . .	. . .	. . .	. . .	. . .	. . .	. . .	. . .
Portfolio investment income	2 339 . .	2	3	2	10	89	87	91	92
Income on equity	2 340 . .	2	3	2	10	2	3	2	1
Income on bonds and notes	2 350 . .	. . .	. . .	. . .	. . .	87	84	89	90
Income on money market instruments	2 360 . .	. . .	. . .	. . .	. . .	. . .	. . .	. . .	. . .
Other investment income	2 370 . .	68	115	62	65	. . .	. . .	. . .	. . .
Investment income, debit	3 320 . .	**–745**	**–835**	**–1,030**	**–939**	**–947**	**–978**	**–1,036**	**–1,036**
Direct investment income	3 330 . .	–187	–174	–314	–335	–337	–398	–468	–480
Dividends and distributed branch profits	3 332 . .	–187	–174	–314	–335	–337	–398	–468	–480
Reinvested earnings and undistributed branch profits	3 333 . .	. . .	. . .	. . .	. . .	. . .	. . .	. . .	. . .
Income on debt (interest)	3 334 . .	. . .	. . .	. . .	. . .	. . .	. . .	. . .	. . .
Portfolio investment income	3 339 . .	–42	–54	–54	–70	–609	–580	–568	–556
Income on equity	3 340 . .	–42	–54	–54	–70	–68	–49	–53	–71
Income on bonds and notes	3 350 . .	. . .	. . .	. . .	. . .	–541	–531	–516	–485
Income on money market instruments	3 360 . .	. . .	. . .	. . .	. . .	. . .	. . .	. . .	. . .
Other investment income	3 370 . .	–517	–607	–662	–535	. . .	. . .	. . .	. . .
D. CURRENT TRANSFERS	4 379 . .	799	774	860	791	832	902	825	982
Credit	2 379 . .	**816**	**805**	**879**	**821**	**852**	**920**	**825**	**958**
General government	2 380 . .	104	25	25	25	60	61	. . .	. . .
Other sectors	2 390 . .	712	779	855	796	792	859	825	958
Workers' remittances	2 391 . .	629	680	736	685	718	761	796	927
Other current transfers	2 392 . .	83	99	119	111	74	98	29	31
Debit	3 379 . .	**–17**	**–31**	**–20**	**–30**	**–20**	**–18**	**. . .**	**24**
General government	3 380 . .	–2	–1	. . .	. . .	–6	–4	29	58
Other sectors	3 390 . .	–15	–30	–20	–30	–14	–13	–29	–34
Workers' remittances	3 391 . .	–11	–21	–11	–20	–8	–8	–21	–21
Other current transfers	3 392 . .	–4	–8	–8	–10	–6	–6	–8	–13
CAPITAL AND FINANCIAL ACCOUNT	4 996 . .	**614**	**893**	**411**	**389**	**687**	**404**	**854**	**890**
CAPITAL ACCOUNT	4 994	**–3**	**32**	**37**	**77**	**61**	**59**	**3**	**53**
Total credit	2 994 . .	*5*	*47*	*46*	*95*	*83*	*72*	*9*	*56*
Total debit	3 994 . .	*–8*	*–15*	*–9*	*–18*	*–22*	*–13*	*–6*	*–3*
Capital transfers, credit	2 400 . .	**5**	**47**	**46**	**95**	**83**	**72**	**9**	**56**
General government	2 401 . .	5	47	46	95	. . .	. . .	9	56
Debt forgiveness	2 402 . .	5	7	7	5	. . .	. . .	. . .	. . .
Other capital transfers	2 410 . .	. . .	39	39	90	. . .	. . .	9	56
Other sectors	2 430 . .	. . .	. . .	. . .	. . .	83	72	. . .	. . .
Migrants' transfers	2 431 . .	. . .	. . .	. . .	. . .	. . .	. . .	. . .	. . .
Debt forgiveness	2 432 . .	. . .	. . .	. . .	. . .	. . .	. . .	. . .	. . .
Other capital transfers	2 440 . .	. . .	. . .	. . .	. . .	83	72	. . .	. . .
Capital transfers, debit	3 400 . .	**–8**	**–15**	**–9**	**–18**	**–22**	**–13**	**–6**	**–3**
General government	3 401 . .	. . .	. . .	. . .	. . .	. . .	. . .	. . .	. . .
Debt forgiveness	3 402 . .	. . .	. . .	. . .	. . .	. . .	. . .	. . .	. . .
Other capital transfers	3 410 . .	. . .	. . .	. . .	. . .	. . .	. . .	. . .	. . .
Other sectors	3 430 . .	–8	–15	–9	–18	–22	–13	–6	–3
Migrants' transfers	3 431 . .	–8	–15	–9	–18	–22	–13	–6	–3
Debt forgiveness	3 432 . .	. . .	. . .	. . .	. . .	. . .	. . .	. . .	. . .
Other capital transfers	3 440 . .	. . .	. . .	. . .	. . .	. . .	. . .	. . .	. . .
Nonproduced nonfinancial assets, credit	2 480 . .	**. . .**	**. . .**	**. . .**	**. . .**	**. . .**	**. . .**	**. . .**	**. . .**
Nonproduced nonfinancial assets, debit	3 480 . .	**. . .**	**. . .**	**. . .**	**. . .**	**. . .**	**. . .**	**. . .**	**. . .**

Table 2 (Continued). STANDARD PRESENTATION, 1994–2001
(Millions of U.S. dollars)

	Code		1994	1995	1996	1997	1998	1999	2000	2001
FINANCIAL ACCOUNT	4 995	. .	**617**	**861**	**374**	**312**	**627**	**345**	**851**	**837**
A. DIRECT INVESTMENT	4 500	. .	426	270	237	333	651	347	751	457
Direct investment abroad	4 505	. .	**–6**	**5**	**–1**	**–6**	**1**	**–3**	**–1**	**–1**
Equity capital	4 510	. .	–6	5	–1	–6	1	–3	–1	–1
Claims on affiliated enterprises	4 515	. .	–6	. . .	–1	–6	. . .	. . .	. . .	. . .
Liabilities to affiliated enterprises	4 520	. .	. . .	5	. . .	. . .	1	–3	–1	–1
Reinvested earnings	4 525	. .	. . .	. . .	. . .	. . .	. . .	. . .	. . .	. . .
Other capital	4 530	. .	. . .	. . .	. . .	. . .	. . .	. . .	. . .	. . .
Claims on affiliated enterprises	4 535	. .	. . .	. . .	. . .	. . .	. . .	. . .	. . .	. . .
Liabilities to affiliated enterprises	4 540	. .	. . .	. . .	. . .	. . .	. . .	. . .	. . .	. . .
Direct investment in Tunisia	4 555	. .	**432**	**264**	**238**	**339**	**650**	**350**	**752**	**457**
Equity capital	4 560	. .	430	271	233	343	648	346	757	459
Claims on direct investors	4 565	. .	. . .	. . .	. . .	. . .	. . .	. . .	. . .	. . .
Liabilities to direct investors	4 570	. .	430	271	233	343	648	346	757	459
Reinvested earnings	4 575	. .	. . .	. . .	. . .	. . .	. . .	. . .	. . .	. . .
Other capital	4 580	. .	2	–6	5	–4	2	4	–4	–1
Claims on direct investors	4 585	. .	. . .	–6	. . .	–4	. . .	. . .	. . .	. . .
Liabilities to direct investors	4 590	. .	2	. . .	5	. . .	2	4	–4	–1
B. PORTFOLIO INVESTMENT	4 600	. .	15	25	62	109	33	10	–20	–15
Assets	4 602	. .	**–1**	**2**	**–5**	**–1**	**. . .**	**. . .**	**. . .**	**. . .**
Equity securities	4 610	. .	1	. . .	. . .	–1	. . .	. . .	. . .	. . .
Monetary authorities	4 611	. .	. . .	. . .	. . .	. . .	. . .	. . .	. . .	. . .
General government	4 612	. .	. . .	. . .	. . .	. . .	. . .	. . .	. . .	. . .
Banks	4 613	. .	. . .	. . .	. . .	. . .	. . .	. . .	. . .	. . .
Other sectors	4 614	. .	1	. . .	. . .	–1	. . .	. . .	. . .	. . .
Debt securities	4 619	. .	–2	2	–5	. . .	. . .	. . .	. . .	. . .
Bonds and notes	4 620	. .	–2	2	–5	. . .	. . .	. . .	. . .	. . .
Monetary authorities	4 621	. .	. . .	. . .	. . .	. . .	. . .	. . .	. . .	. . .
General government	4 622	. .	–2	2	–5	. . .	. . .	. . .	. . .	. . .
Banks	4 623	. .	. . .	. . .	. . .	. . .	. . .	. . .	. . .	. . .
Other sectors	4 624	. .	. . .	. . .	. . .	. . .	. . .	. . .	. . .	. . .
Money market instruments	4 630	. .	. . .	. . .	. . .	. . .	. . .	. . .	. . .	. . .
Monetary authorities	4 631	. .	. . .	. . .	. . .	. . .	. . .	. . .	. . .	. . .
General government	4 632	. .	. . .	. . .	. . .	. . .	. . .	. . .	. . .	. . .
Banks	4 633	. .	. . .	. . .	. . .	. . .	. . .	. . .	. . .	. . .
Other sectors	4 634	. .	. . .	. . .	. . .	. . .	. . .	. . .	. . .	. . .
Liabilities	4 652	. .	**16**	**23**	**67**	**109**	**33**	**10**	**–20**	**–15**
Equity securities	4 660	. .	6	12	29	55	58	–3	–18	–15
Banks	4 663	. .	. . .	. . .	. . .	. . .	. . .	. . .	. . .	. . .
Other sectors	4 664	. .	6	12	29	55	58	–3	–18	–15
Debt securities	4 669	. .	10	12	38	54	–25	13	–3	. . .
Bonds and notes	4 670	. .	. . .	. . .	. . .	. . .	. . .	. . .	. . .	. . .
Monetary authorities	4 671	. .	. . .	. . .	. . .	. . .	. . .	. . .	. . .	. . .
General government	4 672	. .	. . .	. . .	. . .	. . .	. . .	. . .	. . .	. . .
Banks	4 673	. .	. . .	. . .	. . .	. . .	. . .	. . .	. . .	. . .
Other sectors	4 674	. .	. . .	. . .	. . .	. . .	. . .	. . .	. . .	. . .
Money market instruments	4 680	. .	10	12	38	54	–25	13	–3	. . .
Monetary authorities	4 681	. .	. . .	. . .	. . .	. . .	. . .	. . .	. . .	. . .
General government	4 682	. .	10	12	38	54	. . .	19	. . .	. . .
Banks	4 683	. .	. . .	. . .	. . .	. . .	. . .	. . .	. . .	. . .
Other sectors	4 684	. .	. . .	. . .	. . .	. . .	–25	–7	–3	. . .
C. FINANCIAL DERIVATIVES	4 910	. .	. . .	. . .	. . .	. . .	. . .	. . .	. . .	. . .
Monetary authorities	4 911	. .	. . .	. . .	. . .	. . .	. . .	. . .	. . .	. . .
General government	4 912	. .	. . .	. . .	. . .	. . .	. . .	. . .	. . .	. . .
Banks	4 913	. .	. . .	. . .	. . .	. . .	. . .	. . .	. . .	. . .
Other sectors	4 914	. .	. . .	. . .	. . .	. . .	. . .	. . .	. . .	. . .
Assets	4 900	. .	**. . .**	**. . .**	**. . .**	**. . .**	**. . .**	**. . .**	**. . .**	**. . .**
Monetary authorities	4 901	. .	. . .	. . .	. . .	. . .	. . .	. . .	. . .	. . .
General government	4 902	. .	. . .	. . .	. . .	. . .	. . .	. . .	. . .	. . .
Banks	4 903	. .	. . .	. . .	. . .	. . .	. . .	. . .	. . .	. . .
Other sectors	4 904	. .	. . .	. . .	. . .	. . .	. . .	. . .	. . .	. . .
Liabilities	4 905	. .	**. . .**	**. . .**	**. . .**	**. . .**	**. . .**	**. . .**	**. . .**	**. . .**
Monetary authorities	4 906	. .	. . .	. . .	. . .	. . .	. . .	. . .	. . .	. . .
General government	4 907	. .	. . .	. . .	. . .	. . .	. . .	. . .	. . .	. . .
Banks	4 908	. .	. . .	. . .	. . .	. . .	. . .	. . .	. . .	. . .
Other sectors	4 909	. .	. . .	. . .	. . .	. . .	. . .	. . .	. . .	. . .

Table 2 (Concluded). STANDARD PRESENTATION, 1994–2001
(Millions of U.S. dollars)

	Code	1994	1995	1996	1997	1998	1999	2000	2001
D. OTHER INVESTMENT	4 700 . .	703	648	470	207	–245	676	–124	652
Assets	4 703 . .	**–326**	**–327**	**–705**	**–729**	**–508**	**–228**	**–624**	**–416**
Trade credits	4 706 . .	–479	–565	–494	–493	–517	–236	–624	–416
General government	4 707 . .	. . .	. . .	. . .	. . .	. . .	. . .	. . .	. . .
of which: Short-term	4 709 . .	. . .	. . .	. . .	. . .	. . .	. . .	. . .	. . .
Other sectors	4 710 . .	–479	–565	–494	–493	–517	–236	–624	–416
of which: Short-term	4 712 . .	*–479*	*–565*	*–494*	*–493*	*–517*	*–236*	*–624*	*–416*
Loans	4 714 . .	35	43	50	18	10	8	. . .	. . .
Monetary authorities	4 715 . .	. . .	. . .	. . .	. . .	. . .	. . .	. . .	. . .
of which: Short-term	4 718 . .	. . .	. . .	. . .	. . .	. . .	. . .	. . .	. . .
General government	4 719 . .	. . .	. . .	. . .	. . .	. . .	. . .	. . .	. . .
of which: Short-term	4 721 . .	. . .	. . .	. . .	. . .	. . .	. . .	. . .	. . .
Banks	4 722 . .	35	43	50	18	10	8	. . .	. . .
of which: Short-term	4 724 . .	. . .	. . .	. . .	. . .	. . .	. . .	. . .	. . .
Other sectors	4 725 . .	. . .	. . .	. . .	. . .	. . .	. . .	. . .	. . .
of which: Short-term	4 727 . .	. . .	. . .	. . .	. . .	. . .	. . .	. . .	. . .
Currency and deposits	4 730 . .	–26	. . .	–124	–110	. . .	. . .	. . .	. . .
Monetary authorities	4 731 . .	. . .	. . .	. . .	. . .	. . .	. . .	. . .	. . .
General government	4 732 . .	. . .	. . .	. . .	. . .	. . .	. . .	. . .	. . .
Banks	4 733 . .	–26	. . .	–124	–110	. . .	. . .	. . .	. . .
Other sectors	4 734 . .	. . .	. . .	. . .	. . .	. . .	. . .	. . .	. . .
Other assets	4 736 . .	144	195	–137	–144	. . .	. . .	. . .	. . .
Monetary authorities	4 737 . .	86	88	95	14	. . .	. . .	. . .	. . .
of which: Short-term	4 739 . .	*86*	*88*	*95*	*14*	. . .	. . .	. . .	. . .
General government	4 740 . .	. . .	. . .	. . .	. . .	. . .	. . .	. . .	. . .
of which: Short-term	4 742 . .	. . .	. . .	. . .	. . .	. . .	. . .	. . .	. . .
Banks	4 743 . .	58	107	–231	–157	. . .	. . .	. . .	. . .
of which: Short-term	4 745 . .	*58*	*107*	*–231*	*–157*	. . .	. . .	. . .	. . .
Other sectors	4 746 . .	. . .	. . .	. . .	. . .	. . .	. . .	. . .	. . .
of which: Short-term	4 748 . .	. . .	. . .	. . .	. . .	. . .	. . .	. . .	. . .
Liabilities	4 753 . .	**1,029**	**974**	**1,175**	**936**	**263**	**904**	**500**	**1,068**
Trade credits	4 756 . .	284	394	664	473	375	486	277	225
General government	4 757 . .	. . .	. . .	. . .	. . .	. . .	. . .	. . .	. . .
of which: Short-term	4 759 . .	. . .	. . .	. . .	. . .	. . .	. . .	. . .	. . .
Other sectors	4 760 . .	284	394	664	473	375	486	277	225
of which: Short-term	4 762 . .	*284*	*394*	*664*	*473*	*375*	*486*	*277*	*225*
Loans	4 764 . .	577	537	334	344	–112	418	224	843
Monetary authorities	4 765 . .	. . .	–15	–47	–51	–50	–50	–40	–31
of which: Use of Fund credit and loans from the Fund	4 766 . .	. . .	*–15*	*–47*	*–51*	*–50*	*–50*	*–40*	*–31*
of which: Short-term	4 768 . .	. . .	. . .	. . .	. . .	. . .	. . .	. . .	. . .
General government	4 769 . .	411	546	517	324	–49	314	128	752
of which: Short-term	4 771 . .	. . .	. . .	. . .	. . .	. . .	. . .	. . .	. . .
Banks	4 772 . .	. . .	. . .	. . .	. . .	. . .	. . .	. . .	. . .
of which: Short-term	4 774 . .	. . .	. . .	. . .	. . .	. . .	. . .	. . .	. . .
Other sectors	4 775 . .	166	6	–137	71	–13	153	136	122
of which: Short-term	4 777 . .	. . .	. . .	. . .	. . .	. . .	. . .	. . .	. . .
Currency and deposits	4 780 . .	168	43	178	118	. . .	. . .	. . .	. . .
Monetary authorities	4 781 . .	. . .	–1	–11	28	. . .	. . .	. . .	. . .
General government	4 782 . .	. . .	. . .	. . .	. . .	. . .	. . .	. . .	. . .
Banks	4 783 . .	168	44	189	90	. . .	. . .	. . .	. . .
Other sectors	4 784 . .	. . .	. . .	. . .	. . .	. . .	. . .	. . .	. . .
Other liabilities	4 786 . .	. . .	. . .	. . .	. . .	. . .	. . .	. . .	. . .
Monetary authorities	4 787 . .	. . .	. . .	. . .	. . .	. . .	. . .	. . .	. . .
of which: Short-term	4 789 . .	. . .	. . .	. . .	. . .	. . .	. . .	. . .	. . .
General government	4 790 . .	. . .	. . .	. . .	. . .	. . .	. . .	. . .	. . .
of which: Short-term	4 792 . .	. . .	. . .	. . .	. . .	. . .	. . .	. . .	. . .
Banks	4 793 . .	. . .	. . .	. . .	. . .	. . .	. . .	. . .	. . .
of which: Short-term	4 795 . .	. . .	. . .	. . .	. . .	. . .	. . .	. . .	. . .
Other sectors	4 796 . .	. . .	. . .	. . .	. . .	. . .	. . .	. . .	. . .
of which: Short-term	4 798 . .	. . .	. . .	. . .	. . .	. . .	. . .	. . .	. . .
E. RESERVE ASSETS	4 802 . .	–527	–82	–395	–336	187	–688	245	–257
Monetary gold	4 812 . .	. . .	. . .	. . .	. . .	. . .	. . .	. . .	. . .
Special drawing rights	4 811 . .	–1	–5	–9	–1	13	–24	21	1
Reserve position in the Fund	4 810 . .	. . .	. . .	. . .	. . .	. . .	–28	. . .	. . .
Foreign exchange	4 803 . .	–526	–76	–386	–335	174	–636	224	–258
Other claims	4 813 . .	. . .	. . .	. . .	. . .	. . .	. . .	. . .	. . .
NET ERRORS AND OMISSIONS	4 998 . .	**–78**	**–119**	**67**	**206**	**–12**	**38**	**–33**	**–27**

Part 3 of the *Yearbook* contains descriptions of the methodologies, compilation practices, and sources used to compile these data.

Table 3. INTERNATIONAL INVESTMENT POSITION (End–period stocks), 1994–2001

(Millions of U.S. dollars)

	Code	1994	1995	1996	1997	1998	1999	2000	2001
ASSETS	8 995 C.	...	2,953	3,112	3,175	3,313	3,359	3,276	3,281
Direct investment abroad	8 505 . .	**...**	**28**	**29**	**32**	**35**	**34**	**32**	**33**
Equity capital and reinvested earnings	8 506 . .	...	28	29	32	35	34	32	33
Claims on affiliated enterprises	8 507 . .	...	...	...	...	...	...	...	...
Liabilities to affiliated enterprises	8 508 . .	...	28	29	32	35	34	32	33
Other capital	8 530 . .	...	...	...	...	...	...	...	...
Claims on affiliated enterprises	8 535 . .	...	...	...	...	...	...	...	...
Liabilities to affiliated enterprises	8 540 . .	...	...	...	...	...	...	...	...
Portfolio investment	8 602 . .	**...**	**48**	**53**	**50**	**54**	**49**	**45**	**45**
Equity securities	8 610 . .	...	48	53	50	54	49	45	45
Monetary authorities	8 611 . .	...	...	...	...	...	...	...	...
General government	8 612 . .	...	...	...	...	...	...	...	...
Banks	8 613 . .	...	...	...	...	...	...	...	...
Other sectors	8 614 . .	...	48	53	50	54	49	45	45
Debt securities	8 619 . .	...	...	...	...	...	...	...	...
Bonds and notes	8 620 . .	...	...	...	...	...	...	...	...
Monetary authorities	8 621 . .	...	...	...	...	...	...	...	...
General government	8 622 . .	...	...	...	...	...	...	...	...
Banks	8 623 . .	...	...	...	...	...	...	...	...
Other sectors	8 624 . .	...	...	...	...	...	...	...	...
Money market instruments	8 630 . .	...	...	...	...	...	...	...	...
Monetary authorities	8 631 . .	...	...	...	...	...	...	...	...
General government	8 632 . .	...	...	...	...	...	...	...	...
Banks	8 633 . .	...	...	...	...	...	...	...	...
Other sectors	8 634 . .	...	...	...	...	...	...	...	...
Financial derivatives	8 900 . .	**...**	**...**	**...**	**...**	**...**	**...**	**...**	**...**
Monetary authorities	8 901 . .	...	...	...	...	...	...	...	...
General government	8 902 . .	...	...	...	...	...	...	...	...
Banks	8 903 . .	...	...	...	...	...	...	...	...
Other sectors	8 904 . .	...	...	...	...	...	...	...	...
Other investment	8 703 . .	**...**	**1,195**	**1,043**	**1,039**	**1,278**	**911**	**1,300**	**1,162**
Trade credits	8 706 . .	...	563	346	342	518	162	505	517
General government	8 707 . .	...	...	...	...	...	...	...	...
of which: Short-term	8 709 . .	...	...	...	...	...	...	...	...
Other sectors	8 710 . .	...	563	346	342	518	162	505	517
of which: Short-term	8 712 . .	...	*563*	*346*	*342*	*518*	*162*	*505*	*517*
Loans	8 714 . .	...	185	135	75	95	103	99	98
Monetary authorities	8 715 . .	...	...	...	...	...	...	...	...
of which: Short-term	8 718 . .	...	...	...	...	...	...	...	...
General government	8 719 . .	...	...	...	...	...	...	...	...
of which: Short-term	8 721 . .	...	...	...	...	...	...	...	...
Banks	8 722 . .	...	...	...	...	...	...	...	...
of which: Short-term	8 724 . .	...	...	...	...	...	...	...	...
Other sectors	8 725 . .	...	185	135	75	95	103	99	98
of which: Short-term	8 727 . .	...	...	...	...	...	...	...	...
Currency and deposits	8 730 . .	...	...	...	...	...	...	...	...
Monetary authorities	8 731 . .	...	...	...	...	...	...	...	...
General government	8 732 . .	...	...	...	...	...	...	...	...
Banks	8 733 . .	...	...	...	...	...	...	...	...
Other sectors	8 734 . .	...	...	...	...	...	...	...	...
Other assets	8 736 . .	...	447	562	621	665	646	696	547
Monetary authorities	8 737 . .	...	...	...	...	...	...	...	...
of which: Short-term	8 739 . .	...	...	...	...	...	...	...	...
General government	8 740 . .	...	...	...	...	...	...	...	...
of which: Short-term	8 742 . .	...	...	...	...	...	...	...	...
Banks	8 743 . .	...	447	562	621	665	646	696	547
of which: Short-term	8 745 . .	...	*447*	*562*	*621*	*665*	*646*	...	...
Other sectors	8 746 . .	...	...	...	...	...	...	...	...
of which: Short-term	8 748 . .	...	...	...	...	...	...	...	...
Reserve assets	8 802 . .	**...**	**1,681**	**1,987**	**2,054**	**1,947**	**2,366**	**1,898**	**2,042**
Monetary gold	8 812 . .	...	5	4	3	4	3	3	3
Special drawing rights	8 811 . .	3	7	16	16	3	27	4	2
Reserve position in the Fund	8 810 . .	...	...	...	...	...	28	26	25
Foreign exchange	8 803 . .	...	1,669	1,967	2,034	1,940	2,308	1,865	2,012
Other claims	8 813 . .	...	...	...	...	...	...	...	...

Table 3 (Concluded). INTERNATIONAL INVESTMENT POSITION (End–period stocks), 1994–2001
(Millions of U.S. dollars)

	Code	1994	1995	1996	1997	1998	1999	2000	2001
LIABILITIES	8 995 D.	...	22,773	23,382	22,579	24,854	24,295	23,878	24,445
Direct investment in Tunisia	8 555 . .	**...**	**10,967**	**11,201**	**10,629**	**12,237**	**11,463**	**11,452**	**11,671**
Equity capital and reinvested earnings	8 556 . .	...	...	...	...	...	...	11,452	11,671
Claims on direct investors	8 557 . .	...	...	...	...	...	...	...	...
Liabilities to direct investors	8 558 . .	...	...	...	...	...	...	11,452	11,671
Other capital	8 580 . .	...	10,967	11,201	10,629	12,237	11,463	...	...
Claims on direct investors	8 585 . .	...	...	...	...	...	...	...	...
Liabilities to direct investors	8 590 . .	...	10,967	11,201	10,629	12,237	11,463	...	...
Portfolio investment	8 652 . .	**...**	**947**	**1,012**	**1,035**	**1,161**	**1,065**	**975**	**942**
Equity securities	8 660 . .	...	947	1,012	1,035	1,161	1,065	975	942
Banks	8 663 . .	...	...	...	...	...	...	...	...
Other sectors	8 664 . .	...	947	1,012	1,035	1,161	1,065	975	942
Debt securities	8 669 . .	...	...	...	...	...	...	...	...
Bonds and notes	8 670 . .	...	...	...	...	...	...	...	...
Monetary authorities	8 671 . .	...	...	...	...	...	...	...	...
General government	8 672 . .	...	...	...	...	...	...	...	...
Banks	8 673 . .	...	...	...	...	...	...	...	...
Other sectors	8 674 . .	...	...	...	...	...	...	...	...
Money market instruments	8 680 . .	...	...	...	...	...	...	...	...
Monetary authorities	8 681 . .	...	...	...	...	...	...	...	...
General government	8 682 . .	...	...	...	...	...	...	...	...
Banks	8 683 . .	...	...	...	...	...	...	...	...
Other sectors	8 684 . .	...	...	...	...	...	...	...	...
Financial derivatives	8 905 . .	**...**	**...**	**...**	**...**	**...**	**...**	**...**	**...**
Monetary authorities	8 906 . .	...	...	...	...	...	...	...	...
General government	8 907 . .	...	...	...	...	...	...	...	...
Banks	8 908 . .	...	...	...	...	...	...	...	...
Other sectors	8 909 . .	...	...	...	...	...	...	...	...
Other investment	8 753 . .	**...**	**10,860**	**11,170**	**10,914**	**11,456**	**11,766**	**11,451**	**11,831**
Trade credits	8 756 . .	...	370	379	327	354	93	138	216
General government	8 757 . .	...	...	...	...	...	...	...	...
of which: Short-term	8 759 . .	...	...	...	...	...	...	...	...
Other sectors	8 760 . .	...	370	379	327	354	93	138	216
of which: Short-term	8 762 . .	...	*370*	*379*	*327*	*354*	*93*	*138*	*216*
Loans	8 764 . .	...	9,556	9,634	9,430	9,862	10,216	9,861	10,241
Monetary authorities	8 765 . .	...	...	...	...	...	...	...	...
of which: Use of Fund credit and loans from the Fund	8 766 . .	*303*	*293*	*237*	*173*	*129*	*76*	*32*	...
of which: Short-term	8 768 . .	...	...	...	...	...	...	...	...
General government	8 769 . .	...	6,896	6,979	7,014	7,381	7,646	7,318	7,687
of which: Short-term	8 771 . .	...	...	...	...	...	...	...	...
Banks	8 772 . .	...	...	...	...	...	...	...	...
of which: Short-term	8 774 . .	...	...	...	...	...	...	...	...
Other sectors	8 775 . .	...	2,660	2,655	2,416	2,480	2,570	2,542	2,554
of which: Short-term	8 777 . .	...	...	...	...	...	...	...	...
Currency and deposits	8 780 . .	...	934	1,157	1,157	1,240	1,457	1,452	1,374
Monetary authorities	8 781 . .	...	...	...	...	...	...	...	...
General government	8 782 . .	...	...	...	...	...	...	...	...
Banks	8 783 . .	...	934	1,157	1,157	1,240	1,457	1,452	1,374
Other sectors	8 784 . .	...	...	...	...	...	...	...	...
Other liabilities	8 786 . .	...	...	...	...	...	...	...	...
Monetary authorities	8 787 . .	...	...	...	...	...	...	...	...
of which: Short-term	8 789 . .	...	...	...	...	...	...	...	...
General government	8 790 . .	...	...	...	...	...	...	...	...
of which: Short-term	8 792 . .	...	...	...	...	...	...	...	...
Banks	8 793 . .	...	...	...	...	...	...	...	...
of which: Short-term	8 795 . .	...	...	...	...	...	...	...	...
Other sectors	8 796 . .	...	...	...	...	...	...	...	...
of which: Short-term	8 798 . .	...	...	...	...	...	...	...	...
NET INTERNATIONAL INVESTMENT POSITION	8 995 . .	**...**	**-19,820**	**-20,270**	**-19,404**	**-21,541**	**-20,936**	**-20,601**	**-21,163**
Conversion rates: Tunisian dinars per U.S. dollar (end of period)	0 102 . .	**.99120**	**.95080**	**.99850**	**1.14750**	**1.10100**	**1.25250**	**1.38530**	**1.46830**

Table 1. ANALYTIC PRESENTATION, 1994–2001

(Millions of U.S. dollars)

	Code	1994	1995	1996	1997	1998	1999	2000	2001
A. Current Account [1]	4 993 Z.	**2,631**	**–2,338**	**–2,437**	**–2,638**	**1,984**	**–1,360**	**–9,819**	**3,396**
Goods: exports f.o.b	2 100 . .	18,390	21,975	32,067	32,110	30,662	28,842	30,721	34,379
Goods: imports f.o.b	3 100 . .	–22,606	–35,187	–42,681	–47,513	–44,926	–39,326	–53,131	–38,916
Balance on Goods	4 100 . .	*–4,216*	*–13,212*	*–10,614*	*–15,403*	*–14,264*	*–10,484*	*–22,410*	*–4,537*
Services: credit	2 200 . .	10,801	14,606	13,430	19,910	23,879	16,881	20,429	16,059
Services: debit	3 200 . .	–3,782	–5,024	–6,773	–8,998	–10,373	–9,395	–9,061	–6,929
Balance on Goods and Services	4 991 . .	*2,803*	*–3,630*	*–3,957*	*–4,491*	*–758*	*–2,998*	*–11,042*	*4,593*
Income: credit	2 300 . .	890	1,489	1,577	1,900	2,481	2,350	2,836	2,753
Income: debit	3 300 . .	–4,154	–4,693	–4,504	–4,913	–5,466	–5,887	–6,838	–7,753
Balance on Goods, Services, and Income	4 992 . .	*–461*	*–6,834*	*–6,884*	*–7,504*	*–3,743*	*–6,535*	*–15,044*	*–407*
Current transfers: credit	2 379 Z.	3,113	4,512	4,466	4,909	5,861	5,295	5,317	3,861
Current transfers: debit	3 379 . .	–21	–16	–19	–43	–134	–120	–92	–58
B. Capital Account [1]	4 994 Z.	**. . .**	**. . .**	**. . .**	**. . .**	**. . .**	**. . .**	**. . .**	**. . .**
Capital account: credit	2 994 Z.	. . .	. . .	. . .	. . .	. . .	. . .	. . .	. . .
Capital account: debit	3 994 . .	. . .	. . .	. . .	. . .	. . .	. . .	. . .	. . .
Total, Groups A Plus B	4 981 . .	*2,631*	*–2,338*	*–2,437*	*–2,638*	*1,984*	*–1,360*	*–9,819*	*3,396*
C. Financial Account [1]	4 995 W.	**–4,194**	**4,643**	**5,483**	**6,969**	**–840**	**5,085**	**8,610**	**–14,198**
Direct investment abroad	4 505 . .	–49	–113	–110	–251	–367	–645	–870	–497
Direct investment in Turkey	4 555 Z.	608	885	722	805	940	783	982	3,266
Portfolio investment assets	4 602 . .	35	–466	–1,380	–710	–1,622	–759	–594	–788
Equity securities	4 610 . .	5	–75	7	–50	–21	–46	–33	–36
Debt securities	4 619 . .	30	–391	–1,387	–660	–1,601	–713	–561	–752
Portfolio investment liabilities	4 652 Z.	1,123	703	1,950	2,344	–5,089	4,188	1,616	–3,727
Equity securities	4 660 . .	989	195	191	8	–518	428	489	–79
Debt securities	4 669 Z.	134	508	1,759	2,336	–4,571	3,760	1,127	–3,648
Financial derivatives	4 910 . .	. . .	. . .	. . .	. . .	. . .	. . .	. . .	. . .
Financial derivatives assets	4 900 . .	. . .	. . .	. . .	. . .	. . .	. . .	. . .	. . .
Financial derivatives liabilities	4 905 . .	. . .	. . .	. . .	. . .	. . .	. . .	. . .	. . .
Other investment assets	4 703 . .	2,423	–383	331	–1,750	–1,464	–2,198	–1,913	–156
Monetary authorities	4 701 . .	–18	–102	–117	–98	–95	–98	1	–39
General government	4 704 . .	. . .	. . .	. . .	. . .	. . .	. . .	. . .	. . .
Banks	4 705 . .	2,441	–281	1,448	–976	–942	–1,839	–1,574	233
Other sectors	4 728 . .	. . .	. . .	–1,000	–676	–427	–261	–340	–350
Other investment liabilities	4 753 W.	–8,334	4,017	3,970	6,531	6,762	3,716	9,389	–12,296
Monetary authorities	4 753 WA	1,415	1,734	1,380	1,245	760	–160	706	817
General government	4 753 ZB	–2,516	–1,991	–2,108	–1,456	–1,655	–1,932	–883	–1,977
Banks	4 753 ZC	–7,053	1,973	3,046	2,232	3,195	2,655	3,737	–9,644
Other sectors	4 753 ZD	–180	2,301	1,652	4,510	4,462	3,153	5,829	–1,492
Total, Groups A Through C	4 983 . .	*–1,563*	*2,305*	*3,046*	*4,331*	*1,144*	*3,725*	*–1,209*	*–10,802*
D. Net Errors and Omissions	4 998 . .	**1,766**	**2,355**	**1,498**	**–988**	**–703**	**1,629**	**–2,725**	**–2,086**
Total, Groups A Through D	4 984 . .	*203*	*4,660*	*4,544*	*3,343*	*441*	*5,354*	*–3,934*	*–12,888*
E. Reserves and Related Items	4 802 A.	**–203**	**–4,660**	**–4,544**	**–3,343**	**–441**	**–5,354**	**3,934**	**12,888**
Reserve assets	4 802 . .	–547	–5,007	–4,544	–3,316	–217	–5,724	–383	2,718
Use of Fund credit and loans	4 766 . .	344	347	. . .	–27	–224	519	3,316	10,169
Exceptional financing	4 920 . .	. . .	. . .	. . .	. . .	. . .	–150	1,000	. . .
Conversion rates: liras per U.S. dollar	0 101 . .	**29,609**	**45,845**	**81,405**	**151,865**	**260,724**	**418,783**	**625,219**	**1,225,588**

[1] Excludes components that have been classified in the categories of Group E.

Table 2. STANDARD PRESENTATION, 1994–2001
(Millions of U.S. dollars)

	Code			1994	1995	1996	1997	1998	1999	2000	2001
CURRENT ACCOUNT	4	993	. .	**2,631**	**–2,338**	**–2,437**	**–2,638**	**1,984**	**–1,360**	**–9,819**	**3,396**
A. GOODS	4	100	. .	–4,216	–13,212	–10,614	–15,403	–14,264	–10,484	–22,410	–4,537
Credit	2	100	. .	**18,390**	**21,975**	**32,067**	**32,110**	**30,662**	**28,842**	**30,721**	**34,379**
General merchandise: exports f.o.b.	2	110	. .	18,390	21,975	32,067	32,110	30,662	28,842	30,721	34,353
Goods for processing: exports f.o.b.	2	150	. .	. . .	. . .	. . .	. . .	. . .	. . .	. . .	. . .
Repairs on goods	2	160	. .	. . .	. . .	. . .	. . .	. . .	. . .	. . .	. . .
Goods procured in ports by carriers	2	170	. .	. . .	. . .	. . .	. . .	. . .	. . .	. . .	. . .
Nonmonetary gold	2	180	. .	. . .	. . .	. . .	. . .	. . .	. . .	. . .	26
Debit	3	100	. .	**–22,606**	**–35,187**	**–42,681**	**–47,513**	**–44,926**	**–39,326**	**–53,131**	**–38,916**
General merchandise: imports f.o.b.	3	110	. .	–22,126	–33,865	–41,009	–45,646	–43,165	–38,247	–51,231	–37,927
Goods for processing: imports f.o.b.	3	150	. .	. . .	. . .	. . .	. . .	. . .	. . .	. . .	. . .
Repairs on goods	3	160	. .	. . .	. . .	. . .	. . .	. . .	. . .	. . .	. . .
Goods procured in ports by carriers	3	170	. .	. . .	. . .	. . .	. . .	. . .	. . .	. . .	. . .
Nonmonetary gold	3	180	. .	–480	–1,322	–1,672	–1,867	–1,761	–1,079	–1,900	–989
B. SERVICES	4	200	. .	7,019	9,582	6,657	10,912	13,506	7,486	11,368	9,130
Total credit	2	200	. .	*10,801*	*14,606*	*13,430*	*19,910*	*23,879*	*16,881*	*20,429*	*16,059*
Total debit	3	200	. .	*–3,782*	*–5,024*	*–6,773*	*–8,998*	*–10,373*	*–9,395*	*–9,061*	*–6,929*
Transportation services, credit	2	205	. .	**1,221**	**1,712**	**1,756**	**2,193**	**3,120**	**2,900**	**2,955**	**2,854**
Passenger	2	850	. .	. . .	. . .	. . .	. . .	. . .	. . .	. . .	. . .
Freight	2	851	. .	*1,037*	*1,426*	*1,413*	*1,768*	*1,882*	*1,712*	*1,653*	*1,796*
Other	2	852	. .	*184*	*286*	*343*	*425*	*1,238*	*1,188*	*1,302*	*1,058*
Sea transport, passenger	2	207	. .	. . .	. . .	. . .	. . .	. . .	. . .	. . .	. . .
Sea transport, freight	2	208	. .	. . .	. . .	. . .	. . .	. . .	. . .	. . .	. . .
Sea transport, other	2	209	. .	. . .	. . .	. . .	. . .	. . .	. . .	. . .	. . .
Air transport, passenger	2	211	. .	. . .	. . .	. . .	. . .	. . .	. . .	. . .	. . .
Air transport, freight	2	212	. .	. . .	. . .	. . .	. . .	. . .	. . .	. . .	. . .
Air transport, other	2	213	. .	. . .	. . .	. . .	. . .	. . .	. . .	. . .	. . .
Other transport, passenger	2	215	. .	. . .	. . .	. . .	. . .	. . .	. . .	. . .	. . .
Other transport, freight	2	216	. .	. . .	. . .	. . .	. . .	. . .	. . .	. . .	. . .
Other transport, other	2	217	. .	. . .	. . .	. . .	. . .	. . .	. . .	. . .	. . .
Transportation services, debit	3	205	. .	**–953**	**–1,412**	**–1,741**	**–1,870**	**–2,365**	**–2,101**	**–2,463**	**–2,021**
Passenger	3	850	. .	. . .	. . .	. . .	. . .	. . .	. . .	. . .	. . .
Freight	3	851	. .	*–717*	*–1,106*	*–1,348*	*–1,501*	*–1,184*	*–1,049*	*–1,407*	*–1,065*
Other	3	852	. .	*–236*	*–306*	*–393*	*–369*	*–1,181*	*–1,052*	*–1,056*	*–956*
Sea transport, passenger	3	207	. .	. . .	. . .	. . .	. . .	. . .	. . .	. . .	. . .
Sea transport, freight	3	208	. .	. . .	. . .	. . .	. . .	. . .	. . .	. . .	. . .
Sea transport, other	3	209	. .	. . .	. . .	. . .	. . .	. . .	. . .	. . .	. . .
Air transport, passenger	3	211	. .	. . .	. . .	. . .	. . .	. . .	. . .	. . .	. . .
Air transport, freight	3	212	. .	. . .	. . .	. . .	. . .	. . .	. . .	. . .	. . .
Air transport, other	3	213	. .	. . .	. . .	. . .	. . .	. . .	. . .	. . .	. . .
Other transport, passenger	3	215	. .	. . .	. . .	. . .	. . .	. . .	. . .	. . .	. . .
Other transport, freight	3	216		. . .	. . .	. . .	. . .	. . .	. . .	. . .	. . .
Other transport, other	3	217	. .	. . .	. . .	. . .	. . .	. . .	. . .	. . .	. . .
Travel, credit	2	236	. .	**4,321**	**4,957**	**5,650**	**7,002**	**7,177**	**5,203**	**7,636**	**8,090**
Business travel	2	237	. .	258	203	181	1,195	1,366	746	1,488	1,575
Personal travel	2	240	. .	4,063	4,754	5,469	5,807	5,811	4,457	6,148	6,515
Travel, debit	3	236	. .	**–866**	**–911**	**–1,265**	**–1,716**	**–1,754**	**–1,471**	**–1,713**	**–1,738**
Business travel	3	237	. .	–209	–227	–124	–683	–525	–381	393	–685
Personal travel	3	240	. .	–657	–684	–1,141	–1,033	–1,229	–1,090	–1,320	–1,053
Other services, credit	2	200	BA	**5,259**	**7,937**	**6,024**	**10,715**	**13,582**	**8,778**	**9,838**	**5,115**
Communications	2	245	. .	. . .	. . .	. . .	. . .	. . .	. . .	. . .	. . .
Construction	2	249	. .	1,263	1,863	1,967	2,455	2,504	1,176	1,033	685
Insurance	2	253	. .	9	20	24	43	34	30	32	25
Financial	2	260	. .	123	201	293	313	478	319	368	331
Computer and information	2	262	. .	. . .	. . .	. . .	. . .	. . .	. . .	. . .	. . .
Royalties and licence fees	2	266	. .	. . .	. . .	. . .	. . .	. . .	. . .	. . .	. . .
Other business services	2	268	. .	2,152	3,440	2,635	5,499	6,826	4,428	5,562	2,856
Personal, cultural, and recreational	2	287	. .	1,634	2,282	949	2,225	3,580	2,615	2,591	1,072
Government, n.i.e.	2	291	. .	78	131	156	180	160	210	252	146
Other services, debit	3	200	BA	**–1,963**	**–2,701**	**–3,767**	**–5,412**	**–6,254**	**–5,823**	**–4,885**	**–3,170**
Communications	3	245	. .	. . .	. . .	–74	–83	–88	–72	–84	–102
Construction	3	249	. .	–7	–4	–26	–170	–193	–81	–65	–31
Insurance	3	253	. .	–34	–42	–30	–41	–299	–249	–342	–282
Financial	3	260	. .	–288	–350	–484	–603	–590	–631	–671	–722
Computer and information	3	262	. .	. . .	. . .	. . .	. . .	. . .	. . .	. . .	. . .
Royalties and licence fees	3	266	. .	. . .	. . .	–124	–275	–242	–186	–173	–119
Other business services	3	268	. .	–500	–557	–839	–1,185	–1,265	–1,060	–1,480	–1,163
Personal, cultural, and recreational	3	287	. .	–770	–1,378	–1,798	–2,634	–3,158	–3,044	–1,541	–286
Government, n.i.e.	3	291	. .	–364	–370	–392	–421	–419	–500	–529	–465

Table 2 (Continued). STANDARD PRESENTATION, 1994–2001
(Millions of U.S. dollars)

	Code	1994	1995	1996	1997	1998	1999	2000	2001
C. INCOME	4 300 . .	–3,264	–3,204	–2,927	–3,013	–2,985	–3,537	–4,002	–5,000
Total credit	2 300 . .	*890*	*1,489*	*1,577*	*1,900*	*2,481*	*2,350*	*2,836*	*2,753*
Total debit	3 300 . .	*–4,154*	*–4,693*	*–4,504*	*–4,913*	*–5,466*	*–5,887*	*–6,838*	*–7,753*
Compensation of employees, credit	2 310 . .	...	...	...	...	...	...	...	...
Compensation of employees, debit	3 310 . .	...	...	...	...	...	...	...	...
Investment income, credit	2 320 . .	**890**	**1,489**	**1,577**	**1,900**	**2,481**	**2,350**	**2,836**	**2,753**
Direct investment income	2 330 . .	10	41	32	61	101	146	368	361
Dividends and distributed branch profits	2 332 . .	10	41	32	61	101	140	343	324
Reinvested earnings and undistributed branch profits	2 333 . .	...	...	...	...	...	6	25	37
Income on debt (interest)	2 334 . .	...	...	...	...	...	...	...	...
Portfolio investment income	2 339 . .	189	240	379	862	1,284	1,130	1,300	1,253
Income on equity	2 340 . .	2	9	40	66	1	1	...	...
Income on bonds and notes	2 350 . .	187	231	339	796	1,283	1,129	1,300	1,253
Income on money market instruments	2 360 . .	...	...	...	...	...	...	...	...
Other investment income	2 370 . .	691	1,208	1,166	977	1,096	1,074	1,168	1,139
Investment income, debit	3 320 . .	**–4,154**	**–4,693**	**–4,504**	**–4,913**	**–5,466**	**–5,887**	**–6,838**	**–7,753**
Direct investment income	3 330 . .	–112	–312	–207	–203	–328	–313	–279	–309
Dividends and distributed branch profits	3 332 . .	–112	–261	–171	–196	–299	–276	–277	–303
Reinvested earnings and undistributed branch profits	3 333 . .	...	–51	–36	–7	–29	–37	–2	–6
Income on debt (interest)	3 334 . .	...	...	...	...	...	...	...	...
Portfolio investment income	3 339 . .	–731	–981	–896	–915	–1,269	–1,041	–1,734	–1,947
Income on equity	3 340 . .	–91	–48	–52	–55	–200	–79	–58	–124
Income on bonds and notes	3 350 . .	–640	–933	–844	–860	–1,069	–962	–1,676	–1,823
Income on money market instruments	3 360 . .	...	...	...	...	...	...	...	...
Other investment income	3 370 . .	–3,311	–3,400	–3,401	–3,795	–3,869	–4,533	–4,825	–5,497
D. CURRENT TRANSFERS	4 379 . .	3,092	4,496	4,447	4,866	5,727	5,175	5,225	3,803
Credit	2 379 . .	**3,113**	**4,512**	**4,466**	**4,909**	**5,861**	**5,295**	**5,317**	**3,861**
General government	2 380 . .	404	1,087	574	357	293	482	306	265
Other sectors	2 390 . .	2,709	3,425	3,892	4,552	5,568	4,813	5,011	3,596
Workers' remittances	2 391 . .	2,627	3,327	3,542	4,197	5,356	4,529	4,560	2,786
Other current transfers	2 392 . .	82	98	350	355	212	284	451	810
Debit	3 379 . .	**–21**	**–16**	**–19**	**–43**	**–134**	**–120**	**–92**	**–58**
General government	3 380 . .	–21	–16	–19	–43	–134	–120	–92	–58
Other sectors	3 390 . .	...	...	...	...	...	...	...	...
Workers' remittances	3 391 . .	...	...	...	...	...	...	...	...
Other current transfers	3 392 . .	...	...	...	...	...	...	...	...
CAPITAL AND FINANCIAL ACCOUNT	4 996 . .	**–4,397**	**–17**	**939**	**3,626**	**–1,281**	**–269**	**12,544**	**–1,310**
CAPITAL ACCOUNT	4 994 . .	...	...	...	...	...	...	...	...
Total credit	2 994 . .	...	...	...	...	...	...	...	...
Total debit	3 994 . .	...	...	...	...	...	...	...	...
Capital transfers, credit	2 400 . .	...	...	...	...	...	...	...	...
General government	2 401 . .	...	...	...	...	...	...	...	...
Debt forgiveness	2 402 . .	...	...	...	...	...	...	...	...
Other capital transfers	2 410 . .	...	...	...	...	...	...	...	...
Other sectors	2 430 . .	...	...	...	...	...	...	...	...
Migrants' transfers	2 431 . .	...	...	...	...	...	...	...	...
Debt forgiveness	2 432 . .	...	...	...	...	...	...	...	...
Other capital transfers	2 440 . .	...	...	...	...	...	...	...	...
Capital transfers, debit	3 400 . .	...	...	...	...	...	...	...	...
General government	3 401 . .	...	...	...	...	...	...	...	...
Debt forgiveness	3 402 . .	...	...	...	...	...	...	...	...
Other capital transfers	3 410 . .	...	...	...	...	...	...	...	...
Other sectors	3 430 . .	...	...	...	...	...	...	...	...
Migrants' transfers	3 431 . .	...	...	...	...	...	...	...	...
Debt forgiveness	3 432 . .	...	...	...	...	...	...	...	...
Other capital transfers	3 440 . .	...	...	...	...	...	...	...	...
Nonproduced nonfinancial assets, credit	2 480 . .	...	...	...	...	...	...	...	...
Nonproduced nonfinancial assets, debit	3 480 . .	...	...	...	...	...	...	...	...

Table 2 (Continued). STANDARD PRESENTATION, 1994–2001

(Millions of U.S. dollars)

	Code	1994	1995	1996	1997	1998	1999	2000	2001
FINANCIAL ACCOUNT	4 995 . .	**–4,397**	**–17**	**939**	**3,626**	**–1,281**	**–269**	**12,544**	**–1,310**
A. DIRECT INVESTMENT	4 500 . .	559	772	612	554	573	138	112	2,769
Direct investment abroad	4 505 . .	**–49**	**–113**	**–110**	**–251**	**–367**	**–645**	**–870**	**–497**
Equity capital	4 510 . .	–49	–113	–110	–251	–367	–639	–845	–461
Claims on affiliated enterprises	4 515 . .	–49	–113	–110	–251	–367	–639	–845	–461
Liabilities to affiliated enterprises	4 520 . .	...	...	...	...	...	...	...	...
Reinvested earnings	4 525 . .	...	...	...	...	...	–6	–25	–36
Other capital	4 530 . .	...	...	...	...	...	...	...	...
Claims on affiliated enterprises	4 535 . .	...	...	...	...	...	...	...	...
Liabilities to affiliated enterprises	4 540 . .	...	...	...	...	...	...	...	...
Direct investment in Turkey	4 555 . .	**608**	**885**	**722**	**805**	**940**	**783**	**982**	**3,266**
Equity capital	4 560 . .	608	834	686	798	911	746	980	3,260
Claims on direct investors	4 565 . .	...	...	...	...	...	...	...	...
Liabilities to direct investors	4 570 . .	608	834	686	798	911	746	980	3,260
Reinvested earnings	4 575 . .	...	51	36	7	29	37	2	6
Other capital	4 580 . .	...	...	...	...	...	...	...	...
Claims on direct investors	4 585 . .	...	...	...	...	...	...	...	...
Liabilities to direct investors	4 590 . .	...	...	...	...	...	...	...	...
B. PORTFOLIO INVESTMENT	4 600 . .	1,158	237	570	1,634	–6,711	3,429	1,022	–4,515
Assets	4 602 . .	**35**	**–466**	**–1,380**	**–710**	**–1,622**	**–759**	**–594**	**–788**
Equity securities	4 610 . .	5	–75	7	–50	–21	–46	–33	–36
Monetary authorities	4 611 . .	...	...	...	...	...	...	...	...
General government	4 612 . .	–15	–33	–27	–48	–21	–46	–33	–36
Banks	4 613 . .	...	...	...	...	...	...	...	...
Other sectors	4 614 . .	20	–42	34	–2	...	...	...	...
Debt securities	4 619 . .	30	–391	–1,387	–660	–1,601	–713	–561	–752
Bonds and notes	4 620 . .	30	–391	–1,387	–660	–1,601	–713	–561	–752
Monetary authorities	4 621 . .	...	...	...	...	...	...	...	...
General government	4 622 . .	67	...	8	7	...	...	...	...
Banks	4 623 . .	–37	–391	–1,395	–667	–1,791	–812	–680	–281
Other sectors	4 624 . .	...	...	...	...	190	99	119	–471
Money market instruments	4 630 . .	...	...	...	...	...	...	...	...
Monetary authorities	4 631 . .	...	...	...	...	...	...	...	...
General government	4 632 . .	...	...	...	...	...	...	...	...
Banks	4 633 . .	...	...	...	...	...	...	...	...
Other sectors	4 634 . .	...	...	...	...	...	...	...	...
Liabilities	4 652 . .	**1,123**	**703**	**1,950**	**2,344**	**–5,089**	**4,188**	**1,616**	**–3,727**
Equity securities	4 660 . .	989	195	191	8	–518	428	489	–79
Banks	4 663 . .	...	...	...	...	...	...	...	...
Other sectors	4 664 . .	989	195	191	8	–518	428	489	–79
Debt securities	4 669 . .	134	508	1,759	2,336	–4,571	3,760	1,127	–3,648
Bonds and notes	4 670 . .	134	508	1,759	2,336	–4,571	3,760	1,127	–3,648
Monetary authorities	4 671 . .	...	–213	...	...	...	...	...	...
General government	4 672 . .	446	933	1,919	1,915	–4,369	3,677	985	–3,645
Banks	4 673 . .	–312	–212	–160	421	–202	83	142	–3
Other sectors	4 674 . .	...	...	...	...	...	...	...	...
Money market instruments	4 680 . .	...	...	...	...	...	...	...	...
Monetary authorities	4 681 . .	...	...	...	...	...	...	...	...
General government	4 682 . .	...	...	...	...	...	...	...	...
Banks	4 683 . .	...	...	...	...	...	...	...	...
Other sectors	4 684 . .	...	...	...	...	...	...	...	...
C. FINANCIAL DERIVATIVES	4 910 . .	...	...	...	...	...	...	...	...
Monetary authorities	4 911 . .	...	...	...	...	...	...	...	...
General government	4 912 . .	...	...	...	...	...	...	...	...
Banks	4 913 . .	...	...	...	...	...	...	...	...
Other sectors	4 914 . .	...	...	...	...	...	...	...	...
Assets	4 900 . .	**...**	**...**	**...**	**...**	**...**	**...**	**...**	**...**
Monetary authorities	4 901 . .	...	...	...	...	...	...	...	...
General government	4 902 . .	...	...	...	...	...	...	...	...
Banks	4 903 . .	...	...	...	...	...	...	...	...
Other sectors	4 904 . .	...	...	...	...	...	...	...	...
Liabilities	4 905 . .	**...**	**...**	**...**	**...**	**...**	**...**	**...**	**...**
Monetary authorities	4 906 . .	...	...	...	...	...	...	...	...
General government	4 907 . .	...	...	...	...	...	...	...	...
Banks	4 908 . .	...	...	...	...	...	...	...	...
Other sectors	4 909 . .	...	...	...	...	...	...	...	...

Table 2 (Concluded). STANDARD PRESENTATION, 1994–2001
(Millions of U.S. dollars)

	Code	1994	1995	1996	1997	1998	1999	2000	2001
D. OTHER INVESTMENT	4 700	–5,567	3,981	4,301	4,754	5,074	1,887	11,792	–2,283
Assets	4 703	**2,423**	**–383**	**331**	**–1,750**	**–1,464**	**–2,198**	**–1,913**	**–156**
Trade credits	4 706	...	...	...	...	...	...	...	...
General government	4 707	...	...	...	...	...	...	...	...
of which: Short-term	4 709	...	...	...	...	...	...	...	...
Other sectors	4 710	...	...	...	...	...	...	...	...
of which: Short-term	4 712	...	...	...	...	...	...	...	...
Loans	4 714	–38	1,101	–125	–358	–261	–453	117	–734
Monetary authorities	4 715	–28	–48	–63	–60	–71	–68	...	–40
of which: Short-term	4 718	...	...	...	...	...	...	...	...
General government	4 719	...	...	...	...	...	...	...	...
of which: Short-term	4 721	...	...	...	...	...	...	...	...
Banks	4 722	–10	1,149	–62	–298	–190	–385	117	–694
of which: Short-term	4 724	*–10*	*1,219*	*95*	*–134*	*–74*	*–143*	*213*	*–632*
Other sectors	4 725	...	...	...	...	...	...	...	...
of which: Short-term	4 727	...	...	...	...	...	...	...	...
Currency and deposits	4 730	2,451	–1,430	1,510	–678	–752	–1,454	–1,691	927
Monetary authorities	4 731	...	...	...	...	...	...	...	...
General government	4 732	...	...	...	...	...	...	...	...
Banks	4 733	2,451	–1,430	1,510	–678	–752	–1,454	–1,691	927
Other sectors	4 734	...	...	...	...	...	...	...	...
Other assets	4 736	10	–54	–1,054	–714	–451	–291	–339	–349
Monetary authorities	4 737	10	–54	–54	–38	–24	–30	1	1
of which: Short-term	4 739	*10*	*–54*	*–54*	*–38*	*–24*	*–30*	*1*	*1*
General government	4 740	...	...	...	...	...	...	...	...
of which: Short-term	4 742	...	...	...	...	...	...	...	...
Banks	4 743	...	...	...	...	...	...	...	...
of which: Short-term	4 745	...	...	...	...	...	...	...	...
Other sectors	4 746	...	...	–1,000	–676	–427	–261	–340	–350
of which: Short-term	4 748	...	...	*–1,000*	*–676*	*–427*	*–261*	*–340*	*–350*
Liabilities	4 753	**–7,990**	**4,364**	**3,970**	**6,504**	**6,538**	**4,085**	**13,705**	**–2,127**
Trade credits	4 756	–816	1,671	328	572	–40	719	805	–1,930
General government	4 757	...	...	...	...	...	...	...	...
of which: Short-term	4 759	...	...	...	...	...	...	...	...
Other sectors	4 760	–816	1,671	328	572	–40	719	805	–1,930
of which: Short-term	4 762	*–816*	*1,671*	*139*	*316*	*–117*	*771*	*797*	*–1,941*
Loans	4 764	–8,487	53	950	4,837	3,512	3,056	12,833	553
Monetary authorities	4 765	276	340	–81	–29	–227	517	3,313	10,168
of which: Use of Fund credit and loans from the Fund	4 766	*344*	*347*	...	*–27*	*–224*	*519*	*3,316*	*10,169*
of which: Short-term	4 768	...	...	...	...	...	...	...	...
General government	4 769	–2,516	–1,991	–2,108	–1,456	–1,655	–1,932	117	–1,977
of which: Short-term	4 771	...	...	...	...	...	...	*1,000*	*–1,000*
Banks	4 772	–6,883	1,074	1,815	2,384	892	2,187	4,379	–8,076
of which: Short-term	4 774	*–6,601*	*801*	*769*	*724*	*63*	*2,070*	*4,742*	*–7,052*
Other sectors	4 775	636	630	1,324	3,938	4,502	2,284	5,024	438
of which: Short-term	4 777	*–131*	*446*	*7*	*586*	*419*	*–60*	*128*	*183*
Currency and deposits	4 780	1,260	2,462	2,567	876	2,877	239	–20	–832
Monetary authorities	4 781	1,430	1,563	1,336	1,028	574	–229	622	736
General government	4 782	...	...	...	...	...	...	...	...
Banks	4 783	–170	899	1,231	–152	2,303	468	–642	–1,568
Other sectors	4 784	...	...	...	...	...	...	...	...
Other liabilities	4 786	53	178	125	219	189	71	87	82
Monetary authorities	4 787	53	178	125	219	189	71	87	82
of which: Short-term	4 789	*53*	*178*	*125*	*219*	*189*	*71*	*87*	*82*
General government	4 790	...	...	...	...	...	...	...	...
of which: Short-term	4 792	...	...	...	...	...	...	...	...
Banks	4 793	...	...	...	...	...	...	...	...
of which: Short-term	4 795	...	...	...	...	...	...	...	...
Other sectors	4 796	...	...	...	...	...	...	...	...
of which: Short-term	4 798	...	...	...	...	...	...	...	...
E. RESERVE ASSETS	4 802	–547	–5,007	–4,544	–3,316	–217	–5,724	–383	2,718
Monetary gold	4 812	79	27	...	...	...	...	...	...
Special drawing rights	4 811	–1	–2	1	...	–1	1	–29	24
Reserve position in the Fund	4 810	...	...	...	...	...	–111	...	...
Foreign exchange	4 803	–625	–5,032	–4,545	–3,316	–216	–5,614	–354	2,694
Other claims	4 813	...	...	...	...	...	...	...	...
NET ERRORS AND OMISSIONS	4 998	**1,766**	**2,355**	**1,498**	**–988**	**–703**	**1,629**	**–2,725**	**–2,086**

Part 3 of the *Yearbook* contains descriptions of the methodologies, compilation practices, and sources used to compile these data.

Table 3. INTERNATIONAL INVESTMENT POSITION (End–period stocks), 1994–2001

(Millions of U.S. dollars)

	Code	1994	1995	1996	1997	1998	1999	2000	2001
ASSETS	8 995 C.	...	...	...	...	...	...	53,112	51,850
Direct investment abroad	8 505 . .	**...**	**...**	**...**	**...**	**...**	**...**	**3,668**	**3,775**
Equity capital and reinvested earnings	8 506 . .	...	...	...	...	...	...	3,668	3,775
Claims on affiliated enterprises	8 507 . .	...	...	...	...	...	...	3,668	3,775
Liabilities to affiliated enterprises	8 508 . .	...	...	...	...	...	...	...	...
Other capital	8 530 . .	...	...	...	...	...	...	...	...
Claims on affiliated enterprises	8 535 . .	...	...	...	...	...	...	...	...
Liabilities to affiliated enterprises	8 540 . .	...	...	...	...	...	...	...	...
Portfolio investment	8 602 . .	**...**	**...**	**5**	**5**	**5**	**4**	**492**	**1,027**
Equity securities	8 610 . .	...	...	5	5	5	4	492	530
Monetary authorities	8 611 . .	...	...	5	5	5	4	4	4
General government	8 612 . .	...	...	...	...	...	...	488	477
Banks	8 613 . .	...	...	...	...	...	...	...	...
Other sectors	8 614 . .	...	...	...	...	...	...	...	49
Debt securities	8 619 . .	...	...	...	...	...	...	...	497
Bonds and notes	8 620 . .	...	...	...	...	...	...	...	464
Monetary authorities	8 621 . .	...	...	...	...	...	...	...	...
General government	8 622 . .	...	...	...	...	...	...	...	...
Banks	8 623 . .	...	...	...	...	...	...	...	373
Other sectors	8 624 . .	...	...	...	...	...	...	...	91
Money market instruments	8 630 . .	...	...	...	...	...	...	...	33
Monetary authorities	8 631 . .	...	...	...	...	...	...	...	...
General government	8 632 . .	...	...	...	...	...	...	...	...
Banks	8 633 . .	...	...	...	...	...	...	...	2
Other sectors	8 634 . .	...	...	...	...	...	...	...	31
Financial derivatives	8 900 . .	**...**	**...**	**...**	**...**	**...**	**...**	**...**	**...**
Monetary authorities	8 901 . .	...	...	...	...	...	...	...	...
General government	8 902 . .	...	...	...	...	...	...	...	...
Banks	8 903 . .	...	...	...	...	...	...	...	...
Other sectors	8 904 . .	...	...	...	...	...	...	...	...
Other investment	8 703 . .	**11,624**	**13,571**	**9,911**	**10,450**	**13,709**	**25,041**	**25,599**	**27,083**
Trade credits	8 706 . .	...	...	...	...	1,997	2,104	2,697	3,088
General government	8 707 . .	...	...	...	...	...	...	...	...
of which: Short-term	8 709 . .	...	...	...	...	...	...	...	...
Other sectors	8 710 . .	...	...	...	...	1,997	2,104	2,697	3,088
of which: Short-term	8 712 . .	...	...	...	...	*1,997*	*2,104*	*2,697*	*3,088*
Loans	8 714 . .	3,627	3,402	2,557	2,823	2,938	2,292	2,063	2,950
Monetary authorities	8 715 . .	1,061	1,103	1,160	1,211	1,265	297	208	183
of which: Short-term	8 718 . .	...	...	...	...	...	...	...	...
General government	8 719 . .	...	...	...	...	...	...	...	...
of which: Short-term	8 721 . .	...	...	...	...	...	...	...	...
Banks	8 722 . .	2,566	2,299	1,397	1,612	1,673	1,995	1,855	2,767
of which: Short-term	8 724 . .	*1,742*	*1,193*	*347*	*406*	*436*	*559*	*331*	*1,567*
Other sectors	8 725 . .	...	...	...	...	...	...	...	...
of which: Short-term	8 727 . .	...	...	...	...	...	...	...	...
Currency and deposits	8 730 . .	7,997	10,169	7,352	7,625	8,773	19,620	19,654	19,810
Monetary authorities	8 731 . .	...	...	...	...	...	...	...	...
General government	8 732 . .	...	...	...	...	...	...	...	...
Banks	8 733 . .	7,997	10,169	7,352	7,625	8,773	9,569	11,007	10,392
Other sectors	8 734 . .	...	...	...	...	...	10,051	8,647	9,418
Other assets	8 736 . .	...	...	2	2	1	1,025	1,185	1,235
Monetary authorities	8 737 . .	...	...	2	2	1	1,025	1,185	1,235
of which: Short-term	8 739 . .	...	...	...	...	...	...	...	...
General government	8 740 . .	...	...	...	...	...	...	...	...
of which: Short-term	8 742 . .	...	...	...	...	...	...	...	...
Banks	8 743 . .	...	...	...	...	...	...	...	...
of which: Short-term	8 745 . .	...	...	...	...	...	...	...	...
Other sectors	8 746 . .	...	...	...	...	...	...	...	...
of which: Short-term	8 748 . .	...	...	...	...	...	...	...	...
Reserve assets	8 802 . .	**8,570**	**13,825**	**17,704**	**19,587**	**20,780**	**24,343**	**23,353**	**19,965**
Monetary gold	8 812 . .	1,410	1,383	1,383	1,124	1,012	1,011	1,006	1,032
Special drawing rights	8 811 . .	1	3	1	1	1	...	29	4
Reserve position in the Fund	8 810 . .	47	48	46	44	45	155	147	142
Foreign exchange	8 803 . .	7,112	12,391	16,273	18,419	19,721	23,177	22,172	18,787
Other claims	8 813 . .	...	...	...	...	...	...	...	...

Table 3 (Concluded). INTERNATIONAL INVESTMENT POSITION (End–period stocks), 1994–2001

(Millions of U.S. dollars)

	Code	1994	1995	1996	1997	1998	1999	2000	2001
LIABILITIES	8 995 D.	...	...	...	...	...	...	153,387	136,767
Direct investment in Turkey	8 555	...	...	...	...	...	...	**19,209**	**17,521**
Equity capital and reinvested earnings	8 556	...	...	...	...	...	...	19,209	15,891
Claims on direct investors	8 557	...	...	...	...	...	...	...	...
Liabilities to direct investors	8 558	...	...	...	...	...	...	19,209	15,891
Other capital	8 580	...	...	...	...	...	...	...	1,630
Claims on direct investors	8 585	...	...	...	...	...	...	...	...
Liabilities to direct investors	8 590	...	...	...	...	...	...	...	1,630
Portfolio investment	8 652	**13,788**	**14,186**	**16,166**	**19,750**	**17,735**	**38,410**	**36,168**	**25,013**
Equity securities	8 660	...	...	3,085	6,018	3,700	15,358	7,404	5,635
Banks	8 663	...	...	...	...	...	...	...	...
Other sectors	8 664	...	...	3,085	6,018	3,700	15,358	7,404	5,635
Debt securities	8 669	13,788	14,186	13,081	13,732	14,035	23,052	28,764	19,378
Bonds and notes	8 670	13,788	14,186	13,081	13,732	14,035	23,052	28,764	19,378
Monetary authorities	8 671	193	...	...	...	...	...	...	...
General government	8 672	12,407	13,234	12,367	12,658	13,252	22,221	27,536	18,177
Banks	8 673	1,188	952	714	1,074	783	831	1,228	1,201
Other sectors	8 674	...	...	...	...	...	...	...	...
Money market instruments	8 680	...	...	...	...	...	...	...	...
Monetary authorities	8 681	...	...	...	...	...	...	...	...
General government	8 682	...	...	...	...	...	...	...	...
Banks	8 683	...	...	...	...	...	...	...	...
Other sectors	8 684	...	...	...	...	...	...	...	...
Financial derivatives	8 905	...	...	...	...	...	...	...	...
Monetary authorities	8 906	...	...	...	...	...	...	...	...
General government	8 907	...	...	...	...	...	...	...	...
Banks	8 908	...	...	...	...	...	...	...	...
Other sectors	8 909	...	...	...	...	...	...	...	...
Other investment	8 753	**52,239**	**59,829**	**66,126**	**70,539**	**82,349**	**86,717**	**98,010**	**94,233**
Trade credits	8 756	11,049	13,486	6,611	6,653	6,718	7,251	7,863	5,677
General government	8 757	1,876	1,641	...	...	...	...	...	...
of which: Short-term	8 759	...	...	...	...	...	...	...	...
Other sectors	8 760	9,173	11,845	6,611	6,653	6,718	7,251	7,863	5,677
of which: Short-term	8 762	*5,143*	*6,967*	*6,611*	*6,653*	*6,718*	*7,251*	*7,863*	*5,677*
Loans	8 764	29,529	31,403	43,274	48,604	56,405	62,142	74,036	73,884
Monetary authorities	8 765	440	774	712	632	403	905	4,210	14,145
of which: Use of Fund credit and loans from the Fund	8 766	*344*	*685*	*662*	*594*	*388*	*891*	*4,176*	*14,117*
of which: Short-term	8 768	...	...	*42*	*30*	*7*	*6*	*26*	*20*
General government	8 769	19,784	19,787	23,738	22,173	22,391	21,716	23,464	20,992
of which: Short-term	8 771	...	...	...	*54*	...	...	*1,000*	...
Banks	8 772	3,371	4,527	6,630	8,410	9,339	11,989	16,366	7,722
of which: Short-term	8 774	*2,241*	*3,161*	*3,840*	*4,347*	*4,512*	*6,444*	*11,140*	*4,005*
Other sectors	8 775	5,934	6,315	12,194	17,389	24,272	27,532	29,996	31,025
of which: Short-term	8 777	*655*	*1,082*	*1,058*	*1,592*	*1,992*	*1,812*	*1,885*	*1,977*
Currency and deposits	8 780	11,574	14,868	16,241	15,282	19,226	17,324	16,111	14,672
Monetary authorities	8 781	9,131	11,370	11,662	11,126	12,579	10,596	10,351	10,680
General government	8 782	...	...	...	...	...	...	...	...
Banks	8 783	2,443	3,498	4,579	4,156	6,647	6,728	5,760	3,992
Other sectors	8 784	...	...	...	...	...	...	...	...
Other liabilities	8 786	87	72	...	...	...	...	...	...
Monetary authorities	8 787	87	72	...	...	...	...	...	...
of which: Short-term	8 789	*87*	*72*	...	...	...	...	...	...
General government	8 790	...	...	...	...	...	...	...	...
of which: Short-term	8 792	...	...	...	...	...	...	...	...
Banks	8 793	...	...	...	...	...	...	...	...
of which: Short-term	8 795	...	...	...	...	...	...	...	...
Other sectors	8 796	...	...	...	...	...	...	...	...
of which: Short-term	8 798	...	...	...	...	...	...	...	...
NET INTERNATIONAL INVESTMENT POSITION	8 995	...	...	...	...	...	...	**–100,275**	**–84,916**
Conversion rates: liras per U.S. dollar (end of period)	0 102	**38,726**	**59,650**	**107,775**	**205,605**	**314,464**	**541,400**	**673,385**	**1,450,127**

Table 1. ANALYTIC PRESENTATION, 1994–2001
(Millions of U.S. dollars)

	Code	1994	1995	1996	1997	1998	1999	2000	2001
A. Current Account [1]	4 993 Z.	**...**	**...**	**–.2**	**–580.2**	**...**	**...**	**...**	**...**
Goods: exports f.o.b	2 100 . .	...	...	1,692.0	774.2	...	...	...	...
Goods: imports f.o.b	3 100 . .	...	...	–1,388.3	–1,005.1	...	...	...	...
Balance on Goods	4 100 . .	...	...	*303.7*	*–230.9*	...	...	...	...
Services: credit	2 200 . .	...	...	82.5	271.8	...	...	...	...
Services: debit	3 200 . .	...	...	–407.9	–674.6	...	...	...	...
Balance on Goods and Services	4 991 . .	...	...	*–21.8*	*–633.8*	...	...	...	...
Income: credit	2 300 . .	...	...	127.2	156.9	...	...	...	...
Income: debit	3 300 . .	...	...	–110.4	–72.0	...	...	...	...
Balance on Goods, Services, and Income	4 992 . .	...	...	*–5.0*	*–548.9*	...	...	...	...
Current transfers: credit	2 379 Z.	...	...	4.8	49.9	...	...	...	...
Current transfers: debit	3 379 . .	...	...	...	–81.2	...	...	...	...
B. Capital Account [1]	4 994 Z.	**...**	**...**	**–156.9**	**–8.9**	**...**	**...**	**...**	**...**
Capital account: credit	2 994 Z.	...	...	2.8	14.0	...	...	...	...
Capital account: debit	3 994 . .	...	...	–159.7	–22.9	...	...	...	...
Total, Groups A Plus B	4 981 . .	...	...	*–157.1*	*–589.0*	...	...	...	...
C. Financial Account [1]	4 995 W.	**...**	**...**	**113.4**	**1,060.0**	**...**	**...**	**...**	**...**
Direct investment abroad	4 505 . .	...	...	...	...	...	...	...	...
Direct investment in Turkmenistan	4 555 Z.	...	...	108.1	107.9	...	...	...	...
Portfolio investment assets	4 602 . .	...	...	...	–5.4	...	...	...	...
Equity securities	4 610 . .	...	...	...	–5.4	...	...	...	...
Debt securities	4 619 . .	...	...	...	...	...	...	...	...
Portfolio investment liabilities	4 652 Z.	...	...	...	...	...	...	...	...
Equity securities	4 660 . .	...	...	...	...	...	...	...	...
Debt securities	4 669 Z.	...	...	...	...	...	...	...	...
Financial derivatives	4 910 . .	...	...	...	...	...	...	...	...
Financial derivatives assets	4 900 . .	...	...	...	...	...	...	...	...
Financial derivatives liabilities	4 905 . .	...	...	...	...	...	...	...	...
Other investment assets	4 703 . .	...	...	–165.3	205.6	...	...	...	...
Monetary authorities	4 701 . .	...	...	.2	–37.6	...	...	...	...
General government	4 704 . .	...	...	–118.4	127.9	...	...	...	...
Banks	4 705 . .	...	...	–47.1	142.6	...	...	...	...
Other sectors	4 728 . .	...	...	...	–27.2	...	...	...	...
Other investment liabilities	4 753 W.	...	...	170.6	751.9	...	...	...	...
Monetary authorities	4 753 WA	...	...	–3.1	–.3	...	...	...	...
General government	4 753 ZB	...	...	169.2	877.3	...	...	...	...
Banks	4 753 ZC	...	...	4.6	–125.1	...	...	...	...
Other sectors	4 753 ZD	...	...	...	–.1	...	...	...	...
Total, Groups A Through C	4 983 . .	...	...	*–43.7*	*470.9*	...	...	...	...
D. Net Errors and Omissions	4 998 . .	**...**	**...**	**51.6**	**–72.9**	**...**	**...**	**...**	**...**
Total, Groups A Through D	4 984 . .	...	...	*7.9*	*398.0*	...	...	...	...
E. Reserves and Related Items	4 802 A.	**...**	**...**	**–7.9**	**–398.0**	**...**	**...**	**...**	**...**
Reserve assets	4 802 . .	...	...	–4.5	–111.2	...	...	...	...
Use of Fund credit and loans	4 766 . .	...	...	...	...	...	...	...	...
Exceptional financing	4 920 . .	...	...	–3.4	–286.8	...	...	...	...
Conversion rates: manat per U.S. dollar	0 101 . .	**19.2**	**110.9**	**3,257.7**	**4,143.4**	**4,890.2**	**5,200.0**	**5,200.0**	**5,200.0**

[1] Excludes components that have been classified in the categories of Group E.

Table 2. STANDARD PRESENTATION, 1994–2001
(Millions of U.S. dollars)

	Code	1994	1995	1996	1997	1998	1999	2000	2001
CURRENT ACCOUNT	4 993 . .	**. . .**	**. . .**	**–.2**	**–580.2**	**. . .**	**. . .**	**. . .**	**. . .**
A. GOODS	4 100 . .	. . .	. . .	303.7	–230.9	. . .	. . .	. . .	. . .
Credit	2 100 . .	**. . .**	**. . .**	**1,692.0**	**774.2**	**. . .**	**. . .**	**. . .**	**. . .**
General merchandise: exports f.o.b.	2 110 . .	. . .	. . .	1,692.0	743.3	. . .	. . .	. . .	. . .
Goods for processing: exports f.o.b.	2 150 . .	. . .	. . .	. . .	. . .	. . .	. . .	. . .	. . .
Repairs on goods	2 160 . .	. . .	. . .	. . .	. . .	. . .	. . .	. . .	. . .
Goods procured in ports by carriers	2 170 . .	. . .	. . .	. . .	30.9	. . .	. . .	. . .	. . .
Nonmonetary gold	2 180 . .	. . .	. . .	. . .	. . .	. . .	. . .	. . .	. . .
Debit	3 100 . .	**. . .**	**. . .**	**–1,388.3**	**–1,005.1**	**. . .**	**. . .**	**. . .**	**. . .**
General merchandise: imports f.o.b.	3 110 . .	. . .	. . .	–1,388.3	–1,002.6	. . .	. . .	. . .	. . .
Goods for processing: imports f.o.b.	3 150 . .	. . .	. . .	. . .	. . .	. . .	. . .	. . .	. . .
Repairs on goods	3 160 . .	. . .	. . .	. . .	. . .	. . .	. . .	. . .	. . .
Goods procured in ports by carriers	3 170 . .	. . .	. . .	. . .	–2.5	. . .	. . .	. . .	. . .
Nonmonetary gold	3 180 . .	. . .	. . .	. . .	. . .	. . .	. . .	. . .	. . .
B. SERVICES	4 200 . .	. . .	. . .	–325.4	–402.9	. . .	. . .	. . .	. . .
Total credit	2 200 . .	. . .	. . .	*82.5*	*271.8*	. . .	. . .	. . .	. . .
Total debit	3 200 . .	. . .	. . .	*–407.9*	*–674.6*	. . .	. . .	. . .	. . .
Transportation services, credit	2 205 . .	**. . .**	**. . .**	**62.8**	**133.6**	**. . .**	**. . .**	**. . .**	**. . .**
Passenger	2 850 . .	. . .	. . .	*6.2*	*13.1*	. . .	. . .	. . .	. . .
Freight	2 851 . .	. . .	. . .	*56.6*	*120.5*	. . .	. . .	. . .	. . .
Other	2 852 . .	. . .	. . .	. . .	. . .	. . .	. . .	. . .	. . .
Sea transport, passenger	2 207 . .	. . .	. . .	. . .	. . .	. . .	. . .	. . .	. . .
Sea transport, freight	2 208 . .	. . .	. . .	1.5	4.0	. . .	. . .	. . .	. . .
Sea transport, other	2 209 . .	. . .	. . .	. . .	. . .	. . .	. . .	. . .	. . .
Air transport, passenger	2 211 . .	. . .	. . .	6.2	13.1	. . .	. . .	. . .	. . .
Air transport, freight	2 212 . .	. . .	. . .	21.2	23.2	. . .	. . .	. . .	. . .
Air transport, other	2 213 . .	. . .	. . .	. . .	. . .	. . .	. . .	. . .	. . .
Other transport, passenger	2 215 . .	. . .	. . .	. . .	. . .	. . .	. . .	. . .	. . .
Other transport, freight	2 216 . .	. . .	. . .	33.9	93.3	. . .	. . .	. . .	. . .
Other transport, other	2 217 . .	. . .	. . .	. . .	. . .	. . .	. . .	. . .	. . .
Transportation services, debit	3 205 . .	**. . .**	**. . .**	**–162.8**	**–153.4**	**. . .**	**. . .**	**. . .**	**. . .**
Passenger	3 850 . .	. . .	. . .	*–.7*	*–1.8*	. . .	. . .	. . .	. . .
Freight	3 851 . .	. . .	. . .	*–162.1*	*–145.9*	. . .	. . .	. . .	. . .
Other	3 852 . .	. . .	. . .	. . .	*–5.8*	. . .	. . .	. . .	. . .
Sea transport, passenger	3 207 . .	. . .	. . .	. . .	. . .	. . .	. . .	. . .	. . .
Sea transport, freight	3 208 . .	. . .	. . .	–29.2	–19.6	. . .	. . .	. . .	. . .
Sea transport, other	3 209 . .	. . .	. . .	. . .	. . .	. . .	. . .	. . .	. . .
Air transport, passenger	3 211 . .	. . .	. . .	–.7	–1.8	. . .	. . .	. . .	. . .
Air transport, freight	3 212 . .	. . .	. . .	–17.7	–28.1	. . .	. . .	. . .	. . .
Air transport, other	3 213 . .	. . .	. . .	. . .	. . .	. . .	. . .	. . .	. . .
Other transport, passenger	3 215 . .	. . .	. . .	. . .	. . .	. . .	. . .	. . .	. . .
Other transport, freight	3 216 . .	. . .	. . .	–115.2	–98.3	. . .	. . .	. . .	. . .
Other transport, other	3 217 . .	. . .	. . .	. . .	–5.8	. . .	. . .	. . .	. . .
Travel, credit	2 236 . .	**. . .**	**. . .**	**7.3**	**33.3**	**. . .**	**. . .**	**. . .**	**. . .**
Business travel	2 237 . .	. . .	. . .	7.3	33.3	. . .	. . .	. . .	. . .
Personal travel	2 240 . .	. . .	. . .	. . .	. . .	. . .	. . .	. . .	. . .
Travel, debit	3 236 . .	**. . .**	**. . .**	**–73.2**	**–125.3**	**. . .**	**. . .**	**. . .**	**. . .**
Business travel	3 237 . .	. . .	. . .	. . .	. . .	. . .	. . .	. . .	. . .
Personal travel	3 240 . .	. . .	. . .	–73.2	–125.3	. . .	. . .	. . .	. . .
Other services, credit	2 200 BA	**. . .**	**. . .**	**12.4**	**104.8**	**. . .**	**. . .**	**. . .**	**. . .**
Communications	2 245 . .	. . .	. . .	.9	4.0	. . .	. . .	. . .	. . .
Construction	2 249 . .	. . .	. . .	. . .	. . .	. . .	. . .	. . .	. . .
Insurance	2 253 . .	. . .	. . .	.7	. . .	. . .	. . .	. . .	. . .
Financial	2 260 . .	. . .	. . .	. . .	. . .	. . .	. . .	. . .	. . .
Computer and information	2 262 . .	. . .	. . .	. . .	. . .	. . .	. . .	. . .	. . .
Royalties and licence fees	2 266 . .	. . .	. . .	. . .	. . .	. . .	. . .	. . .	. . .
Other business services	2 268 . .	. . .	. . .	6.9	97.7	. . .	. . .	. . .	. . .
Personal, cultural, and recreational	2 287 . .	. . .	. . .	. . .	. . .	. . .	. . .	. . .	. . .
Government, n.i.e.	2 291 . .	. . .	. . .	3.9	3.1	. . .	. . .	. . .	. . .
Other services, debit	3 200 BA	**. . .**	**. . .**	**–171.9**	**–395.9**	**. . .**	**. . .**	**. . .**	**. . .**
Communications	3 245 . .	. . .	. . .	–1.5	–12.0	. . .	. . .	. . .	. . .
Construction	3 249 . .	. . .	. . .	–126.1	–239.5	. . .	. . .	. . .	. . .
Insurance	3 253 . .	. . .	. . .	–27.7	–11.5	. . .	. . .	. . .	. . .
Financial	3 260 . .	. . .	. . .	. . .	. . .	. . .	. . .	. . .	. . .
Computer and information	3 262 . .	. . .	. . .	. . .	. . .	. . .	. . .	. . .	. . .
Royalties and licence fees	3 266 . .	. . .	. . .	. . .	. . .	. . .	. . .	. . .	. . .
Other business services	3 268 . .	. . .	. . .	–11.9	–127.4	. . .	. . .	. . .	. . .
Personal, cultural, and recreational	3 287 . .	. . .	. . .	. . .	. . .	. . .	. . .	. . .	. . .
Government, n.i.e.	3 291 . .	. . .	. . .	–4.7	–5.6	. . .	. . .	. . .	. . .

Table 2 (Continued). STANDARD PRESENTATION, 1994–2001
(Millions of U.S. dollars)

	Code	1994	1995	1996	1997	1998	1999	2000	2001
C. INCOME	4 300 . .	...	...	16.7	84.9	...	...	...	...
Total credit	2 300 . .	...	...	*127.2*	*156.9*	...	...	...	...
Total debit	3 300 . .	...	...	*–110.4*	*–72.0*	...	...	...	...
Compensation of employees, credit	2 310 . .	**...**	**...**	**4.4**	**...**	**...**	**...**	**...**	**...**
Compensation of employees, debit	3 310 . .	**...**	**...**	**–7.3**	**–4.4**	**...**	**...**	**...**	**...**
Investment income, credit	2 320 . .	**...**	**...**	**122.8**	**156.9**	**...**	**...**	**...**	**...**
Direct investment income	2 330 . .	...	...	...	...	...	...	...	...
Dividends and distributed branch profits	2 332 . .	...	...	...	...	...	...	...	...
Reinvested earnings and undistributed branch profits	2 333 . .	...	...	...	...	...	...	...	...
Income on debt (interest)	2 334 . .	...	...	...	...	...	...	...	...
Portfolio investment income	2 339 . .	...	...	...	...	...	...	...	...
Income on equity	2 340 . .	...	...	...	...	...	...	...	...
Income on bonds and notes	2 350 . .	...	...	...	...	...	...	...	...
Income on money market instruments	2 360 . .	...	...	...	...	...	...	...	...
Other investment income	2 370 . .	...	...	122.8	156.9	...	...	...	...
Investment income, debit	3 320 . .	**...**	**...**	**–103.2**	**–67.6**	**...**	**...**	**...**	**...**
Direct investment income	3 330 . .	...	...	–44.9	–6.8	...	...	...	...
Dividends and distributed branch profits	3 332 . .	...	...	–44.9	–6.8	...	...	...	...
Reinvested earnings and undistributed branch profits	3 333 . .	...	...	...	...	...	...	...	...
Income on debt (interest)	3 334 . .	...	...	...	...	...	...	...	...
Portfolio investment income	3 339 . .	...	...	...	...	...	...	...	...
Income on equity	3 340 . .	...	...	...	...	...	...	...	...
Income on bonds and notes	3 350 . .	...	...	...	...	...	...	...	...
Income on money market instruments	3 360 . .	...	...	...	...	...	...	...	...
Other investment income	3 370 . .	...	...	–58.3	–60.8	...	...	...	...
D. CURRENT TRANSFERS	4 379 . .	...	...	4.8	–31.3	...	...	...	...
Credit	2 379 . .	**...**	**...**	**4.8**	**49.9**	**...**	**...**	**...**	**...**
General government	2 380 . .	...	...	4.6	4.7	...	...	...	...
Other sectors	2 390 . .	...	...	.2	45.2	...	...	...	...
Workers' remittances	2 391 . .	...	...	...	...	...	...	...	...
Other current transfers	2 392 . .	...	...	.2	45.2	...	...	...	...
Debit	3 379 . .	**...**	**...**	**...**	**–81.2**	**...**	**...**	**...**	**...**
General government	3 380 . .	...	...	...	...	...	...	...	...
Other sectors	3 390 . .	...	...	...	–81.2	...	...	...	...
Workers' remittances	3 391 . .	...	...	...	...	...	...	...	...
Other current transfers	3 392 . .	...	...	...	–81.2	...	...	...	...
CAPITAL AND FINANCIAL ACCOUNT	4 996 . .	**...**	**...**	**–51.4**	**653.1**	**...**	**...**	**...**	**...**
CAPITAL ACCOUNT	4 994 . .	...	...	**–156.9**	**–8.9**	...	...	...	...
Total credit	2 994 . .	...	...	*2.8*	*14.0*	...	...	...	...
Total debit	3 994 . .	...	...	*–159.7*	*–22.9*	...	...	...	...
Capital transfers, credit	2 400 . .	**...**	**...**	**2.8**	**14.0**	**...**	**...**	**...**	**...**
General government	2 401 . .	...	...	2.8	14.0	...	...	...	...
Debt forgiveness	2 402 . .	...	...	...	...	...	...	...	...
Other capital transfers	2 410 . .	...	...	2.8	14.0	...	...	...	...
Other sectors	2 430 . .	...	...	...	...	...	...	...	...
Migrants' transfers	2 431 . .	...	...	...	...	...	...	...	...
Debt forgiveness	2 432 . .	...	...	...	...	...	...	...	...
Other capital transfers	2 440 . .	...	...	...	...	...	...	...	...
Capital transfers, debit	3 400 . .	**...**	**...**	**–159.7**	**–22.9**	**...**	**...**	**...**	**...**
General government	3 401 . .	...	...	–159.7	–22.9	...	...	...	...
Debt forgiveness	3 402 . .	...	...	–159.7	...	...	...	...	...
Other capital transfers	3 410 . .	...	...	...	–22.9	...	...	...	...
Other sectors	3 430 . .	...	...	...	...	...	...	...	...
Migrants' transfers	3 431 . .	...	...	...	...	...	...	...	...
Debt forgiveness	3 432 . .	...	...	...	...	...	...	...	...
Other capital transfers	3 440 . .	...	...	...	...	...	...	...	...
Nonproduced nonfinancial assets, credit	2 480 . .	**...**	**...**	**...**	**...**	**...**	**...**	**...**	**...**
Nonproduced nonfinancial assets, debit	3 480 . .	**...**	**...**	**...**	**...**	**...**	**...**	**...**	**...**

Table 2 (Continued). STANDARD PRESENTATION, 1994–2001
(Millions of U.S. dollars)

	Code	1994	1995	1996	1997	1998	1999	2000	2001
FINANCIAL ACCOUNT	4 995	**. . .**	**. . .**	**105.5**	**662.0**	**. . .**	**. . .**	**. . .**	**. . .**
A. DIRECT INVESTMENT	4 500	. . .	. . .	108.1	107.9	. . .	. . .	. . .	. . .
Direct investment abroad	4 505	**. . .**	**. . .**	**. . .**	**. . .**	**. . .**	**. . .**	**. . .**	**. . .**
Equity capital	4 510	. . .	. . .	. . .	. . .	. . .	. . .	. . .	. . .
Claims on affiliated enterprises	4 515	. . .	. . .	. . .	. . .	. . .	. . .	. . .	. . .
Liabilities to affiliated enterprises	4 520	. . .	. . .	. . .	. . .	. . .	. . .	. . .	. . .
Reinvested earnings	4 525	. . .	. . .	. . .	. . .	. . .	. . .	. . .	. . .
Other capital	4 530	. . .	. . .	. . .	. . .	. . .	. . .	. . .	. . .
Claims on affiliated enterprises	4 535	. . .	. . .	. . .	. . .	. . .	. . .	. . .	. . .
Liabilities to affiliated enterprises	4 540	. . .	. . .	. . .	. . .	. . .	. . .	. . .	. . .
Direct investment in Turkmenistan	4 555	**. . .**	**. . .**	**108.1**	**107.9**	**. . .**	**. . .**	**. . .**	**. . .**
Equity capital	4 560	. . .	. . .	108.1	84.6	. . .	. . .	. . .	. . .
Claims on direct investors	4 565	. . .	. . .	. . .	. . .	. . .	. . .	. . .	. . .
Liabilities to direct investors	4 570	. . .	. . .	108.1	84.6	. . .	. . .	. . .	. . .
Reinvested earnings	4 575	. . .	. . .	. . .	. . .	. . .	. . .	. . .	. . .
Other capital	4 580	. . .	. . .	. . .	23.3	. . .	. . .	. . .	. . .
Claims on direct investors	4 585	. . .	. . .	. . .	. . .	. . .	. . .	. . .	. . .
Liabilities to direct investors	4 590	. . .	. . .	. . .	23.3	. . .	. . .	. . .	. . .
B. PORTFOLIO INVESTMENT	4 600	. . .	. . .	. . .	–5.4	. . .	. . .	. . .	. . .
Assets	4 602	**. . .**	**. . .**	**. . .**	**–5.4**	**. . .**	**. . .**	**. . .**	**. . .**
Equity securities	4 610	. . .	. . .	. . .	–5.4	. . .	. . .	. . .	. . .
Monetary authorities	4 611	. . .	. . .	. . .	–5.4	. . .	. . .	. . .	. . .
General government	4 612	. . .	. . .	. . .	. . .	. . .	. . .	. . .	. . .
Banks	4 613	. . .	. . .	. . .	. . .	. . .	. . .	. . .	. . .
Other sectors	4 614	. . .	. . .	. . .	. . .	. . .	. . .	. . .	. . .
Debt securities	4 619	. . .	. . .	. . .	. . .	. . .	. . .	. . .	. . .
Bonds and notes	4 620	. . .	. . .	. . .	. . .	. . .	. . .	. . .	. . .
Monetary authorities	4 621	. . .	. . .	. . .	. . .	. . .	. . .	. . .	. . .
General government	4 622	. . .	. . .	. . .	. . .	. . .	. . .	. . .	. . .
Banks	4 623	. . .	. . .	. . .	. . .	. . .	. . .	. . .	. . .
Other sectors	4 624	. . .	. . .	. . .	. . .	. . .	. . .	. . .	. . .
Money market instruments	4 630	. . .	. . .	. . .	. . .	. . .	. . .	. . .	. . .
Monetary authorities	4 631	. . .	. . .	. . .	. . .	. . .	. . .	. . .	. . .
General government	4 632	. . .	. . .	. . .	. . .	. . .	. . .	. . .	. . .
Banks	4 633	. . .	. . .	. . .	. . .	. . .	. . .	. . .	. . .
Other sectors	4 634	. . .	. . .	. . .	. . .	. . .	. . .	. . .	. . .
Liabilities	4 652	**. . .**	**. . .**	**. . .**	**. . .**	**. . .**	**. . .**	**. . .**	**. . .**
Equity securities	4 660	. . .	. . .	. . .	. . .	. . .	. . .	. . .	. . .
Banks	4 663	. . .	. . .	. . .	. . .	. . .	. . .	. . .	. . .
Other sectors	4 664	. . .	. . .	. . .	. . .	. . .	. . .	. . .	. . .
Debt securities	4 669	. . .	. . .	. . .	. . .	. . .	. . .	. . .	. . .
Bonds and notes	4 670	. . .	. . .	. . .	. . .	. . .	. . .	. . .	. . .
Monetary authorities	4 671	. . .	. . .	. . .	. . .	. . .	. . .	. . .	. . .
General government	4 672	. . .	. . .	. . .	. . .	. . .	. . .	. . .	. . .
Banks	4 673	. . .	. . .	. . .	. . .	. . .	. . .	. . .	. . .
Other sectors	4 674	. . .	. . .	. . .	. . .	. . .	. . .	. . .	. . .
Money market instruments	4 680	. . .	. . .	. . .	. . .	. . .	. . .	. . .	. . .
Monetary authorities	4 681	. . .	. . .	. . .	. . .	. . .	. . .	. . .	. . .
General government	4 682	. . .	. . .	. . .	. . .	. . .	. . .	. . .	. . .
Banks	4 683	. . .	. . .	. . .	. . .	. . .	. . .	. . .	. . .
Other sectors	4 684	. . .	. . .	. . .	. . .	. . .	. . .	. . .	. . .
C. FINANCIAL DERIVATIVES	4 910	. . .	. . .	. . .	. . .	. . .	. . .	. . .	. . .
Monetary authorities	4 911	. . .	. . .	. . .	. . .	. . .	. . .	. . .	. . .
General government	4 912	. . .	. . .	. . .	. . .	. . .	. . .	. . .	. . .
Banks	4 913	. . .	. . .	. . .	. . .	. . .	. . .	. . .	. . .
Other sectors	4 914	. . .	. . .	. . .	. . .	. . .	. . .	. . .	. . .
Assets	4 900	**. . .**	**. . .**	**. . .**	**. . .**	**. . .**	**. . .**	**. . .**	**. . .**
Monetary authorities	4 901	. . .	. . .	. . .	. . .	. . .	. . .	. . .	. . .
General government	4 902	. . .	. . .	. . .	. . .	. . .	. . .	. . .	. . .
Banks	4 903	. . .	. . .	. . .	. . .	. . .	. . .	. . .	. . .
Other sectors	4 904	. . .	. . .	. . .	. . .	. . .	. . .	. . .	. . .
Liabilities	4 905	**. . .**	**. . .**	**. . .**	**. . .**	**. . .**	**. . .**	**. . .**	**. . .**
Monetary authorities	4 906	. . .	. . .	. . .	. . .	. . .	. . .	. . .	. . .
General government	4 907	. . .	. . .	. . .	. . .	. . .	. . .	. . .	. . .
Banks	4 908	. . .	. . .	. . .	. . .	. . .	. . .	. . .	. . .
Other sectors	4 909	. . .	. . .	. . .	. . .	. . .	. . .	. . .	. . .

Table 2 (Concluded). STANDARD PRESENTATION, 1994–2001
(Millions of U.S. dollars)

	Code	1994	1995	1996	1997	1998	1999	2000	2001
D. OTHER INVESTMENT	4 700 . .	...	...	1.9	670.7	...	...	...	...
Assets	4 703 . .	**...**	**...**	**–165.3**	**205.6**	**...**	**...**	**...**	**...**
Trade credits	4 706 . .	...	...	...	–276.5	...	...	...	...
General government	4 707 . .	...	...	...	–276.5	...	...	...	...
of which: Short-term	4 709 . .	...	...	...	*–276.5*	...	...	...	...
Other sectors	4 710 . .	...	...	...	...	...	...	...	...
of which: Short-term	4 712 . .	...	...	...	...	...	...	...	...
Loans	4 714 . .	...	...	37.9	148.3	...	...	...	...
Monetary authorities	4 715 . .	...	...	...	...	...	...	...	...
of which: Short-term	4 718 . .	...	...	...	...	...	...	...	...
General government	4 719 . .	...	...	37.9	148.3	...	...	...	...
of which: Short-term	4 721 . .	...	...	*–31.3*	...	...	...	...	...
Banks	4 722 . .	...	...	...	...	...	...	...	...
of which: Short-term	4 724 . .	...	...	...	...	...	...	...	...
Other sectors	4 725 . .	...	...	...	...	...	...	...	...
of which: Short-term	4 727 . .	...	...	...	...	...	...	...	...
Currency and deposits	4 730 . .	...	...	–46.9	77.8	...	...	...	...
Monetary authorities	4 731 . .	...	...	.2	–37.6	...	...	...	...
General government	4 732 . .	...	...	...	...	...	...	...	...
Banks	4 733 . .	...	...	–47.1	142.6	...	...	...	...
Other sectors	4 734 . .	...	...	...	–27.2	...	...	...	...
Other assets	4 736 . .	...	...	–156.2	256.1	...	...	...	...
Monetary authorities	4 737 . .	...	...	...	...	...	...	...	...
of which: Short-term	4 739 . .	...	...	...	...	...	...	...	...
General government	4 740 . .	...	...	–156.2	256.1	...	...	...	...
of which: Short-term	4 742 . .	...	...	*–156.2*	*256.1*	...	...	...	...
Banks	4 743 . .	...	...	...	...	...	...	...	...
of which: Short-term	4 745 . .	...	...	...	...	...	...	...	...
Other sectors	4 746 . .	...	...	...	...	...	...	...	...
of which: Short-term	4 748 . .	...	...	...	...	...	...	...	...
Liabilities	4 753 . .	**...**	**...**	**167.2**	**465.1**	**...**	**...**	**...**	**...**
Trade credits	4 756 . .	...	...	60.1	83.9	...	...	...	...
General government	4 757 . .	...	...	60.1	83.9	...	...	...	...
of which: Short-term	4 759 . .	...	...	*60.1*	...	...	...	...	...
Other sectors	4 760 . .	...	...	...	...	...	...	...	...
of which: Short-term	4 762 . .	...	...	...	...	...	...	...	...
Loans	4 764 . .	...	...	179.4	619.2	...	...	...	...
Monetary authorities	4 765 . .	...	...	...	...	...	...	...	...
of which: Use of Fund credit and loans from the Fund	4 766 . .	...	...	...	...	...	...	...	...
of which: Short-term	4 768 . .	...	...	...	...	...	...	...	...
General government	4 769 . .	...	...	169.4	574.8	...	...	...	...
of which: Short-term	4 771 . .	...	...	...	...	...	...	...	...
Banks	4 772 . .	...	...	10.0	...	...	...	...	...
of which: Short-term	4 774 . .	...	...	*10.0*	...	...	...	...	...
Other sectors	4 775 . .	...	...	...	44.4	...	...	...	...
of which: Short-term	4 777 . .	...	...	...	...	...	...	...	...
Currency and deposits	4 780 . .	...	...	–8.5	–125.4	...	...	...	...
Monetary authorities	4 781 . .	...	...	–3.1	–.3	...	...	...	...
General government	4 782 . .	...	...	...	...	...	...	...	...
Banks	4 783 . .	...	...	–5.4	–125.1	...	...	...	...
Other sectors	4 784 . .	...	...	...	...	...	...	...	...
Other liabilities	4 786 . .	...	...	–63.8	–112.7	...	...	...	...
Monetary authorities	4 787 . .	...	...	...	...	...	...	...	...
of which: Short-term	4 789 . .	...	...	...	...	...	...	...	...
General government	4 790 . .	...	...	–63.8	–112.7	...	...	...	...
of which: Short-term	4 792 . .	...	...	*–63.8*	*–112.7*	...	...	...	...
Banks	4 793 . .	...	...	...	...	...	...	...	...
of which: Short-term	4 795 . .	...	...	...	...	...	...	...	...
Other sectors	4 796 . .	...	...	...	...	...	...	...	...
of which: Short-term	4 798 . .	...	...	...	...	...	...	...	...
E. RESERVE ASSETS	4 802 . .	...	...	–4.5	–111.2	...	...	...	...
Monetary gold	4 812 . .	...	...	...	...	...	...	...	...
Special drawing rights	4 811 . .	...	...	...	...	...	...	...	...
Reserve position in the Fund	4 810 . .	...	...	...	...	...	...	...	...
Foreign exchange	4 803 . .	...	...	–4.5	–111.2	...	...	...	...
Other claims	4 813 . .	...	...	...	...	...	...	...	...
NET ERRORS AND OMISSIONS	4 998 . .	**...**	**...**	**51.6**	**–72.9**	**...**	**...**	**...**	**...**

Part 3 of the *Yearbook* contains descriptions of the methodologies, compilation practices, and sources used to compile these data.

Table 1. ANALYTIC PRESENTATION, 1994–2001
(Millions of U.S. dollars)

	Code		1994	1995	1996	1997	1998	1999	2000	2001
A. Current Account [1]	4 993	Z.	**–207.5**	**–338.9**	**–252.3**	**–366.8**	**–502.6**	**–723.1**	**–850.6**	**–809.5**
Goods: exports f.o.b.	2 100	..	463.0	560.3	639.3	592.6	510.2	483.5	449.9	451.6
Goods: imports f.o.b.	3 100	..	–714.2	–926.8	–986.9	–1,042.6	–1,166.3	–989.1	–949.7	–1,026.6
Balance on Goods	4 100	..	*–251.2*	*–366.5*	*–347.6*	*–449.9*	*–656.1*	*–505.6*	*–499.8*	*–575.0*
Services: credit	2 200	..	64.1	104.0	144.7	164.6	176.3	183.6	184.3	182.6
Services: debit	3 200	..	–436.3	–562.7	–674.6	–668.9	–728.1	–419.2	–455.1	–491.9
Balance on Goods and Services	4 991	..	*–623.4*	*–825.2*	*–877.5*	*–954.2*	*–1,208.0*	*–741.2*	*–770.6*	*–884.3*
Income: credit	2 300	..	13.8	17.7	29.7	40.5	50.7	35.1	53.1	37.3
Income: debit	3 300	..	–71.0	–113.3	–79.2	–55.7	–59.9	–162.5	–165.5	–177.6
Balance on Goods, Services, and Income	4 992	..	*–680.6*	*–920.8*	*–927.0*	*–969.4*	*–1,217.2*	*–868.6*	*–883.0*	*–1,024.6*
Current transfers: credit	2 379	Z.	473.1	581.9	674.7	602.6	714.6	329.7	340.0	583.0
Current transfers: debit	3 379	..	...	...	...	...	...	–184.2	–307.6	–367.9
B. Capital Account [1]	4 994	Z.	**36.1**	**48.3**	**61.4**	**31.9**	**49.5**	**...**	**...**	**...**
Capital account: credit	2 994	Z.	36.1	48.3	61.4	31.9	49.5	...	...	...
Capital account: debit	3 994	..	...	...	...	...	...	...	...	...
Total, Groups A Plus B	4 981	..	*–171.4*	*–290.6*	*–190.9*	*–334.9*	*–453.1*	*–723.1*	*–850.6*	*–809.5*
C. Financial Account [1]	4 995	W.	**76.8**	**210.7**	**140.5**	**298.8**	**372.8**	**253.3**	**320.5**	**499.7**
Direct investment abroad	4 505	..	...	...	...	...	...	...	...	...
Direct investment in Uganda	4 555	Z.	88.2	121.2	121.0	175.0	210.0	140.2	160.7	144.7
Portfolio investment assets	4 602	..	...	...	...	...	...	...	...	...
Equity securities	4 610	..	...	...	...	...	...	...	...	...
Debt securities	4 619	..	...	...	...	...	...	...	...	...
Portfolio investment liabilities	4 652	Z.	...	...	...	...	...	...	...	...
Equity securities	4 660	..	...	...	...	...	...	...	...	...
Debt securities	4 669	Z.	...	...	...	...	...	...	...	...
Financial derivatives	4 910	..	...	...	...	...	...	...	...	...
Financial derivatives assets	4 900	..	...	...	...	...	...	...	...	...
Financial derivatives liabilities	4 905	..	...	...	...	...	...	...	...	...
Other investment assets	4 703	..	–40.3	–9.9	–37.2	–14.0	5.3	–8.2	–.9	–15.0
Monetary authorities	4 701	..	...	...	...	...	...	...	...	...
General government	4 704	..	...	...	...	...	...	...	...	...
Banks	4 705	..	–53.0	12.7	–10.1	–18.2	–29.4	–9.6	–65.8	17.0
Other sectors	4 728	..	12.7	–22.6	–27.1	4.2	34.7	1.4	64.9	–32.0
Other investment liabilities	4 753	W.	28.9	99.4	56.7	137.9	157.5	121.3	160.7	370.0
Monetary authorities	4 753	WA	.9	1.7	1.1	.2	...	...	...	...
General government	4 753	ZB	50.8	111.7	114.4	158.2	178.2	131.1	154.9	327.5
Banks	4 753	ZC	...	...	...	...	...	...	...	...
Other sectors	4 753	ZD	–22.8	–14.0	–58.8	–20.5	–20.7	–9.8	5.8	42.5
Total, Groups A Through C	4 983	..	*–94.6*	*–79.9*	*–50.4*	*–36.1*	*–80.3*	*–469.8*	*–530.1*	*–309.8*
D. Net Errors and Omissions	4 998	..	**32.5**	**28.8**	**41.3**	**–4.8**	**39.7**	**14.4**	**65.8**	**70.9**
Total, Groups A Through D	4 984	..	*–62.1*	*–51.2*	*–9.1*	*–40.9*	*–40.6*	*–455.4*	*–464.3*	*–238.9*
E. Reserves and Related Items	4 802	A.	**62.1**	**51.2**	**9.1**	**40.9**	**40.6**	**455.4**	**464.3**	**238.9**
Reserve assets	4 802	..	–166.9	–140.7	–68.9	–105.2	–91.7	–37.8	–45.1	–175.4
Use of Fund credit and loans	4 766	..	27.1	27.5	13.3	2.5	–12.2	–16.0	–37.4	–29.6
Exceptional financing	4 920	..	201.9	164.3	64.8	143.6	144.4	509.2	546.8	444.0
Conversion rates: Uganda shillings per U.S. dollar	0 101	..	**979.4**	**968.9**	**1,046.1**	**1,083.0**	**1,240.3**	**1,454.8**	**1,644.5**	**1,755.7**

[1] Excludes components that have been classified in the categories of Group E.

Table 2. STANDARD PRESENTATION, 1994–2001

(Millions of U.S. dollars)

	Code		1994	1995	1996	1997	1998	1999	2000	2001
CURRENT ACCOUNT	4 993	. .	**–174.2**	**–281.5**	**–211.5**	**–315.7**	**–363.7**	**–305.6**	**–384.0**	**–440.2**
A. GOODS	4 100	. .	–251.2	–366.5	–347.6	–449.9	–656.1	–505.6	–499.8	–575.0
Credit	2 100	. .	**463.0**	**560.3**	**639.3**	**592.6**	**510.2**	**483.5**	**449.9**	**451.6**
General merchandise: exports f.o.b.	2 110	. .	458.6	554.9	630.0	583.2	499.0	435.5	384.8	390.2
Goods for processing: exports f.o.b.	2 150	. .	. . .	. . .	. . .	. . .	. . .	. . .	. . .	. . .
Repairs on goods	2 160	. .	. . .	. . .	. . .	. . .	. . .	. . .	. . .	. . .
Goods procured in ports by carriers	2 170	. .	4.4	5.4	9.3	9.4	11.2	9.6	9.4	11.0
Nonmonetary gold	2 180	. .	. . .	. . .	. . .	. . .	. . .	38.4	55.7	50.4
Debit	3 100	. .	**–714.2**	**–926.8**	**–986.9**	**–1,042.6**	**–1,166.3**	**–989.1**	**–949.7**	**–1,026.6**
General merchandise: imports f.o.b.	3 110	. .	–714.2	–926.8	–986.9	–1,042.6	–1,166.3	–989.1	–949.7	–1,026.6
Goods for processing: imports f.o.b.	3 150	. .	. . .	. . .	. . .	. . .	. . .	. . .	. . .	. . .
Repairs on goods	3 160	. .	. . .	. . .	. . .	. . .	. . .	. . .	. . .	. . .
Goods procured in ports by carriers	3 170	. .	. . .	. . .	. . .	. . .	. . .	. . .	. . .	. . .
Nonmonetary gold	3 180	. .	. . .	. . .	. . .	. . .	. . .	. . .	. . .	. . .
B. SERVICES	4 200	. .	–372.2	–458.7	–529.9	–504.3	–551.8	–235.6	–270.8	–309.3
Total credit	2 200	. .	*64.1*	*104.0*	*144.7*	*164.6*	*176.3*	*183.6*	*184.3*	*182.6*
Total debit	3 200	. .	*–436.3*	*–562.7*	*–674.6*	*–668.9*	*–728.1*	*–419.2*	*–455.1*	*–491.9*
Transportation services, credit	2 205	. .	**16.8**	**18.6**	**19.8**	**21.8**	**23.6**	**16.8**	**10.9**	**5.3**
Passenger	2 850	. .	. . .	. . .	. . .	. . .	. . .	. . .	. . .	. . .
Freight	2 851	. .	*16.8*	*18.6*	*19.8*	*21.8*	*23.6*	*16.8*	. . .	. . .
Other	2 852	. .	. . .	. . .	. . .	. . .	. . .	. . .	. . .	. . .
Sea transport, passenger	2 207	. .	. . .	. . .	. . .	. . .	. . .	. . .	. . .	. . .
Sea transport, freight	2 208	. .	. . .	. . .	. . .	. . .	. . .	. . .	. . .	. . .
Sea transport, other	2 209	. .	. . .	. . .	. . .	. . .	. . .	. . .	. . .	. . .
Air transport, passenger	2 211	. .	. . .	. . .	. . .	. . .	. . .	. . .	. . .	. . .
Air transport, freight	2 212	. .	11.2	12.4	13.2	14.5	16.0	16.8	. . .	. . .
Air transport, other	2 213	. .	. . .	. . .	. . .	. . .	. . .	. . .	. . .	. . .
Other transport, passenger	2 215	. .	. . .	. . .	. . .	. . .	. . .	. . .	. . .	. . .
Other transport, freight	2 216	. .	5.6	6.2	6.6	7.2	7.6	. . .	. . .	. . .
Other transport, other	2 217	. .	. . .	. . .	. . .	. . .	. . .	. . .	. . .	. . .
Transportation services, debit	3 205	. .	**–165.8**	**–215.1**	**–239.2**	**–241.9**	**–270.6**	**–128.8**	**–149.2**	**–160.0**
Passenger	3 850	. .	. . .	. . .	. . .	. . .	. . .	. . .	. . .	. . .
Freight	3 851	. .	*–165.8*	*–215.1*	*–239.2*	*–241.9*	*–270.6*	*–128.8*	*–149.2*	*–160.0*
Other	3 852	. .	. . .	. . .	. . .	. . .	. . .	. . .	. . .	. . .
Sea transport, passenger	3 207	. .	. . .	. . .	. . .	. . .	. . .	. . .	. . .	. . .
Sea transport, freight	3 208	. .	. . .	. . .	. . .	. . .	. . .	. . .	. . .	. . .
Sea transport, other	3 209	. .	. . .	. . .	. . .	. . .	. . .	. . .	. . .	. . .
Air transport, passenger	3 211	. .	. . .	. . .	. . .	. . .	. . .	. . .	. . .	. . .
Air transport, freight	3 212	. .	. . .	. . .	. . .	. . .	. . .	. . .	. . .	. . .
Air transport, other	3 213	. .	. . .	. . .	. . .	. . .	. . .	. . .	. . .	. . .
Other transport, passenger	3 215	. .	. . .	. . .	. . .	. . .	. . .	. . .	. . .	. . .
Other transport, freight	3 216	. .	. . .	. . .	. . .	. . .	. . .	–128.8	–149.2	–160.0
Other transport, other	3 217	. .	. . .	. . .	. . .	. . .	. . .	. . .	. . .	. . .
Travel, credit	2 236	. .	**40.2**	**78.1**	**117.4**	**135.0**	**144.4**	**149.5**	**155.3**	**157.6**
Business travel	2 237	. .	. . .	. . .	. . .	. . .	. . .	. . .	. . .	. . .
Personal travel	2 240	. .	. . .	. . .	. . .	. . .	. . .	. . .	. . .	. . .
Travel, debit	3 236	. .	**–77.6**	**–80.2**	**–135.3**	**–112.9**	**–94.5**	**. . .**	**. . .**	**. . .**
Business travel	3 237	. .	. . .	. . .	. . .	. . .	. . .	. . .	. . .	. . .
Personal travel	3 240	. .	. . .	. . .	. . .	. . .	. . .	. . .	. . .	. . .
Other services, credit	2 200	BA	**7.1**	**7.3**	**7.5**	**7.9**	**8.2**	**17.3**	**18.1**	**19.7**
Communications	2 245	. .	. . .	. . .	. . .	. . .	. . .	8.9	9.7	11.3
Construction	2 249	. .	. . .	. . .	. . .	. . .	. . .	. . .	. . .	. . .
Insurance	2 253	. .	. . .	. . .	. . .	. . .	. . .	. . .	. . .	. . .
Financial	2 260	. .	. . .	. . .	. . .	. . .	. . .	. . .	. . .	. . .
Computer and information	2 262	. .	. . .	. . .	. . .	. . .	. . .	. . .	. . .	. . .
Royalties and licence fees	2 266	. .	. . .	. . .	. . .	. . .	. . .	. . .	. . .	. . .
Other business services	2 268	. .	7.1	7.3	7.5	7.9	8.2	. . .	. . .	. . .
Personal, cultural, and recreational	2 287	. .	. . .	. . .	. . .	. . .	. . .	. . .	. . .	. . .
Government, n.i.e.	2 291	. .	. . .	. . .	. . .	. . .	. . .	8.4	8.4	8.4
Other services, debit	3 200	BA	**–192.9**	**–267.4**	**–300.1**	**–314.1**	**–363.0**	**–290.4**	**–305.9**	**–331.9**
Communications	3 245	. .	. . .	. . .	. . .	. . .	. . .	–4.8	–5.5	–5.4
Construction	3 249	. .	. . .	. . .	. . .	. . .	. . .	. . .	. . .	. . .
Insurance	3 253	. .	–18.4	–23.9	–26.6	–26.9	–30.1	–12.9	–14.9	–16.0
Financial	3 260	. .	. . .	. . .	. . .	. . .	. . .	. . .	. . .	. . .
Computer and information	3 262	. .	. . .	. . .	. . .	. . .	. . .	. . .	. . .	. . .
Royalties and licence fees	3 266	. .	. . .	. . .	. . .	. . .	. . .	. . .	. . .	. . .
Other business services	3 268	. .	–174.5	–243.5	–273.5	–287.2	–332.9	–272.7	–285.5	–310.5
Personal, cultural, and recreational	3 287	. .	. . .	. . .	. . .	. . .	. . .	. . .	. . .	. . .
Government, n.i.e.	3 291	. .	. . .	. . .	. . .	. . .	. . .	. . .	. . .	. . .

Table 2 (Continued). STANDARD PRESENTATION, 1994–2001
(Millions of U.S. dollars)

	Code	1994	1995	1996	1997	1998	1999	2000	2001
C. INCOME	4 300 . .	–57.2	–95.6	–49.5	–15.2	–9.2	–127.4	–112.4	–140.3
Total credit	2 300 . .	*13.8*	*17.7*	*29.7*	*40.5*	*50.7*	*35.1*	*53.1*	*37.3*
Total debit	3 300 . .	*–71.0*	*–113.3*	*–79.2*	*–55.7*	*–59.9*	*–162.5*	*–165.5*	*–177.6*
Compensation of employees, credit	2 310 . .	**. . .**	**. . .**	**. . .**	**. . .**	**. . .**	**. . .**	**. . .**	**. . .**
Compensation of employees, debit	3 310 . .	**. . .**	**. . .**	**. . .**	**. . .**	**. . .**	**–45.1**	**–45.4**	**–41.0**
Investment income, credit	2 320 . .	**13.8**	**17.7**	**29.7**	**40.5**	**50.7**	**35.1**	**53.1**	**37.3**
Direct investment income	2 330 . .	. . .	. . .	. . .	. . .	. . .	. . .	. . .	. . .
Dividends and distributed branch profits	2 332 . .	. . .	. . .	. . .	. . .	. . .	. . .	. . .	. . .
Reinvested earnings and undistributed branch profits	2 333 . .	. . .	. . .	. . .	. . .	. . .	. . .	. . .	. . .
Income on debt (interest)	2 334 . .	. . .	. . .	. . .	. . .	. . .	. . .	. . .	. . .
Portfolio investment income	2 339 . .	. . .	. . .	. . .	. . .	. . .	. . .	. . .	. . .
Income on equity	2 340 . .	. . .	. . .	. . .	. . .	. . .	. . .	. . .	. . .
Income on bonds and notes	2 350 . .	. . .	. . .	. . .	. . .	. . .	. . .	. . .	. . .
Income on money market instruments	2 360 . .	. . .	. . .	. . .	. . .	. . .	. . .	. . .	. . .
Other investment income	2 370 . .	13.8	17.7	29.7	40.5	50.7	35.1	53.1	37.3
Investment income, debit	3 320 . .	**–71.0**	**–113.3**	**–79.2**	**–55.7**	**–59.9**	**–117.4**	**–120.1**	**–136.6**
Direct investment income	3 330 . .	–20.5	–59.6	–26.2	–10.2	–16.4	–16.7	–19.1	–17.2
Dividends and distributed branch profits	3 332 . .	–10.5	–24.6	–14.7	–7.2	–13.4	. . .	. . .	. . .
Reinvested earnings and undistributed branch profits	3 333 . .	–10.0	–35.0	–11.5	–3.0	–3.0	–16.7	–19.1	–17.2
Income on debt (interest)	3 334 . .	. . .	. . .	. . .	. . .	. . .	. . .	. . .	. . .
Portfolio investment income	3 339 . .	. . .	. . .	. . .	. . .	. . .	. . .	. . .	. . .
Income on equity	3 340 . .	. . .	. . .	. . .	. . .	. . .	. . .	. . .	. . .
Income on bonds and notes	3 350 . .	. . .	. . .	. . .	. . .	. . .	. . .	. . .	. . .
Income on money market instruments	3 360 . .	. . .	. . .	. . .	. . .	. . .	. . .	. . .	. . .
Other investment income	3 370 . .	–50.5	–53.7	–53.0	–45.5	–43.5	–100.7	–101.0	–119.4
D. CURRENT TRANSFERS	4 379 . .	506.4	639.3	715.5	653.7	853.5	563.0	499.0	584.4
Credit	2 379 . .	**506.4**	**639.3**	**715.5**	**653.7**	**853.5**	**747.2**	**806.6**	**952.3**
General government	2 380 . .	251.7	299.8	286.6	277.4	349.3	417.5	466.6	369.3
Other sectors	2 390 . .	254.7	339.5	428.9	376.3	504.1	329.7	340.0	583.0
Workers' remittances	2 391 . .	. . .	. . .	. . .	. . .	. . .	232.6	238.1	482.8
Other current transfers	2 392 . .	254.7	339.5	428.9	376.3	504.1	97.1	101.9	100.2
Debit	3 379 . .	**. . .**	**. . .**	**. . .**	**. . .**	**. . .**	**–184.2**	**–307.6**	**–367.9**
General government	3 380 . .	. . .	. . .	. . .	. . .	. . .	. . .	. . .	. . .
Other sectors	3 390 . .	. . .	. . .	. . .	. . .	. . .	–184.2	–307.6	–367.9
Workers' remittances	3 391 . .	. . .	. . .	. . .	. . .	. . .	–184.2	–307.6	–367.9
Other current transfers	3 392 . .	. . .	. . .	. . .	. . .	. . .	. . .	. . .	. . .
CAPITAL AND FINANCIAL ACCOUNT	4 996 . .	**141.7**	**252.7**	**170.2**	**320.6**	**324.0**	**291.2**	**318.2**	**369.3**
CAPITAL ACCOUNT	4 994 . .	**40.0**	**48.3**	**61.4**	**31.9**	**49.5**	**45.5**	**69.7**	**71.4**
Total credit	2 994 . .	*40.0*	*48.3*	*61.4*	*31.9*	*49.5*	*45.5*	*69.7*	*71.4*
Total debit	3 994 . .	. . .	. . .	. . .	. . .	. . .	. . .	. . .	. . .
Capital transfers, credit	2 400 . .	**40.0**	**48.3**	**61.4**	**31.9**	**49.5**	**45.5**	**69.7**	**71.4**
General government	2 401 . .	34.0	48.3	61.4	31.9	49.5	45.5	69.7	71.4
Debt forgiveness	2 402 . .	3.9	. . .	. . .	. . .	. . .	45.5	69.7	71.4
Other capital transfers	2 410 . .	30.1	48.3	61.4	31.9	49.5	. . .	. . .	. . .
Other sectors	2 430 . .	6.0	. . .	. . .	. . .	. . .	. . .	. . .	. . .
Migrants' transfers	2 431 . .	. . .	. . .	. . .	. . .	. . .	. . .	. . .	. . .
Debt forgiveness	2 432 . .	. . .	. . .	. . .	. . .	. . .	. . .	. . .	. . .
Other capital transfers	2 440 . .	. . .	. . .	. . .	. . .	. . .	. . .	. . .	. . .
Capital transfers, debit	3 400 . .	**. . .**	**. . .**	**. . .**	**. . .**	**. . .**	**. . .**	**. . .**	**. . .**
General government	3 401 . .	. . .	. . .	. . .	. . .	. . .	. . .	. . .	. . .
Debt forgiveness	3 402 . .	. . .	. . .	. . .	. . .	. . .	. . .	. . .	. . .
Other capital transfers	3 410 . .	. . .	. . .	. . .	. . .	. . .	. . .	. . .	. . .
Other sectors	3 430 . .	. . .	. . .	. . .	. . .	. . .	. . .	. . .	. . .
Migrants' transfers	3 431 . .	. . .	. . .	. . .	. . .	. . .	. . .	. . .	. . .
Debt forgiveness	3 432 . .	. . .	. . .	. . .	. . .	. . .	. . .	. . .	. . .
Other capital transfers	3 440 . .	. . .	. . .	. . .	. . .	. . .	. . .	. . .	. . .
Nonproduced nonfinancial assets, credit	2 480 . .	**. . .**	**. . .**	**. . .**	**. . .**	**. . .**	**. . .**	**. . .**	**. . .**
Nonproduced nonfinancial assets, debit	3 480 . .	**. . .**	**. . .**	**. . .**	**. . .**	**. . .**	**. . .**	**. . .**	**. . .**

Table 2 (Continued). STANDARD PRESENTATION, 1994–2001
(Millions of U.S. dollars)

	Code	1994	1995	1996	1997	1998	1999	2000	2001
FINANCIAL ACCOUNT	4 995 . .	**101.7**	**204.4**	**108.8**	**288.6**	**274.5**	**245.7**	**248.5**	**297.9**
A. DIRECT INVESTMENT	4 500 . .	88.2	121.2	121.0	175.0	210.0	140.2	160.7	144.7
Direct investment abroad	4 505 . .	**. . .**	**. . .**	**. . .**	**. . .**	**. . .**	**. . .**	**. . .**	**. . .**
Equity capital	4 510 . .	. . .	. . .	. . .	. . .	. . .	. . .	. . .	. . .
Claims on affiliated enterprises	4 515 . .	. . .	. . .	. . .	. . .	. . .	. . .	. . .	. . .
Liabilities to affiliated enterprises	4 520 . .	. . .	. . .	. . .	. . .	. . .	. . .	. . .	. . .
Reinvested earnings	4 525 . .	. . .	. . .	. . .	. . .	. . .	. . .	. . .	. . .
Other capital	4 530 . .	. . .	. . .	. . .	. . .	. . .	. . .	. . .	. . .
Claims on affiliated enterprises	4 535 . .	. . .	. . .	. . .	. . .	. . .	. . .	. . .	. . .
Liabilities to affiliated enterprises	4 540 . .	. . .	. . .	. . .	. . .	. . .	. . .	. . .	. . .
Direct investment in Uganda	4 555 . .	**88.2**	**121.2**	**121.0**	**175.0**	**210.0**	**140.2**	**160.7**	**144.7**
Equity capital	4 560 . .	78.2	86.2	109.5	172.0	207.0	71.9	82.4	74.2
Claims on direct investors	4 565 . .	. . .	. . .	. . .	. . .	. . .	. . .	. . .	. . .
Liabilities to direct investors	4 570 . .	. . .	. . .	. . .	. . .	. . .	71.9	82.4	74.2
Reinvested earnings	4 575 . .	10.0	35.0	11.5	3.0	3.0	16.7	19.1	17.2
Other capital	4 580 . .	. . .	. . .	. . .	. . .	. . .	51.6	59.2	53.3
Claims on direct investors	4 585 . .	. . .	. . .	. . .	. . .	. . .	. . .	. . .	. . .
Liabilities to direct investors	4 590 . .	. . .	. . .	. . .	. . .	. . .	51.6	59.2	53.3
B. PORTFOLIO INVESTMENT	4 600 . .	. . .	. . .	. . .	. . .	. . .	. . .	. . .	. . .
Assets	4 602 . .	**. . .**	**. . .**	**. . .**	**. . .**	**. . .**	**. . .**	**. . .**	**. . .**
Equity securities	4 610 . .	. . .	. . .	. . .	. . .	. . .	. . .	. . .	. . .
Monetary authorities	4 611 . .	. . .	. . .	. . .	. . .	. . .	. . .	. . .	. . .
General government	4 612 . .	. . .	. . .	. . .	. . .	. . .	. . .	. . .	. . .
Banks	4 613 . .	. . .	. . .	. . .	. . .	. . .	. . .	. . .	. . .
Other sectors	4 614 . .	. . .	. . .	. . .	. . .	. . .	. . .	. . .	. . .
Debt securities	4 619 . .	. . .	. . .	. . .	. . .	. . .	. . .	. . .	. . .
Bonds and notes	4 620 . .	. . .	. . .	. . .	. . .	. . .	. . .	. . .	. . .
Monetary authorities	4 621 . .	. . .	. . .	. . .	. . .	. . .	. . .	. . .	. . .
General government	4 622 . .	. . .	. . .	. . .	. . .	. . .	. . .	. . .	. . .
Banks	4 623 . .	. . .	. . .	. . .	. . .	. . .	. . .	. . .	. . .
Other sectors	4 624 . .	. . .	. . .	. . .	. . .	. . .	. . .	. . .	. . .
Money market instruments	4 630 . .	. . .	. . .	. . .	. . .	. . .	. . .	. . .	. . .
Monetary authorities	4 631 . .	. . .	. . .	. . .	. . .	. . .	. . .	. . .	. . .
General government	4 632 . .	. . .	. . .	. . .	. . .	. . .	. . .	. . .	. . .
Banks	4 633 . .	. . .	. . .	. . .	. . .	. . .	. . .	. . .	. . .
Other sectors	4 634 . .	. . .	. . .	. . .	. . .	. . .	. . .	. . .	. . .
Liabilities	4 652 . .	**. . .**	**. . .**	**. . .**	**. . .**	**. . .**	**. . .**	**. . .**	**. . .**
Equity securities	4 660 . .	. . .	. . .	. . .	. . .	. . .	. . .	. . .	. . .
Banks	4 663 . .	. . .	. . .	. . .	. . .	. . .	. . .	. . .	. . .
Other sectors	4 664 . .	. . .	. . .	. . .	. . .	. . .	. . .	. . .	. . .
Debt securities	4 669 . .	. . .	. . .	. . .	. . .	. . .	. . .	. . .	. . .
Bonds and notes	4 670 . .	. . .	. . .	. . .	. . .	. . .	. . .	. . .	. . .
Monetary authorities	4 671 . .	. . .	. . .	. . .	. . .	. . .	. . .	. . .	. . .
General government	4 672 . .	. . .	. . .	. . .	. . .	. . .	. . .	. . .	. . .
Banks	4 673 . .	. . .	. . .	. . .	. . .	. . .	. . .	. . .	. . .
Other sectors	4 674 . .	. . .	. . .	. . .	. . .	. . .	. . .	. . .	. . .
Money market instruments	4 680 . .	. . .	. . .	. . .	. . .	. . .	. . .	. . .	. . .
Monetary authorities	4 681 . .	. . .	. . .	. . .	. . .	. . .	. . .	. . .	. . .
General government	4 682 . .	. . .	. . .	. . .	. . .	. . .	. . .	. . .	. . .
Banks	4 683 . .	. . .	. . .	. . .	. . .	. . .	. . .	. . .	. . .
Other sectors	4 684 . .	. . .	. . .	. . .	. . .	. . .	. . .	. . .	. . .
C. FINANCIAL DERIVATIVES	4 910 . .	. . .	. . .	. . .	. . .	. . .	. . .	. . .	. . .
Monetary authorities	4 911 . .	. . .	. . .	. . .	. . .	. . .	. . .	. . .	. . .
General government	4 912 . .	. . .	. . .	. . .	. . .	. . .	. . .	. . .	. . .
Banks	4 913 . .	. . .	. . .	. . .	. . .	. . .	. . .	. . .	. . .
Other sectors	4 914 . .	. . .	. . .	. . .	. . .	. . .	. . .	. . .	. . .
Assets	4 900 . .	**. . .**	**. . .**	**. . .**	**. . .**	**. . .**	**. . .**	**. . .**	**. . .**
Monetary authorities	4 901 . .	. . .	. . .	. . .	. . .	. . .	. . .	. . .	. . .
General government	4 902 . .	. . .	. . .	. . .	. . .	. . .	. . .	. . .	. . .
Banks	4 903 . .	. . .	. . .	. . .	. . .	. . .	. . .	. . .	. . .
Other sectors	4 904 . .	. . .	. . .	. . .	. . .	. . .	. . .	. . .	. . .
Liabilities	4 905 . .	**. . .**	**. . .**	**. . .**	**. . .**	**. . .**	**. . .**	**. . .**	**. . .**
Monetary authorities	4 906 . .	. . .	. . .	. . .	. . .	. . .	. . .	. . .	. . .
General government	4 907 . .	. . .	. . .	. . .	. . .	. . .	. . .	. . .	. . .
Banks	4 908 . .	. . .	. . .	. . .	. . .	. . .	. . .	. . .	. . .
Other sectors	4 909 . .	. . .	. . .	. . .	. . .	. . .	. . .	. . .	. . .

Table 2 (Concluded). STANDARD PRESENTATION, 1994–2001
(Millions of U.S. dollars)

	Code	1994	1995	1996	1997	1998	1999	2000	2001
D. OTHER INVESTMENT	4 700 . .	180.4	223.9	56.7	218.8	156.2	143.3	132.9	328.7
Assets	4 703 . .	**–40.3**	**–9.9**	**–37.2**	**–14.0**	**5.3**	**–8.2**	**–.9**	**–15.0**
Trade credits	4 706 . .	4.5	...	...	...	...	...	...	...
General government	4 707 . .	...	...	...	...	...	...	...	...
of which: Short-term	4 709 . .	...	...	...	...	...	...	...	...
Other sectors	4 710 . .	4.5	...	...	...	...	...	...	...
of which: Short-term	4 712 . .	*4.5*	...	...	...	...	...	...	...
Loans	4 714 . .	...	...	...	...	...	...	...	...
Monetary authorities	4 715 . .	...	...	...	...	...	...	...	...
of which: Short-term	4 718 . .	...	...	...	...	...	...	...	...
General government	4 719 . .	...	...	...	...	...	...	...	...
of which: Short-term	4 721 . .	...	...	...	...	...	...	...	...
Banks	4 722 . .	...	...	...	...	...	...	...	...
of which: Short-term	4 724 . .	...	...	...	...	...	...	...	...
Other sectors	4 725 . .	...	...	...	...	...	...	...	...
of which: Short-term	4 727 . .	...	...	...	...	...	...	...	...
Currency and deposits	4 730 . .	–44.8	–9.9	–37.2	–14.0	5.3	–8.2	–.9	–15.0
Monetary authorities	4 731 . .	...	...	...	...	...	...	...	...
General government	4 732 . .	...	...	...	...	...	...	...	...
Banks	4 733 . .	–53.0	12.7	–10.1	–18.2	–29.4	–9.6	–65.8	17.0
Other sectors	4 734 . .	8.2	–22.6	–27.1	4.2	34.7	1.4	64.9	–32.0
Other assets	4 736 . .	...	...	...	...	...	...	...	...
Monetary authorities	4 737 . .	...	...	...	...	...	...	...	...
of which: Short-term	4 739 . .	...	...	...	...	...	...	...	...
General government	4 740 . .	...	...	...	...	...	...	...	...
of which: Short-term	4 742 . .	...	...	...	...	...	...	...	...
Banks	4 743 . .	...	...	...	...	...	...	...	...
of which: Short-term	4 745 . .	...	...	...	...	...	...	...	...
Other sectors	4 746 . .	...	...	...	...	...	...	...	...
of which: Short-term	4 748 . .	...	...	...	...	...	...	...	...
Liabilities	4 753 . .	**220.7**	**233.8**	**93.9**	**232.9**	**150.9**	**151.5**	**133.8**	**343.7**
Trade credits	4 756 . .	–.1	–11.5	–21.8	–.5	–1.7	...	...	...
General government	4 757 . .	...	...	...	...	...	...	...	...
of which: Short-term	4 759 . .	...	...	...	...	...	...	...	...
Other sectors	4 760 . .	–.1	–11.5	–21.8	–.5	–1.7	...	...	...
of which: Short-term	4 762 . .	*–.1*	*–11.5*	*–21.8*	*–.5*	...	...	...	...
Loans	4 764 . .	219.7	221.3	104.9	231.2	166.1	105.3	123.3	340.4
Monetary authorities	4 765 . .	26.6	27.5	13.3	2.5	–12.2	–16.0	–37.4	–29.6
of which: Use of Fund credit and loans from the Fund	4 766 . .	*27.1*	*27.5*	*13.3*	*2.5*	*–12.2*	*–16.0*	*–37.4*	*–29.6*
of which: Short-term	4 768 . .	*–.5*	...	...	...	...	...	...	...
General government	4 769 . .	215.8	196.3	128.7	248.8	197.3	131.1	154.9	327.5
of which: Short-term	4 771 . .	*–1.7*	...	...	...	...	...	...	...
Banks	4 772 . .	...	...	...	...	...	...	...	...
of which: Short-term	4 774 . .	...	...	...	...	...	...	...	...
Other sectors	4 775 . .	–22.7	–2.5	–37.0	–20.1	–19.0	–9.8	5.8	42.5
of which: Short-term	4 777 . .	...	...	...	...	...	...	...	...
Currency and deposits	4 780 . .	...	...	...	...	...	...	...	...
Monetary authorities	4 781 . .	...	...	...	...	...	...	...	...
General government	4 782 . .	...	...	...	...	...	...	...	...
Banks	4 783 . .	...	...	...	...	...	...	...	...
Other sectors	4 784 . .	...	...	...	...	...	...	...	...
Other liabilities	4 786 . .	1.1	24.0	10.8	2.1	–13.5	46.2	10.5	3.3
Monetary authorities	4 787 . .	1.4	1.7	1.1	.2	...	...	...	...
of which: Short-term	4 789 . .	*1.4*	*1.7*	*1.1*	*.2*	...	...	...	...
General government	4 790 . .	–.3	22.3	9.7	1.9	–13.5	46.2	10.5	3.3
of which: Short-term	4 792 . .	*–.3*	*22.3*	*9.7*	*1.9*	*–13.5*	*46.2*	*10.5*	*3.3*
Banks	4 793 . .	...	...	...	...	...	...	...	...
of which: Short-term	4 795 . .	...	...	...	...	...	...	...	...
Other sectors	4 796 . .	...	...	...	...	...	...	...	...
of which: Short-term	4 798 . .	...	...	...	...	...	...	...	...
E. RESERVE ASSETS	4 802 . .	–166.9	–140.7	–68.9	–105.2	–91.7	–37.8	–45.1	–175.4
Monetary gold	4 812 . .	...	...	...	...	...	...	...	...
Special drawing rights	4 811 . .	–3.0	2.7	–.6	–4.4	.6	2.6	–1.4	1.6
Reserve position in the Fund	4 810 . .	...	...	...	...	...	...	...	...
Foreign exchange	4 803 . .	–163.9	–143.4	–68.3	–100.8	–92.3	–40.4	–43.7	–177.0
Other claims	4 813 . .	...	...	...	...	...	...	...	...
NET ERRORS AND OMISSIONS	4 998 . .	**32.5**	**28.8**	**41.3**	**–4.8**	**39.7**	**14.4**	**65.8**	**70.9**

Part 3 of the *Yearbook* contains descriptions of the methodologies, compilation practices, and sources used to compile these data.

Table 3. INTERNATIONAL INVESTMENT POSITION (End–period stocks), 1994–2001

(Millions of U.S. dollars)

	Code	1994	1995	1996	1997	1998	1999	2000	2001
ASSETS	8 995 C.	...	...	...	...	...	...	...	...
Direct investment abroad	8 505 . .	...	...	...	...	...	...	...	...
Equity capital and reinvested earnings	8 506 . .	...	...	...	...	...	...	...	...
Claims on affiliated enterprises	8 507 . .	...	...	...	...	...	...	...	...
Liabilities to affiliated enterprises	8 508 . .	...	...	...	...	...	...	...	...
Other capital	8 530 . .	...	...	...	...	...	...	...	...
Claims on affiliated enterprises	8 535 . .	...	...	...	...	...	...	...	...
Liabilities to affiliated enterprises	8 540 . .	...	...	...	...	...	...	...	...
Portfolio investment	8 602 . .	...	...	...	...	...	**199.8**	**265.6**	**248.6**
Equity securities	8 610 . .	...	...	...	...	...	...	...	...
Monetary authorities	8 611 . .	...	...	...	...	...	...	...	...
General government	8 612 . .	...	...	...	...	...	...	...	...
Banks	8 613 . .	...	...	...	...	...	...	...	...
Other sectors	8 614 . .	...	...	...	...	...	...	...	...
Debt securities	8 619 . .	...	...	...	...	...	199.8	265.6	248.6
Bonds and notes	8 620 . .	...	...	...	...	...	199.8	265.6	248.6
Monetary authorities	8 621 . .	...	...	...	...	...	...	...	...
General government	8 622 . .	...	...	...	...	...	...	...	...
Banks	8 623 . .	...	...	...	...	...	199.8	265.6	248.6
Other sectors	8 624 . .	...	...	...	...	...	...	...	...
Money market instruments	8 630 . .	...	...	...	...	...	...	...	...
Monetary authorities	8 631 . .	...	...	...	...	...	...	...	...
General government	8 632 . .	...	...	...	...	...	...	...	...
Banks	8 633 . .	...	...	...	...	...	...	...	...
Other sectors	8 634 . .	...	...	...	...	...	...	...	...
Financial derivatives	8 900 . .	...	...	...	...	...	...	...	...
Monetary authorities	8 901 . .	...	...	...	...	...	...	...	...
General government	8 902 . .	...	...	...	...	...	...	...	...
Banks	8 903 . .	...	...	...	...	...	...	...	...
Other sectors	8 904 . .	...	...	...	...	...	...	...	...
Other investment	8 703 . .	...	...	...	...	...	...	...	...
Trade credits	8 706 . .	...	...	...	...	...	...	...	...
General government	8 707 . .	...	...	...	...	...	...	...	...
of which: Short-term	8 709 . .	...	...	...	...	...	...	...	...
Other sectors	8 710 . .	...	...	...	...	...	...	...	...
of which: Short-term	8 712 . .	...	...	...	...	...	...	...	...
Loans	8 714 . .	...	...	...	...	...	...	...	...
Monetary authorities	8 715 . .	...	...	...	...	...	...	...	...
of which: Short-term	8 718 . .	...	...	...	...	...	...	...	...
General government	8 719 . .	...	...	...	...	...	...	...	...
of which: Short-term	8 721 . .	...	...	...	...	...	...	...	...
Banks	8 722 . .	...	...	...	...	...	...	...	...
of which: Short-term	8 724 . .	...	...	...	...	...	...	...	...
Other sectors	8 725 . .	...	...	...	...	...	...	...	...
of which: Short-term	8 727 . .	...	...	...	...	...	...	...	...
Currency and deposits	8 730 . .	...	...	...	...	...	...	...	...
Monetary authorities	8 731 . .	...	...	...	...	...	...	...	...
General government	8 732 . .	...	...	...	...	...	...	...	...
Banks	8 733 . .	...	...	...	...	...	...	...	...
Other sectors	8 734 . .	...	...	...	...	...	...	...	...
Other assets	8 736 . .	...	...	...	...	...	...	...	...
Monetary authorities	8 737 . .	...	...	...	...	...	...	...	...
of which: Short-term	8 739 . .	...	...	...	...	...	...	...	...
General government	8 740 . .	...	...	...	...	...	...	...	...
of which: Short-term	8 742 . .	...	...	...	...	...	...	...	...
Banks	8 743 . .	...	...	...	...	...	...	...	...
of which: Short-term	8 745 . .	...	...	...	...	...	...	...	...
Other sectors	8 746 . .	...	...	...	...	...	...	...	...
of which: Short-term	8 748 . .	...	...	...	...	...	...	...	...
Reserve assets	8 802 . .	...	...	...	...	...	**773.2**	**820.5**	**989.1**
Monetary gold	8 812 . .	...	...	...	...	...	...	...	...
Special drawing rights	8 811 . .	3.1	.5	1.1	5.4	5.0	2.3	3.5	1.9
Reserve position in the Fund	8 810 . .	...	...	...	...	...	...	...	...
Foreign exchange	8 803 . .	...	...	...	...	...	770.9	817.0	987.2
Other claims	8 813 . .	...	...	...	...	...	...	...	...

Table 3 (Concluded). INTERNATIONAL INVESTMENT POSITION (End–period stocks), 1994–2001
(Millions of U.S. dollars)

	Code	1994	1995	1996	1997	1998	1999	2000	2001
LIABILITIES	8 995 D.	...	...	...	...	...	...	...	...
Direct investment in Uganda	8 555 ..	...	...	...	...	...	...	...	...
Equity capital and reinvested earnings	8 556 ..	...	...	...	...	...	...	...	...
Claims on direct investors	8 557 ..	...	...	...	...	...	...	...	...
Liabilities to direct investors	8 558 ..	...	...	...	...	...	...	...	...
Other capital	8 580 ..	...	...	...	...	...	...	...	...
Claims on direct investors	8 585 ..	...	...	...	...	...	...	...	...
Liabilities to direct investors	8 590 ..	...	...	...	...	...	...	...	...
Portfolio investment	8 652 ..	...	...	...	...	...	...	...	...
Equity securities	8 660 ..	...	...	...	...	...	...	...	...
Banks	8 663 ..	...	...	...	...	...	...	...	...
Other sectors	8 664 ..	...	...	...	...	...	...	...	...
Debt securities	8 669 ..	...	...	...	...	...	...	...	...
Bonds and notes	8 670 ..	...	...	...	...	...	...	...	...
Monetary authorities	8 671 ..	...	...	...	...	...	...	...	...
General government	8 672 ..	...	...	...	...	...	...	...	...
Banks	8 673 ..	...	...	...	...	...	...	...	...
Other sectors	8 674 ..	...	...	...	...	...	...	...	...
Money market instruments	8 680 ..	...	...	...	...	...	...	...	...
Monetary authorities	8 681 ..	...	...	...	...	...	...	...	...
General government	8 682 ..	...	...	...	...	...	...	...	...
Banks	8 683 ..	...	...	...	...	...	...	...	...
Other sectors	8 684 ..	...	...	...	...	...	...	...	...
Financial derivatives	8 905 ..	...	...	...	...	...	...	...	...
Monetary authorities	8 906 ..	...	...	...	...	...	...	...	...
General government	8 907 ..	...	...	...	...	...	...	...	...
Banks	8 908 ..	...	...	...	...	...	...	...	...
Other sectors	8 909 ..	...	...	...	...	...	...	...	...
Other investment	8 753 ..	...	...	...	...	...	**3,951.7**	**3,720.9**	**3,929.4**
Trade credits	8 756 ..	...	...	...	...	...	...	...	...
General government	8 757 ..	...	...	...	...	...	...	...	...
of which: Short-term	8 759 ..	...	...	...	...	...	...	...	...
Other sectors	8 760 ..	...	...	...	...	...	...	...	...
of which: Short-term	8 762 ..	...	...	...	...	...	...	...	...
Loans	8 764 ..	...	...	...	...	...	3,951.7	3,720.9	3,929.4
Monetary authorities	8 765 ..	...	...	...	...	...	371.7	316.1	275.4
of which: Use of Fund credit and loans from the Fund	8 766 ..	*383.3*	*417.2*	*417.1*	*393.6*	*398.1*	*371.7*	*316.1*	*275.4*
of which: Short-term	8 768 ..	...	...	...	...	...	...	...	...
General government	8 769 ..	...	...	...	...	...	3,580.0	3,404.8	3,654.0
of which: Short-term	8 771 ..	...	...	...	...	...	...	...	...
Banks	8 772 ..	...	...	...	...	...	...	...	...
of which: Short-term	8 774 ..	...	...	...	...	...	...	...	...
Other sectors	8 775 ..	...	...	...	...	...	...	...	...
of which: Short-term	8 777 ..	...	...	...	...	...	...	...	...
Currency and deposits	8 780 ..	...	...	...	...	...	...	...	...
Monetary authorities	8 781 ..	...	...	...	...	...	...	...	...
General government	8 782 ..	...	...	...	...	...	...	...	...
Banks	8 783 ..	...	...	...	...	...	...	...	...
Other sectors	8 784 ..	...	...	...	...	...	...	...	...
Other liabilities	8 786 ..	...	...	...	...	...	...	...	...
Monetary authorities	8 787 ..	...	...	...	...	...	...	...	...
of which: Short-term	8 789 ..	...	...	...	...	...	...	...	...
General government	8 790 ..	...	...	...	...	...	...	...	...
of which: Short-term	8 792 ..	...	...	...	...	...	...	...	...
Banks	8 793 ..	...	...	...	...	...	...	...	...
of which: Short-term	8 795 ..	...	...	...	...	...	...	...	...
Other sectors	8 796 ..	...	...	...	...	...	...	...	...
of which: Short-term	8 798 ..	...	...	...	...	...	...	...	...
NET INTERNATIONAL INVESTMENT POSITION	8 995 ..	...	...	...	...	...	...	...	...
Conversion rates: Uganda shillings per U.S. dollar (end of period)	0 102 ..	**926.8**	**1,009.5**	**1,029.6**	**1,140.1**	**1,362.7**	**1,506.0**	**1,766.7**	**1,727.4**

Table 1. ANALYTIC PRESENTATION, 1994–2001
(Millions of U.S. dollars)

	Code	1994	1995	1996	1997	1998	1999	2000	2001
A. Current Account[1]	4 993 Z.	**–1,163**	**–1,152**	**–1,184**	**–1,335**	**–1,296**	**1,658**	**1,481**	**1,402**
Goods: exports f.o.b	2 100 . .	13,894	14,244	15,547	15,418	13,699	13,189	15,722	17,091
Goods: imports f.o.b	3 100 . .	–16,469	–16,946	–19,843	–19,623	–16,283	–12,945	–14,943	–16,893
Balance on Goods	4 100 . .	*–2,575*	*–2,702*	*–4,296*	*–4,205*	*–2,584*	*244*	*779*	*198*
Services: credit	2 200 . .	2,747	2,846	4,799	4,937	3,922	3,869	3,800	3,995
Services: debit	3 200 . .	–1,538	–1,334	–1,625	–2,268	–2,545	–2,292	–3,004	–3,580
Balance on Goods and Services	4 991 . .	*–1,366*	*–1,190*	*–1,122*	*–1,536*	*–1,207*	*1,821*	*1,575*	*613*
Income: credit	2 300 . .	56	247	102	158	122	98	143	167
Income: debit	3 300 . .	–400	–681	–673	–802	–993	–967	–1,085	–834
Balance on Goods, Services, and Income	4 992 . .	*–1,710*	*–1,624*	*–1,693*	*–2,180*	*–2,078*	*952*	*633*	*–54*
Current transfers: credit	2 379 Z.	583	557	619	942	868	754	967	1,516
Current transfers: debit	3 379 . .	–36	–85	–110	–97	–86	–48	–119	–60
B. Capital Account[1]	4 994 Z.	**97**	**6**	**5**	**. . .**	**–3**	**–10**	**–8**	**3**
Capital account: credit	2 994 Z.	106	6	5	. . .	. . .	. . .	. . .	8
Capital account: debit	3 994 . .	–9	. . .	. . .	. . .	–3	–10	–8	–5
Total, Groups A Plus B	4 981 . .	*–1,066*	*–1,146*	*–1,179*	*–1,335*	*–1,299*	*1,648*	*1,473*	*1,405*
C. Financial Account[1]	4 995 W.	**–557**	**–726**	**317**	**1,413**	**–1,340**	**–879**	**–752**	**–191**
Direct investment abroad	4 505 . .	–8	–10	5	–42	4	–7	–1	–23
Direct investment in Ukraine	4 555 Z.	159	267	521	623	743	496	595	792
Portfolio investment assets	4 602 . .	. . .	–12	–1	–2	–2	–11	–4	1
Equity securities	4 610 . .	. . .	. . .	–11	–14	–3	–5	–2	–1
Debt securities	4 619 . .	. . .	–12	10	12	1	–6	–2	2
Portfolio investment liabilities	4 652 Z.	. . .	16	199	1,605	–1,379	–75	–197	–867
Equity securities	4 660 . .	. . .	. . .	46	248	227	129	–193	–734
Debt securities	4 669 Z.	. . .	16	153	1,357	–1,606	–204	–4	–133
Financial derivatives	4 910 . .	. . .	. . .	. . .	. . .	. . .	. . .	. . .	. . .
Financial derivatives assets	4 900 . .	. . .	. . .	. . .	. . .	. . .	. . .	. . .	. . .
Financial derivatives liabilities	4 905 . .	. . .	. . .	. . .	. . .	. . .	. . .	. . .	. . .
Other investment assets	4 703 . .	–3,026	–1,574	–821	–1,583	–1,321	–2,264	–449	–1,015
Monetary authorities	4 701 . .	. . .	. . .	. . .	. . .	. . .	. . .	–15	1
General government	4 704 . .	. . .	. . .	. . .	. . .	. . .	. . .	1,002	. . .
Banks	4 705 . .	–779	–328	83	–536	–46	51	–64	137
Other sectors	4 728 . .	–2,247	–1,246	–904	–1,047	–1,275	–2,315	–1,372	–1,153
Other investment liabilities	4 753 W.	2,318	587	414	812	615	982	–696	921
Monetary authorities	4 753 WA	. . .	. . .	. . .	. . .	. . .	. . .	. . .	. . .
General government	4 753 ZB	–1,097	–783	–477	–267	–857	–231	–1,457	537
Banks	4 753 ZC	577	724	565	–51	–264	–16	113	139
Other sectors	4 753 ZD	2,838	646	326	1,130	1,736	1,229	648	1,319
Total, Groups A Through C	4 983 . .	*–1,623*	*–1,872*	*–862*	*78*	*–2,639*	*769*	*721*	*1,214*
D. Net Errors and Omissions	4 998 . .	**423**	**248**	**259**	**–781**	**–818**	**–953**	**–148**	**–221**
Total, Groups A Through D	4 984 . .	*–1,200*	*–1,624*	*–603*	*–703*	*–3,457*	*–184*	*573*	*993*
E. Reserves and Related Items	4 802 A.	**1,200**	**1,624**	**603**	**703**	**3,457**	**184**	**–573**	**–993**
Reserve assets	4 802 . .	–549	–469	–894	–385	1,328	–281	–401	–1,609
Use of Fund credit and loans	4 766 . .	368	1,221	776	283	279	75	–603	–86
Exceptional financing	4 920 . .	1,380	871	721	805	1,850	390	431	702
Conversion rates: hryvnias per U.S. dollar	0 101 . .	**.3275**	**1.4731**	**1.8295**	**1.8617**	**2.4495**	**4.1304**	**5.4402**	**5.3722**

[1] Excludes components that have been classified in the categories of Group E.

Table 2. STANDARD PRESENTATION, 1994–2001
(Millions of U.S. dollars)

	Code			1994	1995	1996	1997	1998	1999	2000	2001
CURRENT ACCOUNT	4	993	. .	**–1,163**	**–1,152**	**–1,184**	**–1,335**	**–1,296**	**1,658**	**1,481**	**1,402**
A. GOODS	4	100	. .	–2,575	–2,702	–4,296	–4,205	–2,584	244	779	198
Credit	2	100	. .	**13,894**	**14,244**	**15,547**	**15,418**	**13,699**	**13,189**	**15,722**	**17,091**
General merchandise: exports f.o.b.	2	110	. .	13,221	13,149	13,882	15,381	12,094	11,617	13,775	15,116
Goods for processing: exports f.o.b.	2	150	. .	598	1,046	1,618	. . .	1,478	1,443	1,806	1,823
Repairs on goods	2	160	. .	75	49	47	32	121	122	135	146
Goods procured in ports by carriers	2	170	. .	. . .	. . .	. . .	5	6	7	6	6
Nonmonetary gold	2	180	. .	. . .	. . .	. . .	. . .	. . .	. . .	. . .	. . .
Debit	3	100	. .	**–16,469**	**–16,946**	**–19,843**	**–19,623**	**–16,283**	**–12,945**	**–14,943**	**–16,893**
General merchandise: imports f.o.b.	3	110	. .	–15,705	–15,480	–17,956	–19,413	–15,104	–11,849	–13,788	–15,697
Goods for processing: imports f.o.b.	3	150	. .	–756	–1,376	–1,801	. . .	–1,030	–990	–1,025	–1,091
Repairs on goods	3	160	. .	–8	–61	–38	–34	–16	–10	–11	–13
Goods procured in ports by carriers	3	170	. .	. . .	–29	–48	–176	–133	–96	–119	–92
Nonmonetary gold	3	180	. .	. . .	. . .	. . .	. . .	. . .	. . .	. . .	. . .
B. SERVICES	4	200	. .	1,209	1,512	3,174	2,669	1,377	1,577	796	415
Total credit	2	200	. .	*2,747*	*2,846*	*4,799*	*4,937*	*3,922*	*3,869*	*3,800*	*3,995*
Total debit	3	200	. .	*–1,538*	*–1,334*	*–1,625*	*–2,268*	*–2,545*	*–2,292*	*–3,004*	*–3,580*
Transportation services, credit	2	205	. .	**1,894**	**2,152**	**4,033**	**4,029**	**3,222**	**3,073**	**2,920**	**2,961**
Passenger	2	850	. .	. . .	. . .	*218*	*207*	*224*	*176*	*169*	*186*
Freight	2	851	. .	. . .	. . .	*3,339*	*3,138*	*2,405*	*2,302*	*2,179*	*2,117*
Other	2	852	. .	. . .	. . .	*476*	*684*	*593*	*595*	*572*	*658*
Sea transport, passenger	2	207	. .	. . .	. . .	32	3	5	3	3	. . .
Sea transport, freight	2	208	. .	. . .	. . .	263	127	102	85	80	43
Sea transport, other	2	209	. .	. . .	. . .	336	380	344	373	352	380
Air transport, passenger	2	211	. .	. . .	. . .	70	85	97	92	91	102
Air transport, freight	2	212	. .	. . .	. . .	13	13	43	48	46	47
Air transport, other	2	213	. .	. . .	. . .	57	84	78	79	82	99
Other transport, passenger	2	215	. .	. . .	. . .	116	119	122	81	75	84
Other transport, freight	2	216	. .	. . .	. . .	3,063	2,998	2,260	2,169	2,053	2,027
Other transport, other	2	217	. .	. . .	. . .	83	220	171	143	138	179
Transportation services, debit	3	205	. .	**–244**	**–454**	**–424**	**–476**	**–487**	**–358**	**–390**	**–409**
Passenger	3	850	. .	. . .	. . .	*–97*	*–157*	*–147*	*–96*	*–91*	*–110*
Freight	3	851	. .	. . .	. . .	*–102*	*–81*	*–99*	*–64*	*–91*	*–88*
Other	3	852	. .	. . .	. . .	*–225*	*–238*	*–241*	*–198*	*–208*	*–211*
Sea transport, passenger	3	207	. .	. . .	. . .	–1	. . .	–1	–1	. . .	. . .
Sea transport, freight	3	208	. .	. . .	. . .	–55	–21	–16	–14	–36	–35
Sea transport, other	3	209	. .	. . .	. . .	–81	–70	–77	–55	–75	–94
Air transport, passenger	3	211	. .	. . .	. . .	–20	–58	–50	–42	–46	–53
Air transport, freight	3	212	. .	. . .	. . .	–20	–20	–28	–18	–5	–5
Air transport, other	3	213	. .	. . .	. . .	–78	–58	–48	–48	–51	–52
Other transport, passenger	3	215	. .	. . .	. . .	–76	–99	–96	–53	–45	–57
Other transport, freight	3	216	. .	. . .	. . .	–27	–40	–55	–32	–50	–48
Other transport, other	3	217	. .	. . .	. . .	–66	–110	–116	–95	–82	–65
Travel, credit	2	236	. .	**175**	**191**	**230**	**270**	**315**	**327**	**394**	**573**
Business travel	2	237	. .	. . .	. . .	. . .	. . .	. . .	. . .	. . .	. . .
Personal travel	2	240	. .	. . .	. . .	. . .	. . .	. . .	. . .	. . .	. . .
Travel, debit	3	236	. .	**–141**	**–210**	**–308**	**–305**	**–340**	**–364**	**–470**	**–566**
Business travel	3	237	. .	. . .	. . .	. . .	. . .	. . .	. . .	. . .	. . .
Personal travel	3	240	. .	. . .	. . .	. . .	. . .	. . .	. . .	. . .	. . .
Other services, credit	2	200	BA	**678**	**503**	**536**	**638**	**385**	**469**	**486**	**461**
Communications	2	245	. .	74	176	125	114	102	99	89	93
Construction	2	249	. .	26	31	42	50	41	34	38	27
Insurance	2	253	. .	. . .	. . .	. . .	. . .	. . .	. . .	4	6
Financial	2	260	. .	186	76	26	33	23	19	22	18
Computer and information	2	262	. .	. . .	. . .	. . .	. . .	. . .	. . .	6	7
Royalties and licence fees	2	266	. .	. . .	. . .	. . .	. . .	. . .	. . .	1	5
Other business services	2	268	. .	392	220	343	441	219	317	323	190
Personal, cultural, and recreational	2	287	. .	. . .	. . .	. . .	. . .	. . .	. . .	3	17
Government, n.i.e.	2	291	. .	. . .	. . .	. . .	. . .	. . .	. . .	. . .	98
Other services, debit	3	200	BA	**–1,153**	**–670**	**–893**	**–1,487**	**–1,718**	**–1,570**	**–2,144**	**–2,605**
Communications	3	245	. .	–76	–212	–119	–115	–131	–117	–99	–101
Construction	3	249	. .	–163	–36	–109	–192	–196	–243	–171	–463
Insurance	3	253	. .	. . .	. . .	. . .	. . .	. . .	. . .	–85	–116
Financial	3	260	. .	–215	–98	–42	–80	–90	–83	–74	–35
Computer and information	3	262	. .	. . .	. . .	. . .	. . .	. . .	. . .	–51	–96
Royalties and licence fees	3	266	. .	. . .	. . .	. . .	. . .	. . .	. . .	–663	–183
Other business services	3	268	. .	–699	–324	–623	–1,100	–1,301	–1,127	–576	–1,168
Personal, cultural, and recreational	3	287	. .	. . .	. . .	. . .	. . .	. . .	. . .	–11	–30
Government, n.i.e.	3	291	. .	. . .	. . .	. . .	. . .	. . .	. . .	–414	–413

Table 2 (Continued). STANDARD PRESENTATION, 1994–2001

(Millions of U.S. dollars)

	Code	1994	1995	1996	1997	1998	1999	2000	2001
C. INCOME	4 300 . .	–344	–434	–571	–644	–871	–869	–942	–667
Total credit	2 300 . .	*56*	*247*	*102*	*158*	*122*	*98*	*143*	*167*
Total debit	3 300 . .	*–400*	*–681*	*–673*	*–802*	*–993*	*–967*	*–1,085*	*–834*
Compensation of employees, credit	2 310 . .	**. . .**	**. . .**	**6**	**12**	**12**	**18**	**33**	**56**
Compensation of employees, debit	3 310 . .	**. . .**	**. . .**	**–1**	**–4**	**–3**	**–3**	**–2**	**. . .**
Investment income, credit	2 320 . .	**. . .**	**. . .**	**96**	**146**	**110**	**80**	**110**	**111**
Direct investment income	2 330 . .	. . .	. . .	. . .	1	. . .	3	. . .	. . .
Dividends and distributed branch profits	2 332 . .	. . .	. . .	. . .	. . .	. . .	. . .	. . .	. . .
Reinvested earnings and undistributed branch profits	2 333 . .	. . .	. . .	. . .	. . .	. . .	. . .	. . .	. . .
Income on debt (interest)	2 334 . .	. . .	. . .	. . .	. . .	. . .	. . .	. . .	. . .
Portfolio investment income	2 339 . .	. . .	. . .	3	18	1	. . .	3	2
Income on equity	2 340 . .	. . .	. . .	. . .	. . .	. . .	. . .	. . .	2
Income on bonds and notes	2 350 . .	. . .	. . .	. . .	. . .	1	. . .	3	. . .
Income on money market instruments	2 360 . .	. . .	. . .	. . .	. . .	. . .	. . .	. . .	. . .
Other investment income	2 370 . .	. . .	. . .	93	127	109	77	107	109
Investment income, debit	3 320 . .	**. . .**	**. . .**	**–672**	**–798**	**–990**	**–964**	**–1,083**	**–834**
Direct investment income	3 330 . .	. . .	. . .	–31	–45	–65	–69	–43	–79
Dividends and distributed branch profits	3 332 . .	. . .	. . .	–31	. . .	. . .	. . .	. . .	–79
Reinvested earnings and undistributed branch profits	3 333 . .	. . .	. . .	. . .	. . .	. . .	. . .	. . .	. . .
Income on debt (interest)	3 334 . .	. . .	. . .	. . .	. . .	. . .	. . .	. . .	. . .
Portfolio investment income	3 339 . .	. . .	. . .	–34	–142	–332	–280	–461	–256
Income on equity	3 340 . .	. . .	. . .	. . .	. . .	. . .	. . .	. . .	–14
Income on bonds and notes	3 350 . .	. . .	. . .	. . .	. . .	–332	–280	–461	–242
Income on money market instruments	3 360 . .	. . .	. . .	. . .	. . .	. . .	. . .	. . .	. . .
Other investment income	3 370 . .	. . .	. . .	–607	–611	–593	–615	–579	–499
D. CURRENT TRANSFERS	4 379 . .	547	472	509	845	782	706	848	1,456
Credit	2 379 . .	**583**	**557**	**619**	**942**	**868**	**754**	**967**	**1,516**
General government	2 380 . .	. . .	. . .	. . .	. . .	. . .	. . .	414	413
Other sectors	2 390 . .	. . .	. . .	. . .	. . .	. . .	. . .	553	1,103
Workers' remittances	2 391 . .	. . .	. . .	. . .	. . .	. . .	. . .	. . .	. . .
Other current transfers	2 392 . .	. . .	. . .	. . .	. . .	. . .	. . .	553	1,103
Debit	3 379 . .	**–36**	**–85**	**–110**	**–97**	**–86**	**–48**	**–119**	**–60**
General government	3 380 . .	. . .	. . .	. . .	. . .	. . .	. . .	. . .	. . .
Other sectors	3 390 . .	. . .	. . .	. . .	. . .	. . .	. . .	. . .	. . .
Workers' remittances	3 391 . .	. . .	. . .	. . .	. . .	. . .	. . .	. . .	. . .
Other current transfers	3 392 . .	. . .	. . .	. . .	. . .	. . .	. . .	. . .	. . .
CAPITAL AND FINANCIAL ACCOUNT	4 996 . .	**740**	**904**	**925**	**2,116**	**2,114**	**–705**	**–1,333**	**–1,181**
CAPITAL ACCOUNT	4 994 . .	**97**	**6**	**5**	. . .	**–3**	**–10**	**–8**	**3**
Total credit	2 994 . .	*106*	*6*	*5*	. . .	. . .	. . .	. . .	*8*
Total debit	3 994 . .	*–9*	. . .	. . .	. . .	*–3*	*–10*	*–8*	*–5*
Capital transfers, credit	2 400 . .	**106**	**6**	**5**	**. . .**	**. . .**	**. . .**	**. . .**	**8**
General government	2 401 . .	. . .	6	5	. . .	. . .	. . .	. . .	. . .
Debt forgiveness	2 402 . .	. . .	6	. . .	. . .	. . .	. . .	. . .	. . .
Other capital transfers	2 410 . .	. . .	. . .	5	. . .	. . .	. . .	. . .	. . .
Other sectors	2 430 . .	. . .	. . .	. . .	. . .	. . .	. . .	. . .	8
Migrants' transfers	2 431 . .	. . .	. . .	. . .	. . .	. . .	. . .	. . .	1
Debt forgiveness	2 432 . .	. . .	. . .	. . .	. . .	. . .	. . .	. . .	. . .
Other capital transfers	2 440 . .	. . .	. . .	. . .	. . .	. . .	. . .	. . .	7
Capital transfers, debit	3 400 . .	**–9**	**. . .**	**. . .**	**. . .**	**–3**	**–10**	**–8**	**–5**
General government	3 401 . .	. . .	. . .	. . .	. . .	–3	–10	. . .	. . .
Debt forgiveness	3 402 . .	. . .	. . .	. . .	. . .	. . .	. . .	. . .	. . .
Other capital transfers	3 410 . .	. . .	. . .	. . .	. . .	–3	–10	. . .	. . .
Other sectors	3 430 . .	. . .	. . .	. . .	. . .	. . .	. . .	–8	–5
Migrants' transfers	3 431 . .	. . .	. . .	. . .	. . .	. . .	. . .	–8	–5
Debt forgiveness	3 432 . .	. . .	. . .	. . .	. . .	. . .	. . .	. . .	. . .
Other capital transfers	3 440 . .	. . .	. . .	. . .	. . .	. . .	. . .	. . .	. . .
Nonproduced nonfinancial assets, credit	2 480 . .	**. . .**	**. . .**	**. . .**	**. . .**	**. . .**	**. . .**	**. . .**	**. . .**
Nonproduced nonfinancial assets, debit	3 480 . .	**. . .**	**. . .**	**. . .**	**. . .**	**. . .**	**. . .**	**. . .**	**. . .**

Table 2 (Continued). STANDARD PRESENTATION, 1994–2001
(Millions of U.S. dollars)

	Code	1994	1995	1996	1997	1998	1999	2000	2001
FINANCIAL ACCOUNT	4 995	**643**	**898**	**920**	**2,116**	**2,117**	**–695**	**–1,325**	**–1,184**
A. DIRECT INVESTMENT	4 500	151	257	526	581	747	489	594	769
Direct investment abroad	4 505	**–8**	**–10**	**5**	**–42**	**4**	**–7**	**–1**	**–23**
Equity capital	4 510	...	...	...	...	...	...	...	–23
Claims on affiliated enterprises	4 515	...	...	...	...	...	...	...	...
Liabilities to affiliated enterprises	4 520	...	...	...	...	...	...	...	...
Reinvested earnings	4 525	...	...	...	...	...	...	...	...
Other capital	4 530	...	...	...	...	...	...	...	...
Claims on affiliated enterprises	4 535	...	...	...	...	...	...	...	...
Liabilities to affiliated enterprises	4 540	...	...	...	...	...	...	...	...
Direct investment in Ukraine	4 555	**159**	**267**	**521**	**623**	**743**	**496**	**595**	**792**
Equity capital	4 560	...	...	...	...	...	...	...	...
Claims on direct investors	4 565	...	...	...	...	...	...	...	...
Liabilities to direct investors	4 570	...	...	...	...	...	...	...	...
Reinvested earnings	4 575	...	...	...	...	...	...	...	...
Other capital	4 580	...	...	...	...	...	...	...	...
Claims on direct investors	4 585	...	...	...	...	...	...	...	...
Liabilities to direct investors	4 590	...	...	...	...	...	...	...	...
B. PORTFOLIO INVESTMENT	4 600	...	4	198	1,603	47	–86	–201	–866
Assets	4 602	**...**	**–12**	**–1**	**–2**	**–2**	**–11**	**–4**	**1**
Equity securities	4 610	...	...	–11	–14	–3	–5	–2	–1
Monetary authorities	4 611	...	...	...	...	...	...	...	...
General government	4 612	...	...	...	...	...	...	...	...
Banks	4 613	...	...	...	...	...	...	–2	–1
Other sectors	4 614	...	...	–11	–14	–3	–5	...	...
Debt securities	4 619	...	–12	10	12	1	–6	–2	2
Bonds and notes	4 620	...	–12	10	12	1	–6	–2	2
Monetary authorities	4 621	...	...	...	...	...	...	...	...
General government	4 622	...	...	...	...	...	...	...	...
Banks	4 623	...	–12	10	12	1	–6	–2	3
Other sectors	4 624	...	...	...	...	...	...	...	–1
Money market instruments	4 630	...	...	...	...	...	...	...	...
Monetary authorities	4 631	...	...	...	...	...	...	...	...
General government	4 632	...	...	...	...	...	...	...	...
Banks	4 633	...	...	...	...	...	...	...	...
Other sectors	4 634	...	...	...	...	...	...	...	...
Liabilities	4 652	**...**	**16**	**199**	**1,605**	**49**	**–75**	**–197**	**–867**
Equity securities	4 660	...	...	46	248	227	129	–193	–734
Banks	4 663	...	...	...	...	...	...	...	...
Other sectors	4 664	...	...	46	248	227	129	–193	–734
Debt securities	4 669	...	16	153	1,357	–178	–204	–4	–133
Bonds and notes	4 670	...	16	153	1,357	–178	–204	–4	–133
Monetary authorities	4 671	...	...	...	...	...	...	...	...
General government	4 672	...	16	145	1,357	–178	–204	–4	–133
Banks	4 673	...	...	...	...	...	...	...	...
Other sectors	4 674	...	...	8	...	...	...	...	...
Money market instruments	4 680	...	...	...	...	...	...	...	...
Monetary authorities	4 681	...	...	...	...	...	...	...	...
General government	4 682	...	...	...	...	...	...	...	...
Banks	4 683	...	...	...	...	...	...	...	...
Other sectors	4 684	...	...	...	...	...	...	...	...
C. FINANCIAL DERIVATIVES	4 910	...	...	...	...	...	...	...	...
Monetary authorities	4 911	...	...	...	...	...	...	...	...
General government	4 912	...	...	...	...	...	...	...	...
Banks	4 913	...	...	...	...	...	...	...	...
Other sectors	4 914	...	...	...	...	...	...	...	...
Assets	4 900	**...**	**...**	**...**	**...**	**...**	**...**	**...**	**...**
Monetary authorities	4 901	...	...	...	...	...	...	...	...
General government	4 902	...	...	...	...	...	...	...	...
Banks	4 903	...	...	...	...	...	...	...	...
Other sectors	4 904	...	...	...	...	...	...	...	...
Liabilities	4 905	**...**	**...**	**...**	**...**	**...**	**...**	**...**	**...**
Monetary authorities	4 906	...	...	...	...	...	...	...	...
General government	4 907	...	...	...	...	...	...	...	...
Banks	4 908	...	...	...	...	...	...	...	...
Other sectors	4 909	...	...	...	...	...	...	...	...

Table 2 (Concluded). STANDARD PRESENTATION, 1994–2001
(Millions of U.S. dollars)

	Code	1994	1995	1996	1997	1998	1999	2000	2001
D. OTHER INVESTMENT	4 700 . .	1,040	1,105	1,090	317	–5	–817	–1,317	522
Assets	4 703 . .	**–3,026**	**–1,574**	**–821**	**–1,583**	**–1,321**	**–2,264**	**–449**	**–1,015**
Trade credits	4 706 . .	. . .	. . .	. . .	. . .	. . .	. . .	. . .	. . .
General government	4 707 . .	. . .	. . .	. . .	. . .	. . .	. . .	. . .	. . .
of which: Short-term	4 709 . .	. . .	. . .	. . .	. . .	. . .	. . .	. . .	. . .
Other sectors	4 710 . .	. . .	. . .	. . .	. . .	. . .	. . .	. . .	. . .
of which: Short-term	4 712 . .	. . .	. . .	. . .	. . .	. . .	. . .	. . .	. . .
Loans	4 714 . .	. . .	12	–159	–319	–12	158	12	–4
Monetary authorities	4 715 . .	. . .	. . .	. . .	. . .	. . .	. . .	. . .	. . .
of which: Short-term	4 718 . .	. . .	. . .	. . .	. . .	. . .	. . .	. . .	. . .
General government	4 719 . .	. . .	. . .	. . .	. . .	. . .	. . .	. . .	. . .
of which: Short-term	4 721 . .	. . .	. . .	. . .	. . .	. . .	. . .	. . .	. . .
Banks	4 722 . .	. . .	12	–159	–319	–12	158	12	–4
of which: Short-term	4 724 . .	. . .	*12*	*–159*	*–319*	*–12*	*24*	*9*	*–11*
Other sectors	4 725 . .	. . .	. . .	. . .	. . .	. . .	. . .	. . .	. . .
of which: Short-term	4 727 . .	. . .	. . .	. . .	. . .	. . .	. . .	. . .	. . .
Currency and deposits	4 730 . .	–779	–340	251	–708	–34	–112	–95	143
Monetary authorities	4 731 . .	. . .	. . .	. . .	. . .	. . .	. . .	–15	1
General government	4 732 . .	. . .	. . .	. . .	. . .	. . .	. . .	. . .	. . .
Banks	4 733 . .	–779	–340	242	–217	–34	–107	–76	141
Other sectors	4 734 . .	. . .	. . .	9	–491	. . .	–5	–4	1
Other assets	4 736 . .	–2,247	–1,246	–913	–556	–1,275	–2,310	–366	–1,154
Monetary authorities	4 737 . .	. . .	. . .	. . .	. . .	. . .	. . .	. . .	. . .
of which: Short-term	4 739 . .	. . .	. . .	. . .	. . .	. . .	. . .	. . .	. . .
General government	4 740 . .	. . .	. . .	. . .	. . .	. . .	. . .	1,002	. . .
of which: Short-term	4 742 . .	. . .	. . .	. . .	. . .	. . .	. . .	*1,002*	. . .
Banks	4 743 . .	. . .	. . .	. . .	. . .	. . .	. . .	. . .	. . .
of which: Short-term	4 745 . .	. . .	. . .	. . .	. . .	. . .	. . .	. . .	. . .
Other sectors	4 746 . .	–2,247	–1,246	–913	–556	–1,275	–2,310	–1,368	–1,154
of which: Short-term	4 748 . .	*–2,247*	*–1,246*	*–913*	*–556*	*–1,275*	*–2,310*	*–1,368*	*–1,154*
Liabilities	4 753 . .	**4,066**	**2,679**	**1,911**	**1,900**	**1,316**	**1,447**	**–868**	**1,537**
Trade credits	4 756 . .	. . .	. . .	. . .	. . .	. . .	. . .	. . .	. . .
General government	4 757 . .	. . .	. . .	. . .	. . .	. . .	. . .	. . .	. . .
of which: Short-term	4 759 . .	. . .	. . .	. . .	. . .	. . .	. . .	. . .	. . .
Other sectors	4 760 . .	. . .	. . .	. . .	. . .	. . .	. . .	. . .	. . .
of which: Short-term	4 762 . .	. . .	. . .	. . .	. . .	. . .	. . .	. . .	. . .
Loans	4 764 . .	28	3,732	1,333	983	–39	72	–1,672	392
Monetary authorities	4 765 . .	368	1,221	776	283	279	75	–603	–86
of which: Use of Fund credit and loans from the Fund	4 766 . .	*368*	*1,221*	*776*	*283*	*279*	*75*	*–603*	*–86*
of which: Short-term	4 768 . .	. . .	. . .	. . .	. . .	. . .	. . .	. . .	. . .
General government	4 769 . .	–374	2,259	261	481	–338	118	–1,356	16
of which: Short-term	4 771 . .	. . .	. . .	. . .	. . .	. . .	. . .	. . .	. . .
Banks	4 772 . .	. . .	220	193	–40	–173	–11	18	148
of which: Short-term	4 774 . .	. . .	*220*	*193*	*–40*	*–173*	*–11*	*18*	*148*
Other sectors	4 775 . .	34	32	103	259	193	–110	269	314
of which: Short-term	4 777 . .	. . .	. . .	. . .	. . .	. . .	*81*	*–1*	*82*
Currency and deposits	4 780 . .	577	504	372	–11	–91	–5	95	32
Monetary authorities	4 781 . .	. . .	. . .	. . .	. . .	. . .	. . .	. . .	. . .
General government	4 782 . .	. . .	. . .	. . .	. . .	. . .	. . .	. . .	. . .
Banks	4 783 . .	577	504	372	–11	–91	–5	95	–9
Other sectors	4 784 . .	. . .	. . .	. . .	. . .	. . .	. . .	. . .	41
Other liabilities	4 786 . .	3,461	–1,557	206	928	1,446	1,380	709	1,113
Monetary authorities	4 787 . .	. . .	. . .	. . .	. . .	. . .	. . .	. . .	. . .
of which: Short-term	4 789 . .	. . .	. . .	. . .	. . .	. . .	. . .	. . .	. . .
General government	4 790 . .	658	–2,169	–17	57	–97	41	330	149
of which: Short-term	4 792 . .	*658*	*–2,169*	*–17*	*57*	*–97*	*41*	*330*	*149*
Banks	4 793 . .	. . .	. . .	. . .	. . .	. . .	. . .	. . .	. . .
of which: Short-term	4 795 . .	. . .	. . .	. . .	. . .	. . .	. . .	. . .	. . .
Other sectors	4 796 . .	2,803	612	223	871	1,543	1,339	379	964
of which: Short-term	4 798 . .	*2,803*	*612*	*223*	*871*	*1,543*	*1,339*	*379*	*964*
E. RESERVE ASSETS	4 802 . .	–549	–469	–894	–385	1,328	–281	–401	–1,609
Monetary gold	4 812 . .	–7	. . .	–183	18	4	–15	–87	–5
Special drawing rights	4 811 . .	–183	36	73	–7	–104	114	–187	–12
Reserve position in the Fund	4 810 . .	. . .	. . .	. . .	. . .	. . .	. . .	. . .	. . .
Foreign exchange	4 803 . .	–359	–505	–784	–396	1,428	–380	–127	–1,592
Other claims	4 813 . .	. . .	. . .	. . .	. . .	. . .	. . .	. . .	. . .
NET ERRORS AND OMISSIONS	4 998 . .	**423**	**248**	**259**	**–781**	**–818**	**–953**	**–148**	**–221**

Part 3 of the *Yearbook* contains descriptions of the methodologies, compilation practices, and sources used to compile these data.

Table 3. INTERNATIONAL INVESTMENT POSITION (End–period stocks), 1994–2001
(Millions of U.S. dollars)

	Code	1994	1995	1996	1997	1998	1999	2000	2001
ASSETS	8 995 C.	...	...	...	...	...	...	...	6,223
Direct investment abroad	8 505 . .	...	...	...	...	...	...	...	**158**
Equity capital and reinvested earnings	8 506 . .	...	...	...	...	...	...	...	158
Claims on affiliated enterprises	8 507 . .	...	...	...	...	...	...	...	...
Liabilities to affiliated enterprises	8 508 . .	...	...	...	...	...	...	...	...
Other capital	8 530 . .	...	...	...	...	...	...	...	...
Claims on affiliated enterprises	8 535 . .	...	...	...	...	...	...	...	...
Liabilities to affiliated enterprises	8 540 . .	...	...	...	...	...	...	...	...
Portfolio investment	8 602 . .	...	...	...	...	...	...	...	**31**
Equity securities	8 610 . .	...	...	...	...	...	...	...	21
Monetary authorities	8 611 . .	...	...	...	...	...	...	...	...
General government	8 612 . .	...	...	...	...	...	...	...	...
Banks	8 613 . .	...	...	...	...	...	...	...	2
Other sectors	8 614 . .	...	...	...	...	...	...	...	19
Debt securities	8 619 . .	...	...	...	...	...	...	...	10
Bonds and notes	8 620 . .	...	...	...	...	...	...	...	10
Monetary authorities	8 621 . .	...	...	...	...	...	...	...	...
General government	8 622 . .	...	...	...	...	...	...	...	...
Banks	8 623 . .	...	...	...	...	...	...	...	7
Other sectors	8 624 . .	...	...	...	...	...	...	...	3
Money market instruments	8 630 . .	...	...	...	...	...	...	...	...
Monetary authorities	8 631 . .	...	...	...	...	...	...	...	...
General government	8 632 . .	...	...	...	...	...	...	...	...
Banks	8 633 . .	...	...	...	...	...	...	...	...
Other sectors	8 634 . .	...	...	...	...	...	...	...	...
Financial derivatives	8 900 . .	...	...	...	...	...	...	...	...
Monetary authorities	8 901 . .	...	...	...	...	...	...	...	...
General government	8 902 . .	...	...	...	...	...	...	...	...
Banks	8 903 . .	...	...	...	...	...	...	...	...
Other sectors	8 904 . .	...	...	...	...	...	...	...	...
Other investment	8 703 . .	...	...	...	...	...	...	...	**2,945**
Trade credits	8 706 . .	...	...	...	...	...	...	...	...
General government	8 707 . .	...	...	...	...	...	...	...	...
of which: Short-term	8 709 . .	...	...	...	...	...	...	...	...
Other sectors	8 710 . .	...	...	...	...	...	...	...	...
of which: Short-term	8 712 . .	...	...	...	...	...	...	...	...
Loans	8 714 . .	...	...	...	...	...	...	...	33
Monetary authorities	8 715 . .	...	...	...	...	...	...	...	...
of which: Short-term	8 718 . .	...	...	...	...	...	...	...	...
General government	8 719 . .	...	...	...	...	...	...	...	...
of which: Short-term	8 721 . .	...	...	...	...	...	...	...	...
Banks	8 722 . .	...	...	...	...	...	...	...	33
of which: Short-term	8 724 . .	...	...	...	...	...	...	...	*18*
Other sectors	8 725 . .	...	...	...	...	...	...	...	...
of which: Short-term	8 727 . .	...	...	...	...	...	...	...	...
Currency and deposits	8 730 . .	...	...	...	...	...	...	...	871
Monetary authorities	8 731 . .	...	...	...	...	...	...	...	157
General government	8 732 . .	...	...	...	...	...	...	...	...
Banks	8 733 . .	...	...	...	...	...	...	...	698
Other sectors	8 734 . .	...	...	...	...	...	...	...	16
Other assets	8 736 . .	...	...	...	...	...	...	...	2,041
Monetary authorities	8 737 . .	...	...	...	...	...	...	...	...
of which: Short-term	8 739 . .	...	...	...	...	...	...	...	...
General government	8 740 . .	...	...	...	...	...	...	...	...
of which: Short-term	8 742 . .	...	...	...	...	...	...	...	...
Banks	8 743 . .	...	...	...	...	...	...	...	...
of which: Short-term	8 745 . .	...	...	...	...	...	...	...	...
Other sectors	8 746 . .	...	...	...	...	...	...	...	2,041
of which: Short-term	8 748 . .	...	...	...	...	...	...	...	*2,041*
Reserve assets	8 802 . .	...	...	...	...	...	...	...	**3,089**
Monetary gold	8 812 . .	...	...	...	...	...	...	...	134
Special drawing rights	8 811 . .	181	144	67	71	182	66	249	251
Reserve position in the Fund	8 810 . .	...	...	...	...	...	...	...	...
Foreign exchange	8 803 . .	...	...	...	...	...	...	...	2,704
Other claims	8 813 . .	...	...	...	...	...	...	...	...

Table 3 (Concluded). INTERNATIONAL INVESTMENT POSITION (End–period stocks), 1994–2001
(Millions of U.S. dollars)

	Code	1994	1995	1996	1997	1998	1999	2000	2001
LIABILITIES	8 995 D.	...	...	...	...	...	...	...	25,853
Direct investment in Ukraine	8 555 . .	...	...	...	...	...	...	...	**4,662**
Equity capital and reinvested earnings	8 556 . .	...	...	...	...	...	...	...	4,662
Claims on direct investors	8 557 . .	...	...	...	...	...	...	...	...
Liabilities to direct investors	8 558 . .	...	...	...	...	...	...	...	...
Other capital	8 580 . .	...	...	...	...	...	...	...	...
Claims on direct investors	8 585 . .	...	...	...	...	...	...	...	...
Liabilities to direct investors	8 590 . .	...	...	...	...	...	...	...	...
Portfolio investment	8 652 . .	...	...	...	...	...	...	...	**2,959**
Equity securities	8 660 . .	...	...	...	...	...	...	...	763
Banks	8 663 . .	...	...	...	...	...	...	...	...
Other sectors	8 664 . .	...	...	...	...	...	...	...	763
Debt securities	8 669 . .	...	...	...	...	...	...	...	2,196
Bonds and notes	8 670 . .	...	...	...	...	...	...	...	2,196
Monetary authorities	8 671 . .	...	...	...	...	...	...	...	...
General government	8 672 . .	...	...	...	...	...	...	...	2,196
Banks	8 673 . .	...	...	...	...	...	...	...	...
Other sectors	8 674 . .	...	...	...	...	...	...	...	...
Money market instruments	8 680 . .	...	...	...	...	...	...	...	...
Monetary authorities	8 681 . .	...	...	...	...	...	...	...	...
General government	8 682 . .	...	...	...	...	...	...	...	...
Banks	8 683 . .	...	...	...	...	...	...	...	...
Other sectors	8 684 . .	...	...	...	...	...	...	...	...
Financial derivatives	8 905 . .	...	...	...	...	...	...	...	...
Monetary authorities	8 906 . .	...	...	...	...	...	...	...	...
General government	8 907 . .	...	...	...	...	...	...	...	...
Banks	8 908 . .	...	...	...	...	...	...	...	...
Other sectors	8 909 . .	...	...	...	...	...	...	...	...
Other investment	8 753 . .	...	...	...	...	...	...	...	**18,232**
Trade credits	8 756 . .	...	...	...	...	...	...	...	...
General government	8 757 . .	...	...	...	...	...	...	...	...
of which: Short-term	8 759 . .	...	...	...	...	...	...	...	...
Other sectors	8 760 . .	...	...	...	...	...	...	...	...
of which: Short-term	8 762 . .	...	...	...	...	...	...	...	...
Loans	8 764 . .	...	...	...	...	...	...	...	9,414
Monetary authorities	8 765 . .	...	...	...	...	...	...	...	1,911
of which: Use of Fund credit and loans from the Fund	8 766 . .	*364*	*1,542*	*2,262*	*2,402*	*2,795*	*2,806*	*2,073*	*1,911*
of which: Short-term	8 768 . .	...	...	...	...	...	...	...	...
General government	8 769 . .	...	...	...	...	...	...	...	5,460
of which: Short-term	8 771 . .	...	...	...	...	...	...	...	...
Banks	8 772 . .	...	...	...	...	...	...	...	275
of which: Short-term	8 774 . .	...	...	...	...	...	...	...	*275*
Other sectors	8 775 . .	...	...	...	...	...	...	...	1,768
of which: Short-term	8 777 . .	...	...	...	...	...	...	...	*151*
Currency and deposits	8 780 . .	...	...	...	...	...	...	...	264
Monetary authorities	8 781 . .	...	...	...	...	...	...	...	...
General government	8 782 . .	...	...	...	...	...	...	...	...
Banks	8 783 . .	...	...	...	...	...	...	...	156
Other sectors	8 784 . .	...	...	...	...	...	...	...	108
Other liabilities	8 786 . .	...	...	...	...	...	...	...	8,554
Monetary authorities	8 787 . .	...	...	...	...	...	...	...	...
of which: Short-term	8 789 . .	...	...	...	...	...	...	...	...
General government	8 790 . .	...	...	...	...	...	...	...	626
of which: Short-term	8 792 . .	...	...	...	...	...	...	...	*66*
Banks	8 793 . .	...	...	...	...	...	...	...	...
of which: Short-term	8 795 . .	...	...	...	...	...	...	...	...
Other sectors	8 796 . .	...	...	...	...	...	...	...	7,928
of which: Short-term	8 798 . .	...	...	...	...	...	...	...	*7,652*
NET INTERNATIONAL INVESTMENT POSITION	8 995 . .	...	...	...	...	...	...	...	**–19,630**
Conversion rates: hryvnias per U.S. dollar (end of period)	0 102 . .	**1.0420**	**1.7940**	**1.8890**	**1.8990**	**3.4270**	**5.2163**	**5.4345**	**5.2985**

Table 1. ANALYTIC PRESENTATION, 1994–2001

(Billions of U.S. dollars)

	Code	1994	1995	1996	1997	1998	1999	2000	2001
A. Current Account [1]	4 993 Z.	**-10.23**	**-14.29**	**-13.44**	**-2.85**	**-7.96**	**-31.94**	**-28.82**	**-29.37**
Goods: exports f.o.b	2 100 ..	207.19	242.32	261.25	281.54	271.72	268.88	284.38	275.95
Goods: imports f.o.b	3 100 ..	-224.14	-261.32	-282.48	-301.74	-307.85	-313.18	-330.27	-324.20
Balance on Goods	4 100 ..	*-16.95*	*-19.01*	*-21.23*	*-20.20*	*-36.13*	*-44.29*	*-45.89*	*-48.25*
Services: credit	2 200 ..	69.54	78.78	87.34	97.72	107.23	113.94	116.81	110.55
Services: debit	3 200 ..	-59.77	-65.41	-72.28	-77.20	-86.26	-94.84	-98.71	-94.60
Balance on Goods and Services	4 991 ..	*-7.18*	*-5.64*	*-6.17*	*.32*	*-15.15*	*-25.19*	*-27.80*	*-32.29*
Income: credit	2 300 ..	113.97	138.87	144.49	157.74	171.92	163.10	204.36	201.40
Income: debit	3 300 ..	-108.86	-135.59	-142.72	-151.40	-151.09	-159.04	-190.25	-188.18
Balance on Goods, Services, and Income	4 992 ..	*-2.08*	*-2.35*	*-4.39*	*6.66*	*5.68*	*-21.13*	*-13.68*	*-19.07*
Current transfers: credit	2 379 Z.	17.71	19.70	29.46	21.44	20.59	22.70	18.66	23.30
Current transfers: debit	3 379 ..	-25.86	-31.64	-38.51	-30.95	-34.23	-33.51	-33.80	-33.60
B. Capital Account [1]	4 994 Z.	**.05**	**.84**	**1.14**	**1.32**	**.79**	**1.52**	**2.76**	**2.15**
Capital account: credit	2 994 Z.	1.93	1.84	2.18	2.77	2.44	2.91	4.36	4.06
Capital account: debit	3 994 ..	-1.88	-.99	-1.04	-1.45	-1.65	-1.38	-1.60	-1.91
Total, Groups A Plus B	4 981 ..	*-10.19*	*-13.45*	*-12.30*	*-1.53*	*-7.18*	*-30.42*	*-26.06*	*-27.22*
C. Financial Account [1]	4 995 W.	**4.71**	**7.47**	**7.98**	**-12.16**	**.23**	**30.97**	**26.17**	**23.30**
Direct investment abroad	4 505 ..	-34.90	-45.31	-34.82	-62.44	-122.06	-201.57	-266.25	-34.24
Direct investment in United Kingdom	4 555 Z.	10.73	21.73	27.39	37.38	74.65	89.53	119.93	63.11
Portfolio investment assets	4 602 ..	31.47	-61.69	-93.13	-84.99	-52.98	-33.09	-99.89	-134.34
Equity securities	4 610 ..	-1.47	-13.15	-16.30	7.04	-4.65	-23.37	-28.66	-68.34
Debt securities	4 619 ..	32.95	-48.55	-76.83	-92.03	-48.33	-9.72	-71.23	-66.00
Portfolio investment liabilities	4 652 Z.	47.01	58.79	67.98	43.46	35.28	186.06	258.34	63.88
Equity securities	4 660 ..	7.35	8.07	9.40	7.85	63.09	116.04	179.17	25.99
Debt securities	4 669 Z.	39.66	50.72	58.58	35.61	-27.82	70.02	79.17	37.89
Financial derivatives	4 910 ..	3.67	2.63	1.52	1.90	-5.07	4.41	2.26	12.20
Financial derivatives assets	4 900 ..	...	...	...	...	...	...	...	...
Financial derivatives liabilities	4 905 ..	3.67	2.63	1.52	1.90	-5.07	4.41	2.26	12.20
Other investment assets	4 703 ..	-42.45	-74.90	-215.31	-275.87	-26.84	-94.07	-411.53	-259.02
Monetary authorities	4 701 ..	...	...	...	...	...	...	...	...
General government	4 704 ..	-.69	-.74	-.53	-.07	.25	-1.93	-.42	.02
Banks	4 705 ..	-72.66	-34.91	-102.10	-241.01	-28.36	19.99	-291.77	-125.86
Other sectors	4 728 ..	30.90	-39.25	-112.68	-34.79	1.28	-112.14	-119.34	-133.18
Other investment liabilities	4 753 W.	-10.81	106.22	254.36	328.40	97.24	79.70	423.31	311.71
Monetary authorities	4 753 WA	...	...	...	...	...	...	...	...
General government	4 753 ZB	.86	.59	-1.06	-1.74	.42	.54	...	.12
Banks	4 753 ZC	76.62	41.95	111.45	243.06	78.16	16.41	308.92	183.58
Other sectors	4 753 ZD	-88.29	63.68	143.97	87.09	18.66	62.75	114.39	128.01
Total, Groups A Through C	4 983 ..	*-5.48*	*-5.98*	*-4.31*	*-13.69*	*-6.94*	*.55*	*.10*	*-3.92*
D. Net Errors and Omissions	4 998 ..	**6.98**	**5.13**	**3.66**	**9.79**	**6.68**	**-1.58**	**5.19**	**-.54**
Total, Groups A Through D	4 984 ..	*1.50*	*-.85*	*-.65*	*-3.90*	*-.26*	*-1.04*	*5.30*	*-4.45*
E. Reserves and Related Items	4 802 A.	**-1.50**	**.85**	**.65**	**3.90**	**.26**	**1.04**	**-5.30**	**4.45**
Reserve assets	4 802 ..	-1.48	.90	.65	3.90	.26	1.04	-5.30	4.45
Use of Fund credit and loans	4 766 ..	...	...	...	...	...	...	...	...
Exceptional financing	4 920 ..	-.02	-.04	...	...	...	...	...	...
Conversion rates: pound sterling per U.S. dollar	0 101 ..	**.65343**	**.63367**	**.64096**	**.61084**	**.60382**	**.61806**	**.66093**	**.69466**

[1] Excludes components that have been classified in the categories of Group E.

Table 2. STANDARD PRESENTATION, 1994–2001

(Billions of U.S. dollars)

	Code		1994	1995	1996	1997	1998	1999	2000	2001
CURRENT ACCOUNT	4 993	. .	**–10.23**	**–14.29**	**–13.44**	**–2.85**	**–7.96**	**–31.94**	**–28.82**	**–29.37**
A. GOODS	4 100	. .	–16.95	–19.01	–21.23	–20.20	–36.13	–44.29	–45.89	–48.25
Credit	2 100	. .	**207.19**	**242.32**	**261.25**	**281.54**	**271.72**	**268.88**	**284.38**	**275.95**
General merchandise: exports f.o.b.	2 110	. .	207.19	242.32	261.25	281.54	271.72	268.88	284.38	275.95
Goods for processing: exports f.o.b.	2 150	. .	. . .	. . .	. . .	. . .	. . .	. . .	. . .	. . .
Repairs on goods	2 160	. .	. . .	. . .	. . .	. . .	. . .	. . .	. . .	. . .
Goods procured in ports by carriers	2 170	. .	. . .	. . .	. . .	. . .	. . .	. . .	. . .	. . .
Nonmonetary gold	2 180	. .	. . .	. . .	. . .	. . .	. . .	. . .	. . .	. . .
Debit	3 100	. .	**–224.14**	**–261.32**	**–282.48**	**–301.74**	**–307.85**	**–313.18**	**–330.27**	**–324.20**
General merchandise: imports f.o.b.	3 110	. .	–224.14	–261.32	–282.48	–301.74	–307.85	–313.18	–330.27	–324.20
Goods for processing: imports f.o.b.	3 150	. .	. . .	. . .	. . .	. . .	. . .	. . .	. . .	. . .
Repairs on goods	3 160	. .	. . .	. . .	. . .	. . .	. . .	. . .	. . .	. . .
Goods procured in ports by carriers	3 170	. .	. . .	. . .	. . .	. . .	. . .	. . .	. . .	. . .
Nonmonetary gold	3 180	. .	. . .	. . .	. . .	. . .	. . .	. . .	. . .	. . .
B. SERVICES	4 200	. .	9.77	13.37	15.06	20.52	20.97	19.11	18.10	15.96
Total credit	2 200	. .	*69.54*	*78.78*	*87.34*	*97.72*	*107.23*	*113.94*	*116.81*	*110.55*
Total debit	3 200	. .	*–59.77*	*–65.41*	*–72.28*	*–77.20*	*–86.26*	*–94.84*	*–98.71*	*–94.60*
Transportation services, credit	2 205	. .	**14.56**	**16.10**	**16.89**	**18.30**	**19.18**	**18.80**	**19.06**	**17.58**
Passenger	2 850	. .	*6.13*	*7.14*	*7.65*	*7.96*	*8.27*	*8.09*	*8.21*	*7.10*
Freight	2 851	. .	*5.20*	*5.64*	*5.81*	*6.41*	*6.04*	*5.66*	*5.81*	*5.44*
Other	2 852	. .	*3.23*	*3.32*	*3.43*	*3.93*	*4.87*	*5.05*	*5.04*	*5.05*
Sea transport, passenger	2 207	. .	.92	1.11	1.11	1.16	.77	.76	.96	.81
Sea transport, freight	2 208	. .	3.78	4.09	4.09	4.57	4.15	3.84	4.01	3.85
Sea transport, other	2 209	. .	1.39	1.49	1.48	1.61	1.89	1.72	1.57	1.56
Air transport, passenger	2 211	. .	5.20	5.92	6.42	6.68	7.32	7.12	7.08	6.12
Air transport, freight	2 212	. .	.55	.57	.67	.67	.68	.61	.65	.53
Air transport, other	2 213	. .	1.84	1.83	1.94	2.32	2.98	3.33	3.47	3.49
Other transport, passenger	2 215	. .	. . .	.11	.12	.13	.18	.21	.16	.16
Other transport, freight	2 216	. .	.87	.98	1.06	1.17	1.22	1.20	1.15	1.06
Other transport, other	2 217	. .	. . .	. . .	. . .	. . .	. . .	. . .	. . .	. . .
Transportation services, debit	3 205	. .	**–15.83**	**–16.94**	**–18.60**	**–21.75**	**–22.85**	**–22.94**	**–24.13**	**–22.76**
Passenger	3 850	. .	*–5.74*	*–5.82*	*–6.34*	*–7.43*	*–8.01*	*–8.50*	*–8.75*	*–7.81*
Freight	3 851	. .	*–4.82*	*–5.27*	*–5.60*	*–6.49*	*–7.00*	*–7.38*	*–7.76*	*–8.26*
Other	3 852	. .	*–5.27*	*–5.84*	*–6.67*	*–7.84*	*–7.85*	*–7.06*	*–7.62*	*–6.69*
Sea transport, passenger	3 207	. .	–.84	–.82	–.73	–.94	–.85	–.73	–.65	–.58
Sea transport, freight	3 208	. .	–3.68	–3.85	–4.04	–4.60	–4.77	–4.79	–5.00	–5.22
Sea transport, other	3 209	. .	–1.75	–1.96	–2.35	–2.90	–2.27	–1.66	–1.65	–1.41
Air transport, passenger	3 211	. .	–4.90	–4.91	–5.48	–6.32	–6.95	–7.52	–7.84	–6.99
Air transport, freight	3 212	. .	–.58	–.63	–.75	–.89	–.97	–1.11	–1.11	–1.19
Air transport, other	3 213	. .	–3.52	–3.88	–4.31	–4.94	–5.58	–5.40	–5.97	–5.29
Other transport, passenger	3 215	. .	. . .	–.09	–.13	–.16	–.20	–.25	–.25	–.24
Other transport, freight	3 216	. .	–.57	–.79	–.81	–1.00	–1.26	–1.47	–1.65	–1.85
Other transport, other	3 217	. .	. . .	. . .	. . .	. . .	. . .	. . .	. . .	. . .
Travel, credit	2 236	. .	**16.72**	**20.49**	**21.39**	**22.59**	**23.69**	**22.72**	**21.77**	**18.18**
Business travel	2 237	. .	4.04	5.19	5.17	5.87	6.61	6.65	6.39	5.44
Personal travel	2 240	. .	12.68	15.30	16.22	16.71	17.08	16.06	15.38	12.74
Travel, debit	3 236	. .	**–22.60**	**–24.93**	**–25.96**	**–28.53**	**–33.45**	**–37.03**	**–38.26**	**–37.94**
Business travel	3 237	. .	–4.07	–4.92	–5.46	–5.74	–7.21	–7.36	–7.55	6.76
Personal travel	3 240	. .	–18.53	–20.01	–20.50	–22.78	–26.24	–29.67	–30.71	–31.18
Other services, credit	2 200	BA	**38.27**	**42.20**	**49.06**	**56.83**	**64.37**	**72.43**	**75.98**	**74.79**
Communications	2 245	. .	1.59	1.59	1.65	1.88	2.13	2.48	2.37	1.84
Construction	2 249	. .	.18	.20	.27	.44	.49	.41	.18	.16
Insurance	2 253	. .	2.97	3.71	4.16	5.21	4.71	6.47	6.03	5.52
Financial	2 260	. .	8.77	8.82	10.28	13.46	13.95	16.15	19.38	18.69
Computer and information	2 262	. .	1.18	1.25	1.71	2.06	2.87	3.73	3.83	3.47
Royalties and licence fees	2 266	. .	5.32	6.08	6.66	6.79	7.35	8.09	7.98	8.16
Other business services	2 268	. .	15.39	17.20	21.37	23.80	29.49	31.86	32.72	33.23
Personal, cultural, and recreational	2 287	. .	.87	1.09	1.14	1.34	1.49	1.53	1.71	1.54
Government, n.i.e.	2 291	. .	2.00	2.25	1.84	1.86	1.87	1.72	1.78	2.19
Other services, debit	3 200	BA	**–21.35**	**–23.55**	**–27.72**	**–26.92**	**–29.96**	**–34.86**	**–36.32**	**–33.90**
Communications	3 245	. .	–2.01	–2.10	–2.09	–2.20	–2.50	–2.73	–2.62	–2.51
Construction	3 249	. .	–.13	–.15	–.19	–.27	–.18	–.15	–.08	–.07
Insurance	3 253	. .	–.72	–.78	–.89	–.97	–.97	–.94	–1.05	–1.10
Financial	3 260	. .	–1.72	–1.69	–2.13	–2.54	–2.76	–3.24	–4.21	–4.37
Computer and information	3 262	. .	–.39	–.46	–.52	–.66	–.75	–1.01	–1.22	–1.13
Royalties and licence fees	3 266	. .	–4.47	–5.20	–6.32	–6.14	–6.51	–6.54	–6.14	–5.90
Other business services	3 268	. .	–8.07	–9.24	–10.83	–10.20	–13.01	–15.42	–17.09	–14.79
Personal, cultural, and recreational	3 287	. .	–.59	–.78	–.87	–.89	–.79	–.95	–1.07	–1.01
Government, n.i.e.	3 291	. .	–3.25	–3.15	–3.88	–3.04	–2.50	–3.88	–2.85	–3.03

Table 2 (Continued). STANDARD PRESENTATION, 1994–2001

(Billions of U.S. dollars)

	Code	1994	1995	1996	1997	1998	1999	2000	2001
C. INCOME	4 300 . .	5.10	3.29	1.78	6.34	20.83	4.06	14.12	13.22
Total credit	2 300 . .	*113.97*	*138.87*	*144.49*	*157.74*	*171.92*	*163.10*	*204.36*	*201.40*
Total debit	3 300 . .	*–108.86*	*–135.59*	*–142.72*	*–151.40*	*–151.09*	*–159.04*	*–190.25*	*–188.18*
Compensation of employees, credit	2 310 . .	**1.04**	**1.40**	**1.42**	**1.65**	**1.39**	**1.55**	**1.52**	**1.51**
Compensation of employees, debit	3 310 . .	**–1.31**	**–1.87**	**–1.28**	**–1.51**	**–1.41**	**–1.23**	**–1.32**	**–1.25**
Investment income, credit	2 320 . .	**112.92**	**137.48**	**143.07**	**156.09**	**170.53**	**161.54**	**202.84**	**199.89**
Direct investment income	2 330 . .	33.63	39.06	44.53	48.08	49.41	53.43	67.48	63.13
Dividends and distributed branch profits	2 332 . .	12.62	16.15	16.56	21.78	22.25	16.58	26.08	25.53
Reinvested earnings and undistributed branch profits	2 333 . .	21.18	22.67	26.91	26.28	23.25	34.56	38.16	34.16
Income on debt (interest)	2 334 . .	–.17	.23	1.06	.03	3.91	2.29	3.24	3.44
Portfolio investment income	2 339 . .	25.08	31.13	31.63	39.02	47.98	41.46	49.74	50.24
Income on equity	2 340 . .	5.96	7.03	7.44	8.92	9.93	12.49	14.84	14.96
Income on bonds and notes	2 350 . .	18.06	22.75	23.00	28.56	31.55	25.93	31.06	31.11
Income on money market instruments	2 360 . .	1.07	1.35	1.19	1.54	6.50	3.04	3.85	4.17
Other investment income	2 370 . .	54.21	67.29	66.91	68.99	73.14	66.65	85.62	86.52
Investment income, debit	3 320 . .	**–107.56**	**–133.72**	**–141.44**	**–149.88**	**–149.68**	**–157.81**	**–188.93**	**–186.93**
Direct investment income	3 330 . .	–16.24	–21.82	–26.09	–24.41	–14.47	–27.45	–41.04	–40.47
Dividends and distributed branch profits	3 332 . .	–8.80	–10.54	–12.15	–11.74	–8.06	–15.64	–19.71	–21.67
Reinvested earnings and undistributed branch profits	3 333 . .	–5.96	–8.34	–12.21	–10.43	–2.45	–7.42	–16.56	–13.89
Income on debt (interest)	3 334 . .	–1.48	–2.94	–1.73	–2.23	–3.96	–4.39	–4.77	–4.91
Portfolio investment income	3 339 . .	–26.32	–32.50	–37.13	–43.55	–48.29	–50.50	–46.48	–49.87
Income on equity	3 340 . .	–7.50	–8.85	–11.51	–14.09	–16.45	–21.88	–14.93	–19.56
Income on bonds and notes	3 350 . .	–15.45	–18.12	–19.50	–21.95	–21.94	–20.64	–21.18	–19.35
Income on money market instruments	3 360 . .	–3.37	–5.52	–6.11	–7.51	–9.90	–7.98	–10.37	–10.96
Other investment income	3 370 . .	–64.99	–79.40	–78.22	–81.93	–86.91	–79.86	–101.41	–96.60
D. CURRENT TRANSFERS	4 379 . .	–8.16	–11.94	–9.05	–9.51	–13.64	–10.81	–15.14	–10.30
Credit	2 379 . .	**17.71**	**19.70**	**29.46**	**21.44**	**20.59**	**22.70**	**18.66**	**23.30**
General government	2 380 . .	3.26	2.73	4.41	3.55	3.22	5.74	3.75	7.07
Other sectors	2 390 . .	14.44	16.97	25.05	17.89	17.37	16.96	14.91	16.23
Workers' remittances	2 391 . .	. . .	. . .	. . .	. . .	. . .	. . .	. . .	. . .
Other current transfers	2 392 . .	. . .	. . .	. . .	. . .	. . .	. . .	. . .	. . .
Debit	3 379 . .	**–25.86**	**–31.64**	**–38.51**	**–30.95**	**–34.23**	**–33.51**	**–33.80**	**–33.60**
General government	3 380 . .	–7.56	–7.92	–8.26	–8.60	–11.24	–12.12	–12.16	–10.66
Other sectors	3 390 . .	–18.30	–23.72	–30.25	–22.36	–22.99	–21.39	–21.64	–22.94
Workers' remittances	3 391 . .	. . .	. . .	. . .	. . .	. . .	. . .	. . .	. . .
Other current transfers	3 392 . .	. . .	. . .	. . .	. . .	. . .	. . .	. . .	. . .
CAPITAL AND FINANCIAL ACCOUNT	4 996 . .	**3.26**	**9.16**	**9.78**	**–6.94**	**1.28**	**33.53**	**23.62**	**29.91**
CAPITAL ACCOUNT	4 994 . .	**.05**	**.84**	**1.14**	**1.32**	**.79**	**1.52**	**2.76**	**2.15**
Total credit	2 994 . .	*1.93*	*1.84*	*2.18*	*2.77*	*2.44*	*2.91*	*4.36*	*4.06*
Total debit	3 994 . .	*–1.88*	*–.99*	*–1.04*	*–1.45*	*–1.65*	*–1.38*	*–1.60*	*–1.91*
Capital transfers, credit	2 400 . .	**1.93**	**1.84**	**2.11**	**2.66**	**2.29**	**2.66**	**4.12**	**3.89**
General government	2 401 . .	. . .	. . .	. . .	. . .	. . .	. . .	. . .	. . .
Debt forgiveness	2 402 . .	. . .	. . .	. . .	. . .	. . .	. . .	. . .	. . .
Other capital transfers	2 410 . .	. . .	. . .	. . .	. . .	. . .	. . .	. . .	. . .
Other sectors	2 430 . .	1.93	1.84	2.11	2.66	2.29	2.66	4.12	3.89
Migrants' transfers	2 431 . .	.92	1.07	1.10	1.23	1.60	1.85	2.06	2.30
Debt forgiveness	2 432 . .	. . .	. . .	. . .	. . .	. . .	. . .	. . .	. . .
Other capital transfers	2 440 . .	1.01	.77	1.01	1.43	.69	.81	2.06	1.58
Capital transfers, debit	3 400 . .	**–1.88**	**–.99**	**–.99**	**–1.29**	**–1.42**	**–1.16**	**–1.43**	**–1.42**
General government	3 401 . .	–.32	–.28	–.26	–.32	–.54	–.31	–.37	–.37
Debt forgiveness	3 402 . .	–.04	–.04	–.04	–.04	–.24	–.04	–.03	–.03
Other capital transfers	3 410 . .	–.29	–.24	–.22	–.28	–.30	–.28	–.34	–.34
Other sectors	3 430 . .	–1.56	–.72	–.73	–.97	–.88	–.85	–1.05	–1.05
Migrants' transfers	3 431 . .	–.77	–.72	–.73	–.97	–.88	–.81	–.71	–.62
Debt forgiveness	3 432 . .	–.79	. . .	. . .	. . .	. . .	–.04	–.34	–.43
Other capital transfers	3 440 . .	. . .	. . .	. . .	. . .	. . .	. . .	. . .	. . .
Nonproduced nonfinancial assets, credit	2 480 . .	**. . .**	**. . .**	**.08**	**.11**	**.15**	**.25**	**.24**	**.17**
Nonproduced nonfinancial assets, debit	3 480 . .	**. . .**	**. . .**	**–.05**	**–.17**	**–.23**	**–.23**	**–.18**	**–.49**

Table 2 (Continued). STANDARD PRESENTATION, 1994–2001
(Billions of U.S. dollars)

	Code	1994	1995	1996	1997	1998	1999	2000	2001
FINANCIAL ACCOUNT	4 995 . .	**3.21**	**8.32**	**8.63**	**–8.25**	**.49**	**32.00**	**20.87**	**27.76**
A. DIRECT INVESTMENT	4 500 . .	–24.17	–23.57	–7.43	–25.06	–47.40	–112.04	–146.32	28.87
Direct investment abroad	4 505 . .	**–34.90**	**–45.31**	**–34.82**	**–62.44**	**–122.06**	**–201.57**	**–266.25**	**–34.24**
Equity capital	4 510 . .	–11.99	–12.71	–7.77	–34.86	–78.75	–163.32	–252.68	–27.50
Claims on affiliated enterprises	4 515 . .	–11.99	–12.71	–7.77	–34.86	–78.75	–163.32	–252.68	–27.50
Liabilities to affiliated enterprises	4 520 . .	...	...	...	...	...	...	...	...
Reinvested earnings	4 525 . .	–21.18	–22.67	–26.91	–26.28	–23.25	–34.56	–38.16	–34.16
Other capital	4 530 . .	–1.73	–9.92	–.14	–1.31	–20.06	–3.69	24.59	27.42
Claims on affiliated enterprises	4 535 . .	–6.18	–10.26	–4.36	–10.57	–36.94	–24.67	–27.89	–14.39
Liabilities to affiliated enterprises	4 540 . .	4.45	.34	4.21	9.26	16.88	20.98	52.48	41.80
Direct investment in United Kingdom	4 555 . .	**10.73**	**21.73**	**27.39**	**37.38**	**74.65**	**89.53**	**119.93**	**63.11**
Equity capital	4 560 . .	5.08	20.08	12.78	18.97	46.32	75.80	89.33	18.62
Claims on direct investors	4 565 . .	...	...	...	...	...	...	...	...
Liabilities to direct investors	4 570 . .	5.08	20.08	12.78	18.97	46.32	75.80	89.33	18.62
Reinvested earnings	4 575 . .	5.96	8.34	12.21	10.43	2.45	7.42	16.56	13.89
Other capital	4 580 . .	–.31	–6.68	2.40	7.98	25.88	6.31	14.04	30.61
Claims on direct investors	4 585 . .	–4.39	–7.06	–.81	–4.68	–18.29	–21.27	–7.63	16.67
Liabilities to direct investors	4 590 . .	4.08	.38	3.21	12.65	44.17	27.58	21.66	13.94
B. PORTFOLIO INVESTMENT	4 600 . .	78.48	–2.91	–25.15	–41.53	–17.70	152.97	158.45	–70.46
Assets	4 602 . .	**31.47**	**–61.69**	**–93.13**	**–84.99**	**–52.98**	**–33.09**	**–99.89**	**–134.34**
Equity securities	4 610 . .	–1.47	–13.15	–16.30	7.04	–4.65	–23.37	–28.66	–68.34
Monetary authorities	4 611 . .	...	...	...	...	...	...	...	...
General government	4 612 . .	...	...	...	...	...	...	...	...
Banks	4 613 . .	–2.43	–.25	–7.14	5.20	–7.27	.05	–10.61	1.99
Other sectors	4 614 . .	.96	–12.90	–9.16	1.84	2.62	–23.42	–18.06	–70.32
Debt securities	4 619 . .	32.95	–48.55	–76.83	–92.03	–48.33	–9.72	–71.23	–66.00
Bonds and notes	4 620 . .	26.35	–44.29	–79.57	–76.77	–45.40	12.66	–74.27	–48.92
Monetary authorities	4 621 . .	...	...	...	...	...	...	...	...
General government	4 622 . .	...	...	...	...	...	...	...	...
Banks	4 623 . .	–20.48	–38.17	–29.07	–29.51	–72.80	–19.60	–56.42	–55.63
Other sectors	4 624 . .	46.83	–6.11	–50.50	–47.26	27.40	32.26	–17.86	6.71
Money market instruments	4 630 . .	6.59	–4.26	2.74	–15.26	–2.93	–22.38	3.05	–17.08
Monetary authorities	4 631 . .	...	...	...	...	...	...	...	...
General government	4 632 . .	...	...	...	...	...	...	...	–.64
Banks	4 633 . .	6.46	–2.87	5.35	–12.82	–7.04	–15.47	–1.72	–10.51
Other sectors	4 634 . .	.13	–1.39	–2.61	–2.43	4.11	–6.91	4.77	–5.93
Liabilities	4 652 . .	**47.01**	**58.79**	**67.98**	**43.46**	**35.28**	**186.06**	**258.34**	**63.88**
Equity securities	4 660 . .	7.35	8.07	9.40	7.85	63.09	116.04	179.17	25.99
Banks	4 663 . .	–.80	–1.44	–1.87	–3.52	–4.06	–1.41	2.37	–6.43
Other sectors	4 664 . .	8.15	9.51	11.27	11.37	67.15	117.45	176.80	32.42
Debt securities	4 669 . .	39.66	50.72	58.58	35.61	–27.82	70.02	79.17	37.89
Bonds and notes	4 670	34.70	21.15	37.39	21.75	–1.89	42.99	19.05	5.99
Monetary authorities	4 671 . .	...	...	...	...	...	...	...	...
General government	4 672 . .	8.05	–1.60	9.76	–3.90	3.04	–8.49	–1.13	–5.04
Banks	4 673 . .	13.96	6.93	12.92	9.81	.60	18.16	8.19	7.42
Other sectors	4 674 . .	12.69	15.81	14.71	15.84	–5.53	33.32	12.00	3.62
Money market instruments	4 680 . .	4.95	29.57	21.20	13.86	–25.93	27.03	60.12	31.90
Monetary authorities	4 681 . .	...	...	...	...	...	...	...	...
General government	4 682 . .	–.24	2.09	–.35	–1.49	–2.88	.68	–.44	.29
Banks	4 683 . .	1.64	25.51	18.56	12.52	–27.03	23.54	56.69	31.23
Other sectors	4 684 . .	3.55	1.97	2.98	2.83	3.99	2.80	3.87	.38
C. FINANCIAL DERIVATIVES	4 910 . .	3.67	2.63	1.52	1.90	–5.07	4.41	2.26	12.20
Monetary authorities	4 911 . .	...	...	...	...	...	...	...	...
General government	4 912 . .	...	...	...	...	...	...	...	...
Banks	4 913 . .	...	...	...	...	...	...	...	...
Other sectors	4 914 . .	...	...	...	...	...	...	...	...
Assets	4 900 . .	**...**	**...**	**...**	**...**	**...**	**...**	**...**	**...**
Monetary authorities	4 901 . .	...	...	...	...	...	...	...	...
General government	4 902 . .	...	...	...	...	...	...	...	...
Banks	4 903 . .	...	...	...	...	...	...	...	...
Other sectors	4 904 . .	...	...	...	...	...	...	...	...
Liabilities	4 905 . .	**3.67**	**2.63**	**1.52**	**1.90**	**–5.07**	**4.41**	**2.26**	**12.20**
Monetary authorities	4 906 . .	...	...	...	...	...	...	...	...
General government	4 907 . .	...	...	...	...	...	...	...	...
Banks	4 908 . .	...	...	...	...	...	...	...	...
Other sectors	4 909 . .	...	...	...	...	...	...	...	...

Table 2 (Concluded). STANDARD PRESENTATION, 1994–2001
(Billions of U.S. dollars)

	Code	1994	1995	1996	1997	1998	1999	2000	2001
D. OTHER INVESTMENT	4 700 . .	-53.28	31.27	39.05	52.53	70.40	-14.37	11.77	52.69
Assets	4 703 . .	**-42.45**	**-74.90**	**-215.31**	**-275.87**	**-26.84**	**-94.07**	**-411.53**	**-259.02**
Trade credits	4 706 . .	-.63	-1.92	-3.00	.99	1.92	-1.98	-.32	.13
General government	4 707 . .	-.63	-.70	-.47	-.05	.07	-1.81	-.38	.07
of which: Short-term	4 709 . .	...	...	...	...	...	...	...	...
Other sectors	4 710 . .	...	-1.21	-2.53	1.04	1.85	-.17	.06	.06
of which: Short-term	4 712 . .	*.29*	*-.08*	*-2.56*	*1.04*	*1.85*	*-.17*	*.06*	*.06*
Loans	4 714 . .	5.92	-18.78	-59.84	-51.84	-.31	-26.70	-86.41	-71.58
Monetary authorities	4 715 . .	...	...	...	...	...	...	...	...
of which: Short-term	4 718 . .	...	...	...	...	...	...	...	...
General government	4 719 . .	.08	.09	.07	.08	.29	.03	.04	.03
of which: Short-term	4 721 . .	...	...	...	...	...	...	...	...
Banks	4 722 . .	5.66	-18.67	-59.55	-51.82	-.75	-26.98	-86.71	-71.87
of which: Short-term	4 724 . .	*5.66*	*-18.67*	*-59.55*	*-51.82*	*-.75*	*-26.98*	*-86.71*	*-71.87*
Other sectors	4 725 . .	.18	-.21	-.35	-.10	.15	.25	.26	.26
of which: Short-term	4 727 . .	*.19*	*-.05*	*-.19*	*-.01*	*.23*	...	...	...
Currency and deposits	4 730 . .	-48.39	-54.06	-152.34	-224.91	-28.34	-65.28	-325.07	-187.92
Monetary authorities	4 731 . .	...	...	...	...	...	...	...	...
General government	4 732 . .	...	...	...	...	...	...	...	...
Banks	4 733 . .	-79.11	-16.24	-42.55	-189.18	-27.62	46.97	-205.06	-53.99
Other sectors	4 734 . .	30.72	-37.82	-109.80	-35.73	-.72	-112.26	-120.01	-133.93
Other assets	4 736 . .	.65	-.14	-.13	-.10	-.11	-.11	.26	.35
Monetary authorities	4 737 . .	...	...	...	...	...	...	...	...
of which: Short-term	4 739 . .	...	...	...	...	...	...	...	...
General government	4 740 . .	-.14	-.13	-.13	-.10	-.11	-.15	-.08	-.08
of which: Short-term	4 742 . .	...	...	...	...	...	...	...	...
Banks	4 743 . .	.79	...	...	...	...	...	...	...
of which: Short-term	4 745 . .	*.79*	...	...	...	...	...	...	...
Other sectors	4 746 . .	-.01	-.01	-.01	...	...	.04	.34	.43
of which: Short-term	4 748 . .	*-.01*	*-.01*	*-.01*	...	...	*.04*	*.34*	*.43*
Liabilities	4 753 . .	**-10.83**	**106.17**	**254.36**	**328.40**	**97.24**	**79.70**	**423.31**	**311.71**
Trade credits	4 756 . .	.55	.42	.05	-.01	...	...	...	...
General government	4 757 . .	...	...	...	...	...	...	...	...
of which: Short-term	4 759 . .	...	...	...	...	...	...	...	...
Other sectors	4 760 . .	.55	.42	.05	-.01	...	...	...	...
of which: Short-term	4 762 . .	*.01*	...	*.02*	*-.01*	...	...	...	...
Loans	4 764 . .	-88.78	61.43	131.72	86.13	18.33	63.34	112.31	128.08
Monetary authorities	4 765 . .	...	...	...	...	...	...	...	...
of which: Use of Fund credit and loans from the Fund	4 766 . .	...	...	...	...	...	...	...	...
of which: Short-term	4 768 . .	...	...	...	...	...	...	...	...
General government	4 769 . .	-.34	-.25	-.14	-.50	-.30	-.34	-.45	-.31
of which: Short-term	4 771 . .	...	...	...	...	...	...	...	...
Banks	4 772 . .	...	...	...	...	...	...	...	...
of which: Short-term	4 774 . .	...	...	...	...	...	...	...	...
Other sectors	4 775 . .	-88.44	61.68	131.87	86.63	18.62	63.69	112.76	128.38
of which: Short-term	4 777 . .	*-88.26*	*61.91*	*131.89*	*86.97*	*18.63*	*63.69*	*112.76*	*128.38*
Currency and deposits	4 780 . .	76.62	41.95	111.45	243.06	78.16	16.41	308.92	183.58
Monetary authorities	4 781 . .	...	...	...	...	...	...	...	...
General government	4 782 . .	...	...	...	...	...	...	...	...
Banks	4 783 . .	76.62	41.95	111.45	243.06	78.16	16.41	308.92	183.58
Other sectors	4 784 . .	...	...	...	...	...	...	...	...
Other liabilities	4 786 . .	.78	2.38	11.14	-.77	.76	-.05	2.08	.06
Monetary authorities	4 787 . .	...	...	...	...	...	...	...	...
of which: Short-term	4 789 . .	...	...	...	...	...	...	...	...
General government	4 790 . .	1.18	.82	-.91	-1.24	.72	.88	.45	.43
of which: Short-term	4 792 . .	*1.18*	*.82*	*-.91*	*-1.24*	*.72*	*.88*	*.45*	*.43*
Banks	4 793 . .	...	...	...	...	...	...	...	...
of which: Short-term	4 795 . .	...	...	...	...	...	...	...	...
Other sectors	4 796 . .	-.40	1.55	12.05	.46	.04	-.93	1.63	-.37
of which: Short-term	4 798 . .	*-.40*	*1.55*	*12.05*	*.46*	*.04*	*-.93*	*1.63*	*-.37*
E. RESERVE ASSETS	4 802 . .	-1.48	.90	.65	3.90	.26	1.04	-5.30	4.45
Monetary gold	4 812 . .	-1.12	.11	.03	-1.82	-1.56	.66	1.34	1.13
Special drawing rights	4 811 . .	-.18	.09	.06	-.15	.02	-.06	.17	.02
Reserve position in the Fund	4 810 . .	-.02	-.40	-.09	-.69	-1.25	-1.01	.75	-.93
Foreign exchange	4 803 . .	-.16	1.09	.65	6.56	3.04	1.44	-7.49	4.24
Other claims	4 813 . .	...	...	...	...	...	...	-.07	-.01
NET ERRORS AND OMISSIONS	4 998 . .	**6.98**	**5.13**	**3.66**	**9.79**	**6.68**	**-1.58**	**5.19**	**-.54**

Part 3 of the *Yearbook* contains descriptions of the methodologies, compilation practices, and sources used to compile these data.

Table 3. INTERNATIONAL INVESTMENT POSITION (End-period stocks), 1994–2001
(Billions of U.S. dollars)

	Code	1994	1995	1996	1997	1998	1999	2000	2001
ASSETS	8 995 C.	2,101.90	2,391.34	2,764.53	3,247.52	3,546.24	3,901.19	4,449.02	4,606.31
Direct investment abroad	8 505 . .	**275.23**	**315.74**	**342.31**	**369.24**	**498.36**	**691.91**	**910.12**	**935.77**
Equity capital and reinvested earnings	8 506 . .	257.44	291.33	324.15	354.31	455.33	649.93	894.87	952.09
Claims on affiliated enterprises	8 507 . .	...	...	...	...	...	...	...	...
Liabilities to affiliated enterprises	8 508 . .	...	...	...	...	...	...	...	...
Other capital	8 530 . .	17.79	24.40	18.16	14.93	43.03	41.99	15.25	−16.31
Claims on affiliated enterprises	8 535 . .	...	...	...	...	...	...	...	...
Liabilities to affiliated enterprises	8 540 . .	...	...	...	...	...	...	...	...
Portfolio investment	8 602 . .	**671.53**	**773.94**	**930.84**	**1,076.56**	**1,172.18**	**1,333.57**	**1,343.62**	**1,304.04**
Equity securities	8 610 . .	291.92	336.30	404.67	466.94	505.15	664.31	635.34	558.38
Monetary authorities	8 611 . .	...	...	...	...	...	...	...	...
General government	8 612 . .	...	...	...	...	...	...	...	...
Banks	8 613 . .	5.50	7.45	8.45	4.51	14.70	11.00	29.36	20.78
Other sectors	8 614 . .	286.42	328.86	396.23	462.43	490.45	653.31	605.98	537.60
Debt securities	8 619 . .	379.62	437.63	526.17	609.62	667.03	669.26	708.27	745.67
Bonds and notes	8 620 . .	355.48	407.82	499.57	569.16	624.92	601.96	645.31	667.30
Monetary authorities	8 621 . .	...	...	...	...	...	...	...	...
General government	8 622 . .	...	...	...	...	...	...	...	...
Banks	8 623 . .	188.22	227.06	265.52	303.41	380.44	392.07	430.61	463.69
Other sectors	8 624 . .	167.26	180.76	234.05	265.74	244.47	209.90	214.70	203.61
Money market instruments	8 630 . .	24.14	29.81	26.60	40.46	42.11	67.30	62.96	78.36
Monetary authorities	8 631 . .	...	...	...	...	...	...	...	...
General government	8 632 . .	...	...	...	...	...	...	...	.66
Banks	8 633 . .	16.48	20.68	14.82	27.91	35.96	51.22	52.10	61.01
Other sectors	8 634 . .	7.66	9.13	11.78	12.55	6.15	16.08	10.86	16.69
Financial derivatives	8 900 . .	...	...	...	...	...	...	...	...
Monetary authorities	8 901 . .	...	...	...	...	...	...	...	...
General government	8 902 . .	...	...	...	...	...	...	...	...
Banks	8 903 . .	...	...	...	...	...	...	...	...
Other sectors	8 904 . .	...	...	...	...	...	...	...	...
Other investment	8 703 . .	**1,107.20**	**1,252.52**	**1,444.99**	**1,763.93**	**1,836.86**	**1,839.84**	**2,152.31**	**2,329.26**
Trade credits	8 706 . .	22.85	24.51	19.29	17.86	16.01	15.82	14.64	13.70
General government	8 707 . .	10.88	11.48	13.09	12.80	12.81	12.49	11.50	10.66
of which: Short-term	8 709 . .	...	...	*−.83*	*−.76*	*−.83*	*−.77*	*−.74*	*−1.23*
Other sectors	8 710 . .	11.97	13.03	6.20	5.06	3.21	3.33	3.14	3.04
of which: Short-term	8 712 . .	*2.34*	*2.42*	*5.35*	*4.23*	*2.37*	*2.52*	*2.39*	*2.31*
Loans	8 714 . .	161.42	196.90	261.78	331.86	351.63	364.44	430.83	481.78
Monetary authorities	8 715 . .	...	...	...	...	...	...	...	...
of which: Short-term	8 718 . .	...	...	...	...	...	...	...	...
General government	8 719 . .	.98	.88	.89	.78	.49	.45	.37	.33
of which: Short-term	8 721 . .	...	...	...	...	...	...	...	...
Banks	8 722 . .	157.35	193.39	257.70	328.00	348.40	357.72	425.13	476.18
of which: Short-term	8 724 . .	*157.35*	*193.39*	*257.70*	*328.00*	*348.40*	*357.72*	*425.13*	*476.18*
Other sectors	8 725 . .	3.09	2.63	3.19	3.08	2.73	6.27	5.33	5.27
of which: Short-term	8 727 . .	*1.50*	*.93*	*1.16*	*1.15*	*.96*	*.86*	*.79*	*.77*
Currency and deposits	8 730 . .	919.71	1,028.17	1,160.33	1,410.87	1,464.79	1,455.42	1,702.39	1,829.37
Monetary authorities	8 731 . .	...	...	...	...	...	...	...	...
General government	8 732 . .	...	...	...	...	...	...	...	...
Banks	8 733 . .	719.80	786.38	806.18	1,039.33	1,109.08	1,006.28	1,154.55	1,165.03
Other sectors	8 734 . .	199.91	241.78	354.15	371.54	355.71	449.13	547.83	664.34
Other assets	8 736 . .	3.22	2.95	3.59	3.34	4.42	4.16	4.45	4.40
Monetary authorities	8 737 . .	...	...	...	...	...	...	...	...
of which: Short-term	8 739 . .	...	...	...	...	...	...	...	...
General government	8 740 . .	2.23	2.35	2.71	2.74	2.87	2.94	2.79	2.79
of which: Short-term	8 742 . .	...	...	...	...	...	...	...	...
Banks	8 743 . .	...	...	...	...	...	...	...	...
of which: Short-term	8 745 . .	...	...	...	...	...	...	...	...
Other sectors	8 746 . .	.99	.60	.88	.60	1.55	1.23	1.66	1.61
of which: Short-term	8 748 . .	*.99*	*.60*	*.88*	*.60*	*1.55*	*1.23*	*1.66*	*1.61*
Reserve assets	8 802 . .	**47.93**	**49.15**	**46.39**	**37.79**	**38.84**	**35.86**	**42.97**	**37.24**
Monetary gold	8 812 . .	7.05	7.15	6.80	5.32	6.64	5.97	4.26	3.15
Special drawing rights	8 811 . .	.49	.41	.34	.47	.47	.51	.33	.29
Reserve position in the Fund	8 810 . .	1.99	2.42	2.43	2.97	4.38	5.28	4.28	5.05
Foreign exchange	8 803 . .	38.40	39.17	36.82	29.03	27.35	24.10	33.91	28.18
Other claims	8 813 . .	...	...	...	...	...	...	.19	.57

Table 3 (Concluded). INTERNATIONAL INVESTMENT POSITION (End–period stocks), 1994–2001

(Billions of U.S. dollars)

	Code	1994	1995	1996	1997	1998	1999	2000	2001
LIABILITIES	8 995 D.	2,073.93	2,426.47	2,882.36	3,372.31	3,771.20	4,031.36	4,504.30	4,664.12
Direct investment in United Kingdom	8 555 . .	**203.05**	**226.63**	**259.17**	**287.31**	**355.40**	**404.51**	**457.47**	**503.96**
Equity capital and reinvested earnings	8 556 . .	154.28	184.32	204.73	222.08	265.90	310.94	357.89	377.48
Claims on direct investors	8 557 . .	...	...	...	...	...	...	...	...
Liabilities to direct investors	8 558 . .	...	...	...	...	...	...	...	...
Other capital	8 580 . .	48.77	42.30	54.44	65.24	89.49	93.57	99.57	126.49
Claims on direct investors	8 585 . .	...	...	...	...	...	...	...	...
Liabilities to direct investors	8 590 . .	...	...	...	...	...	...	...	...
Portfolio investment	8 652 . .	**499.95**	**629.75**	**815.00**	**964.63**	**1,155.19**	**1,343.40**	**1,493.50**	**1,420.03**
Equity securities	8 660 . .	197.10	267.66	383.89	499.23	668.90	824.10	901.93	793.68
Banks	8 663 . .	6.83	9.80	16.55	24.42	30.23	34.65	40.10	34.45
Other sectors	8 664 . .	190.26	257.86	367.35	474.81	638.67	789.45	861.83	759.23
Debt securities	8 669 . .	302.85	362.09	431.10	465.40	486.29	519.31	591.58	626.35
Bonds and notes	8 670 . .	224.75	253.72	302.92	322.75	369.19	379.01	393.51	398.38
Monetary authorities	8 671 . .	...	...	...	...	...	...	...	...
General government	8 672 . .	88.45	91.37	107.82	106.46	122.98	98.48	92.51	82.32
Banks	8 673 . .	56.30	63.72	78.23	85.45	96.18	111.83	116.57	123.49
Other sectors	8 674 . .	80.00	98.63	116.87	130.84	150.02	168.70	184.43	192.57
Money market instruments	8 680 . .	78.10	108.38	128.18	142.66	117.11	140.29	198.06	227.96
Monetary authorities	8 681 . .	...	...	...	...	...	...	...	...
General government	8 682 . .	2.86	5.01	5.10	2.93	.69	.34	.04	.12
Banks	8 683 . .	60.23	86.07	103.98	117.63	90.43	111.11	165.59	195.15
Other sectors	8 684 . .	15.01	17.30	19.10	22.10	25.99	28.85	32.43	32.69
Financial derivatives	8 905 . .	...	...	...	...	...	...	...	...
Monetary authorities	8 906 . .	...	...	...	...	...	...	...	...
General government	8 907 . .	...	...	...	...	...	...	...	...
Banks	8 908 . .	...	...	...	...	...	...	...	...
Other sectors	8 909 . .	...	...	...	...	...	...	...	...
Other investment	8 753 . .	**1,370.94**	**1,570.09**	**1,808.19**	**2,120.36**	**2,260.62**	**2,283.45**	**2,553.33**	**2,740.13**
Trade credits	8 756 . .	3.85	4.23	4.52	4.46	4.46	4.39	4.17	4.10
General government	8 757 . .	...	...	...	...	...	...	...	...
of which: Short-term	8 759 . .	...	...	...	...	...	...	...	...
Other sectors	8 760 . .	3.85	4.23	4.52	4.46	4.46	4.39	4.17	4.10
of which: Short-term	8 762 . .	*1.98*	*1.97*	*2.02*	*2.02*	*2.01*	*2.00*	*1.97*	*1.96*
Loans	8 764 . .	238.33	305.72	447.25	509.40	498.09	581.74	632.68	714.47
Monetary authorities	8 765 . .	...	...	...	...	...	...	...	...
of which: Use of Fund credit and loans from the Fund	8 766 . .	...	...	...	...	...	...	...	...
of which: Short-term	8 768 . .	...	...	...	...	...	...	...	...
General government	8 769 . .	3.56	3.37	3.38	2.79	2.68	2.29	2.02	1.64
of which: Short-term	8 771 . .	*.03*	*.03*	...	...	...	...	...	...
Banks	8 772 . .	...	...	...	...	...	...	...	...
of which: Short-term	8 774 . .	...	...	...	...	...	...	...	...
Other sectors	8 775 . .	234.78	302.35	443.87	506.60	495.40	579.45	630.66	712.83
of which: Short-term	8 777 . .	*234.29*	*302.10*	*443.52*	*506.58*	*495.39*	*579.45*	*630.66*	*712.83*
Currency and deposits	8 780 . .	1,114.40	1,242.42	1,329.34	1,578.64	1,730.68	1,672.35	1,891.42	1,997.32
Monetary authorities	8 781 . .	...	...	...	...	...	...	...	...
General government	8 782 . .	...	...	1.82	.51	1.02	2.11	2.74	2.40
Banks	8 783 . .	1,114.40	1,242.42	1,327.38	1,577.98	1,729.50	1,670.07	1,888.51	1,994.76
Other sectors	8 784 . .	...	...	.14	.15	.16	.17	.17	.16
Other liabilities	8 786 . .	14.35	17.72	27.08	27.86	27.38	24.97	25.06	24.25
Monetary authorities	8 787 . .	...	...	...	...	...	...	...	...
of which: Short-term	8 789 . .	...	...	...	...	...	...	...	...
General government	8 790 . .	3.15	3.94	1.35	1.32	1.52	1.23	.97	1.67
of which: Short-term	8 792 . .	*3.15*	*3.94*	*1.35*	*1.32*	*1.52*	*1.23*	*.97*	*1.67*
Banks	8 793 . .	...	...	...	...	...	...	...	...
of which: Short-term	8 795 . .	...	...	...	...	...	...	...	...
Other sectors	8 796 . .	11.20	13.78	25.74	26.54	25.86	23.74	24.10	22.58
of which: Short-term	8 798 . .	*11.20*	*13.78*	*25.74*	*26.54*	*25.86*	*23.74*	*24.10*	*22.58*
NET INTERNATIONAL INVESTMENT POSITION	8 995 . .	**27.96**	**–35.13**	**–117.82**	**–124.79**	**–224.97**	**–130.18**	**–55.29**	**–57.80**
Conversion rates: pound sterling per U.S. dollar (end of period)	0 102 . .	**.64000**	**.64516**	**.58893**	**.60467**	**.60114**	**.61866**	**.67015**	**.68947**

Table 1. ANALYTIC PRESENTATION, 1994–2001

(Billions of U.S. dollars)

	Code	1994	1995	1996	1997	1998	1999	2000	2001
A. Current Account [1]	4 993 Z.	**–118.20**	**–105.82**	**–117.84**	**–128.36**	**–203.85**	**–292.86**	**–410.30**	**–393.39**
Goods: exports f.o.b	2 100 . .	504.93	577.05	614.02	680.33	672.38	686.28	774.64	721.75
Goods: imports f.o.b	3 100 . .	–668.69	–749.38	–803.12	–876.51	–917.12	–1,029.98	–1,224.43	–1,145.98
Balance on Goods	4 100 . .	*–163.76*	*–172.33*	*–189.10*	*–196.18*	*–244.74*	*–343.70*	*–449.79*	*–424.23*
Services: credit	2 200 . .	199.03	217.46	238.17	254.70	260.28	270.90	289.63	276.28
Services: debit	3 200 . .	–131.92	–141.50	–150.91	–166.28	–182.53	–189.47	–218.52	–210.34
Balance on Goods and Services	4 991 . .	*–96.65*	*–96.37*	*–101.84*	*–107.76*	*–166.99*	*–262.27*	*–378.68*	*–358.29*
Income: credit	2 300 . .	165.44	211.54	225.86	260.58	259.40	290.56	353.03	283.76
Income: debit	3 300 . .	–148.75	–186.92	–201.77	–240.39	–251.76	–272.39	–331.22	–269.39
Balance on Goods, Services, and Income	4 992 . .	*–79.96*	*–71.75*	*–77.75*	*–87.57*	*–159.35*	*–244.10*	*–356.87*	*–343.92*
Current transfers: credit	2 379 Z.	6.49	7.68	8.89	8.49	9.19	9.57	10.65	10.47
Current transfers: debit	3 379 . .	–44.73	–41.75	–48.98	–49.28	–53.69	–58.33	–64.08	–59.94
B. Capital Account [1]	4 994 Z.	**–.47**	**.37**	**.69**	**.35**	**.70**	**–3.39**	**.84**	**.83**
Capital account: credit	2 994 Z.	.31	.67	.69	.35	.70	.60	.84	.83
Capital account: debit	3 994 . .	–.77	–.30	. . .	. . .	. . .	–3.99	. . .	. . .
Total, Groups A Plus B	4 981 . .	*–118.67*	*–105.45*	*–117.15*	*–128.01*	*–203.15*	*–296.25*	*–409.46*	*–392.56*
C. Financial Account [1]	4 995 W.	**124.62**	**95.94**	**130.52**	**220.16**	**70.60**	**256.11**	**409.81**	**386.79**
Direct investment abroad	4 505 . .	–80.18	–98.78	–91.88	–104.82	–142.64	–188.91	–178.29	–127.84
Direct investment in United States	4 555 Z.	46.13	57.80	86.52	105.59	179.03	289.44	307.74	130.80
Portfolio investment assets	4 602 . .	–60.31	–122.51	–149.83	–118.98	–136.13	–128.44	–127.50	–94.66
Equity securities	4 610 . .	–48.10	–65.41	–82.85	–57.58	–101.28	–114.31	–103.64	–106.81
Debt securities	4 619 . .	–12.21	–57.10	–66.98	–61.40	–34.85	–14.13	–23.86	12.15
Portfolio investment liabilities	4 652 Z.	139.41	210.36	332.78	333.11	187.58	285.59	419.90	426.06
Equity securities	4 660 . .	.89	16.53	11.06	67.04	41.96	112.29	193.51	121.42
Debt securities	4 669 Z.	138.52	193.83	321.72	266.07	145.62	173.30	226.39	304.64
Financial derivatives	4 910 . .	. . .	. . .	. . .	. . .	. . .	. . .	. . .	. . .
Financial derivatives assets	4 900 . .	. . .	. . .	. . .	. . .	. . .	. . .	. . .	. . .
Financial derivatives liabilities	4 905 . .	. . .	. . .	. . .	. . .	. . .	. . .	. . .	. . .
Other investment assets	4 703 . .	–40.90	–121.38	–178.90	–262.83	–74.21	–169.00	–300.40	–143.54
Monetary authorities	4 701 . .	. . .	. . .	. . .	. . .	. . .	. . .	. . .	. . .
General government	4 704 . .	–.37	–.98	–1.00	.06	–.42	2.75	–.94	–.48
Banks	4 705 . .	–4.20	–75.11	–91.56	–141.13	–35.58	–76.27	–148.66	–128.70
Other sectors	4 728 . .	–36.33	–45.29	–86.34	–121.76	–38.21	–95.48	–150.80	–14.36
Other investment liabilities	4 753 W.	120.46	170.45	131.83	268.09	56.97	167.43	288.36	195.97
Monetary authorities	4 753 WA	9.59	46.73	56.88	–18.86	6.89	24.59	–6.70	35.10
General government	4 753 ZB	2.77	.90	.73	–2.70	–3.26	–.85	–.48	–4.35
Banks	4 753 ZC	108.00	64.19	22.19	171.32	30.27	67.19	122.72	80.39
Other sectors	4 753 ZD	.10	58.63	52.03	118.33	23.07	76.50	172.82	84.83
Total, Groups A Through C	4 983 . .	*5.95*	*–9.51*	*13.37*	*92.15*	*–132.54*	*–40.14*	*.35*	*–5.78*
D. Net Errors and Omissions	4 998 . .	**–11.30**	**19.26**	**–20.04**	**–91.13**	**139.29**	**31.41**	**–.05**	**10.70**
Total, Groups A Through D	4 984 . .	*–5.35*	*9.75*	*–6.67*	*1.02*	*6.74*	*–8.73*	*.30*	*4.93*
E. Reserves and Related Items	4 802 A.	**5.35**	**–9.75**	**6.67**	**–1.02**	**–6.74**	**8.73**	**–.30**	**–4.93**
Reserve assets	4 802 . .	5.35	–9.75	6.67	–1.02	–6.74	8.73	–.30	–4.93
Use of Fund credit and loans	4 766 . .	. . .	. . .	. . .	. . .	. . .	. . .	. . .	. . .
Exceptional financing	4 920 . .	. . .	. . .	. . .	. . .	. . .	. . .	. . .	. . .

[1] Excludes components that have been classified in the categories of Group E.

Table 2. STANDARD PRESENTATION, 1994–2001

(Billions of U.S. dollars)

	Code	1994	1995	1996	1997	1998	1999	2000	2001
CURRENT ACCOUNT	4 993 ..	**–118.20**	**–105.82**	**–117.84**	**–128.36**	**–203.85**	**–292.86**	**–410.30**	**–393.39**
A. GOODS	4 100 ..	–163.76	–172.33	–189.10	–196.18	–244.74	–343.70	–449.79	–424.23
Credit	2 100 ..	**504.93**	**577.05**	**614.02**	**680.33**	**672.38**	**686.28**	**774.64**	**721.75**
General merchandise: exports f.o.b.	2 110 ..	502.78	575.17	611.85	678.35	670.42	683.95	772.00	718.76
Goods for processing: exports f.o.b.	2 150 ..	...	...	...	...	...	...	...	...
Repairs on goods	2 160 ..	2.05	1.84	1.90	1.96	1.96	2.30	2.64	2.99
Goods procured in ports by carriers	2 170 ..	...	...	...	...	...	...	...	...
Nonmonetary gold	2 180 ..	.10	.04	.27	.02	...	.03	...	...
Debit	3 100 ..	**–668.69**	**–749.38**	**–803.12**	**–876.51**	**–917.12**	**–1,029.98**	**–1,224.43**	**–1,145.98**
General merchandise: imports f.o.b.	3 110 ..	–665.94	–746.30	–798.17	–872.96	–914.21	–1,027.26	–1,221.21	–1,143.72
Goods for processing: imports f.o.b.	3 150 ..	...	...	...	...	...	...	...	...
Repairs on goods	3 160 ..	...	...	...	–.02	...	...	...	–.03
Goods procured in ports by carriers	3 170 ..	...	...	...	...	...	...	...	...
Nonmonetary gold	3 180 ..	–2.75	–3.08	–4.95	–3.53	–2.91	–2.72	–3.22	–2.23
B. SERVICES	4 200 ..	67.11	75.96	87.26	88.42	77.75	81.43	71.11	65.94
Total credit	2 200 ..	*199.03*	*217.46*	*238.17*	*254.70*	*260.28*	*270.90*	*289.63*	*276.28*
Total debit	3 200 ..	*–131.92*	*–141.50*	*–150.91*	*–166.28*	*–182.53*	*–189.47*	*–218.52*	*–210.34*
Transportation services, credit	2 205 ..	**40.77**	**45.00**	**46.51**	**47.87**	**45.71**	**46.71**	**50.92**	**46.33**
Passenger	2 850 ..	*17.00*	*18.91*	*20.42*	*20.87*	*20.09*	*19.79*	*20.77*	*18.01*
Freight	2 851 ..	*9.59*	*11.28*	*11.16*	*11.79*	*11.06*	*11.56*	*13.00*	*11.94*
Other	2 852 ..	*14.18*	*14.81*	*14.93*	*15.21*	*14.56*	*15.36*	*17.15*	*16.38*
Sea transport, passenger	2 207 ..	.28	.28	.34	.30	.39	.36	.50	.50
Sea transport, freight	2 208 ..	4.51	5.29	4.71	4.57	3.79	3.94	4.74	4.15
Sea transport, other	2 209 ..	...	...	...	...	...	...	...	...
Air transport, passenger	2 211 ..	16.72	18.63	20.08	20.57	19.70	19.43	20.27	17.51
Air transport, freight	2 212 ..	3.18	3.66	3.96	4.61	4.76	5.05	5.77	5.37
Air transport, other	2 213 ..	...	...	...	...	...	...	...	...
Other transport, passenger	2 215 ..	...	...	...	...	...	...	...	...
Other transport, freight	2 216 ..	1.90	2.33	2.49	2.61	2.51	2.57	2.49	2.42
Other transport, other	2 217 ..	14.18	14.81	14.93	15.21	14.56	15.36	17.15	16.38
Transportation services, debit	3 205 ..	**–39.08**	**–41.71**	**–43.21**	**–47.11**	**–50.35**	**–55.48**	**–65.91**	**–61.23**
Passenger	3 850 ..	*–13.06*	*–14.66*	*–15.81*	*–18.14*	*–19.98*	*–21.32*	*–24.31*	*–22.41*
Freight	3 851 ..	*–16.01*	*–16.47*	*–16.53*	*–17.67*	*–19.42*	*–22.24*	*–27.39*	*–25.66*
Other	3 852 ..	*–10.01*	*–10.58*	*–10.87*	*–11.30*	*–10.95*	*–11.92*	*–14.21*	*–13.16*
Sea transport, passenger	3 207 ..	–.35	–.35	–.44	–.36	–.40	–.37	–.66	–.66
Sea transport, freight	3 208 ..	–11.37	–11.51	–11.26	–11.91	–13.66	–15.73	–20.07	–19.39
Sea transport, other	3 209 ..	...	...	...	...	...	...	...	...
Air transport, passenger	3 211 ..	–12.71	–14.31	–15.37	–17.78	–19.58	–20.95	–23.65	–21.75
Air transport, freight	3 212 ..	–2.92	–3.12	–3.20	–3.55	–3.62	–4.15	–4.74	–3.96
Air transport, other	3 213 ..	...	...	...	...	...	...	...	...
Other transport, passenger	3 215 ..	...	...	...	...	...	...	...	...
Other transport, freight	3 216 ..	–1.72	–1.84	–2.07	–2.21	–2.14	–2.36	–2.58	–2.31
Other transport, other	3 217 ..	–10.01	–10.58	–10.87	–11.30	–10.95	–11.92	–14.21	–13.16
Travel, credit	2 236 ..	**69.31**	**74.81**	**81.80**	**86.18**	**84.96**	**89.28**	**97.82**	**90.09**
Business travel	2 237 ..	2.90	3.02	3.08	3.29	3.43	3.58	3.70	3.80
Personal travel	2 240 ..	66.41	71.79	78.72	82.89	81.53	85.70	94.12	86.29
Travel, debit	3 236 ..	**–44.91**	**–46.21**	**–49.50**	**–53.60**	**–58.28**	**–60.84**	**–67.67**	**–62.67**
Business travel	3 237 ..	–.14	–.16	–.16	–.16	–.17	–.16	–.84	–.17
Personal travel	3 240 ..	–44.77	–46.05	–49.34	–53.44	–58.11	–60.68	–66.83	–62.50
Other services, credit	2 200 BA	**88.95**	**97.65**	**109.86**	**120.65**	**129.61**	**134.91**	**140.89**	**139.86**
Communications	2 245 ..	3.08	3.54	3.56	4.16	5.82	4.78	5.00	5.05
Construction	2 249 ..	2.48	2.55	3.56	3.50	3.88	5.84	2.28	2.61
Insurance	2 253 ..	1.68	1.30	2.18	2.49	2.21	1.02	2.04	...
Financial	2 260 ..	5.76	7.04	8.23	10.25	11.33	13.42	16.31	15.21
Computer and information	2 262 ..	2.33	2.43	2.79	3.48	3.70	4.77	4.90	5.14
Royalties and licence fees	2 266 ..	26.72	30.29	32.46	33.23	35.63	36.90	39.60	38.66
Other business services	2 268 ..	27.63	29.09	33.29	38.74	40.21	42.12	45.76	49.67
Personal, cultural, and recreational	2 287 ..	2.20	2.56	2.83	3.53	4.55	5.63	6.38	6.62
Government, n.i.e.	2 291 ..	17.07	18.85	20.96	21.27	22.28	20.43	18.62	16.90
Other services, debit	3 200 BA	**–47.93**	**–53.58**	**–58.20**	**–65.57**	**–73.90**	**–73.15**	**–84.94**	**–86.44**
Communications	3 245 ..	–7.41	–7.79	–8.80	–8.85	–8.19	–7.06	–5.97	–4.73
Construction	3 249 ..	–.28	–.35	–.47	–.46	–.56	–.52	–.52	–.48
Insurance	3 253 ..	–4.04	–5.35	–3.89	–5.87	–9.25	–2.69	–8.17	–4.89
Financial	3 260 ..	–1.65	–2.48	–2.92	–3.36	–3.58	–3.42	–4.48	–4.01
Computer and information	3 262 ..	–.22	–.28	–.44	–.83	–.99	–1.06	–1.04	–.66
Royalties and licence fees	3 266 ..	–5.85	–6.93	–7.83	–9.17	–11.24	–12.62	–16.13	–16.36
Other business services	3 268 ..	–16.02	–18.04	–20.43	–22.90	–25.45	–29.96	–32.55	–37.53
Personal, cultural, and recreational	3 287 ..	–.14	–.17	–.18	–.15	–.12	–.12	–.14	–.13
Government, n.i.e.	3 291 ..	–12.32	–12.19	–13.24	–13.98	–14.52	–15.70	–15.94	–17.65

Table 2 (Continued). STANDARD PRESENTATION, 1994–2001

(Billions of U.S. dollars)

	Code	1994	1995	1996	1997	1998	1999	2000	2001
C. INCOME	4 300 . .	16.69	24.62	24.09	20.19	7.64	18.17	21.81	14.37
Total credit	2 300 . .	*165.44*	*211.54*	*225.86*	*260.58*	*259.40*	*290.56*	*353.03*	*283.76*
Total debit	3 300 . .	*−148.75*	*−186.92*	*−201.77*	*−240.39*	*−251.76*	*−272.39*	*−331.22*	*−269.39*
Compensation of employees, credit	2 310 . .	**1.55**	**1.76**	**1.76**	**1.80**	**1.94**	**2.22**	**2.35**	**2.38**
Compensation of employees, debit	3 310 . .	**−5.95**	**−6.28**	**−6.30**	**−6.67**	**−7.00**	**−7.95**	**−8.21**	**−8.54**
Investment income, credit	2 320 . .	**163.89**	**209.78**	**224.10**	**258.78**	**257.46**	**288.34**	**350.68**	**281.38**
Direct investment income	2 330 . .	77.34	95.28	102.51	115.34	103.97	128.46	149.69	126.00
Dividends and distributed branch profits	2 332 . .	44.03	38.90	45.62	55.20	56.74	49.00	44.51	42.26
Reinvested earnings and undistributed branch profits	2 333 . .	31.01	53.92	54.69	58.02	44.17	75.52	101.21	79.67
Income on debt (interest)	2 334 . .	2.30	2.46	2.20	2.12	3.06	3.94	3.97	4.07
Portfolio investment income	2 339 . .	40.50	47.67	53.40	61.83	62.72	70.93	78.39	65.07
Income on equity	2 340 . .	14.57	19.37	23.17	27.95	23.47	30.61	35.75	25.17
Income on bonds and notes	2 350 . .	25.93	28.30	30.23	33.88	39.25	40.32	42.64	39.90
Income on money market instruments	2 360 . .	. . .	. . .	. . .	. . .	. . .	. . .	. . .	. . .
Other investment income	2 370 . .	46.05	66.83	68.19	81.61	90.77	88.95	122.60	90.31
Investment income, debit	3 320 . .	**−142.80**	**−180.64**	**−195.47**	**−233.72**	**−244.76**	**−264.44**	**−323.01**	**−260.85**
Direct investment income	3 330 . .	−22.15	−30.33	−33.09	−42.95	−38.41	−53.45	−60.82	−23.39
Dividends and distributed branch profits	3 332 . .	−10.27	−13.76	−15.49	−18.80	−25.21	−33.91	−34.23	−20.40
Reinvested earnings and undistributed branch profits	3 333 . .	−4.88	−8.43	−8.51	−14.97	−2.84	−4.14	−6.52	19.70
Income on debt (interest)	3 334 . .	−7.00	−8.14	−9.09	−9.18	−10.36	−15.40	−20.07	−22.69
Portfolio investment income	3 339 . .	−69.41	−76.75	−91.27	−109.82	−116.52	−122.92	−143.52	−150.33
Income on equity	3 340 . .	−11.21	−12.03	−13.21	−13.98	−15.76	−17.06	−19.56	−20.74
Income on bonds and notes	3 350 . .	−58.20	−64.72	−78.06	−95.84	−100.76	−105.86	−123.96	−129.59
Income on money market instruments	3 360 . .	. . .	. . .	. . .	. . .	. . .	. . .	. . .	. . .
Other investment income	3 370 . .	−51.24	−73.56	−71.11	−80.95	−89.83	−88.07	−118.67	−87.13
D. CURRENT TRANSFERS	4 379 . .	−38.24	−34.07	−40.09	−40.79	−44.50	−48.76	−53.43	−49.47
Credit	2 379 . .	**6.49**	**7.68**	**8.89**	**8.49**	**9.19**	**9.57**	**10.65**	**10.47**
General government	2 380 . .	. . .	. . .	. . .	. . .	. . .	. . .	. . .	. . .
Other sectors	2 390 . .	6.49	7.68	8.89	8.49	9.19	9.57	10.65	10.47
Workers' remittances	2 391 . .	. . .	. . .	. . .	. . .	. . .	. . .	. . .	. . .
Other current transfers	2 392 . .	6.49	7.68	8.89	8.49	9.19	9.57	10.65	10.47
Debit	3 379 . .	**−44.73**	**−41.75**	**−48.98**	**−49.28**	**−53.69**	**−58.33**	**−64.08**	**−59.94**
General government	3 380 . .	−19.53	−14.65	−19.87	−16.67	−17.58	−18.18	−21.53	−17.43
Other sectors	3 390 . .	−25.20	−27.10	−29.11	−32.61	−36.11	−40.15	−42.55	−42.51
Workers' remittances	3 391 . .	−10.94	−11.84	−12.86	−14.14	−15.56	−17.12	−18.61	−19.89
Other current transfers	3 392 . .	−14.26	−15.26	−16.25	−18.47	−20.55	−23.03	−23.94	−22.62
CAPITAL AND FINANCIAL ACCOUNT	4 996 . .	**129.50**	**86.56**	**137.88**	**219.49**	**64.56**	**261.45**	**410.35**	**382.69**
CAPITAL ACCOUNT	4 994 . .	**−.47**	**.37**	**.69**	**.35**	**.70**	**−3.39**	**.84**	**.83**
Total credit	2 994 . .	*.31*	*.67*	*.69*	*.35*	*.70*	*.60*	*.84*	*.83*
Total debit	3 994 . .	*−.77*	*−.30*	. . .	. . .	. . .	*−3.99*	. . .	. . .
Capital transfers, credit	2 400 . .	**.31**	**.67**	**.69**	**.35**	**.70**	**.60**	**.84**	**.83**
General government	2 401 . .	. . .	. . .	. . .	. . .	. . .	. . .	. . .	. . .
Debt forgiveness	2 402 . .	. . .	. . .	. . .	. . .	. . .	. . .	. . .	. . .
Other capital transfers	2 410 . .	. . .	. . .	. . .	. . .	. . .	. . .	. . .	. . .
Other sectors	2 430 . .	. . .	. . .	. . .	. . .	. . .	. . .	. . .	. . .
Migrants' transfers	2 431 . .	. . .	. . .	. . .	. . .	. . .	. . .	. . .	. . .
Debt forgiveness	2 432 . .	. . .	. . .	. . .	. . .	. . .	. . .	. . .	. . .
Other capital transfers	2 440 . .	. . .	. . .	. . .	. . .	. . .	. . .	. . .	. . .
Capital transfers, debit	3 400 . .	**−.77**	**−.30**	**. . .**	**. . .**	**. . .**	**−3.99**	**. . .**	**. . .**
General government	3 401 . .	−.77	−.30	. . .	. . .	. . .	−3.99	. . .	. . .
Debt forgiveness	3 402 . .	−.77	−.30	. . .	. . .	. . .	−3.99	. . .	. . .
Other capital transfers	3 410 . .	. . .	. . .	. . .	. . .	. . .	. . .	. . .	. . .
Other sectors	3 430 . .	. . .	. . .	. . .	. . .	. . .	. . .	. . .	. . .
Migrants' transfers	3 431 . .	. . .	. . .	. . .	. . .	. . .	. . .	. . .	. . .
Debt forgiveness	3 432 . .	. . .	. . .	. . .	. . .	. . .	. . .	. . .	. . .
Other capital transfers	3 440 . .	. . .	. . .	. . .	. . .	. . .	. . .	. . .	. . .
Nonproduced nonfinancial assets, credit	2 480 . .	**. . .**	**. . .**	**. . .**	**. . .**	**. . .**	**. . .**	**. . .**	**. . .**
Nonproduced nonfinancial assets, debit	3 480 . .	**. . .**	**. . .**	**. . .**	**. . .**	**. . .**	**. . .**	**. . .**	**. . .**

Table 2 (Continued). STANDARD PRESENTATION, 1994–2001

(Billions of U.S. dollars)

	Code		1994	1995	1996	1997	1998	1999	2000	2001
FINANCIAL ACCOUNT	4 995	. .	**129.96**	**86.19**	**137.19**	**219.14**	**63.86**	**264.85**	**409.51**	**381.86**
A. DIRECT INVESTMENT	4 500	. .	–34.05	–40.98	–5.36	.77	36.39	100.53	129.45	2.96
Direct investment abroad	4 505	. .	**–80.18**	**–98.78**	**–91.88**	**–104.82**	**–142.64**	**–188.91**	**–178.29**	**–127.84**
Equity capital	4 510	. .	–33.66	–40.48	–27.54	–40.80	–72.44	–79.18	–66.09	–49.83
Claims on affiliated enterprises	4 515	. .	. . .	. . .	. . .	. . .	. . .	. . .	. . .	. . .
Liabilities to affiliated enterprises	4 520	. .	. . .	. . .	. . .	. . .	. . .	. . .	. . .	. . .
Reinvested earnings	4 525	. .	–31.01	–53.92	–54.69	–58.02	–44.17	–75.52	–101.21	–79.67
Other capital	4 530	. .	–15.51	–4.38	–9.65	–6.00	–26.03	–34.21	–10.99	1.66
Claims on affiliated enterprises	4 535	. .	–25.26	–14.46	–13.95	–17.00	–43.29	–49.05	–15.69	–4.05
Liabilities to affiliated enterprises	4 540	. .	9.75	10.08	4.30	11.00	17.26	14.84	4.70	5.71
Direct investment in United States	4 555	. .	**46.13**	**57.80**	**86.52**	**105.59**	**179.03**	**289.44**	**307.74**	**130.80**
Equity capital	4 560	. .	37.21	47.90	63.73	59.50	147.09	221.56	245.94	107.73
Claims on direct investors	4 565	. .	. . .	. . .	. . .	. . .	. . .	. . .	. . .	. . .
Liabilities to direct investors	4 570	. .	. . .	. . .	. . .	. . .	. . .	. . .	. . .	. . .
Reinvested earnings	4 575	. .	4.88	8.43	8.51	14.97	2.84	4.14	6.52	–19.70
Other capital	4 580	. .	4.04	1.47	14.28	31.12	29.10	63.74	55.28	42.77
Claims on direct investors	4 585	. .	–.06	–1.20	–6.84	–5.56	–14.86	–2.72	–19.03	10.90
Liabilities to direct investors	4 590	. .	4.10	2.67	21.12	36.68	43.96	66.46	74.31	31.87
B. PORTFOLIO INVESTMENT	4 600	. .	79.10	87.85	182.95	214.13	51.45	157.15	292.40	331.40
Assets	4 602	. .	**–60.31**	**–122.51**	**–149.83**	**–118.98**	**–136.13**	**–128.44**	**–127.50**	**–94.66**
Equity securities	4 610	. .	–48.10	–65.41	–82.85	–57.58	–101.28	–114.31	–103.64	–106.81
Monetary authorities	4 611	. .	. . .	. . .	. . .	. . .	. . .	. . .	. . .	. . .
General government	4 612	. .	. . .	. . .	. . .	. . .	. . .	. . .	. . .	. . .
Banks	4 613	. .	. . .	. . .	. . .	. . .	. . .	. . .	. . .	. . .
Other sectors	4 614	. .	. . .	. . .	. . .	. . .	. . .	. . .	. . .	. . .
Debt securities	4 619	. .	–12.21	–57.10	–66.98	–61.40	–34.85	–14.13	–23.86	12.15
Bonds and notes	4 620	. .	–12.21	–57.10	–66.98	–61.40	–34.85	–14.13	–23.86	12.15
Monetary authorities	4 621	. .	. . .	. . .	. . .	. . .	. . .	. . .	. . .	. . .
General government	4 622	. .	. . .	. . .	. . .	. . .	. . .	. . .	. . .	. . .
Banks	4 623	. .	. . .	. . .	. . .	. . .	. . .	. . .	. . .	. . .
Other sectors	4 624	. .	. . .	. . .	. . .	. . .	. . .	. . .	. . .	. . .
Money market instruments	4 630	. .	. . .	. . .	. . .	. . .	. . .	. . .	. . .	. . .
Monetary authorities	4 631	. .	. . .	. . .	. . .	. . .	. . .	. . .	. . .	. . .
General government	4 632	. .	. . .	. . .	. . .	. . .	. . .	. . .	. . .	. . .
Banks	4 633	. .	. . .	. . .	. . .	. . .	. . .	. . .	. . .	. . .
Other sectors	4 634	. .	. . .	. . .	. . .	. . .	. . .	. . .	. . .	. . .
Liabilities	4 652	. .	**139.41**	**210.36**	**332.78**	**333.11**	**187.58**	**285.59**	**419.90**	**426.06**
Equity securities	4 660	. .	.89	16.53	11.06	67.04	41.96	112.29	193.51	121.42
Banks	4 663	. .	. . .	. . .	. . .	. . .	. . .	. . .	. . .	. . .
Other sectors	4 664	. .	. . .	. . .	. . .	. . .	. . .	. . .	. . .	. . .
Debt securities	4 669	. .	138.52	193.83	321.72	266.07	145.62	173.30	226.39	304.64
Bonds and notes	4 670	. .	138.52	193.83	321.72	266.07	145.62	173.30	226.39	304.64
Monetary authorities	4 671	. .	. . .	. . .	. . .	. . .	. . .	. . .	. . .	. . .
General government	4 672	. .	100.47	143.95	251.47	199.21	39.66	30.48	59.99	102.68
Banks	4 673	. .	. . .	. . .	. . .	. . .	. . .	. . .	. . .	. . .
Other sectors	4 674	. .	38.05	49.88	70.25	66.86	105.96	142.82	166.40	201.96
Money market instruments	4 680	. .	. . .	. . .	. . .	. . .	. . .	. . .	. . .	. . .
Monetary authorities	4 681	. .	. . .	. . .	. . .	. . .	. . .	. . .	. . .	. . .
General government	4 682	. .	. . .	. . .	. . .	. . .	. . .	. . .	. . .	. . .
Banks	4 683	. .	. . .	. . .	. . .	. . .	. . .	. . .	. . .	. . .
Other sectors	4 684	. .	. . .	. . .	. . .	. . .	. . .	. . .	. . .	. . .
C. FINANCIAL DERIVATIVES	4 910	. .	. . .	. . .	. . .	. . .	. . .	. . .	. . .	. . .
Monetary authorities	4 911	. .	. . .	. . .	. . .	. . .	. . .	. . .	. . .	. . .
General government	4 912	. .	. . .	. . .	. . .	. . .	. . .	. . .	. . .	. . .
Banks	4 913	. .	. . .	. . .	. . .	. . .	. . .	. . .	. . .	. . .
Other sectors	4 914	. .	. . .	. . .	. . .	. . .	. . .	. . .	. . .	. . .
Assets	4 900	. .	**. . .**	**. . .**	**. . .**	**. . .**	**. . .**	**. . .**	**. . .**	**. . .**
Monetary authorities	4 901	. .	. . .	. . .	. . .	. . .	. . .	. . .	. . .	. . .
General government	4 902	. .	. . .	. . .	. . .	. . .	. . .	. . .	. . .	. . .
Banks	4 903	. .	. . .	. . .	. . .	. . .	. . .	. . .	. . .	. . .
Other sectors	4 904	. .	. . .	. . .	. . .	. . .	. . .	. . .	. . .	. . .
Liabilities	4 905	. .	**. . .**	**. . .**	**. . .**	**. . .**	**. . .**	**. . .**	**. . .**	**. . .**
Monetary authorities	4 906	. .	. . .	. . .	. . .	. . .	. . .	. . .	. . .	. . .
General government	4 907	. .	. . .	. . .	. . .	. . .	. . .	. . .	. . .	. . .
Banks	4 908	. .	. . .	. . .	. . .	. . .	. . .	. . .	. . .	. . .
Other sectors	4 909	. .	. . .	. . .	. . .	. . .	. . .	. . .	. . .	. . .

Table 2 (Concluded). STANDARD PRESENTATION, 1994–2001
(Billions of U.S. dollars)

	Code	1994	1995	1996	1997	1998	1999	2000	2001
D. OTHER INVESTMENT	4 700 . .	79.56	49.07	–47.07	5.26	–17.24	–1.57	–12.04	52.43
Assets	4 703 . .	**–40.90**	**–121.38**	**–178.90**	**–262.83**	**–74.21**	**–169.00**	**–300.40**	**–143.54**
Trade credits	4 706 . .	–2.73	–1.84	–2.75	–1.79	.33	–5.43	–.47	5.52
General government	4 707 . .	. . .	. . .	. . .	. . .	. . .	. . .	. . .	. . .
of which: Short-term	4 709 . .	. . .	. . .	. . .	. . .	. . .	. . .	. . .	. . .
Other sectors	4 710 . .	–2.73	–1.84	–2.75	–1.79	.33	–5.43	–.47	5.52
of which: Short-term	4 712 . .	*–2.73*	*–1.84*	*–2.75*	*–1.79*	*.33*	*–5.43*	*–.47*	*5.52*
Loans	4 714 . .	–.30	–.74	–1.10	.02	–.57	3.38	–.91	–.55
Monetary authorities	4 715 . .	. . .	. . .	. . .	. . .	. . .	. . .	. . .	. . .
of which: Short-term	4 718 . .	. . .	. . .	. . .	. . .	. . .	. . .	. . .	. . .
General government	4 719 . .	–.30	–.74	–1.10	.02	–.57	3.38	–.91	–.55
of which: Short-term	4 721 . .	. . .	. . .	. . .	. . .	. . .	. . .	. . .	. . .
Banks	4 722 . .	. . .	. . .	. . .	. . .	. . .	. . .	. . .	. . .
of which: Short-term	4 724 . .	. . .	. . .	. . .	. . .	. . .	. . .	. . .	. . .
Other sectors	4 725 . .	. . .	. . .	. . .	. . .	. . .	. . .	. . .	. . .
of which: Short-term	4 727 . .	. . .	. . .	. . .	. . .	. . .	. . .	. . .	. . .
Currency and deposits	4 730 . .	–4.29	–75.35	–91.46	–141.09	–35.43	–76.90	–148.69	–128.63
Monetary authorities	4 731 . .	. . .	. . .	. . .	. . .	. . .	. . .	. . .	. . .
General government	4 732 . .	–.09	–.24	.10	.04	.15	–.63	–.03	.07
Banks	4 733 . .	–4.20	–75.11	–91.56	–141.13	–35.58	–76.27	–148.66	–128.70
Other sectors	4 734 . .	. . .	. . .	. . .	. . .	. . .	. . .	. . .	. . .
Other assets	4 736 . .	–33.58	–43.45	–83.59	–119.97	–38.54	–90.05	–150.33	–19.88
Monetary authorities	4 737 . .	. . .	. . .	. . .	. . .	. . .	. . .	. . .	. . .
of which: Short-term	4 739 . .	. . .	. . .	. . .	. . .	. . .	. . .	. . .	. . .
General government	4 740 . .	.02	. . .	. . .	. . .	. . .	. . .	. . .	. . .
of which: Short-term	4 742 . .	. . .	. . .	. . .	. . .	. . .	. . .	. . .	. . .
Banks	4 743 . .	. . .	. . .	. . .	. . .	. . .	. . .	. . .	. . .
of which: Short-term	4 745 . .	. . .	. . .	. . .	. . .	. . .	. . .	. . .	. . .
Other sectors	4 746 . .	–33.60	–43.45	–83.59	–119.97	–38.54	–90.05	–150.33	–19.88
of which: Short-term	4 748 . .	*–33.60*	*–43.45*	*–83.59*	*–119.97*	*–38.54*	*–90.05*	*–150.33*	*–19.88*
Liabilities	4 753 . .	**120.46**	**170.45**	**131.83**	**268.09**	**56.97**	**167.43**	**288.36**	**195.97**
Trade credits	4 756 . .	1.21	1.00	1.71	–1.82	.07	1.89	1.43	–2.47
General government	4 757 . .	1.21	1.00	1.71	–1.82	.07	1.89	1.43	–2.47
of which: Short-term	4 759 . .	*1.21*	*1.00*	*1.71*	*–1.82*	*.07*	*1.89*	*1.43*	*–2.47*
Other sectors	4 760 . .	. . .	. . .	. . .	. . .	. . .	. . .	. . .	. . .
of which: Short-term	4 762 . .	. . .	. . .	. . .	. . .	. . .	. . .	. . .	. . .
Loans	4 764 . .	. . .	. . .	. . .	. . .	. . .	. . .	. . .	. . .
Monetary authorities	4 765 . .	. . .	. . .	. . .	. . .	. . .	. . .	. . .	. . .
of which: Use of Fund credit and loans from the Fund	4 766 . .	. . .	. . .	. . .	. . .	. . .	. . .	. . .	. . .
of which: Short-term	4 768 . .	. . .	. . .	. . .	. . .	. . .	. . .	. . .	. . .
General government	4 769 . .	. . .	. . .	. . .	. . .	. . .	. . .	. . .	. . .
of which: Short-term	4 771 . .	. . .	. . .	. . .	. . .	. . .	. . .	. . .	. . .
Banks	4 772 . .	. . .	. . .	. . .	. . .	. . .	. . .	. . .	. . .
of which: Short-term	4 774 . .	. . .	. . .	. . .	. . .	. . .	. . .	. . .	. . .
Other sectors	4 775 . .	. . .	. . .	. . .	. . .	. . .	. . .	. . .	. . .
of which: Short-term	4 777 . .	. . .	. . .	. . .	. . .	. . .	. . .	. . .	. . .
Currency and deposits	4 780 . .	131.40	76.49	39.55	196.10	46.90	89.60	123.85	104.17
Monetary authorities	4 781 . .	23.40	12.30	17.36	24.78	16.63	22.41	1.13	23.78
General government	4 782 . .	. . .	. . .	. . .	. . .	. . .	. . .	. . .	. . .
Banks	4 783 . .	108.00	64.19	22.19	171.32	30.27	67.19	122.72	80.39
Other sectors	4 784 . .	. . .	. . .	. . .	. . .	. . .	. . .	. . .	. . .
Other liabilities	4 786 . .	–12.15	92.96	90.57	73.81	10.00	75.94	163.08	94.27
Monetary authorities	4 787 . .	–13.81	34.43	39.52	–43.64	–9.74	2.18	–7.83	11.32
of which: Short-term	4 789 . .	*–13.81*	*34.43*	*39.52*	*–43.64*	*–9.74*	*2.18*	*–7.83*	*11.32*
General government	4 790 . .	1.56	–.11	–.98	–.88	–3.33	–2.74	–1.91	–1.88
of which: Short-term	4 792 . .	*1.56*	*–.11*	*–.98*	*–.88*	*–3.33*	*–2.74*	*–1.91*	*–1.88*
Banks	4 793 . .	. . .	. . .	. . .	. . .	. . .	. . .	. . .	. . .
of which: Short-term	4 795 . .	. . .	. . .	. . .	. . .	. . .	. . .	. . .	. . .
Other sectors	4 796 . .	.10	58.63	52.03	118.33	23.07	76.50	172.82	84.83
of which: Short-term	4 798 . .	*.10*	*58.63*	*52.03*	*118.33*	*23.07*	*76.50*	*172.82*	*84.83*
E. RESERVE ASSETS	4 802 . .	5.35	–9.75	6.67	–1.02	–6.74	8.73	–.30	–4.93
Monetary gold	4 812 . .	. . .	. . .	. . .	. . .	. . .	. . .	. . .	. . .
Special drawing rights	4 811 . .	–.44	–.81	.37	–.35	–.14	. . .	–.72	–.63
Reserve position in the fund	4 810 . .	.50	–2.47	–1.28	–3.58	–5.07	5.48	2.30	–3.62
Foreign exchange	4 803 . .	5.29	–6.47	7.58	2.91	–1.53	3.26	–1.88	–.68
Other claims	4 813 . .	. . .	. . .	. . .	. . .	. . .	. . .	. . .	. . .
NET ERRORS AND OMISSIONS	4 998 . .	**–11.30**	**19.26**	**–20.04**	**–91.13**	**139.29**	**31.41**	**–.05**	**10.70**

Part 3 of the *Yearbook* contains descriptions of the methodologies, compilation practices, and sources used to compile these data.

Table 3. INTERNATIONAL INVESTMENT POSITION (End-period stocks), 1994–2001

(Billions of U.S. dollars)

	Code	1994	1995	1996	1997	1998	1999	2000	2001
ASSETS	8 995 C.	3,326.66	3,930.28	4,631.28	5,379.14	6,174.46	7,387.01	7,350.86	6,862.95
Direct investment abroad	8 505 . .	**1,114.58**	**1,363.79**	**1,608.34**	**1,879.29**	**2,279.60**	**2,805.22**	**2,674.21**	**2,289.93**
Equity capital and reinvested earnings	8 506 . .	. . .	. . .	. . .	. . .	. . .	. . .	. . .	. . .
Claims on affiliated enterprises	8 507 . .	. . .	. . .	. . .	. . .	. . .	. . .	. . .	. . .
Liabilities to affiliated enterprises	8 508 . .	. . .	. . .	. . .	. . .	. . .	. . .	. . .	. . .
Other capital	8 530 . .	. . .	. . .	. . .	. . .	. . .	. . .	. . .	. . .
Claims on affiliated enterprises	8 535 . .	. . .	. . .	. . .	. . .	. . .	. . .	. . .	. . .
Liabilities to affiliated enterprises	8 540 . .	. . .	. . .	. . .	. . .	. . .	. . .	. . .	. . .
Portfolio investment	8 602 . .	**948.67**	**1,169.64**	**1,467.99**	**1,751.19**	**2,052.93**	**2,583.33**	**2,389.43**	**2,110.52**
Equity securities	8 610 . .	627.46	776.81	1,002.93	1,207.79	1,476.18	2,026.64	1,832.41	1,564.74
Monetary authorities	8 611 . .	. . .	. . .	. . .	. . .	. . .	. . .	. . .	. . .
General government	8 612 . .	. . .	. . .	. . .	. . .	. . .	. . .	. . .	. . .
Banks	8 613 . .	. . .	. . .	. . .	. . .	. . .	. . .	. . .	. . .
Other sectors	8 614 . .	. . .	. . .	. . .	. . .	. . .	. . .	. . .	. . .
Debt securities	8 619 . .	321.21	392.83	465.06	543.40	576.75	556.69	557.02	545.78
Bonds and notes	8 620 . .	321.21	392.83	465.06	543.40	576.75	556.69	557.02	545.78
Monetary authorities	8 621 . .	. . .	. . .	. . .	. . .	. . .	. . .	. . .	. . .
General government	8 622 . .	. . .	. . .	. . .	. . .	. . .	. . .	. . .	. . .
Banks	8 623 . .	. . .	. . .	. . .	. . .	. . .	. . .	. . .	. . .
Other sectors	8 624 . .	. . .	. . .	. . .	. . .	. . .	. . .	. . .	. . .
Money market instruments	8 630 . .	. . .	. . .	. . .	. . .	. . .	. . .	. . .	. . .
Monetary authorities	8 631 . .	. . .	. . .	. . .	. . .	. . .	. . .	. . .	. . .
General government	8 632 . .	. . .	. . .	. . .	. . .	. . .	. . .	. . .	. . .
Banks	8 633 . .	. . .	. . .	. . .	. . .	. . .	. . .	. . .	. . .
Other sectors	8 634 . .	. . .	. . .	. . .	. . .	. . .	. . .	. . .	. . .
Financial derivatives	8 900 . .	**. . .**	**. . .**	**. . .**	**. . .**	**. . .**	**. . .**	**. . .**	**. . .**
Monetary authorities	8 901 . .	. . .	. . .	. . .	. . .	. . .	. . .	. . .	. . .
General government	8 902 . .	. . .	. . .	. . .	. . .	. . .	. . .	. . .	. . .
Banks	8 903 . .	. . .	. . .	. . .	. . .	. . .	. . .	. . .	. . .
Other sectors	8 904 . .	. . .	. . .	. . .	. . .	. . .	. . .	. . .	. . .
Other investment	8 703 . .	**1,100.01**	**1,220.78**	**1,394.21**	**1,613.83**	**1,695.92**	**1,862.01**	**2,158.82**	**2,332.54**
Trade credits	8 706 . .	21.16	23.00	25.75	27.54	27.20	32.63	33.10	27.60
General government	8 707 . .	. . .	. . .	. . .	. . .	. . .	. . .	. . .	. . .
of which: Short-term	8 709 . .	. . .	. . .	. . .	. . .	. . .	. . .	. . .	. . .
Other sectors	8 710 . .	21.16	23.00	25.75	27.54	27.20	32.63	33.10	27.60
of which: Short-term	8 712 . .	. . .	. . .	. . .	. . .	. . .	. . .	. . .	. . .
Loans	8 714 . .	1,078.85	1,197.78	1,368.46	1,586.29	1,668.72	1,829.38	2,125.72	2,304.94
Monetary authorities	8 715 . .	. . .	. . .	. . .	. . .	. . .	. . .	. . .	. . .
of which: Short-term	8 718 . .	. . .	. . .	. . .	. . .	. . .	. . .	. . .	. . .
General government	8 719 . .	83.91	85.06	86.12	86.20	86.77	84.22	85.16	85.65
of which: Short-term	8 721 . .	. . .	. . .	. . .	. . .	. . .	. . .	. . .	. . .
Banks	8 722 . .	693.12	768.15	857.51	982.10	1,020.83	1,100.29	1,252.10	1,416.78
of which: Short-term	8 724 . .	. . .	. . .	. . .	. . .	. . .	. . .	. . .	. . .
Other sectors	8 725 . .	301.82	344.57	424.83	517.99	561.12	644.87	788.46	802.51
of which: Short-term	8 727 . .	. . .	. . .	. . .	. . .	. . .	. . .	. . .	. . .
Currency and deposits	8 730 . .	. . .	. . .	. . .	. . .	. . .	. . .	. . .	. . .
Monetary authorities	8 731 . .	. . .	. . .	. . .	. . .	. . .	. . .	. . .	. . .
General government	8 732 . .	. . .	. . .	. . .	. . .	. . .	. . .	. . .	. . .
Banks	8 733 . .	. . .	. . .	. . .	. . .	. . .	. . .	. . .	. . .
Other sectors	8 734 . .	. . .	. . .	. . .	. . .	. . .	. . .	. . .	. . .
Other assets	8 736 . .	. . .	. . .	. . .	. . .	. . .	. . .	. . .	. . .
Monetary authorities	8 737 . .	. . .	. . .	. . .	. . .	. . .	. . .	. . .	. . .
of which: Short-term	8 739 . .	. . .	. . .	. . .	. . .	. . .	. . .	. . .	. . .
General government	8 740 . .	. . .	. . .	. . .	. . .	. . .	. . .	. . .	. . .
of which: Short-term	8 742 . .	. . .	. . .	. . .	. . .	. . .	. . .	. . .	. . .
Banks	8 743 . .	. . .	. . .	. . .	. . .	. . .	. . .	. . .	. . .
of which: Short-term	8 745 . .	. . .	. . .	. . .	. . .	. . .	. . .	. . .	. . .
Other sectors	8 746 . .	. . .	. . .	. . .	. . .	. . .	. . .	. . .	. . .
of which: Short-term	8 748 . .	. . .	. . .	. . .	. . .	. . .	. . .	. . .	. . .
Reserve assets	8 802 . .	**163.40**	**176.07**	**160.74**	**134.84**	**146.00**	**136.45**	**128.40**	**129.96**
Monetary gold	8 812 . .	100.11	101.28	96.70	75.93	75.29	75.95	71.80	72.33
Special drawing rights	8 811 . .	10.04	11.04	10.31	10.03	10.60	10.35	10.54	10.78
Reserve position in the Fund	8 810 . .	12.03	14.65	15.43	18.07	24.11	17.97	14.82	17.87
Foreign exchange	8 803 . .	41.22	49.10	38.29	30.81	36.00	32.18	31.24	28.98
Other claims	8 813 . .	. . .	. . .	. . .	. . .	. . .	. . .	. . .	. . .

Table 3 (Concluded). INTERNATIONAL INVESTMENT POSITION (End-period stocks), 1994–2001

(Billions of U.S. dollars)

	Code	1994	1995	1996	1997	1998	1999	2000	2001
LIABILITIES	8 995 D.	3,450.40	4,273.60	5,017.81	6,214.33	7,268.62	8,440.52	8,934.03	9,172.06
Direct investment in United States	8 555 ..	**757.85**	**1,005.73**	**1,229.12**	**1,637.41**	**2,179.04**	**2,798.19**	**2,766.04**	**2,526.71**
Equity capital and reinvested earnings	8 556 ..	...	...	...	...	...	...	...	...
Claims on direct investors	8 557 ..	...	...	...	...	...	...	...	...
Liabilities to direct investors	8 558 ..	...	...	...	...	...	...	...	...
Other capital	8 580 ..	...	...	...	...	...	...	...	...
Claims on direct investors	8 585 ..	...	...	...	...	...	...	...	...
Liabilities to direct investors	8 590 ..	...	...	...	...	...	...	...	...
Portfolio investment	8 652 ..	**1,413.55**	**1,851.96**	**2,291.09**	**2,779.96**	**3,217.38**	**3,605.14**	**3,866.35**	**4,132.18**
Equity securities	8 660 ..	397.72	549.51	672.40	952.89	1,250.34	1,611.53	1,625.53	1,533.84
Banks	8 663 ..	...	...	...	...	...	...	...	...
Other sectors	8 664 ..	...	...	...	...	...	...	...	...
Debt securities	8 669 ..	1,015.83	1,302.45	1,618.69	1,827.07	1,967.04	1,993.61	2,240.82	2,598.34
Bonds and notes	8 670 ..	1,015.83	1,302.45	1,618.69	1,827.07	1,967.04	1,993.61	2,240.82	2,598.34
Monetary authorities	8 671 ..	632.57	820.16	1,047.26	1,165.69	1,184.96	1,080.44	1,026.13	1,039.48
General government	8 672 ..	107.55	135.59	163.09	191.17	195.92	241.70	380.15	494.65
Banks	8 673 ..	...	...	...	...	...	...	...	...
Other sectors	8 674 ..	275.71	346.70	408.34	470.21	586.16	671.47	834.54	1,064.21
Money market instruments	8 680 ..	...	...	...	...	...	...	...	...
Monetary authorities	8 681 ..	...	...	...	...	...	...	...	...
General government	8 682 ..	...	...	...	...	...	...	...	...
Banks	8 683 ..	...	...	...	...	...	...	...	...
Other sectors	8 684 ..	...	...	...	...	...	...	...	...
Financial derivatives	8 905 ..	...	...	...	...	...	...	...	...
Monetary authorities	8 906 ..	...	...	...	...	...	...	...	...
General government	8 907 ..	...	...	...	...	...	...	...	...
Banks	8 908 ..	...	...	...	...	...	...	...	...
Other sectors	8 909 ..	...	...	...	...	...	...	...	...
Other investment	8 753 ..	**1,279.00**	**1,415.91**	**1,497.60**	**1,796.96**	**1,872.20**	**2,037.19**	**2,301.64**	**2,513.17**
Trade credits	8 756 ..	10.01	11.01	12.72	10.90	10.98	12.86	14.29	11.82
General government	8 757 ..	...	...	...	...	...	...	...	...
of which: Short-term	8 759 ..	...	...	...	...	...	...	...	...
Other sectors	8 760 ..	10.01	11.01	12.72	10.90	10.98	12.86	14.29	11.82
of which: Short-term	8 762 ..	...	...	...	...	...	...	...	...
Loans	8 764 ..	...	...	...	...	...	...	...	...
Monetary authorities	8 765 ..	...	...	...	...	...	...	...	...
of which: Use of Fund credit and loans from the Fund	8 766 ..	...	...	...	...	...	...	...	...
of which: Short-term	8 768 ..	...	...	...	...	...	...	...	...
General government	8 769 ..	...	...	...	...	...	...	...	...
of which: Short-term	8 771 ..	...	...	...	...	...	...	...	...
Banks	8 772 ..	...	...	...	...	...	...	...	...
of which: Short-term	8 774 ..	...	...	...	...	...	...	...	...
Other sectors	8 775 ..	...	...	...	...	...	...	...	...
of which: Short-term	8 777 ..	...	...	...	...	...	...	...	...
Currency and deposits	8 780 ..	157.19	169.48	186.85	211.63	228.25	250.66	251.79	275.57
Monetary authorities	8 781 ..	157.19	169.48	186.85	211.63	228.25	250.66	251.79	275.57
General government	8 782 ..	...	...	...	...	...	...	...	...
Banks	8 783 ..	...	...	...	...	...	...	...	...
Other sectors	8 784 ..	...	...	...	...	...	...	...	...
Other liabilities	8 786 ..	1,111.80	1,235.42	1,298.03	1,574.43	1,632.97	1,773.67	2,035.56	2,225.78
Monetary authorities	8 787 ..	...	...	...	...	...	...	...	...
of which: Short-term	8 789 ..	...	...	...	...	...	...	...	...
General government	8 790 ..	23.68	23.57	22.59	21.71	18.39	15.65	13.74	11.86
of which: Short-term	8 792 ..	...	...	...	...	...	...	...	...
Banks	8 793 ..	858.31	922.44	941.35	1,104.22	1,139.88	1,206.00	1,306.77	1,421.32
of which: Short-term	8 795 ..	...	...	...	...	...	...	...	...
Other sectors	8 796 ..	229.81	289.41	334.09	448.50	474.70	552.02	715.05	792.60
of which: Short-term	8 798 ..	...	...	...	...	...	...	...	...
NET INTERNATIONAL INVESTMENT POSITION	8 995 ..	**–123.74**	**–343.32**	**–386.53**	**–835.19**	**–1,094.16**	**–1,053.52**	**–1,583.17**	**–2,309.11**

Table 1. ANALYTIC PRESENTATION, 1994–2001
(Millions of U.S. dollars)

	Code	1994	1995	1996	1997	1998	1999	2000	2001
A. Current Account[1]	4 993 Z.	**–438.3**	**–212.5**	**–233.4**	**–287.4**	**–475.5**	**–507.6**	**–566.2**	**–512.5**
Goods: exports f.o.b	2 100 . .	1,917.6	2,147.6	2,448.5	2,793.1	2,829.3	2,290.6	2,383.8	2,143.6
Goods: imports f.o.b	3 100 . .	–2,623.6	–2,710.6	–3,135.4	–3,497.5	–3,601.4	–3,187.2	–3,311.1	–2,914.5
Balance on Goods	4 100 . .	*–706.0*	*–563.0*	*–686.9*	*–704.4*	*–772.1*	*–896.6*	*–927.3*	*–770.9*
Services: credit	2 200 . .	1,330.7	1,359.2	1,398.7	1,424.1	1,319.1	1,261.6	1,275.7	1,132.2
Services: debit	3 200 . .	–861.6	–857.7	–839.0	–888.6	–883.6	–802.3	–881.8	–803.2
Balance on Goods and Services	4 991 . .	*–236.9*	*–61.5*	*–127.2*	*–168.9*	*–336.6*	*–437.3*	*–533.4*	*–441.9*
Income: credit	2 300 . .	282.5	404.3	460.5	547.3	608.0	735.5	781.5	827.3
Income: debit	3 300 . .	–525.1	–631.3	–649.2	–740.0	–805.9	–879.3	–841.8	–941.1
Balance on Goods, Services, and Income	4 992 . .	*–479.5*	*–288.5*	*–315.9*	*–361.6*	*–534.5*	*–581.1*	*–593.7*	*–555.7*
Current transfers: credit	2 379 Z.	49.2	84.0	90.7	83.0	75.0	78.4	48.0	48.0
Current transfers: debit	3 379 . .	–8.0	–8.0	–8.2	–8.8	–16.0	–4.9	–20.5	–4.8
B. Capital Account[1]	4 994 Z.	**. . .**	**. . .**	**. . .**	**. . .**	**. . .**	**. . .**	**. . .**	**. . .**
Capital account: credit	2 994 Z.	. . .	. . .	. . .	. . .	. . .	. . .	. . .	. . .
Capital account: debit	3 994 . .	. . .	. . .	. . .	. . .	. . .	. . .	. . .	. . .
Total, Groups A Plus B	4 981 . .	*–438.3*	*–212.5*	*–233.4*	*–287.4*	*–475.5*	*–507.6*	*–566.2*	*–512.5*
C. Financial Account[1]	4 995 W.	**537.2**	**421.7**	**233.6**	**608.7**	**545.1**	**147.1**	**779.3**	**799.6**
Direct investment abroad	4 505 . .	. . .	. . .	. . .	–13.2	–9.3	. . .	.6	1.1
Direct investment in Uruguay	4 555 Z.	154.5	156.6	136.8	126.4	164.1	235.3	273.5	318.2
Portfolio investment assets	4 602 . .	. . .	. . .	. . .	. . .	. . .	–44.3	–98.1	249.8
Equity securities	4 610 . .	. . .	. . .	. . .	. . .	. . .	. . .	. . .	. . .
Debt securities	4 619 . .	. . .	. . .	. . .	. . .	. . .	–44.3	–98.1	249.8
Portfolio investment liabilities	4 652 Z.	158.1	288.8	179.9	209.6	419.4	128.2	289.5	281.3
Equity securities	4 660 . .	. . .	. . .	. . .	. . .	. . .	. . .	. . .	. . .
Debt securities	4 669 Z.	158.1	288.8	179.9	209.6	419.4	128.2	289.5	281.3
Financial derivatives	4 910 . .	. . .	. . .	. . .	. . .	. . .	. . .	. . .	. . .
Financial derivatives assets	4 900 . .	. . .	. . .	. . .	. . .	. . .	. . .	. . .	. . .
Financial derivatives liabilities	4 905 . .	. . .	. . .	. . .	. . .	. . .	. . .	. . .	. . .
Other investment assets	4 703 . .	–71.8	–961.9	–1,238.5	–626.6	–428.0	–119.3	–690.4	–1,991.1
Monetary authorities	4 701 . .	–10.1	. . .	. . .	. . .	. . .	. . .	.9	–5.3
General government	4 704 . .	. . .	. . .	. . .	. . .	. . .	. . .	. . .	. . .
Banks	4 705 . .	–44.0	–961.3	–1,232.4	–636.4	–428.0	65.4	–549.3	–1,904.8
Other sectors	4 728 . .	–17.7	–.6	–6.1	9.8	. . .	–184.7	–142.0	–81.0
Other investment liabilities	4 753 W.	296.4	938.2	1,155.4	912.5	398.9	–52.8	1,004.2	1,940.3
Monetary authorities	4 753 WA	5.7	–62.5	–10.3	–31.3	–37.2	–135.7	–38.8	–47.0
General government	4 753 ZB	134.0	18.6	20.3	96.8	169.1	260.5	200.7	144.5
Banks	4 753 ZC	99.8	1,017.9	1,112.9	778.9	272.9	–161.3	862.5	1,733.2
Other sectors	4 753 ZD	56.9	–35.8	32.5	68.1	–5.9	–16.3	–20.2	109.6
Total, Groups A Through C	4 983 . .	*98.9*	*209.2*	*.2*	*321.3*	*69.6*	*–360.5*	*213.1*	*287.1*
D. Net Errors and Omissions	4 998 . .	**10.2**	**18.6**	**152.2**	**78.8**	**285.5**	**250.9**	**–46.6**	**16.5**
Total, Groups A Through D	4 984 . .	*109.1*	*227.8*	*152.4*	*400.1*	*355.1*	*–109.6*	*166.5*	*303.6*
E. Reserves and Related Items	4 802 A.	**–109.1**	**–227.8**	**–152.4**	**–400.1**	**–355.1**	**109.6**	**–166.5**	**–303.6**
Reserve assets	4 802 . .	–98.5	–218.0	–140.8	–391.7	–515.2	109.6	–166.5	–303.6
Use of Fund credit and loans	4 766 . .	–10.6	–9.8	–11.6	–8.3	160.1	. . .	. . .	. . .
Exceptional financing	4 920 . .	. . .	. . .	. . .	. . .	. . .	. . .	. . .	. . .
Conversion rates: Uruguayan pesos per U.S. dollar	0 101 . .	**5.0439**	**6.3490**	**7.9718**	**9.4418**	**10.4719**	**11.3393**	**12.0996**	**13.3191**

[1] Excludes components that have been classified in the categories of Group E.

Table 2. STANDARD PRESENTATION, 1994–2001

(Millions of U.S. dollars)

	Code	1994	1995	1996	1997	1998	1999	2000	2001
CURRENT ACCOUNT	4 993 . .	**–438.3**	**–212.5**	**–233.4**	**–287.4**	**–475.5**	**–507.6**	**–566.2**	**–512.5**
A. GOODS	4 100 . .	–706.0	–563.0	–686.9	–704.4	–772.1	–896.6	–927.3	–770.9
Credit	2 100 . .	**1,917.6**	**2,147.6**	**2,448.5**	**2,793.1**	**2,829.3**	**2,290.6**	**2,383.8**	**2,143.6**
General merchandise: exports f.o.b.	2 110 . .	1,913.4	2,106.0	2,397.2	2,729.5	2,768.9	2,236.6	2,299.5	2,060.4
Goods for processing: exports f.o.b.	2 150 . .	. . .	. . .	. . .	. . .	. . .	. . .	. . .	. . .
Repairs on goods	2 160 . .	. . .	. . .	. . .	. . .	. . .	. . .	. . .	. . .
Goods procured in ports by carriers	2 170 . .	4.2	41.6	51.3	63.6	60.4	54.0	84.3	83.2
Nonmonetary gold	2 180 . .	. . .	. . .	. . .	. . .	. . .	. . .	. . .	. . .
Debit	3 100 . .	**–2,623.6**	**–2,710.6**	**–3,135.4**	**–3,497.5**	**–3,601.4**	**–3,187.2**	**–3,311.1**	**–2,914.5**
General merchandise: imports f.o.b.	3 110 . .	–2,599.6	–2,678.3	–3,109.7	–3,477.6	–3,574.3	–3,160.2	–3,276.4	–2,883.8
Goods for processing: imports f.o.b.	3 150 . .	. . .	. . .	. . .	. . .	. . .	. . .	. . .	. . .
Repairs on goods	3 160 . .	. . .	. . .	. . .	. . .	. . .	. . .	. . .	. . .
Goods procured in ports by carriers	3 170 . .	–24.0	–32.3	–25.7	–19.9	–27.1	–27.0	–34.7	–30.7
Nonmonetary gold	3 180 . .	. . .	. . .	. . .	. . .	. . .	. . .	. . .	. . .
B. SERVICES	4 200 . .	469.1	501.5	559.7	535.5	435.5	459.3	393.9	329.0
Total credit	2 200 . .	*1,330.7*	*1,359.2*	*1,398.7*	*1,424.1*	*1,319.1*	*1,261.6*	*1,275.7*	*1,132.2*
Total debit	3 200 . .	*–861.6*	*–857.7*	*–839.0*	*–888.6*	*–883.6*	*–802.3*	*–881.8*	*–803.2*
Transportation services, credit	2 205 . .	**392.7**	**399.3**	**394.1**	**342.8**	**253.0**	**261.0**	**374.3**	**337.1**
Passenger	2 850 . .	*88.7*	*114.1*	*173.1*	*102.7*	. . .	. . .	*114.0*	*82.5*
Freight	2 851 . .	*205.4*	*184.2*	*132.7*	*155.0*	. . .	. . .	*165.7*	*170.5*
Other	2 852 . .	*98.6*	*101.0*	*88.3*	*85.1*	. . .	. . .	*94.6*	*84.1*
Sea transport, passenger	2 207 . .	. . .	51.7	52.2	60.3	. . .	. . .	. . .	. . .
Sea transport, freight	2 208 . .	205.4	184.2	104.1	128.8	. . .	. . .	. . .	. . .
Sea transport, other	2 209 . .	98.6	101.0	37.4	50.7	. . .	. . .	. . .	. . .
Air transport, passenger	2 211 . .	43.6	60.2	117.2	39.6	. . .	. . .	. . .	. . .
Air transport, freight	2 212 . .	. . .	. . .	2.0	2.9	. . .	. . .	. . .	. . .
Air transport, other	2 213 . .	. . .	. . .	47.8	34.1	. . .	. . .	. . .	. . .
Other transport, passenger	2 215 . .	45.1	2.2	3.7	2.8	. . .	. . .	114.0	82.5
Other transport, freight	2 216 . .	. . .	. . .	26.6	23.3	. . .	. . .	165.7	170.5
Other transport, other	2 217 . .	. . .	. . .	3.1	.3	. . .	. . .	94.6	84.1
Transportation services, debit	3 205 . .	**–376.2**	**–376.4**	**–445.9**	**–425.9**	**–362.3**	**–316.8**	**–399.5**	**–359.0**
Passenger	3 850 . .	*–87.0*	*–96.2*	*–146.9*	*–126.7*	. . .	. . .	*–99.8*	*–77.2*
Freight	3 851 . .	*–130.7*	*–120.2*	*–150.3*	*–173.2*	. . .	. . .	*–151.5*	*–136.4*
Other	3 852 . .	*–158.5*	*–160.0*	*–148.7*	*–126.0*	. . .	. . .	*–148.2*	*–145.4*
Sea transport, passenger	3 207 . .	. . .	. . .	–.1	–.1	. . .	. . .	. . .	. . .
Sea transport, freight	3 208 . .	–130.7	–120.2	–117.0	–143.0	. . .	. . .	. . .	. . .
Sea transport, other	3 209 . .	–158.5	–160.0	–94.9	–101.8	. . .	. . .	. . .	. . .
Air transport, passenger	3 211 . .	–84.2	–93.9	–144.8	–124.2	. . .	. . .	. . .	. . .
Air transport, freight	3 212 . .	. . .	. . .	–8.0	–7.2	. . .	. . .	. . .	. . .
Air transport, other	3 213 . .	. . .	. . .	–38.5	–22.0	. . .	. . .	. . .	. . .
Other transport, passenger	3 215 . .	–2.8	–2.3	–2.0	–2.4	. . .	. . .	–99.8	–77.2
Other transport, freight	3 216 . .	. . .	. . .	–25.3	–23.0	. . .	. . .	–151.5	–136.4
Other transport, other	3 217 . .	. . .	. . .	–15.3	–2.2	. . .	. . .	–148.2	–145.4
Travel, credit	2 236 . .	**632.0**	**610.9**	**716.8**	**759.3**	**694.9**	**652.7**	**712.8**	**610.5**
Business travel	2 237 . .	. . .	. . .	. . .	. . .	. . .	. . .	. . .	. . .
Personal travel	2 240 . .	632.0	610.9	716.8	759.3	694.9	652.7	712.8	610.5
Travel, debit	3 236 . .	**–234.0**	**–236.0**	**–192.0**	**–264.1**	**–265.0**	**–279.7**	**–281.4**	**–251.8**
Business travel	3 237 . .	. . .	. . .	. . .	. . .	. . .	. . .	. . .	. . .
Personal travel	3 240 . .	–234.0	–236.0	–192.0	–264.1	–265.0	–279.7	–281.4	–251.8
Other services, credit	2 200 BA	**306.0**	**349.0**	**287.8**	**322.0**	**371.2**	**347.9**	**188.6**	**184.6**
Communications	2 245 . .	. . .	66.8	63.8	58.8	50.0	43.8	27.4	29.7
Construction	2 249 . .	. . .	. . .	. . .	. . .	. . .	. . .	. . .	. . .
Insurance	2 253 . .	16.0	19.5	10.9	39.9	41.0	33.9	32.8	22.1
Financial	2 260 . .	. . .	. . .	56.0	82.4	84.8	73.7	62.0	69.8
Computer and information	2 262 . .	. . .	. . .	. . .	. . .	. . .	13.7	10.0	16.8
Royalties and licence fees	2 266 . .	.5	. . .	. . .	. . .	. . .	. . .	.1	.1
Other business services	2 268 . .	282.7	212.6	146.7	130.0	184.7	155.6	24.4	22.1
Personal, cultural, and recreational	2 287 . .	. . .	. . .	. . .	. . .	.1	.1	4.7	3.7
Government, n.i.e.	2 291 . .	6.8	50.1	10.4	10.9	10.6	27.1	27.2	20.3
Other services, debit	3 200 BA	**–251.4**	**–245.3**	**–201.1**	**–198.6**	**–256.3**	**–205.8**	**–200.9**	**–192.4**
Communications	3 245 . .	. . .	–48.8	–49.4	–48.1	–39.7	–38.9	–22.8	–23.3
Construction	3 249 . .	. . .	. . .	. . .	. . .	. . .	. . .	. . .	. . .
Insurance	3 253 . .	–12.9	–36.9	–44.1	–41.8	–43.0	–43.8	–33.9	–25.8
Financial	3 260 . .	. . .	. . .	–13.8	–20.5	–21.9	–6.1	–18.8	–14.2
Computer and information	3 262 . .	. . .	. . .	. . .	. . .	. . .	–9.5	–1.9	–6.0
Royalties and licence fees	3 266 . .	–5.0	–7.6	–6.3	–7.0	–9.2	–9.3	–6.5	–6.5
Other business services	3 268 . .	–192.6	–108.2	–43.1	–32.3	–64.5	–28.9	–65.0	–61.0
Personal, cultural, and recreational	3 287 . .	. . .	. . .	. . .	. . .	–25.8	–26.5	–12.6	–16.2
Government, n.i.e.	3 291 . .	–40.9	–43.8	–44.4	–48.9	–52.2	–42.8	–39.4	–39.4

Table 2 (Continued). STANDARD PRESENTATION, 1994–2001

(Millions of U.S. dollars)

	Code	1994	1995	1996	1997	1998	1999	2000	2001
C. INCOME	4 300	-242.6	-227.0	-188.7	-192.7	-197.9	-143.8	-60.3	-113.8
Total credit	2 300	*282.5*	*404.3*	*460.5*	*547.3*	*608.0*	*735.5*	*781.5*	*827.3*
Total debit	3 300	*-525.1*	*-631.3*	*-649.2*	*-740.0*	*-805.9*	*-879.3*	*-841.8*	*-941.1*
Compensation of employees, credit	2 310	...	...	...	...	...	...	...	...
Compensation of employees, debit	3 310	...	...	...	...	...	...	...	...
Investment income, credit	2 320	**282.5**	**404.3**	**460.5**	**547.3**	**608.0**	**735.5**	**781.5**	**827.3**
Direct investment income	2 330	.5	.8	...	...	...	...	1.3	1.4
Dividends and distributed branch profits	2 332	.5	.8	...	...	...	...	1.3	1.4
Reinvested earnings and undistributed branch profits	2 333	...	...	...	...	...	...	...	...
Income on debt (interest)	2 334	...	...	...	...	...	...	...	...
Portfolio investment income	2 339	...	...	...	...	...	...	...	...
Income on equity	2 340	...	...	...	...	...	...	...	...
Income on bonds and notes	2 350	...	...	...	...	...	...	...	...
Income on money market instruments	2 360	...	...	...	...	...	...	...	...
Other investment income	2 370	282.0	403.5	460.5	547.3	608.0	735.5	780.2	825.9
Investment income, debit	3 320	**-525.1**	**-631.3**	**-649.2**	**-740.0**	**-805.9**	**-879.3**	**-841.8**	**-941.1**
Direct investment income	3 330	-40.7	-53.7	-36.1	-38.1	-58.4	-135.4	-89.3	-163.9
Dividends and distributed branch profits	3 332	-22.3	-21.5	-12.9	-19.2	-53.1	-19.2	11.7	-10.9
Reinvested earnings and undistributed branch profits	3 333	-18.4	-32.2	-16.7	-17.3	-5.3	-116.2	-101.0	-153.0
Income on debt (interest)	3 334	...	...	-6.5	-1.6	...	...	...	...
Portfolio investment income	3 339	-90.0	-129.5	-136.5	-148.7	-169.1	-169.4	-158.0	-173.7
Income on equity	3 340	...	...	...	...	...	...	...	...
Income on bonds and notes	3 350	-90.0	-129.5	-136.5	-148.7	-169.1	-169.4	-158.0	-173.7
Income on money market instruments	3 360	...	...	...	...	...	...	...	...
Other investment income	3 370	-394.4	-448.1	-476.6	-553.2	-578.4	-574.5	-594.5	-603.5
D. CURRENT TRANSFERS	4 379	41.2	76.0	82.5	74.2	59.0	73.5	27.5	43.2
Credit	2 379	**49.2**	**84.0**	**90.7**	**83.0**	**75.0**	**78.4**	**48.0**	**48.0**
General government	2 380	16.4	42.4	63.4	63.0	...	...	18.0	18.0
Other sectors	2 390	32.8	41.6	27.3	20.0	75.0	78.4	30.0	30.0
Workers' remittances	2 391	...	...	...	...	...	...	...	...
Other current transfers	2 392	32.8	41.6	27.3	20.0	75.0	78.4	30.0	30.0
Debit	3 379	**-8.0**	**-8.0**	**-8.2**	**-8.8**	**-16.0**	**-4.9**	**-20.5**	**-4.8**
General government	3 380	-8.0	-8.0	-8.2	-8.8	...	...	-20.5	-4.8
Other sectors	3 390	...	...	...	...	-16.0	-4.9	...	...
Workers' remittances	3 391	...	...	...	...	...	...	...	...
Other current transfers	3 392	...	...	...	...	-16.0	-4.9	...	...
CAPITAL AND FINANCIAL ACCOUNT	4 996	**428.1**	**193.9**	**81.2**	**208.6**	**190.0**	**256.7**	**612.8**	**496.0**
CAPITAL ACCOUNT	4 994	...	...	...	...	...	...	...	...
Total credit	2 994	...	...	...	...	...	...	...	...
Total debit	3 994	...	...	...	...	...	...	...	...
Capital transfers, credit	2 400	...	...	...	...	...	...	...	...
General government	2 401	...	...	...	...	...	...	...	...
Debt forgiveness	2 402	...	...	...	...	...	...	...	...
Other capital transfers	2 410	...	...	...	...	...	...	...	...
Other sectors	2 430	...	...	...	...	...	...	...	...
Migrants' transfers	2 431	...	...	...	...	...	...	...	...
Debt forgiveness	2 432	...	...	...	...	...	...	...	...
Other capital transfers	2 440	...	...	...	...	...	...	...	...
Capital transfers, debit	3 400	...	...	...	...	...	...	...	...
General government	3 401	...	...	...	...	...	...	...	...
Debt forgiveness	3 402	...	...	...	...	...	...	...	...
Other capital transfers	3 410	...	...	...	...	...	...	...	...
Other sectors	3 430	...	...	...	...	...	...	...	...
Migrants' transfers	3 431	...	...	...	...	...	...	...	...
Debt forgiveness	3 432	...	...	...	...	...	...	...	...
Other capital transfers	3 440	...	...	...	...	...	...	...	...
Nonproduced nonfinancial assets, credit	2 480	...	...	...	...	...	...	...	...
Nonproduced nonfinancial assets, debit	3 480	...	...	...	...	...	...	...	...

Table 2 (Continued). STANDARD PRESENTATION, 1994–2001

(Millions of U.S. dollars)

	Code	1994	1995	1996	1997	1998	1999	2000	2001
FINANCIAL ACCOUNT	4 995 . .	**428.1**	**193.9**	**81.2**	**208.6**	**190.0**	**256.7**	**612.8**	**496.0**
A. DIRECT INVESTMENT	4 500 . .	154.5	156.6	136.8	113.2	154.8	235.3	274.1	319.3
Direct investment abroad	4 505 . .	**. . .**	**. . .**	**. . .**	**–13.2**	**–9.3**	**. . .**	**.6**	**1.1**
Equity capital	4 510 . .	. . .	. . .	. . .	. . .	–9.3	. . .	. . .	. . .
Claims on affiliated enterprises	4 515 . .	. . .	. . .	. . .	. . .	–9.3	. . .	. . .	. . .
Liabilities to affiliated enterprises	4 520 . .	. . .	. . .	. . .	. . .	. . .	. . .	. . .	. . .
Reinvested earnings	4 525 . .	. . .	. . .	. . .	. . .	. . .	. . .	. . .	. . .
Other capital	4 530 . .	. . .	. . .	. . .	–13.2	. . .	. . .	.6	1.1
Claims on affiliated enterprises	4 535 . .	. . .	. . .	. . .	. . .	. . .	. . .	.6	1.1
Liabilities to affiliated enterprises	4 540 . .	. . .	. . .	. . .	–13.2	. . .	. . .	. . .	. . .
Direct investment in Uruguay	4 555 . .	**154.5**	**156.6**	**136.8**	**126.4**	**164.1**	**235.3**	**273.5**	**318.2**
Equity capital	4 560 . .	136.1	124.4	101.2	92.3	158.8	119.1	172.5	165.2
Claims on direct investors	4 565 . .	. . .	. . .	. . .	. . .	. . .	. . .	. . .	. . .
Liabilities to direct investors	4 570 . .	. . .	124.4	101.2	92.3	158.8	119.1	172.5	165.2
Reinvested earnings	4 575 . .	18.4	32.2	16.7	17.3	5.3	116.2	101.0	153.0
Other capital	4 580 . .	. . .	. . .	18.9	16.8	. . .	. . .	. . .	. . .
Claims on direct investors	4 585 . .	. . .	. . .	. . .	. . .	. . .	. . .	. . .	. . .
Liabilities to direct investors	4 590 . .	. . .	. . .	18.9	16.8	. . .	. . .	. . .	. . .
B. PORTFOLIO INVESTMENT	4 600 . .	158.1	288.8	179.9	209.6	419.4	83.9	191.4	531.1
Assets	4 602 . .	**. . .**	**. . .**	**. . .**	**. . .**	**. . .**	**–44.3**	**–98.1**	**249.8**
Equity securities	4 610 . .	. . .	. . .	. . .	. . .	. . .	. . .	. . .	. . .
Monetary authorities	4 611 . .	. . .	. . .	. . .	. . .	. . .	. . .	. . .	. . .
General government	4 612 . .	. . .	. . .	. . .	. . .	. . .	. . .	. . .	. . .
Banks	4 613 . .	. . .	. . .	. . .	. . .	. . .	. . .	. . .	. . .
Other sectors	4 614 . .	. . .	. . .	. . .	. . .	. . .	. . .	. . .	. . .
Debt securities	4 619 . .	. . .	. . .	. . .	. . .	. . .	–44.3	–98.1	249.8
Bonds and notes	4 620 . .	. . .	. . .	. . .	. . .	. . .	. . .	–98.1	249.8
Monetary authorities	4 621 . .	. . .	. . .	. . .	. . .	. . .	. . .	. . .	. . .
General government	4 622 . .	. . .	. . .	. . .	. . .	. . .	. . .	. . .	. . .
Banks	4 623 . .	. . .	. . .	. . .	. . .	. . .	. . .	–98.1	249.8
Other sectors	4 624 . .	. . .	. . .	. . .	. . .	. . .	. . .	. . .	. . .
Money market instruments	4 630 . .	. . .	. . .	. . .	. . .	. . .	–44.3	. . .	. . .
Monetary authorities	4 631 . .	. . .	. . .	. . .	. . .	. . .	. . .	. . .	. . .
General government	4 632 . .	. . .	. . .	. . .	. . .	. . .	. . .	. . .	. . .
Banks	4 633 . .	. . .	. . .	. . .	. . .	. . .	–44.3	. . .	. . .
Other sectors	4 634 . .	. . .	. . .	. . .	. . .	. . .	. . .	. . .	. . .
Liabilities	4 652 . .	**158.1**	**288.8**	**179.9**	**209.6**	**419.4**	**128.2**	**289.5**	**281.3**
Equity securities	4 660 . .	. . .	. . .	. . .	. . .	. . .	. . .	. . .	. . .
Banks	4 663 . .	. . .	. . .	. . .	. . .	. . .	. . .	. . .	. . .
Other sectors	4 664 . .	. . .	. . .	. . .	. . .	. . .	. . .	. . .	. . .
Debt securities	4 669 . .	158.1	288.8	179.9	209.6	419.4	128.2	289.5	281.3
Bonds and notes	4 670 . .	178.0	183.0	284.6	298.6	419.4	128.2	289.5	281.3
Monetary authorities	4 671 . .	. . .	. . .	. . .	. . .	. . .	. . .	. . .	. . .
General government	4 672 . .	178.0	183.0	284.6	298.6	419.4	128.2	289.5	281.3
Banks	4 673 . .	. . .	. . .	. . .	. . .	. . .	. . .	. . .	. . .
Other sectors	4 674 . .	. . .	. . .	. . .	. . .	. . .	. . .	. . .	. . .
Money market instruments	4 680 . .	–19.9	105.8	–104.7	–89.0	. . .	. . .	. . .	. . .
Monetary authorities	4 681 . .	. . .	96.5	–96.5	35.7	. . .	. . .	. . .	. . .
General government	4 682 . .	–19.9	9.3	–8.2	–124.7	. . .	. . .	. . .	. . .
Banks	4 683 . .	. . .	. . .	. . .	. . .	. . .	. . .	. . .	. . .
Other sectors	4 684 . .	. . .	. . .	. . .	. . .	. . .	. . .	. . .	. . .
C. FINANCIAL DERIVATIVES	4 910 . .	. . .	. . .	. . .	. . .	. . .	. . .	. . .	. . .
Monetary authorities	4 911 . .	. . .	. . .	. . .	. . .	. . .	. . .	. . .	. . .
General government	4 912 . .	. . .	. . .	. . .	. . .	. . .	. . .	. . .	. . .
Banks	4 913 . .	. . .	. . .	. . .	. . .	. . .	. . .	. . .	. . .
Other sectors	4 914 . .	. . .	. . .	. . .	. . .	. . .	. . .	. . .	. . .
Assets	4 900 . .	**. . .**	**. . .**	**. . .**	**. . .**	**. . .**	**. . .**	**. . .**	**. . .**
Monetary authorities	4 901 . .	. . .	. . .	. . .	. . .	. . .	. . .	. . .	. . .
General government	4 902 . .	. . .	. . .	. . .	. . .	. . .	. . .	. . .	. . .
Banks	4 903 . .	. . .	. . .	. . .	. . .	. . .	. . .	. . .	. . .
Other sectors	4 904 . .	. . .	. . .	. . .	. . .	. . .	. . .	. . .	. . .
Liabilities	4 905 . .	**. . .**	**. . .**	**. . .**	**. . .**	**. . .**	**. . .**	**. . .**	**. . .**
Monetary authorities	4 906 . .	. . .	. . .	. . .	. . .	. . .	. . .	. . .	. . .
General government	4 907 . .	. . .	. . .	. . .	. . .	. . .	. . .	. . .	. . .
Banks	4 908 . .	. . .	. . .	. . .	. . .	. . .	. . .	. . .	. . .
Other sectors	4 909 . .	. . .	. . .	. . .	. . .	. . .	. . .	. . .	. . .

Table 2 (Concluded). STANDARD PRESENTATION, 1994–2001
(Millions of U.S. dollars)

	Code	1994	1995	1996	1997	1998	1999	2000	2001
D. OTHER INVESTMENT	4 700 . .	214.0	–33.5	–94.7	277.6	131.0	–172.1	313.8	–50.8
Assets	4 703 . .	**–71.8**	**–961.9**	**–1,238.5**	**–626.6**	**–428.0**	**–119.3**	**–690.4**	**–1,991.1**
Trade credits	4 706 . .	–17.7	–.6	–6.1	9.8	. . .	.4	–8.9	. . .
General government	4 707 . .	. . .	. . .	. . .	. . .	. . .	. . .	. . .	. . .
of which: Short-term	4 709 . .	. . .	. . .	. . .	. . .	. . .	. . .	. . .	. . .
Other sectors	4 710 . .	–17.7	–.6	–6.1	9.8	. . .	.4	–8.9	. . .
of which: Short-term	4 712 . .	*–17.7*	*–.6*	*–6.1*	*9.8*	. . .	*.4*	*–8.9*	. . .
Loans	4 714 . .	. . .	–548.8	–290.7	–142.1	–665.0	314.9	113.1	–1,173.5
Monetary authorities	4 715 . .	. . .	. . .	. . .	. . .	. . .	. . .	. . .	. . .
of which: Short-term	4 718 . .	. . .	. . .	. . .	. . .	. . .	. . .	. . .	. . .
General government	4 719 . .	. . .	. . .	. . .	. . .	. . .	. . .	. . .	. . .
of which: Short-term	4 721 . .	. . .	. . .	. . .	. . .	. . .	. . .	. . .	. . .
Banks	4 722 . .	. . .	–548.8	–290.7	–142.1	–665.0	315.4	113.2	–1,173.5
of which: Short-term	4 724 . .	. . .	*–548.8*	*–290.7*	*–142.1*	*–665.0*	*315.4*	*113.2*	*–1,173.5*
Other sectors	4 725 . .	. . .	. . .	. . .	. . .	. . .	–.5	–.1	. . .
of which: Short-term	4 727 . .	. . .	. . .	. . .	. . .	. . .	*–.5*	*–.1*	. . .
Currency and deposits	4 730 . .	–54.1	–412.5	–599.4	–506.9	104.0	–354.2	–850.9	–354.3
Monetary authorities	4 731 . .	–10.1	. . .	. . .	. . .	. . .	. . .	1.7	. . .
General government	4 732 . .	. . .	. . .	. . .	. . .	. . .	. . .	. . .	. . .
Banks	4 733 . .	–44.0	–412.5	–599.4	–506.9	104.0	–166.2	–719.6	–273.3
Other sectors	4 734 . .	. . .	. . .	. . .	. . .	. . .	–188.0	–133.0	–81.0
Other assets	4 736 . .	. . .	. . .	–342.3	12.6	133.0	–80.4	56.3	–463.3
Monetary authorities	4 737 . .	. . .	. . .	. . .	. . .	. . .	. . .	–.8	–5.3
of which: Short-term	4 739 . .	. . .	. . .	. . .	. . .	. . .	. . .	. . .	. . .
General government	4 740 . .	. . .	. . .	. . .	. . .	. . .	. . .	. . .	. . .
of which: Short-term	4 742 . .	. . .	. . .	. . .	. . .	. . .	. . .	. . .	. . .
Banks	4 743 . .	. . .	. . .	–342.3	12.6	133.0	–83.8	57.1	–458.0
of which: Short-term	4 745 . .	. . .	. . .	*–342.3*	*12.6*	*133.0*	*–83.8*	*57.1*	*–458.0*
Other sectors	4 746 . .	. . .	. . .	. . .	. . .	. . .	3.4	. . .	. . .
of which: Short-term	4 748 . .	. . .	. . .	. . .	. . .	. . .	*3.4*	. . .	. . .
Liabilities	4 753 . .	**285.8**	**928.4**	**1,143.8**	**904.2**	**559.0**	**–52.8**	**1,004.2**	**1,940.3**
Trade credits	4 756 . .	92.4	–47.3	–10.7	27.2	38.4	7.3	–3.9	. . .
General government	4 757 . .	. . .	–42.8	–10.9	–43.7	6.1	–11.5	. . .	. . .
of which: Short-term	4 759 . .	. . .	*–42.8*	*–10.9*	*–43.7*	*6.1*	*–11.5*	. . .	. . .
Other sectors	4 760 . .	92.4	–4.5	.2	70.9	32.3	18.8	–3.9	. . .
of which: Short-term	4 762 . .	. . .	*–4.5*	*.2*	*70.9*	*32.3*	*18.8*	*–3.9*	. . .
Loans	4 764 . .	7.1	272.6	514.6	445.8	749.2	103.3	347.6	136.7
Monetary authorities	4 765 . .	–6.6	–72.3	–21.9	–39.6	122.9	–136.6	–36.9	–43.6
of which: Use of Fund credit and loans from the Fund	4 766 . .	*–10.6*	*–9.8*	*–11.6*	*–8.3*	*160.1*	. . .	. . .	. . .
of which: Short-term	4 768 . .	. . .	*–37.9*	*2.8*	*–30.6*	. . .	. . .	. . .	. . .
General government	4 769 . .	134.0	61.4	31.2	140.5	163.0	272.0	200.7	144.5
of which: Short-term	4 771 . .	. . .	. . .	. . .	. . .	. . .	. . .	. . .	. . .
Banks	4 772 . .	–84.8	314.8	473.0	347.7	463.3	3.0	200.1	7.9
of which: Short-term	4 774 . .	*–119.3*	*314.8*	*473.0*	*347.7*	*469.5*	*3.0*	*200.1*	*7.9*
Other sectors	4 775 . .	–35.5	–31.3	32.3	–2.8	. . .	–35.1	–16.3	27.9
of which: Short-term	4 777 . .	. . .	*3.0*	. . .	. . .	. . .	*–35.1*	*–16.3*	*27.9*
Currency and deposits	4 780 . .	184.6	703.1	639.9	431.2	165.9	–259.6	685.9	1,276.8
Monetary authorities	4 781 . .	. . .	. . .	. . .	. . .	. . .	. . .	. . .	. . .
General government	4 782 . .	. . .	. . .	. . .	. . .	. . .	. . .	. . .	. . .
Banks	4 783 . .	184.6	703.1	639.9	431.2	165.9	–259.6	685.9	1,276.8
Other sectors	4 784 . .	. . .	. . .	. . .	. . .	. . .	. . .	. . .	. . .
Other liabilities	4 786 . .	1.7	. . .	. . .	. . .	–394.5	96.2	–25.4	526.8
Monetary authorities	4 787 . .	1.7	. . .	. . .	. . .	. . .	.9	–1.9	–3.4
of which: Short-term	4 789 . .	*27.0*	. . .	. . .	. . .	. . .	*.9*	*–1.9*	*–3.4*
General government	4 790 . .	. . .	. . .	. . .	. . .	. . .	. . .	. . .	. . .
of which: Short-term	4 792 . .	. . .	. . .	. . .	. . .	. . .	. . .	. . .	. . .
Banks	4 793 . .	. . .	. . .	. . .	. . .	–356.3	95.3	–23.5	448.5
of which: Short-term	4 795 . .	. . .	. . .	. . .	. . .	*–356.3*	*95.3*	*–23.5*	*448.5*
Other sectors	4 796 . .	. . .	. . .	. . .	. . .	–38.2	. . .	. . .	81.7
of which: Short-term	4 798 . .	. . .	. . .	. . .	. . .	*–38.2*	. . .	. . .	*81.7*
E. RESERVE ASSETS	4 802 . .	–98.5	–218.0	–140.8	–391.7	–515.2	109.6	–166.5	–303.6
Monetary gold	4 812 . .	. . .	–3.4	–8.2	–8.6	–6.9	18.1	230.3	287.0
Special drawing rights	4 811 . .	.4	–3.5	–.5	3.8	–.7	–.2	.3	–1.4
Reserve position in the Fund	4 810 . .	. . .	. . .	. . .	. . .	. . .	–27.4	. . .	. . .
Foreign exchange	4 803 . .	–228.5	–179.4	–84.7	–415.1	–515.2	26.4	–466.0	–590.9
Other claims	4 813 . .	129.6	–31.7	–47.4	28.2	7.6	92.7	68.9	1.7
NET ERRORS AND OMISSIONS	4 998 . .	**10.2**	**18.6**	**152.2**	**78.8**	**285.5**	**250.9**	**–46.6**	**16.5**

Part 3 of the *Yearbook* contains descriptions of the methodologies, compilation practices, and sources used to compile these data.

Table 3. INTERNATIONAL INVESTMENT POSITION (End-period stocks), 1994–2001

(Millions of U.S. dollars)

	Code	1994	1995	1996	1997	1998	1999	2000	2001
ASSETS	8 995 C.	...	...	...	...	...	12,747.3	13,789.1	15,833.3
Direct investment abroad	8 505 . .	**...**	**...**	**...**	**...**	**...**	**47.2**	**54.0**	**52.9**
Equity capital and reinvested earnings	8 506 . .	...	...	...	...	...	47.2	...	...
Claims on affiliated enterprises	8 507 . .	...	...	...	...	...	47.2	...	...
Liabilities to affiliated enterprises	8 508 . .	...	...	...	...	...	...	...	...
Other capital	8 530 . .	...	...	...	...	...	...	54.0	52.9
Claims on affiliated enterprises	8 535 . .	...	...	...	...	...	...	54.0	52.9
Liabilities to affiliated enterprises	8 540 . .	...	...	...	...	...	...	...	...
Portfolio investment	8 602 . .	**50.4**	**52.4**	**56.9**	**61.7**	**66.9**	**842.3**	**799.0**	**532.6**
Equity securities	8 610 . .	...	...	...	...	...	...	...	...
Monetary authorities	8 611 . .	...	...	...	...	...	...	...	...
General government	8 612 . .	...	...	...	...	...	...	...	...
Banks	8 613 . .	...	...	...	...	...	...	...	...
Other sectors	8 614 . .	...	...	...	...	...	...	...	...
Debt securities	8 619 . .	50.4	52.4	56.9	61.7	66.9	842.3	799.0	532.6
Bonds and notes	8 620 . .	50.4	52.4	56.9	61.7	66.9	842.3	799.0	532.6
Monetary authorities	8 621 . .	50.4	52.4	56.9	61.7	66.9	97.0	59.8	64.8
General government	8 622 . .	...	...	...	...	...	...	...	...
Banks	8 623 . .	...	...	...	...	...	745.3	739.2	467.8
Other sectors	8 624 . .	...	...	...	...	...	...	...	...
Money market instruments	8 630 . .	...	...	...	...	...	...	...	...
Monetary authorities	8 631 . .	...	...	...	...	...	...	...	...
General government	8 632 . .	...	...	...	...	...	...	...	...
Banks	8 633 . .	...	...	...	...	...	...	...	...
Other sectors	8 634 . .	...	...	...	...	...	...	...	...
Financial derivatives	8 900 . .	**...**	**...**	**...**	**...**	**...**	**...**	**...**	**...**
Monetary authorities	8 901 . .	...	...	...	...	...	...	...	...
General government	8 902 . .	...	...	...	...	...	...	...	...
Banks	8 903 . .	...	...	...	...	...	...	...	...
Other sectors	8 904 . .	...	...	...	...	...	...	...	...
Other investment	8 703 . .	**3,892.6**	**4,805.5**	**6,060.9**	**6,718.3**	**7,276.9**	**8,691.9**	**10,158.3**	**12,148.5**
Trade credits	8 706 . .	54.1	54.7	60.8	51.0	55.8	20.4	...	...
General government	8 707 . .	...	...	...	...	...	...	...	...
of which: Short-term	8 709 . .	...	...	...	...	...	...	...	...
Other sectors	8 710 . .	54.1	54.7	60.8	51.0	55.8	20.4	...	...
of which: Short-term	8 712 . .	*54.1*	*54.7*	*60.8*	*51.0*	*55.8*	*20.4*	...	...
Loans	8 714 . .	615.0	637.7	786.5	1,771.2	2,422.7	1,545.7	1,450.6	2,623.3
Monetary authorities	8 715 . .	...	...	...	...	...	...	...	...
of which: Short-term	8 718 . .	...	...	...	...	...	...	...	...
General government	8 719 . .	...	...	...	...	...	...	...	...
of which: Short-term	8 721 . .	...	...	...	...	...	...	...	...
Banks	8 722 . .	615.0	637.7	786.5	1,771.2	2,422.7	1,545.7	1,450.6	2,623.3
of which: Short-term	8 724 . .	*615.0*	*637.7*	*786.5*	*1,771.2*	*2,422.7*	*1,545.7*	*1,450.6*	*2,623.3*
Other sectors	8 725 . .	...	...	...	...	...	...	...	...
of which: Short-term	8 727 . .	...	...	...	...	...	...	...	...
Currency and deposits	8 730 . .	2,392.2	2,804.9	3,404.3	3,911.2	3,807.3	6,934.2	8,444.2	8,798.4
Monetary authorities	8 731 . .	...	...	...	...	...	...	...	...
General government	8 732 . .	...	...	...	...	...	...	...	...
Banks	8 733 . .	2,392.2	2,804.9	3,404.3	3,911.2	3,807.3	3,720.2	4,996.5	5,269.7
Other sectors	8 734 . .	...	...	...	...	...	3,214.0	3,447.7	3,528.7
Other assets	8 736 . .	831.3	1,308.2	1,809.3	984.9	991.1	191.6	263.5	726.8
Monetary authorities	8 737 . .	80.2	83.3	49.1	111.8	113.1	...	103.4	108.7
of which: Short-term	8 739 . .	...	...	...	...	...	...	...	...
General government	8 740 . .	...	...	...	...	...	...	...	...
of which: Short-term	8 742 . .	...	...	...	...	...	...	...	...
Banks	8 743 . .	751.1	1,224.9	1,760.2	873.1	878.0	191.6	160.1	618.1
of which: Short-term	8 745 . .	*751.1*	*1,224.9*	*1,760.2*	*873.1*	*878.0*	*191.6*	*160.1*	*618.1*
Other sectors	8 746 . .	...	...	...	...	...	...	...	...
of which: Short-term	8 748 . .	...	...	...	...	...	...	...	...
Reserve assets	8 802 . .	**2,292.9**	**2,490.6**	**2,600.2**	**2,776.8**	**3,320.6**	**3,165.9**	**2,777.8**	**3,099.3**
Monetary gold	8 812 . .	847.0	864.2	840.2	667.4	674.1	688.8	294.5	2.3
Special drawing rights	8 811 . .	...	3.5	3.9	...	.7	1.0	.5	1.8
Reserve position in the Fund	8 810 . .	22.4	22.9	22.1	20.7	21.6	49.0	46.5	44.8
Foreign exchange	8 803 . .	1,313.7	1,474.9	1,563.3	1,965.7	2,502.8	2,027.2	2,430.9	3,046.7
Other claims	8 813 . .	109.7	125.1	170.6	122.9	121.3	400.0	5.4	3.6

Table 3 (Concluded). INTERNATIONAL INVESTMENT POSITION (End–period stocks), 1994–2001
(Millions of U.S. dollars)

	Code	1994	1995	1996	1997	1998	1999	2000	2001
LIABILITIES	8 995 D.	...	...	...	...	...	14,511.7	15,583.1	18,236.9
Direct investment in Uruguay	8 555	...	...	...	...	...	**1,790.3**	**2,088.0**	**2,406.2**
Equity capital and reinvested earnings	8 556	...	...	...	...	...	1,790.3	2,088.0	2,406.2
Claims on direct investors	8 557	...	...	...	...	...	...	...	...
Liabilities to direct investors	8 558	...	...	...	...	...	1,790.3	2,088.0	2,406.2
Other capital	8 580	...	...	...	...	...	...	...	...
Claims on direct investors	8 585	...	...	...	...	...	...	...	...
Liabilities to direct investors	8 590	...	...	...	...	...	...	...	...
Portfolio investment	8 652	**1,668.6**	**1,858.5**	**2,136.7**	**2,187.3**	**2,606.7**	**2,340.2**	**2,721.1**	**3,115.8**
Equity securities	8 660	...	...	...	...	...	...	...	...
Banks	8 663	...	...	...	...	...	...	...	...
Other sectors	8 664	...	...	...	...	...	...	...	...
Debt securities	8 669	1,668.6	1,858.5	2,136.7	2,187.3	2,606.7	2,340.2	2,721.1	3,115.8
Bonds and notes	8 670	1,668.6	1,858.5	2,136.7	2,151.6	2,566.3	2,340.2	2,721.1	3,115.8
Monetary authorities	8 671	...	...	...	...	...	...	...	...
General government	8 672	1,668.6	1,858.5	2,136.7	2,151.6	2,566.3	2,340.2	2,721.1	3,115.8
Banks	8 673	...	...	...	...	...	...	...	...
Other sectors	8 674	...	...	...	...	...	...	...	...
Money market instruments	8 680	...	...	...	35.7	40.4	...	...	...
Monetary authorities	8 681	...	...	...	35.7	40.4	...	...	...
General government	8 682	...	...	...	...	...	...	...	...
Banks	8 683	...	...	...	...	...	...	...	...
Other sectors	8 684	...	...	...	...	...	...	...	...
Financial derivatives	8 905	...	...	...	...	...	...	...	...
Monetary authorities	8 906	...	...	...	...	...	...	...	...
General government	8 907	...	...	...	...	...	...	...	...
Banks	8 908	...	...	...	...	...	...	...	...
Other sectors	8 909	...	...	...	...	...	...	...	...
Other investment	8 753	**7,501.7**	**8,436.9**	**9,467.3**	**10,297.2**	**11,055.7**	**10,381.2**	**10,774.0**	**12,714.9**
Trade credits	8 756	595.9	555.2	517.6	543.4	570.5	...	22.6	22.6
General government	8 757	...	...	...	...	...	...	...	...
of which: Short-term	8 759	...	...	...	...	...	...	...	...
Other sectors	8 760	595.9	555.2	517.6	543.4	570.5	...	22.6	22.6
of which: Short-term	8 762	...	...	...	...	...	...	*22.6*	*22.6*
Loans	8 764	2,755.5	2,699.3	2,674.5	2,633.0	2,885.7	4,768.5	4,858.7	4,996.0
Monetary authorities	8 765	150.2	68.0	50.3	77.4	232.0	218.9	509.3	460.0
of which: Use of Fund credit and loans from the Fund	8 766	*29.9*	*20.8*	*8.6*	...	*160.8*	*156.7*	*148.8*	*143.5*
of which: Short-term	8 768	*84.1*	*40.6*	*34.0*	*.7*	*.3*	*2.5*	...	...
General government	8 769	1,416.9	1,537.6	1,507.2	1,594.8	1,738.3	1,976.2	1,904.1	2,078.0
of which: Short-term	8 771	...	...	...	...	...	...	...	...
Banks	8 772	...	...	...	32.0	29.4	1,791.3	1,870.4	1,878.0
of which: Short-term	8 774	...	...	...	*32.0*	*29.4*	*1,645.1*	*1,870.4*	*1,878.0*
Other sectors	8 775	1,188.4	1,093.7	1,117.0	928.8	886.0	782.1	574.9	580.0
of which: Short-term	8 777	...	...	...	...	...	...	*574.9*	*580.0*
Currency and deposits	8 780	2,709.3	3,520.7	4,152.5	4,749.5	4,738.4	5,050.6	5,734.6	7,011.4
Monetary authorities	8 781	...	...	...	...	...	...	...	...
General government	8 782	...	...	...	...	...	...	...	...
Banks	8 783	2,709.3	3,520.7	4,152.5	4,749.5	4,738.4	5,050.6	5,734.6	7,011.4
Other sectors	8 784	...	...	...	...	...	...	...	...
Other liabilities	8 786	1,441.0	1,661.7	2,122.7	2,371.3	2,861.1	562.1	158.1	684.9
Monetary authorities	8 787	...	...	...	...	...	...	9.2	5.8
of which: Short-term	8 789	...	...	...	...	...	...	*9.2*	*5.8*
General government	8 790	...	...	...	...	...	...	...	...
of which: Short-term	8 792	...	...	...	...	...	...	...	...
Banks	8 793	1,441.0	1,661.7	2,122.7	2,371.3	2,861.1	69.6	148.9	597.4
of which: Short-term	8 795	*1,441.0*	*1,661.7*	*2,122.7*	*2,371.3*	*2,861.1*	*69.6*	*148.9*	*597.4*
Other sectors	8 796	...	...	...	...	...	492.5	...	81.7
of which: Short-term	8 798	...	...	...	...	...	*492.5*	...	*81.7*
NET INTERNATIONAL INVESTMENT POSITION	8 995	...	...	...	...	...	**–1,764.4**	**–1,794.0**	**–2,403.6**
Conversion rates: Uruguayan pesos per U.S. dollar (end of period)	0 102	**5.6010**	**7.1110**	**8.7130**	**10.0400**	**10.8170**	**11.6150**	**12.5150**	**14.7680**

Table 1. ANALYTIC PRESENTATION, 1994–2001

(Millions of U.S. dollars)

	Code	1994	1995	1996	1997	1998	1999	2000	2001
A. Current Account [1]	4 993 Z.	**–19.78**	**–18.25**	**–26.94**	**–19.34**	**–9.41**	**–33.22**	**–13.65**	**–14.53**
Goods: exports f.o.b	2 100 ..	25.11	28.28	30.20	35.32	33.78	25.66	27.19	19.89
Goods: imports f.o.b	3 100 ..	–74.68	–79.44	–81.11	–78.99	–76.23	–84.46	–76.94	–77.96
Balance on Goods	4 100 ..	*–49.58*	*–51.16*	*–50.91*	*–43.67*	*–42.44*	*–58.80*	*–49.74*	*–58.07*
Services: credit	2 200 ..	78.14	81.65	92.75	87.79	113.95	114.80	129.81	119.26
Services: debit	3 200 ..	–33.44	–35.27	–36.50	–35.95	–56.97	–72.09	–70.15	–72.99
Balance on Goods and Services	4 991 ..	*–4.88*	*–4.78*	*5.34*	*8.16*	*14.55*	*–16.09*	*9.91*	*–11.80*
Income: credit	2 300 ..	9.94	13.07	15.82	15.41	20.98	21.00	18.74	17.23
Income: debit	3 300 ..	–47.36	–49.79	–47.55	–45.68	–29.26	–26.09	–31.71	–21.23
Balance on Goods, Services, and Income	4 992 ..	*–42.30*	*–41.49*	*–26.39*	*–22.11*	*6.26*	*–21.18*	*–3.06*	*–15.80*
Current transfers: credit	2 379 Z.	23.24	23.81	22.39	21.77	15.55	18.72	27.41	39.53
Current transfers: debit	3 379 ..	–.72	–.56	–22.94	–19.00	–31.22	–30.76	–38.00	–38.26
B. Capital Account [1]	4 994 Z.	**37.28**	**31.62**	**4.90**	**–5.46**	**–20.86**	**–49.72**	**–23.58**	**–16.03**
Capital account: credit	2 994 Z.	41.45	38.33	43.38	23.75	25.44	23.94	31.88	46.07
Capital account: debit	3 994 ..	–4.17	–6.71	–38.48	–29.21	–46.29	–73.66	–55.46	–62.10
Total, Groups A Plus B	4 981 ..	*17.50*	*13.38*	*–22.04*	*–24.80*	*–30.27*	*–82.94*	*–37.22*	*–30.57*
C. Financial Account [1]	4 995 W.	**–13.41**	**25.30**	**20.88**	**–16.73**	**17.37**	**56.17**	**19.33**	**12.75**
Direct investment abroad	4 505 ..	...	...	...	...	...	...	...	...
Direct investment in Vanuatu	4 555 Z.	29.79	31.04	32.73	30.23	20.38	13.40	20.26	18.00
Portfolio investment assets	4 602 ..	...	...	...	...	3.45	–1.01	.69	–4.33
Equity securities	4 610 ..	...	...	...	...	...	...	...	...
Debt securities	4 619 ..	...	...	...	...	...	...	...	...
Portfolio investment liabilities	4 652 Z.	...	...	...	...	...	...	...	...
Equity securities	4 660 ..	...	...	...	...	...	...	...	...
Debt securities	4 669 Z.	...	...	...	...	...	...	...	...
Financial derivatives	4 910 ..	...	...	...	...	...	...	...	...
Financial derivatives assets	4 900 ..	...	...	...	...	...	...	...	...
Financial derivatives liabilities	4 905 ..	...	...	...	...	...	...	...	...
Other investment assets	4 703 ..	–45.47	–1.59	–16.63	–23.53	5.12	29.63	–13.55	–11.41
Monetary authorities	4 701 ..	...	...	...	...	...	...	...	...
General government	4 704 ..	–.45	–.30	–.39	–.46	...	...	...	...
Banks	4 705 ..	10.60	–2.18	–16.25	–23.07	5.89	27.05	–13.10	–14.81
Other sectors	4 728 ..	–55.62	.89	...	...	–.77	2.59	–.45	3.40
Other investment liabilities	4 753 W.	2.27	–4.15	4.78	–23.43	–11.58	14.15	11.93	10.48
Monetary authorities	4 753 WA	–.05	.18	–.12	.12	–.11	1.30	–.03	.53
General government	4 753 ZB	2.17	2.21	.45	.68	10.52	5.12	16.36	3.20
Banks	4 753 ZC	.16	–6.54	4.46	–24.23	–20.91	8.73	–4.79	3.05
Other sectors	4 753 ZD	...	...	...	...	–1.09	–1.01	.39	3.70
Total, Groups A Through C	4 983 ..	*4.09*	*38.68*	*1.16*	*–41.53*	*–12.90*	*–26.76*	*–17.89*	*–17.82*
D. Net Errors and Omissions	4 998 ..	**–10.21**	**–33.38**	**–4.14**	**39.37**	**6.01**	**3.57**	**–.88**	**7.55**
Total, Groups A Through D	4 984 ..	*–6.12*	*5.30*	*–5.30*	*–2.16*	*–6.89*	*–23.19*	*–18.77*	*–10.27*
E. Reserves and Related Items	4 802 A.	**6.12**	**–5.30**	**5.30**	**2.16**	**6.89**	**23.19**	**18.77**	**10.27**
Reserve assets	4 802 ..	4.86	–5.30	5.30	2.16	–8.06	3.48	.87	.62
Use of Fund credit and loans	4 766 ..	...	...	...	...	...	...	...	...
Exceptional financing	4 920 ..	1.26	...	...	...	14.95	19.71	17.90	9.64
Conversion rates: vatu per U.S. dollar	0 101 ..	**116.41**	**112.11**	**111.72**	**115.87**	**127.52**	**129.08**	**137.64**	**145.31**

[1] Excludes components that have been classified in the categories of Group E.

Table 2. STANDARD PRESENTATION, 1994–2001
(Millions of U.S. dollars)

	Code	1994	1995	1996	1997	1998	1999	2000	2001
CURRENT ACCOUNT	4 993 . .	**–18.52**	**–18.25**	**–26.94**	**–19.34**	**5.76**	**–13.08**	**4.99**	**1.82**
A. GOODS	4 100 . .	–49.58	–51.16	–50.91	–43.67	–42.44	–58.80	–49.74	–58.07
Credit	2 100 . .	**25.11**	**28.28**	**30.20**	**35.32**	**33.78**	**25.66**	**27.19**	**19.89**
General merchandise: exports f.o.b.	2 110 . .	25.11	28.28	30.20	35.32	33.78	25.66	27.19	19.89
Goods for processing: exports f.o.b.	2 150 . .	. . .	. . .	. . .	. . .	. . .	. . .	. . .	. . .
Repairs on goods	2 160 . .	. . .	. . .	. . .	. . .	. . .	. . .	. . .	. . .
Goods procured in ports by carriers	2 170 . .	. . .	. . .	. . .	. . .	. . .	. . .	. . .	. . .
Nonmonetary gold	2 180 . .	. . .	. . .	. . .	. . .	. . .	. . .	. . .	. . .
Debit	3 100 . .	**–74.68**	**–79.44**	**–81.11**	**–78.99**	**–76.23**	**–84.46**	**–76.94**	**–77.96**
General merchandise: imports f.o.b.	3 110 . .	–74.68	–79.44	–81.11	–78.99	–73.54	–80.53	–74.11	–75.30
Goods for processing: imports f.o.b.	3 150 . .	. . .	. . .	. . .	. . .	. . .	. . .	. . .	. . .
Repairs on goods	3 160 . .	. . .	. . .	. . .	. . .	. . .	. . .	. . .	. . .
Goods procured in ports by carriers	3 170 . .	. . .	. . .	. . .	. . .	–2.68	–3.93	–2.82	–2.66
Nonmonetary gold	3 180 . .	. . .	. . .	. . .	. . .	. . .	. . .	. . .	. . .
B. SERVICES	4 200 . .	44.70	46.38	56.25	51.84	56.99	42.71	59.65	46.27
Total credit	2 200 . .	*78.14*	*81.65*	*92.75*	*87.79*	*113.95*	*114.80*	*129.81*	*119.26*
Total debit	3 200 . .	*–33.44*	*–35.27*	*–36.50*	*–35.95*	*–56.97*	*–72.09*	*–70.15*	*–72.99*
Transportation services, credit	2 205 . .	**10.13**	**11.09**	**9.90**	**8.53**	**22.45**	**23.29**	**28.73**	**26.47**
Passenger	2 850 . .	. . .	. . .	. . .	. . .	*11.97*	*9.41*	*12.72*	*11.73*
Freight	2 851 . .	. . .	. . .	. . .	. . .	*1.34*	*1.36*	*2.31*	*2.31*
Other	2 852 . .	*10.13*	*11.09*	*9.90*	*8.53*	*9.15*	*12.51*	*13.70*	*12.44*
Sea transport, passenger	2 207 . .	. . .	. . .	. . .	. . .	. . .	. . .	. . .	. . .
Sea transport, freight	2 208 . .	. . .	. . .	. . .	. . .	.13	.14	.23	.23
Sea transport, other	2 209 . .	5.06	5.55	4.95	4.27	1.83	2.50	2.74	2.49
Air transport, passenger	2 211 . .	. . .	. . .	. . .	. . .	11.97	9.41	12.72	11.73
Air transport, freight	2 212 . .	. . .	. . .	. . .	. . .	1.20	1.23	2.08	2.08
Air transport, other	2 213 . .	5.06	5.55	4.95	4.27	7.32	10.01	10.96	9.95
Other transport, passenger	2 215 . .	. . .	. . .	. . .	. . .	. . .	. . .	. . .	. . .
Other transport, freight	2 216 . .	. . .	. . .	. . .	. . .	. . .	. . .	. . .	. . .
Other transport, other	2 217 . .	. . .	. . .	. . .	. . .	. . .	. . .	. . .	. . .
Transportation services, debit	3 205 . .	**–18.28**	**–19.40**	**–21.53**	**–20.70**	**–22.66**	**–27.00**	**–23.98**	**–23.63**
Passenger	3 850 . .	*–5.22*	*–5.42*	*–5.44*	*–5.22*	. . .	. . .	. . .	. . .
Freight	3 851 . .	*–13.06*	*–13.97*	*–16.09*	*–15.48*	*–15.06*	*–17.67*	*–14.76*	*–15.41*
Other	3 852 . .	. . .	. . .	. . .	. . .	*–7.60*	*–9.34*	*–9.22*	*–8.22*
Sea transport, passenger	3 207 . .	. . .	. . .	. . .	. . .	. . .	. . .	. . .	. . .
Sea transport, freight	3 208 . .	–13.06	–13.97	–16.09	–15.48	–11.30	–13.25	–11.07	–11.55
Sea transport, other	3 209 . .	. . .	. . .	. . .	. . .	–.76	–.93	–.92	–.82
Air transport, passenger	3 211 . .	–5.22	–5.42	–5.44	–5.22	. . .	. . .	. . .	. . .
Air transport, freight	3 212 . .	. . .	. . .	. . .	. . .	–3.77	–4.42	–3.69	–3.85
Air transport, other	3 213 . .	. . .	. . .	. . .	. . .	–6.84	–8.40	–8.30	–7.40
Other transport, passenger	3 215 . .	. . .	. . .	. . .	. . .	. . .	. . .	. . .	. . .
Other transport, freight	3 216 . .	. . .	. . .	. . .	. . .	. . .	. . .	. . .	. . .
Other transport, other	3 217 . .	. . .	. . .	. . .	. . .	. . .	. . .	. . .	. . .
Travel, credit	2 236 . .	**40.51**	**45.39**	**55.51**	**53.19**	**60.36**	**50.02**	**56.11**	**46.12**
Business travel	2 237 . .	. . .	. . .	. . .	. . .	6.04	5.00	5.61	4.61
Personal travel	2 240 . .	40.51	45.39	55.51	53.19	54.32	45.02	50.50	41.51
Travel, debit	3 236 . .	**–4.34**	**–4.61**	**–4.98**	**–5.03**	**–7.87**	**–9.29**	**–8.90**	**–7.88**
Business travel	3 237 . .	. . .	. . .	. . .	. . .	–5.90	–6.97	–6.67	–5.91
Personal travel	3 240 . .	–4.34	–4.61	–4.98	–5.03	–1.97	–2.32	–2.22	–1.97
Other services, credit	2 200 BA	**27.50**	**25.16**	**27.34**	**26.06**	**31.15**	**41.49**	**44.97**	**46.67**
Communications	2 245 . .	. . .	. . .	4.05	3.92	3.45	5.10	3.37	2.06
Construction	2 249 . .	. . .	. . .	. . .	. . .	.33	.62	.73	.69
Insurance	2 253 . .	. . .	. . .	. . .	. . .	.74	.83	1.66	1.02
Financial	2 260 . .	. . .	. . .	. . .	. . .	4.16	6.51	6.30	6.95
Computer and information	2 262 . .	. . .	. . .	. . .	. . .	. . .	. . .	. . .	. . .
Royalties and licence fees	2 266 . .	. . .	. . .	. . .	. . .	. . .	. . .	. . .	. . .
Other business services	2 268 . .	19.03	18.69	15.55	14.81	16.48	19.20	21.41	28.90
Personal, cultural, and recreational	2 287 . .	. . .	. . .	. . .	. . .	. . .	. . .	. . .	. . .
Government, n.i.e.	2 291 . .	8.47	6.47	7.75	7.32	5.99	9.23	11.49	7.06
Other services, debit	3 200 BA	**–10.82**	**–11.27**	**–9.99**	**–10.22**	**–26.44**	**–35.80**	**–37.27**	**–41.49**
Communications	3 245 . .	. . .	. . .	. . .	. . .	–.86	–1.15	–1.03	–.88
Construction	3 249 . .	. . .	. . .	. . .	. . .	–.30	–.79	–.72	–.40
Insurance	3 253 . .	–1.61	–1.67	–1.60	–1.33	–1.57	–1.65	–2.83	–1.14
Financial	3 260 . .	. . .	. . .	. . .	. . .	–3.93	–2.92	–4.63	–6.95
Computer and information	3 262 . .	. . .	. . .	. . .	. . .	. . .	. . .	. . .	. . .
Royalties and licence fees	3 266 . .	. . .	. . .	. . .	. . .	. . .	. . .	. . .	. . .
Other business services	3 268 . .	–8.71	–9.03	–7.89	–8.07	–15.66	–22.34	–20.39	–25.70
Personal, cultural, and recreational	3 287 . .	. . .	. . .	. . .	. . .	. . .	. . .	. . .	. . .
Government, n.i.e.	3 291 . .	–.50	–.57	–.50	–.82	–4.13	–6.95	–7.68	–6.41

Table 2 (Continued). STANDARD PRESENTATION, 1994–2001
(Millions of U.S. dollars)

	Code		1994	1995	1996	1997	1998	1999	2000	2001
C. INCOME	4 300	. .	–37.42	–36.71	–31.73	–30.28	–8.28	–5.09	–12.97	–4.00
Total credit	2 300	. .	*9.94*	*13.07*	*15.82*	*15.41*	*20.98*	*21.00*	*18.74*	*17.23*
Total debit	3 300	. .	*–47.36*	*–49.79*	*–47.55*	*–45.68*	*–29.26*	*–26.09*	*–31.71*	*–21.23*
Compensation of employees, credit	2 310	. .	**. . .**	**. . .**	**. . .**	**. . .**	**1.56**	**2.13**	**2.54**	**2.62**
Compensation of employees, debit	3 310	. .	**–10.73**	**–11.45**	**–11.19**	**–11.83**	**–2.00**	**–2.75**	**–2.53**	**–1.95**
Investment income, credit	2 320	. .	**9.94**	**13.07**	**15.82**	**15.41**	**19.42**	**18.87**	**16.20**	**14.61**
Direct investment income	2 330	. .	. . .	. . .	. . .	. . .	. . .	. . .	. . .	. . .
Dividends and distributed branch profits	2 332	. .	. . .	. . .	. . .	. . .	. . .	. . .	. . .	. . .
Reinvested earnings and undistributed branch profits	2 333	. .	. . .	. . .	. . .	. . .	. . .	. . .	. . .	. . .
Income on debt (interest)	2 334	. .	. . .	. . .	. . .	. . .	. . .	. . .	. . .	. . .
Portfolio investment income	2 339	. .	. . .	. . .	. . .	. . .	.70	1.27	1.05	.30
Income on equity	2 340	. .	. . .	. . .	. . .	. . .	. . .	. . .	. . .	. . .
Income on bonds and notes	2 350	. .	. . .	. . .	. . .	. . .	. . .	. . .	. . .	. . .
Income on money market instruments	2 360	. .	. . .	. . .	. . .	. . .	. . .	. . .	. . .	. . .
Other investment income	2 370	. .	9.94	13.07	15.82	15.41	18.72	17.60	15.15	14.31
Investment income, debit	3 320	. .	**–36.63**	**–38.33**	**–36.36**	**–33.85**	**–27.27**	**–23.34**	**–29.18**	**–19.28**
Direct investment income	3 330	. .	–34.67	–35.58	–30.74	–28.64	–20.50	–13.68	–21.93	–13.97
Dividends and distributed branch profits	3 332	. .	–5.59	–5.42	. . .	. . .	–2.47	–2.36	–3.53	–2.15
Reinvested earnings and undistributed branch profits	3 333	. .	–29.07	–30.15	–30.74	–28.64	–18.04	–11.31	–18.40	–11.82
Income on debt (interest)	3 334	. .	. . .	. . .	. . .	. . .	. . .	. . .	. . .	. . .
Portfolio investment income	3 339	. .	. . .	. . .	. . .	. . .	. . .	. . .	. . .	. . .
Income on equity	3 340	. .	. . .	. . .	. . .	. . .	. . .	. . .	. . .	. . .
Income on bonds and notes	3 350	. .	. . .	. . .	. . .	. . .	. . .	. . .	. . .	. . .
Income on money market instruments	3 360	. .	. . .	. . .	. . .	. . .	. . .	. . .	. . .	. . .
Other investment income	3 370	. .	–1.96	–2.76	–5.62	–5.20	–6.76	–9.67	–7.25	–5.31
D. CURRENT TRANSFERS	4 379	. .	23.78	23.25	–.55	2.77	–.50	8.11	8.05	17.62
Credit	2 379	. .	**24.50**	**23.81**	**22.39**	**21.77**	**30.72**	**38.86**	**46.05**	**55.88**
General government	2 380	. .	12.22	13.70	22.39	21.77	15.17	20.14	18.64	16.35
Other sectors	2 390	. .	12.28	10.11	. . .	. . .	15.55	18.72	27.41	39.53
Workers' remittances	2 391	. .	5.76	6.13	. . .	. . .	6.22	7.49	10.96	15.81
Other current transfers	2 392	. .	6.52	3.98	. . .	. . .	9.33	11.23	16.45	23.72
Debit	3 379	. .	**–.72**	**–.56**	**–22.94**	**–19.00**	**–31.22**	**–30.76**	**–38.00**	**–38.26**
General government	3 380	. .	–.72	–.56	–.49	–.51	–.94	–1.12	–1.34	–2.87
Other sectors	3 390	. .	. . .	. . .	–22.44	–18.49	–30.29	–29.63	–36.67	–35.39
Workers' remittances	3 391	. .	. . .	. . .	–22.44	–18.49	–12.11	–11.85	–14.67	–14.16
Other current transfers	3 392	. .	. . .	. . .	. . .	. . .	–18.17	–17.78	–22.00	–21.23
CAPITAL AND FINANCIAL ACCOUNT	4 996	. .	**28.72**	**51.63**	**31.08**	**–20.03**	**–11.76**	**9.50**	**–4.12**	**–9.37**
CAPITAL ACCOUNT	4 994	. .	**37.28**	**31.62**	**4.90**	**–5.46**	**–20.86**	**–49.72**	**–23.58**	**–16.03**
Total credit	2 994	. .	*41.45*	*38.33*	*43.38*	*23.75*	*25.44*	*23.94*	*31.88*	*46.07*
Total debit	3 994	. .	*–4.17*	*–6.71*	*–38.48*	*–29.21*	*–46.29*	*–73.66*	*–55.46*	*–62.10*
Capital transfers, credit	2 400	. .	**41.45**	**38.33**	**43.38**	**23.75**	**25.44**	**23.94**	**31.88**	**46.07**
General government	2 401	. .	29.09	30.95	7.81	8.22	11.61	7.59	10.72	11.80
Debt forgiveness	2 402	. .	. . .	. . .	. . .	. . .	. . .	. . .	. . .	. . .
Other capital transfers	2 410	. .	29.09	30.95	7.81	8.22	. . .	. . .	. . .	. . .
Other sectors	2 430	. .	12.36	7.38	35.57	15.53	13.83	16.35	21.16	34.27
Migrants' transfers	2 431	. .	12.36	7.38	35.57	15.53	13.83	16.35	21.16	34.27
Debt forgiveness	2 432	. .	. . .	. . .	. . .	. . .	. . .	. . .	. . .	. . .
Other capital transfers	2 440	. .	. . .	. . .	. . .	. . .	. . .	. . .	. . .	. . .
Capital transfers, debit	3 400	. .	**–4.17**	**–6.71**	**–38.48**	**–29.21**	**–46.29**	**–73.66**	**–55.46**	**–62.10**
General government	3 401	. .	. . .	. . .	. . .	. . .	. . .	. . .	. . .	. . .
Debt forgiveness	3 402	. .	. . .	. . .	. . .	. . .	. . .	. . .	. . .	. . .
Other capital transfers	3 410	. .	. . .	. . .	. . .	. . .	. . .	. . .	. . .	. . .
Other sectors	3 430	. .	–4.17	–6.71	–38.48	–29.21	–46.29	–73.66	–55.46	–62.10
Migrants' transfers	3 431	. .	–4.17	–6.71	–38.48	–29.21	–46.29	–73.66	–55.46	–62.10
Debt forgiveness	3 432	. .	. . .	. . .	. . .	. . .	. . .	. . .	. . .	. . .
Other capital transfers	3 440	. .	. . .	. . .	. . .	. . .	. . .	. . .	. . .	. . .
Nonproduced nonfinancial assets, credit	2 480	. .	**. . .**	**. . .**	**. . .**	**. . .**	**. . .**	**. . .**	**. . .**	**. . .**
Nonproduced nonfinancial assets, debit	3 480	. .	**. . .**	**. . .**	**. . .**	**. . .**	**. . .**	**. . .**	**. . .**	**. . .**

Table 2 (Continued). STANDARD PRESENTATION, 1994–2001
(Millions of U.S. dollars)

	Code	1994	1995	1996	1997	1998	1999	2000	2001
FINANCIAL ACCOUNT	4 995	**–8.55**	**20.01**	**26.18**	**–14.57**	**9.09**	**59.22**	**19.46**	**6.67**
A. DIRECT INVESTMENT	4 500	29.79	31.04	32.73	30.23	20.38	13.40	20.26	18.00
Direct investment abroad	4 505	**. . .**	**. . .**	**. . .**	**. . .**	**. . .**	**. . .**	**. . .**	**. . .**
Equity capital	4 510	. . .	. . .	. . .	. . .	. . .	. . .	. . .	. . .
Claims on affiliated enterprises	4 515	. . .	. . .	. . .	. . .	. . .	. . .	. . .	. . .
Liabilities to affiliated enterprises	4 520	. . .	. . .	. . .	. . .	. . .	. . .	. . .	. . .
Reinvested earnings	4 525	. . .	. . .	. . .	. . .	. . .	. . .	. . .	. . .
Other capital	4 530	. . .	. . .	. . .	. . .	. . .	. . .	. . .	. . .
Claims on affiliated enterprises	4 535	. . .	. . .	. . .	. . .	. . .	. . .	. . .	. . .
Liabilities to affiliated enterprises	4 540	. . .	. . .	. . .	. . .	. . .	. . .	. . .	. . .
Direct investment in Vanuatu	4 555	**29.79**	**31.04**	**32.73**	**30.23**	**20.38**	**13.40**	**20.26**	**18.00**
Equity capital	4 560	. . .	. . .	. . .	. . .	. . .	. . .	. . .	. . .
Claims on direct investors	4 565	. . .	. . .	. . .	. . .	. . .	. . .	. . .	. . .
Liabilities to direct investors	4 570	. . .	. . .	. . .	. . .	. . .	. . .	. . .	. . .
Reinvested earnings	4 575	29.07	30.15	30.74	28.64	18.04	11.31	18.40	11.82
Other capital	4 580	.71	.89	1.99	1.59	2.35	2.09	1.85	6.19
Claims on direct investors	4 585	. . .	. . .	. . .	. . .	. . .	. . .	. . .	. . .
Liabilities to direct investors	4 590	. . .	. . .	. . .	. . .	2.35	2.09	1.85	6.19
B. PORTFOLIO INVESTMENT	4 600	. . .	. . .	. . .	. . .	3.45	–1.01	.69	–4.33
Assets	4 602	**. . .**	**. . .**	**. . .**	**. . .**	**3.45**	**–1.01**	**.69**	**–4.33**
Equity securities	4 610	. . .	. . .	. . .	. . .	. . .	. . .	. . .	. . .
Monetary authorities	4 611	. . .	. . .	. . .	. . .	. . .	. . .	. . .	. . .
General government	4 612	. . .	. . .	. . .	. . .	. . .	. . .	. . .	. . .
Banks	4 613	. . .	. . .	. . .	. . .	. . .	. . .	. . .	. . .
Other sectors	4 614	. . .	. . .	. . .	. . .	. . .	. . .	. . .	. . .
Debt securities	4 619	. . .	. . .	. . .	. . .	. . .	. . .	. . .	. . .
Bonds and notes	4 620	. . .	. . .	. . .	. . .	. . .	. . .	. . .	. . .
Monetary authorities	4 621	. . .	. . .	. . .	. . .	. . .	. . .	. . .	. . .
General government	4 622	. . .	. . .	. . .	. . .	. . .	. . .	. . .	. . .
Banks	4 623	. . .	. . .	. . .	. . .	. . .	. . .	. . .	. . .
Other sectors	4 624	. . .	. . .	. . .	. . .	. . .	. . .	. . .	. . .
Money market instruments	4 630	. . .	. . .	. . .	. . .	. . .	. . .	. . .	. . .
Monetary authorities	4 631	. . .	. . .	. . .	. . .	. . .	. . .	. . .	. . .
General government	4 632	. . .	. . .	. . .	. . .	. . .	. . .	. . .	. . .
Banks	4 633	. . .	. . .	. . .	. . .	. . .	. . .	. . .	. . .
Other sectors	4 634	. . .	. . .	. . .	. . .	. . .	. . .	. . .	. . .
Liabilities	4 652	**. . .**	**. . .**	**. . .**	**. . .**	**. . .**	**. . .**	**. . .**	**. . .**
Equity securities	4 660	. . .	. . .	. . .	. . .	. . .	. . .	. . .	. . .
Banks	4 663	. . .	. . .	. . .	. . .	. . .	. . .	. . .	. . .
Other sectors	4 664	. . .	. . .	. . .	. . .	. . .	. . .	. . .	. . .
Debt securities	4 669	. . .	. . .	. . .	. . .	. . .	. . .	. . .	. . .
Bonds and notes	4 670	. . .	. . .	. . .	. . .	. . .	. . .	. . .	. . .
Monetary authorities	4 671	. . .	. . .	. . .	. . .	. . .	. . .	. . .	. . .
General government	4 672	. . .	. . .	. . .	. . .	. . .	. . .	. . .	. . .
Banks	4 673	. . .	. . .	. . .	. . .	. . .	. . .	. . .	. . .
Other sectors	4 674	. . .	. . .	. . .	. . .	. . .	. . .	. . .	. . .
Money market instruments	4 680	. . .	. . .	. . .	. . .	. . .	. . .	. . .	. . .
Monetary authorities	4 681	. . .	. . .	. . .	. . .	. . .	. . .	. . .	. . .
General government	4 682	. . .	. . .	. . .	. . .	. . .	. . .	. . .	. . .
Banks	4 683	. . .	. . .	. . .	. . .	. . .	. . .	. . .	. . .
Other sectors	4 684	. . .	. . .	. . .	. . .	. . .	. . .	. . .	. . .
C. FINANCIAL DERIVATIVES	4 910	. . .	. . .	. . .	. . .	. . .	. . .	. . .	. . .
Monetary authorities	4 911	. . .	. . .	. . .	. . .	. . .	. . .	. . .	. . .
General government	4 912	. . .	. . .	. . .	. . .	. . .	. . .	. . .	. . .
Banks	4 913	. . .	. . .	. . .	. . .	. . .	. . .	. . .	. . .
Other sectors	4 914	. . .	. . .	. . .	. . .	. . .	. . .	. . .	. . .
Assets	4 900	**. . .**	**. . .**	**. . .**	**. . .**	**. . .**	**. . .**	**. . .**	**. . .**
Monetary authorities	4 901	. . .	. . .	. . .	. . .	. . .	. . .	. . .	. . .
General government	4 902	. . .	. . .	. . .	. . .	. . .	. . .	. . .	. . .
Banks	4 903	. . .	. . .	. . .	. . .	. . .	. . .	. . .	. . .
Other sectors	4 904	. . .	. . .	. . .	. . .	. . .	. . .	. . .	. . .
Liabilities	4 905	**. . .**	**. . .**	**. . .**	**. . .**	**. . .**	**. . .**	**. . .**	**. . .**
Monetary authorities	4 906	. . .	. . .	. . .	. . .	. . .	. . .	. . .	. . .
General government	4 907	. . .	. . .	. . .	. . .	. . .	. . .	. . .	. . .
Banks	4 908	. . .	. . .	. . .	. . .	. . .	. . .	. . .	. . .
Other sectors	4 909	. . .	. . .	. . .	. . .	. . .	. . .	. . .	. . .

Table 2 (Concluded). STANDARD PRESENTATION, 1994–2001
(Millions of U.S. dollars)

	Code		1994	1995	1996	1997	1998	1999	2000	2001
D. OTHER INVESTMENT	4 700	. .	–43.20	–5.74	–11.85	–46.97	–6.69	43.35	–2.36	–7.64
Assets	4 703	. .	**–45.47**	**–1.59**	**–16.63**	**–23.53**	**5.12**	**29.63**	**–13.55**	**–11.41**
Trade credits	4 706	. .	. . .	. . .	. . .	. . .	. . .	. . .	. . .	. . .
General government	4 707	. .	. . .	. . .	. . .	. . .	. . .	. . .	. . .	. . .
of which: Short-term	4 709	. .	. . .	. . .	. . .	. . .	. . .	. . .	. . .	. . .
Other sectors	4 710	. .	. . .	. . .	. . .	. . .	. . .	. . .	. . .	. . .
of which: Short-term	4 712	. .	. . .	. . .	. . .	. . .	. . .	. . .	. . .	. . .
Loans	4 714	. .	2.18	.62	. . .	. . .	. . .	. . .	. . .	. . .
Monetary authorities	4 715	. .	. . .	. . .	. . .	. . .	. . .	. . .	. . .	. . .
of which: Short-term	4 718	. .	. . .	. . .	. . .	. . .	. . .	. . .	. . .	. . .
General government	4 719	. .	. . .	. . .	. . .	. . .	. . .	. . .	. . .	. . .
of which: Short-term	4 721	. .	. . .	. . .	. . .	. . .	. . .	. . .	. . .	. . .
Banks	4 722	. .	1.46	–.27	. . .	. . .	. . .	. . .	. . .	. . .
of which: Short-term	4 724	. .	. . .	. . .	. . .	. . .	. . .	. . .	. . .	. . .
Other sectors	4 725	. .	.71	.89	. . .	. . .	. . .	. . .	. . .	. . .
of which: Short-term	4 727	. .	. . .	. . .	. . .	. . .	. . .	. . .	. . .	. . .
Currency and deposits	4 730	. .	–47.20	–1.90	–16.25	–23.07	5.12	29.63	–13.55	–11.41
Monetary authorities	4 731	. .	. . .	. . .	. . .	. . .	. . .	. . .	. . .	. . .
General government	4 732	. .	. . .	. . .	. . .	. . .	. . .	. . .	. . .	. . .
Banks	4 733	. .	9.13	–1.90	–16.25	–23.07	5.89	27.05	–13.10	–14.81
Other sectors	4 734	. .	–56.33	. . .	. . .	. . .	–.77	2.59	–.45	3.40
Other assets	4 736	. .	–.45	–.30	–.39	–.46	. . .	. . .	. . .	. . .
Monetary authorities	4 737	. .	. . .	. . .	. . .	. . .	. . .	. . .	. . .	. . .
of which: Short-term	4 739	. .	. . .	. . .	. . .	. . .	. . .	. . .	. . .	. . .
General government	4 740	. .	–.45	–.30	–.39	–.46	. . .	. . .	. . .	. . .
of which: Short-term	4 742	. .	. . .	. . .	. . .	. . .	. . .	. . .	. . .	. . .
Banks	4 743	. .	. . .	. . .	. . .	. . .	. . .	. . .	. . .	. . .
of which: Short-term	4 745	. .	. . .	. . .	. . .	. . .	. . .	. . .	. . .	. . .
Other sectors	4 746	. .	. . .	. . .	. . .	. . .	. . .	. . .	. . .	. . .
of which: Short-term	4 748	. .	. . .	. . .	. . .	. . .	. . .	. . .	. . .	. . .
Liabilities	4 753	. .	**2.27**	**–4.15**	**4.78**	**–23.43**	**–11.80**	**13.72**	**11.19**	**3.78**
Trade credits	4 756	. .	. . .	. . .	. . .	. . .	. . .	. . .	. . .	. . .
General government	4 757	. .	. . .	. . .	. . .	. . .	. . .	. . .	. . .	. . .
of which: Short-term	4 759	. .	. . .	. . .	. . .	. . .	. . .	. . .	. . .	. . .
Other sectors	4 760	. .	. . .	. . .	. . .	. . .	. . .	. . .	. . .	. . .
of which: Short-term	4 762	. .	. . .	. . .	. . .	. . .	. . .	. . .	. . .	. . .
Loans	4 764	. .	2.17	2.21	.45	.68	9.21	3.69	16.01	.20
Monetary authorities	4 765	. .	. . .	. . .	. . .	. . .	. . .	. . .	. . .	. . .
of which: Use of Fund credit and loans from the Fund	4 766	. .	. . .	. . .	. . .	. . .	. . .	. . .	. . .	. . .
of which: Short-term	4 768	. .	. . .	. . .	. . .	. . .	. . .	. . .	. . .	. . .
General government	4 769	. .	2.17	2.21	.45	.68	10.30	4.69	15.62	–3.50
of which: Short-term	4 771	. .	. . .	. . .	. . .	. . .	. . .	. . .	. . .	. . .
Banks	4 772	. .	. . .	. . .	. . .	. . .	. . .	. . .	. . .	. . .
of which: Short-term	4 774	. .	. . .	. . .	. . .	. . .	. . .	. . .	. . .	. . .
Other sectors	4 775	. .	. . .	. . .	. . .	. . .	–1.09	–1.01	.39	3.70
of which: Short-term	4 777	. .	. . .	. . .	. . .	. . .	. . .	. . .	. . .	. . .
Currency and deposits	4 780	. .	.10	–6.36	4.34	–24.12	–21.01	10.03	–4.82	3.58
Monetary authorities	4 781	. .	–.05	.18	–.12	.12	–.11	1.30	–.03	.53
General government	4 782	. .	. . .	. . .	. . .	. . .	. . .	. . .	. . .	. . .
Banks	4 783	. .	.16	–6.54	4.46	–24.23	–20.91	8.73	–4.79	3.05
Other sectors	4 784	. .	. . .	. . .	. . .	. . .	. . .	. . .	. . .	. . .
Other liabilities	4 786	. .	. . .	. . .	. . .	. . .	. . .	. . .	. . .	. . .
Monetary authorities	4 787	. .	. . .	. . .	. . .	. . .	. . .	. . .	. . .	. . .
of which: Short-term	4 789	. .	. . .	. . .	. . .	. . .	. . .	. . .	. . .	. . .
General government	4 790	. .	. . .	. . .	. . .	. . .	. . .	. . .	. . .	. . .
of which: Short-term	4 792	. .	. . .	. . .	. . .	. . .	. . .	. . .	. . .	. . .
Banks	4 793	. .	. . .	. . .	. . .	. . .	. . .	. . .	. . .	. . .
of which: Short-term	4 795	. .	. . .	. . .	. . .	. . .	. . .	. . .	. . .	. . .
Other sectors	4 796	. .	. . .	. . .	. . .	. . .	. . .	. . .	. . .	. . .
of which: Short-term	4 798	. .	. . .	. . .	. . .	. . .	. . .	. . .	. . .	. . .
E. RESERVE ASSETS	4 802	. .	4.86	–5.30	5.30	2.16	–8.06	3.48	.87	.62
Monetary gold	4 812	. .	. . .	. . .	. . .	. . .	. . .	. . .	. . .	. . .
Special drawing rights	4 811	. .	–.09	–.11	–.11	–.11	–.12	–.10	–.13	–.11
Reserve position in the Fund	4 810	. .	. . .	. . .	. . .	–.01	. . .	. . .	. . .	. . .
Foreign exchange	4 803	. .	4.95	–5.18	5.41	2.28	–7.94	3.58	1.00	.74
Other claims	4 813	. .	. . .	. . .	. . .	. . .	. . .	. . .	. . .	. . .
NET ERRORS AND OMISSIONS	4 998	. .	**–10.21**	**–33.38**	**–4.14**	**39.37**	**6.01**	**3.57**	**–.88**	**7.55**

Part 3 of the *Yearbook* contains descriptions of the methodologies, compilation practices, and sources used to compile these data.

Table 3. INTERNATIONAL INVESTMENT POSITION (End–period stocks), 1994–2001
(Millions of U.S. dollars)

	Code	1994	1995	1996	1997	1998	1999	2000	2001
ASSETS	8 995 C.	...	...	...	...	237.57	264.79	...	...
Direct investment abroad	8 505 . .	...	...	...	...	...	...	...	...
Equity capital and reinvested earnings	8 506 . .	...	...	...	...	...	...	...	...
Claims on affiliated enterprises	8 507 . .	...	...	...	...	...	...	...	...
Liabilities to affiliated enterprises	8 508 . .	...	...	...	...	...	...	...	...
Other capital	8 530 . .	...	...	...	...	...	...	...	...
Claims on affiliated enterprises	8 535 . .	...	...	...	...	...	...	...	...
Liabilities to affiliated enterprises	8 540 . .	...	...	...	...	...	...	...	...
Portfolio investment	8 602 . .	...	...	...	...	**2.93**	**4.42**	...	...
Equity securities	8 610 . .	...	...	...	...	2.00	3.49	...	...
Monetary authorities	8 611 . .	...	...	...	...	...	...	...	...
General government	8 612 . .	...	...	...	...	...	...	...	...
Banks	8 613 . .	...	...	...	...	...	...	...	...
Other sectors	8 614 . .	...	...	...	...	2.00	3.49	...	...
Debt securities	8 619 . .	...	...	...	...	.92	.93	...	...
Bonds and notes	8 620 . .	...	...	...	...	.92	.93	...	...
Monetary authorities	8 621 . .	...	...	...	...	...	...	...	...
General government	8 622 . .	...	...	...	...	.92	.93	...	...
Banks	8 623 . .	...	...	...	...	...	...	...	...
Other sectors	8 624 . .	...	...	...	...	...	...	...	...
Money market instruments	8 630 . .	...	...	...	...	...	...	...	...
Monetary authorities	8 631 . .	...	...	...	...	...	...	...	...
General government	8 632 . .	...	...	...	...	...	...	...	...
Banks	8 633 . .	...	...	...	...	...	...	...	...
Other sectors	8 634 . .	...	...	...	...	...	...	...	...
Financial derivatives	8 900 . .	...	...	...	...	...	...	...	...
Monetary authorities	8 901 . .	...	...	...	...	...	...	...	...
General government	8 902 . .	...	...	...	...	...	...	...	...
Banks	8 903 . .	...	...	...	...	...	...	...	...
Other sectors	8 904 . .	...	...	...	...	...	...	...	...
Other investment	8 703 . .	...	...	...	...	**189.99**	**219.01**	...	...
Trade credits	8 706 . .	...	...	...	...	...	...	...	...
General government	8 707 . .	...	...	...	...	...	...	...	...
of which: Short-term	8 709 . .	...	...	...	...	...	...	...	...
Other sectors	8 710 . .	...	...	...	...	...	...	...	...
of which: Short-term	8 712 . .	...	...	...	...	...	...	...	...
Loans	8 714 . .	...	...	...	...	...	...	...	...
Monetary authorities	8 715 . .	...	...	...	...	...	...	...	...
of which: Short-term	8 718 . .	...	...	...	...	...	...	...	...
General government	8 719 . .	...	...	...	...	...	...	...	...
of which: Short-term	8 721 . .	...	...	...	...	...	...	...	...
Banks	8 722 . .	...	...	...	...	...	...	...	...
of which: Short-term	8 724 . .	...	...	...	...	...	...	...	...
Other sectors	8 725 . .	...	...	...	...	...	...	...	...
of which: Short-term	8 727 . .	...	...	...	...	...	...	...	...
Currency and deposits	8 730 . .	...	...	...	...	189.99	219.01	...	...
Monetary authorities	8 731 . .	...	...	...	...	...	...	...	...
General government	8 732 . .	...	...	...	...	...	...	...	...
Banks	8 733 . .	...	...	...	...	189.99	164.26	...	...
Other sectors	8 734 . .	...	...	...	...	...	54.74	...	...
Other assets	8 736 . .	...	...	...	...	...	...	...	...
Monetary authorities	8 737 . .	...	...	...	...	...	...	...	...
of which: Short-term	8 739 . .	...	...	...	...	...	...	...	...
General government	8 740 . .	...	...	...	...	...	...	...	...
of which: Short-term	8 742 . .	...	...	...	...	...	...	...	...
Banks	8 743 . .	...	...	...	...	...	...	...	...
of which: Short-term	8 745 . .	...	...	...	...	...	...	...	...
Other sectors	8 746 . .	...	...	...	...	...	...	...	...
of which: Short-term	8 748 . .	...	...	...	...	...	...	...	...
Reserve assets	8 802 . .	...	...	...	...	**44.65**	**41.36**	...	...
Monetary gold	8 812 . .	...	...	...	...	...	...	...	...
Special drawing rights	8 811 . .	.31	.43	.52	.60	.74	.83	.91	.99
Reserve position in the Fund	8 810 . .	3.63	3.70	3.58	3.37	3.51	3.43	3.25	3.14
Foreign exchange	8 803 . .	...	...	...	...	40.39	37.10	...	...
Other claims	8 813 . .	...	...	...	...	...	...	...	...

Table 3 (Concluded). INTERNATIONAL INVESTMENT POSITION (End–period stocks), 1994–2001

(Millions of U.S. dollars)

	Code	1994	1995	1996	1997	1998	1999	2000	2001
LIABILITIES	8 995 D.	...	...	...	...	265.14	280.72	...	...
Direct investment in Vanuatu	8 555 . .	...	...	...	...	**47.62**	**66.53**	...	...
Equity capital and reinvested earnings	8 556 . .	...	...	...	...	43.92	60.71	...	...
Claims on direct investors	8 557 . .	...	...	...	...	...	...	...	...
Liabilities to direct investors	8 558 . .	...	...	...	...	43.92	60.71	...	...
Other capital	8 580 . .	...	...	...	...	3.70	5.82	...	...
Claims on direct investors	8 585 . .	...	...	...	...	...	...	...	...
Liabilities to direct investors	8 590 . .	...	...	...	...	3.70	5.82	...	...
Portfolio investment	8 652 . .	...	...	...	...	...	...	...	...
Equity securities	8 660 . .	...	...	...	...	...	...	...	...
Banks	8 663 . .	...	...	...	...	...	...	...	...
Other sectors	8 664 . .	...	...	...	...	...	...	...	...
Debt securities	8 669 . .	...	...	...	...	...	...	...	...
Bonds and notes	8 670 . .	...	...	...	...	...	...	...	...
Monetary authorities	8 671 . .	...	...	...	...	...	...	...	...
General government	8 672 . .	...	...	...	...	...	...	...	...
Banks	8 673 . .	...	...	...	...	...	...	...	...
Other sectors	8 674 . .	...	...	...	...	...	...	...	...
Money market instruments	8 680 . .	...	...	...	...	...	...	...	...
Monetary authorities	8 681 . .	...	...	...	...	...	...	...	...
General government	8 682 . .	...	...	...	...	...	...	...	...
Banks	8 683 . .	...	...	...	...	...	...	...	...
Other sectors	8 684 . .	...	...	...	...	...	...	...	...
Financial derivatives	8 905 . .	...	...	...	...	...	...	...	...
Monetary authorities	8 906 . .	...	...	...	...	...	...	...	...
General government	8 907 . .	...	...	...	...	...	...	...	...
Banks	8 908 . .	...	...	...	...	...	...	...	...
Other sectors	8 909 . .	...	...	...	...	...	...	...	...
Other investment	8 753 . .	...	...	...	...	**217.52**	**214.19**	...	...
Trade credits	8 756 . .	...	...	...	...	...	...	...	...
General government	8 757 . .	...	...	...	...	...	...	...	...
of which: Short-term	8 759 . .	...	...	...	...	...	...	...	...
Other sectors	8 760 . .	...	...	...	...	...	...	...	...
of which: Short-term	8 762 . .	...	...	...	...	...	...	...	...
Loans	8 764 . .	...	...	...	...	51.93	56.98	...	...
Monetary authorities	8 765 . .	...	...	...	...	...	...	...	...
of which: Use of Fund credit and loans from the Fund	8 766 . .	...	...	...	...	...	...	...	...
of which: Short-term	8 768 . .	...	...	...	...	...	...	...	...
General government	8 769 . .	...	...	...	...	51.93	56.98	...	...
of which: Short-term	8 771 . .	...	...	...	...	...	...	...	...
Banks	8 772 . .	...	...	...	...	...	...	...	...
of which: Short-term	8 774 . .	...	...	...	...	...	...	...	...
Other sectors	8 775 . .	...	...	...	...	...	...	...	...
of which: Short-term	8 777 . .	...	...	...	...	...	...	...	...
Currency and deposits	8 780 . .	...	...	...	...	137.33	121.03	...	...
Monetary authorities	8 781 . .	...	...	...	...	.18	1.70	...	...
General government	8 782 . .	...	...	...	...	...	...	...	...
Banks	8 783 . .	...	...	...	...	137.16	119.33	...	...
Other sectors	8 784 . .	...	...	...	...	...	...	...	...
Other liabilities	8 786 . .	...	...	...	...	28.26	36.19	...	...
Monetary authorities	8 787 . .	...	...	...	...	...	...	...	...
of which: Short-term	8 789 . .	...	...	...	...	...	...	...	...
General government	8 790 . .	...	...	...	...	...	...	...	...
of which: Short-term	8 792 . .	...	...	...	...	...	...	...	...
Banks	8 793 . .	...	...	...	...	25.01	33.92	...	...
of which: Short-term	8 795 . .	...	...	...	...	...	...	...	...
Other sectors	8 796 . .	...	...	...	...	3.25	2.27	...	...
of which: Short-term	8 798 . .	...	...	...	...	*3.25*	*2.27*	...	...
NET INTERNATIONAL INVESTMENT POSITION	8 995 . .	...	...	...	...	**–27.57**	**–15.93**	...	...
Conversion rates: vatu per U.S. dollar (end of period)	0 102 . .	**112.08**	**113.74**	**110.77**	**124.31**	**129.78**	**128.89**	**142.81**	**146.74**

Table 1. ANALYTIC PRESENTATION, 1994–2001
(Millions of U.S. dollars)

	Code	1994	1995	1996	1997	1998	1999	2000	2001
A. Current Account[1]	4 993 Z.	**2,541**	**2,014**	**8,914**	**3,467**	**–3,253**	**3,559**	**13,030**	**3,931**
Goods: exports f.o.b	2 100 . .	16,105	19,082	23,707	23,703	17,576	20,819	32,998	26,726
Goods: imports f.o.b	3 100 . .	–8,480	–12,069	–9,937	–13,678	–15,105	–13,213	–15,491	–17,391
Balance on Goods	4 100 . .	*7,625*	*7,013*	*13,770*	*10,025*	*2,471*	*7,606*	*17,507*	*9,335*
Services: credit	2 200 . .	1,576	1,671	1,573	1,489	1,461	1,310	1,221	1,280
Services: debit	3 200 . .	–4,672	–4,836	–4,842	–5,495	–5,146	–3,772	–4,272	–4,614
Balance on Goods and Services	4 991 . .	*4,529*	*3,848*	*10,501*	*6,019*	*–1,214*	*5,144*	*14,456*	*6,001*
Income: credit	2 300 . .	1,626	1,867	1,579	2,139	2,286	2,159	2,915	2,495
Income: debit	3 300 . .	–3,530	–3,810	–3,304	–4,547	–4,217	–3,684	–4,119	–3,948
Balance on Goods, Services, and Income	4 992 . .	*2,625*	*1,905*	*8,776*	*3,611*	*–3,145*	*3,619*	*13,252*	*4,548*
Current transfers: credit	2 379 Z.	606	413	526	221	275	191	222	196
Current transfers: debit	3 379 . .	–690	–304	–388	–365	–383	–251	–444	–813
B. Capital Account[1]	4 994 Z.	**. . .**	**. . .**	**. . .**	**. . .**	**. . .**	**. . .**	**. . .**	**. . .**
Capital account: credit	2 994 Z.	. . .	. . .	. . .	. . .	. . .	. . .	. . .	. . .
Capital account: debit	3 994 . .	. . .	. . .	. . .	. . .	. . .	. . .	. . .	. . .
Total, Groups A Plus B	4 981 . .	*2,541*	*2,014*	*8,914*	*3,467*	*–3,253*	*3,559*	*13,030*	*3,931*
C. Financial Account[1]	4 995 W.	**–3,204**	**–2,964**	**–1,784**	**1,069**	**1,764**	**–1,010**	**–2,955**	**–811**
Direct investment abroad	4 505 . .	–358	–91	–507	–500	–233	–501	–107	–148
Direct investment in Venezuela	4 555 Z.	813	985	2,183	5,536	4,495	3,290	4,465	3,448
Portfolio investment assets	4 602 . .	–22	–14	–41	–600	1,070	372	–905	–340
Equity securities	4 610 . .	10	–3	–11	–18	–66	70	–87	–117
Debt securities	4 619 . .	–32	–11	–30	–582	1,136	302	–818	–223
Portfolio investment liabilities	4 652 Z.	275	–787	780	1,106	219	1,565	–1,925	936
Equity securities	4 660 . .	585	270	1,318	1,445	186	415	–461	–74
Debt securities	4 669 Z.	–310	–1,057	–538	–339	33	1,150	–1,464	1,010
Financial derivatives	4 910 . .	. . .	. . .	. . .	. . .	. . .	. . .	. . .	. . .
Financial derivatives assets	4 900 . .	. . .	. . .	. . .	. . .	. . .	. . .	. . .	. . .
Financial derivatives liabilities	4 905 . .	. . .	. . .	. . .	. . .	. . .	. . .	. . .	. . .
Other investment assets	4 703 . .	–4,173	–661	–1,592	–3,385	–3,413	–6,371	–4,920	–4,414
Monetary authorities	4 701 . .	. . .	. . .	. . .	. . .	. . .	. . .	. . .	. . .
General government	4 704 . .	–27	240	57	–273	152	240	–195	–1,192
Banks	4 705 . .	–932	216	–53	–25	–169	–228	–46	858
Other sectors	4 728 . .	–3,214	–1,117	–1,596	–3,087	–3,396	–6,383	–4,679	–4,080
Other investment liabilities	4 753 W.	261	–2,396	–2,607	–1,088	–374	635	437	–293
Monetary authorities	4 753 WA	–51	–317	–289	–454	–16	–6	5	8
General government	4 753 ZB	128	–262	–543	–192	260	–315	51	35
Banks	4 753 ZC	–77	52	153	31	–72	–93	244	–70
Other sectors	4 753 ZD	261	–1,869	–1,928	–473	–546	1,049	137	–266
Total, Groups A Through C	4 983 . .	*–663*	*–950*	*7,130*	*4,536*	*–1,489*	*2,549*	*10,075*	*3,120*
D. Net Errors and Omissions	4 998 . .	**–281**	**–494**	**–892**	**–1,461**	**–1,442**	**–1,510**	**–4,250**	**–5,183**
Total, Groups A Through D	4 984 . .	*–944*	*–1,444*	*6,238*	*3,075*	*–2,931*	*1,039*	*5,825*	*–2,063*
E. Reserves and Related Items	4 802 A.	**944**	**1,444**	**–6,238**	**–3,075**	**2,931**	**–1,039**	**–5,825**	**2,063**
Reserve assets	4 802 . .	1,145	1,907	–6,271	–2,624	3,379	–589	–5,316	2,261
Use of Fund credit and loans	4 766 . .	–201	–463	33	–452	–448	–450	–508	–198
Exceptional financing	4 920 . .	. . .	. . .	. . .	. . .	. . .	. . .	. . .	. . .
Conversion rates: bolívares per U.S. dollar	0 101 . .	**148.503**	**176.843**	**417.333**	**488.635**	**547.556**	**605.717**	**679.960**	**723.666**

[1] Excludes components that have been classified in the categories of Group E.

Table 2. STANDARD PRESENTATION, 1994–2001

(Millions of U.S. dollars)

	Code		1994	1995	1996	1997	1998	1999	2000	2001
CURRENT ACCOUNT	4 993	. .	**2,541**	**2,014**	**8,914**	**3,467**	**–3,253**	**3,559**	**13,030**	**3,931**
A. GOODS	4 100	. .	7,625	7,013	13,770	10,025	2,471	7,606	17,507	9,335
Credit	2 100	. .	**16,105**	**19,082**	**23,707**	**23,703**	**17,576**	**20,819**	**32,998**	**26,726**
General merchandise: exports f.o.b.	2 110	. .	15,575	18,656	23,259	23,441	17,063	20,539	32,430	26,317
Goods for processing: exports f.o.b.	2 150	. .	. . .	. . .	. . .	. . .	. . .	. . .	. . .	. . .
Repairs on goods	2 160	. .	13	14	15	4	4	4	4	4
Goods procured in ports by carriers	2 170	. .	187	226	278	256	205	234	340	291
Nonmonetary gold	2 180	. .	330	186	155	2	304	42	224	114
Debit	3 100	. .	**–8,480**	**–12,069**	**–9,937**	**–13,678**	**–15,105**	**–13,213**	**–15,491**	**–17,391**
General merchandise: imports f.o.b.	3 110	. .	–8,346	–11,937	–9,810	–13,641	–15,048	–13,178	–15,463	–17,362
Goods for processing: imports f.o.b.	3 150	. .	. . .	. . .	. . .	. . .	. . .	. . .	. . .	. . .
Repairs on goods	3 160	. .	–56	–62	–56	–17	–12	–10	–8	–8
Goods procured in ports by carriers	3 170	. .	–78	–70	–71	–20	–45	–25	–20	–21
Nonmonetary gold	3 180	. .	. . .	. . .	. . .	. . .	. . .	. . .	. . .	. . .
B. SERVICES	4 200	. .	–3,096	–3,165	–3,269	–4,006	–3,685	–2,462	–3,051	–3,334
Total credit	2 200	. .	*1,576*	*1,671*	*1,573*	*1,489*	*1,461*	*1,310*	*1,221*	*1,280*
Total debit	3 200	. .	*–4,672*	*–4,836*	*–4,842*	*–5,495*	*–5,146*	*–3,772*	*–4,272*	*–4,614*
Transportation services, credit	2 205	. .	**589**	**584**	**484**	**347**	**282**	**331**	**347**	**351**
Passenger	2 850	. .	*132*	*146*	*142*	*35*	*30*	*32*	*25*	*35*
Freight	2 851	. .	*229*	*149*	*117*	*59*	*39*	*92*	*109*	*107*
Other	2 852	. .	*228*	*289*	*225*	*253*	*213*	*207*	*213*	*209*
Sea transport, passenger	2 207	. .	. . .	. . .	. . .	. . .	. . .	. . .	. . .	. . .
Sea transport, freight	2 208	. .	201	115	85	56	38	92	109	107
Sea transport, other	2 209	. .	221	281	139	169	124	130	127	117
Air transport, passenger	2 211	. .	132	146	142	35	30	32	25	35
Air transport, freight	2 212	. .	28	34	32	3	1	. . .	. . .	. . .
Air transport, other	2 213	. .	7	8	14	23	27	22	25	23
Other transport, passenger	2 215	. .	. . .	. . .	. . .	. . .	. . .	. . .	. . .	. . .
Other transport, freight	2 216	. .	. . .	. . .	. . .	. . .	. . .	. . .	. . .	. . .
Other transport, other	2 217	. .	. . .	. . .	72	61	62	55	61	69
Transportation services, debit	3 205	. .	**–1,265**	**–1,430**	**–1,223**	**–1,612**	**–1,589**	**–1,381**	**–1,658**	**–1,862**
Passenger	3 850	. .	*–133*	*–138*	*–103*	*–137*	*–160*	*–139*	*–159*	*–162*
Freight	3 851	. .	*–812*	*–1,067*	*–957*	*–1,330*	*–1,336*	*–1,157*	*–1,358*	*–1,540*
Other	3 852	. .	*–320*	*–225*	*–163*	*–145*	*–93*	*–85*	*–141*	*–160*
Sea transport, passenger	3 207	. .	–17	–13	–13	–15	–13	–8	–9	–8
Sea transport, freight	3 208	. .	–812	–1,067	–957	–1,330	–1,336	–1,157	–1,358	–1,540
Sea transport, other	3 209	. .	–227	–145	–94	–121	–70	–65	–127	–135
Air transport, passenger	3 211	. .	–116	–125	–90	–122	–147	–131	–150	–154
Air transport, freight	3 212	. .	. . .	. . .	. . .	. . .	. . .	. . .	. . .	. . .
Air transport, other	3 213	. .	–93	–80	–69	–24	–23	–20	–14	–25
Other transport, passenger	3 215	. .	. . .	. . .	. . .	. . .	. . .	. . .	. . .	. . .
Other transport, freight	3 216	. .	. . .	. . .	. . .	. . .	. . .	. . .	. . .	. . .
Other transport, other	3 217	. .	. . .	. . .	. . .	. . .	. . .	. . .	. . .	. . .
Travel, credit	2 236	. .	**787**	**849**	**884**	**933**	**961**	**736**	**634**	**682**
Business travel	2 237	. .	301	328	339	429	443	339	292	314
Personal travel	2 240	. .	486	521	545	504	518	397	342	368
Travel, debit	3 236	. .	**–1,950**	**–1,714**	**–2,233**	**–2,552**	**–2,451**	**–1,668**	**–1,705**	**–1,799**
Business travel	3 237	. .	–332	–240	–304	–496	–491	–501	–512	–539
Personal travel	3 240	. .	–1,618	–1,474	–1,929	–2,056	–1,960	–1,167	–1,193	–1,260
Other services, credit	2 200	BA	**200**	**238**	**205**	**209**	**218**	**243**	**240**	**247**
Communications	2 245	. .	29	34	28	11	12	11	11	8
Construction	2 249	. .	. . .	. . .	. . .	. . .	. . .	. . .	. . .	. . .
Insurance	2 253	. .	5	2	2	2	2	2	4	3
Financial	2 260	. .	. . .	. . .	. . .	. . .	. . .	. . .	. . .	. . .
Computer and information	2 262	. .	. . .	. . .	. . .	32	. . .	. . .	. . .	. . .
Royalties and licence fees	2 266	. .	. . .	. . .	. . .	. . .	. . .	. . .	. . .	. . .
Other business services	2 268	. .	44	60	50	39	44	45	55	56
Personal, cultural, and recreational	2 287	. .	. . .	. . .	. . .	. . .	. . .	. . .	. . .	. . .
Government, n.i.e.	2 291	. .	122	142	125	125	160	185	170	180
Other services, debit	3 200	BA	**–1,457**	**–1,692**	**–1,386**	**–1,331**	**–1,106**	**–723**	**–909**	**–953**
Communications	3 245	. .	–31	–28	–28	–43	–46	–41	–79	–105
Construction	3 249	. .	. . .	. . .	. . .	. . .	. . .	. . .	. . .	. . .
Insurance	3 253	. .	–69	–85	–87	–76	–73	–59	–79	–90
Financial	3 260	. .	–40	–35	–50	–98	–42	–53	–28	–69
Computer and information	3 262	. .	. . .	. . .	. . .	. . .	. . .	. . .	. . .	. . .
Royalties and licence fees	3 266	. .	. . .	. . .	–2	. . .	. . .	. . .	. . .	. . .
Other business services	3 268	. .	–1,152	–1,346	–986	–956	–697	–342	–504	–492
Personal, cultural, and recreational	3 287	. .	–18	–16	–16	–16	–18	–19	–20	–25
Government, n.i.e.	3 291	. .	–147	–182	–217	–142	–230	–209	–199	–172

Table 2 (Continued). STANDARD PRESENTATION, 1994–2001

(Millions of U.S. dollars)

	Code		1994	1995	1996	1997	1998	1999	2000	2001
C. INCOME	4 300	. .	–1,904	–1,943	–1,725	–2,408	–1,931	–1,525	–1,204	–1,453
Total credit	2 300	. .	*1,626*	*1,867*	*1,579*	*2,139*	*2,286*	*2,159*	*2,915*	*2,495*
Total debit	3 300	. .	*–3,530*	*–3,810*	*–3,304*	*–4,547*	*–4,217*	*–3,684*	*–4,119*	*–3,948*
Compensation of employees, credit	2 310	. .	**2**	**2**	**4**	**4**	**. . .**	**17**	**16**	**18**
Compensation of employees, debit	3 310	. .	**–11**	**–30**	**–27**	**–28**	**–16**	**–24**	**–28**	**–28**
Investment income, credit	2 320	. .	**1,624**	**1,865**	**1,575**	**2,135**	**2,286**	**2,142**	**2,899**	**2,477**
Direct investment income	2 330	. .	286	265	149	273	444	268	121	639
Dividends and distributed branch profits	2 332	. .	3	14	4	. . .	137	. . .	252	567
Reinvested earnings and undistributed branch profits	2 333	. .	283	251	145	273	307	266	–131	72
Income on debt (interest)	2 334	. .	. . .	. . .	. . .	. . .	. . .	2	. . .	. . .
Portfolio investment income	2 339	. .	323	513	421	743	522	430	583	321
Income on equity	2 340	. .	. . .	. . .	. . .	. . .	. . .	. . .	. . .	. . .
Income on bonds and notes	2 350	. .	. . .	50	20	41	13	27	61	32
Income on money market instruments	2 360	. .	323	463	401	702	509	403	522	289
Other investment income	2 370	. .	1,015	1,087	1,005	1,119	1,320	1,444	2,195	1,517
Investment income, debit	3 320	. .	**–3,519**	**–3,780**	**–3,277**	**–4,519**	**–4,201**	**–3,660**	**–4,091**	**–3,920**
Direct investment income	3 330	. .	–514	–431	–441	–1,031	–1,277	–771	–1,040	–1,106
Dividends and distributed branch profits	3 332	. .	–341	–305	–246	–463	–663	–424	–700	–750
Reinvested earnings and undistributed branch profits	3 333	. .	–173	–126	–195	–568	–609	–347	–340	–356
Income on debt (interest)	3 334	. .	. . .	. . .	. . .	. . .	–5	. . .	. . .	. . .
Portfolio investment income	3 339	. .	–1,577	–1,822	–1,654	–2,402	–1,920	–1,615	–1,739	–1,746
Income on equity	3 340	. .	–175	–189	–133	–922	–404	–118	–49	–131
Income on bonds and notes	3 350	. .	–1,402	–1,633	–1,521	–1,457	–1,501	–1,494	–1,690	–1,615
Income on money market instruments	3 360	. .	. . .	. . .	. . .	–23	–15	–3	. . .	. . .
Other investment income	3 370	. .	–1,428	–1,527	–1,182	–1,086	–1,004	–1,274	–1,312	–1,068
D. CURRENT TRANSFERS	4 379	. .	–84	109	138	–144	–108	–60	–222	–617
Credit	2 379	. .	**606**	**413**	**526**	**221**	**275**	**191**	**222**	**196**
General government	2 380	. .	12	13	11	12	25	30	44	8
Other sectors	2 390	. .	594	400	515	209	250	161	178	188
Workers' remittances	2 391	. .	. . .	. . .	. . .	. . .	. . .	89	115	136
Other current transfers	2 392	. .	594	400	515	209	250	72	63	52
Debit	3 379	. .	**–690**	**–304**	**–388**	**–365**	**–383**	**–251**	**–444**	**–813**
General government	3 380	. .	–25	–46	–36	–84	–73	–18	–52	–52
Other sectors	3 390	. .	–665	–258	–352	–281	–310	–233	–392	–761
Workers' remittances	3 391	. .	–598	–173	–263	–204	–236	–171	–312	–667
Other current transfers	3 392	. .	–67	–85	–89	–77	–74	–62	–80	–94
CAPITAL AND FINANCIAL ACCOUNT	4 996	. .	**–2,260**	**–1,520**	**–8,022**	**–2,006**	**4,695**	**–2,049**	**–8,780**	**1,252**
CAPITAL ACCOUNT	4 994	. .	. . .	. . .	. . .	. . .	. . .	. . .	. . .	. . .
Total credit	2 994	. .	. . .	. . .	. . .	. . .	. . .	. . .	. . .	. . .
Total debit	3 994	. .	. . .	. . .	. . .	. . .	. . .	. . .	. . .	. . .
Capital transfers, credit	2 400	. .	**. . .**	**. . .**	**. . .**	**. . .**	**. . .**	**. . .**	**. . .**	**. . .**
General government	2 401	. .	. . .	. . .	. . .	. . .	. . .	. . .	. . .	. . .
Debt forgiveness	2 402	. .	. . .	. . .	. . .	. . .	. . .	. . .	. . .	. . .
Other capital transfers	2 410	. .	. . .	. . .	. . .	. . .	. . .	. . .	. . .	. . .
Other sectors	2 430	. .	. . .	. . .	. . .	. . .	. . .	. . .	. . .	. . .
Migrants' transfers	2 431	. .	. . .	. . .	. . .	. . .	. . .	. . .	. . .	. . .
Debt forgiveness	2 432	. .	. . .	. . .	. . .	. . .	. . .	. . .	. . .	. . .
Other capital transfers	2 440	. .	. . .	. . .	. . .	. . .	. . .	. . .	. . .	. . .
Capital transfers, debit	3 400	. .	**. . .**	**. . .**	**. . .**	**. . .**	**. . .**	**. . .**	**. . .**	**. . .**
General government	3 401	. .	. . .	. . .	. . .	. . .	. . .	. . .	. . .	. . .
Debt forgiveness	3 402	. .	. . .	. . .	. . .	. . .	. . .	. . .	. . .	. . .
Other capital transfers	3 410	. .	. . .	. . .	. . .	. . .	. . .	. . .	. . .	. . .
Other sectors	3 430	. .	. . .	. . .	. . .	. . .	. . .	. . .	. . .	. . .
Migrants' transfers	3 431	. .	. . .	. . .	. . .	. . .	. . .	. . .	. . .	. . .
Debt forgiveness	3 432	. .	. . .	. . .	. . .	. . .	. . .	. . .	. . .	. . .
Other capital transfers	3 440	. .	. . .	. . .	. . .	. . .	. . .	. . .	. . .	. . .
Nonproduced nonfinancial assets, credit	2 480	. .	**. . .**	**. . .**	**. . .**	**. . .**	**. . .**	**. . .**	**. . .**	**. . .**
Nonproduced nonfinancial assets, debit	3 480	. .	**. . .**	**. . .**	**. . .**	**. . .**	**. . .**	**. . .**	**. . .**	**. . .**

Table 2 (Continued). STANDARD PRESENTATION, 1994–2001
(Millions of U.S. dollars)

	Code	1994	1995	1996	1997	1998	1999	2000	2001
FINANCIAL ACCOUNT	4 995 . .	**–2,260**	**–1,520**	**–8,022**	**–2,006**	**4,695**	**–2,049**	**–8,780**	**1,252**
A. DIRECT INVESTMENT	4 500 . .	455	894	1,676	5,036	4,262	2,789	4,358	3,300
Direct investment abroad	4 505 . .	**–358**	**–91**	**–507**	**–500**	**–233**	**–501**	**–107**	**–148**
Equity capital	4 510 . .	–382	–58	–86	–375	–78	–47	–114	–216
Claims on affiliated enterprises	4 515 . .	–382	–58	–86	–375	–78	–47	–114	–216
Liabilities to affiliated enterprises	4 520 . .	. . .	. . .	. . .	. . .	. . .	. . .	. . .	. . .
Reinvested earnings	4 525 . .	–283	–251	–145	–273	–307	–266	131	–72
Other capital	4 530 . .	307	218	–276	148	152	–188	–124	140
Claims on affiliated enterprises	4 535 . .	319	207	–276	148	152	–188	–124	140
Liabilities to affiliated enterprises	4 540 . .	–12	11	. . .	. . .	. . .	. . .	. . .	. . .
Direct investment in Venezuela	4 555 . .	**813**	**985**	**2,183**	**5,536**	**4,495**	**3,290**	**4,465**	**3,448**
Equity capital	4 560 . .	445	320	901	1,804	2,394	1,025	2,823	1,000
Claims on direct investors	4 565 . .	. . .	. . .	. . .	. . .	. . .	. . .	. . .	. . .
Liabilities to direct investors	4 570 . .	445	320	901	1,804	2,394	1,025	2,823	1,000
Reinvested earnings	4 575 . .	173	126	195	568	609	347	340	356
Other capital	4 580 . .	195	539	1,087	3,164	1,492	1,918	1,302	2,092
Claims on direct investors	4 585 . .	. . .	. . .	. . .	. . .	. . .	. . .	. . .	. . .
Liabilities to direct investors	4 590 . .	195	539	1,087	3,164	1,492	1,918	1,302	2,092
B. PORTFOLIO INVESTMENT	4 600 . .	253	–801	739	506	1,289	1,937	–2,830	596
Assets	4 602 . .	**–22**	**–14**	**–41**	**–600**	**1,070**	**372**	**–905**	**–340**
Equity securities	4 610 . .	10	–3	–11	–18	–66	70	–87	–117
Monetary authorities	4 611 . .	. . .	. . .	. . .	. . .	. . .	. . .	. . .	. . .
General government	4 612 . .	. . .	. . .	. . .	. . .	. . .	. . .	. . .	. . .
Banks	4 613 . .	9	–3	–7	2	3	–1	–11	–1
Other sectors	4 614 . .	1	. . .	–4	–20	–69	71	–76	–116
Debt securities	4 619 . .	–32	–11	–30	–582	1,136	302	–818	–223
Bonds and notes	4 620 . .	–34	–10	1	–93	478	467	–232	–60
Monetary authorities	4 621 . .	. . .	. . .	. . .	–1,130	650	603	. . .	. . .
General government	4 622 . .	. . .	8	. . .	1,130	. . .	. . .	40	5
Banks	4 623 . .	–42	–17	5	–42	–36	–27	–30	–24
Other sectors	4 624 . .	8	–1	–4	–51	–136	–109	–242	–41
Money market instruments	4 630 . .	2	–1	–31	–489	658	–165	–586	–163
Monetary authorities	4 631 . .	. . .	. . .	. . .	. . .	. . .	. . .	. . .	. . .
General government	4 632 . .	. . .	. . .	. . .	. . .	. . .	. . .	. . .	. . .
Banks	4 633 . .	. . .	. . .	–31	–29	69	–98	23	37
Other sectors	4 634 . .	2	–1	. . .	–460	589	–67	–609	–200
Liabilities	4 652 . .	**275**	**–787**	**780**	**1,106**	**219**	**1,565**	**–1,925**	**936**
Equity securities	4 660 . .	585	270	1,318	1,445	186	415	–461	–74
Banks	4 663 . .	8	10	61	206	–63	9	121	–9
Other sectors	4 664 . .	577	260	1,257	1,239	249	406	–582	–65
Debt securities	4 669 . .	–310	–1,057	–538	–339	33	1,150	–1,464	1,010
Bonds and notes	4 670 . .	–266	–1,058	–625	–335	84	1,067	–1,344	1,005
Monetary authorities	4 671 . .	–18	–26	–144	–215	–32	–19	–13	–15
General government	4 672 . .	–248	–832	–413	–694	–1,675	–92	–920	631
Banks	4 673 . .	. . .	. . .	. . .	. . .	. . .	. . .	. . .	. . .
Other sectors	4 674 . .	. . .	200	–68	574	1,791	1,178	–411	389
Money market instruments	4 680 . .	–44	1	87	–4	–51	83	–120	5
Monetary authorities	4 681 . .	–44	1	57	26	–51	–37	. . .	. . .
General government	4 682 . .	. . .	. . .	. . .	. . .	. . .	. . .	. . .	. . .
Banks	4 683 . .	. . .	. . .	. . .	. . .	. . .	. . .	. . .	. . .
Other sectors	4 684 . .	. . .	. . .	30	–30	. . .	120	–120	5
C. FINANCIAL DERIVATIVES	4 910 . .	. . .	. . .	. . .	. . .	. . .	. . .	. . .	. . .
Monetary authorities	4 911 . .	. . .	. . .	. . .	. . .	. . .	. . .	. . .	. . .
General government	4 912 . .	. . .	. . .	. . .	. . .	. . .	. . .	. . .	. . .
Banks	4 913 . .	. . .	. . .	. . .	. . .	. . .	. . .	. . .	. . .
Other sectors	4 914 . .	. . .	. . .	. . .	. . .	. . .	. . .	. . .	. . .
Assets	4 900 . .	**. . .**	**. . .**	**. . .**	**. . .**	**. . .**	**. . .**	**. . .**	**. . .**
Monetary authorities	4 901 . .	. . .	. . .	. . .	. . .	. . .	. . .	. . .	. . .
General government	4 902 . .	. . .	. . .	. . .	. . .	. . .	. . .	. . .	. . .
Banks	4 903 . .	. . .	. . .	. . .	. . .	. . .	. . .	. . .	. . .
Other sectors	4 904 . .	. . .	. . .	. . .	. . .	. . .	. . .	. . .	. . .
Liabilities	4 905 . .	**. . .**	**. . .**	**. . .**	**. . .**	**. . .**	**. . .**	**. . .**	**. . .**
Monetary authorities	4 906 . .	. . .	. . .	. . .	. . .	. . .	. . .	. . .	. . .
General government	4 907 . .	. . .	. . .	. . .	. . .	. . .	. . .	. . .	. . .
Banks	4 908 . .	. . .	. . .	. . .	. . .	. . .	. . .	. . .	. . .
Other sectors	4 909 . .	. . .	. . .	. . .	. . .	. . .	. . .	. . .	. . .

Table 2 (Concluded). STANDARD PRESENTATION, 1994–2001

(Millions of U.S. dollars)

	Code	1994	1995	1996	1997	1998	1999	2000	2001
D. OTHER INVESTMENT	4 700 . .	–4,113	–3,520	–4,166	–4,925	–4,235	–6,186	–4,991	–4,905
Assets	4 703 . .	**–4,173**	**–661**	**–1,592**	**–3,385**	**–3,413**	**–6,371**	**–4,920**	**–4,414**
Trade credits	4 706 . .	–757	–86	–279	517	970	–1,214	–504	1,164
General government	4 707 . .	. . .	. . .	. . .	. . .	. . .	. . .	. . .	–52
of which: Short-term	4 709 . .	. . .	. . .	. . .	. . .	. . .	. . .	. . .	*–52*
Other sectors	4 710 . .	–757	–86	–279	517	970	–1,214	–504	1,216
of which: Short-term	4 712 . .	*–757*	*–86*	*–279*	*517*	*970*	*–1,214*	*–504*	*1,216*
Loans	4 714 . .	78	120	145	132	–48	–613	778	43
Monetary authorities	4 715 . .	. . .	. . .	. . .	. . .	. . .	. . .	. . .	. . .
of which: Short-term	4 718 . .	. . .	. . .	. . .	. . .	. . .	. . .	. . .	. . .
General government	4 719 . .	. . .	. . .	. . .	. . .	. . .	. . .	. . .	. . .
of which: Short-term	4 721 . .	. . .	. . .	. . .	. . .	. . .	. . .	. . .	. . .
Banks	4 722 . .	3	–23	2	. . .	. . .	. . .	. . .	64
of which: Short-term	4 724 . .	*3*	*–8*	*2*	. . .	. . .	. . .	. . .	. . .
Other sectors	4 725 . .	75	143	143	132	–48	–613	778	–21
of which: Short-term	4 727 . .	*12*	*28*	*–2*	*35*	*–115*	*–614*	*729*	. . .
Currency and deposits	4 730 . .	–3,412	–711	–1,416	–3,935	–4,304	–4,442	–5,067	–5,517
Monetary authorities	4 731 . .	. . .	. . .	. . .	. . .	. . .	. . .	. . .	. . .
General government	4 732 . .	3	258	86	–232	182	261	–154	–1,113
Banks	4 733 . .	–930	239	–55	–25	–170	–229	–46	794
Other sectors	4 734 . .	–2,485	–1,208	–1,447	–3,678	–4,316	–4,474	–4,867	–5,198
Other assets	4 736 . .	–82	16	–42	–99	–31	–102	–127	–104
Monetary authorities	4 737 . .	. . .	. . .	. . .	. . .	. . .	. . .	. . .	. . .
of which: Short-term	4 739 . .	. . .	. . .	. . .	. . .	. . .	. . .	. . .	. . .
General government	4 740 . .	–30	–18	–29	–41	–30	–21	–41	–27
of which: Short-term	4 742 . .	. . .	. . .	. . .	. . .	. . .	. . .	. . .	. . .
Banks	4 743 . .	–5	. . .	. . .	. . .	1	1	. . .	. . .
of which: Short-term	4 745 . .	*–5*	. . .	. . .	. . .	*1*	*1*	. . .	. . .
Other sectors	4 746 . .	–47	34	–13	–58	–2	–82	–86	–77
of which: Short-term	4 748 . .	*–33*	*34*	*–10*	*1*	*–2*	*–82*	*–86*	*–77*
Liabilities	4 753 . .	**60**	**–2,859**	**–2,574**	**–1,540**	**–822**	**185**	**–71**	**–491**
Trade credits	4 756 . .	473	–1,102	–113	344	–772	345	–84	–346
General government	4 757 . .	–421	–200	–25	–19	–66	–181	49	65
of which: Short-term	4 759 . .	. . .	. . .	. . .	. . .	. . .	. . .	. . .	. . .
Other sectors	4 760 . .	894	–902	–88	363	–706	526	–133	–411
of which: Short-term	4 762 . .	*897*	*–792*	*11*	*429*	*–637*	*581*	*–126*	*–391*
Loans	4 764 . .	–1,265	–1,249	–1,416	–1,426	61	–311	17	–41
Monetary authorities	4 765 . .	–201	–463	33	–452	–448	–450	–508	–198
of which: Use of Fund credit and loans from the Fund	4 766 . .	*–201*	*–463*	*33*	*–452*	*–448*	*–450*	*–508*	*–198*
of which: Short-term	4 768 . .	. . .	. . .	. . .	. . .	. . .	. . .	. . .	. . .
General government	4 769 . .	170	79	–242	–170	360	–136	–25	–39
of which: Short-term	4 771 . .	. . .	. . .	. . .	. . .	. . .	. . .	. . .	. . .
Banks	4 772 . .	–9	28	190	31	–90	–78	183	–9
of which: Short-term	4 774 . .	*8*	*33*	*158*	*117*	*–131*	*–52*	*169*	*–11*
Other sectors	4 775 . .	–1,225	–893	–1,397	–835	239	353	367	205
of which: Short-term	4 777 . .	*–228*	*163*	*–6*	*3*	*501*	*–447*	*–37*	*51*
Currency and deposits	4 780 . .	–68	24	–37	. . .	18	–16	60	–61
Monetary authorities	4 781 . .	. . .	. . .	. . .	. . .	. . .	. . .	. . .	. . .
General government	4 782 . .	. . .	. . .	. . .	. . .	. . .	. . .	. . .	. . .
Banks	4 783 . .	–68	24	–37	. . .	18	–16	60	–61
Other sectors	4 784 . .	. . .	. . .	. . .	. . .	. . .	. . .	. . .	. . .
Other liabilities	4 786 . .	920	–532	–1,008	–458	–129	167	–64	–43
Monetary authorities	4 787 . .	–51	–317	–289	–454	–16	–6	5	8
of which: Short-term	4 789 . .	*–51*	*–317*	*–289*	*–454*	*–16*	*–6*	*5*	*8*
General government	4 790 . .	379	–141	–276	–3	–34	2	27	9
of which: Short-term	4 792 . .	*379*	*–141*	*–276*	*–3*	*–34*	*2*	*27*	*9*
Banks	4 793 . .	. . .	. . .	. . .	. . .	. . .	1	1	. . .
of which: Short-term	4 795 . .	. . .	. . .	. . .	. . .	. . .	*1*	*1*	. . .
Other sectors	4 796 . .	592	–74	–443	–1	–79	170	–97	–60
of which: Short-term	4 798 . .	*592*	*–74*	*–443*	*–1*	*–47*	*208*	*–97*	*–60*
E. RESERVE ASSETS	4 802 . .	1,145	1,907	–6,271	–2,624	3,379	–589	–5,316	2,261
Monetary gold	4 812 . .	. . .	. . .	. . .	. . .	. . .	. . .	. . .	. . .
Special drawing rights	4 811 . .	51	88	–91	250	79	–27	89	25
Reserve position in the Fund	4 810 . .	. . .	. . .	. . .	. . .	. . .	–244	. . .	. . .
Foreign exchange	4 803 . .	1,197	1,741	–6,180	–2,874	3,300	–318	–5,405	2,236
Other claims	4 813 . .	–103	78	. . .	. . .	. . .	. . .	. . .	. . .
NET ERRORS AND OMISSIONS	4 998 . .	**–281**	**–494**	**–892**	**–1,461**	**–1,442**	**–1,510**	**–4,250**	**–5,183**

Part 3 of the *Yearbook* contains descriptions of the methodologies, compilation practices, and sources used to compile these data.

Table 3. INTERNATIONAL INVESTMENT POSITION (End–period stocks), 1994–2001
(Millions of U.S. dollars)

	Code	1994	1995	1996	1997	1998	1999	2000	2001
ASSETS	8 995 C.	46,634	45,944	. . .	. . .	. . .	. . .	. . .	. . .
Direct investment abroad	8 505 . .	**3,124**	**3,427**	**4,425**	**4,925**	**5,192**	**5,714**	**5,740**	**5,552**
Equity capital and reinvested earnings	8 506 . .	3,124	3,427	3,373	4,021	4,412	4,738	4,641	4,597
Claims on affiliated enterprises	8 507 . .	. . .	. . .	3,373	4,021	4,412	4,738	4,641	4,597
Liabilities to affiliated enterprises	8 508 . .	. . .	. . .	. . .	. . .	. . .	. . .	. . .	. . .
Other capital	8 530 . .	. . .	. . .	1,052	904	780	976	1,099	955
Claims on affiliated enterprises	8 535 . .	. . .	. . .	1,052	904	780	976	1,099	955
Liabilities to affiliated enterprises	8 540 . .	. . .	. . .	. . .	. . .	. . .	. . .	. . .	. . .
Portfolio investment	8 602 . .	**1,796**	**1,530**	**137**	**736**	**597**	**802**	**1,635**	**1,585**
Equity securities	8 610 . .	. . .	. . .	15	36	103	54	36	32
Monetary authorities	8 611 . .	. . .	. . .	. . .	. . .	. . .	. . .	. . .	. . .
General government	8 612 . .	. . .	. . .	. . .	. . .	. . .	. . .	. . .	. . .
Banks	8 613 . .	. . .	. . .	6	4	3	7	18	9
Other sectors	8 614 . .	. . .	. . .	9	32	100	47	18	23
Debt securities	8 619 . .	1,796	1,530	122	700	494	748	1,599	1,553
Bonds and notes	8 620 . .	1,796	1,530	55	146	308	373	563	568
Monetary authorities	8 621 . .	. . .	. . .	. . .	. . .	. . .	. . .	. . .	. . .
General government	8 622 . .	. . .	. . .	. . .	. . .	. . .	. . .	. . .	. . .
Banks	8 623 . .	. . .	. . .	3	46	78	102	132	139
Other sectors	8 624 . .	. . .	. . .	52	100	230	271	431	429
Money market instruments	8 630 . .	. . .	. . .	67	554	186	375	1,036	985
Monetary authorities	8 631 . .	. . .	. . .	. . .	. . .	. . .	. . .	. . .	. . .
General government	8 632 . .	. . .	. . .	. . .	. . .	. . .	. . .	. . .	. . .
Banks	8 633 . .	. . .	. . .	49	77	6	105	104	65
Other sectors	8 634 . .	. . .	. . .	18	477	180	270	932	920
Financial derivatives	8 900 . .	**. . .**	**. . .**	**. . .**	**. . .**	**. . .**	**. . .**	**. . .**	**. . .**
Monetary authorities	8 901 . .	. . .	. . .	. . .	. . .	. . .	. . .	. . .	. . .
General government	8 902 . .	. . .	. . .	. . .	. . .	. . .	. . .	. . .	. . .
Banks	8 903 . .	. . .	. . .	. . .	. . .	. . .	. . .	. . .	. . .
Other sectors	8 904 . .	. . .	. . .	. . .	. . .	. . .	. . .	. . .	. . .
Other investment	8 703 . .	**28,955**	**30,391**	**3,549**	**2,399**	**1,764**	**4,470**	**4,743**	**3,622**
Trade credits	8 706 . .	. . .	. . .	2,138	1,556	584	1,874	2,135	1,069
General government	8 707 . .	. . .	. . .	. . .	. . .	. . .	. . .	. . .	. . .
of which: Short-term	8 709 . .	. . .	. . .	. . .	. . .	. . .	. . .	. . .	. . .
Other sectors	8 710 . .	. . .	. . .	2,138	1,556	584	1,874	2,135	1,069
of which: Short-term	8 712 . .	. . .	. . .	*2,138*	*1,556*	*584*	*1,874*	*2,135*	*1,069*
Loans	8 714 . .	. . .	. . .	51	15	120	730	1	1
Monetary authorities	8 715 . .	. . .	. . .	. . .	. . .	. . .	. . .	. . .	. . .
of which: Short-term	8 718 . .	. . .	. . .	. . .	. . .	. . .	. . .	. . .	. . .
General government	8 719 . .	. . .	. . .	. . .	. . .	. . .	. . .	. . .	. . .
of which: Short-term	8 721 . .	. . .	. . .	. . .	. . .	. . .	. . .	. . .	. . .
Banks	8 722 . .	. . .	. . .	1	. . .	1	1	1	1
of which: Short-term	8 724 . .	. . .	. . .	*1*	. . .	*1*	*1*	*1*	*1*
Other sectors	8 725 . .	. . .	. . .	50	15	119	729	. . .	. . .
of which: Short-term	8 727 . .	. . .	. . .	*50*	*15*	*4*	*729*	. . .	. . .
Currency and deposits	8 730 . .	26,978	28,452	1,337	747	1,019	1,716	2,416	2,323
Monetary authorities	8 731 . .	. . .	. . .	. . .	. . .	. . .	. . .	. . .	. . .
General government	8 732 . .	. . .	. . .	. . .	. . .	. . .	. . .	. . .	. . .
Banks	8 733 . .	3,774	3,586	239	262	435	668	742	1,126
Other sectors	8 734 . .	23,204	24,866	1,098	485	584	1,048	1,674	1,197
Other assets	8 736 . .	1,977	1,939	23	81	41	150	191	229
Monetary authorities	8 737 . .	. . .	. . .	. . .	. . .	. . .	. . .	. . .	. . .
of which: Short-term	8 739 . .	. . .	. . .	. . .	. . .	. . .	. . .	. . .	. . .
General government	8 740 . .	812	874	. . .	. . .	. . .	. . .	. . .	. . .
of which: Short-term	8 742 . .	. . .	. . .	. . .	. . .	. . .	. . .	. . .	. . .
Banks	8 743 . .	. . .	. . .	. . .	. . .	. . .	. . .	. . .	. . .
of which: Short-term	8 745 . .	. . .	. . .	. . .	. . .	. . .	. . .	. . .	. . .
Other sectors	8 746 . .	1,165	1,065	23	81	41	150	191	229
of which: Short-term	8 748 . .	. . .	. . .	*19*	*18*	*41*	*150*	*191*	*229*
Reserve assets	8 802 . .	**12,759**	**10,596**	**16,815**	**19,035**	**15,453**	**16,036**	**21,510**	**18,521**
Monetary gold	8 812 . .	3,439	3,439	3,440	3,440	2,929	2,887	2,794	3,056
Special drawing rights	8 811 . .	463	380	456	183	104	127	36	10
Reserve position in the Fund	8 810 . .	212	215	208	196	204	442	419	405
Foreign exchange	8 803 . .	7,394	5,388	12,711	15,217	12,216	12,580	18,261	15,051
Other claims	8 813 . .	1,252	1,174	. . .	. . .	. . .	. . .	. . .	. . .

Table 3 (Concluded). INTERNATIONAL INVESTMENT POSITION (End–period stocks), 1994–2001
(Millions of U.S. dollars)

	Code	1994	1995	1996	1997	1998	1999	2000	2001
LIABILITIES	8 995 D.	51,730	49,250	...	...	...	...	...	...
Direct investment in Venezuela	8 555 . .	**5,872**	**6,772**	...	...	...	...	...	...
Equity capital and reinvested earnings	8 556 . .	5,872	6,772	...	...	...	...	...	...
Claims on direct investors	8 557 . .	...	...	...	...	...	...	...	...
Liabilities to direct investors	8 558 . .	...	...	...	...	...	...	...	...
Other capital	8 580 . .	...	...	...	...	...	...	...	...
Claims on direct investors	8 585 . .	...	...	...	...	...	...	...	...
Liabilities to direct investors	8 590 . .	...	...	...	...	...	...	...	...
Portfolio investment	8 652 . .	**22,844**	**22,555**	**20,784**	**21,466**	**20,445**	**22,077**	**20,618**	**21,391**
Equity securities	8 660 . .	1,184	1,060	2,487	3,882	1,655	2,148	1,734	1,530
Banks	8 663 . .	...	...	110	269	109	61	55	20
Other sectors	8 664 . .	...	...	2,377	3,613	1,546	2,087	1,679	1,510
Debt securities	8 669 . .	21,660	21,495	18,297	17,584	18,790	19,929	18,884	19,861
Bonds and notes	8 670 . .	21,660	21,495	18,206	17,496	18,754	19,809	18,884	19,861
Monetary authorities	8 671 . .	...	...	...	...	21	16	16	16
General government	8 672 . .	21,295	21,130	16,405	15,123	14,572	14,552	13,957	14,530
Banks	8 673 . .	...	...	...	...	...	...	...	...
Other sectors	8 674 . .	365	365	1,801	2,373	4,161	5,241	4,911	5,315
Money market instruments	8 680 . .	...	...	91	88	36	120	...	...
Monetary authorities	8 681 . .	...	...	61	88	36	...	...	...
General government	8 682 . .	...	...	...	...	...	...	...	...
Banks	8 683 . .	...	...	...	...	...	...	...	...
Other sectors	8 684 . .	...	...	30	...	...	120	...	...
Financial derivatives	8 905 . .	...	...	...	...	...	...	...	...
Monetary authorities	8 906 . .	...	...	...	...	...	...	...	...
General government	8 907 . .	...	...	...	...	...	...	...	...
Banks	8 908 . .	...	...	...	...	...	...	...	...
Other sectors	8 909 . .	...	...	...	...	...	...	...	...
Other investment	8 753 . .	**23,014**	**19,923**	**6,540**	**5,290**	**4,104**	**2,976**	**2,243**	**1,440**
Trade credits	8 756 . .	...	...	931	1,073	851	836	659	263
General government	8 757 . .	...	...	...	...	...	...	...	...
of which: Short-term	8 759 . .	...	...	...	...	...	...	...	...
Other sectors	8 760 . .	...	...	931	1,073	851	836	659	263
of which: Short-term	8 762 . .	...	...	*663*	*871*	*718*	*760*	*631*	*263*
Loans	8 764 . .	16,377	13,559	4,307	3,423	2,974	1,672	1,095	821
Monetary authorities	8 765 . .	2,643	2,239	2,196	1,618	1,225	741	203	...
of which: Use of Fund credit and loans from the Fund	8 766 . .	*2,643*	*2,239*	*2,196*	*1,618*	*1,225*	*741*	*203*	...
of which: Short-term	8 768 . .	...	...	...	...	...	...	...	...
General government	8 769 . .	7,465	7,040	...	...	...	...	...	...
of which: Short-term	8 771 . .	...	...	...	...	...	...	...	...
Banks	8 772 . .	...	...	292	325	239	138	294	286
of which: Short-term	8 774 . .	...	...	*190*	*308*	*181*	*129*	*270*	*259*
Other sectors	8 775 . .	6,269	4,280	1,819	1,480	1,510	793	598	535
of which: Short-term	8 777 . .	*2,978*	*1,740*	*49*	*40*	*528*	*24*	...	...
Currency and deposits	8 780 . .	1,394	1,451	3	4	22	6	65	4
Monetary authorities	8 781 . .	...	...	...	...	...	...	...	...
General government	8 782 . .	...	...	...	...	...	...	...	...
Banks	8 783 . .	1,394	1,451	3	4	22	6	65	4
Other sectors	8 784 . .	...	...	...	...	...	...	...	...
Other liabilities	8 786 . .	5,243	4,913	1,299	790	257	462	424	352
Monetary authorities	8 787 . .	1,603	1,286	995	541	24	19	24	32
of which: Short-term	8 789 . .	*1,603*	*1,286*	*995*	*541*	*24*	*19*	*24*	*32*
General government	8 790 . .	989	969	...	...	...	...	...	...
of which: Short-term	8 792 . .	*989*	*969*	...	...	...	...	...	...
Banks	8 793 . .	...	...	...	...	...	1	1	1
of which: Short-term	8 795 . .	...	...	...	...	...	*1*	*1*	*1*
Other sectors	8 796 . .	2,651	2,658	304	249	233	442	399	319
of which: Short-term	8 798 . .	*414*	*757*	*304*	*249*	*233*	*442*	*399*	*319*
NET INTERNATIONAL INVESTMENT POSITION	8 995 . .	**–5,095**	**–3,306**	...	...	...	...	...	...
Conversion rates: bolívares per U.S. dollar (end of period)	0 102 . .	**170.00**	**290.00**	**476.50**	**504.25**	**564.50**	**648.25**	**699.75**	**763.00**

Table 1. ANALYTIC PRESENTATION, 1994–2001
(Millions of U.S. dollars)

	Code	1994	1995	1996	1997	1998	1999	2000	2001
A. Current Account[1]	4 993 Z.	...	...	**–2,020**	**–1,528**	**–1,074**	**1,177**	**960**	...
Goods: exports f.o.b	2 100 ..	...	...	7,255	9,185	9,361	11,540	14,448	...
Goods: imports f.o.b	3 100 ..	...	...	–10,030	–10,432	–10,350	–10,568	–14,073	...
Balance on Goods	4 100 ..	...	...	*–2,775*	*–1,247*	*–989*	*972*	*375*	...
Services: credit	2 200 ..	...	...	2,243	2,530	2,616	2,493	2,702	...
Services: debit	3 200 ..	...	...	–2,304	–3,153	–3,146	–3,040	–3,252	...
Balance on Goods and Services	4 991 ..	...	...	*–2,836*	*–1,870*	*–1,519*	*425*	*–175*	...
Income: credit	2 300 ..	...	...	140	136	127	142	185	...
Income: debit	3 300 ..	...	...	–524	–679	–804	–571	–782	...
Balance on Goods, Services, and Income	4 992 ..	...	...	*–3,220*	*–2,413*	*–2,196*	*–4*	*–772*	...
Current transfers: credit	2 379 Z.	...	...	1,200	885	1,122	1,181	1,732	...
Current transfers: debit	3 379 ..	...	...	...	...	...	...	...	...
B. Capital Account[1]	4 994 Z.	...	...	...	...	...	...	...	...
Capital account: credit	2 994 Z.	...	...	...	...	...	...	...	...
Capital account: debit	3 994 ..	...	...	...	...	...	...	...	...
Total, Groups A Plus B	4 981 ..	...	...	*–2,020*	*–1,528*	*–1,074*	*1,177*	*960*	...
C. Financial Account[1]	4 995 W.	...	...	**2,909**	**2,125**	**1,646**	**1,058**	**–316**	...
Direct investment abroad	4 505 ..	...	...	...	...	...	...	...	...
Direct investment in Vietnam	4 555 Z.	...	...	2,395	2,220	1,671	1,412	1,298	...
Portfolio investment assets	4 602 ..	...	...	...	...	...	...	...	...
Equity securities	4 610 ..	...	...	...	...	...	...	...	...
Debt securities	4 619 ..	...	...	...	...	...	...	...	...
Portfolio investment liabilities	4 652 Z.	...	...	...	...	...	...	...	...
Equity securities	4 660 ..	...	...	...	...	...	...	...	...
Debt securities	4 669 Z.	...	...	...	...	...	...	...	...
Financial derivatives	4 910 ..	...	...	...	...	...	...	...	...
Financial derivatives assets	4 900 ..	...	...	...	...	...	...	...	...
Financial derivatives liabilities	4 905 ..	...	...	...	...	...	...	...	...
Other investment assets	4 703 ..	...	...	–33	–112	–537	–786	–2,089	...
Monetary authorities	4 701 ..	...	...	...	...	...	...	...	...
General government	4 704 ..	...	...	...	...	...	...	...	...
Banks	4 705 ..	...	...	–33	–112	–537	–786	–2,089	...
Other sectors	4 728 ..	...	...	...	...	...	...	...	...
Other investment liabilities	4 753 W.	...	...	547	17	512	432	475	...
Monetary authorities	4 753 WA	...	...	...	...	...	...	...	...
General government	4 753 ZB	...	...	...	...	...	...	...	...
Banks	4 753 ZC	...	...	...	...	...	...	...	...
Other sectors	4 753 ZD	...	...	547	17	512	432	475	...
Total, Groups A Through C	4 983 ..	...	...	*889*	*597*	*572*	*2,235*	*644*	...
D. Net Errors and Omissions	4 998 ..	...	...	**–611**	**–269**	**–535**	**–925**	**–534**	...
Total, Groups A Through D	4 984 ..	...	...	*278*	*328*	*37*	*1,310*	*110*	...
E. Reserves and Related Items	4 802 A.	...	...	**–278**	**–328**	**–37**	**–1,310**	**–110**	...
Reserve assets	4 802 ..	...	...	–453	–274	41	–1,284	–89	...
Use of Fund credit and loans	4 766 ..	...	...	175	–54	–78	–26	–21	...
Exceptional financing	4 920 ..	...	...	...	...	...	...	...	...
Conversion rates: dong per U.S. dollar	0 101 ..	**10,966**	**11,038**	**11,033**	**11,683**	**13,268**	**13,943**	**14,168**	**14,725**

[1] Excludes components that have been classified in the categories of Group E.

Table 2. STANDARD PRESENTATION, 1994–2001

(Millions of U.S. dollars)

	Code	1994	1995	1996	1997	1998	1999	2000	2001
CURRENT ACCOUNT	4 993 . .	**...**	**...**	**–2,020**	**–1,528**	**–1,074**	**1,177**	**960**	**...**
A. GOODS	4 100 . .	...	...	–2,775	–1,247	–989	972	375	...
Credit	2 100 . .	**...**	**...**	**7,255**	**9,185**	**9,361**	**11,540**	**14,448**	**...**
General merchandise: exports f.o.b.	2 110 . .	...	...	7,255	9,185	9,361	11,540	14,448	...
Goods for processing: exports f.o.b.	2 150 . .	...	...	...	...	...	...	...	...
Repairs on goods	2 160 . .	...	...	...	...	...	...	...	...
Goods procured in ports by carriers	2 170 . .	...	...	...	...	...	...	...	...
Nonmonetary gold	2 180 . .	...	...	...	...	...	...	...	...
Debit	3 100 . .	**...**	**...**	**–10,030**	**–10,432**	**–10,350**	**–10,568**	**–14,073**	**...**
General merchandise: imports f.o.b.	3 110 . .	...	...	–10,030	–10,432	–10,350	–10,568	–14,073	...
Goods for processing: imports f.o.b.	3 150 . .	...	...	...	...	...	...	...	...
Repairs on goods	3 160 . .	...	...	...	...	...	...	...	...
Goods procured in ports by carriers	3 170 . .	...	...	...	...	...	...	...	...
Nonmonetary gold	3 180 . .	...	...	...	...	...	...	...	...
B. SERVICES	4 200 . .	...	...	–61	–623	–530	–547	–550	...
Total credit	2 200 . .	...	...	*2,243*	*2,530*	*2,616*	*2,493*	*2,702*	...
Total debit	3 200 . .	...	...	*–2,304*	*–3,153*	*–3,146*	*–3,040*	*–3,252*	...
Transportation services, credit	2 205 . .	**...**	**...**	**...**	**...**	**...**	**...**	**...**	**...**
Passenger	2 850 . .	...	...	...	...	...	...	...	...
Freight	2 851 . .	...	...	...	...	...	...	...	...
Other	2 852 . .	...	...	...	...	...	...	...	...
Sea transport, passenger	2 207 . .	...	...	...	...	...	...	...	...
Sea transport, freight	2 208 . .	...	...	...	...	...	...	...	...
Sea transport, other	2 209 . .	...	...	...	...	...	...	...	...
Air transport, passenger	2 211 . .	...	...	...	...	...	...	...	...
Air transport, freight	2 212 . .	...	...	...	...	...	...	...	...
Air transport, other	2 213 . .	...	...	...	...	...	...	...	...
Other transport, passenger	2 215 . .	...	...	...	...	...	...	...	...
Other transport, freight	2 216 . .	...	...	...	...	...	...	...	...
Other transport, other	2 217 . .	...	...	...	...	...	...	...	...
Transportation services, debit	3 205 . .	**...**	**...**	**...**	**...**	**...**	**...**	**...**	**...**
Passenger	3 850 . .	...	...	...	...	...	...	...	...
Freight	3 851 . .	...	...	...	...	...	...	...	...
Other	3 852 . .	...	...	...	...	...	...	...	...
Sea transport, passenger	3 207 . .	...	...	...	...	...	...	...	...
Sea transport, freight	3 208 . .	...	...	...	...	...	...	...	...
Sea transport, other	3 209 . .	...	...	...	...	...	...	...	...
Air transport, passenger	3 211 . .	...	...	...	...	...	...	...	...
Air transport, freight	3 212 . .	...	...	...	...	...	...	...	...
Air transport, other	3 213 . .	...	...	...	...	...	...	...	...
Other transport, passenger	3 215 . .	...	...	...	...	...	...	...	...
Other transport, freight	3 216 . .	...	...	...	...	...	...	...	...
Other transport, other	3 217 . .	...	...	...	...	...	...	...	...
Travel, credit	2 236 . .	**...**	**...**	**...**	**...**	**...**	**...**	**...**	**...**
Business travel	2 237 . .	...	...	...	...	...	...	...	...
Personal travel	2 240 . .	...	...	...	...	...	...	...	...
Travel, debit	3 236 . .	**...**	**...**	**...**	**...**	**...**	**...**	**...**	**...**
Business travel	3 237 . .	...	...	...	...	...	...	...	...
Personal travel	3 240 . .	...	...	...	...	...	...	...	...
Other services, credit	2 200 BA	**...**	**...**	**...**	**...**	**...**	**...**	**...**	**...**
Communications	2 245 . .	...	...	...	...	...	...	...	...
Construction	2 249 . .	...	...	...	...	...	...	...	...
Insurance	2 253 . .	...	...	...	...	...	...	...	...
Financial	2 260 . .	...	...	...	...	...	...	...	...
Computer and information	2 262 . .	...	...	...	...	...	...	...	...
Royalties and licence fees	2 266 . .	...	...	...	...	...	...	...	...
Other business services	2 268 . .	...	...	...	...	...	...	...	...
Personal, cultural, and recreational	2 287 . .	...	...	...	...	...	...	...	...
Government, n.i.e.	2 291 . .	...	...	...	...	...	...	...	...
Other services, debit	3 200 BA	**...**	**...**	**...**	**...**	**...**	**...**	**...**	**...**
Communications	3 245 . .	...	...	...	...	...	...	...	...
Construction	3 249 . .	...	...	...	...	...	...	...	...
Insurance	3 253 . .	...	...	...	...	...	...	...	...
Financial	3 260 . .	...	...	...	...	...	...	...	...
Computer and information	3 262 . .	...	...	...	...	...	...	...	...
Royalties and licence fees	3 266 . .	...	...	...	...	...	...	...	...
Other business services	3 268 . .	...	...	...	...	...	...	...	...
Personal, cultural, and recreational	3 287 . .	...	...	...	...	...	...	...	...
Government, n.i.e.	3 291 . .	...	...	...	...	...	...	...	...

Table 2 (Continued). STANDARD PRESENTATION, 1994–2001
(Millions of U.S. dollars)

	Code	1994	1995	1996	1997	1998	1999	2000	2001
C. INCOME	4 300 . .	. . .	. . .	–384	–543	–677	–429	–597	. . .
Total credit	2 300 . .	. . .	. . .	*140*	*136*	*127*	*142*	*185*	. . .
Total debit	3 300 . .	. . .	. . .	*–524*	*–679*	*–804*	*–571*	*–782*	. . .
Compensation of employees, credit	2 310 . .	**. . .**	**. . .**	**. . .**	**. . .**	**. . .**	**. . .**	**. . .**	**. . .**
Compensation of employees, debit	3 310 . .	**. . .**	**. . .**	**. . .**	**. . .**	**. . .**	**. . .**	**. . .**	**. . .**
Investment income, credit	2 320 . .	**. . .**	**. . .**	**. . .**	**. . .**	**. . .**	**. . .**	**. . .**	**. . .**
Direct investment income	2 330 . .	. . .	. . .	. . .	. . .	. . .	. . .	. . .	. . .
Dividends and distributed branch profits	2 332 . .	. . .	. . .	. . .	. . .	. . .	. . .	. . .	. . .
Reinvested earnings and undistributed branch profits	2 333 . .	. . .	. . .	. . .	. . .	. . .	. . .	. . .	. . .
Income on debt (interest)	2 334 . .	. . .	. . .	. . .	. . .	. . .	. . .	. . .	. . .
Portfolio investment income	2 339 . .	. . .	. . .	. . .	. . .	. . .	. . .	. . .	. . .
Income on equity	2 340 . .	. . .	. . .	. . .	. . .	. . .	. . .	. . .	. . .
Income on bonds and notes	2 350 . .	. . .	. . .	. . .	. . .	. . .	. . .	. . .	. . .
Income on money market instruments	2 360 . .	. . .	. . .	. . .	. . .	. . .	. . .	. . .	. . .
Other investment income	2 370 . .	. . .	. . .	. . .	. . .	. . .	. . .	. . .	. . .
Investment income, debit	3 320 . .	**. . .**	**. . .**	**. . .**	**. . .**	**. . .**	**. . .**	**. . .**	**. . .**
Direct investment income	3 330 . .	. . .	. . .	. . .	. . .	. . .	. . .	. . .	. . .
Dividends and distributed branch profits	3 332 . .	. . .	. . .	. . .	. . .	. . .	. . .	. . .	. . .
Reinvested earnings and undistributed branch profits	3 333 . .	. . .	. . .	. . .	. . .	. . .	. . .	. . .	. . .
Income on debt (interest)	3 334 . .	. . .	. . .	. . .	. . .	. . .	. . .	. . .	. . .
Portfolio investment income	3 339 . .	. . .	. . .	. . .	. . .	. . .	. . .	. . .	. . .
Income on equity	3 340 . .	. . .	. . .	. . .	. . .	. . .	. . .	. . .	. . .
Income on bonds and notes	3 350 . .	. . .	. . .	. . .	. . .	. . .	. . .	. . .	. . .
Income on money market instruments	3 360 . .	. . .	. . .	. . .	. . .	. . .	. . .	. . .	. . .
Other investment income	3 370 . .	. . .	. . .	. . .	. . .	. . .	. . .	. . .	. . .
D. CURRENT TRANSFERS	4 379 . .	. . .	. . .	1,200	885	1,122	1,181	1,732	. . .
Credit	2 379 . .	**. . .**	**. . .**	**1,200**	**885**	**1,122**	**1,181**	**1,732**	**. . .**
General government	2 380 . .	. . .	. . .	150	175	172	131	147	. . .
Other sectors	2 390 . .	. . .	. . .	1,050	710	950	1,050	1,585	. . .
Workers' remittances	2 391 . .	. . .	. . .	. . .	. . .	. . .	. . .	. . .	. . .
Other current transfers	2 392 . .	. . .	. . .	. . .	. . .	. . .	. . .	. . .	. . .
Debit	3 379 . .	**. . .**	**. . .**	**. . .**	**. . .**	**. . .**	**. . .**	**. . .**	**. . .**
General government	3 380 . .	. . .	. . .	. . .	. . .	. . .	. . .	. . .	. . .
Other sectors	3 390 . .	. . .	. . .	. . .	. . .	. . .	. . .	. . .	. . .
Workers' remittances	3 391 . .	. . .	. . .	. . .	. . .	. . .	. . .	. . .	. . .
Other current transfers	3 392 . .	. . .	. . .	. . .	. . .	. . .	. . .	. . .	. . .
CAPITAL AND FINANCIAL ACCOUNT	4 996 . .	**. . .**	**. . .**	**2,631**	**1,797**	**1,609**	**–252**	**–426**	**. . .**
CAPITAL ACCOUNT	4 994 . .	**. . .**	**. . .**	**. . .**	**. . .**	**. . .**	**. . .**	**. . .**	**. . .**
Total credit	2 994 . .	. . .	. . .	. . .	. . .	. . .	. . .	. . .	. . .
Total debit	3 994 . .	. . .	. . .	. . .	. . .	. . .	. . .	. . .	. . .
Capital transfers, credit	2 400 . .	**. . .**	**. . .**	**. . .**	**. . .**	**. . .**	**. . .**	**. . .**	**. . .**
General government	2 401 . .	. . .	. . .	. . .	. . .	. . .	. . .	. . .	. . .
Debt forgiveness	2 402 . .	. . .	. . .	. . .	. . .	. . .	. . .	. . .	. . .
Other capital transfers	2 410 . .	. . .	. . .	. . .	. . .	. . .	. . .	. . .	. . .
Other sectors	2 430 . .	. . .	. . .	. . .	. . .	. . .	. . .	. . .	. . .
Migrants' transfers	2 431 . .	. . .	. . .	. . .	. . .	. . .	. . .	. . .	. . .
Debt forgiveness	2 432 . .	. . .	. . .	. . .	. . .	. . .	. . .	. . .	. . .
Other capital transfers	2 440 . .	. . .	. . .	. . .	. . .	. . .	. . .	. . .	. . .
Capital transfers, debit	3 400 . .	**. . .**	**. . .**	**. . .**	**. . .**	**. . .**	**. . .**	**. . .**	**. . .**
General government	3 401 . .	. . .	. . .	. . .	. . .	. . .	. . .	. . .	. . .
Debt forgiveness	3 402 . .	. . .	. . .	. . .	. . .	. . .	. . .	. . .	. . .
Other capital transfers	3 410 . .	. . .	. . .	. . .	. . .	. . .	. . .	. . .	. . .
Other sectors	3 430 . .	. . .	. . .	. . .	. . .	. . .	. . .	. . .	. . .
Migrants' transfers	3 431 . .	. . .	. . .	. . .	. . .	. . .	. . .	. . .	. . .
Debt forgiveness	3 432 . .	. . .	. . .	. . .	. . .	. . .	. . .	. . .	. . .
Other capital transfers	3 440 . .	. . .	. . .	. . .	. . .	. . .	. . .	. . .	. . .
Nonproduced nonfinancial assets, credit	2 480 . .	**. . .**	**. . .**	**. . .**	**. . .**	**. . .**	**. . .**	**. . .**	**. . .**
Nonproduced nonfinancial assets, debit	3 480 . .	**. . .**	**. . .**	**. . .**	**. . .**	**. . .**	**. . .**	**. . .**	**. . .**

Table 2 (Continued). STANDARD PRESENTATION, 1994–2001
(Millions of U.S. dollars)

	Code	1994	1995	1996	1997	1998	1999	2000	2001
FINANCIAL ACCOUNT	4 995	**. . .**	**. . .**	**2,631**	**1,797**	**1,609**	**–252**	**–426**	**. . .**
A. DIRECT INVESTMENT	4 500	. . .	. . .	2,395	2,220	1,671	1,412	1,298	. . .
Direct investment abroad	4 505	**. . .**	**. . .**	**. . .**	**. . .**	**. . .**	**. . .**	**. . .**	**. . .**
Equity capital	4 510	. . .	. . .	. . .	. . .	. . .	. . .	. . .	. . .
Claims on affiliated enterprises	4 515	. . .	. . .	. . .	. . .	. . .	. . .	. . .	. . .
Liabilities to affiliated enterprises	4 520	. . .	. . .	. . .	. . .	. . .	. . .	. . .	. . .
Reinvested earnings	4 525	. . .	. . .	. . .	. . .	. . .	. . .	. . .	. . .
Other capital	4 530	. . .	. . .	. . .	. . .	. . .	. . .	. . .	. . .
Claims on affiliated enterprises	4 535	. . .	. . .	. . .	. . .	. . .	. . .	. . .	. . .
Liabilities to affiliated enterprises	4 540	. . .	. . .	. . .	. . .	. . .	. . .	. . .	. . .
Direct investment in Vietnam	4 555	**. . .**	**. . .**	**2,395**	**2,220**	**1,671**	**1,412**	**1,298**	**. . .**
Equity capital	4 560	. . .	. . .	. . .	. . .	. . .	. . .	. . .	. . .
Claims on direct investors	4 565	. . .	. . .	. . .	. . .	. . .	. . .	. . .	. . .
Liabilities to direct investors	4 570	. . .	. . .	. . .	. . .	. . .	. . .	. . .	. . .
Reinvested earnings	4 575	. . .	. . .	. . .	. . .	. . .	. . .	. . .	. . .
Other capital	4 580	. . .	. . .	. . .	. . .	. . .	. . .	. . .	. . .
Claims on direct investors	4 585	. . .	. . .	. . .	. . .	. . .	. . .	. . .	. . .
Liabilities to direct investors	4 590	. . .	. . .	. . .	. . .	. . .	. . .	. . .	. . .
B. PORTFOLIO INVESTMENT	4 600	. . .	. . .	. . .	. . .	. . .	. . .	. . .	. . .
Assets	4 602	**. . .**	**. . .**	**. . .**	**. . .**	**. . .**	**. . .**	**. . .**	**. . .**
Equity securities	4 610	. . .	. . .	. . .	. . .	. . .	. . .	. . .	. . .
Monetary authorities	4 611	. . .	. . .	. . .	. . .	. . .	. . .	. . .	. . .
General government	4 612	. . .	. . .	. . .	. . .	. . .	. . .	. . .	. . .
Banks	4 613	. . .	. . .	. . .	. . .	. . .	. . .	. . .	. . .
Other sectors	4 614	. . .	. . .	. . .	. . .	. . .	. . .	. . .	. . .
Debt securities	4 619	. . .	. . .	. . .	. . .	. . .	. . .	. . .	. . .
Bonds and notes	4 620	. . .	. . .	. . .	. . .	. . .	. . .	. . .	. . .
Monetary authorities	4 621	. . .	. . .	. . .	. . .	. . .	. . .	. . .	. . .
General government	4 622	. . .	. . .	. . .	. . .	. . .	. . .	. . .	. . .
Banks	4 623	. . .	. . .	. . .	. . .	. . .	. . .	. . .	. . .
Other sectors	4 624	. . .	. . .	. . .	. . .	. . .	. . .	. . .	. . .
Money market instruments	4 630	. . .	. . .	. . .	. . .	. . .	. . .	. . .	. . .
Monetary authorities	4 631	. . .	. . .	. . .	. . .	. . .	. . .	. . .	. . .
General government	4 632	. . .	. . .	. . .	. . .	. . .	. . .	. . .	. . .
Banks	4 633	. . .	. . .	. . .	. . .	. . .	. . .	. . .	. . .
Other sectors	4 634	. . .	. . .	. . .	. . .	. . .	. . .	. . .	. . .
Liabilities	4 652	**. . .**	**. . .**	**. . .**	**. . .**	**. . .**	**. . .**	**. . .**	**. . .**
Equity securities	4 660	. . .	. . .	. . .	. . .	. . .	. . .	. . .	. . .
Banks	4 663	. . .	. . .	. . .	. . .	. . .	. . .	. . .	. . .
Other sectors	4 664	. . .	. . .	. . .	. . .	. . .	. . .	. . .	. . .
Debt securities	4 669	. . .	. . .	. . .	. . .	. . .	. . .	. . .	. . .
Bonds and notes	4 670	. . .	. . .	. . .	. . .	. . .	. . .	. . .	. . .
Monetary authorities	4 671	. . .	. . .	. . .	. . .	. . .	. . .	. . .	. . .
General government	4 672	. . .	. . .	. . .	. . .	. . .	. . .	. . .	. . .
Banks	4 673	. . .	. . .	. . .	. . .	. . .	. . .	. . .	. . .
Other sectors	4 674	. . .	. . .	. . .	. . .	. . .	. . .	. . .	. . .
Money market instruments	4 680	. . .	. . .	. . .	. . .	. . .	. . .	. . .	. . .
Monetary authorities	4 681	. . .	. . .	. . .	. . .	. . .	. . .	. . .	. . .
General government	4 682	. . .	. . .	. . .	. . .	. . .	. . .	. . .	. . .
Banks	4 683	. . .	. . .	. . .	. . .	. . .	. . .	. . .	. . .
Other sectors	4 684	. . .	. . .	. . .	. . .	. . .	. . .	. . .	. . .
C. FINANCIAL DERIVATIVES	4 910	. . .	. . .	. . .	. . .	. . .	. . .	. . .	. . .
Monetary authorities	4 911	. . .	. . .	. . .	. . .	. . .	. . .	. . .	. . .
General government	4 912	. . .	. . .	. . .	. . .	. . .	. . .	. . .	. . .
Banks	4 913	. . .	. . .	. . .	. . .	. . .	. . .	. . .	. . .
Other sectors	4 914	. . .	. . .	. . .	. . .	. . .	. . .	. . .	. . .
Assets	4 900	**. . .**	**. . .**	**. . .**	**. . .**	**. . .**	**. . .**	**. . .**	**. . .**
Monetary authorities	4 901	. . .	. . .	. . .	. . .	. . .	. . .	. . .	. . .
General government	4 902	. . .	. . .	. . .	. . .	. . .	. . .	. . .	. . .
Banks	4 903	. . .	. . .	. . .	. . .	. . .	. . .	. . .	. . .
Other sectors	4 904	. . .	. . .	. . .	. . .	. . .	. . .	. . .	. . .
Liabilities	4 905	**. . .**	**. . .**	**. . .**	**. . .**	**. . .**	**. . .**	**. . .**	**. . .**
Monetary authorities	4 906	. . .	. . .	. . .	. . .	. . .	. . .	. . .	. . .
General government	4 907	. . .	. . .	. . .	. . .	. . .	. . .	. . .	. . .
Banks	4 908	. . .	. . .	. . .	. . .	. . .	. . .	. . .	. . .
Other sectors	4 909	. . .	. . .	. . .	. . .	. . .	. . .	. . .	. . .

Table 2 (Concluded). STANDARD PRESENTATION, 1994–2001
(Millions of U.S. dollars)

	Code		1994	1995	1996	1997	1998	1999	2000	2001
D. OTHER INVESTMENT	4 700	. .	. . .	. . .	689	–149	–103	–380	–1,635	. . .
Assets	4 703	. .	**. . .**	**. . .**	**–33**	**–112**	**–537**	**–786**	**–2,089**	**. . .**
Trade credits	4 706	. .	. . .	. . .	. . .	. . .	. . .	. . .	. . .	. . .
General government	4 707	. .	. . .	. . .	. . .	. . .	. . .	. . .	. . .	. . .
of which: Short-term	4 709	. .	. . .	. . .	. . .	. . .	. . .	. . .	. . .	. . .
Other sectors	4 710	. .	. . .	. . .	. . .	. . .	. . .	. . .	. . .	. . .
of which: Short-term	4 712	. .	. . .	. . .	. . .	. . .	. . .	. . .	. . .	. . .
Loans	4 714	. .	. . .	. . .	. . .	. . .	. . .	. . .	. . .	. . .
Monetary authorities	4 715	. .	. . .	. . .	. . .	. . .	. . .	. . .	. . .	. . .
of which: Short-term	4 718	. .	. . .	. . .	. . .	. . .	. . .	. . .	. . .	. . .
General government	4 719	. .	. . .	. . .	. . .	. . .	. . .	. . .	. . .	. . .
of which: Short-term	4 721	. .	. . .	. . .	. . .	. . .	. . .	. . .	. . .	. . .
Banks	4 722	. .	. . .	. . .	. . .	. . .	. . .	. . .	. . .	. . .
of which: Short-term	4 724	. .	. . .	. . .	. . .	. . .	. . .	. . .	. . .	. . .
Other sectors	4 725	. .	. . .	. . .	. . .	. . .	. . .	. . .	. . .	. . .
of which: Short-term	4 727	. .	. . .	. . .	. . .	. . .	. . .	. . .	. . .	. . .
Currency and deposits	4 730	. .	. . .	. . .	–33	–112	–537	–786	–2,089	. . .
Monetary authorities	4 731	. .	. . .	. . .	. . .	. . .	. . .	. . .	. . .	. . .
General government	4 732	. .	. . .	. . .	. . .	. . .	. . .	. . .	. . .	. . .
Banks	4 733	. .	. . .	. . .	–33	–112	–537	–786	–2,089	. . .
Other sectors	4 734	. .	. . .	. . .	. . .	. . .	. . .	. . .	. . .	. . .
Other assets	4 736	. .	. . .	. . .	. . .	. . .	. . .	. . .	. . .	. . .
Monetary authorities	4 737	. .	. . .	. . .	. . .	. . .	. . .	. . .	. . .	. . .
of which: Short-term	4 739	. .	. . .	. . .	. . .	. . .	. . .	. . .	. . .	. . .
General government	4 740	. .	. . .	. . .	. . .	. . .	. . .	. . .	. . .	. . .
of which: Short-term	4 742	. .	. . .	. . .	. . .	. . .	. . .	. . .	. . .	. . .
Banks	4 743	. .	. . .	. . .	. . .	. . .	. . .	. . .	. . .	. . .
of which: Short-term	4 745	. .	. . .	. . .	. . .	. . .	. . .	. . .	. . .	. . .
Other sectors	4 746	. .	. . .	. . .	. . .	. . .	. . .	. . .	. . .	. . .
of which: Short-term	4 748	. .	. . .	. . .	. . .	. . .	. . .	. . .	. . .	. . .
Liabilities	4 753	. .	**. . .**	**. . .**	**722**	**–37**	**434**	**406**	**454**	**. . .**
Trade credits	4 756	. .	. . .	. . .	. . .	. . .	. . .	. . .	. . .	. . .
General government	4 757	. .	. . .	. . .	. . .	. . .	. . .	. . .	. . .	. . .
of which: Short-term	4 759	. .	. . .	. . .	. . .	. . .	. . .	. . .	. . .	. . .
Other sectors	4 760	. .	. . .	. . .	. . .	. . .	. . .	. . .	. . .	. . .
of which: Short-term	4 762	. .	. . .	. . .	. . .	. . .	. . .	. . .	. . .	. . .
Loans	4 764	. .	. . .	. . .	436	–218	93	–142	15	. . .
Monetary authorities	4 765	. .	. . .	. . .	175	–54	–78	–26	–21	. . .
of which: Use of Fund credit and loans from the Fund	4 766	. .	. . .	. . .	*175*	*–54*	*–78*	*–26*	*–21*	. . .
of which: Short-term	4 768	. .	. . .	. . .	. . .	. . .	. . .	. . .	. . .	. . .
General government	4 769	. .	. . .	. . .	. . .	. . .	. . .	. . .	. . .	. . .
of which: Short-term	4 771	. .	. . .	. . .	. . .	. . .	. . .	. . .	. . .	. . .
Banks	4 772	. .	. . .	. . .	. . .	. . .	. . .	. . .	. . .	. . .
of which: Short-term	4 774	. .	. . .	. . .	. . .	. . .	. . .	. . .	. . .	. . .
Other sectors	4 775	. .	. . .	. . .	261	–164	171	–116	36	. . .
of which: Short-term	4 777	. .	. . .	. . .	. . .	. . .	. . .	. . .	. . .	. . .
Currency and deposits	4 780	. .	. . .	. . .	. . .	. . .	. . .	. . .	. . .	. . .
Monetary authorities	4 781	. .	. . .	. . .	. . .	. . .	. . .	. . .	. . .	. . .
General government	4 782	. .	. . .	. . .	. . .	. . .	. . .	. . .	. . .	. . .
Banks	4 783	. .	. . .	. . .	. . .	. . .	. . .	. . .	. . .	. . .
Other sectors	4 784	. .	. . .	. . .	. . .	. . .	. . .	. . .	. . .	. . .
Other liabilities	4 786	. .	. . .	. . .	286	181	341	548	439	. . .
Monetary authorities	4 787	. .	. . .	. . .	. . .	. . .	. . .	. . .	. . .	. . .
of which: Short-term	4 789	. .	. . .	. . .	. . .	. . .	. . .	. . .	. . .	. . .
General government	4 790	. .	. . .	. . .	. . .	. . .	. . .	. . .	. . .	. . .
of which: Short-term	4 792	. .	. . .	. . .	. . .	. . .	. . .	. . .	. . .	. . .
Banks	4 793	. .	. . .	. . .	. . .	. . .	. . .	. . .	. . .	. . .
of which: Short-term	4 795	. .	. . .	. . .	. . .	. . .	. . .	. . .	. . .	. . .
Other sectors	4 796	. .	. . .	. . .	286	181	341	548	439	. . .
of which: Short-term	4 798	. .	. . .	. . .	. . .	. . .	. . .	. . .	. . .	. . .
E. RESERVE ASSETS	4 802	. .	. . .	. . .	–453	–274	41	–1,284	–89	. . .
Monetary gold	4 812	. .	. . .	. . .	. . .	. . .	. . .	. . .	. . .	. . .
Special drawing rights	4 811	. .	. . .	. . .	–14	3	11	1	1	. . .
Reserve position in the Fund	4 810	. .	. . .	. . .	. . .	. . .	. . .	. . .	. . .	. . .
Foreign exchange	4 803	. .	. . .	. . .	–439	–277	30	–1,285	–90	. . .
Other claims	4 813	. .	. . .	. . .	. . .	. . .	. . .	. . .	. . .	. . .
NET ERRORS AND OMISSIONS	4 998	. .	**. . .**	**. . .**	**–611**	**–269**	**–535**	**–925**	**–534**	**. . .**

Table 1. ANALYTIC PRESENTATION, 1994–2001
(Millions of U.S. dollars)

	Code	1994	1995	1996	1997	1998	1999	2000	2001
A. Current Account [1]	4 993 Z.	**178.3**	**143.7**	**38.8**	**–68.8**	**–303.3**	**577.1**	**1,862.4**	**. . .**
Goods: exports f.o.b.	2 100 . .	1,796.2	1,980.1	2,262.7	2,274.0	1,503.7	2,478.3	4,093.8	. . .
Goods: imports f.o.b.	3 100 . .	–1,522.0	–1,831.5	–2,293.5	–2,406.5	–2,288.8	–2,120.4	–2,484.4	. . .
Balance on Goods	4 100 . .	*274.2*	*148.6*	*–30.8*	*–132.5*	*–785.1*	*357.9*	*1,609.4*	. . .
Services: credit	2 200 . .	148.0	179.4	185.7	207.6	174.4	183.2	210.8	. . .
Services: debit	3 200 . .	–704.3	–639.3	–555.4	–677.4	–692.9	–718.6	–809.3	. . .
Balance on Goods and Services	4 991 . .	*–282.1*	*–311.3*	*–400.5*	*–602.3*	*–1,303.6*	*–177.5*	*1,010.9*	. . .
Income: credit	2 300 . .	22.0	37.4	46.8	69.6	101.1	94.1	297.4	. . .
Income: debit	3 300 . .	–553.9	–598.4	–680.7	–670.6	–276.6	–570.9	–845.4	. . .
Balance on Goods, Services, and Income	4 992 . .	*–814.0*	*–872.3*	*–1,034.4*	*–1,203.3*	*–1,479.1*	*–654.3*	*462.9*	. . .
Current transfers: credit	2 379 Z.	1,062.3	1,080.5	1,140.1	1,177.6	1,223.5	1,262.1	1,471.9	. . .
Current transfers: debit	3 379 . .	–70.0	–64.5	–66.9	–43.1	–47.7	–30.7	–72.4	. . .
B. Capital Account [1]	4 994 Z.	**. . .**	**. . .**	**. . .**	**4,236.2**	**2.2**	**1.5**	**311.8**	**. . .**
Capital account: credit	2 994 Z.	. . .	. . .	. . .	4,236.2	2.2	1.5	391.8	. . .
Capital account: debit	3 994 . .	. . .	. . .	. . .	. . .	. . .	. . .	–80.0	. . .
Total, Groups A Plus B	4 981 . .	*178.3*	*143.7*	*38.8*	*4,167.4*	*–301.1*	*578.6*	*2,174.2*	. . .
C. Financial Account [1]	4 995 W.	**–710.7**	**–858.4**	**–367.8**	**–197.6**	**–468.0**	**–549.8**	**–913.1**	**. . .**
Direct investment abroad	4 505 . .	. . .	. . .	. . .	. . .	. . .	. . .	. . .	. . .
Direct investment in Yemen	4 555 Z.	15.8	–217.7	–60.1	–138.5	–219.4	–194.3	–200.9	. . .
Portfolio investment assets	4 602 . .	2.8	–3.1	.9	5.0	4.9	4.1	.1	. . .
Equity securities	4 610 . .	2.8	–3.1	.9	5.0	4.9	4.1	.1	. . .
Debt securities	4 619 . .	. . .	. . .	. . .	. . .	. . .	. . .	. . .	. . .
Portfolio investment liabilities	4 652 Z.	. . .	. . .	. . .	. . .	. . .	. . .	. . .	. . .
Equity securities	4 660 . .	. . .	. . .	. . .	. . .	. . .	. . .	. . .	. . .
Debt securities	4 669 Z.	. . .	. . .	. . .	. . .	. . .	. . .	. . .	. . .
Financial derivatives	4 910 . .	. . .	. . .	. . .	. . .	. . .	. . .	. . .	. . .
Financial derivatives assets	4 900 . .	. . .	. . .	. . .	. . .	. . .	. . .	. . .	. . .
Financial derivatives liabilities	4 905 . .	. . .	. . .	. . .	. . .	. . .	. . .	. . .	. . .
Other investment assets	4 703 . .	–130.9	158.8	24.0	196.3	10.1	–358.1	–508.9	. . .
Monetary authorities	4 701 . .	. . .	. . .	. . .	. . .	. . .	. . .	. . .	. . .
General government	4 704 . .	1.3	–32.5	–63.7	63.5	70.7	–119.4	. . .	. . .
Banks	4 705 . .	67.8	141.3	7.7	–122.3	–10.6	9.3	–177.9	. . .
Other sectors	4 728 . .	–200.0	50.0	80.0	255.1	–50.0	–248.0	–331.0	. . .
Other investment liabilities	4 753 W.	–598.4	–796.4	–332.6	–260.4	–263.6	–1.5	–203.4	. . .
Monetary authorities	4 753 WA	61.1	4.4	–.6	34.3	–3.0	–23.7	–6.6	. . .
General government	4 753 ZB	–656.6	–626.1	–353.2	–145.7	–250.5	27.1	–207.7	. . .
Banks	4 753 ZC	–1.4	–174.7	21.2	–149.0	–10.1	–4.9	10.9	. . .
Other sectors	4 753 ZD	–1.5	. . .	. . .	. . .	. . .	. . .	. . .	. . .
Total, Groups A Through C	4 983 . .	*–532.4*	*–714.7*	*–329.0*	*3,969.8*	*–769.1*	*28.8*	*1,261.1*	. . .
D. Net Errors and Omissions	4 998 . .	**–189.2**	**186.5**	**–107.0**	**48.4**	**188.2**	**45.2**	**333.3**	**. . .**
Total, Groups A Through D	4 984 . .	*–721.6*	*–528.2*	*–436.0*	*4,018.2*	*–580.9*	*74.0*	*1,594.4*	. . .
E. Reserves and Related Items	4 802 A.	**721.6**	**528.2**	**436.0**	**–4,018.2**	**580.9**	**–74.0**	**–1,594.4**	**. . .**
Reserve assets	4 802 . .	–207.9	–263.1	–415.7	–192.7	210.9	–482.2	–1,429.5	. . .
Use of Fund credit and loans	4 766 . .	. . .	. . .	122.5	139.4	72.3	79.5	–71.0	. . .
Exceptional financing	4 920 . .	929.5	791.3	729.3	–3,964.9	297.7	328.7	–93.9	. . .
Conversion rates: Yemeni rials per U.S. dollar	0 101 . .	**12.010**	**40.839**	**94.157**	**129.281**	**135.882**	**155.718**	**161.718**	**168.672**

[1] Excludes components that have been classified in the categories of Group E.

Table 2. STANDARD PRESENTATION, 1994–2001

(Millions of U.S. dollars)

	Code	1994	1995	1996	1997	1998	1999	2000	2001
CURRENT ACCOUNT	4 993 . .	**249.6**	**183.7**	**106.3**	**22.3**	**–149.4**	**768.6**	**1,862.4**	**. . .**
A. GOODS	4 100 . .	274.2	148.6	–30.8	–132.5	–785.1	357.9	1,609.4	. . .
Credit	2 100 . .	**1,796.2**	**1,980.1**	**2,262.7**	**2,274.0**	**1,503.7**	**2,478.3**	**4,093.8**	**. . .**
General merchandise: exports f.o.b.	2 110 . .	1,796.2	1,980.1	2,262.7	2,274.0	1,501.0	2,466.1	4,077.5	. . .
Goods for processing: exports f.o.b.	2 150 . .	. . .	. . .	. . .	. . .	. . .	. . .	. . .	. . .
Repairs on goods	2 160 . .	. . .	. . .	. . .	. . .	. . .	. . .	. . .	. . .
Goods procured in ports by carriers	2 170 . .	. . .	. . .	. . .	. . .	2.7	12.2	16.3	. . .
Nonmonetary gold	2 180 . .	. . .	. . .	. . .	. . .	. . .	. . .	. . .	. . .
Debit	3 100 . .	**–1,522.0**	**–1,831.5**	**–2,293.5**	**–2,406.5**	**–2,288.8**	**–2,120.4**	**–2,484.4**	**. . .**
General merchandise: imports f.o.b.	3 110 . .	–1,522.0	–1,831.5	–2,293.5	–2,406.5	–2,288.8	–2,120.4	–2,484.4	. . .
Goods for processing: imports f.o.b.	3 150 . .	. . .	. . .	. . .	. . .	. . .	. . .	. . .	. . .
Repairs on goods	3 160 . .	. . .	. . .	. . .	. . .	. . .	. . .	. . .	. . .
Goods procured in ports by carriers	3 170 . .	. . .	. . .	. . .	. . .	. . .	. . .	. . .	. . .
Nonmonetary gold	3 180 . .	. . .	. . .	. . .	. . .	. . .	. . .	. . .	. . .
B. SERVICES	4 200 . .	–556.3	–459.9	–369.7	–469.8	–518.5	–535.4	–598.5	. . .
Total credit	2 200 . .	*148.0*	*179.4*	*185.7*	*207.6*	*174.4*	*183.2*	*210.8*	. . .
Total debit	3 200 . .	*–704.3*	*–639.3*	*–555.4*	*–677.4*	*–692.9*	*–718.6*	*–809.3*	. . .
Transportation services, credit	2 205 . .	**27.0**	**31.0**	**31.0**	**33.5**	**28.3**	**25.9**	**21.5**	**. . .**
Passenger	2 850 . .	. . .	. . .	. . .	. . .	. . .	. . .	. . .	. . .
Freight	2 851 . .	. . .	. . .	. . .	. . .	. . .	. . .	. . .	. . .
Other	2 852 . .	*27.0*	*31.0*	*31.0*	*33.5*	*28.3*	*25.9*	*21.5*	. . .
Sea transport, passenger	2 207 . .	. . .	. . .	. . .	. . .	. . .	. . .	. . .	. . .
Sea transport, freight	2 208 . .	. . .	. . .	. . .	. . .	. . .	. . .	. . .	. . .
Sea transport, other	2 209 . .	27.0	31.0	31.0	33.5	19.0	17.3	19.9	. . .
Air transport, passenger	2 211 . .	. . .	. . .	. . .	. . .	. . .	. . .	. . .	. . .
Air transport, freight	2 212 . .	. . .	. . .	. . .	. . .	. . .	. . .	. . .	. . .
Air transport, other	2 213 . .	. . .	. . .	. . .	. . .	9.3	8.6	1.6	. . .
Other transport, passenger	2 215 . .	. . .	. . .	. . .	. . .	. . .	. . .	. . .	. . .
Other transport, freight	2 216 . .	. . .	. . .	. . .	. . .	. . .	. . .	. . .	. . .
Other transport, other	2 217 . .	. . .	. . .	. . .	. . .	. . .	. . .	. . .	. . .
Transportation services, debit	3 205 . .	**–170.1**	**–215.1**	**–197.3**	**–257.2**	**–290.0**	**–269.0**	**–339.9**	**. . .**
Passenger	3 850 . .	. . .	. . .	. . .	. . .	*–29.5*	*–27.6*	*–57.0*	. . .
Freight	3 851 . .	*–168.3*	*–212.9*	*–194.5*	*–254.3*	*–260.5*	*–241.4*	*–282.9*	. . .
Other	3 852 . .	*–1.8*	*–2.2*	*–2.8*	*–2.9*	. . .	. . .	. . .	. . .
Sea transport, passenger	3 207 . .	. . .	. . .	. . .	. . .	. . .	. . .	. . .	. . .
Sea transport, freight	3 208 . .	–168.3	–212.9	–194.5	–254.3	–260.0	–240.9	–282.3	. . .
Sea transport, other	3 209 . .	–1.8	–2.2	–2.8	–2.9	. . .	. . .	. . .	. . .
Air transport, passenger	3 211 . .	. . .	. . .	. . .	. . .	–29.5	–27.6	–57.0	. . .
Air transport, freight	3 212 . .	. . .	. . .	. . .	. . .	–.5	–.5	–.6	. . .
Air transport, other	3 213 . .	. . .	. . .	. . .	. . .	. . .	. . .	. . .	. . .
Other transport, passenger	3 215 . .	. . .	. . .	. . .	. . .	. . .	. . .	. . .	. . .
Other transport, freight	3 216 . .	. . .	. . .	. . .	. . .	. . .	. . .	. . .	. . .
Other transport, other	3 217 . .	. . .	. . .	. . .	. . .	. . .	. . .	. . .	. . .
Travel, credit	2 236 . .	**18.5**	**49.9**	**54.9**	**69.7**	**84.0**	**61.0**	**72.7**	**. . .**
Business travel	2 237 . .	. . .	. . .	. . .	. . .	. . .	. . .	. . .	. . .
Personal travel	2 240 . .	18.5	49.9	54.9	69.7	84.0	61.0	72.7	. . .
Travel, debit	3 236 . .	**–77.7**	**–75.5**	**–78.2**	**–124.0**	**–129.9**	**–136.4**	**–69.8**	**. . .**
Business travel	3 237 . .	. . .	. . .	. . .	. . .	. . .	. . .	. . .	. . .
Personal travel	3 240 . .	–77.7	–75.5	–78.2	–124.0	–129.9	–136.4	–69.8	. . .
Other services, credit	2 200 BA	**102.5**	**98.5**	**99.8**	**104.4**	**62.1**	**96.3**	**116.6**	**. . .**
Communications	2 245 . .	53.9	54.5	54.9	56.5	20.2	53.9	59.2	. . .
Construction	2 249 . .	. . .	. . .	. . .	. . .	. . .	. . .	. . .	. . .
Insurance	2 253 . .	. . .	. . .	. . .	. . .	. . .	. . .	. . .	. . .
Financial	2 260 . .	. . .	. . .	. . .	. . .	. . .	. . .	. . .	. . .
Computer and information	2 262 . .	. . .	. . .	. . .	. . .	. . .	. . .	. . .	. . .
Royalties and licence fees	2 266 . .	. . .	. . .	. . .	. . .	. . .	. . .	. . .	. . .
Other business services	2 268 . .	5.0	6.0	6.2	8.0	.8	.1	20.9	. . .
Personal, cultural, and recreational	2 287 . .	. . .	. . .	. . .	. . .	. . .	. . .	. . .	. . .
Government, n.i.e.	2 291 . .	43.6	38.0	38.7	39.9	41.1	42.3	36.5	. . .
Other services, debit	3 200 BA	**–456.5**	**–348.7**	**–279.9**	**–296.2**	**–273.0**	**–313.2**	**–399.6**	**. . .**
Communications	3 245 . .	–8.2	–11.6	–11.6	–12.0	–2.4	–12.8	–14.0	. . .
Construction	3 249 . .	–47.1	–56.4	–59.9	–69.0	–94.2	–125.4	–51.0	. . .
Insurance	3 253 . .	–33.7	–42.6	–38.9	–50.9	–52.1	–48.2	–56.4	. . .
Financial	3 260 . .	. . .	. . .	. . .	. . .	. . .	. . .	. . .	. . .
Computer and information	3 262 . .	. . .	. . .	. . .	. . .	. . .	. . .	. . .	. . .
Royalties and licence fees	3 266 . .	. . .	. . .	. . .	. . .	. . .	. . .	. . .	. . .
Other business services	3 268 . .	–326.9	–202.9	–130.6	–118.5	–80.0	–80.0	–226.0	. . .
Personal, cultural, and recreational	3 287 . .	. . .	. . .	. . .	. . .	. . .	. . .	. . .	. . .
Government, n.i.e.	3 291 . .	–40.6	–35.2	–38.9	–45.8	–44.3	–46.8	–52.2	. . .

Table 2 (Continued). STANDARD PRESENTATION, 1994–2001
(Millions of U.S. dollars)

	Code	1994	1995	1996	1997	1998	1999	2000	2001
C. INCOME	4 300 . .	-531.9	-561.0	-633.9	-601.0	-175.5	-476.8	-548.0	...
Total credit	2 300 . .	*22.0*	*37.4*	*46.8*	*69.6*	*101.1*	*94.1*	*297.4*	...
Total debit	3 300 . .	*-553.9*	*-598.4*	*-680.7*	*-670.6*	*-276.6*	*-570.9*	*-845.4*	...
Compensation of employees, credit	2 310 . .	...	...	...	...	...	...	**96.1**	...
Compensation of employees, debit	3 310 . .	...	...	...	...	...	...	**-46.2**	...
Investment income, credit	2 320 . .	**22.0**	**37.4**	**46.8**	**69.6**	**101.1**	**94.1**	**201.3**	...
Direct investment income	2 330 . .	...	...	...	...	...	...	...	...
Dividends and distributed branch profits	2 332 . .	...	...	...	...	...	...	...	...
Reinvested earnings and undistributed branch profits	2 333 . .	...	...	...	...	...	...	...	...
Income on debt (interest)	2 334 . .	...	...	...	...	...	...	...	...
Portfolio investment income	2 339 . .	...	...	...	...	...	...	...	...
Income on equity	2 340 . .	...	...	...	...	...	...	...	...
Income on bonds and notes	2 350 . .	...	...	...	...	...	...	...	...
Income on money market instruments	2 360 . .	...	...	...	...	...	...	...	...
Other investment income	2 370 . .	22.0	37.4	46.8	69.6	101.1	94.1	201.3	...
Investment income, debit	3 320 . .	**-553.9**	**-598.4**	**-680.7**	**-670.6**	**-276.6**	**-570.9**	**-799.2**	...
Direct investment income	3 330 . .	-378.4	-433.4	-541.4	-554.3	-184.2	-480.1	-697.6	...
Dividends and distributed branch profits	3 332 . .	-378.4	-433.4	-541.4	-554.3	-177.6	-456.4	-697.6	...
Reinvested earnings and undistributed branch profits	3 333 . .	...	...	...	...	-6.6	-13.8	...	...
Income on debt (interest)	3 334 . .	...	...	...	...	...	-9.9	...	...
Portfolio investment income	3 339 . .	...	...	...	...	...	...	...	...
Income on equity	3 340 . .	...	...	...	...	...	...	...	...
Income on bonds and notes	3 350 . .	...	...	...	...	...	...	...	...
Income on money market instruments	3 360 . .	...	...	...	...	...	...	...	...
Other investment income	3 370 . .	-175.5	-165.0	-139.3	-116.3	-92.4	-90.8	-101.6	...
D. CURRENT TRANSFERS	4 379 . .	1,063.6	1,056.0	1,140.7	1,225.6	1,329.7	1,422.9	1,399.5	...
Credit	2 379 . .	**1,133.6**	**1,120.5**	**1,207.6**	**1,268.7**	**1,377.4**	**1,453.6**	**1,471.9**	...
General government	2 380 . .	74.3	40.0	73.1	100.1	160.4	193.5	83.8	...
Other sectors	2 390 . .	1,059.3	1,080.5	1,134.5	1,168.6	1,217.0	1,260.1	1,388.1	...
Workers' remittances	2 391 . .	1,059.3	1,080.5	1,134.5	1,168.6	1,202.4	1,223.2	1,288.0	...
Other current transfers	2 392 . .	...	...	...	...	14.6	36.9	100.1	...
Debit	3 379 . .	**-70.0**	**-64.5**	**-66.9**	**-43.1**	**-47.7**	**-30.7**	**-72.4**	...
General government	3 380 . .	-1.6	-3.3	-7.3	-1.7	-5.0	-3.7	-11.9	...
Other sectors	3 390 . .	-68.4	-61.2	-59.6	-41.4	-42.7	-27.0	-60.5	...
Workers' remittances	3 391 . .	-68.4	-61.2	-59.6	-41.4	-42.7	-27.0	-60.5	...
Other current transfers	3 392 . .	...	...	...	...	...	...	...	...
CAPITAL AND FINANCIAL ACCOUNT	4 996 . .	**-60.4**	**-370.2**	**.7**	**-70.7**	**-38.8**	**-813.8**	**-2,195.7**	...
CAPITAL ACCOUNT	4 994 . .	...	...	...	**4,236.2**	**2.2**	**1.5**	**311.8**	...
Total credit	2 994 . .	...	...	...	*4,236.2*	*2.2*	*1.5*	*391.8*	...
Total debit	3 994 . .	...	...	...	...	...	...	*-80.0*	...
Capital transfers, credit	2 400 . .	...	...	...	**4,236.2**	**2.2**	**1.5**	**391.8**	...
General government	2 401 . .	...	...	...	4,236.2	2.2	1.5	338.9	...
Debt forgiveness	2 402 . .	...	...	...	4,236.2	2.2	1.5	338.9	...
Other capital transfers	2 410 . .	...	...	...	...	...	...	...	...
Other sectors	2 430 . .	...	...	...	...	...	...	52.9	...
Migrants' transfers	2 431 . .	...	...	...	...	...	...	52.9	...
Debt forgiveness	2 432 . .	...	...	...	...	...	...	...	...
Other capital transfers	2 440 . .	...	...	...	...	...	...	...	...
Capital transfers, debit	3 400 . .	...	...	...	...	...	...	**-80.0**	...
General government	3 401 . .	...	...	...	...	...	...	...	...
Debt forgiveness	3 402 . .	...	...	...	...	...	...	...	...
Other capital transfers	3 410 . .	...	...	...	...	...	...	...	...
Other sectors	3 430 . .	...	...	...	...	...	...	-80.0	...
Migrants' transfers	3 431 . .	...	...	...	...	...	...	-80.0	...
Debt forgiveness	3 432 . .	...	...	...	...	...	...	...	...
Other capital transfers	3 440 . .	...	...	...	...	...	...	...	...
Nonproduced nonfinancial assets, credit	2 480 . .	...	...	...	...	...	...	...	...
Nonproduced nonfinancial assets, debit	3 480 . .	...	...	...	...	...	...	...	...

Table 2 (Continued). STANDARD PRESENTATION, 1994–2001
(Millions of U.S. dollars)

	Code	1994	1995	1996	1997	1998	1999	2000	2001
FINANCIAL ACCOUNT	4 995 . .	**–60.4**	**–370.2**	**.7**	**–4,306.9**	**–41.0**	**–815.3**	**–2,507.5**	**. . .**
A. DIRECT INVESTMENT	4 500 . .	15.8	–217.7	–60.1	–138.5	–219.4	–194.3	–200.9	. . .
Direct investment abroad	4 505 . .	**. . .**	**. . .**	**. . .**	**. . .**	**. . .**	**. . .**	**. . .**	**. . .**
Equity capital	4 510 . .	. . .	. . .	. . .	. . .	. . .	. . .	. . .	. . .
Claims on affiliated enterprises	4 515 . .	. . .	. . .	. . .	. . .	. . .	. . .	. . .	. . .
Liabilities to affiliated enterprises	4 520 . .	. . .	. . .	. . .	. . .	. . .	. . .	. . .	. . .
Reinvested earnings	4 525 . .	. . .	. . .	. . .	. . .	. . .	. . .	. . .	. . .
Other capital	4 530 . .	. . .	. . .	. . .	. . .	. . .	. . .	. . .	. . .
Claims on affiliated enterprises	4 535 . .	. . .	. . .	. . .	. . .	. . .	. . .	. . .	. . .
Liabilities to affiliated enterprises	4 540 . .	. . .	. . .	. . .	. . .	. . .	. . .	. . .	. . .
Direct investment in Yemen	4 555 . .	**15.8**	**–217.7**	**–60.1**	**–138.5**	**–219.4**	**–194.3**	**–200.9**	**. . .**
Equity capital	4 560 . .	. . .	. . .	. . .	. . .	. . .	7.3	–200.9	. . .
Claims on direct investors	4 565 . .	. . .	. . .	. . .	. . .	. . .	. . .	. . .	. . .
Liabilities to direct investors	4 570 . .	. . .	. . .	. . .	. . .	. . .	7.3	–200.9	. . .
Reinvested earnings	4 575 . .	. . .	. . .	. . .	. . .	6.6	13.8	. . .	. . .
Other capital	4 580 . .	15.8	–217.7	–60.1	–138.5	–226.0	–215.4	. . .	. . .
Claims on direct investors	4 585 . .	. . .	. . .	. . .	. . .	. . .	. . .	. . .	. . .
Liabilities to direct investors	4 590 . .	15.8	–217.7	–60.1	–138.5	–226.0	–215.4	. . .	. . .
B. PORTFOLIO INVESTMENT	4 600 . .	2.8	–3.1	.9	5.0	4.9	4.1	.1	. . .
Assets	4 602 . .	**2.8**	**–3.1**	**.9**	**5.0**	**4.9**	**4.1**	**.1**	**. . .**
Equity securities	4 610 . .	2.8	–3.1	.9	5.0	4.9	4.1	.1	. . .
Monetary authorities	4 611 . .	. . .	. . .	. . .	. . .	. . .	. . .	. . .	. . .
General government	4 612 . .	. . .	. . .	. . .	. . .	. . .	. . .	. . .	. . .
Banks	4 613 . .	2.8	–3.1	.9	5.0	4.9	4.1	.1	. . .
Other sectors	4 614 . .	. . .	. . .	. . .	. . .	. . .	. . .	. . .	. . .
Debt securities	4 619 . .	. . .	. . .	. . .	. . .	. . .	. . .	. . .	. . .
Bonds and notes	4 620 . .	. . .	. . .	. . .	. . .	. . .	. . .	. . .	. . .
Monetary authorities	4 621 . .	. . .	. . .	. . .	. . .	. . .	. . .	. . .	. . .
General government	4 622 . .	. . .	. . .	. . .	. . .	. . .	. . .	. . .	. . .
Banks	4 623 . .	. . .	. . .	. . .	. . .	. . .	. . .	. . .	. . .
Other sectors	4 624 . .	. . .	. . .	. . .	. . .	. . .	. . .	. . .	. . .
Money market instruments	4 630 . .	. . .	. . .	. . .	. . .	. . .	. . .	. . .	. . .
Monetary authorities	4 631 . .	. . .	. . .	. . .	. . .	. . .	. . .	. . .	. . .
General government	4 632 . .	. . .	. . .	. . .	. . .	. . .	. . .	. . .	. . .
Banks	4 633 . .	. . .	. . .	. . .	. . .	. . .	. . .	. . .	. . .
Other sectors	4 634 . .	. . .	. . .	. . .	. . .	. . .	. . .	. . .	. . .
Liabilities	4 652 . .	**. . .**	**. . .**	**. . .**	**. . .**	**. . .**	**. . .**	**. . .**	**. . .**
Equity securities	4 660 . .	. . .	. . .	. . .	. . .	. . .	. . .	. . .	. . .
Banks	4 663 . .	. . .	. . .	. . .	. . .	. . .	. . .	. . .	. . .
Other sectors	4 664 . .	. . .	. . .	. . .	. . .	. . .	. . .	. . .	. . .
Debt securities	4 669 . .	. . .	. . .	. . .	. . .	. . .	. . .	. . .	. . .
Bonds and notes	4 670 . .	. . .	. . .	. . .	. . .	. . .	. . .	. . .	. . .
Monetary authorities	4 671 . .	. . .	. . .	. . .	. . .	. . .	. . .	. . .	. . .
General government	4 672 . .	. . .	. . .	. . .	. . .	. . .	. . .	. . .	. . .
Banks	4 673 . .	. . .	. . .	. . .	. . .	. . .	. . .	. . .	. . .
Other sectors	4 674 . .	. . .	. . .	. . .	. . .	. . .	. . .	. . .	. . .
Money market instruments	4 680 . .	. . .	. . .	. . .	. . .	. . .	. . .	. . .	. . .
Monetary authorities	4 681 . .	. . .	. . .	. . .	. . .	. . .	. . .	. . .	. . .
General government	4 682 . .	. . .	. . .	. . .	. . .	. . .	. . .	. . .	. . .
Banks	4 683 . .	. . .	. . .	. . .	. . .	. . .	. . .	. . .	. . .
Other sectors	4 684 . .	. . .	. . .	. . .	. . .	. . .	. . .	. . .	. . .
C. FINANCIAL DERIVATIVES	4 910 . .	. . .	. . .	. . .	. . .	. . .	. . .	. . .	. . .
Monetary authorities	4 911 . .	. . .	. . .	. . .	. . .	. . .	. . .	. . .	. . .
General government	4 912 . .	. . .	. . .	. . .	. . .	. . .	. . .	. . .	. . .
Banks	4 913 . .	. . .	. . .	. . .	. . .	. . .	. . .	. . .	. . .
Other sectors	4 914 . .	. . .	. . .	. . .	. . .	. . .	. . .	. . .	. . .
Assets	4 900 . .	**. . .**	**. . .**	**. . .**	**. . .**	**. . .**	**. . .**	**. . .**	**. . .**
Monetary authorities	4 901 . .	. . .	. . .	. . .	. . .	. . .	. . .	. . .	. . .
General government	4 902 . .	. . .	. . .	. . .	. . .	. . .	. . .	. . .	. . .
Banks	4 903 . .	. . .	. . .	. . .	. . .	. . .	. . .	. . .	. . .
Other sectors	4 904 . .	. . .	. . .	. . .	. . .	. . .	. . .	. . .	. . .
Liabilities	4 905 . .	**. . .**	**. . .**	**. . .**	**. . .**	**. . .**	**. . .**	**. . .**	**. . .**
Monetary authorities	4 906 . .	. . .	. . .	. . .	. . .	. . .	. . .	. . .	. . .
General government	4 907 . .	. . .	. . .	. . .	. . .	. . .	. . .	. . .	. . .
Banks	4 908 . .	. . .	. . .	. . .	. . .	. . .	. . .	. . .	. . .
Other sectors	4 909 . .	. . .	. . .	. . .	. . .	. . .	. . .	. . .	. . .

Table 2 (Concluded). STANDARD PRESENTATION, 1994–2001
(Millions of U.S. dollars)

	Code	1994	1995	1996	1997	1998	1999	2000	2001
D. OTHER INVESTMENT	4 700 . .	128.9	113.7	475.7	-3,980.7	-37.4	-142.9	-877.2	. . .
Assets	4 703 . .	**-130.9**	**158.8**	**24.0**	**196.3**	**10.1**	**-358.1**	**-508.9**	. . .
Trade credits	4 706 . .	1.3	-32.5	-63.7	63.5	70.7	-119.4	. . .	. . .
General government	4 707 . .	1.3	-32.5	-63.7	63.5	70.7	-119.4	. . .	. . .
of which: Short-term	4 709 . .	*1.3*	*-32.5*	*-63.7*	*63.5*	*70.7*	*-119.4*	. . .	. . .
Other sectors	4 710 . .	. . .	. . .	. . .	. . .	. . .	. . .	. . .	. . .
of which: Short-term	4 712 . .	. . .	. . .	. . .	. . .	. . .	. . .	. . .	. . .
Loans	4 714 . .	. . .	. . .	. . .	. . .	. . .	. . .	. . .	. . .
Monetary authorities	4 715 . .	. . .	. . .	. . .	. . .	. . .	. . .	. . .	. . .
of which: Short-term	4 718 . .	. . .	. . .	. . .	. . .	. . .	. . .	. . .	. . .
General government	4 719 . .	. . .	. . .	. . .	. . .	. . .	. . .	. . .	. . .
of which: Short-term	4 721 . .	. . .	. . .	. . .	. . .	. . .	. . .	. . .	. . .
Banks	4 722 . .	. . .	. . .	. . .	. . .	. . .	. . .	. . .	. . .
of which: Short-term	4 724 . .	. . .	. . .	. . .	. . .	. . .	. . .	. . .	. . .
Other sectors	4 725 . .	. . .	. . .	. . .	. . .	. . .	. . .	. . .	. . .
of which: Short-term	4 727 . .	. . .	. . .	. . .	. . .	. . .	. . .	. . .	. . .
Currency and deposits	4 730 . .	-132.2	191.3	87.7	132.8	-60.6	-238.7	-508.9	. . .
Monetary authorities	4 731 . .	. . .	. . .	. . .	. . .	. . .	. . .	. . .	. . .
General government	4 732 . .	. . .	. . .	. . .	. . .	. . .	. . .	. . .	. . .
Banks	4 733 . .	67.8	141.3	7.7	-122.3	-10.6	9.3	-177.9	. . .
Other sectors	4 734 . .	-200.0	50.0	80.0	255.1	-50.0	-248.0	-331.0	. . .
Other assets	4 736 . .	. . .	. . .	. . .	. . .	. . .	. . .	. . .	. . .
Monetary authorities	4 737 . .	. . .	. . .	. . .	. . .	. . .	. . .	. . .	. . .
of which: Short-term	4 739 . .	. . .	. . .	. . .	. . .	. . .	. . .	. . .	. . .
General government	4 740 . .	. . .	. . .	. . .	. . .	. . .	. . .	. . .	. . .
of which: Short-term	4 742 . .	. . .	. . .	. . .	. . .	. . .	. . .	. . .	. . .
Banks	4 743 . .	. . .	. . .	. . .	. . .	. . .	. . .	. . .	. . .
of which: Short-term	4 745 . .	. . .	. . .	. . .	. . .	. . .	. . .	. . .	. . .
Other sectors	4 746 . .	. . .	. . .	. . .	. . .	. . .	. . .	. . .	. . .
of which: Short-term	4 748 . .	. . .	. . .	. . .	. . .	. . .	. . .	. . .	. . .
Liabilities	4 753 . .	**259.8**	**-45.1**	**451.7**	**-4,177.0**	**-47.5**	**215.2**	**-368.3**	. . .
Trade credits	4 756 . .	-36.4	11.6	123.5	-79.3	-187.2	. . .	-17.7	. . .
General government	4 757 . .	-36.4	11.6	123.5	-79.3	-187.2	. . .	-17.7	. . .
of which: Short-term	4 759 . .	*28.0*	*68.0*	*167.4*	*-79.3*	*-187.2*	. . .	. . .	. . .
Other sectors	4 760 . .	. . .	. . .	. . .	. . .	. . .	. . .	. . .	. . .
of which: Short-term	4 762 . .	. . .	. . .	. . .	. . .	. . .	. . .	. . .	. . .
Loans	4 764 . .	-562.0	-808.0	386.6	1,827.4	158.0	215.2	-1.4	. . .
Monetary authorities	4 765 . .	61.1	4.4	121.9	173.7	69.3	55.8	-77.6	. . .
of which: Use of Fund credit and loans from the Fund	4 766 . .	. . .	. . .	*122.5*	*139.4*	*72.3*	*79.5*	*-71.0*	. . .
of which: Short-term	4 768 . .	*11.7*	*-2.7*	*-1.5*	*5.0*	*7.2*	*-48.7*	*3.7*	. . .
General government	4 769 . .	-620.2	-637.7	243.5	1,802.7	98.8	164.3	65.3	. . .
of which: Short-term	4 771 . .	. . .	. . .	. . .	. . .	. . .	. . .	. . .	. . .
Banks	4 772 . .	-1.4	-174.7	21.2	-149.0	-10.1	-4.9	10.9	. . .
of which: Short-term	4 774 . .	*.4*	*-101.2*	*3.2*	*-7.7*	*-3.2*	*-4.9*	*22.6*	. . .
Other sectors	4 775 . .	-1.5	. . .	. . .	. . .	. . .	. . .	. . .	. . .
of which: Short-term	4 777 . .	. . .	. . .	. . .	. . .	. . .	. . .	. . .	. . .
Currency and deposits	4 780 . .	. . .	. . .	. . .	. . .	. . .	. . .	. . .	. . .
Monetary authorities	4 781 . .	. . .	. . .	. . .	. . .	. . .	. . .	. . .	. . .
General government	4 782 . .	. . .	. . .	. . .	. . .	. . .	. . .	. . .	. . .
Banks	4 783 . .	. . .	. . .	. . .	. . .	. . .	. . .	. . .	. . .
Other sectors	4 784 . .	. . .	. . .	. . .	. . .	. . .	. . .	. . .	. . .
Other liabilities	4 786 . .	858.2	751.3	-58.4	-5,925.1	-18.3	. . .	-349.2	. . .
Monetary authorities	4 787 . .	. . .	. . .	. . .	. . .	. . .	. . .	. . .	. . .
of which: Short-term	4 789 . .	. . .	. . .	. . .	. . .	. . .	. . .	. . .	. . .
General government	4 790 . .	858.2	751.3	-58.4	-5,925.1	-18.3	. . .	-349.2	. . .
of which: Short-term	4 792 . .	*858.2*	*751.3*	*-58.4*	*-5,925.1*	*-18.3*	. . .	*-349.2*	. . .
Banks	4 793 . .	. . .	. . .	. . .	. . .	. . .	. . .	. . .	. . .
of which: Short-term	4 795 . .	. . .	. . .	. . .	. . .	. . .	. . .	. . .	. . .
Other sectors	4 796 . .	. . .	. . .	. . .	. . .	. . .	. . .	. . .	. . .
of which: Short-term	4 798 . .	. . .	. . .	. . .	. . .	. . .	. . .	. . .	. . .
E. RESERVE ASSETS	4 802 . .	-207.9	-263.1	-415.7	-192.7	210.9	-482.2	-1,429.5	. . .
Monetary gold	4 812 . .	. . .	. . .	. . .	. . .	. . .	. . .	. . .	. . .
Special drawing rights	4 811 . .	-46.8	-4.6	5.5	-124.6	-10.9	4.1	83.1	. . .
Reserve position in the Fund	4 810 . .	. . .	. . .	. . .	. . .	. . .	. . .	. . .	. . .
Foreign exchange	4 803 . .	-161.1	-258.5	-421.2	-68.1	221.8	-486.3	-1,512.6	. . .
Other claims	4 813 . .	. . .	. . .	. . .	. . .	. . .	. . .	. . .	. . .
NET ERRORS AND OMISSIONS	4 998 . .	**-189.2**	**186.5**	**-107.0**	**48.4**	**188.2**	**45.2**	**333.3**	. . .

Table 3. INTERNATIONAL INVESTMENT POSITION (End–period stocks), 1994–2001

(Millions of U.S. dollars)

	Code	1994	1995	1996	1997	1998	1999	2000	2001
ASSETS	8 995 C.	...	...	...	...	2,399.0	3,111.1	...	...
Direct investment abroad	8 505 . .	**...**	**...**	**...**	**...**	**...**	**...**	**...**	**...**
Equity capital and reinvested earnings	8 506 . .	...	...	...	...	...	...	...	...
Claims on affiliated enterprises	8 507 . .	...	...	...	...	...	...	...	...
Liabilities to affiliated enterprises	8 508 . .	...	...	...	...	...	...	...	...
Other capital	8 530 . .	...	...	...	...	...	...	...	...
Claims on affiliated enterprises	8 535 . .	...	...	...	...	...	...	...	...
Liabilities to affiliated enterprises	8 540 . .	...	...	...	...	...	...	...	...
Portfolio investment	8 602 . .	**...**	**...**	**...**	**...**	**4.5**	**.4**	**...**	**...**
Equity securities	8 610 . .	...	...	...	...	4.5	.4	...	...
Monetary authorities	8 611 . .	...	...	...	...	...	...	...	...
General government	8 612 . .	...	...	...	...	...	...	...	...
Banks	8 613 . .	...	...	...	...	4.5	.4	...	...
Other sectors	8 614 . .	...	...	...	...	...	...	...	...
Debt securities	8 619 . .	...	...	...	...	...	...	...	...
Bonds and notes	8 620 . .	...	...	...	...	...	...	...	...
Monetary authorities	8 621 . .	...	...	...	...	...	...	...	...
General government	8 622 . .	...	...	...	...	...	...	...	...
Banks	8 623 . .	...	...	...	...	...	...	...	...
Other sectors	8 624 . .	...	...	...	...	...	...	...	...
Money market instruments	8 630 . .	...	...	...	...	...	...	...	...
Monetary authorities	8 631 . .	...	...	...	...	...	...	...	...
General government	8 632 . .	...	...	...	...	...	...	...	...
Banks	8 633 . .	...	...	...	...	...	...	...	...
Other sectors	8 634 . .	...	...	...	...	...	...	...	...
Financial derivatives	8 900 . .	**...**	**...**	**...**	**...**	**...**	**...**	**...**	**...**
Monetary authorities	8 901 . .	...	...	...	...	...	...	...	...
General government	8 902 . .	...	...	...	...	...	...	...	...
Banks	8 903 . .	...	...	...	...	...	...	...	...
Other sectors	8 904 . .	...	...	...	...	...	...	...	...
Other investment	8 703 . .	**...**	**...**	**...**	**...**	**1,381.3**	**1,620.1**	**...**	**...**
Trade credits	8 706 . .	...	...	...	...	...	...	...	...
General government	8 707 . .	...	...	...	...	...	...	...	...
of which: Short-term	8 709 . .	...	...	...	...	...	...	...	...
Other sectors	8 710 . .	...	...	...	...	...	...	...	...
of which: Short-term	8 712 . .	...	...	...	...	...	...	...	...
Loans	8 714 . .	...	...	...	...	...	...	...	...
Monetary authorities	8 715 . .	...	...	...	...	...	...	...	...
of which: Short-term	8 718 . .	...	...	...	...	...	...	...	...
General government	8 719 . .	...	...	...	...	...	...	...	...
of which: Short-term	8 721 . .	...	...	...	...	...	...	...	...
Banks	8 722 . .	...	...	...	...	...	...	...	...
of which: Short-term	8 724 . .	...	...	...	...	...	...	...	...
Other sectors	8 725 . .	...	...	...	...	...	...	...	...
of which: Short-term	8 727 . .	...	...	...	...	...	...	...	...
Currency and deposits	8 730 . .	...	...	...	...	1,381.3	1,620.1	...	...
Monetary authorities	8 731 . .	...	...	...	...	...	...	...	...
General government	8 732 . .	...	...	...	...	...	...	...	...
Banks	8 733 . .	...	...	...	...	454.3	445.1	...	...
Other sectors	8 734 . .	...	...	...	...	927.0	1,175.0	...	...
Other assets	8 736 . .	...	...	...	...	...	...	...	...
Monetary authorities	8 737 . .	...	...	...	...	...	...	...	...
of which: Short-term	8 739 . .	...	...	...	...	...	...	...	...
General government	8 740 . .	...	...	...	...	...	...	...	...
of which: Short-term	8 742 . .	...	...	...	...	...	...	...	...
Banks	8 743 . .	...	...	...	...	...	...	...	...
of which: Short-term	8 745 . .	...	...	...	...	...	...	...	...
Other sectors	8 746 . .	...	...	...	...	...	...	...	...
of which: Short-term	8 748 . .	...	...	...	...	...	...	...	...
Reserve assets	8 802 . .	**...**	**...**	**...**	**...**	**1,013.2**	**1,490.6**	**...**	**...**
Monetary gold	8 812 . .	...	...	...	...	...	...	...	...
Special drawing rights	8 811 . .	48.9	55.0	47.9	167.4	185.2	176.3	84.6	18.5
Reserve position in the Fund	8 810 . .	...	...	...	...	...	...	...	...
Foreign exchange	8 803 . .	...	...	...	...	828.0	1,314.2	...	...
Other claims	8 813 . .	...	...	...	...	...	...	...	...

Table 3 (Concluded). INTERNATIONAL INVESTMENT POSITION (End–period stocks), 1994–2001
(Millions of U.S. dollars)

	Code	1994	1995	1996	1997	1998	1999	2000	2001
LIABILITIES	8 995 D.	...	...	...	...	6,077.9	6,305.5	...	...
Direct investment in Yemen	8 555 ..	...	...	...	...	**1,088.6**	**993.2**	...	...
Equity capital and reinvested earnings	8 556 ..	...	...	...	...	131.1	156.6	...	...
Claims on direct investors	8 557 ..	...	...	...	...	...	...	...	...
Liabilities to direct investors	8 558 ..	...	...	...	...	131.1	156.6	...	...
Other capital	8 580 ..	...	...	...	...	957.5	836.6	...	...
Claims on direct investors	8 585 ..	...	...	...	...	...	...	...	...
Liabilities to direct investors	8 590 ..	...	...	...	...	957.5	836.6	...	...
Portfolio investment	8 652 ..	...	...	...	...	...	...	...	...
Equity securities	8 660 ..	...	...	...	...	...	...	...	...
Banks	8 663 ..	...	...	...	...	...	...	...	...
Other sectors	8 664 ..	...	...	...	...	...	...	...	...
Debt securities	8 669 ..	...	...	...	...	...	...	...	...
Bonds and notes	8 670 ..	...	...	...	...	...	...	...	...
Monetary authorities	8 671 ..	...	...	...	...	...	...	...	...
General government	8 672 ..	...	...	...	...	...	...	...	...
Banks	8 673 ..	...	...	...	...	...	...	...	...
Other sectors	8 674 ..	...	...	...	...	...	...	...	...
Money market instruments	8 680 ..	...	...	...	...	...	...	...	...
Monetary authorities	8 681 ..	...	...	...	...	...	...	...	...
General government	8 682 ..	...	...	...	...	...	...	...	...
Banks	8 683 ..	...	...	...	...	...	...	...	...
Other sectors	8 684 ..	...	...	...	...	...	...	...	...
Financial derivatives	8 905 ..	...	...	...	...	...	...	...	...
Monetary authorities	8 906 ..	...	...	...	...	...	...	...	...
General government	8 907 ..	...	...	...	...	...	...	...	...
Banks	8 908 ..	...	...	...	...	...	...	...	...
Other sectors	8 909 ..	...	...	...	...	...	...	...	...
Other investment	8 753 ..	...	...	...	...	**4,989.3**	**5,312.3**	...	...
Trade credits	8 756 ..	...	...	...	...	137.2	144.6	...	...
General government	8 757 ..	...	...	...	...	137.2	144.6	...	...
of which: Short-term	8 759 ..	...	...	...	...	...	...	...	...
Other sectors	8 760 ..	...	...	...	...	...	...	...	...
of which: Short-term	8 762 ..	...	...	...	...	...	...	...	...
Loans	8 764 ..	...	...	...	...	4,852.1	5,167.7	...	...
Monetary authorities	8 765 ..	...	...	...	...	624.6	664.0	...	...
of which: Use of Fund credit and loans from the Fund	8 766 ..	...	...	*120.8*	*250.1*	*335.6*	*408.5*	*317.3*	*373.7*
of which: Short-term	8 768 ..	...	...	...	...	*177.9*	*129.2*	...	...
General government	8 769 ..	...	...	...	...	4,177.2	4,458.3	...	...
of which: Short-term	8 771 ..	...	...	...	...	...	...	...	...
Banks	8 772 ..	...	...	...	...	50.3	45.4	...	...
of which: Short-term	8 774 ..	...	...	...	...	*15.6*	*10.7*	...	...
Other sectors	8 775 ..	...	...	...	...	...	...	...	...
of which: Short-term	8 777 ..	...	...	...	...	...	...	...	...
Currency and deposits	8 780 ..	...	...	...	...	...	...	...	...
Monetary authorities	8 781 ..	...	...	...	...	...	...	...	...
General government	8 782 ..	...	...	...	...	...	...	...	...
Banks	8 783 ..	...	...	...	...	...	...	...	...
Other sectors	8 784 ..	...	...	...	...	...	...	...	...
Other liabilities	8 786 ..	...	...	...	...	...	...	...	...
Monetary authorities	8 787 ..	...	...	...	...	...	...	...	...
of which: Short-term	8 789 ..	...	...	...	...	...	...	...	...
General government	8 790 ..	...	...	...	...	...	...	...	...
of which: Short-term	8 792 ..	...	...	...	...	...	...	...	...
Banks	8 793 ..	...	...	...	...	...	...	...	...
of which: Short-term	8 795 ..	...	...	...	...	...	...	...	...
Other sectors	8 796 ..	...	...	...	...	...	...	...	...
of which: Short-term	8 798 ..	...	...	...	...	...	...	...	...
NET INTERNATIONAL INVESTMENT POSITION	8 995 ..	...	...	...	...	**–3,678.9**	**–3,194.4**	...	...
Conversion rates: Yemeni rials per U.S. dollar (end of period)	0 102 ..	**12.01**	**50.04**	**126.91**	**130.46**	**141.65**	**159.10**	**165.59**	**173.27**

Table 1. ANALYTIC PRESENTATION, 1994–2001
(Millions of U.S. dollars)

	Code	1994	1995	1996	1997	1998	1999	2000	2001
A. Current Account [1]	4 993 Z.	**. . .**	**. . .**	**. . .**	**–353**	**–573**	**–447**	**–584**	**. . .**
Goods: exports f.o.b	2 100 . .	. . .	. . .	. . .	1,110	818	772	757	. . .
Goods: imports f.o.b	3 100 . .	. . .	. . .	. . .	–1,056	–971	–870	–978	. . .
Balance on Goods	4 100 . .	. . .	. . .	. . .	*54*	*–153*	*–98*	*–221*	. . .
Services: credit	2 200 . .	. . .	. . .	. . .	112	102	107	114	. . .
Services: debit	3 200 . .	. . .	. . .	. . .	–282	–282	–306	–340	. . .
Balance on Goods and Services	4 991 . .	. . .	. . .	. . .	*–115*	*–332*	*–297*	*–447*	. . .
Income: credit	2 300 . .	. . .	. . .	. . .	77	44	44	46	. . .
Income: debit	3 300 . .	. . .	. . .	. . .	–296	–258	–178	–166	. . .
Balance on Goods, Services, and Income	4 992 . .	. . .	. . .	. . .	*–334*	*–546*	*–431*	*–566*	. . .
Current transfers: credit	2 379 Z.	. . .	. . .	. . .	. . .	. . .	. . .	. . .	. . .
Current transfers: debit	3 379 . .	. . .	. . .	. . .	–19	–27	–16	–18	. . .
B. Capital Account [1]	4 994 Z.	**. . .**	**. . .**	**. . .**	**. . .**	**203**	**196**	**153**	**. . .**
Capital account: credit	2 994 Z.	. . .	. . .	. . .	. . .	203	196	153	. . .
Capital account: debit	3 994 . .	. . .	. . .	. . .	. . .	. . .	. . .	. . .	. . .
Total, Groups A Plus B	4 981 . .	. . .	. . .	. . .	*–353*	*–370*	*–251*	*–431*	. . .
C. Financial Account [1]	4 995 W.	**. . .**	**. . .**	**. . .**	**–324**	**–264**	**–174**	**–274**	**. . .**
Direct investment abroad	4 505 . .	. . .	. . .	. . .	. . .	. . .	. . .	. . .	. . .
Direct investment in Zambia	4 555 Z.	. . .	. . .	. . .	207	198	162	122	. . .
Portfolio investment assets	4 602 . .	. . .	. . .	. . .	. . .	. . .	. . .	. . .	. . .
Equity securities	4 610 . .	. . .	. . .	. . .	. . .	. . .	. . .	. . .	. . .
Debt securities	4 619 . .	. . .	. . .	. . .	. . .	. . .	. . .	. . .	. . .
Portfolio investment liabilities	4 652 Z.	. . .	. . .	. . .	1	1	13	–1	. . .
Equity securities	4 660 . .	. . .	. . .	. . .	1	1	13	–1	. . .
Debt securities	4 669 Z.	. . .	. . .	. . .	. . .	. . .	. . .	. . .	. . .
Financial derivatives	4 910 . .	. . .	. . .	. . .	. . .	. . .	. . .	. . .	. . .
Financial derivatives assets	4 900 . .	. . .	. . .	. . .	. . .	. . .	. . .	. . .	. . .
Financial derivatives liabilities	4 905 . .	. . .	. . .	. . .	. . .	. . .	. . .	. . .	. . .
Other investment assets	4 703 . .	. . .	. . .	. . .	–24	–40	–2	–85	. . .
Monetary authorities	4 701 . .	. . .	. . .	. . .	. . .	. . .	. . .	. . .	. . .
General government	4 704 . .	. . .	. . .	. . .	. . .	. . .	. . .	. . .	. . .
Banks	4 705 . .	. . .	. . .	. . .	–24	–40	–2	–85	. . .
Other sectors	4 728 . .	. . .	. . .	. . .	. . .	. . .	. . .	. . .	. . .
Other investment liabilities	4 753 W.	. . .	. . .	. . .	–508	–422	–347	–309	. . .
Monetary authorities	4 753 WA	. . .	. . .	. . .	. . .	. . .	. . .	–7	. . .
General government	4 753 ZB	. . .	. . .	. . .	–192	–136	–259	–290	. . .
Banks	4 753 ZC	. . .	. . .	. . .	19	–2	. . .	. . .	. . .
Other sectors	4 753 ZD	. . .	. . .	. . .	–335	–284	–88	–12	. . .
Total, Groups A Through C	4 983 . .	. . .	. . .	. . .	*–677*	*–634*	*–425*	*–705*	. . .
D. Net Errors and Omissions	4 998 . .	**. . .**	**. . .**	**. . .**	**–255**	**–37**	**–229**	**185**	**. . .**
Total, Groups A Through D	4 984 . .	. . .	. . .	. . .	*–932*	*–671*	*–654*	*–520*	. . .
E. Reserves and Related Items	4 802 A.	**. . .**	**. . .**	**. . .**	**932**	**671**	**654**	**520**	**. . .**
Reserve assets	4 802 . .	. . .	. . .	. . .	–25	194	–1	–90	. . .
Use of Fund credit and loans	4 766 . .	. . .	. . .	. . .	14	. . .	14	26	. . .
Exceptional financing	4 920 . .	. . .	. . .	. . .	944	477	642	584	. . .
Conversion rates: Zambian kwacha per U.S. dollar	0 101 . .	**669.37**	**864.12**	**1,207.90**	**1,314.50**	**1,862.07**	**2,388.02**	**3,110.84**	**3,610.94**

[1] Excludes components that have been classified in the categories of Group E.

Table 2. STANDARD PRESENTATION, 1994–2001

(Millions of U.S. dollars)

	Code	1994	1995	1996	1997	1998	1999	2000	2001
CURRENT ACCOUNT	4 993 . .	**. . .**	**. . .**	**. . .**	**–152**	**–570**	**–386**	**–553**	**. . .**
A. GOODS	4 100 . .	. . .	. . .	. . .	54	–153	–98	–221	. . .
Credit	2 100 . .	**. . .**	**. . .**	**. . .**	**1,110**	**818**	**772**	**757**	**. . .**
General merchandise: exports f.o.b.	2 110 . .	. . .	. . .	. . .	1,110	816	755	746	. . .
Goods for processing: exports f.o.b.	2 150 . .	. . .	. . .	. . .	. . .	. . .	. . .	. . .	. . .
Repairs on goods	2 160 . .	. . .	. . .	. . .	. . .	. . .	. . .	. . .	. . .
Goods procured in ports by carriers	2 170 . .	. . .	. . .	. . .	. . .	2	17	11	. . .
Nonmonetary gold	2 180 . .	. . .	. . .	. . .	. . .	. . .	. . .	. . .	. . .
Debit	3 100 . .	**. . .**	**. . .**	**. . .**	**–1,056**	**–971**	**–870**	**–978**	**. . .**
General merchandise: imports f.o.b.	3 110 . .	. . .	. . .	. . .	–1,056	–971	–870	–978	. . .
Goods for processing: imports f.o.b.	3 150 . .	. . .	. . .	. . .	. . .	. . .	. . .	. . .	. . .
Repairs on goods	3 160 . .	. . .	. . .	. . .	. . .	. . .	. . .	. . .	. . .
Goods procured in ports by carriers	3 170 . .	. . .	. . .	. . .	. . .	. . .	. . .	. . .	. . .
Nonmonetary gold	3 180 . .	. . .	. . .	. . .	. . .	. . .	. . .	. . .	. . .
B. SERVICES	4 200 . .	. . .	. . .	. . .	–170	–179	–199	–226	. . .
Total credit	2 200 . .	. . .	. . .	. . .	*112*	*102*	*107*	*114*	. . .
Total debit	3 200 . .	. . .	. . .	. . .	*–282*	*–282*	*–306*	*–340*	. . .
Transportation services, credit	2 205 . .	**. . .**	**. . .**	**. . .**	**72**	**60**	**51**	**43**	**. . .**
Passenger	2 850 . .	. . .	. . .	. . .	. . .	. . .	. . .	. . .	. . .
Freight	2 851 . .	. . .	. . .	. . .	*72*	*60*	*51*	*43*	. . .
Other	2 852 . .	. . .	. . .	. . .	. . .	. . .	. . .	. . .	. . .
Sea transport, passenger	2 207 . .	. . .	. . .	. . .	. . .	. . .	. . .	. . .	. . .
Sea transport, freight	2 208 . .	. . .	. . .	. . .	. . .	. . .	. . .	. . .	. . .
Sea transport, other	2 209 . .	. . .	. . .	. . .	. . .	. . .	. . .	. . .	. . .
Air transport, passenger	2 211 . .	. . .	. . .	. . .	. . .	. . .	. . .	. . .	. . .
Air transport, freight	2 212 . .	. . .	. . .	. . .	. . .	. . .	. . .	. . .	. . .
Air transport, other	2 213 . .	. . .	. . .	. . .	. . .	. . .	. . .	. . .	. . .
Other transport, passenger	2 215 . .	. . .	. . .	. . .	. . .	. . .	. . .	. . .	. . .
Other transport, freight	2 216 . .	. . .	. . .	. . .	72	60	51	43	. . .
Other transport, other	2 217 . .	. . .	. . .	. . .	. . .	. . .	. . .	. . .	. . .
Transportation services, debit	3 205 . .	**. . .**	**. . .**	**. . .**	**–222**	**–205**	**–202**	**–222**	**. . .**
Passenger	3 850 . .	. . .	. . .	. . .	*–57*	*–57*	*–57*	*–58*	. . .
Freight	3 851 . .	. . .	. . .	. . .	*–116*	*–114*	*–92*	*–109*	. . .
Other	3 852 . .	. . .	. . .	. . .	*–48*	*–33*	*–53*	*–55*	. . .
Sea transport, passenger	3 207 . .	. . .	. . .	. . .	. . .	. . .	. . .	. . .	. . .
Sea transport, freight	3 208 . .	. . .	. . .	. . .	. . .	. . .	. . .	. . .	. . .
Sea transport, other	3 209 . .	. . .	. . .	. . .	. . .	. . .	. . .	. . .	. . .
Air transport, passenger	3 211 . .	. . .	. . .	. . .	. . .	. . .	. . .	. . .	. . .
Air transport, freight	3 212 . .	. . .	. . .	. . .	. . .	. . .	. . .	. . .	. . .
Air transport, other	3 213 . .	. . .	. . .	. . .	. . .	. . .	. . .	. . .	. . .
Other transport, passenger	3 215 . .	. . .	. . .	. . .	–57	–57	–57	–58	. . .
Other transport, freight	3 216 . .	. . .	. . .	. . .	–116	–114	–92	–109	. . .
Other transport, other	3 217 . .	. . .	. . .	. . .	–48	–33	–53	–55	. . .
Travel, credit	2 236 . .	**. . .**	**. . .**	**. . .**	**29**	**40**	**53**	**66**	**. . .**
Business travel	2 237 . .	. . .	. . .	. . .	. . .	. . .	. . .	. . .	. . .
Personal travel	2 240 . .	. . .	. . .	. . .	29	40	53	66	. . .
Travel, debit	3 236 . .	**. . .**	**. . .**	**. . .**	**–26**	**–24**	**–43**	**–44**	**. . .**
Business travel	3 237 . .	. . .	. . .	. . .	–20	–20	–39	–40	. . .
Personal travel	3 240 . .	. . .	. . .	. . .	–6	–4	–4	–4	. . .
Other services, credit	2 200 BA	**. . .**	**. . .**	**. . .**	**11**	**3**	**3**	**5**	**. . .**
Communications	2 245 . .	. . .	. . .	. . .	3	3	2	. . .	. . .
Construction	2 249 . .	. . .	. . .	. . .	. . .	. . .	. . .	. . .	. . .
Insurance	2 253 . .	. . .	. . .	. . .	. . .	. . .	. . .	5	. . .
Financial	2 260 . .	. . .	. . .	. . .	. . .	. . .	. . .	. . .	. . .
Computer and information	2 262 . .	. . .	. . .	. . .	. . .	. . .	. . .	. . .	. . .
Royalties and licence fees	2 266 . .	. . .	. . .	. . .	. . .	. . .	. . .	. . .	. . .
Other business services	2 268 . .	. . .	. . .	. . .	8	. . .	. . .	. . .	. . .
Personal, cultural, and recreational	2 287 . .	. . .	. . .	. . .	. . .	. . .	. . .	. . .	. . .
Government, n.i.e.	2 291 . .	. . .	. . .	. . .	. . .	. . .	. . .	. . .	. . .
Other services, debit	3 200 BA	**. . .**	**. . .**	**. . .**	**–33**	**–53**	**–61**	**–74**	**. . .**
Communications	3 245 . .	. . .	. . .	. . .	–2	–8	–2	–5	. . .
Construction	3 249 . .	. . .	. . .	. . .	–21	–33	–34	–35	. . .
Insurance	3 253 . .	. . .	. . .	. . .	. . .	. . .	–1	–6	. . .
Financial	3 260 . .	. . .	. . .	. . .	. . .	. . .	. . .	. . .	. . .
Computer and information	3 262 . .	. . .	. . .	. . .	. . .	. . .	. . .	. . .	. . .
Royalties and licence fees	3 266 . .	. . .	. . .	. . .	. . .	. . .	. . .	. . .	. . .
Other business services	3 268 . .	. . .	. . .	. . .	–10	–11	–15	–17	. . .
Personal, cultural, and recreational	3 287 . .	. . .	. . .	. . .	. . .	. . .	. . .	. . .	. . .
Government, n.i.e.	3 291 . .	. . .	. . .	. . .	. . .	. . .	–8	–12	. . .

Table 2 (Continued). STANDARD PRESENTATION, 1994–2001

(Millions of U.S. dollars)

	Code	1994	1995	1996	1997	1998	1999	2000	2001
C. INCOME	4 300 . .	. . .	. . .	. . .	–219	–214	–134	–119	. . .
Total credit	2 300 . .	. . .	. . .	. . .	*77*	*44*	*44*	*46*	. . .
Total debit	3 300 . .	. . .	. . .	. . .	*–296*	*–258*	*–178*	*–166*	. . .
Compensation of employees, credit	2 310 . .	**. . .**	**. . .**	**. . .**	**. . .**	**. . .**	**. . .**	**. . .**	**. . .**
Compensation of employees, debit	3 310 . .	**. . .**	**. . .**	**. . .**	**–40**	**–12**	**–6**	**–6**	**. . .**
Investment income, credit	2 320 . .	**. . .**	**. . .**	**. . .**	**77**	**44**	**44**	**46**	**. . .**
Direct investment income	2 330 . .	. . .	. . .	. . .	32	. . .	. . .	. . .	. . .
Dividends and distributed branch profits	2 332 . .	. . .	. . .	. . .	. . .	. . .	. . .	. . .	. . .
Reinvested earnings and undistributed branch profits	2 333 . .	. . .	. . .	. . .	. . .	. . .	. . .	. . .	. . .
Income on debt (interest)	2 334 . .	. . .	. . .	. . .	30	. . .	. . .	. . .	. . .
Portfolio investment income	2 339 . .	. . .	. . .	. . .	. . .	9	9	11	. . .
Income on equity	2 340 . .	. . .	. . .	. . .	. . .	. . .	. . .	. . .	. . .
Income on bonds and notes	2 350 . .	. . .	. . .	. . .	. . .	9	9	11	. . .
Income on money market instruments	2 360 . .	. . .	. . .	. . .	. . .	. . .	. . .	. . .	. . .
Other investment income	2 370 . .	. . .	. . .	. . .	45	35	35	35	. . .
Investment income, debit	3 320 . .	**. . .**	**. . .**	**. . .**	**–256**	**–246**	**–172**	**–160**	**. . .**
Direct investment income	3 330 . .	. . .	. . .	. . .	. . .	. . .	. . .	. . .	. . .
Dividends and distributed branch profits	3 332 . .	. . .	. . .	. . .	. . .	. . .	. . .	. . .	. . .
Reinvested earnings and undistributed branch profits	3 333 . .	. . .	. . .	. . .	. . .	. . .	. . .	. . .	. . .
Income on debt (interest)	3 334 . .	. . .	. . .	. . .	. . .	. . .	. . .	. . .	. . .
Portfolio investment income	3 339 . .	. . .	. . .	. . .	. . .	. . .	. . .	. . .	. . .
Income on equity	3 340 . .	. . .	. . .	. . .	. . .	. . .	. . .	. . .	. . .
Income on bonds and notes	3 350 . .	. . .	. . .	. . .	. . .	. . .	. . .	. . .	. . .
Income on money market instruments	3 360 . .	. . .	. . .	. . .	. . .	. . .	. . .	. . .	. . .
Other investment income	3 370 . .	. . .	. . .	. . .	–256	–246	–172	–160	. . .
D. CURRENT TRANSFERS	4 379 . .	. . .	. . .	. . .	182	–24	45	14	. . .
Credit	2 379 . .	**. . .**	**. . .**	**. . .**	**201**	**3**	**60**	**32**	**. . .**
General government	2 380 . .	. . .	. . .	. . .	201	3	60	32	. . .
Other sectors	2 390 . .	. . .	. . .	. . .	. . .	. . .	. . .	. . .	. . .
Workers' remittances	2 391 . .	. . .	. . .	. . .	. . .	. . .	. . .	. . .	. . .
Other current transfers	2 392 . .	. . .	. . .	. . .	. . .	. . .	. . .	. . .	. . .
Debit	3 379 . .	**. . .**	**. . .**	**. . .**	**–19**	**–27**	**–16**	**–18**	**. . .**
General government	3 380 . .	. . .	. . .	. . .	. . .	. . .	. . .	. . .	. . .
Other sectors	3 390 . .	. . .	. . .	. . .	–19	–27	–16	–18	. . .
Workers' remittances	3 391 . .	. . .	. . .	. . .	–19	–27	–16	–18	. . .
Other current transfers	3 392 . .	. . .	. . .	. . .	. . .	. . .	. . .	. . .	. . .
CAPITAL AND FINANCIAL ACCOUNT	4 996 . .	**. . .**	**. . .**	**. . .**	**407**	**608**	**616**	**368**	**. . .**
CAPITAL ACCOUNT	4 994 . .	**. . .**	**. . .**	**. . .**	**. . .**	**203**	**196**	**153**	**. . .**
Total credit	2 994 . .	. . .	. . .	. . .	. . .	*203*	*196*	*153*	. . .
Total debit	3 994 . .	. . .	. . .	. . .	. . .	. . .	. . .	. . .	. . .
Capital transfers, credit	2 400 . .	**. . .**	**. . .**	**. . .**	**. . .**	**203**	**196**	**153**	**. . .**
General government	2 401 . .	. . .	. . .	. . .	. . .	203	196	153	. . .
Debt forgiveness	2 402 . .	. . .	. . .	. . .	. . .	. . .	. . .	. . .	. . .
Other capital transfers	2 410 . .	. . .	. . .	. . .	. . .	203	196	153	. . .
Other sectors	2 430 . .	. . .	. . .	. . .	. . .	. . .	. . .	. . .	. . .
Migrants' transfers	2 431 . .	. . .	. . .	. . .	. . .	. . .	. . .	. . .	. . .
Debt forgiveness	2 432 . .	. . .	. . .	. . .	. . .	. . .	. . .	. . .	. . .
Other capital transfers	2 440 . .	. . .	. . .	. . .	. . .	. . .	. . .	. . .	. . .
Capital transfers, debit	3 400 . .	**. . .**	**. . .**	**. . .**	**. . .**	**. . .**	**. . .**	**. . .**	**. . .**
General government	3 401 . .	. . .	. . .	. . .	. . .	. . .	. . .	. . .	. . .
Debt forgiveness	3 402 . .	. . .	. . .	. . .	. . .	. . .	. . .	. . .	. . .
Other capital transfers	3 410 . .	. . .	. . .	. . .	. . .	. . .	. . .	. . .	. . .
Other sectors	3 430 . .	. . .	. . .	. . .	. . .	. . .	. . .	. . .	. . .
Migrants' transfers	3 431 . .	. . .	. . .	. . .	. . .	. . .	. . .	. . .	. . .
Debt forgiveness	3 432 . .	. . .	. . .	. . .	. . .	. . .	. . .	. . .	. . .
Other capital transfers	3 440 . .	. . .	. . .	. . .	. . .	. . .	. . .	. . .	. . .
Nonproduced nonfinancial assets, credit	2 480 . .	**. . .**	**. . .**	**. . .**	**. . .**	**. . .**	**. . .**	**. . .**	**. . .**
Nonproduced nonfinancial assets, debit	3 480 . .	**. . .**	**. . .**	**. . .**	**. . .**	**. . .**	**. . .**	**. . .**	**. . .**

Table 2 (Continued). STANDARD PRESENTATION, 1994–2001

(Millions of U.S. dollars)

	Code	1994	1995	1996	1997	1998	1999	2000	2001
FINANCIAL ACCOUNT	4 995 . .	...	...	...	**407**	**405**	**420**	**215**	...
A. DIRECT INVESTMENT	4 500 . .	...	...	...	207	198	162	122	...
Direct investment abroad	4 505 . .	...	...	...	...	...	...	...	...
Equity capital	4 510 . .	...	...	...	...	...	...	...	...
Claims on affiliated enterprises	4 515 . .	...	...	...	...	...	...	...	...
Liabilities to affiliated enterprises	4 520 . .	...	...	...	...	...	...	...	...
Reinvested earnings	4 525 . .	...	...	...	...	...	...	...	...
Other capital	4 530 . .	...	...	...	...	...	...	...	...
Claims on affiliated enterprises	4 535 . .	...	...	...	...	...	...	...	...
Liabilities to affiliated enterprises	4 540 . .	...	...	...	...	...	...	...	...
Direct investment in Zambia	4 555 . .	...	...	...	**207**	**198**	**162**	**122**	...
Equity capital	4 560 . .	...	...	...	197	198	162	122	...
Claims on direct investors	4 565 . .	...	...	...	...	...	...	...	...
Liabilities to direct investors	4 570 . .	...	...	...	197	198	162	122	...
Reinvested earnings	4 575 . .	...	...	...	...	...	...	...	...
Other capital	4 580 . .	...	...	...	10	...	...	...	...
Claims on direct investors	4 585 . .	...	...	...	10	...	...	...	...
Liabilities to direct investors	4 590 . .	...	...	...	...	...	...	...	...
B. PORTFOLIO INVESTMENT	4 600 . .	...	...	...	1	1	13	–1	...
Assets	4 602 . .	...	...	...	...	...	...	...	...
Equity securities	4 610 . .	...	...	...	...	...	...	...	...
Monetary authorities	4 611 . .	...	...	...	...	...	...	...	...
General government	4 612 . .	...	...	...	...	...	...	...	...
Banks	4 613 . .	...	...	...	...	...	...	...	...
Other sectors	4 614 . .	...	...	...	...	...	...	...	...
Debt securities	4 619 . .	...	...	...	...	...	...	...	...
Bonds and notes	4 620 . .	...	...	...	...	...	...	...	...
Monetary authorities	4 621 . .	...	...	...	...	...	...	...	...
General government	4 622 . .	...	...	...	...	...	...	...	...
Banks	4 623 . .	...	...	...	...	...	...	...	...
Other sectors	4 624 . .	...	...	...	...	...	...	...	...
Money market instruments	4 630 . .	...	...	...	...	...	...	...	...
Monetary authorities	4 631 . .	...	...	...	...	...	...	...	...
General government	4 632 . .	...	...	...	...	...	...	...	...
Banks	4 633 . .	...	...	...	...	...	...	...	...
Other sectors	4 634 . .	...	...	...	...	...	...	...	...
Liabilities	4 652 . .	...	...	...	**1**	**1**	**13**	**–1**	...
Equity securities	4 660 . .	...	...	...	1	1	13	–1	...
Banks	4 663 . .	...	...	...	...	...	...	...	...
Other sectors	4 664 . .	...	...	...	1	1	13	–1	...
Debt securities	4 669 . .	...	...	...	...	...	...	...	...
Bonds and notes	4 670 . .	...	...	...	...	...	...	...	...
Monetary authorities	4 671 . .	...	...	...	...	...	...	...	...
General government	4 672 . .	...	...	...	...	...	...	...	...
Banks	4 673 . .	...	...	...	...	...	...	...	...
Other sectors	4 674 . .	...	...	...	...	...	...	...	...
Money market instruments	4 680 . .	...	...	...	...	...	...	...	...
Monetary authorities	4 681 . .	...	...	...	...	...	...	...	...
General government	4 682 . .	...	...	...	...	...	...	...	...
Banks	4 683 . .	...	...	...	...	...	...	...	...
Other sectors	4 684 . .	...	...	...	...	...	...	...	...
C. FINANCIAL DERIVATIVES	4 910 . .	...	...	...	...	...	...	...	...
Monetary authorities	4 911 . .	...	...	...	...	...	...	...	...
General government	4 912 . .	...	...	...	...	...	...	...	...
Banks	4 913 . .	...	...	...	...	...	...	...	...
Other sectors	4 914 . .	...	...	...	...	...	...	...	...
Assets	4 900 . .	...	...	...	...	...	...	...	...
Monetary authorities	4 901 . .	...	...	...	...	...	...	...	...
General government	4 902 . .	...	...	...	...	...	...	...	...
Banks	4 903 . .	...	...	...	...	...	...	...	...
Other sectors	4 904 . .	...	...	...	...	...	...	...	...
Liabilities	4 905 . .	...	...	...	...	...	...	...	...
Monetary authorities	4 906 . .	...	...	...	...	...	...	...	...
General government	4 907 . .	...	...	...	...	...	...	...	...
Banks	4 908 . .	...	...	...	...	...	...	...	...
Other sectors	4 909 . .	...	...	...	...	...	...	...	...

Table 2 (Concluded). STANDARD PRESENTATION, 1994–2001
(Millions of U.S. dollars)

	Code	1994	1995	1996	1997	1998	1999	2000	2001
D. OTHER INVESTMENT	4 700	...	...	...	224	12	247	185	...
Assets	4 703	...	...	...	**–24**	**–40**	**–2**	**–85**	...
Trade credits	4 706	...	...	...	...	...	...	...	...
General government	4 707	...	...	...	...	...	...	...	...
of which: Short-term	4 709	...	...	...	...	...	...	...	...
Other sectors	4 710	...	...	...	...	...	...	...	...
of which: Short-term	4 712	...	...	...	...	...	...	...	...
Loans	4 714	...	...	...	...	...	...	...	...
Monetary authorities	4 715	...	...	...	...	...	...	...	...
of which: Short-term	4 718	...	...	...	...	...	...	...	...
General government	4 719	...	...	...	...	...	...	...	...
of which: Short-term	4 721	...	...	...	...	...	...	...	...
Banks	4 722	...	...	...	...	...	...	...	...
of which: Short-term	4 724	...	...	...	...	...	...	...	...
Other sectors	4 725	...	...	...	...	...	...	...	...
of which: Short-term	4 727	...	...	...	...	...	...	...	...
Currency and deposits	4 730	...	...	...	–24	–40	–2	–85	...
Monetary authorities	4 731	...	...	...	...	...	...	...	...
General government	4 732	...	...	...	...	...	...	...	...
Banks	4 733	...	...	...	–24	–40	–2	–85	...
Other sectors	4 734	...	...	...	...	...	...	...	...
Other assets	4 736	...	...	...	...	...	...	...	...
Monetary authorities	4 737	...	...	...	...	...	...	...	...
of which: Short-term	4 739	...	...	...	...	...	...	...	...
General government	4 740	...	...	...	...	...	...	...	...
of which: Short-term	4 742	...	...	...	...	...	...	...	...
Banks	4 743	...	...	...	...	...	...	...	...
of which: Short-term	4 745	...	...	...	...	...	...	...	...
Other sectors	4 746	...	...	...	...	...	...	...	...
of which: Short-term	4 748	...	...	...	...	...	...	...	...
Liabilities	4 753	...	...	...	**248**	**52**	**248**	**270**	...
Trade credits	4 756	...	...	...	...	...	...	...	...
General government	4 757	...	...	...	...	...	...	...	...
of which: Short-term	4 759	...	...	...	...	...	...	...	...
Other sectors	4 760	...	...	...	...	...	...	...	...
of which: Short-term	4 762	...	...	...	...	...	...	...	...
Loans	4 764	...	...	...	229	54	500	280	...
Monetary authorities	4 765	...	...	...	14	7	21	19	...
of which: Use of Fund credit and loans from the Fund	4 766	...	...	...	*14*	...	*14*	*26*	...
of which: Short-term	4 768	...	...	...	...	*7*	*7*	*–7*	...
General government	4 769	...	...	...	202	77	466	174	...
of which: Short-term	4 771	...	...	...	...	...	...	...	...
Banks	4 772	...	...	...	...	7	5	–4	...
of which: Short-term	4 774	...	...	...	...	*7*	*5*	*–4*	...
Other sectors	4 775	...	...	...	13	–37	7	91	...
of which: Short-term	4 777	...	...	...	*13*	*–37*	*7*	*91*	...
Currency and deposits	4 780	...	...	...	19	–2	...	...	...
Monetary authorities	4 781	...	...	...	...	...	...	...	...
General government	4 782	...	...	...	...	...	...	...	...
Banks	4 783	...	...	...	19	–2	...	...	...
Other sectors	4 784	...	...	...	...	...	...	...	...
Other liabilities	4 786	...	...	...	...	...	–251	–10	...
Monetary authorities	4 787	...	...	...	...	...	...	...	...
of which: Short-term	4 789	...	...	...	...	...	...	...	...
General government	4 790	...	...	...	...	...	–251	–10	...
of which: Short-term	4 792	...	...	...	...	...	*–251*	*–10*	...
Banks	4 793	...	...	...	...	...	...	...	...
of which: Short-term	4 795	...	...	...	...	...	...	...	...
Other sectors	4 796	...	...	...	...	...	...	...	...
of which: Short-term	4 798	...	...	...	...	...	...	...	...
E. RESERVE ASSETS	4 802	...	...	...	–25	194	–1	–90	...
Monetary gold	4 812	...	...	...	...	...	...	...	...
Special drawing rights	4 811	...	...	...	1	...	1	–22	...
Reserve position in the Fund	4 810	...	...	...	...	...	...	...	...
Foreign exchange	4 803	...	...	...	–26	194	–2	–68	...
Other claims	4 813	...	...	...	...	...	...	...	...
NET ERRORS AND OMISSIONS	4 998	...	...	...	**–255**	**–37**	**–229**	**185**	...

Part 3 of the *Yearbook* contains descriptions of the methodologies, compilation practices, and sources used to compile these data.

$195.00 (3 vol set)